# WHITAKER'S
# 2016

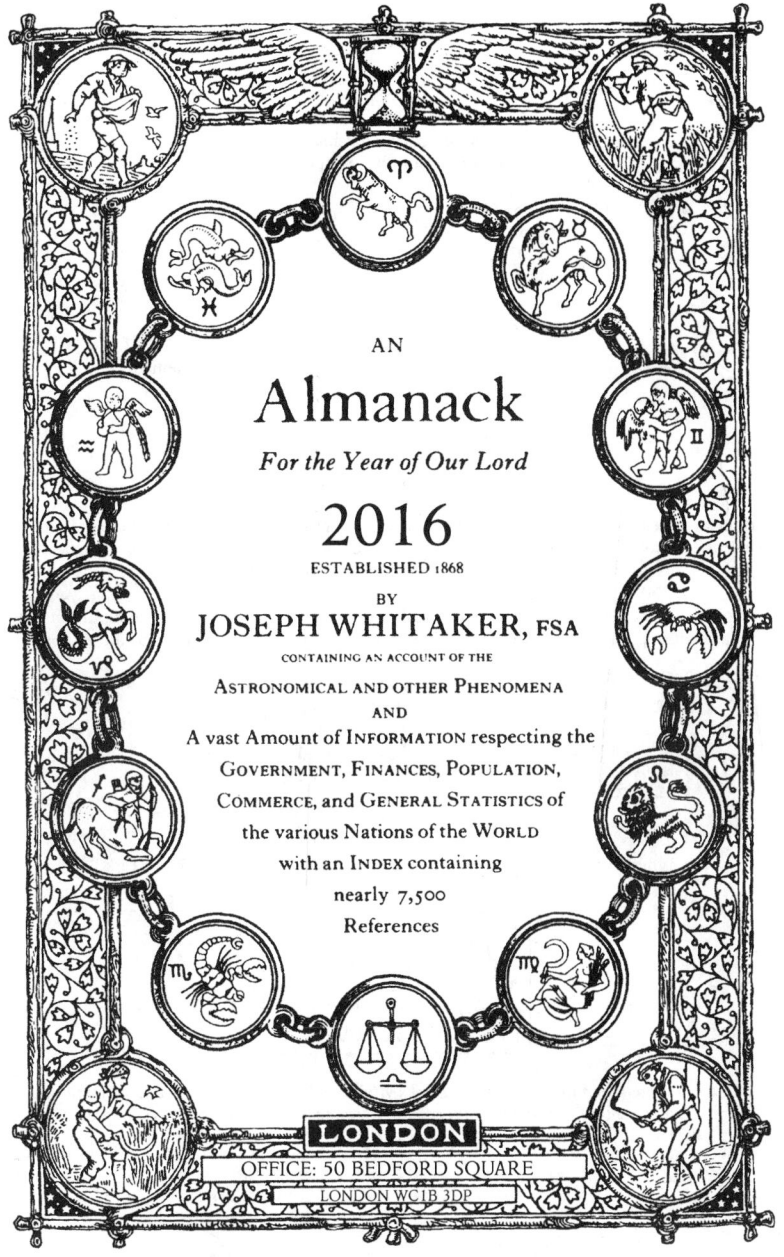

AN

# Almanack

*For the Year of Our Lord*

# 2016

ESTABLISHED 1868

BY

## JOSEPH WHITAKER, FSA

CONTAINING AN ACCOUNT OF THE

ASTRONOMICAL AND OTHER PHENOMENA

AND

A vast Amount of INFORMATION respecting the

GOVERNMENT, FINANCES, POPULATION,

COMMERCE, and GENERAL STATISTICS of

the various Nations of the WORLD

with an INDEX containing

nearly 7,500

References

**LONDON**

OFFICE: 50 BEDFORD SQUARE

LONDON WC1B 3DP

*The traditional design of the title page for Whitaker's Almanack which has appeared in each edition since 1868*

# B L O O M S B U R Y

LONDON · OXFORD · NEW YORK · NEW DELHI · SYDNEY

Bloomsbury Publishing
An imprint of Bloomsbury Publishing Plc

50 Bedford Square
London
WC1B 3DP
UK

1385 Broadway
New York
NY 10018
USA

www.bloomsbury.com

WHITAKER's, the W Trident logo and the Diana logo are trademarks
of Bloomsbury Publishing Plc

Published annually since 1868

148th edition © Bloomsbury Publishing Plc, 2015

British Library Cataloguing-in-Publication Data
A catalogue record for this book is available from the British Library.

ISBN:   HB:                        978-1-4729-0930-5
        Concise Edition PB:        978-1-4729-0932-9

2 4 6 8 10 9 7 5 3 1

Typeset in the UK by RefineCatch Limited, Bungay, Suffolk NR35 1EF
Printed and bound in Italy by L.E.G.O. S.p.A.

MIX
Paper from
responsible sources
FSC® C023419

To find out more about our authors and books visit www.bloomsbury.com. Here you will find
extracts, author interviews, details of forthcoming events and the option to sign up for our
newsletters.

# CONTENTS

4

How fitting to have the 800th anniversary of the sealing of the Magna Carta and a General Election in the same year. When King John sealed the Magna Carta in June 1215, he was presented with at least 13 copies of the manuscript, to be dispatched across his kingdom. Of these originals, only four are known to have survived to the present day and, as part of the celebrations to mark the anniversary of the charter's issue, the manuscripts were brought together at the British Library for the first time since their initial dispersal.

At the start of the election year it seemed a foregone conclusion that we would have another coalition government of some description following the General Election on 7 May. Against all media predictions, and mainly down to the dramatic effect of the Scottish National Party's gains from Labour across Scotland, it was a clear win for the Conservatives, who have a working majority of 16 in the new parliament. Complete election results for every constituency, the current list of MPs, colour infographics depicting turnout and the political landscape of the UK, plus manifesto commitments made by the main parties are all fully detailed in this edition.

Internationally it has been a tumultuous year: the Nepal earthquake in April had devastating effects, the Greek financial crisis and subsequent bailouts and financial restructuring of the country will have a knock-on effect for years to come, and the continuing terrorism of IS in the Middle East and the civil war in Syria has resulted in an unforeseen and unplanned for influx of refugees into Europe. This turmoil in Europe is particularly poignant as 2015 was the 70th anniversary of Victory in Europe Day, which fell on the day after the General Election and was marked by events across the country. A Service of Remembrance at the Cenotaph was attended by the re-elected Prime Minister David Cameron and the now ex-leaders of the main parties who had fallen on their swords following defeat at the polls on the previous day.

Sport provided a welcome relief with the England team beating Germany to finish in third place at the 2015 FIFA Women's World Cup, the best performance by an England team since 1966. This was swiftly followed by England's win in The Ashes and, at the time of writing, the Rugby World Cup 2015 has got off to a great start: the first time the Cup has been hosted solely in England. *Whitaker's 2016* has 27 pages dedicated to sports results, records and events from the past year.

As always I would like to thank our numerous contributors. I would also like to take the opportunity to let our readers know of our new subscription website which will be arriving in Spring 2016. If you would like to be kept informed of developments regarding this, or provide any feedback or comments on this edition, please do email us: whitakersalmanackteam@bloomsbury.com

Ruth Northey
Executive Editor

## JACKET PHOTOGRAPHS

*Main image:* A general view of the Houses of Parliament in Central London © PA

*Top, from left to right:*
1. Seal of King John © Getty Images
2. National banks open for one day to allow Greek pensioners to collect rationed payouts © Getty Images
3. VE Day 70th Anniversary © Getty Images
4. George Ford, England v France – RBS Six Nations © Getty Images

## SOURCES

Whitaker's was compiled with the assistance of HM Revenue and Customs; Keesing's Worldwide; The Met Office; Oxford Cartographers; Press Association; UK Hydrographic Office; WM/Reuters; and The World Bank.

Material was reproduced from (in addition to that indicated): *Abolitionist and Retentionist Countries* © Amnesty International (W www.amnesty.org); *CIA World Factbook 2015*; *Corruption Perceptions Index 2014* © Transparency International (W www.transparency.org); *The Diplomatic List January 2015* © Crown Copyright; *Global Employment Trends 2014* © International Labour Organization; *Human Development Indicators 2014* published by the UN Development Programme and *UN Statistics* published by UN data; *Press Freedom Score 2015* © Reporters Without Borders; Stockholm International Peace Research Institute (SIPRI) 2015; *World Development Indicators 2015* published by The World Bank; *World Economic Outlook Database 2014* © International Monetary Fund; UNESCO Institute for Statistics (UIS) (W www.uis.unesco.org/datacentre); Crown copyright material is reproduced with the permission of the Controller of Her Majesty's Stationery Office.

Government cabinet lists and embassy details are sourced from *People in Power* © Cambridge International Reference on Current Affairs Ltd (W www.circaworld.com). *People in Power* provides a constantly updated service at www.peopleinpower.com

## EDITORIAL STAFF

Executive Editor: Ruth Northey
Senior Project Editor/Infographic Design: Oli Lurie
Assistant Editor: James McCall
Editorial Assistants: Claire Constable; Lucy Thoms
Head of Yearbooks: Katy McAdam

Thanks to Omer Ali, Lucy Beevor, John Bromham, John Flannery, Rob Hardy, Stephen Kershaw, Elizabeth Kingston, Hilary Marsden

CONTRIBUTORS (where not listed)
Sheridan Williams (Astronomy); Anthea Lipsett, Caroline Macready (Education); Graham Bartram (Flags); Clive Longhurst (Insurance); Richard McMeeken, Chris Priestley (Legal Notes); Matthew Chorley (Sports Results); Jill Papworth (Taxation); and Sean Clarke (Weather)

Terrestrial Magnestism data supplied by Dr Susan Macmillan of the British Geological Survey

# THE YEAR 2016

## CHRONOLOGICAL CYCLES AND ERAS

| | |
|---|---:|
| Dominical Letter | CB |
| Epact | 21 |
| Golden Number (Lunar Cycle) | III |
| Julian Period | 6729 |
| Roman Indiction | 9 |
| Solar Cycle | 9 |

| | *Beginning* |
|---|---:|
| *Muslim year AH 1437 | 14 Oct 2015 |
| Japanese year Heisei 28 | 1 Jan |
| Roman year 2769 AUC | 14 Jan |
| Regnal year 65 | 6 Feb |
| Chinese year of the Monkey | 8 Feb |
| Sikh new year | 14 Mar |
| Indian (Saka) year 1938 | 21 Mar |
| Hindu new year (Chaitra) | 8 Apr |
| *Jewish year AM 5777 | 3 Oct |

* Year begins at sunset on the previous day

## RELIGIOUS CALENDARS

### CHRISTIAN

| | |
|---|---:|
| Epiphany | 6 Jan |
| Presentation of Christ in the Temple | 2 Feb |
| Ash Wednesday | 10 Feb |
| The Annunciation | 25 Mar |
| Palm Sunday | 20 Mar |
| Maundy Thursday | 24 Mar |
| Good Friday | 25 Mar |
| Easter Day (western churches) | 27 Mar |
| Easter Day (Eastern Orthodox) | 1 May |
| Rogation Sunday | 1 May |
| Ascension Day | 5 May |
| Pentecost (Whit Sunday) | 15 May |
| Trinity Sunday | 22 May |
| Corpus Christi | 26 May |
| All Saints' Day | 1 Nov |
| Advent Sunday | 27 Nov |
| Christmas Day | 25 Dec |

### HINDU

| | |
|---|---:|
| Makar Sankranti | 14 Jan |
| Vasant Panchami (Sarasvati Puja) | 12 Feb |
| Shivaratri | 8 Mar |
| Holi | 23 Mar |
| Chaitra (Spring new year) | 8 Apr |
| Ram Navami | 15 Apr |
| Raksha-bandhan | 18 Aug |
| Krishna Janmashtami | 25 Aug |
| Ganesh Chaturthi, first day | 5 Sep |
| Navaratri festival (Durga Puja), first day | 1 Oct |
| Dussehra | 11 Oct |
| Diwali (New Year festival of lights), first day | 30 Oct |

### JEWISH

| | |
|---|---:|
| Purim | 24 Mar |
| Pesach (Passover), first day | 23 Apr |
| Shavuot (Feast of Weeks), first day | 12 June |
| Rosh Hashanah (Jewish new year) | 3 Oct |
| Yom Kippur (Day of Atonement) | 12 Oct |
| Succot (Feast of Tabernacles), first day | 17 Oct |
| Hanukkah, first day | 25 Dec |

### MUSLIM†

| | |
|---|---:|
| Al-Hijra (Muslim new year) | 14 Oct 2015 |
| Ashura | 23 Oct 2015 |
| Ramadan, first day | 6 Jun |
| Eid-ul-Fitr | 6 Jul |
| Hajj, first day | 9 Sep |
| Eid-ul-Adha | 11 Sep |

† The Islamic calendar is lunar so religious dates may vary by one or two days locally and according to when the new Moon is first seen

### SIKH

| | |
|---|---:|
| Birthday of Guru Gobind Singh Ji | 5 Jan |
| 1 Chet (Sikh new year) | 14 Mar |
| ‡Hola Mohalla | 24 Mar |
| Baisakhi | 14 Apr |
| Martyrdom of Guru Arjan Dev Ji | 16 Jun |
| ‡Birthday of Guru Nanak Dev Ji | 14 Nov |
| Martyrdom of Guru Tegh Bahadur Ji | 24 Nov |

‡ Currently celebrated according to the lunar, rather than Nanakshahi, calendar, so the date varies annually

## CIVIL CALENDAR

| | |
|---|---:|
| Duchess of Cambridge's birthday | 9 Jan |
| Countess of Wessex's birthday | 20 Jan |
| Accession of the Queen | 6 Feb |
| Duke of York's birthday | 19 Feb |
| St David's Day | 1 Mar |
| Earl of Wessex's birthday | 10 Mar |
| Commonwealth Day | 14 Mar |
| St Patrick's Day | 17 Mar |
| Birthday of the Queen | 21 Apr |
| St George's Day | 23 Apr |
| Europe Day | 9 May |
| Coronation Day | 2 Jun |
| Duke of Edinburgh's birthday | 10 Jun |
| The Queen's Official Birthday | 11 Jun |
| Duke of Cambridge's birthday | 21 Jun |
| Duchess of Cornwall's birthday | 17 Jul |
| Princess Royal's birthday | 15 Aug |
| Lord Mayor's Day | 12 Nov |
| Remembrance Sunday | 13 Nov |
| Prince of Wales' birthday | 14 Nov |
| Wedding Day of the Queen | 20 Nov |
| St Andrew's Day | 30 Nov |

## LEGAL CALENDAR

### LAW TERMS

| | |
|---|---:|
| Hilary Term | 11 Jan to 23 Mar |
| Easter Term | 5 Apr to 27 May |
| Trinity Term | 7 Jun to 29 Jul |
| Michaelmas Term | 3 Oct to 21 Dec |

### QUARTER DAYS

| *England, Wales and Northern Ireland* | TERM DAYS *Scotland* |
|---|---:|
| Lady – 25 Mar | Candlemas – 28 Feb |
| Midsummer – 24 Jun | Whitsunday – 28 May |
| Michaelmas – 29 Sep | Lammas – 28 Aug |
| Christmas – 25 Dec | Martinmas – 28 Nov |

# 2016

| JANUARY | | | | | | |
|---|---|---|---|---|---|---|
| Sunday | | 3 | 10 | 17 | 24 | 31 |
| Monday | | 4 | 11 | 18 | 25 | |
| Tuesday | | 5 | 12 | 19 | 26 | |
| Wednesday | | 6 | 13 | 20 | 27 | |
| Thursday | | 7 | 14 | 21 | 28 | |
| Friday | 1 | 8 | 15 | 22 | 29 | |
| Saturday | 2 | 9 | 16 | 23 | 30 | |

| FEBRUARY | | | | | | |
|---|---|---|---|---|---|---|
| Sunday | | | 7 | 14 | 21 | 28 |
| Monday | | 1 | 8 | 15 | 22 | 29 |
| Tuesday | | 2 | 9 | 16 | 23 | |
| Wednesday | | 3 | 10 | 17 | 24 | |
| Thursday | | 4 | 11 | 18 | 25 | |
| Friday | | 5 | 12 | 19 | 26 | |
| Saturday | | 6 | 13 | 20 | 27 | |

| MARCH | | | | | | |
|---|---|---|---|---|---|---|
| Sunday | | | 6 | 13 | 20 | 27 |
| Monday | | | 7 | 14 | 21 | 28 |
| Tuesday | | 1 | 8 | 15 | 22 | 29 |
| Wednesday | | 2 | 9 | 16 | 23 | 30 |
| Thursday | | 3 | 10 | 17 | 24 | 31 |
| Friday | | 4 | 11 | 18 | 25 | |
| Saturday | | 5 | 12 | 19 | 26 | |

| APRIL | | | | | |
|---|---|---|---|---|---|
| Sunday | | 3 | 10 | 17 | 24 |
| Monday | | 4 | 11 | 18 | 25 |
| Tuesday | | 5 | 12 | 19 | 26 |
| Wednesday | | 6 | 13 | 20 | 27 |
| Thursday | | 7 | 14 | 21 | 28 |
| Friday | 1 | 8 | 15 | 22 | 29 |
| Saturday | 2 | 9 | 16 | 23 | 30 |

| MAY | | | | | | |
|---|---|---|---|---|---|---|
| Sunday | 1 | 8 | 15 | 22 | 29 | |
| Monday | 2 | 9 | 16 | 23 | 30 | |
| Tuesday | 3 | 10 | 17 | 24 | 31 | |
| Wednesday | 4 | 11 | 18 | 25 | | |
| Thursday | 5 | 12 | 19 | 26 | | |
| Friday | 6 | 13 | 20 | 27 | | |
| Saturday | 7 | 14 | 21 | 28 | | |

| JUNE | | | | | |
|---|---|---|---|---|---|
| Sunday | | 5 | 12 | 19 | 26 |
| Monday | | 6 | 13 | 20 | 27 |
| Tuesday | | 7 | 14 | 21 | 28 |
| Wednesday | 1 | 8 | 15 | 22 | 29 |
| Thursday | 2 | 9 | 16 | 23 | 30 |
| Friday | 3 | 10 | 17 | 24 | |
| Saturday | 4 | 11 | 18 | 25 | |

| JULY | | | | | | |
|---|---|---|---|---|---|---|
| Sunday | | 3 | 10 | 17 | 24 | 31 |
| Monday | | 4 | 11 | 18 | 25 | |
| Tuesday | | 5 | 12 | 19 | 26 | |
| Wednesday | | 6 | 13 | 20 | 27 | |
| Thursday | | 7 | 14 | 21 | 28 | |
| Friday | 1 | 8 | 15 | 22 | 29 | |
| Saturday | 2 | 9 | 16 | 23 | 30 | |

| AUGUST | | | | | | |
|---|---|---|---|---|---|---|
| Sunday | | | 7 | 14 | 21 | 28 |
| Monday | | 1 | 8 | 15 | 22 | 29 |
| Tuesday | | 2 | 9 | 16 | 23 | 30 |
| Wednesday | | 3 | 10 | 17 | 24 | 31 |
| Thursday | | 4 | 11 | 18 | 25 | |
| Friday | | 5 | 12 | 19 | 26 | |
| Saturday | | 6 | 13 | 20 | 27 | |

| SEPTEMBER | | | | | | |
|---|---|---|---|---|---|---|
| Sunday | | | 4 | 11 | 18 | 25 |
| Monday | | | 5 | 12 | 19 | 26 |
| Tuesday | | | 6 | 13 | 20 | 27 |
| Wednesday | | | 7 | 14 | 21 | 28 |
| Thursday | | 1 | 8 | 15 | 22 | 29 |
| Friday | | 2 | 9 | 16 | 23 | 30 |
| Saturday | | 3 | 10 | 17 | 24 | |

| OCTOBER | | | | | | |
|---|---|---|---|---|---|---|
| Sunday | | 2 | 9 | 16 | 23 | 30 |
| Monday | | 3 | 10 | 17 | 24 | 31 |
| Tuesday | | 4 | 11 | 18 | 25 | |
| Wednesday | | 5 | 12 | 19 | 26 | |
| Thursday | | 6 | 13 | 20 | 27 | |
| Friday | | 7 | 14 | 21 | 28 | |
| Saturday | 1 | 8 | 15 | 22 | 29 | |

| NOVEMBER | | | | | | |
|---|---|---|---|---|---|---|
| Sunday | | | 6 | 13 | 20 | 27 |
| Monday | | | 7 | 14 | 21 | 28 |
| Tuesday | | 1 | 8 | 15 | 22 | 29 |
| Wednesday | | 2 | 9 | 16 | 23 | 30 |
| Thursday | | 3 | 10 | 17 | 24 | |
| Friday | | 4 | 11 | 18 | 25 | |
| Saturday | | 5 | 12 | 19 | 26 | |

| DECEMBER | | | | | | |
|---|---|---|---|---|---|---|
| Sunday | | | 4 | 11 | 18 | 25 |
| Monday | | | 5 | 12 | 19 | 26 |
| Tuesday | | | 6 | 13 | 20 | 27 |
| Wednesday | | | 7 | 14 | 21 | 28 |
| Thursday | | 1 | 8 | 15 | 22 | 29 |
| Friday | | 2 | 9 | 16 | 23 | 30 |
| Saturday | | 3 | 10 | 17 | 24 | 31 |

| PUBLIC HOLIDAYS | England and Wales | Scotland | Northern Ireland |
|---|---|---|---|
| New Year | 1 January† | 1, 4† January | 1 January† |
| St Patrick's Day | — | — | 17 March |
| *Good Friday | 25 March | 25 March | 25 March |
| Easter Monday | 28 March | — | 28 March |
| Early May | 2 May† | 2 May | 2 May† |
| Spring | 30 May | 30 May† | 30 May |
| Battle of the Boyne | — | — | 12 July‡ |
| Summer | 29 August | 1 August | 29 August |
| St Andrew's Day | — | 30 November§ | — |
| *Christmas | 26, 27 December | 26†, 27 December | 26, 27 December |

* In England, Wales and Northern Ireland, Christmas Day and Good Friday are common law holidays
† Subject to royal proclamation
‡ Subject to proclamation by the Secretary of State for Northern Ireland
§ The St Andrew's Day Holiday (Scotland) Bill was approved by parliament on 29 November 2006; it does not oblige employers to change their existing pattern of holidays but provides the legal framework in which the St Andrew's Day bank holiday could be substituted for an existing local holiday from another date in the year
Note: In the Channel Islands, Liberation Day is a bank and public holiday

# 2017

| JANUARY | | | | | | | FEBRUARY | | | | | | | MARCH | | | | | | |
|---|---|---|---|---|---|---|---|---|---|---|---|---|---|---|---|---|---|---|---|---|
| Sunday | 1 | 8 | 15 | 22 | 29 | | Sunday | | 5 | 12 | 19 | 26 | | Sunday | | 5 | 12 | 19 | 26 | |
| Monday | 2 | 9 | 16 | 23 | 30 | | Monday | | 6 | 13 | 20 | 27 | | Monday | | 6 | 13 | 20 | 27 | |
| Tuesday | 3 | 10 | 17 | 24 | 31 | | Tuesday | | 7 | 14 | 21 | 28 | | Tuesday | | 7 | 14 | 21 | 28 | |
| Wednesday | 4 | 11 | 18 | 25 | | | Wednesday | 1 | 8 | 15 | 22 | | | Wednesday | 1 | 8 | 15 | 22 | 29 | |
| Thursday | 5 | 12 | 19 | 26 | | | Thursday | 2 | 9 | 16 | 23 | | | Thursday | 2 | 9 | 16 | 23 | 30 | |
| Friday | 6 | 13 | 20 | 27 | | | Friday | 3 | 10 | 17 | 24 | | | Friday | 3 | 10 | 17 | 24 | 31 | |
| Saturday | 7 | 14 | 21 | 28 | | | Saturday | 4 | 11 | 18 | 25 | | | Saturday | 4 | 11 | 18 | 25 | | |

| APRIL | | | | | | | MAY | | | | | | | JUNE | | | | | | |
|---|---|---|---|---|---|---|---|---|---|---|---|---|---|---|---|---|---|---|---|---|
| Sunday | | 2 | 9 | 16 | 23 | 30 | Sunday | | 7 | 14 | 21 | 28 | | Sunday | | 4 | 11 | 18 | 25 | |
| Monday | | 3 | 10 | 17 | 24 | | Monday | 1 | 8 | 15 | 22 | 29 | | Monday | | 5 | 12 | 19 | 26 | |
| Tuesday | | 4 | 11 | 18 | 25 | | Tuesday | 2 | 9 | 16 | 23 | 30 | | Tuesday | | 6 | 13 | 20 | 27 | |
| Wednesday | | 5 | 12 | 19 | 26 | | Wednesday | 3 | 10 | 17 | 24 | 31 | | Wednesday | | 7 | 14 | 21 | 28 | |
| Thursday | | 6 | 13 | 20 | 27 | | Thursday | 4 | 11 | 18 | 25 | | | Thursday | 1 | 8 | 15 | 22 | 29 | |
| Friday | | 7 | 14 | 21 | 28 | | Friday | 5 | 12 | 19 | 26 | | | Friday | 2 | 9 | 16 | 23 | 30 | |
| Saturday | 1 | 8 | 15 | 22 | 29 | | Saturday | 6 | 13 | 20 | 27 | | | Saturday | 3 | 10 | 17 | 24 | | |

| JULY | | | | | | | AUGUST | | | | | | | SEPTEMBER | | | | | | |
|---|---|---|---|---|---|---|---|---|---|---|---|---|---|---|---|---|---|---|---|---|
| Sunday | | 2 | 9 | 16 | 23 | 30 | Sunday | | 6 | 13 | 20 | 27 | | Sunday | | 3 | 10 | 17 | 24 | |
| Monday | | 3 | 10 | 17 | 24 | 31 | Monday | | 7 | 14 | 21 | 28 | | Monday | | 4 | 11 | 18 | 25 | |
| Tuesday | | 4 | 11 | 18 | 25 | | Tuesday | 1 | 8 | 15 | 22 | 29 | | Tuesday | | 5 | 12 | 19 | 26 | |
| Wednesday | | 5 | 12 | 19 | 26 | | Wednesday | 2 | 9 | 16 | 23 | 30 | | Wednesday | | 6 | 13 | 20 | 27 | |
| Thursday | | 6 | 13 | 20 | 27 | | Thursday | 3 | 10 | 17 | 24 | 31 | | Thursday | | 7 | 14 | 21 | 28 | |
| Friday | | 7 | 14 | 21 | 28 | | Friday | 4 | 11 | 18 | 25 | | | Friday | 1 | 8 | 15 | 22 | 29 | |
| Saturday | 1 | 8 | 15 | 22 | 29 | | Saturday | 5 | 12 | 19 | 26 | | | Saturday | 2 | 9 | 16 | 23 | 30 | |

| OCTOBER | | | | | | | NOVEMBER | | | | | | | DECEMBER | | | | | | |
|---|---|---|---|---|---|---|---|---|---|---|---|---|---|---|---|---|---|---|---|---|
| Sunday | 1 | 8 | 15 | 22 | 29 | | Sunday | | 5 | 12 | 19 | 26 | | Sunday | | 3 | 10 | 17 | 24 | 31 |
| Monday | 2 | 9 | 16 | 23 | 30 | | Monday | | 6 | 13 | 20 | 27 | | Monday | | 4 | 11 | 18 | 25 | |
| Tuesday | 3 | 10 | 17 | 24 | 31 | | Tuesday | | 7 | 14 | 21 | 28 | | Tuesday | | 5 | 12 | 19 | 26 | |
| Wednesday | 4 | 11 | 18 | 25 | | | Wednesday | 1 | 8 | 15 | 22 | 29 | | Wednesday | | 6 | 13 | 20 | 27 | |
| Thursday | 5 | 12 | 19 | 26 | | | Thursday | 2 | 9 | 16 | 23 | 30 | | Thursday | | 7 | 14 | 21 | 28 | |
| Friday | 6 | 13 | 20 | 27 | | | Friday | 3 | 10 | 17 | 24 | | | Friday | 1 | 8 | 15 | 22 | 29 | |
| Saturday | 7 | 14 | 21 | 28 | | | Saturday | 4 | 11 | 18 | 25 | | | Saturday | 2 | 9 | 16 | 23 | 30 | |

| PUBLIC HOLIDAYS | *England and Wales* | *Scotland* | *Northern Ireland* |
|---|---|---|---|
| New Year | 2 January† | 2, 3† January | 2 January† |
| St Patrick's Day | — | — | 17 March |
| *Good Friday | 14 April | 14 April | 14 April |
| Easter Monday | 17 April | — | 17 April |
| Early May | 1 May† | 1 May | 1 May† |
| Spring | 29 May | 29 May† | 29 May |
| Battle of the Boyne | — | — | 13 July‡ |
| Summer | 28 August | 7 August | 28 August |
| St Andrew's Day | — | 30 November§ | — |
| *Christmas | 25, 26 December | 25†, 26 December | 25, 26 December |

* In England, Wales and Northern Ireland, Christmas Day and Good Friday are common law holidays

† Subject to royal proclamation

‡ Subject to proclamation by the Secretary of State for Northern Ireland

§ The St Andrew's Day Holiday (Scotland) Bill was approved by parliament on 29 November 2006; it does not oblige employers to change their existing pattern of holidays but provides the legal framework in which the St Andrew's Day bank holiday could be substituted for an existing local holiday from another date in the year

*Note:* In the Channel Islands, Liberation Day is a bank and public holiday

# FORTHCOMING EVENTS

\* Provisional dates

## JANUARY 2016
| | |
|---|---|
| 8–17 | London Boat Show, Excel, London Docklands |
| 8–17 | London Short Film Festival |
| 14–31 | Celtic Connections Music Festival, Glasgow |
| 19–21 | UK Open Dance Championships, Bournemouth |
| 20–24 | London Art Fair, Business Design Centre |

## FEBRUARY
| | |
|---|---|
| 3–21 | Leicester Comedy Festival |
| 14 | British Academy Film Awards, Royal Opera House, London |
| 26–6 Mar | Bath Literature Festival |

## MARCH
| | |
|---|---|
| 3 | World Book Day |
| 8 | International Women's Day |
| \*8–15 | Belfast Children's Festival |
| 9–15 | BADA Antiques and Fine Art Fair, Duke of York Square, London |
| 10–13 | Crufts Dog Show, NEC, Birmingham |
| 17 | St Patrick's Day Parade, Piccadilly, London |
| 18–3 Apr | Ideal Home Show, Olympia, London |
| 21 | World Poetry Day |

## APRIL
| | |
|---|---|
| 2–10 | Oxford Literary Festival |
| 12–14 | London Book Fair, Olympia, London |
| 22 | Earth Day |
| \*24–1 May | 9th Stratford-upon-Avon Literary Festival |

## MAY
| | |
|---|---|
| 11–14 | Museums at Night, London |
| 21–28 | 82nd Glyndebourne Festival |
| 24–28 | RHS Chelsea Flower Show, Royal Hospital, London |
| \*25 | Belfast Titanic Maritime Festival |
| 26–5 June | 29th Hay Festival of Literature and the Arts, Hay-on-Wye |

## JUNE
| | |
|---|---|
| 4 | Strawberry Fair, Cambridge |
| 9–12 | Isle of Wight Festival |
| 11 | Trooping the Colour, Horse Guards Parade, London |
| 22–26 | Glastonbury Festival of Contemporary Performing Arts, Somerset |
| 23–26 | 175th Royal Highland Show, Edinburgh |

## JULY
| | |
|---|---|
| 5–10 | RHS Hampton Court Palace Flower Show, Surrey |
| 6–17 | Cheltenham Music Festival |
| \*15–10 Sep | BBC Promenade Concerts, Royal Albert Hall, London |
| 20–24 | RHS Flower Show, Tatton Park, Cheshire |
| Mid-Jul | The Welsh Proms, St David's Hall, Cardiff |
| \*21–24 | WOMAD Festival, Charlton Park, Wiltshire |
| 25–1 Aug | Three Choirs Festival, Gloucester |
| \*28–31 | Cambridge Folk Festival |
| 29–6 Aug | National Eisteddfod of Wales, Monmouthshire |

## AUGUST
| | |
|---|---|
| 5–27 | Edinburgh Military Tattoo, Edinburgh Castle |
| 5–29 | Edinburgh International Festival |
| 7 | Brecon Jazz Festival |
| 21–28 | International Beatles Week, Liverpool |
| \*27–28 | Notting Hill Carnival, London |

## SEPTEMBER
| | |
|---|---|
| \*1 | Brighton Pride, Brighton and Hove |
| 2–6 Nov | Blackpool Illuminations, Blackpool Promenade |
| 3 | Braemar Royal Highland Gathering, Aberdeenshire |
| 8 | International Literacy Day |
| Mid-Sep | TUC Annual Congress |
| 21–26 | Liberal Democrat Party Conference, Brighton |
| Sep–Oct | Labour Party Conference, Liverpool |
| Sep–Oct | Conservative Party Conference, Birmingham |

## OCTOBER
| | |
|---|---|
| 4–8 | Frieze Art Fair, Regent's Park, London |
| Early-Oct | Booker Prize Awards |
| Mid-Oct | BFI London Film Festival |

## NOVEMBER
| | |
|---|---|
| 12 Nov | Lord Mayor's Procession and Show, City of London |
| Mid-Nov | CBI Annual Conference |

# SPORTS EVENTS

**JANUARY 2016**

10–17  Snooker: Masters, Alexandra Palace, London

18–31  Tennis: Australian Open, Melbourne, Australia

**FEBRUARY**

6–19 Mar  Rugby Union: Six Nations Championship, Europe

7  American Football: Super Bowl 50, Santa Clara, USA

8–14  Squash: British National Championships, Manchester

28  Football: League Cup Final, Wembley Stadium, London

**MARCH**

2–6  Cycling: World Track Championships, London

11–3 Apr  Cricket: ICC World Twenty20, India

17–20  Athletics: World Indoor Championships, Portland, USA

**APRIL**

7–9  Horse Racing: Grand National, Aintree, Liverpool

7–10  Golf: Masters, Augusta, Georgia, USA

16–2 May  Snooker: World Championship, Crucible Theatre, Sheffield

24  Athletics: London Marathon

27  Rowing: The Boat Race, Putney to Mortlake, London

**MAY**

4–8  Equestrian: Badminton Horse Trials, Badminton

7  Horse Racing: Kentucky Derby, Louisville, Kentucky

Early May  Horse Racing: Guineas Festival, Newmarket

11–15  Equestrian: Royal Windsor Horse Show, Home Park, Windsor

14  Rugby Union: The European Rugby Champions Cup, Lyon, France

18  Football: UEFA Europa League Final, Basel, Switzerland

22–5 Jun  Tennis: French Open, Paris

21  Football: FA Cup Final, Wembley Stadium, London

21  Football: Scottish Cup Final, Hampden Park, Glasgow

28  Football: UEFA Champions League Final, Milan, Italy

28–10 Jun  Motorcycling: TT Races, Isle of Man

**JUNE**

3–26  Football: Copa America Centenario, USA

4  Horse Racing: The Derby, Epsom Downs

10  Football: 2016 UEFA European Championship, France

13–18  Golf: British Amateur Golf Championship, Royal Porthcawl, South Glamorgan

14–18  Horse Racing: Royal Ascot

16–19  Golf: US Open, Oakmont Country Club, Pennsylvania

27–10 Jul  Tennis: Wimbledon Championship, All England Lawn Tennis Club, London

29–3 Jul  Rowing: Henley Royal Regatta, Henley-on-Thames

**JULY**

2–24  Cycling: Tour de France

6–10  Athletics: European Athletics Championships, Amsterdam, the Netherlands

8  Horse Racing: Cambridgeshire Meeting, Newmarket

14–17  Golf: Open Championship, Royal Troon Golf Club, Ayrshire

23  Horse Racing: King George VI and Queen Elizabeth Diamond Stakes, Ascot

25–31  Golf: PGA Championship, Baltusrol Golf Club, New Jersey, USA

28–31  Golf: Women's British Open, Woburn Golf and Country Club

**AUGUST**

5–21  XXXI Summer Olympic Games, Rio de Janeiro, Brazil

6–13  Sailing: Cowes Week, Isle of Wight

21–28  Rowing: World Rowing Championships, Rotterdam

29  Rugby League: Challenge Cup Final, Wembley Stadium, London

29–11 Sep  Tennis: US Open, New York

**SEPTEMBER**

1–4  Equestrian: Burghley Horse Trials, Stamford, Lincolnshire

7–10  Horse Racing: St Leger, Doncaster

7–18  Summer Paralympic Games, Rio de Janeiro, Brazil

17–1 Oct  Ice Hockey: World Cup of Hockey, Canada

30–2 Oct  Golf: Ryder Cup, Hazeltine National Golf Club, Minnesota, USA

Late Sep–
Early Oct  Athletics: Great North Run, Newcastle

**OCTOBER**

Early Oct  Equestrian: Horse of the Year Show, NEC, Birmingham

Early–Mid-Oct  Rugby League: Super League Final, Old Trafford, Manchester

Mid-Oct  Horse Racing: Champions Meeting, Newmarket

Oct–Nov  Rugby League: Rugby League Four Nations, England

**NOVEMBER**

7–11  Tennis: ATP World Tour Finals, O2 Arena, London

# CENTENARIES

## 2016

**1716**
20 Jan    King Charles III of Spain, born
5 Aug    Silahdar Damat Ali Pasha, Grand Vizier of the Ottoman Empire (1713–16), died

**1816**
20 Mar    Queen Maria I of Portugal, died.
21 Apr    Charlotte Brontë, novelist and poet, born
5 Jun    Giovanni Paisiello, Italian composer, died
30 Jun    Richard Lindon, inventor of the rugby ball, born
9 Jul    Argentina declared independence from Spain
13 Dec    Ernst Werner von Siemens, German inventor and industrialist, born

**1916**
6 Feb    Rubén Darío, Nicaraguan writer, died
21 Feb    Battle of Verdun began
28 Feb    Henry James, writer, died
6 Mar    German car manufacturer BMW, founded
11 Mar    Harold Wilson, prime minister 1974–6, born
5 Apr    Gregory Peck, American actor, born
22 April    Yehudi Menuhin, violinist, born
24 April    Easter Rising began in Ireland
31 May    Battle of Jutland began
4 Jun    The Brusilov Offensive began
5 Jun    Lord Kitchener (1st Earl Kitchener), Secretary of State for War (1914–16), died
8 Jun    Francis Crick, molecular biologist and co-discoverer of the structure of DNA, born
1 Jul    Battle of the Somme began
23 Jul    Sir William Ramsay, Scottish chemist, born
13 Sep    Roald Dahl, children's author, born
11 Oct    King Otto of Bavaria, died
21 Oct    Karl von Stürgkh, Austrian prime minister, assassinated
26 Oct    François Mitterand, President of France 1981–95, born
21 Nov    Emperor Franz Joseph I of Austria, died
22 Nov    Jack London, American author, died
9 Dec    Kirk Douglas, American actor, born
17 Dec    Grigori Rasputin, Russian mystic and private adviser to the Romanovs, murdered

## 2017

**1517**
17 Jan    Henry Grey, 1st Duke of Suffolk and father of Lady Jane Grey, born
31 Oct    Martin Luther posted his Ninety-Five Theses on a church door in Wittenberg
21 Nov    Sikandar Lodi, Sultan of Delhi, died

**1617**
21 Mar    Pocahontas, Native American noblewoman, died
4 Apr    John Napier, mathematician who discovered logarithms, died

**1717**
19 Feb    David Garrick, actor and manager of the Drury Lane Theatre, born
13 May    Maria Theresa, Austrian Holy Roman Empress, born
24 Jun    The first Masonic Grand Lodge was founded in St. Paul's Churchyard
5 Sep    King George I issued the Act of Grace, pardoning all pirates
24 Sep    Horace Walpole, gothic novelist and son of Robert Walpole, born

**1817**
19 Jan    Argentine general José de San Martin lead an army across the Andes into Chile
25 Jan    *The Scotsman* was published for the first time in Edinburgh
8 Mar    The New York Stock Exchange was founded
12 Jul    Henry David Thoreau, American author and naturalist, born
17 Jul    Premier of Handel's *Water Music* in London
18 Jul    Jane Austen, novelist, died
5 Nov    The British East India Company defeated the Maratha Empire at the battle of Khadki
22 Nov    The Roman emerald mines at Sikait, Egypt were discovered
7 Dec    William Bligh, captain of the HMS *Bounty*, died

**1917**
10 Jan    William Frederick Cody, American frontiersman known as Buffalo Bill, died
12 Jan    Maharishi Mahesh Yogi, guru and spiritual leader, born
2 Feb    Bread rationing was introduced in the UK
8 Mar    Ferdinand von Zeppelin, German airship inventor, died
20 Mar    Vera Lynn, actor and singer, born
9 Apr    The First World War Battle of Vimy Ridge began in France
25 Apr    Ella Fitzgerald, American jazz singer, born
29 May    John F. Kennedy, 35th president of the USA, born
7 Jun    Dean Martin, American singer and member of the 'Rat Pack', born
10 June    Eric Hobsbawm, historian, born
17 Jul    The British Royal Family adopted the surname Windsor
31 Jul    Battle of Passchendaele (Third Battle of Ypres) began in Flanders, Belgium
28 Aug    Jack Kirby, American comic book artist, born
8 Nov    Colin Blythe, cricketer, died
16 Dec    Arthur C. Clarke, science fiction author, born

# THE UNITED KINGDOM

# THE UK IN FIGURES

The United Kingdom comprises Great Britain (England, Wales and Scotland) and Northern Ireland. The Isle of Man and the Channel Islands are Crown dependencies with their own legislative systems and are not part of the UK.

ABBREVIATIONS
ONS     Office for National Statistics
NISRA     Northern Ireland Statistics and Research Agency
All data is for the UK unless otherwise stated.

AREA OF THE UNITED KINGDOM

| | Sq. km | Sq. miles |
|---|---|---|
| United Kingdom | 243,122 | 93,870 |
| England | 130,280 | 50,301 |
| Wales | 20,733 | 8,005 |
| Scotland | 77,958 | 30,100 |
| Northern Ireland | 14,150 | 5,463 |

Source: ONS (Crown copyright)

## POPULATION

The first official census of population in England, Wales and Scotland was taken in 1801 and a census has been taken every ten years since, except in 1941 when there was no census because of the Second World War. The last official census in the UK was taken on 27 March 2011.

The first official census of population in Ireland was taken in 1841. However, all figures given below refer only to the area which is now Northern Ireland. Figures for Northern Ireland in 1921 and 1931 are estimates based on the censuses taken in 1926 and 1937 respectively.

Estimates of the population of England before 1801, calculated from the number of baptisms, burials and marriages, are:

| | | | |
|---|---|---|---|
| 1570 | 4,160,221 | 1670 | 5,773,646 |
| 1600 | 4,811,718 | 1700 | 6,045,008 |
| 1630 | 5,600,517 | 1750 | 6,517,035 |

Further details are available on the ONS website (W www.ons.gov.uk).

CENSUS RESULTS *Thousands*

| | United Kingdom | | | England and Wales | | | Scotland | | | Northern Ireland | | |
|---|---|---|---|---|---|---|---|---|---|---|---|---|
| | Total | Male | Female | Total | Male | Female | Total | Male | Female | Total | Male | Female |
| 1801 | — | — | — | 8,893 | 4,255 | 4,638 | 1,608 | 739 | 869 | — | — | — |
| 1811 | 13,368 | 6,368 | 7,000 | 10,165 | 4,874 | 5,291 | 1,806 | 826 | 980 | — | — | — |
| 1821 | 15,472 | 7,498 | 7,974 | 12,000 | 5,850 | 6,150 | 2,092 | 983 | 1,109 | — | — | — |
| 1831 | 17,835 | 8,647 | 9,188 | 13,897 | 6,771 | 7,126 | 2,364 | 1,114 | 1,250 | — | — | — |
| 1841 | 20,183 | 9,819 | 10,364 | 15,914 | 7,778 | 8,137 | 2,620 | 1,242 | 1,378 | 1,649 | 800 | 849 |
| 1851 | 22,259 | 10,855 | 11,404 | 17,928 | 8,781 | 9,146 | 2,889 | 1,376 | 1,513 | 1,443 | 698 | 745 |
| 1861 | 24,525 | 11,894 | 12,631 | 20,066 | 9,776 | 10,290 | 3,062 | 1,450 | 1,612 | 1,396 | 668 | 728 |
| 1871 | 27,431 | 13,309 | 14,122 | 22,712 | 11,059 | 11,653 | 3,360 | 1,603 | 1,757 | 1,359 | 647 | 712 |
| 1881 | 31,015 | 15,060 | 15,955 | 25,974 | 12,640 | 13,335 | 3,736 | 1,799 | 1,936 | 1,305 | 621 | 684 |
| 1891 | 34,264 | 16,593 | 17,671 | 29,003 | 14,060 | 14,942 | 4,026 | 1,943 | 2,083 | 1,236 | 590 | 646 |
| 1901 | 38,237 | 18,492 | 19,745 | 32,528 | 15,729 | 16,799 | 4,472 | 2,174 | 2,298 | 1,237 | 590 | 647 |
| 1911 | 42,082 | 20,357 | 21,725 | 36,070 | 17,446 | 18,625 | 4,761 | 2,309 | 2,452 | 1,251 | 603 | 648 |
| 1921 | 44,027 | 21,033 | 22,994 | 37,887 | 18,075 | 19,811 | 4,882 | 2,348 | 2,535 | 1,258 | 610 | 648 |
| 1931 | 46,038 | 22,060 | 23,978 | 39,952 | 19,133 | 20,819 | 4,843 | 2,326 | 2,517 | 1,243 | 601 | 642 |
| 1951 | 50,225 | 24,118 | 26,107 | 43,758 | 21,016 | 22,742 | 5,096 | 2,434 | 2,662 | 1,371 | 668 | 703 |
| 1961 | 52,709 | 25,481 | 27,228 | 46,105 | 22,304 | 23,801 | 5,179 | 2,483 | 2,697 | 1,425 | 694 | 731 |
| 1971 | 55,515 | 26,952 | 28,562 | 48,750 | 23,683 | 25,067 | 5,229 | 2,515 | 2,714 | 1,536 | 755 | 781 |
| 1981 | 55,848 | 27,104 | 28,742 | 49,155 | 23,873 | 25,281 | 5,131 | 2,466 | 2,664 | 1,533* | 750 | 783 |
| 1991 | 56,467 | 27,344 | 29,123 | 49,890 | 24,182 | 25,707 | 4,999 | 2,392 | 2,607 | 1,578 | 769 | 809 |
| 2001 | 58,789 | 28,581 | 30,208 | 52,042 | 25,327 | 26,715 | 5,062 | 2,432 | 2,630 | 1,685 | 821 | 864 |
| 2011 | 63,182 | 31,028 | 32,153 | 56,076 | 27,574 | 28,502 | 5,295 | 2,567 | 2,728 | 1,810 | 887 | 923 |

* Figure includes 44,500 non-enumerated persons

ISLANDS

| | Isle of Man | | | Jersey | | | Guernsey | | |
|---|---|---|---|---|---|---|---|---|---|
| | Total | Male | Female | Total | Male | Female | Total | Male | Female |
| 1901 | 54,752 | 25,496 | 29,256 | 52,576 | 23,940 | 28,636 | 40,446 | 19,652 | 20,794 |
| 1921 | 60,284 | 27,329 | 32,955 | 49,701 | 22,438 | 27,263 | 38,315 | 18,246 | 20,069 |
| 1951 | 55,123 | 25,749 | 29,464 | 57,296 | 27,282 | 30,014 | 43,652 | 21,221 | 22,431 |
| 1971 | 56,289 | 26,461 | 29,828 | 72,532 | 35,423 | 37,109 | 51,458 | 24,792 | 26,666 |
| 1991 | 69,788 | 33,693 | 36,095 | 84,082 | 40,862 | 43,220 | 58,867 | 28,297 | 30,570 |
| 2001 | 76,315 | 37,372 | 38,943 | 87,186 | 42,485 | 44,701 | 59,807 | 29,138 | 30,669 |
| 2006 | 80,058 | 39,523 | 40,535 | — | — | — | — | — | — |
| 2011 | 84,497 | 41,971 | 42,526 | 97,857 | 48,296 | 49,561 | 62,915 | 31,025 | 31,890 |

Source: Guernsey Annual Publication Bulletin, Isle of Man Government, States of Jersey Statistics Unit

# RESIDENT POPULATION

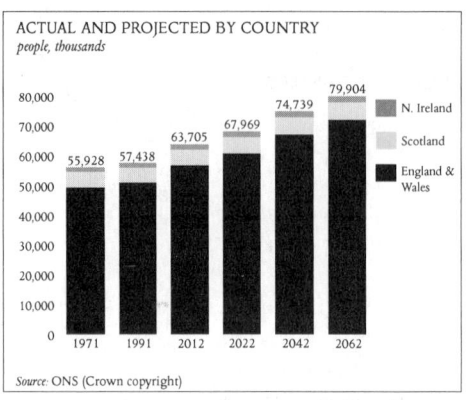

ACTUAL AND PROJECTED BY COUNTRY
*people, thousands*

Source: ONS (Crown copyright)

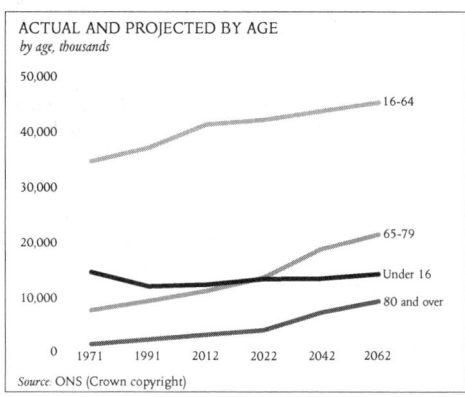

ACTUAL AND PROJECTED BY AGE
*by age, thousands*

Source: ONS (Crown copyright)

## NON-UK BORN RESIDENTS BY COUNTRY OF BIRTH
*thousands*

|                     | 2001 | 2013 |
|---------------------|------|------|
| India               | 468  | 760  |
| Poland              | 61   | 688  |
| Pakistan            | 321  | 516  |
| Republic of Ireland | 534  | 378  |
| Germany             | 266  | 297  |
| Bangladesh          | 154  | 228  |
| South Africa        | 141  | 221  |
| USA                 | 158  | 197  |
| China               | 53   | 191  |
| Nigeria             | 88   | 185  |

Source: ONS (Crown Copyright)

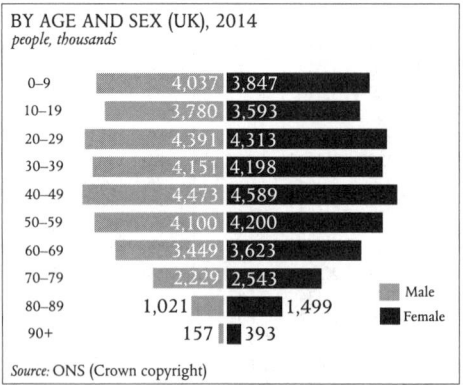

BY AGE AND SEX (UK), 2014
*people, thousands*

| Age | Male | Female |
|-----|------|--------|
| 0–9 | 4,037 | 3,847 |
| 10–19 | 3,780 | 3,593 |
| 20–29 | 4,391 | 4,313 |
| 30–39 | 4,151 | 4,198 |
| 40–49 | 4,473 | 4,589 |
| 50–59 | 4,100 | 4,200 |
| 60–69 | 3,449 | 3,623 |
| 70–79 | 2,229 | 2,543 |
| 80–89 | 1,021 | 1,499 |
| 90+ | 157 | 393 |

Source: ONS (Crown copyright)

# ASYLUM

## NATIONALITIES APPLYING FOR UK ASYLUM
*year ending in March*

| Top 5 Nationalities | 2014  | 2015  |
|---------------------|-------|-------|
| Eritrea             | 1,578 | 3,552 |
| Pakistan            | 3,294 | 2,421 |
| Syria               | 1,709 | 2,222 |
| Iran                | 2,234 | 2,000 |
| Sudan               | 776   | 1,603 |

Source: Home Office, Immigration Statistics

# BIRTHS

|                   | Live births 2014 | Birth rate* 2014 |
|-------------------|------------------|------------------|
| United Kingdom    | 776,352          | 12               |
| England and Wales | 695,233          | 12.1             |
| Scotland          | 56,725           | 10.6             |
| †Northern Ireland | 24,394           | 13.3             |

* Live births per 1,000 population
Source: General Register Office for Scotland, NISRA, ONS (Crown copyright)

## FERTILITY RATES

Total fertility rate is the average number of children which would be born to a woman if she experienced the age-specific fertility rates of the period in question throughout her child-bearing life span. The figures for the years 1960–2 are estimates.

|                   | 1960–2 | 2000 | 2014 |
|-------------------|--------|------|------|
| United Kingdom    | 3.07   | 1.62 | 1.80 |
| England and Wales | 2.77   | 1.65 | 1.83 |
| Scotland          | 2.98   | 1.48 | 1.62 |
| Northern Ireland  | 3.47   | 1.75 | 1.97 |

Source: General Register Office for Scotland, NISRA, ONS (Crown copyright)

## MATERNITY RATES FOR ENGLAND AND WALES 2013

|         | All maternities* | Singleton | All multiple† | Twins  | Triplets |
|---------|------------------|-----------|---------------|--------|----------|
| All ages | 690,820 | 680,037 | 10,783 | 10,593 | 187 |
| <20     | 29,126  | 28,948  | 178    | 176    | 2   |
| 20–24   | 119,208 | 118,144 | 1,064  | 1,052  | 12  |
| 25–29   | 195,032 | 192,550 | 2,482  | 2,446  | 35  |
| 30–34   | 209,515 | 205,884 | 3,631  | 3,574  | 57  |
| 35–39   | 109,546 | 107,037 | 2,509  | 2,451  | 56  |
| 40–44   | 26,551  | 25,807  | 744    | 728    | 16  |
| 45+     | 1,842   | 1,667   | 175    | 166    | 9   |

* Includes stillbirths
† Total includes rates for twins, triplets, quads and above
Source: ONS (Crown copyright)

TOP TEN BABY NAMES (ENGLAND AND WALES)

| | 1984 | | 2014 | |
|---|---|---|---|---|
| | *Girls* | *Boys* | *Girls* | *Boys* |
| 1 | Sarah | Christopher | Amelia | Oliver |
| 2 | Laura | James | Olivia | Jack |
| 3 | Gemma | David | Isla | Harry |
| 4 | Emma | Daniel | Emily | Jacob |
| 5 | Rebecca | Michael | Poppy | Charlie |
| 6 | Clare | Matthew | Ava | Thomas |
| 7 | Victoria | Andrew | Isabella | George |
| 8 | Samantha | Richard | Jessica | Oscar |
| 9 | Rachel | Paul | Lily | James |
| 10 | Amy | Mark | Sophie | William |

*Source:* ONS (Crown copyright)

LIVE BIRTHS (ENGLAND AND WALES)
*by age of mother and registration type*

*Outside marriage/civil partnership*

| Year | under 20 | 20–29 | 30–39 | 40+ | All ages |
|---|---|---|---|---|---|
| 1943 | 6,385 | 25,423 | 10,357 | 1,544 | 43,709 |
| 1963 | 15,603 | 30,505 | 11,197 | 1,799 | 59,104 |
| 1983 | 30,423 | 54,599 | 13,391 | 838 | 99,211 |
| 2003 | 39,898 | 133,972 | 77,003 | 6,352 | 257,225 |
| 2013 | 27,864 | 188,512 | 103,384 | 11,134 | 330,894 |

*Within marriage/civil partnership*

| Year | under 20 | 20–29 | 30–39 | 40+ | All ages |
|---|---|---|---|---|---|
| 1943 | 17,877 | 346,601 | 247,001 | 27,122 | 640,625 |
| 1963 | 56,037 | 500,295 | 216,900 | 21,719 | 794,951 |
| 1983 | 23,636 | 351,371 | 148,882 | 6,034 | 529,923 |
| 2003 | 4,338 | 139,581 | 207,597 | 12,728 | 364,244 |
| 2013 | 1,272 | 127,900 | 220,422 | 18,024 | 367,618 |

*Source:* ONS (Crown copyright)

## MARRIAGE AND DIVORCE

| | Marriages 2014 | Divorces 2014 |
|---|---|---|
| United Kingdom | *299,414 | *130,162 |
| England and Wales | *262,240 | *118,140 |
| Scotland | 29,048 | 9,619 |
| Northern Ireland | 8,126 | 2,403 |

* Figures for England and Wales are for 2012
*Source:* NISRA, ONS (Crown copyright), Scottish Government

## LEGAL ABORTIONS

| | 2003 | 2014 |
|---|---|---|
| England and Wales | 181,582 | 184,571 |
| Scotland | 12,308 | 11,475 |

*Source:* Department of Health, NHS Scotland

## DEATHS

INFANT MORTALITY RATE 2013*

| | |
|---|---|
| United Kingdom | 3.9 |
| England and Wales | 3.8 |
| Scotland | 3.3 |
| Northern Ireland | 4.6 |

* Deaths of infants under one year of age per 1,000 live births
*Source:* NISRA, ONS (Crown copyright), Scottish Government

DEATHS IN THE UK
*people*

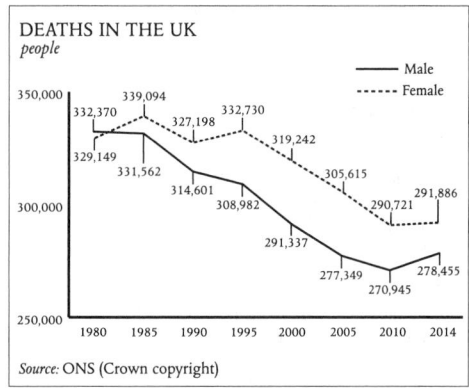

*Source:* ONS (Crown copyright)

## EMPLOYMENT

MEDIAN FULL-TIME GROSS ANNUAL EARNINGS BY REGION (£)

| Region | 2004 | 2014 |
|---|---|---|
| UK | 22,056 | 27,195 |
| England | 22,418 | 27,487 |
| North East | 19,247 | 24,876 |
| North West | 20,717 | 25,229 |
| Yorkshire and the Humber | 20,433 | 24,999 |
| East Midlands | 20,691 | 25,027 |
| West Midlands | 20,765 | 24,920 |
| East | 22,242 | 26,830 |
| London | 28,750 | 35,069 |
| South East | 23,748 | 28,629 |
| South West | 20,694 | 25,571 |
| Wales | 20,085 | 24,384 |
| Scotland | 20,598 | 27,045 |
| Northern Ireland | 19,622 | 24,020 |

*Source:* ONS (Crown Copyright)

## HOUSE PRICES

*Average Price*

| Year | £ | Year | £ |
|---|---|---|---|
| 1930 | 1,000 | 2000 | 102,000 |
| 1950 | 2,000 | 2005 | 191,000 |
| 1960 | 3,000 | 2010 | 251,000 |
| 1970 | 5,000 | 2011 | 245,000 |
| 1980 | 24,000 | 2012 | 246,000 |
| 1990 | 60,000 | 2013 | 251,000 |
| 1995 | 66,000 | 2014 | 267,000 |

*Source:* ONS (Crown Copyright)

## UK RESIDENTS' VISITS ABROAD

| Year | Visits (thousands) | Spending (£m) |
|---|---|---|
| 1980 | 17,507 | 2,738 |
| 1985 | 21,610 | 4,871 |
| 1990 | 31,150 | 9,886 |
| 1995 | 41,345 | 15,386 |
| 2000 | 56,837 | 24,251 |
| 2005 | 66,441 | 32,154 |
| 2010 | 55,562 | 31,820 |
| 2011 | 56,836 | 31,701 |
| 2012 | 56,538 | 32,450 |
| 2013 | 57,792 | 34,510 |
| 2014 | 60,082 | 35,537 |

## DEATHS BY CAUSE, 2014

| | England and Wales | Scotland | N. Ireland |
|---|---:|---:|---:|
| *Total deaths* | 501,424 | 54,239 | 14,678 |
| Deaths from natural causes | 481,564 | 51,678 | 13,977 |
| Certain infectious and parasitic diseases | 5,182 | 716 | 154 |
| Intestinal infectious diseases | 1,272 | 132 | 46 |
| Respiratory and other tuberculosis | 289 | 28 | 6 |
| Meningococcal infection | 44 | 2 | 0 |
| Viral hepatitis | 262 | 22 | 3 |
| Human immunodeficiency virus (HIV) | 159 | 14 | 5 |
| Neoplasms | 147,000 | 16,167 | 4,415 |
| Malignant neoplasms | 143,638 | 15,840 | 4,323 |
| Malignant neoplasm of trachea, bronchus and lung | 30,868 | 4,117 | 978 |
| Malignant melanoma of skin | 2,237 | 176 | 53 |
| Malignant neoplasm of breast | 10,158 | 976 | 323 |
| Malignant neoplasm of cervix uteri | 780 | 88 | 25 |
| Malignant neoplasm of prostate | 10,153 | 906 | 242 |
| Leukaemia | 4,118 | 364 | — |
| Diseases of the blood and blood-forming organs and certain disorders involving the immune mechanism | 960 | 86 | 29 |
| Endocrine, nutritional and metabolic diseases | 7,176 | 1,017 | 284 |
| Diabetes mellitus | 5,314 | 800 | 199 |
| Mental and behavioural disorders | 41,113 | 3,952 | 1,137 |
| Vascular and unspecified dementia | 40,200 | 3,576 | — |
| Diseases of the nervous system | 24,432 | 2,593 | 801 |
| Meningitis (excluding meningococcal) | 150 | 13 | 3 |
| Alzheimer's disease | 11,298 | 1,339 | 406 |
| Diseases of the circulatory system | 135,904 | 15,016 | 3,719 |
| Ischaemic heart diseases | 60,509 | 6,872 | 1,782 |
| Cerebrovascular diseases | 34,157 | 4,123 | 1,002 |
| Diseases of the respiratory system | 66,572 | 6,706 | 2,004 |
| Influenza | 86 | 23 | 4 |
| Pneumonia | 25,336 | 1,719 | 739 |
| Bronchitis, emphysema and other chronic obstructive pulmonary diseases | 26,267 | 3,116 | 728 |
| Asthma | 1,114 | 64 | 30 |
| Diseases of the digestive system | 24,219 | 2,952 | 696 |
| Gastric and duodenal ulcer | 1,870 | 128 | 31 |
| Diseases of the liver | 7,655 | 981 | 177 |
| Diseases of the skin and subcutaneous tissue | 1,753 | 163 | 30 |
| Diseases of the musculo-skeletal system and connective tissue | 3,844 | 327 | 94 |
| Osteoporosis | 1,025 | 48 | 11 |
| Diseases of the genitourinary system | 8,811 | 1,169 | 319 |
| Complications of pregnancy, childbirth and the puerperium | 46 | 5 | 1 |
| Certain conditions originating in the perinatal period* | 195 | 105 | 64 |
| Congenital malformations, deformations and chromosomal abnormalities* | 1,369 | 150 | 85 |
| Symptoms, signs and abnormal findings not classified elsewhere | 11,091 | 549 | 145 |
| Senility | 7,701 | 286 | 104 |
| Sudden infant death syndrome | 129 | 14 | 5 |
| Deaths from external causes | 19,860 | 2,561 | 701 |
| Suicide and intentional self-harm | 4,047 | 549 | 191 |
| Assault | †293 | 52 | 16 |

\* Excludes neonatal deaths (those at age under 28 days): for England and Wales neonatal deaths are included in the total number of deaths but excluded from the cause figures

† This will not be a true figure as registration of homicide and assault deaths in England and Wales is often delayed by adjourned inquests

*Source:* General Register Office for Scotland, NISRA, ONS (Crown copyright)

# THE NATIONAL FLAG

The national flag of the United Kingdom is the Union Flag, generally known as the Union Jack.

The Union Flag is a combination of the cross of St George, patron saint of England, the cross of St Andrew, patron saint of Scotland and the cross of St Patrick, patron saint of Ireland.

*Cross of St George:* cross Gules in a field Argent (red cross on a white ground)

*Cross of St Andrew:* saltire Argent in a field Azure (white diagonal cross on a blue ground)

*Cross of St Patrick:* saltire Gules in a field Argent (red diagonal cross on a white ground)

A flag combining the cross of St George and the cross of St Andrew was first introduced by royal decree in 1606 following the conjoining of the English and Scottish crowns in 1603. In 1707 this flag became the flag of Great Britain after the parliaments of the two kingdoms were united. The cross of St Patrick was added in 1801 after the union of Great Britain and Ireland.

*See also* Flags of the World colour plates.

## FLYING THE UNION FLAG

The correct orientation of the Union Flag when flying is with the broader diagonal band of white uppermost in the hoist (ie near the pole) and the narrower diagonal band of white uppermost in the fly (ie furthest from the pole).

The flying of the Union Flag on government buildings is decided by the Department for Culture, Media and Sport (DCMS) at the Queen's command. There is no formal definition of a government building but it is generally accepted to mean a building owned or used by the Crown and/or predominantly occupied or used by civil servants or the Armed Forces.

The Scottish or Welsh governments are responsible for drawing up their own flag-flying guidance for their buildings. In Northern Ireland, the flying of flags is constrained by The Flags Regulations (Northern Ireland) 2000 and the Police Emblems and Flag Regulations (Northern Ireland) 2002. Individuals, local authorities and other organisations may fly the Union Flag whenever they wish, subject to compliance with any local planning requirement.

## FLAGS AT HALF-MAST

Flags are flown at half-mast (ie two-thirds up between the top and bottom of the flagstaff) on the following occasions:
• from the announcement of the death of the sovereign until the funeral
• the death or funeral of a member of the royal family*
• the funerals of foreign rulers*
• the funerals of prime ministers and ex-prime ministers of the UK*
• the funerals of first ministers and ex-first ministers of Scotland, Wales and Northern Ireland (unless otherwise commanded by the sovereign, this only applies to flags in their respective countries)*
• other occasions by special command from the Queen

* By special command from the Queen in each case

## DAYS FOR FLYING FLAGS

On 25 March 2008 the DCMS announced that UK government departments in England, Scotland and Wales may fly the Union Flag on their buildings whenever they choose and not just on the designated days listed below. In addition, on the patron saints' days of Scotland and Wales, the appropriate national flag may be flown alongside the Union Flag on UK government buildings in the wider Whitehall area. When flying on designated days flags are hoisted from 8am to sunset.

| | |
|---|---|
| Duchess of Cambridge's birthday | 9 Jan |
| Countess of Wessex's birthday | 20 Jan |
| Accession of the Queen | 6 Feb |
| Duke of York's birthday | 19 Feb |
| St David's Day (in Wales only)* | 1 Mar |
| Earl of Wessex's birthday | 10 Mar |
| Commonwealth Day (2016) | 14 Mar |
| St Patrick's Day (in Northern Ireland only)† | 17 Mar |
| The Queen's birthday | 21 Apr |
| St George's Day (in England only)* | 23 Apr |
| Europe Day† | 9 May |
| Coronation Day | 2 Jun |
| Duke of Edinburgh's birthday | 10 Jun |
| The Queen's official birthday (2016) | 11 Jun |
| Duke of Cambridge's birthday | 21 Jun |
| Duchess of Cornwall's birthday | 17 Jul |
| Princess Royal's birthday | 15 Aug |
| Remembrance Day (2016) | 13 Nov |
| Prince of Wales' birthday | 14 Nov |
| Wedding Day of the Queen | 20 Nov |
| St Andrew's Day (in Scotland only)* | 30 Nov |
| Opening of parliament by the Queen‡ | |
| Prorogation of parliament by the Queen‡ | |

* The appropriate national flag, or the European flag, may be flown in addition to the Union Flag (where there are two or more flagpoles), but not in a superior position
† Only the Union Flag should be flown
‡ Only in the Greater London area, whether or not the Queen performs the ceremony in person

## THE ROYAL STANDARD

The Royal Standard comprises four quarterings – two for England (three lions passant), one for Scotland* (a lion rampant) and one for Ireland (a harp).

The Royal Standard is flown when the Queen is in residence at a royal palace, on transport being used by the Queen for official journeys and from Victoria Tower when the Queen attends parliament. It may also be flown on any building (excluding ecclesiastical buildings) during a visit by the Queen. If the Queen is to be present in a building, advice on flag flying can be obtained from the DCMS.

The Royal Standard is never flown at half-mast, even after the death of the sovereign, as the new monarch immediately succeeds to the throne.

* In Scotland a version with two Scottish quarterings is used

# THE ROYAL FAMILY

## THE SOVEREIGN

ELIZABETH II, by the Grace of God, of the United Kingdom of Great Britain and Northern Ireland and of her other Realms and Territories Queen, Head of the Commonwealth, Defender of the Faith
Her Majesty Elizabeth Alexandra Mary of Windsor, elder daughter of King George VI and of HM Queen Elizabeth the Queen Mother
*Born* 21 April 1926, at 17 Bruton Street, London W1
*Ascended the throne* 6 February 1952
*Crowned* 2 June 1953, at Westminster Abbey
*Married* 20 November 1947, in Westminster Abbey, HRH the Prince Philip, Duke of Edinburgh
*Official residences* Buckingham Palace, London SW1A 1AA; Windsor Castle, Berks; Palace of Holyroodhouse, Edinburgh
*Private residences* Sandringham, Norfolk; Balmoral Castle, Aberdeenshire

## HUSBAND OF THE QUEEN

HRH THE PRINCE PHILIP, DUKE OF EDINBURGH, KG, KT, OM, GBE, Royal Victorian Chain, AC, QSO, PC, Ranger of Windsor Park
*Born* 10 June 1921, son of Prince and Princess Andrew of Greece and Denmark, naturalised a British subject 1947, created Duke of Edinburgh, Earl of Merioneth and Baron Greenwich 1947

## CHILDREN OF THE QUEEN

HRH THE PRINCE OF WALES (Prince Charles Philip Arthur George), KG, KT, GCB, OM and Great Master of the Order of the Bath, AK, QSO, PC, ADC(P)
*Born* 14 November 1948, created Prince of Wales and Earl of Chester 1958, succeeded as Duke of Cornwall, Duke of Rothesay, Earl of Carrick and Baron Renfrew, Lord of the Isles and Great Steward of Scotland 1952
*Married* (1) 29 July 1981 Lady Diana Frances Spencer (Diana, Princess of Wales (1961–97), youngest daughter of the 8th Earl Spencer and the Hon. Mrs Shand Kydd), marriage dissolved 1996; (2) 9 April 2005 Mrs Camilla Rosemary Parker Bowles, now HRH the Duchess of Cornwall, GCVO (*born* 17 July 1947, daughter of Major Bruce Shand and the Hon. Mrs Rosalind Shand)
*Residences* Clarence House, London SW1A 1BA; Highgrove, Doughton, Tetbury, Glos GL8 8TN; Birkhall, Ballater, Aberdeenshire
*Issue*
1. HRH Duke of Cambridge (Prince William Arthur Philip Louis), KG, KT *born* 21 June 1982, *created* Duke of Cambridge, Earl of Strathearn and Baron Carrickfergus 2011 *married* 29 April 2011 Catherine Elizabeth Middleton, now HRH the Duchess of Cambridge (*born* 9 January 1982, elder daughter of Michael and Carole Middleton), and has issue, HRH Prince George of Cambridge (Prince George Alexander Louis), *born* 22 July 2013; HRH Princess Charlotte of Cambridge (Princess Charlotte Elizabeth Diana), *born* 2 May 2015
*Residence* Kensington Palace, London W8 4PU; Anmer Hall, Norfolk PE31 6RW
2. HRH Prince Henry of Wales (Prince Henry Charles Albert David), KCVO *born* 15 September 1984
*Residence* Nottingham Cottage, Kensington Palace, London W8 4PU

HRH THE PRINCESS ROYAL (Princess Anne Elizabeth Alice Louise), KG, KT, GCVO
*Born* 15 August 1950, declared the Princess Royal 1987
*Married* (1) 14 November 1973 Captain Mark Anthony Peter Phillips, CVO (*born* 22 September 1948); marriage dissolved 1992; (2) 12 December 1992 Vice-Adm. Sir Timothy James Hamilton Laurence, KCVO, CB, ADC (P) (*born* 1 March 1955)
*Residence* Gatcombe Park, Minchinhampton, Glos GL6 9AT
*Issue*
1. Peter Mark Andrew Phillips, *born* 15 November 1977, *married* 17 May 2008 Autumn Patricia Kelly, and has issue, Savannah Phillips, *born* 29 December 2010; Isla Elizabeth Phillips, *born* 29 March 2012
2. Zara Anne Elizabeth Tindall, MBE, *born* 15 May 1981, *married* 30 July 2011 Michael James Tindall, MBE, and has issue, Mia Grace Tindall, *born* 17 January 2014

HRH THE DUKE OF YORK (Prince Andrew Albert Christian Edward), KG, GCVO, ADC(P)
*Born* 19 February 1960, created Duke of York, Earl of Inverness and Baron Killyleagh 1986
*Married* 23 July 1986 Sarah Margaret Ferguson, now Sarah, Duchess of York (*born* 15 October 1959, younger daughter of Major Ronald Ferguson and Mrs Hector Barrantes), marriage dissolved 1996
*Residence* Royal Lodge, Windsor Great Park, Berks
*Issue*
1. HRH Princess Beatrice of York (Princess Beatrice Elizabeth Mary), *born* 8 August 1988
2. HRH Princess Eugenie of York (Princess Eugenie Victoria Helena), *born* 23 March 1990

HRH THE EARL OF WESSEX (Prince Edward Antony Richard Louis), KG, GCVO, ADC(P)
*Born* 10 March 1964, created Earl of Wessex, Viscount Severn 1999
*Married* 19 June 1999 Sophie Helen Rhys-Jones, now HRH the Countess of Wessex, GCVO (*born* 20 January 1965, daughter of Mr and Mrs Christopher Rhys-Jones)
*Residence* Bagshot Park, Bagshot, Surrey GU19 5HS
*Issue*
1. Lady Louise Mountbatten-Windsor (Louise Alice Elizabeth Mary Mountbatten-Windsor), *born* 8 November 2003
2. Viscount Severn (James Alexander Philip Theo Mountbatten-Windsor), *born* 17 December 2007

## NEPHEW AND NIECE OF THE QUEEN

Children of HRH the Princess Margaret, Countess of Snowdon and the Earl of Snowdon (*see* House of Windsor):

DAVID ALBERT CHARLES ARMSTRONG-JONES, VISCOUNT LINLEY, *born* 3 November 1961, *married* 8 October 1993 Hon. Serena Alleyne Stanhope, and has issue, Hon. Charles Patrick Inigo Armstrong-Jones, *born* 1 July 1999; Hon. Margarita Elizabeth Alleyne Armstrong-Jones, *born* 14 May 2002

LADY SARAH CHATTO (Sarah Frances Elizabeth), *born* 1 May 1964, *married* 14 July 1994 Daniel Chatto, and has issue, Samuel David Benedict Chatto, *born* 28 July 1996; Arthur Robert Nathaniel Chatto, *born* 5 February 1999

# COUSINS OF THE QUEEN

Child of HRH the Duke of Gloucester and HRH Princess Alice, Duchess of Gloucester (*see* House of Windsor):

HRH THE DUKE OF GLOUCESTER (Prince Richard Alexander Walter George), KG, GCVO, Grand Prior of the Order of St John of Jerusalem
*Born* 26 August 1944
*Married* 8 July 1972 Birgitte Eva van Deurs, now HRH the Duchess of Gloucester, GCVO (*born* 20 June 1946, daughter of Asger Henriksen and Vivian van Deurs)
*Residence* Kensington Palace, London W8 4PU
*Issue*
1. Earl of Ulster (Alexander Patrick Gregers Richard), *born* 24 October 1974 *married* 22 June 2002 Dr Claire Alexandra Booth, and has issue, Lord Culloden (Xan Richard Anders), *born* 12 March 2007; Lady Cosima Windsor (Cosima Rose Alexandra), *born* 20 May 2010
2. Lady Davina Lewis (Davina Elizabeth Alice Benedikte), *born* 19 November 1977 *married* 31 July 2004 Gary Christie Lewis, and has issue, Senna Kowhai Lewis, *born* 22 June 2010; Tane Mahuta Lewis, *born* 25 May 2012
3. Lady Rose Gilman (Rose Victoria Birgitte Louise), *born* 1 March 1980 *married* 19 July 2008 George Edward Gilman, and has issue, Lyla Beatrix Christabel Gilman, *born* 30 May 2010; Rufus Gilman, *born* 2 November 2012

Children of HRH the Duke of Kent and Princess Marina, Duchess of Kent (*see* House of Windsor):

HRH THE DUKE OF KENT (Prince Edward George Nicholas Paul Patrick), KG, GCMG, GCVO, ADC(P)
*Born* 9 October 1935
*Married* 8 June 1961 Katharine Lucy Mary Worsley, now HRH the Duchess of Kent, GCVO (*born* 22 February 1933, daughter of Sir William Worsley, Bt.)
*Residence* Wren House, Palace Green, London W8 4PY
*Issue*
1. Earl of St Andrews (George Philip Nicholas), *born* 26 June 1962, *married* 9 January 1988 Sylvana Tomaselli, and has issue, Lord Downpatrick (Edward Edmund Maximilian George), *born* 2 December 1988; Lady Marina-Charlotte Windsor (Marina-Charlotte Alexandra Katharine Helen), *born* 30 September 1992; Lady Amelia Windsor (Amelia Sophia Theodora Mary Margaret), *born* 24 August 1995

2. Lady Helen Taylor (Helen Marina Lucy), *born* 28 April 1964, *married* 18 July 1992 Timothy Verner Taylor, and has issue, Columbus George Donald Taylor, *born* 6 August 1994; Cassius Edward Taylor, *born* 26 December 1996; Eloise Olivia Katharine Taylor, *born* 3 March 2003; Estella Olga Elizabeth Taylor, *born* 21 December 2004
3. Lord Nicholas Windsor (Nicholas Charles Edward Jonathan), *born* 25 July 1970, *married* 4 November 2006 Princess Paola Doimi de Lupis Frankopan Subic Zrinski, and has issue, Albert Louis Philip Edward Windsor, *born* 22 September 2007; Leopold Ernest Augustus Guelph Windsor, *born* 8 September 2009; Louis Arthur Nicholas Felix Windsor, *born* 27 May 2014

HRH PRINCESS ALEXANDRA, THE HON. LADY OGILVY (Princess Alexandra Helen Elizabeth Olga Christabel), KG, GCVO
*Born* 25 December 1936
*Married* 24 April 1963 the Rt. Hon. Sir Angus Ogilvy, KCVO (1928–2004), second son of 12th Earl of Airlie
*Residence* Thatched House Lodge, Richmond Park, Surrey TW10 5HP
*Issue*
1. James Robert Bruce Ogilvy, *born* 29 February 1964, *married* 30 July 1988 Julia Rawlinson, and has issue, Flora Alexandra Ogilvy, *born* 15 December 1994; Alexander Charles Ogilvy, *born* 12 November 1996
2. Marina Victoria Alexandra Ogilvy, *born* 31 July 1966, *married* 2 February 1990 Paul Julian Mowatt (marriage dissolved 1997), and has issue, Zenouska May Mowatt, *born* 26 May 1990; Christian Alexander Mowatt, *born* 4 June 1993

HRH PRINCE MICHAEL OF KENT (Prince Michael George Charles Franklin), GCVO
*Born* 4 July 1942
*Married* 30 June 1978 Baroness Marie-Christine Agnes Hedwig Ida von Reibnitz, now HRH Princess Michael of Kent (*born* 15 January 1945, daughter of Baron Gunther von Reibnitz)
*Residence* Kensington Palace, London W8 4PU
*Issue*
1. Lord Frederick Windsor (Frederick Michael George David Louis), *born* 6 April 1979, *married* 12 September 2009 Sophie Winkleman, and has issue, Maud Elizabeth Daphne Marina, *born* 15 August 2013
2. Lady Gabriella Windsor (Gabriella Marina Alexandra Ophelia), *born* 23 April 1981

# ORDER OF SUCCESSION

The Succession to the Crown Act 2013, received royal assent on 25 April 2013 and makes provision for the order of succession to the Crown not to be dependent on gender and for those members of the royal family married to a Roman Catholic to retain the right of succession to the throne. The provisions of the Act came into force on 26 March 2015, following its ratification by all 15 Realms of the Commonwealth.

On the Act's commencement HRH Prince Michael of Kent and the Earl of St Andrews were restored to the succession. In addition, all male members of the royal family born after 28 October 2011 no longer precede any elder female siblings; and their place in the order of succession changed accordingly.

The following list includes all living descendants of the sons of King George V eligible to succeed to the Crown under the current legislation. Lord Nicholas Windsor, Lord Downpatrick and Lady Marina-Charlotte Windsor renounced their rights to the throne on converting to Roman Catholicism in 2001, 2003 and 2008 respectively. Their children remain in succession provided that they are in communion with the Church of England.

| | | | |
|---|---|---|---|
| 1 | HRH the Prince of Wales | 29 | Senna Lewis |
| 2 | HRH the Duke of Cambridge | 30 | Tane Lewis |
| 3 | HRH Prince George of Cambridge | 31 | Lady Rose Gilman |
| 4 | HRH Princess Charlotte of Cambridge | 32 | Lyla Gilman |
| 5 | HRH Prince Henry of Wales | 33 | Rufus Gilman |
| 6 | HRH the Duke of York | 34 | HRH the Duke of Kent |
| 7 | HRH Princess Beatrice of York | 35 | Earl of St Andrews |
| 8 | HRH Princess Eugenie of York | 36 | Lady Amelia Windsor |
| 9 | HRH the Earl of Wessex | 37 | Albert Windsor |
| 10 | Viscount Severn | 38 | Leopold Windsor |
| 11 | Lady Louise Mountbatten-Windsor | 39 | Louis Windsor |
| 12 | HRH the Princess Royal | 40 | Lady Helen Taylor |
| 13 | Peter Phillips | 41 | Columbus Taylor |
| 14 | Savannah Phillips | 42 | Cassius Taylor |
| 15 | Isla Phillips | 43 | Eloise Taylor |
| 16 | Zara Tindall | 44 | Estella Taylor |
| 17 | Mia Tindall | 45 | HRH Prince Michael of Kent |
| 18 | Viscount Linley | 46 | Lord Frederick Windsor |
| 19 | Hon. Charles Armstrong-Jones | 47 | Maud Windsor |
| 20 | Hon. Margarita Armstrong-Jones | 48 | Lady Gabriella Windsor |
| 21 | Lady Sarah Chatto | 49 | HRH Princess Alexandra, the Hon. Lady Ogilvy |
| 22 | Samuel Chatto | 50 | James Ogilvy |
| 23 | Arthur Chatto | 51 | Alexander Ogilvy |
| 24 | HRH the Duke of Gloucester | 52 | Flora Ogilvy |
| 25 | Earl of Ulster | 53 | Marina Ogilvy |
| 26 | Lord Culloden | 54 | Christian Mowatt |
| 27 | Lady Cosima Windsor | 55 | Zenouska Mowatt |
| 28 | Lady Davina Lewis | | |

# ROYAL HOUSEHOLD

The PRIVATE SECRETARY is responsible for:

- informing and advising the Queen on constitutional, governmental and political matters in the UK, her other Realms and the wider Commonwealth, including communications with the prime minister and government departments
- organising the Queen's domestic and overseas official programme
- the Queen's speeches, messages, patronage, photographs, portraits and official presents
- communications in connection with the role of the royal family
- dealing with correspondence to the Queen from members of the public
- royal travel policy
- coordinating and initiating research to support engagements by members of the royal family

The DIRECTOR OF ROYAL COMMUNICATIONS is in charge of Buckingham Palace's communications office and reports to the Private Secretary. The director is responsible for:

- developing communications strategies to enhance the public understanding of the role of the monarchy
- briefing the British and international media on the role and duties of the Queen and issues relating to the royal family
- responding to media enquiries
- arranging media facilities in the UK and overseas to support royal functions and engagements
- the management of the royal website

The Private Secretary is keeper of the royal archives and is responsible for the care of the records of the sovereign and the royal household from previous reigns, preserved in the royal archives at Windsor. As keeper, it is the Private Secretary's responsibility to ensure the proper management of the records of the present reign with a view to their transfer to the archives as and when appropriate. The Private Secretary is an *ex officio* trustee of the Royal Collection Trust.

The KEEPER OF THE PRIVY PURSE AND TREASURER TO THE QUEEN is responsible for:

- the Sovereign Grant, which is the money paid from the government's Consolidated Fund to meet official expenditure relating to the Queen's duties as Head of State and Head of the Commonwealth and is provided by the government in return for the net surplus from the Crown Estate and other hereditary revenues (*see also* Royal Finances)
- through the Director of Human Resources, the planning and management of personnel policy across the royal household, the allocation of employee and pensioner housing and the administration of all its pension schemes and private estates employees
- information systems and telecommunications
- property services at occupied royal palaces in England, comprising Buckingham Palace, St James's Palace, Clarence House, Marlborough House Mews, the residential and office areas of Kensington Palace, Windsor Castle and buildings in the Home and Great Parks of Windsor and Hampton Court Mews and Paddocks
- audit services
- health and safety; insurance matters
- the privy purse, which is mainly financed by the net income of the Duchy of Lancaster, and meets both official and private expenditure incurred by the Queen

- liaison with other members of the royal family and their households on financial matters
- the Queen's private estates at Sandringham and Balmoral, the Queen's Racing Establishment and the Royal Studs and liaison with the Ascot Authority
- the Home Park at Windsor and liaison with the Crown Estate Commissioners concerning the Home Park and the Great Park at Windsor
- the Royal Philatelic Collection
- administrative aspects of the Military Knights of Windsor
- administration of the Royal Victorian Order, of which the Keeper of the Privy Purse is secretary, Long and Faithful Service Medals, and the Queen's cups, medals and prizes, and policy on commemorative medals

The Keeper of the Privy Purse is one of three royal trustees (in respect of his responsibilities for the Sovereign Grant) and is Receiver-General of the Duchy of Lancaster and a member of the Duchy's Council.

The Keeper of the Privy Purse is an *ex officio* trustee of the Royal Collection Trust and the Historic Royal Palaces Trust.

The DIRECTOR OF THE PROPERTY SECTION has day-to-day responsibility for the royal household's property section:

- fire and health and safety
- repairs and refurbishment of buildings and new building work
- utilities and telecommunications
- putting up stages, tents and other work in connection with ceremonial occasions, garden parties and other official functions

The property section is also responsible, on a sub-contract basis from the DCMS, for the maintenance of Marlborough House (which is occupied by the Commonwealth Secretariat).

The MASTER OF THE HOUSEHOLD is responsible for:

- delivering the majority of the official and private entertaining in the Queen's annual programme across all the occupied palaces and residences in the UK when required
- periodic support for entertaining by all other members of the royal family
- furnishings and internal decorative refurbishment of all the occupied palaces in the UK in conjunction with the Director, Royal Collection Trust
- all operational, domestic and kitchen staff in the royal household

The COMPTROLLER, LORD CHAMBERLAIN'S OFFICE is responsible for:

- the organisation of all ceremonial engagements, including state visits to the Queen in the UK, royal weddings and funerals, the state opening of parliament, Guards of Honour at Buckingham Palace, investitures, and the Garter and Thistle ceremonies
- garden parties at Buckingham Palace and the Palace of Holyroodhouse
- the Crown Jewels, which are part of the Royal Collection, when they are in use on state occasions
- coordination of the arrangements for the Queen to be represented at funerals and memorial services and at the arrival and departure of visiting heads of state
- delivery of all official and approved travel operations

- advising on matters of precedence, style and titles, dress, flying of flags, gun salutes, mourning and other ceremonial issues
- supervising the applications for Royal Warrants of Appointment
- advising on the commercial use of royal emblems and contemporary royal photographs
- the ecclesiastical household, the medical household, the bodyguards and certain ceremonial appointments such as Gentlemen Ushers and Pages of Honour
- the Lords in Waiting, who represent the Queen on various occasions and escort visiting heads of state during incoming state visits
- the Queen's bargemaster and watermen and the Queen's swans
- the Royal Almonry and Royal Maundy Service

The Comptroller is also responsible for the Royal Mews, assisted by the CROWN EQUERRY, who has day-to-day responsibility for:

- the provision of carriage processions for the state opening of parliament, state visits, Trooping of the Colour, Royal Ascot, the Garter Ceremony, the Thistle Service, the presentation of credentials to the Queen by incoming foreign ambassadors and high commissioners, and other state and ceremonial occasions
- the provision of chauffeur-driven cars
- coordinating travel arrangements by road in respect of the royal household
- supervision and administration of the Royal Mews at Buckingham Palace, Windsor Castle, Hampton Court and the Palace of Holyroodhouse

The comptroller also has overall responsibility for the MARSHAL OF THE DIPLOMATIC CORPS, who is responsible for the relationship between the royal household and the Diplomatic Heads of Mission in London; and the SECRETARY OF THE CENTRAL CHANCERY OF THE ORDERS OF KNIGHTHOOD, who administers the Orders of Chivalry, makes arrangements for investitures and the distribution of insignia, and ensures the proper public notification of awards through *The London Gazette;* and the DIRECTOR OF OPERATIONS, ROYAL TRAVEL, who is responsible for the provision of travel arrangements by air and rail.

The DIRECTOR, ROYAL COLLECTION TRUST is responsible for:

- the administration and custodial control of the Royal Collection in all royal residences
- the care, display, conservation and restoration of items in the collection
- initiating and assisting research into the collection and publishing catalogues and books on the collection
- making the collection accessible to the public and educating and informing the public about the collection

The Royal Collection, which contains a large number of works of art, is held by the Queen as sovereign in trust for her successors and the nation and is not owned by her as an individual. The administration, conservation and presentation of the Royal Collection are funded by the Royal Collection Trust solely from income from visitors to Windsor Castle, Buckingham Palace and the Palace of Holyroodhouse. The Royal Collection Trust is chaired by the Prince of Wales. The Lord Chamberlain, the Private Secretary and the Keeper of the Privy Purse are *ex officio* trustees and there are three external trustees appointed by the Queen.

The Director, Royal Collection Trust is also at present the SURVEYOR OF THE QUEEN'S WORKS OF ART, responsible for paintings, miniatures and works of art on paper, including the watercolours, prints and drawings in the Print Room at Windsor Castle, and for the books, manuscripts, coins, medals and insignia in the Royal Library.

Royal Collection Enterprises Limited is the trading subsidiary of the Royal Collection Trust. The company, whose chair is the Keeper of the Privy Purse, is responsible for:

- managing access by the public to Windsor Castle (including Frogmore House), Buckingham Palace (including the Royal Mews and the Queen's Gallery) and the Palace of Holyroodhouse (including the Queen's Gallery)
- running shops at each location
- managing the images and intellectual property rights of the Royal Collection

The Director, Royal Collection Trust is also an *ex officio* trustee of Historic Royal Palaces.

## PRIVATE SECRETARIES

### THE QUEEN
*Office:* Buckingham Palace, London SW1A 1AA **T** 020-7930 4832
*Private Secretary to the Queen,* Rt. Hon. Sir Christopher Geidt, KCB, KCVO, OBE

### PRINCE PHILIP, THE DUKE OF EDINBURGH
*Office:* Buckingham Palace, London SW1A 1AA **T** 020-7930 4832
*Private Secretary,* Brig. Archie Miller-Bakewell

### THE PRINCE OF WALES AND THE DUCHESS OF CORNWALL
*Office:* Clarence House, London SW1A 1BA **T** 020-7930 4832
*Principal Private Secretary,* Clive Alderton, LVO

### THE DUKE AND DUCHESS OF CAMBRIDGE
*Office:* Kensington Palace, Palace Green, London W8 4PU
**T** 020-7930 4832
*Private Secretary to the Duke of Cambridge,* Miguel Head
*Private Secretary to the Duchess of Cambridge,* Rebecca Deacon

### PRINCE HENRY OF WALES
*Office:* Kensington Palace, Palace Green, London W8 4PU
**T** 020-7930 4832
*Private Secretary,* Ed Lane-Fox

### THE DUKE OF YORK
*Office:* Buckingham Palace, London SW1A 1AA **T** 020-7024 4227
*Private Secretary,* Amanda Thirsk, LVO

### THE EARL AND COUNTESS OF WESSEX
*Office:* Bagshot Park, Surrey GU19 5PL **T** 01276-707040
*Private Secretary,* Tim Roberts

### THE PRINCESS ROYAL
*Office:* Buckingham Palace, London SW1A 1AA **T** 020-7024 4199
*Private Secretary,* Capt. N. P. Wright, CVO, RN

### THE DUKE AND DUCHESS OF GLOUCESTER
*Office:* Kensington Palace, London W8 4PU **T** 020-7368 1000
*Private Secretary,* Lt.-Col. Alastair Todd

### THE DUKE OF KENT
*Office:* York House, St James's Palace, London SW1A 1BQ
**T** 020-7930 4872
*Private Secretary,* Nicholas Marden

### THE DUCHESS OF KENT
*Office:* York House, St James's Palace, London SW1A 1BQ
**T** 020-7024 5790
*Personal Secretary,* Serena Brown

**PRINCE AND PRINCESS MICHAEL OF KENT**
*Office:* Kensington Palace, London W8 4PU
W www.princemichael.org.uk
*Private Secretary,* Nicholas Chance, CVO

**PRINCESS ALEXANDRA, THE HON. LADY OGILVY**
*Office:* Buckingham Palace, London SW1A 1AA
T 020-7024 4270
*Private Secretary,* Diane Duke, LVO

## SENIOR MANAGEMENT OF THE ROYAL HOUSEHOLD

*Lord Chamberlain,* Earl Peel, GCVO, PC
HEADS OF DEPARTMENT
*Private Secretary to The Queen,* Rt. Hon. Sir Christopher Geidt, KCB, KCVO, OBE
*Keeper of the Privy Purse,* Sir Alan Reid, GCVO
*Master of the Household,* Vice-Adm. Tony Johnstone-Burt, CB, OBE
*Comptroller, Lord Chamberlain's Office,* Lt.-Col. Sir Andrew Ford, KCVO
*Director of the Royal Collection,* Jonathan Marsden, CVO
NON-EXECUTIVE MEMBERS
*Private Secretary to the Duke of Edinburgh,* Brig. Archie Miller-Bakewell
*Principal Private Secretary to the Prince of Wales and the Duchess of Cornwall,* Clive Alderton, LVO

## ASTRONOMER ROYAL

The post of Astronomer Royal dates back to 1675, when astronomy had many practical applications in navigation. Today the post is largely honorary, although the Astronomer Royal is expected to be available for consultation on scientific matters for as long as the holder remains a professional astronomer. The Astronomer Royal receives a stipend of £100 a year and is a member of the royal household.

*Astronomer Royal,* Lord Rees of Ludlow, OM, *apptd* 1995

## MASTER OF THE QUEEN'S MUSIC

The office of Master of the Queen's Music is an honour conferred on a musician of great distinction. The office was first created in 1626, when the master was responsible for the court musicians. Since the reign of King George V, the position has had no fixed duties, although the Master may choose to produce compositions to mark royal or state occasions. The Master of the Queen's Music is paid an annual stipend of £15,000. In 2004 the length of appointment was changed from life tenure to a ten-year term.

*Master of the Queen's Music,* Judith Weir, CBE, *apptd* 2014

## POET LAUREATE

The post of Poet Laureate was officially established when John Dryden was appointed by royal warrant as Poet Laureate and Historiographer Royal in 1668. The post is attached to the royal household and was originally conferred on the holder for life; in 1999 the length of appointment was changed to a ten-year term. It is customary for the Poet Laureate to write verse to mark events of national importance. The postholder currently receives an honorarium of £5,750 a year.

*The Poet Laureate,* Dame Carol Ann Duffy, DBE, *apptd* 2009

# ROYAL FINANCES

Dating back to the late 17th century the Civil List was originally used by the sovereign to supplement hereditary revenues for paying the salaries of judges, ambassadors and other government officers as well as the expenses of the royal household. In 1760, on the accession of George III, it was decided that the Civil List would be provided by parliament to cover all relevant expenditure in return for the king surrendering the hereditary revenues of the Crown. At that time parliament undertook to pay the salaries of judges, ambassadors etc. In 1831 parliament agreed also to meet the costs of the royal palaces in return for a reduction in the Civil List.

Until 1 April 2012 the Civil List met the central staff costs and running expenses of the Queen's official household. Annual grants-in-aid provided for the maintenance of the occupied royal palaces (see Royal Household for a list of occupied palaces) and royal travel.

## THE SOVEREIGN GRANT

Under the Sovereign Grant Act 2011, which came into force on 1 April 2012, the funding previously provided by the Civil List and the grants-in-aid was consolidated in the Sovereign Grant, which was set at £37.9m for 2014–15. It is provided by HM Treasury from public funds in exchange for the surrender by the Queen of the revenue of the Crown Estate.

Official expenditure met by the Sovereign Grant in 2014–15 amounted to £35.7m. Royal travel accounted for £5.1m of the expenditure and property maintenance for £11.7m. The excess of Sovereign Grant over expenditure of £2.2m was transferred to the Sovereign Grant reserve. The Sovereign Grant is calculated based on 15 per cent of the income account net surplus of the Crown Estate for the two financial years previous. The Crown Estate surplus for the financial year 2012–13 amounted to £252.6m, providing for a Sovereign Grant of £37.9m for 2014–15.

The legislative requirement is for Sovereign Grant accounts to be audited by the Comptroller and Auditor-General, scrutinised by the National Audit Office, and submitted to parliament annually. They are then subjected to the same audit scrutiny as for any other government department. The annual report for the year to 31 March 2015, was published in June 2015.

|  | 2013–14 | 2014–15 |
| --- | --- | --- |
| Sovereign Grant | £36,100,000 | £37,900,000 |
| Draw-down from |  |  |
| (transfer to) the reserve | (£400,000) | (£2,200,000) |
| *Net Funding Receipts* | £35,700,000 | £35,700,000 |
| *Net Expenditure* | (£35,700,000) | (£35,700,000) |

## PARLIAMENTARY ANNUITIES

The Civil List acts provided for other members of the royal family to receive parliamentary annuities from government funds to meet the expenses of carrying out their official duties. Since 1993 these annuities have been a statutory anomaly as the Queen reimbursed HM Treasury for all of them except those paid to the late Queen Elizabeth the Queen Mother and the Duke of Edinburgh. The Sovereign Grant Act 2011 repealed all the parliamentary annuities paid to the royal family, with the exception of the Duke of Edinburgh. The Duke of Edinburgh's annuity (£359,000) is now paid directly from the Consolidated Fund.

## THE PRIVY PURSE

The funds received by the privy purse pay for official expenses incurred by the Queen as head of state and for some of the Queen's private expenditure. The revenues of the Duchy of Lancaster are the principal source of income for the privy purse. The revenues of the Duchy were retained by George III in 1760 when the hereditary revenues were surrendered. The Duchy Council reports to the Chancellor of the Duchy of Lancaster, who is accountable directly to the sovereign rather than to parliament. However the chancellor does answer parliamentary questions on matters relating to the Duchy's responsibilities.

THE DUCHY OF LANCASTER, 1 Lancaster Place, London WC2E 7ED

*Chancellor of the Duchy of Lancaster,* Rt. Hon. Oliver Letwin, MP, *apptd* 2014
*Chair of the Council,* Mark Hudson
*Chief Executive and Clerk,* Nathan Thompson
*Receiver-General,* Sir Alan Reid, GCVO
*Attorney-General,* Robert Miles, QC

### PERSONAL INCOME

The Queen's personal income derives mostly from investments, and is used to meet private expenditure.

## PRINCE OF WALES' FUNDING

The Duchy Estate was created in 1337 by Edward III for his son and heir Prince Edward (the Black Prince) who became the Duke of Cornwall. The Duchy's primary function is to provide an income from its assets for the Prince of Wales. Under a 1337 charter, confirmed by subsequent legislation, the Prince of Wales is not entitled to the proceeds or profit on the sale of Duchy assets but only to the annual income which is generated. The Duchy is responsible for the sustainable and commercial management of its properties, investment portfolio and 53,400.3 hectares of land, based mostly in the south-west of England. The Prince of Wales has chosen to use a proportion of his income to meet the cost of his public and charitable work. The Duchy also funds the public, charitable and private activities of the Duchess of Cornwall, the Duke and Duchess of Cambridge and Prince Henry of Wales.

THE DUCHY OF CORNWALL, 10 Buckingham Gate, London SW1E 6LA T 020-7834 7346 W www.duchyofcornwall.org

*Lord Warden of the Stannaries,* Sir Nicholas Bacon, Bt., OBE
*Receiver-General,* Hon. James Leigh-Pemberton, CVO
*Attorney-General,* Jonathan Crow, QC
*Secretary and Keeper of the Records,* Alastair Martin

## TAXATION

The sovereign is not legally liable to pay income tax or capital gains tax. In 1992 the Queen offered to pay income and capital gains tax on a voluntary basis from 6 April 1993, and the Prince of Wales offered to pay tax on a voluntary basis on his income from the Duchy of Cornwall (he was already taxed in all other respects).

The main provisions for the Queen and the Prince of Wales to pay tax, set out in a Memorandum of Understanding on Royal Taxation presented to parliament on 11 February 1993, are that the Queen will pay income tax and capital gains tax in respect of her private income and assets, and on the proportion of the income and capital gains of the Privy Purse used for private purposes. Inheritance tax will be paid on the Queen's assets, except for those which pass to the next sovereign, whether automatically or by gift or bequest. The Prince of Wales will pay income tax on income from the Duchy of Cornwall used for private purposes.

# ROYAL SALUTES

## ENGLAND

The basic royal salute is 21 rounds with an extra 20 rounds fired at Hyde Park because it is a royal park. At the Tower of London 62 rounds are fired on royal anniversaries (21 plus a further 20 because the Tower is a royal palace and a further 21 'for the City of London') and 41 on other occasions. When the Queen's official birthday coincides with the Duke of Edinburgh's birthday, 124 rounds are fired from the Tower (62 rounds for each birthday). Gun salutes occur on the following royal anniversaries:

• Accession Day
• The Queen's birthday
• Coronation Day
• Duke of Edinburgh's birthday
• The Queen's Official Birthday
• The Prince of Wales' birthday
• State opening of parliament

Gun salutes also occur when parliament is prorogued by the sovereign, on royal births and when a visiting head of state meets the sovereign in London, Windsor or Edinburgh.

In London, salutes are fired at Hyde Park and the Tower of London although on some occasions (state visits, state opening of parliament and the Queen's birthday parade) Green Park is used instead of Hyde Park. Other military saluting stations in England are at Colchester, Dover, Plymouth, Woolwich and York.

*Constable of the Royal Palace and Fortress of London,* Gen. Lord Dannatt, GCB, CBE, MC
*Lieutenant of the Tower of London,* Lt. Gen. Sir Simon Mayall, KBE, CB
*Master Gunner of St James's Park,* Gen. Sir Timothy Granville-Chapman, GBE, KCB, ADC
*Resident Governor and Keeper of the Jewel House,* Col. Richard Harrold, OBE
*Master Gunner within the Tower,* HRH Prince Michael of Kent, GCVO

## SCOTLAND

Royal salutes are authorised at Edinburgh Castle and Stirling Castle. A salute of 21 guns is fired on the following occasions:

• the anniversaries of the birth, accession and coronation of the sovereign
• the anniversary of the birth of the Duke of Edinburgh

A salute of 21 guns is fired in Edinburgh on the occasion of the opening of the general assembly of the Church of Scotland. A salute of 21 guns may also be fired in Edinburgh on the arrival of HM The Queen or a member of the royal family who is a Royal Highness on an official visit.

Military saluting stations are also situated at Cardiff Castle in Wales, Hillsborough Castle in Northern Ireland and in Gibraltar.

# MILITARY RANKS AND TITLES

## THE QUEEN

**ARMY**

*Colonel-in-Chief*

The Life Guards; The Blues and Royals (Royal Horse Guards and 1st Dragoons); The Royal Scots Dragoon Guards (Carabiniers and Greys); The Royal Lancers; Royal Tank Regiment; Corps of Royal Engineers; Grenadier Guards; Coldstream Guards; Scots Guards; Irish Guards; Welsh Guards; The Royal Regiment of Scotland; The Duke of Lancaster's Regiment (King's, Lancashire and Border); The Royal Welsh; Adjutant General's Corps; The Governor General's Horse Guards (of Canada); The King's Own Calgary Regiment (Royal Canadian Armoured Corps); Canadian Forces Military Engineering Branch; Le Royal 22e Regiment (of Canada); The Governor General's Foot Guards (of Canada); The Canadian Grenadier Guards; The Stormont, Dundas and Glengarry Highlanders; Le Régiment de la Chaudière (of Canada); The Royal New Brunswick Regiment; The North Shore (New Brunswick) Regiment; 48th Highlanders of Canada; The Argyll and Sutherland Highlanders of Canada (Princess Louise's); The Calgary Highlanders; Royal Australian Engineers; Royal Australian Infantry Corps; Royal Australian Army Ordnance Corps; Royal Australian Army Nursing Corps; The Corps of Royal New Zealand Engineers; Royal New Zealand Infantry Regiment; Malawi Rifles

*Affiliated Colonel-in-Chief*

The Queen's Gurkha Engineers

*Captain-General*

Royal Regiment of Artillery; The Honourable Artillery Company; Combined Cadet Force; Royal Regiment of Canadian Artillery; Royal Regiment of Australian Artillery; Royal Regiment of New Zealand Artillery; Royal New Zealand Armoured Corps

*Royal Colonel*

Balaklava Company, 5th Battalion The Royal Regiment of Scotland

*Patron*

Royal Army Chaplains' Department

**ROYAL AIR FORCE**

*Air Commodore-in-Chief*

Royal Auxiliary Air Force; Royal Air Force Regiment; Air Reserve (of Canada); Royal Australian Air Force Reserve; Territorial Air Force (of New Zealand)

*Commandant-in-Chief*

RAF College, Cranwell

*Royal Honorary Air Commodore*

RAF Marham; 603 (City of Edinburgh) Squadron Royal Auxiliary Air Force

**TRI-SERVICE**

*Colonel-in-Chief*

The Canadian Armed Forces Legal Branch

## PRINCE PHILIP, DUKE OF EDINBURGH

**ROYAL NAVY**

*Lord High Admiral of the United Kingdom*

*Admiral of the Fleet*

*Admiral of the Fleet, Royal Australian Navy*

*Admiral of the Fleet, Royal New Zealand Navy*

*Admiral, Royal Canadian Navy*

*Admiral, Royal Canadian Sea Cadets*

**ROYAL MARINES**

*Captain-General*

**ARMY**

*Field Marshal*

*Field Marshal, Australian Military Forces*

*Field Marshal, New Zealand Army*

*General, Royal Canadian Army*

*Colonel-in-Chief*

The Queen's Royal Hussars (Queen's Own and Royal Irish); The Rifles; Corps of Royal Electrical and Mechanical Engineers; Intelligence Corps; Army Cadet Force Association; The Royal Canadian Regiment; The Royal Hamilton Light Infantry (Wentworth Regiment of Canada); The Cameron Highlanders of Ottawa; The Queen's Own Cameron Highlanders of Canada; The Seaforth Highlanders of Canada; The Royal Canadian Army Cadets; The Royal Australian Corps of Electrical and Mechanical Engineers; The Australian Army Cadet Corps

*Colonel*

Grenadier Guards

*Royal Colonel*

The Highlanders, 4th Battalion The Royal Regiment of Scotland

*Honorary Colonel*

City of Edinburgh University Officers' Training Corps; The Trinidad and Tobago Regiment

*Member*

Honourable Artillery Company

**ROYAL AIR FORCE**

*Marshal of the Royal Air Force*

*Marshal of the Royal Australian Air Force*

*Marshal of the Royal New Zealand Air Force*

*General, Royal Canadian Air Force*

*Air Commodore-in-Chief*

Air Training Corps; Royal Canadian Air Cadets

*Honorary Air Commodore*

RAF Northolt

## THE PRINCE OF WALES

**ROYAL NAVY**

*Admiral of the Fleet*

*Commodore-in-Chief*

Royal Naval Command Plymouth; Fleet Atlantic, Royal Canadian Navy

**ARMY**

*Field Marshal*

*Colonel-in-Chief*

The Royal Dragoon Guards; The Parachute Regiment; The Royal Gurkha Rifles; Army Air Corps; The Royal Canadian Dragoons; Lord Strathcona's Horse (Royal Canadians); The Royal Regiment of Canada; Royal Winnipeg Rifles; Royal Australian Armoured Corps; The Royal Pacific Islands Regiment; 1st The Queen's Dragoon Guards; The Black Watch (Royal Highland Regiment) of Canada; The Toronto Scottish Regiment (Queen Elizabeth The Queen Mother's Own); The Mercian Regiment; 2nd Battalion The Irish Regiment of Canada

*Royal Colonel*

The Black Watch, 3rd Battalion The Royal Regiment of Scotland; 51st Highland, 7th Battalion The Royal Regiment of Scotland (Territorial Army)

*Colonel*

The Welsh Guards

*Royal Honorary Colonel*

The Queen's Own Yeomanry

**ROYAL AIR FORCE**

*Marshal of the RAF*

*Honorary Air Commodore*

RAF Valley

*Air Commodore-in-Chief*
  Royal New Zealand Air Force
*Colonel-in-Chief*
  Air Reserve Canada

## THE DUCHESS OF CORNWALL
ROYAL NAVY
*Commodore-in-Chief*
  Royal Naval Medical Services; Naval Chaplaincy Services
ARMY
*Colonel-in-Chief*
  Queen's Own Rifles of Canada; Royal Australian Corps of Military Police
*Royal Colonel*
  4th Battalion The Rifles
ROYAL AIR FORCE
*Honorary Air Commodore*
  RAF Halton; RAF Leeming

## THE DUKE OF CAMBRIDGE
ROYAL NAVY
*Lieutenant*
*Commodore-in-Chief*
  Scotland Command; Submarines Command
ARMY
*Colonel*
  Irish Guards
*Captain*
  The Blues and Royals (Royal Horse Guards and 1st Dragoons)
ROYAL AIR FORCE
*Flight Lieutenant*
*Honorary Air Commandant*
  RAF Coningsby

## PRINCE HENRY OF WALES
ROYAL NAVY
*Commodore-in-Chief*
  Small Ships and Diving Command
ARMY
*Captain*
  The Blues and Royals (Royal Horse Guards and 1st Dragoons)
ROYAL AIR FORCE
*Honorary Air Commandant*
  RAF Honington

## THE DUKE OF YORK
ROYAL NAVY
*Vice-Admiral*
*Commodore-in-Chief*
  Fleet Air Arm
*Admiral of the Marine Society and Sea Cadets*
ARMY
*Colonel-in-Chief*
  The Royal Irish Regiment (27th (Inniskilling), 83rd, 87th and The Ulster Defence Regiment); The Yorkshire Regiment (14th/15th, 19th and 33rd/76th Foot); Small Arms School Corps; The Queen's York Rangers (First Americans); Royal New Zealand Army Logistics Regiment; The Royal Highland Fusiliers of Canada; The Princess Louise Fusiliers (Canada)
*Deputy Colonel-in-Chief*
  The Royal Lancers
*Royal Colonel*
  The Royal Highland Fusiliers, 2nd Battalion The Royal Regiment of Scotland
ROYAL AIR FORCE
*Honorary Air Commodore*
  RAF Lossiemouth

## THE EARL OF WESSEX
ROYAL NAVY
*Commodore-in-Chief*
  Royal Fleet Auxiliary
*Patron*
  Royal Fleet Auxiliary Association
ARMY
*Colonel-in-Chief*
  Hastings and Prince Edward Regiment; Saskatchewan Dragoons; Prince Edward Island Regiment
*Royal Colonel*
  2nd Battalion, The Rifles
*Royal Honorary Colonel*
  Royal Wessex Yeomanry; The London Regiment
ROYAL AIR FORCE
*Honorary Air Commodore*
  RAF Waddington

## THE COUNTESS OF WESSEX
ARMY
*Colonel-in-Chief*
  Corps of Army Music; Queen Alexandra's Royal Army Nursing Corps; The Lincoln and Welland Regiment; South Alberta Light Horse Regiment
*Royal Colonel*
  5th Battalion, The Rifles
*Patron*
  Queen Alexandra's Royal Army Nursing Corps Association
ROYAL AIR FORCE
*Honorary Air Commodore*
  RAF Wittering
ROYAL NAVY
*Sponsor*
  HMS *Daring*

## THE PRINCESS ROYAL
ROYAL NAVY
*Admiral (Chief Commandant for Women in the Royal Navy)*
*Commodore-in-Chief*
  HM Naval Base Portsmouth; Fleet Pacific, Royal Canadian Navy
ARMY
*Colonel-in-Chief*
  The King's Royal Hussars; Royal Corps of Signals; Royal Logistic Corps; The Royal Army Veterinary Corps; 8th Canadian Hussars (Princess Louise's); Royal Newfoundland Regiment; Canadian Forces Communications and Electronics Branch; The Grey and Simcoe Foresters; The Royal Regina Rifles; Canadian Forces Medical Branch; Royal Canadian Hussars; Royal Australian Corps of Signals; Royal Australian Corps of Transport; Royal New Zealand Corps of Signals; Royal New Zealand Nursing Corps
*Affiliated Colonel-in-Chief*
  The Queen's Gurkha Signals; The Queen's Own Gurkha Transport Regiment
*Royal Colonel*
  The Royal Scots Borderers, 1st Battalion The Royal Regiment of Scotland; 52nd Lowland, 6th Battalion The Royal Regiment of Scotland
*Colonel*
  The Blues and Royals (Royal Horse Guards and 1st Dragoons)
*Honorary Colonel*
  University of London Officers' Training Corps
*Commandant-in-Chief*
  First Aid Nursing Yeomanry (Princess Royal's Volunteer Corps)

ROYAL AIR FORCE
*Honorary Air Commodore*
   RAF Brize Norton; University of London Air Squadron

## THE DUKE OF GLOUCESTER
ARMY
*Colonel-in-Chief*
   The Royal Anglian Regiment; Royal Army Medical Corps;
   Royal New Zealand Army Medical Corps
*Deputy Colonel-in-Chief*
   The Royal Logistic Corps
*Royal Colonel*
   6th Battalion, The Rifles
*Royal Honorary Colonel*
   Royal Monmouthshire Royal Engineers (Militia)
ROYAL AIR FORCE
*Honorary Air Marshal*
*Honorary Air Commodore*
   RAF Odiham; No. 501 (County of Gloucester) Logistic
   Support Squadron

## THE DUCHESS OF GLOUCESTER
ARMY
*Colonel-in-Chief*
   Royal Army Dental Corps; Royal Australian Army
   Educational Corps; Royal New Zealand Army Educational
   Corps; Royal Canadian Dental Corps; The Bermuda
   Regiment
*Deputy Colonel-in-Chief*
   Adjutant General's Corps
*Royal Colonel*
   7th Battalion, The Rifles
*Vice-Patron*
   Adjutant General's Corps Regimental Association
*Patron*
   Royal Army Educational Corps Association; Army
   Families Federation

## THE DUKE OF KENT
ARMY
*Field Marshal*
*Colonel-in-Chief*
   The Royal Regiment of Fusiliers; Lorne Scots (Peel,
   Dufferin and Hamilton Regiment)
*Deputy Colonel-in-Chief*
   The Royal Scots Dragoon Guards (Carabiniers and Greys)

*Royal Colonel*
   1st Battalion The Rifles
*Colonel*
   Scots Guards
ROYAL AIR FORCE
*Honorary Air Chief Marshal*

## THE DUCHESS OF KENT
ARMY
*Honorary Major-General*
*Deputy Colonel-in-Chief*
   The Royal Dragoon Guards; Adjutant General's Corps;
   The Royal Logistic Corps

## PRINCE MICHAEL OF KENT
ROYAL NAVY
*Honorary Vice-Admiral of the Royal Naval Reserves*
*Commodore-in-Chief of the Maritime Reserves*
ARMY
*Colonel-in-Chief*
   Essex and Kent Scottish Regiment (Ontario)
*Royal Honorary Colonel*
   Honourable Artillery Company
*Senior Colonel*
   King's Royal Hussars
ROYAL AIR FORCE
*Honorary Air Marshal*
   RAF Benson

## PRINCESS ALEXANDRA, THE HON. LADY OGILVY
ROYAL NAVY
*Patron*
   Queen Alexandra's Royal Naval Nursing Service
ARMY
*Colonel-in-Chief*
   The Canadian Scottish Regiment (Princess Mary's)
*Deputy Colonel-in-Chief*
   The Royal Lancers
*Royal Colonel*
   3rd Battalion The Rifles
*Royal Honorary Colonel*
   The Royal Yeomanry
ROYAL AIR FORCE
*Patron and Air Chief Commandant*
   Princess Mary's RAF Nursing Service

# KINGS AND QUEENS

## ENGLISH KINGS AND QUEENS 927 TO 1603

### HOUSES OF CERDIC AND DENMARK

*Reign*

**927–939**    **ÆTHELSTAN**    Son of Edward the Elder, by Ecgwynn, and grandson of Alfred *acceded* to Wessex and Mercia *c.*924, established direct rule over Northumbria 927, effectively creating the Kingdom of England *reigned* 15 years

**939–946**    **EDMUND I**    *born* 921, son of Edward the Elder, by Eadgifu *married* (1) Ælfgifu (2) Æthelflæd *killed* aged 25 *reigned* 6 years

**946–955**    **EADRED**    Son of Edward the Elder, by Eadgifu *reigned* 9 years

**955–959**    **EADWIG**    *born* before 943, son of Edmund and Ælfgifu *married* Ælfgifu *reigned* 3 years

**959–975**    **EDGAR I**    *born* 943, son of Edmund and Ælfgifu *married* (1) Æthelflæd (2) Wulfthryth (3) Ælfthryth *died* aged 32 *reigned* 15 years

**975–978**    **EDWARD I (the Martyr)**    *born* c.962, son of Edgar and Æthelflæd *assassinated* aged c.16 *reigned* 2 years

**978–1016**    **ÆTHELRED (the Unready)**    *born* 968/9, son of Edgar and Ælfthryth *married* (1) Ælfgifu (2) Emma, daughter of Richard I, Count of Normandy, 1013–14 dispossessed of kingdom by Swegn Forkbeard (King of Denmark 987–1014) *died* aged c.47, *reigned* 38 years

**1016**    **EDMUND II (Ironside)**    *born* before 993, **(Apr–Nov)** son of Æthelred and Ælfgifu *married* Ealdgyth died aged over 23 *reigned* 7 months

**1016–1035**    **CNUT (Canute)**    *born* c.995, son of Swegn Forkbeard, King of Denmark, and Gunhild *married* (1) Ælfgifu (2) Emma, widow of Æthelred the Unready. Gained submission of West Saxons 1015, Northumbrians 1016, Mercia 1016, King of all England after Edmund's death, King of Denmark 1019–35, King of Norway 1028–35 *died* aged c.40 *reigned* 19 years

**1035–1040**    **HAROLD I (Harefoot)**    *born* 1016/17, son of Cnut and Ælfgifu *married* Ælfgifu 1035 recognised as regent for himself and his brother Harthacnut; 1037 recognised as king died aged c.23 *reigned* 4 years

**1040–1042**    **HARTHACNUT (Harthacanute)**    *born* c.1018, son of Cnut and Emma. Titular king of Denmark from 1028, acknowledged King of England 1035–7 with Harold I as regent; effective king after Harold's death *died* aged c.24 *reigned* 2 years

**1042–1066**    **EDWARD II (the Confessor)**    *born* between 1002 and 1005, son of Æthelred the Unready and Emma *married* Eadgyth, daughter of Godwine, Earl of Wessex *died* aged over 60 *reigned* 23 years

**1066**    **HAROLD II (Godwinesson)**    *born* c.1020, **(Jan–Oct)** son of Godwine, Earl of Wessex, and Gytha *married* (1) Eadgyth (2) Ealdgyth *killed* in battle aged c.46 *reigned* 10 months

### THE HOUSE OF NORMANDY

**1066–1087**    **WILLIAM I (the Conqueror)**    *born* 1027/8, son of Robert I, Duke of Normandy; obtained the Crown by conquest *married* Matilda, daughter of Baldwin, Count of Flanders *died* aged c.60, *reigned* 20 years

**1087–1100**    **WILLIAM II (Rufus)**    *born* between 1056 and 1060, third son of William I; succeeded his father in England only *killed* aged c.40 *reigned* 12 years

**1100–1135**    **HENRY I (Beauclerk)**    *born* 1068, fourth son of William I *married* (1) Edith or Matilda, daughter of Malcolm III of Scotland (2) Adela, daughter of Godfrey, Count of Louvain *died* aged 67 *reigned* 35 years

**1135–1154**    **STEPHEN**    *born* not later than 1100, third son of Adela, daughter of William I, and Stephen, Count of Blois *married* Matilda, daughter of Eustace, Count of Boulogne. Feb–Nov 1141 held captive by adherents of Matilda, daughter of Henry I, who contested the Crown until 1153 *died* aged over 53 *reigned* 18 years

### THE HOUSE OF ANJOU (PLANTAGENETS)

**1154–1189**    **HENRY II (Curtmantle)**    *born* 1133, son of Matilda, daughter of Henry I, and Geoffrey, Count of Anjou *married* Eleanor, daughter of William, Duke of Aquitaine, and divorced queen of Louis VII of France *died* aged 56 *reigned* 34 years

**1189–1199**    **RICHARD I (Coeur de Lion)**    *born* 1157, third son of Henry II *married* Berengaria, daughter of Sancho VI, King of Navarre *died* aged 42 *reigned* 9 years

**1199–1216**    **JOHN (Lackland)**    *born* 1167, fifth son of Henry II *married* (1) Isabella or Avisa, daughter of William, Earl of Gloucester (divorced) (2) Isabella, daughter of Aymer, Count of Angoulême *died* aged 48 *reigned* 17 years

**1216–1272**    **HENRY III**    *born* 1207, son of John and Isabella of Angoulême *married* Eleanor, daughter of Raymond, Count of Provence *died* aged 65 *reigned* 56 years

**1272–1307**    **EDWARD I (Longshanks)**    *born* 1239, eldest son of Henry III *married* (1) Eleanor, daughter of Ferdinand III, King of Castile (2) Margaret, daughter of Philip III of France *died* aged 68 *reigned* 34 years

**1307–1327**    **EDWARD II**    *born* 1284, eldest surviving son of Edward I and Eleanor *married* Isabella, daughter of Philip IV of France *deposed* Jan 1327 *killed* Sep 1327 aged 43 *reigned* 19 years

**1327–1377**    **EDWARD III**    *born* 1312, eldest son of Edward II *married* Philippa, daughter of William, Count of Hainault *died* aged 64 *reigned* 50 years

**1377–1399**    **RICHARD II**    *born* 1367, son of Edward (the Black Prince), eldest son of Edward III *married* (1) Anne, daughter of Emperor Charles IV (2) Isabelle, daughter of Charles VI of France *deposed* Sep 1399 *killed* Feb 1400 aged 33 *reigned* 22 years

## THE HOUSE OF LANCASTER

**1399–1413  HENRY IV**   *born* 1366, son of John of Gaunt, fourth son of Edward III, and Blanche, daughter of Henry, Duke of Lancaster *married* (1) Mary, daughter of Humphrey, Earl of Hereford (2) Joan, daughter of Charles, King of Navarre, and widow of John, Duke of Brittany *died* aged *c.*47 *reigned* 13 years

**1413–1422  HENRY V**   *born* 1387, eldest surviving son of Henry IV and Mary *married* Catherine, daughter of Charles VI of France *died* aged 34 *reigned* 9 years

**1422–1471  HENRY VI**   *born* 1421, son of Henry V *married* Margaret, daughter of René, Duke of Anjou and Count of Provence *deposed* Mar 1461 *restored* Oct 1470 *deposed* Apr 1471 *killed* May 1471 aged 49 *reigned* 39 years

## THE HOUSE OF YORK

**1461–1483  EDWARD IV**   *born* 1442, eldest son of Richard of York (grandson of Edmund, fifth son of Edward III; and son of Anne, great-granddaughter of Lionel, third son of Edward III) *married* Elizabeth Woodville, daughter of Richard, Lord Rivers, and widow of Sir John Grey *acceded* Mar 1461 *deposed* Oct 1470 *restored* Apr 1471 *died* aged 40 *reigned* 21 years

**1483        EDWARD V**   *born* 1470, eldest son of
**(Apr–Jun)**   Edward IV *deposed* Jun 1483, *died* probably Jul–Sep 1483, aged 12 *reigned* 2 months

**1483–1485  RICHARD III**   *born* 1452, fourth son of Richard of York *married* Anne Neville, daughter of Richard, Earl of Warwick, and widow of Edward, Prince of Wales, son of Henry VI *killed* in battle aged 32 *reigned* 2 years

## THE HOUSE OF TUDOR

**1485–1509  HENRY VII**   *born* 1457, son of Margaret Beaufort (great-granddaughter of John of Gaunt, fourth son of Edward III) and Edmund Tudor, Earl of Richmond *married* Elizabeth, daughter of Edward IV *died* aged 52 *reigned* 23 years

**1509–1547  HENRY VIII**   *born* 1491, second son of Henry VII *married* (1) Catherine, daughter of Ferdinand II, King of Aragon, and widow of his elder brother Arthur (divorced) (2) Anne, daughter of Sir Thomas Boleyn (executed) (3) Jane, daughter of Sir John Seymour (died in childbirth) (4) Anne, daughter of John, Duke of Cleves (divorced) (5) Catherine Howard, niece of the Duke of Norfolk (executed) (6) Catherine, daughter of Sir Thomas Parr and widow of Lord Latimer *died* aged 55 *reigned* 37 years

**1547–1553  EDWARD VI**   *born* 1537, son of Henry VIII and Jane Seymour *died* aged 15 *reigned* 6 years

**1553        JANE**   *born* 1537, daughter of Frances
**\*(6/10–**   (daughter of Mary Tudor, the younger
**19 Jul)**   daughter of Henry VII) and Henry Grey, Duke of Suffolk *married* Lord Guildford Dudley, son of the Duke of Northumberland *deposed*

\* Depending on whether the date of her predecessor's death (6 July) or that of her official proclamation as Queen (10 July) is taken as the beginning of her reign

Jul 1553 *executed* Feb 1554 aged 16 *reigned* 13/9 days

**1553–1558  MARY I**   *born* 1516, daughter of Henry VIII and Catherine of Aragon *married* Philip II of Spain *died* aged 42 *reigned* 5 years

**1558–1603  ELIZABETH I**   *born* 1533, daughter of Henry VIII and Anne Boleyn *died* aged 69 *reigned* 44 years

# BRITISH KINGS AND QUEENS SINCE 1603

## THE HOUSE OF STUART

*Reign*

**1603–1625  JAMES I (VI OF SCOTLAND)**   *born* 1566, son of Mary, Queen of Scots (granddaughter of Margaret Tudor, elder daughter of Henry VII), and Henry Stewart, Lord Darnley *married* Anne, daughter of Frederick II of Denmark *died* aged 58 *reigned* 22 years

**1625–1649  CHARLES I**   *born* 1600, second son of James I *married* Henrietta Maria, daughter of Henry IV of France *executed* 1649 aged 48 *reigned* 23 years

## INTERREGNUM 1649–1660

1649–1653  Government by a council of state
1653–1658  Oliver Cromwell, Lord Protector
1658–1659  Richard Cromwell, Lord Protector

*Reign*

**1660–1685  CHARLES II**   *born* 1630, eldest son of Charles I *married* Catherine, daughter of John IV of Portugal *died* aged 54 *reigned* 24 years

**1685–1688  JAMES II (VII OF SCOTLAND)**   *born* 1633, second son of Charles I *married* (1) Lady Anne Hyde, daughter of Edward, Earl of Clarendon (2) Mary, daughter of Alphonso, Duke of Modena reign ended with flight from kingdom Dec 1688 *died* 1701 aged 67 *reigned* 3 years

## INTERREGNUM

11 Dec 1688 to 12 Feb 1689

*Reign*

**1689–1702  WILLIAM III**   *born* 1650, son of William II, Prince of Orange, and Mary Stuart, daughter of Charles I *married* Mary, elder daughter of James II *died* aged 51 *reigned* 13 years
*and*
**1689–1694  MARY II**   *born* 1662, elder daughter of James II and Anne *died* aged 32 *reigned* 5 years

**1702–1714  ANNE**   *born* 1665, younger daughter of James II and Anne *married* Prince George of Denmark, son of Frederick III of Denmark *died* aged 49 *reigned* 12 years

## THE HOUSE OF HANOVER

**1714–1727  GEORGE I (Elector of Hanover)**   *born* 1660, son of Sophia (daughter of Frederick, Elector Palatine, and Elizabeth Stuart, daughter of James I) and Ernest Augustus, Elector of Hanover *married* Sophia Dorothea, daughter of George William, Duke of Lüneburg-Celle *died* aged 67 *reigned* 12 years

**1727–1760  GEORGE II**   *born* 1683, son of George I *married* Caroline, daughter of John Frederick, Margrave of Brandenburg-Anspach *died* aged 76 *reigned* 33 years

1760–1820   **GEORGE III**   *born* 1738, son of Frederick, eldest son of George II *married* Charlotte, daughter of Charles Louis, Duke of Mecklenburg-Strelitz *died* aged 81 *reigned* 59 years

REGENCY 1811–1820
Prince of Wales regent owing to the insanity of George III

*Reign*
1820–1830   **GEORGE IV**   *born* 1762, eldest son of George III *married* Caroline, daughter of Charles, Duke of Brunswick-Wolfenbüttel *died* aged 67 *reigned* 10 years
1830–1837   **WILLIAM IV**   *born* 1765, third son of George III *married* Adelaide, daughter of George, Duke of Saxe-Meiningen *died* aged 71 *reigned* 7 years
1837–1901   **VICTORIA**   *born* 1819, daughter of Edward, fourth son of George III *married* Prince Albert of Saxe-Coburg and Gotha *died* aged 81 *reigned* 63 years

THE HOUSE OF SAXE-COBURG AND GOTHA
1901–1910   **EDWARD VII**   *born* 1841, eldest son of Victoria and Albert *married* Alexandra, daughter of Christian IX of Denmark *died* aged 68 *reigned* 9 years

THE HOUSE OF WINDSOR
1910–1936   **GEORGE V**   *born* 1865, second son of Edward VII *married* Victoria Mary, daughter of Francis, Duke of Teck *died* aged 70 *reigned* 25 years
1936   **EDWARD VIII**   *born* 1894, eldest son of
(20 Jan–   George V *married* (1937) Mrs Wallis Simpson
11 Dec)   *abdicated* 1936 *died* 1972 aged 77 *reigned* 10 months
1936–1952   **GEORGE VI**   *born* 1895, second son of George V *married* Lady Elizabeth Bowes-Lyon, daughter of 14th Earl of Strathmore and Kinghorne *died* aged 56 *reigned* 15 years
1952–   **ELIZABETH II**   *born* 1926, elder daughter of George VI *married* Philip, son of Prince Andrew of Greece

# KINGS AND QUEENS OF SCOTS 1016 TO 1603

*Reign*
1016–1034   **MALCOLM II**   *born* c.954, son of Kenneth II *acceded* to Alba 1005, secured Lothian c.1016, obtained Strathclyde for his grandson Duncan c.1016, thus reigning over an area approximately the same as that governed by later rulers of Scotland *died* aged c.80 *reigned* 18 years

THE HOUSE OF ATHOLL
1034–1040   **DUNCAN I**   son of Bethoc, daughter of Malcolm II, and Crinan, Mormaer of Atholl *married* a cousin of Siward, Earl of Northumbria *reigned* 5 years
1040–1057   **MACBETH**   *born* c.1005, son of a daughter of Malcolm II and Finlaec, Mormaer of Moray *married* Gruoch, granddaughter of Kenneth III *killed* aged c.52 *reigned* 17 years

1057–1058   **LULACH**   *born* c.1032, son of Gillacomgan,
(Aug–Mar)   Mormaer of Moray, and Gruoch (and stepson of Macbeth) *died* aged c.26 *reigned* 7 months
1058–1093   **MALCOLM III (Canmore)**   *born* c.1031, elder son of Duncan I *married* (1) Ingibiorg (2) Margaret (St Margaret), granddaughter of Edmund II of England *killed* in battle aged c.62 *reigned* 35 years
1093–1097   **DONALD III BÁN**   *born* c.1033, second son of Duncan I *deposed* May 1094 *restored* Nov 1094 *deposed* Oct 1097 *reigned* 3 years
1094   **DUNCAN II**   *born* c.1060, elder son of
(May–Nov)   Malcolm III and Ingibiorg *married* Octreda of Dunbar *killed* aged c.34 *reigned* 6 months
1097–1107   **EDGAR**   *born* c.1074, second son of Malcolm III and Margaret *died* aged c.32 *reigned* 9 years
1107–1124   **ALEXANDER I (the Fierce)**   *born* c.1077, fifth son of Malcolm III and Margaret *married* Sybilla, illegitimate daughter of Henry I of England *died* aged c.47 *reigned* 17 years
1124–1153   **DAVID I (the Saint)**   *born* c.1085, sixth son of Malcolm III and Margaret *married* Matilda, daughter of Waltheof, Earl of Huntingdon *died* aged c.68 *reigned* 29 years
1153–1165   **MALCOLM IV (the Maiden)**   *born* c.1141, son of Henry, Earl of Huntingdon, second son of David I *died* aged c.24 *reigned* 12 years
1165–1214   **WILLIAM I (the Lion)**   *born* c.1142, brother of Malcolm IV *married* Ermengarde, daughter of Richard, Viscount of Beaumont *died* aged c.72 *reigned* 49 years
1214–1249   **ALEXANDER II**   *born* 1198, son of William I *married* (1) Joan, daughter of John, King of England (2) Marie, daughter of Ingelram de Coucy *died* aged 50 *reigned* 34 years
1249–1286   **ALEXANDER III**   *born* 1241, son of Alexander II and Marie *married* (1) Margaret, daughter of Henry III of England (2) Yolande, daughter of the Count of Dreux *killed* accidentally aged 44 *reigned* 36 years
1286–1290   **MARGARET (the Maid of Norway)**   *born* 1283, daughter of Margaret (daughter of Alexander III) and Eric II of Norway *died* aged 7 *reigned* 4 years

FIRST INTERREGNUM 1290–1292
Throne disputed by 13 competitors. Crown awarded to John Balliol by adjudication of Edward I of England

THE HOUSE OF BALLIOL
*Reign*
1292–1296   **JOHN (Balliol)**   *born* c.1250, son of Dervorguilla, great-great-granddaughter of David I, and John de Balliol *married* Isabella, daughter of John, Earl of Surrey *abdicated* 1296 *died* 1313 aged c.63 *reigned* 3 years

SECOND INTERREGNUM 1296–1306
Edward I of England declared John Balliol to have forfeited the throne for contumacy in 1296 and took the government of Scotland into his own hands

THE HOUSE OF BRUCE
*Reign*
1306–1329   **ROBERT I (Bruce)**   *born* 1274, son of Robert Bruce and Marjorie, Countess of Carrick, and great-grandson of the second daughter of David, Earl of Huntingdon,

brother of William I *married* (1) Isabella, daughter of Donald, Earl of Mar (2) Elizabeth, daughter of Richard, Earl of Ulster *died* aged 54 *reigned* 23 years

1329–1371   **DAVID II**   *born* 1324, son of Robert I and Elizabeth *married* (1) Joanna, daughter of Edward II of England (2) Margaret Drummond, widow of Sir John Logie (divorced) *died* aged 46 *reigned* 41 years
1332 (Sep–Dec) Edward Balliol, son of John Balliol
1333–1336 Edward Balliol

THE HOUSE OF STEWART

1371–1390   **ROBERT II (Stewart)**   *born* 1316, son of Marjorie (daughter of Robert I) and Walter, High Steward of Scotland *married* (1) Elizabeth, daughter of Sir Robert Mure of Rowallan (2) Euphemia, daughter of Hugh, Earl of Ross *died* aged 74 *reigned* 19 years

1390–1406   **ROBERT III**   *born* c.1337, son of Robert II and Elizabeth *married* Annabella, daughter of Sir John Drummond of Stobhall *died* aged c.69 *reigned* 16 years

1406–1437   **JAMES I**   *born* 1394, son of Robert III *married* Joan Beaufort, daughter of John, Earl of Somerset *assassinated* aged 42 *reigned* 30 years

1437–1460   **JAMES II**   *born* 1430, son of James I *married* Mary, daughter of Arnold, Duke of Gueldres *killed* accidentally aged 29 *reigned* 23 years

1460–1488   **JAMES III**   *born* 1452, son of James II *married* Margaret, daughter of Christian I of Denmark *assassinated* aged 36 *reigned* 27 years

1488–1513   **JAMES IV**   *born* 1473, son of James III *married* Margaret Tudor, daughter of Henry VII of England *killed* in battle aged 40 *reigned* 25 years

1513–1542   **JAMES V**   *born* 1512, son of James IV *married* (1) Madeleine, daughter of Francis I of France (2) Mary of Lorraine, daughter of the Duc de Guise *died* aged 30 *reigned* 29 years

1542–1567   **MARY**   *born* 1542, daughter of James V and Mary *married* (1) the Dauphin, afterwards Francis II of France (2) Henry Stewart, Lord Darnley (3) James Hepburn, Earl of Bothwell *abdicated* 1567, prisoner in England from 1568, *executed* 1587 *reigned* 24 years

1567–1625   **JAMES VI (and I of England)**   *born* 1566, son of Mary, Queen of Scots, and Henry, Lord Darnley *acceded* 1567 to the Scottish throne *reigned* 58 years *succeeded* 1603 to the English throne, so joining the English and Scottish crowns in one person. The two kingdoms remained distinct until 1707 when the parliaments of the kingdoms became conjoined

## WELSH SOVEREIGNS AND PRINCES

Wales was ruled by sovereign princes from the earliest times until the death of Llywelyn in 1282. The first English Prince of Wales was the son of Edward I, who was born in Caernarvon town on 25 April 1284. According to a discredited legend, he was presented to the Welsh chieftains as their prince, in fulfilment of a promise that they should have a prince who 'could not speak a word of English' and should be native born. This son, who afterwards became Edward II, was created 'Prince of Wales and Earl of Chester' at the Lincoln Parliament on 7 February 1301.

The title Prince of Wales is borne after individual conferment and is not inherited at birth, though some Princes have been declared and styled Prince of Wales but never formally so created (*s.*). The title was conferred on Prince Charles by the Queen on 26 July 1958. He was invested at Caernarvon on 1 July 1969.

INDEPENDENT PRINCES AD 844 TO 1282

| | |
|---|---|
| 844–878 | Rhodri the Great |
| 878–916 | Anarawd, son of Rhodri |
| 916–950 | Hywel Dda, the Good |
| 950–979 | Iago ab Idwal (or Ieuaf) |
| 979–985 | Hywel ab Ieuaf, the Bad |
| 985–986 | Cadwallon, his brother |
| 986–999 | Maredudd ab Owain ap Hywel Dda |
| 999–1005 | Cynan ap Hywel ab Ieuaf |
| 1005–1018 | Aeddan ap Blegywryd |
| 1018–1023 | Llywelyn ap Seisyll |
| 1023–1039 | Iago ab Idwal ap Meurig |
| 1039–1063 | Gruffydd ap Llywelyn ap Seisyll |
| 1063–1075 | Bleddyn ap Cynfyn |
| 1075–1081 | Trahaern ap Caradog |
| 1081–1137 | Gruffydd ap Cynan ab Iago |
| 1137–1170 | Owain Gwynedd |
| 1170–1194 | Dafydd ab Owain Gwynedd |
| 1194–1240 | Llywelyn Fawr, the Great |
| 1240–1246 | Dafydd ap Llywelyn |
| 1246–1282 | Llywelyn ap Gruffydd ap Llywelyn |

ENGLISH PRINCES SINCE 1301

| | |
|---|---|
| 1301 | Edward (Edward II) |
| 1343 | Edward the Black Prince, son of Edward III |
| 1376 | Richard (Richard II), son of the Black Prince |
| 1399 | Henry of Monmouth (Henry V) |
| 1454 | Edward of Westminster, son of Henry VI |
| 1471 | Edward of Westminster (Edward V) |
| 1483 | Edward, son of Richard III (*d.* 1484) |
| 1489 | Arthur Tudor, son of Henry VII |
| 1504 | Henry Tudor (Henry VIII) |
| 1610 | Henry Stuart, son of James I (*d.* 1612) |
| 1616 | Charles Stuart (Charles I) |
| c.1638 (*s.*) | Charles Stuart (Charles II) |
| 1688 (*s.*) | James Francis Edward Stuart (The Old Pretender), son of James II (*d.* 1766) |
| 1714 | George Augustus (George II) |
| 1729 | Frederick Lewis, son of George II (*d.* 1751) |
| 1751 | George William Frederick (George III) |
| 1762 | George Augustus Frederick (George IV) |
| 1841 | Albert Edward (Edward VII) |
| 1901 | George (George V) |
| 1910 | Edward (Edward VIII) |
| 1958 | Charles, son of Elizabeth II |

## PRINCESSES ROYAL

The style Princess Royal is conferred at the sovereign's discretion on his or her eldest daughter. It is an honorary title, held for life, and cannot be inherited or passed on. It was first conferred on Princess Mary, daughter of Charles I, in approximately 1642.

| | |
|---|---|
| c.1642 | Princess Mary (1631–60), daughter of Charles I |
| 1727 | Princess Anne (1709–59), daughter of George II |
| 1766 | Princess Charlotte (1766–1828), daughter of George III |
| 1840 | Princess Victoria (1840–1901), daughter of Victoria |
| 1905 | Princess Louise (1867–1931), daughter of Edward VII |
| 1932 | Princess Mary (1897–1965), daughter of George V |
| 1987 | Princess Anne (*b.* 1950), daughter of Elizabeth II |

# THE HOUSE OF WINDSOR

King George V assumed by royal proclamation (17 July 1917) for his House and family, as well as for all descendants in the male line of Queen Victoria who are subjects of these realms, the name of Windsor.

## KING GEORGE V

(George Frederick Ernest Albert), second son of King Edward VII *born* 3 June 1865 *married* 6 July 1893 HSH Princess Victoria Mary Augusta Louise Olga Pauline Claudine Agnes of Teck (Queen Mary *born* 26 May 1867 *died* 24 March 1953) *succeeded* to the throne 6 May 1910 *died* 20 January 1936. *Issue*

1. HRH PRINCE EDWARD Albert Christian George Andrew Patrick David *born* 23 June 1894 *succeeded* to the throne as King Edward VIII, 20 January 1936 *abdicated* 11 December 1936 *created* Duke of Windsor 1937 *married* 3 June 1937 Mrs Wallis Simpson (Her Grace The Duchess of Windsor *born* 19 June 1896 *died* 24 April 1986) *died* 28 May 1972

2. HRH PRINCE ALBERT Frederick Arthur George *born* 14 December 1895 *created* Duke of York 1920 *married* 26 April 1923 Lady Elizabeth Bowes-Lyon, youngest daughter of the 14th Earl of Strathmore and Kinghorne (HM Queen Elizabeth the Queen Mother *born* 4 August 1900 *died* 30 March 2002) *succeeded* to the throne as King George VI, 11 December 1936 *died* 6 February 1952. *Issue*
   (1) HRH Princess Elizabeth Alexandra Mary *succeeded* to the throne as Queen Elizabeth II, 6 February 1952 (*see* Royal Family)
   (2) HRH Princess Margaret Rose (later HRH The Princess Margaret, Countess of Snowdon) *born* 21 August 1930 *married* 6 May 1960 Anthony Charles Robert Armstrong-Jones, GCVO *created* Earl of Snowdon 1961 (marriage dissolved 1978) *died* 9 February 2002, having had issue (*see* Royal Family)

3. HRH PRINCESS (Victoria Alexandra Alice) MARY *born* 25 April 1897 *created* Princess Royal 1932 *married* 28 February 1922 Viscount Lascelles, later the 6th Earl of Harewood (1882–1947) *died* 28 March 1965. *Issue*

(1) George Henry Hubert Lascelles, 7th Earl of Harewood, KBE *born* 7 February 1923 *died* 11 July 2011 *married* (1) 1949 Maria (Marion) Stein (marriage dissolved 1967) *issue (a)* David Henry George, 8th Earl of Harewood *born* 1950 *(b)* James Edward *born* 1953 *(c)* (Robert) Jeremy Hugh *born* 1955 (2) 1967 Patricia Tuckwell *issue (d)* Mark Hubert *born* 1964
(2) Gerald David Lascelles *born* 21 August 1924 *died* 27 February 1998 *married* (1) 1952 Angela Dowding (marriage dissolved 1978) *issue (a)* Henry Ulick *born* 1953 (2) 1978 Elizabeth Collingwood (Elizabeth Colvin) *issue (b)* Martin David *born* 1962

4. HRH PRINCE HENRY William Frederick Albert *born* 31 March 1900 *created* Duke of Gloucester, Earl of Ulster and Baron Culloden 1928 *married* 6 November 1935 Lady Alice Christabel Montagu-Douglas-Scott, daughter of the 7th Duke of Buccleuch and Queensberry (HRH Princess Alice, Duchess of Gloucester *born* 25 December 1901 *died* 29 October 2004) *died* 10 June 1974. *Issue*
   (1) HRH Prince William Henry Andrew Frederick *born* 18 December 1941 accidentally *killed* 28 August 1972
   (2) HRH Prince Richard Alexander Walter George (HRH The Duke of Gloucester, *see* Royal Family)

5. HRH PRINCE GEORGE Edward Alexander Edmund *born* 20 December 1902 *created* Duke of Kent, Earl of St Andrews and Baron Downpatrick 1934 *married* 29 November 1934 HRH Princess Marina of Greece and Denmark (*born* 30 November 1906 *died* 27 August 1968) *killed* on active service 25 August 1942. *Issue*
   (1) HRH Prince Edward George Nicholas Paul Patrick (HRH The Duke of Kent, *see* Royal Family)
   (2) HRH Princess Alexandra Helen Elizabeth Olga Christabel (HRH Princess Alexandra, the Hon. Lady Ogilvy, *see* Royal Family)
   (3) HRH Prince Michael George Charles Franklin (HRH Prince Michael of Kent, *see* Royal Family)

6. HRH PRINCE JOHN Charles Francis *born* 12 July 1905 *died* 18 January 1919

# DESCENDANTS OF QUEEN VICTORIA

**I. HRH Princess Victoria Adelaide Mary Louisa, Princess Royal (1840–1901) *m* Friedrich III (1831–88), later German Emperor**

**II. HRH Prince Albert Edward (HM KING EDWARD VII) (1841–1910) *succeeded* 22 Jan 1901 *m* HRH Princess Alexandra of Denmark (1844–1925)**

**III. HRH Princess Alice Maud Mary (1843–78) *m* Prince Ludwig (1837–92), later Grand Duke of Hesse**

**IV. HRH Prince Alfred Ernest Albert, Duke of Edinburgh (1844–1900) *succeeded* as Duke of Saxe-Coburg and Gotha 1893 *m* Grand Duchess Marie Alexandrovna of Russia (1853–1920)**

## Column I

1. HIM Wilhelm II (1859–1941), later German Emperor *m* (1) Princess Augusta Victoria of Schleswig-Holstein-Sonderburg-Augustenburg (1858–1921) (2) Princess Hermine of Reuss (1887–1947). *Issue* Wilhelm (1882–1951); Eitel-Friedrich (1883–1942); Adalbert (1884–1948); August Wilhelm (1887–1949); Oskar (1888–1958); Joachim (1890–1920); Viktoria Luise (1892–1980)

2. Charlotte (1860–1919) *m* Bernhard, Duke of Saxe-Meiningen (1851–1928). *Issue* Feodora (1879–1945)

3. Heinrich (1862–1929) *m* Princess Irene of Hesse (*see* III.3). *Issue* Waldemar (1889–1945); Sigismund (1896–1978); Heinrich (1900–4)

4. Sigismund (1864–6)

5. Victoria (1866–1929) *m* (1) Prince Adolf of Schaumburg-Lippe (1859–1916) (2) Alexander Zubkov (1900–36)

6. Waldemar (1868–79)

7. Sophie (1870–1932) *m* Constantine I (1868–1923), later King of the Hellenes. *Issue* George II (1890–1947); Alexander I (1893–1920); Helena (1896–1982); Paul I (1901–64); Irene (1904–74); Katherine (1913–2007)

8. Margarethe (1872–1954) *m* Prince Friedrich Karl of Hesse (1868–1940). *Issue* Friedrich Wilhelm (1893–1916); Maximilian (1894–1914); Philipp (1896–1980); Wolfgang (1896–1989); Richard (1901–69); Christoph (1901–43)

## Column II

1. Albert Victor, Duke of Clarence and Avondale (1864–92)

2. George (HM KING GEORGE V) (1865–1936) (*see* House of Windsor)

3. Louise (1867–1931), later Princess Royal *m* 1st Duke of Fife (1849–1912). *Issue* Alexandra (1891–1959); Maud (1893–1945)

4. Victoria (1868–1935)

5. Maud (1869–1938) *m* Prince Carl of Denmark (1872–1957), later King Haakon VII of Norway. *Issue* Olav V (1903–91)

6. Alexander (6–7 Apr 1871)

## Column III

1. Victoria (1863–1950) *m* Prince Louis of Battenberg (1854–1921), later 1st Marquess of Milford Haven. *Issue* Alice (1885–1969); Louise (1889–1965); George (1892–1938); Louis (1900–79)

2. Elizabeth (1864–1918) *m* Grand Duke Sergius of Russia (1857–1905)

3. Irene (1866–1953) *m* Prince Heinrich of Prussia (*see* I.3)

4. Ernst Ludwig (1868–1937), Grand Duke of Hesse, *m* (1) Princess Victoria Melita of Saxe-Coburg (see IV.3) (2) Princess Eleonore of Solms-Hohensolms-Lich (1871–1937). *Issue* Elizabeth (1895–1903); George (1906–37); Ludwig (1908–68)

5. Frederick William (1870–3)

6. Alix (Tsaritsa of Russia) (1872–1918) *m* Nicholas II, Tsar of All the Russias (1868–1918). *Issue* Olga (1895–1918); Tatiana (1897–1918); Marie (1899–1918); Anastasia (1901–18); Alexis (1904–18)

7. Marie (1874–8)

QUEEN VICTORIA (Alexandrina Victoria) (1819–1901) *succeeded* 20 Jun 1837 *m* (Francis) Albert Augustus Charles Emmanuel, Duke of Saxony, Prince of Saxe-Coburg and Gotha (HRH Albert, Prince Consort) (1819–61)

**VI. HRH Princess Louise Caroline Alberta (1848–1939) *m* Marquess of Lorne (1845–1914), later 9th Duke of Argyll**

**VII. HRH Prince Arthur William Patrick Albert, Duke of Connaught (1850–1942) *m* Princess Louisa of Prussia (1860–1917)**

**VIII. HRH Prince Leopold George Duncan Albert, Duke of Albany (1853–84) *m* Princess Helena of Waldeck (1861–1922)**

**IX. HRH Princess Beatrice Mary Victoria Feodore (1857–1944) *m* Prince Henry of Battenberg (1858–96)**

1. Alfred, Prince of Saxe-Coburg (1874–99)

2. Marie (1875–1938) *m* Ferdinand (1865–1927), later King of Roumania. *Issue* Carol II (1893–1953); Elisabeth (1894–1956); Marie (1900–61); Nicolas (1903–78); Ileana (1909–91); Mircea (1913–16)

3. Victoria Melita (1876–1936) *m* (1) Grand Duke Ernst Ludwig of Hesse (*see* III.4) (2) Grand Duke Kirill of Russia (1876–1938). *Issue* Marie (1907–51); Kira (1909–67); Vladimir (1917–92)

4. Alexandra (1878–1942) *m* Ernst, Prince of Hohenlohe Langenburg (1863–1950). *Issue* Gottfried (1897–1960); Maria (1899–1967); Alexandra (1901–63); Irma (1902–86)

5. Beatrice (1884–1966) *m* Alfonso of Orleans, Infante of Spain (1886–1975). *Issue* Alvaro (1910–97); Alonso (1912–36); Ataulfo (1913–74)

1. Margaret (1882–1920) *m* Crown Prince Gustaf Adolf (1882–1973), later King of Sweden. *Issue* Gustaf Adolf (1906–47); Sigvard (1907–2002); Ingrid (1910–2000); Bertil (1912–97); Count Carl Bernadotte (1916–2012)

2. Arthur (1883–1938) *m* HH Duchess of Fife (1891–1959). *Issue* Alastair Arthur (1914–43)

3. (Victoria) Patricia (1886–1974) *m* Adm. Hon. Sir Alexander Ramsay (1881–1972). *Issue* Alexander (1919–2000)

1. Alice (1883–1981) *m* Prince Alexander of Teck (1874–1957), later 1st Earl of Athlone. *Issue* May (1906–94); Rupert (1907–28); Maurice (Mar–Sep 1910)

2. Charles Edward (1884–1954), Duke of Albany until title suspended 1917, Duke of Saxe-Coburg-Gotha *m* Princess Victoria Adelheid of Schleswig-Holstein-Sonderburg-Glücksburg (1885–1970). *Issue* Johann Leopold (1906–72); Sibylla (1908–72); Dietmar Hubertus (1909–43); Caroline (1912–83); Friedrich Josias (1918–98)

1. Alexander, 1st Marquess of Carisbrooke (1886–1960) *m* Lady Irene Denison (1890–1956). *Issue* Iris (1920–82)

2. Victoria Eugénie (1887–1969) *m* Alfonso XIII, King of Spain (1886–1941). *Issue* Alfonso (1907–38); Jaime (1908–75); Beatriz (1909–2002); Maria (1911–96); Juan (1913–93); Gonzalo (1914–34)

3. Maj. Lord Leopold Mountbatten (1889–1922)

4. Maurice (1891–1914)

**V. HRH Princess Helena Augusta Victoria (1846–1923) *m* Prince Christian of Schleswig-Holstein-Sonderburg-Augustenburg (1831–1917)**

1. Christian Victor (1867–1900)

2. Albert (1869–1931), later Duke of Schleswig-Holstein

3. Helena (1870–1948)

4. Marie Louise (1872–1956), *m* Prince Aribert of Anhalt (1864–1933)

5. Harold (12–20 May 1876)

# PRECEDENCE

## ENGLAND AND WALES

The Sovereign
The Prince Philip, Duke of Edinburgh
The Prince of Wales
The Sovereign's younger sons
The Sovereign's grandsons
The Sovereign's cousins
Archbishop of Canterbury
Lord High Chancellor
Archbishop of York
The Prime Minister
Lord President of the Council
Speaker of the House of Commons
Speaker of the House of Lords
President of the Supreme Court
Lord Chief Justice of England and
  Wales
Lord Privy Seal
Ambassadors and High Commissioners
Lord Great Chamberlain
Earl Marshal
Lord Steward of the Household
Lord Chamberlain of the Household
Master of the Horse
Dukes, according to their patent of
  creation:
  1. of England
  2. of Scotland
  3. of Great Britain
  4. of Ireland
  5. those created since the Union
Eldest sons of Dukes of the Blood
  Royal
Ministers, Envoys, and other important
  overseas visitors
Marquesses, according to their patent
  of creation:
  1. of England
  2. of Scotland
  3. of Great Britain
  4. of Ireland
  5. those created since the Union
Dukes' eldest sons
Earls, according to their patent of
  creation:
  1. of England
  2. of Scotland
  3. of Great Britain
  4. of Ireland
  5. those created since the Union
Younger sons of Dukes of Blood Royal
Marquesses' eldest sons

Dukes' younger sons
Viscounts, according to their patent of
  creation:
  1. of England
  2. of Scotland
  3. of Great Britain
  4. of Ireland
  5. those created since the Union
Earls' eldest sons
Marquesses' younger sons
Bishop of London
Bishop of Durham
Bishop of Winchester
Other English Diocesan Bishops,
  according to seniority of
  consecration
Retired Church of England Diocesan
  Bishops, according to seniority of
  consecration
Suffragan Bishops, according to
  seniority of consecration
Secretaries of State, if of the degree of a
  Baron
Barons, according to their patent of
  creation:
  1. of England
  2. of Scotland (Lords of Parliament)
  3. of Great Britain
  4. of Ireland
  5. those created since the Union,
  including Life Barons
Master of the Rolls
Deputy President of the Supreme
  Court
Justices of the Supreme Court,
  according to seniority of
  appointment
Treasurer of the Household
Comptroller of the Household
Vice-Chamberlain of the Household
Secretaries of State under the degree of
  Baron
Viscounts' eldest sons
Earls' younger sons
Barons' eldest sons
Knights of the Garter
Privy Counsellors
Chancellor of the Order of the Garter
Chancellor of the Exchequer
Chancellor of the Duchy of Lancaster
President of the Queen's Bench
  Division
President of the Family Division

Chancellor of the High Court
Lord Justices of Appeal, according to
  seniority of appointment
Judges of the High Court, according to
  seniority of appointment
Viscounts' younger sons
Barons' younger sons
Sons of Life Peers
Baronets, according to date of patent
Knights of the Thistle
Knights Grand Cross of the Bath
Knights Grand Cross of St Michael and
  St George
Knights Grand Cross of the Royal
  Victorian Order
Knights Grand Cross of the British
  Empire
Knights Commanders of the Bath
Knights Commanders of St Michael
  and St George
Knights Commanders of the Royal
  Victorian Order
Knights Commanders of the British
  Empire
Knights Bachelor
Circuit Judges, according to priority
  and order of their respective
  appointments
Master of the Court of Protection
Companions of the Bath
Companions of St Michael and St
  George
Commanders of the Royal Victorian
  Order
Commanders of the British Empire
Companions of the Distinguished
  Service Order
Lieutenants of the Royal Victorian
  Order
Officers of the British Empire
Companions of the Imperial Service
  Order
Eldest sons of younger sons of peers
Baronets' eldest sons
Eldest sons of knights, in the same
  order as their fathers
Members of the Royal Victorian Order
Members of the British Empire
Baronets' younger sons
Knights' younger sons, in the same
  order as their fathers
Esquires
Gentlemen

## WOMEN

Women take the same rank as their husbands or as their brothers; but the daughter of a peer marrying a commoner retains her title as Lady or Honourable. Daughters of peers rank next immediately after the wives of their elder brothers, and before their younger brothers' wives. Daughters of peers marrying peers of a lower degree take the same order of precedence as that of their husbands; thus the daughter of a

Duke marrying a Baron becomes of the rank of Baroness only, while her sisters married to commoners retain their rank and take precedence over the Baroness. Merely official rank on the husband's part does not give any similar precedence to the wife.

Peeresses in their own right take the same precedence as peers of the same rank, ie from their date of creation.

# SCOTLAND

The Sovereign
The Prince Philip, Duke of Edinburgh
The Lord High Commissioner to the General Assembly of the Church of Scotland (while that assembly is sitting)
The Duke of Rothesay (eldest son of the Sovereign)
The Sovereign's younger sons
The Sovereign's grandsons
The Sovereign's nephews
Lord-Lieutenants
Lord Provosts, during their term of office*
Sheriffs Principal, during their term of office and within the bounds of their respective sheriffdoms
Lord Chancellor of Great Britain
Moderator of the General Assembly of the Church of Scotland
Keeper of the Great Seal of Scotland (the First Minister)
Presiding Officer
The Secretary of State for Scotland
Hereditary High Constable of Scotland
Hereditary Master of the Household in Scotland
Dukes, as in England
Eldest sons of Dukes of the Blood Royal

Marquesses, as in England
Dukes' eldest sons
Earls, as in England
Younger sons of Dukes of Blood Royal
Marquesses' eldest sons
Dukes' younger sons
Lord Justice General
Lord Clerk Register
Lord Advocate
The Advocate General
Lord Justice Clerk
Viscounts, as in England
Earls' eldest sons
Marquesses' younger sons
Lords of Parliament or Barons, as in England
Eldest sons of Viscounts
Earls' younger sons
Eldest sons of Lords of Parliament or Barons
Knights and Ladies of the Garter
Knights and Ladies of the Thistle
Privy Counsellors
Senators of the College of Justice (Lords of Session)
Viscounts' younger sons
Younger sons of Lords of Parliament or Barons
Baronets
Knights and Dames Grand Cross of orders, as in England

Knights and Dames Commanders of orders, as in England
Solicitor-General for Scotland
Lord Lyon King of Arms
Sheriffs Principal, when not within own county
Knights Bachelor
Sheriffs
Companions of Orders, as in England
Commanders of the Royal Victorian Order
Commanders of the British Empire
Lieutenants of the Royal Victorian Order
Companions of the Distinguished Service Order
Officers of the British Empire
Companions of the Imperial Service Order
Eldest sons of younger sons of peers
Eldest sons of baronets
Eldest sons of knights, as in England
Members of the Royal Victorian Order
Members of the British Empire
Baronets' younger sons
Knights' younger sons
Queen's Counsel
Esquires
Gentlemen

* The Lord Provosts of Aberdeen, Dundee, Edinburgh and Glasgow are Lord-Lieutenants for these cities *ex officio* and take precedence as such

# THE PEERAGE

## ABBREVIATIONS AND SYMBOLS

| | | | | |
|---|---|---|---|---|
| S. | Scottish title | | c.p. | civil partnership |
| I. | Irish title | | w. | widower or widow |
| ** | hereditary peer remaining in the House of Lords | | M. | minor |
| ° | there is no 'of' in the title | | † | heir not ascertained at time of going to press |
| b. | born | | F_ | represents forename |
| s. | succeeded | | S_ | represents surname |
| m. | married | | cr. | created |
| § | life peer disqualified from sitting in the House of Lords as a member of the juidiciary | | ¶ | life peer who has resigned permanently from the House of Lords |

The rules which govern the creation and succession of peerages are extremely complicated. There are, technically, five separate peerages, the Peerage of England, of Scotland, of Ireland, of Great Britain, and of the United Kingdom. The Peerage of Great Britain dates from 1707 when an Act of Union combined the two kingdoms of England and Scotland and separate peerages were discontinued. The Peerage of the United Kingdom dates from 1801 when Great Britain and Ireland were combined under an Act of Union. Some Scottish peers have received additional peerages of Great Britain or of the UK since 1707, and some Irish peers additional peerages of the UK since 1801.

The Peerage of Ireland was not entirely discontinued from 1801 but holders of Irish peerages, whether pre-dating or created subsequent to the Union of 1801, were not entitled to sit in the House of Lords if they had no additional English, Scottish, Great Britain or UK peerage. However, they are eligible for election to the House of Commons and to vote in parliamentary elections. An Irish peer holding a peerage of a lower grade which enabled him to sit in the House of Lords was introduced there by the title which enabled him to sit, though for all other purposes he was known by his higher title.

In the Peerage of Scotland there is no rank of Baron; the equivalent rank is Lord of Parliament, abbreviated to 'Lord' (the female equivalent is 'Lady').

All peers of England, Scotland, Great Britain or the UK who are 21 years or over, and of British, Irish or Commonwealth nationality were entitled to sit in the House of Lords until the House of Lords Act 1999, when hereditary peers lost the right to sit. However, section two of the act provided an exception for 90 hereditary peers plus the holders of the office of Earl Marshal and Lord Great Chamberlain to remain as members of the House of Lords for their lifetime or pending further reform. Of the 90 hereditary peers, 75 were elected by the hereditary peers in their political party, or Crossbench grouping, and the remaining 15 by the whole house. Until 7 November 2002 any vacancy arising due to the death of one of the 90 excepted hereditary peers was filled by the runner-up to the original election. From 7 November 2002 any vacancy due to a death has been filled by holding a by-election. By-elections are conducted in accordance with arrangements made by the Clerk of the Parliaments and have to take place within three months of a vacancy occurring. If the vacancy is among the 75, only the excepted hereditary peers in the relevant party or Crossbench grouping are entitled to vote. If the vacancy is among the other 15, the whole house is entitled to vote.

In the list below, peers currently holding one of the 92 hereditary places in the House of Lords are indicated by **.

### HEREDITARY WOMEN PEERS

Most hereditary peerages pass on death to the nearest male heir, but there are exceptions, and several are held by women.

A woman peer in her own right retains her title after marriage, and if her husband's rank is the superior she is designated by the two titles jointly, the inferior one second. Her hereditary claim still holds good in spite of any marriage whether higher or lower. No rank held by a woman can confer any title or even precedence upon her husband but the rank of a hereditary woman peer in her own right is inherited by her eldest son (or in some cases daughter).

After the Peerage Act 1963, hereditary women peers in their own right were entitled to sit in the House of Lords, subject to the same qualifications as men, until the House of Lords Act 1999.

### LIFE PEERS

From 1876 to 2009 non-hereditary or life peerages were conferred on certain eminent judges to enable the judicial functions of the House of Lords to be carried out. These lords were known as Lords of Appeal in Ordinary or law lords. The judicial role of the House of Lords as the highest appeal court in the UK ended on 30 July 2009 and since 1 October 2009, under the Constitutional Reform Act 2005, any peer who holds a senior judicial office is disqualified from sitting in the House of Lords until they retire from that office. In the list of life peerages which follows, members of the judiciary who are currently disqualified from sitting and voting in the House of Lords until retirement, are marked by a '§'.

Under the Constitutional Reform and Governance Act 2010, five peers permanently resigned from the House of Lords.

Since 1958 life peerages have been conferred upon distinguished men and women from all walks of life, giving them seats in the House of Lords in the degree of Baron or Baroness. They are addressed in the same way as hereditary lords and barons, and their children have similar courtesy titles.

### HOUSE OF LORDS REFORM ACT 2014

The House of Lords Reform Act 2014 makes provision for a member of the House of Lords who is a peer to retire or resign by giving notice in writing to the Clerk of Parliaments. Resignations may not be rescinded. A number of life peers and elected hereditary peers have already retired permanently under this provision. The Act also makes provision for the expulsion of peers who do not attend the

House of Lords for an entire parliamentary session which is longer than six months. Peers on leave of absence or subject to a suspension or disqualification which results in absenteeism for an entire session will not be expelled. The House can also resolve that a peer should not be expelled by reason of special circumstances.

All life peers who have resigned permanently from the House of Lords are indicated by a '¶' in the following list

## PEERAGES EXTINCT SINCE THE LAST EDITION
BARONIES: Birdwood (cr. 1938); Strang (cr. 1954)

LIFE PEERAGES: Barnett (cr. 1983); Brittan of Spennithorne (cr. 2000); Gavron (cr. 1999); Griffiths (cr. 1985); James of Holland Park (cr. 1991); Knights (cr. 1987); Mackie of Benshie (cr. 1974); Mason of Barnsley (cr. 1987); Molyneaux of Killead (cr. 1997); Moser (cr. 2001); Mustill (cr. 1992); Platt of Writtle (cr. 1981); Rendell of Babergh (cr. 1997); Sheppard of Didgemere (cr. 1994); Williamson of Horton (cr. 1999)

## DISCLAIMER OF PEERAGES
The Peerage Act 1963 enables peers to disclaim their peerages for life. Peers alive in 1963 could disclaim within twelve months after the passing of the act (31 July 1963); a person subsequently succeeding to a peerage may disclaim within 12 months (one month if an MP) after the date of succession, or of reaching 21, if later. The disclaimer is irrevocable but does not affect the descent of the peerage after the disclaimant's death, and children of a disclaimed peer may, if they wish, retain their precedence and any courtesy titles and styles borne as children of a peer. The disclaimer permitted the disclaimant to sit in the House of Commons if elected as an MP. As the House of Lords Act 1999 removed hereditary peers from the House of Lords, they are now entitled to sit in the House of Commons without having to disclaim their titles.

The following peerages are currently disclaimed:
EARLDOM: Selkirk (1994)
BARONIES: Reith (1972); Sanderson of Ayot (1971); Silkin (2002)
PEERS WHO ARE MINORS (ie under 21 years of age)
BARONS: Hawke (b. 1995); Rodney (b. 1999)

## FORMS OF ADDRESS
Forms of address are given under the style for each individual rank of the peerage. Both formal and social forms of address are given where usage differs; nowadays, the social form is generally preferred to the formal, which increasingly is used only for official documents and on very formal occasions.

## ROLL OF THE PEERAGE
Crown Office, House of Lords, London SW1A 0PW

The Roll of the Peerage is kept at the Crown Office and maintained by the Registrar and Assistant Registrar of the Peerage in accordance with the terms of a 2004 royal warrant. The roll records the names of all living life peers and hereditary peers who have proved their succession to the satisfaction of the Lord Chancellor. The Roll of the Peerage is maintained in addition to the Clerk of the Parliaments' register of hereditary peers eligible to stand for election in House of Lords' by-elections.

A person whose name is not entered on the Roll of the Peerage can not be addressed or mentioned by the title of a peer in any official document.
*Registrar*, Ian Denyer, MVO
*Assistant Registrar*, Grant Bavister

# HEREDITARY PEERS

*as at 31 August 2015*

## PEERS OF THE BLOOD ROYAL

*Style*, His Royal Highness the Duke of _/His Royal Highness the Earl of_/His Royal Highness the Lord_
*Style of address (formal)* May it please your Royal Highness; *(informal)* Sir

| Created | Title, order of succession, name, etc | Heir |
|---|---|---|
| | *Dukes* | |
| 1947 | *Edinburgh (1st)*, HRH the Prince Philip, Duke of Edinburgh | The Prince of Wales * |
| 1337 | *Cornwall*, HRH the Prince of Wales, *s.* 1952 | ‡ |
| 1398 S. | *Rothesay*, HRH the Prince of Wales, *s.* 1952 | ‡ |
| 2011 | *Cambridge (1st)*, HRH Prince William of Wales | HRH Prince George of Cambridge |
| 1986 | *York (1st)*, Prince Andrew, HRH the Duke of York | None |
| 1928 | *Gloucester (2nd)*, Prince Richard, HRH the Duke of Gloucester, *s.* 1974 | Earl of Ulster |
| 1934 | *Kent (2nd)*, Prince Edward, HRH the Duke of Kent, *s.* 1942 | Earl of St Andrews |
| | *Earl* | |
| 1999 | *Wessex (1st)*, Prince Edward, HRH the Earl of Wesex | Viscount Severn |

\* In June 1999 Buckingham Palace announced that the current Earl of Wessex will be granted the Dukedom of Edinburgh when the title reverts to the Crown. The title will only revert to the Crown on both the death of the current Duke of Edinburgh and the Prince of Wales' succession as king
‡ The title is held by the sovereign's eldest son from the moment of his birth or the sovereign's accession

# DUKES

*Coronet*, Eight strawberry leaves

*Style*, His Grace the Duke of _
  *Envelope (formal)*, His Grace the Duke of _; *(social)*, The Duke of _. *Letter (formal)*, My Lord Duke; *(social)*, Dear Duke.
*Spoken (formal)*, Your Grace; *(social)*, Duke
*Wife's style*, Her Grace the Duchess of _
  *Envelope (formal)*, Her Grace the Duchess of _; *(social)*, The Duchess of _. *Letter (formal)*, Dear Madam; *(social)*, Dear
Duchess. *Spoken*, Duchess
*Eldest son's style*, Takes his father's second title as a courtesy title (*see* Courtesy Titles)
*Younger sons' style*, 'Lord' before forename (F_) and surname (S_)
  *Envelope*, Lord F_ S_. *Letter (formal)*, My Lord; *(social)*, Dear Lord F_. *Spoken (formal)*, My Lord; *(social)*, Lord F_
*Daughters' style*, 'Lady' before forename (F_) and surname (S_)
  *Envelope*, Lady F_ S_. *Letter (formal)*, Dear Madam; *(social)*, Dear Lady F_. *Spoken*, Lady F_

| Created | Title, order of succession, name, etc | Heir |
|---|---|---|
| 1868 I. | *Abercorn (5th)*, James Hamilton, KG, *b.* 1934, *s.* 1979, *m.* | Marquess of Hamilton, *b.* 1969 |
| 1701 S. | *Argyll (13th)*, Torquhil Ian Campbell, *b.* 1968, *s.* 2001, *m.* | Marquess of Lorne, *b.* 2004 |
| 1703 S. | *Atholl (12th)*, Bruce George Ronald Murray, *b.* 1960, *s.* 2012, *m.* | Marquis of Tullibardine, *b.* 1985 |
| 1682 | *Beaufort (11th)*, David Robert Somerset, *b.* 1928, *s.* 1984, *m.* | Marquess of Worcester, *b.* 1952 |
| 1694 | *Bedford (15th)*, Andrew Ian Henry Russell, *b.* 1962, *s.* 2003, *m.* | Marquess of Tavistock, *b.* 2005 |
| 1663 S. | *Buccleuch (10th) and Queensberry (12th) (S. 1684)*, Richard Walter John Montagu Douglas Scott, KBE, *b.* 1954, *s.* 2007, *m.* | Earl of Dalkeith, *b.* 1984 |
| 1694 | *Devonshire (12th)*, Peregrine Andrew Morny Cavendish, KCVO, CBE, *b.* 1944, *s.* 2004, *m.* | Earl of Burlington, *b.* 1969 |
| 1900 | *Fife (4th)*, David Charles Carnegie, *b.* 1961, *s.* 2015, *m.* | Earl of Southesk, *b.* 1989 |
| 1675 | *Grafton (12th)*, Henry Oliver Charles FitzRoy, *b.* 1978, *s.* 2011, *m.* | Earl of Euston, *b.* 2012 |
| 1643 S. | *Hamilton (16th) and Brandon (13th) (1711)*, Alexander Douglas Douglas-Hamilton, *b.* 1978, *s.* 2010, *m. Premier Peer of Scotland* | Marquess of Douglas and Clydesdale, *b.* 2012 |
| 1766 I. | *Leinster (9th)*, Maurice FitzGerald, *b.* 1948, *s.* 2004, *m. Premier Duke, Marquess and Earl of Ireland* | Edward F., *b.* 1988 |
| 1719 | *Manchester (13th)*, Alexander Charles David Drogo Montagu, *b.* 1962, *s.* 2002, *m.* | Lord Kimble W. D. M., *b.* 1964 |
| 1702 | *Marlborough (12th)*, Charles James Spencer-Churchill, *b.* 1955, *s.* 2014, *m.* | Marquess of Blandford, *b.* 1992 |
| 1707 S. | ** *Montrose (8th)*, James Graham, *b.* 1935, *s.* 1992, *w.* | Marquis of Graham, *b.* 1973 |
| 1483 | ** *Norfolk (18th)*, Edward William Fitzalan-Howard, *b.* 1956, *s.* 2002, *m. Premier Duke and Earl Marshal* | Earl of Arundel and Surrey, *b.* 1987 |
| 1766 | *Northumberland (12th)*, Ralph George Algernon Percy, *b.* 1956, *s.* 1995, *m.* | Earl Percy, *b.* 1984 |
| 1675 | *Richmond (10th) and Gordon (5th) (1876)*, Charles Henry Gordon Lennox, *b.* 1929, *s.* 1989, *m.* | Earl of March and Kinrara, *b.* 1955 |
| 1707 S. | *Roxburghe (10th)*, Guy David Innes-Ker, *b.* 1954, *s.* 1974, *m. Premier Baronet of Scotland* | Marquis of Bowmont and Cessford, *b.* 1981 |
| 1703 | *Rutland (11th)*, David Charles Robert Manners, *b.* 1959, *s.* 1999, *m.* | Marquess of Granby, *b.* 1999 |
| 1684 | *St Albans (14th)*, Murray de Vere Beauclerk, *b.* 1939, *s.* 1988, *m.* | Earl of Burford, *b.* 1965 |
| 1547 | ** *Somerset (19th)*, John Michael Edward Seymour, *b.* 1952, *s.* 1984, *m.* | Lord Seymour, *b.* 1982 |
| 1833 | *Sutherland (7th)*, Francis Ronald Egerton, *b.* 1940, *s.* 2000, *m.* | Marquess of Stafford, *b.* 1975 |
| 1814 | ** *Wellington (9th)*, Arthur Charles Valerian Wellesley, OBE, *b.* 1945, *s.* 2014, *m.* | Marquess of Douro, *b.* 1978 |
| 1874 | *Westminster (6th)*, Gerald Cavendish Grosvenor, KG, CB, CVO, OBE, TD, *b.* 1951, *s.* 1979, *m.* | Earl Grosvenor, *b.* 1991 |

# MARQUESSES

*Coronet,* Four strawberry leaves alternating with four silver balls

*Style,* The Most Hon. the Marquess (of) _ . In Scotland the spelling 'Marquis' is preferred for pre-Union creations
    *Envelope (formal),* The Most Hon. the Marquess of _; *(social),* The Marquess of _. *Letter (formal),* My Lord; *(social),* Dear Lord _. *Spoken (formal),* My Lord; *(social),* Lord _
*Wife's style,* The Most Hon. the Marchioness (of) _
    *Envelope (formal),* The Most Hon. the Marchioness of _; *(social),* The Marchioness of _. *Letter (formal),* Madam; *(social),* Dear Lady _. *Spoken,* Lady _
*Eldest son's style,* Takes his father's second title as a courtesy title (*see* Courtesy Titles)
*Younger sons' style,* 'Lord' before forename and surname, as for Duke's younger sons
*Daughters' style,* 'Lady' before forename and surname, as for Duke's daughter

| Created | Title, order of succession, name, etc | Heir |
|---|---|---|
| 1915 | Aberdeen and Temair (7th), Alexander George Gordon, b. 1955, s. 2002, m. | Earl of Haddo, b. 1983 |
| 1876 | Abergavenny (6th) and 10th Earl of Abergavenny (1784), Christopher George Charles Nevill, b. 1955, s. 2000, m. | To Earldom only, David M. R. N., b. 1941 |
| 1821 | Ailesbury (8th), Michael Sidney Cedric Brudenell-Bruce, b. 1926, s. 1974 | Earl of Cardigan, b. 1952 |
| 1831 | Ailsa (9th), David Thomas Kennedy, b. 1958, s. 2015, m. | Earl of Cassilis, b. 1995 |
| 1815 | Anglesey (8th), Charles Alexander Vaughan Paget, b. 1950, s. 2013, m. | Earl of Uxbridge, b. 1986 |
| 1789 | Bath (7th), Alexander George Thynn, b. 1932, s. 1992, m. | Viscount Weymouth, b. 1974 |
| 1826 | Bristol (8th), Frederick William Augustus Hervey, b. 1979, s. 1999 | Timothy H. H., b. 1960 |
| 1796 | Bute (7th), John Colum Crichton-Stuart, b. 1958, s. 1993, m. | Earl of Dumfries, b. 1989 |
| 1812 | ° Camden (6th), David George Edward Henry Pratt, b. 1930, s. 1983 | Earl of Brecknock, b. 1965 |
| 1815 | ** Cholmondeley (7th), David George Philip Cholmondeley, KCVO, b. 1960, s. 1990, m. Lord Great Chamberlain | Earl of Rocksavage, b. 2010 |
| 1816 I. | ° Conyngham (8th), Henry Vivian Pierpoint Conyngham, b. 1951, s. 2009, m. | Earl of Mount Charles, b. 1975 |
| 1791 I. | Donegall (8th), Arthur Patrick Chichester, b. 1952, s. 2007, m. | Earl of Belfast, b. 1990 |
| 1789 I. | Downshire (9th), (Arthur Francis) Nicholas Wills Hill, b. 1959, s. 2003, m. | Earl of Hillsborough, b. 1996 |
| 1801 I. | Ely (9th), Charles John Tottenham, b. 1943, s. 2006, m. | Lord Timothy C. T., b. 1948 |
| 1801 | Exeter (8th), (William) Michael Anthony Cecil, b. 1935, s. 1988, m. | Lord Burghley, b. 1970 |
| 1800 I. | Headfort (7th), Thomas Michael Ronald Christopher Taylour, b. 1959, s. 2005, m. | Earl of Bective, b. 1989 |
| 1793 | Hertford (9th), Henry Jocelyn Seymour, b. 1958, s. 1997, m. | Earl of Yarmouth, b. 1993 |
| 1599 S. | Huntly (13th), Granville Charles Gomer Gordon, b. 1944, s. 1987, m. Premier Marquess of Scotland | Earl of Aboyne, b. 1973 |
| 1784 | Lansdowne (9th), Charles Maurice Mercer Nairne Petty-Fitzmaurice, LVO b. 1941, s. 1999, m. | Earl of Kerry, b. 1970 |
| 1902 | Linlithgow (4th), Adrian John Charles Hope, b. 1946, s. 1987, m. | Earl of Hopetoun, b. 1969 |
| 1816 I. | Londonderry (10th), Frederick Aubrey Vane-Tempest-Stewart, b. 1972, s. 2012 | Lord Reginald A. V-T-S, b. 1977 |
| 1701 S. | Lothian (13th) and Baron Kerr of Monteviot (life peerage, 2010), Michael Andrew Foster Jude Kerr (Michael Ancram), PC, QC, b. 1945, s. 2004, m. | Lord Ralph W. F. J. K., b. 1957 |
| 1917 | Milford Haven (4th), George Ivar Louis Mountbatten, b. 1961, s. 1970, m. | Earl of Medina, b. 1991 |
| 1838 | Normanby (5th), Constantine Edmund Walter Phipps, b. 1954, s. 1994, m. | Earl of Mulgrave, b. 1994 |
| 1812 | Northampton (7th), Spencer Douglas David Compton, b. 1946, s. 1978, m. | Earl Compton, b. 1973 |
| 1682 S. | Queensberry (12th), David Harrington Angus Douglas, b. 1929, s. 1954, m. | Viscount Drumlanrig, b. 1967 |
| 1926 | Reading (4th), Simon Charles Henry Rufus Isaacs, b. 1942, s. 1980, m. | Viscount Erleigh, b. 1986 |
| 1789 | Salisbury (7th) and Baron Gascoyne-Cecil (life peerage, 1999), Robert Michael James Gascoyne-Cecil, KCVO, PC, b. 1946, s. 2003, m. | Viscount Cranborne, b. 1970 |
| 1800 I. | Sligo (12th), Sebastian Ulick Browne, b. 1964, s. 2014, m. | Earl of Altamont, b. 1988 |
| 1787 | ° Townshend (8th), Charles George Townshend, b. 1945, s. 2010, m. | Viscount Raynham, b. 1977 |
| 1694 S. | Tweeddale (14th), Charles David Montagu Hay, b. 1947, s. 2005 | (Lord) Alistair J. M. H., b. 1955 |
| 1789 I. | Waterford (9th), Henry Nicholas de la Poer Beresford, b. 1958, s. 2015, m. | Earl of Tyrone, b. 1987 |
| 1551 | Winchester (18th), Nigel George Paulet, b. 1941, s. 1968, m. Premier Marquess of England | Earl of Wiltshire, b. 1969 |
| 1892 | Zetland (4th), Lawrence Mark Dundas, b. 1937, s. 1989, m. | Earl of Ronaldshay, b. 1965 |

# EARLS

*Coronet*, Eight silver balls on stalks alternating with eight gold strawberry leaves

*Style*, The Rt. Hon. the Earl (of) _
    *Envelope (formal)*, The Rt. Hon. the Earl (of) _; *(social)*, The Earl (of) _. *Letter (formal)*, My Lord; *(social)*, Dear Lord
    _. *Spoken (formal)*, My Lord; *(social)*, Lord _.
*Wife's style*, The Rt. Hon. the Countess (of) _
    *Envelope (formal)*, The Rt. Hon. the Countess (of) _; *(social)*, The Countess (of) _. *Letter (formal)*, Madam; *(social)*,
    Lady _. *Spoken (formal)*, Madam; *(social)*, Lady _.
*Eldest son's style*, Takes his father's second title as a courtesy title (*see* Courtesy Titles)
*Younger sons' style*, 'The Hon.' before forename and surname, as for Baron's children
*Daughters' style*, 'Lady' before forename and surname, as for Duke's daughter

| Created | Title, order of succession, name, etc | Heir |
|---|---|---|
| 1639 S. | Airlie (13th), David George Coke Patrick Ogilvy, KT, GCVO, PC, Royal Victorian Chain, b. 1926, s. 1968, m. | Lord Ogilvy, b. 1958 |
| 1696 | Albemarle (10th), Rufus Arnold Alexis Keppel, b. 1965, s. 1979, m. | Viscount Bury, b. 2003 |
| 1952 | ° Alexander of Tunis (2nd), Shane William Desmond Alexander, b. 1935, s. 1969, m. | Hon. Brian J. A., CMG, b. 1939 |
| 1662 S. | Annandale and Hartfell (11th), Patrick Andrew Wentworth Hope Johnstone, b. 1941, s. 1983, m. claim established 1985 | Lord Johnstone, b. 1971 |
| 1789 I. | ° Annesley (12th), Michael Robert Annesley, b. 1933, s. 2011, m. | Viscount Glerawly, b. 1957 |
| 1785 I. | Antrim (9th), Alexander Randal Mark McDonnell, b. 1935, s. 1977, m. | Viscount Dunluce, b. 1967 |
| 1762 I. | ** Arran (9th) and 5th UK Baron Sudley (1884), Arthur Desmond Colquhoun Gore, b. 1938, s. 1983, m. | William H. G., b. 1950 (to the Earldom) |
| 1955 | ° ** Attlee (3rd), John Richard Attlee, b. 1956, s. 1991, m. | None |
| 1714 | Aylesford (12th), Charles Heneage Finch-Knightley, b. 1947, s. 2008, m. | Lord Guernsey, b. 1985 |
| 1937 | ** Baldwin of Bewdley (4th), Edward Alfred Alexander Baldwin, b. 1938, s. 1976, w. | Viscount Corvedale, b. 1973 |
| 1922 | Balfour (5th), Roderick Francis Arthur Balfour, b. 1948, s. 2003, m. | Charles G. Y. B., b. 1951 |
| 1772 | ° Bathurst (9th), Allen Christopher Bertram Bathurst, b. 1961, s. 2011, m. | Lord Apsley, b. 1990 |
| 1919 | ° Beatty (3rd), David Beatty, b. 1946, s. 1972, m. | Viscount Borodale, b. 1973 |
| 1797 I. | ° Belmore (8th), John Armar Lowry-Corry, b. 1951, s. 1960, m. | Viscount Corry, b. 1985 |
| 1739 I. | Bessborough (12th), Myles Fitzhugh Longfield Ponsonby, b. 1941, s. 2002, m. | Viscount Duncannon, b. 1974 |
| 1815 | Bradford (7th), Richard Thomas Orlando Bridgeman, b. 1947, s. 1981, m. | Viscount Newport, b. 1980 |
| 1469 S. | Buchan (17th), Malcolm Harry Erskine, b. 1930, s. 1984, m. | Lord Cardross, b. 1960 |
| 1746 | Buckinghamshire (10th), (George) Miles Hobart-Hampden, b. 1944, s. 1983, m. | Sir John V. Hobart, Bt., b. 1945 |
| 1800 | ° Cadogan (8th), Charles Gerald John Cadogan, KBE, b. 1937, s. 1997, m. | Viscount Chelsea, b. 1966 |
| 1878 | ° Cairns (6th), Simon Dallas Cairns, CVO, CBE, b. 1939, s. 1989, m. | Viscount Garmoyle, b. 1965 |
| 1455 S. | ** Caithness (20th), Malcolm Ian Sinclair, PC, b. 1948, s. 1965, w. | Lord Berriedale, b. 1981 |
| 1800 I. | Caledon (7th), Nicholas James Alexander, KCVO, b. 1955, s. 1980, m. | Viscount Alexander, b. 1990 |
| 1661 | Carlisle (13th), George William Beaumont Howard, b. 1949, s. 1994 | Hon. Philip C. W. H., b. 1963 |
| 1793 | Carnarvon (8th), George Reginald Oliver Molyneux Herbert, b. 1956, s. 2001, m. | Lord Porchester, b. 1992 |
| 1748 I. | Carrick (11th), Arion Thomas Piers Hamilton Butler, b. 1975, s. 2008, m. | Hon. Piers E. T. L. B., b. 1979 |
| 1800 I. | ° Castle Stewart (8th), Arthur Patrick Avondale Stuart, b. 1928, s. 1961, m. | Viscount Stuart, b. 1953 |
| 1814 | °** Cathcart (7th), Charles Alan Andrew Cathcart, b. 1952, s. 1999, m. | Lord Greenock, b. 1986 |
| 1647 I. | Cavan (13th), Roger Cavan Lambart, b. 1944, s. 1988 (claim to the peerage not yet established) | Cavan C. E. L., b. 1957 |
| 1827 | ° Cawdor (7th), Colin Robert Vaughan Campbell, b. 1962, s. 1993, m. | Viscount Emlyn, b. 1998 |
| 1801 | Chichester (9th), John Nicholas Pelham, b. 1944, s. 1944, m. | Richard A. H. P., b. 1952 |
| 1803 I. | ** Clancarty (9th), Nicholas Power Richard Le Poer Trench, b. 1952, s. 1995, m. | None |
| 1776 I. | Clanwilliam (8th), Patrick James Meade, b. 1960, s. 2009, m. | Lord Gillford, b. 1998 |
| 1776 | Clarendon (8th), George Edward Laurence Villiers, b. 1976, s. 2009, m. | Lord Hyde, b. 2008 |
| 1620 I. | Cork and Orrery (15th), John Richard Boyle, b. 1945, s. 2003, m. | Viscount Dungarvan, b. 1978 |
| 1850 | Cottenham (9th), Mark John Henry Pepys, b. 1983, s. 2000, m. | Hon. Sam R. P., b. 1986 |
| 1762 I. | ** Courtown (9th), James Patrick Montagu Burgoyne Winthrop Stopford, b. 1954, s. 1975, m. | Viscount Stopford, b. 1988 |
| 1697 | Coventry (13th), George William Coventry, b. 1939, s. 2004, m. | David D. S. C., b. 1973 |
| 1857 | ° Cowley (7th), Garret Graham Wellesley, b. 1934, s. 1975, m. | Viscount Dangan, b. 1965 |

| | | |
|---|---|---|
| 1892 | *Cranbrook (5th)*, Gathorne Gathorne-Hardy, *b.* 1933, *s.* 1978, *m.* | Lord Medway, *b.* 1968 |
| 1801 | *Craven (9th)*, Benjamin Robert Joseph Craven, *b.* 1989, *s.* 1990 | Rupert J. E. C., *b.* 1926 |
| 1398 S. | *Crawford (29th) and Balcarres (12th) (S. 1651) and Baron Balniel (life peerage, 1974)*, Robert Alexander Lindsay, KT, GCVO, PC, *b.* 1927, *s.* 1975, *m.* Premier Earl on Union Roll | Lord Balniel, *b.* 1958 |
| 1861 | *Cromartie (5th)*, John Ruaridh Blunt Grant Mackenzie, *b.* 1948, *s.* 1989, *m.* | Viscount Tarbat, *b.* 1987 |
| 1901 | *Cromer (4th)*, Evelyn Rowland Esmond Baring, *b.* 1946, *s.* 1991, *m.* | Viscount Errington, *b.* 1994 |
| 1633 S. | *Dalhousie (17th)*, James Hubert Ramsay, *b.* 1948, *s.* 1999, *m. Lord Steward* | Lord Ramsay, *b.* 1981 |
| 1725 I. | *Darnley (11th)*, Adam Ivo Stuart Bligh, *b.* 1941, *s.* 1980, *m.* | Lord Clifton, *b.* 1968 |
| 1711 | *Dartmouth (10th)*, William Legge, MEP, *b.* 1949, *s.* 1997, *m.* | Hon. Rupert L., *b.* 1951 |
| 1761 | ° *De La Warr (11th)*, William Herbrand Sackville, *b.* 1948, *s.* 1988, *m.* | Lord Buckhurst, *b.* 1979 |
| 1622 | *Denbigh (12th) and Desmond (11th) (I. 1622)*, Alexander Stephen Rudolph Feilding, *b.* 1970, *s.* 1995, *m.* | Viscount Feilding, *b.* 2005 |
| 1485 | *Derby (19th)*, Edward Richard William Stanley, *b.* 1962, *s.* 1994, *m.* | Lord Stanley, *b.* 1998 |
| 1553 | *Devon (19th)*, Charles Peregrine Courtenay, *b.* 1975, *s.* 2015, *m.* | Lord Courtenay, *b.* 2009 |
| 1800 I. | *Donoughmore (8th)*, Richard Michael John Hely-Hutchinson, *b.* 1927, *s.* 1981, *w.* | Viscount Suirdale, *b.* 1952 |
| 1661 I. | *Drogheda (12th)*, Henry Dermot Ponsonby Moore, *b.* 1937, *s.* 1989, *m.* | Viscount Moore, *b.* 1983 |
| 1837 | *Ducie (7th)*, David Leslie Moreton, *b.* 1951, *s.* 1991, *m.* | Lord Moreton, *b.* 1981 |
| 1860 | *Dudley (5th)*, William Humble David Jeremy Ward, *b.* 1947, *s.* 2013 | Hon. Leander G. D. W., *b.* 1971 |
| 1660 S. | ** *Dundee (12th)*, Alexander Henry Scrymgeour, *b.* 1949, *s.* 1983, *m.* | Lord Scrymgeour, *b.* 1982 |
| 1669 S. | *Dundonald (15th)*, Iain Alexander Douglas Blair Cochrane, *b.* 1961, *s.* 1986, *m.* | Lord Cochrane, *b.* 1991 |
| 1686 S. | *Dunmore (12th)*, Malcolm Kenneth Murray, *b.* 1946, *s.* 1995, *m.* | Hon. Geoffrey C. M., *b.* 1949 |
| 1833 | *Durham (7th)*, Edward Richard Lambton, *b.* 1961, *s.* 2006, *m.* | Viscount Lambton, *b.* 1985 |
| 1643 S. | *Dysart (13th)*, John Peter Grant of Rothiemurchus, *b.* 1946, *s.* 2011, *m.* | Lord Huntingtower, *b.* 1977 |
| 1837 | *Effingham (7th)*, David Mowbray Algernon Howard, *b.* 1939, *s.* 1996, *m.* | Lord Howard of Effingham, *b.* 1971 |
| 1507 S. | *Eglinton (18th) and Winton (9th) (S. 1600)*, Archibald George Montgomerie, *b.* 1939, *s.* 1966, *m.* | Lord Montgomerie, *b.* 1966 |
| 1821 | *Eldon (5th)*, John Joseph Nicholas Scott, *b.* 1937, *s.* 1976, *m.* | Viscount Encombe, *b.* 1962 |
| 1633 S. | *Elgin (11th) and Kincardine (15th) (S. 1647)*, Andrew Douglas Alexander Thomas Bruce, KT, *b.* 1924, *s.* 1968, *m.* | Lord Bruce, *b.* 1961 |
| 1789 I. | *Enniskillen (7th)*, Andrew John Galbraith Cole, *b.* 1942, *s.* 1989, *m.* | Berkeley A. C., *b.* 1949 |
| 1789 I. | *Erne (6th)*, Henry George Victor John Crichton, KCVO, *b.* 1937, *s.* 1940, *m.* | Viscount Crichton, *b.* 1971 |
| 1452 S. | ** *Erroll (24th)*, Merlin Sereld Victor Gilbert Hay, *b.* 1948, *s.* 1978, *m.* Hereditary Lord High Constable and Knight Marischal of Scotland | Lord Hay, *b.* 1984 |
| 1661 | *Essex (11th)*, Frederick Paul de Vere Capell, *b.* 1944, *s.* 2005 | William J. C., *b.* 1952 |
| 1711 | ° *Ferrers (14th)*, Robert William Saswalo Shirley, *b.* 1952, *s.* 2012, *m.* | Viscount Tamworth, *b.* 1984 |
| 1789 | ° *Fortescue (8th)*, Charles Hugh Richard Fortescue, *b.* 1951, *s.* 1993, *m.* | John A. F. F., *b.* 1955 |
| 1841 | *Gainsborough (6th)*, Anthony Baptist Noel, *b.* 1950, *s.* 2009, *m.* | Viscount Campden, *b.* 1977 |
| 1623 S. | *Galloway (13th)*, Randolph Keith Reginald Stewart, *b.* 1928, *s.* 1978, *w.* | Andrew C. S., *b.* 1949 |
| 1703 S. | ** *Glasgow (10th)*, Patrick Robin Archibald Boyle, *b.* 1939, *s.* 1984, *m.* | Viscount of Kelburn, *b.* 1978 |
| 1806 I. | *Gosford (7th)*, Charles David Nicholas Alexander John Sparrow Acheson, *b.* 1942, *s.* 1966, *m.* | Nicholas H. C. A., *b.* 1947 |
| 1945 | *Gowrie (2nd)*, Alexander Patrick Greysteil Hore Ruthven, PC, *b.* 1939, *s.* 1955, *m.* | Viscount Ruthven of Canberra, *b.* 1964 |
| 1684 I. | *Granard (10th)*, Peter Arthur Edward Hastings Forbes, *b.* 1957, *s.* 1992, *m.* | Viscount Forbes, *b.* 1981 |
| 1833 | ° *Granville (6th)*, Granville George Fergus Leveson-Gower, *b.* 1959, *s.* 1996, *m.* | Lord Leveson, *b.* 1999 |
| 1806 | ° *Grey (7th)*, Philip Kent Grey, *b.* 1940, *s.* 2013, *m.* | Viscount Howick, *b.* 1968 |
| 1752 | *Guilford (10th)*, Piers Edward Brownlow North, *b.* 1971, *s.* 1999, *m.* | Lord North, *b.* 2002 |
| 1619 S. | *Haddington (13th)*, John George Baillie-Hamilton, *b.* 1941, *s.* 1986, *m.* | Lord Binning, *b.* 1985 |
| 1919 | ° *Haig (3rd)*, Alexander Douglas Derrick Haig, *b.* 1961, *s.* 2009, *m.* | None |
| 1944 | *Halifax (3rd)*, Charles Edward Peter Neil Wood, *b.* 1944, *s.* 1980, *m.* | Lord Irwin, *b.* 1977 |
| 1754 | *Hardwicke (10th)*, Joseph Philip Sebastian Yorke, *b.* 1971, *s.* 1974, *m.* | Viscount Royston, *b.* 2009 |
| 1812 | *Harewood (8th)*, David Henry George Lascelles, *b.* 1950, *s.* 2011, *m.* | Viscount Lascelles, *b.* 1978 |
| 1742 | *Harrington (12th)*, Charles Henry Leicester Stanhope, *b.* 1945, *s.* 2009, *m.* | Viscount Petersham, *b.* 1967 |
| 1809 | *Harrowby (8th)*, Dudley Adrian Conroy Ryder, *b.* 1951, *s.* 2007, *m.* | Viscount Sandon, *b.* 1981 |
| 1605 S. | ** *Home (15th)*, David Alexander Cospatrick Douglas-Home, KT, CVO, CBE, *b.* 1943, *s.* 1995, *m.* | Lord Dunglass, *b.* 1987 |
| 1821 | ° ** *Howe (7th)*, Frederick Richard Penn Curzon, PC, *b.* 1951, *s.* 1984, *m.* | Viscount Curzon, *b.* 1994 |
| 1529 | *Huntingdon (16th)*, William Edward Robin Hood Hastings Bass, LVO, *b.* 1948, *s.* 1990, *m.* | Hon. Simon A. R. H. H. B., *b.* 1950 |
| 1885 | *Iddesleigh (5th)*, John Stafford Northcote, *b.* 1957, *s.* 2004, *m.* | Viscount St Cyres, *b.* 1985 |
| 1756 | *Ilchester (10th)*, Robin Maurice Fox-Strangways, *b.* 1942, *s.* 2006, *m.* | Lord Stavordale, *b.* 1972 |
| 1929 | *Inchcape (4th)*, (Kenneth) Peter (Lyle) Mackay, *b.* 1943, *s.* 1994, *m.* | Viscount Glenapp, *b.* 1979 |
| 1919 | *Iveagh (4th)*, Arthur Edward Rory Guinness, *b.* 1969, *s.* 1992, *m.* | Viscount Elveden, *b.* 2003 |
| 1925 | ° *Jellicoe (3rd)*, Patrick John Bernard Jellicoe, *b.* 1950, *s.* 2007 | Hon. Nicholas C. J., *b.* 1953 |

| | | |
|---|---|---|
| 1697 | *Jersey (10th)*, George Francis William Child Villiers, *b.* 1976, *s.* 1998, *m.* | Viscount Villiers, *b.* 2015 |
| 1822 I. | *Kilmorey (6th)*, Sir Richard Francis Needham, PC, *b.* 1942, *s.* 1977, *m.* (Does not use title) | Viscount Newry and Mourne, *b.* 1966 |
| 1866 | *Kimberley (5th)*, John Armine Wodehouse, *b.* 1951, *s.* 2002, *m.* | Lord Wodehouse, *b.* 1978 |
| 1768 I. | *Kingston (12th)*, Robert Charles Henry King-Tenison, *b.* 1969, *s.* 2002, *m.* | Viscount Kingsborough, *b.* 2000 |
| 1633 S. | ** *Kinnoull (16th)*, Charles William Harley Hay, *b.* 1962, *s.* 2013, *m.* | Viscount Dupplin, *b.* 2011 |
| 1677 S. | *Kintore (14th)*, James William Falconer Keith, *b.* 1976, *s.* 2004, *m.* | Lord Inverurie, *b.* 2010 |
| 1624 S. | *Lauderdale (18th)*, Ian Maitland, *b.* 1937, *s.* 2008, *m.* | Viscount Maitland, *b.* 1965 |
| 1837 | *Leicester (8th)*, Thomas Edward Coke, *b.* 1965, *s.* 2015, *m.* | Viscount Coke, *b.* 2003 |
| 1641 S. | *Leven (15th) and Melville (14th) (S. 1690)*, Alexander Ian Leslie Melville, *b.* 1984, *s.* 2012 | Hon. Archibald R. L. M., *b.* 1957 |
| 1831 | *Lichfield (6th)*, Thomas William Robert Hugh Anson, *b.* 1978, *s.* 2005, *m.* | Viscount Anson, *b.* 2011 |
| 1803 I. | *Limerick (7th)*, Edmund Christopher Pery, *b.* 1963, *s.* 2003, *m.* | Viscount Glentworth, *b.* 1991 |
| 1572 | *Lincoln (19th)*, Robert Edward Fiennes-Clinton, *b.* 1972, *s.* 2001 | Hon. William J. Howson, *b.* 1980 |
| 1633 S. | ** *Lindsay (16th)*, James Randolph Lindesay-Bethune, *b.* 1955, *s.* 1989, *m.* | Viscount Garnock, *b.* 1990 |
| 1626 | *Lindsey (14th) and Abingdon (9th) (1682)*, Richard Henry Rupert Bertie, *b.* 1931, *s.* 1963, *m.* | Lord Norreys, *b.* 1958 |
| 1776 I. | *Lisburne (9th)*, David John Francis Malet Vaughan, *b.* 1945, *s.* 2014, *m.* | Hon. Michael J. W. M. V., *b.* 1948 |
| 1822 I. | ** *Listowel (6th)*, Francis Michael Hare, *b.* 1964, *s.* 1997, *m.* | Hon. Timothy P. H., *b.* 1966 |
| 1905 | ** *Liverpool (5th)*, Edward Peter Bertram Savile Foljambe, *b.* 1944, *s.* 1969, *m.* | Viscount Hawkesbury, *b.* 1972 |
| 1945 | ° *Lloyd George of Dwyfor (4th)*, David Richard Owen Lloyd George, *b.* 1951, *s.* 2010, *m.* | Viscount Gwynedd, *b.* 1986 |
| 1785 I. | *Longford (8th)*, Thomas Frank Dermot Pakenham, *b.* 1933, *s.* 2001, *m.* (Does not use title) | Edward M. P., *b.* 1970 |
| 1807 | *Lonsdale (8th)*, Hugh Clayton Lowther, *b.* 1949, *s.* 2006, *m.* | Hon. William J. L., *b.* 1957 |
| 1633 S. | *Loudoun (15th)*, Simon Michael Abney-Hastings, *b.* 1974, *s.* 2012, *m.* | Hon. Marcus W. A.-H., *b.* 1981 |
| 1838 | *Lovelace (5th)*, Peter Axel William Locke King, *b.* 1951, *s.* 1964, *m.* | None |
| 1795 I. | *Lucan (7th)*, Richard John Bingham, *b.* 1934, *s.* 1964, *m.* (missing since 8 November 1974) | Lord Bingham, *b.* 1967 |
| 1880 | ** *Lytton (5th)*, John Peter Michael Scawen Lytton, *b.* 1950, *s.* 1985, *m.* | Viscount Knebworth, *b.* 1989 |
| 1721 | *Macclesfield (9th)*, Richard Timothy George Mansfield Parker, *b.* 1943, *s.* 1992, *m.* | Hon. J. David G. P., *b.* 1945 |
| 1800 | *Malmesbury (7th)*, James Carleton Harris, *b.* 1946, *s.* 2000, *m.* | Viscount FitzHarris, *b.* 1970 |
| 1776 | *Mansfield and Mansfield (8th) (1792)*, William David Mungo James Murray, *b.* 1930, *s.* 1971, *m.* | Viscount Stormont, *b.* 1956 |
| 1565 S. | *Mar (14th) and Kellie (16th) (S. 1616) and Baron Erskine of Alloa Tower (life peerage, 2000)*, James Thorne Erskine, *b.* 1949, *s.* 1994, *m.* | Hon. Alexander D. E., *b.* 1952 |
| 1785 I. | *Mayo (11th)*, Charles Diarmuidh John Bourke, *b.* 1953, *s.* 2006, *m.* | Lord Naas, *b.* 1985 |
| 1627 I. | *Meath (15th)*, John Anthony Brabazon, *b.* 1941, *s.* 1998, *m.* | Lord Ardee, *b.* 1977 |
| 1766 I. | *Mexborough (8th)*, John Christopher George Savile, *b.* 1931, *s.* 1980, *m.* | Viscount Pollington, *b.* 1959 |
| 1813 | *Minto (7th)*, Gilbert Timothy George Lariston Elliot-Murray-Kynynmound, *b.* 1953, *s.* 2005, *m.* | Viscount Melgund, *b.* 1984 |
| 1562 S. | *Moray (21st)*, John Douglas Stuart, *b.* 1966, *s.* 2011, *m.* | Lord Doune, *b.* 2002 |
| 1815 | *Morley (6th)*, John St Aubyn Parker, KCVO, *b.* 1923, *s.* 1962, *m.* | Viscount Boringdon, *b.* 1956 |
| 1458 S. | *Morton (22nd)*, John Charles Sholto Douglas, *b.* 1927, *s.* 1976, *m.* | Lord Aberdour, *b.* 1952 |
| 1789 | *Mount Edgcumbe (8th)*, Robert Charles Edgcumbe, *b.* 1939, *s.* 1982 | Piers V. E., *b.* 1946 |
| 1805 | ° *Nelson (10th)*, Simon John Horatio Nelson, *b.* 1971, *s.* 2009, *m.* | Viscount Merton, *b.* 2010 |
| 1660 S. | *Newburgh (12th)*, Don Filippo Giambattista Camillo Francesco Aldo Maria Rospigliosi, *b.* 1942, *s.* 1986, *m.* | Princess Donna Benedetta F. M. R., *b.* 1974 |
| 1827 I. | *Norbury (7th)*, Richard James Graham-Toler, *b.* 1967, *s.* 2000 | None |
| 1806 I. | *Normanton (6th)*, Shaun James Christian Welbore Ellis Agar, *b.* 1945, *s.* 1967, *m.* | Viscount Somerton, *b.* 1982 |
| 1647 S. | *Northesk (15th)*, Patrick Charles Carnegy, *b.* 1940, *s.* 2010 | Hon. Colin D. C., *b.* 1942 |
| 1801 | *Onslow (8th)*, Rupert Charles William Bullard Onslow, *b.* 1967, *s.* 2011, *m.* | Anthony E. E. O., *b.* 1955 |
| 1696 S. | *Orkney (9th)*, (Oliver) Peter St John, *b.* 1938, *s.* 1998, *m.* | Viscount Kirkwall, *b.* 1969 |
| 1328 I. | *Ormonde and Ossory (I. 1527)*, The 25th/18th Earl (7th Marquess) died in 1988 | †Viscount Mountgarret *b.* 1961 (*see* that title) |
| 1925 | ** *Oxford and Asquith (3rd)*, Raymond Benedict Bartholomew Michael Asquith, OBE, *b.* 1952, *s.* 2011, *m.* | Viscount Asquith, *b.* 1979 |
| 1929 | ° ** *Peel (3rd)*, William James Robert Peel, GCVO, PC, *b.* 1947, *s.* 1969, *m.* *Lord Chamberlain* | Viscount Clanfield, *b.* 1976 |
| 1551 | *Pembroke (18th) and Montgomery (15th) (1605)*, William Alexander Sidney Herbert, *b.* 1978, *s.* 2003, *m.* | Lord Herbert *b.* 2012 |
| 1605 S. | *Perth (18th)*, John Eric Drummond, *b.* 1935, *s.* 2002, *m.* | Viscount Strathallan, *b.* 1965 |
| 1905 | *Plymouth (3rd)*, Other Robert Ivor Windsor-Clive, *b.* 1923, *s.* 1943, *m.* | Viscount Windsor, *b.* 1951 |
| 1785 | *Portarlington (7th)*, George Lionel Yuill Seymour Dawson-Damer, *b.* 1938, *s.* 1959, *m.* | Viscount Carlow, *b.* 1965 |
| 1689 | *Portland (12th)*, Count Timothy Charles Robert Noel Bentinck, *b.* 1953, *s.* 1997, *m.* | Viscount Woodstock, *b.* 1984 |

| 1743 | *Portsmouth (10th)*, Quentin Gerard Carew Wallop, *b.* 1954, *s.* 1984, *m.* | Viscount Lymington, *b.* 1981 |
|---|---|---|
| 1804 | *Powis (8th)*, John George Herbert, *b.* 1952, *s.* 1993, *m.* | Viscount Clive, *b.* 1979 |
| 1765 | *Radnor (9th)*, William Pleydell-Bouverie, *b.* 1955, *s.* 2008, *m.* | Viscount Folkestone, *b.* 1999 |
| 1831 I. | *Ranfurly (7th)*, Gerald Françoys Needham Knox, *b.* 1929, *s.* 1988, *m.* | Viscount Northland, *b.* 1957 |
| 1771 I. | *Roden (10th)*, Robert John Jocelyn, *b.* 1938, *s.* 1993, *m.* | Viscount Jocelyn, *b.* 1989 |
| 1801 | *Romney (8th)*, Julian Charles Marsham, *b.* 1948, *s.* 2004, *m.* | Viscount Marsham, *b.* 1977 |
| 1703 S. | *Rosebery (7th)*, Neil Archibald Primrose, *b.* 1929, *s.* 1974, *m.* | Lord Dalmeny, *b.* 1967 |
| 1806 I. | *Rosse (7th)*, William Brendan Parsons, *b.* 1936, *s.* 1979, *m.* | Lord Oxmantown, *b.* 1969 |
| 1801 | ** *Rosslyn (7th)*, Peter St Clair-Erskine, CVO, QPM, *b.* 1958, *s.* 1977, *m.* | Lord Loughborough, *b.* 1986 |
| 1457 S. | *Rothes (22nd)*, James Malcolm David Leslie, *b.* 1958, *s.* 2005, *m.* | Hon. Alexander J. L., *b.* 1962 |
| 1861 | ° *Russell (7th)*, John Francis Russell, *b.* 1971, *s.* 2014, *m.* | None |
| 1915 | ° *St Aldwyn (3rd)*, Michael Henry Hicks Beach, *b.* 1950, *s.* 1992, *m.* | Hon. David S. H. B., *b.* 1955 |
| 1815 | *St Germans (10th)*, Peregrine Nicholas Eliot, *b.* 1941, *s.* 1988, *m.* | Lord Eliot, *b.* 2004 |
| 1660 | ** *Sandwich (11th)*, John Edward Hollister Montagu, *b.* 1943, *s.* 1995, *m.* | Viscount Hinchingbrooke, *b.* 1969 |
| 1690 | *Scarbrough (13th)*, Richard Osbert Lumley, *b.* 1973, *s.* 2004, *m.* | Hon. Thomas H. L., *b.* 1980 |
| 1701 S. | *Seafield (13th)*, Ian Derek Francis Ogilvie-Grant, *b.* 1939, *s.* 1969, *m.* | Viscount Reidhaven, *b.* 1963 |
| 1882 | ** *Selborne (4th)*, John Roundell Palmer, GBE, *b.* 1940, *s.* 1971, *m.* | Viscount Wolmer, *b.* 1971 |
| 1646 S. | *Selkirk (11th)*, Disclaimed for life 1994 (*see* Lord Selkirk of Douglas, Life Peers) | Master of Selkirk, *b.* 1978 |
| 1672 | *Shaftesbury (12th)*, Nicholas Edmund Anthony Ashley-Cooper, *b.* 1979, *s.* 2005, *m.* | Lord Ashley, *b.* 2011 |
| 1756 I. | *Shannon (10th)*, Richard Henry John Boyle, *b.* 1960, *s.* 2013 | Robert F. B., *b.* 1930 |
| 1442 | ** *Shrewsbury and Waterford (22nd) (I. 1446)*, Charles Henry John Benedict Crofton Chetwynd Chetwynd-Talbot, *b.* 1952, *s.* 1980, *m. Premier Earl of England and Ireland* | Viscount Ingestre, *b.* 1978 |
| 1961 | *Snowdon (1st) and Baron Armstrong-Jones (life peerage, 1999)*, Antony Charles Robert Armstrong-Jones, GCVO, *b.* 1930, *m.* | Viscount Linley, *b.* 1961 |
| 1765 | ° *Spencer (9th)*, Charles Edward Maurice Spencer, *b.* 1964, *s.* 1992, *m.* | Viscount Althorp, *b.* 1994 |
| 1703 S. | ** *Stair (14th)*, John David James Dalrymple, *b.* 1961, *s.* 1996, *m.* | Viscount Dalrymple, *b.* 2008 |
| 1984 | *Stockton (2nd)*, Alexander Daniel Alan Macmillan, *b.* 1943, *s.* 1986, *m.* | Viscount Macmillan of Ovenden, *b.* 1974 |
| 1821 | *Stradbroke (6th)*, Robert Keith Rous, *b.* 1937, *s.* 1983, *m.* | Viscount Dunwich, *b.* 1961 |
| 1847 | *Strafford (8th)*, Thomas Edmund Byng, *b.* 1936, *s.* 1984, *m.* | Viscount Enfield, *b.* 1964 |
| 1606 S. | *Strathmore and Kinghorne (18th) (S. 1677)*, Michael Fergus Bowes Lyon, *b.* 1957, *s.* 1987, *m.* | Lord Glamis, *b.* 1986 |
| 1603 | *Suffolk (21st) and Berkshire (14th) (1626)*, Michael John James George Robert Howard, *b.* 1935, *s.* 1941, *m.* | Viscount Andover, *b.* 1974 |
| 1955 | *Swinton (3rd)*, Nicholas John Cunliffe-Lister, *b.* 1939, *s.* 2006, *m.* | Lord Masham *b.* 1970 |
| 1714 | *Tankerville (10th)*, Peter Grey Bennet, *b.* 1956, *s.* 1980 | Adrian G. B., *b.* 1958 |
| 1822 | ° *Temple of Stowe (9th)*, James Grenville Temple-Gore-Langton, *b.* 1955, *s.* 2013, *m.* | Hon. Robert C. T.-G.-L., *b.* 1957 |
| 1815 | *Verulam (7th)*, John Duncan Grimston, *b.* 1951, *s.* 1973, *m.* | Viscount Grimston, *b.* 1978 |
| 1729 | ° *Waldegrave (13th)*, James Sherbrooke Waldegrave, *b.* 1940, *s.* 1995, *m.* | Viscount Chewton, *b.* 1986 |
| 1759 | *Warwick (9th) and Brooke (9th) (1746)*, Guy David Greville, *b.* 1957, *s.* 1996, *m.* | Lord Brooke, *b.* 1982 |
| 1633 S. | *Wemyss (13th) and March (9th) (S. 1697)*, James Donald Charteris, *b.* 1948, *s.* 2008, *m.* | Lord Elcho, *b.* 1984 |
| 1621 I. | *Westmeath (13th)*, William Anthony Nugent, *b.* 1928, *s.* 1971, *m.* | Sean C. W. N., *b.* 1965 |
| 1624 | *Westmorland (16th)*, Anthony David Francis Henry Fane, *b.* 1951, *s.* 1993, *m.* | Hon. Harry St C. F., *b.* 1953 |
| 1876 | *Wharncliffe (5th)*, Richard Alan Montagu Stuart Wortley, *b.* 1953, *s.* 1987, *m.* | Viscount Carlton, *b.* 1980 |
| 1801 | *Wilton (8th)*, Francis Egerton Grosvenor, *b.* 1934, *s.* 1999, *m.* | Viscount Grey de Wilton, *b.* 1959 |
| 1628 | *Winchilsea (17th) and Nottingham (12th) (1681)*, Daniel James Hatfield Finch Hatton, *b.* 1967, *s.* 1999, *m.* | Viscount Maidstone, *b.* 1998 |
| 1766 I. | ° *Winterton (8th)*, (Donald) David Turnour, *b.* 1943, *s.* 1991, *m.* | Robert C. T., *b.* 1950 |
| 1956 | *Woolton (3rd)*, Simon Frederick Marquis, *b.* 1958, *s.* 1969, *m.* | None |
| 1837 | *Yarborough (8th)*, Charles John Pelham, *b.* 1963, *s.* 1991, *m.* | Lord Worsley, *b.* 1990 |

## COUNTESSES IN THEIR OWN RIGHT

*Style,* The Rt. Hon. the Countess (of) _
 *Envelope (formal),* The Rt. Hon. the Countess (of) _; *(social),* The Countess (of) _. *Letter (formal),* Madam; *(social),* Lady _. *Spoken (formal),* Madam; *(social),* Lady _.
*Husband,* Untitled
*Children's style,* As for children of an Earl

| Created | Title, order of succession, name, etc | Heir |
|---|---|---|
| c.1115 S. | ** *Mar (31st),* Margaret of Mar, *b.* 1940, *s.* 1975, *m. Premier Earldom of Scotland* | Mistress of Mar, *b.* 1963 |
| 1947 | ° *Mountbatten of Burma (2nd),* Patricia Edwina Victoria Knatchbull, CBE, *b.* 1924, *s.* 1979, *w.* | Lord Romsey, (*also* Lord Brabourne (8th) *see* that title) |
| c.1235 S. | *Sutherland (24th),* Elizabeth Millicent Sutherland, *b.* 1921, *s.* 1963, *w.* | Lord Strathnaver, *b.* 1947 |

## VISCOUNTS

*Coronet,* Sixteen silver balls

*Style,* The Rt. Hon. the Viscount _
 *Envelope (formal),* The Rt. Hon. the Viscount _; *(social),* The Viscount _. *Letter (formal),* My Lord; *(social),* Dear Lord _. *Spoken,* Lord _.
*Wife's style,* The Rt. Hon. the Viscountess _
 *Envelope (formal),* The Rt. Hon. the Viscountess _; *(social),* The Viscountess _. *Letter (formal),* Madam; *(social),* Dear Lady _. *Spoken,* Lady _.
*Children's style,* 'The Hon.' before forename and surname, as for Baron's children
In Scotland, the heir apparent to a Viscount may be styled 'The Master of _ (title of peer)'

| Created | Title, order of succession, name, etc | Heir |
|---|---|---|
| 1945 | *Addison (4th),* William Matthew Wand Addison, *b.* 1945, *s.* 1992, *m.* | Hon. Paul W. A., *b.* 1973 |
| 1946 | *Alanbrooke (3rd),* Alan Victor Harold Brooke, *b.* 1932, *s.* 1972 | None |
| 1919 | *Allenby (4th),* Henry Jaffray Hynman Allenby, *b.* 1968, *s.* 2014, *m.* | Hon. Harry M. E. A., *b.* 2000 |
| 1911 | *Allendale (4th),* Wentworth Peter Ismay Beaumont, *b.* 1948, *s.* 2002, *m.* | Hon. Wentworth A. I. B., *b.* 1979 |
| 1642 S. | *of Arbuthnott (17th),* John Keith Oxley Arbuthnott, *b.* 1950, *s.* 2012, *m.* | Master of Arbuthnott, *b.* 1977 |
| 1751 I. | *Ashbrook (11th),* Michael Llowarch Warburton Flower, *b.* 1935, *s.* 1995, *m.* | Hon. Rowland F. W. F., *b.* 1975 |
| 1917 | ** *Astor (4th),* William Waldorf Astor, *b.* 1951, *s.* 1966, *m.* | Hon. William W. A., *b.* 1979 |
| 1781 I. | *Bangor (8th),* William Maxwell David Ward, *b.* 1948, *s.* 1993, *m.* | Hon. E. Nicholas W., *b.* 1953 |
| 1925 | *Bearsted (5th),* Nicholas Alan Samuel, *b.* 1950, *s.* 1996, *m.* | Hon. Harry R. S., *b.* 1988 |
| 1963 | *Blakenham (2nd),* Michael John Hare, *b.* 1938, *s.* 1982, *m.* | Hon. Caspar J. H., *b.* 1972 |
| 1935 | *Bledisloe (4th),* Rupert Edward Ludlow Bathurst, *b.* 1964, *s.* 2009, *m.* | Hon. Benjamin B., *b.* 2004 |
| 1712 | *Bolingbroke (9th) and St John (10th) (1716),* Nicholas Alexander Mowbray St John, *b.* 1974, *s.* 2011, *m.* | German A. St J., *b.* 1980 |
| 1960 | *Boyd of Merton (2nd),* Simon Donald Rupert Neville Lennox-Boyd, *b.* 1939, *s.* 1983, *m.* | Hon. Benjamin A. L.-B., *b.* 1964 |
| 1717 I. | *Boyne (11th),* Gustavus Michael Stucley Hamilton-Russell, *b.* 1965, *s.* 1995, *m.* | Hon. Gustavus A. E. H.-R., *b.* 1999 |
| 1929 | *Brentford (4th),* Crispin William Joynson-Hicks, *b.* 1933, *s.* 1983, *m.* | Hon. Paul W. J.-H., MBE, *b.* 1971 |
| 1929 | ** *Bridgeman (3rd),* Robin John Orlando Bridgeman, *b.* 1930, *s.* 1982, *m.* | Hon. Luke R. O. B., *b.* 1971 |
| 1868 | *Bridport (4th) and 7th Duke, Bronte in Sicily, 1799,* Alexander Nelson Hood, *b.* 1948, *s.* 1969, *m.* | Hon. Peregrine A. N. H., *b.* 1974 |
| 1952 | ** *Brookeborough (3rd),* Alan Henry Brooke, *b.* 1952, *s.* 1987, *m.* | Hon. Christopher A. B., *b.* 1954 |
| 1933 | *Buckmaster (4th),* Adrian Charles Buckmaster, *b.* 1949, *s.* 2007, *m.* | Hon. Andrew N. B., *b.* 1980 |
| 1939 | *Caldecote (3rd),* Piers James Hampden Inskip, *b.* 1947, *s.* 1999, *m.* | Hon. Thomas J. H. I., *b.* 1985 |
| 1941 | *Camrose (4th),* Adrian Michael Berry, *b.* 1937, *s.* 2001, *m.* | Hon. Jonathan W. B., *b.* 1970 |
| 1954 | *Chandos (3rd) and Baron Lyttelton of Aldershot (life peerage, 2000),* Thomas Orlando Lyttelton, *b.* 1953, *s.* 1980, *m.* | Hon. Oliver A. L., *b.* 1986 |

| | | |
|---|---|---|
| 1665 I. | *Charlemont (15th)*, John Dodd Caulfeild, *b.* 1966, *s.* 2001, *m.* | Hon. Shane A. C., *b.* 1996 |
| 1921 | *Chelmsford (4th)* Frederic Corin Piers Thesiger, *b.* 1962, *s.* 1999, *m.* | Hon. Frederic T. *b.* 2006 |
| 1717 I. | *Chetwynd (11th)*, Adam Douglas Chetwynd, *b.* 1969, *s.* 2015, *m.* | Hon. Connor A. C., *b.* 2011 |
| 1911 | *Chilston (4th)*, Alastair George Akers-Douglas, *b.* 1946, *s.* 1982, *m.* | Hon. Oliver I. A.-D., *b.* 1973 |
| 1902 | *Churchill (3rd) and 5th UK Baron Churchill (1815)*, Victor George Spencer, OBE, *b.* 1934, *s.* 1973 | To Barony only, Richard H. R. S., *b.* 1926 |
| 1718 | *Cobham (12th)*, Christopher Charles Lyttelton, *b.* 1947, *s.* 2006, *m.* | Hon. Oliver C. L., *b.* 1976 |
| 1902 | ** *Colville of Culross (5th)*, Charles Mark Townshend Colville, *b.* 1959, *s.* 2010 | Master of Colville, *b.* 1961 |
| 1826 | *Combermere (6th)*, Thomas Robert Wellington Stapleton-Cotton, *b.* 1969, *s.* 2000, *m.* | Hon. Laszlo M. W. S.-C., *b.* 2010 |
| 1917 | *Cowdray (4th)*, Michael Orlando Weetman Pearson, *b.* 1944, *s.* 1995, *m.* | Hon. Peregrine J. D. P., *b.* 1994 |
| 1927 | ** *Craigavon (3rd)*, Janric Fraser Craig, *b.* 1944, *s.* 1974 | None |
| 1943 | *Daventry (4th)*, James Edward FitzRoy Newdegate, *b.* 1960, *s.* 2000, *m.* | Hon. Humphrey J. F. N., *b.* 1995 |
| 1937 | *Davidson (3rd)*, Malcolm William Mackenzie Davidson, *b.* 1934, *s.* 2012, *m.* | Hon. John N. A. D., *b.* 1971 |
| 1956 | *De L'Isle (2nd)*, Philip John Algernon Sidney, MBE, *b.* 1945, *s.* 1991, *m.* | Hon. Philip W. E. S., *b.* 1985 |
| 1776 I. | *de Vesci (7th)*, Thomas Eustace Vesey, *b.* 1955, *s.* 1983, *m.* | Hon. Oliver I. V., *b.* 1991 |
| 1917 | *Devonport (3rd)*, Terence Kearley, *b.* 1944, *s.* 1973, *m.* | Chester D. H. K., *b.* 1932 |
| 1964 | *Dilhorne (2nd)*, John Mervyn Manningham-Buller, *b.* 1932, *s.* 1980, *m.* | Hon. James E. M.-B., *b.* 1956 |
| 1622 I. | *Dillon (22nd)*, Henry Benedict Charles Dillon, *b.* 1973, *s.* 1982 | Thomas A. L. D., *b.* 1983 |
| 1785 I. | *Doneraile (10th)*, Richard Allen St Leger, *b.* 1946, *s.* 1983, *m.* | Hon. Nathaniel W. R. St J. St L., *b.* 1971 |
| 1680 I. | *Downe (12th)*, Richard Henry Dawnay, *b.* 1967, *s.* 2002 | Thomas P. D., *b.* 1978 |
| 1959 | *Dunrossil (3rd)*, Andrew William Reginald Morrison, *b.* 1953, *s.* 2000, *m.* | Hon. Callum A. B. M., *b.* 1994 |
| 1964 | ** *Eccles (2nd)*, John Dawson Eccles, CBE, *b.* 1931, *s.* 1999, *m.* | Hon. William D. E., *b.* 1960 |
| 1897 | *Esher (5th)*, Christopher Lionel Baliol Brett, *b.* 1936, *s.* 2004, *m.* | Hon. Matthew C. A. B., *b.* 1963 |
| 1816 | *Exmouth (10th)*, Paul Edward Pellew, *b.* 1940, *s.* 1970, *m.* | Hon. Edward F. P., *b.* 1978 |
| 1620 S. | ** *of Falkland (15th)*, Lucius Edward William Plantagenet Cary, *b.* 1935, *s.* 1984, *m.* *Premier Scottish Viscount on the Roll* | Master of Falkland, *b.* 1963 |
| 1720 | *Falmouth (9th)*, George Hugh Boscawen, *b.* 1919, *s.* 1962, *w.* | Hon. Evelyn A. H. B., *b.* 1955 |
| 1720 I. | *Gage (8th)*, (Henry) Nicolas Gage, *b.* 1934, *s.* 1993, *m.* | Hon. Henry W. G., *b.* 1975 |
| 1727 I. | *Galway (12th)*, George Rupert Monckton-Arundell, *b.* 1922, *s.* 1980, *m.* | Hon. J. Philip M., *b.* 1952 |
| 1478 I. | *Gormanston (17th)*, Jenico Nicholas Dudley Preston, *b.* 1939, *s.* 1940, *m.* *Premier Viscount of Ireland* | Hon. Jenico F. T. P., *b.* 1974 |
| 1816 I. | *Gort (9th)*, Foley Robert Standish Prendergast Vereker, *b.* 1951, *s.* 1995, *m.* | Hon. Robert F. P. V., *b.* 1993 |
| 1900 | ** *Goschen (4th)*, Giles John Harry Goschen, *b.* 1965, *s.* 1977, *m.* | Hon. Alexander J. E. G., *b.* 2001 |
| 1849 | *Gough (5th)*, Shane Hugh Maryon Gough, *b.* 1941, *s.* 1951 | None |
| 1929 | *Hailsham (3rd) and Baron Hogg (life peerage, 2015)*, Douglas Martin Hogg, PC, QC, *b.* 1945, *s.* 2001, *m.* | Hon. Quintin J. N. M. H., *b.* 1973 |
| 1891 | *Hambleden (5th)*, William Henry Bernard Smith, *b.* 1955, *s.* 2012, *m.* | Hon. Bernardo J. S., *b.* 1957 |
| 1884 | *Hampden (7th)*, Francis Anthony Brand, *b.* 1970, *s.* 2008, *m.* | Hon. Lucian A. B., *b.* 2005 |
| 1936 | ** *Hanworth (3rd)*, David Stephen Geoffrey Pollock, *b.* 1946, *s.* 1996, *m.* | Harold W. C. P., *b.* 1988 |
| 1791 I. | *Harberton (11th)*, Henry Robert Pomeroy, *b.* 1958, *s.* 2004, *m.* | Hon. Patrick C. P., *b.* 1995 |
| 1846 | *Hardinge (8th)*, Thomas Henry de Montarville Hardinge, *b.* 1993, *s.* 2014 | Hon. Jamie A. D. H., *b.* 1996 |
| 1791 I. | *Hawarden (9th)*, (Robert) Connan Wyndham Leslie Maude, *b.* 1961, *s.* 1991, *m.* | Hon. Varian J. C. E. M., *b.* 1997 |
| 1960 | *Head (2nd)*, Richard Antony Head, *b.* 1937, *s.* 1983, *m.* | Hon. Henry J. H., *b.* 1980 |
| 1550 | *Hereford (19th)*, Charles Robin De Bohun Devereux, *b.* 1975, *s.* 2004, *m.* *Premier Viscount of England* | Hon. Henry W. de B. D., *b.* 2015 |
| 1842 | *Hill (9th)*, Peter David Raymond Charles Clegg-Hill, *b.* 1945, *s.* 2003, *m.* | Hon. Michael C. D. C.-H., *b.* 1988 |
| 1796 | *Hood (8th)*, Henry Lyttleton Alexander Hood, *b.* 1958, *s.* 1999, *m.* | Hon. Archibald L. S. H., *b.* 1993 |
| 1945 | *Kemsley (3rd)*, Richard Gomer Berry, *b.* 1951, *s.* 1999, *m.* | Hon. Luke G. B., *b.* 1998 |
| 1911 | *Knollys (3rd)*, David Francis Dudley Knollys, *b.* 1931, *s.* 1966, *m.* | Hon. Patrick N. M. K., *b.* 1962 |
| 1895 | *Knutsford (6th)*, Michael Holland-Hibbert, *b.* 1926, *s.* 1986, *m.* | Hon. Henry T. H.-H., *b.* 1959 |
| 1954 | *Leathers (3rd)*, Christopher Graeme Leathers, *b.* 1941, *s.* 1996, *m.* | Hon. James F. L., *b.* 1969 |
| 1781 I. | *Lifford (9th)*, (Edward) James Wingfield Hewitt, *b.* 1949, *s.* 1987, *m.* | Hon. James T. W. H., *b.* 1979 |
| 1921 | *Long (4th)*, Richard Gerard Long, CBE, *b.* 1929, *s.* 1967, *m.* | Hon. James R. L., *b.* 1960 |
| 1957 | *Mackintosh of Halifax (3rd)*, (John) Clive Mackintosh, *b.* 1958, *s.* 1980, *m.* | Hon. Thomas H. G. M., *b.* 1985 |
| 1955 | *Malvern (3rd)*, Ashley Kevin Godfrey Huggins, *b.* 1949, *s.* 1978 | Hon. M. James H., *b.* 1928 |
| 1945 | *Marchwood (3rd)*, David George Staveley Penny, *b.* 1936, *s.* 1979, *w.* | Hon. Peter G. W. P., *b.* 1965 |
| 1942 | *Margesson (3rd)*, Richard Francis David Margesson, *b.* 1960, *s.* 2014, *m.* | None |
| 1660 I. | *Massereene (14th) and Ferrard (7th) (I. 1797)*, John David Clotworthy Whyte-Melville Foster Skeffington, *b.* 1940, *s.* 1992, *m.* | Hon. Charles J. C. W.-M. F. S., *b.* 1973 |
| 1802 | *Melville (10th)*, Robert Henry Kirkpatrick Dundas, *b.* 1984, *s.* 2011 | Hon. James D. B. D., *b.* 1986 |
| 1916 | *Mersey (5th) and 14th Lord Nairne (S. 1681)*, Edward John Hallam Bigham, *b.* 1966, *s.* 2006, *m.* | Hon. David E. H. B., *b.* 1938 (to Viscountcy); Mistress of Nairne, *b.* 2003 (to Lordship of Nairne) |

| 1717 I. | *Midleton (12th)*, Alan Henry Brodrick, *b.* 1949, *s.* 1988, *m.* | Hon. Ashley R. B., *b.* 1980 |
| 1962 | *Mills (3rd)*, Christopher Philip Roger Mills, *b.* 1956, *s.* 1988, *m.* | None |
| 1716 I. | *Molesworth (12th)*, Robert Bysse Kelham Molesworth, *b.* 1959, *s.* 1997 | Hon. William J. C. M., *b.* 1960 |
| 1801 I. | *Monck (7th)*, Charles Stanley Monck, *b.* 1953, *s.* 1982 (Does not use title) | Hon. George S. M., *b.* 1957 |
| 1957 | *Monckton of Brenchley (3rd)*, Christopher Walter Monckton, *b.* 1952, *s.* 2006, *m.* | Hon. Timothy D. R. M., *b.* 1955 |
| 1946 | *Montgomery of Alamein (2nd)*, David Bernard Montgomery, CMG, CBE, *b.* 1928, *s.* 1976, *m.* | Hon. Henry D. M., *b.* 1954 |
| 1550 I. | *Mountgarret (18th)*, Piers James Richard Butler, *b.* 1961, *s.* 2004, *m.* | Hon. Edmund H. R. B., *b.* 1962 |
| 1952 | *Norwich (2nd)*, John Julius Cooper, CVO, *b.* 1929, *s.* 1954, *m.* | Hon. Jason C. D. B. C., *b.* 1959 |
| 1651 S. | *of Oxfuird (14th)*, Ian Arthur Alexander Makgill, *b.* 1969, *s.* 2003, *m.* | Master of Oxfuird, *b.* 2012 |
| 1873 | *Portman (10th)*, Christopher Edward Berkeley Portman, *b.* 1958, *s.* 1999, *m.* | Hon. Luke O. B. P., *b.* 1984 |
| 1743 I. | *Powerscourt (11th)*, Mervyn Anthony Wingfield, *b.* 1963, *s.* 2015, *m.* | Hon. Guy C. P. W., *b.* 1940 |
| 1900 | ** *Ridley (5th)*, Matthew White Ridley, *b.* 1958, *s.* 2012, *m.* | Hon. Matthew W. R., *b.* 1993 |
| 1960 | *Rochdale (3rd)*, Jonathan Hugo Durival Kemp, *b.* 1961, *s.* 2015, *m.* | George T. K., *b.* 2001 |
| 1919 | *Rothermere (4th)*, (Harold) Jonathan Esmond Vere Harmsworth, *b.* 1967, *s.* 1998, *m.* | Hon. Vere R. J. H. H., *b.* 1994 |
| 1937 | *Runciman of Doxford (3rd)*, Walter Garrison Runciman (Garry), CBE, *b.* 1934, *s.* 1989, *m.* | Hon. David W. R., *b.* 1967 |
| 1918 | *St Davids (4th)*, Rhodri Colwyn Philipps, *b.* 1966, *s.* 2009, *m.* | Hon. Roland A. J. E. P., *b.* 1970 |
| 1801 | *St Vincent (8th)*, Edward Robert James Jervis, *b.* 1951, *s.* 2006, *m.* | Hon. James R. A. J., *b.* 1982 |
| 1937 | *Samuel (5th)*, Jonathan Herbert Samuel, *b.* 1965, *s.* 2014, *m.* | Hon. Benjamin A. S., *b.* 1983 |
| 1911 | *Scarsdale (4th)*, Peter Ghislain Nathaniel Curzon, *b.* 1949, *s.* 2000, *m.* | Hon. David J. N. C., *b.* 1958 |
| 1905 | *Selby (6th)*, Christopher Rolf Thomas Gully, *b.* 1993, *s.* 2001 | Hon. (James) Edward H. G. G., *b.* 1945 |
| 1805 | *Sidmouth (8th)*, Jeremy Francis Addington, *b.* 1947, *s.* 2005, *w.* | Hon. John A., *b.* 1990 |
| 1940 | ** *Simon (3rd)*, Jan David Simon, *b.* 1940, *s.* 1993, *m.* | None |
| 1960 | ** *Slim (2nd)*, John Douglas Slim, OBE, *b.* 1927, *s.* 1970, *m.* | Hon. Mark W. R. S., *b.* 1960 |
| 1954 | *Soulbury (4th)*, Oliver Peter Ramsbotham, *b.* 1943, *s.* 2010, *m.* | Hon. Edward H. R., *b.* 1966 |
| 1776 I. | *Southwell (7th)*, Pyers Anthony Joseph Southwell, *b.* 1930, *s.* 1960, *m.* | Hon. Richard A. P. S., *b.* 1956 |
| 1942 | *Stansgate (3rd)*, Stephen Michael Wedgwood Benn, *b.* 1951, *s.* 2014, *m.* | Hon. Daniel J. W. B., *b.* 1991 |
| 1959 | *Stuart of Findhorn (3rd)*, Dominic Stuart, *b.* 1948, *s.* 1999, *m.* | Hon. Andrew M. S., *b.* 1957 |
| 1957 | *Tenby (3rd)*, William Lloyd George, *b.* 1927, *s.* 1983, *m.* | Hon. Timothy H. G. L. G., *b.* 1962 |
| 1952 | *Thurso (3rd)*, John Archibald Sinclair, PC, *b.* 1953, *s.* 1995, *m.* | Hon. James A. R. S., *b.* 1984 |
| 1721 | *Torrington (11th)*, Timothy Howard St George Byng, *b.* 1943, *s.* 1961, *m.* | Colin H. Cranmer-Byng, *b.* 1960 |
| 1936 | ** *Trenchard (3rd)*, Hugh Trenchard, *b.* 1951, *s.* 1987, *m.* | Hon. Alexander T. T., *b.* 1978 |
| 1921 | ** *Ullswater (2nd)*, Nicholas James Christopher Lowther, LVO, PC, *b.* 1942, *s.* 1949, *m.* | Hon. Benjamin J. L., *b.* 1975 |
| 1642 I. | *Valentia (16th)*, Frances William Dighton Annesley, *b.* 1959, *s.* 2005, *m.* | Hon. Peter J. A., *b.* 1967 |
| 1952 | ** *Waverley (3rd)*, John Desmond Forbes Anderson, *b.* 1949, *s.* 1990, *m.* | Hon. Forbes A. R. A., *b.* 1996 |
| 1938 | *Weir (3rd)*, William Kenneth James Weir, *b.* 1933, *s.* 1975, *m.* | Hon. James W. H. W., *b.* 1965 |
| 1918 | *Wimborne (4th)*, Ivor Mervyn Vigors Guest, *b.* 1968, *s.* 1993 | Hon. Julian J. G., *b.* 1945 |
| 1923 | ** *Younger of Leckie (5th)*, James Edward George Younger, *b.* 1955, *s.* 2003, *m.* | Hon. Alexander W. G. Y., *b.* 1993 |

# BARONS/LORDS

*Coronet*, Six silver balls

*Style*, The Rt. Hon. the Lord _
    *Envelope (formal)*, The Rt. Hon. Lord _; *(social)*, The Lord _. *Letter (formal)*, My Lord; *(social)*, Dear Lord _. *Spoken*, Lord _.
In the Peerage of Scotland there is no rank of Baron; the equivalent rank is Lord of Parliament and Scottish peers should always be styled 'Lord', never 'Baron'.
*Wife's style*, The Rt. Hon. the Lady _
    *Envelope (formal)*, The Rt. Hon. Lady _; *(social)*, The Lady _. *Letter (formal)*, My Lady; *(social)*, Dear Lady _. *Spoken*, Lady _
*Children's style*, 'The Hon.' before forename (F_) and surname (S_)
    *Envelope*, The Hon. F_ S_. *Letter*, Dear Mr/Miss/Mrs S_. *Spoken*, Mr/Miss/Mrs S_
In Scotland, the heir apparent to a Lord may be styled 'The Master of _ (title of peer)'

| *Created* | *Title, order of succession, name, etc* | *Heir* |
|---|---|---|
| 1911 | *Aberconway (4th)*, (Henry) Charles McLaren, *b.* 1948, *s.* 2003, *m.* | Hon. Charles S. M., *b.* 1984 |
| 1873 | ** *Aberdare (5th)*, Alastair John Lyndhurst Bruce, *b.* 1947, *s.* 2005, *m.* | Hon. Hector M. N. B., *b.* 1974 |

| 1835 | *Abinger (9th)*, James Harry Scarlett, *b.* 1959, *s.* 2002, *m.* | Hon. Peter R. S., *b.* 1961 |
|---|---|---|
| 1869 | *Acton (5th)*, John Charles Ferdinand Harold Lyon-Dalberg-Acton, *b.* 1966, *s.* 2010, *m.* | Hon. John C. L.-D.-A., *b.* 1943 |
| 1887 | ** *Addington (6th)*, Dominic Bryce Hubbard, *b.* 1963, *s.* 1982, *m.* | Hon. Michael W. L. H., *b.* 1965 |
| 1896 | *Aldenham (6th) and Hunsdon of Hunsdon (4th) (1923)*, Vicary Tyser Gibbs, *b.* 1948, *s.* 1986, *m.* | Hon. Humphrey W. F. G., *b.* 1989 |
| 1962 | *Aldington (2nd)*, Charles Harold Stuart Low, *b.* 1948, *s.* 2000, *m.* | Hon. Philip T. A. L., *b.* 1990 |
| 1945 | *Altrincham (3rd)*, Anthony Ulick David Dundas Grigg, *b.* 1934, *s.* 2001, *m.* | Hon. (Edward) Sebastian G., *b.* 1965 |
| 1929 | *Alvingham (2nd)*, Maj.-Gen. Robert Guy Eardley Yerburgh, CBE, *b.* 1926, *s.* 1955, *m.* | Capt. Hon. Robert R. G. Y., *b.* 1956 |
| 1892 | *Amherst of Hackney (5th)*, Hugh William Amherst Cecil, *b.* 1968, *s.* 2009, *m.* | Hon. Jack W. A. C., *b.* 2001 |
| 1881 | *Ampthill (5th)*, David Whitney Erskine Russell, *b.* 1947, *s.* 2011, *m.* | Hon. Anthony J. M. R., *b.* 1952 |
| 1947 | *Amwell (3rd)*, Keith Norman Montague, *b.* 1943, *s.* 1990, *m.* | Hon. Ian K. M., *b.* 1973 |
| 1863 | *Annaly (6th)*, Luke Richard White, *b.* 1954, *s.* 1990, *m.* | Hon. Luke H. W., *b.* 1990 |
| 1885 | *Ashbourne (4th)*, Edward Barry Greynville Gibson, *b.* 1933, *s.* 1983, *m.* | Hon. Edward C. d'O. G., *b.* 1967 |
| 1835 | *Ashburton (7th)*, John Francis Harcourt Baring, KG, KCVO, *b.* 1928, *s.* 1991, *m.* | Hon. Mark F. R. B., *b.* 1958 |
| 1892 | *Ashcombe (5th)*, Mark Edward Cubitt, *b.* 1964, *s.* 2013, *m.* | Hon. Richard R. A. C., *b.* 1995 |
| 1911 | ** *Ashton of Hyde (4th)*, Thomas Henry Ashton, *b.* 1958, *s.* 2008, *m.* | Hon. John E. A., *b.* 1966 |
| 1800 I. | *Ashtown (8th)*, Roderick Nigel Godolphin Trench, *b.* 1944, *s.* 2010, *m.* | Hon. Timothy R. H. T., *b.* 1968 |
| 1956 | ** *Astor of Hever (3rd)*, John Jacob Astor, PC, *b.* 1946, *s.* 1984, *m.* | Hon. Charles G. J. A., *b.* 1990 |
| 1789 I. | *Auckland (10th) and Auckland (10th) (1793)*, Robert Ian Burnard Eden, *b.* 1962, *s.* 1997, *m.* | Henry V. E., *b.* 1958 |
| 1313 | *Audley*, Barony in abeyance between three co-heiresses since 1997 | |
| 1900 | ** *Avebury (4th)*, Eric Reginald Lubbock, *b.* 1928, *s.* 1971, *m.* | Hon. Lyulph A. J. L., *b.* 1954 |
| 1718 I. | *Aylmer (14th)*, (Anthony) Julian Aylmer, *b.* 1951, *s.* 2006, *m.* | Hon. Michael H. A., *b.* 1991 |
| 1929 | *Baden-Powell (3rd)*, Robert Crause Baden-Powell, *b.* 1936, *s.* 1962, *w.* | Hon. David M. B.-P., *b.* 1940 |
| 1780 | *Bagot (10th)*, (Charles Hugh) Shaun Bagot, *b.* 1944, *s.* 2001, *m.* | Richard C. V. B., *b.* 1941 |
| 1953 | *Baillieu (3rd)*, James William Latham Baillieu, *b.* 1950, *s.* 1973, *m.* | Hon. Robert L. B., *b.* 1979 |
| 1607 S. | *Balfour of Burleigh (8th)*, Robert Bruce, *b.* 1927, *s.* 1967, *m.* | Hon. Victoria B., *b.* 1973 |
| 1924 | *Banbury of Southam (3rd)*, Charles William Banbury, *b.* 1953, *s.* 1981, *m.* | None |
| 1698 | *Barnard (11th)*, Harry John Neville Vane, TD, *b.* 1923, *s.* 1964 | Hon. Henry F. C. V., *b.* 1959 |
| 1887 | *Basing (6th)*, Stuart Anthony Whitfield Sclater-Booth, *b.* 1969, *s.* 2007, *m.* | Hon. Luke W. S.-B., *b.* 2000 |
| 1917 | *Beaverbrook (3rd)*, Maxwell William Humphrey Aitken, *b.* 1951, *s.* 1985, *m.* | Hon. Maxwell F. A., *b.* 1977 |
| 1647 S. | *Belhaven and Stenton (13th)*, Robert Anthony Carmichael Hamilton, *b.* 1927, *s.* 1961, *m.* | Master of Belhaven, *b.* 1953 |
| 1848 I. | *Bellew (8th)*, Bryan Edward Bellew, *b.* 1943, *s.* 2010, *m.* | Hon. Anthony R. B. B., *b.* 1972 |
| 1856 | *Belper (5th)*, Richard Henry Strutt, *b.* 1941, *s.* 1999, *m.* | Hon. Michael H. S., *b.* 1969 |
| 1421 | *Berkeley (18th) and Gueterbock (life peerage, 2000)*, Anthony Fitzhardinge Gueterbock, OBE, *b.* 1939, *s.* 1992, *m.* | Hon. Thomas F. G., *b.* 1969 |
| 1922 | *Bethell (5th)*, James Nicholas Bethell, *b.* 1967, *s.* 2007, *m.* | Hon. Jacob N. D. B., *b.* 2006 |
| 1938 | *Bicester (4th)*, Hugh Charles Vivian Smith, *b.* 1934, *s.* 2014 | Charles J. V. S., *b.* 1963 |
| 1903 | *Biddulph (5th)*, (Anthony) Nicholas Colin Maitland Biddulph, *b.* 1959, *s.* 1988, *m.* | Hon. Robert J. M. B., *b.* 1994 |
| 1958 | *Birkett (3rd)*, Thomas Birkett, *b.* 1982, *s.* 2015 | None |
| 1907 | *Blyth (5th)*, James Audley Ian Blyth, *b.* 1970, *s.* 2009, *m.* | Hon. Hugo A. J. B., *b.* 2006 |
| 1797 | *Bolton (8th)*, Harry Algar Nigel Orde-Powlett, *b.* 1954, *s.* 2001, *m.* | Hon. Thomas O.-P., MC, *b.* 1979 |
| 1452 S. | *Borthwick (24th)*, John Hugh Borthwick, *b.* 1940, *s.* 1996, *m.* | Hon. James H. A. B. of Glengelt, *b.* 1940 |
| 1922 | ** *Borwick (5th)*, (Geoffrey Robert) James Borwick, *b.* 1955, *s.* 2007, *m.* | Hon. Edwin D. W. B., *b.* 1984 |
| 1761 | *Boston (11th)*, George William Eustace Boteler Irby, *b.* 1971, *s.* 2007, *m.* | Hon. Thomas W. G. B. I., *b.* 1999 |
| 1942 | ** *Brabazon of Tara (3rd)*, Ivon Anthony Moore-Brabazon, PC, *b.* 1946, *s.* 1974, *m.* | Hon. Benjamin R. M.-B., *b.* 1983 |
| 1880 | *Brabourne (8th)*, Norton Louis Philip Knatchbull, *b.* 1947, *s.* 2005, *m.* (also Lord Romsey heir to Countess Mountbatten of Burma, *see* that title) | Hon. Nicholas L. C. N. K., *b.* 1981 |
| 1925 | *Bradbury (3rd)*, John Bradbury, *b.* 1940, *s.* 1994, *m.* | Hon. John B., *b.* 1973 |
| 1962 | *Brain (3rd)*, Michael Cottrell Brain, *b.* 1928, *s.* 2014, *m.* | Hon. Thomas R. B., *b.* 1965 |
| 1938 | *Brassey of Apethorpe (4th)*, Edward Brassey, *b.* 1964, *s.* 2015, *m.* | Hon. Christian B., *b.* 2003 |
| 1788 | *Braybrooke (10th)*, Robin Henry Charles Neville, *b.* 1932, *s.* 1990, *m.* | Richard R. N., *b.* 1977 |
| 1957 | ** *Bridges (2nd)*, Thomas Edward Bridges, GCMG, *b.* 1927, *s.* 1969, *m.* | Hon. Mark T. B., CVO, *b.* 1954 |
| 1945 | *Broadbridge (4th)*, Martin Hugh Broadbridge, *b.* 1929, *s.* 2000, *w.* | Hon. Richard J. M. B., *b.* 1959 |
| 1933 | *Brocket (3rd)*, Charles Ronald George Nall-Cain, *b.* 1952, *s.* 1967, *w.* | Hon. Alexander C. C. N.-C., *b.* 1984 |
| 1860 | ** *Brougham and Vaux (5th)*, Michael John Brougham, CBE, *b.* 1938, *s.* 1967 | Hon. Charles W. B., *b.* 1971 |
| 1776 | *Brownlow (7th)*, Edward John Peregrine Cust, *b.* 1936, *s.* 1978, *m.* | Hon. Peregrine E. Q. C., *b.* 1974 |
| 1942 | *Bruntisfield (3rd)*, Michael John Victor Warrender, *b.* 1949, *s.* 2007, *m.* | Hon. John M. P. C. W., *b.* 1996 |

| | | |
|---|---|---|
| 1950 | *Burden (4th)*, Fraser William Elsworth Burden, *b.* 1964, *s.* 2000, *m.* | Hon. Ian S. B., *b.* 1967 |
| 1529 | *Burgh (8th)*, (Alexander) Gregory Disney Leith, *b.* 1958, *s.* 2001, *m.* | Hon. Alexander J. S. L., *b.* 1986 |
| 1903 | *Burnham (7th)*, Harry Frederick Alan Lawson, *b.* 1968, *s.* 2005 | None |
| 1897 | *Burton (4th)*, Evan Michael Ronald Baillie, *b.* 1949, *s.* 2013, *m.* | Hon. James E. B., *b.* 1975 |
| 1643 | *Byron (13th)*, Robert James Byron, *b.* 1950, *s.* 1989, *m.* | Hon. Charles R. G. B., *b.* 1990 |
| 1937 | *Cadman (3rd)*, John Anthony Cadman, *b.* 1938, *s.* 1966, *m.* | Hon. Nicholas A. J. C., *b.* 1977 |
| 1945 | *Calverley (3rd)*, Charles Rodney Muff, *b.* 1946, *s.* 1971 | Hon. Jonathan E. Brown, *b.* 1975 |
| 1383 | *Camoys (7th)*, (Ralph) Thomas Campion George Sherman Stonor, GCVO, PC, *b.* 1940, *s.* 1976, *m.* | Hon. R. William R. T. S., *b.* 1974 |
| 1715 I. | *Carbery (12th)*, Michael Peter Evans-Freke, *b.* 1942, *s.* 2012, *m.* | Hon. Dominic R. C. E.-F., *b.* 1969 |
| 1834 I. | *Carew (7th) and Carew (7th) (1838)*, Patrick Thomas Conolly-Carew, *b.* 1938, *s.* 1994, *m.* | Hon. William P. C.-C., *b.* 1973 |
| 1916 | *Carnock (5th)*, Adam Nicolson, *b.* 1957, *s.* 2008, *m.* | Hon. Thomas N., *b.* 1984 |
| 1796 I. | *Carrington (6th) and Carrington (6th) (1797) and Carington of Upton (life peerage, 1999)*, Peter Alexander Rupert Carington, KG, GCMG, CH, MC, PC, *b.* 1919, *s.* 1938, *w.* | Hon. Rupert F. J. C., *b.* 1948 |
| 1812 I. | *Castlemaine (8th)*, Roland Thomas John Handcock, MBE, *b.* 1943, *s.* 1973, *m.* | Hon. Ronan M. E. H., *b.* 1989 |
| 1936 | *Catto (3rd)*, Innes Gordon Catto, *b.* 1950, *s.* 2001, *m.* | Hon. Alexander G. C., *b.* 1952 |
| 1918 | *Cawley (4th)*, John Francis Cawley, *b.* 1946, *s.* 2001, *m.* | Hon. William R. H. C., *b.* 1981 |
| 1858 | *Chesham (7th)*, Charles Gray Compton Cavendish, *b.* 1974, *s.* 2009, *m.* | Hon. Oliver N. B. C., *b.* 2007 |
| 1945 | *Chetwode (2nd)*, Philip Chetwode, *b.* 1937, *s.* 1950, *m.* | Hon. Roger C., *b.* 1968 |
| 1945 | *Chorley (2nd)*, Roger Richard Edward Chorley, *b.* 1930, *s.* 1978, *m.* | Hon. Nicholas R. D. C., *b.* 1966 |
| 1858 | *Churston (5th)*, John Francis Yarde-Buller, *b.* 1934, *s.* 1991, *m.* | Hon. Benjamin F. A. Y.-B., *b.* 1974 |
| 1800 I. | *Clanmorris (8th)*, Simon John Ward Bingham, *b.* 1937, *s.* 1988, *m.* | Robert D. de B. B., *b.* 1942 |
| 1672 | *Clifford of Chudleigh (14th)*, Thomas Hugh Clifford, *b.* 1948, *s.* 1988, *m.* | Hon. Alexander T. H. C., *b.* 1985 |
| 1299 | *Clinton (22nd)*, Gerard Nevile Mark Fane Trefusis, *b.* 1934, *s.* 1965, *m.* | Hon. Charles P. R. F. T., *b.* 1962 |
| 1955 | *Clitheroe (2nd)*, Ralph John Assheton, *b.* 1929, *s.* 1984, *m.* | Hon. Ralph C. A., *b.* 1962 |
| 1919 | *Clwyd (4th)*, (John) Murray Roberts, *b.* 1971, *s.* 2006 | Hon. Jeremy T. R., *b.* 1973 |
| 1948 | *Clydesmuir (3rd)*, David Ronald Colville, *b.* 1949, *s.* 1996, *m.* | Hon. Richard C., *b.* 1980 |
| 1960 | *Cobbold (2nd)*, David Antony Fromanteel Lytton Cobbold, *b.* 1937, *s.* 1987, *m.* | Hon. Henry F. L. C., *b.* 1962 |
| 1919 | *Cochrane of Cults (4th)*, (Ralph Henry) Vere Cochrane, *b.* 1926, *s.* 1990, *m.* | Hon. Thomas H. V. C., *b.* 1957 |
| 1954 | *Coleraine (2nd)*, (James) Martin (Bonar) Law, *b.* 1931, *s.* 1980, *m.* | Hon. James P. B. L., *b.* 1975 |
| 1873 | *Coleridge (5th)*, William Duke Coleridge, *b.* 1937, *s.* 1984, *m.* | Hon. James D. C., *b.* 1967 |
| 1946 | *Colgrain (4th)*, Alastair Colin Leckie Campbell, *b.* 1951, *s.* 2008, *m.* | Hon. Thomas C. D. C., *b.* 1984 |
| 1917 | ** *Colwyn (3rd)*, (Ian) Anthony Hamilton-Smith, CBE, *b.* 1942, *s.* 1966, *m.* | Hon. Craig P. H.-S., *b.* 1968 |
| 1956 | *Colyton (2nd)*, Alisdair John Munro Hopkinson, *b.* 1958, *s.* 1996, *m.* | Hon. James P. M. H., *b.* 1983 |
| 1841 | *Congleton (8th)*, Christopher Patrick Parnell, *b.* 1930, *s.* 1967, *m.* | Hon. John P. C. P., *b.* 1959 |
| 1927 | *Cornwallis (4th)*, Fiennes Wykeham Jeremy Cornwallis, *b.* 1946, *s.* 2010, *m.* | Hon. Fiennes A. W. M. C., *b.* 1987 |
| 1874 | *Cottesloe (5th)*, John Tapling Fremantle, *b.* 1927, *s.* 1994, *w.* | Hon. Thomas F. H. F., *b.* 1966 |
| 1929 | *Craigmyle (4th)*, Thomas Columba Shaw, *b.* 1960, *s.* 1998, *m.* | Hon. Alexander F. S., *b.* 1988 |
| 1899 | *Cranworth (3rd)*, Philip Bertram Gurdon, *b.* 1940, *s.* 1964, *m.* | Hon. Sacha W. R. G., *b.* 1970 |
| 1959 | ** *Crathorne (2nd)*, Charles James Dugdale, KCVO, *b.* 1939, *s.* 1977, *w.* | Hon. Thomas A. J. D., *b.* 1977 |
| 1892 | *Crawshaw (5th)*, David Gerald Brooks, *b.* 1934, *s.* 1997, *m.* | Hon. John P. B., *b.* 1938 |
| 1940 | *Croft (3rd)*, Bernard William Henry Page Croft, *b.* 1949, *s.* 1997, *m.* | None |
| 1797 I. | *Crofton (8th)*, Edward Harry Piers Crofton, *b.* 1988, *s.* 2007 | Hon. Charles M. G. C., *b.* 1988 |
| 1375 | ** *Cromwell (7th)*, Godfrey John Bewicke-Copley, *b.* 1960, *s.* 1982, *m.* | Hon. David G. B.-C., *b.* 1997 |
| 1947 | *Crook (3rd)*, Robert Douglas Edwin Crook, *b.* 1955, *s.* 2001, *m.* | Hon. Matthew R. C., *b.* 1990 |
| 1920 | *Cullen of Ashbourne (3rd)*, Edmund Willoughby Marsham Cokayne, *b.* 1916, *s.* 2000, *w.* | Michael J. C., *b.* 1950 |
| 1914 | *Cunliffe (3rd)*, Roger Cunliffe, *b.* 1932, *s.* 1963, *m.* | Hon. Henry C., *b.* 1962 |
| 1332 | *Darcy de Knayth (19th)*, Caspar David Ingrams, *b.* 1962, *s.* 2008, *m.* | Hon. Thomas R. I., *b.* 1999 |
| 1927 | *Daresbury (4th)*, Peter Gilbert Greenall, *b.* 1953, *s.* 1996, *m.* | Hon. Thomas E. G., *b.* 1984 |
| 1924 | *Darling (3rd)*, (Robert) Julian Henry Darling, *b.* 1944, *s.* 2003, *m.* | Hon. Robert J. C. D., *b.* 1972 |
| 1946 | *Darwen (4th)*, Paul Davies, *b.* 1962, *s.* 2011 | Hon. Benjamin D., *b.* 1966 |
| 1932 | *Davies (3rd)*, David Davies, *b.* 1940, *s.* 1944, *m.* | Hon. David D. D., *b.* 1975 |
| 1812 I. | *Decies (7th)*, Marcus Hugh Tristram de la Poer Beresford, *b.* 1948, *s.* 1992, *m.* | Hon. Robert M. D. de la P. B., *b.* 1988 |
| 1299 | *de Clifford (27th)*, John Edward Southwell Russell, *b.* 1928, *s.* 1982, *m.* | Miles E. S. R., *b.* 1966 |
| 1851 | *De Freyne (8th)*, Fulke Charles Arthur John French, *b.* 1957, *s.* 2009, *m.* | Hon. Alexander J. C. F., *b.* 1988 |
| 1821 | *Delamere (5th)*, Hugh George Cholmondeley, *b.* 1934, *s.* 1979, *m.* | Hon. Thomas P. G. C., *b.* 1968 |
| 1838 | ** *de Mauley (7th)*, Rupert Charles Ponsonby, *b.* 1957, *s.* 2002, *m.* | Ashley G. P., *b.* 1959 |
| 1937 | ** *Denham (2nd)*, Bertram Stanley Mitford Bowyer, KBE, PC, *b.* 1927, *s.* 1948, *m.* | Hon. Richard G. G. B., *b.* 1959 |

| | | |
|---|---|---|
| 1834 | *Denman (6th)*, Richard Thomas Stewart Denman, *b.* 1946, *s.* 2012, *m.* | Hon. Robert D., *b.* 1995 |
| 1887 | *De Ramsey (4th)*, John Ailwyn Fellowes, *b.* 1942, *s.* 1993, *m.* | Hon. Freddie J. F., *b.* 1978 |
| 1264 | *de Ros (28th)*, Peter Trevor Maxwell, *b.* 1958, *s.* 1983, *m. Premier Baron of England* | Hon. Finbar J. M., *b.* 1988 |
| 1881 | *Derwent (5th)*, Robin Evelyn Leo Vanden-Bempde-Johnstone, LVO, *b.* 1930, *s.* 1986, *m.* | Hon. Francis P. H. V.-B.-J., *b.* 1965 |
| 1831 | *de Saumarez (7th)*, Eric Douglas Saumarez, *b.* 1956, *s.* 1991, *m.* | Hon. Victor T. S., *b.* 1956 |
| 1910 | *de Villiers (4th)*, Alexander Charles de Villiers, *b.* 1940, *s.* 2001, *m.* | None |
| 1930 | *Dickinson (2nd)*, Richard Clavering Hyett Dickinson, *b.* 1926, *s.* 1943, *m.* | Hon. Martin H. D., *b.* 1961 |
| 1620 I. | *Digby (12th) and Digby (5th) (1765)*, Edward Henry Kenelm Digby, KCVO, *b.* 1924, *s.* 1964, *m.* | Hon. Henry N. K. D., *b.* 1954 |
| 1615 | *Dormer (17th)*, Geoffrey Henry Dormer, *b.* 1920, *s.* 1995, *m.* | Hon. William R. D., *b.* 1960 |
| 1943 | *Dowding (3rd)*, Piers Hugh Tremenheere Dowding, *b.* 1948, *s.* 1992, *m.* | Hon. Mark D. J. D., *b.* 1949 |
| 1439 | *Dudley (15th)*, Jim Anthony Hill Wallace, *b.* 1930, *s.* 2002, *m.* | Hon. Jeremy W. G. W., *b.* 1964 |
| 1800 I. | *Dufferin and Clandeboye (11th)*, John Francis Blackwood, *b.* 1944, *s.* 1991 (claim to the peerage not yet established), *m.* | Hon. Francis S. B., *b.* 1979 |
| 1929 | *Dulverton (3rd)*, (Gilbert) Michael Hamilton Wills, *b.* 1944, *s.* 1992, *m.* | Hon. Robert A. H. W., *b.* 1983 |
| 1800 I. | *Dunalley (7th)*, Henry Francis Cornelius Prittie, *b.* 1948, *s.* 1992, *m.* | Hon. Joel H. P., *b.* 1981 |
| 1324 I. | *Dunboyne (30th)*, Richard Pierce Theobald Butler, *b.* 1983, *s.* 2013, *m.* | Michael J. B., *b.* 1944 |
| 1892 | *Dunleath (6th)*, Brian Henry Mulholland, *b.* 1950, *s.* 1997, *m.* | Hon. Andrew H. M., *b.* 1981 |
| 1439 I. | *Dunsany (21st)*, Randal Plunkett, *b.* 1983, *s.* 2011 | Hon. Oliver P., *b.* 1985 |
| 1780 | *Dynevor (10th)*, Hugo Griffith Uryan Rhys, *b.* 1966, *s.* 2008 | Robert D. A. R., *b.* 1963 |
| 1963 | *Egremont (2nd) and Leconfield (7th) (1859)*, John Max Henry Scawen Wyndham, *b.* 1948, *s.* 1972, *m.* | Hon. George R. V. W., *b.* 1983 |
| 1643 S. | *Elibank (14th)*, Alan D'Ardis Erskine-Murray, *b.* 1923, *s.* 1973, *w.* | Master of Elibank, *b.* 1964 |
| 1802 | *Ellenborough (9th)*, Rupert Edward Henry Law, *b.* 1955, *s.* 2013, *m.* | Hon. James R. T. L., *b.* 1983 |
| 1509 S. | *Elphinstone (19th) and Elphinstone (5th) (1885)*, Alexander Mountstuart Elphinstone, *b.* 1980, *s.* 1994, *m.* | Master of Elphinstone, *b.* 2011 |
| 1934 | ** *Elton (2nd)*, Rodney Elton, TD, *b.* 1930, *s.* 1973, *m.* | Hon. Edward P. E., *b.* 1966 |
| 1627 S. | *Fairfax of Cameron (14th)*, Nicholas John Albert Fairfax, *b.* 1956, *s.* 1964, *m.* | Hon. Edward N. T. F., *b.* 1984 |
| 1961 | *Fairhaven (3rd)*, Ailwyn Henry George Broughton, *b.* 1936, *s.* 1973, *m.* | Maj. Hon. James H. A. B., *b.* 1963 |
| 1916 | *Faringdon (3rd)*, Charles Michael Henderson, KCVO, *b.* 1937, *s.* 1977, *m.* | Hon. James H. H., *b.* 1961 |
| 1756 I. | *Farnham (13th)*, Simon Kenlis Maxwell, *b.* 1933, *s.* 2001, *w.* | Hon. Robin S. M., *b.* 1965 |
| 1856 I. | *Fermoy (6th)*, Maurice Burke Roche, *b.* 1967, *s.* 1984, *m.* | Hon. E. Hugh B. R., *b.* 1972 |
| 1826 | *Feversham (7th)*, Jasper Orlando Slingsby Duncombe, *b.* 1968, *s.* 2009 | Hon. Jake B. D., *b.* 1972 |
| 1798 I. | *ffrench (8th)*, Robuck John Peter Charles Mario ffrench, *b.* 1956, *s.* 1986, *m.* | None |
| 1909 | *Fisher (4th)*, Patrick Vavasseur Fisher, *b.* 1953, *s.* 2012, *m.* | Hon. Benjamin C. V. F., *b.* 1986 |
| 1295 | *Fitzwalter (22nd)*, Julian Brook Plumptre, *b.* 1952, *s.* 2004, *m.* | Hon. Edward B. P., *b.* 1989 |
| 1776 | *Foley (9th)*, Thomas Henry Foley, *b.* 1961, *s.* 2012 | Rupert T. F., *b.* 1970 |
| 1445 S. | *Forbes (23rd)*, Malcolm Nigel Forbes, *b.* 1946, *s.* 2013, *m. Premier Lord of Scotland* | Master of Forbes, *b.* 1970 |
| 1821 | *Forester (9th)*, Charles Richard George Weld-Forester, *b.* 1975, *s.* 2004, *m.* | Hon. Brook G. P. W.-F., *b.* 2014 |
| 1922 | *Forres (3rd)*, Alastair Stephen Grant Williamson, *b.* 1946, *s.* 1978, *m.* | Hon. George A. M. W., *b.* 1972 |
| 1917 | *Forteviot (4th)*, John James Evelyn Dewar, *b.* 1938, *s.* 1993, *w.* | Hon. Alexander J. E. D., *b.* 1971 |
| 1951 | ** *Freyberg (3rd)*, Valerian Bernard Freyberg, *b.* 1970, *s.* 1993, *m.* | Hon. Joseph J. F., *b.* 2007 |
| 1917 | *Gainford (4th)*, George Pease, *b.* 1926, *s.* 2013, *m.* | Hon. Adrian C. P., *b.* 1960 |
| 1818 I. | *Garvagh (6th)*, Spencer George Stratford de Redcliffe Canning, *b.* 1953, *s.* 2013, *w.* | Hon. Stratford G. E. de R. C., *b.* 1990 |
| 1942 | ** *Geddes (3rd)*, Euan Michael Ross Geddes, *b.* 1937, *s.* 1975, *m.* | Hon. James G. N. G., *b.* 1969 |
| 1876 | *Gerard (5th)*, Anthony Robert Hugo Gerard, *b.* 1949, *s.* 1992, *m.* | Hon. Rupert B. C. G., *b.* 1981 |
| 1824 | *Gifford (6th)*, Anthony Maurice Gifford, QC, *b.* 1940, *s.* 1961, *m.* | Hon. Thomas A. G., *b.* 1967 |
| 1917 | *Gisborough (3rd)*, Thomas Richard John Long Chaloner, *b.* 1927, *s.* 1951, *m.* | Hon. T. Peregrine L. C., *b.* 1961 |
| 1960 | *Gladwyn (2nd)*, Miles Alvery Gladwyn Jebb, *b.* 1930, *s.* 1996 | None |
| 1899 | *Glanusk (5th)*, Christopher Russell Bailey, *b.* 1942, *s.* 1997, *m.* | Hon. Charles H. B., *b.* 1976 |
| 1918 | ** *Glenarthur (4th)*, Simon Mark Arthur, *b.* 1944, *s.* 1976, *m.* | Hon. Edward A. A., *b.* 1973 |
| 1911 | *Glenconner (4th)*, Cody Charles Edward Tennant, *b.* 1994, *s.* 2010 | Euan L. T., *b.* 1983 |
| 1964 | *Glendevon (3rd)*, Jonathan Charles Hope, *b.* 1952, *s.* 2009 | None |
| 1922 | *Glendyne (4th)*, John Nivison, *b.* 1960, *s.* 2008 | None |
| 1939 | ** *Glentoran (3rd)*, (Thomas) Robin (Valerian) Dixon, CBE, *b.* 1935, *s.* 1995, *m.* | Hon. Daniel G. D., *b.* 1959 |
| 1909 | *Gorell (5th)*, John Picton Gorell Barnes, *b.* 1959, *s.* 2007, *m.* | Hon. Oliver G. B., *b.* 1993 |
| 1953 | ** *Grantchester (3rd)*, Christopher John Suenson-Taylor, *b.* 1951, *s.* 1995, *m.* | Hon. Jesse D. S.-T., *b.* 1977 |
| 1782 | *Grantley (8th)*, Richard William Brinsley Norton, *b.* 1956, *s.* 1995 | Hon. Francis J. H. N., *b.* 1960 |
| 1794 I. | *Graves (10th)*, Timothy Evelyn Graves, *b.* 1960, *s.* 2002, *m.* | None |
| 1445 S. | *Gray (23rd)*, Andrew Godfrey Diarmid Stuart Campbell-Gray, *b.* 1964, *s.* 2003, *m.* | Master of Gray, *b.* 1996 |
| 1950 | *Greenhill (3rd)*, Malcolm Greenhill, *b.* 1924, *s.* 1989 | None |
| 1927 | ** *Greenway (4th)*, Ambrose Charles Drexel Greenway, *b.* 1941, *s.* 1975, *m.* | Hon. Nigel P. G., *b.* 1944 |

| | | |
|---|---|---|
| 1902 | *Grenfell (3rd) and Grenfell of Kilvey (life peerage, 2000)*, Julian Pascoe Francis St Leger Grenfell, *b.* 1935, *s.* 1976, *m.* | Richard A. St L. G., *b.* 1966 |
| 1944 | *Gretton (4th)*, John Lysander Gretton, *b.* 1975, *s.* 1989 | Hon. John F. B. G., *b.* 2008 |
| 1397 | *Grey of Codnor (6th)*, Richard Henry Cornwall-Legh, *b.* 1936, *s.* 1996, *m.* | Hon. Richard S. C. C.-L., *b.* 1976 |
| 1955 | *Gridley (3rd)*, Richard David Arnold Gridley, *b.* 1956, *s.* 1996, *m.* | Peter A. C. G., *b.* 1940 |
| 1964 | *Grimston of Westbury (3rd)*, Robert John Sylvester Grimston, *b.* 1951, *s.* 2003, *m.* | Hon. Gerald C. W. G., *b.* 1953 |
| 1886 | *Grimthorpe (5th)*, Edward John Beckett, *b.* 1954, *s.* 2003, *m.* | Hon. Harry M. B., *b.* 1993 |
| 1945 | *Hacking (3rd)*, Douglas David Hacking, *b.* 1938, *s.* 1971, *m.* | Hon. Douglas F. H., *b.* 1968 |
| 1950 | *Haden-Guest (5th)*, Christopher Haden-Guest, *b.* 1948, *s.* 1996, *m.* | Hon. Nicholas H.-G., *b.* 1951 |
| 1886 | *Hamilton of Dalzell (5th)*, Gavin Goulburn Hamilton, *b.* 1968, *s.* 2006, *m.* | Hon. Francis A. J. G. H., *b.* 2009 |
| 1874 | *Hampton (7th)*, John Humphrey Arnott Pakington, *b.* 1964, *s.* 2003, *m.* | Hon. Charles R. C. P., *b.* 2005 |
| 1939 | *Hankey (3rd)*, Donald Robin Alers Hankey, *b.* 1938, *s.* 1996, *m.* | Hon. Alexander M. A. H., *b.* 1947 |
| 1958 | *Harding of Petherton (2nd)*, John Charles Harding, *b.* 1928, *s.* 1989, *w.* | Hon. William A. J. H., *b.* 1969 |
| 1910 | *Hardinge of Penshurst (4th)*, Julian Alexander Hardinge, *b.* 1945, *s.* 1997 | Hon. Hugh F. H., *b.* 1948 |
| 1876 | *Harlech (6th)*, Francis David Ormsby-Gore, *b.* 1954, *s.* 1985, *m.* | Hon. Jasset D. C. O.-G., *b.* 1986 |
| 1939 | *Harmsworth (3rd)*, Thomas Harold Raymond Harmsworth, *b.* 1939, *s.* 1990, *m.* | Hon. Dominic M. E. H., *b.* 1973 |
| 1815 | *Harris (8th)*, Anthony Harris, *b.* 1942, *s.* 1996, *m.* | Rear-Adm. Michael G. T. H., *b.* 1941 |
| 1954 | *Harvey of Tasburgh (3rd)*, Charles John Giuseppe Harvey, *b.* 1951, *s.* 2010, *m.* | Hon. John H., *b.* 1993 |
| 1295 | *Hastings (23rd)*, Delaval Thomas Harold Astley, *b.* 1960, *s.* 2007, *m.* | Hon. Jacob A. A., *b.* 1991 |
| 1835 | *Hatherton (8th)*, Edward Charles Littleton, *b.* 1950, *s.* 1985, *m.* | Hon. Thomas E. L., *b.* 1977 |
| 1776 M. | *Hawke (12th)*, William Martin Theodore Hawke, *b.* 1995, *s.* 2010 | None |
| 1927 | *Hayter (4th)*, George William Michael Chubb, *b.* 1943, *s.* 2003, *m.* | Hon. Thomas F. F. C., *b.* 1986 |
| 1945 | *Hazlerigg (3rd)*, Arthur Grey Hazlerigg, *b.* 1951, *s.* 2002, *m.* | Hon. Arthur W. G. H. *b.* 1987 |
| 1943 | *Hemingford (3rd)*, (Dennis) Nicholas Herbert, *b.* 1934, *s.* 1982, *m.* | Hon. Christopher D. C. H., *b.* 1973 |
| 1906 | *Hemphill (6th)*, Charles Andrew Martyn Martyn-Hemphill, *b.* 1954, *s.* 2012, *m.* | Hon. Richard P. L. M.-H., *b.* 1990 |
| 1799 I. | ** *Henley (8th) and Northington (6th) (1885)*, Oliver Michael Robert Eden, PC, *b.* 1953, *s.* 1977, *m.* | Hon. John W. O. E., *b.* 1988 |
| 1800 I. | *Henniker (9th) and Hartismere (6th) (1866)*, Mark Ian Philip Chandos Henniker-Major, *b.* 1947, *s.* 2004, *m.* | Hon. Edward G. M. H.-M., *b.* 1985 |
| 1461 | *Herbert (19th)*, David John Seyfried Herbert, *b.* 1952, *s.* 2002, *m.* Title called out of abeyance 2002 | Hon. Oliver R. S. H., *b.* 1976 |
| 1935 | *Hesketh (3rd)*, Thomas Alexander Fermor-Hesketh, KBE, PC, *b.* 1950, *s.* 1955, *m.* | Hon. Frederick H. F.-H., *b.* 1988 |
| 1828 | *Heytesbury (7th)*, James William Holmes à Court, *b.* 1967, *s.* 2004, *m.* | Peter M. H.. H. à. C., *b.* 1968 |
| 1886 | *Hindlip (6th)*, Charles Henry Allsopp, *b.* 1940, *s.* 1993, *w.* | Hon. Henry W. A., *b.* 1973 |
| 1950 | *Hives (3rd)*, Matthew Peter Hives, *b.* 1971, *s.* 1997 | Hon. Michael B. H., *b.* 1926 |
| 1912 | *Hollenden (4th)*, Ian Hampden Hope-Morley, *b.* 1946, *s.* 1999, *m.* | Hon. Edward H.-M., *b.* 1981 |
| 1897 | *Holm Patrick (4th)*, Hans James David Hamilton, *b.* 1955, *s.* 1991, *m.* | Hon. Ion H. J. H., *b.* 1956 |
| 1797 I. | *Hotham (8th)*, Henry Durand Hotham, *b.* 1940, *s.* 1967, *m.* | Hon. William B. H., *b.* 1972 |
| 1881 | *Hothfield (6th)*, Anthony Charles Sackville Tufton, *b.* 1939, *s.* 1991, *m.* | Hon. William S. T., *b.* 1977 |
| 1930 | *Howard of Penrith (3rd)*, Philip Esme Howard, *b.* 1945, *s.* 1999, *m.* | Hon. Thomas Philip H., *b.* 1974 |
| 1960 | *Howick of Glendale (2nd)*, Charles Evelyn Baring, *b.* 1937, *s.* 1973, *m.* | Hon. David E. C. B., *b.* 1975 |
| 1796 I. | *Huntingfield (7th)*, Joshua Charles Vanneck, *b.* 1954, *s.* 1994, *w.* | Hon. Gerard C. A. V., *b.* 1985 |
| 1866 | ** *Hylton (5th)*, Raymond Hervey Jolliffe, *b.* 1932, *s.* 1967, *m.* | Hon. William H. M. J., *b.* 1967 |
| 1933 | *Iliffe (3rd)*, Robert Peter Richard Iliffe, *b.* 1944, *s.* 1996, *m.* | Hon. Edward R. I., *b.* 1968 |
| 1543 I. | *Inchiquin (18th)*, Conor Myles John O'Brien, *b.* 1943, *s.* 1982, *m.* | Conor J. A. O'B., *b.* 1952 |
| 1962 | *Inchyra (3rd)*, Christian James Charles Hoyer Millar, *b.* 1962, *s.* 2011, *m.* | Hon. Jake C. R. M., *b.* 1996 |
| 1964 | ** *Inglewood (2nd)*, (William) Richard Fletcher-Vane, *b.* 1951, *s.* 1989, *m.* | Hon. Henry W. F. F.-V., *b.* 1990 |
| 1919 | *Inverforth (4th)*, Andrew Peter Weir, *b.* 1966, *s.* 1982 | Hon. Benjamin A. W., *b.* 1997 |
| 1941 | *Ironside (2nd)*, Edmund Oslac Ironside, *b.* 1924, *s.* 1959, *m.* | Hon. Charles E. G. I., *b.* 1956 |
| 1952 | *Jeffreys (3rd)*, Christopher Henry Mark Jeffreys, *b.* 1957, *s.* 1986, *m.* | Hon. Arthur M. H. J., *b.* 1989 |
| 1906 | *Joicey (5th)*, James Michael Joicey, *b.* 1953, *s.* 1993, *m.* | Hon. William J. J., *b.* 1990 |
| 1937 | *Kenilworth (4th)*, (John) Randle Siddeley, *b.* 1954, *s.* 1981, *m.* | Hon. William R. J. S., *b.* 1992 |
| 1935 | *Kennet (3rd)*, William Aldus Thoby Young, *b.* 1957, *s.* 2009, *m.* | Hon. Archibald W. K. Y., *b.* 1992 |
| 1776 I. | *Kensington (8th) and Kensington (5th) (1886)*, Hugh Ivor Edwardes, *b.* 1933, *s.* 1981, *m.* | Hon. W. Owen A. E., *b.* 1964 |
| 1951 | *Kenswood (2nd)*, John Michael Howard Whitfield, *b.* 1930, *s.* 1963, *m.* | Hon. Michael C. W., *b.* 1955 |
| 1788 | *Kenyon (6th)*, Lloyd Tyrell-Kenyon, *b.* 1947, *s.* 1993, *m.* | Hon. Lloyd N. T.-K., *b.* 1972 |
| 1947 | *Kershaw (4th)*, Edward John Kershaw, *b.* 1936, *s.* 1962, *m.* | Hon. John C. E. K., *b.* 1971 |
| 1943 | *Keyes (3rd)*, Charles William Packe Keyes, *b.* 1951, *s.* 2005, *m.* | Hon. (Leopold R.) J. K., *b.* 1956 |
| 1909 | *Kilbracken (4th)*, Christopher John Godley, *b.* 1945, *s.* 2006, *m.* | Hon. James J. G., *b.* 1972 |

| 1900 | *Killanin (4th)*, (George) Redmond Fitzpatrick Morris, *b.* 1947, *s.* 1999, *m.* | Hon. Luke M. G. M., *b.* 1975 |
|------|------|------|
| 1943 | *Killearn (3rd)*, Victor Miles George Aldous Lampson, *b.* 1941, *s.* 1996, *w.* | Hon. Miles H. M. L., *b.* 1977 |
| 1789 I. | *Kilmaine (8th)*, John Francis Sandford Browne, *b.* 1983, *s.* 2013 | Revd Aubrey R. C. B., *b.* 1931 |
| 1831 | *Kilmarnock (8th)*, Dr Robin Jordan Boyd, *b.* 1941, *s.* 2009, *m.* | Hon. Simon J. B., *b.* 1978 |
| 1941 | *Kindersley (4th)*, Rupert John Molesworth Kindersley, *b.* 1955, *s.* 2013, *m.* | Hon. Frederick H. M. K., *b.* 1987 |
| 1223 I. | *Kingsale (36th)*, Nevinson Mark de Courcy, *b.* 1958, *s.* 2005, *m.* Premier Baron of Ireland | Joseph K. C. de C., *b.* 1955 |
| 1902 | *Kinross (5th)*, Christopher Patrick Balfour, *b.* 1949, *s.* 1985, *m.* | Hon. Alan I. B., *b.* 1978 |
| 1951 | *Kirkwood (3rd)*, David Harvie Kirkwood, PHD, *b.* 1931, *s.* 1970, *m.* | Hon. James S. K., *b.* 1937 |
| 1800 I. | *Langford (9th)*, Col. Geoffrey Alexander Rowley-Conwy, OBE, *b.* 1912, *s.* 1953, *m.* | Hon. Owain G. R.-C., *b.* 1958 |
| 1942 | *Latham (2nd)*, Dominic Charles Latham, *b.* 1954, *s.* 1970 | Anthony M. L., *b.* 1954 |
| 1431 | *Latymer (9th)*, Crispin James Alan Nevill Money-Coutts, *b.* 1955, *s.* 2003, *m.* | Hon. Drummond W. T. M.-C., *b.* 1986 |
| 1869 | *Lawrence (5th)*, David John Downer Lawrence, *b.* 1937, *s.* 1968 | None |
| 1947 | *Layton (3rd)*, Geoffrey Michael Layton, *b.* 1947, *s.* 1989, *m.* | Jonathan F. L., *b.* 1942 |
| 1839 | *Leigh (6th)*, Christopher Dudley Piers Leigh, *b.* 1960, *s.* 2003, *m.* | Hon. Rupert D. L., *b.* 1994 |
| 1962 | *Leighton of St Mellons (3rd)*, Robert William Henry Leighton Seager, *b.* 1955, *s.* 1998, *m.* | Hon. Simon J. L. S., *b.* 1957 |
| 1797 | *Lilford (8th)*, Mark Vernon Powys, *b.* 1975, *s.* 2005 | Robert C. L. P., *b.* 1930 |
| 1945 | *Lindsay of Birker (3rd)*, James Francis Lindsay, *b.* 1945, *s.* 1994, *m.* | Alexander S. L., *b.* 1940 |
| 1758 I. | *Lisle (9th)*, (John) Nicholas Geoffrey Lysaght, *b.* 1960, *s.* 2003 | Hon. David J. L., *b.* 1963 |
| 1850 | *Londesborough (9th)*, Richard John Denison, *b.* 1959, *s.* 1968, *m.* | Hon. James F. D., *b.* 1990 |
| 1541 I. | *Louth (17th)*, Jonathan Oliver Plunkett, *b.* 1952, *s.* 2013 | Hon. Matthew O. P., *b.* 1982 |
| 1458 S. | *Lovat (16th) and Lovat (5th) (1837)*, Simon Fraser, *b.* 1977, *s.* 1995 | Hon. Jack F., *b.* 1984 |
| 1946 | *Lucas of Chilworth (3rd)*, Simon William Lucas, *b.* 1957, *s.* 2001, *m.* | Hon. John R. M. L., *b.* 1995 |
| 1663 | ** *Lucas (11th) and Dingwall (14th) (S. 1609)*, Ralph Matthew Palmer, *b.* 1951, *s.* 1991, *m.* | Hon. Lewis E. P., *b.* 1987 |
| 1929 | *Luke (3rd)*, Arthur Charles St John Lawson Johnston, *b.* 1933, *s.* 1996, *m.* | Hon. Ian J. St J. L. J., *b.* 1963 |
| 1914 | ** *Lyell (3rd)*, Charles Lyell, *b.* 1939, *s.* 1943 | None |
| 1859 | *Lyveden (7th)*, Jack Leslie Vernon, *b.* 1938, *s.* 1999, *m.* | Hon. Colin R. V., *b.* 1967 |
| 1959 | *MacAndrew (3rd)*, Christopher Anthony Colin MacAndrew, *b.* 1945, *s.* 1989, *m.* | Hon. Oliver C. J. M., *b.* 1983 |
| 1776 I. | *Macdonald (8th)*, Godfrey James Macdonald of Macdonald, *b.* 1947, *s.* 1970, *m.* | Hon. Godfrey E. H. T. M., *b.* 1982 |
| 1937 | *McGowan (4th)*, Harry John Charles McGowan, *b.* 1971, *s.* 2003, *m.* | Hon. Dominic J. W. M., *b.* 1951 |
| 1922 | *Maclay (3rd)*, Joseph Paton Maclay, *b.* 1942, *s.* 1969, *m.* | Hon. Joseph P. M., *b.* 1977 |
| 1955 | *McNair (3rd)*, Duncan James McNair, *b.* 1947, *s.* 1989, *m.* | Hon. William S. A. M., *b.* 1958 |
| 1951 | *Macpherson of Drumochter (3rd)*, James Anthony Macpherson, *b.* 1979, *s.* 2008, *m.* | Hon. Daniel T. M., *b.* 2013 |
| 1937 | ** *Mancroft (3rd)*, Benjamin Lloyd Stormont Mancroft, *b.* 1957, *s.* 1987, *m.* | Hon. Arthur L. S. M., *b.* 1995 |
| 1807 | *Manners (6th)*, John Hugh Robert Manners, *b.* 1956, *s.* 2008, *m.* | Hon. John A. D. M., *b.* 2011 |
| 1922 | *Manton (4th)*, Miles Ronald Marcus Watson, *b.* 1958, *s.* 2003, *m.* | Hon. Thomas N. C. D. W., *b.* 1985 |
| 1908 | *Marchamley (4th)*, William Francis Whiteley, *b.* 1968, *s.* 1994, *m.* | Hon. Leon W., *b.* 2004 |
| 1965 | *Margadale (3rd)*, Alastair John Morrison, *b.* 1958, *s.* 2003, *m.* | Hon. Declan J. M., *b.* 1993 |
| 1961 | *Marks of Broughton (3rd)*, Simon Richard Marks, *b.* 1950, *s.* 1998, *m.* | Hon. Michael M., *b.* 1989 |
| 1964 | *Martonmere (2nd)*, John Stephen Robinson, *b.* 1963, *s.* 1989 | Hon. James I. R., *b.* 2003 |
| 1776 I. | *Massy (10th)*, David Hamon Somerset Massy, *b.* 1947, *s.* 1995 | Hon. John H. M., *b.* 1950 |
| 1935 | *May (4th)*, Jasper Bertram St John May, *b.* 1965, *s.* 2006 | None |
| 1928 | *Melchett (4th)*, Peter Robert Henry Mond, *b.* 1948, *s.* 1973 | None |
| 1925 | *Merrivale (4th)*, Derek John Philip Duke, *b.* 1948, *s.* 2007, *m.* | Hon. Thomas D., *b.* 1980 |
| 1911 | *Merthyr (5th)*, David Trevor Lewis, *b.* 1977, *s.* 2015, *m.* | Hon. Peter H. L., *b.* 1937 |
| 1919 | *Meston (3rd)*, James Meston, QC, *b.* 1950, *s.* 1984, *m.* | Hon. Thomas J. D. M., *b.* 1977 |
| 1838 | *Methuen (8th)*, James Paul Archibald Methuen-Campbell, *b.* 1952, *s.* 2014 | Thomas R. M. M.-C., *b.* 1977 |
| 1711 | *Middleton (13th)*, Michael Charles James Willoughby, *b.* 1948, *s.* 2011, *m.* | Hon. James W. M. W., *b.* 1976 |
| 1939 | *Milford (4th)*, Guy Wogan Philipps, QC, *b.* 1961, *s.* 1999, *m.* | Hon. Archie S. P., *b.* 1997 |
| 1933 | *Milne (3rd)*, George Alexander Milne, *b.* 1941, *s.* 2005 | Hon. Iain C. L. M., *b.* 1949 |
| 1951 | *Milner of Leeds (3rd)*, Richard James Milner, *b.* 1959, *s.* 2003, *m.* | None |
| 1947 | *Milverton (2nd)*, Revd Fraser Arthur Richard Richards, *b.* 1930, *s.* 1978, *m.* | Hon. Michael H. R., *b.* 1936 |
| 1873 | *Moncreiff (6th)*, Rhoderick Harry Wellwood Moncreiff, *b.* 1954, *s.* 2002, *m.* | Hon. Harry J. W. M., *b.* 1986 |
| 1884 | *Monk Bretton (3rd)*, John Charles Dodson, *b.* 1924, *s.* 1933, *m.* | Hon. Christopher M. D., *b.* 1958 |
| 1885 | *Monkswell (5th)*, Gerard Collier, *b.* 1947, *s.* 1984, *m.* | Hon. James A. C., *b.* 1977 |
| 1728 | *Monson (12th)*, Nicholas John Monson, *b.* 1955, *s.* 2011, *m.* | Hon. Andrew A. J. M., *b.* 1959 |
| 1885 | *Montagu of Beaulieu (4th)*, Ralph Douglas-Scott-Montagu, *b.* 1961, *s.* 2015, *m.* | Hon. Jonathan D. D.-S.-M., *b.* 1975 |
| 1839 | *Monteagle of Brandon (7th)*, Charles James Spring Rice, *b.* 1953, *s.* 2013, *m.* | Hon. Michael S. R., *b.* 1935 |
| 1943 | *Moran (3rd)*, James McMoran Wilson, *b.* 1952, *s.* 2014, *m.* | Hon. David A. M. W., *b.* 1990 |

| | | |
|---|---|---|
| 1918 | *Morris (4th)*, Thomas Anthony Salmon Morris, *b.* 1982, *s.* 2011 | Hon. John M. M., *b.* 1983 |
| 1950 | *Morris of Kenwood (3rd)*, Jonathan David Morris, *b.* 1968, *s.* 2004, *m.* | Hon. Benjamin J. M., *b.* 1998 |
| 1831 | *Mostyn (7th)*, Gregory Philip Roger Lloyd-Mostyn, *b.* 1984, *s.* 2011 | Roger Hugh L.-M., *b.* 1941 |
| 1933 | *Mottistone (6th)*, Christopher David Peter Seely, *b.* 1974, *s.* 2013 | Hon. Richard W. A. S., *b.* 1988 |
| 1945 | ** *Mountevans (4th)*, Jeffrey Richard de Corban Evans, *b.* 1948, *s.* 2014, *m.* | Hon. Alexander R. A. E., *b.* 1975 |
| 1283 | *Mowbray (27th), Segrave (28th) (1295) and Stourton (24th) (1448)*, Edward William Stephen Stourton, *b.* 1953, *s.* 2006, *m.* | Hon. James C. P. S., *b.* 1991 |
| 1932 | *Moyne (3rd)*, Jonathan Bryan Guinness, *b.* 1930, *s.* 1992, *m.* | Hon. Valentine G. B. G., *b.* 1959 |
| 1929 | ** *Moynihan (4th)*, Colin Berkeley Moynihan, *b.* 1955, *s.* 1997, *m.* | Hon. Nicholas E. B. M., *b.* 1994 |
| 1781 I. | *Muskerry (9th)*, Robert Fitzmaurice Deane, *b.* 1948, *s.* 1988, *m.* | Hon. Jonathan F. D., *b.* 1986 |
| 1627 S. | *Napier (15th) and Ettrick (6th) (1872)*, Francis David Charles Napier, *b.* 1962, *s.* 2012, *m.* | Master of Napier, *b.* 1996 |
| 1868 | *Napier of Magdala (6th)*, Robert Alan Napier, *b.* 1940, *s.* 1987, *m.* | Hon. James R. N., *b.* 1966 |
| 1940 | *Nathan (3rd)*, Rupert Harry Bernard Nathan, *b.* 1957, *s.* 2007, *m.* | None |
| 1960 | *Nelson of Stafford (4th)*, Alistair William Henry Nelson, *b.* 1973, *s.* 2006, *m.* | Hon. James J. N., *b.* 1947 |
| 1959 | *Netherthorpe (3rd)*, James Frederick Turner, *b.* 1964, *s.* 1982, *m.* | Hon. Andrew J. E. T., *b.* 1993 |
| 1946 | *Newall (2nd)*, Francis Storer Eaton Newall, *b.* 1930, *s.* 1963, *m.* | Hon. Richard H. E. N., *b.* 1961 |
| 1776 I. | *Newborough (8th)*, Robert Vaughan Wynn, *b.* 1949, *s.* 1998, *m.* | Antony C. V. W., *b.* 1949 |
| 1892 | *Newton (5th)*, Richard Thomas Legh, *b.* 1950, *s.* 1992, *m.* | Hon. Piers R. L., *b.* 1979 |
| 1930 | *Noel-Buxton (4th)*, Charles Connal Noel-Buxton, *b.* 1975, *s.* 2013, *m.* | Hon. Simon C. N.-B., *b.* 1943 |
| 1957 | *Norrie (2nd)*, (George) Willoughby Moke Norrie, *b.* 1936, *s.* 1977, *m.* | Hon. Mark W. J. N., *b.* 1972 |
| 1884 | ** *Northbourne (5th)*, Christopher George Walter James, *b.* 1926, *s.* 1982, *m.* | Hon. Charles W. H. J., *b.* 1960 |
| 1866 | ** *Northbrook (6th)*, Francis Thomas Baring, *b.* 1954, *s.* 1990, *m.* | To the Baronetcy, Peter B., *b.* 1939 |
| 1878 | *Norton (8th)*, James Nigel Arden Adderley, *b.* 1947, *s.* 1993, *m.* | Hon. Edward J. A. A., *b.* 1982 |
| 1906 | *Nunburnholme (6th)*, Stephen Charles Yanath Wilson, *b.* 1973, *s.* 2000 | Hon. David M. W., *b.* 1954 |
| 1950 | *Ogmore (3rd)*, Morgan Rees-Williams, *b.* 1937, *s.* 2004, *m.* | Hon. Tudor D. R.-W., *b.* 1991 |
| 1870 | *O'Hagan (4th)*, Charles Towneley Strachey, *b.* 1945, *s.* 1961, *m.* | Hon. Richard T. S., *b.* 1950 |
| 1868 | *O'Neill (4th)*, Raymond Arthur Clanaboy O'Neill, KCVO, TD, *b.* 1933, *s.* 1944, *m.* | Hon. Shane S. C. O'N., *b.* 1965 |
| 1836 I. | *Oranmore and Browne (5th) and Mereworth (3rd) (1926)*, Dominick Geoffrey Thomas Browne, *b.* 1929, *s.* 2002 | Shaun D. B., *b.* 1964 |
| 1933 | ** *Palmer (4th)*, Adrian Bailie Nottage Palmer, *b.* 1951, *s.* 1990, *m.* | Hon. Hugo B. R. P., *b.* 1980 |
| 1914 | *Parmoor (5th)*, Michael Leonard Seddon Cripps, *b.* 1942, *s.* 2008, *m.* | Hon. Henry W. A. C., *b.* 1976 |
| 1937 | *Pender (3rd)*, John Willoughby Denison-Pender, *b.* 1933, *s.* 1965, *w.* | Hon. Henry J. R. D.-P., *b.* 1968 |
| 1866 | *Penrhyn (7th)*, Simon Douglas-Pennant, *b.* 1938, *s.* 2003, *m.* | Hon. Edward S. D.-P., *b.* 1966 |
| 1603 | *Petre (18th)*, John Patrick Lionel Petre, *b.* 1942, *s.* 1989, *m.* | Hon. Dominic W. P., *b.* 1966 |
| 1918 | *Phillimore (5th)*, Francis Stephen Phillimore, *b.* 1944, *s.* 1994, *m.* | Hon. Tristan A. S. P., *b.* 1977 |
| 1945 | *Piercy (3rd)*, James William Piercy, *b.* 1946, *s.* 1981 | Hon. Mark E. P. P., *b.* 1953 |
| 1827 | *Plunket (9th)*, Tyrone Shaun Terence Plunket, *b.* 1966, *s.* 2013, *m.* | Hon. Rory P. R. P., *b.* 2001 |
| 1831 | *Poltimore (7th)*, Mark Coplestone Bampfylde, *b.* 1957, *s.* 1978, *m.* | Hon. Henry A. W. B., *b.* 1985 |
| 1690 S. | *Polwarth (11th)*, Andrew Walter Hepburne-Scott, *b.* 1947, *s.* 2005, *m.* | Master of Polwarth, *b.* 1973 |
| 1930 | *Ponsonby of Shulbrede (4th) and Ponsonby of Roehampton (life peerage, 2000)*, Frederick Matthew Thomas Ponsonby, *b.* 1958, *s.* 1990, *m.* | Hon. Cameron J. J. P., *b.* 1995 |
| 1958 | *Poole (2nd)*, David Charles Poole, *b.* 1945, *s.* 1993, *m.* | Hon. Oliver J. P., *b.* 1972 |
| 1852 | *Raglan (6th)*, Geoffrey Somerset, *b.* 1932, *s.* 2010, *m.* | Inigo A. F. S., *b.* 2004 |
| 1932 | *Rankeillour (5th)*, Michael Richard Hope, *b.* 1940, *s.* 2005, *m.* | James F. H., *b.* 1968 |
| 1953 | *Rathcavan (3rd)*, Hugh Detmar Torrens O'Neill, *b.* 1939, *s.* 1994, *m.* | Hon. François H. N. O'N., *b.* 1984 |
| 1916 | *Rathcreedan (3rd)*, Christopher John Norton, *b.* 1949, *s.* 1990, *m.* | Hon. Adam G. N., *b.* 1952 |
| 1868 I. | *Rathdonnell (5th)*, Thomas Benjamin McClintock-Bunbury, *b.* 1938, *s.* 1959, *m.* | Hon. William L. M.-B., *b.* 1966 |
| 1911 | *Ravensdale (3rd)*, Nicholas Mosley, MC, *b.* 1923, *s.* 1966, *m.* | Daniel N. M., *b.* 1982 |
| 1821 | *Ravensworth (9th)*, Thomas Arthur Hamish Liddell, *b.* 1954, *s.* 2004, *m.* | Hon. Henry A. T. L., *b.* 1987 |
| 1821 | *Rayleigh (6th)*, John Gerald Strutt, *b.* 1960, *s.* 1988, *m.* | Hon. John F. S., *b.* 1993 |
| 1937 | ** *Rea (3rd)*, John Nicolas Rea, MD, *b.* 1928, *s.* 1981, *m.* | Hon. Matthew J. R., *b.* 1956 |
| 1628 S. | *Reay (15th)*, Aeneas Simon Mackay, *b.* 1965, *s.* 2013, *m.* | Master of Reay, *b.* 2010 |
| 1902 | *Redesdale (6th) and Mitford (life peerage, 2000)*, Rupert Bertram Mitford, *b.* 1967, *s.* 1991, *m.* | Hon. Bertram D. M., *b.* 2000 |
| 1940 | *Reith (2nd)*, Christopher John Reith, *b.* 1928, *s.* 1971, *m.* Disclaimed for life 1972. | Hon. James H. J. R., *b.* 1971 |
| 1928 | *Remnant (3rd)*, James Wogan Remnant, CVO, *b.* 1930, *s.* 1967, *m.* | Hon. Philip J. R., CBE, *b.* 1954 |
| 1806 I. | *Rendlesham (9th)*, Charles William Brooke Thellusson, *b.* 1954, *s.* 1999, *m.* | Hon. Peter R. T., *b.* 1920 |
| 1933 | *Rennell (4th)*, James Roderick David Tremayne Rodd, *b.* 1978, *s.* 2006 | None |
| 1964 | *Renwick (2nd)*, Harry Andrew Renwick, *b.* 1935, *s.* 1973, *m.* | Hon. Robert J. R., *b.* 1966 |
| 1885 | *Revelstoke (7th)*, Alexander Rupert Baring, *b.* 1970, *s.* 2012 | Hon. Thomas J. B., *b.* 1971 |
| 1905 | *Ritchie of Dundee (6th)*, Charles Rupert Rendall Ritchie, *b.* 1958, *s.* 2008, *m.* | Hon. Sebastian R., *b.* 2004 |
| 1935 | *Riverdale (3rd)*, Anthony Robert Balfour, *b.* 1960, *s.* 1998 | Arthur M. B., *b.* 1938 |

| 1961 | *Robertson of Oakridge (3rd)*, William Brian Elworthy Robertson, *b.* 1975, *s.* 2009, *m.* | None |
| 1938 | *Roborough (4th)*, Massey John Henry Lopes, *b.* 1969, *s.* 2015, *m.* | Hon. Henry M. P. L., *b.* 1997 |
| 1931 | *Rochester (2nd)*, Foster Charles Lowry Lamb, *b.* 1916, *s.* 1955, *w.* | Hon. David C. L., *b.* 1944 |
| 1934 | *Rockley (4th)*, Anthony Robert Cecil, *b.* 1961, *s.* 2011, *m.* | Hon. William E. C., *b.* 1996 |
| 1782 M. | *Rodney (11th)*, John George Brydges Rodney, *b.* 1999, *s.* 2011 | Nicholas S. H. R., *b.* 1947 |
| 1651 S. | *Rollo (14th) and Dunning (5th) (1869)*, David Eric Howard Rollo, *b.* 1943, *s.* 1997, *m.* | Master of Rollo, *b.* 1972 |
| 1959 | *Rootes (3rd)*, Nicholas Geoffrey Rootes, *b.* 1951, *s.* 1992, *m.* | William B. R., *b.* 1944 |
| 1796 I. | *Rossmore (7th) and Rossmore (6th) (1838)*, William Warner Westenra, *b.* 1931, *s.* 1958, *m.* | Hon. Benedict W. W., *b.* 1983 |
| 1939 | ** *Rotherwick (3rd)*, (Herbert) Robin Cayzer, *b.* 1954, *s.* 1996, *m.* | Hon. H. Robin C., *b.* 1989 |
| 1885 | *Rothschild (4th)*, (Nathaniel Charles) Jacob Rothschild, OM, GBE, *b.* 1936, *s.* 1990, *m.* | Hon. Nathaniel P. V. J. R., *b.* 1971 |
| 1911 | *Rowallan (4th)*, John Polson Cameron Corbett, *b.* 1947, *s.* 1993, *m.* | Hon. Jason W. P. C. C., *b.* 1972 |
| 1947 | *Rugby (3rd)*, Robert Charles Maffey, *b.* 1951, *s.* 1990, *m.* | Hon. Timothy J. H. M., *b.* 1975 |
| 1919 | ** *Russell of Liverpool (3rd)*, Simon Gordon Jared Russell, *b.* 1952, *s.* 1981, *m.* | Hon. Edward C. S. R., *b.* 1985 |
| 1876 | *Sackville (7th)*, Robert Bertrand Sackville-West, *b.* 1958, *s.* 2004, *m.* | Hon. Arthur S-W., *b.* 2000 |
| 1964 | *St Helens (2nd)*, Richard Francis Hughes-Young, *b.* 1945, *s.* 1980, *m.* | Hon. Henry T. H.-Y., *b.* 1986 |
| 1559 | ** *St John of Bletso (21st)*, Anthony Tudor St John, *b.* 1957, *s.* 1978, *m.* | Hon. Oliver B. St J., *b.* 1995 |
| 1887 | *St Levan (5th)*, James Piers Southwell St Aubyn, *b.* 1950, *s.* 2013, *m.* | Hon. Hugh J. St A., *b.* 1983 |
| 1885 | *St Oswald (6th)*, Charles Rowland Andrew Winn, *b.* 1959, *s.* 1999, *m.* | Hon. Rowland C. S. H. W., *b.* 1986 |
| 1960 | *Sanderson of Ayot (2nd)*, Alan Lindsay Sanderson, *b.* 1931, *s.* 1971, *m.* Disclaimed for life 1971. | Hon. Michael S., *b.* 1959 |
| 1945 | *Sandford (3rd)*, James John Mowbray Edmondson, *b.* 1949, *s.* 2009, *m.* | Hon. Devon J. E., *b.* 1986 |
| 1871 | *Sandhurst (6th)*, Guy Rees John Mansfield, QC, *b.* 1949, *s.* 2002, *m.* | Hon. Edward J. M., *b.* 1982 |
| 1888 | *Savile (4th)*, John Anthony Thornhill Lumley-Savile, *b.* 1947, *s.* 2008, *m.* | Hon. James G. A. L-S., *b.* 1975 |
| 1447 | *Saye and Sele (21st)*, Nathaniel Thomas Allen Fiennes, *b.* 1920, *s.* 1968, *m.* | Hon. Martin G. F., *b.* 1961 |
| 1826 | *Seaford (6th)*, Colin Humphrey Felton Ellis, *b.* 1946, *s.* 1999, *m.* | Hon. Benjamin F. T. E., *b.* 1976 |
| 1932 | ** *Selsdon (3rd)*, Malcolm McEacharn Mitchell-Thomson, *b.* 1937, *s.* 1963, *m.* | Hon. Callum M. M. M.-T., *b.* 1969 |
| 1489 S. | *Sempill (21st)*, James William Stuart Whitemore Sempill, *b.* 1949, *s.* 1995, *m.* | Master of Sempill, *b.* 1979 |
| 1916 | *Shaughnessy (5th)*, Charles George Patrick Shaughnessy, *b.* 1955, *s.* 2007, *m.* | David J. S., *b.* 1957 |
| 1946 | *Shepherd (3rd)*, Graham George Shepherd, *b.* 1949, *s.* 2001, *m.* | Hon. Patrick M. S., *b.* 1980 |
| 1964 | *Sherfield (3rd)*, Dwight William Makins, *b.* 1951, *s.* 2006, *m.* | None |
| 1902 | *Shuttleworth (5th)*, Charles Geoffrey Nicholas Kay-Shuttleworth, KCVO, *b.* 1948, *s.* 1975, *m.* | Hon. Thomas E. K.-S., *b.* 1976 |
| 1950 | *Silkin (3rd)*, Christopher Lewis Silkin, *b.* 1947, *s.* 2001. Disclaimed for life 2002. | Rory L. S., *b.* 1954 |
| 1963 | *Silsoe (3rd)*, Simon Rupert Trustram Eve *b.* 1966, *s.* 2005 | Hon. Peter N. T. E., *b.* 1930 |
| 1947 | *Simon of Wythenshawe (3rd)*, Matthew Simon, *b.* 1955, *s.* 2002, *m.* | Michael B. S., *b.* 1970 |
| 1449 S. | *Sinclair (18th)*, Matthew Murray Kennedy St Clair *b.* 1968, *s.* 2004, *m.* | Master of Sinclair, *b.* 2007 |
| 1957 | *Sinclair of Cleeve (3rd)*, John Lawrence Robert Sinclair, *b.* 1953, *s.* 1985 | None |
| 1919 | *Sinha (6th)*, Arup Kumar Sinha, *b.* 1966, *s.* 1999 | Hon. Dilip K. S., *b.* 1967 |
| 1828 | ** *Skelmersdale (7th)*, Roger Bootle-Wilbraham, *b.* 1945, *s.* 1973, *m.* | Hon. Andrew B.-W., *b.* 1977 |
| 1916 | *Somerleyton (4th)*, Hugh Francis Saville Crossley, *b.* 1971, *s.* 2012, *m.* | Hon. John de B. T. S. C., *b.* 2010 |
| 1784 | *Somers (9th)*, Philip Sebastian Somers Cocks, *b.* 1948, *s.* 1995 | Jonathan B. C., *b.* 1985 |
| 1780 | *Southampton (7th)*, Edward Charles FitzRoy, *b.* 1955, *s.* 2015, *m.* | Hon. Charles E. M. F., *b.* 1983 |
| 1959 | *Spens (4th)*, Patrick Nathaniel George Spens, *b.* 1968, *s.* 2001, *m.* | Hon. Peter L. S., *b.* 2000 |
| 1640 | *Stafford (15th)*, Francis Melfort William Fitzherbert, *b.* 1954, *s.* 1986, *m.* | Hon. Benjamin J. B. F., *b.* 1983 |
| 1938 | *Stamp (4th)*, Trevor Charles Bosworth Stamp, MD, *b.* 1935, *s.* 1987, *m.* | Hon. Nicholas C. T. S., *b.* 1978 |
| 1839 | *Stanley of Alderley (9th)*, Sheffield (9th) (I. 1738) and Eddisbury (8th) (1848), Richard Oliver Stanley, *b.* 1956, *s.* 2013, *m.* | Hon. Charles E. S., *b.* 1960 |
| 1318 | *Strabolgi (12th)*, Andrew David Whitley Kenworthy, *b.* 1967, *s.* 2010, *m.* | Hon. Joel B. K., *b.* 2004 |
| 1628 | *Strange (17th)*, Adam Humphrey Drummond of Megginch, *b.* 1953, *s.* 2005, *m.* | Hon. John A. H. D. of M. *b.* 1992 |
| 1955 | *Strathalmond (3rd)*, William Roberton Fraser, *b.* 1947, *s.* 1976, *m.* | Hon. William G. F., *b.* 1976 |
| 1936 | *Strathcarron (3rd)*, Ian David Patrick Macpherson, *b.* 1949, *s.* 2006, *m.* | Hon. Rory D. A. M., *b.* 1982 |
| 1955 | ** *Strathclyde (2nd)*, Thomas Galloway Dunlop du Roy de Blicquy Galbraith, CH, PC, *b.* 1960, *s.* 1985, *m.* | Hon. Charles W. du R. de B. G., *b.* 1962 |
| 1900 | *Strathcona and Mount Royal (4th)*, Donald Euan Palmer Howard, *b.* 1923, *s.* 1959, *m.* | Hon. D. Alexander S. H., *b.* 1961 |
| 1836 | *Stratheden (7th) and Campbell (7th) (1841)*, David Anthony Campbell, *b.* 1963, *s.* 2011, *m.* | None |
| 1884 | *Strathspey (6th)*, James Patrick Trevor Grant of Grant, *b.* 1943, *s.* 1992, *m.* | Hon. Michael P. F. G., *b.* 1953 |
| 1838 | *Sudeley (7th)*, Merlin Charles Sainthill Hanbury-Tracy, *b.* 1939, *s.* 1941 | Nicholas E. J. H.-T., *b.* 1959 |

| 1786 | *Suffield (12th)*, Charles Anthony Assheton Harbord-Hamond, *b.* 1953, *s.* 2011, *m.* | Hon. John E. R. H.-H., *b.* 1956 |
| 1893 | *Swansea (5th)*, Richard Anthony Hussey Vivian, *b.* 1957, *s.* 2005, *m.* | Hon. James H. H. V., *b.* 1999 |
| 1907 | *Swaythling (5th)*, Charles Edgar Samuel Montagu, *b.* 1954, *s.* 1998, *m.* | Rupert A. S. M., *b.* 1965 |
| 1919 | ** *Swinfen (3rd)*, Roger Mynors Swinfen Eady, *b.* 1938, *s.* 1977, *m.* | Hon. Charles R. P. S. E., *b.* 1971 |
| 1831 I. | *Talbot of Malahide (10th)*, Reginald John Richard Arundell, *b.* 1931, *s.* 1987, *m.* | Hon. Richard J. T. A., *b.* 1957 |
| 1946 | *Tedder (3rd)*, Robin John Tedder, *b.* 1955, *s.* 1994, *m.* | Hon. Benjamin J. T., *b.* 1985 |
| 1884 | *Tennyson (6th)*, David Harold Alexander Tennyson, *b.* 1960, *s.* 2006 | Alan J. D. T., *b.* 1965 |
| 1918 | *Terrington (6th)*, Christopher Richard James Woodhouse, MB, *b.* 1946, *s.* 2001, *m.* | Hon. Jack H. L. W., *b.* 1978 |
| 1940 | *Teviot (2nd)*, Charles John Kerr, *b.* 1934, *s.* 1968, *m.* | Hon. Charles R. K., *b.* 1971 |
| 1616 | *Teynham (20th)*, John Christopher Ingham Roper-Curzon, *b.* 1928, *s.* 1972, *m.* | Hon. David J. H. I. R.-C., *b.* 1965 |
| 1964 | *Thomson of Fleet (3rd)*, David Kenneth Roy Thomson, *b.* 1957, *s.* 2006, *m.* | Hon. Benjamin T., *b.* 2006 |
| 1792 | ** *Thurlow (9th)*, Roualeyn Robert Hovell-Thurlow-Cumming-Bruce, *b.* 1952, *s.* 2013, *m.* | Hon. Nicholas E. H.-T.-C.-B., *b.* 1986 |
| 1876 | *Tollemache (5th)*, Timothy John Edward Tollemache, KCVO, *b.* 1939, *s.* 1975, *m.* | Hon. Edward J. H. T., *b.* 1976 |
| 1564 S. | *Torphichen (15th)*, James Andrew Douglas Sandilands, *b.* 1946, *s.* 1975, *m.* | Robert P. S., *b.* 1950 |
| 1947 | ** *Trefgarne (2nd)*, David Garro Trefgarne, PC, *b.* 1941, *s.* 1960, *m.* | Hon. George G. T., *b.* 1970 |
| 1921 | *Trevethin (5th) and Oaksey (3rd) (1947)*, Patrick John Tristram Lawrence, QC, *b.* 1960, *s.* 2012, *m.* | Hon. Oliver J. T. L., *b.* 1990 |
| 1880 | *Trevor (5th)*, Marke Charles Hill-Trevor, *b.* 1970, *s.* 1997, *m.* | Hon. Iain R. H.-T., *b.* 1971 |
| 1461 I. | *Trimlestown (21st)*, Raymond Charles Barnewall, *b.* 1930, *s.* 1997 | None |
| 1940 | *Tryon (3rd)*, Anthony George Merrik Tryon, OBE, *b.* 1940, *s.* 1976, *w.* | Hon. Charles G. B. T., *b.* 1976 |
| 1935 | *Tweedsmuir (4th)*, John William de l'Aigle (Toby) Buchan, *b.* 1950, *s.* 2008, *m.* | Hon. John A. G. B., *b.* 1986 |
| 1523 | *Vaux of Harrowden (12th)*, Richard Hubert Gordon Gilbey, *b.* 1965, *s.* 2014, *m.* | Hon. Alexander J. C. G., *b.* 2000 |
| 1800 I. | *Ventry (8th)*, Andrew Wesley Daubeny de Moleyns, *b.* 1943, *s.* 1987, *m.* | Hon. Francis W. D. de M., *b.* 1965 |
| 1762 | *Vernon (11th)*, Anthony William Vernon-Harcourt, *b.* 1939, *s.* 2000, *m.* | Hon. Simon A. V-H., *b.* 1969 |
| 1922 | *Vestey (3rd)*, Samuel George Armstrong Vestey, KCVO, *b.* 1941, *s.* 1954, *m.* | Hon. William G. V., *b.* 1983 |
| 1841 | *Vivian (7th)*, Charles Crespigny Hussey Vivian, *b.* 1966, *s.* 2004 | Thomas C. B. V., *b.* 1971 |
| 1934 | *Wakehurst (3rd)*, (John) Christopher Loder, *b.* 1925, *s.* 1970, *m.* | Hon. Timothy W. L., *b.* 1958 |
| 1723 | ** *Walpole (10th) and Walpole of Wolterton (8th) (1756)*, Robert Horatio Walpole, *b.* 1938, *s.* 1989, *m.* | Hon. Jonathan R. H. W., *b.* 1967 |
| 1780 | *Walsingham (9th)*, John de Grey, MC, *b.* 1925, *s.* 1965, *m.* | Hon. Robert de. G., *b.* 1969 |
| 1936 | *Wardington (3rd)*, William Simon Pease, *b.* 1925, *s.* 2005, *m.* | None |
| 1792 I. | *Waterpark (8th)*, Roderick Alexander Cavendish, *b.* 1959, *s.* 2013, *m.* | Hon. Luke F. C., *b.* 1990 |
| 1942 | *Wedgwood (5th)*, Antony John Wedgwood, *b.* 1944, *s.* 2014, *m.* | Hon. Josiah T. A. W., *b.* 1978 |
| 1861 | *Westbury (6th)*, Richard Nicholas Bethell, MBE, *b.* 1950, *s.* 2001, *m.* | Hon. Alexander B., *b.* 1986 |
| 1944 | *Westwood (3rd)*, (William) Gavin Westwood, *b.* 1944, *s.* 1991, *m.* | Hon. W. Fergus W., *b.* 1972 |
| 1544/5 | *Wharton (12th)*, Myles Christopher David Robertson, *b.* 1964, *s.* 2000, *m.* | Hon. Meghan Z. M. R., *b.* 2006 |
| 1935 | *Wigram (2nd)*, (George) Neville (Clive) Wigram, MC, *b.* 1915, *s.* 1960, *w.* | Maj. Hon. Andrew F. C. W., MVO, *b.* 1949 |
| 1491 | ** *Willoughby de Broke (21st)*, Leopold David Verney, *b.* 1938, *s.* 1986, *m.* | Hon. Rupert G. V., *b.* 1966 |
| 1937 | *Windlesham (4th)*, James Rupert Hennessy, *b.* 1968, *s.* 2010, *m.* | Hon. George R. J. H., *b.* 2006 |
| 1951 | *Wise (3rd)*, Christopher John Clayton Wise, *b.* 1949, *s.* 2012 | Hon. Martin H. W., *b.* 1950 |
| 1869 | *Wolverton (8th)*, Miles John Glyn, *b.* 1966, *s.* 2011 | Jonathan C. G., *b.* 1990 |
| 1928 | *Wraxall (3rd)*, Eustace Hubert Beilby Gibbs, KCVO, CMG, *b.* 1929, *s.* 2001, *m.* | Hon. Anthony H. G., *b.* 1958 |
| 1915 | *Wrenbury (4th)*, William Edwards Buckley, *b.* 1966, *s.* 2014, *m.* | Hon. Jamie P. B., *b.* 2001 |
| 1838 | *Wrottesley (6th)*, Clifton Hugh Lancelot de Verdon Wrottesley, *b.* 1968, *s.* 1977, *m.* | Hon. Victor E. F. de V. W., *b.* 2004 |
| 1829 | *Wynford (9th)*, John Philip Robert Best, *b.* 1950, *s.* 2002, *m.* | Hon. Harry R. F. B., *b.* 1987 |
| 1308 | *Zouche (18th)*, James Assheton Frankland, *b.* 1943, *s.* 1965, *m.* | Hon. William T. A. F., *b.* 1984 |

# BARONESSES/LADIES IN THEIR OWN RIGHT

*Style,* The Rt. Hon. the Lady _ , *or* The Rt. Hon. the Baroness _ , according to her preference. Either style may be used, except in the case of Scottish titles (indicated by S.), which are not baronies (*see* page 44) and whose holders are always addressed as Lady.

*Envelope,* may be addressed in same way as a Baron's wife or, if she prefers *(formal),* The Rt. Hon. the Baroness _;   *(social),* The Baroness _. Otherwise as for a Baron's wife

*Husband,* Untitled

*Children's style,* As for children of a Baron

| Created | Title, order of succession, name, etc | Heir |
|---|---|---|
| 1664 | *Arlington (11th),* Jennifer Jane Forwood, *b.* 1939, *s.* 1999, *w.* Title called out of abeyance 1999 | Hon. Patrick J. D. F., *b.* 1967 |
| 1455 | *Berners (16th),* Pamela Vivien Kirkham, *b.* 1929, *s.* 1995, *m.* Title called out of abeyance 1995 | Hon. Rupert W. T. K., *b.* 1953 |
| 1529 | *Braye (8th),* Mary Penelope Aubrey-Fletcher, *b.* 1941, *s.* 1985, *m.* | Linda K. C. Fothergill, *b.* 1930 |
| 1321 | *Dacre (29th),* Emily Beamish, *b.* 1983, *s.* 2014, *m.* | Three co-heiresses |
| 1283 | *Fauconberg (10th) and Conyers (16th) (1509),* Baronies in abeyance between two co-heiresses since 2013 | |
| 1490 S. | *Herries of Terregles (15th),* Mary Katharine Mumford, DCVO, *b.* 1940, *s.* 2014, *w.* | Marchioness of Lothian, *b.* 1945 |
| 1597 | *Howard de Walden (10th),* Mary Hazel Caridwen Czernin, *b.* 1935, *s.* 2004, *m.* Title called out of abeyance 2004 | Hon. Peter J. J. C., *b.* 1966 |
| 1602 S. | *Kinloss (13th),* Teresa Mary Nugent Freeman-Grenville, *b.* 1957, *s.* 2012 | Mistress of Kinloss, *b.* 1960 |
| 1445 S. | *Saltoun (20th),* Flora Marjory Fraser, *b.* 1930, *s.* 1979, *w.* | Hon. Katharine I. M. I. F., *b.* 1957 |
| 1313 | *Willoughby de Eresby (27th),* (Nancy) Jane Marie Heathcote-Drummond-Willoughby, *b.* 1934, *s.* 1983 | Two co-heirs |

# LIFE PEERS

*Style,* The Rt. Hon. the Lord _ / The Rt. Hon. the Lady _ , *or* The Rt. Hon. the Baroness _ , according to her preference
*Envelope (formal),* The Rt. Hon. Lord _/Lady_/ Baroness_; *(social),* The Lord _/Lady_/Baroness_
*Letter (formal),* My Lord/Lady; *(social),* Dear Lord/ Lady _. *Spoken,* Lord/Lady _
*Wife's style,* The Rt. Hon. the Lady _
*Husband,* Untitled
*Children's style,* 'The Hon.' before forename (F_) and surname (S_)
*Envelope,* The Hon. F_ S_. *Letter,* Dear Mr/Miss/Mrs S_. *Spoken,* Mr/Miss/Mrs S_

## NEW LIFE PEERAGES

*1 September 2014 to 31 August 2015:*
Dr Rosalind Altmann; Rt. Hon. James Arbuthnot; Rt. Hon. Gregory Barker; Rt. Hon. Sir Alan Beith; Rt. Hon. David Blunkett; Sharon Bowles; James Bridges, MBE; Sir Malcolm Bruce; Lorely Burt; Rt. Hon. Sir Menzies Campbell, CH, CBE, QC; Rt. Hon. Alistair Darling; Andrew Dunlop; Sir Jonathan Evans, KCB; Catherine Fall; Rt. Hon. Lynne Featherstone; Simone Finn; Rt. Hon. Don Foster; Stephen Gilbert; Sir Andrew Green, KCMG; Rt. Hon. William Hague; Viscount Hailsham; Rt. Hon. Peter Hain; William Hay; Robert Hayward, OBE; Rt. Hon. Dame Tessa Jowell, DBE; Richard Keen, QC; Sir Robert Kerslake; Rt. Hon. Andrew Lansley; Spencer Livermore; James Lupton, CBE; Ruby McGregor-Smith, CBE; Anne McIntosh; Rt. Hon. Francis Maude, Michelle Mone, OBE; TD; Rt. Hon. Peter Murphy; Jonny Oates; Terence O'Neill; James O'Shaughnessy; Emma Pidding, CBE; Stuart Polak, CBE; Cllr Gary Porter; Rt. Hon. Dame Dawn Primarolo, DBE; David Prior; Cllr Elizabeth Redfern; Rt. Hon. Andrew Robathan; Kate Rock; Sir Robert Rogers, KCB; Cllr Jane Scott, OBE; Shas Sheehan; Kevin Shinkwin; Philip Smith, CBE; Philippa Stroud; Rt. Hon. Sir Andrew Stunell, OBE; Dorothy Thornhill, MBE; Dave Watts; Rt. Hon. David Willetts; Alison Wolf, CBE; Rt. Hon. Sir George Young, Bt., CH

## SYMBOLS

\* Hereditary peer who has been granted a life peerage. For further details, please refer to the Hereditary Peers section. For example, life peer *Balniel* can be found under his hereditary title *Earl of Crawford and Balcarres*
§ Members of the Judiciary currently disqualified from sitting or voting in the House of Lords until they retire from that office. For further information *see* Law Courts and Offices
‡ Title not confirmed at time of going to press
¶ Peer who has permanently resigned from the House of Lords

## CREATED UNDER THE APPELLATE JURISDICTION ACT 1876 (AS AMENDED)

BARONS
*Created*
2004    *Brown of Eaton-under-Heywood,* Simon Denis Brown, PC, *b.* 1937, *m.*
1991    *Browne-Wilkinson,* Nicolas Christopher Henry Browne-Wilkinson, PC, *b.* 1930, *m.*
2004    *Carswell,* Robert Douglas Carswell, PC, *b.* 1934, *m.*

2009    *Collins of Mapesbury,* Lawrence Antony Collins, PC, *b.* 1941
1986    *Goff of Chieveley,* Robert Lionel Archibald Goff, PC, *b.* 1926, *m.*
1995    *Hoffmann,* Leonard Hubert Hoffmann, PC, *b.* 1934, *m.*
1997    *Hutton,* (James) Brian (Edward) Hutton, PC, *b.* 1931, *m.*
2009    §*Kerr of Tonaghmore,* Brian Francis Kerr, PC, *b.* 1948, *m.*
1993    ¶*Lloyd of Berwick,* Anthony John Leslie Lloyd, PC, *b.* 1929, *m.*
2005    §*Mance,* Jonathan Hugh Mance, PC, *b.* 1943, *m.*
1998    *Millett,* Peter Julian Millett, PC, *b.* 1932, *m.*
2007    §*Neuberger of Abbotsbury,* David Edmond Neuberger, PC, *b.* 1948, *m.*
1994    *Nicholls of Birkenhead,* Donald James Nicholls, PC, *b.* 1933, *m.*
1999    *Phillips of Worth Matravers,* Nicholas Addison Phillips, KG, PC, *b.* 1938, *m.*
1997    *Saville of Newdigate,* Mark Oliver Saville, PC, *b.* 1936, *m.*
2000    *Scott of Foscote,* Richard Rashleigh Folliott Scott, PC, *b.* 1934, *m.*
1995    *Steyn,* Johan van Zyl Steyn, PC, *b.* 1932, *m.*
2003    *Walker of Gestingthorpe,* Robert Walker, PC, *b.* 1938, *m.*
1992    *Woolf,* Harry Kenneth Woolf, CH, PC, *b.* 1933, *m.*

BARONESSES
2004    §*Hale of Richmond,* Brenda Marjorie Hale, DBE, PC, *b.* 1945, *m.*

## CREATED UNDER THE LIFE PEERAGES ACT 1958

BARONS
*Created*
2001    *Adebowale,* Victor Olufemi Adebowale, CBE, *b.* 1962
2005    *Adonis,* Andrew Adonis, PC, *b.* 1963, *m.*
2011    *Ahmad of Wimbledon,* Tariq Mahmood Ahmad, *b.* 1968, *m.*
1998    *Ahmed,* Nazir Ahmed, *b.* 1957, *m.*
1996    *Alderdice,* John Thomas Alderdice, *b.* 1955, *m.*
2010    *Allan of Hallam,* Richard Beecroft Allan, *b.* 1966
2013    *Allen of Kensington,* Charles Lamb Allen, CBE, *b.* 1957
1998    *Alli,* Waheed Alli, *b.* 1964
2004    *Alliance,* David Alliance, CBE, *b.* 1932
1997    *Alton of Liverpool,* David Patrick Paul Alton, *b.* 1951, *m.*
2005    *Anderson of Swansea,* Donald Anderson, PC, *b.* 1939, *m.*
2015    ‡*Arbuthnot,* James Arbuthnot, PC, *b.* 1952, *m.*
1992    *Archer of Weston-super-Mare,* Jeffrey Howard Archer, *b.* 1940, *m.*
1988    *Armstrong of Ilminster,* Robert Temple Armstrong, GCB, CVO, *b.* 1927, *m.*
1999    \**Armstrong-Jones,* Earl of Snowdon, GCVO, *b.* 1930, *m.* (*see* Hereditary Peers)
2000    ¶*Ashcroft,* Michael Anthony Ashcroft, KCMG, PC, *b.* 1946, *m.*

2001    *Ashdown of Norton-sub-Hamdon,* Jeremy John Durham (Paddy) Ashdown, GCMG, KBE, CH, PC, *b.* 1941, *m.*

1998    *Bach,* William Stephen Goulden Bach, *b.* 1946, *m.*

1997    ¶*Bagri,* Raj Kumar Bagri, CBE, *b.* 1930, *m.*

1997    *Baker of Dorking,* Kenneth Wilfred Baker, CH, PC, *b.* 1934, *m.*

2013    *Balfe,* Richard Andrew Balfe, *b.* 1944, *m.*

1974    *Balniel,* The Earl of Crawford and Balcarres, KT, GCVO, PC *b.* 1927, *m.* (*see* Hereditary Peers)

2013    *Bamford,* Anthony Paul Bamford, *b.* 1945, *m.*

1992    *Barber of Tewkesbury,* Derek Coates Barber, *b.* 1918, *m.*

2015    ‡*Barker,* Gregory Barker, PC, *b.* 1966, *m.*

1997    *Bassam of Brighton,* (John) Steven Bassam, PC, *b.* 1953

2008    *Bates,* Michael Walton Bates, PC, *b.* 1961

2010    *Beecham,* Jeremy Hugh Beecham, *b.* 1944, *m.*

2015    ‡*Beith,* Alan James Beith, PC, *b.* 1943, *m.*

1998    *Bell,* Timothy John Leigh Bell, *b.* 1941, *m.*

2013    *Berkeley of Knighton,* Michael Fitzhardinge Berkeley, CBE, *b.* 1948, *m.*

2001    *Best,* Richard Stuart Best, OBE, *b.* 1945, *m.*

2007    *Bew,* Prof. Paul Anthony Elliott Bew, *b.* 1950, *m.*

2001    *Bhatia,* Amirali Alibhai Bhatia, OBE, *b.* 1932, *m.*

2004    *Bhattacharyya,* Prof. (Sushantha) Kumar Bhattacharyya, CBE *b.* 1932, *m.*

2010    *Bichard,* Michael George Bichard, KCB, *b.* 1947

2006    *Bilimoria,* Karan Faridoon Bilimoria, CBE, *b.* 1961, *m.*

2000    *Birt,* John Francis Hodgess Birt, *b.* 1944, *m.*

2010    *Black of Brentwood,* Guy Vaughan Black, *b.* 1964, *m.*

2001    *Black of Crossharbour,* Conrad Moffat Black, PC (Canadian), *b.* 1944, *m.*

1997    *Blackwell,* Norman Roy Blackwell, *b.* 1952, *m.*

2010    *Blair of Boughton,* Ian Warwick Blair, QPM, *b.* 1953, *m.*

2011    *Blencathra,* David John Maclean, PC, *b.* 1953

2015    ‡*Blunkett,* David Blunkett, PC, *b.* 1947, *m.*

1995    *Blyth of Rowington,* James Blyth, *b.* 1940, *m.*

2010    *Boateng,* Paul Yaw Boateng, PC, *b.* 1951, *m.*

1996    *Borrie,* Gordon Johnson Borrie, QC, *b.* 1931, *w.*

2010    *Boswell of Aynho,* Timothy Eric Boswell, *b.* 1942, *m.*

2013    *Bourne of Aberystwyth,* Nicholas Henry Bourne, *b.* 1952

1996    *Bowness,* Peter Spencer Bowness, CBE, *b.* 1943, *m.*

2003    *Boyce,* Michael Boyce, KG, GCB, OBE, *b.* 1943, *m.*

2006    §*Boyd of Duncansby,* Colin David Boyd, PC, *b.* 1953, *m.*

2006    *Bradley,* Keith John Charles Bradley, PC, *b.* 1950, *m.*

1999    *Bradshaw,* William Peter Bradshaw, *b.* 1936, *m.*

1998    *Bragg,* Melvyn Bragg, *b.* 1939, *m.*

1987    *Bramall,* Edwin Noel Westby Bramall, KG, GCB, OBE, MC, *b.* 1923, *w.*

2000    *Brennan,* Daniel Joseph Brennan, QC, *b.* 1942, *m.*

2015    *Bridges of Headley,* James George Robert Bridges, MBE, *b.* 1970, *m.*

1976    *Briggs,* Asa Briggs, FBA, *b.* 1921, *m.*

2004    *Broers,* Prof. Alec (Nigel) Broers, *b.* 1938, *m.*

1997    *Brooke of Alverthorpe,* Clive Brooke, *b.* 1942, *m.*

2001    *Brooke of Sutton Mandeville,* Peter Leonard Brooke, CH, PC, *b.* 1934, *m.*

1998    *Brookman,* David Keith Brookman, *b.* 1937, *m.*

1979    *Brooks of Tremorfa,* John Edward Brooks, *b.* 1927, *m.*

2006    *Browne of Belmont,* Wallace Hamilton Browne, *b.* 1947

2010    *Browne of Ladyton,* Desmond Henry Browne, PC, *b.* 1952

2001    *Browne of Madingley,* Edmund John Phillip Browne, *b.* 1948

2015    ‡*Bruce,* Malcolm Gray Bruce, *b.* 1944, *m.*

2006    *Burnett,* John Patrick Aubone Burnett, *b.* 1945, *m.*

1998    *Burns,* Terence Burns, GCB, *b.* 1944, *m.*

1998    *Butler of Brockwell,* (Frederick Edward) Robin Butler, KG, GCB, CVO, PC, *b.* 1938, *m.*

2014    *Callanan,* Martin John Callanan, *b.* 1961, *m.*

2004    *Cameron of Dillington,* Ewen (James Hanning) Cameron, *b.* 1949, *m.*

1984    *Cameron of Lochbroom,* Kenneth John Cameron, PC, *b.* 1931, *m.*

2015    ‡*Campbell,* (Walter) Menzies Campbell, CH, CBE, QC, *b.* 1941, *m.*

2001    *Campbell-Savours,* Dale Norman Campbell-Savours, *b.* 1943, *m.*

2002    *Carey of Clifton,* Rt. Revd George Leonard Carey, PC, Royal Victorian Chain, *b.* 1935, *m.*

1999    *Carington of Upton,* Lord Carrington, KG, GCMG, CH, MC, PC, *b.* 1919, *w.* (*see* Hereditary Peers)

1999    *Carlile of Berriew,* Alexander Charles Carlile, QC, *b.* 1948, *m.*

2013    *Carrington of Fulham,* Matthew Hadrian Marshall Carrington, *b.* 1947, *m.*

2008    *Carter of Barnes,* Stephen Andrew Carter, CBE, *b.* 1964, *m.*

2004    *Carter of Coles,* Patrick Robert Carter, *b.* 1946, *m.*

2014    *Cashman,* Michael Maurice Cashman, CBE, *b.* 1950

1990    *Cavendish of Furness,* (Richard) Hugh Cavendish, *b.* 1941, *m.*

1996    *Chadlington,* Peter Selwyn Gummer, *b.* 1942, *m.*

1964    *Chalfont,* (Alun) Arthur Gwynne Jones, OBE, MC, PC, *b.* 1919, *w.*

2005    *Chidgey,* David William George Chidgey, *b.* 1942, *m.*

1998    *Christopher,* Anthony Martin Grosvenor Christopher, CBE, *b.* 1925, *m.*

2001    *Clark of Windermere,* David George Clark, PC, PHD, *b.* 1939, *m.*

1998    *Clarke of Hampstead,* Anthony James Clarke, CBE, *b.* 1932, *m.*

2009    §*Clarke of Stone-Cum-Ebony,* Anthony Peter Clarke, PC, *b.* 1943, *m.*

1998    *Clement-Jones,* Timothy Francis Clement-Jones, CBE, *b.* 1949, *m.*

1990    *Clinton-Davis,* Stanley Clinton Clinton-Davis, PC, *b.* 1928, *m.*

2000    *Coe,* Sebastian Newbold Coe, CH, KBE, *b.* 1956, *m.*

2011    *Collins of Highbury,* Raymond Edward Harry Collins, *b.* 1954

2001    *Condon,* Paul Leslie Condon, QPM, *b.* 1947, *m.*

2014    *Cooper of Windrush,* Andrew Timothy Cooper, *b.* 1963, *m.*

1997    *Cope of Berkeley,* John Ambrose Cope, PC, *b.* 1937, *m.*

2010    *Cormack,* Patrick Thomas Cormack, *b.* 1939, *m.*

2006    *Cotter,* Brian Joseph Michael Cotter, *b.* 1939, *m.*

1991    *Craig of Radley,* David Brownrigg Craig, GCB, OBE, *b.* 1929, *m.*

1987    *Crickhowell,* (Roger) Nicholas Edwards, PC, *b.* 1934, *m.*

2006    *Crisp,* (Edmund) Nigel (Ramsay) Crisp, KCB, *b.* 1952, *m.*

2003    *Cullen of Whitekirk,* William Douglas Cullen, KT, PC, *b.* 1935, *m.*

2005    *Cunningham of Felling,* John Anderson Cunningham, PC, *b.* 1939, *m.*

1996    *Currie of Marylebone,* David Anthony Currie, *b.* 1946, *m.*

2011 *Curry of Kirkharle,* Donald Thomas Younger Curry, CBE, *b.* 1944, *m.*

2011 *Dannatt,* (Francis) Richard Dannatt, GCB, CBE, MC, *b.* 1950, *m.*

2015 ‡*Darling,* Alistair Maclean Darling, PC, *b.* 1953, *m.*

2007 *Darzi of Denham,* Ara Warkes Darzi, KBE, PC, *b.* 1960, *m.*

2006 *Davidson of Glen Clova,* Neil Forbes Davidson, QC, *b.* 1950, *m.*

2009 *Davies of Abersoch,* Evan Mervyn Davies, CBE, *b.* 1952, *m.*

1997 *Davies of Coity,* (David) Garfield Davies, CBE, *b.* 1935, *m.*

1997 *Davies of Oldham,* Bryan Davies, PC, *b.* 1939, *m.*

2010 *Davies of Stamford,* John Quentin Davies, *b.* 1944, *m.*

2006 *Dear,* Geoffrey (James) Dear, QPM, *b.* 1937, *m.*

2010 *Deben,* John Selwyn Gummer, PC, *b.* 1939, *m.*

2012 *Deighton,* Paul Clive Deighton, KBE, *b.* 1956, *m.*

1991 *Desai,* Prof. Meghnad Jagdishchandra Desai, PHD, *b.* 1940, *m.*

1997 *Dholakia,* Navnit Dholakia, OBE, PC, *b.* 1937, *m.*

1997 *Dixon,* Donald Dixon, PC, *b.* 1929, *m.*

1993 *Dixon-Smith,* Robert William Dixon-Smith, *b.* 1934, *m.*

2010 *Dobbs,* Michael John Dobbs, *b.* 1948, *m.*

1985 *Donoughue,* Bernard Donoughue, DPHIL, *b.* 1934

2004 *Drayson,* Paul Rudd Drayson, PC, *b.* 1960, *m.*

1994 *Dubs,* Alfred Dubs, *b.* 1932, *m.*

2015 *Dunlop,* Andrew James Dunlop, *b.* 1959, *m.*

2004 *Dykes,* Hugh John Maxwell Dykes, *b.* 1939, *m.*

1995 *Eames,* Rt. Revd Robert Henry Alexander Eames, OM, PHD, *b.* 1937, *m.*

1992 *Eatwell,* John Leonard Eatwell, PHD, *b.* 1945

1983 ¶*Eden of Winton,* John Benedict Eden, PC, *b.* 1925, *m.*

2011 ¶*Edmiston,* Robert Norman Edmiston, *b.* 1946, *m.*

1999 *Elder,* Thomas Murray Elder, *b.* 1950

1992 *Elis-Thomas,* Dafydd Elis Elis-Thomas, PC, *b.* 1946, *m.*

1981 *Elystan-Morgan,* Dafydd Elystan Elystan-Morgan, *b.* 1932, *m.*

2011 *Empey,* Reginald Norman Morgan Empey, OBE, *b.* 1947, *m.*

2000 *\*Erskine of Alloa Tower,* Earl of Mar and Kellie, *b.* 1949, *m.* (*see* Hereditary Peers)

1997 ¶*Evans of Parkside,* John Evans, *b.* 1930, *m.*

2000 *Evans of Temple Guiting,* Matthew Evans, CBE, *b.* 1941, *m.*

1998 *Evans of Watford,* David Charles Evans, *b.* 1942, *m.*

2014 *Evans of Weardale,* Jonathan Douglas Evans, KCB, *b.* 1958

1983 *Ezra,* Derek Ezra, MBE, *b.* 1919, *m.*

1997 *Falconer of Thoroton,* Charles Leslie Falconer, PC, QC, *b.* 1951, *m.*

2014 *Farmer,* Michael Stahel Farmer, *b.* 1944, *m.*

1999 *Faulkner of Worcester,* Richard Oliver Faulkner, *b.* 1946, *m.*

2010 *Faulks,* Edward Peter Lawless Faulks, QC, *b.* 1950, *m.*

2001 *Fearn,* Ronald Cyril Fearn, OBE, *b.* 1931, *m.*

1996 *Feldman,* Basil Feldman, *b.* 1926, *m.*

2010 *Feldman of Elstree,* Andrew Simon Feldman, PC, *b.* 1966, *m.*

1999 *Fellowes,* Robert Fellowes, GCB, GCVO, PC, *b.* 1941, *m.*

2011 *Fellowes of West Stafford,* Julian Alexander Fellowes, *b.* 1949, *m.*

1999 *Filkin,* David Geoffrey Nigel Filkin, CBE, *b.* 1944

2011 *Fink,* Stanley Fink, *b.* 1957, *m.*

2013 *Finkelstein,* Daniel William Finkelstein, OBE, *b.* 1962, *m.*

2011 *Flight,* Howard Emerson Flight, *b.* 1948, *m.*

1999 *Forsyth of Drumlean,* Michael Bruce Forsyth, PC, *b.* 1954, *m.*

2015 ‡*Foster,* Donald Michael Ellison Foster, PC, *b.* 1947, *m.*

2005 *Foster of Bishop Auckland,* Derek Foster, PC, *b.* 1937, *m.*

1999 ¶*Foster of Thames Bank,* Norman Robert Foster, OM, *b.* 1935, *m.*

2005 *Foulkes of Cumnock,* George Foulkes, PC, *b.* 1942, *m.*

2001 *Fowler,* (Peter) Norman Fowler, PC, *b.* 1938, *m.*

2014 *Fox,* Christopher Francis Fox, *b.* 1957, *m.*

2011 *Framlingham,* Michael Nicholson Lord, *b.* 1938, *m.*

1997 *Freeman,* Roger Norman Freeman, PC, *b.* 1942, *m.*

2009 *Freud,* David Anthony Freud, PC, *b.* 1950 *m.*

2010 *Gardiner of Kimble,* John Gardiner, *b.* 1956, *m.*

1997 *Garel-Jones,* (William Armand) Thomas Tristan Garel-Jones, PC, *b.* 1941, *m.*

1999 *\*Gascoyne-Cecil,* The Marquess of Salisbury, KCVO, PC, *b.* 1946, *m.* (*see* Hereditary Peers)

2010 *German,* Michael James German, OBE, *b.* 1945, *m.*

2004 *Giddens,* Prof. Anthony Giddens, *b.* 1938, *m.*

2015 ‡*Gilbert,* Stephen Gilbert

2011 *Glasman,* Maurice Mark Glasman, *b.* 1961, *m.*

2011 *Glendonbrook,* Michael David Bishop, CBE, *b.* 1942

2014 *Goddard of Stockport,* David Goddard, *b.* 1952

2011 *Gold,* David Laurence Gold, *b.* 1951, *m.*

1999 *Goldsmith,* Peter Henry Goldsmith, PC, QC, *b.* 1950, *m.*

1997 ¶*Goodhart,* William Howard Goodhart, QC, *b.* 1933, *m.*

2005 *Goodlad,* Alastair Robertson Goodlad, KCMG, *b.* 1943, *m.*

1997 *Gordon of Strathblane,* James Stuart Gordon, CBE, *b.* 1936, *m.*

1999 *Grabiner,* Anthony Stephen Grabiner, QC, *b.* 1945, *m.*

2011 *Grade of Yarmouth,* Michael Ian Grade, CBE, *b.* 1943, *m.*

1983 *Graham of Edmonton,* (Thomas) Edward Graham, PC, *b.* 1925, *m.*

2000 *Greaves,* Anthony Robert Greaves, *b.* 1942, *m.*

2014 *Green of Deddington,* Andrew Fleming Green, KCMG, *b.* 1941, *m.*

2010 *Green of Hurstpierpoint,* Stephen Keith Green, *b.* 1948, *m.*

2000 ¶*\*Grenfell of Kilvey,* Lord Grenfell, *b.* 1935, *m.* (*see* Hereditary Peers)

2004 *Griffiths of Burry Port,* Revd Dr Leslie John Griffiths, *b.* 1942, *m.*

1991 *Griffiths of Fforestfach,* Brian Griffiths, *b.* 1941, *m.*

2001 *Grocott,* Bruce Joseph Grocott, PC, *b.* 1940, *m.*

2000 *\*Gueterbock,* Lord Berkeley, OBE, *b.* 1939, *m.* (*see* Hereditary Peers)

2000 *Guthrie of Craigiebank,* Charles Ronald Llewelyn Guthrie, GCB, LVO, OBE, *b.* 1938, *m.*

1995 *Habgood,* Rt. Revd John Stapylton Habgood, PC, PHD, *b.* 1927, *m.*

2015 ‡*Hague,* William Jefferson Hague, PC, *b.* 1961, *m.*

2015 ‡*Hain,* Peter Gerald Hain, PC, *b.* 1950, *m.*

2010 *Hall of Birkenhead,* Anthony William Hall, CBE, *b.* 1951, *m.*

2007 *Hameed,* Dr Khalid Hameed, *b.* 1941, *m.*

| | |
|---|---|
| 2005 | *Hamilton of Epsom,* Archibald Gavin Hamilton, PC, *b.* 1941, *m.* |
| 2001 | *Hannay of Chiswick,* David Hugh Alexander Hannay, GCMG, CH, *b.* 1935, *w.* |
| 1998 | *Hanningfield,* Paul Edward Winston White, *b.* 1940 |
| 1997 | *Hardie,* Andrew Rutherford Hardie, PC, QC, *b.* 1946, *m.* |
| 2006 | *Harries of Pentregarth,* Rt. Revd Richard Douglas Harries, *b.* 1936, *m.* |
| 1998 | *Harris of Haringey,* (Jonathan) Toby Harris, *b.* 1953, *m.* |
| 1996 | *Harris of Peckham,* Philip Charles Harris, *b.* 1942, *m.* |
| 1999 | *Harrison,* Lyndon Henry Arthur Harrison, *b.* 1947, *m.* |
| 2004 | *Hart of Chilton,* Garry Richard Rushby Hart, *b.* 1940, *m.* |
| 1993 | *Haskel,* Simon Haskel, *b.* 1934, *m.* |
| 1998 | *Haskins,* Christopher Robin Haskins, *b.* 1937, *m.* |
| 2005 | *Hastings of Scarisbrick,* Michael John Hastings, CBE, *b.* 1958, *m.* |
| 1997 | *Hattersley,* Roy Sidney George Hattersley, PC, *b.* 1932 |
| 2013 | *Haughey,* William Haughey, OBE, *b.* 1956, *m.* |
| 2004 | *Haworth,* Alan Robert Haworth, *b.* 1948, *m.* |
| 2014 | *Hay of Ballyore,* William Alexander Hay, *b.* 1950, *m.* |
| 2015 | ‡*Hayward,* Robert Antony Hayward, OBE, *b.* 1949 |
| 1992 | *Healey,* Denis Winston Healey, CH, MBE, PC, *b.* 1917, *w.* |
| 2010 | *Hennessy of Nympsfield,* Prof. Peter John Hennessy, *b.* 1947, *m.* |
| 2001 | *Heseltine,* Michael Ray Dibdin Heseltine, CH, PC, *b.* 1933, *m.* |
| 1997 | *Higgins,* Terence Langley Higgins, KBE, PC, *b.* 1928, *m.* |
| 2010 | *Hill of Oareford,* Jonathan Hopkin Hill, CBE, PC, *b.* 1960, *m.* |
| 2000 | *Hodgson of Astley Abbotts,* Robin Granville Hodgson, CBE, *b.* 1942, *m.* |
| 2015 | *‡*Hogg,* Viscount Hailsham, PC, QC, *b.* 1945, *m.* (*see* Hereditary Peers) |
| 1991 | *Hollick,* Clive Richard Hollick, *b.* 1945, *m.* |
| 2013 | *Holmes of Richmond,* Christopher Holmes, MBE, *b.* 1971 |
| 1995 | *Hope of Craighead,* (James Arthur) David Hope, KT, PC, *b.* 1938, *m.* |
| 2005 | ¶*Hope of Thornes,* Rt. Revd David Michael Hope, KCVO, PC, *b.* 1940 |
| 2013 | *Horam,* John Rhodes Horam, *b.* 1939, *m.* |
| 2010 | *Howard of Lympne,* Michael Howard, CH, PC, QC, *b.* 1941, *m.* |
| 2004 | *Howard of Rising,* Greville Patrick Charles Howard, *b.* 1941, *m.* |
| 2005 | *Howarth of Newport,* Alan Thomas Howarth, CBE, PC, *b.* 1944 |
| 1992 | ¶*Howe of Aberavon,* (Richard Edward) Geoffrey Howe, CH, PC, QC, *b.* 1926, *m.* |
| 1997 | *Howell of Guildford,* David Arthur Russell Howell, PC, *b.* 1936, *m.* |
| 1978 | *Howie of Troon,* William Howie, *b.* 1924, *w.* |
| 1997 | *Hoyle,* (Eric) Douglas Harvey Hoyle, *b.* 1930, *w.* |
| 1997 | *Hughes of Woodside,* Robert Hughes, *b.* 1932, *m.* |
| 2000 | *Hunt of Chesterton,* Julian Charles Roland Hunt, CBE, *b.* 1941, *m.* |
| 1997 | *Hunt of Kings Heath,* Philip Alexander Hunt, OBE, PC, *b.* 1949, *m.* |
| 1997 | *Hunt of Wirral,* David James Fletcher Hunt, MBE, PC, *b.* 1942, *m.* |
| 1997 | *Hurd of Westwell,* Douglas Richard Hurd, CH, CBE, PC, *b.* 1930, *w.* |

| | |
|---|---|
| 2011 | *Hussain,* Qurban Hussain, *b.* 1956, *m.* |
| 1978 | *Hutchinson of Lullington,* Jeremy Nicolas Hutchinson, QC, *b.* 1915, *w.* |
| 2010 | *Hutton of Furness,* John Matthew Patrick Hutton, PC, *b.* 1955, *m.* |
| 1999 | *Imbert,* Peter Michael Imbert, CVO, QPM, *b.* 1933, *m.* |
| 1997 | *Inge,* Peter Anthony Inge, KG, GCB, PC, *b.* 1935, *m.* |
| 1987 | *Irvine of Lairg,* Alexander Andrew Mackay Irvine, PC, QC, *b.* 1940, *m.* |
| 2006 | *James of Blackheath,* David Noel James, CBE, *b.* 1937, *m.* |
| 1997 | *Janner of Braunstone,* Greville Ewan Janner, QC, *b.* 1928, *w.* |
| 2007 | *Janvrin,* Robin Berry Janvrin, GCB, GCVO, PC, *b.* 1946, *m.* |
| 2006 | *Jay of Ewelme,* Michael (Hastings) Jay, GCMG, *b.* 1946, *m.* |
| 1987 | ¶*Jenkin of Roding,* (Charles) Patrick (Fleeming) Jenkin, PC, *b.* 1926, *m.* |
| 2000 | ¶*Joffe,* Joel Goodman Joffe, CBE, *b.* 1932, *m.* |
| 2001 | *Jones,* (Stephen) Barry Jones, *b.* 1937, *m.* |
| 2007 | *Jones of Birmingham,* Digby Marritt Jones, *b.* 1955, *m.* |
| 2005 | *Jones of Cheltenham,* Nigel David Jones, *b.* 1948, *m.* |
| 1997 | *Jopling,* (Thomas) Michael Jopling, PC, *b.* 1930, *m.* |
| 2000 | *Jordan,* William Brian Jordan, CBE, *b.* 1936, *m.* |
| 1991 | *Judd,* Frank Ashcroft Judd, *b.* 1935, *m.* |
| 2008 | *Judge,* Igor Judge, PC, *b.* 1941, *m.* |
| 2010 | *Kakkar,* Prof. Ajay Kumar Kakkar, PC, *b.* 1964 |
| 2004 | *Kalms,* Harold Stanley Kalms, *b.* 1931, *m.* |
| 2015 | *Keen of Elie,* richard Sanderson Keen, QC, *b.* 1954, *m.* |
| 2010 | *Kennedy of Southwark,* Roy Francis Kennedy, *b.* 1962 |
| 2004 | *Kerr of Kinlochard,* John (Olav) Kerr, GCMG, *b.* 1942, *m.* |
| 2010 | *Kerr of Monteviot,* Marquess of Lothian (Michael Ancram), PC, QC, *b.* 1945, *m.* (*see* Hereditary Peers) |
| 2015 | *Kerslake,* Robert Walter Kerslake, *b.* 1955, *m.* |
| 2011 | *Kestenbaum,* Jonathan Andrew Kestenbaum, *b.* 1959, *m.* |
| 2001 | *Kilclooney,* John David Taylor, PC (NI), *b.* 1937, *m.* |
| 1996 | *Kilpatrick of Kincraig,* Robert Kilpatrick, CBE, *b.* 1926, *m.* |
| 2001 | *King of Bridgwater,* Thomas Jeremy King, CH, PC, *b.* 1933, *m.* |
| 2013 | *King of Lothbury,* Mervyn Allister King, KG, GBE, *b.* 1948 |
| 2005 | *Kinnock,* Neil Gordon Kinnock, PC, *b.* 1942, *m.* |
| 1999 | *Kirkham,* Graham Kirkham, *b.* 1944, *m.* |
| 1975 | *Kirkhill,* John Farquharson Smith, *b.* 1930, *m.* |
| 2005 | *Kirkwood of Kirkhope,* Archibald Johnstone Kirkwood, *b.* 1946, *m.* |
| 2010 | *Knight of Weymouth,* James Philip Knight, PC, *b.* 1965, *m.* |
| 2007 | *Krebs,* Prof. John (Richard) Krebs, FRS, *b.* 1945, *m.* |
| 2004 | ¶*Laidlaw,* Irvine Alan Stewart Laidlaw, *b.* 1942, *m.* |
| 1999 | *Laird,* John Dunn Laird, *b.* 1944, *m.* |
| 1998 | *Laming,* (William) Herbert Laming, PC, CBE, *b.* 1936, *w.* |
| 1998 | *Lamont of Lerwick,* Norman Stewart Hughson Lamont, PC, *b.* 1942, *m.* |
| 1997 | *Lang of Monkton,* Ian Bruce Lang, PC, *b.* 1940, *m.* |
| 2015 | ‡*Lansley,* Andrew David Lansley, PC, CBE, *b.* 1956, *m.* |
| 1992 | *Lawson of Blaby,* Nigel Lawson, PC, *b.* 1932, *m.* |
| 2000 | *Layard,* Peter Richard Grenville Layard, *b.* 1934, *m.* |

| | |
|---|---|
| 1999 | *Lea of Crondall,* David Edward Lea, OBE, *b.* 1937 |
| 2006 | *Leach of Fairford,* Charles Guy Rodney Leach, *b.* 1934, *m.* |
| 2006 | *Lee of Trafford,* John Robert Louis Lee, *b.* 1942, *m.* |
| 2013 | *Leigh of Hurley,* Howard Darryl Leigh, *b.* 1959, *m.* |
| 2004 | *Leitch,* Alexander Park Leitch, *b.* 1947, *m.* |
| 2014 | *Lennie,* Christopher John Lennie, *b.* 1953, *m.* |
| 1993 | *Lester of Herne Hill,* Anthony Paul Lester, QC, *b.* 1936, *m.* |
| 1997 | *Levene of Portsoken,* Peter Keith Levene, KBE, *b.* 1941, *m.* |
| 1997 | *Levy,* Michael Abraham Levy, *b.* 1944, *m.* |
| 2010 | *Lexden,* Alistair Basil Cooke, OBE, *b.* 1945 |
| 2010 | *Liddle,* Roger John Liddle, *b.* 1947, *m.* |
| 2010 | *Lingfield,* Robert George Alexander Balchin, *b.* 1942, *m.* |
| 1999 | *Lipsey,* David Lawrence Lipsey, *b.* 1948, *m.* |
| 2014 | *Lisvane,* Robert James Rogers, KCB, *b.* 1950, *m.* |
| 2015 | ‡*Livermore,* Spencer Livermore, *b.* 1975 |
| 2013 | *Livingston of Parkhead,* Ian Paul Livingston, *b.* 1964, *m.* |
| 1997 | *Lloyd-Webber,* Andrew Lloyd Webber, *b.* 1948, *m.* |
| 2011 | *Loomba,* Rajinder Paul Loomba, CBE, *b.* 1943, *m.* |
| 2006 | *Low of Dalston,* Prof. Colin MacKenzie Low, CBE, *b.* 1942, *m.* |
| 2000 | *Luce,* Richard Napier Luce, KG, GCVO, PC, *b.* 1936, *m.* |
| 2015 | ‡*Lupton,* James Roger Crompton Lupton, CBE, *b.* 1955, *m.* |
| 2000 | *Lyttelton of Aldershot,* The Viscount Chandos, *b.* 1953, *m.* (*see* Hereditary Peers) |
| 2010 | *McAvoy,* Thomas McLaughlin McAvoy, PC, *b.* 1943, *m.* |
| 1976 | *McCluskey,* John Herbert McCluskey, *b.* 1929, *m.* |
| 1989 | *McColl of Dulwich,* Ian McColl, CBE, FRCS, FRCSE, *b.* 1933, *m.* |
| 2010 | *McConnell of Glenscorrodale,* Dr Jack Wilson McConnell, PC, *b.* 1960, *m.* |
| 2010 | *Macdonald of River Glaven,* Kenneth Donald John Macdonald, QC, *b.* 1953, *m.* |
| 1998 | *Macdonald of Tradeston,* Angus John Macdonald, CBE, PC, *b.* 1940, *m.* |
| 2010 | *McFall of Alcluith,* John Francis McFall, PC, *b.* 1944, *m.* |
| 1991 | *Macfarlane of Bearsden,* Norman Somerville Macfarlane, KT, FRSE, *b.* 1926, *m.* |
| 2001 | *MacGregor of Pulham Market,* John Roddick Russell MacGregor, CBE, PC, *b.* 1937, *m.* |
| 1979 | *Mackay of Clashfern,* James Peter Hymers Mackay, KT, PC, FRSE, *b.* 1927, *m.* |
| 1995 | *Mackay of Drumadoon,* Donald Sage Mackay, PC, *b.* 1946, *m.* |
| 1998 | *MacKenzie of Culkein,* Hector Uisdean MacKenzie, *b.* 1940 |
| 1999 | *Mackenzie of Framwellgate,* Brian Mackenzie, OBE, *b.* 1943, *m.* |
| 2004 | *McKenzie of Luton,* William David McKenzie, *b.* 1946, *m.* |
| 1996 | *MacLaurin of Knebworth,* Ian Charter MacLaurin, *b.* 1937, *m.* |
| 2001 | *Maclennan of Rogart,* Robert Adam Ross Maclennan, PC, *b.* 1936, *m.* |
| 1995 | *McNally,* Tom McNally, PC, *b.* 1943, *m.* |
| 2011 | *Magan of Castletown,* George Morgan Magan, *b.* 1945, *m.* |
| 2001 | *Maginnis of Drumglass,* Kenneth Wiggins Maginnis, *b.* 1938, *m.* |
| 2007 | *Malloch-Brown,* George Mark Malloch Brown, KCMG, PC, *b.* 1953, *m.* |

| | |
|---|---|
| 2008 | *Mandelson,* Peter Benjamin Mandelson, PC, *b.* 1953 |
| 2011 | *Marks of Henley-on-Thames,* Jonathan Clive Marks, QC, *b.* 1952, *m.* |
| 2006 | *Marland,* Jonathan Peter Marland, *b.* 1956, *m.* |
| 1991 | *Marlesford,* Mark Shuldham Schreiber, *b.* 1931, *m.* |
| 2009 | *Martin of Springburn,* Michael Martin, PC, *b.* 1945, *m.* |
| 2015 | *Maude of Horsham,* Francis Anthony Aylmer Maude, PC, TD, *b.* 1953, *m.* |
| 2005 | *Mawhinney,* Brian Stanley Mawhinney, PC, *b.* 1940, *m.* |
| 2007 | *Mawson,* Revd Andrew Mawson, OBE, *b.* 1954, *m.* |
| 2004 | *Maxton,* John Alston Maxton, *b.* 1936, *m.* |
| 2001 | *May of Oxford,* Robert McCredie May, OM, *b.* 1936, *m.* |
| 1997 | ¶*Mayhew of Twysden,* Patrick Barnabas Burke Mayhew, PC, QC, *b.* 1929, *m.* |
| 2013 | *Mendelsohn,* Jonathan Neil Mendelsohn, *b.* 1966, *m.* |
| 2000 | *Mitchell,* Parry Andrew Mitchell, *b.* 1943, *m.* |
| 2000 | *Mitford,* Lord Redesdale, *b.* 1967, *m.* (*see* Hereditary Peers) |
| 2008 | *Mogg,* John (Frederick) Mogg, KCMG, *b.* 1943 *m.* |
| 2010 | *Monks,* John Stephen Monks, *b.* 1945, *m.* |
| 2005 | *Moonie,* Dr. Lewis George Moonie, *b.* 1947, *m.* |
| 1992 | *Moore of Lower Marsh,* John Edward Michael Moore, PC, *b.* 1937, *w.* |
| 2000 | *Morgan,* Kenneth Owen Morgan, *b.* 1934, *m.* |
| 2001 | *Morris of Aberavon,* John Morris, KG, PC, QC, *b.* 1931, *m.* |
| 2006 | *Morris of Handsworth,* William Manuel Morris, *b.* 1938, *m.* |
| 2006 | *Morrow,* Maurice George Morrow, *b.* 1948, *m.* |
| 2015 | ‡*Murphy,* Paul Peter Murphy, PC, *b.* 1948 |
| 2008 | *Myners,* Paul Myners, CBE, *b.* 1948, *m.* |
| 1997 | *Naseby,* Michael Wolfgang Laurence Morris, PC, *b.* 1936, *m.* |
| 2013 | *Nash,* John Alfred Stoddard Nash, *b.* 1949 |
| 1997 | *Neill of Bladen,* (Francis) Patrick Neill, QC, *b.* 1926, *m.* |
| 1997 | *Newby,* Richard Mark Newby, PC, OBE, *b.* 1953, *m.* |
| 1994 | ¶*Nickson,* David Wigley Nickson, KBE, FRSE, *b.* 1929, *m.* |
| 2011 | *Noon,* Gulam Kaderbhoy Noon, MBE, *b.* 1936, *m.* |
| 1998 | *Norton of Louth,* Philip Norton, *b.* 1951 |
| 2000 | *Oakeshott of Seagrove Bay,* Matthew Alan Oakeshott, *b.* 1947, *m.* |
| 2015 | ‡*Oates,* Jonathan Oates, *b.* 1969, *c.p.* |
| 2012 | *O'Donnell,* Augustine Thomas (Gus) O'Donnell, GCB, *b.* 1952, *m.* |
| 2005 | *O'Neill of Clackmannan,* Martin John O'Neill, *b.* 1945, *m.* |
| 2015 | *O'Neill of Gatley,* Terence James O'Neill, PC, *b.* 1957, *m.* |
| 2015 | ‡*O'Shaughnessy,* James O'Shaughnessy |
| 2001 | *Ouseley,* Herman George Ouseley, *b.* 1945, *m.* |
| 1992 | *Owen,* David Anthony Llewellyn Owen, CH, PC, *b.* 1938, *m.* |
| 1999 | *Oxburgh,* Ernest Ronald Oxburgh, KBE, FRS, PHD, *b.* 1934, *m.* |
| 2013 | *Paddick,* Brian Leonard Paddick, *b.* 1958, *m.* |
| 2011 | *Palmer of Childs Hill,* Monroe Edward Palmer, OBE, *b.* 1938, *m.* |
| 1991 | *Palumbo,* Peter Garth Palumbo, *b.* 1935, *m.* |
| 2013 | *Palumbo of Southwark,* James Rudolph Palumbo, *b.* 1963 |
| 2008 | *Pannick,* David Philip Pannick, QC, *b.* 1956, *m.* |
| 2000 | *Parekh,* Bhikhu Chhotalal Parekh, *b.* 1935, *m.* |

1992 ¶*Parkinson,* Cecil Edward Parkinson, PC, *b.* 1931, *m.*

1999 *Patel,* Narendra Babubhai Patel, KT, *b.* 1938

2000 *Patel of Blackburn,* Adam Hafejee Patel, *b.* 1940

2006 *Patel of Bradford,* Prof. Kamlesh Kumar Patel, OBE, *b.* 1960 *m.*

1997 *Patten,* John Haggitt Charles Patten, PC, *b.* 1945, *m.*

2005 *Patten of Barnes,* Christopher Francis Patten, CH, PC, *b.* 1944, *m.*

1996 *Paul,* Swraj Paul, PC, *b.* 1931, *m.*

1990 *Pearson of Rannoch,* Malcolm Everard MacLaren Pearson, *b.* 1942, *m.*

2001 *Pendry,* Thomas Pendry, PC, *b.* 1934, *m.*

1987 *Peston,* Maurice Harry Peston, *b.* 1931, *m.*

1998 ¶*Phillips of Sudbury,* Andrew Wyndham Phillips, OBE, *b.* 1939, *m.*

1992 *Plant of Highfield,* Prof. Raymond Plant, PHD, *b.* 1945, *m.*

1987 *Plumb,* (Charles) Henry Plumb, *b.* 1925, *m.*

2015 ‡*Polak,* Stuart Polak, CBE

2000 *\*Ponsonby of Roehampton,* Lord Ponsonby of Shulbrede, *b.* 1958, *m.* (*see* Hereditary Peers)

2010 *Popat,* Dolar Amarshi Popat, *b.* 1953, *m.*

2015 ‡*Porter,* Gary Porter

2000 *Powell of Bayswater,* Charles David Powell, KCMG, *b.* 1941

2010 *Prescott,* John Leslie Prescott, *b.* 1938, *m.*

1987 *Prior,* James Michael Leathes Prior, PC, *b.* 1927, *m.*

2015 *Prior of Brampton,* David Gifford Leathes Prior, *b.* 1954, *m.*

1982 ¶*Prys-Davies,* Gwilym Prys Prys-Davies, *b.* 1923, *m.*

2013 *Purvis of Tweed,* Jeremy Purvis, *b.* 1974

1997 *Puttnam,* David Terence Puttnam, CBE, *b.* 1941, *m.*

1994 *Quirk,* Prof. (Charles) Randolph Quirk, CBE, FBA, *b.* 1920, *m.*

2001 *Radice,* Giles Heneage Radice, PC, *b.* 1936

2005 *Ramsbotham,* David John Ramsbotham, GCB, CBE, *b.* 1934, *m.*

2004 *Rana,* Dr Diljit Singh Rana, MBE, *b.* 1938, *m.*

1997 *Razzall,* (Edward) Timothy Razzall, CBE, *b.* 1943, *m.*

2005 *Rees of Ludlow,* Prof. Martin John Rees, OM, *b.* 1942, *m.*

2010 *Reid of Cardowan,* Dr John Reid, PC, *b.* 1947, *m.*

1991 *Renfrew of Kaimsthorn,* (Andrew) Colin Renfrew, FBA, *b.* 1937, *m.*

1999 *Rennard,* Christopher John Rennard, MBE, *b.* 1960

1997 *Renton of Mount Harry,* (Ronald) Timothy Renton, PC, *b.* 1932, *m.*

1997 *Renwick of Clifton,* Robin William Renwick, KCMG, *b.* 1937, *m.*

2010 *Ribeiro,* Bernard Francisco Ribeiro, CBE, *b.* 1944, *m.*

1990 *Richard,* Ivor Seward Richard, PC, QC, *b.* 1932, *m.*

2014 *Richards of Herstmonceux,* David Julian Richards, GCB, CBE, DSO, *b.* 1952, *m.*

2010 *Risby,* Richard John Grenville Spring, *b.* 1946, *m.*

1992 *Rix,* Brian Norman Roger Rix, CBE, *b.* 1924, *w.*

2015 ‡*Robathan,* Andrew Robathan, PC, *b.* 1951, *m.*

2004 *Roberts of Llandudno,* Revd John Roger Roberts, *b.* 1935, *m.*

1999 *Robertson of Port Ellen,* George Islay MacNeill Robertson, KT, GCMG, PC, *b.* 1946, *m.*

1992 *Rodgers of Quarry Bank,* William Thomas Rodgers, PC, *b.* 1928, *w.*

1999 *Rogan,* Dennis Robert David Rogan, *b.* 1942, *m.*

1996 *Rogers of Riverside,* Richard George Rogers, CH, RA, RIBA, *b.* 1933, *m.*

2001 *Rooker,* Jeffrey William Rooker, PC, *b.* 1941, *m.*

2000 ¶*Roper,* John Francis Hodgess Roper, PC, *b.* 1935, *m.*

2014 *Rose of Monewden,* Stuart Alan Ransom Rose, *b.* 1949

2004 *Rosser,* Richard Andrew Rosser, *b.* 1944, *m.*

2006 *Rowe-Beddoe,* David (Sydney) Rowe-Beddoe, *b.* 1937, *m.*

2004 *Rowlands,* Edward Rowlands, CBE, *b.* 1940, *m.*

1997 *Ryder of Wensum,* Richard Andrew Ryder, OBE, PC, *b.* 1949, *m.*

1996 *Saatchi,* Maurice Saatchi, *b.* 1946, *w.*

2009 *Sacks,* Chief Rabbi Dr Jonathan Henry Sacks, *b.* 1948, *m.*

1989 *Sainsbury of Preston Candover,* John Davan Sainsbury, KG, *b.* 1927, *m.*

1997 *Sainsbury of Turville,* David John Sainsbury, *b.* 1940, *m.*

1997 ¶*Sandberg,* Michael Graham Ruddock Sandberg, CBE, *b.* 1927, *m.*

1985 *Sanderson of Bowden,* Charles Russell Sanderson, *b.* 1933, *m.*

2010 *Sassoon,* James Meyer Sassoon, *b.* 1955, *m.*

1998 *Sawyer,* Lawrence (Tom) Sawyer, *b.* 1943

2014 *Scriven,* Paul James Scriven, *b.* 1966

1997 *Selkirk of Douglas,* James Alexander Douglas-Hamilton, PC, QC, *b.* 1942, *m.*

1996 ¶*Sewel,* John Buttifant Sewel, CBE, *b.* 1946

2010 *Sharkey,* John Kevin Sharkey, *b.* 1947, *m.*

1999 ¶*Sharman,* Colin Morven Sharman, OBE, *b.* 1943, *m.*

1994 ¶*Shaw of Northstead,* Michael Norman Shaw, *b.* 1920, *m.*

2006 *Sheikh,* Mohamed Iltaf Sheikh, *b.* 1941, *m.*

2001 ¶*Sheldon,* Robert Edward Sheldon, PC, *b.* 1923, *m.*

2013 *Sherbourne of Didsbury,* Stephen Ashley Sherbourne, CBE, *b.* 1945

2015 ‡*Shinkwin,* Kevin Shinkwin

2010 *Shipley,* John Warren Shipley, OBE, *b.* 1946

2000 *Shutt of Greetland,* David Trevor Shutt, OBE, PC, *b.* 1942

1997 *Simon of Highbury,* David Alec Gwyn Simon, CBE, *b.* 1939, *m.*

1997 ¶*Simpson of Dunkeld,* George Simpson, *b.* 1942, *m.*

2011 *Singh of Wimbledon,* Indarjit Singh, CBE, *b.* 1932, *m.*

1991 *Skidelsky,* Robert Jacob Alexander Skidelsky, DPHIL, *b.* 1939, *m.*

2015 ‡*Smith,* Philip Smith, CBE

1997 *Smith of Clifton,* Trevor Arthur Smith, *b.* 1937, *m.*

2005 *Smith of Finsbury,* Christopher Robert Smith, PC, *b.* 1951

2008 *Smith of Kelvin,* Robert (Haldane) Smith, KT, *b.* 1944, *m.*

1999 *Smith of Leigh,* Peter Richard Charles Smith, *b.* 1945, *m.*

2004 *Snape,* Peter Charles Snape, *b.* 1942

2005 *Soley,* Clive Stafford Soley, *b.* 1939

1990 *Soulsby of Swaffham Prior,* Ernest Jackson Lawson Soulsby, PHD, *b.* 1926, *w.*

2010 *Spicer,* (William) Michael Hardy Spicer, PC, *b.* 1943, *m.*

1997 *Steel of Aikwood,* David Martin Scott Steel, KT, KBE, PC, *b.* 1938, *m.*

2011 *Stephen,* Nicol Ross Stephen, *b.* 1960, *m.*

1991 *Sterling of Plaistow,* Jeffrey Maurice Sterling, GCVO, CBE, *b.* 1934, *m.*

2007 *Stern of Brentford,* Nicholas Herbert Stern, *b.* 1946, *m.*

2005 *Stevens of Kirkwhelpington,* John Arthur Stevens, QPM, *b.* 1942, *m.*

1987    *Stevens of Ludgate,* David Robert Stevens,
        *b.* 1936, *m.*
2010    *Stevenson of Balmacara,* Robert Wilfrid Stevenson,
        *b.* 1947, *m.*
1999    *Stevenson of Coddenham,* Henry Dennistoun
        Stevenson, CBE, *b.* 1945, *m.*
1992    *Stewartby,* (Bernard Harold) Ian (Halley) Stewart,
        RD, PC, FBA, FRSE, *b.* 1935, *m.*
2011    *Stirrup,* Graham Eric Stirrup, KG, GCB, AFC,
        *b.* 1949, *m.*
1983    *Stoddart of Swindon,* David Leonard Stoddart,
        *b.* 1926, *m.*
1997    *Stone of Blackheath,* Andrew Zelig Stone,
        *b.* 1942, *m.*
2011    *Stoneham of Droxford,* Benjamin Russell
        Mackintosh Stoneham, *b.* 1940, *m.*
2011    *Storey,* Michael John Storey, CBE, *b.* 1949
2011    *Strasburger,* Paul Cline Strasburger, *b.* 1946
2015    ‡*Stunell,* Andrew Stunell, PC, OBE, *b.* 1942, *m.*
2009    *Sugar,* Alan Michael Sugar, *b.* 1947, *m.*
2014    *Suri,* Ranbir Singh Suri, *b.* 1935
2001    *Sutherland of Houndwood,* Stewart Ross Sutherland,
        KT, *b.* 1941, *m.*
1971    *Tanlaw,* Simon Brooke Mackay, *b.* 1934, *m.*
1996    *Taverne,* Dick Taverne, QC, *b.* 1928, *m.*
1978    *Taylor of Blackburn,* Thomas Taylor, CBE,
        *b.* 1929, *m.*
2010    *Taylor of Goss Moor,* Matthew Owen John Taylor,
        *b.* 1963, *m.*
2006    *Taylor of Holbeach,* John Derek Taylor, PC, CBE,
        *b.* 1943, *m.*
1996    *Taylor of Warwick,* John David Beckett Taylor,
        *b.* 1952, *m.*
1992    *Tebbit,* Norman Beresford Tebbit, CH, PC,
        *b.* 1931, *m.*
2001    *Temple-Morris,* Peter Temple-Morris, *b.* 1938, *m.*
2006    *Teverson,* Robin Teverson, *b.* 1952, *m.*
2013    §*Thomas of Cwmgiedd,* Roger John Laugharne
        Thomas, PC, *b.* 1947, *m., Lord Chief Justice of
        England and Wales*
1996    *Thomas of Gresford,* Donald Martin Thomas, OBE,
        QC, *b.* 1937, *m.*
1997    *Thomas of Macclesfield,* Terence James Thomas,
        CBE, *b.* 1937, *m.*
1981    *Thomas of Swynnerton,* Hugh Swynnerton Thomas,
        *b.* 1931, *m.*
1990    ¶*Tombs,* Francis Leonard Tombs, FENG,
        *b.* 1924, *w.*
1998    *Tomlinson,* John Edward Tomlinson, *b.* 1939
1994    *Tope,* Graham Norman Tope, CBE, *b.* 1943, *m.*
1981    *Tordoff,* Geoffrey Johnson Tordoff, *b.* 1928, *m.*
2010    *Touhig,* James Donnelly Touhig, PC, *b.* 1947, *m.*
2012    *Trees,* Alexander John Trees, PHD, *b.* 1946, *m.*
2004    *Triesman,* David Maxim Triesman, *b.* 1943
2006    *Trimble,* William David Trimble, PC, *b.* 1944, *m.*
2010    *True,* Nicholas Edward True, CBE, *b.* 1951, *m.*
2004    *Truscott,* Dr Peter Derek Truscott, *b.* 1959, *m.*
1993    *Tugendhat,* Christopher Samuel Tugendhat,
        *b.* 1937, *m.*
2004    *Tunnicliffe,* Denis Tunnicliffe, CBE, *b.* 1943, *m.*
2000    *Turnberg,* Leslie Arnold Turnberg, MD,
        *b.* 1934, *m.*
2005    *Turnbull,* Andrew Turnbull, KCB, CVO,
        *b.* 1945, *m.*
2005    *Turner of Ecchinswell,* (Jonathan) Adair Turner,
        *b.* 1955, *m.*
2005    *Tyler,* Paul Archer Tyler, PC, CBE, *b.* 1941, *m.*
2004    *Vallance of Tummel,* Iain (David Thomas) Vallance,
        *b.* 1943, *m.*

2013    *Verjee,* Rumi Verjee, CBE, *b.* 1957
1996    *Vincent of Coleshill,* Richard Frederick Vincent,
        GBE, KCB, DSO, *b.* 1931, *m.*
1985    *Vinson,* Nigel Vinson, LVO, *b.* 1931, *m.*
1990    ¶*Waddington,* David Charles Waddington, GCVO,
        PC, QC, *b.* 1929, *m.*
1990    *Wade of Chorlton,* (William) Oulton Wade,
        *b.* 1932, *m.*
1992    *Wakeham,* John Wakeham, PC, *b.* 1932, *m.*
1999    *Waldegrave of North Hill,* William Arthur
        Waldegrave, PC, *b.* 1946, *m.*
2007    *Walker of Aldringham,* Michael John Dawson
        Walker, GCB, CMG, CBE, *b.* 1944, *m.*
1995    *Wallace of Saltaire,* William John Lawrence Wallace,
        PC, PHD, *b.* 1941, *m.*
2007    *Wallace of Tankerness,* James Robert Wallace, PC,
        QC, *b.* 1954, *m.*
1989    *Walton of Detchant,* John Nicholas Walton, TD,
        FRCP, *b.* 1922, *w.*
1998    *Warner,* Norman Reginald Warner, PC,
        *b.* 1940, *m.*
2011    *Wasserman,* Gordon Joshua Wasserman, *b.* 1938
1997    *Watson of Invergowrie,* Michael Goodall Watson,
        *b.* 1949, *m.*
1999    *Watson of Richmond,* Alan John Watson, CBE,
        *b.* 1941, *m.*
2015    ‡*Watts,* David Leonard Watts, *b.* 1951, *m.*
2010    *Wei,* Nathanael Ming-Yan Wei, *b.* 1977, *m.*
1976    *Weidenfeld,* (Arthur) George Weidenfeld, GBE,
        *b.* 1919, *m.*
2007    *West of Spithead,* Alan William John West, GCB,
        DSC, PC, *b.* 1948, *m.*
2013    *Whitby,* Michael John Whitby, *b.* 1948
1996    *Whitty,* John Lawrence (Larry) Whitty, PC, *b.* 1943,
        *m.*
2011    *Wigley,* Dafydd Wynne Wigley, PC, *b.* 1943, *m.*
2015    ‡*Willetts,* David Lindsay Willetts, *b.* 1956, *m.*
2010    *Williams of Baglan,* Michael Charles Williams,
        *b.* 1949
1985    *Williams of Elvel,* Charles Cuthbert Powell
        Williams, CBE, PC, *b.* 1933, *m.*
2013    *Williams of Oystermouth,* Rt. Revd Rowan Douglas
        Williams, PC, Royal Victorian Chain, DPHIL,
        *b.* 1950, *m.*
2010    *Willis of Knaresborough,* George Philip Willis,
        *b.* 1941, *m.*
2010    *Wills,* Michael David Wills, PC, *b.* 1952, *m.*
2002    *Wilson of Dinton,* Richard Thomas James Wilson,
        GCB, *b.* 1942, *m.*
1992    *Wilson of Tillyorn,* David Clive Wilson, KT,
        GCMG, PHD, *b.* 1935, *m.*
1995    *Winston,* Robert Maurice Lipson Winston, FRCOG,
        *b.* 1940, *m.*
2010    *Wolfson of Aspley Guise,* Simon Adam Wolfson,
        *b.* 1967, *m.*
1991    *Wolfson of Sunningdale,* David Wolfson, *b.* 1935, *m.*
2011    *Wood of Anfield,* Stewart Martin Wood, *b.* 1968, *m.*
1999    *Woolmer of Leeds,* Kenneth John Woolmer,
        *b.* 1940, *m.*
2013    *Wrigglesworth,* Ian William Wrigglesworth,
        *b.* 1939, *m.*
1994    *Wright of Richmond,* Patrick Richard Henry
        Wright, GCMG, *b.* 1931, *m.*
2015    ‡*Young,* George Samuel Knatchbull Young, Bt.,
        CH, PC, *b.* 1941, *m.*
1984    *Young of Graffham,* David Ivor Young, CH, PC,
        *b.* 1932, *m.*
2004    *Young of Norwood Green,* Anthony (Ian) Young,
        *b.* 1942, *m.*

BARONESSES
*Created*

| | |
|---|---|
| 2005 | *Adams of Craigielea,* Katherine Patricia Irene Adams, *b.* 1947, *w.* |
| 2007 | *Afshar,* Prof. Haleh Afshar, OBE, *b.* 1944, *m.* |
| 2015 | *Altmann,* Dr Rosalind Miriam Altmann, CBE, *b.* 1956, *m.* |
| 1997 | *Amos,* Valerie Ann Amos, PC, *b.* 1954 |
| 2000 | *Andrews,* Elizabeth Kay Andrews, OBE, *b.* 1943, *m.* |
| 1996 | *Anelay of St Johns,* Joyce Anne Anelay, DBE, PC, *b.* 1947, *m.* |
| 2010 | *Armstrong of Hill Top,* Hilary Jane Armstrong, PC, *b.* 1945, *m.* |
| 1999 | *Ashton of Upholland,* Catherine Margaret Ashton, GCMG, PC, *b.* 1956, *m.* |
| 2011 | *Bakewell,* Joan Dawson Bakewell, DBE, *b.* 1933 |
| 2013 | *Bakewell of Hardington Mandeville,* Catherine Mary Bakewell, MBE, *b.* 1949 |
| 1999 | *Barker,* Elizabeth Jean Barker, *b.* 1961 |
| 2010 | *Benjamin,* Floella Karen Yunies Benjamin, OBE, *b.* 1949, *m.* |
| 2011 | *Berridge,* Elizabeth Rose Berridge, *b.* 1972 |
| 2000 | *Billingham,* Angela Theodora Billingham, DPHIL, *b.* 1939, *w.* |
| 1987 | *Blackstone,* Tessa Ann Vosper Blackstone, PC, PHD, *b.* 1942 |
| 1999 | *Blood,* May Blood, MBE, *b.* 1938 |
| 2004 | *Bonham-Carter of Yarnbury,* Jane Bonham Carter, *b.* 1957, *w.* |
| 2000 | *Boothroyd,* Betty Boothroyd, OM, PC, *b.* 1929 |
| 2005 | *Bottomley of Nettlestone,* Virginia Hilda Brunette Maxwell Bottomley, PC, *b.* 1948, *m.* |
| 2015 | ‡*Bowles,* Sharon Margaret Bowles, *b.* 1953, *m.* |
| 2014 | *Brady,* Karren Rita Brady, CBE, *b.* 1969, *m.* |
| 2011 | *Brinton,* Sarah Virginia Brinton, *b.* 1955, *m.* |
| 2010 | *Browning,* Angela Frances Browning, *b.* 1946, *m.* |
| 2015 | ‡*Burt,* Lorely Jane Burt, *b.* 1954, *m.* |
| 1998 | *Buscombe,* Peta Jane Buscombe, *b.* 1954, *m.* |
| 2006 | *Butler-Sloss,* (Ann) Elizabeth (Oldfield) Butler-Sloss, GBE, PC *b.* 1933, *m.* |
| 1996 | *Byford,* Hazel Byford, DBE, *b.* 1941, *w.* |
| 2008 | *Campbell of Loughborough,* Susan Catherine Campbell, CBE, *b.* 1948 |
| 2007 | *Campbell of Surbiton,* Jane Susan Campbell, DBE, *b.* 1959, *m.* |
| 1992 | *Chalker of Wallasey,* Lynda Chalker, PC, *b.* 1942 |
| 2014 | *Chisholm of Owlpen,* Caroline Elizabeth (Carlyn) Chisholm, *b.* 1951, *m.* |
| 2005 | §*Clark of Calton,* Dr Lynda Margaret Clark, PC, *b.* 1949 |
| 2000 | *Cohen of Pimlico,* Janet Cohen, *b.* 1940, *m.* |
| 2005 | *Corston,* Jean Ann Corston, PC, *b.* 1942, *w.* |
| 2007 | *Coussins,* Jean Coussins, *b.* 1950 |
| 1982 | *Cox,* Caroline Anne Cox, *b.* 1937, *m.* |
| 1998 | *Crawley,* Christine Mary Crawley, *b.* 1950, *m.* |
| 1990 | *Cumberlege,* Julia Frances Cumberlege, CBE, *b.* 1943, *m.* |
| 1993 | *Dean of Thornton-le-Fylde,* Brenda Dean, PC, *b.* 1943, *m.* |
| 2005 | *Deech,* Ruth Lynn Deech, DBE, *b.* 1943, *m.* |
| 2010 | *Donaghy,* Rita Margaret Donaghy, CBE, *b.* 1944, *m.* |
| 2010 | *Doocey,* Elizabeth Deirdre Doocey, OBE, *b.* 1948, *m.* |
| 2010 | *Drake,* Jean Lesley Patricia Drake, CBE, *b.* 1948 |
| 2004 | *D'Souza,* Dr Frances Gertrude Claire D'Souza, CMG, PC, *b.* 1944, *m. Lord Speaker* |
| 1990 | ¶*Dunn,* Lydia Selina Dunn, DBE, *b.* 1940, *m.* |
| 2010 | *Eaton,* Ellen Margaret Eaton, DBE, *b.* 1942, *m.* |
| 1990 | *Eccles of Moulton,* Diana Catherine Eccles, *b.* 1933, *m.* |
| 1997 | *Emerton,* Audrey Caroline Emerton, DBE, *b.* 1935 |
| 2014 | *Evans of Bowes Park,* Natalie Jessica Evans, *b.* 1975, *m.* |
| 1974 | *Falkender,* Marcia Matilda Falkender, CBE, *b.* 1932 |
| 2004 | *Falkner of Margravine,* Kishwer Falkner, *b.* 1955, *m.* |
| 2015 | ‡*Fall,* Catherine Fall |
| 1994 | *Farrington of Ribbleton,* Josephine Farrington, *b.* 1940, *m.* |
| 2015 | ‡*Featherstone,* Lynne Featherstone, PC, *b.* 1951 |
| 2001 | *Finlay of Llandaff,* Ilora Gillian Finlay, *b.* 1949, *m.* |
| 2015 | ‡*Finn,* Simone Finn |
| 1990 | *Flather,* Shreela Flather, *b.* 1934, *m.* |
| 1997 | *Fookes,* Janet Evelyn Fookes, DBE, *b.* 1936 |
| 2006 | *Ford,* Margaret Anne Ford, *b.* 1957, *m.* |
| 2005 | *Fritchie,* Irene Tordoff Fritchie, DBE, *b.* 1942, *m.* |
| 1999 | *Gale,* Anita Gale, *b.* 1940 |
| 2007 | *Garden of Frognal,* Susan Elizabeth Garden, PC, *b.* 1944, *w.* |
| 1981 | *Gardner of Parkes,* (Rachel) Trixie (Anne) Gardner, *b.* 1927, *w.* |
| 2000 | *Gibson of Market Rasen,* Anne Gibson, OBE, *b.* 1940, *m.* |
| 2013 | *Goldie,* Annabel MacNicholl Goldie, MSP, *b.* 1950 |
| 2001 | *Golding,* Llinos Golding, *b.* 1933, *m.* |
| 1998 | *Goudie,* Mary Teresa Goudie, MSP, *b.* 1946, *m.* |
| 1993 | *Gould of Potternewton,* Joyce Brenda Gould, *b.* 1932, *m.* |
| 2001 | *Greenfield,* Susan Adele Greenfield, CBE, *b.* 1950, *m.* |
| 2000 | *Greengross,* Sally Ralea Greengross, OBE, *b.* 1935, *m.* |
| 2013 | *Grender,* Rosalind Mary Grender, MBE, *b.* 1962 |
| 2010 | *Grey-Thompson,* Tanni Carys Davina Grey-Thompson, DBE, *b.* 1969, *m.* |
| 1991 | *Hamwee,* Sally Rachel Hamwee, *b.* 1947 |
| 1999 | *Hanham,* Joan Brownlow Hanham, CBE, *b.* 1939, *m.* |
| 2014 | *Harding of Winscombe,* Diana Mary (Dido) Harding, *b.* 1967, *m.* |
| 1999 | *Harris of Richmond,* Angela Felicity Harris, *b.* 1944 |
| 1996 | *Hayman,* Helene Valerie Hayman, GBE, PC, *b.* 1949, *m.* |
| 2010 | *Hayter of Kentish Town,* Dr Dianne Hayter, *b.* 1949, *m.* |
| 2014 | *Helic,* Arminka Helic, *b.* 1968 |
| 2010 | *Healy of Primrose Hill,* Anna Healy, *b.* 1955, *m.* |
| 2004 | *Henig,* Ruth Beatrice Henig, CBE, *b.* 1943, *m.* |
| 2011 | *Heyhoe-Flint,* Rachel Heyhoe Flint, OBE, *b.* 1939, *m.* |
| 1991 | *Hilton of Eggardon,* Jennifer Hilton, QPM, *b.* 1936 |
| 2013 | *Hodgson of Abinger,* Fiona Ferelith Hodgson, CBE, *b.* 1954, *m.* |
| 1995 | *Hogg,* Sarah Elizabeth Mary Hogg, *b.* 1946, *m.* |
| 2010 | *Hollins,* Prof. Sheila Clare Hollins, *b.* 1946, *m.* |
| 1990 | *Hollis of Heigham,* Patricia Lesley Hollis, PC, DPHIL, *b.* 1941, *m.* |
| 1985 | *Hooper,* Gloria Dorothy Hooper, CMG, *b.* 1939 |
| 2001 | *Howarth of Breckland,* Valerie Georgina Howarth, OBE, *b.* 1940 |
| 2001 | *Howe of Idlicote,* Elspeth Rosamond Morton Howe, CBE, *b.* 1932, *m.* |
| 1999 | *Howells of St Davids,* Rosalind Patricia-Anne Howells, *b.* 1931, *m.* |
| 2010 | *Hughes of Stretford,* Beverley Hughes, PC, *b.* 1950, *m.* |
| 2013 | *Humphreys,* Christine Mary Humphreys, *b.* 1947 |
| 2010 | *Hussein-Ece,* Meral Hussein Ece, OBE, *b.* 1953 |
| 2014 | *Janke,* Barbara Lilian Janke, *b.* 1947, *m.* |

| | |
|---|---|
| 1992 | *Jay of Paddington,* Margaret Ann Jay, PC, *b.* 1939, *m.* |
| 2011 | *Jenkin of Kennington,* Anne Caroline Jenkin, *b.* 1955, *m.* |
| 2010 | *Jolly,* Judith Anne Jolly, *b.* 1951, *m.* |
| 2013 | *Jones of Moulsecoomb,* Jennifer Helen Jones, *b.* 1949 |
| 2006 | *Jones of Whitchurch,* Margaret Beryl Jones, *b.* 1955 |
| 2015 | ‡*Jowell,* Tessa Jane Helen Douglas Jowell, DBE, PC, *b.* 1947, *m.* |
| 2013 | *Kennedy of Cradley,* Alicia Pamela Kennedy, *b.* 1969, *m.* |
| 1997 | *Kennedy of the Shaws,* Helena Ann Kennedy, QC, *b.* 1950, *m.* |
| 2012 | *Kidron,* Beeban Tania Kidron, OBE, *b.* 1961 *m.* |
| 2011 | *King of Bow,* Oona Tamsyn King, *b.* 1967, *m.* |
| 2006 | *Kingsmill,* Denise Patricia Byrne Kingsmill, CBE, *b.* 1947, *m.* |
| 2009 | *Kinnock of Holyhead,* Glenys Elizabeth Kinnock, *b.* 1944, *m.* |
| 1997 | *Knight of Collingtree,* (Joan Christabel) Jill Knight, DBE, *b.* 1927, *w.* |
| 2010 | *Kramer,* Susan Veronica Kramer, PC, *b.* 1950, *w.* |
| 2013 | *Lane-Fox of Soho,* Martha Lane Fox, CBE, *b.* 1973 |
| 2013 | *Lawrence of Clarendon,* Doreen Delceita Lawrence, OBE, *b.* 1952 |
| 2010 | *Liddell of Coatdyke,* Helen Lawrie Liddell, PC, *b.* 1950, *m.* |
| 1997 | *Linklater of Butterstone,* Veronica Linklater, *b.* 1943, *m.* |
| 2011 | *Lister of Burtersett,* Margot Ruth Aline Lister, CBE, *b.* 1949, *m.* |
| 1978 | *Lockwood,* Betty Lockwood, *b.* 1924, *w.* |
| 1997 | *Ludford,* Sarah Ann Ludford, *b.* 1951 |
| 2004 | *McDonagh,* Margaret Josephine McDonagh, *b.* 1961 |
| 2015 | ‡*McGregor-Smith,* Ruby McGregor-Smith, CBE |
| 2015 | ‡*McIntosh,* Anne Caroline Ballingall McIntosh, *b.* 1954, *m.* |
| 1999 | *McIntosh of Hudnall,* Genista Mary McIntosh, *b.* 1946 |
| 1997 | *Maddock,* Diana Margaret Maddock, *b.* 1945, *m.* |
| 1991 | *Mallalieu,* Ann Mallalieu, QC, *b.* 1945 |
| 2008 | *Manningham-Buller,* Elizabeth (Lydia) Manningham-Buller, LG, DCB, *b.* 1948, *m.* |
| 2013 | *Manzoor,* Zahida Parveen Manzoor, CBE, *b.* 1958, *m.* |
| 1970 | *Masham of Ilton,* Susan Lilian Primrose Cunliffe-Lister, *b.* 1935, *w.* |
| 1999 | *Massey of Darwen,* Doreen Elizabeth Massey, *b.* 1938, *m.* |
| 2006 | *Meacher,* Molly Christine Meacher, *b.* 1940, *m.* |
| 1998 | *Miller of Chilthorne Domer,* Susan Elizabeth Miller, *b.* 1954 |
| 2014 | *Mobarik,* Nosheena Shaheen Mobarik, CBE, *b.* 1957, *m.* |
| 2015 | ‡*Mone,* Michelle Mone, OBE, *b.* 1971 |
| 2004 | *Morgan of Drefelin,* Delyth Jane Morgan, *b.* 1961, *m.* |
| 2011 | *Morgan of Ely,* Mair Eluned Morgan, *b.* 1967, *m.* |
| 2001 | *Morgan of Huyton,* Sally Morgan, *b.* 1959, *m.* |
| 2004 | *Morris of Bolton,* Patricia Morris, OBE, *b.* 1953 |
| 2005 | *Morris of Yardley,* Estelle Morris, PC, *b.* 1952 |
| 2004 | *Murphy,* Elaine Murphy, *b.* 1947, *m.* |
| 2004 | *Neuberger,* Rabbi Julia (Babette Sarah) Neuberger, DBE, *b.* 1950, *m.* |
| 2007 | *Neville-Jones,* (Lilian) Pauline Neville-Jones, DCMG, PC, *b.* 1939 |
| 2013 | *Neville-Rolfe,* Lucy Jeanne Neville-Rolfe, DBE, CMG, *b.* 1953, *m.* |
| 2010 | *Newlove,* Helen Margaret Newlove, b. 1961, *w.* |
| 1997 | *Nicholson of Winterbourne,* Emma Harriet Nicholson, *b.* 1941, *m.* |
| 1982 | *Nicol,* Olive Mary Wendy Nicol, *b.* 1923, *m.* |
| 2000 | *Noakes,* Sheila Valerie Masters, DBE, *b.* 1949, *m.* |
| 2000 | *Northover,* Lindsay Patricia Granshaw, PC, *b.* 1954 |
| 2010 | *Nye,* Susan Nye, *b.* 1955, *m.* |
| 1991 | *O'Cathain,* Detta O'Cathain, OBE, *b.* 1938, *w.* |
| 2009 | *O'Loan,* Nuala Patricia O'Loan, DBE, *b.* 1951, *m.* |
| 1999 | *O'Neill of Bengarve,* Onora Sylvia O'Neill, CH, CBE, FRS, FBA, *b.* 1941 |
| 1989 | *Oppenheim-Barnes,* Sally Oppenheim-Barnes, PC, *b.* 1930, *m.* |
| 2006 | *Paisley of St George's,* Eileen Emily Paisley, *b.* 1931, *w.* |
| 2010 | *Parminter,* Kathryn Jane Parminter, *b.* 1964, *m.* |
| 1991 | *Perry of Southwark,* Pauline Perry, *b.* 1931, *m.* |
| 2015 | ‡*Pidding,* Emma Pidding, CBE |
| 2014 | *Pinnock,* Kathryn Mary Pinnock, *b.* 1946, *m.* |
| 1997 | *Pitkeathley,* Jill Elizabeth Pitkeathley, OBE, *b.* 1940 |
| 1999 | *Prashar,* Usha Kumari Prashar, CBE, PC, *b.* 1948, *m.* |
| 2015 | ‡*Primarolo,* Dawn Primarolo, DBE, PC, *b.* 1954, *m.* |
| 2004 | *Prosser,* Margaret Theresa Prosser, OBE, *b.* 1937 |
| 2006 | *Quin,* Joyce Gwendoline Quin, PC *b.* 1944 |
| 1996 | *Ramsay of Cartvale,* Margaret Mildred (Meta) Ramsay, *b.* 1936 |
| 2011 | *Randerson,* Jennifer Elizabeth Randerson, *b.* 1948, *m.* |
| 1994 | *Rawlings,* Patricia Elizabeth Rawlings, *b.* 1939 |
| 2014 | *Rebuck,* Gail Ruth Rebuck, DBE, *b.* 1952, *m.* |
| 2015 | ‡*Redfern,* Elizabeth Redfern |
| 1998 | *Richardson of Calow,* Kathleen Margaret Richardson, OBE, *b.* 1938, *m.* |
| 2015 | ‡*Rock,* Kate Rock, *m.* |
| 2004 | *Royall of Blaisdon,* Janet Anne Royall, PC, *b.* 1955, *m.* |
| 1997 | *Scotland of Asthal,* Patricia Janet Scotland, PC, QC, *b.* 1955, *m.* |
| 2015 | ‡*Scott,* Jane Antoinette Scott, OBE, *b.* 1947, *m.* |
| 2000 | *Scott of Needham Market,* Rosalind Carol Scott, *b.* 1957 |
| 1991 | *Seccombe,* Joan Anna Dalziel Seccombe, DBE, *b.* 1930, *m.* |
| 2010 | *Shackleton of Belgravia,* Fiona Sara Shackleton, LVO, *b.* 1956, *m.* |
| 1998 | *Sharp of Guildford,* Margaret Lucy Sharp, *b.* 1938, *m.* |
| 1973 | *Sharples,* Pamela Sharples, *b.* 1923, *w.* |
| 2015 | ‡*Sheehan,* Shas Sheehan, *b.* 1959, *m.* |
| 2005 | *Shephard of Northwold,* Gillian Patricia Shephard, PC, *b.* 1940, *m.* |
| 2010 | *Sherlock,* Maeve Christina Mary Sherlock, OBE, *b.* 1960 |
| 2014 | *Shields,* Joanna Shields, OBE, b. 1962, *m.* |
| 2010 | *Smith of Basildon,* Angela Evans Smith, PC, *b.* 1959, *m.* |
| 1995 | *Smith of Gilmorehill,* Elizabeth Margaret Smith, *b.* 1940, *w.* |
| 2014 | *Smith of Newnham,* Dr Julie Elizabeth Smith, *b.* 1969 |
| 2010 | *Stedman-Scott,* Deborah Stedman-Scott, OBE, *b.* 1955 |
| 1999 | *Stern,* Vivien Helen Stern, CBE, *b.* 1941 |
| 2011 | *Stowell of Beeston,* Tina Wendy Stowell, PC, MBE, *b.* 1967 |
| 2015 | ‡*Stroud,* Philippa Stroud, *b.* 1965 |

| 2013 | *Suttie*, Alison Mary Suttie, *b.* 1968 |
| 1996 | *Symons of Vernham Dean*, Elizabeth Conway Symons, PC, *b.* 1951, *m.* |
| 2005 | *Taylor of Bolton*, Winifred Ann Taylor, PC, *b.* 1947, *m.* |
| 1994 | *Thomas of Walliswood*, Susan Petronella Thomas, OBE, *b.* 1935, *m.* |
| 2006 | *Thomas of Winchester*, Celia Marjorie Thomas, MBE, *b.* 1945 |
| 2015 | ‡*Thornhill*, Dorothy Thornhill, MBE, *b.* 1955, *m.* |
| 1998 | *Thornton*, (Dorothea) Glenys Thornton, *b.* 1952, *m.* |
| 2005 | *Tonge*, Dr. Jennifer Louise Tonge, *b.* 1941, *m.* |
| 1980 | *Trumpington*, Jean Alys Barker, DCVO, PC, *b.* 1922, *w.* |
| 1985 | *Turner of Camden*, Muriel Winifred Turner, *b.* 1927, *m.* |
| 2011 | *Tyler of Enfield*, Claire Tyler, *b.* 1957 |
| 1998 | *Uddin*, Manzila Pola Uddin, *b.* 1959, *m.* |
| 2007 | *Vadera*, Shriti Vadera, PC, *b.* 1962 |
| 2005 | *Valentine*, Josephine Clare Valentine, *b.* 1958, *m.* |
| 2006 | *Verma*, Sandip Verma, *b.* 1959, *m.* |
| 2004 | *Wall of New Barnet*, Margaret Mary Wall, *b.* 1941, *m.* |

| 2000 | *Walmsley*, Joan Margaret Walmsley, *b.* 1943 |
| 1985 | ¶*Warnock*, Helen Mary Warnock, DBE, *b.* 1924, *w.* |
| 2007 | *Warsi*, Sayeeda Hussain Warsi, PC, *b.* 1971 |
| 1999 | *Warwick of Undercliffe*, Diana Mary Warwick, *b.* 1945, *m.* |
| 2010 | *Wheatcroft*, Patience Jane Wheatcroft, *b.* 1951, *m.* |
| 2010 | *Wheeler*, Margaret Eileen Joyce Wheeler, MBE, *b.* 1949 |
| 1999 | *Whitaker*, Janet Alison Whitaker, *b.* 1936 |
| 1996 | *Wilcox*, Judith Ann Wilcox, *b.* 1940, *w.* |
| 1999 | ¶*Wilkins*, Rosalie Catherine Wilkins, *b.* 1946 |
| 1993 | *Williams of Crosby*, Shirley Vivien Teresa Brittain Williams, PC, *b.* 1930, *w.* |
| 2013 | *Williams of Trafford*, Susan Frances Maria Williams, *b.* 1967, *m.* |
| 2014 | *Wolf of Dulwich*, Alison Margaret Wolf, CBE, *b.* 1949, *m.* |
| 2011 | *Worthington*, Bryony Katherine Worthington, *b.* 1971, *m.* |
| 2004 | *Young of Hornsey*, Prof. Margaret Omolola Young, OBE, *b.* 1951, *m.* |
| 1997 | *Young of Old Scone*, Barbara Scott Young, *b.* 1948 |

## COURTESY TITLES

The heir apparent to a Duke, Marquess or Earl uses the highest of his father's other titles as a courtesy title. For example, the Marquess of Blandford is heir to the Dukedom of Marlborough, and Viscount Amberley to the Earldom of Russell. Titles of second heirs (when in use) are also given, and the courtesy title of the father of a second heir is indicated by * eg Earl of Mornington, eldest son of *Marquess of Douro.

The holder of a courtesy title is not styled 'the Most Hon.' or 'the Rt. Hon.', and in correspondence 'the' is omitted before the title. The heir apparent to a Scottish title may use the title 'Master'.

### MARQUESSES
*Blandford – *Marlborough*, D.
Bowmont and Cessford – *Roxburghe*, D.
Douglas and Clydesdale – *Hamilton and Brandon*, D.
*Douro – *Wellington*, D.
Graham – *Montrose*, D.
Granby – *Rutland*, D.
*Hamilton – *Abercorn*, D.
Lorne – *Argyll*, D.
Stafford – *Sutherland*, D.
Tavistock – *Bedford*, D.
Tullibardine – *Atholl*, D.
*Worcester – *Beaufort*, D.

### EARLS
*Aboyne – *Huntly*, M.
Altamont – *Sligo*, M.
Arundel and Surrey – *Norfolk*, D.
Bective – *Headfort*, M.
Belfast – *Donegall*, M.
Brecknock – *Camden*, M.
*Burford – *St Albans*, D.
*Burlington – *Devonshire*, D.
*Cardigan – *Ailesbury*, M.
*Cassilis – *Ailsa*, M.
Compton – *Northampton*, M.
*Dalkeith – *Buccleuch*, D.
Dumfries – *Bute*, M.
Euston – *Grafton*, D.
Glamorgan – *Worcester*, M.
Grosvenor – *Westminster*, D.

*Haddo – *Aberdeen and Temair*, M.
Hillsborough – *Downshire*, M.
*Hopetoun – *Linlithgow*, M.
Kerry – *Lansdowne*, M.
*March and Kinrara – *Richmond*, D.
Medina – *Milford Haven*, M.
*Mount Charles – *Conyngham*, M.
Mornington – *Douro*, M.
Mulgrave – *Normanby*, M.
Percy – *Northumberland*, D.
Rocksavage – *Cholmondeley*, M.
Ronaldshay – *Zetland*, M.
*St Andrews – *Kent*, D.
Southesk – *Fife*, D.
*Tyrone – *Waterford*, M.
*Ulster – *Gloucester*, D.
Uxbridge – *Anglesey*, M.
*Wiltshire – *Winchester*, M.
Yarmouth – *Hertford*, M.

### VISCOUNTS
Aithrie – *Hopetoun*, E.
Alexander – *Caledon*, E.
Althorp – *Spencer*, E.
Andover – *Suffolk and Berkshire*, E.
Anson – *Lichfield*, E.
Asquith – *Oxford and Asquith*, E.
Boringdon – *Morley*, E.

Borodale – *Beatty*, E.
Bury – *Albemarle*, E.
Campden – *Gainsborough*, E.
Carlow – *Portarlington*, E.
Carlton – *Wharncliffe*, E.
Chelsea – *Cadogan*, E.
Chewton – *Waldegrave*, E.
Clanfield – *Peel*, E.
Clive – *Powis*, E.
Coke – *Leicester*, E.
Corry – *Belmore*, E.
Corvedale – *Baldwin of Bewdley*, E.
Cranborne – *Salisbury*, M.
Crichton – *Erne*, E.
Curzon – *Howe*, E.
Dalrymple – *Stair*, E.
Dangan – *Cowley*, E.
Drumlanrig – *Queensberry*, M.
Duncannon – *Bessborough*, E.
Dungarvan – *Cork and Orrery*, E.
Dunluce – *Antrim*, E.
Dunwich – *Stradbroke*, E.
Dupplin – *Kinnoull*, E.
Elveden – *Iveagh*, E.
Emlyn – *Cawdor*, E
Encombe – *Eldon*, E.
Enfield – *Strafford*, E.
Erleigh – *Reading*, M.
Errington – *Cromer*, E.
Feilding – *Denbigh and Desmond*, E.

FitzHarris – *Malmesbury*, E.
Folkestone – *Radnor*, E.
Forbes – *Granard*, E.
Formartine – *Haddo*, E.
Garmoyle – *Cairns*, E.
Garnock – *Lindsay*, E.
Glenapp – *Inchcape*, E.
Glentworth – *Limerick*, E.
Glerawly – *Annesley*, E.
Grey de Wilton – *Wilton*, E.
Grimstone – *Verulam*, E.
Gwynedd – *Lloyd George of Dwyfor*, E.
Hawkesbury – *Liverpool*, E.
Hinchingbrooke – *Sandwich*, E.
Howick – *Grey*, E.
Ikerrin – *Carrick*, E.
Ingestre – *Shrewsbury*, E.
Jocelyn – *Roden*, E.
Kelburn – *Glasgow*, E.
Kingsborough – *Kingston*, E.
Kirkwall – *Orkney*, E.
Knebworth – *Lytton*, E.
Lambton – *Durham*, E.
Lascelles – *Harewood*, E.
Linley – *Snowdon*, E.
Lymington – *Portsmouth*, E.
Macmillan of Ovenden – *Stockton*, E.
Maidstone – *Winchilsea*, E
Maitland – *Lauderdale*, E.
Mandeville – *Manchester*, D.
Marsham – *Romney*, E.
Melgund – *Minto*, E.

Merton – *Nelson, E.*
Moore – *Drogheda, E.*
Newport – *Bradford, E.*
Northland – *Ranfurly, E*
Newry and Mourne –
  *Kilmorey, E.*
Petersham – *Harrington, E.*
Pollington – *Mexborough, E*
Raynham – *Townshend, M.*
Reidhaven – *Seafield, E.*
Royston – *Hardwicke, E.*
Ruthven of Canberra –
  *Gowrie, E.*
St Cyres – *Iddesleigh, E.*
Sandon – *Harrowby, E.*
Savernake – *Cardigan, E.*
Severn – *Wessex, E.*
Slane – *Mount Charles, E.*
Somerton – *Normanton, E.*
Stopford – *Courtown, E.*
Stormont – *Mansfield, E.*
Strabane – *Hamilton, M.*
Strathallan – *Perth, E.*
Stuart – *Castle Stewart, E.*
Suirdale – *Donoughmore, E.*
Tamworth – *Ferrers, E.*
Tarbat – *Cromartie, E.*

Villiers – *Jersey, E.*
Weymouth – *Bath, M.*
Windsor – *Plymouth, E.*
Wolmer – *Selborne, E.*
Woodstock – *Portland, E.*

BARONS (LORDS)
Aberdour – *Morton, E.*
Apsley – *Bathurst, E.*
Ardee – *Meath, E.*
Ashley – *Shaftesbury, E.*
Balniel – *Crawford and
  Balcarres, E.*
Berriedale – *Caithness, E.*
Bingham – *Lucan, E.*
Binning – *Haddington, E.*
Brooke – *Warwick, E.*
Bruce – *Elgin, E.*
Buckhurst – *De La Warr, E.*
Burghley – *Exeter, M.*
Cardross – *Buchan, E.*
Cavendish – *Burlington, E.*
Clifton – *Darnley, E.*
Cochrane – *Dundonald, E.*
Courtenay – *Devon, E.*
Culloden – *Ulster, E.*
Dalmeny – *Rosebery, E.*

Doune – *Moray, E.*
Downpatrick – *St Andrews,
  E.*
Dunglass – *Home, E.*
Elcho – *Wemyss and March,
  E.*
Eliot – *St Germans, E.*
Gillford – *Clanwilliam, E.*
Glamis – *Strathmore, E.*
Greenock – *Cathcart, E.*
Guernsey – *Aylesford, E.*
Hay – *Erroll, E.*
Herbert – *Pembroke and
  Montgomery, E.*
Howard of Effingham –
  *Effingham, E.*
Huntingtower – *Dysart, E.*
Hyde – *Clarendon, E.*
Inverurie – *Kintore, E.*
Irwin – *Halifax, E.*
Johnstone – *Annandale and
  Hartfell, E.*
Leveson – *Granville, E*
Loughborough – *Rosslyn, E.*
Masham – *Swinton, E.*
Medway – *Cranbrook, E.*

Montgomerie – *Eglinton and
  Winton, E.*
Moreton – *Ducie, E.*
Naas – *Mayo, E.*
Norreys – *Lindsey and
  Abingdon, E.*
North – *Guilford, E.*
Ogilvy – *Airlie, E.*
Oxmantown – *Rosse, E.*
Porchester – *Carnarvon, E.*
Ramsay – *Dalhousie, E.*
Romsey – *Mountbatten of
  Burma, C.*
St John – *Wiltshire, E.*
Scrymgeour – *Dundee, E.*
Settrington – *March and
  Kinrara, E.*
Seymour – *Somerset, D.*
Stanley – *Derby, E.*
Stavordale – *Ilchester, E.*
Strathavon – *Aboyne, E.*
Strathnaver – *Sutherland, C.*
Vere of Hanworth –
  *Burford, E.*
Wodehouse – *Kimberley, E.*
Worsley – *Yarborough, E.*

## PEERS' SURNAMES

The following symbols
indicate the rank of the
peer holding each title:
  *C.*    Countess
  *D.*    Duke
  *E.*    Earl
  *M.*    Marquess
  *V.*    Viscount
  *    Life Peer
Where no designation is
given, the title is that of a
hereditary Baron or
Baroness.
Abney-Hastings –
  *Loudoun, E.*
Acheson – *Gosford, E.*
Adams – *A. of Craigielea*
Adderley – *Norton*
Addington – *Sidmouth, V.*
Agar – *Normanton, E.*
Ahmad – *A. of Wimbledon*
Aitken – *Beaverbrook*
Akers-Douglas – *Chilston, V.*
Alexander – *A. of Tunis, E.*
Alexander – *Caledon, E.*
Allan – *A. of Hallam*
Allen – *A. of Kensington*
Allsopp – *Hindlip*
Alton – *A. of Liverpool*
Anderson – *A. of Swansea*
Anderson – *Waverley, V.*
Anelay – *A. of St Johns*
Annesley – *Valentia, V.*
Anson – *Lichfield, E.*
Archer – *A. of Weston-super-
  Mare*
Armstrong – *A. of Hill Top*
Armstrong – *A. of Ilminster*

Armstrong-Jones –
  *Snowdon, E.*
Arthur – *Glenarthur*
Arundell – *Talbot of
  Malahide*
Ashdown – *A. of Norton-
  sub-Hamdon*
Ashley-Cooper –
  *Shaftesbury, E.*
Ashton – *A. of Hyde*
Ashton – *A. of Upholland*
Asquith – *Oxford and
  Asquith, E.*
Assheton – *Clitheroe*
Astley – *Hastings*
Astor – *A. of Hever*
Aubrey-Fletcher – *Braye*
Bailey – *Glanusk*
Baillie – *Burton*
Baillie Hamilton –
  *Haddington, E.*
Baker – *B. of Dorking*
Bakewell – *B. of Hardington
  Mandeville*
Balchin – *Lingfield*
Baldwin – *B. of Bewdley, E.*
Balfour – *Kinross*
Balfour – *Riverdale*
Bampfylde – *Poltimore*
Banbury – *B. of Southam*
Barber – *B. of Tewkesbury*
Baring – *Ashburton*
Baring – *Cromer, E.*
Baring – *Howick of
  Glendale*
Baring – *Northbrook*
Baring – *Revelstoke*
Barker – *Trumpington*

Barnes – *Gorell*
Barnewall – *Trimlestown*
Bassam – *B. of Brighton*
Bathurst – *Bledisloe, V.*
Beamish – *Dacre*
Beauclerk – *St Albans, D.*
Beaumont – *Allendale, V.*
Beckett – *Grimthorpe*
Benn – *Stansgate, V.*
Bennet – *Tankerville, E.*
Bentinck – *Portland, E.*
Beresford – *Decies*
Beresford – *Waterford, M.*
Berkeley – *B. of Knighton*
Berry – *Camrose, V.*
Berry – *Kemsley, V.*
Bertie – *Lindsey and
  Abingdon, E.*
Best – *Wynford*
Bethell – *Westbury*
Bewicke-Copley – *Cromwell*
Bigham – *Mersey, V.*
Bingham – *Clanmorris*
Bingham – *Lucan, E.*
Bishop – *Glendonbrook*
Black – *B. of Brentwood*
Black – *B. of Crossharbour*
Blackwood – *Dufferin and
  Clandeboye*
Blair – *B. of Boughton*
Bligh – *Darnley, E.*
Blyth – *B. of Rowington*
Bonham Carter – *B.-C. of
  Yarnbury*
Bootle-Wilbraham –
  *Skelmersdale*
Boscawen – *Falmouth, V.*
Boswell – *B. of Aynho*

Bottomley – *B. of
  Nettlestone*
Bourke – *Mayo, E.*
Bourne – *B. of Aberystwyth*
Bowes Lyon – *Strathmore
  and Kinghorne, E.*
Bowyer – *Denham*
Boyd – *B. of Duncansby*
Boyd – *Kilmarnock*
Boyle – *Cork and Orrery, E.*
Boyle – *Glasgow, E.*
Boyle – *Shannon, E.*
Brabazon – *Meath, E.*
Brand – *Hampden, V.*
Brassey – *B. of Apethorpe*
Brett – *Esher, V.*
Bridgeman – *Bradford, E.*
Brodrick – *Midleton, V.*
Brooke – *Alanbrooke, V.*
Brooke – *B. of Alverthorpe*
Brooke – *B. of Sutton
  Mandeville*
Brooke – *Brookeborough, V.*
Brooks – *B. of Tremorfa*
Brooks – *Crawshaw*
Brougham – *Brougham and
  Vaux*
Broughton – *Fairhaven*
Brown – *B. of Eaton-under-
  Heywood*
Browne – *B. of Belmont*
Browne – *B. of Ladyton*
Browne – *B. of Madingley*
Browne – *Kilmaine*
Browne – *Oranmore and
  Browne*
Browne – *Sligo, M.*
Bruce – *Aberdare*

Macmillan – *Stockton, E.*
Macpherson – *M. of Drumochter*
Macpherson – *Strathcarron*
Maffey – *Rugby*
Magan – *M. of Castletown**
Maginnis – *M. of Drumglass**
Maitland – *Lauderdale, E.*
Makgill – *Oxfuird, V.*
Makins – *Sherfield*
Manners – *Rutland, D.*
Manningham-Buller – *Dilhorne, V.*
Mansfield – *Sandhurst*
Marks – *M. of Broughton*
Marks – *M. of Henley-on-Thames**
Marquis – *Woolton, E.*
Marsham – *Romney, E.*
Martin – *M. of Springburn**
Martyn-Hemphill – *Hemphill*
Massey – *M. of Darwen**
Masters – *Noakes**
Maude – *Hawarden, V.*
Maxwell – *de Ros*
Maxwell – *Farnham*
May – *M. of Oxford**
Mayhew – *M. of Twysden**
Meade – *Clanwilliam, E.*
Mercer Nairne Petty-Fitzmaurice – *Lansdowne, M.*
Methuen-Campbell – *Methuen*
Millar – *Inchyra*
Miller – *M. of Chilthorne Domer**
Milner – *M. of Leeds*
Mitchell-Thomson – *Selsdon*
Mitford – *Redesdale*
Monckton – *M. of Brenchley, V.*
Monckton-Arundell – *Galway, V.*
Mond – *Melchett*
Money-Coutts – *Latymer*
Montagu – *Manchester, D.*
Montagu – *Sandwich, E.*
Montagu – *Swaythling*
Montagu Douglas Scott – *Buccleuch and Queensberry, D.*
Montagu Stuart Wortley – *Wharncliffe, E.*
Montague – *Amwell*
Montgomerie – *Eglinton and Winton, E.*
Montgomery – *M. of Alamein, V.*
Moore – *Drogheda, E.*
Moore – *M. of Lower Marsh**
Moore-Brabazon – *Brabazon of Tara*
Moreton – *Ducie, E.*
Morgan – *M. of Drefelin**
Morgan – *M. of Ely**
Morgan – *M. of Huyton**
Morris – *Killanin*

Morris – *M. of Aberavon**
Morris – *M. of Bolton**
Morris – *M. of Handsworth**
Morris – *M. of Kenwood*
Morris – *M. of Yardley**
Morris – *Naseby**
Morrison – *Dunrossil, V.*
Morrison – *Margadale*
Mosley – *Ravensdale*
Mountbatten – *Milford Haven, M.*
Muff – *Calverley*
Mulholland – *Dunleath*
Mumford – *Herries of Terregles*
Murray – *Atholl, D.*
Murray – *Dunmore, E.*
Murray – *Mansfield and Mansfield, E.*
Nall-Cain – *Brocket*
Napier – *Napier and Ettrick*
Napier – *N. of Magdala*
Needham – *Kilmorey, E.*
Neill – *N. of Bladen**
Nelson – *N. of Stafford*
Neuberger – *N. of Abbotsbury**
Nevill – *Abergavenny, M.*
Neville – *Braybrooke*
Nicholls – *N. of Birkenhead**
Nicolson – *Carnock*
Nicholson – *N. of Winterbourne**
Nivison – *Glendyne*
Noel – *Gainsborough, E.*
North – *Guilford, E.*
Northcote – *Iddesleigh, E.*
Norton – *Grantley*
Norton – *N. of Louth**
Norton – *Rathcreedan*
Nugent – *Westmeath, E.*
Oakeshott – *O. of Seagrove Bay**
O'Brien – *Inchiquin*
Ogilvie-Grant – *Seafield, E.*
Ogilvy – *Airlie, E.*
O'Neill – *O'N. of Bengarve**
O'Neill – *O'N. of Clackmannan**
O'Neill – *Rathcavan*
Orde-Powlett – *Bolton*
Ormsby-Gore – *Harlech*
Paget – *Anglesey, M.*
Paisley – *P. of St George's**
Pakenham – *Longford, E.*
Pakington – *Hampton*
Palmer – *Lucas and Dingwall*
Palmer – *P. of Childs Hill**
Palmer – *Selborne, E.*
Palumbo – *P. of Southwark**
Parker – *Macclesfield, E.*
Parker – *Morley, E.*
Parnell – *Congleton*
Parsons – *Rosse, E.*
Patel – *P. of Blackburn**
Patel – *P. of Bradford**
Patten – *P. of Barnes**
Paulet – *Winchester, M.*

Pearson – *Cowdray, V.*
Pearson – *P. of Rannoch**
Pease – *Gainford*
Pease – *Wardington*
Pelham – *Chichester, E.*
Pelham – *Yarborough, E.*
Pellew – *Exmouth, V.*
Penny – *Marchwood, V.*
Pepys – *Cottenham, E.*
Percy – *Northumberland, D.*
Perry – *P. of Southwark**
Pery – *Limerick, E.*
Philipps – *Milford*
Philipps – *St Davids, V.*
Phillips – *P. of Sudbury**
Phillips – *P. of Worth Matravers**
Phipps – *Normanby, M.*
Plant – *P. of Highfield**
Pleydell-Bouverie – *Radnor, E.*
Plumptre – *Fitzwalter*
Plunkett – *Dunsany*
Plunkett – *Louth*
Pollock – *Hanworth, V.*
Pomeroy – *Harberton, V.*
Ponsonby – *Bessborough, E.*
Ponsonby – *de Mauley*
Ponsonby – *P. of Shulbrede*
Powell – *P. of Bayswater**
Powys – *Lilford*
Pratt – *Camden, M.*
Preston – *Gormanston, V.*
Primrose – *Rosebery, E.*
Prittie – *Dunalley*
Purvis – *P. of Tweed**
Ramsay – *Dalhousie, E.*
Ramsay – *R. of Cartvale**
Ramsbotham – *Soulbury, V.*
Rees – *R. of Ludlow**
Rees-Williams – *Ogmore*
Reid – *R. of Cardowan**
Renfrew – *R. of Kaimsthorn**
Renton – *R. of Mount Harry**
Renwick – *R. of Clifton**
Rhys – *Dynevor*
Richards – *Milverton*
Richards – *R. of Herstmonceux**
Richardson – *R. of Calow**
Ritchie – *R. of Dundee*
Roberts – *Clwyd*
Roberts – *R. of Llandudno**
Robertson – *R. of Oakridge*
Robertson – *R. of Port Ellen**
Robertson – *Wharton*
Robinson – *Martonmere*
Roche – *Fermoy*
Rodd – *Rennell*
Rodgers – *R. of Quarry Bank**
Rogers – *Lisvane**
Rogers – *R. of Riverside**
Roper-Curzon – *Teynham*
Rose – *R. of Monewden**
Rospigliosi – *Newburgh, E.*
Rous – *Stradbroke, E.*

Rowley-Conwy – *Langford*
Royall – *R. of Blaisdon**
Runciman – *R. of Doxford, V.*
Russell – *Ampthill*
Russell – *Bedford, D.*
Russell – *de Clifford*
Russell – *R. of Liverpool*
Ryder – *Harrowby, E.*
Ryder – *R. of Wensum**
Sackville – *De La Warr, E.*
Sackville-West – *Sackville*
Sainsbury – *S. of Preston Candover**
Sainsbury – *S. of Turville**
St Aubyn – *St Levan*
St Clair – *Sinclair*
St Clair-Erskine – *Rosslyn, E.*
St John – *Bolingbroke and St John, V.*
St John – *St John of Bletso*
St Leger – *Doneraile, V.*
Samuel – *Bearsted, V.*
Sanderson – *S. of Ayot*
Sanderson – *S. of Bowden**
Sandilands – *Torphichen*
Saumarez – *de Saumarez*
Savile – *Mexborough, E.*
Saville – *S. of Newdigate**
Scarlett – *Abinger*
Schreiber – *Marlesford**
Sclater-Booth – *Basing*
Scotland – *S. of Asthal**
Scott – *Eldon, E.*
Scott – *S. of Foscote**
Scott – *S. of Needham Market**
Scrymgeour – *Dundee, E.*
Seager – *Leighton of St Mellons*
Seely – *Mottistone*
Seymour – *Hertford, M.*
Seymour – *Somerset, D.*
Shackleton – *S. of Belgravia**
Sharp – *S. of Guildford**
Shaw – *Craigmyle*
Shaw – *S. of Northstead**
Shephard – *S. of Northwold**
Sherbourne – *S. of Didsbury**
Shirley – *Ferrers, E.*
Shutt – *S. of Greetland**
Siddeley – *Kenilworth*
Sidney – *De L'Isle, V.*
Simon – *S. of Highbury**
Simon – *S. of Wythenshawe*
Simpson – *S. of Dunkeld**
Sinclair – *Caithness, E.*
Sinclair – *of Cleeve*
Sinclair – *Thurso, V.*
Singh – *S. of Wimbledon**
Skeffington – *Massereene and Ferrard, V.*
Smith – *Bicester*
Smith – *Hambleden, V.*
Smith – *Kirkhill**
Smith – *S. of Basildon**
Smith – *S. of Clifton**
Smith – *S. of Finsbury**

# LORDS SPIRITUAL

The Lords Spiritual are the Archbishops of Canterbury and York and 24 other diocesan bishops of the Church of England. The Bishops of London, Durham and Winchester always have seats in the House of Lords; the other 21 seats were previously filled by the remaining diocesan bishops in order of seniority. However, the Lords Spiritual (Women) Act 2015 provides for vacancies among the remaining 21 places to be filled by any female diocesan bishop in office at the time and, only if there is no female diocesan bishop, by the longest serving male diocesan bishop. The provision will remain in place for ten years from 2015, equivalent to two fixed-term parliaments. At the end of this period, the provision under the Act will end and the previous arrangements under which vacancies are filled according to length of service as a diocesan bishop will be restored. The Bishop of Sodor and Man and the Bishop of Gibraltar in Europe are not eligible to sit in the House of Lords.

## ARCHBISHOPS

*Style,* The Most Revd and Rt. Hon. the Lord Archbishop of_
*Addressed as* Archbishop *or* Your Grace

INTRODUCED TO HOUSE OF LORDS
2012    *Canterbury* (105th), Justin Portal Welby, *b.* 1956, *m., cons.* 2011, *elected* 2012, *trans.* 2013
2006    *York* (97th), John Mugabi Tucker Sentamu, PHD, *b.* 1949, *m., cons.* 1996, *elected* 2002, *trans.* 2005

## BISHOPS

*Style,* The Rt. Revd the Lord Bishop of _
*Addressed as* Bishop or My Lord
*elected* date of confirmation as diocesan bishop

INTRODUCED TO HOUSE OF LORDS
*as at November 2015*

1996    *London* (132nd), Richard John Carew Chartres, KCVO, PC, *b.* 1947, *m., cons.* 1992, *elected* 1995
2014    *Durham* (74th), Paul Roger Butler, *b.* 1955, *m., cons.* 2004, *elected* 2009, *trans.* 2014
2012    *Winchester* (97th), Timothy John Dakin, *b.* 1958, *m., cons.* 2012, *elected* 2012
2001    *Chester* (40th), Peter Robert Forster, PHD, *b.* 1950, *m., cons.* 1996, *elected* 1996
2004    *Norwich* (71st), Graham Richard James, *b.* 1951, *m., cons.* 1993, *elected* 1999
2009    *Bristol* (55th), Michael Arthur Hill, *b.* 1949, *m., cons.* 1998, *elected* 2003
2010    *Derby* (7th), Alastair Llewellyn John Redfern, PHD, *b.* 1948, *m., cons.* 1997, *elected* 2005
2010    *Birmingham* (9th), David Andrew Urquhart, *b.* 1952, *cons.* 2000, *elected* 2006
2012    *Worcester* (113th), John Geoffrey Inge, PHD, *b.* 1955, *m., cons.* 2003, *elected* 2007

2013    *Coventry* (9th), Christopher John Cocksworth, PHD, *b.* 1959, *m., cons.* 2008, *elected* 2008
2013    *Truro* (15th), Timothy Martin Thornton, *b.* 1957, *m., cons.* 2001, *elected* 2008
2013    *Sheffield* (7th), Stephen John Lindsey Croft, PHD, *b.* 1957, *m., cons.* 2009, *elected* 2009
2013    *Carlisle* (66th), James William Scobie Newcome, *b.* 1953, *m., cons.* 2002, *elected* 2009
2013    *St Albans* (10th), Alan Gregory Clayton Smith, PHD, *b.* 1957, *cons.* 2001, *elected* 2009
2014    *Peterborough* (38th), Donald Spargo Allister, *b.* 1952, *m., cons.* 2010, *elected* 2010
2014    *Portsmouth* (9th), Christopher Richard James Foster, *b.* 1953, *m., cons.* 2001, *elected* 2010
2014    *Chelmsford* (10th), Stephen Geoffrey Cottrell, *b.* 1958, *m., cons.* 2004, *elected* 2010
2014    *Rochester* (107th), James Henry Langstaff, *b.* 1956, *m., cons.* 2004, *elected* 2010
2014    *Ely* (69th), Stephen David Conway, *b.* 1957, *cons.* 2006, *elected* 2010
2014    *Southwark* (10th), Christopher Thomas James Chessun, *b.* 1956, *cons.* 2005, *elected* 2011
2014    *Leeds* (1st), Nicholas Baines, *b.* 1957, *m., cons.* 2003, *elected* 2014
2015    *Salisbury* (78th), Nicholas Roderick Holtam, *b.* 1954, *m., cons.* 2011, *elected* 2011
2015    *Gloucester* (41st), Rachel Treweek, *b.* 1963, *m., cons.* 2015, *elected* 2015
2015    *Lincoln* (71st), Christopher Lowson, *b.* 1953, *m., cons.* 2011, *elected* 2011

BISHOPS AWAITING SEATS, in order of seniority
*as at November 2015*

*Chichester* (103rd), Martin Clive Warner, PHD, *b.* 1958, *cons.* 2010, *elected* 2012
*Blackburn* (9th), Julian Tudor Henderson, *b.* 1954, *m., cons.* 2013, *elected* 2013
*Manchester* (12th), David Stuart Walker, *b.* 1957, *m., cons.* 2000, *elected* 2013
*Bath and Wells* (79th), Peter Hancock, *b.* 1955, *m., cons.* 2010, *elected* 2014
*Exeter* (71st), Robert Ronald Atwell, *b.* 1954, *cons.* 2008, *elected* 2014
*Liverpool* (8th), Paul Bayes, *b.* 1953, *m., cons.* 2010, *elected* 2014
*Hereford* (105th), Richard Michael Cokayne Frith, *b.* 1949, *m., cons.* 1998, *elected* 2014
*Guildford* (10th), Andrew John Watson, *b.* 1961, *m., cons.* 2008, *elected* 2014
*St Edmundsbury and Ipswich* (11th), Martin Alan Seeley, *b.* 1954, *m., cons.* 2015, *elected* 2015
*Southwell and Nottingham* (12th), Paul Gavin Williams, *b.* 1968, *m., cons.* 2009, *elected* 2015
*Newcastle* (12th), Christine Elizabeth Hardman, *b.* 1951, *m., cons.* 2015, *elected* 2015
*Oxford* (43rd), vacant
*Leicester* (7th), vacant
*Lichfield* (99th), vacant

# ORDERS OF CHIVALRY

## THE MOST NOBLE ORDER OF THE GARTER (1348)

KG
*Ribbon,* Blue
*Motto,* Honi soit qui mal y pense
*(Shame on him who thinks evil of it)*

The number of Knights and Ladies Companion is limited to 24

SOVEREIGN OF THE ORDER
The Queen

LADIES OF THE ORDER
HRH The Princess Royal, 1994
HRH Princess Alexandra, The Hon. Lady Ogilvy, 2003

ROYAL KNIGHTS
HRH The Prince Philip, Duke of Edinburgh, 1947
HRH The Prince of Wales, 1958
HRH The Duke of Kent, 1985
HRH The Duke of Gloucester, 1997
HRH The Duke of York, 2006
HRH The Earl of Wessex, 2006
HRH The Duke of Cambridge, 2008

EXTRA KNIGHTS COMPANION AND LADIES
Grand Duke Jean of Luxembourg, 1972
HM The Queen of Denmark, 1979
HM The King of Sweden, 1983
HM King Juan Carlos, 1988
HRH Princess Beatrix of the Netherlands, 1989
HIM The Emperor of Japan, 1998
HM The King of Norway, 2001

KNIGHTS AND LADIES COMPANION
Lord Carrington, 1985
Lord Bramall, 1990
Lord Sainsbury of Preston Candover, 1992
Lord Ashburton, 1994
Sir Ninian Stephen, 1994
Sir Timothy Colman, 1996
Duke of Abercorn, 1999
Sir William Gladstone, 1999
Lord Inge, 2001
Sir Anthony Acland, 2001
Duke of Westminster, 2003
Lord Butler of Brockwell, 2003
Lord Morris of Aberavon, 2003
Sir John Major, 2005
Lord Luce, 2008

Sir Thomas Dunne, 2008
Lord Phillips of Worth Matravers, 2011
Lord Boyce, 2011
Lord Stirrup, 2013
Baroness Manningham-Buller, 2014
Lord King of Lothbury, 2014

*Prelate,* Bishop of Winchester
*Chancellor,* Duke of Abercorn, KG
*Register,* Dean of Windsor
*Garter King of Arms,* Thomas Woodcock, CVO
*Gentleman Usher of the Black Rod,* Lt.-Gen. David Leakey, CMG, CBE
*Secretary,* Patric Dickinson, LVO

## THE MOST ANCIENT AND MOST NOBLE ORDER OF THE THISTLE (REVIVED 1687)

KT
*Ribbon,* Green
*Motto,* Nemo me impune lacessit
*(No one provokes me with impunity)*

The number of Knights and Ladies of the Thistle is limited to 16

SOVEREIGN OF THE ORDER
The Queen

ROYAL KNIGHTS
HRH The Prince Philip, Duke of Edinburgh, 1952
HRH The Prince of Wales, Duke of Rothesay, 1977
HRH The Duke of Cambridge, Earl of Strathearn, 2012

ROYAL LADY OF THE ORDER
HRH The Princess Royal, 2000

KNIGHTS AND LADIES
Earl of Elgin and Kincardine, 1981
Earl of Airlie, 1985
Earl of Crawford and Balcarres, 1996
Lady Marion Fraser, 1996
Lord Macfarlane of Bearsden, 1996
Lord Mackay of Clashfern, 1997
Lord Wilson of Tillyorn, 2000
Lord Sutherland of Houndwood, 2002
Sir Eric Anderson, 2002
Lord Steel of Aikwood, 2004
Lord Robertson of Port Ellen, 2004
Lord Cullen of Whitekirk, 2007
Lord Hope of Craighead, 2009
Lord Patel, 2009

Earl of Home, 2013
Lord Smith of Kelvin, 2013

*Chancellor,* Earl of Airlie, KT, GCVO, PC
*Dean,* Very Revd Prof. Iain Torrance, TD
*Secretary,* Mrs C. Roads, LVO
*Lord Lyon King of Arms,* Dr Joseph Morrow
*Gentleman Usher of the Green Rod,* Rear-Adm. Christopher Layman, CB, DSO, LVO

## THE MOST HONOURABLE ORDER OF THE BATH (1725)

GCB *Military* GCB *Civil*

GCB    Knight (or Dame) Grand Cross
KCB    Knight Commander
DCB    Dame Commander
CB    Companion

*Ribbon,* Crimson
*Motto,* Tria juncta in uno
*(Three joined in one)*

Remodelled 1815, and enlarged many times since. The order is divided into civil and military divisions. Women became eligible for the order from 1 January 1971.

THE SOVEREIGN

GREAT MASTER AND FIRST OR PRINCIPAL KNIGHT GRAND CROSS
HRH The Prince of Wales, KG, KT, GCB, OM

*Dean of the Order,* Dean of Westminster
*Bath King of Arms,* Admiral of the Fleet, the Lord Boyce, KG, GCB, OBE
*Registrar and Secretary,* Rear-Adm. Iain Henderson, CB, CBE
*Genealogist,* Thomas Woodcock, CVO
*Gentleman Usher of the Scarlet Rod,* Maj.-Gen. Charles Vyvyan, CB, CBE
*Deputy Secretary,* Secretary of the Central Chancery of the Orders of Knighthood
*Chancery,* Central Chancery of the Orders of Knighthood, St James's Palace, London SW1A 1BH

# THE ORDER OF MERIT (1902)

OM *Military*     OM *Civil*

OM
*Ribbon,* Blue and crimson

This order is designed as a special distinction for eminent men and women without conferring a knighthood upon them. The order is limited in numbers to 24, with the addition of foreign honorary members.

THE SOVEREIGN

HRH The Prince Philip, Duke of
  Edinburgh, 1968
Sir Michael Atiyah, 1992
Sir Aaron Klug, 1995
Lord Foster of Thames Bank, 1997
Prof. Sir Roger Penrose, 2000
Sir Tom Stoppard, 2000
HRH The Prince of Wales, 2002
Lord May of Oxford, 2002
Lord Rothschild, 2002
Sir David Attenborough, 2005
Baroness Boothroyd, 2005
Sir Michael Howard, 2005
Sir Timothy Berners-Lee, KBE, 2007
Lord Eames, 2007
Lord Rees of Ludlow, 2007
Rt. Hon. Jean Chrétien, QC, 2009
Robert Neil MacGregor, 2010
Hon. John Howard, 2012
David Hockney, 2012
Sir Simon Rattle, 2013
Prof. Sir Magdi Yacoub, 2013

*Secretary and Registrar,* Lord Fellowes,
  GCB, GCVO, PC, QSO
*Chancery,* Central Chancery of the Orders
  of Knighthood, St James's Palace,
  London SW1A 1BH

# THE MOST DISTINGUISHED ORDER OF ST MICHAEL AND ST GEORGE (1818)

GCMG     KCMG

GCMG   Knight (or Dame) Grand
         Cross
KCMG   Knight Commander
DCMG   Dame Commander
CMG    Companion

*Ribbon,* Saxon blue, with scarlet centre
*Motto,* Auspicium melioris aevi
*(Token of a better age)*

THE SOVEREIGN

GRAND MASTER
HRH The Duke of Kent, KG, GCMG,
  GCVO, ADC

*Prelate,* Rt. Revd David Urquhart
*Chancellor,* Lord Robertson of Port
  Ellen, KT, GCMG, PC
*Secretary,* Permanent Under-Secretary
  of State at the Foreign and
  Commonwealth Office and Head of
  the Diplomatic Service
*Registrar,* Sir David Manning, GCMG,
  CVO
*King of Arms,* Sir Jeremy Greenstock,
  GCMG
*Gentleman Usher of the Blue Rod,* vacant
*Dean,* Dean of St Paul's
*Deputy Secretary,* Secretary of the
  Central Chancery of the Orders of
  Knighthood
*Hon. Genealogist,* Timothy Duke
*Chancery,* Central Chancery of the Orders
  of Knighthood, St James's Palace,
  London SW1A 1BH

# THE IMPERIAL ORDER OF THE CROWN OF INDIA (1877) FOR LADIES

CI

*Badge,* the royal cipher of Queen Victoria in jewels within an oval, surmounted by an heraldic crown and attached to a bow of light blue watered ribbon, edged white

The honour does not confer any rank or title upon the recipient

No conferments have been made since 1947

HM The Queen, 1947

# THE ROYAL VICTORIAN ORDER (1896)

GCVO     KCVO

GCVO   Knight or Dame Grand
         Cross
KCVO   Knight Commander
DCVO   Dame Commander
CVO    Commander
LVO    Lieutenant
MVO    Member

*Ribbon,* Blue, with red and white edges
*Motto,* Victoria

THE SOVEREIGN
GRAND MASTER
HRH The Princess Royal, KG, KT,
  GCVO

*Chancellor,* Lord Chamberlain
*Secretary,* Keeper of the Privy Purse
*Registrar,* Secretary of the Central
  Chancery of the Orders of
  Knighthood
*Chaplain,* Chaplain of the Queen's
  Chapel of the Savoy
*Hon. Genealogist,* David White

## THE MOST EXCELLENT ORDER OF THE BRITISH EMPIRE (1917)

GBE                    KBE

The order was divided into military and civil divisions in December 1918

GBE    Knight or Dame Grand Cross
KBE    Knight Commander
DBE    Dame Commander
CBE    Commander
OBE    Officer
MBE    Member

*Ribbon,* Rose pink edged with pearl grey with vertical pearl stripe in centre (military division); without vertical pearl stripe (civil division)
*Motto,* For God and the Empire

THE SOVEREIGN

GRAND MASTER
HRH The Prince Philip, Duke of Edinburgh, KG, KT, OM, GBE, PC

*Prelate,* Bishop of London
*King of Arms,* vacant
*Registrar,* Secretary of the Central Chancery of the Orders of Knighthood
*Secretary,* Secretary of the Cabinet and Head of the Home Civil Service
*Dean,* Dean of St Paul's
*Lady Usher of the Purple Rod,* Dame Amelia Chilcott Fawcett, DBE
*Chancery,* Central Chancery of the Orders of Knighthood, St James's Palace, London SW1A 1BH

## ORDER OF THE COMPANIONS OF HONOUR (1917)

CH

*Ribbon,* Carmine, with gold edges

This order consists of one class only and carries with it no title. The number of awards is limited to 65 (excluding honorary members).

Anthony, John, 1981
Ashdown of Norton-sub-Hamdon, Lord, 2015
Attenborough, Sir David, 1995
Baker, Dame Janet, 1993
Baker of Dorking, Lord, 1992
Birtwistle, Sir Harrison, 2000
Brenner, Sydney, 1986
Brook, Peter, 1998
Brooke of Sutton Mandeville, Lord, 1992
Campbell, Sir Menzies, 2013
Carrington, Lord, 1983
Clarke, Kenneth, 2014
Coe, Lord, 2012
De Chastelain, Gen. John, 1999
Dench, Dame Judi, 2005
Hannay of Chiswick, Lord, 2003
Hawking, Prof. Stephen, 1989
Healey, Lord, 1979
Heseltine, Lord, 1997
Higgs, Prof. Peter, 2012
Hockney, David, 1997
Hodgkin, Sir Howard, 2002
Howard, Sir Michael, 2002
Howard of Lympne, Lord, 2011
Howe of Aberavon, Lord, 1996
Hurd of Westwell, Lord, 1995
King of Bridgwater, Lord, 1992
Lovelock, Prof. James, 2002
McKellen, Sir Ian Murray, 2008
McKenzie, Prof. Dan Peter, 2003
Major, Sir John, 1998
Marriner, Sir Neville, 2015
Maxwell Davies, Sir Peter, 2013
O'Neill of Bengarve, Baroness, 2013
Owen, Lord, 1994
Patten of Barnes, Lord, 1997
Peters, Dame Mary, 2015
Riley, Bridget, 1998
Rogers of Riverside, Lord, 2008
Serota, Sir Nicholas, 2013
Smith, Dame Margaret (Maggie), 2014
Somare, Sir Michael, 1978
Strathclyde, Lord, 2013
Tebbit, Lord, 1987
Woolf, Lord, 2015
Young, Sir George, 2012
Young of Graffham, Lord, 2015

*Honorary Members,* Prof. Amartya Sen, 2000; Bernard Haitink, 2002
*Secretary and Registrar,* Secretary of the Central Chancery of the Orders of Knighthood

## THE DISTINGUISHED SERVICE ORDER (1886)

DSO

*Ribbon,* Red, with blue edges

Bestowed in recognition of especial services in action of commissioned officers in the Navy, Army and Royal Air Force and (since 1942) Mercantile Marine. The members are Companions only. A bar may be awarded for any additional act of service.

## THE IMPERIAL SERVICE ORDER (1902)

ISO

*Ribbon,* Crimson, with blue centre

Appointment as companion of this order is open to members of the civil services whose eligibility is determined by the grade they hold. The order consists of the sovereign and companions to a number not exceeding 1,900, of whom 1,300 may belong to the home civil services and 600 to overseas civil services. The then prime minister announced in March 1993 that he would make no further recommendations for appointments to the order.

*Secretary,* Head of the Home Civil Service
*Registrar,* Secretary of the Central Chancery of the Orders of Knighthood

## THE ROYAL VICTORIAN CHAIN (1902)

It confers no precedence on its holders

HM THE QUEEN

HM The King of Thailand, 1960
HM The Queen of Denmark, 1974
HM The King of Sweden, 1975
HRH Princess Beatrix of the Netherlands, 1982
Gen. Antonio Eanes, 1985
HM King Juan Carlos, 1986
HM The King of Norway, 1994
Earl of Airlie, 1997
Rt. Revd and Rt. Hon. Lord Carey of Clifton, 2002
HRH Prince Philip, Duke of Edinburgh, 2007
HM The Sultan of Oman, 2010
Rt. Revd and Rt. Hon. Lord Williams of Oystermouth, 2012

# BARONETAGE AND KNIGHTAGE

## BARONETS

*Style,* 'Sir' before forename and surname, followed by 'Bt'.
  *Envelope,* Sir F_ S_, Bt. *Letter (formal),* Dear Sir; *(social),* Dear Sir F_. *Spoken,* Sir F_
*Wife's style,* 'Lady' followed by surname
  *Envelope,* Lady S_. *Letter (formal),* Dear Madam; *(social),* Dear Lady S_. *Spoken,* Lady S_
*Style of Baronetess,* 'Dame' before forename and surname, followed by 'Btss.' (*see also* Dames)

There are five different creations of baronetcies: Baronets of England (creations dating from 1611); Baronets of Ireland (creations dating from 1619); Baronets of Scotland or Nova Scotia (creations dating from 1625); Baronets of Great Britain (creations after the Act of Union 1707 which combined the kingdoms of England and Scotland); and Baronets of the United Kingdom (creations after the union of Great Britain and Ireland in 1801).

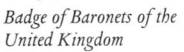

*Badge of Baronets of the United Kingdom*

*Badge of Baronets of Nova Scotia*

*Badge of Ulster*

The patent of creation limits the destination of a baronetcy, usually to male descendants of the first baronet. In some cases, however, special remainders have allowed baronetcies to pass, in the absence of sons, to another relative. In the case of baronetcies of Scotland or Nova Scotia, a special remainder of 'heirs male and of tailzie' allows the baronetcy to descend to heirs general, including women. There are four existing Scottish baronetcies with such a remainder.

The Official Roll of the Baronetage is kept at the Crown Office and maintained by the Registrar and Assistant Registrar of the Baronetage. Anyone who considers that he or she is entitled to be entered on the roll may apply through the Crown Office to prove their succession. Every person succeeding to a baronetcy must exhibit proofs of succession to the Lord Chancellor. A person whose name is not entered on the official roll will not be addressed or mentioned by the title of baronet or baroness in any official document, nor will he or she be accorded precedence as a baronet or baroness.

BARONETCIES EXTINCT SINCE THE LAST EDITION
Dodds (cr. 1964); Hawley (cr. 1795)

OFFICIAL ROLL OF THE BARONETAGE, Crown Office,
House of Lords, London SW1A 0PW T 020-7219 2632
*Registrar,* Ian Denyer, MVO
*Assistant Registrar,* Grant Bavister

## KNIGHTS

*Style,* 'Sir' before forename and surname, followed by appropriate post-nominal initials if a Knight Grand Cross or Knight Commander
  *Envelope,* Sir F_ S_. *Letter (formal),* Dear Sir; *(social),* Dear Sir F_. *Spoken,* Sir F_
*Wife's style,* 'Lady' followed by surname
  *Envelope,* Lady S_. *Letter (formal),* Dear Madam; *(social),* Dear Lady S_. *Spoken,* Lady S_

The prefix 'Sir' is not used by knights who are clerics of the Church of England, who do not receive the accolade. Their wives are entitled to precedence as the wife of a knight but not to the style of 'Lady'.

ORDERS OF KNIGHTHOOD
Knight Grand Cross and Knight Commander are the higher classes of the Orders of Chivalry (*see* Orders of Chivalry). Honorary knighthoods of these orders may be conferred on men who are citizens of countries of which the Queen is not head of state. As a rule, the prefix 'Sir' is not used by honorary knights.

KNIGHTS BACHELOR

The Knights Bachelor do not constitute a royal order, but comprise the surviving representation of the ancient state orders of knighthood. The Register of Knights Bachelor, instituted by James I in the 17th century, lapsed, and in 1908 a voluntary association under the title of the Society of Knights (now the Imperial Society of Knights Bachelor) was formed with the primary objectives of continuing the various registers dating from 1257 and obtaining the uniform registration of every created Knight Bachelor. In 1926 a design for a badge to be worn by Knights Bachelor was approved and adopted; in 1974 a neck badge and miniature were added.

THE IMPERIAL SOCIETY OF KNIGHTS BACHELOR,
Magnesia House, 56 Playhouse Yard, London EC4V 5EX
*Knight Principal,* Sir Colin Berry
*Prelate,* Rt. Revd and Rt. Hon. Bishop of London
*Registrar,* Sir Gavyn Arthur
*Hon. Treasurer,* Sir Jeremy Elwes, CBE
*Clerk to the Council,* Col. Simon Doughty

# LIST OF BARONETS AND KNIGHTS *as at 31 August 2015*

| † | Not registered on the Official Roll of the Baronetage at the time of going to press |
|---|---|
| ( ) | The date of creation of the baronetcy is given in parentheses |
| I | Baronet of Ireland |
| NS | Baronet of Nova Scotia |
| S | Baronet of Scotland |

*A full entry in italic type* indicates that the recipient of a knighthood died during the year in which the honour was conferred. The name is included for purposes of record. Peers are not included in this list.

Aaronson, Sir Michael John, Kt., CBE
Abbott, *Adm.* Sir Peter Charles, GBE, KCB
†Abdy, Sir Robert Etienne Eric, Bt. (1850)
Abed, *Dr* Sir Fazle Hasan, KCMG
Acher, Sir Gerald, Kt., CBE, LVO
Ackroyd, Sir Timothy Robert Whyte, Bt. (1956)
Acland, Sir Antony Arthur, KG, GCMG, GCVO
Acland, *Lt.-Col.* Sir (Christopher) Guy (Dyke), Bt. (1890), MVO
†Acland, Sir Dominic Dyke, Bt. (1678)
Adam, Sir Kenneth Hugo, Kt., OBE
Adams, Sir Geoffrey Doyne, KCMG
Adams, Sir William James, KCMG
Adsetts, Sir William Norman, Kt., OBE
Adye, Sir John Anthony, KCMG
Aga Khan IV, HH Prince Karim, KBE
Agnew, Sir Crispin Hamlyn, Bt. (S. 1629)
Agnew, Sir George Anthony, Bt. (1895)
Agnew, Sir Rudolph Ion Joseph, Kt.
Agnew, Sir Theodore, Kt.
Agnew-Somerville, Sir James Lockett Charles, Bt. (1957)
Ah Koy, Sir James Michael, KBE
Aikens, *Rt. Hon.* Sir Richard John Pearson, Kt.
Ainslie, Sir Charles Benedict, Kt., CBE
†Ainsworth, Sir Anthony Thomas Hugh, Bt. (1917)
Aird, Sir (George) John, Bt. (1901)
Airy, *Maj.-Gen.* Sir Christopher John, KCVO, CBE
Aitchison, Sir Charles Walter de Lancey, Bt. (1938)
Ajegbo, Sir Keith Onyema, Kt., OBE
Akenhead, *Hon.* Sir Robert, Kt.
Akers-Jones, Sir David, KBE, CMG
Alberti, *Prof.* Sir Kurt George Matthew Mayer, Kt.
Albu, Sir George, Bt. (1912)
Alcock, *Air Chief Marshal* Sir (Robert James) Michael, GCB, KBE
Aldous, *Rt. Hon.* Sir William, Kt.
Aldridge, Sir Rodney Malcolm, Kt., OBE
Alexander, *Rt. Hon.* Sir Daniel (Grian), Kt.
Alexander, Sir Douglas, Bt. (1921)
Alexander, Sir Richard, Bt. (1945)
Alghanim, Sir Kutayba Yusuf, KCMG
Allan, *Hon.* Sir Alexander Claud Stuart, KCB
Allen, Sir Errol Newton Fitzrose, KCMG
Allen, *Prof.* Sir Geoffrey, Kt., PHD, FRS
Allen, Sir John Derek, Kt., CBE
Allen, Sir Mark John Spurgeon, Kt., CMG

Allen, *Hon.* Sir Peter Austin Philip Jermyn, Kt.
Allen, Sir Thomas Boaz, Kt., CBE
Allen, *Hon.* Sir William Clifford, KCMG
Allen, Sir William Guilford, Kt.
Alleyne, Sir George Allanmoore Ogarren, Kt.
Alleyne, *Revd* John Olpherts Campbell, Bt. (1769)
Allinson, Sir (Walter) Leonard, KCVO, CMG
Alliott, *Hon.* Sir John Downes, Kt.
Allison, *Air Chief Marshal* Sir John Shakespeare, KCB, CBE
Amess, Sir David Anthony Andrew, Kt.
Amet, *Hon.* Sir Arnold Karibone, Kt.
Amory, Sir Ian Heathcoat, Bt. (1874)
Anderson, *Dr* Sir James Iain Walker, Kt., CBE
Anderson, Sir John Anthony, KBE
Anderson, Sir Leith Reinsford Steven, Kt., CBE
Anderson, *Prof.* Sir Roy Malcolm, Kt.
Anderson, *Air Marshal* Sir Timothy Michael, KCB, DSO
Anderson, Sir (William) Eric Kinloch, KT
Anderton, Sir (Cyril) James, Kt., CBE, QPM
Andrew, Sir Robert John, KCB
Andrew, Sir Warwick, Kt.
Andrews, Sir Derek Henry, KCB, CBE
Andrews, Sir Ian Charles Franklin, Kt., CBE, TD
Angest, Sir Henry, Kt.
Annesley, Sir Hugh Norman, Kt., QPM
Anson, Sir John, KCB
Anson, *Rear-Adm.* Sir Peter, Bt. (1831), CB
Anstruther, Sir Sebastian Paten Campbell, Bt. (S. 1694 and S. 1700)
Anstruther-Gough-Calthorpe, Sir Euan Hamilton, Bt. (1929)
Antrobus, Sir Edward Philip, Bt. (1815)
Appleyard, Sir Leonard Vincent, KCMG
Appleyard, Sir Raymond Kenelm, KBE
Arbib, Sir Martyn, Kt.
Arbuthnot, Sir Keith Robert Charles, Bt. (1823)
Arbuthnot, Sir William Reierson, Bt. (1964)
Arbuthnott, *Prof.* Sir John Peebles, Kt., PHD, FRSE
†Archdale, Sir Nicholas Edward, Bt. (1928)
Arculus, Sir Ronald, KCMG, KCVO
Arculus, Sir Thomas David Guy, Kt.
Armitage, *Air Chief Marshal* Sir Michael John, KCB, CBE

Armitt, Sir John Alexander, Kt., CBE
Armour, *Prof.* Sir James, Kt., CBE
Armstrong, Sir Christopher John Edmund Stuart, Bt. (1841), MBE
Armstrong, Sir Patrick John, Kt., CBE
Armstrong, Sir Richard, Kt., CBE
Armytage, Sir John Martin, Bt. (1738)
Arnold, *Hon.* Sir Richard David, Kt.
Arnold, Sir Thomas Richard, Kt.
Arnott, Sir Alexander John Maxwell, Bt. (1896)
†Arthur, Sir Benjamin Nathan, Bt. (1841)
Arthur, Sir Gavyn Farr, Kt.
Arthur, *Lt.-Gen.* Sir (John) Norman Stewart, KCB, CVO
Arthur, Sir Michael Anthony, KCMG
Arulkumaran, *Prof.* Sir Sabaratnam, Kt.
Asbridge, Sir Jonathan Elliott, Kt.
Ash, *Prof.* Sir Eric Albert, Kt., CBE, FRS, FRENG
Ashburnham, Sir James Fleetwood, Bt. (1661)
Ashmore, *Admiral of the Fleet* Sir Edward Beckwith, GCB, DSC
Ashworth, *Dr* Sir John Michael, Kt.
Aske, Sir Robert John Bingham, Bt. (1922)
Askew, Sir Bryan, Kt.
Asquith, *Hon.* Sir Dominic Anthony Gerard, KCMG
Astill, *Hon.* Sir Michael John, Kt.
Astley-Cooper, Sir Alexander Paston, Bt. (1821)
Astwood, *Hon.* Sir James Rufus, KBE
Atcherley, Sir Harold Winter, Kt.
Atiyah, Sir Michael Francis, Kt., OM, PHD, FRS
Atkins, *Rt. Hon.* Sir Robert James, Kt.
Atkinson, *Prof.* Sir Anthony Barnes, Kt.
Atkinson, Sir Frederick John, KCB
Atkinson, Sir William Samuel, Kt.
Atopare, Sir Sailas, GCMG
Attenborough, Sir David Frederick, Kt., OM, CH, CVO, CBE, FRS
Aubrey-Fletcher, Sir Henry Egerton, Bt. (1782)
Audland, Sir Christopher John, KCMG
Augier, *Prof.* Sir Fitzroy Richard, Kt.
Auld, *Rt. Hon.* Sir Robin Ernest, Kt.
Austin, Sir Anthony Leonard, Bt. (1894)
Austin, *Air Marshal* Sir Roger Mark, KCB, AFC
Austen-Smith, *Air Marshal* Sir Roy David, KBE, CB, CVO, DFC
Avei, Sir Moi, KBE
Ayaz, *Dr* Sir Iftikhar Ahmad, KBE
Ayckbourn, Sir Alan, Kt., CBE
Aykroyd, Sir Henry Robert George, Bt. (1920)

Aykroyd, Sir James Alexander Frederic, Bt. (1929)
Aylmer, Sir Richard John, Bt. (I. 1622)
Aylward, *Prof.* Sir Mansel, Kt., CB
Aynsley-Green, *Prof.* Sir Albert, Kt.

Bacha, Sir Bhinod, Kt., CMG
Backhouse, Sir Alfred James Stott, Bt. (1901)
Bacon, Sir Nicholas Hickman Ponsonby, Bt., OBE (1611 and 1627), *Premier Baronet of England*
Baddeley, Sir John Wolsey Beresford, Bt. (1922)
Badge, Sir Peter Gilmour Noto, Kt.
Baer, Sir Jack Mervyn Frank, Kt.
Bagge, Sir (John) Jeremy Picton, Bt. (1867)
Baggott, Sir Matthew David, Kt., CBE, QPM
Bagnall, *Air Chief Marshal* Sir Anthony, GBE, KCB
Bai, Sir Brown, KBE
Bailey, Sir Alan Marshall, KCB
Bailey, Sir Brian Harry, Kt., OBE
Bailey, Sir John Bilsland, KCB
Bailey, Sir John Richard, Bt. (1919)
Bailhache, Sir Philip Martin, Kt.
Baillie, Sir Adrian Louis, Bt. (1823)
Bain, *Prof.* Sir George Sayers, Kt.
Baird, Sir Charles William Stuart, Bt. (1809)
†Baird, Sir James Andrew Gardiner, Bt. (S. 1695)
Baird, *Air Marshal* Sir John Alexander, KBE
Baird, *Vice-Adm.* Sir Thomas Henry Eustace, KCB
Bairsto, *Air Marshal* Sir Peter Edward, KBE, CB
Baker, Sir Bryan William, Kt.
Baker, *Hon.* Sir Jeremy Russell, Kt.
Baker, *Prof.* Sir John Hamilton, Kt., QC
Baker, Sir John William, Kt., CBE
Baker, *Hon.* Sir Jonathan Leslie, Kt.
Baker, *Rt. Hon.* Sir (Thomas) Scott (Gillespie), Kt.
Baldry, Sir Antony Brian, Kt.
Baldwin, *Prof.* Sir Jack Edward, Kt., FRS
Ball, Sir Christopher John Elinger, Kt.
Ball, *Prof.* Sir John Macleod, Kt.
Ball, Sir Richard Bentley, Bt. (1911)
Ball, *Prof.* Sir Robert James, Kt., PHD
Ballantyne, *Dr* Sir Frederick Nathaniel, GCMG
Band, *Adm.* Sir Jonathon, GCB
Banham, Sir John Michael Middlecott, Kt.
Bannerman, Sir David Gordon, Bt. (S. 1682), OBE
Bannister, Sir Roger Gilbert, Kt., CBE, DM, FRCP
Barber, Sir Brendan, Kt.
Barber, Sir Michael Bayldon, Kt.
Barber, Sir (Thomas) David, Bt. (1960)
Barclay, Sir Robert Colraine, Bt. (S. 1668)
Barclay, Sir David Rowat, Kt.
Barclay, Sir Frederick Hugh, Kt.
Barder, Sir Brian Leon, KCMG
Baring, Sir John Francis, Bt. (1911)
Barker, Sir Colin, Kt.

Barker, *Hon.* Sir (Richard) Ian, Kt.
Barling, *Hon.* Sir Gerald Edward, Kt.
Barlow, Sir Christopher Hilaro, Bt. (1803)
Barlow, Sir Frank, Kt., CBE
Barlow, Sir James Alan, Bt. (1902)
Barlow, Sir John Kemp, Bt. (1907)
Barnes, *The Most Revd* Brian James, KBE
Barnes, Sir (James) David (Francis), Kt., CBE
Barnett, *Hon.* Sir Michael Lancelot Patrick, Kt.
Barnett, *Prof.* Sir Richard Robert, Kt.
Barnewall, Sir Reginald Robert, Bt. (I. 1623)
Baron, Sir Thomas, Kt., CBE
†Barran, Sir John Ruthven, Bt. (1895)
Barrett, Sir Stephen Jeremy, KCMG
Barrett-Lennard, Sir Peter John, Bt. (1801)
Barrington, Sir Benjamin, Bt. (1831)
Barrington, Sir Nicholas John, KCMG, CVO
Barrington-Ward, *Rt. Revd* Simon, KCMG
Barron, Sir Donald James, Kt.
Barron, *Rt. Hon.* Sir Kevin, Kt.
Barrons, *Gen.* Sir Richard, KCB, CBE, ADC
Barrow, Sir Anthony John Grenfell, Bt. (1835)
Barrow, Sir Timothy Earle, KCMG, LVO, MBE
Barry, Sir (Lawrence) Edward (Anthony Tress), Bt. (1899)
Barter, Sir Peter Leslie Charles, Kt., OBE
Bartlett, Sir Andrew Alan, Bt. (1913)
Barttelot, *Col.* Sir Brian Walter de Stopham, Bt. (1875), OBE
Bate, *Prof.* Sir Andrew Jonathan, Kt., CBE
Bates, Sir James Geoffrey, Bt. (1880)
Bates, Sir Richard Dawson Hoult, Bt. (1937)
Bateson, *Prof.* Sir Patrick, Kt.
Bather, Sir John Knollys, KCVO
Batho, Sir Peter Ghislain, Bt. (1928)
Bathurst, *Admiral of the Fleet* Sir (David) Benjamin, GCB
Battersby, *Prof.* Sir Alan Rushton, Kt., FRS
Battishill, Sir Anthony Michael William, GCB
Baulcombe, *Prof.* Sir David Charles, Kt., FRS
Baxendell, Sir Peter Brian, Kt., CBE, FRENG
Bayley, Sir Hugh Nigel Edward, Kt.
Bayne, Sir Nicholas Peter, KCMG
Baynes, Sir Christopher Rory, Bt. (1801)
Bazalgette, Sir Peter Lytton, Kt.
Bazley, Sir Thomas John Sebastian, Bt. (1869)
Beach, *Gen.* Sir (William Gerald) Hugh, GBE, KCB, MC
Beache, *Hon.* Sir Vincent Ian, KCMG
Beale, *Lt.-Gen.* Sir Peter John, KBE, FRCP
Beamish, Sir Adrian John, KCMG
Bean, *Dr* Sir Charles Richard, Kt.

Bean, *Rt. Hon.* Sir David Michael, Kt.
Bear, Sir Michael David, Kt.
Beatson, *Rt. Hon.* Sir Jack, Kt.
Beavis, *Air Chief Marshal* Sir Michael Gordon, KCB, CBE, AFC
Beck, Sir Edgar Philip, Kt.
Beckett, Sir Richard Gervase, Bt. (1921), QC
Beckwith, Sir John Lionel, Kt., CBE
Beddington, *Prof.* Sir John Rex, Kt., CMG
Beecham, Sir Robert Adrian, Bt. (1914)
Beetham, *Marshal of the Royal Air Force* Sir Michael James, GCB, CBE, DFC, AFC
Beevor, Sir Thomas Agnew, Bt. (1784)
Beldam, *Rt. Hon.* Sir (Alexander) Roy (Asplan), Kt.
Belgrave, *HE* Sir Elliott Fitzroy, GCMG
Bell, Sir David Charles Maurice, Kt.
Bell, Sir David Robert, KCB
Bell, *Prof.* Sir John Irving, GBE
Bell, Sir John Lowthian, Bt. (1885)
Bell, *Prof.* Sir Peter Robert Frank, Kt.
Bell, *Hon.* Sir Rodger, Kt.
Bellamy, *Hon.* Sir Christopher William, Kt.
Bellingham, Sir Anthony Edward Norman, Bt. (1796)
Bender, Sir Brian Geoffrey, KCB
Benn, Sir (James) Jonathan, Bt. (1914)
Bennett, *Air Vice-Marshal* Sir Erik Peter, KBE, CB
Bennett, *Hon.* Sir Hugh Peter Derwyn, Kt.
Bennett, *Gen.* Sir Phillip Harvey, KBE, DSO
Bennett, Sir Ronald Wilfrid Murdoch, Bt. (1929)
Benson, Sir Christopher John, Kt.
Beresford, Sir (Alexander) Paul, Kt.
Beresford-Peirse, Sir Henry Njers de la Poer, Bt. (1814)
Berghuser, *Hon.* Sir Eric, Kt., MBE
Beringer, *Prof.* Sir John Evelyn, Kt., CBE
Berman, Sir Franklin Delow, KCMG
Berners-Lee, Sir Timothy John, OM, KBE, FRS
Bernard, Sir Dallas Edmund, Bt. (1954)
Berney, Sir Julian Reedham Stuart, Bt. (1620)
Bernstein, Sir Howard, Kt.
Berragan, *Lt.-Gen.* Sir Gerald William, KBE, CB
Berridge, *Prof.* Sir Michael John, Kt., FRS
Berriman, Sir David, Kt.
Berry, *Prof.* Sir Colin Leonard, Kt., FRCPATH
Berry, *Prof.* Sir Michael Victor, Kt., FRS
Berthoud, Sir Martin Seymour, KCVO, CMG
Berwick, *Prof.* Sir George Thomas, Kt., CBE
Best-Shaw, Sir Thomas Joshua, Bt. (1665)
Bethel, Sir Baltron Benjamin, KCMG
Bethlehem, Sir Daniel, KCMG
Bett, Sir Michael, Kt., CBE
Bettison, Sir Norman George, Kt., QPM

Bevan, Sir James David, KCMG
Bevan, Sir Martyn Evan Evans, Bt. (1958)
Bevan, Sir Nicolas, Kt., CB
Bevan, Sir Timothy Hugh, Kt.
Beverley, *Lt.-Gen.* Sir Henry York La Roche, KCB, OBE, RM
Bhadeshia, *Prof.* Sir Harshad Kumar Dharamshi, Kt., FRS
Bibby, Sir Michael James, Bt. (1959)
Bickersteth, *Rt. Revd* John Monier, KCVO
Biddulph, Sir Ian D'Olier, Bt. (1664)
Biggam, Sir Robin Adair, Kt.
Bilas, Sir Angmai Simon, Kt., OBE
Bill, *Lt.-Gen.* Sir David Robert, KCB
Billière, *Gen.* Sir Peter Edgar de la Cour de la, KCB, KBE, DSO, MC
Bindman, Sir Geoffrey Lionel, Kt.
Bingham, *Hon.* Sir Eardley Max, Kt.
Birch, Sir John Allan, KCVO, CMG
Birch, Sir Roger, Kt., CBE, QPM
Bird, *Prof.* Sir Adrian Peter, Kt., CBE, FRS, FRSE
Bird, Sir Richard Geoffrey Chapman, Bt. (1922)
Birkett, Sir Peter, Kt.
Birkin, Sir John Christian William, Bt. (1905)
Birkin, Sir (John) Derek, Kt., TD
Birkmyre, Sir James, Bt. (1921)
Birrell, Sir James Drake, Kt.
Birss, *Hon.* Sir Colin Ian, Kt.
Birt, Sir Michael, Kt.
Birtwistle, Sir Harrison, Kt., CH
Bischoff, Sir Winfried Franz Wilhelm, Kt.
Black, *Adm.* Sir (John) Jeremy, GBE, KCB, DSO
Black, Sir Robert David, Bt. (1922)
Blackburn, *Vice-Adm.* Sir David Anthony James, KCVO, CB
Blackburne, *Hon.* Sir William Anthony, Kt.
Blackett, Sir Hugh Francis, Bt. (1673)
Blackham, *Vice-Adm.* Sir Jeremy Joe, KCB
Blackman, Sir Frank Milton, KCVO, OBE
†Blair, Sir Patrick David Hunter, Bt. (1786)
Blair, *Hon.* Sir William James Lynton, Kt.
Blake, Sir Anthony Teilo Bruce, Bt. (I. 1622)
Blake, Sir Francis Michael, Bt. (1907)
Blake, *Hon.* Sir Nicholas John Gorrod, Kt.
Blake, Sir Peter Thomas, Kt., CBE
Blake, Sir Quentin Saxby, Kt., CBE
Blakemore, *Prof.* Sir Colin Brian, Kt., FRS
Blaker, Sir John, Bt. (1919)
Blakiston, Sir Ferguson Arthur James, Bt. (1763)
Blanch, Sir Malcolm, KCVO
Bland, Sir (Francis) Christopher (Buchan), Kt.
Bland, *Lt.-Col.* Sir Simon Claud Michael, KCVO
Blank, Sir Maurice Victor, Kt.
Blatherwick, Sir David Elliott Spiby, KCMG, OBE

Blelloch, Sir John Nial Henderson, KCB
Blennerhassett, Sir (Marmaduke) Adrian Francis William, Bt. (1809)
Blewitt, *Maj.* Sir Shane Gabriel Basil, GCVO
Blofeld, *Hon.* Sir John Christopher Calthorpe, Kt.
Blois, Sir Charles Nicholas Gervase, Bt. (1686)
Blom-Cooper, Sir Louis Jacques, Kt., QC
Blomefield, Sir Thomas Charles Peregrine, Bt. (1807)
Blundell, *Prof.* Sir Richard William, Kt., CBE, FBA
Bloom, *Prof.* Sir Stephen Robert, Kt.
Bloomfield, Sir Kenneth Percy, KCB
Blundell, *Prof.* Sir Richard William, Kt., CBE, FBA
Blundell, Sir Thomas Leon, Kt., FRS
†Blunden, Sir Hubert Chisholm, Bt. (I. 1766)
Blunt, Sir David Richard Reginald Harvey, Bt. (1720)
Blyth, Sir Charles (Chay), Kt., CBE, BEM
Boardman, *Prof.* Sir John, Kt., FSA, FBA
Bodey, *Hon.* Sir David Roderick Lessiter, Kt.
Bodmer, Sir Walter Fred, Kt., PHD, FRS
Body, Sir Richard Bernard Frank Stewart, Kt.
Bogle, Sir Nigel, Kt.
Bogan, Sir Nagora, KBE
Boileau, Sir Nicolas Edmond George, Bt. (1838)
Boles, Sir Richard Fortescue, Bt. (1922)
Bona, Sir Kina, KBE
Bonallack, Sir Michael Francis, Kt., OBE
Bond, Sir John Reginald Hartnell, Kt.
Bond, *Prof.* Sir Michael Richard, Kt., FRCPSYCH, FRCPGLAS, FRCSE
Bone, *Prof.* Sir (James) Drummond, Kt., FRSE
Bone, Sir Roger Bridgland, KCMG
Bonfield, Sir Peter Leahy, Kt., CBE, FRENG
Bonham, Sir George Martin Antony, Bt. (1852)
Bonington, Sir Christian John Storey, Kt., CVO, CBE
Bonsor, Sir Nicholas Cosmo, Bt. (1925)
Boord, Sir Nicolas John Charles, Bt. (1896)
Boorman, *Lt.-Gen.* Sir Derek, KCB
Booth, Sir Clive, Kt.
Booth, Sir Douglas Allen, Bt. (1916)
Boothby, Sir Brooke Charles, Bt. (1660)
Bore, Sir Albert, Kt.
Boreel, Sir Stephan Gerard, Bt. (1645)
Borthwick, Sir Anthony Thomas, Bt. (1908)
Borysiewicz, *Prof.* Sir Leszek Krzysztof, Kt.
Bosher, Sir Robin, Kt.
Bossom, *Hon.* Sir Clive, Bt. (1953)
Bostock, Sir David John, KCMG
Boswell, *Lt.-Gen.* Sir Alexander Crawford Simpson, KCB, CBE

Botham, Sir Ian Terence, Kt., OBE
Bottomley, Sir Peter James, Kt.
Bottoms, *Prof.* Sir Anthony Edward, Kt.
Boughey, Sir John George Fletcher, Bt. (1798)
Boulton, Sir Clifford John, GCB
†Boulton, Sir John Gibson, Bt. (1944)
Bouraga, Sir Phillip, KBE
Bourn, Sir John Bryant, KCB
Bowater, Sir Euan David Vansittart, Bt. (1939)
†Bowater, Sir Michael Patrick, Bt. (1914)
Bowden, Sir Andrew, Kt., MBE
Bowden, Sir Nicholas Richard, Bt. (1915)
Bowen, Sir Barry Manfield, KCMG
Bowen, Sir Geoffrey Fraser, Kt.
Bowen, Sir George Edward Michael, Bt. (1921)
Bowes Lyon, Sir Simon Alexander, KCVO
Bowlby, Sir Richard Peregrine Longstaff, Bt. (1923)
Bowman, Sir Edwin Geoffrey, KCB
Bowman, Sir Jeffery Haverstock, Kt.
Bowness, Sir Alan, Kt., CBE
Bowyer-Smyth, Sir Thomas Weyland, Bt. (1661)
Boyce, Sir Graham Hugh, KCMG
Boyce, Sir Robert Charles Leslie, Bt. (1952)
Boyd, Sir Alexander Walter, Bt. (1916)
Boyd, Sir John Dixon Iklé, KCMG
Boyd, Sir Michael, Kt.
Boyd, *Prof.* Sir Robert David Hugh, Kt.
Boyd-Carpenter, Sir (Marsom) Henry, KCVO
Boyd-Carpenter, *Lt.-Gen. Hon.* Sir Thomas Patrick John, KBE
Boyle, *Prof.* Sir Roger Michael, Kt., CBE
Boyle, Sir Simon Hugh Patrick, KCVO
Boyle, Sir Stephen Gurney, Bt. (1904)
Bracewell-Smith, Sir Charles, Bt. (1947)
Bradbeer, Sir John Derek Richardson, Kt., OBE, TD
Bradford, Sir Edward Alexander Slade, Bt. (1902)
Bradshaw, *Lt-Gen.* Sir Adrian, KCB, OBE
Brady, *Prof.* Sir John Michael, Kt., FRS
Brailsford, Sir David John, Kt., CBE
Braithwaite, Sir Rodric Quentin, GCMG
Bramley, *Prof.* Sir Paul Anthony, Kt.
Branagh, Sir Kenneth Charles, Kt.
Branson, Sir Richard Charles Nicholas, Kt.
Braithwaite, *Rt. Hon.* Sir Nicholas Alexander, Kt., OBE
Bratza, *Hon.* Sir Nicolas Dušan, Kt.
Breckenridge, *Prof.* Sir Alasdair Muir, Kt., CBE
Brennan, *Hon.* Sir (Francis) Gerard, KBE
Brenton, Sir Anthony Russell, KCMG
Brewer, Sir David William, Kt., CMG
Brierley, Sir Ronald Alfred, Kt.
Briggs, *Rt. Hon.* Sir Michael Townley Featherstone, Kt.

Brighouse, *Prof.* Sir Timothy Robert Peter, Kt.

Bright, Sir Graham Frank James, Kt.

Bright, Sir Keith, Kt.

Brigstocke, *Adm.* Sir John Richard, KCB

Brinckman, Sir Theodore George Roderick, Bt. (1831)

†Brisco, Sir Campbell Howard, Bt. (1782)

Briscoe, Sir Brian Anthony, Kt.

Briscoe, Sir John Geoffrey James, Bt. (1910)

Brittan, Sir Samuel, Kt.

Britton, Sir Paul John James, Kt., CB

†Broadbent, Sir Andrew George, Bt. (1893)

Broadbent, Sir Richard John, KCB

Brocklebank, Sir Aubrey Thomas, Bt. (1885)

Brodie, Sir Benjamin David Ross, Bt. (1834)

Bromhead, Sir John Desmond Gonville, Bt. (1806)

Bromley, Sir Michael Roger, KBE

Bromley, Sir Rupert Charles, Bt. (1757)

Bromley-Davenport, Sir William Arthur, KCVO

Brook, *Prof.* Sir Richard John, Kt. OBE

Brooke, Sir Alistair Weston, Bt. (1919)

Brooke, Sir Francis George Windham, Bt. (1903)

Brooke, *Rt. Hon.* Sir Henry, Kt.

Brooke, Sir Richard Christopher, Bt. (1662)

Brooke, Sir Rodney George, Kt., CBE

Brooking, Sir Trevor David, Kt., CBE

Brooksbank, Sir (Edward) Nicholas, Bt. (1919)

Broomfield, Sir Nigel Hugh Robert Allen, KCMG

†Broughton, Sir David Delves, Bt. (1661)

Broughton, Sir Martin Faulkner, Kt.

Broun, Sir Wayne Hercules, Bt. (S. 1686)

Brown, Sir (Austen) Patrick, KCB

Brown, *Adm.* Sir Brian Thomas, KCB, CBE

Brown, Sir David, Kt.

Brown, *Hon.* Sir Douglas Dunlop, Kt.

Brown, Sir Ewan, Kt., CBE

Brown, Sir George Francis Richmond, Bt. (1863)

Brown, Sir Mervyn, KCMG, OBE

Brown, Sir Peter Randolph, Kt.

Brown, *Rt. Hon.* Sir Stephen, GBE

Brownrigg, Sir Nicholas (Gawen), Bt. (1816)

Browse, *Prof.* Sir Norman Leslie, Kt., MD, FRCS

Bruce, Sir (Francis) Michael Ian, Bt. (S. 1628)

Bruce-Clifton, Sir Hervey Hamish Peter, Bt. (1804)

Bruce-Gardner, Sir Robert Henry, Bt. (1945)

Brunner, Sir Hugo Laurence Joseph, KCVO

Brunner, Sir John Henry Kilian, Bt. (1895)

Brunton, Sir Gordon Charles, Kt.

†Brunton, Sir James Lauder, Bt. (1908)

Bryant, *Air Chief Marshal* Sir Simon, KCB, CBE, ADC

Bubb, Sir Stephen John Limrick, Kt.

Buchan-Hepburn, Sir John Alastair Trant Kidd, Bt. (1815)

Buchanan, Sir Andrew George, Bt. (1878), KCVO

Buchanan-Jardine, Sir John Christopher Rupert, Bt. (1885)

Buckland, Sir Ross, Kt.

Buckley, *Dr* Sir George William, Kt.

Buckley, Sir Michael Sidney, Kt.

Buckley, *Lt.-Cdr.* Sir (Peter) Richard, KCVO

Buckley, *Hon.* Sir Roger John, Kt.

Bucknall, *Lt.-Gen.* Sir James Jeffrey Corfield, KCB, CBE

†Buckworth-Herne-Soame, Sir Richard John, Bt. (1697)

Budd, Sir Alan Peter, GBE

Budd, Sir Colin Richard, KCMG

Bull, Sir George Jeffrey, Kt.

Bull, Sir Simeon George, Bt. (1922)

Bullock, Sir Stephen Michael, Kt.

Bultin, Sir Bato, Kt., MBE

Bunbury, Sir Michael William, Bt. (1681), KCVO

Bunyard, Sir Robert Sidney, Kt., CBE, QPM

Burbidge, Sir Peter Dudley, Bt. (1916)

Burden, Sir Anthony Thomas, Kt., QPM

Burdett, Sir Savile Aylmer, Bt. (1665)

Burgen, Sir Arnold Stanley Vincent, Kt., FRS

Burgess, Sir (Joseph) Stuart, Kt., CBE, PHD, FRSC

Burgess, *Prof.* Sir Robert George, Kt.

Burke, Sir James Stanley Gilbert, Bt. (I. 1797)

Burke, Sir (Thomas) Kerry, Kt.

Burn, *Prof.* Sir John, Kt.

Burns, *Rt. Hon.* Sir Simon Hugh McGuigan, Kt.

Burnell-Nugent, *Vice-Adm.* Sir James Michael, KCB, CBE, ADC

Burnett, Sir Charles David, Bt., (1913)

Burnett, *Rt. Hon.* Sir Ian Duncan, Kt.

Burnett, Sir Walter John, Kt.

Burney, Sir Nigel Dennistoun, Bt. (1921)

Burns, *Dr* Sir Henry, Kt.

Burns, Sir (Robert) Andrew, KCMG

Burnton, *Rt. Hon.* Sir Stanley Jeffrey, Kt.

Burrell, Sir Charles Raymond, Bt. (1774)

Burridge, *Air Chief Marshal* Sir Brian Kevin, KCB, CBE, ADC

Burt, Sir Peter Alexander, Kt.

Burton, *Lt.-Gen.* Sir Edmund Fortescue Gerard, KBE

Burton, Sir Graham Stuart, KCMG

Burton, *Hon.* Sir Michael John, Kt.

Burton, Sir Michael St Edmund, KCVO, CMG

Butler, *Hon.* Sir Arlington Griffith, KCMG

Butler, *Dr* Sir David Edgeworth, Kt., CBE

Butler, Sir Percy James, Kt., CBE

Butler, Sir Reginald Richard Michael, Bt. (1922)

Butler, Sir Richard Pierce, Bt. (I. 1628)

Butterfield, *Hon.* Sir Alexander Neil Logie, Kt.

Butterfill, Sir John Valentine, Kt.

Buxton, Sir Crispin Charles Gerard, Bt. (1840)

Buxton, *Rt. Hon.* Sir Richard Joseph, Kt.

Buzzard, Sir Anthony Farquhar, Bt. (1929)

Byatt, Sir Ian Charles Rayner, Kt.

Byford, Sir Lawrence, Kt., CBE, QPM

Byron, *Rt. Hon.* Sir Charles Michael Dennis, Kt.

Cable, *Rt. Hon.* Sir (John) Vincent, Kt., PHD

†Cable-Alexander, Sir Patrick Desmond William, Bt. (1809)

Cadbury, Sir (Nicholas) Dominic, Kt.

Cadogan, *Prof.* Sir John Ivan George, Kt., CBE, FRS, FRSE

Cahn, Sir Albert Jonas, Bt. (1934)

Cahn, Sir Andrew Thomas, KCMG

Caine, Sir Michael (Maurice Micklewhite), Kt., CBE

Caines, Sir John, KCB

Cairns, *Very Revd* John Ballantyne, KCVO

Caldwell, Sir Edward George, KCB

Callaghan, Sir William Henry, Kt.

Callan, Sir Ivan Roy, KCVO, CMG

Callman, *His Hon.* Sir Clive Vernon, Kt.

Calman, *Prof.* Sir Kenneth Charles, KCB, MD, FRCP, FRCS, FRSE

Calne, *Prof.* Sir Roy Yorke, Kt., FRS

Calvert-Smith, Sir David, Kt., QC

Cameron, Sir Hugh Roy Graham, Kt., QPM

Campbell, *Prof.* Sir Colin Murray, Kt.

Campbell, Sir Ian Tofts, Kt., CBE, VRD

Campbell, Sir Ilay Mark, Bt. (1808)

Campbell, Sir James Alexander Moffat Bain, Bt. (S. 1668)

Campbell, Sir Lachlan Philip Kemeys, Bt. (1815)

Campbell, *Dr.* Sir Philip Henry Montgomery, Kt.

Campbell, Sir Roderick Duncan Hamilton, Bt. (1831)

Campbell, Sir Robin Auchinbreck, Bt. (S. 1628)

Campbell, *Dr* Sir Simon Fraser, Kt., CBE

Campbell, *Rt. Hon.* Sir William Anthony, Kt.

Campbell-Orde, Sir John Alexander, Bt. (1790)

Cannadine, *Prof.* Sir David Nicholas, Kt.

Capewell, *Lt.-Gen.* Sir David Andrew, KCB, OBE, RM

†Carden, Sir Christopher Robert, Bt. (1887)

†Carden, Sir John Craven, Bt. (I. 1787)

Carew, Sir Rivers Verain, Bt. (1661)

Carey, Sir de Vic Graham, Kt.

Carleton-Smith, *Maj.-Gen.* Sir Michael Edward, Kt., CBE

Carlisle, Sir James Beethoven, GCMG
Carlisle, Sir John Michael, Kt.
Carlisle, Sir Kenneth Melville, Kt.
Carnegie, Sir Roderick Howard, Kt.
Carnwath, *Rt. Hon.* Sir Robert John Anderson, Kt., CVO (Lord Carnwath of Notting Hill)
Carr, *Very Revd Dr* Arthur Wesley, KCVO
Carr, Sir Peter Derek, Kt., CBE
Carr, Sir Roger Martyn, Kt.
Carrick, *Hon.* Sir John Leslie, KCMG
Carrick, Sir Roger John, KCMG, LVO
Carruthers, Sir Ian James, Kt., OBE
Carsberg, *Prof.* Sir Bryan Victor, Kt.
Carter, Sir Andrew Nicholas, Kt., OBE
Carter, Sir David Anthony, Kt.
Carter, *Prof.* Sir David Craig, Kt., FRCSE, FRCSGLAS, FRCPE
Carter, Sir John Alexander, Kt.
Carter, Sir John Gordon Thomas, Kt.
Carter, *Lt-Gen.* Sir Nicholas Patrick, KCB, CBE, DSO
Cartledge, Sir Bryan George, KCMG
Caruna, *Hon.* Sir Peter Richard, KCMG, QC
†Cary, Sir Nicholas Robert Hugh, Bt. (1955)
Cash, Sir Andrew John, Kt., OBE
Cash, Sir William Nigel Paul, Kt.
Cass, Sir Geoffrey Arthur, Kt.
Cassel, Sir Timothy Felix Harold, Bt. (1920)
Cassels, Sir John Seton, Kt., CB
Cassels, *Adm.* Sir Simon Alastair Cassillis, KCB, CBE
Cassidi, *Adm.* Sir (Arthur) Desmond, GCB
Castell, Sir William Martin, Kt.
Catto, *Prof.* Sir Graeme Robertson Dawson, Kt.
Cave, Sir John Charles, Bt. (1896)
Cave-Browne-Cave, Sir John Robert Charles, Bt. (1641)
Cayley, Sir Digby William David, Bt. (1661)
Cazalet, *Hon.* Sir Edward Stephen, Kt.
Cazalet, Sir Peter Grenville, Kt.
Cecil, *Rear-Adm.* Sir (Oswald) Nigel Amherst, KBE, CB
Chadwick, *Rt. Hon.* Sir John Murray, Kt.
Chadwick, Sir Joshua Kenneth Burton, Bt. (1935)
Chadwyck-Healey, Sir Charles Edward, Bt. (1919)
Chakrabarti, Sir Sumantra, KCB
Chalmers, Sir Iain Geoffrey, Kt.
Chalmers, Sir Neil Robert, Kt.
Chalstrey, Sir (Leonard) John, Kt., MD, FRCS
Chan, *Rt. Hon.* Sir Julius, GCMG, KBE
Chan, Sir Thomas Kok, Kt., OBE
Chance, Sir (George) Jeremy ffolliott, Bt. (1900)
Chandler, Sir Colin Michael, Kt.
Chantler, *Prof.* Sir Cyril, Kt., MD, FRCP
Chaplin, Sir Malcolm Hilbery, Kt., CBE
Chapman, Sir David Robert Macgowan, Bt. (1958)
Chapman, Sir Frank, Kt.

Chapman, Sir George Alan, Kt.
Chapple, *Field Marshal* Sir John Lyon, GCB, CBE
Charles, *Hon.* Sir Arthur William Hessin, Kt.
Charlton, Sir Robert (Bobby), Kt., CBE
Charnley, Sir (William) John, Kt., CB, FRENG
Chartres, *Rt. Revd and Rt. Hon.* Richard John Carew, KCVO
†Chaytor, Sir Bruce Gordon, Bt. (1831)
Checketts, *Sqn. Ldr.* Sir David John, KCVO
Checkland, Sir Michael, Kt.
Cheshire, Sir Ian Michael, Kt.
Cheshire, *Air Chief Marshal* Sir John Anthony, KBE, CB
Chessells, Sir Arthur David (Tim), Kt.
†Chetwynd, Sir Peter James Talbot, Bt. (1795)
Cheyne, Sir Patrick John Lister, Bt. (1908)
Chichester, Sir James Henry Edward, Bt. (1641)
Chichester-Clark, Sir Robin, Kt.
Chilcot, *Rt. Hon.* Sir John Anthony, GCB
Child, Sir (Coles John) Jeremy, Bt. (1919)
Chilwell, *Hon.* Sir Muir Fitzherbert, Kt.
Chinn, Sir Trevor Edwin, Kt., CVO
†Chinubhai, Sir Prashat, Bt. (1913)
Chipperfield, *Prof.* Sir David Alan, Kt., CBE
Chipperfield, Sir Geoffrey Howes, KCB
Chisholm, Sir John Alexander Raymond, Kt., FRENG
†Chitty, Sir Andrew Edward Willes, Bt. (1924)
Cholmeley, Sir Hugh John Frederick Sebastian, Bt. (1806)
Chow, Sir Chung Kong, Kt.
Chow, Sir Henry Francis, Kt., OBE
Christopher, Sir Duncan Robin Carmichael, KBE, CMG
Chung, Sir Sze-yuen, GBE, FRENG
Clark, *Prof.* Sir Christopher Munro, Kt.
Clark, Sir Francis Drake, Bt. (1886)
Clark, Sir John Arnold, Kt.
Clark, Sir Jonathan George, Bt. (1917)
Clark, Sir Terence Joseph, KBE, CMG, CVO
Clark, Sir Timothy Charles, KBE
Clarke, Sir (Charles Mansfield) Tobias, Bt. (1831)
Clarke, *Rt. Hon.* Sir Christopher Simon Courtenay Stephenson, Kt.
Clarke, *Hon.* Sir David Clive, Kt.
Clarke, Sir Jonathan Dennis, Kt.
Clarke, Sir Paul Robert Virgo, KCVO
Clarke, Sir Robert Cyril, Kt.
Clarke, Sir Rupert Grant Alexander, Bt. (1882)
Clay, Sir Edward, KCMG
Clay, Sir Richard Henry, Bt. (1841)
Clayton, Sir David Robert, Bt. (1732)
Cleaver, Sir Anthony Brian, Kt.
Clementi, Sir David Cecil, Kt.
Clerk, Sir Robert Maxwell, Bt. (S. 1679), OBE
Clerke, Sir Francis Ludlow Longueville, Bt. (1660)

Clifford, Sir Roger Joseph, Bt. (1887)
Clifford, Sir Timothy Peter Plint, Kt.
Coates, Sir Anthony Robert Milnes, Bt. (1911)
Coates, Sir David Frederick Charlton, Bt. (1921)
Coats, Sir Alastair Francis Stuart, Bt. (1905)
Cobb, *Hon.* Sir Stephen William Scott, Kt.
Cochrane, Sir (Henry) Marc (Sursock), Bt. (1903)
†Cockburn, Sir Charles Christopher, Bt. (S. 1671)
Cockburn-Campbell, Sir Alexander Thomas, Bt. (1821)
Cockell, Sir Merrick, Kt.
Cockshaw, Sir Alan, Kt., FRENG
Codrington, Sir Christopher George Wayne, Bt. (1876)
Codrington, Sir Giles Peter, Bt. (1721)
Codron, Sir Michael Victor, Kt., CBE
Coghill, Sir Patrick Kendal Farley, Bt. (1778)
Coghlin, *Rt. Hon.* Sir Patrick, Kt.
Cohen, Sir Ivor Harold, Kt., CBE, TD
Cohen, *Prof.* Sir Philip, Kt., PHD, FRS
Cohen, Sir Ronald, Kt.
Cole, Sir (Robert) William, Kt.
Coleman, Sir Robert John, KCMG
Coleridge, *Hon.* Sir Paul James Duke, Kt.
Coles, Sir (Arthur) John, GCMG
Colfox, Sir Philip John, Bt. (1939)
Collas, Sir Richard John, Kt.
Collett, Sir Ian Seymour, Bt. (1934)
Collier, Sir Paul, Kt., CBE
Collins, Sir Alan Stanley, KCVO, CMG
Collins, *Hon.* Sir Andrew David, Kt.
Collins, Sir Bryan Thomas Alfred, Kt., OBE, QFSM
Collins, Sir John Alexander, Kt
Collins, Sir Kenneth Darlingston, Kt.
Collins, *Dr* Sir Kevan Arthur, Kt.
Collins, *Prof.* Sir Rory Edwards, Kt.
Collyear, Sir John Gowen, Kt.
Colman, *Hon.* Sir Anthony David, Kt.
Colman, Sir Michael Jeremiah, Bt. (1907)
Colman, Sir Timothy, KG
Colquhoun of Luss, Sir Malcolm Rory, Bt. (1786)
Colt, Sir Edward William Dutton, Bt. (1694)
Colthurst, Sir Charles St John, Bt. (I. 1744)
Conant, Sir John Ernest Michael, Bt. (1954)
Conner, *Rt. Revd* David John, KCVO
Connery, Sir Sean, Kt.
Connor, Sir William Joseph, Kt.
Conran, Sir Terence Orby, Kt.
Cons, *Hon.* Sir Derek, Kt.
Constantinou, Sir Kosta George, Kt., OBE
Constantinou, Sir Theophilus George, Kt., CBE
Conway, *Prof.* Sir Gordon Richard, KCMG, FRS
Cook, Sir Christopher Wymondham Rayner Herbert, Bt. (1886)

Cook, *Prof.* Sir Peter Frederic Chester, Kt.

Cooke, *Col.* Sir David William Perceval, Bt. (1661)

Cooke, *Hon.* Sir Jeremy Lionel, Kt.

Cooke, *Prof.* Sir Ronald Urwick, Kt.

Cooksey, Sir David James Scott, GBE

Cooper, *Prof.* Sir Cary Lynn, Kt., CBE

Cooper, *Gen.* Sir George Leslie Conroy, GCB, MC

Cooper, Sir Richard Adrian, Bt. (1905)

Cooper, Sir Robert Francis, KCMG, MVO

Cooper, *Maj.-Gen.* Sir Simon Christie, GCVO

Cooper, Sir William Daniel Charles, Bt. (1863)

Coote, Sir Christopher John, Bt. (I. 1621), *Premier Baronet of Ireland*

Copisarow, Sir Alcon Charles, Kt.

Corbett, *Maj.-Gen.* Sir Robert John Swan, KCVO, CB

Cordy-Simpson, *Lt.-Gen.* Sir Roderick Alexander, KBE, CB

Corfield, Sir Kenneth George, Kt., FRENG

Corness, Sir Colin Ross, Kt.

Corry, Sir James Michael, Bt. (1885)

Cortazzi, Sir (Henry Arthur) Hugh, GCMG

Cory, Sir (Clinton Charles) Donald, Bt. (1919)

Cory-Wright, Sir Richard Michael, Bt. (1903)

Cossons, Sir Neil, Kt., OBE

Cotter, Sir Patrick Laurence Delaval, Bt. (I. 1763)

Cotterell, Sir John Henry Geers, Bt. (1805)

†Cotts, Sir Richard Crichton Mitchell, Bt. (1921)

Coulson, *Hon.* Sir Peter David William, Kt.

Couper, Sir James George, Bt. (1841)

Courtenay, Sir Thomas Daniel, Kt.

Cousins, *Air Chief Marshal* Sir David, KCB, AFC

Coville, *Air Marshal* Sir Christopher Charles Cotton, KCB

Cowan, *Gen.* Sir Samuel, KCB, CBE

Coward, *Lt-Gen.* Sir Gary Robert, KBE, CB, OBE

Coward, *Vice-Adm.* Sir John Francis, KCB, DSO

Cowper-Coles, Sir Sherard Louis, KCMG, LVO

Cox, Sir Alan George, Kt., CBE

Cox, *Prof.* Sir David Roxbee, Kt.

Cox, Sir George Edwin, Kt.

Craft, *Prof.* Sir Alan William, Kt.

Cragnolini, Sir Luciano, Kt.

Craig, Sir (Albert) James (Macqueen), GCMG

Craig-Cooper, Sir (Frederick Howard) Michael, Kt., CBE, TD

Crane, *Prof.* Sir Peter Robert, Kt.

Cranston, *Hon.* Sir Ross Frederick, Kt.

Craufurd, Sir Robert James, Bt. (1781)

Craven, Sir John Anthony, Kt.

Craven, Sir Philip Lee, Kt., MBE

Crawford, *Prof.* Sir Frederick William, Kt., FRENG

Crawford, Sir Robert William Kenneth, Kt. CBE

Crawley-Boevey, Sir Thomas Michael Blake, Bt. (1784)

Cresswell, *Hon.* Sir Peter John, Kt.

Crew, Sir (Michael) Edward, Kt., QPM

Crewe, *Prof.* Sir Ivor Martin, Kt.

Crisp, Sir John Charles, Bt. (1913)

Critchett, Sir Charles George Montague, Bt. (1908)

Crittin, *Hon.* Sir John Luke, KBE

Croft, Sir Owen Glendower, Bt. (1671)

Croft, Sir Thomas Stephen Hutton, Bt. (1818)

†Crofton, Sir Hugh Denis, Bt. (1801)

†Crofton, Sir Julian Malby, Bt. (1838)

Crombie, Sir Alexander, Kt.

Crompton, Sir Dan, Kt., CBE, QPM

Cropper, Sir James Anthony, KCVO

Crossley, Sir Sloan Nicholas, Bt. (1909)

Crowe, Sir Brian Lee, KCMG

Cruickshank, Sir Donald Gordon, Kt.

Cruthers, Sir James Winter, Kt.

Cubie, *Dr* Sir Andrew, Kt., CBE

Cubitt, Sir Hugh Guy, Kt., CBE

Cubitt, *Maj.-Gen.* Sir William George, KCVO, CBE

Cullen, Sir (Edward) John, Kt., FRENG

Culme-Seymour, Sir Michael Patrick, Bt. (1809)

Culpin, Sir Robert Paul, Kt.

Cummins, Sir Michael John Austin, Kt.

Cunliffe, *Prof.* Sir Barrington, Kt., CBE

Cunliffe, Sir David Ellis, Bt. (1759)

Cunliffe, Sir Jonathan Stephen, Kt., CB

Cunliffe-Owen, Sir Hugo Dudley, Bt. (1920)

Cunningham, *Lt.-Gen.* Sir Hugh Patrick, KBE

Cunningham, *Prof.* Sir John, KCVO

Cunningham, Sir Roger Keith, Kt., CBE

Cunningham, Sir Thomas Anthony, Kt.

Cunynghame, Sir Andrew David Francis, Bt. (S. 1702)

†Currie, Sir Bradley Mark Higgins, Bt. (1847)

Curtain, Sir Michael, KBE

Curtis, Sir Barry John, Kt.

Curtis, *Hon.* Sir Richard Herbert, Kt.

Curtis, Sir Edward Philip, Bt. (1802)

Cuschieri, *Prof.* Sir Alfred, Kt.

Dain, Sir David John Michael, KCVO

Dales, Sir Richard Nigel, KCVO

Dalrymple-Hay, Sir Malcolm John Robert, Bt. (1798)

†Dalrymple-White, Sir Jan Hew, Bt. (1926)

Dalton, Sir David Nigel, Kt.

Dalton, *Vice-Adm.* Sir Geoffrey Thomas James Oliver, GCB

Dalton, Sir Richard John, KCMG

Dalton, *Air Chief Marshal* Sir Stephen Gary George, GCB

Dalyell, Sir Tam (Thomas), Bt. (NS 1685)

Dancer, Sir Eric, KCVO, CBE

Dangoor, Sir Naim Eliahou, Kt., CBE

Daniel, Sir John Sagar, Kt., DSC

Darell, Sir Guy Jeffrey Adair, Bt. (1795)

Darrington, Sir Michael John, Kt.

Darroch, Sir Nigel Kim, KCMG

Dasgupta, *Prof.* Sir Partha Sarathi, Kt.

Dashwood, *Prof.* Sir (Arthur) Alan, KCMG, CBE, QC

Dashwood, Sir Edward John Francis, Bt. (1707), *Premier Baronet of Great Britain*

Dashwood, Sir Frederick George Mahon, Bt. (1684)

Daunt, Sir Timothy Lewis Achilles, KCMG

David, *His Hon.* Sir Robin (Robert) Daniel George, Kt.

Davidson, Sir Martin Stuart, KCMG

Davies, *Prof.* Sir David Evan Naughton, Kt., CBE, FRS, FRENG

Davies, Sir David John, Kt.

Davies, Sir Frank John, Kt., CBE

Davies, *Prof.* Sir Graeme John, Kt., FRENG

Davies, Sir John Howard, Kt.

Davies, Sir John Michael, KCB

Davies, Sir Rhys Everson, Kt., QC

Davis, Sir Andrew Frank, Kt., CBE

Davis, Sir Crispin Henry Lamert, Kt.

Davis, Sir John Gilbert, Bt. (1946)

Davis, Sir Michael Lawrence, Kt.

Davis, *Rt. Hon.* Sir Nigel Anthony Lambert, Kt.

Davis, Sir Peter John, Kt.

Davis, *Hon.* Sir William Easthorpe, Kt., QC

Davis-Goff, Sir Robert (William), Bt. (1905)

†Davson, Sir George Trenchard Simon, Bt. (1927)

Dawanincura, Sir John Norbert, Kt., OBE

Dawbarn, Sir Simon Yelverton, KCVO, CMG

Dawson, *Hon.* Sir Daryl Michael, KBE, CB

Dawson, Sir Nicholas Antony Trevor, Bt. (1920)

Dawtry, Sir Alan (Graham), Kt., CBE, TD

Day, Sir Barry Stuart, Kt., OBE

Day, *Air Chief Marshal* Sir John Romney, KCB, OBE, ADC

Day, Sir (Judson) Graham, Kt.

Day, Sir Michael John, Kt., OBE

Day, Sir Simon James, Kt.

Day-Lewis, Sir Daniel Michael Blake, Kt.

Deane, *Hon.* Sir William Patrick, KBE

Dearlove, Sir Richard Billing, KCMG, OBE

†Debenham, Sir Thomas Adam, Bt. (1931)

de Deney, Sir Geoffrey Ivor, KCVO

Deegan, Sir Michael, Kt., CBE

Deeny, *Hon.* Sir Donnell Justin Patrick, Kt.

De Haan, Sir Roger Michael, Kt., CBE

De Halpert, *Rear-Adm.* Sir Jeremy Michael, KCVO, CB

de Hoghton, Sir (Richard) Bernard (Cuthbert), Bt. (1611)

De la Bère, Sir Cameron, Bt. (1953)

de la Rue, Sir Andrew George Ilay, Bt. (1898)

Dellow, Sir John Albert, Kt., CBE

Delves, *Lt.-Gen.* Sir Cedric Norman George, KBE

Denholm, Sir John Ferguson (Ian), Kt., CBE

Denison-Smith, *Lt.-Gen.* Sir Anthony Arthur, KBE

Denny, Sir Charles Alistair Maurice, Bt. (1913)

†Denny, Sir Piers Anthony de Waltham, Bt. (I. 1782)

Derbyshire, Sir Andrew George, Kt.

De Silva, *Rt. Hon.* Sir (George) Desmond Lorenz, Kt., QC

de Trafford, Sir John Humphrey, Bt. (1841)

Devane, Sir Ciaran Gearoid, Kt.

Deverell, *Lt-Gen.* Sir Christopher Michael, KCB, MBE

Deverell, *Gen.* Sir John Freegard, KCB, OBE

De Ville, Sir Harold Godfrey Oscar, Kt., CBE

Devine, *Prof.* Sir Thomas Martin, Kt., OBE, FRSE

Devitt, Sir James Hugh Thomas, Bt. (1916)

de Waal, Sir (Constant Henrik) Henry, KCB, QC

Dewey, Sir Anthony Hugh, Bt. (1917)

De Witt, Sir Ronald Wayne, Kt.

Diamond, *Prof.* Sir Ian David, Kt., FRSE

Dick-Lauder, Sir Piers Robert, Bt. (S. 1690)

Dilke, Revd Charles John Wentworth, Bt. (1862)

Dilnot, Sir Andrew William, Kt., CBE

Dillon, Sir Andrew Patrick, Kt., CBE

Dilley, Sir Philip Graham, Kt.

Dillwyn-Venables-Llewelyn, Sir John Michael, Bt. (1890)

Dingemans, *Hon.* Sir James Michael, Kt.

Dixon, Sir Jeremy, Kt.

Dixon, Sir Jonathan Mark, Bt. (1919)

Dixon, *Dr* Sir Michael, Kt.

Dixon, Sir Peter John Bellett, Kt.

Djanogly, Sir Harry Ari Simon, Kt., CBE

Dobson, *Vice-Adm.* Sir David Stuart, KBE

Dollery, Sir Colin Terence, Kt.

Don-Wauchope, Sir Roger (Hamilton), Bt. (S. 1667)

Donald, Sir Alan Ewen, KCMG

Donaldson, *Prof.* Sir Liam Joseph, Kt.

Donaldson, *Prof.* Sir Simon Kirwan, Kt.

Donne, Sir John Christopher, Kt.

Donnelly, Sir Joseph Brian, KBE, CMG

Dorman, Sir Philip Henry Keppel, Bt. (1923)

Douglas, *Prof.* Sir Neil James, Kt.

Douglas, *Hon.* Sir Roger Owen, Kt.

Dove, *Hon.* Sir Ian Williams, Kt., QC

Dowell, Sir Anthony James, Kt., CBE

Dowling, Sir Robert, Kt.

Downes, *Prof.* Sir Charles Peter, Kt., OBE, FRSE

Downey, Sir Gordon Stanley, KCB

Doyle, Sir Reginald Derek Henry, Kt., CBE

D'Oyly, Sir Hadley Gregory Bt. (1663)

Drewry, *Lt.-Gen.* Sir Christopher Francis, KCB, CBE

Drinkwater, Sir John Muir, Kt., QC

Dryden, Sir John Stephen Gyles, Bt. (1733 and 1795)

Duberly, Sir Archibald Hugh, KCVO, CBE

du Cann, *Rt. Hon.* Sir Edward Dillon Lott, KBE

Duckworth, Sir James Edward Dyce, Bt. (1909)

du Cros, Sir Julian Claude Arthur Mallet, Bt. (1916)

Dudley-Williams, Sir Alastair Edgcumbe James, Bt. (1964)

Duff, *Prof.* Sir Gordon William, Kt.

Duff-Gordon, Sir Andrew Cosmo Lewis, Bt. (1813)

Duffell, *Lt.-Gen.* Sir Peter Royson, KCB, CBE, MC

Duffy, Sir (Albert) (Edward) Patrick, Kt., PHD

†Dugdale, Sir (William) Matthew Stratford, Bt. (1936)

Duggin, Sir Thomas Joseph, Kt.

Dunbar, Sir Archibald Ranulph, Bt. (S. 1700)

Dunbar, Sir James Michael, Bt. (S. 1694)

Dunbar, Sir Robert Drummond Cospatrick, Bt. (S. 1698)

Dunbar of Hempriggs, Sir Richard Francis, Bt. (S. 1706)

Dunbar-Nasmith, *Prof.* Sir James Duncan, Kt., CBE

Duncan, Sir James Blair, Kt.

Dunford, *Dr* Sir John Ernest, Kt., OBE

Dunlop, Sir Thomas, Bt. (1916)

Dunne, Sir Martin, KCVO

Dunne, Sir Thomas Raymond, KG, KCVO

Dunning, Sir Simon William Patrick, Bt. (1930)

Dunnington-Jefferson, Sir John Alexander, Bt. (1958)

Dunstone, Sir Charles William, Kt., CVO

Dunt, *Vice-Adm.* Sir John Hugh, KCB

Duntze, Sir Daniel Evans, Bt. (1774)

Dupre, Sir Tumun, Kt., MBE

Durand, Sir Edward Alan Christopher David Percy, Bt. (1892)

Durant, Sir (Robert) Anthony (Bevis), Kt.

Durie, Sir David Robert Campbell, KCMG

Durrant, Sir William Alexander Estridge, Bt. (1784)

Duthie, Sir Robert Grieve (Robin), Kt., CBE

Dutton, *Lt.-Gen.* Sir James Benjamin, KCB, CBE

Dwyer, Sir Joseph Anthony, Kt.

Dyke, Sir David William Hart, Bt. (1677)

Dymock, *Vice-Adm.* Sir Anthony Knox, KBE, CB

Dyson, Sir James, Kt., CBE (Lord Dyson)

Dyson, *Rt. Hon.* Sir John Anthony, Kt.

Eady, *Hon.* Sir David, Kt.

†Eardley-Wilmot, Sir Benjamin John Assheton, Bt. (1821)

Earle, Sir (Hardman) George (Algernon), Bt. (1869)

Eastwood, *Prof.* Sir David Stephen, Kt.

Eaton, *Adm.* Sir Kenneth John, GBE, KCB

Eberle, *Adm.* Sir James Henry Fuller, GCB

Ebrahim, Sir (Mahomed) Currimbhoy, Bt. (1910)

Eddington, Sir Roderick Ian, Kt.

Eder, *Hon.* Sir Henry Bernard, Kt.

Edis, *Hon.* Sir Andrew Jeremy Coulter, Kt., QC

Edge, *Capt.* Sir (Philip) Malcolm, KCVO

†Edge, Sir William, Bt. (1937)

Edmonstone, Sir Archibald Bruce Charles, Bt. (1774)

Edward, *Rt. Hon.* Sir David Alexander Ogilvy, KCMG

Edwardes, Sir Michael Owen, Kt.

Edwards, Sir Christopher John Churchill, Bt. (1866)

Edwards, *Prof.* Sir Christopher Richard Watkin, Kt.

Edwards, Sir Gareth Owen, Kt., CBE

Edwards, Sir Llewellyn Roy, Kt.

Edwards, *Prof.* Sir Michael, OBE

Edwards, Sir Robert Paul, Kt.

†Edwards-Moss, Sir David John, Bt. (1868)

Edwards-Stuart, *Hon.* Sir Antony James Cobham, Kt.

Egan, Sir John Leopold, Kt.

Egerton, Sir William de Malpas, Bt. (1617)

Ehrman, Sir William Geoffrey, KCMG

Eichelbaum, *Rt. Hon.* Sir Thomas, GBE

Elder, Sir Mark Philip, Kt., CBE

Eldon, Sir Stewart Graham, KCMG, OBE

Elias, *Rt. Hon.* Sir Patrick, Kt.

Eliott of Stobs, Sir Charles Joseph Alexander, Bt. (S. 1666)

Elliot, Sir Gerald Henry, Kt.

Elliott, Sir Clive Christopher Hugh, Bt. (1917)

Elliott, Sir David Murray, KCMG, CB

Elliott, *Prof.* Sir John Huxtable, Kt., FBA

Elliott, *Prof.* Sir Roger James, Kt., FRS

Ellis, Sir Herbert Douglas, Kt., OBE

Ellis, Sir Vernon James, Kt.

Ellwood, Sir Peter Brian, Kt., CBE

†Elphinstone, Sir Alexander, Bt. (S. 1701)

Elphinstone, Sir John Howard Main, Bt. (1816)

Elton, Sir Arnold, Kt., CBE

Elton, Sir Charles Abraham Grierson, Bt. (1717)

Elvidge, Sir John, KCB

Elwes, *Dr* Sir Henry William, KCVO

Elwes, Sir Jeremy Vernon, Kt., CBE

Elwood, Sir Brian George Conway, Kt., CBE

Elworthy, *Air Cdre. Hon.* Sir Timothy Charles, KCVO, CBE

Enderby, *Prof.* Sir John Edwin, Kt. CBE, FRS

Engle, Sir George Lawrence Jose, KCB, QC

English, Sir Terence Alexander Hawthorne, KBE, FRCS

Ennals, Sir Paul Martin, Kt., CBE

Epstein, *Prof.* Sir (Michael) Anthony, Kt., CBE, FRS

Errington, *Col.* Sir Geoffrey Frederick, Bt. (1963), OBE

Erskine, Sir (Thomas) Peter Neil, Bt. (1821)

Erskine-Hill, Sir Alexander Rodger, Bt. (1945)

Esmonde, Sir Thomas Francis Grattan, Bt. (I. 1629)

Esplen, Sir John Graham, Bt. (1921)

Esquivel, *Rt. Hon.* Sir Manuel, KCMG

Essenhigh, *Adm.* Sir Nigel Richard, GCB

Etherington, Sir Stuart James, Kt.

Etherton, *Rt. Hon.* Sir Terence Michael Elkan Barnet, Kt.

Evans, Sir Anthony Adney, Bt. (1920)

Evans, *Rt. Hon.* Sir Anthony Howell Meurig, Kt., RD

Evans, *Prof.* Sir Christopher Thomas, Kt., OBE

Evans, *Air Chief Marshal* Sir David George, GCB, CBE

Evans, *Hon.* Sir David Roderick, Kt.

Evans, Sir Harold Matthew, Kt.

Evans, *Prof.* Sir John Grimley, Kt., FRCP

Evans, Sir John Stanley, Kt., QPM

Evans, *Prof.* Sir Martin John, Kt., FRS

Evans, Sir Richard Harry, Kt., CBE

Evans, *Prof.* Sir Richard John, Kt.

Evans, Sir Robert, Kt., CBE, FRENG

Evans-Lombe, *Hon.* Sir Edward Christopher, Kt.

†Evans-Tipping, Sir David Gwynne, Bt. (1913)

Everard, Sir Henry Peter Charles, Bt. (1911)

Everington, *Dr.* Sir Anthony Herbert, Kt., OBE

Every, Sir Henry John Michael, Bt. (1641)

Ewart, Sir William Michael, Bt. (1887)

Eyre, Sir Reginald Edwin, Kt.

Eyre, Sir Richard Charles Hastings, Kt., CBE

Fagge, Sir John Christopher Frederick, Bt. (1660)

Fahy, Sir Peter, Kt., QPM

Fairbairn, Sir (James) Brooke, Bt. (1869)

Fairlie-Cuninghame, Sir Robert Henry, Bt. (S. 1630)

Fairweather, Sir Patrick Stanislaus, KCMG

Faldo, Sir Nicholas Alexander, Kt., MBE

†Falkiner, Sir Benjamin Simon Patrick, Bt. (I. 1778)

Fall, Sir Brian James Proetel, GCVO, KCMG

Fang, *Prof.* Sir Harry, Kt., CBE

Fareed, Sir Djamil Sheik, Kt.

Farmer, Sir Thomas, Kt., CVO, CBE

Farquhar, Sir Michael Fitzroy Henry, Bt. (1796)

Farquharson, Sir Angus Durie Miller, KCVO, OBE

Farrell, Sir Terence, Kt., CBE

Farrer, Sir (Charles) Matthew, GCVO

Farrington, Sir Henry William, Bt. (1818)

Fat, Sir (Maxime) Edouard (Lim Man) Lim, Kt.

Faulkner, Sir (James) Dennis (Compton), Kt., CBE, VRD

Fay, Sir (Humphrey) Michael Gerard, Kt.

Fayrer, Sir John Lang Macpherson, Bt. (1896)

Feachem, *Prof.* Sir Richard George Andrew, KBE

Fean, Sir Thomas Vincent, KCVO

Feilden, Sir Henry Rudyard, Bt. (1846)

Feldmann, *Prof.* Sir Marc, Kt.

Fell, Sir David, KCB

Fender, Sir Brian Edward Frederick, Kt., CMG, PHD

Fenn, Sir Nicholas Maxted, GCMG

Fenwick, Sir Leonard Raymond, Kt., CBE

Fergus, Sir Howard Archibald, KBE

Ferguson, Sir Alexander Chapman, Kt., CBE

Ferguson-Davie, Sir Michael, Bt. (1847)

Fergusson of Kilkerran, Sir Charles, Bt. (S. 1703)

Fergusson, Sir Ewan Alastair John, GCMG, GCVO

Ferris, *Hon.* Sir Francis Mursell, Kt., TD

Fersht, *Prof.* Sir Alan Roy, Kt., FRS

ffolkes, Sir Robert Francis Alexander, Bt. (1774), OBE

Field, Sir Malcolm David, Kt.

Field, *Hon.* Sir Richard Alan, Kt.

Fielding, Sir Leslie, KCMG

Fields, Sir Allan Clifford, KCMG

Fieldsend, *Hon.* Sir John Charles Rowell, KBE

Fiennes, Sir Ranulph Twisleton-Wykeham, Bt. (1916), OBE

Figgis, Sir Anthony St John Howard, KCVO, CMG

Finch, Sir Robert Gerard, Kt.

Finlay, Sir David Ronald James Bell, Bt. (1964)

Finlayson, Sir Garet Orlando, KCMG, OBE

Fish, *Hon.* Sir David Royden, Kt.

†Fison, Sir Charles William, Bt. (1905)

FitzGerald, Sir Adrian James Andrew, Bt. (1880)

†Fitzgerald, *Revd* Daniel Patrick, Bt. (1903)

FitzHerbert, Sir Richard Ranulph, Bt. (1784)

Fitzpatrick, *Air Marshal* Sir John Bernard, KBE, CB

Flanagan, Sir Ronald, GBE, QPM

Flaux, *Hon.* Sir Julian Martin, Kt.

Floud, *Prof.* Sir Roderick Castle, Kt.

Floyd, *Rt. Hon.* Sir Christopher David, Kt.

Floyd, Sir Giles Henry Charles, Bt. (1816)

Foley, *Lt.-Gen.* Sir John Paul, KCB, OBE, MC

Follett, *Prof.* Sir Brian Keith, Kt., FRS

Forbes of Craigievar, Sir Andrew Iain Ochoncar, Bt. (S. 1630)

Forbes, *Adm.* Sir Ian Andrew, KCB, CBE

Forbes, Sir James Thomas Stewart, Bt. (1823)

Forbes, *Vice-Adm.* Sir John Morrison, KCB

Forbes, *Hon.* Sir Thayne John, Kt.

†Forbes Adam, Revd Stephen Timothy Beilby, Bt. (1917)

Forbes-Leith, Sir George Ian David, Bt. (1923)

Ford, *Lt.-Col.* Sir Andrew Charles, KCVO

Ford, Sir Andrew Russell, Bt. (1929)

Ford, Sir David Robert, KBE, LVO

Ford, Sir John Archibald, KCMG, MC

Ford, *Gen.* Sir Robert Cyril, GCB, CBE

Forestier-Walker, Sir Michael Leolin, Bt. (1835)

Forrest, *Prof.* Sir (Andrew) Patrick (McEwen), Kt.

Forsyth-Johnson, Sir Bruce Joseph, Kt., CBE (Bruce Forsyth)

Forte, *Hon.* Sir Rocco John Vincent, Kt.

Forwood, Sir Peter Noel, Bt. (1895)

Foskett, *Hon.* Sir David Robert, Kt.

Foster, Sir Andrew William, Kt.

Foster, *Prof.* Sir Christopher David, Kt.

†Foster, Sir Saxby Gregory, Bt. (1930)

Foulkes, Sir Arthur Alexander, GCMG

Fountain, *Hon.* Sir Cyril Stanley Smith, Kt.

Fowke, Sir David Frederick Gustavus, Bt. (1814)

Fowler, Sir (Edward) Michael Coulson, Kt.

Fox, Sir Christopher, Kt., QPM

Fox, Sir Paul Leonard, Kt., CBE

Francis, Sir Horace William Alexander, Kt., CBE, FRENG

Francis, Sir Robert Anthony, Kt., QC

Frank, Sir Robert Andrew, Bt. (1920)

Franklin, Sir Michael David Milroy, KCB, CMG

Fraser, Sir Charles Annand, KCVO

Fraser, Sir Iain Michael Duncan, Bt. (1943)

Fraser, Sir James Murdo, KBE

Fraser, Sir Simon James, KCMG

Fraser, Sir William Kerr, GCB

Frayling, *Prof.* Sir Christopher John, Kt.

Frederick, Sir Christopher St John, Bt. (1723)

Freedman, *Rt. Hon. Prof.* Sir Lawrence David, KCMG, CBE

Freeman, Sir James Robin, Bt. (1945)

French, *Air Marshal* Sir Joseph Charles, KCB, CMG

Frere, *Vice-Adm.* Sir Richard Tobias, KCB

Fretwell, Sir (Major) John (Emsley), GCMG

Friend *Prof.* Sir Richard Henry, Kt.

Froggatt, Sir Peter, Kt.

Fry, Sir Graham Holbrook, KCMG

Fry, *Lt.-Gen.* Sir Robert Allan, KCB, CBE

Fry, *Dr* Sir Roger Gordon, Kt., OBE

Fulford, *Rt. Hon.* Sir Adrian Bruce, Kt.

Fuller, Sir James Henry Fleetwood, Bt. (1910)

Fulton, *Lt.-Gen.* Sir Robert Henry Gervase, KBE

Furness, Sir Stephen Roberts, Bt. (1913)

Gage, *Rt. Hon.* Sir William Marcus, Kt., QC
Gains, Sir John Christopher, Kt.
Gainsford, Sir Ian Derek, Kt.
Gale, Sir Roger James, Kt.
Galsworthy, Sir Anthony Charles, KCMG
Galway, Sir James, Kt., OBE
Gamble, Sir David Hugh Norman, Bt. (1897)
Gambon, Sir Michael John, Kt., CBE
Gammell, Sir William Benjamin Bowring, Kt.
Gardiner, Sir John Eliot, Kt., CBE
Gardner, *Prof.* Sir Richard Lavenham, Kt.
Gardner, Sir Roy Alan, Kt.
Garland, *Hon.* Sir Patrick Neville, Kt.
Garland, *Hon.* Sir Ransley Victor, KBE
Garland, *Dr* Sir Trevor, KBE
Garnett, *Adm.* Sir Ian David Graham, KCB
Garnier, Sir Edward Henry, Kt., QC
Garnier, *Rear-Adm.* Sir John, KCVO, CBE
Garrard, Sir David Eardley, Kt.
Garrett, Sir Anthony Peter, Kt., CBE
Garrick, Sir Ronald, Kt., CBE, FRENG
Garthwaite, Sir (William) Mark (Charles), Bt. (1919)
Gass, Sir Simon Lawrance, KCMG, CVO
Geidt, *Rt. Hon.* Sir Christopher, KCB, KCVO, OBE
Geim, *Prof.* Sir Andre Konstantin, Kt.
Geno, Sir Makena Viora, KBE
Gent, Sir Christopher Charles, Kt.
George, *Prof.* Sir Charles Frederick, Kt., MD, FRCP
George, Sir Richard William, Kt., CVO
Gerken, *Vice-Adm.* Sir Robert William Frank, KCB, CBE
Gershon, Sir Peter Oliver, Kt., CBE
Gethin, Sir Richard Joseph St Lawrence, Bt. (I. 1665)
Gibbings, Sir Peter Walter, Kt.
Gibbons, Sir William Edward Doran, Bt. (1752)
Gibbs, *Hon.* Sir Richard John Hedley, Kt.
Gibbs, Sir Roger Geoffrey, Kt.
†Gibson, *Revd* Christopher Herbert, Bt. (1931)
Gibson, Sir Ian, Kt., CBE
Gibson, Sir Kenneth Archibald, Kt.
Gibson, *Rt. Hon.* Sir Peter Leslie, Kt.
Gibson-Craig-Carmichael, Sir David Peter William, Bt. (S. 1702 and 1831)
Gieve, Sir Edward John Watson, KCB
Giffard, Sir (Charles) Sydney (Rycroft), KCMG
Gifford, Sir Michael Roger, Kt.
Gilbart, *Hon.* Sir Andrew James, Kt., QC
Gilbart-Denham, *Lt.-Col.* Sir Seymour Vivian, KCVO
Gilbert, *Air Chief Marshal* Sir Joseph Alfred, KCB, CBE
†Gilbey, Sir Walter Gavin, Bt. (1893)
Gill, Sir Anthony Keith, Kt.
Gill, Sir Robin Denys, KCVO

Gillam, Sir Patrick John, Kt.
Gillen, *Hon.* Sir John de Winter, Kt.
Gillett, Sir Nicholas Danvers Penrose, Bt. (1959)
Gillinson, Sir Clive Daniel, Kt., CBE
Gilmore, *Prof.* Sir Ian Thomas, Kt.
Gilmour, *Hon.* Sir David Robert, Bt. (1926)
Gilmour, Sir John Nicholas, Bt. (1897)
Gina, Sir Lloyd Maepeza, KBE
Giordano, Sir Richard Vincent, KBE
Girolami, Sir Paul, Kt.
Girvan, *Rt. Hon.* Sir (Frederick) Paul, Kt.
Gladstone, Sir (Erskine) William, Bt. (1846), KG
Glean, Sir Carlyle Arnold, GCMG
Glidewell, *Rt. Hon.* Sir Iain Derek Laing, Kt.
Globe, *Hon.* Sir Henry Brian, Kt.
Glover, Sir Victor Joseph Patrick, Kt.
Glyn, Sir Richard Lindsay, Bt. (1759 and 1800)
Gobbo, Sir James Augustine, Kt., AC
Goldberg, *Prof.* Sir David Paul Brandes, Kt.
Goldring, *Rt. Hon.* Sir John Bernard, Kt.
Gomersall, Sir Stephen John, KCMG
Gonsalves-Sabola, *Hon.* Sir Joaquim Claudino, Kt
Gooch, Sir Arthur Brian Sherlock Heywood, Bt. (1746)
Gooch, Sir Miles Peter, Bt. (1866)
Good, Sir John James Griffen, Kt. CBE
Goodall, Sir (Arthur) David Saunders, GCMG
Goodall, *Air Marshal* Sir Roderick Harvey, KBE, CB, AFC
Goode, *Prof.* Sir Royston Miles, Kt., CBE, QC
Goodenough, Sir Anthony Michael, KCMG
Goodenough, Sir William McLernon, Bt. (1943)
Goodhart, Sir Robert Anthony Gordon, Bt. (1911)
Goodison, Sir Nicholas Proctor, Kt.
Çoodman, Sir Patrick Ledger, Kt., CBE
Goodson, Sir Alan Reginald, Bt. (1922)
Goodwin, Sir Frederick, KBE
Goold, Sir George William, Bt. (1801)
Gordon, Sir Donald, Kt.
Gordon, Sir Gerald Henry, Kt., CBE, QC
Gordon, Sir Robert James, Bt. (S. 1706)
Gordon-Cumming, Sir Alexander Penrose, Bt. (1804)
Gore, Sir Hugh Frederick Corbet, Bt. (I. 1622)
Gore-Booth, Sir Josslyn Henry Robert, Bt. (I. 1760)
Goring, Sir William Burton Nigel, Bt. (1678)
Gormley, Sir Antony Mark David, Kt., OBE
Gormley, Sir Paul Brendan, KCMG, MBE
Goschen, Sir (Edward) Alexander, Bt. (1916)

Gosling, Sir (Frederick) Donald, KCVO
Goss, *Hon.* Sir James Richard William, Kt., QC
Goulden, Sir (Peter) John, GCMG
Goulding, Sir (William) Lingard Walter, Bt. (1904)
Gourlay, Sir Simon Alexander, Kt.
Gowans, Sir James Learmonth, Kt., CBE, FRCP, FRS
Gowers, *Prof.* Sir William Timothy, Kt.
Gozney, Sir Richard Hugh Turton, KCMG
Graaff, Sir De Villiers, Bt. (1911)
Graham, Sir Alexander Michael, GBE
Graham, Sir James Bellingham, Bt. (1662)
Graham, Sir James Fergus Surtees, Bt. (1783)
Graham, Sir James Thompson, Kt., CMG
Graham, Sir John Alexander Noble, Bt. (1906), GCMG
Graham, Sir John Alistair, Kt.
Graham, Sir John Moodie, Bt. (1964)
Graham, Sir Peter, KCB, QC
Graham, *Lt.-Gen.* Sir Peter Walter, KCB, CBE
†Graham, Sir Ralph Stuart, Bt. (1629)
Graham-Moon, Sir Peter Wilfred Giles, Bt. (1855)
Graham-Smith, *Prof.* Sir Francis, Kt.
Grange, Sir Kenneth Henry, Kt., CBE
Grant, Sir Archibald, Bt. (S. 1705)
Grant, Sir Ian David, Kt., CBE
Grant, Sir (John) Anthony, Kt.
Grant, Sir John Douglas Kelso, KCMG
Grant, *Prof.* Sir Malcolm John, Kt., CBE
Grant, Sir Patrick Alexander Benedict, Bt. (S. 1688)
Grant, Sir Paul Joseph Patrick, Kt.
Grant, *Lt.-Gen.* Sir Scott Carnegie, KCB
Grant-Suttie, Sir James Edward, Bt. (S. 1702)
Granville-Chapman, *Gen.* Sir Timothy John, GBE, KCB, ADC
Grattan-Bellew, Sir Henry Charles, Bt. (1838)
Gray, Sir Bernard Peter, Kt.
Gray, *Hon.* Sir Charles Anthony St John, Kt.
Gray, Sir Charles Ireland, Kt., CBE
Gray, *Prof.* Sir Denis John Pereira, Kt., OBE, FRCGP
Gray, *Dr.* Sir John Armstrong Muir, Kt., CBE
Gray, Sir Robert McDowall (Robin), Kt.
Gray, Sir William Hume, Bt. (1917)
Graydon, *Air Chief Marshal* Sir Michael James, GCB, CBE
Grayson, Sir Jeremy Brian Vincent Harrington, Bt. (1922)
Green, Sir Allan David, KCB, QC
Green, Sir Edward Patrick Lycett, Bt. (1886)
Green, Sir Gregory David, KCMG
Green, *Hon.* Sir Guy Stephen Montague, KBE
Green, *Prof.* Sir Malcolm, Kt.
Green, *Hon.* Sir Nicholas Nigel, Kt., QC
Green, Sir Owen Whitley, Kt.
Green, Sir Philip Green, Kt.
Green-Price, Sir Robert John, Bt. (1874)

Greenaway, *Prof.* Sir David, Kt.
Greenaway, Sir Thomas Edward Burdick, Bt. (1933)
Greenbury, Sir Richard, Kt.
Greener, Sir Anthony Armitage, Kt.
Greengross, Sir Alan David, Kt.
Greenstock, Sir Jeremy Quentin, GCMG
Greenwell, Sir Edward Bernard, Bt. (1906)
Greenwood, *Prof.* Sir Brian Mellor, Kt., CBE
Greenwood, *Prof.* Sir Christopher John, Kt., CMG
Gregory, *Prof.* Sir Michael John, Kt., CBE
Gregson, Sir Peter John, Kt.
Gregson, Sir Peter Lewis, GCB
Grey, Sir Anthony Dysart, Bt. (1814)
Griffiths, Sir Michael, Kt.
Grigson, *Hon.* Sir Geoffrey Douglas, Kt.
Grimshaw, Sir Nicholas Thomas, Kt., CBE
Grimstone, Sir Gerald Edgar, Kt.
Grimwade, Sir Andrew Sheppard, Kt., CBE
Grose, *Vice-Adm.* Sir Alan, KBE
Gross, *Rt. Hon.* Sir Peter Henry, Kt.
Grossart, Sir Angus McFarlane McLeod, Kt., CBE
Grotrian, Sir Philip Christian Brent, Bt. (1934)
Grove, Sir Charles Gerald, Bt. (1874)
Grundy, Sir Mark, Kt.
Guinness, Sir Howard Christian Sheldon, Kt., VRD
Guinness, Sir John Ralph Sidney, Kt., CB
Guinness, Sir Kenelm Edward Lee, Bt. (1867)
Guise, Sir Christopher James, Bt. (1783)
Gull, Sir Rupert William Cameron, Bt. (1872)
Gumbs, Sir Emile Rudolph, Kt.
Gunn, Sir Robert Norman, Kt.
Gunning, Sir Charles Theodore, Bt. (1778)
Gunston, Sir John Wellesley, Bt. (1938)
Gurdon, *Prof.* Sir John Bertrand, Kt., DPHIL, FRS
Guthrie, Sir Malcolm Connop, Bt. (1936)

Haddacks, *Vice-Adm.* Sir Paul Kenneth, KCB
Haddon-Cave, *Hon.* Sir Charles Anthony, Kt.
Hadlee, Sir Richard John, Kt., MBE
Hagart-Alexander, Sir Claud, Bt. (1886)
Haines, *Prof.* Sir Andrew Paul, Kt.
Haji-Ioannou, Sir Stelios, Kt.
Halberg, Sir Murray Gordon, Kt., MBE
Hall, *Dr* Sir Andrew James, Kt.
Hall, Sir David Christopher, Bt. (1923)
Hall, *Prof.* Sir David Michael Baldock, Kt.
Hall, Sir Ernest, Kt., OBE
Hall, Sir Geoffrey, Kt.
Hall, Sir Graham Joseph, Kt.
Hall, Sir Iain Robert, Kt.

Hall, Sir John, Kt.
Hall, Sir John Bernard, Bt. (1919)
Hall, Sir John Douglas Hoste, Bt. (S. 1687)
Hall, HE *Prof.* Sir Kenneth Octavius, GCMG
Hall, Sir Peter Edward, KBE, CMG
Hall, Sir Peter Reginald Frederick, Kt., CBE
Hall, *Revd* Wesley Winfield, Kt.
Hall, Sir William Joseph, KCVO
Halpern, Sir Ralph Mark, Kt.
Halsey, *Revd* John Walter Brooke, Bt. (1920)
Halstead, Sir Ronald, Kt., CBE
Hamblen, *Hon.* Sir Nicholas Archibald, Kt.
Hambling, Sir Herbert Peter Hugh, Bt. (1924)
Hamilton, Sir Andrew Caradoc, Bt. (S. 1646)
Hamilton, Sir Nigel, KCB
Hamilton-Dalrymple, *Maj.* Sir Hew Fleetwood, Bt. (S. 1698), GCVO
Hamilton-Spencer-Smith, Sir John, Bt. (1804)
Hammick, Sir Jeremy Charles, Bt. (1834)
Hammond, Sir Anthony Hilgrove, KCB, QC
Hampel, Sir Ronald Claus, Kt.
Hampson, Sir Stuart, Kt.
Hampton, Sir (Leslie) Geoffrey, Kt.
Hampton, Sir Philip Roy, Kt.
Hanbury-Tenison, Sir Richard, KCVO
Hanham, Sir William John Edward, Bt. (1667)
Hankes-Drielsma, Sir Claude Dunbar, KCVO
Hanley, *Rt. Hon.* Sir Jeremy James, KCMG
Hanmer, Sir Wyndham Richard Guy, Bt. (1774)
Hannam, Sir John Gordon, Kt.
Hanson, Sir (Charles) Rupert (Patrick), Bt. (1918)
Hanson, Sir John Gilbert, KCMG, CBE
Harcourt-Smith, *Air Chief Marshal* Sir David, GBE, KCB, DFC
Hardie Boys, *Rt. Hon.* Sir Michael, GCMG
Harding, Sir George William, KCMG, CVO
Harding, *Marshal of the Royal Air Force* Sir Peter Robin, GCB
Hardy, Sir David William, Kt.
Hardy, Sir James Gilbert, Kt., OBE
Hardy, Sir Richard Charles Chandos, Bt. (1876)
Hare, Sir David, Kt., FRSL
Hare, Sir Nicholas Patrick, Bt. (1818)
Haren, *Dr* Sir Patrick Hugh, Kt.
Harford, Sir Mark John, Bt. (1934)
Harington, Sir Nicholas John, Bt. (1611)
Harkness, *Very Revd* James, KCVO, CB, OBE
Harley, *Gen.* Sir Alexander George Hamilton, KBE, CB
Harman, *Hon.* Sir Jeremiah LeRoy, Kt.
Harman, Sir John Andrew, Kt.
Harmsworth, Sir Hildebrand Harold, Bt. (1922)

Harper, *Air Marshal* Sir Christopher Nigel, KBE
Harper, Sir Ewan William, Kt., CBE
Harper, *Prof.* Sir Peter Stanley, Kt., CBE
Harris, Sir Christopher John Ashford, Bt. (1932)
Harris, *Air Marshal* Sir John Hulme, KCB, CBE
Harris, *Prof.* Sir Martin Best, Kt., CBE
Harris, Sir Michael Frank, Kt.
Harris, Sir (Theodore) Wilson, Kt.
Harris, Sir Thomas George, KBE, CMG
Harrison, *Prof.* Sir Brian Howard, Kt.
Harrison, Sir David, Kt., CBE, FRENG
Harrison, *Hon.* Sir Michael Guy Vicat, Kt.
Harrison, Sir Michael James Harwood, Bt. (1961)
Harrison, Sir (Robert) Colin, Bt. (1922)
Harrison, Sir Terence, Kt., FRENG
Harrop, Sir Peter John, KCB
Hart, *Hon.* Sir Anthony Ronald, Kt.
Hart, Sir Graham Allan, KCB
Hartwell, Sir (Francis) Anthony Charles Peter, Bt. (1805)
Harvey, Sir Charles Richard Musgrave, Bt. (1933)
Harvey, Sir Nicholas Barton, Kt.
Harvie, Sir John Smith, Kt., CBE
Harvie-Watt, Sir James, Bt. (1945)
Harwood, Sir Ronald, Kt., CBE
Haselhurst, *Rt. Hon.* Sir Alan Gordon Barraclough, Kt.
Haskard, Sir Cosmo Dugal Patrick Thomas, KCMG, MBE
Hastie, *Cdre* Sir Robert Cameron, KCVO, CBE, RD
Hastings, Sir Max Macdonald, Kt.
Hastings, *Dr* Sir William George, Kt., CBE
Hatter, Sir Maurice, Kt.
Havelock-Allan, Sir (Anthony) Mark David, Bt. (1858)
Hawkes, Sir John Garry, Kt., CBE
Hawkhead, Sir Anthony Gerard, Kt., CBE
Hawkins, Sir Richard Caesar, Bt. (1778)
Hawley, Sir James Appleton, KCVO, TD
Haworth, Sir Philip, Bt. (1911)
Hay, Sir David Russell, Kt., CBE, FRCP, MD
Hay, Sir John Erroll Audley, Bt. (S. 1663)
†Hay, Sir Ronald Frederick Hamilton, Bt. (S. 1703)
Hayden, *Hon.* Sir Anthony Paul, Kt.
Hayes, Sir Brian, Kt., CBE, QPM
Hayes, Sir Brian David, GCB
Hayman-Joyce, *Lt.-Gen.* Sir Robert John, KCB, CBE
Hayter, Sir Paul David Grenville, KCB, LVO
Head, Sir Patrick, Kt.
Head, Sir Richard Douglas Somerville, Bt. (1838)
Heald, Sir Oliver, Kt.
Heap, Sir Peter William, KCMG
Heap, *Prof.* Sir Robert Brian, Kt., CBE, FRS

Hearne, Sir Graham James, Kt., CBE

†Heathcote, Sir Mark Simon Robert, Bt. (1733), OBE

†Heathcote, Sir Timothy Gilbert, Bt. (1733)

Heatley, Sir Peter, Kt., CBE

Heber-Percy, Sir Algernon Eustace Hugh, KCVO

Hedley *Hon.* Sir Mark, Kt.

Hegarty, Sir John Kevin, Kt.

Heiser, Sir Terence Michael, GCB

Heller, Sir Michael Aron, Kt.

Henderson, Sir Denys Hartley, Kt.

Henderson, *Hon.* Sir Launcelot Dinadan James, Kt.

Henderson, *Maj.* Sir Richard Yates, KCVO

Hendry, *Prof.* Sir David Forbes, Kt.

Hendy, Sir Peter Gerard, Kt., CBE

Hennessy, Sir James Patrick Ivan, KBE, CMG

†Henniker, Sir Adrian Chandos, Bt. (1813)

Henniker-Heaton, Sir Yvo Robert, Bt. (1912)

Henriques, *Hon.* Sir Richard Henry Quixano, Kt.

Henry, Sir Lenworth George, Kt., CBE

†Henry, Sir Patrick Denis, Bt. (1923)

Henshaw, Sir David George, Kt.

Herbecq, Sir John Edward, KCB

Herbert, *Adm.* Sir Peter Geoffrey Marshall, KCB, OBE

Heron, Sir Conrad Frederick, KCB, OBE

Heron-Maxwell, Sir Nigel Mellor, Bt. (S. 1683)

Hervey, Sir Roger Blaise Ramsay, KCVO, CMG

Hervey-Bathurst, Sir Frederick William John, Bt. (1818)

Heseltine, *Rt. Hon.* Sir William Frederick Payne, GCB, GCVO

Hewetson, Sir Christopher Raynor, Kt., TD

Hewett, Sir Richard Mark John, Bt. (1813)

Hewitt, Sir (Cyrus) Lenox (Simson), Kt., OBE

Hewitt, Sir Nicholas Charles Joseph, Bt. (1921)

Heygate, Sir Richard John Gage, Bt. (1831)

Heywood, Sir Jeremy John, KCB, CVO

Heywood, Sir Peter, Bt. (1838)

Hickey, Sir John Tongri, Kt., CBE

Hickinbottom, *Hon.* Sir Gary Robert, Kt.

Hickman, Sir (Richard) Glenn, Bt. (1903)

Hicks, Sir Robert, Kt.

Hidden, *Hon.* Sir Anthony Brian, Kt.

Hielscher, Sir Leo Arthur, Kt.

Higgins, Sir David Hartmann, Kt.

Higgins, *Rt. Hon.* Sir Malachy Joseph, Kt.

Hildyard, *Hon.* Sir Robert Henry Thoroton, Kt.

Hill, Sir Brian John, Kt.

Hill, *Rt. Revd Dr.* Christopher John, KCVO

Hill, *Prof.* Sir Geoffrey William, Kt.

Hill, Sir James Frederick, Bt. (1917)

Hill, Sir John Alfred Rowley, Bt. (I. 1779)

Hill, *Vice-Adm.* Sir Robert Charles Finch, KBE, FRENG

Hill-Norton, *Vice-Adm. Hon.* Sir Nicholas John, KCB

Hill-Wood, Sir Samuel Thomas, Bt. (1921)

Hillhouse, Sir (Robert) Russell, KCB

Hillier, *Air Marshal* Sir Stephen John, KCB, CBE, DFC

Hills, Sir John Robert, Kt., CBE

Hilly, Sir Francis Billy, KCMG

Hine, *Air Chief Marshal* Sir Patrick Bardon, GCB, GBE

Hintze, Sir Michael, Kt.

Hirsch, *Prof.* Sir Peter Bernhard, Kt., PHD, FRS

Hirst, Sir Michael William, Kt.

Hoare, *Prof.* Sir Charles Anthony Richard, Kt., FRS

Hoare, Sir Charles James, Bt. (I. 1784)

Hoare, Sir David John, Bt. (1786)

Hobart, Sir John Vere, Bt. (1914)

Hobbs, *Maj.-Gen.* Sir Michael Frederick, KCVO, CBE

Hobhouse, Sir Charles John Spinney, Bt. (1812)

Hobson, Sir Ronald, KCVO

†Hodge, Sir Andrew Rowland, Bt. (1921)

Hodge, Sir James William, KCVO, CMG

Hodgkin, Sir (Gordon) Howard (Eliot), Kt., CH, CBE

Hodgkinson, Sir Michael Stewart, Kt.

Hodson, Sir Michael Robin Adderley, Bt. (I. 1789)

Hogan-Howe, Sir Bernard, Kt., QPM

Hogg, Sir Christopher Anthony, Kt.

Hogg, Sir Piers Michael James, Bt. (1846)

Hohn, Sir Christopher, KCMG

Holcroft, Sir Charles Anthony Culcheth, Bt. (1921)

Holden, Sir John David, Bt. (1919)

Holden, Sir Paul, Bt. (1893)

Holden-Brown, Sir Derrick, Kt.

Holder, Sir John Henry, Bt. (1898)

Holderness, Sir Martin William, Bt. (1920)

Holdgate, Sir Martin Wyatt, Kt., CB, PHD

Holgate, *Hon.* Sir David John, Kt., QC

Holland, *Hon.* Sir Alan Douglas, Kt.

Holland, *Hon.* Sir Christopher John, Kt.

Holland, Sir Geoffrey, KCB

Holland, Sir John Anthony, Kt.

Holliday, *Prof.* Sir Frederick George Thomas, Kt., CBE, FRSE

Holm, Sir Ian (Holm Cuthbert), Kt., CBE

Holman, *Hon.* Sir (Edward) James, Kt.

Holman, *Prof.* Sir John Stranger, Kt.

Holmes, Sir John Eaton, GCVO, KBE, CMG

Holroyd, Sir Michael De Courcy Fraser, Kt., CBE

Holroyde, *Hon.* Sir Timothy Victor, Kt.

Home, Sir William Dundas, Bt. (S. 1671)

Honywood, Sir Filmer Courtenay William, Bt. (1660)

†Hood, Sir John Joseph Harold, Bt. (1922)

Hooper, *Rt. Hon.* Sir Anthony, Kt.

Hope, Sir Alexander Archibald Douglas, Bt. (S. 1628)

Hope-Dunbar, Sir David, Bt. (S. 1664)

Hopkin, *Prof.* Sir Deian Rhys, Kt.

Hopkin, Sir Royston Oliver, KCMG

Hopkins, Sir Anthony Philip, Kt., CBE

Hopkins, Sir Michael John, Kt., CBE, RA, RIBA

Hopwood, *Prof.* Sir David Alan, Kt., FRS

Hordern, *Rt. Hon.* Sir Peter Maudslay, Kt.

Horlick, *Vice-Adm.* Sir Edwin John, KBE, FRENG

Horlick, Sir James Cunliffe William, Bt. (1914)

Horn-Smith, Sir Julian Michael, Kt.

Horne, Sir Alan Gray Antony, Bt. (1929)

Horne, *Dr* Sir Alistair Allan, Kt. CBE

Horner, *Hon.* Sir Thomas Mark, Kt.

Horsbrugh-Porter, Sir Andrew Alexander Marshall, Bt. (1902)

Horsfall, Sir Edward John Wright, Bt. (1909)

Hort, Sir Andrew Edwin Fenton, Bt. (1767)

Hosker, Sir Gerald Albery, KCB, QC

Hoskins, *Prof.* Sir Brian John, Kt. CBE, FRS

Hoskyns, Sir Robin Chevallier, Bt. (1676)

Hotung, Sir Joseph Edward, Kt.

Houghton, *Gen.* Sir John Nicholas Reynolds, GCB, CBE

Houghton, Sir John Theodore, Kt., CBE, FRS

Houghton, Sir Stephen Geoffrey, Kt., CBE

Houldsworth, Sir Richard Thomas Reginald, Bt. (1887)

Hourston, Sir Gordon Minto, Kt.

Housden, Sir Peter James, KCB

House, Sir Stephen, Kt., QPM

Houssemayne du Boulay, Sir Roger William, KCVO, CMG

Houstoun-Boswall, Sir (Thomas) Alford, Bt. (1836)

Howard, Sir David Howarth Seymour, Bt. (1955)

Howard, *Prof.* Sir Michael Eliot, Kt., OM, CH, CBE, MC

Howard-Lawson, Sir John Philip, Bt. (1841)

Howarth, Sir (James) Gerald Douglas, Kt.

Howells, Sir Eric Waldo Benjamin, Kt., CBE

Howes, Sir Christopher Kingston, KCVO, CB

Howlett, *Gen.* Sir Geoffrey Hugh Whitby, KBE, MC

Hoy, Sir Christopher Andrew, Kt., MBE

Hugh-Jones, Sir Wynn Normington, Kt., LVO

Kay, *Rt. Hon.* Sir Maurice Ralph, Kt.
Kaye, Sir Paul Henry Gordon, Bt.
　(1923)
Keane, Sir John Charles, Bt. (1801)
Kearney, *Hon.* Sir William John Francis,
　Kt., CBE
Keegan, *Dr* Sir Donal Arthur John,
　KCVO, OBE
Keehan, *Hon.* Sir Michael Joseph, Kt.
Keene, *Rt. Hon.* Sir David Wolfe, Kt.
Keith, *Hon.* Sir Brian Richard, Kt.
Keith, *Rt. Hon.* Sir Kenneth, KBE
†Kellett, Sir Stanley Charles, Bt.
　(1801)
Kelly, Sir Christopher William, KCB
Kelly, Sir David Robert Corbett, Kt.,
　CBE
Kemakeza, Sir Allan, Kt.
Kemball, *Air Marshal* Sir (Richard)
　John, KCB, CBE
Kemp-Welch, Sir John, Kt.
Kendall, Sir Peter Ashley, Kt.
Kenilorea, *Rt. Hon.* Sir Peter, KBE
Kennaway, Sir John Lawrence, Bt.
　(1791)
Kennedy, Sir Francis, KCMG, CBE
†Kennedy, Sir George Matthew Rae,
　Bt. (1836)
Kennedy, *Hon.* Sir Ian Alexander, Kt.
Kennedy, *Prof.* Sir Ian McColl, Kt.
Kennedy, *Rt. Hon.* Sir Paul Joseph
　Morrow, Kt.
Kenny, Sir Anthony John Patrick, Kt.,
　DPHIL, DLITT, FBA
Kenny, *Gen.* Sir Brian Leslie Graham,
　GCB, CBE
Kenny, Sir Paul Stephen, Kt.
Kentridge, Sir Sydney Woolf, KCMG,
　QC
Kenyon, Sir Nicholas Roger, Kt.,
　CBE
Keogh, *Prof.* Sir Bruce Edward, KBE
Kere, *Dr* Sir Nathan, KCMG
Kere, *Adm.* Sir John BevKere *Hon.* Sir
　Nathan, KCMGerley, GCB
Kerr, Sir Ronald James, Kt., CB
Kerr, *Hon.* Sir Timothy Julian, Kt., QC
Kershaw, *Prof.* Sir Ian, Kt.
Keswick, Sir Henry Neville Lindley, Kt.
Keswick, Sir John Chippendale
　Lindley, Kt.
Kevau, *Prof.* Sir Isi Henao, Kt., CBE
Khaw, *Prof.* Sir Peng Tee, Kt.
Kibble, *Prof.* Sir Thomas Walter
　Bannerman, Kt., CBE, FRS
Kikau, *Ratu* Sir Jone Latianara, KBE
Kimber, Sir Rupert Edward Watkin, Bt.
　(1904)
King, *Prof.* Sir David Anthony, Kt.,
　FRS
King, Sir James Henry Rupert, Bt.
　(1888)
King, Sir Julian Beresford, KCVO,
　CMG
King, *Hon.* Sir Timothy Roger Alan,
　Kt.
King, Sir Wayne Alexander, Bt. (1815)
Kingman, *Prof.* Sir John Frank Charles,
　Kt., FRS
Kingsley, Sir Ben, Kt.
Kinloch, Sir David, Bt. (S. 1686)
Kinloch, Sir David Oliphant, Bt.
　(1873)

Kipalan, Sir Albert, Kt.
Kirch, Sir David Roderick, KBE
Kirkpatrick, Sir Ivone Elliott, Bt.
　(S. 1685)
Kiszely, *Lt.-Gen.* Sir John Panton, KCB,
　MC
Kitchin, *Rt. Hon.* Sir David James
　Tyson, Kt.
Kitson, *Gen.* Sir Frank Edward, GBE,
　KCB, MC
Kitson, Sir Timothy Peter Geoffrey, Kt.
Kleinwort, Sir Richard Drake, Bt.
　(1909)
Klug, Sir Aaron, Kt., OM
Knight, *Rt. Hon.* Sir Gregory, Kt.
Knight, Sir Kenneth John, Kt., CBE,
　QFSM
Knight, *Air Chief Marshal* Sir Michael
　William Patrick, KCB, AFC
Knight, *Prof.* Sir Peter, Kt.
Knill, Sir Thomas John Pugin
　Bartholomew, Bt. (1893)
Knowles, Sir Charles Francis, Bt. (1765)
Knowles, Sir Durward Randolph, Kt.,
　OBE
Knowles, Sir Nigel Graham, Kt.
Knowles, *Hon.* Sir Robin St John, Kt.
Knox, Sir David Laidlaw, Kt.
Knox-Johnston, Sir William Robert
　Patrick (Sir Robin), Kt., CBE, RD
Kohn, *Dr* Sir Ralph, Kt.
Koraea, Sir Thomas, Kt.
Kornberg, *Prof.* Sir Hans Leo, Kt., DSc,
　SCD, PHD, FRS
Korowi, Sir Wiwa, GCMG
Kroto, *Prof.* Sir Harold Walter, Kt.,
　FRS
Kulukundis, Sir Elias George (Eddie),
　Kt., OBE
Kulunga, Sir Toami, Kt., OBE, QPM
Kwok-Po Li, *Dr* Sir David, Kt., OBE

Lachmann, *Prof.* Sir Peter Julius, Kt.
Lacon, Sir, Edmund Richard Vere,
　Bt. (1818)
Lacy, Sir Patrick Brian Finucane, Bt.
　(1921)
Laing, Sir (John) Martin (Kirby), Kt.,
　CBE
Laird, Sir Gavin Harry, Kt., CBE
Lake, Sir Edward Geoffrey, Bt. (1711)
Lakin, Sir Richard Anthony, Bt.
　(1909)
Lamb, Sir Albert Thomas, KBE, CMG,
　DFC
Lamb, *Lt.-Gen.* Sir Graeme Cameron
　Maxwell, KBE, CMG, DSO
Lambert, *Vice-Adm.* Sir Paul, KCB
†Lambert, Sir Peter John Biddulph, Bt.
　(1711)
Lambert, Sir Richard Peter, Kt.
Lampl, Sir Peter, Kt., OBE
Lamport, Sir Stephen Mark Jeffrey,
　KCVO
Landale, Sir David William Neil,
　KCVO
Landau, Sir Dennis Marcus, Kt.
Lander, Sir Stephen James, KCB
Lane, Prof. Sir David Philip, Kt.
Langham, Sir John Stephen, Bt. (1660)
Langlands, Sir Robert Alan, Kt.
Langley, *Hon.* Sir Gordon Julian Hugh,
　Kt.

Langrishe, Sir James Hercules, Bt.
　(I. 1777)
Langstaff, *Hon.* Sir Brian Frederick
　James, Kt.
Lankester, Sir Timothy Patrick, KCB
Lapli, Sir John Ini, GCMG
Lapthorne, Sir Richard Douglas, Kt.,
　CBE
Large, Sir Andrew McLeod Brooks,
　Kt.
Latasi, *Rt. Hon.* Sir Kamuta, KCMG,
　OBE
Latham, *Rt. Hon.* Sir David Nicholas
　Ramsey, Kt.
Latham, Sir Michael Anthony, Kt.
Latham, Sir Richard Thomas Paul,
　Bt. (1919)
Latimer, Sir Graham Stanley, KBE
Latour-Adrien, *Hon.* Sir Maurice, Kt.
Laughton, Sir Anthony Seymour, Kt.
Laurence, *Vice-Adm.* Sir Timothy James
　Hamilton, KCVO, CB, ADC
Laurie, Sir Robert Bayley Emilius, Bt.
　(1834)
Lauterpacht, Sir Elihu, Kt., CBE, QC
Lawler, Sir Peter James, Kt., OBE
†Lawrence, Sir Aubrey Lyttelton
　Simon, Bt. (1867)
Lawrence, Sir Clive Wyndham, Bt.
　(1906)
Lawrence, Sir Edmund Wickham,
　GCMG, OBE
Lawrence, Sir Henry Peter, Bt. (1858)
Lawrence, Sir Ivan John, Kt., QC
Lawrence-Jones, Sir Christopher, Bt.
　(1831)
Laws, *Rt. Hon.* Sir John Grant
　McKenzie, Kt.
Laws, Sir Stephen Charles, KCB
Lawson, Sir Charles John Patrick, Bt.
　(1900)
Lawson, *Gen.* Sir Richard George,
　KCB, DSO, OBE
Lawson-Tancred, Sir Andrew Peter,
　Bt. (1662)
Lawton, *Prof.* Sir John Hartley, Kt.,
　CBE, FRS
Layard, *Adm.* Sir Michael Henry
　Gordon, KCB, CBE
Lea, Sir Thomas William, Bt. (1892)
Leahy, Sir Daniel Joseph, Kt.
Leahy, Sir John Henry Gladstone,
　KCMG
Leahy, Sir Terence Patrick, Kt.
Learmont, *Gen.* Sir John Hartley, KCB,
　CBE
Leaver, Sir Christopher, GBE
Le Cheminant, *Air Chief Marshal* Sir
　Peter de Lacey, GBE, KCB, DFC
Lechler, *Prof.* Sir Robert Ian, Kt.
Lechmere, Sir Nicholas Anthony
　Hungerford, Bt. (1818)
†Leeds, Sir John Charles Hildyard, Bt.
　(1812)
Lees, Sir David Bryan, Kt.
Lees, Sir Thomas Edward, Bt. (1897)
Lees, Sir Thomas Harcourt Ivor, Bt.
　(1804)
Lees, Sir (William) Antony Clare, Bt.
　(1937)
Leese, Sir Richard Charles, Kt., CBE
Leeson, *Air Marshal* Sir Kevin James,
　KCB, CBE

le Fleming, Sir David Kelland, Bt. (1705)
Legard, Sir Charles Thomas, Bt. (1660)
Legg, Sir Thomas Stuart, KCB, QC
Leggatt, Rt. Hon. Sir Andrew Peter, Kt.
Leggatt, Hon. George Andrew Midsomer, Kt.
Leggett, Prof. Sir Anthony James, KBE
Le Grand, Prof. Sir Julian Ernest, Kt.
Leigh, Sir Edward Julian Egerton, Kt.
Leigh, Sir Geoffrey Norman, Kt.
Leigh, Dr Sir Michael, KCMG
Leigh, Sir Richard Henry, Bt. (1918)
Leighton, Sir John Mark Nicholas, Kt.
Leighton, Sir Michael John Bryan, Bt. (1693)
Leith-Buchanan, Sir Gordon Kelly McNicol, Bt. (1775)
Le Marchant, Sir Francis Arthur, Bt. (1841)
Lennox-Boyd, Hon. Sir Mark Alexander, Kt.
Leon, Sir John Ronald, Bt. (1911)
Lepping, Sir George Geria Dennis, GCMG, MBE
Leslie, Sir John Norman Ide, Bt. (1876)
Lester, Sir James Theodore, Kt.
Lethbridge, Sir Thomas Periam Hector Noel, Bt. (1804)
Lever, Sir Jeremy Frederick, KCMG, QC
Lever, Sir Paul, KCMG
Lever, Sir (Tresham) Christopher Arthur Lindsay, Bt. (1911)
Leveson, Rt. Hon. Sir Brian Henry, Kt.
Levi, Sir Wasangula Noel, Kt., CBE
Levinge, Sir Richard George Robin, Bt. (I. 1704)
Lewinton, Sir Christopher, Kt.
Lewis, Hon. Sir Clive Buckland, Kt.
Lewis, Sir David Thomas Rowell, Kt.
Lewis, Sir John Anthony, Kt., OBE
Lewis, Sir Leigh Warren, KCB
Lewis, Sir Terence Murray, Kt., OBE, GM, QPM
Lewison, Rt. Hon. Sir Kim Martin Jordan, Kt.
Ley, Sir Ian Francis, Bt. (1905)
Li, Sir Ka-Shing, KBE
Lickiss, Sir Michael Gillam, Kt.
Liddington, Sir Bruce, Kt.
Lightman, Hon. Sir Gavin Anthony, Kt.
Lighton, Sir Thomas Hamilton, Bt. (I. 1791)
Likierman, Prof. Sir John Andrew, Kt.
Lilleyman, Prof. Sir John Stuart, Kt.
Lindblom, Hon. Sir Keith John, Kt.
†Lindsay, Sir James Martin Evelyn, Bt. (1962)
Lindsay, Hon. Sir John Edmund Frederic, Kt.
†Lindsay-Hogg, Sir Michael Edward, Bt. (1905)
Lipton, Sir Stuart Anthony, Kt.
Lipworth, Sir (Maurice) Sydney, Kt.
Lister-Kaye, Sir John Phillip Lister, Bt. (1812)
Lithgow, Sir William James, Bt. (1925)
Llewellyn, Sir Roderic Victor, Bt. (1922)
Llewellyn-Smith, Prof. Sir Christopher Hubert, Kt.

Lloyd, Prof. Sir Geoffrey Ernest Richard, Kt., FBA
Lloyd, Sir Nicholas Markley, Kt.
Lloyd, Rt. Hon. Sir Peter Robert Cable, Kt.
Lloyd, Sir Richard Ernest Butler, Bt. (1960)
Lloyd, Rt. Hon. Sir Timothy Andrew Wigram, Kt.
Lloyd-Edwards, Capt. Sir Norman, KCVO, RD
Lloyd Jones, Rt. Hon. Sir David, Kt.
Loader, Air Marshal Sir Clive Robert, KCB, OBE
Lobban, Sir Iain Robert, KCMG, CB
Lockett, Sir Michael Vernon, KCVO
Lockhead, Sir Moir, Kt., OBE
Loder, Sir Edmund Jeune, Bt. (1887)
Logan, Sir David Brian Carleton, KCMG
Longley, Hon. Sir Hartman Godfrey, Kt.
Longmore, Rt. Hon. Sir Andrew Centlivres, Kt.
Lorimer, Sir (Thomas) Desmond, Kt.
Los, Hon. Sir Kubulan, Kt., CBE
Loughran, Sir Gerald Finbar, KCB
Lourdenadin, Sir Ninian Mogan, KCMG, KBE
Lovill, Sir John Roger, Kt., CBE
Lowa, Rt. Revd Sir Samson, KBE
Lowe, Air Chief Marshal Sir Douglas Charles, GCB, DFC, AFC
Lowe, Sir Frank Budge, Kt.
Lowe, Sir Philip Martin, KCMG
Lowe, Sir Thomas William Gordon, Bt. (1918)
Lowson, Sir Ian Patrick, Bt. (1951)
Lowther, Col. Sir Charles Douglas, Bt. (1824)
Loyd, Sir Julian St John, KCVO
Lu, Sir Tseng Chi, Kt.
Lucas, Prof. Sir Colin Renshaw, Kt.
Lucas, Sir Thomas Edward, Bt. (1887)
Lucas-Tooth, Sir (Hugh) John, Bt. (1920)
Luff, Sir Peter James, Kt.
Lumsden, Sir David James, Kt.
Lushington, Sir John Richard Castleman, Bt. (1791)
Lyall Grant, Sir Mark Justin, KCMG
Lyle, Sir Gavin Archibald, Bt. (1929)
Lynch-Blosse, Capt. Sir Richard Hely, Bt. (I. 1622)
Lynch-Robinson, Sir Dominick Christopher, Bt. (1920)
Lyne, Rt. Hon. Sir Roderic Michael John, KBE, CMG
Lyons, Sir John, Kt.
Lyons, Sir Michael Thomas, Kt.

McAllister, Sir Ian Gerald, Kt., CBE
McAlpine, Sir William Hepburn, Bt. (1918)
McCaffrey, Sir Thomas Daniel, Kt.
McCamley, Sir Graham Edward, KBE
McCarthy, Sir Callum, Kt.
McCartney, Rt. Hon. Sir Ian, Kt.
McCartney, Sir (James) Paul, Kt., MBE
Macartney, Sir John Ralph, Bt. (I. 1799)
McClement, Vice-Admiral Sir Timothy Pentreath, KCB, OBE

McClintock, Sir Eric Paul, Kt.
McCloskey, Hon. Sir John Bernard, Kt.
McColl, Sir Colin Hugh Verel, KCMG
McColl, Gen. Sir John Chalmers, KCB, CBE, DSO
McCollum, Rt. Hon. Sir William, Kt.
McCombe, Rt. Hon. Sir Richard George Bramwell, Kt.
McConnell, Sir Robert Shean, Bt. (1900)
†McCowan, Sir David William, Bt. (1934)
MacCulloch, Prof. Sir Diarmaid Ninian John, Kt.
McCulloch, Rt. Revd Nigel Simeon, KCVO
McCullough, Hon. Sir (Iain) Charles (Robert), Kt.
MacDermott, Rt. Hon. Sir John Clarke, Kt.
Macdonald, Sir Alasdair Uist, Kt., CBE
MacDonald, Hon. Sir Alistair William, Kt., QC
McDonald of Sleat, Sir Ian Godfrey Bosville, Bt. (S. 1625)
McDonald, Prof. Sir James, Kt.
Macdonald, Sir Kenneth Carmichael, KCB
McDonald, Sir Simon Gerard, KCMG, KCVO
McDonald, Sir Trevor, Kt., OBE
McDowell, Sir Eric Wallace, Kt., CBE
MacDuff, Hon. Sir Alistair Geoffrey, Kt.
Mace, Lt.-Gen. Sir John Airth, KBE, CB
McEwen, Sir John Roderick Hugh, Bt. (1953)
MacFadyen Air Marshal Sir Ian David, KCVO, CB, OBE
McFarland, Sir John Talbot, Bt. (1914)
MacFarlane, Prof. Sir Alistair George James, Kt., CBE, FRS
McFarlane, Rt. Hon. Sir Andrew Ewart, Kt.
Macfarlane, Sir (David) Neil, Kt.
McGeechan, Sir Ian Robert, Kt., OBE
McGrath, Sir Brian Henry, GCVO
Macgregor, Sir Ian Grant, Bt. (1828)
MacGregor of MacGregor, Sir Malcolm Gregor Charles, Bt. (1795)
McGrigor, Sir James Angus Rhoderick Neil, Bt. (1831)
McIntosh, Sir Neil William David, Kt., CBE
McIntosh, Sir Ronald Robert Duncan, KCB
McIntyre, Sir Donald Conroy, Kt., CBE
McIntyre, Sir Meredith Alister, Kt.
Mackay, Hon. Sir Colin Crichton, Kt.
MacKay, Prof. Sir Donald Iain, Kt.
MacKay, Sir Francis Henry, Kt.
McKay, Sir Neil Stuart, Kt., CB
McKay, Sir William Robert, KCB
Mackay-Dick, Maj.-Gen. Sir Iain Charles, KCVO, MBE
Mackechnie, Sir Alistair John, Kt.
McKellen, Sir Ian Murray, Kt., CH, CBE
Mackenzie, Sir (James William) Guy, Bt. (1890)
Mackenzie, Gen. Sir Jeremy John George, GCB, OBE

†Mackenzie, Sir Peter Douglas, Bt. (S. 1673)
†Mackenzie, Sir Roderick McQuhae, Bt. (S. 1703)
Mackeson, Sir Rupert Henry, Bt. (1954)
McKillop, Sir Thomas Fulton Wilson, Kt.
McKinnon, *Rt. Hon.* Sir Donald Charles, GCVO
McKinnon, Sir James, Kt.
McKinnon, *Hon.* Sir Stuart Neil, Kt.
Mackintosh, Sir Cameron Anthony, Kt.
Mackworth, Sir Digby (John), Bt. (1776)
McLaughlin, Sir Richard, Kt.
Maclean of Dunconnell, Sir Charles Edward, Bt. (1957)
Maclean, *Hon.* Sir Lachlan Hector Charles, Bt., CVO (NS 1631)
Maclean, Sir Murdo, Kt.
†McLeod, Sir James Roderick Charles, Bt. (1925)
MacLeod, Sir (John) Maxwell Norman, Bt. (1924)
Macleod, Sir (Nathaniel William) Hamish, KBE
McLintock, Sir Michael William, Bt. (1934)
McLoughlin, Sir Francis, Kt., CBE
Maclure, Sir John Robert Spencer, Bt. (1898)
McMahon, Sir Brian Patrick, Bt. (1817)
McMahon, Sir Christopher William, Kt.
McMaster, Sir Brian John, Kt., CBE
McMichael, *Prof.* Sir Andrew James, Kt., FRS
MacMillan *Very Rvd.* Gilleasbuig Iain, KCVO
McMillan, Sir Iain Macleod, Kt., CBE
Macmillan, *Dr* Sir James Loy, Kt., CBE
MacMillan, *Lt.-Gen.* Sir John Richard Alexander, KCB, CBE
McMullin, *Rt. Hon.* Sir Duncan Wallace, Kt.
McMurtry, Sir David, Kt., CBE
Macnaghten, Sir Malcolm Francis, Bt. (1836)
McNair-Wilson, Sir Patrick Michael Ernest David, Kt.
Macnaughton, *Prof.* Sir Malcolm Campbell, Kt.
McNee, Sir David Blackstock, Kt., QPM
McNulty, Sir (Robert William) Roy, Kt., CBE
MacPhail, Sir Bruce Dugald, Kt.
Macpherson, Sir Nicholas Ian, GCB
Macpherson of Cluny, *Hon.* Sir William Alan, Kt., TD
McQuarrie, Sir Albert, Kt.
MacRae, Sir (Alastair) Christopher (Donald Summerhayes), KCMG
Macready, Sir Charles Nevil, Bt. (1923)
MacSween, *Prof.* Sir Roderick Norman McIver, Kt.
Mactaggart, Sir John Auld, Bt. (1938)
McVicar, Sir David, Kt.
McWilliam, Sir Michael Douglas, KCMG
McWilliams, Sir Francis, GBE
Madden, Sir Charles Jonathan, Bt. (1919)

Madden, Sir David Christopher Andrew, KCMG
Maddison, *Hon.* Sir David George, Kt.
Madejski, Sir John Robert, Kt., OBE
Madel, Sir (William) David, Kt.
Magee, Sir Ian Bernard Vaughan, Kt., CB
Magnus, Sir Laurence Henry Philip, Bt. (1917)
Maguire, *Hon.* Sir Paul Richard, Kt.
Mahon, Sir William Walter, Bt. (1819), LVO
Maiden, Sir Colin James, Kt., DPHIL
Maini, *Prof.* Sir Ravinder Nath, Kt.
Maino, Sir Charles, KBE
†Maitland, Sir Charles Alexander, Bt. (1818)
Major, *Rt. Hon.* Sir John, KG, CH
Malbon, *Vice-Adm.* Sir Fabian Michael, KBE
Malcolm, Sir Alexander James Elton, Bt. (S. 1665), OBE
Malcolm, *Dr* Noel Robert, Kt., FBA
Males, *Hon.* Sir Stephen Martin, Kt.
Malet, Sir Harry Douglas St Lo, Bt. (1791)
Mallaby, Sir Christopher Leslie George, GCMG, GCVO
Mallick, *Prof.* Sir Netar Prakash, Kt.
Mallinson, Sir William James, Bt. (1935)
Malpas, Sir Robert, Kt., CBE
Mancham, Sir James Richard Marie, KBE
Mander, Sir (Charles) Nicholas, Bt. (1911)
Manduell, Sir John, Kt., CBE
Mann, *Hon.* Sir George Anthony, Kt.
Mann, Sir Rupert Edward, Bt. (1905)
Manning, Sir David Geoffrey, GCMG, KCVO
Mano, Sir Koitaga, Kt., MBE
Mans, *Lt.-Gen.* Sir Mark Francis Noel, KCB, CBE
Mansel, Sir Philip, Bt. (1622)
Mansfield, *Prof.* Sir Peter, Kt.
Manuella, Sir Tulaga, GCMG, MBE
Mara, Sir Nambuga, KBE
Margetson, Sir John William Denys, KCMG
Margetts, Sir Robert John, Kt., CBE
Markesinis, *Prof.* Sir Basil Spyridonos, Kt. QC
Markham, *Prof.* Sir Alexander Fred, Kt.
Markham, Sir (Arthur) David, Bt. (1911)
Marling, Sir Charles William Somerset, Bt. (1882)
Marmot, *Prof.* Sir Michael Gideon, Kt.
Marr, Sir Leslie Lynn, Bt. (1919)
Marriner, Sir Neville, Kt., CBE, CH
†Marsden, Sir Tadgh Orlando Denton, Bt. (1924)
Marsh, *Prof.* Sir John Stanley, Kt., CBE
Marshall, Sir Michael John, Kt., CBE
Marshall, *Prof.* Sir (Oshley) Roy, Kt., CBE
Marshall, Sir Peter Harold Reginald, KCMG
Marshall, *Prof. Emeritus* Sir Woodville Kemble, Kt.

Martin, Sir Clive Haydon, Kt., OBE
Martin, Sir George Henry, Kt., CBE
Martin, Sir Gregory Michael Gerard, Kt.
Martin, *Prof.* Sir Laurence Woodward, Kt.
Martin, Sir (Robert) Bruce, Kt., QC
Marychurch, Sir Peter Harvey, KCMG
Masefield, Sir Charles Beech Gordon, Kt.
Mason, *Hon.* Sir Anthony Frank, KBE
Mason, *Prof.* Sir David Kean, Kt., CBE
Mason, Sir Peter James, KBE
Mason, *Prof.* Sir Ronald, KCB, FRS
Massey, *Vice-Adm.* Sir Alan, KCB, CBE, ADC
Massie, Sir Herbert William, Kt., CBE
Matane, HE Sir Paulias Nguna, GCMG, OBE
Matheson of Matheson, Sir Fergus John, Bt. (1882)
Mathews, *Vice-Adm.* Sir Andrew David Hugh, KCB
Mathewson, Sir George Ross, Kt., CBE, PHD, FRSE
Matthews, Sir Terence Hedley, Kt., OBE
Maughan, Sir Deryck, Kt.
Mawer, Sir Philip John Courtney, Kt.
Maxwell, Sir Michael Eustace George, Bt. (S. 1681)
Maxwell Davies, Sir Peter, Kt., CH, CBE
Maxwell Macdonald (formerly Stirling-Maxwell), Sir John Ronald, Bt. (NS 1682)
Maxwell-Scott, Sir Dominic James, Bt. (1642)
May, *Rt. Hon.* Sir Anthony Tristram Kenneth, Kt.
Mayall, *Lt-Gen.* Sir Simon Vincent, KBE, CB
Mayfield, Sir Andrew Charles, Kt.
Meadow, *Prof.* Sir (Samuel) Roy, Kt., FRCP, FRCPE
Meale, Sir Joseph Alan, Kt.
Medlycott, Sir Mervyn Tregonwell, Bt. (1808)
Meeran, *His Hon.* Sir Goolam Hoosen Kader, Kt.
Meldrum, Sir Graham, Kt., CBE, QFSM
Melhuish, Sir Michael Ramsay, KBE, CMG
Mellars, *Prof.* Sir Paul Anthony, Kt., FBA
Mellon, Sir James, KCMG
Melmoth, Sir Graham John, Kt.
Melville, *Prof.* Sir David, Kt., CBE
Merifield, Sir Anthony James, KCVO, CB
Metcalf, *Prof.* Sir David Harry, Kt., CBE
†Meyer, Sir (Anthony) Ashley Frank, Bt. (1910)
Meyer, Sir Christopher John Rome, KCMG
†Meyrick, Sir Timothy Thomas Charlton, Bt. (1880)
Miakwe, *Hon.* Sir Akepa, KBE
Michael, Sir Duncan, Kt.
Michael, *Dr* Sir Jonathan, Kt.
Michael, Sir Peter Colin, Kt., CBE

Michels, Sir David Michael Charles, Kt.

Middleton, Sir John Maxwell, Kt.

Middleton, Sir Peter Edward, GCB

Miers, Sir (Henry) David Alastair Capel, KBE, CMG

Milbank, Sir Anthony Frederick, Bt. (1882)

Milborne-Swinnerton-Pilkington, Sir Thomas Henry, Bt. (S. 1635)

Milburn, Sir Anthony Rupert, Bt. (1905)

†Miles, Sir Philip John, Bt. (1859)

Millais, Sir Geoffrey Richard Everett, Bt. (1885)

Millar, *Prof.* Sir Fergus Graham Burtholme, Kt.

Miller, Sir Albert Joel, KCMG, LVO, MBE, QPM, CPM

Miller, Sir Donald John, Kt., FRSE, FRENG

Miller, *Air Marshal* Sir Graham Anthony, KBE

Miller, Sir Anthony Thomas, Bt. (1705)

Miller, Sir Jonathan Wolfe, Kt., CBE

Miller, Sir Peter North, Kt.

Miller, Sir Robin Robert William, Kt.

Miller, Sir Ronald Andrew Baird, Kt., CBE

Miller of Glenlee, Sir Stephen William Macdonald, Bt. (1788)

Mills, Sir Ian, Kt.

Mills, Sir Jonathan Edward Harland (John), Kt., FRSE

Mills, Sir Keith Edward, GBE

Mills, Sir Peter Frederick Leighton, Bt. (1921)

Milman, Sir David Patrick, Bt. (1800)

Milne, Sir John Drummond, Kt.

Milne-Watson, Sir Andrew Michael, Bt. (1937)

Milner, Sir Timothy William Lycett, Bt. (1717)

Mirrlees, *Prof.* Sir James Alexander, Kt., FBA

Mitchell, *Rt. Hon.* Sir James FitzAllen, KCMG

Mitchell, *Very Revd* Patrick Reynolds, KCVO

Mitchell, *Hon.* Sir Stephen George, Kt.

Mitting, *Hon.* Sir John Edward, Kt.

Moate, Sir Roger Denis, Kt.

Moberly, Sir Patrick Hamilton, KCMG

Moffat, Sir Brian Scott, Kt., OBE

Moir, Sir Christopher Ernest, Bt. (1916)

Molesworth-St Aubyn, Sir William, Bt. (1689)

†Molony, Sir Peter John, Bt. (1925)

Moncada, *Prof.* Sir Salvador, Kt.

Montagu, Sir Nicholas Lionel John, KCB

Montagu-Pollock, Sir Giles Hampden, Bt. (1872)

Montague, Sir Adrian Alastair, Kt., CBE

Montgomery, Sir (Basil Henry) David, Bt. (1801), CVO

Montgomery, *Vice-Adm.* Sir Charles Percival Ross, KBE, ADC

Montgomery-Cuninghame, Sir John Christopher Foggo, Bt. (NS 1672)

Moody-Stuart, Sir Mark, KCMG

Moollan, Sir Abdool Hamid Adam, Kt.

†Moon, Sir Roger, Bt. (1887)

Moor, *Hon.* Sir Philip Drury, Kt.

Moorcroft, Sir William, KBE

Moore, *Most Revd* Desmond Charles, KBE

Moore, Sir Francis Thomas, Kt.

Moore, Sir John Michael, KCVO, CB, DSC

Moore, *Vice Adm.* Sir Michael Antony Claës, KBE, LVO

Moore, *Prof.* Sir Norman Winfrid, Bt. (1919)

Moore, Sir Roger George, KBE

Moore, Sir William Roger Clotworthy, Bt. (1932), TD

Moore-Bick, *Rt. Hon.* Sir Martin James, Kt.

Moores, Sir Peter, Kt., CBE

Morauta, Sir Mekere, KCMG

Mordaunt, Sir Richard Nigel Charles, Bt. (1611)

Morgan, *Vice-Adm.* Sir Charles Christopher, KBE

Morgan, *Rt. Hon.* Sir (Charles) Declan, Kt.

Morgan, Sir Graham, Kt.

Morgan, *Hon.* Sir Paul Hyacinth, Kt.

Morison, *Hon.* Sir Thomas Richard Atkin, Kt.

Moritz, Sir Michael Jonathan, KBE

Morland, *Hon.* Sir Michael, Kt.

Morland, Sir Robert Kenelm, Kt.

†Morris, Sir Allan Lindsay, Bt. (1806)

Morris, Sir Andrew Valentine, Kt., OBE

Morris, *Air Marshal* Sir Arnold Alec, KBE, CB

Morris, Sir Derek James, Kt.

Morris, Sir Keith Elliot Hedley, KBE, CMG

Morris, *Prof.* Sir Peter John, Kt.

Morris, Sir Trefor Alfred, Kt., CBE, QPM

Morrison, Sir (Alexander) Fraser, Kt., CBE

Morrison, Sir George Ivan, Kt., OBE

Morrison, Sir Kenneth Duncan, Kt., CBE

Morrison-Bell, Sir William Hollin Dayrell, Bt. (1905)

Morrison-Low, Sir Richard Walter, Bt. (1908)

Morritt, *Rt. Hon.* Sir (Robert) Andrew, Kt., CVO

Morse, Sir Amyas Charles Edward, KCB

Morse, Sir Christopher Jeremy, KCMG

Moses, *Rt. Hon.* Sir Alan George, Kt.

Moses, *Very Revd* Dr John Henry, KCVO

Moss, Sir David Joseph, KCVO, CMG

Moss, Sir Stephen Alan, Kt.

Moss, Sir Stirling Craufurd, Kt., OBE

Mostyn, *Hon.* Sir Nicholas Anthony Joseph Ghislain, Kt.

Mostyn, Sir William Basil John, Bt. (1670)

Motion, Sir Andrew, Kt.

†Mott, Sir David Hugh, Bt. (1930)

Mottram, Sir Richard Clive, GCB

†Mount, Sir (William Robert) Ferdinand, Bt. (1921)

Mountain, Sir Edward Brian Stanford, Bt. (1922)

Mowbray, Sir John Robert, Bt. (1880)

Moylan, *Hon.* Sir Andrew John Gregory, Kt.

Moynihan, *Dr* Sir Daniel, Kt.

†Muir, Sir Richard James Kay, Bt. (1892)

Muir-Mackenzie, Sir Alexander Alwyne Henry Charles Brinton, Bt. (1805)

Mulcahy, Sir Geoffrey John, Kt.

Mummery, *Rt. Hon.* Sir John Frank, Kt.

Munby, *Rt. Hon.* Sir James Lawrence, Kt.

Munro, Sir Alan Gordon, KCMG

†Munro, Sir Ian Kenneth, Bt. (S. 1634)

Munro, Sir Keith Gordon Ian, Bt. (1825)

Muria, *Hon.* Sir Gilbert John Baptist, Kt.

Murphy, Sir Jonathan Michael, Kt., QPM

Murray, Sir David Edward, Kt.

Murray, *Rt. Hon.* Sir Donald Bruce, Kt.

Murray, Sir Nigel Andrew Digby, Bt. (S. 1628)

Murray, Sir Patrick Ian Keith, Bt. (S. 1673)

Murray, Sir Robert Sydney, Kt., CBE

Murray, Sir Robin MacGregor, Kt.

†Murray, Sir Rowland William, Bt. (S. 1630)

Musgrave, Sir Christopher John Shane, Bt. (I. 1782)

Musgrave, Sir Christopher Patrick Charles, Bt. (1611)

Myers, Sir Derek John, Kt.

Myers, *Prof.* Sir Rupert Horace, KBE

Mynors, Sir Richard Baskerville, Bt. (1964)

Naipaul, Sir Vidiadhar Surajprasad, Kt.

Nairn, Sir Michael, Bt. (1904)

Naish, Sir (Charles) David, Kt.

Nalau, Sir Jerry Kasip, KBE

Nall, Sir Edward William Joseph Bt. (1954)

Namaliu, *Rt. Hon.* Sir Rabbie Langanai, KCMG

Napier, Sir Charles Joseph, Bt. (1867)

Napier, Sir John Archibald Lennox, Bt. (S. 1627)

Narey, Sir Martin James, Kt.

Naylor, Sir Robert, Kt.

Naylor-Leyland, Sir Philip Vyvyan, Bt. (1895)

Neal, Sir Eric James, Kt., CVO

Neale, Sir Gerrard Anthony, Kt.

Neave, Sir Paul Arundell, Bt. (1795)

Neill, *Rt. Hon.* Sir Brian Thomas, Kt.

Neill, Sir (James) Hugh, KCVO, CBE, TD

†Nelson, Sir Jamie Charles Vernon Hope, Bt. (1912)

Nelson, *Hon.* Sir Robert Franklyn, Kt.

New, *Maj.-Gen.* Sir Laurence Anthony Wallis, Kt., CB, CBE

Newbigging, Sir David Kennedy, OBE

Newby, *Prof.* Sir Howard Joseph, Kt., CBE

Newey, *Hon.* Sir Guy Richard, Kt.

Newington, Sir Michael John, KCMG

Newman, Sir Francis Hugh Cecil, Bt. (1912)

Newman, Sir Geoffrey Robert, Bt. (1836)

Newman, *Hon.* Sir George Michael, Kt.

Newman, Sir Kenneth Leslie, GBE, QPM

Newman, *Vice-Adm.* Sir Roy Thomas, KCB

Newman Taylor, *Prof.* Sir Anthony John, Kt., CBE

Newsam, Sir Peter Anthony, Kt.

Newson-Smith, Sir Peter Frank Graham, Bt. (1944)

Newton, *Revd* George Peter Howgill, Bt. (1900)

Newton, Sir John Garnar, Bt. (1924)

Newton, *Lt-Gen.* Sir Paul Raymond, KBE

Newton, *Hon.* Sir Roderick Brian, Kt.

Nice, Sir Geoffrey, Kt., QC

Nickell, *Prof.* Sir Stephen John, Kt., CBE, FBA

Nicol, *Hon.* Sir Andrew George Lindsay, Kt.

Nichol, Sir Duncan Kirkbride, Kt., CBE

Nicholas, Sir David, Kt., CBE

Nicholas, Sir John William, KCVO, CMG

Nicholls, Sir Nigel Hamilton, KCVO, CBE

Nichols, Sir Richard Everard, Kt.

Nicholson, Sir Bryan Hubert, GBE, Kt.

Nicholson, Sir Charles Christian, Bt. (1912)

Nicholson, Sir David, KCB, CBE

Nicholson, *Rt. Hon.* Sir Michael, Kt.

Nicholson, Sir Paul Douglas, KCVO, Kt.

Nicholson, Sir Robin Buchanan, Kt., PHD, FRS, FRENG

Nicoll, Sir William, KCMG

Nightingale, Sir Charles Manners Gamaliel, Bt. (1628)

Nixon, Sir Simon Michael Christopher, Bt. (1906)

Noble, Sir David Brunel, Bt. (1902)

Noble, Sir Timothy Peter, Bt. (1923)

Nombri, Sir Joseph Karl, Kt., ISO, BEM

Norman, Sir Nigel James, Bt. (1915)

Norman, Sir Ronald, Kt., OBE

Norman, Sir Torquil Patrick Alexander, Kt., CBE

Normington, Sir David John, GCB

Norrington, Sir Roger Arthur Carver, Kt., CBE

Norris, *Hon.* Sir Alastair Hubert, Kt.

Norriss, *Air Marshal* Sir Peter Coulson, KBE, CB, AFC

North, *Air Marshal.* Sir Barry Mark, KCB, MBE

North, Sir Peter Machin, Kt., CBE, QC, DCL, FBA

North, Sir Thomas Lindsay, Kt.

North, Sir (William) Jonathan (Frederick), Bt. (1920)

Norton, Barry, Kt.

Norton, *Maj.-Gen.* Sir George Pemberton Ross, KCVO, CBE

Norton-Griffiths, Sir John, Bt. (1922)

Nossal, Sir Gustav Joseph Victor, Kt., CBE

Nott, *Rt. Hon.* Sir John William Frederic, KCB

Nourse, *Rt. Hon.* Sir Martin Charles, Kt.

Novoselov, *Prof.* Sir Konstantin, Kt.

Nugee, *Hon.* Sir Chrisstopher George, Kt.

†Nugent, Sir Christopher George Ridley, Bt. (1806)

Nugent, Sir Nicholas Myles John, Bt. (I. 1795)

Nugent, Sir (Walter) Richard Middleton, Bt. (1831)

Nunn, Sir Trevor Robert, Kt., CBE

Nunneley, Sir Charles Kenneth Roylance, Kt.

Nursaw, Sir James, KCB, QC

Nurse, Sir Paul Maxime, Kt.

Nuttall, Sir Harry, Bt. (1922)

Nutting, Sir John Grenfell, Bt. (1903), QC

Oakeley, Sir John Digby Atholl, Bt. (1790)

Oakes, Sir Christopher, Bt. (1939)

Oakshott, Sir Thomas Hendrie, Bt. (1959)

O'Brien, Sir Robert Stephen, Kt., CBE

O'Brien, Sir Timothy John, Bt. (1849)

O'Brien, Sir William, Kt.

O'Brien, *Adm.* Sir William Donough, KCB, DSC

O'Connell, Sir Bernard, Kt.

O'Connell, Sir Maurice James Donagh MacCarthy, Bt. (1869)

O'Connor, Sir Denis Francis, Kt., CBE, QPM

Odell, Sir Stanley John, Kt.

Odgers, Sir Graeme David William, Kt.

O'Donnell, Sir Christopher John, Kt.

O'Donoghue, *Lt.-Gen.* Sir Kevin, KCB, CBE

O'Dowd, Sir David Joseph, Kt., CBE, QPM

Ogden, *Dr* Sir Peter James, Kt.

Ogden, Sir Robert, Kt., CBE

Ogilvy, Sir Francis Gilbert Arthur, Bt. (S. 1626)

Ogilvy-Wedderburn, Sir Andrew John Alexander, Bt. (1803)

Ogio, *HE* Sir Michael, GCMG, CBE

Ognall, *Hon.* Sir Harry Henry, Kt.

Ohlson, Sir Brian Eric Christopher, Bt. (1920)

Oldham, *Dr* Sir John, Kt., OBE

Oliver, Sir James Michael Yorrick, Kt.

Oliver, Sir Stephen John Lindsay, Kt., QC

O'Hara *Hon.* Sir John Ailbe

†O'Loghlen, Sir Michael, Bt. (1838)

Olver, Sir Richard Lake, Kt.

Omand, Sir David Bruce, GCB

Ondaatje, Sir Christopher, Kt., CBE

O'Nions, Prof. Sir Robert Keith, Kt., FRS, PHD

Onslow, Sir Richard Paul Atherton, Bt. (1797)

Oppenheimer, Sir Michael Bernard Grenville, Bt. (1921)

Oppenshaw, Sir Charles Peter Lawford, Kt., QC

O'Rahilly, *Prof.* Sir Stephen Patrick, Kt., FRS

Orde, Sir Hugh Stephen Roden, Kt., OBE, QPM

O'Regan, *Dr* Sir Stephen Gerard (Tipene), Kt.

O'Reilly, Sir Anthony John Francis, Kt.

O'Reilly, *Prof.* Sir John James, Kt.

Orr, Sir John, Kt., OBE

Orr-Ewing, Sir (Alistair) Simon, Bt. (1963)

Orr-Ewing, Sir Archibald Donald, Bt. (1886)

Osborn, Sir John Holbrook, Kt.

Osborn, Sir Richard Henry Danvers, Bt. (1662)

Osborne, Sir Peter George, Bt. (I. 1629)

O'Shea, *Prof.* Sir Timothy Michael Martin, Kt.

Osmotherly, Sir Edward Benjamin Crofton, Kt., CB

Oswald, Sir (William Richard) Michael, KCVO

Ottaway *Rt. Hon.* Sir Richard Geoffrey James, Kt.

Otton, Sir Geoffrey John, KCB

Otton, *Rt. Hon.* Sir Philip Howard, Kt.

Oulton, Sir Antony Derek Maxwell, GCB, QC

Ouseley, *Hon.* Sir Brian Walter, Kt.

Outram, Sir Alan James, Bt. (1858)

Owen, Sir Geoffrey, Kt.

Owen, *Prof.* Sir Michaael John, Kt.

Owen, *Hon.* Sir Robert Michael, Kt.

Owen-Jones, Sir Lindsay Harwood, KBE

Packer, Sir Richard John, KCB

Paget, Sir Julian Tolver, Bt. (1871), CVO

Paget, Sir Richard Herbert, Bt. (1886)

Paice, *Rt. Hon.* Sir James Edward Thornton, Kt.

Paine, Sir Christopher Hammon, Kt., FRCP, FRCR

Pakenham, *Hon.* Sir Michael Aiden, KBE, CMG

Palin, *Air Chief Marshal* Sir Roger Hewlett, KCB, OBE

Palmer, Sir Albert Rocky, Kt.

Palmer, Sir (Charles) Mark, Bt. (1886)

Palmer, Sir Geoffrey Christopher John, Bt. (1660)

Palmer, *Rt. Hon.* Sir Geoffrey Winston Russell, KCMG

Palmer, *Prof.* Sir Godfrey Henry Oliver, Kt., OBE

Palmer, Sir John Edward Somerset, Bt. (1791)

Palmer, *Maj.-Gen.* Sir (Joseph) Michael, KCVO

Palmer, Sir Reginald Oswald, GCMG, MBE

Paniguian, Sir Richard Leon, Kt., CBE

Panter, Sir Howard Hugh, Kt.

Pappano, Sir Antonio, Kt.

Parbo, Sir Arvi Hillar, Kt.

Park, *Hon.* Sir Andrew Edward Wilson, Kt.

Parker, Sir Alan, Kt.

Parker, Sir Alan William, Kt., CBE

Parker, *Rt. Hon.* Sir Jonathan Frederic, Kt.

Parker, *Hon.* Sir Kenneth Blades, Kt.

Parker, *Maj.* Sir Michael John, KCVO, CBE

Parker, *Gen.* Sir Nicholas Ralph, KCB, CBE

Parker, Sir Richard (William) Hyde, Bt. (1681)

Parker, Sir (Thomas) John, GBE

Parker, Sir William Peter Brian, Bt. (1844)

Parkes, Sir Edward Walter, Kt., FRENG

Parkinson, Sir Michael, Kt., CBE

Parry, *Prof.* Sir Eldryd Hugh Owen, KCMG, OBE

Parry, Sir Emyr Jones, GCMG

Parry-Evans, *Air Chief Marshal* Sir David, GCB, CBE

Parsons, Sir John Christopher, KCVO

Parsons, Sir Richard Edmund (Clement Fownes), KCMG

Partridge, Sir Michael John Anthony, KCB

Partridge, Sir Nicholas Wyndham, Kt., OBE

Pascoe, *Gen.* Sir Robert Alan, KCB, MBE

Pasley, Sir Robert Killigrew Sabine, Bt. (1794)

Paston-Bedingfeld, Sir Henry Edgar, Bt. (1661)

Paterson, Sir Dennis Craig, Kt.

Patey, Sir William Charters, KCMG

Patten, *Rt. Hon.* Sir Nicholas John, Kt.

Pattie, *Rt. Hon.* Sir Geoffrey Edwin, Kt.

Pattison, *Prof.* Sir John Ridley, Kt., DM, FRCPATH

Pattullo, Sir (David) Bruce, Kt., CBE

Pauncefote-Duncombe, Sir David Philip Henry, Bt. (1859)

Payne, *Prof.* Sir David Neil, Kt., CBE, FRS

Peace, Sir John Wilfrid, Kt.

Peach, Sir Leonard Harry, Kt.

Peach, *Air Chief Marshal* Sir Stuart William, KCB, CBE

Pearce, Sir (Daniel Norton) Idris, Kt., CBE, TD

Pearse, Sir Brian Gerald, Kt.

Pearson, Sir Francis Nicholas Fraser, Bt. (1964)

Pearson, Sir Keith, Kt.

Pearson, *Gen.* Sir Thomas Cecil Hook, KCB, CBE, DSO

Peart, *Prof.* Sir William Stanley, Kt., MD, FRS

Pease, Sir Joseph Gurney, Bt. (1882)

Pease, Sir Richard Thorn, Bt. (1920)

Peat, Sir Gerrard Charles, KCVO

Peat, Sir Michael Charles Gerrard, GCVO

Peckham, *Prof.* Sir Michael John, Kt.

Peek, Sir Richard Grenville, Bt. (1874)

Pelgen, Sir Harry Friedrich, Kt., MBE

Pelham, *Dr* Sir Hugh Reginald Brentnall, Kt., FRS

Pelly, Sir Richard John, Bt. (1840)

Pendry, *Prof.* Sir John Brian, Kt., FRS

Penny, *Dr* Nicholas Beaver, Kt., FBA

Penrose, *Prof.* Sir Roger, Kt., OM, FRS

Penry-Davey, *Hon.* Sir David Herbert, Kt.

Pepper, *Dr.* Sir David Edwin, KCMG

Pepper, *Prof.* Sir Michael, Kt.

Pepys, *Prof.* Sir Mark Brian, Kt.

Perowne, *Vice-Adm.* Sir James Francis, KBE

Perring, Sir John Raymond, Bt. (1963)

Perris, Sir David (Arthur), Kt., MBE

Perry, Sir David Howard, KCB

Perry, Sir Michael Sydney, GBE

Pervez, Sir Mohammed Anwar, Kt., OBE

Peters, *Prof.* Sir David Keith, Kt., FRCP

Pethica, *Prof.* Sir John Bernard, Kt., FRS

Petit, Sir Dinshaw Manockjee, Bt. (1890)

Peto, Sir Francis Michael Morton, Bt. (1855)

Peto, Sir Henry Christopher Morton Bampfylde, Bt. (1927)

Peto, *Prof.* Sir Richard, Kt., FRS

Petrie, Sir Peter Charles, Bt. (1918), CMG

Pettigrew, Sir Russell Hilton, Kt.

†Philipson-Stow, Sir (Robert) Matthew, Bt. (1907)

Phillips, Sir (Gerald) Hayden, GCB

Phillips, Sir John David, Kt., QPM

Phillips, Sir Jonathan, KCB

Phillips, Sir Peter John, Kt., OBE

Phillips, Sir Robin Francis, Bt. (1912)

Phillips *Hon.* Sir Stephen Edmund, Kt.

Phillips, Sir Tom Richard Vaughan, KCMG

Pickard, Sir (John) Michael, Kt.

Picken, *Hon.* Sir Simon Derek, Kt., QC

Pickles, *Rt. Hon.* Sir Eric Jack, Kt.

Pickthorn, Sir James Francis Mann, Bt. (1959)

Pidgeon, Sir John Allan Stewart, Kt.

†Piers, Sir James Desmond, Bt. (I. 1661)

Piggott-Brown, Sir William Brian, Bt. (1903)

Pigot, Sir George Hugh, Bt. (1764)

Pigott, *Lt.-Gen.* Sir Anthony David, KCB, CBE

Pigott, Sir Berkeley Henry Sebastian, Bt. (1808)

Pike, *Lt.-Gen.* Sir Hew William Royston, KCB, DSO, MBE

Pike, Sir Michael Edmund, KCVO, CMG

Pile, Sir Anthony John Devereux, Bt. (1900)

Pilditch, Sir John Richard, Bt. (1929)

Pill, *Rt. Hon.* Sir Malcolm Thomas, Kt.

Pilling, Sir Joseph Grant, KCB

Pinsent, Sir Matthew Clive, Kt., CBE

†Pinsent, Sir Thomas Benjamin Roy, Kt.

Pirmohamed, *Prof.* Sir Hussein Munir, Kt.

Pissarides, *Prof.* Sir Christopher Antoniou, Kt., FBA

Pitcher, Sir Desmond Henry, Kt.

Pitchers, *Hon.* Sir Christopher (John), Kt.

Pitchford, *Rt. Hon.* Sir Christopher John, Kt.

Pitoi, Sir Sere, Kt., CBE

Pitt, Sir Michael Edward, Kt.

Plastow, Sir David Arnold Stuart, Kt.

Platt, Sir Martin Philip, Bt. (1959)

Pledger, *Air Chief Marshal* Sir Malcolm David, KCB, OBE, AFC

Plender, *Hon.* Sir Richard Owen, Kt.

Plumbly, Sir Derek John, KCMG

Pocock, *Dr* Sir Andrew John, KCMG

Pohai, Sir Timothy, Kt., MBE

Pole, Sir John Chandos, Bt. (1791)

Poliakoff, *Prof.* Sir Martyn, Kt., CBE

Pole, Sir (John) Richard (Walter Reginald) Carew, Bt. (1628)

Polkinghorne, *Revd Canon* John Charlton, KBE

Pollard, Sir Charles, Kt.

†Pollen, Sir Richard John Hungerford, Bt. (1795)

Pollock, Sir George Frederick, Bt. (1866)

Pomeroy, Sir Brian Walter, Kt., CBE

Ponder, *Prof.* Sir Bruce Anthony John, Kt.

Ponsonby, Sir Charles Ashley, Bt. (1956)

Poon, Sir Dickson, Kt., CBE

Poore, Sir Roger Ricardo, Bt. (1795)

Popplewell, *Hon.* Sir Andrew John, Kt.

Popplewell, *Hon.* Sir Oliver Bury, Kt.

†Porritt, *Hon.* Sir Jonathon Espie, Bt. (1963), CBE

Portal, Sir Jonathan Francis, Bt. (1901)

Porter, *Prof.* Sir Keith Macdonald, Kt.

Potter, *Rt. Hon.* Sir Mark Howard, Kt.

Pound, Sir John David, Bt. (1905)

Povey, Sir Keith, Kt., QPM

Powell, Sir John Christopher, Kt.

Powell, Sir Nicholas Folliott Douglas, Bt. (1897)

Power, Sir Alastair John Cecil, Bt. (1924)

Pownall, Sir Michael Graham, KCB

Prance, *Prof.* Sir Ghillean Tolmie, Kt., FRS

Prendergast, Sir (Walter) Kieran, KCVO, CMG

Prescott, Sir Mark, Bt. (1938)

Preston, Sir Philip Charles Henry Hulton, Bt. (1815)

Prevost, Sir Christopher Gerald, Bt. (1805)

Price, Sir Francis Caradoc Rose, Bt. (1815)

Price, Sir Frank Leslie, Kt.

†Prichard-Jones, Sir David John Walter, Bt. (1910)

Priestly, Sir Julian Gordon, KCMG

†Primrose, Sir John Ure, Bt. (1903)

Pringle, *Hon.* Sir John Kenneth, Kt.

†Pringle, Sir Simon Robert, Bt. (S. 1683)

Proby, Sir William Henry, Bt. (1952)

Proctor-Beauchamp, Sir Christopher Radstock, Bt. (1745)

Prosser, Sir David John, Kt.

Prosser, Sir Ian Maurice Gray, Kt.

Pryke, Sir Christopher Dudley, Bt. (1926)

Puapua, *Rt. Hon.* Sir Tomasi, GCMG, KBE

Pulford, *Air Marshal* Sir Andrew Douglas, KCB, CBE

Purves, Sir William, Kt., CBE, DSO

Purvis, *Vice-Adm.* Sir Neville, KCB

Quan, Sir Henry (Francis), KBE

Quilter, Sir Guy Raymond Cuthbert, Bt. (1897)

Radcliffe, Sir Sebastian Everard, Bt. (1813)

Radda, *Prof.* Sir George Karoly, Kt., CBE, FRS

Rae, Sir William, Kt., QPM

Raeburn, Sir Michael Edward Norman, Bt. (1923)

Rake, Sir Michael Derek Vaughan, Kt.

Ralli, Sir David Charles, Bt. (1912)

Ramakrishnan, *Dr* Sir Venkatraman, Kt.

Ramdanee, Sir Mookteswar Baboolall Kailash, Kt.

Ramphal, Sir Shridath Surendranath, GCMG

Ramphul, Sir Baalkhristna, Kt.

Ramphul, Sir Indurduth, Kt.

Ramsay, Sir Alexander William Burnett, Bt. (1806)

Ramsay, Sir Allan John (Hepple), KBE, CMG

Ramsay-Fairfax-Lucy, Sir Edmund John William Hugh, Bt. (1836)

Ramsden, Sir David Edward John, Kt., CBE

Ramsden, Sir John Charles Josslyn, Bt. (1689)

Ramsey, *Dr* Sir Frank Cuthbert, KCMG

Ramsey, *Hon.* Sir Vivian Arthur, Kt.

Randall, *Rt. Hon.* Sir (Alexander) John, Kt.

Rankin, Sir Ian Niall, Bt. (1898)

Rasch, Sir Simon Anthony Carne, Bt. (1903)

Rashleigh, Sir Richard Harry, Bt. (1831)

Ratcliffe, *Prof.* Sir Peter John, Kt., FRS

Ratford, Sir David John Edward, KCMG, CVO

Rattee, *Hon.* Sir Donald Keith, Kt.

Rattle, Sir Simon Dennis, Kt., OM, CBE

Rawlins, *Hon.* Sir Hugh Anthony, Kt.

Rawlins, *Prof.* Sir Michael David, Kt., FRCP, FRCPED

Rawlinson, Sir Anthony Henry John, Bt. (1891)

Rea, *Prof.* Sir Desmond, Kt., OBE

Read, *Prof.* Sir David John, Kt.

Reardon-Smith, Sir (William) Antony (John), Bt. (1920)

Reddaway, Sir David Norman, KCMG, MBE

Redgrave, Sir Steven Geoffrey, Kt., CBE

Redmayne, Sir Giles Martin, Bt. (1964)

Redmond, Sir Anthony Gerard, Kt.

Redwood, Sir Peter Boverton, Bt. (1911)

Reed, *Prof.* Sir Alec Edward, Kt., CBE

Reedie, Sir Craig Collins, Kt., CBE

Rees, Sir David Allan, Kt., PHD, DSC, FRS

Rees, Sir Richard Ellis Meuric, Kt., CBE

Reffell, *Adm.* Sir Derek Roy, KCB

Reich, Sir Erich Arieh, Kt.

Reid, Sir Alexander James, Bt. (1897)

Reid, Sir David Edward, Kt.

Reid, *Rt. Hon.* Sir George, Kt.

Reid, Sir (Philip) Alan, GCVO

Reid, Sir Robert Paul, Kt.

Reid, Sir William Kennedy, KCB

Reiher, Sir Frederick Bernard Carl, KCMG, KBE

Reilly, *Lt.-Gen.* Sir Jeremy Calcott, KCB, DSO

Renals, Sir Stanley, Bt. (1895)

Renouf, Sir Clement William Bailey, Kt.

Renshaw, Sir John David Bine, Bt. (1903)

Renwick, Sir Richard Eustace, Bt. (1921)

†Reynolds, Sir James Francis, Bt. (1923)

Reynolds, Sir Peter William John, Kt., CBE

Rhodes, Sir John Christopher Douglas, Bt. (1919)

Rice, *Prof.* Sir Charles Duncan, Kt.

Rice, *Maj.-Gen.* Sir Desmond Hind Garrett, KCVO, CBE

Rice, Sir Timothy Miles Bindon, Kt.

Richard, Sir Cliff, Kt., OBE

Richards, Sir Brian Mansel, Kt., CBE, PHD

Richards, *Hon.* Sir David Anthony Stewart, Kt.

Richards, Sir David Gerald, Kt.

Richards, Sir Francis Neville, KCMG, CVO

Richards, *Prof.* Sir Michael Adrian, Kt., CBE

Richards, Sir Rex Edward, Kt., DSC, FRS

Richards, *Rt. Hon.* Sir Stephen Price, Kt.

Richardson, Sir Anthony Lewis, Bt. (1924)

Richardson, Sir John Patrick, KBE

Richardson, Sir Thomas Legh, KCMG

Richardson-Bunbury, Sir (Richard David) Michael, Bt. (I. 1787)

Richmond, Sir David Frank, KBE, CMG

Richmond, *Prof.* Sir Mark Henry, Kt., FRS

Ricketts, Sir Peter Forbes, GCMG, GCVO

Ricketts, Sir Stephen Tristram, Bt. (1828)

Ricks, *Prof.* Sir Christopher Bruce, Kt.

Riddell, Sir Walter John, Bt. (S. 1628)

Ridgway, *Lt.-Gen.* Sir Andrew Peter, KBE, CB

Ridley, Sir Adam (Nicholas), Kt.

Ridley, Sir Michael Kershaw, KCVO

Rifkind, *Rt. Hon.* Sir Malcolm Leslie, KCMG

Rigby, Sir Anthony John, Bt. (1929)

Rigby, Sir Peter, Kt.

Rimer, *Rt. Hon.* Sir Colin Percy Farquharson, Kt.

Ripley, Sir William Hugh, Bt. (1880)

Ritako, Sir Thomas Baha, Kt., MBE

Ritblat, Sir John Henry, Kt.

Ritchie, *Prof.* Sir Lewis Duthie, Kt., OBE

Rivett-Carnac, Sir Jonathan James, Bt. (1836)

Rix, *Rt. Hon.* Sir Bernard Anthony, Kt.

Robb, Sir John Weddell, Kt.

Roberts, Sir Derek Harry, Kt., CBE, FRS, FRENG

Roberts, *Prof.* Sir Edward Adam, KCMG

Roberts, Sir Gilbert Howland Rookehurst, Bt. (1809)

Roberts, Sir Hugh Ashley, GCVO

Roberts, Sir Ivor Anthony, KCMG

Roberts, *Dr* Sir Richard John, Kt.

Roberts, Sir Samuel, Bt. (1919)

Roberts, *Maj.-Gen.* Sir Sebastian John Lechmere, KCVO, OBE

†Roberts-Buchanan, Sir James Elton Denby, Bt. (1909)

Robertson, Sir Simon Manwaring, Kt.

Robins, Sir Ralph Harry, Kt., FRENG

Robinson, Sir Anthony, Kt.

Robinson, Sir Bruce, KCB

†Robinson, Sir Christopher Philipse, Bt. (1854)

Robinson, Sir Gerrard Jude, Kt.

Robinson, Sir Ian, Kt.

Robinson, Sir John James Michael Laud, Bt. (1660)

Robinson, *Dr* Sir Kenneth, Kt.

Robinson, Sir Peter Frank, Bt. (1908)

Robson, Sir John Adam, KCMG

Robson, Sir Stephen Arthur, Kt., CB

Roch, *Rt. Hon.* Sir John Ormond, Kt.

Roche, Sir David O'Grady, Bt. (1838)

Roche, Sir Henry John, Kt.

Rodgers, Sir (Andrew) Piers (Wingate Aikin-Sneath), Bt. (1964)

Rodley, *Prof.* Sir Nigel, KBE

Rogers, *Air Chief Marshal* Sir John Robson, KCB, CBE

Rogers, Sir Peter, Kt.

Rollo, *Lt.-Gen.* Sir William Raoul, KCB, CBE

Ropner, Sir John Bruce Woollacott, Bt. (1952)

Ropner, Sir Robert Clinton, Bt. (1904)

Rose, Sir Arthur James, Kt., CBE

Rose, *Rt. Hon.* Sir Christopher Dudley Roger, Kt.

Rose, Sir Clive Martin, GCMG

Rose, Sir David Lancaster, Bt. (1874)

Rose, *Gen.* Sir (Hugh) Michael, KCB, CBE, DSO, QGM

Rose, Sir John Edward Victor, Kt.

Rose, Sir Julian Day, Bt. (1872 and 1909)

Rosenthal, Sir Norman Leon, Kt.

Ross, *Maj.* Sir Andrew Charles Paterson, Bt. (1960)

Ross, *Lt.-Gen.* Sir Robert Jeremy, KCB, OBE

Ross, *Lt.-Col.* Sir Walter Hugh Malcolm, GCVO, OBE

Ross, Sir Walter Robert Alexander, KCVO

Rossi, Sir Hugh Alexis Louis, Kt.

Roth, *Hon.* Sir Peter Marcel, Kt.

Rothschild, Sir Evelyn Robert Adrian de, Kt.

Rove, *Revd* Ikan, KBE

Rowe, *Rear-Adm.* Sir Patrick Barton, KCVO, CBE

Rowe-Ham, Sir David Kenneth, GBE

Rowland, Sir Geoffrey Robert, Kt.

Rowland, Sir (John) David, Kt.

Rowley, Sir Richard Charles, Bt. (1786 and 1836)

Rowling, Sir John Reginald, Kt.

Rowlinson, *Prof.* Sir John Shipley, Kt., FRS

Royce, *Hon.* Sir Roger John, Kt.

Royden, Sir Christopher John, Bt. (1905)

Rubin, *Prof.* Sir Peter Charles, Kt.

Rudd, Sir (Anthony) Nigel (Russell), Kt.

Ruddock, Sir Paul, Kt.

Rudge, Sir Alan Walter, Kt., CBE, FRS

Rugge-Price, Sir James Keith Peter, Bt. (1804)

Ruggles-Brise, Sir Timothy Edward, Bt. (1935)

Rumbold, Sir Henry John Sebastian, Bt. (1779)

Rushdie, Sir (Ahmed) Salman, Kt.

†Russell, Sir (Arthur) Mervyn, Bt. (1812)

Russell, Sir Charles Dominic, Bt. (1916)

Russell, Sir George, Kt., CBE

Russell, Sir Muir, KCB

Russell, Sir Robert, Kt.

Rutter, *Prof.* Sir Michael Llewellyn, Kt., CBE, MD, FRS

Ryan, Sir Derek Gerald, Bt. (1919)

Rycroft, Sir Richard John, Bt. (1784)

Ryder, *Rt. Hon.* Sir Ernest Nigel, Kt., TD

Sacranie, Sir Iqbal Abdul Karim Mussa, Kt., OBE

Sainsbury, *Rt. Hon.* Sir Timothy Alan Davan, Kt.

St Clair-Ford, Sir Robin Sam, Bt. (1793)

St George, Sir John Avenel Bligh, Bt. (I. 1766)

St John-Mildmay, Sir Walter John Hugh, Bt. (1772)

St Omer, *Hon. Dr* Sir Dunstan Gerbert Raphael, KCMG

Sainty, Sir John Christopher, KCB

Sakora, *Hon.* Sir Bernard Berekia, KBE

Sales, *Rt. Hon.* Sir Philip James, Kt.

Salika, Sir Gibuna Gibbs, KBE

Salisbury, Sir Robert William, Kt.

Salt, Sir Patrick MacDonnell, Bt. (1869)

Salt, Sir (Thomas) Michael John, Bt. (1899)

Salusbury-Trelawny, Sir John William Richard, Bt. (1628)

Salz, Sir Anthony Michael Vaughan, Kt.

Samani, *Prof.* Sir Nilesh Jayantilal, Kt.

Sampson, Sir Colin, Kt., CBE, QPM

Samuel, Sir John Michael Glen, Bt. (1898)

Samuelson, Sir James Francis, Bt. (1884)

Samuelson, Sir Sydney Wylie, Kt., CBE

Samworth, Sir David Chetwode, Kt., CBE

Sanders, Sir Robert Tait, KBE, CMG

Sanders, Sir Ronald Michael, KCMG

Sanderson, Sir Frank Linton, Bt. (1920)

Sands, Sir Roger Blakemore, KCB

Sants, Sir Hector William Hepburn, Kt.

Sarei, Sir Alexis Holyweek, Kt., CBE

Sargent, Sir William Desmond, Kt., CBE

Satchwell, Sir Kevin Joseph, Kt.

Saunders, Sir Bruce Joshua, KBE

Saunders, *Hon.* Sir John Henry Boulton, Kt.

Savill, *Prof.* Sir John Stewart, Kt.

Savory, Sir Michael Berry, Kt.

Sawers, Sir Robert John, GCMG

Saxby, *Prof.* Sir Robin Keith, Kt.

Scarlett, Sir John McLeod, KCMG, OBE

Schiemann, *Rt. Hon.* Sir Konrad Hermann Theodor, Kt.

Schiff, Sir András, Kt.

Scholar, Sir Michael Charles, KCB

Scholey, Sir David Gerald, Kt., CBE

Schubert, Sir Sydney, Kt.

Scipio, Sir Hudson Rupert, Kt.

Scott, Sir Anthony Percy, Bt. (1913)

Scott, Sir David Richard Alexander, Kt., CBE

Scott, *Prof.* Sir George Peter, Kt.

Scott, Sir James Jervoise, Bt. (1962)

Scott, Sir John Hamilton, KCVO

Scott, Sir Kenneth Bertram Adam, KCVO, CMG

Scott, Sir Oliver Christopher Anderson, Bt. (1909)

Scott, *Prof.* Sir Philip John, KBE

Scott, Sir Ridley, Kt.

Scott, Sir Robert David Hillyer, Kt.

Scott, Sir Walter John, Bt. (1907)

Scott-Lee, Sir Paul Joseph, Kt., QPM

Seale, Sir Clarence David, Kt.

Seale, Sir John Henry, Bt. (1838)

Sealy, Sir Austen Llewellyn, Kt.

Sebastian, Sir Cuthbert Montraville, GCMG, OBE

†Sebright, Sir Rufus Hugo Giles, Bt. (1626)

Seccombe, Sir (William) Vernon Stephen, Kt.

Seconde, Sir Reginald Louis, KCMG, CVO

Sedley, *Rt. Hon.* Sir Stephen John, Kt.

Seely, Sir Nigel Edward, Bt. (1896)

Seeto, Sir Ling James, Kt., MBE

Seeyave, Sir Rene Sow Choung, Kt., CBE

Seldon, *Dr* Sir Anthony Francis, Kt.

Semple, Sir John Laughlin, KCB

Sergeant, Sir Patrick, Kt.

Serota, *Hon.* Sir Nicholas Andrew, Kt., CH

Setchell, Sir Marcus Edward, KCVO

†Seton, Sir Charles Wallace, Bt. (S. 1683)

Seton, Sir Iain Bruce, Bt. (S. 1663)

Severne, *Air Vice-Marshal* Sir John de Milt, KCVO, OBE, AFC

Seymour, Sir Julian Roger, Kt., CBE

Shadbolt, *Prof.* Sir Nigel Richard, Kt.

Shaffer, Sir Peter Levin, Kt., CBE

Shakerley, Sir Nicholas Simon Adam, Bt. (1838)

Shakespeare, Sir Thomas William, Bt. (1942)

Sharp, Sir Adrian, Bt. (1922)

Sharp, Sir Leslie, Kt., QPM

Sharp, Sir Sheridan Christopher Robin, Bt. (1920)

Sharples, Sir James, Kt., QPM

Shaw, Sir Charles De Vere, Bt. (1821)

Shaw, *Prof.* Sir John Calman, Kt., CBE

Shaw, Sir Neil McGowan, Kt.

Shaw-Stewart, Sir Ludovic Houston, Bt. (S. 1667)

Shebbeare, Sir Thomas Andrew, KCVO

Sheehy, Sir Patrick, Kt.

Sheffield, Sir Reginald Adrian Berkeley, Bt. (1755)

Shehadie, Sir Nicholas Michael, Kt., OBE

Sheil, *Rt. Hon.* Sir John, Kt.

Sheinwald, Sir Nigel Elton, GCMG

Shelley, Sir John Richard, Bt. (1611)

Shepherd, Sir Colin Ryley, Kt.

Shepherd, Sir John Alan, KCVO, CMG

Shepherd, Sir Richard Charles Scrimgeour, Kt.

Sher, Sir Antony, KBE

Sherlock, Sir Nigel, KCVO, OBE

Sherston-Baker, Sir Robert George Humphrey, Bt. (1796)

Shiffner, Sir Henry David, Bt. (1818)

Shinwell, Sir (Maurice) Adrian, Kt.

Shirreff, *Gen.* Sir Alexander Richard David, KCB, CBE

Shock, Sir Maurice, Kt.

Shortridge, Sir Jon Deacon, KCB

Shuckburgh, Sir James Rupert Charles, Bt. (1660)

Sieff, *Hon.* Sir David, Kt.

Silber, *Rt. Hon.* Sir Stephen Robert, Kt.

Silk, Sir Evan Paul, KCB

†Simeon, Sir Stephen George Barrington, Bt. (1815)

Simmonds, *Rt. Hon. Dr* Sir Kennedy Alphonse, KCMG

Simmons, *Air Marshal* Sir Michael George, KCB, AFC

Simmons, Sir Stanley Clifford, Kt.

Simms, Sir Neville Ian, Kt., FRENG

Simon, *Hon.* Sir Peregrine Charles Hugh, Kt.

Simonet, Sir Louis Marcel Pierre, Kt., CBE

Simpson, Sir Peter Austin, Kt., OBE

Simpson, *Dr* Sir Peter Jeffery, Kt.

Sims, Sir Roger Edward, Kt.

Sinclair, Sir Clive Marles, Kt.

Sinclair, Sir Robert John, Kt.

Sinclair, Sir William Robert Francis, Bt. (S. 1704)

Sinclair-Lockhart, Sir Simon John Edward Francis, Bt. (S. 1636)

Singer, *Hon.* Sir Jan Peter, Kt.

Singh, *His Hon.* Sir Mota, Kt., QC

Singh, Sir Pritpal, Kt.

Singh, *Hon.* Sir Rabinder, Kt.

Singleton, Sir Roger, Kt., CBE

Sione, Sir Tomu Malaefone, GCMG, OBE

Sissons, *Prof.* Sir (John Gerald) Patrick, Kt.

†Sitwell, Sir George Reresby Sacheverell, Bt. (1808)

Skeggs, Sir Clifford George, Kt.

Skehel, Sir John James, Kt., FRS

Skingsley, *Air Chief Marshal* Sir Anthony Gerald, GBE, KCB

Skinner, Sir (Thomas) Keith (Hewitt), Bt. (1912)

Skipwith, Sir Patrick Alexander d'Estoteville, Bt. (1622)

Slack, Sir William Willatt, KCVO, FRCS

Slade, Sir Benjamin Julian Alfred, Bt. (1831)

Slade, *Rt. Hon.* Sir Christopher John, Kt.

Slaney, *Prof.* Sir Geoffrey, KBE

Slater, *Adm.* Sir John (Jock) Cunningham Kirkwood, GCB, LVO

Sleight, Sir Richard, Bt. (1920)

Smiley, *Lt.-Col.* Sir John Philip, Bt. (1903)

Smith, *Prof.* Sir Adrian Frederick Melhuish, Kt., FRS

Smith, *Hon.* Sir Andrew Charles, Kt.

Smith, Sir Andrew Thomas, Bt. (1897)

Smith, *Prof.* Sir David Cecil, Kt., FRS

Smith, Sir David Iser, KCVO

Smith, Sir Dudley (Gordon), Kt.

Smith, *Prof.* Sir Eric Brian, Kt., PHD

Smith, Sir John Alfred, Kt., QPM

Smith, Sir Joseph William Grenville, Kt.

Smith, Sir Kevin, Kt., CBE

Smith, Sir Martin Gregory, Kt.

Smith, Sir Michael John Llewellyn, KCVO, CMG

Smith, Sir (Norman) Brian, Kt., CBE, PHD

Smith, Sir Paul Brierley, Kt., CBE

Smith, *Hon.* Sir Peter (Winston), Kt.

Smith, Sir Robert Courtney, Kt., CBE

Smith, Sir Robert Hill, Bt. (1945)

Smith, *Gen.* Sir Rupert Anthony, KCB, DSO, OBE, QGM

Smith, Sir Steven Murray, Kt.

Smith-Dodsworth, Sir David John, Bt. (1784)

Smith-Gordon, Sir (Lionel) Eldred (Peter), Bt. (1838)

Smith-Marriott, Sir Peter Francis, Bt. (1774)

Smurfit, *Dr.* Sir Michael William Joseph, KBE

Smyth, Sir Timothy John, Bt. (1956)

Snowden, *Prof.* Sir Christopher Maxwell, Kt.

Snowden, *Hon.* Sir Richard Andrew, Kt., QC

Snyder, Sir Michael John, Kt.

Soames, *Rt. Hon.* Sir (Arthur) Nicholas Winston, Kt.

Soar, *Adm.* Sir Trevor Alan, KCB, OBE

Sobers, Sir Garfield St Auburn, Kt.

Solomon, Sir Harry, Kt.

Somare, *Rt. Hon.* Sir Michael Thomas, GCMG, CH

Somerville, *Brig.* Sir John Nicholas, Kt., CBE

Songo, Sir Bernard Paul, Kt., CMG, OBE

Sorabji, *Prof.* Sir Richard Rustom Kharsedji, Kt., CBE

Sorrell, Sir John William, Kt., CBE

Sorrell, Sir Martin Stuart, Kt.

Sosa, Sir Manuel, Kt.

Soulsby, Sir Peter Alfred, Kt.

Soutar, *Air Marshal* Sir Charles John Williamson, KBE

Souter, Sir Brian, Kt.

Southby, Sir John Richard Bilbe, Bt. (1937)

Southern, *Prof.* Sir Edwin Mellor, Kt.

Southgate, Sir Colin Grieve, Kt.

Southgate, Sir William David, Kt.

Southward, *Dr* Sir Nigel Ralph, KCVO

Sowrey, *Air Marshal* Sir Frederick Beresford, KCB, CBE, AFC

Sparrow, Sir John, Kt.

Spearman, Sir Alexander Young Richard Mainwaring, Bt. (1840)

Speed, Sir (Herbert) Keith, Kt., RD

Spencer, Sir Derek Harold, Kt., QC

Spencer, *Vice-Adm.* Sir Peter, KCB

Spencer, *Hon.* Sir Robin Godfrey, Kt.

Spencer-Nairn, Sir Robert Arnold, Bt. (1933)

Spicer, Sir Nicholas Adrian Albert, Bt. (1906)

Spiegelhalter *Prof.* Sir David John, Kt., OBE, FRS

Spiers, Sir Donald Maurice, Kt., CB, TD

Spooner, Sir James Douglas, Kt.

Spring, Sir Dryden Thomas, Kt.

Spurling, Sir John Damian, KCVO, OBE

Squire, *Air Chief Marshal* Sir Peter Ted, GCB, DFC, AFC, ADC

Stadlen, *Hon.* Sir Nicholas Felix, Kt.

Stagg, Sir Charles Richard Vernon, KCMG

Staite, Sir Richard John, Kt., OBE

Stamer, Sir Peter Tomlinson, Bt. (1809)

Stanhope, *Adm.* Sir Mark, GCB, OBE, ADC

Stanier, Sir Beville Douglas, Bt. (1917)

Stanley, *Rt. Hon.* Sir John Paul, Kt.

Starkey, Sir John Philip, Bt. (1935)

Starmer, Sir Keir, KCB, QC

Stear, *Air Chief Marshal* Sir Michael James Douglas, KCB, CBE

Steel, *Vice-Adm.* Sir David George, KBE

Steel, *Hon.* Sir David William, Kt.

Steer, Sir Alan William, Kt.

Stephen, *Rt. Hon.* Sir Ninian Martin, KG, GCMG, GCVO, KBE

Stephens, Sir (Edwin) Barrie, Kt.

Stephens, Sir Jonathan Andrew de Sievrac, KCB

Stephens, Sir William Benjamin Synge, Kt.

Stephenson, Sir Henry Upton, Bt. (1936)

Stephenson, Sir Paul Robert, Kt., QPM

Sterling, Sir Michael John Howard, Kt.

Sternberg, Sir Sigmund, Kt.

Stevenson, Sir Hugh Alexander, Kt.

Stevenson, Sir Simpson, Kt.

Stewart, Sir Alan d'Arcy, Bt. (I. 1623)

Stewart, Sir Brian John, Kt., CBE

Stewart, Sir David James Henderson, Bt. (1957)

Stewart, Sir David John Christopher, Bt. (1803)

Stewart, Sir James Moray, KCB

Stewart, Sir (John) Simon (Watson), Bt. (1920)

Stewart, Sir John Young, Kt., OBE

Stewart, Sir Patrick, Kt., OBE

Stewart, *Lt.-Col.* Sir Robert Christie, KCVO, CBE, TD

Stewart, Sir Robin Alastair, Bt. (1960)

Stewart, *Hon.* Sir Stephen Paul, Kt.

Stewart, *Prof.* Sir William Duncan Paterson, Kt., FRS, FRSE

Stewart-Clark, Sir John, Bt. (1918)

Stewart-Richardson, Sir Simon Alaisdair, Bt. (S. 1630)

Stilgoe, Sir Richard Henry Simpson, Kt., OBE

Stirling, Sir Angus Duncan Aeneas, Kt.

Stirling of Garden, *Col.* Sir James, KCVO, CBE, TD

Stirling-Hamilton, Sir Malcolm William Bruce, Bt. (S. 1673)

Stockdale, Sir Thomas Minshull, Bt. (1960)

Stoddart, *Prof.* Sir James Fraser, Kt.

Stone, Sir Christopher, Kt.

Stonhouse, *Revd* Michael Philip, Bt. (1628 and 1670)

Stonor, *Air Marshal* Sir Thomas Henry, KCB

Stoppard, Sir Thomas, Kt., OM, CBE

Storey, *Hon.* Sir Richard, Bt., CBE (1960)

Stothard, Sir Peter Michael, Kt.

Stott, Sir Adrian George Ellingham, Bt. (1920)

Stoute, Sir Michael Ronald, Kt.

Stracey, Sir John Simon, Bt. (1818)

Strachan, Sir Curtis Victor, Kt., CVO

Strachan, Sir Hew Francis Anthony, Kt.

Strachey, Sir Charles, Bt. (1801)

Straker, Sir Louis Hilton, KCMG

Strang Steel, Sir (Fiennes) Michael, Bt. (1938), CBE

Stratton, *Prof.* Sir Michael Rudolf, Kt., FRS

Street, *Hon.* Sir Laurence Whistler, KCMG

Streeton, Sir Terence George, KBE, CMG

Strickland-Constable, Sir Frederic, Bt. (1641)

Stringer, Sir Donald Edgar, Kt., CBE

Stringer, Sir Howard, Kt.

Strong, Sir Roy Colin, Kt., PHD, FSA

Stronge, Sir James Anselan Maxwell, Bt. (1803)

Stuart, Sir James Keith, Kt.

Stuart, Sir Kenneth Lamonte, Kt.

†Stuart, Sir Phillip Luttrell, Bt. (1660)

†Stuart-Forbes, Sir William Daniel, Bt. (S. 1626)

Stuart-Menteth, Sir Charles Greaves, Bt. (1838)

Stuart-Paul, *Air Marshal* Sir Ronald Ian, KBE

Stuart-Smith, *Hon.* Sir Jeremy Hugh, Kt.

Stuart-Smith, *Rt. Hon.* Sir Murray, KCMG, Kt.

Stubbs, Sir William Hamilton, Kt., PHD

Stucley, *Lt.* Sir Hugh George Coplestone Bampfylde, Bt. (1859)

Studd, Sir Edward Fairfax, Bt. (1929)

Studholme, Sir Henry William, Bt. (1956)

Stunell, *Rt. Hon.* Sir Robert Andrew, Kt., OBE

Sturridge, Sir Nicholas Anthony, KCVO

Stuttard, Sir John Boothman, Kt.

†Style, Sir William Frederick, Bt. (1627)

Sullivan, *Rt. Hon.* Sir Jeremy Mirth, Kt.

Sullivan, Sir Richard Arthur, Bt. (1804)

Sulston, Sir John Edward, Kt.

Sunderland, Sir John Michael, Kt.

Supperstone, *Hon.* Sir Michael Alan, Kt.

Sutherland, Sir John Brewer, Bt. (1921)

Sutherland, Sir William George MacKenzie, Kt.

Sutton, Sir Richard Lexington, Bt. (1772)

Swan, Sir Conrad Marshall John Fisher, KCVO, PHD

Swan, Sir John William David, KBE

Swann, Sir Michael Christopher, Bt. (1906), TD

Sweeney, Sir George, Kt.

Sweeney, *Hon.* Sir Nigel Hamilton, Kt.

Sweeting, *Prof.* Sir Martin Nicholas, Kt., OBE, FRS

Swinburn, *Lt.-Gen.* Sir Richard Hull, KCB

Swinnerton-Dyer, *Prof.* Sir (Henry) Peter (Francis), Bt. (1678), KBE, FRS

Swinton, *Maj.-Gen.* Sir John, KCVO, OBE

Swire, Sir Adrian Christopher, Kt.

Swire, Sir John Anthony, Kt., CBE

Sykes, Sir David Michael, Bt. (1921)

Sykes, Sir Francis John Badcock, Bt. (1781)

Sykes, Sir Hugh Ridley, Kt.

Sykes, *Prof.* Sir (Malcolm) Keith, Kt.

Sykes, Sir Richard, Kt.

Sykes, Sir Tatton Christopher Mark, Bt. (1783)

Symons, *Vice-Adm.* Sir Patrick Jeremy, KBE

†Synge, Sir Allen James Edward, Bt. (1801)

Tang, Sir David Wing-cheung, KBE

Tanner, Sir David Whitlock, Kt., CBE

Tapps-Gervis-Meyrick, Sir George Christopher Cadafael, Bt. (1791)

Tapsell, *Rt. Hon.* Sir Peter Hannay Bailey, Kt.

†Tate, Sir Edward Nicolas, Bt. (1898)

Taureka, *Dr* Sir Reubeh, KBE

Tauvasa, Sir Joseph James, KBE

Taylor, Sir Cyril Julian Hebden, GBE

Taylor, Sir Edward Macmillan (Teddy), Kt.

Taylor, Sir Hugh Henderson, KCB

Taylor, *Rt. Revd* John Bernard, KCVO

Taylor, *Dr* Sir John Michael, Kt., OBE

Taylor, *Prof.* Sir Martin John, Kt., FRS

Taylor, Sir Nicholas Richard Stuart, Bt. (1917)

Taylor, *Prof.* Sir William, Kt., CBE

Taylor, Sir William George, Kt.

Teagle, *Vice-Adm.* Sir Somerford Francis, KBE

Teare, *Hon.* Sir Nigel John Martin, Kt.

Teasdale, *Prof.* Sir Graham Michael, Kt.

Tebbit, Sir Kevin Reginald, KCB, CMG

Temple, *Prof.* Sir John Graham, Kt.

Temple, Sir Richard Carnac Chartier, Bt. (1876)

Temu, *Hon. Dr* Sir Puka, KBE, CMG

Tennyson-D'Eyncourt, Sir Mark Gervais, Bt. (1930)

Terry, *Air Marshal* Sir Colin George, KBE, CB

Terry, *Air Chief Marshal* Sir Peter David George, GCB, AFC

Thatcher, *Hon.* Sir Mark, Bt. (1990)

Thomas, Sir David John Godfrey, Bt. (1694)

Thomas, Sir Derek Morison David, KCMG

Thomas, *Prof.* Sir Eric Jackson, Kt.

Thomas, Sir Gilbert Stanley, Kt., OBE

Thomas, Sir Jeremy Cashel, KCMG

Thomas, Sir (John) Alan, Kt.

Thomas, *Prof.* Sir John Meurig, Kt., FRS

Thomas, Sir Keith Vivian, Kt.

Thomas, *Dr* Sir Leton Felix, KCMG, CBE

Thomas, Sir Philip Lloyd, KCVO, CMG

Thomas, Sir Quentin Jeremy, Kt., CB

Thomas, *Rt. Hon.* Sir Swinton Barclay, Kt.

Thomas, Sir William Michael, Bt. (1919)

Thompson, Sir Christopher Peile, Bt. (1890)

Thompson, Sir Clive Malcolm, Kt.

Thompson, Sir David Albert, KCMG

Thompson, *Prof.* Sir Michael Warwick, Kt., DSc

Thompson, Sir Nicholas Annesley, Bt. (1963)

Thompson, Sir Nigel Cooper, KCMG, CBE

Thompson, Sir Paul Anthony, Bt. (1963)

Thompson, Sir Peter Anthony, Kt.

Thompson, *Dr* Sir Richard Paul Hepworth, KCVO

Thompson, Sir Thomas d'Eyncourt John, Bt. (1806)

Thomson, Sir Adam McClure, KCMG

Thomson, Sir (Frederick Douglas) David, Bt. (1929)

Thomson, Sir John Adam, GCMG

Thomson, Sir Mark Wilfrid Home, Bt. (1925)

Thorne, Sir Neil Gordon, Kt., OBE, TD

Thornton, *Air Marshal* Sir Barry Michael, KCB

Thornton, Sir (George) Malcolm, Kt.

†Thorold, Sir (Anthony) Oliver, Bt. (1642)

Thorpe, *Rt. Hon.* Sir Mathew Alexander, Kt.

Thrift, *Prof.* Sir Nigel John, Kt.

Thurecht, Sir Ramon Richard, Kt., OBE

Thwaites, Sir Bryan, Kt., PHD

Tickell, Sir Crispin Charles Cervantes, GCMG, KCVO

Tidmarsh, Sir James Napier, KCVO, MBE

Tilt, Sir Robin Richard, Kt.

Tiltman, Sir John Hessell, KCVO

Timmins, *Col.* Sir John Bradford, KCVO, OBE, TD

Tims, Sir Michael David, KCVO

Tindle, Sir Ray Stanley, Kt., CBE

Tirvengadum, Sir Harry Krishnan, Kt.

Tjoeng, Sir James Neng, KBE

Tod, *Vice-Adm.* Sir Jonathan James Richard, KCB, CBE

Todd, *Prof.* Sir David, Kt., CBE

Toka, Sir Mahuru Dadi, Kt., MBE

Tollemache, Sir Lyonel Humphry John, Bt. (1793)

Tomkys, Sir (William) Roger, KCMG

Tomlinson, *Prof.* Sir Bernard Evans, Kt., CBE

Tomlinson, Sir John Rowland, Kt., CBE

Tomlinson, Sir Michael John, Kt., CBE

Tomlinson, *Rt. Hon.* Sir Stephen Miles, Kt.

Tooke, *Prof.* Sir John Edward, Kt.

Tooley, Sir John, Kt.

ToRobert, Sir Henry Thomas, KBE

Torpy, *Air Chief Marshal* Sir Glenn Lester, GCB, CBE, DSO

Torry, Sir Peter James, GCVO, KCMG

Touche, Sir Anthony George, Bt. (1920)

Touche, Sir Rodney Gordon, Bt. (1962)

Toulson, *Rt. Hon.* Sir Roger Grenfell, Kt. (Lord Toulson)

Tovadek, Sir Martin, Kt. CMG

Tovey, Sir Brian John Maynard, KCMG

Tovua, Sir Paul Joshua, KCMG

ToVue, Sir Ronald, Kt., OBE

Towneley, Sir Simon Peter Edmund Cosmo William, KCVO

Townsley, Sir John Arthur, Kt.

Traill, Sir Alan Towers, GBE

Trawen, Sir Andrew Sean, Kt., CMG, MBE

Trainor, *Prof.* Sir Richard Hughes, KBE

Treacher, *Adm.* Sir John Devereux, KCB

Treacy, *Rt. Hon.* Sir Colman Maurice, Kt.

Treacy, *Hon.* Sir (James Mary) Seamus, Kt.

Treitel, *Prof.* Sir Guenter Heinz, Kt., FBA, QC

Trescowthick, Sir Donald Henry, KBE

†Trevelyan, Sir Andrew John, Bt. (1662 and 1874)

Trezise, Sir Kenneth Bruce, Kt., OBE

Trippier, Sir David Austin, Kt., RD

Tritton, Sir Jeremy Ernest, Bt. (1905)

Trollope, Sir Anthony Simon, Bt. (1642)

Trotman-Dickenson, Sir Aubrey Fiennes, Kt.

Trotter, Sir Neville Guthrie, Kt.

Troubridge, Sir Thomas Richard, Bt. (1799)

Trousdell, *Lt.-Gen.* Sir Philip Charles Cornwallis, KBE, CB

Truscott, Sir Ralph Eric Nicholson, Bt. (1909)

Tsang, Sir Donald Yam-keun, KBE

Tuck, Sir Bruce Adolph Reginald, Bt. (1910)

Tucker, Sir Paul, Kt.

Tucker, *Hon.* Sir Richard Howard, Kt.
Tuckey, *Rt. Hon.* Sir Simon Lane, Kt.
Tugendhat, *Hon.* Sir Michael George, Kt.
Tuite, Sir Christopher Hugh, Bt. (I. 1622), PHD
Tuivaga, Sir Timoci Uluiburotu, Kt.
Tully, Sir William Mark, KBE
Tunstall, Sir Craig, Kt.
Tupper, Sir Charles Hibbert, Bt. (1888)
Turbott, Sir Ian Graham, Kt., CMG, CVO
Turing, Sir John Dermot, Bt. (S. 1638)
Turner, *Hon.* Sir Mark George, Kt.
Turner, *Hon.* Sir Michael John, Kt.
Turnquest, Sir Orville Alton, GCMG, QC
Tusa, Sir John, Kt.
Tweedie, *Prof.* Sir David Philip, Kt.
Tyrwhitt, Sir Reginald Thomas Newman, Bt. (1919)

Udny-Lister, Sir Edward Julian, Kt.
Ullman, Sir Anthony, Kt.
Underhill, *Rt. Hon.* Sir Nicholas Edward, Kt.
Underwood, *Prof.* Sir James Cressee Elphinstone, Kt.
Unwin, Sir (James) Brian, KCB
Ure, Sir John Burns, KCMG, LVO
Urquhart, Sir Brian Edward, KCMG, MBE
Urwick, Sir Alan Bedford, KCVO, CMG
Usher, Sir Andrew John, Bt. (1899)
Utting, Sir William Benjamin, Kt., CB

Vardy, Sir Peter, Kt.
Varney, Sir David Robert, Kt.
Vassar-Smith, Sir John Rathbone, Bt. (1917)
Vavasour, Sir Eric Michael Joseph Marmaduke, Bt. (1828)
Veness, Sir David, Kt., CBE, QPM
Venner, Sir Kenneth Dwight Vincent, KBE
Vereker, Sir John Michael Medlicott, KCB
Verey, Sir David John, Kt.
Verity, Sir Gary Keith, Kt.
Verney, Sir Edmund Ralph, Bt. (1818)
†Verney, Sir John Sebastian, Bt. (1946)
Vernon, Sir James William, Bt. (1914)
Vestey, Sir Paul Edmund, Bt. (1921)
Vickers, *Prof.* Sir Brian William, Kt.
Vickers, Sir John Stuart, Kt.
Vickers, *Lt.-Gen.* Sir Richard Maurice Hilton, KCB, CVO, OBE
Vickers, Sir Roger Henry, KCVO
Viggers, *Lt-Gen.* Sir Frederick Richard, KCB, CMG, MBE
Viggers, Sir Peter John, Kt.
Vincent, Sir William Percy Maxwell, Bt. (1936)
Vineall, Sir Anthony John Patrick, Kt.
Virdee, *Prof.* Sir Tejinder Singh, Kt.
Vos, *Rt. Hon.* Sir Geoffrey Michael, Kt.
†Vyvyan, Sir Ralph Ferrers Alexander, Bt. (1645)

Waena, Sir Nathaniel Rahumaea, GCMG

Waine, *Rt. Revd* John, KCVO
Waite, *Rt. Hon.* Sir John Douglas, Kt.
Waka, Sir Lucas Joseph, Kt., OBE
Wake, Sir Hereward, Bt. (1621), MC
Wakefield, Sir (Edward) Humphry (Tyrell), Bt. (1962)
Wakefield, Sir Norman Edward, Kt.
Wakeford, Sir Geoffrey Michael Montgomery, Kt., OBE
Wakeham, *Prof.* Sir William Arnot, Kt.
†Wakeley, Sir Nicholas Jeremy, Bt. (1952)
Wald, *Prof.* Sir Nicholas John, Kt.
Wales, Sir Robert Andrew, Kt.
Waley-Cohen, Sir Stephen Harry, Bt. (1961)
Walford, Sir Christopher Rupert, Kt.
Walker, *Gen.* Sir Antony Kenneth Frederick, Kt.
Walker, Sir Christopher Robert Baldwin, Bt. (1856)
Walker, Sir David Alan, Kt.
Walker, *Air Vice-Marshal* Sir David Allan, KCVO, OBE
Walker, Sir Harold Berners, KCMG
Walker, Sir John Ernest, Kt., DPHIL, FRS
Walker, *Air Marshal* Sir John Robert, KCB, CBE, AFC
Walker, Sir Miles Rawstron, Kt., CBE
Walker, Sir Patrick Jeremy, KCB
Walker, *Hon.* Sir Paul James, Kt.
Walker, Sir Rodney Myerscough, Kt.
Walker, Sir Roy Edward, Bt. (1906)
Walker, *Hon.* Sir Timothy Edward, Kt.
Walker, Sir Victor Stewart Heron, Bt. (1868)
Walker-Okeover, Sir Andrew Peter Monro, Bt. (1886)
Walker-Smith, *Hon.* Sir John Jonah, Bt. (1960)
Wall, Sir (John) Stephen, GCMG, LVO
Wall, *Rt. Hon.* Sir Nicholas Peter Rathbone, Kt.
Wall, *Gen.* Sir Peter Anthony, GCB, CBE, ADC
Wallace, *Lt.-Gen.* Sir Christopher Brooke Quentin, KBE
Wallace, *Prof.* Sir David James, Kt., CBE, FRS
Waller, *Rt. Hon.* Sir (George) Mark, Kt.
Waller, Sir John Michael, Bt. (I. 1780)
Wallis, Sir Peter Gordon, KCVO
Wallis, Sir Timothy William, Kt.
Walmsley, *Vice-Adm.* Sir Robert, KCB
Walport, *Dr* Sir Mark Jeremy, Kt.
†Walsham, Sir Gerald Percy Robert, Bt. (1831)
Walters, Sir Dennis Murray, Kt., MBE
Walters, Sir Frederick Donald, Kt.
Walters, Sir Peter Ingram, Kt.
Wamiri, Sir Akapite, KBE
Warby, *Hon.* Sir Mark David John, Kt., QC
Ward, *Rt. Hon.* Sir Alan Hylton, Kt.
Ward, Sir Austin, Kt., QC
Ward, *Hon.* Sir (Frederik) Gordon (Roy), Kt., OBE
Ward, *Prof.* Sir John MacQueen, Kt., CBE
Ward, Sir Joseph James Laffey, Bt. (1911)
Ward, Sir Timothy James, Kt.

Wardale, Sir Geoffrey Charles, KCB
Wardlaw, Sir Henry Justin, Bt. (NS. 1631)
Waring, Sir (Alfred) Holburt, Bt. (1935)
Warmington, Sir Rupert Marshall, Bt. (1908)
Warner, Sir Gerald Chierici, KCMG
Warner, Sir Philip Courtenay Thomas, Bt. (1910)
Warren, Sir David Alexander, KCMG
Warren, Sir (Frederick) Miles, KBE
Warren, Sir Kenneth Robin, Kt.
Warren, Sir Nicholas Roger, Kt.
Wass, Sir Douglas William Gretton, GCB
Waterlow, Sir Christopher Rupert, Bt. (1873)
Waterlow, Sir (Thomas) James, Bt. (1930)
Waters, *Gen.* Sir (Charles) John, GCB, CBE
Waters, Sir (Thomas) Neil (Morris), Kt.
Waterworth, Sir Alan William, KCVO
Wates, Sir Christopher Stephen, Kt.
Watson, Sir Graham Robert, Kt.
Watson, Sir (James) Andrew, Bt. (1866)
Watson, *Prof.* Sir Robert Tony, Kt., CMG
Watson, Sir Ronald Matthew, Kt., CBE
Watson, Sir Simon Conran Hamilton, Bt. (1895)
Watt, *Gen.* Sir Charles Redmond, KCB, KCVO, CBE, ADC
Watts, Sir Philip Beverley, KCMG
Weatherall, *Prof.* Sir David John, Kt., FRS
Weatherall, *Vice-Adm.* Sir James Lamb, KCVO, KBE
Weatherup, *Hon.* Sir Ronald Eccles, Kt.
Webb, *Prof.* Sir Adrian Leonard, Kt.
Webb-Carter, *Maj.-Gen.* Sir Evelyn John, KCVO, OBE
Webster, *Vice-Adm.* Sir John Morrison, KCB
Wedgwood, Sir Ralph Nicholas, Bt. (1942)
Weekes, Sir Everton DeCourcey, KCMG, OBE
Weinberg, Sir Mark Aubrey, Kt.
Weir, *Hon.* Sir Reginald George, Kt.
Weir, Sir Roderick Bignell, Kt.
Welby, Sir (Richard) Bruno Gregory, Bt. (1801)
Welch, Sir John Reader, Bt. (1957)
Weldon, Sir Anthony William, Bt. (I. 1723)
Wellend, *Prof.* Sir Mark Edward, Kt.
Weller, *Prof.* Sir Ian Vincent Derrick, Kt.
Weller, Sir Nicholas John, Kt.
†Wells, Sir Christopher Charles, Bt. (1944)
Wells, Sir John Julius, Kt.
Wells, Sir William Henry Weston, Kt., FRICS
Wesker, Sir Arnold, Kt.
Wessely, *Prof.* Sir Simon Charles, Kt.
Westmacott, Sir Peter John, KCMG
Weston, Sir Michael Charles Swift, KCMG, CVO
Weston, Sir (Philip) John, KCMG
Whalen, Sir Geoffrey Henry, Kt., CBE

Wheeler, *Rt. Hon.* Sir John Daniel, Kt.

Wheeler, Sir John Frederick, Bt. (1920)

Wheeler, *Gen.* Sir Roger Neil, GCB, CBE

Wheeler-Booth, Sir Michael Addison John, KCB

Wheler, Sir Trevor Woodford, Bt. (1660)

Whitaker, Sir John James Ingham (Jack), Bt. (1936)

Whitbread, Sir Samuel Charles, KCVO

Whitchurch, Sir Graeme Ian, Kt., OBE

White, Sir Adrian Edwin, Kt., CBE

White, *Prof.* Sir Christopher John, Kt., CVO

White, Sir Christopher Robert Meadows, Bt. (1937)

White, Sir David (David Jason), Kt., OBE

White, Sir David Harry, Kt.

White, Sir George Stanley James, Bt. (1904)

White, Sir John Woolmer, Bt. (1922)

White, Sir Nicholas Peter Archibald, Bt. (1802)

White, Sir Willard Wentworth, Kt., CBE

White-Spunner, *Lt.-Gen.* Sir Barnabas William Benjamin, KCB, CBE

Whitehead, Sir Philip Henry Rathbone, Bt. (1889)

Whiteley, *Gen.* Sir Peter John Frederick, GCB, OBE, RM

Whitfield, Sir William, Kt., CBE

Whitmore, Sir Clive Anthony, GCB, CVO

Whitmore, Sir John Henry Douglas, Bt. (1954)

Whitson, Sir Keith Roderick, Kt.

Whittam Smith, Sir Andreas, Kt., CBE

Wickerson, Sir John Michael, Kt.

Wicks, Sir Nigel Leonard, GCB, CVO, CBE

Wigan, Sir Michael Iain, Bt. (1898)

Wiggin, Sir Richard Edward John, Bt. (1892)

Wiggins, Sir Bradley Marc, Kt., CBE

Wigram, Sir John Woolmore, Bt. (1805)

Wilbraham, Sir Richard Baker, Bt. (1776)

Wild, Sir John Ralston, Kt., CBE

Wiles, *Prof.* Sir Andrew John, KBE

Wilkie, *Hon.* Sir Alan Fraser, Kt.

Wilkins, Sir Michael, Kt.

Wilkinson, Sir (David) Graham (Brook) Bt. (1941)

Wilkinson, *Prof.* Sir Denys Haigh, Kt., FRS

Willcocks, Sir David Valentine, Kt., CBE, MC

Willcocks, *Lt.-Gen.* Sir Michael Alan, KCB, CVO

Williams, Sir Anthony Geraint, Bt. (1953)

Williams, Sir (Arthur) Gareth Ludovic Emrys Rhys, Bt. (1918)

Williams, Sir Charles Othniel, Kt.

Williams, Sir Daniel Charles, GCMG, QC

Williams, Sir David Reeve, Kt., CBE

Williams, Sir Donald Mark, Bt. (1866)

Williams, *Prof.* Sir (Edward) Dillwyn, Kt., FRCP

Williams, Sir Francis Owen Garbett, Kt., CBE

Williams, *Hon.* Sir (John) Griffith, Kt.

Williams, Sir (Lawrence) Hugh, Bt. (1798)

Williams, Sir Nicholas Stephen, Kt.

Williams, *Prof.* Sir Norman Stanley, Kt.

Williams, Sir Paul Michael, Kt., OBE

Williams, Sir Peter Michael, Kt.

Williams, Sir (Robert) Philip Nathaniel, Bt. (1915)

Williams, *HE Dr* Sir Rodney Errey Lawrence, GCMG

Williams, *Prof.* Sir Roger, Kt.

Williams, Sir (William) Maxwell (Harries), Kt.

Williams, *Hon.* Sir Wyn Lewis, Kt.

Williams-Bulkeley, Sir Richard Thomas, Bt. (1661)

Williams-Wynn, Sir David Watkin, Bt. (1688)

Williamson, Sir George Malcolm, Kt.

Williamson, *Marshal of the Royal Air Force* Sir Keith Alec, GCB, AFC

Williamson, Sir Robert Brian, Kt., CBE

Willink, Sir Edward Daniel, Bt. (1957)

Wills, Sir David James Vernon, Bt. (1923)

Wills, Sir David Seton, Bt. (1904)

Wilmot, Sir David, Kt., QPM

Wilmot, Sir Henry Robert, Bt. (1759)

Wilmut, *Prof.* Sir Ian, Kt., OBE

Wilsey, *Gen.* Sir John Finlay Willasey, GCB, CBE

Wilshaw, Sir Michael, Kt.

Wilson, *Prof.* Sir Alan Geoffrey, Kt.

Wilson, *Vice-Adm.* Sir Barry Nigel, KCB

Wilson, Sir David Mackenzie, Kt.

Wilson, Sir James William Douglas, Bt. (1906)

Wilson, *Brig.* Sir Mathew John Anthony, Bt. (1874), OBE, MC

Wilson, *Rt. Hon.* Sir Nicholas Allan Roy, Kt. (Wilson of Culworth)

Wilson, *Prof.* Sir Robert James Timothy, Kt.

Wilson, Sir Robert Peter, KCMG

Wilson, *Air Chief Marshal* Sir (Ronald) Andrew (Fellowes), KCB, AFC

Wilson, Sir Thomas David, Bt. (1920)

Wingate, *Capt.* Sir Miles Buckley, KCVO

Winkley, Sir David Ross, Kt.

Winnington, Sir Anthony Edward, Bt. (1755)

Winship, Sir Peter James Joseph, Kt., CBE

Winsor, Sir Thomas Philip, Kt.

Winter, *Dr* Sir Gregory Winter, Kt., CBE

Winterton, Sir Nicholas Raymond, Kt.

Wiseman, Sir John William, Bt. (1628)

Witty, Sir Andrew, Kt.

Wolfendale, *Prof.* Sir Arnold Whittaker, Kt., FRS

Wolseley, Sir Charles Garnet Richard Mark, Bt. (1628)

†Wolseley, Sir James Douglas, Bt. (I. 1745)

†Wombwell, Sir George Philip Frederick, Bt. (1778)

Womersley, Sir Peter John Walter, Bt. (1945)

Woo, Sir Leo Joseph, Kt., MBE

Woo, Sir Po-Shing, Kt.

Wood, Sir Andrew Marley, GCMG

Wood, Sir Anthony John Page, Bt. (1837)

Wood, Sir Ian Clark, Kt., CBE

Wood, Sir James Sebastian Lamin, KCMG

Wood, Sir Martin Francis, Kt., OBE

Wood, Sir Michael Charles, KCMG

Wood, *Hon.* Sir Roderic Lionel James, Kt.

Woodard, *Rear Adm.* Sir Robert Nathaniel, KCVO

Woodhead, *Vice-Adm.* Sir (Anthony) Peter, KCB

Woods, *Prof.* Sir Kent Linton, Kt.

Woods, Sir Robert Kynnersley, Kt., CBE

Woodward, Sir Clive Ronald, Kt., OBE

Woodward, Sir Thomas Jones (Tom Jones), Kt., OBE

Wootton, Sir David Hugh, Kt.

Worsley, Sir William Ralph, Bt. (1838)

Worsthorne, Sir Peregrine Gerard, Kt.

Worthington, Sir Mark, Kt., OBE

Wratten, *Air Chief Marshal* Sir William John, GBE, CB, AFC

Wraxall, Sir Charles Frederick Lascelles, Bt. (1813)

Wrey, Sir George Richard Bourchier, Bt. (1628)

Wright, Sir Allan Frederick, KBE

Wright, Sir David John, GCMG, LVO

Wright, *Hon.* Sir (John) Michael, Kt.

Wright, *Prof.* Sir Nicholas Alcwyn, Kt.

Wright, Sir Peter Robert, Kt., CBE

Wright, *Air Marshal* Sir Robert Alfred, KBE, AFC

Wright, Sir Stephen John Leadbetter, KCMG

Wrightson, Sir Charles Mark Garmondsway, Bt. (1900)

Wrigley, *Prof.* Sir Edward Anthony (Sir Tony), Kt., PHD, PBA

Wrixon-Becher, Sir John William Michael, Bt. (1831)

Wroughton, Sir Philip Lavallin, KCVO

Wu, Sir Gordon Ying Sheung, KCMG

Wynne, Sir Graham Robert, Kt., CBE

Yacoub, *Prof.* Sir Magdi Habib, Kt., OM, FRCS

Yaki, Sir Roy, KBE

Yang, *Hon.* Sir Ti Liang, Kt.

Yarrow, Sir Eric Grant, Bt. (1916), MBE

Yassaie, *Dr* Sir Hossein, Kt.

Yocklunn, Sir John (Soong Chung), KCVO

Yoo Foo, Sir (François) Henri, Kt.

Young, Sir Brian Walter Mark, Kt.

Young, Sir Colville Norbert, GCMG, MBE

Young, Sir Dennis Charles, KCMG
Young, Sir Jimmy Leslie Ronald, Kt.,
   CBE
Young, Sir John Kenyon Roe, Bt.
   (1821)
Young, Sir John Robertson, GCMG
Young, Sir Leslie Clarence, Kt., CBE
Young, Sir Nicholas Charles, Kt.
Young, Sir Robin Urquhart, KCB
Young, Sir Roger William, Kt.

Young, Sir Stephen Stewart Templeton,
   Bt. (1945)
Young, Sir William Neil, Bt. (1769)
Younger, *Capt.* Sir John David
   Bingham, KCVO
Younger, Sir Julian William Richard, Bt.
   (1911)
Yuwi, Sir Matiabe, KBE

Zacca, *Rt. Hon.* Sir Edward, KCMG

Zambellas, *Adm.* Sir George Michael,
   KCB, DSC
Zeeman, *Prof.* Sir (Erik) Christopher,
   Kt., FRS
Zissman, Sir Bernard Philip, Kt.
Zunz, Sir Gerhard Jacob (Jack), Kt.,
   FRENG
Zurenuoc, Sir Manasupe Zure, Kt.,
   OBE
Zurenuoc, Sir Zibang, KBE

# THE ORDER OF ST JOHN

THE MOST VENERABLE ORDER OF THE HOSPITAL
OF ST JOHN OF JERUSALEM (1888)

| | |
|---|---|
| GCStJ | Bailiff/Dame Grand Cross |
| KStJ | Knight of Justice/Grace |
| DStJ | Dame of Justice/Grace |
| CStJ | Commander |
| OStJ | Officer |
| SBStJ | Serving Brother |
| SSStJ | Serving Sister |

*Motto,* Pro Fide, Pro Utilitate Hominum
*(For the faith and in the service of humanity)*

The Order of St John, founded in the early 12th century
in Jerusalem, was a religious order with a particular duty
to care for the sick. In Britain the order was dissolved
by Henry VIII in 1540 but the British branch was revived
in the early 19th century. The branch was not accepted
by the Grand Magistracy of the Order in Rome but its
search for a role in the tradition of the hospitallers led to
the founding of the St John Ambulance Association in 1877
and later the St John Ambulance Brigade; in 1882 the St
John Ophthalmic Hospital was founded in Jerusalem. A
royal charter was granted in 1888 establishing the Order
of St John as a British Order of Chivalry with the sovereign
as its head.

Since October 1999 the whole order worldwide has been
governed by a Grand Council which includes a representative
from each of the 11 priories (England, Scotland, Wales,
Hong Kong, Kenya, Singapore, South Africa, New Zealand,
Canada, Australia and the USA). In addition there are also
five commanderies in Northern Ireland, Jersey, Guernsey,
the Isle of Man and Western Australia. There are also
branches in about 30 other Commonwealth countries. Apart
from St John Ambulance, the Order is also responsible for the
Eye Hospital in Jerusalem. Admission to the order is usually
conferred in recognition of service to either one of these
institutions. Membership does not confer any rank, style, title
or precedence on a recipient.

SOVEREIGN HEAD OF THE ORDER
HM The Queen

GRAND PRIOR
HRH The Duke of Gloucester, KG, GCVO

*Lord Prior,* vacant
*Prelate,* vacant
*Sub Prior,* Stuart Shilson, LVO
*Chancellor,* Patrick Burgess, OBE
*Secretary General,* vacant
*International Office,* 3 Charterhouse Mews, London EC1M 6BB
   T 020-7251 3292 W www.stjohninternational.org

# DAMES

*Style,* 'Dame' before forename and surname, followed by appropriate post-nominal initials. Where such an award is made to a lady already in possession of a higher title, the appropriate initials follow her name
*Envelope,* Dame F_ S_, followed by appropriate post-nominal letters. *Letter (formal),* Dear Madam; *(social),* Dear Dame F_. *Spoken,* Dame F_
*Husband,* Untitled

Dame Grand Cross and Dame Commander are the higher classes for women of the Order of the Bath, the Order of St Michael and St George, the Royal Victorian Order, and the Order of the British Empire. Dames Grand Cross rank after the wives of Baronets and before the wives of Knights Grand Cross. Dames Commanders rank after the wives of Knights Grand Cross and before the wives of Knights Commanders.

Honorary damehoods may be conferred on women who are citizens of countries of which the Queen is not head of state.

LIST OF DAMES *As at 31 August 2015*

Women peers in their own right and life peers are not included in this list. Female members of the royal family are not included in this list; details of the orders they hold can be found within the Royal Family section.

If a dame has a double barrelled or hyphenated surname, she is listed under the first element of the name.

Abaijah, Dame Josephine, DBE
Abramsky, Dame Jennifer Gita, DBE
Acland Hood Gass, Lady (Elizabeth Periam), DCVO
Airlie, The Countess of, DCVO
Alexander, Dame Helen Anne, DBE
Allen, *Prof.* Dame Ingrid Victoria, DBE
Andrews, *Hon.* Dame Geraldine Mary, DBE
Andrews, Dame Julie, DBE
Angiolini, *Rt. Hon.* Dame Elish, DBE, QC
Anglesey, Shirley, Marchioness of, DBE
Anson, Lady (Elizabeth Audrey), DBE
Anstee, Dame Margaret Joan, DCMG
Archer, *Dr* Dame Mary Doreen, DBE
Arden, *Rt. Hon.* Dame Mary Howarth (Mrs Mance), DBE
Ashcroft, *Prof.* Dame Frances Mary, DBE, FRS
Asplin, *Hon.* Dame Sarah Jane (Mrs Sherwin), DBE
Atkins, Dame Eileen, DBE
August, Dame Kathryn, DBE
Bacon, Dame Patricia Anne, DBE
Bailey, *Prof.* Dame Susan Mary, DBE
Baker, Dame Janet Abbott (Mrs Shelley), CH, DBE
Barbour, Dame Margaret (Mrs Ash), DBE
Barker, Dame Katharine Mary, DBE
Barker-Welch, *Hon.* Dame Maizie Irene, DBE
Barrow, Dame Jocelyn Anita (Mrs Downer), DBE
Barstow, Dame Josephine Clare (Mrs Anderson), DBE
Bassey, Dame Shirley, DBE
Beasley, *Prof.* Dame Christine Joan, DBE
Beaurepaire, Dame Beryl Edith, DBE
Beckett, *Rt. Hon.* Dame Margaret Mary, DBE
Beer, *Prof.* Dame Gillian Patricia Kempster, DBE, FBA
Begg, Dame Anne, DBE
Beral, *Prof.* Dame Valerie, DBE
Bertschinger, *Dr* Dame Claire, DBE
Bevan, Dame Yasmin, DBE
Bewley, Dame Beulah Rosemary, DBE

Bibby, Dame Enid, DBE
Black, *Prof.* Dame Carol Mary, DBE
Black, *Rt. Hon.* Dame Jill Margaret, DBE
Blackadder, Dame Elizabeth Violet, DBE
Blaize, Dame Venetia Ursula, DBE
Blaxland, Dame Helen Frances, DBE
Blume, Dame Hilary Sharon Braverman, DBE
Booth, *Hon.* Dame Margaret Myfanwy Wood, DBE
Bourne, Dame Susan Mary (Mrs Bourne), DBE
Bowe, *Dr* Dame (Mary) Colette, DBE
Bowtell, Dame Ann Elizabeth, DCB
Braddock, *Dr* Dame Christine, DBE
Brain, Dame Margaret Anne (Mrs Wheeler), DBE
Breakwell, *Prof.* Dame Glynis Marie, DBE
Brennan, Dame Maureen, DBE
Brennan, Dame Ursula, DCB
Brewer, *Dr* Dame Nicola Mary, DCMG
Bridges, Dame Mary Patricia, DBE
Brindley, Dame Lynne Janie, DBE
Brittan, Dame Diana (Lady Brittan of Spennithorne), DBE
Brooke, *Rt. Hon.* Dame Annette (Lesley), DBE
Browne, Lady Moyra Blanche Madeleine, DBE
Bruce, Dame Susan Margaret, DBE
Bruce, *Prof.* Dame Victoria Geraldine, DBE, FBA, FRSE
Buckland, Dame Yvonne Helen Elaine, DBE
Burnell, *Prof.* Dame Susan Jocelyn Bell, DBE
Burslem, Dame Alexandra Vivien, DBE
Butler, Dame Rosemary Janet Mair, DBE
Byatt, Dame Antonia Susan, DBE, FRSL
Caldicott, Dame Fiona, DBE, FRCP, FRCPSYCH
Cairncross, Dame Frances Anne, DBE, FRSE
Cameron, *Prof.* Dame Averil Millicent, DBE
Campbell-Preston, Dame Frances Olivia, DCVO
Carnall, Dame Ruth, DBE
Carnwath, Dame Alison Jane, DBE
Carr, *Hon.* Dame Sue Lascelles (Mrs Birch), DBE
Cartwright, Dame Silvia Rose, DBE
Clark, *Prof.* Dame Jill MacLeod, DBE
Clark, *Prof.* Dame (Margaret) June, DBE, PHD
Cleverdon, Dame Julia Charity, DCVO, CBE
Coates, Dame Sally, DBE
Collarbone, Dame Patricia, DBE
Collins, Dame Joan Henrietta, DBE
Contreras, *Prof.* Dame Marcela, DBE
Corner, *Prof.* Dame Jessica Lois, DBE
Corsar, *Hon.* Dame Mary Drummond, DBE
Coward, Dame Pamela Sarah, DBE
Cowley, *Prof.* Dame Sarah Ann, DBE
Cox, *Hon.* Dame Laura Mary, DBE
Cramp, *Prof.* Dame Rosemary Jean, DBE
Cullum, *Prof.* Dame Nicola Anne, DBE
Dacon, Dame Monica Jessie, DBE, CMG
Davies, *Prof.* Dame Kay Elizabeth, DBE
Davies, Dame Laura Jane, DBE
Davies, *Hon.* Dame Nicola Velfor, DBE
Davies, *Prof.* Dame Sally Claire, DBE
Davies, Dame Wendy Patricia, DBE
Davis, Dame Karlene Cecile, DBE
Dawson, *Prof.* Dame Sandra Jane Noble, DBE
De Souza, Dame Rachel Mary, DBE
Dell, Dame Miriam Patricia, DBE
Dench, Dame Judith Olivia (Mrs Williams), CH, DBE
Descartes, Dame Marie Selipha Sesenne, DBE, BEM
Dethridge, Dame Kate, DBE

Digby, The Lady, DBE
Dobbs, *Hon.* Dame Linda Penelope, DBE
Docherty, Dame Jacqueline, DBE
Donald, *Prof.* Dame Athene Margaret, DBE, FRS
Dowling, *Prof.* Dame Ann Patricia, DBE
Duffield, Dame Vivien Louise, DBE
Duffy, Dame Carol Ann, DBE
Dumont, Dame Ivy Leona, DCMG
Dunnell, Dame Karen, DCB
Dyche, Dame Rachael Mary, DBE
Elcoat, Dame Catherine Elizabeth, DBE
Ellis, Dame Diana Margaret (Mrs Ellis), DBE
Ellison, Dame Jill, DBE
Elton, Dame Susan Richenda (Lady Elton), DCVO
Engel, Dame Pauline Frances (Sister Pauline Engel), DBE
Esteve-Coll, Dame Elizabeth Anne Loosemore, DBE
Evans, Dame Anne Elizabeth Jane, DBE
Evans, Dame Madeline Glynne Dervel, DBE, CMG
Evans, Dame Oremi, DBE
Fagan, Dame (Florence) Mary, DCVO
Farnham, Dame Marion (Lady Farnham), DCVO
Fawcett, Dame Amelia Chilcott, DBE
Fielding, Dame Pauline, DBE
Finch, *Prof.* Dame Janet Valerie, DBE
Fisher, Dame Jacqueline, DBE
Forgan, Dame Elizabeth Anne Lucy, DBE
Fradd, Dame Elizabeth, DBE
Fraser, Lady Antonia, DBE
Fraser, Dame Dorothy Rita, DBE
Fry, Dame Margaret Louise, DBE
Furse, Dame Clara Hedwig Frances, DBE
Gaymer, Dame Janet Marion, DBE, QC
Ghosh, Dame Helen Frances, DCB
Gibb, Dame Moira Margaret, DBE
Glenn, *Prof.* Dame Hazel Gillian, DBE
Glennie, *Dr* Dame Evelyn Elizabeth Ann, DBE
Gloster, *Rt. Hon.* Dame Elizabeth (Lady Popplewell), DBE
Glover, Dame Audrey Frances, DBE, CMG
Glover, *Prof.* Dame Lesley Anne, DBE, FRSE
Goad, Dame Sarah Jane Frances, DCVO
Goodall, *Dr* Dame (Valerie) Jane, DBE
Goodfellow, *Prof.* Dame Julia Mary, DBE
Gordon, Dame Minita Elmira, GCMG, GCVO
Gordon, *Hon.* Dame Pamela Felicity, DBE
Gow, Dame Jane Elizabeth (Mrs Whiteley), DBE
Grafton, Ann, The Duchess of, GCVO
Grant, Dame Mavis, DBE
Green, Dame Pauline, DBE
Grey, Dame Beryl Elizabeth (Mrs Svenson), DBE
Griffiths, Dame Anne, DCVO
Grimthorpe, Elizabeth, The Lady, DCVO
Guilfoyle, Dame Margaret Georgina Constance, DBE
Guthardt, *Revd Dr* Dame Phyllis Myra, DBE
Hadid, Dame Zaha, DBE
Hakin, *Dr* Dame Barbara Ann, DBE
Hall, *Prof.* Dame Wendy, DBE
Hallett, *Rt. Hon.* Dame Heather Carol, DBE
Hallett, Dame Nancy Karen, DBE
Harbison, Dame Joan Irene, DBE
Harper, Dame Elizabeth Margaret Way, DBE
Harris, Dame Pauline (Lady Harris of Peckham), DBE
Harris, Dame Philippa Jill Olivier, DBE
Hassan, Dame Anna Patricia Lucy, DBE
Hay, Dame Barbara Logan, DCMG, MBE
Henderson, Dame Fiona Douglas, DCVO
Hercus, *Hon.* Dame (Margaret) Ann, DCMG
Higgins, *Prof.* Dame Joan Margaret, DBE
Higgins, *Prof.* Dame Julia Stretton, DBE, FRS
Higgins, *Prof.* Dame Rosalyn, DBE, QC

Hill, *Air Cdre* Dame Felicity Barbara, DBE
Hill, *Prof.* Dame Judith Eileen, DBE
Hine, Dame Deirdre Joan, DBE, FRCP
Hodge, *Rt. Hon.* Lady Margaret (Eve), DBE
Hodgson, Dame Patricia Anne, DBE
Hogg, *Hon.* Dame Mary Claire (Mrs Koops), DBE
Holborow, Lady Mary Christina, DCVO
Hollows, Dame Sharon, DBE
Holmes, Dame Kelly, DBE
Holroyd, Lady (Margaret Drabble), DBE
Holt, Dame Denise Mary, DCMG
Hoodless, Dame Elisabeth Anne, DBE
Hoyles, *Prof.* Dame Celia Mary, DBE
Hufton, *Prof.* Dame Olwen, DBE
Humphrey, *Prof.* Dame Caroline (Lady Rees of Ludlow), DBE
Husband, *Prof.* Dame Janet Elizabeth Siarey, DBE
Hussey, Dame Susan Katharine (Lady Hussey of North Bradley), GCVO
Hutton, Dame Deirdre Mary, DBE
Hyde, Dame Helen, DBE
Imison, Dame Tamsyn, DBE
Ion, *Dr* Dame Susan Elizabeth, DBE
Isaacs, Dame Albertha Madeline, DBE
James, Dame Naomi Christine (Mrs Haythorne), DBE
Jenkins, Dame (Mary) Jennifer (Lady Jenkins of Hillhead), DBE
John, Dame Susan, DBE
Johnson, *Prof.* Dame Anne Mandall, DBE
Jones, Dame Gwyneth (Mrs Haberfeld-Jones), DBE
Jordan, *Prof.* Dame Carole, DBE
Joseph, Dame Monica Theresa, DBE
Jowell, *Rt. Hon.* Dame Tessa Jane, DBE
Julius, *Dr* Dame DeAnne Shirley, DCMG, CBE
Karika, Dame Pauline Margaret Rakera George (Mrs Taripo), DBE
Keeble, *Dr* Dame Reena, DBE
Keegan, Dame Elizabeth Mary, DBE
Keegan, Dame Geraldine Mary Marcella, DBE
Keith, Dame Penelope Anne Constance (Mrs Timson), DBE
Kekedo, Dame Rosalina Violet, DBE
Kelleher, Dame Joan, DBE
Kelly, Dame Barbara Mary, DBE
Kelly, Dame Lorna May Boreland, DBE
Kendrick, Dame Fiona Marie, DBE
Kershaw, Dame Janet Elizabeth Murray (Dame Betty), DBE
Kettlewell, *Comdt.* Dame Marion Mildred, DBE
Kharas, Dame Zarine, DBE
Khemka, Dame Asha, DBE
Kidu, Lady, DBE
King, *Rt. Hon.* Dame Eleanor Warwick, DBE
King, *Prof.* Dame Julia Elizabeth, DBE
Kinnair, Dame Donna, DBE
Kirby, Dame Carolyn Emma, DBE
Kirby, Dame Georgina Kamiria, DBE
Kirwan, *Prof.* Dame Frances Clare, DBE, FRS
Kramer, *Prof.* Dame Leonie Judith, DBE
La Grenade, *HE.* Dame Cécile Ellen Fleurette, GCMG, OBE
Laine, Dame Cleo (Clementine) Dinah (Lady Dankworth), DBE
Laing, *Hon.* Dame Elisabeth Mary Caroline, DBE
Lake-Tack, *HE* Dame Louise Agnetha, GCMG
Lamb, Dame Dawn Ruth, DBE
Lang, *Hon.* Dame Beverley Ann Macnaughton, DBE
Lansbury Shaw, Dame Angela Brigid, DBE
Lavender, *Prof.* Dame Tina, DBE
Leather, Dame Susan Catherine, DBE
Lee, *Prof.* Dame Hermione, DBE
Legge-Bourke, *Hon.* Dame Elizabeth Shân Josephine, DCVO
Leslie, Dame Alison Mariot, DCMG

Leslie, Dame Ann Elizabeth Mary, DBE
Lewis, Dame Edna Leofrida (Lady Lewis), DBE
Lively, Dame Penelope Margaret, DBE
Lott, Dame Felicity Ann Emwhyla (Mrs Woolf), DBE
Louisy, Dame (Calliopa) Pearlette, GCMG
Lynn, Dame Vera (Mrs Lewis), DBE
Lynne, Dame Gillian Barbara, DBE
MacArthur, Dame Ellen Patricia, DBE
Macdonald, Dame Mary Beaton, DBE
McDonald, Dame Mavis, DCB
McGowan, *Hon.* Dame Maura Patricia, DBE
McGuire, *Rt. Hon.* Dame Anne Catherine, DBE
MacIntyre, *Prof.* Dame Sarah Jane, DBE
Macmillan of Ovenden, Katharine, Viscountess, DBE
Macur, *Rt. Hon.* Dame Julia Wendy, DBE
McVittie, Dame Joan Christine, DBE
Mayhew, Jonas, Dame Judith, DBE
Major, Dame Malvina Lorraine (Mrs Fleming), DBE
Major, Dame Norma Christina Elizabeth, DBE
Makin, *Dr* Dame Pamela Louise, DBE
Mantel, *Dr.* Dame Hiliary Mary, DBE
Marsden, *Dr* Dame Rosalind Mary, DCMG
Marsh, Dame Mary Elizabeth, DBE
Mason, Dame Monica Margaret, DBE
Matheson, Dame Jilian Norma, DCB
Mellor, Dame Julie Thérèse Mellor, DBE
Metge, *Dr* Dame (Alice) Joan, DBE
Middleton, Dame Elaine Madoline, DCMG, MBE
Mills, *Prof.* Dame Anne Jane, DCMG, CBE
Mirren, Dame Helen, DBE
Monroe, *Prof.* Dame Barbara, DBE
Moore, Dame Julie, DBE
Moores, Dame Yvonne, DBE
Morgan, *Dr* Dame Gillian Margaret, DBE
Morris, Dame Sylvia Ann, DBE
Morrison, *Hon.* Dame Mary Anne, GCVO
Muirhead, Dame Lorna Elizabeth Fox, DBE
Mullally, *Rt. Revd* Dame Sarah Elisabeth, DBE
Murray, Dame Jennifer Susan, DBE
Nelson, *Prof.* Dame Janet Laughland, DBE
Nelson-Taylor, Dame Nicola Jane, DBE
Neville, Dame Elizabeth, DBE, QPM
Newell, Dame Priscilla Jane, DBE
O'Brien, Dame Una, DCB
Ogilvie, Dame Bridget Margaret, DBE, PHD, DSc
Oliver, Dame Gillian Frances, DBE
Owers, Dame Anne Elizabeth (Mrs Cook), DBE
Oxenbury, Dame Shirley Ann, DBE
Palmer, Dame Felicity Joan, DBE
Paraskeva, *Rt. Hon.* Dame Janet, DBE
Park, Dame Merle Florence (Mrs Bloch), DBE
Parker, *Hon.* Dame Judith Mary Frances, DBE
Partridge, *Prof.* Dame Linda, DBE
Patel, Dame Indira, DBE
Paterson, Dame Vicki, DBE
Patterson, *Hon.* Dame Frances Silvia, DBE
Pauffley, *Hon.* Dame Anna Evelyn Hamilton, DBE
Peacock, Dame Alison Margaret, DBE
Pearce, *Prof.* Dame Shirley, DBE
Penhaligon, Dame Annette (Mrs Egerton), DBE
Pereira, *Hon.* Dame Janice Mesadis, DBE
Perkins, Dame Mary Lesley, DBE
Peters, Dame Mary Elizabeth, DBE, CH
Pienaar, Dame Erica, DBE
Pindling, Lady (Marguerite Matilda), GCMG
Platt, Dame Denise, DBE
Plotnikoff, Dame Joyce Evelyn, DBE
Plowright, Dame Joan Ann, DBE
Plunket Greene, Dame Barbara Mary, DBE

Poole, Dame Avril Anne Barker, DBE
Porter, Dame Shirley (Lady Porter), DBE
Powell, Dame Sally Ann Vickers, DBE
Pringle, Dame Anne Fyfe, DCMG
Proudman, *Hon.* Dame Sonia Rosemary Susan, DBE
Pugh, *Dr* Dame Gillian Mary, DBE
Quinn, Dame Sheila Margaret Imelda, DBE
Rafferty, *Rt. Hon.* Dame Anne Judith, DBE
Rantzen, Dame Esther Louise (Mrs Wilcox), DBE
Rawson, *Prof.* Dame Jessica Mary, DBE
Rees, *Prof.* Dame Judith Anne, DBE
Rees, *Prof.* Dame Lesley Howard, DBE
Rees, *Prof.* Dame Teresa Lesley, DBE
Reeves, Dame Helen May, DBE
Rego, Dame Paula Figueiroa, DBE
Reid, Dame Seona Elizabeth, DBE
Reynolds, Dame Fiona Claire, DBE
Rhodes, Dame Zandra Lindsey, DBE
Richard, Dame Alison (Fettes), DBE
Richardson, Dame Mary, DBE
Rigg, Dame Diana, DBE
Rimington, Dame Stella, DCB
Ritterman, Dame Janet, DBE
Roberts, Dame Jane Elisabeth, DBE
Roberts, *Hon.* Dame Jennifer Mary, DBE
Roberts, *Hon.* Dame Priscilla Jane Stephanie (Lady Roberts),
     DCVO
Robins, Dame Ruth Laura, DBE
Robinson, *Prof.* Dame Carol Vivien, DBE
Robottom, Dame Marlene, DBE
Roe, Dame Marion Audrey, DBE
Roe, Dame Raigh Edith, DBE
Ronson, Dame Gail, DBE
Rose, *Hon.* Dame Vivien Judith, DBE
Ross-Wawrzynski, Dame Dana (Mrs Ross-Wawrzynski), DBE
Rothwell, *Prof.* Dame Nancy Jane, DBE
Ruddock, *Rt. Hon.* Dame Joan Mary, DBE
Runciman of Doxford, The Viscountess, DBE
Russell, *Hon.* Dame Alison Hunter, DBE
Russell, *Dr* Dame Philippa Margaret, DBE
Sackler, Dame Theresa, DBE
Salas, Dame Margaret Laurence, DBE
Salmond, *Prof.* Dame Mary Anne, DBE
Savill, Dame Rosalind Joy, DBE
Sawyer, *Rt. Hon.* Dame Joan Augusta, DBE
Scardino, Dame Marjorie, DBE
Scott, Dame Catherine Margaret (Mrs Denton), DBE
Scott Thomas, Dame Kristin, DBE
Seward, Dame Margaret Helen Elizabeth, DBE
Shafik, *Dr.* Dame Nemat Talaat, DBE
Sharp, *Rt. Hon.* Dame Victoria Madeleine, DBE
Shaw, *Prof.* Dame Pamela Jean, DBE
Sheldrick, *Dr* Dame Daphne Marjorie, DBE
Shirley, Dame Stephanie, DBE
Shovelton, Dame Helena, DBE
Sibley, Dame Antoinette (Mrs Corbett), DBE
Sills, *Prof.* Dame Eileen, DBE
Silver, *Dr* Dame Ruth Muldoon, DBE
Simler, *Hon.* Dame Ingrid Ann (Mrs Bernstein), DBE
Slade, *Hon.* Dame Elizabeth Ann, DBE
Slingo, *Prof.* Dame Julia Mary, DBE
Smith, Dame Dela, DBE
Smith, *Rt. Hon.* Dame Janet Hilary (Mrs Mathieson), DBE
Smith, *Hon.* Dame Jennifer Meredith, DBE
Smith, Dame Margaret Natalie (Maggie) (Mrs Cross),
     CH, DBE
Southgate, *Prof.* Dame Lesley Jill, DBE
Spencer, Dame Rosemary Jane, DCMG
Steel, *Hon.* Dame (Anne) Heather (Mrs Beattie), DBE

Stocking, Dame Barbara Mary, DBE
Storey, Dame Sarah Joanne, DBE
Strachan, Dame Valerie Patricia Marie, DCB
Strathern, *Prof.* Dame Anne Marilyn, DBE
Street, Dame Susan Ruth, DCB
Stringer, *Prof.* Dame Joan Kathleen, DBE
Sutherland, Dame Veronica Evelyn, DBE, CMG
Suzman, Dame Janet, DBE
Swift, *Hon.* Dame Caroline Jane (Mrs Openshaw), DBE
Symmonds, Dame Olga Patricia, DBE
Tanner, *Dr* Dame Mary Elizabeth, DBE
Taylor, Dame Meg, DBE
Te Kanawa, Dame Kiri Janette, DBE
Theis, *Hon.* Dame Lucy Morgan, DBE
Thirlwall, *Hon.* Dame Kathryn Mary, DBE
Thomas, *Prof.* Dame Jean Olwen, DBE
Thomas, Dame Maureen Elizabeth (Lady Thomas), DBE
Thompson, Dame Ila Dianne, DBE
Thornton, *Prof.* Dame Janet Maureen, DBE
Tickell, Dame Clare Oriana, DBE
Tinson, Dame Sue, DBE
Tizard, Dame Catherine Anne, GCMG, GCVO, DBE
Tokiel, Dame Rosa, DBE
Trotter, Dame Janet Olive, DBE
Turner-Warwick, Dame Margaret Elizabeth Harvey,
    DBE, FRCP, FRCPED
Twelftree, Dame Marcia, DBE
Uchida, Dame Mitsuko, DBE

Uprichard, Dame Mary Elizabeth, DBE
Varley, Dame Joan Fleetwood, DBE
Wagner, Dame Gillian Mary Millicent (Lady Wagner),
    DBE
Wall, Dame (Alice) Anne, (Mrs Michael Wall), DCVO
Wallace, *Prof.* Dame Helen Sarah, DBE, CMG
Wallis, Dame Sheila Ann, DBE
Walter, Dame Harriet Mary, DBE
Warner, *Prof.* Dame Marina Sarah, DBE, FBA
Waterhouse, Dr Dame Rachel Elizabeth, DBE
Waterman, *Dr* Dame Fanny, DBE
Watkinson, Dame Angela Eileen, DBE
Webb, *Prof.* Dame Patricia, DBE
Weir, Dame Gillian Constance (Mrs Phelps), DBE
Weller, Dame Rita, DBE
Weston, Dame Margaret Kate, DBE
Westwood, Dame Vivienne Isabel, DBE
Whitehead, *Hon.* Dame Annabel Alice Hoyer, DCVO
Williams, Dame Josephine, DBE
Willmot, Dame Glenis, DBE
Wilson, Dame Jacqueline, DBE
Wilson-Barnett, *Prof.* Dame Jenifer, DBE
Winstone, Dame Dorothy Gertrude, DBE, CMG
Wolfson de Botton, Dame Janet (Mrs Wolfson de Botton),
    DBE
Wong Yick-ming, Dame Rosanna, DBE
Woolf, Dame Catherine Fiona, DBE
Zaffar, Dame Naila, DBE

# DECORATIONS AND MEDALS

## PRINCIPAL DECORATIONS AND MEDALS
IN ORDER OF WEAR

VICTORIA CROSS (VC), 1856 (*see* below)
GEORGE CROSS (GC), 1940 (*see* below)

BRITISH ORDERS OF KNIGHTHOOD (*see also* Orders of Chivalry)
*Order of the Garter*
*Order of the Thistle*
*Order of St Patrick*
*Order of the Bath*
*Order of Merit*
*Order of the Star of India*
*Order of St Michael and George*
*Order of the Indian Empire*
*Order of the Crown of India*
*Royal Victorian Order (Classes I, II and III)*
*Order of the British Empire (Classes I, II and III)*
*Order of the Companions of Honour*
*Distinguished Service Order*
*Royal Victorian Order (Class IV)*
*Order of the British Empire (Class IV)*
*Imperial Service Order*
*Royal Victorian Order (Class V)*
*Order of the British Empire (Class V)*

BARONET'S BADGE

KNIGHT BACHELOR'S BADGE

INDIAN ORDER OF MERIT (MILITARY)

DECORATIONS
*Conspicuous Gallantry Cross* (CGC), 1995
*Royal Red Cross* Class I (RRC), 1883
*Distinguished Service Cross* (DSC), 1914
*Military Cross* (MC), December 1914
*Distinguished Flying Cross* (DFC), 1918
*Air Force Cross* (AFC), 1918
*Royal Red Cross* Class II (ARRC)
*Order of British India*
*Kaisar-i-Hind Medal*
*Order of St John*

MEDALS FOR GALLANTRY AND DISTINGUISHED CONDUCT
*Union of South Africa Queen's Medal for Bravery,* in Gold
*Distinguished Conduct Medal* (DCM), 1854
*Conspicuous Gallantry Medal* (CGM), 1874
*Conspicuous Gallantry Medal (Flying)*
*George Medal* (GM), 1940
*Queen's Police Medal for Gallantry*
*Queen's Fire Service Medal for Gallantry*
*Royal West African Frontier Force Distinguished Conduct Medal*
*King's African Rifles Distinguished Conduct Medal*
*Indian Distinguished Service Medal*
*Union of South Africa Queen's Medal for Bravery,* in Silver
*Distinguished Service Medal* (DSM), 1914
*Military Medal* (MM), 1916
*Distinguished Flying Medal* (DFM), 1918
*Air Force Medal* (AFM)
*Constabulary Medal (Ireland)*

*Medal for Saving Life at Sea (Sea Gallantry Medal)*
*Indian Order of Merit* (Civil)
*Indian Police Medal for Gallantry*
*Ceylon Police Medal for Gallantry*
*Sierra Leone Police Medal for Gallantry*
*Sierra Leone Fire Brigades Medal for Gallantry*
*Overseas Territories Police Medal for Gallantry*
*Queen's Gallantry Medal* (QGM), 1974
*Royal Victorian Medal* (RVM), Gold, Silver and Bronze
*British Empire Medal* (BEM)
*Canada Medal*
*Queen's Police Medal for Distinguished Service* (QPM)
*Queen's Fire Service Medal for Distinguished Service* (QFSM)
*Queen's Volunteer Reserves Medal*
*Queen's Medal for Chiefs*

CAMPAIGN MEDALS AND STARS
Including authorised United Nations, European Community/Union and North Atlantic Treaty Organisation medals (in order of date of campaign for which awarded)

*Iraq Reconstruction Service Medal*
*Civilian Service Medal (Afghanistan)*

POLAR MEDALS (in order of date)

IMPERIAL SERVICE MEDAL

POLICE MEDALS FOR VALUABLE SERVICE
*Indian Police Medal for Meritorious Service*
*Ceylon Police Medal for Merit*
*Sierra Leone Police Medal for Meritorious Service*
*Sierra Leone Fire Brigades Medal for Meritorious Service*
*Overseas Territories Police Medal for Meritorious Service*

BADGE OF HONOUR

JUBILEE, CORONATION AND DURBAR MEDALS
*Queen Victoria, King Edward VII, King George V, King George VI, Queen Elizabeth II, Visit Commemoration and Long and Faithful Service Medals*

EFFICIENCY AND LONG SERVICE DECORATIONS AND MEDALS
*Medal for Meritorious Service*
*Accumulated Campaign Service Medal*
*Medal for Long Service and Good Conduct* (Military)
*Naval Long Service and Good Conduct Medal*
*Medal for Meritorious Service* (Royal Navy 1918–28)
*Indian Long Service and Good Conduct Medal*
*Indian Meritorious Service Medal*
*Royal Marines Meritorious Service Medal* (1849–1947)
*Royal Air Force Meritorious Service Medal* (1918–1928)
*Royal Air Force Long Service and Good Conduct Medal*
*Medal for Long Service and Good Conduct (Ulster Defence Regiment)*
*Indian Long Service and Good Conduct Medal*
*Royal West African Frontier Force Long Service and Good Conduct Medal*
*Royal Sierra Leone Military Forces Long Service and Good Conduct Medal*
*King's African Rifles Long Service and Good Conduct Medal*

Indian Meritorious Service Medal
Police Long Service and Good Conduct Medal
Fire Brigade Long Service and Good Conduct Medal
African Police Medal for Meritorious Service
Royal Canadian Mounted Police Long Service Medal
Ceylon Police Long Service Medal
Ceylon Fire Services Long Service Medal
Sierra Leone Police Long Service Medal
Overseas Territories Police Long Service Medal
Sierra Leone Fire Brigades Long Service Medal
Mauritius Police Long Service and Good Conduct Medal
Mauritius Fire Services Long Service and Good Conduct Medal
Mauritius Prisons Service Long Service and Good Conduct
   Medal
Overseas Territories Fire Brigades Long Service Medal
Overseas Territories Prison Service Medal
Hong Kong Disciplined Services Medal
Army Emergency Reserve Decoration (ERD)
Volunteer Officers' Decoration (VD)
Volunteer Long Service Medal
Volunteer Officers' Decoration (for India and the Colonies)
Volunteer Long Service Medal (for India and the Colonies)
Colonial Auxiliary Forces Officers' Decoration
Colonial Auxiliary Forces Long Service Medal
Medal for Good Shooting (Naval)
Militia Long Service Medal
Imperial Yeomanry Long Service Medal
Territorial Decoration (TD), 1908
Ceylon Armed Services Long Service Medal
Efficiency Decoration (ED)
Territorial Efficiency Medal
Efficiency Medal
Special Reserve Long Service and Good Conduct Medal
Decoration for Officers of the Royal Navy Reserve (RD), 1910
Decoration for Officers of the Royal Naval Volunteer Reserve
   (VRD)
Royal Naval Reserve Long Service and Good Conduct Medal
Royal Naval Volunteer Reserve Long Service and Good Conduct
   Medal
Royal Naval Auxiliary Sick Berth Reserve Long Service and
   Good Conduct Medal
Royal Fleet Reserve Long Service and Good Conduct Medal
Royal Naval Wireless Auxiliary Reserve Long Service and Good
   Conduct Medal
Royal Naval Auxiliary Service Medal
Air Efficiency Award (AE), 1942
Volunteer Reserves Service Medal
Ulster Defence Regiment Medal
Northern Ireland Home Service Medal
Queen's Medal (for Champion Shots of the RN and RM)
Queen's Medal (for Champion Shots of the New Zealand
   Naval Forces)
Queen's Medal (for Champion Shots in the Military Forces)
Queen's Medal (for Champion Shots of the Air Forces)
Cadet Forces Medal, 1950
HM Coastguard Long Service and Good Conduct Medal
Special Constabulary Long Service Medal
Canadian Forces Decoration
Royal Observer Corps Medal
Civil Defence Long Service Medal
Ambulance Service (Emergency Duties) Long Service and Good
   Conduct Medal
Royal Fleet Auxiliary Service Medal
Prison Services (Operational Duties) Long Service and Good
   Conduct Medal
Jersey Honorary Police Long Service and Good Conduct Medal
Merchant Navy Medal for Meritorious Service
Ebola Medal for Service in West Africa
Rhodesia Medal

Royal Ulster Constabulary Service Medal
Northern Ireland Prison Service Medal
Union of South Africa Commemoration Medal
Indian Independence Medal
Pakistan Medal
Ceylon Armed Services Inauguration Medal
Ceylon Police Independence Medal (1948)
Sierra Leone Independence Medal
Jamaica Independence Medal
Uganda Independence Medal
Malawi Independence Medal
Fiji Independence Medal
Papua New Guinea Independence Medal
Solomon Islands Independence Medal
Service Medal of the Order of St John
Badge of the Order of the League of Mercy
Voluntary Medical Service Medal (1932)
Women's Royal Voluntary Service Medal
South African Medal for War Services
Overseas Territories Special Constabulary Medal

HONORARY MEMBERSHIP OF COMMONWEALTH
ORDERS

OTHER COMMONWEALTH MEMBERS' ORDERS,
DECORATIONS AND MEDALS

FOREIGN ORDERS

FOREIGN DECORATIONS

FOREIGN MEDALS

## THE VICTORIA CROSS (1856)
FOR CONSPICUOUS BRAVERY

VC

*Ribbon,* Crimson, for all Services (until 1918 it was blue for
the Royal Navy)

Instituted on 29 January 1856, the Victoria Cross was
awarded retrospectively to 1854, the first being held by Lt.
C. D. Lucas, RN, for bravery in the Baltic Sea on 21 June
1854 (gazetted 24 February 1857). The first 62 crosses were
presented by Queen Victoria in Hyde Park, London, on 26
June 1857.
   The Victoria Cross is worn before all other decorations,
on the left breast, and consists of a cross-pattée of bronze,
3.8cm in diameter, with the royal crown surmounted by
a lion in the centre, and beneath there is the inscription *For
Valour.* Holders of the VC currently receive a tax-free annuity
of £2,149, irrespective of need or other conditions. In 1911,
the right to receive the cross was extended to Indian soldiers,
and in 1920 to matrons, sisters and nurses, the staff of the
nursing services and other services pertaining to hospitals
and nursing, and to civilians of either sex regularly or
temporarily under the orders, direction or supervision of the
naval, military, or air forces of the crown.

SURVIVING RECIPIENTS OF THE VICTORIA CROSS
*as at 31 August 2015*

Apiata, *Cpl.* B. H., VC (New Zealand Special Air Service)
   2004 *Afghanistan*

Beharry, *LSgt.* J. G., VC  (Princess of Wales's Royal Regiment)
   2005 *Iraq*
Cruickshank, *Flt. Lt.* J. A., VC  (RAFVR)
   1944 *World War*
Donaldson, *Cpl.* M. G. S., VC  (Australian Special Air Service)
   2008 *Afghanistan*
Keighran, *Cpl.* D. A., VC  (Royal Australian Regiment)
   2012 *Afghanistan*
Leakey, *Lance Cpl.* J. M., VC  (Parachute Regiment)
   2015 *Afghanistan*
Payne, *WO* K., VC, DSC (USA) (Australian Army Training
   Team)
   1969 *Vietnam*
Rambahadur Limbu, *Capt.,* VC, MVO (10th Princess Mary's
   Gurkha Rifles)
   1965 *Sarawak*
Roberts-Smith, *Cpl.* B., VC  (Australian Special Air Service)
   2010 *Afghanistan*
Speakman, *Sgt.* W., VC  (Black Watch, attached KOSB)
   1951 *Korea*

# THE GEORGE CROSS (1940)
FOR GALLANTRY

GC

*Ribbon,* Dark blue, threaded through a bar adorned with
   laurel leaves
Instituted   24   September   1940   (with   amendments,
   3 November 1942)

The George Cross is worn before all other decorations
(except the VC) on the left breast (when worn by a woman it
may be worn on the left shoulder from a ribbon of the same
width and colour fashioned into a bow). It consists of a plain
silver cross with four equal limbs, the cross having in the
centre a circular medallion bearing a design showing St
George and the Dragon. The inscription *For Gallantry*
appears round the medallion and in the angle of each limb of
the cross is the royal cypher 'G VI' forming a circle
concentric with the medallion. The reverse is plain and bears
the name of the recipient and the date of the award. The
cross is suspended by a ring from a bar adorned with laurel
leaves on dark blue ribbon 3.8cm wide.
   The cross is intended primarily for civilians; awards to the
fighting services are confined to actions for which purely
military honours are not normally granted. It is awarded only
for acts of the greatest heroism or of the most conspicuous
courage in circumstances of extreme danger. From 1 April
1965, holders of the cross have received a tax-free annuity,
which is currently £2,149. The cross has twice been awarded
collectively rather than to an individual: to Malta (1942) and
the Royal Ulster Constabulary (1999).
   In October 1971 all surviving holders of the Albert Medal
and the Edward Medal exchanged those decorations for the
George Cross.

SURVIVING RECIPIENTS OF THE GEORGE CROSS
*as at 31 August 2015*

If the recipient originally received the Albert Medal (AM) or
the Edward Medal (EM), this is indicated by the initials in
parentheses.

Bamford, J., GC, 1952
Beaton, J., GC, CVO, 1974
Croucher, *Lance Cpl.* M., GC, 2008
Finney,  C., GC, 2003
Flintoff, H. H., GC (EM), 1944
Gledhill, A. J., GC, 1967
Gregson, J. S., GC (AM), 1943
Haberfield, *Csgt.* K. H., GC, 2005
Hughes, *WO2* K. S., GC, 2010
Johnson, *WO1 (SSM)* B., GC, 1990
Kinne, D. G., GC, 1954
Lowe, A. R., GC (AM), 1949
Norton, *Maj.* P. A., GC, 2006
Pratt, M. K., GC, 1978
Purves, Mrs M., GC (AM), 1949
Raweng, Awang anak, GC, 1951
Shephard, S. J., GC, 2014
Stevens, H. W., GC, 1958
Walker, C., GC, 1972
Wooding, E. A., GC (AM), 1945

# THE ELIZABETH CROSS (2009)

EC

Instituted 1 July 2009

The Elizabeth Cross consists of a silver cross with a laurel
wreath passing between the arms, which bear the floral
symbols of England (rose), Scotland (thistle), Ireland
(shamrock) and Wales (daffodil). The centre of the cross bears
the royal cypher and the reverse is inscribed with the name
of the person for whom it is in honour. The cross is
accompanied by a memorial scroll and a miniature.
   The cross was created to commemorate UK armed forces
personnel who have died on operations or as a result of an
act of terrorism. It may be granted to and worn by the next of
kin of any eligible personnel who died from 1 January 1948
to date. It offers the wearer no precedence. Those who are
eligible include the next of kin of personnel who died while
serving on a medal earning operation, as a result of an act of
terrorism, or on a non-medal earning operation where death
was caused by the inherent high risk of the task.
   The Elizabeth Cross is not intended as a posthumous
medal for the fallen but as an emblem of national recognition
of the loss and sacrifice made by the personnel and their
families.

# CHIEFS OF CLANS IN SCOTLAND

Only chiefs of whole Names or Clans are included, except certain special instances (marked *) who, though not chiefs of a whole Name, were or are for some reason (eg the Macdonald forfeiture) independent. Under decision (*Campbell-Gray*, 1950) that a bearer of a 'double or triple-barrelled' surname cannot be held chief of a part of such, several others cannot be included in the list at present.

THE ROYAL HOUSE: HM The Queen

AGNEW: Sir Crispin Agnew of Lochnaw, Bt., QC
ANSTRUTHER: Tobias Anstruther of Anstruther and Balcaskie
ARBUTHNOTT: Viscount of Arbuthnott
BANNERMAN: Sir David Bannerman of Elsick, Bt.
BARCLAY: Peter C. Barclay of Towie Barclay and of that Ilk
BORTHWICK: Lord Borthwick
BOYLE: Earl of Glasgow
BRODIE: Alexander Brodie of Brodie
BROUN OF COLSTOUN: Sir Wayne Broun of Colstoun, Bt.
BRUCE: Earl of Elgin and Kincardine, KT
BUCHAN: David Buchan of Auchmacoy
BURNETT: James C. A. Burnett of Leys
CAMERON: Donald Cameron of Lochiel
CAMPBELL: Duke of Argyll
CARMICHAEL: Richard Carmichael of Carmichael
CARNEGIE: Duke of Fife
CATHCART: Earl Cathcart
CHARTERIS: Earl of Wemyss and March
CLAN CHATTAN: K. Mackintosh of Clan Chattan
CHISHOLM: Hamish Chisholm of Chisholm (*The Chisholm*)
COCHRANE: Earl of Dundonald
COLQUHOUN: Sir Malcolm Rory Colquhoun of Luss, Bt.
CRANSTOUN: David Cranstoun of that Ilk
CUMMING: Sir Alastair Cumming of Altyre, Bt.
DARROCH: Duncan Darroch of Gourock
DEWAR: Michael Dewar of that Ilk and Vogrie
DRUMMOND: Earl of Perth
DUNBAR: Sir James Dunbar of Mochrum, Bt.
DUNDAS: David Dundas of Dundas
DURIE: Andrew Durie of Durie, CBE
ELIOTT: Mrs Margaret Eliott of Redheugh
ERSKINE: Earl of Mar and Kellie
FARQUHARSON: Capt. Alwyne Farquharson of Invercauld, MC
FERGUSSON: Sir Charles Fergusson of Kilkerran, Bt.
FORBES: Lord Forbes
FORSYTH: Alistair Forsyth of that Ilk
FRASER: Lady Saltoun
*FRASER (OF LOVAT): Lord Lovat
GAYRE: Reinold Gayre of Gayre and Nigg
GORDON: Marquess of Huntly
GRAHAM: Duke of Montrose
GRANT: Lord Strathspey
GUTHRIE: Alexander Guthrie of Guthrie
HAIG: Earl Haig
HALDANE: Martin Haldane of Gleneagles
HANNAY: David Hannay of Kirkdale and of that Ilk
HAY: Earl of Erroll

HENDERSON: Alistair Henderson of Fordell
HUNTER: Pauline Hunter of Hunterston
IRVINE OF DRUM: David Irvine of Drum
JARDINE: Sir William Jardine of Applegirth, Bt.
JOHNSTONE: Earl of Annandale and Hartfell
KEITH: Earl of Kintore
KENNEDY: Marquess of Ailsa
KERR: Marquess of Lothian, PC
KINCAID: Madam Arabella Kincaid of Kincaid
LAMONT: Revd Peter Lamont of that Ilk
LEASK: Jonathan Leask of that Ilk
LENNOX: Edward Lennox of that Ilk
LESLIE: Earl of Rothes
LINDSAY: Earl of Crawford and Balcarres, KT, GCVO, PC
LIVINGSTONE (or MACLEA): Niall Livingstone of the Bachuil
LOCKHART: Angus Lockhart of the Lee
LUMSDEN: Gillem Lumsden of that Ilk and Blanerne
MACALESTER: William St J. McAlester of Loup and Kennox
MACARTHUR; John MacArthur of that Ilk
MCBAIN: James H. McBain of McBain
MACDONALD: Lord Macdonald (*The Macdonald of Macdonald*)
*MACDONALD OF CLANRANALD: Ranald Macdonald of Clanranald
*MACDONALD OF KEPPOCH: Ranald MacDonald of Keppoch
*MACDONALD OF SLEAT (CLAN HUSTEAIN): Sir Ian Macdonald of Sleat, Bt.
*MACDONELL OF GLENGARRY: Ranald MacDonell of Glengarry
MACDOUGALL: Morag MacDougall of MacDougall
MACDOWALL: Fergus Macdowall of Garthland
MACGREGOR: Sir Malcolm MacGregor of MacGregor, Bt.
MACINTYRE: Donald MacIntyre of Glenoe
MACKAY: Lord Reay
MACKENZIE: Earl of Cromartie
MACKINNON: Anne Mackinnon of Mackinnon
MACKINTOSH: John Mackintosh of Mackintosh (*The Mackintosh of Mackintosh*)
MACLACHLAN: Euan MacLachlan of MacLachlan
MACLAREN: Donald MacLaren of MacLaren and Achleskine
MACLEAN: Hon. Sir Lachlan Maclean of Duart, Bt., CVO
MACLENNAN: Ruaraidh MacLennan of MacLennan
MACLEOD: Hugh MacLeod of MacLeod
MACMILLAN: George MacMillan of MacMillan

MACNAB: James W. A. Macnab of Macnab (*The Macnab*)
MACNAGHTEN: Sir Malcolm Macnaghten of Macnaghten and Dundarave, Bt.
MACNEACAIL: John Macneacail of Macneacail and Scorrybreac
MACNEIL OF BARRA: Rory Macneil of Barra (*The Macneil of Barra*)
MACPHERSON: Hon. Sir William Macpherson of Cluny, TD
MACTAVISH: Steven MacTavish of Dunardry
MACTHOMAS: Andrew MacThomas of Finegand
MAITLAND: Earl of Lauderdale
MAKGILL: Viscount of Oxfuird
MALCOLM (MACCALLUM): Robin N. L. Malcolm of Poltalloch
MAR: Countess of Mar
MARJORIBANKS: Andrew Marjoribanks of that Ilk
MATHESON: Maj. Sir Fergus Matheson of Matheson, Bt.
MENZIES: David Menzies of Menzies
MOFFAT: Madam Moffat of that Ilk
MONCREIFFE: Hon. Peregrine Moncreiffe of that Ilk
MONTGOMERIE: Earl of Eglinton and Winton
MORRISON: Dr John Ruairidh Morrison of Ruchdi
MUNRO: Hector Munro of Foulis
MURRAY: Duke of Atholl
NESBITT (or NISBET): Mark Nesbitt of that Ilk
OGILVY: Earl of Airlie, KT, GCVO, PC
OLIPHANT: Richard Oliphant of that Ilk
RAMSAY: Earl of Dalhousie
RIDDELL: Sir Walter Riddell of Riddell, Bt.
ROBERTSON: Alexander Robertson of Struan (*Struan-Robertson*)
ROLLO: Lord Rollo
ROSS: David Ross of that Ilk and Balnagowan
RUTHVEN: Earl of Gowrie, PC
SCOTT: Duke of Buccleuch and Queensberry, KBE
SCRYMGEOUR: Earl of Dundee
SEMPILL: Lord Sempill
SHAW: John Shaw of Tordarroch
SINCLAIR: Earl of Caithness, PC
SKENE: Danus Skene of Skene
STIRLING: Fraser Stirling of Cader
STRANGE: Maj. Timothy Strange of Balcaskie
SUTHERLAND: Countess of Sutherland
SWINTON: John Swinton of that Ilk
TROTTER: Alexander Trotter of Mortonhall, CVO
URQUHART: Wilkins F. Urquhart of Urquhart
WALLACE: Ian Wallace of that Ilk
WEDDERBURN: Master of Dundee
WEMYSS: Michael Wemyss of that Ilk

# THE PRIVY COUNCIL

The sovereign in council, or Privy Council, was the chief source of executive power until the system of cabinet government developed in the 18th century. Now the Privy Council's main functions are to advise the sovereign and to exercise its own statutory responsibilities independent of the sovereign in council.

Membership of the Privy Council is automatic upon appointment to certain government and judicial positions in the UK, eg cabinet ministers must be Privy Counsellors and are sworn in on first assuming office. Membership is also accorded by the Queen to eminent people in the UK and independent countries of the Commonwealth of which she is Queen, on the recommendation of the prime minister. Membership of the council is retained for life, except for very occasional removals.

The administrative functions of the Privy Council are carried out by the Privy Council Office under the direction of the president of the council, who is always a member of the cabinet. (*See also* Parliament)

*President of the Council*, Rt. Hon. Chris Grayling, MP
*Clerk of the Council*, Richard Tilbrook

*Style The Right (or Rt.) Hon._*
  *Envelope, The Right (or Rt.) Hon. F_ S_*
  *Letter, Dear Mr/Miss/Mrs S_*
  *Spoken, Mr/Miss/Mrs S_*
It is incorrect to use the letters PC after the name in conjunction with the prefix The Rt. Hon., unless the Privy Counsellor is a peer below the rank of Marquess and so is styled The Rt. Hon. because of his/her rank.

## MEMBERS *as at August 2015*

HRH The Duke of Edinburgh, 1951
HRH The Prince of Wales, 1977

Abernethy, *Hon.* Lord (Alastair
  Cameron), 2005
Adonis, Lord, 2009
Aikens, Sir Richard, 2008
Ainsworth, Robert, 2005
Airlie, Earl of, 1984
Aldous, Sir William, 1995
Alebua, Ezekiel, 1988
Alexander, Douglas, 2005
Alexander, Sir Danny, 2010
Amos, Baroness, 2003
Anderson of Swansea, Lord, 2000
Anelay of St Johns, Baroness, 2009
Angiolini, Dame Elish, 2006
Anthony, Douglas, 1971
Arbuthnot, Lord, 1998
Arden, Dame Mary, 2000
Armstrong of Hill Top, Baroness, 1999
Arthur, *Hon.* Owen, 1995
Ashdown of Norton-sub-Hamdon,
  Lord, 1989
Ashcroft, Lord, 2012
Ashton of Upholland, Baroness, 2006
Astor of Hever, Lord, 2015
Atkins, Sir Robert, 1995
Auld, Sir Robin, 1995
Baker, Norman, 2014
Baker, Sir Thomas, 2002
Baker of Dorking, Lord, 1984
Baldry, Sir Tony, 2013
Balls, Ed, 2007
Barker, Lord, 2012
Barron, Sir Kevin, 2001
Bassam of Brighton, Lord, 2009
Bates, Sir David, 2014
Battle, John, 2002
Bean, Sir David, 2014
Beatson, Sir Jack, 2013
Beckett, Dame Margaret, 1993
Beith, Lord, 1992
Beldam, Sir Roy, 1989
Benn, Hilary, 2003
Bercow, John, 2009

Birch, William, 1992
Black, Dame Jill, 2011
Blackstone, Baroness, 2001
Blair, Anthony, 1994
Blanchard, Peter, 1998
Blears, Hazel, 2005
Blencathra, Lord, 1995
Blunkett, Lord, 1997
Boateng, Lord, 1999
Bolger, James, 1991
Bonomy, *Hon.* Lord (Iain Bonomy),
  2010
Boothroyd, Baroness, 1992
Bottomley of Nettlestone, Baroness,
  1992
Boyd of Duncansby, Lord, 2000
Brabazon of Tara, Lord, 2013
Bracadale, *Hon.* Lord
  (Alistair Campbell), 2013
Bradley, Lord, 2001
Bradshaw, Ben, 2009
Brake, Thomas, 2011
Brathwaite, Sir Nicholas, 1991
Briggs, Sir Michael, 2013
Brodie, *Hon.* Lord (Philip Brodie),
  2013
Brokenshire, James, 2015
Brooke, Annette, 2014
Brooke, Sir Henry, 1996
Brooke of Sutton Mandeville, Lord,
  1988
Brown, Gordon, 1996
Brown, Nicholas, 1997
Brown, Sir Stephen, 1983
Brown of Eaton-under-Heywood,
  Lord, 1992
Browne of Ladyton, Lord, 2005
Browne-Wilkinson, Lord, 1983
Bruce, Sir Malcolm, 2006
Burnett, Sir Ian, 2014
Burnham, Andy, 2007
Burns, Simon, 2011
Burnton, Sir Stanley, 2008
Burstow, Paul, 2012
Burt, Alistair, 2013
Butler of Brockwell, Lord, 2004

Butler-Sloss, Baroness, 1988
Buxton, Sir Richard, 1997
Byers, Stephen, 1998
Byrne, Liam, 2008
Byron, Sir Dennis, 2004
Cable, Sir Vincent, 2010
Caborn, Richard, 1999
Caithness, Earl of, 1990
Cameron, David, 2005
Cameron of Lochbroom, Lord, 1984
Camoys, Lord, 1997
Campbell, Alan, 2014
Campbell, Lord, 1999
Campbell, Sir William, 1999
Canterbury, Archbishop of, 2013
Carey of Clifton, Lord, 1991
Carloway, *Hon.* Lord (Colin
  Sutherland), 2008
Carmichael, Alistair, 2010
Carnwath of Notting Hill, Lord, 2002
Carrington, Lord, 1959
Carswell, Lord, 1993
Chadwick, Sir John, 1997
Chalfont, Lord, 1964
Chalker of Wallasey, Baroness, 1987
Chan, Sir Julius, 1981
Chilcot, Sir John, 2004
Christie, Perry, 2004
Clark, Greg, 2010
Clark, Helen, 1990
Clark of Carlton, Baroness, 2013
Clark of Windermere, Lord, 1997
Clarke, Charles, 2001
Clarke, Sir Christopher, 2013
Clarke, Kenneth, 1984
Clarke, *Hon.* Lord (Matthew Clarke),
  2008
Clarke, Thomas, 1997
Clarke of Stone-Cum-Ebony, Lord,
  1998
Clegg, Nicholas, 2008
Clinton-Davis, Lord, 1998
Clwyd, Ann, 2004
Coghlin, Sir Patrick, 2009
Collins of Mapesbury, Lord, 2007
Cooper, Yvette, 2007

Cope of Berkeley, Lord, 1988
Corston, Baroness, 2003
Cosgrove, *Hon.* Lady (Hazel Cosgrove), 2003
Coulsfield, *Hon.* Lord (John Coulsfield), 2000
Crabb, Stephen, 2014
Crawford and Balcarres, Earl of, 1972
Creech, *Hon.* Wyatt, 1999
Crickhowell, Lord, 1979
Cullen of Whitekirk, Lord, 1997
Cunningham of Felling, Lord, 1993
Curry, David, 1996
Darling, Lord, 1997
Darzi of Denham, Lord, 2009
Davey, Edward, 2012
Davies, Denzil, 1978
Davies, Ronald, 1997
Davies of Oldham, Lord, 2006
Davis, David, 1997
Davis, Sir Nigel, 2011
Davis, Terence, 1999
de la Bastide, Michael, 2004
de Silva, Sir Desmond, 2011
Dean of Thornton-le-Fylde, Baroness, 1998
Deben, Lord, 1985
Denham, John, 2000
Denham, Lord, 1981
Dholakia, Lord, 2010
Dixon, Lord, 1996
Dobson, Frank, 1997
Dodds, Nigel, 2010
Donaldson, Jeffrey, 2007
Dorrell, Stephen, 1994
Dorrian, *Hon.* Lady (Leona Dorrian), 2013
Douglas, *Dr* Denzil, 2011
Drayson, Lord, 2008
Drummond Young, *Hon.* Lord (James Drummond Young), 2013
D'Souza, Baroness, 2009
du Cann, Sir Edward, 1964
Duncan, Alan, 2010
Duncan Smith, Iain, 2001
Dyson, Lord, 2001
Eassie, *Hon.* Lord (Ronald Mackay), 2006
East, Paul, 1998
Eden of Winton, Lord, 1972
Edward, Sir David, 2005
Eggar, Timothy, 1995
Eichelbaum, Sir Thomas, 1989
Elias, Sir Patrick, 2009
Elias, *Hon.* Dame, Sian, 1999
Elis-Thomas, Lord, 2004
Emslie, *Hon.* Lord (George Emslie), 2011
Esquivel, Manuel, 1986
Etherton, Sir Terence, 2008
Evans, Sir Anthony, 1992
Evennett, David, 2015
Falconer of Thoroton, Lord, 2003
Fallon, Michael, 2012
Featherstone, Baroness, 2014
Feldman of Elstree, Lord, 2015
Fellowes, Lord, 1990
Fergusson, Alexander, 2010
Field, Frank, 1997

Flint, Caroline, 2008
Floyd, Sir Christopher, 2013
Forsyth of Drumlean, Lord, 1995
Foster, Lord, 2010
Foster of Bishop Auckland, Lord, 1993
Foulkes of Cumnock, Lord, 2002
Fowler, Lord, 1979
Fox, Liam, 2010
Francois, Mark, 2010
Freedman, Sir Lawrence, 2009
Freeman, Lord, 1993
Freud, Lord, 2015
Fulford, Sir Adrian, 2013
Gage, Sir William, 2004
Garden of Frognal, Baroness, 2015
Garel-Jones, Lord, 1992
Garnier, Sir Edward, 2015
Geidt, Sir Christopher, 2007
George, Bruce, 2000
Gibson, Sir Peter, 1993
Gill, *Hon.* Lord (Brian Gill), 2002
Gillan, Cheryl, 2010
Gillen, Sir John, 2014
Girvan, Sir (Frederick) Paul, 2007
Glidewell, Sir Iain, 1985
Gloster, Dame Elizabeth, 2013
Goff of Chieveley, Lord, 1982
Goldring, Sir John, 2008
Goldsmith, Lord, 2002
Goodlad, Lord, 1992
Gove, Michael, 2010
Gowrie, Earl of, 1984
Graham, Sir Douglas, 1998
Graham of Edmonton, Lord, 1998
Grayling, Chris, 2010
Green, Damian, 2012
Greening, Justine, 2011
Grieve, Dominic, 2010
Grocott, Lord, 2002
Gross, Sir Peter, 2011
Habgood, Lord, 1983
Hague, Lord, 1995
Hailsham, Viscount, 1992
Hain, Lord, 2001
Hale of Richmond, Baroness, 1999
Halfron, Robert, 2015
Hallett, Dame Heather, 2005
Hamilton, *Hon.* Lord (Arthur Hamilton), 2002
Hamilton of Epsom, Lord, 1991
Hammond, Philip, 2010
Hancock, Matthew, 2014
Hands, Gregory, 2014
Hanley, Sir Jeremy, 1994
Hanson, David, 2007
Hardie, Lord, 1997
Hardie Boys, Sir Michael, 1989
Harman, Harriet, 1997
Harper, Mark, 2015
Haselhurst, Sir Alan, 1999
Hattersley, Lord, 1975
Hayes, John, 2013
Hayman, Baroness, 2000
Healey, John, 2008
Healey, Lord, 1964
Heath, David, 2015
Heathcoat-Amory, David, 1996
Hendry, Charles, 2015
Henley, Lord, 2013

Henry, John, 1996
Herbert, Nick, 2010
Heseltine, Lord, 1979
Heseltine, Sir William, 1986
Hesketh, Lord, 1991
Hewitt, Patricia, 2001
Higgins, Lord, 1979
Higgins, Sir Malachy, 2007
Hill, Keith, 2003
Hill of Oareford, Lord, 2013
Hodge, Lord, 2013
Hodge, Margaret, 2003
Hoffmann, Lord, 1992
Hollis of Heigham, Baroness, 1999
Hoon, Geoffrey, 1999
Hooper, Sir Anthony, 2004
Hope of Craighead, Lord, 1989
Hope of Thornes, Lord, 1991
Hordern, Sir Peter, 1993
Howard of Lympne, Lord, 1990
Howarth, George, 2005
Howarth of Newport, Lord, 2000
Howe, Earl, 2013
Howe of Aberavon, Lord, 1972
Howell of Guildford, Lord, 1979
Howells, Kim, 2009
Hoyle, Lindsay, 2013
Hughes, Simon, 2010
Hughes of Ombersley, Lord, 2006
Hughes of Stretford, Baroness, 2004
Hunt, Jeremy, 2010
Hunt, Jonathon, 1989
Hunt of Kings Heath, Lord, 2009
Hunt of Wirral, Lord, 1990
Hurd of Westwell, Lord, 1982
Hutchison, Sir Michael, 1995
Hutton, Lord, 1988
Hutton of Furness, Lord, 2001
Inge, Lord, 2004
Ingraham, Hubert, 1993
Ingram, Adam, 1999
Irvine of Lairg, Lord, 1997
Jack, Michael, 1997
Jackson, Sir Rupert, 2008
Jacob, Sir Robert, 2004
Jacobs, Francis, 2005
Janvrin, Lord, 1998
Javid, Sajid, 2014
Jay of Paddington, Baroness, 1998
Jenkin of Roding, Lord, 1973
Johnson, Alan, 2003
Jones, Carwyn, 2010
Jones, David, 2012
Jones, Lord, 1999
Jopling, Lord, 1979
Jowell, Baroness, 1998
Judge, Lord, 1996
Jugnauth, Sir Aneerood, 1987
Kakkar, Lord, 2014
Kaufman, Sir Gerald, 1978
Kay, Sir Maurice, 2004
Keene, Sir David, 2000
Keith, Sir Kenneth, 1998
Kelly, Ruth, 2004
Kenilorea, Sir Peter, 1979
Kennedy, Jane, 2003
Kennedy, Sir Paul, 1992
Kerr of Tonaghmore, Lord, 2004
Khan, Sadiq, 2009

Ross, *Hon.* Lord (Donald MacArthur), 1985
Royall of Blaisdon, Baroness, 2008
Rudd, Amber, 2015
Ruddock, Dame Joan, 2010
Ryan, Joan, 2007
Ryder, Sir Ernest, 2013
Ryder of Wensum, Lord, 1990
Sainsbury, Sir Timothy, 1992
Sales, Sir Philip, 2014
Salisbury, Marquess of, 1994
Salmond, Alex, 2007
Sandiford, Erskine, 1989
Saville of Newdigate, Lord, 1994
Sawyer, Dame Joan, 2004
Schiemann, Sir Konrad, 1995
Scotland of Asthal, Baroness, 2001
Scott of Foscote, Lord, 1991
Seaga, Edward, 1981
Sedley, Sir Stephen, 1999
Selkirk of Douglas, Lord, 1996
Shapps, Grant, 2010
Sharp, Dame Victoria, 2013
Sheldon, Lord, 1977
Shephard of Northwold, Baroness, 1992
Sheil, Sir John, 2005
Shipley, Jennifer, 1998
Short, Clare, 1997
Shutt of Greetland, Lord, 2009
Simmonds, Sir Kennedy, 1984
Simmonds, Mark, 2014
Simpson, Keith, 2015
Sinclair, Ian, 1977
Slade, Sir Christopher, 1982
Smith, Andrew, 1997
Smith, Dame Janet, 2002
Smith, *Hon.* Lady (Anne Smith), 2013
Smith, Jacqueline, 2003
Smith of Basildon, Baroness, 2009
Smith of Finsbury, Lord, 1997
Soames, *Hon.* (Arthur) Nicholas, 2011
Somare, Sir Michael, 1977
Soubry, Anna, 2015
Spellar, John, 2001
Spelman, Caroline, 2010

Spicer, Lord, 2013
Stanley, Sir John, 1984
Steel of Aikwood, Lord, 1977
Stephen, Sir Ninian, 1979
Stewartby, Lord, 1989
Steyn, Lord, 1992
Stowell of Beeston, Baroness, 2014
Strang, Gavin, 1997
Strathclyde, Lord, 1995
Straw, Jack, 1997
Stuart, Freundel, 2013
Stuart-Smith, Sir Murray, 1988
Stunnell, Lord, 2012
Sturgeon, Nicola, 2014
Sullivan, Sir Jeremy, 2009
Sumption, Lord, 2011
Sutherland, *Hon.* Lord (Ranald Sutherland), 2000
Swayne, Desmond, 2011
Swire, Hugo, 2010
Symons of Vernham Dean, Baroness, 2001
Tapsell, Sir Peter, 2011
Taylor of Bolton, Baroness, 1997
Taylor of Holbeach, Lord, 2014
Tebbit, Lord, 1981
Thomas, Edmund, 1996
Thomas, Sir Swinton, 1994
Thomas of Cwmgiedd, Lord, 2003
Thorpe, Sir Matthew, 1995
Thurso, Viscount, 2014
Timms, Stephen, 2006
Tipping, Andrew, 1998
Tizard, Robert, 1986
Tomlinson, Sir Stephen, 2011
Touhig, Lord, 2006
Toulson, Lord, 2007
Treacy, Sir Colman, 2012
Trefgarne, Lord, 1989
Trimble, Lord, 1997
Trumpington, Baroness, 1992
Truss, Elizabeth, 2014
Tuckey, Sir Simon, 1998
Tyler, Lord, 2014
Tyrie, Andrew, 2015
Ullswater, Viscount, 1994

Underhill, Sir Nicholas, 2013
Upton, Simon, 1999
Vadera, Baroness, 2009
Vaz, Keith, 2006
Villiers, Theresa, 2010
Vos, Sir Geoffrey, 2013
Waddington, Lord, 1987
Waite, Sir John, 1993
Wakeham, Lord, 1983
Waldegrave of North Hill, Lord, 1990
Walker of Gestingthorpe, Lord, 1997
Wall, Sir Nicholas, 2004
Wallace of Saltaire, Lord, 2012
Wallace of Tankerness, Lord, 2000
Waller, Sir Mark, 1996
Ward, Sir Alan, 1995
Warner, Lord, 2006
Warsi, Baroness, 2010
Webb, Steve, 2014
West of Spithead, Lord, 2010
Wheatley, *Hon.* Lord (John Wheatley), 2007
Wheeler, Sir John, 1993
Whittingdale, John, 2015
Whitty, Lord, 2005
Widdecombe, Ann, 1997
Wigley, Lord, 1997
Willetts, Lord, 2010
Williams of Crosby, Baroness, 1974
Williams of Elvel, Lord, 2013
Williams of Oystermouth, Lord, 2002
Williamson, Gavin, 2015
Willott, Jennifer, 2014
Wills, Lord, 2008
Wilson, Brian, 2003
Wilson of Culworth, Lord, 2005
Winterton, Rosie, 2006
Wingti, Paias, 1987
Woodward, Shaun, 2007
Woolf, Lord, 1986
Wright, Jeremy, 2014
York, Archbishop of, 2005
Young, Lord, 1993
Young of Graffham, Lord, 1984
Zacca, Edward, 1992

## PRIVY COUNCIL OF NORTHERN IRELAND

The Privy Council of Northern Ireland had responsibilities in Northern Ireland similar to those of the Privy Council in Great Britain until the Northern Ireland Act 1974. Membership of the Privy Council of Northern Ireland is retained for life. Since the Northern Ireland Constitution Act 1973 no further appointments have been made. The postnominal initials PC (NI) are used to differentiate its members from those of the Privy Council.

MEMBERS *as at August 2015*
Bailie, Robin, 1971
Bleakley, David, 1971
Dobson, John, 1969
Kilclooney, Lord, 1970

# PARLIAMENT

The UK constitution is not contained in any single document but has evolved over time, formed by statute, common law and convention. A constitutional monarchy, the UK is governed by ministers of the crown in the name of the sovereign, who is head both of the state and of the government.

The organs of government are the legislature (parliament), the executive and the judiciary. The executive comprises HM government (the cabinet and other ministers), government departments and local authorities (see Government Departments, Public Bodies and Local Government). The judiciary (see Law Courts and Offices) pronounces on the law, both written and unwritten, interprets statutes and is responsible for the enforcement of the law; the judiciary is independent of both the legislature and the executive.

## THE MONARCHY

The sovereign personifies the state and is, in law, an integral part of the legislature, head of the executive, head of the judiciary, commander-in-chief of all armed forces of the crown and supreme governor of the Church of England. In the Channel Islands and the Isle of Man, which are crown dependencies, the sovereign is represented by a lieutenant-governor. In the member states of the Commonwealth of which the sovereign is head of state, her representative is a governor-general; in UK overseas territories the sovereign is usually represented by a governor, who is responsible to the British government.

Although in practice the powers of the monarchy are now very limited, and restricted mainly to the advisory and ceremonial, there are important acts of government which require the participation of the sovereign. These include summoning, proroguing and dissolving parliament, giving royal assent to bills passed by parliament, appointing important office-holders, eg government ministers, judges, bishops and governors, conferring peerages, knighthoods and other honours, and granting pardon to a person wrongly convicted of a crime. The sovereign appoints the prime minister; by convention this office is held by the leader of the political party which enjoys, or can secure, a majority of votes in the House of Commons. In international affairs the sovereign, as head of state, has the power to declare war and make peace, to recognise foreign states and governments, to conclude treaties and to annex or cede territory. However, as the sovereign entrusts executive power to ministers of the crown and acts on the advice of her ministers, which she cannot ignore, royal prerogative powers are in practice exercised by ministers, who are responsible to parliament.

Ministerial responsibility does not diminish the sovereign's importance to the smooth working of government. She holds meetings of the Privy Council (see below), gives audiences to her ministers and other officials at home and overseas, receives accounts of cabinet decisions, reads dispatches and signs state papers; she must be informed and consulted on every aspect of national life; and she must show complete impartiality.

### COUNSELLORS OF STATE
If the sovereign travels abroad for more than a few days or suffers from a temporary illness, it is necessary to appoint members of the royal family, known as counsellors of state, under letters patent to carry out the chief functions of the monarch, including the holding of Privy Councils and giving royal assent to acts passed by parliament. The normal procedure is to appoint three or four members of the royal family among those members remaining in the UK, provided they are over 21. There are currently five counsellors of state.

In the event of the sovereign on accession being under the age of 18 years, or by infirmity of mind or body, rendered incapable of performing the royal functions, provision is made for a regency.

## THE PRIVY COUNCIL

The sovereign in council, or Privy Council, was the chief source of executive power until the system of cabinet government developed. Its main function today is to advise the sovereign on the approval of various statutory functions and acts of the royal prerogative. These powers are exercised through orders in council and royal proclamations, approved by the Queen at meetings of the Privy Council. The council is also able to exercise a number of statutory duties without approval from the sovereign, including powers of supervision over the registering bodies for the medical and allied professions. These duties are exercised through orders of council.

Although appointment as a privy counsellor is for life, only those who are currently government ministers are involved in the day-to-day business of the council. A full council is summoned only on the death of the sovereign or when the sovereign announces his or her intention to marry. (For a full list of privy counsellors, see the Privy Council section.)

There are a number of advisory Privy Council committees whose meetings the sovereign does not attend. Some are prerogative committees, such as those dealing with legislative matters submitted by the legislatures of the Channel Islands and the Isle of Man or with applications for charters of incorporation; and some are provided for by statute, eg those for the universities of Oxford and Cambridge and some Scottish universities.

Administrative work is carried out by the Privy Council Office under the direction of the Lord President of the Council, a cabinet minister.

### JUDICIAL COMMITTEE OF THE PRIVY COUNCIL
Supreme Court Building, Parliament Square, London SW1P 3BD
T 020-7960 1500 W www.jcpc.uk

The Judicial Committee of the Privy Council is the court of final appeal from courts of the UK dependencies, courts of independent Commonwealth countries which have retained the right of appeal and courts of the Channel Islands and the Isle of Man. It also hears very occasional appeals from a number of ancient and ecclesiastical courts.

The committee is composed of privy counsellors who hold, or have held, high judicial office. Only three or five judges hear each case, and these are usually justices of the supreme court.
*Chief Executive,* Jenny Rowe, CB

## PARLIAMENT

Parliament is the supreme law-making authority and can legislate for the UK as a whole or for any parts of it separately (the Channel Islands and the Isle of Man are crown dependencies and not part of the UK). The main functions of parliament are to pass laws, to enable the government to raise taxes and to scrutinise government policy and administration, particularly proposals for expenditure. International treaties and agreements are customarily presented to parliament before ratification.

Parliament can trace its roots to two characteristics of Anglo-Saxon rule: the *witan* (a meeting of the king, nobles and advisors) and the *moot* (county meetings where local matters were discussed). However, it was the parliament that Simon de Montfort called in 1265 that is accepted as the forerunner to modern parliament, as it included non-noble representatives from counties, cities and towns alongside the nobility. The nucleus of early parliaments at the beginning of the 14th century were the officers of the king's household and the king's judges, joined by such ecclesiastical and lay magnates as the king might summon to form a prototype 'House of Lords', and occasionally by the knights of the shires, burgesses and proctors of the lower clergy. By the end of Edward III's reign a 'House of Commons' was beginning to appear; the first known Speaker was elected in 1377.

Parliamentary procedure is based on custom and precedent, partly formulated in the standing orders of both houses of parliament. Each house has the right to control its own internal proceedings and to commit for contempt. The system of debate in the two houses is similar; when a motion has been moved, the Speaker proposes the question as the subject of a debate. Members speak from wherever they have been sitting. Questions are decided by a vote on a simple majority. Draft legislation is introduced, in either house, as a bill. Bills can be introduced by a government minister or a private member, but in practice the majority of bills which become law are introduced by the government. To become law, a bill must be passed by each house (for parliamentary stages, *see* Parliamentary Information) and then sent to the sovereign for the royal assent, after which it becomes an act of parliament.

Proceedings of both houses are public, except on extremely rare occasions. The minutes (called *Votes and Proceedings in the Commons*, and *Minutes of Proceedings in the Lords)* and the speeches *(The Official Report of Parliamentary Debates,* Hansard) are published daily. Proceedings are also recorded for transmission on radio and television and stored in the Parliamentary Recording Unit before transfer to the National Sound Archive. Television cameras have been allowed into the House of Lords since 1985 and into the House of Commons since 1989; committee meetings may also be televised.

The Fixed Term Parliament Act 2011 fixed the duration of a parliament at five years in normal circumstances, the term being reckoned from the date given on the writs for the new parliament. The term of a parliament has been prolonged by legislation in such rare circumstances as the two World Wars (31 January 1911 to 25 November 1918; 26 November 1935 to 15 June 1945). The life of a parliament is divided into sessions, usually of one year in length, beginning and ending most often in May.

DEVOLUTION
The Scottish parliament and the National Assembly for Wales have legislative power over all devolved matters, ie matters not reserved to Westminster or otherwise outside its powers. The Northern Ireland Assembly has legislative authority in the fields previously administered by the Northern Ireland departments. The assembly was suspended in October 2002 and dissolved in April 2003, before being reinstated on 8 May 2007. For further information, *see* Devolved Government.

## THE HOUSE OF LORDS
London SW1A 0PW
T 020-7219 3107
E hlinfo@parliament.uk W www.parliament.uk

The House of Lords is the second chamber, or 'Upper House', of the UK's bicameral parliament. Until the beginning of the 20th century, the House of Lords had considerable power, being able to veto any bill submitted to it by the House of Commons. Since the introduction of the Parliament Acts 1911 and 1949, however, it has no powers over money bills and its power of veto over public legislation has been reduced over time to the power to delay bills for up to one session of parliament (usually one year). Today the main functions of the House of Lords are to contribute to the legislative process, to act as a check on the government, and to provide a forum of expertise. Its judicial role as final court of appeal ended in 2009 with the establishment of a new UK Supreme Court (*see* Law Courts and Offices section).

The House of Lords has a number of select committees. Some relate to the internal affairs of the house – such as its management and administration – while others carry out important investigative work on matters of public interest. The main committees are: the Communications Committee; the Constitution Committee; the Economic Affairs Committee; the European Union Committee; and the Science and Technology Committee. House of Lords' investigative committees look at broad issues and do not mirror government departments as the select committees in the House of Commons do.

The Constitutional Reform Act 2005 significantly altered the judicial function of the House of Lords and the role of the Lord Chancellor as a judge and its presiding officer. The Lord Chancellor is no longer the presiding officer of the House of Lords nor head of the judiciary in England and Wales, but remains a cabinet minister (the Lord Chancellor and Secretary of State for Justice), and is currently a member of the House of Commons. The function of the presiding officer of the House of Lords was devolved to the newly created post of the Speaker of the House of Lords, commonly known as Lord Speaker. The first Lord Speaker elected by the House was the Rt. Hon. Baroness Hayman on 4 July 2006.

Membership of the House of Lords comprises mainly of life peers created under the Life Peerages Act 1958, along with 92 hereditary peers and a small number of Lords of Appeal in Ordinary, ie law lords, who were created under the Appellate Jurisdiction Act 1876*. The Archbishops of Canterbury and York, the Bishops of London, Durham and Winchester, and the 21 senior diocesan bishops of the Church of England are also members.

The House of Lords Act 1999 provides for 92 hereditary peers to remain in the House of Lords until further reform of the House has been carried out. Of these, 75 (42 Conservative, 28 crossbench, three Liberal Democrat and two Labour) are elected by hereditary peers in their political party or crossbench grouping. In addition, 15 office holders were elected by the whole house. Two hereditary peers with royal duties, the Earl Marshal and the Lord Great Chamberlain, have also remained members. Since November 2002, by-elections have been held to fill vacancies left by deaths of hereditary peers and are now held within three months following the permanent retirement of an elected hereditary peer; the by-elections take place under the Alternative Vote System and must occur within three months of the death of the hereditary peer (*see also* The Peerage).

Peers are disqualified from sitting in the house if they are:
• aliens, ie any peer who is not a British citizen, a Commonwealth citizen (under the British Nationality Act 1981) or a citizen of the Republic of Ireland

- under the age of 21
- undischarged bankrupts or, in Scotland, those whose estate is sequestered
- holders of a disqualifying judicial office
- members of the European parliament
- convicted of treason

Bishops cease to be members of the house when they retire.

Members who do not wish to attend sittings of the House of Lords may apply for leave of absence for the duration of a parliament. Since the passage of the House of Lords Reform Act 2014, members of the House may also retire permanently by giving notice in writing to the Clerk of the Parliaments.

Members of the House of Lords, who are not paid a salary, may claim a daily allowance of £300 (or may elect to claim a reduced daily allowance of £150) per sitting day – but only if they attend a sitting of the House and/or committee proceedings.

* Although the office of Lord of Appeal in Ordinary no longer exists, law lords created under the Appellate Jurisdiction Act 1876 remain members of the House. Those in office at the time of the establishment of the Supreme Court became justices of the UK Supreme Court and are not permitted to sit or vote in the House of Lords until they retire.

## COMPOSITION *as at 1 September 2015*

| | |
|---|---|
| Archbishops and bishops | 25 |
| Life peers under the Appellate Jurisdiction Act 1876 and the Life Peerages Act 1958 | 664 |
| Peers under the House of Lords Act 1999 | 86 |
| *Total* | 775 |

## STATE OF THE PARTIES *as at 1 September 2015*†

| | |
|---|---|
| Conservative | 225 |
| Labour | 211 |
| Liberal Democrat | 101 |
| Crossbench | 176 |
| Archbishops and bishops | 25 |
| Non-affiliated | 20 |
| Other parties | 17 |
| *Total* | 775 |

† Excluding 34 peers on leave of absence and eight disqualified as senior members of the judiciary

## HOUSE OF LORDS PAY FOR SENIOR STAFF 2015–16
Senior staff are placed in the following pay bands according to their level of responsibility and taking account of other factors such as experience and marketability.

| | |
|---|---|
| Judicial group 4 | £176,226 |
| Senior band 3 | £104,000–£139,829 |
| Senior band 2 | £85,000–£124,845 |
| Senior band 1A | £69,000–£105,560 |
| Senior band 1 | £63,500–£93,380 |
| Band A1 | £60,824–£74,998 |
| Band A2 | £49,329–£61,741 |

## OFFICERS AND OFFICIALS
The house is presided over by the Lord Speaker, whose powers differ from those of the Speaker of the House of Commons. The Lord Speaker has no power to rule on matters of order because the House of Lords is self-regulating. The maintenance of the rules of debate is the responsibility of all the members who are present.

A panel of deputy speakers is appointed by Royal Commission. The first deputy speaker is the Chair of Committees, a salaried officer of the house appointed at the beginning of each session. He or she chairs a number of 'domestic' committees relating to the internal affairs of the house . The first deputy speaker is assisted by a panel of deputy chairs, headed by the salaried Principal Deputy Chair of Committees, who is also chair of the European Union Committee of the house.

The Clerk of the Parliaments is the accounting officer and the chief permanent official responsible for the administration of the house. The Gentleman Usher of the Black Rod is responsible for security and other services and also has royal duties as secretary to the Lord Great Chamberlain.

*Lord Speaker* (£101,664), Rt. Hon. Baroness D'Souza, CMG
*Chair of Committees* (£84,524), Rt. Hon. Lord Laming, CBE
*Principal Deputy Chair of Committees* (£79,076), Lord Boswell of Aynho
*Clerk of the Parliaments* (Judicial Group 4), David Beamish
*Clerk Assistant* (Senior Band 3), Edward Ollard
*Reading Clerk and Clerk of the Overseas Office* (Senior Band 3), Simon Burton
*Gentleman Usher of the Black Rod and Serjeant-at-Arms* (Senior Band 2), Lt.-Gen. David Leakey, CMG, CBE
*Yeoman Usher of the Black Rod and Deputy Serjeant-at-Arms* (Band A1), Neil Baverstock
*Commissioner for Lords' Standards,* Paul Kernagham, CBE, QPM
*Counsel to the Chair of Committees* (Senior Band 2), Peter Milledge; P. Hardy
*Registrar of Lords' Interests* (Senior Band 1A), Brendan Keith
*Clerk of Committees* (Senior Band 2), Dr F. P. Tudor
*Legal Adviser to the Human Rights Committee* (Senior Band 2), Murray Hunt
*Director of Information Services and Librarian* (Senior Band 2), Dr Elizabeth Hallam Smith
*Director of Facilities* (Senior Band 2), Carl Woodall
*Finance Director* (Senior Band 1A), Andrew Makower
*Director of Parliamentary Digital Service* (Senior Band 1A), Rob Greig
*Director of Human Resources* (Senior Band 1A), Tom Mohan
*Clerk of Legislation* (Senior Band 1A), Jake Vaughan
*Principal Clerk of Select Committees* (Senior Band 1A), Christopher Johnson, DPHIL
*Director of Parliamentary Archives* (Senior Band 1), Adrian Brown

## LORD GREAT CHAMBERLAIN'S OFFICE
*Lord Great Chamberlain,* Marquess of Cholmondeley, KCVO
*Secretary to the Lord Great Chamberlain,* Lt.-Gen. David Leakey, CMG, CBE

## SELECT COMMITTEES
The main House of Lords select committees, as at July 2015, are as follows:
*Administration and Works – Chair,* Rt. Hon. Lord Laming, CBE; *Clerk,* Chris Atkinson
*Communications – Chair,* Lord Best, OBE; *Clerk,* Anna Murphy
*Constitution – Chair,* Lord Lang of Monkton, PC; *Clerk,* Antony Willott
*Delegated Powers and Regulatory Reform – Chair,* Baroness Fookes, DBE; *Clerk,* Christine Salmon Percival
*Economic Affairs – Chair,* Lord Hollick; *Clerk,* Ayeesha Waller
*Equality Act 2010 and Disability – Chair,* Baroness Deech, DBE; *Clerk,* Michael Collon
*European Union – Chair,* Lord Boswell of Aynho; *Principal Clerk,* Christopher Johnson, DPHIL; *Clerk,* Stuart Stoner
*European Union – Sub-committees:*
*Energy and Environment – Chair,* Baroness Scott of Needham Market; *Clerk,* Patrick Milner
*External Affairs – Chair,* Lord Tugendhat; *Clerk,* Eva George
*Financial Affairs – Chair,* Baroness Falkner of Margravine; *Clerk,* John Turner

*Home Affairs – Chair,* Baroness Prashar; *Clerk,* Theodore Pembroke

*Internal Market – Chair,* Lord Whitty; *Clerk,* Alicia Cunningham

*Justice – Chair,* Baroness Kennedy of the Shaws; *Clerk,* Megan Conway

*House – Chair,* Baroness D'Souza, CMG, PC; *Clerk,* Rob Whiteway

*Hybrid Instruments – Chair,* Rt. Hon. Lord Laming, CBE; *Clerk,* vacant

*Information – Chair,* Baroness Donaghy, CBE; *Clerk,*

*Liaison – Chair,* Rt. Hon. Lord Laming, CBE; *Clerk,* Philippa Tudor

*National Policy for the Built Environment – Chair,* Baroness O'Cathain, OBE; *Clerk,* Matthew Smith

*Privileges and Conduct – Chair,* Rt. Hon. Lord Laming, CBE; *Clerk,* Chloe Mawson

*Procedure – Chair,* Rt. Hon. Lord Laming, CBE; *Clerk,* Chloe Mawson

*Refreshment – Chair,* Rt. Hon. Lord Laming, CBE; *Clerk,* Chris Atkinson

*Science and Technology – Chair,* Earl of Selborne, GBE; *Clerk,* Chris Clarke

*Secondary Legislation Scrutiny – Chair,* Lord Trefgarne, PC; *Clerk,* vacant

*Selection Committee – Chair,* Rt. Hon. Lord Laming, CBE; *Clerk,* vacant

*Sexual Violence in Conflict – Chair,* Baroness Nicholson of Winterbourne; *Clerk,* Aaron Speer

*Social Mobility – Chair,* Baroness Corston, PC; *Clerk,* Luke Hussey

*Standing Orders (Private Bills) – Chair,* Rt. Hon. Lord Laming, CBE; *Clerk,* vacant

*Joint Committees:*
*Consolidation Bills*
*Human Rights*
*National Security Strategy*
*Palace of Westminster*
*Statutory Instruments – Chair,* Derek Twigg; *Clerk,* Amelia Aspden

## THE HOUSE OF COMMONS
London SW1A 0AA
T 020-7219 3000 **W** www.parliament.uk

### HOUSE OF COMMONS INFORMATION OFFICE
14 Tothill Street, London SW1H 9NB
T 020-7219 4272 **E** hcinfo@parliament.uk

The members of the House of Commons are elected by universal adult suffrage. For electoral purposes, the UK is divided into constituencies, each of which returns one member to the House of Commons, the member being the candidate who obtains the largest number of votes cast in the constituency. To ensure equitable representation, the four Boundary Commissions keep constituency boundaries under review and recommend any redistribution of seats which may seem necessary because of population movements etc. At the 2010 general election the number of seats increased from 646 to 650. Of the present 650 seats, there are 533 for England, 40 for Wales, 59 for Scotland and 18 for Northern Ireland.

### NUMBER OF SEATS IN THE HOUSE OF COMMONS BY COUNTRY

|                  | 2005 | 2015 |
|------------------|------|------|
| England          | 529  | 533  |
| Wales            | 40   | 40   |
| Scotland         | 59   | 59   |
| Northern Ireland | 18   | 18   |
| *Total*          | 646  | 650  |

### ELECTIONS
Elections are by secret ballot, each elector casting one vote; voting is not compulsory. (For entitlement to vote in parliamentary elections, *see* Legal Notes.) When a seat becomes vacant between general elections, a by-election is held.

British subjects and citizens of the Irish Republic can stand for election as MPs provided they are 18 or over and not subject to disqualification. Those disqualified from sitting in the house include:

- undischarged bankrupts
- people sentenced to more than one year's imprisonment
- members of the House of Lords (but hereditary peers not sitting in the Lords are eligible)
- holders of certain offices listed in the House of Commons Disqualification Act 1975, eg members of the judiciary, civil service, regular armed forces, police forces, some local government officers and some members of public corporations and government commissions

A candidate does not require any party backing but his or her nomination for election must be supported by the signatures of ten people registered in the constituency. A candidate must also deposit £500 with the returning officer, which is forfeit if the candidate does not receive more than 5 per cent of the votes cast. All election expenses at a general election, except the candidate's personal expenses, are subject to a statutory limit of £8,700, plus six pence for each elector in a borough constituency or nine pence for each elector in a county constituency.

*See* pages 128–173 for an alphabetical list of MPs and results of the general election in 2015.

### STATE OF THE PARTIES *as at 1 September 2015**

| Party | Seats |
|-------|-------|
| Conservative | 330 |
| Labour | 232 |
| Scottish National Party | 56 |
| Democratic Unionist Party | 8 |
| Liberal Democrats | 8 |
| Sinn Fein (have not taken their seats) | 4 |
| Plaid Cymru | 3 |
| Social Democratic & Labour Party | 3 |
| Ulster Unionist Party | 2 |
| Green | 1 |
| Independent | 1 |
| The Speaker | 1 |
| UK Independence Party | 1 |
| *Total* | 650 |

* Working majority of 16; 330 Conservative MPs less all other parties (exlcuding the speaker, deputy speakers and Sinn Fein)

### BUSINESS
The week's business of the house is outlined each Thursday by the leader of the house, after consultation between the chief government whip and the chief opposition whip. A quarter to a third of the time will be taken up by the government's legislative programme and the rest by other business. As a rule, bills likely to raise political controversy are introduced in the Commons before going on to the Lords, and the Commons claims exclusive control in respect of national taxation and expenditure. Bills such as the finance bill, which imposes taxation, and the consolidated fund bills, which authorise expenditure, must begin in the Commons. A bill of which the financial provisions are subsidiary may begin in the Lords, and the Commons may waive its rights in regard to Lords' amendments affecting finance.

The Commons has a public register of MPs' financial and certain other interests; this is published annually as a House of Commons paper. Members must also disclose any relevant financial interest or benefit in a matter before the house when taking part in a debate, in certain other proceedings of the house, or in consultations with other MPs, with ministers or with civil servants.

## MEMBERS' PAY AND ALLOWANCES

Since 1911 members of the House of Commons have received salary payments; facilities for free travel were introduced in 1924. Salary rates for the last 30 years are as follows:

| | | | |
|---|---|---|---|
| 1985 Jan | £16,904 | 2000 Apr | £48,371 |
| 1986 Jan | 17,702 | 2001 Apr | 49,822 |
| 1987 Jan | 18,500 | 2002 Apr | 55,118 |
| 1988 Jan | 22,548 | 2003 Apr | 56,358 |
| 1989 Jan | 24,107 | 2004 Apr | 57,485 |
| 1990 Jan | 26,701 | 2005 Apr | 59,095 |
| 1991 Jan | 28,970 | 2006 Apr | 59,686 |
| 1992 Jan | 30,854 | 2007 Apr | 61,181 |
| 1993 Jan | 30,854 | 2008 Apr | 63,291 |
| 1994 Jan | 31,687 | 2009 Apr | 64,766 |
| 1995 Jan | 33,189 | 2010 Apr | 65,738 |
| 1996 Jan | 34,085 | 2011 Apr | 65,738 |
| 1996 Jul | 43,000 | 2012 Apr | 65,738 |
| 1997 Apr | 43,860 | 2013 Apr | 66,396 |
| 1998 Apr | 45,066 | 2014 Apr | 67,060 |
| 1999 Apr | 47,008 | 2015 May | 74,000 |

The Independent Parliamentary Standards Authority (IPSA) was established under the Parliamentary Standards Act 2009 and is responsible for the independent regulation and administration of the MPs' Scheme of Business Costs and Expenses, as well as for paying the salaries of MPs and their staff members. Since May 2011, the IPSA has also been responsible for determining MPs' pay and setting the level of any increase to their salary.

For 2015–16, the office costs expenditure budget is £26,050 for London area MPs and £23,400 for non-London area MPs. The maximum annual staff budget for London area MPs is £147,000 and £140,000 for non-London area MPs.

Since 1972 MPs have been able to claim reimbursement for the additional cost of staying overnight away from their main residence while on parliamentary business. This is not payable to London area MPs and those MPs who reside in 'grace and favour' accommodation. Accommodation expenses for MPs claiming rental payments in the London area is capped at £20,600 a year; outside of the London area each constituency is banded according to rental values in the area and capped accordingly; annual caps range from £10,400 to £15,650 across five bands. For MPs who own their own homes, mortgage interest and associated expenses up to £8,850 are payable.

For ministerial salaries see Government Departments.

## MEMBERS' PENSIONS

Pension arrangements for MPs were first introduced in 1964. Under the Parliamentary Contributory Pension Fund CARE (career-averaged revalued earnings) scheme, MPs receive a pension on retirement based upon accumulating proportions of pensionable earnings over each year of membership. MPs contributions are payable at a rate of 11.09 per cent of pay. Exchequer contributions are paid at a rate recommended by the Government Actuary and meet the balance of the cost of providing MPs' retirement benefits. Pensions are normally payable upon retirement at age 65 to those who are no longer MPs. Abated pensions may be payable to members aged 55 or over. Pensions are also payable to spouses and other qualifying partners of deceased scheme members at the rate of three-eighths of the deceased member's pension. In the case of members who are in service, an enhanced spouse's or partner's pension and a lump sum equal to two times pensionable salary is payable. There are also provisions in place for dependants and MPs of any age who retire due to ill health. All pensions are CPI index-linked.

## HOUSE OF COMMONS PAY BANDS FOR SENIOR STAFF

Senior Staff are placed in the following Senior Civil Service pay bands. These pay bands apply to the most senior staff in departments and agencies.

| Pay Band 1 | £63,500–£93,380 |
|---|---|
| Pay Band 1A | £67,600–£105,560 |
| Pay Band 2 | £85,000–£124,845 |
| Pay Band 3 | £104,000–£139,829 |

## OFFICERS AND OFFICIALS

The House of Commons is presided over by the Speaker, who has considerable powers to maintain order. A deputy speaker, called the Chairman of Ways and Means, and two deputy chairs may preside over sittings of the House of Commons; they are elected by the house, and, like the Speaker, neither speak nor vote other than in their official capacity.

The staff of the house are employed by a commission chaired by the Speaker. The heads of the six House of Commons departments are permanent officers of the house, not MPs. The Clerk of the House is the principal adviser to the Speaker on the privileges and procedures of the house, the conduct of the business of the house, and committees. The Serjeant-at-Arms is responsible for security and ceremonial functions of the house.

Speaker (£142,826)*, Rt. Hon. John Bercow, MP
Chairman of Ways and Means (£107,108), Rt. Hon. Lindsay Hoyle, MP
First Deputy Chairman of Ways and Means (£102,098), Eleanor Laing, MP
Second Deputy Chairman of Ways and Means (£102,098), Natascha Engel, MP
House of Commons Commission, Rt, Hon. John Bercow, MP (chair); Sir Paul Beresford, MP; Angela Eagle, MP; Rt. Hon. Chris Grayling, MP
Secretary of the Commission, Robert Twigger
* Salaries in parentheses are the maximum available. The Speaker and Deputies have opted not to take the statutory increases awarded to them each year as office holders.

## OFFICE OF THE SPEAKER

Speaker's Secretary, Peter Barratt
Assistant Secretary to the Speaker, Ian Davies, MBE
Trainbearer, Jim Davey
Speaker's Counsel, Michael Carpenter, CB
Chaplain to the Speaker, Revd Rose Hudson-Wilkin

## OFFICE OF THE CLERK OF THE HOUSE

Clerk of the House, David Natzler
Private Secretary, Lloyd Owen

## PARLIAMENTARY COMMISSIONER FOR STANDARDS

Parliamentary Commissioner for Standards, Kathryn Hudson
Registrar of Members' Financial Interests, Heather Wood

## PARLIAMENTARY SECURITY DIRECTOR

Parliamentary Security Director, Paul Martin, CBE
Deputy Parliamentary Security Director, Emily Baldock

## OFFICE OF THE CHAIRMAN OF WAYS AND MEANS

Secretary to the Chairman of Ways and Means, Joanna Dodd

GOVERNANCE OFFICE
*Head of Office,* Tom Goldsmith
*Corporate Risk Management Facilitator,* Rachel Harrison
*Head of Central Communications,* Marianne Cwynarski
*Head of Internal Audit,* Paul Dillon-Robinson
*Head of Parliamentary Programme and Project Assurance,*
Jane Rumsam
*Strategy, Planning and Performance Manager,* Jane Hough

DEPARTMENT OF CHAMBER AND COMMITTEE
SERVICES
*Acting Clerk Assistant and Acting Director General,*
Jacqy Sharpe
*Director of Departmental Services,* Elizabeth Hunt

OVERSEAS OFFICE
*Principal Clerk,* Crispin Poyser
*Delegation Secretary,* Nick Wright
*Inward Visits Manager,* Alison Game, MBE
*National Parliament Representative (Brussels),* Alison Grove

COMMITTEE OFFICE
*Clerk of Committees,* Andrew Kennon
*Principal Clerk of Select Committees,* Mark Hutton; Colin Lee;
Simon Patrick
*Business Managers,* Anita Fuki; Richard Dawson
*Operations Manager,* Karen Saunders

DEPARTMENTAL SELECT COMMITTEES
*Backbench Business – Chair,* Ian Mearns; *Clerk,* Mike
Hennessy
*Business, Innovation and Skills – Chair,* Iain Wright;
*Clerk,* Jessica Montgomery
*Communities and Local Government – Chair,* Clive Betts;
*Clerk,* Dr Anna Dickson
*Culture, Media and Sport – Chair,* Jesse Norman;
*Clerk,* Elizabeth Flood
*Defence – Chair,* Dr Julian Lewis; *Clerk,* James Davies
*Education – Chair,* Neil Carmichael; *Clerk,* Lynn Gardner
*Energy and Climate Change – Chair,* Angus Brendan MacNeil;
*Clerk,* Dr Farrah Bhatti
*Environment, Food and Rural Affairs – Chair,* Neil Parish;
*Clerks,* David Weir
*Foreign Affairs – Chair,* Crispin Blunt; *Clerk,* Kenneth Fox
*Health – Chair,* Dr Sarah Wollaston; *Clerk,* Huw Yardley
*High Speed Rail Bill – Chair,* Robert Syms; *Clerk,* Neil
Caulfield
*Home Affairs – Chair,* Keith Vaz; *Clerk,* Carol Oxborough
*International Development – Chair,* Stephen Twigg; *Clerk,*
Kate Emms
*Justice – Chair,* Robert Neill; *Clerk,* Nick Walker
*Northern Ireland Affairs – Chair,* Laurence Robertson;
*Clerk,* Mike Clark
*Procedure – Chair,* Charles Walker; *Clerk,* Martyn Atkins
*Science and Technology – Chair,* Nicola Blackwood; *Clerk,*
Simon Fiander
*Scottish Affairs – Chair,* Pete Wishart; *Clerk,* Jyoti Chandola
*Standards – Chair,* Kevin Barron; *Clerk,* Eve Samson
*Statutory Instruments – Chair,* Derek Twigg; *Clerk,* Amelia
Aspden
*Transport – Chair,* Louise Ellman; *Clerk,* Gordon Clarke
*Treasury – Chair,* Andrew Tyrie; *Clerk,* James Rhys
*Welsh Affairs – Chair,* David Davies; *Clerk,* Richard Ward
*Women and Equalities – Chair,* Maria Miller; *Clerk,* Gosia
McBride
*Work and Pensions – Chair,* Frank Field; *Clerk,* Adam
Mellows-Facer

DOMESTIC COMMITTEES
*Administration – Chair,* Sir Paul Beresford; Clerks, Sarah
Heath; Helen Wood
*Finance – Chair,* Nicholas Brown; *Clerk,* Robert Twigger
*Members' Expenses – Chair,* vacant; *Clerk,* Robert Twigger

OTHER COMMITTEES
*Environmental Audit – Chair,* Huw Irranca-Davies;
*Clerk,* David Slater
*Liaison – Chair,* vacant; *Clerk,* Andrew Kennon
*Petitions Committee – Chair,* Helen Jones; *Clerk,* Anne-Marie
Griffiths
*Public Accounts – Chair,* Meg Hillier; *Clerk,* Sarah Petit
*Public Administration and Constitutional Affairs – Chair,*
Bernard Jenkin; *Clerks,* Dr Rebecca Davies; Sian
Woodward
*Regulatory Reform – Chair,* vacant; *Clerk,* Jessica Montgomery
*European Scrutiny Committee – Chair,* Sir William Cash;
*Clerk,* Sarah Davies

SCRUTINY UNIT
*Head of Unit,* Jessica Mulley
*Deputy Head of Unit,* Larry Honeysett

VOTE OFFICE
*Deliverer of the Vote,* Catherine Fogarty
*Deputy Deliverer of the Vote,* Owen Sweeney
*Head of Procedural Publishing,* Tom McVeagh
*Procedural Publishing Operations Manager,* Stuart Miller

CHAMBER BUSINESS DIRECTORATE
*Acting Clerk of Legislation,* Liam Laurence Smyth
*Principal Clerks*
*Table Office,* Philippa Helme
*Journals,* Paul Evans
*Bills,* Matthew Hamlyn

OFFICIAL REPORT DIRECTORATE
*Editor,* Lorraine Sutherland
*Deputy Editor,* Alex Newton
*Director of Broadcasting,* John Angeli

SERJEANT-AT-ARMS DIRECTORATE
*Serjeant-at-Arms,* Lawrence Ward
*Deputy Serjeant-at-Arms,* Richard Latham
*Assistant Serjeant-at-Arms,* Lesley Scott

OFFICE OF SPEAKER'S COUNSEL
*Speaker's Counsel and Head of Legal Services Office,* Michael
Carpenter, CB
*Counsel for European Legislation,* Arnold Ridout
*Assistant Counsel for European Legislation,* Joanne Dee
*Counsel for Domestic Legislation,* Peter Davis
*Deputy Counsel for Domestic Legislation,* Peter Brooksbank;
Philip Davies; Daniel Greenberg
*Principal Assistant Counsel,* Helen Emes
*Legal Assistants,* Ami Cochrane; Emma Johnston

DEPARTMENT OF FACILITIES
*Director-General,* John Borley, CB
*Director of Business Management,* Della Herd
*Acting Parliamentary Director of Estates,* Brian Finnimore
*Director of Accommodation and Logistics Services,* Fiona
Channon
*Director of Facilities Finance,* Philip Collins
*Executive Officer,* Katie Phelan-Molloy
*Director of Catering Services,* Richard Tapner-Evans
*Operations Manager,* Robert Gibbs
*Executive Chef,* Mark Hill

## DEPARTMENT OF FINANCE

*Director of Finance,* Myfanwy Barrett
*Chief Accountant,* Alex Mills
*Head of Financial Planning,* Amanda Colledge
*Head of Financial Accounting,* Debra Shirtcliffe
*Head of Financial Services,* Sam Rao

## DEPARTMENT OF HUMAN RESOURCES AND CHANGE

*Director-General of HR and Change,* Andrew J. Walker
*Director of HR Services,* Alix Langley
*Occupational Health and Wellbeing Manager,* Anne Mossop
*Head of Safety,* Dr Marianne McDougall

## DEPARTMENT OF INFORMATION SERVICES

*Director-General and Librarian,* Penny Young
*Director of Service Delivery,* John Benger
*Head of Central Support Services,* Grahame Allen
*Curator of Works of Art,* Malcolm Hay
*Head of Customer Services,* Dr Patsy Richards

## PARLIAMENTARY INFORMATION AND COMMUNICATION TECHNOLOGY (ICT)

*Director of Parliamentary Digital Service,* Rob Greig
*Director of Technology,* Steve O'Connor
*Director of Operations and Members Services,* Rob Sanders
*Director of Resources,* Tracey Jessup
*Director of Programmes and Projects,* Steven Mark
*Head of the Web and Intranet Service,* Tracy Green

## OTHER PRINCIPAL OFFICERS

*Clerk of the Crown in Chancery,* Dame Ursula Brennan
*Parliamentary and Health Service Ombudsman,* Dame Julie Mellor

## NATIONAL AUDIT OFFICE

157–197 Buckingham Palace Road, London SW1W 9SP
T 020-7798 7000
E enquiries@nao.gsi.gov.uk W www.nao.org.uk

The National Audit Office came into existence under the National Audit Act 1983 to replace and continue the work of the former Exchequer and Audit Department. The act reinforced the office's total financial and operational independence from the government and brought its head, the Comptroller and Auditor-General, into a closer relationship with parliament as an officer of the House of Commons.

The National Audit Office (NAO) scrutinises public spending on behalf of parliament, helping it to hold government departments to account and helping public service managers improve performance and service delivery. The NAO audits the financial statements of all government departments and a wide range of other public bodies. It regularly publishes 'value for money' reports on the efficiency and effectiveness of how public resources are used. *Comptroller and Auditor-General,* Amyas Morse
*Assistant Auditors-General,* Sue Higgins; Sally Howes; Martin Sinclair; John Thorpe
*Chief Operating Officer,* Michael Whitehouse

## PARLIAMENTARY INFORMATION

The following is a short glossary of aspects of the work of parliament. Unless otherwise stated, references are to House of Commons procedures.

BILL – Proposed legislation is termed a bill. The stages of a public bill (for private bills, *see* below) in the House of Commons are as follows:

*First reading:* This stage introduces the legislation to the house and, for government bills, merely constitutes an order to have the bill printed.

*Second reading:* The debate on the principles of the bill.

*Committee stage:* The detailed examination of a bill, clause by clause. In most cases this takes place in a public bill committee, or the whole house may act as a committee. Public bill committees may take evidence before embarking on detailed scrutiny of the bill. Very rarely, a bill may be examined by a select committee.

*Report stage:* Detailed review of a bill as amended in committee, on the floor of the house, and an opportunity to make further changes.

*Third reading:* Final debate on the full bill in the Commons.

Public bills go through the same stages in the House of Lords, but with important differences: the committee stage is taken in committee of the whole house or in a grand committee, in which any peer may participate. There are no time limits, all amendments are debated, and further amendments can be made at third reading.

A bill may start in either house, and has to pass through both houses to become law. Both houses have to agree the final text of a bill, so that amendments made by the second house are then considered in the originating house, and if not agreed, sent back or themselves amended, until agreement is reached.

CHILTERN HUNDREDS – A nominal office of profit under the crown, the acceptance of which requires an MP to vacate his/her seat. The Manor of Northstead is similar. These are the only means by which an MP may resign.

CONSOLIDATED FUND BILL – A bill to authorise the issue of money to maintain government services. The bill is dealt with without debate.

EARLY DAY MOTION – A motion put on the notice paper by an MP without, in general, the real prospect of its being debated. Such motions are expressions of back-bench opinion.

FATHER OF THE HOUSE – The MP whose continuous service in the House of Commons is the longest. The present Father of the House is the Rt. Hon. Sir Gerald Kaufman, MP.

GRAND COMMITTEES – There are three grand committees in the House of Commons, one each for Northern Ireland, Scotland and Wales; they consider matters relating specifically to that country. In the House of Lords, bills may be sent to a grand committee instead of a committee of the whole house (*see also* Bill).

HOURS OF MEETING – The House of Commons normally meets on Mondays at 2.30pm, Tuesdays and Wednesdays at 11.30am, Thursdays at 9.30am and some Fridays at 9.30am. (*See also* Westminster Hall Sittings, below.) The House of Lords normally meets at 2.30pm Mondays and Tuesdays, 3pm on Wednesdays and at 11am on Thursdays. The House of Lords occasionally sits on Fridays at 10am.

LEADER OF THE OPPOSITION – In 1937 the office of leader of the opposition was recognised and a salary was assigned to the post. In 2015–16 this is £135,776 (including a parliamentary salary of £74,000). The present leader of the opposition is the Rt. Hon. Jeremy Corbyn, MP.

THE LORD CHANCELLOR – The office of Lord High Chancellor of Great Britain was significantly altered by the Constitutional Reform Act 2005. Previously, the Lord Chancellor was (*ex officio*) the Speaker of the House of Lords, and took part in debates and voted in divisions in the House of Lords. The Department for Constitutional Affairs was created in 2003, and became the Ministry of Justice in 2007, incorporating most of the responsibilities of the Lord Chancellor's department. The role of Speaker has been transferred to the post of Lord Speaker. The Constitutional

Reform Act 2005 also brought to an end the Lord Chancellor's role as head of the judiciary. A Judicial Appointments Commission was created in April 2006, and a supreme court (separate from the House of Lords) was established in 2009.

THE LORD GREAT CHAMBERLAIN – The Lord Great Chamberlain is a Great Officer of State, the office being hereditary since the grant of Henry I to the family of De Vere, Earls of Oxford. It is now a joint hereditary office rotating on the death of the sovereign between the Cholmondeley, Carington and Ancaster families.

The Lord Great Chamberlain, currently the Marquess of Cholmondeley, is responsible for the royal apartments in the Palace of Westminster, the Royal Gallery, the administration of the Chapel of St Mary Undercroft and, in conjunction with the Lord Speaker and the Speaker of the House of Commons, Westminster Hall. The Lord Great Chamberlain has the right to perform specific services at a coronation and has particular responsibility for the internal administrative arrangements within the House of Lords for state openings of parliament.

THE LORD SPEAKER – The first Lord Speaker of the House of Lords, the Rt. Hon. Baroness Hayman, took up office on 4 July 2006. The Lord Speaker is independent of the government and elected by members of the House of Lords rather than appointed by the prime minister. Although the Lord Speaker's primary role is to preside over proceedings in the House of Lords, she does not have the same powers as the Speaker of the House of Commons. For example, the Lord Speaker is not responsible for maintaining order during debates, as this is the responsibility of the house as a whole. The Lord Speaker sits in the Lords on one of the woolsacks, which are couches covered in red cloth and stuffed with wool.

OPPOSITION DAY – A day on which the topic for debate is chosen by the opposition. There are 20 such days in a normal session. On 17 days, subjects are chosen by the leader of the opposition; on the remaining three days by the leader of the next largest opposition party.

PARLIAMENT ACTS 1911 AND 1949 – Under these acts, bills may become law without the consent of the Lords, though the House of Lords has the power to delay a public bill for a parliamentary session.

PRIME MINISTER'S QUESTIONS – The prime minister answers questions from 12 to 12.30pm on Wednesdays.

PRIVATE BILL – A bill promoted by a body or an individual to give powers additional to, or in conflict with, the general law, and to which a special procedure applies to enable people affected to object.

PRIVATE MEMBER'S BILL – A public bill promoted by an MP or peer who is not a member of the government.

PRIVATE NOTICE QUESTION – A question adjudged of urgent importance on submission to the Speaker (in the Lords, the Lord Speaker), answered at the end of oral questions.

PRIVILEGE – The House of Commons has rights and immunities to protect it from obstruction in carrying out its duties. These are known as parliamentary privilege and enable Members of Parliament to debate freely. The most important privilege is that of freedom of speech. MPs cannot be prosecuted for sedition or sued for libel or slander over anything said during proceedings in the house. This enables them to raise in the house questions affecting the public good which might be difficult to raise outside owing to the possibility of legal action against them. The House of Lords has similar privileges.

QUESTION TIME – Oral questions are answered by ministers in the Commons from 2.30 to 3.30pm on Mondays, 11.30am to 12.30pm on Tuesdays and Wednesdays, and 9.30 to 10.30am on Thursdays. Questions are also taken for half an hour at the start of the Lords sittings.

ROYAL ASSENT – The royal assent is signified by letters patent to such bills and measures as have passed both Houses of Parliament (or bills which have been passed under the Parliament Acts 1911 and 1949). The sovereign has not given royal assent in person since 1854. On occasion, for instance in the prorogation of parliament, royal assent may be pronounced to the two houses by Lords Commissioners. More usually royal assent is notified to each house sitting separately in accordance with the Royal Assent Act 1967. The old French formulae for royal assent are then endorsed on the acts by the Clerk of the Parliaments.

The power to withhold assent resides with the sovereign but has not been exercised in the UK since 1707.

SELECT COMMITTEES – Consisting usually of 10 to 15 members of all parties, select committees are a means used by both houses in order to investigate certain matters.

Most select committees in the House of Commons are tied to departments: each committee investigates subjects within a government department's remit. There are other select committees dealing with matters such as public accounts (ie the spending by the government of money voted by parliament) and European legislation, and also committees advising on procedures and domestic administration of the house. Major select committees usually take evidence in public; their evidence and reports are published on the parliament website and in hard copy by The Stationery Office (TSO). House of Commons select committees are reconstituted after a general election.

In the House of Lords, select committees do not mirror government departments but cover broader issues. There is a select committee on the European Union (EU), which has six sub-committees dealing with specific areas of EU policy, a select committee on science and technology, a select committee on economic affairs and also one on the constitution. There is also a select committee on delegated powers and regulatory reform and one on privileges and conduct. In addition, ad hoc select committees have been set up from time to time to investigate specific subjects. There are also joint committees of the two houses, eg the committees on statutory instruments and on human rights.

THE SPEAKER – The Speaker of the House of Commons is the spokesperson and chair of the Chamber. He or she is elected by the house at the beginning of each parliament or when the previous Speaker retires or dies. The Speaker neither speaks in debates nor votes in divisions except when the voting is equal.

VACANT SEATS – When a vacancy occurs in the House of Commons during a session of parliament, the writ for the by-election is moved by a whip of the party to which the member whose seat has been vacated belonged. If the house is in recess, the Speaker can issue a warrant for a writ, should two members certify to him that a seat is vacant.

WESTMINSTER HALL SITTINGS – Following a report by the Modernisation of the House of Commons Select Committee, the Commons decided in May 1999 to set up a second debating forum. It is known as 'Westminster Hall' and sittings are in the Grand Committee Room on some Mondays from 4.30pm to 7.30pm, Tuesdays and Wednesdays from 9.30am to 11.30am and from 2pm to 5pm, and Thursdays from 1.30pm to 4.30pm. Sittings are open to the public at the times indicated.

WHIPS – In order to secure the attendance of members of a particular party in parliament, particularly on the occasion of an important vote, whips (originally known as 'whippers-in') are appointed. The written appeal or circular letter issued by them is also known as a 'whip', its urgency being denoted by the number of times it is underlined. Failure to respond to a three-line whip is tantamount in the Commons to secession (at any rate temporarily) from the party. Whips are provided with office accommodation in both houses, and government and some opposition whips receive salaries from public funds.

## PARLIAMENTARY ARCHIVES
Houses of Parliament, London SW1A 0PW
**T** 020-7219 3074 **E** archives@parliament.uk
**W** www.parliament.uk/archives

Since 1497, the records of parliament have been kept within the Palace of Westminster. They are in the custody of the Clerk of Parliaments. In 1946 the House of Lords Record Office, which became the Parliamentary Archives in 2006, was established to supervise their preservation and their availability to the public. Some 3 million documents are preserved, including acts of parliament from 1497, journals of the House of Lords from 1510, minutes and committee proceedings from 1610, and papers laid before parliament from 1531. Among the records are the Petition of Right, the death warrant of Charles I, the Declaration of Breda, and the Bill of Rights. Records are made available through a public search room.
*Director of the Parliamentary Archives,* Adrian Brown

## GOVERNMENT OFFICE

The government is the body of ministers responsible for the administration of national affairs, determining policy and introducing into parliament any legislation necessary to give effect to government policy. The majority of ministers are members of the House of Commons but members of the House of Lords, or of neither house, may also hold ministerial responsibility. The prime minister is, by current convention, always a member of the House of Commons.

### THE PRIME MINISTER
The office of prime minister, which had been in existence for nearly 200 years, was officially recognised in 1905 and its holder was granted a place in the table of precedence. The prime minister, by tradition also First Lord of the Treasury and Minister for the Civil Service, is appointed by the sovereign and is usually the leader of the party which enjoys, or can secure, a majority in the House of Commons. Other ministers are appointed by the sovereign on the recommendation of the prime minister, who also allocates functions among ministers and has the power to dismiss ministers from their posts.

The prime minister informs the sovereign on state and political matters, advises on the dissolution of parliament, and makes recommendations for important crown appointments, ie the award of honours, etc.

As the chair of cabinet meetings and leader of a political party, the prime minister is responsible for translating party policy into government activity. As leader of the government, the prime minister is responsible to parliament and to the electorate for the policies and their implementation.

The prime minister also represents the nation in international affairs, eg summit conferences.

### THE CABINET
The cabinet developed during the 18th century as an inner committee of the Privy Council, which was the chief source of executive power until that time. The cabinet is composed of about 20 ministers chosen by the prime minister, usually the heads of government departments (generally known as secretaries of state unless they have a special title, eg Chancellor of the Exchequer), the leaders of the two houses of parliament, and the holders of various traditional offices.

The cabinet's functions are the final determination of policy, control of government and coordination of government departments. The exercise of its functions is dependent upon the incumbent party's (or parties') majority support in the House of Commons. Cabinet meetings are held in private, taking place once or twice a week during parliamentary sittings and less often during a recess. Proceedings are confidential, the members being bound by their oath as privy counsellors not to disclose information about the proceedings.

The convention of collective responsibility means that the cabinet acts unanimously even when cabinet ministers do not all agree on a subject. The policies of departmental ministers must be consistent with the policies of the government as a whole, and once the government's policy has been decided, each minister is expected to support it or resign.

The convention of ministerial responsibility holds a minister, as the political head of his or her department, accountable to parliament for the department's work. Departmental ministers usually decide all matters within their responsibility, although on matters of political importance they normally consult their colleagues collectively. A decision by a departmental minister is binding on the government as a whole.

## POLITICAL PARTIES

Before the reign of William and Mary, the principal officers of state were chosen by and were responsible to the sovereign alone, and not to parliament or the nation at large. Such officers acted sometimes in concert with one another but more often independently, and the fall of one did not, of necessity, involve that of others, although all were liable to be dismissed at any moment.

In 1693 the Earl of Sunderland recommended to William III the advisability of selecting a ministry from the political party which enjoyed a majority in the House of Commons, and the first united ministry was drawn in 1696 from the Whigs, to which party the king owed his throne. This group became known as the 'junto' and was regarded with suspicion as a novelty in the political life of the nation, being a small section meeting in secret apart from the main body of ministers. It may be regarded as the forerunner of the cabinet and in the course of time it led to the establishment of the principle of joint responsibility of ministers, so that internal disagreement caused a change of personnel or resignation of the whole body of ministers.

The accession of George I, who was unfamiliar with the English language, led to a disinclination on the part of the sovereign to preside at meetings of his ministers and caused the emergence of a prime minister, a position first acquired by Robert Walpole in 1721 and retained by him without interruption for 20 years and 326 days. The office of prime minister was formally recognised in 1905 when it was established by royal warrant.

### DEVELOPMENT OF PARTIES
In 1828 the Whigs became known as Liberals, a name originally given by opponents to imply laxity of principles, but gradually accepted by the party to indicate its claim to be pioneers and champions of political reform and progressive legislation. In 1861 a Liberal Registration Association was founded and Liberal Associations became widespread. In 1877 a National Liberal Federation was formed, with its headquarters in London. The Liberal Party was in power for long periods during the second half of the 19th century and

for several years during the first quarter of the 20th century, but after a split in the party in 1931, the numbers elected remained small. In 1988 a majority of the Liberals agreed on a merger with the Social Democratic Party under the title Social and Liberal Democrats; since 1989 they have been known as the Liberal Democrats. A minority continue separately as the Liberal Party.

Soon after the change from Whig to Liberal, the Tory Party became known as Conservative, a name believed to have been invented by John Wilson Croker in 1830 and to have been generally adopted around the time of the passing of the Reform Act of 1832 – to indicate that the preservation of national institutions was the leading principle of the party. After the Home Rule crisis of 1886 the dissentient Liberals entered into a compact with the Conservatives, under which the latter undertook not to contest their seats, but a separate Liberal Unionist organisation was maintained until 1912, when it was united with the Conservatives.

Labour candidates for parliament made their first appearance at the general election of 1892, when there were 27 standing as Labour or Liberal-Labour. In 1900 the Labour Representation Committee (LRC) was set up in order to establish a distinct Labour group in parliament, with its own whips, its own policy, and a readiness to cooperate with any party which might be engaged in promoting legislation in the direct interests of labour. In 1906 the LRC became known as the Labour Party.

The Green Party was founded in 1973 and campaigns for social and environmental justice. The party began as 'People', was renamed the Ecology Party, and became the Green Party in 1985.

The UK Independence Party (UKIP) was founded in 1993 by members of the Anti-Federalist League. It is a right-wing populist party with one key policy – to leave the European Union. In the 2014 European elections, UKIP became the first party, other than the Conservatives or Labour to win a national election in over a century.

Plaid Cymru was founded in 1926 to provide an independent political voice for Wales and to campaign for self-government in Wales.

The Scottish National Party (SNP) was founded in 1934 to campaign for independence for Scotland and a referendum on the subject was held in September 2014 which culminated in a 'no' to independence result.

The Social Democratic and Labour Party (SDLP) was founded in 1970, emerging from the civil rights movement of the 1960s, with the aim of promoting reform, reconciliation and partnership across the sectarian divide in Northern Ireland, and of opposing violence from any quarter.

The Democratic Unionist Party (DUP) was founded in 1971 to resist moves by the Ulster Unionist Party which were considered a threat to the Union. Its aim is to maintain Northern Ireland as an integral part of the UK.

The Alliance Party of Northern Ireland was formed in 1970 as a non-sectarian unionist party.

Sinn Fein first emerged in the 1900s as a federation of nationalist clubs. It is a left-wing republican and labour party that seeks to end British governance in Ireland and achieve a 32-county republic.

## GOVERNMENT AND OPPOSITION

The government is formed by the party which wins the largest number of seats in the House of Commons at a general election, or which has the support of a majority of members in the House of Commons. By tradition, the leader of the majority party is asked by the sovereign to form a government, while the largest minority party becomes the official opposition with its own leader and a shadow cabinet.

Leaders of the government and opposition sit on the front benches of the Commons with their supporters (the backbenchers) sitting behind them.

## FINANCIAL SUPPORT

Financial support for opposition parties in the House of Commons was introduced in 1975 and is commonly known as Short Money, after Edward Short, the leader of the house at that time, who introduced the scheme. Short Money is only payable to those parties that secured either one seat or two seats and more than 150,000 votes at the previous general election, and is only intended to provide assistance for parliamentary duties. The amount payable is £16,956.86 for every seat won at the most recent general election plus £33.86 for every 200 votes gained by the party. Short Money approximations for 2015–16 are:

| DUP | £166,000 |
| Green | £212,000 |
| Labour | £6,200,000 |
| Liberal Democrats | £540,000 |
| Plaid Cymru | £81,000 |
| SDLP | £70,000 |
| SNP | £1,200,000 |
| UKIP | £650,000 |

* The sum paid to Sinn Fein and any other party that may choose not to take their seats in the House of Commons is calculated on the same basis as Short Money, but is known as Representative Money.

A specific allocation of around £777,500, for the leader of the opposition's office was introduced in April 1999.

Financial support for opposition parties in the House of Lords was introduced in 1996 and is commonly known as Cranborne Money, after former leader of the house, Viscount Cranborne.

The following list of political parties are those with at least one MP or sitting member of the House of Lords in the present parliament.

## ALLIANCE PARTY OF NORTHERN IRELAND

88 University Street, Belfast BT7 1HE
T 028-9032 4274 E alliance@allianceparty.org
W www.allianceparty.org
*Party Leader,* David Ford
*Deputy Party Leader,* Naomi Long, MP
*President,* Andrew Muir
*Chair,* Neil Kelly

## CONSERVATIVE PARTY

Conservative Campaign Headquarters, 4 Matthew Parker Street, London SW1H 9HQ
T 020-7222 9000 W www.conservatives.com
*Parliamentary Party Leader,* Rt. Hon. David Cameron, MP
*Leader in the Lords and Lord Privy Seal,* Rt. Hon. Baroness Stowell of Beeston, MBE
*Leader in the Commons and Lord President of the Council,* Rt. Hon. Chris Grayling, MP
*Deputy Leader in the Commons,* Dr Thérèse Coffey, MP
*Chair,* Lord Feldman of Elstree
*Party Treasurer,* Michael Farmer

## GREEN PARTY

Development House, 56–64 Leonard Street, London, EC2A 4LT
T 020-7549 0310 E office@greenparty.org.uk
W www.greenparty.org.uk
*Party Leader,* Natalie Bennett

*Deputy Leaders,* Shahrar Ali; Amelia Womack
*Chair,* Richard Mallender
*Finance Coordinator,* Michael Coffey

## LABOUR PARTY

Labour Central, Kings Manor, Newcastle upon Tyne NE1 6PA
T 0845-092 2299 W www.labour.org.uk
*General Secretary,* Iain McNicol
*General Secretary, Welsh Labour,* Dave Hagendyk
*General Secretary, Scottish Labour Party,* Brian Roy

SHADOW CABINET *as at September 2015*
*Leader of the Opposition,* Rt. Hon. Jeremy Corbyn, MP
*Deputy Leader,* Tom Watson, MP
*Chancellor of the Exchequer,* John McDonnell, MP
*Secretary of State for Foreign Affairs,* Rt. Hon. Hilary Benn, MP
*Secretary of State for the Home Department,* Rt. Hon. Andy Burnham, MP
*First Secretary of State for Business, Innovation and Skills,* Angela Eagle, MP
*Secretary of State for Communities and Local Government and Minister for Constitutional Convention,* Jon Trickett, MP
*Secretary of State for Culture, Media and Sport,* Michael Dugher, MP
*Secretary of State for Defence,* Maria Eagle, MP
*Secretary of State for Education,* Lucy Powell, MP
*Secretary of State for Energy and Climate Change,* Lisa Nandy, MP
*Secretary of State for Environment, Food and Rural Affairs,* Kerry McCarthy, MP
*Secretary of State for Health,* Heidi Alexander, MP
*Minister for Mental Health,* Luciana Berger, MP
*Minister for Housing and Planning,* Rt. Hon. John Healey, MP
*Secretary of State for International Development,* Diane Abbott, MP
*Lord Chancellor and Secretary of State for Justice,* Rt. Hon. Lord Falconer of Thoroton, QC
*Secretary of State for Northern Ireland,* Vernon Coaker, MP
*Secretary of State for Scotland,* Ian Murray, MP
*Secretary of State for Transport,* Lilian Greenwood, MP
*Chief Secretary to the Treasury,* Seema Malhotra, MP
*Minister for Women and Equalities,* Kate Green, MP
*Secretary of State for Wales,* Nia Griffith, MP
*Secretary of State for Work and Pensions,* Owen Smith, MP
*Minister for Young People and Voter Registration,* Gloria De Piero, MP
*Leader of the House of Commons,* Chris Bryant, MP
*Leader of the House of Lords,* Rt. Hon. Baroness Smith of Basildon
*Attorney-General,* Catherine McKinnell, MP
*Minister without Portfolio,* Jonathan Ashworth, MP

LABOUR WHIPS
*Commons Chief Whip,* Rt. Hon. Rosie Winterton, MP
*Lords Chief Whip,* Rt. Hon. Lord Bassam of Brighton

## LIBERAL DEMOCRATS

8–10 Great George Street, London SW1P 3AE
T 020-7022 0988 E info@libdems.org.uk W www.libdems.org.uk
*Parliamentary Party Leader,* Tim Farron, MP
*Deputy Party Leader,* Rt. Hon. Malcolm Bruce, MP
*Leader in the Lords,* Rt. Hon. Lord Wallace
*President,* Sarah Brinton
*Chief Executive,* Tim Gordon
*Hon. Treasurer,* Lord Wrigglesworth

## NORTHERN IRELAND DEMOCRATIC UNIONIST PARTY

91 Dundela Avenue, Belfast BT4 3BU
T 028-9047 1155
E info@mydup.com W www.mydup.com
*Parliamentary Party Leader,* Rt. Hon. Peter Robinson, MLA
*Deputy Leader,* Rt. Hon Nigel Dodds, OBE, MP, MLA
*Chair,* Lord Morrow, MLA

## PLAID CYMRU – THE PARTY OF WALES

Ty Gwynfor, Anson Court, Atlantic Wharf, Caerdydd CF10 4AL
T 029-2047 2272 E post@plaidcymru.org W www.partyof.wales
*Party Leader,* Leanne Wood, AM
*Hon. Party President,* Rt. Hon. Lord Wigley
*Parliamentary Group Leader,* Jonathan Edwards, MP
*Chair,* Dafydd Trystan Davies
*Chief Executive,* Rhuanedd Richards

## SCOTTISH NATIONAL PARTY

Gordon Lamb House, 3 Jackson's Entry, Edinburgh EH8 8PJ
T 0800-633 5432 E info@snp.org W www.snp.org
*Westminster Parliamentary Party Leader,* Angus Robertson, MP
*Westminster Parliamentary Party Chief Whip,* Stewart Hosie, MP
*\*Scottish Parliamentary Party Leader and Leader of the SNP,* Rt. Hon. Nicola Sturgeon, MSP
*Deputy Leader and Deputy First Minister of Scotland,* Stewart Hosie, MP
*Party President,* Ian Hudghton, MEP
*National Treasurer,* Colin Beattie, MSP
*Chief Executive,* Peter Murrell

## SINN FEIN

53 Falls Road, Belfast BT12 4PD
T 028-9034 7350 E admin@sinnfein.ie W www.sinnfein.ie
*Party President,* Gerry Adams
*Vice-President,* Mary Lou McDonald
*Chair,* Declan Kearney

## SOCIAL DEMOCRATIC AND LABOUR PARTY

121 Ormeau Road, Belfast BT7 1SH
T 028-9024 7700 E info@sdlp.ie W www.sdlp.ie
*Parliamentary Party Leader,* Dr Alisdair McDonnell, MP, MLA
*Deputy Leader,* Dolores Kelly, MLA
*Party Whip,* Pat Ramsey, MLA
*Chair,* Joe Byrne, MLA
*Treasurer,* Peter McEvoy

## ULSTER UNIONIST PARTY

Strandtown Hall, 2–4 Belmont Road, Belfast BT4 2AN
T 028-9047 4630
E uup@uup.org W www.uup.org
*Party Leader,* Mike Nesbitt, MLA
*Chair,* Lord Empey of Shandon, OBE
*Hon. Treasurer,* Cllr Mark Cosgrove

## UK INDEPENDENCE PARTY

Lexdrum House, King Charles Business Park, Newton Abbot, Devon TQ12 9BG
T 01626-831290
E mail@ukip.org W www.ukip.org
*Party Leader,* Nigel Farage, MEP
*Deputy Leader,* Paul Nuttall
*Chair,* Steve Crowther
*Treasurer,* Hugh Williams
*Party Secretary,* Matt Richardson

# MEMBERS OF PARLIAMENT *as at May 2015*

\* Denotes new MP in the 2015 parliament

**Abbott**, Diane (*b.* 1953) *Lab., Hackney North & Stoke Newington*, Maj. 24,008

**Abrahams**, Debbie (*b.* 1960) *Lab., Oldham East & Saddleworth*, Maj. 6,002

**Adams**, Nigel (*b.* 1966) *C., Selby & Ainsty*, Maj. 13,557

**Afriyie**, Adam (*b.* 1965) *C., Windsor*, Maj. 25,083

**\*Ahmed-Sheikh**, Tasmina (*b.* 1970) *SNP, Ochil & Perthshire South*, Maj. 10,168

**Aldous**, Peter (*b.* 1961) *C., Waveney*, Maj. 2,408

**Alexander**, Heidi (*b.* 1975) *Lab., Lewisham East*, Maj. 14,333

**Ali**, Rushanara (*b.* 1975) *Lab., Bethnal Green & Bow*, Maj. 24,317

**\*Allan**, Lucy (*b.* 1964) *C., Telford*, Maj. 730

**Allen**, Graham (*b.* 1953) *Lab., Nottingham North*, Maj. 11,860

**\*Allen**, Heidi (*b.* 1975) *C., Cambridgeshire South*, Maj. 20,594

**Amess**, Sir David (*b.* 1952) *C., Southend West*, Maj. 14,021

**Anderson**, David (*b.* 1953) *Lab., Blaydon*, Maj. 14,227

**Andrew**, Stuart (*b.* 1971) *C., Pudsey*, Maj. 4,501

**\*Ansell**, Caroline (*b.* 1972) *C., Eastbourne*, Maj. 733

**\*Argar**, Edward (*b.* 1977) *C., Charnwood*, Maj. 16,931

**\*Arkless**, Richard (*b.* 1975) *SNP, Dumfries & Galloway*, Maj. 6,514

**Ashworth**, Jonathan (*b.* 1978) *Lab. Co-op, Leicester South*, Maj. 17,865

**\*Atkins**, Victoria (*b.* 1976) *C., Louth & Horncastle*, Maj. 14,977

**Austin**, Ian (*b.* 1965) *Lab., Dudley North*, Maj. 4,181

**Bacon**, Richard (*b.* 1962) *C., Norfolk South*, Maj. 20,493

**Bailey**, Adrian (*b.* 1945) *Lab. Co-op, West Bromwich West*, Maj. 7,742

**Baker**, Steve (*b.* 1971) *C., Wycombe*, Maj. 14,856

**Baldwin**, Harriett (*b.* 1960) *C., Worcestershire West*, Maj. 22,578

**Barclay**, Steve (*b.* 1972) *C., Cambridgeshire North East*, Maj. 16,874

**\*Bardell,** Hannah (*b.* 1984) *SNP, Livingston*, Maj. 16,843

**Baron**, John (*b.* 1959) *C., Basildon & Billericay*, Maj. 12,482

**Barron**, Rt. Hon. Sir Kevin (*b.* 1946) *Lab., Rother Valley*, Maj. 7,297

**Barwell**, Gavin (*b.* 1972) *C., Croydon Central*, Maj. 165

**Bebb**, Guto (*b.* 1968) *C., Aberconwy*, Maj. 3,999

**Beckett**, Rt. Hon. Dame Margaret (*b.* 1943) *Lab., Derby South*, Maj. 8,828

**Bellingham**, Henry (*b.* 1955) *C., Norfolk North West*, Maj. 13,948

**Benn**, Rt. Hon. Hilary (*b.* 1953) *Lab., Leeds Central*, Maj. 16,967

**Benyon**, Richard (*b.* 1960) *C., Newbury*, Maj. 26,368

**Bercow**, Rt. Hon. John (*b.* 1963) *The Speaker, Buckingham*, Maj. 22,942

**Beresford**, Sir Paul (*b.* 1946) *C., Mole Valley*, Maj. 25,453

**Berger**, Luciana (*b.* 1981) *Lab. Co-op, Liverpool Wavertree*, Maj. 24,303

**Berry**, Jake (*b.* 1978) *C., Rossendale & Darwen*, Maj. 5,654

**\*Berry**, James (*b.* 1984) *C., Kingston & Surbiton*, Maj. 2,834

**Betts**, Clive (*b.* 1950) *Lab., Sheffield South East*, Maj. 12,311

**Bingham**, Andrew (*b.* 1962) *C., High Peak*, Maj. 4,894

**\*Black**, Mhairi (*b.* 1994) *SNP, Paisley & Renfrewshire South*, Maj. 5,684

**\*Blackford**, Ian (*b.* 1961) *SNP, Ross, Skye & Lochaber*, Maj. 5,124

**Blackman**, Bob (*b.* 1956) *C., Harrow East*, Maj. 4,757

**\*Blackman**, Kirsty (*b.* 1986) *SNP, Aberdeen North*, Maj. 13,396

**Blackman-Woods**, Dr Roberta (*b.* 1957) *Lab., Durham, City of*, Maj. 11,439

**Blackwood**, Nicola (*b.* 1979) *C., Oxford West & Abingdon*, Maj. 9,582

**Blenkinsop**, Tom (*b.* 1980) *Lab., Middlesbrough South & Cleveland East*, Maj. 2,268

**Blomfield**, Paul (*b.* 1953) *Lab., Sheffield Central*, Maj. 17,309

**Blunt**, Crispin (*b.* 1960) *C., Reigate*, Maj. 22,334

**Boles**, Nick (*b.* 1965) *C., Grantham & Stamford*, Maj. 18,989

**Bone**, Peter (*b.* 1952) *C., Wellingborough*, Maj. 16,397

**\*Borwick**, Lady (Victoria) (*b.* 1956) *C., Kensington*, Maj. 7,361

**\*Boswell**, Phil (*b.* 1963) *SNP, Coatbridge, Chryston & Bellshill*, Maj. 11,501

**Bottomley**, Sir Peter (*b.* 1944) *C., Worthing West*, Maj. 16,855

**Bradley**, Karen (*b.* 1970) *C., Staffordshire Moorlands*, Maj. 10,174

**Bradshaw**, Rt. Hon. Ben (*b.* 1960) *Lab., Exeter*, Maj. 7,183

**Brady**, Graham (*b.* 1967) *C., Altrincham & Sale West*, Maj. 13,290

**\*Brady**, Mickey (*b.* 1950) *SF, Newry & Armagh*, Maj. 4,176

**Brake**, Rt. Hon. Tom (*b.* 1962) *LD, Carshalton & Wallington*, Maj. 1,510

**Brazier**, Julian (*b.* 1953) *C., Canterbury*, Maj. 9,798

**Brennan**, Kevin (*b.* 1959) *Lab., Cardiff West*, Maj. 6,789

**Bridgen**, Andrew (*b.* 1964) *C., Leicestershire North West*, Maj. 11,373

**Brine**, Steve (*b.* 1974) *C., Winchester*, Maj. 16,914

**\*Brock**, Deidre (*b.* 1961) *SNP, Edinburgh North & Leith*, Maj. 5,597

**Brokenshire**, James (*b.* 1968) *C., Old Bexley & Sidcup*, Maj. 15,803

**\*Brown**, Alan (*b.* 1970), *SNP, Kilmarnock & Loudoun*, Maj. 13,638

**Brown**, Lyn (*b.* 1960) *Lab., West Ham*, Maj. 27,986

**Brown**, Rt. Hon. Nicholas (*b.* 1950) *Lab., Newcastle upon Tyne East*, Maj. 12,494

**Bruce**, Fiona (*b.* 1957) *C., Congleton*, Maj. 16,773

**Bryant**, Chris (*b.* 1962) *Lab., Rhondda*, Maj. 7,455

**Buck**, Karen (*b.* 1958) *Lab., Westminster North*, Maj. 1,977

**Buckland**, Robert (*b.* 1968) *C., Swindon South*, Maj. 5,785

**Burden**, Richard (*b.* 1954) *Lab., Birmingham Northfield*, Maj. 2,509

**\*Burgon**, Richard (*b.* 1980) *Lab., Leeds East*, Maj. 12,533

**Burnham**, Rt. Hon. Andy (*b.* 1970) *Lab., Leigh*, Maj. 14,096

**Burns**, Conor (*b.* 1972) *C., Bournemouth West*, Maj. 12,410

**Burns**, Rt. Hon. Sir Simon (*b.* 1952) *C., Chelmsford*, Maj. 18,250

**Burrowes**, David (*b.* 1969) *C., Enfield Southgate*, Maj. 4,753

**Burt**, Rt. Hon. Alistair (*b.* 1955) *C., Bedfordshire North East*, Maj. 25,644

**\*Butler**, Dawn (*b.* 1969) *Lab., Brent Central*, Maj. 19,649

**Byrne**, Rt. Hon. Liam (*b.* 1970) *Lab., Birmingham Hodge Hill*, Maj. 23,362

**\*Cadbury**, Ruth (*b.* 1959) *Lab., Brentford & Isleworth*, Maj. 465

**Cairns**, Alun (*b.* 1970) *C., Vale of Glamorgan*, Maj. 6,880

**Cameron**, Rt. Hon. David (*b.* 1966) *C., Witney*, Maj. 25,155

**\*Cameron**, Dr Lisa (*b.* 1972) *SNP, East Kilbride, Strathaven & Lesmahagow*, Maj. 16,527

**Campbell**, Rt. Hon. Alan (*b.* 1957) *Lab., Tynemouth*, Maj. 8,240

**Campbell**, Gregory (*b.* 1953) *DUP, Londonderry East,*
Maj. 7,804
**Campbell**, Ronnie (*b.* 1943) *Lab., Blyth Valley,* Maj. 9,229
**Carmichael**, Rt. Hon. Alistair (*b.* 1965) *LD, Orkney &*
*Shetland,* Maj. 817
**Carmichael**, Neil (*b.* 1961) *C., Stroud,* Maj. 4,866
**Carswell**, Douglas (*b.* 1971) *UKIP, Clacton,* Maj. 3,437
\***Cartlidge**, James (*b.* 1974) *C., Suffolk South,* Maj. 17,545
**Cash**, Sir William (*b.* 1940) *C., Stone,* Maj. 16,250
\***Caulfield**, Maria (*b.* 1974) *C., Lewes,* Maj. 1,083
\***Chalk**, Alex (*b.* 1977) *C., Cheltenham,* Maj. 6,516
**Champion**, Sarah (*b.* 1969) *Lab., Rotherham,* Maj. 8,446
\***Chapman**, Douglas (*b.* 1955) *SNP, Dunfermline &*
*Fife West,* Maj. 10,352
**Chapman**, Jenny (*b.* 1973) *Lab., Darlington,* Maj. 3,158
\***Cherry**, Joanna (*b.* 1966) *SNP, Edinburgh South West,*
Maj. 8,135
**Chishti**, Rehman (*b.* 1978) *C., Gillingham & Rainham,*
Maj. 10,530
**Chope**, Christopher (*b.* 1947) *C., Christchurch,* Maj. 18,224
\***Churchill**, Jo (*b.* 1964) *C., Bury St Edmunds,* Maj. 21,301
**Clark**, Rt. Hon. Greg (*b.* 1967) *C., Tunbridge Wells,*
Maj. 22,874
**Clarke**, Rt. Hon. Kenneth (*b.* 1940) *C., Rushcliffe,*
Maj. 13,829
**Clegg**, Rt. Hon. Nick (*b.* 1967) *LD, Sheffield Hallam,*
Maj. 2,353
\***Cleverly**, James (*b.* 1969) *C., Braintree,* Maj. 17,610
**Clifton-Brown**, Geoffrey (*b.* 1953) *C., The Cotswolds,*
Maj. 21,477
**Clwyd**, Rt. Hon. Ann (*b.* 1937) *Lab., Cynon Valley,*
Maj. 9,406
**Coaker**, Vernon (*b.* 1953) *Lab., Gedling,* Maj. 2,986
**Coffey**, Ann (*b.* 1946) *Lab., Stockport,* Maj. 10,061
**Coffey**, Dr Thérèse (*b.* 1971) *C., Suffolk Coastal,*
Maj. 18,842
**Collins**, Damian (*b.* 1974) *C., Folkestone & Hythe,*
Maj. 13,797
**Colvile**, Oliver (*b.* 1959) *C., Plymouth Sutton & Devonport,*
Maj. 523
\***Cooper**, Julie (*b.* 1960) *Lab., Burnley,* Maj. 3,244
**Cooper**, Rosie (*b.* 1950) *Lab., Lancashire West,* Maj. 8,360
**Cooper**, Rt. Hon. Yvette (*b.* 1969) *Lab., Normanton,*
*Pontefract & Castleford,* Maj. 15,428
**Corbyn**, Jeremy (*b.* 1949) *Lab., Islington North,* Maj. 21,194
\***Costa**, Alberto (*b.* 1971) *C., Leicestershire South,* Maj. 16,824
\***Cowan**, Ronnie (*b.* 1959) *SNP, Inverclyde,* Maj. 11,063
**Cox**, Geoffrey (*b.* 1960) *C., Devon West & Torridge,*
Maj. 18,403
\***Cox**, Jo (*b.* 1974) *Lab., Batley & Spen,* Maj. 6,057
\***Coyle**, Neil (*b.* 1978) *Lab., Bermondsey & Old Southwark,*
Maj. 4,489
**Crabb**, Rt. Hon. Stephen (*b.* 1973) *C., Preseli Pembrokeshire,*
Maj. 4,969
**Crausby**, David (*b.* 1946) *Lab., Bolton North East,* Maj. 4,377
\***Crawley**, Angela (*b.* 1987) *SNP, Lanark & Hamilton East,*
Maj. 10,100
**Creagh**, Mary (*b.* 1967) *Lab., Wakefield,* Maj. 2,613
**Creasy**, Stella (*b.* 1977) *Lab. Co-op, Walthamstow,*
Maj. 23,195
**Crouch**, Tracey (*b.* 1975) *C., Chatham & Aylesford,*
Maj. 11,455
**Cruddas**, Jon (*b.* 1965) *Lab., Dagenham & Rainham,*
Maj. 4,980
**Cryer**, John (*b.* 1964) *Lab., Leyton & Wanstead,* Maj. 14,919
\***Cummins**, Judith (*b.* 1967) *Lab., Bradford South,*
Maj. 6,450
**Cunningham**, Alex (*b.* 1955) *Lab., Stockton North,*
Maj. 8,367

**Cunningham**, Jim (*b.* 1941) *Lab., Coventry South,*
Maj. 3,188
**Dakin**, Nic (*b.* 1955) *Lab., Scunthorpe,* Maj. 3,134
**Danczuk**, Simon (*b.* 1966) *Lab., Rochdale,* Maj. 12,442
**David**, Wayne (*b.* 1957) *Lab., Caerphilly,* Maj. 10,073
\***Davies**, Byron (*b.* 1952) *C., Gower,* Maj. 27
\***Davies**, Chris (*b.* 1967) *C., Brecon & Radnorshire,*
Maj. 5,102
**Davies**, David (*b.* 1970) *C., Monmouth,* Maj. 10,982
**Davies**, Geraint (*b.* 1960) *Lab. Co-op, Swansea West,*
Maj. 7,036
**Davies**, Glyn (*b.* 1944) *C., Montgomeryshire,* Maj. 5,325
\***Davies**, James (*b.* 1980) *C., Vale of Clwyd,* Maj. 237
\***Davies**, Mims (*b.* 1975) *C., Eastleigh,* Maj. 9,147
**Davies**, Philip (*b.* 1972) *C., Shipley,* Maj. 9,624
**Davis**, Rt. Hon. David (*b.* 1948) *C., Haltemprice & Howden,*
Maj. 16,195
\***Day**, Martyn (*b.* 1971) *SNP, Linlithgow & Falkirk East,*
Maj. 12,934
**De Piero**, Gloria (*b.* 1972) *Lab., Ashfield,* Maj. 8,820
\***Debbonaire**, Thangam (*b.* 1966) *Lab., Bristol West,*
Maj. 5,673
**Dinenage**, Caroline (*b.* 1971) *C., Gosport,* Maj. 17,098
**Djanogly**, Jonathan (*b.* 1965) *C., Huntingdon,* Maj. 19,404
\***Docherty**, Martin (*b.* 1971) *SNP, Dunbartonshire West,*
Maj. 14,171
**Dodds**, Rt. Hon. Nigel (*b.* 1958) *DUP, Belfast North,*
Maj. 5,326
**Doherty**, Pat (*b.* 1945) *SF, Tyrone West,* Maj. 10,060
**Donaldson**, Rt. Hon. Jeffrey (*b.* 1962) *DUP, Lagan Valley,*
Maj. 13,000
\***Donaldson**, Stuart (*b.* 1992) *SNP, Aberdeenshire West &*
*Kincardine,* Maj. 7,033
\***Donelan**, Michelle (*b.* 1984) *C., Chippenham,* Maj. 10,076
**Dorries**, Nadine (*b.* 1958) *C., Bedfordshire Mid,* Maj. 23,327
\***Double**, Steve (*b.* 1966) *C., St Austell & Newquay,*
Maj. 8,173
**Doughty**, Stephen (*b.* 1980) *Lab. Co-op, Cardiff South &*
*Penarth,* Maj. 7,453
**Dowd**, Jim (*b.* 1951) *Lab., Lewisham West & Penge,*
Maj. 12,714
\***Dowd**, Peter (*b.* 1957) *Lab., Bootle,* Maj. 28,704
\***Dowden**, Oliver (*b.* 1978) *C., Hertsmere,* Maj. 18,461
**Doyle-Price**, Jackie (*b.* 1969) *C., Thurrock,* Maj. 536
**Drax**, Richard (*b.* 1958) *C., Dorset South,* Maj. 11,994
**Dromey**, Jack (*b.* 1948) *Lab., Birmingham Erdington,*
Maj. 5,129
\***Drummond**, Flick (*b.* 1962) *C., Portsmouth South,*
Maj. 5,241
**Duddridge**, James (*b.* 1971) *C., Rochford & Southend East,*
Maj. 9,476
**Dugher**, Michael (*b.* 1975) *Lab., Barnsley East,* Maj. 12,034
**Duncan**, Rt. Hon. Sir Alan (*b.* 1957) *C., Rutland & Melton,*
Maj. 21,705
**Duncan Smith**, Rt. Hon. Iain (*b.* 1954) *C., Chingford &*
*Woodford Green,* Maj. 8,386
**Dunne**, Philip (*b.* 1958) *C., Ludlow,* Maj. 18,929
**Durkan**, Mark (*b.* 1960) *SDLP, Foyle,* Maj. 6,046
**Eagle**, Angela (*b.* 1961) *Lab., Wallasey,* Maj. 16,348
**Eagle**, Maria (*b.* 1961) *Lab., Garston & Halewood,*
Maj. 27,146
**Edwards**, Jonathan (*b.* 1976) *PC, Carmarthen East &*
*Dinefwr,* Maj. 5,599
**Efford**, Clive (*b.* 1958) *Lab., Eltham,* Maj. 2,693
**Elliott**, Julie (*b.* 1963) *Lab., Sunderland Central,* Maj. 11,179
\***Elliott**, Tom (*b.* 1963) *UUP, Fermanagh & South Tyrone,*
Maj. 530
**Ellis**, Michael (*b.* 1967) *C., Northampton North,* Maj. 3,245
**Ellison**, Jane (*b.* 1964) *C., Battersea,* Maj. 7,938

**Ellman**, Louise (b. 1945) Lab. Co-op, Liverpool Riverside, Maj. 24,463

**Ellwood**, Tobias (b. 1966) C., Bournemouth East, Maj. 14,612

**Elphicke**, Charlie (b. 1971) C., Dover, Maj. 6,294

**Engel**, Natascha (b. 1967) Lab., Deputy Speaker, Derbyshire North East, Maj. 1,883

**Esterson**, Bill (b. 1966) Lab., Sefton Central, Maj. 11,846

**Eustice**, George (b. 1971) C., Camborne & Redruth, Maj. 7,004

**Evans**, Chris (b. 1976) Lab. Co-op, Islwyn, Maj. 10,404

**Evans**, Graham (b. 1963) C., Weaver Vale, Maj. 806

**Evans**, Nigel (b. 1957) C., Ribble Valley, Maj. 13,606

**Evennett**, Rt. Hon. David (b. 1949) C., Bexleyheath & Crayford, Maj. 9,192

**Fabricant**, Michael (b. 1950) C., Lichfield, Maj. 18,189

**Fallon**, Rt. Hon. Michael (b. 1952) C., Sevenoaks, Maj. 19,561

**Farrelly**, Paul (b. 1962) Lab., Newcastle-under-Lyme, Maj. 650

**Farron**, Tim (b. 1970) LD, Westmorland & Lonsdale, Maj. 8,949

*****Fellows**, Marion (b. 1949) SNP, Motherwell & Wishaw, Maj. 11,898

*****Fernandes**, Suella (b. 1980) C., Fareham, Maj. 22,262

*****Ferrier**, Margaret (b. 1960) SNP, Rutherglen & Hamilton West, Maj. 9,975

**Field**, Rt. Hon. Frank (b. 1942) Lab., Birkenhead, Maj. 20,652

**Field**, Rt. Hon. Mark (b. 1964) C., Cities of London & Westminster, Maj. 9,671

**Fitzpatrick**, Jim (b. 1952) Lab., Poplar & Limehouse, Maj. 16,924

**Flello**, Robert (b. 1966) Lab., Stoke-on-Trent South, Maj. 2,539

*****Fletcher**, Colleen (b. 1954) Lab., Coventry North East, Maj. 12,274

**Flint**, Rt. Hon. Caroline (b. 1961) Lab., Don Valley, Maj. 8,885

**Flynn**, Paul (b. 1935) Lab., Newport West, Maj. 3,510

*****Foster**, Kevin (b. 1978) C., Torbay, Maj. 3,286

**Fovargue**, Yvonne (b. 1956) Lab., Makerfield, Maj. 13,155

**Fox**, Rt. Hon. Dr Liam (b. 1961) C., Somerset North, Maj. 23,099

*****Foxcroft**, Vicky (b. 1977) Lab., Lewisham Deptford, Maj. 21,516

**Francois**, Rt. Hon. Mark (b. 1965) C., Rayleigh & Wickford, Maj. 17,230

*****Frazer**, Lucy (b. 1972) C., Cambridgeshire South East, Maj. 16,837

**Freeman**, George (b. 1967) C., Norfolk Mid, Maj. 17,276

**Freer**, Mike (b. 1960) C., Finchley & Golders Green, Maj. 5,662

**Fuller**, Richard (b. 1962) C., Bedford, Maj. 1,097

*****Fysh**, Marcus (b. 1970) C., Yeovil, Maj. 5,313

**Gale**, Sir Roger (b. 1943) C., Thanet North, Maj. 10,948

**Gapes**, Mike (b. 1952) Lab. Co-op, Ilford South, Maj. 19,777

**Gardiner**, Barry (b. 1957) Lab., Brent North, Maj. 10,834

**Garnier**, Rt. Hon. Sir Edward (b. 1952) C., Harborough, Maj. 19,632

**Garnier**, Mark (b. 1963) C., Wyre Forest, Maj. 12,871

**Gauke**, David (b. 1971) C., Hertfordshire South West, Maj. 23,263

*****Gethins**, Stephen (b. 1976) SNP, Fife North East, Maj. 4,344

*****Ghani**, Nusrat (b. 1972) C., Wealden, Maj. 22,967

**Gibb**, Nick (b. 1960) C., Bognor Regis & Littlehampton, Maj. 13,944

*****Gibson**, Patricia (b. 1968) SNP, Ayrshire North & Arran, Maj. 13,573

**Gillan**, Rt. Hon. Cheryl (b. 1952) C., Chesham & Amersham, Maj. 23,920

**Glass**, Pat (b. 1956) Lab., Durham North West, Maj. 10,056

**Glen**, John (b. 1974) C., Salisbury, Maj. 20,421

**Glindon**, Mary (b. 1957) Lab., Tyneside North, Maj. 17,194

**Godsiff**, Roger (b. 1946) Lab., Birmingham Hall Green, Maj. 19,818

**Goldsmith**, Zac (b. 1975) C., Richmond Park, Maj. 23,015

**Goodman**, Helen (b. 1958) Lab., Bishop Auckland, Maj. 3,508

**Goodwill**, Robert (b. 1956) C., Scarborough & Whitby, Maj. 6,200

**Gove**, Rt. Hon. Michael (b. 1967) C., Surrey Heath, Maj. 24,804

*****Grady**, Patrick (b. 1980) SNP, Glasgow North, Maj. 9,295

**Graham**, Richard (b. 1958) C., Gloucester, Maj. 7,251

**Grant**, Helen (b. 1961) C., Maidstone & The Weald, Maj. 10,709

*****Grant**, Peter (b. 1961) SNP, Glenrothes, Maj. 13,897

**Gray**, James (b. 1954) C., Wiltshire North, Maj. 21,046

*****Gray**, Neil (b. 1986) SNP, Airdrie & Shotts, Maj. 8,779

**Grayling**, Rt. Hon. Chris (b. 1962) C., Epsom & Ewell, Maj. 24,443

*****Green**, Chris (b. 1973) C., Bolton West, Maj. 801

**Green**, Rt. Hon. Damian (b. 1956) C., Ashford, Maj. 19,296

**Green**, Kate (b. 1960) Lab., Stretford & Urmston, Maj. 11,685

**Greening**, Rt. Hon. Justine (b. 1969) C., Putney, Maj. 10,180

**Greenwood**, Lilian (b. 1966) Lab., Nottingham South, Maj. 6,936

*****Greenwood**, Margaret (b. 1959) Lab., Wirral West, Maj. 417

**Grieve**, Rt. Hon. Dominic (b. 1956) C., Beaconsfield, Maj. 26,311

**Griffith**, Nia (b. 1956) Lab., Llanelli, Maj. 7,095

**Griffiths**, Andrew (b. 1970) C., Burton, Maj. 11,252

**Gummer**, Ben (b. 1978) C., Ipswich, Maj. 3,733

**Gwynne**, Andrew (b. 1974) Lab., Denton & Reddish, Maj. 10,511

**Gyimah**, Sam (b. 1976) C., Surrey East, Maj. 22,658

*****Haigh**, Louise (b. 1987) Lab., Sheffield Heeley, Maj. 12,954

**Halfon**, Rt. Hon. Robert (b. 1969) C., Harlow, Maj. 8,350

*****Hall**, Luke (b. 1986) C., Thornbury & Yate, Maj. 1,495

**Hamilton**, Fabian (b. 1955) Lab., Leeds North East, Maj. 7,250

**Hammond**, Rt. Hon. Philip (b. 1955) C., Runnymede & Weybridge, Maj. 22,134

**Hammond**, Stephen (b. 1962) C., Wimbledon, Maj. 12,619

**Hancock**, Rt. Hon. Matthew (b. 1978) C., Suffolk West, Maj. 14,984

**Hands**, Rt. Hon. Greg (b. 1965) C., Chelsea & Fulham, Maj. 16,022

**Hanson**, Rt. Hon. David (b. 1957) Lab., Delyn, Maj. 2,930

**Harman**, Rt. Hon. Harriet (b. 1950) Lab., Camberwell & Peckham, Maj. 25,824

**Harper**, Rt. Hon. Mark (b. 1970) C., Forest of Dean, Maj. 10,987

*****Harpham**, Harry (b. 1954) Lab., Sheffield Brightside & Hillsborough, Maj. 13,807

**Harrington**, Richard (b. 1957) C., Watford, Maj. 9,794

*****Harris**, Carolyn (b. 1960) Lab., Swansea East, Maj. 12,028

**Harris**, Rebecca (b. 1967) C., Castle Point, Maj. 8,934

**Hart**, Simon (b. 1963) C., Carmarthen West & Pembrokeshire South, Maj. 6,054

**Haselhurst**, Rt. Hon. Sir Alan (b. 1937) C., Saffron Walden, Maj. 24,991

*****Hayes**, Helen (b. 1974) Lab., Dulwich & West Norwood, Maj. 16,122

**Hayes**, Rt. Hon. John (*b.* 1958) *C., South Holland & The Deepings*, Maj. 18,567

*****Hayman**, Sue (*b.* 1962) *Lab., Workington*, Maj. 4,686

**Heald**, Sir Oliver (*b.* 1954) *C., Hertfordshire North East*, Maj. 19,080

**Healey**, Rt. Hon. John (*b.* 1960) *Lab., Wentworth & Dearne*, Maj. 13,838

*****Heappey**, James (*b.* 1981) *C., Wells*, Maj. 7,585

**Heaton-Harris**, Chris (*b.* 1967) *C., Daventry*, Maj. 21,059

*****Heaton-Jones**, Peter (*b.* 1963) *C., Devon North*, Maj. 6,936

**Henderson**, Gordon (*b.* 1948) *C., Sittingbourne & Sheppey*, Maj. 12,168

**Hendrick**, Mark (*b.* 1958) *Lab. Co-op, Preston*, Maj. 12,067

*****Hendry**, Drew (*b.* 1964) *SNP, Inverness, Nairn, Badenoch & Strathspey*, Maj. 10,809

**Hepburn**, Stephen (*b.* 1959) *Lab., Jarrow*, Maj. 13,881

**Herbert**, Rt. Hon. Nick (*b.* 1963) *C., Arundel & South Downs*, Maj. 26,177

**Hermon**, Lady (Sylvia) (*b.* 1956) *Ind., Down North*, Maj. 9,202

**Hillier**, Meg (*b.* 1969) *Lab. Co-op, Hackney South & Shoreditch*, Maj. 24,243

**Hinds**, Damian (*b.* 1969) *C., Hampshire East*, Maj. 25,147

*****Hoare**, Simon (*b.* 1969) *C., Dorset North*, Maj. 21,118

**Hodge**, Rt. Hon. Margaret (*b.* 1944) *Lab., Barking*, Maj. 15,272

**Hodgson**, Sharon (*b.* 1966) *Lab., Washington & Sunderland West*, Maj. 13,157

**Hoey**, Kate (*b.* 1946) *Lab., Vauxhall*, Maj. 12,708

*****Hollern**, Kate (*b.* 1955) *Lab., Blackburn*, Maj. 12,760

**Hollingbery**, George (*b.* 1963) *C., Meon Valley*, Maj. 23,913

*****Hollinrake**, Kevin (*b.* 1963) *C., Thirsk & Malton*, Maj. 19,456

**Hollobone**, Philip (*b.* 1964) *C., Kettering*, Maj. 12,590

**Holloway**, Adam (*b.* 1965) *C., Gravesham*, Maj. 8,380

**Hopkins**, Kelvin (*b.* 1941) *Lab., Luton North*, Maj. 9,504

**Hopkins**, Kris (*b.* 1963) *C., Keighley*, Maj. 3,053

**Hosie**, Stewart (*b.* 1963) *SNP, Dundee East*, Maj. 19,162

**Howarth**, Rt. Hon. George (*b.* 1949) *Lab., Knowsley*, Maj. 34,655

**Howarth**, Sir Gerald (*b.* 1947) *C., Aldershot*, Maj. 14,901

**Howell**, John (*b.* 1955) *C., Henley*, Maj. 25,375

*****Howlett**, Ben (*b.* 1986) *C., Bath*, Maj. 3,833

**Hoyle**, Rt. Hon. Lindsay (*b.* 1957) *Lab., Deputy Speaker, Chorley*, Maj. 4,530

*****Huddleston**, Nigel (*b.* 1970) *C., Worcestershire Mid*, Maj. 20,532

**Hunt**, Rt. Hon. Jeremy (*b.* 1966) *C., Surrey South West*, Maj. 28,556

**Hunt**, Tristram (*b.* 1974) *Lab., Stoke-on-Trent Central*, Maj. 5,179

*****Huq**, Rupa (*b.* 1972) *Lab., Ealing Central & Acton*, Maj. 274

**Hurd**, Nick (*b.* 1962) *C., Ruislip, Northwood & Pinner*, Maj. 20,224

*****Hussain**, Imran (*b.* 1978) *Lab., Bradford East*, Maj. 7.084

**Irranca-Davies**, Huw (*b.* 1963) *Lab., Ogmore*, Maj. 13,043

**Jackson**, Stewart (*b.* 1965) *C., Peterborough*, Maj. 1,925

**James**, Margot (*b.* 1957) *C., Stourbridge*, Maj. 6,694

**Jarvis**, Dan (*b.* 1972) *Lab., Barnsley Central*, Maj. 12,435

**Javid**, Rt. Hon. Sajid (*b.* 1969) *C., Bromsgrove*, Maj. 16,529

*****Jayawardena**, Ranil (*b.*1986) *C., Hampshire North East*, Maj. 29,916

**Jenkin**, Bernard (*b.* 1959) *C., Harwich & Essex North*, Maj. 15,174

*****Jenkyns**, Andrea (*b.* 1974) *C., Morley & Outwood*, Maj. 422

**Jenrick**, Robert (*b.* 1982) *C., Newark*, Maj. 18,474

**Johnson**, Rt. Hon. Alan (*b.* 1950) *Lab., Hull West & Hessle*, Maj. 9,333

*****Johnson**, Boris (*b.* 1964) *C., Uxbridge & Ruislip South*, Maj. 10,695

**Johnson**, Diana (*b.* 1966) *Lab., Hull North*, Maj. 12,899

**Johnson**, Gareth (*b.* 1969) *C., Dartford*, Maj. 12,345

**Johnson**, Joseph (*b.* 1971) *C., Orpington*, Maj. 19,979

**Jones**, Andrew (*b.* 1963) *C., Harrogate & Knaresborough*, Maj. 16,371

**Jones**, Rt. Hon. David (*b.* 1952) *C., Clwyd West*, Maj. 6,730

*****Jones**, Gerald (*b.* 1970) *Lab., Merthyr Tydfil & Rhymney*, Maj. 11,513

**Jones**, Graham (*b.* 1966) *Lab., Hyndburn*, Maj. 4,400

**Jones**, Helen (*b.* 1954) *Lab., Warrington North*, Maj. 8,923

**Jones**, Kevan (*b.* 1964) *Lab., Durham North*, Maj. 13,644

**Jones**, Marcus (*b.* 1974) *C., Nuneaton*, Maj. 4,882

**Jones**, Susan (*b.* 1968) *Lab., Clwyd South*, Maj. 2,402

**Kane**, Mike (*b.* 1969) *Lab., Wythenshawe & Sale East*, Maj. 10,569

**Kaufman**, Rt. Hon. Sir Gerald (*b.* 1930) *Lab., Manchester Gorton*, Maj. 24,079

**Kawczynski**, Daniel (*b.* 1972) *C., Shrewsbury & Atcham*, Maj. 9,565

**Keeley**, Barbara (*b.* 1952) *Lab., Worsley & Eccles South*, Maj. 5,946

**Kendall**, Liz (*b.* 1971) *Lab., Leicester West*, Maj. 7,203

*****Kennedy**, Seema (*b.* 1974) *C., South Ribble*, Maj. 5,945

*****Kerevan**, George (*b.* 1949) *SNP, East Lothian*, Maj. 6,803

*****Kerr**, Calum (*b.* 1972) *SNP, Berwickshire, Roxburgh & Selkirk*, Maj. 328

**Khan**, Rt. Hon. Sadiq (*b.* 1970) *Lab., Tooting*, Maj. 2,842

*****Kinahan**, Danny (*b.*1958) *UUP, Antrim South*, Maj. 949

*****Kinnock**, Stephen (*b.* 1970) *Lab., Aberavon*, Maj. 10,445

**Kirby**, Simon (*b.* 1964) *C., Brighton Kemptown*, Maj. 690

**Knight**, Rt. Hon. Sir Greg (*b.* 1949) *C., Yorkshire East*, Maj. 14,933

*****Knight**, Julian (*b.* 1972) *C., Solihull*, Maj. 12,902

**Kwarteng**, Kwasi (*b.* 1975) *C., Spelthorne*, Maj. 14,152

*****Kyle**, Peter (*b.* 1970) *Lab., Hove*, Maj. 1,236

**Laing**, Eleanor (*b.* 1958) *C., Deputy Speaker, Epping Forest*, Maj. 17,978

**Lamb**, Rt. Hon. Norman (*b.* 1957) *LD, Norfolk North*, Maj. 4,043

**Lammy**, Rt. Hon. David (*b.* 1972) *Lab., Tottenham*, Maj. 23,564

**Lancaster**, Mark (*b.* 1970) *C., Milton Keynes North*, Maj. 9,753

**Latham**, Pauline (*b.* 1948) *C., Derbyshire Mid*, Maj. 12,774

**Lavery**, Ian (*b.* 1962) *Lab., Wansbeck*, Maj. 10,881

*****Law**, Chris (*b.* 1969) *SNP, Dundee West*, Maj. 17,092

**Leadsom**, Andrea (*b.* 1963) *C., Northamptonshire South*, Maj. 26,416

**Lee**, Dr Phillip (*b.* 1970) *C., Bracknell*, Maj. 20,650

**Lefroy**, Jeremy (*b.* 1959) *C., Stafford*, Maj. 9,177

**Leigh**, Sir Edward (*b.* 1950) *C., Gainsborough*, Maj. 15,449

**Leslie**, Charlotte (*b.* 1978) *C., Bristol North West*, Maj. 4,944

**Leslie**, Chris (*b.* 1972) *Lab. Co-op, Nottingham East*, Maj. 11,894

**Letwin**, Rt. Hon. Oliver (*b.* 1956) *C., Dorset West*, Maj. 16,130

**Lewell-Buck**, Emma (*b.* 1978) *Lab., South Shields*, Maj. 10,614

**Lewis**, Brandon (*b.* 1971) *C., Great Yarmouth*, Maj. 6,154

*****Lewis**, Clive (*b.* 1971) *Lab., Norwich South*, Maj. 7,654

**Lewis**, Ivan (*b.* 1967) *Lab., Bury South*, Maj. 4,922

**Lewis**, Dr Julian (*b.* 1951) *C., New Forest East*, Maj. 19,162

**Liddell-Grainger**, Ian (*b.* 1959) *C., Bridgwater & Somerset West*, Maj. 14,583

Lidington, Rt. Hon. David (b. 1956) C., Aylesbury, Maj. 17,158

Lilley, Rt. Hon. Peter (b. 1943) C., Hitchin & Harpenden, Maj. 20,055

*Long Bailey, Rebecca (b. 1979) Lab., Salford & Eccles, Maj. 12,541

Lopresti, Jack (b. 1969) C., Filton & Bradley Stoke, Maj. 9,838

Lord, Jonathan (b. 1962) C., Woking, Maj. 20,810

Loughton, Tim (b. 1962) C., Worthing East & Shoreham, Maj. 14,949

Lucas, Caroline (b. 1960) Green, Brighton Pavilion, Maj. 7,967

Lucas, Ian (b. 1960) Lab., Wrexham, Maj. 1,831

Lumley, Karen (b. 1964) C., Redditch, Maj. 7,054

*Lynch, Holly (b. 1986) Lab., Halifax, Maj. 428

McCabe, Steve (b. 1955) Lab., Birmingham Selly Oak, Maj. 8,447

*McCaig, Callum (b. 1985) SNP, Aberdeen South, Maj. 7,230

McCarthy, Kerry (b. 1965) Lab., Bristol East, Maj. 3,980

McCartney, Jason (b. 1968) C., Colne Valley, Maj. 5,378

McCartney, Karl (b. 1968) C., Lincoln, Maj. 1,443

McDonagh, Siobhain (b. 1960) Lab., Mitcham & Morden, Maj. 16,922

McDonald, Andy (b. 1958) Lab., Middlesbrough, Maj. 12,477

*McDonald, Stewart (b. 1986) SNP, Glasgow South, Maj. 12,269

*McDonald, Stuart (b. 1978) SNP, Cumbernauld, Kilsyth & Kirkintilloch East, Maj. 14,752

McDonnell, Dr Alasdair (b. 1949) SDLP, Belfast South, Maj. 906

McDonnell, John (b. 1951) Lab., Hayes & Harlington, Maj. 15,700

McFadden, Rt. Hon. Pat (b. 1965) Lab., Wolverhampton South East, Maj. 10,778

*McGarry, Natalie (b. 1981) SNP, Glasgow East, Maj. 10,387

*McGinn, Conor (b. 1984) Lab., St Helens North, Maj. 17,291

McGovern, Alison (b. 1980) Lab., Wirral South, Maj. 4,599

*McInnes, Liz (b. 1959) Lab., Heywood & Middleton, Maj. 5,299

*Mackinlay, Craig (b. 1967) C., Thanet South, Maj. 2,812

McKinnell, Catherine (b. 1976) Lab., Newcastle upon Tyne North, Maj. 10,153

*Mackintosh, David (b. 1979) C., Northampton South, Maj. 3,793

*McLaughlin, Anne (b. 1966) SNP, Glasgow North East, Maj. 9,222

McLoughlin, Rt. Hon. Patrick (b. 1957) C., Derbyshire Dales, Maj. 14,044

*McNally, John (b. 1951) SNP, Falkirk, Maj. 19,701

MacNeil, Angus (b. 1970) SNP, Na h-Eileanan an Iar, Maj. 4,102

McPartland, Stephen (b. 1976) C., Stevenage, Maj. 4,955

Mactaggart, Rt. Hon. Fiona (b. 1953) Lab., Slough, Maj. 7,336

*Madders, Justin (b. 1972) Lab., Ellesmere Port & Neston, Maj. 6,275

Mahmood, Khalid (b. 1961) Lab., Birmingham Perry Barr, Maj. 14,828

Mahmood, Shabana (b. 1980) Lab., Birmingham Ladywood, Maj. 21,868

Main, Anne (b. 1957) C., St Albans, Maj. 12,732

*Mak, Alan (b. 1983) C., Havant, Maj. 13,920

Malhotra, Seema (b. 1972) Lab. Co-op, Feltham & Heston, Maj. 11,463

*Malthouse, Kit (b. 1966) C., Hampshire North West, Maj. 23,943

Mann, John (b. 1960) Lab., Bassetlaw, Maj. 8,843

*Mann, Scott (b. 1977) C., Cornwall North, Maj. 6,621

*Marris, Rob (b. 1955) Lab., Wolverhampton South West, Maj. 801

Marsden, Gordon (b. 1953) Lab., Blackpool South, Maj. 2,585

*Maskell, Rachael (b. 1972) Lab., Co-op, York Central, Maj. 6,716

Maskey, Paul (b. 1967) SF, Belfast West, Maj. 12,365

*Matheson, Chris (b. 1968) Lab., Chester, City of, Maj. 93

*Mathias, Tania (b. 1964) C., Twickenham, Maj. 2,017

May, Rt. Hon. Theresa (b. 1956) C., Maidenhead, Maj. 29,059

Maynard, Paul (b. 1975) C., Blackpool North & Cleveleys, Maj. 3,340

Meacher, Rt. Hon. Michael (b. 1939) Lab., Oldham West & Royton, Maj. 14,738

Meale, Sir Alan (b. 1949) Lab., Mansfield, Maj. 5,315

Mearns, Ian (b. 1957) Lab., Gateshead, Maj. 14,784

Menzies, Mark (b. 1971) C., Fylde, Maj. 13,224

*Mercer, Johnny (b. 1981) C., Plymouth Moor View, Maj. 1,026

*Merriman, Huw (b. 1973) C., Bexhill & Battle, Maj. 20,075

Metcalfe, Stephen (b. 1966) C., Basildon South & Thurrock East, Maj. 7,691

Miliband, Rt. Hon. Edward (b. 1969) Lab., Doncaster North, Maj. 11,780

Miller, Rt. Hon. Maria (b. 1964) C., Basingstoke, Maj. 11,063

*Milling, Amanda (b. 1975) C., Cannock Chase, Maj. 4,923

Mills, Nigel (b. 1974) C., Amber Valley, Maj. 4,205

Milton, Rt. Hon. Anne (b. 1955) C., Guildford, Maj. 22,448

Mitchell, Rt. Hon. Andrew (b. 1956) C., Sutton Coldfield, Maj. 16,417

Molloy, Francie (b. 1950) SF, Ulster Mid, Maj. 13,617

*Monaghan, Carol (b. 1972) SNP, Glasgow North West, Maj. 10,364

*Monaghan, Dr Paul (b. 1966) SNP, Caithness, Sutherland & Easter Ross, Maj. 3,844

Moon, Madeleine (b. 1950) Lab., Bridgend, Maj. 1,927

Mordaunt, Penny (b. 1973) C., Portsmouth North, Maj. 10,537

Morden, Jessica (b. 1968) Lab., Newport East, Maj. 4,705

Morgan, Rt. Hon. Nicky (b. 1972) C., Loughborough, Maj. 9,183

Morris, Anne Marie (b. 1957) C., Newton Abbot, Maj. 11,288

Morris, David (b. 1966) C., Morecambe & Lunesdale, Maj. 4,590

Morris, Grahame (b. 1961) Lab., Easington, Maj. 14,641

Morris, James (b. 1967) C., Halesowen & Rowley Regis, Maj. 3,082

*Morton, Wendy (b. 1967) C., Aldridge-Brownhills, Maj. 11,723

Mowat, David (b. 1957) C., Warrington South, Maj. 2,750

Mulholland, Greg (b. 1970) LD, Leeds North West, Maj. 2,907

*Mullin, Roger (b. 1948) SNP, Kirkcaldy & Cowdenbeath, Maj. 9,974

Mundell, Rt. Hon. David (b. 1962) C., Dumfriesshire, Clydesdale & Tweeddale, Maj. 798

Murray, Ian (b. 1976) Lab., Edinburgh South, Maj. 2,637

Murray, Sheryll (b. 1956) C., Cornwall South East, Maj. 16,995

Murrison, Dr Andrew (b. 1961) C., Wiltshire South West, Maj. 18,168

Nandy, Lisa (*b.* 1979) *Lab., Wigan,* Maj. 14,236

Neill, Robert (*b.* 1952) *C., Bromley & Chislehurst,* Maj. 13,564

*Newlands, Gavin (*b.* 1980) *SNP, Paisley & Renfrewshire North,* Maj. 9,076

Newton, Sarah (*b.* 1962) *C., Truro & Falmouth,* Maj. 14,000

*Nicolson, John (*b.* 1961) *SNP, Dunbartonshire East,* Maj. 2,167

Nokes, Caroline (*b.* 1972) *C., Romsey & Southampton North,* Maj. 17,712

Norman, Jesse (*b.* 1962) *C., Hereford & Herefordshire South,* Maj. 16,890

Nuttall, David (*b.* 1962) *C., Bury North,* Maj. 378

Offord, Dr Matthew (*b.* 1969) *C., Hendon,* Maj. 3,724

*O'Hara, Brendan (*b.* 1964) *SNP, Argyll & Bute,* Maj. 8,473

*Onn, Melanie (*b.* 1979) *Lab., Great Grimsby,* Maj. 4,540

Onwurah, Chi (*b.* 1965) *Lab., Newcastle upon Tyne Central,* Maj. 12,673

Opperman, Guy (*b.* 1965) *C., Hexham,* Maj. 12,031

*Osamor, Kate (*b.* 1968) *Lab. Co-op, Edmonton,* Maj. 15,419

Osborne, Rt. Hon. George (*b.* 1971) *C., Tatton,* Maj. 18,241

*Oswald, Kirsten (*b.* 1972) *SNP, Renfrewshire East,* Maj. 3,718

Owen, Albert (*b.* 1960) *Lab., Ynys Mon,* Maj. 229

Paisley, Ian (*b.* 1966) *DUP, Antrim North,* Maj. 11,546

Parish, Neil (*b.* 1956) *C., Tiverton & Honiton,* Maj. 20,173

Patel, Rt. Hon. Priti (*b.* 1972) *C., Witham,* Maj. 19,554

Paterson, Rt. Hon. Owen (*b.* 1956) *C., Shropshire North,* Maj. 16,494

*Paterson, Steven (*b.* 1975) *SNP, Stirling,* Maj. 10,480

Pawsey, Mark (*b.* 1957) *C., Rugby,* Maj. 10,345

Pearce, Teresa (*b.* 1955) *Lab., Erith & Thamesmead,* Maj. 9,525

Penning, Rt. Hon. Mike (*b.* 1957) *C., Hemel Hempstead,* Maj. 14,420

*Pennycook, Matthew (*b.* 1982) *Lab., Greenwich & Woolwich,* Maj. 11,946

Penrose, John (*b.* 1964) *C., Weston-super-Mare,* Maj. 15,609

Percy, Andrew (*b.* 1977) *C., Brigg & Goole,* Maj. 11,176

Perkins, Toby (*b.* 1970) *Lab., Chesterfield,* Maj. 13,598

Perry, Claire (*b.* 1964) *C., Devizes,* Maj. 20,751

*Phillips, Jess (*b.* 1981) *Lab., Birmingham Yardley,* Maj. 6,595

Phillips, Stephen (*b.* 1970) *C., Sleaford & North Hykeham,* Maj. 24,115

Phillipson, Bridget (*b.* 1983) *Lab., Houghton & Sunderland South,* Maj. 12,938

*Philp, Chris (*b.* 1976) *C., Croydon South,* Maj. 17,140

Pickles, Rt. Hon. Sir Eric (*b.* 1952) *C., Brentwood & Ongar,* Maj. 21,810

Pincher, Christopher (*b.* 1969) *C., Tamworth,* Maj. 11,302

Poulter, Dr Daniel (*b.* 1978) *C., Suffolk Central & Ipswich North,* Maj. 20,144

Pound, Stephen (*b.* 1948) *Lab., Ealing North,* Maj. 12,326

*Pow, Rebecca (*b.* 1960) *C., Taunton Deane,* Maj. 15,491

Powell, Lucy (*b.* 1974) *Lab. Co-op, Manchester Central,* Maj. 21,639

*Prentis, Victoria (*b.* 1971) *C., Banbury,* Maj. 18,395

Prisk, Mark (*b.* 1962) *C., Hertford & Stortford,* Maj. 21,509

Pritchard, Mark (*b.* 1966) *C., The Wrekin,* Maj. 10,743

Pugh, Dr John (*b.* 1948) *LD, Southport,* Maj. 1,322

*Pursglove, Tom (*b.* 1988) *C., Corby,* Maj. 2,412

*Quin, Jeremy (*b.* 1968) *C., Horsham,* Maj. 24,658

*Quince, Will (*b.* 1982) *C., Colchester,* Maj. 5,575

Qureshi, Yasmin (*b.* 1963) *Lab., Bolton South East,* Maj. 10,928

Raab, Dominic (*b.* 1974) *C., Esher & Walton,* Maj. 28,616

*Rayner, Angela (*b.* 1980) *Lab., Ashton-under-Lyne,* Maj. 10,756

Redwood, Rt. Hon. John (*b.* 1951) *C., Wokingham,* Maj. 24,197

Reed, Jamie (*b.* 1973) *Lab., Copeland,* Maj. 2,564

Reed, Steve (*b.* 1963) *Lab. Co-op, Croydon North,* Maj. 21,364

*Rees, Christina (*b.* 1954) *Lab., Neath,* Maj. 9,548

Rees-Mogg, Jacob (*b.* 1969) *C., Somerset North East,* Maj. 12,749

Reeves, Rachel (*b.* 1979) *Lab., Leeds West,* Maj. 10,727

Reynolds, Emma (*b.* 1977) *Lab., Wolverhampton North East,* Maj. 5,495

Reynolds, Jonathan (*b.* 1980) *Lab. Co-op, Stalybridge & Hyde,* Maj. 6,686

*Rimmer, Marie (*b.* 1947) *Lab., St Helens South & Whiston,* Maj. 21,243

Ritchie, Margaret (*b.* 1958) *SDLP, Down South,* Maj. 5,891

Robertson, Angus (*b.* 1969) *SNP, Moray,* Maj. 9,065

Robertson, Laurence (*b.* 1958) *C., Tewkesbury,* Maj. 21,972

*Robinson, Gavin (*b.* 1985) *DUP, Belfast East,* Maj. 2,597

Robinson, Geoffrey (*b.* 1938) *Lab., Coventry North West,* Maj. 4,509

*Robinson, Mary (*b.* 1955) *C., Cheadle,* Maj. 6,453

Rosindell, Andrew (*b.* 1966) *C., Romford,* Maj. 13,859

Rotheram, Steve (*b.* 1961) *Lab., Liverpool Walton,* Maj. 27,777

Rudd, Rt. Hon. Amber (*b.* 1963) *C., Hastings & Rye,* Maj. 4,796

Rutley, David (*b.* 1961) *C., Macclesfield,* Maj. 14,811

*Ryan, Rt. Hon. Joan (*b.* 1955) *Lab., Enfield North,* Maj. 1,086

*Salmond, Alex (*b.* 1954) *SNP, Gordon,* Maj. 8,687

*Sandbach, Antoinette (*b.* 1969) *C., Eddisbury,* Maj. 12,974

*Saville-Roberts, Liz (*b.* 1964) *PC, Dwyfor Meirionnydd,* Maj. 5,261

*Scully, Paul (*b.* 1968) *C., Sutton & Cheam,* Maj. 3,921

Selous, Andrew (*b.* 1962) *C., Bedfordshire South West,* Maj. 17,813

*Shah, Naseem (*b.* 1973) *Lab., Bradford West,* Maj. 11,420

Shannon, Jim (*b.* 1955) *DUP, Strangford,* Maj. 10,185

Shapps, Rt. Hon. Grant (*b.* 1968) *C., Welwyn Hatfield,* Maj. 12,153

Sharma, Alok (*b.* 1967) *C., Reading West,* Maj. 6,650

Sharma, Virendra (*b.* 1947) *Lab., Ealing Southall,* Maj. 18,760

Sheerman, Barry (*b.* 1940) *Lab. Co-op, Huddersfield,* Maj. 7,345

Shelbrooke, Alec (*b.* 1976) *C., Elmet & Rothwell,* Maj. 8,490

*Sheppard, Tommy (*b.* 1959) *SNP, Edinburgh East,* Maj. 9,106

*Sherriff, Paula (*b.* 1975) *Lab., Dewsbury,* Maj. 1,451

Shuker, Gavin (*b.* 1981) *Lab. Co-op, Luton South,* Maj. 5,711

*Siddiq, Tulip (*b.* 1982) *Lab., Hampstead & Kilburn,* Maj. 1,138

Simpson, David (*b.* 1959) *DUP, Upper Bann,* Maj. 2,264

Simpson, Rt. Hon. Keith (*b.* 1949) *C., Broadland,* Maj. 16,838

Skidmore, Chris (*b.* 1981) *C., Kingswood,* Maj. 9,006

Skinner, Dennis (*b.* 1932) *Lab., Bolsover,* Maj. 11,778

Slaughter, Andy (*b.* 1960) *Lab., Hammersmith,* Maj. 6,518

*Smeeth, Ruth (*b.* 1979) *Lab., Stoke-on-Trent North,* Maj. 4,836

Smith, Rt. Hon. Andrew (*b.* 1951) *Lab., Oxford East,* Maj. 15,280

Smith, Angela (*b.* 1961) *Lab., Penistone & Stocksbridge,* Maj. 6,723

*Smith, Catherine (*b.* 1985) *Lab., Lancaster & Fleetwood,* Maj. 1,265
Smith, Chloe (*b.* 1982) *C., Norwich North,* Maj. 4,463
Smith, Henry (*b.* 1969) *C., Crawley,* Maj. 6,526
*Smith, Jeff (*b.* 1963) *Lab., Manchester Withington,* Maj. 14,873
Smith, Julian (*b.* 1971) *C., Skipton & Ripon,* Maj. 20,761
Smith, Nick (*b.* 1960) *Lab., Blaenau Gwent,* Maj. 12,703
Smith, Owen (*b.* 1970) *Lab., Pontypridd,* Maj. 8,985
*Smith, Royston (*b.* 1964) *C., Southampton Itchen,* Maj. 2,316
*Smyth, Karin (*b.* 1964) *Lab., Bristol South,* Maj. 7,128
Soames, Rt. Hon. Sir Nicholas (*b.* 1948) *C., Sussex Mid,* Maj. 24,286
*Solloway, Amanda (*b.* 1961) *C., Derby North,* Maj. 41
Soubry, Rt. Hon. Anna (*b.* 1956) *C., Broxtowe,* Maj. 4,287
Spellar, Rt. Hon. John (*b.* 1947) *Lab., Warley,* Maj. 14,702
Spelman, Rt. Hon. Caroline (*b.* 1958) *C., Meriden,* Maj. 18,795
Spencer, Mark (*b.* 1970) *C., Sherwood,* Maj. 4,647
*Starmer, Sir Keir (*b.* 1962) *Lab., Holborn & St Pancras,* Maj. 17,048
*Stephens, Christopher (*b.* 1973) *SNP, Glasgow South West,* Maj. 9,950
Stephenson, Andrew (*b.* 1981) *C., Pendle,* Maj. 5,453
*Stevens, Jo (*b.* 1966) *Lab., Cardiff Central,* Maj. 4,981
Stevenson, John (*b.* 1963) *C., Carlisle,* Maj. 2,774
Stewart, Bob (*b.* 1949) *C., Beckenham,* Maj. 18,471
Stewart, Iain (*b.* 1972) *C., Milton Keynes South,* Maj. 8,672
Stewart, Rory (*b.* 1973) *C., Penrith & The Border,* Maj. 19,894
Streeter, Gary (*b.* 1955) *C., Devon South West,* Maj. 20,109
*Streeting, Wes (*b.* 1983) *Lab., Ilford North,* Maj. 589
Stride, Mel (*b.* 1961) *C., Devon Central,* Maj. 21,265
Stringer, Graham (*b.* 1950) *Lab., Blackley & Broughton,* Maj. 16,874
Stuart, Gisela (*b.* 1955) *Lab., Birmingham Edgbaston,* Maj. 2,706
Stuart, Graham (*b.* 1962) *C., Beverley & Holderness,* Maj. 12,203
Sturdy, Julian (*b.* 1971) *C., York Outer,* Maj. 13,129
*Sunak, Rishi (*b.* 1980) *C., Richmond (Yorks),* Maj. 19,550
Swayne, Rt. Hon. Desmond (*b.* 1956) *C., New Forest West,* Maj. 20,604
Swire, Rt. Hon. Hugo (*b.* 1959) *C., Devon East,* Maj. 12,261
Syms, Robert (*b.* 1956) *C., Poole,* Maj. 15,789
Tami, Mark (*b.* 1963) *Lab., Alyn & Deeside,* Maj. 3,343
*Thewliss, Alison (*b.* 1982) *SNP, Glasgow Central,* Maj. 7,662
*Thomas, Derek (*b.* 1972) *C., St Ives,* Maj. 2,469
Thomas, Gareth (*b.* 1967) *Lab. Co-op, Harrow West,* Maj. 2,208
*Thomas-Symonds, Nick (*b.* 1980) *Lab., Torfaen,* Maj. 8,169
*Thompson, Owen (*b.* 1978) *SNP, Midlothian,* Maj. 9,859
*Thomson, Michelle (*b.* 1965) *SNP, Edinburgh West,* Maj. 3,210
Thornberry, Emily (*b.* 1960) *Lab., Islington South & Finsbury,* Maj. 12,708
*Throup, Maggie (*b.* 1957) *C., Erewash,* Maj. 3,584
Timms, Rt. Hon. Stephen (*b.* 1955) *Lab., East Ham,* Maj. 34,252
Timpson, Edward (*b.* 1973) *C., Crewe & Nantwich,* Maj. 3,620
*Tolhurst, Kelly (*b.* 1978) *C., Rochester & Strood,* Maj. 7,133
Tomlinson, Justin (*b.* 1976) *C., Swindon North,* Maj. 11,786
*Tomlinson, Michael (*b.* 1977) *C., Dorset Mid & Poole North,* Maj. 10,530
*Tracey, Craig (*b.* 1974) *C., Warwickshire North,* Maj. 2,973

Tredinnick, David (*b.* 1950) *C., Bosworth,* Maj. 10,988
*Trevelyan, Anne-Marie (*b.* 1969) *C., Berwick-upon-Tweed,* Maj. 4,914
Trickett, Jon (*b.* 1950) *Lab., Hemsworth,* Maj. 12,078
Truss, Rt. Hon. Elizabeth (*b.* 1975) *C., Norfolk South West,* Maj. 13,861
*Tugendhat, Tom (*b.* 1973) *C., Tonbridge & Malling,* Maj. 23,734
*Turley, Anna (*b.* 1978) *Lab. Co-op, Redcar,* Maj. 10,388
Turner, Andrew (*b.* 1953) *C., Isle of Wight,* Maj. 13,703
Turner, Karl (*b.* 1971) *Lab., Hull East,* Maj. 10,319
Twigg, Derek (*b.* 1959) *Lab., Halton,* Maj. 20,285
Twigg, Stephen (*b.* 1966) *Lab. Co-op, Liverpool West Derby,* Maj. 27,367
Tyrie, Rt. Hon. Andrew (*b.* 1957) *C., Chichester,* Maj. 24,413
Umunna, Chuka (*b.* 1978) *Lab., Streatham,* Maj. 13,934
Vaizey, Edward (*b.* 1969) *C., Wantage,* Maj. 21,749
Vara, Shailesh (*b.* 1960) *C., Cambridgeshire North West,* Maj. 19,795
Vaz, Rt. Hon. Keith (*b.* 1956) *Lab., Leicester East,* Maj. 18,352
Vaz, Valerie (*b.* 1954) *Lab., Walsall South,* Maj. 6,007
Vickers, Martin (*b.* 1950) *C., Cleethorpes,* Maj. 7,893
Villiers, Rt. Hon. Theresa (*b.* 1968) *C., Chipping Barnet,* Maj. 7,656
Walker, Charles (*b.* 1967) *C., Broxbourne,* Maj. 16,723
Walker, Robin (*b.* 1978) *C., Worcester,* Maj. 5,646
Wallace, Ben (*b.* 1970) *C., Wyre & Preston North,* Maj. 14,151
*Warburton, David (*b.* 1965) *C., Somerton & Frome,* Maj. 20,268
*Warman, Matt (*b.* 1981) *C., Boston & Skegness,* Maj. 4,336
Watkinson, Dame Angela (*b.* 1941) *C., Hornchurch & Upminster,* Maj. 13,074
Watson, Tom (*b.* 1967) *Lab., West Bromwich East,* Maj. 9,470
Weir, Mike (*b.* 1957) *SNP, Angus,* Maj. 11,230
*West, Catherine (*b.* 1966) *Lab., Hornsey & Wood Green,* Maj. 11,058
Wharton, James (*b.* 1984) *C., Stockton South,* Maj. 5,046
*Whately, Helen (*b.* 1976) *C., Faversham & Kent Mid,* Maj. 16,652
Wheeler, Heather (*b.* 1959) *C., Derbyshire South,* Maj. 11,471
White, Chris (*b.* 1967) *C., Warwick & Leamington,* Maj. 6,606
Whiteford, Dr Eilidh (*b.* 1969) *SNP, Banff & Buchan,* Maj. 14,339
Whitehead, Dr Alan (*b.* 1950) *Lab., Southampton Test,* Maj. 3,810
*Whitford, Dr Philippa (*b.* 1959) *SNP, Ayrshire Central,* Maj. 13,589
Whittaker, Craig (*b.* 1962) *C., Calder Valley,* Maj. 4,427
Whittingdale, Rt. Hon. John (*b.* 1959) *C., Maldon,* Maj. 22,070
Wiggin, Bill (*b.* 1966) *C., Herefordshire North,* Maj. 19,996
*Williams, Craig (*b.* 1985) *C., Cardiff North,* Maj. 2,137
Williams, Hywel (*b.* 1953) *PC, Arfon,* Maj. 3,668
Williams, Mark (*b.* 1966) *LD, Ceredigion,* Maj. 3,067
Williamson, Rt. Hon. Gavin (*b.* 1976) *C., Staffordshire South,* Maj. 20,371
*Wilson, Corri (*b.* 1963) *SNP, Ayr, Carrick & Cumnock,* Maj. 11,265
Wilson, Phil (*b.* 1959) *Lab., Sedgefield,* Maj. 6,843
Wilson, Rob (*b.* 1965) *C., Reading East,* Maj. 6,520
Wilson, Sammy (*b.* 1953) *DUP, Antrim East,* Maj. 5,795
Winnick, David (*b.* 1933) *Lab., Walsall North,* Maj. 1,937

**Winterton**, Rt. Hon. Rosie (*b.* 1958) *Lab., Doncaster Central,* Maj. 10,093

**Wishart**, Pete (*b.* 1962) *SNP, Perth & Perthshire North,* Maj. 9,641

**Wollaston**, Dr Sarah (*b.* 1962) *C., Totnes,* Maj. 18,285

*****Wood**, Mike (*b.* 1976) *C., Dudley South,* Maj. 4,270

**Woodcock**, John (*b.* 1978) *Lab. Co-op, Barrow & Furness,* Maj. 795

*****Wragg**, William (*b.* 1987) *C., Hazel Grove,* Maj. 6,552

**Wright**, Iain (*b.* 1972) *Lab., Hartlepool,* Maj. 3,024

**Wright**, Rt. Hon. Jeremy (*b.* 1972) *C., Kenilworth & Southam,* Maj. 21,002

**Zahawi**, Nadhim (*b.* 1967) *C., Stratford-on-Avon,* Maj. 22,876

*****Zeichner**, Daniel (*b.* 1956) *Lab., Cambridge,* Maj. 599

# GENERAL ELECTION RESULTS

The results of voting in each of the 650 parliamentary constituencies at the general election of 7 May 2015 are given below.

KEY
* New MP
E. Electorate      T. Turnout

swing N/A   Indicates a constituency for which the swing data cannot be calculated because one of the top two parties in the General Election 2015 did not field a candidate in the seat in 2010.

*Abbreviations*

| | |
|---|---|
| 30-50 | The 30-50 Coalition |
| Above | Above and Beyond |
| Active Dem. | Movement for Active Democracy |
| AD | Apolitical Democrats |
| Alliance | Alliance Party of Northern Ireland |
| AP | All People's Party |
| APNI | APNI Party |
| Atom | Children of the Atom |
| AWP | Animal Welfare Party |
| Beer | Reduce Tax on Beer Party |
| Beer BS | Beer, Baccy and Scratchings Party |
| Birthday | The Birthday Party |
| BNP | British National Party |
| Bournemouth | Bournemouth Independent Alliance |
| Brit. Dem. | British Democratic Party |
| Brit. Ind. | British Independents |
| Bristol | Independents for Bristol |
| C. | Conservative |
| Campaign | Campaign Party |
| Change | Alter Change |
| Ch. M. | Christian Movement for Great Britain |
| Ch. P. | The Christian Party |
| CISTA | Cannabis is Safer than Alcohol |
| Class War | Class War |
| Comm. | Communist Party of Britain |
| Comm. Lge | Communist League |
| Community | Communities United Party |
| Consensus | Consensus |
| CPA | Christian People's Alliance |
| Croydon | Putting Croydon First |
| CSP | Common Sense Party |
| Dem. Ref. | Democratic Reform Party |
| Digital | Digital Democracy |
| DP | The Democratic Party |
| DUP | Democratic Unionist Party |
| Eccentric | The Eccentric Party of Great Britain |
| Elmo | Give Me Back Elmo |
| Eng. Dem. | English Democrats |
| EP | Europeans Party |
| FPT | Free Public Transport Party |
| FUKP | Free United Kingdom Party |
| Green | Green Party |
| Green Soc. | Alliance for Green Socialism |
| Guildford | Guildford Greenbelt Group |
| Hoi | Hoi Polloi Party |
| Hospital | Save Hartlepool Hospital |
| Humanity | Humanity |

| | |
|---|---|
| IASI | Independents Against Social Injustice |
| IE | Independence from Europe |
| Ind. | Independent |
| Ind. CHC | Independent Community and Health Concern |
| IPAP | The Independent Political Alliance Party |
| ISWSL | Independent Save Withybush Save Lives |
| IZB | Islam Zinda Baad Platform |
| JACP | Justice & Anti-Corruption Party |
| JMB | Justice for Men & Boys |
| Lab. | Labour |
| Lab. Co-op | Labour and Co-operative |
| LD | Liberal Democrat |
| Lib. | The Liberal Party |
| Lib. GB | Liberty Great Britain |
| Lincs Ind. | Lincolnshire Independents |
| Loony | Monster Raving Loony Party |
| LP | Land Party |
| LU | Left Unity |
| Magna Carta | Magna Carta Conservation Party Great Britain |
| Mainstream | Mainstream Party |
| Manston | Manston Airport Independent Party |
| MC | The Magna Carta Party |
| Meb. Ker. | Mebyon Kernow |
| Nat. Lib. | National Liberal Party |
| ND | No description |
| NE | The North East Party |
| New IC | New Independent Centralists |
| NF | National Front |
| NHAP | National Health Action Party |
| Northern | Northern Party |
| Patria | Patria |
| PBP | People Before Profit Alliance |
| PC | Plaid Cymru |
| Peace | Peace Party |
| PF | People First |
| Pilgrim | The Pilgrim Party |
| Pirate | Pirate Party UK |
| Plural | The Pluralist Party |
| Poole | The Party for Poole People Ltd |
| PPP | The Principles of Politics Party |
| PP UK | Population Party UK |
| PSP | Patriotic Socialist Party |
| Real | Keep It Real Party |
| Realist | The Realists' Party |

| | |
|---|---|
| Reality | We are the Reality Party |
| Reboot | Rebooting Democracy |
| Rep. Soc. | The Republican Socialist Party |
| Respect | The Respect Party |
| Restore | Restore the Family for Children's Sake |
| RFAC | Red Flag Anti-Corruption |
| Rochdale | Rochdale First Party |
| Roman | The Roman Party |
| S. New | Something New |
| Scot. Green | Scottish Green Party |
| SCP | Scottish Christian Party |
| SDLP | Social Democratic and Labour Party |
| SEP | Socialist Equality Party |
| SF | Sinn Fein |
| SNP | Scottish National Party |
| Soc. | Socialist Party |
| Soc. Dem. | Social Democratic Party |
| Soc. Lab. | Socialist Labour Party |
| Song | World Peace Through Song |
| Southport | The Southport Party |
| Speaker | The Speaker |
| SPGB | The Socialist Party of Great Britain |
| SSP | Scottish Socialist Party |
| TEP | The Evolution Party |
| Thanet | Party for a United Thanet |
| TSPP | The Sustainable Population Party |
| TUSC | Trade Unionist and Socialist Coalition |
| TUV | Traditional Unionist Voice |
| U Party | Universal Party |
| Ubuntu | Ubuntu |
| UKIP | UK Independence Party |
| UKPDP | UK Progressive Democracy Party |
| UUP | Ulster Unionist Party |
| Uttlesford | Residents for Uttlesford |
| Vapers | Vapers in Power |
| VAT | Reduce VAT in Sport |
| Wessex Reg. | Wessex Regionalists |
| Whig | Whig Party |
| Wigan | Wigan Independents |
| Worth | The New Society of Worth |
| WP | Workers' Party |
| WRP | Workers' Revolutionary Party |
| WVPTFP | War Veteran's Pro-Traditional Family Party |
| Yorks | Yorkshire First |
| Young | Young People's Party |
| Zeb | Al-Zebabist Nation of Ooog |

# PARLIAMENTARY CONSTITUENCIES AS AT 7 MAY 2015 GENERAL ELECTION

*UK Turnout*
E. 46,424,006  T. 30,697,845 (66.1%)

## ENGLAND

**ALDERSHOT**
E. 72,434    T. 46,191 (63.77%)    C. hold
Gerald Howarth, C.                     23,369
Gary Puffett, Lab.                      8,468
Bill Walker, UKIP                       8,253
Alan Hilliar, LD                        4,076
Carl Hewitt, Green                      2,025
C. majority 14,901 (32.26%)
1.18% swing C. to Lab.
(2010: C. majority 5,586 (12.31%))

**ALDRIDGE-BROWNHILLS**
E. 60,215    T. 39,497 (65.59%)    C. hold
*Wendy Morton, C.                      20,558
John Fisher, Lab.                       8,835
Anthony Thompson, UKIP                  7,751
Ian Garrett, LD                         1,330
Martyn Curzey, Green                      826
Mark Beech, Loony                         197
C. majority 11,723 (29.68%)
4.92% swing C. to Lab.
(2010: C. majority 15,266 (39.51%))

**ALTRINCHAM & SALE WEST**
E. 72,004    T. 50,517 (70.16%)    C. hold
Graham Brady, C.                       26,771
James Wright, Lab.                     13,481
Jane Brophy, LD                         4,235
Chris Frost, UKIP                       4,047
Nick Robertson-Brown, Green             1,983
C. majority 13,290 (26.31%)
0.11% swing C. to Lab.
(2010: C. majority 11,595 (23.47%))

**AMBER VALLEY**
E. 70,226    T. 45,717 (65.10%)    C. hold
Nigel Mills, C.                        20,106
Kevin Gillott, Lab.                    15,901
Stuart Bent, UKIP                       7,263
Kate Smith, LD                          1,360
John Devine, Green                      1,087
C. majority 4,205 (9.20%)
4.02% swing Lab. to C.
(2010: C. majority 536 (1.17%))

**ARUNDEL & SOUTH DOWNS**
E. 77,272    T. 56,477 (73.09%)    C. hold
Nick Herbert, C.                       34,331
Peter Grace, UKIP                       8,154
Christopher Wellbelove, Lab.            6,324
Shweta Kapadia, LD                      4,062
Isabel Thurston, Green                  3,606
C. majority 26,177 (46.35%)
2.87% swing C. to UKIP
(2010: C. majority 16,691 (29.81%))

**ASHFIELD**
E. 77,126    T. 47,409 (61.47%)    Lab. hold
Gloria De Piero, Lab.                  19,448
Helen Harrison, C.                     10,628
Simon Ashcroft, UKIP                   10,150
Philip Smith, LD                        7,030
Mike Buchanan, JMB                        153
Lab. majority 8,820 (18.60%)
3.55% swing C. to Lab.
(2010: Lab. majority 192 (0.40%))

**ASHFORD**
E. 85,189    T. 57,372 (67.35%)    C. hold
Damian Green, C.                       30,094
Gerald O'Brien, UKIP                   10,798
Brendan Chilton, Lab.                  10,580
Debbie Enever, LD                       3,433
Mandy Rossi, Green                      2,467
C. majority 19,296 (33.63%)
7.98% swing C. to UKIP
(2010: C. majority 17,297 (31.34%))

**ASHTON-UNDER-LYNE**
E. 67,714    T. 38,918 (57.47%)    Lab. hold
*Angela Rayner, Lab.                   19,366
Tracy Sutton, C.                        8,610
Maurice Jackson, UKIP                   8,468
Charlotte Hughes, Green                 1,531
Carly Hicks, LD                           943
Lab. majority 10,756 (27.64%)
1.99% swing C. to Lab.
(2010: Lab. majority 9,094 (23.66%))

**AYLESBURY**
E. 80,611    T. 55,419 (68.75%)    C. hold
David Lidington, C.                    28,083
Chris Adams, UKIP                      10,925
Will Cass, Lab.                         8,391
Steven Lambert, LD                      5,885
David Lyons, Green                      2,135
C. majority 17,158 (30.96%)
7.21% swing C. to UKIP
(2010: C. majority 12,618 (23.73%))

**BANBURY**
E. 86,420    T. 58,008 (67.12%)    C. hold
*Victoria Prentis, C.                  30,749
Sean Woodcock, Lab.                    12,354
Dickie Bird, UKIP                       8,050
John Howson, LD                         3,440
Ian Middleton, Green                    2,686
Roseanne Edwards, NHAP                    729
C. majority 18,395 (31.71%)
0.97% swing C. to Lab.
(2010: C. majority 18,227 (32.41%))

**BARKING**
E. 74,004    T. 43,023 (58.14%)    Lab. hold
Margaret Hodge, Lab.                   24,826
Roger Gravett, UKIP                     9,554
Mina Rahman, C.                         7,019
Tony Rablen, Green                        879
Peter Wilcock, LD                         562
Joseph Mambuliya, TUSC                    183
Lab. majority 15,272 (35.50%)
7.98% swing Lab. to UKIP
(2010: Lab. majority 16,555 (36.51%))

**BARNSLEY CENTRAL**
E. 64,534    T. 36,560 (56.65%)    Lab. hold
Dan Jarvis, Lab.                       20,376
Lee Hunter, UKIP                        7,941
Kay Carter, C.                          5,485
Michael Short, Green                      938
David Ridgway, LD                         770
Dave Gibson, TUSC                         573
Ian Sutton, Eng. Dem.                     477
Lab. majority 12,435 (34.01%)
4.29% swing Lab. to UKIP
(2010: Lab. majority 11,093 (29.98%))
(2011: Lab. majority 11,771 (48.60%))

**BARNSLEY EAST**
E. 69,135    T. 38,517 (55.71%)    Lab. hold
Michael Dugher, Lab.                   21,079
Robert Swiffen, UKIP                    9,045
Katharine Harborne, C.                  5,622
Ruth Coleman-Taylor, LD                 1,217
Tony Devoy, Yorks                         647
Kevin Riddiough, Eng. Dem.                440
Ralph Dyson, TUSC                         364
Billy Marsden, Vapers                     103
Lab. majority 12,034 (31.24%)
5.65% swing Lab. to UKIP
(2010: Lab. majority 11,090 (28.89%))

**BARROW & FURNESS**
E. 68,338    T. 43,275 (63.32%)
                          Lab. Co-op hold
John Woodcock, Lab. Co-op              18,320
Simon Fell, C.                         17,525
Nigel Cecil, UKIP                       5,070
Clive Peaple, LD                        1,169
Robert O'Hara, Green                    1,061
Ian Jackson, Ind.                         130
Lab. Co-op majority 795 (1.84%)
4.98% swing Lab. Co-op to C.
(2010: Lab. Co-op majority 5,208
(11.80%))

**BASILDON & BILLERICAY**
E. 68,459    T. 43,028 (62.85%)    C. hold
John Baron, C.                         22,668
Gavin Callaghan, Lab.                  10,186
George Konstantinidis, UKIP             8,538
Martin Thompson, LD                     1,636
C. majority 12,482 (29.01%)
0.34% swing C. to Lab.
(2010: C. majority 12,338 (29.68%))

**BASILDON SOUTH & THURROCK EAST**
E. 73,210    T. 45,593 (62.28%)    C. hold
Stephen Metcalfe, C.                   19,788
Ian Luder, UKIP                        12,097
Mike Le-Surf, Lab.                     11,493
Geoff Williams, LD                      1,356
Kerry Smith, Ind.                         401
None Of The Above X, ND                   253
Stuart Hooper, Ind.                       205
C. majority 7,691 (16.87%)
10.55% swing C. to UKIP
(2010: C. majority 5,772 (12.90%))

**BASINGSTOKE**
E. 79,662    T. 53,076 (66.63%)    C. hold
Maria Miller, C.                       25,769
Paul Harvey, Lab.                      14,706
Alan Stone, UKIP                        8,290
Janice Spalding, LD                     3,919
Omar Selim, Ind.                          392
C. majority 11,063 (20.84%)
4.64% swing C. to Lab.
(2010: C. majority 13,176 (26.01%))

**BASSETLAW**
E. 77,480    T. 49,289 (63.62%)    Lab. hold
John Mann, Lab.                        23,965
Sarah Downes, C.                       15,122
David Scott, UKIP                       7,865
Leon Duveen, LD                         1,331
Kris Wragg, Green                       1,006
Lab. majority 8,843 (17.94%)
0.69% swing C. to Lab.
(2010: Lab. majority 8,215 (16.57%))

BATH
E. 60,869   T. 47,167 (77.49%)   C. gain
*Ben Howlett, C.   17,833
Steve Bradley, LD   14,000
Ollie Middleton, Lab.   6,216
Dominic Tristram, Green   5,634
Julian Deverell, UKIP   2,922
Loraine Morgan-Brinkhurst, Ind.   499
Jenny Knight, Eng. Dem.   63
C. majority 3,833 (8.13%)
16.68% swing LD to C.
(2010: LD majority 11,883 (25.24%))

BATLEY & SPEN
E. 78,373   T. 50,479 (64.41%)   Lab. hold
*Jo Cox, Lab.   21,826
Imtiaz Ameen, C.   15,769
Aleks Lukic, UKIP   9,080
John Lawson, LD   2,396
Ian Bullock, Green   1,232
Dawn Wheelhouse, TUSC   123
Karl Varley, PSP   53
Lab. majority 6,057 (12.00%)
1.69% swing C. to Lab.
(2010: Lab. majority 4,406 (8.62%))

BATTERSEA
E. 76,106   T. 51,031 (67.05%)   C. hold
Jane Ellison, C.   26,730
Will Martindale, Lab.   18,792
Luke Taylor, LD   2,241
Joe Stuart, Green   1,682
Christopher Howe, UKIP   1,586
C. majority 7,938 (15.56%)
1.65% swing Lab. to C.
(2010: C. majority 5,977 (12.25%))

BEACONSFIELD
E. 76,380   T. 53,163 (69.60%)   C. hold
Dominic Grieve, C.   33,621
Tim Scott, UKIP   7,310
Tony Clements, Lab.   6,074
Peter Chapman, LD   3,927
Dave Hampton, Green   2,231
C. majority 26,311 (49.49%)
3.31% swing C. to UKIP
(2010: C. majority 21,782 (41.50%))

BECKENHAM
E. 67,436   T. 48,803 (72.37%)   C. hold
Bob Stewart, C.   27,955
Marina Ahmad, Lab.   9,484
Rob Bryant, UKIP   6,108
Anuja Prashar, LD   3,378
Ruth Fabricant, Green   1,878
C. majority 18,471 (37.85%)
2.78% swing C. to Lab.
(2010: C. majority 17,784 (37.29%))

BEDFORD
E. 69,311   T. 46,086 (66.49%)   C. hold
Richard Fuller, C.   19,625
Patrick Hall, Lab.   18,528
Charlie Smith, UKIP   4,434
Mahmud Henry Rogers, LD   1,958
Ben Foley, Green   1,412
Faruk Choudhury, Ind.   129
C. majority 1,097 (2.38%)
0.31% swing C. to Lab.
(2010: C. majority 1,353 (3.00%))

BEDFORDSHIRE MID
E. 81,144   T. 58,060 (71.55%)   C. hold
Nadine Dorries, C.   32,544
Charlynne Pullen, Lab.   9,217
Nigel Wickens, UKIP   8,966
Linda Jack, LD   4,193
Gareth Ellis, Green   2,462
Tim Ireland, Ind.   384
Ann Kelly, Loony   294
C. majority 23,327 (40.18%)
1.23% swing Lab. to C.
(2010: C. majority 15,152 (27.60%))

BEDFORDSHIRE NORTH EAST
E. 83,551   T. 58,672 (70.22%)   C. hold
Alistair Burt, C.   34,891
Saqhib Ali, Lab.   9,247
Adrianne Smyth, UKIP   8,579
Peter Morris, LD   3,418
Mark Bowler, Green   2,537
C. majority 25,644 (43.71%)
2.02% swing Lab. to C.
(2010: C. majority 18,942 (34.10%))

BEDFORDSHIRE SOUTH WEST
E. 79,664   T. 51,304 (64.40%)   C. hold
Andrew Selous, C.   28,212
Daniel Scott, Lab.   10,399
John Van Weenen, UKIP   7,941
Stephen Rutherford, LD   2,646
Emily Lawrence, Green   2,106
C. majority 17,813 (34.72%)
0.75% swing Lab. to C.
(2010: C. majority 16,649 (32.79%))

BERMONDSEY & OLD SOUTHWARK
E. 80,604   T. 51,424 (63.80%)   Lab. gain
*Neil Coyle, Lab.   22,146
Simon Hughes, LD   17,657
JP Floru, C.   6,051
Andrew Beadle, UKIP   3,254
William Lavin, Green   2,023
Kingsley Abrams, TUSC   142
Lucy Hall, Ind.   72
Donald Cole, AP   59
Steve Freeman, Rep. Soc.   20
Lab. majority 4,489 (8.73%)
13.92% swing LD to Lab.
(2010: LD majority 8,530 (19.10%))

BERWICK-UPON-TWEED
E. 58,098   T. 40,423 (69.58%)   C. gain
*Anne-Marie Trevelyan, C.   16,603
Julie Porksen, LD   11,689
Scott Dickinson, Lab.   6,042
Nigel Coghill-Marshall, UKIP   4,513
Rachael Roberts, Green   1,488
Neil Humphrey, Eng. Dem.   88
C. majority 4,914 (12.16%)
9.58% swing LD to C.
(2010: LD majority 2,690 (7.00%))

BETHNAL GREEN & BOW
E. 82,825   T. 52,924 (63.90%)   Lab. hold
Rushanara Ali, Lab.   32,387
Matt Smith, C.   8,070
Alistair Polson, Green   4,906
Paula McQueen, UKIP   3,219
Teena Lashmore, LD   2,395
Glyn Robbins, TUSC   949
M. Rowshan Ali, Community   356
Jonathan Dewey, CISTA   303
Alasdair Henderson, Whig   203
Elliot Ball, 30-50   78
Jason Pavlou, RFAC   58
Lab. majority 24,317 (45.95%)
8.47% swing C. to Lab.
(2010: Lab. majority 11,574 (22.82%))

BEVERLEY & HOLDERNESS
E. 80,822   T. 52,677 (65.18%)   C. hold
Graham Stuart, C.   25,363
Margaret Pinder, Lab.   13,160
Gary Shores, UKIP   8,794
Denis Healy, LD   2,900
Richard Howarth, Green   1,802
Lee Walton, Yorks   658
C. majority 12,203 (23.17%)
1.42% swing C. to Lab.
(2010: C. majority 12,987 (24.41%))

BEXHILL & BATTLE
E. 78,796   T. 55,218 (70.08%)   C. hold
*Huw Merriman, C.   30,245
Geoffrey Bastin, UKIP   10,170
Michelle Thew, Lab.   7,797
Rachel Sadler, LD   4,199
Jonathan Kent, Green   2,807
C. majority 20,075 (36.36%)
swing N/A
(2010: C. majority 12,880 (23.60%))

BEXLEYHEATH & CRAYFORD
E. 64,828   T. 43,685 (67.39%)   C. hold
David Evennett, C.   20,643
Stef Borella, Lab.   11,451
Chris Attard, UKIP   9,182
Richard Davis, LD   1,308
Stella Gardiner, Green   950
Maggi Young, Eng. Dem.   151
C. majority 9,192 (21.04%)
1.46% swing C. to Lab.
(2010: C. majority 10,344 (23.95%))

BIRKENHEAD
E. 62,438   T. 37,680 (60.35%)   Lab. hold
Frank Field, Lab.   26,468
Clark Vasey, C.   5,816
Wayne Harling, UKIP   3,838
Allan Brame, LD   1,396
Kenny Peers, Green   162
Lab. majority 20,652 (54.81%)
5.61% swing C. to Lab.
(2010: Lab. majority 15,395 (43.58%))

BIRMINGHAM EDGBASTON
E. 65,591   T. 41,293 (62.96%)   Lab. hold
Gisela Stuart, Lab.   18,518
Luke Evans, C.   15,812
Graham Short, UKIP   4,154
Phil Simpson, Green   1,371
Lee Dargue, LD   1,184
Gabriel Ukandu, Ch. P.   163
Henna Rai, Ind.   91
Lab. majority 2,706 (6.55%)
1.74% swing C. to Lab.
(2010: Lab. majority 1,274 (3.06%))

BIRMINGHAM ERDINGTON
E. 65,128   T. 34,684 (53.26%)   Lab. hold
Jack Dromey, Lab.   15,824
Robert Alden, C.   10,695
Andrew Garcarz, UKIP   6,040
Ann Holtom, LD   965
Joe Belcher, Green   948
Ted Woodley, TUSC   212
Lab. majority 5,129 (14.79%)
2.78% swing C. to Lab.
(2010: Lab. majority 3,277 (9.22%))

**BIRMINGHAM HALL GREEN**
E. 76,330   T. 47,046 (61.64%)   Lab. hold
Roger Godsiff, Lab.                           28,147
James Bird, C.                                  8,329
Jerry Evans, LD                                 5,459
Elly Stanton, Green                             2,200
Rashpal Mondair, UKIP                           2,131
Shiraz Peer, Respect                              780
Lab. majority 19,818 (42.12%)
12.12% swing C. to Lab.
(2010: Lab. majority 3,799 (7.80%))

**BIRMINGHAM HODGE HILL**
E. 75,302   T. 41,039 (54.50%)   Lab. hold
Liam Byrne, Lab.                              28,069
Kieran Mullan, C.                              4,707
Albert Duffen, UKIP                            4,651
Phil Bennion, LD                               2,624
Chris Nash, Green                                835
Andy Chaffer, Comm.                              153
Lab. majority 23,362 (56.93%)
8.28% swing C. to Lab.
(2010: Lab. majority 10,302 (24.26%))

**BIRMINGHAM LADYWOOD**
E. 68,128   T. 35,916 (52.72%)   Lab. hold
Shabana Mahmood, Lab.                         26,444
Isabel Sigmac, C.                              4,576
Clair Braund, UKIP                             1,805
Margaret Okole, Green                          1,501
Shazad Iqbal, LD                               1,374
Timothy Burton, Lib. GB                          216
Lab. majority 21,868 (60.89%)
8.57% swing C. to Lab.
(2010: Lab. majority 10,105 (28.20%))

**BIRMINGHAM NORTHFIELD**
E. 71,428   T. 42,461 (59.45%)   Lab. hold
Richard Burden, Lab.                          17,673
Rachel Maclean, C.                            15,164
Keith Rowe, UKIP                               7,106
Steven Haynes, LD                              1,349
Anna Masters, Green                            1,169
Lab. majority 2,509 (5.91%)
0.37% swing Lab. to C.
(2010: Lab. majority 2,782 (6.65%))

**BIRMINGHAM PERRY BARR**
E. 69,943   T. 41,260 (58.99%)   Lab. hold
Khalid Mahmood, Lab.                          23,697
Charlotte Hodivala, C.                         8,869
Harjinder Singh, UKIP                          5,032
Arjun Singh, LD                                2,001
James Lovatt, Green                            1,330
Robert Punton, TUSC                              331
Lab. majority 14,828 (35.94%)
3.48% swing C. to Lab.
(2010: Lab. majority 11,908 (28.32%))

**BIRMINGHAM SELLY OAK**
E. 75,092   T. 45,294 (60.32%)   Lab. hold
Steve McCabe, Lab.                            21,584
Alex Boulter, C.                              13,137
Steven Brookes, UKIP                           5,755
Colin Green, LD                                2,517
Clare Thomas, Green                            2,301
Lab. majority 8,447 (18.65%)
5.59% swing C. to Lab.
(2010: Lab. majority 3,482 (7.48%))

**BIRMINGHAM YARDLEY**
E. 72,146   T. 41,151 (57.04%)   Lab. gain
*Jess Phillips, Lab.                          17,129
John Hemming, LD                              10,534
Paul Clayton, UKIP                             6,637
Arun Photay, C.                                5,760
Grant Bishop, Green                              698
Teval Stephens, Respect                          187
Eamonn Flynn, TUSC                               135
Peter Johnson, Soc. Dem.                          71
Lab. majority 6,595 (16.03%)
11.69% swing LD to Lab.
(2010: LD majority 3,002 (7.35%))

**BISHOP AUCKLAND**
E. 66,089   T. 39,389 (59.60%)   Lab. hold
Helen Goodman, Lab.                           16,307
Christopher Adams, C.                         12,799
Rhys Burriss, UKIP                             7,015
Stephen White, LD                              1,723
Thom Robinson, Green                           1,545
Lab. majority 3,508 (8.91%)
1.89% swing Lab. to C.
(2010: Lab. majority 5,218 (12.68%))

**BLACKBURN**
E. 73,265   T. 43,999 (60.05%)   Lab. hold
*Kate Hollern, Lab.                           24,762
Bob Eastwood, C.                              12,002
Dayle Taylor, UKIP                             6,280
Gordon Lishman, LD                               955
Lab. majority 12,760 (29.00%)
3.67% swing C. to Lab.
(2010: Lab. majority 9,856 (21.66%))

**BLACKLEY & BROUGHTON**
E. 71,900   T. 37,112 (51.62%)   Lab. hold
Graham Stringer, Lab.                         22,982
Martin Power, UKIP                             6,108
Michelle Tanfield-Johnson, C.                 5,581
David Jones, Green                             1,567
Richard Gadsden, LD                              874
Lab. majority 16,874 (45.47%)
3.09% swing Lab. to UKIP
(2010: Lab. majority 12,303 (35.97%))

**BLACKPOOL NORTH & CLEVELEYS**
E. 62,469   T. 39,393 (63.06%)   C. hold
Paul Maynard, C.                              17,508
Sam Rushworth, Lab.                           14,168
Simon Noble, UKIP                              5,823
Sue Close, LD                                    948
John Warnock, Green                              889
James Walsh, Northern                             57
C. majority 3,340 (8.48%)
1.59% swing Lab. to C.
(2010: C. majority 2,150 (5.30%))

**BLACKPOOL SOUTH**
E. 57,411   T. 32,436 (56.50%)   Lab. hold
Gordon Marsden, Lab.                          13,548
Peter Anthony, C.                             10,963
Peter Wood, UKIP                               5,613
Duncan Royle, Green                              841
Bill Greene, LD                                  743
Andy Higgins, Ind.                               655
Lawrence Chard, Ind.                              73
Lab. majority 2,585 (7.97%)
1.35% swing Lab. to C.
(2010: Lab. majority 1,851 (5.26%))

**BLAYDON**
E. 67,706   T. 44,936 (66.37%)   Lab. hold
David Anderson, Lab.                          22,090
Mark Bell, UKIP                                7,863
Alison Griffiths, C.                           7,838
Jonathan Wallace, LD                           5,497
Paul McNally, Green                            1,648
Lab. majority 14,227 (31.66%)
swing N/A
(2010: Lab. majority 9,117 (20.30%))

**BLYTH VALLEY**
E. 63,958   T. 38,461 (60.13%)   Lab. hold
Ronnie Campbell, Lab.                         17,813
Barry Elliott, UKIP                            8,584
Greg Munro, C.                                 8,346
Philip Latham, LD                              2,265
Dawn Furness, Green                            1,453
Lab. majority 9,229 (24.00%)
8.09% swing Lab. to UKIP
(2010: Lab. majority 6,668 (17.29%))

**BOGNOR REGIS & LITTLEHAMPTON**
E. 73,095   T. 47,116 (64.46%)   C. hold
Nick Gibb, C.                                 24,185
Graham Jones, UKIP                            10,241
Alan Butcher, Lab.                             6,508
Francis Oppler, LD                             4,240
Simon McDougall, Green                         1,942
C. majority 13,944 (29.60%)
7.67% swing C. to UKIP
(2010: C. majority 13,063 (27.88%))

**BOLSOVER**
E. 71,976   T. 43,998 (61.13%)   Lab. hold
Dennis Skinner, Lab.                          22,542
Peter Bedford, C.                             10,764
Ray Calladine, UKIP                            9,228
David Lomax, LD                                1,464
Lab. majority 11,778 (26.77%)
0.67% swing C. to Lab.
(2010: Lab. majority 11,182 (25.42%))

**BOLTON NORTH EAST**
E. 67,901   T. 43,161 (63.56%)   Lab. hold
David Crausby, Lab.                           18,541
James Daly, C.                                14,164
Harry Lamb, UKIP                               8,117
Stephen Rock, LD                               1,236
Laura Diggle, Green                            1,103
Lab. majority 4,377 (10.14%)
0.35% swing C. to Lab.
(2010: Lab. majority 4,084 (9.44%))

**BOLTON SOUTH EAST**
E. 69,692   T. 40,743 (58.46%)   Lab. hold
Yasmin Qureshi, Lab.                          20,555
Jeff Armstrong, UKIP                           9,627
Mudasir Dean, C.                               8,289
Alan Johnson, Green                            1,200
Darren Reynolds, LD                            1,072
Lab. majority 10,928 (26.82%)
8.33% swing Lab. to UKIP
(2010: Lab. majority 8,634 (21.80%))

**BOLTON WEST**
E. 72,727   T. 48,592 (66.81%)   C. gain
*Chris Green, C.                              19,744
Julie Hilling, Lab.                           18,943
Bob Horsefield, UKIP                           7,428
Andrew Martin, LD                              1,947
Andy Smith, Ind.                                 321
John Vickers, TUSC                               209
C. majority 801 (1.65%)
0.92% swing Lab. to C.
(2010: Lab. majority 92 (0.19%))

BOOTLE
E. 70,137   T. 45,152 (64.38%)   Lab. hold
*Peter Dowd, Lab.                      33,619
Paul Nuttall, UKIP                      4,915
Jade Marsden, C.                        3,639
Lisa Tallis, Green                      1,501
David Newman, LD                          978
Pete Glover, TUSC                         500
Lab. majority 28,704 (63.57%)
1.61% swing UKIP to Lab.
(2010: Lab. majority 21,181 (51.31%))

BOSTON & SKEGNESS
E. 67,834   T. 43,339 (63.89%)   C. hold
*Matt Warman, C.                       18,981
Robin Hunter-Clarke, UKIP              14,645
Paul Kenny, Lab.                        7,142
David Watts, LD                         1,015
Victoria Percival, Green                  800
Chris Pain, IE                            324
Peter Johnson, ND                         170
Lyn Luxton, Pilgrim                       143
Robert West, BNP                          119
C. majority 4,336 (10.00%)
14.99% swing C. to UKIP
(2010: C. majority 12,426 (28.81%))

BOSWORTH
E. 79,742   T. 53,582 (67.19%)   C. hold
David Tredinnick, C.                   22,939
Michael Mullaney, LD                   11,951
Chris Kealey, Lab.                      9,354
David Sprason, UKIP                     9,338
C. majority 10,988 (20.51%)
5.62% swing LD to C.
(2010: C. majority 5,032 (9.27%))

BOURNEMOUTH EAST
E. 71,956   T. 44,827 (62.30%)   C. hold
Tobias Ellwood, C.                     22,060
Peter Stokes, Lab.                      7,448
David Hughes, UKIP                      7,401
Jon Nicholas, LD                        3,752
Alasdair Keddie, Green                  3,263
David Ross, Bournemouth                   903
C. majority 14,612 (32.60%)
1.29% swing C. to Lab.
(2010: C. majority 7,728 (17.55%))

BOURNEMOUTH WEST
E. 72,082   T. 41,773 (57.95%)   C. hold
Conor Burns, C.                        20,155
Martin Houlden, UKIP                    7,745
David Stokes, Lab.                      7,386
Mike Plummer, LD                        3,281
Elizabeth McManus, Green                3,107
Dick Franklin, Patria                      99
C. majority 12,410 (29.71%)
4.12% swing C. to UKIP
(2010: C. majority 5,583 (13.40%))

BRACKNELL
E. 78,131   T. 53,086 (67.94%)   C. hold
Phillip Lee, C.                        29,606
James Walsh, Lab.                       8,956
Richard Thomas, UKIP                    8,339
Patrick Smith, LD                       3,983
Derek Florey, Green                     2,202
C. majority 20,650 (38.90%)
1.64% swing Lab. to C.
(2010: C. majority 15,704 (30.12%))

BRADFORD EAST
E. 66,123   T. 41,406 (62.62%)   Lab. gain
*Imran Hussain, Lab.                   19,312
David Ward, LD                         12,228
Iftikhar Ahmed, C.                      4,682
Owais Rajput, UKIP                      4,103
Dave Stevens, Green                       871
James Lewthwaite, Brit. Dem.              210
Lab. majority 7,084 (17.11%)
9.01% swing LD to Lab.
(2010: LD majority 365 (0.90%))

BRADFORD SOUTH
E. 63,670   T. 37,600 (59.05%)   Lab. hold
*Judith Cummins, Lab.                  16,328
Tanya Graham, C.                        9,878
Jason Smith, UKIP                       9,057
Andrew Robinson, Green                  1,243
Andrew Tear, LD                         1,094
Lab. majority 6,450 (17.15%)
2.49% swing C. to Lab.
(2010: Lab. majority 4,622 (12.16%))

BRADFORD WEST
E. 63,371   T. 40,290 (63.58%)   Lab. gain
*Naseem Shah, Lab.                     19,977
George Galloway, Respect                8,557
George Grant, C.                        6,160
Harry Boota, UKIP                       3,140
Alun Griffiths, LD                      1,173
Celia Hickson, Green                    1,085
James Kirkcaldy, Ind.                     100
Therese Hirst, Eng. Dem.                   98
Lab. majority 11,420 (28.34%)
swing N/A
(2010: Lab. majority 5,763 (14.20%))
(2012: Respect majority 10,140 (30.90%))

BRAINTREE
E. 73,557   T. 50,283 (68.36%)   C. hold
*James Cleverly, C.                    27,071
Richard Bingley, UKIP                   9,461
Malcolm Fincken, Lab.                   9,296
Matthew Klesel, LD                      2,488
Paul Jeater, Green                      1,564
Toby Pereira, Ind.                        295
Paul Hooks, Ind.                          108
C. majority 17,610 (35.02%)
6.29% swing C. to UKIP
(2010: C. majority 16,121 (32.76%))

BRENT CENTRAL
E. 77,038   T. 47,032 (61.05%)   Lab. gain
*Dawn Butler, Lab.                     29,216
Alan Mendoza, C.                        9,567
Lauren Keith, LD                        3,937
Shahrar Ali, Green                      1,912
Stephen Priestley, UKIP                 1,850
John Boyle, TUSC                          235
Kamran Malik, Community                   170
Noel Coonan, Ind.                         145
Lab. majority 19,649 (41.78%)
28.36% swing LD to Lab.
(2010: LD majority 1,345 (2.97%))

BRENT NORTH
E. 82,196   T. 52,235 (63.55%)   Lab. hold
Barry Gardiner, Lab.                   28,351
Luke Parker, C.                        17,517
Paul Lorber, LD                         2,607
Alan Craig, UKIP                        2,024
Scott Bartle, Green                     1,539
Elcena Jeffers, Ind.                      197
Lab. majority 10,834 (20.74%)
2.70% swing C. to Lab.
(2010: Lab. majority 8,028 (15.35%))

BRENTFORD & ISLEWORTH
E. 84,557   T. 57,355 (67.83%)   Lab. gain
*Ruth Cadbury, Lab.                    25,096
Mary Macleod, C.                       24,631
Richard Hendron, UKIP                   3,203
Joe Bourke, LD                          2,305
Daniel Goldsmith, Green                 2,120
Lab. majority 465 (0.81%)
2.23% swing C. to Lab.
(2010: C. majority 1,958 (3.64%))

BRENTWOOD & ONGAR
E. 72,461   T. 51,897 (71.62%)   C. hold
Eric Pickles, C.                       30,534
Michael McGough, UKIP                   8,724
Liam Preston, Lab.                      6,492
David Kendall, LD                       4,577
Reza Hossain, Green                     1,397
Robin Tilbrook, Eng. Dem.                 173
C. majority 21,810 (42.03%)
5.43% swing C. to UKIP
(2010: C. majority 16,921 (33.45%))

BRIDGWATER & SOMERSET WEST
E. 80,491   T. 54,447 (67.64%)   C. hold
Ian Liddell-Grainger, C.               25,020
Stephen Fitzgerald, UKIP               10,437
Mick Lerry, Lab.                        9,589
Theodore Butt Phillip, LD               6,765
Julie Harvey-Smith, Green               2,636
C. majority 14,583 (26.78%)
6.86% swing C. to UKIP
(2010: C. majority 9,249 (16.97%))

BRIGG & GOOLE
E. 68,486   T. 43,270 (63.18%)   C. hold
Andrew Percy, C.                       22,946
Jacky Crawford, Lab.                   11,770
David Jeffreys, UKIP                    6,694
Natalie Hurst, Green                      915
Liz Leffman, LD                           764
Trevor Dixon, Ind.                        153
Ray Spalding, IE                           28
C. majority 11,176 (25.83%)
7.05% swing Lab. to C.
(2010: C. majority 5,147 (11.73%))

BRIGHTON KEMPTOWN
E. 67,858   T. 45,306 (66.77%)   C. hold
Simon Kirby, C.                        18,428
Nancy Platts, Lab.                     17,738
Ian Buchanan, UKIP                      4,446
Davy Jones, Green                       3,187
Paul Chandler, LD                       1,365
Jacqueline Shodeke, SPGB                   73
Matt Taylor, Ind.                          69
C. majority 690 (1.52%)
0.79% swing C. to Lab.
(2010: C. majority 1,328 (3.11%))

BRIGHTON PAVILION
E. 76,557  T. 54,676 (71.42%)  Green hold
Caroline Lucas, Green                  22,871
Purna Sen, Lab.                        14,904
Clarence Mitchell, C.                  12,448
Nigel Carter, UKIP                      2,724
Chris Bowers, LD                        1,525
Nick Yeomans, Ind.                        116
Howard Pilott, SPGB                        88
Green majority 7,967 (14.57%)
6.08% swing Lab. to Green
(2010: Green majority 1,252 (2.42%))

## BRISTOL EAST
E. 71,965   T. 46,213 (64.22%)   Lab. hold
| | |
|---|---|
| Kerry McCarthy, Lab. | 18,148 |
| Theo Clarke, C. | 14,168 |
| James McMurray, UKIP | 7,152 |
| Lorraine Francis, Green | 3,827 |
| Abdul Malik, LD | 2,689 |
| Matt Gordon, TUSC | 229 |

Lab. majority 3,980 (8.61%)
0.17% swing C. to Lab.
(2010: Lab. majority 3,722 (8.27%))

## BRISTOL NORTH WEST
E. 76,626   T. 51,805 (67.61%)   C. hold
| | |
|---|---|
| Charlotte Leslie, C. | 22,767 |
| Darren Jones, Lab. | 17,823 |
| Michael Frost, UKIP | 4,889 |
| Clare Campion-Smith, LD | 3,214 |
| Justin Quinnell, Green | 2,952 |
| Anne Lemon, TUSC | 160 |

C. majority 4,944 (9.54%)
1.24% swing C. to Lab.
(2010: C. majority 3,274 (6.50%))

## BRISTOL SOUTH
E. 81,996   T. 50,842 (62.01%)   Lab. hold
| | |
|---|---|
| *Karin Smyth, Lab. | 19,505 |
| Isobel Grant, C. | 12,377 |
| Steve Wood, UKIP | 8,381 |
| Tony Dyer, Green | 5,861 |
| Mark Wright, LD | 4,416 |
| Tom Baldwin, TUSC | 302 |

Lab. majority 7,128 (14.02%)
0.76% swing Lab. to C.
(2010: Lab. majority 4,734 (9.79%))

## BRISTOL WEST
E. 89,198   T. 64,218 (71.99%)   Lab. gain
| | |
|---|---|
| *Thangam Debbonaire, Lab. | 22,900 |
| Darren Hall, Green | 17,227 |
| Stephen Williams, LD | 12,103 |
| Claire Hiscott, C. | 9,752 |
| Paul Turner, UKIP | 1,940 |
| Dawn Parry, Bristol | 204 |
| Stewart Weston, LU | 92 |

Lab. majority 5,673 (8.83%)
18.67% swing LD to Lab.
(2010: LD majority 11,366 (20.54%))

## BROADLAND
E. 74,680   T. 53,089 (71.09%)   C. hold
| | |
|---|---|
| Keith Simpson, C. | 26,808 |
| Chris Jones, Lab. | 9,970 |
| Stuart Agnew, UKIP | 8,881 |
| Steve Riley, LD | 5,178 |
| Andrew Boswell, Green | 2,252 |

C. majority 16,838 (31.72%)
0.33% swing C. to Lab.
(2010: C. majority 7,292 (13.84%))

## BROMLEY & CHISLEHURST
E. 65,476   T. 44,066 (67.30%)   C. hold
| | |
|---|---|
| Robert Neill, C. | 23,343 |
| John Courtneidge, Lab. | 9,779 |
| Emmett Jenner, UKIP | 6,285 |
| Sam Webber, LD | 2,836 |
| Roisin Robertson, Green | 1,823 |

C. majority 13,564 (30.78%)
3.09% swing C. to Lab.
(2010: C. majority 13,900 (31.56%))

## BROMSGROVE
E. 73,329   T. 52,245 (71.25%)   C. hold
| | |
|---|---|
| Sajid Javid, C. | 28,133 |
| Tom Ebbutt, Lab. | 11,604 |
| Stuart Cross, UKIP | 8,163 |
| Bart Ricketts, LD | 2,616 |
| Spoz Esposito, Green | 1,729 |

C. majority 16,529 (31.64%)
4.87% swing Lab. to C.
(2010: C. majority 11,308 (21.90%))

## BROXBOURNE
E. 72,944   T. 46,024 (63.09%)   C. hold
| | |
|---|---|
| Charles Walker, C. | 25,797 |
| David Platt, UKIP | 9,074 |
| Edward Robinson, Lab. | 8,470 |
| Anthony Rowlands, LD | 1,467 |
| Russell Secker, Green | 1,216 |

C. majority 16,723 (36.34%)
9.16% swing C. to UKIP
(2010: C. majority 18,804 (41.18%))

## BROXTOWE
E. 71,865   T. 53,440 (74.36%)   C. hold
| | |
|---|---|
| Anna Soubry, C. | 24,163 |
| Nick Palmer, Lab. | 19,876 |
| Frank Dunne, UKIP | 5,674 |
| Stan Heptinstall, LD | 2,120 |
| David Kirwan, Green | 1,544 |
| Ray Barry, JMB | 63 |

C. majority 4,287 (8.02%)
3.64% swing Lab. to C.
(2010: C. majority 389 (0.74%))

## BUCKINGHAM
E. 77,572   T. 53,692 (69.22%)
| | |
|---|---|
| | Speaker hold |
| John Bercow, Speaker | 34,617 |
| David Fowler, UKIP | 11,675 |
| Alan Francis, Green | 7,400 |

Speaker majority 22,942 (42.73%)
swing N/A
(2010: Speaker majority 12,529 (25.92%))

## BURNLEY
E. 64,486   T. 39,746 (61.64%)   Lab. gain
| | |
|---|---|
| *Julie Cooper, Lab. | 14,951 |
| Gordon Birtwistle, LD | 11,707 |
| Tom Commis, UKIP | 6,864 |
| Sarah Cockburn-Price, C. | 5,374 |
| Mike Hargreaves, Green | 850 |

Lab. majority 3,244 (8.16%)
6.25% swing LD to Lab.
(2010: LD majority 1,818 (4.34%))

## BURTON
E. 75,300   T. 49,334 (65.52%)   C. hold
| | |
|---|---|
| Andrew Griffiths, C. | 24,736 |
| Jon Wheale, Lab. | 13,484 |
| Mike Green, UKIP | 8,658 |
| David MacDonald, LD | 1,232 |
| Sam Patrone, Green | 1,224 |

C. majority 11,252 (22.81%)
5.08% swing Lab. to C.
(2010: C. majority 6,304 (12.65%))

## BURY NORTH
E. 67,580   T. 45,230 (66.93%)   C. hold
| | |
|---|---|
| David Nuttall, C. | 18,970 |
| James Frith, Lab. | 18,592 |
| Ian Henderson, UKIP | 5,595 |
| John Southworth, Green | 1,141 |
| Richard Baum, LD | 932 |

C. majority 378 (0.84%)
2.08% swing Lab. to C.
(2010: C. majority 2,243 (4.99%))

## BURY ST EDMUNDS
E. 85,993   T. 59,341 (69.01%)   C. hold
| | |
|---|---|
| *Jo Churchill, C. | 31,815 |
| Bill Edwards, Lab. | 10,514 |
| John Howlett, UKIP | 8,739 |
| Helen Geake, Green | 4,692 |
| David Chappell, LD | 3,581 |

C. majority 21,301 (35.90%)
2.52% swing Lab. to C.
(2010: C. majority 12,380 (21.08%))

## BURY SOUTH
E. 73,883   T. 47,215 (63.91%)   Lab. hold
| | |
|---|---|
| Ivan Lewis, Lab. | 21,272 |
| Daniel Critchlow, C. | 16,350 |
| Seamus Martin, UKIP | 6,299 |
| Paul Ankers, LD | 1,690 |
| Glyn Heath, Green | 1,434 |
| Valerie Morris, Eng. Dem. | 170 |

Lab. majority 4,922 (10.42%)
1.80% swing C. to Lab.
(2010: Lab. majority 3,292 (6.82%))

## CALDER VALLEY
E. 77,753   T. 53,541 (68.86%)   C. hold
| | |
|---|---|
| Craig Whittaker, C. | 23,354 |
| Josh Fenton-Glynn, Lab. | 18,927 |
| Paul Rogan, UKIP | 5,950 |
| Alisdair Calder McGregor, LD | 2,666 |
| Jenny Shepherd, Green | 2,090 |
| Rod Sutcliffe, Yorks | 389 |
| Joe Stead, Song | 165 |

C. majority 4,427 (8.27%)
2.08% swing C. to Lab.
(2010: C. majority 6,431 (12.42%))

## CAMBERWELL & PECKHAM
E. 80,507   T. 51,561 (64.05%)   Lab. hold
| | |
|---|---|
| Harriet Harman, Lab. | 32,614 |
| Naomi Newstead, C. | 6,790 |
| Amelia Womack, Green | 5,187 |
| Yahaya Kiingi, LD | 2,580 |
| David Kurten, UKIP | 2,413 |
| Prem Goyal, AP | 829 |
| Rebecca Fox, NHAP | 466 |
| Nick Wrack, TUSC | 292 |
| Alex Robertson, CISTA | 197 |
| Joshua Ogunleye, WRP | 107 |
| Felicity Anscomb, Whig | 86 |

Lab. majority 25,824 (50.08%)
1.96% swing C. to Lab.
(2010: Lab. majority 17,187 (36.84%))

## CAMBORNE & REDRUTH
E. 66,944   T. 45,868 (68.52%)   C. hold
| | |
|---|---|
| George Eustice, C. | 18,452 |
| Michael Foster, Lab. | 11,448 |
| Bob Smith, UKIP | 6,776 |
| Julia Goldsworthy, LD | 5,687 |
| Geoff Garbett, Green | 2,608 |
| Loveday Jenkin, Meb. Ker. | 897 |

C. majority 7,004 (15.27%)
2.98% swing C. to Lab.
(2010: C. majority 66 (0.16%))

## CAMBRIDGE
E. 83,384   T. 51,774 (62.09%)   Lab. gain
| | |
|---|---|
| *Daniel Zeichner, Lab. | 18,646 |
| Julian Huppert, LD | 18,047 |
| Chamali Fernando, C. | 8,117 |
| Rupert Read, Green | 4,109 |
| Patrick O'Flynn, UKIP | 2,668 |
| Keith Garrett, Reboot | 187 |

Lab. majority 599 (1.16%)
8.01% swing LD to Lab.
(2010: LD majority 6,792 (13.55%))

**CAMBRIDGESHIRE NORTH EAST**
E. 82,990    T. 51,780 (62.39%)    C. hold
Stephen Barclay, C.                           28,524
Andrew Charalambous, UKIP            11,650
Ken Rustidge, Lab.                              7,476
Lucy Nethsingha, LD                           2,314
Helen Scott-Daniels, Green                 1,816
C. majority 16,874 (32.59%)
6.54% swing C. to UKIP
(2010: C. majority 16,425 (31.43%))

**CAMBRIDGESHIRE NORTH WEST**
E. 91,783    T. 61,100 (66.57%)    C. hold
Shailesh Vara, C.                              32,070
Peter Reeve, UKIP                             12,275
Nick Thulbourn, Lab.                         10,927
Nicholas Sandford, LD                         3,479
Nicola Day, Green                              2,159
Fay Belham, CPA                                 190
C. majority 19,795 (32.40%)
4.90% swing C. to UKIP
(2010: C. majority 16,677 (28.61%))

**CAMBRIDGESHIRE SOUTH**
E. 84,132    T. 61,540 (73.15%)    C. hold
*Heidi Allen, C.                               31,454
Dan Greef, Lab.                               10,860
Sebastian Kindersley, LD                     9,368
Marion Mason, UKIP                            6,010
Simon Saggers, Green                          3,848
C. majority 20,594 (33.46%)
1.87% swing C. to Lab.
(2010: C. majority 7,838 (13.27%))

**CAMBRIDGESHIRE SOUTH EAST**
E. 84,570    T. 59,506 (70.36%)    C. hold
*Lucy Frazer, C.                              28,845
Jonathan Chatfield, LD                      12,008
Huw Jones, Lab.                                9,013
Deborah Rennie, UKIP                          6,593
Clive Semmens, Green                          3,047
C. majority 16,837 (28.29%)
8.99% swing LD to C.
(2010: C. majority 5,946 (10.32%))

**CANNOCK CHASE**
E. 74,531    T. 47,099 (63.19%)    C. hold
*Amanda Milling, C.                          20,811
Janos Toth, Lab.                             15,888
Grahame Wiggin, UKIP                          8,224
Ian Jackson, LD                               1,270
Paul Woodhead, Green                           906
C. majority 4,923 (10.45%)
1.72% swing Lab. to C.
(2010: C. majority 3,195 (7.01%))

**CANTERBURY**
E. 83,481    T. 53,465 (64.04%)    C. hold
Julian Brazier, C.                           22,918
Hugh Lanning, Lab.                           13,120
Jim Gascoyne, UKIP                            7,289
James Flanagan, LD                            6,227
Stuart Jeffery, Green                         3,746
Robert Cox, SPGB                               165
C. majority 9,798 (18.33%)
5.17% swing C. to Lab.
(2010: C. majority 6,048 (12.29%))

**CARLISLE**
E. 65,827    T. 42,587 (64.70%)    C. hold
John Stevenson, C.                           18,873
Lee Sherriff, Lab.                           16,099
Fiona Mills, UKIP                             5,277
Helen Davison, Green                          1,125
Loraine Birchall, LD                         1,087
Alfred Okam, Ind.                              126
C. majority 2,774 (6.51%)
2.25% swing Lab. to C.
(2010: C. majority 853 (2.02%))

**CARSHALTON & WALLINGTON**
E. 69,866    T. 47,613 (68.15%)    LD hold
Tom Brake, LD                                16,603
Matthew Maxwell Scott, C.                    15,093
Siobhan Tate, Lab.                            7,150
Bill Main-Ian, UKIP                           7,049
Ross Hemingway, Green                         1,492
Ashley Dickenson, CPA                          177
Richard Edmonds, NF                             49
LD majority 1,510 (3.17%)
4.14% swing LD to C.
(2010: LD majority 5,260 (11.46%))

**CASTLE POINT**
E. 68,170    T. 45,450 (66.67%)    C. hold
Rebecca Harris, C.                           23,112
Jamie Huntman, UKIP                          14,178
Joe Cooke, Lab.                               6,283
Dominic Ellis, Green                          1,076
Sereena Davey, LD                              801
C. majority 8,934 (19.66%)
swing N/A
(2010: C. majority 7,632 (16.95%))

**CHARNWOOD**
E. 77,269    T. 52,261 (67.64%)    C. hold
*Edward Argar, C.                            28,384
Sean Kelly-Walsh, Lab.                       11,453
Lynton Yates, UKIP                            8,330
Simon Sansome, LD                             3,605
Cathy Duffy, BNP                               489
C. majority 16,931 (32.40%)
1.23% swing Lab. to C.
(2010: C. majority 15,029 (28.07%))

**CHATHAM & AYLESFORD**
E. 68,625    T. 43,073 (62.77%)    C. hold
Tracey Crouch, C.                            21,614
Tristan Osborne, Lab.                        10,159
Ian Wallace, UKIP                             8,581
Thomas Quinton, LD                            1,360
Luke Balnave, Green                           1,101
John-Wesley Gibson, CPA                        133
Ivor Riddell, TUSC                             125
C. majority 11,455 (26.59%)
6.37% swing Lab. to C.
(2010: C. majority 6,069 (13.85%))

**CHEADLE**
E. 73,239    T. 53,095 (72.50%)    C. gain
*Mary Robinson, C.                           22,889
Mark Hunter, LD                              16,436
Martin Miller, Lab.                           8,673
Shaun Hopkins, UKIP                           4,423
Matthew Torbitt, Ind.                          390
Drew Carswell, Above                           208
Helen Bashford, IE                              76
C. majority 6,453 (12.15%)
9.19% swing LD to C.
(2010: LD majority 3,272 (6.23%))

**CHELMSFORD**
E. 78,580    T. 53,817 (68.49%)    C. hold
Simon Burns, C.                              27,732
Chris Vince, Lab.                             9,482
Mark Gough, UKIP                              7,652
Stephen Robinson, LD                          6,394
Angela Thomson, Green                         1,892
Henry Boyle, Lib.                              665
C. majority 18,250 (33.91%)
0.65% swing C. to Lab.
(2010: C. majority 5,110 (9.36%))

**CHELSEA & FULHAM**
E. 63,478    T. 40,226 (63.37%)    C. hold
Greg Hands, C.                               25,322
Alexandra Sanderson, Lab.                     9,300
Simon Bailey, LD                              2,091
Adrian Noble, UKIP                            2,039
Guy Rubin, Green                              1,474
C. majority 16,022 (39.83%)
1.06% swing C. to Lab.
(2010: C. majority 16,722 (41.96%))

**CHELTENHAM**
E. 77,286    T. 53,735 (69.53%)    C. gain
*Alex Chalk, C.                              24,790
Martin Horwood, LD                           18,274
Paul Gilbert, Lab.                            3,902
Christina Simmonds, UKIP                      3,808
Adam Van Coevorden, Green                     2,689
Richard Lupson-Darnell, Ind.                   272
C. majority 6,516 (12.13%)
10.72% swing LD to C.
(2010: LD majority 4,920 (9.32%))

**CHESHAM & AMERSHAM**
E. 73,423    T. 52,731 (71.82%)    C. hold
Cheryl Gillan, C.                            31,138
Alan Stevens, UKIP                            7,218
Benjamin Davies, Lab.                         6,712
Kirsten Johnson, LD                           4,761
Gill Walker, Green                            2,902
C. majority 23,920 (45.36%)
5.47% swing C. to UKIP
(2010: C. majority 16,710 (31.86%))

**CHESTER, CITY OF**
E. 72,269    T. 51,161 (70.79%)    Lab. gain
*Chris Matheson, Lab.                        22,118
Stephen Mosley, C.                           22,025
Stephen Ingram, UKIP                          4,148
Bob Thompson, LD                              2,870
Lab. majority 93 (0.18%)
2.85% swing C. to Lab.
(2010: C. majority 2,583 (5.52%))

**CHESTERFIELD**
E. 72,078    T. 45,567 (63.22%)    Lab. hold
Toby Perkins, Lab.                           21,829
Mark Vivis, C.                                8,231
Stuart Yeowart, UKIP                          7,523
Julia Cambridge, LD                           6,301
Matthew Genn, Green                           1,352
Matt Whale, TUSC                               202
Tommy Holgate, Peace                           129
Lab. majority 13,598 (29.84%)
3.27% swing C. to Lab.
(2010: Lab. majority 549 (1.20%))

**CHICHESTER**
E. 83,575    T. 57,139 (68.37%)    C. hold
Andrew Tyrie, C.                             32,953
Andrew Moncreiff, UKIP                        8,540
Mark Farwell, Lab.                            6,933
Andrew Smith, LD                              4,865
Jasper Richmond, Green                        3,742
Andrew Emerson, Patria                         106
C. majority 24,413 (42.73%)
2.90% swing C. to UKIP
(2010: C. majority 15,877 (27.96%))

**CHINGFORD & WOODFORD GREEN**
E. 66,691   T. 43,804 (65.68%)   C. hold
Iain Duncan Smith, C.                    20,999
Bilal Mahmood, Lab.                      12,613
Freddy Vachha, UKIP                       5,644
Anne Crook, LD                            2,400
Rebecca Tully, Green                      1,854
Len Hockey, TUSC                            241
Lisa McKenzie, Class War                     53
C. majority 8,386 (19.14%)
5.46% swing C. to Lab.
(2010: C. majority 12,963 (30.07%))

**CHIPPENHAM**
E. 74,225   T. 55,407 (74.65%)   C. gain
*Michelle Donelan, C.                    26,354
Duncan Hames, LD                         16,278
Julia Reid, UKIP                          5,884
Andy Newman, Lab.                         4,561
Tina Johnston, Green                      2,330
C. majority 10,076 (18.19%)
11.45% swing LD to C.
(2010: LD majority 2,470 (4.72%))

**CHIPPING BARNET**
E. 77,853   T. 53,013 (68.09%)   C. hold
Theresa Villiers, C.                     25,759
Amy Trevethan, Lab.                      18,103
Victor Kaye, UKIP                         4,151
A Poppy, Green                            2,501
Marisha Ray, LD                           2,381
Mehdi Akhavan, ND                           118
C. majority 7,656 (14.44%)
4.56% swing C. to Lab.
(2010: C. majority 11,927 (23.57%))

**CHORLEY**
E. 74,679   T. 51,712 (69.25%)   Lab. hold
Lindsay Hoyle, Lab.                      23,322
Rob Loughenbury, C.                      18,792
Mark Smith, UKIP                          6,995
Stephen Fenn, LD                          1,354
Alistair Straw, Green                     1,111
Adrian Maudsley, Ind.                       138
Lab. majority 4,530 (8.76%)
1.78% swing C. to Lab.
(2010: Lab. majority 2,593 (5.21%))

**CHRISTCHURCH**
E. 69,302   T. 49,707 (71.73%)   C. hold
Christopher Chope, C.                    28,887
Robin Grey, UKIP                         10,663
Andrew Satherley, Lab.                    4,745
Andy Canning, LD                          3,263
Shona Dunn, Green                         2,149
C. majority 18,224 (36.66%)
5.64% swing C. to UKIP
(2010: C. majority 15,410 (31.18%))

**CITIES OF LONDON & WESTMINSTER**
E. 60,992   T. 36,185 (59.33%)   C. hold
Mark Field, C.                           19,570
Nik Slingsby, Lab.                        9,899
Belinda Brooks-Gordon, LD                 2,521
Hugh Small, Green                         1,953
Robert Stephenson, UKIP                   1,894
Edouard-Henri Desforges, CISTA             160
Jill McLachlan, CPA                         129
Adam Clifford, Class War                     59
C. majority 9,671 (26.73%)
1.63% swing C. to Lab.
(2010: C. majority 11,076 (29.99%))

**CLACTON**
E. 68,936   T. 44,207 (64.13%)   UKIP hold
Douglas Carswell, UKIP                   19,642
Giles Watling, C.                        16,205
Tim Young, Lab.                           6,364
Chris Southall, Green                     1,184
David Grace, LD                             812
UKIP majority 3,437 (7.77%)
swing N/A
(2010: C. majority 12,068 (27.99%))
(2014: UKIP majority 12,404 (35.10%))

**CLEETHORPES**
E. 70,514   T. 45,089 (63.94%)   C. hold
Martin Vickers, C.                       21,026
Peter Keith, Lab.                        13,133
Stephen Harness, UKIP                     8,356
Roy Horobin, LD                           1,346
Carol Thornton, Green                     1,013
Malcolm Morland, TUSC                       215
C. majority 7,893 (17.51%)
3.97% swing Lab. to C.
(2010: C. majority 4,298 (9.56%))

**COLCHESTER**
E. 74,203   T. 48,593 (65.49%)   C. gain
*Will Quince, C.                         18,919
Bob Russell, LD                          13,344
Jordan Newell, Lab.                       7,852
John Pitts, UKIP                          5,870
Mark Goacher, Green                       2,499
Ken Scrimshaw, CPA                          109
C. majority 5,575 (11.47%)
13.30% swing LD to C.
(2010: LD majority 6,982 (15.13%))

**COLNE VALLEY**
E. 82,510   T. 56,800 (68.84%)   C. hold
Jason McCartney, C.                      25,246
Jane East, Lab.                          19,868
Melanie Roberts, UKIP                     5,734
Cahal Burke, LD                           3,407
Chas Ball, Green                          1,919
Paul Salveson, Yorks                        572
Melodie Staniforth, ND                       54
C. majority 5,378 (9.47%)
0.56% swing C. to Lab.
(2010: C. majority 4,837 (8.75%))

**CONGLETON**
E. 72,398   T. 50,976 (70.41%)   C. hold
Fiona Bruce, C.                          27,164
Darren Price, Lab.                       10,391
Lee Slaughter, UKIP                       6,922
Peter Hirst, LD                           4,623
Alec Heath, Green                         1,876
C. majority 16,773 (32.90%)
2.17% swing Lab. to C.
(2010: C. majority 7,063 (13.91%))

**COPELAND**
E. 62,119   T. 39,631 (63.80%)   Lab. hold
Jamie Reed, Lab.                         16,750
Stephen Haraldsen, C.                    14,186
Michael Pye, UKIP                         6,148
Danny Gallagher, LD                       1,368
Allan Todd, Green                         1,179
Lab. majority 2,564 (6.47%)
1.24% swing Lab. to C.
(2010: Lab. majority 3,833 (8.96%))

**CORBY**
E. 79,775   T. 56,174 (70.42%)   C. gain
*Tom Pursglove, C.                       24,023
Andy Sawford, Lab. Co-op                 21,611
Margot Parker, UKIP                       7,708
Peter Harris, LD                          1,458
Jonathan Hornett, Green                   1,374
C. majority 2,412 (4.29%)
0.40% swing Lab. to C.
(2010: C. majority 1,895 (3.49%))
(2012: Lab. majority 7,791 (21.84%))

**CORNWALL NORTH**
E. 67,192   T. 48,245 (71.80%)   C. gain
*Scott Mann, C.                          21,689
Dan Rogerson, LD                         15,068
Julie Lingard, UKIP                       6,121
John Whitby, Lab.                         2,621
Amanda Pennington, Green                  2,063
Jeremy Jefferies, Meb. Ker.                 631
John Allman, Restore                         52
C. majority 6,621 (13.72%)
10.91% swing LD to C.
(2010: LD majority 2,981 (6.36%))

**CORNWALL SOUTH EAST**
E. 71,071   T. 50,498 (71.05%)   C. hold
Sheryll Murray, C.                       25,516
Phil Hutty, LD                            8,521
Bradley Monk, UKIP                        7,698
Declan Lloyd, Lab.                        4,692
Martin Corney, Green                      2,718
Andrew Long, Meb. Ker.                    1,003
George Trubody, Ind.                        350
C. majority 16,995 (33.65%)
13.58% swing LD to C.
(2010: C. majority 3,220 (6.49%))

**COTSWOLDS, THE**
E. 78,292   T. 56,667 (72.38%)   C. hold
Geoffrey Clifton-Brown, C.               32,045
Paul Hodgkinson, LD                      10,568
Chris Harlow, UKIP                        6,188
Manjinder Kang, Lab.                      5,240
Penny Burgess, Green                      2,626
C. majority 21,477 (37.90%)
7.22% swing LD to C.
(2010: C. majority 12,864 (23.46%))

**COVENTRY NORTH EAST**
E. 76,401   T. 42,231 (55.28%)   Lab. hold
*Colleen Fletcher, Lab.                  22,025
Michelle Lowe, C.                         9,751
Avtar Taggar, UKIP                        6,278
Russell Field, LD                         2,007
Matthew Handley, Green                    1,245
Nicky Downes, TUSC                          633
William Sidhu, Ch. M.                       292
Lab. majority 12,274 (29.06%)
0.96% swing C. to Lab.
(2010: Lab. majority 11,775 (27.14%))

**COVENTRY NORTH WEST**
E. 74,597   T. 45,246 (60.65%)   Lab. hold
Geoffrey Robinson, Lab.                  18,557
Parvez Akhtar, C.                        14,048
Harjinder Singh Sehmi, UKIP               7,101
Laura Vesty, Green                        1,961
Andrew Furse, LD                          1,810
Dave Nellist, TUSC                        1,769
Lab. majority 4,509 (9.97%)
1.77% swing Lab. to C.
(2010: Lab. majority 6,288 (13.51%))

**COVENTRY SOUTH**
E. 71,380   T. 43,699 (61.22%)   Lab. hold
Jim Cunningham, Lab.                 18,472
Gary Ridley, C.                      15,284
Mark Taylor, UKIP                     5,709
Greg Judge, LD                        1,779
Benjamin Gallaher, Green              1,719
Judy Griffiths, TUSC                    650
Chris Rooney, Mainstream                 86
Lab. majority 3,188 (7.30%)
0.54% swing Lab. to C.
(2010: Lab. majority 3,845 (8.37%))

**CRAWLEY**
E. 73,940   T. 48,550 (65.66%)   C. hold
Henry Smith, C.                      22,829
Chris Oxlade, Lab.                   16,303
Chris Brown, UKIP                     6,979
Sarah Osborne, LD                     1,339
Guy Hudson, Green                     1,100
C. majority 6,526 (13.44%)
0.48% swing Lab. to C.
(2010: C. majority 5,928 (12.48%))

**CREWE & NANTWICH**
E. 74,039   T. 49,896 (67.39%)   C. hold
Edward Timpson, C.                   22,445
Adrian Heald, Lab.                   18,825
Richard Lee, UKIP                     7,252
Roy Wood, LD                          1,374
C. majority 3,620 (7.26%)
2.29% swing C. to Lab.
(2010: C. majority 6,046 (11.84%))

**CROYDON CENTRAL**
E. 78,171   T. 52,941 (67.72%)   C. hold
Gavin Barwell, C.                    22,753
Sarah Jones, Lab.                    22,588
Peter Staveley, UKIP                  4,810
Esther Sutton, Green                  1,454
James Robert Fearnley, LD             1,152
April Ashley, TUSC                      127
Martin Camden, UKPDP                     57
C. majority 165 (0.31%)
2.83% swing C. to Lab.
(2010: C. majority 2,969 (5.97%))

**CROYDON NORTH**
E. 85,951  T. 53,522 (62.27%)
                          Lab. Co-op hold
Steve Reed, Lab. Co-op               33,513
Vidhi Mohan, C.                      12,149
Winston McKenzie, UKIP                2,899
Shasha Khan, Green                    2,515
Joanna Corbin, LD                     1,919
Glen Hart, TUSC                         261
Lee Berks, Ind.                         141
Ben Stevenson, Comm.                    125
Lab. Co-op majority 21,364 (39.92%)
4.01% swing C. to Lab.
(2010: Lab. majority 16,483 (31.90%))
(2012: Lab. majority 11,761 (47.87%))

**CROYDON SOUTH**
E. 82,010   T. 57,712 (70.37%)   C. hold
*Chris Philp, C.                     31,448
Emily Benn, Lab.                     14,308
Kathleen Garner, UKIP                 6,068
Gill Hickson, LD                      3,448
Peter Underwood, Green                2,154
Mark Samuel, Croydon                    221
Jon Bigger, Class War                    65
C. majority 17,140 (29.70%)
0.59% swing C. to Lab.
(2010: C. majority 15,818 (28.08%))

**DAGENHAM & RAINHAM**
E. 69,049   T. 43,050 (62.35%)   Lab. hold
Jon Cruddas, Lab.                    17,830
Peter Harris, UKIP                   12,850
Julie Marson, C.                     10,492
Kate Simpson, Green                     806
Denise Capstick, LD                     717
Tess Culnane, BNP                       151
Terry London, ND                        133
Kim Gandy, Eng. Dem.                     71
Lab. majority 4,980 (11.57%)
12.58% swing Lab. to UKIP
(2010: Lab. majority 2,630 (5.95%))

**DARLINGTON**
E. 65,832   T. 41,141 (62.49%)   Lab. hold
Jenny Chapman, Lab.                  17,637
Peter Cuthbertson, C.                14,479
David Hodgson, UKIP                   5,392
Anne-Marie Curry, LD                  1,966
Michael Cherrington, Green            1,444
Alan Docherty, TUSC                     223
Lab. majority 3,158 (7.68%)
0.11% swing Lab. to C.
(2010: Lab. majority 3,388 (7.90%))

**DARTFORD**
E. 76,686   T. 52,418 (68.35%)   C. hold
Gareth Johnson, C.                   25,670
Simon Thomson, Lab.                  13,325
Elizabeth Jones, UKIP                10,434
Simon Beard, LD                       1,454
Andy Blatchford, Green                1,324
Steve Uncles, Eng. Dem.                 211
C. majority 12,345 (23.55%)
1.16% swing Lab. to C.
(2010: C. majority 10,628 (21.22%))

**DAVENTRY**
E. 72,753   T. 52,518 (72.19%)   C. hold
Chris Heaton-Harris, C.              30,550
Abigail Campbell, Lab.                9,491
Michael Gerard, UKIP                  8,296
Callum Delhoy, LD                     2,352
Steve Whiffen, Green                  1,829
C. majority 21,059 (40.10%)
0.31% swing C. to Lab.
(2010: C. majority 19,188 (37.06%))

**DENTON & REDDISH**
E. 66,574   T. 38,681 (58.10%)   Lab. hold
Andrew Gwynne, Lab.                  19,661
Lana Hempsall, C.                     9,150
Andrew Fairfoull, UKIP                7,225
Nick Koopman, Green                   1,466
Mark Jewell, LD                         957
Victoria Lofas, Ind.                    222
Lab. majority 10,511 (27.17%)
0.53% swing C. to Lab.
(2010: Lab. majority 9,831 (26.12%))

**DERBY NORTH**
E. 64,739   T. 44,745 (69.12%)   C. gain
*Amanda Solloway, C.                 16,402
Chris Williamson, Lab.               16,361
Tilly Ward, UKIP                      6,532
Lucy Care, LD                         3,832
Alice Mason-Power, Green              1,618
C. majority 41 (0.09%)
0.73% swing Lab. to C.
(2010: Lab. majority 613 (1.36%))

**DERBY SOUTH**
E. 70,247   T. 40,820 (58.11%)   Lab. hold
Margaret Beckett, Lab.               20,007
Evonne Williams, C.                  11,179
Victor Webb, UKIP                     6,341
Joe Naitta, LD                        1,717
David Foster, Green                   1,208
Chris Fernandez, TUSC                   225
David Gale, Brit. Ind.                  143
Lab. majority 8,828 (21.63%)
3.38% swing C. to Lab.
(2010: Lab. majority 6,122 (14.86%))

**DERBYSHIRE DALES**
E. 63,470   T. 47,361 (74.62%)   C. hold
Patrick McLoughlin, C.               24,805
Andy Botham, Lab.                    10,761
John Young, UKIP                      5,508
Benjamin Fearn, LD                    3,965
Ian Wood, Green                       2,173
Amila Y'Mech, Humanity                  149
C. majority 14,044 (29.65%)
1.54% swing C. to Lab.
(2010: C. majority 13,866 (29.64%))

**DERBYSHIRE MID**
E. 67,576   T. 47,729 (70.63%)   C. hold
Pauline Latham, C.                   24,908
Nicola Heaton, Lab.                  12,134
Martin Fitzpatrick, UKIP              6,497
Hilary Jones, LD                      2,292
Sue MacFarlane, Green                 1,898
C. majority 12,774 (26.76%)
1.46% swing Lab. to C.
(2010: C. majority 11,292 (23.85%))

**DERBYSHIRE NORTH EAST**
E. 71,456  T. 47,948 (67.10%)   Lab. hold
Natascha Engel, Lab.                 19,488
Lee Rowley, C.                       17,605
James Bush, UKIP                      7,631
David Batey, LD                       2,004
David Kesteven, Green                 1,059
Rob Lane, Ind.                          161
Lab. majority 1,883 (3.93%)
0.64% swing Lab. to C.
(2010: Lab. majority 2,445 (5.20%))

**DERBYSHIRE SOUTH**
E. 74,395   T. 50,762 (68.23%)   C. hold
Heather Wheeler, C.                  25,066
Cheryl Pidgeon, Lab.                 13,595
Alan Graves, UKIP                     8,998
Lorraine Johnson, LD                  1,887
Marianne Bamkin, Green                1,216
C. majority 11,471 (22.60%)
4.23% swing Lab. to C.
(2010: C. majority 7,128 (14.14%))

**DEVIZES**
E. 69,211   T. 49,006 (70.81%)   C. hold
Claire Perry, C.                     28,295
David Pollitt, UKIP                   7,544
Chris Watts, Lab.                     6,360
Manda Rigby, LD                       3,954
Emma Dawnay, Green                    2,853
C. majority 20,751 (42.34%)
4.12% swing C. to UKIP
(2010: C. majority 13,005 (28.06%))

**DEVON CENTRAL**
E. 72,737   T. 54,448 (74.86%)   C. hold
Mel Stride, C.                                    28,436
John Conway, UKIP                              7,171
Lynne Richards, Lab.                          6,985
Alex White, LD                                    6,643
Andy Williamson, Green                      4,866
Arthur Price, Ind.                                 347
C. majority 21,265 (39.06%)
3.55% swing C. to UKIP
(2010: C. majority 9,230 (17.13%))

**DEVON EAST**
E. 74,224   T. 54,717 (73.72%)   C. hold
Hugo Swire, C.                                    25,401
Claire Wright, Ind.                             13,140
Andrew Chapman, UKIP                        6,870
Steve Race, Lab.                                  5,591
Stuart Mole, LD                                   3,715
C. majority 12,261 (22.41%)
swing N/A
(2010: C. majority 9,114 (17.17%))

**DEVON NORTH**
E. 74,737   T. 52,320 (70.01%)   C. gain
*Peter Heaton-Jones, C.                      22,341
Nick Harvey, LD                                 15,405
Steve Crowther, UKIP                          7,719
Mark Cann, Lab.                                   3,699
Ricky Knight, Green                            3,018
Gerrard Sables, Comm.                          138
C. majority 6,936 (13.26%)
12.30% swing LD to C.
(2010: LD majority 5,821 (11.34%))

**DEVON SOUTH WEST**
E. 71,035   T. 50,372 (70.91%)   C. hold
Gary Streeter, C.                                28,500
Chaz Singh, Lab.                                  8,391
Robin Julian, UKIP                              7,306
Tom Davies, LD                                    3,767
Win Scutt, Green                                2,408
C. majority 20,109 (39.92%)
1.82% swing C. to Lab.
(2010: C. majority 15,874 (31.84%))

**DEVON WEST & TORRIDGE**
E. 78,582   T. 56,584 (72.01%)   C. hold
Geoffrey Cox, C.                                 28,774
Derek Sargent, UKIP                          10,371
Paula Dolphin, LD                              7,483
Mike Sparling, Lab.                             6,015
Cathrine Simmons, Green                    3,941
C. majority 18,403 (32.52%)
3.83% swing C. to UKIP
(2010: C. majority 2,957 (5.35%))

**DEWSBURY**
E. 79,765   T. 53,630 (67.24%)   Lab. gain
*Paula Sherriff, Lab.                          22,406
Simon Reevell, C.                               20,955
Mark Thackray, UKIP                          6,649
Ednan Hussain, LD                             1,924
Adrian Cruden, Green                        1,366
Richard Carter, Yorks                            236
Steve Hakes, CPA                                   94
Lab. majority 1,451 (2.71%)
2.77% swing C. to Lab.
(2010: C. majority 1,526 (2.83%))

**DON VALLEY**
E. 71,299   T. 42,486 (59.59%)   Lab. hold
Caroline Flint, Lab.                           19,621
Carl Jackson, C.                                 10,736
Guy Aston, UKIP                                 9,963
Rene Paterson, LD                              1,487
Steve Williams, TUSC                             437
Louise Dutton, Eng. Dem.                     242
Lab. majority 8,885 (20.91%)
6.32% swing C. to Lab.
(2010: Lab. majority 3,595 (8.28%))

**DONCASTER CENTRAL**
E. 71,136   T. 40,420 (56.82%)   Lab. hold
Rosie Winterton, Lab.                        19,840
Chris Hodgson, UKIP                          9,747
Zoe Metcalfe, C.                                 8,386
John Brown, LD                                   1,717
Mev Akram, TUSC                                  421
David Burnett, Eng. Dem.                      309
Lab. majority 10,093 (24.97%)
5.66% swing Lab. to UKIP
(2010: Lab. majority 6,229 (14.92%))

**DONCASTER NORTH**
E. 70,898   T. 39,501 (55.72%)   Lab. hold
Ed Miliband, Lab.                               20,708
Kim Parkinson, UKIP                          8,928
Mark Fletcher, C.                                7,235
Penny Baker, LD                                 1,005
Peter Kennedy, Green                           757
David Allen, Eng. Dem.                         448
Mary Jackson, TUSC                             258
Nick The Flying Brick, Loony             162
Lab. majority 11,780 (29.82%)
6.59% swing Lab. to UKIP
(2010: Lab. majority 10,909 (26.30%))

**DORSET MID & POOLE NORTH**
E. 68,917   T. 46,499 (67.47%)   C. gain
*Michael Tomlinson, C.                      23,639
Vikki Slade, LD                                 13,109
Richard Turner, UKIP                          5,663
Patrick Canavan, Lab.                         2,767
Mark Chivers, Green                           1,321
C. majority 10,530 (22.65%)
11.61% swing LD to C.
(2010: LD majority 269 (0.57%))

**DORSET NORTH**
E. 74,576   T. 53,385 (71.58%)   C. hold
*Simon Hoare, C.                               30,227
Steve Unwin, UKIP                              9,109
Hugo Mieville, LD                              6,226
Kim Fendley, Lab.                               4,785
Richard Barrington, Green                 3,038
C. majority 21,118 (39.56%)
3.15% swing C. to UKIP
(2010: C. majority 7,625 (14.08%))

**DORSET SOUTH**
E. 71,974   T. 48,597 (67.52%)   C. hold
Richard Drax, C.                                23,756
Simon Bowkett, Lab.                         11,762
Malcolm Shakesby, UKIP                    7,304
Howard Legg, LD                                2,901
Jane Burnet, Green                            2,275
Mervyn Stewkesbury, Ind.                    435
Andy Kirkwood, Active Dem.                164
C. majority 11,994 (24.68%)
4.94% swing Lab. to C.
(2010: C. majority 7,443 (14.79%))

**DORSET WEST**
E. 78,427   T. 56,458 (71.99%)   C. hold
Oliver Letwin, C.                               28,329
Ros Kayes, LD                                    12,199
David Glossop, UKIP                          7,055
Rachel Rogers, Lab.                            5,633
Peter Barton, Green                           3,242
C. majority 16,130 (28.57%)
10.86% swing LD to C.
(2010: C. majority 3,923 (6.84%))

**DOVER**
E. 72,929   T. 50,224 (68.87%)   C. hold
Charlie Elphicke, C.                          21,737
Clair Hawkins, Lab.                           15,443
David Little, UKIP                             10,177
Sarah Smith, LD                                 1,572
Jolyon Trimingham, Green                 1,295
C. majority 6,294 (12.53%)
1.03% swing Lab. to C.
(2010: C. majority 5,274 (10.47%))

**DUDLEY NORTH**
E. 60,718   T. 37,992 (62.57%)   Lab. hold
Ian Austin, Lab.                                 15,885
Les Jones, C.                                      11,704
Bill Etheridge, UKIP                          9,113
Will Duckworth, Green                         517
Mike Collins, LD                                   478
Rehan Afzal, APNI                                156
Dave Pitt, TUSC                                    139
Lab. majority 4,181 (11.00%)
4.66% swing C. to Lab.
(2010: Lab. majority 649 (1.68%))

**DUDLEY SOUTH**
E. 60,363   T. 38,210 (63.30%)   C. hold
*Mike Wood, C.                                 16,723
Natasha Millward, Lab.                      12,453
Paul Brothwood, UKIP                        7,236
Vicky Duckworth, Green                        970
Martin Turner, LD                                 828
C. majority 4,270 (11.18%)
0.54% swing C. to Lab.
(2010: C. majority 3,856 (10.10%))

**DULWICH & WEST NORWOOD**
E. 75,244   T. 51,362 (68.26%)   Lab. hold
*Helen Hayes, Lab.                            27,772
Resham Kotecha, C.                          11,650
James Barber, LD                               5,055
Rashid Nix, Green                              4,844
Rathy Alagaratnam, UKIP                   1,606
Steve Nally, TUSC                                248
David Lambert, Ind.                              125
Amadu Kanumansa, AP                         62
Lab. majority 16,122 (31.39%)
3.48% swing C. to Lab.
(2010: Lab. majority 9,365 (19.42%))

**DURHAM, CITY OF**
E. 68,741   T. 45,669 (66.44%)   Lab. hold
Roberta Blackman-Woods, Lab.         21,596
Rebecca Coulson, C.                         10,157
Liam Clark, UKIP                                5,232
Craig Martin, LD                                5,153
Jonathan Elmer, Green                      2,687
John Marshall, Ind.                               649
Jon Collings, Ind.                                  195
Lab. majority 11,439 (25.05%)
2.99% swing Lab. to C.
(2010: Lab. majority 3,067 (6.63%))

DURHAM NORTH
E. 65,373   T. 40,146 (61.41%)   Lab. hold
Kevan Jones, Lab. 22,047
Laetitia Glossop, C. 8,403
Malcolm Bint, UKIP 6,404
Peter Maughan, LD 2,046
Vicki Nolan, Green 1,246
Lab. majority 13,644 (33.99%)
2.25% swing C. to Lab.
(2010: Lab. majority 12,076 (29.48%))

DURHAM NORTH WEST
E. 69,817   T. 42,818 (61.33%)   Lab. hold
Pat Glass, Lab. 20,074
Charlotte Haitham-Taylor, C. 10,018
Bruce Reid, UKIP 7,265
Owen Temple, LD 3,894
Mark Shilcock, Green 1,567
Lab. majority 10,056 (23.49%)
0.59% swing C. to Lab.
(2010: Lab. majority 7,612 (17.37%))

EALING CENTRAL & ACTON
E. 71,238   T. 50,894 (71.44%)   Lab. gain
*Rupa Huq, Lab. 22,002
Angie Bray, C. 21,728
Jon Ball, LD 3,106
Peter Florence, UKIP 1,926
Tom Sharman, Green 1,841
Jonathan Notley, Ind. 125
Scott Dore, WRP 73
Tammy Rendle, Above 54
Andrzej Rygielski, EP 39
Lab. majority 274 (0.54%)
4.21% swing C. to Lab.
(2010: C. majority 3,716 (7.87%))

EALING NORTH
E. 73,836   T. 48,510 (65.70%)   Lab. hold
Stephen Pound, Lab. 26,745
Thomas O'Malley, C. 14,419
Afzal Akram, UKIP 3,922
Meena Hans, Green 1,635
Kevin McNamara, LD 1,575
David Hofman, TUSC 214
Lab. majority 12,326 (25.41%)
2.95% swing C. to Lab.
(2010: Lab. majority 9,301 (19.51%))

EALING SOUTHALL
E. 65,495   T. 43,321 (66.14%)   Lab. hold
Virendra Sharma, Lab. 28,147
James Symes, C. 9,387
Jaspreet Mahal, Green 2,007
John Poynton, UKIP 1,769
Kavya Kaushik, LD 1,550
Jagdeesh Singh, Nat. Lib. 461
Lab. majority 18,760 (43.30%)
10.79% swing C. to Lab.
(2010: Lab. majority 9,291 (21.73%))

EASINGTON
E. 61,675   T. 34,624 (56.14%)   Lab. hold
Grahame Morris, Lab. 21,132
Jonathan Arnott, UKIP 6,491
Chris Hampsheir, C. 4,478
Luke Armstrong, LD 834
Susan McDonnell, NE 810
Martie Warin, Green 733
Steve Colborn, SPGB 146
Lab. majority 14,641 (42.29%)
5.99% swing Lab. to UKIP
(2010: Lab. majority 14,982 (42.91%))

EAST HAM
E. 87,378   T. 52,290 (59.84%)   Lab. hold
Stephen Timms, Lab. 40,563
Samir Jassal, C. 6,311
Daniel Oxley, UKIP 2,622
Tamsin Omond, Green 1,299
David Thorpe, LD 856
Mohammed Aslam, Community 409
Lois Austin, TUSC 230
Lab. majority 34,252 (65.50%)
5.13% swing C. to Lab.
(2010: Lab. majority 27,826 (55.24%))

EASTBOURNE
E. 78,262   T. 52,907 (67.60%)   C. gain
*Caroline Ansell, C. 20,934
Stephen Lloyd, LD 20,201
Nigel Jones, UKIP 6,139
Jake Lambert, Lab. 4,143
Andrew Durling, Green 1,351
Paul Howard, Ind. 139
C. majority 733 (1.39%)
3.99% swing LD to C.
(2010: LD majority 3,435 (6.59%))

EASTLEIGH
E. 79,609   T. 55,505 (69.72%)   C. gain
*Mims Davies, C. 23,464
Mike Thornton, LD 14,317
Patricia Culligan, UKIP 8,783
Mark Latham, Lab. 7,181
Ron Meldrum, Green 1,513
Ray Hall, Beer BS 133
Declan Clune, TUSC 114
C. majority 9,147 (16.48%)
11.84% swing LD to C.
(2010: LD majority 3,864 (7.20%))
(2013: LD majority 1,771 (4.26%))

EDDISBURY
E. 68,636   T. 47,352 (68.99%)   C. hold
*Antoinette Sandbach, C. 24,167
James Laing, Lab. 11,193
Rob Millington, UKIP 5,778
Ian Priestner, LD 4,289
Andrew Garman, Green 1,624
George Antar, CISTA 301
C. majority 12,974 (27.40%)
1.36% swing C. to Lab.
(2010: C. majority 13,255 (29.19%))

EDMONTON
E. 66,015   T. 41,338 (62.62%)
                                Lab. Co-op hold
*Kate Osamor, Lab. Co-op 25,388
Gonul Daniels, C. 9,969
Neville Watson, UKIP 3,366
Douglas Coker, Green 1,358
David Schmitz, LD 897
Lewis Peacock, TUSC 360
Lab. Co-op majority 15,419 (37.30%)
6.75% swing C. to Lab.
(2010: Lab. Co-op majority 9,613
(23.81%))

ELLESMERE PORT & NESTON
E. 68,134   T. 46,727 (68.58%)   Lab. hold
*Justin Madders, Lab. 22,316
Katherine Fletcher, C. 16,041
Jonathan Starkey, UKIP 5,594
Trish Derraugh, LD 1,563
Michelle Palmer, Green 990
Felicity Dowling, TUSC 192
John Dyer, ND 31
Lab. majority 6,275 (13.43%)
1.82% swing C. to Lab.
(2010: Lab. majority 4,331 (9.79%))

ELMET & ROTHWELL
E. 79,143   T. 57,797 (73.03%)   C. hold
Alec Shelbrooke, C. 27,978
Veronica King, Lab. 19,488
Paul Spivey, UKIP 6,430
Stewart Golton, LD 2,640
Dave Brooks, Green 1,261
C. majority 8,490 (14.69%)
3.29% swing Lab. to C.
(2010: C. majority 4,521 (8.10%))

ELTHAM
E. 63,998   T. 43,157 (67.43%)   Lab. hold
Clive Efford, Lab. 18,393
Spencer Drury, C. 15,700
Peter Whittle, UKIP 6,481
Alex Cunliffe, LD 1,308
James Parker, Green 1,275
Lab. majority 2,693 (6.24%)
1.14% swing C. to Lab.
(2010: Lab. majority 1,663 (3.96%))

ENFIELD NORTH
E. 68,119   T. 46,137 (67.73%)   Lab. gain
*Joan Ryan, Lab. 20,172
Nick de Bois, C. 19,086
Deborah Cairns, UKIP 4,133
David Flint, Green 1,303
Cara Jenkinson, LD 1,059
Yemi Awolola, CPA 207
Joe Simpson, TUSC 177
Lab. majority 1,086 (2.35%)
3.08% swing C. to Lab.
(2010: C. majority 1,692 (3.81%))

ENFIELD SOUTHGATE
E. 64,938   T. 45,812 (70.55%)   C. hold
David Burrowes, C. 22,624
Bambos Charalambous, Lab. 17,871
David Schofield, UKIP 2,109
Jean Robertson-Molloy, Green 1,690
Paul Smith, LD 1,518
C. majority 4,753 (10.38%)
3.41% swing C. to Lab.
(2010: C. majority 7,626 (17.19%))

EPPING FOREST
E. 73,545   T. 49,348 (67.10%)   C. hold
Eleanor Laing, C. 27,027
Andrew Smith, UKIP 9,049
Gareth Barrett, Lab. 7,962
Jon Whitehouse, LD 3,448
Anna Widdup, Green 1,782
Mark Wadsworth, Young 80
C. majority 17,978 (36.43%)
6.79% swing C. to UKIP
(2010: C. majority 15,131 (32.48%))

EPSOM & EWELL
E. 78,633   T. 57,143 (72.67%)   C. hold
Chris Grayling, C. 33,309
Sheila Carlson, Lab. 8,866
Robert Leach, UKIP 7,117
Stephen Gee, LD 5,002
Susan McGrath, Green 2,116
Lionel Blackman, Ind. 612
Gareth Harfoot, ND 121
C. majority 24,443 (42.78%)
0.75% swing C. to Lab.
(2010: C. majority 16,134 (29.36%))

**EREWASH**
E. 71,937   T. 48,322 (67.17%)   C. hold
*Maggie Throup, C.   20,636
Catherine Atkinson, Lab.   17,052
Philip Rose, UKIP   7,792
Martin Garnett, LD   1,658
Ralph Hierons, Green   1,184
C. majority 3,584 (7.42%)
1.08% swing Lab. to C.
(2010: C. majority 2,501 (5.25%))

**ERITH & THAMESMEAD**
E. 69,787   T. 42,617 (61.07%)   Lab. hold
Teresa Pearce, Lab.   21,209
Anna Firth, C.   11,684
Ronie Johnson, UKIP   7,368
Simon Waddington, LD   972
Ann Garrett, Green   941
Sidney Cordle, CPA   255
Graham Moore, Eng. Dem.   188
Lab. majority 9,525 (22.35%)
4.46% swing C. to Lab.
(2010: Lab. majority 5,703 (13.43%))

**ESHER & WALTON**
E. 79,894   T. 56,976 (71.31%)   C. hold
Dominic Raab, C.   35,845
Francis Eldergill, Lab.   7,229
Nicholas Wood, UKIP   5,551
Andrew Davis, LD   5,372
Olivia Palmer, Green   2,355
Matt Heenan, CISTA   396
Della Reynolds, Ind.   228
C. majority 28,616 (50.22%)
1.00% swing Lab. to C.
(2010: C. majority 18,593 (34.09%))

**EXETER**
E. 76,964   T. 54,018 (70.19%)   Lab. hold
Ben Bradshaw, Lab.   25,062
Dom Morris, C.   17,879
Keith Crawford, UKIP   5,075
Diana Moore, Green   3,491
Joel Mason, LD   2,321
Edmund Potts, TUSC   190
Lab. majority 7,183 (13.30%)
4.04% swing C. to Lab.
(2010: Lab. majority 2,721 (5.21%))

**FAREHAM**
E. 77,233   T. 54,700 (70.82%)   C. hold
*Suella Fernandes, C.   30,689
Malcolm Jones, UKIP   8,427
Stuart Rose, Lab.   7,800
Matt Winnington, LD   4,814
Miles Grindey, Green   2,129
Nick Gregory, Ind.   705
Harvey Hines, Ind.   136
C. majority 22,262 (40.70%)
5.23% swing C. to UKIP
(2010: C. majority 17,092 (31.45%))

**FAVERSHAM & KENT MID**
E. 69,523   T. 45,803 (65.88%)   C. hold
*Helen Whately, C.   24,895
Peter Edwards-Daem, UKIP   8,243
Michael Desmond, Lab.   7,403
David Naghi, LD   3,039
Tim Valentine, Green   1,768
Hairy Knorm Davidson, Loony   297
Gary Butler, Eng. Dem.   158
C. majority 16,652 (36.36%)
8.08% swing C. to UKIP
(2010: C. majority 17,088 (36.58%))

**FELTHAM & HESTON**
E. 82,328   T. 49,405 (60.01%)   Lab. Co-op hold
Seema Malhotra, Lab. Co-op   25,845
Simon Nayyar, C.   14,382
Peter Dul, UKIP   6,209
Roger Crouch, LD   1,579
Tony Firkins, Green   1,390
Lab. Co-op majority 11,463 (23.20%)
6.80% swing C. to Lab.
(2010: Lab. Co-op majority 4,658 (9.60%))
(2011: Lab. majority 6,203 (26.71%))

**FILTON & BRADLEY STOKE**
E. 70,722   T. 49,101 (69.43%)   C. hold
Jack Lopresti, C.   22,920
Ian Boulton, Lab.   13,082
Ben Walker, UKIP   7,261
Peter Bruce, LD   3,581
Diana Warner, Green   2,257
C. majority 9,838 (20.04%)
2.86% swing Lab. to C.
(2010: C. majority 6,914 (14.31%))

**FINCHLEY & GOLDERS GREEN**
E. 72,049   T. 50,759 (70.45%)   C. hold
Mike Freer, C.   25,835
Sarah Sackman, Lab.   20,173
Richard King, UKIP   1,732
Jonathan Davies, LD   1,662
Adele Ward, Green   1,357
C. majority 5,662 (11.15%)
0.58% swing C. to Lab.
(2010: C. majority 5,809 (12.32%))

**FOLKESTONE & HYTHE**
E. 83,612   T. 55,010 (65.79%)   C. hold
Damian Collins, C.   26,323
Harriet Yeo, UKIP   12,526
Claire Jeffrey, Lab.   7,939
Lynne Beaumont, LD   4,882
Martin Whybrow, Green   2,956
Seth Cruse, TUSC   244
Rohen Kapur, Young   72
Andy Thomas, SPGB   68
C. majority 13,797 (25.08%)
9.87% swing C. to UKIP
(2010: C. majority 10,122 (19.17%))

**FOREST OF DEAN**
E. 69,882   T. 49,520 (70.86%)   C. hold
Mark Harper, C.   23,191
Steve Parry-Hearn, Lab.   12,204
Steve Stanbury, UKIP   8,792
James Greenwood, Green   2,703
Christopher Coleman, LD   2,630
C. majority 10,987 (22.19%)
0.25% swing C. to Lab.
(2010: C. majority 11,064 (22.69%))

**FYLDE**
E. 65,679   T. 43,557 (66.32%)   C. hold
Mark Menzies, C.   21,406
Jed Sullivan, Lab.   8,182
Paul White, UKIP   5,569
Mike Hill, Ind.   5,166
Fred van Mierlo, LD   1,623
Bob Dennett, Green   1,381
Elizabeth Clarkson, Northern   230
C. majority 13,224 (30.36%)
1.07% swing C. to Lab.
(2010: C. majority 13,185 (30.18%))

**GAINSBOROUGH**
E. 73,212   T. 49,261 (67.29%)   C. hold
Edward Leigh, C.   25,949
David Prescott, Lab.   10,500
John Saxon, UKIP   7,727
Lesley Rollings, LD   3,290
Geoffrey Barnes, Green   1,290
Christopher Darcel, Lincs Ind.   505
C. majority 15,449 (31.36%)
1.14% swing C. to Lab.
(2010: C. majority 10,559 (21.44%))

**GARSTON & HALEWOOD**
E. 74,063   T. 48,983 (66.14%)   Lab. hold
Maria Eagle, Lab.   33,839
Martin Williams, C.   6,693
Carl Schears, UKIP   4,482
Anna Martin, LD   2,279
William Ward, Green   1,690
Lab. majority 27,146 (55.42%)
6.01% swing C. to Lab.
(2010: Lab. majority 16,877 (39.41%))

**GATESHEAD**
E. 63,910   T. 38,009 (59.47%)   Lab. hold
Ian Mearns, Lab.   21,549
John Tennant, UKIP   6,765
Thomas Smith, C.   5,562
Frank Hindle, LD   2,585
Andy Redfern, Green   1,548
Lab. majority 14,784 (38.90%)
6.18% swing Lab. to UKIP
(2010: Lab. majority 12,549 (32.80%))

**GEDLING**
E. 70,046   T. 47,998 (68.52%)   Lab. hold
Vernon Coaker, Lab.   20,307
Carolyn Abbott, C.   17,321
Lee Waters, UKIP   6,930
Robert Swift, LD   1,906
Jim Norris, Green   1,534
Lab. majority 2,986 (6.22%)
1.18% swing C. to Lab.
(2010: Lab. majority 1,859 (3.86%))

**GILLINGHAM & RAINHAM**
E. 72,609   T. 47,078 (64.84%)   C. hold
Rehman Chishti, C.   22,590
Paul Clark, Lab.   12,060
Mark Hanson, UKIP   9,199
Paul Chaplin, LD   1,707
Neil Williams, Green   1,133
Jacqui Berry, TUSC   273
Roger Peacock, ND   72
Mike Walters, ND   44
C. majority 10,530 (22.37%)
1.91% swing Lab. to C.
(2010: C. majority 8,680 (18.55%))

**GLOUCESTER**
E. 82,949   T. 52,575 (63.38%)   C. hold
Richard Graham, C.   23,837
Sophy Gardner, Lab.   16,586
Richard Ford, UKIP   7,497
Jeremy Hilton, LD   2,828
Jonathan Ingleby, Green   1,485
George Ridgeon, Loony   227
Sue Powell, TUSC   115
C. majority 7,251 (13.79%)
4.51% swing Lab. to C.
(2010: C. majority 2,420 (4.77%))

GOSPORT
E. 73,271    T. 47,665 (65.05%)    C. hold
Caroline Dinenage, C.    26,364
Christopher Wood, UKIP    9,266
Alan Durrant, Lab.    6,926
Rob Hylands, LD    3,298
Monica Cassidy, Green    1,707
Jeffrey Roberts, ND    104
C. majority 17,098 (35.87%)
6.36% swing C. to UKIP
(2010: C. majority 14,413 (30.71%))

GRANTHAM & STAMFORD
E. 81,151    T. 53,755 (66.24%)    C. hold
Nick Boles, C.    28,399
Marietta King, UKIP    9,410
Barrie Fairbairn, Lab.    9,070
Harrish Bisnauthsing, LD    3,263
Aidan Campbell, Green    1,872
Ian Selby, Ind.    1,017
Jan Hansen, Lincs Ind.    724
C. majority 18,989 (35.33%)
5.96% swing C. to UKIP
(2010: C. majority 14,826 (28.08%))

GRAVESHAM
E. 74,307    T. 50,149 (67.49%)    C. hold
Adam Holloway, C.    23,484
Tanmanjit Singh Dhesi, Lab.    15,114
Sean Marriott, UKIP    9,306
Mark Lindop, Green    1,124
Anne-Marie Bunting, LD    1,111
C. majority 8,370 (16.71%)
1.49% swing C. to Lab.
(2010: C. majority 9,312 (19.69%))

GREAT GRIMSBY
E. 58,484    T. 33,731 (57.68%)    Lab. hold
*Melanie Onn, Lab.    13,414
Marc Jones, C.    8,874
Victoria Ayling, UKIP    8,417
Steve Beasant, LD    1,680
Vicky Dunn, Green    783
Gary Calder, Ind.    390
Val O'Flynn, TUSC    173
Lab. majority 4,540 (13.46%)
5.65% swing C. to Lab.
(2010: Lab. majority 714 (2.17%))

GREAT YARMOUTH
E. 69,793    T. 44,469 (63.72%)    C. hold
Brandon Lewis, C.    19,089
Lara Norris, Lab.    12,935
Alan Grey, UKIP    10,270
James Joyce, LD    1,030
Harry Webb, Green    978
Samuel George Townley, CISTA    167
C. majority 6,154 (13.84%)
1.95% swing Lab. to C.
(2010: C. majority 4,276 (9.93%))

GREENWICH & WOOLWICH
E. 73,315    T. 46,716 (63.72%)    Lab. hold
*Matthew Pennycook, Lab.    24,384
Matt Hartley, C.    12,438
Ryan Acty, UKIP    3,888
Abideen Akinoshun, Green    2,991
Tom Holder, LD    2,645
Lynne Chamberlain, TUSC    370
Lab. majority 11,946 (25.57%)
0.46% swing C. to Lab.
(2010: Lab. majority 10,153 (24.65%))

GUILDFORD
E. 76,554    T. 53,986 (70.52%)    C. hold
Anne Milton, C.    30,802
Kelly-Marie Blundell, LD    8,354
Richard Wilson, Lab.    6,534
Harry Aldridge, UKIP    4,774
John Pletts, Green    2,558
Susan Parker, Guildford    538
John Morris, Peace    230
Gerri Smyth, CISTA    196
C. majority 22,448 (41.58%)
13.79% swing LD to C.
(2010: C. majority 7,782 (14.00%))

HACKNEY NORTH & STOKE
NEWINGTON
E. 83,195    T. 49,887 (59.96%)    Lab. hold
Diane Abbott, Lab.    31,357
Amy Gray, C.    7,349
Heather Finlay, Green    7,281
Simon de Deney, LD    2,492
Keith Fraser, UKIP    1,085
Jon Homan, AWP    221
Jonathan Silberman, Comm. Lge    102
Lab. majority 24,008 (48.12%)
3.85% swing C. to Lab.
(2010: Lab. majority 14,461 (31.11%))

HACKNEY SOUTH & SHOREDITCH
E. 79,962    T. 47,610 (59.54%)
    Lab. Co-op hold
Meg Hillier, Lab. Co-op    30,663
Jack Tinley, C.    6,420
Charlotte George, Green    5,519
Ben Mathis, LD    2,186
Angus Small, UKIP    1,818
Brian Debus, TUSC    302
Paul Birch, CISTA    297
Taiwo Adewuyi, CPA    236
Russell Higgs, Ind.    78
Bill Rogers, WRP    63
Gordon Shrigley, Campaign    28
Lab. Co-op majority 24,243 (50.92%)
4.36% swing C. to Lab.
(2010: Lab. majority 14,288 (33.34%))

HALESOWEN & ROWLEY REGIS
E. 74,203    T. 43,818 (59.05%)    C. hold
James Morris, C.    18,933
Stephanie Peacock, Lab.    15,851
Dean Perks, UKIP    7,280
Peter Tyzack, LD    905
John Payne, Green    849
C. majority 3,082 (7.03%)
1.22% swing Lab. to C.
(2010: C. majority 2,023 (4.60%))

HALIFAX
E. 70,461    T. 43,753 (62.10%)    Lab. hold
*Holly Lynch, Lab.    17,506
Philip Allott, C.    17,078
Liz Phillips, UKIP    5,621
Mohammad Ilyas, LD    1,629
Gary Scott, Green    1,142
Asama Javed, Respect    465
Trevor Bendrien, Ch. P.    312
Lab. majority 428 (0.98%)
1.20% swing Lab. to C.
(2010: Lab. majority 1,472 (3.38%))

HALTEMPRICE & HOWDEN
E. 71,205    T. 48,757 (68.47%)    C. hold
David Davis, C.    26,414
Edward Hart, Lab.    10,219
John Kitchener, UKIP    6,781
Carl Minns, LD    3,055
Tim Greene, Green    1,809
Diana Wallis, Yorks    479
C. majority 16,195 (33.22%)
0.68% swing C. to Lab.
(2010: C. majority 11,602 (23.81%))

HALTON
E. 72,818    T. 45,023 (61.83%)    Lab. hold
Derek Twigg, Lab.    28,292
Matthew Lloyd, C.    8,007
Glyn Redican, UKIP    6,333
Ryan Bate, LD    1,097
David Melvin, Green    1,017
Vic Turton, Ind.    277
Lab. majority 20,285 (45.05%)
3.77% swing C. to Lab.
(2010: Lab. majority 15,504 (37.51%))

HAMMERSMITH
E. 72,254    T. 47,960 (66.38%)    Lab. hold
Andy Slaughter, Lab.    23,981
Charlie Dewhirst, C.    17,463
Millicent Scott, LD    2,224
David Akan, Green    2,105
Richard Wood, UKIP    2,105
Stephen Brennan, ND    82
Lab. majority 6,518 (13.59%)
3.06% swing C. to Lab.
(2010: Lab. majority 3,549 (7.48%))

HAMPSHIRE EAST
E. 72,600    T. 51,649 (71.14%)    C. hold
Damian Hinds, C.    31,334
Peter Baillie, UKIP    6,187
Richard Robinson, LD    5,732
Alex Wilks, Lab.    5,220
Peter Bisset, Green    3,176
C. majority 25,147 (48.69%)
2.61% swing C. to UKIP
(2010: C. majority 13,497 (26.30%))

HAMPSHIRE NORTH EAST
E. 74,025    T. 54,000 (72.95%)    C. hold
*Ranil Jayawardena, C.    35,573
Graham Cockarill, LD    5,657
Amran Hussain, Lab.    5,290
Robert Blay, UKIP    4,732
Andrew Johnston, Green    2,364
Mad Max Bobetsky, Loony    384
C. majority 29,916 (55.40%)
10.14% swing LD to C.
(2010: C. majority 18,597 (35.13%))

HAMPSHIRE NORTH WEST
E. 79,223    T. 55,195 (69.67%)    C. hold
*Kit Malthouse, C.    32,052
Sue Perkins, UKIP    8,109
Andrew Adams, Lab.    7,342
Alex Payton, LD    5,151
Dan Hill, Green    2,541
C. majority 23,943 (43.38%)
4.88% swing C. to UKIP
(2010: C. majority 18,583 (34.87%))

HAMPSTEAD & KILBURN
E. 80,241   T. 53,964 (67.25%)   Lab. hold
*Tulip Siddiq, Lab.                     23,977
Simon Marcus, C.                        22,839
Maajid Nawaz, LD                         3,039
Rebecca Johnson, Green                   2,387
Magnus Nielsen, UKIP                     1,532
The Eurovisionary Carroll, Ind.            113
Robin Ellison, U Party                      77
Lab. majority 1,138 (2.11%)
1.01% swing C. to Lab.
(2010: Lab. majority 42 (0.08%))

HARBOROUGH
E. 77,760   T. 52,471 (67.48%)   C. hold
Edward Garnier, C.                      27,675
Sundip Meghani, Lab.                     8,043
Mark Hunt, UKIP                          7,539
Zuffar Haq, LD                           7,037
Darren Woodiwiss, Green                  2,177
C. majority 19,632 (37.41%)
0.59% swing Lab. to C.
(2010: C. majority 9,797 (17.83%))

HARLOW
E. 67,994   T. 44,251 (65.08%)   C. hold
Robert Halfon, C.                       21,623
Suzy Stride, Lab.                       13,273
Sam Stopplecamp, UKIP                    7,208
Murray Sackwild, Green                     954
Geoff Seeff, LD                            904
David Brown, TUSC                          174
Eddy Butler, Eng. Dem.                     115
C. majority 8,350 (18.87%)
3.82% swing Lab. to C.
(2010: C. majority 4,925 (11.22%))

HARROGATE & KNARESBOROUGH
E. 77,379   T. 53,376 (68.98%)   C. hold
Andrew Jones, C.                        28,153
Helen Flynn, LD                         11,782
David Simister, UKIP                     5,681
Jan Williams, Lab.                       5,409
Shan Oakes, Green                        2,351
C. majority 16,371 (30.67%)
14.36% swing LD to C.
(2010: C. majority 1,039 (1.96%))

HARROW EAST
E. 70,980   T. 49,000 (69.03%)   C. hold
Bob Blackman, C.                        24,668
Uma Kumaran, Lab.                       19,911
Aidan Powlesland, UKIP                   2,333
Ross Barlow, LD                          1,037
Emma Wallace, Green                        846
Nana Asante, TUSC                          205
C. majority 4,757 (9.71%)
1.31% swing Lab. to C.
(2010: C. majority 3,403 (7.09%))

HARROW WEST
E. 69,643 T. 46,603 (66.92%)
                              Lab. Co-op hold
Gareth Thomas, Lab. Co-op               21,885
Hannah David, C.                        19,677
Mohammad Ali Bhatti, UKIP                2,047
Chris Noyce, LD                          1,567
Rowan Langley, Green                     1,310
Kailash Trivedi, Ind.                      117
Lab. Co-op majority 2,208 (4.74%)
1.04% swing Lab. to C.
(2010: Lab. Co-op majority 3,143 (6.82%))

HARTLEPOOL
E. 69,516   T. 39,490 (56.81%)   Lab. hold
Iain Wright, Lab.                       14,076
Phillip Broughton, UKIP                 11,052
Richard Royal, C.                        8,256
Stephen Picton, Ind.                     2,954
Michael Holt, Green                      1,341
Sandra Allison, Hospital                   849
Hilary Allen, LD                           761
John Hobbs, Ind.                           201
Lab. majority 3,024 (7.66%)
13.93% swing Lab. to UKIP
(2010: Lab. majority 5,509 (14.41%))

HARWICH & ESSEX NORTH
E. 69,289   T. 48,432 (69.90%)   C. hold
Bernard Jenkin, C.                      24,722
Edward Carlsson Browne, Lab.             9,548
Mark Hughes, UKIP                        8,464
Dominic Graham, LD                       3,576
Christopher Flossman, Green              2,122
C. majority 15,174 (31.33%)
2.17% swing Lab. to C.
(2010: C. majority 11,447 (23.36%))

HASTINGS & RYE
E. 75,095   T. 50,927 (67.82%)   C. hold
Amber Rudd, C.                          22,686
Sarah Owen, Lab. Co-op                  17,890
Andrew Michael, UKIP                     6,786
Jake Bowers, Green                       1,951
Nick Perry, LD                           1,614
C. majority 4,796 (9.42%)
2.71% swing Lab. to C.
(2010: C. majority 1,993 (4.00%))

HAVANT
E. 70,573   T. 44,828 (63.52%)   C. hold
*Alan Mak, C.                           23,159
John Perry, UKIP                         9,239
Graham Giles, Lab.                       7,149
Steve Sollitt, LD                        2,929
Tim Dawes, Green                         2,352
C. majority 13,920 (31.05%)
7.05% swing C. to UKIP
(2010: C. majority 12,160 (27.70%))

HAYES & HARLINGTON
E. 74,875   T. 45,056 (60.17%)   Lab. hold
John McDonnell, Lab.                    26,843
Pearl Lewis, C.                         11,143
Cliff Dixon, UKIP                        5,388
Satnam Khalsa, LD                          888
Alick Munro, Green                         794
Lab. majority 15,700 (34.85%)
4.73% swing C. to Lab.
(2010: Lab. majority 10,824 (25.39%))

HAZEL GROVE
E. 63,098   T. 43,219 (68.50%)   C. gain
*William Wragg, C.                      17,882
Lisa Smart, LD                          11,330
Michael Taylor, Lab.                     7,584
Darran Palmer, UKIP                      5,283
Graham Reid, Green                       1,140
C. majority 6,552 (15.16%)
15.17% swing LD to C.
(2010: LD majority 6,371 (15.18%))

HEMEL HEMPSTEAD
E. 74,616   T. 49,633 (66.52%)   C. hold
Mike Penning, C.                        26,245
Tony Breslin, Lab.                      11,825
Howard Koch, UKIP                        7,249
Rabi Martins, LD                         2,402
Alan Borgars, Green                      1,660
Brian Hall, Ind.                           252
C. majority 14,420 (29.05%)
0.05% swing C. to Lab.
(2010: C. majority 13,406 (27.10%))

HEMSWORTH
E. 72,714   T. 42,406 (58.32%)   Lab. hold
Jon Trickett, Lab.                      21,772
Chris Pearson, C.                        9,694
Steve Ashton, UKIP                       8,565
Mary Macqueen, LD                        1,357
Martin Roberts, Yorks                    1,018
Lab. majority 12,078 (28.48%)
3.01% swing C. to Lab.
(2010: Lab. majority 9,844 (22.45%))

HENDON
E. 74,658   T. 49,630 (66.48%)   C. hold
Matthew Offord, C.                      24,328
Andrew Dismore, Lab.                    20,604
Raymond Shamash, UKIP                    2,595
Alasdair Hill, LD                        1,088
Ben Samuel, Green                        1,015
C. majority 3,724 (7.50%)
3.64% swing Lab. to C.
(2010: C. majority 106 (0.23%))

HENLEY
E. 78,243   T. 55,236 (70.60%)   C. hold
John Howell, C.                         32,292
Sam Juthani, Lab.                        6,917
Susan Cooper, LD                         6,205
Christopher Jones, UKIP                  6,007
Mark Stevenson, Green                    3,815
C. majority 25,375 (45.94%)
0.34% swing Lab. to C.
(2010: C. majority 16,588 (30.99%))

HEREFORD & HEREFORDSHIRE
SOUTH
E. 70,711   T. 47,257 (66.83%)   C. hold
Jesse Norman, C.                        24,844
Nigel Ely, UKIP                          7,954
Anna Coda, Lab.                          6,042
Lucy Hurds, LD                           5,002
Diana Toynbee, Green                     3,415
C. majority 16,890 (35.74%)
3.55% swing C. to UKIP
(2010: C. majority 2,481 (5.13%))

HEREFORDSHIRE NORTH
E. 66,683   T. 48,023 (72.02%)   C. hold
Bill Wiggin, C.                         26,716
Jonathan Oakton, UKIP                    6,720
Jeanie Falconer, LD                      5,768
Sally Prentice, Lab.                     5,478
Daisy Blench, Green                      3,341
C. majority 19,996 (41.64%)
2.23% swing C. to UKIP
(2010: C. majority 9,887 (20.78%))

HERTFORD & STORTFORD
E. 78,906   T. 56,277 (71.32%)   C. hold
Mark Prisk, C.                          31,593
Katherine Chibah, Lab.                  10,084
Adrian Baker, UKIP                       7,534
Michael Green, LD                        4,385
Sophie Christophy, Green                 2,681
C. majority 21,509 (38.22%)
0.93% swing C. to Lab.
(2010: C. majority 15,437 (27.88%))

### HERTFORDSHIRE NORTH EAST
E. 73,944    T. 52,287 (70.71%)    C. hold
Oliver Heald, C.                                    28,949
Chris York, Lab.                                     9,869
William Compton, UKIP                                6,728
Joe Jordan, LD                                       3,952
Mario May, Green                                     2,789
C. majority 19,080 (36.49%)
0.30% swing C. to Lab.
(2010: C. majority 15,194 (30.13%))

### HERTFORDSHIRE SOUTH WEST
E. 79,666    T. 57,267 (71.88%)    C. hold
David Gauke, C.                                     32,608
Simon Diggins, Lab.                                  9,345
Mark Anderson, UKIP                                  6,603
Nigel Quinton, LD                                    5,872
Charlotte Pardy, Green                               2,583
Graham Cartmell, CSP                                   256
C. majority 23,263 (40.62%)
1.05% swing C. to Lab.
(2010: C. majority 14,920 (26.29%))

### HERTSMERE
E. 73,753    T. 50,091 (67.92%)    C. hold
*Oliver Dowden, C.                                  29,696
Richard Butler, Lab.                                11,235
Frank Ward, UKIP                                     6,383
Sophie Bowler, LD                                    2,777
C. majority 18,461 (36.85%)
0.19% swing C. to Lab.
(2010: C. majority 17,605 (37.24%))

### HEXHAM
E. 60,614    T. 43,345 (71.51%)    C. hold
Guy Opperman, C.                                    22,834
Liam Carr, Lab.                                     10,803
David Nicholson, UKIP                                4,302
Jeff Reid, LD                                        2,961
Lee Williscroft-Ferris, Green                        2,445
C. majority 12,031 (27.76%)
1.76% swing Lab. to C.
(2010: C. majority 5,788 (13.31%))

### HEYWOOD & MIDDLETON
E. 79,989    T. 48,538 (60.68%)    Lab. hold
*Liz McInnes, Lab.                                  20,926
John Bickley, UKIP                                  15,627
Iain Gartside, C.                                    9,268
Anthony Smith, LD                                    1,607
Abi Jackson, Green                                   1,110
Lab. majority 5,299 (10.92%)
13.28% swing Lab. to UKIP
(2010: Lab. majority 5,971 (12.95%))
(2014: Lab. majority 617 (2.17%))

### HIGH PEAK
E. 73,336    T. 50,789 (69.26%)    C. hold
Andrew Bingham, C.                                  22,836
Caitlin Bisknell, Lab.                              17,942
Ian Guiver, UKIP                                     5,811
Stephen Worrall, LD                                  2,389
Charlotte Farrell, Green                             1,811
C. majority 4,894 (9.64%)
0.17% swing Lab. to C.
(2010: C. majority 4,677 (9.29%))

### HITCHIN & HARPENDEN
E. 74,839    T. 55,375 (73.99%)    C. hold
Peter Lilley, C.                                    31,488
Rachel Burgin, Lab.                                 11,433
John Stocker, UKIP                                   4,917
Pauline Pearce, LD                                   4,484
Richard Wise, Green                                  3,053
C. majority 20,055 (36.22%)
2.42% swing C. to Lab.
(2010: C. majority 15,271 (27.91%))

### HOLBORN & ST PANCRAS
E. 86,864    T. 54,917 (63.22%)    Lab. hold
*Keir Starmer, Lab.                                 29,062
Will Blair, C.                                      12,014
Natalie Bennett, Green                               7,013
Jill Fraser, LD                                      3,555
Maxine Spencer, UKIP                                 2,740
Shane O'Donnell, CISTA                                 252
Vanessa Hudson, AWP                                   173
David O'Sullivan, SEP                                 108
Lab. majority 17,048 (31.04%)
2.65% swing C. to Lab.
(2010: Lab. majority 9,942 (18.19%))

### HORNCHURCH & UPMINSTER
E. 79,331    T. 55,236 (69.63%)    C. hold
Angela Watkinson, C.                                27,051
Lawrence Webb, UKIP                                 13,977
Paul McGeary, Lab.                                  11,103
Jonathan Mitchell, LD                                1,501
Melanie Collins, Green                               1,411
Paul Borg, BNP                                         193
C. majority 13,074 (23.67%)
11.22% swing C. to UKIP
(2010: C. majority 16,371 (30.66%))

### HORNSEY & WOOD GREEN
E. 79,241    T. 57,785 (72.92%)    Lab. gain
*Catherine West, Lab.                               29,417
Lynne Featherstone, LD                              18,359
Suhail Rahuja, C.                                    5,347
Gordon Peters, Green                                 3,146
Clive Morrison, UKIP                                 1,271
Helen Spiby-Vann, CPA                                 118
Frank Sweeney, WRP                                     82
Geoff Moseley, Hoi                                     45
Lab. majority 11,058 (19.14%)
15.81% swing LD to Lab.
(2010: LD majority 6,875 (12.49%))

### HORSHAM
E. 78,181    T. 56,925 (72.81%)    C. hold
*Jeremy Quin, C.                                    32,627
Roger Arthur, UKIP                                   7,969
Morwen Millson, LD                                   6,647
Martyn Davis, Lab.                                   6,499
Darrin Green, Green                                  2,198
James Smith, S. New                                   375
Jim Duggan, Peace                                     307
Jim Rae, Ind.                                         303
C. majority 24,658 (43.32%)
2.17% swing C. to UKIP
(2010: C. majority 11,460 (20.52%))

### HOUGHTON & SUNDERLAND SOUTH
E. 68,316    T. 38,489 (56.34%)    Lab. hold
Bridget Phillipson, Lab.                            21,218
Richard Elvin, UKIP                                  8,280
Stewart Hay, C.                                      7,105
Alan Robinson, Green                                 1,095
Jim Murray, LD                                         791
Lab. majority 12,938 (33.61%)
7.01% swing Lab. to UKIP
(2010: Lab. majority 10,990 (28.91%))

### HOVE
E. 73,505    T. 52,214 (71.03%)    Lab. gain
*Peter Kyle, Lab.                                   22,082
Graham Cox, C.                                      20,846
Christopher Hawtree, Green                           3,569
Kevin Smith, UKIP                                    3,265
Peter Lambell, LD                                    1,861
Jenny Barnard-Langston, Ind.                          322
Dave Hill, TUSC                                       144
The Dame Dixon, Loony                                 125
Lab. majority 1,236 (2.37%)
3.06% swing C. to Lab.
(2010: C. majority 1,868 (3.75%))

### HUDDERSFIELD
E. 65,265 T. 40,478 (62.02%)
                                     Lab. Co-op hold
Barry Sheerman, Lab. Co-op                          18,186
Itrat Ali, C.                                       10,841
Rob Butler, UKIP                                     5,948
Andrew Cooper, Green                                 2,798
Zulfiqar Ali, LD                                     2,365
Mike Forster, TUSC                                    340
Lab. Co-op majority 7,345 (18.15%)
3.56% swing C. to Lab.
(2010: Lab. majority 4,472 (11.04%))

### HULL EAST
E. 65,606  T. 35,144 (53.57%)    Lab. hold
Karl Turner, Lab.                                   18,180
Richard Barrett, UKIP                                7,861
Christine Mackay, C.                                 5,593
David Nolan, LD                                      2,294
Sarah Walpole, Green                                  806
Martin Clayton, Yorks                                 270
Mike Cooper, NF                                        86
Val Hoodless, Soc. Dem.                                54
Lab. majority 10,319 (29.36%)
5.27% swing Lab. to UKIP
(2010: Lab. majority 8,597 (25.15%))

### HULL NORTH
E. 63,650  T. 35,336 (55.52%)    Lab. hold
Diana Johnson, Lab.                                 18,661
Sergi Singh, UKIP                                    5,762
Dehenna Davison, C.                                  5,306
Mike Ross, LD                                        3,175
Martin Deane, Green                                  2,066
Vicky Butler, Yorks                                   366
Lab. majority 12,899 (36.50%)
0.70% swing UKIP to Lab.
(2010: Lab. majority 641 (1.93%))

### HULL WEST & HESSLE
E. 59,008  T. 31,803 (53.90%)    Lab. hold
Alan Johnson, Lab.                                  15,646
Paul Salvidge, UKIP                                  6,313
Jo Barker, C.                                        5,561
Claire Thomas, LD                                    3,169
Angela Needham, Green                                 943
Paul Spooner, TUSC                                    171
Lab. majority 9,333 (29.35%)
3.88% swing Lab. to UKIP
(2010: Lab. majority 5,742 (18.23%))

### HUNTINGDON
E. 82,404    T. 55,926 (67.87%)    C. hold
Jonathan Djanogly, C.                               29,652
Nik Johnson, UKIP                                   10,248
Paul Bullen, UKIP                                    9,473
Rod Cantrill, LD                                     4,375
Tom MacLennan, Green                                 2,178
C. majority 19,404 (34.70%)
1.57% swing C. to Lab.
(2010: C. majority 10,819 (19.94%))

### HYNDBURN
E. 68,341  T. 42,887 (62.75%)    Lab. hold
Graham Jones, Lab.                                  18,076
Kevin Horkin, C.                                    13,676
Janet Brown, UKIP                                    9,154
Kerry Gormley, Green                                 1,122
Alison Firth, LD                                      859
Lab. majority 4,400 (10.26%)
1.51% swing C. to Lab.
(2010: Lab. majority 3,090 (7.24%))

ILFORD NORTH
E. 78,162    T. 48,932 (62.60%)    Lab. gain
*Wes Streeting, Lab.                          21,463
Lee Scott, C.                                 20,874
Philip Hyde, UKIP                              4,355
Rich Clare, LD                                 1,130
David Reynolds, Green                          1,023
Doris Osen, Ind.                                  87
Lab. majority 589 (1.20%)
6.35% swing C. to Lab.
(2010: C. majority 5,404 (11.49%))

ILFORD SOUTH
E. 95,023    T. 51,912 (54.63%)
                              Lab. Co-op hold
Mike Gapes, Lab. Co-op                        33,232
Chris Chapman, C.                             13,455
Amjad Khan, UKIP                               2,705
RoseMary Warrington, Green                     1,506
Ashburn Holder, LD                             1,014
Lab. Co-op majority 19,777 (38.10%)
8.02% swing C. to Lab.
(2010: Lab. Co-op majority 11,287
(22.05%))

IPSWICH
E. 74,498    T. 48,694 (65.36%)    C. hold
Ben Gummer, C.                                21,794
David Ellesmere, Lab.                         18,061
Maria Vigneau, UKIP                            5,703
Barry Broom, Green                             1,736
Chika Akinwale, LD                             1,400
C. majority 3,733 (7.67%)
1.62% swing Lab. to C.
(2010: C. majority 2,079 (4.43%))

ISLE OF WIGHT
E. 108,804    T. 70,300 (64.61%)    C. hold
Andrew Turner, C.                             28,591
Iain McKie, UKIP                              14,888
Vix Lowthion, Green                            9,404
Stewart Blackmore, Lab.                        8,984
David Goodall, LD                              5,235
Ian Stephens, Ind.                             3,198
C. majority 13,703 (19.49%)
11.87% swing C. to UKIP
(2010: C. majority 10,527 (14.98%))

ISLINGTON NORTH
E. 73,325    T. 49,234 (67.14%)    Lab. hold
Jeremy Corbyn, Lab.                           29,659
Alex Burghart, C.                              8,465
Caroline Russell, Green                        5,043
Julian Gregory, LD                             3,984
Gregory Clough, UKIP                           1,971
Bill Martin, SPGB                                112
Lab. majority 21,194 (43.05%)
1.39% swing C. to Lab.
(2010: Lab. majority 12,401 (27.83%))

ISLINGTON SOUTH & FINSBURY
E. 68,127    T. 44,270 (64.98%)    Lab. hold
Emily Thornberry, Lab.                        22,547
Mark Lim, C.                                   9,839
Terry Stacy, LD                                4,829
Pete Muswell, UKIP                             3,375
Charlie Kiss, Green                            3,371
Jay Kirton, CISTA                                309
Lab. majority 12,708 (28.71%)
2.92% swing C. to Lab.
(2010: Lab. majority 3,569 (8.19%))

JARROW
E. 63,882    T. 38,564 (60.37%)    Lab. hold
Stephen Hepburn, Lab.                         21,464
Steven Harrison, UKIP                          7,583
Nick Mason, C.                                 6,584
David Herbert, Green                           1,310
Stan Collins, LD                               1,238
Norman Hall, TUSC                                385
Lab. majority 13,881 (35.99%)
swing N/A
(2010: Lab. majority 12,908 (33.28%))

KEIGHLEY
E. 68,865    T. 49,123 (71.33%)    C. hold
Kris Hopkins, C.                              21,766
John Grogan, Lab.                             18,713
Paul Latham, UKIP                              5,662
Ros Brown, Green                               1,661
Gareth Epps, LD                                1,321
C. majority 3,053 (6.22%)
0.03% swing Lab. to C.
(2010: C. majority 2,940 (6.16%))

KENILWORTH & SOUTHAM
E. 65,245    T. 48,791 (74.78%)    C. hold
Jeremy Wright, C.                             28,474
Bally Singh, Lab.                              7,472
Harry Cottam, UKIP                             5,467
Richard Dickson, LD                            4,913
Rob Ballantyne, Green                          1,956
Nick Blunderbuss Green, Loony                    370
Jon Foster-Smith, Digital                        139
C. majority 21,002 (43.04%)
1.91% swing Lab. to C.
(2010: C. majority 12,552 (25.92%))

KENSINGTON
E. 61,333    T. 34,828 (56.79%)    C. gain
*Lady (Victoria) Borwick, C.                  18,199
Rod Abouharb, Lab.                            10,838
Robin McGhee, LD                               1,962
Robina Rose, Green                             1,765
Jack Bovill, UKIP                              1,557
Tony Auguste, CISTA                              211
Andrew Knight, AWP                               158
Toby Abse, Green Soc.                            115
Roland Courtenay, New IC                          23
C. majority 7,361 (21.14%)
1.69% swing C. to Lab.
(2010: C. majority 8,616 (24.51%))

KETTERING
E. 70,155    T. 47,218 (67.31%)    C. hold
Philip Hollobone, C.                          24,467
Rhea Keehn, Lab.                              11,877
Jonathan Bullock, UKIP                         7,600
Rob Reeves, Green                              1,633
Chris McGlynn, LD                              1,490
Derek Hilling, Eng. Dem.                         151
C. majority 12,590 (26.66%)
3.72% swing Lab. to C.
(2010: C. majority 9,094 (19.21%))

KINGSTON & SURBITON
E. 81,277    T. 59,253 (72.90%)    C. gain
*James Berry, C.                              23,249
Ed Davey, LD                                  20,415
Lee Godfrey, Lab.                              8,574
Ben Roberts, UKIP                              4,321
Clare Keogh, Green                             2,322
Daniel Gill, CPA                                 198
Laurel Fogarty, TUSC                             174
C. majority 2,834 (4.78%)
9.01% swing LD to C.
(2010: LD majority 7,560 (13.24%))

KINGSWOOD
E. 67,992    T. 48,125 (70.78%)    C. hold
Chris Skidmore, C.                            23,252
Jo McCarron, Lab.                             14,246
Duncan Odgers, UKIP                            7,133
Adam Boyden, LD                                1,827
Cezara Nanu, Green                             1,370
Julie Lake, BNP                                  164
Richard Worth, TUSC                               84
Liam Bryan, Vapers                                49
C. majority 9,006 (18.71%)
6.81% swing Lab. to C.
(2010: C. majority 2,445 (5.10%))

KNOWSLEY
E. 79,109    T. 50,728 (64.12%)    Lab. hold
George Howarth, Lab.                          39,628
Louise Bours, UKIP                             4,973
Alice Bramall, C.                              3,367
Carl Cashman, LD                               1,490
Vikki Gregorich, Green                         1,270
Lab. majority 34,655 (68.32%)
swing N/A
(2010: Lab. majority 25,686 (57.52%))

LANCASHIRE WEST
E. 70,945    T. 49,676 (70.02%)    Lab. hold
Rosie Cooper, Lab.                            24,474
Paul Greenall, C.                             16,114
Jack Sen, UKIP                                 6,058
Ben Basson, Green                              1,582
Daniel Lewis, LD                               1,298
David Braid, WVPTFP                               150
Lab. majority 8,360 (16.83%)
3.93% swing C. to Lab.
(2010: Lab. majority 4,343 (8.96%))

LANCASTER & FLEETWOOD
E. 60,883    T. 41,738 (68.55%)    Lab. gain
*Cat Smith, Lab.                              17,643
Eric Ollerenshaw, C.                          16,378
Matthew Atkins, UKIP                           4,060
Chris Coates, Green                            2,093
Robin Long, LD                                 1,390
Harold Elletson, Northern                        174
Lab. majority 1,265 (3.03%)
1.91% swing C. to Lab.
(2010: C. majority 333 (0.78%))

LEEDS CENTRAL
E. 81,799    T. 45,048 (55.07%)    Lab. hold
Hilary Benn, Lab.                             24,758
Nicola Wilson, C.                              7,791
Luke Senior, UKIP                              7,082
Michael Hayton, Green                          3,558
Emma Spriggs, LD                               1,529
Liz Kitching, TUSC                               330
Lab. majority 16,967 (37.66%)
4.27% swing C. to Lab.
(2010: Lab. majority 10,645 (28.47%))

LEEDS EAST
E. 64,754    T. 38,196 (58.99%)    Lab. hold
*Richard Burgon, Lab.                         20,530
Ryan Stephenson, C.                            7,997
Mark Maniatt, UKIP                             7,256
Ed Sanderson, LD                               1,296
Kate Bisson, Green                             1,117
Lab. majority 12,533 (32.81%)
2.80% swing C. to Lab.
(2010: Lab. majority 10,293 (27.22%))

**LEEDS NORTH EAST**
E. 69,097  T. 48,291 (69.89%)  Lab. hold
Fabian Hamilton, Lab.                23,137
Simon Wilson, C.                     15,887
Warren Hendon, UKIP                   3,706
Aqila Choudhry, LD                    2,569
Emma Carter, Green                    2,541
Celia Foote, Green Soc.                 451
Lab. majority 7,250 (15.01%)
2.73% swing C. to Lab.
(2010: Lab. majority 4,545 (9.56%))

**LEEDS NORTH WEST**
E. 61,974  T. 43,357 (69.96%)  LD hold
Greg Mulholland, LD                  15,948
Alex Sobel, Lab.                     13,041
Alex Story, C.                        8,083
Tim Goodall, Green                    3,042
Julian Metcalfe, UKIP                 2,997
Bob Buxton, Yorks                       143
Mike Davies, Green Soc.                  79
Mark Flanagan, Above                     24
LD majority 2,907 (6.70%)
9.90% swing LD to Lab.
(2010: LD majority 9,103 (20.93%))

**LEEDS WEST**
E. 64,950  T. 38,423 (59.16%)  Lab. hold
Rachel Reeves, Lab.                  18,456
Alex Pierre-Traves, C.                7,729
Anne Murgatroyd, UKIP                 7,104
Andrew Pointon, Green                 3,217
Laura Coyle, LD                       1,495
Matthew West, CISTA                     217
Ben Mayor, TUSC                         205
Lab. majority 10,727 (27.92%)
2.67% swing C. to Lab.
(2010: Lab. majority 7,016 (18.10%))

**LEICESTER EAST**
E. 75,430  T. 48,068 (63.73%)  Lab. hold
Keith Vaz, Lab.                      29,386
Kishan Devani, C.                    11,034
Susanna Steptoe, UKIP                 4,290
Nimit Jethwa, Green                   1,468
Dave Raval, LD                        1,233
Michael Barker, TUSC                    540
Tom Darwood, ND                         117
Lab. majority 18,352 (38.18%)
4.42% swing C. to Lab.
(2010: Lab. majority 14,082 (29.34%))

**LEICESTER SOUTH**
E. 73,518  T. 45,962 (62.52%)
                         Lab. Co-op hold
Jon Ashworth, Lab. Co-op            27,473
Leon Hadji-Nikolaou, C.              9,628
Peter Stone, UKIP                     3,832
Gabby Garcia, Green                   2,533
Anita Prabhakar, LD                   2,127
Andrew Walton, TUSC                     349
Lab. Co-op majority 17,845 (38.87%)
7.32% swing C. to Lab.
(2010: Lab. majority 8,808 (18.69%))
(2011: Lab. majority 12,078 (35.34%))

**LEICESTER WEST**
E. 63,204  T. 34,522 (54.62%)  Lab. hold
Liz Kendall, Lab.                    16,051
Paul Bessant, C.                      8,848
Stuart Young, UKIP                    5,950
Peter Hague, Green                    1,878
Ian Bradwell, LD                      1,507
Heather Rawling, TUSC                   288
Lab. majority 7,203 (20.86%)
4.83% swing C. to Lab.
(2010: Lab. majority 4,017 (11.21%))

**LEICESTERSHIRE NORTH WEST**
E. 72,194  T. 51,548 (71.40%)  C. hold
Andrew Bridgen, C.                   25,505
Jamie McMahon, Lab. Co-op            14,132
Andy McWilliam, UKIP                  8,704
Mark Argent, LD                       2,033
Benjamin Gravestock, Green            1,174
C. majority 11,373 (22.06%)
3.80% swing Lab. to C.
(2010: C. majority 7,511 (14.46%))

**LEICESTERSHIRE SOUTH**
E. 76,877  T. 53,926 (70.15%)  C. hold
*Alberto Costa, C.                   28,700
Amanda Hack, Lab.                    11,876
Barry Mahoney, UKIP                   9,363
Geoffrey Welsh, LD                    3,987
C. majority 16,824 (31.20%)
1.30% swing Lab. to C.
(2010: C. majority 15,524 (28.44%))

**LEIGH**
E. 75,974  T. 45,123 (59.39%)  Lab. hold
Andy Burnham, Lab.                   24,312
Louisa Townson, C.                   10,216
Les Leggett, UKIP                     8,903
Bill Winlow, LD                       1,150
Stephen Hall, TUSC                      542
Lab. majority 14,096 (31.24%)
2.07% swing Lab. to C.
(2010: Lab. majority 12,011 (27.09%))

**LEWES**
E. 69,481  T. 50,540 (72.74%)  C. gain
*Maria Caulfield, C.                 19,206
Norman Baker, LD                     18,123
Ray Finch, UKIP                       5,427
Lloyd Russell-Moyle, Lab.             5,000
Alfie Stirling, Green                 2,784
C. majority 1,083 (2.14%)
8.70% swing LD to C.
(2010: LD majority 7,647 (15.27%))

**LEWISHAM DEPTFORD**
E. 73,426  T. 47,426 (64.59%)  Lab. hold
*Vicky Foxcroft, Lab.                28,572
Bim Afolami, C.                       7,056
John Coughlin, Green                  5,932
Michael Bukola, LD                    2,497
Massimo Dimambro, UKIP                2,013
Helen Mercer, PBP                       666
Malcolm Martin, CPA                     300
Chris Flood, TUSC                       286
Phillip Badger, Dem. Ref.                74
David Harvey, ND                         30
Lab. majority 21,516 (45.37%)
2.57% swing C. to Lab.
(2010: Lab. majority 12,499 (30.32%))

**LEWISHAM EAST**
E. 73,428  T. 42,923 (58.46%)  Lab. hold
Heidi Alexander, Lab.                23,907
Peter Fortune, C.                     9,574
Anne Marie Waters, UKIP               3,886
Julia Fletcher, LD                    2,455
Storm Poorun, Green                   2,429
Nick Long, PBP                          390
Maureen Martin, CPA                     282
Lab. majority 14,333 (33.39%)
6.97% swing C. to Lab.
(2010: Lab. majority 6,216 (14.90%))

**LEWISHAM WEST & PENGE**
E. 72,289  T. 48,125 (66.57%)  Lab. hold
Jim Dowd, Lab.                       24,347
Russell Jackson, C.                  11,633
Tom Chance, Green                     4,077
Gary Harding, UKIP                    3,764
Alex Feakes, LD                       3,709
Martin Powell-Davies, TUSC              391
David Hansom, Ind.                      160
George Whale, Lib. GB                    44
Lab. majority 12,714 (26.42%)
5.42% swing C. to Lab.
(2010: Lab. majority 5,828 (12.94%))

**LEYTON & WANSTEAD**
E. 64,746  T. 40,705 (62.87%)  Lab. hold
John Cryer, Lab.                     23,858
Matthew Scott, C.                     8,939
Ashley Gunstock, Green                2,974
Rosamund Beattie, UKIP                2,341
Carl Quilliam, LD                     2,304
Mahtab Aziz, Ind.                       289
Lab. majority 14,919 (36.65%)
7.64% swing C. to Lab.
(2010: Lab. majority 6,416 (15.98%))

**LICHFIELD**
E. 83,339  T. 51,467 (61.76%)  C. hold
Michael Fabricant, C.                28,389
Chris Worsey, Lab.                   10,200
John Rackham, UKIP                    8,082
Paul Ray, LD                          2,700
Robert Pass, Green                    1,976
Andy Bennetts, Class War                120
C. majority 18,189 (35.34%)
0.39% swing Lab. to C.
(2010: C. majority 17,683 (34.29%))

**LINCOLN**
E. 74,121  T. 46,852 (63.21%)  C. hold
Karl McCartney, C.                   19,976
Lucy Rigby, Lab.                     18,533
Nick Smith, UKIP                      5,721
Ross Pepper, LD                       1,992
Elaine Smith, TUSC                      344
Helen Powell, Lincs Ind.                286
C. majority 1,443 (3.08%)
0.38% swing Lab. to C.
(2010: C. majority 1,058 (2.31%))

**LIVERPOOL RIVERSIDE**
E. 70,950  T. 44,263 (62.39%)
                         Lab. Co-op hold
Louise Ellman, Lab. Co-op            29,835
Martin Dobson, Green                  5,372
Jackson Ng, C.                        4,245
Joe Chiffers, UKIP                    2,510
Paul Childs, LD                       1,719
Tony Mulhearn, TUSC                     582
Lab. Co-op majority 24,463 (55.27%)
0.26% swing Lab. to Green
(2010: Lab. majority 14,173 (36.53%))

**LIVERPOOL WALTON**
E. 62,868  T. 38,403 (61.09%)  Lab. hold
Steve Rotheram, Lab.                 31,222
Steve Flatman, UKIP                   3,445
Norsheen Bhatti, C.                   1,802
Jonathan Clatworthy, Green              956
Pat Moloney, LD                         899
Alexander Karran, Ind.                   56
Jonathan Dzon, Plural                    23
Lab. majority 27,777 (72.33%)
1.49% swing UKIP to Lab.
(2010: Lab. majority 19,818 (57.72%))

LIVERPOOL WAVERTREE
E. 61,731 T. 40,974 (66.38%)
Lab. Co-op hold
Luciana Berger, Lab. Co-op          28,401
James Pearson, C.                    4,098
Adam Heatherington, UKIP             3,375
Leo Evans, LD                        2,454
Peter Cranie, Green                  2,140
Dave Walsh, TUSC                       362
Niamh McCarthy, Ind.                   144
Lab. Co-op majority 24,303 (59.31%)
6.84% swing C. to Lab.
(2010: Lab. Co-op majority 7,167
(18.90%))

LIVERPOOL WEST DERBY
E. 63,875 T. 41,031 (64.24%)
Lab. Co-op hold
Stephen Twigg, Lab. Co-op           30,842
Neil Miney, UKIP                     3,475
Ed McRandal, C.                      2,710
Steve Radford, Lib.                  2,049
Rebecca Lawson, Green                  996
Paul Twigger, LD                       959
Lab. Co-op majority 27,367 (66.70%)
2.80% swing UKIP to Lab.
(2010: Lab. Co-op majority 18,467
(51.61%))

LOUGHBOROUGH
E. 72,644   T. 52,020 (71.61%)   C. hold
Nicky Morgan, C.                    25,762
Matthew O'Callaghan, Lab.           16,579
Bill Piper, UKIP                     5,704
Steve Coltman, LD                    2,130
Matt Sisson, Green                   1,845
C. majority 9,183 (17.65%)
5.28% swing Lab. to C.
(2010: C. majority 3,744 (7.09%))

LOUTH & HORNCASTLE
E. 74,280   T. 50,336 (67.77%)   C. hold
*Victoria Atkins, C.                25,755
Colin Mair, UKIP                    10,778
Matthew Brown, Lab.                  9,077
Lisa Gabriel, LD                     2,255
Romy Rayner, Green                   1,549
Daniel Simpson, Lincs Ind.             659
Peter Hill, Loony                      263
C. majority 14,977 (29.75%)
7.78% swing C. to UKIP
(2010: C. majority 13,871 (27.47%))

LUDLOW
E. 66,423   T. 48,063 (72.36%)   C. hold
Philip Dunne, C.                    26,093
David Kelly, UKIP                    7,164
Charlotte Barnes, LD                 6,469
Simon Slater, Lab.                   5,902
Janet Phillips, Green                2,435
C. majority 18,929 (39.38%)
4.52% swing C. to UKIP
(2010: C. majority 9,749 (20.01%))

LUTON NORTH
E. 66,533   T. 42,571 (63.98%)   Lab. hold
Kelvin Hopkins, Lab.                22,243
Dean Russell, C.                    12,739
Allan White, UKIP                    5,318
Aroosa Ulzaman, LD                   1,299
Sofiya Ahmed, Green                    972
Lab. majority 9,504 (22.33%)
2.42% swing C. to Lab.
(2010: Lab. majority 7,520 (17.48%))

LUTON SOUTH
E. 67,234 T. 42,216 (62.79%)
Lab. Co-op hold
Gavin Shuker, Lab. Co-op            18,660
Katie Redmond, C.                   12,949
Yasin Rehman, UKIP                   5,129
Ashuk Ahmed, LD                      3,183
Simon Hall, Green                    1,237
Attiq Malik, Ind.                      900
Paul Weston, Lib. GB                   158
Lab. Co-op majority 5,711 (13.53%)
4.01% swing C. to Lab.
(2010: Lab. Co-op majority 2,329 (5.52%))

MACCLESFIELD
E. 71,580   T. 49,598 (69.29%)   C. hold
David Rutley, C.                    26,063
Tim Roca, Lab.                      11,252
Adrian Howard, UKIP                  6,037
Neil Christian, LD                   3,842
Joan Plimmer, Green                  2,404
C. majority 14,811 (29.86%)
1.61% swing Lab. to C.
(2010: C. majority 11,959 (23.89%))

MAIDENHEAD
E. 74,963   T. 53,855 (71.84%)   C. hold
Theresa May, C.                     35,453
Charles Smith, Lab.                  6,394
Tony Hill, LD                        5,337
Herbie Crossman, UKIP                4,539
Emily Blyth, Green                   1,915
Ian Taplin, Ind.                       162
Joe Wilcox, Class War                   55
C. majority 29,059 (53.96%)
0.79% swing Lab. to C.
(2010: C. majority 16,769 (31.22%))

MAIDSTONE & THE WEALD
E. 73,181   T. 50,010 (68.34%)   C. hold
Helen Grant, C.                     22,745
Jasper Gerard, LD                   12,036
Eddie Powell, UKIP                   7,930
Allen Simpson, Lab.                  5,268
Hannah Patton, Green                 1,396
Paul Hobday, NHAP                      583
Robin Kinrade, Ind.                     52
C. majority 10,709 (21.41%)
4.69% swing LD to C.
(2010: C. majority 5,889 (12.04%))

MAKERFIELD
E. 74,370   T. 44,788 (60.22%)   Lab. hold
Yvonne Fovargue, Lab.               23,208
Andrew Collinson, UKIP              10,053
Zehra Zaidi, C.                      8,752
John Skipworth, LD                   1,639
Philip Mitchell, Green               1,136
Lab. majority 13,155 (29.37%)
swing N/A
(2010: Lab. majority 12,490 (28.53%))

MALDON
E. 69,455   T. 48,045 (69.17%)   C. hold
John Whittingdale, C.               29,112
Beverley Acevedo, UKIP               7,042
Peter Edwards, Lab.                  5,690
Ken Martin, LD                       2,424
Zoe O'Connell, LD                    2,157
Robert Graves, Green                 1,504
John Marett, TSPP                      116
C. majority 22,070 (45.94%)
4.40% swing C. to UKIP
(2010: C. majority 19,407 (40.52%))

MANCHESTER CENTRAL
E. 98,435 T. 45,331 (46.05%)
Lab. Co-op hold
Lucy Powell, Lab. Co-op             27,772
Xingang Wang, C.                     6,133
Myles Power, UKIP                    5,033
Kieran Turner-Dave, Green            3,838
John Reid, LD                        1,867
Loz Kaye, Pirate                       346
Alex Davidson, TUSC                    270
Paul Davies, Comm. Lge                  72
Lab. Co-op majority 21,639 (47.74%)
3.39% swing C. to Lab.
(2010: Lab. majority 10,439 (26.15%)
(2012: Lab. majority 9,936 (59.68%))

MANCHESTER GORTON
E. 72,959   T. 42,019 (57.59%)   Lab. hold
Gerald Kaufman, Lab.                28,187
Laura Bannister, Green               4,108
Mo Afzal, C.                         4,063
Phil Eckersley, UKIP                 3,434
Dave Page, LD                        1,782
Simon Hickman, TUSC                    264
Cris Chesha, Pirate                    181
Lab. majority 24,079 (57.31%)
4.96% swing Green to Lab.
(2010: Lab. majority 6,703 (17.49%))

MANCHESTER WITHINGTON
E. 80,590   T. 49,966 (62.00%)   Lab. gain
*Jeff Smith, Lab.                   26,843
John Leech, LD                      11,970
Robert Manning, C.                   4,872
Lucy Bannister, Green                4,048
Mark Davies, UKIP                    2,172
Marcus Farmer, Ind.                     61
Lab. majority 14,873 (29.77%)
16.99% swing LD to Lab.
(2010: LD majority 1,894 (4.21%))

MANSFIELD
E. 77,534   T. 47,193 (60.87%)   Lab. hold
Sir Alan Meale, Lab.                18,603
Andrea Clarke, C.                   13,288
Sid Pepper, UKIP                    11,850
Tony Rogers, LD                      1,642
Paul Frost, Green                    1,486
Karen Seymour, TUSC                    324
Lab. majority 5,315 (11.26%)
0.58% swing Lab. to C.
(2010: Lab. majority 6,012 (12.42%))

MEON VALLEY
E. 72,738   T. 51,717 (71.10%)   C. hold
George Hollingbery, C.              31,578
Dave Alexander, UKIP                 7,665
Gemma McKenna, Lab.                  5,656
Chris Carrigan, LD                   4,987
Diana Korchien, Green                1,831
C. majority 23,913 (46.24%)
3.55% swing C. to UKIP
(2010: C. majority 12,125 (23.66%))

MERIDEN
E. 81,079   T. 52,603 (64.88%)   C. hold
Caroline Spelman, C.                28,791
Tom McNeil, Lab.                     9,996
Mick Gee, UKIP                       8,908
Ade Adeyemo, LD                      2,638
Alison Gavin, Green                  2,170
Chris Booth, IE                        100
C. majority 18,795 (35.73%)
2.29% swing Lab. to C.
(2010: C. majority 16,253 (31.16%))

MIDDLESBROUGH
E. 61,868   T. 32,706 (52.86%)   Lab. hold
Andy McDonald, Lab.                     18,584
Nigel Baker, UKIP                         6,107
Simon Clarke, C.                          5,388
Hannah Graham, Green                      1,407
Richard Kilpatrick, LD                    1,220
Lab. majority 12,477 (38.15%)
2.02% swing Lab. to UKIP
(2010: Lab. majority 8,689 (25.97%))
(2012: Lab. majority 8,211 (47.7%))

MIDDLESBROUGH SOUTH &
CLEVELAND EAST
E. 71,153   T. 45,677 (64.20%)   Lab. hold
Tom Blenkinsop, Lab.                    19,193
Will Goodhand, C.                       16,925
Steve Turner, UKIP                       6,935
Ben Gibson, LD                           1,564
Martin Brampton, Green                   1,060
Lab. majority 2,268 (4.97%)
0.67% swing C. to Lab.
(2010: Lab. majority 1,677 (3.63%))

MILTON KEYNES NORTH
E. 84,892   T. 57,692 (67.96%)   C. hold
Mark Lancaster, C.                      27,244
Emily Darlington, Lab.                  17,491
David Reilly, UKIP                       6,852
Paul Graham, LD                          3,575
Jennifer Marklew, Green                  2,255
Katie Simpson, TUSC                        163
David Mortimer, Ind.                       112
C. majority 9,753 (16.91%)
0.14% swing Lab. to C.
(2010: C. majority 8,961 (16.63%))

MILTON KEYNES SOUTH
E. 87,968   T. 59,019 (67.09%)   C. hold
Iain Stewart, C.                        27,671
Andrew Pakes, Lab. Co-op                18,929
Vince Peddle, UKIP                       7,803
Lisa Smith, LD                           2,309
Samantha Pancheri, Green                 1,936
Stephen Fulton, Ind.                       255
Matthew Gibson, Real                       116
C. majority 8,742 (14.81%)
2.71% swing Lab. to C.
(2010: C. majority 5,201 (9.40%))

MITCHAM & MORDEN
E. 68,474   T. 45,142 (65.93%)   Lab. hold
Siobhain McDonagh, Lab.                 27,380
Paul Holmes, C.                         10,458
Richard Hilton, UKIP                     4,287
Mason Redding, Green                     1,422
Diana Coman, LD                          1,378
Des Coke, CPA                              217
Lab. majority 16,922 (37.49%)
3.14% swing C. to Lab.
(2010: Lab. majority 13,666 (31.20%))

MOLE VALLEY
E. 74,317   T. 55,140 (74.20%)   C. hold
Paul Beresford, C.                      33,434
Paul Kennedy, LD                         7,981
Paul Oakley, UKIP                        6,181
Len Amos, Lab.                           4,565
Jacquetta Fewster, Green                 2,979
C. majority 25,453 (46.16%)
8.67% swing LD to C.
(2010: C. majority 15,653 (28.81%))

MORECAMBE & LUNESDALE
E. 66,476   T. 43,242 (65.05%)   C. hold
David Morris, C.                        19,691
Amina Lone, Lab.                        15,101
Steve Ogden, UKIP                        5,358
Matthew Severn, LD                       1,612
Phil Chandler, Green                     1,395
Michael Dawson, ND                          85
C. majority 4,590 (10.61%)
4.31% swing Lab. to C.
(2010: C. majority 866 (1.99%))

MORLEY & OUTWOOD
E. 76,179   T. 48,250 (63.34%)   C. gain
*Andrea Jenkyns, C.                     18,776
Ed Balls, Lab. Co-op                    18,354
David Dews, UKIP                         7,951
Rebecca Taylor, LD                       1,426
Martin Hemingway, Green                  1,264
Arnie Craven, Yorks                        479
C. majority 422 (0.87%)
1.56% swing Lab. to C.
(2010: Lab. Co-op majority 1,101 (2.25%))

NEW FOREST EAST
E. 72,720   T. 49,447 (68.00%)   C. hold
Julian Lewis, C.                        27,819
Roy Swales, UKIP                         8,657
Andrew Pope, Lab.                        6,018
Bruce Tennent, LD                        4,626
Sally May, Green                         2,327
C. majority 19,162 (38.75%)
4.53% swing C. to UKIP
(2010: C. majority 11,307 (22.60%))

NEW FOREST WEST
E. 68,465   T. 47,410 (69.25%)   C. hold
Desmond Swayne, C.                      28,420
Paul Bailey, UKIP                        7,816
Lena Samuels, Lab.                       5,133
Imogen Shepherd-DuBey, LD                3,293
Janet Richards, Green                    2,748
C. majority 20,604 (43.46%)
4.75% swing C. to UKIP
(2010: C. majority 16,896 (35.52%))

NEWARK
E. 73,724   T. 52,302 (70.94%)   C. hold
Robert Jenrick, C.                      29,834
Michael Payne, Lab.                     11,360
Brian Mapletoft, UKIP                    6,294
David Dobbie, LD                         2,385
Elayne Forster, Green                    1,792
Helen Tyrer, Consensus                     637
C. majority 18,474 (35.32%)
1.90% swing Lab. to C.
(2010: C. majority 16,152 (31.53%))
(2014: C. majority 7,403 (19.13%))

NEWBURY
E. 79,058   T. 57,300 (72.48%)   C. hold
Richard Benyon, C.                      34,973
Judith Bunting, LD                       8,605
Catherine Anderson, UKIP                 6,195
Jonny Roberts, Lab.                      4,837
Paul Field, Green                        2,324
Peter Norman, AD                           228
Barrie Singleton, Ind.                      85
Andrew Stott, PSP                           53
C. majority 26,368 (46.02%)
12.56% swing LD to C.
(2010: C. majority 12,248 (20.90%))

NEWCASTLE-UNDER-LYME
E. 66,752   T. 42,997 (64.41%)   Lab. hold
Paul Farrelly, Lab.                     16,520
Tony Cox, C.                            15,870
Phil Wood, UKIP                          7,252
Ian Wilkes, LD                           1,826
Sam Gibbons, Green                       1,246
David Nixon, Ind.                          283
Lab. majority 650 (1.51%)
1.04% swing Lab. to C.
(2010: Lab. majority 1,552 (3.59%))

NEWCASTLE UPON TYNE CENTRAL
E. 61,061   T. 35,085 (57.46%)   Lab. hold
Chi Onwurah, Lab.                       19,301
Simon Kitchen, C.                        6,628
Daniel Thompson, UKIP                    5,214
Nick Cott, LD                            2,218
Alexander Johnson, Green                 1,724
Lab. majority 12,673 (36.12%)
4.76% swing C. to Lab.
(2010: Lab. majority 7,466 (21.86%))

NEWCASTLE UPON TYNE EAST
E. 74,112   T. 39,222 (52.92%)   Lab. hold
Nick Brown, Lab.                        19,378
Duncan Crute, C.                         6,884
David Robinson-Young, UKIP               4,910
Wendy Taylor, LD                         4,332
Andrew Gray, Green                       3,426
Paul Phillips, TUSC                        170
Mollie Stevenson, Comm.                    122
Lab. majority 12,494 (31.85%)
1.43% swing C. to Lab.
(2010: Lab. majority 4,453 (11.77%))

NEWCASTLE UPON TYNE NORTH
E. 67,267   T. 44,891 (66.74%)   Lab. hold
Catherine McKinnell, Lab.               20,689
Stephen Bates, C.                       10,536
Tim Marron, UKIP                         7,447
Anita Lower, LD                          4,366
Alison Whalley, Green                    1,515
Violet Rook, NE                            338
Lab. majority 10,153 (22.62%)
0.05% swing Lab. to C.
(2010: Lab. majority 3,414 (7.77%))

NEWTON ABBOT
E. 69,743   T. 48,199 (69.11%)   C. hold
Anne Marie Morris, C.                   22,794
Richard Younger-Ross, LD                11,506
Rod Peers, UKIP                          6,726
Roy Freer, Lab.                          4,736
Steven Smyth-Bonfield, Green             2,216
Sean Brogan, TUSC                          221
C. majority 11,288 (23.42%)
11.17% swing LD to C.
(2010: C. majority 523 (1.08%))

NORFOLK MID
E. 76,975   T. 52,212 (67.83%)   C. hold
George Freeman, C.                      27,206
Anna Coke, UKIP                          9,930
Harry Clarke, Lab.                       9,585
Paul Speed, LD                           3,300
Simeon Jackson, Green                    2,191
C. majority 17,276 (33.09%)
5.44% swing C. to UKIP
(2010: C. majority 13,856 (27.29%))

**NORFOLK NORTH**
E. 68,958  T. 49,414 (71.66%)  LD hold
Norman Lamb, LD                    19,299
Ann Steward, C.                    15,256
Michael Baker, UKIP                 8,328
Denise Burke, Lab.                  5,043
Michael Macartney-Filgate, Green    1,488
LD majority 4,043 (8.18%)
7.61% swing LD to C.
(2010: LD majority 11,626 (23.41%))

**NORFOLK NORTH WEST**
E. 72,400  T. 47,371 (65.43%)  C. hold
Henry Bellingham, C.               24,727
Jo Rust, Lab.                      10,779
Toby Coke, UKIP                     8,412
Michael de Whalley, Green           1,780
Hugh Lanham, LD                     1,673
C. majority 13,948 (29.44%)
5.74% swing C. to Lab.
(2010: C. majority 14,810 (30.98%))

**NORFOLK SOUTH**
E. 78,885  T. 57,123 (72.41%)  C. hold
Richard Bacon, C.                  30,995
Deborah Sacks, Lab.                10,502
Barry Cameron, UKIP                 7,847
Jacqueline Howe, LD                 4,689
Catherine Rowett, Green             3,090
C. majority 20,493 (35.88%)
0.14% swing C. to Lab.
(2010: C. majority 10,940 (19.89%))

**NORFOLK SOUTH WEST**
E. 76,970  T. 50,110 (65.10%)  C. hold
Elizabeth Truss, C.                25,515
Paul Smyth, UKIP                   11,654
Peter Smith, Lab.                   8,649
Rupert Moss-Eccardt, LD             2,217
Sandra Walmsley, Green              2,075
C. majority 13,861 (27.66%)
7.22% swing C. to UKIP
(2010: C. majority 13,140 (26.73%))

**NORMANTON, PONTEFRACT & CASTLEFORD**
E. 82,592  T. 45,897 (55.57%)  Lab. hold
Yvette Cooper, Lab.                25,213
Nathan Garbutt, UKIP                9,785
Beth Prescott, C.                   9,569
Edward McMillan-Scott, LD           1,330
Lab. majority 15,428 (33.61%)
swing N/A
(2010: Lab. majority 10,979 (23.74%))

**NORTHAMPTON NORTH**
E. 59,147  T. 39,411 (66.63%)  C. hold
Michael Ellis, C.                  16,699
Sally Keeble, Lab.                 13,454
Tom Rubython, UKIP                  6,354
Tony Clarke, Green                  1,503
Angela Paterson, LD                 1,401
C. majority 3,245 (8.23%)
1.71% swing Lab. to C.
(2010: C. majority 1,936 (4.81%))

**NORTHAMPTON SOUTH**
E. 61,284  T. 38,884 (63.45%)  C. hold
*David Mackintosh, C.              16,163
Kevin McKeever, Lab.               12,370
Rose Gibbins, UKIP                  7,114
Sadik Chaudhury, LD                 1,673
Julie Hawkins, Green                1,403
Kevin Willsher, Ind.                  161
C. majority 3,793 (9.75%)
2.82% swing C. to Lab.
(2010: C. majority 6,004 (15.40%))

**NORTHAMPTONSHIRE SOUTH**
E. 85,092  T. 60,862 (71.52%)  C. hold
Andrea Leadsom, C.                 36,607
Lucy Mills, Lab.                   10,191
Roger Clark, UKIP                   8,204
Tom Snowdon, LD                     3,613
Damon Boughen, Green                2,247
C. majority 26,416 (43.40%)
2.75% swing Lab. to C.
(2010: C. majority 20,478 (34.19%))

**NORWICH NORTH**
E. 65,136  T. 43,592 (66.92%)  C. hold
Chloe Smith, C.                    19,052
Jessica Asato, Lab.                14,589
Glenn Tingle, UKIP                  5,986
Adrian Holmes, Green                1,939
James Wright, LD                    1,894
Mick Hardy, Ind.                      132
C. majority 4,463 (10.24%)
0.54% swing Lab. to C.
(2010: C. majority 3,901 (9.16%))

**NORWICH SOUTH**
E. 74,875  T. 48,463 (64.73%)  Lab. gain
*Clive Lewis, Lab.                 19,033
Lisa Townsend, C.                  11,379
Lesley Grahame, Green               6,749
Simon Wright, LD                    6,607
Steve Emmens, UKIP                  4,539
David Peel, Class War                  96
Cengiz Ceker, Ind.                     60
Lab. majority 7,654 (15.79%)
13.15% swing LD to Lab.
(2010: LD majority 310 (0.65%))

**NOTTINGHAM EAST**
E. 60,464  T. 35,209 (58.23%)  Lab. Co-op hold
Chris Leslie, Lab. Co-op           19,208
Garry Hickton, C.                   7,314
Fran Loi, UKIP                      3,501
Antonia Zenkevitch, Green           3,473
Tadeusz Jones, LD                   1,475
Seb Soar, Ind.                        141
James Stephenson, Ind.                 97
Lab. Co-op majority 11,894 (33.78%)
6.05% swing C. to Lab.
(2010: Lab. Co-op majority 6,969 (21.05%))

**NOTTINGHAM NORTH**
E. 65,918  T. 35,343 (53.62%)  Lab. hold
Graham Allen, Lab.                 19,283
Louise Burfitt-Dons, C.             7,423
Stephen Crosby, UKIP                6,542
Katharina Boettge, Green            1,088
Tony Sutton, LD                       847
Cathy Meadows, TUSC                   160
Lab. majority 11,860 (33.56%)
4.91% swing C. to Lab.
(2010: Lab. majority 8,138 (23.74%))

**NOTTINGHAM SOUTH**
E. 68,987  T. 43,465 (63.00%)  Lab. hold
Lilian Greenwood, Lab.             20,697
Jane Hunt, C.                      13,761
David Hollas, UKIP                  4,900
Adam McGregor, Green                2,345
Deborah Newton-Cook, LD             1,532
Andrew Clayworth, TUSC                230
Lab. majority 6,936 (15.96%)
5.81% swing C. to Lab.
(2010: Lab. majority 1,772 (4.34%))

**NUNEATON**
E. 68,032  T. 45,749 (67.25%)  C. hold
Marcus Jones, C.                   20,827
Vicky Fowler, Lab.                 15,945
Alwyn Waine, UKIP                   6,582
Keith Kondakor, Green               1,281
Christina Jebb, LD                    816
Paul Reilly, TUSC                     194
Stephen Paxton, Eng. Dem.             104
C. majority 4,882 (10.67%)
3.02% swing Lab. to C.
(2010: C. majority 2,069 (4.63%))

**OLD BEXLEY & SIDCUP**
E. 66,035  T. 46,748 (70.79%)  C. hold
James Brokenshire, C.              24,682
Ibrahim Mehmet, Lab.                8,879
Catherine Reilly, UKIP              8,528
Jennifer Keen, LD                   1,644
Derek Moran, Green                  1,336
Bob Gill, NHAP                      1,216
Laurence Williams, Ch. P.             245
Nicola Finch, BNP                     218
C. majority 15,803 (33.80%)
0.53% swing C. to Lab.
(2010: C. majority 15,857 (34.86%))

**OLDHAM EAST & SADDLEWORTH**
E. 72,005  T. 44,483 (61.78%)  Lab. hold
Debbie Abrahams, Lab.              17,529
Sajjad Hussain, C.                 11,527
Peter Klonowski, UKIP               8,557
Richard Marbrow, LD                 5,718
Miranda Meadowcroft, Green          1,152
Lab. majority 6,002 (13.49%)
4.04% swing C. to Lab.
(2010: Lab. majority 103 (0.23%))
(2011: Lab. majority 3,558 (10.23%))

**OLDHAM WEST & ROYTON**
E. 72,341  T. 43,137 (59.63%)  Lab. hold
Michael Meacher, Lab.              23,630
Francis Arbour, UKIP                8,892
Kamran Ghafoor, C.                  8,187
Garth Harkness, LD                  1,589
Simeon Hart, Green                    839
Lab. majority 14,738 (34.17%)
4.03% swing Lab. to UKIP
(2010: Lab. majority 9,352 (21.79%))

**ORPINGTON**
E. 68,129  T. 49,032 (71.97%)  C. hold
Joseph Johnson, C.                 28,152
Idham Ramadi, UKIP                  8,173
Nigel de Gruchy, Lab.               7,645
Peter Brooks, LD                    3,330
Tamara Galloway, Green              1,732
C. majority 19,979 (40.75%)
8.09% swing C. to UKIP
(2010: C. majority 17,200 (35.17%))

**OXFORD EAST**
E. 78,974  T. 50,689 (64.18%)  Lab. hold
Andrew Smith, Lab.                 25,356
Melanie Magee, C.                  10,076
Ann Duncan, Green                   5,890
Alasdair Murray, LD                 5,453
Ian Macdonald, UKIP                 3,451
Chaka Artwell, Ind.                   160
Mad Hatter, Loony                     145
James Morbin, TUSC                    108
Kevin Parkin, SPGB                     50
Lab. majority 15,280 (30.14%)
3.25% swing C. to Lab.
(2010: Lab. majority 4,581 (8.87%))

**OXFORD WEST & ABINGDON**
E. 79,767   T. 57,247 (71.77%)   C. hold
Nicola Blackwood, C.            26,153
Layla Moran, LD                16,571
Sally Copley, Lab.              7,274
Alan Harris, UKIP               3,963
Larry Sanders, Green            2,497
Helen Salisbury, NHAP             723
Mike Foster, SPGB                  66
C. majority 9,582 (16.74%)
8.21% swing LD to C.
(2010: C. majority 176 (0.31%))

**PENDLE**
E. 64,657   T. 44,448 (68.74%)   C. hold
Andrew Stephenson, C.          20,978
Azhar Ali, Lab.                15,525
Mick Waddington, UKIP           5,415
Graham Roach, LD                1,487
Laura Fisk, Green               1,043
C. majority 5,453 (12.27%)
2.15% swing Lab. to C.
(2010: C. majority 3,585 (7.96%))

**PENISTONE & STOCKSBRIDGE**
E. 71,048   T. 46,854 (65.95%)   Lab. hold
Angela Smith, Lab.             19,691
Steven Jackson, C.             12,968
Graeme Waddicar, UKIP          10,738
Rosalyn Gordon, LD              2,957
Colin Porter, Eng. Dem.           500
Lab. majority 6,723 (14.35%)
3.90% swing C. to Lab.
(2010: Lab. majority 3,049 (6.55%))

**PENRITH & THE BORDER**
E. 65,209   T. 43,921 (67.35%)   C. hold
Rory Stewart, C.               26,202
Lee Rushworth, Lab.             6,308
John Stanyer, UKIP              5,353
Neil Hughes, LD                 3,745
Bryan Burrow, Green             2,313
C. majority 19,894 (45.29%)
2.42% swing Lab. to C.
(2010: C. majority 11,241 (24.93%))

**PETERBOROUGH**
E. 72,521   T. 47,075 (64.91%)   C. hold
Stewart Jackson, C.            18,684
Lisa Forbes, Lab.              16,759
Mary Herdman, UKIP              7,485
Darren Fower, LD                1,774
Darren Bisby-Boyd, Green        1,218
Chris Ash, Lib.                   639
John Fox, Ind.                    516
C. majority 1,925 (4.09%)
3.37% swing C. to Lab.
(2010: C. majority 4,861 (10.82%))

**PLYMOUTH MOOR VIEW**
E. 69,146   T. 42,606 (61.62%)   C. gain
*Johnny Mercer, C.             16,020
Alison Seabeck, Lab.           14,994
Penny Mills, UKIP               9,152
Stuart Bonar, LD                1,265
Ben Osborn, Green               1,023
Louise Parker, TUSC               152
C. majority 1,026 (2.41%)
3.12% swing Lab. to C.
(2010: Lab. majority 1,588 (3.82%))

**PLYMOUTH SUTTON & DEVONPORT**
E. 69,146   T. 47,963 (69.36%)   C. hold
Oliver Colvile, C.             18,120
Luke Pollard, Lab. Co-op       17,597
Roy Kettle, UKIP                6,731
Libby Brown, Green              3,401
Graham Reed, LD                 2,008
Laura-Jane Rossington, Comm.      106
C. majority 523 (1.09%)
0.76% swing C. to Lab.
(2010: C. majority 1,149 (2.62%))

**POOLE**
E. 72,557   T. 47,393 (65.32%)   C. hold
Robert Syms, C.                23,745
David Young, UKIP               7,956
Helen Rosser, Lab.              6,102
Philip Eades, LD                5,572
Adrian Oliver, Green            2,198
Mark Howell, Poole              1,766
Ian Northover, ND                  54
C. majority 15,789 (33.32%)
4.45% swing C. to UKIP
(2010: C. majority 7,541 (15.90%))

**POPLAR & LIMEHOUSE**
E. 82,076   T. 51,044 (62.19%)   Lab. hold
Jim Fitzpatrick, Lab.          29,886
Christopher Wilford, C.        12,962
Nicholas McQueen, UKIP          3,128
Maureen Childs, Green           2,463
Elaine Bagshaw, LD              2,149
Hugo Pierre, TUSC                 367
Rene Mugenzi, RFAC                 89
Lab. majority 16,924 (33.16%)
10.12% swing C. to Lab.
(2010: Lab. majority 6,030 (12.91%))

**PORTSMOUTH NORTH**
E. 73,105   T. 45,390 (62.09%)   C. hold
Penny Mordaunt, C.             21,343
John Ferrett, Lab.             10,806
Mike Fitzgerald, UKIP           8,660
Darren Sanders, LD              2,828
Gavin Ellis, Green              1,450
Jon Woods, TUSC                   231
Steven George, JACP                72
C. majority 10,537 (23.21%)
3.35% swing Lab. to C.
(2010: C. majority 7,289 (16.52%))

**PORTSMOUTH SOUTH**
E. 71,639   T. 41,903 (58.49%)   C. gain
*Flick Drummond, C.            14,585
Gerald Vernon-Jackson, LD       9,344
Sue Castillon, Lab.             8,184
Steve Harris, UKIP              5,595
Ian McCulloch, Green            3,145
Mike Hancock, Ind.                716
Sean Hoyle, TUSC                  235
Don Jerrard, JACP                  99
C. majority 5,241 (12.51%)
12.55% swing LD to C.
(2010: LD majority 5,200 (12.60%))

**PRESTON**
E. 59,981   T. 33,469 (55.80%)
                          Lab. Co-op hold
Mark Hendrick, Lab. Co-op      18,755
Richard Holden, C.              6,688
James Barker, UKIP              5,139
Gemma Christie, Green           1,643
Jo Barton, LD                   1,244
Lab. Co-op majority 12,067 (36.05%)
4.79% swing C. to Lab.
(2010: Lab. Co-op majority 7,733
(23.79%))

**PUDSEY**
E. 70,533   T. 50,927 (72.20%)   C. hold
Stuart Andrew, C.              23,637
Jamie Hanley, Lab.             19,136
Roger Tattersall, UKIP          4,689
Ryk Downes, LD                  1,926
Claire Allen, Green             1,539
C. majority 4,501 (8.84%)
2.73% swing Lab. to C.
(2010: C. majority 1,659 (3.38%))

**PUTNEY**
E. 63,918   T. 42,813 (66.98%)   C. hold
Justine Greening, C.           23,018
Sheila Boswell, Lab.           12,838
Andy Hallett, LD                2,717
Chris Poole, Green              2,067
Tricia Ward, UKIP               1,989
Guy Dessoy, AWP                   184
C. majority 10,180 (23.78%)
0.44% swing C. to Lab.
(2010: C. majority 10,053 (24.65%))

**RAYLEIGH & WICKFORD**
E. 77,870   T. 53,220 (68.34%)   C. hold
Mark Francois, C.              29,088
John Hayter, UKIP              11,858
David Hough, Lab.               6,705
Linda Kendall, Ind.             2,418
Mike Pitt, LD                   1,622
Sarah Yapp, Green               1,529
C. majority 17,230 (32.38%)
10.60% swing C. to UKIP
(2010: C. majority 22,338 (42.68%))

**READING EAST**
E. 74,651   T. 50,494 (67.64%)   C. hold
Rob Wilson, C.                 23,217
Matt Rodda, Lab.               16,697
Jenny Woods, LD                 3,719
Christine Forrester, UKIP       3,647
Rob White, Green                3,214
C. majority 6,520 (12.91%)
2.09% swing C. to Lab.
(2010: C. majority 7,605 (15.21%))

**READING WEST**
E. 72,302   T. 48,404 (66.95%)   C. hold
Alok Sharma, C.                23,082
Victoria Groulef, Lab.         16,432
Malik Azam, UKIP                4,826
Meri O'Connell, LD              2,355
Miriam Kennet, Green            1,406
Suzie Ferguson, Ind.              156
Neil Adams, TUSC                   83
Philip West, Roman                 64
C. majority 6,650 (13.74%)
0.55% swing Lab. to C.
(2010: C. majority 6,004 (12.63%))

**REDCAR**
E. 64,825   T. 40,919 (63.12%)
                          Lab. Co-op gain
*Anna Turley, Lab. Co-op       17,946
Josh Mason, LD                  7,558
Chris Gallacher, UKIP           7,516
Jacob Young, C.                 6,630
Peter Pinkney, Green              880
Philip Lockey, NE                 389
Lab. Co-op majority 10,388 (25.39%)
18.91% swing LD to Lab.
(2010: LD majority 5,214 (12.43%))

REDDITCH
E. 65,529   T. 44,098 (67.30%)   C. hold
Karen Lumley, C.                        20,771
Rebecca Blake, Lab.                     13,717
Peter Jewell, UKIP                       7,133
Hilary Myers, LD                         1,349
Kevin White, Green                         960
Seth Colton, Ind.                          168
C. majority 7,054 (16.00%)
1.39% swing Lab. to C.
(2010: C. majority 5,821 (13.22%))

REIGATE
E. 73,429   T. 51,349 (69.93%)   C. hold
Crispin Blunt, C.                       29,151
Joseph Fox, UKIP                         6,817
Ali Aklakul, Lab.                        6,578
Anna Tarrant, LD                         5,369
Jonathan Essex, Green                    3,434
C. majority 22,334 (43.49%)
2.86% swing C. to UKIP
(2010: C. majority 13,591 (27.19%))

RIBBLE VALLEY
E. 77,873   T. 52,243 (67.09%)   C. hold
Nigel Evans, C.                         25,404
David Hinder, Lab.                      11,798
Shirley Parkinson, UKIP                  8,250
Jackie Pearcey, LD                       2,756
Graham Sowter, Green                     2,193
David Brass, Ind.                        1,498
Grace Astley, Ind.                         288
Tony Johnson, IPAP                          56
C. majority 13,606 (26.04%)
1.10% swing C. to Lab.
(2010: C. majority 14,769 (28.25%))

RICHMOND (YORKS)
E. 83,451   T. 53,999 (64.71%)   C. hold
*Rishi Sunak, C.                        27,744
Matthew Cooke, UKIP                      8,194
Mike Hill, Lab.                          7,124
John Harris, LD                          3,465
John Blackie, Ind.                       3,348
Leslie Rowe, Green                       2,313
Robin Scott, Ind.                        1,811
C. majority 19,550 (36.20%)
swing N/A
(2010: C. majority 23,336 (43.69%))

RICHMOND PARK
E. 77,297   T. 59,101 (76.46%)   C. hold
Zac Goldsmith, C.                       34,404
Robin Meltzer, LD                       11,389
Sachin Patel, Lab.                       7,296
Andree Frieze, Green                     3,548
Sam Naz, UKIP                            2,464
C. majority 23,015 (38.94%)
16.02% swing LD to C.
(2010: C. majority 4,091 (6.90%))

ROCHDALE
E. 79,170   T. 45,430 (57.38%)   Lab. hold
Simon Danczuk, Lab.                     20,961
Mohammed Masud, UKIP                     8,519
Azi Ahmed, C.                            7,742
Andy Kelly, LD                           4,667
Farooq Ahmed, Rochdale                   1,535
Mark Hollinrake, Green                   1,382
Kevin Bryan, NF                            433
Mohammed Salim, IZB                        191
Lab. majority 12,442 (27.39%)
2.32% swing Lab. to UKIP
(2010: Lab. majority 889 (1.94%))

ROCHESTER & STROOD
E. 79,000   T. 52,516 (66.48%)   C. gain
*Kelly Tolhurst, C.                     23,142
Mark Reckless, UKIP                      16,009
Naushabah Khan, Lab.                     10,396
Clive Gregory, Green                     1,516
Prue Bray, LD                            1,251
Dan Burn, TUSC                             202
C. majority 7,133 (13.58%)
swing N/A
(2010: C. majority 9,953 (20.75%))
(2014: UKIP majority 2,920 (7.29%))

ROCHFORD & SOUTHEND EAST
E. 71,935   T. 43,608 (60.62%)   C. hold
James Duddridge, C.                     20,241
Ian Gilbert, Lab.                       10,765
Floyd Waterworth, UKIP                   8,948
Simon Cross, Green                       2,195
Peter Gwizdala, LD                       1,459
C. majority 9,476 (21.73%)
2.41% swing C. to Lab.
(2010: C. majority 11,050 (26.54%))

ROMFORD
E. 72,594   T. 49,178 (67.74%)   C. hold
Andrew Rosindell, C.                    25,067
Gerard Batten, UKIP                     11,208
Sam Gould, Lab.                         10,268
Ian Sanderson, LD                        1,413
Lorna Tooley, Green                      1,222
C. majority 13,859 (28.18%)
11.71% swing C. to UKIP
(2010: C. majority 16,954 (36.48%))

ROMSEY & SOUTHAMPTON NORTH
E. 66,519   T. 48,398 (72.76%)   C. hold
Caroline Nokes, C.                      26,285
Ben Nicholls, LD                         8,573
Darren Paffey, Lab.                      5,749
Sandra James, UKIP                       5,511
Ian Callaghan, Green                     2,280
C. majority 17,712 (36.60%)
14.05% swing LD to C.
(2010: C. majority 4,156 (8.49%))

ROSSENDALE & DARWEN
E. 84,011   T. 49,024 (58.35%)   C. hold
Jake Berry, C.                          22,847
Will Straw, Lab.                        17,193
Clive Balchin, UKIP                      6,862
Karen Pollard-Rylance, Green             1,046
Afzal Anwar, LD                            806
Kevin Scranage, Ind.                       122
Simon Thomas, TUSC                         103
Shaun Hargreaves, Northern                  45
C. majority 5,654 (11.53%)
1.00% swing Lab. to C.
(2010: C. majority 4,493 (9.53%))

ROTHER VALLEY
E. 74,275   T. 47,019 (63.30%)   Lab. hold
Kevin Barron, Lab.                      20,501
Allen Cowles, UKIP                      13,204
Gareth Streeter, C.                     10,945
Robert Teal, LD                          1,992
Sharon Pilling, Eng. Dem.                  377
Lab. majority 7,297 (15.52%)
9.92% swing Lab. to UKIP
(2010: Lab. majority 5,866 (12.55%))

ROTHERHAM
E. 63,698   T. 37,823 (59.38%)   Lab. hold
Sarah Champion, Lab.                    19,860
Jane Collins, UKIP                      11,414
Sebastian Lowe, C.                       4,656
Janice Middleton, LD                     1,093
Pat McLaughlin, TUSC                       409
Adam Walker, BNP                           225
Dean Walker, Eng. Dem.                     166
Lab. majority 8,446 (22.33%)
8.19% swing Lab. to UKIP
(2010: Lab. majority 10,462 (27.89%))
(2012: Lab. majority 5,318 (24.79%))

RUGBY
E. 79,557   T. 49,006 (61.60%)   C. hold
Mark Pawsey, C.                         24,040
Claire Edwards, Lab.                    13,695
Gordon Davies, UKIP                      6,855
Ed Goncalves, LD                         2,776
Terence White, Green                     1,415
Pete McLaren, TUSC                         225
C. majority 10,345 (21.11%)
4.23% swing Lab. to C.
(2010: C. majority 6,000 (12.64%))

RUISLIP, NORTHWOOD & PINNER
E. 73,219   T. 51,222 (69.96%)   C. hold
Nick Hurd, C.                           30,521
Michael Borio, Lab.                     10,297
Gerard Barry, UKIP                       5,598
Joshua Dixon, LD                         2,537
Karen Pillai, Green                      1,801
Wally Kennedy, TUSC                        302
Sockalingam Yogalingam, Nat. Lib.          166
C. majority 20,224 (39.48%)
0.76% swing Lab. to C.
(2010: C. majority 19,060 (37.96%))

RUNNYMEDE & WEYBRIDGE
E. 73,744   T. 50,052 (67.87%)   C. hold
Philip Hammond, C.                      29,901
Arran Neathey, Lab.                      7,767
Joe Branco, UKIP                         6,951
John Vincent, LD                         3,362
Rustam Majainah, Green                   2,071
C. majority 22,134 (44.22%)
0.86% swing Lab. to C.
(2010: C. majority 16,509 (34.29%))

RUSHCLIFFE
E. 73,294   T. 55,164 (75.26%)   C. hold
Kenneth Clarke, C.                      28,354
David Mellen, Lab.                      14,525
Matthew Faithfull, UKIP                  5,943
Richard Mallender, Green                 3,559
Bob Johnston, LD                         2,783
C. majority 13,829 (25.07%)
2.69% swing C. to Lab.
(2010: C. majority 15,811 (29.45%))

RUTLAND & MELTON
E. 79,789   T. 54,603 (68.43%)   C. hold
Alan Duncan, C.                         30,383
Richard Billington, UKIP                 8,678
James Moore, Lab.                        8,383
Ed Reynolds, LD                          4,407
Alastair McQuillan, Green                2,325
Marilyn Gordon, Ind.                       427
C. majority 21,705 (39.75%)
3.40% swing C. to UKIP
(2010: C. majority 14,000 (25.35%))

### SAFFRON WALDEN
E. 80,615    T. 57,563 (71.40%)    C. hold
| | |
|---|---|
| Sir Alan Haselhurst, C. | 32,926 |
| Peter Day, UKIP | 7,935 |
| Jane Berney, Lab. | 6,791 |
| Mike Hibbs, LD | 6,079 |
| Karmel Stannard, Green | 2,174 |
| Heather Asker, Uttlesford | 1,658 |

C. majority 24,991 (43.42%)
3.98% swing C. to UKIP
(2010: C. majority 15,242 (28.03%))

### ST ALBANS
E. 72,507    T. 54,433 (75.07%)    C. hold
| | |
|---|---|
| Anne Main, C. | 25,392 |
| Kerry Pollard, Lab. | 12,660 |
| Sandy Walkington, LD | 10,076 |
| Chris Wright, UKIP | 4,271 |
| Jack Easton, Green | 2,034 |

C. majority 12,732 (23.39%)
0.11% swing Lab. to C.
(2010: C. majority 2,305 (4.36%))

### ST AUSTELL & NEWQUAY
E. 76,607    T. 50,361 (65.74%)    C. gain
| | |
|---|---|
| *Stephen Double, C. | 20,250 |
| Stephen Gilbert, LD | 12,077 |
| David Mathews, UKIP | 8,503 |
| Deborah Hopkins, Lab. | 5,150 |
| Steve Slade, Green | 2,318 |
| Dick Cole, Meb. Ker. | 2,063 |

C. majority 8,173 (16.23%)
9.50% swing LD to C.
(2010: LD majority 1,312 (2.78%))

### ST HELENS NORTH
E. 75,262    T. 46,256 (61.46%)    Lab. hold
| | |
|---|---|
| *Conor McGinn, Lab. | 26,378 |
| Paul Richardson, C. | 9,087 |
| Ian Smith, UKIP | 6,983 |
| Denise Aspinall, LD | 2,046 |
| Elizabeth Ward, Green | 1,762 |

Lab. majority 17,291 (37.38%)
3.99% swing C. to Lab.
(2010: Lab. majority 13,101 (29.40%))

### ST HELENS SOUTH & WHISTON
E. 77,720    T. 48,397 (62.27%)    Lab. hold
| | |
|---|---|
| *Marie Rimmer, Lab. | 28,950 |
| Gillian Keegan, C. | 7,707 |
| John Beirne, UKIP | 6,766 |
| Brian Spencer, LD | 2,737 |
| James Chan, Green | 2,237 |

Lab. majority 21,243 (43.89%)
4.42% swing C. to Lab.
(2010: Lab. majority 14,122 (30.65%))

### ST IVES
E. 65,570    T. 48,312 (73.68%)    C. gain
| | |
|---|---|
| *Derek Thomas, C. | 18,491 |
| Andrew George, LD | 16,022 |
| Graham Calderwood, UKIP | 5,720 |
| Cornelius Olivier, Lab. | 4,510 |
| Tim Andrewes, Green | 3,051 |
| Rob Simmons, Meb. Ker. | 518 |

C. majority 2,469 (5.11%)
4.43% swing LD to C.
(2010: LD majority 1,719 (3.74%))

### SALFORD & ECCLES
E. 74,290    T. 43,261 (58.23%)    Lab. hold
| | |
|---|---|
| *Rebecca Long Bailey, Lab. | 21,364 |
| Greg Downes, C. | 8,823 |
| Paul Doyle, UKIP | 7,806 |
| Emma Van Dyke, Green | 2,251 |
| Charlie Briggs, LD | 1,614 |
| Bez Berry, Reality | 703 |
| Noreen Bailey, TUSC | 517 |
| Sam Clark, Pirate | 183 |

Lab. majority 12,541 (28.99%)
4.67% swing C. to Lab.
(2010: Lab. majority 5,725 (13.78%))

### SALISBURY
E. 69,590    T. 50,705 (72.86%)    C. hold
| | |
|---|---|
| John Glen, C. | 28,192 |
| Tom Corbin, Lab. | 7,771 |
| Paul Martin, UKIP | 6,152 |
| Reetendra Nath Banerji, LD | 5,099 |
| Alison Craig, Green | 2,762 |
| King Arthur Pendragon, Ind. | 729 |

C. majority 20,421 (40.27%)
0.66% swing C. to Lab.
(2010: C. majority 5,966 (12.31%))

### SCARBOROUGH & WHITBY
E. 73,511    T. 47,739 (64.94%)    C. hold
| | |
|---|---|
| Robert Goodwill, C. | 20,613 |
| Ian McInnes, Lab. | 14,413 |
| Samuel Cross, UKIP | 8,162 |
| David Malone, Green | 2,185 |
| Michael Beckett, LD | 2,159 |
| Juliet Boddington, Green Soc. | 207 |

C. majority 6,200 (12.99%)
1.75% swing C. to Lab.
(2010: C. majority 8,130 (16.50%))

### SCUNTHORPE
E. 64,010    T. 36,941 (57.71%)    Lab. hold
| | |
|---|---|
| Nic Dakin, Lab. | 15,393 |
| Jo Gideon, C. | 12,259 |
| Stephen Howd, UKIP | 6,329 |
| Des Comerford, Ind. | 1,097 |
| Martin Dwyer, Green | 887 |
| Simon Dodd, LD | 770 |
| Paul Elsom, Ind. | 206 |

Lab. majority 3,134 (8.48%)
0.80% swing C. to Lab.
(2010: Lab. majority 2,549 (6.88%))

### SEDGEFIELD
E. 62,860    T. 38,716 (61.59%)    Lab. hold
| | |
|---|---|
| Phil Wilson, Lab. | 18,275 |
| Scott Wood, C. | 11,432 |
| John Leathley, UKIP | 6,426 |
| Stephen Glenn, LD | 1,370 |
| Greg Robinson, Green | 1,213 |

Lab. majority 6,843 (17.67%)
1.97% swing Lab. to C.
(2010: Lab. majority 8,696 (21.62%))

### SEFTON CENTRAL
E. 67,746    T. 49,021 (72.36%)    Lab. hold
| | |
|---|---|
| Bill Esterson, Lab. | 26,359 |
| Valerie Allen, C. | 14,513 |
| Tim Power, UKIP | 4,879 |
| Paula Keaveney, LD | 2,086 |
| Lindsay Melia, Green | 1,184 |

Lab. majority 11,846 (24.17%)
8.10% swing C. to Lab.
(2010: Lab. majority 3,862 (7.97%))

### SELBY & AINSTY
E. 76,082    T. 52,804 (69.40%)    C. hold
| | |
|---|---|
| Nigel Adams, C. | 27,725 |
| Mark Hayes, Lab. | 14,168 |
| Colin Heath, UKIP | 7,389 |
| Nicola Turner, LD | 1,920 |
| Ian Richards, Green | 1,465 |
| Ian Wilson, TUSC | 137 |

C. majority 13,557 (25.67%)
0.98% swing Lab. to C.
(2010: C. majority 12,265 (23.71%))

### SEVENOAKS
E. 70,741    T. 50,124 (70.86%)    C. hold
| | |
|---|---|
| Michael Fallon, C. | 28,531 |
| Steve Lindsay, UKIP | 8,970 |
| Chris Clark, Lab. | 6,448 |
| Alan Bullion, LD | 3,937 |
| Amelie Boleyn, Green | 2,238 |

C. majority 19,561 (39.03%)
7.10% swing C. to UKIP
(2010: C. majority 17,515 (35.45%))

### SHEFFIELD BRIGHTSIDE & HILLSBOROUGH
E. 73,090    T. 40,053 (54.80%)    Lab. hold
| | |
|---|---|
| *Harry Harpham, Lab. | 22,663 |
| John Booker, UKIP | 8,856 |
| Elise Dunweber, C. | 4,407 |
| Jonathan Harston, LD | 1,802 |
| Christine Gilligan Kubu, Green | 1,712 |
| Maxine Bowler, TUSC | 442 |
| Justin Saxton, Eng. Dem. | 171 |

Lab. majority 13,807 (34.47%)
8.21% swing Lab. to UKIP
(2010: Lab. majority 13,632 (35.03%))

### SHEFFIELD CENTRAL
E. 77,014    T. 44,173 (57.36%)    Lab. hold
| | |
|---|---|
| Paul Blomfield, Lab. | 24,308 |
| Jillian Creasy, Green | 6,999 |
| Stephanie Roe, C. | 4,917 |
| Joe Otten, LD | 4,278 |
| Dominic Cook, UKIP | 3,296 |
| Steve Andrew, Comm. | 119 |
| Andy Halsall, Pirate | 113 |
| Elizabeth Breed, Eng. Dem. | 68 |
| Thom Brown, Above | 42 |
| Michael Driver, WRP | 33 |

Lab. majority 17,309 (39.18%)
swing N/A
(2010: Lab. majority 165 (0.40%))

### SHEFFIELD HALLAM
E. 73,658    T. 55,481 (75.32%)    LD hold
| | |
|---|---|
| Nick Clegg, LD | 22,215 |
| Oliver Coppard, Lab. | 19,862 |
| Ian Walker, C. | 7,544 |
| Joseph Jenkins, UKIP | 3,575 |
| Peter Garbutt, Green | 1,772 |
| Carlton Reeve, Ind. | 249 |
| Steven Clegg, Eng. Dem. | 167 |
| Jim Stop the fiasco Wild, Ind. | 97 |

LD majority 2,353 (4.24%)
16.55% swing LD to Lab.
(2010: LD majority 15,284 (29.89%))

### SHEFFIELD HEELEY
E. 69,265    T. 42,048 (60.71%)    Lab. hold
| | |
|---|---|
| *Louise Haigh, Lab. | 20,269 |
| Howard Denby, UKIP | 7,315 |
| Stephen Castens, C. | 6,792 |
| Simon Clement-Jones, LD | 4,746 |
| Rita Wilcock, Green | 2,566 |
| Alan Munro, TUSC | 238 |
| David Haslett, Eng. Dem. | 122 |

Lab. majority 12,954 (30.81%)
4.02% swing Lab. to UKIP
(2010: Lab. majority 5,807 (14.21%))

SHEFFIELD SOUTH EAST
E. 70,422   T. 41,685 (59.19%)   Lab. hold
Clive Betts, Lab.                        21,439
Steve Winstone, UKIP                      9,128
Matt Sleat, C.                            7,242
Gail Smith, LD                            2,226
Linda Duckenfield, Green                  1,117
Jen Battersby, CISTA                        207
Ian Whitehouse, TUSC                        185
Matthew Roberts, Eng. Dem.                  141
Lab. majority 12,311 (29.53%)
7.31% swing Lab. to UKIP
(2010: Lab. majority 10,505 (25.37%))

SHERWOOD
E. 73,334   T. 50,698 (69.13%)   C. hold
Mark Spencer, C.                         22,833
Leonie Mathers, Lab.                     18,186
Sally Chadd, UKIP                         7,399
Lydia Davies-Bright, Green                1,108
Dan Mosley, LD                            1,094
Dave Perkins, Class War                      78
C. majority 4,647 (9.17%)
4.36% swing Lab. to C.
(2010: C. majority 214 (0.44%))

SHIPLEY
E. 70,466   T. 50,542 (71.73%)   C. hold
Philip Davies, C.                        25,269
Steve Clapcote, Lab.                     15,645
Waqas Khan, UKIP                          4,479
Kevin Warnes, Green                       2,657
Andrew Martin, LD                         1,949
Darren Hill, Yorks                          543
C. majority 9,624 (19.04%)
0.54% swing C. to Lab.
(2010: C. majority 9,944 (20.12%))

SHREWSBURY & ATCHAM
E. 76,460   T. 54,102 (70.76%)   C. hold
Daniel Kawczynski, C.                    24,628
Laura Davies, Lab.                       15,063
Suzanne Evans, UKIP                       7,813
Christine Tinker, LD                      4,268
Emma Bullard, Green                       2,247
Stirling McNeillie, Atom                     83
C. majority 9,565 (17.68%)
2.85% swing C. to Lab.
(2010: C. majority 7,944 (14.98%))

SHROPSHIRE NORTH
E. 78,910   T. 52,573 (66.62%)   C. hold
Owen Paterson, C.                        27,041
Graeme Currie, Lab.                      10,547
Andrea Allen, UKIP                        9,262
Tom Thornhill, LD                         3,148
Duncan Kerr, Green                        2,575
C. majority 16,494 (31.37%)
0.98% swing C. to Lab.
(2010: C. majority 15,828 (30.52%))

SITTINGBOURNE & SHEPPEY
E. 76,018   T. 49,378 (64.96%)   C. hold
Gordon Henderson, C.                     24,425
Richard Palmer, UKIP                     12,257
Guy Nicholson, Lab.                       9,673
Keith Nevols, LD                          1,563
Gary Miller, Green                        1,185
Mad Mike Young, Loony                       275
C. majority 12,168 (24.64%)
10.02% swing C. to UKIP
(2010: C. majority 12,383 (25.49%))

SKIPTON & RIPON
E. 76,243   T. 54,559 (71.56%)   C. hold
Julian Smith, C.                         30,248
Malcolm Birks, Lab.                       9,487
Alan Henderson, UKIP                      7,651
Jacquie Bell, LD                          4,057
Andy Brown, Green                         3,116
C. majority 20,761 (38.05%)
1.25% swing C. to Lab.
(2010: C. majority 9,950 (18.18%))

SLEAFORD & NORTH HYKEHAM
E. 88,188   T. 61,944 (70.24%)   C. hold
Stephen Phillips, C.                     34,805
Jason Pandya-Wood, Lab.                  10,690
Steven Hopkins, UKIP                      9,716
Matthew Holden, LD                        3,500
Marianne Overton, Lincs Ind.             3,233
C. majority 24,115 (38.93%)
2.11% swing Lab. to C.
(2010: C. majority 19,905 (33.44%))

SLOUGH
E. 86,366   T. 48,275 (55.90%)   Lab. hold
Fiona Mactaggart, Lab.                   23,421
Gurcharan Singh, C.                      16,085
Diana Coad, UKIP                          6,274
Tom McCann, LD                            1,275
Julian Edmonds, Green                     1,220
Lab. majority 7,336 (15.20%)
1.81% swing C. to Lab.
(2010: Lab. majority 5,523 (11.57%))

SOLIHULL
E. 77,251   T. 54,779 (70.91%)   C. gain
*Julian Knight, C.                       26,956
Lorely Burt, LD                          14,054
Phil Henrick, UKIP                        6,361
Nigel Knowles, Lab.                       5,693
Howard Allen, Green                       1,632
Mike Nattrass, IE                            50
Matthew Ward, DP                             33
C. majority 12,902 (23.55%)
11.94% swing LD to C.
(2010: LD majority 175 (0.32%))

SOMERSET NORTH
E. 80,115   T. 58,942 (73.57%)   C. hold
Liam Fox, C.                             31,540
Greg Chambers, Lab.                       8,441
Ian Kealey, UKIP                          7,669
Marcus Kravis, LD                         7,486
David Derbyshire, Green                   3,806
C. majority 23,099 (39.19%)
0.52% swing Lab. to C.
(2010: C. majority 7,862 (13.57%))

SOMERSET NORTH EAST
E. 69,380   T. 51,110 (73.67%)   C. hold
Jacob Rees-Mogg, C.                      25,439
Todd Foreman, Lab.                       12,690
Ernie Blaber, UKIP                        6,150
Wera Hobhouse, LD                         4,029
Katy Boyce, Green                         2,802
C. majority 12,749 (24.94%)
7.67% swing Lab. to C.
(2010: C. majority 4,914 (9.60%))

SOMERTON & FROME
E. 83,527   T. 60,309 (72.20%)   C. gain
*David Warburton, C.                     31,960
David Rendel, LD                         11,692
Alan Dimmick, UKIP                        6,439
Theo Simon, Green                         5,434
David Oakensen, Lab.                      4,419
Ian Angell, Ind.                            365
C. majority 20,268 (33.61%)
18.30% swing LD to C.
(2010: LD majority 1,817 (3.00%))

SOUTH HOLLAND & THE DEEPINGS
E. 77,015   T. 49,207 (63.89%)   C. hold
John Hayes, C.                           29,303
David Parsons, UKIP                      10,736
Matthew Mahabadi, Lab.                    6,122
Daniel Wilshire, Green                    1,580
George Smid, LD                           1,466
C. majority 18,567 (37.73%)
7.43% swing C. to UKIP
(2010: C. majority 21,880 (43.60%))

SOUTH RIBBLE
E. 76,489   T. 52,370 (68.47%)   C. hold
*Seema Kennedy, C.                       24,313
Veronica Bennett, Lab.                   18,368
David Gallagher, UKIP                     7,377
Sue McGuire, LD                           2,312
C. majority 5,945 (11.35%)
0.28% swing Lab. to C.
(2010: C. majority 5,554 (10.79%))

SOUTH SHIELDS
E. 62,730   T. 36,265 (57.81%)   Lab. hold
Emma Lewell-Buck, Lab.                   18,589
Norman Dennis, UKIP                       7,975
Robert Oliver, C.                         6,021
Shirley Ford, Green                       1,614
Lisa Nightingale, Ind.                    1,427
Gita Gordon, LD                             639
Lab. majority 10,614 (29.27%)
swing N/A
(2010: Lab. majority 11,109 (30.42%))
(2013: Lab. majority 6,505 (26.30%))

SOUTHAMPTON ITCHEN
E. 72,309   T. 44,710 (61.83%)   C. gain
*Royston Smith, C.                       18,656
Rowenna Davis, Lab. Co-op                16,340
Kim Rose, UKIP                            6,010
John Spottiswoode, Green                  1,876
Eleanor Bell, LD                          1,595
Sue Atkins, TUSC                            233
C. majority 2,316 (5.18%)
2.81% swing Lab. to C.
(2010: Lab. majority 192 (0.43%))

SOUTHAMPTON TEST
E. 70,285   T. 43,652 (62.11%)   Lab. hold
Alan Whitehead, Lab.                     18,017
Jeremy Moulton, C.                       14,207
Pearline Hingston, UKIP                   5,566
Angela Mawle, Green                       2,568
Adrian Ford, LD                           2,121
Chris Davis, Ind.                           770
Nick Chaffey, TUSC                          403
Lab. majority 3,810 (8.73%)
1.63% swing C. to Lab.
(2010: Lab. majority 2,413 (5.46%))

SOUTHEND WEST
E. 66,876   T. 44,509 (66.55%)   C. hold
David Amess, C.                          22,175
Julian Ware-Lane, Lab.                    8,154
Brian Otridge, UKIP                       7,803
Paul Collins, LD                          4,129
Jonathan Fuller, Green                    2,083
Jeremy Moss, Eng. Dem.                      165
C. majority 14,021 (31.50%)
0.57% swing C. to Lab.
(2010: C. majority 7,270 (16.67%))

SOUTHPORT
E. 67,328   T. 44,101 (65.50%)   LD hold
John Pugh, LD                    13,652
Damien Moore, C.                 12,330
Liz Savage, Lab.                  8,468
Terry Durrance, UKIP              7,429
Laurence Rankin, Green            1,230
Jacqueline Barlow, Southport        992
LD majority 1,322 (3.00%)
5.38% swing LD to C.
(2010: LD majority 6,024 (13.77%))

SPELTHORNE
E. 71,592   T. 49,079 (68.55%)   C. hold
Kwasi Kwarteng, C.               24,386
Redvers Cunningham, UKIP         10,234
Rebecca Geach, Lab.               9,114
Rosie Shimell, LD                 3,163
Paul Jacobs, Green                1,724
Juliet Griffith, ND                 230
Paul Couchman, TUSC                 228
C. majority 14,152 (28.84%)
4.87% swing C. to UKIP
(2010: C. majority 10,019 (21.18%))

STAFFORD
E. 68,705   T. 48,767 (70.98%)   C. hold
Jeremy Lefroy, C.                23,606
Kate Godfrey, Lab.               14,429
Edward Whitfield, UKIP            6,293
Karen Howell, NHAP                1,701
Mike Shone, Green                 1,390
Keith Miller, LD                  1,348
C. majority 9,177 (18.82%)
3.98% swing Lab. to C.
(2010: C. majority 5,460 (10.87%))

STAFFORDSHIRE MOORLANDS
E. 63,104   T. 42,587 (67.49%)   C. hold
Karen Bradley, C.                21,770
Trudie McGuinness, Lab.          11,596
George Langley-Poole, UKIP        6,236
John Redfern, LD                  1,759
Brian Smith, Green                1,226
C. majority 10,174 (23.89%)
4.31% swing Lab. to C.
(2010: C. majority 6,689 (15.27%))

STAFFORDSHIRE SOUTH
E. 84,243   T. 49,598 (58.87%)   C. hold
Gavin Williamson, C.             29,478
Kevin McElduff, Lab.              9,107
Lyndon Jones, UKIP                8,267
Robert Woodthorpe Browne, LD      1,448
Claire McIlvenna, Green           1,298
C. majority 20,371 (41.07%)
4.09% swing Lab. to C.
(2010: C. majority 16,590 (32.89%))

STALYBRIDGE & HYDE
E. 69,081  T. 41,034 (59.40%)
                    Lab. Co-op hold
Jonathan Reynolds, Lab. Co-op    18,447
Martin Riley, C.                 11,761
Angela McManus, UKIP              7,720
Jenny Ross, Green                 1,850
Pete Flynn, LD                    1,256
Lab. Co-op majority 6,686 (16.29%)
4.79% swing C. to Lab.
(2010: Lab. majority 2,744 (6.71%))

STEVENAGE
E. 70,597   T. 47,799 (67.71%)   C. hold
Stephen McPartland, C.           21,291
Sharon Taylor, Lab. Co-op        16,336
David Collins, UKIP               6,864
Susan Van De Ven, LD              1,582
Graham White, Green               1,369
Trevor Palmer, TUSC                 175
Charles Vickers, Eng. Dem.          115
David Cox, Ind.                      67
C. majority 4,955 (10.37%)
1.18% swing Lab. to C.
(2010: C. majority 3,578 (8.01%))

STOCKPORT
E. 63,931   T. 39,649 (62.02%)   Lab. hold
Ann Coffey, Lab.                 19,771
Daniel Hamilton, C.               9,710
Steven Woolfe, UKIP               5,206
Daniel Hawthorne, LD              3,034
Gary Lawson, Green                1,753
John Pearson, LU                    175
Lab. majority 10,061 (25.38%)
4.02% swing C. to Lab.
(2010: Lab. majority 6,784 (17.34%))

STOCKTON NORTH
E. 66,126   T. 39,571 (59.84%)   Lab. hold
Alex Cunningham, Lab.            19,436
Chris Daniels, C.                11,069
Mandy Boylett, UKIP               7,581
Anthony Sycamore, LD                884
John Tait, NE                       601
Lab. majority 8,367 (21.14%)
2.12% swing C. to Lab.
(2010: Lab. majority 6,676 (16.90%))

STOCKTON SOUTH
E. 75,109   T. 51,797 (68.96%)   C. hold
James Wharton, C.                24,221
Louise Baldock, Lab. Co-op       19,175
Ted Strike, UKIP                  5,480
Drew Durning, LD                  1,366
Jacqui Lovell, Green                952
Steve Walmsley, IASI                603
C. majority 5,046 (9.74%)
4.54% swing Lab. to C.
(2010: C. majority 332 (0.66%))

STOKE-ON-TRENT CENTRAL
E. 62,250   T. 31,084 (49.93%)   Lab. hold
Tristram Hunt, Lab.              12,220
Mick Harold, UKIP                 7,041
Liam Ascough, C.                  7,008
Mark Breeze, Ind.                 2,120
Zulfiqar Ali, LD                  1,296
Jan Zablocki, Green               1,123
Ali Majid, CISTA                    244
Paul Toussaint, Ubuntu               32
Lab. majority 5,179 (16.66%)
8.92% swing Lab. to UKIP
(2010: Lab. majority 5,566 (17.14%))

STOKE-ON-TRENT NORTH
E. 72,689   T. 38,654 (53.18%)   Lab. hold
*Ruth Smeeth, Lab.               15,429
Ben Adams, C.                    10,593
Geoffrey Locke, UKIP              9,542
Paul Roberts, LD                  1,137
Sean Adam, Green                  1,091
John Millward, Ind.                 508
Craig Pond, Ind.                    354
Lab. majority 4,836 (12.51%)
3.99% swing Lab. to C.
(2010: Lab. majority 8,235 (20.49%))

STOKE-ON-TRENT SOUTH
E. 68,788   T. 39,107 (56.85%)   Lab. hold
Rob Flello, Lab.                 15,319
Joe Rich, C.                     12,780
Tariq Mahmood, UKIP               8,298
Peter Andras, LD                  1,309
Luke Bellamy, Green               1,029
Matt Wright, TUSC                   372
Lab. majority 2,539 (6.49%)
1.94% swing Lab. to C.
(2010: Lab. majority 4,130 (10.36%))

STONE
E. 67,339   T. 47,031 (69.84%)   C. hold
Bill Cash, C.                    25,733
Sam Hale, Lab.                    9,483
Andrew Illsley, UKIP              7,620
Martin Lewis, LD                  2,473
Wenslie Naylon, Green             1,191
John Coutouvidis, Ind.              531
C. majority 16,250 (34.55%)
2.33% swing Lab. to C.
(2010: C. majority 13,292 (28.14%))

STOURBRIDGE
E. 69,077   T. 46,029 (66.63%)   C. hold
Margot James, C.                 21,195
Pete Lowe, Lab.                  14,501
James Carver, UKIP                7,774
Chris Bramall, LD                 1,538
Christian Kiever, Green           1,021
C. majority 6,694 (14.54%)
1.81% swing Lab. to C.
(2010: C. majority 5,164 (10.93%))

STRATFORD-ON-AVON
E. 70,914   T. 51,459 (72.57%)   C. hold
Nadhim Zahawi, C.                29,674
Edward Fila, UKIP                 6,798
Jeff Kenner, Lab.                 6,677
Elizabeth Adams, LD               6,182
Dominic Giles, Green              2,128
C. majority 22,876 (44.45%)
1.72% swing C. to UKIP
(2010: C. majority 11,346 (22.45%))

STREATHAM
E. 78,673   T. 49,933 (63.47%)   Lab. hold
Chuka Umunna, Lab.               26,474
Kim Caddy, C.                    12,540
Amna Ahmad, LD                    4,491
Jonathan Bartley, Green           4,421
Bruce Machan, UKIP                1,602
Artificial Beast, CISTA             192
Unjum Mirza, TUSC                   164
Deon Gayle, WRP                      49
Lab. majority 13,934 (27.91%)
1.72% swing C. to Lab.
(2010: Lab. majority 3,259 (6.96%))

STRETFORD & URMSTON
E. 69,490   T. 46,386 (66.75%)   Lab. hold
Kate Green, Lab.                 24,601
Lisa Cooke, C.                   12,916
Kalvin Chapman, UKIP              5,068
Geraldine Coggins, Green          2,187
Louise Ankers, LD                 1,362
Paul Bradley-Law, Whig              169
Paul Carson, PP UK                   83
Lab. majority 11,685 (25.19%)
2.65% swing C. to Lab.
(2010: Lab. majority 8,935 (19.90%))

STROUD
E. 80,522    T. 60,819 (75.53%)    C. hold
Neil Carmichael, C.    27,813
David Drew, Lab. Co-op    22,947
Caroline Stephens, UKIP    4,848
Sarah Lunnon, Green    2,779
Adrian Walker-Smith, LD    2,086
Rich Wilson, Ind.    246
David Michael, FPT    100
C. majority 4,866 (8.00%)
2.88% swing Lab. to C.
(2010: C. majority 1,299 (2.24%))

SUFFOLK CENTRAL & IPSWICH
NORTH
E. 78,782    T. 54,089 (68.66%)    C. hold
Daniel Poulter, C.    30,317
Jack Abbott, Lab.    10,173
Mark Cole, UKIP    7,459
Jon Neal, LD    3,314
Rhodri Griffiths, Green    2,664
Tony Holyoak, Eng. Dem.    162
C. majority 20,144 (37.24%)
1.32% swing Lab. to C.
(2010: C. majority 13,786 (25.81%))

SUFFOLK COASTAL
E. 78,782    T. 55,594 (70.57%)    C. hold
Therese Coffey, C.    28,855
Russell Whiting, Lab.    10,013
Daryll Pitcher, UKIP    8,655
James Sandbach, LD    4,777
Rachel Smith-Lyte, Green    3,294
C. majority 18,842 (33.89%)
1.77% swing Lab. to C.
(2010: C. majority 9,128 (16.63%))

SUFFOLK SOUTH
E. 73,220    T. 51,907 (70.89%)    C. hold
*James Cartlidge, C.    27,546
Jane Basham, Lab.    10,001
Steven Whalley, UKIP    7,897
Grace Weaver, LD    4,044
Robert Lindsay, Green    2,253
Stephen Todd, CPA    166
C. majority 17,545 (33.80%)
0.19% swing Lab. to C.
(2010: C. majority 8,689 (16.90%))

SUFFOLK WEST
E. 76,197    T. 49,232 (64.61%)    C. hold
Matthew Hancock, C.    25,684
Julian Flood, UKIP    10,700
Michael Jefferys, Lab.    8,604
Elfreda Tealby-Watson, LD    2,465
Niall Pettitt, Green    1,779
C. majority 14,984 (30.44%)
6.85% swing C. to UKIP
(2010: C. majority 13,050 (27.14%))

SUNDERLAND CENTRAL
E. 72,933    T. 41,762 (57.26%)    Lab. hold
Julie Elliott, Lab.    20,959
Jeffrey Townsend, C.    9,780
Bryan Foster, UKIP    7,997
Rachel Featherstone, Green    1,706
Adrian Page, LD    1,105
Joseph Young, ND    215
Lab. majority 11,179 (26.77%)
5.47% swing C. to Lab.
(2010: Lab. majority 6,725 (15.84%))

SURREY EAST
E. 79,654    T. 56,103 (70.43%)    C. hold
Sam Gyimah, C.    32,211
Helena Windsor, UKIP    9,553
Matt Wilson, Lab.    6,627
David Lee, LD    5,189
Nicky Dodgson, Green    2,159
Sandy Pratt, Ind.    364
C. majority 22,658 (40.39%)
4.73% swing C. to UKIP
(2010: C. majority 16,874 (30.88%))

SURREY HEATH
E. 79,515    T. 54,431 (68.45%)    C. hold
Michael Gove, C.    32,582
Paul Chapman, UKIP    7,778
Laween Atroshi, Lab.    6,100
Ann-Marie Barker, LD    4,937
Kimberley Lawson, Green    2,400
Juliana Brimicombe, Ch. P.    361
Bob Smith, Ind.    273
C. majority 24,804 (45.57%)
2.88% swing C. to UKIP
(2010: C. majority 17,289 (31.81%))

SURREY SOUTH WEST
E. 77,050    T. 57,119 (74.13%)    C. hold
Jeremy Hunt, C.    34,199
Mark Webber, UKIP    5,643
Howard Kaye, Lab.    5,415
Louise Irvine, NHAP    4,851
Patrick Haveron, LD    3,586
Susan Ryland, Green    3,105
Paul Robinson, S. New    320
C. majority 28,556 (49.99%)
3.05% swing C. to UKIP
(2010: C. majority 16,318 (28.50%))

SUSSEX MID
E. 79,520    T. 57,492 (72.30%)    C. hold
Nicholas Soames, C.    32,268
Greg Mountain, Lab.    7,982
Toby Brothers, UKIP    6,898
Daisy Cooper, LD    6,604
Miranda Diboll, Green    2,453
Beki Adam, Ind.    958
Baron Von Thunderclap, Loony    329
C. majority 24,286 (42.24%)
0.94% swing C. to Lab.
(2010: C. majority 7,402 (13.25%))

SUTTON & CHEAM
E. 69,160    T. 49,905 (72.16%)    C. gain
*Paul Scully, C.    20,732
Paul Burstow, LD    16,811
Emily Brothers, Lab.    5,546
Angus Dalgleish, UKIP    5,341
Maeve Tomlinson, Green    1,051
Dave Ash, NHAP    345
Pauline Gorman, TUSC    79
C. majority 3,921 (7.86%)
5.59% swing LD to C.
(2010: LD majority 1,608 (3.31%))

SUTTON COLDFIELD
E. 74,956    T. 50,854 (67.85%)    C. hold
Andrew Mitchell, C.    27,782
Rob Pocock, Lab.    11,365
Marcus Brown, UKIP    7,489
Richard Brighton-Knight, LD    2,627
David Ratcliff, Green    1,426
Mark Sleigh, Ubuntu    165
C. majority 16,417 (32.28%)
0.67% swing C. to Lab.
(2010: C. majority 17,005 (33.61%))

SWINDON NORTH
E. 81,005    T. 52,242 (64.49%)    C. hold
Justin Tomlinson, C.    26,295
Mark Dempsey, Lab.    14,509
James Faulkner, UKIP    8,011
Poppy Hebden-Leeder, Green    1,723
Janet Ellard, LD    1,704
C. majority 11,786 (22.56%)
4.26% swing Lab. to C.
(2010: C. majority 7,060 (14.04%))

SWINDON SOUTH
E. 73,956    T. 49,263 (66.61%)    C. hold
Robert Buckland, C.    22,777
Anne Snelgrove, Lab.    16,992
John Short, UKIP    5,920
Damon Hooton, LD    1,817
Talis Kimberley-Fairbourn, Green    1,757
C. majority 5,785 (11.74%)
2.11% swing Lab. to C.
(2010: C. majority 3,544 (7.52%))

TAMWORTH
E. 71,912    T. 47,174 (65.60%)    C. hold
Christopher Pincher, C.    23,606
Carol Dean, Lab.    12,304
Jan Higgins, UKIP    8,727
Jenny Pinkett, LD    1,427
Nicola Holmes, Green    1,110
C. majority 11,302 (23.96%)
5.42% swing Lab. to C.
(2010: C. majority 6,090 (13.13%))

TATTON
E. 64,512    T. 45,298 (70.22%)    C. hold
George Osborne, C.    26,552
David Pinto-Duschinsky, Lab.    8,311
Stuart Hutton, UKIP    4,871
Gareth Wilson, LD    3,850
Tina Louise Rothery, Green    1,714
C. majority 18,241 (40.27%)
1.47% swing Lab. to C.
(2010: C. majority 14,487 (32.03%))

TAUNTON DEANE
E. 81,830    T. 57,887 (70.74%)    C. gain
*Rebecca Pow, C.    27,849
Rachel Gilmour, LD    12,358
Laura Bailhache, UKIP    6,921
Neil Guild, Lab.    5,347
Clive Martin, Green    2,630
Mike Rigby, Ind.    2,568
Stephen German, TUSC    118
Bruce Gauld, Ind.    96
C. majority 15,491 (26.76%)
16.81% swing LD to C.
(2010: LD majority 3,993 (6.87%))

TELFORD
E. 66,166    T. 40,645 (61.43%)    C. gain
*Lucy Allan, C.    16,094
David Wright, Lab.    15,364
Denis Allen, UKIP    7,330
Peter Hawkins, Green    930
Ian Croll, LD    927
C. majority 730 (1.80%)
2.08% swing Lab. to C.
(2010: Lab. majority 978 (2.37%))

TEWKESBURY
E. 78,500　T. 55,344 (70.50%)　C. hold
Laurence Robertson, C.　30,176
Ed Buxton, Lab.　8,204
Alistair Cameron, LD　7,629
Stuart Adair, UKIP　7,128
Jemma Clarke, Green　2,207
C. majority 21,972 (39.70%)
2.04% swing Lab. to C.
(2010: C. majority 6,310 (11.69%))

THANET NORTH
E. 70,504　T. 47,053 (66.74%)　C. hold
Roger Gale, C.　23,045
Piers Wauchope, UKIP　12,097
Frances Rehal, Lab.　8,411
Ed Targett, Green　1,719
George Cunningham, LD　1,645
Cemanthe McKenzie, Thanet　136
C. majority 10,948 (23.27%)
11.45% swing C. to UKIP
(2010: C. majority 13,528 (31.21%))

THANET SOUTH
E. 70,182　T. 49,401 (70.39%)　C. hold
*Craig Mackinlay, C.　18,838
Nigel Farage, UKIP　16,026
Will Scobie, Lab.　11,740
Ian Driver, Green　1,076
Russ Timpson, LD　932
Al Murray, FUKP　318
Ruth Bailey, Manston　191
Nigel Askew, Reality　126
Grahame Birchall, Thanet　63
Dean McCastree, Ind.　61
Zebadiah Abu-Obadiah, Zeb　30
C. majority 2,812 (5.69%)
18.40% swing C. to UKIP
(2010: C. majority 7,617 (16.58%))

THIRSK & MALTON
E. 77,451　T. 52,365 (67.61%)　C. hold
*Kevin Hollinrake, C.　27,545
Alan Avery, Lab.　8,089
Toby Horton, UKIP　7,805
Dinah Keal, LD　4,703
Chris Newsam, Green　2,404
John Clark, Lib.　1,127
Philip Tate, Ind.　692
C. majority 19,456 (37.15%)
1.08% swing C. to Lab.
(2010: C. majority 11,281 (29.58%))

THORNBURY & YATE
E. 65,884　T. 48,570 (73.72%)　C. gain
*Luke Hall, C.　19,924
Steve Webb, LD　18,429
Russ Martin, UKIP　5,126
Hadleigh Roberts, Lab.　3,775
Iain Hamilton, Green　1,316
C. majority 1,495 (3.08%)
8.92% swing LD to C.
(2010: LD majority 7,116 (14.76%))

THURROCK
E. 77,569　T. 49,564 (63.90%)　C. hold
Jackie Doyle-Price, C.　16,692
Polly Billington, Lab.　16,156
Tim Aker, UKIP　15,718
Rhodri Jamieson-Ball, LD　644
Jamie Barnes, CISTA　244
Daniel Munyambu, ND　79
Aba Kristilolu, AP　31
C. majority 536 (1.08%)
0.44% swing Lab. to C.
(2010: C. majority 92 (0.20%))

TIVERTON & HONITON
E. 76,270　T. 53,763 (70.49%)　C. hold
Neil Parish, C.　29,030
Graham Smith, UKIP　8,857
Caroline Kolek, Lab.　6,835
Stephen Kearney, LD　5,626
Paul Edwards, Green　3,415
C. majority 20,173 (37.52%)
3.41% swing C. to UKIP
(2010: C. majority 9,320 (16.98%))

TONBRIDGE & MALLING
E. 74,877　T. 53,670 (71.68%)　C. hold
*Thomas Tugendhat, C.　31,887
Robert Izzard, UKIP　8,153
Claire Leigh, Lab.　7,604
Mary Varrall, LD　3,660
Howard Porter, Green　2,366
C. majority 23,734 (44.22%)
4.99% swing C. to UKIP
(2010: C. majority 18,178 (35.43%))

TOOTING
E. 76,778　T. 53,529 (69.72%)　Lab. hold
Sadiq Khan, Lab.　25,263
Dan Watkins, C.　22,421
Esther Obiri-Darko, Green　2,201
Philip Ling, LD　2,107
Przemek Skwirczynski, UKIP　1,537
Lab. majority 2,842 (5.31%)
0.16% swing C. to Lab.
(2010: Lab. majority 2,524 (4.98%))

TORBAY
E. 76,259　T. 48,079 (63.05%)　C. gain
*Kevin Foster, C.　19,551
Adrian Sanders, LD　16,265
Tony McIntyre, UKIP　6,540
Su Maddock, Lab.　4,166
Paula Hermes, Green　1,557
C. majority 3,286 (6.83%)
7.56% swing LD to C.
(2010: LD majority 4,078 (8.29%))

TOTNES
E. 68,630　T. 47,097 (68.62%)　C. hold
Sarah Wollaston, C.　24,941
Justin Haque, UKIP　6,656
Nicky Williams, Lab.　5,988
Gill Coombs, Green　4,845
Julian Brazil, LD　4,667
C. majority 18,285 (38.82%)
0.50% swing C. to UKIP
(2010: C. majority 4,927 (10.30%))

TOTTENHAM
E. 70,809　T. 42,558 (60.10%)　Lab. hold
David Lammy, Lab.　28,654
Stefan Mrozinski, C.　5,090
Dee Searle, Green　3,931
Turhan Ozen, LD　1,756
Tariq Saeed, UKIP　1,512
Jenny Sutton, TUSC　1,324
Tania Mahmood, Peace　291
Lab. majority 23,564 (55.37%)
5.49% swing C. to Lab.
(2010: Lab. majority 16,931 (41.61%))

TRURO & FALMOUTH
E. 73,601　T. 51,544 (70.03%)　C. hold
Sarah Newton, C.　22,681
Simon Rix, LD　8,681
Stuart Roden, Lab.　7,814
John Hyslop, UKIP　5,967
Karen Westbrook, Green　4,483
Loic Rich, Ind.　792
Stephen Richardson, Meb. Ker.　563
Rik Evans, NHAP　526
Stanley Guffogg, PPP　37
C. majority 14,000 (27.16%)
13.13% swing LD to C.
(2010: C. majority 435 (0.89%))

TUNBRIDGE WELLS
E. 73,429　T. 51,428 (70.04%)　C. hold
Greg Clark, C.　30,181
Kevin Kerrigan, Lab.　7,307
Colin Nicholson, UKIP　6,481
James MacCleary, LD　4,342
Marie Jones, Green　2,659
Graham Naismith, Ind.　458
C. majority 22,874 (44.48%)
0.47% swing C. to Lab.
(2010: C. majority 15,576 (30.95%))

TWICKENHAM
E. 80,242　T. 62,004 (77.27%)　C. gain
*Tania Mathias, C.　25,580
Vince Cable, LD　23,563
Nick Grant, Lab.　7,129
Barry Edwards, UKIP　3,069
Tanya Williams, Green　2,463
Dominic Stockford, Ch. P.　174
David Wedgwood, MC　26
C. majority 2,017 (3.25%)
11.79% swing LD to C.
(2010: LD majority 12,140 (20.33%))

TYNEMOUTH
E. 77,523　T. 53,495 (69.01%)　Lab. hold
Alan Campbell, Lab.　25,791
Glenn Hall, C.　17,551
Gary Legg, UKIP　6,541
Julia Erskine, Green　2,017
John Paton-Day, LD　1,595
Lab. majority 8,240 (15.40%)
2.25% swing C. to Lab.
(2010: Lab. majority 5,739 (10.90%))

TYNESIDE NORTH
E. 79,286　T. 46,818 (59.05%)　Lab. hold
Mary Glindon, Lab.　26,191
Martin McGann, C.　8,997
Scott Hartley, UKIP　7,618
John Appleby, LD　2,075
Martin Collins, Green　1,442
Tim Wall, TUSC　304
Bob Batten, NF　191
Lab. majority 17,194 (36.73%)
2.21% swing C. to Lab.
(2010: Lab. majority 12,884 (27.76%))

UXBRIDGE & RUISLIP SOUTH
E. 70,634   T. 44,811 (63.44%)   C. hold
*Boris Johnson, C.                22,511
Chris Summers, Lab.               11,816
Jack Duffin, UKIP                  6,346
Mike Cox, LD                       2,215
Graham Lee, Green                  1,414
Gary Harbord, TUSC                   180
Jenny Thompson, Ind.                  84
Howling Laud Hope, Loony              72
Sabrina Moosun, Community             52
Lord Toby Jug, Eccentric              50
Michael Doherty, Ind.                 39
Jane Lawrence, Realist                18
James Jackson, ND                     14
C. majority 10,695 (23.87%)
0.51% swing C. to Lab.
(2010: C. majority 11,216 (24.88%))

VAUXHALL
E. 81,698   T. 47,941 (58.68%)   Lab. hold
Kate Hoey, Lab.                   25,778
James Bellis, C.                  13,070
Gulnar Hasnain, Green              3,658
Adrian Hyyrylainen-Trett, LD       3,312
Ace Nnorom, UKIP                   1,385
Mark Chapman, Pirate                 201
Simon Hardy, LU                      188
Louis Jensen, CISTA                  164
Waleed Salman Ghani, Whig            103
Danny Lambert, SPGB                   82
Lab. majority 12,708 (26.51%)
0.87% swing Lab. to C.
(2010: Lab. majority 10,651 (24.66%))

WAKEFIELD
E. 70,521   T. 42,973 (60.94%)   Lab. hold
Mary Creagh, Lab.                 17,301
Antony Calvert, C.                14,688
Alan Hazelhurst, UKIP              7,862
Finbarr Cronin, LD                 1,483
Rebecca Thackray, Green            1,069
Mick Griffiths, TUSC                 287
Elliot Barr, CISTA                   283
Lab. majority 2,613 (6.08%)
1.23% swing C. to Lab.
(2010: Lab. majority 1,613 (3.63%))

WALLASEY
E. 65,495   T. 43,366 (66.21%)   Lab. hold
Angela Eagle, Lab.                26,176
Chris Clarkson, C.                 9,828
Geoff Caton, UKIP                  5,063
Julian Pratt, Green                1,288
Kris Brown, LD                     1,011
Lab. majority 16,348 (37.70%)
8.64% swing C. to Lab.
(2010: Lab. majority 8,507 (20.42%))

WALSALL NORTH
E. 67,080   T. 36,883 (54.98%)   Lab. hold
David Winnick, Lab.               14,392
Douglas Hansen-Luke, C.           12,455
Liz Hazell, UKIP                   8,122
Nigel Jones, LD                      840
Pete Smith, TUSC                     545
Mike Harrison, Green                 529
Lab. majority 1,937 (5.25%)
1.26% swing C. to Lab.
(2010: Lab. majority 990 (2.74%))

WALSALL SOUTH
E. 67,743   T. 41,838 (61.76%)   Lab. hold
Valerie Vaz, Lab.                 19,740
Sue Arnold, C.                    13,733
Derek Bennett, UKIP                6,540
Charlotte Fletcher, Green          1,149
Joel Kenrick, LD                     676
Lab. majority 6,007 (14.36%)
5.03% swing C. to Lab.
(2010: Lab. majority 1,755 (4.29%))

WALTHAMSTOW
E. 67,289   T. 41,796 (62.11%)
                          Lab. Co-op hold
Stella Creasy, Lab. Co-op         28,779
Molly Samuel-Leport, C.            5,584
Michael Gold, Green                2,661
Paul Hillman, UKIP                 2,507
Steven Cheung, LD                  1,661
Nancy Taaffe, TUSC                   394
Ellie Merton, ND                     129
Jonty Leff, WRP                       81
Lab. Co-op majority 23,195 (55.50%)
8.82% swing C. to Lab.
(2010: Lab. majority 9,478 (23.12%))

WANSBECK
E. 63,273   T. 38,528 (60.89%)   Lab. hold
Ian Lavery, Lab.                  19,267
Chris Galley, C.                   8,386
Melanie Hurst, UKIP                7,014
Tom Hancock, LD                    2,407
Christopher Hedley, Green          1,454
Lab. majority 10,881 (28.24%)
0.03% swing Lab. to C.
(2010: Lab. majority 7,031 (18.37%))

WANTAGE
E. 83,516   T. 58,320 (69.83%)   C. hold
Ed Vaizey, C.                     31,092
Stephen Webb, Lab.                 9,343
Alex Meredith, LD                  7,611
Lee Upcraft, UKIP                  7,288
Kate Prendergast, Green            2,986
C. majority 21,749 (37.29%)
0.37% swing C. to Lab.
(2010: C. majority 13,547 (24.04%))

WARLEY
E. 63,740   T. 37,829 (59.35%)   Lab. hold
John Spellar, Lab.                22,012
Tom Williams, C.                   7,310
Pete Durnell, UKIP                 6,237
Robert Buckman, Green              1,465
Catherine Smith, LD                  805
Lab. majority 14,702 (38.86%)
5.38% swing C. to Lab.
(2010: Lab. majority 10,756 (28.11%))

WARRINGTON NORTH
E. 72,632   T. 45,419 (62.53%)   Lab. hold
Helen Jones, Lab.                 21,720
Richard Short, C.                 12,797
Trevor Nicholls, UKIP              7,757
Stefan Krizanac, LD                1,881
Sarah Hayes, Green                 1,264
Lab. majority 8,923 (19.65%)
2.17% swing C. to Lab.
(2010: Lab. majority 6,771 (15.32%))

WARRINGTON SOUTH
E. 85,566   T. 59,353 (69.37%)   C. hold
David Mowat, C.                   25,928
Nick Bent, Lab.                   23,178
Malcolm Lingley, UKIP              4,909
Bob Barr, LD                       3,335
Stephanie Davies, Green            1,765
Kevin Bennett, TUSC                  238
C. majority 2,750 (4.63%)
0.90% swing Lab. to C.
(2010: C. majority 1,553 (2.83%))

WARWICK & LEAMINGTON
E. 71,570   T. 50,581 (70.67%)   C. hold
Chris White, C.                   24,249
Lynnette Kelly, Lab.              17,643
Alastair MacBrayne, UKIP           4,183
Haseeb Arif, LD                    2,512
Azzees Minott, Green               1,994
C. majority 6,606 (13.06%)
2.95% swing Lab. to C.
(2010: C. majority 3,513 (7.16%))

WARWICKSHIRE NORTH
E. 70,152   T. 47,377 (67.53%)   C. hold
*Craig Tracey, C.                 20,042
Mike O'Brien, Lab.                17,069
William Cash, UKIP                 8,256
Alan Beddow, LD                      978
Ian Bonner, Green                    894
Eileen Hunter, TUSC                  138
C. majority 2,973 (6.28%)
3.08% swing Lab. to C.
(2010: C. majority 54 (0.11%))

WASHINGTON & SUNDERLAND WEST
E. 68,188   T. 37,257 (54.64%)   Lab. hold
Sharon Hodgson, Lab.              20,478
Aileen Casey, UKIP                 7,321
Bob Dhillon, C.                    7,033
Anthony Murphy, Green              1,091
Dominic Haney, LD                    993
Gary Duncan, TUSC                    341
Lab. majority 13,157 (35.31%)
6.92% swing Lab. to UKIP
(2010: Lab. majority 11,458 (30.69%))

WATFORD
E. 84,270   T. 56,149 (66.63%)   C. hold
Richard Harrington, C.            24,400
Matt Turmaine, Lab.               14,606
Dorothy Thornhill, LD             10,152
Nick Lincoln, UKIP                 5,481
Aidan Cottrell-Boyce, Green        1,332
Mark O'Connor, TUSC                  178
C. majority 9,794 (17.44%)
4.61% swing Lab. to C.
(2010: C. majority 1,425 (2.58%))

WAVENEY
E. 80,171   T. 52,196 (65.11%)   C. hold
Peter Aldous, C.                  22,104
Bob Blizzard, Lab.                19,696
Simon Tobin, UKIP                  7,580
Graham Elliott, Green              1,761
Steve Gordon, LD                   1,055
C. majority 2,408 (4.61%)
1.55% swing Lab. to C.
(2010: C. majority 769 (1.50%))

WEALDEN
E. 80,252   T. 57,017 (71.05%)   C. hold
*Nus Ghani, C.                          32,508
Peter Griffiths, UKIP                    9,541
Solomon Curtis, Lab.                     6,165
Giles Goodall, LD                        5,180
Mark Smith, Green                        3,623
C. majority 22,967 (40.28%)
5.12% swing C. to UKIP
(2010: C. majority 17,179 (31.25%))

WEAVER VALE
E. 68,407   T. 46,867 (68.51%)   C. hold
Graham Evans, C.                        20,227
Julia Tickridge, Lab.                   19,421
Amos Wright, UKIP                        4,547
Mary Di Mauro, LD                        1,395
Chris Copeman, Green                     1,183
Joseph Whyte, TUSC                          94
C. majority 806 (1.72%)
0.27% swing C. to Lab.
(2010: C. majority 991 (2.25%))

WELLINGBOROUGH
E. 77,127   T. 50,430 (65.39%)   C. hold
Peter Bone, C.                          26,265
Jonathan Munday, UKIP                    9,868
Richard Garvie, Lab.                     9,839
Chris Nelson, LD                         2,240
Marion Turner-Hawes, Green               2,218
C. majority 16,397 (32.51%)
6.28% swing C. to UKIP
(2010: C. majority 11,787 (22.82%))

WELLS
E. 79,405   T. 56,904 (71.66%)   C. gain
*James Heappey, C.                      26,247
Tessa Munt, LD                          18,662
Helen Hims, UKIP                         5,644
Chris Inchley, Lab.                      3,780
Jon Cousins, Green                       2,331
Paul Arnold, ND                             83
Dave Dobbs, Birthday                        81
Gypsy Watkins, Ind.                         76
C. majority 7,585 (13.33%)
7.38% swing LD to C.
(2010: LD majority 800 (1.43%))

WELWYN HATFIELD
E. 73,264   T. 50,205 (68.53%)   C. hold
Grant Shapps, C.                        25,281
Anawar Miah, Lab.                       13,128
Arthur Stevens, UKIP                     6,556
Hugh Annand, LD                          3,140
Marc Scheimann, Green                    1,742
Michael Green, Ind.                        216
Richard Shattock, TUSC                     142
C. majority 12,153 (24.21%)
5.69% swing C. to Lab.
(2010: C. majority 17,423 (35.58%))

WENTWORTH & DEARNE
E. 74,283   T. 43,189 (58.14%)   Lab. hold
John Healey, Lab.                       24,571
Mike Hookem, UKIP                       10,733
Michael Naughton, C.                     6,441
Edwin Simpson, LD                        1,135
Alan England, Eng. Dem.                    309
Lab. majority 13,838 (32.04%)
5.23% swing Lab. to UKIP
(2010: Lab. majority 13,920 (33.06%))

WEST BROMWICH EAST
E. 63,641   T. 37,492 (58.91%)   Lab. hold
Tom Watson, Lab.                        18,817
Olivia Seccombe, C.                      9,347
Steve Latham, UKIP                       7,949
Flo Clucas, LD                             751
Barry Lim, Green                           628
Lab. majority 9,470 (25.26%)
3.81% swing C. to Lab.
(2010: Lab. majority 6,696 (17.64%))

WEST BROMWICH WEST
E. 65,533 T. 35,026 (53.45%)
                          Lab. Co-op hold
Adrian Bailey, Lab. Co-op               16,578
Graham Eardley, UKIP                     8,836
Paul Ratner, C.                          8,365
Mark Redding, Green                        697
Karen Trench, LD                           550
Lab. Co-op majority 7,742 (22.10%)
9.26% swing Lab. to UKIP
(2010: Lab. majority 5,651 (15.62%))

WEST HAM
E. 90,634   T. 52,793 (58.25%)   Lab. hold
Lyn Brown, Lab.                         36,132
Festus Akinbusoye, C.                    8,146
Jamie McKenzie, UKIP                     3,950
Rachel Collinson, Green                  2,651
Paul Reynolds, LD                        1,430
Andy Uzoka, CPA                            369
Cydatty Bogie, Community                   115
Lab. majority 27,986 (53.01%)
2.51% swing C. to Lab.
(2010: Lab. majority 22,534 (47.99%))

WESTMINSTER NORTH
E. 62,346   T. 39,514 (63.38%)   Lab. hold
Karen Buck, Lab.                        18,504
Lindsey Hall, C.                        16,527
Nigel Sussman, UKIP                      1,489
Kirsty Allan, LD                         1,457
Jennifer Nadel, Green                    1,322
Gabriela Fajardo, Ch. P.                   152
Nicholas Ward, Ind.                         63
Lab. majority 1,977 (5.00%)
0.18% swing Lab. to C.
(2010: Lab. majority 2,126 (5.37%))

WESTMORLAND & LONSDALE
E. 65,857   T. 48,929 (74.30%)   LD hold
Tim Farron, LD                          25,194
Ann Myatt, C.                           16,245
Alan Piper, UKIP                         3,031
John Bateson, Lab.                       2,661
Chris Loynes, Green                      1,798
LD majority 8,949 (18.29%)
2.76% swing LD to C.
(2010: LD majority 12,264 (23.82%))

WESTON-SUPER-MARE
E. 79,493   T. 52,552 (66.11%)   C. hold
John Penrose, C.                        25,203
Tim Taylor, Lab.                         9,594
Ernie Warrender, UKIP                    9,366
John Munro, LD                           5,486
Richard Lawson, Green                    2,592
Ronald Lavelle, Eng. Dem.                  311
C. majority 15,609 (29.70%)
1.83% swing C. to Lab.
(2010: C. majority 2,691 (5.10%))

WIGAN
E. 76,068   T. 45,293 (59.54%)   Lab. hold
Lisa Nandy, Lab.                        23,625
Caroline Kerswell, C.                    9,389
Mark Bradley, UKIP                       8,818
Will Patterson, Green                    1,273
Mark Clayton, LD                         1,255
Gareth Fairhurst, Wigan                    768
Brian Parr, Ind.                           165
Lab. majority 14,236 (31.43%)
3.84% swing C. to Lab.
(2010: Lab. majority 10,487 (23.76%))

WILTSHIRE NORTH
E. 67,858   T. 50,556 (74.50%)   C. hold
James Gray, C.                          28,938
Brian Mathew, LD                         7,892
Patricia Bryant, UKIP                    5,813
Peter Baldrey, Lab.                      4,930
Phil Chamberlain, Green                  2,350
Simon Killane, Ind.                        390
Giles Wareham, Ind.                        243
C. majority 21,046 (41.63%)
13.13% swing LD to C.
(2010: C. majority 7,483 (15.37%))

WILTSHIRE SOUTH WEST
E. 73,030   T. 51,643 (70.71%)   C. hold
Andrew Murrison, C.                     27,198
Matthew Brown, UKIP                      9,030
George Aylett, Lab.                      6,948
Trevor Carbin, LD                        5,482
Phil Randle, Green                       2,985
C. majority 18,168 (35.18%)
5.50% swing C. to UKIP
(2010: C. majority 10,367 (21.15%))

WIMBLEDON
E. 65,853   T. 48,422 (73.53%)   C. hold
Stephen Hammond, C.                     25,225
Andrew Judge, Lab.                      12,606
Shas Sheehan, LD                         6,129
Peter Bucklitsch, UKIP                   2,476
Charles Barraball, Green                 1,986
C. majority 12,619 (26.06%)
0.38% swing C. to Lab.
(2010: C. majority 11,408 (24.07%))

WINCHESTER
E. 74,119   T. 55,316 (74.63%)   C. hold
Steve Brine, C.                         30,425
Jackie Porter, LD                       13,511
Mark Chaloner, UKIP                      4,613
Martin Lyon, Lab.                        4,122
Michael Wilks, Green                     2,645
C. majority 16,914 (30.58%)
12.56% swing LD to C.
(2010: C. majority 3,048 (5.45%))

WINDSOR
E. 74,119   T. 50,160 (67.67%)   C. hold
Adam Afriyie, C.                        31,797
Fiona Dent, Lab.                         6,714
Tariq Malik, UKIP                        4,992
George Fussey, LD                        4,323
Derek Wall, Green                        1,834
Wisdom Da Costa, Ind.                      500
C. majority 25,083 (50.01%)
0.47% swing C. to Lab.
(2010: C. majority 19,054 (38.42%))

**WIRRAL SOUTH**
E. 56,956   T. 41,837 (73.45%)   Lab. hold
Alison McGovern, Lab.                     20,165
John Bell, C.                             15,566
David Scott, UKIP                          3,737
Elizabeth Jewkes, LD                       1,474
Paul Cartlidge, Green                        895
Lab. majority 4,599 (10.99%)
4.83% swing C. to Lab.
(2010: Lab. majority 531 (1.33%))

**WIRRAL WEST**
E. 55,377   T. 41,858 (75.59%)   Lab. gain
*Margaret Greenwood, Lab.                 18,898
Esther McVey, C.                          18,481
Hilary Jones, UKIP                         2,772
Peter Reisdorf, LD                         1,433
David James, ND                              274
Lab. majority 417 (1.00%)
3.59% swing C. to Lab.
(2010: C. majority 2,436 (6.19%))

**WITHAM**
E. 67,090   T. 47,168 (70.31%)   C. hold
Priti Patel, C.                           27,123
Garry Cockrill, UKIP                       7,569
John Clarke, Lab.                          7,467
Jo Hayes, LD                               2,891
James Abbott, Green                        2,038
Doreen Scrimshaw, CPA                         80
C. majority 19,554 (41.46%)
2.11% swing C. to UKIP
(2010: C. majority 15,196 (32.45%))

**WITNEY**
E. 79,767   T. 58,482 (73.32%)   C. hold
David Cameron, C.                         35,201
Duncan Enright, Lab.                      10,046
Simon Strutt, UKIP                         5,352
Andrew Graham, LD                          3,953
Stuart Macdonald, Green                    2,970
Clive Peedell, NHAP                          616
Colin Bex, Wessex Reg.                       110
Chris Tompson, Ind.                           94
Vivien Saunders, VAT                          56
Bobby Smith, Elmo                             37
Deek Jackson, LP                              35
Nathan Handley, ND                            12
C. majority 25,155 (43.01%)
1.40% swing C. to Lab.
(2010: C. majority 22,740 (39.36%))

**WOKING**
E. 74,287   T. 51,964 (69.95%)   C. hold
Jonathan Lord, C.                         29,199
Jill Rawling, Lab.                         8,389
Chris Took, LD                             6,047
Rob Burberry, UKIP                         5,873
Martin Robson, Green                       2,109
Declan Wade, CISTA                           229
Ruth Temple, Magna Carta                      77
Angela Woolford, TEP                          41
C. majority 20,810 (40.05%)
1.10% swing C. to Lab.
(2010: C. majority 6,807 (12.90%))

**WOKINGHAM**
E. 77,881   T. 55,999 (71.90%)   C. hold
John Redwood, C.                          32,329
Andy Croy, Lab.                            8,132
Clive Jones, LD                            7,572
Philip Cunnington, UKIP                    5,516
Adrian Windisch, Green                     2,092
Kaz Lokuciewski, Ind.                        358
C. majority 24,197 (43.21%)
0.30% swing Lab. to C.
(2010: C. majority 13,492 (24.74%))

**WOLVERHAMPTON NORTH EAST**
E. 61,073   T. 34,003 (55.68%)   Lab. hold
Emma Reynolds, Lab.                       15,669
Darren Henry, C.                          10,174
Star Etheridge, UKIP                       6,524
Ian Jenkins, LD                              935
Becky Cooper, Green                          701
Lab. majority 5,495 (16.16%)
4.52% swing C. to Lab.
(2010: Lab. majority 2,484 (7.12%))

**WOLVERHAMPTON SOUTH EAST**
E. 62,561   T. 34,764 (55.57%)   Lab. hold
Pat McFadden, Lab.                        18,539
Suria Photay, C.                           7,761
Barry Hodgson, UKIP                        7,061
Ian Griffiths, LD                            798
Geeta Kauldhar, Green                        605
Lab. majority 10,778 (31.00%)
6.00% swing C. to Lab.
(2010: Lab. majority 6,593 (19.00%))

**WOLVERHAMPTON SOUTH WEST**
E. 60,375   T. 40,209 (66.60%)   Lab. gain
*Rob Marris, Lab.                         17,374
Paul Uppal, C.                            16,573
David Everett, UKIP                        4,310
Andrea Cantrill, Green                     1,058
Neale Upstone, LD                            845
Brian Booth, Ind.                             49
Lab. majority 801 (1.99%)
1.86% swing C. to Lab.
(2010: C. majority 691 (1.72%))

**WORCESTER**
E. 71,003   T. 49,723 (70.03%)   C. hold
Robin Walker, C.                          22,534
Joy Squires, Lab.                         16,888
James Goad, UKIP                           6,378
Louis Stephen, Green                       2,024
Federica Smith, LD                         1,677
Pete McNally, TUSC                           153
Mark Shuker, Ind.                             69
C. majority 5,646 (11.35%)
2.63% swing Lab. to C.
(2010: C. majority 2,982 (6.09%))

**WORCESTERSHIRE MID**
E. 73,069   T. 52,225 (71.47%)   C. hold
*Nigel Huddleston, C.                     29,763
Richard Keel, UKIP                         9,231
Robin Lunn, Lab.                           7,548
Margaret Rowley, LD                        3,750
Neil Franks, Green                         1,933
C. majority 20,532 (39.31%)
4.61% swing C. to UKIP
(2010: C. majority 15,864 (31.15%))

**WORCESTERSHIRE WEST**
E. 73,415   T. 54,100 (73.69%)   C. hold
Harriett Baldwin, C.                      30,342
Richard Chamings, UKIP                     7,764
Daniel Walton, Lab.                        7,244
Dennis Wharton, LD                         5,245
Julian Roskams, Green                      3,505
C. majority 22,578 (41.73%)
2.33% swing C. to UKIP
(2010: C. majority 6,754 (12.49%))

**WORKINGTON**
E. 58,672   T. 38,463 (65.56%)   Lab. hold
*Sue Hayman, Lab.                         16,282
Rozila Kana, C.                           11,596
Mark Jenkinson, UKIP                       7,538
Phill Roberts, LD                          1,708
Jill Perry, Green                          1,149
Roy Ivinson, ND                              190
Lab. majority 4,686 (12.18%)
0.26% swing C. to Lab.
(2010: Lab. majority 4,575 (11.65%))

**WORSLEY & ECCLES SOUTH**
E. 72,174   T. 42,048 (58.26%)   Lab. hold
Barbara Keeley, Lab.                      18,600
Iain Lindley, C.                          12,654
Owen Hammond, UKIP                         7,688
Christopher Bertenshaw, Green              1,242
Kate Clarkson, LD                          1,100
Steve North, TUSC                            380
Mags McNally, Reality                        200
Geoffrey Berg, Ind.                          184
Lab. majority 5,946 (14.14%)
1.87% swing C. to Lab.
(2010: Lab. majority 4,337 (10.40%))

**WORTHING EAST & SHOREHAM**
E. 74,272   T. 49,898 (67.18%)   C. hold
Tim Loughton, C.                          24,686
Tim Macpherson, Lab.                       9,737
Mike Glennon, UKIP                         8,267
Bob Smytherman, LD                         3,360
James Doyle, Green                         2,605
Carl Walker, NHAP                          1,243
C. majority 14,949 (29.96%)
0.90% swing C. to Lab.
(2010: C. majority 11,105 (22.95%))

**WORTHING WEST**
E. 75,617   T. 50,763 (67.13%)   C. hold
Peter Bottomley, C.                       26,124
Tim Cross, UKIP                            9,269
Jim Deen, Lab.                             7,955
Hazel Thorpe, LD                           4,477
David Aherne, Green                        2,938
C. majority 16,855 (33.20%)
6.29% swing C. to UKIP
(2010: C. majority 11,729 (23.88%))

**WREKIN, THE**
E. 65,942   T. 45,437 (68.90%)   C. hold
Mark Pritchard, C.                        22,579
Katrina Gilman, Lab.                      11,836
Jill Seymour, UKIP                         7,620
Rod Keyes, LD                              1,959
Cath Edwards, Green                        1,443
C. majority 10,743 (23.64%)
1.54% swing Lab. to C.
(2010: C. majority 9,450 (20.56%))

**WYCOMBE**
E. 76,371   T. 51,439 (67.35%)   C. hold
Steven Baker, C.                          26,444
David Williams, Lab.                      11,588
David Meacock, UKIP                        5,198
Steve Guy, LD                              4,546
Jem Bailey, Green                          3,086
David Fitton, Ind.                           577
C. majority 14,856 (28.88%)
1.24% swing C. to Lab.
(2010: C. majority 9,560 (19.85%))

## WYRE & PRESTON NORTH
E. 70,697　T. 49,893 (70.57%)　C. hold

| | |
|---|---|
| Ben Wallace, C. | 26,528 |
| Ben Whittingham, Lab. | 12,377 |
| Kate Walsh, UKIP | 6,577 |
| John Potter, LD | 2,712 |
| Anne Power, Green | 1,699 |

C. majority 14,151 (28.36%)
1.36% swing C. to Lab.
(2010: C. majority 15,844 (30.88%))

## WYRE FOREST
E. 77,451　T. 49,440 (63.83%)　C. hold

| | |
|---|---|
| Mark Garnier, C. | 22,394 |
| Matt Lamb, Lab. | 9,523 |
| Michael Wrench, UKIP | 7,967 |
| Richard Taylor, Ind. CHC | 7,211 |
| Andy Crick, LD | 1,228 |
| Natalie McVey, Green | 1,117 |

C. majority 12,871 (26.03%)
1.72% swing Lab. to C.
(2010: C. majority 2,643 (5.19%))

## WYTHENSHAWE & SALE EAST
E. 75,980　T. 43,263 (56.94%)　Lab. hold

| | |
|---|---|
| Mike Kane, Lab. | 21,693 |
| Fiona Green, C. | 11,124 |
| Lee Clayton, UKIP | 6,354 |
| Victor Chamberlain, LD | 1,927 |
| Jess Mayo, Green | 1,658 |
| Johnny Disco, Loony | 292 |
| Lynn Worthington, TUSC | 215 |

Lab. majority 10,569 (24.43%)
2.92% swing C. to Lab.
(2010: Lab. majority 7,575 (18.59%))
(2014: Lab. majority 8,960 (37.54%))

## YEOVIL
E. 82,446　T. 56,933 (69.05%)　C. gain

| | |
|---|---|
| *Marcus Fysh, C. | 24,178 |
| David Laws, LD | 18,865 |
| Simon Smedley, UKIP | 7,646 |
| Sheena King, Lab. | 4,053 |
| Emily McIvor, Green | 2,191 |

C. majority 5,313 (9.33%)
16.07% swing LD to C.
(2010: LD majority 13,036 (22.81%))

## YORK CENTRAL
E. 75,351　T. 47,677 (63.27%)

Lab. Co-op hold

| | |
|---|---|
| *Rachael Maskell, Lab. Co-op | 20,212 |
| Robert McIlveen, C. | 13,496 |
| Ken Guest, UKIP | 4,795 |
| Jonathan Tyler, Green | 4,791 |
| Nick Love, LD | 3,804 |
| Chris Whitwood, Yorks | 291 |
| Megan Ollerhead, TUSC | 288 |

Lab. Co-op majority 6,716 (14.09%)
0.10% swing C. to Lab.
(2010: Lab. majority 6,451 (13.88%))

## YORK OUTER
E. 78,561　T. 53,903 (68.61%)　C. hold

| | |
|---|---|
| Julian Sturdy, C. | 26,477 |
| Joe Riches, Lab. | 13,348 |
| James Blanchard, LD | 6,269 |
| Paul Abbott, UKIP | 5,251 |
| Ginnie Shaw, Green | 2,558 |

C. majority 13,129 (24.36%)
0.77% swing C. to Lab.
(2010: C. majority 3,688 (6.92%))

## YORKSHIRE EAST
E. 81,030　T. 49,991 (61.69%)　C. hold

| | |
|---|---|
| Greg Knight, C. | 25,276 |
| Kevin Hickson, Lab. | 10,343 |
| Stephanie Todd, UKIP | 8,955 |
| Robert Adamson, LD | 2,966 |
| Mark Maloney, Green | 1,731 |
| Stewart Arnold, Yorks | 720 |

C. majority 14,933 (29.87%)
1.35% swing Lab. to C.
(2010: C. majority 13,486 (26.31%))

# WALES

## ABERAVON
E. 49,821　T. 31,523 (63.27%)　Lab. hold

| | |
|---|---|
| *Stephen Kinnock, Lab. | 15,416 |
| Peter Bush, UKIP | 4,971 |
| Edward Yi He, C. | 3,742 |
| Duncan Higgitt, PC | 3,663 |
| Helen Ceri Clarke, LD | 1,397 |
| Captain Beany, Ind. | 1,137 |
| Jonathan Tier, Green | 711 |
| Andrew Jordan, Soc. Lab. | 352 |
| Owen Herbert, TUSC | 134 |

Lab. majority 10,445 (33.13%)
8.60% swing Lab. to UKIP
(2010: Lab. majority 11,039 (35.66%))

## ABERCONWY
E. 45,540　T. 30,148 (66.20%)　C. hold

| | |
|---|---|
| Guto Bebb, C. | 12,513 |
| Mary Wimbury, Lab. | 8,514 |
| Dafydd Meurig, PC | 3,536 |
| Andrew Haigh, UKIP | 3,467 |
| Victor Babu, LD | 1,391 |
| Petra Haig, Green | 727 |

C. majority 3,999 (13.26%)
0.96% swing Lab. to C.
(2010: C. majority 3,398 (11.34%))

## ALYN & DEESIDE
E. 62,016　T. 41,314 (66.62%)　Lab. hold

| | |
|---|---|
| Mark Tami, Lab. | 16,540 |
| Laura Knightly, C. | 13,197 |
| Blair Smillie, UKIP | 7,260 |
| Tudor Jones, LD | 1,733 |
| Jacqueline Hurst, PC | 1,608 |
| Alasdair Ibbotson, Green | 976 |

Lab. majority 3,343 (8.09%)
0.39% swing C. to Lab.
(2010: Lab. majority 2,919 (7.31%))

## ARFON
E. 40,492　T. 26,837 (66.28%)　PC hold

| | |
|---|---|
| Hywel Williams, PC | 11,790 |
| Alun Pugh, Lab. | 8,122 |
| Anwen Barry, C. | 3,521 |
| Simon Wall, UKIP | 2,277 |
| Mohammed Shultan, LD | 718 |
| Kathrine Jones, Soc. Lab. | 409 |

PC majority 3,668 (13.67%)
4.04% swing Lab. to PC
(2010: PC majority 1,455 (5.58%))

## BLAENAU GWENT
E. 51,332　T. 31,683 (61.72%)　Lab. hold

| | |
|---|---|
| Nick Smith, Lab. | 18,380 |
| Susan Boucher, UKIP | 5,677 |
| Tracey West, C. | 3,419 |
| Steffan Lewis, PC | 2,849 |
| Mark Pond, Green | 738 |
| Sam Rees, LD | 620 |

Lab. majority 12,703 (40.09%)
5.40% swing Lab. to UKIP
(2010: Lab. majority 10,516 (32.46%))

## BRECON & RADNORSHIRE
E. 54,311　T. 40,074 (73.79%)　C. gain

| | |
|---|---|
| *Chris Davies, C. | 16,453 |
| Roger Williams, LD | 11,351 |
| Matthew Dorrance, Lab. | 5,904 |
| Darran Thomas, UKIP | 3,338 |
| Freddy Greaves, PC | 1,767 |
| Chris Carmichael, Green | 1,261 |

C. majority 5,102 (12.73%)
11.19% swing LD to C.
(2010: LD majority 3,747 (9.65%))

## BRIDGEND
E. 59,998　T. 39,453 (65.76%)　Lab. hold

| | |
|---|---|
| Madeleine Moon, Lab. | 14,624 |
| Meirion Jenkins, C. | 12,697 |
| Caroline Jones, UKIP | 5,911 |
| James Radcliffe, PC | 2,784 |
| Anita Davies, LD | 1,648 |
| Les Tallon-Morris, Ind. | 763 |
| Tony White, Green | 736 |
| Aaron David, TUSC | 118 |
| David Elston, Pirate | 106 |
| Adam Lloyd, NF | 66 |

Lab. majority 1,927 (4.88%)
0.51% swing Lab. to C.
(2010: Lab. majority 2,263 (5.90%))

## CAERPHILLY
E. 62,793　T. 40,283 (64.15%)　Lab. hold

| | |
|---|---|
| Wayne David, Lab. | 17,864 |
| Sam Gould, UKIP | 7,791 |
| Leo Docherty, C. | 6,683 |
| Beci Newton, PC | 5,895 |
| Katy Beddoe, Green | 937 |
| Aladdin Ayesh, LD | 935 |
| Jaime Davies, TUSC | 178 |

Lab. majority 10,073 (25.01%)
8.61% swing Lab. to UKIP
(2010: Lab. majority 10,755 (27.58%))

CARDIFF CENTRAL
E. 57,454   T. 38,646 (67.26%)   Lab. gain
*Jo Stevens, Lab.                        15,462
Jenny Willott, LD                        10,481
Richard Hopkin, C.                        5,674
Anthony Raybould, UKIP                    2,499
Christopher von Ruhland, Green            2,461
Martin Pollard, PC                        1,925
Steve Williams, TUSC                        110
Kazimir Hubert, Ind.                         34
Lab. majority 4,981 (12.89%)
12.77% swing LD to Lab.
(2010: LD majority 4,576 (12.66%))

CARDIFF NORTH
E. 67,193   T. 51,151 (76.13%)   C. hold
*Craig Williams, C.                      21,709
Mari Williams, Lab.                      19,572
Ethan Wilkinson, UKIP                     3,953
Elin Walker Jones, PC                     2,301
Elizabeth Clark, LD                       1,953
Ruth Osner, Green                         1,254
Jeff Green, Ch. P.                          331
Shaun Jenkins, Change                        78
C. majority 2,137 (4.18%)
1.89% swing Lab. to C.
(2010: C. majority 194 (0.41%))

CARDIFF SOUTH & PENARTH
E. 75,714 T. 46,667 (61.64%)
                         Lab. Co-op hold
Stephen Doughty, Lab. Co-op              19,966
Emma Warman, C.                          12,513
John Rees-Evans, UKIP                     6,423
Ben Foday, PC                             3,443
Nigel Howells, LD                         2,318
Anthony Slaughter, Green                  1,746
Ross Saunders, TUSC                         258
Lab. Co-op majority 7,453 (15.97%)
2.68% swing C. to Lab.
(2010: Lab. Co-op majority 4,710 (10.62%))
(2012: Lab. majority 5,334 (27.44%))

CARDIFF WEST
E. 66,758   43,792 (65.60%)   Lab. hold
Kevin Brennan, Lab.                      17,803
James Taghdissian, C.                    11,014
Neil McEvoy, PC                           6,096
Brian Morris, UKIP                        4,923
Cadan ap Tomos, LD                        2,069
Ken Barker, Green                         1,704
Helen Jones, TUSC                           183
Lab. majority 6,789 (15.50%)
1.95% swing C. to Lab.
(2010: Lab. majority 4,750 (11.60%))

CARMARTHEN EAST & DINEFWR
E. 55,750   T. 39,399 (70.67%)   PC hold
Jonathan Edwards, PC                     15,140
*Calum Higgins, Lab.                      9,541
Matthew Paul, C.                          8,336
Norma Woodward, UKIP                      4,363
Ben Rice, Green                           1,091
Sara Lloyd-Williams, LD                     928
PC majority 5,599 (14.21%)
2.53% swing Lab. to PC
(2010: PC majority 3,481 (9.16%))

CARMARTHEN WEST &
PEMBROKESHIRE SOUTH
E. 57,755   T. 40,350 (69.86%)   C. hold
Simon Hart, C.                           17,626
Delyth Evans, Lab.                       11,572
John Atkinson, UKIP                       4,698
Elwyn Williams, PC                        4,201
Gary Tapley, Green                        1,290
Selwyn Runnett, LD                          963
C. majority 6,054 (15.00%)
3.28% swing Lab. to C.
(2010: C. majority 3,423 (8.45%))

CEREDIGION
E. 54,215   T. 37,416 (69.01%)   LD hold
Mark Williams, LD                        13,414
Mike Parker, PC                          10,347
Henrietta Hensher, C.                     4,123
Gethin James, UKIP                        3,829
Huw Thomas, Lab.                          3,615
Daniel Thompson, Green                    2,088
LD majority 3,067 (8.20%)
6.78% swing LD to PC
(2010: LD majority 8,324 (21.76%))

CLWYD SOUTH
E. 54,996   T. 35,064 (63.76%)   Lab. hold
Susan Elan Jones, Lab.                   13,051
David Nicholls, C.                       10,649
Mandy Jones, UKIP                         5,480
Mabon ap Gwynfor, PC                      3,620
Bruce Roberts, LD                         1,349
Duncan Rees, Green                          915
Lab. majority 2,402 (6.85%)
0.66% swing Lab. to C.
(2010: Lab. majority 2,834 (8.17%))

CLWYD WEST
E. 58,657   T. 38,028 (64.83%)   C. hold
David Jones, C.                          16,463
Gareth Thomas, Lab.                       9,733
Warwick Nicholson, UKIP                   4,988
Marc Jones, PC                            4,651
Sarah Lesiter-Burgess, LD                 1,387
Bob English, Soc. Lab.                      612
Rory Jepson, Above                          194
C. majority 6,730 (17.70%)
0.43% swing Lab. to C.
(2010: C. majority 6,419 (16.84%))

CYNON VALLEY
E. 51,421   T. 30,472 (59.26%)   Lab. hold
Ann Clwyd, Lab.                          14,532
Cerith Griffiths, PC                      5,126
Rebecca Rees-Evans, UKIP                  4,976
Keith Dewhurst, C.                        3,676
Angharad Jones, LD                          830
John Matthews, Green                        799
Chris Beggs, Soc. Lab.                      533
Lab. majority 9,406 (30.87%)
0.66% swing Lab. to PC
(2010: Lab. majority 9,617 (32.19%))

DELYN
E. 53,639   T. 37,457 (69.83%)   Lab. hold
David Hanson, Lab.                       15,187
Mark Isherwood, C.                       12,257
Nigel Williams, UKIP                      6,150
Paul Rowlinson, PC                        1,803
Tom Rippeth, LD                           1,380
Kay Roney, Green                            680
Lab. majority 2,930 (7.82%)
0.84% swing C. to Lab.
(2010: Lab. majority 2,272 (6.14%))

DWYFOR MEIRIONNYDD
E. 44,395   T. 28,913 (65.13%)   PC hold
*Liz Saville-Roberts, PC                 11,811
Neil Fairlamb, C.                         6,550
Mary Griffiths Clarke, Lab.               3,904
Christopher Gillibrand, UKIP              3,126
Louise Hughes, Ind.                       1,388
Steve Churchman, LD                       1,153
Marc Fothergill, Green                      981
PC majority 5,261 (18.20%)
1.92% swing PC to C.
(2010: PC majority 6,367 (22.03%))

GOWER
E. 61,820   T. 42,758 (69.17%)   C. gain
*Byron Davies, C.                        15,862
Liz Evans, Lab.                          15,835
Colin Beckett, UKIP                       4,773
Darren Thomas, PC                         3,051
Mike Sheehan, LD                          1,552
Julia Marshall, Green                     1,161
Baron Barnes Von Claptrap, Loony            253
Steve Roberts, Ind.                         168
Mark Evans, TUSC                            103
C. majority 27 (0.06%)
3.25% swing Lab. to C.
(2010: Lab. majority 2,683 (6.44%))

ISLWYN
E. 55,075   T. 35,401 (64.28%)
                         Lab. Co-op hold
Chris Evans, Lab. Co-op                  17,336
Joe Smyth, UKIP                           6,932
Laura Jones, C.                           5,366
Lyn Ackerman, PC                          3,794
Brendan D'Cruz, LD                          950
Peter Varley, Green                         659
Baron Von Magpie, Loony                     213
Josh Rawcliffe, TUSC                        151
Lab. Co-op majority 10,404 (29.39%)
8.56% swing Lab. to UKIP
(2010: Lab. Co-op majority 12,215
(35.21%))

LLANELLI
E. 59,314   T. 38,574 (65.03%)   Lab. hold
Nia Griffith, Lab.                       15,948
Vaughan Williams, PC                      8,853
Ken Rees, UKIP                            6,269
Selaine Saxby, C.                         5,534
Cen Phillips, LD                            751
Guy Smith, Green                            689
Sian Caiach, PF                             407
Scott Jones, TUSC                           123
Lab. majority 7,095 (18.39%)
2.92% swing PC to Lab.
(2010: Lab. majority 4,701 (12.55%))

MERTHYR TYDFIL & RHYMNEY
E. 61,719   T. 32,715 (53.01%)   Lab. hold
*Gerald Jones, Lab.                      17,619
David Rowlands, UKIP                      6,106
Bill Rees, C.                             3,292
Rhayna Mann, PC                           3,099
Bob Griffin, LD                           1,351
Elspeth Parris, Green                       603
Eddy Blanche, Ind.                          459
Robert Griffiths, Comm.                     186
Lab. majority 11,513 (35.19%)
2.88% swing Lab. to UKIP
(2010: Lab. majority 4,056 (12.64%))

MONMOUTH
E. 65,706    T. 47,462 (72.23%)    C. hold
David Davies, C.                    23,701
Ruth Jones, Lab.                    12,719
Gareth Dunn, UKIP                    4,942
Veronica German, LD                  2,496
Jonathan Clark, PC                   1,875
Christopher Were, Green              1,629
Stephen Morris, Eng. Dem.             100
C. majority 10,982 (23.14%)
0.36% swing Lab. to C.
(2010: C. majority 10,425 (22.41%))

MONTGOMERYSHIRE
E. 48,491    T. 33,757 (69.61%)    C. hold
Glyn Davies, C.                     15,204
Jane Dodds, LD                       9,879
Des Parkinson, UKIP                  3,769
Martyn Singleton, Lab.               1,900
Ann Griffith, PC                     1,745
Richard Chaloner, Green              1,260
C. majority 5,325 (15.77%)
6.14% swing LD to C.
(2010: C. majority 1,184 (3.50%))

NEATH
E. 56,099    T. 37,135 (66.20%)    Lab. hold
*Christina Rees, Lab.               16,270
Daniel Thomas, PC                    6,722
Richard Pritchard, UKIP              6,094
Ed Hastie, C.                        5,691
Catrin Brock, Green                  1,185
Clare Bentley, LD                    1,173
Lab. majority 9,548 (25.71%)
0.31% swing Lab. to PC
(2010: Lab. majority 9,775 (26.33%))

NEWPORT EAST
E. 56,018    T. 35,108 (62.67%)    Lab. hold
Jessica Morden, Lab.                14,290
Natasha Asghar, C.                   9,585
David Stock, UKIP                    6,466
Paul Halliday, PC                    2,251
Tony Salkeld, PC                     1,231
David Mclean, Green                    887
Shangara Singh Bhatoe, Soc. Lab.      398
Lab. majority 4,705 (13.40%)
0.30% swing Lab. to C.
(2010: Lab. majority 1,650 (4.79%))

NEWPORT WEST
E. 62,145    T. 40,347 (64.92%)    Lab. hold
Paul Flynn, Lab.                    16,633
Nick Webb, C.                       13,123
Gordon Norrie, UKIP                  6,134
Simon Coopey, PC                     1,604
Ed Townsend, LD                      1,581
Pippa Bartolotti, Green              1,272
Lab. majority 3,510 (8.70%)
0.11% swing Lab. to C.
(2010: Lab. majority 3,544 (8.92%))

OGMORE
E. 55,320    T. 35,250 (63.72%)    Lab. hold
Huw Irranca-Davies, Lab.            18,663
Jane March, C.                       5,620
Glenda Davies, UKIP                  5,420
Tim Thomas, PC                       3,556
Gerald Francis, LD                   1,072
Laurie Brophy, Green                   754
Emma Saunders, TUSC                    165
Lab. majority 13,043 (37.00%)
0.61% swing Lab. to C.
(2010: Lab. majority 13,246 (38.23%))

PONTYPRIDD
E. 58,929    T. 37,882 (64.28%)    Lab. hold
Owen Smith, Lab.                    15,554
Ann-Marie Mason, C.                  6,569
Andrew Tomkinson, UKIP               5,085
Mike Powell, LD                      4,904
Osian Lewis, PC                      4,348
Katy Clay, Green                       992
Damien Biggs, Soc. Lab.                332
Esther Pearson, TUSC                    98
Lab. majority 8,985 (23.72%)
0.56% swing C. to Lab.
(2010: Lab. majority 2,785 (7.59%))

PRESELI PEMBROKESHIRE
E. 57,291    T. 40,556 (70.79%)    C. hold
Stephen Crabb, C.                   16,383
Paul Miller, Lab.                   11,414
Howard Lillyman, UKIP                4,257
Chris Overton, ISWSL                 3,729
John Osmond, PC                      2,518
Frances Bryant, Green                1,452
Nick Tregoning, LD                     780
Rodney Maile, Worth                     23
C. majority 4,969 (12.25%)
0.31% swing Lab. to C.
(2010: C. majority 4,605 (11.63%))

RHONDDA
E. 51,809    T. 31,538 (60.87%)    Lab. hold
Chris Bryant, Lab.                  15,976
Shelley Rees-Owen, PC                8,521
Ron Hughes, UKIP                     3,998
Lyn Hudson, C.                       2,116
George Summers, LD                     474
Lisa Rapado, Green                     453
Lab. majority 7,455 (23.64%)
6.77% swing Lab. to PC
(2010: Lab. majority 11,553 (37.18%))

SWANSEA EAST
E. 58,011    T. 33,618 (57.95%)    Lab. hold
*Carolyn Harris, Lab.               17,807
Cliff Johnson, UKIP                  5,779
Altaf Hussain, C.                    5,142
Dic Jones, PC                        3,498
Amina Jamal, LD                      1,392
Lab. majority 12,028 (35.78%)
6.56% swing Lab. to UKIP
(2010: Lab. majority 10,838 (33.17%))

SWANSEA WEST
E. 58,776    T. 35,156 (59.81%)
                            Lab. Co-op hold
Geraint Davies, Lab. Co-op          14,967
Emma Lane, C.                        7,931
Martyn Ford, UKIP                    4,744
Chris Holley, LD                     3,178
Harri Roberts, PC                    2,266
Ashley Wakeling, Green               1,784
Ronnie Job, TUSC                       159
Maxwell Rosser, Ind.                    78
Brian Johnson, SPGB                     49
Lab. Co-op majority 7,036 (20.01%)
3.08% swing C. to Lab.
(2010: Lab. majority 504 (1.42%))

TORFAEN
E. 61,896    T. 37,937 (61.29%)    Lab. hold
*Nick Thomas-Symonds, Lab.          16,938
Graham Smith, C.                     8,769
Ken Beswick, UKIP                    7,203
Boydd Hackley-Green, PC              2,169
Alison Willott, LD                   1,271
Matt Cooke, Green                      746
John Cox, Soc. Lab.                    697
Mark Griffiths, Comm.                  144
Lab. majority 8,169 (21.53%)
1.60% swing Lab. to C.
(2010: Lab. majority 9,306 (24.72%))

VALE OF CLWYD
E. 56,505    T. 35,261 (62.40%)    C. gain
*James Davies, C.                   13,760
Chris Ruane, Lab.                   13,523
Paul Davies-Cooke, UKIP              4,577
Mair Rowlands, PC                    2,486
Gwyn Williams, LD                      915
C. majority 237 (0.67%)
3.87% swing Lab. to C.
(2010: Lab. majority 2,509 (7.06%))

VALE OF GLAMORGAN
E. 72,187    T. 51,293 (71.06%)    C. hold
Alun Cairns, C.                     23,607
Chris Elmore, Lab.                  16,727
Kevin Mahoney, UKIP                  5,489
Ian Johnson, PC                      2,869
David Morgan, LD                     1,309
Alan Armstrong, Green                1,054
Steve Reed, CISTA                      238
C. majority 6,880 (13.41%)
2.28% swing Lab. to C.
(2010: C. majority 4,307 (8.85%))

WREXHAM
E. 50,992    T. 32,719 (64.16%)    Lab. hold
Ian Lucas, Lab.                     12,181
Andrew Atkinson, C.                 10,350
Niall Plevin-Kelly, UKIP             5,072
Carrie Harper, PC                    2,501
Rob Walsh, LD                        1,735
David Munnerley, Green                 669
Brian Edwards, Ind.                    211
Lab. majority 1,831 (5.60%)
2.94% swing Lab. to C.
(2010: Lab. majority 3,658 (11.09%))

YNYS MON
E. 49,944    T. 34,926 (69.93%)    Lab. hold
Albert Owen, Lab.                   10,871
John Rowlands, PC                   10,642
Michelle Willis, C.                  7,393
Nathan Gill, UKIP                    5,121
Mark Rosenthal, LD                     751
Liz Screen, Soc. Lab.                  148
Lab. majority 229 (0.66%)
3.24% swing Lab. to PC
(2010: Lab. majority 2,461 (7.14%))

# SCOTLAND

## ABERDEEN NORTH
E. 67,745   T. 43,936 (64.85%)   SNP gain
*Kirsty Blackman, SNP                         24,793
Richard Baker, Lab. Co-op                     11,397
Sanjoy Sen, C.                                 5,304
Euan Davidson, LD                              2,050
Tyrinne Rutherford, TUSC                         206
Christopher Willett, NF                          186
SNP majority 13,396 (30.49%)
26.33% swing Lab. to SNP
(2010: Lab. majority 8,361 (22.18%))

## ABERDEEN SOUTH
E. 68,056   T. 48,551 (71.34%)   SNP gain
*Callum McCaig, SNP                           20,221
Anne Begg, Lab.                               12,991
Ross Thomson, C.                              11,087
Denis Rixon, LD                                2,252
Dan Yeats, Scot. Green                           964
Sandra Skinner, UKIP                             897
Christopher Gray, Ind.                           139
SNP majority 7,230 (14.89%)
19.78% swing Lab. to SNP
(2010: Lab. majority 3,506 (8.15%))

## ABERDEENSHIRE WEST & KINCARDINE
E. 73,445   T. 55,196 (75.15%)   SNP gain
*Stuart Donaldson, SNP                        22,949
Alexander Burnett, C.                         15,916
Robert Smith, LD                              11,812
Barry Black, Lab.                              2,487
David Lansdell, UKIP                           1,006
Richard Openshaw, Scot. Green                    885
Graham Reid, Ind.                                141
SNP majority 7,033 (12.74%)
21.46% swing LD to SNP
(2010: LD majority 3,684 (8.15%))

## AIRDRIE & SHOTTS
E. 66,715   T. 44,286 (66.38%)   SNP gain
*Neil Gray, SNP                               23,887
Pamela Nash, Lab.                             15,108
Eric Holford, C.                               3,389
Matt Williams, UKIP                            1,088
John Love, LD                                    678
Deryck Beaumont, Ind.                            136
SNP majority 8,779 (19.82%)
27.22% swing Lab. to SNP
(2010: Lab. majority 12,408 (34.61%))

## ANGUS
E. 65,792   T. 44,485 (67.61%)   SNP hold
Mike Weir, SNP                                24,130
Derek Wann, C.                                12,900
Gerard McMahon, Lab.                           3,919
Calum Walker, UKIP                             1,355
Sanjay Samani, LD                              1,216
David Mumford, Scot. Green                       965
SNP majority 11,230 (25.24%)
8.30% swing C. to SNP
(2010: SNP majority 3,282 (8.65%))

## ARGYLL & BUTE
E. 68,875   T. 51,883 (75.33%)   SNP gain
*Brendan O'Hara, SNP                          22,959
Alan Reid, LD                                 14,486
Alastair Redman, C.                            7,733
Mary Galbraith, Lab.                           5,394
Caroline Santos, UKIP                          1,311
SNP majority 8,473 (16.33%)
14.50% swing LD to SNP
(2010: LD majority 3,431 (7.59%))

## AYR, CARRICK & CUMNOCK
E. 72,985   T. 52,209 (71.53%)   SNP gain
*Corri Wilson, SNP                            25,492
Sandra Osborne, Lab.                          14,227
Lee Lyons, C.                                 10,355
Joseph Adam-Smith, UKIP                        1,280
Richard Brodie, LD                               855
SNP majority 11,265 (21.58%)
25.34% swing Lab. to SNP
(2010: Lab. majority 9,911 (21.60%))

## AYRSHIRE CENTRAL
E. 69,982   T. 50,774 (72.55%)   SNP gain
*Philippa Whitford, SNP                       26,999
Brian Donohoe, Lab.                           13,410
Marc Hope, C.                                  8,803
Gordon Bain, LD                                  917
Veronika Tudhope, Scot. Green                    645
SNP majority 13,589 (26.76%)
27.71% swing Lab. to SNP
(2010: Lab. majority 12,007 (27.34%))

## AYRSHIRE NORTH & ARRAN
E. 75,772   T. 53,869 (71.09%)   SNP gain
*Patricia Gibson, SNP                         28,641
Katy Clark, Lab.                              15,068
Jamie Greene, C.                               7,968
Sharon McGonigal, UKIP                         1,296
Ruby Kirkwood, LD                                896
SNP majority 13,573 (25.20%)
23.33% swing Lab. to SNP
(2010: Lab. majority 9,895 (21.46%))

## BANFF & BUCHAN
E. 68,609   T. 45,629 (66.51%)   SNP hold
Eilidh Whiteford, SNP                         27,487
Alex Johnstone, C.                            13,148
Sumon Hoque, Lab.                              2,647
David Evans, LD                                2,347
SNP majority 14,339 (31.43%)
10.48% swing C. to SNP
(2010: SNP majority 4,027 (10.47%))

## BERWICKSHIRE, ROXBURGH & SELKIRK
E. 74,179   T. 55,038 (74.20%)   SNP gain
*Calum Kerr, SNP                              20,145
John Lamont, C.                               19,817
Michael Moore, LD                             10,294
Kenryck Lloyd-Jones, Lab.                      2,700
Peter Neilson, UKIP                            1,316
Pauline Stewart, Scot. Green                     631
Jesse Rae, Ind.                                  135
SNP majority 328 (0.60%)
27.04% swing LD to SNP
(2010: LD majority 5,675 (11.58%))

## CAITHNESS, SUTHERLAND & EASTER ROSS
E. 47,558   T. 34,186 (71.88%)   SNP gain
*Paul Monaghan, SNP                           15,831
John Thurso, LD                               11,987
John Erskine, Lab.                             3,061
Alastair Graham, C.                            2,326
Ann Therese Murray, UKIP                         981
SNP majority 3,844 (11.24%)
16.73% swing LD to SNP
(2010: LD majority 4,826 (16.78%))

## COATBRIDGE, CHRYSTON & BELLSHILL
E. 73,813   T. 50,698 (68.68%)   SNP gain
*Phil Boswell, SNP                            28,696
Tom Clarke, Lab.                              17,195
Mhairi Fraser, C.                              3,209
Scott Cairns, UKIP                             1,049
Robert Simpson, LD                               549
SNP majority 11,501 (22.69%)
36.22% swing Lab. to SNP
(2010: Lab. majority 20,714 (49.75%))

## CUMBERNAULD, KILSYTH & KIRKINTILLOCH EAST
E. 67,009   T. 49,382 (73.69%)   SNP gain
*Stuart McDonald, SNP                         29,572
Gregg McClymont, Lab.                         14,820
Malcolm Mackay, C.                             3,891
John Duncan, LD                                1,099
SNP majority 14,752 (29.87%)
31.65% swing Lab. to SNP
(2010: Lab. majority 13,755 (33.43%))

## DUMFRIES & GALLOWAY
E. 75,249   T. 56,602 (75.22%)   SNP gain
*Richard Arkless, SNP                         23,440
Finlay Carson, C.                             16,926
Russell Brown, Lab.                           13,982
Geoff Siddall, UKIP                            1,301
Andrew Metcalf, LD                               953
SNP majority 6,514 (11.51%)
25.16% swing Lab. to SNP
(2010: Lab. majority 7,449 (14.28%))

## DUMFRIESSHIRE, CLYDESDALE & TWEEDDALE
E. 68,483   T. 52,134 (76.13%)   C. hold
David Mundell, C.                             20,759
Emma Harper, SNP                              19,961
Archie Dryburgh, Lab.                          7,711
Kevin Newton, UKIP                             1,472
Amanda Kubie, LD                               1,392
Jody Jamieson, Scot. Green                       839
C. majority 798 (1.53%)
12.87% swing C. to SNP
(2010: C. majority 4,194 (9.14%))

## DUNBARTONSHIRE EAST
E. 66,966   T. 54,871 (81.94%)   SNP gain
*John Nicolson, SNP                           22,093
Jo Swinson, LD                                19,926
Amanjit Jhund, Lab.                            6,754
Andrew Polson, C.                              4,727
Ross Greer, Scot. Green                          804
Wilfred Arasaratnam, UKIP                        567
SNP majority 2,167 (3.95%)
16.05% swing LD to SNP
(2010: LD majority 2,184 (4.55%))

## DUNBARTONSHIRE WEST
E. 69,193   T. 51,141 (73.91%)   SNP gain
*Martin Docherty, SNP                         30,198
Gemma Doyle, Lab. Co-op                       16,027
Maurice Corry, C.                              3,597
Aileen Morton, LD                                816
Claire Muir, Ind.                                503
SNP majority 14,171 (27.71%)
34.45% swing Lab. to SNP
(2010: Lab. Co-op majority 17,408 (41.19%))

**DUNDEE EAST**
E. 66,960  T. 48,185 (71.96%)  SNP hold

| | |
|---|---|
| Stewart Hosie, SNP | 28,765 |
| Lesley Brennan, Lab. | 9,603 |
| Bill Bowman, C. | 7,206 |
| Craig Duncan, LD | 1,387 |
| Helen Grayshan, Scot. Green | 895 |
| Lesley Parker-Hamilton, CISTA | 225 |
| Carlo Morelli, TUSC | 104 |

SNP majority 19,162 (39.77%)
17.64% swing Lab. to SNP
(2010: SNP majority 1,821 (4.49%))

**DUNDEE WEST**
E. 66,287  T. 44,714 (67.46%)  SNP gain

| | |
|---|---|
| *Chris Law, SNP | 27,684 |
| Michael Marra, Lab. | 10,592 |
| Nicola Ross, C. | 3,852 |
| Pauline Hinchion, Scot. Green | 1,225 |
| Daniel Coleman, LD | 1,057 |
| Jim McFarlane, TUSC | 304 |

SNP majority 17,092 (38.23%)
28.91% swing Lab. to SNP
(2010: Lab. majority 7,278 (19.60%))

**DUNFERMLINE & FIFE WEST**
E. 78,037  T. 55,890 (71.62%)  SNP gain

| | |
|---|---|
| *Douglas Chapman, SNP | 28,096 |
| Thomas Docherty, Lab. | 17,744 |
| James Reekie, C. | 6,623 |
| Gillian Cole-Hamilton, LD | 2,232 |
| Lewis Campbell, Scot. Green | 1,195 |

SNP majority 10,352 (18.52%)
27.07% swing Lab. to SNP
(2010: Lab. majority 5,470 (11.18%))

**EAST KILBRIDE, STRATHAVEN & LESMAHAGOW**
E. 83,071  T. 60,539 (72.88%)  SNP gain

| | |
|---|---|
| *Lisa Cameron, SNP | 33,678 |
| Michael McCann, Lab. | 17,151 |
| Graham Simpson, C. | 7,129 |
| Robert Sale, UKIP | 1,221 |
| Paul McGarry, LD | 1,042 |
| John Houston, Ind. | 318 |

SNP majority 16,527 (27.30%)
27.88% swing Lab. to SNP
(2010: Lab. majority 14,503 (28.47%))

**EAST LOTHIAN**
E. 79,481  T. 59,014 (74.25%)  SNP gain

| | |
|---|---|
| *George Kerevan, SNP | 25,104 |
| Fiona O'Donnell, Lab. | 18,301 |
| David Roach, C. | 11,511 |
| Ettie Spencer, LD | 1,517 |
| Jason Rose, Scot. Green | 1,245 |
| Oluf Marshall, UKIP | 1,178 |
| Mike Allan, Ind. | 158 |

SNP majority 6,803 (11.53%)
20.04% swing Lab. to SNP
(2010: Lab. majority 12,258 (24.93%))

**EDINBURGH EAST**
E. 66,178  T. 47,089 (71.16%)  SNP gain

| | |
|---|---|
| *Tommy Sheppard, SNP | 23,188 |
| Sheila Gilmore, Lab. | 14,082 |
| James McMordie, C. | 4,670 |
| Peter McColl, Scot. Green | 2,809 |
| Karen Utting, LD | 1,325 |
| Oliver Corbishley, UKIP | 898 |
| Ayesha Saleem, TUSC | 117 |

SNP majority 9,106 (19.34%)
21.18% swing Lab. to SNP
(2010: Lab. majority 9,181 (23.03%))

**EDINBURGH NORTH & LEITH**
E. 80,978  T. 58,008 (71.63%)  SNP gain

| | |
|---|---|
| *Deidre Brock, SNP | 23,742 |
| Mark Lazarowicz, Lab. Co-op | 18,145 |
| Iain McGill, C. | 9,378 |
| Sarah Beattie-Smith, Scot. Green | 3,140 |
| Martin Veart, LD | 2,634 |
| Alan Melville, UKIP | 847 |
| Bruce Whitehead, TUSC | 122 |

SNP majority 5,597 (9.65%)
18.73% swing Lab. to SNP
(2010: Lab. Co-op majority 1,724 (3.64%))

**EDINBURGH SOUTH**
E. 65,846  T. 49,286 (74.85%)  Lab. hold

| | |
|---|---|
| Ian Murray, Lab. | 19,293 |
| Neil Hay, SNP | 16,656 |
| Miles Briggs, C. | 8,626 |
| Phyl Meyer, Scot. Green | 2,090 |
| Pramod Subbaraman, LD | 1,823 |
| Paul Marshall, UKIP | 601 |
| Colin Fox, SSP | 197 |

Lab. majority 2,637 (5.35%)
swing N/A
(2010: Lab. majority 316 (0.72%))

**EDINBURGH SOUTH WEST**
E. 72,178  T. 51,602 (71.49%)  SNP gain

| | |
|---|---|
| *Joanna Cherry, SNP | 22,168 |
| Ricky Henderson, Lab. | 14,033 |
| Gordon Lindhurst, C. | 10,444 |
| Alan Doherty, Scot. Green | 1,965 |
| Daniel Farthing-Sykes, LD | 1,920 |
| Richard Lucas, UKIP | 1,072 |

SNP majority 8,135 (15.76%)
23.22% swing Lab. to SNP
(2010: Lab. majority 8,447 (18.58%))

**EDINBURGH WEST**
E. 71,749  T. 54,858 (76.46%)  SNP gain

| | |
|---|---|
| *Michelle Thomson, SNP | 21,378 |
| Michael Crockart, LD | 18,168 |
| Lindsay Paterson, C. | 6,732 |
| Cammy Day, Lab. | 6,425 |
| Pat Black, Scot. Green | 1,140 |
| Otto Inglis, UKIP | 1,015 |

SNP majority 3,210 (5.85%)
14.30% swing LD to SNP
(2010: LD majority 3,803 (8.19%))

**FALKIRK**
E. 83,380  T. 60,340 (72.37%)  SNP gain

| | |
|---|---|
| *John McNally, SNP | 34,831 |
| Karen Whitefield, Lab. | 15,130 |
| Alison Harris, C. | 7,325 |
| David Coburn, UKIP | 1,829 |
| Galen Milne, LD | 1,225 |

SNP majority 19,701 (32.65%)
24.05% swing Lab. to SNP
(2010: Lab. majority 7,843 (15.45%))

**FIFE NORTH EAST**
E. 62,003  T. 45,263 (73.00%)  SNP gain

| | |
|---|---|
| *Stephen Gethins, SNP | 18,523 |
| Tim Brett, LD | 14,179 |
| Huw Bell, C. | 7,373 |
| Brian Thomson, Lab. | 3,476 |
| Andy Collins, Scot. Green | 1,387 |
| Mike Scott-Hayward, Ind. | 325 |

SNP majority 4,344 (9.60%)
19.87% swing LD to SNP
(2010: LD majority 9,048 (22.58%))

**GLASGOW CENTRAL**
E. 70,945  T. 39,318 (55.42%)  SNP gain

| | |
|---|---|
| *Alison Thewliss, SNP | 20,658 |
| Anas Sarwar, Lab. | 12,996 |
| Simon Bone, C. | 2,359 |
| Cass MacGregor, Scot. Green | 1,559 |
| Stuart Maskell, UKIP | 786 |
| Chris Young, LD | 612 |
| James Marris, CISTA | 171 |
| Andrew Elliott, TUSC | 119 |
| Katie Rhodes, SEP | 58 |

SNP majority 7,662 (19.49%)
27.00% swing Lab. to SNP
(2010: Lab. majority 10,551 (34.50%))

**GLASGOW EAST**
E. 70,378  T. 42,417 (60.27%)  SNP gain

| | |
|---|---|
| *Natalie McGarry, SNP | 24,116 |
| Margaret Curran, Lab. | 13,729 |
| Andy Morrison, C. | 2,544 |
| Arthur Thackeray, UKIP | 1,105 |
| Kim Long, Scot. Green | 381 |
| Gary McLelland, LD | 318 |
| Liam McLaughlan, SSP | 224 |

SNP majority 10,387 (24.49%)
30.65% swing Lab. to SNP
(2010: Lab. majority 11,840 (36.81%))

**GLASGOW NORTH**
E. 58,875  T. 36,922 (62.71%)  SNP gain

| | |
|---|---|
| *Patrick Grady, SNP | 19,610 |
| Ann McKechin, Lab. | 10,315 |
| Lauren Hankinson, C. | 2,901 |
| Martin Bartos, Scot. Green | 2,284 |
| Jade O'Neil, LD | 1,012 |
| Jamie Robertson, UKIP | 486 |
| Angela McCormick, TUSC | 160 |
| Russell Benson, CISTA | 154 |

SNP majority 9,295 (25.17%)
28.88% swing Lab. to SNP
(2010: Lab. majority 3,898 (13.16%))

**GLASGOW NORTH EAST**
E. 66,678  T. 37,857 (56.78%)  SNP gain

| | |
|---|---|
| *Anne McLaughlin, SNP | 21,976 |
| Willie Bain, Lab. | 12,754 |
| Annie Wells, C. | 1,769 |
| Zara Kitson, Scot. Green | 615 |
| Eileen Baxendale, LD | 300 |
| Geoff Johnson, CISTA | 225 |
| Jamie Cocozza, TUSC | 218 |

SNP majority 9,222 (24.36%)
39.28% swing Lab. to SNP
(2010: Lab. majority 15,942 (54.21%))

**GLASGOW NORTH WEST**
E. 68,418  T. 43,854 (64.10%)  SNP gain

| | |
|---|---|
| *Carol Monaghan, SNP | 23,908 |
| John Robertson, Lab. | 13,544 |
| Roger Lewis, C. | 3,692 |
| James Harrison, LD | 1,194 |
| Moira Crawford, Scot. Green | 1,167 |
| Chris MacKenzie, CISTA | 213 |
| Zoe Streatfield, Comm. | 136 |

SNP majority 10,364 (23.63%)
31.21% swing Lab. to SNP
(2010: Lab. majority 13,611 (38.25%))

**GLASGOW SOUTH**
E. 74,051  T. 48,778 (65.87%)  SNP gain

| | |
|---|---|
| *Stewart McDonald, SNP | 26,773 |
| Tom Harris, Lab. | 14,504 |
| Kyle Thornton, C. | 2,620 |
| Alastair Whitelaw, Scot. Green | 1,431 |
| Ewan Hoyle, LD | 1,019 |
| Brian Smith, TUSC | 299 |

SNP majority 12,269 (25.15%)
28.36% swing Lab. to SNP
(2010: Lab. majority 12,658 (31.57%))

GLASGOW SOUTH WEST
E. 66,209  T. 40,921 (61.81%)  SNP gain
*Christopher Stephens, SNP        23,388
Ian Davidson, Lab. Co-op          13,438
Gordon McCaskill, C.               2,036
Sarah Hemy, UKIP                     970
Sean Templeton, Scot. Green          507
Isabel Nelson, LD                    406
Bill Bonnar, SSP                     176
SNP majority 9,950 (24.32%)
35.24% swing Lab. to SNP
(2010: Lab. Co-op majority 14,671
(46.16%))

GLENROTHES
E. 69,781  T. 47,598 (68.21%)  SNP gain
*Peter Grant, SNP                 28,459
Melanie Ward, Lab. Co-op          14,562
Alex Stewart-Clark, C.             3,685
Jane Ann Liston, LD                 892
SNP majority 13,897 (29.20%)
34.90% swing Lab. to SNP
(2010: Lab. majority 16,448 (40.61%))

GORDON
E. 79,393  T. 58,161 (73.26%)  SNP gain
*Alex Salmond, SNP                27,717
Christine Jardine, LD             19,030
Colin Clark, C.                    6,807
Braden Davy, Lab.                  3,441
Emily Santos, UKIP                 1,166
SNP majority 8,687 (14.94%)
14.39% swing LD to SNP
(2010: LD majority 6,748 (13.83%))

INVERCLYDE
E. 59,350  T. 44,607 (75.16%)  SNP gain
*Ronnie Cowan, SNP                24,585
Iain McKenzie, Lab.               13,522
George Jabbour, C.                 4,446
John Watson, LD                    1,106
Michael Burrows, UKIP               715
Craig Hamilton, CISTA               233
SNP majority 11,063 (24.80%)
31.63% swing Lab. to SNP
(2010: Lab. majority 14,426 (38.47%))
(2011: Lab. majority 5,838 (20.78%))

INVERNESS, NAIRN, BADENOCH &
STRATHSPEY
E. 77,268  T. 57,613 (74.56%)  SNP gain
*Drew Hendry, SNP                 28,838
Danny Alexander, LD               18,029
Mike Robb, Lab.                    4,311
Edward Mountain, C.                3,410
Isla O'Reilly, Scot. Green         1,367
Les Durance, UKIP                  1,236
Donald Boyd, SCP                    422
SNP majority 10,809 (18.76%)
20.39% swing LD to SNP
(2010: LD majority 8,765 (18.61%))

KILMARNOCK & LOUDOUN
E. 75,233  T. 53,903 (71.65%)  SNP gain
*Alan Brown, SNP                  30,000
Cathy Jamieson, Lab. Co-op        16,362
Brian Whittle, C.                  6,752
Rod Ackland, LD                     789
SNP majority 13,638 (25.30%)
25.95% swing Lab. to SNP
(2010: Lab. Co-op majority 12,378
(26.59%))

KIRKCALDY & COWDENBEATH
E. 75,941  T. 52,892 (69.65%)  SNP gain
*Roger Mullin, SNP                27,628
Kenny Selbie, Lab. Co-op          17,654
Dave Dempsey, C.                   5,223
Jack Neill, UKIP                   1,237
Callum Leslie, LD                  1,150
SNP majority 9,974 (18.86%)
34.55% swing Lab. to SNP
(2010: Lab. majority 23,009 (50.24%))

LANARK & HAMILTON EAST
E. 78,846  T. 55,258 (70.08%)  SNP gain
*Angela Crawley, SNP              26,976
Jim Hood, Lab.                    16,876
Alex Allison, C.                   8,772
Donald MacKay, UKIP                1,431
Gregg Cullen, LD                   1,203
SNP majority 10,100 (18.28%)
23.61% swing Lab. to SNP
(2010: Lab. majority 13,478 (28.95%))

LINLITHGOW & FALKIRK EAST
E. 86,955  T. 61,597 (70.84%)  SNP gain
*Martyn Day, SNP                  32,055
Michael Connarty, Lab.            19,121
Sandy Batho, C.                    7,384
Alistair Forrest, UKIP             1,682
Emma Farthing-Sykes, LD            1,252
Neil McIvor, NF                     103
SNP majority 12,934 (21.00%)
22.70% swing Lab. to SNP
(2010: Lab. majority 12,553 (24.40%))

LIVINGSTON
E. 82,373  T. 57,547 (69.86%)  SNP gain
*Hannah Bardell, SNP              32,736
Graeme Morrice, Lab.              15,893
Chris Donnelly, C.                 5,929
Nathan Somerville, UKIP            1,757
Charles Dundas, LD                 1,232
SNP majority 16,843 (29.27%)
25.90% swing Lab. to SNP
(2010: Lab. majority 10,791 (22.52%))

MIDLOTHIAN
E. 67,875  T. 48,331 (71.21%)  SNP gain
*Owen Thompson, SNP               24,453
Kenny Young, Lab.                 14,594
Michelle Ballantyne, C.            5,760
Ian Baxter, Scot. Green            1,219
Gordon Norrie, UKIP                1,173
Aisha Mir, LD                      1,132
SNP majority 9,859 (20.40%)
23.39% swing Lab. to SNP
(2010: Lab. majority 10,349 (26.37%))

MORAY
E. 71,685  T. 49,280 (68.75%)  SNP hold
Angus Robertson, SNP              24,384
Douglas Ross, C.                  15,319
Sean Morton, Lab.                  4,898
Robert Scorer, UKIP                1,939
Jamie Paterson, LD                 1,395
James MacKessack-Leitch, Scot.
Green                              1,345
SNP majority 9,065 (18.39%)
swing N/A
(2010: SNP majority 5,590 (13.63%))

MOTHERWELL & WISHAW
E. 70,269  T. 48,237 (68.65%)  SNP gain
*Marion Fellows, SNP              27,275
Frank Roy, Lab.                   15,377
Meghan Gallacher, C.               3,695
Neil Wilson, UKIP                  1,289
Ross Laird, LD                      601
SNP majority 11,898 (24.67%)
33.81% swing Lab. to SNP
(2010: Lab. majority 16,806 (42.96%))

NA H-EILEANAN AN IAR
E. 21,744  T. 15,938 (73.30%)  SNP hold
Angus MacNeil, SNP                 8,662
Alasdair Morrison, Lab.            4,560
Mark Brown, C.                     1,215
John Cormack, SCP                  1,045
Ruaraidh Ferguson, LD               456
SNP majority 4,102 (25.74%)
6.46% swing Lab. to SNP
(2010: SNP majority 1,885 (12.81%))

OCHIL & PERTHSHIRE SOUTH
E. 77,370  T. 57,871 (74.80%)  SNP gain
*Tasmina Ahmed-Sheikh, SNP        26,620
Gordon Banks, Lab.                16,452
Luke Graham, C.                   11,987
Iliyan Stefanov, LD                1,481
Martin Gray, TUSC                  1,331
SNP majority 10,168 (17.57%)
13.92% swing Lab. to SNP
(2010: Lab. majority 5,187 (10.28%))

ORKNEY & SHETLAND
E. 34,551  T. 22,728 (65.78%)  LD hold
Alistair Carmichael, LD            9,407
Danus Skene, SNP                   8,590
Donald Cameron, C.                 2,025
Gerry McGarvey, Lab.               1,624
Robert Smith, UKIP                 1,082
LD majority 817 (3.59%)
23.91% swing LD to SNP
(2010: LD majority 9,928 (51.32%))

PAISLEY & RENFREWSHIRE NORTH
E. 66,206  T. 50,462 (76.22%)  SNP gain
*Gavin Newlands, SNP              25,601
Jim Sheridan, Lab.                16,525
John Anderson, C.                  6,183
James Speirs, LD                   1,055
Ryan Morrison, Scot. Green          703
Andy Doyle, CISTA                   202
Jim Halfpenny, TUSC                 193
SNP majority 9,076 (17.99%)
26.47% swing Lab. to SNP
(2010: Lab. majority 15,280 (34.96%))

PAISLEY & RENFREWSHIRE SOUTH
E. 61,281  T. 46,226 (75.43%)  SNP gain
*Mhairi Black, SNP                23,548
Douglas Alexander, Lab.           17,864
Fraser Galloway, C.                3,526
Eileen McCartin, LD                1,010
Sandra Webster, SSP                 278
SNP majority 5,684 (12.30%)
26.92% swing Lab. to SNP
(2010: Lab. majority 16,614 (41.54%))

PERTH & PERTHSHIRE NORTH
E. 72,447  T. 54,200 (74.81%)  SNP hold
Pete Wishart, SNP                    27,379
Alexander Stewart, C.                17,738
Scott Nicholson, Lab.                 4,413
Peter Barrett, LD                     2,059
Louise Ramsay, Scot. Green            1,146
John Myles, UKIP                      1,110
Xander McDade, Ind.                     355
SNP majority 9,641 (17.79%)
4.36% swing C. to SNP
(2010: SNP majority 4,379 (9.07%))

RENFREWSHIRE EAST
E. 69,982  T. 56,730 (81.06%)  SNP gain
*Kirsten Oswald, SNP                 23,013
Jim Murphy, Lab.                     19,295
David Montgomery, C.                 12,465
Graeme Cowie, LD                      1,069
Robert Malyn, UKIP                      888
SNP majority 3,718 (6.55%)
24.23% swing Lab. to SNP
(2010: Lab. majority 10,420 (20.36%))

ROSS, SKYE & LOCHABER
E. 54,169  T. 41,811 (77.19%)  SNP gain
*Ian Blackford, SNP                  20,119
Charles Kennedy, LD                  14,995
Lindsay McCallum, C.                  2,598
Chris Conniff, Lab.                   2,043
Anne Thomas, Scot. Green              1,051
Philip Anderson, UKIP                   814
Ronnie Campbell, Ind.                   191
SNP majority 5,124 (12.26%)
24.89% swing LD to SNP
(2010: LD majority 13,070 (37.52%))

RUTHERGLEN & HAMILTON WEST
E. 82,701  T. 57,615 (69.67%)  SNP gain
*Margaret Ferrier, SNP               30,279
Tom Greatrex, Lab. Co-op             20,304
Taylor Muir, C.                       4,350
Janice MacKay, UKIP                   1,301
Tony Hughes, LD                       1,045
Yvonne Maclean, CISTA                   336
SNP majority 9,975 (17.31%)
31.01% swing Lab. to SNP
(2010: Lab. Co-op majority 21,002
(44.70%))

STIRLING
E. 67,236  T. 52,135 (77.54%)  SNP gain
*Steven Paterson, SNP                23,783
Johanna Boyd, Lab.                   13,303
Stephen Kerr, C.                     12,051
Mark Ruskell, Scot. Green             1,606
Elisabeth Wilson, LD                  1,392
SNP majority 10,480 (20.10%)
22.30% swing Lab. to SNP
(2010: Lab. majority 8,354 (17.85%))

# NORTHERN IRELAND

ANTRIM EAST
E. 62,810  T. 33,497 (53.33%)  DUP hold
Sammy Wilson, DUP                    12,103
Roy Beggs, UUP                        6,308
Stewart Dickson, Alliance             5,021
Noel Jordan, UKIP                     3,660
Oliver McMullan, SF                   2,314
Ruth Wilson, TUV                      1,903
Margaret Anne McKillop, SDLP          1,639
Alex Wilson, C.                         549
DUP majority 5,795 (17.30%)
swing N/A
(2010: DUP majority 6,770 (22.20%))

ANTRIM NORTH
E. 75,874  T. 41,907 (55.23%)  DUP hold
Ian Paisley, DUP                     18,107
Timothy Gaston, TUV                   6,561
Daithi McKay, SF                      5,143
Robin Swann, UUP                      5,054
Declan O'Loan, SDLP                   2,925
Jayne Dunlop, Alliance                2,351
Robert Hill, UKIP                     1,341
Carol Freeman, C.                       368
Thomas Palmer, Ind.                      57
DUP majority 11,546 (27.55%)
1.03% swing DUP to TUV
(2010: DUP majority 12,558 (29.62%))

ANTRIM SOUTH
E. 67,423  T. 36,523 (54.17%)  UUP gain
*Danny Kinahan, UUP                  11,942
William McCrea, DUP                  10,993
Declan Kearney, SF                    4,699
Neil Kelly, Alliance                  3,576
Roisin Lynch, SDLP                    2,990
Richard Cairns, TUV                   1,908
Alan Dunlop, C.                         415
UUP majority 949 (2.60%)
swing N/A
(2010: DUP majority 1,183 (3.48%))

BELFAST EAST
E. 63,154  T. 39,682 (62.83%)  DUP gain
*Gavin Robinson, DUP                 19,575
Naomi Long, Alliance                 16,978
Neil Wilson, C.                       1,121
Ross Brown, Green                     1,058
Niall O Donnghaile, SF                 823
Mary Muldoon, SDLP                     127
DUP majority 2,597 (6.54%)
5.49% swing Alliance to DUP
(2010: Alliance majority 1,533 (4.45%))

BELFAST NORTH
E. 68,552  T. 40,593 (59.21%)  DUP hold
Nigel Dodds, DUP                     19,096
Gerry Kelly, SF                      13,770
Alban Maginness, SDLP                 3,338
Jason O'Neill, Alliance               2,941
Gemma Weir, WP                          919
Fra Hughes, Ind.                        529
DUP majority 5,326 (13.12%)
3.55% swing SF to DUP
(2010: DUP majority 2,224 (6.01%))

BELFAST SOUTH
E. 64,912  T. 38,957 (60.02%)  SDLP hold
Alasdair McDonnell, SDLP              9,560
Jonathan Bell, DUP                    8,654
Paula Bradshaw, Alliance              6,711
Mairtin O Muilleoir, SF               5,402
Rodney McCune, UUP                    3,549
Clare Bailey, Green                   2,238
Bob Stoker, UKIP                      1,900
Ben Manton, C.                          582
Lily Kerr, WP                           361
SDLP majority 906 (2.33%)
7.50% swing SDLP to DUP
(2010: SDLP majority 5,926 (17.33%))

BELFAST WEST
E. 62,685  T. 35,329 (56.36%)  SF hold
Paul Maskey, SF                      19,163
Gerry Carroll, PBP                    6,798
Alex Attwood, SDLP                    3,475
Frank McCoubrey, DUP                  2,773
Bill Manwaring, UUP                   1,088
Brian Higginson, UKIP                  765
Gerard Catney, Alliance                636
John Lowry, WP                         597
Paul Shea, C.                           34
SF majority 12,365 (35.00%)
swing N/A
(2010: SF majority 17,579 (54.71%))
(2011: SF majority 13,123 (50.6%))

DOWN NORTH
E. 64,207  T. 35,947 (55.99%)  Ind. hold
Lady (Sylvia) Hermon, Ind.           17,689
Alex Easton, DUP                      8,487
Andrew Muir, Alliance                 3,086
Steven Agnew, Green                   1,958
Mark Brotherston, C.                  1,593
Jonny Lavery, UKIP                    1,482
William Cudworth, TUV                   686
Tom Woolley, SDLP                       355
Glenn Donnelly, CISTA                  338
Therese McCartney, SF                  273
Ind. majority 9,202 (25.60%)
swing N/A
(2010: Ind. majority 14,364 (42.90%))

DOWN SOUTH
E. 75,215  T. 42,697 (56.77%)  SDLP hold
Margaret Ritchie, SDLP               18,077
Chris Hazzard, SF                    12,186
Harold McKee, UUP                     3,964
Jim Wells, DUP                        3,486
Henry Reilly, UKIP                    3,044
Martyn Todd, Alliance                 1,622
Felicity Buchan, C.                     318
SDLP majority 5,891 (13.80%)
2.98% swing SDLP to SF
(2010: SDLP majority 8,412 (19.75%))

FERMANAGH & SOUTH TYRONE
E. 70,106  T. 50,864 (72.55%)  UUP gain
*Tom Elliott, UUP                    23,608
Michelle Gildernew, SF               23,078
John Coyle, SDLP                      2,732
Tanya Jones, Green                      788
Hannah Su, Alliance                    658
UUP majority 530 (1.04%)
swing N/A
(2010: SF majority 4 (0.01%))

FOYLE
E. 70,035  T. 37,002 (52.83%)  SDLP hold
Mark Durkan, SDLP                    17,725
Gearoid O hEara, SF                  11,679
Gary Middleton, DUP                   4,573
Julia Kee, UUP                        1,226
David Hawthorne, Alliance               835
Kyle Thompson, UKIP                     832
Hamish Badenoch, C.                     132
SDLP majority 6,046 (16.34%)
1.80% swing SF to SDLP
(2010: SDLP majority 4,824 (12.73%))

LAGAN VALLEY
E. 71,140  T. 39,795 (55.94%)  DUP hold
| Jeffrey Donaldson, DUP | 19,055 |
| Alex Redpath, UUP | 6,055 |
| Trevor Lunn, Alliance | 5,544 |
| Pat Catney, SDLP | 2,500 |
| Alan Love, UKIP | 2,200 |
| Samuel Morrison, TUV | 1,887 |
| Jacqui McGeough, SF | 1,144 |
| Jonny Orr, Ind. | 756 |
| Helen Osborne, C. | 654 |
DUP majority 13,000 (32.67%)
swing N/A
(2010: DUP majority 10,486 (28.70%))

LONDONDERRY EAST
E. 66,925  T. 34,714 (51.87%)  DUP hold
| Gregory Campbell, DUP | 14,663 |
| Caoimhe Archibald, SF | 6,859 |
| William McCandless, UUP | 5,333 |
| Gerry Mullan, SDLP | 4,268 |
| Yvonne Boyle, Alliance | 2,642 |
| Neil Paine, CISTA | 527 |
| Liz St Clair-Legge, C. | 422 |
DUP majority 7,804 (22.48%)
3.58% swing SF to DUP
(2010: DUP majority 5,355 (15.32%))

NEWRY & ARMAGH
E. 77,622  T. 49,877 (64.26%)  SF hold
| *Mickey Brady, SF | 20,488 |
| Danny Kennedy, UUP | 16,312 |
| Justin McNulty, SDLP | 12,026 |
| Kate Nicholl, Alliance | 841 |
| Robert Rigby, C. | 210 |
SF majority 4,176 (8.37%)
swing N/A
(2010: SF majority 8,331 (18.55%))

STRANGFORD
E. 64,286  T. 33,924 (52.77%)  DUP hold
| Jim Shannon, DUP | 15,053 |
| Robert Burgess, UUP | 4,868 |
| Kellie Armstrong, Alliance | 4,687 |
| Joe Boyle, SDLP | 2,335 |
| Joe Jordan, UKIP | 2,237 |
| Johnny Andrews, C. | 2,167 |
| Stephen Cooper, TUV | 1,701 |
| Sheila Bailie, SF | 876 |
DUP majority 10,185 (30.02%)
swing N/A
(2010: DUP majority 5,876 (18.08%))

TYRONE WEST
E. 63,854  T. 38,654 (60.53%)  SF hold
| Pat Doherty, SF | 16,807 |
| Tom Buchanan, DUP | 6,747 |
| Daniel McCrossan, SDLP | 6,444 |
| Ross Hussey, UUP | 6,144 |
| Stephen Donnelly, Alliance | 869 |
| Ciaran McClean, Green | 780 |
| Barry Brown, CISTA | 528 |
| Claire-Louise Leyland, C. | 169 |
| Susan-Anne White, Ind. | 166 |
SF majority 10,060 (26.03%)
1.32% swing SF to DUP
(2010: SF majority 10,685 (28.67%))

ULSTER MID
E. 67,831  T. 40,922 (60.33%)  SF hold
| Francie Molloy, SF | 19,935 |
| Sandra Overend, UUP | 6,318 |
| Ian McCrea, DUP | 5,465 |
| Malachy Quinn, SDLP | 5,055 |
| Gareth Ferguson, TUV | 1,892 |
| Alan Day, UKIP | 863 |
| Eric Bullick, Alliance | 778 |
| Hugh Scullion, WP | 496 |
| Lucille Nicholson, C. | 120 |
SF majority 13,617 (33.28%)
swing N/A
(2010: SF majority 15,363 (37.62%))
(2013: SF majority 4,681 (12.58%))

UPPER BANN
E. 80,052  T. 47,219 (58.99%)  DUP hold
| David Simpson, DUP | 15,430 |
| Jo-Anne Dobson, UUP | 13,166 |
| Catherine Seeley, SF | 11,593 |
| Dolores Kelly, SDLP | 4,238 |
| Peter Lavery, Alliance | 1,780 |
| Martin Kelly, CISTA | 460 |
| Damien Harte, WP | 351 |
| Amandeep Singh Bhogal, C. | 201 |
DUP majority 2,264 (4.79%)
swing N/A
(2010: DUP majority 3,361 (8.12%))

# MANIFESTO COMMITMENTS

## THE CONSERVATIVE PARTY MANIFESTO 2015

Below are selected key commitments made by the Conservative Party in their 2015 manifesto.

### ECONOMY AND TAXATION
- Increase the income tax personal allowance to £12,500
- Increase the higher rate income tax threshold to £50,000
- Freeze income tax, national insurance and VAT rates for the duration of the next parliament
- Reduce government spending by 1 per cent in real terms for the first two years of the next parliament
- Increase annual tax charges paid by those with non-domiciled status
- Invest in infrastructure and devolve power to support industry growth and jobs in the English regions

### HEALTH
- Provide an additional £8bn of real terms funding to NHS England over the five years to 2020
- Ensure everyone can access a GP and necessary hospital care seven days a week by 2020
- Guarantee same-day GP appointments for those aged 75 and over if they need one
- Continue to invest in the Cancer Drugs Fund and deliver earlier detection and diagnosis, and better treatment and care for cancer and dementia patients
- Increase funding for mental health care and enforce new access and waiting time standards for those with mental ill-health

### EDUCATION
- Train an extra 17,500 maths and physics teachers over the next five years
- Create 3 million new apprenticeships
- Ensure there is no cap on university places
- Turn every 'failing' secondary school into an academy
- Support the delivery of free schools for parents and communities that want them

### LAW AND ORDER
- Replace the Human Rights Act with a British Bill of Rights; curtailing the role of the European Court of Human Rights and making the UK Supreme Court arbiter of human rights matters in the UK
- Develop the role of Police and Crime Commissioners
- Prioritise victim support
- Deploy new technology to monitor offenders in the community and to bring persistent offenders to justice quickly
- Continue to reform the police and prison systems

### SOCIETY
- Support museums, libraries, media, press freedom, creative industries and tourism
- Introduce three days a year paid volunteering leave for those in the public sector and with big companies
- Guarantee a place on the National Citizen Service scheme for every 16 and 17-year-old who wants one

- Build 200,000 new starter homes for first-time buyers aged under 40
- Increase the state pension by at least 2.5 per cent, in line with inflation, or in line with earnings – whichever is higher

### IMMIGRATION
- Continue to work towards the goal of reducing annual net migration to under 100,000 a year*
- Maintain an annual cap of 20,700 on the number of skilled migrants who can come to the UK from outside the EU
- Reform welfare rules so that EU migrants have to be resident in the UK for at least four years before they can claim certain benefits or social housing
- End the provision of out of work benefits for all EU migrants
- Migrants will be required to leave the UK if they have not found a job within six months
- Enhance border security and strengthen the enforcement of immigration rules

\* For the year ending December 2014 net migration stood at 318,000 (*Source:* ONS)

### POLITICAL REFORM
- Maintain the Westminster Parliament as the UK's law-making body
- Give English MPs a veto over matters only affecting England
- Introduce a Scotland bill, to ensure that more than 50 per cent of the Scottish parliament's budget is funded from revenues raised in Scotland and also devolve further powers in welfare, taxation and spending to the Scottish parliament
- Devolve new powers to the Welsh Assembly, including control over its name, size, assembly electoral system and voting age
- Fully implement the Stormont House Agreement in Northern Ireland

### ENVIRONMENT
- Establishing a new 'Blue Belt' category to protect marine habitats
- Spend £3bn over this parliament enhancing England's countryside
- Build 1,400 new flood defence schemes to protect 300,000 homes
- Work with the natural capital committee on a 25-year plan to restore the UK's biodiversity
- Phase-out public subsidies for new onshore wind farms

### DEFENCE AND FOREIGN AFFAIRS
- Give the UK people a say in whether we should remain in the EU, with an 'in-out' referendum by 2017
- Work for peace and stability in Iraq and Syria; pursuing a comprehensive political and military strategy to defeat IS
- Uphold the sovereignty of Ukraine by continuing to reject Russia's illegal annexation of Crimea
- Invest at least £160bn in new military equipment over the next decade
- Spend 0.7 per cent of GNI on international development

# POLITICAL PARTIES' KEY PLEDGES

Includes the political parties which are represented by at least one MP in the current parliament (*see* State of the Parties, page 120). The parties are ordered by number of seats held and then alphabetical order if tied.

## CONSERVATIVES
- Eliminate the deficit and be running a surplus by the end of the parliament
- Provide an extra £8bn above inflation for the NHS by 2020
- Extend the right-to-buy scheme to housing association tenants in England
- Introduce legislation so that those working 30 hours a week on the minimum wage are not eligible for tax
- 30 hours of free childcare a week for working parents of all three- and four-year-olds
- Referendum on the UK's EU membership

## LABOUR
- Cut the deficit every year; balance the books as soon as possible in next parliament
- An extra £2.5bn for the NHS, largely paid for by a mansion tax on properties valued at over £2m
- Increase the hourly minimum wage to more than £8 by 2019
- No increases in VAT, national insurance or basic and higher rates of income tax
- Access to childcare from 8am to 6pm for parents of primary school children
- A freeze on energy bills until 2017 and new powers to the energy regulator to reduce bills for winter 2015

## SCOTTISH NATIONAL PARTY
- Increase government spending by 0.5 per cent a year to enable £140bn extra investment in the economy and public services
- Annual UK target of 100,000 affordable homes
- Increase the hourly minimum wage to £8.70 by 2020
- Restore the 50 per cent income tax rate for those earning over £150,000
- Build an alliance against the renewal of the Trident nuclear weapons system
- Retain the triple lock on pensions and protect the winter fuel allowance

## DEMOCRATIC UNIONIST PARTY
- Grow the Northern Ireland economy by making the region an attractive option for foreign investment
- Deliver world class public services
- Create a society based on fairness and opportunity for everyone
- Make politics and government work better in Northern Ireland and enhance British identity

## LIBERAL DEMOCRATS
- Balance the budget fairly through a mixture of cuts and taxes on higher earners
- Increase the tax-free allowance to £12,500
- Guarantee education funding for all from nursery age to 19 years and ensure every school-aged child is taught by a qualified teacher

- Invest £8bn in the NHS and bring mental health care in line with that provided for physical health
- Five new laws to protect the natural environment and fight climate change

## SINN FEIN
- End austerity – negotiate an extra £1.5bn for job creation and strong public services in Northern Ireland
- Return economic powers for a fair recovery, including full control over income tax
- Fully implement the welfare protection outlined in the Stormont House Agreement
- Continue to campaign for a referendum on Irish unity

## PLAID CYMRU
- Living wage for all employees by 2020
- Extra 1,000 doctors for Wales NHS
- Devolve control of the criminal justice system – including policing – to Wales
- Oppose renewal of the Trident nuclear weapons system
- Wales to get the same devolved powers and similar funding to Scotland – an additional £1.2bn a year

## SOCIAL DEMOCRATIC AND LABOUR PARTY
- A Scottish-style commission on devolving fiscal powers to Northern Ireland
- A prosperity process rather than continued austerity
- VAT in the hospitality and tourism industry reduced to 5 per cent
- Opposition to further welfare spending cuts

## ULSTER UNIONIST PARTY
- Reduce the rate of corporation tax in Northern Ireland to encourage economic growth and create tens of thousands of new jobs
- An integrated education system in Northern Ireland where children mix from age four to ensure against sectarianism
- Benchmark the performance of the NHS in Northern Ireland against the best performing aspects of the NHS in other parts of the UK
- Improve mental health and wellbeing

## GREEN
- End austerity and restore the public sector, creating jobs that pay at least a living wage
- End privatisation of the NHS and re-nationalise the railways
- Work with other countries on climate change to ensure global temperature increases do not exceed 2°C
- Invest £85bn in a public programme of renewable fuel generation, flood defences and building insulation
- Provide 500,000 social homes for rent by 2020 and introduce rent caps

## UK INDEPENDENCE PARTY
- Hold a referendum on the UK's membership of the European Union
- Limit immigration to 50,000 skilled workers a year and implement a five-year ban on unskilled immigration
- Provide an additional £3bn a year of funding for the NHS in England
- No tax on the minimum wage
- Meet the NATO target of spending 2 per cent of GDP on defence, and look to increase this target substantially

# THE GOVERNMENT

*as at 1 September 2015*

## THE CABINET

*Prime Minister, First Lord of the Treasury and Minister for the Civil Service*
Rt. Hon. David Cameron, MP
*Chancellor of the Exchequer and First Secretary of State*
Rt. Hon. George Osborne, MP
*Secretary of State for Foreign and Commonwealth Affairs*
Rt. Hon. Philip Hammond, MP
*Secretary of State for the Home Department*
Rt. Hon. Theresa May, MP
*Lord Chancellor and Secretary of State for Justice*
Rt. Hon. Michael Gove, MP
*Secretary of State for Defence*
Rt. Hon. Michael Fallon, MP
*Secretary of State for Work and Pensions*
Rt. Hon. Iain Duncan Smith, MP
*Secretary of State for Health*
Rt. Hon. Jeremy Hunt, MP
*Lord President of the Council and Leader of the House of Commons*
Rt. Hon. Chris Grayling, MP
*Secretary of State for International Development*
Rt. Hon. Justine Greening, MP
*Secretary of State for Education and Minister for Women and Equalities*
Rt. Hon. Nicky Morgan, MP
*Lord Privy Seal and Leader of the House of Lords*
Rt. Hon. Baroness Stowell of Beeston, MBE
*Secretary of State for Transport*
Rt. Hon. Patrick McLoughlin, MP
*Secretary of State for Business, Innovation and Skills and President of the Board of Trade*
Rt. Hon. Sajid Javid, MP
*Secretary of State for Northern Ireland*
Rt. Hon. Theresa Villiers, MP
*Secretary of State for Environment*
Rt. Hon. Theresa Villiers, MP
*Secretary of State for Environment, Food and Rural Affairs*
Rt. Hon. Elizabeth Truss, MP
*Secretary of State for Communities and Local Government*
Rt. Hon. Greg Clark, MP
*Secretary of State for Wales*
Rt. Hon. Stephen Crabb, MP
*Chancellor of the Duchy of Lancaster*
Rt. Hon. Oliver Letwin, MP
*Secretary of State for Culture, Media and Sport*
Rt. Hon. John Whittingdale, MP
*Secretary of State for Scotland*
David Mundell, MP
*Secretary of State for Energy and Climate Change*
Rt. Hon. Amber Rudd, MP

### ALSO ATTENDING CABINET MEETINGS
*Attorney-General*
Rt. Hon. Jeremy Wright, QC, MP
*Minister for the Cabinet Office and Paymaster General*
Rt. Hon. Matthew Hancock, MP
*Chief Secretary to the Treasury*
Rt. Hon. Greg Hands, MP
*Minister for Small Business, Industry and Enterprise*
Rt. Hon. Anna Soubry, MP

*Minister without Portfolio*
Rt. Hon. Robert Halfon, MP
*Parliamentary Secretary to the Treasury and Chief Whip*
Rt. Hon. Mark Harper, MP
*Minister of State at the Foreign and Commonwealth Office*
Rt. Hon. Baroness Anelay of St Johns, DBE
*Minister of State for Employment*
Rt. Hon. Priti Patel, MP

## LAW OFFICERS

*Attorney-General*
Rt. Hon. Jeremy Wright, QC, MP
*Solicitor-General*
Robert Buckland, QC, MP
*Advocate-General for Scotland*
Rt. Hon. Lord Keen of Elie, QC

## MINISTERS OF STATE

*Business, Innovation and Skills*
Jo Johnson, MP
*Ed Vaizey, MP
†Rt. Hon. Lord Maude of Horsham
‡Nick Boles, MP
*Communities and Local Government*
Rt. Hon. Mark Francois, MP
Brandon Lewis, MP
*Culture, Media and Sport*
§Ed Vaizey, MP
*Defence*
Philip Dunne, MP
Penny Mordaunt, MP
Rt. Hon. Earl Howe
*Education*
§Nick Boles, MP
Nick Gibb, MP
Edward Timpson, MP
*Energy and Climate Change*
Andrea Leadsom, MP
*Enivronment, Food and Rural Affairs*
George Eustice, MP
*Foreign and Commonwealth Office*
Rt. Hon. David Lidington, MP
Rt. Hon. Hugo Swire, MP
§Rt. Hon. Lord Maude of Horsham
**Rt. Hon. Baroness Anelay of St Johns, DBE
Rt. Hon. Grant Shapps, MP
*Health*
Rt. Hon. Alistair Burt, MP
*Home Office*
Rt. Hon. Mike Penning, MP
Rt. Hon. John Hayes, MP
James Brokenshire, MP
Rt. Hon. Lord Bates
*Justice*
Rt. Hon. Mike Penning, MP
Rt. Hon. Lord Faulks, QC
*International Development*
Rt. Hon. Grant Shapps, MP
Rt. Hon. Desmond Swayne, TD, MP

*Work and Pensions*
Rt. Hon. Priti Patel, MP
Rt. Hon. Lord Freud
Baroness Altmann, CBE
*UK Export Finance*
**Lord Maude of Horsham

* position held jointly with the Department for Culture, Media and Sport
† position held jointly with the Foreign and Commonwealth Office (FCO)
‡ position held jointly with the Department for Education
§ position held jointly with the Department for Business, Innovation and Skills (BIS)
** position held jointly between the FCO and the BIS

## UNDER-SECRETARIES OF STATE

*Business, Innovation and Skills*
*George Freeman, MP
Baroness Neville-Rolfe, DBE, CMG
*Communities and Local Government*
Marcus Jones, MP
James Wharton, MP
Baroness Williams of Trafford
*Culture, Media and Sport*
Richard Harrington, MP
Baroness Neville-Rolfe, DBE, CMG
Tracey Crouch, MP
Baroness Shields, OBE
*Defence*
Mark Lancaster, TD, MP
Julian Brazier, MP
*Education*
Caroline Dinenage, MP
Sam Gyimah, MP
Lord Nash
*Energy and Climate Change*
Lord Bourne of Aberystwyth
*Environment, Food and Rural Affairs*
Rory Stewart, MP
*Foreign and Commonwealth Office*
Tobias Ellwood, MP
*Health*
Ben Gummer, MP
Jane Ellison, MP
†George Freeman, MP
Lord Prior of Brampton
*Home Office*
Karen Bradley, MP
Lord Ahmad of Wimbledon
Richard Harrington, MP
*International Development*
Baroness Verma
Richard Harrington, MP
*Justice*
Caroline Dinenage, MP
Dominic Raab, MP
Andrew Selous, MP
Shailesh Vara, MP
*Northern Ireland Office*
Ben Wallace, MP
*Scotland Office*
Lord Dunlop
*Transport*
Robert Goodwill, MP
Claire Perry, MP

Andrew Jones, MP
Lord Ahmad of Wimbledon
*Wales Office*
Alun Cairns, MP
Lord Bourne of Aberystwyth
*Work and Pensions*
Justin Tomlinson, MP
Shailesh Vara, MP

* Jointly with the Department for Health
† Jointly with BIS

## OTHER MINISTERS

*Cabinet Office*
Rob Wilson, MP *(Parliamentary Secretary)*
John Penrose, MP *(Parliamentary Secretary)*
Lord Bridges of Headley *(Parliamentary Secretary)*
*Office of the Leader of the House of Commons*
Thérèse Coffey, MP
*(Parliamentary Secretary and Deputy Leader of the Commons)*
*Office of the Leader of the House of Lords*
Rt. Hon. Earl Howe *(Deputy Leader of the House of Lords)*
*Treasury*
Damian Hinds, MP *(Exchequer Secretary)*
David Gauke, MP *(Financial Secretary)*
Harriet Baldwin, MP *(Economic Secretary)*
Lord O'Neill of Gatley *(Commercial Secretary)*

## GOVERNMENT WHIPS

### HOUSE OF LORDS
*Lords Chief Whip and Captain of the Honourable Corps of Gentlemen-at-Arms*
Lord Taylor of Holbeach, CBE
*Deputy Chief Whip and Captain of the Queen's Bodyguard of the Yeomen of the Guard*
Lord Gardiner of Kimble
*Lords-in-Waiting*
Lord Ashton of Hyde
Lord Bourne of Aberystwyth
Viscount Young of Leckie
Earl of Courtown
*Baronesses-in-Waiting*
Baroness Chisholm of Owlpen
Baroness Evans of Bowes Park

### HOUSE OF COMMONS
*Chief Whip and Parliamentary Secretary to the Treasury*
Rt. Hon. Mark Harper, MP
*Deputy Chief Whip and Treasurer of HM Household*
Anne Milton, MP
*Deputy Chief Whip and Comptroller of HM Household*
Gavin Barwell, MP
*Government Whip and Vice-Chamberlain of HM Household*
Kris Hopkins, MP
*Lords Commissioners of HM Treasury (Whips)*
David Evennett, MP; John Penrose, MP; *Alun Cairns, MP;
Charlie Elphicke, MP; Mel Stride, MP;
George Hollingberry, MP
*Assistant Whips* Guy Opperman, MP; Julian Smith, MP;
Margot James, MP; Sarah Newton, MP;
Stephen Barclay, MP; Simon Kirby, MP;
Jackie Doyle-Price, MP

* alongside role as Under-Secretary of State at the Wales Office

# GOVERNMENT DEPARTMENTS

## THE CIVIL SERVICE

The civil service helps the government develop and deliver its policies as effectively as possible. It works in three types of organisations – departments, executive agencies, and non-departmental government bodies (NDPBs). Under the Next Steps programme, launched in 1988, many semi-autonomous executive agencies were established to carry out much of the work of the civil service. Executive agencies operate within a framework set by the responsible minister which specifies policies, objectives and available resources. All executive agencies are set annual performance targets by their minister. Each agency has a chief executive, who is responsible for the day-to-day operations of the agency and who is accountable to the minister for the use of resources and for meeting the agency's targets. The minister accounts to parliament for the work of the agency.

There are currently 412,000 civil servants on a full-time equivalent (FTE) basis and 447,000 on a headcount basis. FTE is a measure that counts staff according to the proportion of full-time hours that they work. Almost three-quarters of all civil servants work outside London and the south-east. All government departments and executive agencies are responsible for their own pay and grading systems for civil servants outside the senior civil service.

### SALARIES 2015–16

MINISTERIAL SALARIES *from 31 July 2015 until May 2020*
Ministers who are members of the House of Commons receive a parliamentary salary of £74,000 in addition to their ministerial salary.

| | |
|---|---|
| Prime minister | £75,440 |
| Cabinet minister (Commons) | £67,505 |
| Cabinet minister (Lords) | £101,038 |
| Minister of state (Commons) | £31,680 |
| Minister of state (Lords) | £78,891 |
| Parliamentary under-secretary (Commons) | £22,375 |
| Parliamentary under-secretary (Lords) | £68,710 |

SPECIAL ADVISERS' SALARIES *from 1 April 2015*
Special advisers to government ministers are paid out of public funds; their salaries are negotiated individually, but are usually in the range of £40,352 to £106,864.

CIVIL SERVICE SALARIES *from 1 April 2015*

| *Senior Civil Servants* | |
|---|---|
| Permanent secretary | £142,000–£200,000 |
| Band 3 | £105,000–£208,100 |
| Band 2 | £86,000–£162,500 |
| Band 1 | £63,000–£117,800 |

Staff are placed in pay bands according to their level of responsibility and taking account of other factors such as experience and marketability. Movement within and between bands is based on performance. Following the delegation of responsibility for pay and grading to government

departments and agencies from 1 April 1996, it is no longer possible to show service-wide pay rates for staff outside the Senior Civil Service.

## GOVERNMENT DEPARTMENTS

For more information on government departments, *see* W www.gov.uk/government/ministers

### ATTORNEY-GENERAL'S OFFICE

Attorney-General's Office, 20 Victoria Street, London SW1H 0NF
T 020-7271 2492 E correspondence@attorneygeneral.gsi.gov.uk
W www.gov.uk/government/organisations/attorney-generals-office

The law officers of the crown for England and Wales are the Attorney-General and the Solicitor-General. The Attorney-General, assisted by the Solicitor-General, is the chief legal adviser to the government and is also ultimately responsible for all crown litigation. He has overall responsibility for the work of the Law Officers' Departments (the Treasury Solicitor's Department, the Crown Prosecution Service – incorporating the Revenue and Customs Prosecutions Office – and the Serious Fraud Office, and HM Crown Prosecution Service Inspectorate). The Attorney-General also oversees the armed forces' prosecuting authority and the government legal service. He has a specific statutory duty to superintend the discharge of their duties by the Director of Public Prosecutions (who heads the Crown Prosecution Service) and the Director of the Serious Fraud Office. The Attorney-General has specific responsibilities for the enforcement of the criminal law and also performs certain public interest functions, eg protecting charities and appealing unduly lenient sentences. He also deals with questions of law arising in bills and with issues of legal policy.

Following the devolution of power to the Northern Ireland Assembly on 12 April 2010, the assembly now appoints the Attorney General for Northern Ireland. The Attorney General for England and Wales holds the office of Advocate General for Northern Ireland, with significantly reduced responsibilities in Northern Ireland.
*Attorney-General,* Rt. Hon. Jeremy Wright, QC, MP
*Parliamentary Private Secretary,* Rehman Chishti, MP
*Solicitor-General,* Robert Buckland, QC, MP
*Director-General,* Rowena Collins Rice

### DEPARTMENT FOR BUSINESS, INNOVATION AND SKILLS

1 Victoria Street, London SW1H 0ET
T 020-7215 5000
W www.gov.uk/government/organisations/department-for-business-innovation-skills

The Department for Business, Innovation and Skills (BIS) was established in June 2009 by merging the Department for Business, Enterprise and Regulatory Reform and the Department for Innovation, Universities and Skills. BIS is the department for economic growth which invests in skills and education to promote trade, boost innovation and help people to start and grow a business. BIS also protects consumers and reduces the impact of regulation.
*Secretary of State for Business, Innovation and Skills and President of the Board of Trade,* Rt. Hon. Sajid Javid, MP*

*Parliamentary Private Secretary,* John Glen, MP
*Principal Private Secretary,* Emma Squire
*Senior Private Secretary,* Emily Shirtcliff
*Special Advisers,* Nick King; Salma Shah; Daniel Gilbert
*Minister of State,* Jo Johnson, MP *(Universities and Science)*
*Parliamentary Private Secretary,* Anne Marie Morris, MP
*Senior Private Secretary,* Hannah Nicholls
*Minister of State,* Rt. Hon. Lord Maude of Horsham *(Trade and Investment)*\*
*Senior Private Secretary,* John Frew
*Special Adviser,* Simone Finn
*Minister of State,* Rt. Hon. Anna Soubry, MP *(Small Business, Industry and Enterprise)*
*Parliamentary Private Secretary,* Mark Pawsey, MP
*Senior Private Secretary,* Claire Rannard
*Special Adviser,* Elliott Burton
*Minister of State,* Ed Vaizey, MP *(Culture and the Digital Economy)*†
*Parliamentary Private Secretary,* Sheryll Murray, MP
*Private Secretary,* Jack Hindley
*Minister of State,* Nick Boles, MP *(Skills)*‡
*Parliamentary Private Secretary,* Anne Marie Morris, MP
*Senior Private Secretary,* Rose McNamee
*Parliamentary Under-Secretary of State,* George Freeman, MP *(Life Sciences)*§
*Senior Private Secretary,* Rebecca Molyneux
*Parliamentary Under-Secretary of State,* Baroness Neville-Rolfe, DBE, CMG *(Minister for Intellectual Property)*†
*Private Secretary,* Harriet Smith
*Permanent Secretary,* Martin Donnelly
*Senior Private Secretary,* Casey Malynn
*Head of Parliamentary Unit,* Georgina Holme-Skelton

\* Jointly with UK Export Finance
† Jointly with the Department for Culture, Media and Sport
‡ Jointly with the Department for Education
§ Jointly with the Department of Health

DEPARTMENTAL BOARD
*Chair,* Rt. Hon. Sajid Javid, MP *(Secretary of State)*
*Members,* Sam Beckett *(Economics and Markets);* Gareth Davies *(Knowledge and Innovation);* Martin Donnelly *(Permanent Secretary);* Dominic Jermey *(Chief Executive, UK Trade and Investment);* Bernadette Kelly *(Business and Local Growth);* Philippa Lloyd *(People and Strategy);* Howard Orme *(Finance and Commercial);* Rachel Sandby-Thomas, CB *(Enterprise and Skills and Legal)*
*Non-Executive Members,* Stephen Bligh; Allan Cook *(Lead);* Prof. Dame Ann Dowling, DBE; Juergen Maier; Dale Murray; Dalton Philips; Prof. Wendy Purcell

BETTER REGULATION EXECUTIVE
1 Victoria Street, London SW1 0ET
T 020-7215 5000 E betterregulation@bis.gsi.gov.uk
W www.gov.uk/government/policy-teams/better-regulation-executive

The Better Regulation Executive (BRE) is a joint BIS/Cabinet Office unit which leads on delivering the government's manifesto commitment to reduce the overall burden on business, in order to increase growth and create jobs. Each government department is however responsible for delivering its part of the deregulation agenda within the framework put in place by the BRE.
*Non-Executive Chair,* Lord Curry of Kirkharle, CBE
*Chief Executive,* Graham Turnock

SHAREHOLDER EXECUTIVE
1 Victoria Street, London SW1H 0ET
T 020-7215 5000
W www.shareholderexecutive.gov.uk

The Shareholder Executive was set up in September 2003 to work with other departments in government to improve the government's capabilities and performance as a shareholder, and to offer corporate finance expertise and advice across government. Its goal is to create a climate of ownership that, while challenging, is genuinely supportive and provides the framework for the 23 businesses under its remit to be successful. In addition, the Shareholder Executive's Government Property Unit is responsible for maximising value from the state's property portfolio.
*Chair,* Robert Swannell
*Chief Executive,* Mark Russell

# CABINET OFFICE
70 Whitehall, London SW1A 2AS
T 020-7276 1234
W www.gov.uk/government/organisations/cabinet-office

The Cabinet Office, alongside the Treasury, sits at the centre of the government, with an overarching purpose of making government work better. It supports the prime minister and the cabinet, helping to ensure effective development, coordination and implementation of policy and operations across all government departments. The Cabinet Office also leads work to ensure that the Civil Service provides the most effective and efficient support to the government to meet its objectives. The department is headed by the Minister for the Cabinet Office.
*Prime Minister, First Lord of the Treasury and Minister for the Civil Service,* Rt. Hon. David Cameron, MP
*Parliamentary Private Secretary,* Gavin Williamson, MP
*Principal Private Secretary,* Chris Martin
*Chancellor of the Duchy of Lancaster,* Rt. Hon. Oliver Letwin, MP
*Parliamentary Private Secretary,* Alok Sharma, MP
*Minister for the Cabinet Office and Paymaster General,* Rt. Hon. Matthew Hancock, MP
*Parliamentary Private Secretary,* Gareth Johnson, MP
*Principal Private Secretary,* Athith Shetty
*Private Secretaries,* Helen Devanny, Miriam Laurance, Joe Taylor
*Lord President of the Council,* Rt. Hon. Chris Grayling, MP
*Parliamentary Private Secretary,* Mike Freer, MP
*Minister for Civil Society,* Rob Wilson, MP
*Private Secretary,* Elizabeth Jacobs
*Minister for Constitutional Reform,* John Penrose, MP
*Parliamentary Secretary,* Lord Bridges of Headley
*Private Secretary,* Luke Montague
*Minister without Portfolio,* Rt. Hon. Robert Halfon, MP
*Parliamentary Private Secretary,* Andrew Stephenson, MP
*Head of the Civil Service and Cabinet Secretary,* Sir Jeremy Heywood, KCB, CVO
*Chief Executive of the Civil Service,* John Manzoni
*Permanent Secretary and First Parliamentary Counsel,* Richard Heaton, CB
*Chair of the Joint Intelligence Committee,* Jon Day
*National Security Adviser,* Sir Kim Darroch
*Head of European and Global Issues,* Tom Scholar

MANAGEMENT BOARD
*Chair,* Rt. Hon. Francis Maude, MP
*Board Members,* Melanie Dawes *(Director-General, Economic and Domestic Affairs Secretariat);* Sue Gray

*(Director-General, Propriety and Ethics Team, and Head of Private Offices Group);* Richard Heaton, CB *(Permanent Secretary and First Parliamentary Counsel);* Sir Jeremy Heywood, KCB, CVO *(Cabinet Secretary);* Nick Hurd, MP *(Minister for Civil Society);* Bruce Mann, CB *(Finance Director)*
*Non-Executive Directors,* Lord Browne of Madingley; Ian Davis; Rona Fairhead; Dame Barbara Stocking, DBE

## HONOURS AND APPOINTMENTS SECRETARIAT
Room G-39, Horse Guards Road, London SW1A 2HQ
T 020-7276 2777
*Head,* Richard Tilbrook

## OFFICE OF THE LEADER OF THE HOUSE OF COMMONS
1 Horse Guards Road, London SW1A 2HQ
T 020-7276 1005 E commonsleader@cabinetoffice.gov.uk
W www.gov.uk/government/organisations/the-office-of-the-leader-of-the-house-of-commons

The Office of the Leader of the House of Commons is responsible for the arrangement of government business in the House of Commons and for planning and supervising the government's legislative programme. The Leader of the House of Commons upholds the rights and privileges of the house and acts as a spokesperson for the government as a whole.

The leader reports regularly to the cabinet on parliamentary business and the legislative programme. In his capacity as leader of the house, he is a member of the House of Commons Commission. He also chairs the cabinet committee on the legislative programme. As Lord President of the Council, he is a member of the cabinet and in charge of the Office of the Privy Council.

The Deputy Leader of the House of Commons supports the leader in handling the government's business in the house. He is responsible for monitoring MPs' and peers' correspondence.

*Leader of the House of Commons and Lord Privy Seal,*
  Rt. Hon. Chris Grayling, MP
*Parliamentary Private Secretary,* Mike Freer, MP
*Head of Office,* Mike Winter
*Deputy Head of Office,* Christine Hill
*Assistant Private Secretaries,* James Waddington *(Parliamentary Business);* Mark Fernandes *(Parliamentary Reform)*
*Deputy Leader of the House of Commons,* Dr Thérèse Coffey, MP
*Private Secretary,* Mark Fernandes

## OFFICE OF THE LEADER OF THE HOUSE OF LORDS
House of Lords, London SW1A 0PW
T 020-7219 3200 E psleaderofthelords@cabinet-office.x.gsi.gov.uk
W www.gov.uk/government/organisations/office-of-the-leader-of-the-house-of-lords

The Office of the Leader of the House of Lords provides support to the leader in their parliamentary and ministerial duties, which include leading the government benches in the House of Lords; the delivery of the government's business in the Lords; taking part in formal ceremonies such as the state opening of parliament; and giving guidance to the House of Lords on matters of procedure and order.

*Lord Privy Seal, Leader of the House of Lords,*
  Rt. Hon. Baroness Stowell of Beeston, MBE
*Parliamentary Private Secretary,* Kwasi Kwarteng, MP
*Deputy Leader of the House of Lords,* Rt. Hon. Earl Howe

## GOVERNMENT POLICY
## PRIME MINISTER'S OFFICE
10 Downing Street, London SW1A 2AA
T 020-7930 4433
W www.number-10.gov.uk
*Prime Minister,* Rt. Hon. David Cameron, MP
*Parliamentary Private Secretary,* Gavin Williamson, MP
*Principal Private Secretary,* Chris Martin
*Private Secretaries,* Nigel Casey *(Foreign Affairs);* Kate Joseph *(Home Affairs);* Ed Whiting *(Foreign Affairs and Development)*
*Speech Writer to the Prime Minister,* Tim Kiddell
*Director of Communications,* Craig Oliver
*Director of External Relations,* Gabby Bertin
*Director of Operations and Campaigns,* Liz Sugg
*Director of Strategy,* Ameet Gill
*Prime Minister's Official Spokesman,* Helen Bower
*Chief of Staff,* Ed Llewellyn
*Deputy Chief of Staff,* Catherine Fall
*Press Secretary to the Prime Minister,* Graeme Wilson
*Head of Policy Unit,* Camilla Cavendish
*Head of Implementation Unit,* Antonia Romeo
*Head of Corporate Services,* Helen Lederer

## CIVIL SERVICE REFORM
*Director-General,* Oliver Robbins, CB

## ECONOMIC AND DOMESTIC AFFAIRS SECRETARIAT
*Director-General,* Antonia Romeo

## IMPLEMENTATION GROUP
*Executive Director,* Simon Case

## PRIVATE OFFICES GROUP
*Director-General, Propriety and Ethics and Head of Private Offices Group,* Sue Gray

## UK GOVERNANCE GROUP
*Second Permanent Secretary and Head of UK Governance Group,* Philip Rycroft

## CABINET OFFICE CORPORATE SERVICES
*Executive Director, Government Communications,* Alex Aiken
*Finance Director,* Guy Lester
*Human Resources Directors,* Crystal Akass; Ruth Bailey

## NATIONAL SECURITY
Comprises the National Security Secretariat and the Joint Intelligence Organisation. The National Security Secretariat is responsible for providing policy advice to the National Security Council, where ministers discuss national security issues at a strategic level; coordinating and developing foreign and defence policy across government; coordinating policy, ethical and legal issues across the intelligence community, managing its funding and priorities, and dealing with the Intelligence and Security Committee which calls it to account; developing effective protective security policies and capabilities for government; improving the UK's resilience to respond to and recover from emergencies, and maintaining facilities for the effective coordination of government response to crises; and providing strategic leadership for cyber security in the UK, in line with the National Cyber Security Strategy.

## NATIONAL SECURITY SECRETARIAT
*National Security Adviser,* Sir Mark Lyall Grant
*Deputy National Security Adviser,* Julian Miller, CB

## JOINT INTELLIGENCE ORGANISATION
*Chair, Joint Intelligence Committee,* Jon Day

EFFICIENCY AND REFORM GROUP
*Chief Procurement Officer,* Bill Crothers, CB
*Deputy Chief Procurement Officer,* Sally Collier

INDEPENDENT OFFICES

CIVIL SERVICE COMMISSION
1 Horse Guards Road, London SW1A 2HQ
T 020-7271 0831
W http://civilservicecommission.independent.gov.uk

The Civil Service Commission regulates the requirement that selection for appointment to the Civil Service must be on merit on the basis of fair and open competition; the commission publishes its recruitment principles and audit departments and agencies' performance against these. Commissioners personally chair competitions for the most senior jobs in the civil service. In addition, the commission hears complaints from civil servants under the Civil Service Code.

The commission was established as a statutory body in November 2010 under the provisions of the Constitutional Reform and Governance Act 2010.
*First Commissioner (part-time),* Sir David Normington, GCB
*Commissioners,* Jonathan Baume; Kathryn Bishop; Andrew Flanagan; Dame Moira Gibb, DBE; Wanda Goldwag; Angela Sarkis, CBE

THE COMMISSIONER FOR PUBLIC APPOINTMENTS
G/8, 1 Horse Guards Road, London SW1A 2HQ
T 020-7271 0831 E publicappointments@csc.gsi.gov.uk
W http://publicappointmentscommissioner.independent.gov.uk

The Commissioner for Public Appointments is responsible for monitoring, regulating and reporting on ministerial appointments (including those made by Welsh government ministers) to public bodies. The commissioner can investigate complaints about the way in which appointments were made.
*Commissioner for Public Appointments,* Sir David Normington, GCB
*Chief Executive Commission Secretariat,* Clare Salters

OFFICE OF THE PARLIAMENTARY COUNSEL
1 Horse Guards Road, London SW1A 2HQ
T 02-7276 6586 E goodlaw@cabinet-office.gsi.gov.ukk
W www.gov.uk/government/organisations/office-of-the-parliamentary-counsel

The Office of the Parliamentary Counsel is a group of government lawyers who specialise in drafting government bills; advising departments on the rules and procedures of Parliament; reviewing orders and regulations which amend Acts of Parliament; and assisting the government on a range of legal and constitutional issues.
*First Parliamentary Counsel,* Richard Heaton, CB
*Chief Executive,* Jim Barron, CBE

## DEPARTMENT FOR COMMUNITIES AND LOCAL GOVERNMENT
2 Marsham Street, London SW1P 4DF
T 0303-444 0000
W www.gov.uk/government/organisations/department-for-communities-and-local-government

The Department for Communities and Local Government was formed in May 2006 with a remit to promote community cohesion and prevent extremism, and was given responsibility for housing, urban regeneration and planning. It unites the communities and civil renewal functions previously undertaken by the Home Office, with responsibility for regeneration, neighbourhood renewal and local government (previously

held by the Office of the Deputy Prime Minister, which was abolished following a cabinet reshuffle in May 2006). The department ensures that the Fire and Rescue services have the resources they need to reduce the number of deaths from fire, promote fire prevention activity and respond swiftly to national emergencies. The department also has responsibility for equality policy on race and faith (functions that were previously split between several government departments).
*Secretary of State for Communities and Local Government and Minister for Faith,* Rt. Hon. Greg Clark, MP
*Parliamentary Private Secretary,* Henry Smith, MP
*Principal Private Secretary,* Alex Williams
*Special Advisers,* Megan Powell-Chandler; Jacob Willmer
*Minister of State,* Brandon Lewis, MP *(Housing and Planning)*
*Parliamentary Private Secretary,* Andrew Griffiths, MP
*Private Secretary,* Ruth Long
*Minister of State,* Rt. Hon. Mark Francois, MP *(Communities and Resilience)*
*Parliamentary Private Secretary,* Andrew Griffiths, MP
*Private Secretary,* Lucy Yates
*Parliamentary Under-Secretary of State,* Marcus Jones, MP *(Local Government)*
*Private Secretary,* Peter Fenn
*Parliamentary Under-Secretary of State,* James Wharton, MP *(Local Growth and the Northern Powerhouse)*
*Private Secretary,* Kerr McKendrick
*Parliamentary Under-Secretary of State,* Baroness Williams of Trafford
*Private Secretary,* Shamila Meadows

MANAGEMENT BOARD
*Permanent Secretary,* Melanie Dawes, CB
*Members,* Stephen Aldridge, CB; Dawn Brodrick, CB; Andrew Campbell, CB; Louise Casey, CB; Helen Edwards, CBE; David Hill; Jacinda Humphry; Peter Schofield
*Non-Executive Members,* Stephen Hay; Nick Markham; Grenville Turner; Sara Weller *(Lead)*

## DEPARTMENT FOR CULTURE, MEDIA AND SPORT
100 Parliament Street, London SW1A 2BQ
T 020-7211 6000 E enquiries@culture.gov.uk
W www.gov.uk/government/organisations/department-for-culture-media-sport

The Department for Culture, Media and Sport (DCMS) was established in July 1997 and aims to improve the quality of life for all those in the UK through cultural and sporting activities while championing the tourism, creative and leisure industries. It is responsible for government policy relating to the arts, sport, the National Lottery, tourism, libraries, museums and galleries, broadcasting, creative industries – including film and the music industry – press freedom and regulation, licensing, gambling, the historic environment, telecommunications and online and media ownership and mergers.

The department is also responsible for 41 agencies and public bodies that help deliver the department's strategic aims and objectives, the listing of historic buildings and scheduling of ancient monuments, the export licensing of cultural goods, and the management of the Government Art Collection and the Royal Parks (its sole executive agency). It has the responsibility for humanitarian assistance in the event of a disaster, as well as for the organisation of the annual Remembrance Day ceremony at the Cenotaph. In September 2012, the Government Equalities Office became part of DCMS, having previously been part of the Home Office.
*Secretary of State for Culture, Media and Sport,* Rt. Hon. John Whittingdale, MP

*Parliamentary Private Secretary*, Heather Wheeler, MP
*Principal Private Secretary*, Ben Dean
*Minister of State*, Ed Vaizey, MP *(Culture and the Digital Economy)**
*Parliamentary Private Secretary*, Sheryll Murray, MP
*Private Secretary*, Jack Hindley
*Parliamentary Under-Secretary of State*, Tracey Crouch, MP *(Sport, Tourism and Heritage)*
*Private Secretary*, Philip Bland
*Parliamentary Under-Secretary of State*, Baroness Neville-Rolfe, DBE, CMG *(Minister for Intellectual Property)**
*Private Secretary*, Lizzie Glithero-West
*Parliamentary Under-Secretary of State*, Baroness Shields *(Internet Safety and Security)*
*Private Secretary*, Saskia Bradbury

*Jointly with the Department for Business, Innovation and Skills

MANAGEMENT BOARD
*Permanent Secretary*, Sue Owen
*Members*, Hugh Harris; Sarah Healey; Clare Pillman; Alison Pritchard; David Rossington; Chris Townsend; Andrea Young
*Non-Executive Members*, Ajay Chowdhury; Dr Tracy Long; Ruby McGregor-Smith, CBE; Sir David Verey

GOVERNMENT EQUALITIES OFFICE (GEO)
100 Parliament Street, London SW1A 2BQ T 020-7211 6000
E enquiries@culture.gsi.gov.uk
W www.gov.uk/government/organisations/government-equalities-office

The GEO is responsible for the government's overall strategy on equality. Its work includes leading the development of a more integrated approach on equality across government with the aim of improving equality and reducing discrimination and disadvantage for all. The office is also responsible for leading policy on gender equality, sexual orientation and transgender equality matters.
*Minister for Women and Equality*, Rt. Hon. Nicky Morgan, MP
*Parliamentary Under-Secretary of State*, Caroline Dinenage, MP *(Women, Equalities and Family Justice)*
*Director*, Alison Pritchard

## MINISTRY OF DEFENCE
*see* Defence Chapter

## DEPARTMENT FOR EDUCATION
Piccadilly Gate, Store Street, Manchester M1 2WD
T 0370-000 2288
W www.gov.uk/government/organisations/department-for-education

The Department for Education (DfE) was established in May 2010 in place of the Department for Children, Schools and Families (DCSF), in order to refocus the department on its core purpose of supporting teaching and learning. The department is responsible for education and children's services, while the Department for Business, Innovation and Skills is responsible for higher education. The DfE is supported by nine executive agencies and public bodies.
 The department's objectives include the expansion of the academies programme, to allow schools to apply to become independent of their local authority, and the introduction of the free schools programme, to allow any suitable proposers, such as parents, businesses or charities, to set up their own school.
*Secretary of State for Education and Minister for Women and Equalities*, Rt. Hon. Nicky Morgan, MP
*Parliamentary Private Secretary*, Robin Walker, MP
*Principal Private Secretary*, Rose Pennells
*Special Advisers*, Lee Davis; George Looker; Luke Tryl

*Minister of State*, Nick Boles, MP *(Skills)**
*Parliamentary Private Secretary*, Anne Marie Morris, MP
*Senior Private Secretary*, Rose McNamee
*Minister of State*, Nick Gibb, MP *(Schools)*
*Parliamentary Private Secretary*, Stephen Metcalfe, MP
*Private Secretary*, Huw Leslie
*Minister of State*, Edward Timpson, MP *(Children and Families)*
*Parliamentary Private Secretary*, Stephen Metcalfe, MP
*Private Secretary*, Holly Jones
*Parliamentary Under-Secretary of State*, Lord Nash *(Schools)*
*Private Secretary*, Bonnie Wang
*Parliamentary Under-Secretary of State*, Caroline Dinenage, MP *(Women, Equalities and Family Justice)†*
*Private Secretary*, Ben Charnock
*Parliamentary Under-Secretary of State*, Sam Gyimah, MP *(Childcare and Education)*
*Private Secretary*, Hannah Maher

* Jointly with the Department for Business, Innovation and Skills
†Jointly with the Ministry of Justice

MANAGEMENT BOARD
*Permanent Secretary*, Chris Wormald
*Members*, Shona Dunn; Simon Fryer; Simon Judge; Paul Kissack; Peter Lauener; Andrew McCully; Tom Shinner
*Non-Executive Members*, Paul Marshall *(Lead)*; David Meller; Marion Plant, OBE

## DEPARTMENT OF ENERGY AND CLIMATE CHANGE
3 Whitehall Place, London SW1A 2AW
T 0300-060 4000 E correspondence@decc.gsi.gov.uk
W www.gov.uk/government/organisations/department-of-energy-climate-change

The Department of Energy and Climate Change (DECC) was formed in 2008 to ensure that the UK has secure, clean, affordable energy supplies and to promote international action to mitigate climate change. It is supported by nine agencies and public bodies.
*Secretary of State for the Department of Energy and Climate Change*, Rt. Hon. Amber Rudd, MP
*Parliamentary Private Secretary*, Paul Maynard, MP
*Private Secretary*, Tim Lord
*Minister of State*, Andrea Leadsom, MP
*Parliamentary Private Secretary*, Sheryll Murray, MP
*Private Secretary*, Stephen Burke
*Parliamentary Under-Secretary of State*, Lord Bourne of Aberystwyth*
*Private Secretary*, Edward Hogg
*Jointly with the Wales Office

MANAGEMENT BOARD
*Permanent Secretary*, Stephen Lovegrove
*Members*, Prof. John Loughhead *(Chief Scientific Adviser)*; Clive Maxwell *(Director-General, Consumers and Households)*; Angie Ridgwell *(Director-General, Finance and Corporate Services)*; Jeremy Pocklington *(Director-General, Markets and Infrastructure)*; Katrina Williams *(Director-General, International, Science and Resilience)*

## DEPARTMENT FOR ENVIRONMENT, FOOD AND RURAL AFFAIRS
Nobel House, 17 Smith Square, London SW1P 3JR
T 03459-335577
E defra.helpline@defra.gsi.gov.uk
W www.gov.uk/government/organisations/department-for-environment-food-rural-affairs

The Department for Environment, Food and Rural Affairs (DEFRA) is responsible for government policy on the environment, rural matters and farming and food production. In association with the agriculture departments of the Scottish government, the National Assembly for Wales and the Northern Ireland Office, the department is responsible for negotiations in the EU on the common agricultural and fisheries policies, and for single European market questions relating to its responsibilities. Its remit includes international agricultural and food trade policy.

The department's five strategic priorities are climate change adaptation; sustainable consumption and production; the protection of natural resources and the countryside; sustainable rural communities; and sustainable farming and food, including animal health and welfare. DEFRA, which is supported by 34 executive agencies and public bodies, is also the lead government department for emergencies in animal and plant diseases, flooding, food and water supply, dealing with the consequences of a chemical, biological, radiological or nuclear incident, and other threats to the environment.

*Secretary of State for Environment, Food and Rural Affairs,* Rt. Hon. Elizabeth Truss, MP
*Parliamentary Private Secretary,* Mark Spencer, MP
*Principal Private Secretary,* Dr Jeremy Marlow
*Senior Private Secretary,* Stuart Colville
*Private Secretaries,* Emma Southard; Adam Stevens
*Parliamentary Under-Secretary of State,* Rory Stewart, MP *(Natural Environment, Floods and Water, Resource and Environmental Management, Rural Affairs, Lead responsibility for the Environment Agency, Natural England and the Forestry Commission and Deputy for the Secretary of State on Environment Council)*
*Senior Private Secretary,* Suzie Pinkett
*Minister of State,* George Eustice, MP *(Farming, Food and the Marine Environment)*
*Parliamentary Private Secretary,* Matthew Offord
*Senior Private Secretary,* Matthew Sabourin
*Private Secretaries,* Yasmin Hussain; James Turner; David How
*Spokesman in the House of Lords,* Lord Gardiner of Kimble
*Permanent Secretary,* Bronwyn Hill, CBE
*Private Secretary,* Linda Kiff

SUPERVISORY BOARD
*Chair,* Bronwyn Hill *(Permanent Secretary)*
*Members,* Betsy Bassis *(Chief Operating Officer);* Prof Ian Boyd *(Chief Scientific Adviser);* Alastair Bridges *(Finance);* Nick Joicey *(Strategy, International and Biosecurity);* Sonia Phippard *(Policy Delivery)*
*Non-Executive Members,* Catherine Doran; Iain Ferguson; Sir Tony Hawkhead, CBE; Paul Rew

# FOREIGN AND COMMONWEALTH OFFICE
King Charles Street, London SW1A 2AH
T 020-7008 1500 E fcocorrespondence@fco.gov.uk
W www.gov.uk/government/organisations/foreign-commonwealth-office

The Foreign and Commonwealth Office (FCO) provides the means of communication between the British government and other governments – and international governmental organisations – on all matters falling within the field of international relations. The FCO employs over 14,000 people in nearly 270 places across the world through a network of embassies and consulates, which help to protect and promote national interests. FCO diplomats are skilled in understanding and influencing what is happening abroad, supporting British citizens who are travelling and living overseas, helping to manage migration into Britain, promoting British trade and other interests abroad and

encouraging foreign investment in the UK. The FCO is supported by 11 executive agencies and public bodies.
*Secretary of State for Foreign and Commonwealth Affairs,* Rt. Hon. Philip Hammond, MP
*Parliamentary Private Secretary,* Christopher Pincher, MP
*Principal Private Secretary,* Martin Reynolds
*Special Advisers,* Graham Hook; Hayden Allan; Duncan McCourt
*Minister of State,* Rt. Hon. David Lidington, MP *(Europe)*
*Parliamentary Private Secretary,* James Morris, MP
*Private Secretary,* Jennifer MacNaughton
*Minister of State,* Rt. Hon. Hugo Swire, MP
*Parliamentary Private Secretary,* Pauline Latham, MP
*Private Secretary,* Fergus Eckersley
*Minister of State,* Rt. Hon. Lord Maude of Horsham *(Trade and Investment)**
*Private Secretary,* Nick Whittingham
*Minister of State,* Rt. Hon. Baroness Anelay of St Johns, DBE
*Private Secretary,* Kate English
*Minister of State,* Rt. Hon. Grant Shapps, MP†
*Private Secretary,* Iain Griffiths
*Parliamentary Under-Secretary of State,* Tobias Ellwood, MP
*Private Secretary,* Sharon Wilkins
*Special Representatives,* Rt. Hon. Baroness Anelay of St Johns, DBE *(Prime Minister's Special Representative on Preventing Sexual Violence in Conflict);* Sir Andrew Burns *(Post-Holocaust Issues);* Rt. Hon. Sir Alan Duncan, MP *(Special Envoy to Oman and Yemen);* Owen Jenkins *(Afghanistan and Pakistan);* Matthew Cannell *(Sudan and South Sudan);* Sir David King *(Climate Change)*

* Jointly with the Department for Business, Innovation and Skills and UK Export Finance
†Jointly with the Department for International Development

BOARD
*Permanent Under-Secretary and Head of the Diplomatic Service,* Sir Simon Fraser, KCMG
*Members,* Deborah Bronnert; Sir Simon Gass *(Political);* Dominic Jermey, OBE *(Chief Executive, UK Trade and Investment);* Julian King, KCVO, CMG *(Economic and Consular);* Sara Mackintosh *(Defence and Intelligence)*
*Non-Executive Members,* Julia Bond; Prof. Robin Grimes; Sir Richard Lambert *(Lead);* Rudy Markham

# DEPARTMENT OF HEALTH
Richmond House, 79 Whitehall, London SW1A 2NS
T 020-7210 4850
W https://www.gov.uk/government/organisations/department-of-health

The Department of Health (DH) leads, shapes and funds health and care in England, making sure people have the support, care and treatment they need and that this is delivered in a compassionate, respectful and dignified manner.

The DH leads across health and care by creating national policies and legislation to meet current and future challenges. It provides funding, assures the delivery and continuity of services and accounts to parliament in a way that represents the best interests of the patient, public and taxpayer. 26 executive agencies and public bodies support the DH.
*Secretary of State for Health,* Rt. Hon. Jeremy Hunt, MP
*Parliamentary Private Secretary,* Steve Brine, MP
*Principal Private Secretary,* Kristen McLeod
*Private Secretary,* Andrew Edmunds
*Minister of State,* Rt. Hon. Alistair Burt, MP *(Community and Social Care)*
*Parliamentary Private Secretary,* Karen Lumley

*Private Secretary,* Claire McAvinchey
*Parliamentary Under-Secretary of State,* Ben Gummer, MP
 *(Care Quality)*
*Private Secretary,* Alex Wallace
*Parliamentary Under-Secretary of State,* Jane Ellison, MP
 *(Public Health)*
*Private Secretary,* Kirsty Bell
*Parliamentary Under-Secretary of State,* Lord Prior of
 Brampton *(NHS Productivity)*
*Private Secretary,* Ilaria Regondi
*Parliamentary Under-Secretary of State,* George Freeman, MP
 *(Life Sciences)\**
*Private Secretary,* Rebecca Molyneux

\* Jointly with the Department for Business, Innovation and Skills

DEPARTMENTAL BOARD
*Chair,* Rt. Hon. Jeremy Hunt, MP
*Members,* Rt. Hon. Alistair Burt MP; Will Cavendish
 *(Innovation, Growth and Technology);* Prof. Dame Sally
 Davies, DBE *(Chief Medical Officer);* Jane Ellison, MP;
 Tamara Finkelstein *(Chief Operating Officer);* Ben
 Gummer, MP; Felicity Harvey, CBE *(Public Health);*
 Charlie Massey *(Strategy and External Relations);* Dame
 Una O'Brien, DCB *(Permanent Secretary);* Dr Daniel
 Poulter, MP; Lord Prior; Jon Rouse *(Social Care, Local
 Government and Care Partnerships);* David Williams
 *(Finance and NHS)*
*Non-Executive Members,* Dr Catherine Bell; Gerry Murphy;
 Chris Pilling; Peter Sands *(Lead)*

## HOME OFFICE
2 Marsham Street, London SW1P 4DF
T 020-7035 4848 E public.enquiries@homeoffice.gsi.gov.uk
W www.gov.uk/government/organisations/home-office

The Home Office deals with those internal affairs in England and Wales which have not been assigned to other government departments. The Secretary of State for the Home Department is the link between the Queen and the public, and exercises certain powers on her behalf, including that of the royal pardon.

The Home Office aims to build a safe, just and tolerant society and to maintain and enhance public security and protection; to support and mobilise communities so that they are able to shape policy and improvement for their locality, overcome nuisance and anti-social behaviour, maintain and enhance social cohesion and enjoy their homes and public spaces peacefully; to deliver departmental policies and responsibilities fairly, effectively and efficiently; and to make the best use of resources. These objectives reflect the priorities of the government and the home secretary in areas of crime, citizenship and communities, namely to work on the problems caused by illegal drug use; shape the alcohol strategy, policy and licensing conditions; keep the UK safe from the threat of terrorism; reduce and prevent crime, and ensure people feel safe in their homes and communities; secure the UK border and control immigration; consider applications to enter and stay in the UK; issue passports and visas; and to support visible, responsible and accountable policing by empowering the public and freeing up the police to fight crime.

The Home Office delivers these aims through the immigration services, its 29 executive agencies and non-departmental public bodies, and by working with partners in private, public and voluntary sectors, individuals and communities. The home secretary is also the link between the UK government and the governments of the Channel Islands and the Isle of Man.

*Secretary of State for the Home Department,* Rt. Hon. Theresa
 May, MP
*Parliamentary Private Secretary,* Michael Ellis, MP
*Principal Private Secretary,* Andrew Scurry
*Special Advisers,* Alex Dawson; Stephen Parkinson; Liz
 Sanderson
*Minister of State,* Mike Penning, MP *(Policing, Crime and
 Criminal Justice and Victims)\**
*Parliamentary Private Secretary,* Chris White, MP
*Private Secretary,* Sarah Phillips
*Minister of State,* Rt. Hon. John Hayes, MP *(Security)*
*Parliamentary Private Secretary,* Chris White, MP
*Minister of State,* James Brokenshire, MP *(Immigration)*
*Parliamentary Private Secretary,* Craig Whittaker, MP
*Private Secretary,* Jon Rosenorn-Lanng
*Minister of State,* Rt. Hon. Lord Bates
*Private Secretary,* Moore Flannery
*Parliamentary Under-Secretary of State,* Karen Bradley, MP
 *(Preventing Abuse and Exploitation)*
*Parliamentary Under-Secretary of State,* Lord Ahmad of
 Wimbledon *(Countering Extremism)*

\*Jointly with the Ministry of Justice

MANAGEMENT BOARD
*Permanent Secretary,* Mark Sedwill
*Members,* Mary Calam *(Crime and Policing Group);* Mandie
 Campbell *(Immigration Enforcement);* Charles Farr
 *(Office for Security and Counter Terrorism);* Peter Fish
 *(Legal);* Sir Charles Montgomery *(Border Force);* Mike
 Parsons *(Chief Operating Officer, Home Office);* Sarah
 Rapson *(UK Visas and Immigration);* Prof. Bernard
 Silverman *(Chief Scientific Adviser);* Peter Storr
 *(International and Immigration Policy);* Julie Taylor
 *(Transformation);* Mark Thomson *(HM Passport Office);*
 Kevin White, CB *(Human Resources);* Simon Wren
 *(Communications)*

## DEPARTMENT FOR INTERNATIONAL DEVELOPMENT
22 Whitehall, London SW1A 2EG T 020-7023 0000
Abercrombie House, Eaglesham Road, East Kilbride, Glasgow
G75 8EA T 01355-844000
Public Enquiries 0845-300 4100 E enquiry@dfid.gov.uk
W www.gov.uk/government/organisations/department-for-international-development

The Department for International Development (DFID) is responsible for promoting sustainable development and reducing poverty. The central focus of the government's policy, based on the 1997, 2000, 2006 and 2009 white papers on international development, is a commitment to the internationally agreed Millennium Development Goals, to be achieved by 2015. These seek to eradicate extreme poverty and hunger; achieve universal primary education; promote gender equality and empower women; reduce child mortality; improve maternal health; combat HIV/AIDS, malaria and other diseases; improve sanitation and access to clean water; ensure environmental sustainability; and encourage a global partnership for development.

DFID's assistance is concentrated in the poorest countries of sub-Saharan Africa and Asia, but also contributes to poverty reduction and sustainable development in middle-income countries, including those in Latin America and Eastern Europe. It also responds to overseas emergencies. The department works in partnership with governments of developing countries, charities, non-governmental organisations and businesses. It also works with multilateral institutions, including the World Bank, United Nations

agencies and the European Commission. The department, which is supported by two executive agencies and public bodies, has headquarters in London and East Kilbride, offices in many developing countries, and staff based in British embassies and high commissions around the world.
*Secretary of State for International Development,*
  Rt. Hon. Justine Greening, MP
*Parliamentary Private Secretary,* Andrew Bingham, MP
*Principal Private Secretary,* Jonathan Baxter
*Special Advisers,* Simon Bishop; Aline Nassif
*Minister of State,* Rt. Hon. Grant Shapps, MP*
*Parliamentary Private Secretary,* Charlotte Leslie, MP
*Private Secretary,* Vicky Seymour
*Minister of State,* Rt. Hon. Desmond Swayne, TD, MP
*Parliamentary Private Secretary,* Charlotte Leslie, MP
*Private Secretary,* Heather Opie
*Parliamentary Under-Secretary of State,* Baroness Verma
*Private Secretary,* Zoe Ware

*Jointly with the Foreign and Commonwealth Office

### MANAGEMENT BOARD
*Chair,* Rt. Hon. Justine Greening, MP
*Members,* Richard Calvert *(Finance and Corporate Performance);* Nick Dyer *(acting Policy and Global Programmes);* Joy Hutcheon *(Country Programmes);* David Kennedy *(Economic Development);* Mark Lowcock *(Permanent Secretary);* Rt. Hon. Grant Shapps, MP; Rt. Hon. Desmond Swayne, TD, MP; Baroness Verma
*Non-Executive Members,* Vivienne Cox *(Lead);* Richard Keys; Tim Robinson; Eric Salama

### CDC GROUP
123 Victoria Street, London SW1E 6DE
**T** 020-7963 4700 **E** enquiries@cdcgroup.com
**W** www.cdcgroup.com

Founded in 1948, CDC is the UK's Development Finance Institution wholly owned by the UK government. It invests to create jobs and build businesses in developing countries in Africa and South Asia. In 2014 CDC made 19 new investment commitments which totalled £296.8m across these regions. CDC is a public limited company with net assets of £3,369m.
*Chair,* Graham Wrigley
*Chief Executive,* Diana Noble

## MINISTRY OF JUSTICE
102 Petty France, London SW1H 9AJ
**T** 020-3334 3555 **E** general.queries@justice.gsi.gov.uk
**W** www.gov.uk/government/organisations/ministry-of-justice

The Ministry of Justice (MoJ) was established in May 2007. MoJ is headed by the Lord Chancellor and Secretary of State for Justice who is responsible for improvements in the justice system so that it better serves the public. He is also responsible for some areas of constitutional policy (those not covered by the Deputy Prime Minister).

The MoJ established five key priorities for 2014. These were to reduce reoffending by using the skills of the public, private and voluntary sectors; reduce youth crime by putting education at the centre of youth justice; build a prison system that delivers maximum value for money; reduce the cost of legal aid and ensure it helps those cases that genuinely require it; and to improve the way the courts are run and put the needs of victims first. The MoJ has a budget of around £9bn and is supported by 38 executive agencies and public bodies to achieve its targets.

The Lord Chancellor and Secretary of State for Justice is the government minister responsible to parliament for the

judiciary, the court system and prisons and probation. The Lord Chief Justice has been the head of the judiciary since 2006.

MoJ incorporates the National Offender Management Service; the HM Prison Service and the National Probation Service; Her Majesty's Courts and Tribunals Service; the Legal Aid Agency; and the Youth Justice Board.

MoJ has several associated departments, non-departmental public bodies and executive agencies, including the National Archives and the Office of the Public Guardian.
*Lord Chancellor and Secretary of State for Justice,*
  Rt. Hon. Michael Gove, MP
*Parliamentary Private Secretary,* Robert Jenrick, MP
*Principal Private Secretary,* Amy Rees
*Minister of State,* Rt. Hon. Mike Penning, MP
  *(Policing, Crime and Criminal Justice and Victims)**
*Parliamentary Private Secretary,* Chris White, MP
*Private Secretary,* Marc Attwell
*Minister of State,* Lord Edward Faulks, QC *(Civil Justice)*
*Private Secretary,* Elaine Cobb
*Parliamentary Under-Secretary of State,* Shailesh Vara, MP
  *(Courts and Legal Aid)*
*Private Secretary,* Stephen Doney
*Parliamentary Under-Secretary of State,* Andrew Selous, MP
  *(Prisons, Probation, Rehabilitation and Sentencing)*
*Private Secretary,* Catherine Bennion
*Parliamentary Under-Secretary of State,* Caroline Dinenage,
  MP *(Women, Equalities and Family Justice)†*
*Private Secretary,* Ben Charnock
*Parliamentary Under-Secretary of State,* Dominic Raab, MP
  *(Human Rights)*
*Private Secretary,* Mary Jones

*Jointly with the Home Office
†Jointly with the Department for Education

### MANAGEMENT BOARD
*Permanent Secretary,* Ursula Brennan
*Members,* Ann Beasley *(Director-General, Finance);* Matthew Coats *(Director-General, Legal Aid Agency and Corporate Services Group);* Catherine Lee *(Director-General, Law and Access to Justice Group);* Michael Spurr *(Chief Executive, National Offender Management Service)*
*Non-Executive Member,* Sir Theodore Agnew

## NORTHERN IRELAND OFFICE
1 Horse Guards Road, London SW1A 2HQ
Stormont House, Stormont Estate, Belfast BT4 3SH
**T** 028-9052 0700 **E** nioweb.editor@nio.x.gsi.gov.uk
**W** www.gov.uk/government/organisations/northern-ireland-office

The Northern Ireland Office was established in 1972, when the Northern Ireland (Temporary Provisions) Act transferred the legislative and executive powers of the Northern Ireland parliament and government to the UK parliament and a secretary of state. Under the terms of the 1998 Good Friday Agreement, power was devolved to the Northern Ireland Assembly in 1999. The assembly took on responsibility for the relevant areas of work previously undertaken by the departments of the Northern Ireland Office, covering agriculture and rural development, the environment, regional development, social development, education, higher education, training and employment, enterprise, trade and investment, culture, arts and leisure, health, social services, public safety and finance and personnel. In October 2002 the Northern Ireland Assembly was suspended and Northern Ireland returned to direct rule, but despite repeated setbacks, devolution was restored on 8 May 2007. For further details, *see* Regional Government.

The Northern Ireland Office is supported by three executive agencies and public bodies and is currently responsible for overseeing the devolution settlement; representing Northern Ireland interests within the UK government and similarly representing the UK government in Northern Ireland; working in partnership with the Northern Ireland Executive for a stable, prosperous Northern Ireland; and supporting and implementing political agreements to increase stability.

*Secretary of State for Northern Ireland,* Rt. Hon. Theresa Villiers, MP
*Parliamentary Private Secretary,* Rebecca Harris, MP
*Parliamentary Under-Secretary of State,* Ben Wallace, MP
*Private Secretary,* Andy Monaghan
*Permanent Secretary,* Sir Jonathan Stephens

## OFFICE OF THE ADVOCATE-GENERAL FOR SCOTLAND

Dover House, Whitehall, London SW1A 2AU
T 020-7270 6770
Office of the Solicitor to the Advocate-General, Victoria Quay, Edinburgh EH6 6QQ
T 0131-244 0359 E enquiries@advocategeneral.gsi.gov.uk
W www.gov.uk/government/organisations/office-of-the-advocate-general-for-scotland

The Advocate-General for Scotland is one of the three law officers of the crown, alongside the Attorney-General and the Solicitor-General for England and Wales. He is the legal adviser to the UK government on Scottish law and is supported by staff in the Office of the Advocate-General for Scotland. The office is divided into the Legal Secretariat, based mainly in London, and the Office of the Solicitor to the Advocate-General, based in Edinburgh.

The post was created as a consequence of the constitutional changes set out in the Scotland Act 1998, which created a devolved Scottish parliament. The Lord Advocate and the Solicitor-General for Scotland then became part of the Scottish government and the Advocate-General took over their previous role as legal adviser to the UK government on Scots law. *See also* Regional Government *and* Ministry of Justice.

*Advocate-General for Scotland,* Lord Keen of Elie, QC
*Private Secretary,* Craig Chalcraft

MANAGEMENT BOARD
*Direcor and Solicitor,* Michael Chalmers
*Members,* Jim Logie; Ruraidh Macniven; Fiona Robertson; Neil Taylor

## SCOTLAND OFFICE

Dover House, Whitehall, London SW1A 2AU
1 Melville Crescent, Edinburgh EH3 7HW
T 0131-244 9010 E enquiries@scotlandoffice.gsi.gov.uk
W www.gov.uk/government/organisations/scotland-office

The Scotland Office is the department of the Secretary of State for Scotland which represents Scottish interests within the UK government in matters reserved to the UK parliament. The Secretary of State for Scotland maintains the stability of the devolution settlement for Scotland; delivers secondary legislation under the Scotland Act 1998; is responsible for the conduct and funding of the Scottish parliament elections; manages the Scottish vote provision and authorises the monthly payment of funds from the UK consolidated fund to the Scottish consolidated fund; and publishes regular information on the state of the Scottish economy.

Matters reserved to the UK parliament include the constitution, foreign affairs, defence, international development, the civil service, financial and economic matters, national security, immigration and nationality, misuse of drugs, trade and industry, various aspects of energy regulation (eg coal, electricity, oil, gas and nuclear energy), various aspects of transport, social security, employment, abortion, genetics, surrogacy, medicines, broadcasting and equal opportunities. Devolved matters include health and social work, education and training, local government and housing, justice and police, agriculture, forestry, fisheries, the environment, tourism, sports, heritage, economic development and internal transport. *See also* Regional Government *and* Ministry of Justice.

*Secretary of State for Scotland,* Rt. Hon. David Mundell, MP
*Parliamentary Private Secretary,* Iain Stewart, MP
*Principal Private Secretary,* Chris Flatt
*Parliamentary Under-Secretary of State,* Lord Dunlop
*Private Secretary,* Stephanie Sandison

MANAGEMENT BOARD
*Director,* Francesca Osowska, OBE
*Members,* Colin Faulkner; Chris Flatt; Helena Gray; Glenn Preston

## DEPARTMENT FOR TRANSPORT

Great Minster House, 33 Horseferry Road, London SW1P 4DR
T 0300-330 3000
W www.gov.uk/government/organisations/department-for-transport

The Department for Transport (DfT) works with its agencies and partners to support the transport network that helps the UK's businessees and gets people and goods travelling around the country. The DfT plans and invests in transport infrastructure to keep the UK on the move. DFT is supported by 19 executive agencies and public bodies.

*Secretary of State for Transport,* Rt. Hon. Patrick McLoughlin, MP
*Parliamentary Private Secretary,* Stuart Andrew, MP
*Principal Private Secretary,* Phil West
*Parliamentary Under-Secretary of State,* Robert Goodwill, MP
*Private Secretary,* Alex Philpott
*Parliamentary Under-Secretary of State,* Andrew Jones, MP
*Private Secretary,* Rory Sedgley
*Parliamentary Under-Secretary of State,* Claire Perry, MP
*Private Secretary,* Matthew Eglinton
*Parliamentary Under-Secretary of State,* Lord Ahmad of Wimbledon
*Private Secretary,* Fiona Douglas
*Permanent Secretary,* Philip Rutnam
*Private Secretary,* Natalie Golding

MANAGEMENT BOARD
*Chair,* Rt. Hon. Patrick McLoughlin, MP *(Secretary of State)*
*Members,* Lord Ahmad of Wimbledon; Lucy Chadwick *(Director-General, International, Security and Environment);* John Dowie *(Director-General, Roads, Traffic and Local);* Robert Goodwill, MP; Andrew Jones, MP; Jonathan Moor, CBE *(Director-General, Resources and Strategy);* Clare Moriarty *(Director-General, Rail Executive);* Nick Olley *(General Counsel);* Claire Perry, MP; David Prout *(Director-General, High Speed 2);* Philip Rutnam *(Permanent Secretary)*

# HM TREASURY

1 Horse Guards Road, London SW1A 2HQ
T 020-7270 5000 E public.enquiries@hmtreasury.gsi.gov.uk
W www.gov.uk/government/organisations/hm-treasury

HM Treasury is the country's economics and finance ministry, and is responsible for formulating and implementing the government's financial and economic policy. It aims to raise the rate of sustainable growth, boost prosperity, and provide the conditions necessary for universal economic and employment opportunities. The Office of the Lord High Treasurer has been continuously in commission for over 200 years. The Lord High Commissioners of HM Treasury are the First Lord of the Treasury (who is also the prime minister), the Chancellor of the Exchequer and five junior lords. This board of commissioners is assisted at present by the chief secretary, the parliamentary secretary who is also the government chief whip in the House of Commons), the financial secretary, the economic secretary, the exchequer secretary and the commercial secretary. The prime minister as first lord is not primarily concerned with the day-to-day aspects of Treasury business; neither are the parliamentary secretary and the junior lords as government whips. Treasury business is managed by the Chancellor of the Exchequer and the other Treasury ministers, assisted by the permanent secretary.

The chief secretary is responsible for public expenditure, including spending reviews and strategic planning; in-year control; public-sector pay and pensions; Annually Managed Expenditure and welfare reform; efficiency in public services; procurement and capital investment. He also has responsibility for the Treasury's interest in devolution.

The financial secretary has responsibility for financial services policy including banking and financial services reform and regulation; financial stability; city competitiveness; wholesale and retail markets in the UK, Europe and internationally; and the Financial Services Authority. His other responsibilities include banking support; bank lending; UK Financial Investments; Equitable Life; and personal savings and pensions policy. He also provides support to the chancellor on EU and wider international finance issues.

The exchequer secretary is a title only used occasionally, normally when the post of paymaster-general is allocated to a minister outside of the Treasury (as it is at present; the Rt. Hon. Matthew Hancock, MP was appointed paymaster-general and minister of the Cabinet Office in May 2015). The exchequer secretary's responsibilities include strategic oversight of the UK tax system; corporate and small business taxation, with input from the commercial secretary; departmental minister for HM Revenue and Customs and the Valuation Office Agency; and lead minister on European and international tax issues.

The economic secretary's responsibilities include environmental issues such as taxation of transport, international climate change and energy; North Sea oil taxation; tax credits and child poverty; assisting the chief secretary on welfare reform; charities and the voluntary sector; excise duties and gambling; stamp duty land tax; EU Budget; the Royal Mint; and departmental minister for HM Treasury Group.

The role of commercial secretary was created in 2010. Responsibilities include enterprise and productivity; corporate finance; assisting the financial secretary on financial services, banking policy promoting the government's financial services policies and the competitiveness of the UK; asset freezing and financial crime; foreign exchange reserves and debt management policy; National Savings and Investments; and the Debt Management Office. The

commercial secretary is also the treasury spokesperson in the House of Lords.
Prime Minister and First Lord of the Treasury, Rt. Hon. David Cameron, MP
Chancellor of the Exchequer, Rt. Hon. George Osborne, MP
Parliamentary Private Secretary, Chris Skidmore, MP
Principal Private Secretary, Clare Lombardelli
Private Secretary, Melanie Pitt
Special Advisers to the Chancellor of the Exchequer, James Chapman; Matt Cook; Thea Rogers
Council of Economic Advisers, Lisa Buckland; Richard Davies; Simon Glasson; Neil O'Brien; Eleanor Wolfson
Chief Secretary to the Treasury, Rt. Hon. Greg Hands, MP
Parliamentary Private Secretary, Jake Berry, MP
Private Secretary, Alex Furse
Special Adviser to the Chief Secretary, Jennifer Donnellan
Financial Secretary to the Treasury, David Gauke, MP
Parliamentary Private Secretary, Conor Burns, MP
Exchequer Secretary to the Treasury, Damian Hinds, MP
Private Secretary, David Pares
Economic Secretary to the Treasury, Harriet Baldwin, MP
Private Secretary, Luke Seaman
Commercial Secretary to the Treasury, Lord O'Neill of Gatley
Private Secretary, Zoe NcNulty
Lords Commissioners of HM Treasury (Whips), Alun Cairns, MP; Charlie Elphicke, MP; David Evennett, MP; George Hollingbery, MP; John Penrose, MP; Mel Stride, MP
Assistant Whips, Stephen Barclay, MP; Jackie Doyle-Price, MP; Margot James, MP; Simon Kirby, MP; Sarah Newton, MP; Guy Opperman, MP; Julian Smith, MP

## MANAGEMENT BOARD

Chair, Sir Nicholas Macpherson, GCB (Permanent Secretary)
Executive Members, Mark Bowman (Director-General, International and EU); James Bowler (Director-General, Tax and Welfare); Julian Kelly (Public Spending and Finance); John Kingman (Second Permanent Secretary); Sir Dave Ramsden, CBE (Chief Economic Adviser); Charles Roxburgh (Director-General, Financial Services)

## ROYAL MINT LTD

PO Box 500, Llantrisant, Pontyclun CF72 8YT
T 01443-222111 W www.royalmint.com

From 1975 the Royal Mint operated as a trading fund and was established as an executive agency in 1990. Since 2010 it has operated as Royal Mint Ltd, a company 100 per cent owned by HM Treasury, with an exclusive contract to supply all coinage for the UK.

The Royal Mint actively competes in world markets for a share of the available circulating coin business and about half of the coins and blanks it produces annually are exported. It is the leading export mint, accounting for around 15 per cent of the world market. The Royal Mint also manufactures special proof and uncirculated quality coins in gold, silver and other metals; military and civil decorations and medals; commemorative and prize medals; and royal and official seals.
Master of the Mint, Chancellor of the Exchequer (ex officio)
Chair, Peter Warry
Chief Executive, Adam Lawrence

## UK EXPORT FINANCE

1 Horse Guards Road, London SW1A 2HQ
T 020-7271 8000 E contact-us@ukef.gsi.gov.uk
W www.gov.uk/government/organisations/uk-export-finance

UK Export Finance is the UK's export credit agency. It helps UK exporters by providing insurance to them and guarantees to banks to share the risks of providing export finance.

Additionally, it can make loans to overseas buyers of goods and services from the UK. UK Export Finance is the operating name of the Export Credits Guarantee Department.

The priorities of UK Export Finance are to fulfil its statutory remit to support exports; operate within the policy and financial objectives established by the government, which includes international obligations; and to recover the maximum amount of debt in respect of claims paid, taking account of the government's policy on debt forgiveness. It is supported by the Export Guarantees Advisory Council.

*Secretary of State for Business, Innovation and Skills and President of the Board of Trade,* Rt. Hon. Sajid Javid, MP*
*Senior Private Secretary,* Emily Shirtcliffe
*Minister of State,* Rt. Hon. Lord Maude of Horsham *(Trade and Investment)*\*†
*Private Secretary,* Nick Whittingham

\*Jointly with the Department for Business, Innovation, and Skills
†Jointly with the Foreign and Commonwealth Office

### MANAGEMENT BOARD
*Members,* Steve Dodgson *(Business Group);* Cameron Fox *(Finance);* David Godfrey *(Chief Executive);* David Havelock *(Credit Risk Group);* Lucy Wylde *(General Counsel)*
*Non-Executive Members,* Guy Beringer; Roger Lowe; Amin Mawji, OBE; Jane Owen; Sir Eric Peacock

## WALES OFFICE
Gwydyr House, Whitehall, London SW1A 2NP
T 029-2092 4220 E correspondence@walesoffice.gsi.gov.uk
W www.gov.uk/wales-office

The Wales Office was established in 1999 when most of the powers of the Welsh Office were handed over to the National Assembly for Wales. It is the department of the Secretary of State for Wales, who is the key government figure liaising with the devolved government in Wales and who represents Welsh interests in the cabinet and parliament. The secretary of state has the right to attend and speak at sessions of the National Assembly (and must consult the assembly on the government's legislative programme). *See also* Regional Government *and* Ministry of Justice.

*Secretary of State for Wales,* Rt. Hon. Stephen Crabb, MP
*Parliamentary Private Secretary,* David Morris, MP
*Special Adviser,* Emily Poole
*Parliamentary Under-Secretary of State,* Alun Cairns, MP
*Private Secretary,* Elizabeth Allen
*Parliamentary Under-Secretary of State,* Lord Bourne of Aberystwyth*
*Private Secretary,* Elizabeth Allen
*Director of Office,* Glynne Jones

\*Jointly with the Department of Energy and Climate Change

## DEPARTMENT FOR WORK AND PENSIONS
Caxton House, Tothill Street, London SW1H 9NA
T 020-7340 4000 E ministers@dwp.gsi.gov.uk
W www.gov.uk/government/organisations/department-for-work-pensions

The Department for Work and Pensions was formed in June 2001 from parts of the former Department of Social Security, the Department for Education and Employment and the Employment Service. The department helps unemployed people of working age into work, helps employers to fill their vacancies and provides financial support to people unable to help themselves, through back-to-work programmes. The department also administers the child support system, social security benefits and the social fund. In addition, the department has reciprocal social security arrangements with other countries.

*Secretary of State for Work and Pensions,* Rt. Hon. Iain Duncan Smith, MP
*Parliamentary Private Secretary,* David Rutley, MP
*Principal Private Secretary,* Paul McComb
*Private Secretaries,* Rob Cook; David Slovak
*Minister of State,* Rt. Hon. Priti Patel, MP *(Employment)*
*Parliamentary Private Secretary,* Alec Shelbrooke, MP
*Private Secretary,* Mike Maynard
*Assistant Private Secretaries,* Tia Priest; Nicholas Slim; Sam Gilbert
*Minister of State,* Baroness Altmann, CBE *(Pensions)*
*Private Secretary,* Michael Dynan-Oakley
*Assistant Private Secretaries,* Yasna Reynolds; Victoria Oliphant; Ella Taylor
*Parliamentary Under-Secretary,* Justin Tomlinson, MP *(Disabled People)*
*Private Secretary,* Jack Goodwin
*Assistant Private Secretaries,* Heather Lockley; Frank Shields; Joanna Ziff
*Minister of State,* Lord Freud *(Welfare Reform)*
*Private Secretary,* Becky Richards
*Assistant Private Secretaries,* Gemma Alcorn; Chris Ramm; Sarah Gaskell
*Permanent Secretary,* Robert Devereux

### MANAGEMENT BOARD
*Permanent Secretary and Head of Department,* Robert Devereux
*Members,* Debbie Alder *(Director-General, Human Resources);* Neil Couling, CBE *(Director-General, Universal Credit);* Kevin Cunnington *(Director-General, Digital Transformation);* Mike Driver *(Director-General, Finance);* Jeremy Moore *(Director-General, Strategy, Policy and Analysis);* Mayank Prakash *(Director-General, Technology);* Noel Shanahan, CB *(Director-General, Operations)*

## EXECUTIVE AGENCIES

Executive agencies are well-defined business units that carry out services with a clear focus on delivering specific outputs within a framework of accountability to ministers. They can be set up or disbanded without legislation, and they are organisationally independent from the department they are answerable to. In the following list the agencies are shown in the accounts of their sponsor departments. Legally they act on behalf of the relevant secretary of state. Their chief executives also perform the role of accounting officers, which means they are responsible for the money spent by their organisations. Staff employed by agencies are civil servants.

## DEPARTMENT FOR BUSINESS, INNOVATION AND SKILLS

### COMPANIES HOUSE
Crown Way, Cardiff CF14 3UZ
T 0303-123 4500 E enquiries@companies-house.gov.uk
W www.companies-house.gov.uk

Companies House incorporates and dissolves companies, examines and stores company information delivered under the Companies Act and related legislation; and makes this information available to the public.

*Registrar of Companies for England and Wales and Chief Executive,* Tim Moss
*Registrar of Companies for Scotland,* Aoife Ann Martin
*Registrar of Companies for Northern Ireland,* Helen Shilliday

## THE INSOLVENCY SERVICE

4 Abbey Orchard Street, London SW1P 2HT
T 020-7637 1110 E redundancyclaims@insolvency.gsi.gov.uk
W www.bis.gov.uk/insolvency

The role of the service includes administration and investigation of the affairs of bankrupts, individuals subject to debt relief orders, partnerships and companies in compulsory liquidation; dealing with the disqualification of directors in all corporate failures; authorising and regulating the insolvency profession; providing banking and investment services for bankruptcy and liquidation estate funds; assessing and paying statutory entitlement to redundancy payments when an employer cannot, or will not, pay its employees; and advising ministers on insolvency, redundancy and related issues. The service has around 1,700 staff, operating from 21 locations across Great Britain.
*Inspector-General and Chief Executive,* Sarah Albon
*Deputy Chief Executive,* Graham Horne

## INTELLECTUAL PROPERTY OFFICE

Concept House, Cardiff Road, Newport NP10 8QQ
T 0300-300 2000 E information@ipo.gov.uk
W www.gov.uk/government/organisations/intellectual-property-office

The Intellectual Property Office (an operating name of the Patent Office) was set up in 1852 to act as the UK's sole office for the granting of patents. It was established as an executive agency in 1990 and became a trading fund in 1991. The office is responsible for the granting of intellectual property (IP) rights which include patents, trade marks, designs and copyright.
*Comptroller-General and Chief Executive,* John Alty

## MET OFFICE

FitzRoy Road, Exeter, Devon EX1 3PB
T 01392-885680 E enquiries@metoffice.gov.uk
W www.metoffice.gov.uk

The Met Office is the UK's National Weather Service, operating as an executive agency of BIS, having transferred from the MoD in July 2011. It is a world leader in providing weather and climate services, using over 10 million weather observations a day, and employs more than 1,700 people at 60 locations throughout the world.
*Chief Executive,* Rob Varley
*Chief Scientist,* Prof. Julia Slingo, OBE

## NATIONAL MEASUREMENT AND REGULATION OFFICE

Stanton Avenue, Teddington, Middx TW11 0JZ
T 020-8943 7272 E info@nmro.gov.uk
W www.gov.uk/nmro

The National Measurement and Regulation Office (NMRO), formerly the National Measurement Office, aims to simplify technical regulation for the benefit of British business. The work of the NMRO should reduce unnecessary costs and give businesses greater confidence to invest and grow.
*Chief Executive (acting),* Richard Sanders

## SKILLS FUNDING AGENCY

Cheylesmore House, Quinton Road, Coventry CV1 2WT
T 0345-377 5000 E info@skillsfundingagency.bis.gov.uk
W www.gov.uk/sfa

The Skills Funding Agency (SFA) funds skills training for further education (FE) in England, including traineeships and apprenticeships. The SFA supports over 1,000 colleges, private training organisations and employers with more than £4bn of funding annually. It is responsible for giving colleges, training organisations and employers the right funding to help adults, young people, the unemployed and those with low skill levels the opportunity to obtain the skills they require for employment.
*Chief Executive,* Peter Lauener

## UK SPACE AGENCY

Polaris House, North Star Avenue, Swindon, Wiltshire SN2 1SZ
T 020-7215 5000 E info@ukspaceagency.bis.gsi.gov.uk
W www.gov.uk/uk-space-agency

The UK Space Agency was established on 23 March 2010 and became an executive agency on 1 April 2011. It was created to provide a single voice for UK space ambitions, and is responsible for all strategic decisions on the UK civil space programme. Responsibilities of the UK Space Agency include coordinating UK civil space activity; supporting academic research; nurturing the UK space industry; raising the profile of UK space activities at home and abroad; working to increase understanding of space science and its practical benefits; and inspiring the next generation of UK scientists and engineers. It aims to capture 10 per cent of the global market for space by 2030.
*Chief Executive,* Dr David Parker

# CABINET OFFICE

## CROWN COMMERCIAL SERVICE

Floor 9, The Capital Building, Old Hall Street, Liverpool L3 9PP
T 0345-410 2222 E info@crowncommercial.gov.uk
W www.gov.uk/government/organisations/crown-commercial-service

The Crown Commercial Service (CCS) is an executive agency of the Cabinet Office, bringing together policy, advice and direct buying; providing commercial services to the public sector and saving money for the taxpayer. The CCS works with over 1,400 organisations in the public sector.
*Chair,* Ed Smith
*Chief Executive,* Sally Collier

# DEPARTMENT FOR COMMUNITIES AND LOCAL GOVERNMENT

## PLANNING INSPECTORATE

Temple Quay House, 2 The Square, Temple Quay, Bristol BS1 6PN
T 0303-444 5000 E enquiries@pins.gsi.gov.uk
W www.gov.uk/government/organisations/planning-inspectorate; www.planningportal.gov.uk/planning/planninginspectorate

The main work of the inspectorate consists of national infrastructure planning under the Planning Act 2008 as amended by the Localism Act 2011, the processing of planning and enforcement appeals, and holding examinations into development plan documents. It also deals with listed building consent appeals; advertisement appeals; rights of way cases; cases arising from the Environmental Protection and Water acts, the Transport and Works Act 1992 and other highways legislation; and reporting on planning applications called in for decision by the Department for Communities and Local Government and the Welsh government.
*Chief Executive,* Simon Ridley

## THE QUEEN ELIZABETH II CONFERENCE CENTRE
Broad Sanctuary, London SW1P 3EE
**T** 020-7798 4000 **W** www.qeiicentre.london

The centre provides secure conference facilities for national and international government and private sector use.
*Chief Executive*, Mark Taylor

## DEPARTMENT FOR CULTURE, MEDIA AND SPORT
### THE ROYAL PARKS
The Old Police House, Hyde Park, London W2 2UH
**T** 0300-061 2000 **E** hq@royalparks.gsi.gov.uk
**W** www.royalparks.org.uk

Royal Parks is responsible for maintaining and developing over 2,000 hectares (5,000 acres) of urban parkland contained within the eight royal parks in London: Bushy Park (with the Longford river); Green Park; Greenwich Park; Hyde Park; Kensington Gardens; Regent's Park (with Primrose Hill); Richmond Park and St James's Park.
*Chief Executive*, Andrew Scattergood

## MINISTRY OF DEFENCE
*see* Defence chapter

## DEPARTMENT FOR EDUCATION

### THE EDUCATION FUNDING AGENCY
Sanctuary Buildings, 20 Great Smith Street, London SW1P 3BT
**T** 0370-000 2288
**W** www.gov.uk/government/organisations/education-funding-agency

Formed on 1 April 2012, the Education Funding Agency (EFA) is the DFE's delivery agency for funding and compliance. It manages £54m of funding each year to support all state-provided education for 8 million children aged 3 to 16, and 1.6 million young people aged 16 to 19. The EFA also supports the delivery of building and maintenance programmes for schools, academies, free schools and sixth-form colleges.
*Chief Executive*, Peter Lauener

### NATIONAL COLLEGE FOR TEACHING AND LEADERSHIP
Piccadilly Gate, Store Street, Manchester M1 2WD
**T** 0370-000 2288 **E** enquiries@nationalcollege.org.uk
**W** www.gov.uk/government/organisations/national-college-for-teaching-and-leadership

On 1 April 2013 the National College merged with the Teaching Agency to become the National College for Teaching and Leadership. It has two key aims: improving the quality of the workforce; and helping schools to help each other to improve. It is also the awarding body for Qualified Teacher Status (QTS).
*Chief Executive*, Charlie Taylor

### STANDARDS AND TESTING AGENCY
53–55 Butts Road, Earlsdon Park, Coventry CV1 3BH
**T** 0300-303 3013 **E** assessments@education.gov.uk
**W** www.gov.uk/government/organisations/standards-and-testing-agency

The Standards and Testing Agency (STA) opened on 1 October 2011 and is responsible for the development and delivery of all statutory assessments from early years to the end of Key Stage 2.
*Chief Executive*, Claire Burton

## DEPARTMENT FOR ENVIRONMENT, FOOD AND RURAL AFFAIRS

### ANIMAL AND PLANT HEALTH AGENCY
Woodham Lane, New Haw, Addlestone, Surrey KT15 3NB
**T** 01932-341 111 **E** apha.corporate_centre@apha.gsi.gov.uk
**W** www.gov.uk/government/organisations/animal-and-plant-health-agency

The Animal and Plant Health Agency (APHA) was launched on 1 October 2014. It merged the former Animal Health and Veterinary Laboratories Agency with parts of the Food and Environment Research Agency responsible for plant and bee health to create a single agency responsible for animal, plant and bee health.

APHA is responsible for identifying and controlling endemic and exotic diseases and pests in animals, plants and bees, and surveillance of new and emerging pests and diseases; scientific research in areas such as bacterial, viral, prion and parasitic diseases, vaccines and food safety and act as an international reference laboratory for many farm animal diseases; facilitating international trade in animals, products of animal origin, and plants; protecting endangered wildlife through licensing and registration; managing a programme of apiary inspections, diagnostics, research and development, training and advice; and regulating the safe disposal of animal by-products to reduce the risk of potentially dangerous substances entering the food chain.

The agency provides all or some of these services to DEFRA and the Scottish and Welsh governments.
*Chief Executive*, Chris Hadkiss

### CENTRE FOR ENVIRONMENT, FISHERIES AND AQUACULTURE SCIENCE (CEFAS)
Pakefield Road, Lowestoft, Suffolk NR33 0HT
**T** 01502-562244 **W** www.cefas.gov.uk

Established in April 1997, the agency provides research and consultancy services in fisheries science and management, aquaculture, fish health and hygiene, environmental impact assessment, and environmental quality assessment.
*Chief Executive*, Tom Karsten

### RURAL PAYMENTS AGENCY
PO Box 69, Reading RG1 3YD
**T** 0300-0200 301 **E** ruralpayments@defra.gsi.gov.uk
**W** www.gov.uk/government/organisations/rural-payments-agency

The RPA was established in 2001. It pays out over £2bn each year to support the farming and food sector and is responsible for Common Agricultural Policy (CAP) schemes in England. In addition it manages over 40 other rural economy and community schemes. It is also responsible for operating cattle tracing services across Great Britain; conducting inspections of farms, processing plants and fresh produce markets in England; and managing the Rural Land Register.
*Chief Executive*, Mark Grimshaw

### VETERINARY MEDICINES DIRECTORATE
Woodham Lane, New Haw, Addlestone, Surrey KT15 3LS
**T** 01932-336911 **E** postmaster@vmd.defra.gsi.gov.uk
**W** www.gov.uk/government/organisations/veterinary-medicines-directorate

The Veterinary Medicines Directorate is responsible for all aspects of the authorisation and control of veterinary medicines, including post-authorisation surveillance of residues in animals and animal products. It is also responsible for the development and enforcement of legislation concerning veterinary medicines and the provision of policy advice to ministers.
*Chief Executive*, Prof. Pete Borriello

# FOREIGN AND COMMONWEALTH OFFICE

## FCO SERVICES
Hanslope Park, Milton Keynes MK19 7BH
T 01908-515 789 E fcoservices.customercontactcentre@fco.gov.uk
W www.fcoservices.gov.uk

FCO Services was established as an executive agency in April 2006 and became a trading fund in April 2008. It operates as the service delivery arm of the FCO, keeping their people, assets and information across the globe safe and secure from the threats they face. FCO Services also works with central government departments, law enforcement, HM government abroad, local government and the UK's critical national infrastructure.
*Chief Executive*, Danny Payne

## WILTON PARK CONFERENCE CENTRE
Wiston House, Steyning, W. Sussex BN44 3DZ
T 01903-815020 W www.wiltonpark.org.uk

Wilton Park organises international affairs conferences and is hired out to government departments and commercial users.
*Chair*, Iain Ferguson
*Chief Executive*, Richard Burge

# DEPARTMENT OF HEALTH

## MEDICINES AND HEALTHCARE PRODUCTS REGULATORY AGENCY (MHRA)
151 Buckingham Palace Road, London SW1W 9SZ
E info@mhra.gsi.gov.uk
W www.gov.uk/government/organisations/medicines-and-healthcare-products-regulatory-agency

The MHRA is a centre of the Medicines and Healthcare Products Regulatory Agency which also includes the National Institute for Biological Standards and Control (NIBSC) and the Clinical Practice Research Datalink (CPRD). The MHRA is responsible for regulating all medicines and medical devices in the UK by ensuring they work and are acceptably safe.
*Chair*, Sir Michael Rawlins
*Chief Executive*, Dr Ian Hudson

## PUBLIC HEALTH ENGLAND
Wellington House, 133–155 Waterloo Road, London SE1 8UG
T 020-7654 8000 E enquiries@phe.gov.uk
W www.gov.uk/government/organisations/public-health-england

Public Health England (PHE) began operating on 1 April 2013 with a remit to protect and improve the health and wellbeing of people within the UK, and reducing health inequalities. PHE employs 5,000 staff who are mostly scientists, researchers and public health professionals. It has 15 local centres and four regions in England and works closely with public health profesionals in Wales, Scotland, Northern Ireland and internationally.
*Chair*, Prof. David Heymann, CBE
*Chief Executive*, Duncan Selbie

# MINISTRY OF JUSTICE

## CRIMINAL INJURIES COMPENSATION AUTHORITY (CICA)
Tay House, 300 Bath Street, Glasgow G2 4LN
T 0300-003 3601
W www.gov.uk/goverment/organisations/criminal-injuries-compensation-authority

CICA is the executive agency responsible for administering the Criminal Injuries Compensation Scheme in England, Scotland and Wales (separate arrangements apply in Northern Ireland). CICA handles up to 40,000 applications for compensation each year, covering every aspect of compensation under the 1996, 2001 and 2008 Criminal Injuries Compensation Schemes. Appeals against decisions made by CICA can be put to the First-tier Tribunal (Criminal Injuries Compensation) *see* Tribunals.
*Chief Executive*, Carole Oatway

## HER MAJESTY'S COURTS AND TRIBUNALS SERVICE
*see* Law Courts and Offices

## LEGAL AID AGENCY
Berkley Way, Viking Business Park, Jarrow, South Tyneside NE31 1SF
T 0300-200 2020 E contactcivil@legalaid.gsi.gov.uk
W www.gov.uk/government/organisations/legal-aid-agency

The Legal Aid Agency provides civil and criminal legal aid and advice in England and Wales. Formed on 1 April 2013 as part of the Legal Aid, Sentencing and Punishment of Offenders Act 2012, the agency replaces the Legal Services Commission, a non-departmental public body of the MoJ.
*Chief Executive*, Matthew Coats

## NATIONAL OFFENDER MANAGEMENT SERVICE
*see* The Prison Service

## OFFICE OF THE PUBLIC GUARDIAN
PO Box 16185, Birmingham B2 2WH
T 0300-456 0300 E customerservices@publicguardian.gsi.gov.uk
W www.gov.uk/government/organisations/office-of-the-public-guardian

The Office of the Public Guardian (OPG) works within the Mental Capacity Act 2005 to support and protect those who lack the mental capacity to make decisions for themselves. It supports the Public Guardian in the registration of Enduring Powers of Attorney (EPA) and Lasting Powers of Attorney (LPA), and the supervision of deputies appointed by the Court of Protection. The OPG also has responsibility for investigating and acting on allegations of abuse by attorneys and deputies. The OPG's responsibility extends across England and Wales.
*Chief Executive and Public Guardian*, Alan Eccles, CBE

# DEPARTMENT FOR TRANSPORT

## DRIVER AND VEHICLE LICENSING AGENCY (DVLA)
Longview Road, Swansea SA6 7JL
W www.gov.uk/government/organisations/driver-and-vehicle-licensing-agency

The DVLA, established as an executive agency in 1990, maintains registers of drivers and vehicles in Great Britain. The information collated by the DVLA helps to improve road safety, reduce vehicle related crime, support environmental initiatives and limit vehicle tax evasion. The DVLA maintains over 45 million driver records and over 38 million vehicle records and collects over £6bn a year in vehicle tax.
*Chief Executive*, Oliver Morley

## DRIVER AND VEHICLE STANDARDS AGENCY
Berkeley House, Croydon Street, Bristol BS5 0DA
T 0300-123 9000 E inform@vosa.gov.uk
W www.gov.uk/government/organisations/driver-and-vehicle-standards-agency

Formed by the merger of the Driving Standards Agency and the Vehicle and Operator Services Agency in 2014, the Driver and Vehicle Standards Agency (DVSA) is responsible for improving road safety in the UK by setting standards for driving and motorcycling, and ensuring drivers, vehicle

operators and MOT garages understand and comply with roadworthiness standards. It additionally provides a range of licensing, testing, education and enforcement services.
*Chief Executive,* Alastair Peoples

## MARITIME AND COASTGUARD AGENCY
Spring Place, 105 Commercial Road, Southampton SO15 1EG
T 023-8032 9100
W www.gov.uk/government/organisations/maritime-and-coastguard-agency

The agency's aims are to prevent loss of life, continuously improve maritime safety and protect the marine environment.
*Chief Executive,* Sir Alan Massey
*Chief Coastguard,* Keith Oliver

## VEHICLE CERTIFICATION AGENCY
1 Eastgate Office Centre, Eastgate Road, Bristol BS5 6XX
T 0300-330 5797 E enquiries@vca.gov.uk W www.dft.gov.uk/vca

The agency is the UK authority responsible for ensuring that new road vehicles, agricultural tractors, off-road vehicles and vehicle parts have been designed and constructed to meet internationally agreed standards of safety and environmental protection.
*Chief Executive,* Paul Markwick

## HM TREASURY

### UK DEBT MANAGEMENT OFFICE
Eastcheap Court, 11 Philpot Lane, London EC3M 8UD
T 020-7862 6500 W www.gov.uk/government/organisations/uk-debt-management-office

The UK Debt Management Office (DMO) was launched as an exec'utive agency of HM Treasury in April 1998. The Chancellor of the Exchequer determines the policy and financial framework within which the DMO operates, but delegates operational decisions on debt and cash management and the day-to-day running of the office to the chief executive. The DMO's remit is to carry out the government's debt management policy of minimising financing costs over the long term, and to minimise the cost of offsetting the government's net cash flows over time, while operating at a level of risk approved by ministers in both cases. The DMO is also responsible for providing loans to local authorities through the Public Works Loan Board, and for managing the assets of certain public-sector bodies through the Commissioners for the Reduction of the National Debt.
*Chief Executive,* Robert Stheeman

## NON-MINISTERIAL GOVERNMENT DEPARTMENTS

Non-ministerial government departments are part of central government but are not headed by a minister and are not funded by a sponsor department. They are created to implement specific legislation, but do not have the ability to change it. Departments may have links to a minister, but the minister is not responsible for the department's overall performance. Staff employed by non-ministerial departments are civil servants.

## CHARITY COMMISSION
PO Box 1227, Liverpool L69 3UG
T 0845-300 0218
W www.gov.uk/government/organisations/charity-commission

The Charity Commission is established by law as the independent regulator and registrar of charities in England

and Wales. Its aim is to provide the best possible regulation of these charities in order to ensure their legal compliance and increase their efficiency, accountability and effectiveness, as well as to encourage public trust and confidence in them. The commission maintains a register of over 160,000 charities. It is accountable to both parliament and the First-tier Tribunal (Charity), and the chamber of the Upper Tribunal or high court for decisions made in exercising the commission's legal powers. The Charity Commission has offices in London, Liverpool, Taunton and Newport.
*Chair,* William Shawcross, CVO
*Chief Executive,* Paula Sussex

## COMPETITION AND MARKETS AUTHORITY
Victoria House, Southampton Row, London WC1B 4AD
T 020-3738 6000 E general.enquiries@cma.gsi.gov.uk
W www.gov.uk/cma

The Competition and Markets Authority (CMA) is the UK's primary competition and consumer authority. It is an independent non-ministerial government department with responsibility for carrying out investigations into mergers, markets and the regulated industries and enforcing competition and consumer law. From 1 April 2014 it took over the functions of the Competition Commission and the competition and certain consumer functions of the Office of Fair Trading under the Enterprise Act 2002, as amended by the Enterprise and Regulatory Reform Act 2013.
*Chair,* David Currie
*Chief Executive,* Alex Chisholm

## CROWN PROSECUTION SERVICE
Rose Court, 2 Southwark Bridge Road, London SE1 9HS
T 020-3357 0000 E enquiries@cps.gsi.gov.uk
W www.cps.gov.uk

The Crown Prosecution Service (CPS) is the independent body responsible for prosecuting people in England and Wales. The CPS was established as a result of the Prosecution of Offences Act 1985. It works closely with the police to advise on lines of inquiry and to decide on appropriate charges and other disposals in all but minor cases. *See also* Law Courts and Offices.
*Director of Public Prosecutions,* Alison Saunders, CB
*Chief Executive,* Peter Lewis, CB

## FOOD STANDARDS AGENCY
Aviation House, 125 Kingsway, London WC2B 6NH
T 020-7276 8829 E helpline@foodstandards.gsi.gov.uk
W www.food.gov.uk

Established in April 2000, the FSA is a UK-wide non-ministerial government body responsible for food safety and hygiene. The agency has the general function of developing policy in these areas and provides information and advice to the government, other public bodies and consumers. The FSA also works with local authorities to enforce food safety regulations and has staff working in UK meat plants to check that the requirements of the regulations are being met.
*Chair,* Tim Bennett
*Chief Executive,* Catherine Brown

FOOD STANDARDS AGENCY NORTHERN IRELAND,
10C Clarendon Road, Belfast BT1 3BG  T 028-9041 7700
E infosani@foodstandards.gsi.gov.uk
FOOD STANDARDS AGENCY WALES, 11th Floor, South Gate House, Wood Street, Cardiff CF10 1EW T 029-2067 8999
E wales@foodstandards.gsi.gov.uk

## FORESTRY COMMISSION

Silvan House, 231 Corstorphine Road, Edinburgh EH12 7AT
T 0300-067 4321 E enquiries@forestry.gsi.gov.uk
W www.forestry.gov.uk

The Forestry Commission is the government department responsible for forestry policy in England and Scotland. It is divided into Forestry Commission England and Forestry Commission Scotland, which report to forestry ministers (the Secretary of State for Environment, Food & Rural Affairs in the UK government, and to ministers in the Scottish government), to whom it is responsible for advice on and implementation of forestry policy. It has an agency, Forest Research, which carries out scientific research and technical development relevant to forestry. The public forests are managed through two additional executive agencies, known as Forest Enterprise England and Forest Enterprise Scotland.

On 1 April 2013 the functions of its Welsh division, Forestry Commission Wales, were subsumed into Natural Resources Wales, a new body established by the Welsh government to regulate and manage natural resources in Wales.

The commission's principal objectives are to protect and expand England's and Scotland's forests and woodlands; enhance the economic value of forest resources; conserve and improve the biodiversity, landscape and cultural heritage of forests and woodlands; develop opportunities for woodland recreation; and increase public understanding of, and community participation in, forestry. It does this by managing public forests in its care to implement these objectives; by supporting other woodland owners with grants, regulation, advice and tree felling licences; and, through its Forest Research agency, by carrying out scientific research and technical development in support of these objectives.

*Chair (2014–17),* Sir Harry Studholme, Bt.
*Deputy Chair and Director, England,* Ian Gambles
*Forestry Commissioner, Scotland,* Dr Bob McIntosh

FORESTRY COMMISSION ENGLAND, 620 Bristol Business Park, Coldharbour Lane, Bristol BS16 1EJ T 0117-906 6000
FORESTRY COMMISSION SCOTLAND, Silvan House, 231 Corstorphine Road, Edinburgh EH12 7AT T 0845-367 3787

## GOVERNMENT ACTUARY'S DEPARTMENT

Finlaison House, 15–17 Furnival Street, London EC4A 1AB
T 020-7211 2601
Belford House, 59 Belford Road, Edinburgh EH4 3UE
T 0131-467 0324
E enquiries@gad.gov.uk W www.gov.uk/gad

The Government Actuary's Department (GAD) was established in 1919 and provides actuarial advice to the public sector in the UK and overseas, and also to the private sector, where consistent with government policy. The GAD provides advice on occupational pension schemes, social security and National Insurance, investment and strategic risk management, insurance analysis and advice, financial risk management, and healthcare financing.

*Government Actuary,* Martin Clarke
*Deputy Government Actuaries,* George Russell; Colin Wilson
*Chief Actuaries,* Sandra Bell; Ian Boonin; Tracey Cutler; Adrian Hale; Stephen Humphrey; Ken Kneller; Ian Rogers; Aidan Smith; Sue Vivian; Matt Wood

## GOVERNMENT LEGAL DEPARTMENT

1 Kemble Street, London WC2B 4TS
T 020-7210 3000
E thetreasurysolicitor@governmentlegal.gov.uk
W www.gov.uk/gld

The Treasury Solicitor's Department became the Government Legal Department (GLD) on 1 April 2015. The department provides legal advice to government on the development, design and implementation of government policies and decisions, and represents the government in court. It is superintended by the Attorney-General. The permanent secretary of the GLD, the Treasury Solicitor, is also the Queen's Proctor, and is responsible for collecting ownerless goods *(bona vacantia)* on behalf of the crown.

*HM Procurator-General and Treasury Solicitor,* Jonathan Jones
*Directors-General,* Stephen Braviner-Roman; Peter Fish; Claire Johnston
*Head of Bona Vacantia,* Mayur Patel

## HM REVENUE AND CUSTOMS (HMRC)

100 Parliament Street, London SW1A 2BQ
Income Tax Enquiries 0300-200 3300
National Insurance Enquiries 0300-200 3500
VAT Enquiries 0300-200 3700
W www.gov.uk/government/organisations/hm-revenue-customs

HMRC was formed following the integration of the Inland Revenue and HM Customs and Excise, which was made formal by parliament in April 2005. It collects and administers direct taxes (capital gains tax, corporation tax, income tax, inheritance tax and national insurance contributions) and indirect taxes (excise duties, insurance premium tax, petroleum revenue tax, stamp duty, stamp duty land tax, stamp duty reserve tax and value-added tax). HMRC also pays and administers child benefit, tax credits and the Child Trust Fund, in addition to being responsible for environmental taxes, national minimum wage enforcement, recovery of student loans, the climate change levy and landfill tax. HMRC also administers the Government Banking Service.

*Chief Executive and Permanent Secretary,* Lin Homer
*Tax Assurance Commissioner and Second Permanent Secretary,* Edward Troup

## VALUATION OFFICE AGENCY

Wingate House, 93–107 Shaftesbury Avenue, London W1D 5BU
T 0300-050 0385 W www.voa.gov.uk

Established in 1991, the Valuation Office is an executive agency of HM Revenue and Customs. It is responsible for compiling and maintaining the business rating and council tax valuation lists for England and Wales; valuing property throughout Great Britain for the purposes of taxes administered by HMRC; providing statutory and non-statutory property valuation services in England, Wales and Scotland; and giving policy advice to ministers on property valuation matters. In April 2009 the VOA assumed responsibility for the functions of The Rent Service, which provided a rental valuation service to local authorities in England, and fair rent determinations for landlords and tenants.

*Chief Executive,* Penny Ciniewicz

## LAND REGISTRY

Trafalgar House, 1 Bedford Park, Croydon CR0 2AQ
T 0300-006 0411
W www.gov.uk/government/organisations/land-registry

A government department and trading fund of BIS, Land Registry maintains the Land Register – the definitive source of information for more than 24 million property titles in England and Wales. The Land Register has been open to public inspection since 1990.

*Chief Land Registrar and Chief Executive,* Graham Farrant

## NATIONAL ARCHIVES
NATIONAL ARCHIVES
Kew, Richmond, Surrey TW9 4DU
T 020-8876 3444 W www.nationalarchives.gov.uk

The National Archives is a non-ministerial government department of the Ministry of Justice. It incorporates the Public Record Office, Historical Manuscripts Commission, Office of Public Sector Information and Her Majesty's Stationery Office. As the official archive of the UK government, it preserves, protects and makes accessible the historical collection of official records.

The National Archives also manages digital information including the UK government web archive which contains over one billion digital documents, and devises solutions for keeping government records readable now and in the future.

The organisation administers the UK's public records system under the Public Records Acts of 1958 and 1967. The records it holds span 1,000 years – from the Domesday Book to the latest government papers to be released – and fill more than 167km (104 miles) of shelving.
*Chief Executive and Keeper,* Jeff James

## NATIONAL CRIME AGENCY
Units 1–6 Citadel Place, Tinworth Street, London SE11 5EF
T 0370-496 7622 E communication@nca.x.gsi.gov.uk
W www.nationalcrimeagency.gov.uk

The National Crime Agency (NCA) is an operational crime fighting agency introduced under the Crime and Courts Act 2013, which became fully operational in October 2013. The NCA's remit is to fight organised crime, strengthen UK borders, tackle fraud and cyber crime and protect children and young people. The agency employs over 4,000 officers and provides leadership through its organised crime, border policing, economic crime and Child Exploitation and Online Protection Centre commands, the National Cyber Crime Unit and specialist capability teams.
Chair, Keith Bristow, QPM

## NATIONAL SAVINGS AND INVESTMENTS
Glasgow G58 1SB
T 0500-007 007 W www.nsandi.com

NS&I (National Savings and Investments) came into being in 1861 when the Palmerston government set up the Post Office Savings Bank, a savings scheme which aimed to encourage ordinary wage earners 'to provide for themselves against adversity and ill health'. NS&I was established as a government department in 1969. It is responsible for the design, marketing and administration of savings and investment products for personal savers and investors. It has over 25 million customers and more than £110bn invested.
*See also* Banking and Finance, National Savings.
*Chief Executive,* Jane Platt, CBE

## OFFICE OF GAS AND ELECTRICITY MARKETS (OFGEM)
9 Millbank, London SW1P 3GE
T 020-7901 7295 W www.ofgem.gov.uk

OFGEM is the regulator for Britain's gas and electricity industries. Its role is to protect and advance the interests of consumers by promoting competition where possible, and through regulation only where necessary. OFGEM operates under the direction and governance of the Gas and Electricity Markets Authority, which makes all major decisions and sets policy priorities for OFGEM. OFGEM's powers are provided for under the Gas Act 1986 and the Electricity Act 1989, as amended by the Utilities Act 2000. It also has enforcement powers under the Competition Act 1998 and the Enterprise Act 2002.
*Chair,* David Gray
*Chief Executive,* Dermot Nolan

## OFFICE OF QUALIFICATIONS AND EXAMINATIONS REGULATION (OFQUAL)
Spring Place, Herald Avenue, Coventry CV5 6UB
T 0300-303 3344 E public.enquiries@ofqual.gov.uk
W www.gov.uk/government/organisations/ofqual

OFQUAL became the independent regulator of qualifications, examinations and assessments on 1 April 2010. It is responsible for maintaining standards, improving confidence and distributing information about qualifications and examinations, as well as regulating general and vocational qualifications in England and vocational qualifications in Northern Ireland.
*Chief Executive,* Glenys Stacey

## OFFICE OF RAIL REGULATION
1 Kemble Street, London WC2B 4AN
T 020-7282 2000 E contact.cct@orr.gsi.gov.uk
W www.orr.gov.uk

The Office of the Rail and Road (ORR) is the operating name of the Office of Rail Regulation. The Office of Rail Regulation was established on 5 July 2004 under the Railways and Transport Safety Act 2003. It replaced the Office of the Rail Regulator.

On 1 April 2006, ORR assumed new responsibilities as a combined safety and economic regulator under the Railways Act 2005. It also has concurrent jurisdiction with Competition and Market Authority under the Competition Act 1998 as the competition authority for the railways.

As the railway industry's independent health and safety and econimic regulator, its principal functions are to: ensure that Network Rail and HS1 manage the national network efficiently and in a way that meets the needs of its users; encourage continuous health and safety performance; secure compliance with relevant health and safety law, including taking enforcement action as necessary; develop policy and enhance relevant railway health and safety legislation; and license operators of railway assets, setting the terms for access by operators to the network and other railway facilities, and enforce competition and consumer law in the rail sector.

On 1 April 2015, under the Infrastructure Act 2015, ORR assumed responsibility for monitoring Highways England's management and development of the strategic road network – the motorways and main 'A' roads in England. In this role ORR ensures that the network is managed efficiently, safely and sustainably, for the benefit of road users and the public.

On 16 March 2015, ORR signed an agreement with the French rail regulator ARAF to establish a collaborative regulatory approach for consistent independent regulation across the Channel tunnel network.

ORR is led by a board appointed by the Secretary of State for Transport.
*Chair,* Anna Walker

## OFFICE FOR STANDARDS IN EDUCATION, CHILDREN'S SERVICES AND SKILLS (OFSTED)
Piccadilly Gate, Store Street, Manchester M1 2WD
T 0300-123 1231 E enquiries@ofsted.gov.uk
W www.gov.uk/government/organisations/ofsted

Ofsted was established under the Education (Schools Act) 1992 and was relaunched on 1 April 2007 with a wider remit, bringing together four formerly separate inspectorates. It works to raise standards in services through the inspection

and regulation of care for children and young people, and inspects education and training for children of all ages. *See also* Education.
*HM Chief Inspector,* Sir Michael Wilshaw
*Chair,* David Hoare

## ORDNANCE SURVEY
Adanac Drive, Southampton SO16 0AS
T 0845-605 0505
E customerservices@os.uk
W www.ordnancesurvey.co.uk

Ordnance Survey is the national mapping agency for Great Britain. It is a government department and executive agency operating as a trading fund since 1999.
*Director-General and Chief Executive,* Nigel Clifford

## SERIOUS FRAUD OFFICE
2–4 Cockspur Street, London SW1Y 5BS
T 020-7239 7272 E public.enquiries@sfo.gsi.gov.uk
W www.sfo.gov.uk

The Serious Fraud Office is an independent government department that investigates and, where appropriate, prosecutes serious or complex fraud, bribery and corruption. It is part of the UK criminal justice system with jurisdiction over England, Wales and Northern Ireland but not Scotland, the Isle of Man or the Channel Islands. The office is headed by a director who is superintended by the Attorney-General.
*Director,* David Green, CB, QC

## SUPREME COURT OF THE UNITED KINGDOM
*see* Law Courts and Offices

## UK STATISTICS AUTHORITY
Drummond Gate, London SW1V 2QQ
T 0845-604 1857 E authority.enquiries@statistics.gsi.gov.uk
W www.statisticsauthority.gov.uk

The UK Statistics Authority was established on 1 April 2008 by the Statistics and Registration Service Act 2007 as an independent body operating at arm's length from government, reporting to the UK parliament and the devolved legislatures. Its overall objective is to promote and safeguard the production and publication of official statistics and ensure their quality and comprehensiveness. The authority's main functions are the oversight of the Office for National Statistics (ONS); monitoring and reporting on all UK official statistics, which includes around 30 central government departments and the devolved administrations; and the production of a code of practice for statistics and the assessment of official statistics against the code.

BOARD
*Chair,* Sir Andrew Dilnot, CBE
*Board Members,* Dr Dame Colette Bowe, DBE; Carolyn Fairbairn; Dame Moira Gibb, DBE; Prof. David Hand; Ed Humpherson *(Director-General, Regulation);* Dr David

Levy; John Pullinger *(National Statistician);* Prof. Sir Adrian Smith, FRS *(Deputy Chair, ONS);* Glen Watson *(Deputy National Statistician)*

## OFFICE FOR NATIONAL STATISTICS (ONS)
Cardiff Road, Newport NP10 8XG
T 0845-601 3034 E info@statistics.gov.uk W www.ons.gov.uk

The ONS was created in 1996 by the merger of the Central Statistical Office and the Office of Population Censuses and Surveys. On 1 April 2008 it became the executive office of the UK Statistics Authority. As part of these changes, the office's responsibility for the General Register Office transferred to HM Passport Office of the Home Office.

The ONS is responsible for preparing, interpreting and publishing key statistics on the government, economy and society of the UK. Its key responsibilities include designing, managing and running the Census and providing statistics on health and other demographic matters in England and Wales; the production of the UK National Accounts and other economic indicators; the organisation of population censuses in England and Wales and surveys for government departments and public bodies.
*National Statistician,* John Pullinger
*Director-Generals,* Jonathan Athow; Heather Savory; Glen Watson

## UK TRADE AND INVESTMENT
1 Victoria Street, London SW1H 0ET
T 020-7215 5000 E enquiries@ukti.gsi.gov.uk
W www.gov.uk/government/organisations/uk-trade-investment

UK Trade and Investment is a government organisation that helps UK-based companies succeed in international markets. It assists overseas companies to bring high quality investment to the UK economy.
*Chief Executive,* Dominic Jermey, OBE, CVO

## WATER SERVICES REGULATION AUTHORITY (OFWAT)
Centre City Tower, 7 Hill Street, Birmingham B5 4UA
T 0121-644 7500 E mailbox@ofwat.gsi.gov.uk
W www.ofwat.gov.uk

OFWAT is the independent economic regulator of the water and sewerage companies in England and Wales. It is responsible for ensuring that the water industry in England and Wales provides household and business customers with a good quality service and value for money. This is done by ensuring that the companies provide customers with a good quality, efficient service at a fair price; limiting the prices companies can charge; monitoring the companies' performance and taking action, including enforcement, to protect customers' interests; settting the companies efficiency targets; making sure the companies deliver the best for consumers and the environment in the long term; and encouraging competition where it benefits consumers.
*Chair,* Jonson Cox
*Chief Executive,* Cathryn Ross

# PUBLIC BODIES

The following section is a listing of public bodies and other civil service organisations: it is not a complete list of these organisations.

Whereas executive agencies are either part of a government department or are one in their own right (*see* Government Departments), public bodies carry out their functions to a greater or lesser extent at arm's length from central government. Ministers are ultimately responsible to parliament for the activities of the public bodies sponsored by their department and in almost all cases (except where there is separate statutory provision) ministers make the appointments to their boards. Departments are responsible for funding and ensuring good governance of their public bodies.

The term 'public body' is a general one which includes public corporations, such as the BBC; NHS bodies; and non-departmental public bodies (NDPBs).

In October 2010, the government announced proposals to drastically reform public bodies or 'quangos' (quasi-autonomous non-governmental organisations, another term for NDPBs). In total, 901 bodies were reviewed – 679 NDPBs and 222 other statutory bodies. Consequently, the government introduced the Public Bodies Bill, which received royal assent on 14 December 2011 and became the Public Bodies act 2011, allowing the government to abolish, merge or transfer the functions of the public bodies listed in the appropriate schedules to the Act.

## ADJUDICATOR'S OFFICE
PO Box 10280, Nottingham NG2 9PF
T 0300-057 1111 W www.adjudicatorsoffice.gov.uk

The Adjudicator's Office investigates complaints from individuals and businesses about the way that HM Revenue and Customs, the Valuation Office Agency and the Insolvency Service have handled a person's affairs. The Adjudicator's Office will only consider a complaint after the respective organisation's internal complaints procedure has been exhausted.
*The Adjudicator,* Judy Clements, OBE

## ADVISORY, CONCILIATION AND ARBITRATION SERVICE (ACAS)
22nd Floor, Euston Tower, 286 Euston Road, London NW1 3JJ
T 0300-123 1100 W www.acas.org.uk

The Advisory, Conciliation and Arbitration Service was set up under the Employment Protection Act 1975 (the provisions now being found in the Trade Union and Labour Relations (Consolidation) Act 1992).

ACAS is largely funded by the Department for Business, Innovation and Skills. A council sets its strategic direction, policies and priorities, and ensures that the agreed strategic objectives and targets are met. It consists of a chair and 11 employer, trade union and independent members, appointed by the Secretary of State for Business, Innovation and Skills.

ACAS aims to improve organisations and working life through better employment relations, to provide up-to-date information, independent advice and high-quality training, and to work with employers and employees to solve problems and improve performance.

ACAS has regional offices, in Birmingham, Bristol, Bury St Edmunds, Cardiff, Fleet, Glasgow, Leeds, Liverpool, Manchester, Newcastle upon Tyne and Nottingham. The head office is in London.
*Chair,* Sir Brendan Barber
*Chief Executive,* Anne Sharp

## ADVISORY COUNCIL ON NATIONAL RECORDS AND ARCHIVES
The National Archives, Kew, Surrey TW9 4DU
T 020-8392 5337
W www.nationalarchives.gov.uk/advisorycouncil

The Advisory Council on National Records and Archives advises the Lord Chancellor on issues relating to public records that are over 30 years old including public access to them. The council meets four times a year, and its main task is to consider requests for the extended closure of public records; it also reaches decisions regarding government departments that want to keep records.

The Forum on Historical Manuscripts and Academic Research, a sub-committee of the Advisory Council, provides advice to the Lord Chancellor on matters relating to historical manuscripts, records and archives, other than public records.
*Chair,* Rt. Hon. Lord Dyson, PC *(Master of the Rolls)*

## AGRICULTURE AND HORTICULTURE DEVELOPMENT BOARD
Stoneleigh Park, Kenilworth, Warwickshire CV8 2TL
T 02476-692051 E info@ahdb.org.uk W www.ahdb.org.uk

The Agriculture and Horticulture Development Board (AHDB) is funded by the agriculture and horticulture industries through statutory levies, with the duty to improve efficiency and competitiveness within six sectors: pig meat in England; milk in Great Britain; beef and lamb in England; commercial horticulture in Great Britain; cereals and oilseeds in the UK; and potatoes in Great Britain. The AHDB represents about 75 per cent of total UK agricultural output. Levies raised from the six sectors are ring-fenced to ensure that they can only be used to the benefit of the sectors from which they were raised.
*Chair,* Sir Peter Kendall
*Independent members,* Prof. Ian Crute, CBE; Will Lifford; George Lyon
*Sector members,* Gary Taylor, MBE *(horticulture);* Stuart Roberts *(beef and lamb);* Meryl Ward, MBE *(pig meat);* Fiona Fell *(potatoes);* Paul Temple *(cereals and oilseeds);* Gwyn Howells *(milk)*
*Chief Executive,* Jane King

## ARCHITECTURE AND DESIGN SCOTLAND
Bakehouse Close, 146 Canongate, Edinburgh EH8 8DD
T 0131-556 6699
W www.ads.org.uk

Architecture and Design Scotland (A+DS) was established in 2005 by the Scottish government as the national champion for good architecture, urban design and planning in the built environment; it works with a wide range of organisations at national, regional and local levels.
*Chair,* Karen Anderson
*Chief Executive,* Jim MacDonald

## ARMED FORCES' PAY REVIEW BODY
8th Floor, Fleetbank House, 2-6 Salisbury Square, London EC4Y 8JX
**T** 020-7211 8315 **W** www.ome.uk.com

The Armed Forces' Pay Review Body was appointed in
1971. It advises the prime minister and the Secretary of State
for Defence on the pay and allowances of members of naval,
military and air forces of the Crown.
*Chair,* John Steele
*Members,* Brendan Connor; Tim Flesher, CB; Paul
  Kernaghan, CBE, QPM; Judy McKnight, CBE; Ken
  Mayhew; Vilma Patterson, MBE; Jon Westbrook, CBE

## ARTS COUNCIL ENGLAND
21 Bloomsbury Street, London WC1B 3HF
**T** 0845-300 6200 **W** www.artscouncil.org.uk

Arts Council England is the national development agency
for the arts in England. Using public money from government and the National Lottery, it supports a range of artistic
activities, including theatre, music, literature, dance,
photography, digital art, carnival and crafts. Between 2015
and 2018, Arts Council England is investing £1.1bn of
public money from the government and around £700m from
the National Lottery.
   The governing body, the national council, comprises 14
members, who are appointed by the Secretary of State for
Culture, Media and Sport usually for a term of four years.
There are also five councils, responsible for the agreement of
area strategies, plans and priorities for action within the
national framework.
*National Council Chair,* Sir Peter Bazalgette
*National Council Members,* Maria Balshaw; Matthew
  Bowcock, CBE; David Bryan; Prof. Jon Cook; Joe
  Docherty; Sheila Healy; David Joseph; Sir Nicholas
  Kenyon; Nazo Moosa; Peter Phillips; Alistair Spalding,
  CBE; Rosemary Squire, OBE; Veronica Wadley
*Chief Executive,* Darren Henley

## ARTS COUNCIL OF NORTHERN IRELAND
77 Malone Road, Belfast BT9 6AQ
**T** 028-9038 5200 **E** info@artscouncil-ni.org
**W** www.artscouncil-ni.org

The Arts Council of Northern Ireland is the prime distributor
of government funds in support of the arts in Northern
Ireland. It is funded by the Department of Culture, Arts and
Leisure and from National Lottery funds.
*Chair,* Bob Collins
*Members,* David Alderdice; Anna Carragher; Damien Coyle;
  Eibhlinn Ni Dhochartaigh; Noelle McAlinden; Katherine
  McCloskey; Prof. Ian Montgomery; Paul Mullan;
  Prof. Paul Seawright; Conor Shields; Brian Sore; Nisha
  Tandon; Dr Siún Hanrahan; Dr Leon Litvack
*Chief Executive,* Roisin McDonough

## ARTS COUNCIL OF WALES
Bute Place, Cardiff CF10 5AL
**T** 0845-873 4900 **E** information@artscouncilofwales.org.uk
**W** www.artswales.org.uk

The Arts Council of Wales was established in 1994 by royal
charter and is the development body for the arts in Wales.
It funds arts organisations with funding from the Welsh
government and is the distributor of National Lottery funds
to the arts in Wales.
*Chair,* Prof. Dai Smith
*Members,* John Geraint; Michael Griffiths; Melanie
  Hawthorne; Dr Lesley Hodgson; Margaret Jervis, MBE;
  Marian Wyn Jones; Andrew Miller; Richard Turner; Alan

Watkin; Prof. Gerwyn Wiliams; John Carey Williams; Dr
  Kate Woodward
*Chief Executive,* Nick Capaldi

## AUDIT SCOTLAND
102 West Port, Edinburgh EH3 9DN
**T** 0131-625 1500 **E** info@audit-scotland.gov.uk
**W** www.audit-scotland.gov.uk

Audit Scotland was set up in 2000 to provide services to the
Accounts Commission and the Auditor-General for Scotland.
Together they help to ensure that public-sector bodies in
Scotland are held accountable for the proper, efficient and
effective use of public funds.
   Audit Scotland's work covers about 200 bodies including
local authorities; health boards; further education colleges;
Scottish Water; the Scottish government; government
agencies such as the Prison Service and non-departmental
public bodies such as the Scottish Police Authority and the
Scottish Fire and Rescue Service.
   Audit Scotland carries out financial and regularity audits
to ensure that public-sector bodies adhere to the highest
standards of financial management and governance. It also
carries out performance audits to ensure that these bodies
achieve the best value for money. All of Audit Scotland's
work in connection with local authorities is carried out for
the Accounts Commission; its other work is undertaken
for the Auditor-General.
*Auditor-General,* Caroline Gardner
*Chair of the Accounts Commission,* Douglas Sinclair

## BANK OF ENGLAND
Threadneedle Street, London EC2R 8AH
**T** 020-7601 4444 **E** enquiries@bankofengland.co.uk
**W** www.bankofengland.co.uk

The Bank of England was incorporated in 1694 under royal
charter. It was nationalised in 1946 under the Bank of
England Act of that year which gave HM Treasury statutory
powers over the bank. It is the banker of the government
and it manages the issue of banknotes. Since 1998 it has
been operationally independent and its Monetary Policy
Committee has been responsible for setting short-term
interest rates to meet the government's inflation target. Its
responsibility for banking supervision was transferred to the
Financial Services Authority in the same year. As the central
reserve bank of the country, the Bank of England keeps the
accounts of British banks, and of most overseas central
banks; the larger banks and building societies are required to
maintain with it a proportion of their cash resources. The
bank's core purposes are monetary stability and financial
stability. The Banking Act 2009 increased the responsibilities
of the bank, including giving it a new financial stability
objective and creating a special resolution regime for dealing
with failing banks.
   In 2013, through the Prudential Regulation Authority
(PRA), the bank became responsible for the prudential
regulation and supervision of banks, building societies, credit
unions, insurers and major investment firms.
*Governor,* Mark Carney
*Deputy Governors,* Andrew Bailey; Dr Ben Broadbent;
  Sir John Cunliffe; Nemat Shafik
*Court of Directors,* The Governor; Anthony Habgood
  (Chair of Court); the Deputy Governors; Michael Cohrs;
  Bradley Fried; Tim Frost; Baroness Harding of
  Winscombe; Dave Prentis; Don Robert; John Stewart;
  Dorothy Thompson
*Monetary Policy Committee,* The Governor; Dr Ben
  Broadbent; Nemat Shafik; Sir Jon Cunliffe; Andy Haldane;
  Kristin Forbes; Prof. David Miles; Ian McCafferty; Dr
  Martin Weale

*Financial Policy Committee,* The Governor; Andrew Bailey; Dr Ben Broadbent; Sir John Cunliffe; Alex Brazier; Dame Clara Furse, DBE; Donald Kohn; Richard Sharp; Martin Taylor; Martin Wheatley
*Chief Legal Adviser,* Sonya Branch
*Director for Banknotes and Chief Cashier,* Victoria Cleland
*The Auditor,* Stephen Brown

## BIG LOTTERY FUND

1 Plough Place, London EC4A 1DE
**T** 020-7211 1800 **Advice Line** 0845-410 2030
**E** general.enquiries@biglotteryfund.org.uk
**W** www.biglotteryfund.org.uk

The Big Lottery Fund is responsible for distributing 40 per cent of all funds raised for good causes by the National Lottery, amounting to around £650m to 12,000 projects a year across the UK. It is responsible for supporting health, education, environmental and charitable projects.
*Chair,* Peter Ainsworth
*Vice-Chair,* Tony Burton, CBE
*Regional Chairs,* Frank Hewitt *(Northern Ireland);* Maureen McGinn *(Scotland);* Nat Sloane, *(England);* Sir Adrian Webb *(Wales)*
*Chief Executive,* Dawn Austwick

## BOUNDARY COMMISSIONS

ENGLAND
2nd Floor, 35 Great Smith Street, London SW1P 3BQ
**T** 020-7276 1102
**E** information@boundarycommissionengland.gov.uk
**W** www.independent.gov.uk/boundarycommissionforengland
*Deputy Chair,* Hon. Mrs Justice Patterson

WALES
Hastings House, Fitzalan Court, Cardiff CF24 0BL
**T** 029-2046 4819 **E** bcomm.wales@wales.gsi.gov.uk
**W** www.bcomm-wales.gov.uk
*Deputy Chair,* Hon. Mr Justice Williams

SCOTLAND
Thistle House, 91 Haymarket Terrace, Edinburgh EH12 5HD
**T** 0131-538 7510 **E** bcs@scottishboundaries.gov.uk
**W** www.bcomm-scotland.gov.uk
*Deputy Chair,* Hon. Lord Woolman

NORTHERN IRELAND
Forestview, Purdy's Lane, Belfast BT8 7AR
**T** 028-9069 4800 **E** bcni@belfast.org.uk
**W** www.boundarycommission.org.uk
*Deputy Chair,* Hon. Mr Justice McCloskey

The commissions, established in 1944, are constituted under the Parliamentary Constituencies Act 1986 (as amended). The Speaker of the House of Commons is the *ex officio* chair of all four commissions in the UK.

The next reviews of UK parliament constituencies will be undertaken using the electoral register from 1 December 2015; these reviews must be submitted before 1 October 2018.

## BRITISH BROADCASTING CORPORATION (BBC)

BBC Broadcasting House, Portland Place, London W1A 1AA
**W** www.bbc.co.uk

The BBC was incorporated under royal charter in 1926 as successor to the British Broadcasting Company Ltd. The BBC's current charter, which came into force on 1 January 2007

and extends to 31 December 2016, recognises the BBC's editorial independence and sets out its public purposes. The BBC Trust was formed under the new charter and replaces the Board of Governors; it sets the strategic direction of the BBC and has a duty to represent the interests of licence fee payers. The chair, vice-chair and other trustees are appointed by the Queen-in-Council. The BBC is financed by television licence revenue and by grant-in-aid from parliament for the World Service (radio). *See* Broadcasting.

BBC TRUST MEMBERS
*Chair,* Rona Fairhead
*National Trustees,* Mark Florman *(England);* Aideen McGinley, OBE *(Northern Ireland);* Bill Matthews *(Scotland);* Elan Closs Stephens *(Wales)*
*Trustees,* Sonita Alleyne, OBE; Richard Ayre; Sir Roger Carr; Mark Damazer; Nicholas Prettejohn; Suzanna Taverne; Lord Williams of Baglan

EXECUTIVE BOARD
*Director-General,* Lord Hall of Birkenhead
*Directors,* Helen Boaden *(Radio);* Anne Bulford, OBE *(Finance and Operations);* Danny Cohen *(Television);* Tim Davie *(CEO: BBC Worldwide, Director: Global);* James Harding *(News and Current Affairs);* Rt. Hon. James Purnell *(Strategy & Digital)*
*Non-Executive Directors,* Simon Burke; Sir Nicholas Hytner; Dharmish Mistry; Alice Perkins; Dame Fiona Reynolds, DBE; Sir Howard Stringer

STATION CONTROLLERS
*BBC1,* Charlotte Moore
*BBC2 and BBC4,* Kim Shillinglaw
*BBC3,* Damian Kavanagh
*BBC News Channel,* Sam Taylor
*BBC Parliament,* Peter Knowles
*BBC Northern Ireland,* Peter Johnston
*BBC Scotland,* Ken MacQuarrie
*BBC Wales,* Rhodri Talfan-Davies
*CBBC,* Cheryl Taylor
*CBeebies,* Kay Benbow
*Radio 1 and 1Xtra,* Ben Cooper
*Radio 2, 6 Music and Asian Network,* Bob Shennan
*Radio 3,* vacant
*Radio 4,* Gwyneth Williams
*Radio 5 Live and 5 Live Sports Extra,* Jonathan Wall

## BRITISH COUNCIL

Bridgewater House, 58 Whitworth Street, Manchester M1 6BB
**T** 0161-957 7755 **E** general.enquiries@britishcouncil.org
**W** www.britishcouncil.org

The British Council was established in 1934, incorporated by royal charter in 1940 and granted a supplemental charter in 1993. It is an independent, non-political organisation which promotes Britain abroad and is the UK's international organisation for educational and cultural relations. The British Council is represented in over 200 towns and cities in over 100 countries.
*Chair,* Sir Vernon Ellis
*Chief Executive,* Sir Ciarán Devne

## BRITISH FILM INSTITUTE

21 Stephen Street, London W1T 1LN
**T** 020-7255 1444 **W** www.bfi.org.uk

The BFI, established in 1933, offers opportunities for people throughout the UK to experience, learn and discover more about the world of film and moving image culture. It incorporates the BFI National Archive, the BFI Reuben

Library, BFI Southbank, BFI Distribution, the annual BFI London Film Festival as well as the BFI London Lesbian and Gay Film Festival, and the BFI IMAX cinema. It also publishes the monthly *Sight and Sound* magazine and provides advice and support for regional cinemas and film festivals across the UK.

Following the closure of the UK Film Council in April 2011, the BFI became the lead body for film in the UK, in charge of allocating lottery money for the development and production of new British films.

*Chair,* Greg Dyke
*Chief Executive,* Amanda Nevill

## BRITISH LIBRARY

96 Euston Road, London NW1 2DB
T 0843-208 1144 E customer-services@bl.uk
W www.bl.uk

The British Library was established in 1973. It is the UK's national library and one of the world's greatest research libraries. It aims to serve scholarship, research, industry, commerce and all other major users of information. The Library's collection has developed over 250 years and exceeds 150 million separate items, including books, journals, manuscripts, maps, stamps, music, patents, newspapers and sound recordings in all written and spoken languages. The library is now based at three sites: London (St Pancras and Colindale) and Boston Spa, W. Yorks. The library's sponsoring department is the Department for Culture, Media and Sport. Up to 10 million people visit the British Library website every year, where up to 4 million digitised collection items are available to view.

BRITISH LIBRARY BOARD
*Chair,* Rt. Hon. Baroness Blackstone
*Members,* David Barclay; Dr Robert Black, CBE, FRSE; Jonathan Callaway; Tracey Chevalier, FRSL; Martin Dickson; Rt. Hon. Lord Fellowes, GCB, GCVO; Roly Keating; Dr Stephen Page; Patrick Plant; Sir John Ritblat; Dr Simon Thurley, CBE; Prof. Dame Helen Wallace

EXECUTIVE
*Chief Executive,* Roly Keating
*Director, Collections,* Caroline Brazier
*Chief Operating Officer,* Phil Spence

BRITISH LIBRARY NEWSPAPERS
Colindale Avenue, London NW9 5HE
T 020-7412 7353

BRITISH LIBRARY, BOSTON SPA
Boston Spa, Wetherby, W. Yorks LS23 7BQ
T 01937-546070

## BRITISH MUSEUM

Great Russell Street, London WC1B 3DG
T 020-7323 8000 E information@britishmuseum.org
W www.britishmuseum.org

The British Museum houses the national collection of antiquities, ethnography, coins and paper money, medals, prints and drawings. The British Museum dates from 7 June 1753, when parliament approved the holding of a public lottery to raise funds for the purchase of the collections of Sir Hans Sloane and the Harleian manuscripts, and for their proper housing and maintenance. The building (Montagu House) was opened in 1759. The existing buildings were erected between 1823 and the present day, and the original collection has increased to its current dimensions by gifts and purchases. Total government grant-in-aid for 2014–15 is £43.2m.

*Chair,* Sir Richard Lambert
*Trustees,* Karen Armstrong; Hon. Nigel Boardman; Cheryl Carolus; Patricia Cumper, MBE; Dame Liz Forgan, DBE; Prof. Clive Gamble; Penny Hughes, CBE; Sir George Iacobescu, CBE; Wasfi Kani, OBE; Sir Richard Lambert; James Lupton, CBE; Sir Deryck Maughan; John Micklethwait; Sir Paul Nurse, PRS; Gavin Patterson; Grayson Perry, CBE; Rt. Hon. Lord Sassoon, KT; Prof. Amartya Sen; Ahdaf Soueif; Lord Stern of Brentford, FBA; Lord Turner of Ecchinswell; Baroness Wheatcroft

OFFICERS
*Director,* Neil MacGregor, OM, FSA
*Deputy Directors,* Joanna Mackle; Jonathan Williams; Christopher Yates; Marilyn Standley

KEEPERS
*Keeper of Africa, Oceania and the Americas,* Lissant Bolton
*Keeper of Ancient Egypt and Sudan,* Neal Spencer
*Keeper of Asia,* Jane Portal
*Keeper of Coins and Medals,* Philip Attwood
*Keeper of Greece and Rome,* J. Lesley Fitton
*Keeper of the Middle East,* Jonathan Tubb
*Keeper of Britain, Europe and Prehistory,* Roger Bland
*Keeper of Prints and Drawings,* Hugo Chapman

## BRITISH PHARMACOPOEIA COMMISSION

151 Buckingham Palace Road, London SW1W 9SZ
T 020-3080 6561 E bpcom@mhra.gsi.gov.uk
W www.pharmacopoeia.com

The British Pharmacopoeia Commission sets standards for medicinal products used in human and veterinary medicines and is responsible for publication of the *British Pharmacopoeia* (a publicly available statement of the standard that a medicinal substance or product must meet throughout its shelf-life), the *British Pharmacopoeia (Veterinary)* and the *British Approved Names*. It has 17 members, including two lay members, who are appointed on behalf of the Secretary of State for Health by the Department of Health.

*Chair,* Prof. Kevin Taylor
*Vice-Chair,* Prof. A. Davidson
*Secretary and Scientific Director,* Dr Samantha Atkinson

## CARE QUALITY COMMISSION

Citygate, Gallowgate, Newcastle upon Tyne NE1 4PA
T 0300-061 6161 E enquiries@cqc.org.uk W www.cqc.org.uk

The Care Quality Commission (CQC) is the independent regulator of health and adult social care services in England, ensuring health and social care services provide people with safe, effective, compassionate, high-quality care and encouraging them to improve. CQC monitors, inspects and regulates services to make sure they meet fundamental standards of quality and safety and publishes performance ratings to help people choose care.

*Chair,* Hon. David Prior
*Board Members,* Prof. Louis Appleby; Paul Rew; Sir Robert Francis, QC; Anna Bradley; Camilla Cavendish; Paul Corrigan; Dr Jennifer Dixon; Michael Mire; Kay Sheldon
*Chief Executive,* David Behan, CBE

## CENTRAL ARBITRATION COMMITTEE

22nd Floor, Euston Tower, 286 Euston Road, London NW1 3JJ
T 020-7904 2300 E enquiries@cac.gov.uk W www.cac.gov.uk

The Central Arbitration Committee (CAC) is a permanent independent body with statutory powers whose main function is to adjudicate on applications relating to the statutory recognition and de-recognition of trade unions for collective bargaining purposes, where such recognition or de-recognition cannot be agreed voluntarily. In addition, the CAC has a statutory role in determining disputes between trade unions and employers over the disclosure of information for collective bargaining purposes, and in resolving applications and complaints under the information and consultation regulations, and performs a similar role in relation to the legislation on the European Works Council, European companies, European cooperative societies and cross-border mergers. The CAC and its predecessors have also provided voluntary arbitration in collective disputes, but this role has not been used for some years.

*Chair,* Sir Michael Burton
*Chief Executive,* Simon Gouldstone

## CERTIFICATION OFFICE FOR TRADE UNIONS AND EMPLOYERS' ASSOCIATIONS

Euston Tower, 286 Euston Road, London NW1 3JJ
T 020-7210 3734 E info@certoffice.org
W www.gov.uk/certificationofficer

The Certification Office is an independent statutory authority. The Certification Officer is appointed by the Secretary of State for Business, Innovation and Skills and is responsible for maintaining a list of trade unions and employers' associations; ensuring compliance with statutory requirements and keeping available for public inspection annual returns from trade unions and employers' associations; determining complaints concerning trade union elections, certain ballots and certain breaches of trade union rules; ensuring observance of statutory requirements governing mergers between trade unions and employers' associations; overseeing the political funds and finances of trade unions and employers' associations; and for certifying the independence of trade unions.

*Certification Officer,* David Cockburn

## CHURCH COMMISSIONERS

Church House, Great Smith Street, London SW1P 3AZ
T 020-7898 1000 E commissioners.enquiry@churchofengland.org
W www.churchofengland.org/about-us/structure/churchcommissioners

The Church Commissioners were established in 1948 by the amalgamation of Queen Anne's Bounty (established 1704) and the Ecclesiastical Commissioners (established 1836). They are responsible for the management of some of the Church of England's assets, the income from which is predominantly used to help pay for the stipend and pension of the clergy and to support the church's work throughout the country. The commissioners own UK and global company shares, over 43,000ha (106,000 acres) of agricultural land, a residential estate in central London, and commercial property across Great Britain, plus an interest in overseas property via managed funds. They also carry out administrative duties in connection with pastoral reorganisation and closed churches.

The 33 commissioners are: the Archbishops of Canterbury and of York; eleven people elected by the General Synod, comprising four bishops, three clergy and four lay persons; three Church Estates Commissioners; two cathedral deans; nine people appointed by the crown and the archbishops; six holders of state office, comprising the Prime Minister, the Lord Chancellor, the Lord President of the Council, the Secretary of State for Culture, Media and Sport, the Speaker of the House of Commons and the Lord Speaker.

CHURCH ESTATES COMMISSIONERS
*First,* Andreas Whittam Smith, CBE
*Second,* Rt. Hon. Caroline Spelman, MP
*Third,* Andrew Mackie

OFFICERS
*Chief Executive,* Andrew Brown
*Official Solicitor,* Stephen Slack

## COAL AUTHORITY

200 Lichfield Lane, Mansfield, Notts NG18 4RG
T 01623-637000 E thecoalauthority@coal.gov.uk
W coal.decc.gov.uk/coalauthority

The Coal Authority was established under the Coal Industry Act 1994 to manage certain functions previously undertaken by British Coal, including ownership of unworked coal. It is responsible for licensing coal mining operations and for providing information on coal reserves and past and future coal mining. It settles subsidence damage claims which are not the responsibility of licensed coal mining operators. It deals with the management and disposal of property, and with surface hazards such as abandoned coal mine entries and mine water discharges. The Coal Authority's powers were extended alongside the Energy Act 2011 to enable it to deal with metal mine subsidence issues and deliver a metal mine water treatment programme when the necessary funding is made available.

*Chair,* Stephen Dingle
*Chief Executive,* Philip Lawrence

## COMMITTEE ON STANDARDS IN PUBLIC LIFE

1 Horseguards Road, London SW1A 2HQ
T 020-7271 2948 E public@public-standards.gov.uk
W www.gov.uk/government/organisations/the-committee-on-standards-in-public-life

The Committee on Standards in Public Life (CSPL) was set up in October 1994. It is formed of 9 people appointed by the prime minister, comprising the chair, three political members nominated by the leaders of the three main political parties and five independent members. The CSPL advises the prime minister on ethical standards across the whole of public life in the UK. It monitors and reports on issues relating to the standards of conduct of all public office holders. It is responsible for promoting the 7 principles of public life, being: selflessness; integrity; objectivity; accountability; openness; honesty; and leadership.

*Chair,* Lord Bew
*Members,* Lord Alderdice; Rt. Hon. Dame Margaret Beckett, DBE, MP; Carolyn Fairbairn; David Prince, CBE; Patricia Moberly; Sheila Drew Smith, OBE; Richard Thomas; Dame Angela Watkinson, DBE, MP

## COMMONWEALTH WAR GRAVES COMMISSION

2 Marlow Road, Maidenhead, Berks SL6 7DX
T 01628-634221 W www.cwgc.org

The Commonwealth War Graves Commission (formerly Imperial War Graves Commission) was founded by royal charter in 1917. It is responsible for the commemoration of around 1.7 million members of the forces of the Commonwealth who lost their lives in the two world wars. More than one million graves are maintained in over 23,000 burial grounds across 153 countries. Over three-quarters of a million men and women who have no known grave or who were cremated are commemorated by name on memorials built by the commission.

The funds of the commission are derived from the six participating governments: the UK, Canada, Australia, New Zealand, South Africa and India.

*President,* HRH The Duke of Kent, KG, GCMG, GCVO, ADC

*Chair,* Secretary of State for Defence (UK)
*Vice-Chair,* Air Chief Marshal Sir Joe French, KCB, CBE
*Members,* High Commissioners in London for Australia, Canada, India, New Zealand and South Africa; Edward Chaplin, CMG, OBE; Robert Fox, MBE; Kevan Jones, MP; Hon. Ros Kelly; Vice-Adm. Sir Tim Laurence, KCVO, CB; Lt.-Gen. Sir William Rollo, KCB, CBE; Keith Simpson, MP; Prof. Sir Hew Strachan, FRSE
*Director-General and Secretary to the Commission,* Victoria Wallace
*Director of Legal Services,* Gillian Stedman

## COMPETITION SERVICE

Victoria House, Bloomsbury Place, London WC1A 2EB
T 020-7979 7979 E info@catribunal.org.uk
W www.catribunal.org.uk

The Competition Service is the financial corporate body by which the Competition Appeal Tribunal is administered and through which it receives funding for the performance of its judicial functions.
*Registrar,* Charles Dhanowa, OBE, QC

## CONSUMER COUNCIL FOR WATER

7th Floor, Embassy House, 60 Church Street, Birmingham B3 2DJ
T 0121-345 1000 E enquiries@ccwater.org.uk
W www.ccwater.org.uk

The Consumer Council for Water was established in 2005 under the Water Act 2003 to represent consumers' interests in respect of price, service and value for money from their water and sewerage services, and to investigate complaints from customers about their water company. There are four regional committees in England and one in Wales.
*Chair,* Alan Lovell

## CORPORATION OF TRINITY HOUSE

Trinity House, Tower Hill, London EC3N 4DH
T 020-7481 6900 E enquiries@thls.org
W www.trinityhouse.co.uk

The Corporation of Trinity House of Deptford Strond is the UK's largest-endowed maritime charity, established formally by Royal Charter by Henry VIII in 1514, with statutory duties as the General Lighthouse Authority (GLA) for England, Wales, the Channel Islands and Gibraltar. Its remit is to assist the safe passage of a variety of vessels through some of the busiest sea-lanes in the world; it does this by deploying and maintaining approximately 600 aids to navigation, ranging from lighthouses to a satellite navigation service. The corporation also has certain statutory jurisdiction over aids to navigation maintained by local harbour authorities and is responsible for marking or dispersing wrecks dangerous to navigation, except those occurring within port limits or wrecks of HM ships.
   The statutory duties of Trinity House are funded by the General Lighthouse Fund, which is provided from light dues levied on ships calling at ports of the UK and the Republic of Ireland. The corporation is a deep-sea pilotage authority, authorised by the Secretary of State for Transport to license deep-sea pilots. In addition Trinity House is a charitable organisation that maintains a number of retirement homes for mariners and their dependants, funds a four-year training scheme for those seeking a career in the merchant navy, and also dispenses grants to a wide range of maritime charities. The charity work is wholly funded by its own activities.
   The corporation is controlled by a court of 31 Elder Brethren; a separate board controls the Lighthouse Service. The Elder Brethren also act as nautical assessors in marine cases in the Admiralty Division of the High Court.

### ELDER BRETHREN

*Master,* HRH the Princess Royal, KG, KT, GCVO
*Deputy Master,* Capt. Ian McNaught
*Wardens,* Simon Sherrard *(Rental)*; Capt. Nigel Palmer, OBE *(Nether)*
*Elder Brethren,* HRH the Duke of Edinburgh, KG, KT, OM, GBE; HRH the Prince of Wales, KG, KT, GCB; HRH the Duke of York, KG, GCVO, ADC; Capt. Roger Barker; Adm. Lord Boyce, KG, GCB, OBE; Lord Browne of Madingley; Capt. John Burton-Hall, RD; Lord Carrington, KG, GCMG, CH, PC; Viscount Cobham; Capt. Sir Malcolm Edge, KCVO; Capt. Ian Gibb, MBE; Capt. Duncan Glass, OBE; Capt. Stephen Gobbi; Lord Greenway; Rear-Adm. Sir Jeremy de Halpert, KCVO, CB; Capt. Nigel Hope, RD; Lord Mackay of Clashfern, KT; Sir John Major, KG, CH; Capt. Peter Mason, CBE; Cdre. Peter Melson, CVO, CBE, RN; Capt. David Orr; Sir John Parker, GBE; Douglas Potter; Capt. Nigel Pryke; Capt. Derek Richards, RD; Lord Robertson of Port Ellen, KT, GCMG, PC; Rear-Adm. Sir Patrick Rowe, KCVO, CBE; Cdre. James Scorer; Adm. Sir Jock Slater, GCB, LVO; Cdre. David Squire, CBE, RFA; Rear-Adm. Lord Sterling of Plaistow, GCVO, CBE, RNR; Capt. Colin Stewart, LVO; Sir Adrian Swire, KT, AE; Capt. Sir Miles Wingate, KCVO; Capt. Thomas Woodfield, OBE; Capt. Richard Woodman, LVO; Rear-Adm. David Snelson, CB; Cdre. William Walworth, CBE

### OFFICERS

*Secretary,* Cdr Graham Hockley, RN
*Director of Finance & Support Services,* Jerry Wedge
*Director of Navigational Requirements,* Capt. Roger Barker
*Director of Operations,* vacant

## CREATIVE SCOTLAND

Waverley Gate, 2–4 Waterloo Place, Edinburgh EH1 3EG
T 0330-333 2000 E enquiries@creativescotland.com
W www.creativescotland.com

Creative Scotland is the organisation tasked with leading the development of the arts, creative and screen industries across Scotland. It was created in 2010 as an amalgamation of the Scottish Arts Council and Scottish Screen, and it encourages and sustains the arts through investment in the form of grants, bursaries, loans and equity. It aims to invest in talent; artistic production; audiences, access and participation; and the cultural economy. Total Scottish government grant-in-aid for 2015–16 is £50m.
*Chair,* Richard Findlay
*Board,* Steve Grimmond; Sandra Gunn; Prof. Robin MacPherson; May Miller; Fergus Muir; Barclay Price; Richard Scott; Dr Gary West; Ruth Wishart
*Chief Executive,* Janet Archer

## CRIMINAL CASES REVIEW COMMISSION

5 St Philip's Place, Birmingham B3 2PW
T 0121-233 1473 E info@ccrc.x.gsi.gov.uk
W www.ccrc.gov.uk

The Criminal Cases Review Commission is the independent body set up under the Criminal Appeal Act 1995. It is a non-departmental public body reporting to parliament via the Lord Chancellor and Secretary of State for Justice. It is responsible for investigating possible miscarriages of justice in England, Wales and Northern Ireland, and deciding whether or not to refer cases back to an appeal court. Members of the commission are appointed in accordance with the Commissioner for Public Appointments' code of practice.

*Chair,* Richard Foster, CBE
*Members,* Liz Calderbank; Jim England; Julie Goulding; Celia Hughes; Stephen Leach, CB; Alexandra Marks; Dr Sharon Persaud; Andrew Rennison; David Smith; Ewen Smith; Ranjit Sondhi
*Chief Executive,* Karen Kneller

## CROFTING COMMISSION

Great Glen House, Leachkin Road, Inverness IV3 8NW
T 01463-663439 E info@crofting.scotland.gov.uk
W www.crofting.scotland.gov.uk

The Crofting Commission was established on 1 April 2012, taking over the regulation of crofting from the Crofters Commission. The aim of the Crofting Commission is to regulate crofting, to promote the occupancy of crofts, active land use, and shared management of the land by crofters, as a means of sustaining and enhancing rural communities in Scotland.
*Chief Executive,* Catriona Maclean

## CROWN ESTATE

16 New Burlington Place, London W1S 2HX
T 020-7851 5000 E enquiries@thecrownestate.co.uk
W www.thecrownestate.co.uk

The Crown Estate is part of the hereditary possessions of the sovereign 'in right of the crown', managed under the provisions of the Crown Estate Act 1961. It had a capital value of £9.9bn in 2014, and includes substantial blocks of urban property, primarily in London, almost 144,000 hectares (356,000 acres) of rural land, over half of the foreshore, and the seabed out to the 12 nautical mile territorial limit throughout the UK. The Crown Estate has a duty to maintain and enhance the capital value of estate and the income obtained from it. Under the terms of the act, the estate pays its revenue surplus to the Treasury every year.
*Chair and First Commissioner,* Sir Stuart Hampson
*Chief Executive and Second Commissioner,* Alison Nimmo, CBE, FRICS

## DISCLOSURE AND BARRING SERVICE

PO Box 3961, Wootton Bassett SN4 4HF
T 0300-020 0190 E customerservices@dbs.gsi.gov.uk
W https://www.gov.uk/government/organisations/disclosure-and-barring-service

The Disclosure and Barring Service (DBS) is an executive non-departmental public body of the Home Office. It helps employers make safer recruitment decisions and prevent unsuitable people from working with vulnerable groups, including children. It was formed on 1 December 2012 and replaced the Criminal Records Bureau (CRB) and Independent Safeguarding Authority (ISA). The DBS is responsible for the children's barred list and adults' barred list for England, Wales and Northern Ireland.
*Chair,* Bill Griffiths
*Chief Executive,* Adriènne Kelbie

## ENVIRONMENT AGENCY

PO Box 544, Rotherham S60 1BY
T 0370-850 6506 E enquiries@environment-agency.gov.uk,
Incident Hotline 0800-807060
W www.environment-agency.gov.uk

Established in 1996 under the Environment Act 1995, the Environment Agency is a non-departmental public body sponsored by the Department for Environment, Food and Rural Affairs. On 1 April 2013, Natural Resources Wales took over the Environment Agency's responsibilities in Wales. Around 70 per cent of the agency's funding is from the government, with the rest raised from various charging schemes. The agency is responsible for pollution prevention and control in England and for the management and use of water resources, including flood defences, fisheries and navigation. Its remit also includes: scrutinising potentially hazardous business operations; helping businesses to use resources more efficiently; taking action against those who do not take environmental responsibilities seriously; looking after wildlife; working with farmers; helping people get the most out of their environment; and improving the quality of inner city areas and parks by restoring rivers and lakes.

The Environment Agency has head offices in Bristol and London has offices across England divided into 16 regions. Its total grant-in-aid for 2015–16 is £738m.
*Chair,* Sir Philip Dilley
*Deputy Chair,* Emma Howard Boyd
*Board Members,* Peter Ainsworth; Karen Burrows; Clive Elphick; Lynne Frostick; Richard Leafe; Richard MacDonald; John Varley; Gill Weeks
*Chief Executive,* Dr Paul Leinster, CBE

## EQUALITY AND HUMAN RIGHTS COMMISSION

Arndale House, The Arndale Centre, Manchester M4 3AQ
T 0161-829 8100 E correspondence@equalityhumanrights.com
W www.equalityhumanrights.com

The Equality and Human Rights Commission (EHRC) is a statutory body, established under the Equality Act 2006 and launched in October 2007. It inherited the responsibilities of the Commission for Racial Equality, the Disability Rights Commission and the Equal Opportunities Commission. The EHRC's purpose is to reduce inequality, eliminate discrimination, strengthen relations between people, and promote and protect human rights. It enforces equality legislation on age, disability and health, gender, race, religion and belief, sexual orientation or transgender status, and encourages compliance with the Human Rights Act 1998 throughout England, Wales and Scotland.
*Chair,* Baroness O'Neill of Bengarve, CH, CBE, PHD
*Deputy Chair,* Caroline Waters, OBE
*Commissioners,* Sarah Anderson, CBE; Evelyn Asante-Mensah, OBE; Ann Beynon, OBE *(Wales Commissioner)*; Laura Carstensen; Lord Holmes of Richmond, MBE *(Disability Commissioner)*; Kaliani Lyle *(Scotland Commissioner)*; Prof. Sarwan Singh; Sarah Veale, CBE; Susan Johnson, OBE; Lorna McGregor
*Chief Executive,* Mark Hammond

## EQUALITY COMMISSION FOR NORTHERN IRELAND

Equality House, 7–9 Shaftesbury Square, Belfast BT2 7DP
T 028-9050 0600 **Textphone** 028-9050 0589
E information@equalityni.org W www.equalityni.org

The Equality Commission was set up in 1999 under the Northern Ireland Act 1998 and is responsible for promoting equality, keeping the relevant legislation under review, eliminating discrimination on the grounds of race, disability, sexual orientation, gender (including marital and civil partner status), age, religion and political opinion and for overseeing the statutory duties on public authorities to promote equality of opportunity and good relations.
*Chief Commissioner,* Dr Michael Wardlow
*Deputy Chief Commissioner,* Revd Dr Lesley Carroll
*Chief Executive,* Evelyn Collins, CBE, FRSA

## GAMBLING COMMISSION

Victoria Square House, Victoria Square, Birmingham B2 4BP
T 0121-230 6666 E info@gamblingcommission.gov.uk
W www.gamblingcommission.gov.uk

The Gambling Commission was established under the Gambling Act 2005, and took over the role previously occupied by the Gaming Board for Great Britain in regulating and licensing all commercial gambling – apart from spread betting and the National Lottery – ie casinos, bingo, betting, remote gambling, gaming machines and lotteries. It also advises local and central government on related issues, and is responsible for the protection of children and the vulnerable from being harmed by gambling. In October 2013, the Gambling Commission took over all the responsibilities of the National Lottery Commission in regulating the National Lottery. The commission is sponsored by the Department for Culture, Media and Sport, with its work funded by licence fees paid by the gambling industry.

*Chair,* Philip Graf, CBE
*Chief Executive,* Jenny Williams

## HEALTH AND SAFETY EXECUTIVE

Redgrave Court, Merton Road, Bootle, Merseyside L20 7HS
T 0845-300 9923 W www.hse.gov.uk

The Health and Safety Commission (HSC) and the Health and Safety Executive (HSE) merged on 1 April 2008 to form a single national regulatory body – the HSE – responsible for promoting the cause of better health and safety at work. The HSE is sponsored by the Department for Work and Pensions.

HSE regulates all industrial and commercial sectors except operations in the air and at sea. This includes agriculture, construction, manufacturing, services, transport, mines, offshore oil and gas, quarries and major hazard sites in chemicals and petrochemicals.

HSE is responsible for developing and enforcing health and safety law; providing guidance and advice; commissioning research; conducting inspections and accident and ill-health investigations; developing standards; and licensing or approving some work activities such as asbestos removal. The HSE's nuclear directorate merged with a number of other bodies on 1 April 2011 to form the Office for Nuclear Regulation, an agency of the HSE.

*Chair,* Judith Hackitt, CBE
*Board Members,* Nick Baldwin; Jonathan Baume; George Brechin; Isobel Garner; Paul Kenny; John Morgan; Frances Outram; Sarah Pinch; Martyn Thomas; Sarah Veale, CBE
*Chief Executive,* Richard Judge

## HER MAJESTY'S OFFICERS OF ARMS

COLLEGE OF ARMS (HERALDS' COLLEGE)
130 Queen Victoria Street, London EC4V 4BT
T 020-7248 2762 E enquiries@college-of-arms.gov.uk
W www.college-of-arms.gov.uk

The Sovereign's Officers of Arms (Kings, Heralds and Pursuivants of Arms) were first incorporated by Richard III in 1484. The powers vested by the crown in the Earl Marshal (the Duke of Norfolk) with regard to state ceremonial are largely exercised through the college. The college is also the official repository of the arms and pedigrees of English, Welsh, Northern Irish and Commonwealth (except Canadian) families and their descendants, and its records include official copies of the records of the Ulster King of Arms, the originals of which remain in Dublin. The 13 officers of the college specialise in genealogical and heraldic work for their respective clients.

Arms have long been, and still are, granted by letters patent from the Kings of Arms. A right to arms can only be established by the registration in the official records of the College of Arms of a pedigree showing direct male line descent from an ancestor already appearing therein as being entitled to arms, or by making application through the College of Arms for a grant of arms. Grants are made to corporations as well as to individuals.

*Earl Marshal,* the Duke of Norfolk

KINGS OF ARMS
*Garter,* Thomas Woodcock, CVO, FSA
*Clarenceux,* Patric Dickinson, LVO
*Norroy and Ulster,* Timothy Duke

HERALDS
*Chester,* vacant
*Lancaster,* Robert Noel
*Windsor,* William Hunt, TD
*Somerset (and Registrar),* David White
*Richmond (and Earl Marshal's Secretary),* Clive Cheesman, FSA
*York,* Michael O'Donoghue

PURSUIVANTS
*Portcullis,* Hon. Christopher Fletcher-Vane
*Rouge Croix,* John Allen-Petrie

### COURT OF THE LORD LYON
HM New Register House, Edinburgh EH1 3YT
T 0131-556 7255 W www.lyon-court.com

Her Majesty's Officers of Arms in Scotland perform ceremonial duties and in addition may be consulted by members of the public on heraldic and genealogical matters in a professional capacity.

KING OF ARMS
*Lord Lyon King of Arms,* Dr Joseph Morrow

HERALDS
*Rothesay,* Sir Crispin Agnew of Lochnaw, Bt., QC
*Snawdoun,* Elizabeth Roads, LVO, FSA, FSA SCOT
*Marchmont,* Hon. Adam Bruce, WS

PURSUIVANTS
*Ormond,* Mark Dennis
*Dingwall,* Yvonne Holton
*Unicorn,* John Malden

EXTRAORDINARY OFFICERS
*Orkney Herald Extraordinary,* Sir Malcolm Innes of Edingight, KCVO, WS
*Angus Herald Extraordinary,* Robin Blair, CVO, WS
*Islay Herald Extraordinary,* David Sellar, MVO
*Ross Herald Extraordinary,* Charles Burnett, FSA SCOT

## HIGHLANDS AND ISLANDS ENTERPRISE

Fraser House, Friar's Lane, Inverness IV1 1BA
T 01463-234171 E info@hient.co.uk W www.hie.co.uk

Highlands and Islands Enterprise (HIE) was set up under the Enterprise and New Towns (Scotland) Act 1991. Its role is to deliver community and economic development in line with the Scottish government economic strategy. It focuses on four priorities: supporting businesses and social enterprises; strengthening communities and fragile areas; developing growth sectors; and creating the conditions for a competitive and low carbon region. HIE's draft budget for 2015–16 is £97.7m.

*Chair,* Prof. Lorne Crerar
*Chief Executive,* Alex Paterson

## HISTORIC ENGLAND

1 Waterhouse Square, 138–142 Holborn, London EC1N 2ST
T 020-7973 3700 E customers@historicengland.org.uk
W www.historicengland.org.uk

Historic England was established as an executive non-departmental public body on 1 April 2015, having previously been known as English Heritage (following the National Heritage Act 1983). Its remit is to look after England's historic environment and has five key objectives: to champion historic places; to identify and protect England's heritage; to support change, including giving advice on over 20,000 applications for planning permission or listed building consent; to understand historic places; and to provide expertise at a local level. In 2015–16 Historic England will receive £88.5m in grant-in-aid from the Department for Culture, Media and Sport.

*Chair,* Sir Laurie Magnus
*Commissioners,* Lynda Addison, OBE; Sally Balcombe;
    Alex Balfour; Prof. Martin Daunton; Prof. Michael
    Fulford, CBE; Victoria Harley; Martin Moore; Michael
    Morrison; Baroness Young of Hornsey, OBE
*Chief Executive,* Duncan Wilson, OBE

## HISTORIC ROYAL PALACES

Apartment 39A, Hampton Court Palace, Surrey KT8 9AU
T 0844-482 7777 E operators@hrp.org.uk W www.hrp.org.uk

Historic Royal Palaces was established in 1998 as a royal charter body with charitable status and is contracted by the Secretary of State for Culture, Media and Sport to manage the palaces on his behalf. The palaces – the Tower of London, Hampton Court Palace, the Banqueting House, Kensington Palace and Kew Palace – are owned by the Queen on behalf of the nation. Since 1 April 2014, Historic Royal Palaces is also responsible for the management of Hillsborough Castle in Northern Ireland under contract with the Secretary of State for Northern Ireland.

The organisation is governed by a board comprising a chair and 11 non-executive trustees. The chief executive is accountable to the board of trustees and ultimately to parliament. Historic Royal Palaces receives no funding from the government or the Crown.

TRUSTEES
*Chair,* Rupert Gavin
*Appointed by the Queen,* Val Gooding, CBE; Sir Trevor
    McDonald, OBE; Jonathan Marsden, CVO, FSA;
    Mike Stephens
*Appointed by the Secretary of State,* Dawn Austwick, OBE;
    Prof. Sir David Cannadine; Bruce Carnegie-Brown;
    Liz Cleaver; Jane Kennedy; Louise Wilson, FRSA
*Ex officio,* Gen. Lord Dannatt, GCB, CBE, MC *(159th
    Constable of the Tower of London)*

OFFICER
*Chief Executive,* Michael Day, CVO

## HOMES AND COMMUNITIES AGENCY

Fry Building, 2 Marsham Street, London W1T 7BN
T 0300-500 1234 E mail@homesandcommunities.gsi.gov.uk
W www.gov.uk/hca

The Homes and Communities Agency (HCA) is the national housing regeneration agency for England. The HCA invests mostly in building new homes, but also in creating employment floorspace nationwide. The HCA also brings forward public land for development and increases the speed with which it is made available.
*Chair,* Robert Napier, CBE
*Chief Executive,* Andy Rose

## HUMAN TISSUE AUTHORITY (HTA)

151 Buckingham Palace Road, London SW1W 9SZ
T 020-7269 1900 E enquiries@hta.gov.uk
W www.hta.gov.uk

The Human Tissue Authority (HTA) was established on 1 April 2005 under the Human Tissue Act 2004, and is sponsored and part-funded by the Department of Health. It regulates organisations that remove, store and use tissue for research, medical treatment, post-mortem examination, teaching and display in public. The HTA also gives approval for organ and bone marrow donations from living people. Under the EU tissues and cells directives, the HTA is one of the two designated competent authorities for the UK responsible for regulating tissues and cells. The HTA is also the sole competent authority for the UK under the EU organ donation directive.
*Chair,* Sharmila Nebhrajani, OBE
*Chief Executive,* Allan Marriott-Smith

## IMPERIAL WAR MUSEUMS (IWM)

Lambeth Road, London SE1 6HZ
T 020-7416 5000 E mail@iwm.org.uk
W www.iwm.org.uk

IWM is the world's leading authority on conflict and its impact, focusing on Britain, its former empire and the Commonwealth, from the First World War to the present. IWM aims to enrich people's understanding of the causes, course and consequences of war and conflict.

IWM comprises the organisation's flagship, IWM London; IWM North in Trafford, Manchester; IWM Duxford in Cambridgeshire; the Churchill War Rooms in Whitehall; and HMS *Belfast* in the Pool of London.

The total grant-in-aid for 2015–16 is £19.8m.

OFFICERS
*President,* HRH the Duke of Kent, KG, GCMG, GCVO, ADC
*Chair,* Sir Francis Richards, KCMG, CVO
*Trustees,* Rt. Hon. Lord Ashcroft, KCMG; Rear-Adm. Amjad
    Hussain, CB; Dame Judith Mayhew, DBE; Air Chief
    Marshal Sir Stuart Peach, KCB, CBE, FRAES; Sir John
    Scarlett, KCMG, OBE; Prof. Sir Hew Strachan, FRSE;
    Tamsin Todd; Peter Watkins, CBE; Matthew Westerman;
    Sir Nick Williams; HE Hon. Alexander Downer; HE
    Gordon Campbell; HE Ranjan Mathai; HE Hon. Sir
    Lockwood Smith; HE Syed Ibne Abbas; HE Obed Mlaba;
    HE Dr Chris Nonis
*Director-General,* Diane Lees, CBE
*Directors,* Jon Card *(Executive Director of Collections and
    Governance);* Samantha Heywood *(Director of Special
    Projects);* Phil Reed *(Director of Museums and Executive
    Vice President American Air Museum);* Graeme Etheridge
    *(Change Director)*

## INFORMATION COMMISSIONER'S OFFICE

Wycliffe House, Water Lane, Wilmslow, Cheshire SK9 5AF
T 0303-123 1113 W www.ico.org.uk

The Information Commissioner's Office (ICO) oversees and enforces the Freedom of Information Act 2000 and the Data Protection Act 1998, with the objective of promoting public access to official information and protecting personal information.

The Data Protection Act 1998 sets out rules for the processing of personal information and applies to records held on computers and some paper files. The Freedom of Information Act 2000 is designed to help end the culture of unnecessary secrecy and open up the inner workings of the public sector to citizens and businesses.

The ICO also enforces and oversees the privacy and electronic communications regulations 2003 and the environmental regulations 2004. It also has limited responsibilities under the INSPIRE regulations 2009.

The Information Commissioner reports annually to parliament on the performance of his/her functions under the acts and has obligations to assess breaches of the acts. As of April 2010, the ICO has been able to fine organisations up to £500,000 for serious breaches of the Data Protection Act. The budget for 2013–14 was £20m.

*Information Commissioner,* Christopher Graham

## INDUSTRIAL INJURIES ADVISORY COUNCIL

First Floor, Caxton House, Tothill Street, London SW1H 9NA
T 020-7449 5618 E iiac@dwp.gsi.gov.uk
W www.gov.uk/iiac

The Industrial Injuries Advisory Council was established under the National Insurance (Industrial Injuries) Act 1946, which came into effect on 5 July 1948. Statutory provisions governing its work are set out in the Social Security Administration Act 1992 and corresponding Northern Ireland legislation. The council currently consists of 17 independent members, including a chair, appointed by the Secretary of State for Work and Pensions, and has three roles: to advise on the prescription of diseases; to consider and advise on draft regulations and proposals concerning the industrial injuries disablement benefit scheme referred to it by the Secretary of State for Work and Pensions or the Department for Social Development in Northern Ireland; and to advise on any other matter concerning the scheme or its administration.

*Chair,* Prof. Keith Palmer

## JOINT NATURE CONSERVATION COMMITTEE

Monkstone House, City Road, Peterborough PE1 1JY
T 01733-562626 E comment@jncc.gov.uk
W www.jncc.defra.gov.uk

The committee was established under the Environmental Protection Act 1990 and was reconstituted by the Natural Environment and Rural Communities Act 2006. It advises the government and devolved administrations on UK and international nature conservation issues. Its work contributes to maintaining and enriching biological diversity, conserving geological features and sustaining natural systems.
*Chair,* Prof. Chris Gilligan
*Chief Executive,* Marcus Yeo

## LAW COMMISSION

1st Floor, Tower, 52 Queen Anne's Gate, London SW1H 9AG
T 020-3334 0200 E enquiries@lawcommission.gsi.gov.uk
W www.lawcom.gov.uk

The Law Commission was set up under the Law Commissions Act 1965 to make proposals to the government for the examination of the law in England and Wales and for its revision where it is unsuited for modern requirements, obscure or otherwise unsatisfactory. It recommends to the lord chancellor programmes for the examination of different branches of the law and suggests whether the examination should be carried out by the commission itself or by some other body. The commission is also responsible for the preparation of Consolidation and Statute Law (Repeals) Bills.
*Chair,* Rt. Hon. Lord Justice David Bean
*Commissioners,* Prof. Nicholas Hopkins; Stephen Lewis; Prof. David Ormerod QC; Nicholas Paines, QC
*Chief Executive,* Elaine Lorimer

## NATIONAL ARMY MUSEUM

Royal Hospital Road, London SW3 4HT
T 020-7730 0717 E info@nam.ac.uk
W www.nam.ac.uk

The National Army Museum explores the impact of the British Army on the story of Britain, Europe and the world. It was established by royal charter in 1960 and moved to its current site in Chelsea in 1970. The museum houses a wide array of artefacts, paintings, photographs, uniforms and equipment. The museum is closed for major refurbishment until late 2016.
*Chair,* General Sir Richard Shirreff, KCB, CBE
*Council Members,* Keith Baldwin; Patrick Bradley; Algy Cluff; Brig. Douglas Erskine Crum; Rt. Hon. Lord Hamilton of Epsom; Prof. William Philpott; Lt.-Gen Sir Barney White-Spunner, KCB, CBE; Caroline Wyatt, CB, CBE; Deborah Younger
*Director-General,* Janice Murray, FRSA

## NATIONAL GALLERIES OF SCOTLAND

73 Belford Road, Edinburgh EH4 3DS
T 0131-624 6200 E enquiries@nationalgalleries.org
W www.nationalgalleries.org

The National Galleries of Scotland comprise three galleries in Edinburgh: the National Gallery of Scotland, the Scottish National Portrait Gallery and the Scottish National Gallery of Modern Art. There are also partner galleries at Paxton House, Berwickshire, and Duff House, Banffshire.

TRUSTEES
*Chair,* Ben Thomson
*Trustees,* Tricia Bey; Alistair Dodds; Edward Green; Benny Higgins; Lesley Knox; Prof. Nicholas Pearce; Tari Lang; Catherine Muirden; Willy Watt; Nicky Wilson

OFFICERS
*Director-General,* Sir John Leighton
*Directors,* Christopher Baker *(Scottish National Portrait Gallery);* Michael Clarke, CBE *(National Gallery of Scotland);* Nicola Catterall *(Chief Operating Officer);* Dr Simon Groom *(Scottish National Gallery of Modern Art);* Jacqueline Ridge *(Keeper of Conservation)*

## NATIONAL GALLERY

Trafalgar Square, London WC2N 5DN
T 020-7747 2885 E information@ng-london.org.uk
W www.nationalgallery.org.uk

The National Gallery, which houses a collection of paintings in the western European tradition from the 13th to the 20th century, was founded in 1824, following a parliamentary grant of £60,000 for the purchase and exhibition of the Angerstein collection of pictures. The present site was first occupied in 1838; an extension to the north of the building with a public entrance in Orange Street was opened in 1975; the Sainsbury Wing was opened in 1991; and the Getty Entrance opened off Trafalgar Square at the east end of the main building in 2004. Total government grant-in-aid for 2015–16 is £24.17m.

BOARD OF TRUSTEES
*Chair,* Mark Getty
*Trustees,* Lance Batchelor; Gautam Dalal; Prof. Dexter Dalwood; Lady Heseltine; Sir Michael Hintze; Prof. Anya Hurlbert; Lord King of Lothbury, KG, GBE, FBA; John Nelson; Hannah Rothschild; Charles Sebag-Montefiore; Monisha Shah; John Singer; Caroline Thomson

OFFICERS
*Director,* Dr Sir Nicholas Penny
*Director of Public Engagement and Deputy Director,* Dr Susan Foister
*Director of Finance and Operations,* Chris Walker
*Director of Collections,* Dr Ashok Roy

## NATIONAL HERITAGE MEMORIAL FUND
7 Holbein Place, London SW1W 8NR
T 020-7591 6044 E NHMF_Enquiries@nhmf.org.uk
W www.nhmf.org.uk

The National Heritage Memorial Fund was set up under the National Heritage Act 1980 in memory of people who have given their lives for the United Kingdom. The fund provides grants to organisations based in the UK, mainly so that they can buy items of outstanding interest and of importance to the national heritage. These must either be at risk or have a memorial character. The fund is administered by a chair and 14 trustees who are appointed by the prime minister.

The National Heritage Memorial Fund receives an annual grant from the Department for Culture, Media and Sport. Under the National Lottery etc Act 1993, the trustees of the fund became responsible for the distribution of funds for both the National Heritage Memorial Fund and the Heritage Lottery Fund.

*Chair,* Sir Peter Luff
*Trustees,* David Heathcoat-Amory; Jim Dixon; Dr Angela Dean; Sandie Dawe, CBE; Sir Roger De Haan; Perdita Hunt, OBE; Steve Miller; Richard Morris, OBE; Atul Patel; Dame Seona Reid, DBE; Virginia Tandy, OBE; Dr Tom Tew
*Chief Executive,* Carole Souter, CBE

## NATIONAL LIBRARY OF SCOTLAND
George IV Bridge, Edinburgh EH1 1EW
T 0131-623 3700 E enquiries@nls.uk W www.nls.uk

The library, which was founded as the Advocates' Library in 1682, became the National Library of Scotland (NLS) in 1925. Funded by the Scottish government, it contains about 24 million printed items: two million maps, 25,000 newspaper and magazine titles and over 100,000 manuscripts, including the John Murray Archive. The library receives around 300,000 new items every year and has material in 490 languages. It has an unrivalled Scottish collection as well as online catalogues and digital resources which can be accessed through the NLS website. Material can be consulted in the reading rooms, which are open to anyone with a valid library card.

The National Library of Scotland Act 2012 modernised the make-up and responsibilities of the board of trustees. At present there are 14, one of whom is nominated by the Faculty of Advocates. All of them are appointed by the Scottish ministers.

*Chair,* James Boyle
*National Librarian and Chief Executive,* Dr John Scally
*Heads of Department,* John Coll *(Access);* Graeme Forbes *(Ingest);* Anthony Gillespie *(Finance);* Murat Guven *(Resources);* Alexandra Miller *(Communications and Enterprise);* Robin Smith *(Collections and Interpretation)*

## NATIONAL LIBRARY OF WALES/ LLYFRGELL GENEDLAETHOL CYMRU
Aberystwyth, Ceredigion, Wales SY23 3BU
T 01970-632800 W www.llgc.org.uk

The National Library of Wales was founded by royal charter in 1907, and is funded by the Welsh government. It contains about five million printed books, 40,000 manuscripts, four million deeds and documents, numerous maps, prints and drawings, and a sound and moving image collection. It specialises in manuscripts and books relating to Wales and the Celtic peoples. It is the repository for pre-1858 Welsh probate records, manorial records and tithe documents, and certain legal records. Admission is by reader's ticket to the reading rooms but entry to the exhibition programme is free.

Total grant-in-aid from the Welsh government for 2014–15 was £15.13m.

*Trustees,* Lord Aberdare; Tricia Carter *(Vice-President);* Philip Cooper; Susan Davies; Roy Evans; Sir Deian Hopkin *(President);* Colin John *(Treasurer);* Wyn Penri Jones; Enid Morgan; Roy Roberts; David Hugh Thomas; Michael Trickey; Gareth Haulfryn Williams; Huw Williams
*Librarian and Chief Executive,* Aled Gruffydd Jones

## NATIONAL MUSEUM OF THE ROYAL NAVY
HM Naval Base (PP66), Portsmouth PO1 3NH
T 023-9272 7574
W www.nmrn.org.uk

The National Museum of the Royal Navy comprises six museums: HMS *Victory,* the National Museum of the Royal Navy Portsmouth, the Fleet Air Arm Museum, the Royal Navy Submarine Museum, the Royal Marines Museum and Explosion! Museum of Naval Firepower. The Fleet Air Museum is located at RNAS Yeovilton, Somerset, while the other four are situated in Portsmouth and Gosport.

*Chair,* Adm. Sir Jonathon Band, GCB
*Trustees,* M. Bedingfield; John Brookes, OBE; Prof. John Craven, CBE; Sir Robert Crawford, CBE; Neil Davidson, FCA; Lieut.-Gen. Sir Robert Fulton, KBE; M. Gambazzi; Vice-Adm. Sir Adrian Johns, KCB, CBE, ADC; Rear-Adm. Terry Loughran, CB; Vice-Adm. Sir Tim McClement, KCB, OBE; Kim Marshall; Tim Schadla-Hall; Dr Caroline Williams, C. Wilson
*Director-General,* Prof. Dominic Tweddle

## NATIONAL MUSEUM WALES/AMGUEDDFA CYMRU
Cathays Park, Cardiff CF10 3NP
T 029-2039 7951
W www.museumwales.ac.uk

National Museum Wales – Amgueddfa Cymru (also known as Amgueddfa Cymru) is the body that runs Wales's seven national museums. It comprises National Museum Cardiff; St Fagans: National History Museum; Big Pit: National Coal Museum, Blaenafon; National Roman Legion Museum, Caerleon; National Slate Museum, Llanberis; National Wool Museum, Dre-fach Felindre; National Waterfront Museum, Swansea; and National Collections Centre, Nantgarw. Total funding from the Welsh government for 2014–15 was £26m.

*Trustees,* Elisabeth Elias *(President);* Dr Haydn Ellis Edwards *(Vice President);* Laurence Pavelin, CBE *(Treasurer);* Baroness Andrews, OBE; Prof. Tony Atkins; Dr Carol Bell; Miriam Hazell Griffiths; Dr Glenda Jones; Emeritus Prof. R. Gareth Wyn Jones, FLSW; Dr Hywel Ceri Jones, CMG; Christina Macaulay; Prof. Robert Pickard; Victoria Mary Provis; Keshav Singhal, MBE
*Director-General,* David Anderson

## NATIONAL MUSEUMS LIVERPOOL
127 Dale Street, Liverpool L2 2JH
T 0151-207 0001 W www.liverpoolmuseums.org.uk

National Museums Liverpool is a group of museums and collections including the World Museum, the Merseyside Maritime Museum (also home to the Border Force National

Museum), the Lady Lever Art Gallery, the Walker Art Gallery, Sudley House, the International Slavery Museum and the Museum of Liverpool.

*Chair,* Prof. Phil Redmond, CBE

*Trustees,* Carmel Booth; Laura Carstensen; Clive Elphick; Andrew McCluskey; Philip Price; Dr Nicola Thorp

*Director,* Dr David Fleming, OBE

*Director of Art Galleries,* Sandra Penketh

*Director, World Museum Liverpool,* Steve Judd

*Director, Museum of Liverpool,* Janet Dugdale

*Head of International Slavery Museum,* Dr Richard Benjamin

## NATIONAL MUSEUMS NORTHERN IRELAND

Cultra, Holywood, Northern Ireland BT18 0EU

T 0845-608 0000 W www.nmni.com

Across three unique sites National Museums Northern Ireland cares for and presents inspirational collections reflecting the creativity, innovation, history, culture and people of Northern Ireland and beyond.

Together the Ulster Museum, Ulster Folk and Transport Museum and Ulster American Folk Park offer a unique opportunity to experience the heritage and way of life of Northern Ireland.

*Chair,* Miceal McCoy

*Trustees,* Prof. Michael Catto; Prof. Garth Earls; Prof. Karen Fleming; Hazel Francey; Daphne Harshaw; Dr Rosemary Kelly; Dr Leon Litvack; Alan McFarland; Dr George McIlroy; Catherine Molloy; Annette Moor; Joseph Rice; Dr Margaret Ward

*Chief Executive (acting),* Jude Helliker

## NATIONAL MUSEUMS SCOTLAND

Chambers Street, Edinburgh EH1 1JF

T 0300-123 6789 E info@nms.ac.uk W www.nms.ac.uk

National Museums Scotland provides advice, expertise and support to the museums community across Scotland, and undertakes fieldwork that often involves collaboration at local, national and international levels. National Museums Scotland comprises the National Museum of Scotland, the National War Museum, the National Museum of Rural Life, the National Museum of Flight and the National Museums Collection Centre. Its collections represent more than two centuries of collecting and include Scottish and classical archaeology, decorative and applied arts, world cultures and social history and science, technology and the natural world.

Up to 15 trustees can be appointed by the Minister for Culture and External Affairs for a term of four years, and may serve a second term.

*Chair,* Bruce Minto

*Trustees,* Dr Isabel Bruce, OBE, FRSSA; Prof. Chris Breward; Gordon Drummond; Chris Fletcher; Dr Anna Gregor, CBE, FRCR, FRCP; Andrew Holmes; Dr Brian Lang, FRSE; Lynda Logan; Dr Catriona Macdonald; Miller McLean, FCIBS, FIB; Prof. Walter Nimmo, FRCA, FRCP, FRSE; James Troughton, RIBA; Eilidh Wiseman

*Director,* Dr Gordon Rintoul

## NATIONAL PORTRAIT GALLERY

St Martin's Place, London WC2H 0HE

T 020-7306 0055 W www.npg.org.uk

The National Portrait Gallery was formed after a grant was made in 1856 to form a gallery of the portraits of the most eminent persons in British history. Today the gallery collects portraits of those who have made, or are making, a significant contribution to British history and culture. The collection includes works across all media, from painting and sculpture to photography and digital portraits. The gallery stages a range of exhibitions, displays, talks and events throughout the year which explore the nature of portraiture. The present building was opened in 1896 and the Ondaatje Wing (including the Balcony Gallery, Tudor Gallery, Digital Space, Ondaatje Wing Theatre and roof-top Portrait Restaurant) opened in May 2000. There are three principle partnerships displaying portraits at Montacute House, Beningbrough Hall and Bodelwyddan Castle. Total government grant-in-aid for 2015–16 is £6.74m.

BOARD OF TRUSTEES

*Chair,* Sir William Proby, Bt., CBE

*Trustees,* Dr Brian Allen; Allegra Berman; Prof. Dame Carol Black, DBE; Dr Rosalind P. Blakesley; Dr Augustus Casely-Hayford; Kim Evans, OBE; Rt. Hon. Nick Clegg, MP; Rt. Hon. Lord Janvrin, GCB, GCVO, QSO; Christopher Le Brun, PRA; Mary McCartney; David Ross; Stephan Shakespeare; Marina Warner, CBE, FBA

*Director,* Dr Nicholas Cullinan

## NATURAL ENGLAND

4th Floor, Foss House, King's Pool, 1-2 Peasholme Green, York YO1 7PX

T 0300-060 6000 E enquiries@naturalengland.org.uk

W www.gov.uk/natural-england

Natural England is the government's adviser on the natural environment, providing practical scientific advice on how to look after England's landscapes and wildlife.

The organisation's remit is to ensure sustainable stewardship of the land and sea so that people and nature can thrive.

Natural England works with farmers and land managers; business and industry; planners and developers; national and local government; charities and conservationists; interest groups and local communities to help them improve their local environment.

*Chair,* Andrew Sells

*Chief Executive,* James Cross

## NATURAL HISTORY MUSEUM

Cromwell Road, London SW7 5BD

T 020-7942 5000 W www.nhm.ac.uk

The Natural History Museum, which houses 80 million natural history specimens, originates from the natural history departments of the British Museum, which grew extensively during the 19th century; in 1860 it was agreed that the natural history collections should be separated from the British Museum's collections of books, manuscripts and antiquities. Part of the site of the 1862 International Exhibition in South Kensington was acquired for the new museum, and the museum opened to the public in 1881. In 1963 the Natural History Museum became completely independent with its own board of trustees. The Natural History Museum at Tring, bequeathed by the second Lord Rothschild, has formed part of the museum since 1937. The Geological Museum merged with the Natural History Museum in 1985. In September 2009 the Natural History Museum opened the Darwin Centre, which contains public galleries, a high-tech interactive area known as the Attenborough Studio, scientific research facilities and storage for 28 million zoological specimens, 17 million entomology specimens and three million botanical specimens. Total government grant-in-aid for 2015–16 is £41.9m

*Chair,* Lord Green of Hurstpierpoint

*Trustees,* Prof. Sir Roy Anderson, FRS, FMEDSCI; Prof. Sir John Beddington, CMG, FRS; Prof. David Drewry; Prof. Christopher Gilligan; Prof. Sir John Holman; Dr

Derek Langslow, CBE; Hilary Newiss; Simon Patterson; Prof. Stephen Sparks, FRS, CBE; Dr Kim Winser, OBE
*Museum Director,* Dr Michael Dixon
*Directors,* Neil Greenwood *(Finance and Corporate Services);* Dr Justin Morris *(Public Engagement);* Prof. Ian Owens *(Science)*

## NATURAL RESOURCES WALES

Ty Cambria, 29 Newport Road, Cardiff CF24 0TP
T 0300-065 3000 E enquiries@naturalresources.gov.uk
W www.naturalresources.wales

Natural Resources Wales is the principal adviser to the Welsh government on the environment. It became operational on 1 April 2013 following a merger of the Countryside Council for Wales, Environment Agency Wales and the Forestry Commission Wales. It is responsible for ensuring that the natural resources of Wales are sustainably maintained, enhanced and used; now and in the future.
*Chair,* Prof. Peter Matthews, FRSC, FCIWEM, FIWO
*Board Members,* Harry Legge-Bourke; Revd Hywel Davies; Dr Ruth Hall; Dr Madeleine Havard; Andy Middleton; Nigel Reader, CBE; Prof. Lynda Warren; Sir Paul Williams, OBE
*Chief Executive,* Dr Emyr Roberts

## NHS PAY REVIEW BODY

8th Floor, Fleetbank House, 2-6 Salisbury Square, London EC4Y 8JX
T 020-7211 8295 W www.gov.uk/government/organisations/nhs-pay-review-body

The NHS Pay Review Body (NHSPRB) makes recommendations to the prime minister, Secretary of State for Health and ministers in Scotland, Wales and Northern Ireland on the remuneration of all paid staff under agenda for change and employed in the NHS. The review body was established in 1983 for nurses and allied health professionals. Its remit has since expanded to cover over 1.8 million staff; ie almost all staff in the NHS, with the exception of dentists, doctors and very senior managers.
*Chair,* Jerry Cope
*Members,* Prof. David Blackaby; Joan Ingram; Graham Jagger; Colin Kennedy; Janet Rubin, MBE; Prof. Anna Vignoles

## NORTHERN IRELAND HUMAN RIGHTS COMMISSION

Temple Court, 39 North Street, Belfast BT1 1NA
T 028-9024 3987 E information@nihrc.org W www.nihrc.org

The Northern Ireland Human Rights Commission is a non-departmental public body, established by the Northern Ireland Act 1998 and set up in March 1999. Its purpose is to protect and promote human rights in Northern Ireland. Its main functions include reviewing the law and practice relating to human rights, advising government and the Northern Ireland Assembly, and promoting an awareness of human rights. It can also investigate human rights violations and take cases to court. The members of the commission are appointed by the Secretary of State for Northern Ireland.
*Chief Commissioner,* Les Allamby
*Commissioners,* John Corey; Christine Collins; Milton Kerr, QPM; Grainia Long; Alan McBride; Marion Reynolds; Paul Yam
*Director,* Virginia McVea

## NORTHERN LIGHTHOUSE BOARD

84 George Street, Edinburgh EH2 3DA
T 0131-473 3100 E enquiries@nlb.org.uk W www.nlb.org.uk

The Northern Lighthouse Board is the general lighthouse authority for Scotland and the Isle of Man and owes its origin to an act of parliament passed in 1786. At present there are 19 commissioners who operate under the Merchant Shipping Act 1995.

The commissioners control 206 lighthouses, many lighted and unlighted buoys, a DGPS (differential global positioning system) station and an ELORAN (long-range navigation) system. *See also* Transport.
*Chair,* Capt. Alistair Mackenzie
*Commissioners,* Lord Advocate; Solicitor-General for Scotland; Lord Provosts of Edinburgh, Glasgow and Aberdeen; Convener of Highland Council; Convener of Argyll and Bute Council; Sheriffs-Principal of North Strathclyde, Tayside, Central and Fife, Grampian, Highlands and Islands, South Strathclyde, Dumfries and Galloway, Lothians and Borders and Glasgow and Strathkelvin; Capt. Alastair Beveridge; Capt. Michael Brew; Graham Crerar; Capt. H. Michael Close; John Ross, CBE
*Chief Executive,* Mike Bullock, MBE

## NUCLEAR DECOMMISSIONING AUTHORITY

Herdus House, Westlakes Science and Technology Park, Moor Row, Cumbria CA24 3HU
T 01925-802077 E enquiries@nda.gov.uk W www.nda.gov.uk

The Nuclear Decommissioning Authority (NDA) was created under the Energy Act 2004. It is a strategic authority that owns 19 sites and associated civil nuclear liabilities and assets of the public sector, previously under the control of the UK Energy Authority and British Nuclear Fuels. The NDA's responsibilities include decommissioning and cleaning up civil nuclear facilities; ensuring the safe management of waste products, both radioactive and non-radioactive; implementing government policy on the long-term management of nuclear waste; and developing UK-wide low-level waste strategy plans.

Total planned expenditure for 2015–16 is £3.31bn, with total grant-in-aid standing at £2.09bn. The remaining £1.22bn will come from commercial operations.
*Chair,* Stephen Henwood
*Chief Executive,* John Clarke

## OFFICE FOR BUDGET RESPONSIBILITY

20 Victoria Street, London SW1H 0NF
T 020-7271 2520 E obrenquiries@obr.gsi.gov.uk
W budgetresponsibility.org.uk

The Office for Budget Responsibility (OBR) was created in 2010 to provide independent and authoritative analysis of the UK's public finances. It has four main roles: producing forecasts for the economy and public finances; judging progress towards the government's fiscal targets; assessing the long-term sustainability of the public finances; and scrutinising HM Treasury's costing of tax and welfare spending measures.
*Chair,* Robert Chote
*Committee Members,* Steve Nickell, CBE; Graham Parker, CBE

## OFFICE OF COMMUNICATIONS (OFCOM)

Riverside House, 2A Southwark Bridge Road, London SE1 9HA
T 0300-123 3000 W www.ofcom.org.uk

OFCOM was established in 2003 under the Office of Communications Act 2002 as the independent regulator and competition authority for the UK communications industries with responsibility for television, radio, telecommunications and wireless communications services.

Following the passing of the Postal Services Act 2011, OFCOM has assumed regulatory responsibility for postal services from Postcomm, the Postal Services Commission.

*Chair,* Dame Patricia Hodgson, DBE
*Deputy Chair,* Baroness Noakes, DBE
*Board Members,* Dame Lynne Brindley, DBE; Tim Gardam; Stephen Hill; Graham Mather; Mike McTighe; Jonathan Oxley; Dr Stephen Unger
*Chief Executive,* Sharon White

## OFFICE OF TAX SIMPLIFICATION

HM Treasury, 1 Horse Guards Road, London SW1A 2HQ
E ots@ots.gsi.gov.uk W www.gov.uk/government/organisations/office-of-tax-simplification

The chancellor and exchequer secretary to HM Treasury launched the Office of Tax Simplification (OTS) on 20 July 2010 to provide the government with independent advice on simplifying the UK tax system. The OTS is an independent office of HM Treasury that provides the government with independent advice on simplifying the UK tax system. It carries out projects investigating complex areas of the tax system and makes recommendations to the chancellor in reports which are published on its website.
*Chair,* Rt. Hon. Michael Jack
*Tax Director,* John Whiting

## OFFICE OF MANPOWER ECONOMICS (OME)

8th Floor, Fleetbank House, 2–6 Salisbury Square, London EC4Y 8JX
T 020-7211 8165 W www.gov.uk/government/organisations/office-of-manpower-economics

The Office of Manpower Economics (OME) was established in 1971. It is an independent non-statutory organisation which is responsible for servicing eight independent review bodies which make recommendations impacting 2.5m workers – around 45 per cent of public sector staff – and a pay bill of £100bn.
*OME Director,* Martin Williams
*Directors,* Jenny Eastabrook *(National Crime Agency Remuneration Review Body, Police Remuneration Review Body, and School Teachers' Review Body);* Margaret McEvoy *(Chief Economist and Research and Analysis Group);* Stuart Sarson *(Prison Service Pay Review Body and Armed Forces' Pay Review Body);* Ffiona Kyte *(Senior Salaries Review Body, NHS Pay Review Body, and Review Body on Doctors' and Dentists' Remuneration)*

## PARADES COMMISSION

Andras House, 60 Great Victoria Street, Belfast BT2 7BB
T 028-9089 5900 E info@paradescommissionni.org
W www.paradescommission.org

The Parades Commission was set up under the Public Processions (Northern Ireland) Act 1998. Its function is to encourage and facilitate local accommodation of contentious parades; where this is not possible, the commission is empowered to make legal determinations about such parades, which may include imposing conditions on aspects of the notified parade (such as restrictions on routes/areas and exclusion of certain groups with a record of bad behaviour).
     The chair and members are appointed by the Secretary of State for Northern Ireland; the membership must, as far as is practicable, be representative of the community in Northern Ireland.
*Chair,* Anne Henderson
*Members,* Sarah Havlin; Paul Hutchinson; Colin Kennedy; Frances McCartney; Anne Marshall

## PAROLE BOARD FOR ENGLAND AND WALES

52 Queen Anne's Gate, London SW1H 9AG
T 020-3334 4402 E info@paroleboard.gsi.gov.uk
W www.gov.uk/government/organisations/parole-board

The Parole Board was established in 1968 under the Criminal Justice Act 1967 and became an independent executive non-departmental public body on 1 July 1996 under the Criminal Justice and Public Order Act 1994. It is the body that protects the public by making risk assessments about prisoners to decide who may safely be released into the community and who must remain in, or be returned to, custody. Board decisions are taken at two main types of panels of up to three members: 'paper panels' for the majority of cases, or oral hearings for decisions concerning prisoners serving life or indeterminate sentences for public protection. The budget for 2014–15 was £14.2m.
*Chair,* Sir David Calvert-Smith
*Chief Executive,* Claire Bassett

## PAROLE BOARD FOR SCOTLAND

Saughton House, Broomhouse Drive, Edinburgh EH11 3XD
T 0131-244 8373
E paroleboardforscotlandexecutive@scotland.gsi.gov.uk
W www.scottishparoleboard.gov.uk

The board directs and advises the Scottish ministers on the release of prisoners on licence, and related matters.
*Chair,* John Watt

## PENSION PROTECTION FUND (PPF)

Renaissance, 12 Dingwall Road, Croydon CR0 2NA
T 0845-600 2541 E information@ppf.gsi.gov.uk
W www.pensionprotectionfund.org.uk

The PPF became operational in 2005. It was established to pay compensation to members of eligible defined-benefit pension schemes where a qualifying insolvency event in relation to the employer occurs and where there is a lack of sufficient assets in the pension scheme. The PPF also administers the Financial Assistance Scheme, which helps members whose schemes wound-up before 2005. It is also responsible for the Fraud Compensation Fund (which provides compensation to occupational pension schemes that suffer a loss that can be attributed to dishonesty). The chair and board of the PPF are appointed by, and accountable to, the Secretary of State for Work and Pensions, and are responsible for paying compensation, calculating annual levies (which help fund the PPF), and setting and overseeing investment strategy.
*Chair,* Lady Judge, CBE
*Chief Executive,* Alan Rubenstein

## PENSIONS REGULATOR

Napier House, Trafalgar Place, Brighton BN1 4DW
T 0845-600 0707 E customersupport@tpr.gov.uk
W www.thepensionsregulator.gov.uk

The Pensions Regulator was established in 2005 as the regulator of work-based pension schemes in the UK, replacing the Occupational Pensions Regulatory Authority (OPRA). It aims to protect the benefits of occupational and personal pension scheme members by working with trustees, employers, pension providers and advisors. The regulator's work focuses on encouraging better management and administration of schemes, ensuring that final salary schemes have a sensible funding plan, and encouraging money purchase schemes to provide members with the information

that they need to make informed choices about their pension fund. The Pensions Act 2004 and the Pensions Act 2008 gave the regulator a range of powers which can be used to protect scheme members, but a strong emphasis is placed on educating and enabling those responsible for managing pension schemes, and powers are used only where necessary. The regulator offers three free online resources to help trustees, employers, professionals and advisors understand their role, duties and obligations.
*Chair,* Mark Boyle
*Chief Executive,* Lesley Titcomb

## POLICE ADVISORY BOARD FOR ENGLAND AND WALES

Home Office, 6th Floor Fry, 2 Marsham Street, London SW1P 4DF
T 020-7271 0472 W www.gov.uk/government/organisations/
police-advisory-board-for-england-and-wales

The Police Advisory Board for England and Wales was established in 1965 and provides advice to the home secretary on general questions affecting the police in England and Wales. It also considers draft regulations which the secretary of state proposes to make with respect to matters other than hours of duty, leave, pay and allowances or the issue, use and return of police clothing, personal equipment and other effects.
*Independent Chair,* Elizabeth France
*Independent Deputy Chair,* Prof. Gillian Morris

## PRISON SERVICE PAY REVIEW BODY

8th Floor, Fleetbank House, 2-6 Salisbury Square, London EC4Y 8JX
T 020-7211 8259 W www.gov.uk/government/organisations/
prison-services-pay-review-body

The Prison Service Pay Review Body was set up in 2001. It makes independent recommendations on the pay of prison governors, operational managers, prison officers and related grades for the Prison Service in England and Wales and for the Northern Ireland Prison Service.
*Chair,* Dr Peter Knight, CBE
*Members,* Prof. John Beath; Nicholas Caton; Elaine Hartin; Karen Heaton; Esmond Lindop; Peter Maddison, QPM

## PRIVY COUNCIL OFFICE

2 Carlton Gardens, London SW1Y 5AA
T 020-7747 5310 E pcosecretariat@pco.gov.uk
W http://privycouncil.independent.gov.uk

The primary function of the office is to act as the secretariat to the Privy Council. It is responsible for the arrangements leading to the making of all royal proclamations and orders in council; for certain formalities connected with ministerial changes; for considering applications for the granting (or amendment) of royal charters; for the scrutiny and approval of by-laws and statutes of chartered institutions and of the governing instruments of universities and colleges; and for the appointment of high sheriffs and Privy Council appointments to governing bodies. Under the relevant acts, the office is responsible for the approval of certain regulations and rules made by the regulatory bodies of the medical and certain allied professions.

The Lord President of the Council is the ministerial head of the office and presides at meetings of the Privy Council. The Clerk of the Council is the administrative head of the Privy Council office.
*Lord President of the Council and Leader of the House of Commons,* Rt. Hon. Chris Grayling, MP
*Clerk of the Council,* Richard Tilbrook

*Head of Secretariat and Deputy Clerk,* Ceri King
*Deputy Clerk,* Christopher Berry

## REVIEW BODY ON DOCTORS' AND DENTISTS' REMUNERATION

8th Floor, Fleetbank House, 2-6 Salisbury Square, London EC4Y 8JX
T 020-7211 8809
W www.gov.uk/government/organisations/review-body-on-doctors-and-dentists-remuneration

The Review Body on Doctors' and Dentists' Remuneration was set up in 1971. It advises the prime minister, first ministers in Scotland, Wales and Northern Ireland, and the ministers for Health, in England, Scotland, Wales and Northern Ireland on the remuneration of doctors and dentists taking any part in the National Health Service.
*Chair,* Prof. Paul Curnan
*Members,* Lucinda Bolton; Mark Butler; John Glennie, OBE; Alan Henry, OBE; Prof. Kevin Lee; Prof. Steve Thompson; Nigel Turner, OBE

## ROYAL AIR FORCE MUSEUM

Grahame Park Way, London NW9 5LL
T 020-8205 2266 E london@rafmuseum.org
W www.rafmuseum.org.uk

The museum has two sites, one at the former airfield at Hendon and the second at Cosford, in the West Midlands, both of which illustrate the development of aviation from before the Wright brothers to the present-day RAF. The museum's collection across both sites consists of over 170 aircraft, as well as artefacts, aviation memorabilia, fine art and photographs.
*Chair,* Air Chief Marshal Sir Glenn Torpy, GCB, CBE, DSO
*Trustees,* Dr Carol Cole; Brendan Connor; Alan Coppin; Dr Rodney Eastwood, MBE; Rt. Hon. Lord Hutton of Furness; Gerry Grimstone; Richard Holman; Hon. John Michaelson; Andrew Reid; Michael Schindler; Robin Southwell; Alan Spence; Malcolm G. F. White, OBE
*Director-General,* Air Vice-Marshal Peter Dye, OBE
*Chief Executive,* Maggie Appleton, MBE

## ROYAL BOTANIC GARDEN EDINBURGH

20A Inverleith Row, Edinburgh EH3 5LR
T 0131-552 7171 W www.rbge.org.uk

The Royal Botanic Garden Edinburgh (RBGE) originated as the Physic Garden, established in 1670 beside the Palace of Holyroodhouse. The garden moved to its present 28ha site at Inverleith, Edinburgh, in 1821. There are also three regional gardens: Benmore Botanic Garden, near Dunoon, Argyll; Logan Botanic Garden, near Stranraer, Wigtownshire; and Dawyck Botanic Garden, near Stobo, Peeblesshire. Since 1986 RBGE has been administered by a board of trustees established under the National Heritage (Scotland) Act 1985. It receives an annual grant from the Scottish government's Rural and Environmental Research and Analysis Directorate.

The RBGE is an international centre for scientific research on plant diversity and for horticulture education and conservation. It has an extensive library, a herbarium with almost three million preserved plant specimens, and over 15,000 species in the living collections.
*Chair,* Sir Muir Russell, KCB, FRSE
*Trustees,* Sir Beverley Glover; Prof. Iain Gordon, FRSE; Patricia Henton, FRSE; Angela McNaught; Prof. Thomas Meagher; Diana Murray; Tim Rollinson, CBE; Prof. Ian Wall, FRSE
*Regius Keeper and Queen's Botanist in Scotland,* Simon Milne, MBE

## ROYAL BOTANIC GARDENS, KEW

Kew Gardens, Richmond, Surrey TW9 3AB
T 020-8332 5655 E info@kew.org
Wakehurst, Ardingly, W. Sussex RH17 6TN
T 01444-894066
E wakehurstinfo@kew.org W www.kew.org

Kew Gardens was originally laid out as a private garden for the now demolished White House for George III's mother, Princess Augusta, in 1759. The gardens were much enlarged in the 19th century, notably by the inclusion of the grounds of the former Richmond Lodge. In 1965 Kew acquired the gardens at Wakehurst on a long lease from the National Trust. Under the National Heritage Act 1983 a board of trustees was set up to administer the gardens, which in 1984 became an independent body supported by grant-in-aid from the Department for Environment, Food and Rural Affairs.

The functions of RBG, Kew are to carry out research into plant sciences, to disseminate knowledge about plants and to provide the public with the opportunity to gain knowledge and enjoyment from the gardens' collections. There are extensive national reference collections of living and preserved plants and a comprehensive library and archive. The main emphasis is on plant conservation and biodiversity; Wakehurst houses the Millennium Seed Bank Partnership, which is the largest *ex situ* conservation project in the world – its aim is to save seed from 25 per cent of the earth's wild plant species by 2020.

*Chair,* Marcus Agius
*Trustees,* Catherine Dugmore; Valerie Gooding; Ian Karet; Dr Geoffrey Hawtin; Sir Henry Keswick; George Loudon; Sir Derek Myers; Prof. Malcolm Press; Prof. Nicola Spence; Jennifer Ullman
*Director,* Richard Deverell

## ROYAL COMMISSION ON THE ANCIENT AND HISTORICAL MONUMENTS OF SCOTLAND

John Sinclair House, 16 Bernard Terrace, Edinburgh EH8 9NX
T 0131-662 1456 W www.rcahms.gov.uk

The Royal Commission on the Ancient and Historical Monuments of Scotland (RCAHMS) was established by a royal warrant in 1908, which was revised in 1992, and is appointed to provide for the collecting, recording and interpretation of information on the architectural, industrial, archaeological and maritime heritage of Scotland, to give a picture of the human influence on Scotland's places from the earliest times to the present day. It is funded by the Scottish government. More than 15 million items, including photographs, maps, drawings and documents, are available through the search room, and online databases provide access to over 600,000 images and information on 300,000 buildings and sites. RCAHMS also holds Scotland's national collection of historical aerial photography as well as The Aerial Reconnaissance Archives (TARA) of international wartime photography.
*Chair,* Prof. John Hume, OBE, FSA SCOT
*Commissioners,* Dr Kate Byrne, FRSA; Tom Dawson, FSA SCOT; Mark Hopton, FSA SCOT; Dr Jeremy Huggett, FSA, FSA SCOT; Prof. John Hunter, OBE, FSA, FSA SCOT; Paul Jardine; Dr Gordon Masterton, OBE, FICE, FIES; Jude Quartson-Mochrie; Elspeth Reid
*Chief Executive,* Diana Murray, FSA, FSA SCOT

## ROYAL COMMISSION ON THE ANCIENT AND HISTORICAL MONUMENTS OF WALES

Crown Building, Plas Crug, Aberystwyth SY23 1NJ
T 01970-621200 E nmr.wales@rcahmw.gov.uk
W www.rcahmw.gov.uk

The Royal Commission on the Ancient and Historical Monuments of Wales, established in 1908, is the investigation body and national archive for the historic environment of Wales. It has the lead role in ensuring that Wales's archaeological, built and maritime heritage is authoritatively recorded, and seeks to promote the understanding and appreciation of this heritage nationally and internationally. The commission is funded by the Welsh government.
*Chair,* Dr Eurwyn Wiliam, FSA
*Vice-Chair,* Henry Owen-John, FSA
*Commissioners,* Catherine S. Hardman; Jonathan Hudson; Thomas O. S. Lloyd, OBE, FSA; Dr Mark Redknap, FSA; Prof. Christopher Williams, FRHISTS
*Chief Executive,* Christopher Catling

## ROYAL MUSEUMS GREENWICH

National Maritime Museum, Greenwich, London SE10 9NF
T 020-8858 4422 W www.rmg.co.uk

Royal Museums Greenwich comprises the National Maritime Museum, the Queen's House and the Royal Observatory Greenwich. It also works in collaboration with the Cutty Sark Trust. The National Maritime Museum provides information on the maritime history of Great Britain and is the largest institution of its kind in the world, with over two million items in its collections related to seafaring, navigation and astronomy. Originally the home of Charles I's Queen, Henrietta Maria, the Queen's House was designed by Inigo Jones and built between 1616–18, although it was structurally altered between 1629–35. It now contains a fine-art collection. The Royal Observatory, Greenwich is the home of Greenwich Mean Time and the prime meridian of the world. It also contains London's only planetarium, Harrison's timekeepers and the UK's largest refracting telescope.
*Director,* Kevin Fewster, FRSA
*Chair,* Sir Charles Dunstone
*Trustees,* Eleanor Boddington; Sir Robert Crawford, CBE; Linda Hutchinson; Prof. Christopher Lintott; Joyce Bridges, CBE; Carol Marlow; Jonathan Ofer; Eric Reynolds; Gerald Russell; Prof. Alison Bashford; Jeremy Penn; Adm. Sir Mark Stanhope, GCB, OBE

## SCHOOL TEACHERS' REVIEW BODY

8th Floor, Fleetbank House, 2-6 Salisbury Square, London EC4Y 8JX
T 020-7211 8463
W www.gov.uk/government/organisations/school-teachers-review-body

The School Teachers' Review Body was set up under the School Teachers' Pay and Conditions Act 1991. It is required to examine and report on such matters relating to the statutory conditions of employment of school teachers in England and Wales as may be referred to it by the education secretary.
*Chair,* Dr Patricia Rice
*Members,* Peter Batley; Jonathan Crossley-Holland; Daniel Flint; Ken Clark; Debbie Meech; Jill Pullen; Mike Redhouse

## SCIENCE MUSEUM

Exhibition Road, London SW7 2DD
T 0870-870 4868 E info@sciencemuseum.org.uk
W www.sciencemuseum.org.uk

The Science Museum, part of the Science Museum Group (SMG), houses the national collections of science, technology, industry and medicine. The museum began as the science collection of the South Kensington Museum and first opened in 1857. In 1883 it acquired the collections of the Patent Museum and in 1909 the science collections were transferred to the new Science Museum, leaving the art collections with the Victoria and Albert Museum. The Wellcome Wing was opened in July 2000.

The SMG also incorporates the National Railway Museum, York; the National Media Museum, Bradford; Locomotion: the National Railway Museum at Shildon; and the Museum of Science and Industry, Manchester.

Total government grant-in-aid for 2015–16 is £38.87m.
*Chair,* Dame Mary Archer
*Trustees,* Howard Covington; Matthew D'Ancona; Prof. Dame Athene Donald, DBE, FRS; Lord Faulkner of Worcester; Sharon Flood; Prof. Russell Foster, CBE; Andreas Goss; Lord Grade of Yarmouth, CBE; Prof. Ludmilla Jordanova; Simon Linnett; Prof. Averil Macdonald; Prof. David Phoenix, OBE; Dr Gill Samuels, CBE; Anton Valk, CBE; Dame Fiona Woolf, CBE; Rt. Hon. David Willetts
*Director of SMG,* Ian Blatchford
*Director of Science Museum,* Ian Blatchford
*Director of Museum of Science & Industry,* Sally MacDonald
*Director of National Media Museum,* Jo Quinton-Tulloch
*Director of National Railway Museum,* Paul Kirkman

## SCOTTISH CRIMINAL CASES REVIEW COMMISSION
5th Floor, Portland House, 17 Renfield Street, Glasgow G2 5AH
T 0141-270 7030 E info@sccrc.org.uk W www.sccrc.org.uk

The commission is a non-departmental public body, funded by the Scottish Government Criminal Justice Directorate, and established by Act of Parliament in April 1999. It assumed the role previously performed by the Secretary of State for Scotland to consider alleged miscarriages of justice in Scotland and refer cases meeting the relevant criteria to the high court for determination. Members are appointed by the Queen on the recommendation of the first minister; senior executive staff are appointed by the commission.
*Chair,* Jean Couper, CBE
*Members,* Gerrard Bann; Peter Ferguson, QC; Prof. George Irving, CBE; Frances McMenamin, QC
*Chief Executive,* Gerard Sinclair

## SCOTTISH ENTERPRISE
Atrium Court, 50 Waterloo Street, Glasgow G2 6HQ
T 0845-607 8787 E enquiries@scotent.co.uk
W www.scottish-enterprise.com

Scottish Enterprise was established in 1991 and its purpose is to stimulate the sustainable growth of Scotland's economy. It is mainly funded by the Scottish government and is responsible to the Scottish ministers. Working in partnership with the private and public sectors, Scottish Enterprise will invest £321.2m in 2015–16 to further the development of Scotland's economy by helping ambitious and innovative businesses grow and become more successful. Scottish Enterprise is particularly interested in supporting companies that provide renewable energy, encourage trade overseas, increase innovation, and those that will help Scotland become a low-carbon economy. Its grant-in-aid allocation (capital and resource allocation) for 2015–16 is £243.5m.
*Chair,* Crawford Gillies
*Chief Executive,* Dr Lena Wilson

## SCOTTISH ENVIRONMENT PROTECTION AGENCY (SEPA)
Erskine Court, Castle Business Park, Stirling FK9 4TZ
T 0300-099 6699
W www.sepa.org.uk

SEPA was established in 1996 and is the public body responsible for environmental protection in Scotland. It regulates potential pollution to land, air and water; the storage, transport and disposal of controlled waste; and the safe-keeping and disposal of radioactive materials. It does this within a complex legislative framework of acts of parliament, EU directives and regulations, granting licences to operations of industrial processes and waste disposal. SEPA also operates Floodline (T 0845-988 1188), a public service providing information on the possible risk of flooding 24 hours a day, 365 days a year.
*Chair,* David Sigsworth
*Chief Executive,* Terry A'Hearn
*Directors,* Calum MacDonald *(Operations);* David Pirie *(Science and Strategy)*

## SCOTTISH LAW COMMISSION
140 Causewayside, Edinburgh EH9 1PR
T 0131-668 2131 E info@scotlawcom.gsi.gov.uk
W www.scotlawcom.gov.uk

The Scottish Law Commission, established in 1965, keeps the law in Scotland under review and makes proposals for its development and reform. It is responsible to the Scottish ministers through the Scottish government justice directorate.
*Chair (part-time),* Hon. Lord Pentland
*Chief Executive,* Malcolm McMillan
*Commissioners,* C. Drummond; D. Johnston, QC; Prof. H. MacQueen; Dr A. Steven

## SCOTTISH LEGAL AID BOARD
Thistle House, 91 Haymarket Terrace, Edinburgh EH12 5HE
T 0131-226 7061 Helpline 0845-122 8686
E general@slab.org.uk W www.slab.org.uk

The Scottish Legal Aid Board was set up under the Legal Aid (Scotland) Act 1986 to manage legal aid in Scotland. It reports to the Scottish government. Board members are appointed by Scottish ministers.
*Chair,* Iain Robertson, CBE
*Members,* Les Campbell; Rani Dhir; Alastair Kinroy, QC; Denise Loney; Ray MacFarlane; Vincent McGovern; Bill McQueen, CBE; Ros Micklem; Derek Ogg, QC; Sheriff Ray Small; Graham Watson
*Chief Executive,* Lindsay Montgomery, CBE

## SCOTTISH NATURAL HERITAGE (SNH)
Great Glen House, Leachkin Road, Inverness IV3 8NW
T 01463-725000 E enquiries@snh.gov.uk
W www.snh.org.uk

SNH was established in 1992 under the Natural Heritage (Scotland) Act 1991. It is the government's adviser on all aspects of nature and landscape across Scotland and its role is to help the public understand, value and enjoy Scotland's nature, as well as to support those people and organisations that manage it.
*Chair,* Ian Ross
*Acting Chief Executive,* Susan Davies
*Directors,* Nick Halfhide *(Operations);* Andrew Bachell *(Policy and Advice);* Joe Moore *(Corporate Services)*

## SEAFISH
18 Logie Mill, Logie Green Road, Edinburgh EH7 4HS
T 0131-558 3331 E seafish@seafish.co.uk
W www.seafish.org

Established under the Fisheries Act 1981, Seafish works with all sectors of the UK seafood industry to satisfy consumers, raise standards, improve efficiency and secure a sustainable and profitable future. Services range from research and development, economic consulting, market research and training and accreditation through to legislative advice for the seafood industry. It is sponsored by the four UK fisheries departments, which appoint the board, and is funded by a levy on seafood.

*Chair,* Elaine Hayes

*Chief Executive,* Dr Paul Williams

## SECURITY AND INTELLIGENCE SERVICES

### GOVERNMENT COMMUNICATIONS HEADQUARTERS (GCHQ)

Hubble Road, Cheltenham GL51 0EX
**T** 01242-221491 **W** www.gchq.gov.uk

GCHQ produces signals intelligence in support of national security and the UK's economic wellbeing, and in the prevention or detection of serious crime. Additionally, GCHQ's Information Security arm, CESG, is the national technical authority for information assurance, and provides advice and assistance to government departments, the armed forces and other national infrastructure bodies on the security of their communications and information systems. GCHQ was placed on a statutory footing by the Intelligence Services Act 1994 and is headed by a director who is directly accountable to the foreign secretary.

*Director,* Robert Hannigan, CMG

### SECRET INTELLIGENCE SERVICE (MI6)

PO Box 1300, London SE1 1BD
**W** www.sis.gov.uk

Established in 1909 as the Foreign Section of the Secret Service Bureau, the Secret Intelligence Service produces secret intelligence in support of the government's security, defence, foreign and economic policies. It was placed on a statutory footing by the Intelligence Services Act 1994 and is headed by a chief, known as 'C', who is directly accountable to the foreign secretary.

*Chief,* Alex Younger

### SECURITY SERVICE (MI5)

PO Box 3255, London SW1P 1AE
**T** 020-7930 9000 **W** www.mi5.gov.uk

The Security Service is responsible for security intelligence work against covertly organised threats to the UK. It is organised into seven branches, each with dedicated areas of responsibility, which include countering terrorism, espionage and the proliferation of weapons of mass destruction. The Security Service also provides security advice to a wide range of organisations to help reduce vulnerability to threats from individuals, groups or countries hostile to UK interests. The home secretary has parliamentary accountability for the Security Service. There is a network of regional offices around the UK plus a Northern Ireland headquarters.

*Director-General,* Andrew Parker

## SENIOR SALARIES REVIEW BODY

8th Floor, Fleetbank House, 2-6 Salisbury Square, London EC4Y 8JX
**T** 020-7211 8315 **W** www.ome.uk.com

The Senior Salaries Review Body (formerly the Top Salaries Review Body) was set up in 1971 to advise the prime minister on the remuneration of the judiciary, senior civil servants, senior officers of the armed forces and very senior managers in the NHS. In 1993 its remit was extended to cover the pay, pensions and allowances of MPs, ministers and others whose pay is determined by the Ministerial and Other Salaries Act 1975, and also the allowances of peers. If asked, it advises on the pay of officers and members of the devolved parliament and assemblies.

*Chair,* Dr Martin Read, DPHIL, FIET

*Members,* Margaret Edwards; Dame Hazel Genn, DBE, QC; David Lebrecht; John Steele

## STUDENT LOANS COMPANY LTD

100 Bothwell Street, Glasgow G2 7JD
**T** 0141-306 2000 **W** www.slc.co.uk

The Student Loans Company (SLC) is owned by the Department for Business, Innovation and Skills and the Secretary of State for Scotland. It processes and administers financial assistance, in the form of grants and loans, for undergraduates who have secured a place at university or college. The SLC also provides loans for tuition fees, which are paid directly to the university or college. In the year 2013–14 the SLC supported around 1.43 million students.

*Chair,* Christian Brodie

*Chief Executive,* Mick Laverty

## TATE

**W** www.tate.org.uk

### TATE BRITAIN

Millbank, London SW1P 4RG
**T** 020-7887 8888 **E** visiting.britain@tate.org.uk

### TATE MODERN

Bankside, London SE1 9TG
**T** 020-7887 8888 **E** visiting.modern@tate.org.uk

### TATE LIVERPOOL

Albert Dock, Liverpool L3 4BB
**T** 0151-702 7400 **E** visiting.liverpool@tate.org.uk

### TATE ST IVES

Porthmeor Beach, St Ives, Cornwall TR26 1TG
**T** 01736-796226 **E** visiting.stives@tate.org.uk

Tate comprises four art galleries: Tate Britain and Tate Modern in London, Tate Liverpool and Tate St Ives.

Tate Britain, which opened in 1897, displays the national collection of British art from 1500 to the present day – with special attention and dedicated space given to Blake, Turner and Constable. A £45m renovation of Tate Britain was completed in 2013.

Opened in May 2000, Tate Modern displays the Tate collection of international modern art dating from 1900 to the present day. It includes works by Dalí, Picasso, Matisse and Warhol as well as many contemporary works. It is housed in the former Bankside Power Station in London, which was redesigned by the Swiss architects Herzog and de Meuron.

Tate Liverpool opened in 1988 and houses mainly 20th-century art and Tate St Ives, which features work by artists from and working in St Ives and includes the Barbara Hepworth Museum and Sculpture Garden, opened in 1993.

### BOARD OF TRUSTEES

*Chair,* Lord Browne of Madingley

*Trustees,* John Akomfrah; Lionel Barber; Tom Bloxham, MBE; Mala Gaonkar; Maja Hoffman; Lisa Milroy; Elisabeth Murdoch; Franck Petitgas; Dame Seona Reid, DBE; Hannah Rothschild; Monisha Shah; Gareth Thomas; Stephen Witherford

OFFICERS
*Director, Tate,* Sir Nicholas Serota, CH
*Directors,* Dr Penelope Curtis *(Tate Britain);* Chris Dercon
*(Tate Modern);* Caroline Collier *(Tate National);* Andrea
Nixon *(Tate Liverpool);* Mark Osterfield *(Tate St Ives)*

## TOURISM BODIES

Visit Britain, Visit Scotland, Visit Wales and the Northern
Ireland Tourist Board are responsible for developing and
marketing the tourist industry in their respective regions.
Visit Wales is not listed here as it is part of the Welsh
government, within the Department for Heritage, and not a
public body.

VISITBRITAIN
Sanctuary Buildings, 20 Great Smith Street, London SW1P 3BT
T 020-7578 1000 E industry.relations@visitbritain.org
W www.visitbritain.com
*Chair,* Christopher Rodrigues, CBE
*Chief Executive,* Sally Balcombe

VISIT SCOTLAND
Ocean Point One, 94 Ocean Drive, Edinburgh EH6 6JH
T 0131-472 2222
E info@visitscotland.com W www.visitscotland.com
*Chair,* Dr Mike Cantlay, OBE
*Chief Executive,* Malcolm Roughead, OBE

NORTHERN IRELAND TOURIST BOARD
St. Anne's Court, 59 North Street, Belfast BT1 1NB
T 028-9023 1221 E info@tourismni.com W www.nitb.com
*Chair,* Terence Brannigan
*Chief Executive,* John McGrillen

## TRANSPORT FOR LONDON (TFL)

Windsor House, 42–50 Victoria Street, London SW1H 0TL
E enquire@tfl.gov.uk W www.tfl.gov.uk

TfL was created in July 2000 and is the integrated body
responsible for the capital's transport system. Its role is to
implement the Mayor of London's transport strategy and
manage the transport services across London for which the
mayor has responsibility. These services include London's
buses, London Underground, London Overground, London
Docklands Light Railway (DLR), Tramlink, London River
Services and Victoria Coach Station. TfL also runs the
Emirates Air Line and the London Transport Museum. In
a joint venture with the Department for Transport, TfL is
responsible for the construction of Crossrail - a new railway
linking Maidenhead and Heathrow in the west, to Shenfield
and Abbey Wood in the east. The central section of Crossrail
is expected to be completed by the end of 2018.
  TfL is responsible for managing the Congestion Charging
scheme and for maintaining 360 miles (580km) of main
roads and all of London's 6,000+ traffic lights. It also
regulates the city's taxis and private hire vehicles. TfL runs
the Santander Cycle Hire scheme, allowing customers to hire
a bicycle from £2, and the Dial-a-ride scheme, a door-to-
door service for disabled people unable to use buses, trams or
the London Underground.
*Chair,* Boris Johnson
*Members,* Peter Anderson; Sir John Armitt, CBE;
  Sir Brendan Barber; Richard Barnes; Charles Belcher;
  Roger Burnley; Brian Cooke; Isabel Dedring *(Deputy
  Chair);* Baroness Grey-Thompson, DBE; Angela Knight;
  Michael Liebreich; Eva Lindholm; Daniel Moylan;
  Bob Oddy; Keith Williams; Steve Wright, MBE
*Commissioner,* Mike Brown

## UK ATOMIC ENERGY AUTHORITY

Culham Science Centre, Abingdon, Oxfordshire OX14 3DB
T 01235-528822 W www.gov.uk/government/organisations/uk-
atomic-energy-authority

The UK Atomic Energy Authority (UKAEA) was established
by the Atomic Energy Authority Act 1954 and took
over responsibility for the research and development of the
civil nuclear power programme. The UKAEA reports to
the Department for Business, Innovation and Skills and is
responsible for managing UK fusion research including
operating the Joint European Torus (JET) on behalf of
the UKAEA's European partners at its site in Culham,
Oxfordshire. In October 2009, as part of the government's
Operation Efficiency Programme, the authority sold its
commercial arm, UKAEA Limited; as a result, the UKAEA no
longer provides nuclear decommissioning services.
*Chair,* Prof. Roger Cashmore, CMG, FRS
*Chief Executive,* Prof. Steven Cowley

## UK SPORT

21 Bloomsbury Street, London WC1B 3HF
T 020-7211 5100 E info@uksport.gov.uk W www.uksport.gov.uk

UK Sport was established by royal charter in 1997 and is
accountable to parliament through the Department for
Culture, Media and Sport. Its mission is to lead sport in the
UK to world-class success. This means working with partner
organisations to deliver medals at the Olympic and
Paralympic Games and organising, bidding for and staging
major sporting events in the UK; increasing the UK's
sporting activity and influence overseas; and promoting
sporting conduct, ethics and diversity in society. UK Sport
is funded by a mix of grant-in-aid and National Lottery
income. For 2014–15 projected grant-in-aid and National
Lottery funding amounted to approximately £111m.
*Chair,* Rod Carr, CBE
*Chief Executive,* Liz Nicholl, OBE

## VICTORIA AND ALBERT MUSEUM

Cromwell Road, London SW7 2RL
T 020-7942 2000 W www.vam.ac.uk

The Victoria and Albert Museum (V&A) is the national
museum of art, design and performance. It descends directly
from the Museum of Manufactures, which opened in
Marlborough House in 1852 after the Great Exhibition of
1851. The museum was moved in 1857 to become part of
the South Kensington Museum. It was renamed the Victoria
and Albert Museum in 1899. It also houses the National Art
Library and Print Room.
  The museum's collections span over 5,000 years of human
creativity, including paintings, sculpture, architecture,
ceramics, furniture, fashion and textiles, theatre and
performance, photography, glass, jewellery and metalwork.
Materials relating to childhood are displayed at the V&A
Museum of Childhood at Bethnal Green, which opened in
1872 and is the most important surviving example of the
type of glass and iron construction used by Joseph Paxton
for the Great Exhibition. The V&A also houses the National
Art Library which holds over 950,000 books dedicated to
the study of fine and decorative arts from around the world.
*Chair,* Nicholas Coleridge, CBE
*Trustees,* Joao Baptista; Mark Damazer; Prof. Margot
  Finn; Andrew Hochhauser, QC; Stephen McGuckin;
  Dame Theresa Sackler, DBE; Mark Sebba; Caroline Silver;
  Sir John Sorrell; Dr Paul Thompson; Edmund de Waal,
  OBE; Prof. Evelyn Welch
*Director,* Prof. Martin Roth

# WALLACE COLLECTION

Hertford House, Manchester Square, London W1U 3BN
T 020-7563 9500 E collections@wallacecollection.org
W www.wallacecollection.org

The Wallace Collection was bequeathed to the nation by the widow of Sir Richard Wallace, in 1897, and Hertford House was subsequently acquired by the government. The collection contains works by Titian and Rembrandt, and includes porcelain, furniture and an array of arms and armour.

*Chair,* António Horta Osório
*Trustees,* Prof. Jasper Conran, OBE; Prof. Frances Corner, OBE; Duke of Devonshire, KCVO, CBE; Jennifer Eady, QC; Rupert Hambro; Jagdip Jagpal; Denise Lewis; Jessica Pulay; Sir Hugh Roberts, GCVO, FSA; Kate de Rothschild Agius; Dr Ashok Roy; Adrian Sassoon; Timothy Schrofer
*Director,* Dr Christoph Vogtherr

# WALES

## WELSH GOVERNMENT

Cathays Park, Cardiff CF10 3NQ
T 0845-010 3300 W http://wales.gov.uk

The Welsh government is the devolved government of Wales. It is accountable to the National Assembly for Wales, the Welsh legislature which represents the interests of the people of Wales, and makes laws for Wales. The Welsh government and the National Assembly for Wales were established as separate institutions under the Government of Wales Act 2006.

The Welsh government comprises the first minister, who is usually the leader of the largest party in the National Assembly for Wales; up to 14 ministers and deputy ministers; and a counsel general (the chief legal adviser).

Following the referendum on 3 March 2011 on granting further law-making powers to the National Assembly, the Welsh government's functions now include the ability to propose bills to the National Assembly on subjects within 20 set areas of policy. Subject to limitations prescribed by the Government of Wales Act 2006, acts of the National Assembly may make any provision that could be made by act of parliament. The 20 areas of responsibility devolved to the National Assembly for Wales (and within which Welsh ministers exercise executive functions) are: agriculture, fisheries, forestry and rural development; ancient monuments and historic buildings; culture; economic development; education and training; environment; fire and rescue services and promotion of fire safety; food; health and health services; highways and transport; housing; local government; the National Assembly for Wales; public administration; social welfare; sport and recreation; tourism; town and country planning; water and flood defence; and the Welsh language.

*First Minister of Wales,* Rt. Hon. Carwyn Jones, AM
*Minister for Communities and Tackling Poverty,* Lesley Griffiths, AM
*Minister for Economy, Science and Transport,* Edwina Hart, MBE, AM
*Minister for Education and Skills,* Huw Lewis, AM
*Minister for Finance and Government Business,* Jane Hutt, AM
*Minister for Health and Social Services,* Mark Drakeford, AM
*Minister for Natural Resources,* Carl Sargeant, AM
*Minister for Public Services,* Leighton Andrews, AM
*Deputy Minister for Health,* Vaughan Gething, AM
*Deputy Minister for Culture, Sport and Tourism,* Ken Skates, AM
*Deputy Minister for Farming and Food,* Rebecca Evans, AM
*Deputy Minister for Skills and Technology,* Julie James, AM
*Counsel General of Wales,* Theodore Huckle, QC
*Chief Whip,* Janice Gregory, AM

### MANAGEMENT BOARD

*Permanent Secretary,* Sir Derek Jones, KCB
*Director-General, Finance and Corporate Services,* Michael Hearty
*Director-General, Economy, Science and Transport,* James Price
*Director-General, Education and Skills,* Owen Evans
*Director-General, Health, Social Services and Children and Chief Executive of NHS Wales,* Andrew Goodall
*Director-General, Local Government and Communities,* Dr June Milligan
*Director-General, People, Places and Corporate Services,* Bernard Galton

*Director-General, Natural Resources,* Gareth Jones
*Non-Executive Directors,* Elan Closs Stephens; James Turner; Adrian Webb

### DEPARTMENTS

Department for Education and Skills
Department for Health and Social Services
Department for Economy, Science and Transport
Department for Finance and Corporate Services
Department for Local Government and Communities
Department for Natural Resources
Permanent Secretary's Division (Office of the First Minister; Legal Services Department; European and External Affairs Division; Constitutional Affairs and Inter-governmental Relations Division)
Sustainable Futures

### ASSEMBLY COMMITTEES

Children, Young People and Education
Communities, Equality and Local Government
Constitutional and Legislative Affairs
Enterprise and Business
Environment and Sustainability
Finance
Health and Social Care
Petitions
Public Accounts
Scrutiny of the First Minister
Standards of Conduct

### ASSEMBLY COMMISSION

The Assembly Commission was created under the Government of Wales Act 2006 to ensure that the assembly is provided with the property, staff and services required for it to carry out its functions. The commission also sets the National Assembly's strategic aims, objectives, standards and values. The Assembly Commission consists of the presiding officer, plus four other assembly members, one nominated by each of the four party groups. The five commissioners are accountable to the National Assembly.

*Presiding Officer,* Dame Rosemary Butler, DBE, AM
*Commissioners,* Peter Black, Angela Burns, Rhodri Glyn Thomas, Sandy Mewies
*Chief Executive and Clerk of the Assembly,* Claire Clancy

## NATIONAL ASSEMBLY FOR WALES

Cardiff Bay, Cardiff CF99 1NA
T 0845-010 5500 W www.assemblywales.org

In July 1997 the government announced plans to establish a National Assembly for Wales. In a referendum in September 1997 about 50 per cent of the electorate voted, of whom 50.3 per cent voted in favour of a national assembly. Elections are held every four years and the first election took place on 6 May 1999. The fourth election took place on 5 May 2011. There has been a minority Labour administration since the 2011 elections.

National Assembly members are elected using the additional member system. Voters are given two votes: one for a constituency member and one for a regional member. The constituency members are elected under the first-past-the-post system, also used to elect constituency members to the London Assembly. Four regional members in each of the five constituencies are then chosen from party lists or independent candidates using a form of proportional representation.

Until 2007 the National Assembly for Wales was a corporate body comprising both the executive and legislative branches of government. It had no primary law-making powers and only had responsibility for exercising and implementing ministerial functions which had previously been vested in the Secretary of State for Wales.

The Government of Wales Act 2006 introduced a radical change to the functions and status of the National Assembly for Wales. With effect from 25 May 2007 the act formally separated the National Assembly for Wales (the legislature – made up of 60 elected assembly members) and the Welsh government (the executive – comprising the first minister, Welsh ministers, deputy Welsh ministers and the counsel general). It also made changes to the electoral process: candidates are no longer permitted to stand as both constituency and regional members. The act enabled the National Assembly for Wales to formulate its own legislation (assembly measures) on the 20 devolved areas for which it has responsibility (*see* Welsh government); the assembly was given legislative competence (the legal authority to pass measures) on a case-by-case basis by the UK parliament.

The act also included a mechanism that would allow for full transfer of legislative powers relating to all devolved matters to the National Assembly, provided that the people of Wales voted for such a proposal in a referendum. In a referendum held on 3 March 2011, 63.5 per cent voted in favour of giving the National Assembly full legislative powers for all devolved matters. The National Assembly for Wales can now pass legislation (assembly acts) on the 20 devolved areas for which it has responsibility. An assembly act has the same powers as an act of the UK parliament and may be proposed by the Welsh government, assembly committees, an assembly member or the assembly commission.

The National Assembly for Wales also scrutinises and monitors the Welsh government. It meets in plenary in the Senedd debating chamber. The 60 assembly members examine and approve assembly bills and approve certain items of subordinate legislation; approve the Welsh government and assembly commission's budget; hold Welsh ministers to account; and analyse and debate their decisions and policies.

*Presiding Officer*, Dame Rosemary Butler, DBE, AM
*Deputy Presiding Officer*, David Melding, AM

| SALARIES *2015–16* | |
| --- | --- |
| First Minister* | £80,870 |
| Minister/Presiding Officer* | £41,949 |
| Deputy Minister/Deputy Presiding Officer* | £26,385 |
| Assembly Member (AM)† | £54,391 |

\* Also receives the assembly member salary
† Reduced by two-thirds if the member is also an MP or an MEP

## MEMBERS OF THE NATIONAL ASSEMBLY FOR WALES
*as at 1 September 2015*

**Andrews**, Leighton, *Lab., Rhondda,* Maj. 6,739
**Antoniw**, Mick, *Lab., Pontypridd,* Maj. 7,694
**ap Iorwerth, Rhun**, *PC, Ynys Môn,* Maj. 9,166
**Asghar**, Mohammad, *C., South Wales East region*
**Black**, Peter, *LD, South Wales West region*
**Burns**, Angela, *C., Carmarthen West and South Pembrokeshire,* Maj. 1,504
**Butler**, Dame Rosemary, DBE, *Lab., Newport West,* Maj. 4,220
**Chapman**, Christine, *Lab., Cynon Valley,* Maj. 6,515
**Cuthbert**, Jeff, *Lab., Caerphilly,* Maj. 4,924

**Davies**, Alun, *Lab., Blaenau Gwent,* Maj. 9,120
**Davies**, Andrew R. T., *C., South Wales Central region*
**Davies**, Jocelyn, *PC, South Wales East region*
**Davies**, Keith, *Lab., Llanelli,* Maj. 80
**Davies**, Paul, *C., Preseli Pembrokeshire,* Maj. 2,175
**Davies**, Suzy, *C., South Wales West region*
**Drakeford**, Mark, *Lab., Cardiff West,* Maj. 5,901
**Elis-Thomas**, Rt. Hon. Lord, *PC, Dwyfor Meirionnydd,* Maj. 5,417
**Evans**, Rebecca, *Lab., Mid and West Wales region*
**Finch-Saunders**, Janet, *C., Aberconwy,* Maj. 1,567
**George**, Russell, *C., Montgomeryshire,* Maj. 2,324
**Gething**, Vaughan, *Lab., Cardiff South and Penarth,* Maj. 6,259
**Graham**, William, *C., South Wales East region*
**Gregory**, Janice, *Lab., Ogmore,* Maj. 9,576
**Griffiths**, John, *Lab., Newport East,* Maj. 5,388
**Griffiths**, Lesley, *Lab., Wrexham,* Maj. 3,337
**Hart**, Edwina, *Lab., Gower,* Maj. 4,864
**Haworth**, Janet, *C., North Wales region*
**Hedges**, Mike, *Lab., Swansea East,* Maj. 8,281
**Hussain**, Altaf, *C., South Wales West region*
**Hutt**, Jane, *Lab., Vale of Glamorgan,* Maj. 3,775
**Huws Gruffydd**, Llyr, *PC, North Wales region*
**Isherwood**, Mark, *C., North Wales region*
**James**, Julie, *Lab., Swansea West,* Maj. 4,654
**Jenkins**, Bethan, *PC, South Wales West region*
**Jones**, Alun Ffred, *PC, Arfon,* Maj. 5,394
**Jones**, Ann, *Lab., Vale of Clwyd,* Maj. 4,011
**Jones**, Rt. Hon. Carwyn, *Lab., Bridgend,* Maj. 6,775
**Jones**, Elin, *PC, Ceredigion,* Maj. 1,777
**Lewis**, Huw, *Lab., Merthyr Tydfil and Rhymney,* Maj. 7,051
**Melding**, David, *C., South Wales Central region*
**Mewies**, Sandra, *Lab., Delyn,* Maj. 2,881
**Millar**, Darren, *C., Clwyd West,* Maj. 4,248
**Morgan**, Julie, *Lab., Cardiff North,* Maj. 1,782
**Neagle**, Lynne, *Lab., Torfaen,* Maj. 6,088
**Parrott**, Eluned, *LD, South Wales Central region*
**Powell**, William, *LD, Mid and West Wales region*
**Price**, Gwyn, *Lab., Islwyn,* Maj. 7,589
**Ramsay**, Nicholas, *C., Monmouth,* Maj. 6,117
**Rathbone**, Jenny, *Lab., Cardiff Central,* Maj. 38
**Rees**, David, *Lab., Aberavon,* Maj. 9,311
**Roberts**, Aled, *LD, North Wales region*
**Sargeant**, Carl, *Lab., Alyn and Deeside,* Maj. 5,581
**Skates**, Ken, *Lab., Clwyd South,* Maj. 2,659
**Thomas**, Gwenda, *Lab., Neath,* Maj. 6,390
**Thomas**, Rhodri Glyn, *PC, Carmarthen East and Dinefwr,* Maj. 4,148
**Thomas**, Simon, *PC, Mid and West Wales region*
**Watson**, Joyce, *Lab., Mid and West Wales region*
**Whittle**, Lindsay, *PC, South Wales East region*
**Williams**, Kirsty, *LD, Brecon and Radnorshire,* Maj. 2,757
**Wood**, Leanne, *PC, South Wales Central region*

### STATE OF THE PARTIES
*as at 1 September 2015*

| | Constituency AMs | Regional AMs | AM total |
| --- | --- | --- | --- |
| Labour (Lab.) | 28* | 2 | 30 |
| Conservative (C.) | 6 | 8† | 14 |
| Plaid Cymru (PC) | 5 | 6 | 11 |
| Liberal Democrats (LD) | 1 | 4 | 5 |
| Total | 40 | 20 | 60 |

\* Includes the Presiding Officer
† Includes the Deputy Presiding Officer

## NATIONAL ASSEMBLY ELECTION RESULTS
*As at 5 May 2011*
E. Electorate  T. Turnout
*See* General Election Results for a list of party abbreviations

CONSTITUENCIES
E. 2,289,555  T. 41.5%

ABERAVON (S. WALES WEST)
E. 50,754  T. 18,879 (37.20%)
David Rees, Lab.                    12,104
Paul Nicholls-Jones, PC              2,793
Tamojen Morgan, C.                   2,704
Helen Ceri Clarke, LD                1,278
*Lab. majority* 9,311 (49.32%)
8.65% swing PC to Lab.

ABERCONWY (WALES N.)
E. 44,978  T. 20,288 (45.11%)
Janet Finch-Saunders, C.             6,888
Iwan Huws, PC                        5,321
Eifion Wyn Williams, Lab.            5,206
Mike Priestley, LD                   2,873
*C. majority* 1,567 (7.72%)
7.95% swing PC to C.

ALYN AND DEESIDE (WALES N.)
E. 61,751  T. 22,769 (36.87%)
Carl Sargeant, Lab.                 11,978
John Bell, C.                        6,397
Pete Williams, LD                    1,725
Shane Brennan, PC                    1,710
Michael Whitby, BNP                    959
*Lab. majority* 5,581 (24.51%)
4.29% swing C. to Lab.

ARFON (WALES N.)
E. 41,093  T. 17,664 (42.99%)
Alun Ffred Jones, PC                10,024
Christina Rees, Lab.                 4,630
Aled Davies, C.                      2,209
Rhys Jones, LD                         801
*PC majority* 5,394 (30.54%)
2.45% swing Lab. to PC

BLAENAU GWENT
(S. WALES EAST)
E. 53,230  T. 20,211 (37.97%)
Alun Davies, Lab.                   12,926
Jayne Sullivan, Ind.                 3,806
Darren Jones, PC                     1,098
Bob Hayward, C.                      1,066
Brian Urch, BNP                        948
Martin Blakeborough, LD                367
*Lab. majority* 9,120 (45.12%)
33.95% swing Ind. to Lab.

BRECON AND RADNORSHIRE
(WALES MID AND W.)
E. 53,546  T. 28,348 (52.94%)
Kirsty Williams, LD                 12,201
Chris Davies, C.                     9,444
Christopher Lloyd, Lab.              4,797
Gary Price, PC                       1,906
*LD majority* 2,757 (9.73%)
4.45% swing LD to C.

BRIDGEND (S. WALES WEST)
E. 59,104  T. 24,035 (40.67%)
Carwyn Jones, Lab.                  13,499
Alex Williams, C.                    6,724
Tim Thomas, PC                       2,076
Briony Davies, LD                    1,736
*Lab. majority* 6,775 (28.19%)
8.89% swing C. to Lab.

CAERPHILLY (S. WALES EAST)
E. 62,049  T. 25,570 (41.21%)
Jeff Cuthbert, Lab.                 12,521
Ron Davies, PC                       7,597
Owen Meredith, C.                    3,368
Kay David, LD                        1,062
Anthony King, BNP                    1,022
*Lab. majority* 4,924 (19.26%)
5.25% swing PC to Lab.

CARDIFF CENTRAL
(S. WALES CENTRAL)
E. 64,347  T. 23,628 (36.72%)
Jenny Rathbone, Lab.                 8,954
Nigel Howells, LD                    8,916
Matt Smith, C.                       3,559
Chris Williams, PC                   1,690
Mathab Khan, Ind.                      509
*Lab. majority* 38 (0.16%)
14.74% swing LD to Lab.

CARDIFF NORTH
(S. WALES CENTRAL)
E. 66,934  T. 34,431 (51.44%)
Julie Morgan, Lab.                  16,384
Jonathan Morgan, C.                 14,602
Ben Foday, PC                        1,850
Matt Smith, LD                       1,595
*Lab. majority* 1,782 (5.18%)
9.77% swing C. to Lab.

CARDIFF SOUTH AND PENARTH
(S. WALES CENTRAL)
E. 75,038  T. 27,479 (36.62%)
Vaughan Gething, Lab.               13,814
Ben Gray, C.                         7,555
Liz Musa, PC                         3,324
Sian Cliff, LD                       2,786
*Lab. majority* 6,259 (22.78%)
6.24% swing C. to Lab.

CARDIFF WEST
(S. WALES CENTRAL)
E. 64,219  T. 27,726 (43.17%)
Mark Drakeford, Lab.                13,067
Craig Williams, C.                   7,167
Neil McEvoy, PC                      5,551
David Morgan, LD                     1,942
*Lab. majority* 5,901 (21.28%)
3.77% C. to Lab.

CARMARTHEN EAST AND
DINEFWR (WALES MID AND W.)
E. 54,243  T. 27,828 (51.30%)
Rhodri Glyn Thomas, PC              12,501
Anthony Jones, Lab.                  8,353
Henrietta Hensher, C.                5,635
Will Griffiths, LD                   1,339
*PC majority* 4,148 (14.91%)
7.01% swing PC to Lab.

CARMARTHEN WEST AND
SOUTH PEMBROKESHIRE
(WALES MID AND W.)
E. 58,435  T. 28,156 (48.18%)
Angela Burns, C.                    10,095
Christine Gwyther, Lab.              8,591
Nerys Evans, PC                      8,373
Selwyn Runnett, LD                   1,097
*C. majority* 1,504 (5.34%)
2.50% swing Lab. to C.

CEREDIGION
(WALES MID AND W.)
E. 56,983  T. 29,076 (51.03%)
Elin Jones, PC                      12,020
Liz Evans, LD                       10,243
Luke Evetts, C.                      2,755
Richard Boudier, Lab.                2,544
Chris Simpson, Green                 1,514
*PC majority* 1,777 (6.11%)
3.51% swing PC to LD

CLWYD SOUTH (WALES N.)
E. 54,499  T. 19,498 (37.59%)
Ken Skates, Lab.                     8,500
Paul Rogers, C.                      5,841
Mabon ap Gwynfor, PC                 3,719
Bruce Roberts, LD                    1,977
*Lab. majority* 2,659 (13.27%)
3.77% swing C. to Lab.

CLWYD WEST (WALES N.)
E. 57,980  T. 25,153 (43.38%)
Darren Millar, C.                   10,890
Crispin Jones, Lab.                  6,642
Eifion Lloyd Jones, PC               5,775
Brian Cossey, LD                     1,846
*C. majority* 4,248 (16.89%)
5.40% swing Lab. to C.

CYNON VALLEY
(S. WALES CENTRAL)
E. 52,133  T. 18,760 (35.98%)
Christine Chapman, Lab.             11,626
Dafydd Trystan Davies, PC            5,111
Dan Saxton, C.                       1,531
Ian Walton, LD                         492
*Lab. majority* 6,515 (34.73%)
2.96% swing PC to Lab.

DELYN (WALES N.)
E. 53,996  T. 23,194 (42.96%)
Sandy Mewies, Lab.                  10,695
Matt Wright, C.                      7,814
Carrie Harper, PC                    2,918
Michele Jones, LD                    1,767
*Lab. majority* 2,881 (12.42%)
5.03% swing C. to Lab.

DWYFOR MEIRONNYDD
(WALES MID AND W.)
E. 44,669  T. 20,743 (46.44%)
| | |
|---|---|
| Dafydd Elis-Thomas, PC | 9,656 |
| Simon Baynes, C. | 4,239 |
| Louise Hughes, Llais Gwynedd | 3,225 |
| Martyn Stuart Singleton, Lab. | 2,623 |
| Steven William Churchman, LD | 1,000 |
*PC majority* 5,417 (26.11%)
6.99% swing PC to C.

GOWER (S. WALES WEST)
E. 61,909  T. 26,773 (43.25%)
| | |
|---|---|
| Edwina Hart, Lab. | 12,866 |
| Caroline Jones, C. | 8,002 |
| Darren Price, PC | 3,249 |
| Peter May, LD | 2,656 |
*Lab. majority* 4,864 (18.17%)
6.92% swing C. to Lab.

ISLWYN (S. WALES EAST)
E. 54,893  T. 20,908 (38.09%)
| | |
|---|---|
| Gwyn Price, Lab. | 12,116 |
| Steffan Lewis, PC | 4,527 |
| David Chipp, C. | 2,497 |
| Peter Whalley, BNP | 1,115 |
| Tom Sullivan, LD | 653 |
*Lab. majority* 7,589 (36.30%)
10.09% swing PC to Lab.

LLANELLI (WALES MID AND W.)
E. 58,838  T. 26,070 (44.31%)
| | |
|---|---|
| Keith Davies, Lab. | 10,359 |
| Helen Mary Jones, PC | 10,279 |
| Andrew Morgan, C. | 2,880 |
| Sian Caiach, Putting Llanelli First | 2,004 |
| Cheryl Philpott, LD | 548 |
*Lab. majority* 80 (0.31%)
7.19% swing PC to Lab.

MERTHYR TYDFIL AND
RHYMNEY (S. WALES EAST)
E. 55,031  T. 19,320 (35.11%)
| | |
|---|---|
| Huw Lewis, Lab. | 10,483 |
| Tony Rogers, Ind. | 3,432 |
| Amy Kitcher, LD | 2,480 |
| Noel Turner, PC | 1,701 |
| Chris O'Brien, C. | 1,224 |
*Lab. majority* 7,051 (36.50%)
0.14% swing Ind. to Lab.

MONMOUTH (S. WALES EAST)
E. 64,857  T. 30,001 (46.26%)
| | |
|---|---|
| Nick Ramsay, C. | 15,087 |
| Mark Whitcutt, Lab. | 8,970 |
| Janet Ellard, LD | 2,937 |
| Fiona Cross, PC | 2,263 |
| Steve Uncles, Eng. Dem. | 744 |
*C. majority* 6,117 (20.39%)
4.13% swing C. to Lab.

MONTGOMERYSHIRE
(WALES MID AND W.)
E. 48,675  T. 22,933 (47.11%)
| | |
|---|---|
| Russell George, C. | 10,026 |
| Wyn Williams, LD | 7,702 |
| Nick Colbourne, Lab. | 2,609 |
| David Senior, PC | 2,596 |
*C. majority* 2,324 (10.13%)
9.50% swing LD to C.

NEATH (S. WALES WEST)
E. 57,533  T. 23,849 (41.45%)
| | |
|---|---|
| Gwenda Thomas, Lab. | 12,736 |
| Alun Llewelyn, PC | 6,346 |
| Alex Powell, C. | 2,780 |
| Michael Green, BNP | 1,004 |
| Mathew McCarthy, LD | 983 |
*Lab. majority* 6,390 (26.79%)
9.54% swing PC to Lab.

NEWPORT EAST (S. WALES EAST)
E. 55,120  T. 19,460 (35.30%)
| | |
|---|---|
| John Griffiths, Lab. | 9,888 |
| Nick Webb, C. | 4,500 |
| Ed Townsend, LD | 3,703 |
| Chris Paul, PC | 1,369 |
*Lab. majority* 5,388 (27.69%)
9.11% swing C. to Lab.

NEWPORT WEST (S. WALES EAST)
E. 63,180  T. 23,014 (36.43%)
| | |
|---|---|
| Rosemary Butler, Lab. | 12,011 |
| David Williams, C. | 7,791 |
| Lyndon Binding, PC | 1,626 |
| Liz Newton, LD | 1,586 |
*Lab. majority* 4,220 (18.34%)
6.21% swing C. to Lab.

OGMORE (S. WALES WEST)
E. 55,442  T. 20,264 (36.55%)
| | |
|---|---|
| Janice Gregory, Lab. | 12,955 |
| Danny Clark, PC | 3,379 |
| Martyn Hughes, C. | 2,945 |
| Gerald Francis, LD | 985 |
*Lab. majority* 9,576 (47.26%)
6.28% swing PC to Lab.

PONTYPRIDD
(S. WALES CENTRAL)
E. 60,028  T. 23,333 (38.87%)
| | |
|---|---|
| Mick Antoniw, Lab. | 11,864 |
| Michael Powell, LD | 4,170 |
| Joel James, C. | 3,659 |
| Ioan Bellin, PC | 3,139 |
| Ken Owen, ND | 501 |
*Lab. majority* 7,694 (32.97%)
9.28% swing LD to Lab.

PRESELI PEMBROKESHIRE
(WALES MID AND W.)
E. 57,758  T. 27,218 (47.12%)
| | |
|---|---|
| Paul Davies, C. | 11,541 |
| Terry Mills (Lab.) | 9,366 |
| Rhys Sinnett, PC | 4,226 |
| Rob Kilmister, LD | 2,085 |
*C. majority* 2,175 (7.99%)
1.58% swing C. to Lab.

RHONDDA (S. WALES CENTRAL)
E. 52,532  T. 20,027 (38.12%)
| | |
|---|---|
| Leighton Andrews, Lab. | 12,650 |
| Sarah Evans-Fear, PC | 5,911 |
| James Jeffreys, C. | 969 |
| George Summers, LD | 497 |
*Lab. majority* 6,739 (33.65%)
2.77% swing PC to Lab.

SWANSEA EAST (S. WALES WEST)
E. 60,246  T. 18,910 (58.36%)
| | |
|---|---|
| Mike Hedges, Lab. | 11,035 |
| Daniel Boucher, C. | 2,754 |
| Dic Jones, PC | 2,346 |
| Sam Samuel, LD | 1,673 |
| Joanne Shannon, BNP | 1,102 |
*Lab. majority* 8,281 (43.79%)
6.05% swing C. to Lab.

SWANSEA WEST (S. WALES WEST)
E. 62,345  T. 21,805 (34.97%)
| | |
|---|---|
| Julie James, Lab. | 9,885 |
| Steve Jenkins, C. | 5,231 |
| Rob Speht, LD | 3,654 |
| Carl Harris, PC | 3,035 |
*Lab. majority* 4,654 (21.34%)
4.09% swing C. to Lab.

TORFAEN (S. WALES EAST)
E. 61,126  T. 22,328 (36.53%)
| | |
|---|---|
| Lynne Neagle, Lab. | 10,318 |
| Elizabeth Haynes, Ind. | 4,230 |
| Natasha Asghar, C. | 3,306 |
| Jeff Rees, PC | 2,716 |
| Susan Harwood, BNP | 906 |
| Will Griffiths, LD | 852 |
*Lab. majority* 6,088 (27.27%)
0.52% swing Lab. to Ind.

VALE OF CLWYD (WALES N.)
E. 56,232  T. 23,056 (41.00%)
| | |
|---|---|
| Ann Jones, Lab. | 11,691 |
| Ian Gunning, C. | 7,680 |
| Alun Lloyd Jones, PC | 2,597 |
| Heather Prydderch, LD | 1,088 |
*Lab. majority* 4,011 (17.40%)
8.49% swing C. to Lab.

VALE OF GLAMORGAN
(S. WALES CENTRAL)
E. 71,602  T. 33,254 (46.80%)
| | |
|---|---|
| Jane Hutt, Lab. | 15,746 |
| Angela Jones-Evans, C. | 11,971 |
| Ian Johnson, PC | 4,024 |
| Damian Chick, LD | 1,513 |
*Lab. majority* 3,775 (11.35%)
5.55% swing C. to Lab.

WREXHAM (WALES N.)
E. 53,516  T. 18,687 (34.92%)
| | |
|---|---|
| Lesley Griffiths, Lab. | 8,368 |
| John Marek, C. | 5,031 |
| Bill Brereton | 2,692 |
| Marc Jones, PC | 2,596 |
*Lab. majority* 3,337 (17.86%)
3.15% swing C. to Lab.

YNYS MON (WALES N.)
E. 49,431  T. 24,067 (48.69%)
| | |
|---|---|
| Ieuan Wyn Jones, PC | 9,969 |
| Paul Williams, C. | 7,032 |
| Joe Lock, Lab. | 6,307 |
| Rhys Taylor, LD | 759 |
*PC majority* 2,937 (12.20%)
7.27% swing PC to C.

REGIONS
E. 2,289,555  T. 41.4%

MID AND WEST WALES
E. 433,147  T. 210,352 (48.56%)

| | | |
|---|---|---|
| PC | 56,384 | (26.7%) |
| C. | 52,905 | (25.1%) |
| Lab. | 47,348 | (22.5%) |
| LD | 26,847 | (12.7%) |
| UKIP | 9,211 | (4.4%) |
| Green | 8,660 | (4.1%) |
| Soc. Lab. | 3,951 | (1.9%) |
| BNP | 2,821 | (1.3%) |
| Welsh Christian Party | 1,630 | (0.8%) |
| Comm. Brit. | 595 | (0.3%) |

PC majority 3,479 (1.65%)
3.25% swing PC to C. (2007 PC majority 17,652)

ADDITIONAL MEMBERS

| | |
|---|---|
| Rebecca Evans, Lab. | William Powell, LD |
| Joyce Watson, Lab. | Simon Thomas, PC |

NORTH WALES
E. 473,296  T. 194,798 (41.16%)

| | | |
|---|---|---|
| Lab. | 62,677 | (32.2%) |
| C. | 52,201 | (26.8%) |
| PC | 41,701 | (21.4%) |
| LD | 11,507 | (5.9%) |
| UKIP | 9,608 | (4.9%) |
| Soc. Lab. | 4,895 | (2.5%) |
| BNP | 4,785 | (2.5%) |
| Green | 4,406 | (2.3%) |
| Welsh Christian Party | 1,401 | (0.7%) |
| Ind. | 1,094 | (0.6%) |
| Comm. Brit. | 523 | (0.3%) |

Lab. majority 10,476 (5.38%)
5.05% swing PC to Lab. (2007 Lab. majority 1,273)

ADDITIONAL MEMBERS

| | |
|---|---|
| Mark Isherwood, C. | Aled Roberts, LD |
| Antoinette Sandbach, C. | Llyr Huws Griffiths, PC |

SOUTH WALES CENTRAL
E. 506,293  T. 208,333 (41.15%)

| | | |
|---|---|---|
| Lab. | 85,445 | (41.0%) |
| C. | 45,751 | (22.0%) |
| PC | 28,606 | (13.7%) |
| LD | 16,514 | (7.9%) |
| Green | 10,774 | (5.2%) |
| UKIP | 8,292 | (4.0%) |
| Soc. Lab. | 4,690 | (2.3%) |
| BNP | 3,805 | (1.8%) |
| Welsh Christian Party | 1,873 | (0.9%) |
| Loony | 1,237 | (0.6%) |
| TUSC | 830 | (0.4%) |
| Comm. Brit. | 516 | (0.2%) |

Lab. majority 39,694 (19.05%)
6.55% swing LD to C. (2007 Lab. majority 25,652)

ADDITIONAL MEMBERS

| | |
|---|---|
| David Melding, C. | Leanne Wood, PC |
| Andrew Davies, C. | John Dixon, LD |

SOUTH WALES EAST
E. 469,486  T. 181,024 (38.56%)

| | | |
|---|---|---|
| Lab. | 82,699 | (45.7%) |
| C. | 35,459 | (19.6%) |
| PC | 21,851 | (12.1%) |
| LD | 10,798 | (6.0%) |
| UKIP | 9,526 | (5.3%) |
| BNP | 6,485 | (3.6%) |
| Green | 4,857 | (2.7%) |
| Soc. Lab. | 4,427 | (2.4%) |
| Welsh Christian Party | 2,441 | (1.3%) |
| Eng. Dem. | 1,904 | (1.1%) |
| Comm. Brit. | 578 | (0.3%) |

Lab. majority 47,240 (26.10%)
5.95% swing LD to Lab. (2007 Lab. majority 30,063)

ADDITIONAL MEMBERS

| | |
|---|---|
| William Graham, C. | Jocelyn Davies, PC |
| Mohammad Asghar, C. | Lindsay Whittle, PC |

SOUTH WALES WEST
E. 407,333  T. 154,381 (37.90%)

| | | |
|---|---|---|
| Lab. | 71,766 | (46.5%) |
| Con. | 27,457 | (17.8%) |
| PC | 21,258 | (13.8%) |
| LD | 10,683 | (6.9%) |
| UKIP | 6,619 | (4.3%) |
| Soc. Lab. | 5,057 | (3.3%) |
| BNP | 4,714 | (3.1%) |
| Green | 3,952 | (2.6%) |
| Welsh Christian Party | 1,602 | (1.0%) |
| TUSC | 809 | (0.5%) |
| Comm. Brit. | 464 | (0.3%) |

Lab. majority 44,309 (28.70%)
8.10% swing LD to Lab. (2007 Lab. majority 29,528)

ADDITIONAL MEMBERS

| | |
|---|---|
| Suzy Davies, C. | Peter Black, LD |
| Byron Davies, C. | Bethan Jenkins, PC |

# SCOTLAND

## SCOTTISH GOVERNMENT

Andrew's House, Regent Road, Edinburgh EH1 3DG
T 0300-244 4000
E ceu@scotland.gsi.gov.uk W www.gov.scot

The devolved government for Scotland is responsible for most of the issues of day-to-day concern to the people of Scotland, including health, education, justice, rural affairs and transport.

The Scottish government was known as the Scottish executive when it was established in 1999, following the first elections to the Scottish parliament. There has been a majority Scottish National Party administration since the elections in May 2011.

The government is led by a first minister who is nominated by the parliament and in turn appoints the other Scottish ministers who make up the cabinet.

Civil servants in Scotland are accountable to Scottish ministers, who are themselves accountable to the Scottish parliament.

### CABINET

*First Minister,* Rt. Hon. Nicola Sturgeon, MSP
*Deputy First Minister and Cabinet Secretary for Finance, Constitution and Economy,* John Swinney, MSP
*Cabinet Secretary for Infrastructure, Investment and Cities,* Keith Brown, MSP
*Cabinet Secretary for Culture, Europe and External Affairs,* Fiona Hyslop, MSP
*Cabinet Secretary for Education and Lifelong Learning,* Angela Constance, MSP
*Cabinet Secretary for Health and Wellbeing,* Shona Robison, MSP
*Cabinet Secretary for Rural Affairs and the Environment,* Richard Lochhead, MSP
*Cabinet Secretary for Justice,* Michael Matheson, MSP
*Cabinet Secretary for Social Justice, Communities and Pensioners' Rights,* Angela Constance, MSP
*Cabinet Secretary for Fair Work, Skills and Training,* Roseanna Cunningham
*Minister for Children and Young People,* Aileen Campbell, MSP
*Minister for Community Safety and Legal Affairs,* Paul Wheelhouse, MSP
*Minister for Business, Energy, and Tourism,* Fergus Ewing, MSP
*Minister for Environment, Climate Change and Land Reform,* Aileen McLeod, MSP
*Minister for Europe and International Development,* Humza Yousaf, MSP
*Minister for Housing and Welfare,* Margaret Burgess, MSP
*Minister for Learning, Science and Scotland's Languages,* Alasdair Allan, MSP
*Minister for Local Government and Community Empowerment,* Marco Biagi, MSP
*Minister for Parliamentary Business,* Joe Fitzpatrick, MSP
*Minister for Public Health,* Maureen Watt, MSP
*Minister for Transport and Islands,* Derek Mackay, MSP
*Minister for Youth and Women's Employment,* Annabelle Ewing, MSP
*Minister for Sport and Health Improvement,* Jamies Hepburn, MSP

### LAW OFFICERS

*Lord Advocate,* Frank Mulholland, QC
*Solicitor-General for Scotland,* Lesley Thomson

## STRATEGIC BOARD

*Permanent Secretary,* Leslie Evans
*Director-General Communities,* Sarah Davidson
*Director-General, Enterprise, Environment and Digital,* Graeme Dickson
*Director-General, Finance,* Alyson Stafford
*Director-General, Health and Social Care,* Paul Gray
*Director-General, Learning and Justice,* Paul Johnston
*Director-General, Strategy and External Affairs,* Ken Thomson

## GOVERNMENT DEPARTMENTS

### DIRECTOR-GENERAL ENTERPRISE, ENVIRONMENT AND INNOVATION

St Andrew's House, Edinburgh EH1 3DG
*Directorates:* Agriculture, Food and Rural Affairs; Chief Scientific Adviser for Rural Affairs and the Environment; Chief Economist; Economic Development; Energy and Climate Change; Environment and Forestry; Marine Scotland; Scottish Development International
*Director-General,* Graeme Dickson
*Executive Agencies*
Accountant in Bankruptcy
Drinking Water Quality Regulator
James Hutton Institute
Moredun Research Institute
Scottish Agricultural College
Transport Scotland
Waterwatch Scotland

### DIRECTOR-GENERAL FINANCE

Victoria Quay, Edinburgh EH6 6QQ
*Directorates:* Legal Services (Solicitor to the Scottish Government), Financial Management; Financial Strategy; Office of the Scottish Parliamentary Counsel; Scottish Procurement and Commercial; Internal Audit
*Director-General,* Alyson Stafford
*Executive Agencies*
Audit Scotland
Scottish Public Pensions Agency

### DIRECTOR-GENERAL COMMUNITIES

Saughton House, Broomhouse Drive, Edinburgh, EH11 3XD
*Directorates:* Digital; Housing, Regeneration and Welfare; Local Government and Communities
*Director-General,* Sarah Davidson
*Executive Agency*
Scottish Housing Regulator

### DIRECTOR-GENERAL HEALTH AND SOCIAL CARE

St Andrew's House, Regent Road, Edinburgh EH1 3DG
*Directorates:* Chief Medical Officer; Chief Nursing Officer; Children and Families; Finance, eHealth and Analytics; Health and Social Care Integration; Healthcare Quality and Strategy; Office of the Director-General Health and Social Care and Chief Executive NHS Scotland; Performance and Delivery; Population Health Improvement
*Director-General Health and Social Care and Chief Executive NHS Scotland,* Paul Gray
*Executive Agencies*
Disclosure Scotland
Scottish Children's Reporters Administration

### DIRECTOR-GENERAL LEARNING AND JUSTICE

St Andrew's House, Edinburgh EH1 3DG

*Directorates:* Advance Learning and Science; Education Analytical Services; Fair Work; Justice; Learning; Safer Communities
*Director-General,* Paul Johnston
*Executive Agencies*
Education Scotland
HM Chief Inspector of Prosecution in Scotland
HM Inspectorate of Constabulary
HM Inspectorate of Prisons
Inspectorate of Prosecution in Scotland
Justices of the Peace Advisory Committee
Scottish Prison Service
Student Awards Agency for Scotland
Visiting Committees for Scottish Penal Establishments

DIRECTOR-GENERAL STRATEGY AND EXTERNAL AFFAIRS
St Andrew's House, Edinburgh EH1 3DG
*Directorates:* Communications and Ministerial Support; Culture, Europe and External Affairs; People; Strategy and Constitution
*Executive Agency*
Historic Scotland

NON-MINISTERIAL DEPARTMENTS

FOOD STANDARDS SCOTLAND
Pilgrim House, Old Ford Road, Aberdeen AB11 5RL
T 01224-285100
*Chief Executive,* Geoff Ogle

NATIONAL RECORDS OF SCOTLAND
General Register House, 2 Princes Street, Edinburgh EH1 3YY
T 0131-535 1314 W www.nationalrecordsofscotland.gov.uk
*Registrar General and Keeper of the Records of Scotland,* Tim Ellis

OFFICE OF THE SCOTTISH CHARITY REGULATOR
2nd Floor, Quadrant House, 9 Riverside Drive, Dundee DD1 4NY
T 01382-220446 W www.oscr.org.uk
*Chief Executive,* David Robb

REGISTERS OF SCOTLAND
Meadowbank House, 153 London Road, Edinburgh, Midlothian EH8 7AU T 0845-607 0161 W www.ros.gov.uk
*Keeper,* Sheenagh Adams

REVENUE SCOTLAND
PO Box 24068, Victoria Quay, Edinburgh EH6 9BR
T 0300-020 0310 W www.revenue.scot
*Chief Executive,* Eleanor Emberson

SCOTTISH COURTS AND TRIBUNALS SERVICE
Saughton House, Broomhouse Drive, Edinburgh EH11 3XD
T 0131-444 3352 W www.scotcourts.gov.uk
*Chief Executive,* Eric McQueen

SCOTTISH HOUSING REGULATOR
Highlander House, 58 Waterloo Street, Glasgow G2 7DA
T 0141-271 3810 W www.scottishhousingregulator.gov.uk
*Chief Executive,* Michael Cameron

## SCOTTISH PARLIAMENT
Edinburgh EH99 1SP
T 0131-348 5000/ 0800-092 7500
E sp.info@scottish.parliament.uk
W www.scottish.parliament.uk

In July 1997 the government announced plans to establish a Scottish parliament. In a referendum on 11 September 1997 about 60 per cent of the electorate voted. Of those who voted, 74.3 per cent voted in favour of the parliament and 63.5 per cent voted in support of granting the parliament

having tax-raising powers. Elections are normally held every four years, but the current session is scheduled to last five years in order to avoid it falling at the same time as the UK General Election 2015. The first elections were held on 6 May 1999, when around 59 per cent of the electorate voted. The first meeting was held on 12 May 1999 and the Scottish parliament was officially opened on 1 July 1999 at the Assembly Hall, Edinburgh. A new building to house the parliament was opened, in the presence of the Queen, at Holyrood on 9 October 2004. On 5 May 2011 the fourth elections to the Scottish parliament took place.

The Scottish parliament normally 129 members (including the presiding officer), comprising 73 constituency members and 56 additional regional members, mainly from party lists. There are currently 128 members –until the Scottish parliament elections in May 2016 – following the death of Margo MacDonald, who was an independent regional MSP, in 2014. It can introduce primary legislation and has the power to raise or lower the basic rate of income tax by up to three pence in the pound. Members of the Scottish parliament are elected using the additional member system, the same system used to elect London Assembly and Welsh Assembly members.

The areas for which the Scottish parliament is responsible include: civil and criminal justice; education; health; environment; economic development; local government; housing; police; fire services; planning; financial assistance to industry; tourism; heritage and the arts; agriculture; social work; sports; public registers and records; forestry; food standards; and some aspects of transport.

| SALARIES *as at 1 April 2015* | |
| --- | --- |
| First Minister* | £85,598 |
| Cabinet Secretary | £44,406 |
| Lord Advocate* | £58,013 |
| Solicitor-General for Scotland* | £41,951 |
| Minister* | £27,816 |
| MSP† | £59,089 |
| Presiding Officer* | £44,406 |
| Deputy Presiding Officer* | £27,816 |

* In addition to the MSP salary
† Reduced by two-thirds if the member is also an MP or an MEP

## MEMBERS OF THE SCOTTISH PARLIAMENT
*as at 1 September 2015*
**Adam**, George, *SNP, Paisley,* Maj. 248
**Adamson**, Clare, *SNP, Central Scotland region*
**Allan**, Alasdair, *SNP, Na h-Eileanan an Iar,* Maj. 4,772
**Allard**, Christian, *SNP, North East Scotland region*
**Baillie**, Jackie, *Lab., Dumbarton,* Maj. 1,639
**Baker**, Claire, *Lab., Mid Scotland and Fife region*
**Baker**, Richard, *Lab., North East Scotland region*
**Baxter**, Jayne, *Lab., Mid Scotland and Fife region*
**Beamish**, Claudia, *Lab., South Scotland region*
**Beattie**, Colin, *SNP, Midlothian North and Musselburgh,* Maj. 2,996
**Biagi**, Marco, *SNP, Edinburgh Central,* Maj. 237
**Bibby**, Neil, *Lab., West Scotland region*
**Boyack**, Sarah, *Lab., Lothian region*
**Brodie**, Chic, *SNP, South Scotland region*
**Brown**, Gavin, *C., Lothian region*
**Brown**, Keith, *SNP, Clackmannanshire and Dunblane,* Maj. 3,609
**Buchanan**, Cameron, *C., Lothian region*
**Burgess**, Margaret, *SNP, Cunninghame South,* Maj. 2,348
**Campbell**, Aileen, *SNP, Clydesdale,* Maj. 4,216
**Campbell**, Roderick, *SNP, North East Fife,* Maj. 2,592
**Carlaw**, Jackson, *C., West Scotland region*

**Chisholm**, Malcolm, *Lab., Edinburgh Northern and Leith,* Maj. 595

**Coffey**, Willie, *SNP, Kilmarnock and Irvine Valley,* Maj. 5,993

**Constance**, Angela, *SNP, Almond Valley,* Maj. 5,542

**Crawford**, Bruce, *SNP, Stirling,* Maj. 5,671

**Cunningham**, Roseanna, *SNP, Perthshire South and Kinross-shire,* Maj. 7,166

**Davidson**, Ruth, *C., Glasgow region*

**Dey**, Graeme, *SNP, Angus South,* Maj. 10,583

**Don**, Nigel, *SNP, Angus North and Mearns,* Maj. 7,286

**Doris**, Bob, *SNP, Glasgow region*

**Dornan**, James, *SNP, Glasgow Cathcart,* Maj. 1,592

**Dugdale**, Kezia, *Lab., Lothian region*

**Eadie**, Jim, *SNP, Edinburgh Southern,* Maj. 693

**Ewing**, Annabelle, *SNP, Mid Scotland and Fife region*

**Ewing**, Fergus, *SNP, Inverness and Nairn,* Maj. 9,745

**Fabiani**, Linda, *SNP, East Kilbride,* Maj. 1,949

**Fee**, Mary, *Lab., West Scotland region*

**Ferguson**, Patricia, *Lab., Glasgow Maryhill and Springburn,* Maj. 1,252

**Fergusson**, Rt. Hon. Alex, *C., Galloway and West Dumfries,* Maj. 862

**Findlay**, Neil, *Lab., Lothian region*

**Finnie**, John, *Ind., Highlands and Islands region*

**FitzPatrick**, Joe, *SNP, Dundee City West,* Maj. 6,405

**Fraser**, Murdo, *C., Mid Scotland and Fife region*

**Gibson**, Kenneth, *SNP, Cunninghame North,* Maj. 6,117

**Gibson**, Rob, *SNP, Caithness, Sutherland and Ross,* Maj. 7,458

**Goldie**, Baroness, *C., West Scotland region*

**Grahame**, Christine, *SNP, Midlothian South, Tweeddale and Lauderdale,* Maj. 4,924

**Grant**, Rhoda, *Lab., Highlands and Islands region*

**Gray**, Iain, *Lab., East Lothian,* Maj. 151

**Griffin**, Mark, *Lab., Central Scotland region*

**Harvie**, Patrick, *Green, Glasgow region*

**Henry**, Hugh, *Lab., Renfrewshire South,* Maj. 2,577

**Hepburn**, Jamie, *SNP, Cumbernauld and Kilsyth,* Maj. 3,459

**Hilton**, Cara, *Lab., Dunfermline,* Maj. 2,873

**Hume**, Jim, *LD, South Scotland region*

**Hyslop**, Fiona, *SNP, Linlithgow,* Maj. 4,091

**Ingram**, Adam, *SNP, Carrick, Cumnock and Doon Valley,* Maj. 2,581

**Johnstone**, Alex, *C., North East Scotland region*

**Johnstone**, Alison, *Green, Lothian region*

**Keir**, Colin, *SNP, Edinburgh West,* Maj. 2,689

**Kelly**, James, *Lab., Rutherglen,* Maj. 1,779

**Kidd**, Bill, *SNP, Glasgow Anniesland,* Maj. 7

**Lamont**, Johann, *Lab., Glasgow Pollok,* Maj. 623

**Lamont**, John, *C., Ettrick, Roxburgh and Berwickshire,* Maj. 5,334

**Lochhead**, Richard, *SNP, Moray,* Maj. 10,944

**Lyle**, Richard, *SNP, Central Scotland region*

**McAlpine**, Joan, *SNP, South Scotland region*

**McArthur**, Liam, *LD, Orkney,* Maj. 860

**MacAskill**, Kenny, *SNP, Edinburgh Eastern,* Maj. 2,233

**McCulloch**, Margaret, *Lab., Central Scotland region*

**MacDonald**, Angus, *SNP, Falkirk East,* Maj. 3,535

**MacDonald**, Gordon, *SNP, Edinburgh Pentlands,* Maj. 1,758

**Macdonald**, Lewis, *Lab., North East Scotland region*

**McDonald**, Mark, *SNP, Aberdeen Donside,* Maj. 2,025

**McDougall**, Margaret, *Lab., West Scotland region*

**McGrigor**, Jamie, *C., Highlands and Islands region*

**McInnes**, Alison, *LD, North East Scotland region*

**Macintosh**, Ken, *Lab., Eastwood,* Maj. 2,012

**Mackay**, Derek, *SNP Renfrewshire North and West,* Maj. 1,564

**McKelvie**, Christina, *SNP, Hamilton, Larkhall and Stonehouse,* Maj. 2,213

**MacKenzie**, Mike, *SNP, Highlands and Islands region*

**McLeod**, Aileen, *SNP, South Scotland region*

**McLeod**, Fiona, *SNP, Strathkelvin and Bearsden,* Maj. 1,802

**McMahon**, Michael, *Lab., Uddingston and Bellshill,* Maj. 714

**McMahon**, Siobhan, *Lab., Central Scotland region*

**McMillan**, Stuart, *SNP, West Scotland region*

**McNeil**, Duncan, *Lab., Greenock and Inverclyde,* Maj. 511

**McTaggart**, Anne, *Lab., Glasgow region*

**Malik**, Hanzala, *Lab., Glasgow region*

**Marra**, Jenny, *Lab., North East Scotland region*

**Martin**, Paul, *Lab., Glasgow Provan,* Maj. 2,079

**Marwick**, Rt. Hon. Tricia, *SNP, Mid Fife and Glenrothes,* Maj. 4,188

**Mason**, John, *SNP, Glasgow Shettleston,* Maj. 586

**Matheson**, Michael, *SNP, Falkirk West,* Maj. 5,745

**Maxwell**, Stewart, *SNP, West Scotland region*

**Milne**, Nanette, *C., North East Scotland region*

**Mitchell**, Margaret, *C., Central Scotland region*

**Murray**, Elaine, *Lab., Dumfriesshire,* Maj. 3,156

**Neil**, Alex, *SNP, Airdrie and Shotts,* Maj. 2,001

**Paterson**, Gil, *SNP, Clydebank and Milngavie,* Maj. 714

**Pearson**, Graeme, *Lab, South Scotland region*

**Pentland**, John, *Lab., Motherwell and Wishaw,* Maj. 587

**Rennie**, Willie, *LD, Mid Scotland and Fife region*

**Robertson**, Dennis, *SNP, Aberdeenshire West,* Maj. 4,112

**Robison**, Shona, *SNP, Dundee City East,* Maj. 10,679

**Rowley**, Alex, *Lab., Cowdenbeath,* Maj. 5,488

**Russell**, Michael, *SNP, Argyll and Bute,* Maj. 8,543

**Salmond**, Rt. Hon. Alex, *SNP, Aberdeenshire East,* Maj. 15,295

**Scanlon**, Mary, *C., Highlands and Islands region*

**Scott**, John, *C., Ayr,* Maj. 1,113

**Scott**, Tavish, *LD, Shetland Islands,* Maj. 1,617

**Simpson**, Richard, *Lab., Mid Scotland and Fife region*

**Smith**, Drew, *Lab., Glasgow region*

**Smith**, Elaine, *Lab., Coatbridge and Chryston,* Maj. 2,741

**Smith**, Liz, *C., Mid Scotland and Fife region*

**Stevenson**, Stewart, *SNP, Banffshire and Buchan Coast,* Maj. 12,220

**Stewart**, David, *Lab., Highlands and Islands region*

**Stewart**, Kevin, *SNP, Aberdeen Central,* Maj. 617

**Sturgeon**, Nicola, *SNP, Glasgow Southside,* Maj. 4,349

**Swinney**, John, *SNP, Perthshire North,* Maj. 10,353

**Thompson**, Dave, *SNP, Skye, Lochaber and Badenoch* Maj. 4,995

**Torrance**, David, *SNP, Kirkcaldy,* Maj. 182

**Urquhart**, Jean, *Ind., Highlands and Islands region*

**Watt**, Maureen, *SNP, Aberdeen South and North Kincardine,* Maj. 6,323

**Wheelhouse**, Paul, *SNP, South Scotland region*

**White**, Sandra, *SNP, Glasgow Kelvin,* Maj. 882

**Wilson**, John, *Ind., Central Scotland region*

**Yousaf**, Humza, *SNP, Glasgow region*

## STATE OF THE PARTIES
*as at 1 September 2015*

| | Constituency MSPs | Regional MSPs | Total |
|---|---|---|---|
| Scottish National Party (SNP) | 51 | 13 | 64 |
| Scottish Labour Party (Lab.) | 16 | 22 | 38 |
| Scottish Conservative and Unionist Party (C.) | 3 | 12 | 15 |
| Scottish Liberal Democrats (LD) | 2 | 3 | 5 |
| Scottish Green Party (Green) | 0 | 2 | 2 |
| Independent (Ind.) | 0 | 3 | 3 |
| *Presiding Officer | 1 | 0 | 1 |
| Total | 73 | 55 | 128 |

*The presiding officer was elected as a constituency member for the SNP but has no party affiliation while in post

*The Presiding Officer,* Rt. Hon. Tricia Marwick, MSP
*Deputy Presiding Officers,* John Scott, MSP *(C.);* Elaine Smith, MSP *(Lab.)*

## SCOTTISH PARLIAMENT ELECTION RESULTS

*as at 5 May 2011*
Electorate (E.) 3,985,161 Turnout (T.) 50.4%
*See* General Election Results for a list of party abbreviations

**ABERDEEN CENTRAL**
*(Scotland North East Region)*
E. 57,396  T. 25,149 (43.82%)
| | |
|---|---|
| Kevin Stewart, SNP | 10,058 |
| Lewis Macdonald, Lab. | 9,441 |
| Sandy Wallace, C. | 3,100 |
| Sheila Thomson, LD | 2,349 |
| Mike Phillips, NF | 201 |
*SNP majority* 617 (2.45%)
0.54% swing Lab. to SNP

**ABERDEEN DONSIDE**
*(Scotland North East Region)*
E. 56,145  T. 26,761 (47.66%)
| | |
|---|---|
| Brian Adam, SNP | 14,790 |
| Barney Crockett, Lab. | 7,615 |
| Ross Thomson, C. | 2,166 |
| Millie McLeod, LD. | 1,606 |
| David Henderson, Ind. | 371 |
| Christopher Willett, NF | 213 |
*SNP majority* 7,175 (26.81%)
6.87% swing Lab. to SNP

**ABERDEEN SOUTH &
KINCARDINE NORTH**
*(Scotland North East Region)*
E. 54,338  T. 28,697 (52.81%)
| | |
|---|---|
| Maureen Watt, SNP | 11,947 |
| Greg Williams, Lab. | 5,624 |
| John Sleigh, LD | 4,994 |
| Stewart Whyte, C. | 4,058 |
*SNP majority* 6,323 (22.03%)
15.77% swing LD to SNP

**ABERDEENSHIRE EAST**
*(Scotland North East Region)*
E. 57,591  T. 30,286 (52.59%)
| | |
|---|---|
| Alex Salmond, SNP | 19,533 |
| Alison McInnes, LD | 4,238 |
| Geordie Burnett Stuart, C. | 4,211 |
| Peter Smyth, Lab. | 2,304 |
*SNP majority* 15,295 (50.5%)
19.53% swing LD to SNP

**ABERDEENSHIRE WEST**
*(Scotland North East Region)*
E. 53,779  T. 28,636 (53.25%)
| | |
|---|---|
| Dennis Robertson, SNP | 12,186 |
| Mike Rumbles, LD | 8,074 |
| Nanette Milne, C. | 6,027 |
| Jean Morrison, Lab. | 2,349 |
*SNP majority* 4,112 (14.36%)
13.45% swing LD to SNP

**AIRDRIE & SHOTTS**
*(Scotland Central Region)*
E. 51,336  T. 23,894 (46.54%)
| | |
|---|---|
| Alex Neil, SNP | 11,984 |
| Karen Whitefield, Lab. | 9,983 |
| Robert Crozier, C. | 1,396 |
| John Love, LD | 531 |
*SNP majority* 2,001 (8.37%)
5.50% swing Lab. to SNP

**ALMOND VALLEY**
*(Lothian Region)*
E. 59,896  T. 30,737 (51.32%)
| | |
|---|---|
| Angela Constance, SNP | 16,704 |
| Lawrence Fitzpatrick, Lab. | 11,162 |
| Andrew Hardie, C. | 1,886 |
| Emma Sykes, LD | 656 |
| Neil McIvor, NF | 329 |
*SNP majority* 5,542 (18.03%)
9.01% swing Lab. to SNP

**ANGUS NORTH & MEARNS**
*(Scotland North East Region)*
E. 52,124  T. 24,920 (47.81%)
| | |
|---|---|
| Nigel Don, SNP | 13,660 |
| Alex Johnstone, C. | 6,374 |
| Kevin Hutchens, Lab. | 3,160 |
| Sanjay Samani, LD | 1,726 |
*SNP majority* 7,286 (29.24%)
4.15% swing C. to SNP

**ANGUS SOUTH**
*(Scotland North East Region)*
E. 54,922  T. 27,643 (50.33%)
| | |
|---|---|
| Graeme Dey, SNP | 16,164 |
| Hughie Campbell Adamson, C. | 5,581 |
| William Campbell, Lab. | 3,703 |
| David Fairweather, AIR | 1,321 |
| Clive Sneddon, LD | 874 |
*SNP majority* 10,583 (38.28%)
9.31% swing C. to SNP

**ARGYLL & BUTE**
*(Highlands and Islands Region)*
E. 49,028  T. 26,476 (54.00%)
| | |
|---|---|
| Michael Russell, SNP | 13,390 |
| Jamie McGrigor, C. | 4,847 |
| Mick Rice, Lab. | 4,041 |
| Alison Hay, LD | 3,220 |
| George Doyle, Ind. | 542 |
| George White, Lib. | 436 |
*SNP majority* 8,543 (32.27%)
8.52% swing C. to SNP

**AYR**
*(Scotland South Region)*
E. 61,563  T. 33,373 (54.21%)
| | |
|---|---|
| John Scott, C. | 12,997 |
| Chic Brodie, SNP | 11,884 |
| Gordon McKenzie, Lab. | 7,779 |
| Eileen Taylor, LD | 713 |
*C. majority* 1,113 (3.34%)
5.16% swing C. to SNP

**BANFFSHIRE & BUCHAN COAST**
*(Scotland North East Region)*
E. 53,698  T. 25,004 (46.56%)
| | |
|---|---|
| Stewart Stevenson, SNP | 16,812 |
| Michael Watt, C. | 4,592 |
| Alan Duffill, Lab. | 2,642 |
| Galen Milne, LD | 958 |
*SNP majority* 12,220 (48.87%)
3.48% swing C. to SNP

**CAITHNESS, SUTHERLAND &
ROSS**
*(Highlands and Islands Region)*
E. 55,116  T. 28,600 (51.89%)
| | |
|---|---|
| Rob Gibson, SNP | 13,843 |
| Robbie Rowantree, LD | 6,385 |
| John MacKay, Lab. | 5,438 |
| Edward Mountain, C. | 2,934 |
*SNP majority* 7,458 (26.08%)
17.32% swing LD to SNP

**CARRICK, CUMNOCK &
DOON VALLEY**
*(Scotland South Region)*
E. 59,368  T. 28,703 (48.35%)
| | |
|---|---|
| Adam Ingram, SNP | 13,250 |
| Richard Leonard, Lab. | 10,669 |
| Peter Kennerley, C. | 4,160 |
| Andrew Chamberlain, LD | 624 |
*SNP majority* 2,581 (8.99%)
11.77% swing Lab. to SNP

**CLACKMANNANSHIRE &
DUNBLANE**
*(Mid Scotland and Fife Region)*
E. 49,415  T. 27,416 (55.48%)
| | |
|---|---|
| Keith Brown, SNP | 13,253 |
| Richard Simpson, Lab. | 9,644 |
| Callum Campbell, C. | 3,501 |
| Tim Brett, LD | 1,018 |
*SNP majority* 3,609 (13.16%)
5.20% swing Lab. to SNP

**CLYDEBANK & MILNGAVIE**
*(Scotland West Region)*
E. 53,018  T. 28,369 (53.51%)
| | |
|---|---|
| Gils Paterson, SNP | 12,278 |
| Des McNulty, Lab. | 11,564 |
| Alice Struthers, C. | 2,758 |
| John Duncan, LD | 1,769 |
*SD majority* 714 (2.52%)
6.56% swing Lab. to SNP

**CLYDESDALE**
*(Scotland South Region)*
E. 56,828  T. 29,937 (52.68%)
| | |
|---|---|
| Aileen Campbell, SNP | 14,931 |
| Karen Gillon, Lab. | 10,715 |
| Colin McGavigan, C. | 4,291 |
*SNP majority* 4,216 (14.08%)
8.89% swing Lab. to SNP

**COATBRIDGE & CHRYSTON**
*(Scotland Central Region)*
E. 51,206  T. 23,279 (45.46%)
| | |
|---|---|
| Elaine Smith, Lab. | 12,161 |
| John Wilson, SNP | 9,420 |
| Jason Lingiah, C. | 1,317 |
| Rod Ackland, LD | 381 |
*Lab. majority* 2,741 (11.77%)
3.28% swing Lab. to SNP

COWDENBEATH
*(Mid Scotland and Fife Region)*
E. 54,284  T. 25,670 (47.29%)
Helen Eadie, Lab.                    11,926
Ian Chisholm, SNP                    10,679
Belinda Don, C.                       1,792
Keith Legg, LD                          997
Mike Heenan, Land Party                 276
*Lab. majority* 1,247 (4.86%)
4.85% swing Lab. to SNP

CUMBERNAULD & KILSYTH
*(Scotland Central Region)*
E. 48,006  T. 25,254 (52.61%)
Jamie Hepburn, SNP                   13,595
Cathie Craigie, Lab.                 10,136
James Boswell, C.                     1,156
Martin Oliver, LD                       367
*SNP majority* 3,459 (13.7%)
10.79% Lab. to SNP

CUNNINGHAME NORTH
*(Scotland West Region)*
E. 56,548  T. 29,536 (52.23%)
Kenneth Gibson, SNP                  15,539
Allan Wilson, Lab.                    9,422
Maurice Golden, C.                    4,032
Mallika Punukollu, LD                   543
*SNP majority* 6,117 (20.71%)
10.29% swing Lab. to SNP

CUNNINGHAME SOUTH
*(Scotland South Region)*
E. 50,926  T. 22,056 (43.31%)
Margaret Burgess, SNP                10,993
Irene Oldfather, Lab.                 8,645
Alistair Haw, C.                      1,871
Ruby Kirkwood, LD                       547
*SNP majority* 2,348 (10.65%)
9.93% swing Lab. to SNP

DUMBARTON
*(Scotland West Region)*
E. 53,470  T. 28,508 (53.32%)
Jackie Baillie, Lab.                 12,562
Iain Robertson, SNP                  10,923
Graham Smith, C.                      3,395
Helen Watt, LD                          858
George Rice, Ind.                       770
*Lab. majority* 1,639 (5.75%)
0.24% swing SNP to Lab.

DUMFRIESSHIRE
*(Scotland South Region)*
E. 59,716  T. 31,895 (53.41%)
Elaine Murray, Lab.                  12,624
Gill Dykes, C.                        9,468
Aileen Orr, SNP                       8,384
Richard Brodie, LD                    1,419
*Lab. majority* 3,156 (9.89%)
5.99% swing C. to Lab.

DUNDEE EAST
*(Scotland North East Region)*
E. 54,404  T. 25,753 (47.34%)
Shona Robison, SNP                   16,541
Mohammed Asif, Lab.                   5,862
Brian Docherty, C.                    2,550
Allan Petrie, LD                        800
*SNP majority* 10,679 (41.47%)
12.47% swing Lab. to SNP

DUNDEE WEST
*(Scotland North East Region)*
E. 53,841  T. 24,461 (45.43%)
Joe Fitzpatrick, SNP                 14,089
Richard McCready, Lab.                7,684
Colin Stewart, C.                     1,625
Alison Burns, LD                      1,063
*SNP majority* 6,405 (26.18%)
8.88% swing Lab. to SNP

DUNFERMLINE
*(Scotland Mid and Fife Region)*
E. 55,479  T. 29,299 (52.81%)
Bill Walker, SNP                     11,010
Alex Rowley, Lab.                    10,420
Jim Tolson, LD                        5,776
James Reekie, C.                      2,093
*SNP majority* 599 (2.01%)
13.41% swing LD to SNP

EAST KILBRIDE
*(Scotland Central Region)*
E. 58,251  T. 29,911 (51.35%)
Linda Fabiani, SNP                   14,359
Andy Kerr, Lab.                      12,410
Graham Simpson, C.                    2,260
Douglas Herbison, LD                    468
John Houston, Ind.                      414
*SNP majority* 1,949 (6.52%)
6.64% swing Lab. to SNP

EAST LOTHIAN
*(Scotland South Region)*
E. 56,333  T. 32,177 (57.12%)
Iain Gray, Lab.                      12,536
David Berry, SNP                     12,385
Derek Brownlee, C.                    5,344
Ettie Spencer, LD                     1,912
*Lab. majority* 151 (0.47%)
3.12% swing Lab to SNP

EASTWOOD
*(Scotland West Region)*
E. 50,476  T. 31,924 (63.25%)
Ken Macintosh, Lab.                  12,662
Jackson Carlaw, C.                   10,650
Stewart Maxwell, SNP                  7,777
Gordon Cochrane, LD                     835
*Lab. majority* 2,012 (6.3%)
8.74% swing C. to Lab.

EDINBURGH CENTRAL
*(Lothian Region)*
E. 53,606  T. 29,014 (54.12%)
Marco Biagi, SNP                      9,480
Sarah Boyack, Lab.                    9,243
Alex Cole-Hamilton, LD                5,937
Iain McGill, C.                       4,354
*SNP majority* 237 (0.82%)
10.16% swing Lab. to SNP

EDINBURGH EASTERN
*(Lothian Region)*
E. 55,773  T. 30,728 (55.09%)
Kenny MacAskill, SNP                 14,552
Ewan Aitken, Lab.                    12,319
Cameron Buchanan, C.                  2,630
Martin Veart, LD                      1,227
*SNP majority* 2,233 (7.27%)
4.53% swing Lab. to SNP

EDINBURGH NORTHERN & LEITH
*(Lothian Region)*
E. 59,138  T. 30,885 (52.23%)
Malcolm Chisholm, Lab.               12,858
Shirley-Anne Somerville,
SNP                                  12,263
Sheila Low, C.                        2,928
Don Farthing, LD                      2,836
*Lab. majority* 595 (1.93%)
2.66% swing Lab. to SNP

EDINBURGH PENTLANDS
*(Lothian Region)*
E. 52,620  T. 30,049 (57.11%)
Gordon MacDonald, SNP                11,197
David McLetchie, C.                   9,439
Ricky Henderson, Lab.                 7,993
Simon Clark, LD                       1,420
*SNP majority* 1,758 (5.85%)
7.42% swing C. to SNP

EDINBURGH SOUTHERN
*(Lothian Region)*
E. 54,868  T. 33,796 (61.60%)
Jim Eadie, SNP                        9,947
Paul Godzik, Lab.                     9,254
Mike Pringle, LD                      8,297
Gavin Brown, C.                       6,298
*SNP majority* 693 (2.05%)
12.06% swing LD to SNP

EDINBURGH WESTERN
*(Lothian Region)*
E. 56,338  T. 33,452 (59.38%)
Colin Keir, SNP                      11,965
Margaret Smith, LD                    9,276
Lesley Hinds, Lab.                    7,164
Gordon Lindhurst, C.                  5,047
*SNP majority* 2,689 (8.04%)
12.60% swing LD to SNP

ETTRICK, ROXBURGH &
BERWICKSHIRE
*(Scotland South Region)*
E. 54,327  T. 28,816 (53.04%)
John Lamont, C.                      12,933
Paul Wheelhouse, SNP                  7,599
Euan Robson, LD                       4,990
Rab Stewart, Lab.                     2,986
Jesse Rae, Ind.                         308
*C. majority* 5,334 (18.51%)
1.39% swing C. to SNP

FALKIRK EAST
*(Scotland Central Region)*
E. 56,408  T. 28,168 (49.94%)
Angus MacDonald, SNP                 14,302
Cathy Peattie, Lab.                  10,767
Lynn Munro, C.                        2,372
Ross Laird, LD                          727
*SNP majority* 3,535 (12.55%)
9.33% swing Lab. to SNP

FALKIRK WEST
*(Scotland Central Region)*
E. 55,739  T. 28,199 (50.59%)

| | |
|---|---|
| Michael Matheson, SNP | 15,607 |
| Dennis Goldie, Lab. | 9,862 |
| Allan Finnie, C. | 2,086 |
| Callum Chomczuk, LD | 644 |

*SNP majority* 5,745 (20.37%)
8.91% swing Lab. to SNP

FIFE MID & GLENROTHES
*(Scotland Mid and Fife Region)*
E. 53,701  T. 26,313 (49.0%)

| | |
|---|---|
| Tricia Marwick, SNP | 13,761 |
| Claire Baker, Lab. | 9,573 |
| Allan Smith, C. | 1,676 |
| Jim Parker, ASPP | 673 |
| Callum Leslie, LD | 630 |

*SNP majority* 4,188 (15.92%)
3.43% swing Lab. to SNP

FIFE NORTH EAST
*(Scotland Mid and Fife Region)*
E. 58,858  T. 29,676 (50.42%)

| | |
|---|---|
| Roderick Campbell, SNP | 11,029 |
| Iain Smith, LD | 8,437 |
| Miles Briggs, C. | 5,618 |
| Colin Davidson, Lab. | 3,613 |
| Mike Scott-Hayward, UKIP | 979 |

*SNP majority* 2,592 (8.73%)
15.02% swing LD to SNP

GALLOWAY & WEST
DUMFRIES
*(Scotland South Region)*
E. 56,611  T. 29,997 (52.99%)

| | |
|---|---|
| Alex Fergusson, C. | 11,071 |
| Aileen McLeod, SNP | 10,209 |
| Willie Scobie, Lab. | 7,954 |
| Joe Rosiejak, LD | 763 |

*C. majority* 862 (2.87%)
2.40% swing C. to SNP

GLASGOW ANNIESLAND
*(Glasgow Region)*
E. 55,411  T. 23,918 (43.16%)

| | |
|---|---|
| Bill Kidd, SNP | 10,329 |
| Bill Butler, Lab. | 10,322 |
| Matthew Smith, C. | 2,011 |
| Paul McGarry, LD | 1,000 |
| Marc Livingstone, Comm. Brit. | 256 |

*SNP majority* 7 (0.03%)
10.09% swing Lab. to SNP

GLASGOW CATHCART
*(Glasgow Region)*
E. 58,525  T. 26,222 (44.8%)

| | |
|---|---|
| James Dornan, SNP | 11,918 |
| Charlie Gordon, Lab. | 10,326 |
| Richard Sullivan, C. | 2,410 |
| Eileen Baxendale, LD | 1,118 |
| John McKee, Ind. | 450 |

*SNP majority* 1,592 (6.07%)
6.53% swing Lab. to SNP

GLASGOW KELVIN
*(Glasgow Region)*
E. 61,893  T. 24,548 (39.66%)

| | |
|---|---|
| Sandra White, SNP | 10,640 |
| Pauline McNeil, Lab. | 9,758 |
| Natalie McKee, LD | 1,900 |
| Ruth Davidson, C. | 1,845 |
| Tom Muirhead, Ind. | 405 |

*SNP majority* 882 (3.59%)
4.03% swing Lab. to SNP

GLASGOW MARYHILL &
SPRINGBURN
*(Glasgow Region)*
E. 56,622  T. 20,531 (36.26%)

| | |
|---|---|
| Patricia Ferguson, Lab. | 9,884 |
| Bob Doris, SNP | 8,592 |
| Stephanie Murray, C. | 1,222 |
| Sophie Bridger, LD | 833 |

*Lab. majority* 1,292 (6.29%)
5.43% swing Lab. to SNP

GLASGOW POLLOK
*(Glasgow Region)*
E. 58,429  T. 22,915 (39.22%)

| | |
|---|---|
| Johann Lamont, Lab. | 10,875 |
| Chris Stephens, SNP | 10,252 |
| Andrew Morrison, C. | 1,298 |
| Isabel Nelson, LD | 490 |

*Lab. majority* 623 (2.72%)
8.53% swing Lab. to SNP

GLASGOW PROVAN
*(Glasgow Region)*
E. 55,118  T. 19,185 (34.81%)

| | |
|---|---|
| Paul Martin, Lab. | 10,037 |
| Anne McLaughlin, SNP | 7,958 |
| Majid Hussain, C. | 777 |
| Michael O'Donnell, LD | 413 |

*Lab. majority* 2,079 (10.84%)
8.68% swing Lab. to SNP

GLASGOW SHETTLESTON
*(Glasgow Region)*
E. 55,874  T. 21,204 (37.95%)

| | |
|---|---|
| John Mason, SNP | 10,128 |
| Frank McAveety, Lab. | 9,542 |
| David Wilson, C. | 1,163 |
| Ruaraidh Dobson, LD | 371 |

*SNP majority* 586 (2.76%)
12.61% swing Lab. to SNP

GLASGOW SOUTHSIDE
*(Glasgow Region)*
E. 52,325  T. 22,608 (43.21%)

| | |
|---|---|
| Nicola Sturgeon, SNP | 12,306 |
| Stephen Curran, Lab. | 7,957 |
| David Meikle, C. | 1,733 |
| Kenneth Elder, LD | 612 |

*SNP majority* 4,349 (19.24%)
9.68% swing Lab. to SNP

GREENOCK & INVERCLYDE
*(Scotland West Region)*
E. 56,989  T. 28,298 (49.50%)

| | |
|---|---|
| Duncan McNeil, Lab. | 12,387 |
| Stuart McMillan, SNP | 11,876 |
| Graeme Brooks, C. | 2,011 |
| Ross Finnie, LD | 1,934 |

*Lab. majority* 511 (1.81%)
6.90% swing Lab. to SNP

HAMILTON, LARKHALL &
STONEHOUSE
*(Scotland Central Region)*
E. 56,123  T. 25,354 (45.18%)

| | |
|---|---|
| Christina McKelvie, SNP | 12,202 |
| Tom McCabe, Lab. | 9,989 |
| Margaret Mitchell, C. | 2,547 |
| Ewan Hoyle, LD | 616 |

*SNP majority* 2,213 (8.73%)
10.99% swing Lab. to SNP

INVERNESS & NAIRN
*(Highlands and Islands Region)*
E. 62,168  T. 32,731 (52.65%)

| | |
|---|---|
| Fergus Ewing, SNP | 16,870 |
| David Stewart, Lab. | 7,125 |
| Mary Scanlon, C. | 3,797 |
| Christine Jardine, LD | 3,763 |
| Donald Boyd, Christian Party | 646 |
| Ross Durance, UKIP | 530 |

*SNP majority* 9,745 (29.77%)
4.85% swing Lab. to SNP

KILMARNOCK & IRVINE VALLEY
*(Scotland Central Region)*
E. 63,257  T. 31,858 (50.36%)

| | |
|---|---|
| Willie Coffey, SNP | 16,964 |
| Matt McLaughlin, Lab. | 10,971 |
| Grant Fergusson, C. | 3,309 |
| Robbie Simpson, LD | 614 |

*SNP majority* 5,993 (18.81%)
7.40% swing Lab. to SNP

KIRKCALDY
*(Scotland Mid and Fife Region)*
E. 60,079  T. 27,803 (46.28%)

| | |
|---|---|
| David Torrance, SNP | 12,579 |
| Marilyn Livingstone, Lab. | 12,397 |
| Ian McFarlane, C. | 2,007 |
| John Mainland, LD | 820 |

*SNP majority* 182 (0.65%)
6.19% swing Lab. to SNP

LINLITHGOW
*(Lothian Region)*
E. 65,025  T. 34,182 (52.57%)

| | |
|---|---|
| Fiona Hyslop, SNP | 17,027 |
| Mary Mulligan, Lab. | 12,936 |
| Christopher Donnelly, C. | 2,646 |
| Jennifer Lang, LD | 1,015 |
| Mike Coyle, NF | 558 |

*SNP majority* 4,091 (11.97%)
6.42% swing Lab. to SNP

MIDLOTHIAN NORTH &
MUSSELBURGH
*(Lothian Region)*
E. 58,246  T. 29,818 (51.19%)
Colin Beattie, SNP             14,079
Bernard Harkins, Lab.          11,083
Scott Douglas, C.               2,541
Ian Younger, LD                 1,254
Alan Hay, Ind.                    861
*SNP majority* 2,996 (10.05%)
7.61% swing Lab. to SNP

MIDLOTHIAN SOUTH,
TWEEDDALE & LAUDERDALE
*(Lothian Region)*
E. 57,781  T. 31,841 (55.11%)
Christine Grahame, SNP         13,855
Jeremy Purvis, LD               8,931
Ian Miller, Lab.                5,312
Peter Duncan, C.                3,743
*SNP majority* 4,924 (15.46%)
5.87% swing LD to SNP

MORAY
*(Highlands and Islands Region)*
E. 56,215  T. 28,596 (50.87%)
Richard Lochhead, SNP          16,817
Douglas Ross, C.                5,873
Kieron Green, Lab.              3,580
Jamie Paterson, LD              1,327
Donald Gatt, UKIP                 999
*SNP majority* 10,944 (38.27%)
6.19% swing C. to SNP

MOTHERWELL & WISHAW
*(Scotland Central Region)*
E. 53,610  T. 24,451 (45.61%)
John Pentland, Lab.            10,713
Clare Adamson, SNP             10,126
Bob Burgess, C.                 1,753
John Swinburne, ASPP              945
Tom Selfridge, Christian          547
Party
Beverley Hope, LD                367
*Lab. majority* 587 (2.4%)
10.20% swing Lab. to SNP

NA H-EILEANAN AN IAR
*(Highlands and Islands Region)*
E. 21,834  T. 13,011 (59.59%)
Alasdair Allan, SNP             8,496
Donald Crichton, Lab.           3,724
Charlie McGrigor, C.              563
Peter Morrison, LD               228
*SNP majority* 4,772 (36.68%)
15.82% swing Lab. to SNP

ORKNEY
*(Highlands and Islands Region)*
E. 16,393  T. 8,152 (49.73%)
Liam McArthur, LD               2,912
James Stockan, Ind.             2,052
George Adam, SNP                2,044
Jamie Halcro Johnston, C.         686
William Sharkey, Lab.             458
*LD majority* 860 (10.55%)
17.70% swing LD to Ind.

PAISLEY
*(Scotland West Region)*
E. 52,066  T. 25,590 (49.15%)
George Adam, SNP               10,913
Evan Williams, Lab.            10,665
Malcolm MacAskill, C.           2,229
Eileen McCartin, LD             1,783
*SNP majority* 248 (0.97%)
7.80% swing Lab. to SNP

PERTHSHIRE NORTH
*(Scotland and Mid Fife Region)*
E. 53,412  T. 29,953 (56.08%)
John Swinney, SNP              18,219
Murdo Fraser, C.                7,866
Pete Cheema, Lab.               2,672
Victor Clements, LD             1,196
*SNP majority* 10,353 (34.56%)
6.53% swing C. to SNP

PERTHSHIRE SOUTH &
KINROSS-SHIRE
*(Scotland and Mid Fife Region)*
E. 58,093  T. 31,216 (53.73%)
Roseanna Cunningham, SNP       16,073
Liz Smith, C.                   8,907
Tricia Duncan, Lab.             3,980
Willie Robertson, LD            2,256
*SNP majority* 7,166 (22.96%)
9.25% swing C. to SNP

RENFREWSHIRE NORTH & WEST
*(Scotland West Region)*
E. 49,060  T. 27,495 (56.04%)
Derek Mackay, SNP              11,510
Stuart Clark, Lab.              9,946
Annabel Goldie, C.              5,489
Andrew Page, LD                  550
*SNP majority* 1,564 (5.69%)
8.42% swing Lab. to SNP

RENFREWSHIRE SOUTH
*(Scotland West Region)*
E. 50,221  T. 26,908 (53.58%)
Hugh Henry, Lab.               12,933
Andrew Doig, SNP               10,356
Alistair Campbell, C.           2,917
Gordon Anderson, LD              702
*Lab. majority* 2,577 (9.58%)
5.41% swing Lab. to SNP

RUTHERGLEN
*(Glasgow Region)*
E. 57,777  T. 27,122 (46.94%)
James Kelly, Lab.              12,489
Jim McGuigan, SNP              10,710
Martyn McIntyre, C.             2,096
Lisa Strachan, LD               1,174
Caroline Johnstone, Ind.          633
*Lab. majority* 1,779 (6.56%)
7.43% swing Lab. to SNP

SHETLAND ISLANDS
*(Highlands and Islands Region)*
E. 17,505  T. 9,391 (53.65%)
Tavish Scott, LD                4,462
Billy Fox, Ind.                 2,845
Jean Urquhart, SNP              1,134
Jamie Kerr, Lab.                  620
Sandy Cross, C.                   330
*LD majority* 1,617 (17.22%)
5.5% swing LD to Ind.

SKYE, LOCHABER & BADENOCH
*(Highlands and Islands Region)*
E. 57,024  T. 31,915 (55.97%)
Dave Thompson, SNP             14,737
Alan MacRae, LD                 9,742
Linda Stewart, Lab.             4,112
Kerensa Carr, C.                2,834
Ronnie Campbell, Ind.             490
*SNP majority* 4,995 (15.65%)
12.97% swing LD to SNP

STIRLING
*(Scotland and Mid Fife Region)*
E. 51,458  T. 30,406 (59.09%)
Bruce Crawford, SNP            14,859
John Hendry, Lab.               9,188
Neil Benny, C.                  4,610
Graham Reed, LD                 1,296
Jack Black, Ind.                  454
*SNP majority* 5,671 (18.65%)
9.93% swing Lab. to SNP

STRATHKELVIN & BEARSDEN
*(Scotland West Region)*
E. 59,323  T. 33,752 (56.90%)
Fiona McLeod, SNP              14,258
David Whitton, Lab.            12,456
Jean Turner, Ind.               6,742
Stephanie Fraser, C.            4,438
Gordon Macdonald, LD            2,600
*SNP majority* 1,802 (5.34%)
7.69% swing Lab. to SNP

UDDINGSTON & BELLSHILL
*(Central Scotland Region)*
E. 55,584  T. 24,995 (44.97%)
Michael McMahon, Lab.          11,531
Richard Lyle, SNP              10,817
Mark Brown, C.                  2,117
Fraser Macgregor, LD              530
*Lab majority* 714 (2.86%)
9.04% swing Lab. to SNP

REGIONS
E. 3,985,161  T. 50.4%

GLASGOW
E. 514,393  T. 208,712 (40.57%)

| SNP | 83,109 | (39.8%) |
|---|---|---|
| Lab. | 73,031 | (35.0%) |
| C. | 12,749 | (6.1%) |
| Green | 12,454 | (6.0%) |
| Respect | 6,972 | (3.3%) |
| LD | 5,312 | (2.5%) |
| ASPP | 3,750 | (1.8%) |
| BNP | 2,424 | (1.2%) |
| Socialist Labour | 2,276 | (1.1%) |
| Christian Party | 1,501 | (0.7%) |
| Scottish Unionist Party | 1,447 | (0.7%) |
| SSP | 1,362 | (0.7%) |
| UKIP | 1,123 | (0.5%) |
| Pirate | 581 | (0.3%) |
| Ind. Johnstone | 338 | (0.2%) |
| SHP | 283 | (0.1%) |

Lab. majority 10,078 (4.83%)
8.04% swing Lab. to SNP (2007 Lab. majority 23,006)

ADDITIONAL MEMBERS
Humza Yousaf, SNP
Bob Doris, SNP
Hanzala Malik, Lab.
Drew Smith, Lab.
Anne McTaggert, Lab.
Ruth Davidson, C.
Patrick Harvie, Green

HIGHLANDS AND ISLANDS
E. 337,588  T. 179,010 (53.03%)

| SNP | 85,082 | (47.5%) |
|---|---|---|
| Lab. | 25,884 | (14.5%) |
| C. | 21,729 | (12.1%) |
| LD | 20,843 | (11.6%) |
| Green | 9,076 | (5.1%) |
| Christian Party | 3,541 | (2%) |
| UKIP | 3,372 | (1.9%) |
| ASPP | 2,770 | (1.5%) |
| Ban Bankers Bonuses | 1,764 | (1%) |
| Lib. | 1,696 | (0.9%) |
| Soc. Lab. | 1,406 | (0.8%) |
| BNP | 1,134 | (0.6%) |
| SSP | 509 | (0.3%) |
| Solidarity | 204 | (0.1%) |

SNP majority 59,198 (33.07%)
8.16% swing Lab. to SNP (2007 SNP majority 26,978)

ADDITIONAL MEMBERS
John Finnie, SNP
Jean Urquhart, SNP
Mike MacKenzie, SNP
Rhoda Grant, Lab.
David Stewart, Lab.
Jamie McGrigor, C.
Mary Scanlon, C.

LOTHIAN
E. 515,978  T. 283,203 (54.89%)

| SNP | 110,953 | (39.2%) |
|---|---|---|
| Lab. | 70,544 | (24.9%) |
| C. | 33,019 | (11.7%) |
| Green | 21,505 | (7.6%) |
| Ind. MacDonald | 18,732 | (6.6%) |
| LD | 15,588 | (5.5%) |
| ASPP | 3,218 | (1.1%) |
| BNP | 1,978 | (0.7%) |
| UKIP | 1,822 | (0.6%) |
| Soc. Lab. | 1,681 | (0.6%) |
| SSP | 1,183 | (0.4%) |
| Christian Party | 914 | (0.3%) |
| Lib. | 697 | (0.2%) |
| CPA | 553 | (0.2%) |
| Solidarity | 327 | (0.1%) |
| Ind. Hogg | 294 | (0.1%) |
| Ind. O'Neill | 134 | (0.1%) |
| Ind. Brown | 61 | (0.1%) |

SNP majority 40,409 (14.27%)
7.0% swing Lab. to SNP (2007 SNP majority 524)

ADDITIONAL MEMBERS
Sarah Boyack, Lab.
Kezia Dugdale, Lab.
Neil Findlay, Lab.
David McLetchie, C.
Gavin Brown, C.
Alison Johnstone, Green
Margo MacDonald, Ind.

SCOTLAND CENTRAL
E. 497,737  T. 233,560 (46.92%)

| SNP | 108,261 | (46.4%) |
|---|---|---|
| Lab. | 82,459 | (35.3%) |
| C. | 14,870 | (6.4%) |
| ASPP | 5,793 | (2.5%) |
| Green | 5,634 | (2.4%) |
| LD | 3,318 | (1.4%) |
| Christian Party | 3,173 | (1.4%) |
| Soci. Lab. | 2,483 | (1.1%) |
| BNP | 2,214 | (0.9%) |
| Scottish Unionist Party | 1,555 | (0.7%) |
| UKIP | 1,263 | (0.5%) |
| Ind. O'Donnell | 821 | (0.4%) |
| SSP | 820 | (0.4%) |
| Solidarity | 559 | (0.2%) |
| SHP | 337 | (0.1%) |

Lab. majority 25,802 (11.05%)
10.08% swing Lab. to SNP (2007 Lab. majority 23,386)

ADDITIONAL MEMBERS
Richard Lyle, SNP
John Wilson, SNP
Clare Adamson, SNP
Siobhan McMahon, Lab.
Mark Griffin, Lab.
Margaret McCulloch, Lab.
Margaret Mitchell, C.

SCOTLAND MID AND FIFE
E. 503,559  T. 258,163 (51.27%)

| | | |
|---|---|---|
| *SNP* | 116,691 | (45.2%) |
| *Lab.* | 64,623 | (25.0%) |
| *C.* | 36,458 | (14.1%) |
| *LD* | 15,103 | (5.9%) |
| *Green* | 10,914 | (4.2%) |
| *ASPP* | 4,113 | (1.6%) |
| *UKIP* | 2,838 | (1.1%) |
| *Soc. Lab.* | 1,771 | (0.7%) |
| *BNP* | 1,726 | (0.7%) |
| *Ind. Rodger* | 1,466 | (0.6%) |
| *SSP* | 834 | (0.3%) |
| *Christian Party* | 786 | (0.3%) |
| *CPA* | 638 | (0.2%) |
| *Solidarity* | 202 | (0.1%) |

*SNP majority* 52,068 (10.9%)
7.43% swing Lab. to SNP (2007 Lab. majority 18,168)

ADDITIONAL MEMBERS
Annabelle Ewing, *SNP*
John Park, *Lab.*
Claire Baker, *Lab.*
Richard Simpson, *Lab.*
Murdo Fraser, *C.*
Liz Smith, *C.*
Willie Rennie, *LD*

SCOTLAND NORTH EAST
E. 550,162  T. 267,045 (48.54%)

| | | |
|---|---|---|
| *SNP* | 140,749 | (52.7%) |
| *Lab.* | 43,893 | (16.4%) |
| *C.* | 37,681 | (14.1%) |
| *LD* | 18,178 | (6.8%) |
| *Green* | 10,407 | (3.9%) |
| *ASPP* | 4,420 | (1.7%) |
| *UKIP* | 2,477 | (0.9%) |
| *Christian Party* | 2,159 | (0.8%) |
| *BNP* | 1,925 | (0.7%) |
| *Soc. Lab.* | 1,459 | (0.5%) |
| *Ind. Cox* | 758 | (0.3%) |
| *NF* | 640 | (0.2%) |
| *AIR* | 471 | (0.2%) |
| *Solidarity* | 286 | (0.1%) |
| *Ind. Henderson* | 237 | (0.1%) |
| *Ind. McBride* | 190 | (0.1%) |

*SNP majority* 96,856 (36.27%)
7.68% swing Lab. to SNP (2007 SNP majority 53,140)

ADDITIONAL MEMBERS
Mark McDonald, *SNP*
Richard Baker, *Lab.*
Jenny Marra, *Lab.*
Lewis McDonald, *Lab.*
Alex Johnstone, *C.*
Nanette Milne, *C.*
Alison McInnes, *LD*

SCOTLAND SOUTH
E. 529,682  T. 278,987 (52.67%)

| | | |
|---|---|---|
| *SNP* | 114,270 | (41.0%) |
| *Lab.* | 70,595 | (25.3%) |
| *C.* | 54,352 | (19.5%) |
| *LD* | 15,096 | (5.4%) |
| *Green* | 8,656 | (3.1%) |
| *ASPP* | 4,418 | (1.6%) |
| *UKIP* | 3,243 | (1.2%) |
| *Soc. Lab.* | 2,906 | (1.0%) |
| *BNP* | 2,017 | (0.7%) |
| *Christian Party* | 1,924 | (0.7%) |
| *Solidarity* | 813 | (0.3%) |
| *SSP* | 697 | (0.2%) |

*SNP majority* 43,675 (15.66%)
7.95% swing Lab. to SNP (2007 Lab. majority 2,709)

ADDITIONAL MEMBERS
Joan McAlpine, *SNP*
Aileen McLeod, *SNP*
Paul Wheelhouse, *SNP*
Chic Brodie, *SNP*
Claudia Beamish, *Lab.*
Graeme Pearson, *Lab.*
Jim Hume, *LD*

SCOTLAND WEST
E. 536,062  T. 282,371 (52.68%)

| | | |
|---|---|---|
| *SNP* | 117,306 | (41.5%) |
| *Lab.* | 92,530 | (32.8%) |
| *C.* | 35,995 | (12.7%) |
| *LD* | 9,148 | (3.2%) |
| *Green* | 8,414 | (3.0%) |
| *ASPP* | 4,771 | (1.7%) |
| *Soc. Lab.* | 2,865 | (1.0%) |
| *Christian Party* | 2,468 | (0.9%) |
| *BNP* | 2,162 | (0.8%) |
| *UKIP* | 2,000 | (0.7%) |
| *SSP* | 1,752 | (0.6%) |
| *Ban Bankers Bonuses* | 1,204 | (0.4%) |
| *Pirate* | 850 | (0.3%) |
| *Ind. Vassie* | 460 | (0.2%) |
| *Solidarity* | 446 | (0.2%) |

*SNP majority* 24,776 (8.77%)
7.4% swing Lab. to SNP (2007 Lab. majority 15,772)

ADDITIONAL MEMBERS
Stewart Maxwell, *SNP*
Stuart McMillan, *SNP*
Mary Fee, *Lab.*
Neil Bibby, *Lab.*
Margaret McDougall, *Lab.*
Annabel Goldie, *C.*
Jackson Carlaw, *C.*

# THE SCOTTISH REFERENDUM

## THE ROAD TO REFERENDUM

Following the establishment of a majority Scottish National Party (SNP) government at Holyrood in May 2011, the SNP officially launched its independence bid at its annual party conference in October the same year. In May 2012 the UK government published the results of the Scottish referendum consultation, which showed strong levels of support for a single clear question on independence. On 25 May 2012 the 'Yes Scotland' campaign launched with the aim of encouraging 1 million Scots to sign a declaration of independence prior to a referendum.

## THE EDINBURGH AGREEMENT

A series of talks between the Scottish government's deputy first minister Nicola Sturgeon and the Secretary of State for Scotland Michael Moore resulted in the Edinburgh Agreement. The agreement was signed by prime minister David Cameron and first minister Alex Salmond on 15 October 2012 and set out a timetable for a referendum vote to be held in autumn 2014.

## SHOULD SCOTLAND BE AN INDEPENDENT COUNTRY?

On 30 January 2013 the wording of the independence referendum question was finalised as a simple yes/no question: 'Should Scotland be an independent country?'

## THOSE AGED 16 GET TO VOTE

On 12 March 2013 the Scottish independence referendum (franchise) bill was brought before parliament to ensure that all those aged 16 and over on the date of the referendum were entitled to vote.

## THE DATE IS SET

On the 21 March 2013 the date of the referendum was revealed as 18 September 2014. On 26 November 2013 Alex Salmond launched his government's independence blueprint, a 667-page white paper entitled *Scotland's Future: Your guide to an independent Scotland*. On 13 February 2014 the UK Chancellor of the Exchequer, George Osborne ruled out a formal currency union in the event of independence. The formal 16-week campaign period, during which the amount of money registered campaigners can spend was limited, began at the start of May 2014.

## REFERENDUM RESULTS *18 September 2014*

SHOULD SCOTLAND BE AN INDEPENDENT COUNTRY?

| NO | YES |
|---|---|
| 2,001,926 votes | 1,617,989 votes |
| (55.3%) | (44.7%) |
| Turnout 84.6% | |

PERCENTAGE OF VOTE BY REGION

Only four of the 32 Scottish local authority areas voted in favour of independence: Dundee City, Glasgow, North Lanarkshire and West Dunbartonshire.

| Local Authority Area | No (%) | Yes (%) |
|---|---|---|
| Aberdeen City | 58.6 | 41.4 |
| Aberdeenshire | 60.4 | 39.6 |
| Angus | 56.3 | 43.7 |
| Argyll and Bute | 58.5 | 41.5 |
| Clackmannanshire | 53.8 | 46.2 |
| Dumfries and Galloway | 65.7 | 34.3 |
| Dundee City | 42.7 | 57.3 |
| East Ayrshire | 52.8 | 47.2 |
| East Dunbartonshire | 61.2 | 38.8 |
| East Lothian | 61.7 | 38.3 |
| East Renfrewshire | 63.2 | 36.8 |
| Edinburgh City | 61.1 | 38.9 |
| Falkirk | 53.5 | 46.5 |
| Fife | 55.0 | 45.0 |
| Glasgow City | 46.5 | 53.5 |
| Highland | 52.9 | 47.1 |
| Inverclyde | 50.1 | 49.9 |
| Midlothian | 56.3 | 43.7 |
| Moray | 57.6 | 42.4 |
| North Ayrshire | 51.0 | 49.0 |
| North Lanarkshire | 48.9 | 51.1 |
| Orkney | 67.2 | 32.8 |
| Perth and Kinross | 60.2 | 39.8 |
| Renfrewshire | 52.8 | 47.2 |
| Scottish Borders | 66.6 | 33.4 |
| Shetland | 63.7 | 36.3 |
| South Ayrshire | 57.9 | 42.1 |
| South Lanarkshire | 54.7 | 45.3 |
| Stirling | 59.8 | 40.2 |
| West Dunbartonshire | 46.0 | 54.0 |
| Western Isles (Eilean Siar) | 53.4 | 46.6 |
| West Lothian | 55.2 | 44.8 |

# NORTHERN IRELAND

## NORTHERN IRELAND EXECUTIVE
Stormont Castle, Stormont, Belfast BT4 3TT
T 028-9052 8400
W www.northernireland.gov.uk

The first minister and deputy first minister head the executive committee of ministers and, acting jointly, determine the total number of ministers in the executive. First and deputy first ministers are elected by Northern Ireland assembly members through a formula of parallel consent that requires a majority of designated unionists, a majority of designated nationalists and a majority of the whole assembly to vote in favour. The parties elected to the assembly select ministerial portfolios in proportion to party strengths using the d'Hondt nominating procedure.

The executive committee includes five DUP ministers, four SF ministers, two Alliance members, one Social Democratic and Labour Party minister and one Ulster Unionist minister alongside the acting first minister Arlene Foster, MLA of the DUP and the deputy first minister, Martin McGuinness, MLA, of SF.

### EXECUTIVE COMMITTEE
*Acting First Minister,* Arlene Foster, MLA
*Deputy First Minister,* Martin McGuinness, MLA
*Junior Ministers,* Jennifer McCann, MLA; Michelle McIlveen, MLA
*Minister for Agriculture and Rural Development,* Michelle O'Neill, MLA
*Minister for Culture, Arts and Leisure,* Carál Ní Chuilín, MLA
*Minister for Education,* John O'Dowd, MLA
*Minister for Employment and Learning,* Dr Stephen Farry, MLA
*Minister for Enterprise, Trade and Investment,* Jonathan Bell, MLA
*Minister for Environment,* Mark Durkan, MLA
*Minister for Finance and Personnel,* Arlene Foster, MLA
*Minister for Health, Social Services and Public Safety,* Simon Hamilton, MLA
*Minister for Justice,* David Ford, MLA
*Minister for Regional Development,* vacant
*Minister for Social Development,* Mervyn Storey, MLA

## OFFICE OF THE FIRST MINISTER AND DEPUTY FIRST MINISTER
Stormont Castle, Stormont, Belfast BT4 3TT
T 028-9052 8400 W www.ofmdfmni.gov.uk

## DEPARTMENT OF AGRICULTURE AND RURAL DEVELOPMENT
Dundonald House, Upper Newtownards Road, Belfast BT4 3SB
T 028-9052 0100 W www.dardni.gov.uk

### EXECUTIVE AGENCIES
Forest Service
Rivers Agency

## DEPARTMENT OF CULTURE, ARTS AND LEISURE
Causeway Exchange, 1–7 Bedford Street, Belfast BT1 7FB
T 028-9025 8825 W www.dcalni.gov.uk

## DEPARTMENT OF EDUCATION
Rathgael House, Balloo Road, Bangor, Co. Down BT19 7PR
T 028-9127 9279 W www.deni.gov.uk

## DEPARTMENT FOR EMPLOYMENT AND LEARNING
Adelaide House, 39–49 Adelaide Street, Belfast BT2 8FD
T 028-9025 7777 W www.delni.gov.uk

## DEPARTMENT OF ENTERPRISE, TRADE AND INVESTMENT
Netherleigh, Massey Avenue, Belfast BT4 2JP T 028-9052 9900
W www.detini.gov.uk

## DEPARTMENT OF THE ENVIRONMENT
Goodwood House, 45–58 May Street, Belfast BT1 4NN
W www.doeni.gov.uk

### EXECUTIVE AGENCIES
Driver and Vehicle Agency (DVA)
NI Environment Agency (NIEA)

## DEPARTMENT OF FINANCE AND PERSONNEL
Rathgael House, Balloo Road, Bangor BT19 7NA T 028-9185 8111
W www.dfpni.gov.uk

### EXECUTIVE AGENCIES
Northern Ireland Statistics and Research Agency (NISRA)

## DEPARTMENT OF HEALTH, SOCIAL SERVICES AND PUBLIC SAFETY
Castle Buildings, Stormont, Belfast BT4 3SJ T 028-9052 0500
W www.dhsspsni.gov.uk

## DEPARTMENT OF JUSTICE
Block B, Castle Buildings, Stormont Estate, Belfast BT4 3SG
T 028-9076 3000 W www.dojni.gov.uk

### EXECUTIVE AGENCIES
Forensic Service Northern Ireland
Legal Services Agency
Northern Ireland Courts and Tribunals Service
Northern Ireland Prison Service
Youth Justice Agency

## DEPARTMENT FOR REGIONAL DEVELOPMENT
Clarence Court, 10–18 Adelaide Street, Belfast BT2 8GB
T 028-9054 0540 W www.drdni.gov.uk

## DEPARTMENT FOR SOCIAL DEVELOPMENT
Lighthouse Building, 1 Cromac Place, Gasworks Business Park, Ormeau Road, Belfast BT7 2JB T 028-9082 9000
W www.dsdni.gov.uk

### EXECUTIVE AGENCIES
Northern Ireland Central Investment Fund for Charities

## NORTHERN IRELAND AUDIT OFFICE
106 University Street, Belfast BT7 1EU
T 028-9025 1000 E info@niauditoffice.gov.uk
W www.niauditoffice.gov.uk
*Comptroller and Auditor-General,* Kieran Donnelly

## NORTHERN IRELAND AUTHORITY FOR UTILITY REGULATION
Queens House, 14 Queen Street, Belfast BT1 6ED
T 028-9031 1575 E info@uregni.gov.uk W www.uregni.gov.uk
*Chair,* Dr Bill Emery

## NORTHERN IRELAND ASSEMBLY

Parliament Buildings, Stormont, Belfast BT4 3XX
T 028-9052 1137 E info@niassembly.gov.uk
W www.niassembly.gov.uk

The Northern Ireland Assembly was established as a result of the Belfast Agreement (also known as the Good Friday Agreement) in April 1998. The agreement was endorsed through a referendum held in May 1998 and subsequently given legal force through the Northern Ireland Act 1998.

The Northern Ireland Assembly has full legislative and executive authority for all matters that are the responsibility of the government's Northern Ireland departments – known as transferred matters. Excepted and reserved matters are defined in schedules 2 and 3 of the Northern Ireland Act 1998 and remain the responsibility of UK parliament.

The first assembly election occurred on 25 June 1998 and the 108 members elected met for the first time on 1 July 1998. Members of the Northern Ireland Assembly are elected by the single transferable vote system from 18 constituencies – six per constituency. Under the single transferable vote system every voter has a single vote that can be transferred from one candidate to another. Voters number their candidates in order of preference. Where candidates reach their quota of votes and are elected, surplus votes are transferred to other candidates according to the next preference on each voter's ballot slip. The candidate in each round with the fewest votes is eliminated and their surplus votes are redistributed according to the voter's next preference. The process is repeated until the required number of members are elected.

On 29 November 1999 the assembly appointed ten ministers as well as the chairs and deputy chairs for the ten statutory departmental committees. Devolution of powers to the Northern Ireland Assembly occurred on 2 December 1999, following several delays concerned with Sinn Fein's inclusion in the executive while Irish Republican Army (IRA) weapons were yet to be decommissioned.

Since the devolution of powers, the assembly has been suspended by the Secretary of State for Northern Ireland on four occasions. The first was between 11 February and 30 May 2000, with two 24-hour suspensions on 10 August and 22 September 2001 – all owing to a lack of progress in decommissioning. The final suspension took place on 14 October 2002 after unionists walked out of the executive following a police raid on Sinn Fein's office investigating alleged intelligence gathering.

The assembly was formally dissolved in April 2003 in anticipation of an election, which eventually took place on 26 November 2003. The results of the election changed the balance of power between the political parties, with an increase in the number of seats held by the Democratic Unionist Party (DUP) and Sinn Fein (SF), so that they became the largest parties. The assembly was restored to a state of suspension following the November election while political parties engaged in a review of the Belfast Agreement aimed at fully restoring the devolved institutions.

In July 2005 the leadership of the IRA formally ordered an end to its armed campaign; it authorised a representative to engage with the Independent International Commission on Decommissioning in order to verifiably put the arms beyond use. On 26 September 2005 General John de Chastelain, the chair of the commission, along with two independent church witnesses confirmed that the IRA's entire arsenal of weapons had been decommissioned.

Following the passing of the Northern Ireland Act 2006 the secretary of state created a non-legislative fixed-term assembly, whose membership consisted of the 108 members elected in the 2003 election. It first met on 15 May 2006 with the remit of making preparations for the restoration of devolved government; its discussions informed the next round of talks called by the British and Irish governments held at St Andrews. The St Andrews agreement of 13 October 2006 led to the establishment of the transitional assembly.

The Northern Ireland (St Andrews Agreement) Act 2006 set out a timetable to restore devolution, and also set the date for the third election to the assembly as 7 March 2007. The DUP and SF again had the largest number of Members of the Legislative Assembly (MLAs) elected, and although the initial restoration deadline of 26 March was missed, the leaders of the DUP and SF (Revd Dr Ian Paisley, MP, MLA and Gerry Adams, MLA, respectively) took part in a historic meeting and made a joint commitment to establish an executive committee in the assembly to which devolved powers were restored on 8 May 2007. After completing a full four-year mandate, new assembly elections took place on 5 May 2011 to elect the 108 members of the legislative assembly.

| SALARIES | |
| --- | --- |
| | 2015–16 |
| First Minister/Deputy First Minister | £120,000 |
| Minister | £86,000 |
| MLA | £48,000 |

## NORTHERN IRELAND ASSEMBLY MEMBERS

* Previously MLA for another party
*as at June 2015*

**Agnew**, Steven, *Green, North Down*
**Allister**, Jim, *TUV, North Antrim*
**Anderson**, Sydney, *DUP, Upper Bann*
**Attwood**, Alex, *SDLP, Belfast West*
**Beggs**, Roy, *UUP, East Antrim*
**Bell**, Jonathan, *DUP, Strangford*
**Boylan**, Cathal, *SF, Newry and Armagh*
**Boyle**, Michaela, *SF, West Tyrone*
**Bradley**, Dominic, *SDLP, Newry and Armagh*
**Bradley**, Paula, *DUP, Belfast North*
**Brady**, Mickey, *SF, Newry and Armagh*
**Buchanan**, Thomas, *DUP, West Tyrone*
**Byrne**, Joe, *SDLP, West Tyrone*
**Cameron**, Pam, *DUP, South Antrim*
**Campbell**, Gregory, *DUP, East Londonderry*
**Clarke**, Trevor, *DUP, South Antrim*
**Cochrane**, Judith, *Alliance, Belfast East*
**Copeland**, Michael, *UUP, Belfast East*
**Craig**, Jonathan, *DUP, Lagan Valley*
**Cree**, Leslie, *UUP, North Down*
**Dallat**, John, *SDLP, East Londonderry*
**Dickson**, Stewart, *Alliance, East Antrim*
**Dobson**, Jo-Anne, *UUP, Upper Bann*
**Douglas**, Sammy, *DUP, Belfast East*
**Dunne**, Gordon, *DUP, North Down*
**Durkan**, Mark, *SDLP, Foyle*
**Easton**, Alex, *DUP, North Down*
**Eastwood**, Colum, *SDLP, Foyle*
**Elliot**, Tom, *UUP, Fermanagh and South Tyrone*
**Farry**, Stephen, *Alliance, North Down*
**Fearon**, Megan, *SF, Newry and Armagh*
**Flanagan**, Phil, *SF, Fermanagh and South Tyrone*
**Ford**, David, *Alliance, South Antrim*
**Foster**, Arlene, *DUP, Fermanagh and South Tyrone*
**Frew**, Paul, *DUP, North Antrim*
**Gardiner**, Samuel, *UUP, Upper Bann*
**Girvan**, Paul, *DUP, South Antrim*
**Givan**, Paul, *DUP, Lagan Valley*

Hale, Brenda, *DUP, Lagan Valley*
Hamilton, Simon, *DUP, Strangford*
Hazzard, Chris, *SF, South Down*
Hilditch, David, *DUP, East Antrim*
Humphrey, William, *DUP, Belfast North*
Hussey, Ross, *UUP, West Tyrone*
Irwin, William, *DUP, Newry and Armagh*
Kelly, Dolores, *SDLP, Upper Bann*
Kelly, Gerry, *SF, Belfast North*
Kennedy, Danny, *UUP, Newry and Armagh*
Kinahan, Danny, *UUP, South Antrim*
Lo, Anna, *Alliance, Belfast South*
Lunn, Trevor, *Alliance, Lagan Valley*
Lynch, Sean, *SF, Fermanagh and South Tyrone*
Lyttle, Chris, *Alliance, Belfast East*
Maginness, Alban, *SDLP, Belfast North*
Maskey, Alex, *SF, Belfast South*
McAleer, Declan, *SF, West Tyrone*
*McCallister, John, *NI21, South Down*
McCann, Fra, *SF, Belfast West*
McCann, Jennifer, *SF, Belfast West*
McCarthy, Kieran, *Alliance, Strangford*
McCartney, Raymond, *SF, Foyle*
McCausland, Nelson, *DUP, Belfast North*
McCorley, Rosaleen, *SF, Belfast West*
*McCrea, Basil, *NI21, Lagan Valley*
McCrea, Ian, *DUP, Mid Ulster*
McDonnell, Dr Alasdair, *SDLP, Belfast South*
McElduff, Barry, *SF, West Tyrone*
McGahan, Bronwyn, *SF, Fermanagh and South Tyrone*
McGimpsey, Michael, *UUP, Belfast South*
McGlone, Patsy, *SDLP, Mid Ulster*
McGuinness, Martin, *SF, Mid Ulster*
McIlveen, David, *DUP, North Antrim*
McIlveen, Michelle, *DUP, Strangford*
McKay, Daithi, *SF, North Antrim*
McKevitt, Karen, *SDLP, South Down*
McKinney, Fearghal, *SDLP, Belfast South*
McLaughlin, Maeve, *SF, Foyle*
McLaughlin, Mitchel, *SF, South Antrim*
McMullan, Oliver, *SF, East Antrim*
*McNarry, David, *UKIP, Strangford*
McQuillan, Adrian, *DUP, East Londonderry*

Middleton, Gary, *DUP, Foyle*
Milne, Ian, *SF, Mid Ulster*
Morrow, Lord, *DUP, Fermanagh and South Tyrone*
Moutray, Stephen, *DUP, Upper Bann*
Murphy, Conor, *SF, Newry and Armagh*
Nesbitt, Mike, *UUP, Strangford*
Newton, Robin, *DUP, Belfast East*
Ni Chuilin, Caral, *SF, Belfast North*
O'Dowd, John, *SF, Upper Bann*
O'Neill, Michelle, *SF, Mid Ulster*
O hOisin, Cathal, *SF, East Londonderry*
Overend, Sandra, *UUP, Mid Ulster*
Poots, Edwin, *DUP, Lagan Valley*
Ramsey, Pat, *SDLP, Foyle*
Ramsey, Sue, *SF, Belfast West*
Robinson, George, *DUP, East Londonderry*
Robinson, Rt. Hon. Peter, *DUP, Belfast East*
Rodgers, Sean, *SDLP, South Down*
Ross, Alastair, *DUP, East Antrim*
Ruane, Caitriona, *SF, South Down*
Sheehan, Pat, *SF, Belfast West*
Spratt, Jimmy, *DUP, Belfast South*
Storey, Mervyn, *DUP, North Antrim*
Sugden, Claire, *Ind., East Londonderry*
Swann, Robin, *UUP, North Antrim*
Weir, Peter, *DUP, North Down*
Wells, Jim, *DUP, South Down*
Wilson, Sammy, *DUP, East Antrim*

STATE OF THE PARTIES *as at 1 September 2014*

| Party | Seats |
| --- | --- |
| Democratic Unionist Party (DUP) | 38 |
| Sinn Fein (SF) | 29 |
| Social Democratic and Labour Party (SDLP) | 14 |
| Ulster Unionist Party (UUP) | 13 |
| Alliance Party (Alliance) | 8 |
| NI21 | 2 |
| Green Party | 1 |
| Independent (Ind.) | 1 |
| Traditional Unionist Voice (TUV) | 1 |
| UK Independence Party (UKIP) | 1 |
| Total | 108 |

## NORTHERN IRELAND ASSEMBLY ELECTION RESULTS

*As at 5 May 2011*
E. 1,210,009   T. 55.64%

E. Electorate   T. Turnout
*First* = first-preference votes
*Final* = final total for that candidate, after all necessary transfers of lower-preference votes
*R.* = round
* = eliminated last
*See* General Election Results for a list of party abbreviations

### ANTRIM EAST
E. 61,617   T. 29,430 (47.76%)

| | First | Final | Elected (R.) |
|---|---|---|---|
| Sammy Wilson, DUP | 7,181 | 7,181 | First (1) |
| David Hilditch, DUP | 3,288 | 4,219 | Second (2) |
| Roy Beggs, UUP | 3,042 | 4,194 | Fifth (9) |
| Stewart Dickson, Alliance | 2,889 | 4,777 | Fourth (9) |
| Oliver McMullan, SF | 2,369 | 3,389 | Sixth (10) |
| *Rodney McCune, UUP | 1,851 | 2,890 | |
| Gerardine Mulvenna, Alliance | 1,620 | | |
| Alastair Ross, DUP | 1,608 | 4,267 | Third (6) |
| Ruth Wilson, TUV | 1,346 | | |
| Justin McCamphill, SDLP | 1,333 | | |
| Gordon Lyons, DUP | 1,321 | | |
| Daniel Donnelly, Green | 664 | | |
| Steven Moore, BNP | 511 | | |

### ANTRIM NORTH
E. 74,760   T. 40,983 (54.82%)

| | First | Final | Elected (R.) |
|---|---|---|---|
| Paul Frew, DUP | 6,581 | 6,581 | First (1) |
| Daithi McKay, SF | 6,152 | 6,152 | Second (1) |
| Mervyn Storey, DUP | 6,083 | 6,083 | Third (1) |
| Jim Allister, TUV | 4,061 | 5,430 | Sixth (9) |
| *Declan O'Loan, SDLP | 3,682 | 4,816 | |
| David McIlveen, DUP | 3,275 | 6,594 | Fourth (8) |
| Evelyne Robinson, DUP | 3,256 | | |
| Robin Swann, UUP | 2,518 | 5,557 | Fifth (9) |
| Bill Kennedy, UUP | 2,189 | | |
| Jayne Dunlop, Alliance | 1,848 | | |
| Audrey Patterson, TUV | 668 | | |

### ANTRIM SOUTH
E. 65,231   T. 32,652 (50.06%)

| | First | Final | Elected (R.) |
|---|---|---|---|
| Paul Girvan, DUP | 4,844 | 4,844 | First (1) |
| Mitchel McLaughlin, SF | 4,662 | 4,662 | Second (1) |
| Trevor Clarke, UUP | 4,607 | 4,607 | Third (1) |
| David Ford, Alliance | 4,554 | 4,660 | Fourth (2) |
| Danny Kinahan, UUP | 3,445 | 5,585 | Fifth (3) |
| *Thomas Burns, SDLP | 3,406 | 3,591 | |
| Pam Lewis, DUP | 2,866 | 4,668 | Sixth (4) |
| Adrian Cochrane-Watson, UUP | 2,285 | | |
| Mel Lucas, TUV | 1,091 | | |
| Stephen Parkes, BNP | 404 | | |

### BELFAST EAST
E. 61,263   T. 32,828 (53.59%)

| | First | Final | Elected (R.) |
|---|---|---|---|
| Peter Robinson, DUP | 9,149 | 9,149 | First (1) |
| Judith Cochrane, Alliance | 4,329 | 4,755 | Third (7) |
| Chris Lyttle, Alliance | 4,183 | 4,696 | Fourth (9) |
| Sammy Douglas, DUP | 2,668 | 4,783 | Fifth (11) |
| Robin Newton, DUP | 2,436 | 4,801 | Second (2) |
| Michael Copeland, UUP | 2,194 | 3,723 | Sixth (11) |
| *Dawn Purvis, Ind. | 1,702 | 2,789 | |
| Brian Ervine, PUP | 1,493 | | |
| Niall O'Donnghaile, SF | 1,030 | | |
| Philip Robinson, UUP | 943 | | |
| Harry Toan, TUV | 712 | | |
| Martin Gregg, Green | 572 | | |
| Ann Cooper, BNP | 337 | | |
| Magdalena Wolska, SDLP | 250 | | |
| Tommy Black, SP | 201 | | |
| Kevin McNally, WP | 102 | | |
| Stephen Stewart, Ind. | 46 | | |

### BELFAST NORTH
E. 68,119   T. 34,280 (50.32%)

| | First | Final | Elected (R.) |
|---|---|---|---|
| Gerry Kelly, SF | 6,674 | 6,674 | First (1) |
| Nelson McCausland, DUP | 5,200 | 5,200 | Second (1) |
| Alban Maginness, SDLP | 4,025 | 5,004 | Fourth (6) |
| William Humphrey, DUP | 3,724 | 4,332 | Fifth (7) |
| Paula Bradley, DUP | 3,488 | 4,065 | Sixth (7) |
| Caral Ni Chuilin, SF | 2,999 | 4,868 | Third (6) |
| *Fred Cobain, UUP | 2,758 | 3,623 | |
| Billy Webb, Alliance | 2,096 | | |
| Raymond McCord, Ind. | 1,176 | | |
| JJ Magee, SF | 998 | | |
| John Lavery, WP | 332 | | |

### BELFAST SOUTH
E. 62,484   T. 32,752 (52.42%)

| | First | Final | Elected (R.) |
|---|---|---|---|
| Anna Lo, Alliance | 6,390 | 6,390 | First (1) |
| Dr Alasdair McDonnell, SDLP | 4,527 | 4,916 | Second (2) |
| Jimmy Spratt, DUP | 4,045 | 4,281 | Sixth (5) |
| Alex Maskey, SF | 4,038 | 4,452 | Fourth (5) |
| *Ruth Patterson, DUP | 3,800 | 4,163 | |
| Connall McDevitt, SDLP | 3,191 | 4,445 | Fifth (5) |
| Michael McGimpsey, UUP | 2,988 | 4,622 | Third (5) |
| Mark Finlay, UUP | 1,394 | | |
| Claire Bailey, Green | 889 | | |
| Brian Faloon, PBP | 414 | | |
| Paddy Meehan, SP | 234 | | |
| Nico Torregrosa, UKIP | 234 | | |
| Paddy Lynn, WP | 135 | | |
| Charles Smyth, Pro-Capitalism | 29 | | |

BELFAST WEST
E. 61,520  T. 35,618 (57.89%)

| | First | Final | Elected (R.) |
|---|---|---|---|
| Paul Maskey, SF | 5,343 | 5,343 | First (1) |
| Jennifer McCann, SF | 5,239 | 5,239 | Second (1) |
| Fra McCann, SF | 4,481 | 5,167 | Third (10) |
| Sue Ramsey, SF | 4,116 | 4,823 | Fifth (11) |
| Alex Attwood, SDLP | 3,765 | 5,152 | Fourth (10) |
| Pat Sheehan, SF | 3,723 | 4,327 | Sixth (11) |
| *Brian Kingston, DUP | 2,587 | 3,867 | |
| Gerry Carroll, PBP | 1,661 | | |
| Bill Manwaring, UUP | 1,471 | | |
| Colin Keenan, SDLP | 802 | | |
| John Lowry, WP | 586 | | |
| Pat Lawlor, SP | 384 | | |
| Dan McGuinness, Alliance | 365 | | |
| Brian Pelan, Ind. | 122 | | |

DOWN NORTH
E. 62,170  T. 28,528 (45.89%)

| | First | Final | Elected (R.) |
|---|---|---|---|
| Alex Easton, DUP | 5,175 | 5,175 | First (1) |
| Gordon Dunne, DUP | 3,741 | 4,121 | Second (2) |
| Peter Weir, DUP | 3,496 | 4,101 | Third (2) |
| Stephen Farry, Alliance | 3,131 | 4,078 | Fourth (10) |
| Steven Agnew, Green | 2,207 | 3,229 | Sixth (11) |
| *Anne Wilson, Alliance | 2,100 | 3,130 | |
| Alan McFarland, Ind. | 1,879 | | |
| Alan Chambers, Ind. | 1,765 | | |
| Leslie Cree, UUP | 1,585 | 4,015 | Fifth (10) |
| Colin Breen, UUP | 1,343 | | |
| Liam Logan, SDLP | 768 | | |
| Fred McGlade, UKIP | 615 | | |
| Conor Keenan, SF | 293 | | |

DOWN SOUTH
E. 73,240  T. 42,551 (58.10%)

| | First | Final | Elected (R.) |
|---|---|---|---|
| Margaret Ritchie, SDLP | 8,506 | 8,506 | First (1) |
| Catriona Ruane, SF | 5,955 | 6,192 | Second (2) |
| Jim Wells, DUP | 5,200 | 6,543 | Third (5) |
| John McCallister, UUP | 4,409 | 6,240 | Fourth (6) |
| Willie Clarke, SF | 3,882 | 6,777 | Fifth (7) |
| Karen McKevitt, SDLP | 3,758 | 5,347 | Sixth (9) |
| Naomi Bailie, SF | 3,050 | | |
| *Eamonn O'Neill, SDLP | 2,663 | 4,883 | |
| Henry Reilly, UKIP | 2,332 | | |
| Cadogan Enright, Green | 1,107 | | |
| David Griffin, Alliance | 864 | | |

FERMANAGH AND SOUTH TYRONE
E. 70,985  T. 48,949 (68.96%)

| | First | Final | Elected (R.) |
|---|---|---|---|
| Michelle Gildernew, SF | 9,110 | 9,110 | First (1) |
| Tom Elliott, UUP | 6,896 | 6,896 | Second (1) |
| Arlene Foster, DUP | 6,876 | 6,876 | Third (3) |
| Sean Lynch, SF | 5,146 | 6,476 | Fifth (6) |
| Phil Flanagan, SF | 5,082 | 6,137 | Sixth (6) |
| Maurice Morrow, DUP | 4,844 | 7,229 | Fourth (5) |
| *Tommy Gallagher, SDLP | 4,606 | 6,075 | |
| Kenny Donaldson, UUP | 2,366 | | |
| Alex Elliott, TUV | 1,231 | | |
| Pat Cox, Ind. | 997 | | |
| Hannah Su, Alliance | 845 | | |

FOYLE
E. 68,663  T. 39,686 (57.80%)

| | First | Final | Elected (R.) |
|---|---|---|---|
| William Hay, DUP | 7,154 | 7,154 | First (1) |
| Martina Anderson, SF | 6,950 | 6,950 | Second (1) |
| Mark Durkan, SDLP | 4,970 | 5,794 | Third (4) |
| Raymond McCartney, SF | 3,638 | 6,245 | Fourth (7) |
| Pat Ramsey, SDLP | 3,138 | 4,876 | Sixth (7) |
| *Eamonn McCann (PBP) | 3,120 | 3,916 | |
| Colum Eastwood, SDLP | 2,967 | 5,563 | Fifth (7) |
| Pol Callaghan, SDLP | 2,624 | | |
| Paul Fleming, SF | 2,612 | | |
| Paul McFadden, Ind. | 1,280 | | |
| Keith McGrellis, Alliance | 334 | | |
| Terry Doherty, Ind. | 60 | | |

LAGAN VALLEY
E. 67,532  T. 35,842 (53.07%)

| | First | Final | Elected (R.) |
|---|---|---|---|
| Edwin Poots, DUP | 7,329 | 7,329 | First (1) |
| Basil McCrea, UUP | 5,771 | 5,771 | Second (1) |
| Trevor Lunn, Alliance | 4,389 | 5,120 | Fourth (6) |
| Paul Givan, DUP | 4,352 | 5,518 | Fifth (7) |
| Jonathan Craig, DUP | 4,263 | 5,081 | Third (5) |
| Brenda Hale, DUP | 2,910 | 4,791 | Sixth (7) |
| *Pat Catney, SDLP | 2,165 | 3,406 | |
| Mark Hill, UUP | 1,482 | | |
| Mary-Kate Quinn, SF | 1,203 | | |
| Lyle Rea, TUV | 1,031 | | |
| Conor Quinn, Green | 592 | | |

LONDONDERRY EAST
E. 65,226  T. 35,303 (54.12%)

| | First | Final | Elected (R.) |
|---|---|---|---|
| Gregory Campbell, DUP | 6,319 | 6,319 | First (1) |
| Cathal O hOisin, SF | 4,681 | 4,962 | Third (6) |
| George Robinson, DUP | 3,855 | 4,823 | Fourth (7) |
| David McClarty (Ind.) | 3,003 | 4,405 | Fifth (7) |
| John Dallat, SDLP | 2,967 | 5,207 | Second (6) |
| Bernadette Archibald, SF | 2,639 | | |
| Adrian McQuillan, DUP | 2,633 | 3,782 | Sixth (7) |
| Thomas Conway | 2,222 | | |
| Barney Fitzpatrick, Alliance | 1,905 | | |
| Boyd Douglas, TUV | 1,568 | | |
| Lesley Macaulay, UUP | 1,472 | | |
| *David Harding, UUP | 1,458 | 3,460 | |

NEWRY AND ARMAGH
E. 77,544  T. 47,562 (61.34%)

| | First | Final | Elected (R.) |
|---|---|---|---|
| Conor Murphy, SF | 9,127 | 9,127 | First (1) |
| Danny Kennedy, UUP | 8,718 | 8,718 | Second (1) |
| Dominic Bradley, SDLP | 7,123 | 7,123 | Third (1) |
| Cathal Boylan, SF | 6,614 | 8,092 | Fourth (2) |
| William Irwin, DUP | 6,101 | 7,502 | Fifth (3) |
| *Thomas O'Hanlon, SDLP | 3,825 | 5,014 | |
| Mickey Brady, SF | 3,254 | 5,625 | Sixth (6) |
| Barrie Halliday, TUV | 830 | | |
| David Murphy, Alliance | 734 | | |
| Robert Woods, UKIP | 98 | | |
| James Malone, ND | 90 | | |

STRANGFORD
E. 62,178  T. 30,186 (48.55%)

| | First | Final | Elected (R.) |
|---|---|---|---|
| Michelle McIlveen, DUP | 4,573 | 4,573 | First (1) |
| Kieran McCarthy, Alliance | 4,284 | 4,284 | Second (1) |
| Jonathan Bell, DUP | 4,265 | 4,265 | Third (1) |
| Simon Hamilton, DUP | 3,456 | 5,745 | Fourth (5) |
| Mike Nesbitt, UUP | 3,273 | 4,072 | Fifth (6) |
| David McNarry, UUP | 2,733 | 3,767 | Sixth (6) |
| *Joe Boyle, SDLP | 2,525 | 3,308 | |
| Billy Walker, DUP | 2,175 | | |
| Mickey Coogan, SF | 902 | | |
| Terry Williams, TUV | 841 | | |
| Cecil Andrews, UKIP | 601 | | |

TYRONE WEST
E. 62,970  T. 40,323 (64.04%)

| | First | Final | Elected (R.) |
|---|---|---|---|
| Barry McElduff, SF | 6,008 | 6,008 | First (1) |
| Pat Doherty, SF | 5,630 | 5,630 | Second (1) |
| Michaela Boyle, SF | 5,053 | 7,792 | Third (4) |
| Tom Buchanan, DUP | 5,027 | 5,162 | Fifth (5) |
| Ross Hussey, UUP | 4,072 | 4,398 | Sixth (5) |
| *Allan Bresland, DUP | 4,059 | 4,124 | |
| Joe Byrne, SDLP | 3,353 | 5,321 | Fourth (5) |
| Declan McAleer, SF | 3,008 | | |
| Paddy McGowan, Ind. | 1,145 | | |
| Eugene McMenamin, Ind. | 1,096 | | |
| Eric Bullick, Ind. | 852 | | |

ULSTER MID
E. 66,602  T. 43,522 (65.35%)

| | First | Final | Elected (R.) |
|---|---|---|---|
| Martin McGuinness, SF | 8,957 | 8,957 | First (1) |
| Ian McCrea, DUP | 7,127 | 7,127 | Second (1) |
| Michelle O'Neill, SF | 5,178 | 5,735 | Sixth (7) |
| Patsy McGlone, SDLP | 5,065 | 6,110 | Third (5) |
| Sandra Overend, UUP | 4,409 | 7,130 | Fourth (6) |
| Francie Molloy, SF | 4,263 | 5,191 | Fifth (7) |
| *Ian Milne, SF | 2,635 | 4,412 | |
| Walter Millar, TUV | 2,075 | | |
| Austin Kelly, SDLP | 1,214 | | |
| Hugh McCloy, Ind. | 933 | | |
| Michael McDonald, Alliance | 398 | | |
| Harry Hutchinson, PBP | 243 | | |
| Gary McCann, Ind. | 241 | | |

UPPER BANN
E. 77,905  T. 43,113 (55.34%)

| | First | Final | Elected (R.) |
|---|---|---|---|
| John O'Dowd, SF | 6,649 | 6,649 | First (1) |
| Sydney Anderson, DUP | 5,584 | 6,163 | Second (5) |
| Stephen Moutray, DUP | 5,645 | 6,085 | Third (5) |
| *Johnny McGibbon, SF | 4,879 | 5,438 | |
| Dolores Kelly, SDLP | 4,846 | 5,787 | Sixth (7) |
| Sam Gardiner, UUP | 3,676 | 6,012 | Fourth (7) |
| Colin McCusker, UUP | 3,402 | | |
| Joanne Dobson, UUP | 3,348 | 5,827 | Fifth (7) |
| Harry Hamilton, Alliance | 1,979 | | |
| David Vance, TUV | 1,026 | | |
| Sheila McQuaid, Alliance | 786 | | |
| Barbara Trotter, UKIP | 272 | | |

# REGIONAL GOVERNMENT

## LONDON

### GREATER LONDON AUTHORITY (GLA)
City Hall, The Queen's Walk, London SE1 2AA
T 020-7983 4000 E mayor@london.gov.uk
W www.london.gov.uk

On 7 May 1998 London voted in favour of the formation of the Greater London Authority (GLA). The first elections to the GLA took place on 4 May 2000 and the new authority took over its responsibilities on 3 July 2000. In July 2002 the GLA moved to one of London's most spectacular buildings, newly built on a brownfield site on the south bank of the Thames, adjacent to Tower Bridge. The fourth and most recent election to the GLA took place on 3 May 2012.

The structure and objectives of the GLA stem from its main areas of responsibility: transport, policing, fire and emergency planning, economic development, planning, culture and health. There are four functional bodies which form part of the wider GLA group and report to the GLA: the Mayor's Office for Policing and Crime (MOPAC), Transport for London (TfL), the London Fire and Emergency Planning Authority (LFEPA) and the London Legacy Development Corporation, established in 2012.

The GLA consists of a directly elected mayor, the Mayor of London, and a separately elected assembly, the London Assembly. The mayor has the key role in decision making, with the assembly responsible for regulating and scrutinising these decisions, and investigating issues of importance to Londoners. In addition, the GLA has around 600 permanent staff to support the activities of the mayor and the assembly, which are overseen by a head of paid service. The mayor may appoint two political advisers and not more than ten other members of staff, though he does not necessarily exercise this power, but he does not appoint the chief executive, the monitoring officer or the chief finance officer. These must be appointed jointly by the assembly and the mayor.

Every aspect of the assembly and its activities must be open to public scrutiny and therefore accountable. The assembly holds the mayor to account through scrutiny of his strategies, decisions and actions. Mayor's Question Time, conducted on ten occasions a year at City Hall, is carried out by direct questioning at assembly meetings and by conducting detailed investigations in committee.

People's Question Time, held twice a year, and Talk London (W www.talklondon.london.gov.uk) give Londoners the chance to question and express their opinions to the mayor and the assembly about plans, priorities and policies for London.

The role of the mayor can be broken down into a number of key areas:
• to represent and promote London at home and abroad and speak up for Londoners
• to devise strategies and plans to tackle London-wide issues, such as crime, transport, housing, planning, economic development and regeneration, environment, public services, society and culture, sport and health; and to set budgets for TfL, MOPAC, LFEPA and the London Legacy Development Corporation
• the mayor is chair of TfL, and is responsible for the Metropolitan Police's priorities and performance

The role of the assembly can be broken down into a number of key areas:
• to hold the mayor to account by examining his decisions and actions
• to have the power to amend the mayor's budget by a majority of two-thirds
• to have the power to summon the mayor, senior staff of the GLA and functional bodies
• to investigate issues of London-wide significance and make proposals to appropriate stakeholders
• to examine the work of MOPAC and to review the police and crime plan for London through the Police and Crime Committee

*Mayor,* Boris Johnson
*Deputy Mayors,* Roger Evans, AM *(Statutory Deputy Mayor)*; Richard Blakeway *(Housing, Land and Property)*; Isabel Dedring *(Transport)*; Stephen Greenhalgh *(Policing and Crime)*; Sir Edward Lister *(Policy and Planning, and Chief of Staff)*; Munira Mirza *(Education and Culture)*; Matthew Pencharz *(Environment and Energy)*
*Chair of the London Assembly,* Jennette Arnold, OBE, AM
*Deputy Chair of the Assembly,* Tony Arbour, AM

### ELECTIONS AND VOTING SYSTEMS
The assembly is elected every four years at the same time as the mayor, and consists of 25 members. There is one member from each of the 14 GLA constituencies topped up with 11 London-wide members who are either representatives of political parties or individuals standing as independent candidates. The last election was on 3 May 2012.

Two distinct voting systems are used to appoint the existing mayor and the assembly. The mayor is elected using the supplementary vote system (SVS). With SVS, electors have two votes: one to give a first choice for mayor and one to give a second choice; they cannot vote twice for the same candidate. If one candidate gets more than half of all the first-choice votes, he or she becomes mayor. If no candidate gets more than half of the first-choice votes, the two candidates with the most first-choice votes remain in the election and all the other candidates drop out. The second-choice votes on the ballot papers for the candidates who are then counted. Where these second-choice votes are for the two remaining candidates they are added to the first-choice votes these candidates already have. The candidate with the most first- and second-choice votes combined becomes the Mayor of London.

The assembly is appointed using the additional member system (AMS). Under AMS, electors have two votes. The first vote is for a constituency candidate. The second vote is for a party list or individual candidate contesting the London-wide assembly seats. The 14 constituency members are elected under the first-past-the-post system, the same system used in general and local elections. Electors vote for one candidate and the candidate with the most votes wins. The additional members are drawn from party lists or are independent candidates who stand as London members; they are chosen using a form of proportional representation.

The Greater London Returning Officer (GLRO) is the independent official responsible for running the election in London. He is supported in this by returning officers in each of the 14 London constituencies.
*GLRO,* Jeff Jacobs

## TRANSPORT FOR LONDON (TFL)

TfL is the integrated body responsible for London's transport system. Its role is to implement the mayor's transport strategy for London and manage transport services across the capital for which the mayor has responsibility. TfL is directed by a management board whose members are chosen for their understanding of transport matters and are appointed by the mayor, who chairs the board. TfL's role is:
• to manage the London Underground, buses, Croydon Tramlink, London Overground and the Docklands Light Railway (DLR)
• to manage a 580km network of main roads and all 6,000 of London's traffic lights
• to regulate taxis and minicabs
• to run the London River Services, Victoria Coach Station and London Transport Museum
• to help to coordinate the Dial-a-Ride, Capital Call and Taxicard schemes for door-to-door services for transport users with mobility problems

The London Borough Councils maintain the role of highway and traffic authorities for 95 per cent of London's roads. A congestion charge for motorists driving into central London between the hours of 7am and 6.30pm, Monday to Friday (excluding public holidays) was introduced on 17 February 2003. On 19 February 2007, the charge zone roughly doubled in size after a westward expansion and the charging hours were shortened, to finish at 6pm. On 4 January 2011, the westward expansion was removed from the charging zone and an automated payment system was also introduced. As at September 2015 the daily congestion charge was £11.50 (£10.50 if paid via the automated service).

TfL introduced a low emission zone (LEZ) for London on 4 February 2008 which is in constant operation. Following tougher emissions standards introduced on 3 January 2012 there is a daily charge for polluting vehicles entering the zone (which covers most of Greater London) that do not meet Euro 3 or Euro 4 emissions standards. With the exception of minibuses, vehicles over three-and-a-half tonnes such as lorries, buses and coaches, face a daily charge of £200. Vehicles up to three-and-a-half tonnes and minibuses (with more than eight passenger seats) up to five tonnes pay a daily charge of £100. For further information see W www.tfl.gov.uk/lez

Since 2 January 2009, Londoners over pensionable age (or over 60 if born before 1950) and those with eligible disabilities are entitled to free travel on the capital's transport network at any time. War veterans who are receiving ongoing payments under the war pensions scheme, or those receiving guaranteed income payments under the armed forces compensation scheme can travel free at any time on bus, underground, DLR, tram and London Overground services and at certain times on National Rail services.

In the summer of 2010, the London cycle hire scheme launched with 6,000 new bicycles for hire from 400 docking stations across eight boroughs, the City and the Royal parks. The scheme has been expanded and there are now around 10,000 bicycles available and over 700 docking stations.

*Commissioner of TfL (interim),* Mike Brown, MVO

## MAYOR'S OFFICE FOR POLICING AND CRIME (MOPAC)

The Mayor's Office for Policing and Crime (MOPAC) was set up in response to the Police Reform and Social Responsibility Act 2011, replacing the Metropolitan Police Authority. MOPAC is headed by the mayor, or the appointed statutory deputy mayor for policing and crime. Operational responsibility for policing in London belongs to the Metropolitan Police Commissioner. The major areas of focus of MOPAC are:

• operational policing and crime reduction including counter terrorism
• ensuring the Metropolitan Police effectively reduce gang crime and violence in London and coordinating support for communities and local organisations to prevent gang activities
• criminal justice, including preventing reoffending, reducing crime and decreasing demand within the criminal justice system in addition to reducing alcohol and drug abuse.

The Police and Crime Committee consisting of nine elected members of the London Assembly scrutinises the work of MOPAC and meets regularly to hold to account the Deputy Mayor for Policing and Crime.

*Deputy Mayor for Policing and Crime,* Stephen Greenhalgh

## LONDON FIRE AND EMERGENCY PLANNING AUTHORITY (LFEPA)

In July 2000 the London Fire and Civil Defence Authority became the London Fire and Emergency Planning Authority. It consists of 17 members, eight drawn from the assembly, seven from the London boroughs and two mayoral appointees. The role of the LFEPA is:
• to set the strategy for the provision of fire services
• to ensure that the fire brigade can meet all the normal requirements efficiently
• to ensure that effective arrangements are made for the fire brigade to receive emergency calls and deal with them promptly
• to ensure members of the fire brigade are properly trained and equipped
• to ensure that information useful to the development of the fire brigades is gathered
• to ensure arrangements for advice and guidance on fire protection are made

*Chair,* Gareth Bacon

## LONDON LEGACY DEVELOPMENT CORPORATION

Following the London 2012 Olympic Games, the London Legacy Development Corporation was made responsible for the long-term planning, development, management and maintenance of the Queen Elizabeth Olympic Park (formerly the Olympic Park) and its facilities. The organisation is tasked with transforming the area into a thriving neighbourhood.

*Chair,* Neale Coleman, CBE

| SALARIES *as at August 2015* | |
| --- | --- |
| *Mayor* | £143,911 |
| *Chief of Staff and Deputy Mayor of Policy* | |
| *and Planning* | £168,924 |
| *Deputy Mayors* | |
| Housing, Land and Property | £146,245 |
| Transport | £146,245 |
| Policing and Crime | £146,245 |
| Education and Culture | £145,345 |
| Environment and Energy | £107,017 |
| Statutory Deputy Mayor | £99,188 |
| *Chair of the Assembly* | £66,168 |
| *Assembly Member* | £55,161 |

## LONDON ASSEMBLY COMMITTEES

*Chair, Audit Panel,* Valerie Shawcross, CBE
*Chair, Budget and Performance Committee,* John Biggs
*Chair, Budget Monitoring Sub-Committee,* John Biggs
*Chair, Confirmation Hearings Committee,* various
*Chair, Devolution Working Group,* Darren Johnson
*Chair, Economy Committee,* Fiona Twycross
*Chair, Education Panel,* Jennette Arnold, OBE

*Chair, Environment Committee,* Darren Johnson
*Chair, GLA Oversight Committee,* Len Duvall
*Chair, Health Committee,* Dr Onkar Sahota
*Chair, Housing Committee,* Tom Copley, AM
*Chair, Online Crime Working Group,* Roger Evans
*Chair, Planning Committee,* Nicky Gavron
*Chair, Police and Crime Committee,* Joanne McCartney
*Chair, Regeneration Committee,* Gareth Bacon
*Chair, Transport Committee,* Valerie Shawcross, CBE

## LONDON ASSEMBLY MEMBERS
*as at 3 May 2012*
**Arbour,** Tony, *C., South West,* Maj. 19,262
**Arnold,** Jennette, *Lab. North East,* Maj. 66,188
**Bacon,** Gareth, *C., London List*
**Biggs,** John, *Lab., City and East,* Maj. 82,744
**Boff,** Andrew, *C., London List*
**Borwick,** Victoria, *C., London List*
**Cleverly,** James, *C., Bexley and Bromley,* Maj. 47,768
**Copley,** Tom, *Lab. London List*
**Dismore,** Andrew, *Lab., Barnet and Camden,* Maj. 21,299
**Duvall,** Len, *Lab., Greenwich and Lewisham,* Maj. 38,037
**Evans,** Roger, *C., Havering and Redbridge,* Maj. 3,899
**Gavron,** Nicky, *Lab., London List*
**Johnson,** Darren, *Green, London List*
**Jones,** Jenny, *Green, London List*
**Knight,** Stephen, *LD, London List*
**Malthouse,** Kit, *C., West Central,* Maj. 29,131
**McCartney,** Joanne, *Lab., Enfield and Haringey,* Maj. 36,741
**O'Connell,** Steve, *C., Croydon and Sutton,* Maj. 9,418
**Pidgeon,** Caroline, *LD, London List*
**Qureshi,** Murad, *Lab., London List*
**Sahota,** Dr Onkar, *Lab., Ealing and Hillingdon,* Maj. 3,110
**Shah,** Navin, *Lab., Brent and Harrow,* Maj. 29,796
**Shawcross,** Valerie, *Lab., Lambeth and Southwark,* Maj. 52,702
**Tracey,** Richard, *C., Merton and Wandsworth,* Maj. 9,981
**Twycross,** Fiona, *Lab., London List*

STATE OF THE PARTIES *as at 3 May 2012*

| Party | Seats |
|---|---|
| Conservative (C.) | 9 |
| Labour (Lab.) | 12 |
| Liberal Democrats (LD) | 2 |
| Green | 2 |

## MAYORAL ELECTION RESULTS
*as at 3 May 2012*

Electorate 5,910,460          Turnout 38%

*Change in turnout from 2008:* -7.33%
*Good votes:* 1st choice 2,208,475 (98.21%); 2nd choice 1,763,009 (79.83%)
*Rejected votes:* 1st choice 40,210 (1.79%); 2nd choice 445,466 (20.17%)

| First | Party | Votes | % |
|---|---|---|---|
| Boris Johnson | C. | 971,931 | 44.01 |
| Ken Livingstone | Lab. | 889,918 | 40.30 |
| Jenny Jones | Green | 98,913 | 4.48 |
| Brian Paddick | LD | 91,774 | 4.16 |
| Siobhan Benita | Ind. | 83,914 | 3.80 |
| Lawrence Webb | UKIP | 43,274 | 1.96 |
| Carlos Cortiglia | BNP | 28,751 | 1.30 |

| Second | Party | Votes | % |
|---|---|---|---|
| Brian Paddick | LD | 363,692 | 20.63 |
| Jenny Jones | Green | 363,193 | 20.60 |
| Ken Livingstone | Lab. | 335,398 | 19.02 |
| Boris Johnson | C. | 253,709 | 14.39 |
| Siobhan Benita | Ind. | 212,412 | 12.05 |
| Lawrence Webb | UKIP | 161,252 | 9.15 |
| Carlos Cortiglia | BNP | 73,353 | 4.16 |

## LONDON ASSEMBLY ELECTION RESULTS
*as at 3 May 2012*
E. Electorate  T. Turnout
*See* General Election Results for a list of party abbreviations

CONSTITUENCIES
E. 5,910,460  T. 38%

BARNET AND CAMDEN
E. 446,248  T. 38%

| | |
|---|---:|
| Andrew Dismore, Lab. | 74,677 |
| Brian Coleman, C. | 53,378 |
| Audrey Poppy, Green | 17,904 |
| Chris Richards, LD | 13,800 |
| Michael Corby, UKIP | 7,331 |

*Lab. majority* 21,299

BEXLEY AND BROMLEY
E. 447,465  T. 38.1%

| | |
|---|---:|
| James Cleverly, C. | 88,482 |
| Josie Channer, Lab. | 40,714 |
| Sam Webber, LD, | 11,396 |
| David Cobum, UKIP | 10,771 |
| Jonathan Rooks, Green | 9,209 |
| Donna Treanor, BNP | 7,563 |

*C. majority* 47,768

BRENT AND HARROW
E. 389,737  T. 38%

| | |
|---|---:|
| Navin Shah, Lab. | 70,400 |
| Sachin Rajput, C. | 40,604 |
| Charlotte Henry, LD | 15,690 |
| Shahrar Ali, Green | 10,546 |
| Mick McGough, UKIP | 7,830 |

*Lab. majority* 29,796

CITY AND EAST
E. 500,427  T. 34.8%

| | |
|---|---:|
| John Biggs, Lab. | 107,667 |
| John Moss, C. | 24,923 |
| Chris Smith, Green | 10,891 |
| Richard Macmillan, LD | 7,351 |
| Paul Borg, BNP | 7,031 |
| Kamran Malik, CUP | 6,774 |
| Steven Woolfe, UKIP | 5,243 |
| Paul Davies, Comm. Lge | 1,108 |

*Lab. majority* 82,744

CROYDON AND SUTTON
E. 436,451  T. 35.7%

| | |
|---|---:|
| Stephen O'Connell, C. | 60,152 |
| Louisa Woodley, Lab. | 50,734 |
| Abigail Lock, LD | 21,889 |
| Winston McKenzie, UKIP | 10,757 |
| Gordon Ross, Green | 10,287 |

*C. majority* 9,418

EALING AND HILLINGDON
E. 439,143  T. 37.9%

| | |
|---|---:|
| Onkar Sahota, Lab. | 65,584 |
| Richard Barnes, C. | 62,474 |
| Michael Cox, LD | 11,805 |
| Mike Harling, Green | 10,877 |
| Helen Knight, UKIP | 6,750 |
| Dave Furness, BNP | 4,284 |
| Ian Edward, NF | 2,035 |

*Lab. majority* 3,110

ENFIELD AND HARINGEY
E. 383,623  T. 38.3%

| | |
|---|---:|
| Joanne McCartney, Lab. | 74,034 |
| Andy Hemsted, C. | 37,293 |
| Dawn Barnes, LD | 13,601 |
| Peter Krakowiak, Green | 12,278 |
| Peter Staveley, UKIP | 4,298 |
| Marie Nicholas, BNP | 3,081 |

*Lab. majority* 36,741

GREENWICH AND LEWISHAM
E. 359,742  T. 37.2%

| | |
|---|---:|
| Len Duvall, Lab. | 65,366 |
| Alex Wilson, C. | 27,329 |
| Roger Sedgley, Green | 12,427 |
| John Russell, LD | 9,393 |
| Barbara Raymond, PBP | 6,873 |
| Paul Oakley, UKIP | 4,997 |
| Roberta Woods, BNP | 3,551 |
| Tess Culnane, NF | 1,816 |

*Lab. majority* 38,037

HAVERING AND REDBRIDGE
E. 389,814  T. 36.9%

| | |
|---|---:|
| Roger Evans, C. | 53,285 |
| Mandy Richards, Lab. | 49,386 |
| Lawrence Webb, UKIP | 9,471 |
| Melvin Brown, RAL | 8,239 |
| Farrukh Islam, LD | 6,435 |
| Robert Taylor, BNP | 5,234 |
| Haroon Saad, Green | 5,207 |
| Mark Twiddy, Eng. Dem. | 2,573 |
| Richard Edmonds, NF | 1,936 |

*C. majority* 3,899

LAMBETH AND SOUTHWARK
E. 422,981  T. 37.8%

| | |
|---|---:|
| Valerie Shawcross, Lab. | 83,239 |
| Michael Mitchell, C. | 30,537 |
| Rob Blackie, LD | 18,359 |
| Jonathan Bartley, Green | 18,144 |
| James Fluss, UKIP | 4,395 |
| Daniel Lambert, Soc. | 2,938 |

*Lab. majority* 52,702

MERTON AND WANDSWORTH
E. 376,365  T. 40.9%

| | |
|---|---:|
| Richard Tracey, C. | 65,197 |
| Leonie Cooper, Lab. | 55,216 |
| Lisa Smart, LD | 11,904 |
| Roy Vickery, Green | 11,307 |
| Mazhar Manzoor, UKIP | 3,717 |
| Thamilini Kulendran, Ind. | 2,424 |
| James Martin, Soc. | 1,343 |

*C. majority* 9,981

NORTH EAST
E. 499,418  T. 39.1%

| | |
|---|---:|
| Jennette Arnold, Lab. | 101,902 |
| Naomi Newstead, C. | 35,714 |
| Caroline Allen, Green | 29,677 |
| Farooq Qureshi, LD | 13,237 |
| Paul Wiffen, UKIP | 6,623 |
| Ijaz Hayat, Ind. | 4,842 |

*Lab. majority* 66,188

SOUTH WEST
E. 437,945  T. 40.2%

| | |
|---|---:|
| Tony Arbour, C. | 69,151 |
| Lisa Homan, Lab. | 49,889 |
| Munira Wilson, LD | 28,947 |
| Daniel Goldsmith, Green | 17,070 |
| Jeff Bolter, UKIP | 8,505 |

*C. majority* 19,262

WEST CENTRAL
E. 381,101  T. 39.2%

| | |
|---|---:|
| Kit Malthouse, C. | 73,761 |
| Todd Foreman, Lab. | 44,630 |
| Susanna Rustin, Green | 12,799 |
| Layla Moran, LD | 10,035 |
| Elizabeth Jones, UKIP | 5,161 |

*C. majority* 29,131

LONDON-WIDE MEMBERS

| *Conservative* | *Labour Party* |
|---|---|
| Gareth Bacon | Tom Copley |
| Andrew Boff | Nicky Gavron |
| Victoria Borwick | Murad Qureshi |
| | Fiona Twycross |

| *Green Party* | *Liberal Democrat* |
|---|---|
| Darren Johnson | Stephen Knight |
| Jenny Jones | Caroline Pidgeon |

# EUROPEAN PARLIAMENT

European parliament elections take place at five-yearly intervals; the first direct elections to the parliament were held in 1979. In mainland Britain, members of the European parliament (MEPs) were elected in all constituencies on a first-past-the-post basis until 1999, when a regional system of proportional representation was introduced; in Northern Ireland three MEPs have been elected by the single transferable vote system of proportional representation since 1979. Under the terms of the Lisbon Treaty, the UK gained an extra seat in December 2011, taking the total to 73. This seat was added to the West Midlands region and filled by the highest-ranked losing candidate standing for the region in the 2009 European parliament elections.

At the 2014 European parliament elections all UK MEPs were elected under a 'closed-list' regional system of proportional representation, with England being divided into nine regions (residents of Gibraltar vote in the South West region) and Scotland, Wales and Northern Ireland each constituting a single region each. Parties submitted a list of candidates for each region in their own order of preference. Votes were cast for a party or an independent candidate, and the first seat in each region was allocated to the party or candidate with the highest number of votes. The rest of the seats in each region were then allocated broadly in proportion to each party's share of the vote. Each region returned the following number of members: East Midlands, 5; Eastern, 7; London, 8; North East, 3; North West, 8; South East, 10; South West, 6; West Midlands, 7; Yorkshire and the Humber, 6; Wales, 4; Northern Ireland, 3; Scotland, 6.

If a vacancy occurs due to the resignation or death of an MEP, it is filled by the next available person on that party's list. If an independent MEP resigns or dies, a by-election is held. Where an MEP leaves the party on whose list he/she was elected, there is no requirement to resign the post of MEP.

British subjects and nationals of member states of the European Union are eligible for election to the European parliament provided they are aged 18 or over and not subject to disqualification. Since 1994, eligible citizens have had the right to vote in elections to the European parliament in the UK as long as they are entered on the electoral register.

In July 2009 an MEP statute introduced a uniform salary for all MEPs, set at a rate of 38.5 per cent of the basic salary of a European court of justice judge. As at May 2015 this equated to an annual salary of €96,246.36 (approximately £68,000, depending on the monthly exchange rate). Member states can also subject the salary to national taxes. In the UK the salary is taxed by HM Revenue and Customs in order to bring the total tax paid up to the level of taxation payable by a UK resident.

The 2014 UK component of the European parliament was won by UKIP, who claimed 24 seats. It was the first time a party other than the Conservatives or Labour had won the largest number of seats in a general election since the December 1910 general election.

The next elections to the European parliament will take place in 2019. For further information visit the UK's European parliament website (W www.europarl.org.uk).

## UK MEMBERS as at June 2015

\* Denotes membership of the last European parliament
† Previously sat as a member of the Conservative party
‡ Previously sat as a member of UKIP
§ Previously sat as a member of UCUNF

\*Agnew, Stuart (b. 1949), UKIP, Eastern
Aker, Tim (b. 1985), UKIP, Eastern
Anderson, Lucy, Lab., London
\*Anderson, Martina (b. 1962), SF, Northern Ireland
Arnott, Jonathan (b. 1981), UKIP, North East
\*Ashworth, Richard (b. 1947), C., South East
Atkinson, Janice (b. 1962), Ind., South East
Bashir, Amjad (b. 1952), UKIP, Yorkshire and the Humber
\*Batten, Gerard (b. 1954), UKIP, London
\*Bearder, Catherine (b. 1949), LD, South East
Bours, Louise (b. 1968), UKIP, North West
Brannen, Paul (b. 1962), Lab., North East
\*‡Campbell Bannerman, David (b. 1960), C., Eastern
Carver, Jim (b. 1969), UKIP, West Midlands
Coburn, David (b. 1958), UKIP, Scotland
Collins, Jane (b. 1962), UKIP, Yorkshire and the Humber
Corbett, Richard (b. 1955), Lab., Yorkshire and the Humber
Dalton, Daniel (b. 1974), C., West Midlands
Dance, Seb (b. 1981), Lab., London
\*Dartmouth, Earl of (b. 1949), UKIP, South West
\*Deva, Nirj (b. 1948), C., South East
Dodds, Anneliese (b. 1978), Lab., South East
\*Dodds, Diane (b. 1958), DUP, Northern Ireland
Duncan, Ian (b. 1973), C., Scotland
Etheridge, Bill (b. 1970), UKIP, West Midlands
\*Evans, Jill (b. 1959), PC, Wales
\*Farage, Nigel (b. 1964), UKIP, South East
Finch, Ray (b. 1963), UKIP, South East
\*Ford, Vicky (b. 1967), C., Eastern
\*Foster, Jacqueline (b. 1947), C., North West
\*Fox, Ashley (b. 1969), C., South West
Gill, Nathan (b. 1973), UKIP, Wales
Gill, Neena (b. 1957), Lab., West Midlands
\*Girling, Julie (b. 1956), C., South West
Griffin, Theresa (b. 1962), Lab., North West
\*Hannan, Daniel (b. 1971), C., South East
\*†Helmer, Roger (b. 1944), UKIP, East Midlands
\*Honeyball, Mary (b. 1952), Lab., London
Hookem, Mike (b. 1953), UKIP, Yorkshire and the Humber
\*Howitt, Richard (b. 1961), Lab., Eastern
\*Hudghton, Ian (b. 1951), SNP, Scotland
James, Diane (b. 1959), UKIP, South East
\*Kamall, Dr Syed (b. 1967), C., London
\*Karim, Sajjad (b. 1970), C., North West
Khan, Afzal (b. 1960), Lab., North West
\*Kirkhope, Timothy (b. 1945), C., Yorkshire and the Humber
Kirton-Darling, Judith (b. 1977), Lab., North East
\*Lambert, Jean (b. 1950), Green, London
Lewer, Andrew (b. 1971), C., East Midlands
\*McAvan, Linda (b. 1962), Lab., Yorkshire and the Humber
\*McClarkin, Emma (b. 1978), C., East Midlands
\*McIntyre, Anthea (b. 1954), C., West Midlands
\*Martin, David (b. 1954), Lab., Scotland
Moody, Clare (b. 1965), Lab., South West
\*Moraes, Claude (b. 1965), Lab., London
\*Nicholson, James (b. 1945), UUP, Northern Ireland
\*Nuttall, Paul (b. 1976), UKIP, North West
O'Flynn, Patrick (b. 1965), UKIP, Eastern
Parker, Margot (b. 1943), UKIP, East Midlands
Reid, Julia (b. 1952), UKIP, South West
Scott Cato, Molly (b. 1963), Green, South West
Seymour, Jill (b. 1958), UKIP, West Midlands
Simon, Siôn (b. 1968), Lab., West Midlands
\*Smith, Alyn (b. 1973), SNP, Scotland

**\*Stihler,** Catherine (*b.* 1973), *Lab., Scotland*
**\*Swinburne,** Dr Kay (*b.* 1967), *C., Wales*
**\*Tannock,** Dr Charles (*b.* 1957), *C., London*
**\*Taylor,** Keith (*b.* 1953), *Green, South East*
**\*Van Orden,** Geoffrey (*b.* 1945), *C., Eastern*
**\*Vaughan,** Derek (*b.* 1961), *Lab., Wales*
**Ward,** Julie (*b.* 1957), *Lab., North West*
**\*Willmott,** Glenis (*b.* 1951), *Lab., East Midlands*
**Woolfe,** Steven (*b.* 1967), *UKIP, North West*

STATE OF THE PARTIES *as at June 2015*

| *Party* | *Seats* |
|---|---|
| UK Independence Party (UKIP) | 24 |
| Labour (Lab.) | 20 |
| Conservative (C.) | 19 |
| Green Party (Green) | 3 |
| Scottish National Party (SNP) | 2 |
| Others* | 5 |
| *Total* | 73 |

\* The Democratic Unionist Party (DUP), Liberal Democrats (LD) Plaid Cymru (PC), the Ulster Unionist Party (UUP) and Sinn Fein (SF) have one seat each.

## UK REGIONS *as at 22 May 2014 election*

*Abbreviations*

| | |
|---|---|
| *4FP* | 4 Freedoms Party (UK EPP) |
| *AIFE* | An Independence from Europe |
| *AW* | Animal Welfare |
| *BF* | Britain First |
| *CPA* | Christian Peoples Alliance |
| *EP* | Europeans Party |
| *Harmony* | Harmony Party |
| *Liberty* | Liberty GB |
| *NLP* | National Liberal Party |
| *NI21* | NI21 |
| *No2EU* | No2EU Yes to Democracy |
| *Peace* | Peace Party |
| *Roman* | Roman Party |
| *SGB* | Socialist Party of Great Britain |
| *SLP* | Socialist Labour Party |
| *TUV* | Traditional Unionist Voice (NI) |
| *UUP* | Ulster Unionist Party |
| *WDR* | We Demand a Referendum |
| *Your* | YOURvoice |
| *YF* | Yorkshire First |

For other abbreviations, *see* UK General Election Results.

| | |
|---|---|
| E. 46,615,585 | T. 35.32% |

### EASTERN
(Bedfordshire, Cambridgeshire, Essex, Hertfordshire, Luton, Norfolk, Peterborough, Southend-on-Sea, Suffolk, Thurrock)

| | | |
|---|---|---|
| E. 4,369,382 | | T. 36.19% |
| *UKIP* | 542,812 | (34.5%) |
| *C.* | 446,569 | (28.4%) |
| *Lab.* | 271,601 | (17.2%) |
| *Green* | 133,331 | (8.5%) |
| *LD* | 108,010 | (6.9%) |
| *AIFE* | 26,564 | (1.7%) |
| *Eng. Dem.* | 16,497 | (1.0%) |
| *BNP* | 12,465 | (0.8%) |
| *CPA* | 11,627 | (0.7%) |
| *No2EU* | 4,870 | (0.3%) |
| *UKIP majority* | | 96,243 |
| (June 2009, C. maj. 186,410) | | |

MEMBERS ELECTED
1. P. O'Flynn, *UKIP* 2. *V. Ford, *C.*
3. *R. Howitt, *Lab.* 4. *S. Agnew, *UKIP*
5. *G. Van Orden, *C.* 6. T. Aker, *UKIP*
7. *‡ D. Campbell Bannerman, *C.*

### EAST MIDLANDS
(Derby, Derbyshire, Leicester, Leicestershire, Lincolnshire, Northamptonshire, Nottingham, Nottinghamshire, Rutland)

| | | |
|---|---|---|
| E. 3,437,794 | | T. 32.6% |
| *UKIP* | 368,734 | (32.9%) |
| *C.* | 291,270 | (26.0%) |
| *Lab.* | 279,363 | (24.9%) |
| *Green* | 67,066 | (6.0%) |
| *LD* | 60,773 | (5.4%) |
| *AIFE* | 21,384 | (1.9%) |
| *BNP* | 18,326 | (1.6%) |
| *Eng. Dem.* | 11,612 | (1.0%) |
| *Harmony* | 2,194 | (0.2%) |
| *UKIP majority* | | 77,464 |
| (June 2009, C. maj. 163,330) | | |

MEMBERS ELECTED
1. *†R. Helmer, *UKIP* 2.*E. McClarkin, *C.* 3. *G. Willmott, *Lab.* 4. M. Parker, *UKIP* 5. A. Lewer, *C.*

### LONDON

| | | |
|---|---|---|
| E. 5,490,248 | | T. 40.5% |
| *Lab.* | 806,959 | (36.7%) |
| *C.* | 495,639 | (22.5%) |
| *UKIP* | 371,133 | (16.9%) |
| *Green* | 196,419 | (8.9%) |
| *LD* | 148,013 | (6.7%) |
| *4FP* | 28,014 | (1.3%) |
| *AIFE* | 26,675 | (1.2%) |
| *CPA* | 23,702 | (1.1%) |
| *NHA* | 23,253 | (1.1%) |
| *AW* | 21,092 | (1.0%) |
| *BNP* | 19,246 | (0.9%) |
| *EP* | 10,712 | (0.5%) |
| *Eng. Dem.* | 10,142 | (0.5%) |
| *CUP* | 6,951 | (0.3%) |
| *NLP* | 6,736 | (0.3%) |
| *No2EU* | 3,804 | (0.2%) |
| *Harmony* | 1,985 | (0.1%) |
| *Lab. majority* | | 311,320 |
| (June 2009, C. maj. 106,447) | | |

MEMBERS ELECTED
1. *C. Moraes, *Lab.* 2. *S. Kamall, *C.*
3. *M. Honeyball, *Lab.* 4. *G. Batten, *UKIP* 5. L. Anderson, *Lab.*
6. *C. Tannock, *C.* 7. S. Dance, *Lab.*
8. *J. Lambert, *Green*

### NORTH EAST
(Co. Durham, Darlington, Hartlepool, Middlesbrough, Northumberland, Redcar and Cleveland, Stockton-on-Tees, Tyne and Wear)

| | | |
|---|---|---|
| E. 1,968,780 | | T. 31.0% |
| *Lab.* | 221,988 | (36.5%) |
| *UKIP* | 177,660 | (29.2%) |
| *C.* | 107,733 | (17.7%) |
| *LD* | 36,093 | (5.9%) |
| *Green* | 31,605 | (5.2%) |
| *AIFE* | 13,934 | (2.3%) |
| *BNP* | 10,360 | (1.7%) |
| *Eng. Dem.* | 9,279 | (1.5%) |
| *Lab. majority* | | 44,328 |
| (June 2009, Lab. maj. 30,427) | | |

MEMBERS ELECTED
1. J. Darling, *Lab.* 2. J. Arnott, *UKIP* 3. P. Brannen, *Lab.*

### NORTHERN IRELAND
(Northern Ireland forms a three-member seat with a single transferable vote system)

| | | |
|---|---|---|
| E. 1,225,771 | | T. 51.84% |
| | | *1st Pref. Votes* |
| Martina Anderson, *SF* | | 159,813 (25.5%) |
| Diane Dodds, *DUP* | | 131,163 (20.9%) |
| Jim Nicholson, *UUP* | | 83,438 (13.3%) |
| Alex Attwood, *SDLP* | | 81,594 (13%) |
| Jim Allister, *TUV* | | 75,806 (12.1%) |
| Anna Lo, *Alliance* | | 44,432 (7.1%) |
| Henry Reilly, *UKIP*, | | 24,584 (3.9%) |
| Ross Brown, *Green* | | 10,598 (1.7%) |
| Tina McKenzie, *NI21* | | 10,553 (1.7%) |
| Mark Brotherston, *C.* | | 4,144 (0.7%) |

MEMBERS ELECTED
1. *M. Anderson, *SF* 2. *D. Dodds, *DUP* 3. *§ J. Nicholson, *UUP*

## NORTH WEST
Blackburn-with-Darwen, Blackpool,
Cheshire, Cumbria, Greater
Manchester, Halton, Lancashire,
Merseyside, Warrington)

| | |
|---|---|
| E. 5,267,777 | T. 33.68% |
| Lab. | 594,063 (33.9%) |
| UKIP | 481,932 (27.5%) |
| C. | 351,985 (20.1%) |
| Green | 123,075 (7.0%) |
| LD | 105,487 (6.0%) |
| BNP | 32,826 (1.9%) |
| AIFE | 26,731 (1.5%) |
| Eng. Dem. | 19,522 (1.1%) |
| Pirate | 8,597 (0.5%) |
| No2EU | 5,402 (0.3%) |
| EP | 5,067 (0.3%) |
| Lab. majority | 112,131 |
| (June 2009, C. maj. 86,343) | |

MEMBERS ELECTED
1. T. Griffin, Lab. 2.*P. Nuttall, UKIP
3. *J. Foster, C. 4. A. Khan, Lab.
5. L. Bours, UKIP 6. J. Ward, Lab.
7. *S. Karim, C. 8. S. Woolfe, UKIP

## SCOTLAND

| | |
|---|---|
| E. 4,016,735 | T. 33.5% |
| SNP | 389,503 (29.0%) |
| Lab. | 348,219 (25.9%) |
| C. | 231,330 (17.2%) |
| UKIP | 140,534 (10.5%) |
| Green | 108,305 (8.7%) |
| LD | 95,319 (7.1%) |
| BF | 13,639 (1.0%) |
| BNP | 10,216 (0.8%) |
| No2EU | 6,418 (0.5%) |
| SNP majority | 41,284 |
| (June 2009, SNP. maj. 91,154) | |

MEMBERS ELECTED
1. *I. Hudghton, SNP 2. *D. Martin,
Lab. 3. I. Duncan, C. 4. *A. Smith, SNP
5. *C. Stihler, Lab. 6. D. Coburn, UKIP

## SOUTH EAST
Bracknell Forest, Brighton and Hove,
Buckinghamshire, East Sussex,
Hampshire, Isle of Wight, Kent,
Medway, Milton Keynes, Newbury,
Oxfordshire, Portsmouth, Reading,
Slough, Southampton, Surrey, West
Sussex, Windsor and Maidenhead,
Wokingham)

| | |
|---|---|
| E. 6,441,003 | T. 36.46% |
| UKIP | 751,439 (32.1%) |
| C. | 723,571 (31.0%) |
| Lab. | 342,775 (14.7%) |
| Green | 211,706 (9.1%) |
| LD | 187,876 (8.0%) |
| AIFE | 45,199 (1.9%) |
| Eng. Dem. | 17,771 (0.8%) |
| BNP | 16,909 (0.7%) |
| CPA | 14,893 (0.6%) |
| Peace | 10,130 (0.4%) |
| SGB | 5,454 (0.2%) |
| Roman | 2,997 (0.1%) |
| Your | 2,932 (0.1%) |
| Liberty | 2,494 (0.1%) |
| Harmony | 1,904 (0.1%) |
| UKIP majority | 27,868 |
| (June 2009, C. maj. 372,286) | |

MEMBERS ELECTED
1. *N. Farage, UKIP 2. *D. Hannan, C.
3. J. Atkinson, UKIP 4. *N. Deva, C.
5. A. Dodds, Lab. 6. D. James, UKIP
7. *R. Ashworth, C. 8. *K.Taylor, Green
9. * C. Bearder, LD 10. R. Finch, UKIP

## SOUTH WEST
(Bath and North East Somerset,
Bournemouth, Bristol, Cornwall,
Devon, Dorset, Gloucestershire, North
Somerset, Plymouth, Poole, Somerset,
South Gloucestershire, Swindon,
Torbay, Wiltshire, Isles of Scilly,
Gibraltar)

| | |
|---|---|
| E. 4,059,889 | T. 37.03% |
| UKIP | 484,184 (32.3%) |
| C. | 433,151 (28.9%) |
| Lab. | 206,124 (13.8%) |
| Green | 166,447 (11.1%) |
| LD | 160,376 (10.7%) |
| AIFE | 23,169 (1.6%) |
| Eng. Dem. | 15,081 (1.0%) |
| BNP | 10,910 (0.7%) |
| UKIP majority | 51,033 |
| (June 2009, C. maj. 126,627) | |

MEMBERS ELECTED
1. *W. Dartmouth, UKIP 2. *A. Fox, C.
3. J. Reid, UKIP 4. *J. Girling, C.
5. C. Moody, Lab. 6. M. Scott Cato,
Green

## WALES

| | |
|---|---|
| E. 2,327,175 | T. 31.50% |
| Lab. | 206,332 (28.2%) |
| UKIP | 201,983 (27.6%) |
| C. | 127,742 (17.4%) |
| PC | 111,864 (15.3%) |
| Green | 33,275 (4.5%) |
| LD | 28,930 (4.0%) |
| BNP | 7,655 (1.0%) |
| BF | 6,633 (0.9%) |
| SLP | 4,459 (0.6%) |
| No2EU | 2,803 (0.4%) |
| SGB | 1,384 (0.2%) |
| Lab. majority | 4,349 |
| (June 2004, Lab. maj. 120,039) | |

MEMBERS ELECTED
1. *D. Vaughan, Lab. 2. N. Gill, UKIP
3. *K. Swinburne, C. 4. *J. Evans, PC

## WEST MIDLANDS
(Herefordshire, Shropshire,
Staffordshire, Stoke-on-Trent, Telford
and Wrekin, Warwickshire, West
Midlands Metropolitan area,
Worcestershire)

| | |
|---|---|
| E. 4,105,305 | T. 33.31% |
| UKIP | 428,010 (28.1%) |
| Lab. | 363,033 (21.3%) |
| C. | 330,470 (17.0%) |
| LD | 75,648 (12.0%) |
| Green | 71,464 (8.6%) |
| AIFE | 27,171 (6.2%) |
| WDR | 23,426 (2.3%) |
| BNP | 20,643 (1.3%) |
| Eng. Dem. | 12,832 (1.0%) |
| No2EU | 4,653 (0.9%) |
| Harmony | 1,857 (0.6%) |
| UKIP majority | 64,977 |
| (June 2009, C. maj. 96,016) | |

MEMBERS ELECTED
1. J Seymour, UKIP 2. N. Gill, Lab.
3. *P. Bradbourn, C. 4. J. Carver, UKIP
5. S. Simon, Lab. 6. *A. McIntyre, C.
7. B. Etheridge, UKIP

## YORKSHIRE AND THE HUMBER
(East Riding of Yorkshire,
Kingston-upon-Hull, North East
Lincolnshire, North Lincolnshire,
North Yorkshire, South Yorkshire,
West Yorkshire, York)

| | |
|---|---|
| E. 3,905,726 | T. 33.2% |
| UKIP | 403,630 (31.1%) |
| Lab. | 380,189 (29.3%) |
| C. | 248,945 (19.2%) |
| Green | 102,282 (7.9%) |
| LD | 81,108 (6.3%) |
| AIFE | 24,297 (1.9%) |
| BNP | 20,138 (1.6%) |
| YF | 19,017 (1.5%) |
| Eng. Dem. | 13,288 (1.0%) |
| No2EU | 3,807 (0.3%) |
| UKIP majority | 23,441 |
| (June 2009, C. maj. 69,793) | |

MEMBERS ELECTED
1. J. Collins, UKIP 2. *L. McAvan, Lab.
3. *T. Kirkhope, C. 4. A. Bashir, UKIP
5. R. Corbett, Lab. 6. M. Hookem,
UKIP

# LOCAL GOVERNMENT

Major changes in local government were introduced in England and Wales in 1974 and in Scotland in 1975 by the Local Government Act 1972 and the Local Government (Scotland) Act 1973. Further significant alterations were made in England by the Local Government Acts of 1985, 1992 and 2000.

The structure in England was based on two tiers of local authorities (county councils and district councils) in the non-metropolitan areas; and a single tier of metropolitan councils in the six metropolitan areas of England and London borough councils in London.

Following reviews of the structure of local government in England by the Local Government Commission (now the Boundary Commission for England), 46 unitary (all-purpose) authorities were created between April 1995 and April 1998 to cover certain areas in the non-metropolitan counties. The remaining county areas continue to have two tiers of local authorities. The county and district councils in the Isle of Wight were replaced by a single unitary authority on 1 April 1995; the former counties of Avon, Cleveland, Humberside and Berkshire were replaced by unitary authorities; and Hereford & Worcester was replaced by a new county council for Worcestershire (with district councils) and a unitary authority for Herefordshire. On 1 April 2009 the county areas of Cornwall, Durham, Northumberland, Shropshire and Wiltshire were given unitary status and two new unitary authorities were created for Bedfordshire (Bedford and Central Bedfordshire) and Cheshire (Cheshire East and Cheshire West & Chester) replacing the two-tier county/district system in these areas.

The Local Government (Wales) Act 1994 and the Local Government etc (Scotland) Act 1994 abolished the two-tier structure in Wales and Scotland with effect from 1 April 1996, replacing it with a single tier of unitary authorities. In June 2015 the Welsh government published a proposal to reduce the number of local authorities in Wales from 22 to eight or nine.

In Northern Ireland a reform programme to reduce the number of local authorities from 26 to 11 began in 2012 when legislation finalising the boundaries of the new 11 local government district authorities was approved by the Northern Ireland Assembly. The Local Government Act (Northern Ireland) 2014 received royal assent on 12 May 2014, providing the legislative framework for the 11 new councils. On 1 April 2015 additional functions, that were previously the responsibility of the Northern Ireland executive, fully transferred to the new district authorities.

## ELECTIONS

Local elections are normally held on the first Thursday in May. Generally, all citizens of the UK, the Republic of Ireland, Commonwealth and other European Union citizens who are 18 years or over and resident on the qualifying date in the area for which the election is being held, are entitled to vote at local government elections. A register of electors is prepared and published annually by local electoral registration officers.

A returning officer has the overall responsibility for an election. Voting takes place at polling stations, arranged by the local authority and under the supervision of a presiding officer specially appointed for the purpose. Candidates, who are subject to various statutory qualifications and disqualifications designed to ensure that they are suitable to hold office, must be nominated by electors for the electoral area concerned.

In England, the Local Government Boundary Commission for England is responsible for carrying out periodic reviews of electoral arrangements, to consider whether the boundaries of wards or divisions within a local authority need to be altered to take account of changes in electorate; structural reviews, to consider whether a single, unitary authority should be established in an area instead of an existing two-tier system; and administrative boundary reviews of district or county authorities.

The Local Democracy and Boundary Commission for Wales, the Local Government Boundary Commission for Scotland and the local government boundary commissioner for Northern Ireland (appointed when required by the Boundary Commission for Northern Ireland) are responsible for reviewing the electoral arrangements and boundaries of local authorities within their respective regions.

The Local Government Act 2000 provided for the secretary of state to change the frequency and phasing of elections in England and Wales.

**LOCAL GOVERNMENT BOUNDARY COMMISSION FOR ENGLAND**, 14th Floor, Millbank Tower, London SW1P 4QP **T** 0330-500 1525 **E** reviews@lgbce.org.uk **W** www.lgbce.org.uk

**LOCAL DEMOCRACY AND BOUNDARY COMMISSION FOR WALES**, Ground Floor, Hastings House, Fitzalan Court, Cardiff CF24 0BL **T** 029-2046 4819 **E** ldbc.wales@wales.gsi.gov.uk **W** www.lgbc-wales.gov.uk

**LOCAL GOVERNMENT BOUNDARY COMMISSION FOR SCOTLAND**, Thistle House, 91 Haymarket Terrace, Edinburgh EH12 5HD **T** 0131-538 7510 **E** lgbcs@scottishboundaries.gov.uk **W** www.lgbc-scotland.gov.uk

**BOUNDARY COMMISSION FOR NORTHERN IRELAND**, Stormont House, Stormont Estate, Belfast BT4 3SH **T** 028-9069 4800 **E** bcni@belfast.org.uk **W** www.boundarycommission.org.uk

## INTERNAL ORGANISATION

The council as a whole is the final decision-making body within any authority. Councils are free to a great extent to make their own internal organisational arrangements. The Local Government Act, given royal assent on 28 July 2000, allows councils to adopt one of three broad categories of constitution which include a separate executive:
• A directly elected mayor with a cabinet selected by the mayor
• A cabinet, either elected by the council or appointed by its leader
• A directly elected mayor and council manager
Normally, questions of policy are settled by the full council while the administration of the various services is the responsibility of committees of councillors. Day-to-day decisions are delegated to the council's officers, who act within the policies laid down by the councillors.

## FINANCE

Local government in England, Wales and Scotland is financed from four sources: council tax, non-domestic rates, government grants and income from fees and charges for services.

## COUNCIL TAX

Council tax is a local tax levied by each local council. Liability for the council tax bill usually falls on the owner-occupier or tenant of a dwelling which is their sole or main residence. Council tax bills may be reduced because of the personal circumstances of people resident in a property and there are discounts in the case of dwellings occupied by fewer than two adults.

In England, unitary and metropolitan authorities are responsible for collecting their own council tax. In areas where there are two tiers of local authority, each county and district authority sets its own council tax rate; the district authorities collect the combined council tax and the county councils claim their share from the district councils' collection funds. In Wales, each unitary authority sets its own council tax rate and is responsible for collection. In Scotland, each local authority sets its own rate of council tax.

The tax relates to the value of the dwelling. In England and Scotland each dwelling is placed in one of eight valuation bands, ranging from A to H, based on the property's estimated market value as at 1 April 1991. In Wales there are nine bands, ranging from A to I, based on the estimated market value of property as at 1 April 2003.

The valuation bands and ranges of values in England, Wales and Scotland are:

### England

| | | | |
|---|---|---|---|
| A | Up to £40,000 | E | £88,001–£120,000 |
| B | £40,001–£52,000 | F | £120,001–£160,000 |
| C | £52,001–£68,000 | G | £160,001–£320,000 |
| D | £68,001–£88,000 | H | Over £320,001 |

### Wales

| | | | |
|---|---|---|---|
| A | Up to £44,000 | F | £162,001–£223,000 |
| B | £44,001–£65,000 | G | £223,001–£324,000 |
| C | £65,001–£91,000 | H | £324,001–£424,000 |
| D | £91,001–£123,000 | I | Over £424,001 |
| E | £123,001–£162,000 | | |

### Scotland

| | | | |
|---|---|---|---|
| A | Up to £27,000 | E | £58,001–£80,000 |
| B | £27,001–£35,000 | F | £80,001–£106,000 |
| C | £35,001–£45,000 | G | £106,001–£212,000 |
| D | £45,001–£58,000 | H | Over £212,001 |

The council tax within a local area varies between the different bands according to proportions laid down by law. The charge attributable to each band as a proportion of the Band D charge set by the council is approximately:

| | | | |
|---|---|---|---|
| A | 67% | F | 144% |
| B | 78% | G | 167% |
| C | 89% | H | 200% |
| D | 100% | I | 233%* |
| E | 122% | | |

*Wales only

The average Band D council tax bill for each authority area is given in the tables starting on page 264. There may be variations from the given figure within each district council area because of different parish or community precepts being levied.

## NON-DOMESTIC RATES

Non-domestic (business) rates are collected by billing authorities; these are the district councils in those areas of England with two tiers of local government and are unitary authorities in other parts of England, in Wales and in Scotland. In respect of England and Wales, the Local Government Finance Act 1988 provides for liability for rates to be assessed on the basis of a poundage (multiplier) tax on the rateable value of property (hereditaments). Separate multipliers are set by the Department for Communities and Local Government (CLG) in England, the Welsh government and the Scottish government. Rates are collected by the billing authority for the area where a property is located. Rate income collected by billing authorities is paid into a national non-domestic rating (NNDR) pool and redistributed to individual authorities on the basis of the adult population figure as prescribed by CLG, the Welsh government or the Scottish government. The rates pools are maintained separately in England, Wales and Scotland. Actual payment of rates in certain cases is subject to transitional arrangements, to phase in the larger increases and reductions in rates resulting from the effects of the latest revaluation.

Rateable values for the 2010 rating lists for England, Wales and Scotland came into effect on 1 April 2010. They are derived from the rental value of property as at 1 April 2003 and determined on certain statutory assumptions by the Valuation Office Agency in England and Wales, and by local area assessors in Scotland. New property which is added to the list, and significant changes to existing property, necessitate amendments to the rateable value on the same basis. Rating lists (valuation rolls in Scotland) remain in force until the next general revaluation, which usually take place every five years to reflect changes in the property market. The next revaluations for England, Wales and Scotland are scheduled for 2017.

A revaluation of non-domestic properties in Northern Ireland was completed at the start of 2015 and since 1 April 2015 the rateable value of all non-domestic properties in Northern Ireland is based on the rental value of the property as at 1 April 2013; there is no date scheduled for the next revaluation.

Certain types of property are exempt from rates, eg agricultural land and buildings, certain businesses and some places of public religious worship. Charities and other non-profit-making organisations may receive full or partial relief and relief schemes for small businesses are available in England, Wales, Scotland and Northern Ireland. Empty commercial property in England and Wales is exempt from business rates for the first three months that the property is vacant (six months for some types of property such as industrial premises and listed buildings), after which full business rates are normally payable. In Scotland an empty commercial property is exempt from business rates for the first three months and entitled to a 10 per cent discount thereafter, except for empty industrial and listed buildings and properties with a rateable value of less than £1,700, which are entirely exempt.

## COMPLAINTS

### ENGLAND

In England the Local Government Ombudsman investigates complaints of injustice arising from maladministration by local authorities and certain other bodies. The Local Government Ombudsman will not usually consider a complaint unless the local authority concerned has had an opportunity to investigate and reply to a complainant.

LOCAL GOVERNMENT OMBUDSMAN, PO Box 4771, Coventry CV4 0EH T 0300-061 0614 W www.lgo.org.uk
*Ombudsman,* Dr Jane Martin

## WALES

The office of Public Services Ombudsman for Wales came into force on 1 April 2006, incorporating the functions of the Local Government Ombudsman for Wales.

PUBLIC SERVICES OMBUDSMAN FOR WALES,
1 Ffordd yr Hen Gae, Pencoed CF35 5LJ T 0300-790 0203
W www.ombudsman-wales.org.uk
*Ombudsman,* Nick Bennett

## SCOTLAND

The Scottish Public Services Ombudsman is responsible for complaints regarding the maladministration of local government in Scotland.

SCOTTISH PUBLIC SERVICES OMBUDSMAN,
4 Melville Street, Edinburgh EH3 7NS T 0800-377 7330
W www.spso.org.uk
*Ombudsman,* Jim Martin

## NORTHERN IRELAND

The Northern Ireland Ombudsman (also known as the Northern Ireland Commissioner for Complaints) fulfils a similar function in Northern Ireland, investigating complaints about local authorities and certain public bodies. Complaints are made to the relevant local authority in the first instance but may also be made directly to the ombudsman.

NORTHERN IRELAND COMMISSIONER FOR
COMPLAINTS, 33 Wellington Place, Belfast BT1 6HN
T 028-9023 3821 E ombudsman@ni-ombudsman.org.uk
W www.ni-ombudsman.org.uk
*Ombudsman,* Dr Tom Frawley, CBE

## THE QUEEN'S REPRESENTATIVES

The lord-lieutenant of a county is the permanent local representative of the Crown in that county. The appointment of lord-lieutenants is now regulated by the Lieutenancies Act 1997. They are appointed by the sovereign on the recommendation of the prime minister. The retirement age is 75. The office of lord-lieutenant dates from 1551, and its holder was originally responsible for maintaining order and for local defence in the county. The duties of the post include attending on royalty during official visits to the county, performing certain duties in connection with the armed forces (and in particular the reserve forces), and making presentations of honours and awards on behalf of the Crown. In England, Wales and Northern Ireland, the lord-lieutenant usually also holds the office of *Custos Rotulorum.* As such, he or she acts as head of the county's commission of the peace (which recommends the appointment of magistrates).

The office of sheriff (from the Old English *shire-reeve*) of a county was created in the tenth century. The sheriff was the special nominee of the sovereign, and the office reached the peak of its influence under the Norman kings. The Provisions of Oxford (1258) laid down a yearly tenure of office. Since the mid-16th century the office has been purely civil, with military duties taken over by the lord-lieutenant of the county. The sheriff (commonly known as 'high sheriff') attends on royalty during official visits to the county, acts as the returning officer during parliamentary elections in county constituencies, attends the opening ceremony when a high court judge goes on circuit, executes high court writs, and appoints under-sheriffs to act as deputies. The appointments and duties of the sheriffs in England and Wales are laid down by the Sheriffs Act 1887.

The serving high sheriff submits a list of names of possible future sheriffs to a tribunal, which chooses three names to put to the sovereign. The tribunal nominates the high sheriff annually on 12 November and the sovereign picks the name of the sheriff to succeed in the following year. The term of office runs from 25 March to the following 24 March (the civil and legal year before 1752). No person may be chosen twice in three years if there is any other suitable person in the county.

## CIVIC DIGNITIES

District councils in England and local councils in Wales may petition for a royal charter granting borough or 'city' status to the council.

In England and Wales the chair of a borough or county borough council may be called a mayor, and the chair of a city council may be called a lord mayor (if lord mayoralty has been conferred on that city). Parish councils in England and community councils in Wales may call themselves 'town councils', in which case their chair is the town mayor.

In Scotland the chair of a local council may be known as a convenor; a provost is the mayoral equivalent. The chair of the councils for the cities of Aberdeen, Dundee, Edinburgh and Glasgow are lord provosts.

## ENGLAND

There are 27 counties, divided into 201 districts, 55 unitary authorities (plus the Isles of Scilly) and 36 metropolitan boroughs.

The populations of most of the unitary authorities are in the range of 100,000 to 300,000. The district councils have populations broadly in the range of 60,000 to 150,000; some, however, have larger populations, because of the need to avoid dividing large towns, and some in mainly rural areas have smaller populations.

The main conurbations outside Greater London – Tyne and Wear, West Midlands, Merseyside, Greater Manchester, West Yorkshire and South Yorkshire – are divided into 36 metropolitan boroughs, most of which have a population of over 200,000.

### ELECTIONS

For districts, counties and for 8,810 parishes, there are elected councils, consisting of directly elected councillors. The councillors elect one of their number as chair annually.

In general, councils can have whole council elections, elections by thirds or elections by halves. However all metropolitan authorities must hold elections by thirds. The electoral cycle of any new unitary authority is specified in the appropriate statutory order under which it is established.

### FUNCTIONS

In areas with a two-tier system of local governance, functions are divided between the district and county authorities, with those functions affecting the larger area or population generally being the responsibility of the county council. A few functions continue to be exercised over the larger area by joint bodies, made up of councillors from each authority within the area.

Generally the allocation of functions is as follows:
*County councils:* education; strategic planning; traffic, transport and highways; fire service; consumer protection; refuse disposal; smallholdings; social care; libraries
*District councils:* local planning; housing; highways (maintenance of certain urban roads and off-street car parks); building regulations; environmental health; refuse collection; cemeteries and crematoria; collection of council tax and non-domestic rates
*Unitary and metropolitan councils:* their functions are all those listed above, except that the fire service is exercised by a joint body

*Concurrently by county and district councils:* recreation (parks, playing fields, swimming pools); museums; encouragement of the arts, tourism and industry

## PARISH COUNCILS

Parish or town councils are the most local tier of government in England. There are currently around 10,000 parishes in England, of which around 8,810 have councils. Since 15 February 2008 local councils have been able to create new parish councils without seeking approval from the government. Around 80 per cent of parish councils represent populations of less than 2,500; parishes with no parish council can be grouped with neighbouring parishes under a common parish council. A parish council comprises at least five members, the number being fixed by the district council. Elections are held every four years, at the time of the election of the district councillor for the ward including the parish. Full parish councils must be formed for those parishes with more than 999 electors – below this number, parish meetings comprising the electors of the parish must be held at least twice a year.

Parish council functions include: allotments; encouragement of arts and crafts; community halls, recreational facilities (eg open spaces, swimming pools), cemeteries and crematoria; and many minor functions. They must also be given an opportunity to comment on planning applications. They may, like county and district councils, spend limited sums for the general benefit of the parish. They levy a precept on the district councils for their funds. Parish precepts for 2015–16 totalled £409m, an increase of 5.2 per cent on 2014–15.

## FINANCE

Local government revenue expenditure is budgeted to be £9.54bn in 2015–16; of this £24.7bn is to be raised through council tax, £11.9bn from the business rate retention scheme and £56.6bn from government grants. The remainder will be drawn down from local authority reserves.

Since April 2013 local authorities retain a share of business rates and keep the growth on that share (the 'rate retention scheme'). Revenue support grant is paid to local authorities to enable all authorities in the same class to broadly set the same council tax; in 2015–16 revenue support grant totals £9.5bn. In addition central government pays specific grants in support of revenue expenditure on particular services. Police grant totals £7.4bn in 2015–16.

In England, the average council tax per dwelling for 2014–15 is £1,051. The average council tax bill for a Band D dwelling (occupied by two adults, including parish precepts) for 2015–16 is £1,484, an increase of 1.1 per cent from 2014–15. The average Band D council tax is £1,547 in shire districts, £1,451 in metropolitan areas, £1,520 in unitary authority areas and £1,298 in London. Since 2006–7 the London figure has included a levy to fund the 2012 Olympic Games, which equates to a £20 a year increase on a Band D council tax. This levy is expected to continue until 2016–17.

The non-domestic rating multiplier for England for 2015–16 is 49.3p (48.0p for small businesses). The City of London is able to set a different multiplier from the rest of England; for 2015–16 this is 49.7p (48.4p for small businesses).

Under the Local Government and Housing Act 1989, local authorities have four main ways of paying for capital expenditure: borrowing and other forms of extended credit; capital grants from central government towards some types of capital expenditure; 'usable' capital receipts from the sale of land, houses and other assets; and revenue.

The amount of capital expenditure which a local authority can finance by borrowing (or other forms of credit) is effectively limited by the credit approvals issued to it by central government. Most credit approvals can be used for any kind of local authority capital expenditure; these are known as basic credit approvals. Others (supplementary credit approvals) can be used only for the kind of expenditure specified in the approval, and so are often given to fund particular projects or services.

Local authorities can use all capital receipts from the sale of property or assets for capital spending, except in the case of sales of council houses. Generally, the 'usable' part of a local authority's capital receipts consists of 25 per cent of receipts from the sale of council houses and 50 per cent of other housing assets such as shops or vacant land. The balance has to be set aside as provision for repaying debt and meeting other credit liabilities.

## EXPENDITURE

Budgeted revenue expenditure for 2015–16 is:

| Service | £ million |
|---|---|
| *Education | 34,976 |
| Highways and transport | 4,922 |
| Social care | 21,779 |
| Public health | 3,321 |
| Housing (excluding HRA) | 1,742 |
| Cultural, environment and planning | 8,695 |
| Police | 10,951 |
| Fire and rescue | 2,080 |
| Central services | 3,112 |
| Mandatory housing benefits | 21,094 |
| Other services | 281 |
| *Less* appropriations from accumulated absences account | (6) |
| *Net current expenditure* | 113,089 |
| Capital financing | 4,463 |
| Capital expenditure charged to revenue account | 1,320 |
| Discretionary non-domestic rate relief | – |
| Bad debt provision | 57 |
| Flood defence payments to Environment Agency | 30 |
| Private Finance Initiative schemes | 4 |
| Carbon Reduction Commitment | 25 |
| *Less* adjustments permitted by regulation | (20) |
| *Less* interest receipts | (793) |
| *Less* specific grants outside AEF | (22,427) |
| *Less* Business Rates Supplement | (223) |
| *Less* Community Infrastructure Levy | (87) |
| REVENUE EXPENDITURE | 95,437 |

HRA = Housing Revenue Account
AEF = aggregate external finance
* Education expenditure is not comparable to previous years due to a number of schools becoming centrally funded academies

# LONDON

The Greater London Council was abolished in 1986 and London was divided into 32 borough councils, which have a status similar to the metropolitan borough councils in the rest of England, and the City of London Corporation.

In March 1998 the government announced proposals for a Greater London Authority (GLA) covering the area of the 32 London boroughs and the City of London, which would comprise a directly elected mayor and a 25-member assembly. A referendum was held in London on 7 May 1998 and 72 per cent of voters balloted in favour of the GLA. A London mayor was elected on 4 May 2000 and the authority assumed its responsibilities on 3 July 2000 (*see also* Regional Government).

## LONDON BOROUGH COUNCILS

The London boroughs have whole council elections every four years, in the year immediately following the county council election year. The most recent elections took place on 22 May 2014.

The borough councils have responsibility for the following functions: building regulations, cemeteries and crematoria, consumer protection, education, youth employment, environmental health, electoral registration, food, drugs, housing, leisure services, libraries, local planning, local roads, museums, parking, recreation (parks, playing fields, swimming pools), refuse collection and street cleaning, social services, town planning and traffic management.

## CITY OF LONDON CORPORATION

The City of London Corporation is the local authority for the City of London. Its legal definition is the 'Mayor and Commonalty and Citizens of the City of London'. It is governed by the court of common council, which consists of the lord mayor, 25 other aldermen and 100 common councilmen. The lord mayor and two sheriffs are nominated annually by the City guilds (the livery companies) and elected by the court of aldermen. Aldermen and councilmen are elected from the 25 wards into which the City is divided; councilmen must stand for re-election annually. The council is a legislative assembly, and there are no political parties.

The corporation has the same functions as the London borough councils. In addition, it runs the City of London Police; is the health authority for the Port of London; has health control of animal imports throughout Greater London, including at Heathrow airport; owns and manages public open spaces throughout Greater London; runs the central criminal court; and runs Billingsgate, New Spitalfields and Smithfield markets.

## THE CITY GUILDS (LIVERY COMPANIES)

The livery companies of the City of London grew out of early medieval religious fraternities and began to emerge as trade and craft guilds, retaining their religious aspect, in the 12th century. From the early 14th century, only members of the trade and craft guilds could call themselves citizens of the City of London. The guilds began to be called livery companies, because of the distinctive livery worn by the most prosperous guild members on ceremonial occasions, in the late 15th century.

By the early 19th century the power of the companies within their trades had begun to wane, but those wearing the livery of a company continued to play an important role in the government of the City of London. Liverymen still have the right to nominate the lord mayor and sheriffs, and most members of the court of common council are liverymen.

## WALES

The Local Government (Wales) Act 1994 abolished the two-tier structure of eight county and 37 district councils which had existed since 1974, and replaced it, from 1 April 1996, with 22 unitary authorities. The new authorities were elected in May 1995. Each unitary authority inherited all the functions of the previous county and district councils, except fire services (which are provided by three combined fire authorities, composed of representatives from the unitary authorities) and national parks (which are the responsibility of three independent national park authorities). In June 2015 the Welsh government published plans to reduce the number of local authorities from 22 to eight or nine.

## COMMUNITY COUNCILS

In Wales communities are the equivalent of parishes in England. Unlike England, where many areas are not in any parish, communities have been established for the whole of Wales, approximately 865 communities in all. Community meetings may be convened as and when desired.

Community or town councils exist in around 730 of the communities and further councils may be established at the request of a community meeting. Community councils have broadly the same range of powers as English parish councils. Community councillors are elected for a term of four years.

## ELECTIONS

Elections take place every four years; the last elections took place in May 2012.

## FINANCE

Total budgeted revenue expenditure for 2015–16 is £7.8bn, a decrease of 1.6 per cent on 2014–15. Total budget requirement, which excludes expenditure financed by specific and special government grants and any use of reserves, is £6bn. This comprises revenue support grant of £3.3bn, support from the national non-domestic rate pool of £1bn, police grant of £221m and £1.6bn to be raised through council tax. The non-domestic rating multiplier for Wales for 2015–16 is 48.2p. The average Band D council tax levied in Wales for 2015–16 is £1,328, comprising unitary authorities £1,088, police and crime commissioners £211 and community councils £29.

## EXPENDITURE

Local authority budgeted revenue expenditure for 2015–16 is:

| Service | £ million |
|---|---|
| Education | 2,555.1 |
| Social services | 1,639.0 |
| Council fund housing | 1,141.2 |
| Local environmental services | 377.8 |
| Roads and transport | 286.5 |
| Libraries, culture, heritage, sport and recreation | 218.6 |
| Planning, economic and community development | 80.6 |
| Council tax collection | 36.2 |
| Debt financing | 338.3 |
| Central administrative and other revenue expenditure | 313.3 |
| Police | 666.9 |
| Fire | 144.8 |
| National parks | 14.5 |
| *Gross revenue expenditure* | 7,812.8 |
| *Less* specific and special government grants | (1,935.1) |
| *Net revenue expenditure* | 5,877.7 |
| *Less* appropriations from reserves | (84.5) |
| Council tax reduction scheme | 255.7 |
| BUDGET REQUIREMENT | 6,048.9 |

## SCOTLAND

The Local Government etc (Scotland) Act 1994 abolished the two-tier structure of nine regional and 53 district councils which had existed since 1975 and replaced it, from 1 April 1996, with 29 unitary authorities on the mainland; the three islands councils remained. The new authorities were elected in April 1995.

In July 1999 the Scottish parliament assumed responsibility for legislation on local government.

## ELECTIONS

The unitary authorities consist of directly elected councillors. The Scottish Local Government (Elections) Act 2002 moved elections from a three-year to a four-year cycle, but to avoid the local authority elections coinciding with the Scottish parliament elections in May 2011, the last local authority elections took place in May 2012.

## FUNCTIONS
The functions of the councils and islands councils are: education; social work; strategic planning; the provision of infrastructure such as roads; consumer protection; flood prevention; coast protection; valuation and rating; the police and fire services; civil defence; electoral registration; public transport; registration of births, deaths and marriages; housing; leisure and recreation; development and building control; environmental health; licensing; allotments; public conveniences; and the administration of district courts.

## COMMUNITY COUNCILS
Scottish community councils differ from those in England and Wales. Their purpose as defined in statute is to ascertain and express the views of the communities they represent, and to take in the interests of their communities such action as appears to be expedient or practicable. Around 1,200 community councils have been established under schemes drawn up by local authorities in Scotland.

## FINANCE
Budgeted total revenue support for 2015–16 is £10.0bn, comprising £7.1bn general resource grant, non-domestic rate income of £2.8bn and specific revenue grants of £90.9m. The non-domestic rate multiplier or poundage for 2015–16 is 48.0p. Larger businesses in 2015–16 (rateable value in excess of £35,000) pay a poundage supplement of 1.3p, which contributes towards the cost of the small business bonus scheme. Non-domestic properties with a rateable value of £18,000 or less may be eligible for non-domestic rates relief – ranging from 25 to 100 per cent – from the small business bonus scheme. The average Band D council tax for 2015–16 is £1,149.

## EXPENDITURE
Local authority budgeted net expenditure for 2015–16 is:

| Service | £ million |
| --- | --- |
| Education | 4,764.7 |
| Cultural and related services | 583.2 |
| Social work services | 3,106.3 |
| Roads and transport | 457.7 |
| Environmental services | 680.7 |
| Planning and development services | 278.8 |
| Other | 2,005.7 |
| TOTAL | 11,877.1 |

## NORTHERN IRELAND

In 2012 a reform programme began to reduce the number of district councils from 26 to 11. The Local Government Act (Northern Ireland) received royal assent on 12 May 2014 providing new governance arrangements for local councils and made transitional provisions for the transfer of staff, assets and liabilities etc to the new 11 councils. On 1 April 2015 additional functions, that were previously the responsibility of the Northern Ireland executive, fully transferred to the new district authorities.

## ELECTIONS
Elections to the 11 councils took place on 22 May 2014.

## FUNCTIONS
The councils are responsible for approving business and financial plans, setting domestic and non-domestic rates. From April 2016 councils will also be responsible for urban regeneration and community development.

The district councils are responsible for:
*Direct Service Provision* of a wide range of local services, including: building control-inspection and the regulation of new buildings; byelaw enforcement; cemeteries; community centres; cultural facilities; dog control; environmental health; food safety; health and safety; local economic development; local planning; off-street parking (except park and ride schemes); parks, open spaces and playgrounds; public conveniences; recycling and waste management; registration of births, deaths and marriages; sport, leisure and recreational facilities; and street cleaning. District councils also have a role in community development and safety; sports development; summer schemes; and tourism.

*Representation:* nominating representatives to sit as members of the various statutory bodies responsible for the administration of regional services such as education, health and social services, libraries and road safety committees

## FINANCE
Government in Northern Ireland is part-funded by a system of rates, which supplement the Northern Ireland budget from the UK government. The ratepayer receives a combined tax bill consisting of the regional rate, set by the Northern Ireland executive, and the district rate, which is set by each district council. The regional and district rates are both collected by the Land and Property Services Agency (formerly the Rate Collection Agency). The product of the district rates is paid over to each council while the product of the regional rate supports expenditure by the departments of the executive and assembly.

Since April 2007 domestic rates bills have been based on the capital value of a property, rather than the rental value. The capital value is defined as the price the property might reasonably be expected to realise had it been sold on the open market on 1 January 2005. Non-domestic rates bills are based on 2001 rental values.

Rate bills are calculated by multiplying the property's net annual rental value (in the case of non-domestic property), or capital value (in the case of domestic property), by the regional and district rate poundages respectively.

For 2015–16 the overall average domestic poundage is 0.7490p compared to 0.7387p in 2014–15. The overall average non-domestic rate poundage in 2015–16 is 55.47p compared to 59.17p in 2014–15.

# POLITICAL COMPOSITION OF LOCAL COUNCILS

*as at May 2015*

*Abbreviations*

| | |
|---|---|
| All. | Alliance |
| BNP | British National Party |
| C. | Conservative |
| DUP | Democratic Unionist Party |
| Green | Green |
| Ind. | Independent |
| Ind. Un. | Independent Unionist |
| Lab. | Labour |
| LD | Liberal Democrat |
| Lib. | Liberal |
| O. | Other |
| PC | Plaid Cymru |
| PUP | Progressive Unionist Party of Northern Ireland |
| R. | Residents Associations/Ratepayers |
| SD | Social Democrat |
| SDLP | Social Democratic and Labour Party |
| SF | Sinn Fein |
| SNP | Scottish National Party |
| Soc. | Socialist |
| TUV | Traditional Unionist Voice |
| UKIP | UK Independence Party |
| UUP | Ulster Unionist Party |
| v. | vacant |

Total number of seats is given in parentheses after council name.

## ENGLAND

### COUNTY COUNCILS

Buckinghamshire (49) — C. 37; LD 4; UKIP 4; Ind. 2; Lab. 1; O. 1

Cambridgeshire (69) — C. 33; LD 13; UKIP 11; Lab. 8; Ind. 4

Cumbria (84) — Lab. 36; C. 26; LD 15; Ind. 5; O. 2; v. 2

Derbyshire (64) — Lab. 43; C. 17; LD 3; v. 1

Devon (62) — C. 38; LD 9; Lab. 7; UKIP 4; Ind. 3; Green 1

Dorset (45) — C. 27; LD 12; Lab. 5; UKIP. 1

East Sussex (49) — C. 20; LD 10; Lab. 7; UKIP 7; Ind. 3; O. 2

Essex (75) — C. 44; Lab. 9; LD 9; UKIP 6; O. 4; Green 2; Ind. 1

Gloucestershire (53) — C. 24; LD 14; Lab. 9; UKIP 3; Green 1; Ind. 1; O. 1

Hampshire (78) — C. 46; LD 16; UKIP 9; Lab. 4; Ind. 2; O. 1

Hertfordshire (77) — C. 46; LD 16; Lab. 15

Kent (84) — C. 46; UKIP 16; Lab. 13; LD 7; Green 1; Ind. 1

Lancashire (84) — Lab. 39; C. 35; LD 6; Ind. 3; Green 1

Leicestershire (55) — C. 30; LD 13; Lab. 10; UKIP 2

Lincolnshire (77) — C. 34; Lab. 12; UKIP 12; O. 11; LD 4; Ind. 3; v. 1

Norfolk (84) — C. 40; UKIP 14; Lab. 13; LD 10; Green 4; O. 1; v. 2

North Yorkshire (72) — C. 45; Ind. 10; Lab. 7; LD 6; Lib. 2; UKIP 2

Northamptonshire (57) — C. 36; Lab. 11; LD 6; UKIP 3; Ind. 1

Nottinghamshire (67) — Lab. 32; C. 21; LD 7; O. 4; Ind. 3

Oxfordshire (63) — C. 31; Lab. 15; LD 11; Ind. 4; Green 2

Somerset (55) — C. 31; LD 15; Lab. 3; Ind. 3; UKIP 3

Staffordshire (62) — C. 34; Lab. 23; O. 3; Ind. 1; UKIP 1

Suffolk (75) — C. 38; Lab. 15; UKIP 9; LD 7; Ind. 4; Green 2

Surrey (81) — C. 58; LD. 9; R. 9; UKIP 3; Green 1; Lab. 1

Warwickshire (62) — C. 26; Lab. 22; LD 9; Ind. 3; Green 2

West Sussex (71) — C. 44; UKIP 10; LD 7; Lab. 6; Ind. 4

Worcestershire (57) — C. 31; Lab. 11; LD 4; Ind. 3; O. 3; Green 2; UKIP 2; R. 1

### DISTRICT COUNCILS

Adur (30) — C. 21; UKIP 6; Ind. 2; Lab. 1

Allerdale (56) — Lab. 28; C. 17; Ind. 4; O. 4; UKIP 3

Amber Valley (45) — C. 24; Lab. 23

Arun (54) — C. 42; LD 5; UKIP 4; Ind. 2; Lab. 1

Ashfield (35) — Lab. 22; LD 5; C. 4; Ind. 3; O. 1

Ashford (43) — C. 34; Lab. 4; Ind. 3; LD 1; UKIP 1

Aylesbury Vale (59) — C. 43; LD 9; UKIP 4; Lab. 2; Ind. 1

Babergh (43) — C. 31; Ind. 8; LD 3; Lab. 1

Barrow-in-Furness (36) — Lab. 27; C. 9

Basildon (42) — C. 18; UKIP 11; Lab. 9; O. 2; Green 1; LD 1

Basingstoke and Deane (60) — C. 32; Lab. 17; LD 7; Ind. 4

Bassetlaw (48) — Lab. 33; C. 12; Ind. 3

Blaby (39) — C. 29; Lab. 6; LD 4

Bolsover (37) — Lab. 32; Ind. 4; O. 1

Boston (30) — C. 13; UKIP 12; Ind. 2; Lab. 2; O. 1

Braintree (49) — C. 44; Lab. 2; R. 2; Green 1

Breckland (49) — C. 42; UKIP 4; Lab. 2; Ind. 1

Brentwood (37) — C. 23; LD 11; Lab. 2; Ind. 1

Broadland (47) — C. 43; LD 4

Bromsgrove (31) — C. 18; Lab. 7; Ind. 3; R. 3

Broxbourne (30) — C. 24; Lab. 3; O. 2; UKIP 1

Broxtowe (44) — C. 27; Lab. 12; LD 4; Ind. 1

Burnley (45) — Lab. 30; LD 10; C. 5

Cambridge (42) — Lab. 24; LD 14; Ind. 2; C. 1; Green 1

Cannock Chase (41) — Lab. 22; C. 12; UKIP 5; Ind. 1; LD 1

Canterbury (39) — C. 31; Lab. 3; LD 3; UKIP 2

Carlisle (52) — Lab. 29; C. 20; Ind. 2; LD 1

Castle Point (41) — C. 23; O. 13; UKIP 3; Ind. 2

Charnwood (52) — C. 41; Lab. 9; Ind. 1; LD 1

Chelmsford (57) — C. 52; LD 5

Cheltenham (40) — LD 24; C. 11; O. 4; Ind. 1

Cherwell (50) — C. 41; Lab. 7; LD 1; Ind. 1; O. 1

Chesterfield (48) — Lab. 34; LD 11; Ind. 2; UKIP 1

Chichester (48) — C. 42; Ind. 3; LD 3

Chiltern (40) — C. 35; LD 3; Ind. 2

Chorley (47) — Lab. 31; C. 14; Ind. 2

Christchurch (24) — C. 21; Ind. 2; UKIP 1

Colchester (60)   C. 27; LD 20; Lab. 9; O. 4
Copeland (51)   Lab. 29; C. 17; Ind. 5
Corby (29)   Lab. 24; C. 5
Cotswolds (34)   C. 24; LD 10
Craven (30)   C. 20; Ind. 6; LD 2; Lab. 1;
   UKIP 1
Crawley (37)   Lab. 19; C. 18
Dacorum (51)   C. 46; LD 3; Lab. 2
Dartford (44)   C. 34; Lab. 7; R. 3
Daventry (36)   C. 31; Lab. 2; UKIP 2; LD 1
Derbyshire Dales (39)   C. 29; Lab. 5; LD 3; Ind. 1; O. 1
Dover (45)   C. 25; Lab. 17; UKIP 3
East Cambridgeshire (39)   C. 36; LD 2; Ind. 1
East Devon (59)   C. 37; Ind. 15; LD 6; O. 1
East Dorset (29)   C. 25; LD 3; Ind. 1
East Hampshire (44)   C. 42; LD 2
East Hertfordshire (50)   C. 50
East Lindsey (55)   C. 33; UKIP 8; Ind. 6; Lab. 4;
   O. 3; LD 1
East Northamptonshire   C. 37; Ind. 2; LD 1
   (40)
East Staffordshire (39)   C. 25; Lab. 12; LD 1; UKIP 1
Eastbourne (27)   LD 18; C. 9
Eastleigh (44)   LD 38; C. 6
Eden (38)   C. 21; Ind. 10; LD 7
Elmbridge (60)   C. 33; R. 19; LD 7; O. 1
Epping Forest (58)   C. 38; R. 12; LD 3; Ind. 2;
   UKIP 2; Green 1
Epsom and Ewell (38)   R. 31; C. 4; Lab. 3
Erewash (47)   C. 30; Lab. 17
Exeter (40)   Lab. 29; C. 10; LD 1
Fareham (31)   C. 24; LD 4; Ind. 2; UKIP 1
Fenland (39)   C. 34; Ind. 3; LD 2
Forest Heath (27)   C. 23; Ind. 2; Lab. 1; LD 1
Forest of Dean (48)   C. 21; Lab. 13; UKIP 7; Ind. 5;
   Green 2
Fylde (51)   C. 32; Ind. 12; LD 2; O. 2; R. 2;
   Lab. 1
Gedling (41)   Lab. 25; C. 15; LD 1
Gloucester (36)   C. 20; Lab. 9; LD 7
Gosport (34)   C. 21; Lab. 6; LD 6; UKIP 1
Gravesham (44)   C. 23; Lab. 21
Great Yarmouth (39)   C. 14; Lab. 14; UKIP 10; Ind. 1
Guildford (48)   C. 35; LD 9; O. 3; Lab. 1
Hambleton (28)   C. 27; UKIP 1
Harborough (37)   C. 29; LD 8
Harlow (33)   Lab. 19; C. 12; UKIP 2
Harrogate (54)   C. 35; LD 15; Ind. 2; O. 2
Hart (33)   C. 16; LD 8; O. 8; Ind. 1
Hastings (32)   Lab. 24; C. 8
Havant (38)   C. 31; Lab. 4; UKIP 2; LD 1
Hertsmere (39)   C. 37; Lab. 2
High Peak (43)   C. 23; Lab. 17; LD 2; Ind. 1
Hinckley and Bosworth   C. 21; LD 12; Lab. 1
   (34)
Horsham (44)   C. 39; LD 4; Ind. 1
Huntingdonshire (52)   C. 35; Ind. 5; UKIP 5; LD 4;
   Lab. 2; O. 1
Hyndburn (34)   Lab. 25; C. 7; UKIP 2
Ipswich (48)   Lab. 31; C. 15; LD 2
Kettering (36)   C. 25; Lab. 7; Ind. 1; v. 3
King's Lynn and West   C. 50; Lab. 10; Ind. 2
   Norfolk (62)
Lancaster (60)   Lab. 29; C. 19; Green 9; Ind. 2;
   O. 1
Lewes (41)   C. 24; LD 11; Green 3; Ind. 2;
   UKIP 1
Lichfield (47)   C. 41; Lab. 4; LD 1; UKIP 1
Lincoln City (33)   Lab. 27; C. 6

Maidstone (55)   C. 25; LD 20; Ind. 6; Lab. 2;
   UKIP 2
Maldon (31)   C. 28; Ind. 2; UKIP 1
Malvern Hills (38)   C. 23; Ind. 7; LD 5; Green 3
Mansfield (36)   Lab. 18; Ind. 16; UKIP 2
Melton (28)   C. 26; Ind. 2
Mendip (47)   C. 32; LD 11; Green 3; Ind. 1
Mid Devon (42)   C. 28; Ind. 6; LD 5; UKIP 2;
   Lib. 1
Mid Suffolk (40)   C. 29; Green 5; LD 4; Ind. 2
Mid Sussex (54)   C. 54
Mole Valley (41)   C. 23; LD 10; Ind. 6; v. 2
New Forest (60)   C. 58; LD 2
Newark and Sherwood   C. 24; Lab. 12; Ind. 3
   (39)
Newcastle-under-Lyme   Lab. 28; C. 20; LD 5;
   (60)   Ind. 4; UKIP 2; Green 1
North Devon (43)   C. 19; LD 12; Ind. 10; O. 1;
   UKIP 1
North Dorset (33)   C. 27; LD 4; Ind. 2
North East Derbyshire   Lab. 34; C. 18; Ind. 1
   (53)
North Hertfordshire (49)   C. 36; Lab. 11; LD 2
North Kesteven (43)   C. 28; O. 15
North Norfolk (48)   C. 33; LD 15
North Warwickshire (35)   C. 22; Lab. 13
North West   C. 25; Lab. 10; Ind. 2; LD 1
   Leicestershire (38)
Northampton (45)   C. 26; Lab. 17; LD 2
Norwich (39)   Lab. 22; Green 14; LD 3
Nuneaton and   Lab. 28; C. 3; Green 2; Ind. 1
   Bedworth (34)
Oadby and Wigston (26)   LD 19; C. 6; Lab. 1
Oxford (48)   Lab. 33; LD 8; Green 6; Ind. 1
Pendle (49)   C. 19; Lab. 18; LD 11; BNP 1
Preston (57)   Lab. 32; C. 19; LD 5; Ind. 1
Purbeck (25)   C. 20; LD 4; Ind. 1
Redditch (29)   Lab. 15; C. 13; UKIP 1
Reigate and Banstead   C. 40; R. 7; Green 2; LD 1;
   (51)   UKIP 1
Ribble Valley (40)   C. 35; LD 4; Lab. 1
Richmondshire (34)   C. 21; Ind. 11; LD 2
Rochford (39)   C. 28; Green 4; UKIP 3; LD 2;
   Lab. 1; O. 1
Rossendale (36)   Lab. 19; C. 15; Ind. 1; O. 1
Rother (38)   C. 31; O. 3; LD 2; Ind. 1; Lab. 1
Rugby (42)   C. 22; Lab. 9; LD 8; Ind. 3
Runnymede (42)   C. 36; R. 6
Rushcliffe (44)   C. 34; Lab. 4; Green 2; Ind. 2;
   LD 2
Rushmoor (39)   C. 26; Lab. 11; UKIP 2
Ryedale (30)   C. 20; Ind. 5; Lib. 3; LD 2
St Albans (58)   C. 32; LD 16; Lab. 8; Green 1;
   Ind. 1
St Edmundsbury (45)   C. 36; UKIP 4; Ind. 2; Lab. 2;
   Green 1; Ind. 1
Scarborough (50)   C. 26; Lab. 14; UKIP 5; Ind. 3;
   Green 2
Sedgemoor (48)   C. 35; Lab. 10; UKIP 2; LD 1
Selby (31)   C. 22; Lab. 8; Ind. 1
Sevenoaks (54)   C. 49; LD 2; Ind. 1; Lab. 1;
   UKIP 1
Shepway (30)   C. 22; UKIP 7; Lab. 1
South Bucks (28)   C. 27; Ind. 1
South Cambridgeshire   C. 38; LD 11; Ind. 7; Lab. 1
   (57)
South Derbyshire (36)   C. 24; Lab. 12
South Hams (31)   C. 25; Green 3; LD 2; Lab. 1
South Holland (37)   C. 28; Ind. 7; UKIP 2

South Kesteven (58)    C. 45; Ind. 5; Lab. 3; O. 2;
UKIP 1; v. 2
South Lakeland (51)    LD 32; C. 15; Lab. 3; Ind. 1
South Norfolk (46)    C. 40; LD 6
South Northamptonshire    C. 35; Lab. 4; LD 3
(42)
South Oxfordshire (36)    C. 33; Lab. 1; LD 1; R 1
South Ribble (50)    C. 29; Lab. 19; LD 2
South Somerset (60)    LD 29; C. 28; Ind. 3
South Staffordshire (49)    C. 43; Ind. 4; Lab. 1; UKIP 1
Spelthorne (39)    C. 35; LD 3; Lab. 1
Stafford (40)    C. 29; Lab. 9; Ind. 2
Staffordshire Moorlands    C. 41; Lab. 7; O. 6; LD 2
(56)
Stevenage (39)    Lab. 30; C. 6; LD 3
Stratford-on-Avon (36)    C. 31; LD 3; Ind. 1; Lab. 1
Stroud (51)    C. 23; Lab. 18; Green 6; LD 3;
O. 1
Suffolk Coastal (42)    C. 37; Ind. 2; LD 2; Lab. 1
Surrey Heath (40)    C. 36; Ind. 2; Lab. 1; LD 1
Swale (47)    C. 32; UKIP 9; Lab. 4; Ind. 2
Tamworth (30)    C. 18; Lab. 11; UKIP 1
Tandridge (42)    C. 35; LD 6; Ind. 1
Taunton Deane (56)    C. 36; LD 14; Ind. 3; Lab. 2;
UKIP 1
Teignbridge (46)    C. 30; LD 11; Ind. 5
Tendring (60)    C. 23; UKIP 16; Ind. 11; Lab. 4;
R. 3; LD 1; O. 1; v. 1
Test Valley (48)    C. 38; LD 9; Ind. 1
Tewkesbury (38)    C. 33; Ind. 2; LD 2; O. 1
Thanet (56)    UKIP 33; C. 18; Lab. 4; Ind. 1
Three Rivers (39)    LD 19; C. 17; Lab. 3
Tonbridge and Malling    C. 48; LD 4; Ind. 2
(54)
Torridge (36)    C. 19; O. 10; UKIP 7
Tunbridge Wells (48)    C. 42; LD 3; Lab. 2; Ind. 1
Uttlesford (39)    C. 23; O. 9; LD 6; Ind. 1
Vale of White Horse (38)    C. 29; LD 9
Warwick (46)    C. 31; Lab. 9; R. 3; LD 2; Green 1
Watford (36)    LD 18; Lab. 13; C. 5
Waveney (48)    C. 27; Lab. 20; Green 1
Waverley (57)    C. 53; R. 3; Ind. 1
Wealden (55)    C. 50; Ind. 5
Wellingborough (36)    C. 27; Lab. 9
Welwyn and    C. 31; Lab. 15; LD 2
Hatfield (48)
West Devon (31)    C. 21; Ind. 9; LD 1
West Dorset (42)    C. 30; LD 12
West Lancashire (54)    Lab. 30; C. 23; O. 1
West Lindsey (36)    C. 24; LD 7; Lab. 3; Ind. 2
West Oxfordshire (49)    C. 40; Lab. 4; LD 4; Ind. 1
West Somerset (28)    C. 21; Ind. 3; UKIP 3; Lab. 1
Weymouth and Portland    C. 14; Lab. 13; LD 6; Ind. 3
(36)
Winchester (57)    C. 33; LD 22; Lab. 2
Woking (36)    C. 24; LD 9; Lab. 2; Ind. 1
Worcester (35)    C. 19; Lab. 15; Green 1
Worthing (37)    C. 30; LD 4; UKIP 2; Green 1
Wychavon (45)    C. 38; LD 5; UKIP 1; v. 1
Wycombe (60)    C. 47; Lab. 6; O. 3; Ind. 2; LD 1;
UKIP 1
Wyre (50)    C. 36; Lab. 14
Wyre Forest (33)    C. 23; Ind. 5; Lab. 3; LD 1;
UKIP 1

## LONDON BOROUGH COUNCILS

Barking and Dagenham    Lab. 51
(51)
Barnet (63)    C. 32; Lab. 30; LD 1

Bexley (63)    C. 45; Lab. 15; UKIP 3
Brent (63)    Lab. 56; C. 6; LD 1
Bromley (60)    C. 51; Lab. 7; UKIP 2
Camden (54)    Lab. 40; C. 12; Green 1; LD 1
Croydon (70)    Lab. 40; C. 30
Ealing (69)    Lab. 53; C. 12; LD 4
Enfield (63)    Lab. 39; C. 22; Ind. 2
Greenwich (51)    Lab. 43; C. 8
Hackney (57)    Lab. 50; C. 4; LD 3
Hammersmith and    Lab. 26; C. 20
Fulham (46)
Haringey (57)    Lab. 48; LD 9
Harrow (63)    Lab. 34; C. 26; Ind. 2; LD 1
Havering (54)    Ind. 24; C. 22; UKIP 7; Lab. 1
Hillingdon (65)    C. 42; Lab. 23
Hounslow (60)    Lab. 47; C. 11; Ind. 1; v. 1
Islington (48)    Lab. 47; Green 1
Kensington and Chelsea    C. 37; Lab. 12; LD 1
(50)
Kingston upon Thames    C. 28; LD 18; Lab. 2
(48)
Lambeth (63)    Lab. 59; C. 3; Green 1
Lewisham (55)    Lab. 54; Green 1
Merton (60)    Lab. 36; C. 20; R. 3; O. 1
Newham (60)    Lab. 60
Redbridge (63)    Lab. 35; C. 25; LD 3
Richmond upon Thames    C. 39; LD 15
(54)
Southwark (63)    Lab. 48; LD 13; C. 2
Sutton (54)    LD 43; C. 8; Ind. 2; v. 1
Tower Hamlets (45)    Lab. 22; Ind. 17; C. 5; v. 1
Waltham Forest (60)    Lab. 44; C. 16
Wandsworth (60)    C. 39; Lab. 19; O. 2
Westminster (60)    C. 44; Lab. 16

## METROPOLITAN BOROUGHS

Barnsley (63)    Lab. 55; C. 4; Ind. 4
Birmingham (120)    Lab. 79; C. 30; LD 11
Bolton (60)    Lab. 39; C. 15; LD 3; UKIP 3
Bradford (90)    Lab. 46; C. 23; LD 9; O. 8;
Green 3; Ind. 1
Bury (51)    Lab. 35; C. 12; LD 2; Green 1;
Ind. 1
Calderdale (51)    Lab. 24; C. 21; LD 5; Ind. 1
Coventry (54)    Lab. 41; C. 13
Doncaster (63)    Lab. 42; C. 8; O. 3; UKIP 2; Ind. 1
Dudley (72)    Lab. 38; C. 25; UKIP 7; Green 1;
Ind. 1
Gateshead (66)    Lab. 56; LD 10
Kirklees (69)    Lab. 34; C. 18; LD 10; Green 4;
Ind. 3
Knowsley (63)    Lab. 63
Leeds (99)    Lab. 63; C. 19; LD 9; O. 5;
Green 3
Liverpool (90)    Lab. 81; Green 4; LD 2; O. 2;
Ind. 1
Manchester (96)    Lab. 96
Newcastle-upon-Tyne    Lab. 53; LD 22; Ind. 3
(78)
North Tyneside (60)    Lab. 49; C. 9; LD 2
Oldham (60)    Lab. 45; LD 10; C. 2; UKIP 2;
Ind. 1
Rochdale (60)    Lab. 47; C. 11; LD 2
Rotherham (63)    Lab. 48; UKIP 12; Ind. 2; C. 1
St Helens (48)    Lab. 42; C. 3; LD 3
Salford (60)    Lab. 52; C. 8
Sandwell (72)    Lab. 68; Ind. 2; UKIP 1; v. 1
Sefton (66)    Lab. 42; LD 16; C. 7; O. 1
Sheffield (84)    Lab. 59; LD 17; Green 4; UKIP 4

olihull (51) — C. 32; Green 9; LD 6; UKIP 2; Ind. 1; Lab. 1

outh Tyneside (54) — Lab. 52; C. 1; Ind. 1

tockport (63) — LD 26; Lab. 21; C. 13; Ind. 3

underland (75) — Lab. 66; C. 6; Ind. 3

ameside (57) — Lab. 52; C. 5

rafford (63) — C. 34; Lab. 26; LD 3

Wakefield (63) — Lab. 53; C. 6; Ind. 2; UKIP 2

Valsall (60) — Lab. 27; C. 25; UKIP 3; Ind. 2; LD 2; O. 1

Vigan (75) — Lab. 64; Ind. 8; C. 3

Virral (66) — Lab. 38; C. 21; LD 5; Green 1; Ind. 1

Volverhampton (60) — Lab. 48; C. 10; LD 1; UKIP 1

## UNITARY COUNCILS

ath and North East Somerset (65) — C. 37; LD 15; Lab. 6; Ind. 5; Green 2

edford (40) — C. 15; Lab. 14; LD 9; Ind. 2

lackburn with Darwen (64) — Lab. 47; C. 14; LD 3

lackpool (42) — Lab. 29; C. 13; LD 1; v. 1

ournemouth (54) — C. 51; Green 1; Ind. 1; UKIP 1

racknell Forest (42) — C. 41; Lab. 1

righton and Hove (54) — Lab. 23; C. 20; Green 11

ristol (70) — Lab. 30; C. 16; Green 14; LD 9; UKIP 1

entral Bedfordshire (59) — C. 53; Ind. 3; Lab. 2; LD 1

heshire East (82) — C. 53; Lab. 16; O. 7; R. 3; LD 2; Ind. 1

heshire West and Chester (75) — Lab. 38; C. 36; Ind. 1

ornwall (123) — LD 37; Ind. 36; C. 29; Lab. 8; UKIP 6; O. 5; Green 1; v. 1

arlington (50) — Lab. 29; C. 17; LD 3; Ind. 1

erby (51) — Lab. 27; C. 14; LD 7; UKIP 2; Ind. 1

urham (126) — Lab. 96; Ind. 17; LD 9; C. 4

ast Riding of Yorkshire (67) — C. 51; Lab. 6; Ind. 5; UKIP 3; LD 2

alton (56) — Lab. 52; LD 2; C. 2

artlepool (33) — Lab. 22; C. 3; Ind. 3; O. 3; UKIP 2

erefordshire (58) — C. 27; Ind. 13; O. 13; LD 3; Green 2

Isles of Scilly (21) — Ind. 19; v. 2

sle of Wight (40) — Ind. 21; C. 14; Lab. 2; UKIP 2; LD 1

ingston-upon-Hull (59) — Lab. 40; LD 15; C. 2; O. 1; UKIP 1

eicester (54) — Lab. 52; C. 1; LD 1

uton (48) — Lab. 35; LD 8; C. 5

edway (55) — C. 36; Lab. 15; UKIP 3; Ind. 1

iddlesbrough (47) — Lab. 34; O. 6; C. 4; Ind. 3

ilton Keynes (57) — Lab. 23; C. 22; LD 12

orth East Lincolnshire (42) — Lab. 19; C. 10; UKIP 9; LD 3; v. 1

orth Lincolnshire (43) — C. 26; Lab. 17

orth Somerset (50) — C. 36; Ind. 7; LD 4; Lab. 3

orthumberland (68) — Lab. 32; C. 21; LD 10; Ind. 2; O. 2; v. 1

ottingham (55) — Lab. 52; C. 3

eterborough (57) — C. 26; Lab. 22; Ind. 6; O. 4; LD 4; UKIP 4; v. 1

lymouth (57) — Lab. 28; C. 26; UKIP 3

oole (42) — C. 32; LD 6; O. 3; UKIP 1

ortsmouth (42) — C. 18; LD 15; Lab. 4; UKIP 4; Ind. 1

Reading (46) — Lab. 31; C. 10; Green 3; LD 2

Redcar and Cleveland (59) — Lab. 29; LD 11; C. 10; Ind. 8; UKIP 1

Rutland (26) — C. 17; Ind. 7; LD 2

Shropshire (74) — C. 47; LD 13; Lab. 9; O. 4; Ind. 1

Slough (42) — Lab. 30; C. 10; UKIP 2

South Gloucestershire (70) — C. 40; LD 16; Lab. 14

Southampton (48) — Lab. 25; C. 20; O. 2; Ind. 1

Southend-on-Sea (51) — C. 22; Ind. 11; Lab. 9; LD 4; O. 3; UKIP 2

Stockton-on-Tees (56) — Lab. 32; C. 13; O. 10; LD 1

Stoke-on-Trent (44) — Lab. 21; Ind. 14; C. 7; UKIP 2

Swindon (57) — C. 32; Lab. 23; LD 2

Telford and Wrekin (54) — Lab. 27; C. 22; LD 3; Ind. 2

Thurrock (49) — Lab. 18; C. 17; UKIP 12; Ind. 2

Torbay (37) — C. 26; LD 7; Ind. 3; UKIP 1

Warrington (57) — Lab. 42; LD 9; C. 5; O. 1

West Berkshire (52) — C. 48; LD 4

Wiltshire (98) — C. 60; LD 21; Ind. 12; Lab. 4; UKIP 1

Windsor and Maidenhead (57) — C. 54; R. 2; LD 1

Wokingham (54) — C. 47; LD 5; Ind. 1; Lab. 1

York (47) — Lab. 15; C. 14; LD 12; Green 4; Ind. 2

* Thirteen councillors are elected by the residents of the isle of St Mary's and two councillors each are elected by the residents of the four other islands (Bryher, St Agnes, St Martins and Tresco)

## WALES

Blaenau Gwent (42) — Lab. 32; Ind. 10

Bridgend (54) — Lab. 38; Ind. 11; LD 3; C. 1; PC 1

Caerphilly (73) — Lab. 47; PC 20; Ind. 3; v. 3

Cardiff (80) — Lab. 51; LD 15; C. 9; PC 3; Ind. 2

Carmarthenshire (74) — PC 29; Lab. 22; Ind. 21; O. 2

Ceredigion (42) — PC 19; Ind. 11; LD 7; O. 5

Conwy (59) — Ind. 19; C. 13; PC 12; Lab. 11; LD 4

Denbighshire (47) — Lab. 18; Ind. 13; C. 8; PC 8

Flintshire (70) — Lab. 33; O. 17; C. 8; Ind. 6; LD 6

Gwynedd (75) — PC 37; Ind. 18; O. 12; Lab. 5; LD 2; v. 1

Merthyr Tydfil (33) — Lab. 25; Ind. 8

Monmouthshire (43) — C. 19; Lab. 11; Ind. 10; LD 3

Neath Port Talbot (64) — Lab. 50; PC 8; Ind. 6

Newport (50) — Lab. 37; C. 10; Ind. 2; LD 1

Pembrokeshire (60) — Ind. 31; O. 16; Lab. 6; PC 4; C. 3

Powys (73) — O. 35; Ind. 13; C. 11; LD 8; Lab. 6

Rhondda Cynon Taff (75) — Lab. 60; PC 9; Ind. 4; C. 1; LD 1

Swansea (72) — Lab. 48; LD 12; Ind. 8; C. 4

Torfaen (44) — Lab. 30; Ind. 8; C. 4; PC 2

Vale of Glamorgan (47) — Lab. 21; C. 12; PC 6; Ind. 4; O. 3; UKIP 1

Wrexham (52) — Ind. 27; Lab. 13; O. 5; LD 5; PC 2

Ynys Mon (Isle of Anglesey) (30) — Ind. 12; PC 12; O. 3; Lab. 2; LD 1

## SCOTLAND

Aberdeen (43) — Lab. 17; SNP 13; LD 5; Ind. 3; C. 2; O. 1; v. 2

Aberdeenshire (68) — SNP 28; C. 13; Ind. 13; LD 11; Lab. 2; Green 1

Angus (29) — SNP 14; Ind. 9; C. 4; LD 1; Lab. 1

| | |
|---|---|
| Argyll and Bute (36) | Ind. 17; SNP 9; C. 4; LD 4; Lab. 1; O. 1 |
| Clackmannanshire (18) | Lab. 8; SNP 8; C. 1; Ind. 1 |
| Dumfries and Galloway (47) | Lab. 15; C. 14; SNP 10; Ind. 5; O. 3 |
| Dundee (29) | SNP 16; Lab. 10; C. 1; Ind. 1; LD 1 |
| East Ayrshire (32) | SNP 15; Lab. 14; C. 2; Ind. 1 |
| East Dunbartonshire (24) | Lab. 9; SNP 8; LD 3; C. 2; Ind. 2 |
| East Lothian (23) | Lab. 10; SNP 8; C. 3; Ind. 2 |
| East Renfrewshire (20) | Lab. 8; C. 6; SNP 4; Ind. 2 |
| Edinburgh (58) | Lab. 20; SNP 17; C. 11; Green 6; LD 3; Ind. 1 |
| Eilean Siar (Western Isles) (31) | Ind. 23; SNP 6; Lab. 2 |
| Falkirk (31) | Lab. 14; SNP 12; Ind. 3; C. 2 |
| Fife (78) | Lab. 33; SNP 27; LD 10; Ind. 4; C. 3; O. 1 |
| Glasgow (79) | Lab. 45; SNP 27; Green 5; C. 1; LD 1 |
| Highland (80) | Ind. 32; SNP 21; LD 11; Lab. 8; O. 8 |
| Inverclyde (20) | Lab. 9; SNP 6; Ind. 2; LD 2; C. 1 |
| Midlothian (18) | Lab. 8; SNP 8; Green 1; Ind. 1 |
| Moray (26) | SNP 11; Ind. 10; C. 3; Lab. 2 |
| North Ayrshire (30) | SNP 12; Lab. 11; Ind. 6; C. 1 |
| North Lanarkshire (70) | Lab. 43; SNP 21; Ind. 6 |
| Orkney Islands (21) | Ind. 18; O. 3 |
| Perth and Kinross (41) | SNP 18; C. 10; LD 5; Lab. 4; Ind. 4 |
| Renfrewshire (40) | Lab. 22; SNP 15; C. 1; Ind. 1; LD 1 |
| Scottish Borders (34) | Ind. 10; C. 9; SNP 9; LD 6 |
| Shetland Islands (22) | Ind. 22 |
| South Ayrshire (30) | C. 10; Lab. 9; SNP 9; Ind. 2 |
| South Lanarkshire (67) | Lab. 38; SNP 21; C. 3; Ind. 3; LD 1; O. 1 |
| Stirling (22) | SNP 9; Lab. 8; C. 4; Green 1 |
| West Dunbartonshire (22) | Lab. 12; SNP 6; Ind. 3; O. 1 |
| West Lothian (33) | Lab. 16; SNP 15; C. 1; Ind. 1 |

## NORTHERN IRELAND

| | |
|---|---|
| Antrim and Newtownabbey (40) | DUP 15; UUP 11; All. 4; SDLP 4; SF 3; TUV 2; v. 1 |
| Armagh, Banbridge and Craigavon (41) | DUP 13; UUP 12; SF 8; SDLP 6; Ind. 1; UKIP 1 |
| Belfast (60) | SF 19; DUP 13; All. 8; SDLP 7; UUP 7; PUP 3; Green 1; O. 1; TUV 1 |
| Causeway Coast and Glens (40) | DUP 11; UUP 9; SF 7; SDLP 6; TUV 3; All. 1; Ind. 1; Ind. Un. 1; PUP 1 |
| Derry and Strabane (40) | SF 16; SDLP 10; DUP 8; Ind. 4; UUP 2 |
| Fermanagh and Omagh (40) | SF 17; UUP 9; SDLP 8; DUP 5; Ind. 1 |
| Lisburn and Castlereagh (40) | DUP 20; UUP 8; All. 7; SDLP 3; O. 1; TUV 1 |
| Mid and East Antrim (40) | DUP 18; UUP 10; TUV 5; All. 3; SF 3; Ind. 2; SDLP 1; UKIP 1 |
| Mid Ulster (40) | SF 18; DUP 8; UUP 7; SDLP 6; Ind. 1 |
| Newry, Mourne and Down (41) | SF 14; SDLP 13; Ind. 5; DUP 4; UUP 3; All. 1; UKIP 1 |
| North Down and Ards (40) | DUP 17; UUP 9; All. 7; Ind. 3; Green 2; SDLP 1; TUV 1 |

# ENGLAND

The country of England lies between 55° 46' and 49° 57' 30" N. latitude (from a few miles north of the mouth of the Tweed to the Lizard), and between 1° 46' E. and 5° 43' W. longitude (from Lowestoft to Land's End). England is bounded on the north by the Cheviot Hills; on the south by the English Channel; on the east by the Straits of Dover (Pas de Calais) and the North Sea; and on the west by the Atlantic Ocean, Wales and the Irish Sea. It has a total area of 130,432 sq. km (50,360 sq. miles): land 130,279 sq. km (50,301 sq. miles); inland water 153 sq. km (59 sq. miles).

## POPULATION
The population at the 2011 census was 53,012,456 (men 26,069,148; women 26,943,308). The average density of the population in 2011 was 406 persons per sq. km (1,053 per sq. mile).

## FLAG
The flag of England is the cross of St George, a red cross on a white field (cross gules in a field argent). The cross of St George, the patron saint of England, has been used since the 13th century.

## RELIEF
There is a marked division between the upland and lowland areas of England. In the extreme north the Cheviot Hills highest point, the Cheviot, 815m/2,674ft) form a natural boundary with Scotland. Running south from the Cheviots, though divided from them by the Tyne Gap, is the Pennine range (highest point, Cross Fell, 893m/2,930ft), the main orological feature of the country. The Pennines culminate in the Peak District of Derbyshire (Kinder Scout, 636m/ 2,088ft). West of the Pennines are the Cumbrian mountains, which include Scafell Pike (978m/3,210ft), the highest peak in England, and to the east are the Yorkshire Moors, their highest point being Urra Moor (454m/1,490ft).

In the west, the foothills of the Welsh mountains extend into the bordering English counties of Shropshire (the Wrekin, 407m/1,334ft; Long Mynd, 516m/1,694ft) and Hereford and Worcester (the Malvern Hills – Worcestershire Beacon, 425m/1,394ft). Extensive areas of highland and moorland are also to be found in the south-western peninsula formed by Somerset, Devon and Cornwall, principally Exmoor (Dunkery Beacon, 519m/1,704ft), Dartmoor (High Willhays, 621m/2,038ft) and Bodmin Moor (Brown Willy, 420m/1,377ft). Ranges of low, undulating hills run across the south of the country, including the Cotswolds in the Midlands and south-west, the Chilterns to the north of London, and the North (Kent) and South (Sussex) Downs of the south-east coastal areas.

The lowlands of England lie in the Vale of York, East Anglia and the area around the Wash. The lowest-lying are the Cambridgeshire Fens in the valleys of the Great Ouse and the river Nene, which are below sea-level in places. Since the 17th century extensive drainage has brought much of the Fens under cultivation. The North Sea coast between the Thames and the Humber, low-lying and formed of sand and shingle for the most part, is subject to erosion and defences against further incursion have been built along many stretches.

## HYDROGRAPHY
The Severn is the longest river in Great Britain, rising on the north-eastern slopes of Plynlimon (Wales) and entering England in Shropshire, with a total length of 354km (220

miles) from its source to its outflow into the Bristol Channel, where it receives the Bristol Avon on the east and the Wye on the west; its other tributaries are the Vyrnwy, Tern, Stour, Teme and Upper (or Warwickshire) Avon. The Severn is tidal below Gloucester, and a high bore or tidal wave sometimes reverses the flow as high as Tewkesbury (21.75km/13.5 miles above Gloucester). The scenery of the greater part of the river is very picturesque, and the Severn is a noted salmon river, with some of its tributaries being famous for trout. Navigation is assisted by the Gloucester and Berkeley Ship Canal (26km/16.25 miles), which admits vessels of 350 tons to Gloucester. The Severn Tunnel was begun in 1873 and completed in 1886 at a cost of £2m and after many difficulties caused by flooding. It is 7km (4 miles 628 yards) in length (of which 3.67km/2.25 miles are under the river). The Severn road bridge between Haysgate, Gwent, and Almondsbury, Glos, with a centre span of 988m (3,240ft), was opened in 1966.

The longest river wholly in England is the Thames, with a total length of 346km (215 miles) from its source in the Cotswold hills to the Nore, and is navigable by ocean-going ships to London Bridge. The Thames is tidal to Teddington (111km/69 miles from its mouth) and forms county boundaries almost throughout its course; on its banks are situated London, Windsor Castle, Eton College and Oxford University. Of the remaining English rivers, those flowing into the North Sea are the Tyne, Wear, Tees, Ouse and Trent from the Pennine Range, the Great Ouse (257km/160 miles), which rises in Northamptonshire, and the Orwell and Stour from the hills of East Anglia. Flowing into the English Channel are the Sussex Ouse from the Weald, the Itchen from the Hampshire hills, and the Axe, Teign, Dart, Tamar and Exe from the Devonian hills. Flowing into the Irish Sea are the Mersey, Ribble and Eden from the western slopes of the Pennines and the Derwent from the Cumbrian mountains.

The English Lakes, notable for their picturesque scenery and poetic associations, lie in Cumbria's Lake District; the largest are Windermere (14.7 sq. km/5.7 sq. miles), Ullswater (8.8 sq. km/3.4 sq. miles) and Derwent Water (5.3 sq. km/2.0 sq. miles).

## ISLANDS
The Isle of Wight is separated from Hampshire by the Solent. The capital, Newport, stands at the head of the estuary of the Medina, and Cowes (at the mouth) is the chief port. Other centres are Ryde, Sandown, Shanklin, Ventnor, Freshwater, Yarmouth, Totland Bay, Seaview and Bembridge.

Lundy (the name is derived from the Old Norse for 'puffin island'), 18km (11 miles) north-west of Hartland Point, Devon, is around 5km (3 miles) long and almost 1km (half a mile) wide on average, with a total area of around 452 hectares (1,116 acres), and a population of 27. It became the property of the National Trust in 1969 and is now principally a bird sanctuary and the UK's first marine conservation zone.

The Isles of Scilly comprise around 140 islands and skerries (total area, 10 sq. km/6 sq. miles) situated 45 km (28 miles) south-west of Land's End in Cornwall. Only five are inhabited: St Mary's, St Agnes, Bryher, Tresco and St Martin's. The population at the 2011 census was 2,200. The entire group has been designated an Area of Outstanding Natural Beauty because of its unique flora and fauna. Tourism and the winter/spring flower trade for the home market form the basis of the economy of the islands. The island group is a recognised rural development area.

# EARLY HISTORY

Archaeological evidence suggests that England has been inhabited since at least the Palaeolithic period, though the extent of the various Palaeolithic cultures was dependent upon the degree of glaciation. The succeeding Neolithic and Bronze Age cultures have left abundant remains throughout the country; the best-known of these are the henges and stone circles of Stonehenge (ten miles north of Salisbury, Wilts) and Avebury (Wilts), both of which are believed to have been of religious significance. In the latter part of the Bronze Age the Goidels, a people of the Celtic race, invaded the country and brought with them Celtic civilisation and dialects; as a result place names in England bear witness to the spread of the invasion across the whole region.

## THE ROMAN CONQUEST

The Roman conquest of Gaul (57–50 BC) brought Britain into close contact with Roman civilisation, but although Julius Caesar raided the south of Britain in 55 and 54 BC, conquest was not undertaken until nearly 100 years later. In AD 43 the Emperor Claudius dispatched Aulus Plautius, with a well-equipped force of 40,000, and himself followed with reinforcements in the same year. Success was delayed by the resistance of Caratacus (Caractacus), the British leader from AD 48–51, who was finally captured and sent to Rome, and by a great revolt in AD 61 led by Boudicca (Boadicea), Queen of the Iceni, but the south of Britain was secured by AD 70, and Wales and the area north to the Tyne by about AD 80.

In AD 122, the Emperor Hadrian visited Britain and built a continuous rampart, since known as Hadrian's Wall, from Wallsend to Bowness (Tyne to Solway). The work was entrusted by the Emperor Hadrian to Aulus Platorius Nepos, legate of Britain from AD 122 to 126, and it was intended to form the northern frontier of the Roman Empire.

The Romans administered Britain as a province under a governor, with a well-defined system of local government, each Roman municipality ruling itself and its surrounding territory, while London was the centre of the road system and the seat of the financial officials of the Province of Britain. Colchester, Lincoln, York, Gloucester and St Albans stand on the sites of five Roman municipalities, and Wroxeter, Caerleon, Chester, Lincoln and York were at various times the sites of legionary fortresses. Well-preserved Roman towns have been uncovered at or near Silchester *(Calleva Atrebatum),* ten miles south of Reading, Wroxeter *(Viroconium Cornoviorum),* near Shrewsbury, and St Albans *(Verulamium)* in Hertfordshire.

Four main groups of roads radiated from London, and a fifth (the Fosse) ran obliquely from Lincoln through Leicester, Cirencester and Bath to Exeter. Of the four groups radiating from London, one ran south-east to Canterbury and the coast of Kent, a second to Silchester and thence to parts of western Britain and south Wales, a third (later known as Watling Street) ran through St Albans to Chester, with various branches, and the fourth reached Colchester, Lincoln, York and the eastern counties.

In the fourth century Britain was subjected to raids along the east coast by Saxon pirates, which led to the establishment of a system of coastal defences from the Wash to Southampton Water, with forts at Brancaster, Burgh Castle (Yarmouth), Walton (Felixstowe), Bradwell, Reculver, Richborough, Dover, Lympne, Pevensey and Porchester (Portsmouth). The Irish (Scoti) and Picts in the north were also becoming more aggressive and from around AD 350 incursions became more frequent and more formidable. As the Roman Empire came increasingly under attack towards the end of the fourth century, many troops were removed from Britain for service in other parts of the empire. The island was eventually cut off from Rome by the Teutonic conquest of Gaul, and with the withdrawal of the last Roman garrison early in the fifth century, the Romano-British were left to themselves.

## SAXON SETTLEMENT

According to legend, the British King Vortigern called in the Saxons to defend his lands against the Picts. The Saxon chieftains Hengist and Horsa landed at Ebbsfleet, Kent, and established themselves in the Isle of Thanet, but the events during the one-and-a-half centuries between the final break with Rome and the re-establishment of Christianity are unclear. However, it would appear that over the course of this period the raids turned into large-scale settlement by invaders traditionally known as Angles (England north of the Wash and East Anglia), Saxons (Essex and southern England) and Jutes (Kent and the Weald), which pushed the Romano-British into the mountainous areas of the north and west. Celtic culture outside Wales and Cornwall survives only in topographical names. Various kingdoms established at this time attempted to claim overlordship of the whole country, hegemony finally being achieved by Wessex (with the capital at Winchester) in the ninth century. This century also saw the beginning of raids by the Vikings (Danes), which were resisted by Alfred the Great (871–899), who fixed a limit on the advance of Danish settlement by the Treaty of Wedmore (878), giving them the area north and east of Watling Street on the condition that they adopt Christianity.

In the tenth century the kings of Wessex recovered the whole of England from the Danes, but subsequent rulers were unable to resist a second wave of invaders. England paid tribute *(Danegeld)* for many years, and was invaded in 1013 by the Danes and ruled by Danish kings (including Cnut) from 1016 until 1042, when Edward the Confessor was recalled from exile in Normandy. On Edward's death in 1066 Harold Godwinson (brother-in-law of Edward and son of Earl Godwin of Wessex) was chosen to be King of England. After defeating (at Stamford Bridge, Yorkshire, 25 September 1066) an invading army under Harald Hadraada, King of Norway (aided by the outlawed Earl Tostig of Northumbria, Harold's brother), Harold was himself defeated at the Battle of Hastings on 14 October 1066, and the Norman conquest secured the throne of England for Duke William of Normandy, a cousin of Edward the Confessor.

## CHRISTIANITY

Christianity reached the Roman province of Britain from Gaul in the third century (or possibly earlier). Alban, traditionally Britain's first martyr, was put to death as a Christian during the persecution of Diocletian (22 June 303) at his native town *Verulamium,* and the bishops of *Londinium, Eboracum* (York), and *Lindum* (Lincoln) attended the Council of Arles in 314. However, the Anglo-Saxon invasions submerged the Christian religion in England until the sixth century: conversion was undertaken in the north from 563 by Celtic missionaries from Ireland led by St Columba, and in the south by a mission sent from Rome in 597 which was led by St Augustine, who became the first archbishop of Canterbury. England appears to have been converted again by the end of the seventh century and followed, after the Council of Whitby in 663, the practices of the Roman Church, which brought the kingdom into the mainstream of European thought and culture.

# PRINCIPAL CITIES

There are 51 cities in England and space constraints prevent us from including profiles of them all. Below is a selection of

England's principal cities with the date on which city status was conferred in parentheses. Other cities are Bradford (pre-1900), Chelmsford (2012), Chichester (pre-1900), Coventry (pre-1900), Derby (1977), Ely (pre-1900), Exeter (pre-1900), Gloucester (pre-1900), Hereford (pre-1900), Kingston-upon-Hull (pre-1900), Lancaster (1937), Lichfield (pre-1900), London (pre-1900), Peterborough (pre-1900), Plymouth (1928), Portsmouth (1926), Preston (2002), Ripon (pre-1900), Salford (1926), Stoke-on-Trent (1925), Sunderland (1992), Truro (pre-1900), Wakefield (pre-1900), Wells (pre-1900), Westminster (pre-1900), Wolverhampton (2000) and Worcester (pre-1900).

Certain cities have also been granted a lord mayoralty – this grant confers no additional powers or functions and is purely honorific. Cities with lord mayors are Birmingham, Bradford, Bristol, Canterbury, Chester, Coventry, Exeter, Kingston-upon-Hull, Leeds, Leicester, Liverpool, London, Manchester, Newcastle-upon-Tyne, Norwich, Nottingham, Oxford, Plymouth, Portsmouth, Sheffield, Stoke-on-Trent, Westminster and York.

## BATH (PRE-1900)

Bath stands on the river Avon between the Cotswold hills to the north and the Mendips to the south, and was originally a small Roman town *(Aquae Sulis)* with a baths and temple complex built around naturally occurring hot springs. In the early 18th century Bath became England's premier spa town where the rich and celebrated members of fashionable society gathered to 'take the waters' and enjoy the town's theatres and concert rooms. During this period the architect John Wood laid the foundations of a new Georgian city built using the honey-coloured stone for which Bath is famous today. Since 1987 the city has been listed as a UNESCO World Heritage Site.

Contemporary Bath is a thriving tourist destination and remains a leading cultural, religious and historical centre with many art galleries and historic sites including the Pump Room (1790); the Royal Crescent (1767); the Circus (1754); the 18th-century Assembly Rooms (housing the Museum of Costume); Pulteney Bridge (1771); the Guildhall and the Abbey, now over 500 years old, which is built on the site of a Saxon monastery. In 2006 the Bath Thermae Spa was completed and the hot springs reopened to the public for the first time since 1978.

## BIRMINGHAM (PRE-1900)

Birmingham is Britain's second largest city, with a population of over one million. The generally accepted derivation of 'Birmingham' is the *ham* (dwelling-place) of the *ing* (family) of *Beorma*, presumed to have been Saxon. During the Industrial Revolution the town grew into a major manufacturing centre, known as the 'city of a thousand trades', and in 1889 was granted city status. By the 18th century, Birmingham was the main European producer of items such as buckles, medals and coins. Today, around 40 per cent of all the UK's handmade jewellery is produced in Birmingham's Jewellery Quarter. Another product of the Industrial Revolution are the city's 34 miles (56km) of canals.

Recent developments include Millennium Point, which houses Thinktank, the Birmingham science museum, and Brindleyplace, a development of shops, offices and leisure facilities on a former industrial site clustered around canals. In 2003 the Bullring shopping centre was officially opened as part of the city's urban regeneration programme.

The principal buildings are the Town Hall (1834–50), the Council House (1879), Victoria Law Courts (1891), the University of Birmingham (1906–9), the 13th-century Church of St Martin in the Bull Ring (rebuilt 1873), the

cathedral (formerly St Philip's Church) (1711), the Roman Catholic cathedral of St Chad (1839–41), the Assay Office (1773), the Rotunda (1964) and the National Exhibition Centre (1976).

## BRIGHTON AND HOVE (2000)

Brighton and Hove is situated on the south coast of England, around 96 km (60 miles) south of London. Originally a fishing village called Brighthelmstone, it was transformed into a fashionable seaside resort in the 18th century when Dr Richard Russell popularised the benefits of his 'sea-water cure'; as one of the closest beaches to London, Brighton began to attract wealthy visitors. One of these was the Prince Regent (the future King George IV), who first visited in 1783 and became so fond of the city that in 1807 he bought the former farmhouse he had been renting, and gradually turned it into Brighton's most recognisable building, the Royal Pavilion. The Pavilion is renowned for its Indo-Saracenic exterior, featuring minarets and an enormous central dome designed by John Nash, combined with the lavish chinoiserie of Frederick Crace's and Robert Jones' interiors. Queen Victoria sold the Pavilion to Brighton's municipal authority in 1850.

Brighton and Hove's Regency heritage can also be seen in the numerous elegant squares and crescents designed by Amon Wilds and Augustin Busby that dominate the seafront.

## BRISTOL (PRE-1900)

Bristol was a royal borough before the Norman conquest. The earliest form of the name is *Bricgstow*. Due to the city's position close to the mouth of the River Avon, it was an important location for marine trade for centuries and prospered greatly from the transatlantic slave trade during the 18th century.

The principal buildings include the 12th-century Cathedral with Norman chapter house and gateway; the 14th-century Church of St Mary Redcliffe; Wesley's Chapel, Broadmead; the Merchant Venturers' Almshouses; the Council House (1956); the Guildhall; the Exchange (erected from the designs of John Wood in 1743); Cabot Tower; the University and Clifton College.

The Clifton Suspension Bridge, with a span of 214m (702ft) over the Avon, was projected by Isambard Kingdom Brunel in 1836 but was not completed until 1864. Brunel's SS *Great Britain,* the first ocean-going propeller-driven ship, now forms a museum at the Western Dockyard, from where she was originally launched in 1843. The docks themselves have been extensively restored and redeveloped; the 19th-century two-storey former tea warehouse is now the Arnolfini centre for contemporary arts, and an 18th-century sail-loft houses the Architecture Centre. On Princes Wharf, 1950s transit sheds have been renovated and converted into the museum of Bristol, M Shed, which opened in 2011.

## CAMBRIDGE (1951)

Cambridge, a settlement far older than its ancient university, lies on the River Cam (or Granta). Its industries include technology research and development, and biotechnology. Among its open spaces are Jesus Green, Sheep's Green, Coe Fen, Parker's Piece, Christ's Pieces, the University Botanic Garden, and the 'Backs' – lawns and gardens through which the Cam winds behind the principal line of college buildings. Historical sites east of the Cam include King's Parade, Great St Mary's Church, Gibbs' Senate House and King's College Chapel.

University and college buildings provide the outstanding features of Cambridge's architecture but several churches (especially St Bene't's, the oldest building in the city, and Holy Sepulchre or the Round Church) are also notable. The

Guildhall (1937) stands on a site of which at least part has held municipal buildings since 1224. In 2009 the University of Cambridge celebrated its 800th anniversary.

## CANTERBURY (PRE-1900)

Canterbury, seat of the Archbishop of Canterbury, the primate of the Church of England, dates back to prehistoric times. It was the Roman *Durovernum Cantiacorum* and the Saxon *Cant-wara-byrig* (stronghold of the men of Kent). It was here in 597 that St Augustine began the conversion of the English to Christianity, when Ethelbert, King of Kent, was baptised.

Of the Benedictine St Augustine's Abbey, burial place of the Jutish kings of Kent, only ruins remain. According to Bede, St Martin's Church, on the eastern outskirts of the city, was the place of worship of Queen Bertha, the Christian wife of King Ethelbert, before the advent of St Augustine.

In 1170 the rivalry of Church and State culminated in the murder of Archbishop Thomas Becket in Canterbury Cathedral, by Henry II's knights. His shrine became a great centre of pilgrimage, as described in Chaucer's *Canterbury Tales*. After the Reformation pilgrimages ceased, but the prosperity of the city was strengthened by an influx of Huguenot refugees, who introduced weaving. The poet and playwright Christopher Marlowe was born and raised in Canterbury and the city is home to the 1,200-seat Marlowe Theatre, which reopened to the public in 2011, following an extensive £25m rebuild.

The cathedral, its architecture ranging from the 11th to the 15th centuries, is famous worldwide. Visitors are attracted particularly to the Martyrdom, the Black Prince's Tomb and the Warriors' Chapel.

The medieval city walls are built on Roman foundations and the 14th-century West Gate is one of the finest buildings of its kind in the country.

## CHESTER (PRE-1900)

Chester is situated on the River Dee. Its recorded history dates from the first century when the Romans founded the fortress of *Deva.* The city's name is derived from the Latin *castra* (a camp or encampment). During the Middle Ages, Chester was the principal port of north-west England but declined with the silting of the Dee estuary and competition from Liverpool. The city was also an important military centre, notably during Edward I's Welsh campaigns and the Elizabethan Irish campaigns. During the Civil War, Chester supported the King and was besieged from 1643 to 1646. Chester's first charter was granted *c.*1175 and the city was incorporated in 1506. The office of sheriff is the earliest created in the country (1120s), and in 1992 the mayor, who also enjoys the title 'Admiral of the Dee', was made a lord mayor.

The city's architectural features include the city walls (an almost complete two-mile circuit), the unique 13th-century Rows (covered galleries above the street-level shops), the Victorian Gothic town hall (1869), the castle (rebuilt 1788 and 1822) and numerous half-timbered buildings. The cathedral was a Benedictine abbey until the dissolution of the monasteries. Chester racecourse is the oldest racecourse in Britain, believed to have origins in the 13th century. The first recorded horserace was in 1539, during the reign of Henry VIII. Chester also houses the ruins of a Roman amphitheatre, built in the late first century AD.

## DURHAM (PRE-1900)

The city of Durham's prominent Norman cathedral and castle are set high on a wooded peninsula overlooking the river Wear. The cathedral was founded as a shrine for the body of St Cuthbert in 995. The present building dates from 1093 and among its many treasures is the tomb of the Venerable Bede (673–735). Durham's prince bishops had unique powers up to 1836, being lay rulers as well as religious leaders. As a palatinate, Durham could have its own army, nobility, coinage and courts. The castle was the main seat of the prince bishops for nearly 800 years; it is now used as a college by the University of Durham. The university, founded in the early 19th century on the initiative of Bishop William Van Mildert, is England's third oldest.

Annual events include Durham's regatta in June (claimed to be the oldest rowing event in Britain) and the annual Gala (formerly Durham Miners' Gala) in July. Durham County Cricket Club was established in 1882.

## LEEDS (PRE-1900)

Leeds, situated in the lower Aire valley, was first incorporated by Charles I in 1626. The earliest forms of the name are *Loidis* or *Ledes,* the origins of which are obscure.

The principal buildings are the Civic Hall (1933), the Town Hall (1858), the Municipal Buildings and Art Gallery (1884) with the Henry Moore Gallery (1982), the Corn Exchange (1863) and the University. The parish church of St Peter was rebuilt in 1841 and granted minster status in 2012. The 17th-century St John's Church has a fine interior with a famous English Renaissance screen; the last remaining 18th-century church in the city is Holy Trinity in Boar Lane (1727). Kirkstall Abbey (about three miles from the centre of the city), founded by Henry de Lacy in 1152, is one of the most complete examples of a Cistercian house now remaining. The Royal Armouries Museum forms part of a group of museums that house the national collection of antique arms and armour. The Grand Theatre and Opera House is home to Northern Ballet and Opera North.

## LEICESTER (1919)

Leicester is situated in central England. The city was an important Roman settlement and also one of the five 'burghs' or boroughs of the Danelaw. In 1485 Richard III was buried in Leicester following his death at the nearby Battle of Bosworth. In 1589 Queen Elizabeth I granted a charter to the city and the ancient title was confirmed by letters patent in 1919.

The textile industry was responsible for Leicester's early expansion and the city still maintains a strong manufacturing base. Cotton mills and factories are now undergoing extensive regeneration and are being converted into offices, apartments, bars and restaurants. The principal buildings include the two universities (the University of Leicester and De Montfort University), as well as the Town Hall, the 13th-century Guildhall, De Montfort Hall, Leicester Cathedral, the Jewry Wall (the UK's highest standing Roman wall), St Nicholas Church and St Mary de Castro church. The motte and Great Hall of Leicester can be seen from the castle gardens, situated next to the River Soar.

## LINCOLN (PRE-1900)

Situated 64km (40 miles) inland on the river Witham, Lincoln derives its name from a contraction of *Lindum Colonia,* the settlement founded in AD 48 by the Romans to command the crossing of Ermine Street and Fosse Way. Sections of the third-century Roman city wall can be seen, including an extant gateway (Newport Arch). The Romans also drained the surrounding fenland and created a canal system, laying the foundations of Lincoln's agricultural prosperity and also the city's importance in the medieval wool trade as a port and staple town.

As one of the five 'burghs' or boroughs of the Danelaw, Lincoln was an important trading centre in the ninth and tenth centuries and prosperity from the wool trade lasted until the 14th century. This wealth enabled local merchants to build parish churches, of which three survive, and there are also remains of a 12th-century Jewish community. However, the removal of the staple to Boston in 1369 heralded a decline, from which the city only recovered fully in the 19th century, when improved fen drainage made Lincoln agriculturally important. Improved canal and rail links led to industrial development, mainly in the manufacture of machinery and engineering products.

The castle was built shortly after the Norman Conquest and is unusual in having two mounds; on one motte stands a keep (Lucy's Tower) added in the 12th century. It currently houses one of the four surviving copies of the Magna Carta. The cathedral was begun c.1073 but was mostly destroyed by fire and earthquake in the 12th century. Rebuilding was begun by St Hugh and completed over a century later. Other notable architectural features are the 12th-century High Bridge, the oldest in Britain still to carry buildings, and the Guildhall, situated above the 15th-century Stonebow gateway.

## LIVERPOOL (PRE-1900)

Liverpool, on the north bank of the river Mersey, 5km (3 miles) from the Irish Sea, is the UK's foremost port for Atlantic trade.

There are 2,100 acres of dockland on both sides of the river and the Gladstone and Royal Seaforth Docks can accommodate tanker-sized vessels. Liverpool Free Port was opened in 1984.

Liverpool was created a free borough in 1207 and was given city status in 1880. From the early 18th century it expanded rapidly with the growth of industrialisation and the transatlantic slave trade. Surviving buildings from this period include the Bluecoat Chambers (1717, formerly the Bluecoat School), and the Town Hall (1754, rebuilt to the original design 1795). Notable from the 19th and 20th centuries are the Anglican cathedral (built from the designs of Sir Giles Gilbert Scott, it took 74 years to construct), and the Catholic Metropolitan Cathedral (designed by Sir Frederick Gibberd, consecrated 1967). Both of these cathedrals are situated on Hope Street, named after the merchant William Hope, which is the only street in the UK with a cathedral at either end. The refurbished Albert Dock (designed by Jesse Hartley) contains the Merseyside Maritime Museum, the International Slavery Museum, the Beatles Story and the Tate Liverpool art gallery. The Museum of Liverpool opened in 2011.

## MANCHESTER (PRE-1900)

Manchester (the *Mamucium* of the Romans, who occupied it in AD 79) is a commercial and industrial centre connected with the sea by the Manchester Ship Canal, 57km (35.5 miles) long, opened in 1894, and accommodating ships up to 15,000 tons. During the Industrial Revolution the city had a thriving cotton industry and by 1853 there were over 100 cotton mills which dominated the city's landscape.

The principal buildings are the Town Hall, erected in 1877 from the designs of Alfred Waterhouse, with a large extension of 1938; the Royal Exchange (1869, enlarged 1921); the Central Library (1934); Heaton Hall; the 17th-century Chetham Library; the Rylands Library (1900), which includes the Althorp collection; the university precinct; the 15th-century cathedral (formerly the parish church); the Manchester Central conference and exhibition centre and the Bridgewater Hall (1996) concert venue. Manchester is the home of the Hallé Orchestra, the Royal Northern College of Music, the Royal Exchange Theatre and numerous public art galleries.

The town received its first charter of incorporation in 1838 and was created a city in 1853.

## NEWCASTLE UPON TYNE (PRE-1900)

Newcastle upon Tyne, on the north bank of the River Tyne, is 13km (8 miles) from the North Sea. A cathedral and university city, it is the administrative, commercial and cultural centre for north-east England and the principal port.

The principal buildings include the Castle Keep (12th century), Black Gate (13th century), Blackfriars (13th century), West Walls (13th century), St Nicholas's Cathedral (15th century, fine lantern tower), St Andrew's Church (12th–14th century), St John's (14th–15th century), All Saints (1786 by Stephenson), St Mary's Roman Catholic Cathedral (1844), Trinity House (17th century), Sandhill (16th-century houses), Guildhall (Georgian), Grey Street (1834–9), Central Station (1846–50) and the Central Library (1969). Open spaces include the Town Moor (927 acres).

Numerous bridges span the Tyne at Newcastle, including the Tyne Bridge (1928) and the tilting Millennium Bridge (2001) which links the city with Gateshead to the south.

The city's name is derived from the 'new castle' (1080) erected as a defence against the Scots. In 1265 defensive walls over two miles in length were built around the city as further protection; parts of these walls remain today and can be found to the west of the city centre.

## NORWICH (PRE-1900)

Norwich grew from an early Anglo-Saxon settlement near the confluence of the rivers Yare and Wensum, and now serves as the provincial capital for the predominantly agricultural region of East Anglia. The name is thought to relate to the most northerly of a group of Anglo-Saxon villages or *wics*. The city's first known charter was granted in 1158 by Henry II.

Norwich serves its surrounding area as a market town and commercial centre. From the 14th century until the Industrial Revolution, Norwich was the regional centre of the woollen industry. Now the biggest single industry is financial services and principal trades are engineering, printing and shoemaking. The University of East Anglia is on the city's western boundary and admitted its first students in 1963. Norwich is accessible to seagoing vessels by means of the river Yare, entered at Great Yarmouth, 32km (20 miles) to the east.

Among many historic buildings are the cathedral (completed in the 12th century and surmounted by a 15th-century spire 96m (315ft) in height); the keep of the Norman castle (now a museum and art gallery); the 15th-century flint-walled Guildhall; some 30 medieval parish churches; St Andrew's and Blackfriars' Halls; the Tudor houses preserved in Elm Hill and the Georgian Assembly House.

## NOTTINGHAM (PRE-1900)

Nottingham stands on the river Trent. *Snotingaham* or *Notingeham*, the 'homestead of the people of Snot', is the Anglo-Saxon name for the Celtic settlement of *Tigguocobauc*, or the house of caves. In 878, Nottingham became one of the five 'burghs' or boroughs of the Danelaw. William the Conqueror ordered the construction of Nottingham Castle, while the town itself developed rapidly under Norman rule. Its laws and rights were formally recognised by Henry II's charter in 1155. The castle became a favoured residence of King John. In 1642 Charles I raised his personal standard at Nottingham Castle at the start of the Civil War.

Architecturally, Nottingham has a wealth of notable buildings, particularly those designed in the Victorian era by T. C. Hine and Watson Fothergill. The city council owns the castle, of Norman origin but restored in 1878, Wollaton Hall (1580–8), Newstead Abbey (once the home of Lord Byron), the Guildhall (1888) and the Council House (1929). St Mary's, St Peter's and St Nicholas' churches are of interest, as is the Roman Catholic cathedral (Pugin, 1842–4). Nottingham was granted city status in 1897.

## OXFORD (PRE-1900)

Oxford is a university city, an important industrial centre and a market town.

Oxford is known for its architecture, its oldest specimens being the reputedly Saxon tower of St Michael's Church, the remains of the Norman castle and city walls, and the Norman church at Iffley. It also has many Gothic buildings, such as the Divinity Schools, the Old Library at Merton College, William of Wykeham's New College, Magdalen and Christ Church colleges and many other college buildings. Later centuries are represented by the Laudian quadrangle at St John's College, the Renaissance Sheldonian Theatre by Sir Christopher Wren, Trinity College Chapel, All Saints Church, Hawksmoor's mock-Gothic at All Souls College, and the 18th-century Queen's College. In addition to individual buildings, High Street and Radcliffe Square both form interesting architectural compositions. Most of the colleges have gardens, those of Magdalen, New College, St John's and Worcester being the largest.

The Oxford University Museum of Natural History, renowned for its spectacular neo-gothic architecture, houses the university's scientific collections of zoological, entomological and geological specimens and is attached to the neighbouring Pitt Rivers Museum, which houses ethnographic and archaeological objects from around the world. The Ashmolean is the city's museum of art and archaeology and Modern Art Oxford hosts a programme of contemporary art exhibitions.

## ST ALBANS (PRE-1900)

The origins of St Albans, situated on the river Ver, stem from the Roman town of *Verulamium*. Named after the first Christian martyr in Britain, who was executed there, St Albans has developed around the Norman abbey and cathedral church (consecrated 1115), which was built partly of materials from the old Roman city. The museums house Iron Age and Roman artefacts and the Roman theatre, unique in Britain, has a stage as opposed to an amphitheatre. Archaeological excavations in the city centre have revealed evidence of pre-Roman, Saxon and medieval occupation.

The town's significance grew to the extent that it was a signatory and venue for the drafting of the Magna Carta. It was also the scene of riots during the Peasants' Revolt, the French King John was imprisoned there after the Battle of Poitiers, and heavy fighting took place there during the Wars of the Roses.

Previously controlled by the Abbot, the town achieved a charter in 1553 and city status in 1877. The street market, first established in 1553, is still an important feature of the city, as are many hotels and inns, surviving from the days when St Albans was an important coach stop. St Albans is also noted for its Clock Tower, built between 1403 and 1412, the only remaining medieval town belfry in England.

## SALISBURY (PRE-1900)

The history of Salisbury centres around the cathedral and cathedral close. The city evolved from an Iron Age camp a mile to the north of its current position which was strengthened by the Romans and called *Serviodunum*. The Normans built a castle and cathedral on the site and renamed it Sarum. In 1220 Bishop Richard Poore and the architect Elias de Derham decided to build a new Gothic-style cathedral. The cathedral was completed 38 years later and a community known as New Sarum, now called Salisbury, grew around it. Originally the cathedral had a squat tower; the 123m (404ft) spire that makes the cathedral the tallest

medieval structure in the world was added c.1315. A walled close with houses for the clergy was built around the cathedral; the Medieval Hall still stands today, alongside buildings dating from the 13th to the 20th century, including some designed by Sir Christopher Wren.

A prosperous wool and cloth trade allowed Salisbury to flourish until the 17th century. When the wool trade declined new crafts were established, including cutlery, leather and basket work, saddlery, lacemaking, joinery and malting. By 1750 it had become an important road junction and coaching centre and in the Victorian era the railways enabled a new age of expansion and prosperity.

## SHEFFIELD (PRE-1900)

Sheffield is situated at the confluence of the rivers Sheaf, Porter, Rivelin and Loxley with the river Don and was created a city in 1893.

The parish church of St Peter and St Paul, founded in the 12th century, became the cathedral church of the diocese of Sheffield in 1914. The Roman Catholic Cathedral Church of St Marie (founded 1847) was created a cathedral for the new diocese of Hallam in 1980; parts of the present building date from c.1435. The principal buildings are the Town Hall (1897), the Cutlers' Hall (1832), City Hall (1932), Graves Art Gallery (1934), Mappin Art Gallery, the Crucible Theatre and the restored Lyceum theatre, which dates from 1897 and was reopened in 1990. Three major sporting and entertainment venues were opened between 1990 and 1991: Sheffield Arena, Don Valley Stadium (closed 2013) and Pond's Forge. The Millennium Galleries opened in 2001. The Leadmill, Sheffield's longest-running independent live music venue, opened in 1980.

## SOUTHAMPTON (1964)

Southampton is a major seaport on the south coast of England, situated between the mouths of the Test and Itchen rivers. Southampton's natural deep-water harbour has made the area an important settlement since the Romans built the first port (known as *Clausentum*) in the first century, and Southampton's port has witnessed several important departures, including those of Henry V in 1415 for the Battle of Agincourt, the *Mayflower* in 1620, and the RMS *Titanic* in 1912.

The city's strategic importance, not only as a seaport but also as a centre for aircraft production, meant that it was heavily bombed during the Second World War. However, many historically significant structures remain, including the Wool House, dating from 1417 and now used as the Maritime Museum; parts of the Norman city walls, which are among the most complete in the UK; the Bargate, which was originally the main gateway into the city; God's House Tower, now the Museum of Archaeology; St Michael's, the city's oldest church; and the Tudor Merchants Hall.

## WINCHESTER (PRE-1900)

Winchester, the ancient capital of England, is situated on the river Itchen. The city is rich in architecture of all types, and especially notable is the cathedral. Built in 1079–93 the cathedral exhibits examples of Norman, early English and Perpendicular styles and is the burial place of author Jane Austen. Winchester College, founded in 1382, is one of the country's most famous public schools, and the original building (1393) remains largely unaltered. St Cross Hospital, another great medieval foundation, lies one mile south of the city. The almshouses were founded in 1136 by Bishop Henry de Blois, and Cardinal Henry Beaufort added a new almshouse of 'Noble Poverty' in 1446. The chapel and dwellings are of great architectural interest, and visitors may still receive the 'Wayfarer's Dole' of bread and ale, a tradition now 900 years old.

Excavations have done much to clarify the origins and development of Winchester. Part of the forum and several of the streets from the Roman town have been discovered. Excavations in the cathedral close have uncovered the entire site of the Anglo-Saxon cathedral (known as the Old Minster) and parts of the New Minster which was built by Alfred the Great's son, Edward the Elder, and is the burial place of the Alfredian dynasty. The original burial place of St Swithun, before his remains were translated to a site in the present cathedral, was also uncovered.

Excavations in other parts of the city have cast much light on Norman Winchester, notably on the site of the Royal Castle (adjacent to which the new Law Courts have been built) and in the grounds of Wolvesey Castle, where the great house built by Bishops Giffard and Henry de Blois in the 12th century has been uncovered. The Great Hall, built by Henry III between 1222 and 1236, survives and houses the Arthurian Round Table.

## YORK (PRE-1900)

The city of York is an archiepiscopal seat. Its recorded history dates from AD 71, when the Roman Ninth Legion established a base under Petilius Cerealis that would later become the fortress of *Eburacum,* or *Eboracum.* In Anglo-Saxon times the city was the royal and ecclesiastical centre of Northumbria, and after capture by a Viking army in AD 866 it became the capital of the Viking kingdom of Jorvik. By the 14th century the city had become a great mercantile centre, mainly because of its control of the wool trade, and was used as the chief base against the Scots. Under the Tudors its fortunes declined, although Henry VIII made it the headquarters of the Council of the North. Excavations on many sites, including Coppergate, have greatly expanded knowledge of Roman, Viking and medieval urban life.

The city is rich in examples of architecture of all periods. The earliest church was built in AD 627 and, from the 12th to 15th centuries, the present Minster was built in a succession of styles.

# LORD-LIEUTENANTS AND HIGH SHERIFFS

| Area | Lord-Lieutenant | High Sheriff (2015–16) |
|---|---|---|
| Bedfordshire | Helen Nellis | The Countess of Erroll |
| Berkshire | James Puxley | David Albermarle Bertie |
| Bristol | Mary Prior, MBE | Dr Rosalind Kennedy |
| Buckinghamshire | Sir Henry Aubrey-Fletcher, Bt. | Anna Skelton |
| Cambridgeshire | Sir Hugh Duberly, KCVO, CBE | Capt. Victor Lucas |
| Cheshire | David Briggs, MBE | Charles Holroyd, CBE |
| Cornwall | Col. Edward Bolitho, OBE | Anthony Fortescue |
| Cumbria | Claire Hensman | Samuel Rayner |
| Derbyshire | William Tucker | Oliver Stephenson |
| Devon | David Fursdon | Adm. Sir James Burnell-Nugent, KCB, CBE |
| Dorset | Angus Campbell | Jennifer Coombs |
| Durham | Susan Snowdon | James Featherstone Fenwick |
| East Riding of Yorkshire | Hon. Susan Cunliffe-Lister | James Dick, OBE |
| East Sussex | Peter Field | Juliet Smith |
| Essex | Lord Petre | Gerald Thompson |
| Gloucestershire | Dame Janet Trotter, DBE | Roger Head |
| Greater London | Kenneth Olisa, OBE | Dr Ghazala Afzal |
| Greater Manchester | Warren Smith | Mrs Sharman Birtles |
| Hampshire | Nigel Atkinson | Lady Portal, MBE |
| Herefordshire | Countess of Darnley | Edward Harley |
| Hertfordshire | Countess of Verulam | Jonathan Gosselin Trower |
| Isle of Wight | Maj.-Gen. Martin White, CB, CBE | Ronald Holland |
| Kent | Viscount De L'Isle, MBE | William Alexander |
| Lancashire | Lord Shuttleworth, KCVO | Amanda Parker |
| Leicestershire | Lady Gretton | Gordon Arthur |
| Lincolnshire | Toby Dennis | Air Vice-Marshal Hector Mackay, CB, OBE, AFC |
| Merseyside | Dame Lorna Fox Muirhead, DBE | Robert Owen |
| Norfolk | Richard Jewson | Nicholas Hedley Pratt |
| North Yorkshire | Barry Dodd, CBE | Charles Forbes Adam |
| Northamptonshire | David Laing | Dr Ahmed Mukhtar |
| Northumberland | Duchess of Northumberland | Lucy Maxwell Carroll |
| Nottinghamshire | Sir John Peace | Dr Jaswant Bilkhu |
| Oxfordshire | Tim Stevenson, OBE | Thomas Birch Reynardson |
| Rutland | Dr Laurence Howard, OBE | Andrew Brown Williamson-Noble |
| Shropshire | Sir Algernon Heber-Percy, KCVO | David Stacey |
| Somerset | Anne Maw | Hon. Mrs James Nelson |
| South Yorkshire | Andrew Coombe | John Holt |
| Staffordshire | Ian Dudson, CBE | John Leavesley |
| Suffolk | Countess of Euston | Judith Shallow |
| Surrey | Michael More-Molyneux | Elizabeth Stafford Kennedy |
| Tyne and Wear | Susan Winfield, OBE | Kathryn Hay Winksell, OBE |
| Warwickshire | Timothy Cox | Janet Bell-Smith |
| West Midlands | vacant | Edward Turpie, MBE |
| West Sussex | Susan Pyper | Denise Patterson |
| West Yorkshire | Dr Ingrid Roscoe | Edmund Anderson |
| Wiltshire | Sarah Troughton | Lady Gooch |
| Worcestershire | Lt.-Col. Patrick Holcroft, LVO, OBE | Sir Anthony Winnington, Bt. |

# COUNTY COUNCILS

| Council & Administrative Headquarters | Telephone | Population* | Council Tax† | Chief Executive‡ |
|---|---|---|---|---|
| Buckinghamshire, Aylesbury | 01296-395000 | 521,922 | £1,116 | Chris Williams |
| Cambridgeshire, Cambridge | 0345-045 5200 | 639,818 | £1,144 | Mark Lloyd |
| Cumbria, Carlisle | 01228-606060 | 497,874 | £1,185 | Diane Wood |
| Derbyshire, Matlock | 01629-580000 | 779,804 | £1,120 | Ian Stephenson |
| Devon, Exeter | 0345-155 1015 | 765,302 | £1,161 | Phil Norrey |
| Dorset, Dorchester | 01305-221000 | 418,269 | £1,215 | Debbie Ward |
| East Sussex, Lewes | 0345-608 0190 | 539,766 | £1,204 | Becky Shaw |
| Essex, Chelmsford | 0845-7430 430 | 1,431,953 | £1,087 | vacant |
| Gloucestershire, Gloucester | 01452-425000 | 611,332 | £1,091 | Peter Bungard |
| Hampshire, Winchester | 0300-555 1375 | 1,346,136 | £1,038 | Andrew Smith, OBE |
| Hertfordshire, Hertford | 0300-123 4040 | 1,154,766 | £1,141 | John Wood |
| Kent, Maidstone | 0300-041 4141 | 1,510,354 | £1,090 | David Cockburn |
| Lancashire, Preston | 0300-123 6701 | 1,184,735 | £1,130 | Jo Turton |
| Leicestershire, Leicester | 0116-232 3232 | 667,905 | £1,084 | John Sinnott |
| Lincolnshire, Lincoln | 01522-552222 | 731,516 | £1,086 | Tony McArdle |
| Norfolk, Norwich | 0344-800 8020 | 877,710 | £1,145 | Wendy Thomson |
| North Yorkshire, Northallerton | 01609-780780 | 601,536 | £1,100 | Richard Flinton |
| Northamptonshire, Northampton | 0300-126 1000 | 714,392 | £1,069 | Paul Blantern |
| Nottinghamshire, Nottingham | 0115-982 3823 | 801,390 | £1,241 | Anthony May |
| Oxfordshire, Oxford | 01865-792422 | 672,516 | £1,232 | Joanna Simons |
| Somerset, Taunton | 0300-123 2224 | 541,609 | £1,027 | Patrick Flaherty |
| Staffordshire, Stafford | 0300-111 8000 | 860,165 | £1,047 | John Henderson, CB |
| Suffolk, Ipswich | 0345-606 6067 | 738,512 | £1,127 | Deborah Cadman |
| Surrey, Kingston upon Thames | 0345-600 9009 | 1,161,256 | £1,220 | David McNulty |
| Warwickshire, Warwick | 01926-410410 | 551,594 | £1,201 | Jim Graham |
| West Sussex, Chichester | 01243-777100 | 828,398 | £1,162 | Diane Ashby |
| Worcestershire, Worcester | 01905-763763 | 575,421 | £1,080 | Clare Marchant |

\* Source: Office for National Statistics – Mid-2014 Population Estimates (Crown copyright)
† Average 2015–16 Band D council tax in the county area exclusive of precepts for fire authorities and Police Crime Commissioners. County councils claim their share of the combined council tax from the collection funds of the district authorities within their area. Average Band D council tax bills for the billing authority are given on the following pages
‡ Or equivalent postholder

# LONDON BOROUGH COUNCILS

| Council | Telephone | Population* | Council Tax‡ | Chief Executive‡ |
|---|---|---|---|---|
| Barking and Dagenham | 020-8592 4500 | 198,294 | £1,332 | Chris Naylor |
| Barnet | 020-8359 2000 | 374,915 | £1,397 | Andrew Travers |
| Bexley | 020-8303 7777 | 239,865 | £1,446 | Will Tuckley |
| Brent | 020-8937 1234 | 320,762 | £1,354 | Christine Gilbert (acting) |
| Bromley | 020-8464 3333 | 321,278 | £1,325 | Doug Patterson |
| Camden | 020-7974 4444 | 234,846 | £1,337 | Mike Cooke |
| CITY OF LONDON CORPORATION | 020-7606 3030 | 8,072 | £943 | John Barradell, OBE |
| Croydon | 020-8726 6000 | 376,040 | £1,466 | Nathan Elvery |
| Ealing | 020-8825 5000 | 342,118 | £1,355 | Martin Smith |
| Enfield | 020-8379 1000 | 324,574 | £1,395 | Rob Leak |
| Greenwich | 020-8854 8888 | 268,678 | £1,276 | John Comber |
| Hackney | 020-8356 5000 | 263,150 | £1,293 | Tim Shields |
| Hammersmith and Fulham | 020-8748 3020 | 178,365 | £1,023 | Nigel Pallace |
| Haringey | 020-8489 0000 | 267,541 | £1,479 | Nick Walkley |
| Harrow | 020-8863 5611 | 246,011 | £1,529 | Michael Lockwood |
| Havering | 01708-434343 | 245,974 | £1,514 | Cheryl Coppell |
| Hillingdon | 01895-250111 | 292,690 | £1,408 | Fran Beasley |
| Hounslow | 020-8583 2000 | 265,568 | £1,375 | Mary Harpley |
| Islington | 020-7527 2000 | 221,030 | £1,276 | Lesley Seary |
| Kensington and Chelsea | 020-7361 3000 | 156,190 | £1,078 | Nicholas Holgate |
| Kingston upon Thames | 020-8547 5000 | 169,958 | £1,675 | Bruce McDonald |
| Lambeth | 020-7926 1000 | 318,216 | £1,239 | Sean Harriss |
| Lewisham | 020-8314 6000 | 291,933 | £1,355 | Barry Quirk, CBE |
| Merton | 020-8274 4901 | 203,515 | £1,401 | Ged Curran |
| Newham | 020-8430 2000 | 324,322 | £1,241 | Kim Bromley-Derry |
| Redbridge | 020-8554 5000 | 293,055 | £1,391 | Roger Hampson |
| Richmond upon Thames | 020-8891 1411 | 193,585 | £1,582 | Gillian Norton |
| Southwark | 020-7525 5000 | 302,538 | £1,207 | Eleanor Kelly |
| Sutton | 020-8770 5000 | 198,134 | £1,459 | Niall Bolger |
| Tower Hamlets | 020-7364 5000 | 284,015 | £1,181 | Stephen Halsey |
| Waltham Forest | 020-8496 3000 | 268,020 | £1,447 | Martin Esom |
| Wandsworth | 020-8871 6000 | 312,145 | £683 | Paul Martin |
| WESTMINSTER | 020-7641 6000 | 233,292 | £674 | Charlie Parker |

# DISTRICT COUNCILS

| District Council | Telephone | Population* | Council Tax‡ | Chief Executive‡ |
|---|---|---|---|---|
| Adur | 01903-239999 | 63,176 | £1,596 | Alex Bailey |
| Allerdale | 01900-702702 | 96,471 | £1,613 | Ian Frost |
| Amber Valley | 01773-570222 | 123,942 | £1,559 | Julian Townsend |
| Arun | 01903-737500 | 154,414 | £1,531 | Nigel Lynn |
| Ashfield | 01623-450000 | 122,508 | £1,669 | Robert Mitchell |
| Ashford | 01233-331111 | 123,285 | £1,482 | John Bunnett |
| Aylesbury Vale | 01296-585858 | 184,560 | £1,551 | Andrew Grant |
| Babergh | 01473-822801 | 88,845 | £1,516 | Charlie Adan |
| Barrow-in-Furness | 01229-876543 | 67,648 | £1,619 | Phil Huck |
| Basildon | 01268-533333 | 180,521 | £1,560 | Bala Mahendran |
| Basingstoke and Deane | 01256-844844 | 172,870 | £1,379 | Melbourne Barrett |
| Bassetlaw | 01909-533533 | 114,143 | £1,676 | Neil Taylor |
| Blaby | 0116-275 0555 | 95,851 | £1,548 | Sandra Whiles |
| Bolsover | 01246-242424 | 77,155 | £1,635 | Wesley Lumley |
| Boston | 01205-314200 | 66,458 | £1,471 | Phil Drury |
| Braintree | 01376-552525 | 149,985 | £1,494 | Nicola Beach |
| Breckland | 01362-656870 | 133,986 | £1,500 | Anna Graves |
| Brentwood | 01277-312500 | 75,645 | £1,480 | Philip Ruck |
| Broadland | 01603-431133 | 125,961 | £1,533 | Phil Kirby |
| Bromsgrove | 01527-881288 | 95,485 | £1,564 | Kevin Dicks |
| Broxbourne | 01992-785555 | 95,748 | £1,402 | Jeff Stack |
| Broxtowe | 0115-917 7777 | 111,780 | £1,674 | Ruth Hyde, OBE |
| Burnley | 01282-425011 | 87,291 | £1,630 | Pam Smith |
| CAMBRIDGE | 01223-457000 | 128,515 | £1,567 | Antoinette Jackson |
| Cannock Chase | 01543-462621 | 98,549 | £1,516 | Tony McGovern |
| CANTERBURY | 01227-862000 | 157,649 | £1,509 | Colin Carmichael |
| CARLISLE | 01228-817000 | 108,022 | £1,605 | Jason Gooding |
| Castle Point | 01268-882200 | 88,907 | £1,542 | David Marchant |
| Charnwood | 01509-263151 | 173,545 | £1,502 | Geoffrey Parker |
| CHELMSFORD | 01245-606606 | 171,633 | £1,508 | Steve Packham |
| Cheltenham | 01242-262626 | 116,495 | £1,490 | Andrew North |
| Cherwell | 01295-252535 | 144,494 | £1,604 | Sue Smith |
| Chesterfield | 01246-345345 | 104,288 | £1,522 | Huw Bowen |
| Chichester | 01243-785166 | 115,527 | £1,495 | Diane Shepherd |
| Chiltern | 01494-729000 | 93,972 | £1,561 | Alan Goodrum |
| Chorley | 01257-515151 | 111,607 | £1,547 | Gary Hall |
| Christchurch | 01202-495000 | 48,895 | £1,657 | David McIntosh |
| Colchester | 01206-282222 | 180,420 | £1,497 | Adrian Pritchard |
| Copeland | 0845-054 8600 | 69,832 | £1,630 | Paul Walker |
| Corby | 01536-464000 | 65,434 | £1,452 | Norman Stronach |
| Cotswold | 01285-623000 | 84,637 | £1,486 | David Neudegg |
| Craven | 01756-700600 | 55,696 | £1,585 | Paul Shevlin |
| Crawley | 01293-438000 | 109,883 | £1,494 | Lee Harris |
| Dacorum | 01442-228000 | 149,741 | £1,480 | Sally Marshall |
| Dartford | 01322-343434 | 102,234 | £1,504 | Graham Harris |
| Daventry | 01327-871100 | 79,036 | £1,475 | Ian Vincent |
| Derbyshire Dales | 01629-761100 | 71,281 | £1,600 | Dorcas Bunton |
| Dover | 01304-821199 | 113,066 | £1,537 | Nadeem Aziz |
| East Cambridgeshire | 01353-665555 | 86,685 | £1,591 | John Hill |
| East Devon | 01395-516551 | 136,374 | £1,573 | Mark Williams |
| East Dorset | 01202-886201 | 88,186 | £1,720 | David McIntosh |
| East Hampshire | 01730-266551 | 117,483 | £1,458 | Sandy Hopkins |
| East Hertfordshire | 01279-655261 | 143,021 | £1,508 | vacant |
| East Lindsey | 01507-601111 | 137,623 | £1,443 | Stuart Davy |
| East Northamptonshire | 01832-742000 | 88,872 | £1,482 | David Oliver |
| East Staffordshire | 01283-508000 | 115,663 | £1,504 | Andy O'Brien |
| Eastbourne | 01323-410000 | 101,547 | £1,657 | Robert Cottrill |
| Eastleigh | 023-8068 8000 | 128,877 | £1,450 | Nick Tustian |
| Eden | 01768-817817 | 52,630 | £1,614 | Robin Hooper |
| Elmbridge | 01372-474474 | 132,769 | £1,639 | Robert Moran |
| Epping Forest | 01992-564000 | 128,777 | £1,511 | Glen Chipp |
| Epsom and Ewell | 01372-732000 | 78,318 | £1,613 | Frances Rutter |
| Erewash | 0115-907 2244 | 114,048 | £1,537 | Jeremy Jaroszek |
| EXETER | 01392-277888 | 124,328 | £1,544 | Karime Hassan |
| Fareham | 01329-236100 | 114,331 | £1,397 | Peter Grimwood |
| Fenland | 01354-654321 | 97,732 | £1,671 | Paul Medd |
| Forest Heath | 01638-719000 | 62,812 | £1,520 | Ian Gallin |
| Forest of Dean | 01594-810000 | 83,674 | £1,525 | Sue Pangbourne |
| Fylde | 01253-658658 | 77,042 | £1,568 | Allan Oldfield |
| Gedling | 0115-901 3901 | 115,638 | £1,658 | John Robinson |

| District Council | Telephone | Population* | Council Tax‡ | Chief Executive‡ |
|---|---|---|---|---|
| GLOUCESTER | 01452-396396 | 125,649 | £1,485 | – |
| Gosport | 023-9258 4242 | 84,287 | £1,459 | Ian Lycett |
| Gravesham | 01474-564422 | 105,261 | £1,497 | David Hughes |
| Great Yarmouth | 01493-856100 | 98,172 | £1,512 | Gordon Mitchell |
| Guildford | 01483-505050 | 142,958 | £1,613 | Sue Sturgeon |
| Hambleton | 01619-779977 | 89,828 | £1,504 | Phillip Morton |
| Harborough | 01858-828282 | 88,008 | £1,523 | Beverley Jolly & Norman Proudfoot |
| Harlow | 01279-446655 | 84,564 | £1,563 | Malcolm Morley |
| Harrogate | 01423-500600 | 157,267 | £1,608 | Wallace Sampson |
| Hart | 01252-622122 | 93,325 | £1,470 | Patricia Hughes & Daryl Phillips |
| Hastings | 01424-451066 | 91,093 | £1,673 | Neil Dart |
| Havant | 023-9244 6019 | 122,210 | £1,449 | Sandy Hopkins |
| Hertsmere | 020-8207 2277 | 102,427 | £1,470 | Donald Graham |
| High Peak | 0345-129 7777 | 91,364 | £1,556 | Simon Baker |
| Hinckley and Bosworth | 01455-238141 | 107,722 | £1,480 | Steve Atkinson |
| Horsham | 01403-215100 | 134,158 | £1,489 | Tom Crowley |
| Huntingdonshire | 01480-388388 | 173,605 | £1,609 | Jo Lancaster |
| Hyndburn | 01254-388111 | 80,208 | £1,585 | David Welsby |
| Ipswich | 01473-432000 | 134,966 | £1,625 | Russell Williams |
| Kettering | 01536-410333 | 96,945 | £1,484 | David Cook, MBE |
| King's Lynn and West Norfolk | 01553-616200 | 150,026 | £1,516 | Ray Harding |
| LANCASTER | 01524-582000 | 141,277 | £1,571 | Mark Cullinan |
| Lewes | 01273-471600 | 100,229 | £1,702 | Jenny Rowlands |
| Lichfield | 01543-308000 | 102,093 | £1,488 | Diane Tilley |
| LINCOLN | 01522-881188 | 96,202 | £1,533 | Angela Andrews *(acting)* |
| Maidstone | 01622-602000 | 161,819 | £1,568 | Alison Broom |
| Maldon | 01621-854477 | 62,767 | £1,523 | Fiona Marshall |
| Malvern Hills | 01684-862151 | 75,911 | £1,538 | Jack Hegarty |
| Mansfield | 01623-463463 | 105,893 | £1,677 | Ruth Marlow |
| Melton | 01664-502502 | 50,969 | £1,535 | Lynn Aisbett |
| Mendip | 0300-3038588 | 110,844 | £1,496 | Stuart Brown |
| Mid Devon | 01884-255255 | 79,198 | £1,633 | Kevin Finan |
| Mid Suffolk | 01449-720711 | 99,121 | £1,514 | Charlie Adan |
| Mid Sussex | 01444-458166 | 144,377 | £1,515 | Kathryn Hall |
| Mole Valley | 01306-885001 | 86,234 | £1,601 | Yvonne Rees |
| New Forest | 023-8028 5000 | 178,907 | £1,482 | David Yates |
| Newark and Sherwood | 01636-650000 | 117,758 | £1,718 | Andrew Muter |
| Newcastle-under-Lyme | 01782-717717 | 126,052 | £1,479 | John Sellgren |
| North Devon | 01271-327711 | 94,059 | £1,623 | Mike Mansell |
| North Dorset | 01258-454111 | 70,043 | £1,675 | Matt Prosser |
| North East Derbyshire | 01246-231111 | 99,352 | £1,635 | Wes Lumley |
| North Hertfordshire | 01462-474000 | 131,046 | £1,517 | David Scholes |
| North Kesteven | 01529-414155 | 111,046 | £1,502 | Ian Fytche |
| North Norfolk | 01263-513811 | 102,867 | £1,540 | Sheila Oxtoby |
| North Warwickshire | 01827-715341 | 62,468 | £1,641 | Jerry Hutchinson |
| North West Leicestershire | 01530-454545 | 95,882 | £1,552 | Christine Fisher |
| Northampton | 0300-330 7000 | 219,495 | £1,494 | David Kennedy |
| NORWICH | 0344-980 3333 | 137,472 | £1,593 | Laura McGillivray |
| Nuneaton and Bedworth | 024-7637 6376 | 126,174 | £1,601 | Alan Franks |
| Oadby and Wigston | 0116-288 8961 | 55,928 | £1,527 | Mark Hall |
| OXFORD | 01865-249811 | 157,997 | £1,679 | Peter Sloman |
| Pendle | 01282-661661 | 89,840 | £1,624 | Dean Langton |
| PRESTON | 01772-906900 | 140,452 | £1,644 | Lorraine Norris |
| Purbeck | 01929-556561 | 45,679 | £1,713 | Steve Mackenzie |
| Redditch | 01527-64252 | 84,471 | £1,560 | Kevin Dicks |
| Reigate and Banstead | 01737-276000 | 143,094 | £1,647 | John Jory |
| Ribble Valley | 01200-425111 | 58,091 | £1,511 | Marshall Scott |
| Richmondshire | 01748-829100 | 52,729 | £1,607 | Tony Clark |
| Rochford | 01702-318111 | 84,776 | £1,549 | Amar Dave |
| Rossendale | 01706-217777 | 69,168 | £1,610 | Stuart Sugarman |
| Rother | 01424-787000 | 92,130 | £1,649 | Malcolm Johnston & Anthony Leonard |
| Rugby | 01788-533533 | 102,500 | £1,578 | Ian Davis & Adam Norburn |
| Runnymede | 01932-838383 | 84,584 | £1,580 | Paul Turrell |
| Rushcliffe | 0115-981 9911 | 113,670 | £1,670 | Allen Graham |
| Rushmoor | 01252-398398 | 95,296 | £1,441 | Andrew Colver |
| Ryedale | 01653-600666 | 52,655 | £1,592 | Janet Waggott |
| ST ALBANS | 01727-866100 | 144,834 | £1,497 | James Blake |
| St Edmundsbury | 01284-763233 | 112,073 | £1,519 | Ian Gallin |
| Scarborough | 01723-232323 | 108,006 | £1,610 | Jim Dillon |

| District Council | Telephone | Population* | Council Tax‡ | Chief Executive‡ |
|---|---|---|---|---|
| Sedgemoor | 0845-408 2540 | 119,057 | £1,472 | Mr Kerry Rickards |
| Selby | 01757-705101 | 85,355 | £1,592 | Mary Weastell |
| Sevenoaks | 01732-227000 | 117,811 | £1,575 | Dr Pav Ramewal |
| Shepway | 01303-853000 | 109,452 | £1,593 | Alistair Stewart |
| South Bucks | 01895-837200 | 68,512 | £1,541 | Alan Goodrum |
| South Cambridgeshire | 0345-045 0500 | 153,281 | £1,591 | Jean Hunter |
| South Derbyshire | 01283-595795 | 98,374 | £1,536 | Frank McArdle |
| South Hams | 01803-861234 | 84,108 | £1,601 | Alan Robinson & Tracy Winser |
| South Holland | 01775-761161 | 90,419 | £1,471 | Anna Graves |
| South Kesteven | 01476-406080 | 137,981 | £1,455 | Beverly Agass |
| South Lakeland | 01539-733333 | 103,271 | £1,605 | Lawrence Conway |
| South Norfolk | 01508-533633 | 129,226 | £1,551 | Sandra Dinneen |
| South Northamptonshire | 01327-322322 | 88,164 | £1,511 | Sue Smith |
| South Oxfordshire | 01235-520202 | 137,015 | £1,585 | David Buckle |
| South Ribble | 01772-421491 | 109,077 | £1,570 | Mike Nuttall |
| South Somerset | 01935-462462 | 164,569 | £1,502 | Mark Williams |
| South Staffordshire | 01902-696000 | 110,692 | £1,439 | Steve Winterflood |
| Spelthorne | 01784-451499 | 98,106 | £1,618 | Roberto Tambini |
| Stafford | 01785-619000 | 132,241 | £1,457 | Ian Thompson |
| Staffordshire Moorlands | 0345-605 3010 | 97,763 | £1,477 | Simon Baker |
| Stevenage | 01438-242242 | 85,997 | £1,477 | Scott Crudgington |
| Stratford-on-Avon | 01789-267575 | 121,056 | £1,572 | Paul Lankester |
| Stroud | 01453-766321 | 115,093 | £1,555 | David Hagg |
| Suffolk Coastal | 01394-383789 | 124,776 | £1,503 | Stephen Baker |
| Surrey Heath | 01276-707100 | 87,533 | £1,651 | Karen Whelan |
| Swale | 01795-417850 | 140,836 | £1,489 | Abdool Kara |
| Tamworth | 01827-709709 | 77,112 | £1,452 | Tony Goodwin |
| Tandridge | 01883-722000 | 85,374 | £1,649 | Louise Round |
| Taunton Deane | 01823-356356 | 112,817 | £1,433 | Penny James |
| Teignbridge | 01626-361101 | 127,357 | £1,613 | Nicola Bulbeck |
| Tendring | 01255-686868 | 139,916 | £1,479 | Ian Davidson |
| Test Valley | 01264-368000 | 119,332 | £1,415 | Roger Tetstall |
| Tewkesbury | 01684-295010 | 85,784 | £1,452 | Michael Dawson |
| Thanet | 01843-577000 | 138,410 | £1,539 | Madeline Homer |
| Three Rivers | 01923-776611 | 90,423 | £1,486 | Dr Steven Halls |
| Tonbridge and Malling | 01732-844522 | 124,426 | £1,539 | Julie Beilby |
| Torridge | 01237-428700 | 65,618 | £1,602 | Jenny Wallace |
| Tunbridge Wells | 01892-526121 | 116,105 | £1,513 | William Benson |
| Uttlesford | 01799-510510 | 84,042 | £1,513 | John Mitchell |
| Vale of White Horse | 01235-520202 | 124,852 | £1,576 | David Buckle |
| Warwick | 01926-410410 | 139,396 | £1,560 | Chris Elliott |
| Watford | 01923-226400 | 95,505 | £1,539 | Manny Lewis |
| Waveney | 01502-562111 | 115,919 | £1,461 | Stephen Baker |
| Waverley | 01483-523333 | 122,860 | £1,646 | Paul Wenham |
| Wealden | 01323-443322 | 154,767 | £1,698 | Charles Lant |
| Wellingborough | 01933-229777 | 76,446 | £1,421 | John Campbell |
| Welwyn & Hatfield | 01707-357000 | 116,024 | £1,524 | Michel Saminaden |
| West Devon | 01822-813600 | 54,260 | £1,678 | Sophie Hosking & Steve Jordan |
| West Dorset | 01305-251010 | 100,474 | £1,680 | Matt Prosser |
| West Lancashire | 01695-577177 | 111,940 | £1,552 | Gill Rowe & Kim Webber |
| West Lindsey | 01427-676676 | 91,787 | £1,530 | Manjeet Gill |
| West Oxfordshire | 01993-861000 | 108,158 | £1,552 | Elaine Nicklin |
| West Somerset | 01643-703704 | 34,323 | £1,486 | Penny James |
| Weymouth and Portland | 01305-838000 | 64,992 | £1,756 | Matt Prosser |
| WINCHESTER | 01962-840222 | 119,218 | £1,452 | Simon Eden |
| Woking | 01483-755855 | 99,426 | £1,652 | Ray Morgan, OBE |
| WORCESTER | 01905-722233 | 100,842 | £1,512 | Lesley Meagher *(acting)* |
| Worthing | 01903-239999 | 106,863 | £1,522 | Alex Bailey |
| Wychavon | 01386-565000 | 119,752 | £1,497 | Jack Hegarty |
| Wycombe | 01494-461000 | 174,878 | £1,505 | Karen Satterford |
| Wyre | 01253-891000 | 108,742 | £1,548 | Garry Payne |
| Wyre Forest | 01562-732928 | 98,960 | £1,563 | Ian Miller |

# METROPOLITAN BOROUGH COUNCILS

| Metropolitan Borough Council | Telephone | Population* | Council Tax‡ | Chief Executive‡ |
|---|---|---|---|---|
| Barnsley | 01226-770770 | 237,843 | £1,470 | Diana Terris |
| BIRMINGHAM | 0121-303 1111 | 1,101,360 | £1,320 | Mark Rogers |
| Bolton | 01204-333333 | 280,439 | £1,492 | Paul Najsarek |
| BRADFORD | 01274-432001 | 528,155 | £1,361 | Kersten England |
| Bury | 0161-253 5000 | 187,474 | £1,514 | Mike Owen *(acting)* |
| Calderdale | 01422-288001 | 207,376 | £1,459 | Merran McRae |
| COVENTRY | 0500-834 333 | 337,428 | £1,537 | Martin Reeves |
| Doncaster | 01302-736000 | 304,185 | £1,384 | Johanna Miller |
| Dudley | 0300-555 2345 | 315,799 | £1,287 | Sarah Norman |
| Gateshead | 0191-433 3000 | 200,505 | £1,634 | Jane Robinson |
| Kirklees | 01484-221000 | 431,020 | £1,471 | Adrian Lythgo |
| Knowsley | 0151-489 6000 | 146,407 | £1,507 | Mike Harden |
| LEEDS | 0113-222 4444 | 766,399 | £1,375 | Tom Riordan |
| LIVERPOOL | 0151-233 3000 | 473,073 | £1,616 | Ged Fitzgerald |
| MANCHESTER | 0161-234 5000 | 520,215 | £1,382 | Sir Howard Bernstein |
| NEWCASTLE UPON TYNE | 0191-278 7878 | 289,835 | £1,545 | Pat Ritchie |
| North Tyneside | 0191-643 5991 | 202,744 | £1,491 | Patrick Melia |
| Oldham | 0161-770 3000 | 228,765 | £1,607 | Carolyn Wilkins |
| Rochdale | 01706-647474 | 212,962 | £1,540 | Steve Rumbelow |
| Rotherham | 01709-382121 | 260,070 | £1,526 | Stella Manzie, CBE |
| St Helens | 01744-676789 | 177,188 | £1,451 | Carole Hudson, CBE |
| SALFORD | 0161-794 4711 | 242,040 | £1,536 | Jim Taylor |
| Sandwell | 0121-569 2200 | 316,719 | £1,337 | Jan Britton |
| Sefton | 0151-922 4040 | 273,531 | £1,560 | Margaret Carney |
| SHEFFIELD | 0114-273 4567 | 563,749 | £1,526 | John Mothersole |
| Solihull | 0121-704 8001 | 209,890 | £1,351 | Nick Page |
| South Tyneside | 0191-427 7000 | 148,740 | £1,480 | Martin Swales |
| Stockport | 0161-480 4949 | 286,755 | £1,607 | Eamonn Boylan |
| SUNDERLAND | 0191-520 5555 | 276,889 | £1,350 | Dave Smith |
| Tameside | 0161-342 8355 | 220,771 | £1,443 | Steven Pleasant |
| Trafford | 0161-912 2000 | 232,458 | £1,316 | Theresa Grant |
| WAKEFIELD | 0845-850 6506 | 331,379 | £1,393 | Joanne Roney, OBE |
| Walsall | 01922-650000 | 274,173 | £1,600 | Paul Sheehan |
| Wigan | 01942-244991 | 320,975 | £1,403 | Donna Hall |
| Wirral | 0151-606 2000 | 320,914 | £1,509 | Eric Robinson |
| WOLVERHAMPTON | 01902-551155 | 252,987 | £1,531 | Keith Ireland |

# UNITARY COUNCILS

| Unitary Council | Telephone | Population* | Council Tax‡ | Chief Executive‡ |
|---|---|---|---|---|
| Bath and North East Somerset | 01225-477000 | 182,021 | £1,479 | Dr Jo Farrar |
| Bedford | 01234-267422 | 163,924 | £1,599 | Philip Simpkins |
| Blackburn with Darwen | 01254-585585 | 146,743 | £1,495 | Harry Catherall |
| Blackpool | 01253-477477 | 140,501 | £1,530 | Neil Jack |
| Bournemouth | 01202-451451 | 191,390 | £1,499 | Tony Williams |
| Bracknell Forest | 01344-352000 | 118,025 | £1,383 | Timothy Wheadon |
| BRIGHTON AND HOVE | 01273-290000 | 281,076 | £1,569 | Penny Thompson, CBE |
| BRISTOL | 0117-922 2000 | 442,474 | £1,660 | Nicola Yates |
| Central Bedfordshire | 0300-300 8000 | 269,076 | £1,688 | Richard Carr |
| Cheshire East | 0300-123 5500 | 374,179 | £1,483 | Mike Suarez |
| Cheshire West and Chester | 0300-123 8123 | 332,210 | £1,525 | Steve Robinson |
| Cornwall | 0300-123 4100 | 545,335 | £1,550 | Andrew Kerr |
| Darlington | 01325-380651 | 105,367 | £1,524 | Ada Burns |
| DERBY | 01332-293111 | 252,463 | £1,432 | Paul Robison (acting) |
| DURHAM | 0300-026000 | 517,773 | £1,675 | George Garlick |
| East Riding of Yorkshire | 01482-393939 | 337,115 | £1,518 | Nigel Pearson |
| Halton | 0303-333 4300 | 126,354 | £1,433 | David Parr |
| Hartlepool | 01429-266522 | 92,590 | £1,696 | Gill Alexander |
| Herefordshire | 01432-260000 | 187,160 | £1,584 | Alastair Neill |
| Isle of Wight | 01983-821000 | 139,105 | £1,547 | Dave Burbage |
| Isles of Scilly§ | 01720-424000 | 2,280 | £1,241 | Theo Leijser |
| KINGSTON-UPON-HULL | 01482-609100 | 257,710 | £1,420 | Darryl Stephenson |
| LEICESTER | 0116-254 1000 | 337,653 | £1,542 | Andy Keeling |
| Luton | 01582-546000 | 210,962 | £1,514 | Trevor Holden |
| Medway | 01634-333333 | 274,015 | £1,410 | Neil Davies |
| Middlesbrough | 01642-245432 | 139,119 | £1,657 | Mike Robinson |
| Milton Keynes | 01908-691691 | 259,245 | £1,451 | Carole Mills |
| North East Lincolnshire | 01472-313131 | 159,804 | £1,569 | Rob Walsh |
| North Lincolnshire | 01724-296296 | 169,247 | £1,571 | Simon Driver |
| North Somerset | 01934-888888 | 208,154 | £1,459 | Mike Jackson |
| Northumberland | 0345-600 6400 | 315,987 | £1,591 | Steven Mason |
| NOTTINGHAM | 0115-915 5555 | 314,268 | £1,709 | Ian Curryer |
| PETERBOROUGH | 01733-747474 | 190,461 | £1,383 | Gillian Beasley |
| PLYMOUTH | 01752-668000 | 261,546 | £1,568 | Tracey Lee |
| Poole | 01202-633633 | 150,109 | £1,465 | Andrew Flockhart (acting) |
| PORTSMOUTH | 023-9282 2251 | 209,085 | £1,390 | David Williams |
| Reading | 0118-937 3787 | 160,825 | £1,589 | Ian Wardle |
| Redcar and Cleveland | 0164-277 4774 | 135,042 | £1,668 | Amanda Skelton |
| Rutland | 01572-722577 | 38,022 | £1,710 | Helen Briggs |
| Shropshire | 0345-678 9000 | 310,121 | £1,504 | Clive Wright |
| Slough | 01753-475111 | 144,575 | £1,403 | Ruth Bagley, OBE |
| South Gloucestershire | 01454-868009 | 271,556 | £1,550 | Amanda Deeks |
| SOUTHAMPTON | 023-8083 3000 | 245,290 | £1,532 | Dawn Baxendale |
| Southend-on-Sea | 01702-215000 | 177,931 | £1,380 | Robert Tinlin |
| Stockton-on-Tees | 01642-393939 | 194,119 | £1,627 | Neil Schneider |
| STOKE-ON-TRENT | 01782-234567 | 251,027 | £1,430 | John van de Laarschot |
| Swindon | 01793-463000 | 215,799 | £1,404 | Gavin Jones |
| Telford and Wrekin | 01952-380000 | 169,440 | £1,492 | Richard Partington |
| Thurrock | 01375-652652 | 163,270 | £1,338 | David Bull (acting) |
| Torbay | 01803-201201 | 132,984 | £1,514 | Steve Parrock |
| Warrington | 01925-443322 | 206,428 | £1,456 | Steven Broomhead |
| West Berkshire | 01635-42400 | 155,732 | £1,546 | Nick Carter |
| Wiltshire | 0300-456 0100 | 483,143 | £1,534 | C. Brand, C. Godfrey & M. Rae |
| Windsor and Maidenhead | 01628-683800 | 147,400 | £1,150 | Alison Alexander |
| Wokingham | 0118-974 6000 | 159,097 | £1,525 | Andy Couldrick |
| YORK | 01904-551550 | 204,439 | £1,453 | Kersten England |

* Source: Office for National Statistics – Mid-2014 Population Estimates (Crown copyright)
‡ Average Band D council tax bill for 2015–16
‡ Or equivalent postholder
§ Under the Isles of Scilly Clause the council has additional functions to other unitary authorities
Councils in CAPITAL LETTERS have city status

# MAP OF COUNCILS IN ENGLAND

1 Stockton-on-Tees
2 Middlesbrough
3 Blackpool
4 Blackburn
   with Darwen
5 Bolton
6 Bury
7 Rochdale
8 Salford
9 Oldham
10 Liverpool
11 Knowsley
12 St Helens
13 Halton
14 Warrington
15 Trafford
16 Manchester
17 Tameside
18 Stockport
19 Nottingham
20 Telford and
   Wrekin
21 Wolverhampton

22 Walsall
23 Sandwell
24 Dudley
25 Birmingham
26 Solihull
27 Coventry
28 Peterborough
29 South Glos
30 Bristol
31 Bath and
   NE Somerset
32 Windsor and
   Maidenhead
33 Slough
34 Reading
35 Wokingham
36 Bracknell Forest
37 Thurrock
38 Southend
39 Medway
40 Plymouth
41 Torbay
42 Bournemouth

LONDON

1 Hillingdon
2 Harrow
3 Barnet
4 Enfield
5 Waltham Forest
6 Redbridge
7 Barking and Dagenham
8 Havering
9 Ealing
10 Brent
11 Camden
12 Haringey
13 Islington
14 Hackney
15 Newham
16 Hounslow
17 Hammersmith and Fulham
18 Kensington and Chelsea
19 City of Westminster
20 City of London
21 Tower Hamlets
22 Richmond upon Thames
23 Wandsworth
24 Lambeth
25 Southwark
26 Lewisham
27 Greenwich
28 Bexley
29 Kingston upon Thames
30 Merton
31 Sutton
32 Croydon
33 Bromley

# LONDON

## THE CITY OF LONDON CORPORATION

The City of London is the historic centre at the heart of London known as 'the square mile', around which the vast metropolis has grown over the centuries. The City's residential population was 7,400 at the 2011 census and in addition, around 400,000 people work in the City. The civic government is carried on by the City of London Corporation through the court of Common Council.

The City is an international financial and business centre, generating about £30bn a year for the British economy. It includes the head offices of the principal banks, insurance companies and mercantile houses, in addition to buildings ranging from the historic Roman Wall and the 15th-century Guildhall, to the massive splendour of St Paul's Cathedral and the architectural beauty of Wren's spires.

The City of London was described by Tacitus in AD 62 as a busy emporium for trade and traders'. Under the Romans it became an important administration centre and hub of the road system. Little is known of London in Saxon times, when it formed part of the kingdom of the East Saxons. In 886 Alfred recovered London from the Danes and reconstituted it a burgh under his son-in-law. In 1066 the citizens submitted to William the Conqueror who in 1067 granted them a charter, which is still preserved, establishing them in the rights and privileges they had hitherto enjoyed.

### THE MAYORALTY

The mayoralty was probably established about 1189, the first mayor being Henry Fitz Ailwyn who filled the office for 23 years and was succeeded by Fitz Alan (1212–14). A new charter was granted by King John in 1215, directing the mayor to be chosen annually, which has been done ever since, though in early times the same individual often held the office more than once. A familiar instance is that of Whittington, thrice Lord Mayor of London' (in reality four times: 1397, 1398, 1406 and 1419); and many modern cases have occurred. The earliest instance of the phrase 'lord mayor' in English is in 1414. It was used more generally in the latter part of the 15th century and became invariable from 1535 onwards. At Michaelmas the liverymen in Common Hall choose two aldermen who have served the office of sheriff for presentation to the Court of Aldermen, and one is chosen to be lord mayor for the following mayoral year.

### LORD MAYOR'S DAY

The lord mayor of London was previously elected on the feast of St Simon and St Jude (28 October), and from the time of Edward I, at least, was presented to the King or to the Barons of the Exchequer on the following day, unless that day was a Sunday. The day of election was altered to 16 October in 1346, and after some further changes was fixed for Michaelmas Day in 1546, but the ceremonies of admittance and swearing-in of the lord mayor continued to take place on 28 and 29 October respectively until 1751. In 1752, at the reform of the calendar, the lord mayor was continued in office until 8 November, the 'new style' equivalent of 28 October. The lord mayor is now presented to the lord chief justice at the royal courts of justice on the second Saturday in November to make the final declaration of office, having been sworn in at Guildhall on the preceding day. The procession to the royal courts of justice is popularly known as the Lord Mayor's Show.

## REPRESENTATIVES

Aldermen are mentioned in the 11th century and their office is of Saxon origin. They were elected annually between 1377 and 1394, when an act of parliament of Richard II directed them to be chosen for life. Aldermen now serve a six-year term of office before submitting themselves for re-election.

The Common Council was, at an early date, substituted for a popular assembly called the *Folkmote*. At first only two representatives were sent from each ward, but now each of the City's 25 wards is represented by an alderman and at least two Common Councilmen (the number depending on the size of the ward). Common Councilmen are elected every four years.

## OFFICERS

Sheriffs were Saxon officers; their predecessors were the *wic-reeves* and *portreeves* of London and Middlesex. At first they were officers of the Crown, and were named by the Barons of the Exchequer; but Henry I (in 1132) gave the citizens permission to choose their own sheriffs, and the annual election of sheriffs became fully operative under King John's charter of 1199. The citizens lost this privilege, as far as the election of the sheriff of Middlesex was concerned, by the Local Government Act 1888; but the liverymen continue to choose two sheriffs of the City of London, who are appointed on Midsummer Day and take office at Michaelmas.

The office of chamberlain is an ancient one, the first contemporary record of which is 1237. The town clerk (or common clerk) is first mentioned in 1274.

## ACTIVITIES

The work of the City of London Corporation is assigned to a number of committees which present reports to the Court of Common Council. These committees are: Audit and Risk Management; Barbican Centre; Barbican Residential; Board of Governors of the City of London Freeman's School, the City of London School, the City of London School for Girls and the Guildhall School of Music and Drama; City Bridge Trust; Community and Children's Services; Culture, Heritage and Libraries; Education; Epping Forest and Commons; Establishment; Finance; Freedom Applications; Gresham (City Side); Guildhall Improvement; Hampstead Heath, Highgate Wood and Queen's Park; Health and Wellbeing; Investment; Licensing; Livery; Markets; Open Spaces and City Gardens; Pensions Board; Planning and Transportation; Police; Policy and Resources; Port Health and Environmental Services; Standards Committees; and West Ham Park.

The City's estate, in the possession of which the City of London Corporation differs from other municipalities, is managed by the City Lands and Bridge House Estates Committee, the chairmanship of which carries with it the title of chief commoner.

The Honourable the Irish Society, which manages the City Corporation's estates in Ulster, consists of a governor and five other aldermen, the recorder, and 19 common councilmen, of whom one is elected deputy governor.

## THE LORD MAYOR 2015–16

*The Rt. Hon. the Lord Mayor,* Lord Mountevans*
*Private Secretary,* William Chapman
* Provisional at time of going to press

THE SHERIFFS 2015–16
Alderman Charles Bowman (Lime Street); Dr Christine Rigden

OFFICERS, ETC
*Town Clerk,* John Barradell
*Chamberlain,* Peter Kane
*Chief Commoner (2015),* Deputy William Dove, OBE
*Clerk, The Honourable the Irish Society,* C. Fisher

THE ALDERMEN
*with office held and date of appointment to that office*

| Name and Ward | Common Councilman | Alderman | Sheriff | Lord Mayor |
|---|---|---|---|---|
| Sir David Howard, Bt., *Cornhill* | 1972 | 1986 | 1997 | 2000 |
| Ian Luder, *Castle Baynard* | 1998 | 2005 | 2007 | 2008 |
| Nicholas Anstee, *Aldersgate* | 1987 | 1996 | 2003 | 2009 |
| Sir Michael Bear, *Portsoken* | 2003 | 2005 | 2007 | 2010 |
| Sir David Wootton, *Langbourn* | 2002 | 2005 | 2009 | 2011 |
| Sir Roger Gifford, *Cordwainer* | – | 2004 | 2008 | 2012 |
| Dame Fiona Woolf, DBE, *Candlewick* | – | 2007 | 2010 | 2013 |
| Alan Yarrow, *Bridge & Bridge Wt.* | – | 2007 | 2011 | 2014 |
| Lord Mountevans, *Cheap* | – | 2007 | 2012 | 2015 |

*All the above have passed the Civic Chair*

| | | | | |
|---|---|---|---|---|
| Dr Andrew Parmley, *Vintry* | 1992 | 2001 | 2014 | |
| Alison Gowman, *Dowgate* | 1991 | 2002 | – | |
| Gordon Haines, *Queenhithe* | – | 2004 | – | |
| Jeffrey Evans, *Cheap* | – | 2007 | 2012 | |
| Sir Paul Judge, *Tower* | – | 2007 | 2013 | |
| David Graves, *Cripplegate* | | 2008 | – | |
| John Garbutt, *Walbrook* | | 2009 | – | |
| Neil Redcliffe, *Bishopsgate* | – | 2009 | – | |
| Peter Hewitt, *Aldgate* | – | 2012 | – | |
| Timothy Hailes, *Bassishaw* | – | 2013 | – | |
| Julian Malins, QC, *Farringdon Wt.* | – | 2013 | – | |
| Matthew Richardson, *Billingsgate* | 2009 | 2012 | – | |
| William Russell, *Bread Street* | – | 2013 | – | |
| Peter Estlin, *Coleman Street* | – | 2013 | – | |
| Charles Bowman, *Lime Street* | – | 2013 | – | |
| Timothy Hailes, *Bassishaw* | – | 2013 | – | |
| Julian Malins, QC, *Farringdon Wt.* | 1981 | 2013 | – | |
| Prof. Michael Mainelli, *Broad Street* | – | 2013 | – | |
| Vincent Keaveny, *Farringdon Wn* | – | 2013 | – | |
| Peter Estlin, *Coleman Street* | – | 2013 | – | |

THE COMMON COUNCIL
*Deputy:* each common councilman so described serves a deputy to the alderman of her/his ward.

| | |
|---|---|
| Abrahams, G. C. (2000) | *Farringdon Wt.* |
| Absalom, *Deputy* J. D. (1994) | *Farringdon Wt.* |
| Anderson, R. K. (2013) | *Aldersgate* |
| Bain-Stewart, A. (2005) | *Farringdon Wn.* |
| Barker, *Deputy* J. A., OBE (1981) | *Cripplegate Wn.* |
| Barrow, *Deputy* D. (2007) | *Aldgate* |
| Bennett, *Deputy* J. A. (2005) | *Broad Street* |
| Benstead-Smith, N. M. (2014) | *Cheap* |
| Boden, C. P. (2013) | *Castle Baynard* |
| Boleat, M. J. (2002) | *Cordwainer* |
| Bottomley, K. D. F. (2015) | *Bridge & Bridge Wt* |
| Bradshaw, D. J. (1991) | *Cripplegate Wn.* |
| Campbell-Taylor, Revd W. G. (2014) | *Portsoken* |
| Cassidy, *Deputy* M. J., CBE (1980) | *Coleman Street* |
| Chadwick, R. A. H. (1994) | *Tower* |
| Challis, N. K. (2005) | *Castle Baynard* |
| Chapman, *Deputy* J. D. (2006) | *Langbourn* |
| Colthurst, H. N. A. (2013) | *Lime Street* |
| Cotgrove, D. (1991) | *Lime Street* |
| De Sausmarez, H. J. (2015) | *Candlewick* |
| Deane, *Deputy* A. J. C. (2011) | *Farringdon Wt.* |
| Dostalova, K. (2013) | *Farringdon Wn.* |
| Dove, *Deputy* W. H., OBE (1993) | *Bishopsgate Wt.* |
| Duckworth, S. D., OBE (2000) | *Bishopsgate Wn.* |
| Dudley, Revd Dr M. R. (2002) | *Aldersgate* |
| Dunphy, P. G. (2009) | *Cornhill* |
| Edham, E. (2014) | *Castle Baynard* |
| Eskenzi, *Deputy* A. N., CBE (1970) | *Farringdon Wn.* |
| Everett, K. M. (1984) | *Candlewick* |
| Fernandes, S. A. (2009) | *Coleman Street* |
| Fletcher, J. W. (2011) | *Portsoken* |
| Fraser, S. J., CBE (1993) | *Coleman Street* |
| Fraser, *Deputy* W. B., OBE (1981) | *Vintry* |
| Fredericks, M. B. (2008) | *Tower* |
| Frew, L. (2013) | *Walbrook* |
| Gillon, G. M. F. (1995) | *Cordwainer* |
| Ginsburg, *Deputy* S. (1990) | *Bishopsgate Wn.* |
| Haines, *Deputy* Revd S. D. (2005) | *Cornhill* |
| Harris, B. N. (2004) | *Bridge & Bridge Wt* |
| Harrower, G. G. (2015) | *Bassishaw* |
| Haywood, C. M. (2013) | *Broad Street* |
| Hoffman, T. D. D. (2002) | *Vintry* |
| Holmes, A. (2013) | *Farringdon Wn.* |
| Howard, *Deputy* R. P. S. (2011) | *Lime Street* |
| Hudson, M. (2007) | *Castle Baynard* |
| Hyde, W. (2011) | *Bishopsgate Wt.* |
| Ingham Clark, J. (2013) | *Billingsgate* |
| James, Clare (2008) | *Farringdon Wn.* |
| Jones, G. P., QC (2013) | *Farringdon Wt.* |
| Jones, *Deputy* H. L. M. (2004) | *Portsoken* |
| King, *Deputy* A. J. N. (1999) | *Queenhithe* |
| Lawrence, G. A. (2002) | *Farringdon Wt.* |
| Littlechild, V. (2009) | *Cripplegate Wn.* |
| Lodge, O. A. W., TD (2009) | *Bread Street* |
| Lord, C. E., OBE (2001) | *Farringdon Wt.* |
| Lumley, Prof. J. S. P. (2013) | *Aldersgate* |
| McGuinness, *Deputy* C. S. (1997) | *Castle Baynard* |
| McMurtie, A. S. (2013) | *Coleman Street* |
| Martinelli, P. N. (2009) | *Farringdon Wn.* |
| Mayhew, J. P. (1996) | *Aldersgate* |
| Mead, W. (1997) | *Farringdon Wt.* |
| Merrett, R. A. (2009) | *Bassishaw* |

Mooney, B. D. F. (1998) · *Queenhithe*
Moore, G. W. (2009) · *Cripplegate Wt.*
Morris, H. F. (2008) · *Aldgate*
Moss, *Deputy* A. M. (2013) · *Cheap*
Moys, S. D. (2001) · *Aldgate*
Nash, *Deputy* J. C., OBE (1983) · *Aldersgate*
Newman, B. P., CBE (1989) · *Aldersgate*
Packham, G. D. (2013) · *Castle Baynard*
Patel, D. (2013) · *Aldgate*
Pembroke, A. M. F. (1978) · *Cheap*
Pleasance, J. L. (2013) · *Langbourn*
Pollard, *Deputy* J. H. G. (2002) · *Dowgate*
Price, E. C. L. (2013) · *Farringdon Wt.*
Priest, H. J. S. (2009) · *Castle Baynard*
Pulman, *Deputy* G. A. G. (1983) · *Tower*
Punter, C. (1993) · *Cripplegate Wt.*
Quilter, S. D. (1998) · *Cripplegate Wt.*
Regan, *Deputy* R. D., OBE (1998) · *Farringdon Wn.*
Regis, D. (2009) · *Portsoken*
Richardson, A. F. M. (2013) · *Farringdon Wt.*
Rogula, E. (2008) · *Lime Street*
Rounding, V. (2011) · *Farringdon Wn.*
Scott, J. G. S. (1999) · *Broad Street*
Seaton, I. (2009) · *Cornhill*
Shilson, *Deputy*, G. R. E., DPHIL (2009) · *Bread Street*
Simons, J. L. (2004) · *Castle Baynard*
Sleigh, T. C. C. (2013) · *Bishopsgate Wt.*
Smith, G. M. (2013) · *Farringdon Wn.*
Snyder, *Deputy* Sir Michael (1986) · *Cordwainer*
Starling, A. M. (2006) · *Cripplegate Wn.*
Streeter, P. T. (2013) · *Bishopsgate Wn.*
Thompson, D. J. (2004) · *Aldgate*
Thomson, *Deputy* J. M. D. (2013) · *Walbrook*
Tomlinson, *Deputy* J. (2004) · *Cripplegate Wt.*
Tumbridge, J. R. (2009) · *Tower*
Welbank, *Deputy* M., MBE (2005) · *Billingsgate*
Wheatley, M. R. P. H. D. (2013) · *Dowgate*
Woodhouse, P. (2013) · *Langbourn*

## THE CITY GUILDS (LIVERY COMPANIES)

The constitution of the livery companies has been unchanged for centuries. There are three ranks of membership: freemen, liverymen and assistants. A person can become a freeman by patrimony (through a parent having been a freeman); by servitude (through having served an apprenticeship to a freeman); or by redemption (by purchase).

Election to the livery is the prerogative of the company, who can elect any of its freemen as liverymen. Assistants are usually elected from the livery and form a Court of Assistants which is the governing body of the company. The master (in some companies called the prime warden) is elected annually from the assistants.

The register for 2015–16 lists 25,510 liverymen of the guilds entitled to vote at elections at Common Hall.

The order of precedence, omitting extinct companies, is given in parentheses after the name of each company in the list below. In certain companies the election of master or prime warden for the year does not take place until the autumn. In such cases the master or prime warden for 2014–15, rather than 2015–16, is given.

### THE TWELVE GREAT COMPANIES
*In order of civic precedence*

MERCERS *(1)*. *Hall*, Mercers' Hall, Ironmonger Lane, London EC2V 8HE *Livery*, 247. *Clerk*, Menna McGregor *Master*, Timothy Haywood, CBE

GROCERS *(2)*. *Hall*, Grocers' Hall, Princes Street, London EC2R 8AD *Livery*, 348. *Clerk*, Brig. Robert Pridham, OBE *Master*, Charles McAndrew

DRAPERS *(3)*. *Hall*, Drapers' Hall, Throgmorton Avenue, London EC2N 2DQ *Livery*, 317. *Clerk*, Col. Richard Winstanley, OBE *Master*, John Giffard, CBE, QPM

FISHMONGERS *(4)*. *Hall*, Fishmongers' Hall, London Bridge, London EC4R 9EL *Livery*, 388. *Clerk*, Maj.-Gen. Colin Boag, CB, CBE *Prime Warden*, Michael McLaren

GOLDSMITHS *(5)*. *Hall*, Goldsmiths' Hall, Foster Lane, London EC2V 6BN *Livery*, 285. *Clerk*, Rear-Adm. Richard Melly *Prime Warden*, Timothy Schroder

MERCHANT TAYLORS *(6/7)*. *Hall*, Merchant Taylors' Hall, 30 Threadneedle Street, London EC2R 8JB *Livery*, 340. *Clerk*, Rear-Adm. Nicholas Harris, CB, MBE *Master*, P. T. E. Massey

SKINNERS *(6/7)*. *Hall*, Skinners' Hall, 8 Dowgate Hill, London EC4R 2SP *Livery*, 400. *Clerk*, Maj.-Gen. Brian Plummer, CBE *Master*, The Hon. Emmeline Winterbotham

HABERDASHERS *(8)*. *Hall*, Haberdashers' Hall, 18 West Smithfield, London EC1A 9HQ *Livery*, 320. *Clerk*, Cdre Philip Thicknesse, RN *Master*, Audley Twiston-Davies

SALTERS *(9)*. *Hall*, Salters' Hall, 4 Fore Street, London EC2Y 5DE *Livery*, 176. *Clerk*, Capt. David Morris, RN *Master*, Col. David Woodd

IRONMONGERS *(10)*. *Hall*, Ironmongers' Hall, 1 Shaftesbury Place, London EC2Y 8AA *Livery*, 146. *Clerk*, Col. Hamon Massey *Master*, George Bastin

VINTNERS *(11)*. *Hall*, Vintners' Hall, Upper Thames Street, London EC4V 3BG *Livery*, 369. *Clerk*, Brig. Jonathan Bourne-May *Master*, Simon Leschallas

CLOTHWORKERS *(12)*. *Hall*, Clothworkers' Hall, Dunster Court, Mincing Lane, London EC3R 7AH *Livery*, 200. *Clerk*, Mr Andrew Blessley *Master*, Melville Haggard

### OTHER CITY GUILDS
*In alphabetical order*

ACTUARIES *(91)*. Cheapside House, 138 Cheapside, London EC2V 6BW *Livery*, 220. *Clerk*, David Johnson *Master*, Peter Thompson

AIR PILOTS AND AIR NAVIGATORS *(81)*. *Hall*, Cobham House, 9 Warwick Court, Gray's Inn, London WC1R 5DJ *Livery*, 600. *Clerk*, Paul Tacon *Grand Master*, HRH the Duke of York, KG, GCVO, ADC(P) *Master*, Sqn Ldr Chris Ford

APOTHECARIES *(58)*. *Hall*, Apothecaries' Hall, 14 Black Friars Lane, London EC4V 6EJ *Livery*, 1,215. *Clerk*, A. Wallington-Smith *Master*, Dr R. N. Palmer

ARBITRATORS *(93)*. 98 Elm Road, Kingston-upon-Thames, Surrey KT2 6HU *Livery*, 180. *Clerk*, Elinor Pritchard *Master*, Michael Goodridge, MBE

ARMOURERS AND BRASIERS *(22)*. *Hall*, Armourers' Hall, 81 Coleman Street, London EC2R 5BJ *Livery*, 130. *Clerk*, Peter Bateman *Master*, Col. David Wynne Davies

ART SCHOLARS *(110)*. Furniture Makers' Hall, 12 Austin Friars, London EC2N 2HE *Livery*, 85. *Clerk*, Georgina Gough *Master*, Alistair Leslie

BAKERS *(19)*. *Hall*, Bakers' Hall, 9 Harp Lane, London EC3R 6DP *Livery*, 350. *Clerk*, Cdre Martin Westwood *Master*, Colin Reese, QC

BARBERS *(17)*. *Hall*, Barber-Surgeons' Hall, Monkwell Square, Wood Street, London EC2Y 5BL *Livery*, 220. *Clerk*, Col. Peter Durrant, MBE *Master*, Geoffrey Preston

BASKETMAKERS *(52)*. 56 Victoria Way, Liphook, Hampshire GU30 7NJ *Livery*, 300. *Clerk*, Fiona Janczur *Prime Warden*, Richard Boucher-Giles

BLACKSMITHS *(40)*. 9 Little Trinity Lane, London EC4V 2AD *Livery*, 246. *Clerk*, Wg Cdr M. A. Heath *Prime Warden*, Nigel Whitehead

BOWYERS *(38)*. 46 The Haydens, Tonbridge, Kent TN9 1NS, *Livery*, 88. *Clerk*, Brian Francois *Master*, Revd John Hayton, TD

BREWERS *(14)*. *Hall*, Brewers' Hall, Aldermanbury Square, London EC2V 7HR *Livery*, 200. *Clerk*, Col. Michael O'Dwyer, OBE *Master*, Miles Jenner, DL

BRODERERS *(48)*. Ember House, 35–37 Creek Road, East Molesey, Surrey KT8 9BE *Livery*, 126. *Clerk*, Peter J. C. Crouch *Master*, Nicholas Bagshawe

BUILDERS MERCHANTS *(88)*. 4 College Hill, London EC4R 2RB *Livery*, 208. *Clerk*, T. Statham *Master*, Leo Martin

BUTCHERS *(24)*. *Hall*, Butchers' Hall, 87 Bartholomew Close, London EC1A 7EB *Livery*, 638. *Clerk*, Maj.-Gen. J. S. Mason, MBE *Master*, Patricia Dart

CARMEN *(77)*. Five Kings House, 1 Queen Street Place, London EC4R 1QS *Livery*, 500. *Clerk*, Walter Gill *Master*, Mark Roderick Winton Griffiths

CARPENTERS *(26)*. *Hall*, Carpenters' Hall, 1 Throgmorton Avenue, London EC2N 2JJ *Livery*, 150. *Clerk*, Brig. Tim Gregson, MBE *Master*, Michael Neal

CHARTERED ACCOUNTANTS *(86)*. Larksfield, Kent Hatch Road, Crockham Hill, Edenbridge, Kent TN8 6SX *Livery*, 365. *Clerk*, Peter Dickinson *Master*, David Illingworth

CHARTERED ARCHITECTS *(98)*. 164 Stockbridge Road, Winchester SO22 6RW *Livery*, 165. *Clerk*, Ian Head *Master*, Dr Geoffrey Purves

CHARTERED SECRETARIES AND ADMINISTRATORS *(87)*. 3rd Floor, Saddlers' House, 40 Gutter Lane, London EC2V 6BR *Livery*, 240. *Clerk*, Erica Lee *Master*, Patricia Day

CHARTERED SURVEYORS *(85)*. 75 Meadway Drive, Horsell, Woking, Surrey GU21 4TF *Livery*, 365. *Clerk*, Amanda Jackson *Master*, Graham Chase

CLOCKMAKERS *(61)*. 1 Throgmorton Avenue, London EC2N 2BY *Livery*, 289. *Clerk*, Lt.-Col. Oliver Bartrum, MBE *Master*, Philip Whyte

COACHMAKERS AND COACH-HARNESS MAKERS *(72)*. The Old Barn, Church Lane, Glentham Market Rasen, Lincolnshire LN8 2EL *Livery*, 500. *Clerk*, Cdr Mark Leaning, RN *Master*, Michael Kimber

CONSTRUCTORS *(99)*. 5 Delft Close, Locks Heath, Southampton SO31 7TQ *Livery*, 145. *Clerk*, Kim Tyrrell *Master*, Graeme Monteith

COOKS *(35)*. 18 Solent Drive, Warsash, Southampton SO31 9HB *Livery*, 75. *Clerk*, Vice-Adm. P. J. Wilkinson, CB, CVO *Master*, Donald Hodgson

COOPERS *(36)*. *Hall*, Coopers' Hall, 13 Devonshire Square, London EC2M 4TH *Livery*, 260. *Clerk*, Lt.-Col. Adrian Carroll *Master*, Vivian Bairstow

CORDWAINERS *(27)*. Clothworkers' Hall, Dunster Court, Mincing Lane, London EC3R 7AH *Livery*, 182. *Clerk*, John Miller *Master*, John Rubinstein

CURRIERS *(29)*. Oak Lodge, 4 Greenhill Lane, Wimborne, Dorset BH21 2RN *Livery*, 105. *Clerk*, Adrian Rafferty *Master*, J. Allen

CUTLERS *(18)*. *Hall*, Cutlers' Hall, Warwick Lane, London EC4M 7BR *Livery*, 100. *Clerk*, Rupert Meacher *Master*, J. C. W. Wichtowski

DISTILLERS *(69)*. 1 The Sanctuary, Westminster, London SW1P 3JT *Livery*, 260. *Clerk*, Edward Macey-Dare *Master*, Douglas Morton

DYERS *(13)*. *Hall*, Dyers' Hall, 10 Dowgate Hill, London EC4R 2ST *Livery*, 136. *Clerk*, J. R. Vaizey *Prime Warden*, A. C. S. Macpherson

EDUCATORS *(109)*. 8 Little Trinity Lane, London EC4V 2AN *Livery*, 275. *Clerk*, Dr Misha Hebel *Master*, John Leighfield, CBE

ENGINEERS *(94)*. Wax Chandlers' Hall, 6 Gresham Street, London EC2V 7AD *Livery*, 320. *Clerk*, A. G. Willenbruch *Master*, Air Vice-Marshal P. J. O'Reilly, CB

ENVIRONMENTAL CLEANERS *(97)*. 64 Ravensfield Gardens, Epsom, Surrey KT19 0SR *Livery*, 185. *Clerk*, Maureen Marden *Master*, Timothy Doyle

FAN MAKERS *(76)*. Skinners' Hall, 8 Dowgate Hill, London EC4R 2SP *Livery*, 180. *Clerk*, Martin Davies *Master*, John Naylor

FARMERS *(80)*. *Hall*, The Farmers' and Fletchers' Hall, 3 Cloth Street, London EC1A 7LD *Livery*, 350. *Clerk*, Col. David King, OBE *Master*, A. J. Alston

FARRIERS *(55)*. 19 Queen Street, Chipperfield, Kings Langley, Herts WD4 9BT *Livery*, 351. *Clerk*, Charlotte Clifford *Master*, Guy Hurst

FELTMAKERS *(63)*. Post Cottage, Greywell, Hook, Hants RG29 1DA *Livery*, 190. *Clerk*, Maj. J. T. H. Coombs *Master*, Peter Simeons

FIREFIGHTERS *(103)*. The Insurance Hall, 20 Aldermanbury, London EC2V 7GF *Livery*, 121. *Clerk*, Steven Tamcken *Master*, Ron Murray

FLETCHERS *(39)*. *Hall*, The Farmers' and Fletchers' Hall, 3 Cloth Street, London EC1A 7LD *Livery*, 143. *Clerk*, Kate Pink *Master*, Adrian Knight

FOUNDERS *(33)*. *Hall*, Founders' Hall, 1 Cloth Fair, London EC1A 7JQ *Livery*, 175. *Clerk*, J. P. Knight *Master*, P. A. Draycott

FRAMEWORK KNITTERS *(64)*. The Grange, Kimcote, Lutterworth LE17 5RU *Livery*, 200. *Clerk*, Capt. Shaun Mackaness *Master*, David Miller

FRUITERERS *(45)*. Chapelstones, 84 High Street, Codford St Mary, Warminster BA12 0ND *Livery*, 283. *Clerk*, Lt.-Col. L. French *Master*, R. Best

FUELLERS *(95)*. Skinners' Hall, 8 Dowgate Hill, London EC4R 2SP *Livery*, 141. *Clerk*, Cdre Bill Walworth *Master*, Neville Chamberlain, OBE

FURNITURE MAKERS *(83)*. *Hall*, Furniture Makers' Hall, 12 Austin Friars, London EC2N 2HE *Livery*, 205. *Clerk*, Jonny Westbrooke *Master*, David Dewing

GARDENERS *(66)*. 25 Luke Street, London EC2A 4AR *Livery*, 298. *Clerk*, Maj. Jeremy Herrtage *Master*, Bernard Williams

GIRDLERS *(23)*. *Hall*, Girdlers' Hall, Basinghall Avenue, London EC2V 5DD *Livery*, 80. *Clerk*, Brig. Ian Rees *Master*, Patrick Reeve

GLASS SELLERS *(71)*. 17 The Ryde, Hatfield, Herts AL9 5DQ *Livery*, 230. *Clerk*, Caroline Gillett *Master*, William Knocker

GLAZIERS AND PAINTERS OF GLASS *(53)*. *Hall*, Glaziers' Hall, 9 Montague Close, London SE1 9DD *Livery*, 292. *Clerk*, Cdr Andrew Gordon-Lennox, RN *Master*, Duncan Gee

GLOVERS *(62)*. Seniors Farmhouse, Semley, Shaftesbury, Dorset SP7 9AX *Livery*, 245. *Clerk*, Lt.-Col. Mark Butler *Master*, Michael Orr

GOLD AND SILVER WYRE DRAWERS *(74)*. 9A Prince of Wales Mansions, Prince of Wales Drive, London SW11 4BG *Livery*, 280. *Clerk*, Cdr. R. House *Master*, Michael F. Powell

GUNMAKERS *(73)*. The Proof House, 48–50 Commercial Road, London E1 1LP *Livery*, 350. *Clerk*, John Allen *Master*, J. F. Jackman

HACKNEY CARRIAGE DRIVERS *(104)*. 25 The Grove, Parkfield, Latimer, Bucks HP5 1UE *Livery*, 105. *Clerk*, Mary Whitworth *Master*, Colin Evans

HORNERS *(54)*. 12 Coltsfoot Close, Ixworth, Suffolk IP31 2NJ *Livery*, 225. *Clerk*, Jonathan Mead *Master*, Raymond Layard

INFORMATION TECHNOLOGISTS *(100)*. *Hall*, Information Technologists' Hall, 39A Bartholomew Close, London EC1A 7JN *Livery*, 349. *Clerk*, Mike Jenkins *Master*, Nicholas Birtles

INNHOLDERS *(32)*. *Hall,* Innholders' Hall, 30 College Street, London EC4R 2RH *Livery,* 150. *Clerk,* Dougal Bulger *Master,* Julia Sibley, MBE

INSURERS *(92)*. Insurance Hall, 20 Aldermanbury, London EC2V 7HY *Livery,* 341. *Clerk,* Sarah Clark *Master,* Andrew Hubbard, FCA

INTERNATIONAL BANKERS *(106)*. 12 Austin Friars, London EC2N 2HE *Livery,* 223. *Clerk,* Nicholas Westgarth *Master,* Michael Llewelyn-Jones

JOINERS AND CEILERS *(41)*. 75 Meadway Drive, Horsell, Woking, Surrey GU21 4TF *Livery,* 115. *Clerk,* Amanda Jackson *Master,* Mark Snelling

LAUNDERERS *(89)*. *Hall,* Launderers' Hall, 9 Montague Close, London Bridge, London SE1 9DD *Livery,* 175. *Clerk,* Margaret Campbell *Master,* Paul Higgs

LEATHERSELLERS *(15)*. 21 Garlick Hill, London EC4V 2AU *Livery,* 150. *Clerk,* Brig. David Santa-Olalla, DSO, MC *Master,* His Hon. Anthony Thornton, QC

LIGHTMONGERS *(96)*. 1 Manor House Garden, High Street, Wanstead, London E11 2RU *Livery,* 168. *Clerk,* Phillip Hyde *Master,* Rod Bennion

LORINERS *(57)*. 30 Elm Park, Royal Wootton Bassett, Wiltshire SN4 7TA *Livery,* 400. *Clerk,* Honor Page *Master,* Graham Flight

MAKERS OF PLAYING CARDS *(75)*. 256 St David's Square, London E14 3WE *Livery,* 147. *Clerk,* David Barrett *Master,* Capt. Michael Davis-Marks, OBE

MANAGEMENT CONSULTANTS *(105)*. Skinners' Hall, 8 Dowgate Hill, London EC4R 2SP *Livery,* 197. *Clerk,* Julie Fox *Master,* David Peregrine-Jones

MARKETORS *(90)*. Plaisterers' Hall, One London Wall, London EC2Y 5JU *Livery,* 250. *Clerk,* John Hammond *Master,* Andrew Marsden

MASONS *(30)*. 8 Little Trinity Lane, London EC4V 2AN *Livery,* 163. *Clerk,* Maj. Giles Clapp *Master,* William Gloyn

MASTER MARINERS *(78)*. *Hall,* HQS Wellington, Temple Stairs, Victoria Embankment, London WC2R 2PN *Livery,* 160. *Clerk,* Cdre Angus Menzies, RN *Master,* Capt. Jim Conybeare

MUSICIANS *(50)*. 1 Speed Highwalk, Barbican, London EC2Y BDX *Livery,* 420. *Clerk,* Hugh Lloyd *Master,* Kathleen Duncan, OBE

NEEDLEMAKERS *(65)*. PO Box 3682, Windsor, Berkshire SL4 3WR *Livery,* 200. *Clerk,* Philip Grant *Master,* Geoffrey Lewis, FRICS

PAINTER-STAINERS *(28)*. *Hall,* Painters' Hall, 9 Little Trinity Lane, London EC4V 2AD *Livery,* 310. *Clerk,* C. J. Twyman *Master,* A. J. Ward

PATTENMAKERS *(70)*. 3 The High Street, Sutton Valence, Kent ME17 3AG *Livery,* 200. *Clerk,* Col. R. W. Murfin, TD *Master,* Nicholas Andrews

PAVIORS *(56)*. Paviors' House, Charter House, Charterhouse Square, London EC1M 6AN *Livery,* 285. *Clerk,* John Freestone *Master,* Terry Last

PEWTERERS *(16)*. *Hall,* Pewterers' Hall, Oat Lane, London EC2V 7DE *Livery,* 98. *Clerk,* Capt. Paddy Watson, RN *Master,* Mark Chambers

PLAISTERERS *(46)*. *Hall,* Plaisterers' Hall, 1 London Wall, London EC2Y 5JU *Livery,* 236. *Clerk,* Nigel Bamping *Master,* Bill Mahoney

PLUMBERS *(31)*. Wax Chandlers' Hall, 6 Gresham Street, London EC2V 7AD *Livery,* 360. *Clerk,* Air Cdre Paul Nash, OBE *Master,* Stephen Hodkinson

POULTERS *(34)*. 57 Cullum Welch House, Golden Lane Estate, London EC17 0SH *Livery,* 204. *Clerk,* Vernon Ashford *Master,* Rowland Hughes

SADDLERS *(25)*. *Hall,* Saddlers' Hall, 40 Gutter Lane, London EC2V 6BR *Livery,* 75. *Clerk,* Col. Nigel Lithgow, CBE *Master,* C. E. Barclay

SCIENTIFIC INSTRUMENT MAKERS *(84)*. 9 Montague Close, London SE1 9DD *Livery,* 185. *Clerk,* N. J. Watson *Master,* C. J. Sawyer

SCRIVENERS *(44)*. HQS Wellington, Temple Stairs, Victoria Embankment, London WC2R 2PN *Livery,* 191. *Clerk,* Giles Cole *Master,* Jeremy Burgess

SECURITY PROFESSIONALS *(108)*. 34 Tye Green, Glemsford, Suffolk CO10 7RG *Livery,* 150. *Clerk,* Patricia Boswell *Master,* Stewart Seymour, CSyP

SHIPWRIGHTS *(59)*. Ironmongers Hall, Shaftesbury Place, London EC2Y 8AA *Livery,* 450. *Clerk,* Lt.-Col. Richard Cole-Mackintosh *Prime Warden,* Douglas Barrow, PC *Grand Master,* HRH the Prince of Wales, KG, KT, GCB

SOLICITORS *(79)*. 4 College Hill, London EC4R 2RB *Livery,* 350. *Clerk,* Neil Cameron *Master,* Dame Fiona Woolf

SPECTACLE MAKERS *(60)*. Apothecaries' Hall, Black Friars Lane, London EC4V 6EL *Livery,* 400. *Clerk,* Helen Perkins, FCIS, FCSI *Master,* Edward Middleton, FCA

STATIONERS AND NEWSPAPER MAKERS *(47)*. *Hall,* Stationers' Hall, Ave Maria Lane, London EC4M 7DD *Livery,* 540. *Clerk,* William Alden, MBE *Master,* Helen Esmonde

TALLOW CHANDLERS *(21)*. *Hall,* Tallow Chandlers' Hall, 4 Dowgate Hill, London EC4R 2SH *Livery,* 180. *Clerk,* Brig. D. Homer, MBE *Master,* Nicholas Bull, FCA

TAX ADVISERS *(107)*. 191 West End Road, Ruislip, Middx HA4 6LD *Freemen,* 145. *Clerk,* Paul Herbage, MBE *Master,* Anthony Thomas

TIN PLATE WORKERS (ALIAS WIRE WORKERS) *(67)*. PO Box 71002, London W4 9FH *Livery,* 200. *Clerk,* Piers Baker *Master,* Ian Makowski

TOBACCO PIPE MAKERS AND TOBACCO BLENDERS *(82)*. 14 Montpelier Road, Sutton, Surrey SM1 4QE *Livery,* 138. *Clerk,* Sandra Stocker *Master,* Christopher Allen

TURNERS *(51)*. Skinner's Hall, 8 Dowgate Hill, London EC4R 2SP *Livery,* 186. *Clerk,* Alex Robertson *Master,* Nicholas Edwards

TYLERS AND BRICKLAYERS *(37)*. 3 Farmers' Way, Seer Green, Bucks HP9 2YY *Livery,* 158. *Clerk,* John Brooks *Master,* Tom Rider

UPHOLDERS *(49)*. E clerk@upholders.co.uk *Livery,* 175. *Clerk,* Susan Nevard *Master,* Wynne Gilham

WATER CONSERVATORS *(102)*. The Lark, 2 Bell Lane, Worlington, Bury St Edmunds, Suffolk IP28 8SE *Livery,* 212. *Clerk,* Ralph Riley *Master,* Peter Hall

WAX CHANDLERS *(20)*. *Hall,* Wax Chandlers' Hall, 6 Gresham Street, London EC2V 7AD *Livery,* 110. *Clerk,* Georgina Brown *Master,* Dr Andrew Mair

WEAVERS *(42)*. Saddlers' House, Gutter Lane, London EC2V 6BR *Livery,* 125. *Clerk,* John Snowdon *Upper Bailiff,* John Nugee

WHEELWRIGHTS *(68)*. 16 Gordon Avenue, Twickenham TW1 1NQ *Livery,* 220. *Clerk,* Bridget Hynard *Master,* G. I. A. Armfield

WOOLMEN *(43)*. 52 Cumberland Drive, Bexleyheath, Kent DA7 5LB *Livery,* 150. *Clerk,* Maj. Steve Wake *Master,* John Brewer

WORLD TRADERS *(101)*. 13 Hall Gardens, Colney Heath, St. Albans, Herts AL4 0QF *Livery,* 240. *Clerk,* Mrs Gaye Duffy *Master,* Wendy Hyde, C.C.

PARISH CLERKS *(No Livery\*)*. Acreholt, 33 Medstead Road, Beech, Alton, Hants GU34 4AD *Members,* 91. *Clerk,* Alana Coombes *Master,* Martin Woods

WATERMEN AND LIGHTERMEN *(No Livery\*)*. *Hall,* Watermen's Hall, 16–18 St Mary at Hill, London EC3R 8EF *Craft Owning Freemen,* 381. *Clerk,* Colin Middlemiss *Master,* Richard Springford

\* Parish Clerks and Watermen and Lightermen have requested to remain with no livery

# WALES

*Cymru*

The principality of Wales (Cymru) occupies the extreme west of the central southern portion of the island of Great Britain, with a total area of 20,778 sq. km (8,022 sq. miles): land 20,733 sq. km (8,005 sq. miles); inland water 45 sq. km (17 sq. miles). It is bordered in the north by the Irish Sea, in the south by the Bristol Channel, in the east by the English counties of Cheshire West and Chester, Shropshire, Herefordshire and Gloucestershire, and in the west by St George's Channel.

Across the Menai Straits is Ynys Mon (Isle of Anglesey) (715 sq. km/276 sq. miles), communication with which is facilitated by the Menai Suspension Bridge (305m/1,000ft long) built by Telford in 1826, and by the Britannia Bridge (351m/1,151ft), a two-tier road and rail truss arch design, rebuilt in 1972 after a fire destroyed the original tubular railway bridge built by Stephenson in 1850. Holyhead harbour, on Holy Isle (north-west of Anglesey), provides ferry services to Dublin (113km/70 miles).

## POPULATION
The population at the 2011 census was 3,063,456 (men 1,504,228; women 1,559,228). The average density of population in 2011 was 147 persons per sq. km (382 per sq. mile).

## RELIEF
Wales is a country of extensive tracts of high plateau and shorter stretches of mountain ranges deeply dissected by river valleys. Lower-lying ground is largely confined to the coastal belt and the lower parts of the valleys. The highest mountains are those of Snowdonia in the north-west (Snowdon, 1,085m/3,559ft and Aran Fawddwy, 906m/2,971ft). Snowdonia is also home to Cader Idris (Pen y Gadair, 892m/2,928ft). Other high peaks are to be found in the Cambrian range (Plynlimon, 752m/2,467ft), and the Black Mountains, Brecon Beacons and Black Forest ranges in the south-east (Pen y Fan, 886m/2,906ft; Waun Fâch, 811m/2,660ft; Carmarthen Van, 802m/2,630ft).

## HYDROGRAPHY
The principal river in Wales is the Severn, which flows from the slopes of Plynlimon to the English border. The Wye (209km/130 miles) also rises on the slopes of Plynlimon. The Usk (90km/56 miles) flows into the Bristol Channel through Gwent. The Dee (113km/70 miles) rises in Bala Lake and flows through the Vale of Llangollen, where an aqueduct (built by Telford in 1805) carries the Pontcysyllte branch of the Shropshire Union Canal across the valley. The estuary of the Dee is the navigable portion; it is 23km (14 miles) in length and about 8km (5 miles) in breadth. Towy (109km/68 miles), Teifi (80km/50 miles), Taff (64km/40 miles), Dovey (48km/30 miles), Taf (40km/25 miles) and Conway (39km/24 miles) are wholly Welsh rivers.

The largest natural lake is Bala (Llyn Tegid) in Gwynedd, nearly 7km (4 miles) long and 1.6km (1 mile) wide. Lake Vyrnwy is an artificial reservoir, about the size of Bala, and forms the water supply of Liverpool; Birmingham's water is supplied from reservoirs in the Elan and Claerwen valleys.

## WELSH LANGUAGE
According to the 2011 census results, the percentage of people aged three years and over who are able to speak Welsh is:

| | | | |
|---|---|---|---|
| Blaenau Gwent | 7.8 | Neath Port Talbot | 15.3 |
| Bridgend | 9.7 | Newport | 9.3 |
| Caerphilly | 11.2 | Pembrokeshire | 19.2 |
| Cardiff | 11.1 | Powys | 18.6 |
| Carmarthenshire | 43.9 | Rhondda Cynon Taf | 12.3 |
| Ceredigion | 47.3 | Swansea | 11.4 |
| Conwy | 27.4 | Torfaen | 9.8 |
| Denbighshire | 24.6 | Vale of Glamorgan | 10.8 |
| Flintshire | 13.2 | Wrexham | 12.9 |
| Gwynedd | 65.4 | Ynys Mon | |
| Merthyr Tydfil | 8.9 | (Isle of Anglesey) | 57.2 |
| Monmouthshire | 9.9 | *Total in Wales* | 19.0 |

## FLAG
The flag of Wales, the Red Dragon *(Y Ddraig Goch)*, is a red dragon on a field divided white over green (per fess argent and vert a dragon passant gules). The flag was augmented in 1953 by a royal badge on a shield encircled with a riband bearing the words *Ddraig Goch Ddyry Cychwyn* and imperially crowned, but this augmented flag is rarely used.

## EARLY HISTORY

The earliest inhabitants of whom there is any record appear to have been subdued or exterminated by the Goidels (a people of Celtic race) in the Bronze Age. A further invasion of Celtic Brythons and Belgae followed in the ensuing Iron Age. The Roman conquest of southern Britain and Wales then, for some time successfully opposed by Caratacus (Caractacus or Caradog), chieftain of the Catuvellauni and son of Cunobelinus (Cymbeline). South-east Wales was subjugated and the legionary fortress at Caerleon-on-Usk established by around AD 75–7; the conquest of Wales was completed by Agricola around AD 78. Communications were opened up by the construction of military roads from Chester to Caerleon-on-Usk and Caerwent, and from Chester to Conwy (and thence to Carmarthen and Neath). Christianity was introduced in the fourth century, during the Roman occupation.

## ANGLO-SAXON ATTACKS
The Anglo-Saxon invaders of southern Britain drove the Celts into the mountain stronghold of Wales, and into Strathclyde (Cumberland and south-west Scotland) and Cornwall, giving them the name of *Waelisc* (Welsh), meaning 'foreign'. The West Saxons' victory of Deorham (AD 577) isolated Wales from Cornwall and the battle of Chester (AD 613) cut off communication with Strathclyde and northern Britain. In the eighth century the boundaries of the Welsh were further restricted by the annexations of Offa, King of Mercia, and counter-attacks were largely prevented by the construction of an artificial boundary from the Dee to the Wye (Offa's Dyke).

In the ninth century Rhodri Mawr (844–878) united the country and successfully resisted further incursions of the Saxons by land and raids of Norse and Danish pirates by sea, but at his death his three provinces of Gwynedd (north), Powys (central) and Deheubarth (south) were divided among his three sons, Anarawd, Mervyn and Cadell. Cadell's son Hywel Dda ruled a large part of Wales and codified its laws but the provinces were not united again until the rule of Llewelyn ap Seisyllt (husband of the heiress of Gwynedd) from 1018 to 1023.

## THE NORMAN CONQUEST

After the Norman conquest of England, William I created palatine counties along the Welsh frontier, and the Norman barons began to make encroachments into Welsh territory. The Welsh princes recovered many of their losses during the civil wars of Stephen's reign (1135–54), and in the early 13th century Owen Gruffydd, prince of Gwynedd, was the dominant figure in Wales. Under Llywelyn ap Iorwerth 1194–1240) the Welsh united in powerful resistance to English incursions and Llywelyn's privileges and *de facto* independence were recognised in the Magna Carta. His grandson, Llywelyn ap Gruffydd, was the last native prince; he was killed in 1282 during hostilities between the Welsh and English, allowing Edward I of England to establish his authority over the country. On 7 February 1301, Edward of Caernarvon, son of Edward I, was created Prince of Wales, a title subsequently borne by the eldest son of the sovereign.

Strong Welsh national feeling continued, expressed in the early 15th century in the rising led by Owain Glyndwr, but the situation was altered by the accession to the English throne in 1485 of Henry VII of the Welsh House of Tudor. Wales was politically annexed by England under the Act of Union of 1535, which extended English laws to the principality and gave it parliamentary representation for the first time.

## EISTEDDFOD

The Welsh are a distinct nation, with a language and literature of their own; the national bardic festival (Eisteddfod), instituted by Prince Rhys ap Griffith in 1176, is still held annually.

# PRINCIPAL CITIES

There are six cities in Wales (with date city status conferred): Bangor (pre-1900), Cardiff (1905), Newport (2002), St Asaph (2012), St David's (1994) and Swansea (1969).

Cardiff and Swansea have also been granted lord mayoralities.

## CARDIFF

Cardiff *(Caerdydd)*, at the mouth of the rivers Taff, Rhymney and Ely, is the capital city of Wales and at the 2011 census had a population of 346,090. The city has changed dramatically in recent years following the regeneration of Cardiff Bay and construction of a barrage, which has created a permanent freshwater lake and waterfront for the city. As the capital city, Cardiff is home to the National Assembly for Wales and is a major administrative, retail, business and cultural centre.

The city is home to many fine buildings, including the City Hall, Cardiff Castle, Llandaff Cathedral, the National Museum of Wales, university buildings, law courts and the Temple of Peace and Health. The Millennium Stadium opened in 1999 and has hosted high-profile events since 2001.

## SWANSEA

Swansea *(Abertawe)* is a seaport with a population of 239,023 at the 2011 census. The Gower peninsula was brought within the city boundary under local government reform in 1974.

The principal buildings are the Norman castle (rebuilt *c.*1330), the Royal Institution of South Wales, founded in 1835 (including library), the University of Wales Swansea at Singleton and the Guildhall, containing Frank Brangwyn's British Empire panels. The Dylan Thomas Centre, formerly the old Guildhall, was restored in 1995. More recent buildings include the County Hall, the Maritime Quarter Marina, the Wales National Pool and the National Waterfront Museum.

Swansea was chartered by the Earl of Warwick (1158–84), and further charters were granted by King John, Henry III, Edward II, Edward III and James II, Oliver Cromwell and the Marcher Lord William de Breos. It was formally invested with city status in 1969.

# LORD-LIEUTENANTS AND HIGH SHERIFFS

| Area | Lord-Lieutenant | High Sheriff (2015–16) |
| --- | --- | --- |
| Clwyd | Henry Fetherstonhaugh, OBE | Janet Evans |
| Dyfed | Hon. Robin Lewis, OBE | James Lewis |
| Gwent | Sir Simon Boyle, KCVO | Lt.-Col. Andrew Tuggey |
| Gwynedd | Edmund Bailey | Dr Elizabeth Nesbit Andrews, MBE |
| Mid Glamorgan | Kate Thomas, CVO | Jayne James |
| Powys | Hon. Dame Elizabeth Legge-Bourke, DCVO | Lt.-Col. Michael Ledston Lewis |
| South Glamorgan | Dr Peter Beck, MD, FRCP | Prof. Heather Stevens, CBE |
| West Glamorgan | D. Byron Lewis | Robert Redfern |

# LOCAL COUNCILS

| Council | Administrative Headquarters | Telephone | Population* | Council Tax† | Chief Executive |
|---|---|---|---|---|---|
| Blaenau Gwent | Ebbw Vale | 01495-311556 | 69,674 | £1,635 | David Waggett |
| Bridgend | Bridgend | 01656-643643 | 141,214 | £1,483 | Darren Mepham |
| Caerphilly | Hengoed | 01443-815588 | 179,941 | £1,215 | Chris Burns |
| CARDIFF | Cardiff | 029-2087 2087 | 354,294 | £1,224 | Paul Orders |
| Carmarthenshire | Carmarthen | 01267-234567 | 184,898 | £1,348 | Mark James, CBE |
| Ceredigion | Aberaeron | 01545-570881 | 75,425 | £1,300 | Bronwen Morgan |
| Conwy | Conwy | 01492-574000 | 116,287 | £1,286 | Iwan Davies |
| Denbighshire | Ruthin | 01824-706101 | 94,791 | £1,422 | Dr Mohammed Mehmet |
| Flintshire | Mold | 01352-752121 | 153,804 | £1,301 | Colin Everett |
| Gwynedd | Caernarfon | 01766-771000 | 122,273 | £1,430 | Dilwyn Williams |
| Merthyr Tydfil | Merthyr Tydfil | 01685-725000 | 59,065 | £1,554 | Gareth Chapman |
| Monmouthshire | Cwmbran | 01633-644644 | 92,336 | £1,349 | Paul Matthews |
| Neath Port Talbot | Port Talbot | 01639-686868 | 140,490 | £1,609 | Steven Phillips |
| NEWPORT | Newport | 01633-656656 | 146,841 | £1,154 | Will Godfrey |
| Pembrokeshire | Haverfordwest | 01437-764551 | 123,666 | £1,029 | Ian Westley |
| Powys | Llandrindod Wells | 01597-827460 | 132,675 | £1,287 | Jeremy Patterson |
| Rhondda Cynon Taff | Tonypandy | 01443-425005 | 236,888 | £1,519 | Steve Merritt |
| SWANSEA | Swansea | 01792-636000 | 241,297 | £1,342 | Jack Straw |
| Torfaen | Pontypool | 01495-762200 | 91,609 | £1,352 | Alison Ward |
| Vale of Glamorgan | Barry | 01446-700111 | 127,685 | £1,312 | Neil Moore |
| Wrexham | Wrexham | 01978-292000 | 136,714 | £1,276 | Dr Helen Paterson |
| Ynys Mon (Isle of Anglesey) | Ynys Mon | 01248-750057 | 70,169 | £1,296 | vacant |

* *Source:* Office for National Statistics – *Mid-2014 Population Estimates* (Crown copyright)
† Average Band D council tax bill 2015–16
Councils in CAPITAL LETTERS have city status

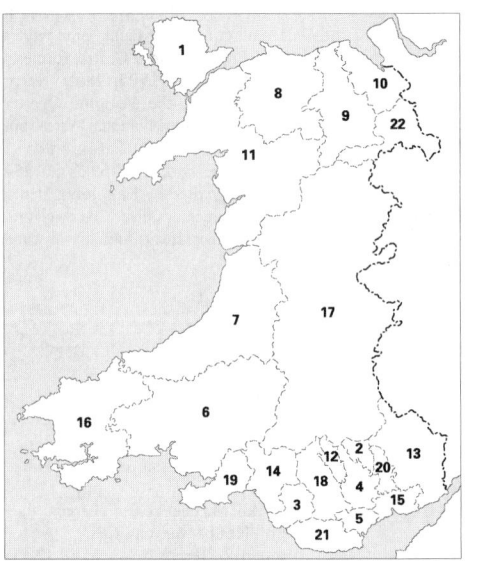

| Key | Council | Key | Council |
|---|---|---|---|
| 1 | Anglesey (Ynys Mon) | 12 | Merthyr Tydfil |
| 2 | Blaenau Gwent | 13 | Monmouthshire |
| 3 | Bridgend | 14 | Neath Port Talbot |
| 4 | Caerphilly | 15 | Newport |
| 5 | Cardiff | 16 | Pembrokeshire |
| 6 | Carmarthenshire | 17 | Powys |
| 7 | Ceredigion | 18 | Rhondda Cynon Taff |
| 8 | Conwy | 19 | Swansea |
| 9 | Denbighshire | 20 | Torfaen |
| 10 | Flintshire | 21 | Vale of Glamorgan |
| 11 | Gwynedd | 22 | Wrexham |

# SCOTLAND

Scotland occupies the northern portion of the main island of Great Britain and includes the Inner and Outer Hebrides, Orkney, Shetland and many other islands. It lies between 0° 51′ 30″ and 54° 38′ N. latitude and between 1° 45′ 32″ and 6° 14′ W. longitude, with England to the south-east, the North Channel and the Irish Sea to the south-west, the Atlantic Ocean on the north and west, and the North Sea on the east.

The greatest length of the mainland (Cape Wrath to the Mull of Galloway) is 441km (274 miles), and the greatest breadth (Buchan Ness to Applecross) is 248km (154 miles). The customary measurement of the island of Great Britain from the site of John o' Groats house, near Duncansby Head, Caithness, to Land's End, Cornwall, a total distance of 970km (603 miles) in a straight line and approximately 1,448km (900 miles) by road.

The total area of Scotland is 78,807 sq. km (30,427 sq. miles): land 77,907 sq. km (30,080 sq. miles), inland water 900 sq. km (347 sq. miles).

## POPULATION
The population at the 2011 census was 5,295,403 (men 2,567,444; women 2,727,959). The average density of the population in 2011 was 67 persons per sq. km (174 per sq. mile).

## RELIEF
There are three natural orographic divisions of Scotland. The southern uplands have their highest points in Merrick 843m/2,766ft), Rhinns of Kells (814m/2,669ft) and Cairnsmuir of Carsphairn (797m/2,614ft), in the west; and the Tweedsmuir Hills in the east (Broad Law 840m/2,756ft; Dollar Law 817m/2,682ft; Hartfell 808m/2,651ft).

The central lowlands, formed by the valleys of the Clyde, Forth and Tay, divide the southern uplands from the Highlands, which extend from close to the extreme north of the mainland to the central lowlands, and are divided into a northern and a southern system by the Great Glen.

The Grampian Mountains, the southern Highland system, include in the west Ben Nevis (1,343m/4,406ft), the highest point in the British Isles, and in the east the Cairngorm Mountains (Ben Macdui 1,309m/4,296ft; Braeriach 1,295m/4,248ft; Cairn Gorm 1,245m/4,084ft). The north-west Highlands contain the mountains of Wester and Easter Ross (Carn Eige 1,183m/3,880ft; Sgurr na Lapaich 1,151m/3,775ft).

Created, like the central lowlands, by a major geological fault, the Great Glen (97km/60 miles long) runs between Inverness and Fort William, and contains Loch Ness, Loch Oich and Loch Lochy. These are linked to each other and to the north-east and south-west coasts of Scotland by the Caledonian Canal, providing a navigable passage between the Moray Firth and the Inner Hebrides.

## HYDROGRAPHY
The western coast is fragmented by peninsulas and islands, and indented by fjords (sea-lochs), the longest of which is Loch Fyne (68km/42 miles long) in Argyll. Although the east coast tends to be less fractured and lower, there are several great drowned inlets (firths), including the Firth of Forth, Firth of Tay and the Moray Firth, as well as the Firth of Clyde in the west.

The lochs are the principal hydrographic feature. The largest in Scotland and in Britain is Loch Lomond (70 sq. km/

27 sq. miles), in the Grampian valleys, and the longest and deepest is Loch Ness (39km/24 miles long and 244m/800ft deep), in the Great Glen.

The longest river is the Tay (188km/117 miles), noted for its salmon. It flows into the North Sea, with Dundee on the estuary, which is spanned by the Tay Bridge (3,136m/10,289ft) opened in 1887 and the Tay Road Bridge (2,245m/7,365ft) opened in 1966. Other noted salmon rivers are the Dee (145km/90 miles) which flows into the North Sea at Aberdeen, and the Spey (177km/110 miles), the swiftest flowing river in the British Isles, which flows into the Moray Firth. The Tweed, which gave its name to the woollen cloth produced along its banks, marks in the lower stretches of its 154km (96 mile) course the border between Scotland and England.

The most important river commercially is the Clyde (171km/106 miles), formed by the junction of the Daer and Portrail water, which flows through the city of Glasgow to the Firth of Clyde. During its course it passes over the picturesque Falls of Clyde, Bonnington Linn (9m/30ft), Corra Linn (26m/84ft), Dundaff Linn (3m/10ft) and Stonebyres Linn (24m/80ft), above and below Lanark. The Forth (106km/66 miles), upon which stands Edinburgh, the capital, is spanned by the Forth Railway Bridge (1890), which is 1,625m (5,330ft) long, and the Forth Road Bridge (1964), which has a total length of 1,876m (6,156ft) (over water) and a single span of 914m (3,000ft).

The highest waterfall in Scotland, and the British Isles, is Eas a'Chùal Aluinn with a total height of 201m (658ft), which falls from Glas Bheinn in Sutherland. The Falls of Glomach, on a head-stream of the Elchaig in Wester Ross, have a drop of 113m (370ft).

## GAELIC LANGUAGE
According to the 2011 census, 1.1 per cent (58,000 people) of the population of Scotland aged three and over were able to speak the Scottish form of Gaelic. This was a slight decrease from the 1.2 per cent recorded at the 2001 census.

## LOWLAND SCOTTISH LANGUAGE
Several regional lowland Scottish dialects, known variously as Scots, Lallans or Doric, are widely spoken. According to the 2011 census, 43 per cent of the population of Scotland aged three and over stated they could do one or a combination of read, write, speak or understand Scots. A question on Scots was not included in the 2001 census.

## FLAG
The flag of Scotland is known as the Saltire. It is a white diagonal cross on a blue field (saltire argent in a field azure) and represents St Andrew, the patron saint of Scotland.

## THE SCOTTISH ISLANDS

### ORKNEY
The Orkney Islands (total area 972 sq. km/376 sq. miles) lie about 10km (six miles) north of the mainland, separated from it by the Pentland Firth. Of the 90 islands and islets (holms and skerries) in the group, about one-third are inhabited.

The total population at the 2011 census was 21,349; the 2011 populations of the islands shown here include those of smaller islands forming part of the same council district.

| | | |
|---|---|---|
| Mainland, 17,162 | Inner Holm, 1 | |
| Auskerry, 4 | North Ronaldsay, 72 | |
| Burray, 409 | Papa Westray, 90 | |
| Eday, 160 | Rousay, 216 | |
| Egilsay, 26 | Sanday, 494 | |
| Flotta, 8 | Shapinsay, 307 | |
| Gairsay, 3 | South Ronaldsay, 909 | |
| Graemsay, 28 | Stronsay, 349 | |
| Holm of Grimbister, 3 | Westray, 588 | |
| Hoy, 419 | Wyre, 29 | |

The islands are rich in prehistoric and Scandinavian remains, the most notable being the Stone Age village of Skara Brae, the burial chamber of Maes Howe, the many brochs (towers) and the 12th-century St Magnus Cathedral. Scapa Flow, between the Mainland and Hoy, was the war station of the British Grand Fleet from 1914 to 1919 and the scene of the scuttling of the surrendered German High Seas Fleet (21 June 1919).

Most of the islands are low-lying and fertile, and farming (principally beef cattle) is the main industry. Flotta, to the south of Scapa Flow, is the site of the oil terminal for the Piper, Claymore and Tartan fields in the North Sea.

The capital is Kirkwall (population 7,045) situated on Mainland.

## SHETLAND
The Shetland Islands have a total area of 1,427 sq. km (551 sq. miles) and had a population at the 2011 census of 23,167. They lie about 80km (50 miles) north of the Orkneys, with Fair Isle about half way between the two groups. Out Stack, off Muckle Flugga, 1.6km (one mile) north of Unst, is the most northerly part of the British Isles (60° 51' 30" N. lat.).

There are over 100 islands, of which 16 are inhabited. Populations at the 2011 census were:

| | |
|---|---|
| Mainland, 18,765 | Muckle Roe, 130 |
| Bressay, 368 | Papa Stour, 15 |
| Bruray, 24 | Trondra, 135 |
| East Burra, 76 | Unst, 632 |
| Fair Isle, 68 | Vaila, 2 |
| Fetlar, 61 | West Burra, 776 |
| Foula, 38 | Whalsay, 1,061 |
| Housay, 50 | Yell, 966 |

Shetland's many archaeological sites include Jarlshof, Mousa and Clickhimin, and its long connection with Scandinavia has resulted in a strong Norse influence on its place names and dialect.

Industries include fishing, knitwear and farming. In addition to the fishing fleet there are fish processing factories, and the traditional handknitting of Fair Isle and Unst is now supplemented with machine-knitted garments. Farming is mainly crofting, with sheep being raised on the moorland and hills of the islands. Latterly the islands have become a centre of the North Sea oil industry, with pipelines from the Brent and Ninian fields running to the terminal at Sullom Voe, the largest of its kind in Europe.

The capital is Lerwick (population 6,958) situated on Mainland. Lerwick is the main centre for supply services for offshore oil exploration and development.

## THE HEBRIDES
Until the late 13th century the Hebrides included other Scottish islands in the Firth of Clyde, the peninsula of Kintyre (Argyll), the Isle of Man and the (Irish) Isle of Rathlin. The origin of the name is probably the Greek *Eboudai,* latinised as *Hebudes* by Pliny, and corrupted to its present form. The Norwegian name *Sudreyjar* (Southern Islands) was latinised as *Sodorenses,* a name that survives in the Anglican bishopric of Sodor and Man.

There are over 500 islands and islets, of which about 100 are inhabited, though mountainous terrain and extensive peat bogs mean that only a fraction of the total area is under cultivation. Stone, Bronze and Iron Age settlement has left many remains, including those at Callanish on Lewis and Norse colonisation influenced language, customs and place names. Occupations include farming (mostly crofting and stock-raising), fishing and the manufacture of tweeds and other woollens. Tourism is also an important part of the economy.

The Inner Hebrides lie off the west coast of Scotland and are relatively close to the mainland. The largest and best-known is Skye (area 1,665 sq. km/643 sq. miles; pop. 10,008; chief town, Portree), which contains the Cuillin Hills (Sgurr Alasdair, 993m/3,257ft), Bla Bheinn (928m/3,046ft), the Storr (719m/2,358ft) and the Red Hills (Beinn na Caillich, 732m/2,403ft). Other islands in the Highland council area include Raasay (pop. 161), Eigg (pop. 83), Muck (pop. 27) and Rhum (pop. 22).

Further south the Inner Hebridean islands include Arran (pop. 4,629), containing Goat Fell (874m/2,868ft); Coll (pop. 195) and Tiree (pop. 653); Colonsay (pop. 124) and Oronsay (pop. 8); Easdale (pop. 59); Gigha (pop. 163); Islay (area 608 sq. km/235 sq. miles; pop. 3,228); Jura (area 414 sq. km/160 sq. miles; pop. 196), with a range of hills culminating in the Paps of Jura (Beinn-an-Oir, 785m/2,576ft, and Beinn Chaolais, 755m/2,477ft); Lismore (pop. 192); Luing (pop. 195); and Mull (area 950 sq. km/367 sq. miles; pop. 2,800; chief town Tobermory), containing Ben More (967m/3,171ft).

The Outer Hebrides, separated from the mainland by the Minch, now form the Eilean Siar (Western Isles) council area (area 2,897 sq. km/1,119 sq. miles; pop. 27,684). The main islands are Lewis with Harris (area 1,994 sq. km/770 sq. miles, pop. 21,031), whose chief town, Stornoway, is the administrative headquarters; North Uist (pop. 1,254); South Uist (pop. 1,754); Benbecula (pop. 1,303) and Barra (pop. 1,174). Other inhabited islands include Great Bernera (252), Berneray (138), Eriskay (143), Grimsay (169), Scalpay (291) and Vatersay (90).

## EARLY HISTORY

There is evidence of human settlement in Scotland dating from the third millennium BC, the earliest settlers being Mesolithic hunters and fishermen. Early in the second millennium BC, Neolithic farmers began to cultivate crops and rear livestock; their settlements were on the west coast and in the north, and included Skara Brae and Maeshowe (Orkney). Settlement by the early Bronze Age 'Beaker Folk' so-called from the shape of their drinking vessels, in eastern Scotland dates from about 1800 BC. Further settlement is believed to have occurred from 700 BC onwards, as tribes were displaced from further south by new incursions from the Continent and the Roman invasions from AD 43.

Julius Agricola, the Roman governor of Britain AD 77–84, extended the Roman conquests in Britain by advancing into Caledonia, culminating in a victory at Mons Graupius probably in AD 84; he was recalled to Rome shortly afterwards and his forward policy was not pursued. Hadrian's Wall, mostly completed by AD 30, marked the northern frontier of the Roman empire except for the period between about AD 144 and 190 when the frontier moved north to the Forth-Clyde isthmus and a turf wall, the Antonine Wall, was manned.

After the Roman withdrawal from Britain, there were centuries of warfare between the Picts, Scots, Britons, Angles nd Vikings. The Picts, generally accepted to be descended rom the indigenous Iron Age people of northern Scotland, )ccupied the area north of the Forth. The Scots, a Gaelic-peaking people of northern Ireland, colonised the area of Argyll and Bute (the kingdom of Dalriada) in the fifth entury AD and then expanded eastwards and northwards. The Britons, speaking a Brythonic Celtic language, colonised Scotland from the south from the first century BC; they lost ontrol of south-eastern Scotland (incorporated into the cingdom of Northumbria) to the Angles in the early seventh entury but retained Strathclyde (south-western Scotland and Cumbria). Viking raids from the late eighth century were ollowed by Norse settlement in the western and northern sles, Argyll, Caithness and Sutherland from the mid-ninth entury onwards.

## UNIFICATION

The union of the areas which now comprise Scotland began n AD 843 when Kenneth MacAlpin, king of the Scots from ;834, also became king of the Picts, joining the two lands to orm the kingdom of Alba (comprising Scotland north of a ine between the Forth and Clyde rivers). Lothian, the eastern part of the area between the Forth and the Tweed, seems to have been leased to Kenneth II of Alba (reigned 971–995) by Edgar of England c.973, and Scottish possession was onfirmed by Malcolm II's victory over a Northumbrian rmy at Carham c.1016. At about this time Malcolm II reigned 1005–34) placed his grandson Duncan on the throne of the British kingdom of Strathclyde, bringing under Scots rule virtually all of what is now Scotland.

The Norse possessions were incorporated into the cingdom of Scotland from the 12th century onwards. An uprising in the mid-12th century drove the Norse from most of mainland Argyll. The Hebrides were ceded to Scotland by the Treaty of Perth in 1266 after a Norwegian expedition in 1263 failed to maintain Norse authority over the islands. Orkney and Shetland fell to Scotland in 1468–9 as a pledge for the unpaid dowry of Margaret of Denmark, wife of James III, although Danish claims of suzerainty were relinquished only with the marriage of Anne of Denmark to James VI in 1590.

From the 11th century, there were frequent wars between Scotland and England over territory and the extent of England's political influence. The failure of the Scottish royal ine with the death of Margaret of Norway in 1290 led to disputes over the throne which were resolved by the adjudication of Edward I of England. He awarded the throne to John Balliol in 1292 but Balliol's refusal to be a puppet cing led to war. Balliol surrendered to Edward I in 1296 and Edward attempted to rule Scotland himself. Resistance to Scotland's loss of independence was led by William Wallace, who defeated the English at Stirling Bridge (1297), and Robert Bruce, crowned in 1306, who held most of Scotland by 1311 and routed Edward II's army at Bannockburn (1314). England recognised the independence of Scotland in the Treaty of Northampton in 1328. Subsequent clashes include the disastrous battle of Flodden (1513) in which James IV and many of his nobles fell.

## THE UNION

In 1603 James VI of Scotland succeeded Elizabeth I on the throne of England (his mother, Mary Queen of Scots, was the great-granddaughter of Henry VII), his successors reigning as sovereigns of Great Britain. Political union of the two countries did not occur until 1707.

## THE JACOBITE REVOLTS

After the abdication (by flight) in 1688 of James VII and II, the crown devolved upon William III (grandson of Charles I)

and Mary II (elder daughter of James VII and II). In 1689 Graham of Claverhouse roused the Highlands on behalf of James VII and II, but died after a military success at Killiecrankie.

After the death of Anne (younger daughter of James VII and II), the throne devolved upon George I (great-grandson of James VI and I). In 1715, armed risings on behalf of James Stuart (the Old Pretender, son of James VII and II) led to the indecisive battle of Sheriffmuir, and the Jacobite movement died down until 1745, when Charles Stuart (the Young Pretender) defeated the Royalist troops at Prestonpans and advanced to Derby (1746). From Derby, the adherents of 'James VIII and III' (the title claimed for his father by Charles Stuart) fell back on the defensive and were finally crushed at Culloden (16 April 1746) by an army led by the Duke of Cumberland, son of George II.

## PRINCIPAL CITIES

### ABERDEEN

Aberdeen, 209km (130 miles) north-east of Edinburgh, received its charter as a Royal Burgh in 1124. Scotland's third largest city, Aberdeen lies between two rivers, the Dee and the Don, facing the North Sea; the city has a strong maritime history and is today a major centre for offshore oil exploration and production. It is also an ancient university town and distinguished research centre. Other industries include engineering, food processing, textiles, paper manufacturing and chemicals.

Places of interest include King's College, St Machar's Cathedral, Brig o' Balgownie, Duthie Park and Winter Gardens, Hazlehead Park, the Kirk of St Nicholas, Mercat Cross, Marischal College and Marischal Museum, Provost Skene's House, Aberdeen Art Gallery, Gordon Highlanders Museum, Satrosphere Science Centre, and Aberdeen Maritime Museum.

### DUNDEE

The Royal Burgh of Dundee is situated on the north bank of the Tay estuary. The city's port and dock installations are important to the offshore oil industry and the airport also provides servicing facilities. Principal industries include textiles, biotechnology and digital media, lasers, printing, tyre manufacture, food processing, engineering and tourism.

The unique City Churches – three churches under one roof, together with the 15th-century St Mary's Tower – are the most prominent architectural feature. Dundee is home to two historic ships: the Dundee-built RRS *Discovery* which took Capt. Scott to the Antarctic alongside Discovery Quay, and the frigate *Unicorn,* the only British-built wooden warship still afloat, is moored in Victoria Dock. Places of interest include Mills Public Observatory, the Tay road and rail bridges, Dundee Contemporary Arts centre, McManus Galleries, Claypotts Castle, Broughty Castle, Verdant Works (textile heritage centre) and the Sensation Science Centre.

### EDINBURGH

Edinburgh is the capital city and seat of government in Scotland. The new Scottish parliament building designed by Enric Miralles was completed in 2004 and is open to visitors. The city is built on a group of hills and both the Old and New Towns are inscribed on the UNESCO World Cultural and Natural Heritage List for their cultural significance.

Other places of interest include the castle, which houses the Stone of Scone and also includes St Margaret's Chapel, the oldest building in Edinburgh, and near it, the Scottish National War Memorial; the Palace of Holyroodhouse, the Queen's official residence in Scotland; Parliament House, the present seat of the judicature; Princes Street; three universities (Edinburgh, Heriot-Watt, Napier); St Giles' Cathedral; St Mary's (Scottish Episcopal) Cathedral (Sir George Gilbert Scott); the General Register House (Robert Adam); the National and Signet libraries; the National Gallery of Scotland; the Royal Scottish Academy; the Scottish National Portrait Gallery and the Edinburgh International Conference Centre.

## GLASGOW

Glasgow, a Royal Burgh, is Scotland's largest city and its principal commercial and industrial centre. The city occupies the north and south banks of the Clyde, formerly one of the chief commercial estuaries in the world. The main industries include engineering, electronics, finance, chemicals and printing. The city is also a key tourist and conference destination.

The chief buildings are the 13th-century Gothic cathedral, the university (Sir George Gilbert Scott), the City Chambers, the Royal Concert Hall, St Mungo Museum of Religious Life and Art, Pollok House, the School of Art (Charles Rennie Mackintosh), Kelvingrove Art Gallery and Museum, the Gallery of Modern Art, the Riverside Museum: Scotland's Museum of Transport and Travel (Zaha Hadid), the Burrell Collection museum and the Mitchell Library. The city is home to the Royal Scottish National Orchestra, Scottish Opera, Scottish Ballet, BBC Scotland and Scottish Television (STV).

## INVERNESS

Inverness was granted city status in 2000. The city's name is derived from the Gaelic for 'the mouth of the Ness', referring to the river on which it lies. Inverness is recorded as being at the junction of trade routes since AD 565. Today the city is the main administrative centre for the north of Scotland and is the capital of the Highlands. Tourism is one of the city's main industries.

Among the city's most notable buildings is Abertarff House, built in 1593 and the oldest secular building remaining in Inverness. Balnain House, built as a town house in 1726, is a fine example of early Georgian architecture. The Old High Church, on St Michael's Mount, is the original parish church of Inverness and is built on the site of the earliest Christian church in the city. Parts of the church date back to the 14th century.

Stirling was granted city status in 2002 and Perth in 2012. Aberdeen, Dundee, Edinburgh and Glasgow have also been granted lord mayoralty/lord provostship.

## LORD-LIEUTENANTS

| Title | Name |
| --- | --- |
| Aberdeen City* | Lord Provost George Adam |
| Aberdeenshire | James Ingleby |
| Angus | Georgiana Osborne |
| Argyll and Bute | Patrick Stewart, MBE |
| Ayrshire and Arran | John Duncan, QPM |
| Banffshire | Clare Russell |
| Berwickshire | Jeannna Swan |
| Caithness | M. Anne Dunnett |
| Clackmannanshire | Lt.-Col. John Stewart |
| Dumfries | Jean Tulloch |
| Dunbartonshire | Rear-Adm. Michael Gregory, OBE |
| Dundee City* | Lord Provost Robert Duncan |
| East Lothian | Maj. Michael Williams, MBE |
| Edinburgh City* | Rt. Hon. Lord Provost Donald Wilson |
| Eilean Siar (Western Isles) | Alexander Matheson, OBE |
| Fife | Robert Balfour |
| Glasgow City* | Rt. Hon. Lord Provost Sadie Docherty |
| Inverness | Donald Cameron of Lochiel |
| Kincardineshire | Carol Kinghorn |
| Lanarkshire | Mushtaq Ahmad, OBE |
| Midlothian | Sir Robert Maxwell Clerk, Bt., OBE |
| Moray | Lt.-Col. Grenville Shaw Johnston, OBE, TD |
| Nairn | Ewen Brodie of Lethen, CVO |
| Orkney | Bill Spence |
| Perth and Kinross | Brig. Melville Jameson, CBE |
| Renfrewshire | Guy Clark |
| Ross and Cromarty | Janet Bowen |
| Roxburgh, Ettrick and Lauderdale | Capt. Hon. Gerald Maitland-Carew |
| Shetland | Robert Hunter |
| Stirling and Falkirk | Marjory McLachlan |
| Sutherland | Dr Monica Main |
| The Stewartry of Kirkcudbright | Lt.-Col. Sir Malcolm Ross, GCVO, OBE |
| Tweeddale | Prof. Sir Hew Strachan |
| West Lothian | Isobel Brydie, MBE |
| Wigtown | John Ross |

* The Lord Provosts of the four cities of Aberdeen, Dundee, Edinburgh and Glasgow are Lord-Lieutenants *ex officio* for those districts

# LOCAL COUNCILS

| Council | Administrative Headquarters | Telephone | Population* | Council Tax† | Chief Executive |
|---|---|---|---|---|---|
| ABERDEEN | Aberdeen | 01224-522000 | 228,990 | £1,230 | Angela Scott |
| Aberdeenshire | Aberdeen | 08456-081207 | 260,500 | £1,141 | Jim Savege |
| Angus | Forfar | 0845-277 7778 | 116,660 | £1,072 | Richard Stiff |
| Argyll and Bute | Lochgilphead | 01546-602127 | 87,660 | £1,178 | Sally Loudon |
| Clackmannanshire | Alloa | 01259-450000 | 51,190 | £1,148 | Elaine McPherson |
| Dumfries and Galloway | Dumfries | 030-3333 3000 | 149,940 | £1,049 | Gavin Stevenson |
| DUNDEE | Dundee | 01382-434000 | 148,260 | £1,211 | David Martin |
| East Ayrshire | Kilmarnock | 01563-576000 | 122,150 | £1,189 | Fiona Lees |
| East Dunbartonshire | Kirkintilloch | 0300-123 4510 | 106,730 | £1,142 | Gerry Cornes |
| East Lothian | Haddington | 01620-827827 | 102,050 | £1,118 | Angela Leitch |
| East Renfrewshire | Giffnock | 0141-577 3000 | 92,380 | £1,126 | Lorraine McMillan |
| EDINBURGH | Edinburgh | 0131-200 2000 | 492,680 | £1,169 | Dame Sue Bruce, DBE |
| Eilean Siar (Western Isles) | Stornoway | 01851-703773 | 27,250 | £1,024 | Malcolm Burr |
| Falkirk | Falkirk | 01324-506070 | 157,640 | £1,070 | Mary Pitcaithly, OBE |
| Fife | Glenrothes | 0345-155 0000 | 367,260 | £1,118 | Steve Grimmond |
| GLASGOW | Glasgow | 0141-287 2000 | 599,650 | £1,213 | Annemarie O'Donnell |
| Highland | Inverness | 01349-886606 | 233,100 | £1,163 | Steve Barron |
| Inverclyde | Greenock | 01475-717171 | 79,860 | £1,198 | John Mundell |
| Midlothian | Dalkeith | 0131-270 7500 | 86,210 | £1,210 | Kenneth Lawrie |
| Moray | Elgin | 01343-543451 | 94,750 | £1,135 | Roddy Burns |
| North Ayrshire | Irvine | 0845-603 0590 | 136,450 | £1,152 | Elma Murray |
| North Lanarkshire | Motherwell | 01698-403200 | 337,950 | £1,098 | Gavin Whitefield |
| Orkney | Kirkwall | 01856-873535 | 21,590 | £1,037 | Alistair Buchan |
| Perth and Kinross | Perth | 01738-475000 | 148,880 | £1,158 | Bernadette Malone |
| Renfrewshire | Paisley | 0300-300 0300 | 174,230 | £1,165 | Sandra Black |
| Scottish Borders | Melrose | 01835-824000 | 114,030 | £1,084 | Tracey Logan |
| Shetland | Lerwick | 01595-693535 | 23,230 | £1,053 | Mark Boden |
| South Ayrshire | Ayr | 0300-123 0900 | 112,510 | £1,154 | Eileen Howat |
| South Lanarkshire | Hamilton | 0303-123 1015 | 315,360 | £1,101 | Lindsay Freeland |
| STIRLING | Stirling | 0845-277 7000 | 91,580 | £1,197 | Stewart Carruth |
| West Dunbartonshire | Dumbarton | 01389-737000 | 89,730 | £1,163 | Joyce White |
| West Lothian | Livingston | 01506-280000 | 177,150 | £1,128 | Graham Hope |

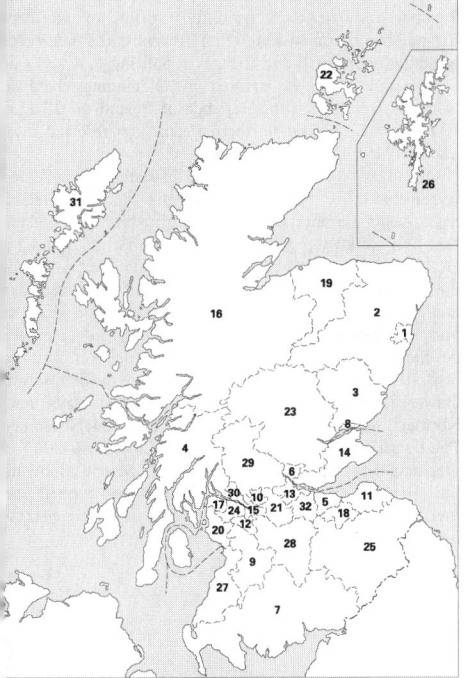

| Key | Council | Key | Council |
|---|---|---|---|
| 1 | Aberdeen City | 17 | Inverclyde |
| 2 | Aberdeenshire | 18 | Midlothian |
| 3 | Angus | 19 | Moray |
| 4 | Argyll and Bute | 20 | North Ayrshire |
| 5 | City of Edinburgh | 21 | North Lanarkshire |
| 6 | Clackmannanshire | 22 | Orkney |
| 7 | Dumfries and Galloway | 23 | Perth and Kinross |
| 8 | Dundee City | 24 | Renfrewshire |
| 9 | East Ayrshire | 25 | Scottish Borders |
| 10 | East Dunbartonshire | 26 | Shetland |
| 11 | East Lothian | 27 | South Ayrshire |
| 12 | East Renfrewshire | 28 | South Lanarkshire |
| 13 | Falkirk | 29 | Stirling |
| 14 | Fife | 30 | West Dunbartonshire |
| 15 | Glasgow City | 31 | Western Isles (Eilean Siar) |
| 16 | Highland | 32 | West Lothian |

* *Source:* Office for National Statistics – *Mid-2014 Population Estimates* (Crown copyright)
† Average Band D council tax bill 2015–16
Councils in CAPITAL LETTERS have city status

# NORTHERN IRELAND

Northern Ireland has a total area of 14,149 sq. km (5,463 sq. miles): land, 13,576 sq. km (5,242 sq. miles); inland water, 573 sq. km (221 sq. miles).

The population of Northern Ireland at the 2011 census was 1,810,863 (men 887,323; women 923,540). The average density of population in 2011 was 128 persons per sq. km (331 per sq. mile).

## FLAG

The official national flag of Northern Ireland is the Union Flag.

## PRINCIPAL CITIES

In addition to Belfast and Londonderry, three other places in Northern Ireland have been granted city status: Armagh (1994), Lisburn (2002) and Newry (2002).

### BELFAST

Belfast, the administrative centre of Northern Ireland, is situated at the mouth of the River Lagan at its entrance to Belfast Lough. The city grew to be a great industrial centre, owing to its easy access by sea to Scottish coal and iron.

The principal buildings are of a relatively young age and include the parliament buildings at Stormont, the City Hall, Waterfront Hall, the Law Courts, the Public Library and the Museum and Art Gallery. In March 2012, a new museum, Titanic Belfast, opened on the banks of the Lagan River – the site where RMS *Titanic* was built and launched. The museum forms the centrepiece of a new mixed-use maritime quarter.

Belfast received its first charter of incorporation in 1613 and was created a city in 1888; the title of lord mayor was conferred in 1892.

### LONDONDERRY

Londonderry (originally Derry) is situated on the River Foyle, and has important associations with the City of London. The Irish Society was created by the City of London in 1610, and under its royal charter of 1613 it fortified the city and was for a long time closely associated with its administration. Because of this connection the city was incorporated in 1613 under the new name of Londonderry.

The city is famous for the great siege of 1688–9, when for 105 days the town held out against the forces of James II. The city walls are still intact and form a circuit of 1.6 km (one mile) around the old city.

Interesting buildings are the Protestant cathedral of St Columb's (1633) and the Guildhall, reconstructed in 1912 and containing a number of beautiful stained glass windows, many of which were presented by the livery companies of London.

## CONSTITUTIONAL HISTORY

Northern Ireland is subject to the same fundamental constitutional provisions which apply to the rest of the UK. It had its own parliament and government from 1921 to 1972, but after increasing civil unrest the Northern Ireland (Temporary Provisions) Act 1972 transferred the legislative and executive powers of the Northern Ireland parliament and government to the UK parliament and a secretary of state. The Northern Ireland Constitution Act 1973 provided for devolution in Northern Ireland through an assembly and executive, but a power-sharing executive formed by the Northern Ireland political parties in January 1974 collapsed in May 1974. Following the collapse of the power-sharing executive Northern Ireland returned to direct rule governance under the provisions of the Northern Ireland Act 1974, placing the Northern Ireland department under the direction and control of the Northern Ireland secretary.

In December 1993 the British and Irish governments published the Joint Declaration, complementing their political talks and making clear that any settlement would need to be founded on principles of democracy and consent.

On 12 January 1998 the British and Irish governments issued a joint document, *Propositions on Heads of Agreement*, proposing the establishment of various new cross-border bodies; further proposals were presented on 27 January. A draft peace settlement was issued by the talks' chairman, US Senator George Mitchell, on 6 April 1998 but was rejected by the Unionists the following day. On 10 April agreement was reached between the British and Irish governments and the eight Northern Ireland political parties still involved in the talks (the Good Friday Agreement). The agreement provided for an elected Northern Ireland Assembly, a North/South Ministerial Council, and a British-Irish Council comprising representatives of the British, Irish, Channel Islands and Isle of Man governments and members of the new assemblies for Scotland, Wales and Northern Ireland. Further points included the abandonment of the Republic of Ireland's constitutional claim to Northern Ireland, the decommissioning of weapons, the release of paramilitary prisoners and changes in policing.

The agreement was ratified in referendums held in Northern Ireland and the Republic of Ireland on 22 May 1998. In the UK, the Northern Ireland Act received royal assent in November 1998.

On 28 April 2003 the secretary of state again assumed responsibility for the direction of the Northern Ireland departments on the dissolution of the Northern Ireland Assembly, following its initial suspension from midnight on 14 October 2002. In 2006, following the passing of the Northern Ireland Act, the secretary of state created a non-legislative fixed-term assembly which would cease to operate either when the political parties agreed to restore devolution, or on 24 November 2006 (whichever occurred first). In October 2006 a timetable to restore devolution was drawn up (St Andrews Agreement) and a transitional Northern Ireland Assembly was formed on 24 November. The transitional assembly was dissolved in January 2007 in preparation for elections to be held on 7 March; following the elections a power-sharing executive was formed and the new 108-member Northern Ireland Assembly became operational on 8 May 2007.

*See also* Regional Government.

# LORD-LIEUTENANTS AND HIGH SHERIFFS

| County | Lord-Lieutenant | High Sheriff (2015) |
| --- | --- | --- |
| Antrim | Joan Christie, OBE | John Pinkerton |
| Armagh | Earl of Caledon, KCVO | Anna Shepherd |
| Belfast City | Fionnuala Mary Jay-O'Boyle, CBE | Councillor Gareth McKee |
| Down | David Lindsay | Patrick Cross |
| Fermanagh | Viscount Brookeborough | Hope Kerr |
| Londonderry | Denis Desmond, CBE | Helen Mark |
| Londonderry City | Dr Angela Josepha Garvey | Mrs Harvinder Torney |
| Tyrone | Robert Scott, OBE | Dr Lisheen Webb |

# LOCAL COUNCILS

| Council | Telephone | Population* | Chief Executive |
| --- | --- | --- | --- |
| Antrim & Newtownabbey | 028-9448 1311 | 139,966 | Jacqui Dixon |
| Armagh, Banbridge & Craigavon | 0300-030 0900 | 205,711 | Roger Wilson |
| Belfast | 028-9027 0549 | 336,830 | Suzanne Wylie |
| Causeway Coast & Glens | 028-7034 7034 | 142,303 | David Jackson, MBE |
| Derry & Strabane | 028-7138 2204 | 149,198 | John Kelpie |
| Fermanagh & Omagh | 0300-303 1777 | 114,992 | Brendan Hegarty |
| Lisburn & Castlereagh | 028-9250 9250 | 138,627 | Theresa Donaldson |
| Mid & East Antrim | 028-9335 8000 | 136,642 | Anne Donaghy |
| Mid Ulster | 0300-013 2132 | 142,895 | Anthony Tohill |
| Newry, Mourne & Down | 028-3031 3037 | 175,403 | Liam Hannaway |
| North Down & Ards | 0300-013 3333 | 157,930 | Stephen Reid |

* Source: NISRA – Mid-year Population Estimates 2014

# THE ISLE OF MAN

*Ellan Vannin*

The Isle of Man is an island situated in the Irish Sea, at latitude 54° 3'–54° 25' N. and longitude 4° 18'–4° 47' W., nearly equidistant from England, Scotland and Ireland. Although the early inhabitants were of Celtic origin, the Isle of Man was part of the Norwegian Kingdom of the Hebrides until 1266, when this was ceded to Scotland. Subsequently granted to the Stanleys (Earls of Derby) in the 15th century and later to the Dukes of Atholl, it was brought under the administration of the Crown in 1765. The island forms the bishopric of Sodor and Man.

The total land area is 572 sq. km (221 sq. miles). The 2011 census showed a resident population of 84,497 (men, 41,971; women, 42,526). The main language in use is English. Around 1,660 people are able to speak the Manx Gaelic language.

CAPITAL – ΨDouglas; population, 27,938 (2011). ΨCastletown (3,097) is the ancient capital; the other towns are ΨPeel (5,093) and ΨRamsey (7,821)

FLAG – A red flag charged with three conjoined armoured legs in white and gold

NATIONAL DAY – 5 July (Tynwald Day)

## GOVERNMENT

The Isle of Man is a self-governing Crown dependency, with its own parliamentary, legal and administrative system. The British government is responsible for international relations and defence. Under the UK Act of Accession, Protocol 3, the island's relationship with the European Union is limited to trade alone and does not extend to financial aid. The Lieutenant-Governor is the Queen's personal representative on the island.

The legislature, Tynwald, is the oldest parliament in the world in continuous existence. It has two branches: the Legislative Council and the House of Keys. The council consists of the President of Tynwald, the Bishop of Sodor and Man, the Attorney-General (who does not have a vote) and eight members elected by the House of Keys. The House of Keys has 24 members, elected by universal adult suffrage. The branches sit separately to consider legislation and sit together, as Tynwald Court, for most other parliamentary purposes.

The presiding officer of Tynwald Court is the President of Tynwald, elected by the members, who also presides over sittings of the Legislative Council. The presiding officer of the House of Keys is the Speaker, who is elected by members of the house.

The principal members of the Manx government are the chief minister and eight departmental ministers, who comprise the Council of Ministers.

*Lieutenant-Governor,* HE Adam Wood
*President of Tynwald,* Hon. Clare Christian

*Speaker, House of Keys,* Hon. Steve Rodan, SHK
*The First Deemster and Clerk of the Rolls,* His Hon. David Doyle
*Clerk of Tynwald, Secretary to the House of Keys and Counsel to the Speaker,* Roger Phillips
*Clerk of the Legislative Council and Deputy Clerk of Tynwald,* Jonathan King
*Attorney-General,* Stephen Harding
*Chief Minister,* Hon. Allan Bell, MHK
*Chief Secretary,* Will Greenhow

## ECONOMY

Much of the income generated in the island is earned in the services sector with financial and professional services accounting for 43 per cent of the national income. E-gaming is also a significant sector, contributing 13.5 per cent to national income. Under the terms of protocol 3, the island has tariff-free access to EU markets for the products of its engineering, farming and fishing industries.

In May 2015 the island's unemployment rate was 1.7 per cent and the rate of inflation (RPI) was 2.1 per cent.

## FINANCE

The budget for 2015–16 provides for net revenue expenditure of £545.2m. The principal sources of government revenue are taxes on income and expenditure. Income tax is payable at a rate of 10 per cent on the first £10,500 of taxable income for single resident individuals and 20 per cent on the balance, after personal allowances of £9,500. These bands are doubled for married couples. The rate of income tax for trading companies is zero per cent except for income from banking and major retail operations which is taxed at 10 per cent, and income from land and property which is taxed at 20 per cent. By agreement with the British government, the island keeps most of its rates of indirect taxation (VAT and duties) the same as those in the UK. However, VAT on tourist accommodation, property, repairs and renovations is charged at 5 per cent. A reciprocal agreement on national insurance benefits and pensions exists between the governments of the Isle of Man and the UK. Taxes are also charged on property (rates), but these are comparatively low.

The major government expenditure items are social care, health and education, which account for 50 per cent of the government budget. The island makes an annual contribution to the UK for defence and other external services.

The island has a special relationship with the European Union and neither contributes money to nor receives funds from the EU budget.

Ψ = sea port

# THE CHANNEL ISLANDS

The Channel Islands, situated off the north-west coast of France (at a distance of 16km (10 miles) at their closest point), are the only portions of the Dukedom of Normandy still belonging to the Crown, to which they have been attached since the Norman Conquest of 1066. They were the only British territory to come under German occupation during the Second World War, following invasion on 30 June and 1 July 1940. Guernsey and Jersey were relieved by British forces on 9 May 1945, Sark on 10 May 1945 and Alderney on 16 May 1945; 9 May (Liberation Day) is now observed as a bank and public holiday in Guernsey and Jersey.

The islands consist of Jersey (11,630ha/28,717 acres), Guernsey (6,340ha/15,654 acres), and the dependencies of Guernsey: Alderney (795ha/1,962 acres), Brecqhou (30ha/74 acres), Great Sark (419ha/1,035 acres), Little Sark (97ha/239 acres), Herm (130ha/320 acres), Jethou (18ha/44 acres) and Lihou (15ha/38 acres) – a total of 19,474ha/48,083 acres, or 195 sq. km/75 sq. miles.

The 2011 census (taken in March) showed the population of Jersey as 97,857. Guernsey did not complete the same census, but the most recent official records for Guernsey and Alderney estimated the populations at 62,732 and 1,903 respectively. Sark's population is estimated to be around 600. The official language is English but French is often used for ceremonial purposes. In country districts of Jersey and Guernsey and throughout Sark a Norman-French *patois* is also in use, though to a lesser extent.

## GOVERNMENT
The islands are Crown dependencies with their own legislative assemblies (the States of Jersey and the States of Alderney, the States of Deliberation in Guernsey and the Chief Pleas in Sark), systems of local administration and law, and their own courts. *Projets de Loi* (Acts) passed by the States require the sanction of the Queen-in-council. The UK government is responsible for defence and international relations, although the islands are increasingly entering into agreements with other countries in their own right. The Channel Islands are not members of the European Union but, under protocol 3 of the UK's Treaty of Accession, have trading rights with the free movement of goods within the EU. A common customs tariff, levies and agricultural and import measures apply to trade between the islands and non-member countries.

In both Jersey and Guernsey bailiwicks the Lieutenant-Governor and Commander-in-Chief, who is appointed by the Crown, is the personal representative of the Queen and the official channel of communication between the Crown (via the Privy Council) and the islands' governments.

The head of government in both Jersey and Guernsey is the Chief Minister. Jersey has a ministerial system of government; the executive comprises the Council of Ministers and consists of a chief minister and ten other ministers. The ministers are assisted by up to ten assistant ministers. Members of the States who are not in the executive are able to sit on a number of scrutiny panels and the Public Accounts Committee to examine the policy of the executive and hold ministers to account. Guernsey is administered by a number of departments and committees. There are ten States departments with mandated responsibilities, each department is constituted of a minister and four members of the States. Each of the ministers has a seat on the Policy Council

which is presided over by the Chief Minister. The States of Deliberation, the island's parliamentary assembly, is the overarching executive. There are also five parliamentary committees, each led by a chair, responsible for scrutinising policy, finance and legislation, parliamentary procedural matters and public sector pay negotiations. Alderney has a legislature comprising a President and ten members elected by universal suffrage. Sark has a directly elected legislature of 28 members *(conseillers)* who serve on a number of committees.

Justice is administered by the royal courts of Jersey and Guernsey, each consisting of the bailiff and 12 elected jurats. The bailiffs of Jersey and Guernsey, appointed by the Crown, are presidents of the royal courts of their respective islands. Each bailiff is the *ex-officio* presiding officer in their respective parliaments and, by convention, the civic head.

Each bailiwick constitutes a deanery under the administration of the Diocese of Winchester. Since January 2014 episcopal oversight for the Channel Islands has been delegated, on a temporary basis, to the Bishop of Dover (Diocese of Canterbury).

## ECONOMY
A mild climate and good soil have led to the development of intensive systems of agriculture and horticulture, which form a significant part of the economy. Equally important are earnings from tourism and banking and finance: the low rates of income and corporation tax and the absence of death duties make the islands an important offshore financial centre. The financial services sector contributes over 50 per cent of GDP in Jersey and around 40 per cent in Guernsey. In addition, there is no VAT or equivalent tax in Guernsey and only small goods and services tax in Jersey (5 per cent since 1 June 2011). The Channel Islands stock exchange is located in Guernsey, which also has a thriving e-gaming sector.

Principal exports are agricultural produce and flowers; imports are chiefly machinery, manufactured goods, food, fuel and chemicals. Trade with the UK is regarded as internal.

British currency is legal tender in the Channel Islands but each bailiwick issues its own coins and notes (*see* Currency section). They also issue their own postage stamps; UK stamps are not valid.

## JERSEY

*Lieutenant-Governor and Commander-in-Chief of Jersey,*
  HE Gen. Sir John McColl, KCB, CBE, DSO, *apptd* 2011
*Chief of Staff,* Maj. Justin Oldridge
*Bailiff of Jersey,* William J. Bailhache
*Deputy Bailiff,* Timothy J. Le Cocq
*Attorney-General,* Robert J. MacRae, QC
*Receiver-General,* David Pett
*Solicitor-General,* Mark Temple
*Greffier of the States,* Michael N. de la Haye, OBE
*States Treasurer,* Richard Bell
*Chief Minister,* Senator Ian Gorst

| FINANCE | 2013 | 2014 |
| --- | --- | --- |
| Revenue income | £1,283,412,000 | £1,158,308,000 |
| Revenue expenditure | £1,004,863,000 | £1,151,886,000 |
| Capital expenditure | £51,507,000 | £65,484,000 |

CHIEF TOWN – ΨSt Helier, on the south coast
FLAG – A white field charged with a red saltire cross, and the arms of Jersey in the upper centre

# GUERNSEY AND DEPENDENCIES

*Lieutenant-Governor and Commander-in-Chief of the Bailiwick of Guernsey and its Dependencies,* vacant
*Presiding Officer of the Royal Court and of the States of Deliberation,* Bailiff Richard Collas
*Deputy Presiding Officer of the Royal Court and States of Deliberation,* Deputy Bailiff Richard McMahon, QC
*HM Procureur and Receiver-General (Attorney-General),* Howard Roberts, QC
*HM Comptroller (Solicitor-General),* Megan Pullum, QC

## GUERNSEY

*Chief Minister,* Deputy Jonathan Le Tocq
*Chief Executive,* Paul Whitfield

| FINANCE | 2013 | 2014 |
| --- | --- | --- |
| Revenue income | £361,257,000 | £384,550,000 |
| Revenue expenditure | £345,698,000 | £355,900,000 |
| Capital expenditure | £13,362,000 | £7,300,000 |

CHIEF TOWNS – ΨSt Peter Port, on the east coast of Guernsey; St Anne on Alderney

FLAG – White, bearing a red cross of St George, with a gold cross of Normandy overall in the centre

## ALDERNEY

*President of the States,* Stuart Trought
*Chief Executive,* Victor Brownlees
*Greffier,* Sarah Kelly

## SARK

Sark was the last European territory to abolish feudal parliamentary representation. Elections for a democratic legislative assembly took place in December 2008, with the *conseillers* taking their seats in the newly constituted Chief Pleas in January 2009.
*Seigneur of Sark,* John Beaumont, OBE
*Seneschal,* Jeremy la Trobe-Bateman
*President,* Lt.-Col. Reg Guille, MBE
*Greffier,* Trevor Hamon

## OTHER DEPENDENCIES

Herm and Lihou are owned by the States of Guernsey; Herm is leased, Lihou is uninhabited. Jethou is leased by the Crown to the States of Guernsey and is sub-let by the States. Brecqhou is within the legislative and judicial territory of Sark.

Ψ = seaport

# LAW COURTS AND OFFICES

## SUPREME COURT OF THE UNITED KINGDOM

The Supreme Court of the United Kingdom is the highest domestic judicial authority; it replaced the appellate committee of the House of Lords (the house functioning in its judicial capacity) on 1 October 2009. It is the final court of appeal for cases heard in Great Britain and Northern Ireland (except for criminal cases from Scotland). Cases concerning the interpretation and application of European Union law, including preliminary rulings requested by British courts and tribunals, which are decided by the Court of Justice of the European Union (CJEU) (see European Union), and the supreme court can make a reference to the CJEU in appropriate cases. Additionally, in giving effect to rights contained in the European Convention on Human Rights, the supreme court must take account of any decision of the European Court of Human Rights.

The supreme court also assumed jurisdiction in relation to devolution matters under the Scotland Act 1998 (now partly superseded by the Scotland Act 2012), the Northern Ireland Act 1988 and the Government of Wales Act 2006; these powers were transferred from the Judicial Committee of the Privy Council. Ten of the 12 Lords of Appeal in Ordinary (Law Lords) from the House of Lords transferred to the 12-member supreme court when it came into operation (at the same time one law lord retired and another was appointed Master of the Rolls). All new justices of the supreme court are now appointed by an independent selection commission, and, although styled Rt. Hon. Lord, are not members of the House of Lords. Peers who are members of the judiciary are disqualified from sitting or voting in the House of Lords until they retire from their judicial office. See Life Peers (page 60) for a list of such peers (§).

*President of the Supreme Court* (£220,655), Rt. Hon. Lord Neuberger of Abbotsbury, *born* 1948, *apptd* 2012
*Deputy President of the Supreme Court* (£213,125), Rt. Hon. Lady Hale of Richmond, *born* 1945, *apptd* 2013

JUSTICES OF THE SUPREME COURT *as at September 2015* (each £213,125)
*Style,* The Rt. Hon. Lord/Lady–

Rt. Hon. Lord Mance, *born* 1943, *apptd* 2005
Rt. Hon. Lord Kerr of Tonaghmore, *born* 1948, *apptd* 2009
Rt. Hon. Lord Clarke of Stone-cum-Ebony, *born* 1943, *apptd* 2009
Rt. Hon. Lord Wilson of Culworth, *born* 1945, *apptd* 2011
Rt. Hon. Lord Sumption, *born* 1948, *apptd* 2012
Rt. Hon. Lord Reed, *born* 1956, *apptd* 2012
Rt. Hon. Lord Carnwath of Notting Hill, CVO, *born* 1945, *apptd* 2012
Rt. Hon. Lord Hughes of Ombersley, *born* 1948, *apptd* 2013
Rt. Hon. Lord Toulson, *born* 1946, *apptd* 2013
Rt. Hon. Lord Hodge, *born* 1953, *apptd* 2013

UNITED KINGDOM SUPREME COURT
Parliament Square, London SW1P 3BD T 020-7960 1900
*Chief Executive,* Mark Ormerod, CB

## JUDICATURE OF ENGLAND AND WALES

The legal system in England and Wales is divided into criminal law and civil law. Criminal law is concerned with

acts harmful to the community and the rules laid down by the state for the benefit of citizens, whereas civil law governs the relationships and transactions between individuals. Administrative law is a kind of civil law usually concerning the interaction of individuals and the state, and most cases are heard in tribunals specific to the subject (see Tribunals section). Scotland and Northern Ireland possess legal systems that differ from the system in England and Wales in law, judicial procedure and court structure, but retain the distinction between criminal and civil law.

Under the provisions of the Criminal Appeal Act 1995, a commission was set up to direct and supervise investigations into possible miscarriages of justice and to refer cases to the appeal courts on the grounds of conviction and sentence; these functions were formerly the responsibility of the home secretary.

### SENIOR COURTS OF ENGLAND AND WALES
The senior courts of England and Wales (until September 2009 known as the supreme court of judicature of England and Wales) comprise the high court, the crown court and the court of appeal. The President of the Courts of England and Wales, a new title given to the Lord Chief Justice under the Constitutional Reform Act 2005, is the head of the judiciary.

The high court was created in 1875 and combined many previously separate courts. Sittings are held at the royal courts of justice in London or at around 120 district registries outside the capital. It is the superior civil court and is split into three divisions – the chancery division, the Queen's bench division and the family division – each of which is further divided. The chancery division is headed by the Chancellor of the High Court and is concerned mainly with equity, trusts, tax and bankruptcy, while also including two specialist courts, the patents court and the companies court. The Queen's bench division (QBD) is the largest of the three divisions, and is headed by its own president. It deals with common law (ie tort, contract, debt and personal injuries), some tax law, eg VAT tribunal appeals, and encompasses the admiralty court and the commercial court. The QBD also administers the technology and construction court. The family division was created in 1970 and is headed by its own president, who is also Head of Family Justice, and hears cases concerning divorce, access to and custody of children, and other family matters. The divisional court of the high court sits in the family and chancery divisions, and hears appeals from the magistrates' courts and county courts.

The crown court was set up in 1972 and sits at 77 centres throughout England and Wales. It deals with more serious (indictable) criminal cases, which are triable before a judge and jury, including treason, murder, rape, kidnapping, armed robbery and Official Secrets Act offences. It also handles cases transferred from the magistrates' courts where the magistrate decides his or her own power of sentence is inadequate, or where someone appeals against a magistrate's decision, or in a case that is triable 'either way' where the accused has chosen a jury trial. The crown court centres are divided into three tiers: high court judges, circuit judges and sometimes recorders (part-time circuit judges), sit in first-tier centres, hearing the most serious criminal offences (eg murder, treason, rape, manslaughter) and some civil high court cases. The second-tier centres are presided over by high court judges, circuit judges or recorders and also deal with the most serious criminal cases. Third-tier courts deal with the remaining criminal offences, with circuit judges or recorders presiding.

## HIERARCHY OF ENGLISH AND WELSH COURTS

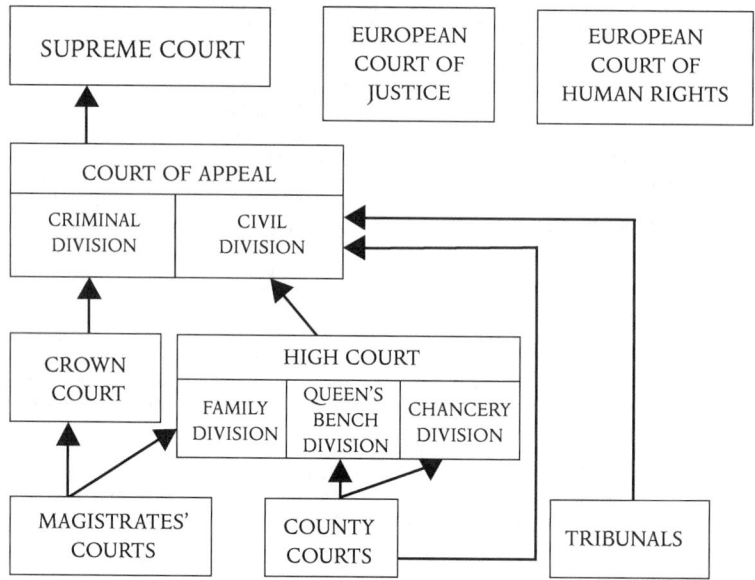

The court of appeal hears appeals against both fact and law, and was last restructured in 1966 when it replaced the court of criminal appeal. It is split into the civil division (which hears appeals from the high court, tribunals and in certain cases, the county courts) and the criminal division (which hears appeals from the crown court). Cases are heard by Lords Justices of Appeal and high court judges if deemed suitable for reconsideration.

The Constitutional Reform Act 2005 instigated several key changes to the judiciary in England and Wales. These included the establishment of the independent supreme court, which opened in October 2009; the reform of the post of Lord Chancellor, transferring its judicial functions to the President of the Courts of England and Wales; a duty on government ministers to uphold the independence of the judiciary by barring them from trying to influence judicial decisions through any special access to judges; the formation of a fully transparent and independent Judicial Appointments Commission that is responsible for selecting candidates to recommend for judicial appointment to the Lord Chancellor and Secretary of State for Justice; and the creation of the post of Judicial Appointments and Conduct Ombudsman.

### CRIMINAL CASES

In criminal matters the decision to prosecute (in the majority of cases) rests with the Crown Prosecution Service (CPS), which is the independent prosecuting body in England and Wales. The CPS is headed by the director of public prosecutions, who works under the superintendence of the Attorney-General. Certain categories of offence continue to require the Attorney-General's consent for prosecution.

Most minor criminal cases (summary offences) are dealt with in magistrates' courts, usually by a bench of three unpaid lay magistrates (justices of the peace) sitting without a jury and assisted on points of law and procedure by a legally trained clerk. As at 1 April 2015, there were around 23,000 justices of the peace. In some courts a full-time, salaried and legally qualified district judge (magistrates' court) – formerly known as a stipendiary judge – presides alone. There are 138 district judges and 115 deputy district judges operating

in around 330 magistrates' courts in England and Wales. Magistrates' courts oversee the completion of 90 per cent of all criminal cases. Magistrates' courts also house some family proceedings courts (which deal with relationship breakdown and childcare cases) and youth courts. Cases of medium seriousness (known as 'offences triable either way') where the defendant pleads not guilty can be heard in the crown court for a trial by jury, if the defendant so chooses. Preliminary proceedings in a serious case to decide whether there is evidence to justify committal for trial in the crown court are dealt with in the magistrates' courts.

The 77 centres that the crown court sits in are divided into seven regions. There are 640 circuit judges and 1,031 recorders (part-time circuit judges); they must sit a minimum of 15 days per year and are usually subject to a maximum of 30. A jury is present in all trials that are contested.

Appeals from magistrates' courts against sentence or conviction are made to the crown court, and appeals upon a point of law are made to the high court, which may ultimately be appealed to the supreme court. Appeals from the crown court, either against sentence or conviction, are made to the court of appeal (criminal division). Again, these appeals may be brought to the supreme court if a point of law is contested, and if the house considers it is of sufficient importance.

### CIVIL CASES

Most minor civil cases – including contract, tort (especially personal injuries), property, divorce and other family matters, bankruptcy etc – are dealt with by the county courts, of which there are 216 (see **W** www.justice.gov.uk for further details). Cases are heard by circuit judges, recorders or district judges. For cases involving small claims (with certain exceptions, where the amount claimed is £5,000 or less) there are informal and simplified procedures designed to enable parties to present their cases themselves without recourse to lawyers. Where there are financial limits on county court jurisdiction, claims that exceed those limits may be tried in the county courts with the consent of the parties, subject to the court's agreement, or in certain circumstances on transfer from the high court. Outside London, bankruptcy proceedings can be heard in designated county courts. Magistrates' courts also deal with certain classes of civil case, and committees of magistrates license public houses, clubs and betting shops. For the implementation of the Children Act 1989, a new structure of hearing centres was set up in 1991 for family proceedings cases, involving magistrates' courts (family proceedings courts), divorce county courts, family hearing centres and care centres.

Appeals in certain family matters heard in the family proceedings courts go to the family division of the high court. Appeals from county courts may be heard in the court of appeal (civil division) or the high court, and may go on to the supreme court.

## CORONERS' COURTS
The coroners' courts investigate violent and unnatural deaths or sudden deaths where the cause is unknown. Doctors, the police, various public authorities or members of the public may bring cases before a local coroner (a senior lawyer or doctor), in order to determine whether further criminal investigation is necessary. Where a death is sudden and the cause is unknown, the coroner may order a post-mortem examination to determine the cause of death rather than hold an inquest in court. An inquest must be held, however, if a person died in a violent or unnatural way, or died in prison or other unusual circumstances. If the coroner suspects murder, manslaughter or infanticide, he or she must summon a jury.

## SENIOR JUDICIARY OF ENGLAND AND WALES
*Lord Chief Justice of England and Wales and Head of Criminal Justice* (£247,112), Rt. Hon. Lord Thomas of Cwmgiedd, *born* 1947, *apptd* 2013
*Master of the Rolls and Head of Civil Justice* (£220,655), Rt. Hon. Lord Dyson, *born* 1943, *apptd* 2012
*President of the Queen's Bench Division* (£213,125), Rt. Hon. Sir Brian Leveson, *born* 1949, *apptd* 2013
*President of the Family Division and Head of Family Justice* (£213,125), Rt. Hon. Sir James Munby, *born* 1948, *apptd* 2013
*Chancellor of the High Court* (£213,125), Rt. Hon. Sir Terence Etherton, *born* 1951, *apptd* 2013

## SENIOR COURTS OF ENGLAND AND WALES
### COURT OF APPEAL
*Presiding Judge, Criminal Division*, Lord Chief Justice of England and Wales
*Presiding Judge, Civil Division*, Master of the Rolls
*Vice-President, Civil Division* (£202,668), Rt. Hon. Sir Martin Moore-Bick, *born* 1946, *apptd* 2014
*Vice-President, Criminal Division* (£202,668), Rt. Hon. Dame Heather Hallett, DBE, *born* 1949, *apptd* 2013

LORD JUSTICES OF APPEAL *as at September 2015* (each £202,668)
*Style,* The Rt. Hon. Lord/Lady Justice [surname]

Rt. Hon. Sir John Laws, *born* 1945, *apptd* 1999
Rt. Hon. Dame Mary Arden, DBE, *born* 1947, *apptd* 2000
Rt. Hon. Sir Andrew Longmore, *born* 1944, *apptd* 2001
Rt. Hon. Sir Martin Moore-Bick, *born* 1948, *apptd* 2005
Rt. Hon. Sir Stephen Richards, *born* 1950, *apptd* 2005
Rt. Hon. Dame Heather Hallett, DBE, *born* 1949, *apptd* 2005
Rt. Hon. Sir Rupert Jackson, *born* 1948, *apptd* 2008
Rt. Hon. Sir Richard Aikens, *born* 1948, *apptd* 2008
Rt. Hon. Sir Jeremy Sullivan, *born* 1945, *apptd* 2009

Rt. Hon. Sir Patrick Elias, *born* 1947, *apptd* 2009
Rt. Hon. Sir Nicholas Patten, *born* 1950, *apptd* 2009
Rt. Hon. Sir Christopher Pitchford, *born* 1947, *apptd* 2010
Rt. Hon. Dame Jill Black, DBE, *born* 1954, *apptd* 2010
Rt. Hon. Sir Stephen Tomlinson, *born* 1952, *apptd* 2010
Rt. Hon. Sir Peter Gross, *born* 1952, *apptd* 2010
Rt. Hon. Dame Anne Rafferty, DBE, *born* 1950, *apptd* 2011
Rt. Hon. Sir Andrew McFarlane, *born* 1954, *apptd* 2011
Rt. Hon. Sir Nigel Davis, *born* 1951, *apptd* 2011
Rt. Hon. Sir Kim Lewison, *born* 1952, *apptd* 2011
Rt. Hon. Sir David Kitchin, *born* 1955, *apptd* 2011
Rt. Hon. Sir David Lloyd Jones, *born* 1952, *apptd* 2012
Rt. Hon. Sir Colman Treacy, *born* 1949, *apptd* 2012
Rt. Hon. Sir Richard McCombe, *born* 1952, *apptd* 2012
Rt. Hon. Sir Jack Beatson, *born* 1948, *apptd* 2013
Rt. Hon. Dame Elizabeth Gloster, DBE, *born* 1949, *apptd* 2013
Rt. Hon. Sir Ernest Ryder, TD, *born* 1957, *apptd* 2013
Rt. Hon. Sir Nicholas Underhill, *born* 1952, *apptd* 2013
Rt. Hon. Sir Michael Briggs, *born* 1954, *apptd* 2013
Rt. Hon. Sir Christopher Floyd, *born* 1951, *apptd* 2013
Rt. Hon. Sir Adrian Fulford, *born* 1953, *apptd* 2013
Rt. Hon. Dame Julia Macur, DBE, *born* 1957, *apptd* 2013
Rt. Hon. Sir Christopher Clarke, *born* 1947, *apptd* 2013
Rt. Hon. Dame Victoria Sharp, DBE, *born* 1956, *apptd* 2013
Rt. Hon. Sir Geoffrey Vos, *born* 1855, *apptd* 2013
Rt. Hon. Sir David Bean, *born* 1954, *apptd* 2014
Rt. Hon. Dame Eleanor King, DBE, *born* 1957, *apptd* 2014
Rt. Hon. Sir Ian Burnett, *born* 1958, *apptd* 2014
Rt. Hon. Sir Philip Sales, *born* 1962, *apptd* 2014
*Ex Officio Judges,* Lord Chief Justice of England and Wales; Master of the Rolls; President of the Queen's Bench Division; President of the Family Division; Chancellor of the High Court

### COURTS-MARTIAL APPEAL COURT
*Judges,* Lord Chief Justice of England and Wales; Master of the Rolls; Lord Justices of Appeal; Judges of the High Court of Justice

## HIGH COURT
### CHANCERY DIVISION
*Chancellor of the High Court* (£213,125), Rt. Hon. Sir Terence Etherton, *born* 1951, *apptd* 2013
*Personal Secretary,* Elaine Harbert
*Legal Secretary,* Vannina Ettori
*Clerk,* Amanda Collins

JUDGES *as at September 2015* (each £177,988)
*Style,* The Hon. Mr/Mrs Justice [surname]

Hon. Sir Peter Smith, *born* 1952, *apptd* 2002
Hon. Sir David Richards, *born* 1951, *apptd* 2003
Hon. Sir George Mann, *born* 1951, *apptd* 2004
Hon. Sir Nicholas Warren, *born* 1949, *apptd* 2005
Hon. Sir Launcelot Henderson, *born* 1951, *apptd* 2007
Hon. Sir Paul Morgan, *born* 1952, *apptd* 2007
Hon. Sir Alastair Norris, *born* 1950, *apptd* 2007
Hon. Sir Gerald Barling, *born* 1949, *apptd* 2007
Hon. Dame Sonia Proudman, DBE, *born* 1949, *apptd* 2008
Hon. Sir Richard Arnold, *born* 1961, *apptd* 2008
Hon. Sir Peter Roth, *born* 1952, *apptd* 2009
Hon. Sir Guy Newey, *born* 1959, *apptd* 2010
Hon. Sir Robert Hildyard, *born* 1952, *apptd* 2011
Hon. Dame Sarah Asplin, DBE, *born* 1959, *apptd* 2012
Hon. Sir Colin Birss, *born* 1964, *apptd* 2013
Hon. Dame Vivien Rose, DBE, *born* 1960, *apptd* 2013
Hon. Sir Christopher Nugee, *born* 1959, *apptd* 2013
Hon. Sir Andrew Snowden, *born* 1962, *apptd* 2015

The Chancery Division also includes three specialist courts: the Companies Court, the Patents Court and the Bankruptcy Court.

## QUEEN'S BENCH DIVISION
*President* (£213,125), Rt. Hon. Sir Brian Leveson, *born* 1949, *apptd* 2013
*Vice-President* (£202,668), Rt. Hon. Sir Nigel Davis, *born* 1951, *apptd* 2014

JUDGES *as at September 2015* (each £177,988)
*Style,* The Hon. Mr/Mrs Justice [surname]

Hon. Sir Andrew Collins, *born* 1942, *apptd* 1994
Hon. Sir William Charles, *born* 1948, *apptd* 1998
Hon. Sir Michael Burton, *born* 1946, *apptd* 1998
Hon. Sir Andrew Smith, *born* 1947, *apptd* 2000
Hon. Sir Duncan Ouseley, *born* 1950, *apptd* 2000
Hon. Sir John Mitting, *born* 1947, *apptd* 2001
Hon. Sir Jeremy Cooke, *born* 1949, *apptd* 2001
Hon. Sir Peregrine Simon, *born* 1950, *apptd* 2002
Hon. Dame Laura Cox, DBE, *born* 1951, *apptd* 2002
Hon. Sir Alan Wilkie, *born* 1947, *apptd* 2004
Hon. Sir Paul Walker, *born* 1954, *apptd* 2004
Hon. Sir Charles Openshaw, *born* 1947, *apptd* 2005
Hon. Dame Caroline Swift, DBE, *born* 1955, *apptd* 2005
Hon. Sir Brian Langstaff, *born* 1948, *apptd* 2005
Hon. Sir Stephen Irwin, *born* 1953, *apptd* 2006
Hon. Sir Nigel Teare, *born* 1952, *apptd* 2006
Hon. Sir Wyn Williams, *born* 1951, *apptd* 2007
Hon. Sir Timothy King, *born* 1949, *apptd* 2007
Hon. Sir John Saunders, *born* 1949, *apptd* 2007
Hon. Sir Julian Flaux, *born* 1955, *apptd* 2007
Hon. Sir David Foskett, *born* 1949, *apptd* 2007
Hon. Sir Robert Akenhead, *born* 1949, *apptd* 2007
Hon. Sir Nicholas Blake, *born* 1949, *apptd* 2007
Hon. Sir Ross Cranston, *born* 1948, *apptd* 2007
Hon. Sir Peter Coulson, *born* 1958, *apptd* 2008
Hon. Sir William Blair, *born* 1950, *apptd* 2008
Hon. Sir Nigel Sweeney, *born* 1954, *apptd* 2008
Hon. Dame Elizabeth Slade, DBE, *born* 1949, *apptd* 2008
Hon. Sir Nicholas Hamblen, *born* 1957, *apptd* 2008
Hon. Sir Gary Hickinbottom, *born* 1955, *apptd* 2009
Hon. Sir Timothy Holroyde, *born* 1955, *apptd* 2009
Hon. Sir Andrew Nicol, *born* 1951, *apptd* 2009
Hon. Sir Kenneth Parker, *born* 1945, *apptd* 2009
Hon. Sir Antony Edwards-Stuart, *born* 1946, *apptd* 2009
Hon. Dame Nicola Davies, DBE, *born* 1953, *apptd* 2010
Hon. Dame Kathryn Thirlwall, DBE, *born* 1957, *apptd* 2010
Hon. Sir Michael Supperstone, *born* 1950, *apptd* 2010
Hon. Sir Robin Spencer, *born* 1955, *apptd* 2010
Hon. Sir Keith Lindblom, *born* 1956, *apptd* 2010
Hon. Sir Henry Globe, *born* 1949, *apptd* 2011
Hon. Sir Andrew Popplewell, *born* 1959, *apptd* 2011
Hon. Sir Rabinder Singh, *born* 1964, *apptd* 2011
Hon. Dame Beverley Lang, DBE, *born* 1955, *apptd* 2011
Hon. Sir Charles Haddon-Cave, *born* 1956, *apptd* 2011
Hon. Sir Stephen Males, *born* 1955, *apptd* 2012
Hon. Sir Jeremy Stuart-Smith, *born* 1955, *apptd* 2012
Hon. Sir George Leggatt, *born* 1957, *apptd* 2012
Hon. Sir Mark Turner, *born* 1959, *apptd* 2013
Hon. Sir Jeremy Baker, *born* 1958, *apptd* 2013
Hon. Sir Stephen Stewart, *born* 1953, *apptd* 2013
Hon. Sir Robert Jay, QC, *born* 1959, *apptd* 2013
Hon. Sir James Dingemans, *born* 1964, *apptd* 2013
Hon. Sir Clive Lewis, *born* 1960, *apptd* 2013
Hon. Dame Sue Carr, DBE, *born* 1964, *apptd* 2013
Hon. Sir Stephen Phillips, *born* 1961, *apptd* 2013
Hon. Dame Geraldine Andrews, DBE, *born* 1959, *apptd* 2013

Hon. Dame Frances Patterson, DBE, *born* 1955, *apptd* 2013
Hon. Sir Nicholas Green, QC, *born* 1958, *apptd* 2013
Hon. Dame Ingrid Simler, DBE, *born* 1963, *apptd* 2013
Hon. Dame Elisabeth Laing, DBE, *born* 1956, *apptd* 2014
Hon. Sir William Davis, QC, *born* 1954, *apptd* 2014
Hon. Sir Mark Warby, QC, *born* 1958, *apptd* 2014
Hon. Sir Andrew Edis, *born* 1957, *apptd* 2014
Hon. Dame Maura McGowan, *born* 1957, *apptd* 2014
Hon. Sir James Goss, *born* 1953, *apptd* 2014
Hon. Sir Robin Knowles, *born* 1960, *apptd* 2014
Hon. Sir Ian Dove, *born* 1963, *apptd* 2014
Hon. Sir Andrew Gilbart, *born* 1950, *apptd* 2014
Hon. Sir David Holgate, *born* 1956, *apptd* 2014
Hon. Sir Timothy Kerr, *born* 1958, *apptd* 2015
Hon. Sir Simon Picken, *born* 1966, *apptd* 2015

The Queen's Bench Division also includes the Divisional Court, the Admiralty Court, Commercial Court and Technology and Construction Court.

## FAMILY DIVISION
*President* (£213,125), Rt. Hon. Sir James Munby, *born* 1948, *apptd* 2013
*Secretary,* Mrs Sarah Leung
*Clerk,* George Pitchley

JUDGES *as at September 2015* (each £177,988)
*Style,* The Hon. Mr/Mrs Justice [surname]

Hon. Sir Edward Holman, *born* 1947, *apptd* 1995
Hon. Dame Mary Hogg, DBE, *born* 1947, *apptd* 1995
Hon. Sir David Bodey, *born* 1947, *apptd* 1999
Hon. Dame Anna Pauffley, DBE, *born* 1956, *apptd* 2003
Hon. Sir Roderic Wood, *born* 1951, *apptd* 2004
Hon. Sir Andrew Moylan, *born* 1953, *apptd* 2007
Hon. Dame Judith Parker, DBE, *born* 1950, *apptd* 2008
Hon. Sir Jonathan Baker, *born* 1955, *apptd* 2009
Hon. Sir Nicholas Mostyn, *born* 1957, *apptd* 2010
Hon. Sir Peter Arthur Jackson, *born* 1955, *apptd* 2010
Hon. Dame Lucy Theis, DBE, *born* 1960, *apptd* 2010
Hon. Sir Philip Moor, *born* 1959, *apptd* 2011
Hon. Sir Stephen Cobb, *born* 1960, *apptd* 2013
Hon. Sir Michael Keehan, *born* 1960, *apptd* 2013
Hon. Sir Anthony Hayden, *born* 1961, *apptd* 2013
Hon. Dame Alison Russell, DBE, *born* 1958, *apptd* 2014
Hon. Roderick Newton, *born* 1958, *apptd* 2014
Hon. Dame Jennifer Roberts, *born* 1953, *apptd* 2014
Hon. Sir Alistair MacDonald, *born* 1970, *apptd* 2015

## DEPARTMENTS AND OFFICES OF THE SENIOR COURTS OF ENGLAND AND WALES
Royal Courts of Justice, London WC2A 2LL
T 020-7947 6000

## ADMINISTRATIVE COURT OFFICE
T 020-7947 6655
*Judge in charge of the Administrative Court* (£177,988), Hon. Sir Duncan Ouseley
*Master of the Crown Office, and Queen's Coroner and Attorney* (£106,040), M. Egan, QC
*Deputy Master of the Crown Office,* Mrs L. G. Knapman
*Court Manager,* Miss A. Lee

## ADMIRALTY, COMMERCIAL AND LONDON MERCANTILE COURT
Ground Floor, 7 Rolls Buildings, London EC4A 1NL
T 020-7947 6112
*Registrar* (£106,040), J. Kay, QC
*Admiralty Marshal,* M. Parker
*Admiralty Court Manager,* W. Lusty

*Judge in charge of the Commercial Court* (£177,988), Hon. Sir Julian Flaux
*Commercial Court Senior Lists Officer,* J. Kelly

**BANKRUPTCY AND COMPANIES COURT REGISTRY**
7 Rolls Building, Fetter Lane, London EC4A 1NL T 020-7947 6294
*Chief Registrar* (132,184), S. Baister
*Bankruptcy Registrars* (£106,040), S. Barber; Briggs; C. Derrett; C. Jones
*Court Manager,* T. Pollen

**CENTRAL OFFICE OF THE QUEEN'S BENCH DIVISION**
*Senior Master and Queen's Remembrancer* (£132,184), B. Fontaine
*Masters of the Queen's Bench Division* (£106,040), J. D. Cook; R. Eastman; Gidden; J. K. Kay, QC; Leslie; V. McCloud; R. R. Roberts; B. Yoxall
*Court Manager,* Miss A. Lee

**CHANCERY CHAMBERS**
7 Rolls Building, Fetter Lane, London EC4A 1NL T 020-7947 7391
*Chief Master* (£132,184), M. Marsh
*Masters Chancery* (£106,040), T. J. Bowles; J. E. Clark; N. S. Price; P. R. Teverson
*Court Manager,* T. Pollen

**COSTS OFFICE**
T 020-7947 6423
*Senior Costs Judge* (£132,184), A. Gordon-Saker
*Masters of the Senior Courts* (£106,040), C. D. N. Campbell; P. Haworth; C. Leonard; J. E. O'Hare; J. Rowley; J. Simons
*Court Manager,* S. Christou

**COURT OF APPEAL CIVIL DIVISION**
T 020-7947 6915
*Deputy Registrars,* Marie Bancroft-Rimmer; Sally Meacher
*Court Manager,* Miss K. Langan

**COURT OF APPEAL CRIMINAL DIVISION**
T 020-7947 6011
*Registrar* (£106,040), M. Egan, QC
*Deputy Registrar,* Mrs L. G. Knapman
*Court Manager,* Miss C. Brownbill

**COURT OF PROTECTION**
First Avenue House, 42–49 High Holborn, London WC1V 6NP
T 0300-456 4600
*Senior Judge* (£132,184), D. Lush
*Court Manager,* J. Matthews

**ELECTION PETITIONS OFFICE**
Room E113, Royal Courts of Justice, Strand, London WC2A 2LL
T 020-7947 6877

The office accepts petitions and deals with all matters relating to the questioning of parliamentary, European parliament, local government and parish elections, and with applications for relief under the 'representation of the people' legislation.
*Prescribed Officer, The Senior Master and Senior Remembrancer* (£132,184), B. Fontaine
*Chief Clerk,* Geraint Evans

**EXAMINERS OF THE COURT**
Empowered to take examination of witnesses in all divisions of the High Court.

**PRINCIPAL REGISTRY (FAMILY DIVISION)**
First Avenue House, 42–49 High Holborn, London WC1V 6NP
T 020-7421 8594
*Senior District Judge* (£132,184), P. Waller
*District Judges* (£106,040), Mrs A. Aitken; Ms Y. Gibson; Mrs L. Gordon-Saker; Harper; Ms H. Macgregor; R. Robinson; C. Simmonds

**TECHNOLOGY AND CONSTRUCTION COURT (TCC)**
Ground Floor, 7 Rolls Building, Fetter Lane, London EC4A 1NL
T 020-7947 7156
*Judge in charge of the TCC* (£177,988), Hon. Mr Justice Edwards-Stuart
*Court Manager,* W. Lusty
*List Officer,* S. Gibbon

**COURT FUNDS OFFICE**
Glasgow G58 1AB T 0300-020 0199

The Court Funds Office (CFO), established in 1726, provides a banking and administration service for the civil courts throughout England and Wales, including the High Court.
*Head of CFO,* Eddie Bloomfield

**OFFICIAL SOLICITOR AND PUBLIC TRUSTEE**
Victory House, 30–34 Kingsway, London WC2B 6EX

The Official Solicitor and the Public Trustee are independent statutory office holders. Their office (OSPT) is an arms-length body of the Ministry of Justice that exists to support their work.The Official Solicitor provides access to the justice system to those who are vulnerable by virtue of minority or lack of mental capacity. The Public Trustee acts as executor or administrator of estates and as the appointed trustee of settlements, providing an effective executor and trustee service of last resort.
*Official Solicitor to the Senior Courts,* Alistair Pitblado
*Public Trustee,* Eddie Bloomfield

**PROBATE SERVICE**
London Probate Department
PRFD, 7th Floor, First Avenue House, 42–49 High Holborn, London WC1V 6NP T 020-7421 8500
*Probate Manager,* Ms T. Constantinou

**DISTRICT PROBATE REGISTRIES**
*Birmingham District*
*Brighton District*
*Bristol District*
*Cardiff District (Wales)*
*Ipswich District*
*Leeds District*
*Liverpool District*
*Manchester District*
*Newcastle District*
*Oxford District*
*Winchester District*

**JUDGE ADVOCATES GENERAL**
The Judge Advocate General is the judicial head of the Service justice system, and the leader of the judges who preside over trials in the court martial and other Service courts. The defendants are service personnel from the Royal Navy, the army and the Royal Air Force, and civilians accompanying them overseas.

JUDGE ADVOCATE GENERAL OF THE FORCES
9th Floor, Thomas More Building, Royal Courts of Justice, Strand, London WC2A 2LL
T 020-7218 8095
*Judge Advocate General* (£151,112), His Hon. Judge Blackett
*Vice Judge Advocate General* (£124,445), Michael Hunter
*Assistant Judge Advocates General* (£106,040), J. P. Camp;
M. R. Elsom; R. D. Hill; A. M. Large; A. J. B. McGrigor;
E. Peters
*Style,* Judge [surname]

## HIGH COURT AND CROWN COURT CENTRES

First-tier centres deal with both civil and criminal cases and are served by high court and circuit judges. Second-tier centres deal with criminal cases only and are served by high court and circuit judges. Third-tier centres deal with criminal cases only and are served only by circuit judges.

LONDON REGION
*First-tier* – None
*Second-tier* – Central Criminal Court
*Third-tier* – Blackfriars, Croydon, Harrow, Inner London, Isleworth, Kingston upon Thames, Snaresbrook, Southwark, Wood Green, Woolwich
*Delivery Director,* Sheila Proudlock, 3rd Floor, Rose Court, 2 Southwark Bridge, London SE1 9HS

The high court (first-tier) in Greater London sits at the Royal Courts of Justice.

MIDLANDS REGION
*First-tier* – Birmingham, Lincoln, Nottingham, Stafford, Warwick
*Second-tier* – Leicester, Northampton, Shrewsbury, Worcester, Wolverhampton
*Third-tier* – Coventry, Derby, Hereford, Stoke on Trent
*Delivery Director,* Lucy Garrod, 6th Floor, Temple Court, Bull Street, Birmingham B4 6WF

NORTH-EAST REGION
*First-tier* – Leeds, Newcastle upon Tyne, Sheffield, Teesside
*Second-tier* – Bradford, York
*Third-tier* – Doncaster, Durham, Kingston upon Hull, Great Grimsby
*Delivery Director,* Mark Swales, 17th Floor, West Riding House, Albion Street, Leeds LS1 5AA T 0113-251 1204

NORTH-WEST REGION
*First-tier* – Carlisle, Chester, Liverpool, Manchester (Crown Square), Preston
*Third-tier* – Barrow in Furness, Bolton, Burnley, Knutsford, Lancaster, Manchester (Minshull Street), Warrington
*Delivery Director,* Gill Hague, Manchester Civil Justice Centre, 1 Bridge Street West, Manchester M60 1UR T 0161-240 5000

SOUTH-EAST REGION
*First-tier* – Cambridge, Chelmsford, Lewes, Norwich, Oxford
*Second-tier* – Guildford, Ipswich, Luton, Maidstone, Reading, St Albans
*Third-tier* – Aylesbury, Basildon, Canterbury, Chichester, Croydon, King's Lynn, Peterborough, Southend
*Delivery Director,* Chris Jennings, 9th Floor, 102 Petty France, London SW1H 9AJ T 020-3206 0627

SOUTH-WEST REGION
*First-tier* – Bristol, Exeter, Truro, Winchester
*Second-tier* – Dorchester & Weymouth, Gloucester, Plymouth

*Third-tier* – Barnstaple, Bournemouth, Newport (IoW), Portsmouth, Salisbury, Southampton, Swindon, Taunton
*Delivery Director,* Sandra Aston, PO Box 484, Queensway House, Weston-super-Mare, N. Somerset BS23 9BJ
T 01934 528668

WALES REGION
*First-tier* – Caernarfon, Cardiff, Merthyr Tydfil, Mold, Swansea
*Second-tier* – Carmarthen, Newport, Welshpool
*Third-tier* – Dolgellau, Haverfordwest
*Delivery Director,* Luigi Strinati, Wales Support Unit, 2nd Floor, Cardiff and Vale of Glamorgan Magistrates' Court, Fitzalan Place, Cardiff CF24 0RZ T 029-2067 8311

## CIRCUIT JUDGES

Circuit judges are barristers of at least seven years' standing or recorders of at least five years' standing. Circuit judges serve in the county courts and the crown court.
*Style,* His/Her Hon. Judge [surname]
*Senior Presiding Judge,* Rt. Hon. Lord Justice Gross
*Senior Circuit Judges,* each £142,745
*Circuit Judges at the Central Criminal Court, London (Old Bailey Judges),* each £142,745
*Circuit Judges,* each £132,184

MIDLAND CIRCUIT
*Presiding Judges,* Hon. Mr Justice Haddon-Cave; Hon. Mrs Justice Thirlwall

NORTH-EASTERN CIRCUIT
*Presiding Judges,* Hon. Mr Justice Globe; Hon. Mr Justice Males

NORTHERN CIRCUIT
*Presiding Judges,* Hon. Mr Justice Holroyde; Hon. Mr Justice Turner

SOUTH-EASTERN CIRCUIT
*Presiding Judges,* Hon. Mr Justice Singh; Hon. Mr Justice Spencer; Hon. Mr Justice Stuart-Smith; Hon. Mr Justice Sweeney

WALES CIRCUIT
*Presiding Judges,* Hon. Mrs Justice Davies; Hon. Mr Justice Williams

WESTERN CIRCUIT
*Presiding Judges,* Hon. Mr Justice Dingemans; Hon. Mr Justice Teare

## DISTRICT JUDGES

District judges, formerly known as registrars of the court, are solicitors of at least seven years' standing and serve in county courts.
*District Judges,* each £106,040

## DISTRICT JUDGES (MAGISTRATES' COURTS)

District judges (magistrates' courts), formerly known as stipendiary magistrates, serve in magistrates courts where they hear criminal cases, youth cases and some civil proceedings. Many also hear family cases in the single family court. Some may be authorised to handle extradition proceedings and terrorist cases. District judges (magistrates' courts) are appointed following competition conducted by the Judicial Appointments Commission.
*District Judges (Magistrates' Courts),* each £106,040

**OFFICE OF THE CHIEF MAGISTRATE**
181 Marylebone Road, London NW1 5BR
T 020-3126 3100

The Chief Magistrate (senior district judge) is responsible for hearing many of the sensitive or complex cases – extradition and special jurisdiction cases in particular – in the magistrates' courts. The Chief Magistrate also supports and guides district judges (magistrates' court), and liaises with the senior judiciary and presiding judges on matters pertaining to magistrates' courts.
The Office of the Chief Magistrate provides administrative support to both the Chief Magistrate and to all the district judges sitting at magistrates' courts in England and Wales.
*Chief Magistrate,* Howard Riddle
*Deputy Chief Magistrate,* Emma Arbuthnot

**CROWN PROSECUTION SERVICE**
Rose Court, 2 Southwark Bridge Road, London SE1 9HS
T 020-3357 0000 E enquiries@cps.gsi.gov.uk W www.cps.gov.uk

The Crown Prosecution Service (CPS) is responsible for prosecuting cases investigated by the police in England and Wales, with the exception of cases conducted by the Serious Fraud Office and certain minor offences.
The CPS is headed by the director of public prosecutions (DPP), who works under the superintendence of the attorney-general. The service is divided into 13 areas across England and Wales, with each area led by a chief crown prosecutor.
*Director of Public Prosecutions,* Alison Saunders, CB
*Chief Executive,* Peter Lewis, CB
*Chief Operating Officer,* Jim Brisbane
*Principal Legal Adviser,* Alison Levitt, QC
*Directors,* Jim Brisbane *(Operations);* Helen Kershaw *(Private Office);* Joanna Millington *(Communication);* Paul Staff *(Corporate Services and Finance);* Mark Summerfield *(Human Resources)*

**CPS AREAS**
EAST MIDLANDS, 2 King Edward Court, King Edward Street, Nottingham NG1 1EL T 0115-852 3300
*Chief Crown Prosecutor,* Steve Chappell
EASTERN, County House, 100 New London Road, Chelmsford, Essex CM2 0RG T 01245-455800
*Chief Crown Prosecutor,* Jenny Hopkins
LONDON, 5th Floor, Rose Court, 2 Southwark Bridge, London SE1 9HS T 020-3357 0000
*Chief Crown Prosecutor,* Baljit Ubhey, OBE
MERSEY–CHESHIRE, 2nd Floor, Walker House, Exchange Flags, Liverpool L2 3YL T 0151-239 6400
*Chief Crown Prosecutor,* Claire Lindley
NORTH EAST, St Ann's Quay, 112 Quayside, Newcastle Upon Tyne, NE1 3BD T 0191-260 4200
*Chief Crown Prosecutor,* Gerry Wareham
NORTH WEST, 1st Floor, Stocklund House, Castle Street, Carlisle CA3 8SY T 01228-882900
*Chief Crown Prosecutor (acting),* Ian Rushton
SOUTH EAST, Riding Gate House, 37 Old Dover Road, Canterbury, Kent CT1 3JG T 01227-866000
*Chief Crown Prosecutor,* Jaswant Narwal
SOUTH WEST, 5th Floor, Kite Wing, Temple Quay House, 2 The Square, Bristol BS1 6PN T 0117-930 2800
*Chief Crown Prosecutor,* Barry Hughes
THAMES AND CHILTERN, Eaton Court, 112 Oxford Road, Reading, Berks RG1 7LL T 0118-951 3600
*Chief Crown Prosecutor,* Adrian Foster
WALES, 20th Floor, Capital Tower, Greyfriars Road, Cardiff CF10 3PL T 029-2080 3800
*Chief Crown Prosecutor,* Ed Beltrami

WESSEX, 3rd Floor, Black Horse House, 8–10 Leigh Road, Eastleigh, Hants SO50 9FH T 02380-673 800
*Chief Crown Prosecutor,* Kate Brown
WEST MIDLANDS, Colmore Gate, 2 Colmore Row, Birmingham B3 2QA T 0121-262 1300
*Chief Crown Prosecutor,* Grace Ononiwu, OBE
YORKSHIRE AND HUMBERSIDE, 27 Park Place, Leeds LS1 2SZ T 0113-290 2700
*Chief Crown Prosecutor,* Martin Goldman

**HER MAJESTY'S COURTS AND TRIBUNALS SERVICE**
1st Floor, 102 Petty France, London SW1H 9AJ
W www.justice.gov.uk

Her Majesty's Courts Service and the Tribunals Service merged on 1 April 2011 to form HM Courts and Tribunals Service. It is an agency of the Ministry of Justice, operating as a partnership between the Lord Chancellor, the Lord Chief Justice and the Senior President of Tribunals. It is responsible for administering the criminal, civil and family courts and tribunals in England and Wales and non-devolved tribunals in Scotland and Northern Ireland.
*Chief Executive,* Natalie Ceeney

**JUDICIAL APPOINTMENTS COMMISSION**
1st Floor, Zone A, 102 Petty France, London SW1H 9AJ
T 020-3334 0123 E jaas@jac.gsi.gov.uk
W jjac.judiciary.gov.uk

The Judicial Appointments Commission was established as an independent non-departmental public body in April 2006 by the Constitutional Reform Act 2005. Its role is to select judicial office holders independently of government (a responsibility previously held by the Lord Chancellor) for courts and tribunals in England and Wales, and for some tribunals whose jurisdiction extends to Scotland or Northern Ireland. It has a statutory duty to encourage diversity in the range of persons available for selection and is sponsored by the Ministry of Justice and accountable to parliament through the Lord Chancellor. It is made up of 15 commissioners, including a chair.
*Chair,* Christopher Stephens
*Commissioners,* Martin Forde, QC; Debra van Gene; Prof. Emily Jackson; Prof. Noel Lloyd, CBE; Rt. Hon. Dame Julia Macur, DBE; Alexandra Marks; Katharine Rainsford; Lt.-Gen. Sir Andrew Ridgway, KBE, CB; Lucy Scott-Moncrieff, CBE; District Judge Simmonds; Dame Valerie Strachan, DCB; Hon. Sir Alan Wilkie
*Chief Executive,* Nigel Reeder

**DIRECTORATE OF JUDICIAL OFFICES**
The Judicial Office was established in April 2006 to support the judiciary in discharging its responsibilities under the Constitutional Reform Act 2005. It is led by a chief executive, who reports to the Lord Chief Justice rather than to ministers, and its work is directed by the judiciary rather than by the administration of the day. The Judicial Office incorporates the Judicial College, sponsorship of the Family and Civil Justice Councils, the Office for Judicial Complaints and Office of the Chief Coroner.

CHIEF EXECUTIVE'S OFFICE
T 020-7947 7598
*Chief Executive,* Jillian Kay

**JUDICIAL COMMITTEE OF THE PRIVY COUNCIL**

The Judicial Committee of the Privy Council is the final court of appeal for the United Kingdom overseas territories (*see* UK Overseas Territories section), crown dependencies and those independent Commonwealth countries which have retained this avenue of appeal and the sovereign base areas of Akrotiri and Dhekelia in Cyprus. The committee also hears appeals against pastoral schemes under the Pastoral Measure 1983, and deals with appeals from veterinary disciplinary bodies.

Until October 2009, the Judicial Committee of the Privy Council was the final arbiter in disputes as to the legal competence of matters done or proposed by the devolved legislative and executive authorities in Scotland, Wales and Northern Ireland. This is now the responsibility of the UK Supreme Court.

Between 1 April 2014 and 31 March 2015 the Judicial Committee heard a total of 58 appeals.

The members of the Judicial Committee are the justices of the supreme court, and Privy Counsellors who hold or have held high judicial office in the United Kingdom or in certain designated courts of Commonwealth countries from which appeals are taken to committee.

**JUDICIAL COMMITTEE OF THE PRIVY COUNCIL**
Parliament Square, London SW1A 2AJ T 020-7960 1500
W www.jcpc.uk
*Registrar of the Privy Council,* Louise di Mambro

## SCOTTISH JUDICATURE

Scotland has a legal system separate from, and differing greatly from, the English legal system in enacted law, judicial procedure and the structure of courts.

In Scotland the system of public prosecution is headed by the Lord Advocate and is independent of the police, who have no say in the decision to prosecute. The Lord Advocate, discharging his functions through the Crown Office in Edinburgh, is responsible for prosecutions in the high court, sheriff courts and justice of the peace courts. Prosecutions in the high court are prepared by the Crown Office and conducted in court by one of the law officers, by an advocate-depute, or by a solicitor advocate. In the inferior courts the decision to prosecute is made and prosecution is preferred by procurators fiscal, who are lawyers and full-time civil servants subject to the directions of the Crown Office. A permanent legally qualified civil servant, known as the crown agent, is responsible for the running of the Crown Office and the organisation of the Procurator Fiscal Service, of which he or she is the head.

Scotland is divided into six sheriffdoms, each with a full-time sheriff principal. The sheriffdoms are further divided into sheriff court districts, each of which has a legally qualified resident sheriff or sheriffs, who are the judges of the court.

In criminal cases sheriffs principal and sheriffs have the same powers; sitting with a jury of 15 members, they may try more serious cases on indictment, or, sitting alone, may try lesser cases under summary procedure. Minor summary offences are dealt with in justice of the peace courts, which replaced district courts formerly operated by local authorities, and presided over by lay justices of the peace (of whom some 500 regularly sit in court) and, in Glasgow only, by stipendiary magistrates. Juvenile offenders (children under 16) may be brought before an informal children's hearing comprising three local lay people. The superior criminal court is the high court of justiciary which is both a trial and an appeal court. Cases on indictment are tried by a high court judge, sitting with a jury of 15, in Edinburgh and on circuit in other towns. Appeals from the lower courts against conviction or sentence are also heard by the high court,

which sits as an appeal court only in Edinburgh. There is no further appeal to the UK supreme court in criminal cases.

In civil cases the jurisdiction of the sheriff court extends to most kinds of action. Appeals against decisions of the sheriff may be made to the sheriff principal and thence to the court of session, or direct to the court of session, which sits only in Edinburgh. The court of session is divided into the inner and the outer house. The outer house is a court of first instance in which cases are heard by judges sitting singly, sometimes with a jury of 12. The inner house, itself subdivided into two divisions of equal status, is mainly an appeal court. Appeals may be made to the inner house from the outer house as well as from the sheriff court. An appeal may be made from the inner house to the UK supreme court.

The judges of the court of session are the same as those of the high court of justiciary, with the Lord President of the court of session also holding the office of Lord Justice General in the high court. Senators of the College of Justice are Lords Commissioners of Justiciary as well as judges of the court of session. On appointment, a senator takes a judicial title, which is retained for life. Although styled The Hon./Rt. Hon. Lord, the senator is not a peer, although some judges are peers in their own right.

The office of coroner does not exist in Scotland. The local procurator fiscal inquires privately into sudden or suspicious deaths and may report findings to the crown agent. In some cases a fatal accident inquiry may be held before the sheriff.

## COURT OF SESSION AND HIGH COURT OF JUSTICIARY

*The Lord President and Lord Justice General* (£220,655),
   Rt. Hon. Lord Gill, *born* 1942, *apptd* 2012
*Private Secretary,* P. Gilmour

INNER HOUSE
*Lords of Session* (each £202,668)

FIRST DIVISION
*The Lord President*

Rt. Hon. Lord Eassie (Ronald Mackay), *born* 1945,
   *apptd* 2006
Rt. Hon. Lord Menzies (Duncan Menzies), *born* 1953,
   *apptd* 2012
Rt. Hon. Lady Smith (Anne Smith), *born* 1955, *apptd* 2012
Rt. Hon. Lord Brodie (Philip Brodie), *born* 1950, *apptd* 2012
Rt. Hon. Lady Clark of Calton (Lynda Clark), *born* 1949,
   *apptd* 2013

SECOND DIVISION
*Lord Justice Clerk* (£213,125), Rt. Hon. Lord Carloway,
   *born* 1954, *apptd* 2012
Rt. Hon. Lady Paton (Ann Paton), *born* 1952, *apptd* 2007
Rt. Hon. Lady Dorrian (Leona Dorrian), *born* 1957, *apptd*
   2012
Rt. Hon. Lord Bracadale (Alistair Campbell), *born* 1949,
   *apptd* 2013
Rt. Hon. Lord Drummond Young (James Drummond Young),
   *born* 1950, *apptd* 2013
Rt. Hon. Lord Malcolm (Colin M. Campbell), *born* 1953,
   *apptd* 2007

OUTER HOUSE
*Lords of Session* (each £177,988)
Hon. Lord Glennie (Angus Glennie), *born* 1950, *apptd* 2005
Hon. Lord Kinclaven (Alexander F. Wylie), *born* 1951,
   *apptd* 2005
Hon. Lord Turnbull (Alan Turnbull), *born* 1958, *apptd* 2006

Hon. Lord Brailsford (Sidney Brailsford), *born* 1954, *apptd* 2006
Hon. Lord Uist (Roderick Macdonald), *born* 1951, *apptd* 2006
Hon. Lord Matthews (Hugh Matthews), *born* 1953, *apptd* 2007
Hon. Lord Woolman (Stephen Woolman), *born* 1953, *apptd* 2008
Hon. Lord Pentland (Paul Cullen), *born* 1957, *apptd* 2008
Hon. Lord Bannatyne (Iain Peebles), *born* 1954, *apptd* 2008
Hon. Lady Stacey (Valerie E. Stacey), *born* 1954, *apptd* 2009
Hon. Lord Tyre (Colin Tyre), *born* 1956, *apptd* 2010
Hon. Lord Doherty (Raymond Doherty), *born* 1958, *apptd* 2010
Hon. Lord Stewart (Angus Stewart), *born* 1946, *apptd* 2010
Rt. Hon. Lord Boyd of Duncansby (Colin Boyd), *born* 1953, *apptd* 2012
Hon. Lord Jones (Michael Jones), *born* 1948, *apptd* 2012
Hon. Lord Burns (David Burns), *born* 1952, *apptd* 2012
Hon. Lady Scott (Margaret Scott), *born* 1960, *apptd* 2012
Hon. Lady Wise (Morag Wise), *born* 1963, *apptd* 2013
Hon. Lord Armstrong (Iain Armstrong), *born* 1956, *apptd* 2013
Hon. Lady Rae (Rita Rae), *born* 1950, *apptd* 2014
Hon. Lady Wolffe (Sarah Wolffe), *apptd* 2014

## COURT OF SESSION AND HIGH COURT OF JUSTICIARY
Parliament House, Parliament Square, Edinburgh EH1 1RQ
T 0131-225 2595

*Principal Clerk of Session and Justiciary,* G. Marwick
*Deputy Principal Clerk of Session and Principal Extractor,* G. Prentice
*Deputy Principal Clerk of Justiciary,* J. Moyes
*Depute in Charge of Offices of Court,* Y. Anderson
*Officer in Charge of Justiciary Office,* Roddy MacPherson
*Keeper of the Rolls,* G. Combe
*Depute Clerks,* D. Cullen; A. Hutchison; C. Reid
*Appeal Manager,* F. Merrilees
*Clerking Service Manager,* D. MacLeod
*Depute Clerks of Session and Justiciary,* L. Alexander; N. Boyle; R. Broome; G. Burton; Z. Conway; L. Curran; H. Fraser; A. Galloway; K. Keir; T. Kell; A. Lynch; N. Marchant; R. Martin; M. McGrane; G. McLeod; L. McNamara; L. Morgan; D. Morrison; C. Munn; K. Neal; R. Newlands; K. O'Hare; C. Scott; G. Scott; L. Sexto; C. Stark; P. Weir

## JUDICIAL APPOINTMENTS BOARD FOR SCOTLAND
38–39 Drumsheugh Gardens, Edinburgh EH3 7SW
T 0131-528 5101 W www.judicialappointmentsscotland.org.uk

The board's remit is to provide the first minister with the names of candidates recommended for appointment to the posts of senator of the college of justice, chair of the Scottish Land Court, sheriff principal, sheriff and part-time sheriff.
*Chair,* Sir Muir Russell, KCB, FRSE

## JUDICIAL OFFICE FOR SCOTLAND
Parliament House, Edinburgh EH1 1RQ
T 0131-240 6677 W www.scotland-judiciary.org.uk

The Judicial Office for Scotland came into being on 1 April 2010 as part of the changes introduced by the Judiciary and Courts (Scotland) Act 2008. It provides support for the Lord President in his role as head of the Scottish judiciary with responsibility for the training, welfare, deployment and conduct of judges and the efficient disposal of business in the courts.
*Executive Director,* Steve Humphreys

## SCOTTISH COURT SERVICE
Saughton House, Broomhouse Drive, Edinburgh EH11 3XD
T 0131-444 3300 W www.scotcourts.gov.uk

The Scottish Court Service is responsible for the provision of staff, buildings and technology to support Scotland's courts, the independent judiciary, the courts' Rules Councils and the Office of the Public Guardian. On 1 April 2010 it was established by the Judiciary and Courts (Scotland) Act 2008 as an independent body, governed by a corporate board and chaired by the Lord President.
*Chief Executive,* Eric McQueen

## SCOTTISH GOVERNMENT JUSTICE DIRECTORATE
Legal System Division, Room 2W, St Andrew's House, Edinburgh EH1 3DG
T 0131-556 8400

The Justice Directorate is responsible for the appointment of judges and sheriffs to meet the needs of the business of the supreme and sheriffs court in Scotland. It is also responsible for providing resources for the efficient administration of certain specialist courts and tribunals.
*Director (acting),* Neil Rennick

## SCOTTISH LAND COURT
126 George Street, Edinburgh EH2 4HH
T 0131-271 4360

The court deals with disputes relating to agricultural and crofting land in Scotland.
*Chair* (£142,745), Hon. Lord McGhie (James McGhie), QC
*Deputy Chair,* R. J. Macleod
*Members,* A. Macdonald *(part-time)*; J. A. Smith *(part-time)*
*Principal Clerk,* Barbara Brown

## SHERIFF COURT OF CHANCERY
27 Chambers Street, Edinburgh EH1 1LB
T 0131-225 2525

The court deals with service of heirs and completion of title in relation to heritable property.
*Sheriff of Chancery,* M. Stephen

## SHERIFF COURTS
The majority of cases in Scotland are handled by one of the 39 sheriff courts. Criminal cases are heard by a sheriff and a jury (solemn procedure) but can be heard by a sheriff alone (summary procedure). Civil cases are heard by a single sheriff.

Scotland is split into six sheriffdoms, each headed by a sheriff principal.

### SALARIES
Sheriff Principal, £142,745
Sheriff, £132,184

### SHERIFFDOMS
GLASGOW AND STRATHKELVIN
*Sheriff Principal,* C. A. L. Scott, QC
GRAMPIAN, HIGHLAND AND ISLANDS
*Sheriff Principal,* D. C. W. Pyle
LOTHIAN AND BORDERS
*Sheriff Principal,* M. M. Stephen, QC
NORTH STRATHCLYDE
*Sheriff Principal,* D. L. Murray
SOUTH STRATHCLYDE, DUMFRIES AND GALLOWAY
*Sheriff Principal,* I. R. Abercrombie, QC
TAYSIDE, CENTRAL AND FIFE
*Sheriff Principal,* W. M. Lewis

## JUSTICE OF THE PEACE COURTS

Justice of the peace courts replaced district courts and are a unique feature of Scotland's judicial system. Justices of the peace are lay magistrates who either sit alone, or in a bench of three, and deal with summary crimes such as speeding and careless driving. In court, justices have access to solicitors, who fulfill the role of legal advisers or clerks of court.

A justice of the peace court can be presided over by a stipendiary magistrate – a legally qualified solicitor or advocate who sits alone. They deal with more serious summary business similar to sheriffs, such as drink driving and assault. All sheriffs principal have powers to appoint stipendiary magistrates, but at present they have only been appointed in the justice of the peace court in the Sheriffdom of Glasgow and Strathkelvin.

## CROWN OFFICE AND PROCURATOR FISCAL SERVICE

CROWN OFFICE
25 Chambers Street, Edinburgh EH1 1LA
T 01389-739557 W www.crownoffice.gov.uk
*Chief Executive and Crown Agent*, Catherine Dyer

PROCURATORS FISCAL

PAY BAND AND SALARY SCALE: £75,000–£162,500

NORTH FEDERATION
*Area Procurator Fiscal*, Liam Murphy
EAST FEDERATION
*Area Procurator Fiscal*, John Dunn
WEST FEDERATION
*Area Procurator Fiscal*, David Harvie
NATIONAL FEDERATION
*Director of Serious Casework*, John Logue

## COURT OF THE LORD LYON

HM New Register House, Edinburgh EH1 3YT
T 0131-556 7255 W www.lyon-court.com

The Court of the Lord Lyon is the Scottish Court of Chivalry (including the genealogical jurisdiction of the *Ri-Sennachie* of Scotland's Celtic kings). The Lord Lyon King of Arms has jurisdiction, subject to appeal to the Court of Session and the House of Lords, in questions of heraldry and the right to bear arms. The court also administers the Public Register of All Arms and Bearings and the Public Register of All Genealogies in Scotland. Pedigrees are established by decrees of Lyon Court and by letters patent. As Royal Commissioner in Armory, the Lord Lyon grants patents of arms to virtuous and well-deserving Scots and to petitioners (personal or corporate) in the Queen's overseas realms of Scottish connection, and also issues birthbrieves. For information on Her Majesty's Officers of Arms in Scotland, *see* the Court of the Lord Lyon in the Public Bodies section.
*Lord Lyon King of Arms*, Dr Joseph J. Morrow
*Lyon Clerk and Keeper of the Records*, Mrs C. G. W. Roads, LVO, FSA SCOT, FSA
*Procurator Fiscal*, Alexander M. S. Green
*Macer*, Roderick Macpherson

## NORTHERN IRELAND JUDICATURE

In Northern Ireland the legal system and the structure of courts closely resemble those of England and Wales; there are, however, often differences in enacted law.

The court of judicature of Northern Ireland comprises the court of appeal, the high court of justice and the crown court.

The practice and procedure of these courts is similar to that in England. The superior civil court is the high court of justice, from which an appeal lies to the Northern Ireland court of appeal; the UK supreme court is the final civil appeal court.

The crown court, served by high court and county court judges, deals with criminal trials on indictment. Cases are heard before a judge and, except those certified by the Director of Public Prosecutions under the Justice and Security Act 2007, a jury. Appeals from the crown court against conviction or sentence are heard by the Northern Ireland court of appeal; the UK supreme court is the final court of appeal.

The decision to prosecute in criminal cases in Northern Ireland rests with the Director of Public Prosecutions.

Minor criminal offences are dealt with in magistrates' courts by a legally qualified district judge (magistrates' courts) and, where an offender is under the age of 18, by youth courts each consisting of a district judge (magistrates' courts) and two lay magistrates (at least one of whom must be a woman). As at 1 June 2015 there were 210 lay magistrates in Northern Ireland. Appeals from magistrates' courts are heard by the county court, or by the court of appeal on a point of law or an issue as to jurisdiction.

Magistrates' courts in Northern Ireland can deal with certain classes of civil case but most minor civil cases are dealt with in county courts. Judgments of all civil courts are enforceable through a centralised procedure administered by the Enforcement of Judgments Office.

## COURT OF JUDICATURE

The Royal Courts of Justice, Chichester Street, Belfast BT1 3JF
T 0300-200 7812
*Lord Chief Justice of Northern Ireland* (£220,655),
Rt. Hon. Sir Declan Morgan, *born* 1952, *apptd* 2009
*Principal Private Secretary*, Laurene McAlpine

LORDS JUSTICES OF APPEAL (£202,668)
*Style*, The Rt. Hon. Lord Justice [surname]

Rt. Hon. Sir Paul Girvan, *born* 1948, *apptd* 2007
Rt. Hon. Sir Patrick Coghlin, *born* 1945, *apptd* 2008
Rt. Hon. Sir John Gillen, *born* 1947, *apptd* 2014

HIGH COURT JUDGES (£177,988)
*Style*, The Hon. Mr Justice [surname]

Hon. Sir Ronald Weatherup, *born* 1947, *apptd* 2001
Hon. Sir Reginald Weir, *born* 1947, *apptd* 2003
Hon. Sir Donnell Deeny, *born* 1950, *apptd* 2004
Hon. Sir Benjamin Stephens, *born* 1954, *apptd* 2007
Hon. Sir Seamus Treacy, *born* 1956, *apptd* 2007
Hon. Sir Bernard McCloskey, *born* 1956, *apptd* 2008
Hon. Sir Paul Maguire, *born* 1952, *apptd* 2012
Hon. Sir Mark Horner, *born* 1956, *apptd* 2012
Hon. Sir John O'Hara, *born* 1956, *apptd* 2013

MASTERS OF THE HIGH COURT (£106,040)
Master Bell, *apptd* 2006; Master Hardstaff, *apptd* 2014; Master Kelly, *apptd* 2005; Master McCorry, *apptd* 2011; Master Sweeney, *apptd* 2015; Master A. Wells, *apptd* 2013; Master H. Wells, *apptd* 2005

OFFICIAL SOLICITOR
*Official Solicitor to the Court of Judicature*, Miss B. M. Donnelly

COUNTY COURTS

JUDGES (£132,184†)
*Style,* His/Her Hon. Judge [surname]

Judge Babington; Judge Devlin; Judge Finnegan, QC; Judge Fowler, QC; Judge Grant; Judge Kerr, QC; Judge Kinney; Judge Lynch, QC; Judge McColgan; Judge McFarland; Judge McReynolds; Judge Marrinan; Judge Miller, QC; Judge Philpott, QC; Judge Ramsay; Judge Sherrard; Judge Smyth

† County court judges are paid £142,745 so long as they are required to carry out significantly different work from their counterparts elsewhere in the UK

RECORDERS
*Belfast* (£154,165), Judge McFarland
*Londonderry* (£142,745), Judge Babington

DISTRICT JUDGES (£106,040)
Only barristers and solicitors with ten years' standing are eligible to become district judges. There are four district judges in Northern Ireland.

MAGISTRATES' COURTS

DISTRICT JUDGES (MAGISTRATES' COURTS)
(£106,040)
There are 21 district judges (magistrates' courts) in Northern Ireland.

NORTHERN IRELAND COURTS AND TRIBUNALS SERVICE
23–27 Oxford Street, Belfast BT1 3LA
T 0300-200 7812 W www.courtsni.gov.uk
*Chief Executive,* Ronnie Armour

CROWN SOLICITOR'S OFFICE
Royal Courts of Justice, Chichester Street, Belfast BT1 3JE
T 028-9054 2555
*Crown Solicitor,* J. Conn

PUBLIC PROSECUTION SERVICE
Linum Chambers, 2 Bedford Square, Belfast BT2 7ES
T 028-9089-7100 W www.ppsni.gov.uk
*Director of Public Prosecutions,* Barra McGrory, QC

# TRIBUNALS

Information on all the tribunals listed here, with the exception of the independent tribunals and the tribunals based in Scotland, Wales and Northern Ireland, can be found on the Ministry of Justice website (W www.justice.gov.uk/tribunals).

## HM COURTS AND TRIBUNALS SERVICE

102 Petty France, London SW1H 9AJ
W www.justice.gov.uk and
W https://courttribunalfinder.service.gov.uk
HM Courts Service and the Tribunals Service merged on 1 April 2011 to form HM Courts and Tribunals Service, an integrated agency providing support for the administration of justice in courts and tribunals. It is an agency within the Ministry of Justice, operating as a partnership between the Lord Chancellor, the Lord Chief Justice and the Senior President of Tribunals. It is responsible for the administration of the criminal, civil and family courts and tribunals in England and Wales and non-devolved tribunals in Scotland

and Northern Ireland. The agency's work is overseen by a board headed by an independent chair working with non-executive, executive and judicial members.

A two-tier tribunal system, comprising the First-tier Tribunal and Upper Tribunal, was established on 3 November 2008 as a result of radical reform under the Tribunals, Courts and Enforcement Act 2007. Both of these tiers are split into a number of separate chambers. These chambers group together individual tribunals (also known as 'jurisdictions') which deal with similar work or require similar skills. Cases start in the First-tier Tribunal and there is a right of appeal to the Upper Tribunal. Some tribunals transferred to the new two-tier system immediately, with more transferring between 2009 and 2011. The exception is employment tribunals, which remain outside this structure. The Act also allowed legally qualified tribunal chairs and adjudicators to swear the judicial oath and become judges.
*Senior President,* Rt. Hon. Sir Ernest Ryder, TD
*Chief Executive,* Natalie Ceeney, CBE

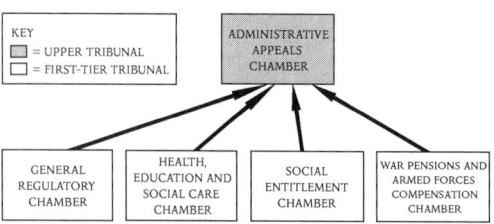

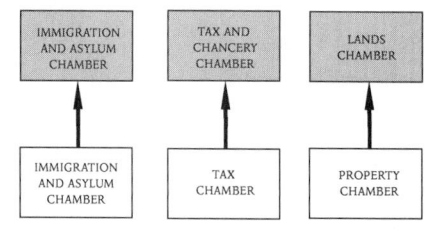

## FIRST-TIER TRIBUNAL

The main function of the First-tier Tribunal is to hear appeals by citizens against decisions of the government. In most cases appeals are heard by a panel made up of one judge and two specialists in their relevant field, known as 'members'. Both judges and members are appointed through the Independent Judicial Appointments Commission. Most of the tribunals administered by central government are part of the First-tier Tribunal, which is split into seven separate chambers.

### GENERAL REGULATORY CHAMBER
For all jurisdictions: General Regulatory Chamber, HMCTS, PO Box 9300, Leicester LE1 8DJ T 0300-123 4504
E grc@hmcts.gsi.gov.uk
*Chamber President,* Judge Lane*
*Judicial Leads,* Judge Brodrick (Transport); Judge McKenna (Charity)

*Acts as judicial lead for all jurisdictions with the exception of the ones specified above

### CHARITY
Under the Charities Act 2011 (only applicable to England and Wales), First-tier Tribunal (Charity) hears appeals against the decisions of the Charity Commission, applications for the review of decisions made by the Charity Commission and considers references from the Attorney-General or the Charity Commission on points of law.

### CLAIMS MANAGEMENT SERVICES
Under section 13 of the Compensation Act 2006, Claims Management Services hears appeals pertaining to decisions

made by the claims regulator, such as the regulator's decision to cancel or suspend a claims management licence, refuse authorisation for claims managment services or add conditions to a claims management licence. Claims management services include all companies and individuals that offer a service for people hoping to claim compensation for personal injury, mis-sold financial products and services, redundancy, criminial or industrial injury and housing disrepair.

### COMMUNITY RIGHT TO BID
The Community Right to Bid jurisdiction of the General Regulatory Chamber was established in January 2013 and hears appeals against review decisions made by local authorities to list your property as a community asset and give local communities the right to bid for it if you decide to sell. Individuals have the right to appeal against a listing decision under the Localism Act 2011 and the assets of community value (England) regulations 2012.

### COPYRIGHT LICENSING
Under the copyright (regulation of relevant licensing bodies) regulations 2014 a copyright licensing body may appeal to a First-tier Tribunal (Copyright Licensing) against a government decision to fine or impose a code of conduct on their organisation.

### ELECTRONIC COMMUNICATIONS AND POSTAL SERVICES
Hears appeals against decisions made by the Interception of Communications Commissioner under the Regulation of Investigatory Powers (Monetary Penalty Notices and Consents for Interceptions) Regulations 2011.

## ENVIRONMENT

First-tier Tribunal (Environment) was created to decide appeals regarding civil sanctions made by environmental regulators. Established in April 2010, the jurisdiction of the tribunal extends to England and Wales.

## ESTATE AGENTS

First-tier Tribunal (Estate Agents) hears appeals, under the Estate Agents Act 1979, against decisions made by the Office of Fair Trading pertaining to orders prohibiting a person from being employed as an estate agent when that person has been, for example, convicted of fraud or another offence involving dishonesty. The tribunal also hears appeals relating to decisions refusing to revoke or vary a prohibition order or warning order, as well as appeals regarding the issuing of a warning order when a person has not fulfilled their obligations under the Act.

## EXAM BOARD

Under the Education Act 1997 regulated awarding organisations can appeal to the Exam Board tribunal if they disagree with a decision by OFQUAL or the Welsh government to impose a fine, the amount of the fine, or to recover the costs of taking enforcement action. The board is an independent tribunal and hears appeals across England and Wales.

## FOOD

The food jurisdiction of the General Regulatory Chamber was established in January 2013 and hears appeals against some of the decisions taken by the Food Standards Agency, Department for Environment, Food and Rural Affairs and local authority trading standards departments. It also deals with appeals against decisions under the Fish Labelling (England) Regulations.

## GAMBLING

First-tier Tribunal (Gambling) hears and decides appeals against decisions made by the Gambling Commission under the Gambling Act 2005.

## IMMIGRATION SERVICES

First-tier Tribunal (Immigration Services) is an independent judicial body established in 2000. It hears appeals against decisions made by the Office of the Immigration Services Commissioner and considers disciplinary charges brought against immigration advisers by the Commissioner. The tribunal does not deal with immigration and asylum cases.

## INFORMATION RIGHTS

First-tier Tribunal (Information Rights) determines appeals against notices issued by the Information Commissioner under the Freedom of Information Act 2000 and other regulations.

When a minister of the crown issues a certificate on the grounds of national security, the appeal must be transferred to the Administrative Appeals Chamber of the Upper Tribunal on receipt.

## LETTING OR MANAGING AGENTS

First-tier Tribunal (Letting or Managing Agents) hears appeals against a decision by a local authority or the Trading Standards Office to impose a fine on an agent for not being a member of an approved complaints scheme or for not clearly publicising fees under The Redress Schemes for Lettings Agency Work and Property Management Work (Requirements to Belong to a Scheme etc) (England) Order 2014 and schedule 9 of the Consumer Rights Act 2015.

## MICROCHIPPING DOGS

Established under the Microchipping of Dogs (England) Regulations 2015, appeals can be made to First-Tier Tribunal (Microchipping Dogs) against a decision by the Department for the Environment and Rural Affairs to ban or stop an individual from microchipping dogs or from running a database on microchipped dogs.

## PENSIONS REGULATION

First-tier Tribunal (Pensions) hears appeals against decisions made by the Pensions Regulator under section 44 of the Pensions Act 2008. Appeals under section 102 of the Act are heard by the Tax and Chancery Chamber of the Upper Tribunal.

## PROFESSIONAL REGULATION

The professional regulation jurisdiction hears appeals against decisions made by the Council for Licensed Conveyancers under the Legal Services Act 2007.

## TRANSPORT

First-tier Tribunal (Transport) hears appeals against decisions made by the Registrar of Approved Driving Instructors under the Road Traffic Act 1988, Transport Act 2000 and the Motor Cars (Driving Instruction) Regulations 2005. Its jurisdiction covers England, Scotland and Wales.

# HEALTH, EDUCATION AND SOCIAL CARE CHAMBER

*Chamber President,* His Hon. Judge Sycamore
*Deputy Chamber Presidents,* Judge Hinchliffe (Mental Health); Judge Tudur (Special Educational Needs and Disability, Care Standards and Primary Health Lists)

## CARE STANDARDS

First-tier Tribunal (Care Standards), 1st Floor Darlington Magistrates' Court, Parkgate DL1 1RU
T 01325-289350 E cst@hmcts.gsi.gov.uk
First-tier Tribunal (Care Standards) was established under the Protection of Children Act 1999 and considers appeals in relation to decisions made by the Secretary of State for Education, the Secretary of State for Health, OFSTED, OFQUAL or the Care Council Wales about the inclusion of individuals' names on the list of those considered unsuitable to work with children or vulnerable adults, restrictions from teaching and employment in schools/further education institutions, and the registration of independent schools. It also deals with general registration decisions made about care homes, children's homes, childcare providers, nurses' agencies, social workers, residential family centres, independent hospitals and fostering agencies.

## MENTAL HEALTH

PO Box 8793, 5th Floor, Leicester LE1 8BN
T 0300-123 2201 E mhrtenquiries@hmcts.gsi.gov.uk
The First-tier Tribunal (Mental Health) hears applications and references for people detained under the Mental Health Act 1983 (as amended by the Mental Health Act 2007). There are separate mental health tribunals for Wales and Scotland.

## PRIMARY HEALTH LISTS

First-tier Tribunal (Primary Health Lists), 1st Floor Darlington Magistrates' Court, Parkgate DL1 1RU
T 01325-289350
First-tier Tribunal (Primary Health Lists) hears appeals against decisions made by the NHS Commissioning Board to not include, to remove or to change the conditions of inclusion for medical practitioners and providers on the NHS medical, dental, opthalmic or pharmaceutical lists.

## SPECIAL EDUCATIONAL NEEDS AND DISABILITY
First-tier Tribunal (SEND), 1st Floor Darlington Magistrates' Court, Parkgate DL1 1RU
T 01325-289350 E sendistqueries@hmcts.gsi.gov.uk
First-tier Tribunal (Special Educational Needs and Disability) considers parents' appeals against the decisions of local authorities about children's special educational needs if parents cannot reach agreement with the local authority. It also considers claims of disability discrimination in schools.

## IMMIGRATION AND ASYLUM CHAMBER
*Chamber President,* Judge Clements
PO Box 6987, Leicester LE1 6ZX
T 0300-123 1711 E customer.service@hmcts.gsi.gov.uk
The Immigration and Asylum Chamber is an independent tribunal dealing with appeals against decisions made by the Home Office concerning immigration, asylum and nationality matters.

## PROPERTY CHAMBER
*Chamber President,* Judge McGrath
10 Alfred Place, London WC1E 7LR
T 020-7446 7700 E rplondon@hmcts.gsi.gov.uk
The First-tier Tribunal (Property Chamber) Residential Property serves the private-rented and leasehold property market in England by resolving disputes between leaseholders, tenants and landlords.

## SOCIAL ENTITLEMENT CHAMBER
*Chamber President,* His Hon. Judge Aitken
*Judicial Leads,* His Hon. Judge Aitken (Social Security and Child Support); Sehba Storey (Asylum Support and Criminal Injuries Compensation)

ASYLUM SUPPORT
2nd Floor, Anchorage House, 2 Clove Crescent, London E14 2BE
T 020-7538 6171
First-tier Tribunal (Asylum Support) deals with appeals against decisions made by the Home Office. The Home Office decides whether asylum seekers, failed asylum seekers and/or their dependants are entitled to support and accommodation on the grounds of destitution, as provided by the Immigration and Asylum Act 1999. The tribunal can only consider appeals against a refusal or termination of support. It can, if appropriate, require the Secretary of State for the Home Department to reconsider the original decision, substitute the original decision with the tribunal's own decision or dismiss the appeal.

CRIMINAL INJURIES COMPENSATION
3rd Floor Wellington House, 134–136 Wellington Street, Glasgow G2 2XL T 0141-354 8555 E cic.enquiries@hmcts.gsi.gov.uk
First-tier Tribunal (Criminal Injuries Compensation) determines appeals against review decisions made by the Criminal Injuries Compensation Authority on applications for compensation made by victims of violent crime. It only considers appeals on claims made on or after 1 April 1996 under the Criminal Injuries Compensation Scheme.

SOCIAL SECURITY AND CHILD SUPPORT
England and Wales, T 0300-123 1142
Scotland, T 0141-354 8400
First-tier Tribunal (Social Security and Child Support) arranges and hears appeals against decisions made by the Department for Work and Pensions and HM Revenue and Customs regarding social security benefits. Appeals considered include those concerned with: attendance, bereavement and carer's allowances; child benefit; child support; the compensation recovery scheme (including NHS recovery claims); diffuse mesotheliomia and the industrial injuries disablement benefit payment schemes; income support; jobseeker's allowance; tax credits; universal credit; and vaccine damage payment.

## TAX CHAMBER
*Chamber President,* Judge Bishopp

MP EXPENSES
PO Box 16972, Birmingham B16 6TZ
T 0300-123 1024 E taxappeals@hmcts.gsi.gov.uk
First-tier Tribunal (MP Expenses) hears appeals against certain decisions made by the Compliance Officer, an independent office holder appointed by the Independent Parliamentary Standards Authority, the organisation responsible for determining and paying MP expenses. Appeals can be made by current or former MPs under the Parliamentary Standards Act 2009. The jurisdiction is UK-wide.

TAX
PO Box 16972, Birmingham B4 6EQ
T 0300-123 1024 E taxappeals@hmcts.gsi.gov.uk
First-tier Tribunal (Tax) hears most appeals against decisions made by HM Revenue and Customs in relation to income tax, corporation tax, capital gains tax, inheritance tax, stamp duty land tax, statutory sick and maternity pay, national insurance contributions and VAT or duties. The tribunal also hears some appeals relating to goods seized by either HM Revenue and Customs or Border Force and against some decisions made by the National Crime Agency. Appeals can be made by individuals or organisations, single taxpayers or large multinational companies. The jurisdiction is UK-wide.

## WAR PENSIONS AND ARMED FORCES COMPENSATION CHAMBER
*Chamber President,* Judge McKenna
5th Floor, Fox Court, 14 Gray's Inn Road, London WC1X 8HN
T 020-3206 0701 E armedforces.chamber@hmcts.gsi.gov.uk
The War Pensions and Armed Forces Compensation Chamber of the First-tier Tribunal hears appeals brought by ex-servicemen and women against decisions by Veterans UK regarding pensions, compensation and other amounts under the war pensions legislation for injuries sustained before 5 April 2005, and under the armed forces compensation scheme for injuries after that date.

## UPPER TRIBUNAL

Comprising four separate chambers, the Upper Tribunal deals mostly with appeals from, and enforcement of, decisions taken by the First-tier Tribunal, but it also handles some cases that do not go through the First-tier Tribunal. Additionally, it has assumed some of the supervisory powers of the courts to deal with the actions of tribunals, government departments and some other public authorities. All the decision-makers of the Upper Tribunal are judges or expert members sitting in a panel chaired by a judge, and are specialists in the areas of law they handle. Over time their decisions are expected to build comprehensive case law for each area covered by the tribunals.

## ADMINISTRATIVE APPEALS CHAMBER
*Chamber President,* Hon. Sir Willim Charles
General Enquiries, E adminappeals@hmcts.gsi.gov.uk
England and Wales, 5th Floor, 7 Rolls Buildings, London EC4A 1NL T 020-7071 5662
Scotland, George House, 126 George Street, Edinburgh EH2 4HH
T 0131-271 4310

Northern Ireland, Tribunal Hearing Centre, 2nd Floor Royal Courts of Justice, Chichester Street, Belfast BT1 3JF

T 028-9072 4848

The Administrative Appeals Chamber considers appeals against most of the decisions of the following First-tier chambers: General Regulatory; Health, Education and Social Care; Social Entitlement; and War Pensions and Armed Forces Compensation. It also considers appeals against decisions of the Disclosure and Barring Service (England and Wales), Traffic Commissioners (England, Wales and Scotland) and appeals from decisions of a number of independent tribunals in Northern Ireland, Scotland and Wales. Its judges also decide Forfeiture Act references (England, Wales and Scotland).

## IMMIGRATION AND ASYLUM CHAMBER

*Chamber President,* Hon. Sir Bernard McCloskey

15–25 Bream's Buildings, London EC4A 1DZ

T 0300-123 1711 E fieldhousecorrespondence@hmcts.gsi.gov.uk

The Immigration and Asylum Chamber hears appeals against decisions made by the Immigration and Asylum Chamber in the First-tier Tribunal relating to visa and asylum applications and the right to enter or stay in the UK. The chamber also deals with applications for judicial review of certain decisions made by the Home Office relating to immigration, asylum and human rights claims.

## LANDS CHAMBER

*Chamber President,* Hon. Sir Keith Lindblom

5th Floor, 7 Rolls Buildings, London EC4A 1NL

T 020-7612 9710 E lands@hmcts.gsi.gov.uk

The Lands Chamber determines questions relating to the valuation of land, rating appeals from valuation tribunals, appeals from the First-tier (Property Chamber), applications to discharge or modify restrictions on the use of land, and compulsory purchase compensation. The tribunal may also arbitrate under a reference by consent.

## TAX AND CHANCERY CHAMBER

*Chamber President,* Hon. Dame Vivien Rose, DBE

5th Floor, 7 Rolls Buildings, London EC4A 1NL

T 020-7612 9700 E uttc@hmcts.gsi.gov.uk

The Tax and Chancery Chamber hears appeals against decisions made by the First-tier Tribunal (Tax), the land registration division of the First-tier Tribunal (Property Chamber) and the General Regulatory Chamber in cases relating to charities. The chamber also hears appeals against decisions issued by the Financial Conduct Authority, the Prudential Regulation Authority, the Pensions Regulator, the Bank of England, HM Treasury and OFGEM.

## SPECIAL IMMIGRATION APPEALS COMMISSION

15–25 Bream's Buildings, London EC4A 1DZ

T 0300-123 1711 E customer.service@hmcts.gsi.gov.uk

The commission was set up under the Special Immigration Appeals Commission Act 1997. It remains separate from the First-tier and Upper Tribunal structure but is part of HM Courts and Tribunals Service. Its main function is to consider appeals against orders for deportation or exclusion, or orders withdrawing or refusing British nationality, in cases which involve considerations of national security.

*Chair,* Hon. Sir Stephen Irwin

## EMPLOYMENT TRIBUNALS

Employment Tribunal Central Office England and Wales, PO Box 10218, Leicester LE1 8EG Public Enquiry Line: 0300-123 1024

Employment Tribunal Central Office Scotland, PO Box 27105, Glasgow G2 9JR Public Enquiry Line: 0141-354 8574

Employment tribunals hear claims regarding matters of employment law, redundancy, dismissal, contract disputes, sexual, racial and disability discrimination and related areas of dispute which may arise in the workplace. A public register of judgments in England and Wales is held at Triton House, St Andrew's Street North, Bury St Edmunds, Suffolk IP33 1TR and in Scotland at the central office in Glasgow.

*President (England and Wales),* Brian Doyle

*President (Scotland),* Shona Simon

## EMPLOYMENT APPEAL TRIBUNAL

*Employment Appeal Tribunal England and Wales,* 2nd Floor, Fleetbank House, 2–6 Salisbury Square, London EC4Y 8AE

T 020-7273 1041 E londoneat@hmcts.gsi.gov.uk

*Employment Appeal Tribunal Scotland,* 52 Melville Street, Edinburgh EH3 7HF T 0131-225 3963

E edinburgheat@hmcts.gsi.gov.uk

The Employment Appeal Tribunal hears appeals (on points of law only) arising from decisions made by employment tribunals.

*President,* Hon. Sir Brian Langstaff

## SCOTTISH COURTS AND TRIBUNALS SERVICE

First Floor, Bothwell House, Hamilton Business Park, Caird Park, Hamilton ML3 0QA T 0800-345 7060 W www.scotland.gov.uk

*Director of Tribunals Operations,* Martin McKenna

The Scottish Courts and Tribunals Service currently provides administrative support for the following Scottish tribunals:

THE ADDITIONAL SUPPORT NEEDS TRIBUNAL FOR SCOTLAND, Europa Building, 450 Argyle Street, Glasgow G2 8LH T 0845-120 2906

E asntsinquiries@scotland.gsi.gov.uk

W www.asntscotland.gov.uk

*President,* May Dunsmuir

COUNCIL TAX REDUCTION REVIEW PANEL, Europa Building, 450 Argyle Street, Glasgow G2 8LH

T 0141-242 0223 E ctrrpadmin@scotland.gsi.gov.uk

W www.counciltaxreductionreview.scotland.gov.uk

*Senior Convener,* Donald Ferguson

HOMEOWNER HOUSING PANEL, Europa Building, 450 Argyle Street, Glasgow G2 8LH T 0141-242 0175

E hohpadmin@scotland.gsi.gov.uk

W www.hohp.scotland.gov.uk

*President,* Aileen Devanny

THE LANDS TRIBUNAL FOR SCOTLAND, George House, 126 George Street, Edinburgh EH2 4HH T 0131-271 4350

E mailbox@lands-tribunal-scotland.org.uk

W www.lands-tribunal-scotland.org.uk

*President,* Hon. Lord Minginish (Roderick MacLeod), QC

THE MENTAL HEALTH TRIBUNAL FOR SCOTLAND, Bothwell House, First Floor, Hamilton Business Park, Caird Park, Hamilton ML3 0QA T 0800-345 7060

E mhts@scotland.gsi.gov.uk W www.mhtscotland.gov.uk

*President,* Dr Joe Morrow

THE PENSIONS APPEAL TRIBUNAL SCOTLAND, George House, 126 George Street, Edinburgh EH2 4HH

T 0131-271 4340 E info@patscotland.org.uk

W www.patscotland.org.uk

*President,* Marion Caldwell, QC

THE PRIVATE RENTED HOUSING PANEL, Europa Building, 450 Argyle Street, Glasgow G2 8LH

T 0141-242 0142 E prhpadmin@scotland.gsi.gov.uk

W www.prhpscotland.gov.uk

*President,* Aileen Devanny

THE SCOTTISH CHARITY APPEALS PANEL,
George House, 126 George Street, Edinburgh EH2 4HH
T 0131-271 4340 E scap@scotland.gsi.gov.uk
W www.scap.gov.uk
*Chairs,* Aileen Devanny; Joseph Hughes; Gary McIlravey;
John Walker

## NORTHERN IRELAND COURTS AND TRIBUNALS SERVICE

Laganside House, 23–27 Oxford Street, Belfast BT1 3LA
T 028-9032 8594 W www.courtsni.gov.uk
*Lord Chief Justice of Northern Ireland,* Rt. Hon. Sir Declan Morgan

The Northern Ireland Courts and Tribunals Service currently provides administrative support for the following Northern Ireland tribunals:

THE APPEALS SERVICE, Cleaver House,
3 Donegall Square North, Belfast BT1 5GA
T 028-9051 8518 E appeals.service.belfast@dsdni.gov.uk
*President of the Appeal Tribunals,* John Duffy
THE CARE TRIBUNAL, 2nd Floor, Royal Courts of Justice,
Chichester Street, Belfast BT1 3JF T 028-9072 4857
E tribunalsunit@courtsni.gov.uk
*Chair,* Diane Drennan
THE CHARITY TRIBUNAL, 2nd Floor,
Royal Courts of Justice, Chichester Street, Belfast BT1 3JF
T 028-9072 4857 E tribunalsunit@courts.ni.gov.uk
*President,* Damien McMahon
CRIMINAL INJURIES COMPENSATION APPEALS
PANEL NORTHERN IRELAND, 2nd Floor,
Royal Courts of Justice, Chichester Street, Belfast BT1 3JF
T 028-9072 4823 E cicapnicustomer@courtsni.gov.uk
*Chair,* Patricia McKaigue
LANDS TRIBUNAL, 2nd Floor, Royal Courts of Justice,
Chichester Street, Belfast BT1 3JF T 028-9032 7703
E landstribunal@courtsni.gov.uk
*Valuation Member,* Henry Spence
MENTAL HEALTH REVIEW TRIBUNAL, 2nd Floor,
Royal Courts of Justice, Chichester Street, Belfast BT1 3JF
T 028-9072 4843 E tribunalsunit@courtsni.gov.uk
*Chair,* Attracta Wilson
NORTHERN IRELAND HEALTH AND SAFETY
TRIBUNAL, 2nd Floor, Royal Courts of Justice,
Chichester Street, Belfast BT1 3JF T 028-9072 4857
E tribunalsunit@courtsni.gov.uk
*Chairs,* James Leonard; Damian McMahon;
Petra Shiels
NORTHERN IRELAND TRAFFIC PENALTY
TRIBUNAL, 2nd Floor, Royal Courts of Justice,
Chichester Street, Belfast BT1 3JF T 028-9072 4888
E tribunalsunit@courtsni.gov.uk
*Adjudicators,* Michael Bready; Maura Hutchinson;
Julie McGrath; Patrick McGurgan
NORTHERN IRELAND VALUATION TRIBUNAL,
2nd Floor, Royal Courts of Justice, Chichester Street,
Belfast BT1 3JF T 028-9072 4857
E tribunalsunit@courtsni.gov.uk
*President,* James Leonard
OFFICE OF SOCIAL SECURITY COMMISSIONERS
AND CHILD SUPPORT COMMISSIONERS,
2nd Floor, Royal Courts of Justice, Chichester Street,
Belfast BT1 3JF T 028-9072 4883
E tribunalsunit@courtsni.gov.uk
*Chief Commissioner,* Dr Kenneth Mullan

PAROLE COMMISSIONERS FOR NORTHERN
IRELAND, Linum Chambers, 9th Floor, 2 Bedford Square,
Bedford Street, Belfast BT2 7ES T 028-9054 5900
E pcniinfo@dojni.x.gsi.gov.uk W www.parolecomni.org.uk
*Chief Commissioner,* Ms Christine Glenn
PENSIONS APPEAL COMMISSIONERS, 2nd Floor,
Royal Courts of Justice, Chichester Street, Belfast BT1 3JF
T 028-9072 4883 E tribunalsunit@courtsni.gov.uk
*Chief Commissioner,* Dr Kenneth Mullan
PENSIONS APPEAL TRIBUNAL, 2nd Floor,
Royal Courts of Justice, Chichester Street, Belfast BT1 3JF
T 028-9072 4883 E tribunalsunit@courtsni.gov.uk
*President,* Dr Kenneth Mullan
RENT ASSESSMENT PANEL, Cleaver House,
3 Donegall Square North, Belfast BT1 5GA T 028-9051 8518
E appeals.service.belfast@dsdni.gov.uk
SPECIAL EDUCATIONAL NEEDS AND DISABILITY
TRIBUNAL, 2nd Floor, Royal Courts of Justice,
Chichester Street, Belfast BT1 3JF T 028-9072 4887
E tribunalsunit@courtsni.gov.uk
*President,* Damian G. McCormick

## INDEPENDENT TRIBUNALS

The following represents a selection of tribunals not administered by HM Courts and Tribunals Service.

### CIVIL AVIATION AUTHORITY
CAA House, 45–59 Kingsway, London WC2B 6TE
T 020-7379 7311 E infoservices@caa.co.uk
W www.caa.co.uk
The Civil Aviation Authority (CAA) does not have a separate tribunal department as such, but for certain purposes the CAA must conform to tribunal requirements, for example, to deal with appeals against the refusal or revocation of aviation licences and certificates issued by the CAA, and the allocation of routes outside of the EU to airlines.
The chair and five non-executive members who may sit on panels for tribunal purposes are appointed by the Secretary of State for Transport.
*Chair,* Dame Deirdre Hutton, DBE

### COMPETITION APPEAL TRIBUNAL
Victoria House, Bloomsbury Place, London WC1A 2EB
T 020-7979 7979 E info@catribunal.org.uk
W www.catribunal.org.uk
The Competition Appeal Tribunal (CAT) is a specialist tribunal established to hear certain cases in the sphere of UK competition and economic regulatory law. It hears appeals against decisions of the Competition and Markets Authority (CMA) and the sectoral regulators in respect of infringements of competition law and with respect to mergers and markets. The CAT also has jurisdiction to award damages in respect of infringements of EU or UK competition law and to hear appeals against decisions of the Office of Communications (OFCOM) in telecommunications matters.
*President,* Hon. Sir Peter Roth

### COPYRIGHT TRIBUNAL
4 Abbey Orchard Street, London SW1P 2HT
T 020-7034 2836 E copyright.tribunal@ipo.gov.uk
W www.ipo.gov.uk/ctribunal
The Copyright Tribunal resolves disputes over the terms and conditions of licences offered by, or licensing schemes operated by, collective management organisations in the copyright and related rights area. Its decisions are appealable to the high court on points of law only.
*Chair,* Hon. Mr Justice Hacon

## INDUSTRIAL TRIBUNALS AND THE FAIR EMPLOYMENT TRIBUNAL (NORTHERN IRELAND)

Killymeal House, 2 Cromac Quay, Ormeau Road, Belfast BT7 2JD
T 028-9032 7666 E mail@employmenttribunalsni.org
W www.employmenttribunalsni.co.uk
The industrial tribunal system in Northern Ireland was set up in 1965 and has a similar remit to the employment tribunals in the rest of the UK. There is also a Fair Employment Tribunal, which hears and determines individual cases of alleged religious or political discrimination in employment. Employers can appeal to the Fair Employment Tribunal if they consider the directions of the Equality Commission to be unreasonable, inappropriate or unnecessary, and the Equality Commission can make application to the tribunal for the enforcement of undertakings or directions with which an employer has not complied.

*President,* Eileen McBride

## INVESTIGATORY POWERS TRIBUNAL

PO Box 33220, London SW1H 9ZQ
T 020-7035 3711 E info@ipt-uk.com W www.ipt-uk.com
The Investigatory Powers Tribunal replaced the Interception of Communications Tribunal, the Intelligence Services Tribunal, the Security Services Tribunal and the complaints function of the commissioner appointed under the Police Act 1997.

The Regulation of Investigatory Powers Act 2000 (RIPA) provides for a tribunal made up of senior members of the legal profession, independent of the government and appointed by the Queen, to consider all complaints against the intelligence services and those against public authorities in respect of powers covered by RIPA; and to consider proceedings brought under section 7 of the Human Rights Act 1998 against the intelligence services and law enforcement agencies in respect of these powers.

*President,* Sir Michael Burton

## NATIONAL HEALTH SERVICE TRIBUNAL (SCOTLAND)

Anderson Strathern LLP, Lomond House, 9 George Square, Glasgow G2 1DY
T 0141-242 7974 E nhstribunal@nhs.net
The Scottish National Health Service Tribunal considers representations that the continued inclusion of a family health service practitioner (eg a doctor, dentist, optometrist or pharmacist) on a health board's list would be prejudicial to the efficiency of the service concerned, by virtue either of fraudulent practices or unsatisfactory personal or professional conduct. If this is established, the tribunal has the power to disqualify practitioners from working in the NHS family health services.

*Chair,* J. Michael Graham

## SOLICITORS' DISCIPLINARY TRIBUNAL

5th Floor, Gate House, 1 Farringdon Street, London EC4M 7LG
T 020-7329 4808 E enquiries@solicitorsdt.com
W www.solicitorstribunal.org.uk
The Solicitors' Disciplinary Tribunal is an independent statutory body whose members are appointed by the Master of the Rolls. The tribunal adjudicates upon alleged breaches of the rules and regulations applicable to solicitors and their firms, including the Solicitors' Code of Conduct 2007. It also decides applications by former solicitors for restoration to the Roll.

*President,* Andrew Spooner

## SOLICITORS' DISCIPLINE TRIBUNAL (SCOTTISH)

Unit 3.5, The Granary Business Centre, Coal Road, Cupar, Fife KY15 5YQ
T 01334-659088 E enquiries@ssdt.org.uk W www.ssdt.org.uk
The Scottish Solicitors' Discipline Tribunal is an independent statutory body with a panel of 24 members, 12 of whom are solicitors appointed by the Lord President of the Court of Session. Its principal function is to consider complaints of misconduct against solicitors in Scotland.

*Chair,* Alaistair Cockburn

## TRAFFIC PENALTY TRIBUNAL

Springfield House, Water Lane, Wilmslow, Cheshire SK9 5BG
T 01625-445555 E info@trafficpenaltytribunal.gov.uk
W www.trafficpenaltytribunal.gov.uk
The Traffic Penalty Tribunal adjudicators consider appeals in relation to penalty charge notices issued by local authorities in England (outside London) and Wales for parking and bus lane contraventions and, additionally in Wales, moving traffic contraventions. The tribunal also considers appeals in relation to penalties issued by the Secretary of State for Transport for failing to pay a charge at the Dartford river crossing and by Durham County Council in the Durham congestion charging zone.

*Chief Adjudicator,* Caroline Sheppard

## VALUATION TRIBUNAL FOR ENGLAND

2nd Floor, 120 Leman Street, London E1 8EU
T 020-7246 3900 W www.valuationtribunal.gov.uk
The Valuation Tribunal for England (VTE) came into being on 1 October 2009, replacing 56 valuation tribunals in England. Provision for the VTE was made in the Local Government and Public Involvement in Health Act 2007. The VTE hears appeals concerning council tax and non-domestic (business) rates, as well as a small number of appeals against drainage boards' assessments of drainage rates. A separate panel is constituted for each hearing, and consists of a chair and usually one or two other members.

The Valuation Tribunal Service (VTS) was created as a corporate body by the Local Government Act 2003, and is responsible for providing or arranging the services required for the operation of the Valuation Tribunal for England. The VTS board consists of a chair and members appointed by the secretary of state. The VTS is sponsored by the Department for Communities and Local Government.

*President (VTE),* Prof. Graham Zellick, CBE, QC
*Chair (VTS),* Anne Galbraith, CBE

## VALUATION TRIBUNAL FOR WALES

Government Buildings, Block A (L1), Sarn Mynach, Llandudno Junction LL31 9RZ
T 0300-062 5350 E VTWalesnorth@vtw.gsi.gov.uk
W www.valuation-tribunals-wales.org.uk
The Valuation Tribunal for Wales (VTW) was established by the Valuation Tribunal for Wales Regulations 2010, and hears and determines appeals concerning council tax, non-domestic rating and drainage rates in Wales. The governing council, comprising the president, four regional representatives and one member who is appointed by the Welsh government, performs the management functions on behalf of the tribunal.

*President,* Miss C. Cobert

# OMBUDSMAN SERVICES

The following section is a listing of selected ombudsman services. Ombudsmen are a free, independent and impartial means of resolving certain disputes outside of the courts. These disputes are, in the majority of cases, concerned with whether something has been badly or unfairly handled (for example owing to delay, neglect, inefficiency or failure to follow proper procedures). Most ombudsman schemes are established by statute; they cover various public and private bodies and generally examine matters only after the relevant body has been given a reasonable opportunity to deal with the complaint.

After conducting an investigation an ombudsman will usually issue a written report, which normally suggests a resolution to the dispute and often includes recommendations concerning the improvement of procedures.

## OMBUDSMAN ASSOCIATION

56 Cambridge Road, Carshalton, Surrey SM5 3QS
T 020-8894 9272 E secretary@ombudsmanassociation.org
W www.ombudsmanassociation.org

The Ombudsman Association was established in 1994 and exists to provide information to the government, public bodies and the public about ombudsmen and other complaint-handling services in the UK and Ireland. An ombudsman scheme must meet four criteria in order to attain full Ombudsman Association membership: independence from the organisations the ombudsman has the power to investigate, fairness, effectiveness and public accountability. Complaint Handler membership is open to complaint-handling bodies that do not meet these criteria in full. Ombudsmen schemes from the UK, Ireland, British crown dependencies and overseas territories may apply to the Ombudsman Association for membership. The Ombudsman Association publishes a triannual newsletter containing news about ombudsmen and complaint-handling services in the UK, Ireland and overseas, along with topical articles of interest to members of the Association.
*Chair*, Lewis Shand Smith

The following is a selection of organisations that are members of the Ombudsman Association.

### FINANCIAL OMBUDSMAN SERVICE
Exchange Tower, London E14 9SR
T 020-7964 1000 E complaint.info@financial-ombudsman.org.uk
W www.financial-ombudsman.org.uk

The Financial Ombudsman Service settles individual disputes between businesses providing financial services and their customers. The service answers around a million enquiries every year and deals with over 250,000 disputes. The service examines complaints about most financial matters, including banking, insurance, mortgages, pensions, savings, loans and credit cards. *See also* Banking and Finance.
*Chief Ombudsman and Chief Executive*, Caroline Wayman

### HOUSING OMBUDSMAN SERVICE
81 Aldwych, London WC2B 4HN
T 0300-111 3000 E info@housing-ombudsman.org.uk
W www.housing-ombudsman.org.uk

The Housing Ombudsman Service was established in 1997 to deal with complaints and disputes involving tenants and housing associations and social landlords, certain private-sector landlords and managing agents. The ombudsman has a

statutory jurisdiction over all registered social landlords in England. Private and other landlords can join the service on a voluntary basis. On 1 April 2013 a new Housing Ombudsman Service was launched with an extended jurisdiction covering all housing associations and local authorities.
*Ombudsman*, Denise Fowler

### INDEPENDENT POLICE COMPLAINTS COMMISSION (IPCC)
90 High Holborn, London WC1V 6BH
T 0300-020 0096 E enquiries@ipcc.gsi.gov.uk
W www.ipcc.gov.uk

The IPCC succeeded the Police Complaints Authority in 2004. It was established under the Police Reform Act 2002. The IPCC is responsible for carrying out independent investigations into serious incidents or allegations of misconduct by those serving with the police in England and Wales. The IPCC's chair and commissioners must not have worked for the police in any capacity prior to their appointment. It has the power to initiate, undertake and oversee investigations and is also responsible for the way in which complaints are handled by local police forces. The IPCC is also responsible for serious complaints and conduct matters relating to staff at the National Crime Agency (NCA), Her Majesty's Revenue and Customs (HMRC), and the Home Office immigration and enforcement staff. In 2011 the IPCC became responsible for investigating allegations against the Police and Crime Commissioner for each police force area in England and Wales (established 2011) and against the equivalent for the Metropolitan Police, the Mayor's Office for Policing and Crime (MOPAC), set up in 2012.
*Chair*, Dame Anne Owers
*Deputy Chairs*, Rachel Cerfontyne; Sarah Green
*Chief Executive*, Lesley Longstone

### LEGAL OMBUDSMAN
PO Box 6806, Wolverhampton WV1 9WJ
T 0300-555 0333 E enquiries@legalombudsman.org.uk
W www.legalombudsman.org.uk

The Legal Ombudsman was set up by the Office for Legal Complaints under the Legal Services Act 2007 and is the single body for all consumer legal complaints in England and Wales. It replaced the Office of the Legal Services Ombudsman in 2010. The Legal Ombudsman aims to resolve disputes between individuals and authorised legal practitioners, including barristers, law cost draftsmen, legal executives, licensed conveyancers, notaries, patent attorneys, probate practitioners, registered European lawyers, solicitors and trade mark attorneys. The Legal Ombudsman is an independent and impartial organisation and deals with various types of complaints against legal services, such as wills, family issues, personal injury and buying or selling a house.
*Chief Ombudsman (acting)*, Kathryn King

### LOCAL GOVERNMENT OMBUDSMAN
PO Box 4771, Coventry CV4 0EH
T 0300-061 0614 W www.lgo.org.uk

The Local Government Ombudsman deals with complaints about councils and service failure by local authorities, schools and care providers.

There are two ombudsmen in England, each with responsibility for different regions; they aim to provide satisfactory redress for complainants and better administration by the authorities. The ombudsmen investigate complaints about most council matters, including housing, planning, education, social care, housing benefit, transport and highways, environment and waste, and council tax. See also Local Government.

*Local Government Ombudsman,* Dr Jane Martin

## NORTHERN IRELAND OMBUDSMAN

33 Wellington Place, Belfast BT1 6HN
T 028-9023 3821 E ombudsman@ni-ombudsman.org.uk
W www.ni-ombudsman.org.uk

The Northern Ireland Ombudsman (also known as the Assembly Ombudsman and the Northern Ireland Commissioner for Complaints) is appointed under legislation with powers to investigate complaints by people claiming to have sustained injustice arising from action taken by a Northern Ireland government department, their agencies or any other public body within his remit. Public bodies include all local authorities, education and library boards and organisations providing health and social care.

*Ombudsman,* Dr Tom Frawley, CBE
*Deputy Ombudsman,* Marie Anderson

## OFFICE OF THE PENSIONS OMBUDSMAN

11 Belgrave Road, London SW1V 1RB
T 020-7630 2200 E enquiries@pensions-ombudsman.org.uk
W www.pensions-ombudsman.org.uk

The Pensions Ombudsman is appointed by the Secretary of State for Work and Pensions, under the Pension Schemes Act 1993 as amended by the Pensions Act 1995. He investigates and decides complaints and disputes about the way that personal and occupational pension schemes are run and between members of pensions schemes and their beneficiaries, employers, trustees, managers and scheme administrators. As the ombudsman for the Board of the Pension Protection Fund, he can deal with disputes about the decisions made by the board or the actions of their staff. He also deals with appeals against decisions made by the scheme manager under the Financial Assistance Scheme.

*Pensions Ombudsman,* Anthony Arter
*Deputy Pensions Ombudsman,* Karen Johnston

## OMBUDSMAN SERVICES

The Brew House, Wilderspool Park, Greenalls Avenue,
Warrington WA4 6HL
W www.ombudsman-services.org

Ombudsman Services was founded in 2002 and provides independent dispute resolution for the communications, copyright licensing, energy and property sectors.

Ombudsman Services: Communications investigates complaints from consumers about companies which provide communication services to the public.

Ombudsman Services: Copyright Licensing helps to resolve complaints about bodies that either own or administer, on behalf of third parties, the licensing of copyright materials.

Ombudsman Services: Energy helps to resolve complaints from consumers about energy (gas and electricity companies). This service is also responsible for handling investigations concerning the government's Green Deal policy, which launched in 2013, and offers long-term loans towards energy-saving home improvements.

Ombudsman Services: Property investigates complaints from consumers about chartered surveying companies, surveyors, estate agents and other property professionals.

*Chair,* Dame Janet Finch
*Chief Ombudsman,* Lewis Shand Smith

## OMBUDSMAN SERVICES: COMMUNICATIONS

PO Box 730, Warrington WA4 6WU
T 0330-440 1614

## OMBUDSMAN SERVICES: COPYRIGHT LICENSING

PO Box 1124, Warrington WA4 9GH
T 0330-440 1601

## OMBUDSMAN SERVICES: ENERGY

PO Box 966, Warrington WA4 9DF
T 0330-440 1624

## OMBUDSMAN SERVICES: PROPERTY

PO Box 1021, Warrington WA4 9FE
T 0330-440 1634

## PARLIAMENTARY AND HEALTH SERVICE OMBUDSMAN

Millbank Tower, Millbank, London SW1P 4QP
T 0345-015 4033
W www.ombudsman.org.uk

The Parliamentary Commissioner for Administration (commonly known as the Parliamentary Ombudsman) is independent of government and is an officer of Parliament. She is responsible for investigating complaints referred to her by MPs from members of the public who claim to have sustained injustice in consequence of maladministration by or on behalf of government departments and certain non-departmental public bodies in the UK. Certain types of action by government departments or bodies are excluded from investigation.

The Health Service Ombudsman is responsible for investigating complaints about services funded by the National Health Service in England that have not been dealt with by the service providers to the satisfaction of the complainant. This includes complaints about doctors, dentists, pharmacists and opticians. Complaints can be referred directly by the member of the public who claims to have sustained injustice or hardship in consequence of the failure in a service provided by a relevant organisation.

The two offices of the Parliamentary and Health Service Ombudsman are traditionally held by the same person.

*Parliamentary Ombudsman and Health Service Ombudsman,* Dame Julie Mellor, DBE

## PRISONS AND PROBATION OMBUDSMAN

PO Box 70769, London SE1P 4XY
T 020-7633 4100 E mail@ppo.gsi.gov.uk
W www.ppo.gov.uk

The Prisons and Probation Ombudsman investigates complaints from prisoners, people on probation and immigration detainees, deaths of prisoners, residents of probation-service Approved Premises and those held in immigration removal centres. The ombudsman is appointed by the Secretary of State for Justice and works closely with the Ministry of Justice. All deaths that occur in prison are investigated and an anonymised fatal incident report is written after each investigation.

*Ombudsman,* Nigel Newcomen, CBE

## PROPERTY OMBUDSMAN

Milford House, 43–55 Milford Street, Salisbury SP1 2BP
T 01722-333306
W www.tpos.co.uk

The Property Ombudsman (TPO) scheme was established in 1998 and provides a free, impartial and independent service for dealing with unresolved disputes between property agents and buyers, sellers, tenants and landlords of property in the UK.

The ombudsman's role is to consider complaints against the agents' obligation to act in accordance with the TPO codes of practice and to propose a full and final resolution to the dispute. Consumers are not bound by the Ombudsman's decision, but registered agents are.

With over 12,800 estate agent offices and 11,500 lettings offices registered, TPO is the primary dispute-resolution service for the property industry.
*Ombudsman,* Katrine Sporle, CBE

## PUBLIC SERVICES OMBUDSMAN FOR WALES
1 Ffordd yr Hen Gae, Pencoed CF35 5LJ
T 0300-790 0203
W www.ombudsman-wales.org.uk

The office of Public Services Ombudsman for Wales was established, with effect from 1 April 2006, by the Public Services Ombudsman (Wales) Act 2005. The ombudsman, who is appointed by the Queen, investigates complaints of injustice caused by maladministration or service failure by public services such as the Assembly Commission (and public bodies sponsored by the assembly); Welsh government; National Health Service bodies, including GPs, family health service providers and hospitals; registered social landlords; local authorities, including community councils; fire and rescue authorities; police authorities; the Arts Council of Wales; national park authorities; and countryside and environmental organisations.
*Ombudsman,* Nick Bennett

## REMOVALS INDUSTRY OMBUDSMAN SCHEME
PO Box 6412, Leighton Buzzard, Beds LU7 6EG
T 01525-850054 E ombudsman@removalsombudsman.co.uk
W www.removalsombudsman.org.uk

The Removals Industry Ombudsman Scheme was established to resolve disputes between removal companies that are members of the scheme and their clients, both domestic and commercial. It comprises a board of four members, only one of whom has any connection with the removals industry. The ombudsman investigates complaints such as breaches of contract, unprofessional conduct, delays, excessive charges or breaches in the code of practice. The National Guild of Removers and Storers is currently the principal member.
*Ombudsman,* Lynne Stone

## SCOTTISH PUBLIC SERVICES OMBUDSMAN
4 Melville Street, Edinburgh EH3 7NS
T 0800-377 7330
W www.spso.org.uk

The Scottish Public Services Ombudsman (SPSO) was established in 2002. The SPSO is the final stage for complaints about public services in Scotland. Its service is free and independent. SPSO investigates complaints about the Scottish government, its agencies and departments; the Scottish Parliamentary Corporate Body; colleges and universities; councils; housing associations; NHS Scotland; prisons; some water and sewerage service providers; and most other Scottish public bodies. The ombudsman looks at complaints regarding poor service or administrative failure and can usually only look at those that have been through the formal complaints process of the organisation concerned. It also has a statutory function in improving complaints handling in public services, which it carries out through its Complaints Standards Authority.
*Scottish Public Services Ombudsman,* Jim Martin

## WATERWAYS OMBUDSMAN
PO Box 854, Altrincham WA15 5JS
T 0161-980 4858 E enquiries@waterways-ombudsman.org
W www.waterways-ombudsman.org

Since July 2012, the Waterways Ombudsman has investigated complaints about the Canal and River Trust and its subsidiaries (such as British Waterways Marinas Limited). The ombudsman does not consider complaints about canals in Scotland, which are the responsibility of the Scottish Public Services Ombudsman.
*Ombudsman,* Andrew Walker

# THE POLICE SERVICE

There are 45 police forces in the United Kingdom: 43 in England and Wales, including the Metropolitan Police and the City of London Police, Police Scotland and the Police Service of Northern Ireland. The Isle of Man, Jersey and Guernsey have their own forces responsible for policing in their respective islands and bailiwicks. The National Crime Agency, which became operational in October 2013, is responsible for preventing organised crime and strengthening UK borders.

Since 1964, police authorities – separate independent bodies for each police force – were responsible for the supervision of local policing in England and Wales. Following the government's white paper *Policing in the 21st Century* it was concluded that, in order to make the police more accountable, police authorities should be replaced with a directly elected commissioner for each force, supported by a police and crime panel. In November 2012, following the enactment of the Police Reform and Social Responsibility Act 2011, elections to install police and crime commissioners (PCCs) were held in 41 police force areas across England and Wales. The PCCs are responsible for appointing the chief constable of their force, establishing local priorities and setting budgets. The PCCs are not in place to run their local force but rather to hold them to account. The Mayor of London, supported by the Mayor's Office for Policing and Crime (MOPAC), acts as the PCC for the Metropolitan Police. The City of London Corporation acts as the police authority for the City of London Police.

In England the police and crime panels are made up of representatives from each local authority in a police force area. In Wales they are independent public bodies, established and maintained by the secretary of state, rather than local authority committees.

Under the Police and Fire Reform (Scotland) Act 2012, Police Scotland was established on 1 April 2013, merging the eight separate territorial police forces, the Scottish Crime and Drug Enforcement Agency and the Association of Chief Police Officers in Scotland. Responsible for policing the whole of Scotland, Police Scotland is the second largest force in the UK after the Metropolitan Police. The service is led by a chief constable who is supported by a team of four deputy constables, assistant chief constables and three directors. The Scottish Police Authority, established in October 2012, is responsible for maintaining policing, promoting policing principles, the continuous improvement of policing and holds the Chief Constable to account. In Northern Ireland, the Northern Ireland Policing Board, an independent public body consisting of 19 political and independent members, fulfils a similar role.

Police forces in England, Scotland and Wales are financed by central and local government grants and a precept on the council tax. The Police Service of Northern Ireland is wholly funded by central government.

The home secretary, the Scottish government and the Northern Ireland Minister of Justice are responsible for the organisation, administration and operation of the police service. They regulate police ranks, discipline, hours of duty and pay and allowances. All police forces are subject to inspection by HM Inspectorate of Constabulary, which reports to the home secretary and the Northern Ireland Minister of Justice. Police forces in Scotland are inspected by HM Inspectorate of Constabulary for Scotland which operates independently of the Scottish government.

## COMPLAINTS

The Independent Police Complaints Commission (IPCC) was established under the Police Reform Act 2002. The IPCC is responsible for overseeing the whole of the police complaints system in England and Wales. It has the power to initiate, undertake and oversee investigations and is also responsible for the way in which complaints are handled by local police forces. In addition the IPCC is responsible for dealing with serious complaints and conduct matters relating to staff at the National Crime Agency, HM Revenue and Customs and Home Office immigration and enforcement staff. The most recent responsibility assigned to the IPCC is to decide whether investigations should be made regarding any allegations of criminal offence against MOPAC, the PCCs or their deputies.

Complaints about the police must first be recorded with the relevant police force; the local force will attempt to resolve complaints internally and an official investigation might not be required. Certain complaints, such as an allegation that an officer has seriously assaulted someone, are automatically referred to the IPCC. The IPCC or police force may refer the case to the Crown Prosecution Service, which will decide whether to bring criminal charges against the officer/s involved. An officer who is dismissed, required to resign or reduced in rank, whether as a result of a complaint or not, can appeal to a police appeals tribunal established by the relevant police authority.

On 1 April 2013, under the Police and Fire Reform (Scotland) Act 2012 which brought together Scotland's eight police services into the single Police Service of Scotland, the remit of the Police Complaints Commissioner for Scotland (PCCS) was expanded to include investigations into the most serious incidents concerning the police. To reflect this change, the PCCS was renamed the Police Investigations and Review Commissioner (PIRC).

The Police Ombudsman for Northern Ireland provides an independent police complaints system for Northern Ireland, dealing with all stages of the complaints procedure. Complaints that cannot be resolved informally are investigated and the ombudsman recommends a suitable course of action to the Chief Constable of the Police Service of Northern Ireland or the Northern Ireland Policing Board based on the investigation's findings. The ombudsman may recommend that a police officer be prosecuted, but the decision to prosecute a police officer rests with the Director of Public Prosecutions.

INDEPENDENT POLICE COMPLAINTS
COMMISSION, PO Box 473, Sale M33 0BW
T 0300-020 0096 E enquiries@ipcc.gsi.gov.uk
W www.ipcc.gov.uk
POLICE INVESTIGATIONS AND REVIEW
COMMISSIONER, Hamilton House, Hamilton Business Park,
Caird Park, Hamilton ML3 0QA T 0808-178 5577
E enquiries@pirc.gsi.gov.uk W www.pirc.scotland.gov.uk
*Police Investigations and Review Commissioner,*
Kate Frame
POLICE OMBUDSMAN FOR NORTHERN IRELAND,
New Cathedral Buildings, Writers' Square, 11 Church Street,
Belfast BT1 1PG T 028-9082 8600
E info@policeombudsman.org W www.policeombudsman.org
*Police Ombudsman,* Dr Michael Maguire

# POLICE SERVICES

## COLLEGE OF POLICING

Leamington Road, Ryton-on-Dunsmore, Coventry CV8 3EN
T 0800-496 3322 E contactus@college.pnn.police.uk
W www.college.police.uk

The College of Policing was established in December 2012 as the first professional body set up for policing. It works on behalf of the public to raise professional standards in policing and to assist forces to reduce crime and protect the public. It engages with the public through the Police and Crime Commissioners to ensure that it is responsive to the issues of greatest concern.

The government has designated the college as a centre for reviewing and testing practices and interventions to identify which are effective in reducing crime. It makes this information accessible for all in policing, particularly frontline practitioners. The college also supports continuous professional development and sets national standards for promotion and progression.

*Chief Executive,* Alex Marshall, QPM
*Chair,* Prof. Dame Shirley Pearce, DBE

## NATIONAL CRIME AGENCY

Units 1–6 Citadel Place, Tinworth Street, London SE11 5EF
T 0370-496 7622
E communication@nca.x.gsi.gov.uk
W www.nationalcrimeagency.gov.uk

Established under the Crime and Courts Act 2013 the National Crime Agency (NCA) became fully operational in October 2013. The NCA is a non-ministerial government department.

In order to carry out its remit to fight organised crime, strengthen UK borders, tackle fraud and cyber crime and protect children and young people the agency is organised into four separate commands: Border Policing, Child Exploitation and Online Protection, Economic Crime and Organised Crime; and a specialist National Cyber Crime Unit.

The director-general has independent operational direction and control over the NCA's activities and, through the home secretary, is accountable to parliament.

*Director-General,* Keith Bristow, QPM

## UK MISSING PERSONS BUREAU

Albert Day Building, Sunningdale Park, Ascot, Berks SL5 0QE
T 0845-000 5481 E missingpersonsbureau@nca.x.gsi.gov.uk
W www.missingpersons.police.uk

The UK Missing Persons Bureau, which is now part of the National Crime Agency, acts as the centre for the exchange of information connected with the search for missing persons nationally and internationally alongside the police and other related organisations. The unit focuses on cross-matching missing persons with unidentified persons or bodies by maintaining records, including a dental index of ante-mortem chartings of long-term missing persons and post-mortem chartings from unidentified bodies.

Information is supplied and collected for all persons who have been missing in the UK for over 72 hours (or fewer where police deem appropriate), foreign nationals reported missing in the UK, UK nationals reported missing abroad and all unidentified bodies and persons found within the UK.

# SPECIALIST FORCES

## BRITISH TRANSPORT POLICE

25 Camden Road, London NW1 9LN T 0800-405040
W www.btp.police.uk

*Strength (March 2015),* 2,876
British Transport Police is the national police force for the railways in England, Wales and Scotland, including the London Underground system, Docklands Light Railway, Glasgow Subway, Midland Metro tram system, Sunderland Metro, London Tramlink and the Emirates Air Line cable car. The chief constable reports to the British Transport Police Authority. The members of the authority are appointed by the transport secretary and include representatives from the rail industry as well as independent members. Officers are paid the same salary as those in other police forces.
*Chief Constable,* Paul Crowther, OBE

## CIVIL NUCLEAR CONSTABULARY

Building F6, Culham Science Centre, Abingdon,
Oxfordshire OX14 3DB T 01235-466606
W www.gov.uk/government/organisations/civil-nuclear-constabulary

*Strength (July 2015),* c.1,500
The Civil Nuclear Constabulary (CNC) operates under the strategic direction of the Department of Energy and Climate Change. The CNC is a specialised armed force that protects civil nuclear sites and nuclear materials. The constabulary is responsible for policing UK civil nuclear industry facilities and for escorting nuclear material between establishments within the UK and worldwide.
*Chief Constable,* Michael Griffiths, CBE
*Deputy Chief Constable,* Simon Chesterton, QPM

## MINISTRY OF DEFENCE POLICE

Ministry of Defence Police HQ, Wethersfield, Braintree, Essex
CM7 4AZ T 01371-854000 W www.mod.police.uk

*Strength (July 2015),* c.2,650
Part of the Ministry of Defence Police and Guarding Agency, the Ministry of Defence Police is a statutory civil police force with particular responsibility for the security and policing of the MoD environment. It contributes to the physical protection of property and personnel within its jurisdiction and provides a comprehensive police service to the MoD as a whole.
*Chief Constable,* Alf Hitchcock, QPM
*Deputy Chief Constable,* Gerard McAuley

## THE SPECIAL CONSTABULARY

Darby House, 162 Bletchingley Road, Merstham, Surrey RH1 3DN
W www.policespecials.com

*Strength (June 2015),* c.20,000
The Special Constabulary is a force of trained volunteers who support and work with their local police force, usually for a minimum of 16 hours a month. Special constables are thoroughly grounded in the basic aspects of police work, such as self-defence, powers of arrest, common crimes and preparing evidence for court, before they can begin to carry out any police duties. Once they have completed their training, they have the same powers as a regular officer and wear a similar uniform.

# POLICE FORCES

The telephone number for each local police force in England, Wales, Scotland and Northern Ireland is T 101

## ENGLAND

| Force | Strength† | Chief Constable | Police and Crime Commissioner |
|---|---|---|---|
| Avon and Somerset | 2,716 | John Long *(acting)*, QPM | Sue Mountstevens |
| Bedfordshire | 1,161 | Colette Paul, QPM | Olly Martins |
| Cambridgeshire | 1,337 | Simon Parr, QPM | Sir Graham Bright |
| Cheshire | 1,878 | Simon Byrne | John Dwyer |
| Cleveland | 1,434 | Jacqui Cheer, QPM | Barry Coppinger |
| Cumbria | 1,137 | Jeremy Graham | Richard Rhodes |
| Derbyshire | 1,889 | Mick Creedon, QPM | Alan Charles |
| Devon and Cornwall | 3,073 | Shaun Sawyer | Tony Hogg |
| Dorset | 1,268 | Debbie Simpson, QPM | Martyn Underhill |
| Durham | 1,199 | Mike Barton, QPM | Ron Hogg |
| Essex | 3,090 | Stephen Kavanagh | Nick Alston |
| Gloucestershire | 1,178 | Suzette Davenport | Martin Surl |
| Greater Manchester | 6,749 | Sir Peter Fahy, QPM | Tony Lloyd |
| Hampshire | 3,283 | Andy Marsh | Simon Hayes |
| Hertfordshire | 1,923 | Andy Bliss, QPM | David Lloyd |
| Humberside | 1,760 | Justine Curran, QPM | Matthew Grove |
| Kent | 3,196 | Alan Pughsley, QPM | Ann Barnes |
| Lancashire | 3,059 | Steve Finnigan, CBE, QPM | Clive Grunshaw |
| Leicestershire | 2,072 | Simon Cole, QPM | Sir Clive Loader |
| Lincolnshire | 1,108 | Neil Rhodes | Alan Hardwick |
| Merseyside | 3,978 | Sir Jon Murphy, QPM | Jane Kennedy |
| Norfolk | 1,551 | Simon Bailey | Stephen Bett |
| North Yorkshire | 1,392 | Dave Jones | Julia Mulligan |
| Northamptonshire | 1,364 | Adrian Lee | Adam Simmonds |
| Northumbria | 3,506 | Sue Sim | Vera Baird |
| Nottinghamshire | 2,106 | Chris Eyre, QPM | Paddy Tipping |
| South Yorkshire | 2,690 | David Crompton, QPM | Dr Alan Billings |
| Staffordshire | 1,684 | Jane Sawyers | Matthew Ellis |
| Suffolk | 1,180 | Douglas Paxton, QPM | Tim Passmore |
| Surrey | 1,941 | Lynne Owens, QPM | Kevin Hurley |
| Sussex | 2,831 | Giles York, QPM | Katy Bourne |
| Thames Valley | 4,209 | Sara Thornton, CBE, QPM | Anthony Stansfeld |
| Warwickshire | 791 | Andy Parker, QPM | Ron Ball |
| West Mercia | 1,902 | David Shaw | Bill Longmore |
| West Midlands | 7,401 | Chris Sims, OBE, QPM | David Jamieson |
| West Yorkshire | 4,774 | Mark Gilmore, QPM | Mark Burns-Williamson, OBE |
| Wiltshire | 1,022 | Patrick Geenty | Angus Macpherson |
| WALES | | | |
| Dyfed-Powys | 1,094 | Simon Prince, QPM | Christopher Salmon |
| Gwent | 1,272 | Jeffrey Farrar, QPM | Ian Johnston |
| North Wales | 1,515 | Mark Polin, QPM | Winston Roddick |
| South Wales | 2,853 | Peter Vaughan, QPM | Rt. Hon. Alun Michael |
| POLICE SCOTLAND | 17,234 | vacant | – |
| POLICE SERVICE OF NORTHERN IRELAND | 7,791 | George Hamilton, QPM | – |

| ISLANDS | Strength† | Chief Constable | Telephone |
|---|---|---|---|
| Isle of Man | 210 | Gary Roberts | 01624-631212 |
| States of Jersey | 230 | Mike Bowron, QPM | 01534-612612 |
| Guernsey | 148 | Patrick Rice | 01481-725111 |

† Size of force (full-time equivalent) as at March 2015
*Sources:* R. Hazell & Co, Sweet & Maxwell *Police and Constabulary Almanac 2015*

# LONDON FORCES

## CITY OF LONDON POLICE

37 Wood Street, London EC2P 2NQ T 020-7601 2222
W www.cityoflondon.police.uk
*Strength (March 2015),* 750

The City of London has one of the most important financial centres in the world and the force has particular expertise in fraud investigation. The force concentrates on: economic crime, counter terrorism and community policing. It has a wholly elected police authority, the police committee of the City of London Corporation, which appoints the commissioner.

*Commissioner,* Adrian Leppard, QPM
*Assistant Commissioner,* Ian Dyson
*Commanders,* Wayne Chance *(Operations);* Steve Head *(Economic Crime)*

## METROPOLITAN POLICE SERVICE
New Scotland Yard, Broadway, London SW1H 0BG
T 020-7230 1212 W www.met.police.uk
*Strength (March 2015),* 39,548
*Commissioner,* Sir Bernard Hogan-Howe, QPM
*Deputy Commissioner,* Craig Mackey, QPM

The Metropolitan Police Service is divided into three main areas for operational purposes:

TERRITORIAL POLICING
Most of the day-to-day policing of London is carried out by 32 borough operational command units operating within the same boundaries as the London borough councils.
*Assistant Commissioner,* Helen King, QPM

SPECIALIST CRIME AND OPERATIONS (SC&O)
SC&O provides two main services: reducing the harm caused by serious crime and criminal networks and providing specialist policing services across London. SC&O provides specialist training to detectives, and conducts forensic examinations of crime scenes in the capital.
*Assistant Commissioner,* Patricia Gallan

SPECIALIST OPERATIONS
• *Counter Terrorism Command* is responsible for the prevention and disruption of terrorist activity, domestic extremism and related offences within London and nationally. It provides an explosives disposal and chemical, biological, radiological and nuclear capability in London, assists the security services in fulfilling their roles and provides a point of contact for international partners
• *Protection Command* is responsible for the protection and security of high-profile persons, including the royal family and the prime minister. It is also responsible for protecting royal residences and embassies, providing residential protection for visiting heads of state, heads of government and foreign ministers and advising the diplomatic community on security
• *Security Command* works with authorities at the Houses of Parliament to provide security for peers, MPs, employees and visitors to the Palace of Westminster. It is also responsible for policing Heathrow and London City airports
*Assistant Commissioner,* Mark Rowley, QPM

PROFESSIONALISM
The Directorate of Professionalism's key aims are to uphold and improve professional standards across the Metropolitan Police Service. The directorate works with the IPCC to establish good practice, reduce bureaucracy and review decision making. It also works with the Crown Prosecution Service to ensure timely and professional investigations of complaints and conduct matters.
*Assistant Commissioner,* Martin Hewitt

## STAFF ASSOCIATIONS

Police officers are not permitted to join a trade union or to take strike action. All ranks have their own staff associations.
NATIONAL POLICE CHIEFS' COUNCIL (NPPC),
10 Victoria Street, London SW1H 0NN T 020-7084 8950
*Chair,* Sara Thornton

### ENGLAND AND WALES
POLICE FEDERATION OF ENGLAND AND WALES,
Federation House, Highbury Drive, Leatherhead,
Surrey KT22 7UY T 01372-352000 W www.polfed.org
*General Secretary,* Andy Fittes
POLICE SUPERINTENDENTS' ASSOCIATION OF
ENGLAND AND WALES, 67A Reading Road, Pangbourne,
Reading RG8 7JD T 0118-984 4005 W www.policesupers.com
*National Secretary,* Chief Supt. Tim Jackson

### SCOTLAND
ASSOCIATION OF SCOTTISH POLICE
SUPERINTENDENTS, Scottish Police College,
Tulliallan Castle, Kincardine, Fife FK10 4BE T 01259-732123
W www.scottishpolicesupers.org.uk
*General Secretary,* Craig Suttie
SCOTTISH POLICE FEDERATION, 5 Woodside Place,
Glasgow G3 7QF T 0300-303 0027 W www.spf.org.uk
*General Secretary,* Calum Steele

### NORTHERN IRELAND
POLICE FEDERATION FOR NORTHERN IRELAND,
77–79 Garnerville Road, Belfast BT4 2NX T 028-9076 4200
W www.policefed-ni.org.uk
*Secretary,* Marty Whittle
SUPERINTENDENTS' ASSOCIATION OF NORTHERN
IRELAND, PSNI College, Garnerville Road, Belfast BT4 2NX
T 028-9092 2201 W www.policesuperintendentsni.org
*Hon. Secretary,* vacant

## RATES OF PAY *from September 2015*

| | |
|---|---:|
| Chief Constables of Greater Manchester and West Midlands* | £186,954 |
| Chief Constable | £133,983–£174,491 |
| Deputy Chief Constable | £112,173–£143,334 |
| Assistant Chief Constable and Commanders | £96,596–£109,055 |
| Chief Superintendent | £79,557–£83,925 |
| Superintendent Range *in rank on or after* 1 April 2014 | £64,188–£75,816 |
| Superintendent *in rank before* 1 April 2014 | £64,188–£74,784 |
| Chief Inspector‡ | £53,358 (£55,485)–£55,554 (£57,675)† |
| Inspector‡ | £48,207 (£50,319)–£52,290 (£54,420)† |
| Sergeant | £38,910–£42,285† |
| Constable *apptd on or after 1 April 2013* | £19,578–£37,626 |
| Constable *apptd before 1 April 2013* | £23,964–£37,626† |

*Metropolitan Police*

| | |
|---|---:|
| Commissioner | £267,970 |
| Deputy Commissioner | £221,229 |

*City of London Police*

| | |
|---|---:|
| Commissioner | £165,777 |
| Assistant Commissioner | £136,734 |

*Police Scotland*

| | |
|---|---:|
| Chief Constable | £208,100 |
| Deputy Chief Constable | £169,600 |
| Assistant Chief Constable | £115,000 |

*Police Service of Northern Ireland*

| | |
|---|---:|
| Chief Constable | £199,413 |
| Deputy Chief Constable | £162,020 |

* Also applicable to the four Assistant Commissioners of the Metropolitan Police Service
† Officers on this pay point may additionally receive a competence-related threshold payment of £300 in 2015–16. This payment will be abolished from 1 April 2016
‡ London salary in parentheses. All other officers (not Metropolitan or City of London Commissioners) working in London receive an additional payment of £2,349 per annum

# THE PRISON SERVICE

The prison services in the UK are the responsibility of the Secretary of State for Justice, the Scottish Secretary for Justice and the Minister of Justice in Northern Ireland. The chief executive (director-general in Northern Ireland), officers of the National Offender Management Service (NOMS), the Scottish Prison Service (SPS) and the Northern Ireland Prison Service are responsible for the day-to-day running of the system.

There are 122 prison establishments in England and Wales, 15 in Scotland and three in Northern Ireland. Convicted prisoners are classified according to their assessed security risk and are housed in establishments appropriate to that level of security. There are no open prisons in Northern Ireland. Female prisoners are housed in women's establishments or in separate wings of mixed prisons. Remand prisoners are, where possible, housed separately from convicted prisoners. Offenders under the age of 21 are usually detained in a Young Offender Institution, which may be a separate establishment or part of a prison. Appellant and failed asylum seekers are held in Immigration Removal Centres, or in separate units of other prisons.

Fourteen prisons are now run by the private sector in England and Wales, and in England, Wales and Scotland all escort services have been contracted out to private companies. In Scotland, two prisons (Kilmarnock and Addiewell) were built and financed by the private sector and are being operated by private contractors.

There are independent prison inspectorates in England, Wales and Scotland which report annually on conditions and the treatment of prisoners. The Chief Inspector of Criminal Justice in Northern Ireland and HM Inspectorate of Prisons for England and Wales perform an inspectorate role for prisons in Northern Ireland. Every prison establishment also has an independent monitoring board made up of local volunteers.

Any prisoner whose complaint is not satisfied by the internal complaints procedures may complain to the prisons and probation ombudsman for England and Wales, the Scottish public services ombudsman or the prisoner ombudsman for Northern Ireland. The prisons and probation inspectors, the prisons ombudsman and the independent monitoring boards report to the home secretary and to the Minister of Justice in Northern Ireland.

## PRISON STATISTICS

The projected 'high scenario' prison population for 2020 in England and Wales is 98,900; the 'low scenario' is 81,400.

PRISON POPULATION (UK) *as at June 2015*

| | Remand | Sentenced | Other |
| --- | --- | --- | --- |
| ENGLAND AND WALES | 11,785 | 72,659 | 1,749 |
| Male | 11,159 | 69,404 | 1,726 |
| Female | 626 | 3,255 | 23 |
| SCOTLAND* | 1,365 | 6,062 | – |
| Male | 1,283 | 5,757 | – |
| Female | 82 | 305 | – |
| N. IRELAND | 373 | 1,292 | 0 |
| Male | 355 | 1,253 | 0 |
| Female | 18 | 39 | 0 |
| UK TOTAL | 13,523 | 80,013 | 1,749 |

* Figures from August 2015
*Sources:* MoJ; Scottish Prison Service; NI Prison Service

PRISON CAPACITY (ENGLAND AND WALES)
*as at August 2015*

| | |
| --- | --- |
| Male prisoners | 82,041 |
| Female prisoners | 3,910 |
| *Total* | 85,951 |
| Useable operational capacity | 88,242 |
| Under home detention curfew supervision | 2,127 |

*Source:* MoJ – *Prisons and Probation Statistics*

SENTENCED PRISON POPULATION BY SEX AND OFFENCE (ENGLAND AND WALES)
*as at 30 June 2015*

| | Male | Female |
| --- | --- | --- |
| Violence against the person | 17,664 | 873 |
| Sexual offences | 11,402 | 88 |
| Robbery | 7,934 | 312 |
| Theft offences | 10,825 | 742 |
| Criminal damage and arson | 1,066 | 115 |
| Fraud offences | 1,227 | 182 |
| Drugs offences | 10,013 | 429 |
| Possession of weapons | 1,697 | 56 |
| Public order offences | 1,153 | 37 |
| Miscellaneous crimes against society | 3,008 | 217 |
| Summary non-motoring | 2,568 | 139 |
| Summary motoring | 374 | 7 |
| Offence not recorded | 379 | 45 |
| *Total* | 69,310 | 3,242 |

*Source:* MoJ – *Prisons and Probation Statistics*

SENTENCED POPULATION BY LENGTH OF SENTENCE (ENGLAND AND WALES)
*as at 30 June 2015*

| | British | Other Nationalities or Not Recorded |
| --- | --- | --- |
| Less than 12 months | 5,347 | 843 |
| 12 months to less than 4 years | 16,958 | 1,650 |
| 4 years to less than life | 25,794 | 3,013 |
| Indeterminate | 11,020 | 1,033 |
| *Total** | 59,119 | 6,539 |

* Figures do not include civil (non-criminal) prisoners or fine defaulters
*Source:* MoJ – *Prisons and Probation Statistics*

AVERAGE DAILY POPULATION BY TYPE OF CUSTODY 2014–15 (SCOTLAND)

| | |
| --- | --- |
| Remand: sub total | 1,525 |
| Persons under sentence: sub total | 6,205 |
| Under 4 years | 3,385 |
| 4 years and over | 2,820 |
| *Total* | 7,730 |

*Source:* SPS – *Annual Report and Accounts 2014–15*

SUICIDES IN PRISON IN 2014 (ENGLAND AND WALES)

| | |
| --- | --- |
| *Total* | 82 |

*Source:* MoJ

# THE PRISON SERVICES

## NATIONAL OFFENDER MANAGEMENT SERVICE

Clive House, 70 Petty France, London SW1H 9EX
T 0300-047 6325 E public.enquiries@noms.gsi.gov.uk
W www.gov.uk/government/organisations/national-offender-management-service

HM Prison Service became part of the National Offender Management Service (NOMS) on 1 April 2008 as part of the reorganisation of the Ministry of Justice (MoJ).

### SALARIES (ENGLAND AND WALES)
*from 1 April 2015*
All salary ranges given are for the average across England and Wales (includes inner and outer London salaries) and are based on a 37-hour-week inclusive of the required hours allowance (Governors, Deputy Governors and Heads of Function) or the additional 17 per cent unsocial hours payment for all other grades.

| | |
|---|---|
| Governor | £63,411–£86,075 |
| Deputy Governor | £44,972–£69,124 |
| Head of Function | £38,569–£53,970 |
| Custodial Manager | £29,562–£33,334 |
| Supervising/Specialist Officer | £26,183–£29,221 |
| Prison Officer | £20,545–£22,892 |
| Operational Support Grade | £17,386–£18,622 |

### THE NOMS BOARD
*Chief Executive,* Michael Spurr
*Director of Commissioning and Commercial,* Ian Blakeman
*Director of Probation,* Colin Allars
*Director of National Operational Services,* Digby Griffith
*Director of Public Sector Prisons,* Phil Copple
*Director of Human Resources,* Carol Carpenter
*Director, National Offender Management Service in Wales,* Sarah Payne
*Director of Finance and Analysis,* Andrew Emmett
*Director of Digital and Change,* Bryan Clarke
*Director of Commissioning and Contract Management,* Ian Porée

### DEPUTY DIRECTORS OF CUSTODY
Paul Baker *(East Midlands and West Midlands);* Ian Barrow *(Wales);* Michelle Jarman-Howe *(Kent and Sussex);* Ian Mulholland *(Public Service Prisons);* Nick Pascoe *(London);* Neil Richards *(Yorkshire and Humberside);* Andy Rogers *(South-West);* Alan Scott *(North-West);* Adrian Smith *(East of England);* Claudia Sturt *(South-Central);* Alan Tallentire *(North-East);* Richard Vince *(High Security)*

### OPERATING COSTS OF NOMS 2014–15
| | |
|---|---|
| Staff costs | £1,864,683,000 |
| Operating income | (£313,596,000) |
| Net operating costs (before tax) | £3,762,100,000 |
| Net operating costs (after tax) | £3,761,676,000 |
*Source:* NOMS – *Annual Report 2014–15*

## SCOTTISH PRISON SERVICE (SPS)
Calton House, 5 Redheughs Rigg, Edinburgh EH12 9HW
T 0131-244 8745 E gaolinfo@sps.pnn.gov.uk
W www.sps.gov.uk

### SALARIES *from October 2015*
| | |
|---|---|
| Governor in Charge | £62,160–£70,509 |
| Deputy Governor | £50,323–£58,424 |
| Head of Operations | £40,654–£48,579 |
| Unit Manager | £32,778–£41,269 |
| First Line Manager | £26,717–£34,430 |
| Residential Officer | £22,427–£28,891 |
| Operations Officer | £17,521–£22,245 |

### SPS BOARD
*Chief Executive,* Colin McConnell
*Directors,* Ian Davidson *(Strategy and Innovation);* Eric Murch *(Operations);* Catherine Topley *(Corporate Services)*
*Non-Executive Directors,* S. Browell; A. Burns; H. McGuigan; A. Macmillan; J. Martin; S. Matheson, OBE; H. Monro; Z. Van Zwanenberg

### OPERATING COSTS OF SPS 2014–15
| | |
|---|---|
| Total income | (£7,491,000) |
| Total expenditure | £310,081,000 |
| Staff costs | £163,029,000 |
| Running costs | £115,513,000 |
| Other current expenditure | £31,539,000 |
| Operating cost | £302,590,000 |
| Interest payable and similar charges | £11,181,000 |
| Net operating cost | £313,771,000 |
*Source:* SPS – *Annual Report and Accounts 2014–15*

## NORTHERN IRELAND PRISON SERVICE
Dundonald House, Upper Newtownards Road, Belfast BT4 3SU
T 028-9052 2922 E info@niprisonservice.gov.uk
W www.dojni.gov.uk

### SALARIES *as at April 2015*
| | |
|---|---|
| Governor 1 | £74,747–£81,356 |
| Governor in Charge | £64,900–£72,900 |
| Head of Function | £53,300–£57,050 |
| Head of Unit | £47,150–£51,055 |
| Senior Prison Officer | £33,400–£38,000 |
| Main Grade Prison Officer | £22,397–£30,406 |
| Operational Support Grade | £20,297 |

### SENIOR STAFF
*Director-General,* Sue McAllister
*Executive,* Mark Adam *(Human Resources and Corporate Services);* Brian McCaughey *(Rehabilitation);* Max Murray *(Estates Management)*

### OPERATING COSTS OF NORTHERN IRELAND PRISON SERVICE 2013–14
| | |
|---|---|
| Staff costs | £76,682,000 |
| Net running costs | £31,706,000 |
| Depreciation | £11,999,000 |
| *Operating expenditure* | £120,387,000 |
| *Net operating costs for the year* | £122,798,000 |
*Source:* NI Prison Service – *Annual Report and Accounts 2013–14*

# PRISON ESTABLISHMENTS

## ENGLAND AND WALES *as at June 2015*

| Prison | Address | Capacity | Prisoners | Governor/Director |
|---|---|---|---|---|
| ALTCOURSE (private prison) | Liverpool L9 7WU | 1,093 | 1,090 | Dave Thompson |
| ASHFIELD (private prison) | Bristol BS16 9QJ | 400 | 391 | Ray Duckworth |
| *‡ASKHAM GRANGE | York YO23 3FT | 128 | 87 | Diane Pellew |
| ‡AYLESBURY | Bucks HP20 1EH | 444 | 383 | Kevin Leggett |
| BEDFORD | Bedford MK40 1HG | 506 | 489 | Ian Blakeman |
| BELMARSH | London SE28 0EB | 906 | 867 | Phil Wragg |
| BIRMINGHAM | Birmingham B18 4AS | 1,450 | 1,426 | Peter Small |
| BLANTYRE HOUSE | Kent TN17 2NH | 0 | 0 | James Bourke |
| †‡BRINSFORD | Wolverhampton WV10 7PY | 455 | 386 | Carl Hardwick |
| ‡BRISTOL | Bristol BS7 8PS | 614 | 594 | Andrea Albutt |
| ‡BRIXTON | London SW2 5XF | 798 | 795 | Edmond Tullett |
| *BRONZEFIELD (private prison) | Middlesex TW15 3JZ | 527 | 491 | Charlotte Pattison-Rideout |
| BUCKLEY HALL | Lancs OL12 9DP | 445 | 446 | Susan Kennedy |
| BULLINGDON | Oxon OX25 1PZ | 1,114 | 1,079 | Ian Blakeman |
| BURE | Norfolk NR10 5GB | 624 | 622 | Sue Doolan |
| †CARDIFF | Cardiff CF24 0UG | 820 | 815 | Steve Cross |
| CHANNINGS WOOD | Devon TQ12 6DW | 731 | 720 | Gavin O'Malley |
| ‡CHELMSFORD | Essex CM2 6LQ | 745 | 690 | Helen Carter |
| COLDINGLEY | Surrey GU24 9EX | 519 | 516 | Glenn Knight |
| ‡COOKHAM WOOD | Kent ME1 3LU | 188 | 173 | Jonathan French |
| DARTMOOR | Devon PL20 6RR | 660 | 633 | Terry Witton |
| ‡DEERBOLT | Co. Durham DL12 9BG | 513 | 360 | Gabrielle Lee |
| ‡DONCASTER (private prison) | Doncaster DN5 8UX | 1,145 | 1,107 | John Biggin |
| DOVEGATE (private prison) | Staffs ST14 8XR | 1,133 | 1,103 | Craig Thomson |
| §DOVER | Kent CT17 9DR | 401 | 370 | Sara Pennington |
| *DOWNVIEW | Surrey SM2 5PD | 0 | 0 | Jonathan French |
| *‡DRAKE HALL | Staffs ST21 6LQ | 340 | 300 | Paul Newton |
| DURHAM | Durham DH1 3HU | 995 | 948 | Tim Allen |
| *‡EAST SUTTON PARK | Kent ME17 3DF | 100 | 94 | James Bourke |
| *‡EASTWOOD PARK | Glos GL12 8DB | 363 | 330 | Simon Beecroft |
| ELMLEY | Kent ME12 4DZ | 1,175 | 1,152 | Jim Carmichael |
| ERLESTOKE | Wilts SN10 5TU | 524 | 514 | Andy Rogers |
| †‡EXETER | Devon EX4 4EX | 561 | 524 | Jeannine Hendrick |
| FEATHERSTONE | Wolverhampton WV10 7PU | 687 | 677 | Deborah Butler |
| †‡FELTHAM | Middx TW13 4ND | 594 | 496 | Glenn Knight |
| FORD | W. Sussex BN18 0BX | 524 | 512 | Sharon Williams |
| ‡FOREST BANK (private prison) | Manchester M27 8FB | 1,460 | 1,434 | Trevor Shortt |
| *FOSTON HALL | Derby DE65 5DN | 345 | 290 | Ken Kan |
| FRANKLAND | Durham DH1 5YD | 844 | 834 | Paddy Fox |
| FULL SUTTON | York YO41 1PS | 616 | 585 | Paul Foweather |
| GARTH | Preston PR26 8NE | 773 | 795 | Steve Lawrence |
| GARTREE | Leics LE16 7RP | 708 | 710 | Ian Telfer |
| †‡GLEN PARVA | Leicester LE18 4TN | 728 | 554 | Michael Wood |
| GRENDON/SPRING HILL | Bucks HP18 0TL | 568 | 529 | Jamie Bennett |
| ‡GUYS MARSH | Dorset SP7 0AH | 579 | 564 | Duncan Burles |
| §HASLAR | Hampshire PO12 2AW | 0 | 0 | Paul Millett |
| HAVERIGG | Cumbria LA18 4NA | 644 | 622 | Tony Corcoran |
| HEWELL | Worcs B97 6QS | 1,279 | 1,261 | Nigel Atkinson |
| HIGH DOWN | Surrey SM2 5PJ | 1,163 | 1,147 | Ian Bickers |
| HIGHPOINT | Suffolk CB8 9YG | 1,300 | 1,298 | Nigel Smith |
| †‡HINDLEY | Lancs WN2 5TH | 398 | 436 | Peter Francis |
| ‡HOLLESLEY BAY | Suffolk IP12 3JW | 424 | 391 | Declan Moore |
| *‡HOLLOWAY | London N7 0NU | 591 | 518 | Julia Killick |
| HOLME HOUSE | Stockton-on-Tees TS18 2QU | 1,210 | 1,199 | Jenny Mooney |
| ‡HULL | Hull HU9 5LS | 1,044 | 995 | Norman Griffin |
| HUMBER | E. Yorks HU15 | 1,026 | 1,008 | Ian Telfer |
| ‡HUNTERCOMBE | Oxon RG9 5SB | 430 | 427 | Nigel Atkinson |
| ISIS | Thamesmead SE28 0NZ | 622 | 614 | Grahame Hawkings |
| ISLE OF WIGHT | Isle of Wight PO30 5RS | 1,097 | 1,079 | Andy Lattimore |
| KENNET | Merseyside L31 1HX | 342 | 290 | Steve Valentine |
| KIRKHAM | Lancs PR4 2RN | 657 | 606 | Graham Beck |
| KIRKLEVINGTON GRANGE | Cleveland TS15 9PA | 283 | 274 | Steve Robson |
| †‡LANCASTER FARMS | Lancaster LA1 3QZ | 549 | 535 | Derek Harrison |
| LEEDS | Leeds LS12 2TJ | 1,212 | 1,189 | Susan Kennedy |
| LEICESTER | Leicester LE2 7AJ | 411 | 340 | Ali Dodds |
| ‡LEWES | E. Sussex BN7 1EA | 722 | 649 | Nigel Foote |
| LEYHILL | Glos GL12 8BT | 527 | 494 | Chantel King |
| LINCOLN | Lincoln LN2 4BD | 729 | 643 | Peter Wright |
| LINDHOLME | Doncaster DN7 6EE | 1,010 | 990 | Steve Robson |
| LITTLEHEY | Cambs PE28 0SR | 1,219 | 1,210 | David Taylor |
| LIVERPOOL | Liverpool L9 3DF | 1,386 | 1,193 | John Illingsworth |
| LONG LARTIN | Worcs WR11 8TZ | 625 | 616 | Nick Dann |
| *‡LOW NEWTON | Durham DH1 5YA | 344 | 297 | Alan Richer |

| Prison | Address | Capacity | Prisoners | Governor/Director |
|---|---|---|---|---|
| LOWDHAM GRANGE (private prison) | Notts NG14 7DA | 920 | 914 | Trish Mitchell |
| MAIDSTONE | Kent ME14 1UZ | 600 | 599 | Dave Atkinson |
| MANCHESTER | Manchester M60 9AH | 1,286 | 1,090 | Hannah Lane |
| ‡MOORLAND/HATFIELD | Doncaster DN7 6BW | 1,006 | 970 | David Bamford |
| §MORTON HALL | Lincoln LN6 9PT | 392 | 373 | Karen Head |
| MOUNT | Herts HP3 0NZ | 1,020 | 1,020 | Steven Bradford |
| *‡NEW HALL | W. Yorks WF4 4XX | 425 | 386 | Diane Pellew |
| NORTH SEA CAMP | Lincs PE22 0QX | 420 | 307 | Paul Yates |
| ‡NORTHUMBERLAND | Northumberland NE65 9XF | 1,348 | 1,329 | Matt Spencer |
| ‡NORWICH | Norfolk NR1 4LU | 769 | 737 | Will Styles |
| NOTTINGHAM | Notts NG5 3AG | 1,060 | 1,049 | James Shanley |
| OAKWOOD | W. Midlands WV10 7QD | 1,605 | 1,599 | John McLaughlin |
| ONLEY | Warks CV23 8AP | 747 | 720 | Stephen Ruddy |
| †‡PARC (private prison) | Bridgend CF35 6AP | 1,723 | 1,687 | Janet Wallsgrove |
| ‡PENTONVILLE | London N7 8TT | 1,316 | 1,297 | Kevin Reilly |
| *†PETERBOROUGH (private prison) | Peterborough PE3 7PD | 1,252 | 1,188 | Nick Leader |
| ‡PORTLAND | Dorset DT5 1DL | 531 | 486 | James Lucas |
| PRESTON | Lancs PR1 5AB | 790 | 707 | Paul Holland |
| RANBY | Notts DN22 8EU | 1,098 | 1,065 | Susan Howard |
| RISLEY | Cheshire WA3 6BP | 1,095 | 1,081 | Jerry Spencer |
| ‡ROCHESTER | Kent ME1 3QS | 738 | 735 | Andy Hudson |
| RYE HILL (private prison) | Warks CV23 8SZ | 625 | 625 | Dave Thompson, OBE |
| *SEND | Surrey GU23 7LJ | 282 | 278 | Dave Charity *(acting)* |
| STAFFORD | Stafford ST16 3AW | 741 | 738 | Bridie Oakes-Richards |
| STANDFORD HILL | Kent ME12 4AA | 464 | 456 | Sarah Coccia |
| STOCKEN | Leics LE15 7RD | 713 | 683 | Michael Wood |
| ‡STOKE HEATH | Shropshire TF9 2JL | 782 | 748 | John Huntington |
| *‡STYAL | Cheshire SK9 4HR | 485 | 471 | John Hewitson |
| SUDBURY | Derbys DE6 5HW | 600 | 447 | Adrian Turner |
| SWALESIDE | Kent ME12 4AX | 1,112 | 1,108 | Sarah Coccia |
| †‡SWANSEA | Swansea SA1 3SR | 455 | 429 | Lauren Watson |
| ‡SWINFEN HALL | Staffs WS14 9QS | 594 | 578 | Teresa Clarke |
| THAMESIDE | London SE28 0FJ | 1,080 | 1,009 | Guy Baulf |
| ‡THORN CROSS | Cheshire WA4 4RL | 381 | 339 | Pia Sinha |
| USK/PRESCOED | Monmouthshire NP15 1XP | 503 | 499 | Steve Cross |
| VERNE | Dorset DT5 1EQ | 580 | 491 | David Ward |
| WAKEFIELD | W. Yorks WF2 9AG | 730 | 722 | Susan Howard |
| WANDSWORTH | London SW18 3HS | 1,658 | 1,593 | Kenny Brown |
| ‡WARREN HILL | Suffolk IP12 3JW | 212 | 157 | Bev Bevan |
| WAYLAND | Norfolk IP25 6RL | 1,015 | 1,000 | Steve Rodford, OBE |
| WEALSTUN | W. Yorks LS23 7AZ | 833 | 807 | Andrew Dickinson |
| ‡WERRINGTON | Stoke-on-Trent ST9 0DX | 160 | 114 | Babafemi Dada |
| ‡WETHERBY | W. Yorks LS22 5ED | 336 | 278 | Sara Snell |
| WHATTON | Nottingham NG13 9FQ | 841 | 838 | Lynn Saunders |
| WHITEMOOR | Cambs PE15 0PR | 458 | 447 | Paul Cawkwell |
| WINCHESTER | Winchester SO22 5DF | 685 | 681 | David Rogers |
| WOODHILL | Bucks MK4 4DA | 727 | 706 | Rob Davis |
| WORMWOOD SCRUBS | London W12 0AE | 1,279 | 1,241 | Gary Monaghan |
| WYMOTT | Preston PR26 8LW | 1,143 | 1,130 | Terry Williams |

## SCOTLAND *as at July 2015*

| Prison | Address | Average Daily | Maximum Number | Governor/Director |
|---|---|---|---|---|
| ADDIEWELL (private prison) | West Lothian EH55 8QA | 700 | 710 | Audrey Park |
| †BARLINNIE | Glasgow G33 2QX | 1,303 | 1,433 | Ian Whitehead |
| *†‡CORNTON VALE | Stirling FK9 5NU | 213 | 264 | Allister Purdie |
| †DUMFRIES | Dumfries DG2 9AX | 174 | 186 | Rhona Hotchkiss |
| †EDINBURGH | Edinburgh EH11 3LN | 864 | 931 | Teresa Medhurst |
| GLENOCHIL | Tullibody FK10 3AD | 635 | 678 | Nigel Ironside |
| GRAMPIAN | Aberdeenshire AB42 2YY | 291 | 395 | Jim Farish |
| †‡GREENOCK | Greenock PA16 9AH | 235 | 248 | William Stuart |
| *†INVERNESS | Inverness IV2 3HH | 120 | 141 | Andrew Hodge |
| †‡KILMARNOCK (private prison) | Kilmarnock KA1 5AA | 501 | 518 | Craig Thomson |
| LOW MOSS | Glasgow G64 2PZ | 737 | 764 | Sharanne Findley *(acting)* |
| OPEN ESTATE | Angus DD8 3QY | 252 | 276 | Jacqui Clinton |
| †PERTH | Perth PH2 8AT | 643 | 689 | Tom McMurchie *(acting)* |
| †‡POLMONT | Falkirk FK2 0AB | 501 | 546 | Sue Brookes |
| SHOTTS | Lanarkshire ML7 4LE | 531 | 540 | James Kerr |

## NORTHERN IRELAND *as at June 2015*

| Prison | Address | Prisoners | Governor/Director |
|---|---|---|---|
| *†‡HYDEBANK WOOD | Belfast BT8 8NA | 153 | Austin Treacy |
| †§MAGHABERRY | Co. Antrim BT28 2NF | 974 | Pat Maguire |
| MAGILLIGAN | Co. Londonderry BT49 0LR | 538 | Alan Longwell |

* Women's establishment or establishment with units for women; † Remand Centre or establishment with units for remand prisoners; ‡ Young Offender Institution or establishment with units for young offenders; § Immigration Removal Centre or establishment with units for immigration detainees

# DEFENCE

The armed forces of the UK comprise the Royal Navy, the Army and the Royal Air Force (RAF). The Queen is Commander-in-Chief of all the armed forces. The Secretary of State for Defence is responsible for the formulation and content of defence policy and for providing the means by which it is conducted. The formal legal basis for the conduct of defence in the UK rests on a range of powers vested by statute and letters patent in the Defence Council, chaired by the Secretary of State for Defence. Beneath the ministers lies the top management of the Ministry of Defence (MoD), headed jointly by the Permanent Secretary and the Chief of Defence Staff. The Permanent Secretary is the government's principal civilian adviser on defence and has the primary responsibility for policy, finance, management and administration. The Permanent Secretary is also personally accountable to parliament for the expenditure of all public money allocated to defence purposes. The Chief of Defence Staff is the professional head of the armed forces in the UK and the principal military adviser to the secretary of state and the government.

The Defence Board is the executive of the Defence Council. Chaired by the Permanent Secretary, it acts as the main executive board of the Ministry of Defence, providing senior level leadership and strategic management of defence.

The Central Staff, headed by the Vice-Chief of the Defence Staff and the Second Permanent Under-Secretary of State, is the policy core of the department. Defence Equipment and Support, headed by the Chief of Defence Materiel, is responsible for purchasing defence equipment and providing logistical support to the armed forces.

A permanent Joint Headquarters for the conduct of joint operations was set up at Northwood in 1996. The Joint Headquarters connects the policy and strategic functions of the MoD head office with the conduct of operations and is intended to strengthen the policy/executive division.

The UK pursues its defence and security policies through its membership of NATO (to which most of its armed forces are committed), the European Union, the Organisation for Security and Cooperation in Europe and the UN (*see* International Organisations section).

## STRENGTH OF THE REGULAR ARMED FORCES

|  | Royal Navy | Army | RAF | All Services |
|---|---|---|---|---|
| 1975 strength | 76,200 | 167,100 | 95,000 | 338,300 |
| 2000 strength | 42,850 | 110,050 | 54,720 | 207,620 |
| 2005 strength | 39,940 | 109,290 | 51,870 | 201,100 |
| 2006 strength | 39,390 | 107,730 | 48,730 | 195,850 |
| 2007 strength | 38,850 | 106,340 | 45,480 | 190,670 |
| 2008 strength | 38,560 | 104,980 | 43,370 | 186,910 |
| 2009 strength | 38,340 | 106,700 | 43,560 | 188,600 |
| 2010 strength | 38,730 | 108,920 | 44,050 | 191,700 |
| 2011 strength | 37,660 | 106,240 | 42,460 | 186,360 |
| 2012 strength | 35,540 | 104,250 | 40,000 | 179,800 |
| 2013 strength | 33,960 | 99,730 | 37,030 | 170,710 |
| 2014 strength | 33,330 | 91,070 | 35,230 | 159,630 |
| 2015 strength | 32,740 | 87,060 | 33,930 | 153,720 |

*Source:* MoD – *Defence Statistics (Tri-Service)*

## SERVICE PERSONNEL BY RANK AND GENDER 2015

|  | Males | Females |
|---|---|---|
| Officers | 23,760 | 3,470 |
| Other Ranks | 114,410 | 12,080 |

*Source:* MoD – *Defence Statistics (Tri-Service)*

UK regular forces include trained and untrained personnel and nursing services, but exclude Gurkhas, full-time reserve service personnel, mobilised reservists and naval activated reservists. As at 1 April 2015 these groups provisionally numbered:

| | |
|---|---|
| All Gurkhas | 2,870 |
| Full-time reserve service | 3,750 |
| Mobilised reservists | |
| Army | 310 |
| RAF | 70 |
| Naval activated reservists | 30 |

*Source:* MoD – *Defence Statistics (Tri-Service)*

## CIVILIAN PERSONNEL

| | |
|---|---|
| 2000 level | 121,300 |
| 2001 level | 118,200 |
| 2002 level | 110,100 |
| 2003 level | 107,600 |
| 2004 level | 108,990 |
| 2005 level | 107,680 |
| 2006 level | 102,970 |
| 2007 level | 95,790 |
| 2008 level | 88,690 |
| 2009 level | 86,620 |
| 2010 level | 85,850 |
| 2011 level | 83,060 |
| 2012 level | 70,940 |
| 2013 level | 65,400 |
| 2014 level | 62,340 |
| 2015 level | 58,200 |

*Source:* MoD – *Defence Statistics (Tri-Service)*

## UK REGULAR FORCES: DEATHS

In 2014 there were a total of 68 deaths among the UK regular armed forces, of which 12 were serving in the Royal Navy and Royal Marines, 40 in the Army and 16 in the RAF. The largest single cause of death was land transport accidents, which accounted for 31 deaths (31 per cent of total) in 2014. Cancer accounted for 15 deaths (22 per cent) and other accidents accounted for a further 12 deaths (18 per cent). For the first time since 2002, there were no deaths as a result of hostile action. Suicides and open verdicts accounted for six deaths.

## NUMBER OF DEATHS AND MORTALITY RATES

|  | 2010 | 2011 | 2012 | 2013 | 2014 |
|---|---|---|---|---|---|
| Total number | 187 | 132 | 130 | 86 | 68 |
| Royal Navy | 30 | 19 | 20 | 13 | 12 |
| Army | 136 | 98 | 95 | 63 | 40 |
| RAF | 21 | 15 | 15 | 10 | 16 |
| *Mortality rates per thousand* | | | | | |
| Tri-service rate | 0.97 | 0.69 | 0.72 | 0.50 | 0.42 |
| Navy | 0.77 | 0.52 | 0.59 | 0.42 | 0.35 |
| Army | 1.16 | 0.88 | 0.89 | 0.65 | 0.42 |
| RAF | 0.50 | 0.33 | 0.42 | 0.23 | 0.40 |

*Source:* MoD *National Statistics*

## NUCLEAR FORCES

The Vanguard Class SSBN (ship submersible ballistic nuclear) provides the UK's strategic nuclear deterrent. Each Vanguard Class submarine is capable of carrying 16 Trident D5 missiles equipped with nuclear warheads.

There is a ballistic missile early warning system station at RAF Fylingdales in North Yorkshire.

## ARMS CONTROL

The 1990 Conventional Armed Forces in Europe (CFE) Treaty, which commits all NATO and former Warsaw Pact members to limiting their holdings of five major classes of conventional weapons, has been adapted to reflect the changed geo-strategic environment and negotiations continue for its implementation. The Open Skies Treaty, which the UK signed in 1992 and entered into force in 2002, allows for the overflight of states parties by other states parties using unarmed observation aircraft.

The UN Convention on Certain Conventional Weapons (as amended 2001), which bans or restricts the use of specific types of weapons that are considered to cause unnecessary or unjustifiable suffering to combatants, or to affect civilians indiscriminately, was ratified by the UK in 1995. In 1968 the UK signed and ratified the Nuclear Non-Proliferation Treaty, which came into force in 1970 and was indefinitely and unconditionally extended in 1995. In 1996 the UK signed the Comprehensive Nuclear Test Ban Treaty and ratified it in 1998. The UK is a party to the 1972 Biological and Toxin Weapons Convention, which provides for a worldwide ban on biological weapons, and the 1993 Chemical Weapons Convention, which came into force in 1997 and provides for a verifiable worldwide ban on chemical weapons.

## DEFENCE BUDGET DEPARTMENTAL EXPENDITURE LIMITS £ billion

|  | 2015–16 |
| --- | --- |
| Resource DEL | 28.1 |
| Capital DEL | 6.8 |
| Total | 34.9 |

Source: HM Treasury – Summer Budget 2015 (Crown copyright)

## MINISTRY OF DEFENCE

Main Building, Whitehall, London SW1A 2HB
T 020-7218 9000
W www.gov.uk/government/organisations/ministry-of-defence

Secretary of State for Defence, Rt. Hon. Michael Fallon, MP
Parliamentary Private Secretary, Graham Evans, MP
Private Secretary, Luke Dearden
Special Advisers, Ben Mascall; James Wild
Minister of State (Defence Procurement), Philip Dunne, MP
Parliamentary Private Secretary, Oliver Colville, MP
Minister of State (Armed Forces), Penny Mordaunt, MP
Parliamentary Private Secretary, Oliver Colville, MP
Parliamentary Under-Secretary of State and Minister for Defence, Personnel and Veterans, Mark Lancaster, TD, MP
Parliamentary Under-Secretary of State and Minister for Reserves, Julian Brazier, MP
Private Secretary, Emma Frost
Parliamentary Under-Secretary of State and Lords Spokesman, Rt. Hon. Earl Howe

## CHIEFS OF STAFF

Chief of the Defence Staff, Gen. Sir Nicholas Houghton, GCB, CBE, ADC
Vice Chief of the Defence Staff, Air Chief Marshal Sir Stuart Peach, KCB, CBE, ADC

Chief of the Naval Staff and First Sea Lord, Adm. Sir George Zambellas, KCB, DSC, ADC
Second Sea Lord, Rear-Adm. (Simon) Jonathan Woodcock, OBE
Chief of the General Staff, Gen. Sir Nicholas Carter, KCB, CBE, DSO, ADC
Assistant Chief of the General Staff, Maj.-Gen. David Cullen, OBE
Chief of the Air Staff, Air Chief Marshal Sir Andrew Pulford, KCB, CBE, ADC
Assistant Chief of the Air Staff, Air Vice-Marshal Richard Knighton

## SENIOR OFFICIALS

Permanent Under-Secretary of State, Jon Thompson
Chief of Defence Materiel, Sir Bernard Gray
Chief Scientific Adviser, Prof. Vernon Gibson, FRS
Director-General Finance, Louise Tulett

## THE DEFENCE COUNCIL

The Defence Council is chaired by the Secretary of State, and comprises the other ministers, the Permanent Under-Secretary, the Chief of Defence Staff and senior service officers and officials who head the armed services and the department's major corporate functions. It provides the formal legal basis for the conduct of UK defence through a range of powers vested in it by statute and letters patent.

## THE DEFENCE BOARD

Chaired by the Secretary of State, the Defence Board is the main corporate board of the MoD, providing senior level leadership and strategic management of defence. The current membership of the Defence Board is: the Secretary of State; the Minister of State for Defence Procurement; the Permanent Secretary (the most senior civilian in the MoD); the Chief of Defence Staff (the professional head of the armed forces); the Vice-Chief of the Defence Staff (the chief operating officer for the armed forces element of defence business); the Chief of Defence Materiel (the head of Defence Equipment and Support); the Director-General Finance; and three non-executive members.

## CENTRAL STAFF

Vice-Chief of the Defence Staff, Air Chief Marshal Sir Stuart Peach, KCB, CBE, ADC

## JOINT FORCES COMMAND

Commander Joint Forces Command, Gen. Sir Richard Barrons, KCB, CBE, ADC
Chief of Joint Operations, Lt.-Gen. John Lorimer, MBE, DSO
Chief of Staff (Operations), Air Vice-Marshal Stuart Atha, DSO
Chief of Staff HQ, Rear-Adm. Paul Bennett, OBE

## FLEET COMMAND

First Sea Lord, Adm. Sir George Zambellas, KCB, DSC, ADC
Fleet Commander and Deputy Chief of Naval Staff, Vice-Adm. Sir Philip Jones, KCB

## NAVAL HOME COMMAND

Second Sea Lord, Rear-Adm. (Simon) Jonathan Woodcock, OBE

## LAND FORCES

Commander Land Forces, Lt.-Gen. James Everard, CBE
Chief of Staff Land Forces, Maj.-Gen. Timothy Robinson, CBE

## AIR COMMAND

*Deputy Commander Operations,* Air Marshal Greg Bagwell, CB, CBE

*Deputy Commander Capability and Air Member for Personnel and Capability,* Air Marshal Sir Barry North, OBE

## DEFENCE EQUIPMENT AND SUPPORT

*Chief of Defence Materiel,* Sir Bernard Gray
*Chief of Materiel (Fleet),* Vice-Adm. Simon Lister, CB, OBE
*Chief of Materiel (Land),* Lt.-Gen. Sir Christopher Deverell, KCB, MBE
*Chief of Materiel (Air),* Air Marshal Sir Simon Bollom, CB

## EXECUTIVE AGENCIES

## DEFENCE ELECTRONICS AND COMPONENTS AGENCY

Welsh Road, Deeside, Flintshire CH5 2LS **T** 01244-847745
**E** decainfo@deca.mod.uk
**W** www.gov.uk/government/organisations/defence-electronics-and-components-agency
*Director Support Services,* Ian Doughty

## DEFENCE SCIENCE AND TECHNOLOGY LABORATORY

Porton Down, Salisbury, Wiltshire SP4 0JQ **T** 01980-613000
**E** centralenquiries@dstl.gov.uk
**W** www.gov.uk/government/organisations/defence-science-and-technology-laboratory
*Chief Executive,* Jonathan Lyle

## UK HYDROGRAPHIC OFFICE

Admiralty Way, Taunton, Somerset TA1 2DN **T** 01823-337900
**E** customerservices@ukho.gov.uk
**W** www.gov.uk/government/organisations/uk-hydrographic-office
*Chief Executive,* John Humphrey

## ARMED FORCES TRAINING AND RECRUITMENT

Flag Officer Sea Training (FOST) is responsible for all Royal Navy and Royal Fleet Auxiliary operational sea training. FOST's International Defence Training provides the focal point for all aspects of naval training. Training is divided into five streams: Naval Core Training (responsible for new entry, command, leadership and management training); Royal Marine; Submarine; Surface and Aviation.

The Army Recruiting and Training Division (ARTD) is responsible for the four key areas of army training: soldier initial training, at the School of Infantry or at one of the army's four other facilities; officer initial training at the Royal Military Academy Sandhurst; trade training at one of the army's specialist facilities; and resettlement training for those about to leave the army. Trade training facilities include: the Armour Centre; the Infantry Battle School; the Infantry Training Centre, Catterick; the Royal School of Military Engineering and the Army Aviation Centre.

The Royal Air Force No. 22 (Training) Group exists to recruit RAF personnel and provide trained specialist personnel to the armed forces as a whole, such as providing the army air corps with trained helicopter pilots. The group is split into five areas: RAF College Cranwell; the Air Cadet Organisation (ACO); the Directorate of Flying Training (DFT); the Directorate of Ground Training; and the Defence College of Technical Training.

The Defence College of Technical Training provides technical training to all three services and includes the Defence School of Aeronautical Engineering (DSAE); the Defence School of Communications and Information Systems (DSCIS); the Defence School of Electronic and Mechanical Engineering (DSEME); and the Defence School of Marine Engineering (DSMarE).

## USEFUL WEBSITES

**W** www.royalnavy.mod.uk
**W** www.army.mod.uk
**W** www.raf.mod.uk

# THE ROYAL NAVY

*In Order of Seniority*

## LORD HIGH ADMIRAL OF THE UNITED KINGDOM

HRH The Prince Philip, Duke of Edinburgh, KG, KT, OM, GBE, AC, QSO, PC, *apptd* 2011

## ADMIRALS OF THE FLEET

HRH The Prince Philip, Duke of Edinburgh, KG, KT, OM, GBE, AC, QSO, PC, *apptd* 1953
Sir Edward Ashmore, GCB, DSC, *apptd* 1977
Sir Benjamin Bathurst, GCB, *apptd* 1995
HRH The Prince of Wales, KG, KT, GCB, OM, AK, QSO, PC, ADC, *apptd* 2012
Lord Boyce, KG, GCB, OBE, *apptd* 2014

## ADMIRALS

(Former Chiefs or Vice Chiefs of Defence Staff and First Sea Lords who remain on the active list)
Slater, Sir Jock, GCB, LVO, *apptd* 1991
Abbott, Sir Peter, GBE, KCB, *apptd* 1995
Essenhigh, Sir Nigel, GCB, *apptd* 1998
West of Spithead, Lord, GCB, DSC, PC, *apptd* 2000

Band, Sir Jonathon, GCB, *apptd* 2002
Stanhope, Sir Mark, GCB, OBE, *apptd* 2004

## ADMIRALS

HRH The Princess Royal, KG, KT, GCVO, QSO *(Cdre-in-Chief HM Naval Base Portsmouth)*
Zambellas, Sir George, KCB, DSC, ADC *(First Sea Lord and Chief of Naval Staff)*

## VICE-ADMIRALS

HRH The Duke of York, KG, GCVO, ADC *(Adm. of the Sea Cadet Corps and Cdre-in-Chief Fleet Air Arm)*
Jones, Sir Philip, KCB *(Fleet Commander, Deputy Chief of Naval Staff and Chief Naval Warfare Officer)*
Hudson, Peter, CB, CBE *(Cdr Maritime Command)*
Corder, Ian, CB *(UK Military Representative to NATO and the EU)*
Lister, Simon, CB, OBE *(Chief of Materiel (Fleet), Chief of Fleet Support to the Navy Board and Chief Naval Engineering Officer)*
Potts, Duncan, CB *(Director-General Joint Force Development and Director Defence Academy)*
Woodcock, (Simon) Jonathan, OBE *(Second Sea Lord)*

## REAR-ADMIRALS

Parr, Matthew, CB *(Cdr (Operations) and Rear-Adm. Submarines (Head of Fighting Arm))*

Fraser, Timothy, CB *(Assistant Chief of Defence Staff (Capability and Force Design))*

Parker, Henry *(Director Ship Acquisition and Deputy Director Ships)*

Beverstock, Mark *(Assistant Chief of Defence Staff (Nuclear and Chemical, Biological))*

Morse, James *(Assistant Chief of Naval Staff (Capability) and Controller of the Navy)*

Lowe, Timothy *(National Hydrographer and Deputy Chief Executive (Hydrography))*

Williams, Simon *(Naval Secretary and Assistant Chief of Naval Staff (Personnel))*

Bennett, Paul, OBE *(Chief of Staff Joint Forces Command)*

Wareham, Michael *(Director Submarines)*

Cree, Malcolm *(Chief of Staff (Integrated Change Programme))*

Ancona, Simon *(Assistant Chief of Defence Staff (Defence Engagement))*

Kingwell, John *(Director Concepts and Doctrine)*

Mackay, Graeme *(Director Carrier Strike)*

Clink, John, OBE *(Flag Officer Sea Training)*

Burton, Alexander *(Assistant Chief of Naval Staff (Surface Ships))*

Beckett, Keith CBE *(Chief Strategic Systems Executive)*

Radakin, Antony *(Cdr UK Maritime Forces and Rear-Adm. Surface Ships (Head of Fighting Arm))*

Stokes, Richard *(Assistant Chief of Naval Staff (Support))*

Weale, John, OBE *(Flag Officer Scotland and Northern Ireland and Assistant Chief of Naval Staff (Submarines))*

Blount, Keith, OBE *(Assistant Chief of Naval Staff (Aviation, Amphibious Capability and Carriers) and Rear-Adm. Fleet Air Arm (Head of Fighting Arm))*

McAlpine, Paul, OBE *(Deputy Cdr Strike Force NATO)*

Hine, Nicholas *(Assistant Chief of Naval Staff (Policy))*

## MEDICAL

Walker, Alasdair, OBE, QHS *(Surgeon Rear-Adm., Director Medical Policy and Operational Capability and Medical Director General (Naval))*

## ROYAL MARINES

### CAPTAIN-GENERAL

HRH The Prince Philip, Duke of Edinburgh, KG, KT, OM, GBE, AC, QSO, PC

### LIEUTENANT-GENERAL

Messenger, Gordon, CB, DSO\*, OBE *(Deputy Chief of Defence Staff (Military Strategic Operations))*

Davis, Edward, CB, CBE *(Deputy Cdr Land Command, Izmir)*

### MAJOR-GENERAL

Smith, Martin, MBE *(Cdr UK Amphibious Forces and Commandant-General Royal Marines)*

The Royal Marines were formed in 1664 and are part of the Naval Service. Their primary purpose is to conduct amphibious and land warfare. The principal operational units are:

• Three Commando Brigade, an amphibious all-arms brigade trained to operate in arduous environments (a core element of the UK's Joint Rapid Reaction Force). The commando units, 40 Commando, 42 Commando and 45 Commando each have a strength of around 700 and are based in Taunton, Plymouth and Arbroath, respectively. 43 Commando Fleet Protection Group is over 500 strong

and is based at HM Naval Base Clyde on the west coast of Scotland.

• 1 Assault Group, which has its headquarters located in Devonport, Plymouth is responsible for ten landing craft training squadron at Poole, Dorset and 11 amphibious trials and training squadron at Instow, Devon

The Royal Marines also provide detachments for warships and land-based naval parties as required.

## ROYAL MARINES RESERVES (RMR)

The Royal Marines Reserve is a commando-trained volunteer force with the principal role, when mobilised, of supporting the Royal Marines. The RMR consists of approximately 600 trained ranks who are distributed between the four RMR centres in the UK. Approximately 10 per cent of the RMR are working with the regular corps on long-term attachments within all of the Royal Marines regular units.

## OTHER PARTS OF THE NAVAL SERVICE

### FLEET AIR ARM

The Fleet Air Arm (FAA) provides the Royal Navy with a multi-role aviation combat capability able to operate autonomously at short notice worldwide in all environments, over the sea and land. The FAA numbers some 6,200 people, which comprises 11.5 per cent of the total Royal Naval strength. It operates some 200 combat aircraft and more than 50 support/training aircraft.

### ROYAL FLEET AUXILIARY SERVICE (RFA)

The Royal Fleet Auxiliary Service is a civilian-manned flotilla of 13 ships owned by the MoD. Its primary role is to supply the Royal Navy and host nations while at sea with fuel, ammunition, food and spares, enabling them to maintain operations away from their home ports. It also provides amphibious support and secure sea transport for military units and their equipment. The ships routinely support and embark Royal Naval Air Squadrons.

### ROYAL NAVAL RESERVE (RNR)

The Royal Naval Reserve is an integral part of the Naval Service. It is a part-time force of 2,300 trained men and women who are deployed with the Royal Navy in times of tension, humanitarian crisis or conflict.

The Royal Naval Reserve has 18 units throughout the UK; 17 of these provide initial training while one other specialist unit, HMS *Ferret,* provides intelligence training. Basic training is provided at HMS *Raleigh,* Torpoint in Cornwall for ratings and at the Britannia Royal Naval College, Dartmouth in Devon for officers; both these and most other RNR courses are of two weeks' duration or less.

### QUEEN ALEXANDRA'S ROYAL NAVAL NURSING SERVICE

The first nursing sisters were appointed to naval hospitals in 1884 and the Queen Alexandra's Royal Naval Nursing Service (QARNNS) gained its current title in 1902. Nursing ratings were introduced in 1960 and men were integrated into the service in 1982; QARNNS recruits qualified nurses as both officers and ratings, and student nurse training can be undertaken in the service.

*Patron,* HRH Princess Alexandra, the Hon. Lady Ogilvy, KG, GCVO

*Head of the Naval Nursing Service,* Capt. Steve Spencer, QHNS, QARNNS

## HM FLEET
*as at September 2015*

### Submarines
| | |
|---|---|
| Vanguard Class | Vanguard, Vengeance, Victorious, Vigilant |
| Trafalgar Class | Talent, Torbay, Trenchant, Triumph |
| Astute Class | Astute, Ambush, Artful |
| *Landing Platform Helicopter* | Ocean |
| *Landing Platform Dock* | Albion, Bulwark |

### Destroyers
| | |
|---|---|
| Type 45 | Daring, Dauntless, Defender, Diamond, Dragon, Duncan |

### Frigates
| | |
|---|---|
| Type 23 | Argyll, Iron Duke, Kent, Lancaster, Monmouth, Montrose, Northumberland, Portland, Richmond, St Albans, Somerset, Sutherland, Westminster |

### Mine Warfare Vessels
| | |
|---|---|
| Hunt Class | Atherstone, Brocklesby, Cattistock, Chiddingfold, Hurworth, Ledbury, Middleton, Quorn |
| Sandown Class | Bangor, Blyth, Grimsby, Pembroke, Penzance, Ramsey, Shoreham |

### Patrol Vessels
| | |
|---|---|
| Archer Class P2000 Training Boats | Archer, Biter, Blazer, Charger, Dasher, Example, Exploit, Explorer, Express, Puncher, Pursuer, Raider, Ranger, Smiter, Tracker, Trumpeter |
| Gibraltar Squadron 16m Fast Patrol Boats | Sabre, Scimitar |
| River Class | Clyde, Mersey, Severn, Tyne |

### Survey Vessels
| | |
|---|---|
| Ice Patrol Ships | Protector |
| Ocean Survey Vessel | Scott |
| Coastal Survey Vessel | Gleaner |
| Multi-Role Survey Vessels | Echo, Enterprise |

## ROYAL FLEET AUXILIARY
| | |
|---|---|
| Landing Ship Dock (Auxiliary) Wave Class | RFA Cardigan Bay, RFA Mounts Bay, RFA Lyme Bay RFA Wave Knight, RFA Wave Ruler |
| Rover Class | RFA Black Rover, RFA Gold Rover |
| Leaf Class | RFA Orangeleaf |
| Fort Class | RFA Fort Austin, RFA Fort Rosalie, RFA Fort Victoria |
| Forward Repair Ship | RFA Diligence |
| Joint Casualty Treatment Ship/Maritime Afloat Training Capability | RFA Argus |

---

# THE ARMY

*In Order of Seniority*

### THE QUEEN

### FIELD MARSHALS
HRH The Prince Philip, Duke of Edinburgh, KG, KT, OM, GBE, AC, QSO, PC, *apptd* 1953
Lord Bramall, KG, GCB, OBE, MC, *apptd* 1982
Lord Vincent of Coleshill, GBE, KCB, DSO, *apptd* 1991

Sir John Chapple, GCB, CBE, *apptd* 1992
HRH The Duke of Kent, KG, GCMG, GCVO, ADC, *apptd* 1993
Lord Inge, KG, GCB, PC, *apptd* 1994
HRH The Prince of Wales, KG, KT, GCB, OM, AK, QSO, PC, ADC, *apptd* 2012
Lord Guthrie of Craigiebank, GCB, LVO, OBE, *apptd* 2012
Lord Walker of Aldringham, GCB, CMG, CBE, *apptd* 2014

### FORMER CHIEFS OF STAFF
Gen. Sir Roger Wheeler, GCB, CBE, *apptd* 1997
Gen. Sir Mike Jackson, GCB, CBE, DSO, *apptd* 2003
Gen. Sir Timothy Granville-Chapman, GBE, KCB, *apptd* 2005
Gen. Lord Dannatt, GCB, CBE, MC, *apptd* 2006
Gen. Lord Richards of Herstmonceux, GCB, CBE, DSO, ADC, *apptd* 2009
Gen. Sir Peter Wall, GCB, CBE, *apptd* 2010

### GENERALS
Houghton, Sir Nicholas, GCB, CBE, ADC *(Chief of the Defence Staff)*

Barrons, Sir Richard, KCB, CBE, ADC *(Cdr Joint Force Command)*
Bradshaw Sir Adrian, KCB, OBE *(Deputy Supreme Allied Cdr Europe)*
Carter, Sir Nicholas, KCB, CBE, DSO, ADC *(Chief of the General Staff)*

### LIEUTENANT-GENERALS
Deverell, Sir Christopher, KCB, MBE *(Chief of Materiel (Land) and Quartermaster General)*
Berragan, Sir Gerald, KBE, CB *(pending retirement)*
Everard, J., CBE *(Cdr Land Forces)*
Gregory, A., CB *(Chief of Defence People)*
Lorimer, J., MBE, DSO *(Chief of Joint Operations, Permanent Joint HQ)*
Evans, T., CBE, DSO *(Cdr Allied Rapid Reaction Corps)*
Jones, P., CB, CBE *(Chief of Staff Supreme Allied Command Transformation)*
Poffley, M., OBE *(Deputy Chief of the General Staff)*
Beckett, T., CBE *(Defence Senior Adviser to the Middle East)*
Bashall, J., CBE *(Cdr Personnel and Support Command)*
Radford, T., OBE, DSO *(Deputy Cdr, Resolute Support)*

### MAJOR-GENERALS
Foster, A., CMG, MBE *(Deputy Military Adviser UNHQ)*
Conway, M., CB *(pending retirement)*
Jaques, P., CBE *(Director Land Equipment, Defence Equipment and Support)*
Norton, Sir George, KCVO, CBE *(Deputy Cdr NATO Rapid Deployment Corps, Naples)*
Ashmore, N., OBE *(Military Secretary/General Officer Scotland)*

Cullen, D., CB, OBE *(Assistant Chief of the General Staff)*
Storrie, A., CBE *(Deputy Commandant, Royal College of Defence Studies)*
Pope, N., CBE *(Director Capability and Master of Signals)*
Rowan, J., OBE, QHS *(Director Army Medical Services)*
Carleton-Smith, M., CBE *(Director Strategy)*
Free, J., CBE *(Commandant Joint Services Command and Staff College)*
Nugee, R., CBE *(Assistant Chief of Defence Staff (Personnel Capability) and Defence Services Secretary)*
Weighill, R., CBE *(pending retirement)*
Munro, R., CBE, TD *(Deputy Cdr Land Forces (Reserves))*
Chiswell, J., CBE, MC *(appointment withheld)*
Smyth-Osbourne, E., CBE *(GOC London District and Maj.-Gen. Commanding the Household Division)*
Urch, T., CBE *(GOC Force Troops Command)*
Cripwell, R., CBE *(Head of British Defence Staff (USA)))*
Sanders, P., CBE, DSO *(GOC 3rd (UK) Division)*
Crackett, J., CB, TD *(Assistant Chief of Defence Staff (Reserves and Cadets))*
Hockenhull, J., OBE *(Director DC13, Defence Intelligence Staff)*
Nitsch, R., CBE *(Director Personnel)*
Skeates, S., CBE *(Standing Joint Force Cdr)*
Tickell, C., CBE *(Director Army Recruiting and Training)*
Semple, R., CBE *(Director Information)*
Felton, R., CBE *(Cdr Joint Helicopter Command)*
Talbot Rice, R. *(Head of Armoured Vehicle Programmes)*
Bathurst, B., CBE *(pending assignment)*
Dickinson, A., CBE *(Director Army Basing and Infrastructure)*
Welch, N., OBE *(Chief of Staff, HQ Allied Rapid Reaction Corps)*
Fattorini, C., *(Senior British Loan Service Officer (Oman))*
Coulter, D., QHC, CF *(Revd Doctor – Chaplain-General)*
Hooper, I. *(Director Service Operations, Information Systems and Services)*
Lawrence, J., CBE *(Director Joint Warfare)*
Patterson, J. *(Director Capability, Joint Forces Command)*
Bruce, R., DSO *(Deputy Cdr Combined Joint Task Force Kuwait)*
Fay, A., *(Assistant Chief of Defence Staff (Logistic Operations))*
Gaunt, M., *(Director Support)*
Hill, G., CBE *(GOC 1st (UK) Division)*
Robinson, T., CBE *(Chief of Staff Land Forces)*
Bramble, W., CBE *(Deputy Adviser Ministry of Interior, HQ Resolute Support)*
Stanford, R., MBE *(GOC Support Command)*
Cave, I., *(Deputy Chief of Staff (Plans), Joint Force Command Naples)*
Nanson, P., CBE *(Commandant Royal Military Academy Sandhurst)*

## CONSTITUTION OF THE ARMY

The army consists of the Regular Army, the Regular Reserve and the Territorial Army (TA). It is commanded by the Chief of the General Staff, who is the professional Head of Service and Chair of the Executive Committee of the Army Board, which provides overall strategic policy and direction to the Commander Land Forces (formerly Commander-in-Chief, Land Forces). There are four subordinate commands that report to the Commander Land Forces: the Field Army; Support Command, headed by the Adjutant General; Force Development and Capability Command and the Joint Helicopter Command. The army is divided into functional arms and services, subdivided into regiments and corps (listed below in order of precedence). During 2008, as part of the Future Army Structure (FAS) reform programme, the infantry was re-structured into large multi-battalion regiments, which involved amalgamations and changes in

title for some regiments. The 2010 Strategic Defence and Security Review laid out the commitments expected of the UK Armed Forces and, as a result, Army 2020 was created to replace FAS. The main changes at divisional, brigade and unit level occurred largely between mid-2014 and mid-2015.

All enquiries with regard to records of serving personnel (Regular and Territorial Army) should be directed to The Army Personnel Centre Help Desk, Kentigern House, 65 Brown Street, Glasgow G2 8EX T 0845-600 9663. Enquirers should note that the Army is governed in the release of personal information by various acts of parliament.

## ORDER OF PRECEDENCE OF CORPS AND REGIMENTS OF THE BRITISH ARMY

ARMS

HOUSEHOLD CAVALRY
The Life Guards
The Blues and Royals (Royal Horse Guards and 1st Dragoons)

ROYAL HORSE ARTILLERY
(when on parade, the Royal Horse Artillery take precedence over the Household Cavalry)

ROYAL ARMOURED CORPS
1st the Queen's Dragoon Guards
The Royal Scots Dragoon Guards (Carabiniers and Greys)
The Royal Dragoon Guards
The Queen's Royal Hussars (The Queen's Own and Royal Irish)
The Royal Lancers
The King's Royal Hussars
The Light Dragoons
Royal Tank Regiment

ROYAL REGIMENT OF ARTILLERY
(with the exception of the Royal Horse Artillery (*see* above))

CORPS OF ROYAL ENGINEERS

ROYAL CORPS OF SIGNALS

REGIMENTS OF FOOT GUARDS
Grenadier Guards
Coldstream Guards
Scots Guards
Irish Guards
Welsh Guards

REGIMENTS OF INFANTRY
The Royal Regiment of Scotland
The Princess of Wales's Royal Regiment (Queen and Royal Hampshire's)
The Duke of Lancaster's Regiment (King's, Lancashire and Border)
The Royal Regiment of Fusiliers
The Royal Anglian Regiment
The Rifles
The Yorkshire Regiment
The Mercian Regiment
The Royal Welsh
The Royal Irish Regiment
The Parachute Regiment
The Royal Gurkha Rifles

SPECIAL AIR SERVICE

ARMY AIR CORPS

SERVICES

ROYAL ARMY CHAPLAINS' DEPARTMENT
THE ROYAL LOGISTIC CORPS
ROYAL ARMY MEDICAL CORPS
CORPS OF ROYAL ELECTRICAL AND MECHANICAL
    ENGINEERS
ADJUTANT-GENERAL'S CORPS
ROYAL ARMY VETERINARY CORPS
SMALL ARMS SCHOOL CORPS
ROYAL ARMY DENTAL CORPS
INTELLIGENCE CORPS
ROYAL ARMY PHYSICAL TRAINING CORPS
QUEEN ALEXANDRA'S ROYAL ARMY NURSING
    CORPS
CORPS OF ARMY MUSIC

THE ROYAL MONMOUTHSHIRE ROYAL ENGINEERS
    (MILITIA) (THE ARMY RESERVE)

THE HONOURABLE ARTILLERY COMPANY (THE
    ARMY RESERVE)

REST OF THE ARMY RESERVE

## THE ARMY RESERVE

The Army Reserve (formerly the Territorial Army (TA)) is part of the UK's reserve land forces and provides support to the regular army at home and overseas. The Army Reserve is divided into three types of unit: national, regional, and sponsored. Army Reserve soldiers serving in regional units complete a minimum of 27 days training a year, comprising some evenings, weekends and an annual two-week camp. National units normally specialise in a specific role or trade, such as logistics, IT, communications or medical services. Members of national units have a lower level of training commitment and complete 19 days training a year. Sponsored reserves are individuals who will serve, as members of the workforce of a company contracted to the MoD, in a military capacity and have agreed to accept a reserve liability to be called up for active service in a crisis. In 2012 the Secretary of State for Defence issued a consultation paper *Future Reserves 2020: Delivering the Nation's Security Together,* which outlined plans to invest an additional £1.8bn in the Reserve Forces over the next ten years, for the Reserve Forces to be more integrated with the regular forces and to have a more significant role within the armed forces as a whole.

## QUEEN ALEXANDRA'S ROYAL ARMY NURSING CORPS

The Queen Alexandra's Royal Army Nursing Corps (QARANC) was founded in 1902 as Queen Alexandra's Imperial Military Nursing Service and gained its present title in 1949. The QARANC has trained nurses for the register since 1950 and also trains and employs health care assistants up to diploma level 3 in Health and Social Care. The corps also recruits qualified nurses as officers and other ranks and in 1992 male nurses already serving in the army were transferred to the QARANC.
*Colonel-in-Chief,* HRH The Countess of Wessex, GCVO
*Colonels Commandant,* Col. Sue Bush; Col. Jane Davis, OBE, QVRM, TD

# THE ROYAL AIR FORCE

*In Order of Seniority*

THE QUEEN
MARSHALS OF THE ROYAL AIR FORCE
HRH The Prince Philip, Duke of Edinburgh, KG, KT, OM,
    GBE, AC, QSO, PC, *apptd* 1953
HRH The Prince of Wales, KG, KT, GCB, OM, AK, QSO,
    PC, ADC, *apptd* 2012

FORMER CHIEFS OF THE AIR STAFF

MARSHALS OF THE ROYAL AIR FORCE
Sir Michael Beetham, GCB, CBE, DFC, AFC, *apptd* 1982
Sir Keith Williamson, GCB, AFC, *apptd* 1985
Lord Craig of Radley, GCB, OBE, *apptd* 1988
Lord Stirrup, KG, GCB, AFC, *apptd* 2003

AIR CHIEF MARSHALS
Sir Michael Graydon, GCB, CBE, *apptd* 1991
Sir Richard Johns, GCB, KCVO, OBE, *apptd* 1994
Sir Peter Squire, GCB, DFC, AFC, *apptd* 1999
Sir Glenn Torpy, GCB, CBE, DSO, *apptd* 2006
Sir Stephen Dalton, GCB, *apptd* 2009

AIR RANK LIST

AIR CHIEF MARSHALS
Peach, Sir Stuart, KCB, CBE, ADC *(Vice Chief of the Defence
    Staff)*
Pulford, Sir Andrew, KCB, CBE, ADC *(Chief of the Air Staff)*

AIR MARSHALS
Harper, Sir Christopher, KBE *(Director-General International
    Military Staff)*
Garwood, R., CB, CBE, DFC *(Director-General of the
    Military Aviation Authority)*
Hillier, Sir Stephen, KCB, CBE, DFC *(Deputy Chief of the
    Defence Staff (Military Capability))*
Bollom, S., CB *(Chief of Materiel (Air) and Air Member for
    Materiel)*
Bagwell, G., CB, CBE *(Deputy Cdr Operations and Air
    Member for Operations)*
Stacey, G., CB, MBE *(Deputy Cdr Joint Force Command,
    Brunssum)*
North, Sir Barry, KCB, OBE *(Deputy Cdr Capability and Air
    Member for Personnel and Capability)*
Evans, C., CB, QHP *(Surgeon-General HQ Joint Medical
    Command)*
Osborne, P., CBE *(Chief of Defence Intelligence)*

AIR VICE-MARSHALS
Irvine, L., CB *(Director RAF Legal Services)*
Young, J., CB, OBE *(Director Technical, Defence Equipment
    and Support)*
Chaffey, J., QHC *(Chaplain Chief and Director-General
    Chaplaincy Services)*
Howard, G., CB *(Assistant Chief of the Defence Staff Logistics
    Operations)*
Atha, S., CB, DSO *(Chief of Staff (Operations), Permanent
    Joint HQ)*
Morrison, I., CBE *(Director-General, Saudi Armed Forces
    Project)*

Clark, M. *(Director Technical in the Military Aviation Authority)*

Farnell, G., CB, OBE *(General-Manager, NATO Eurofighter and Typhoon Management Agency)*

Atherton, P., OBE *(Director Operations, Military Aviation Authority)*

Brecht, M. *(Chief of Staff Capability, Air Command)*

Stringer, E., CBE *(Assistant Chief of the Defence Staff (Operations))*

Bishop, T., OBE *(Air Officer Commanding No. 38 Group)*

Evans, S., CBE *(Senior British Military Adviser to the United States Central Command, Tampa)*

Gray, S., OBE *(Director Combat Air, Defence Equipment and Support)*

Turner, A., CBE *(Air Officer Commanding No. 22 Group and Chief of Staff Training)*

Stubbs, D., OBE *(Chief of Staff Personnel and Air Secretary)*

West, M., CBE *(Director of Projects and Programme Delivery, Defence Infrastructure Organisation)*

Waterfall, G., CBE *(Air Officer Commanding No.1 Group)*

Neal, M., OBE *(Director Service Design, Information Services and Systems)*

Broadbridge, Hon. R., QHS *(Director Healthcare Delivery and Training)*

Wigston, M., CBE *(Commander British Forces Cyprus and Administer of the Sovereign Base Area)*

Knighton, R. *(Assistant Chief of the Air Staff)*

Parker, G., OBE *(Air Officer Commanding No. 2 Group)*

## CONSTITUTION OF THE RAF

The RAF consists of a single command, Air Command, based at RAF High Wycombe. RAF Air Command was formed on 1 April 2007 from the amalgamation of Strike Command and Personnel and Training Command.

Air Command consists of three groups, each organised around specific operational duties. No. 1 Group is the coordinating organisation for the tactical fast-jet forces responsible for attack, offensive support and air defence operations. No. 2 Group provides air combat support including air transport and air-to-air refuelling; intelligence surveillance; targeting and reconnaissance; and force protection. No. 22 (Training) Group recruits personnel and provides trained specialist personnel to the RAF, as well as to the Royal Navy and the Army (*see also* Armed Forces Training and Recruitment).

## RAF EQUIPMENT

### AIRCRAFT

| | |
|---|---|
| Combat Aircraft | Lightening II, Tornado GR4, Typhoon FGR4 |
| Training Aircraft | Hawk T1, Hawk T2, King Air B200, Tucano T1, Tutor T1, Vigilant T1, Viking T1 |
| Surveillance Aircraft | Reaper MQ9A RPAS, RC-135W Rivet Joint, Sentinel R1, E-3D Sentry AEW1, Shadow R1 |

### HELICOPTERS

| | |
|---|---|
| Helicopters | Chinook, Griffin HAR2, Merlin HC3 Puma HC2, Sea King HAR3/3A |
| Training Helicopters | Griffin HT1, Squirrel HT1 |

## ROYAL AUXILIARY AIR FORCE

The Auxiliary Air Force was formed in 1924 to train an elite corps of civilians to serve their country in flying squadrons in their spare time. In 1947 the force was awarded the prefix 'royal' in recognition of its distinguished war service and the Sovereign's Colour for the RAuxAF was presented in 1989. The RAuxAF continues to recruit civilians who undertake military training in their spare time, with a standard minimum commitment of 27 days a year. With the amendments to the reserve service made under the Defence Reform Act 2014, reservists can now be employed to support the RAF across the full spectrum of military tasks. There are currently 27 squadrons with the RAuxAF, with a total establishment of just under 3,200 posts, with reservist posts being available in the majority of trades.

*Air Commodore-in-Chief,* HM The Queen

*Honorary Inspector-General (Air Vice-Marshal) Royal Auxiliary Air Force,* Lord Beaverbrook

*Inspector Royal Auxiliary Air Force,* Gp Capt. Gavin Hellard, ADC

## PRINCESS MARY'S ROYAL AIR FORCE NURSING SERVICE

The Princess Mary's Royal Air Force Nursing Service (PMRAFNS) was formed on 1 June 1918 as the Royal Air Force Nursing Service. In June 1923, His Majesty King George V gave his royal assent for the Royal Air Force Nursing Service to be known as the Princess Mary's Royal Air Force Nursing Service. Men were integrated into the PMRAFNS in 1980.

*Patron and Air Chief Commandant,* HRH Princess Alexandra, The Hon. Lady Ogilvy, KG, GCVO

*Director of Nursing Services and Matron-in-Chief,* Gp Capt. Phil Spragg

# SERVICE SALARIES

The following rates of pay apply from 1 April 2015 and are rounded to the nearest pound.

The pay rates shown are for army personnel. The rates also apply to personnel of equivalent rank and pay band in the other services *(see* below for table of relative ranks).

| Rank | Annual salary |
| --- | --- |
| SECOND LIEUTENANT | £25,472 |
| LIEUTENANT | |
| On appointment | £30,617 |
| After 1 year in rank | £31,426 |
| After 2 years in rank | £32,231 |
| After 3 years in rank | £33,032 |
| After 4 years in rank | £33,842 |
| CAPTAIN | |
| On appointment | £39,236 |
| After 1 year in rank | £40,287 |
| After 2 years in rank | £41,351 |
| After 3 years in rank | £42,419 |
| After 4 years in rank | £43,474 |
| After 5 years in rank | £44,538 |
| After 6 years in rank | £45,592 |
| After 7 years in rank | £46,131 |
| After 8 years in rank | £46,660 |
| MAJOR | |
| On appointment | £49,424 |
| After 1 year in rank | £50,644 |
| After 2 years in rank | £51,856 |
| After 3 years in rank | £53,085 |
| After 4 years in rank | £54,301 |
| After 5 years in rank | £55,530 |
| After 6 years in rank | £56,750 |
| After 7 years in rank | £57,966 |
| After 8 years in rank | £59,191 |
| LIEUTENANT-COLONEL | |
| On appointment | £69,366 |
| After 1 year in rank | £70,285 |
| After 2 years in rank | £71,196 |
| After 3 years in rank | £72,108 |
| After 4 years in rank | £73,019 |
| After 5 years in rank | £77,212 |
| After 6 years in rank | £78,242 |
| After 7 years in rank | £79,281 |
| After 8 years in rank | £80,320 |
| COLONEL | |
| On appointment | £84,037 |
| After 1 year in rank | £85,079 |
| After 2 years in rank | £86,124 |
| After 3 years in rank | £87,166 |
| After 4 years in rank | £88,207 |
| After 5 years in rank | £89,248 |
| After 6 years in rank | £90,290 |
| After 7 years in rank | £91,335 |
| After 8 years in rank | £92,381 |
| BRIGADIER | |
| On appointment | £100,146 |
| After 1 year in rank | £101,158 |
| After 2 years in rank | £102,170 |
| After 3 years in rank | £103,178 |
| After 4 years in rank | £104,198 |

## PAY SYSTEM FOR SENIOR MILITARY OFFICERS

Pay rates effective from 1 April 2015 for all military officers of 2* rank and above (excluding medical and dental officers). All pay rates are rounded to the nearest pound.

| Rank | Annual salary |
| --- | --- |
| MAJOR-GENERAL (2*) | |
| Scale 1 | £111,567 |
| Scale 2 | £113,747 |
| Scale 3 | £115,972 |
| Scale 4 | £118,241 |
| Scale 5 | £120,555 |
| Scale 6 | £122,914 |
| LIEUTENANT-GENERAL (3*) | |
| Scale 1 | £129,810 |
| Scale 2 | £136,174 |
| Scale 3 | £142,856 |
| Scale 4 | £148,468 |
| Scale 5 | £152,845 |
| Scale 6 | £157,355 |
| GENERAL (4*) | |
| Scale 1 | £170,292 |
| Scale 2 | £174,549 |
| Scale 3 | £178,913 |
| Scale 4 | £183,386 |
| Scale 5 | £187,054 |
| Scale 6 | £190,795 |

Field Marshal – appointments to this rank will not usually be made in peacetime. The salary for holders of the rank is equivalent to the salary of a 5-star General, a salary created only in times of war. In peacetime, the equivalent rank to Field Marshal is the Chief of the Defence Staff. From 1 April 2015, the annual salary range for the Chief of the Defence Staff is £245,338–£260,355.

## OFFICERS COMMISSIONED FROM THE SENIOR RANKS

| Rank | Annual salary |
| --- | --- |
| Level 15 | £52,445 |
| Level 14 | £52,101 |
| Level 13 | £51,741 |
| Level 12 | £51,042 |
| Level 11 | £50,347 |
| Level 10 | £49,644 |
| Level 9 | £48,945 |
| Level 8 | £48,246 |
| Level 7* | £47,373 |
| Level 6 | £46,834 |
| Level 5 | £46,287 |
| Level 4† | £45,207 |
| Level 3 | £44,669 |
| Level 2 | £44,118 |
| Level 1‡ | £43,041 |

* Officers commissioned from the ranks with more than 15 years' service enter on level 7

† Officers commissioned from the ranks with between 12 and 15 years' service enter on level 4

‡ Officers commissioned from the ranks with less than 12 years' service enter on level 1

## SOLDIERS' SALARIES

Under the Pay 2000 scheme, personnel are paid in either a high or low band in accordance with how their trade has been allocated to those bands at each rank. Pay is based on trade and rank, not on individual appointment, or in response to temporary changes in role.

Rates of pay effective from 1 April 2015 (rounded to the nearest pound) are:

| Rank | Lower band | Higher band |
| --- | --- | --- |
| PRIVATE | | |
| Level 1 | £18,125 | £18,125 |
| Level 2 | £18,612 | £19,498 |
| Level 3 | £19,099 | £21,473 |
| Level 4 | £20,727 | £22,531 |
| LANCE CORPORAL (levels 5–7 also applicable to Privates) | | |
| Level 5 | £21,816 | £24,913 |
| Level 6 | £22,188 | £26,125 |
| Level 7 | £23,138 | £27,324 |
| Level 8 | £24,197 | £28,553 |
| Level 9 | £25,074 | £29,947 |
| CORPORAL | | |
| Level 1 | £27,324 | £28,553 |
| Level 2 | £28,553 | £29,947 |
| Level 3 | £29,947 | £31,414 |
| Level 4 | £30,176 | £32,147 |
| Level 5 | £30,413 | £32,922 |
| Level 6 | £30,655 | £33,604 |
| Level 7 | £30,879 | £34,338 |

| Rank | Lower band | Higher band |
| --- | --- | --- |
| SERGEANT | | |
| Level 1 | £31,058 | £33,897 |
| Level 2 | £31,871 | £34,774 |
| Level 3 | £32,672 | £35,655 |
| Level 4 | £33,003 | £36,105 |
| Level 5 | £33,863 | £36,808 |
| Level 6 | £35,032 | £37,511 |
| Level 7 | £35,300 | £38,215 |
| STAFF SERGEANT | | |
| Level 1 | £34,380 | £38,240 |
| Level 2 | £34,829 | £39,164 |
| Level 3 | £35,961 | £40,101 |
| Level 4 | £36,804 | £41,029 |
| WARRANT OFFICER II (levels 5–7 also applicable to Staff Sergeants) | | |
| Level 5 | £37,304 | £41,961 |
| Level 6 | £38,990 | £42,889 |
| Level 7 | £39,588 | £43,508 |
| Level 8 | £40,101 | £44,127 |
| Level 9 | £41,008 | £44,758 |
| WARRANT OFFICER I | | |
| Level 1 | £39,944 | £43,546 |
| Level 2 | £40,719 | £44,402 |
| Level 3 | £41,541 | £45,165 |
| Level 4 | £42,364 | £45,995 |
| Level 5 | £43,190 | £46,817 |
| Level 6 | £44,402 | £47,652 |
| Level 7 | £45,656 | £48,381 |

## RELATIVE RANK – ARMED FORCES

| Royal Navy | Army | Royal Air Force |
| --- | --- | --- |
| 1 Admiral of the Fleet | 1 Field Marshal | 1 Marshal of the RAF |
| 2 Admiral (Adm.) | 2 General (Gen.) | 2 Air Chief Marshal |
| 3 Vice-Admiral (Vice-Adm.) | 3 Lieutenant-General (Lt.-Gen.) | 3 Air Marshal |
| 4 Rear-Admiral (Rear-Adm.) | 4 Major-General (Maj.-Gen.) | 4 Air Vice-Marshal |
| 5 Commodore (Cdre) | 5 Brigadier (Brig.) | 5 Air Commodore (Air Cdre) |
| 6 Captain (Capt.) | 6 Colonel (Col.) | 6 Group Captain (Gp Capt.) |
| 7 Commander (Cdr) | 7 Lieutenant-Colonel (Lt.-Col.) | 7 Wing Commander (Wg Cdr) |
| 8 Lieutenant-Commander (Lt.-Cdr) | 8 Major (Maj.) | 8 Squadron Leader (Sqn Ldr) |
| 9 Lieutenant (Lt.) | 9 Captain (Capt.) | 9 Flight Lieutenant (Flt Lt) |
| 10 Sub-Lieutenant (Sub-Lt.) | 10 Lieutenant (Lt.) | 10 Flying Officer (FO) |
| 11 Midshipman | 11 Second Lieutenant (2nd Lt.) | 11 Pilot Officer (PO) |

## SERVICE RETIRED PAY *on compulsory retirement*

Those that leave the service having served at least two years, but not long enough to qualify for the appropriate immediate pension, qualify for a preserved pension and terminal grant, both of which are payable from age 60, for service before 6 April 2006, and age 65 for service after 6 April 2006. The tax-free resettlement grants shown below are payable on release to those that have completed nine years' service (officers) or 12 years (other ranks).

The annual rates for army personnel are given. The rates also apply to personnel of equivalent rank in the other services, including the nursing services.

### OFFICERS

The rates shown below are applicable to officers who give full pay service on the active list on or after 31 March 2015, Pensionable earnings for senior officers (*) is defined as the total amount of basic pay received during the year ending on the day prior to retirement, or the amount of basic pay received during any 12-month period within three years prior to retirement, whichever is the higher. Figures for senior officers are percentage rates of pensionable earnings on final salary arrangements on or after 31 March 2015.

| No. of years reckonable service | Capt. and below | Major | Lt.-Col. | Colonel | Brigadier | Major-General* | Lieutenant-General* | General* |
|---|---|---|---|---|---|---|---|---|
| 16 | £12,994 | £15,476 | £20,291 | £24,545 | £29,118 | — | — | — |
| 17 | £13,593 | £16,211 | £21,238 | £25,671 | £30,254 | — | — | — |
| 18 | £14,192 | £16,946 | £22,365 | £26,796 | £31,389 | — | — | — |
| 19 | £14,791 | £17,681 | £23,402 | £27,922 | £32,524 | — | — | — |
| 20 | £15,389 | £18,416 | £24,439 | £29,047 | £33,659 | — | — | — |
| 21 | £15,988 | £19,151 | £25,475 | £30,173 | £34,794 | — | — | — |
| 22 | £16,587 | £19,886 | £26,512 | £31,298 | £35,930 | — | — | — |
| 23 | £17,186 | £20,622 | £27,549 | £32,424 | £37,065 | — | — | — |
| 24 | £17,785 | £21,357 | £28,586 | £33,549 | £38,200 | 38.5% | — | — |
| 25 | £18,384 | £22,092 | £29,623 | £34,675 | £39,335 | 39.7% | — | — |
| 26 | £18,983 | £22,827 | £30,660 | £35,800 | £40,471 | 40.8% | — | — |
| 27 | £19,582 | £23,562 | £31,697 | £36,926 | £41,606 | 42.0% | 42.0% | — |
| 28 | £20,181 | £24,297 | £32,734 | £38,052 | £42,741 | 43.1% | 43.1% | — |
| 29 | £20,780 | £25,032 | £33,771 | £39,177 | £43,876 | 44.3% | 44.3% | — |
| 30 | £21,378 | £25,767 | £34,808 | £40,303 | £45,011 | 45.4% | 45.4% | 45.4% |
| 31 | £21,977 | £26,502 | £35,844 | £41,428 | £46,147 | 46.6% | 46.6% | 46.6% |
| 32 | £22,576 | £27,238 | £36,881 | £42,554 | £47,282 | 47.7% | 47.7% | 47.7% |
| 33 | £23,175 | £27,973 | £37,918 | £43,679 | £48,417 | 48.9% | 48.9% | 48.9% |
| 34 | £23,774 | £28,708 | £38,955 | £44,805 | £49,552 | 50.0% | 50.0% | 50.0% |

### WARRANT OFFICERS, NCOS AND PRIVATES
(Applicable to soldiers who give full pay service on or after 31 March 2015)

| No. of years reckonable service | Below Corporal | Corporal | Sergeant | Staff Sergeant | Warrant Officer Level II | Warrant Officer Level I |
|---|---|---|---|---|---|---|
| 22 | £7,690 | £9,920 | £10,875 | £12,388 | £13,226 | £14,064 |
| 23 | £7,958 | £10,266 | £11,255 | £12,821 | £13,688 | £14,555 |
| 24 | £8,227 | £10,612 | £11,635 | £13,253 | £14,149 | £15,045 |
| 25 | £8,495 | £10,958 | £12,014 | £13,685 | £14,611 | £15,536 |
| 26 | £8,763 | £11,305 | £12,394 | £14,118 | £15,073 | £16,027 |
| 27 | £9,032 | £11,651 | £12,773 | £14,550 | £15,534 | £16,518 |
| 28 | £9,300 | £11,997 | £13,153 | £14,983 | £15,996 | £17,009 |
| 29 | £9,569 | £12,343 | £13,533 | £15,415 | £16,457 | £17,500 |
| 30 | £9,837 | £12,690 | £13,912 | £15,847 | £16,919 | £17,991 |
| 31 | £10,105 | £13,036 | £14,292 | £16,280 | £17,381 | £18,482 |
| 32 | £10,374 | £13,382 | £14,671 | £16,712 | £17,842 | £18,973 |
| 33 | £10,642 | £13,728 | £15,051 | £17,145 | £18,304 | £19,463 |
| 34 | £10,911 | £14,075 | £15,431 | £17,577 | £18,766 | £19,954 |
| 35 | £11,179 | £14,421 | £15,810 | £18,010 | £19,227 | £20,445 |
| 36 | £11,448 | £14,767 | £16,190 | £18,442 | £19,689 | £20,936 |
| 37 | £11,716 | £15,113 | £16,569 | £18,874 | £20,151 | £21,427 |

### GRANTS AND GRATUITIES

Terminal grants are in each case three times the rate of retired pay or pension. There are special rates of retired pay for certain other ranks not shown above. Lower rates are payable in cases of voluntary retirement.

A gratuity of £4,420 is payable for officers with short service commissions for each year completed. Resettlement grants are £15,197 for officers and £10,387 for other ranks.

# EDUCATION

## THE UK EDUCATION SYSTEM

The structure of the education system in the UK is a devolved matter with each of the countries of the UK having separate systems under separate governments. There are differences between the school systems in terms of the curriculum, examinations and final qualifications and, at university level, in terms of the nature of some degrees and in the matter of tuition fees. The systems in England, Wales and Northern Ireland are similar and have more in common with one another than the Scottish system, which differs significantly.

Education in England is overseen by the Department for Education (DfE) and the Department for Business, Innovation and Skills (BIS).

In Wales, responsibility for education lies with the Department for Education and Skills (DfES) within the Welsh government. Ministers in the Scottish government are responsible for education in Scotland, led by the directorates of Learning and Lifelong Learning, while in Northern Ireland responsibility lies with the Department of Education (DENI) and the Department for Employment and Learning (DELNI) within the Northern Ireland government.

DEPARTMENT FOR EDUCATION T 0370-000 2288
  W www.gov.uk/government/organisations/department-for-education
DEPARTMENT FOR BUSINESS, INNOVATION AND SKILLS T 020-7215 5000
  W www.gov.uk/government/organisations/department-for-business-innovation-skills
DEPARTMENT FOR EDUCATION AND SKILLS (DFES) T 0300-060 3300
  W www.wales.gov.uk/topics/educationandskills
SCOTTISH GOVERNMENT – EDUCATION
  T 0131-244 4000; 0300-244 4000
  W www.gov.scot/Topics/Education
DEPARTMENT OF EDUCATION (NI) T 028-9127 9279
  W www.deni.gov.uk
DEPARTMENT FOR EMPLOYMENT AND LEARNING
  (NI) T 028-9025 7777 W www.delni.gov.uk

## RECENT DEVELOPMENTS

In England, reform of the national curriculum, initial teacher training and apprenticeships continued under the former coalition government. Since May 2015, the new Conservative government announced plans to replace maintenance grants for students in England with loans of up to £8,200 from 2016–17 and proposed a bill to raise standards and turn 'coasting' schools into academies. Elsewhere in the UK, there were also plans for curriculum and assessment change and proposals to raise standards. Changes made or announced include:

ENGLAND
- Since September 2015, Ofsted inspect good schools and further education and skills providers once every 3 years under a new short (one-day) inspection model. Inspectors focus on ensuring standards are being maintained and check that leaders have identified areas of concern and have the capacity to address them
- Pupils starting secondary school in September 2015 must study the English Baccalaureate (EBacc) subjects of English, maths, science, history or geography, and a language at GCSE

- The achievement of a level 5 on the new 1 to 9 grading scale at GCSE (a low B or high C under the old grading system) will be considered the new 'good pass' used to hold the government and schools to account
- A school behaviour expert will draw up plans to help teachers deal with low-level disruption in classrooms
- Six new core maths qualifications are to be included in school and college performance tables from 2017 and be part of the TechBacc measure from 2016
- A new college of teaching, revised standards for school leaders, a working group on improving initial teacher training and a review of standards for teaching assistants
- 'Degree apprenticeships', designed by industry and funded by BIS (two-thirds) and employers (one-third), will be available from September 2015 in thirteen subjects including chartered surveying, aerospace engineering and laboratory science
- The cap is lifted on university student numbers but controls are placed on some private higher education providers from 2015–16
- In Research Excellence Framework assessments, 30 per cent of UK university research was judged to be world-leading and 46 per cent internationally excellent. A complementary Teaching Excellence Framework is proposed to improve the standing of university teaching in England

WALES
- New curriculum and assessment changes set out in *Successful Futures* accepted in full. Children and young people will be supported to be ambitious, capable learners; enterprising, creative contributors; ethical, informed citizens of Wales and the world; and healthy, confident individuals. Implementation plans were due in autumn 2015
- Plans set out to revise professional teaching standards and drive up the quality of initial teacher training, by overhauling the teaching qualification and accreditation process
- Qualifications Wales, a new body to oversee qualifications, regulation and assessment in Wales, started work in September 2015
- New *Digital Competence Framework* will help schools embed digital competency into their teaching and learning from September 2016
- Financial incentives introduced (up to £20,000) for top graduates to study to teach the priority subjects of Welsh, Maths, Physics and Chemistry at secondary school level
- *Qualified for Life*, an education improvement plan for Wales up to 2020, sets out four strategic objectives: an excellent professional workforce; engaging curriculum; credible qualifications; education leaders improving the system
- Skills Implementation Plan launched to respond to the needs of local employers with industry-led skills and training solutions

SCOTLAND
- Funding pledges include £2m for 250 extra teacher training places, £2.7m for pre-school programmes to improve literacy, £1m to develop the early years workforce a doubling of spending on early years and childcare and £12m for clinical research fellowships
- Creative industries skills investment plan announced, the latest in a series which since March 2014 has included construction, chemical sciences, energy, highlands and

islands, engineering, life sciences, ICT and digital, finance and tourism

• Education (Scotland) Bill to place a statutory duty on councils to narrow the attainment gap, require councils and ministers to report on progress, promote Gaelic education and ensure teachers and school leaders are appropriately trained and qualified. A Masters qualification for headship introduced in 2015 will be mandatory for all new headteachers from 2018–19

• From 2015–16 all pupils should be studying for the new Higher qualifications

NORTHERN IRELAND

• Addition of £80m to the schools budget for 2015–16, and £2.5m to the pre-school education programme

• Practical assessments of science subjects will remain as part of the overall grade at A-level. The weighting of AS-levels will be changed to 40 per cent and A2 levels to 60 per cent

• New higher level apprenticeships in Finance and Accountancy and Applied Industrial and Life Science (equivalent to a Foundation degree) to be piloted as part of *Securing our Success* strategy

# STATE SCHOOL SYSTEM

## PRE-SCHOOL

Pre-school education is not compulsory. In England, a free place is available for every 3- and 4-year-old whose parents want one, although parents may use as little or as much of their entitlement as they choose. All 3- and 4-year-olds, and disadvantaged 2-year-olds, are entitled to 15 hours a week of free early education over 38 weeks of the year until they reach compulsory school age (the term following their fifth birthday). This is delivered flexibly over a minimum of two days each week during normal term times. Free places are funded by local authorities and are delivered by a range of providers in the maintained and non-maintained sectors – nursery schools; nursery classes in primary schools; private schools; private day nurseries; voluntary playgroups; preschools; and registered childminders. In order to receive funding, providers must be working towards the early learning goals and other features of the Early Years Foundation Stage curriculum, must be inspected on a regular basis by Ofsted and must meet any conditions set by the local authority.

In Wales, every child is entitled to receive free Foundation Phase education for a minimum of two hours a day from the term following their third birthday.

In Scotland, councils have a duty to provide a pre-school education for all 3- and 4-year-olds whose parents request one. Education authorities must offer each child at least 600 hours of free pre-school education a year, although they may provide more if they choose.

In Northern Ireland, the Department of Education aims to provide a funded place for all 3- and 4-year-old children in their final pre-school year. All places offer 2.5 hours a day, five days a week for at least 38 weeks a year.

## PRIMARY AND SECONDARY SCHOOLS

By law, full-time education starts at the age of five for children in England, Scotland and Wales and at the age of four in Northern Ireland. In practice, most children in the UK start school before their fifth birthday: in England all children are entitled to a primary school place from the September after their fourth birthday.

Children in England are required to stay in education or training until the end of the academic year in which they turn 18 (from September 2015). In all other parts of the UK, compulsory schooling ends at age 16, but children born between certain dates may leave school before their 16th birthday. Most young people stay in some form of education until 17 or 18.

Primary education consists mainly of infant schools for children aged 5 to 7, junior schools for those aged 7 to 11, and combined infant and junior schools for both age groups. First schools in some parts of England cater for ages 5 to 10 as the first stage of a three-tier system of first (lower), middle and secondary (upper) schools. Scotland has only primary schools with no infant/junior division.

Children usually leave primary school and move on to secondary school at the age of 11 (or 12 in Scotland). In the few areas of England that have a three-tier system of schools, middle schools cater for children after they leave first schools for three to four years between the ages of 8 and 14, depending on the local authority.

Secondary schools cater for children aged 11 to 16 and, if they have a sixth form, for those who choose to stay on to the age of 18. From the age of 16, students may move instead to further education colleges or work-based training.

Most UK secondary schools are co-educational. The largest secondary schools have more than 1,500 pupils and around 60 per cent of secondary pupils in the UK are in schools that take more than 1,000 pupils.

Most state-maintained secondary schools in England, Wales and Scotland are comprehensive schools, which admit pupils without reference to ability. In England there remain some areas with grammar schools, catering for pupils aged 11 to 18, which select pupils on the basis of high academic ability. Over half of state secondary schools in England (61 per cent in January 2015) are now academies: academies are funded directly by the state rather than being maintained by local authorities. Northern Ireland still has 68 grammar schools; the 11-plus has been officially discontinued but schools, or consortia of schools, use their own unregulated entry tests.

More than 90 per cent of pupils in the UK attend publicly funded schools and receive free education. The rest attend privately funded 'independent' schools, which charge fees, or are educated at home.

The bulk of the UK government's expenditure on school education is through local authorities (Education and Library Boards (ELBs) in Northern Ireland), who pass on state funding to schools and other educational institutions.

## SPECIAL EDUCATION

Schools and local authorities in England and Wales, Education and Library Boards (ELBs) in Northern Ireland and education authorities in Scotland are required to identify and secure provision for children with special educational needs and to involve parents in decisions. The majority of children with special educational needs are educated in ordinary mainstream schools, sometimes with supplementary help from outside specialists. Parents of children with special educational needs (referred to as additional support needs in Scotland) have a right of appeal to independent tribunals if their wishes are not met.

Special educational needs provision may be made in maintained special schools, special units attached to mainstream schools or in mainstream classes themselves, all funded by local authorities. There are also non-maintained special schools run by voluntary bodies, mainly charities, who may receive grants from central government for capital expenditure and equipment but whose other costs are met primarily from the fees charged to local authorities for pupils placed in the schools. Some independent schools also provide education wholly or mainly for children with special educational needs.

ADDITIONAL SUPPORT NEEDS TRIBUNALS FOR
SCOTLAND T 0845-120 2906 W www.asntscotland.gov.uk
FIRST-TIER TRIBUNAL (SPECIAL EDUCATIONAL
NEEDS AND DISABILITY) T 020-7843 6958
W www.gov.uk/special-educational-needs-disability-tribunal
INFORMATION ADVICE AND SUPPORT SERVICES
NETWORK FOR SEND E iassn@ncb.org.uk
W www.iassnetwork.org.uk
SPECIAL EDUCATIONAL NEEDS TRIBUNAL FOR
WALES T 01597-829800 W sentw.gov.uk

## HOME EDUCATION

In England and Wales parents have the right to educate their
children at home and do not have to be qualified teachers to
do so. Home-educated children do not have to follow the
National Curriculum or take national tests nor do they need
a fixed timetable, formal lessons or to observe school hours,
days or terms. However, by law parents must ensure that
the home education provided is full-time and suitable for the
child's age, ability and aptitude and, if appropriate, for any
special educational needs. Parents have no legal obligation to
notify the local authority that a child is being educated at
home, but if they take a child out of school, they must notify
the school in writing and the school must report this to the
local authority. Local authorities can make informal enquiries
of parents to establish that a suitable education is being
provided. For children in special schools, parents must seek
the consent of the local authority before taking steps to
educate them at home.

In Northern Ireland, ELBs monitor the quality of home
provision and provide general guidance on appropriate
materials and exam types through regular home visits.

The home schooling law in Scotland is similar to that of
England. One difference, however, is that if parents wish to
take a child out of school they must have permission from the
local education authority.

HOME EDUCATION ADVISORY SERVICE
T 01707-371854 W www.heas.org.uk
HOME EDUCATION IN NORTHERN IRELAND
W www.hedni.org
SCHOOLHOUSE HOME EDUCATION ASSOCIATION
(SCOTLAND) T 01307-463120 W www.schoolhouse.org.uk

## FURTHER EDUCATION

In the UK, further education (FE) is generally understood as
post-secondary education, ie any education undertaken after
an individual leaves school that is below higher education
level. FE therefore embraces a wide range of general and
vocational study undertaken by people of all ages from 16
upwards, full-time or part-time, who may be self-funded,
employer-funded or state-funded.

FE in the UK is often undertaken at further education
colleges, although some takes place on employers' premises.
Many of these colleges offer some courses at higher
education level; some FE colleges teach certain subjects to
14- to 16-year-olds under collaborative arrangements with
schools. Colleges' income comes from public funding,
student fees and work for and with employers.

## HIGHER EDUCATION

Higher education (HE) in the UK describes courses of
study, provided in universities, specialist colleges of higher
education and in some FE colleges, where the level of
instruction is above that of A-level or equivalent exams.

All UK universities and colleges that provide HE are
autonomous bodies with their own internal systems of
governance. They are not owned by the state. However, most
receive a portion of their income from state funds distributed
by the separate HE funding councils for England, Scotland

and Wales, and the Department for Employment and
Learning in Northern Ireland. The rest of their income
comes from a number of sources including fees from home
and overseas students, government funding for research,
endowments and work with or for business.

## EXPENDITURE

UK-MANAGED EXPENDITURE ON EDUCATION
(Real terms adjusted to 2014–15 price levels) £bn

| | | | |
|---|---|---|---|
| 2005–6 | 85.4 | 2010–11 | 97.9 |
| 2006–7 | 86.9 | 2011–12 | 91.4 |
| 2007–8 | 91.0 | 2012–13 | 90.0 |
| 2008–9 | 93.7 | 2013–14 | 90.4 |
| 2009–10 | 97.3 | 2014–15 (est) | 84.3 |

*Source:* HM Treasury – Public Spending Statistics July 2015

## SCHOOLS

### ENGLAND AND WALES

In England and Wales, publicly funded schools are referred to
as 'state schools'. The four main categories of state school –
Community, Foundation, Voluntary-aided and Voluntary-
controlled – are maintained by local authorities which have a
duty to ensure there is a suitable place for every school-age
child resident in their area. Each school has a governing
body, made up of volunteers elected or appointed by
parents, staff, the community and the local authority,
which is responsible for strategic management, ensuring
accountability, monitoring school performance, setting
budgets and appointing the headteacher and senior staff.
The headteacher is responsible for the school's day-to-day
management and operations and for decisions requiring
professional teaching expertise.

In *Community schools,* which are non-denominational, local
authorities are the employers of the staff, own the land and
buildings and set the admissions criteria.

In *Foundation schools,* the governing body employs the staff
and sets the admissions criteria. The land and buildings
are usually owned by the governing body or a charitable
foundation. A Foundation school may have a religious
character, although most do not. A *Trust school* is a distinct
type of foundation school that forms a charitable trust with
an outside partner – for example, a business, a university,
an educational charity or simply another school – that
shares the school's aspirations. The decision to become a
Trust school is taken by the governing body while taking
account of parents' views. Community schools can take on
Foundation status and set up a trust in a single process.

Most *Voluntary-aided schools* are religious schools founded
by Christian denominations or other faiths. As with
Foundation schools, the governing body employs the staff
and sets the admissions criteria, which may include priority
for members of the faith or denomination. The school
buildings and land are normally owned and provided by a
charitable foundation, often a religious organisation, which
appoints a majority of the school's governors and makes a
small contribution to major building costs.

*Voluntary-controlled schools* are similar to Voluntary-aided
schools in that they often have a particular religious ethos,
commonly Church of England, and the school land and
buildings are normally owned by a charity. However, as with
Community schools, the local authority employs the school's
staff, sets the admissions criteria and bears all the costs.

Among the local authority-maintained schools are some
with particular characteristics:

• *Community and Foundation special schools* cater for children
with specific special educational needs, which may include
physical disabilities or learning difficulties

- *Grammar schools* are secondary schools catering for pupils aged 11 to 18 that select all of their pupils based on academic ability. In England there are 164 grammar schools, concentrated in certain local authority areas. Wales has none
- *Maintained boarding schools* are state-funded and offer free tuition but charge fees for board and lodging

In Wales, Welsh-medium primary and secondary schools were first established in the 1950s and 1960s, originally in response to the wishes of Welsh-speaking parents who wanted their children to be educated through the medium of the Welsh language. Now, many children who are not from Welsh-speaking homes also attend Welsh-medium and bilingual schools throughout Wales. There are 444 Welsh-medium primary schools, where the main or sole medium of instruction is in the Welsh language, two Welsh-medium middle schools and 52 Welsh-medium secondary schools, where more than half of foundation subjects (other than English and Welsh) and religious education are taught wholly or partly in Welsh.

England now has increasing numbers of *Academies*. Those set-up before the Academies Act 2010 were sponsored by business, faith or voluntary groups who contributed to funding their land and buildings, while the government covered the running costs at a level comparable to other local schools. The Academies Act 2010 streamlined the process of becoming an academy, enabled high-performing schools to convert without a sponsor and allowed primary and special schools to become academies. All academies now receive funding from central government at the level they would have received if still maintained by their local authority, with extra funding only to cover those services the local authority no longer provides. Academies have greater freedoms over how they use their budgets, set staff pay and conditions and deliver the curriculum. As at June 2015 there were 4,675 open academies, of which 2,546 were primaries.

## SCOTLAND

Most schools in Scotland, known as 'publicly funded' schools, are state-funded and charge no fees. Funding is met from resources raised by the Scottish local authorities and from an annual grant from the Scottish government. Scotland does not have school governing bodies like the rest of the UK: local authorities retain greater responsibility for the management and performance of publicly funded schools. Headteachers manage at least 80 per cent of a school's budget, covering staffing, furnishings, repairs, supplies, services and energy costs. Spending on new buildings, modernisation projects and equipment is financed by the local authority within the limits set by the Scottish government.

Scotland has 370 state-funded *faith schools*, the majority of which are Catholic. It has no grammar schools.

*Integrated community schools* form part of the Scottish government's strategy to promote social inclusion and to raise educational standards. They encourage closer and better joint working among education, health and social work agencies and professionals, greater pupil and parental involvement in schools, and improved support and service provision for vulnerable children and young people.

Scotland has a number of *grant-aided schools* that are independent of local authorities but supported financially by the Scottish government. These schools are managed by boards and most of them provide education for children and young people with special educational needs.

## NORTHERN IRELAND

Most schools in Northern Ireland are maintained by the state and generally charge no fees, though fees may be charged in preparatory departments of some grammar schools. There are different types of state-funded schools, each under the control of management committees, which also employ the teachers.

*Controlled schools* (nursery, primary, special, secondary and grammar schools) are managed by Northern Ireland's five ELBs through boards of governors consisting of teachers, parents, members of the ELB and transferor representatives (mainly from the Protestant churches).

*Catholic maintained schools* (nursery, primary, special and secondary) are under the management of boards of governors consisting of teachers, parents and members nominated by the employing authority, the Council for Catholic Maintained Schools (CCMS).

*Other maintained schools* (primary, special and secondary) are, in the main, Irish-medium schools that provide education in an Irish-speaking environment. The Department of Education has a duty to encourage and facilitate the development of Irish-medium education. Northern Ireland has 29 standalone Irish-medium schools, most of them primary schools, and ten Irish-medium units attached to English-medium host schools.

*Voluntary schools* are mainly grammar schools, which select most pupils according to academic ability. They are managed by boards of governors consisting of teachers, parents and, in most cases, representatives from the Department of Education and the ELB.

*Integrated schools* (primary and secondary) educate pupils from both the Protestant and Catholic communities as well as those of other faiths and no faith; each school is managed by a board of governors. There are at present 62 integrated schools maintained by the state, 24 of which are controlled schools.

Since 2013 all pupils are guaranteed access to a wide range of courses, with a minimum of 24 courses at Key Stage 4, and 27 at post-16. At least one-third of the courses on offer will be academic and another third will be vocational. Schools work with other schools, FE colleges and other providers to widen the range of courses on offer.

## INDEPENDENT SCHOOLS

Around 6 per cent of UK schoolchildren are educated by privately funded 'independent' schools that charge fees and set their own admissions policies. Independent schools are required to meet certain minimum standards but need not teach the National Curriculum. *See also* Independent Schools.

## UK SCHOOLS BY CATEGORY (2013–14)

| | England | Wales |
|---|---|---|
| *Maintained nursery schools | 414 | 17 |
| †Maintained primary and secondary schools | 16,290 | 1,574 |
| Community | 9,342 | – |
| Voluntary-aided | 3,760 | – |
| Voluntary-controlled | 2,369 | – |
| Foundation | 961 | – |
| Pupil Referral Units | 371 | – |
| Maintained Special schools | 964 | 42 |
| ‡Non-maintained Special schools | 69 | – |
| ‡Academies | 3,827 | – |
| Independent schools | 2,411 | 66 |
| *Total* | 24,346 | 1,699 |

\* Includes one direct grant school in England
† Includes four middle schools in Wales
‡ Includes City Technology Colleges, University Technology Colleges, studio schools and free schools; excludes voluntary and private pre-school education centres
*Source:* DfE; Welsh government

*Scotland*

| | |
|---|---|
| Publicly funded schools | 2,560 |
| Primary | 2,055 |
| Secondary | 363 |
| Special | 142 |
| Independent schools | 100 |
| Total | 2,660 |

*Source:* Scottish government

*Northern Ireland*

| | |
|---|---|
| State-maintained nursery schools | 96 |
| State-maintained primary and secondary schools | 1,035 |
| Controlled | 440 |
| Voluntary | 51 |
| Catholic maintained | 452 |
| Other maintained | 30 |
| Integrated | 62 |
| Special schools | 40 |
| Independent schools | 15 |
| Total | 1,186 |

*Source:* DENI

## INSPECTION

### ENGLAND

The Office for Standards in Education, Children's Services and Skills (Ofsted) is the main body responsible for inspecting education in English schools. As well as inspecting all publicly funded and some independent schools, Ofsted inspects a range of other services in England, including childcare, children's homes, pupil referral units, local authority children's services, further education, initial teacher training and publicly funded adult skills training.

Ofsted is an independent, non-ministerial government department that reports directly to parliament, headed by Her Majesty's Chief Inspector (HMCI). Ofsted is required to promote improvement in the public services that it inspects; ensure that these services focus on the interests of their users – children, parents, learners and employers; and see that these services are efficient, effective and promote value for money. A new 'common inspection regime' came into effect in September 2015 *(see* Recent Developments) to make inspections of different settings with similar age groups more coherent.

Ofsted publishes the findings of its inspection reports, its recommendations and statistical information on its website.
OFFICE FOR STANDARDS IN EDUCATION,
CHILDREN'S SERVICES AND SKILLS **T** 0300-123 1231
    **W** www.gov.uk/government/organisations/ofsted

### WALES

Estyn is the office of Her Majesty's Inspectorate for Education and Training in Wales. It is independent of, but funded by, the Welsh government and is led by Her Majesty's Chief Inspector of Education and Training in Wales.

Estyn's role is to inspect quality and standards in education and training in Wales, including in primary, secondary, special and independent schools, and pupil referral units, publicly funded nursery schools and settings, further education, adult community-based and work-based learning, local authorities and teacher education and training.

Estyn also provides advice on quality and standards in education and training to the Welsh government and others and its remit includes making public good practice based on inspection evidence. Estyn publishes the findings of its inspection reports, its recommendations and statistical information on its website.
HER MAJESTY'S INSPECTORATE FOR EDUCATION
    AND TRAINING IN WALES **T** 029-2044 6446
    **W** www.estyn.gov.uk

### SCOTLAND

HM Inspectorate of Education (HMIE) merged with Learning and Teaching Scotland in July 2011 to become Education Scotland, an executive agency of the Scottish government. Education Scotland operates independently and impartially while being directly accountable to Scottish ministers for the standards of its work. The agency's core business is inspection and review. It is responsible for delivering measurable year-on-year improvements, with maximum efficiency, by promoting excellence, building on strengths, and identifying and addressing under-performance. Since August 2015, inspections take account of national expectations of progress in implementing Curriculum for Excellence (CfE).

Inspection reports and reviews, recommendations, examples of good practice and statistical information are published on Education Scotland's website.
EDUCATION SCOTLAND **T** 0141 282 5000
    **W** www.educationscotland.gov.uk

### NORTHERN IRELAND

The Education and Training Inspectorate (ETINI) provides inspection services for the Department of Education and Employment and Learning Northern Ireland.

ETINI carries out inspections of all schools, pre-school services, special education, further education colleges, initial teacher training, training organisations, and curriculum advisory and support services. Since September 2013 regional colleges of further education have received four weeks' notification of inspection, while all other organisations have received two weeks' notification of inspection.

The inspectorate's role is to improve services and it provides evidence-based advice to ministers in order to assist in the formulation of policies. It publishes the findings of its inspection reports, its recommendations and statistical information on its website.
EDUCATION AND TRAINING INSPECTORATE
    **T** 028-9127 9726 **W** www.etini.gov.uk

## THE NATIONAL CURRICULUM

### ENGLAND

The National Curriculum, first introduced in 1988, is mandatory in all state schools for children from age 5 onwards.

Until age 5, or the end of Reception Year in primary school, children are in the Early Years Foundation Stage (EYFS), which has its own learning and development requirements for children in nursery and primary schools. Changes to the EYFS came into effect in 2012 and 2014. These included simplifying the statutory assessment of children's development at age five; reducing the number of early learning goals from 69 to 17; focusing on seven areas of learning and development (prime areas: communication and language, physical development and personal, social and emotional development; and specific areas: literacy, mathematics, understanding the world, and expressive arts and design) and, for parents, a new progress check at age two on their child's development.

Following the EYFS, the National Curriculum is organised into 'Key Stages', and sets out the core subjects that must be taught and the standards or attainment targets for each subject at each Key Stage.
- Key Stage 1 covers Years 1 and 2 of primary school, for children aged 5–7
- Key Stage 2 covers Years 3 to 6 of primary school, for children aged 7–11
- Key Stage 3 covers Years 7 to 9 of secondary school, for children aged 11–14
- Key Stage 4 covers Years 10 and 11 of secondary school, for children aged 14–16

Within the framework of the National Curriculum, schools may plan and organise teaching and learning in the way that best meets the needs of their pupils, but maintained schools are expected to follow the programmes of study associated with particular subjects. The programmes of study describe the subject knowledge, skills and understanding that pupils are expected to have developed by the end of each Key Stage.

The former coalition government brought in a new National Curriculum for England, to be taught in all maintained primary and secondary schools from September 2014, however pupils in Years 10 and 11 continued to be taught English, mathematics and science on the old programmes of study until new, more demanding GCSEs in these subjects were ready for them to take. Since September 2015 all maintained secondary schools in England have had to teach the Key Stage 4 programmes of study for English and mathematics in Year 10. From September 2015 they must teach the new programmes for English and mathematics in Year 11 and science in Year 10, and from September 2017 schools must teach all the programmes of study to all Key Stage 4 pupils.

| KEY STAGES 1 AND 2 COMPULSORY SUBJECTS | |
|---|---|
| English | Design and technology |
| Mathematics | Geography |
| Science | History |
| Art and design | Music |
| Computing | Physical education |

Foreign languages will be compulsory in Key Stage 2, but not Key Stage 1: schools can choose from French, German, Italian, Mandarin, Spanish, Latin or Ancient Greek.

In Key Stage 3, compulsory subjects include those listed above for Key Stage 2 (though the language taught should be a modern foreign language) plus citizenship.

Pupils in Key Stage 4 study a mix of compulsory and optional subjects in preparation for national examinations such as GCSEs. Pupils at this key stage also have to undertake careers education and work-related learning. In addition, schools must offer at least one subject from each of four 'entitlement' areas: arts (art and design, music, dance, drama and media arts); design and technology; humanities (history and geography); and modern foreign languages. To meet the entitlement requirements, schools must ensure that courses in these areas lead to approved qualifications, and allow pupils to take courses in all four areas if they wish to do so.

| KEY STAGE 4 COMPULSORY SUBJECTS | |
|---|---|
| English | Citizenship |
| Mathematics | Computing |
| Science | Physical education |

Schools must teach religious education (RE) at all key stages, although parents have the right to withdraw children for all or part of the RE curriculum. Secondary schools must provide sex and relationship education.

Statutory assessment must be undertaken for all pupils in publicly funded schools in the relevant years. It first takes place towards the end of the Early Years Foundation Stage, when children's level of development is compared to and recorded against a Foundation Stage Profile (this will no longer be a statutory requirement from September 2016). Pupils receive a phonics screening check at the end of the first year in Key Stage 1, repeated the following year if necessary. Teacher assessments in English, mathematics and science take place at the end of Key Stage 1 (Year 2) and Key Stage 2 (Year 6); at the end of Key Stage 3 (Year 9) teachers assess progress in all subjects being studied. National tests in

English and mathematics take place in Year 6. At Key Stage 4, national examinations are the main form of assessment.

The assessment process for English at the end of Key Stage 2 now involves three elements. Reading comprehension is assessed by an external national test. Written comprehension is subject only to teacher assessment. Grammar, punctuation and spelling are assessed by a new external test introduced in May 2013.

Each year the DfE publishes on its website performance tables covering every school, college and local authority. The primary school tables are based mainly on the results of the tests taken by children at the end of Key Stage 2 when they are usually aged 11; since 2010 teacher assessment results are also included. Pupils at the end of Key Stage 2 will take new-style tests in English, mathematics and science, based on the new National Curriculum, for the first-time in summer 2016. The tables for secondary schools and attainment post-16 rely mainly on the results of national examinations. All tables include indicators of the progress that pupils have made since their last assessment. From 2016 the tables will identify 'coasting' schools that are not pushing every pupil to reach their potential.

DEPARTMENT FOR EDUCATION T 0370-000 2288
W www.education.gov.uk

## WALES

Wales is reviewing its National Curriculum and assessment from Foundation Phase to Key Stage 4. An implementation plan for the curriculum and assessment changes set out in *Successful Futures (see* Recent Developments) was due in autumn 2015. *Successful Futures* states that the purpose of the curriculum in Wales should be that children and young people develop as:

- Ambitious, capable learners, ready to learn throughout their lives
- Enterprising, creative contributors, ready to play a full part in life and work
- Ethical, informed citizens of Wales and the world
- Healthy, confident individuals, ready to lead fulfilling lives as valued members of society

It also sets out that the new national curriculum in Wales for 3- to 16-year-olds should be organised into areas of learning and experience that establish the breadth of the curriculum. These areas should provide rich contexts for developing the four curriculum purposes, be internally coherent, employ distinctive ways of thinking, and have an identifiable core of disciplinary or instrumental knowledge. There should be seven areas of learning and experience: expressive arts; health and well-being; humanities; languages, literacy and communication; mathematics and numeracy; and science and technology. Cross-curricular, all teachers should be responsible for developing literacy, numeracy and digital competence.

Initially a Foundation Phase curriculum for 3- to 7-year-olds was introduced in September 2008. The emphasis is on learning-by-doing and children's skills and knowledge are planned across seven areas of learning. They are:

- Personal and social development, well-being and cultural diversity
- Language, literacy and communication skills
- Mathematical development
- Welsh language development
- Knowledge and understanding of the world
- Physical development
- Creative development

Full details of the Foundation Phase can be found in *Framework for Children's Learning for 3- to 7-year-olds in Wales*, available on the Welsh government website (*see* below).

Currently the National Curriculum is for 7- to 16-year-olds. Originally it was broadly similar to that of England, with distinctive characteristics for Wales reflected in the programmes of study. From September 2008 a revised school curriculum was implemented, consisting of the National Curriculum subjects together with non-statutory frameworks for personal and social education, the world of work, religious education and skills.

The National Curriculum in Wales includes the following subjects:
• *Key Stage 2* – English, Welsh, mathematics, science, design and technology, ICT, history, geography, art and design, music, and physical education
• *Key Stage 3* – as Key Stage 2, plus a modern foreign language
• *Key Stage 4* – English, Welsh, mathematics, science and physical education
Welsh is compulsory for pupils at all key stages, either as a first or as a second language. In 2010, 16.5 per cent of pupils were taught Welsh as a first language. In April 2012, the Minister for Education and Skills approved the implementation of an action plan to raise standards and attainment in Welsh second language education.

Statutory testing at the end of Key Stage 2 was removed for pupils in Wales from 2004–5. Only statutory teacher assessment remains. It is also done at the end of Key Stage 1 (in future, the Foundation Phase) and Key Stage 3, and is being strengthened by moderation and accreditation arrangements.

The new National Literacy and Numeracy Framework (LNF), outlining the skills 5- to 15-year-olds are expected to acquire, became statutory from September 2013. For literacy, this means children should become accomplished in reading for information, writing for information and expressing themselves fluently and grammatically in speech. In numeracy, children are expected to develop numerical reasoning and use number skills, measuring skills and data skills.

New national reading and numeracy tests for pupils in Years 2 to 9 took place for the first time in Wales in May 2013. The tests are designed to give teachers a clearer insight into a learner's development and progress, to allow them to intervene at an earlier stage if learners are falling behind.

The reading test includes a statutory 'core' test, and a set of optional test materials to help teachers to investigate learners' strengths and development needs in more depth.

The numeracy test is split into two papers: numerical procedures and numerical reasoning. The procedural paper consists of a set of questions designed to assess the basic, essential numeracy skills such as addition, multiplication and division.

The numerical reasoning paper was introduced in May 2014. It will assess learners' ability to find the most effective ways to solve everyday numeracy problems.

Learners in Welsh medium schools will take a reading test in Welsh only in Years 2 and 3, but in both English and Welsh from Year 4 onwards. Schools will have the option to use both tests in Year 3. Learners will take the numeracy test in either English or Welsh.

THE WELSH GOVERNMENT – EDUCATION AND SKILLS
W www.wales.gov.uk/topics/educationandskills/schoolshome/curriculuminwales/arevisedcurriculumforwales
W www.learning.wales.gov.uk

## SCOTLAND

The curriculum in Scotland is not prescribed by statute but is the responsibility of education authorities and individual schools. However, schools and authorities are expected to follow the Scottish government's guidance on management and delivery of the curriculum.

Advice and guidance are provided by the Scottish government primarily through Education Scotland.

Scotland is now implementing *Curriculum for Excellence*, which aims to provide more autonomy for teachers, greater choice and opportunity for pupils and a single coherent curriculum for all children and young people aged 3 to 18.

The purpose of Curriculum for Excellence is encapsulated in 'the four capacities': to enable each child or young person to be a successful learner, a confident individual, a responsible citizen and an effective contributor. It focuses on providing a broad curriculum that develops skills for learning, skills for life and skills for work, with a sustained focus on literacy and numeracy. The period of education from pre-school through to the end of secondary stage 3, when pupils reach age 14, has the particular purpose of providing each young person in Scotland with this broad general education.

Curriculum for Excellence sets out 'experiences and outcomes', which describe broad areas of learning and what is to be achieved within them. They are:
• Expressive arts (including art and design, dance, drama, music)
• Health and wellbeing (including physical education, food and health, relationships and sexual health and mental, physical and social wellbeing)
• Languages
• Mathematics
• Religious and moral education
• Sciences
• Social studies (including history, geography, society and economy)
• Technologies (including business, computing, food and textiles, craft, design, engineering and graphics)
The experiences and outcomes are written at five levels with progression to examinations and qualifications during the senior phase, which covers secondary stages 4 to 6 when students are generally aged 14 to 17. The framework is designed to be flexible so that pupils can progress at their own pace.

| Level | Stage |
|---|---|
| Early | The pre-school years and primary 1 (ages 3–5), or later for some |
| First | To the end of primary 4 (age 8), but earlier or later for some |
| Second | To the end of primary 7 (age 11), but earlier or later for some |
| Third and Fourth | Secondary 1 to secondary 3 (ages 12–14), but earlier for some. The fourth level experiences and outcomes are intended to provide possibilities for choice and young people's programmes will not include all of the fourth level outcomes |
| Senior phase | Secondary 4 to secondary 6 (ages 15–18), and college or other means of study |

Under the new curriculum, assessment of students' progress and achievements from ages 3 to 15 is carried out by teachers who base their assessment judgments on a range of evidence rather than single assessment instruments such as tests. Teachers have access to an online National Assessment Resource (NAR), which provides a range of assessment material and national exemplars across the curriculum areas.

In the senior phase, young people aged 16 to 18, including those studying outside school, build up a portfolio of national qualifications, awarded by the Scottish Qualifications Authority (SQA).

Provision is made for teaching in Gaelic in many parts of Scotland and the number of pupils, from nursery to secondary, in Gaelic-medium education is growing.

EDUCATION SCOTLAND T 0141-282 5000
W www.educationscotland.gov.uk

SCOTTISH QUALIFICATIONS AUTHORITY
T 0845-279 1000 W www.sqa.org.uk

## NORTHERN IRELAND

In September 2009 Northern Ireland put in place across Years 1 to 12 a revised statutory curriculum placing greater emphasis on developing skills and preparing young people for life and work.

This curriculum includes a new Foundation Stage to cover Years 1 and 2 of primary school, so as to allow a more appropriate learning style for the youngest pupils and to ease the transition from pre-school. Key Stage 1 covers primary Years 3 and 4, until children are 8, and Key Stage 2 covers primary Years 5, 6 and 7, until children are 11. Post-primary, Key Stage 3 covers Years 8, 9 and 10 and Key Stage 4 Years 11 and 12.

The current primary curriculum is made up of the following areas of learning:
• Language and literacy
• Mathematics and numeracy
• The arts
• The world around us
• Personal development and mutual understanding
• Physical education
• Religeous education

The current post-primary curriculum includes a new area of learning for life and work, made up of employability, personal development, local and global citizenship and home economics (at Key Stage 3). It is also made up of RE and the following areas of learning:
• Language and literacy
• Mathematics and numeracy
• Modern languages
• The arts
• Environment and society
• Physical education
• Science and technology

At Key Stage 4, there are nine areas of learning, but statutory requirements have been significantly reduced to: learning for life and work, physical education and RE. The aim is to provide greater choice and flexibility for pupils and allow them access to a wider range of academic and vocational courses provided under the revised curriculum's 'Entitlement Framework' (EF).

Since September 2013, schools have been required to provide pupils with access to at least 18 courses at Key Stage 4 and 21 courses at post-16. This increased to 24 and 27 courses respectively in September 2015. At least one third of the courses must be 'general' with one third 'applied'. The remaining third is at the discretion of each school. Individual pupils decide on the number and mix of courses they wish to follow.

RE is a compulsory part of the Northern Ireland curriculum, although parents have the right to withdraw their children from part or all of RE or collective worship. Schools have to provide RE in accordance with a core syllabus drawn up by the province's four main churches (Church of Ireland, Presbyterian, Methodist and Roman Catholic) and specified by the Department of Education.

Revised assessment and reporting arrangements were introduced when the curriculum was revised. The focus from Foundation to Key Stage 3 is on 'Assessment for Learning'. This programme includes classroom-based teacher assessment, computer-based assessment of literacy and numeracy and pupils deciding on their strengths and weaknesses and how they might progress to achieve their potential. Assessment information is given to parents in an annual report. Pupils at Key Stage 4 and beyond continue to be assessed through public examinations.

The Council for the Curriculum, Examinations and Assessment (CCEA), a non-departmental public body reporting to the Department of Education in Northern Ireland, is unique in the UK in combining the functions of a curriculum advisory body, an awarding body and a qualifications regulatory body. It advises the government on what should be taught in Northern Ireland's schools and colleges, ensures that the qualifications and examinations offered by awarding bodies in Northern Ireland are of an appropriate quality and standard and, as the leading awarding body itself, offers a range of qualifications including GCSEs, A-levels and AS-levels.

The CCEA hosts a dedicated curriculum website covering all aspects of the revised curriculum, assessment and reporting.

COUNCIL FOR THE CURRICULUM, EXAMINATIONS AND ASSESSMENT T 028-9026 1200 W www.ccea.org.uk
NORTHERN IRELAND CURRICULUM
T 028-9028 1200 W www.nicurriculum.org.uk

## QUALIFICATIONS

### ENGLAND, WALES AND NORTHERN IRELAND

There is a very wide range of public examinations and qualifications available, accredited by the Office of Qualifications and Examinations Regulation (OFQUAL) in England, the Department for Education and Skills (DfES) in Wales, and the Council for the Curriculum, Examinations and Assessment (CCEA) in Northern Ireland. Up-to-date information on all accredited qualifications and awarding bodies is available online at the Register of Regulated Qualifications website.

The qualifications frameworks group all accredited qualifications into levels, up to level 8. All the qualifications within a level place similar demands on individuals as learners. Entry level, for example, covers basic knowledge and skills in English, maths and ICT not geared towards specific occupations, level 3 includes qualifications such as A-levels which are appropriate for those wishing to go on to higher education, level 7 covers Master's degrees and vocational qualifications appropriate for senior professionals and managers and level 8 is equivalent to a doctorate.

Young people aged 14 to 19 in schools or (post-16) colleges or apprenticeships may gain academic qualifications such as GCSEs, AS-levels and A-levels; qualifications linked to particular career fields, like diplomas; vocational qualifications such as BTECs and NVQs; and functional key or basic skills qualifications.

The National Qualifications Framework (NQF) formerly used in England, Wales and Northern Ireland has now been replaced by the Qualifications and Credit Framework (QCF) for England and Northern Ireland and the Credit and Qualifications Framework for Wales (CQFW). There is also a Framework for Higher Education Qualifications (FHEQ) for England, Wales and Northern Ireland.

#### QUALIFICATIONS AND CREDIT FRAMEWORK (QCF)

This framework, originally designed for vocational qualifications, has now been broadened to include all accredited academic, vocational or other qualifications taken in schools, further education, higher education or elsewhere. The QCF goes from entry level up to level 8. Qualifications in the QCF are built up of units of learning, and every qualification or unit recognised in the framework has a credit value, showing how long it takes to complete. One credit is equivalent to ten hours. As each unit and the credits can be transferred, the system enables learners to complete qualifications at their own pace. When an individual takes QCF units or qualifications, their learning is 'banked' and stored on their personal learner record.

QCF qualifications include GCSEs and A-levels; International Baccalaureate; BTEC courses; English for Speakers of Other Languages (ESOL); Skills for Life; Foundation Learning; National Vocational Qualifications (NVQs); Cambridge Nationals; Higher National Certificates (HNC); and Higher National Diplomas (HND).

## FRAMEWORK FOR HIGHER EDUCATION QUALIFICATIONS (FHEQ)

This framework applies to degrees, diplomas, certificates and other academic awards (other than honorary degrees and higher doctorates) granted by a higher education provider in the exercise of its degree awarding powers. It starts at QCF level 4 and goes up to level 8 and includes the following qualifications: Certificate of Higher Education; Diploma of Higher Education; Bachelor's degrees; Master's degrees; and Doctoral degrees.

## COUNCIL FOR THE CURRICULUM, EXAMINATIONS AND ASSESSMENT (NORTHERN IRELAND)
T 028-9026 1200 W www.ccea.org.uk

## DEPARTMENT FOR EDUCATION AND SKILLS (DfES)
T 0300-0603300; 0845-010 3300
W http://wales.gov.uk/topics/educationandskills

## REGISTER OF REGULATED QUALIFICATIONS
T 0300-303 3346 W http://register.ofqual.gov.uk

## OFFICE OF QUALIFICATIONS AND EXAMINATIONS REGULATION (OFQUAL) T 0300-303 3344
W www.ofqual.gov.uk

## GCSE

The vast majority of pupils in their last year of compulsory schooling in England, Wales and Northern Ireland take at least one General Certificate of Secondary Education (GCSE) exam, though GCSEs may be taken at any age. GCSEs assess the performance of pupils on a subject-specific basis and are mostly taken after a two-year course. They are available in more than 50 subjects, most of them academic subjects, though some, known as vocational or applied GCSEs, involve the study of a particular area of employment and the development of work-related skills. Some subjects are also offered as short-course qualifications, equivalent to half a standard GCSE, or as double awards, equivalent to two GCSEs.

For many years GCSEs have been assessed on coursework completed by students during the course as well as exams at the end and GCSE certificates have been awarded on an eight-point scale from A* to G. In most subjects two different papers, foundation and higher, are provided for different ranges of ability, with grades A*–D available to students taking the higher paper and grades C–G available from the foundation paper.

Major changes to GCSEs are taking place in England. From 2015, GCSEs no longer involve modules and coursework, just exams at the end of the two-year course. The pass mark will be higher and the qualifications will be graded 9 to 1, rather than A* to G. There will no longer be controlled assessments (coursework done under exam conditions) and final exams will be essay-based. Changes will initially be for nine core GCSE subjects. Revised GCSEs in English language, English literature and mathematics began in September 2015 and those in chemistry, biology, physics,

science (double award), geography, history and modern foreign languages will be taught from September 2016. Revised GCSEs in art and design, computer science, citizenship, dance, design and technology, drama, music, physical education and religious studies will also be ready for teaching from September 2016. The remaining subjects will either be reformed for teaching from 2017 or withdrawn.
W www.gov.uk/government/collections/gcse-subject-content

All GCSE specifications, assessments and grading procedures are monitored by OFQUAL, DfES and the CCEA.

Since September 2010 the government has allowed state schools to offer pupils International GCSE (iGCSE) exams in key subjects including English, mathematics, science and ICT. The iGCSEs do not include coursework and some experts consider them more rigorous than traditional GCSEs.

## GCE A-LEVEL AND AS-LEVEL

GCE (General Certificate of Education) Advanced levels (A-levels) are the qualifications used by most young people in England, Wales and Northern Ireland to gain entry to university.

A-levels are subject-based qualifications. They are mostly taken by UK students aged 16 to 19 over a two-year course in school sixth forms or at college, but can be taken at any age. They are available in more than 45, mostly academic, subjects, though there are some A-levels in vocational areas, often termed 'applied A-levels'.

Traditionally, A-level qualifications consists of two parts: advanced subsidiary (AS) and A2 units. The AS has traditionally been a standalone qualification normally consisting of two units, assessed at the standard expected for a learner half way through an A-level course, that together contribute 50 per cent towards the full A-level. The A2 is the second half of a full A-level qualification. It normally consists of two units, assessed at the standard expected for a learner at the end of a full A-level course, that together make-up the remaining 50 per cent of the full A-level qualification. Most units are assessed by examination. Each unit is graded A–E. Since 2010 an A* grade has been awarded to exceptional candidates.

An extended project was introduced in September 2008 as a separate qualification. It is a single piece of work on a topic of the student's own choosing that requires a high degree of planning, preparation, research and autonomous working. Awards are graded A–E and the extended project is accredited as half an A-level.

Since September 2013, students in England in their first or second year of A-level studies can no longer sit A-level exams in January. A-levels are still examined unit by unit, but all exams are taken in the summer.

From 2015, revised AS and A-levels are being introduced in phases until 2017. All assessment of the new A-levels will take place at the end of the two-year course and the AS will become an entirely standalone qualification rather than contributing to a full A-level qualification.

Since September 2015 students have been taught the new-style AS-level and A-level in art and design, biology, business, chemistry, computer science, economics, English language, English language and literature, English literature, history, physics, psychology and sociology. The new AS and A-levels in ancient languages, dance, drama and theatre, geography, modern foreign languages (French, German and Spanish), music, physical education and religious studies will be taught from September 2016.

Further subjects in the new AS and A-level will be ready for teaching from September 2017.
W www.gov.uk/government/collections/gce-as-and-a-level-subject-content

## INTERNATIONAL BACCALAUREATE

The International Baccalaureate (IB) offers four educational programmes for students aged 3 to 19: IB primary years programme, IB middle years programme, IB diploma programme, IB career-related certificate.

Some 155 'IB World Schools' in the UK offer at least one IB programme.

The IB diploma programme for students aged 16 to 19 is based around detailed academic study of a wide range of subjects, including languages, the arts, science, maths, history and geography, this leads to a single qualification recognised by UK universities.

The IB diploma is made up of a compulsory 'core' plus six separate subjects where individuals have some choice over what they study. The compulsory core contains three elements: theory of knowledge; creativity, action and service; and a 4,000-word extended essay.

The diploma normally takes two years to complete and most of the assessment is done through externally marked examinations. Candidates are awarded points for each part of the programme, up to a maximum of 45. A candidate must score 24 points or more to achieve a full diploma.

Successfully completing the diploma earns points on the 'UCAS tariff', the UK system for allocating points to qualifications used for entry to higher education. An IB diploma total of 24 points is worth 260 UCAS points – the same as a B and two C grades at A-level. The maximum of 45 points earns 720 UCAS points – equivalent to six A-levels at grade A.

## WELSH BACCALAUREATE

The Welsh Baccalaureate Qualification (WBQ), available for 14- to 19-year-olds in Wales, combines a compulsory core, which incorporates personal development skills, with options from existing academic and vocational qualifications, such as A-levels, GCSEs and NVQs, to make one broader award. The WBQ can be studied in English or Welsh, or a combination of the two. Candidates who meet the requirements of the compulsory core and options relevant to each level of the qualification are awarded the Welsh Baccalaureate Foundation, Intermediate or Advanced Diploma as appropriate.

WJEC (Welsh Joint Education Committee), which administers the WBQ, has also developed two new WBQs at level 1 and level 2 suitable for delivery over one year and with a particular focus on employability. These are currently only available as a pilot in some colleges or work-based learning providers.

A revised and more rigorous Welsh Baccalaureate has been taught since September 2015. It is based on a Skills Challenge Certificate, which will be graded, and supporting qualifications. The aim is to enable learners to develop and demonstrate an understanding of, and proficiency in, essential and employability skills: communication, numeracy, digital Literacy, planning and organisation, creativity and innovation, critical thinking and problem solving, and personal effectiveness. The emphasis is on applied and purposeful learning and opportunities for assessment in a range of real life contexts through three 'challenge briefs' and an individual project.

## BTECS, OCR NATIONALS AND OTHER VOCATIONAL QUALIFICATIONS

Vocational qualifications can range from general qualifications where a person learns skills relevant to a variety of jobs, to specialist qualifications designed for a particular sector. They are available from several awarding bodies, such as City & Guilds, Edexcel and OCR, and can be taken at many different levels. All vocational and work-related qualifications fit into the Qualifications and Credit Framework (QCF).

BTEC qualifications and OCR Nationals are particular types of work-related qualifications, available in a wide range of subjects, including: art and design, business, health and social care, information technology, media, public services, science and sport. The qualifications offer a mix of theory and practice, can include work experience and can take be part of an Apprenticeship. They can be studied full-time at college or school, or part-time at college.

Learners complete a range of assignments, case studies and practical activities, as well as a portfolio of evidence that shows what work has been completed.

From 2016, the quality and assessment of all vocational courses offered by schools and colleges to 14- to 19-year-olds will be strengthened. The standards of reformed BTECs, along with Cambridge OCR National Certificates and Vocational Certificates (V-Certs), will equal those of GCSE A*–C grades. All vocational qualifications will be graded (previously many were simply pass/fail) and all will have a 25 per cent externally examined component.

## NVQS

A National Vocational Qualification (NVQ) is a 'competence-based' qualification that is recognised by employers. Individuals learn practical, work-related tasks designed to help them develop the skills and knowledge to do a particular job effectively. NVQs can be taken in school, at college or by people already in work. There are more than 1,300 different NVQs available from the vast majority of business sectors. NVQs exist at levels 1 to 5 on the QCF. An NVQ qualification at level 2 or 3 can also be taken as part of an Apprenticeship.

## FUNCTIONAL SKILLS

Functional skills qualifications were launched during 2010, for all learners aged 14 and above. They test practical skills that allow people to work confidently, effectively and independently in life, and are available only in England. Wales and Northern Ireland have literacy and numeracy qualifications known as 'essential skills'.

Following a review by OFQUAL, the functional skills qualifications in English and mathematics are changing. Assessment materials will be improved, the risk of malpractice will be reduced, standard setting procedures will be strengthened and there will be better evaluation of how well the qualifications meet user needs.

## APPRENTICESHIPS

Apprenticeships combine on-the-job training with nationally recognised qualifications, allowing individuals to gain skills and qualifications while working and earning a wage. More than 200 different types of apprenticeships are available, offering over 1,500 job roles; they take between one and five years to complete. There are four levels available:

- Intermediate Apprenticeships – at level 2 on the National Qualifications Framework (NQF), they are equivalent to five good GCSE passes
- Advanced Apprenticeships – at level 3 on the NQF, they are equivalent to two A-level passes
- Higher Apprenticeships – lead to qualifications at NVQ Level 4 or, in some cases, a foundation degree
- Degree Apprenticeships – added in 2015 *(see* Recent Developments)

In England, the National Apprenticeship Service (NAS), launched in 2009, is responsible for the delivery of apprenticeships and provides an online vacancy matching system. In 2013–14, some 440,000 young people (53 per cent women and 47 per cent men) started apprenticeships in England. The Welsh government and the Department for

Employment and Learning (DEL) are responsible for the apprenticeship programmes in Wales and Northern Ireland respectively.

NATIONAL APPRENTICESHIP SERVICE (NAS)
T 02476-826482 W www.apprenticeships.gov.uk

## SCOTLAND

Scotland has its own system of public examinations and qualifications. The Scottish Qualifications Authority (SQA) is Scotland's national body for qualifications, responsible for developing, accrediting, assessing and certificating all Scottish qualifications apart from university degrees and some professional body qualifications.

There are qualifications at all levels of attainment. Almost all school candidates gain SQA qualifications in the fourth year of secondary school and most obtain further qualifications in the fifth or sixth year or in further education colleges. Increasingly, people also take them in the workplace.

SQA, with partners such as Universities Scotland, has introduced the Scottish Credit and Qualifications Framework (SCQF) as a way of comparing and understanding Scottish qualifications. It includes qualifications across academic and vocational sectors and compares them by giving a level and credit points. There are 12 levels in the SCQF, level 1 being the least difficult and level 12 the most difficult. The number of SCQF credit points shows how much learning has to be done to achieve the qualification. For instance, one SCQF credit point equals about 10 hours of learning including assessment.

- Standard Grades are taken over the third and fourth years at secondary school. Students often choose to study seven or eight subjects, of which Mathematics and English are compulsory. There are three levels of study at Standard Grade: Foundation, General and Credit. Students usually sit exams at two levels – either Foundation/General or General/Credit – to ensure they have the best chance of achieving as high a grade as possible.
- National Units are the building blocks of National Courses, but they are also recognised qualifications in their own right and are designed to take approximately 40 hours of teaching time to complete.
- National Courses usually comprise three National Units and an externally marked assessment. National Courses are available at a number of levels including Access 1, Access 2, Access 3, Intermediate 1, Intermediate 2, Higher and Advanced Higher.
- Skills for Work courses encourage school pupils to become familiar with the world of work. They involve a strong element of learning through involvement in practical and vocational activities and develop knowledge, skills and experience that are related to employment. They are available at a number of levels and are frequently delivered in partnership between schools and colleges.
- Wider Achievement qualifications provide young people with the opportunity to have learning and skills formally recognised, whether developed in or outside the classroom. Available at a number of levels in subjects including Employability, Leadership and Enterprise, these qualifications help schools deliver skills for learning, life and work.
- Scottish Baccalaureates consist of a coherent group of Higher and Advanced Higher qualifications and, uniquely, an interdisciplinary project of candidates' own choosing which is marked at Advanced Higher level in one of four broad topics – languages, science, expressive arts or social studies. Aimed at high-achieving candidates in their sixth year, the Scottish Baccalaureate is designed to encourage personalised, in-depth study and interdisciplinary learning in the later stages of secondary school.

As part of the Curriculum for Excellence programme (see above) SQA has developed new National qualifications that became available in schools from August 2013, replacing Standard Grade, Intermediate and Access qualifications at all levels. New Higher qualifications became available from August 2014 and Advanced Higher qualifications will be available from August 2015:

| SCQF Level | New national qualifications | Replaces |
|---|---|---|
| 1 and 2 | National 1 and 2 | Access 1 and Access 2 |
| 3 | National 3 | Access 3 Standard Grade (Foundation Level) |
| 4 | National 4 | Standard Grade (General Level) Intermediate 1 |
| 5 | National 5 | Standard Grade (Credit Level) Intermediate 2 |
| 6 | Higher (new) | Higher |
| 7 | Advanced Higher (new) | Advanced Higher |

All new qualifications will run concurrently with existing qualifications until 2015/16. Final results for existing Access, Intermediate, Higher and Advanced Higher qualifications were issued in August 2015.

SQA has also developed five new Awards – in modern languages, personal achievement, personal development, religion and wellbeing – that cover work from across different subject areas, and are shorter than traditional courses and recognise success across different levels of difficulty. These started in August 2012 and are marked and assessed by schools and colleges rather than by external assessment or exams. New Awards in Cycling and Scottish Studies began in August 2013.

### SQA QUALIFICATIONS

#### HIGHER NATIONAL CERTIFICATES AND HIGHER NATIONAL DIPLOMAS

Higher National Certificates and Higher National Diplomas (HNCs and HNDs) are offered by colleges, some universities and many other training providers – including employers. Both HNCs and HNDs are comprised of Higher National Units and cover a wide range of subject areas. Many HNDs allow the holder entry to the second or third year of a degree course. HNCs are available at SCQF level 7, HNDs at level 8.

#### NATIONAL QUALIFICATION GROUP AWARDS

National Certificates and National Progression Awards are designed to prepare people for employment, career development or progression to more advanced study at HNC/HND level. They also aim to develop a range of transferable knowledge including core skills. These certificates are aimed at 16- to 18-year-olds or adults in full-time education and are at SCQF levels 2 to 6. Each one has specific aims relating to a subject or occupational area.

#### SCOTTISH VOCATIONAL QUALIFICATIONS

Scottish Vocational Qualifications (SVQs) are based on national standards drawn up by people from industry, commerce and education. Possession of an SVQ demonstrates ability to perform in a job to agreed national standards. Primarily delivered to candidates in full-time employment, SVQs are available at SCQF levels 4 to 12.

#### PROFESSIONAL DEVELOPMENT AWARDS

Professional Development Awards (PDAs) are designed to develop and deliver high-level skills in a sharp, flexible and focused way. They are for people already in work who wish to extend or broaden their skills. Candidates often take an

PDA after completing a degree or vocational qualification. PDAs are available at SCQF levels 6 to 12.

THE SCOTTISH QUALIFICATIONS AUTHORITY (SQA) T 0845-279 1000 W www.sqa.org.uk
SCOTTISH CREDIT AND QUALIFICATIONS FRAMEWORK (SCQF) T 0845-270 7371 W www.scqf.org.uk

# FURTHER EDUCATION AND LIFELONG LEARNING

## ENGLAND

The further education (FE) system in England provides a wide range of education and training opportunities for young people and adults. From the age of 16, young people who wish to remain in education, but not in a school setting, can undertake further education (including skills training) in an FE college. There are two main types of college in the FE sector: sixth form colleges and general further education (GFE) colleges. Some FE colleges focus on a particular area, such as art and design or agriculture and horticulture. Each institution decides its own range of subjects and courses. Students at FE colleges can study for a wide and growing range of academic and/or work-related qualifications, from entry level to higher education level.

Though the Department for Business, Innovation and Skills is responsible for the FE sector and for funding FE for adults (19 or over), the Department for Education funds all education and training for 16- to 18-year-olds.

The proportion of 16- to 18-year-olds in education or training has risen steadily over recent years. Those in full-time education increased to a high of 71.5 per cent in 2014, driven by increase in state-funded schools and higher education, and is expected to increase to 100 per cent in 2015 as the education-leaving age in England becomes 18. It is assumed that most of the additional students will go into FE or work-based training rather than staying on at school.

The 'September Guarantee', introduced in 2007, offers a place in post-16 education or training to all 16- and 17-year-olds who want one. In 2014, 93.2 per cent of 16- and 17-year-olds in England received an offer of a place. A new Education Funding Agency (EFA) was established in April 2012 as an executive agency of the Department for Education (DfE). It is responsible for education funding for 16- to 19-year-olds as well as academies.

The FE sector in England, as in other parts of the UK, also provides a range of opportunities for adults.

The Skills Funding Agency (SFA), part of the Department for Business, Innovation and Skills, is presently responsible for funding and regulating education and training for adults. It will invest government funding of around £3.86bn in FE and skills training places in 2015–16.

In November 2010, the government announced a new strategy for FE, including more adult apprenticeships (provision for 200,000 adults by 2014–15); fully funded training for 19- to 24-year-olds undertaking their first full level 2 (GCSE equivalent) or first level 3 qualification when they do not already have one; and fully funded basic skills for people who left school without basic skills in reading, writing and mathematics. 'Train to Gain', the programme that funded trainees sponsored by employers, was replaced in July 2011 by a programme focused on helping small employers to train low-skilled staff. This was followed in December 2011 by a plan to reform FE that focuses on students and in April 2012 by the creation of a National Careers Service.

In April 2013, the government announced plans to make the skills system more 'responsive' and to create new traineeships.

From 2014, Tech-levels will take as long to complete as A-Levels and will need to be endorsed by either a professional association or by five employers registered with Companies House. These qualifications will focus on hands-on practical training leading to recognised occupations for example in engineering, computing, accounting or hospitality.

Applied General Qualifications will take the same time to complete as AS-levels and will focus on broader study of a technical area, not directly linked to an occupation. These qualifications will need backing from three universities to count in the school and college performance tables.

A Tech-level along with a core maths qualification, for example AS-level maths, and an extended project will amount to an over-arching Technical Baccalaureate.

New Substantial Vocational Qualifications at level 2 will provide 16- to 19-year-old students seeking entry at a more basic level to a skilled trade or occupation with qualifications that are valued by employers.

There are currently 19 centres of training excellence called National Skills Academies, led, funded and designed by employers, in various stages of development. Each academy offers specialist training in a key sector of the economy, working in partnership with colleges, schools and independent training providers.

Among the many voluntary bodies providing adult education, the Workers' Educational Association (WEA) is the UK's largest, operating throughout England and Scotland. It provides part-time courses to adults in response to local need in community centres, village halls, schools, pubs or workplaces. Similar but separate WEA organisations operate in Wales and Northern Ireland.

The National Institute of Adult Continuing Education (NIACE), a charitable non-governmental organisation, promotes lifelong learning opportunities for adults in England and Wales.

NATIONAL INSTITUTE OF ADULT CONTINUING EDUCATION (NIACE) T 0116-204 4200 W www.niace.org.uk
THE SKILLS FUNDING AGENCY T 0345-377 5000 W www.gov.uk/government/organisations/skills-funding-agency
WORKERS' EDUCATIONAL ASSOCIATION (WEA) T 020-7426 3450 W www.wea.org.uk

## WALES

In Wales, the aims and makeup of the FE system are similar to those outlined for England. The Welsh government funds a wide range of learning programmes for young people through its 15 FE colleges, and local authorities and private organisations. The Welsh government has set out plans to improve learning opportunities for all post-16 learners in the shortest possible time, to increase the engagement of disadvantaged young people in the learning process, and to transform the learning network to increase learner choice, reduce duplication of provision and encourage higher-quality learning and teaching in all post-16 provision. One goal is to ensure that, by 2015, 95 per cent of young people will be ready for high-skilled employment or higher education by the age of 25.

In Wales, responsibility for adult and continuing education lies with the Department for Education and Skills (DfES) within the Welsh government. Wales operates a range of programmes to support skills development, including subsidised work-based training courses for employees and the Workforce Development Programme, where employers can use the free services of experienced skills advisers to develop staff training plans.

COLLEGES WALES T 029-2052 2500 W www.collegeswales.ac.uk

COLEG HARLECH WEA **T** 01248-353254
**W** www.harlech.ac.uk/en
NIACE DYSGU CYMRU **T** 029-2037 0900
**W** www.niacedc.org.uk
WEA SOUTH WALES **T** 029-2023 5277
**W** www.swales.wea.org.uk

## SCOTLAND

Following a series of mergers, Scotland now has 27 FE colleges (known simply as colleges) which are at the forefront of lifelong learning, education, training and skills in Scotland. Colleges cater for the needs of learners both in and out of employment, at all stages in their lives from middle secondary school and earlier to retirement. Colleges' courses span much of the range of learning needs, from specialised vocational education and training through to general educational programmes. The level of provision ranges from essential life skills and provision for students with learning difficulties to HNCs and HNDs. Some colleges, notably those in the Highlands and Islands, also deliver degrees and postgraduate qualifications.

A shift in study patterns is taking place within the college sector as colleges concentrate on full-time courses aimed at helping people gain employment and no longer fund short courses lasting less than ten hours. Overall figures are stable but this change has led to a decline in part-time study and an increase in full-time study.

The Scottish Funding Council (SFC) is the statutory body responsible for funding teaching and learning provision, research and other activities in Scotland's colleges. Overall strategic direction for the sector is provided by the Lifelong Learning Directorate of the Scottish government, which provides annual guidance to the SFC and liaises closely with bodies such as Colleges Scotland, the Scottish Qualifications Authority and the FE colleges themselves to ensure that policies remain relevant and practical.

The Scottish government takes responsibility for community learning and development in Scotland while Skills Development Scotland, a non-departmental public body, is charged with improving Scotland's skills performance by linking skills supply and demand and helping people and organisations to learn, develop and make use of these skills to greater effect. ILA Scotland is a Scottish government scheme delivered by Skills Development Scotland that provides funding for training to individuals over the age of 16 with an income of less than £22,000 a year.
ILA SCOTLAND **T** 0800-917 8000
**W** www.myworldofwork.co.uk/section/funding
COLLEGES SCOTLAND **T** 01786-892100
**W** www.collegesscotland.ac.uk
SCOTTISH FUNDING COUNCIL **T** 0131-313 6500
**W** www.sfc.ac.uk
SKILLS DEVELOPMENT SCOTLAND **T** 0141-285 6000
**W** www.skillsdevelopmentscotland.co.uk

## NORTHERN IRELAND

FE in Northern Ireland is provided through six regional multi-campus colleges and the College of Agriculture, Food and Rural Affairs (CAFRE). Most secondary schools also have a sixth form which students may attend for two additional years to complete their AS-levels and A-levels.

Colleges Northern Ireland (CNI) acts as the representative body for the six FE colleges which, like their counterparts in the rest of the UK, are independent corporate bodies each managed by their own governing body. The range of courses that they offer spans essential skills, a wide choice of vocational and academic programmes and higher education programmes. Most full-time students in the six colleges are aged 16 to 19, while most part-time students are over 19.

The Department for Employment and Learning (DELNI) is responsible for the policy, strategic development and financing of the statutory FE sector and for lifelong learning, and also provides support to a small number of non-statutory FE providers. The Educational Guidance Service for Adults (EGSA), an independent, not-for-profit organisation, has a network of local offices based across Northern Ireland which provide services to adult learners, learning advisers, providers, employers and others interested in improving access to learning for adults.
COLLEGES NORTHERN IRELAND (CNI)
**T** 028-9068 2296 **W** www.anic.ac.uk
THE EDUCATIONAL GUIDANCE SERVICE FOR ADULTS **W** www.egsa.org.uk
WEA NORTHERN IRELAND **T** 028-9032 9718
**W** www.wea-ni.com

## FINANCIAL SUPPORT

England has a bursary scheme of up to £1,200 a year for full-time 16- to 19-year-old students facing financial hardship. Two types of bursary exist: vulnerable student bursary and discretionary bursary. Help with transport costs is also possible for some students. This scheme replaced the Education Maintenance Allowance (EMA) which gave 16- to 19-year-olds from low-income families a weekly allowance to continue in education.

There are EMA schemes in Scotland, Wales and Northern Ireland, but with slightly different eligibility conditions. Students must apply to the EMA scheme for the part of the UK where they intend to study. In Northern Ireland 16- to 19-year-old students, who meet the relevant criteria, and live in a household that has an annual income of £20,500 or less a year (£22,500 if there is more than one young person in the household who qualifies for child benefit) automatically get £30 a week in 2015–16.

Colleges and learning providers award learner support funds directly to new students aged 19 and over.

*Care to Learn* is available in England to help young parents under the age of 20, who are caring for their own child or children while they are in some form of publicly funded learning (below higher education level), with the costs of childcare and travel. The scheme is not income assessed and pays up to £160 a week (£175 in London) to cover costs.

*Dance and Drama Awards* (DaDA) are state-funded scholarships for students over the age of 16 enrolled at one of 19 private dance and drama schools in England, who are taking specified courses at National Certificate or National Diploma level. Awards, based on household income, cover some of students' tuition fees and up to £5,185 maintenance in 2015–16.

Young people studying away from home because their chosen course is not available locally may qualify for the *Residential Support Scheme*.

Information and advice on funding support and applications are available from the Learner Support helpline (**T** 0800-121 8989) or on the GOV.UK website (*see* below).

*Discretionary Support Funds* (DSF) are available in colleges and school sixth forms to help students who have trouble meeting the costs of participating in further education.

In Wales, students aged 19 or over on FE courses may be eligible for the *Welsh Government Learning Grant FE* (previously the *Assembly Learning Grant for Further Education*). This is a means-tested payment of up to £1,500 for full-time students and up to £750 for those studying part-time. *Discretionary Financial Contingency Funds* are also available to all students in Wales suffering hardship and are administered by the institutions themselves.

In Scotland, FE students can apply to their college for discretionary support in the form of *Further Education*

*Bursaries.* These can include allowances for maintenance, travel, study, childcare and additional support needs. *Individual Learning Accounts* provide up to £200 for those with incomes of less than £22,000.

In Northern Ireland, FE students may be eligible for *Further Education Awards,* non-refundable assistance administered on behalf of the five Education and Library Boards by the Western Education and Library Board.

UK FE students over 18 whose costs are not fully met from the grants described above may also be eligible for *Professional and Career Development Loans.* These loans – also available to HE students – cover up to 80 per cent of course fees (up to 100 per cent for those unemployed for three months); other course costs, such as books, travel and childcare; and living expenses, such as rent, food and clothing (for those who are unemployed or working fewer than 30 hours a week). The loans, of between £300 and £10,000, are available from participating high street banks. The Skills Funding Agency (SFA) pays the interest on the loan while the student is studying and for one month afterwards. Once students complete their courses, they must pay interest at the rate fixed when they took out the loan, which will be competitive with other commercially available 'unsecured' personal loans.
CAREERS SCOTLAND **W** www.careers-
scotland.org.uk/Education/Funding/Funding.asp
GOV.UK **W** www.gov.uk/further-education-courses/financial-help
STUDENT FINANCE WALES **T** 0845-602 8845
**W** www.studentfinancewales.co.uk
WESTERN EDUCATION AND LIBRARY BOARD
**T** 028-8241 1411 **W** www.welbni.org

# HIGHER EDUCATION

Publicly funded higher education (HE) in the UK is provided in 334 universities, higher education colleges and other specialist HE institutions, and a significant number of FE colleges offering higher education courses.

The Higher Education Funding Council for England (HEFCE) funds teaching and research in 121 English higher education institutions (HEIs), of which 103 have university status, and 205 FE colleges.

The Higher Education Funding Council for Wales (HEFCW) distributes funding for HE in Wales through Wales's 10 HEIs and some FE colleges.

The Scottish Funding Council (SFC) – which is also responsible for FE in Scotland – is the national strategic body responsible for funding HE teaching and research in Scotland's 19 HEIs and 27 colleges.

In Northern Ireland, HE is provided by two universities, two university colleges, six regional institutes of further and higher education and the Open University (OU), which operates UK-wide. Unlike other parts of the UK, Northern Ireland has no higher education funding council; the Department for Employment and Learning fulfils that role.

All UK universities and a number of HE colleges award their own degrees and other HE qualifications. HE providers who do not have their own degree-awarding powers offer degrees under 'validation arrangements' with other institutions that do have those powers. The OU, for example, runs a validation service which enables a number of other institutions to award OU degrees, after the OU has assured itself that the academic standards of their courses are as high as the OU's own standards.

Each HE institution is responsible for the standards of the awards it makes and the quality of the education it provides to its students, and each has its own internal quality assurance procedures. External quality assurance for HE institutions throughout the UK is provided by the Quality Assurance Agency for Higher Education (QAA).

The QAA is independent of government, funded by subscriptions from all publicly funded UK universities and colleges of HE. Its main role is to safeguard the standards of HE qualifications. It does this by defining standards for HE through a framework known as the academic infrastructure. QAA carries out reviews of the quality of UK HE institutions via a system known as 'institutional audits'. QAA also advises government on a range of HE quality issues, including applications for the grant of degree-awarding powers. It publishes reports on its review activities on its website.
DEPARTMENT FOR EMPLOYMENT AND LEARNING
**T** 028-9025 7777 **W** www.delni.gov.uk
HIGHER EDUCATION FUNDING COUNCIL FOR
ENGLAND **T** 0117-931 7317 **W** www.hefce.ac.uk
HIGHER EDUCATION FUNDING COUNCIL FOR
WALES **T** 029-2076 1861 **W** www.hefcw.ac.uk
SCOTTISH FUNDING COUNCIL **T** 0131-313 6500
**W** www.sfc.ac.uk
THE QUALITY ASSURANCE AGENCY FOR HIGHER
EDUCATION **T** 01452-557000 **W** www.qaa.ac.uk
*See also* Universities for information on the 2014 Research Excellence Framework (which replaced the Research Assessment Exercise) and listings of universities in the UK.

| STUDENTS APPLYING TO UNIVERSITY | | | |
|---|---|---|---|
| | *2014* | *2015* | *Difference* |
| Total applicants | 634,610 | 647,610 | 2% |
| *Source:* UCAS | | | |

| STUDENTS IN HIGHER EDUCATION (2013–14)* | | | |
|---|---|---|---|
| | *Full-time* | *Part-time* | *Total* |
| HE students | 1,696,030 | 603,325 | 2,299,355 |
| Postgraduate students | 304,445 | 234,995 | 539,440 |
| Undergraduate students | 1,391,585 | 368,330 | 1,759,915 |
| *Includes UK, EU and non-EU students | | | |
| *Source:* Higher Education Statistics Agency (HESA) 2014 | | | |

| UK HIGHER EDUCATION QUALIFICATIONS AWARDED (2013–14) | | |
|---|---|---|
| | *Full-time* | *Part-time* |
| First degrees | 383,630 | 38,220 |
| Other undergraduate qualifications | 53,875 | 44,145 |
| Postgraduate Certificate in Education (PGCE) | 21,305 | 1,055 |
| Other postgraduate qualifications | 14,570 | 32,345 |
| Total higher degrees including doctorates | 146,900 | 41,770 |
| *Source:* HESA 2014 | | |

## COURSES

HE institutions in the UK mainly offer courses leading to the following qualifications. These qualifications go from levels 4 to 8 on England's Qualifications and Credit Framework, levels 7 to 12 on Scotland's Credit and Qualifications Framework. Individual HEIs may not offer all of these.

*Certificates of Higher Education* (CertHE) are awarded after one year's full-time study (or equivalent). If available to students on longer courses, they certify that students have reached a minimum standard in their first year.

*Diplomas of Higher Education* (DipHE) and other *Higher Diplomas* are awarded after two to three years' full-time study (or equivalent). They certify that a student has achieved a minimum standard in first- and second-year courses and, in the case of nursing, third-year courses. They can often be used for entry to the third year of a related degree course.

*Foundation degrees* are awarded after two years of full-time study (or equivalent). These degrees combine academic study with work-based learning, and have been designed jointly by universities, colleges and employers with a particular area of work in mind. They are usually accepted as a basis for entry to the third year of a related degree course.

*Bachelor's degrees*, also referred to as *first degrees*, have different titles, Bachelor of Arts (BA) and Bachelor of Science (BSc) being the most common. In England, Wales and Northern Ireland most Bachelor's degree courses are 'with Honours' and awarded after three years of full-time study, although in some subjects the courses last longer. In Scotland, where young people often leave school and go to university a year younger, HE institutions typically offer Ordinary Bachelor's degrees after three years' study and Bachelor's degrees with Honours after four years. Honours degrees are graded as first, upper-second (2:1), lower second (2:2), or third. HEIs in England, Wales and Northern Ireland may allow students who fail the first year of an Honours degree by a small margin to transfer to an Ordinary degree course, if they have one. Ordinary degrees may also be awarded to Honours degree students who do not finish an Honours degree course but complete enough of it to earn a pass.

*Postgraduate* or *Higher degrees*. Graduates may go on to take *Master's degrees*, which involve one or two years' work and can be taught or research-based. They may also take one-year postgraduate diplomas and certificates, often linked to a specific profession, such as the *Postgraduate Certificate in Education* (PGCE) required to become a state school teacher. A *doctorate*, leading to a qualification such as Doctor of Philosophy – a PHD or DPHIL – usually involves at least three years of full-time research.

The framework for HE qualifications in England, Wales and Northern Ireland (FHEQ) and the framework for qualifications of HE institutions in Scotland, can both be found on the QAA website, which describes the achievement represented by HE qualifications.

## ADMISSIONS

When preparing to apply to a university or other HE college, individuals can compare facts and figures on institutions and courses using the government's Unistats website. This includes details of students' views from the annual National Student Survey.

For the vast majority of full-time undergraduate courses, individuals need to apply online through UCAS, the organisation responsible for managing applications to HE courses in the UK. More than half a million people wanting to study at a university or college each year use this UCAS service, which has useful online tools to help students find the right course.

UCAS also provides two specialist applications services used by more than 50,000 people each year: the Conservatoires UK Admissions Service (CUKAS), for those applying to UK music conservatoires, and the Graduate Teacher Training Registry (GTTR), for postgraduate applications for initial teacher training courses in England and Wales and some in Scotland. Details of initial teacher training courses in Scotland can also be obtained from Universities Scotland and from Teach in Scotland, the website created by the Scottish government to promote teaching.

Each university or college sets its own entry requirements. These can be in terms of particular exam grades or total points on the 'UCAS tariff' (UCAS's system for allocating points to different qualifications on a common basis), or be non-academic, like having a health check. HEIs will make 'firm offers' to candidates who have already gained the qualifications they present for entry, and 'conditional offers'

to those who have yet to take their exams or obtain their results. Conditional offers often require a minimum level of achievement in a specified subject, for example '300 points to include grade A at A-level Chemistry'. If candidates' achievements are lower than specified in their conditional offers, the university or college may not accept them; then, if they still wish to go into HE, they need to find another institution through the UCAS 'clearing' process.

The OU conducts its own admissions. It is the UK's only university dedicated to distance learning and the UK's largest for part-time HE. Because it is designed to be 'open' to all, no qualifications are needed for entry to the majority of its courses.

Individuals can search over 58,000 UK postgraduate courses and research opportunities on UK graduate careers website Prospects. The application process for postgraduate places can vary between institutions. Most universities and colleges accept direct applications and many accept applications through UKPASS, a free, centralised online service run by UCAS that allows individuals to submit up to ten different applications, track their progress and attach supporting material, such as references.

UNISTATS W http://unistats.direct.gov.uk
UCAS T 0371-468 0468 W www.ucas.com
UNIVERSITIES SCOTLAND T 0131-226 1111
    W www.universities-scotland.ac.uk
TEACH IN SCOTLAND T 0845-345 4745
    W www.teachinscotland.com
PROSPECTS T 0161-277 5200 W www.prospects.ac.uk
UKPASS T 0371-334 4447 W http://ukpass.ac.uk

## TUITION FEES AND STUDENT SUPPORT
### TUITION FEES

HE institutions in England, Wales and Northern Ireland are allowed to charge variable tuition fees for full-time HE courses. Although students from outside the EU can be charged the full cost of their courses, the amount that HEIs may charge students from the UK and other EU countries was capped from 2006 at £3,000 a year plus inflationary increases. From September 2012, universities have been able to charge up to £9,000 a year in tuition fees. The exact fee depends on the course studied and the institution attended. Full-time students do not have to pay their fees before or during their course, as tuition fee loans are available to cover the full cost; these do not have to be repaid until the student is working (*see* below).

In recent years, Scottish HE institutions have charged flat rate fees, set by the Scottish government, to undergraduate students classed as being ordinarily resident in England, Wales or Northern Ireland; though, as explained above, students can get repayable tuition fee loans to cover the cost. Since 2012 universities can set their own fees, up to £9,000 a year, for undergraduates starting courses. On average, Scottish universities have opted to charge £6,841. However, undergraduate students classed as being ordinarily resident in Scotland or another EU country do not have to pay tuition fees at Scottish HE institutions. All tuition fees are paid on their behalf by the Scottish government through the Student Awards Agency for Scotland (SAAS); students must apply for this funding every year.

In the July 2015 Budget it was announced that from 2017–18 universities with 'high quality' teaching will be able to raise tuition fees in-line with inflation.

### STUDENT LOANS, GRANTS AND BURSARIES
#### ENGLAND

All students starting a full-time HE course in 2015–16 can apply through Student Finance England for financial support. Two student loans are available from the government: a *tuition fee loan* of up to £9,000 for 2015–16; and a *maintenance loan* (for students aged under 60) to help with living expenses of up to £5,740 for those living away from home (£8,009 if studying away from home in London) and £4,565 for those living with their parents during term time, or £6,820 if living and studying abroad for at least one term.

The tuition fee loan is not affected by household income and is paid directly to the relevant HE institution. A proportion (currently 65 per cent) of the maximum maintenance loan is available irrespective of household income while the rest depends on an income assessment. Student Finance England usually pays the money into the student's own bank account in three instalments, one at the start of each term.

Repayment of both loans does not start until the April after the student has left university or college, or before they are earning more than £21,000 a year.

At this point the individual's employer will deduct 9 per cent of any salary above the starting limit through the Pay As You Earn (PAYE) system. The self-employed make repayments through their tax returns. Someone earning £21,702 a year, the average starting salary for graduates entering full-time employment, will have to pay back £5.27 a week. Student loans accrue interest from the date they are paid out, up until they are repaid in full. Generally, the interest rate for student loans is set in September each year. The latest rate can be found online (W www.studentloanrepayment.co.uk/interest).

In 2015–16, full-time HE students with a household income of £25,000 or under can apply for a *maintenance grant* towards living expenses, which does not have to be repaid. The maximum grant available is £3,387 for the academic year. Those with a household income of £42,620 or under receive a partial grant. If a student is eligible for the maintenance grant, their maintenance loan is reduced by £1 for every £1 of maintenance grant that they are entitled to (up to a maximum of £1,354). This means that students from lower income households generally have less to repay when they finish studying and start work. Some students who claim means-tested state benefits, such as single parents and students with certain disabilities, are entitled to the *special support grant,* also worth up to £3,387, instead of the maintenance grant. If a student receives the special support grant it does not effect the amount of maintenance loan that he or she receives.

For all new full-time students starting HE from September 2016, maintenance grants are to be replaced by loans (*see* Recent Developments). Students whose family income is up to £42,620 will be able to apply from January 2016 for maintenance loans of up to £8,200 a year (£10,702 in London) – the maximum amount applying only to students with a household income of less than £25,000 a year. Special support grants will also be replaced by maintenance loans.

Students needing extra help may also be entitled to receive disabled students' allowance (DSA), adult dependants' grant, childcare grant or parents' learning allowance. These grants will remain available to full-time students starting HE from September 2016 at the 2015–16 levels. DSA is also available to part-time and postgraduate students.

*Part-time Higher Education Students* in England are entitled to tuition fee loans (which replaced grants) of up to £6,750 in 2015–16. Following government changes to student finance, the maximum universities and colleges can charge part-time students in tuition fees is £6,750. Part-time students who earn over £21,000 a year have to start paying back their loans after four years even if their course has not finished.

Details are available on the Student Finance England website (W www.gov.uk/student-finance/loans-and-grants). There is a student finance calculator on the website to work out what financial support is available.

Universities and other higher education providers offer their own grants and bursaries, with differing criteria. Bursaries do not have to be repaid. Students should always check with the institution they are planning to attend to find out what extra financial support may be available.

If the student's chosen HE institution runs the *additional fee support scheme,* it could provide extra financial help if the student is on a low income and in certain other circumstances. Help may also be available through the institution's *access to learning fund,* for students in financial difficulty.

## WALES

Welsh students starting a full-time HE course in 2015–16 can apply through Student Finance Wales for the forms of financial support described below.

A similar system of tuition fee and maintenance loans and grants operates in Wales as in England but Welsh students can also receive a substantial tuition *fee grant.* Maximum maintenance loans are: up to £5,376 for students living away from home (£7,532 if studying away from home in London) and £4,162 for those living with their parents during term time. From September 2015, eligible Welsh students can access a non means-tested tuition fee loan of up to £3,810 and grant of up to £5,190 to cover the exact amount that the institution charges for a course.

Welsh-domiciled students may apply for an *Welsh government learning grant* of up to £5,161 to help meet general living costs. This is paid in three instalments, one at the start of each term, like the student maintenance loan. The amount that a student gets depends on household income. The maximum grant is available to those with a household income of £18,370 or under. Those with an income of £50,020 or under receive a partial grant.

There is also a *special support grant* for single parents, student parents or those with disabilities, which is worth up to £5,161 a year in 201–16. It is paid directly to students and is not offset against student loan borrowing.

Students needing extra help may also be entitled to adult dependants' grant, childcare grant, parents' learning allowance and disabled students' allowance. These grants may also be available to part-time students.

Students can use the student finance calculator on the Student Finance Wales website to work out what financial support they may be entitled to.

Welsh HE institutions also hold financial contingency funds to provide discretionary assistance to students experiencing financial difficulties.

From September 2015 part-time undergraduate higher education students studying at least 50 per cent of an equivalent full-time course are entitled to receive a fee loan of £2,625 (£6,750 for a course at a publicly funded university or college elsewhere in the UK, or £4,500 at a private university or college).

A *course grant* of up to £1,155 for books, travel and other course-related costs is available for part-time students. This course grant depends on household income.

Recipients must be studying at an average course intensity of at least 50 per cent to get it, as for the fee grant. The *course grant* is paid into the student's bank account in one lump sum. It is not usually available to those who already have a UK honours degree.

Continuing part-time students get a *fee grant* of up to £1,025, depending on their household income (partial fee grant is available for those with household incomes up to £25,435).

STUDENT FINANCE WALES T 0300-200 4050
  W www.studentfinancewales.co.uk

## SCOTLAND

All students starting a full-time HE course in 2015–16 can apply through the Student Awards Agency for Scotland for financial support. Living cost support is mainly provided through a *student loan*, the majority of which is income-assessed. The maximum loan for 2015–16 is £5,750.

The *young students' bursary* (YSB) is available to young students from low-income backgrounds and is non-repayable. Eligible students receive this bursary instead of part of the student loan, thus reducing their level of repayable debt. In 2015–16 the maximum annual support provided through YSB is £1,750 if household income is £17,000 or less a year.

The *independent students' bursary* (ISB) similarly replaces part of the loan and reduces repayable debt for low-income students classed as 'independent' of parental support. The maximum paid is £750 a year to those whose household income is £17,000 or less a year.

Travel expenses are included within the student loan. There are also *supplementary grants* available to certain categories of students such as lone parents (£2,640) and those with dependants (£1,305). Extra help is also available to those who have a disability, learning difficulty or mental health problem.

**STUDENT AWARDS AGENCY FOR SCOTLAND**
T 0300-555 0505
W www.saas.gov.uk/forms/funding_guide.pdf

## NORTHERN IRELAND

All students starting a full-time HE course in 2015–16 can apply through Student Finance Northern Ireland for financial support. The arrangements for both full-time and part-time students are similar to those for England. The main difference is that the income-assessed *maintenance grant* (or *special support grant* for students on certain income-assessed benefits) for new full-time students studying at UK universities and colleges is worth up to £3,475 (for household incomes of £19,203 or less). Loans are available for living costs, £3,750 for study in Northern Ireland, £4,840 for study elsewhere in the UK (£6,780 in London) and £4,840 for study in the Republic of Ireland.

**STUDENT FINANCE NORTHERN IRELAND**
T 0300-100 0077 W www.studentfinanceni.co.uk

## DISABLED STUDENTS' ALLOWANCES

*Disabled Students' Allowances* (DSAs) are grants available throughout the UK to help meet the extra course costs that students can face as a direct result of a disability, ongoing health condition, mental health condition or specific learning difficulty. They help disabled people to study in HE on an equal basis with other students. They are paid on top of the standard student finance package and do not have to be repaid. The amount that an individual gets depends on the type of extra help needed, not on household income. This amounts to £5,212 for specialist equipment for the entire course, non-medical helper allowance of £20,725 a year and a general allowance of £1,741 a year. Eligible individuals should apply as early as possible to the relevant UK awarding authority.

## POSTGRADUATE AWARDS

In general, postgraduate students do not qualify for mandatory support like student loans. An exception to this is students taking a Postgraduate Certificate in Education (PGCE), who can qualify for the finance package usually available only to undergraduates. There are also bursaries available for social work and some medical students.

There is heavy competition for any postgraduate funding available. Individuals can search for postgraduate awards and scholarships on two websites: Hot Courses and Prospects.

They can also search for grants available from educational trusts, often reserved for students from poorer backgrounds or for those who have achieved academic excellence, on W www.gov.uk/grant-bursary-adult-learners or the Family Action website. Otherwise they need to fund their own fees and living expenses.

Postgraduates from Scotland can get £3,400 towards tuition fees but no support for living costs. In Northern Ireland, the Department for Employment and Learning and the Education and Library Boards provide postgraduate funding for certain courses. Postgraduate students with an impairment, health condition or learning difficulty can apply for disabled students' allowances (*see* above) for both taught courses and research places. For both full-time and part-time postgraduate students there is a single allowance of up to £10,362 a year.

**DEPARTMENT FOR EMPLOYMENT AND LEARNING (DELNI)** T 028-9025 7777 W www.delni.gov.uk
**FAMILY ACTION** T 020-7254 6251 W www.family-action.org.uk
**HOT COURSES** W www.hotcourses.com
**SCHOLARSHIP SEARCH** W www.scholarship-search.org.uk
**PROSPECTS** W www.prospects.ac.uk
**STUDENT AWARDS AGENCY FOR SCOTLAND (SAAS)**
T 0300-555 0505 W www.student-support-saas.gov.uk

# TEACHER TRAINING

*See* Professional Education.

# EMPLOYEES AND SALARIES

## EMPLOYEES

**QUALIFIED TEACHERS IN MAINTAINED SCHOOLS (NOVEMBER 2013–14)**
*Full-time equivalent, thousands*

|  | England | Wales | Scotland | NI | UK |
|---|---|---|---|---|---|
| Nursery and primary schools | 215.5* | 13.7 | 24.2 | 8.2 | 261.6 |
| Secondary schools | 213.4* | 12.6 | 23.0 | 9.4 | 258.4 |
| Special schools | 21.3 | 0.7 | 2.0 | 0.8 | 24.8 |
| *Total* | 450.2 | 27.0 | 49.2 | 18.4 | 544.8 |

* Includes academies and city technology colleges in England

**SUPPORT STAFF IN MAINTAINED SCHOOLS, ENGLAND AND WALES (2013–14)**
*Full-time equivalent, thousands*

|  | England | Wales |
|---|---|---|
| *Total support staff* | 398.8* | 23.5 |
| Teaching assistants | 255.1 | – |
| Other support staff | 143.7* | – |

* Includes academies and city technology colleges in England

**ACADEMIC STAFF IN UK HIGHER EDUCATION INSTITUTIONS (2013–14)**

|  | Full-time | Part-time | Total |
|---|---|---|---|
| Professors | 15,705 | 4,040 | 19,745 |
| Non-professors | 112,465 | 62,030 | 174,495 |
| Teaching only | 12,475 | 40,100 | 52,575 |
| Teaching and research | 77,170 | 17,310 | 94,480 |
| Research only | 37,455 | 8,130 | 45,585 |
| Neither teaching nor research | 1,075 | 535 | 1,610 |

*Source:* HESA 2014

## SALARIES

State school teachers in England and Wales are employed by local authorities or the governing bodies of their schools. All teachers are eligible for membership of the Teachers' Pension Scheme.

There are teaching and learning responsibility payments for specific posts, special needs work and recruitment and retention factors which may be awarded at the discretion of the school governing body or the local authority. There are separate pay ranges for Headteachers and other school leaders. Academies are free to set their own salaries.

In 2014, the average salary for all full- and part-time classroom teachers was £34,300 (£100 less than in 2013). The average salary for all full- and part-time leadership group teachers was £56,500 in 2014 (£500 more than in 2013). Overall, the average salary for all teachers was the same, at £37,400, as in 2013.

In local authority maintained nursery and primary schools the average salary for all teachers was £33,100, compared with £31,600 in primary academies. The average salary for all classroom teachers in local authority maintained secondary schools was £36,300; an increase of £100 from 2013, whereas, in secondary academies, it was £35,100; a decrease of £200 from the 2013 average.

In 2013 every school was required to revise its pay and appraisal policies, setting out how pay progression would, in future, be linked to a teacher's performance. The first decisions on pay progression under the new provisions were decided in September 2014, based on appraisals at the end of the 2013–14 cycle. Also in September 2014, school governing bodies were given more flexibility, within the national pay ranges, to determine the pay of headteachers and other school leaders. The pay of school leaders ranges from £38,215 to £107,210 a year outside London and from £45,436 to £114,437 a year in Inner London.

After completing initial teacher training (ITT) and achieving qualified teacher status (QTS), newly qualified teachers (NQTs) in maintained schools can expect to start on a salary of £21,804 a year in England and Wales (or £27,270 in inner London). The current pay ranges for teachers in England and Wales are:

*Main pay range (including NQTs)*

| | |
|---|---|
| London fringe | £23,082–£33,244 |
| Outer London | £25,623–£35,823 |
| Inner London | £27,543–£37,119 |
| Rest of England and Wales | £22,023–£32,187 |

*Upper pay range*

| | |
|---|---|
| London fringe | £35,927–£38,555 |
| Outer London | £38,355–£41,274 |
| Inner London | £42,332–£45,905 |
| Rest of England and Wales | £34,869–£37,496 |

In March 2014 the Scottish Negotiating Committee for Teachers agreed a two-year pay deal, backdated to 1 April 2013. The agreement provides for pay increases of 1 per cent from 1 April 2013, followed by a 1 per cent increase from 1 April 2014. Teachers are paid on a seven-point scale where the entry point is for newly qualified teachers undertaking their probationary year. Experienced, ambitious teachers who reach the top of the main pay scale are eligible to become chartered teachers and earn more on a separate pay spine. However, to do so they must study for further professional qualifications. Headteachers and deputies have a separate pay spine as do 'principals' or heads of department. Additional allowances are payable to teachers under a range of circumstances, such as working in distant islands and remote schools.

Salary scales for teachers in Scotland remain at 2014 levels:

| | |
|---|---|
| Headteacher/deputy headteacher | £43,137–£84,201 |
| Principal teacher | £38,034–£49,086 |
| Chartered teacher | £35,964–£42,768 |
| Main grade | £21,867–£34,887 |

Teachers in Northern Ireland have broadly similar payscales to teachers in England and Wales. Classroom teachers who take on teaching and learning responsibilities outside their normal classroom duties may be awarded one of five teaching allowances. A two-year pay freeze was imposed for 2011 and 2012, except for those earning £21,000 or less, who received an increase of at least £250 a year. A 1 per cent pay increase, across all salary scales, was awarded in September 2013. In July 2015 a further 1 per cent increase to salary scales was announced; this increase was backdated to September 2014. As at September 2015, salary scales in Northern Ireland stood at:

| | |
|---|---|
| Principal (headteacher) | £43,231–£107,209 |
| Classroom teacher (upper pay scale) | £34,868–£37,495 |
| Classroom teacher (main pay scale) | £22,022–£32,187 |
| Unqualified teacher | £14,121 |
| Teaching allowances | £1,884–£12,150 |

Since 2007, most academic staff in HE across the UK are paid on a single national pay scale as a result of a national framework agreement negotiated by the HE unions and HE institutions. Staff are paid according to rates on a 51-point national pay spine and academic and academic-related staff are graded according to a national grading structure. In 2014–15 the pay spine ranged from £13,953 to £58,172. From August 2015 employers have proposed to raise pay by 1 per cent (and by between 1.2 per cent and 2.65 per cent from pay scale point 8 to 1), but union representatives have not accepted this offer. As HE institutions are autonomous employers, precise job grades and salaries may vary but the following table outlines salaries that typically tally with certain job roles in HE.

| | |
|---|---|
| Principal lecturer | £47,328–£54,841 |
| Senior lecturer | £37,394–£45,954 |
| Lecturer | £31,342–£36,309 |
| Junior researcher | £24,775–£30,434 |

# UNIVERSITIES

The following is a list of universities, which are those institutions that have been granted degree-awarding powers by either a royal charter or an act of parliament, or have been permitted to use the word 'university' (or 'university college') by the Privy Council. There are other recognised bodies in the UK with degree-awarding powers, as well as institutions offering courses leading to a degree from a recognised body. Further information is available at W www.gov.uk/recognised-uk-degrees

Student figures represent the number of undergraduate (UG) and postgraduate (PG) students based on information available at July 2015.

For information on tuition fees and student loans, *see* Education, Higher Education.

## RESEARCH EXCELLENCE FRAMEWORK

The research excellence framework (REF) is the new system for assessing the quality of research in UK higher education institutions. It replaced the research assessment exercise (RAE), last conducted in 2008. The 2014 REF was conducted jointly by the Higher Education Funding Council for England (HEFCE), the Scottish Funding Council (SFC), the Higher Education Funding Council for Wales (HEFCW) and the Department for Employment and Learning (DEL), Northern Ireland. The primary purpose of REF 2014 was to assess the quality of research and produce outcomes for each submission made by institutions. The table below shows the top five universities or specialist colleges for each discipline based on the mean average ranking of the overall quality of their research.

| Subject | Universities or university colleges |
|---|---|
| Agriculture, Veterinary & Food Science | Aberdeen (1), Warwick (2), Glasgow (3), Stirling (4), Queen's Belfast (5) |
| Anthropology | Oxford (1), Manchester: Anthropology (2), Manchester: Development Studies (3), UEA (4), LSE (5) |
| Architecture | Bath (1), Glasgow (1), Cambridge (3), Sheffield (4), Loughborough (5) |
| Area Studies | LSE (1), Birmingham (2), Exeter (3), London Met (4), UEA (5), Aston (5) |
| Art & Design | Reading (1), Courtauld (2), Westminster (3), St Andrews (4), York (5) |
| Biological Sciences | Institute of Cancer Research (1), Dundee (2), Edinburgh (3), Imperial (4), Oxford (5), Sheffield (5), Newcastle (5) |
| Business & Management | LSE (1), Cambridge (2), Imperial (3), Oxford (4), London Business School (5) |
| Chemistry | Cambridge (1), Liverpool (2), Oxford (3), Bristol (4), Durham (5) |
| Classics | Cambridge (1), Durham (2), St Andrews (2), Oxford (4), Birmingham (5) |
| Clinical Medicine | Oxford (1), Cambridge (2), King's (3), Imperial (4), Institute of Cancer Research (4) |
| Computer Science | UCL (1), Warwick (2), Imperial (3), Manchester (4), Sheffield (5) |
| Dentistry, Nursing & Pharmacy | Sheffield (1), Swansea (2), Southampton (3), Cardiff (4), Nottingham (4) |
| Earth Systems & Environmental Sciences | Oxford (1), Bristol (2), Cambridge (3), Southampton (4), Leeds (5) |
| Economics | UCL (1), LSE (2), Oxford (3), Cambridge (4), Warwick (5) |
| Education | Oxford (1), King's (2), Nottingham (3), Sheffield (4), Cambridge (5), Durham (5), Cardiff (5) |
| Engineering (Civil & Construction) | Cardiff (1), Imperial (2), Dundee (3), Sheffield (4), Manchester (5) |
| Engineering (Electronic) | Cambridge (1), Oxford (2), Imperial: Electrical and Electronic (3), Imperial: Metallurgy & Materials (4), Leeds (5) |
| Engineering (General) | Cambridge (1), Imperial (2), Manchester (3), Birmingham (4), Leeds (4) |
| English | Warwick (1), York (2), Newcastle (3), Durham (4), Queen Mary (5) |
| Geography, Environment & Archaeology | Bristol (1), Cambridge (2), Royal Holloway (2), LSE (4), St Andrews (5) |
| History | Birmingham (1), York (2), Southampton (3), Sheffield (3), King's (5), Hertfordshire (5) |
| Law | King's (1), LSE (2), Durham (3), Ulster (4), UCL (5), York (5) |
| Maths | Oxford (1), Cambridge (2), Warwick (3), Imperial (4), Bristol (5), Lancaster (5) |
| Modern Languages | Queen Mary (1), Edinburgh (2), Kent (3), Queen Margaret (3), Southampton (5), Queen's Belfast (5) |
| Philosophy | Oxford (1), Birmingham (2), King's (3), Warwick (4), St Andrew's (5), LSE (5) |
| Physics | Strathclyde (1), Oxford (2), Edinburgh (3), Nottingham (3), St Andrews (3) |
| Politics & International Studies | Essex (1), LSE (2), Sheffield (3), Oxford (4), UCL (5) |
| Psychology, Psychiatry & Neuroscience | Oxford (1), Cardiff (1), Cambridge (3), York (4), Birkbeck (5) |
| Public Health, Health Services & Primary Care | Oxford (1), Imperial (2), Cambridge (3), Bristol (4), Queen Mary (5) |
| Social Work and Social Policy | Oxford (1), LSE (2), York (3), UEA (4), Kent (5) |
| Sociology | York (1), Manchester (2), Cardiff (3), Lancaster (4), Oxford (5) |
| Sports-related subjects | Bristol (1), Liverpool John Moores (2), Leeds (3), Birmingham (4), Bath (5) |
| Theology & Religious Studies | Durham (1), Birmingham (2), Lancaster (3), Leeds (3), UCL (3) |

## UNIVERSITY OF ABERDEEN (1495)

King's College, Aberdeen AB24 3FX T 01224-272000
W www.abdn.ac.uk
*Fee:* £9,000 *Students:* 10,375 UG; 3,450 PG
*Chancellor,* HRH the Duchess of Rothesay, GCVO
*Vice-Chancellor,* Prof. Sir Ian Diamond, FRSE
*University Secretary,* Caroline Inglis

UNIVERSITY OF ABERTAY DUNDEE (1994)
Bell Street, Dundee DD1 1HG T 01382-308000
W www.abertay.ac.uk
Fee: £7,250 Students: 4,345 UG; 410 PG
Chancellor, Lord Cullen of Whitekirk, KT, PC, FRSE
Vice-Chancellor, Prof. Nigel Seaton, FRENG
Registrar, Susan Campbell

ABERYSTWYTH UNIVERSITY (1872)
Penglais, Aberystwyth SY23 3FL T 01970-623111
W www.aber.ac.uk
Fee: £9,000 Students: 9,560 UG; 1,610 PG
Vice-Chancellor, Prof. April McMahon, FRSE, FBA
University Secretary, Geraint Pugh

ANGLIA RUSKIN UNIVERSITY (1992)
Chelmsford Campus, Bishop Hall Lane, Chelmsford CM1 1SQ
T 0845-271 3333 W www.anglia.ac.uk
Fee: £9,000 Students: 17,290 UG; 3,410 PG
Chancellor, Lord Ashcroft, KCMG, PC
Vice-Chancellor, Prof. Michael Thorne, PHD, FRSA
Secretary and Clerk, Stephen Bennett

ARTS UNIVERSITY BOURNEMOUTH (2012)
Wallisdown, Poole BH12 5HH T 01202-533011
W www.aub.ac.uk
Fee: £9,000 Students: 2,865 UG; 75 PG
Chancellor, Prof. Sir Christopher Frayling
Vice-Chancellor, Prof. Stuart Bartholomew, CBE
University Secretary, Jon Renyard

UNIVERSITY OF THE ARTS LONDON (2003)
Formerly The London Institute (1986), renamed 2004)
272 High Holborn, London WC1V 7EY T 020-7514 6000
W www.arts.ac.uk
Fee: £9,000 Students: 14,035 UG; 3,105 PG
Chancellor, Grayson Perry, CBE
Vice-Chancellor, Nigel Carrington
Secretary and Registrar, Stephen Marshall

COLLEGES
CAMBERWELL COLLEGE OF ARTS (1898)
40–65 Peckham Road, London SE5 8UF T 020-7514 6301
W www.arts.ac.uk/camberwell
Head of College, Prof. Chris Wainwright
CENTRAL SAINT MARTINS COLLEGE OF ART AND
DESIGN (1854)
Granary Building, 1 Granary Square, London N1C 4AA
T 020-7514 7444 W www.arts.ac.uk/csm
Head of College, Jeremy Till
CHELSEA COLLEGE OF ARTS (1895)
16 John Islip Street, London SW1P 4JU T 020-7514 7751
W www.arts.ac.uk/chelsea
Head of College, Prof. Chris Wainwright
LONDON COLLEGE OF COMMUNICATION (1894)
Elephant and Castle, London SE1 6SB T 020-7514 6500
W www.arts.ac.uk/lcc
Head of College, Natalie Brett
LONDON COLLEGE OF FASHION (1963)
20 John Prince's Street, London W1G 0BJ T 020-7514 7400
W www.arts.ac.uk/fashion
Head of College, Prof. Frances Corner, OBE
WIMBLEDON COLLEGE OF ART (1930)
Merton Hall Road, London SW19 3QA T 020-7514 9641
W www.arts.ac.uk/wimbledon
Head of College, Chris Wainwright

ASTON UNIVERSITY (1966)
Aston Triangle, Birmingham B4 7ET T 0121-204 3000
W www.aston.ac.uk

Fee: £9,000 Students: 8,130 UG; 2,855 PG
Chancellor, Sir John Sunderland
Vice-Chancellor, Prof. Dame Julia King, DBE, FRENG, FRSA
Registrar, Alison Levey

BANGOR UNIVERSITY (1884)
Gwynedd LL57 2DG T 01248-351151 W www.bangor.ac.uk
Fee: £9,000 Students: 8,030 UG; 2,615 PG
Vice-Chancellor, Prof. John Hughes
University Secretary, Dr Kevin Mundy

UNIVERSITY OF BATH (1966)
Claverton Down, Bath BA2 7AY T 01225-388388
W www.bath.ac.uk
Fee: £9,000 Students: 10,810 UG; 4,345 PG
Chancellor, HRH the Earl of Wessex, KG, GCVO
Vice-Chancellor, Prof. Dame Glynis Breakwell, DBE, FRSA
University Secretary, Mark Humphriss

BATH SPA UNIVERSITY (2005)
Newton Park, Newton St Loe, Bath BA2 9BN T 01225-875875
W www.bathspa.ac.uk
Fee: £9,000 Students: 5,220 UG; 1,990 PG
Vice-Chancellor, Prof. Christina Slade
Academic Registrar, Christopher Ellicott

UNIVERSITY OF BEDFORDSHIRE (1993)
University Square, Luton LU1 3JU T 01234-400400
W www.beds.ac.uk
Fee: £9,000 Students: 12,900 UG; 4,940 PG
Chancellor, Rt. Hon. John Bercow, MP
Vice-Chancellor, Bill Rammell
Registrar, Jenny Jenkin

UNIVERSITY OF BIRMINGHAM (1900)
Edgbaston, Birmingham B15 2TT T 0121-414 3344
W www.birmingham.ac.uk
Fee: £9,000 Students: 19,185 UG; 13,150 PG
Chancellor, Lord Bilimoria, CBE
Vice-Chancellor and Principal, Prof. Sir David Eastwood
Registrar and Secretary, Lee Sanders

BIRMINGHAM CITY UNIVERSITY (1992)
City North Campus, Birmingham B42 2SU T 0121-331 5000
W www.bcu.ac.uk
Fee: £9,000 Students: 18,770 UG; 3,770 PG
Chancellor, Lord Mayor of Birmingham (Raymond Hassall
2015–16)
Vice-Chancellor, Prof. Cliff Allan
University Secretary, Ms Christine Abbott

UNIVERSITY COLLEGE BIRMINGHAM (2012)
Summer Rowe, Birmingham B3 1JB T 0121-604 1000
W www.ucb.ac.uk
Fee: £8,558 Students: 4,510 UG; 485 PG
Vice-Chancellor, Ray Linforth

BISHOP GROSSETESTE UNIVERSITY (2013)
Longdales Road, Lincoln LN1 3DY T 01522-527347
W www.bishopg.ac.uk
Fee: £9,000 Students: 1,730 UG; 670 PG
Chancellor, Dame Judith Mayhew, DBE
Vice-Chancellor, Revd. Canon Prof. Peter Neil
Registrar and University Secretary, Dr Anne Craven

UNIVERSITY OF BOLTON (2005)
Deane Road, Bolton BL3 5AB T 01204-900600
W www.bolton.ac.uk

*Fee:* £9,000 *Students:* 5,740 UG; 1,055 PG
*Chancellor,* Lord Justice Ryder, PC
*Vice-Chancellor,* Prof George Holmes
*Registrar and Secretary,* Sue Duncan

BOURNEMOUTH UNIVERSITY (1992)
Fern Barrow, Poole, Dorset BH12 5BB T 01202-524111
W www.bournemouth.ac.uk
*Fee:* £9,000 *Students:* 14,910 UG; 2,825 PG
*Chancellor,* Lord Phillips of Worth Matravers, KG, PC
*Vice-Chancellor,* Prof. John Vinney
*Clerk,* Deborah Wakeley

UNIVERSITY OF BRADFORD (1966)
Richmond Road, Bradford BD7 1DP T 01274-232323
W www.bradford.ac.uk
*Fee:* £9,000 *Students:* 9,775 UG; 2,730 PG
*Chancellor,* Kate Swann
*Vice-Chancellor and Principal,* Prof. Brian Cantor, CBE
*University Secretary,* Alison Jones

UNIVERSITY OF BRIGHTON (1992)
Mithras House, Lewes Road, Brighton BN2 4AT T 01273-600900
W www.brighton.ac.uk
*Fee:* £9,000 *Students:* 16,655 UG; 4,045 PG
*Vice-Chancellor,* Prof. Julian Crampton
*Registrar,* Carol Burns

UNIVERSITY OF BRISTOL (1909)
Senate House, Tyndall Avenue, Bristol BS8 1TH T 0117-928 9000
W www.bris.ac.uk
*Fee:* £9,000 *Students:* 14,930 UG; 5,190 PG
*Chancellor,* Baroness Hale of Richmond, DBE, PC
*Vice-Chancellor,* Prof. Hugh Brady
*Registrar,* Robin Geller

BRUNEL UNIVERSITY LONDON (1966)
Kingston Lane, Uxbridge, Middx UB8 3PH T 01895-274000
W www.brunel.ac.uk
*Fee:* £9,000 *Students:* 10,075 UG; 4,255 PG
*Chancellor,* Sir Richard Sykes
*Vice-Chancellor,* Prof. Julia Buckingham, PHD, DSc, FRSA

UNIVERSITY OF BUCKINGHAM (1983)
Buckingham MK18 1EG T 01280-814080
W www.buckingham.ac.uk
*Fee:* £6,444 *Students:* 1,260 UG; 985 PG
*Chancellor,* Lady Keswick
*Vice-Chancellor,* Sir Anthony Seldon, PHD, FRSA
*Registrar,* Anne Miller

BUCKS NEW UNIVERSITY (2007)
High Wycombe Campus, Queen Alexandra Road, High Wycombe
HP11 2JZ T 01494-522141 W www.bucks.ac.uk
*Fee:* £9,000 *Students:* 7,990. UG; 1,095 PG
*Vice-Chancellor,* Prof. Rebecca Bunting

UNIVERSITY OF CAMBRIDGE (1209)
The Old Schools, Trinity Lane, Cambridge CB2 1TN
T 01223-337733 W www.cam.ac.uk
*Fee:* £9,000 *Students:* 12,155 UG; 7,425 PG
*Chancellor,* Lord Sainsbury of Turville, FRS (King's)
*Vice-Chancellor,* Prof. Sir Leszek Borysiewicz, FRS
(Wolfson)
*High Steward,* Lord Watson of Richmond, CBE (Jesus)
*Deputy High Steward,* Mrs A. Lonsdale, CBE (Murray
Edwards)
*Commissary,* Lord Mackay of Clashfern, KT, PC, FRSE
(Trinity)

*Pro-Vice-Chancellors,* Dr J. C. Barnes (Murray Edwards);
Prof. L. F. Gladden, CBE, FRS (Trinity); Prof. D. Maskell,
FMedSci (Wolfson); Prof. J. K. M. Sanders, FRS (Selwyn);
Prof. G. J. Virgo (Downing); Prof. S. J. Young, FRENG
(Emmanuel)
*Proctors (2015–16),* D. Goode (Wolfson); R. Taplin (Gonville
and Caius)
*Deputy Proctors (2015–16),* J. M. Holmes (Queens');
R. K. Taplin (Downing)
*Orator,* Dr R. J. E. Thompson (Selwyn)
*Registrar,* Dr J. W. Nicholls (Emmanuel)
*Librarian,* Mrs A. E. Jarvis (Wolfson)
*Director of the Fitzwilliam Museum,* T. Knox (Gonville and
Caius)
*Academic Secretary,* G. P. Allen (Wolfson)
*Director of Finance,* A. M. Reid (Wolfson)
*Executive Director of Development,* Ms A. Traub
*Esquire Bedells,* Mrs N. Hardy (Jesus); Ms S. V. Scarlett
(Lucy Cavendish)
*University Advocate,* C. F. Forsyth (Robinson)
*Deputy University Advocate,* J. K. Seymour (Sidney Sussex)

COLLEGES AND HALLS *with dates of foundation*
CHRIST'S (1505)
*Master,* Prof. F. P. Kelly, CBE, FRS
CHURCHILL (1960)
*Master,* Prof. Dame Athene Donald, DBE, FRS
CLARE (1326)
*Master,* Lord Grabiner, QC
CLARE HALL (1966)
*President,* Prof. D. J. Ibbetson, FBA
CORPUS CHRISTI (1352)
*Master,* S. Laing
DARWIN (1964)
*Master,* C. M. R. Fowler
DOWNING (1800)
*Master,* Prof. G. R. Grimmett
EMMANUEL (1584)
*Master,* Dame Fiona Reynolds, DBE
FITZWILLIAM (1966)
*Master,* Mrs N. M. Padfield
GIRTON (1869)
*Mistress,* Prof. S. J. Smith, FBA
GONVILLE AND CAIUS (1348)
*Master,* Prof. Sir Alan Fersht, FRS
HOMERTON (1976)
*Principal,* Prof. G. Ward
HUGHES HALL (1885)
*President,* Dr Anthony Freeling
JESUS (1496)
*Master,* Prof. I. H. White
KING'S (1441)
*Provost,* Prof. M. R. E. Proctor, FRS
LUCY CAVENDISH (1965)
*President,* Prof. J. M. Todd, OBE
MAGDALENE (1542)
*Master,* Rt. Revd Lord Williams of Oystermouth, PC, DPHIL,
FBA
MURRAY EDWARDS (1954)
*President,* Dame Barbara Stocking, DBE
NEWNHAM (1871)
*Principal,* Prof. Dame Carol Black, DBE, FRCP
PEMBROKE (1347)
*Master,* Sir Richard Dearlove, KCMG, OBE
PETERHOUSE (1284)
*Master,* Prof. A. K. Dixon, FRCP
QUEENS' (1448)
*President,* Prof. Lord Eatwell
ROBINSON (1979)
*Warden,* Prof. A. D. Yates

ST CATHARINE'S (1473)
*Master,* Prof. Dame Jean Thomas, DBE, FRS
ST EDMUND'S (1896)
*Master,* Matthew Bullock
ST JOHN'S (1511)
*Master,* Prof. C. M. Dobson, FRS
SELWYN (1882)
*Master,* Roger Mosey
SIDNEY SUSSEX (1596)
*Master,* Prof. R. V. Penty
TRINITY (1546)
*Master,* Sir Gregory Winter, CBE, FRS
TRINITY HALL (1350)
*Master,* Revd. Dr Jeremy Morris
WOLFSON (1965)
*President,* Prof. Sir Richard Evans, FBA

CANTERBURY CHRIST CHURCH UNIVERSITY (2005)
North Holmes Road, Canterbury CT1 1QU T 01227-767700
W www.canterbury.ac.uk
*Fee:* £9,000 *Students:* 13,945 UG; 3,480 PG
*Chancellor,* Most Revd and Rt. Hon. Archbishop of Canterbury
*Vice-Chancellor,* Prof. Rama Thirunamachandran
*Academic Registrar,* Lorri Curri

CARDIFF METROPOLITAN UNIVERSITY (2011)
Western Avenue, Cardiff CF5 2YB T 029-2041 6138
W www.cardiffmet.ac.uk
*Fee:* £9,000 *Students:* 8,730 UG; 4,665 PG
*Vice-Chancellor and Principal,* Prof. Anthony Chapman

CARDIFF UNIVERSITY (1883)
Cardiff CF10 3XQ T 029-2087 4000 W www.cardiff.ac.uk
*Fee:* £9,000 *Students:* 21,495 UG; 8,635 PG
*Chancellor,* Prof. Sir Martin Evans, FRS
*Vice-Chancellor,* Prof. Colin Riordan
*Chief Operating Officer,* Jayne Dowden

UNIVERSITY OF CENTRAL LANCASHIRE (1992)
Preston PR1 2HE T 01772-201201 W www.uclan.ac.uk
*Fee:* £9,000 *Students:* 21,995 UG; 4,590 PG
*Chancellor,* Sir Richard Evans, CBE
*Vice-Chancellor,* Prof. Gerry Kelleher

UNIVERSITY OF CHESTER (2005)
Parkgate Road, Chester CH1 4BJ T 01244-511000
W www.chester.ac.uk
*Fee:* £9,000 *Students:* 10,725 UG; 4,015 PG
*Chancellor,* Duke of Westminster, KG, CB, CVO, OBE
*Vice-Chancellor,* Canon Prof. Tim Wheeler
*Registrar,* Jonathan Moores

UNIVERSITY OF CHICHESTER (2005)
College Lane, Chichester PO19 6PE T 01243-816000
W www.chi.ac.uk
*Fee:* £9,000 *Students:* 4,790 UG; 845 PG
*Vice-Chancellor,* Prof. Clive Behagg, PHD
*Secretary,* Isabel Cherrett

CITY UNIVERSITY LONDON (1966)
Northampton Square, London EC1V 0HB T 020-7040 5060
W www.city.ac.uk
*Fee:* £9,000 *Students:* 9,645 UG; 8,500 PG
*Chancellor,* Alan Yarrow
*Vice-Chancellor,* Prof. Paul Curran
*Secretary,* Frank Toop

COVENTRY UNIVERSITY (1992)
Priory Street, Coventry CV1 5FB T 024-7688 7688
W www.coventry.ac.uk
*Fee:* £9,000 *Students:* 20,310 UG; 5,525 PG
*Chancellor,* Sir John Egan
*Vice-Chancellor,* John Latham
*Registrar,* Kate Quantrell

CRANFIELD UNIVERSITY (1969)
Cranfield, Bedfordshire MK43 0AL T 01234-750111
W www.cranfield.ac.uk
*Students:* 4,205 PG (postgraduate only)
*Chancellor,* Baroness Young of Old Scone
*Vice-Chancellor,* Prof. Sir Peter Gregson

UNIVERSITY FOR THE CREATIVE ARTS (2008)
Falkner Road, Farnham GU9 7DS T 01252-722441
W www.ucreative.ac.uk
*Fee:* £9,000 *Students:* 4,825 UG; 255 PG
*Chancellor,* Dame Zandra Rhodes, DBE
*Vice-Chancellor,* Dr Simon Ofield-Kerr
*University Secretary,* Marion Wilks

UNIVERSITY OF CUMBRIA (2007)
Fusehill Street, Carlisle CA1 2HH T 01228-616234
W www.cumbria.ac.uk
*Fee:* £9,000 *Students:* 7,695 UG; 1,930 PG
*Chancellor,* Most Revd and Rt. Hon. Archbishop of York
*Vice-Chancellor,* Prof. Peter Strike
*Registrar and Secretary,* Neil Harris

DE MONTFORT UNIVERSITY (1992)
The Gateway, Leicester LE1 9BH T 0116-255 1551
W www.dmu.ac.uk
*Fee:* £9,000 *Students:* 16,410 UG; 3,235 PG
*Chancellor,* Lord Alli
*Vice-Chancellor,* Prof. Dominic Shellard

UNIVERSITY OF DERBY (1992)
Kedleston Road, Derby DE22 1GB T 01332-590500
W www.derby.ac.uk
*Fee:* £9,000 *Students:* 13,565 UG; 2,820 PG
*Chancellor,* Duke of Devonshire, KCVO, CBE
*Vice-Chancellor,* Prof. John Coyne
*Registrar,* June Hughes

UNIVERSITY OF DUNDEE (1967)
Nethergate, Dundee DD1 4HN T 01382-383000
W www.dundee.ac.uk
*Fee:* £9,000 *Students:* 10,310 UG; 4,883 PG
*Chancellor,* Lord Patel, KT, FRSE
*Vice-Chancellor and Principal,* Prof. Pete Downes, OBE, FRSE
*University Secretary,* Dr Jim McGeorge

DURHAM UNIVERSITY (1832)
The Palatine Centre, Stockton Road, Durham DH1 3LE
T 0191-334 2000 W www.dur.ac.uk
*Fee:* £9,000 *Students:* 12,540 UG; 4,655 PG
*Chancellor,* Sir Thomas Allen, CBE
*Vice-Chancellor,* Prof. Ray Hudson, DSc, DLITT, FBA
*Registrar and Treasurer (acting),* Paulina Lubacz

COLLEGES
COLLINGWOOD (1972)
*Principal,* Prof. J. Elliott
GREY (1959)
*Master,* Prof. T. Allen
HATFIELD (1846)
*Master,* Prof. T. P. Burt

JOHN SNOW (2001)
*Principal*, Prof. C. Summerbell
JOSEPHINE BUTLER (2006)
*Principal*, A. Simpson
ST AIDAN'S (1947)
*Principal*, Dr S. F. Frenk
ST CHAD'S (1904)
*Principal*, Revd Dr J. P. M. Cassidy
ST CUTHBERT'S SOCIETY (1888)
*Principal*, Prof. E. Archibald
ST HILD AND ST BEDE (1839)
*Principal*, Prof. A. Darnell
ST JOHN'S (1909)
*Principal*, Revd Dr D. Wilkinson
ST MARY'S (1899)
*Principal*, Prof. S. Hackett
STEPHENSON (2001)
*Principal*, Prof. J. Ashworth
TREVELYAN (1966)
*Principal*, Prof. H. M. Evans
UNIVERSITY (1832)
*Master*, Prof. D. Held
USTINOV (2003)
*Principal*, Prof. G. McGregor
VAN MILDERT (1965)
*Principal*, Prof. D. Harper


UNIVERSITY OF EAST ANGLIA (1963)
Norwich Research Park, Norwich NR4 7TJ **T** 01603-456161
**W** www.uea.ac.uk
*Fee:* £9,000 *Students:* 12,090 UG; 5,055 PG
*Chancellor*, Rose Tremain, CBE
*Vice-Chancellor*, Prof. David Richardson
*Registrar and Secretary*, Brian Summers


UNIVERSITY OF EAST LONDON (1898)
University Way, London E16 2RD **T** 020-8223 3000
**W** www.uel.ac.uk
*Fee:* £9,000 *Students:* 12,900 UG; 4,275 PG
*Chancellor*, Lord Noon, MBE
*Vice-Chancellor*, Prof. John Joughin
*Deputy Vice-Chancellor*, Dusty Amroliwala


EDGE HILL UNIVERSITY (2006)
St Helens Road, Ormskirk, Lancs L39 4QP **T** 01695-575171
**W** www.edgehill.ac.uk
*Fee:* £9,000 *Students:* 12,670 UG; 4,110 PG
*Chancellor*, Prof. Tanya Byron
*Vice-Chancellor*, Dr John Cater
*University Secretary*, Lynda Brady


UNIVERSITY OF EDINBURGH (1583)
Old College, South Bridge, Edinburgh EH8 9YL **T** 0131-650 1000
**W** www.ed.ac.uk
*Fee:* £9,000 *Students:* 19,015 UG; 3,605 PG
*Chancellor*, HRH the Princess Royal, KG, KT, GCVO
*Vice-Chancellor and Principal*, Prof. Sir Timothy O'Shea,
    FRSE
*University Secretary*, Sarah Smith


EDINBURGH NAPIER UNIVERSITY (1992)
Sighthill Campus, Edinburgh EH11 4BN **T** 0333-900 6040
**W** www.napier.ac.uk
*Fee:* £9,000 *Students:* 10,605 UG; 2,085 PG
*Chancellor*, Tim Waterstone
*Vice-Chancellor*, Prof. Andrea Nolan, OBE
*Secretary*, Dr Gerry Webber


UNIVERSITY OF ESSEX (1965)
Wivenhoe Park, Colchester CO4 3SQ **T** 01206-873333
**W** www.essex.ac.uk
*Fee:* £9,000 *Students:* 10,840 UG; 3,140 PG
*Chancellor*, Shami Chakrabarti, CBE
*Vice-Chancellor*, Prof. Anthony Forster, DPHIL
*Registrar*, Bryn Morris


UNIVERSITY OF EXETER (1955)
Stocker Road, Exeter EX4 4PY **T** 01392-661000
**W** www.exeter.ac.uk
*Fee:* £9,000 *Students:* 15,030 UG; 4,470 PG
*Chancellor*, Baroness Benjamin, OBE
*Vice-Chancellor*, Prof. Sir Steve Smith, PHD
*Chief Operating Officer*, Geoff Pringle


FALMOUTH UNIVERSITY (2012)
Falmouth Campus, Woodlane, Falmouth TR11 4RH
**T** 01326-211077 **W** www.falmouth.ac.uk
*Fee:* £9,000 *Students:* 3,715 UG; 300 PG
*Chancellor*, Dawn French
*Vice-Chancellor*, Prof. Anne Carlisle


UNIVERSITY OF GLASGOW (1451)
University Avenue, Glasgow G12 8QQ **T** 0141-330 2000
**W** www.gla.ac.uk
*Fee:* £9,000 *Students:* 19,850 UG; 7,540 PG
*Chancellor*, Prof. Sir Kenneth Calman, KCB, FRCS, FRSE
*Vice-Chancellor*, Prof. Anton Muscatelli, FRSE
*Registrar*, David Bennion


GLASGOW CALEDONIAN UNIVERSITY (1993)
City Campus, Cowcaddens Road, Glasgow G4 0BA
**T** 0141-331 3000 **W** www.gcu.ac.uk
*Fee:* £7,000 *Students:* 13,825 UG; 2,925 PG
*Chancellor*, Prof. Muhammad Yunus
*Vice-Chancellor*, Prof. Pamela Gillies, CBE, FRSE
*University Secretary*, Jan Hulme


UNIVERSITY OF GLOUCESTERSHIRE (2001)
The Park, Cheltenham GL50 2RH **T** 0844-801 0001
**W** www.glos.ac.uk
*Fee:* £9,000 *Students:* 6,710 UG; 1,260 PG
*Chancellor*, Baroness Fritchie, DBE
*Vice-Chancellor*, Stephen Marston
*Registrar*, Julie Thackray


GLYNDWR UNIVERSITY (2008)
Mold Road, Wrexham LL11 2AW **T** 01978-290666
**W** www.glyndwr.ac.uk
*Fee:* £8,450 *Students:* 7,100 UG; 1,305 PG
*Chancellor*, Sir John Shortridge, KCB
*Vice-Chancellor*, Prof. Graham Upton


UNIVERSITY OF GREENWICH (1992)
Old Royal Naval College, Park Row, London SE10 9LS
**T** 020-8331 8000 **W** www.gre.ac.uk
*Fee:* £9,000 *Students:* 17,020 UG; 4,930 PG
*Chancellor*, Baroness Scotland of Asthal, PC, QC
*Vice-Chancellor*, Prof. David Maguire
*Secretary*, Louise Nadal


HARPER ADAMS UNIVERSITY (2012)
Newport, Shropshire TF10 8NB **T** 01952-820280
**W** www.harper-adams.ac.uk
*Fee:* £9,000 *Students:* 4,415 UG; 385 PG
*Chancellor*, HRH the Princess Royal, KG, KT, GCVO
*Vice-Chancellor*, Dr David Llewellyn
*University Secretary*, Dr Catherine Baxter

HERIOT-WATT UNIVERSITY (1966)
Edinburgh EH14 4AS T 0131-449 5111 W www.hw.ac.uk
*Fee:* £9,000 *Students:* 7,315 UG; 3,575 PG
*Chancellor,* Dr Robert Buchan
*Vice-Chancellor and Principal,* Prof. Julian Jones, OBE,
   FRSE
*Secretary,* Ann Marie Dalton

UNIVERSITY OF HERTFORDSHIRE (1992)
Hatfield AL10 9AB T 01707-284000 W www.herts.ac.uk
*Fee:* £9,000 *Students:* 19,760 UG; 5,535 PG
*Chancellor,* Marquess of Salisbury, KCVO, PC
*Vice-Chancellor,* Prof. Quintin McKellar, CBE
*Registrar,* Sue Grant

UNIVERSITY OF THE HIGHLANDS AND ISLANDS
(2011)
Ness Walk, Inverness IV3 5SQ T 01463-279000
W www.uhi.ac.uk
*Fee:* £9,000 *Students:* 7,000 UG; 465 PG
*Chancellor,* HRH the Princess Royal, KG, KT, GCVO
*Vice-Chancellor,* Prof. Clive Mulholland
*University Secretary,* Fiona Larg

UNIVERSITY OF HUDDERSFIELD (1992)
Queensgate, Huddersfield HD1 3DH T 01484-422288
W www.hud.ac.uk
*Fee:* £9,000 *Students:* 14,965 UG; 4,210 PG
*Chancellor,* Prof. Sir Patrick Stewart, OBE
*Vice-Chancellor,* Prof. Bob Cryan, CBE, PHD, DSc
*University Secretary,* Michaela Boryslawskyj

UNIVERSITY OF HULL (1927)
Cottingham Road, Hull HU6 7RX T 01482-346311
W www.hull.ac.uk
*Fee:* £9,000 *Students:* 14,285 UG; 3,730 PG
*Chancellor,* Baroness Bottomley of Nettlestone, PC
*Vice-Chancellor,* Prof. Calie Pistorius, PHD
*Registrar,* Jeannette Strachan

IMPERIAL COLLEGE LONDON (1907)
South Kensington, London SW7 2AZ T 020-7589 5111
W www.imperial.ac.uk
*Fee:* £9,000 *Students:* 8,885 UG; 7,340 PG
*Rector,* Alice Gast
*Deputy Rector,* Prof. Stephen Richardson
*Registrar,* John Neilson

KEELE UNIVERSITY (1962)
Keele, Staffs ST5 5BG T 01782-732000 W www.keele.ac.uk
*Fee:* £9,000 *Students:* 7,555 UG; 2,425 PG
*Chancellor,* Jonathon Porritt, CBE
*Vice-Chancellor,* Prof. Nick Foskett, PHD

UNIVERSITY OF KENT (1965)
Canterbury CT2 7NZ T 01227-764000 W www.kent.ac.uk
*Fee:* £9,000 *Students:* 15,200 UG; 3,805 PG
*Chancellor,* Gavin Esler
*Vice-Chancellor,* Prof. Dame Julia Goodfellow, DBE, PHD

KINGSTON UNIVERSITY (1992)
River House, 53–57 High Street, Kingston upon Thames
KT1 1LQ T 020-8417 9000 W www.kingston.ac.uk
*Fee:* £9,000 *Students:* 17,790 UG; 5,270 PG
*Chancellor,* Bonnie Greer, OBE
*Vice-Chancellor,* Prof. Julius Weinberg
*Academic Registrar,* Matthew Hilton

UNIVERSITY OF LANCASTER (1964)
Bailrigg, Lancaster LA1 4YW T 01524-65201
W www.lancaster.ac.uk
*Fee:* £9,000 *Students:* 9,410 UG; 3,670 PG
*Chancellor,* Rt. Hon. Alan Milburn
*Vice-Chancellor,* Prof. Mark E. Smith
*University Secretary,* Fiona Aiken

UNIVERSITY OF LEEDS (1904)
Leeds LS2 9JT T 0113-243 1751 W www.leeds.ac.uk
*Fee:* £9,000 *Students:* 23,265 UG; 7,710 PG
*Chancellor,* Lord Bragg
*Vice-Chancellor,* Sir Alan Langlands
*Registrar,* Roger Gair

LEEDS BECKETT UNIVERSITY (1992)
City Campus, Leeds LS1 3HE T 0113-812 0000
W www.leedsbeckett.ac.uk
*Fee:* £9,000 *Students:* 20,935 UG; 3,970 PG
*Chancellor,* Sir Bob Murray, CBE
*Vice-Chancellor,* Prof. Susan Price
*Secretary and Registrar,* Jenny Share

LEEDS TRINITY UNIVERSITY (2012)
Brownberrie Lane, Leeds LS18 5HD T 0113-283 7100
W www.leedstrinity.ac.uk
*Fee:* £9,000 *Students:* 2,750 UG; 570 PG
*Chancellor,* Gabby Logan
*Vice-Chancellor,* Prof. Margaret House
*Secretary,* Howard Nelson

UNIVERSITY OF LEICESTER (1957)
University Road, Leicester LE1 7RH T 0116-252 2522
W www.le.ac.uk
*Fee:* £9,000 *Students:* 10,905 UG; 5,845 PG
*Chancellor,* Lord Grocott, PC
*Vice-Chancellor,* Prof. Paul Boyle, FBA, FRSE
*Registrar,* Dave Hall

UNIVERSITY OF LINCOLN (1992)
Brayford Pool, Lincoln LN6 7TS T 01522-882000
W www.lincoln.ac.uk
*Fee:* £9,000 *Students:* 11,210 UG; 2,190 PG
*Chancellor,* Lord Adebowale, CBE
*Vice-Chancellor,* Prof. Mary Stuart
*Registrar,* Chris Spendlove

UNIVERSITY OF LIVERPOOL (1903)
Brownlow Hill, Liverpool L69 7ZX T 0151-794 2000
W www.liv.ac.uk
*Fee:* £9,000 *Students:* 16,860 UG; 4,490 PG
*Chancellor,* Sir David King, FRS
*Vice-Chancellor,* Prof. Janet Beer

LIVERPOOL HOPE UNIVERSITY (2005)
Hope Park, Liverpool L16 9JD T 0151-291 3000
W www.hope.ac.uk
*Fee:* £9,000 *Students:* 4,315 UG; 1,925 PG
*Chancellor,* Lord Guthrie of Craigiebank, GCB, LVO, OBE
*Vice-Chancellor and Rector,* Prof. Gerald Pillay
*Registrar,* Neil McLaughlin-Cook

LIVERPOOL JOHN MOORES UNIVERSITY (1992)
Kingsway House, 2nd Floor, Hatton Garden, Liverpool L3 2AJ
T 0151-231 2121 W www.ljmu.ac.uk
*Fee:* £9,000 *Students:* 18, 450 UG; 2,865 PG
*Chancellor,* Rt. Hon. Sir Brian Leveson
*Vice-Chancellor,* Prof. Nigel Weatherill, DSc, FRENG
*Secretary,* Denise Tipping

## UNIVERSITY OF LONDON (1836)
Senate House, Malet Street, London WC1E 7HU
T 020-7862 8000 W www.london.ac.uk
*Fee:* £9,000
*Chancellor,* HRH the Princess Royal, KG, KT, GCVO
*Vice-Chancellor,* Prof. Sir Adrian Smith, FRS
*University Secretary,* Chris Cobb

### COLLEGES
**BIRKBECK COLLEGE**
Malet Street, London WC1E 7HX
*Students:* 10,805 UG; 4,740 PG
*President,* Baroness Bakewell, DBE
*Master,* Prof. David Latchman, CBE
**COURTAULD INSTITUTE OF ART**
Somerset House, Strand, London WC2R 0RN
*Students:* 155 UG; 305 PG
*Director,* Prof. Deborah Swallow
**GOLDSMITHS COLLEGE**
New Cross, London SE14 6NW
*Students,* 5,030 UG; 3,080 PG
*Warden,* Patrick Loughrey
**HEYTHROP COLLEGE**
Kensington Square, London W8 5HN
*Students:* 415 UG; 335 PG
*Principal,* Michael Holman, SJ
**INSTITUTE OF CANCER RESEARCH**
15 Cotswold Road, Sutton, Surrey SM2 5NG
*Students:* (postgraduate only) 290 PG
*Chief Executive,* Prof. Paul Workman
**KING'S COLLEGE LONDON** (includes Guy's, King's and St Thomas's Schools of Medicine, Dentistry and Biomedical Sciences)
Strand, London WC2R 2LS
*Students:* 16,410 UG; 11,235 PG
*Principal,* Prof. Edward Byrne
**LONDON BUSINESS SCHOOL**
Regent's Park, London NW1 4SA
*Students:* 1,905 PG (postgraduate only)
*Dean,* Prof. Sir Andrew Likierman
**LONDON SCHOOL OF ECONOMICS AND POLITICAL SCIENCE**
Houghton Street, London WC2A 2AE
*Students:* 4,035 UG; 6,115 PG
*Director,* Prof. Craig Calhoun
**LONDON SCHOOL OF HYGIENE AND TROPICAL MEDICINE**
Keppel Street, London WC1E 7HT
*Students:* (postgraduate only) 1,250 PG
*Director,* Prof. Peter Piot, CMG, PHD, MD
**QUEEN MARY** (incorporating St Bartholomew's and the London School of Medicine and Dentistry)
Mile End Road, London E1 4NS
*Students:* 11,200 UG; 4,220 PG
*Principal,* Prof. Simon Gaskell
**ROYAL ACADEMY OF MUSIC**
Marylebone Road, London NW1 5HT
*Students:* 350 UG; 395 PG
*Principal,* Prof. Jonathan Freeman-Attwood
**ROYAL CENTRAL SCHOOL OF SPEECH AND DRAMA**
Eton Avenue, London NW3 3HY
*Students:* 630 UG; 355 PG
*President,* Michael Grandage, CBE
*Principal,* Prof. Gavin Henderson, CBE
**ROYAL HOLLOWAY**
Egham Hill, Egham, Surrey TW20 0EX
*Students:* 7,160 UG; 2,515 PG
*Principal,* Prof. Paul Layzell

**ROYAL VETERINARY COLLEGE**
Royal College Street, London NW1 0TU
*Students:* 1,595 UG; 560 PG
*Principal,* Prof. Stuart Reid
**ST GEORGE'S**
Cranmer Terrace, London SW17 0RE
*Students:* 4,590 UG; 915 PG
*Principal,* Prof. Peter Kopelman
**SCHOOL OF ADVANCED STUDY**
Senate House, Malet Street, London WC1E 7HU
*Dean and Chief Executive,* Prof. Roger Kain, CBE, FBA
**SCHOOL OF ORIENTAL AND AFRICAN STUDIES**
Thornhaugh Street, Russell Square, London WC1H 0XG
*Students:* 2,975 UG; 2,435 PG
*Director,* Prof. Paul Webley
**UNIVERSITY COLLEGE LONDON** (including the Institute of Neurology, Eastman Dental Institute, School of Pharmacy and Institute of Education)
Gower Street, London WC1E 6BT
*Students:* 15,415 UG; 13,015 PG
*Provost and President,* Prof. Michael Arthur, FRCP, FMedSci
**UNIVERSITY OF LONDON INSTITUTE IN PARIS**
9–11 rue de Constantine, 75340 Paris Cedex 07, France
*Dean,* Prof. Andrew Hussey, OBE

### INSTITUTES
**INSTITUTE OF ADVANCED LEGAL STUDIES**
Charles Clore House, 17 Russell Square, London WC1B 5DR
*Director,* Jules Winterton
**INSTITUTE OF CLASSICAL STUDIES**
Senate House, Malet Street, London WC1E 7HU
*Director,* Prof. Greg Woolf, FSA
**INSTITUTE OF COMMONWEALTH STUDIES**
Senate House, Malet Street, London WC1E 7HU
*Director,* Prof. Rick Rylance
**INSTITUTE OF ENGLISH STUDIES**
Senate House, Malet Street, London WC1E 7HU
*Director,* Prof. Philip Murphy
**INSTITUTE OF HISTORICAL RESEARCH**
Senate House, Malet Street, London WC1E 7HU
*Director,* Prof. Lawrence Goldman
**INSTITUTE OF LATIN AMERICAN STUDIES**
Senate House, Malet Street, London WC1E 7HU
*Director,* Prof. Linda Newson
**INSTITUTE OF MODERN LANGUAGES RESEARCH**
Senate House, Malet Street, London WC1E 7HU
*Director,* Prof. Catherine Davies
**INSTITUTE OF MUSICAL RESEARCH**
Senate House, Malet Street, London WC1E 7HU
*Director,* Dr Paul Archbold
**INSTITUTE OF PHILOSOPHY**
Senate House, Malet Street, London WC1E 7HU
*Director,* Prof. Barry Smith
**WARBURG INSTITUTE**
Woburn Square, London WC1H 0AB
*Director,* Prof. David Freedberg

## LONDON METROPOLITAN UNIVERSITY (2002)
166–220 Holloway Road, London N7 8DB
T 020-7423 0000 W www.londonmet.ac.uk
*Fee:* £9,000 *Students:* 13,100 UG; 3,155 PG
*Patron,* HRH the Duke of York, KG, GCVO
*Vice-Chancellor,* Prof. John Raftery
*University Secretary,* Alison Wells

## LONDON SOUTH BANK UNIVERSITY (1992)
103 Borough Road, London SE1 0AA T 020-7815 7815
W www.lsbu.ac.uk

*Fee:* £9,000 *Students:* 17,005 UG; 4,220 PG
*Chancellor,* Richard Farleigh
*Vice-Chancellor,* Prof. David Phoenix
*University Secretary,* James Stevenson

## LOUGHBOROUGH UNIVERSITY (1966)
Epinal Way, Loughborough, Leics LE11 3TU T 01509-222222
W www.lboro.ac.uk
*Fee:* £9,000 *Students:* 12,005 UG; 3,955 PG
*Chancellor,* Sir Nigel Rudd
*Vice-Chancellor and President,* Prof. Robert Allison
*Chief Operating Officer,* Richard Taylor

## UNIVERSITY OF MANCHESTER (2004)
Formed by the amalgamation of Victoria University of
Manchester (1851; reorganised 1880 and 1903) and the
University of Manchester Institute of Science and
Technology (1824))
Oxford Road, Manchester M13 9PL T 0161-306 6000
W www.manchester.ac.uk
*Fee:* £9,000 *Students:* 26,485 UG; 11,440 PG
*Chancellor,* Tom Bloxham, MBE
*Vice-Chancellor,* Prof. Dame Nancy Rothwell, DBE, FRS
*Registrar,* Will Spinks

## MANCHESTER METROPOLITAN UNIVERSITY (1992)
All Saints, Manchester M15 6BH T 0161-247 2000
W www.mmu.ac.uk
*Fee:* £9,000 *Students:* 26,635 UG; 5.525 PG
*Chancellor,* Dianne Thompson, CBE
*Vice-Chancellor,* Prof. John Brooks, DSc
*Registrar,* Karen Moore

## MIDDLESEX UNIVERSITY (1992)
Hendon Campus, The Burroughs, London NW4 4BT
T 020-8411 5555 W www.mdx.ac.uk
*Fee:* £9,000 *Students:* 15,645 UG; 4,235 PG
*Chancellor,* Dame Janet Ritterman, DBE
*Vice-Chancellor,* Prof. Michael Driscoll

## NEWCASTLE UNIVERSITY (1963)
Newcastle upon Tyne NE1 7RU T 0191-208 6000
W www.ncl.ac.uk
*Fee:* £9,000 *Students:* 16,290 UG; 6,120 PG
*Chancellor,* Prof. Sir Liam Donaldson
*Vice-Chancellor,* Prof. Chris Brink, FRS, DPHIL
*Registrar,* Dr John Hogan

## NEWMAN UNIVERSITY, BIRMINGHAM (2013)
Genners Lane, Bartley Green, Birmingham B32 3NT
T 0121-476 1181 W www.newman.ac.uk
*Fee:* £9,000 *Students:* 2,250 UG; 603 PG
*Vice-Chancellor,* Prof. Peter Lutzeier
*University Secretary,* Heather Somerfield

## UNIVERSITY OF NORTHAMPTON (2005)
Park Campus, Boughton Green Road, Northampton NN2 7AL
T 01604-735500 W www.northampton.ac.uk
*Fee:* £9,000 *Students:* 10,975 UG; 2,315 PG
*Chancellor,* David Laing
*Vice-Chancellor,* Prof. Nick Petford, PHD, DSc
*Registrar,* Jane Bunce

## NORTHUMBRIA UNIVERSITY AT NEWCASTLE (1992)
Ellison Building, Ellison Place, Newcastle upon Tyne NE1 8ST
T 0191-232 6002 W www.northumbria.ac.uk
*Fee:* £9,000 *Students:* 23,065 UG; 4,500 PG
*Chancellor,* Lord Stevens of Kirkwhelpington, QPM
*Vice-Chancellor,* Prof. Andrew Wathey, DPHIL
*Chief Operating Officer,* Chris Reilly

## NORWICH UNIVERSITY OF THE ARTS (2012)
Francis House, 3–7 Redwell Street, Norwich NR2 4SN
T 01603-610561 W www.nua.ac.uk
*Fee:* £9,000 *Students:* 1,705 UG; 60 PG
*Chancellor,* Sir John Hurt, CBE
*Vice-Chancellor,* Prof. John Last
*Registrar,* Angela Tubb

## UNIVERSITY OF NOTTINGHAM (1948)
University Park, Nottingham NG7 2RD T 0115-951 5151
W www.nottingham.ac.uk
*Fee:* £9,000 *Students:* 24,885 UG; 8,385 PG
*Chancellor,* Sir Andrew Witty
*Vice-Chancellor,* Prof. David Greenaway
*Registrar,* Dr Paul Greatrix

## NOTTINGHAM TRENT UNIVERSITY (1992)
Burton Street, Nottingham NG1 4BU T 0115-941 8418
W www.ntu.ac.uk
*Fee:* £9,000 *Students:* 21,670 UG; 5,175 PG
*Chancellor,* Kevin Cahill, CBE
*Vice-Chancellor,* Prof. Edward Peck

## OPEN UNIVERSITY (1969)
Walton Hall, Milton Keynes MK7 6AA T 01908-274066
W www.open.ac.uk
*Fee:* £6,000 *Students:* 138,605 UG; 12,230 PG
*Chancellor,* Baroness Lane-Fox of Soho, CBE
*Vice-Chancellor,* Peter Horrocks
*University Secretary,* Fraser Woodburn

## UNIVERSITY OF OXFORD (c.12th century)
University Offices, Wellington Square, Oxford OX1 2JD
T 01865-270000 W www.ox.ac.uk
*Fee:* £9,000 *Students:* 16,655 UG; 9,250 PG
*Chancellor,* Lord Patten of Barnes, CH, PC (Balliol,
St Antony's)
*Vice-Chancellor,* Prof. Louise Richardson, FRSE
*Pro-Vice-Chancellors,* Dr S. J. Goss (Wadham); Prof. W. James
(Brasenose); Prof. S. L. Mapstone (St Hilda's); Prof. J. N. P.
Rawlins (Wolfson); Prof. A. Trefethen (St Cross); Prof. I. A.
Walmsley (St. Hugh's)
*Registrar,* Prof. E. G. McKendrick (Lady Margaret Hall)
*Deputy Registrar,* M. Sibly (St Anne's)
*Public Orator,* R. H. A. Jenkyns (Lady Margaret Hall)
*Director of University Library Services and Bodley's Librarian,*
R. Ovenden (Balliol)
*Director of the Ashmolean Museum,* Dr A. Sturgis (Worcester)
*Keeper of Archives,* S. Bailey (Linacre)
*Director of Estates,* P. Goffin
*Director of Finance,* G. F. B. Kerr (Keble)

COLLEGES AND HALLS *with dates of foundation*
ALL SOULS (1438)
*Warden,* Prof. Sir John Vickers, FBA
BALLIOL (1263)
*Master,* Prof. Sir Drummond Bone, FRSE
BLACKFRIARS (1221)
*Regent,* Very Revd Dr Simon Gaine
BRASENOSE (1509)
*Principal,* John Bowers, QC
CAMPION HALL (1896)
*Master,* Revd James Hanvey
CHRIST CHURCH (1546)
*Dean,* Very Revd Christopher Lewis
CORPUS CHRISTI (1517)
*President,* Prof. Richard Carwardine, FBA
EXETER (1314)
*Rector,* Prof. Sir Rick Trainor, KBE

GREEN TEMPLETON (2008)
*Principal,* Prof. Denise Lievesley, CBE
HARRIS MANCHESTER (1889)
*Principal,* Revd Dr Ralph Waller, FRSE
HERTFORD (1740)
*Principal,* Will Hutton
JESUS (1571)
*Principal,* Prof. Sir Nigel Shadbolt, FRENG
KEBLE (1870)
*Warden,* Sir Jonathan Phillips, KCB
KELLOGG (1990)
*President,* Prof. Jonathan M. Michie
LADY MARGARET HALL (1878)
*Principal,* Alan Rusbridger
LINACRE (1962)
*Principal,* Dr Nick Brown
LINCOLN (1427)
*Rector,* Prof. Henry Woudhuysen, FBA
MAGDALEN (1458)
*President,* Prof. David Clary, FRS
MANSFIELD (1886)
*Principal,* Baroness Kennedy of the Shaws, QC
MERTON (1264)
*Warden,* Prof. Sir Martin Taylor, FRS
NEW COLLEGE (1379)
*Warden,* Prof. Curtis Price
NUFFIELD (1958)
*Warden,* Sir Andrew Dilnot, CBE
ORIEL (1326)
*Provost,* Moira Wallace, OBE
PEMBROKE (1624)
*Master,* Dame Lynne Brindley, DBE
QUEEN'S (1341)
*Provost,* Prof. Paul Madden, FRS, FRSE
REGENT'S PARK (1810)
*Principal,* Revd Dr Robert Ellis
ST ANNE'S (1878)
*Principal,* Tim Gardam
ST ANTONY'S (1953)
*Warden,* Prof. Margaret MacMillan
ST BENET'S HALL (1897)
*Master,* Prof. Werner Jeanrond
ST CATHERINE'S (1963)
*Master,* Prof. Roger Ainsworth
ST CROSS (1965)
*Master,* Sir Mark Jones, FRSE
ST EDMUND HALL (*c.*1278)
*Principal,* Prof. Keith Gull, CBE, FRS, FMedSci
ST HILDA'S (1893)
*Principal,* Prof. Sir Gordon Duff, FRCP, FRSE, FMedSci
ST HUGH'S (1886)
*Principal,* Rt. Hon. Dame Elish Angiolini, DBE, QC
ST JOHN'S (1555)
*President,* Prof. Margaret J. Snowling, FBA, FMedSci
ST PETER'S (1929)
*Principal,* Mark Damazer, CBE
ST STEPHEN'S HOUSE (1876)
*Principal,* Revd Dr Robin Ward
SOMERVILLE (1879)
*Principal,* Dr Alice Prochaska
TRINITY (1554)
*President,* Sir Ivor Roberts, KCMG
UNIVERSITY (1249)
*Master,* Sir Ivor Crewe
WADHAM (1610)
*Warden,* Lord Macdonald of River Glaven, QC
WOLFSON (1981)
*President,* Prof. Dame Hermione Lee, DBE, FBA, FRSL

WORCESTER (1714)
*Provost,* Prof. Sir Jonathan Bate, CBE, FBA, FRSL
WYCLIFFE HALL (1877)
*Principal,* Revd Michael Lloyd

OXFORD BROOKES UNIVERSITY (1992)
Gipsy Lane, Oxford OX3 0BP T 01865-741111
W www.brookes.ac.uk
*Fee:* £9,000 *Students:* 13,715 UG; 4,185 PG
*Chancellor,* Dr Katherine Granger, CBE
*Vice-Chancellor,* Prof. Alistair Fitt
*Registrar,* Paul Large

UNIVERSITY OF PLYMOUTH (1992)
Drake Circus, Plymouth PL4 8AA T 01752-600600
W www.plymouth.ac.uk
*Fee:* £9,000 *Students:* 23,585 UG; 3,345 PG
*Chancellor,* Lord Kestenbaum
*Vice-Chancellor,* Prof. David Coslett
*University Secretary,* Jane Hopkinson

UNIVERSITY OF PORTSMOUTH (1992)
University House, Winston Churchill Avenue, Portsmouth PO1 2UP
T 023-9284 8484 W www.port.ac.uk
*Fee:* £9,000 *Students:* 18,380 UG; 3,520 PG
*Chancellor,* Sandi Toksvig, OBE
*Vice-Chancellor,* Prof. Graham Galbraith, PHD
*Registrar,* Stephen Wiggins

QUEEN MARGARET UNIVERSITY (2007)
Musselburgh, Edinburgh EH21 6UU T 0131-474 0000
W www.qmu.ac.uk
*Fee:* £7,000 *Students:* 3,520 UG; 1,695 PG
*Chancellor,* Sir Tom Farmer, CVO, CBE
*Vice-Chancellor,* Prof. Petra Wend, FRSE
*Secretary,* Irene Hynd

QUEEN'S UNIVERSITY BELFAST (1908)
University Road, Belfast BT7 1NN T 028-9024 5133
W www.qub.ac.uk
*Fee:* £9,000 *Students:* 18,370 UG; 4,950 PG
*Chancellor,* Thomas Moran
*Vice-Chancellor,* Prof. Patrick Johnston
*Registrar,* James O'Kane

UNIVERSITY OF READING (1926)
Whiteknights, PO Box 217, Reading RG6 6AH T 0118-987 5123
W www.reading.ac.uk
*Fee:* £9,000 *Students:* 9,320 UG; 4,275 PG
*Chancellor,* Sir John Madejski, OBE
*Vice-Chancellor,* Sir David Bell, KCB
*University Secretary,* Dr Richard Messer

ROBERT GORDON UNIVERSITY (1992)
Schoolhill, Aberdeen AB10 1FR T 01224-262000
W www.rgu.ac.uk
*Fee:* £8,500 *Students:* 9,360 UG; 4,030 PG
*Chancellor,* Sir Ian Wood, CBE
*Vice-Chancellor,* Prof. Ferdinand von Prondzynski
*Academic Registrar,* Hilary Douglas

ROEHAMPTON UNIVERSITY (2004)
Erasmus House, Roehampton Lane, London SW15 5PU
T 020-8392 3000 W www.roehampton.ac.uk
*Fee:* £9,000 *Students:* 6,110 UG; 2,420 PG
*Chancellor,* Dame Jacqueline Wilson, DBE, FRSL
*Vice-Chancellor,* Prof. Paul O'Prey
*Registrar,* Laurence Benson

**ROYAL AGRICULTURAL UNIVERSITY (2013)**
Stroud Road, Cirencester GL7 6JS
T 01285-652531 W www.rau.ac.uk
*Fee:* £9,000 *Students:* 955 UG; 200 PG
*Principal,* Prof. Chris Gaskell
*Secretary,* Theresa Chapman

**ROYAL COLLEGE OF ART (1967)**
Kensington Gore, London SW7 2EU T 020-7590 4444
W www.rca.ac.uk
*Students:* 1,670 PG (postgraduate only)
*Provost,* Sir James Dyson, CBE, FRS, FRENG
*Rector,* Dr Paul Thompson
*Registrar,* Corinne Smith

**ROYAL COLLEGE OF MUSIC (1882)**
Prince Consort Road, London SW7 2BS T 020-7591 4300
W www.rcm.ac.uk
*Fee:* £9,000 *Students:* 415 UG; 375 PG
*President,* HRH the Prince of Wales, KG, KT, GCB, OM
*Director,* Prof. Colin Lawson
*Registrar,* Elly Taylor

**UNIVERSITY OF ST ANDREWS (1413)**
St Andrews, Fife KY16 9AJ T 01334-476161
W www.st-andrews.ac.uk
*Fee:* £9,000 *Students:* 7,610 UG; 2,125 PG
*Chancellor,* Rt. Hon. Sir Menzies Campbell, CH, CBE, QC
*Vice-Chancellor and Principal,* Prof. Louise Richardson,
 FRSE
*Academic Registrar,* Ester Ruskuc

**UNIVERSITY OF ST MARK AND ST JOHN (2012)**
Derriford Road, Plymouth PL6 8BH T 01752-636700
W www.marjon.ac.uk
*Fee:* £9,000 *Students:* 2,215 UG; 540 PG
*Vice-Chancellor,* Prof. Cara Aitchison
*Secretary,* Dr Karen Cook

**UNIVERSITY OF SALFORD (1967)**
The Crescent, Salford M5 4WT
T 0161-295 5000 W www.salford.ac.uk
*Fee:* £9,000 *Students:* 14,910 UG; 3,575 PG
*Chancellor,* Dr Irene Khan
*Vice-Chancellor,* Prof. Martin Hall

**UNIVERSITY OF SHEFFIELD (1905)**
Western Bank, Sheffield S10 2TN T 0114-222 2000
W www.sheffield.ac.uk
*Fee:* £9,000 *Students:* 18,590 UG; 8,010 PG
*Chancellor,* Sir Peter Middleton, GCB
*Vice-Chancellor,* Prof. Sir Keith Burnett, CBE, DPHIL, FRS
*Registrar and Secretary,* vacant

**SHEFFIELD HALLAM UNIVERSITY (1992)**
City Campus, Howard Street, Sheffield S1 1WB T 0114-225 5555
W www.shu.ac.uk
*Fee:* £9,000 *Students:* 25,985 UG; 7,115 PG
*Chancellor,* Prof. Lord Winston, FRCOG, FRCP, FMedSci
*Vice-Chancellor,* Prof. Philip Jones
*Secretary and Registrar,* Elizabeth Winders

**UNIVERSITY OF SOUTH WALES (1992)**
Pontypridd CF37 1DL T 0345-576 0101 W www.southwales.ac.uk
*Fee:* £9,000 *Students:* 23,890 UG; 5,310 PG
*Chancellor,* Rt. Revd and Rt. Hon. Lord Williams of
 Oystermouth, PC, DPHIL
*Vice-Chancellor,* Prof. Julie Lydon, OBE
*University Secretary,* William Callaway

**UNIVERSITY OF SOUTHAMPTON (1952)**
University Road, Southampton SO17 1BJ T 023-8059 5000
W www.southampton.ac.uk
*Fee:* £9,000 *Students:* 16,195 UG; 7,840 PG
*Chancellor,* Dame Helen Alexander, DBE
*Vice-Chancellor,* Prof. Don Nutbeam
*Registrar,* Tessa Harrison

**SOUTHAMPTON SOLENT UNIVERSITY (2005)**
East Park Terrace, Southampton SO14 0YN T 023-8031 9039
W www.solent.ac.uk
*Fee:* £9,000 *Students:* 11,285 UG; 440 PG
*Chancellor,* Adm. Lord West of Spithead, GCB, DSC, PC
*Vice-Chancellor,* Prof. Graham Baldwin

**STAFFORDSHIRE UNIVERSITY (1992)**
College Road, Stoke-on-Trent ST4 2DE T 01782-294000
W www.staffs.ac.uk
*Fee:* £9,000 *Students:* 16,490 UG; 3,655 PG
*Chancellor,* Lord Stafford
*Vice-Chancellor,* Prof. Michael Gunn
*University Secretary,* Ken Sproston

**UNIVERSITY OF STIRLING (1967)**
Stirling FK9 4LA T 01786-473171 W www.stir.ac.uk
*Fee:* £6,750 *Students:* 7,675 UG; 3,415 PG
*Chancellor,* James Naughtie, OBE
*Vice-Chancellor,* Prof. Gerry McCormac, FRSE
*University Secretary,* Eileen Schofield

**UNIVERSITY OF STRATHCLYDE (1964)**
16 Richmond Street, Glasgow G1 1XQ T 0141-552 4400
W www.strath.ac.uk
*Fee:* £9,000 *Students:* 14,070 UG; 5,920 PG
*Chancellor,* Lord Smith of Kelvin, KT
*Vice-Chancellor,* Prof. Sir Jim McDonald, FRSE,
 FRENG
*Chief Operating Officer,* Hugh Hall

**UNIVERSITY OF SUNDERLAND (1992)**
Edinburgh Building, Chester Road, Sunderland SR1 3SD
T 0191-515 2000 W www.sunderland.ac.uk
*Fee:* £8,750 *Students:* 12,255 UG; 3,765 PG
*Chancellor,* Steve Cram, MBE
*Vice-Chancellor,* Shirley Atkinson

**UNIVERSITY OF SURREY (1966)**
Guildford GU2 7XH T 01483-300800 W www.surrey.ac.uk
*Fee:* £9,000 *Students:* 10,035 UG; 4.030 PG
*Chancellor,* HRH the Duke of Kent, KG, GCMG, GCVO
*Vice-Chancellor,* Prof. Sir Christopher Snowden, FRS,
 FRENG
*Registrar,* Dr David Ashton

**UNIVERSITY OF SUSSEX (1961)**
Sussex House, Brighton BN1 9RH T 01273-606755
W www.sussex.ac.uk
*Fee:* £9,000 *Students:* 10,145 UG; 3,490 PG
*Chancellor,* Sanjeev Bhaskar, OBE
*Vice-Chancellor,* Prof. Michael Farthing, FRCP
*Registrar,* John Duffy

**SWANSEA UNIVERSITY (1920)**
Singleton Park, Swansea SA2 8PP T 01792-205678
W www.swansea.ac.uk
*Fee:* £9,000 *Students:* 12,405 UG; 2,415 PG
*Chancellor,* Rt. Hon. Rhodri Morgan
*Vice-Chancellor,* Prof. Richard Davies
*Registrar,* Raymond Ciborowski

TEESSIDE UNIVERSITY (1992)
Middlesbrough TS1 3BA T 01642-218121
W www.tees.ac.uk
*Fee:* £9,000 *Students:* 16,070 UG; 1,995 PG
*Chancellor,* Lord Sawyer
*Vice-Chancellor,* Prof. Paul Croney, CBE
*University Secretary,* Prof. Liz Holey

UNIVERSITY OF ULSTER (1984)
Cromore Road, Coleraine, Co. Londonderry BT52 1SA
T 028-7012 3456 W www.ulster.ac.uk
*Fee:* £6,200 *Students:* 20,335 UG; 5,865 PG
*Chancellor,* James Nesbitt
*Vice-Chancellor,* Prof. Alastair Adair
*University Secretary,* Eamon Mullan

UNIVERSITY OF WALES, TRINITY SAINT DAVID
(1828)
Carmarthen Campus, Carmarthen SA31 3EP
T 01267-676767 W www.uwtsd.ac.uk
*Fee:* £9,000 *Students:* 9,280 UG; 2,040 PG
*Chancellor,* HRH the Prince of Wales, KG, KT, GCB, OM
*Vice-Chancellor,* Prof. Medwin Hughes

UNIVERSITY OF WARWICK (1965)
Coventry CV4 7AL T 024-7652 3523 W www.warwick.ac.uk
*Fee:* £9,000 *Students:* 14,725 UG; 10,520 PG
*Chancellor,* Sir Richard Lambert
*Vice-Chancellor,* Prof. Sir Nigel Thrift, PHD, DSc, FBA
*Registrar,* Ken Sloan

UNIVERSITY OF WEST LONDON (1992)
St Mary's Road, Ealing, London W5 5RF T 0800-036 8888
W www.uwl.ac.uk
*Fee:* £9,000 *Students:* 9,785 UG; 1,520 PG
*Chancellor,* Laurence Geller, CBE
*Vice-Chancellor,* Prof. Peter John
*Registrar,* Prof. Kathryn Mitchell

UNIVERSITY OF WESTMINSTER (1992)
309 Regent Street, London W1B 2HW T 020-7911 5000
W www.westminster.ac.uk
*Fee:* £9,000 *Students:* 15,733 UG; 4,460 PG
*Chancellor,* Lord Paul, PC
*Vice-Chancellor and Rector,* Prof. Geoffrey Petts
*Registrar and Secretary,* Suzanne Enright

UNIVERSITY OF THE WEST OF ENGLAND (1992)
Frenchay Campus, Coldharbour Lane, Bristol BS16 1QY
T 0117-965 6261 W www.uwe.ac.uk

*Fee:* £9,000 *Students:* 21,500 UG; 5,545 PG
*Chancellor,* Sir Ian Carruthers, OBE
*Vice-Chancellor,* Prof. Steve West

UNIVERSITY OF THE WEST OF SCOTLAND (2007)
(Formed by the merger of the University of Paisley (1992)
with Bell College, Hamilton)
Paisley PA1 2BE T 0141-848 3000 W www.uws.ac.uk
*Fee:* £7,000 *Students:* 13,630 UG; 1,630 PG
*Chancellor,* Rt. Hon. Dame Elish Angiolini, DBE, QC
*Vice-Chancellor and Principal,* Prof. Craig Mahoney
*Registrar and Secretary,* Donna McMillan

UNIVERSITY OF WINCHESTER (2005)
Winchester SO22 4NR T 01962-841515 W www.winchester.ac.uk
*Fee:* £9,000 *Students:* 5,620 UG; 1,260 PG
*Chancellor,* Dame Mary Fagan, DCVO
*Vice-Chancellor,* Prof. Joy Carter
*Director of Student Recruitment and Marketing,* Dr Karen
  Pendlebury

UNIVERSITY OF WOLVERHAMPTON (1992)
Wulfruna Street, Wolverhampton WV1 1LY T 01902-321000
W www.wlv.ac.uk
*Fee:* £9,000 *Students:* 16,160 UG; 2,940 PG
*Chancellor,* Lord Paul, PC
*Vice-Chancellor,* Prof. Geoff Layer, OBE, FRSA
*Registrar,* Dr Emma Wedge

UNIVERSITY OF WORCESTER (2005)
Henwick Grove, Worcester WR2 6AJ T 01905-855000
W www.worcester.ac.uk
*Fee:* £9,000 *Students:* 8,885 UG; 1,410 PG
*Chancellor,* HRH the Duke of Gloucester, KG, GCVO
*Vice-Chancellor,* Prof. David Green
*Registrar,* John Ryan

UNIVERSITY OF YORK (1963)
Heslington, York YO10 5DD T 01904-320000 W www.york.ac.uk
*Fee:* £9,000 *Students:* 12,695 UG; 3,935 PG
*Chancellor,* Prof. Sir Malcolm Grant, CBE
*Vice-Chancellor,* Prof. Koen Lamberts, PHD
*Registrar,* Dr David Duncan, PHD

YORK ST JOHN UNIVERSITY (2006)
Lord Mayor's Walk, York YO31 7EX T 01904-624624
W www.yorksj.ac.uk
*Fee:* £9,000 *Students:* 5,535 UG; 885 PG
*Chancellor,* Most Revd and Rt. Hon. Archbishop of York
*Vice-Chancellor,* Prof. Karen Stanton
*Registrar,* Alison Kennel

# PROFESSIONAL EDUCATION

The organisations selected below provide specialist training, conduct examinations or are responsible for maintaining a register of those with professional qualifications in their sector, thereby controlling entry into a profession.

## EU RECOGNITION

It is possible for those with professional qualifications obtained in the UK to have these recognised in other European countries. Further information can be obtained from:
UK NARIC, Oriel House, Oriel Road, Cheltenham GL50 1XP
T 0871-330 7033 W www.ecctis.co.uk

## ACCOUNTANCY

*Salary range for chartered accountants:*
Certified £25,000 (starting), rising to £26,000–£45,000+ (qualified), £40,000–£100,000+ at senior levels
Management £28,000 (starting), £61,000 (average), £46,000–£129,000+ at senior levels
Public finance £18,000–£30,000 (starting), £32,000–£65,000 (qualified), £80,000+ at senior levels

Chartered Accountancy trainees can be school-leavers or graduates. They usually undertake a three-year training contract with an approved employer culminating in professional exams provided by ICAEW, ICAS or ICAI. Success in the exams and membership of one of the professional bodies – which includes continuous professional development and regulation – allows them to use the designation 'chartered accountant' and the letters ACA, FCA or CA.

The Association of Chartered Certified Accountants (ACCA) is the global body for professional accountants. The ACCA aims to offer business-relevant qualifications to students in a range of business sectors and countries seeking a career in accountancy, finance and management. The ACCA Qualification consists of up to 14 examinations, practical experiences and a professional ethics module. Chartered certified accountants can use the designatory letters ACCA.

Chartered global management accountants focus on accounting for businesses, and most do not work in accountancy practices but in industry, commerce, not-for-profit and public-sector organisations. Graduates who have not studied a business or accounting degree must complete the Chartered Institute of Management Accountants (CIMA) Certificate in Business Accounting before progressing to the CIMA Professional Qualification, which requires three years of practical experience, nine examinations and a pass in the Institute's Test of Professional Competence in Management Accounting (TOPCIMA). In May 2011, CIMA and the American Institute of Certified Public Accountants (AICPA) agreed on the creation of a new professional designation, the Chartered Global Management Accountant (CGMA), which represents a worldwide standard of professional excellence in management accounting.

The Chartered Institute of Public Finance and Accountancy (CIPFA) is the professional body for people working in public finance. Chartered public finance accountants usually work for public bodies, but they can also work in the private sector. To gain chartered public finance accountant status (CPFA), trainees must complete a professional qualification in public sector accountancy. In addition, CIPFA also offers a postgraduate diploma for those already working in leadership positions.

ASSOCIATION OF CHARTERED CERTIFIED ACCOUNTANTS (ACCA), 29 Lincoln's Inn Fields, London WC2A 3EE T 0141-582 2000 E info@accaglobal.com W www.accaglobal.com
*Chief Executive,* Helen Brand
CHARTERED INSTITUTE OF MANAGEMENT ACCOUNTANTS (CIMA), 26 Chapter Street, London SW1P 4NP T 020-8849 2251
E cima.contact@cimaglobal.com W www.cimaglobal.com
*Chief Executive,* Charles Tilley
CHARTERED INSTITUTE OF PUBLIC FINANCE AND ACCOUNTANCY (CIPFA), 77 Mansell Street, London E1 8AN T 020-7543 5600 E customerliaison@cipfa.org W www.cipfa.org
*Chief Executive,* Rob Whiteman
INSTITUTE OF CHARTERED ACCOUNTANTS IN ENGLAND AND WALES (ICAEW), Chartered Accountants' Hall, Moorgate Place, London EC2R 6EA T 020-7920 8100 E contactus@icaew.com W www.icaew.com
*Chief Executive,* Michael Izza
INSTITUTE OF CHARTERED ACCOUNTANTS IN IRELAND (ICAI), 47 Pearse Street, Dublin T 0353-1637 7200 W www.charteredaccountants.ie
*Chief Executive,* Pat Costello
INSTITUTE OF CHARTERED ACCOUNTANTS OF SCOTLAND (ICAS), CA House, 21 Haymarket Yards, Edinburgh EH12 5BH T 0131-347 0100 E enquiries@icas.org.uk W www.icas.com
*Chief Executive,* Anton Colella

## ACTUARIAL SCIENCE

*Salary range:* £25,000–£35,000 for graduate trainees; £40,000–£55,000 after qualification; £60,000–£100,000+ for senior roles; £185,000+ for senior directors

Actuaries apply financial and statistical theories to solve business problems. These problems usually involve analysing future financial events in order to assess investment risks. To qualify, graduate trainees must complete 15 exams and three years worth of actuarial work-based training; most graduate trainees take between three and six years to qualify. Students can become Associate members of the Institute and Faculty of Actuaries (IFoA) and gain the right to describe themselves as an actuary and to use the letters AIA or AFA. Members of the profession who wish to continue their studies to an advanced level, or who specialise in a particular actuarial field, may take further specialist exams to qualify as a Fellow and bear the designations FIA or FFA.

The IFoA is the UK's chartered professional body dedicated to educating, developing and regulating actuaries based both in the UK and internationally. The IFoA represent and regulate their members and oversee their education at all stages of qualification and development throughout their careers.

The Financial Reporting Council (FRC) is the unified independent regulator for corporate reporting, auditing, actuarial practice, corporate governance and the professionalism of accountants and actuaries. The FRC's Board for Actuarial Standards sets and maintains technical actuarial standards independently of the profession, while the Professional Oversight Board of the FRC oversees the regulation of the accountancy and actuarial professions by their respective professional bodies. The Accountancy and

Actuarial Discipline Board operates an investigation and discipline scheme for members of the profession who wish to raise issues affecting UK public interest.

**FINANCIAL REPORTING COUNCIL (FRC)**, 8th Floor, 125 London Wall, London EC2Y 5AS **T** 020-7492 2300 **E** enquiries@frc.org.uk **W** www.frc.org.uk
*Chief Executive*, Stephen Haddrill

**INSTITUTE AND FACULTY OF ACTUARIES**, Staple Inn Hall, High Holborn, London WC1V 7QJ **T** 020-7632 2100 **W** www.actuaries.org.uk
*Chief Executive*, Derek Cribb

## ARCHITECTURE
*Salary range:* £15,000–£26,000 during training; newly registered £26,000–£35,000; project architect and senior roles £35,000–£80,000+

It takes a minimum of seven years to become an architect, involving three stages: a three-year first degree, a two-year second degree or diploma and two years of professional experience followed by the successful completion of a professional practice examination.

The Architects Registration Board (ARB) is the independent regulator for the profession. It was set up by an act of parliament in 1997 and is responsible for maintaining the register of UK architects, prescribing qualifications that lead to registration as an architect, investigating complaints about the conduct and competence of architects and ensuring that only those who are registered with ARB offer their services as an architect. It is only following registration with ARB that an architect can apply for chartered membership of the Royal Institute of British Architects (RIBA). RIBA, the UK body for architecture and the architectural profession, received its royal charter in 1837 and validates courses at over 40 schools of architecture in the UK; it also validates overseas courses. RIBA provides support and guidance for its members in the form of training, technical services and events and sets standards for the education of architects.

The Chartered Institute of Architectural Technologists is the international qualifying body for Chartered Architectural Technologists (MCIAT) and Architectural Technicians (TCIAT).

**ARCHITECTS REGISTRATION BOARD (ARB)** 8 Weymouth Street, London W1W 5BU **T** 020-7580 5861 **E** info@arb.org.uk **W** www.arb.org.uk
*Registrar and Chief Executive*, Karen Holmes

**CHARTERED INSTITUTE OF ARCHITECTURAL TECHNOLOGISTS** 397 City Road, London EC1V 1NH **T** 020-7278 2206 **E** info@ciat.org.uk **W** www.ciat.org.uk
*Chief Executive*, Francesca Berriman

**ROYAL INCORPORATION OF ARCHITECTS IN SCOTLAND** 15 Rutland Square, Edinburgh EH1 2BE **T** 0131-229 7545 **E** info@rias.org.uk **W** www.rias.org.uk
*Secretary*, Neil Baxter

**ROYAL INSTITUTE OF BRITISH ARCHITECTS (RIBA)** 66 Portland Place, London W1B 1AD **T** 020-7580 5533 **E** info@riba.org **W** www.architecture.com
*Chief Executive*, Harry Rich

## ENGINEERING
*Salary range:*
Civil/structural £23,500–£32,000 (graduate); £40,000–£70,000 with experience (chartered status, in senior posts)
Chemical £29,500 average (graduate); £70,000+ (chartered)
Electrical £20,000–£25,000 (graduate); £28,000–£40,000 with experience; £40,000–£55,000+ (chartered)

The Engineering Council holds the national registers of Engineering Technicians (EngTech), Incorporated Engineers (IEng), Chartered Engineers (CEng) and Information and Communication Technology Technicians (ICTTech). It also sets and maintains the internationally recognised standards of competence and ethics that govern the award and retention of these titles.

To apply for the EngTech, IEng, CEng or ICTTech titles an individual must be a member of one of the 36 engineering institutions and societies (listed below) currently licensed by the Engineering Council to assess candidates. Applicants must demonstrate that they possess a range of technical and personal competences and are committed to keeping these up-to-date.

**ENGINEERING COUNCIL**, Aldgate House, 33 Aldgate High Street, London EC3N 1EN **T** 020-3206 0500 **E** info@engc.org.uk **W** www.engc.org.uk
*Chief Executive*, Jon Prichard

### LICENSED MEMBERS
*BCS – The Chartered Institute for IT* **W** www.bcs.org
*British Institute of Non-Destructive Testing* **W** www.bindt.org
*Chartered Institute of Plumbing and Heating Engineering* **W** www.ciphe.org.uk
*Chartered Institution of Building Services Engineers* **W** www.cibse.org
*Chartered Institution of Highways and Transportation* **W** www.ciht.org.uk
*Chartered Institution of Water and Environmental Management* **W** www.ciwem.org.uk
*Energy Institute* **W** www.energyinst.org
*Institute of Acoustics* **W** www.ioa.org.uk
*Institute of Cast Metals Engineers* **W** www.icme.org.uk
*Institute of Healthcare Engineering and Estate Management* **W** www.iheem.org.uk
*Institute of Highway Engineers* **W** www.theihe.org
*Institute of Marine Engineering, Science and Technology* **W** www.imarest.org
*Institute of Materials, Minerals and Mining* **W** www.iom3.org
*Institute of Measurement and Control* **W** www.instmc.org.uk
*Institute of Physics* **W** www.iop.org
*Institute of Physics and Engineering in Medicine* **W** www.ipem.ac.uk
*Institute of Water* **W** www.instituteofwater.org.uk
*Institution of Agricultural Engineers* **W** www.iagre.org
*Institution of Chemical Engineers* **W** www.icheme.org
*Institution of Civil Engineers* **W** www.ice.org.uk
*Institution of Diesel and Gas Turbine Engineers* **W** www.idgte.org
*Institution of Engineering Designers* **W** www.ied.org.uk
*Institution of Engineering and Technology* **W** www.theiet.org
*Institution of Fire Engineers* **W** www.ife.org.uk
*Institution of Gas Engineers and Managers* **W** www.igem.org.uk
*Institution of Lighting Professionals* **W** www.theilp.org
*Institution of Mechanical Engineers* **W** www.imeche.org
*Institution of Railway Signal Engineers* **W** www.irse.org
*Institution of Royal Engineers* **W** www.instre.org
*Institution of Structural Engineers* **W** www.istructe.org
*Nuclear Institute* **W** www.nuclearinst.com
*Royal Aeronautical Society* **W** www.aerosociety.com
*Royal Institution of Naval Architects* **W** www.rina.org.uk
*Society of Environmental Engineers* **W** www.environmental.org.uk
*Society of Operations Engineers* **W** www.soe.org.uk
*The Welding Institute* **W** www.theweldinginstitute.com

## HEALTHCARE
### CHIROPRACTIC
*Salary range:* £20,000–£40,000 starting salary; with own practice £50,000–£70,000

Chiropractors diagnose and treat conditions caused by problems with joints, ligaments, tendons and nerves of the body. The General Chiropractic Council (GCC) is the independent statutory regulatory body for chiropractors and its role and remit is defined in the Chiropractors Act 1994. The GCC sets the criteria for the recognition of chiropractic degrees and for standards of proficiency and conduct. Details of the institutions offering degree programmes are available on the GCC website (see below). It is illegal for anyone in the UK to use the title 'chiropractor' unless registered with the GCC.

The British Chiropractic Association, Scottish Chiropractic Association, McTimoney Chiropractic Association and United Chiropractic Association are the representative bodies for the profession and are sources of further information.

**BRITISH CHIROPRACTIC ASSOCIATION,**
59 Castle Street, Reading RG1 7SN **T** 0118-950 5950
**E** enquiries@chiropractic-uk.co.uk
**W** www.chiropractic-uk.co.uk
*Executive Director,* Satjit Singh
**GENERAL CHIROPRACTIC COUNCIL (GCC),**
44 Wicklow Street, London WC1X 9HL **T** 020-7713 5155
**E** enquiries@gcc-uk.org **W** www.gcc-uk.org
*Chief Executive and Registrar,* David Howell, CB, OBE
**SCOTTISH CHIROPRACTIC ASSOCIATION,** 1 Chisholm
Avenue, Bishopton, Renfrewshire PA7 5JH **T** 0141-404 0260
**E** admin@sca-chiropractic.org **W** www.sca-chiropractic.org
*Administrator,* Morag Cairns

**DENTISTRY**
*Salary range: see* Health: Employees and Salaries

The General Dental Council (GDC) is the organisation that regulates dental professionals in the UK. All dentists, dental hygienists, dental therapists, dental technicians, clinical dental technicians, dental nurses and orthodontic therapists must be registered with the GDC to work in the UK.

There are various different routes to qualify for registration as a dentist, including holding a degree from a UK university, completing the GDC's qualifying examination or holding a relevant European Economic Area or overseas diploma. The GDC's purpose is to protect the public through the regulation of UK dental professionals. It keeps up-to-date registers of dental professionals, works to set standards of dental practice, behaviour and education, and helps to protect patients by hearing complaints and taking action against professionals where necessary.

Founded in 1880, the British Dental Association (BDA) is the professional association and trade union for dentists in the UK. It represents dentists working in general practice, in community and hospital settings, in academia, research and the armed forces, and includes dental students.

**BRITISH DENTAL ASSOCIATION (BDA),**
64 Wimpole Street, London W1G 8YS **T** 020-7935 0875
**E** enquiries@bda.org **W** www.bda.org
*Chief Executive,* Peter Ward
**GENERAL DENTAL COUNCIL (GDC),** 37 Wimpole Street,
London W1G 8DQ **T** 020-7167 6000 **E** information@gdc-uk.org
**W** www.gdc-uk.org
*Chief Executive,* Evlynne Gilvarry

**MEDICINE**
*Salary range: see* Health: Employees and Salaries

The General Medical Council (GMC) regulates medical education and training in the UK. This covers undergraduate study (usually five years), the two-year foundation programme taken by doctors directly after graduation and all subsequent postgraduate study, including specialty and GP training.

All doctors must be registered with the GMC, which is responsible for protecting the public. It does this by promoting high standards of medical education and training, fostering good medical practice, keeping a register of qualified doctors and taking action where a doctor's fitness to practise is in doubt. Doctors are eligible for full registration upon successful completion of the first year of training after graduation.

Following the foundation programme, many doctors undertake specialist training (provided by the colleges and faculties listed below) to become either a consultant or a GP. Once specialist training has been completed, doctors are awarded the Certificate of Completion of Training (CCT) and are eligible to be placed on either the GMC's specialist register or its GP register.

**GENERAL MEDICAL COUNCIL (GMC),** 350 Euston Road,
London NW1 3JN **T** 0161-923 6602 **E** gmc@gmc-uk.org
**W** www.gmc-uk.org
*Chief Executive,* Niall Dickson
**WORSHIPFUL SOCIETY OF APOTHECARIES OF**
**LONDON,** Black Friars Lane, London EC4V 6EJ
**T** 020-7236 1189 **E** clerk@apothecaries.org
**W** www.apothecaries.org
*Master,* Dr J. Moore-Gillon

**SPECIALIST TRAINING COLLEGES AND FACULTIES**
*College of Emergency Medicine* **W** www.rcem.ac.uk
*Faculty of Pharmaceutical Medicine* **W** www.fpm.org.uk
*Faculty of Public Health* **W** www.fph.org.uk
*Royal College of Anaesthetists* **W** www.rcoa.ac.uk
*Royal College of General Practitioners* **W** www.rcgp.org.uk
*Royal College of Obstetricians and Gynaecologists*
**W** www.rcog.org.uk
*Royal College of Opthalmologists* **W** www.rcophth.ac.uk
*Royal College of Paediatrics and Child Health*
**W** www.rcpch.ac.uk
*Royal College of Pathologists* **W** www.rcpath.org
*Royal College of Physicians, London* **W** www.rcplondon.ac.uk
*Royal College of Physicians and Surgeons of Glasgow*
**W** www.rcpsg.ac.uk
*Royal College of Physicians of Edinburgh* **W** www.rcpe.ac.uk
*Royal College of Psychiatrists* **W** www.rcpsych.ac.uk
*Royal College of Radiologists* **W** www.rcr.ac.uk
*Royal College of Surgeons of Edinburgh* **W** www.rcsed.ac.uk
*Royal College of Surgeons of England* **W** www.rcseng.ac.uk

**MEDICINE, SUPPLEMENTARY PROFESSIONS**
The standard of professional education for arts therapists, biomedical scientists, chiropodists and podiatrists, clinical scientists, dietitians, hearing aid dispensers, occupational therapists, operating department practitioners, orthoptists, paramedics, physiotherapists, practitioner psychologists, prosthetists and orthotists, radiographers, social workers in England and speech and language therapists are regulated by the Health and Care Professions Council (HCPC), which only registers those practitioners who meet certain standards of training, professional skills, behaviour and health. The HCPC can take action against professionals who do not meet these standards or falsely declare they are registered. Each profession regulated by the HCPC has at least one professional title that is protected by law.

**HEALTH AND CARE PROFESSIONS COUNCIL (HCPC),**
Park House, 184 Kennington Park Road, London SE11 4BU
**T** 0845-300 6184 **E** registration@hcpc-uk.org
**W** www.hcpc-uk.org
*Chief Executive and Registrar,* Marc Seale

## ART, DRAMA AND MUSIC THERAPIES

*Salary range:* £25,500–£34,500 (starting); £39,000–£47,000 with experience

An art, drama or music therapist encourages people to express their feelings and emotions through art, such as painting and drawing, drama or music. A postgraduate qualification in the relevant therapy is required. Details of accredited training programmes in the UK can be obtained from the following organisations:

BRITISH ASSOCIATION FOR MUSIC THERAPY,
24–27 White Lion Street, London N1 9PD **T** 020-7837 6100
**E** info@bamt.org **W** www.bamt.org
*Chair,* Donald Wetherick

BRITISH ASSOCIATION OF ART THERAPISTS,
24–27 White Lion Street, London N1 9PD **T** 020-7686 4216
**E** info@baat.org **W** www.baat.org
*Chief Executive,* Val Huet

BRITISH ASSOCIATION OF DRAMA THERAPISTS,
Waverley, Battledown Approach, Cheltenham,
Gloucestershire GL52 6RE **T** 0124-2235 5155
**E** info@badth.org.uk **W** www.badth.org.uk
*Chair,* John Hazlett Dickinson

## BIOMEDICAL SCIENCES

*Salary range:* £21,000–£28,000 (starting); £25,700–£34,500 with experience; £30,700–40,500 for senior roles

The Institute of Biomedical Science (IBMS) is the professional body for biomedical scientists in the UK. Biomedical scientists carry out investigations on tissue and body fluid samples to diagnose disease and monitor the progress of a patient's treatment. The IBMS sets quality standards for the profession through training, education, assessments, examinations and continuous professional development.

INSTITUTE OF BIOMEDICAL SCIENCE (IBMS),
12 Coldbath Square, London EC1R 5HL **T** 020-7713 0214
**E** mail@ibms.org **W** www.ibms.org
*Chief Executive,* Jill Rodney

## CHIROPODY AND PODIATRY

*Salary range:* £21,500–£40,500

Chiropodists and podiatrists assess, diagnose and treat problems of the lower leg and foot. The Society of Chiropodists and Podiatrists is the professional body and trade union for the profession. Qualifications granted and degrees recognised by the society are approved by the HCPC. HCPC registration is required in order to use the titles chiropodist and podiatrist.

SOCIETY OF CHIROPODISTS AND PODIATRISTS,
1 Fellmonger's Path, Tower Bridge Road, London SE1 3LY
**T** 020-7234 8620 **W** www.scpod.org
*Chief Executive,* Joanna Brown

## CLINICAL SCIENCE

*Salary range:* £25,500–£97,000+

Clinical scientists conduct tests in laboratories in order to diagnose and manage disease. The Association of Clinical Scientists is responsible for setting the criteria for competence of applicants to the HCPC's register and to present a Certificate of Attainment to candidates following a successful assessment. This certificate will allow direct registration with the HCPC.

ASSOCIATION OF CLINICAL SCIENTISTS,
c/o Association for Clinical Biochemistry, 130–132 Tooley Street,
London SE1 2TU **T** 020-7940 8960 **E** info@assclinsci.org
**W** www.assclinsci.org
*Chair,* Prof. Richard Lerski

## DIETETICS

*Salary range:* £21,500–£40,500

Dietitians advise patients on how to improve their health and counter specific health problems through diet. The British Dietetic Association, established in 1936, is the professional association for dietitians. Full membership is open to UK-registered dietitians, who must also be registered with the HCPC.

BRITISH DIETETIC ASSOCIATION, 5th Floor,
Charles House, 148–149 Great Charles Street Queensway,
Birmingham B3 3HT **T** 0121-200 8080 **E** info@bda.uk.com
**W** www.bda.uk.com
*Chief Executive,* Andy Burman

## OCCUPATIONAL THERAPY

*Salary range:* £21,400–£40,500; £63,000–£79,000 for consultancy roles

Occupational therapists work with people who have physical, mental and/or social problems, either from birth or as a result of accident, illness or ageing, and aim to make them as independent as possible. The professional qualification and eligibility for registration may be obtained upon successful completion of a validated course in any of the educational institutions approved by the College of Occupational Therapists, which is the professional body for occupational therapy in the UK. The courses are normally degree-level and based in higher education institutions.

COLLEGE OF OCCUPATIONAL THERAPISTS,
106–114 Borough High Street, London SE1 1LB
**T** 020-7357 6480 **W** www.cot.org.uk
*Chief Executive,* Julia Scott

## MENTAL HEALTH

*Salary range:*
Clinical psychologist £25,800, rising to £45,700–£81,000+ at senior levels
Counselling psychologist £25,800–£34,500 (starting), rising to £30,700–£40,500 (qualified) and up to £81,600 at senior levels
Educational psychologist £22,000, rising to £46,000 (fully qualified) and up to £63,500 at senior levels
Psychotherapist £21,600–£28,000 (starting), rising to £47,500 with experience

Psychologists and counsellors are mental health professionals who can work in a range of settings including prisons, schools and hospitals. The British Psychological Society (BPS) is the representative body for psychology and psychologists in the UK. The BPS is responsible for the development, promotion and application of psychology for the public good. The Association of Educational Psychologists (AEP) represents the interests of educational psychologists. The British Association for Counselling and Psychotherapy (BACP) sets educational standards and provides professional support to counsellors, pyschotherapists and others working in counselling, pyschotherapy or counselling-related roles. The BPS website provides more information on the different specialisations that may be pursued by psychologists.

ASSOCIATION OF EDUCATIONAL PSYCHOLOGISTS
(AEP), 4 The Riverside Centre, Frankland Lane, Durham
DH1 5TA **T** 0191-384 9512 **E** enquiries@aep.org.uk
**W** www.aep.org.uk
*General Secretary,* Kate Fallon

BRITISH ASSOCIATION FOR COUNSELLING
AND PSYCHOTHERAPY (BACP), BACP House,
15 St John's Business Park, Lutterworth, Leicestershire LE17 4HB
**T** 01455-883300 **E** bacp@bacp.co.uk **W** www.bacp.co.uk
*President,* Dr Michael Shooter, CBE

BRITISH PSYCHOLOGICAL SOCIETY (BPS),
St Andrews House, 48 Princess Road East, Leicester LE1 7DR
T 0116-254 9568 E enquiries@bps.org.uk W www.bps.org.uk
*President,* Prof. Jamie Hacker Hughes

ORTHOPTICS
*Salary range:* £21,500 (graduate), rising to £30,700–£81,500 in senior posts

Orthoptists undertake the diagnosis and treatment of all types of squint and other anomalies of binocular vision, working in close collaboration with ophthalmologists. The all-graduate workforce comes from three universities: the University of Liverpool, the University of Sheffield and Glasgow Caledonian University.
BRITISH AND IRISH ORTHOPTIC SOCIETY,
Salisbury House, Station Road, Cambridge CB1 2LA
T 01353-665541 E bios@orthoptics.org.uk
W www.orthoptics.org.uk
*Chair,* Lesley-Anne Baxter

PARAMEDICAL SERVICES
*Salary range:* £21,500–£34,500

Paramedics deal with accidents and emergencies, assessing patients and carrying out any specialist treatment and care needed in the first instance. The body that represents ambulance professionals is the College of Paramedics.
COLLEGE OF PARAMEDICS, The Exchange, Express Park,
Bristol Road, Bridgwater TA6 4RR T 01278-420014
E membership@collegeofparamedics.co.uk
W www.collegeofparamedics.co.uk
*Chief Executive,* Dave Hodge

PHYSIOTHERAPY
*Salary range:* £21,500–£40,500

Physiotherapists are concerned with movement and function and deal with problems arising from injury, illness and ageing. Full-time three- or four-year degree courses are available at around 36 higher education institutions in the UK. Information about courses leading to state registration is available from the Chartered Society of Physiotherapy.
CHARTERED SOCIETY OF PHYSIOTHERAPY,
14 Bedford Row, London WC1R 4ED T 020-7306 6666
W www.csp.org.uk
*Chief Executive,* Karen Middleton, CBE

PROSTHETICS AND ORTHOTICS
*Salary range:* £21,000 on qualification, up to £67,000 as a consultant

Prosthetists provide artificial limbs, while orthotists provide devices to support or control a part of the body. It is necessary to obtain an honours degree to become a prosthetist or orthotist. Training is centred at the University of Salford and the University of Strathclyde.
BRITISH ASSOCIATION OF PROSTHETISTS AND
ORTHOTISTS, Sir James Clark Building,
Abbey Mill Business Centre, Paisley PA1 1TJ T 0141-561 7217
E enquiries@bapo.com W www.bapo.com
*Chair,* Lynne Rowley

RADIOGRAPHY
*Salary range:* £21,000–£40,000, rising to £67,800 in senior posts

In order to practise both diagnostic and therapeutic radiography in the UK, it is necessary to have successfully completed a course of education and training recognised by the HCPC. Such courses are offered by around 24 universities throughout the UK and lead to the award of a degree in radiography. Further information is available from the Society and College of Radiographers, the trade union and professional body which represents the whole of the radiographic workforce in the UK.
SOCIETY AND COLLEGE OF RADIOGRAPHERS,
207 Providence Square, Mill Street, London SE1 2EW
T 020-7740 7200 W www.sor.org
*Chief Executive,* Richard Evans

SPEECH AND LANGUAGE THERAPY
*Salary range:* £21,500–£40,500

Speech and language therapists (SLTs) work with people with communication, swallowing, eating and drinking problems. The Royal College of Speech and Language Therapists is the professional body for speech and language therapists and support workers. Alongside the HCPC, it accredits education and training courses leading to qualification.
ROYAL COLLEGE OF SPEECH AND LANGUAGE
THERAPISTS, 2 White Hart Yard, London SE1 1NX
T 020-7378 1200 E info@rcslt.org W www.rcslt.org
*Chief Executive,* Kamini Gadhok, MBE

NURSING
*Salary range: see* Health: Employees and Salaries

In order to practise in the UK, all nurses and midwives must be registered with the Nursing and Midwifery Council (NMC). The NMC is a statutory regulatory body that establishes and maintains standards of education, training, conduct and performance for nursing and midwifery. Courses leading to registration are currently at a minimum of degree level. All take a minimum of three years if undertaken full-time. The NMC approves programmes run jointly by higher education institutions with their healthcare service partners who offer clinical placements. The nursing part of the register has four fields of practice: adult, children's (paediatric), learning disability and mental health nursing. In most cases students must select one specific field to study before applying to an institution. Some universities run courses which offer the simultaneous study of two nursing fields. In addition, those studying to become adult nurses gain experience of nursing in relation to medicine, surgery, maternity care and nursing in the home. The NMC also sets standards for programmes leading to registration as a midwife and a range of post-registration courses including specialist practice programmes, nurse prescribing and those for teachers of nursing and midwifery. The NMC has a part of the register for specialist community public health nurses and approves programmes for health visitors, occupational health nurses and school nurses.
The Royal College of Nursing is the largest professional union for nursing in the UK, representing qualified nurses, midwives, healthcare assistants and nursing students in the NHS and the independent sector.
NURSING AND MIDWIFERY COUNCIL (NMC),
23 Portland Place, London W1B 1PZ T 020-7637 7181
E communications@nmc-uk.org W www.nmc-uk.org
*Chief Executive and Registrar,* Dame Janet Finch
ROYAL COLLEGE OF NURSING,
20 Cavendish Square, London W1G 0RN
T 020-7409 3333 W www.rcn.org.uk
*Chief Executive and General Secretary,* Dr Peter Carter

## OPTOMETRY AND DISPENSING OPTICS

*Salary range:*
Optometrist £17,000–£60,000+, up to £81,500 for consultant posts
Dispensing Optician £16,000–£35,000+

There are various routes to qualification as a dispensing optician. Qualification takes three years in total, and can be completed by combining a distance learning course or day release while working as a trainee under the supervision of a qualified and registered optician. Alternatively, students can do a two-year full-time course followed by one year of supervised practice with a qualified and registered optician. Training must be done at a training establishment approved by the regulatory body – the General Optical Council (GOC). There are five training establishments which are approved by the GOC: ABDO (Association of British Dispensing Opticians) College, Anglia Ruskin University, Bradford College, City and Islington College and Glasgow Caledonian University. After the completion of training to fit contact lenses and attaining the ABDO Level 6 certificate in contact lens practice qualification, a Contact Lens Optician may apply to be included in the GOC Speciality Register. Students are also able to complete a Foundation or Undergraduate degree in Ophthalmic Dispensing, offered by ABDO in conjunction with Canterbury Christ Church University. All routes are concluded by professional qualifying examinations, successful completion of which leads to the awarding of the Level 6 Fellowship Diploma of the Association of British Dispensing Opticians (FBDO) by ABDO. FBDO holders are able to register with the GOC following the awarding of their diploma, with registration being compulsory for all practising dispensing opticians.

Continuing Education and Training (CET) is a statutory requirement for all registered dispensing opticians and contact lens opticians to retain GOC registration.

ASSOCIATION OF BRITISH DISPENSING OPTICIANS (ABDO), Godmersham Park, Godmersham, Canterbury, Kent CT4 7DT T 01227-738 829 E general@abdo.org.uk
W www.abdo.org.uk
*General Secretary,* Sir Anthony Garrett, CBE
COLLEGE OF OPTOMETRISTS, 42 Craven Street, London WC2N 5NG T 020-7839 6000
W www.college-optometrists.org
*Chief Executive,* Bryony Pawinska
GENERAL OPTICAL COUNCIL (GOC), 41 Harley Street, London W1G 8DJ T 020-7580 3898 E goc@optical.org
W www.optical.org
*Chair,* Gareth Hadley

## OSTEOPATHY

*Salary Range:* £20,000–£100,000+

Osteopathy is a system of diagnosis and treatment for a wide range of conditions. It works with the structure and function of the body, and is based on the principle that the well-being of an individual depends on the skeleton, muscles, ligaments and connective tissues functioning smoothly together. The General Osteopathic Council (GOsC) regulates the practice of osteopathy in the UK and maintains a register of those entitled to practise. It is a criminal offence for anyone to describe themselves as an osteopath unless they are registered with the GOsC.

To gain entry to the register, applicants must hold a recognised qualification from an osteopathic education institute accredited by the GOsC; this involves a four- to five-year honours degree programme combined with clinical training.

GENERAL OSTEOPATHIC COUNCIL (GOsC),
Osteopathy House, 176 Tower Bridge Road, London SE1 3LU
T 020-7357 6655 W www.osteopathy.org.uk
*Chief Executive and Registrar,* Tim Walker

## PHARMACY

*Salary range:* £20,000–£68,000+

Pharmacists are involved in the preparation and use of medicines, from the discovery of their active ingredients to their use by patients. Pharmacists also monitor the effects of medicines, both for patient care and for research purposes.

The General Pharmaceutical Council (GPhC) is the independent regulatory body for pharmacists in England, Scotland and Wales, having taken over the regulating function of the Royal Pharmaceutical Society in 2010. The GPhC maintains the register of pharmacists, pharmacy technicians and pharmacy premises; it also sets national standards for training, ethics, proficiency and continuing professional development. The Pharmaceutical Society of Northern Ireland (PSNI) performs the same role in Northern Ireland. In order to register, students must complete a four-year degree in pharmacy that is accredited by either the GPhC or the PSNI, followed by one year of pre-registration training at an approved pharmacy; they must then pass an entrance examination.

GENERAL PHARMACEUTICAL COUNCIL (GPhC),
25 Canada Square, London, E14 5LQ T 020-3713 8000
W www.pharmacyregulation.org
*Chief Executive and Registrar,* Duncan Rudkin
PHARMACEUTICAL SOCIETY OF NORTHERN
IRELAND (PSNI), 73 University Street, Belfast BT7 1HL
T 028-9032 6927 W www.psni.org.uk
*Chief Executive,* Trevor Patterson
ROYAL PHARMACEUTICAL SOCIETY,
66-68 East Smithfield, London, E1W 1AW T 020-7572 2737
E support@rpharms.com W www.rpharms.com
*Chief Executive,* Helen Gordon

## INFORMATION MANAGEMENT

*Salary range:* Archivist £21,000–£30,000 (starting), £30,000–£55,000+ in senior posts
Information Officer £17,000–£28,000 (starting); £26,000–£50,000+ in senior posts
Librarian £19,500–£23,500 (newly qualified); £23,500–£32,000 (chartered); £50,000+ in senior posts

The Chartered Institute of Library and Information Professionals (CILIP) is the leading professional body for librarians, information specialists and knowledge managers. The Archives and Records Association is the professional body for archivists and record managers. The Association of Special Libraries and Information Bureau (ASLIB) is a member association for people who manage information and knowledge in organisations across all sectors. ASLIB provides its members with access to leading publications in information and knowledge management, networking opportunities and professional development.

ARCHIVES AND RECORDS ASSOCIATION,
Prioryfield House, 20 Canon Street, Taunton, Somerset
TA1 1SW T 01823-327077 E ara@archives.org.uk
W www.archives.org.uk
*Chief Executive,* John Chambers
ASLIB, Howard House, Wagon Lane, Bingley, W. Yorks BD16 1WA
T 01274-777700 E support@aslib.com W www.aslib.com
*Director,* Rebecca Marsh

CHARTERED INSTITUTE OF LIBRARY AND
INFORMATION PROFESSIONALS (CILIP),
7 Ridgmount Street, London WC1E 7AE T 020-7255 0500
E info@cilip.org.uk W www.cilip.org.uk
*Chief Executive,* Nick Poole

## JOURNALISM

*Salary range:* £12,000–£15,000 (trainee); £22,250 for established journalists, rising to £35,000–£40,000 for those with over a decade's experience

The National Council for the Training of Journalists (NCTJ) accredits 83 courses for journalists run by a number of different education providers throughout the United Kingdom; it also provides professional support to journalists.
The Broadcast Journalism Training Council (BJTC) is an association of the UK's main broadcast journalism employers and accredits courses in broadcast journalism.
BROADCAST JOURNALISM TRAINING COUNCIL (BJTC), 130 East Hill, London, SW18 2HF
T 0845-600 8789 E sec@bjtc.org.uk W www.bjtc.org.uk
*Chair,* Jon Godel
NATIONAL COUNCIL FOR THE TRAINING OF
JOURNALISTS (NCTJ), The New Granary, Station Road, Newport, Saffron Walden, Essex CB11 3PL T 01799-544014
E info@nctj.com W www.nctj.com
*Chief Executive,* Joanne Butcher

## LAW

There are three types of practising lawyers: barristers, notaries and solicitors. Solicitors tend to work as a group in firms, and can be approached directly by individuals. They advise on a variety of legal issues and must decide the most appropriate course of action, if any. Notaries have all the powers of a solicitor other than the conduct of litigation. Most of them are primarily concerned with the preparation and authentication of documents for use abroad. Barristers are usually self-employed. If a solicitor believes that a barrister is required, he or she will instruct one on behalf of the client; the client will not have contact with the barrister without the solicitor being present.
When specialist expertise is needed, barristers give opinions on complex matters of law, and when clients require representation in the higher courts (crown courts, the high court, the court of appeal and the supreme court), barristers provide a specialist advocacy service. However, solicitors – who represent their clients in the lower courts such as magistrates' courts and county courts – can also apply for advocacy rights in the higher courts instead of briefing a barrister.

### THE BAR

*Salary range:* £12,000–£65,000 (pupillage); £25,000–£300,000 (qualified); £1,000,000+ with ten years experience

The governing body of the Bar of England and Wales is the General Council of the Bar, also known as the Bar Council. Since January 2006, the regulatory functions of the Bar Council (including regulating the education and training requirements for those wishing to enter the profession) have been undertaken by the Bar Standards Board.
In the first (or 'academic') stage of training, aspiring barristers must obtain a law degree of a good standard (at least second class). Alternatively, those with a non-law degree (at least second class) may complete a one-year full-time or two-year part-time Common Professional Examination (CPE) or Graduate Diploma in Law (GDL).
The second (vocational) stage is the completion of the Bar Professional Training Course (BPTC), which is available

at a number of validated institutions in the UK and must be applied for around one year in advance. All barristers must join one of the four Inns of Court prior to commencing the BPTC.
Students are 'called to the Bar' by their Inn after completion of the vocational stage, but cannot practise as a barrister until completion of the third stage, which is called 'pupillage'. Being called to the Bar does not entitle a person to practise as a barrister – successful completion of pupillage is now a prerequisite. Pupillage lasts for two six-month periods: the 'non-practising six' and the 'practising six'. The former consists of shadowing an experienced barrister, while the latter involves appearing in court as a barrister.
Admission to the Bar of Northern Ireland is controlled by the General Council of the Bar of Northern Ireland; admission as an Advocate to the Scottish Bar is through the Faculty of Advocates.
FACULTY OF ADVOCATES, Parliament House,
Edinburgh EH1 1RF T 0131-226 5071
W www.advocates.org.uk
*Dean,* Richard Keen, QC
GENERAL COUNCIL OF THE BAR (THE BAR
COUNCIL), 289–293 High Holborn, London WC1V 7HZ
T 020-7242 0082 E contactus@barcouncil.org.uk
W www.barcouncil.org.uk
*Chief Executive,* Stephen Crowne
BAR STANDARDS BOARD address as above
E contactus@barstandardsboard.org.uk
W www.barstandardsboard.org.uk
*Chair of the Bar Council,* Sir Andrew Burns, KCMG
GENERAL COUNCIL OF THE BAR OF NORTHERN
IRELAND, The Bar Library, 91 Chichester Street,
Belfast BT1 3JQ T 028-9024 1523 E contatc@barofni.com
W www.barlibrary.com
*Chief Executive,* David Mulholland

### THE INNS OF COURT

HONOURABLE SOCIETY OF GRAY'S INN,
8 South Square, London WC1R 5ET T 020-7458 7800
W www.graysinn.org.uk
*Under-Treasurer,* Brig. Anthony Faith, CBE
HONOURABLE SOCIETY OF LINCOLN'S INN,
Treasury Office, Lincoln's Inn, London WC2A 3TL
T 020-7405 1393 E mail@lincolnsinn.org.uk
W www.lincolnsinn.org.uk
*Under-Treasurer,* Mary Kerr
HONOURABLE SOCIETY OF THE INNER TEMPLE,
Inner Temple, London EC4Y 7HL T 020-7797 8250
W www.innertemple.org.uk
*Treasurer,* Rt. Hon. Lord Justice Moore-Bick
HONOURABLE SOCIETY OF THE MIDDLE TEMPLE,
Middle Temple Lane, London EC4Y 9AT T 020-7427 4800
E members@middletemple.org.uk
W www.middletemple.org.uk
*Chief Executive,* Guy Perricone

### NOTARIES PUBLIC

Notaries are qualified lawyers with a postgraduate diploma in notarial practice. Once a potential notary has passed the postgraduate diploma, they can petition the Court of Faculties for a 'faculty'. After the faculty is granted, the notary is able to practise; however, for the first two years this must be under the supervision of an experienced notary. The admission and regulation of notaries in England and Wales is a statutory function of the Faculty Office. This jurisdiction was confirmed by the Courts and Legal Services Act 1990. The Notaries Society of England and Wales is the representative body for practising notaries.

THE FACULTY OFFICE, 1 The Sanctuary, Westminster, London SW1P 3JT T 020-7222 5381
E faculty.office@1thesanctuary.com
W www.facultyoffice.org.uk
*Registrars,* Peter Beesley; Howard Dellar
THE NOTARIES SOCIETY OF ENGLAND AND WALES, PO Box 1023, Ipswich IP1 9XB
E admin@thenotariessociety.org.uk
W www.thenotariessociety.org.uk
*Secretary,* Christopher Vaughan

## SOLICITORS

*Salary range:* Trainee solicitors paid at least the national minimum wage; £25,000–£75,000 after qualification; £100,000+ (associate or partner)

Graduates from any discipline can train to be a solicitor; however, if the undergraduate degree is not in law, a one-year conversion course – either the Common Professional Examination (CPE) or the Graduate Diploma in Law (GDL) – must be completed. The next stage, and the beginning of the vocational phase, is the Legal Practice Course (LPC), which takes one year and is obligatory for both law and non-law graduates. The LPC provides professional instruction for prospective solicitors and can be completed on a full-time or part-time basis. Trainee solicitors then enter the final stage, which is a paid period of supervised work that lasts two years for full-time contracts. The employer that provides the training contract must be authorised by the Solicitors Regulation Authority (SRA) (the regulatory body of the Law Society of England and Wales), the Law Society of Scotland or the Law Society of Northern Ireland. The SRA also monitors the training contract to ensure that it provides the trainee with the expertise to qualify as a solicitor.

Conveyancers are specialist property lawyers, dealing with the legal processes involved in transferring buildings, land and associated finances from one owner to another. This was the sole responsibility of solicitors until 1987 but under current legislation it is now possible for others to train as conveyancers.
COUNCIL FOR LICENSED CONVEYANCERS (CLC), 16 Glebe Road, Chelmsford, Essex CM1 1QG T 01245-349599
E clc@clc-uk.org W www.clc-uk.org
*Chief Executive,* Sheila Kumar
THE LAW SOCIETY OF ENGLAND AND WALES, The Law Society's Hall, 113 Chancery Lane, London WC2A 1PL
T 020-7242 1222 W www.lawsociety.org.uk
*Chief Executive,* Catherine Dixon
LAW SOCIETY OF NORTHERN IRELAND, 96 Victoria Street, Belfast BT1 3GN T 028-9023 1614
W www.lawsoc-ni.org
*Chief Executive,* Alan Hunter
LAW SOCIETY OF SCOTLAND, 26 Drumsheugh Gardens, Edinburgh EH3 7YR T 0131-226 7411
E lawscot@lawscot.org.uk W www.lawscot.org.uk
*Chief Executive,* Lorna Jack
SOLICITORS REGULATION AUTHORITY (SRA), The Cube, 199 Wharfside Street, Birmingham B1 1RN
T 0370-606 2555 W www.sra.org.uk
*Chief Executive,* Paul Philip

## SOCIAL WORK

*Salary range:* £25,000–£34,000 (starting), rising to £42,000 as an experienced manager; £57,000+ at senior levels

Social workers tend to specialise in either adult or children's services. The HCPC obtained regulatory responsibility from the General Social Care Council in August 2012 and is responsible for setting standards of conduct and practice for social care workers and their employers; regulating the workforce and social work education and training. A degree or postgraduate qualification is needed in order to become a social worker. For more information *see* Social Welfare.
HEALTH AND CARE PROFESSIONS COUNCIL (HCPC), Park House, 184 Kennington Park Road, London SE11 4BU
T 0845-300 6184 W www.hcpc-uk.org
*Chief Executive and Registrar,* Marc Seale

## SURVEYING

*Salary range:* £18,500–£22,000 (starting); £45,000 (senior); up to £100,000 (partners and directors)

The Royal Institution of Chartered Surveyors (RICS) is the professional body that represents and regulates property professionals including land surveyors, valuers, auctioneers, quantity surveyors and project managers. Entry to the institution, following completion of a RICS-accredited degree, is through completion of the Assessment of Professional Competence (APC), which involves a period of practical training concluded by a final assessment of competence. Entry as a technical surveyor requires completion of the Assessment of Technical Competence (ATC), which mirrors the format of the APC. The different levels of RICS membership are MRICS (member) or FRICS (fellow) for chartered surveyors, and AssocRICS for associate members.

Relevant courses can also be accredited by the Chartered Institute of Building (CIOB), which represents managers working in a range of construction disciplines. The CIOB offers four levels of membership to those who satisfy its requirements: FCIOB (fellow), MCIOB (member), ICIOB (incorporated) and ACIOB (associate).
CHARTERED INSTITUTE OF BUILDING (CIOB), 1 Arlington Square, Downshire Way, Bracknell RG12 1WA
T 01344-630700 E reception@ciob.org.uk W www.ciob.org.uk
*Chief Executive,* Chris Blythe
ROYAL INSTITUTION OF CHARTERED SURVEYORS (RICS), RICS HQ, Parliament Square, London SW1P 3AD
T 024-7686 8555 E contactrics@rics.org W www.rics.org
*Chief Executive,* Sean Tompkins

## TEACHING

*Salary range:* £22,000–£57,000; headteacher £43,000–£113,000 (for more detailed information *see* Education: Employees and Salaries)

The General Teaching Councils (GTCs) for Northern Ireland, Scotland and Wales maintain registers of qualified teachers in their respective countries, and registration is a legal requirement in order to teach in local authority schools. On 1 April 2013, the Teaching Agency merged with the National College to form the National College for Teaching and Leadership (NCTL), an executive agency of the Department for Education, which became the awarding body for Qualified Teacher Status (QTS). UCAS Teacher Training (UTT) has replaced the Graduate Teacher Training Registry (GTTR) as the body through which to apply for postgraduate teacher training in the UK. To become a qualified teacher, all entrants must have a degree and gain QTS, which includes a minimum of 24 weeks in at least two different schools and academic study of teaching. Another route is through School-centred Initial Teacher Training (SCITT), where practical, hands-on teacher training is delivered by experienced, practising teachers in their own government-approved school.

Many courses also award an academic qualification known as the Postgraduate Certificate in Education (PGCE) in England and Wales and the Professional Graduate Diploma in Education (PGDE) in Scotland. Once training is completed, applicants spend a year in school as a newly qualified teacher (NQT).

Teachers in Further Education (FE) need not have QTS, though new entrants to FE may be required to work towards a specified FE qualification by employers. A range of courses are offered and usually require one year of study in addition to 100 hours of teaching experience. Similarly, academic staff in Higher Education require no formal teaching qualification, but are expected to obtain a qualification that meets standards set by the Higher Education Academy.

Details of routes to gaining QTS are available in England from the NCTL, the Department for Education and UTT, in Wales from the Teacher Training & Education Recruitment Forum Wales, in Scotland from Teach in Scotland and in Northern Ireland from the Department of Education.

The College of Teachers, under the terms of its royal charter, provides professional qualifications and membership to teachers and those involved in education in the UK and overseas.

COLLEGE OF TEACHERS, Institute of Education, 20 Bedford Way, London WC1H 0AL T 020-7911 5536 W www.collegeofteachers.ac.uk
*Chief Executive and Registrar,* Angela McFarlane
DEPARTMENT OF EDUCATION NORTHERN IRELAND, Rathgael House, Balloo Road, Bangor BT19 7PR T 028-9127 9279 E mail@deni.gov.uk W www.deni.gov.uk
*Permanent Secretary,* Paul Sweeney
GENERAL TEACHING COUNCIL FOR NORTHERN IRELAND, 3rd Floor, Albany House, 73–75 Great Victoria Street, Belfast BT2 7AF T 028-9033 3390 E info@gtcni.org.uk W www.gtcni.org.uk
*Chair,* Ivan Arbuthnot
GENERAL TEACHING COUNCIL FOR SCOTLAND, Clerwood House, 96 Clermiston Road, Edinburgh EH12 6UT T 0131-314 6000 E gtcs@gtcs.org.uk W www.gtcs.org.uk
*Chief Executive,* Kenneth Muir
EDUCATION WORKFORCE COUNCIL, 9th Floor, Eastgate House, 35–43 Newport Road, Cardiff CF24 0AB T 029-2046 0099 E information@ewc.wales W www.ewc.wales
*Chair,* Hayden Llewellyn
UCAS TEACHER TRAINING (UTT), Rosehill, New Barn Lane, Cheltenham GL52 3LZ T 0371-468 0469 W www.ucas.com/teacher-training
*Chief Executive,* Mary Curnock Cook, OBE

HIGHER EDUCATION ACADEMY, Innovation Way, York Science Park, Heslington, York YO10 5BR T 01904-717500 E enquiries@heacademy.ac.uk W www.heacademy.ac.uk
*Chief Executive,* Prof. Stephanie Marshall
NATIONAL COLLEGE FOR TEACHING AND LEADERSHIP, Triumph Road, Nottingham NG8 1DH T 0345-609 0009 E college.enquiries@bt.com W www.nationalcollege.org.uk
*Chief Executive,* Charlie Taylor

## VETERINARY MEDICINE
*Salary range:* £21,000–£53,000+

The regulatory body for veterinary surgeons in the UK is the Royal College of Veterinary Surgeons (RCVS), which keeps the register of those entitled to practise veterinary medicine, the register of veterinary nurses and veterinary practice premises (on behalf of the Veterinary Medicines Directorate). Holders of recognised degrees from any of the seven UK university veterinary schools that have been approved by the RCUS or from certain EU or overseas universities are entitled to be registered, and holders of certain other degrees may take a statutory membership examination. The UK's RCUS-approved veterinary schools are located at the University of Bristol, the University of Cambridge, the University of Edinburgh, the University of Glasgow, the University of Liverpool, the University of Nottingham and the Royal Veterinary College in London; all veterinary degrees last for five years except that offered at Cambridge, which lasts for six.

The British Veterinary Association is the national representative body for the UK veterinary profession. The British Veterinary Nursing Association is the professional body representing veterinary nurses.
BRITISH VETERINARY ASSOCIATION, 7 Mansfield Street, London W1G 9NQ T 020-7636 6541 E bvahq@bva.co.uk W www.bva.co.uk
*Chief Executive,* David Calpin
BRITISH VETERINARY NURSING ASSOCIATION, 82 Greenway Business Centre, Harlow Business Park, Harlow CM19 5QE T 01279-408644 E bvna@bvna.co.uk W www.bvna.org.uk
*Honorary Secretary,* Lucy Hayne
ROYAL COLLEGE OF VETERINARY SURGEONS (RCVS), Belgravia House, 62–64 Horseferry Road, London SW1P 2AF T 020-7222 2001 E info@rcvs.org.uk W www.rcvs.org.uk
*Registrar,* Nick Stace

# INDEPENDENT SCHOOLS

Independent schools (non-maintained mainstream schools) charge fees and are owned and managed under special trusts, with profits being used for the benefit of the schools concerned. In 2013–14 there were 2,497 non-maintained mainstream schools in the UK, educating around 623,000 pupils, or around 6.3 per cent of the total school-age population. The number of pupils at non-maintained mainstream schools as at January 2015 was:

| | |
|---|---|
| UK | 623,186 |
| England | 582,866 |
| Wales | 8,991 |
| Scotland | 30,687 |
| Northern Ireland | 642 |

The Independent Schools Council (ISC), formed in 1974, acts on behalf of the seven independent schools' associations which constitute it. These associations are:

Association of Governing Bodies of Independent Schools (AGBIS)
Girls' Schools Association (GSA)
Headmasters' & Headmistresses' Conference (HMC)
Independent Association of Prep Schools (IAPS)
Independent Schools Association (ISA)
Independent Schools' Bursars Association (ISBA)
The Society of Heads

In 2014–15 there were 517,113 pupils being educated in 1,267 schools in membership of associations within the Independent Schools Council (ISC). Most schools not in membership of an ISC association are likely to be privately owned. The Independent Schools Inspectorate (ISI) was demerged from ISC with effect from 1 January 2008 and is legally and operationally independent of ISC. ISI works as an accredited inspectorate of schools in membership of the ISC associations under a framework agreed with the Department for Education (DfE). A school must pass an ISI accreditation inspection to qualify for membership of an association within ISC.

In 2014 at GCSE 60.6 per cent of all exams taken by candidates in ISC associations' member schools achieved either an A\* or A grade (compared to the national average of 21.3 per cent), and at A-level 19.2 per cent of entries were awarded an A\* grade (national average, 8.2 per cent). In 2014–15 a total of 167,798 (33.3 per cent) pupils at schools in ISC associations received help with their fees, mainly in the form of bursaries and scholarships from the schools. ISC schools provided more than £700m of assistance with fees.

INDEPENDENT SCHOOLS COUNCIL
First Floor, 27 Queen Anne's Gate, London SW1H 9BU
T 020-7766 7070 W www.isc.co.uk

The list of schools below was compiled from the Independent Schools Yearbook 2014–15 (ed. Judy Mott, published by Bloomsbury Publishing) which includes schools whose heads are members of one of the ISC's five Heads' Associations. Further details are available online (W www.isyb.co.uk).

The fees shown below represent the upper limit payable for the year 2014–15.

| School | Web Address | Termly Fees Day | Board | Head |
|---|---|---|---|---|
| **ENGLAND** | | | | |
| Abbey Gate College, Cheshire | www.abbeygatecollege.co.uk | £3,677 | – | Mrs T. Pollard |
| The Abbey School, Berks | www.theabbey.co.uk | £4,830 | – | Mrs R. Dent |
| Abbots Bromley School, Staffs | www.abbotsbromley.net | £5,119 | £8,575 | Mrs V. Musgrave |
| Abbot's Hill School, Herts | www.abbotshill.herts.sch.uk | £5,444 | – | Mrs E. Thomas |
| Abbotsholme School, Derbys | www.abbotsholme.co.uk | £6,735 | £9,890 | S. Fairclough |
| Abingdon School, Oxon | www.abingdon.org.uk | £5,550 | £11,730 | Miss O. Lusk |
| Ackworth School, W. Yorks | www.ackworthschool.com | £4,285 | £7,703 | A. Maree |
| Adcote School, Shrops | www.adcoteschool.co.uk | £4,573 | £8,351 | G. Wright |
| AKS, Lancs | www.arnoldkeqms.com | £3,264 | – | M. Walton |
| Aldenham School, Herts | www.aldenham.com | £6,663 | £9,707 | J. Fowler |
| Alderley Edge School for Girls, Cheshire | www.aesg.co.uk | £3,426 | – | Mrs S. Goff |
| Alleyn's School, London SE22 | www.alleyns.org.uk | £5,529 | – | Dr G. Savage |
| Ampleforth College, N. Yorks | www.college.ampleforth.org.uk | £7,047 | £10,441 | D. Lambon |
| Ardingly College, W. Sussex | www.ardingly.com | £7,505 | £10,120 | B. Figgis |
| Ashford School, Kent | www.ashfordschool.co.uk | £5,200 | £10,450 | M. Buchanan |
| Ashville College, N. Yorks | www.ashville.co.uk | £4,220 | £8,420 | D. Lauder |
| Austin Friars St Monica's School, Cumbria | www.austinfriars.cumbria.sch.uk | £4,193 | – | M. Harris |
| Bablake School, W. Midlands | www.bablake.com | £3,400 | – | J. Watson |
| Badminton School, Bristol | www.badmintonschool.co.uk | £5,810 | £11,010 | Mrs R. Tear |
| Bancroft's School, Essex | www.bancrofts.org | £5,016 | – | Mrs M. Ireland |
| Barnard Castle School, Durham | www.barnardcastleschool.org.uk | £7,391 | £4,117 | A. Stevens |
| Bedales School, Hants | www.bedales.org.uk | £8,590 | £10,930 | K. Budge |
| Bede's Senior School, E. Sussex | www.bedes.org | £6,640 | £10,055 | Dr R. Maloney |
| Bedford Girls' School, Beds | www.bedfordgirlsschool.co.uk | £3,960 | – | Miss J. MacKenzie |
| Bedford Modern School, Beds | www.bedmod.co.uk | £3,982 | – | M. Hall |

| | | | | |
|---|---|---|---|---|
| Bedford School, Beds | www.bedfordschool.org.uk | £5,708 | £9,654 | J. Hodgson |
| Bedstone College, Shrops | www.bedstone.org | £4,555 | £8,255 | D. Gajadharsingh |
| Beechwood Sacred Heart School, Kent | www.beechwood.org.uk | £5,312 | £8,820 | A. Lennon |
| Benenden School, Kent | www.benenden.kent.sch.uk | – | £11,150 | Mrs S. Price |
| Berkhamsted School, Herts | www.berkhamstedschool.org | £6,180 | £9,843 | M. Steed |
| Bethany School, Kent | www.bethanyschool.org.uk | £5,457 | £9,246 | M. Healy |
| Birkdale School, S. Yorks | www.birkdaleschool.org.uk | £3,850 | – | Dr P. Owen |
| Birkenhead School, Merseyside | www.birkenheadschool.co.uk | £3,580 | – | D. Edmunds |
| Bishop's Stortford College, Herts | www.bishopsstortfordcollege.org | £5,484 | £8,238 | J. Gladwin |
| Blackheath High School, London SE3 | www.blackheathhighschool.gdst.net | £4,693 | – | Mrs C. Chandler-Thompson |
| Bloxham School, Oxon | www.bloxhamschool.com | £7,890 | £10,195 | P. Sanderson |
| Blundell's School, Devon | www.blundells.org | £6,545 | £10,175 | Mrs N. Huggett |
| Bolton School Boys' Division, Lancs | www.boltonschool.org/seniorboys | £3,632 | – | P. Britton |
| Bolton School Girls' Division, Lancs | www.boltonschool.org/seniorgirls | £3,632 | – | Miss S. Hincks |
| Bootham School, N. Yorks | www.boothamschool.com | £5,505 | £9,495 | J. Taylor |
| Bournemouth Collegiate School, Dorset | www.bournemouthcollegiateschool.co.uk | £4,400 | £8,400 | R. Slatford |
| Box Hill School, Surrey | www.boxhillschool.com | £5,700 | £9,980 | C. Lowde |
| Bradfield College, Berks | www.bradfieldcollege.org.uk | £8,880 | £11,100 | S. Henderson |
| Bradford Grammar School, W. Yorks | www.bradfordgrammar.com | £3,930 | – | K. Riley |
| Brentwood School, Essex | www.brentwoodschool.co.uk | £5,331 | £10,463 | D. Davies |
| Brighton & Hove High School, E. Sussex | www.bhhs.gdst.net | £4,155 | – | Ms J. Smith |
| Brighton College, E. Sussex | www.brightoncollege.net | £7,080 | £11,320 | R. Cairns |
| Bristol Grammar School, Bristol | www.bristolgrammarschool.co.uk | £4,365 | – | R. MacKinnon |
| Bromley High School, Kent | www.bromleyhigh.gdst.net | £4,896 | – | Mrs A. Drew |
| Bromsgrove School, Worcs | www.bromsgrove-school.co.uk | £4,845 | £10,395 | P. Clague |
| Bruton School for Girls, Somerset | www.brutonschool.co.uk | £4,850 | £8,858 | Mrs N. Botterill |
| Bryanston School, Dorset | www.bryanston.co.uk | £9,153 | £11,162 | Ms S. Thomas |
| Burgess Hill School for Girls, W. Sussex | www.burgesshill-school.com | £5,100 | £9,000 | Mrs K. Bell |
| Bury Grammar School Boys, Lancs | www.bgsboys.co.uk | £3,266 | – | R. Marshall |
| Bury Grammar School Girls, Lancs | www.bgsg.bury.sch.uk | £3,266 | – | Mrs R. Georghiou |
| Canford School, Dorset | www.canford.com | £7,954 | £10,374 | B. Vessey |
| Caterham School, Surrey | www.caterhamschool.co.uk | £5,361 | £10,003 | J. Thomas |
| Channing School, London N6 | www.channing.co.uk | £5,340 | – | Mrs B. Elliott |
| Charterhouse, Surrey | www.charterhouse.org.uk | £8,273 | £11,415 | R. Pleming |
| Cheadle Hulme School, Cheshire | www.cheadlehulmeschool.co.uk | £3,552 | – | Miss L. Pearson |
| Cheltenham College, Glos | www.cheltenhamcollege.org | £8,496 | £11,238 | Dr A. Peterken |
| Cheltenham Ladies' College, Glos | www.cheltladiescollege.org | £8,039 | £11,862 | Ms E. Jardine-Young |
| Chetham's School of Music, Greater Manchester | www.chethams.com | – | – | Mrs C. Moreland |
| Chigwell School, Essex | www.chigwell-school.org | £5,115 | £8,560 | M. Punt |
| Christ's Hospital, W. Sussex | www.christs-hospital.org.uk | £6,400 | £9,850 | J. Franklin |
| Churcher's College, Hants | www.churcherscollege.com | £4,352 | – | S. Williams |
| City of London Freemen's School, Surrey | www.clfs.surrey.sch.uk | £5,175 | £8,370 | P. MacDonald |
| City of London School, London EC4 | www.clsb.org.uk | £4,771 | – | Mrs S. Fletcher |
| City of London School for Girls, London EC2 | www.clsg.org.uk | £4,803 | – | Mrs E. Harrop |
| Claremont Fan Court School, Surrey | www.claremont-school.co.uk | £5,090 | – | J. Insall-Reid |
| Clayesmore School, Dorset | www.clayesmore.com | £7,783 | £10,639 | M. Cooke |
| Clifton College, Bristol | www.cliftoncollege.com | £7,875 | £11,450 | M. Moore |
| Clifton High School, Bristol | www.cliftonhigh.bristol.sch.uk | £4,270 | – | Dr A. Neill |
| Cobham Hall, Kent | www.cobhamhall.com | £6,526 | £9,817 | P. Mitchell |
| Cokethorpe School, Oxon | www.cokethorpe.org.uk | £5,550 | – | D. Ettinger |
| Colfe's School, London SE12 | www.colfes.com | £4,917 | – | R. Russell |
| Colston's School, Bristol | www.colstons.bristol.sch.uk | £4,045 | – | J. McCullough |
| Concord College, Shrops | www.concordcollegeuk.com | £4,182 | £10,800 | N. Hawkins |
| Cranford House School, Oxon | www.cranfordhouse.net | £5,020 | – | Dr J. Raymond |
| Cranleigh, Surrey | www.cranleigh.org | £8,910 | £10,930 | M. Reader |
| Croydon High School, Surrey | www.croydonhigh.gdst.net | £4,818 | – | Mrs D. Leonard |
| Culford School, Suffolk | www.culford.co.uk | £5,780 | £9,330 | J. Johnson-Munday |
| Dame Allan's Boys' School, Tyne and Wear | www.dameallans.co.uk | £3,756 | – | Dr J. Hind |
| Dame Allan's Girls' School, Tyne and Wear | www.dameallans.co.uk | £3,756 | – | Dr J. Hind |

| | | | | |
|---|---|---|---|---|
| Dauntsey's School, Wilts | www.dauntseys.org | £5,600 | £10,850 | M. Lascelles |
| Dean Close School, Glos | www.deanclose.org.uk | £7,360 | £10,680 | J. Lancashire |
| Denstone College, Staffs | www.denstonecollege.org | £4,568 | £7,954 | D. Derbyshire |
| Derby Grammar School, Derbys | www.derbygrammar.co.uk | £3,916 | – | R. Paine |
| Derby High School, Derbys | www.derbyhigh.derby.sch.uk | £3,760 | – | Mrs D. Gould |
| Dodderhill School, Worcs | www.dodderhill.co.uk | £3,350 | – | Mrs C. Mawston |
| Dover College, Kent | www.dovercollege.org.uk | £4,750 | £9,300 | G. Holden |
| d'Overbroeck's, Oxon | www.doverbroecks.com | £6,860 | £10,560 | S. Cohen |
| Downe House, Berks | www.downehouse.net | £7,910 | £10,930 | Mrs E. McKendrick |
| Dulwich College, London SE21 | www.dulwich.org.uk | £5,801 | £12,108 | Dr J. Spence |
| Dunottar School, Surrey | www.dunottarschool.com | £4,700 | – | Mrs R. Cole |
| Durham High School for Girls, Durham | www.dhsfg.org.uk | £3,750 | – | Mrs L. Renwick |
| Durham School, Durham | www.durhamschool.co.uk | £5,280 | £8,645 | K. McLaughlin |
| Eastbourne College, E. Sussex | www.eastbourne-college.co.uk | £6,860 | £10,410 | S. Davies |
| Edgbaston High School, W. Midlands | www.edgbastonhigh.co.uk | £3,729 | – | Dr R. Weeks |
| Ellesmere College, Shrops | www.ellesmere.com | £5,598 | £9,717 | B. Wignall |
| Eltham College, London SE9 | www.eltham-college.org.uk | £4,916 | – | G. Sanderson |
| Emanuel School, London SW11 | www.emanuel.org.uk | £5,468 | – | M. Hanley-Browne |
| Epsom College, Surrey | www.epsomcollege.org.uk | £7,335 | £10,730 | J. Piggott |
| Eton College, Berks | www.etoncollege.com | – | £11,478 | A. Little |
| Ewell Castle School, Surrey | www.ewellcastle.co.uk | £4,560 | – | P. Harris |
| Exeter School, Devon | www.exeterschool.org.uk | £3,765 | – | R. Griffin |
| Farlington School, W. Sussex | www.farlingtonschool.net | £5,385 | £8,890 | Miss L. Higson |
| Farnborough Hill, Hants | www.farnborough-hill.org.uk | £4,230 | – | Mrs S. Buckle |
| Farringtons School, Kent | www.farringtons.org.uk | £4,390 | £8,610 | Mrs D. Nancekievill |
| Felsted School, Essex | www.felsted.org | £6,975 | £9,990 | Dr M. Walker |
| Forest School, London E17 | www.forest.org.uk | £5,238 | – | Mrs S. Kerr-Dineen |
| Framlingham College, Suffolk | www.framcollege.co.uk | £5,929 | £9,222 | P. Taylor |
| Francis Holland School, London NW1 | www.francisholland.org.uk | £5,560 | – | Mrs V. Durham |
| Francis Holland School, London SW1 | www.francisholland.org.uk | £5,790 | – | Mrs L. Elphinstone |
| Frensham Heights, Surrey | www.frensham.org | £6,110 | £9,045 | A. Fisher |
| Friends' School, Essex | www.friends.org.uk | £5,305 | £8,590 | Mrs A. Chaudhri |
| Fulneck School, W. Yorks | www.fulneckschool.co.uk | £3,950 | £7,425 | Mrs D. Newman |
| Gateways School, W. Yorks | www.gatewaysschool.co.uk | £3,940 | – | Dr T. Johnson |
| Giggleswick School, N. Yorks | www.giggleswick.org.uk | £6,769 | £9,884 | M. Turnbull |
| The Godolphin and Latymer School, London W6 | www.godolphinandlatymer.com | £6,060 | – | Mrs R. Mercer |
| The Godolphin School, Wilts | www.godolphin.org | £6,176 | £9,359 | Mrs E. Hattersley |
| The Grange School, Cheshire | www.grange.org.uk | £3,435 | – | C. Jeffery |
| Greenacre School for Girls, Surrey | www.greenacre.surrey.sch.uk | £5,094 | – | Mrs L. Redding |
| Gresham's School, Norfolk | www.greshams.com | £7,620 | £10,230 | D. Robb |
| Guildford High School, Surrey | www.guildfordhigh.surrey.sch.uk | £4,988 | – | Mrs F. Boulton |
| The Haberdashers' Aske's Boys' School, Herts | www.habsboys.org.uk | £5,554 | – | P. Hamilton |
| Haberdashers' Aske's School for Girls, Herts | www.habsgirls.org.uk | £4,834 | – | Miss B. O'Connor |
| Haileybury, Herts | www.haileybury.com | £7,546 | £10,046 | J. Davies |
| Halliford School, Middx | www.hallifordschool.co.uk | £4,315 | – | S. Wilson |
| Hampshire Collegiate School, Hants | www.hampshirecs.org.uk | £4,715 | £8,874 | Mrs E. Henry |
| Hampton School, Middx | www.hamptonschool.org.uk | £5,585 | – | K. Knibbs |
| Harrogate Ladies' College, N. Yorks | www.hlc.org.uk | £4,935 | £10,695 | Mrs S. Brett |
| Harrow School, Middx | www.harrowschool.org.uk | – | £11,530 | J. Hawkins |
| Headington School, Oxon | www.headington.org | £5,480 | £10,700 | Mrs C. Jordan |
| Heathfield School, Berks | www.heathfieldschool.net | £7,525 | £10,750 | Mrs J. Heywood |
| Hereford Cathedral School, Herefords | www.herefordcs.com | £4,213 | – | P. Smith |
| Hethersett Old Hall School, Norfolk | www.hohs.co.uk | £4,300 | £8,100 | S. Crump |
| Highgate School, London N6 | www.highgateschool.org.uk | £6,055 | – | A. Pettitt |
| Hill House School, S. Yorks | www.hillhouse.doncaster.sch.uk | £3,670 | – | D. Holland |
| Hull Collegiate School, E. Yorks | www.hullcollegiateschool.co.uk | £3,571 | – | Mrs R. Glover |
| Hurstpierpoint College, W. Sussex | www.hppc.co.uk | £6,975 | £10,375 | T. Manly |
| Hymers College, E. Yorks | www.hymerscollege.co.uk | £3,333 | – | D. Elstone |
| Immanuel College, Herts | www.immanuelcollege.co.uk | £4,999 | – | C. Dormer |
| Ipswich High School, Suffolk | www.ipswichhighschool.co.uk | £4,107 | – | Ms O. Carlin |
| Ipswich School, Suffolk | www.ipswich.suffolk.sch.uk | £4,351 | £8,054 | N. Weaver |

| | | | | |
|---|---|---|---|---|
| James Allen's Girls' School (JAGS), London SE22 | www.jags.org.uk | £5,080 | – | Mrs M. Gibbs |
| The John Lyon School, Middx | www.johnlyon.org | £5,188 | – | Miss K. Haynes |
| Kent College, Kent | www.kentcollege.com | £5,613 | £10,358 | Dr D. Lamper |
| Kent College Pembury, Kent | www.kent-college.co.uk | £6,515 | £9,633 | Mrs S. Huang |
| Kimbolton School, Cambs | www.kimbolton.cambs.sch.uk | £4,615 | £7,685 | J. Belbin |
| King Edward VI High School for Girls, W. Midlands | www.kehs.org.uk | £3,750 | – | Mrs A. Clark |
| King Edward VI School, Hants | www.kes.hants.sch.uk | £4,605 | – | A. Thould |
| King Edward's School, Somerset | www.kesbath.com | £4,200 | – | M. Boden |
| King Edward's School, W. Midlands | www.kes.org.uk | £3,860 | – | J. Claughton |
| King Edward's, Surrey | www.kesw.org | £6,650 | £9,500 | J. Attwater |
| King Henry VIII School, W. Midlands | www.khviii.com | £3,400 | – | J. Slack |
| King William's College, Isle of Man | www.kwc.im | £6,773 | £9,860 | M. Humphreys |
| Kingham Hill School, Oxon | www.kinghamhill.org.uk | £5,680 | £9,490 | Revd N. Seward |
| King's College School, London SW19 | www.kcs.org.uk | £6,485 | – | A. Halls |
| King's College, Somerset | www.kings-taunton.co.uk | £6,650 | £9,800 | R. Biggs |
| King's High School, Warwicks | www.kingshighwarwick.co.uk | £3,623 | – | Mrs E. Surber |
| King's School, Somerset | www.kingsbruton.com | £6,868 | £9,642 | I. Wilmshurst |
| The King's School, Kent | www.kings-school.co.uk | £8,430 | £11,120 | P. Roberts |
| The King's School, Cheshire | www.kingschester.co.uk | £3,986 | – | C. Ramsey |
| King's Ely, Cambs | www.kingsely.org | £6,177 | £8,942 | Mrs S. Freestone |
| The King's School, Glos | www.thekingsschool.co.uk | £5,895 | – | A. Macnaughton |
| The King's School, Cheshire | www.kingsmac.co.uk | £3,770 | – | Dr S. Hyde |
| King's Rochester, Kent | www.kings-rochester.co.uk | £5,680 | £9,225 | J. Walker |
| The King's School, Worcs | www.ksw.org.uk | £4,021 | – | M. Armstrong |
| Kingsley School, Devon | www.kingsleyschoolbideford.co.uk | £4,170 | £9,770 | S. Woolcott |
| The Kingsley School, Warwicks | www.thekingsleyschool.com | £3,820 | – | Ms H. Owens |
| Kingston Grammar School, Surrey | www.kgs.org.uk | £5,535 | – | S. Lehec |
| Kingswood School, Somerset | www.kingswood.bath.sch.uk | £4,465 | £9,624 | S. Morris |
| Kirkham Grammar School, Lancs | www.kirkhamgrammar.co.uk | £3,338 | £6,340 | R. Laithwaite |
| The Lady Eleanor Holles School, Middx | www.lehs.org.uk | £5,800 | – | Mrs H. Hanbury |
| Lancing College, W. Sussex | www.lancingcollege.co.uk | £7,480 | £10,650 | D. Oliver |
| Langley School, Norfolk | www.langleyschool.co.uk | £4,395 | £8,930 | D. Findlay |
| Latymer Upper School, London W6 | www.latymer-upper.org | £5,770 | – | D. Goodhew |
| Lavant House, W. Sussex | www.lavanthouse.org.uk | £4,500 | £7,100 | Mrs C. Horton |
| The Grammar School at Leeds, W. Yorks | www.gsal.org.uk | £4,038 | – | M. Gibbons |
| Leicester Grammar School, Leics | www.leicestergrammar.org.uk | £3,859 | – | C. King |
| Leicester High School for Girls, Leics | www.leicesterhigh.co.uk | £3,625 | – | A. Whelpdale |
| Leighton Park School, Berks | www.leightonpark.com | £6,548 | £10,197 | N. Williams |
| Leweston School, Dorset | www.leweston.co.uk | £5,928 | £9,576 | A. Aylward |
| The Leys, Cambs | www.theleys.net | £6,395 | £9,610 | M. Priestley |
| Lichfield Cathedral School, Staffs | www.lichfieldcathedralschool.com | £6,450 | £6,110 | Mrs S. Hannam |
| Lincoln Minster School, Lincs | www.lincolnminsterschool.co.uk | £4,159 | £9,952 | C. Rickart |
| Longridge Towers School, Northumberland | www.lts.org.uk | £3,992 | £8,132 | T. Manning |
| Lord Wandsworth College, Hants | www.lordwandsworth.org | £6,840 | £9,660 | F. Livingstone |
| Loughborough Grammar School, Leics | www.lesgrammar.org | £3,682 | £7,969 | P. Fisher |
| Loughborough High School, Leics | www.leshigh.org | £3,553 | – | Mrs G. Byrom |
| Luckley House School, Berks | www.luckleyhouseschool.org | £5,029 | £8,801 | Mrs J. Tudor |
| LVS Ascot (The Licensed Victuallers' School), Berks | www.lvs.ascot.sch.uk | £5,128 | £9,010 | Mrs C. Cunniffe |
| Magdalen College School, Oxon | www.mcsoxford.org | £5,140 | – | Dr T. Hands |
| Malvern College, Worcs | www.malverncollege.org.uk | £7,558 | £11,801 | A. Clark |
| The Manchester Grammar School, Greater Manchester | www.mgs.org | £3,800 | – | Dr M. Boulton |
| Manchester High School for Girls, Greater Manchester | www.manchesterhigh.co.uk | £3,546 | – | Mrs A. Hewitt |
| Manor House School, Surrey | www.manorhouseschool.org | £5,050 | – | Miss Z. Axton |
| The Marist Senior School, Berks | www.themaristschools.com | £4,200 | – | K. McCloskey |
| Marlborough College, Wilts | www.marlboroughcollege.org | £9,375 | £11,030 | J. Leigh |
| Marymount International School, Surrey | www.marymountlondon.com | £6,890 | £11,635 | Ms S. Gallagher |
| Mayfield School, E. Sussex | www.mayfieldgirls.org | £6,250 | £10,000 | Miss A. Beary |

| School | Website | Fee 1 | Fee 2 | Head |
|---|---|---|---|---|
| The Maynard School, Devon | www.maynard.co.uk | £3,906 | – | Ms B. Hughes |
| Merchant Taylors' Boys' School, Merseyside | www.merchanttaylors.com | £3,508 | – | D. Cook |
| Merchant Taylors' Girls' School, Merseyside | www.merchanttaylors.com | £3,508 | – | Mrs L. Robinson |
| Merchant Taylors' School, Middx | www.mtsn.org.uk | £6,017 | – | S. Everson |
| Mill Hill School, London NW7 | www.millhill.org.uk | £6,082 | £9,609 | Dr D. Luckett |
| Millfield, Somerset | millfieldschool.com | £7,500 | £11,150 | C. Considine |
| Milton Abbey School, Dorset | www.miltonabbey.co.uk | £5,495 | £10,690 | M. Bashaarat |
| Moira House Girls School, E. Sussex | www.moirahouse.co.uk | £5,110 | £9,900 | J. Sheridan |
| Monkton Combe School, Somerset | www.monktoncombeschool.com | £6,312 | £9,772 | R. Backhouse |
| More House School, London SW1 | www.morehouse.org.uk | £5,500 | – | Mrs A. Leach |
| Moreton Hall, Shrops | www.moretonhall.org | £8,320 | £10,100 | J. Forster |
| Mount Kelly, Devon | www.mountkelly.com | £5,330 | £9,310 | M. Semmence |
| Mount St Mary's College, Derbys | www.msmcollege.com | £3,490 | £8,704 | Dr N. Cuddihy |
| The Mount School, N. Yorks | www.mountschoolyork.co.uk | £5,515 | £8,729 | Ms J. Lodrick |
| New Hall School, Essex | www.newhallschool.co.uk | £5,739 | £8,811 | Mrs K. Jeffrey |
| Newcastle High School for Girls, Tyne and Wear | www.newcastlehigh.gdst.net | £3,896 | – | Mrs H. French |
| Newcastle School for Boys, Tyne and Wear | www.newcastleschool.co.uk | £3,910 | – | D. Tickner |
| Newcastle-under-Lyme School, Staffs | www.nuls.org.uk | £3,626 | – | N. Rugg |
| North Cestrian Grammar School, Cheshire | www.ncgs.co.uk | £3,142 | – | L. Bergin |
| North London Collegiate School, Middx | www.nlcs.org.uk | £5,875 | – | Mrs B. McCabe |
| Northampton High School, Northants | www.northamptonhigh.gdst.net | £4,335 | – | Mrs S. Dixon |
| Northwood College for Girls, Middx | www.northwoodcollege.gdst.net | £4,982 | – | Miss J. Pain |
| Norwich High School, Norfolk | www.norwichhigh.gdst.net | £4,119 | – | J. Morrow |
| Norwich School, Norfolk | www.norwich-school.org.uk | £4,565 | – | S. Griffiths |
| Notre Dame School, Surrey | www.notredame.co.uk | £4,875 | – | D. Plummer |
| Notting Hill and Ealing High School, London W13 | www.nhehs.gdst.net | £5,250 | – | Ms L. Hunt |
| Nottingham Girls' High School, Notts | www.nottinghamgirlshigh.gdst.net | £3,932 | – | Mrs S. Gorham |
| Nottingham High School, Notts | www.nottinghamhigh.co.uk | £4,281 | – | K. Fear |
| Oakham School, Rutland | www.oakham.rutland.sch.uk | £5,990 | £9,980 | N. Lashbrook |
| Ockbrook School, Derbys | www.ockbrooksch.co.uk | £3,755 | £7,135 | T. Brooksby |
| Oldham Hulme Grammar School, Lancs | www.ohgs.co.uk | £3,345 | – | C. Mairs |
| The Oratory School, Oxon | www.oratory.co.uk | £7,450 | £10,245 | C. Dytor |
| Oswestry School, Shrops | www.oswestryschool.org.uk | £4,610 | £8,595 | J. Noad |
| Oundle School, Northants | www.oundleschool.org.uk | £6,875 | £10,720 | C. Bush |
| Our Lady's Abingdon Senior School, Oxon | www.olab.org.uk | £4,348 | – | S. Oliver |
| Oxford High School, Oxon | www.oxfordhigh.gdst.net | £4,341 | – | Mrs J. Carlisle |
| Palmers Green High School, London N21 | www.pghs.co.uk | £4,465 | – | Mrs C. Edmundson |
| Pangbourne College, Berks | www.pangbournecollege.com | £7,193 | £10,172 | T. Garnier |
| The Perse Upper School, Cambs | www.perse.co.uk | £4,970 | – | E. Elliott |
| The Peterborough School, Cambs | www.thepeterboroughschool.co.uk | £4,526 | – | A. Meadows |
| Pipers Corner School, Bucks | www.piperscorner.co.uk | £5,100 | – | Mrs H. Ness-Gifford |
| Pitsford School, Northants | www.pitsfordschool.com | £4,333 | – | N. Toone |
| Plymouth College, Devon | www.plymouthcollege.com | £4,920 | £9,420 | J. Standen |
| Pocklington School, E. Yorks | www.pocklingtonschool.com | £4,296 | £8,099 | M. Ronan |
| Portland Place School, London W1 | www.portland-place.co.uk | £6,035 | – | D. Hyman |
| The Portsmouth Grammar School, Hants | www.pgs.org.uk | £4,567 | – | J. Priory |
| Portsmouth High School, Hants | www.portsmouthhigh.co.uk | £4,089 | – | Mrs J. Prescott |
| Princess Helena College, Herts | www.princesshelenacollege.co.uk | £5,995 | £9,705 | Mrs S. Wallace-Woodroffe |
| Princethorpe College, Warwicks | www.princethorpe.co.uk | £3,536 | – | E. Hester |
| Prior Park College, Somerset | www.thepriorfoundation.com | £4,975 | £9,210 | J. Murphy-O'Connor |
| Prior's Field, Surrey | www.priorsfieldschool.com | £5,395 | £8,910 | Mrs J. Roseblade |
| The Purcell School, Herts | www.purcell-school.org | £8,259 | £10,562 | D. Thomas |
| Putney High School, London SW15 | www.putneyhigh.gdst.net | £5,290 | – | Dr D. Lodge |
| Queen Anne's School, Berks | www.qas.org.uk | £6,770 | £9,975 | Mrs J. Harrington |

| School | Website | | | Head |
|---|---|---|---|---|
| Queen Elizabeth's Hospital (QEH), Bristol | www.qehbristol.co.uk | £4,231 | – | S. Holliday |
| Queen Margaret's School, N. Yorks | www.queenmargarets.com | £6,125 | £9,530 | Mrs J. Miles |
| Queen Mary's School, N. Yorks | www.queenmarys.org | £5,390 | £6,990 | R. Johnston |
| Queen's College, London, London W1 | www.qcl.org.uk | £5,410 | – | Dr F. Ramsey |
| Queen's College, Somerset | www.queenscollege.org.uk | £5,470 | £10,050 | C. Alcock |
| Queen's Gate School, London SW7 | www.queensgate.org.uk | £5,850 | – | Mrs R. Kamaryc |
| Queenswood School, Herts | www.queenswood.org | £8,150 | £10,750 | Mrs P. Edgar |
| Radley College, Oxon | www.radley.org.uk | – | £11,075 | J. Moule |
| Ratcliffe College, Leics | www.ratcliffe-college.co.uk | £4,955 | £8,748 | G. Lloyd |
| The Read School, N. Yorks | www.readschool.co.uk | £3,580 | £8,610 | J. Sweetman |
| Reading Blue Coat School, Berks | www.rbcs.org.uk | £4,860 | – | M. Windsor |
| The Red Maids' School, Bristol | www.redmaids.co.uk | £4,090 | – | Mrs I. Tobias |
| Redland High School for Girls, Bristol | www.redlandhigh.com | £3,880 | – | Mrs C. Bateson |
| Reed's School, Surrey | www.reeds.surrey.sch.uk | £7,315 | £9,680 | M. Hoskins |
| Reigate Grammar School, Surrey | www.reigategrammar.org | £5,330 | – | S. Fenton |
| Rendcomb College, Glos | www.rendcombcollege.org.uk | £6,910 | £9,505 | R. Martin |
| Repton School, Derbys | www.repton.org.uk | £7,825 | £10,547 | Mrs S. Tennant |
| Rishworth School, W. Yorks | www.rishworth-school.co.uk | £3,795 | £8,160 | A. Gloag |
| Roedean School, E. Sussex | www.roedean.co.uk | £6,300 | £11,200 | O. Blond |
| Rossall School, Lancs | www.rossallschool.org.uk | £4,060 | £11,500 | Ms E. Purves |
| Royal Grammar School, Surrey | www.rgs-guildford.co.uk | £5,100 | – | Dr J. Cox |
| Royal Grammar School, Tyne and Wear | www.rgs.newcastle.sch.uk | £3,731 | – | Dr B. Trafford |
| RGS Worcester, Worcs | www.rgsw.org.uk | £3,620 | – | J. Pitt |
| The Royal High School Bath, Somerset | www.royalhighbath.gdst.net | £4,050 | £8,499 | Mrs J. Duncan |
| The Royal Hospital School, Suffolk | www.royalhospitalschool.org | £4,730 | £9,070 | J. Lockwood |
| The Royal Masonic School for Girls, Herts | www.royalmasonic.herts.sch.uk | £4,970 | £8,600 | Mrs D. Rose |
| Royal Russell School, Surrey | www.royalrussell.co.uk | £5,295 | £10,475 | C. Hutchinson |
| The Royal School, Wolverhampton, W. Midlands | www.theroyalschool.co.uk | £4,410 | £9,610 | M. Heywood |
| Rugby School, Warwicks | www.rugbyschool.net | £6,698 | £10,675 | P. Green |
| Ryde School with Upper Chine, Isle of Wight | www.rydeschool.org.uk | £3,850 | £8,105 | M. Waldron |
| Rye St Antony, Oxon | www.ryestantony.co.uk | £4,475 | £7,355 | Miss A. Jones |
| St Albans High School for Girls, Herts | www.stahs.org.uk | £4,825 | – | Mrs J. Brown |
| St Albans School, Herts | www.st-albans.herts.sch.uk | £5,292 | – | J. Gillespie |
| St Augustine's Priory School, London W5 | www.saintaugustinespriory.org.uk | £4,200 | – | Mrs S. Raffray |
| St Bede's College, Greater Manchester | www.stbedescollege.co.uk | £3,300 | – | R. Robson |
| St Benedict's School, London W5 | www.stbenedicts.org.uk | £4,620 | – | C. Cleugh |
| St Catherine's School, Surrey | www.stcatherines.info | £5,535 | £9,115 | Mrs A. Phillips |
| St Catherine's School, Middx | www.stcatherineschool.co.uk | £4,405 | – | Sr P. Thomas |
| St Christopher School, Herts | www.stchris.co.uk | £5,615 | £9,935 | R. Palmer |
| St Columba's College, Herts | www.stcolumbascollege.org | £4,390 | – | D. Buxton |
| St Dominic's Brewood, Staffs | www.stdominicsbrewood.co.uk | £3,875 | £7,167 | H. Trump |
| St Dominic's Priory School, Staffs | www.stdominicspriory.co.uk | £3,482 | £8,000 | Mrs R. Harrison |
| St Dunstan's College, London SE6 | www.stdunstans.org.uk | £5,020 | – | N. Hewlett |
| St Edmund's College, Herts | www.stedmundscollege.org | £5,238 | £8,836 | P. Durn |
| St Edmund's School, Kent | www.stedmunds.org.uk | £6,217 | £9,927 | Mrs L. Moelwyn-Hughes |
| St Edward's, Oxford, Oxon | www.stedwardsoxford.org | £8,891 | £11,111 | S. Jones |
| St Edward's School, Glos | www.stedwards.co.uk | £4,900 | – | Mrs P. Clayfield |
| Saint Felix School, Suffolk | www.stfelix.co.uk | £4,845 | £8,465 | Miss M. D'Alcorn |
| St Gabriel's, Berks | www.stgabriels.co.uk | £4,960 | – | A. Jones |
| St George's College, Surrey | www.stgeorgesweybridge.com | £5,550 | – | J. Peake |
| St George's School, W. Midlands | www.sgse.co.uk | £3,255 | – | G. Neal |
| St George's, Ascot, Berks | www.stgeorges-ascot.org.uk | £6,750 | £10,375 | Mrs R. Owens |
| St Helen & St Katharine, Oxon | www.shsk.org.uk | £4,510 | – | Mrs R. Dougall |
| St Helen's School, Middx | www.sthelens.london | £4,977 | – | Dr M. Short |
| St James Senior Boys' School, Surrey | www.stjamesboys.co.uk | £5,090 | £7,260 | D. Brazier |
| St James Senior Girls' School, London W14 | www.stjamesgirls.co.uk | £5,400 | – | Mrs S. Labram |

| School | Website | Fee 1 | Fee 2 | Head |
|---|---|---|---|---|
| St John's College, Hants | www.stjohnscollege.co.uk | £3,550 | £8,240 | G. Best |
| St John's School, Surrey | www.stjohnsleatherhead.co.uk | £7,155 | £9,035 | M. Collier |
| St Joseph's College, Suffolk | www.stjos.co.uk | £4,365 | £9,420 | Mrs D. Clarke |
| St Lawrence College, Kent | www.slcuk.com | £5,643 | £9,985 | A. Spencer |
| St Margaret's School, Herts | www.stmargaretsbushey.co.uk | £4,910 | £9,200 | Mrs R. Hardy |
| St Margaret's School, London NW3 | www.st-margarets.co.uk | £4,020 | – | M. Webster |
| St Martha's, Herts | www.st-marthas.co.uk | £4,345 | – | M. Burke |
| Saint Martin's, W. Midlands | www.saintmartins-school.com | £3,749 | – | Miss N. Edgar |
| St Mary's Calne, Wilts | www.stmaryscalne.org | £8,450 | £11,300 | Dr F. Kirk |
| St Mary's School, Cambs | www.stmaryscambridge.co.uk | £4,638 | £9,902 | Ms C. Avery |
| St Mary's School, Essex | www.stmaryscolchester.org.uk | £4,100 | – | Mrs H. Vipond |
| St Mary's College, Merseyside | www.stmarys.ac | £3,338 | – | M. Kennedy |
| St Mary's School, Bucks | www.stmarysschool.co.uk | £4,652 | – | Mrs J. Ross |
| St Mary's School Ascot, Berks | www.st-marys-ascot.co.uk | £7,800 | £10,950 | Mrs M. Breen |
| St Mary's School, Dorset | www.st-marys-shaftesbury.co.uk | £6,195 | £8,990 | R. James |
| St Nicholas' School, Hants | www.st-nicholas.hants.sch.uk | £4,265 | – | Mrs A. Whatmough |
| St Paul's Girls' School, London W6 | www.spgs.org | £6,958 | – | Ms C. Farr |
| St Paul's School, London SW13 | www.stpaulsschool.org.uk | £7,264 | £10,880 | M. Bailey |
| St Peter's School, York, N. Yorks | www.stpetersyork.org.uk | £5,310 | £8,770 | L. Winkley |
| St Swithun's School, Hants | www.stswithuns.com | £6,150 | £9,855 | Ms J. Gandee |
| Scarborough College N. Yorks | www.scarboroughcollege.co.uk | £4,331 | £8,110 | Mrs I. Nixon |
| Seaford College, W. Sussex | www.seaford.org | £6,150 | £9,690 | J. Green |
| Sevenoaks School, Kent | www.sevenoaksschool.org | £7,554 | £11,526 | Mrs C. Ricks |
| Shebbear College, Devon | www.shebbearcollege.co.uk | £3,950 | £7,790 | S. Weale |
| Sheffield High School, S. Yorks | www.sheffieldhighschool.org.uk | £3,805 | – | Mrs V. Dunsford |
| Sherborne Girls, Dorset | www.sherborne.com | £7,505 | £10,330 | Mrs J. Dwyer |
| Sherborne School, Dorset | www.sherborne.org | £8,865 | £10,950 | R. Barlow |
| Shiplake College, Oxon | www.shiplake.org.uk | £6,450 | £9,560 | A. Davies |
| Shrewsbury High School, Shrops | www.shrewsburyhigh.gdst.net | £4,136 | – | M. Getty |
| Shrewsbury School, Shrops | www.shrewsbury.org.uk | £7,385 | £10,545 | M. Turner |
| Sibford School, Oxon | www.sibfordschool.co.uk | £4,400 | £8,549 | M. Goodwin |
| Sidcot School, Somerset | www.sidcot.org.uk | £5,200 | £9,340 | I. Kilpatrick |
| Silcoates School, W. Yorks | www.silcoates.org.uk | £4,210 | – | D. Wideman |
| Solihull School, W. Midlands | www.solsch.org.uk | £3,741 | – | D. Lloyd |
| South Hampstead High School, London NW3 | www.shhs.gdst.net | £5,074 | – | Miss H. Pike |
| Stafford Grammar School, Staffs | www.staffordgrammar.co.uk | £3,666 | – | M. Darley |
| Stamford High School, Lincs | www.ses.lincs.sch.uk | £4,482 | £8,303 | S. Roberts |
| Stamford School, Lincs | www.ses.lincs.sch.uk | £4,482 | £8,303 | S. Roberts |
| The Stephen Perse Foundation, Cambs | www.stephenperse.com | £5,135 | – | Miss P. Kelleher |
| Stockport Grammar School, Cheshire | www.stockportgrammar.co.uk | £3,450 | – | A. Chicken |
| Stonar, Wilts | www.stonarschool.com | £4,965 | £8,960 | Dr S. Divall |
| Stonyhurst College, Lancs | www.stonyhurst.ac.uk | £5,628 | £10,111 | A. Johnson |
| Stover School, Devon | www.stover.co.uk | £3,996 | £8,178 | R. Notman |
| Stowe School, Bucks | www.stowe.co.uk | £7,770 | £10,700 | Dr A. Wallersteiner |
| Streatham & Clapham High School, London SW16 | www.schs.gdst.net | £5,013 | – | Dr M. Sachania |
| Sunderland High School, Tyne and Wear | www.sunderlandhigh.co.uk | £3,077 | – | Dr A. Slater |
| Surbiton High School, Surrey | www.surbitonhigh.com | £4,931 | – | Ms E. Haydon |
| Sutton High School, Surrey | www.suttonhigh.gdst.net | £4,929 | – | Mrs K. Crouch |
| Sutton Valence School, Kent | www.svs.org.uk | £6,435 | £9,885 | B. Grindlay |
| Sydenham High School, London SE26 | www.sydenhamhighschool.gdst.net | £4,864 | – | Mrs K. Pullen |
| Talbot Heath, Dorset | www.talbotheath.org | £4,113 | £7,250 | Mrs A. Holloway |
| Taunton School, Somerset | www.tauntonschool.co.uk | £5,675 | £10,600 | Dr J. Newton |
| Tettenhall College, W. Midlands | www.tettenhallcollege.co.uk | £4,200 | £8,833 | D. Williams |
| Thetford Grammar School, Norfolk | www.thetgram.norfolk.sch.uk | £4,109 | – | G. Price |
| Tonbridge School, Kent | www.tonbridge-school.co.uk | £8,790 | £11,721 | T. Haynes |
| Tormead School, Surrey | www.tormeadschool.org.uk | £4,550 | – | Mrs C. Foord |
| Tring Park School for the Performing Arts, Herts | www.tringpark.com | £7,110 | £10,640 | S. Anderson |
| Trinity School, Surrey | www.trinity-school.org | £4,820 | – | M. Bishop |
| Trinity School, Devon | www.trinityschool.co.uk | £3,785 | £8,340 | T. Waters |
| Truro High School for Girls, Cornwall | www.trurohigh.co.uk | £3,851 | £7,438 | Dr G. Moodie |
| Truro School, Cornwall | www.truroschool.com | £4,075 | £7,900 | A. Gordon-Brown |
| Tudor Hall, Oxon | www.tudorhallschool.com | £6,420 | £10,070 | Miss W. Griffiths |

| School | Website | Fee 1 | Fee 2 | Head |
|---|---|---|---|---|
| University College School, London NW3 | www.ucs.org.uk | £5,945 | – | M. Beard |
| Uppingham School, Rutland | www.uppingham.co.uk | £7,665 | £10,950 | R. Harman |
| Walthamstow Hall, Kent | www.walthamstow-hall.co.uk | £5,750 | – | Mrs J. Milner |
| Warminster School, Wilts | www.warminsterschool.org.uk | £4,650 | £8,875 | M. Mortimer |
| Warwick School, Warwicks | www.warwickschool.org | £3,791 | £8,090 | A. Lock |
| Welbeck - The Defence Sixth Form College, Leics | www.dsfc.ac.uk | – | – | J. Middleton |
| Wellingborough School, Northants | www.wellingboroughschool.org | £4,473 | – | G. Bowe |
| Wellington College, Berks | www.wellingtoncollege.org.uk | £8,350 | £11,375 | Dr A. Seldon |
| Wellington School, Somerset | www.wellington-school.org.uk | £4,553 | £9,395 | H. Price |
| Wells Cathedral School, Somerset | www.wells-cathedral-school.com | £5,547 | £9,283 | Mrs E. Cairncross |
| West Buckland School, Devon | www.westbuckland.devon.com | £4,420 | £8,200 | J. Vick |
| Westfield School, Tyne and Wear | www.westfield.newcastle.sch.uk | £3,915 | – | Mrs C. Jawaheer |
| Westholme School, Lancs | www.westholmeschool.com | £3,200 | – | Mrs L. Horner |
| Westminster School, London SW1 | www.westminster.org.uk | £8,456 | £11,264 | P. Derham |
| Westonbirt School, Glos | www.westonbirt.org | £7,100 | £10,995 | Mrs N. Dangerfield |
| Whitgift School, Surrey | www.whitgift.co.uk | £5,780 | £11,132 | Dr C. Barnett |
| Wimbledon High School, London SW19 | www.wimbledonhigh.gdst.net | £5,250 | – | Mrs J. Lunnon |
| Winchester College, Hants | www.winchestercollege.org | – | £11,580 | R. Townsend |
| Windermere School, Cumbria | www.windermereschool.co.uk | £5,378 | £9,632 | I. Lavender |
| Wisbech Grammar School, Cambs | WisbechGrammar.com | £3,885 | – | C. Staley |
| Withington Girls' School, Greater Manchester | www.wgs.org | £3,600 | – | Mrs S. Marks |
| Woldingham School, Surrey | www.woldinghamschool.co.uk | £6,965 | £11,225 | Mrs J. Triffitt |
| Wolverhampton Grammar School, W. Midlands | www.wgs.org.uk | £4,085 | – | Mrs K. Crewe-Read |
| Woodbridge School, Suffolk | www.woodbridge.suffolk.sch.uk | £4,944 | £9,167 | N. Tetley |
| Woodhouse Grove School, W. Yorks | www.woodhousegrove.co.uk | £3,940 | £8,020 | D. Humphreys |
| Worksop College, Notts | www.wsnl.co.uk | £5,410 | £8,650 | G. Horgan |
| Worth School, W. Sussex | www.worthschool.co.uk | £7,085 | £9,990 | G. Carminati |
| Wrekin College, Shrops | www.wrekincollege.com | – | – | Dr H. Griffiths |
| Wychwood School, Oxon | www.wychwoodschool.org | £4,550 | £7,150 | Mrs A. Johnson |
| Wycliffe College, Glos | www.wycliffe.co.uk | £5,995 | £9,850 | Mrs M. Burnet Ward |
| Wycombe Abbey, Bucks | www.wycombeabbey.com | £8,645 | £11,525 | Mrs R. Wilkinson |
| Wykeham House School, Hants | www.wykehamhouse.com | £3,990 | – | Mrs L. Clarke |
| Yarm School, Cleveland | www.yarmschool.org | £3,867 | – | D. Dunn |
| The Yehudi Menuhin School, Surrey | www.yehudimenuhinschool.co.uk | – | – | Dr R. Hillier |

## WALES

| School | Website | Fee 1 | Fee 2 | Head |
|---|---|---|---|---|
| The Cathedral School Llandaff, Cardiff | www.cathedral-school.co.uk | £3,740 | – | S. Morris |
| Christ College, Brecon | www.christcollegebrecon.com | £5,395 | £8,335 | Mrs E. Taylor |
| Haberdashers' Monmouth School for Girls, Monmouth | www.habs-monmouth.org | £4,419 | £9,085 | Mrs C. Pascoe |
| Howell's School Llandaff, Cardiff | www.howells-cardiff.gdst.net | £4,169 | – | Mrs S. Davis |
| Monmouth School, Monmouth | www.habs-monmouth.org | £4,729 | £9,085 | Dr S. Connors |
| Rougemont School, Newport | www.rougemontschool.co.uk | £3,996 | – | R. Carnevale |
| Ruthin School, Ruthin | www.ruthinschool.co.uk | £3,917 | £8,167 | T. Belfield |
| Rydal Penrhos School, Colwyn Bay | www.rydalpenrhos.com | £5,070 | £10,105 | P. Lee-Browne |

## SCOTLAND

| School | Website | Fee 1 | Fee 2 | Head |
|---|---|---|---|---|
| Dollar Academy, Dollar | www.dollaracademy.org.uk | £3,678 | £8,508 | D. Knapman |
| The High School of Dundee, Dundee | www.highschoolofdundee.org.uk | £3,690 | – | Dr J. Halliday |
| The Edinburgh Academy, Edinburgh | www.edinburghacademy.org.uk | £4,164 | – | M. Longmore |
| Fettes College, Edinburgh | www.fettes.com | £7,730 | £10,060 | M. Spens |
| George Heriot's School, Edinburgh | www.george-heriots.com | £3,565 | – | C. Wyllie |
| The Glasgow Academy, Glasgow | www.theglasgowacademy.org.uk | £3,468 | – | P. Brodie |
| The High School of Glasgow, Glasgow | www.glasgowhigh.com | £3,659 | – | C. Mair |
| Glenalmond College, Perth | www.glenalmondcollege.co.uk | £6,880 | £10,100 | G. Woods |
| Hutchesons' Grammar School, Glasgow | www.hutchesons.org | £3,477 | – | Dr K. Greig |
| Kelvinside Academy, Glasgow | www.kelvinsideacademy.org.uk | £3,720 | – | R. Karling |
| Kilgraston, Bridge of Earn | www.kilgraston.com | £5,225 | £8,925 | Mrs D. MacGinty |
| Lomond School, Helensburgh | www.lomondschool.com | £3,454 | £7,670 | Mrs J. Urquhart |
| Loretto School, Musselburgh | www.loretto.com | £6,670 | £9,820 | G. Hawley |
| The Mary Erskine School, Edinburgh | www.esms.org.uk | £3,355 | £6,731 | J. Gray |

| Merchiston Castle School, Edinburgh | www.merchiston.co.uk | £7,015 | £9,520 | A. Hunter |
|---|---|---|---|---|
| Morrison's Academy, Crieff | www.morrisonsacademy.org | £3,790 | – | G. Pengelley |
| Robert Gordon's College, Aberdeen | www.rgc.aberdeen.sch.uk | £3,870 | – | S. Mills |
| St Aloysius' College, Glasgow | www.staloysius.org | £3,438 | – | J. Browne |
| St Columba's School, Kilmacolm | www.st-columbas.org | £3,533 | – | D. Girdwood |
| St Leonards School, St Andrews | www.stleonards-fife.org | £3,999 | £9,753 | Dr M. Carslaw |
| St Margaret's School for Girls, Aberdeen | www.st-margaret.aberdeen.sch.uk | £3,734 | – | Miss A. Tomlinson |
| Stewart's Melville College, Edinburgh | www.esms.org.uk | £3,355 | £6,563 | J. Gray |
| Strathallan School, Perth | www.strathallan.co.uk | £6,570 | £9,682 | B. Thompson |

## NORTHERN IRELAND

| Bangor Grammar School, Bangor | www.bangorgrammarschool.com | – | – | Mrs E. Huddleson |
|---|---|---|---|---|
| Belfast Royal Academy, Belfast | www.belfastroyalacademy.com | £47 | – | J. Dickson |
| Campbell College, Belfast | www.campbellcollege.co.uk | £2,460 | £5,740 | R. Robinson |
| The Royal School Dungannon, Dungannon | www.royaldungannon.com | £50 | £5,117 | D. Burnett |

## CHANNEL ISLANDS

| Elizabeth College, Guernsey | www.elizabethcollege.gg | £3,205 | – | G. Hartley |
|---|---|---|---|---|
| Victoria College, Jersey | www.victoriacollege.je | £1,612 | – | A. Watkins |

# NATIONAL ACADEMIES OF SCHOLARSHIP

The national academies are self-governing bodies whose members are elected as a result of achievement and distinction in the academy's field. Within their discipline, the academies provide advice, support education and exceptional scholars, stimulate debate, promote UK research worldwide and collaborate with international counterparts.

Three of the national academies – the Royal Society, the British Academy and the Royal Academy of Engineering – receive grant-in-aid funding from the Department for Business, Innovation and Skills (BIS). The Academy of Medical Sciences receives core funding from the Department of Health and since 2014 an additional programme grant (£0.47m in 2015–16) from BIS. The Royal Society of Edinburgh is aided by funds provided by the Scottish government. In addition to government funding, the national academies generate additional income from donations, membership contributions, trading and investments.

## SCIENCE BUDGET ALLOCATIONS
*£ thousands*

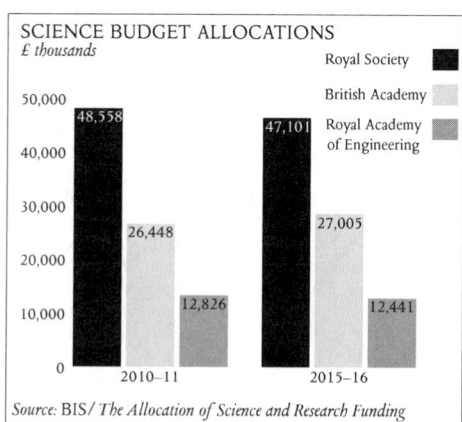

Source: BIS/ *The Allocation of Science and Research Funding*

## ACADEMY OF MEDICAL SCIENCES (1998)
41 Portland Place, London W1B 1QH
T 020-3176 2150 W www.acmedsci.ac.uk

Founded in 1998, the Academy of Medical Sciences is the independent body in the UK representing the diversity of medical science. The Academy seeks to improve health through research, as well as to promote medical science and its translation into benefits for society.

The academy is self-governing and receives funding from a variety of sources, including the fellowship, charitable donations, government and industry.

Fellows are elected from a broad range of medical sciences: biomedical, clinical and population based. The academy includes in its remit veterinary medicine, dentistry, nursing, medical law, economics, sociology and ethics. Elections are from nominations put forward by existing fellows.

As at May 2015 there were 1,094 fellows and 39 honorary fellows.

*President,* Prof. Sir John Tooke, PMEDSCI
*Executive Director,* Dr Helen Munn

## BRITISH ACADEMY (1902)
10–11 Carlton House Terrace, London SW1Y 5AH
T 020-7969 5200 W www.britac.ac.uk

The British Academy is an independent, self-governing learned society for the promotion of the humanities and social sciences. It was founded in 1901 and granted a royal charter in 1902. The British Academy supports advanced academic research and is a channel for the government's support of research in those disciplines.

The fellows are scholars who have attained distinction in one of the branches of study that the academy exists to promote. Candidates must be nominated by existing fellows. There are around 930 fellows, 20 honorary fellows and 300 corresponding fellows overseas.

*President,* Lord Stern of Brentford
*Chief Executive,* Alun Evans

## ROYAL ACADEMY OF ENGINEERING (1976)
3 Carlton House Terrace, London SW1Y 5DG
T 020-7766 0600 W www.raeng.org.uk

The Royal Academy of Engineering was established as the Fellowship of Engineering in 1976. It was granted a royal charter in 1983 and its present title in 1992. It is an independent, self-governing body whose object is the pursuit, encouragement and maintenance of excellence in the whole field of engineering, in order to promote the advancement of the science, art and practice of engineering for the benefit of the public.

Election to the fellowship is by invitation only, from nominations supported by the body of fellows. There are around 1,370 fellows, 42 honorary fellows and 102 international fellows. The Duke of Edinburgh is the senior fellow and the Princess Royal and the Duke of Kent are both royal fellows.

*President,* Dame Ann Dowling, DBE, FRENG, FRS
*Chief Executive,* Philip Greenish, CBE

## ROYAL SOCIETY (1660)
6–9 Carlton House Terrace, London SW1Y 5AG
T 020-7451 2500 W www.royalsociety.org

The Royal Society is an independent academy promoting the natural and applied sciences. Founded in 1660 and granted a royal charter in 1662, the society has three roles: as the UK academy of science, as a learned society and as a funding agency. It is an independent, self-governing body under a royal charter, promoting and advancing all fields of physical and biological sciences, of mathematics and engineering, medical and agricultural sciences and their application.

Fellows are elected for their contributions to science, both in fundamental research resulting in greater understanding, and also in leading and directing scientific and technological progress in industry and research establishments. Each year up to 52 new fellows, who must be citizens or residents of the Commonwealth or Ireland, and up to ten foreign members may be elected. In addition one honorary fellow may also be elected annually from those not eligible for election as fellows or foreign members. There are around 1,430 fellows, 165 foreign members and six honorary members covering all scientific disciplines. The Queen is the patron of the Royal Society, and there are also six royal fellows.

*President,* Sir Venkatraman Ramakrishnan
*Executive Director,* Dr Julie Maxton

## ROYAL SOCIETY OF EDINBURGH (1783)
22–26 George Street, Edinburgh EH2 2PQ
T 0131-240 5000 W www.royalsoced.org.uk

The Royal Society of Edinburgh (RSE) is an educational charity and Scotland's national academy. An independent body with charitable status, its multidisciplinary membership represents a knowledge resource for the people of Scotland. Granted its royal charter in 1783 for the 'advancement of learning and useful knowledge', the society organises conferences, debates and lectures; conducts independent inquiries; facilitates international collaboration and showcases the country's research and development capabilities; provides educational activities for primary and secondary school students; and awards prizes and medals. The society also awards over £2m annually to Scotland's top researchers and entrepreneurs working in Scotland.

As at May 2015 there were 1,606 fellows, comprising 1,463 fellows, 70 honorary fellows and 73 corresponding fellows overseas.

*President,* Prof. Dame Jocelyn Bell Burnell, DBE, FRS, FRSE
*General Secretary,* Prof. Alan Alexander, OBE, FRSE

## PRIVATELY FUNDED ARTS ACADEMIES

The Royal Academy and the Royal Scottish Academy support the visual arts community in the UK, hold educational events and promote interest in the arts. They are entirely privately funded through contributions by 'friends' (regular donors who receive benefits such as free entry, previews and magazines), bequests, corporate donations and exhibitions.

## ROYAL ACADEMY OF ARTS (1768)
Burlington House, Piccadilly, London W1J 0BD
T 020-7300 8000 W www.royalacademy.org.uk

Founded by George III in 1768, the Royal Academy of Arts is an independent, self-governing society devoted to the encouragement and promotion of the fine arts.

Membership of the academy is limited to 80 academicians, all of whom are either painters, engravers, printmakers, draughtsmen, sculptors or architects. There must always be at least 14 sculptors, 12 architects and eight printmakers among the academicians. Candidates must be professionally active in the UK and are nominated and elected by the existing academicians. The members are known as royal academicians (RAs) and are responsible for both the governance and direction of the academy. When RAs reach the age of 75, they become senior academicians and can no longer serve as officers or on the committees.

The title of honorary academician is awarded to a small number of distinguished artists who are not resident in the UK; as at April 2015, there were 29 honorary academicians. Unlike the RAs, they do not take part in the governance of the academy and are unable to vote.

*President,* Christopher Le Brun, PRA
*Secretary and Chief Executive,* Dr Charles Saumarez Smith, CBE

## ROYAL SCOTTISH ACADEMY (1838)
The Mound, Edinburgh EH2 2EL
T 0131-225 6671 W www.royalscottishacademy.org

Founded in 1826 and led by a body of academicians comprising eminent artists and architects, the Royal Scottish Academy (RSA) is an independent voice for cultural advocacy and one of the largest supporters of artists in Scotland. The Academy administers a number of scholarships, awards and residencies and has a historic collection of Scottish artworks, recognised by the Scottish government as being of national significance. The Academy is independent from local or national government funding, relying instead on bequests, legacies, sponsorship and earned income.

Academicians have to be Scots by birth or domicile, and are elected from the disciplines of art and architecture following nominations put forward by the existing membership. There are also a small number of honorary academicians – distinguished artists and architects, writers, historians and musicians – who do not have to be Scottish. As at May 2015 there were 111 academicians and 31 honorary academicians.

*President,* Arthur Watson, PRSA
*Secretary,* Marion Smith, RSA
*Treasurer,* Gareth Fisher, RSA

375

# RESEARCH COUNCILS

The government funds basic and applied civil science research, mostly through seven research councils, which are established under royal charter and supported by the Department for Business, Innovation and Skills (BIS). Research Councils UK is the strategic partnership of these seven councils* (for further information *see* W www.rcuk.ac.uk). The councils support research and training in universities and other higher education and research facilities.

The science budget, administered by BIS, is the main source of public sector funding for research councils, with further public funds provided through the Large Facilities Capital Fund and the Higher Education Innovation Fund. Additional funds may also be provided by other government departments, devolved administrations, the European Commission and other international bodies. The councils also receive income for research specifically commissioned by government departments and the private sector, and income from charitable sources.

## GOVERNMENT SCIENCE BUDGET
*£ thousand*

| | 2014–15 | 2015–16 |
| --- | --- | --- |
| Arts and Humanities Research Council | 98,521 | 98,300 |
| Biotechnology and Biological Sciences Research Council | 391,271 | 432,300 |
| Economic and Social Research Council | 166,186 | 178,400 |
| Engineering and Physical Sciences Research Council | 780,150 | 898,100 |
| Medical Research Council | 649,370 | 810,000 |
| Natural Environment Research Council | 347,929 | 365,000 |
| Science and Technology Facilities Council* | 527,708 | 612,300 |
| Higher Education Innovation Fund (HEIF)† | 113,000 | 113,800 |

* Includes cross-council facilities and international subscriptions, which are managed by STFC on behalf of all research councils
† The research contribution to the HEIF, the Higher Education Funding Council for England (HEFCE) can add additional funding
*Source: BIS – The Allocation of Science and Research Funding 2015/16*

## ARTS AND HUMANITIES RESEARCH COUNCIL*
Polaris House, North Star Avenue, Swindon SN2 1FL
T 01793-416000 W www.ahrc.ac.uk

The AHRC is the successor organisation to the Arts and Humanities Research Board and was incorporated by royal charter and established in 2005. It provides funding for postgraduate training and research in the arts and humanities; in any one year, the AHRC makes approximately 700 research awards and around 2,000 postgraduate scholarships. Awards are made after a rigorous peer review system, which ensures the quality of applications.
*Chair,* Prof. Sir Drummond Bone, FRSE
*Chief Executive,* Prof. Rick Rylance, FRSA

## BIOTECHNOLOGY AND BIOLOGICAL SCIENCES RESEARCH COUNCIL*
Polaris House, North Star Avenue, Swindon SN2 1UH
T 01793-413200 W www.bbsrc.ac.uk

Established by royal charter in 1994, the BBSRC is the UK funding agency for research in the non-clinical life sciences. It funds research into how all living organisms function and behave, benefiting the agriculture, food, health, pharmaceutical and chemical sectors. To deliver its mission, the BBSRC supports research and training in universities and research centres throughout the UK, including providing strategic research grants to the institutes listed below. In June 2015, the institutes founded the National Institutes of Bioscience (NIB) partnership in order to increase the impact of bioscience research and to strengthen the UK's reputation in the field.
*Chair,* Prof. Sir Tom Blundell
*Chief Executive,* Prof. Jackie Hunter

### INSTITUTES
BABRAHAM INSTITUTE, Babraham Hall, Babraham, Cambridge CB22 3AT T 01223-496000
*Director,* Prof. Michael Wakelam
GENOME ANALYSIS CENTRE, Norwich Research Park, Colney, Norwich NR4 7UH T 01603-450861
*Director,* Dr Mario Caccamo
INSTITUTE FOR BIOLOGICAL, ENVIRONMENTAL AND RURAL SCIENCES (ABERYSTWYTH UNIVERSITY), Penglais, Aberystwyth SY23 3DA T 01970-621986
*Director,* Prof. Mike Gooding
INSTITUTE OF FOOD RESEARCH, Norwich Research Park, Colney Lane, Norwich NR4 7UA T 01603-255000
*Director,* Prof. Ian Charles
JOHN INNES CENTRE, Norwich Research Park, Colney, Norwich NR4 7UH T 01603-450000
*Director,* Prof. Dale Sanders
PIRBRIGHT INSTITUTE, Pirbright Laboratory, Ash Road, Pirbright, Surrey GU24 0NF T 01483-232441
*Director,* Prof. John Fazakerley
ROSLIN INSTITUTE (UNIVERSITY OF EDINBURGH), Easter Bush, Midlothian EH25 9RG T 0131-651 9100
*Director,* Prof. David Hume
ROTHAMSTED RESEARCH, Harpenden, Herts AL5 2JQ T 01582-763133
*Director,* Prof. Achim Dobermann

## ECONOMIC AND SOCIAL RESEARCH COUNCIL*
Polaris House, North Star Avenue, Swindon SN2 1UJ
T 01793-413000 E comms@esrc.ac.uk
W www.esrc.ac.uk

The ESRC was established by royal charter in 1965 as an organisation for funding and promoting research and postgraduate training in the social sciences. It also provides advice, disseminates knowledge and promotes public understanding in these areas. The ESRC provides core funding to the centres listed below.
*Chair,* Dr Alan Gillespie, CBE
*Chief Executive,* Prof. Jane Elliott

### RESEARCH CENTRES
CENTRE FOR CLIMATE CHANGE, ECONOMICS AND POLICY, LSE, Houghton Street, London WC2A 2AE T 020-7107 5433
*Directors,* Dr Simon Dietz; Prof. Andy Gouldson

CENTRE FOR CORPUS APPROACHES TO SOCIAL SCIENCE (CASS), FASS Building, Lancaster University, Lancaster, Lancashire LA1 4YW E CASS@lancs.ac.uk
*Director,* Prof. Tony McEnery
CENTRE FOR LANGUAGE AND COMMUNICATIVE DEVELOPMENT, University of Manchester, Manchester M13 9PL T 0161-275 7342
*Director,* Prof. Elena Lieven
CENTRE FOR LONGITUDINAL STUDIES, Institute of Education, 20 Bedford Way, London WC1H 0AL T 020-7612 6875
*Director (acting),* Prof. Alissa Goodman
CENTRE FOR MACROECONOMICS, LSE, Houghton Street, London WC2A 2AE T 020-3486 2818
*Directors,* Prof. Wouter Den Haan; Prof. Morten Ravn
CENTRE FOR MAINTAINING FUNCTION AND WELLBEING IN LATER LIFE, Bangor University, Holyhead Road, Bangor LL57 2PZ T 01248-383968
*Director,* Bob Woods
CENTRE FOR MICRODATA METHODS AND PRACTICE, Institute for Fiscal Studies, 7 Ridgmount Street, London WC1E 7AE T 020-7291 4800
*Director,* Andrew Chesher
CENTRE ON DYNAMICS OF ETHNICITY, University of Manchester, Oxford Road, Manchester M13 9PL T 0161-275 4579
*Director,* Prof. James
NATIONAL CENTRE FOR RESEARCH METHODS, Social Sciences, Room 4139, Murray Building, University of Southampton, Southampton SO17 1BJ T 0238-059 8199
*Director,* Prof. Patrick Sturgis
SYSTEMIC RISK CENTRE, LSE, Houghton Street, London WC2A 2AE E scr@lse.ac.uk
*Directors,* Dr Jon Danielsson; Dr Jean-Pierre Zigrand
TAX ADMINISTRATION RESEARCH CENTRE, University of Exeter, Streatham Court, Rennes Drive, Exeter EX4 4ST T 01392-726286
*Director,* Prof. Gareth Myles
UK ENERGY RESEARCH CENTRE, 11 Princes Gardens, London SW7 1NA T 020-7594 1574
*Director,* Jim Watson

# ENGINEERING AND PHYSICAL SCIENCES RESEARCH COUNCIL*
Polaris House, North Star Avenue, Swindon SN2 1ET
T 01793-444000 W www.epsrc.ac.uk

Formed in 1994 by royal charter, the EPSRC is the UK government's main agency for funding research and training in engineering and the physical sciences in universities and other organisations throughout the UK. It also provides advice, disseminates knowledge and promotes public understanding in these areas.
*Chair,* Paul Golby, FRENG
*Chief Executive,* Prof. Philip Nelson, FRENG

# MEDICAL RESEARCH COUNCIL*
Polaris House, North Star Avenue, Swindon SN2 1FL
T 01793-416200 W www.mrc.ac.uk

The MRC is a publicly funded organisation dedicated to improving human health. The MRC supports research across the entire spectrum of medical sciences, in universities, hospitals, centres and institutes.
*Chair,* Donald Brydon, CBE
*Chief Executive,* Prof. Sir John Savill
*Chair, Infections and Immunity Board,* Prof. Paul Moss
*Chair, Molecular and Cellular Medicine Board,* Prof. Patrick Maxwell

*Chair, Neurosciences and Mental Health Board,* Prof. Hugh Perry
*Chair, Population Health Sciences Group,* Prof. Debbie Lawlor
*Chair, Population and Systems Medicine Board,* Prof. David Lomas

MRC UNITS, CENTRES AND INSTITUTES
*Asthma UK Centre in Allergic Mechanisms of Asthma*
   W www.asthma-allergy.ac.uk
*Behavioural and Clinical Neuroscience Institute (BCNI)*
   W http://research.psychol.cam.ac.uk/~bcni
*Biostatistics Unit* W www.mrc-bsu.cam.ac.uk
*Brain Network Dynamics Unit* W www.mrcbndu.ox.ac.uk
*Cancer Unit* W www.mrc-cu.cam.ac.uk
*Centre for Brain Ageing and Vitality* W www.ncl.ac.uk/cbav
*Centre for Cognitive Ageing and Cognitive Epidemiology*
   W www.ccace.ed.ac.uk
*Centre for Developmental Neurobiology*
   W www.kcl.ac.uk/oppn/depts/devneuro
*Centre for Drug Safety Science* W www.liv.ac.uk/drug-safety
*Centre for Environment and Health*
   W www.environment-health.ac.uk
*Centre for Genomics and Global Health* W www.cggh.org
*Centre for Immune Regulation* W www.birmingham.ac.uk/
   research/activity/mds/centres/mrc-immune
*Centre for Inflammation Research* W www.cir.ed.ac.uk
*Centre for Integrated Research into Musculoskeletal Ageing*
   W www.cimauk.org
*Centre for Medical Molecular Virology*
   W www.ucl.ac.uk/infection-immunity/mrc_ucl-centre
*Centre for Molecular Bacteriology and Infection*
   W www3.imperial.ac.uk/cmbi
*Centre for Mouse Genetics* W www.rc-harwell.ac.uk
*Centre for Musculoskeletal Ageing Research*
   W www.birmingham.ac.uk/generic/mrc-aruk
*Centre for Musculoskeletal Health and Work*
   W www.mrc.soton.ac.uk/cmhw
*Centre for Neuromuscular Diseases* W www.cnmd.ac.uk
*Centre for Neuropsychiatric Genetics and Genomics*
   W http://medicine.cardiff.ac.uk/cngg
*Centre for Outbreak Analysis and Modelling*
   W www1.imperial.ac.uk/medicine/about/institutes/outbreaks
*Centre for Regenerative Medicine* W www.crm.ed.ac.uk
*Centre for Reproductive Health (CRH)*
   W www.crh.ed.ac.uk
*Centre for Transplantation* W http://transplantation.kcl.ac.uk
*Centre for Virus Research*
   W www.gla.ac.uk/researchinstitutes/iii/cvr
*Clinical Sciences Center* W www.csc.mrc.ac.uk
*Clinical Trial Services and Epidemiological Studies Unit*
   W www.ctsu.ox.ac.uk
*Clinical Trials Unit* W www.ctu.mrc.ac.uk
*Cognition and Brain Sciences Unit* W www.mrc-cbu.cam.ac.uk
*Epidemiology Unit* W www.mrc-epid.cam.ac.uk
*Francis Crick Institute* W www.crick.ac.uk
*Functional Genomics Unit* W www.mrcfgu.ox.ac.uk
*Genome Damage and Stability Centre* W www.sussex.ac.uk/gdsc
*Human Genetics Unit* W www.hgu.mrc.ac.uk
*Human Immunology Unit*
   W www.imm.ox.ac.uk/mrc-human-immunology-unit
*Human Nutrition Research Unit* W www.mrc-hnr.cam.ac.uk
*Institute of Genetics and Molecular Medicine*
   W www.igmm.ac.uk
*Institute of Hearing Research* W www.ihr.mrc.ac.uk
*Institute of Radiation Oncology and Biology*
   W www.rob.ox.ac.uk
*Integrative Epidemiology Unit*
   W www.bristol.ac.uk/integrative-epidemiology

*Laboratory of Molecular Biology* W www2.mrc-lmb.cam.ac.uk
*Laboratory for Molecular Cell Biology* W www.ucl.ac.uk/lmcb
*Lifecourse Epidemiology Unit* W www.mrc.soton.ac.uk
*Lifelong Health and Ageing Unit* W www.nshd.mrc.ac.uk
*Metabolic Diseases Unit* W www.mrc-cord.org
*Mitochondrial Biology Unit* W www.mrc-mbu.cam.ac.uk
*Molecular Haemotology Unit*
  W www.imm.ox.ac.uk/mrc-molecular-haematology-unit
*National Institute for Medical Research (NIMR)*
  W www.nimr.mrc.ac.uk
*Prion Unit* W www.prion.ucl.ac.uk
*Protein Phosphorylation and Ubiquitylation Unit*
  W www.ppu.mrc.ac.uk
*Research Complex at Harwell (RCaH)* W www.rc-harwell.ac.uk
*Scottish Collaboration for Public Health Research and Policy*
  W www.scphrp.ac.uk
*Social and Public Health Sciences Unit* W www.sphsu.mrc.ac.uk
*Social, Genetic and Developmental Psychiatry Centre*
  W www.kcl.ac.uk/iop/depts/mrc
*Stem Cell Institute* W www.stemcells.cam.ac.uk
*Toxicology Unit* W www.tox.mrc.ac.uk
*Weatherall Institute of Molecular Medicine (WIMM)*
  W www.imm.ox.ac.uk

*MRC The Gambia* W www.mrc.gm
*Uganda Research Unit on AIDS* W www.mrcuganda.org

## NATIONAL PHYSICAL LABORATORY
Hampton Road, Teddington, Middx TW11 0LW
T 020-8977 3222 W www.npl.co.uk

The National Physical Laboratory (NPL) was established in 1900 and is the UK's national measurement institute. On 1 January 2015 it became a wholly owned government company, part of the Department for Business, Innovation and Skills. It develops, maintains and disseminates national measurement standards for physical quantities such as mass, length, time, temperature, voltage and force. It also conducts underpinning research on engineering materials and information technology, and disseminates good measurement practice.
*Chief Executive,* Dr Peter Thompson

## ASSOCIATION OF INNOVATION, RESEARCH AND TECHNOLOGY ORGANISATIONS LIMITED (AIRTO)
T 020-8943 6600 E enquiries@airto.co.uk W www.airto.co.uk

AIRTO is a membership body, based at the NPL, for organisations operating in the UK's innovation, research and technology sector and represents around 80 per cent of organisations in this sector. AIRTO's members deliver vital innovation and knowledge transfer services which include applied and collaborative research and development (frequently in conjunction with universities), consultancy, technology validation and testing, incubation of commercialisation opportunities and early stage financing. AIRTO members have a combined turnover of over £5.5bn from clients inside and outside the UK, and together employ over 47,000 scientists, technologists and engineers. For a full list of members, *see* AIRTO's website.
*President,* Prof. Richard Brook, OBE, FRENG

## NATURAL ENVIRONMENT RESEARCH COUNCIL*
Polaris House, North Star Avenue, Swindon SN2 1EU
T 01793-411500 W www.nerc.ac.uk

NERC is the leading funder of independent research, training and innovation in environmental science in the UK. Its work covers the full range of atmospheric, earth, biological, terrestrial and aquatic sciences. NERC invests public money in research exploring how we can sustainably benefit from our natural resources, predict and respond to natural hazards and understand environmental change. NERC works closely with policymakers and industry to support sustainable economic growth in the UK and around the world.
*Chair,* Sir Anthony Cleaver
*Chief Executive,* Prof. Duncan Wingham

RESEARCH CENTRES
BRITISH ANTARCTIC SURVEY, High Cross, Madingley Road, Cambridge CB3 0ET T 01223-221400
  *Director,* Prof. Jane Francis
BRITISH GEOLOGICAL SURVEY, Kingsley Dunham Centre, Keyworth, Nottingham NG12 5GG T 0115-936 3100
  *Executive Director,* Prof. John Ludden
CENTRE FOR ECOLOGY AND HYDROLOGY, Maclean Building, Benson Lane, Crowmarsh Gifford, Wallingford OX10 8BB T 01491-838800
  *Director,* Prof. Mark J. Bailey
NATIONAL CENTRE FOR ATMOSPHERIC SCIENCE, NCAS Headquarters, School of Earth and Environment, University of Leeds, Leeds LS2 9JT T 0113-343 6408
  *Director,* Prof. Stephen Mobbs
NATIONAL CENTRE FOR EARTH OBSERVATION, Michael Atiyah Building, University of Leicester, University Road, Leicester LE1 7RH T 0116-252 2016
  *Director,* Prof. John Remedios
NATIONAL OCEANOGRAPHY CENTRE, University of Southampton Waterfront Campus, European Way, Southampton SO14 3ZH T 023-8059 6666
  *Director,* Prof. Ed Hill, OBE

## SCIENCE AND TECHNOLOGY FACILITIES COUNCIL*
Polaris House, North Star Avenue, Swindon SN2 1SZ
T 01793-442000 W www.stfc.ac.uk

Formed by royal charter in 2007, through the merger of the Council for the Central Laboratory of the Research Councils and the Particle Physics and Astronomy Research Council, the STFC is a non-departmental public body reporting to BIS.

The STFC invests in large national and international research facilities, while delivering science and technology expertise for the UK. The council is involved in research projects such as the Diamond Light Source Synchrotron and the Large Hadron Collider, and develops new areas of science and technology. The EPSRC has transferred its responsibility for nuclear physics to the STFC.
*Chair,* Prof. Michael Sterling, FRENG
*Chief Executive,* Prof. John Womersley

RESEARCH CENTRES
BOULBY UNDERGROUND SCIENCE FACILITY, Boulby Mine, Loftus, Saltburn-by-the-Sea, Cleveland TS13 4UZ
  T 01287-646300
CHILBOLTON OBSERVATORY, Chilbolton, Stockbridge, Hampshire SO20 6BJ T 01264-860391
DARESBURY LABORATORY, SciTech Daresbury, Warrington WA4 4AD T 01925-603000
RUTHERFORD APPLETON LABORATORY, Harwell Oxford, Didcot OX11 0QX T 01235-445000
UK ASTRONOMY TECHNOLOGY CENTRE, Royal Observatory Edinburgh, Blackford Hill, Edinburgh EH9 3HJ
  T 0131-668 8100

# HEALTH

## NATIONAL HEALTH SERVICE

The National Health Service (NHS) came into being on 5 July 1948 under the National Health Service Act 1946, covering England and Wales and, under separate legislation, Scotland and Northern Ireland. The NHS is now administered by the Secretary of State for Health (in England), the Welsh government, the Scottish government and the Northern Ireland Executive.

The function of the NHS is to provide a comprehensive health service designed to secure improvement in the physical and mental health of the people and to prevent, diagnose and treat illness. It was founded on the principle that treatment should be provided according to clinical need rather than ability to pay, and should be free at the point of delivery.

Hospital, mental, dental, nursing, ophthalmic and ambulance services and facilities for the care of expectant and nursing mothers and young children are provided by the NHS to meet all reasonable requirements. Rehabilitation services such as occupational therapy, physiotherapy, speech therapy and surgical and medical appliances are supplied where appropriate. Specialists and consultants who work in NHS hospitals can also engage in private practice, including the treatment of their private patients in NHS hospitals.

### STRUCTURE

The structure of the NHS remained relatively stable for the first 30 years of its existence. In 1974, a three-tier management structure comprising regional health authorities, area health authorities and district management teams was introduced in England, and the NHS became responsible for community health services. In 1979, area health authorities were abolished and district management teams were replaced by district health authorities.

The National Health Service and Community Care Act 1990 provided for more streamlined regional health authorities and district health authorities, and for the establishment of family health services authorities (FHSAs) and NHS trusts. The concept of the 'internal market' was introduced into health care, whereby care was provided through NHS contracts where health authorities or boards and GP fundholders (the purchasers) were responsible for buying health care from hospitals, non-fundholding GPs, community services and ambulance services (the providers). The Act also paved the way for the community care reforms, which were introduced in April 1993, and changed the way care is administered for older people, the mentally ill, the physically disabled and people with learning disabilities.

### ENGLAND

Under the Health and Social Care Act 2012, which gained royal assent in March 2012, the NHS in England is undergoing a complete operational and budgetary restructure at a cost of approximately £1.4bn. The full implementation of all the changes will not be complete for some time.

Hospitals will be extensively affected by the overhaul, with the cap on income from private hospital patients rising from 1.5 per cent to 49 per cent. All hospitals will become foundation trusts, competing for treatment contracts from clinical commissioning groups (CCGs).

On 1 April 2013 the new commissioning board, NHS England, took on full statutory responsibilities; at the same time, strategic health authorities (SHAs) and primary care trusts (PCTs) which, alongside the Department of Health (DoH), had been responsible for NHS planning and delivery, were abolished. NHS England is an executive non-departmental public body of the DoH with a remit to:
• provide national leadership to improve the quality of care
• oversee the operation of clinical commissioning groups
• allocate resources to clinical commissioning groups
• commission primary care and specialist services

The secretary of state has ultimate responsibility for the provision of a comprehensive health service in England and for ensuring the system works to its optimum capacity to meet the needs of its patients. The DoH is responsible for strategic leadership of the health and social care systems, but will cease to be the headquarters of the NHS, nor will it directly manage any NHS organisations.

In October 2014, NHS England published *Five Year Forward View* which committed the organisation to further change, including additional decentralisation and a greater emphasis on out-of-hospital care and preventative medicine.

NHS ENGLAND, PO Box 16738, Redditch B97 9PT
T 0300-311 2233 W www.england.nhs.uk
*Chief Executive*, Simon Stevens

### CLINICAL COMMISSIONING GROUPS (CCGS)

On 1 April 2013, PCTs, which controlled 80 per cent of the NHS budget and commissioned most NHS services, were abolished. They were replaced with CCGs which took on many of the functions of the PCTs in addition to some functions previously assumed by the Department of Health. All GP practices now belong to a CCG which also includes other health professionals, such as nurses. CCGs commission most services, including:
• mental health and learning disability services
• planned hospital care
• rehabilitative care
• urgent and emergency care (including out-of-hours)
• most community health services

CCGs can commission any service provider that meets NHS standards and costs. These can be NHS hospitals, social enterprises, charities, or private-sector providers. There are 210 CCGs, which together are responsible for around 60 per cent of the NHS budget, around £69bn in 2015–16. In April 2015, 64 CCGs were approved to take on the additional responsibility for commissioning GP services within their area.

### HEALTH AND WELLBEING BOARDS

Every upper-tier local authority hasestablished a health and wellbeing board to act as a forum for local commissioners across the NHS, social care, public health and other services. The 152 boards are intended to:
• encourage integrated commissioning of health and social care services
• increase democratic input into strategic decisions about health and wellbeing services
• strengthen working relationships between health and social care

### PUBLIC HEALTH ENGLAND (PHE)

This new organisation was established on 1 April 2013. It provides national leadership and expert services to support public health and also works with local government and the NHS to respond to emergencies. PHE's responsibilities are to:

- coordinate a national public health service
- support the public to make healthier choices
- provide leadership to the public health delivery system
- support the development of the public health workforce

## REGULATION

Since the restructuring of the NHS in England began in April 2013, some elements of the regulation system have changed. Responsibility for the regulation of particular aspects of care is shared across a number of different bodies, including the Care Quality Commission (CQC), Monitor, and individual professional regulatory bodies, such as the General Medical Council, Nursing and Midwifery Council, General Dental Council and the Health and Care Professions Council.

### CARE QUALITY COMMISSION (CQC)

The CQC regulates all health and social care services in England, including those provided by the NHS, local authorities, private companies or voluntary organisations. In addition it protects the interests of people detained under the Mental Health Act. The CQC ensures that all essential standards of quality and safety are met where care is provided, from hospitals to private care homes. By law all NHS providers (such as hospitals and ambulance services) must register with the CQC to show they are protecting people from the risk of infection. The CQC possesses a range of legal powers and duties and will take action if providers do not meet essential standards of quality or safety.

### MONITOR

Monitor is the sector regulator for health services in England. Their job is to protect and promote the interests of patients. Monitor's aim is to promote competition, regulate prices and ensure the continuity of services for NHS foundation trusts. Under the new structure, most NHS providers need to be registered with both the CQC and Monitor to be able to legally provide services.

### HEALTHWATCH

Healthwatch England was established in October 2012 following the restructuring of the NHS. The organisation functions at a national and local level as an independent consumer body, gathering and representing the views of the public about health and social care services in England.
CARE QUALITY COMMISSION, Finsbury Tower,
    103–105 Bunhill Row, London EC1Y 8TG T 03000-616161
    W www.cqc.org.uk
    *Chief Executive*, David Behan
MONITOR, Wellington House, 133–155 Waterloo Road,
    London SE1 8UG T 020-3747 0000
    W www.monitor-nhsft.gov.uk
    *Chief Executive*, Dr David Bennett
HEALTHWATCH, Citygate, Gallowgate, Newcastle upon Tyne
    NE1 4PA T 03000-683000 W www.healthwatch.co.uk
    *Chief Executive*, Dr Katherine Rake, OBE

## AUTHORITIES AND TRUSTS

Overseen by the NHS Trust Development Authority all NHS trusts are expected to eventually become foundation trusts.

### ACUTE TRUSTS

Hospitals in England are managed by acute trusts. There are 161 acute trusts, of which 102 have foundation trust status. Acute trusts ensure hospitals provide high-quality healthcare and spend money efficiently. They employ a large sector of the NHS workforce, including doctors, nurses, pharmacists, midwives, and health visitors. Acute trusts also employ those in supplementary medical professions, such as physiotherapists, radiographers and podiatrists, in addition to many other non-medical staff.

### AMBULANCE TRUSTS

There are 10 ambulance services (five foundation trusts) in England, providing emergency services to healthcare.

### CLINICAL SENATES AND STRATEGIC CLINICAL NETWORKS

Clinical senates are advisory groups of experts from across health and social care. There are 12 senates covering England comprising clinical leaders from across the healthcare system, in addition to members from social care and public health.

There are 12 strategic clinical networks across England, comprising groups of clinical experts covering a particular disease, patient or professional group. They offer advice to CCGs and NHS England.

Neither organisation is a statutory body, and although they comment on CCG plans to NHS England, they are unable to veto them.

### FOUNDATION TRUSTS

NHS foundation trusts are independent legal entities with unique governance arrangements. Each NHS foundation trust has a duty to consult and involve a board of governors in the strategic planning of its organisation. They have financial freedoms and can raise capital from both the public and private sectors within borrowing limits determined by projected cash flows and based on affordability. They are overseen by Monitor.

### MENTAL HEALTH TRUSTS

There are 59 mental health trusts in England, 43 of which have foundation trust status. They provide health and social care services for people with mental health problems.

### NHS TRUST DEVELOPMENT AUTHORITY (TDA)

Following the abolition of SHAs in 2013, the TDA became responsible for overseeing the performance, management and governance of NHS trusts, including clinical quality, and managing their progress towards foundation trust status.

### SPECIAL HEALTH AUTHORITIES

There are 12 Special health authorities with a nationwide remit, including:
- The National Blood and Transplant Authority
- NHS Business Services Authority
- NHS Litigation Authority

## WALES

The NHS Wales was reorganised according to Welsh Assembly commitments laid out in the *One Wales* strategy which came into effect in October 2009. There are now seven local health boards (LHBs) that are responsible for delivering all health care services within a geographical area, rather than the trust and local health board system that existed previously. Community health councils (CHCs) are statutory lay bodies that represent the public for the health service in their region. There are currently eight CHCs.

### NHS TRUSTS

There are three NHS trusts in Wales. The Welsh Ambulance Services NHS Trust is for emergency services; the Velindre NHS Trust offers specialist services in cancer care; while Public Health Wales serves as a unified public health organisation for Wales.

### LOCAL HEALTH BOARDS

The websites of the seven LHBs, and contact details for community health councils and NHS trusts, are available in the *NHS Wales Directory* on the NHS Wales website (W www.wales.nhs.uk).

ABERTAWE BRO MORGANNWG UNIVERSITY HEALTH BOARD, One Talbot Gateway, Baglan Energy Park, Baglan, Port Talbot SA12 7BR T 01639-683344
*Chief Executive*, Paul Roberts

ANEURIN BEVAN HEALTH BOARD, Headquarters, Lodge Road, Caerleon, Newport NP18 3XQ T 01873-732732
*Chief Executive*, Judith Paget

BETSI CADWALADR UNIVERSITY HEALTH BOARD, Ysbyty Gwynedd, Penrhosgarnedd, Bangor, Gwynedd LL57 2PW T 01248-384384
*Chief Executive (interim)*, Simon Dean

CARDIFF AND VALE UNIVERSITY HEALTH BOARD, Cardigan House, University Hospital of Wales, Heath Park, Cardiff CF14 4XW T 029-2074 7747
*Chief Executive*, Adam Cairns

CWM TAF HEALTH BOARD, Ynysmeurig House, Navigation Park, Abercynon CF45 4SN T 01443-744800
*Chief Executive*, Allison Williams

HYWEL DDA HEALTH BOARD, Corporate Offices, Ystwyth Building, Hafan Derwen, Jobswell Road, Carmarthen SA31 3BB T 01267-235151
*Chief Executive*, Steve Moore

POWYS TEACHING HEALTH BOARD, Mansion House, Bronllys, Brecon, Powys LD3 0LS T 01874-771661
*Chief Executive*, Carol Shillabeer

## SCOTLAND

The Scottish government Health Directorate is responsible both for NHS Scotland and for the development and implementation of health and community care policy. The chief executive of NHS Scotland leads the central management of the NHS, is accountable to ministers for the efficiency and performance of the service and heads the Health Department which oversees the work of the 14 regional health boards. These boards provide strategic management for the entire local NHS system and are responsible for ensuring that services are delivered effectively and efficiently.

In addition to the 14 regional health boards there are a further seven special boards and one public health body, which provide national services, such as the Scottish ambulance service and NHS Health Scotland. Healthcare Improvement Scotland, was formed on 1 April 2011 by the Public Services Reform Act 2010 to improve the quality of Scottish healthcare.

## REGIONAL HEALTH BOARDS

AYRSHIRE AND ARRAN, Eglinton House, Ailsa Hospital, Dalmellington Road, Ayr KA6 6AB T 0800-169 1441
W www.nhsaaa.net
*Chief Executive*, John Burns

BORDERS, Borders General Hospital, Melrose, Roxburghshire TD6 9DA T 01896-826000 W www.nhsborders.org.uk
*Chief Executive*, Jane Davidson

DUMFRIES AND GALLOWAY, Ryan North, Crichton Hall, Dumfries DG1 4TG T 01387-246246
W www.nhsdg.scot.nhs.uk
*Chief Executive*, Jeff Ace

EILEAN SIAR (WESTERN ISLES), 37 South Beach Street, Stornoway, Isle of Lewis HS1 2BB T 01851-702997
W www.wihb.scot.nhs.uk
*Chief Executive*, Gordon Jamieson

FIFE, Hayfield House, Hayfield Road, Kirkcaldy, Fife KY2 5AH T 01592-643355 W www.nhsfife.org
*Chief Executive*, John Wilson

FORTH VALLEY, Carseview House, Castle Business Park, Stirling FK9 4SW T 01786-463031 W www.nhsforthvalley.com
*Chief Executive*, Jane Grant

GRAMPIAN, Summerfield House, 2 Eday Road, Aberdeen AB15 6RE T 0845-456 6000 W www.nhsgrampian.org
*Chief Executive*, Malcolm Wright

GREATER GLASGOW AND CLYDE, J B Russell House, Gartnavel Royal Hospital Campus, 1055 Great Western Road, Glasgow G12 0XH T 0141-201 4444 W www.nhsgg.org.uk
*Chief Executive*, Robert Calderwood

HIGHLAND, Assynt House, Beechwood Park, Inverness IV2 3BW T 01463-717123 W www.nhshighland.scot.nhs.uk
*Chief Executive*, Elaine Mead

LANARKSHIRE, Kirklands, Fallside Road, Bothwell G71 8BB T 01236-748748 W www.nhslanarkshire.org.uk
*Chief Executive*, Calum Campbell

LOTHIAN, Waverley Gate, 2–4 Waterloo Place, Edinburgh EH1 3EG T 0131-536 9000 W www.nhslothian.scot.nhs.uk
*Chief Executive*, Tim Davison

ORKNEY, Garden House, New Scapa Road, Kirkwall, Orkney KW15 1BQ T 01856-888000 W www.ohb.scot.nhs.uk
*Chief Executive*, Cathie Cowan

SHETLAND, Upper Floor Montfield, Burgh Road, Lerwick ZE1 0LA T 01595-743060 W www.shb.scot.nhs.uk
*Chief Executive*, Ralph Roberts

TAYSIDE, Level 10, Ninewells Hospital, Dundee DD1 9SY T 01382-660111 W www.nhstayside.scot.nhs.uk
*Chief Executive*, Lesley McLay

## NORTHERN IRELAND

On 1 April 2009 the four health and social services boards in Northern Ireland were replaced by a single health and social care board for the whole of Northern Ireland. The new board together with its local commissioning groups (whose boundaries are subject to review pending the outcome of local government reform) are responsible for improving the health and social wellbeing of people in the area for which they are responsible, planning and commissioning services, and coordinating the delivery of services in a cost-effective manner.

HEALTH AND SOCIAL CARE BOARD, 12–22 Linenhall Street, Belfast BT2 8BS T 030-0555 0115
W www.hscboard.hscni.net
*Chief Executive*, Valerie Watts

## FINANCE

The NHS is still funded mainly through general taxation, although in recent years more reliance has been placed on the NHS element of national insurance contributions, patient charges and other sources of income.

Funding for NHS England was set at £98.84bn for 2015–16. Expenditure for the NHS in Wales, Scotland and Northern Ireland is set by the devolved governments.

## EMPLOYEES AND SALARIES

NHS HEALTH SERVICE STAFF 2015 (ENGLAND)
*Full-time equivalent*

| | |
|---|---|
| All hospital, community and dental staff | 1,218,911 |
| Consultants | 43,766 |
| Registrars | 39,976 |
| Qualified nursing and midwifery staff | 357,548 |
| Qualified scientific, therapeutic and technical staff | 155,603 |

*Source*: Health and Social Care Information Centre *NHS Hospital and Community Health Service: Monthly Workforce Statistics*

## SALARIES

Many general practitioners (GPs) are self-employed and hold contracts, either on their own or as part of a Clinical Commissioning Group (CCG). The profit of GPs varies according to the services they provide for their patients and the way they choose to provide these services. Salaried GPs who are part of a CCG earn between £55,412 and £83,617. Most NHS dentists are self-employed contractors. A contract for dentists was introduced on 1 April 2006 which provides dentists with an annual income in return for carrying out an agreed amount, or units, of work. A salaried dentist employed by the NHS, who works mainly with community dental services earn between £38,095 and £81,480.

## BASIC SALARIES FOR HOSPITAL MEDICAL AND DENTAL STAFF

*from 1 April 2015*

From 1 April 2015 to 31 March 2016 staff who are on the top salary in their pay band will receive a non-consolidated lump sum, payable in monthly instalments, of either 1 or 2 per cent of their basic pay dependent on the length of time they have been on the top salary in their pay band. The figures below do not include merit awards, discretionary points or banding supplements.

| | |
|---|---|
| Consultant (2003 contract) | £75,249–£101,451 |
| Specialist registrar | £31,301–£47,175 |
| Speciality registrar (full) | £30,002–£47,175 |
| Speciality registrar (fixed term) | £30,002–£39,693 |
| Foundation house officer year 2 | £28,076–£31,748 |
| Foundation house officer year 1 | £22,636–£25,461 |

## NURSES

From 1 December 2004 the *Agenda for Change* pay system was introduced throughout the UK for all NHS staff with the exception of medical and dental staff, doctors in public health medicine and the community health service. Nurses' salaries are incorporated in the *Agenda for Change* nine pay band structure, which provides additional payments for flexible working such as providing out-of-hours services, working weekends and nights and being on-call. There is also additional payments for those staff who work in high-cost areas such as London.

## SALARIES FOR NURSES AND MIDWIVES

*from 1 April 2015*

| | |
|---|---|
| Nurse/Midwife consultant | £39,632–£67,805 |
| Modern matron | £39,632–£47,559 |
| Nurse advanced/team manager | £31,072–£40,964 |
| Midwife higher level | £31,072–£40,964 |
| Nurse specialist/team leader | £26,041–£34,876 |
| Hospital/community midwife | £26,041–£34,876 |
| Registered nurse/entry level midwife* | £21,692–£28,180 |

*Starting salaries in Wales and Norther Ireland are currently the same as in England. The starting salary in Scotland is £21,602

# HEALTH SERVICES

## PRIMARY CARE

Primary care comprises the services provided by general practitioners, community health centres, pharmacies, dental practices and opticians. Primary nursing care includes the work carried out by practice nurses, community nurses, community midwives and health visitors.

## PRIMARY MEDICAL SERVICES

In England, primary medical services (PMS) are provided by 66,846 registerd GPs, working in around 8,000 GP practices, with 56.6 million registered patients.

In Wales, responsibility for primary medical services rests with local health boards (LHBs), in Scotland with the 14 regional health boards and in Northern Ireland with the health and social care board.

Any vocationally trained doctor may provide general or personal medical services. GPs may also have private fee-paying patients, but not if that patient is already an NHS patient on that doctor's patient list.

A person who is ordinarily resident in the UK is eligible to register with a GP (or PMS provider) for free primary care treatment. Should a patient have difficulty in registering with a doctor, he or she should contact the local CCG for help. When a person is away from home he/she can still access primary care treatment from a GP if they ask to be treated as a temporary resident. In an emergency any doctor in the service will give treatment and advice.

GPs or CCGs are responsible for the care of their patients 24 hours a day, seven days a week, but can fulfil the terms of their contract by delegating or transferring responsibility for out-of-hours care to an accredited provider.

In addition, NHS walk-in centres (WICs) throughout England are usually open seven days a week, from early in the morning until late in the evening. They are nurse-led and provide treatment for minor illnesses and injuries, health information and self-help advice. Some WICs are not able to treat young children.

## HEALTH COSTS

Some people are exempt from, or entitled to help with, health costs such as prescription charges, ophthalmic and dental costs, and in some cases help towards travel costs to and from hospital.

The following list is intended as a general guide to those who may be entitled to help, or who are exempt from some of the charges relating to the above:

- children under 16 and young people in full-time education who are under 19
- people aged 60 or over
- pregnant women and women who have had a baby in the last 12 months and have a valid maternity exemption certificate (MatEx)
- people, or their partners, who are in receipt of income support, income-based jobseeker's allowance and/or income-based employment and support allowance
- people in receipt of the pension credit
- diagnosed glaucoma patients, people who have been advised by an ophthalmologist that they are at risk of glaucoma and people aged 40 or over who have an immediate family member who is a diagnosed glaucoma patient
- NHS in-patients
- NHS out-patients for all prescribed contraceptives, medication given at a hospital, NHS walk-in centre, personally administered by a GP or supplied at a hospital or primary care trust clinic for the treatment of tuberculosis or a sexually transmissible infection
- out-patients of the NHS Hospital Dental Service
- people registered blind or partially sighted
- people who need complex lenses
- war pensioners whose treatment/prescription is for their accepted disablement and who have a valid exemption certificate
- people who are entitled to, or named on, a valid NHS tax credit exemption or HC2 certificate
- people who have a medical exemption (MedEx) certificate, including those with cancer or diabetes

People in other circumstances may also be eligible for help; *see* booklet HC12 (England) and HCS2 (Scotland) for further information.

## WALES

On 1 April 2007 all prescription charges (including those for medical supports and appliances and wigs) for people living in Wales were abolished. The above guide still applies for NHS dental and optical charges although all people aged under 25 living in Wales are also entitled to free dental examinations.

## SCOTLAND

On 1 April 2011 all prescription charges in Scotland were abolished. Those entitled to free prescriptions in Scotland include patients registered with a Scottish GP and receiving a prescription from a Scottish pharmacy, and Scottish patients who have an English GP and an entitlement card.

## NORTHERN IRELAND

On 1 April 2010 all prescription charges in Northern Ireland were abolished. All prescriptions dispensed in Northern Ireland are free, even for patients visiting from England, Wales or Scotland.

## PHARMACEUTICAL SERVICES

Patients may obtain medicines and appliances under the NHS from any pharmacy whose owner has entered into arrangements with the CCG to provide this service. There are also some suppliers who only provide special appliances. In rural areas, where access to a pharmacy may be difficult, patients may be able to obtain medicines, etc, from a dispensing doctor.

In England, a charge of £8.20 is payable for each item supplied (except for contraceptives for which there is no charge), unless the patient is exempt and the declaration on the back of the prescription form is completed. Prescription prepayment certificates (£29.10 valid for three months, £104 valid for a year) may be purchased by those patients not entitled to exemption who require frequent prescriptions.

## DENTAL SERVICES

Dentists, like doctors, may take part in the NHS and also have private patients. Dentists are responsible to the local health provider in whose areas they provide services. Patients may go to any dentist who is taking part in the NHS and is willing to accept them. There is a three-tier payment system based on the individual course of treatment required.

## NHS DENTAL CHARGES
*from 1 April 2015*

| | England/Wales |
|---|---|
| Band 1* – Examination, diagnosis, preventive care (eg x-rays, scale and polish) | £18.80/£13.50 |
| Band 2 – Band 1 + basic additional treatment (eg fillings and extractions) | £51.30/£43.00 |
| Band 3 – Bands 1 and 2 + all other treatment (eg crowns, dentures and bridges) | £222.50/£185.00 |

* Urgent and out-of-hours treatment is also charged at this payment tier

The cost of individual treatment plans should be known prior to treatment and some dental practices may require payment in advance. There is no charge for writing a prescription or removing stitches and only one charge is payable for each course of treatment even if more than one visit to the dentist is required. If additional treatment is required within two months of visiting the dentist and this is covered by the course of treatment most recently paid for (eg payment was made for the second tier of treatment but an additional filling is required) then this will be provided free of charge.

## SCOTLAND AND NORTHERN IRELAND

Scotland and Northern Ireland have yet to simplify their charging systems. NHS dental patients pay 80 per cent of the cost of the individual items of treatment provided up to a maximum of £384. Patients in Scotland are entitled to free basic and extensive examinations.

## GENERAL OPHTHALMIC SERVICES

General ophthalmic services are administered by local health providers. Testing of sight may be carried out by any ophthalmic medical practitioner or ophthalmic optician (optometrist). The optician must give the prescription to the patient, who can take this to any supplier of glasses to have them dispensed. Only registered opticians can supply glasses to children and to people registered as blind or partially sighted.

Free eyesight tests and help towards the cost are available to people in certain circumstances. Help is also available for the purchase of glasses or contact lenses (*see* Health Costs). In Scotland eye examinations, which include a sight test, are free to all UK residents. Help is also available for the purchase of glasses or contact lenses to those entitled to help with health costs in the same way it is available to those in England and Wales.

## CHILD HEALTH SERVICES

Pre-school services at GP surgeries or child health clinics provide regular monitoring of children's physical, mental and emotional health and development and advise parents on their children's health and welfare.

## NHS 111, NHS DIRECT AND NHS 24

NHS Direct Wales is a website and 24-hour nurse-led advice telephone service for Wales. It provides medical advice as well as directing people to the appropriate part of the NHS for treatment if necessary (T 0845 46 47 W www.nhsdirect.wales.nhs.uk). NHS Direct had also operated in England but closed on 31 March 2014. Non-urgent 24-hour nurse-led advice in England can be accessed via the NHS 111 service (T 111).

NHS 24 provides an equivalent service for Scotland (T 0845-424 2424 W www.nhs24.com).

# SECONDARY CARE AND OTHER SERVICES

## HOSPITALS

NHS hospitals provide acute and specialist care services, treating conditions which normally cannot be dealt with by primary care specialists, and provide for medical emergencies.

## NUMBER OF BEDS 2014–15

| | Average daily | |
|---|---|---|
| | available beds | occupation of beds |
| England | 137,088 | 121,391 |
| Wales* | 11,241 | 9,653 |
| Scotland* | 16,059 | 13,650 |
| Northern Ireland | 6,034 | 5,020 |

* Figures are for 2013–14

*Sources:* NHS England, Welsh government, ISD Scotland, NI Direct

## HOSPITAL CHARGES

Acute or foundation trusts can provide hospital accommodation in single rooms or small wards, if not required for patients who need privacy for medical reasons. The patient is still an NHS patient, but there may be a charge for these additional facilities. Acute or foundation trusts can charge for certain patient services that are considered to be additional treatments over and above the normal hospital service provision. There is no blanket policy to cover this and each case is considered in the light of the patient's clinical need. However, if an item or service is considered to be an integral part of a patient's treatment by their clinician, then a charge should not be made.

In some NHS hospitals, accommodation and services are available for the treatment of private patients where it does not interfere with care for NHS patients. Income generated by treating private patients is then put back into local NHS services. Private patients undertake to pay the full costs of medical treatment, accommodation, medication and other related services. Charges for private patients are set locally.

## WAITING LISTS

*England*

For June 2015, 328,565 referral to treatment (RTT) patients started admitted treatment and 970,070 started non-admitted treatment. Of the admitted patients, 90 per cent were treated within 18 weeks, and for non-admitted patients 92 per cent were treated within 18 weeks.

*Wales*

In June 2015, 76.9 per cent of 90,012 patients were treated within 26 weeks and 89.1 per cent were treated within 36 weeks of the date the referral letter was received in hospital. There are also operational standards for maximum waiting times for first out-patient appointments and in-patient or day-case treatment but these are not set targets. The standards are 14 weeks for in-patient or day case treatment, and ten weeks for a first out-patient appointment.

*Scotland*

In March 2015, 88.5 per cent of patients on an 18 week referral to treatment pathway were reported as being seen within 18 weeks, a decrease from 89.6 per cent in March 2014.

*Northern Ireland*

From March 2015 the aim was for at least 70 per cent of patients to wait no longer than nine weeks for a first out-patient appointment, with no patient waiting longer than 18 weeks. The total number of people waiting for a first out-patient appointment at the end of March 2015 was 191,779, of these 56.3 per cent had been waiting over nine weeks, compared with just 31.3 per cent at the end of March 2014. The number of people waiting for in-patient treatment at the end of March 2015 was 57,934 – of these, 48 per cent had been waiting for more than 13 weeks.

### AMBULANCE SERVICE

The NHS provides emergency ambulance services free of charge via the 999 emergency telephone service. Air ambulances, provided through local charities and partially funded by the NHS, are used throughout the UK. They assist with cases where access may be difficult or heavy traffic could hinder road progress. Non-emergency ambulance services are provided free to patients who are deemed to require them on medical grounds.

Since 1 April 2001 all services have had a system of call prioritisation. Since 2013–14, ambulances have been expected to reach Red 1 – calls requiring a defibrillator – and Red 2 emergency calls within eight minutes, at least 75 per cent of the time. Non-emergency calls are categorised as Green 1, 2, 3 or 4, with category Green 4 calls being the least serious. Green calls are generally responded to between 20 minutes and one hour.

In April 2015, the NHS employed 18,798 qualified ambulance staff in England earning between £19,027 (ambulance practitioner) and £34,876 (senior paramedic).

### BLOOD AND TRANSPLANT SERVICES

There are four national bodies which coordinate the blood donor programme and transplant and related services in the

UK. Donors give blood at local centres on a voluntary basis.

NHS BLOOD AND TRANSPLANT, Oak House, Reeds Crescent, Watford, Herts WD24 4QN **T** 0300-123 2323 **W** www.nhsbt.nhs.uk

WELSH BLOOD SERVICE, Ely Valley Road, Talbot Green, Pontyclun CF72 9WB **T** 01443-622000 **W** www.welsh-blood.org.uk

SCOTTISH NATIONAL BLOOD TRANSFUSION SERVICE, 21 Ellen's Glen Road, Edinburgh EH17 7QT **T** 0131-314536 5510 **W** www.scotblood.co.uk

NORTHERN IRELAND BLOOD TRANSFUSION SERVICE, Lisburn Road, Belfast BT9 7TS **T** 028-9032 1414 **W** www.nibts.org

### HOSPICES

Hospice or palliative care may be available for patients with life-threatening illnesses. It may be provided at the patient's home in a voluntary or NHS hospice or in hospital, and is intended to ensure the best possible quality of life for the patient, and to provide help and support to both the patient and the patient's family. The National Council for Palliative Care coordinates NHS and voluntary services in England, Wales and Northern Ireland; the Scottish Partnership for Palliative Care performs the same function in Scotland.

NATIONAL COUNCIL FOR PALLIATIVE CARE, The Fitzpatrick Building, 188–194 York Way, London N7 9AS **T** 020-7697 1520 **W** www.ncpc.org.uk

SCOTTISH PARTNERSHIP FOR PALLIATIVE CARE, CBC House, 24 Canning Street, Edinburgh EH3 8EG **T** 0131-272 2735 **W** www.palliativecarescotland.org.uk

## COMPLAINTS

Patient advice and liaison services (PALS) have been established for every NHS and PCT in England. PALS can give advice on local complaints procedure, or resolve concerns informally. If the case is not resolved locally or the complainant is not satisfied with the way a local NHS body or practice has dealt with their complaint, they may approach the Parliamentary and Health Service Ombudsman in England, the Scottish Public Services Ombudsman, Public Services Ombudsman for Wales or the Northern Ireland Commissioner for Complaints.

## HEALTH ADVICE AND MEDICAL TREATMENT ABROAD

### IMMUNISATION

Country-by-country guidance is set out on the website **W** www.fitfortravel.nhs.uk.

### RECIPROCAL ARRANGEMENTS

The European Health Insurance Card (EHIC) allows UK residents access to state-provided health care while temporarily travelling in all European Economic Area countries and Switzerland either free or at a reduced cost. A card is free, valid for up to five years and should be obtained before travelling. Applications can be made by telephone (**T** 0300 330 1350) online (**W** www.ehic.org.uk) or by post (a form is available from the post office).

The UK also has bilateral agreements with several other countries, including Australia and New Zealand, for the free provision of urgent medical treatment.

European Economic Area nationals visiting the UK and visitors from other countries with which the UK has bilateral health care agreements are able to receive emergency health care on the NHS on the same terms as available to UK residents.

# SOCIAL WELFARE

## SOCIAL SERVICES

The Secretary of State for Health (in England), the Welsh government, the Scottish government and the Secretary of State for Northern Ireland are responsible, under the Local Authority Social Services Act 1970, for the provision of social services for older people, disabled people, families and children, and those with mental disorders. Personal social services are administered by local authorities according to policies, with standards set by central and devolved government. Each authority has a director and a committee responsible for the social services functions placed upon them. Local authorities provide, enable and commission care after assessing the needs of their population. The private and voluntary sectors also play an important role in the delivery of social services, and an estimated 7 million people in the UK provide substantial regular care for a member of their family.

The Care Quality Commission (CQC) was established in April 2009, bringing together the independent regulation of health, mental health and adult social care. Prior to 1 April 2009 this work was carried out by three separate organisations: the Healthcare Commission, the Mental Health Act Commission and the Commission for Social Care Inspection. The CQC is responsible for the registration of health and social care providers, the monitoring and inspection of all health and adult social care, issuing fines, public warnings or closures if standards are not met and for undertaking regular performance reviews. Since April 2007 the Office for Standards in Education, Children's Services and Skills (Ofsted) has been responsible for inspecting and regulating all care services for children and young people in England. Both Ofsted and CQC collate information on local care services and make this information available to the public.

The Care and Social Services Inspectorate Wales (CSSIW), an operationally independent part of the Welsh government, is responsible for the regulation and inspection of all social care services in Wales. A new unified body, the Care Inspectorate, was established on 1 April 2011, replacing the Scottish Commission for the Regulation of Care (the Care Commission) and is now the independent care services regulator for Scotland.

The Department of Health, Social Services and Public Safety is responsible for social care in Northern Ireland.

CARE QUALITY COMMISSION (CQC), Citygate, Gallowgate, Newcastle upon Tyne NE1 4PA T 0300-061 6161 W www.cqc.org.uk

OFFICE FOR STANDARDS IN EDUCATION, CHILDREN'S SERVICES AND SKILLS (Ofsted), Piccadilly Gate, Store Street, Manchester M1 2WD T 0300-123 1231 E enquiries@ofsted.gov.uk W www.ofsted.gov.uk

CARE AND SOCIAL SERVICES INSPECTORATE WALES (CSSIW), Welsh Government Office, Rhydcar Business Park, Merthyr Tydfil CF48 1UZ T 0300-790 0126 E cssiw@wales.gsi.gov.uk W www.cssiw.org.uk

CARE INSPECTORATE, Compass House, 11 Riverside Drive, Dundee DD1 4NY T 0845-600 9527 E enquiries@careinspectorate.com W www.scswis.com

DEPARTMENT OF HEALTH, SOCIAL SERVICES AND PUBLIC SAFETY, Castle Buildings, Stormont, Belfast BT4 3SQ T 028-9052 0500 E webmaster@dhsspsni.gov.uk W www.dhsspsni.gov.uk

### STAFF

| | |
|---|---|
| Total Social Services Staff (England, full-time) | 130,100 |
| Community | 42,933 |
| Residential | 29,923 |
| Other | 26,020 |
| Domiciliary | 18,214 |
| Day | 13,010 |

Source: Health and Social Care Information Centre 2015

### OLDER PEOPLE

Services for older people are designed to enable them to remain living in their own homes for as long as possible. Local authority services include advice, domestic help, meals in the home, alterations to the home to aid mobility, emergency alarm systems, day and/or night attendants, laundry services and the provision of day centres and recreational facilities. Charges may be made for these services. Respite care may also be provided in order to allow carers temporary relief from their responsibilities.

Local authorities and the private sector also provide 'sheltered housing' for older people, sometimes with resident wardens.

If an older person is admitted to a residential home, charges are made according to a means test; if the person cannot afford to pay, the costs are met by the local authority.

### DISABLED PEOPLE

Services for disabled people are designed to enable them to remain living in their own homes wherever possible. Local authority services include advice, adaptations to the home, meals in the home, help with personal care, occupational therapy, educational facilities and recreational facilities. Respite care may also be provided in order to allow carers temporary relief from their responsibilities.

Special housing may be available for disabled people who can live independently, and residential accommodation for those who cannot.

### FAMILIES AND CHILDREN

Local authorities are required to provide services aimed at safeguarding the welfare of children in need and, wherever possible, allowing them to be brought up by their families. Services include advice, counselling, help in the home and the provision of family centres. Many authorities also provide short-term refuge accommodation for women and children.

### DAY CARE

In allocating day care places to children, local authorities give priority to children with special needs, whether in terms of their health, learning abilities or social needs. Since September 2001, Ofsted has been responsible for the regulation and registration of all early years childcare and education provision in England (previously the responsibility of the local authorities). All day care and childminding services that care for children under eight years of age for more than two hours a day must register with Ofsted and are inspected at least every two years. As at 31 March 2015, there were 89,117 providers in England.

### CHILD PROTECTION

Children considered to be at risk of physical injury, neglect or sexual abuse are placed on the local authority's child protection register. Local authority social services staff, schools, health visitors and other agencies work together to prevent and detect cases of abuse. As at 31 March 2014, there was a total of 56,231 children on child protection registers or subject to a child protection plan in the UK. In England, there were 48,300 children on child protection registers, of these, 20,980 were at risk of neglect, 4,770 of physical abuse, 2,210 of sexual abuse and 15,870 of emotional abuse. At 31 March (July in Scotland) 2014 there were 3,135 children on child protection registers in Wales, 2,882 in Scotland and 1,914 in Northern Ireland.

## LOCAL AUTHORITY CARE

Local authorities are required to provide accommodation for children who have no parents or guardians or whose parents or guardians are unable or unwilling to care for them. A family proceedings court may also issue a care order where a child is being neglected or abused, or is not attending school; the court must be satisfied that this would positively contribute to the well-being of the child.

The welfare of children in local authority care must be properly safeguarded. Children may be placed with foster families, who receive payments to cover the expenses of caring for the child or children, or in residential care.

Children's homes may be run by the local authority or by the private or voluntary sectors; all homes are subject to inspection procedures. As at 31 March 2014, 68,840 children in the UK were in the care of local authorities, of these, 51,340 were in foster placements and 6,360 were in children's homes, hostels or secure units.

## ADOPTION

Local authorities are required to provide an adoption service, either directly or via approved voluntary societies. In 2013–14, 5,050 children in local authority care were adopted.

## PEOPLE WITH LEARNING DISABILITIES

Services for people with learning disabilities are designed to enable them to remain living in the community wherever possible. Local authority services include short-term care, support in the home, the provision of day care centres, and help with other activities outside the home. Residential care is provided for the severely or profoundly disabled.

## MENTALLY ILL PEOPLE

Under the care programme approach, mentally ill people should be assessed by specialist services and receive a care plan. A key worker should be appointed for each patient and regular reviews of the person's progress should be conducted. Local authorities provide help and advice to mentally ill people and their families, and places in day centres and social centres. Social workers can apply for a mentally disturbed person to be compulsorily detained in hospital. Where appropriate, mentally ill people are provided with accommodation in special hospitals, local authority accommodation, or at homes run by private or voluntary organisations. Patients who have been discharged from hospitals may be placed on a supervision register.

# NATIONAL INSURANCE

The National Insurance (NI) scheme operates under the Social Security Contributions and Benefits Act 1992 and the Social Security Administration Act 1992, and orders and regulations made thereunder. The scheme is financed by contributions payable by earners, employers and others (*see* below). Money collected under the scheme is used to finance the National Insurance Fund (from which contributory benefits are paid) and to contribute to the cost of the National Health Service.

## NATIONAL INSURANCE FUND

Estimated receipts, payments and statement of balances of the National Insurance Fund for 2015–16:

| Receipts | £ million |
| --- | --- |
| Net national insurance contributions | 86,265 |
| Compensation from the Consolidated Fund for statutory sick, maternity, paternity and adoption pay recoveries | 2,545 |
| Income from investments | 95 |
| State scheme premiums | 49 |
| Other receipts | 34 |
| TOTAL RECEIPTS | 88,989 |

| Payments | £ million |
| --- | --- |
| Benefits | |
| At present rates | 93,780 |
| Increase due to proposed rate changes | 1,966 |
| Personal and stakeholder pensions contracted-out rebates | 0 |
| Administration costs | 939 |
| Redundancy fund payments | 330 |
| Transfer to Northern Ireland | 386 |
| Other payments | 175 |
| TOTAL PAYMENTS | 97,576 |

| Balances | £ million |
| --- | --- |
| Balance at the beginning of the year | 17,965 |
| Excess of receipts over payments | (8,587) |
| BALANCE AT END OF YEAR | 9,378 |

## CONTRIBUTIONS

There are six classes of National Insurance contributions (NICs):

| | |
| --- | --- |
| Class 1 | paid by employees and their employers |
| Class 1A | paid by employers who provide employees with certain benefits in kind for private use, such as company cars |
| Class 1B | paid by employers who enter into a pay as you earn (PAYE) settlement agreement (PSA) with HM Revenue and Customs |
| Class 2 | paid by self-employed people |
| Class 3 | voluntary contributions paid to protect entitlement to the state pension for those who do not pay enough NI contributions in another class |
| Class 4 | paid by the self-employed on their taxable profits over a set limit. These are normally paid by self-employed people in addition to class 2 contributions. Class 4 contributions do not count towards benefits. |

The lower and upper earnings limits and the percentage rates referred to below apply from April 2015 to April 2016.

## CLASS 1

Class 1 contributions are paid where a person:
- is an employed earner (employee), office holder (eg company director) or employed under a contract of service in Great Britain or Northern Ireland
- is 16 or over and under state pension age
- earns at or above the earnings threshold of £155 per week (including overtime pay, bonus, commission, etc, without deduction of superannuation contributions)

Class 1 contributions are made up of primary and secondary contributions. Primary contributions are those paid by the employee and these are deducted from earnings by the employer. Since 6 April 2001 the employee's and employer's earnings thresholds have been the same and are referred to as the earnings threshold. Primary contributions are not paid on earnings below the earnings threshold of £155 per week. However, between the lower earnings limit of £112 per week and the earnings threshold of £155 per week, NI contributions are treated as having been paid to protect the benefit entitlement position of lower earners. Contributions are payable at the rate of 12 per cent on earnings between the earnings threshold and the upper earnings limit of £815 per week (10.6 per cent for contracted-out employment). Above the upper earnings limit 2 per cent is payable.

Some married women or widows pay a reduced rate of 5.85 per cent on earnings between the earnings threshold and upper earnings limits and 2 per cent above this. It is no longer possible to elect to pay the reduced rate but those who had reduced liability before 12 May 1977 may retain it for as long as certain conditions are met.

Secondary contributions are paid by employers of employed earners at the rate of 13.8 per cent on all earnings above the earnings threshold of £155 per week. There is no upper earnings limit for employers' contributions. Employers operating contracted-out salary related schemes pay reduced contributions of 10.4 per cent. The contracted-out rate applies only to that portion of earnings between the earnings threshold and the upper earnings limit. Employers' contributions below and above those respective limits are assessed at the appropriate not contracted-out rate.

### CLASS 2

Class 2 contributions are paid where a person is self-employed and is 16 or over and under state pension age. Contributions are paid at a flat rate of £2.80 per week regardless of the amount earned. However, those with earnings of less than £5,965 a year can apply for small earnings exception. Those granted exemption from class 2 contributions may pay class 2 or class 3 contributions voluntarily. Self-employed earners (whether or not they pay class 2 contributions) may also be liable to pay class 4 contributions based on profits. There are special rules for those who are concurrently employed and self-employed.

Married women and widows can no longer choose not to pay class 2 contributions but those who elected not to pay class 2 contributions before 12 May 1977 may retain the right for as long as certain conditions are met.

Class 2 contributions are collected by the national insurance contributions department of HM Revenue and Customs (HMRC), by direct debit or quarterly bills.

### CLASS 3

Class 3 contributions are voluntary flat-rate contributions of £14.10 per week payable by persons over the age of 16 who would otherwise be unable to qualify for retirement pension and certain other benefits because they have an insufficient record of class 1 or class 2 contributions. This may include those who are not working, those not liable for class 1 or class 2 contributions, or those excepted from class 2 contributions. Married women and widows who on or before 11 May 1977 elected not to pay class 1 (full rate) or class 2 contributions cannot pay class 3 contributions while they retain this right. Class 3 contributions are collected by HMRC by quarterly bills or direct debit.

### CLASS 4

Self-employed people whose profits and gains are over £8,060 a year pay class 4 contributions in addition to class 2 contributions. This applies to self-employed earners over 16 and under the state pension age. Class 4 contributions are calculated at 9 per cent of annual profits or gains between £8,060 and £42,385 and 2 per cent above. Class 4 contributions are assessed and collected by HMRC. It is

possible, in some circumstances, to apply for exceptions from liability to pay class 4 contributions or to have the amount of contribution reduced.

# PENSIONS

Many people will qualify for a state pension; however, there are further pension choices available, such as workplace, personal and stakeholder pensions. There are also other non-pension savings and investment options. The following section provides background information on existing pension schemes.

## STATE PENSION

From April 2016, the system of basic and additional state pension will be replaced with a new scheme for people reaching state pension age after that date (ie men born on or after 6 April 1951, and women born on or after 6 April 1953).

Current pensioners and those reaching state pension age before the introduction of the new state pension will continue to receive their state pension in line with existing rules. Information about the new state pension can be found online: (W www.gov.uk/new-state-pension).

Currently the state pension does not have to be claimed at state pension age, people can delay claiming it to earn weekly state pension or a lump sum payment. Different rules apply to the new scheme from 6 April 2016. People will only earn weekly new state pension if they delay their claim.

## CURRENT STATE PENSION SCHEME

The current system consists of:
• basic state pension
• additional state pension

People may be able to get both or either when they reach state pension age and meet the qualifying conditions.

*Basic State Pension*

The amount of basic state pension paid is dependent on the number of 'qualifying years' a person has established during their working life. In 2015–16, the full basic state pension is £115.95 a week (*see also* Benefits, State Pension: Categories A and B).

*Working Life*

The working life is from the start of the tax year (6 April) in which a person reaches 16 to the end of the tax year (5 April) before the one in which they reach state pension age (*see* State Pension Age).

*Qualifying Years*

A 'qualifying year' is a tax year in which a person has sufficient earnings upon which they have paid, are treated as having paid, or have been credited with national insurance (NI) contributions (*see* National Insurance Credits).

From 6 April 2010 to 5 April 2016, a person who has 30 qualifying years will be entitled to a full basic state pension. Someone with less than 30 qualifying years will be entitled to a proportion of the full basic state pension based on the number of qualifying years they have. Just one qualifying year, achieved through paid or credited contributions, will give entitlement to the basic state pension worth one-thirtieth of the full basic state pension.

Until 6 April 2010, women normally needed 39 qualifying years for a full basic state pension (£115.95 in 2015–16) and men normally needed 44 qualifying years. A reduced-rate basic state pension was payable if the number of qualifying years was less than 90 per cent of the working life, but to receive any basic state pension at all, a person must have had enough qualifying years, normally 10 or 11, to receive a basic state pension of at least 25 per cent of the full rate.

The full rate of the new state pension will be finalised closer to its introduction. It will be set at a level that is above the basic level of means-tested support, the standard minimum guarantee in pension credit (£151.20 in 2015–16 for a single person).

The amounts of state pension people will receive under the new system will also be based on their NI record, with NI contributors or credits made prior to 6 April 2016 recognised under transitional arrangements.

NI contributions and credits will be used to calculate a 'starting amount' under the new system. An individual's starting amount will be the higher of either:
• the value of NI contributions under the current state pension rules (basic state pension, additional state pension and graduated retirement benefit)
• the value of NI contributions if the new state pension had been in place at the start of their working life
A deduction may be made to these amounts for periods an individual was contracted out of the additional state pension before 6 April 2016.

A minimum of 10 qualifying years will usually be needed to get any new state pension.

### National Insurance Credits

Those in receipt of carer's allowance, working tax credit (with a disability element), jobseeker's allowance, incapacity benefit, employment support allowance, unemployability supplement, statutory sick pay, statutory maternity pay or statutory adoption pay may have class 1 NI contributions credited to them each week. People may also get credits if they are unemployed and looking for work or too sick to work, even if they are not in receipt of any benefit, although the credits must be applied for in these circumstances. Since April 2010, spouses and civil partners of members of HM forces may get credits if they are on an accompanied assignment outside the UK. A new measure will allow those who reach state pension age on or after 6 April 2016 to apply for NI credits for periods before April 2010 during which they were married to, or in a civil partnership with, a member of HM forces and accompanied them on a posting outside the UK. Persons undertaking certain training courses or jury service or who have been wrongly imprisoned for a conviction which is quashed on appeal may also get class 1 NI credits for each week they fulfil certain conditions. Class 1 credits may also be available to men approaching state pension age. Until 5 April 2010, these credits were awarded for the tax years in which they reached age 60 and continued until age 64, if they were not liable to pay contributions and were not absent from the UK for more than six months in any tax year. Since 6 April 2010 these credits are being phased out in line with the increase in women's state pension age. Class 1 NI credits count toward all future contributory benefits. A class 3 NI credit for basic state pension and bereavement benefit purposes is awarded, where required, for each week the working tax credit (without a disability element) has been received or child benefit, for a child under 12, has been received. Class 3 credits may also be awarded, on application, to approved foster carers and people caring for at least 20 hours a week. Since 6 April 2011, class 3 credits have been available to adults under state pension age who care for a family member under 12. In certain cases people may also get a credit towards their state second pension.

### State Pension Age

State pension age is currently 65 for men born before 6 December 1953 and 60 for women born before 6 April 1950. Women's state pension age will equalise with men's at 65 in 2018 and this will increase to age 66 for both men and women by October 2020. The Pensions Act 2014 makes provision for a regular review of state pension age. Reviews will take place at least once every six years and will take into account up-to-date life expectancy data and the findings of an independently led review, which will consider wider factors such as variation in life expectancy and employment opportunities for older workers. Further information can be obtained from the online state pension calculator (W www.gov.uk/calculate-state-pension).

### Using the NI Contribution Record of Another Person to Claim a State Pension

Married people or civil partners whose own NI record is incomplete may get a lower-rate basic state pension calculated using their partner's NI contribution record. This can be up to £69.50 a week in 2015–16, including any basic state pension of their own. Married men, members of married same-sex couples and civil partners may only qualify if their spouse or civil partner was born on or after 6 April 1950 (this rule does not apply to a married woman whose spouse has legally changed gender from male to female during the marriage). Widows, widowers, surviving civil partners, and people who are divorced or whose civil partnership has been dissolved may qualify for up to a full basic state pension based on their late or ex-spouse's/civil partner's NI contributions.

People who reach state pension age before 6 April 2016 will continue to be able to use these provisions, even if their spouse or civil partner reaches state pension age on or after that date. However, contributions their spouse or civil partner pays, or is credited with, following implementation of the new system will only count towards their own state pension. This means that only the NI record of the spouse or civil partner up to and including 2015–16 will be used to calculate any derived entitlement.

People reaching state pension age on or after 6 April 2016 will not be able to claim state pension on their spouse's or civil partner's NI record. There will be special arrangements for women who had opted to pay the married women's and widows reduced rate contributions before May 1977.

### Non-contributory State Pensions

A non-contributory state pension may be payable to those aged 80 or over who live in England, Scotland or Wales, and have done so for a total of ten years or more for any continuous period in the 20 years after their 60th birthday, if they are not entitled to another category of state pension, or are entitled to one below the rate of £69.50 a week in 2015–16 (see also Benefits, State Pension for people aged 80 and over).

### Graduated Retirement Benefit

Graduated Retirement Benefit (GRB) is based on the amount of graduated NI contributions paid into the GRB scheme between April 1961 and April 1975 (see also Benefits, Graduated Retirement Benefit). It is normally paid as an increase to a main state pension. For those reaching state pension age under the new state pension rules, it will be included in the calculation of their basic amount.

### Home Responsibilities Protection

From 6 April 1978 until 5 April 2010, it was possible for people who had low income or were unable to work because they cared for children or a sick or disabled person at home to reduce the number of qualifying years required for basic state pension. This was called home responsibilities protection (HRP); the number of years for which HRP was given was deducted from the number of qualifying years needed. HRP could, in some cases, also qualify the recipient for additional state pension. From April 2003 to April 2010 HRP was also available to approved foster carers.

From 6 April 2010, HRP was replaced by weekly credits for parents and carers. A class 3 national insurance credit is given, where eligible, towards basic state pension and bereavement benefits for spouses and civil partners. An earnings factor credit towards additional state pension is also awarded. Any years of HRP accrued before 6 April 2010 have been converted into qualifying years of credits for people reaching state pension age after that date, up to a maximum of 22 years for basic state pension purposes.

*Additional State Pension*
The amount of additional state pension paid depends on the amount of earnings a person has, or is treated as having, between the lower and upper earnings limits (from April 2009, the upper accruals point replaced the upper earnings limit for additional pension) for each complete tax year between 6 April 1978 (when the scheme started) and the tax year before they reach state pension age. The right to additional state pension does not depend on the person's right to basic state pension.

From 1978 to 2002, additional state pension was called the State Earnings-Related Pension Scheme (SERPS). SERPS covered all earnings by employees from 6 April 1978 to 5 April 1997 on which standard rate class 1 NI contributions had been paid, and earnings between 6 April 1997 and 5 April 2002 if the standard rate class 1 NI contributions had been contracted-in.

In 2002, SERPS was reformed through the state second pension, by improving the pension available to low and moderate earners and extending access to certain carers and people with long-term illness or disability. If earnings on which class 1 NI contributions have been paid or can be treated as paid are above the annual NI lower earnings limit (£5,824 for 2015–16) but below the statutory low earnings threshold (£15,300 for 2015–16), the state second pension regards this as earnings of £15,300 and it is treated as equivalent. Certain carers and people with long-term illness and disability will be considered as having earned at the low earnings threshold for each complete tax year since 2002–3 even if they do not work at all, or earn less than the annual NI lower earnings limit.

The amount of additional state pension paid also depends on when a person reaches state pension age; changes phased in from 6 April 1999 mean that pensions are calculated differently from that date.

*Additional State Pension Inheritance*
Men or women widowed before 6 October 2002 may inherit all of their late spouse's SERPS pension. From 6 October 2002, the maximum percentage of SERPS pension that a person can inherit from a late spouse or civil partner depends on their late spouse's or civil partner's date of birth:

| Maximum SERPS entitlement | d.o.b (men) | d.o.b (women) |
|---|---|---|
| 100% | 5/10/37 or earlier | 5/10/42 or earlier |
| 90% | 6/10/37 to 5/10/39 | 6/10/42 to 5/10/44 |
| 80% | 6/10/39 to 5/10/41 | 6/10/44 to 5/10/46 |
| 70% | 6/10/41 to 5/10/43 | 6/10/46 to 5/10/48 |
| 60% | 6/10/43 to 5/10/45 | 6/10/48 to 5/7/50 |
| 50% | 6/10/45 or later | 6/7/50 or later |

The maximum state second pension a person can inherit from a spouse or civil partner is 50 per cent. If a person is bereaved before they have reached their state pension age, inherited SERPS or state second pension can be paid as part of widowed parent's allowance (in the case of a person who has dependent children) or otherwise only from state pension age. If they remarry or form a new civil partnership before

state pension age they lose the right to inherit any state pension.

*New State Pension Inheritance*
A person who reaches state pension age before 6 April 2016 will still be able to inherit additional state pension under the existing rules. However, if their late spouse or civil partner reaches state pension age on or after that date, the amount they can inherit will be based on the deceased's contributions up to 5 April 2016 only.

A person reaching state pension age on or after 6 April 2016 whose deceased spouse or civil partner reached state pension age or died before that date will be able to inherit additional state pension under the current rules. If the deceased spouse or civil partner is also in the new state pension the survivor may inherit half of any 'protected payment'. A person will have a protected payment if their state pension calculated under current rules is more than the full rate of new state pension at April 2016. The protected payment is the amount of the excess.

In order for a person reaching state pension age on or after 6 April 2016 to qualify for an inherited amount the marriage or civil partnership must have begun before that date; and, in the case of a person widowed under state pension age, they must not remarry or form a new civil partnership before state pension age.

*State Pension Statements*
The Department for Work and Pensions provide state pension statements. These statements give an estimate of the state pension an individual may get based on their current NI contribution record (W www.gov.uk/state-pension-statement).

There is also an online state pension calculator. Individuals can use this to find out their state pension age and, based on information they provide, get an estimate of their basic state pension (W www.gov.uk/calculate-state-pension).

## PRIVATE PENSIONS

### CONTRACTED-OUT PENSIONS
'Contracting-out' means leaving the additional state pension and joining a workplace, company or occupational pension scheme to build up benefits into an alternative pension scheme.

*Contracting-Out with an Occupational Pension Scheme*
An occupational pension scheme is an arrangement some employers set up to give their employees a pension when they retire. The government is gradually introducing a requirement for all employers to provide their workers with a workplace pension. All employers will be included by 2018.

Providing that a company pension scheme meets certain conditions, it can be used to contract employees out of the additional state pension. Employees who join a scheme that is contracted-out will automatically be contracted-out of the additional state pension.

Employers providing such contracted-out schemes pay lower rate of National Insurance contributions for those employees who join their schemes, and employees themselves also pay reduced-rate contributions.

*Contracted-Out Salary-Related (COSR) Scheme*
• these schemes (also known as contracted-out defined benefit (DB) or final salary schemes) provide a pension related to earnings and the length of pensionable service
• any notional additional state pension built up from 6 April 1978 to 5 April 1997 will be reduced by the amount of guaranteed minimum pension (GMP) accrued during that period (the contracted-out deduction). GMP is payable at 65 for men and 60 for women

- since 6 April 1997 these schemes no longer provide a GMP. Instead, as a condition of contracting-out they have to ensure that the benefits provided are at least as good as a prescribed standard (known as the Reference Scheme Test)
- when someone contracts-out of the additional state pension through these schemes, both the scheme member and the employer pay a reduced rate of NI contributions (known as the contracted-out rebate) to compensate for the additional state pension given up

*Changes to contracted-out pensions from 2012*
The rules for contracting-out of the additional state pension changed from 6 April 2012. The changes means contracting-out will not be possible through:
- a money purchase (defined contribution) occupational pension scheme
- a personal pension or stakeholder pension
From that date, employees have not been able to contract-out of the state second pension on a money purchase basis. Anyone contracted-out through this basis from that date was automatically contracted back into the additional state pension. Those rights built up before the abolition date will be used to provide pension benefits. These changes have not affected contracting-out via a salary-related occupational pension scheme. However, the introduction of the single-tier pension scheme in April 2016 will close the additional state pension for those reaching state pension age after this date, and contracting out on a DB basis will end.

### STAKEHOLDER PENSION SCHEMES
Introduced in 2001, stakeholder pensions are available to everyone but are principally for moderate earners who do not have access to a good value company pension scheme. Stakeholder pensions must meet minimum standards to make sure they are flexible, portable and annual management charges are capped. The minimum contribution is £20.

As with personal pensions it is possible to invest up to £3,600 (including tax relief) into stakeholder pensions each year without evidence of earnings. Contributions can be made on someone else's behalf, eg a non-working partner.

### AUTOMATIC ENROLMENT INTO WORKPLACE PENSIONS
Since October 2012, employers must automatically enrol their workers who meet the age and earnings criteria into a workplace pension. This applies to people who are not already in a workplace pension scheme and who:
- earn over £10,000 per annum
- are aged 22 or over
- are under state pension age
- work in the UK
Employees who meet the above requirements are entitled to opt out of the scheme if they wish to. If remains in the scheme, they, together with their employer, will pay into it every month. The government will also contribute through tax relief. Further information is available at W www.gov.uk/workplace-pensions

### COMPLAINTS
The Pensions Advisory Service provides information and guidance to members of the public, on state, company, personal and stakeholder schemes. They also help any member of the public who has a problem, complaint or dispute with their occupational or personal pensions.

There are two bodies for pension complaints. The Financial Ombudsman Service deals with complaints which predominantly concern the sale and/or marketing of occupational, stakeholder and personal pensions. The Pensions Ombudsman deals with complaints which pre-dominantly concern the management (after sale or marketing) of occupational, stakeholder and personal pensions.

The Pensions Regulator is the UK regulator for work-based pension schemes; it concentrates its resources on schemes where there is the greatest risk to the security of members' benefits, promotes good administration practice for all work-based schemes and works with trustees, employers and professional advisers to put things right when necessary.

## WAR PENSIONS AND THE ARMED FORCES COMPENSATION SCHEME
Veterans UK is part of the Ministry of Defence. It was formed on 1 April 2007 to provide services to both serving personnel and veterans.

Veterans UK is responsible for the administration of the war pensions scheme and the armed forces compensation scheme (AFCS) to members of the armed forces in respect of disablement or death due to service. There is also a scheme for civilians and civil defence workers in respect of the Second World War, and other schemes for groups such as merchant seamen and Polish armed forces who served under British command during the Second World War. They are also responsible for the administration of the armed forces pension scheme (AFPS), which provides occupational pensions for ex-service personnel *(see* Defence).

### THE WAR PENSIONS SCHEME
War disablement pension is awarded for the disabling effects of any injury, wound or disease which was the result of, or was aggravated by, service in the armed forces prior to 6 April 2005. Claims are only considered once the person has left the armed forces. The amount of pension paid depends on the severity of disablement, which is assessed by comparing the health of the claimant with that of a healthy person of the same age and sex. The person's earning capacity or occupation are not taken into account in this assessment. A pension is awarded if the person has a disablement of 20 per cent or more and a lump sum is usually payable to those with a disablement of less than 20 per cent. No award is made for noise-induced sensorineural hearing loss where the assessment of disablement is less than 20 per cent. Where an assessment of disablement is at 40 per cent or more, an age addition is automatically given when the pensioner reaches 65.

A pension is payable to war widows, widowers and surviving civil partners where the spouse's or civil partner's death was due to, or hastened by, service in the armed forces prior to 6 April 2005 or where the spouse or civil partner was in receipt of a war disablement pension constant attendance allowance (or would have been if not in hospital) at the time of death. A pension is also payable to widows, widowers or surviving civil partners if the spouse or civil partner was receiving the war disablement pension at the 80 per cent rate or higher in conjunction with unemployability supplement at the time of death. War widows, widowers and surviving civil partners receive a standard rank-related rate, but a lower weekly rate is payable to war widows, widowers and surviving civil partners of personnel of the rank of Major or below who are under the age of 40, without children and capable of maintaining themselves. This is increased to the standard rate at age 40. Allowances are paid for children and adult dependants. An age allowance is automatically given when the widow, widower or surviving civil partner reaches 65 and increased at ages 70 and 80.

Pensioners living overseas receive the same pension rates as those living in the UK. All war disablement pensions and allowances and pensions for war widows, widowers and surviving civil partners are tax-free in the UK; this does not always apply in overseas countries due to different tax laws.

## SUPPLEMENTARY ALLOWANCES

A number of supplementary allowances may be awarded to a war pensioner and are intended to meet various needs. The principal supplementary allowances are unemployability supplement, allowance for lowered standard of occupation, constant attendance allowance and war pensions mobility supplement. Others include exceptionally severe disablement allowance, severe disablement occupational allowance, treatment allowance, comforts allowance, clothing allowance, age allowance and widow/widower/surviving civil partner's age allowance. Rent and children's allowances are also available with pensions for war widows, widowers and surviving civil partners.

## ARMED FORCES COMPENSATION SCHEME

The armed forces compensation scheme (AFCS) became effective on 6 April 2005 and covers all regular (including Gurkhas) and reserve personnel whose injury, ill health or death is caused predominantly by service on or after 6 April 2005. There are time limits under this scheme and generally claims must be made within seven years of the injury occurring or from first seeking medical advice about an illness. There are some exceptions to this time limit, the main one being for a late-onset illness. Claims for a late-onset illness can be made at any time after the event to which it relates, providing the claim is made within three years of medical advice being sought.

The AFCS provides compensation where service in the armed forces is the only or predominant cause of injury, illness or death. Any other personal accident cover held by the individual is not taken into account when determining an AFCS award. Under the terms of the scheme a tax-free lump sum is payable to service or ex-service personnel based on a 15-level tariff, graduated according to the seriousness of the injury. If multiple injuries are sustained in the same incident compensation for each injury, up to the scheme maximum, is awarded. For those with the most serious injuries and illness a tax-free, index-linked monthly payment – a guaranteed income payment or GIP – is paid for life from the point of discharge. A survivor's GIP (SGIP) will also be paid to surviving spouses, civil partners and unmarried partners who meet certain criteria. GIP and SGIP are calculated by multiplying the pensionable pay of the service person by a factor that depends on the age at the person's last birthday. The younger the person, the higher the factor, because there are more years to normal retirement age.

## ARMED FORCES INDEPENDENCE PAYMENT

Armed forces independence payment (AFIP) is designed to provide financial support for service personnel and veterans who have been seriously injured to cover the extra costs they may incur as a result of their injury. It is administered by Veterans UK as part of AFCS although payments are made by the Department for Work and Pensions (DWP). It is non-taxable and non-means-tested.

Service personnel and veterans awarded a GIP of 50 per cent or higher under the AFCS are eligible. Those eligible for AFIP are not required to undergo an assessment and will keep the payment for as long as they are entitled to receive a GIP of 50 per cent or higher.

## DEPARTMENT FOR WORK AND PENSIONS BENEFITS

Payments under the AFCS and the war pensions scheme may affect income related benefits from the DWP. In particular any supplementary allowances in payment with war pensions. Any state pension for which a war widow, widower or surviving civil partner qualifies for on their own NI contribution record can be paid in addition to monies received under the war pensions scheme.

## CLAIMS AND QUESTIONS

Further information on the war pensions scheme, the AFCS and the nearest Veterans' Welfare Office can be obtained from Veterans UK (T 0808-191 4218, if calling from the UK or, if living overseas, T (+44) (1253) 866-043).

VETERANS UK, Norcross Lane, Thornton-Cleveleys FY5 3WP
  E veterans-uk@mod.uk
  W www.gov.uk/government/organisations/veterans-uk

## TAX CREDITS

Tax credits are administered by HM Revenue and Customs (HMRC). They are based on an individual's or couple's household income and current circumstances. Adjustments can be made during the year to reflect changes in income and/or circumstances. Further information regarding the qualifying conditions for tax credits, how to claim and the rates payable is available online on the HMRC website (W www.hmrc.gov.uk/taxcredits).

### WORKING TAX CREDIT

Working tax credit is a payment from the government to support people on low incomes. It may be claimed by:
- those aged 25 or over who work at least 30 hours a week
- those aged 16 or over who work at least 16 hours a week, who are responsible for a child or young person, or have a disability that puts them at a disadvantage of getting a job
- those aged 60 or over, who work at least 16 hours a week
- couples who are responsible for a child or young person, who work at least 24 hours per week between them with one partner working at least 16 hours a week

The amount received depends on the circumstances and number of hours worked a week.

### WORKING TAX CREDIT FOR INDIVIDUALS WITHOUT CHILDREN 2015–16

The amounts shown in the table below, presume a single person is over 25 years of age and working 30 or more hours a week, that a couple includes one person over 25 years of age who is working 30 or more hours a week and that a single adult with a disability is over 16 years of age and working 16–29 hours a week.

| Annual Income/Status | Tax Credit per annum |
|---|---|
| £5,500 | |
| *Single | – |
| *Couple | – |
| Single adult with a disability | £4,935 |
| £9,850 | |
| Single | £1,370 |
| Couple | £3,380 |
| Single adult with a disability | £3,530 |
| £10,000 | |
| Single | £1,305 |
| Couple | £3,320 |
| Single adult with a disability | £3,465 |
| £12,000 | |
| Single | £485 |
| Couple | £2,500 |
| Single adult with a disability | £2,645 |
| £16,000 | |
| Single | – |
| Couple | £860 |
| Single adult with a disability | £1,005 |

* No amounts are shown here as this income would be under the minimum wage for 2015–16 of £5,491.20 per annum for an adult (aged 21 and above) working 16 hours a week (six months at £6.50/hour (minimum wage October 2014 to September 2015), plus six months at £6.70 (minimum wage from October 2015))

## CHILDCARE

In families with children where a lone parent works at least 16 hours a week, or couples who work at least 24 hours a week between them with one partner working at least 16 hours a week, or where one partner works at least 16 hours a week and the other is disabled, an in-patient in hospital, or in prison, the family is entitled to the childcare element of working tax credit. Depending on circumstances this payment can contribute up to £175 of childcare costs for one child and up to £300 a week for two or more children. Families can only claim if they use an approved or registered childcare provider.

## CHILD TAX CREDIT

Child tax credit combines all income-related support for children and is paid direct to the main carer. The credit is made up of a main 'family' payment with additional payments for each extra child in the household, for children with a disability and an extra payment for children who are severely disabled. Child tax credit is available to households where:
• there is at least one dependant under 16
• there is at least one dependant between 16 and 20 who is in relevant education or training or is registered for work, education or training with an approved body

# BENEFITS

The following is intended as a general guide to the benefits system. Conditions of entitlement and benefit rates change annually and all prospective claimants should check exact entitlements and rates of benefit directly with their local Jobcentre Plus office, pension centre or online (W www.gov.uk). Leaflets relating to the various benefits and contribution conditions for different benefits are available from local Jobcentre Plus offices.

## UNIVERSAL CREDIT

From 29 April 2013, Universal Credit began to gradually be introduced in certain areas of the country. Universal Credit is a single new payment for those looking for work or on a low income. Universal Credit will eventually replace:
• Income-based jobseekers allowance
• Income-related employment support allowance
• Income support
• Child tax credit
• Working tax credit
• Housing benefit
For more information go to W www.gov.uk/universalcredit

## CONTRIBUTORY BENEFITS

Entitlement to contributory benefits depends on national insurance contribution conditions being satisfied either by the claimant or by someone on the claimant's behalf (depending on the kind of benefit). The class or classes of national insurance contribution relevant to each benefit is:

| | |
|---|---|
| Jobseeker's allowance (contribution-based) | Class 1 |
| Employment and Support Allowance (contributory) | Class 1 or 2 |
| Widow's benefit and bereavement benefit | Class 1, 2 or 3 |
| State pensions, categories A and B | Class 1, 2 or 3 |

The system of contribution conditions relates to yearly levels of earnings on which national insurance (NI) contributions have been paid.

## JOBSEEKER'S ALLOWANCE

Jobseeker's allowance (JSA) replaced unemployment benefit and income support for unemployed people under state pension age from 7 October 1996. There are two routes of entitlement. Contribution-based JSA is paid at a personal rate (i.e. additional benefit for dependants is not paid) to those who have made sufficient NI contributions in two particular tax years. Savings and partner's earnings are not taken into account and payment can be made for up to six months. Rates of JSA correspond to income support rates.

Claims are made through Jobcentre Plus. A person wishing to claim JSA must generally be unemployed or working on average less than 16 hours a week, capable of work and available for any work which he or she can reasonably be expected to do, usually for at least 40 hours a week. The claimant must agree and sign a 'jobseeker's agreement', which will set out his or her plans to find work, and must actively seek work. If the claimant refuses work or training the benefit may be sanctioned for between one and 26 weeks.

A person will be sanctioned from JSA for up to 26 weeks if he or she has left a job voluntarily without just cause or through misconduct. In these circumstances, it may be possible to receive hardship payments, particularly where the claimant or the claimant's family is vulnerable, eg if sick or pregnant, or with children or caring responsibilities.

*Weekly Rates from April 2015*

| | |
|---|---|
| Person aged 18–24 | £57.90 |
| Person aged 25 to state pension age* | £73.10 |

* Since October 2003 people aged between 60 and state pension age can choose to claim pension credits instead of JSA

## EMPLOYMENT AND SUPPORT ALLOWANCE

From 27 October 2008, employment and support allowance (ESA) replaced incapacity benefit and income support paid on the grounds of incapacity or disability. The benefit consists of two strands, contribution-based benefit and income-related benefit, so that people no longer need to make two claims for benefit in order to gain their full entitlement. Contributory ESA is available to those who have limited capability for work but cannot get statutory sick pay from their employer. Those over pensionable age are not entitled to ESA. Apart from those who qualify under the special provisions for people incapacitated in youth, entitlement to contributory ESA is based on a person's NI contribution record. In order to qualify for contributory ESA, two contribution conditions, based on the last three years before the tax year in which benefit is claimed, must be satisfied. The amount of contributory ESA payable may be reduced where the person receives more than a specified amount of occupational or personal pension. Contributory ESA is paid only in respect of the person claiming the benefit – there are no additional amounts for dependants.

At the outset, new claimants are paid a basic allowance (the same rate as jobseeker's allowance) for 13 weeks while their medical condition is assessed and a work capability assessment is conducted. Following the completion of the assessment phase those claimants capable of engaging in work-related activities will receive a work-related activity component on top of the basic rate. The work-related activity component can be subject to sanctions if the claimant does not engage in the conditionality requirements without good reason. The maximum sanction is equal to the value of the work-related activity component of the benefit.

Those with the most severe health conditions or disabilities will receive the support component, which is more than the work-related activity component. Claimants in receipt of the support component are not required to engage in work-related activities, although they can volunteer to do so or undertake permitted work if their condition allows.

*Weekly Rates from April 2015*

| | |
|---|---|
| ESA plus work-related activity component | up to £102.15 |
| ESA plus support component | up to £109.30 |

## BEREAVEMENT BENEFITS

Bereavement benefits replaced widow's benefit on 9 April 2001. Those claiming widow's benefit before this date will continue to receive it under the old scheme for as long as they qualify. The new system provides bereavement benefits for widows, widowers and, from 5 December 2005, surviving civil partners (providing that their deceased spouse or civil partner paid NI contributions). The new system offers benefits in three forms:

• *Bereavement payment* – may be received by a man or woman who is under the state pension age at the time of their spouse or civil partner's death, or whose husband, wife or civil partner was not entitled to a category A retirement pension when he or she died. It is a single tax-free lump sum of £2,000 payable immediately on widowhood or loss of a civil partner

• *Widowed parent's allowance* – a taxable benefit payable to the surviving partner if he or she is entitled or treated as entitled to child benefit, or to a widow if she is expecting her husband's baby at the time of his death

• *Bereavement allowance* – a taxable weekly benefit paid for 52 weeks after the spouse or civil partner's death. If aged over 55 and under state pension age the full allowance is payable, if aged between 45 and 54 a percentage of the full rate is paid. A widow, widower or surviving civil partner may receive this allowance if his or her widowed parent's allowance ends before 52 weeks

It is not possible to receive widowed parent's allowance and bereavement allowance at the same time. Bereavement benefits and widow's benefit, in any form, cease upon remarriage or a new civil partnership or are suspended during a period of cohabitation as partners without being legally married or in a civil partnership.

*Weekly Rates from April 2015*

| | |
|---|---|
| Bereavement payment (lump sum) | £2,000 |
| Widowed parent's allowance (or widowed mother's allowance) | £112.55 |
| Bereavement allowance (or widow's pension), full entitlement (aged 55 and over at time of spouse's or civil partner's death) | £112.55 |

Amount of bereavement allowance (or widow's pension) by age of widow/widower or surviving civil partner at spouse's or civil partner's death:

| | |
|---|---|
| aged 54 | £104.67 |
| aged 53 | £96.79 |
| aged 52 | £88.91 |
| aged 51 | £81.04 |
| aged 50 | £73.16 |
| aged 49 | £65.28 |
| aged 48 | £57.40 |
| aged 47 | £49.52 |
| aged 46 | £41.64 |
| aged 45 | £33.77 |

## STATE PENSION: CATEGORIES A AND B

Category A pension is payable for life to men and women who reach state pension age, who satisfy the contributions conditions and who claim for it. Category B pension may be payable to married women, married men and civil partners who are not entitled to a basic state pension on their own NI contributions or whose own basic state pension entitlement is less than £69.50 a week in 2015–16. It is based on their wife's, husband's or civil partner's NI contributions and is payable when both members of the couple have reached state pension age. Married men and civil partners may only be able to qualify for a category B pension if their wife or civil partner was born on or after 6 April 1950. Category B

pension is also payable to widows, widowers and surviving civil partners who are bereaved before state pension age if they were previously entitled to widowed parent's allowance or bereavement allowance based on their late spouse's or civil partner's NI contributions. If they were receiving widowed parent's allowance on reaching state pension age, they could qualify for a category B pension payable at the same rate as their widowed parent's allowance comprising a basic pension, plus, if applicable, the appropriate share of their late spouse's or late civil partner's additional state pension. If their widowed parent's allowance had stopped before they reached state pension age, or they had been getting bereavement allowance at any time before state pension age, their category B pension will consist of inheritable additional state pension only. No basic state pension is included, although they may qualify for a basic state pension or have their own basic state pension improved by substituting their late spouse's or late civil partner's NI records for their own.

Widows who are bereaved when over state pension age can qualify for a category B pension regardless of the age of their husband when he died. This is payable at the same rate as the basic state pension the widow's late husband was entitled to (or would have been entitled to) at the time of his death. It can also be paid to widowers and civil partners who are bereaved when over state pension age if their wife or civil partner had reached state pension age when they died. Widowers and surviving civil partners who reached state pension age on or after 6 April 2010 and bereaved when over state pension age can qualify for a category B pension regardless of the age of their wife or civil partner when they died.

Where a person is entitled to both a category A and category B pension then they can be combined to give a composite pension, but this cannot be more than the full rate pension. Where a person is entitled to more than one category A or category B pension then only one can be paid. In such cases the person can choose which to get; if no choice is made, the most favourable one is paid.

A person may defer claiming their pension beyond state pension age. In doing so they may earn increments which will increase the weekly amount paid by 1 per cent per five weeks of deferral (equivalent to 10.4 per cent/year) when they claim their state pension. If a person delays claiming for at least 12 months they are given the option of a one-off taxable lump sum, instead of a pension increase, based on the weekly pension deferred, plus interest of at least 2 per cent above the Bank of England base rate. Since 6 April 2010, a category B pension has been treated independently of the spouse's or partner's pension. It is possible to take a category B pension even if the spouse or partner has deferred theirs.

It is no longer possible to claim an increase on a state pension for another adult (known as adult dependency increase). Those who received the increase before April 2010 can keep receiving it until the conditions are no longer met or until 5 April 2020, whichever is first.

Provision for children is made through child tax credits. An age addition of 25p a week is payable with a state pension if a pensioner is aged 80 or over.

Since 1989 pensioners have been allowed to have unlimited earnings without affecting their state pension. *See* Pensions.

*Weekly Rates from April 2015*

| | |
|---|---|
| Category A or B pension for a single person | £115.95 |
| Category B pension based on husband's/wife's/ civil partner's NI contributions | £69.50 |

## GRADUATED RETIREMENT BENEFIT

Graduated retirement benefit (GRB) is based on the amount of graduated NI contributions paid into the GRB scheme between April 1961 and April 1975; however, it is still paid in addition to any state pension to those who made the relevant contributions. A person will receive graduated retirement benefit based on their own contributions, even if not entitled to a basic state pension. Widows, widowers and surviving civil partners may inherit half of their deceased spouse's or civil partner's entitlement, but none that the deceased spouse or civil partner may have been eligible for from a former spouse or civil partner. If a person defers making a claim beyond state pension age, they may earn an increase or a one-off lump sum payment in respect of their deferred graduated retirement benefit; calculated in the same way as for category A or B state pension.

## NON-CONTRIBUTORY BENEFITS
These benefits are paid from general taxation and are not dependent on NI contributions.

### JOBSEEKER'S ALLOWANCE (INCOME-BASED)
Those who do not qualify for contribution-based jobseeker's allowance (JSA), those who have exhausted their entitlement to contribution-based JSA or those for whom contribution-based JSA provides insufficient income may qualify for income-based JSA. The amount paid depends on age, whether they are single or a couple and amount of income and savings. To get income-based JSA the claimant must usually be aged 18 or over but below state pension age, although there are some exceptions for 16- or 17-year-olds. Since April 2003, child dependants have been provided for through the child tax credit system.

The rules of entitlement are the same as for contribution-based JSA.

If one person in a couple was born after 28 October 1957 and neither person in the couple has responsibility for a child or children, then the couple will have to make a joint claim for JSA if they wish to receive income-based JSA.

*Weekly Rates from April 2015*

| | |
|---|---|
| Person aged 18–24 | £57.90 |
| Person aged 25 to state pension age | £73.10 |
| Couple, both aged 18 to state pension age | £114.85 |

### MATERNITY ALLOWANCE
Maternity allowance (MA) is a benefit available for pregnant women who cannot get statutory maternity pay (SMP) from their employer or have been employed/self-employed during or close to their pregnancy. In order to qualify for payment, a woman must have been employed and/or self-employed for at least 26 weeks in the 66-week period up to and including the week before the baby is due (test period). These weeks do not have to be in a row and any part weeks worked will count towards the 26 weeks. She must also have an average weekly earning of at least £30 (maternity allowance threshold) over any 13 weeks of the woman's choice within the test period.

Self-employed women who pay class 2 NI contributions or who hold a small earnings exception certificate are deemed to have enough earnings to qualify for MA.

A woman can choose to start receiving MA from the 11th week before the week in which the baby is due (if she stops work before then) up to the day following the day of birth. The exact date MA starts will depend on when the woman stops work to have her baby or if the baby is born before she stops work. However, where the woman is absent from work wholly or partly due to her pregnancy in the four weeks before the week the baby is due to be born, MA will start the day following the first day of absence from work. MA is paid for a maximum of 39 weeks.

Women who are not eligible for statutory maternity pay or the higher amount of MA may be eligible for a reduced rate of MA for a 14-week period. For example, women who take part in the business of their self-employed spouse or civil partner, for at least 26 weeks in the 66 weeks before their baby is due, and the work they do is unpaid.

*Weekly Rate from April 2015*

| | |
|---|---|
| Standard rate | £139.58 or 90 per cent of the woman's average weekly earnings if less than £139.58 |
| 14-week reduced rate | £27 |

### CHILD BENEFIT
Child benefit is payable for virtually all children aged under 16 and for those aged 16 and 17 if they are in relevant education or training or are registered for work, education or training with an approved body.

*Weekly Rates at April 2015*

| | |
|---|---|
| Eldest/only child | £20.70 |
| Each subsequent child | £13.70 |

### GUARDIAN'S ALLOWANCE
Guardian's allowance is payable to a person who is bringing up a child or young person because the child's parents have died, or in some circumstances, where only one parent has died. To receive the allowance the person must be in receipt of child benefit for the child or young person, although they do not have to be the child's legal guardian.

*Weekly Rate (in addition to child benefit) from April 2015*

| | |
|---|---|
| Each child | £16.55 |

### CARER'S ALLOWANCE
Carer's allowance (CA) is a benefit payable to people who spend at least 35 hours a week caring for a severely disabled person. To qualify for CA a person must be caring for someone in receipt of one of the following benefits:
• attendance allowance
• personal independence payment
• constant attendance allowance, paid at not less than the normal maximum rate with an industrial injuries disablement payment or basic (full-day) rate, under the industrial injuries or war pension schemes.
• armed forces independence payment (AFIP)

*Weekly Rate from April 2015*

| | |
|---|---|
| Carer's allowance | £62.10 |

### ATTENDANCE ALLOWANCE
This may be payable to people aged 65 or over who need help with personal care because they are physically or mentally disabled, and who have needed help for a period of at least six months. Attendance allowance has two rates: the lower rate is for day or night care, and the higher rate is for day and night care. People not expected to live for more than six months because of a progressive disease can receive the highest rate of attendance allowance straight away.

*Weekly Rates from April 2015*

| | |
|---|---|
| Higher rate | £82.30 |
| Lower rate | £55.10 |

### PERSONAL INDEPENDENCE PAYMENT (PIP)
Personal independence payment (PIP) replaced disability living allowance (DLA) for people aged 16 to 64 on 8 April 2013. PIP has two components: the daily living component and the mobility component, with each offering two different benefit rates: standard and enhanced. Whether one or both components are claimed depends on the requirements of the individual. Claimants are assessed on their

ability to carry out everyday activities, with the majority of claims evaluated via an interview. Claimants with a terminal illness automatically receive the enhanced daily living component.

*Weekly Rates from April 2015*
*Daily living component*

| | |
|---|---|
| Standard | £55.10 |
| Enhanced | £82.30 |

*Mobility component*

| | |
|---|---|
| Standard | £21.80 |
| Enhanced | £57.45 |

## STATE PENSION FOR PEOPLE AGED 80 AND OVER

A state pension, also referred to as category D pension, is provided for people aged 80 and over if they are not entitled to another category of state pension or are entitled to a state pension that is less than £69.50 a week. The person must also live in Great Britain and have done so for a period of ten years or more in any continuous 20-year period since their 60th birthday.

*Weekly Rate from April 2015*

| | |
|---|---|
| Single person | £69.50 |
| Age addition | £0.25 |

## INCOME SUPPORT

Broadly speaking income support is a benefit for those between age 16 and the age they can receive pension credit, whose income is below a certain level, who work on average less than 16 hours a week and who are:
• bringing up children alone
• registered sick or disabled
• a student who is also a lone parent or disabled
• caring for someone who is sick or elderly

Income support is not payable if the claimant, or claimant and partner, have capital or savings in excess of £16,000 – and deductions are made for capital and savings in excess of £6,000. For people permanently in residential care and nursing homes deductions apply for capital over £10,000.

Sums payable depend on fixed allowances laid down by law for people in different circumstances. If both partners are eligible for income support, either may claim it for the couple. People receiving income support may be able to receive housing benefit, help with mortgage or home loan interest and help with healthcare. They may also be eligible for help with exceptional expenses from the Social Fund. Special rates may apply to some people living in residential care or nursing homes.

## INCOME SUPPORT PREMIUMS

Income support premiums are extra weekly payments for those with additional needs. People qualifying for more than one premium will normally only receive the highest single premium for which they qualify. However, family premium, disabled child premium, severe disability premium and carer premium are payable in addition to other premiums.

Child tax credit replaced premiums for people with children for all new income support claims from 6 April 2004. People with children who were already in receipt of income support in April 2004 and have not claimed child tax credit may qualify for:
• the family premium if they have at least one child
• the disabled child premium if they have a child who receives disability living allowance or is registered blind
• the enhanced disability child premium if they have a child in receipt of the higher rate disability living allowance care component

Carers may qualify for:
• the carer premium if they or their partner are in receipt of carer's allowance

Long-term sick or disabled people may qualify for:
• the disability premium if they or their partner are receiving certain benefits because they are disabled or cannot work; are registered blind; or if the claimant has been incapable of work or receiving statutory sick pay for at least 364 days (196 days if the person is terminally ill), including periods of incapacity separated by eight weeks or less
• the severe disability premium if the person lives alone and receives the middle or higher rate of disability living allowance care component and no one receives carer's allowance for caring for that person
• the enhanced disability premium if the person is in receipt of the higher rate disability living allowance care component

People with a partner aged over 60 may qualify for:
• the pensioner premium

## WEEKLY RATES OF INCOME SUPPORT
*from April 2015*

*Single person*

| | |
|---|---|
| aged 16–24 | £57.90 |
| aged 25+ | £73.10 |
| aged 16–17 and a single parent | £57.90 |
| aged 18+ and a single parent | £73.10 |

*Couples*

| | |
|---|---|
| Both under 18 | £57.90 |
| Both under 18, in certain circumstances | £87.50 |
| One under 18, one aged 18–24 | £57.90 |
| One under 18, one aged 25+ | £73.10 |
| Both aged 18+ | £114.85 |

*Premiums*

| | |
|---|---|
| Carer premium | £34.60 |
| Severe disability premium | £61.85 |
| Enhanced disability premium | |
| Single person | £15.75 |
| Couples | £22.60 |
| Pensioner premium (couple) | £116.00 |

## PENSION CREDIT

Pension credit was introduced on 6 October 2003 and replaced income support for those aged 60 and over. Between April 2010 and April 2020 the pension credit qualifying age is increasing from 60 to 65 alongside the increase in women's state pension age.

There are two elements to pension credit:

## THE GUARANTEE CREDIT

The guarantee credit guarantees a minimum income of £151.20 for single people and £230.85 for couples, with additional elements for people who have:
• eligible housing costs
• severe disabilities
• caring responsibilities

Income from state pension, private pensions, earnings, working tax credit and certain benefits are taken into account when calculating the pension credit. For savings and capital in excess of £10,000, £1 for every £500 or part of £500 held is taken into account as income when working out entitlement to pension credit.

People receiving the guarantee credit element of pension credit will be able to receive housing benefit, council tax benefit and help with healthcare costs.

*Weekly Rates from April 2015*
Additional amount for severe disability

| | |
|---|---|
| Single person | £61.85 |
| Couple (one qualifies) | £61.85 |
| Couple (both qualify) | £123.70 |
| Additional amount for carers | £34.60 |

## THE SAVINGS CREDIT

Single people aged 65 or over (and couples where one member is 65 or over) may be entitled to a savings credit which provides additional support for pensioners who have made modest provision towards their retirement. The savings credit is calculated by taking into account any qualifying income above the savings credit threshold. For 2015–16 the threshold is £126.50 for single people and £201.80 for couples. The maximum savings credit is £14.82 a week (£17.43 a week for couples).

Income that qualifies towards the savings credit includes state pensions, earnings, second pensions and income taken into account from capital above £10,000.

Some people will be entitled to the guarantee credit, some to the savings credit and some to both.

Where only the savings credit is in payment, people need to claim standard housing benefit or council tax benefit. Although local authorities take any savings credit into account in the housing benefit or council tax benefit assessment, for people aged 65 and over housing benefit or council tax benefit is enhanced to ensure that gains in pension credit are not depleted.

## HOUSING BENEFIT

Housing benefit is designed to help people with rent (including rent for accommodation in guesthouses, lodgings or hostels). It does not cover mortgage payments. The amount of benefit paid depends on:

- the income of the claimant, and partner if there is one, including earned income, unearned income (any other income including some other benefits) and savings
- number of dependants
- certain extra needs of the claimant, partner or any dependants
- number and gross income of people sharing the home who are not dependent on the claimant
- how much rent is paid

Housing benefit is not payable if the claimant, or claimant and partner, have savings in excess of £16,000. The amount of benefit is affected if savings held exceed £6,000 (£10,000 for people living in residential care and nursing homes). Housing benefit is not paid for meals, fuel or certain service charges that may be included in the rent. Deductions are also made for most non-dependants who live in the same accommodation as the claimant (and their partner). If the claimant is living with a partner or civil partner there can only be one claim.

The maximum amount of benefit (which is not necessarily the same as the amount of rent paid) may be paid where the claimant is in receipt of income support, income-based jobseeker's allowance, the guarantee element of pension credit or where the claimant's income is less than the amount allowed for their needs. Any income over that allowed for their needs will mean that their benefit is reduced.

### LOCAL HOUSING ALLOWANCE

Local housing allowance (LHA), which was rolled out nationally from 7 April 2008, is a way of calculating the rent element of housing benefit based on the area in which a person lives and household size. It affects people in the deregulated private rented sector who make a new claim for housing benefit or existing recipients who move address. LHA ensures that tenants in similar circumstances in the same area receive the same amount of financial support for their housing costs. It does not affect the way a person's income or capital is taken into account. LHA is paid to the tenant rather than the landlord in most circumstances. A weekly limit on payments is now in place so LHA does not exceed:

- £260.64 for a one bedroom property
- £302.33 for a two bedroom property
- £354.46 for a three bedroom property
- £417.02 for a four bedroom property

### COUNCIL TAX REDUCTION

From April 2013, council tax benefit was replaced by council tax reduction. Nearly all the rules that apply to housing benefit apply to council tax reduction, which helps people on low incomes to pay council tax bills. The amount payable depends on how much council tax is paid and who lives with the claimant. The benefit may be available to those receiving income support, income-based jobseeker's allowance, the guarantee element of pension credit or to those whose income is less than that allowed for their needs. Any income over that allowed for their needs will mean that they will receive less help with their council tax reduction. Deductions are made for non-dependants.

A full council tax bill is based on at least two adults living in a home. Residents may receive a 25 per cent reduction on their bill if they count as an adult for council tax and live on their own. If the property is the resident's main home and there is no-one who counts as an adult, the reduction is 50 per cent.

## THE SOCIAL FUND

### REGULATED PAYMENTS

*Sure Start Maternity Grant*

Sure start maternity grant (SSMG) is a one-off payment of £500 to help people on low incomes pay for essential items for new babies that are expected, born, adopted, the subject of a parental order (following a surrogate birth) or, in certain circumstances, the subject of a residency order. SSMG can be claimed any time from within 11 weeks of the expected birth and up to three months after the birth, adoption or date of parental or residency order. Those eligible are people in receipt of income support, income-based jobseeker's allowance, pension credit, child tax credit at a rate higher than the family element or working tax credit where a disability or severe disability element is in payment. Since 11 April 2011, new rules have been applied for babies due, born or adopted on this date. These are that SSMG is only available if there are no other children under 16 in the family or in the case of a dependent child's new baby, SSMG is only available if the dependent is under the age of 20 and has no other children.

*Funeral Payments*

Payable to help cover the necessary cost of burial or cremation, a new burial plot with an exclusive right of burial (where burial is chosen), certain other expenses, and up to £700 for any other funeral expenses, such as the funeral director's fees, the coffin or flowers. Those eligible are people receiving income support, income-based jobseeker's allowance, pension credit, child tax credit at a higher rate than the family element, working tax credit where a disability or severe disability element is in payment, council tax benefit or housing benefit who have good reason for taking responsibility for the funeral expenses. These payments are recoverable from any estate of the deceased.

*Cold Weather Payments*

A payment of £25 per seven-day period between 1 November and 31 March when the average temperature is recorded at or forecast to be 0°C or below over seven consecutive days in the qualifying person's area. Payments are made to people on pension credit or child tax credit with a disability element, those on income support whose benefit includes a pensioner or disability premium, and those on income-based jobseeker's allowance or employment and support allowance who have a child who is disabled or under the age of five. Payments are made automatically and do not have to be repaid.

*Winter Fuel Payments*
For 2015–16 the winter fuel payment is set at £200 for households with someone aged 62–79 and £300 for households with someone aged 80 or over. The rate paid is based on the person's age and circumstances in the 'qualifying week' between 21 and 27 September 2015. The majority of eligible people are paid automatically before Christmas, although a few need to claim. Payments do not have to be repaid.

*Christmas Bonus*
The Christmas bonus is a one-off tax-free £10 payment made before Christmas to those people in receipt of a qualifying benefit in the qualifying week.

## DISCRETIONARY PAYMENTS
*Community Care Grants*
These are intended to help people in Northern Ireland (they are no longer available in the rest of the UK) in receipt of income support, income-based jobseeker's allowance or employment and support allowance, pension credit, or payments on account of such benefits (or those likely to receive these benefits within the next six weeks because they are leaving residential or institutional accommodation) to live as independently as possible in the community; ease exceptional pressures on families; care for a prisoner or young offender released on temporary licence; help people set up home as part of a resettlement programme and/or assist with certain travelling expenses. They do not have to be repaid.

*Budgeting Loans*
These are interest-free loans to people who have been receiving income support, income-based jobseeker's allowance or employment and support allowance, pension credit or payments on account of such benefits for at least 26 weeks, for intermittent expenses that may be difficult to budget for. The smallest amount available to borrow is £100.

*Crisis Loans*
These are interest-free loans available to anyone in Northern Ireland aged 16 or over (they are no longer available in the rest of the UK), whether receiving benefits or not, who is without resources in an emergency or due to a disaster, where there is no other means of preventing serious damage or serious risk to their or their family members' health or safety.

## SAVINGS
Savings over £500 (£1,000 for people aged 62 or over) are taken into account for community care grants and savings of £1,000 (£2,000 for people aged 62 or over) are taken into account for budgeting loans. All savings are taken into account for crisis loans. Savings are not taken into account for sure start maternity grant, funeral payments, cold weather payments, winter fuel payments or the Christmas bonus.

## INDUSTRIAL INJURIES AND DISABLEMENT BENEFITS
The Industrial Injuries Scheme, administered under the Social Security Contributions and Benefits Act 1992, provides a range of benefits designed to compensate for disablement resulting from an industrial accident (ie an accident arising out of and in the course of an earner's employment) or from a prescribed disease due to the nature of a person's employment. Those who are self-employed are not covered by this scheme.

## INDUSTRIAL INJURIES DISABLEMENT BENEFIT
A person may be able to claim industrial injuries disablement benefit if they are ill or disabled due to an accident or incident that happened at work or in connection with work in England, Scotland or Wales. The amount of benefit awarded depends on the person's age and the degree of disability as assessed by a doctor.

The benefit is payable whether the person works or not and those who are incapable of work are entitled to draw other benefits, such as statutory sick pay or incapacity benefit, in addition to industrial injuries disablement benefit. It may also be possible to claim the following allowances:
- reduced earnings allowance for those who are unable to return to their regular work or work of the same standard and who had their accident (or whose disease started) before 1 October 1990. At state pension age this is converted to retirement allowance
- constant attendance allowance for those with a disablement of 100 per cent who need constant care. There are four rates of allowance depending on how much care the person needs
- exceptionally severe disablement allowance can be claimed in addition to constant care attendance allowance at one of the higher rates for those who need constant care permanently

*Weekly Rates of Benefit from April 2015*

| Degree of disablement | Aged 18+ or with dependants |
|---|---|
| 100 per cent | £168.00 |
| 90 | £151.20 |
| 80 | £134.40 |
| 70 | £117.60 |
| 60 | £100.80 |
| 50 | £84.00 |
| 40 | £67.20 |
| 30 | £50.40 |
| 20 | £33.60 |
| Unemployability supplement | £103.85 |
| Reduced earnings allowance (maximum) | £67.20 |
| Retirement allowance (maximum) | £16.80 |
| Constant attendance allowance (normal maximum rate) | £67.20 |
| Exceptionally severe disablement allowance | £67.20 |

## OTHER BENEFITS
People who are disabled because of an accident or disease that was the result of work that they did before 5 July 1948 are not entitled to industrial injuries disablement benefit. They may, however, be entitled to payment under the Workmen's Compensation Scheme or the Pneumoconiosis, Byssinosis and Miscellaneous Diseases Benefit Scheme. People who suffer from certain industrial diseases caused by dust can make a claim for an additional payment under the Pneumoconiosis Act 1979 if they are unable to get damages from the employer who caused or contributed to the disease.

*Diffuse Mesothelioma Payments (2008 Scheme)*
Since 1 October 2008 any person suffering from the asbestos-related disease, diffuse mesothelioma, who is unable to make a claim under the Pneumoconiosis Act 1979, have not received payment in respect of the disease from an employer, via a civil claim or elsewhere, and are not entitled to compensation from a MoD scheme, can claim a one-off

lump sum payment. The scheme covers people whose exposure to asbestos occurred in the UK and was not as a result of their work as an employee (ie they lived near a factory using asbestos). The amount paid depends on the age of the person when the disease was diagnosed, or the date of the claim if the diagnosis date is not known. The current rate is £85,580 for those aged 37 and under to £13,295 for persons aged 77 and over. From 1 October 2009 claims must be received within 12 months of the date of diagnosis. If the sufferer has died, their dependants may be able to claim, but must do so within 12 months of the date of death.

## CLAIMS AND QUESTIONS
Entitlement to benefit and regulated Social Fund payments is determined by a decision maker on behalf of the Secretary of State for the Department for Work and Pensions. A claimant who is dissatisfied with that decision can ask for an explanation. He or she can dispute the decision by applying to have it revised or, in particular circumstances, superseded. The claimant can appeal to the First Tier-tribunal (Social Security and Child Support). There is a further right of appeal to the Administrative and Appeals Chamber of the Upper Tribunal (*see* Tribunals).

Decisions on claims and applications for housing benefit and council tax benefit are made by local authorities. The explanation, dispute and appeals process is the same as for other benefits.

All decisions on applications to the discretionary Social Fund are made by Jobcentre Plus Social Fund decision makers. Applicants can ask for a review of the decision within 28 days of the date on the decision letter. As above, the claimant has a right of appeal to the First-tier Tribunal (Social Security and Child Support).

## EMPLOYER PAYMENTS

### STATUTORY MATERNITY PAY
Employers pay statutory maternity pay (SMP) to pregnant women who have been employed by them full or part-time continuously for at least 26 weeks into the 15th week before the week the baby is due, and whose earnings on average at least equal the lower earnings limit applied to NI contributions (£112 a week if the end of the qualifying week is in the 2015–16 tax year). SMP can be paid for a maximum period of up to 39 weeks. If the qualifying conditions are met women will receive a payment of 90 per cent of their average earnings for the first six weeks, followed by 33 weeks at £139.58 or 90 per cent of the woman's average weekly earnings if this is less than £139.58. SMP can be paid, at the earliest, 11 weeks before the week in which the baby is due, up to the day following the birth. Women can decide when they wish their maternity leave and pay to start and can work until the baby is born. However, where the woman is absent from work wholly or partly due to her pregnancy in the four weeks before the week the baby is due to be born, SMP will start the day following the first day of absence from work.

Employers are reimbursed for 92 per cent of the SMP they pay. Small employers with annual gross NI payments of £45,000 or less recover 103 per cent of the SMP paid out.

### STATUTORY PATERNITY PAY
*Ordinary Statutory Paternity Pay*
Employers pay ordinary statutory paternity pay (OSPP) to employees who are taking leave when a child is born or placed for adoption. To qualify the employee must:
• have responsibility for the child's upbringing
• be the biological father of the child (or the child's adopter), or the spouse/civil partner/partner of the mother or adopter
• have been employed by the same employer for at least 26 weeks ending with the 15th week before the baby is due

(or the week in which the adopter is notified of having been matched with a child)
• continue working for the employer up to the child's birth (or placement for adoption)
• be earning an average of at least £112 a week (before tax)
Employees who meet these conditions receive payment of £139.58 or 90 per cent of the employee's average weekly earnings if this is less than £139.58. The employee can choose to be paid for one or two consecutive weeks. The earliest the OSPP period can begin is the date of the child's birth or placement for adoption. The OSPP period must be completed within eight weeks of that date. OSPP is not payable for any week in which the employee works. Employers are reimbursed in the same way as for statutory maternity pay.

*Additional Paternity Leave and Pay*
### ADDITIONAL PATERNITY LEAVE AND PAY
Regulations introduced on 6 April 2010 give parents greater flexibility in how they use their maternity and paternity provisions. For births from 3 April 2011, additional paternity leave (APL) entitles eligible fathers to take up to 26 weeks' additional paternity leave, allowing for up to a total of one year's leave to be shared between the couple. APL entitlement requires the mother to have returned to work; it must also be taken between 20 weeks and one year after the child is born. APL may be paid if taken during the mother's statutory maternity pay period or maternity allowance period.

The APL entitlement will also apply to husbands, partners or civil partners who are not the child's father but expect to have the main responsibility (apart from the mother) for the child's upbringing.

The current rate of additional statutory paternity pay is £139.58 a week or 90 per cent of the emplyee's average weekly earnings if this is less than £139.58.

### STATUTORY ADOPTION PAY
Employers pay statutory adoption pay (SAP) to employees taking adoption leave from their employers. To qualify for SAP the employee must:
• be newly matched with a child by an adoption agency
• have been employed by the same employer for at least 26 weeks ending the week in which they have been notified of being matched with a child
• be earning an average of at least £112 a week (before tax)
Employees who meet these conditions receive payment of £139.58 or 90 per cent of their average weekly earnings if this is less than £139.58 for up to 39 weeks. The earliest SAP can be paid from is two weeks before the expected date of placement; the latest it can start is the date of the child's placement. Where a couple adopt a child, only one of them may receive SAP, the other may be able to receive statutory paternity pay if they meet the eligibility criteria. Employers are reimbursed in the same way as for statutory maternity pay.

The additional paternity leave entitlement (*see* above) will also apply to adoptions where adoptive parents are notified of a match on or after 3 April 2011.

### STATUTORY SICK PAY
Employers pay statutory sick pay (SSP) for up to a maximum of 28 weeks to any employee incapable of work for four or more consecutive days. Employees must have done some work under their contract of service and have average weekly earnings of at least £112 from April 2014. SSP is a daily payment and is usually paid for the days that an employee would normally work, these days are known as qualifying days. SSP is not paid for the first three qualifying days in a period of sickness. SSP is paid at £88.45 per week and is subject to PAYE and NI contributions. Employees who cannot obtain SSP may be able to claim incapacity benefit. Employers may be able to recover some SSP costs.

# THE WATER INDUSTRY

In the UK, the water industry provides clean and safe drinking water for homes and businesses to over 63 million people and has an annual turnover of around £10bn. It supplies around 17 billion litres of water a day to domestic and commercial customers and collects and treats more than 16 billion litres of wastewater a day. It also manages assets that include around 1,400 water treatment and 9,350 wastewater treatment works, 550 impounding reservoirs, over 6,500 service reservoirs/water towers and 800,000km of water mains and sewers.

Water services in England and Wales are provided by private companies. In Scotland and Northern Ireland there are single authorities, Scottish Water and Northern Ireland Water, that are publicly owned companies answerable to their respective governments. In drinking water quality tests carried out in 2013 by the Drinking Water Inspectorate, the water industry in England and Wales achieved 99.97 per cent compliance with the standards required by the EU Drinking Water Directive; Scotland achieved 99.86 per cent and Northern Ireland 99.81 per cent.

Water UK is the industry association that represents all UK water and wastewater service suppliers at national and European level and is funded directly by its members, who are the service suppliers for England, Scotland, Wales and Northern Ireland; every member has a seat on the Water UK Council.

WATER UK, 3rd Floor, 36 Broadway, London SW1H 0BH
T 020-7344 1844 W www.water.org.uk
*Chief Executive,* Pamela Taylor, OBE

## ENGLAND AND WALES

In England and Wales, the Secretary of State for Environment, Food and Rural Affairs and the Welsh government have overall responsibility for water policy and oversee environmental standards for the water industry.

The statutory consumer representative body for water services is the Consumer Council for Water.

CONSUMER COUNCIL FOR WATER, 1st Floor,
Victoria Square House, Victoria Square, Birmingham B2 4AJ
T 0121-345 1000 E enquiries@ccwater.org.uk
W www.ccwater.org.uk

### REGULATORY BODIES

The Water Services Regulation Authority (OFWAT) was established in 1989 when the water and sewerage industry in England and Wales was privatised. Its statutory role and duties are laid out under the Water Industry Act 1991 and it is the independent economic regulator of the water and sewerage companies in England and Wales. OFWAT's main duties are to ensure that the companies can finance and carry out their statutory functions and to protect the interests of water customers. OFWAT is a non-ministerial government department headed by a board following a change in legislation introduced by the Water Act 2003.

Under the Competition Act 1998, from 1 March 2000 the Competition Appeal Tribunal has heard appeals against the regulator's decisions regarding anti-competitive agreements and abuse of a dominant position in the marketplace. The Water Act 2003 placed a new duty on OFWAT to contribute to the achievement of sustainable development.

The Environment Agency has statutory duties and powers in relation to water resources, pollution control, flood defence, fisheries, recreation, conservation and navigation in England and Wales. It is also responsible for issuing permits, licences, consents and registrations such as industrial licences to extract water and fishing licences.

The Drinking Water Inspectorate (DWI) is the drinking water quality regulator for England and Wales, responsible for assessing the quality of the drinking water supplied by the water companies and investigating any incidents affecting drinking water quality, initiating prosecution where necessary. The DWI science and strategy group provides scientific advice on drinking water policy issues to DEFRA and the Welsh government.

OFWAT, Centre City Tower, 7 Hill Street, Birmingham B5 4UA
T 0121-644 7500 E mailbox@ofwat.gsi.gov.uk
W www.ofwat.gov.uk
*Chair,* Jonson Cox
*Chief Executive,* Cathryn Ross

### METHODS OF CHARGING

In England and Wales, most domestic customers still pay for domestic water supply and sewerage services through charges based on the rateable value of their property. OFWAT estimated that the proportion of household customers in England and Wales to have metered supplies was around 50 per cent in 2014–15. Nearly all non-household customers are charged according to consumption.

Under the Water Industry Act 1999, water companies can continue basing their charges on the old rateable value of the property. Domestic customers can continue paying on an unmeasured basis unless they choose to pay according to consumption. After having a meter installed (which is free of charge), a customer can revert to unmeasured charging within 12 months. However, water companies may charge by meter for new homes, or homes where there is a high discretionary use of water. Domestic, school and hospital customers cannot be disconnected for non-payment.

In December 2014, OFWAT finalised its 2014 price review decisions for household water bills for the five-year period to 2020. With the exception of Bristol Water, all the water and sewerage, and water only companies confirmed acceptance of OFWAT's price decisions by the 12 February 2015 deadline. This means that average bills for water and waste-water customers in England and Wales will decrease by around 5 per cent, before adjustments for inflation, between 2015 and 2020; an average decrease of around £20, from £396 to £376 per annum.

AVERAGE HOUSEHOLD BILLS 2014–20 *(£)*

WATER AND SEWERAGE COMPANIES

| | 2014–15 (£) | 2019–20 (£) | 5-year change (%) |
|---|---|---|---|
| Anglian | 431 | 390 | −10 |
| Dwr Cymru | 440 | 416 | −5 |
| Northumbrian | 388 | 382 | −1 |
| Severn Trent | 333 | 316 | −5 |
| South West | 545 | 506 | −7 |
| Southern | 437 | 403 | −8 |
| Thames* | 370 | 353 | −5 |
| United Utilities | 410 | 398 | −3 |
| Wessex | 485 | 442 | −9 |
| Yorkshire | 373 | 361 | −3 |

* Includes the cost for the preparatory works to build the Thames Tideway Tunnel – a 25km sewer to resolve the problem of too much sewage overflowing into the River Thames

## WATER ONLY COMPANIES

| | 2014–15 (£) | 2019–20 (£) | 5-year change (%) |
|---|---|---|---|
| Affinity | 176 | 163 | −7 |
| Bristol* | 202 | 160 | −21 |
| Dee Valley | 152 | 149 | −2 |
| Portsmouth | 97 | 96 | −1 |
| Bournemouth | 153 | 134 | −12 |
| South East | 201 | 194 | −3 |
| South Staffordshire | 141 | 135 | −4 |
| Sutton and East Surrey | 186 | 180 | −3 |

\* Bristol Water has referred OFWAT's price decision to the Competition Markets Authority

*Source:* OFWAT

## SCOTLAND

In 2002 the three existing water authorities in Scotland (East of Scotland Water, North of Scotland Water and West of Scotland Water) merged to form Scottish Water. Scottish Water, which serves more than 2.4 million households and provides 1.3 billion litres of water per day while removing 847 million litres of waste water, is a public sector company, structured and managed like a private company, but remains answerable to the Scottish parliament. Scottish Water is regulated by the Water Industry Commission for Scotland (established under the Water Services (Scotland) Act 2005), the Scottish Environment Protection Agency (SEPA) and the Drinking Water Quality Regulator for Scotland. The Water Industry Commissioner is responsible for regulating all aspects of economic and customer service performance, including water and sewerage charges. SEPA, created under the Environment Act 1995, is responsible for environmental issues, including controlling pollution and promoting the cleanliness of Scotland's rivers, lochs and coastal waters. The Public Services Reform (Scotland) Act 2010 transferred the complaints handling function of Waterwatch Scotland regarding Scottish Water, to the Scottish Public Services Ombudsman. Consumer Futures represented the views and interests of Scottish Water customers but became part of Citizens Advice Scotland in 2014.

### METHODS OF CHARGING
Scottish Water sets charges for domestic and non-domestic water and sewerage provision through charges schemes which are regulated by the Water Industry Commission for Scotland. In February 2004 the harmonisation of all household charges across the country was completed following the merger of the separate authorities under Scottish Water. In November 2014 the Water Industry Commission for Scotland published *The Strategic Review of Charges 2015–2021*, stating that annual price rises would not increase at a rate higher than that of consumer price inflation during this six-year period. For the year 2015–16, the combined service charge, covering the water supply and waste water collection, increased by 1.6 per cent; resulting in an annual average household bill of £346.

CITIZENS ADVICE SCOTLAND, T 0808-800 9060
W www.cas.org.uk
DRINKING WATER QUALITY REGULATOR FOR
SCOTLAND, Area 1-D South, Victoria Quay,
Edinburgh EH6 6QQ T 0131-244 0190 W www.dwqr.org.uk
SCOTTISH ENVIRONMENT PROTECTION AGENCY,
Erskine Court, Castle Business Park, Stirling FK9 4TZ
T 01786-457700 W www.sepa.org.uk
SCOTTISH WATER, Castle House, 6 Castle Drive,
Dunfermline KY11 8GG T 0345-601 8855
W www.scottishwater.co.uk
*Chief Executive,* Douglas Millican

WATER INDUSTRY COMMISSION FOR SCOTLAND,
First Floor, Moray House, Forthside Way, Stirling FK8 1QZ
T 01786-430200 W www.watercommission.co.uk

## NORTHERN IRELAND

Formerly an executive agency of the Department for Regional Development, Northern Ireland Water is a government-owned company but with substantial independence from government. Northern Ireland Water was set up as a result of government reform of water and sewerage services in April 2007. It is responsible for policy and coordination with regard to the supply, distribution and cleanliness of water, and the provision and maintenance of sewerage services. The Northern Ireland Authority for Utility Regulation (known as the Utility Regulator) is responsible for regulating the water services provided by Northern Ireland Water. The Drinking Water Inspectorate, a unit in the Northern Ireland Environment Agency (NIEA), regulates drinking water quality. Another NIEA unit, the Water Management Unit, has responsibility for the protection of the aquatic environment. The Consumer Council for Northern Ireland is the consumer representative body for water services.

### METHODS OF CHARGING
The water and sewerage used by domestic customers in Northern Ireland is currently paid for by the Department for Regional Development (DRD), a system which will continue at least through the end of 2015; however the future of the subsidy is uncertain. Non-domestic customers in Northern Ireland became subject to water and sewerage charges and trade effluent charges where applicable in April 2008.

CONSUMER COUNCIL FOR NORTHERN IRELAND,
Seatem House, 28–32 Alfred Street, Belfast BT2 8EN
T 028-9025 1600 W www.consumercouncil.org.uk
NORTHERN IRELAND AUTHORITY FOR UTILITY
REGULATION, Queens House, 14 Queen Street, Belfast
BT1 6ED T 028-9031 1575 W www.uregni.gov.uk
NORTHERN IRELAND WATER, PO Box 1026, Belfast
BT1 9DJ T 0345-744 0088 W www.niwater.com
*Chief Executive,* Sara Venning

## WATER SERVICE COMPANIES

*(\* associate member of Water UK)*

AFFINITY WATER, Tamblin Way, Hatfield, Herts AL10 9EZ
T 01707-268111 W www.affinitywater.co.uk
ALBION WATER LTD, Forest House, 3–5 Horndean Road,
Bracknell RG12 0XQ T 0330-024 2020
W www.albionwater.co.uk
ANGLIAN WATER SERVICES LTD, PO Box 10642, Harlow
CM20 9HA T 03457-919155 W www.anglianwater.co.uk
BOURNEMOUTH WATER, George Jessel House,
Francis Avenue, Bournemouth, Dorset BH11 8NX
T 01202-590059 W www.bournemouthwater.co.uk
BRISTOL WATER PLC, Bridgwater Road, Bristol BS13 7AT
T 0345-702 3797 W www.bristolwater.co.uk
CAMBRIDGE WATER PLC, 90 Fulbourn Road, Cambridge
CB1 9JN T 01223-706050 W www.cambridge-water.co.uk
\*CHOLDERTON & DISTRICT WATER COMPANY LTD,
Estate Office, Cholderton, Salisbury, Wiltshire SP4 0DR
T 01980-629203 W www.choldertonwater.co.uk
DEE VALLEY WATER PLC, Packsaddle, Wrexham Road,
Rhostyllen, Wrexham LL14 4EH T 01978-846946
W www.deevalleywater.co.uk
DWR CYMRU (WELSH WATER), Pentwyn Road, Nelson,
Treharris, Mid Glamorgan CF46 6LY T 0800-052 0145
W www.dwrcymru.co.uk

ESSEX & SUFFOLK WATER PLC (subsidiary of Northumbrian Water Ltd), Customer Centre, PO Box 292, Durham DH1 9TX **T** 0845-782 0111 **W** www.eswater.co.uk

NORTHUMBRIAN WATER LTD, Abbey Road, Pity Me, Durham DH1 5FJ **T** 0845-604 7468 **W** www.nwl.co.uk

PORTSMOUTH WATER PLC, PO Box 8, West Street, Havant, Hants PO9 1LG **T** 023-9249 9888 **W** www.portsmouthwater.co.uk

SEVERN TRENT WATER LTD, 2 St Johns Street, Coventry CV1 2LZ **T** 024-7771 5000 **W** www.stwater.co.uk

SOUTH EAST WATER LTD, Rocfort Road, Snodland, Kent ME6 5AH **T** 0333-000 0001 **W** www.southeastwater.co.uk

SOUTH STAFFORDSHIRE WATER PLC, Green Lane, Walsall WS2 7PD **T** 0845-607 0456 **W** www.south-staffs-water.co.uk

SOUTH WEST WATER LTD, Peninsula House, Rydon Lane, Exeter EX2 7HR **T** 01392-443020 **W** www.southwestwater.co.uk

SOUTHERN WATER SERVICES LTD, PO Box 41, Worthing BN13 3NZ **T** 01903-264444 **W** www.southernwater.co.uk

SUTTON AND EAST SURREY WATER PLC, London Road, Redhill, Surrey RH1 1LJ **T** 01737-772000 **W** www.waterplc.com

THAMES WATER UTILITIES LTD, PO Box 286, Swindon SN38 2RA **T** 0800-980 8800 **W** www.thameswater.co.uk

UNITED UTILITIES WATER PLC, Haweswater House, Lingley Mere Business Park, Great Sankey, Warrington WA5 3LP **T** 0845-746 2200 **W** www.unitedutilities.com

WESSEX WATER SERVICES LTD, Claverton Down, Bath BA2 7WW **T** 01225-526000 **W** www.wessexwater.co.uk

YORKSHIRE WATER SERVICES LTD, Western House, Western Way, Bradford BD6 2LZ **T** 01274-691111 **W** www.yorkshirewater.com

## ISLAND WATER AUTHORITIES
*(not members of Water UK)*

COUNCIL OF THE ISLES OF SCILLY, Town Hall, St Mary's, Isles of Scilly TR21 0LW **T** 01720-424000 **W** www.scilly.gov.uk

GUERNSEY WATER, PO Box 30, Brickfield House, St Andrew, Guernsey GY1 3AS **T** 01481-239500 **W** www.water.gg

MANX UTILITIES, PO Box 177, Douglas, Isle of Man IM99 1PS **T** 01624-687687 **W** www.manxutilities.im

JERSEY WATER, PO Box 69, Mulcaster House, Westmount Road, St Helier, Jersey JE1 1DG **T** 01534-707300 **W** www.jerseywater.je

THE INCOMPETENT COOK
IVOR THOMAS
ILLUSTRATIONS BY TOM WATSON



Awarded Johansens
Small Hotel of the Year
AWARD WINNER

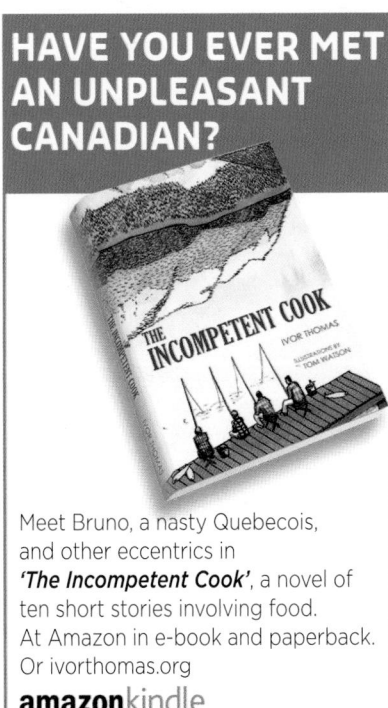

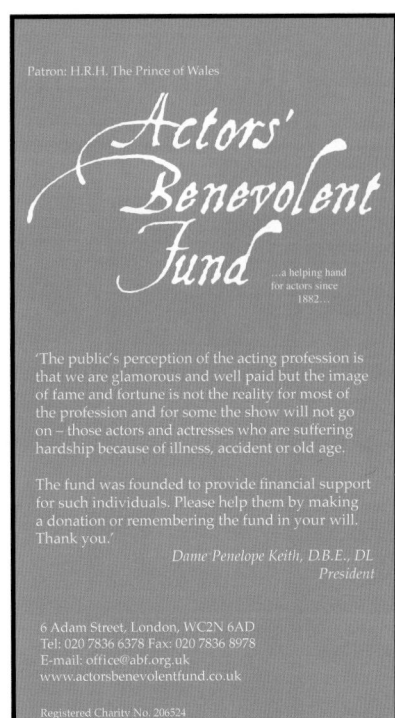

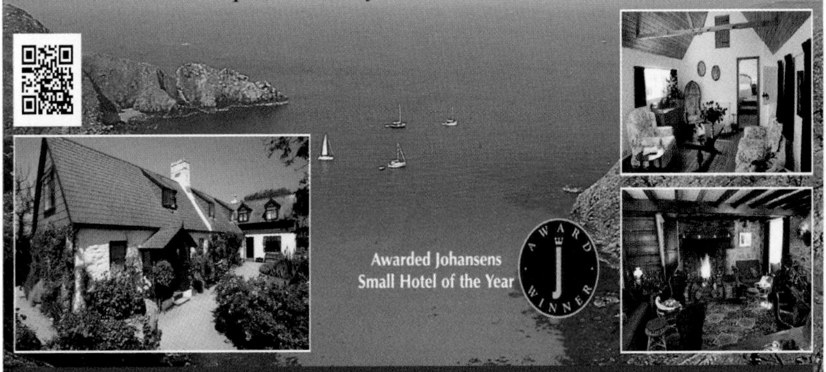

# We've helped improve the lives of many kidney patients...

# but we'd like to do more...

## BKPA Legacy Appeal

To find out how you can help please visit
www.britishkidney-pa.co.uk or call us on
**01420 541424**

**BRITISH KIDNEY**
*Patient* **ASSOCIATION**
*improving life for kidney patients*

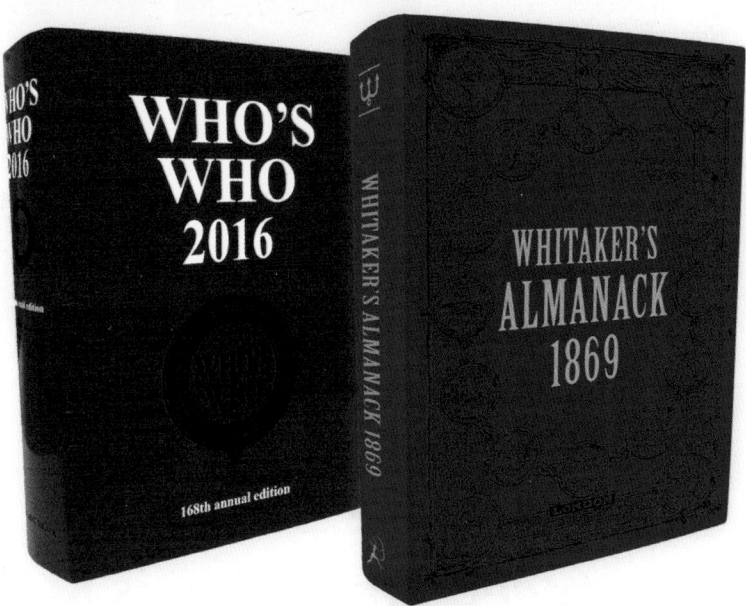
 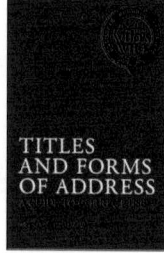  

# ENERGY

The main primary sources of energy in Britain are coal, oil, natural gas, renewables and nuclear power. The main secondary sources are electricity, coke and smokeless fuels and petroleum products. The UK was a net importer of fuels in the 1970s, however as a result of growth in oil and gas production from the North Sea, the UK became a net exporter of energy for most of the 1980s. Output decreased in the late 1980s following the Piper Alpha disaster until the mid-1990s, after which the UK again became a net exporter. Since 2004, the UK reverted back to become a net importer of energy. In 2014, the UK net import gap decreased to 94 million tonnes of oil equivalent – from 102 million tonnes of oil equivalent in the previous year – accounting for 46.2 per cent of the total energy used in the UK. In value terms, on an Overseas Trade Statistics (OTS) basis, the total fuel deficit for 2014 was £13.7bn, 25 per cent less than in 2013, due to substantial reduction in crude oil and natural gas prices. The deficit of crude oil and petroleum products, on the same basis, in 2014 was £5.8bn (1.1 per cent more than in 2013) compared with a £2.2bn surplus in 2004. The Department of Energy and Climate Change (DECC) is responsible for promoting energy efficiency.

## INDIGENOUS PRODUCTION OF PRIMARY FUELS
*Million tonnes of oil equivalent*

|  | 2013 | 2014 |
|---|---|---|
| Primary oils | 44.5 | 43.7 |
| Natural gas | 36.5 | 36.6 |
| Primary electricity | 18.5 | 17.5 |
| Coal | 8.0 | 7.3 |
| Bioenergy and waste | 7.5 | 7.9 |
| Total | 115.0 | 113.0 |

*Source: DECC*

## INLAND ENERGY CONSUMPTION BY PRIMARY FUEL
*Million tonnes of oil equivalent, temperature adjusted*

|  | 2013 | 2014 |
|---|---|---|
| Natural gas | 70.5 | 69.6 |
| Petroleum | 66.1 | 65.8 |
| Coal | 38.3 | 33.4 |
| Nuclear electricity | 15.4 | 13.9 |
| Bioenergy and waste | 9.4 | 10.7 |
| Wind and hydro electricity | 3.0 | 3.6 |
| Net Imports | 1.2 | 1.8 |
| Total | 203.9 | 198.8 |

*Source: DECC*

## TRADE IN FUELS AND RELATED MATERIALS (2014)

|  | Quantity, million tonnes of oil equivalent | Value £m |
|---|---|---|
| *Imports* | | |
| Crude oil | 51.0 | 21,553 |
| Petroleum products | 33.3 | 16,455 |
| Natural gas | 41.0 | 6,750 |
| Coal and other solid fuel | 26.2 | 2,539 |
| Electricity | 2.0 | 1,022 |
| Total | 153.6 | 48,319 |
| *Exports* | | |
| Crude oil | 41.5 | 18,160 |
| Petroleum products | 30.2 | 14,080 |
| Natural gas | 11.0 | 2,106 |
| Coal and other solid fuel | 0.6 | 118 |
| Electricity | 0.2 | 123 |
| Total | 83.5 | 34,587 |

*Source: HMRC/DECC, ONS*

## OIL

Until the 1960s Britain imported almost all its oil supplies. In 1969 oil was discovered in the Arbroath field in the North Sea. The first oilfield to be brought into production was Argyll in 1975, and since the mid-1970s Britain has been a major producer of crude oil.

To date, the UK has produced around 3.6 billion tonnes of oil. It is estimated that there are around 716 million tonnes remaining to be produced. Licences for exploration and production are granted to companies by the DECC. As at July 2015, 678 offshore production licences and 138 onshore petroleum exploration and development licences had been awarded. At the end of 2014, there were a total of 338 offshore oil and gas fields in production. Total UK oil production peaked in 1999 but is now declining. Production stood at 39.9 million tonnes in 2014, just under a third of the 1999 level. Profits from oil production are subject to a special tax regime with different taxes applying depending on the date of approval of each field.

## DRILLING ACTIVITY (2014)
*by number of wells started*

|  | Offshore | Onshore |
|---|---|---|
| Exploration | 14 | 0 |
| Appraisal | 18 | 0 |
| Exploration and appraisal | 32 | 8 |
| Development | 126 | 11 |

*Source: DECC*

## INDIGENOUS PRODUCTION AND REFINERY RECEIPTS
*Thousand tonnes*

|  | 2013 | 2014 |
|---|---|---|
| Indigenous production | 40,646 | 39,928 |
| Crude oil | 38,456 | 37,474 |
| *NGLs | 2,190 | 2,453 |
| Refinery receipts | 65,687 | 60,823 |

* Natural Gas Liquids: condensates and petroleum gases derived at onshore treatment plants
*Source: DECC*

## DELIVERIES OF PETROLEUM PRODUCTS FOR INLAND CONSUMPTION BY ENERGY USE
*Thousand tonnes*

|  | 2013 | 2014 |
|---|---|---|
| Transport | 47,222 | 47,648 |
| Industry | 4,016 | 4,033 |
| Domestic | 2,580 | 2,299 |
| Other | 1,365 | 1,379 |
| Total | 55,183 | 55,359 |

*Source: DECC*

## COAL

Mines were in private ownership until 1947 when they were nationalised and came under the management of the National Coal Board, later the British Coal Corporation. The corporation held a near monopoly on coal production until 1994 when the industry was restructured. Under the Coal Industry Act 1994, the Coal Authority was established to take over ownership of coal reserves and to issue licences to private mining companies. The Coal Authority is also responsible for the physical legacy of mining, eg subsidence damage claims that are not the responsibility of licensees, and for holding and making available all existing records. It also publishes current data on the coal industry on its website (W www.gov.uk/government/organisations/the-coal-authority).

The mines owned by the British Coal Corporation were sold as five separate businesses in 1994 and coal production is now undertaken entirely in the private sector. Coal output was around 50 million tonnes a year in 1994 but has since declined. In 2014, coal output stood at around 11.6 million tonnes. Deep mine production decreased by 9.9 per cent in 2014 due to the closure of a number of mines and geological conditions at some others. Surface mine production also decreased by 7.2 per cent due to geological conditions at some mines and the liquidation of Scottish Coal Company. As at 31 December 2014, there were ten deep mines and 22 surface mines in production in the UK.

The main consumer of coal in the UK is the electricity supply industry. Coal still supplies over a third of the UK's electricity needs but as indigenous production has declined, imports have continued to make up the shortfall and now represent around 86 per cent of UK coal supply, 42 per cent of which is currently supplied from Russia.

UK government policy is to meet the long-term challenges posed by climate change while continuing to ensure secure, clean and affordable energy. Coal's availability, flexibility and reliability compared to other sources mean that it is expected to continue to play an important role in the future generating mix, but its carbon emissions will need to be managed through the introduction of abatement technologies including carbon capture and storage (CCS).

CCS attempts to mitigate the effects of global warming by capturing the carbon dioxide emissions from power stations that burn fossil fuels, preventing the gas from being released into the atmosphere, and storing it in underground geological formations. CCS is still in its infancy and only through its successful demonstration and development will it be possible for coal to remain a part of a low-carbon UK energy mix. The government is committed to public sector investment in CCS technology on four power stations and has made it clear that there can be no new coal power stations in England and Wales without CCS on a defined amount of capacity. As part of a wider package of reforms to the electricity market, the government will also be introducing an Emissions Performance Standard, which will limit the emissions from new fossil fuel power stations.

### COAL PRODUCTION AND FOREIGN TRADE
*Thousand tonnes*

|  | 2013 | 2014 |
|---|---|---|
| Surface mining | 8,679 | 7,962 |
| Deep-mined | 4,089 | 3,685 |
| Imports | 49,402 | 41,765 |
| Exports | (593) | (425) |
| *Total supply | 60,248 | 48,658 |
| Total demand | 60,425 | 48,500 |

\* Includes an estimate for slurry and stock change
*Source:* DECC

### INLAND COAL USE
*Thousand tonnes*

|  | 2013 | 2014 |
|---|---|---|
| *Fuel producers* |  |  |
| Electricity generators | 50,041 | 38,400 |
| Coke manufacture | 5,288 | 4,977 |
| Blast furnaces | 1,411 | 1,513 |
| Heat generation | 609 | 516 |
| Patent fuel manufacture | 259 | 259 |
| *Final consumption* |  |  |
| Industry | 2,134 | 2,241 |
| Transport | 14 | 13 |
| Domestic | 636 | 547 |
| Public administration | 22 | 23 |
| Commercial | 5 | 5 |
| Agriculture | 0 | 0 |
| Miscellaneous | 7 | 6 |

*Source:* DECC

## GAS

From the late 18th century gas in Britain was produced from coal. In the 1960s town gas began to be produced from oil-based feedstocks using imported oil. In 1965 gas was discovered in the North Sea in the West Sole field, which became the first gasfield in production in 1967, and from the late 1960s natural gas began to replace town gas. From October 1998 Britain was connected to the continental European gas system via a pipeline from Bacton, Norfolk to Zeebrugge, Belgium. Gas is transported through 278,000km of mains pipeline including 7,600km of high-pressure gas pipelines owned and operated in the UK by National Grid Gas plc.

The gas industry in Britain was nationalised in 1949 and operated as the Gas Council. The Gas Council was replaced by the British Gas Corporation in 1972 and the industry became more centralised. The British Gas Corporation was privatised in 1986 as British Gas plc. In 1993 the Monopolies and Mergers Commission found that British Gas's integrated business in Great Britain as a gas trader and the owner of the gas transportation system could operate against the public interest. In February 1997, British Gas demerged its trading arm to become two separate companies, BG plc and Centrica plc. BG Group, as the company is now known, is an international natural gas company whose principal business is finding and developing gas reserves and building gas markets. Its core operations are located in the UK, South America, Egypt, Trinidad and Tobago, Kazakhstan and India. Centrica runs the trading and services operations under the British Gas brand name in Great Britain. In October 2000 BG demerged its pipeline business, Transco, which became part of Lattice Group, finally merging with the National Grid Group in 2002 to become National Grid Transco plc.

In July 2005 National Grid Transco plc changed its name to National Grid plc and Transco plc became National Grid Gas plc. In the same year National Grid Gas also completed the sale of four of its eight gas distribution networks. The distribution networks transport gas at lower pressures, which eventually supply the consumers such as domestic customers. The Scotland and south-east of England networks were sold to Scotia Gas Networks. The Wales and south-west network was sold to Wales & West Utilities and the network in the north-east to Northern Gas Networks. This was the biggest change in the corporate structure of gas infrastructure since privatisation in 1986.

Competition was gradually introduced into the industrial gas market from 1986. Supply of gas to the domestic market was opened to companies other than British Gas, starting in

April 1996 with a pilot project in the West Country and Wales, with the rest of the UK following soon after.

Declines in UK indigenous gas production and increasing demand led to the UK becoming a net importer of gas once more in 2004. With the depletion of the UK Continental Shelf reserves, UK gas production has seen growing rates of decline. As part of the Energy Act 2008, the government planned to strengthen regulation of the offshore gas supply infrastructure, to allow private sector investment to help maintain UK energy supplies.

BG GROUP PLC, Thames Valley Park Drive, Reading RG6 1PT
   T 0118-935 3222 W www.bg-group.com
Chief Executive, Helge Lund

CENTRICA PLC, Millstream, Maidenhead Road, Windsor, Berkshire SL4 5GD T 01753-494000 W www.centrica.com
Chair, Rick Haythornthwaite
Chief Executive, Iain Conn

NATIONAL GRID PLC, National Grid House, Warwick Technology Park, Gallows Hill, Warwick CV34 6DA
   T 01926-653000 W www.nationalgrid.com
Chair, Sir Peter Gershon, CBE
Chief Executive, Steve Holliday

UK GAS CONSUMPTION BY INDUSTRY
GWh

|  | 2013 | 2014 |
|---|---|---|
| Domestic | 342,501 | 278,101 |
| Industry | 93,005 | 92,493 |
| Public administration | 44,419 | 36,969 |
| Commercial | 57,791 | 48,443 |
| Agriculture | 1,096 | 886 |
| Non-energy use | 5,598 | 5,430 |
| Miscellaneous | 12,065 | 10,079 |
| Total gas consumption | 556,475 | 472,401 |

Source: DECC

# ELECTRICITY

The first power station in Britain generating electricity for public supply began operating in 1882. In the 1930s a national transmission grid was developed and it was reconstructed and extended in the 1950s and 1960s. Power stations were operated by the Central Electricity Generating Board.

Under the Electricity Act 1989, 12 regional electricity companies, responsible for the distribution of electricity from the national grid to consumers, were formed from the former area electricity boards in England and Wales. Four companies were formed from the Central Electricity Generating Board: three generating companies (National Power plc, Nuclear Electric plc and Powergen plc) and the National Grid Company plc, which owned and operated the transmission system in England and Wales. National Power and Powergen were floated on the stock market in 1991.

National Power was demerged in October 2000 to form two separate companies: International Power plc and Innogy plc, which manages the bulk of National Power's UK assets. Nuclear Electric was split into two parts in 1996.

The National Grid Company was floated on the stock market in 1995 and formed a new holding company, National Grid Group. National Grid Group completed a merger with Lattice in 2002 to form National Grid Transco, a public limited company (see Gas).

Following privatisation, generators and suppliers in England and Wales traded via the Electricity Pool. A competitive wholesale trading market known as NETA (New Electricity Trading Arrangements) replaced the Electricity Pool in March 2001, and was extended to include Scotland via the British Electricity Transmissions and Trading Arrangements (BETTA) in 2005. As part of BETTA, National Grid became the system operator for all transmission. The introduction of competition into the domestic electricity market was completed in May 1999. Since competition was introduced, over 19 million of Britain's 28 million electricity customers have switched their supplier.

In Scotland, three new companies were formed under the Electricity Act 1989: Scottish Power plc and Scottish Hydro-Electric plc, which were responsible for generation, transmission, distribution and supply; and Scottish Nuclear Ltd. Scottish Power and Scottish Hydro-Electric were floated on the stock market in 1991. Scottish Hydro-Electric merged with Southern Electric in 1998 to become Scottish and Southern Energy plc. Scottish Nuclear was incorporated into British Energy in 1996. BETTA opened the Scottish market to the same competition that had applied in England and Wales.

In Northern Ireland, Northern Ireland Electricity plc (NIE) was set up in 1993 under a 1991 Order in Council. In 1993 it was floated on the stock market and in 1998 it became part of the Viridian Group and was responsible for distribution and supply until NIE was sold to ESB Independent Energy in December 2010. In June 2010, Airtricity became the first new electricity supplier since the Northern Ireland electricity market was opened to competition in 2007.

On 12 July 2011, the government published Planning Our Electric Future: a White Paper for Secure, Affordable and Low-carbon Electricity in response to the challenges set by increasing electricity demands. It was agreed that extensive investment is needed to update the grid and build new power stations. Currently, 16 per cent of the UK electricity supply comes from nuclear reactors. While nuclear power stations will close gradually over the next decade, with only one expected to produce power beyond 2025, there are plans in place for a new generation of reactors to be built, potentially running by 2018.

On 30 September 2003 the Electricity Association, the industry's main trade association, was replaced with three separate trade bodies: the Association of Electricity Producers; the Energy Networks Association; and the Energy Retail Association. In April 2012, following a merger between the Association of Electricity Producers, the Energy Retail Association and the UK Business Council for Sustainable Energy, Energy UK – the new trade association for the gas and electricity sector – was established.

ENERGY NETWORKS ASSOCIATION, 6th floor, Dean Bradley House, 52 Horseferry Road, London SW1P 2AF
   T 020-7706 5100 W www.energynetworks.org
Chief Executive, David Smith
ENERGY UK, Charles House, 5–11 Regent Street, London SW1Y 4LR T 020-7930 9390 W www.energy-uk.org.uk
Chief Executive, Lawrence Slade

## ELECTRICITY PRODUCTION, SUPPLY AND CONSUMPTION
*GWh*

|  | 2013 | 2014 |
|---|---|---|
| *Electricity produced* | | |
| Nuclear | 70,607 | 63,748 |
| Hydro | 4,702 | 5,885 |
| Wind, wave and solar photovoltaics | 30,417 | 36,068 |
| Coal | 130,768 | 100,707 |
| Oil | 2,091 | 1,881 |
| Gas | 96,028 | 100,928 |
| Other renewables | 18,159 | 22,702 |
| Other | 3,493 | 4,125 |
| *Total* | 356,265 | 336,045 |
| | | |
| *Electricity supplied* | | |
| Production | 356,264 | 336,043 |
| *Other sources | 2,904 | 2,883 |
| Imports | 17,533 | 23,230 |
| Exports | (3,103) | (2,720) |
| *Total* | 373,598 | 359,436 |
| | | |
| *Electricity consumed* | | |
| Industry | 97,669 | 93,373 |
| Transport | 4,268 | 4,259 |
| Other | 215,040 | 205,777 |
| Domestic | 113,445 | 108,881 |
| Public administration | 18,820 | 18,203 |
| Commercial | 78,901 | 74,965 |
| Agriculture | 3,874 | 3,728 |
| *Total* | 316,977 | 303,409 |

\* Pumped storage production
*Source:* DECC

## GAS AND ELECTRICITY SUPPLIERS

With the gas and electricity markets open, most suppliers offer their customers both services. The majority of gas/electricity companies have become part of larger multi-utility companies, often operating internationally.

As part of measures to reduce the UK's carbon output, the government has outlined plans to introduce 'smart meters' to all UK homes. Smart meters perform the traditional meter function of measuring energy consumption, in addition to more advanced functions such as allowing energy suppliers to communicate directly with their customers and removing the need for meter readings and bill estimates. The meters also allow domestic customers to have direct access to energy consumption information.

The following list comprises a selection of suppliers offering gas and electricity. Organisations in italics are subsidiaries of the companies listed in capital letters directly above.

### ENGLAND, SCOTLAND AND WALES
CENTRICA PLC, Millstream, Maidenhead Road, Windsor, Berkshire SL4 5GD T 01753-494000 W www.centrica.com
*British Gas*, PO Box 4805, Worthing BN11 9QW T 0800-048 0202 W www.britishgas.co.uk
EDF ENERGY, Osprey House, Osprey Road, Exeter, EX2 7WN T 0800-056 7777 W www.edfenergy.com
E.ON, 6th Floor, 100 Pall Mall, London SW1Y 5NQ T 024-7618 3843 W www.eonenergy.com
NORTHERN POWERGRID, Houghton le Spring DH4 7LA T 0845-070 7172 W www.northernpowergrid.com
NPOWER, PO Box 93, Peterlee SR8 2XX T 0800-073 3000 W www.npower.com
SCOTTISHPOWER, PO Box 8729, Bellshill ML4 3YD T 0845-270 0700 W www.scottishpower.co.uk
SSE PLC, Inveralmond House, 200 Dunkeld Road, Perth PH1 3AQ T 0800-980 8831 W www.sse.com

*Scottish Hydro*, T 0800-980 8754 W www.hydro.co.uk
*Southern Electric*, T 0800-980 8476 W www.southern-electric.co.uk
SWALEC, T 0800-980 9041 W www.swalec.co.uk

### NORTHERN IRELAND
AIRTRICITY (a member of Scottish and Southern Energy), Red Oak South, South County Business Park, Leopardstown, Dublin 18 T 0345-864 3546 W www.sseairtricity.com
ELECTRIC IRELAND, Forsyth House, Cromac Square, Belfast BT2 8LA T 0845-600 5335 W www.electricireland.ie
VIRIDIAN GROUP PLC, Greenwood House, 64 Newforge Lane, Belfast BT9 5NF T 028-9066 8416 W www.viridiangroup.co.uk
*Energia*, 3rd Floor, Mill House, Ashtowngate, Navan Road, Dublin 15 T 1850-363744 W www.energia.ie

## REGULATION OF THE GAS AND ELECTRICITY INDUSTRIES

The Office of the Gas and Electricity Markets (OFGEM) regulates the gas and electricity industries in Great Britain. It was formed in 1999 by the merger of the Office of Gas Supply and the Office of Electricity Regulation. OFGEM's overriding aim is to protect and promote the interests of all gas and electricity customers by promoting competition and regulating monopolies. It is governed by an authority and its powers are provided for under the Gas Act 1986, the Electricity Act 1989, the Competition Act 1998, the Utilities Act 2000 and the Enterprise Act 2002. Energywatch was the independent gas and electricity watchdog, set up in November 2000 through the Utility Act to protect and promote the interests of gas and electricity consumers. In October 2008 Energywatch merged with Postwatch and the National Consumer Council to form a new advocacy body, Consumer Focus. In October 2010, the government announced that Consumer Focus would be abolished and some of its functions would transfer to Citizens Advice, Citizens Advice Scotland and the Consumer Council for Northern Ireland. This transfer began in April 2013 and full responsibility was transferred to Citizens Advice following the abolition of Consumer Focus on 1 April 2014.

CITIZENS ADVICE, 3rd Floor North, 200 Aldersgate Street, London EC1A 4HD T 0300-023 1231 W www.citizensadvice.org.uk
CITIZENS ADVICE SCOTLAND, 1st Floor, Spectrum House, 2 Powderhall Road, Edinburgh EH7 4GB T 0808-800 9060 W www.cas.org.uk
CONSUMER COUNCIL FOR NORTHERN IRELAND, 116 Holywood Road, Belfast BT4 1NY T 028-9067 2488 W www.consumercouncil.org.uk
THE OFFICE OF THE GAS AND ELECTRCITY MARKETS (OFGEM), 9 Millbank, London SW1 3GE T 020-7901 7000 W www.ofgem.gov.uk

## NUCLEAR POWER

Nuclear reactors began to supply electricity to the national grid in 1956. Nuclear power is currently generated in the UK at nine sites: one magnox reactor (Wylfa 1, possible generation extension to December 2015) following the closure of Oldbury nuclear power station in February 2012, seven advanced gas-cooled reactors (AGR) and one pressurised water reactor (PWR), Sizewell 'B' in Suffolk. The AGRs and PWR are owned by a private company, EDF Energy, while the magnox reactor is state-owned by the Nuclear Decommissioning Authority. The first of a series of new-generation plants is expected to come on-line around

2018; all but one of the current sites (Sizewell 'B') will be shut down by 2035.

In April 2005 the responsibility for the decommissioning of civil nuclear reactors and other nuclear facilities used in research and development was handed to the Nuclear Decommissioning Authority (NDA). The NDA is a non-departmental public body, funded mainly by the DECC. The total planned expenditure for the NDA in 2015–16 was £3.31bn. Until April 2007, UK Nirex was responsible for the disposal of intermediate and some low-level nuclear waste. After this date Nirex was integrated into the NDA and renamed the Radioactive Waste Management directorate.

There are currently 17 nuclear sites owned by the NDA that are in various stages of decommissioning, including the world's first commercial power station at Calder Hall on the Sellafield site in Cumbria. The decommissioning of these sites is scheduled for completion within the next 15 to 20 years. In the case of the Dounreay research facility in Scotland, controls on access to contaminated land are expected to remain in place until around 2300.

In 2014 electricity supplied from nuclear sources accounted for 18.9 per cent of the total electricity supply. The 2008 Energy bill paved the way for the construction of up to ten new nuclear power stations by 2020. Eight sites have been assessed as potentially suitable for the development of new power stations in England and Wales before the end of 2025. A number of factors have led to government backing for nuclear power: domestic gas supplies are running low; oil and gas prices are high; carbon emissions must be cut to comply with EU legislation and meet global climate change targets; and a number of coal-fired power stations that fail to meet clean air requirements are due to be closed.

Nuclear power has its advantages: reactors emit virtually no carbon dioxide and uranium prices remain relatively steady. However, the advantages of low emissions are countered by the high costs of construction and difficulties in disposing of nuclear waste. Currently, the only method is to store it securely until it has slowly decayed to safe levels. Public distrust persists despite the advances in safety technology.

SAFETY AND REGULATION

The Office for Nuclear Regulation (ONR), a public corporation of the Department for Work and Pensions, is the nuclear industry's regulator. Operations at the 37 UK nuclear power stations are governed by a site licence which is issued under the Nuclear Installations Act. The ONR monitors compliance and has the jurisdiction to close down a reactor if the terms of the licence are breached. The DECC is responsible for security at all the UK's nuclear power stations, which are policed by the Civil Nuclear Constabulary, a specialised armed force created in April 2005. In 2009 Magnox Electric Ltd was found guilty of breaking the Radioactive Substances Act 2003: it had left a radioactive leak on a holding tank at Bradwell power station, Essex, unchecked for 14 years.

RENEWABLE SOURCES

Renewable sources of energy principally include biofuels, hydro, wind and solar. Renewable sources produced 14.3 million tonnes of oil equivalent for primary energy usage in 2014; of this, 10.1 million tonnes was used to generate electricity, 2.9 million tonnes to generate heat and 1.2 million tonnes was used as transport fuels. In 2014, the UK generated 19.1 per cent of its total electricity production from renewable sources, compared with 14.9 per cent in 2013. Heat from renewable sources increased by 4.6 per cent during 2014 to 2.7 million tonnes of oil equivalent. Overall,

in 2014 renewable energy accounted for 7 per cent of final energy consumption as measured using the 2009 Renewable Energy Directive (RED) methodology, an increase from 5.6 per cent in 2013. Averaged over 2013 and 2014, the UK has now achieved 6.3 per cent renewable energy, in excess of the interim target which was set at 5.4 per cent.

The government's principal mechanisms for developing renewable energy sources are the Renewables Obligation (RO) and the Renewable Heat Incentive (RHI). The RO aims to increase the contribution of electricity from renewables in the UK. There are seperate RO schemes for England and Wales, Scotland and Northern Ireland. For both England and Wales and Scotland, the RO was set so that 15.4 per cent of licensed electricity sales should be from renewable sources eligible for the RO by 2015/16 – 6.3 per cent in Northern Ireland. In 2014, renewable sources accounted for 19.8 per cent of sales on an RO basis, an increase from 15.6 per cent in 2013.

A Renewables Obligation has been in place in England and Wales since April 2002 to give incentives to generators to supply progressively higher levels of renewable energy over time. These measures included exempting renewable energy sources from the climate change levy, capital grants, enhanced research funding and regional planning to meet renewables targets.

In addition to the RO, in April 2010, the government launched a Feed-in Tariff (FIT) scheme in Great Britain to encourage the uptake of small-scale low carbon electricity generation technologies, principally renewables such as solar photovoltaics, wind and hydro-electricity.

The RHI was originally introduced in November 2011 to provide a long-term financial incentive to support the uptake of renewable heat in the non-domestic sector. In April 2014, the RHI was extended to cover the domestic sector replacing the renewable heat premium payment scheme which closed in March 2013. Participants of the scheme receive tarifff payments for the heat generated from an eligible renewable heating system which is heating a single dwelling.

The government approved an EU-wide agreement in March 2007 to generate 20 per cent of energy production from renewable sources by 2020. It has since negotiated down the national share in this target to 15 per cent of energy production by 2020. In July 2009 the government published a Renewable Energy Strategy in order to meet this target. Other impediments to the expansion of renewable energy production include planning restrictions, rising raw material prices, and the possible redirection of funds to develop CCS technology and nuclear energy sources.

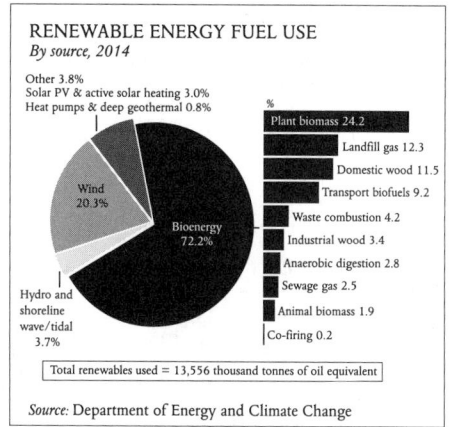

RENEWABLE ENERGY FUEL USE
By source, 2014

Other 3.8%
Solar PV & active solar heating 3.0%
Heat pumps & deep geothermal 0.8%

Wind 20.3%
Bioenergy 72.2%
Hydro and shoreline wave/tidal 3.7%

Plant biomass 24.2
Landfill gas 12.3
Domestic wood 11.5
Transport biofuels 9.2
Waste combustion 4.2
Industrial wood 3.4
Anaerobic digestion 2.8
Sewage gas 2.5
Animal biomass 1.9
Co-firing 0.2

Total renewables used = 13,556 thousand tonnes of oil equivalent

Source: Department of Energy and Climate Change

# TRANSPORT

## CIVIL AVIATION

Since the privatisation of British Airways in 1987, UK airlines have been operated entirely by the private sector. In 2014, total capacity of British airlines amounted to 50.5 billion tonne-km, of which 41 billion tonne-km was on scheduled services. UK airlines carried around 141 million passengers; 125 million on scheduled services and 16 million on charter flights. Passenger traffic through UK airports increased by 0.44 per cent in 2014. Traffic at the six main London area airports (Gatwick, Heathrow, London City, Luton, Southend and Stansted) increased by 5 per cent over 2014 and other UK regional airports saw an increase of 3 per cent.

Leading British airlines include British Airways, EasyJet, Monarch, Thomas Cook Airlines, Thomson Airways and Virgin Atlantic. Irish airline Ryanair also operates frequent flights from the UK.

There are around 140 licensed civil aerodromes in Britain, with Heathrow and Gatwick handling the highest volume of passengers.

The Civil Aviation Authority (CAA), an independent statutory body, is responsible for the regulation of UK airlines. This includes economic and airspace regulation, air safety, consumer protection and environmental research and consultancy. All commercial airline companies must be granted an air operator's certificate, which is issued by the CAA to operators meeting the required safety standards. The CAA issues airport safety licences, which must be obtained by any airport used for public transport and training flights. All British-registered aircraft must be granted an airworthiness certificate, and the CAA issues professional licences to pilots, flight crew, ground engineers and air traffic controllers. The CAA also manages the Air Travel Organiser's Licence (ATOL), the UK's principal travel protection scheme. The CAA's costs are met entirely from charges on those whom it regulates; there is no direct government funding of the CAA's work.

The Transport Act 2000 separated the CAA from its subsidiary, National Air Traffic Services (NATS), which provides air traffic control services to aircraft flying in UK airspace and over the eastern part of the North Atlantic. NATS is a public private partnership (PPP) between the Airline Group (a consortium of UK airlines), which holds 42 per cent of the shares; NATS staff, who hold 5 per cent; UK airport operator LHR Airports Limited, which holds 4 per cent, and the government, which holds 49 per cent and a golden share. In 2013–14 NATS handled a total of 2,153,995 flights, an increase of 0.4 per cent on 2012–13 figures.

### AIR PASSENGERS 2014

| | |
|---|---|
| *All UK Airports: Total* | 238,557,866 |
| Aberdeen | 3,723,662 |
| Barra | 10,521 |
| Belfast City | 2,555,145 |
| Belfast International | 4,033,954 |
| Benbecula | 31,213 |
| Birmingham | 9,705,955 |
| Blackpool | 223,998 |
| Bournemouth | 661,584 |
| Bristol | 6,339,805 |
| Cambridge | 20,663 |
| Campbeltown | 9,365 |

| | |
|---|---|
| Cardiff | 1,023,932 |
| City of Derry (Eglinton) | 350,257 |
| Doncaster Sheffield | 724,885 |
| Dundee | 22,069 |
| Durham Tees Valley | 142,379 |
| East Midlands | 4,510,544 |
| Edinburgh | 10,160,004 |
| Exeter | 767,404 |
| Gatwick | 38,103,667 |
| Glasgow | 7,715,988 |
| Gloucestershire | 15,172 |
| Heathrow | 73,405,330 |
| Humberside | 239,173 |
| Inverness | 612,725 |
| Islay | 27,659 |
| Isle of Man | 729,703 |
| Isles of Scilly (St Mary's) | 90,944 |
| Kent International | 12,508 |
| Kirkwall | 161,347 |
| Lands End (St Just) | 44,475 |
| Leeds Bradford | 2,274,474 |
| Lerwick (Tingwall) | 3,739 |
| Liverpool | 3,986,654 |
| London City | 3,647,824 |
| Luton | 10,484,938 |
| Lydd | 1,227 |
| Manchester | 21,989,682 |
| Newcastle | 4,516,739 |
| Newquay | 221,047 |
| Norwich | 458,968 |
| Oxford (Kidlington) | 1,194 |
| Prestwick | 913,685 |
| Scatsta | 279,799 |
| Shoreham | 452 |
| Southampton | 1,831,700 |
| Southend | 1,102,358 |
| Stansted | 19,965,093 |
| Stornoway | 129,481 |
| Sumburgh | 264,521 |
| Tiree | 9,322 |
| Wick | 28,145 |
| *Channel Islands Airports: Total* | 2,451,626 |
| Alderney | 61,317 |
| Guernsey | 894,602 |
| Jersey | 1,495,707 |

*Source:* Civil Aviation Authority

CAA, CAA House, 45–59 Kingsway, London WC2B 6TE
T 020-7379 7311 W www.caa.co.uk

| | |
|---|---|
| *Heathrow Airport* | T 0844-335 1801 |
| *Gatwick Airport* | T 0844-892 0322 |
| *Manchester Airport* | T 0871-271 0711 |
| *Stansted Airport* | T 0844-335 1803 |

### BRITISH AIRLINES
BRITISH AIRWAYS, PO Box 365, Waterside, Harmondsworth UB7 0GB T 0844-493 0787 W www.britishairways.com
EASYJET, Hangar 89, London Luton Airport LU2 9PF T 0330-365 5000 W www.easyjet.com
MONARCH, Prospect House, Prospect Way, London Luton Airport LU2 9NU T 0333-003 0100 W www.monarch.co.uk

THOMAS COOK AIRLINES, Thomas Cook Business Park, Coningsby Road, Peterborough PE3 8SB **T** 01733-224 800 **W** www.thomascook.com

THOMSON AIRWAYS, Wigmore House, Wigmore Place, Wigmore Lane, Luton, Beds LU2 9TN **T** 0203-451 2688 **W** www.thomson.co.uk

VIRGIN ATLANTIC, The Office, Manor Royal, Crawley, W. Sussex RH10 9NU **T** 0344-811 0000 **W** www.virgin-atlantic.com

# RAILWAYS

The railway network in Britain was developed by private companies in the 19th century. In 1948 the main railway companies were nationalised and were run by a public authority, the British Transport Commission. The commission was replaced by the British Railways Board in 1963, operating as British Rail. On 1 April 1994, responsibility for managing the track and railway infrastructure passed to a newly formed company, Railtrack plc. In October 2001 Railtrack was put into administration under the Railways Act 1993. In October 2002 Railtrack was taken out of administration and replaced by the not-for-profit company Network Rail. The British Railways Board continued as operator of all train services until 1996–7, when they were sold or franchised to the private sector.

The Strategic Rail Authority (SRA) was created to provide strategic leadership to the rail industry and formally came into being on 1 February 2001 following the passing of the Transport Act 2000. In January 2002 it published its first strategic plan, setting out the strategic priorities for Britain's railways over the next ten years. In addition to its coordinating role, the SRA was responsible for allocating government funding to the railways and awarding and monitoring the franchises for operating rail services.

On 15 July 2004 the transport secretary announced a new structure for the rail industry in the white paper *The Future of Rail*. These proposals were implemented under the Railways Act 2005, which abolished the SRA, passing most of its functions to the Department for Transport; established the Rail Passengers Council as a single national body, dissolving the regional committees; and gave devolved governments in Scotland and Wales more say in decisions at a local level. In addition, responsibility for railway safety regulation was transferred to the Office of Rail Regulation from the Health and Safety Executive.

## OFFICE OF RAIL AND ROAD

The Office of Rail and Road (ORR), previously known as the Office of Rail Regulation, was established on 5 July 2004 by the Railways and Transport Safety Act 2003, replacing the Office of the Rail Regulator. In April 2015 it acquired responsibility for monitoring Highways England in addition to its existing role as the railway industry's economic and safety regulator and changed its name to better reflect its functions. The ORR regulates Network Rail's stewardship of the national network, licenses operators, approves network access agreements, and enforces domestic competition law. The ORR is led by a board appointed by the Secretary of State for Transport and chaired by Anna Walker.

## SERVICES

For privatisation, under the Railways Act 1993, domestic passenger services were divided into 25 train operating units, which were franchised to private sector operators via a competitive tendering process. The train operators formed the Association of Train Operating Companies (ATOC) to act as the official voice of the passenger rail industry and provide its members with a range of services enabling them to comply with conditions imposed on them through their franchise agreements and operating licences.

As at July 2015 there were 25 passenger train operating companies: Abellio Greater Anglia, Arriva Trains Wales, c2c, Caledonian Sleeper, Chiltern Railways, CrossCountry, East Midlands Trains, Eurostar, First Great Western, First Hull Trains, First TransPennine Express, Grand Central, Great Northern, Heathrow Express, London Midland, London Overground, Merseyrail, Northern, ScotRail, South West Trains, Southeastern, Southern, Thameslink, Virgin Trains and Virgin Trains East Coast.

Network Rail publishes a national timetable which contains details of rail services operated over the UK network and sea ferry services which provide connections with Ireland, the Isle of Man, the Isle of Wight, the Channel Islands and some European destinations.

The national rail enquiries service offers information about train times and fares for any part of the country, Transport for London (TfL) provides London-specific travel information for all modes of travel and Eurostar provides information for international channel tunnel rail services:

### NATIONAL RAIL ENQUIRIES
**T** 0345-748 4950 **W** www.nationalrail.co.uk
### TRANSPORT FOR LONDON
**T** 0343-222 1234 **W** www.tfl.gov.uk
### EUROSTAR
**T** 03432-186186 **W** www.eurostar.com

### TRANSPORT FOCUS AND LONDON TRAVELWATCH

Previously known as Passenger Focus, Transport Focus is the national consumer watchdog for bus, tram, coach and rail passengers in England. Under The Infrastructure Act 2015 Transport Focus's role was expanded to also represent users of the strategic road network. The entity is funded by the Department for Transport and is an executive non-departmental public body.

Established in July 2000, London TravelWatch is the operating name of the official watchdog organisation representing the interests of transport users in and around the capital. Officially known as the London Transport Users' Committee, it is sponsored and funded by the London Assembly and is independent of the transport operators. London TravelWatch represents users of buses, the Underground, river and rail services in and around London, including Eurostar and Heathrow Express, Croydon Tramlink and the Docklands Light Railway. The interests of pedestrians, cyclists and motorists are also represented, as are those of taxi users.

### FREIGHT

On privatisation in 1996, British Rail's bulk freight operations were sold to North and South Railways – subsequently called English, Welsh and Scottish Railways (EWS). In 2007, EWS was bought by Deutsche Bahn and in January 2009 was re-named DB Schenker. The other major companies in the rail freight sector are: Colas Rail, Direct Rail Services, Freightliner and GB Railfreight (GBRf). In 2014–15 freight moved by rail amounted to 22.2 billion tonne-kilometres, a 2.2 per cent decrease from 2013–14.

### NETWORK RAIL

Network Rail is responsible for the tracks, bridges, tunnels, level crossings, viaducts and 18 main stations that form Britain's rail network. In addition to providing the timetables for the passenger and freight operators, Network Rail is also responsible for all the signalling and electrical control equipment needed to operate the rail network and for monitoring and reporting performance across the industry.

In September 2014, Network Rail was reclassified as a public body after being privately run since 2002 as a commercial business which was directly accountable to its members. The members had similar rights to those of shareholders in a public company except they did not receive dividends or share capital and thereby had no financial interest in Network Rail. On 1 July 2015 the 46 public members were dismissed and the company is now accountable directly to parliament through the Secretary of State for Transport. Network Rail is regulated by the ORR and all of its profits are reinvested into maintaining and upgrading the rail infrastructure. In 2014–15 a total of 1,656 million passenger journeys were made on the rail network.

### ASSOCIATION OF TRAIN OPERATING COMPANIES,
ATOC Ltd, 2nd Floor, 200 Aldersgate Street, London EC1A 4HD
T 020-7841 8000 W www.atoc.org
LONDON TRAVELWATCH, 169 Union Street, London
SE1 0LL T 020-3176 2999 W www.londontravelwatch.org.uk
NETWORK RAIL, 1 Eversholt Street, London NW1 2DN
T 020-7557 8000 W www.networkrail.co.uk
OFFICE OF RAIL REGULATION, 1 Kemble Street,
London WC2B 4AN T 020-7282 2018 W www.orr.gov.uk
TRANSPORT FOCUS, 2-6 Salisbury Square, London EC4Y 8JX
T 0300-123 0860 W www.transportfocus.org.uk

### RAIL SAFETY
On 1 April 2006 responsibility for health and safety policy and enforcement on the railways transferred from the Health and Safety Executive to the Office of Rail Regulation (ORR). In 2014–15 a total of 39 passengers, railway staff and other members of the public were fatally injured in all rail incidents (excluding suicides), compared with 37 in 2013–14.

### ACCIDENTS ON RAILWAYS

|                              | 2013–14 | 2014–15 |
|------------------------------|---------|---------|
| *Rail incident fatalities*   | 37      | 39      |
| Passengers                   | 4       | 3       |
| Railway employees            | 3       | 3       |
| Public                       | 30      | 33      |
| *Rail incident major injuries* | 498   | 521     |
| Passengers                   | 276     | 296     |
| Railway employees            | 177     | 175     |
| Public                       | 45      | 50      |

### SUICIDES AND ATTEMPTED SUICIDES 2014–15
Fatalities             293
Major Injuries         38
*Source: RSSB – Annual Safety Performance Report 2014–15*

### OTHER RAIL SYSTEMS
Responsibility for the London Underground passed from the government to the Mayor and Transport for London on 15 July 2003, with a public-private partnership already in place. Plans for a public-private partnership for London Underground were pushed through by the government in February 2002 despite opposition from the Mayor of London and a range of transport organisations. Under the PPP, long-term contracts with private companies were estimated to enable around £16bn to be invested in renewing and upgrading the London Underground's infrastructure over 15 years. In July 2007, Metronet, which was responsible for two of three PPP contracts, went into administration; TfL took over both contracts. Responsibility for stations, trains, operations, signalling and safety remains in the public sector. In 2014–15 there were more than 1,300 million passenger journeys on the London Underground.

In addition to Glasgow Subway, which is classified as an underground system (13 million passenger journeys in

2014–15), Britain has eight other light rail and tram systems: Blackpool Tramway, Docklands Light Railway (DLR), London Tramlink, Manchester Metrolink, Midland Metro, Nottingham Express Transit (NET), Sheffield Supertram and Tyne and Wear Metro.

In 2014–15 there were 240 million passenger light rail and tram journeys in Great Britain; an increase of 5.6 per cent on 2013–14 figures.

### THE CHANNEL TUNNEL
The earliest recorded scheme for a submarine transport connection between Britain and France was in 1802. Tunnelling began simultaneously on both sides of the Channel three times: in 1881, in the early 1970s, and on 1 December 1987, when construction workers bored the first of the three tunnels which form the Channel Tunnel. Engineers 'holed through' the first tunnel (the service tunnel) on 1 December 1990 and tunnelling was completed in June 1991. The tunnel was officially inaugurated by the Queen and President Mitterrand of France on 6 May 1994.

The submarine link comprises two rail tunnels, each carrying trains in one direction, which measure 7.6m (24.93ft) in diameter. Between them lies a smaller service tunnel, measuring 4.8m (15.75ft) in diameter. The service tunnel is linked to the rail tunnels by 130 cross-passages for maintenance and safety purposes. The tunnels are 50km (31 miles) long, 38km (24 miles) of which is under the seabed at an average depth of 40m (132ft). The rail terminals are situated at Folkestone and Calais, and the tunnels go underground at Shakespeare Cliff, Dover and Sangatte, west of Calais.

### RAIL LINKS
The British Channel Tunnel Rail Link route runs from Folkestone to St Pancras station, London, with intermediate stations at Ashford and Ebbsfleet in Kent and more recently, Stratford International.

Construction of the rail link was financed by the private sector with a substantial government contribution. A private sector consortium, London and Continental Railways Ltd (LCR), comprising Union Railways and the UK operator of Eurostar, owns the rail link and was responsible for its design and construction. The rail link was constructed in two phases: phase one, from the Channel Tunnel to Fawkham Junction, Kent, began in October 1998 and opened to fare-paying passengers on 28 September 2003; phase two, from Southfleet Junction to St Pancras, was completed in November 2007.

There are direct services from the UK to Calais, Disneyland Paris, Lille and Paris in France and Brussels in Belgium. There are also direct services to Avignon in the south of France between July and September and during the winter months (December to April) to the French Alps. High-speed trains also run from Lille to the south of France.

Eurostar, the high-speed passenger train service, connects London with Paris in 2 hours 15 minutes, Brussels in 1 hour 51 minutes and Lille in 1 hour 20 minutes. There are Eurostar terminals at London St Pancras, Ashford and Ebbsfleet in Kent, Paris Gare Du Nord and Lille in France, and Brussels-South in Belgium.

# ROADS

### HIGHWAY AUTHORITIES
The powers and responsibilities of highway authorities in England and Wales are set out in the Highways Act 1980; for Scotland there is separate legislation.

Responsibility for motorways and other trunk roads in Great Britain rests in England with the Secretary of State for

Transport, in Scotland with the Scottish government, and in Wales with the Welsh government. The highway authority for non-trunk roads in England, Wales and Scotland is, in general, the local authority in whose area the roads lie. With the establishment of the Greater London Authority in July 2000, Transport for London became the highway authority for roads in London.

In Northern Ireland the Department for Regional Development is the statutory road authority responsible for public roads and their maintenance and construction; the Transport NI executive agency (formerly known as the Roads Service) carries out these functions on behalf of the department.

## FINANCE

In England all aspects of trunk road and motorway funding are provided directly by the government to Highways England, which operates, maintains and improves a network of motorways and trunk roads around 6,920km (4,300 miles) long, on behalf of the secretary of state. Since 2001 the length of the network that the Highways England is responsible for has been decreasing owing to a policy of de-trunking, which transfers responsibility for non-core roads to local authorities. For the financial year 2015–16 Highways England's total budget, excluding depreciation, is £2,854m: £979m for maintenance, £1,036m for major schemes and the remainder for traffic management, technology improvements, other programmes and administration costs.

Government support for local authority capital expenditure on roads and other transport infrastructure is provided through grant and credit approvals as part of the Local Transport Plan (LTP). Local authorities bid for resources on the basis of a five-year programme built around delivering integrated transport strategies. As well as covering the structural maintenance of local roads and the construction of major new road schemes, LTP funding also includes smaller-scale safety and traffic management measures with associated improvements for public transport, cyclists and pedestrians.

Total expenditure by the Welsh government in 2014–15 to improve and maintain the motorway and trunk road network in Wales was £271.7m. Total budgeted expenditure for the motorway and trunk road network in 2015–16 is £275.3m.

Since 1 July 1999 all decisions on Scottish transport expenditure have been devolved to the Scottish government. Total expenditure on motorways and trunk roads in Scotland during 2014–15 was £717.5m.

In Northern Ireland total expenditure by the Roads Service on all roads in 2014–15 was £178.4m, with £88m spent on trunk roads and motorways. Planned expenditure for 2015–16 is £97.1m, of which £69.9m is allocated for trunk roads and motorways.

The Transport Act 2000 gave English and Welsh local authorities (outside London) powers to introduce road-user charging or workplace parking levy schemes. The act requires that the net revenue raised is used to improve local transport services and facilities for at least ten years. The aim is to reduce congestion and encourage greater use of alternative modes of transport. Schemes developed by local authorities require government approval. The UK's first toll road, the M6 Toll, opened in December 2003 and runs for 43.5km (27 miles) around Birmingham from junction 3a to junction 11a on the M6.

Charging schemes in London are allowed under the 1999 Greater London Authority Act. The Central London Congestion Charge Scheme began on 17 February 2003 (see also Regional Government).

## ROAD LENGTHS 2014
*Miles*

|  | England | Wales | Scotland | Great Britain |
|---|---|---|---|---|
| Major Roads | 20,085 | 2,600 | 6,384 | 29,071 |
| Motorways | 1,893 | 88 | 284 | 2,265 |
| Minor Roads | 165,858 | 18,387 | 30,246 | 214,491 |
| *Total* | 187,838 | 21,075 | 36,914 | 245,827 |

*Source*: Department for Transport

## BUSES

The majority of bus services outside London are provided on a commercial basis by private operators. Local authorities have powers to subsidise services where needs are not being met by a commercial service.

Since April 2008 men and women who have attained the state pension age and disabled people who qualify under the categories listed in the Transport Act 2000 have been able to travel for free on any local bus across England between 9.30am and 11pm Monday to Friday and all day on weekends and bank holidays. Local authorities recompense operators for the reduced fare revenue. The age of eligibility for concessionary travel currently stands at 60 but will increase in line with the state pension age, which is expected to reach 65 by 2018. A similar scheme operates in Wales and within London, although there is no time restriction. In Scotland, people aged 60 and over and disabled people have been able to travel for free on any local or long-distance bus since April 2006.

In London, Transport for London (TfL) has overall responsibility for setting routes, service standards and fares for the bus network. Almost all routes are competitively tendered to commercial operators.

In Northern Ireland, passenger transport services are provided by Ulsterbus and Metro (formerly Citybus), two wholly owned subsidiaries of the Northern Ireland Transport Holding Company. Along with Northern Ireland Railways, Ulsterbus and Metro operate under the brand name of Translink and are publicly owned. Ulsterbus is responsible for virtually all bus services in Northern Ireland except Belfast city services, which are operated by Metro. People living in Northern Ireland aged 65 and over can travel on buses and trains for free once they have obtained a Senior Citizen SmartPass from Translink.

## LOCAL BUS PASSENGER JOURNEYS 2014–15

|  | No. of journeys (millions) |
|---|---|
| England | 4,700 |
| London | 2,390 |
| Scotland | 420 |
| Wales | 100 |
| *Total* | 5,220 |

*Source*: Department for Transport

## TAXIS AND PRIVATE HIRE VEHICLES

A taxi is a public transport vehicle with fewer than nine passenger seats, which is licensed to 'ply for hire'. This distinguishes taxis from private hire vehicles (PHVs) which must be booked in advance through an operator. In London, taxis and private hire vehicles are licensed by the Public Carriage Office (PCO), part of TfL. There are currently around 22,500 taxis and 62,800 PHVs licensed in London. Outside London, local authorities are responsible for the licensing of taxis and private hire vehicles operational in their respective administrative areas. At the end of March 2015 there were 76,100 licensed taxis and 166,100 PHVs in England. In 2014 there were 34,519 taxis and PHVs licensed in Scotland.

## ROAD TRAFFIC BY VEHICLE TYPE (GREAT BRITAIN) 2014

| | Million vehicle miles |
|---|---|
| All motor vehicles | 311,100 |
| Cars | 244,500 |
| Light goods vehicles | 45,000 |
| Heavy goods vehicles | 16,000 |
| Buses and coaches | 2,800 |
| Motorcycles | 2,800 |
| Pedal cycles | 3,200 |

Source: Department for Transport

## ROAD SAFETY

In May 2011, the government published *The Strategic Framework for Road Safety* which identified key indicators at national and local level intended to monitor the progress towards improving safety and decreasing the number of fatalities and seriously injured casualties on Great Britain's roads.

The key findings from the Department for Transport's 2014 annual road casualty report found that the number of people killed in road accidents reported to the police had increased, by 4 per cent, from 1,713 in 2013 to 1,775 in 2014; it is the third lowest figure after 2012 and 2013. The total number of reported casualties in Great Britain (slight injuries, serious injuries and fatalities) also increased by 6 per cent, from 183,670 in 2013 to 194,477 in 2014. Total reported child casualties (0–15 years) increased by 6 per cent in 2014 to 16,727, with the number of children killed or seriously injured also increasing by 5 per cent to 2,082 in 2014.

## ROAD ACCIDENT CASUALTIES 2014

| | Killed | Serious | Slight | Total |
|---|---|---|---|---|
| Average for 2005–9 | 2,816 | 27,225 | 216,010 | 246,050 |
| England | 1,472 | 19,953 | 153,604 | 175,029 |
| Wales | 103 | 1,160 | 6,945 | 8,208 |
| Scotland | 200 | 1,694 | 9,346 | 11,290 |
| Great Britain | 1,775 | 22,807 | 169,895 | 194,477 |

Source: Department for Transport

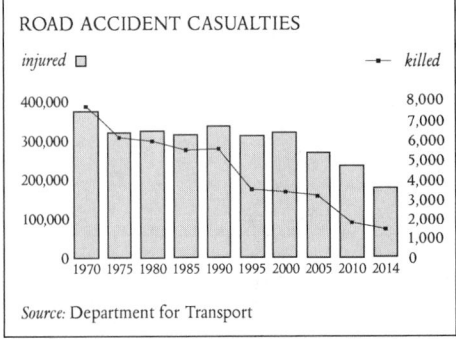

ROAD ACCIDENT CASUALTIES

injured □          —•— killed

Source: Department for Transport

## DRIVING LICENCES

It is necessary to hold a valid full licence in order to drive unaccompanied on public roads in the UK. Learner drivers must obtain a provisional driving licence before starting to learn to drive and must then pass theory and practical tests to obtain a full driving licence.

There are separate tests for driving motorcycles, cars, passenger-carrying vehicles (PCVs) and large goods vehicles

(LGVs). Drivers must hold full car entitlement before they can apply for PCV or LGV entitlements.

The Driver and Vehicle Licensing Agency (DVLA) ceased the issue of paper licences in March 2000, but those currently in circulation will remain valid until they expire or the details on them change. The photocard driving licence was introduced to comply with the second EC directive on driving licences. This requires a photograph of the driver to be included on all UK licences issued from July 2001. The photocard licence must be renewed every ten years, with fines of up to £1,000 for failure to do so.

To apply for a first photocard driving licence, individuals are required to either apply online or complete the form *Application for a Driving Licence* (D1) and submit by post.

The minimum age for driving motor cars, light goods vehicles up to 3.5 tonnes and motorcycles is 17 (moped, 16). Since June 1997, drivers who collect six or more penalty points within two years of qualifying lose their licence and are required to take another test. Forms and leaflets are available from post offices and online (W www.gov.uk/dvlaforms or W www.gov.uk/government/organisations/driver-and-vehicle-licensing-agency).

The DVLA is responsible for issuing driving licences, registering and licensing vehicles, and collecting excise duty in Great Britain. The Driver and Vehicle Agency (DVA), has similar responsibilities in Northern Ireland.

## DRIVING LICENCE FEES
*As at August 2015*

| | online fee / postal fee* |
|---|---|
| Provisional licence | |
| Car, motorcycle or moped | £34/£43 |
| Bus or lorry | Free |
| After disqualification until passing re-test | Free |
| Changing a provisional licence to a full licence | Free |
| Renewal | |
| Renewing an expired licence (must be renewed every 10 years) | £14/£17 |
| At age 70 and over | Free |
| For medical reasons | Free |
| Bus or lorry driver entitlement | Free |
| After disqualification | £65 |
| After disqualification for some drink driving offences† | £90 |
| After revocation (under the New Drivers Act) | £50 |
| Replacing a lost, stolen, defaced or destroyed licence | £20/£20 |
| Adding an entitlement to a full licence | Free |
| Removing expired endorsements | £20 |
| Exchanging | |
| a paper licence for a photocard licence‡ | £20/£20 |
| a full Northern Ireland licence for a full GB licence | Free |
| a full GB licence for a full EU/EEA or other foreign licence (including Channel Islands and Isle of Man) | Free |
| a full EU/EEA or other foreign licence (including Channel Islands and Isle of Man) for a full GB licence | £43 |
| Changing | |
| name or address (existing licence must be surrendered)† | Free |
| photo | £14/£17 |

* Not all services are available online; in these instances just the postal fee is shown. Licence fees differ in Northern Ireland (W www.nidirect.gov.uk/the-cost-of-a-driving-licence).

† For an alcohol-related offence where the DVLA need to arrange medical enquiries

‡ If a paper licence is exchanged for a photocard at the same time as name or address details are changed there is no charge

## DRIVING TESTS

The Driver and Vehicle Standards Agency (DVSA) is responsible for improving road safety in Great Britain by setting standards for driving and motorcycling and making sure drivers, vehicle operators and MOT garages understand and follow roadworthiness standards. The agency also provides a range of licensing, testing, education and enforcement services.

## DRIVING TESTS TAKEN AND PASSED
*April 2014–March 2015*

| | Number Taken | Percentage Passed |
|---|---|---|
| *Practical Test* | | |
| Car | 1,532,504 | 46.9 |
| Motorcycle Module 1 | 52,005 | 69.7 |
| Motorcycle Module 2 | 49,194 | 70.2 |
| LGV/PCV | 63,392 | 55.5 |
| Driver CPC* | 20,709 | 87.6 |
| *Theory Test* | | |
| Car | 1,680,268 | 51.0 |
| Motorcycle | 62,807 | 74.1 |
| LGV/PCV | | |
| Multiple choice | 49,908 | 66.4 |
| Hazard perception | 44,309 | 79.1 |
| Driver CPC* | 33,393 | 61.6 |

LGV = Large goods vehicle; PCV = Passenger-carrying vehicle
* Driver Certificate of Professional Competence – legal requirement for all professional bus, coach and lorry drivers
*Source:* DVSA

The theory and practical driving tests can be booked online (W www.gov.uk/book-practical-driving-test) or by phone (T 0300-200 1122).

## DRIVING TEST FEES (WEEKDAY/EVENING* AND WEEKEND)
*As at July 2015*

| Theory tests | |
|---|---|
| Car and motorcycle | £25.00 |
| Bus and lorry | |
| Multiple choice | £28.00 |
| Hazard perception | £12.00 |
| Driver CPC | £24.00 |
| Practical tests | |
| Car | £62.00/£75.00 |
| Tractor and other specialist vehicles | £62.00/£75.00 |
| Motorcycle | |
| Module 1 (off-road) | £15.50/£15.50 |
| Module 2 (on-road) | £75.00/£88.50 |
| Lorry and bus | £115.00/£141.00 |
| Driver CPC | £55.00/£63.00 |
| Car and trailer | £115.00/£141.00 |
| Extended tests for disqualified drivers | |
| Car | £124.00/£150.00 |
| Motorcycle Module 1 (on-road) | £150.00/£177.00 |

* After 4.30pm

## VEHICLE LICENCES

Registration and first licensing of vehicles is through local offices of the DVLA in Swansea. Local facilities for relicensing are available at any post office which deals with vehicle licensing. Applicants will need to take their vehicle registration document (V5C) or, if this is not available, the applicant must complete form V62. Forms are available at post offices and online (W www.gov.uk/dvlaforms)

## MOTOR VEHICLES LICENSED (GREAT BRITAIN)
*As at 31 March 2015*

| | Thousands |
|---|---|
| All cars | 29,766 |
| Light goods vehicles | 3,508 |
| Motorcycles | 1,205 |
| Heavy goods vehicles | 473 |
| Buses and coaches | 163 |
| Other vehicles* | 696 |
| Total | 35,811 |

* Includes rear diggers, lift trucks, rollers, ambulances, Hackney Carriages, three-wheelers and agricultural vehicles
*Source:* Department for Transport

## VEHICLE EXCISE DUTY

Details of the present duties chargeable on motor vehicles are available at post offices and online (W www.gov.uk/government/publications/rates-of-vehicle-tax-v149). The Vehicle Excise and Registration Act 1994 provides *inter alia* that any vehicle kept on a public road but not used on roads is chargeable to excise duty as if it were in use. All non-commercial vehicles constructed before 1 January 1973 are exempt from vehicle excise duty. Any vehicle licensed on or after 31 January 1998, not in use and not kept on public roads must be registered as SORN (Statutory Off Road Notification) to be exempted from vehicle excise duty. From 1 January 2004 the registered keeper of a vehicle remains responsible for taxing a vehicle or making a SORN declaration until that liability is formally transferred to a new keeper.

## RATES OF DUTY *from 1 April 2015*

| | 6 months | 12 months |
|---|---|---|
| *Cars registered before 1 March 2001* | | |
| Under 1,549cc | £79.75 | £145.00 |
| Over 1,549cc | £126.50 | £230.00 |
| *Light goods vehicles registered on or after 1 March 2001* | | |
| | £123.75 | £225.00 |
| *Euro 4 light goods vehicles registered between 1 March 2003 and 31 December 2006* | £77.00 | £140.00 |
| *Euro 5 light goods vehicles registered between 1 January 2009 and 31 December 2010* | £77.00 | £140.00 |
| *Motorcycles (with or without sidecar)* | | |
| Not over 150cc | – | £17.00 |
| 151–400cc | – | £38.00 |
| 401–600cc | £32.45 | £59.00 |
| 600cc+ | £44.55 | £81.00 |
| *Tricycles* | | |
| Not over 150cc | – | £17.00 |
| All others | £44.55 | £81.00 |

## MOT TESTING

Cars, motorcycles, motor caravans, light goods and dual-purpose vehicles more than three years old must be covered by a current MOT test certificate. However, some vehicles (ie minibuses, ambulances and taxis) may require a certificate at one year old. All certificates must be renewed annually. Only MOT testing stations showing a blue sign with three triangles and an official 'MOT: Test: Fees and Appeals' poster may carry out an approved MOT. The MOT testing scheme is administered by the Driver and Vehicle Standards Agency (DVSA) on behalf of the Secretary of State for Transport.

RATES OF DUTY *from 1 April 2015*
All rates of duty can also be paid by direct debit – the 6-month direct debit rate is slightly cheaper than the non-direct debit rate listed below. There is also the option to pay vehicle duty by direct debit monthly installments.

*Cars registered on or after 1 March 2001 and first-year\* rates*

| Band | $CO_2$ | Petrol and Diesel Car | | | Alternative Fuel Car | | |
|------|--------|----------|-----------|---|----------|-----------|---|
| | Emissions (g/km) | 6 months | 12 months | | 6 months | 12 months | |
| A | Up to 100 | – | £0.00 | | – | £0.00 | |
| B | 101–110 | – | £20.00 | | – | £10.00 | |
| C | 111–120 | – | £30.00 | | – | £20.00 | |
| D | 121–130 | £60.50 | £110.00 | | £55.00 | £100.00 | |
| E | 131–140 | £71.50 | £130.00 | | £66.00 | £120.00 | |
| F | 141–150 | £79.75 | £145.00 | | £74.25 | £135.00 | |
| G | 151–165 | £99.00 | £180.00 | | £93.50 | £170.00 | |
| H | 166–175 | £112.75 | £205.00 | (£295.00) | £107.25 | £195.00 | (£285.00) |
| I | 176–185 | £123.75 | £225.00 | (£350.00) | £118.25 | £215.00 | (£340.00) |
| J | 186–200 | £145.75 | £265.00 | (£490.00) | £140.25 | £255.00 | (£480.00) |
| K† | 201–225 | £159.50 | £290.00 | (£640.00) | £154.00 | £280.00 | (£630.00) |
| L | 226–255 | £269.50 | £490.00 | (£870.00) | £264.00 | £480.00 | (£860.00) |
| M | 255+ | £277.75 | £505.00 | (£1,100.00) | £272.25 | £495.00 | (£1,090.00) |

\* First-year rates (figures in parentheses) are payable for some vehicles' first tax disc taken out at first registration
† Includes cars that have a $CO_2$ emission figure over 225g/km but were registered before 23 March 2006

A fee is payable to MOT testing stations. The current maximum fees are:

| | |
|---|---|
| For cars, private hire and public service vehicles, motor caravans, dual purpose vehicles, ambulances and taxis (all up to eight passenger seats) | £54.85 |
| For motorcycles | £29.65 |
| For motorcycles with sidecar | £37.80 |
| For three-wheeled vehicles (up to 450kg unladen weight) | £37.80 |
| \*Private passenger vehicles and ambulances with: | |
| 9–12 passenger seats | £57.30 (£64.00) |
| 13–16 passenger seats | £59.55 (£80.50) |
| 16+ passenger seats | £80.65 (£124.50) |
| Goods vehicles (3,000–3,500kg) | £58.60 |

\* Figures in parentheses include seatbelt installation check

## SHIPPING AND PORTS

Sea trade has always played a central role in Britain's economy. By the 17th century Britain had built up a substantial merchant fleet and by the early 20th century it dominated the world shipping industry. Between 1997 and 2009, the size and tonnage of the UK-registered trading fleet saw substantial growth however between 2009 and 2014 this had begun to slow and decrease. By the end of 2014 the number of ships in the UK-flagged merchant fleet had increased by 20 per cent while gross tonnage had more than quadrupled since 1999. The UK-flagged merchant fleet now constitutes 0.8 per cent of the world merchant fleet in terms of vessels and 1.1 per cent in terms of gross tonnage.

Freight is carried by liner and bulk services, almost all scheduled liner services being containerised. About 95 per cent by weight of Britain's overseas trade is carried by sea; this amounts to 75 per cent of its total value. Passengers and vehicles are carried by roll-on, roll-off ferries, hovercraft, hydrofoils and high-speed catamarans. There were around 43 million ferry passengers in 2013, of whom 22 million travelled internationally.

Lloyd's of London provides the most comprehensive shipping intelligence service in the world. *Lloyd's Shipping Index,* published daily, lists some 25,000 ocean-going vessels and gives the latest known report of each.

### PORTS
There are more than 650 ports in Great Britain for which statutory harbour powers have been granted. Over 100 of these are active in cargo trade. The largest ports in terms of freight tonnage in 2014 were Grimsby and Immingham (59 million tonnes), London (44 million tonnes), Tees and Hartlepool (40 million tonnes), Southampton (37 million tonnes), Milford Haven (34 million tonnes), Liverpool (31 million tonnes), Felixstowe (28 million tonnes), Dover (28 million tonnes) and Forth (25 million tonnes). Belfast (17 million tonnes) is the principal freight port in Northern Ireland.

Broadly speaking, ports are owned and operated by private companies, local authorities or self-owning bodies, known as trust ports. The largest operator is Associated British Ports which owns 21 ports. Port traffic results show that 503 million tonnes were handled by UK ports in 2014, remaining stable compared to the previous year's.

### MARINE SAFETY
The Maritime and Coastguard Agency (MCA) is an executive agency of the Department for Transport responsible for implementing the government's maritime safety policy in the UK and works to prevent the loss of life on the coast and at sea.

HM Coastguard maintains a 24-hour search and rescue response and coordination capability for the whole of the UK coast and the internationally agreed search and rescue region. HM Coastguard is responsible for mobilising and organising resources in response to people in distress at sea, or at risk of injury or death on the UK's cliffs or shoreline.

The MCA also inspects and surveys ships to ensure that they are meeting UK and international safety rules, provides certification to seafarers, registers vessels and responds to pollution from shipping and offshore installations.

Locations hazardous to shipping in coastal waters are marked by lighthouses and other lights and buoys. The lighthouse authorities are the Corporation of Trinity House (for England, Wales and the Channel Islands), the Northern Lighthouse Board (for Scotland and the Isle of Man), and the Commissioners of Irish Lights (for Northern Ireland and the Republic of Ireland). Trinity House maintains 66 lighthouses, eight light vessels/floats, 450 buoys, 21 beacons, 52 radar beacons, eight DGPS (differential global positioning system) stations* and three AIS (automatic identification system) stations. The Northern Lighthouse Board maintains 206 lighthouses, 165 buoys, 26 beacons, 29 radar beacons, 35 AIS stations, four DGPS stations and one LORAN (long-range navigation) station; and Irish Lights looks after 71 lighthouses, 117 buoys, 24 beacons, and three DGPS stations, with AIS in operation on 37 lighthouses.

Harbour authorities are responsible for pilotage within their harbour areas; and the Ports Act 1991 provides for the transfer of lights and buoys to harbour authorities where these are used mainly for local navigation.

\* DGPS is a satellite-based navigation system

## UK-OWNED TRADING VESSELS
*500 gross tons and over, as at end 2014*

| Type of vessel | No. | Gross tonnage |
|---|---|---|
| Tankers | 98 | 3,684,000 |
| Fully cellular container | 100 | 5,009,000 |
| Dry bulk carriers | 74 | 2,955,000 |
| Ro-Ro (passenger and cargo) | 85 | 1,293,000 |
| Passenger | 30 | 1,642,000 |
| Other general cargo | 95 | 446,000 |
| Specialised carriers | 26 | 1,249,000 |
| *All vessels* | 508 | 16,278,000 |

*Source:* Department for Transport

## UK SEA PASSENGER* MOVEMENTS 2013

| Type of journey | No. of passenger movements |
|---|---|
| International | |
| Ro-Ro Passengers on short sea routes | 20,490,000 |
| Passengers on cruises beginning or ending at UK ports* | 1,906,000 |
| Passengers on long sea journeys | 34,000 |
| *Total* | 22,430,000 |

\* Passengers are included at both departure and arrival if their journeys begin and end at a UK seaport

*Source:* Department for Transport

# UK SHIPPING FORECAST AREAS

Weather bulletins for shipping are broadcast daily on BBC Radio 4 at 00h 48m, 05h 20m, 12h 01m and 17h 54m. All transmissions are broadcast on long wave at 1515m (198kHz) and the 00h 48m and 05h 20m transmissions are also broadcast on FM. The bulletins consist of a gale warning summary, general synopsis, sea-area forecasts and coastal station reports. In addition, gale warnings are broadcast at the first available programme break after receipt. If this does not coincide with a news bulletin, the warning is repeated after the next news bulletin. Shipping forecasts and gale warnings are also available on the Met Office and BBC Weather websites.

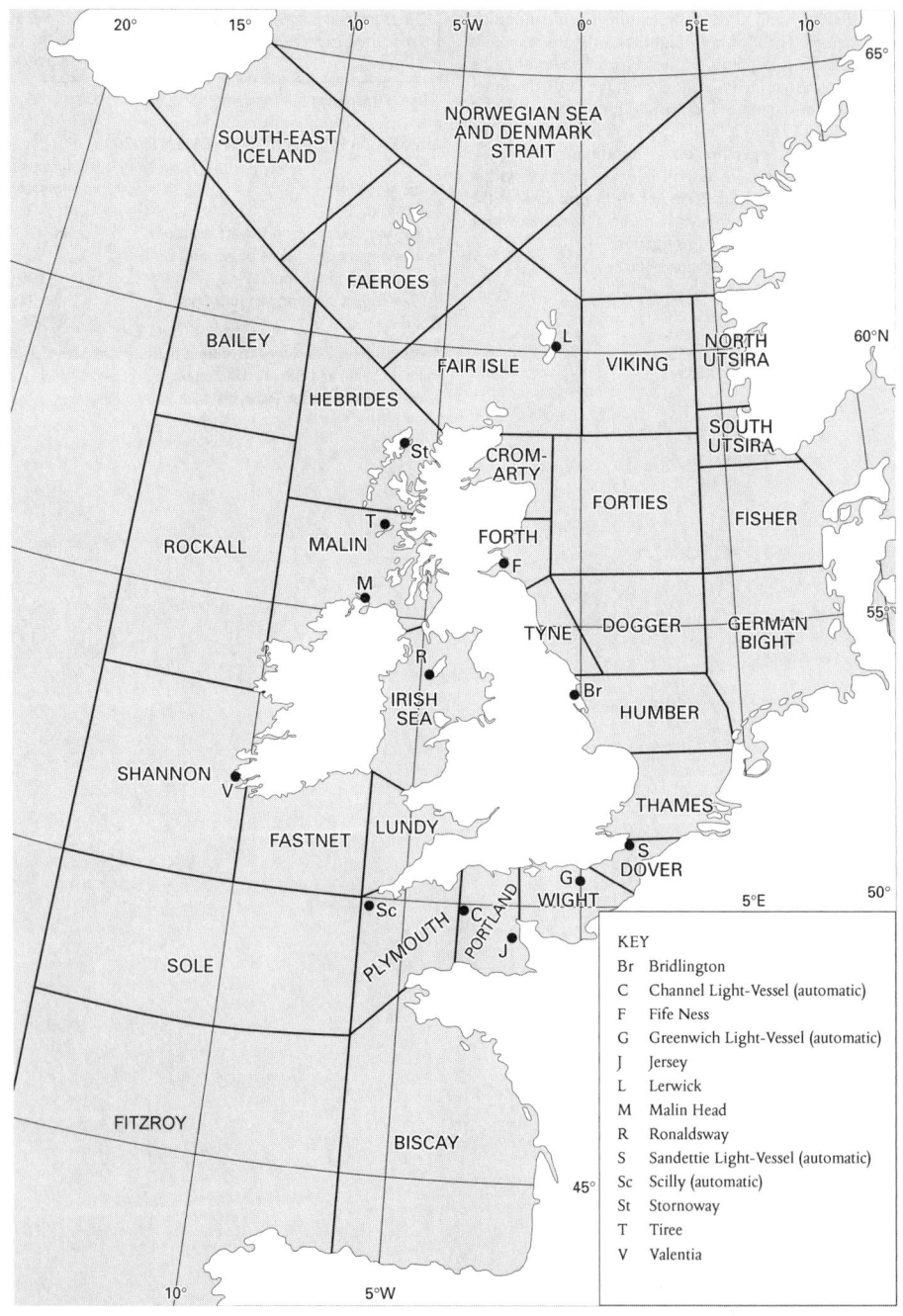

KEY

| | |
|---|---|
| Br | Bridlington |
| C | Channel Light-Vessel (automatic) |
| F | Fife Ness |
| G | Greenwich Light-Vessel (automatic) |
| J | Jersey |
| L | Lerwick |
| M | Malin Head |
| R | Ronaldsway |
| S | Sandettie Light-Vessel (automatic) |
| Sc | Scilly (automatic) |
| St | Stornoway |
| T | Tiree |
| V | Valentia |

# RELIGION IN THE UK

The 2011 census in England and Wales included a voluntary question on religion; 92.8 per cent of the population chose to answer the question. Christianity remained the largest religion, despite a decrease of 4 million people from the 2001 census, to 33.2 million adherents, or 59.3 per cent of the population. The second largest religious group were Muslims with 2.7 million people identifying themselves as such, an increase of 1.2 million since 2001. The number of people reporting that they had 'no religion' was 14.1 million, around a quarter of the population. Of those reporting that they had no religion, the majority identified themselves as white (93 per cent) and born in the UK (also 93 per cent); in terms of age, the largest demographic were those aged 20 to 24 (1.4 million or 10 per cent). More than 240,000 people listed 'other religion' on the census, which included, among many others, 176,632 Jedi Knights, 56,620 Pagans and 39,061 Spiritualists. Norwich remained the city with the highest proportion reporting no religion (42.5 per cent), while London was the most diverse region with the largest proportion of people classifying themselves as Buddhist, Hindu, Jewish and Muslim. Knowsley, in Merseyside, was the local authority with the highest proportion of Christians at 80.9 per cent, while Tower Hamlets in London had the highest population of Muslims at 34.5 per cent.

In Northern Ireland, the religion question was phrased differently; 738,033 (41 per cent) identified themselves as Roman Catholic, 752,555 (42 per cent) as 'Protestant and other Christian', 14,859 (0.8 per cent) belonged to an 'other religion' and 183,164 (10 per cent) stated they had no religion.

CENSUS 2011 RESULTS – RELIGION IN ENGLAND, WALES AND SCOTLAND*

| | thousands | per cent |
|---|---|---|
| Christian | 36,093 | 58.8 |
| Buddhist | 261 | 0.4 |
| Hindu | 833 | 1.4 |
| Jewish | 269 | 0.4 |
| Muslim | 2,783 | 4.5 |
| Sikh | 432 | 0.7 |
| Other religion | 256 | 0.4 |
| *All religions* | 40,927 | 66.6 |
| No religion | 16,038 | 26.1 |
| Not stated | 4,406 | 7.2 |
| *All no religion / not stated* | 20,444 | 33.3 |
| TOTAL | 61,371 | 100 |

* Figures from the 2011 census for Northern Ireland did not contain a full breakdown of each major religion
*Source:* Census 2011

## INTER-CHURCH AND INTER-FAITH COOPERATION

The main umbrella body for the Christian churches in the UK is Churches Together in Britain and Ireland. There are also ecumenical bodies in each of the constituent countries of the UK: Churches Together in England, Action of Churches Together in Scotland, CYTUN (Churches Together in Wales), and the Irish Council of Churches. The Free Churches Group (formerly the Free Churches Council), which is closely associated with Churches Together in England, represents

most of the free churches in England and Wales, and the Evangelical Alliance represents evangelical Christians.

The Inter Faith Network for the United Kingdom promotes cooperation between faiths, and the Council of Christians and Jews works to improve relations between the two religions. Churches Together in Britain and Ireland also has a commission on inter-faith relations.

ACTION OF CHURCHES TOGETHER IN SCOTLAND, Inglewood House, Alloa, Clackmannanshire FK10 2HU T 01259-216980 W www.acts-scotland.org
*General Secretary,* Revd Matthew Ross
CHURCHES TOGETHER IN BRITAIN AND IRELAND, 39 Ecclestone Square, London SW1V 1BX T 0845-680 6851 E info@ctbi.org.uk W www.ctbi.org.uk
*General Secretary,* Revd Bob Fyffe
CHURCHES TOGETHER IN ENGLAND, 27 Tavistock Square, London WC1H 9HH T 020-7529 8131 E office@cte.org.uk W www.cte.org.uk
*General Secretary,* Revd Dr David Cornick
COUNCIL OF CHRISTIANS AND JEWS, Collaboration House, 77–79 Charlotte Street, London W1T 4PW T 020-3515 3003 E cjrelations@ccj.org.uk W www.ccj.org.uk
*Director,* Jane Clements
CYTUN (CHURCHES TOGETHER IN WALES), 58 Richmond Road, Cardiff CF24 3UR T 029-2046 4204 E post@cytun.org.uk W www.cytun.org.uk
*Chief Executive,* Revd Canon Aled Edwards, OBE
EVANGELICAL ALLIANCE, 176 Copenhagen Street, London N1 0ST T 020-7520 3830 E info@eauk.org W www.eauk.org
*General Director,* Steve Clifford
FREE CHURCHES GROUP, 27 Tavistock Square, London WC1H 9HH T 020-3651 8334 E info@freechurches.org.uk W www.freechurches.org.uk
*Secretary,* vacant
INTERFAITH NETWORK FOR THE UK, 2 Grosvenor Gardens, London SW1W 0DH T 020-7730 0410 W www.interfaith.org.uk
*Director,* Dr Harriet Crabtree
IRISH COUNCIL OF CHURCHES, Inter-Church Centre, 48 Elmwood Avenue, Belfast BT9 6AZ T 028-9066 3145 E info@irishchurches.org W www.irishchurches.org
*Executive Officer,* Mervyn McCullagh

## RELIGIONS AND BELIEFS

### BAHA'I FAITH
*Baha'u'llah* ('Glory of God'), the founder of the Baha'i faith, was born in Iran in 1817. He was imprisoned in 1852 for advocating the teachings of the Bab ('Gate'), a prophet who was martyred in 1850. Baha'u'llah was persecuted and sent into successive stages of exile, first to Baghdad – where in 1863 he announced that he was the 'promised one' foretold by the Bab – and then to Constantinople, Adrianople and eventually Acre, in present day Israel. He died in 1892 and was succeeded by his son, Abdu'l-Baha, as head of the Baha'i faith, under whose guidance the faith spread to Europe and North America. He was in turn succeeded by Shoghi Effendi, his grandson, who oversaw the establishment of the administrative order and the spread of the faith around the world until his death in 1957. The Universal House

of Justice, an elected international governing council, was formed in 1963 in accordance with Baha'u'llah's teachings.

The Baha'i faith espouses the oneness of humanity and of religion and teaches that there is only one God, whose will has been revealed to mankind by a series of messengers, such as Zoroaster, Abraham, Moses, Buddha, Krishna, Christ, Muhammad, the Bab and Baha'u'llah, who were seen as the founders of separate religions, but whose common purpose was to bring God's message to mankind. The Baha'i faith attributes the differences in teachings between religions to humanity's changing needs. Baha'i teachings include that all races and both sexes are equal and deserving of equal opportunities and treatment, that education is a fundamental right and that extremes of wealth and poverty should be eliminated. In addition, the faith exhorts mankind to establish a world federal system to promote peace and unity.

In an effort to translate these principles into action, Baha'is have initiated an educational process across the world that seeks to raise the capacity of people of all ages and from all backgrounds to contribute towards the betterment of society. There is no clergy; each local community elects a local spiritual assembly to tend to its administrative needs. A national spiritual assembly is elected annually by locally elected delegates, and every five years the national spiritual assemblies meet together to elect the Universal House of Justice, the supreme international governing body of the Baha'i Faith. Worldwide there are over 13,000 local spiritual assemblies and more than 5 million members.

BAHA'I COMMUNITY OF THE UK, 27 Rutland Gate,
London SW7 1PD T 020-7584 2566 E nsa@bahai.org.uk
W www.bahai.org.uk
*Director, Office of Public Affairs,* Dr Kishan Manocha

## BUDDHISM

Buddhism originated in what is now the Bihar area of northern India in the teachings of Siddhartha Gautama, who became the *Buddha* ('Enlightened One'). In the Thai or Suriyakati calendar the beginning of the Buddhist era is dated from the death of Buddha; the year 2015 is therefore 2558 by the Thai Buddhist reckoning.

Fundamental to Buddhism is the concept of rebirth, whereby each life carries with it the consequences of the conduct of earlier lives (known as the law of *karma*) and this cycle of death and rebirth is broken only when the state of *nirvana* has been reached. Buddhism steers a middle path between belief in personal continuity and the belief that death results in total extinction.

While doctrine does not have a pivotal position in Buddhism, a statement of four 'Noble Truths' is common to all its schools and varieties. These are: suffering is inescapable in even the most fortunate of existences; craving is the root cause of suffering; abandonment of the selfish mindset is the way to end suffering; and bodily and mental discipline, accompanied by the cultivation of wisdom and compassion, provides the spiritual path ('Noble Eightfold Path') to accomplish this. Buddhists deny the idea of a creator and prefer to emphasise the practical aspects of moral and spiritual development.

The schools of Buddhism can be broadly divided into three: *Theravada,* the generally monastic-led tradition practised in Sri Lanka and South East Asia; *Mahayana,* the philosophical and popular traditions of the Far East; and *Esoteric,* the Tantric-derived traditions found in Tibet and Mongolia and, to a lesser extent, China and Japan. The extensive Theravada scriptures are contained in the *Pali Canon,* which dates in its written form from the first century BC. Mahayana and Esoteric schools have Sanskrit-derived translations of these plus many more additional scriptures as well as exegetical material.

In the East the new and full moons and the lunar quarter days were (and to a certain extent, still are) significant in determining the religious calendar. Most private homes contain a shrine where offerings, worship and other spiritual practices (such as meditation, chanting or mantra recitation) take place on a daily basis. Buddhist festivals vary according to local traditions within the different schools and there is little uniformity – even in commemorating the birth, enlightenment and death of the Buddha.

There is no governing authority for Buddhism in the UK. Communities representing all schools of Buddhism operate independently. The Buddhist Society was established in 1924; it runs courses, lectures and meditation groups, and publishes books about Buddhism. The Network of Buddhist Organisations was founded in 1993 to promote fellowship and dialogue between Buddhist organisations and to facilitate cooperation in matters of common interest.

There are estimated to be at least 375 million Buddhists worldwide. Of the 248,000 Buddhists in England and Wales (according to the 2011 census), 72,000 are white British (the majority are converts), 49,000 Chinese, 93,000 'other Asian' and 36,000 are 'other ethnic'.

THE BUDDHIST SOCIETY, 58 Eccleston Square,
London SW1V 1PH T 020-7834 5858
E info@thebuddhistsociety.org W www.thebuddhistsociety.org
LONDON BUDDHIST CENTRE, 51 Roman Road,
London E2 0HU T 020-8981 1225 E info@lbc.org.uk
W www.lbc.org.uk
*Chair,* Dharmachari Jnanavaca
THE NETWORK OF BUDDHIST ORGANISATIONS,
PO Box 4147, Maidenhead SL60 1DN T 0845-345 8978
E secretary@nbo.org.uk W www.nbo.org.uk
THE OFFICE OF TIBET, Tibet House, 1 Culworth Street,
London NW8 7AF T 020-7722 5378 E info@otlondon.org
W www.tibet.org
*Representative of HH the Dalai Lama,* Chonpel Tsering
SOKA GAKKAI UK, Taplow Court Grand Cultural Centre,
Cliveden Road, Taplow, Berkshire SL6 0ER T 01628-773163
W www.sgi-uk.org

## CHRISTIANITY

Christianity is a monotheistic faith based on the person and teachings of Jesus Christ, and all Christian denominations claim his authority. Central to its teaching is the concept of God and his son Jesus Christ, who was crucified and resurrected in order to enable mankind to attain salvation.

The Jewish scriptures predicted the coming of a *Messiah,* an 'anointed one', who would bring salvation. To Christians, Jesus of Nazareth, a Jewish rabbi (teacher) who was born in Palestine, was the promised Messiah. Jesus' birth, teachings, crucifixion and subsequent resurrection are recorded in the *Gospels,* which, together with other scriptures that summarise Christian belief, form the *New Testament.* This, together with the Hebrew scriptures – entitled the *Old Testament* by Christians – makes up the Bible, the sacred texts of Christianity.

Christians believe that sin distanced mankind from God, and that Jesus was the son of God, sent to redeem mankind from sin by his death. In addition, many believe that Jesus will return again at some future date, triumph over evil and establish a kingdom on earth, thus inaugurating a new age. The Gospel assures Christians that those who believe in Jesus and obey his teachings will be forgiven their sins and will be resurrected from the dead.

The Apostles were Jesus' first converts and are recognised by Christians as the founders of the Christian community. Early Christianity spread rapidly throughout the eastern provinces of the Roman Empire but was subjected to great persecution until AD 313, when Emperor Constantine's

Edict of Toleration confirmed its right to exist. Christianity was established as the religion of the Roman Empire in AD 381.

Between AD 325 and 787 there were seven Oecumenical Councils at which bishops from the entire Christian world assembled to resolve various doctrinal disputes. The estrangement between East and West began after Constantine moved the centre of the Roman Empire from Rome to Constantinople, and it grew after the division of the Roman Empire into eastern and western halves. Linguistic and cultural differences between Greek East and Latin West served to encourage separate ecclesiastical developments which became pronounced in the tenth and early 11th centuries. Administration of the church was divided between five ancient patriarchates: Rome and all the West, Constantinople (the imperial city – the 'New Rome'), Jerusalem and all of Palestine, Antioch and all the East, and Alexandria and all of Africa. Of these, only Rome was in the Latin West and after the schism in 1054, Rome developed a structure of authority centralised on the Papacy, while the Orthodox East maintained the style of localised administration. Papal authority over the doctrine and jurisdiction of the church in Western Europe was unrivalled after the split with the Eastern Orthodox Church until the Protestant Reformation in the 16th century.

Christian practices vary widely between different Christian churches, but prayer, charity and giving (for the maintenance of the church buildings, for the work of the church, and to those in need) are common to all. In addition, certain days of observance, ie the *Sabbath, Easter* and *Christmas,* are celebrated by most Christians. The Orthodox, Roman Catholic and Anglican churches celebrate many more days of observance, based on saints and significant events in the life of Jesus. The belief in sacraments, physical signs believed to have been ordained by Jesus Christ to symbolise and convey spiritual gifts, varies greatly between Christian denominations; *baptism* and the *Eucharist* are practised by most Christians. Baptism, symbolising repentance and faith in Jesus, is an act marking entry into the Christian community; the Eucharist, the ritual re-enactment of the Last Supper, Jesus' final meal with his disciples, is also practised by most denominations. Other sacraments, such as anointing the sick, the laying on of hands to symbolise the passing on of the office of priesthood or to heal the sick, and speaking in tongues, where it is believed that the person is possessed by the Holy Spirit, are less common. In denominations where infant baptism is practised, confirmation (where the person confirms the commitments made on their behalf in infancy) is common. Matrimony and the ordination of priests are also widely believed to be sacraments. Many Protestants regard only baptism and the Eucharist to be sacraments; the Quakers and the Salvation Army reject the use of sacraments.

*See* Churches for contact details of the Church of England, the Roman Catholic Church and other Christian churches in the UK.

# HINDUISM

Hinduism has no historical founder but had become highly developed in India by *c.*2500 BC. Its adherents originally called themselves Aryans; Muslim invaders first called the Aryans 'Hindus' (derived from 'Sindhu', the name of the river Indus) in the eighth century.

Most Hindus hold that *satya* (truthfulness), honesty, sincerity and devotion to God are essential for good living. They believe in one supreme spirit *(Brahman),* and in the transmigration of *atman* (the soul). Most Hindus accept the doctrine of *karma* (consequences of actions), the concept of *samsara* (successive lives) and the possibility of all atmans achieving *moksha* (liberation from samsara) through *jnana*

(knowledge), *yoga* (meditation), *karma* (work or action) and *bhakti* (devotion).

Most Hindus offer worship to *murtis* (images of deities) representing different incarnations or aspects of Brahman, and follow their *dharma* (religious and social duty) according to the traditions of their *varna* (social class), *ashrama* (stage in life), *jaiti* (caste) and *kula* (family).

Hinduism's sacred texts are divided into *shruti* ('that which is heard'), including the *Vedas,* and *smriti* ('that which is remembered'), including the *Ramayana,* the *Mahabharata,* the *Puranas* (ancient myths), and the sacred law books. Most Hindus recognise the authority of the *Vedas,* the oldest holy books, and accept the philosophical teachings of the *Upanishads,* the *Vedanta Sutras* and the *Bhagavad-Gita.*

Hindus believe Brahman to be omniscient, omnipotent, limitless and all-pervading. Brahman is usually worshipped in its deity form. Brahma, Vishnu and Shiva are the most important deities or aspects of Brahman worshipped by Hindus; their respective consorts are Saraswati, Lakshmi and Durga or Parvati, also known as Shakti. There are believed to have been ten *avatars* (incarnations) of Vishnu, of whom the most important are Rama and Krishna. Other popular gods are Ganesha, Hanuman and Subrahmanyam. All Hindu gods are seen as aspects of the supreme spirit (Brahman), not as competing deities.

Orthodox Hindus revere all gods and goddesses equally, but there are many denominations, including the Hare-Krishna movement (ISKCon), the Arya Samaj and the Swaminarayan Hindu mission, in which worship is concentrated on one deity. The *guru* (spiritual teacher) is seen as the source of spiritual guidance.

Hinduism does not have a centrally trained and ordained priesthood. The pronouncements of the *shankaracharyas* (heads of monasteries) of Shringeri, Puri, Dwarka and Badrinath are heeded by the orthodox but may be ignored by the various sects.

The commonest form of worship is *puja,* in which water, flowers, food, fruit, incense and light are offered to the deity. Puja may be done either in a home shrine or a *mandir* (temple). Many British Hindus celebrate *samskars* (purification rites), to name a baby, for the sacred thread (an initiation ceremony), marriage and cremation.

The largest communities of Hindus in Britain are in Leicester, London, Birmingham and Bradford, and developed as a result of immigration from India, eastern Africa and Sri Lanka.

There are an estimated 800 million Hindus worldwide; there are around 817,000 adherents, according to the 2011 census in England and Wales, and around 135 temples in the UK.

**ARYA SAMAJ LONDON,** 69 Argyle Road, London W13 0LY
**T** 020-8991 1732 **E** aryasamajlondon@yahoo.co.uk
**W** aryasamajlondon.org.uk
*General Secretary,* Amrit Lal Bhardwaj
**BHARATIYA VIDYA BHAVAN,** 4A Castletown Road, London W14 9HE **T** 020-7381 3086 **E** info@bhavan.net
**W** www.bhavan.net
*Executive Director,* Dr M. N. Nandakumara
**INTERNATIONAL SOCIETY FOR KRISHNA CONSCIOUSNESS (ISKCON),** Bhaktivedanta Manor, Dharam Marg, Hilfield Lane, Aldenham, Watford, Herts WD25 8EZ **T** 01923-851000 **E** info@krishnatemple.com
**W** www.krishnatemple.com
*Temple President,* Sruti Dharma Das
**NATIONAL COUNCIL OF HINDU TEMPLES (UK),**
c/o Shree Sanatan Mandir, 84 Weymouth Street, Leicester LE4 6FQ **T** 0776-317 8628 **E** info@nchtuk.org
**W** www.nchtuk.org
*General Secretary,* Satish K. Sharma

SWAMINARAYAN HINDU MISSION (SHRI SWAMINARAYAN MANDIR), 105–119 Brentfield Road, London NW10 8LD **T** 020-8965 2651 **E** info@londonmandir.baps.org **W** www.mandir.org

## HUMANISM

Humanism traces its roots back to ancient times, with Chinese, Greek, Indian and Roman philosophers expressing Humanist ideas some 2,500 years ago. Confucius, the Chinese philosopher who lived *c.*500 BC, believed that religious observances should be replaced with moral values as the basis of social and political order and that 'the true way' is based on reason and humanity. He also stressed the importance of benevolence and respect for others, and believed that the individual situation should be considered rather than the global application of traditional rules.

Humanists believe that there is no God or other supernatural being, that humans have only one life (Humanists do not believe in an afterlife or reincarnation) and that humans can live ethical and fulfilling lives without religious beliefs through a moral code derived from a shared history, personal experience and thought. There are no sacred Humanist texts. Particular emphasis is placed on science as the only reliable source of knowledge of the universe. Many Humanists recognise a need for ceremonies to mark important occasions in life and the British Humanist Association has a network of celebrants who are trained and accredited to conduct baby namings, weddings and funerals. The British Humanist Association's campaigns for a secular state (a state based on freedom of religious or non-religious belief with no privileges for any particular set of beliefs) are based on equality and human rights. The association also campaigns for inclusive schools that meet the needs of all parents and pupils, regardless of their religious or non-religious beliefs. According to figures from the 2011 census, there are just over 15,000 Humanists in England and Wales.

BRITISH HUMANIST ASSOCIATION, 39 Moreland Street, London EC1V 8BB **T** 020-7324 3060 **E** info@humanism.org.uk **W** www.humanism.org.uk

*Chief Executive,* Andrew Copson

## ISLAM

Islam (which means 'peace arising from submission to the will of Allah' in Arabic) is a monotheistic religion which was taught in Arabia by the Prophet Muhammad, who was born in Mecca (Al-Makkah) in 570 AD. Islam spread to Egypt, north Africa, Spain and the borders of China in the century following the Prophet's death, and is now the predominant religion in Indonesia, the near and Middle East, northern and parts of western Africa, Pakistan, Bangladesh, Malaysia and some of the former Soviet republics. There are also large Muslim communities in other countries.

For Muslims (adherents of Islam), there is one God *(Allah)*, who holds absolute power. Muslims believe that Allah's commands were revealed to mankind through the prophets, who include Abraham, Moses and Jesus, but that Allah's message was gradually corrupted until revealed finally and in perfect form to Muhammad through the angel *Jibril* (Gabriel) over a period of 23 years. This last, incorruptible message is said to have been recorded in the *Qur'an* (Koran), which contains 114 divisions called *surahs,* each made up of *ayahs* of various lengths, and is held to be the essence of all previous scriptures. The *Ahadith* are the records of the Prophet Muhammad's deeds and sayings (the *Sunnah*) as practised and recounted by his immediate followers. A culture and a system of law and theology gradually developed to form a distinctive Islamic civilisation. Islam makes no distinction between sacred and worldly affairs and provides rules for every aspect of human life. The *Shariah* is the sacred law of Islam based primarily upon prescriptions derived from the *Qur'an* and the *Sunnah* of the Prophet.

The 'five pillars of Islam' are *shahadah* (a declaration of faith in the oneness and supremacy of Allah and the messengership of Muhammad); *salat* (formal prayer, to be performed five times a day facing the *Ka'bah* (the most sacred shrine in the holy city of Mecca)); *zakat* (welfare due, paid annually on all savings at the rate of 2.5 per cent); *sawm* (fasting during the month of Ramadan from dawn until sunset); and *hajj* (pilgrimage to Mecca made once in a lifetime if the believer is financially and physically able). Some Muslims would add *jihad* as the sixth pillar (striving for the cause of good and resistance to evil).

Two main groups developed among Muslims. *Sunni* Muslims accept the legitimacy of Muhammad's first four *caliphs* (successors as head of the Muslim community) and of the authority of the Muslim community as a whole. About 90 per cent of Muslims are Sunni Muslims.

*Shi'ites* recognise only Muhammad's son-in-law Ali as his rightful successor and the *Imams* (descendants of Ali, not to be confused with *imams,* who are prayer leaders or religious teachers) as the principal legitimate religious authority. The largest group within Shi'ism is *Twelver Shi'ism,* which has been the official school of law and theology in Iran since the 16th century; other subsects include the *Ismailis,* the *Druze* and the *Alawis,* the latter two differing considerably from the main body of Muslims. The *Ibadis* of Oman are neither Sunni nor Shia, deriving from the strictly observant *Khariji* (Seceders). There is no organised priesthood, but learned men such as imams, *ulama,* and *ayatollahs* are accorded great respect. The *Sufis* are the mystics of Islam. Mosques are centres for worship and teaching and also for social and welfare activities.

Islam was first recorded in western Europe in the eighth century AD when 800 years of Muslim rule began in Spain. Later, Islam spread to eastern Europe. More recently, Islam came to Europe from Africa, the Middle East and Asia in the late 19th century. Both the Sunni and Shia traditions are represented in Britain, but the majority of Muslims in Britain adhere to Sunni Islam. Efforts to establish a representative national body for Muslims in Britain resulted in the founding, in 1997, of the Muslim Council of Britain. In addition, there are many other Muslim organisations in the UK. There are around 1.6 billion Muslims worldwide, with around 2.8 million adherents in England, Wales and Scotland and about 1,500 mosques in the UK.

ISLAMIC CULTURAL CENTRE – THE LONDON CENTRAL MOSQUE, 146 Park Road, London NW8 7RG **T** 020-7724 3363 **E** info@iccuk.org **W** www.iccuk.org *Director-General,* Dr Ahmad Al-Dubayan
MUSLIM COUNCIL OF BRITAIN, PO Box 57330, London E1 2WJ **T** 0845-262 6786 **E** admin@mcb.org.uk **W** www.mcb.org.uk *Secretary-General,* Dr Shuja Shafi
MUSLIM LAW (SHARIAH) COUNCIL UK, PO Box 851, Wembley, Middx HA9 1BE **T** 0771-265 4880 **E** msraza@shariahcouncil.org.uk **W** www.shariahcouncil.org *Chair,* Dr Sheikh Gamal Solaiman Manna
MUSLIM WORLD LEAGUE LONDON, 46 Goodge Street, London W1T 4LU **T** 020-7636 7568 **E** infor@mwllo.org.uk **W** www.mwllo.org.uk *Director,* Dr Ahmed Makhdoom

## JAINISM

Jainism traces its history to Vardhamana Jnatriputra, known as *Tirthankara Mahavira* ('the Great Hero') whose traditional dates were 599–527 BC. Jains believe he was the last of the current era in a series of 24 *Jinas* (those who overcome all passions and desires) or *Tirthankaras* (those who show a way across the ocean of life) stretching back to remote antiquity. Born to a noble family in north-eastern India (presently the state of Bihar), he renounced the world for the life of a wandering ascetic and after 12 years of austerity and meditation he attained enlightenment. He then preached his message until, at the age of 72, he left the mortal world and achieved total liberation *(moksha)* from the cycle of death and rebirth.

Jains declare that the Hindu rituals of transferring merit are not acceptable as each living being is responsible for its own actions. They recognise some of the minor deities of the Hindu pantheon, but the supreme objects of worship are the Tirthankaras. The pious Jain does not ask favours from the Tirthankaras, but seeks to emulate their example in his or her own life.

Jains believe that the universe is eternal and self-subsisting, that there is no omnipotent creator God ruling it and the destiny of the individual is in his or her own hands. *Karma,* the fruit of past actions, is believed to determine the place of every living being and rebirth may be in the heavens, on earth as a human, an animal or other lower being, or in the hells. The ultimate goal of existence for Jains is *moksha,* a state of perfect knowledge and tranquillity for each individual soul, which can be achieved only by gaining enlightenment.

The Jainist path to liberation is defined by the three jewels: *Samyak Darshan* (right perception), *Samyak Jnana* (right knowledge) and *Samyak Charitra* (right conduct). Of the five fundamental precepts of the Jains, *Ahimsa* (non-injury to any form of being, in any mode: thought, speech or action) is the first and foremost, and was popularised by Gandhi as *Ahimsa paramo dharma* (non-violence is the supreme religion).

The largest population of Jains can be found in India but there are approximately 30,000 Jains in Britain, with sizeable communities in North America, East Africa, Australia and smaller groups in many other countries.

**INSTITUTE OF JAINOLOGY,** Unit 18, Silicon Business Centre, 28 Wadsworth Road, Perivale, Greenford, Middx UB6 7JZ **T** 020-8997 2300 **E** info@jainology.org
**W** www.jainology.org
*Deputy Chair,* Dr Harshad Sanghrajka

## JUDAISM

Judaism is the oldest monotheistic faith. The primary text of Judaism is the Hebrew bible or *Tanakh,* which records how the descendants of Abraham were led by Moses out of their slavery in Egypt to Mount Sinai where God's law *(Torah)* was revealed to them as the chosen people. The *Talmud,* which consists of commentaries on the *Mishnah* (the first text of rabbinical Judaism), is also held to be authoritative, and may be divided into two main categories: the *halakah* (dealing with legal and ritual matters) and the *aggadah* (dealing with theological and ethical matters not directly concerned with the regulation of conduct). The *midrash* comprises rabbinic writings containing biblical inter-pretations in the spirit of the aggadah. The halakah has become a source of division: orthodox Jews regard Jewish law as derived from God and therefore unalterable; progressive Jews seek to interpret it in the light of contemporary considerations; and conservative Jews aim to maintain most of the traditional rituals but to allow changes in accordance with tradition. Reconstructionist Judaism, a 20th-century movement, regards Judaism as a culture rather than a theological system and accepts all forms of Jewish practice.

The family is the basic unit of Jewish ritual, with the synagogue playing an important role as the centre for public worship and religious study. A synagogue is led by a group of laymen who are elected to office. The Rabbi is primarily a teacher and spiritual guide. The *Sabbath* is the central religious observance. Most British Jews are descendants of either the *Ashkenazim* of central and eastern Europe or the *Sephardim* of Spain, Portugal and the Middle East.

The Chief Rabbi of the United Hebrew Congregations of the Commonwealth is appointed by a Chief Rabbinate Conference, and is the rabbinical authority of the mainstream Orthodox sector of the Ashkenazi Jewish community, the largest body of which is the United Synagogue. His formal ecclesiastical authority is not recognised by the Reform Synagogues of Great Britain (the largest progressive group), the Union of Liberal and Progressive Synagogues, the Spanish and Portuguese Jews' Congregation or the Assembly of Masorti Synagogues. He is, however, generally recognised both outside the Jewish community and within it as the public religious representative of the totality of British Jewry. The Chief Rabbi is President of the London *Beth Din* (Court of Judgment), a rabbinic court. The *Dayanim* (Judges) adjudicate in disputes or on matters of Jewish law and tradition; they also oversee dietary law administration, marriage, divorce and issues of personal status.

The Board of Deputies of British Jews, established in 1760, is the representative body of British Jewry. The basis of representation is through the election of deputies by synagogues and communal organisations. It protects and promotes the interests of British Jewry, acts as the central voice of the community and seeks to counter anti-Jewish discrimination and anti-Semitic activities.

There are approximately 13.9 million Jews worldwide; in the UK there are an estimated 290,000 adherents and over 400 synagogues.

**OFFICE OF THE CHIEF RABBI,** 305 Ballards Lane, London N12 8GB **T** 020-8343 6301 **E** info@chiefrabbi.org
**W** www.chiefrabbi.org
*Chief Rabbi,* Ephraim Mirvis
**BETH DIN (COURT OF THE CHIEF RABBI),** 305 Ballards Lane, London N12 8GB **T** 020-8343 6270 **E** info@bethdin.org.uk **W** www.theus.org.uk
*Registrar,* David Frei
*Dayanim,* Yonason Abraham; Menachem Gelley *(Rosh Beth Din);* Ivan Binstock; Shmuel Simons
**MASORTI JUDAISM,** Alexander House, 3 Shakespeare Road, London N3 1XE **T** 020-8349 6650 **E** enquiries@masorti.org.uk
**W** www.masorti.org.uk
*Executive Director,* Matt Plen
**BOARD OF DEPUTIES OF BRITISH JEWS,** 37 Kentish Town, London NW1 8NX **T** 020-7543 5400 **E** info@bod.org.uk **W** www.bod.org.uk
*Chief Executive,* Gillian Merron
**FEDERATION OF SYNAGOGUES,** 65 Watford Way, London NW4 3AQ **T** 020-8202 2263 **E** info@federationofsynagogues.com
**W** www.federationofsynagogues.com
*Chief Executive,* Rabbi Ari Lazarus
**LIBERAL JUDAISM,** The Montagu Centre, 21 Maple Street, London W1T 4BE **T** 020-7580 1663 **W** www.liberaljudaism.org
*Chief Executive,* Rabbi Danny Rich
**THE MOVEMENT FOR REFORM JUDAISM,** The Sternberg Centre for Judaism, 80 East End Road, London N3 2SY **T** 020-8349 5640 **E** admin@reformjudaism.org.uk
**W** www.reformjudaism.org.uk
*Senior Rabbi,* Laura Janner-Klausner
**SPANISH AND PORTUGUESE JEWS' CONGREGATION,** 2 Ashworth Road, London W9 1JY **T** 020-7289 2573 **E** admin@spsyn.org.uk **W** www.sandp.org.uk
*Administrator,* Alison Rosen
**UNION OF ORTHODOX HEBREW CONGREGATIONS,** 140 Stamford Hill, London N16 6QT **T** 020-8802 6226 *Executive Coordinator,* Chanoch Kesselman

UNITED SYNAGOGUE HEAD OFFICE, Adler House,
735 High Road, London N12 0US T 020-8343 8989
W www.theus.org.uk
Chief Executive, Dr Stephen Wilson

## PAGANISM

Paganism draws on the ideas of the Celtic people of pre-Roman Europe and is closely linked to Druidism. The first historical record of Druidry comes from classical Greek and Roman writers of the third century BC, who noted the existence of Druids among a people called the Keltoi who inhabited central and southern Europe. The word druid may derive from the Indo-European 'dreo-vid', meaning 'one who knows the truth'. In practice it was probably understood to mean something like 'wise-one' or 'philosopher-priest'.

Paganism is a pantheistic nature-worshipping religion which incorporates beliefs and ritual practices from ancient times. Pagans place much emphasis on the natural world and the ongoing cycle of life and death is central to their beliefs. Most Pagans believe that they are part of nature and not separate from, or superior to it, and seek to live in a way that minimises harm to the natural environment (the word Pagan derives from the Latin *Paganus,* meaning 'rural'). Paganism strongly emphasises the equality of the sexes, with women playing a prominent role in the modern Pagan movement and goddess worship featuring in most ceremonies. Paganism cannot be defined by any principal beliefs because it is shaped by each individual's experiences.

The Pagan Federation was founded in 1971 to provide information on Paganism, campaigns on issues which affect Paganism and provides support to members of the Pagan community. Within the UK the Pagan Federation is divided into 13 districts each with a district manager, regional and local coordinators. Local meetings are called 'moots' and take place in private homes, pubs or coffee bars. The Pagan Federation publishes a quarterly journal, *Pagan Dawn,* formerly *The Wiccan* (founded in 1968). The federation also publishes other material, arranges members-only and public events and maintains personal contact by letter with individual members and the wider Pagan community. Regional gatherings and conferences are held throughout the year.

THE PAGAN FEDERATION, BM Box 7097, London
WC1N 3XX E info@paganfederation.co.uk
W www.paganfed.org
President, Mike Stygal

## SIKHISM

The Sikh religion dates from the birth of Guru Nanak in the Punjab in 1469. 'Guru' means teacher but in Sikh tradition has come to represent the divine presence of God giving inner spiritual guidance. Nanak's role as the human vessel of the divine guru was passed on to nine successors, the last of whom (Guru Gobind Singh) died in 1708. The immortal guru is now held to reside in the sacred scripture, *Guru Granth Sahib,* and so to be present in all Sikh gatherings.

Guru Nanak taught that there is one God and that different religions are like different roads leading to the same destination. He condemned religious conflict, ritualism and caste prejudices. The fifth Guru, Guru Arjan Dev, largely compiled the Sikh Holy scripture, a collection of hymns *(gurbani)* known as the *Adi Granth.* It includes the writings of the first five gurus and the ninth guru, and selected writings of Hindu and Muslim saints whose views are in accord with the gurus' teachings. Guru Arjan Dev also built the Golden Temple at Amritsar, the centre of Sikhism. The tenth guru, Guru Gobind Singh, passed on the guruship to the sacred scripture, Guru Granth Sahib, and founded the *Khalsa,* an order intended to fight against tyranny and injustice. Male initiates to the order added 'Singh' to their given names and

women added 'Kaur'. Guru Gobind Singh also made the wearing of five symbols obligatory: *kaccha* (a special undergarment), *kara* (a steel bangle), *kirpan* (a small sword), *kesh* (long unshorn hair, and consequently the wearing of a turban) and *kangha* (a comb). These practices are still compulsory for those Sikhs who are initiated into the Khalsa (the *Amritdharis*). Those who do not seek initiation are known as *Sehajdharis.*

There are no professional priests in Sikhism; anyone with a reasonable proficiency in the Punjabi language can conduct a service. Worship can be offered individually or communally, and in a private house or a *gurdwara* (temple). Sikhs are forbidden to eat meat prepared by ritual slaughter; they are also asked to abstain from smoking, alcohol and other intoxicants. Such abstention is compulsory for the Amritdharis.

There are about 24 million Sikhs worldwide and, according to the 2011 census, there are 432,000 adherents in England, Wales and Scotland. Every gurdwara manages its own affairs; there is no central body in the UK. The Sikh Missionary Society provides an information service.

SIKH MISSIONARY SOCIETY UK, 10 Featherstone Road,
Southall, Middx UB2 5AA T 020-8574 1902
E info@sikhmissionarysociety.org
W www.sikhmissionarysociety.org
Hon. General Secretary, Bahadur Singh

## ZOROASTRIANISM

Zoroastrians are followers of the Iranian prophet Spitaman Zarathushtra (or Zoroaster in its hellenised form) who lived c.1200–1500 BC. Zoroastrians were persecuted in Iran following the Arab invasion of Persia in the seventh century AD and a group (who are known as Parsis) migrated to India in the ninth century AD to avoid harassment and persecution. Zarathushtra's words are recorded in 17 hymns called the *Gathas,* which, together with other scriptures, form the *Avesta.*

Zoroastrianism teaches that there is one God, *Ahura Mazda* ('Wise Lord'), and that all creation stems ultimately from God; the Gathas teach that human beings have free will, are responsible for their own actions and can choose between good and evil. It is believed that choosing *Asha* (truth or righteousness), with the aid of *Vohu Manah* (good mind), leads to happiness for the individual and society, whereas choosing evil leads to unhappiness and conflict. The *Gathas* also encourage hard work, good deeds and charitable acts. Zoroastrians believe that after death the immortal soul is judged by God, and is then sent to paradise or hell, where it will stay until the end of time to be resurrected for the final judgment.

In Zoroastrian places of worship, an urn containing fire is the central feature; the fire symbolises purity, light and truth and is a visible symbol of the *Fravashi* or *Farohar* (spirit), the presence of Ahura Mazda in every human being. Zoroastrians respect nature and much importance is attached to cultivating land and protecting air, earth and water.

The Zoroastrian Trust Funds of Europe is the main body for Zoroastrians in the UK. Founded in 1861 as the Religious Funds of the Zoroastrians of Europe, it disseminates information on the Zoroastrian faith, provides a place of worship and maintains separate burial grounds for Zoroastrians. It also holds religious and social functions and provides assistance to Zoroastrians as considered necessary, including the provision of loans and grants to students of Zoroastrianism, and participates in inter-faith educational activities.

There are approximately 150,000 Zoroastrians worldwide, of which around 4,000 reside in England and Wales, mainly in London and the South East.

ZOROASTRIAN TRUST FUNDS OF EUROPE, Zoroastrian
Centre, 440 Alexandra Avenue, Harrow, Middx HA2 9TL
T 020-8866 0765 E secretary@ztfe.com W www.ztfe.com
President, Malcolm Deboo

# CHURCHES

There are two established (ie state) churches in the UK: the Church of England and the Church of Scotland. There are no established churches in Wales or Northern Ireland, though the Church in Wales, the Scottish Episcopal Church and the Church of Ireland are members of the Anglican Communion.

## CHURCH OF ENGLAND

The Church of England is divided into the two provinces of Canterbury and York, each under an archbishop. The two provinces are subdivided into 42 dioceses, the newest of which came into existence on 20 April 2014. The new diocese is known as West Yorkshire and the Dales – officially entitled the Diocese of Leeds – and was formed by the amalgamation of the former dioceses of Bradford, Ripon and Leeds and Wakefield.

Legislative provision for the Church of England is made by the General Synod, established in 1970. It also discusses and expresses opinion on any other matter of religious or public interest. The General Synod has 467 members in total, divided between three houses: the House of Bishops, the House of Clergy and the House of Laity. It is presided over jointly by the Archbishops of Canterbury and York and normally meets twice a year. The synod has the power, delegated by parliament, to frame statute law (known as a measure') on any matter concerning the Church of England. A measure must be laid before both houses of parliament, who may accept or reject it but cannot amend it. Once accepted the measure is submitted for royal assent and then has the full force of law. In addition to the General Synod, there are synods at diocesan level. The entire General Synod is re-elected once every five years. The tenth General Synod was inaugurated by the Queen on 23 November 2015.

The Archbishops' Council was established in January 1999. Its creation was the result of changes to the Church of England's national structure proposed in 1995 and subsequently approved by the synod and parliament. The council's purpose, set out in the National Institutions Measure 1998, is 'to coordinate, promote and further the work and mission of the Church of England'. It reports to the General Synod. The Archbishops' Council comprises the Archbishops of Canterbury and York, ex officio, the prolocutors elected by the convocations of Canterbury and York, the chair and vice-chair of the House of Laity, two bishops, two clergy and two lay persons elected by their respective houses of the General Synod, the Church Estates Commissioner, and up to six persons appointed jointly by the two archbishops.

There are also a number of national boards, councils and other bodies working on matters such as social responsibility, mission, Christian unity and education, which report to the General Synod through the Archbishops' Council.

**GENERAL SYNOD OF THE CHURCH OF ENGLAND/ ARCHBISHOPS' COUNCIL**, Church House, Great Smith Street, London SW1P 3NZ T 020-7898 1000
*Secretary-General*, William Fittall

### THE ORDINATION AND CONSECRATION OF WOMEN
The canon making it possible for women to be ordained to the priesthood was promulgated in the General Synod in February 1994 and the first 32 women priests were ordained on 12 March 1994.

On 14 July 2014 the General Synod approved the Bishops and Priests (Consecration and Ordination of Women) Measure which makes provision for the consecration of women as bishops and for the continuation of provision for the ordination of women. The Revd Elizabeth Lane was consecrated as the first female bishop on 26 January 2015 when she became Bishop Suffragan of Stockport in the diocese of Chester. The first female diocesan bishop, Rachel Treweek, was consecrated as the 41st Bishop of Gloucester on 22 July 2015.

### PORVOO DECLARATION
The Porvoo Declaration was approved by the General Synod of the Church of England in July 1995. Churches that approve the declaration regard baptised members of each other's churches as members of their own, and allow free interchange of episcopally ordained ministers within the rules of each church.

### MEMBERSHIP AND MINISTRY
In 2013, 132,990 people were baptised, 49,690 people were married in parish churches, the Church of England had an electoral roll membership of 1.2 million, and each week an average 1.01 million people attended services. As at December 2013 there were 15,799 churches and places of worship. As at December 2012* there were 358 senior clergy (including bishops, archdeacons and cathedral clergy); 7,195 full-time parochial stipendiary clergy; 245 full-time non-parochial stipendiary clergy; 3,148 self-supporting ministers; 1,520 chaplains and other ministers; 262 lay workers and Church Army evangelists; 6,623 licensed readers and 2,777 readers with permission to officiate and active emeriti; and approximately 5,700 active retired ordained clergy.

| | Full-time Equivalent Diocesan Clergy 2012* | | Electoral Roll Membership |
|---|---|---|---|
| | Male | Female | 2013 |
| Bath and Wells | 144 | 53 | 32,400 |
| Birmingham | 115 | 48 | 15,100 |
| Blackburn | 148 | 20 | 29,300 |
| †Bradford | 69 | 18 | 9,900 |
| Bristol | 86 | 19 | 14,300 |
| Canterbury | 105 | 27 | 18,900 |
| Carlisle | 98 | 26 | 19,400 |
| Chelmsford | 265 | 89 | 43,400 |
| Chester | 168 | 56 | 38,600 |
| Chichester | 253 | 22 | 48,400 |
| Coventry | 99 | 18 | 15,300 |
| Derby | 104 | 45 | 15,900 |
| Durham | 132 | 33 | 20,500 |
| Ely | 81 | 46 | 17,900 |
| Europe | 110 | 14 | 9,600 |
| Exeter | 168 | 38 | 28,400 |
| Gloucester | 93 | 32 | 22,200 |
| Guildford | 136 | 34 | 29,500 |
| Hereford | 57 | 33 | 15,600 |
| Leicester | 95 | 41 | 16,000 |
| Lichfield | 241 | 51 | 37,600 |
| Lincoln | 112 | 35 | 22,500 |
| Liverpool | 150 | 56 | 23,500 |
| London | 450 | 80 | 68,300 |
| Manchester | 158 | 66 | 29,200 |

| | Full-time Equivalent Diocesan Clergy 2012* | | Electoral Roll Membership |
|---|---|---|---|
| | Male | Female | 2013 |
| Newcastle | 88 | 28 | 15,200 |
| Norwich | 145 | 37 | 17,900 |
| Oxford | 293 | 98 | 51,900 |
| Peterborough | 100 | 37 | 18,500 |
| Portsmouth | 76 | 22 | 16,200 |
| †Ripon and Leeds | 81 | 40 | 15,000 |
| Rochester | 158 | 42 | 25,500 |
| St Albans | 168 | 71 | 32,500 |
| St Edmundsbury and Ipswich | 94 | 39 | 20,700 |
| Salisbury | 142 | 50 | 36,300 |
| Sheffield | 107 | 38 | 15,300 |
| Sodor and Man | 13 | 2 | 2,200 |
| Southwark | 264 | 82 | 46,700 |
| Southwell and Nottingham | 92 | 43 | 16,900 |
| Truro | 73 | 21 | 15,200 |
| †Wakefield | 100 | 35 | 16,100 |
| Winchester | 137 | 33 | 36,700 |
| Worcester | 86 | 27 | 15,500 |
| York | 163 | 36 | 29,100 |
| ‡*Total* | 6,017 | 1,781 | 1,085,600 |

\* 2013 figures for the ministry were not available from the Church of England at the time of going to press

† Now part of the new Diocese of Yorkshire and the Dales (also known as the Diocese of Leeds)

‡ Figures are rounded to the nearest 10 and may not add up as a result.

STIPENDS

| | 2015–16 |
|---|---|
| Archbishop of Canterbury | £77,810 |
| Archbishop of York | £66,680 |
| Bishop of London | £61,120* |
| Other diocesan bishops | £42,240* |
| Suffragan bishops | £34,460* |
| Assistant bishops (full-time) | £33,350* |
| Deans | £34,460* |
| Archdeacons | £33,670* |
| Residentiary canons | £26,660† |
| Incumbents and clergy of similar status | £24,690† |

\* For those appointed on or after 1 April 2004; transitional arrangements are in place for those appointed prior to this date

† National stipend benchmark: adjusted regionally to reflect variations in the cost of living

## CANTERBURY
### 105TH ARCHBISHOP AND PRIMATE OF ALL ENGLAND
Most Revd and Rt. Hon. Justin Welby, *cons.* 2011, *apptd* 2013; Lambeth Palace, London SE1 7JU
*Signs* Justin Cantuar:

BISHOPS SUFFRAGAN
\**Dover*, Rt. Revd Trevor Willmott, *cons.* 2002, *apptd* 2009; Upway, St Martin's Hill, Canterbury, Kent CT1 1PR
*Ebbsfleet*, Rt. Revd Jonathan Goodall, *cons.* 2013, *apptd* 2013; Hill House, Treetops, The Mount, Caversham, Reading RG4 7RE
*Richborough*, Rt. Revd Norman Banks, *cons.* 2011, *apptd* 2011; Parkside House, Abbey Mill Lane, St Albans AL3 4HE

\*Temporarily responsible for episcopal oversight of the Channel Islands as Assistant Bishop of Winchester

DEAN
Very Revd Robert Willis, *apptd* 2001

*Organist*, D. Flood, FRCO, *apptd* 1988

ARCHDEACONS
*Ashford*, Ven. Philip Down, *apptd* 2011
*Canterbury*, Ven. Sheila Watson, *apptd* 2007
*Maidstone*, Ven. Stephen Taylor, *apptd* 2011

*Vicar-General of Province and Diocese*, Chancellor Sheila Cameron, QC
*Commissary-General*, Morag Ellis, QC
*Joint Registrars of the Province*, Canon John Rees; Stephen Slack
*Diocesan Registrar and Legal Adviser*, Owen Carew Jones
*Diocesan Secretary*, Julian Hills, Diocesan House, Lady Wootton's Green, Canterbury CT1 1NQ T 01227-459401

## YORK
### 97TH ARCHBISHOP AND PRIMATE OF ENGLAND
Most Revd and Rt. Hon. Dr John Sentamu, *cons.* 1996, *trans.* 2005; Bishopthorpe, York YO23 2GE
*Signs* Sentamu Ebor:

BISHOPS SUFFRAGAN
*Hull*, Rt. Revd Alison White, *cons.* 2015, *apptd* 2015; Hullen House, Woodfield Lane, Hessle, Hull HU13 0ES
*Selby*, Rt. Revd John Thomson, *cons.* 2014, *apptd* 2014; 6 Pinfold Garth, Malton YO17 7XQ
*Whitby*, Rt. Revd Paul Fergson, *cons.* 2014, *apptd* 2014; 21 Thornton Road, Stainton TS8 9DS

PRINCIPAL EPISCOPAL VISITOR
*Beverley*, Rt. Revd Glyn Webster, *cons.* 2013, *apptd* 2013; Holy Trinity Rectory, Micklegate, York YO1 6LE

DEAN
Very Revd Vivienne Faull, *apptd* 2012

*Director of Music*, Robert Sharpe, *apptd* 2008

ARCHDEACONS
*Cleveland*, Ven. Samantha Rushton, *apptd* 2015
*East Riding*, Ven. Andy Broom, *apptd* 2014
*York*, Ven. Sarah Bullock, *apptd* 2013

*Chancellor of the Diocese*, His Hon. Judge Collier, QC, *apptd* 2006
*Registrar and Legal Secretary*, Caroline Mockford
*Diocesan Secretary*, Peter Warry, Diocesan House, Aviator Court, Clifton Moor, York YO30 4WJ T 01904-699500

## LONDON *(CANTERBURY)*
### 132ND BISHOP
Rt. Revd and Rt. Hon. Richard Chartres, KCVO, *cons.* 1992, *apptd* 1995; The Old Deanery, Dean's Court, London EC4V 5AA
*Signs* Richard Londin:

AREA BISHOPS
*Edmonton*, vacant
*Kensington*, vacant
*Stepney*, Rt. Revd Adrian Newman, *cons.* 2011, *apptd* 2011; 63 Coburn Road, London E3 2DB
*Willesden*, Rt. Revd Peter Broadbent, *cons.* 2001, *apptd* 2001; 173 Willesden Lane, London NW6 7YN

BISHOP SUFFRAGAN
*Fulham*, Rt. Revd Jonathan Baker, *cons.* 2011, *apptd* 2013; The Old Deanery, Dean's Court, London EC4V 5AA

DEAN OF ST PAUL'S
Very Revd Dr David Ison, PHD, *apptd* 2012; Parkside House, Abbey Mill Lane, St Albans AL3 4HE

*Director of Music*, Andrew Carwood, *apptd* 2007

ARCHDEACONS
*Charing Cross,* vacant
*Hackney,* vacant
*Hampstead,* Ven. Luke Miller, *apptd* 2010
*London,* vacant
*Middlesex,* Ven. Stephan Welch, *apptd* 2006
*Northolt,* Ven. Duncan Green, *apptd* 2013

*Chancellor,* Nigel Seed, QC, *apptd* 2002
*Registrar and Legal Secretary,* Paul Morris
*Diocesan Secretary,* Andrew Brookes, London
Diocesan House, 36 Causton Street, London SW1P 4AU
T 020-7932 1100

## DURHAM *(YORK)*
74TH BISHOP
Rt. Revd Paul Butler, *cons.* 2004, *trans.* 2013; Auckland Castle,
Bishop Auckland DL14 7NR
*Signs* Paul Dunelm:

BISHOP SUFFRAGAN
*Jarrow,* Rt. Revd Mark Bryant, *cons.* 2007, *apptd* 2007;
Bishop's House, 25 Ivy Lane, Low Fell, Gateshead NE9 6QD

DEAN
Very Revd Michael Sadgrove, *apptd* 2003

*Organist,* James Lancelot, FRCO, *apptd* 1985

ARCHDEACONS
*Auckland,* Ven. Nicholas Barker, *apptd* 2007
*Durham,* Ven. Ian Jagger, *apptd* 2006
*Sunderland,* Ven. Stuart Bain, *apptd* 2002

*Chancellor,* His Hon. Judge Bursell, QC, *apptd* 1989
*Registrar and Legal Secretary,* Hilary Monckton-Milnes
*Diocesan Secretary,* Andrew Thurston, Diocesan Office,
Auckland Castle, Bishop Auckland DL14 7QJ
T 01388-660010

## WINCHESTER *(CANTERBURY)*
97TH BISHOP
Rt. Revd Tim Dakin, cons. 2012, *apptd* 2011; Wolvesey,
Winchester SO23 9ND
*Signs* Tim Winton:

BISHOPS SUFFRAGAN
*Basingstoke,* Rt. Revd David Williams, *cons.* 2014,
*apptd* 2014; Bishop's Office, Old Alresford Place, Alresford,
Hants SO24 9DH
*Southampton,* Rt. Revd Jonathan Frost, *cons.* 2010,
*apptd* 2010; Bishop's House, St Mary's Church Close,
Wessex Lane, Southampton SO18 2ST

DEANS
*Dean of Winchester,* Very Revd James Atwell, *apptd* 2005
*Dean of Jersey (A Peculiar),* Very Revd Robert Key,
*apptd* 2005
*Dean of Guernsey (A Peculiar),* vacant
*Director of Music,* Andrew Lumsden, *apptd* 2002

ARCHDEACONS
*Bournemouth,* Ven. Dr Peter Rouch, *apptd* 2011
*Winchester,* Ven. Michael Harley, *apptd* 2009

*Chancellor,* His Hon. Judge Clark, QC, *apptd* 1993
*Acting Registrar and Legal Secretary,* Sue de Candole
*Chief Executive,* Andrew Robinson, Old Alresford Place,
Alresford, Hants SO24 9DH T 01962-737300

## BATH AND WELLS *(CANTERBURY)*
79TH BISHOP
Rt. Revd Peter Hancock, *cons.* 2010, *apptd* 2014; The Bishop's
Palace, Wells, Somerset BA5 2PD
*Signs* Peter Bath & Wells:

BISHOP SUFFRAGAN
*Taunton,* vacant

DEAN
Very Revd John Clarke, *apptd* 2004

*Organist,* Matthew Owens, *apptd* 2005

ARCHDEACONS
*Bath,* Ven. Andrew Piggott, *apptd* 2005
*Taunton,* Ven. John Reed, *apptd* 1999
*Wells,* Ven. Nicola Sullivan, *apptd* 2006

*Chancellor,* Timothy Briden, *apptd* 1993
*Registrar and Legal Secretary,* Roland Callaby
*Diocesan Secretary,* Nick May, The Old Deanery, St Andrew's
Street, Wells, Somerset BA5 2UG T 01749-670777

## BIRMINGHAM *(CANTERBURY)*
9TH BISHOP
Rt. Revd David Urquhart, *cons.* 2000, *apptd* 2006; Bishop's
Croft, Old Church Road, Harborne, Birmingham B17 0BG
*Signs* David Birmingham:

BISHOP SUFFRAGAN
*Aston,* vacant

DEAN
Very Revd Catherine Ogle, *apptd* 2010

*Director of Music,* Marcus Huxley, FRCO, *apptd* 1986

ARCHDEACONS
*Aston,* Ven. Simon Heathfield, *apptd* 2014
*Birmingham,* Ven. Hayward Osborne, *apptd* 2001

*Chancellor,* Mark Powell, QC, *apptd* 2012
*Registrar and Legal Secretary,* Hugh Carslake
*Diocesan Secretary,* Andrew Halstead, 1 Colmore Row,
Birmingham B3 2BJ T 0121-426 0400

## BLACKBURN *(YORK)*
9TH BISHOP
Rt. Revd Julian Henderson, *cons.* 2013, *apptd* 2013;
Bishop's House, Ribchester Road, Blackburn BB1 9EF
*Signs* Julian Blackburn

BISHOPS SUFFRAGAN
*Burnley,* Rt. Revd Philip North, *cons.* 2015, *apptd* 2015;
Dean House, 449 Padiham Road, Burnley BB12 6TE
*Lancaster,* Rt. Revd Geoffrey Pearson, *cons.* 2006,
*apptd* 2006; The Vicarage, Whinney Brow Lane, Shireshead,
Forton, Preston PR3 0AE

DEAN
Very Revd Christopher Armstrong, *apptd* 2001

*Organist and Director of Music,* Samuel Holden

ARCHDEACON
*Blackburn,* vacant
*Lancaster,* Ven. Michael Everitt, *apptd* 2011

*Chancellor,* His Hon. Judge Bullimore, *apptd* 1990
*Registrar and Legal Secretary,* Stephen Crossley

*Diocesan Secretary,* Graeme Pollard, Diocesan Office, Clayton House, Walker Office Park, Blackburn BB1 5AA
T 01254-503070

## BRISTOL *(CANTERBURY)*
55TH BISHOP
Rt. Revd Michael Hill, *cons.* 1998, *apptd* 2003;
58A High Street, Winterbourne, Bristol BS36 1JQ
*Signs* Michael Bristol

BISHOP SUFFRAGAN
*Swindon,* Rt. Revd Dr Lee Rayfield, *cons.* 2005, *apptd* 2005;
Mark House, Field Rise, Swindon, Wiltshire SN1 4HP

DEAN
Very Revd David Hoyle, *apptd* 2010

*Organist and Director of Music,* Mark Lee, *apptd* 1998

ARCHDEACONS
*Bristol,* vacant
*Malmesbury,* Ven. Christine Froude, *apptd* 2011

*Chancellor,* The Worshipful Revd Justin Gau
*Registrar and Legal Secretary,* Roland Callaby
*Diocesan Secretary,* Oliver Home, First Floor, Hillside House, 1500 Parkway North, Stoke Gifford, Bristol BS34 8YU
T 0117-9060100

## CARLISLE *(YORK)*
67TH BISHOP
Rt. Revd James Newcome, *cons.* 2002, *apptd* 2009;
Bishop's House, Ambleside Road, Keswick CA12 4DD
*Signs* James Carliol

BISHOP SUFFRAGAN
*Penrith,* Rt. Revd Robert Freeman, *cons.* 2011, *apptd* 2011;
Holm Croft, Castle Road, Kendal, Cumbria LA9 7AU

DEAN
Very Revd Mark Boyling, *apptd* 2004

*Organist,* Jeremy Suter, FRCO, *apptd* 1991

ARCHDEACONS
*Carlisle,* Ven. Kevin Roberts, *apptd* 2009
*West Cumberland,* Ven. Dr Richard Pratt, *apptd* 2009
*Westmorland and Furness,* Ven. Penny Driver, *apptd* 2012

*Chancellor,* Geoffrey Tattersall, QC, *apptd* 2003
*Registrar and Legal Secretary,* Jane Lowdon
*Diocesan Secretary,* Derek Hurton, Church House, West Walls, Carlisle CA3 8UE T 01228-522573

## CHELMSFORD *(CANTERBURY)*
10TH BISHOP
Rt. Revd Stephen Cottrell, *cons.* 2004, *apptd* 2010;
Bishopscourt, Main Road, Margaretting, Ingatestone, Essex CM4 0HD
*Signs* Stephen Chelmsford

BISHOPS SUFFRAGAN
*Barking,* Rt. Revd Peter Hill, *cons.* 2014, *apptd* 2014;
Barking Lodge, Verulam Avenue, London E17 8ES
*Bradwell,* Rt. Revd John Wraw, *cons.* 2012, *apptd* 2012;
Bishop's House, Orsett Road, Horndon-on-the-Hill, Stanford-le-Hope, Essex SS17 8NS
*Colchester,* Rt. Revd Roger Morris, *cons.* 2014, *apptd* 2014;
1 Fitzwater Road, Colchester, Essex CO3 3SS

DEAN
Very Revd Nicholas Henshall, *apptd* 2013

*Director of Music,* James Davy, *apptd* 2012

ARCHDEACONS
*Barking,* Ven. Dr John Perumbalath, *apptd* 2013
*Chelmsford,* Ven. David Lowman, *apptd* 2013
*Colchester,* Ven. Annette Cooper, *apptd* 2004
*Harlow,* Ven. Martin Webster, *apptd* 2009
*Southend,* Ven. Mina Smallman, *apptd* 2013
*Stansted,* Ven. Robin King, *apptd* 2013
*West Ham,* Ven. Elwin Cockett, *apptd* 2007

*Chancellor,* George Pulman, QC, *apptd* 2001
*Registrar and Legal Secretary,* Aiden Hargreaves-Smith
*Chief Executive,* John Ball, 53 New Street, Chelmsford, Essex CM1 1AT T 01245-294400

## CHESTER *(YORK)*
40TH BISHOP
Rt. Revd Peter Forster, PHD, *cons.* 1996, *apptd* 1996;
Bishop's House, Abbey Square, Chester CH1 2JD
*Signs* Peter Cestr:

BISHOPS SUFFRAGAN
*Birkenhead,* Rt. Revd Keith Sinclair, *cons.* 2007, *apptd* 2007;
Bishop's Lodge, 67 Bidston Road, Prenton CH43 6TR
*Stockport,* Rt. Revd Elizabeth Lane, *cons.* 2015, *apptd* 2015;
Bishop's Lodge, Back Lane, Dunham, Altrincham WA14 4SG

DEAN
Very Revd Dr Gordon McPhate, *apptd* 2002

*Organist and Director of Music,* Philip Rushforth, FRCO, *apptd* 2008

ARCHDEACONS
*Chester,* Ven. Dr Michael Gilbertson, *apptd* 2010
*Macclesfield,* Ven. Ian Bishop, *apptd* 2011

*Chancellor,* His Hon. Judge Turner, QC, *apptd* 1998
*Registrar and Legal Secretary,* Helen McFall
*Diocesan Secretary,* George Colville, Church House, 5500 Daresbury Park, Daresbury, Warrington WA4 4GE
T 01928-718834

## CHICHESTER *(CANTERBURY)*
103RD BISHOP
Rt. Revd Dr Martin Warner, *cons.* 2010, *apptd* 2012;
The Palace, Chichester PO19 1PY
*Signs* Martin Cicestr:

BISHOPS SUFFRAGAN
*Horsham,* Rt. Revd Mark Sowerby, *cons.* 2009, *apptd* 2009;
21 Guildford Road, Horsham, W. Sussex RH12 1LU
*Lewes,* Rt. Revd Richard Jackson, *cons.* 2014, *apptd* 2014;
c/o Church House, 211 New Church Road, Hove BN3 4ED

DEAN
Very Revd Stephen Waine, *apptd* 2015

*Organist,* Charles Harrison, *apptd* 2014

ARCHDEACONS
*Brighton and Lewes,* Ven. Martin Lloyd Williams, *apptd* 2015
*Chichester,* Ven. Douglas McKittrick, *apptd* 2002
*Horsham,* Ven. Fiona Windsor, *apptd* 2014
*Hastings,* Ven. Philip Jones, *apptd* 2005

*Chancellor,* Prof. Mark Hill, QC
*Registrar and Legal Secretary,* Matthew Chinery

*Diocesan Secretary,* Gabrielle Higgins, Diocesan Church House, 211 New Church Road, Hove, E. Sussex BN3 4ED T 01273-421021

## COVENTRY *(CANTERBURY)*
9TH BISHOP
Rt. Revd Dr Christopher Cocksworth, *cons.* 2008, *apptd* 2008; The Bishop's House, 23 Davenport Road, Coventry CV5 6PW
*Signs* Christopher Coventry

BISHOP SUFFRAGAN
*Warwick,* Rt. Revd John Stroyan, *cons.* 2005, *apptd* 2005; Warwick House, 139 Kenilworth Road, Coventry CV4 7AP

DEAN
Very Revd John Witcombe, *apptd* 2013

*Director of Music,* Mr Kerry Beaumont, *apptd* 2006

ARCHDEACONS
*Coventry,* Ven. John Green, CB, *apptd* 2013
*Warwick,* Ven. Morris Rodham, *apptd* 2010

*Chancellor,* Stephen Eyre, *apptd* 2009
*Registrar and Legal Secretary,* Mary Allanson
*Diocesan Secretary,* Simon Lloyd, Cathedral & Diocesan Offices, 1 Hilltop, Coventry CV1 5AB T 024-7652 1200

## DERBY *(CANTERBURY)*
7TH BISHOP
Rt. Revd Dr Alastair Redfern, *cons.* 1997, *apptd* 2005; The Bishop's House, 6 King Street, Duffield, Belper, Derbyshire DE56 4EU
*Signs* Alastair Derby

BISHOP SUFFRAGAN
*Repton,* vacant

DEAN
Very Revd Dr John Davies, *apptd* 2010

*Organist,* Hugh Morris, *apptd* 2015

ARCHDEACONS
*Chesterfield,* Ven. Christine Wilson, *apptd* 2010
*Derby,* Ven. Dr Christopher Cunliffe, *apptd* 2006

*Chancellor,* His Hon. Judge Bullimore, *apptd* 1981
*Registrar and Legal Secretary,* Mrs Nadine Waldron
*Diocesan Secretary,* Maureen Cole, Derby Church House, Full Street, Derby DE1 3DR T 01332-388650

## ELY *(CANTERBURY)*
69TH BISHOP
Rt. Revd Stephen Conway, *cons.* 2006, *apptd* 2011; The Bishop's House, Ely CB7 4DW
*Signs* Stephen Ely

BISHOP SUFFRAGAN
*Huntingdon,* Rt. Revd David Thomson, DPHIL, *cons.* 2008, *apptd* 2008; 14 Lynn Road, Ely, Cambs CB6 1DA

DEAN
Very Revd Mark Bonney, *apptd* 2012

*Director of Music,* Paul Trepte, FRCO, *apptd* 1991

ARCHDEACONS
*Cambridge,* Ven. Alex Hughes, *apptd* 2014
*Huntingdon and Wisbech,* Ven. Hugh McCurdy, *apptd* 2005

*Chancellor,* His Hon. Judge Leonard, QC
*Registrar,* Howard Dellar
*Diocesan Secretary,* Paul Evans, Bishop Woodford House, Barton Road, Ely, Cambs CB7 4DX T 01353-652702

## EXETER *(CANTERBURY)*
71ST BISHOP
Rt. Revd Robert Atwell, *cons.* 2008, *apptd* 2014; The Palace, Exeter EX1 1HY
*Signs* Robert Exon:

BISHOPS SUFFRAGAN
*Crediton,* Rt. Revd Dame Sarah Mullally, DBE, *cons.* 2015, *apptd* 2015; 32 The Avenue, Tiverton EX16 4HW
*Plymouth,* Rt. Revd Nick McKinnel, *cons.* 2012, *trans.* 2015; 108 Molesworth Road, Stoke, Plymouth PL3 4AQ

DEAN
Very Revd Jonathan Draper, *apptd* 2012

*Director of Music,* Andrew Millington, *apptd* 1999

ARCHDEACONS
*Barnstaple,* Ven. Mark Butchers, *apptd* 2015
*Exeter,* Ven. Christopher Futcher, *apptd* 2012
*Plymouth,* Ven. Ian Chandler, *apptd* 2010
*Totnes,* Ven. Douglas Dettmer, *apptd* 2015

*Chancellor,* Hon. Sir Andrew McFarlane
*Registrar and Legal Secretary,* M. Follett
*Diocesan Secretary,* Mark Beedell, The Old Deanery, The Cloisters, Exeter EX1 1HS T 01392-272686

## GIBRALTAR IN EUROPE *(CANTERBURY)*
4TH BISHOP
Rt. Revd Robert Innes, PHD, *cons.* 2014, *apptd* 2014; 47, rue Capitaine Crespel – boite 49, 1050 Brussels, Belgium

BISHOP SUFFRAGAN
*In Europe,* Rt. Revd David Hamid, *cons.* 2002, *apptd* 2002; 14 Tufton Street, London SW1P 3QZ

*Dean, Cathedral Church of the Holy Trinity, Gibraltar,* Very Revd Dr John Paddock

*Chancellor, Pro-Cathedral of St Paul, Valletta, Malta,* Canon Simon Godfrey
*Chancellor, Pro-Cathedral of the Holy Trinity, Brussels, Belgium,* Revd Dr Paul Vrolijk

ARCHDEACONS
*Eastern,* Ven. Patrick Curran
*North-West Europe,* Canon Meurig Williams *(acting)*
*France,* Ven. Ian Naylor
*Gibraltar,* Canon Geoffrey Johnston *(acting)*
*Italy,* Ven. Jonathan Boardman
*Germany and Northern Europe,* Ven. Peter Potter *(acting)*
*Switzerland,* Ven. Peter Potter

*Chancellor,* Prof. Mark Hill, QC
*Registrar and Legal Secretary,* Aiden Hargreaves-Smith
*Diocesan Secretary,* Adrian Mumford, 14 Tufton Street, London SW1P 3QZ T 020-7898 1155

## GLOUCESTER *(CANTERBURY)*
41ST BISHOP
Rt. Revd Rachel Treweek, *cons.* 2015, *apptd* 2015; 2 College Green, Gloucester GL1 2LR
*Signs* Rachel Gloucestr

BISHOP SUFFRAGAN
*Tewkesbury,* Rt. Revd Martyn Snow, *cons.* 2013, *apptd* 2013; 2 College Green, Gloucester GL1 2LR

DEAN
Very Revd Stephen Lake, *apptd* 2011

*Director of Music,* Adrian Partington, *apptd* 2007

ARCHDEACONS
*Cheltenham,* Ven. Robert Springett, *apptd* 2010
*Gloucester,* Ven. Jackie Searle, *apptd* 2012

*Chancellor and Vicar-General,* June Rodgers, *apptd* 1990
*Registrar and Legal Secretary,* Jos Moule
*Diocesan Secretary,* Ben Preece Smith, Church House,
  College Green, Gloucester GL1 2LY T 01452-410022

## GUILDFORD *(CANTERBURY)*
10TH BISHOP
Rt. Revd Andrew Watson, *cons.* 2008, *apptd* 2014;
  Willow Grange, Woking Road, Guildford, Surrey GU4 7QS
  *Signs* Andrew Guildford

BISHOP SUFFRAGAN
*Dorking,* vacant

DEAN
Very Revd Dianna Gwilliams, *apptd* 2013

*Organist,* Katherine Dienes-Williams, *apptd* 2007

ARCHDEACONS
*Dorking,* Ven. Paul Bryer, *apptd* 2014
*Surrey,* Ven. Stuart Beake, *apptd* 2005

*Chancellor,* Andrew Jordan
*Registrars and Legal Secretaries,* Lee Coley; Howard
  Dellar
*Diocesan Secretary,* vacant, Diocesan House, Quarry Street,
  Guildford GU1 3XG T 01483-790300

## HEREFORD *(CANTERBURY)*
105TH BISHOP
Rt. Revd Richard Frith, cons. 1998, apptd 2014;
  Bishop's House, The Palace, Hereford HR4 9BN
  *Signs* Richard Hereford

BISHOP SUFFRAGAN
*Ludlow,* Rt. Revd Alistair Magowan, *cons.* 2009, *apptd* 2009;
  Bishop's House, Corvedale Road, Craven Arms,
  Shropshire SY7 9BT

DEAN
Very Revd Michael Tavinor, *apptd* 2002

*Organist and Director of Music,* Geraint Bowen, FRCO,
  *apptd* 2001

ARCHDEACONS
*Hereford,* Ven. Paddy Benson, *apptd* 2011
*Ludlow,* Rt. Revd Alistair Magowan, *apptd* 2009

*Chancellor,* His Hon. Judge Kaye, QC
*Registrar and Legal Secretary,* Howard Dellar
*Diocesan Secretary,* John Clark, The Palace, Hereford HR4 9BL
  T 01432-373300

## LEICESTER *(CANTERBURY)*
7TH BISHOP
vacant

ASSISTANT BISHOP
Rt. Revd Christopher Boyle, *cons.* 2000, *apptd* 2009;
  St Martins House, 7 Peacock Lane, Leicester LE1 5PZ

DEAN
Very Revd David Monteith, *apptd* 2013

*Director of Music,* Dr Christopher Johns

ARCHDEACONS
*Leicester,* Ven. Timothy Stratford, *apptd* 2012
*Loughborough,* Ven. David Newman, *apptd* 2009

*Chancellor,* Mark Blackett-Ord
*Registrar and Legal Secretary,* Revd Trevor Kirkman
*Diocesan Secretary,* Carol Gibbons, St Martin's House,
  7 Peacock Lane, Leicester LE1 5PZ T 0116-261 5200

## LICHFIELD *(CANTERBURY)*
99TH BISHOP
vacant

BISHOPS SUFFRAGAN
*Shrewsbury,* Rt. Revd Mark Rylands, *cons.* 2009,
  *apptd* 2009; Athlone House, 66 London Road,
  Shrewsbury SY2 6PG
*Stafford,* Rt. Revd Geoffrey Annas, *cons.* 2010, *apptd* 2010;
  Ash Garth, Broughton Crescent, Barlaston, Stoke-on-Trent
  ST12 9DD
*Wolverhampton,* Rt. Revd Clive Gregory, *cons.* 2007,
  *apptd* 2007; 61 Richmond Road, Wolverhampton WV3 9JH

DEAN
Very Revd Adrian Dorber, *apptd* 2005

*Directors of Music,* Ben and Cathy Lamb, *apptd* 2010
*Organist,* Martyn Rawles, *apptd* 2010

ARCHDEACONS
*Lichfield,* Ven. Simon Baker, *apptd* 2013
*Salop,* Ven. Paul Thomas, *apptd* 2011
*Stoke-on-Trent,* Ven. Matthew Parker, *apptd* 2013
*Walsall,* Ven. Dr Susan Weller, *apptd* 2015

*Chancellor,* His Hon. Judge Stephen Eyre, QC, *apptd* 2012
*Registrar and Legal Secretary,* N. Blackie
*Diocesan Secretary,* Julie Jones, St Mary's House, The Close,
  Lichfield, Staffs WS13 7LD T 01543-306030

## LINCOLN *(CANTERBURY)*
72ND BISHOP
Rt. Revd Christopher Lowson, *cons.* 2011, *apptd* 2011;
  Bishop's Office, The Old Palace, Minster Yard, Lincoln LN2 1PU
  *Signs* Christopher Lincoln

BISHOPS SUFFRAGAN
*Grantham,* vacant
*Grimsby,* Rt. Revd Dr David Court, *cons.* 2014, *apptd* 2014;
  The Old Palace, Minster Yard, Lincoln LN2 1PU

DEAN
Very Revd Philip Buckler, *apptd* 2007

*Director of Music,* Aric Prentice, *apptd* 2003

ARCHDEACONS
*Boston,* Ven. Dr Justine Allain Chapman, *apptd* 2013
*Lincoln,* Ven. Timothy Barker, *apptd* 2009
*Stow and Lindsey,* vacant

*Chancellor,* His Hon. Judge Bishop
*Registrar and Legal Secretary,* Julie Robinson
*Diocesan Secretary,* Angela Sibson, OBE, Edward King House,
  Minster Yard, Lincoln LN2 1PU T 01522-504050

**LIVERPOOL** *(YORK)*
8TH BISHOP
Rt. Revd Paul Bayes, *cons.* 2010, *apptd* 2014; Bishop's Lodge, Woolton Park, Liverpool L25 6DT
*Signs* Paul Liverpool

BISHOP SUFFRAGAN
*Warrington,* Rt. Revd Richard Blackburn, *cons.* 2009, *apptd* 2009; 34 Central Avenue, Eccleston Park, Liverpool L34 2QP

DEAN
Very Revd Pete Wilcox, *apptd* 2012

*Director of Music,* David Poulter, *apptd* 2008

ARCHDEACONS
*Liverpool,* Ven. Richard Panter, *apptd* 2002
*Warrington,* vacant

*Chancellor,* Hon. Sir Mark Hedley
*Registrar and Legal Secretary,* Howard Dellar
*Diocesan Secretary,* Mike Eastwood, St James House, 20 St James Street, Liverpool L1 7BY **T** 0151-709 9722

**MANCHESTER** *(YORK)*
12TH BISHOP
Rt. Revd Dr David Walker, *cons.* 2000, *apptd* 2013; Bishopscourt, Bury New Road, Salford M7 4LE
*Signs* David Manchester

BISHOPS SUFFRAGAN
*Bolton,* Rt. Revd Christopher Edmondson, *cons.* 2008, *apptd* 2008; Bishop's Lodge, Walkden Road, Worsley, Manchester M28 2WH
*Middleton,* Rt. Revd Mark Davies, *cons.* 2008, *apptd* 2008; The Hollies, Manchester Road, Rochdale OL11 3QY

DEAN
Very Revd Rogers Govender, *apptd* 2006

*Organist,* Christopher Stokes, *apptd* 1992

ARCHDEACONS
*Bolton,* Ven. David Bailey, *apptd* 2008
*Manchester,* Ven. Mark Ashcroft, *apptd* 2009
*Rochdale,* Ven. Cherry Vann, *apptd* 2008
*Salford,* Ven. David Sharples, *apptd* 2009

*Chancellor,* Geoffrey Tattersall, QC
*Registrar and Legal Secretary,* Jane Monks
*Diocesan Secretary,* Martin Miller, Diocesan Church House, 90 Deansgate, Manchester M3 2GH **T** 0161-828 1400

**NEWCASTLE** *(YORK)*
12TH BISHOP
Rt. Revd Christine Elizabeth Hardman, *cons.* 2015, *apptd* 2015
*Signs* Christine Newcastle

ASSISTANT BISHOP
Rt. Revd Frank White, *cons.* 2002, *apptd* 2010

DEAN
Very Revd Christopher C. Dalliston, *apptd* 2003

*Director of Music,* Michael Stoddart, *apptd* 2009

ARCHDEACONS
*Lindisfarne,* Ven. Dr Peter Robinson, *apptd* 2008
*Northumberland,* Ven. Geoffrey Miller, *apptd* 2004

*Chancellor,* Euan Duff, *apptd* 2013
*Registrar and Legal Secretary,* Jane Lowdon
*Diocesan Secretary,* Shane Waddle, Church House, St John's Terrace, North Shields NE29 6HS **T** 0191-270 4100

**NORWICH** *(CANTERBURY)*
71ST BISHOP
Rt. Revd Graham R. James, *cons.* 1993, *apptd* 2000; Bishop's House, Norwich NR3 1SB
*Signs* Graham Norvic:

BISHOPS SUFFRAGAN
*Lynn,* Rt. Revd Jonathan Meyrick, *cons.* 2011, *apptd* 2011; The Old Vicarage, Castle Acre, King's Lynn PE32 2AA
*Thetford,* Rt. Revd Alan Winton, PHD, *cons.* 2009, *apptd* 2009; The Red House, 53 Norwich Road, Stoke Holy Cross, Norwich NR14 8AB

DEAN
Very Revd Jane Hedges, *apptd* 2014

*Master of Music,* Ashley Grote, *apptd* 2012

ARCHDEACONS
*Lynn,* Ven. John Ashe, *apptd* 2009
*Norfolk,* Ven. Steven Betts, *apptd* 2012
*Norwich,* Ven. Jan McFarlane, *apptd* 2008

*Chancellor,* Ruth Arlow, *apptd* 2012
*Registrar and Legal Secretary,* Stuart Jones
*Diocesan Secretary,* Richard Butler, Diocesan House, 109 Dereham Road, Easton, Norwich, Norfolk NR9 5ES **T** 01603-880853

**OXFORD** *(CANTERBURY)*
43RD BISHOP
vacant

AREA BISHOPS
*Buckingham,* Rt. Revd Dr Alan Wilson, *cons.* 2003, *apptd* 2003; Sheridan, Grimms Hill, Great Missenden, Bucks HP16 9BD
*Dorchester,* Rt. Revd Colin Fletcher, *cons.* 2000, *apptd* 2000; Arran House, Sandy Lane, Yarnton, Oxon OX5 1PB
*Reading,* Rt. Revd Andrew Proud, *cons.* 2011, *apptd* 2011; Bishop's House, Tidmarsh Lane, Tidmarsh, Reading RG8 8HA

DEAN OF CHRIST CHURCH
Very Revd Martyn Percy, PHD, *apptd* 2014

*Organist,* Dr Stephen Darlington, FRCO, *apptd* 1985

ARCHDEACONS
*Berkshire,* Ven. Olivia Graham, *apptd* 2013
*Buckingham,* Ven. Karen Gorham, *apptd* 2007
*Oxford,* Ven. Martin Gorick, *apptd* 2013

*Chancellor,* Revd Alex McGregor, *apptd* 2013
*Registrar and Legal Secretary,* Revd Canon John Rees
*Diocesan Secretary,* Rosemary Pearce, Diocesan Church House, North Hinksey, Oxford OX2 0NB **T** 01865-208202

**PETERBOROUGH** *(CANTERBURY)*
38TH BISHOP
Rt. Revd Donald Allister, *cons.* 2010, *apptd* 2009; Bishop's Lodging, The Palace, Peterborough PE1 1YA
*Signs* Donald Petriburg:

BISHOP SUFFRAGAN
*Brixworth,* Rt. Revd John Holbrook, *cons.* 2011, *apptd* 2011; Orchard Acre, 11 North Street, Mears Ashby, Northants NN6 0DW

DEAN
Very Revd Charles Taylor, *apptd* 2007

*Director of Music,* Stephen Grahl, *apptd* 2014

ARCHDEACONS
*Northampton,* Ven. Richard Ormston, *apptd* 2014
*Oakham,* Ven. Gordon Steele, *apptd* 2012

*Chancellor,* David Pittaway, QC, *apptd* 2005
*Registrar and Legal Secretary,* Anna Spriggs
*Diocesan Secretary,* Andrew Roberts, Diocesan Office,
The Palace, Peterborough PE1 1YB **T** 01733-887000

## PORTSMOUTH *(CANTERBURY)*
9TH BISHOP
Rt. Revd Christopher Foster, *cons.* 2010, *apptd* 2010;
Bishopsgrove, 26 Osborn Road, Fareham, Hants PO16 7DQ
*Signs* Christopher Portsmouth

DEAN
Very Revd David Brindley, *apptd* 2002

*Organist,* David Price, *apptd* 1996

ARCHDEACONS
*Isle of Wight,* Ven. Peter Sutton, *apptd* 2012
*Portsdown,* Ven. Joanne Grenfell, *apptd* 2013
*The Meon,* Ven. Gavin Collins, *apptd* 2011

*Chancellor,* His Hon. Judge Waller, CBE
*Registrar and Legal Secretary,* Hilary Tyler
*Diocesan Secretary,* Wendy Kennedy, Diocesan Offices, 1st Floor,
Peninsular House, Wharf Road, Portsmouth PO2 8HB
**T** 023-9289 9664

## ROCHESTER *(CANTERBURY)*
107TH BISHOP
Rt. Revd James Langstaff, *cons.* 2004, *apptd* 2010;
Bishopscourt, 24 St Margaret's Street, Rochester ME1 1TS
*Signs,* James Roffen:

BISHOP SUFFRAGAN
*Tonbridge,* Rt. Revd Dr Brian Castle, *cons.* 2002, *apptd* 2002;
Bishop's Lodge, 48 St Botolph's Road, Sevenoaks TN13 3AG

DEAN
vacant

*Director of Music,* Scott Farrell, *apptd* 2008

ARCHDEACONS
*Bromley & Bexley,* Ven. Dr Paul Wright, *apptd* 2003
*Rochester,* Ven. Simon Burton-Jones, *apptd* 2010
*Tonbridge,* Ven. Clive Mansell, *apptd* 2002

*Chancellor,* The Worshipful John Gallagher
*Registrar and Legal Secretary,* Owen Carew-Jones
*Diocesan Secretary,* Geoff Marsh, St Nicholas Church, Boley Hill,
Rochester ME1 1SL **T** 01634-560000

## ST ALBANS *(CANTERBURY)*
10TH BISHOP
Rt. Revd Dr Alan Smith, *cons.* 2001, *apptd* 2009, *trans.*
2009; Abbey Gate House, St Albans AL3 4HD
*Signs* Alan St Albans

BISHOPS SUFFRAGAN
*Bedford,* Rt. Revd Richard Atkinson, OBE, *cons.* 2012,
*apptd* 2012; Bishop's Lodge, Bedford Road, Cardington,
Bedford MK44 3SS

*Hertford,* Rt. Revd Michael Beasley, *cons.* 2015, *apptd* 2015;
Bishopswood, 3 Stobarts Close, Knebworth SG3 6ND

DEAN
Very Revd Dr Jeffrey John, *apptd* 2004

*Organist,* Andrew Lucas, *apptd* 1998

ARCHDEACONS
*Bedford,* Ven. Paul Hughes, *apptd* 2004
*Hertford,* Ven. Dr Trevor Jones, *apptd* 1997
*St Albans,* Ven. Jonathan Smith, *apptd* 2008

*Chancellor,* Roger Kaye, *apptd* 2002
*Registrar and Legal Secretary,* Lee Coley
*Diocesan Secretary,* Susan Pope, Holywell Lodge, 41 Holywell Hill,
St Albans AL1 1HE **T** 01727-854532

## ST EDMUNDSBURY AND IPSWICH *(CANTERBURY)*
11TH BISHOP
Rt. Revd Martin Seeley, *cons.* 2015, *apptd* 2015;
The Bishop's House, 4 Park Road, Ipswich IP1 3ST
*Signs* Martin St Edmundsbury and Ipswich

BISHOP SUFFRAGAN
*Dunwich,* vacant

DEAN
Very Revd Frances Ward, *apptd* 2010

*Director of Music,* James Thomas, *apptd* 1997

ARCHDEACONS
*Sudbury,* Ven. Dr David Jenkins, *apptd* 2010
*Suffolk,* Ven. Ian Morgan, *apptd* 2012

*Chancellor,* David Etherington, QC
*Registrar and Legal Secretary,* James Hall
*Diocesan Secretary,* Nicholas Edgell, Diocesan Office,
St Nicholas Centre, 4 Cutler Street, Ipswich IP1 1UQ
**T** 01473-298500

## SALISBURY *(CANTERBURY)*
78TH BISHOP
Rt. Revd Nicholas Holtam, *cons.* 2011, *apptd* 2011;
South Canonry, 71 The Close, Salisbury SP1 2ER
*Signs* Nicholas Sarum

BISHOPS SUFFRAGAN
*Ramsbury,* Rt. Revd Edward Condry, DPHIL, *cons.* 2012,
*apptd* 2012; Bishop's Office, Southbroom House,
London Road, Devizes SN10 1LT
*Sherborne,* vacant

DEAN
Very Revd June Osborne, *apptd* 2004

*Organist,* David Halls, *apptd* 2005

ARCHDEACONS
*Dorset,* Ven. Antony Macrow-Wood, *apptd* 2015
*Sarum,* Ven. Alan Jeans, *apptd* 2003
*Sherborne,* Ven. Paul Taylor, *apptd* 2004
*Wilts,* Ven. Ruth Worsley, *apptd* 2012

*Chancellor,* His Hon. Judge Wiggs, *apptd* 1997
*Acting Registrar and Legal Secretary,* Sue de Candole
*Diocesan Secretary,* Lucinda Herklots, Church House,
Crane Street, Salisbury SP1 2QB **T** 01722-411922

**SHEFFIELD** *(YORK)*
7TH BISHOP
Rt. Revd Steven Croft, PHD, *cons.* 2009, *apptd* 2008;
Bishopscroft, Snaithing Lane, Sheffield S10 3LG
*Signs* Steven Sheffield

BISHOP SUFFRAGAN
*Doncaster,* Rt. Revd Peter Burrows, *cons.* 2012, *apptd* 2011;
Doncaster House, Church Lane, Fishlake, Doncaster DN7 5JW

DEAN
Very Revd Peter Bradley, *apptd* 2003

*Master of Music,* Neil Taylor, *apptd* 1997

ARCHDEACONS
*Doncaster,* Ven. Steve Wilcockson, *apptd* 2012
*Sheffield and Rotherham,* Ven. Malcolm Chamberlain,
*apptd* 2013
*Chancellor,* Her Hon. Judge Sarah Singleton, QC, *apptd* 2014
*Registrar and Legal Secretary,* Andrew Vidler
*Diocesan Secretary,* Malcolm Fair, Church House,
95–99 Effingham Street, Rotherham S65 1BL T 01709-309100

**SODOR AND MAN** *(YORK)*
81ST BISHOP
Rt. Revd Robert Paterson, *cons.* 2008, *apptd* 2008;
Thie yn Aspick, 4 The Falls, Douglas, Isle of Man IM4 4PZ
*Signs* Robert Sodor as Mannin

ARCHDEACON OF MAN
Ven. Andrew Brown, *apptd* 2011

*Vicar-General and Chancellor,* Geoffrey Tattersall, QC
*Registrar,* Lionel Lennox
*Diocesan Secretary,* Andrew Swithinbank, Thie yn Aspick,
4 The Falls, Douglas, Isle of Man IM4 4PZ T 07624-314590

**SOUTHWARK** *(CANTERBURY)*
10TH BISHOP
Rt. Revd Christopher Chessun, *cons.* 2005, *apptd* 2011;
Trinity House, 4 Chapel Court, Borough High Street,
London SE1 1HW
*Signs* Christopher Southwark

AREA BISHOPS
*Croydon,* Rt. Revd Jonathan Clark, *cons.* 2012, *apptd* 2012;
St Matthew's House, 100 George Street, London CR0 1PE
*Kingston upon Thames,* Rt. Revd Dr Richard Cheetham,
*cons.* 2002, *apptd* 2002; 620 Kingston Road, Raynes Park,
London SW20 8DN
*Woolwich,* Rt. Revd Dr Michael Ipgrave, OBE, *cons.* 2012,
*apptd* 2012; Trinity House, 4 Chapel Court, Borough High
Street, London SE1 1HW

DEAN
Very Revd Andrew Nunn, *apptd* 2011

*Organist,* Peter Wright, FRCO, *apptd* 1989

ARCHDEACONS
*Croydon,* Ven. Christopher Skilton, *apptd* 2013
*Lambeth,* Ven. Simon Gates, *apptd* 2013
*Lewisham & Greenwich,* Ven. Alastair Cutting, *apptd* 2013
*Reigate,* Ven. Daniel Kajumba, *apptd* 2001
*Southwark,* Ven. Dr Jane Steen, *apptd* 2013
*Wandsworth,* vacant

*Chancellor,* Philip Petchey
*Registrar and Legal Secretary,* Paul Morris

*Diocesan Secretary,* Ruth Martin, Trinity House, 4 Chapel Court,
Borough High Street, London SE1 1HW T 020-7939 9400

**SOUTHWELL AND NOTTINGHAM** *(YORK)*
12TH BISHOP
Rt. Revd Paul Williams, *cons.* 2009, *trans.* 2015;
Bishop's Manor, Southwell, Nottinghamshire NG25 0JR
*Signs* Paul Southwell and Nottingham

BISHOP SUFFRAGAN
*Sherwood,* Rt. Revd Anthony Porter, *cons.* 2006, *apptd* 2006;
Jubilee House, Westgate, Southwell NG25 0JH

DEAN
vacant

*Organist,* Paul Hale, *apptd* 1989

ARCHDEACONS
*Newark,* Ven. David Picken, *apptd* 2012
*Nottingham,* Ven. Sarah Clark, *apptd* 2014

*Chancellor,* Linda Box, *apptd* 2005
*Registrar and Legal Secretary,* Amanda Redgate
*Chief Executive,* Nigel Spraggins, Jubilee House, Westgate,
Southwell, Notts NG25 0JH T 01636-814331

**TRURO** *(CANTERBURY)*
15TH BISHOP
Rt. Revd Tim Thornton, *cons.* 2001, *apptd* 2008; Lis Escop,
Truro TR3 6QQ
*Signs* Tim Truro

BISHOP SUFFRAGAN
*St Germans,* Rt. Revd Christopher Goldsmith, DPHIL,
*cons.* 2013, *apptd* 2013; Vounder, Tresillian, Truro TR2 4BW

DEAN
Very Revd Roger Bush, *apptd* 2012

*Organist and Director of Music,* Chris Gray, *apptd* 2008

ARCHDEACONS
*Bodmin,* Ven. Audrey Elkington, *apptd* 2011
*Cornwall,* Ven. Bill Stuart-White, *apptd* 2012

*Chancellor,* Timothy Briden, *apptd* 1998
*Registrar and Legal Secretary,* Martin Follett
*Diocesan Secretary,* Esther Pollard, Church House, Woodlands
Court, Truro Business Park, Threemilestone, Truro TR4 9NH
T 01872-274351

**WEST YORKSHIRE AND THE DALES***
*(YORK)*
1ST BISHOP OF LEEDS*
Rt. Revd Nicholas Baines, *cons.* 2003, *apptd* 2014;
Hollin House, Weetwood Avenue, Leeds LS16 5NG
*Signs* Nicholas Leeds

AREA BISHOPS
*Bradford,* Rt. Revd Toby Howarth, *cons.* 2014, *apptd* 2014;
c/o Bradford Cathedral, 1 Stott Hill, Bradford BD1 4EH
*Huddersfield,* Rt. Revd Jonathan Gibbs, *cons.* 2014,
*apptd* 2014; 2 Bullace Trees Lane, Roberttown WF15 7PF
*Ripon,* Rt. Revd James Bell, *cons.* 2004, *apptd* 2014;
Thistledown, Main Street, Exelby, Bedale DL8 2HD
*Wakefield,* Rt. Revd Anthony Robinson, *cons.* 2002,
*apptd* 2014; Pontefract House 181A Manygates Lane,
Sandal, Wakefield WF2 7DR

SUFFRAGAN BISHOP
*Richmond,* Rt. Revd Paul Slater, *cons.* 2015, *apptd* 2015

DEANS
*Bradford,* Very Revd Jerry Lepine, *apptd* 2013
*Ripon,* Very Revd John Dobson, *apptd* 2014
*Wakefield,* Very Revd Jonathan Greener, *apptd* 2007

*Directors of Music,* Andrew Bryden (Ripon), *apptd* 2003; Thomas Moore (Wakefield), *apptd* 2010; Alexander Woodrow (Bradford), *apptd* 2012

ARCHDEACONS
*Bradford,* Ven. Dr David Lee, *apptd* 2004
*Halifax,* Ven. Dr Anne Dawtry, *apptd* 2011
*Leeds,* Ven. Paul Hooper, *apptd* 2012
*Richmond,* vacant
*Pontefract,* Ven. Peter Townley, *apptd* 2008

*Chancellor,* Prof. Mark Hill, QC
*Registrars and Legal Secretaries,* Peter Foskett
*Diocesan Secretaries,* Debbie Child; Ashley Ellis
*Bradfield Office,* Kadugli House, Elmsley St, Steeton, Keighly, W. Yorks BD20 6SE **T** 01535-650555
*Leeds Office,* St Mary's Street, Leeds LS9 7DP **T** 0113-2000540
*Wakefield Office,* Church House, 1 South Parade, Wakefield WF1 1LP **T** 01924-371802

\* The official name of the diocese is The Diocese of Leeds

## WORCESTER *(CANTERBURY)*
113TH BISHOP
Rt. Revd Dr John Inge, *cons.* 2003, *apptd* 2007; The Bishop's Office, The Old Palace, Deansway, Worcester WR1 2JE
*Signs* John Wigorn

SUFFRAGAN BISHOP
*Dudley,* Rt. Revd Graham Usher, *cons.* 2014, *apptd* 2014; Bishop's House, 60 Bishop's Walk, Cradley Heath, West Midlands B64 7RH

DEAN
Very Revd Peter Atkinson, *apptd* 2006

*Organist,* Dr Peter Nardone, *apptd* 2012

ARCHDEACONS
*Dudley,* Ven. Nikki Groarke, *apptd* 2014
*Worcester,* Ven. Robert Jones, *apptd* 2014

*Chancellor,* Charles Mynors, *apptd* 1999
*Registrar and Legal Secretary,* Michael Huskinson
*Diocesan Secretary,* Robert Higham, The Old Palace, Deansway, Worcester WR1 2JE **T** 01905-20537

## ROYAL PECULIARS
WESTMINSTER
*The Collegiate Church of St Peter*
*Dean,* Very Revd Dr John Hall
*Canon Steward,* Revd Canon Jane Sinclair
*Chapter Clerk, Receiver-General and Registrar,* Sir Stephen Lamport, KCVO, Chapter Office, 20 Dean's Yard, London SW1P 3PA
*Organist,* James O'Donnell, *apptd* 1999
*Legal Secretary,* Christopher Vyse, *apptd* 2000

WINDSOR
*The Queen's Free Chapel of St George within Her Castle of Windsor*
*Dean,* Rt. Revd David Conner, KCVO, *apptd* 1998
*Chapter Clerk,* Charlotte Manley, LVO, OBE, *apptd* 2003; Chapter Office, The Cloisters, Windsor Castle, Windsor, Berks SL4 1NJ
*Director of Music,* James Vivian, *apptd* 2013

# OTHER ANGLICAN CHURCHES

## THE CHURCH IN WALES
The Anglican Church was the established church in Wales from the 16th century until 1920, when the estrangement of the majority of Welsh people from Anglicanism resulted in disestablishment. Since then the Church in Wales has been an autonomous province consisting of six sees. The bishops are elected by an electoral college comprising elected lay and clerical members, who also elect one of the diocesan bishops as Archbishop of Wales.

The legislative body of the Church in Wales is the Governing Body, which has 144 members divided between the three orders of bishops, clergy and laity. Its president is the Archbishop of Wales and it meets twice annually. Its decisions are binding upon all members of the church. The church's property and finances are the responsibility of the Representative Body. There are 53,262 members of the Church in Wales, with 443 stipendiary clergy and 836 parishes.

THE REPRESENTATIVE BODY OF THE CHURCH IN WALES, 39 Cathedral Road, Cardiff CF11 9XF

**T** 029-2034 8200 *Secretary,* John Shirley

12TH ARCHBISHOP OF WALES, Most Revd Dr Barry Morgan (Bishop of Llandaff), *elected* 2003
*Signs* Barry Cambrensis

BISHOPS
*Bangor* (81st), Rt. Revd Andrew John, *b.* 1964, *cons.* 2008, *elected* 2008; Ty'r Esgob, Bangor, Gwynedd LL57 2SS
*Signs* Andrew Bangor. *Stipendiary clergy,* 49
*Llandaff* (102nd), Most Revd Dr Barry Morgan (*also* Archbishop of Wales), *b.* 1947, *cons.* 1993, *trans.* 1999; Llys Esgob, The Cathedral Green, Llandaff, Cardiff CF5 2YE
*Signs* Barry Cambrensis. *Stipendiary clergy,* 111
*Monmouth* (10th), Rt. Revd Richard Pain, *b.* 1956, *cons.* 2013, *elected* 2013; Bishopstow, Stow Hill, Newport NP20 4EA *Signs* Richard Monmouth.
*Stipendiary clergy,* 87
*St Asaph* (76th), Rt. Revd Gregory Cameron, *b.* 1959, *cons.* 2009, *elected* 2009; Esgobty, Upper Denbigh Road, St Asaph, Denbighshire LL17 0TW *Signs* Gregory Llanelwy.
*Stipendiary clergy,* 100
*St David's* (128th), Rt. Revd (John) Wyn Evans, *b.* 1946, *cons.* 2008, *elected* 2008; Llys Esgob, Abergwili, Carmarthen SA31 2JG *Signs* Wyn St Davids.
*Stipendiary clergy,* 98
*Swansea and Brecon* (9th), Rt. Revd John Davies, *b.* 1953, *cons.* 2008, *elected* 2008; Ely Tower, Castle Square, Brecon, Powys LD3 9DJ
*Signs* John Swansea & Brecon. *Stipendiary clergy,* 65

The stipend for a diocesan bishop of the Church in Wales is £42,587 a year for 2015–16.

## SCOTTISH EPISCOPAL CHURCH
The Scottish Episcopal Church was founded after the Act of Settlement (1690) established the presbyterian nature of the Church of Scotland. The Scottish Episcopal Church is a member of the worldwide Anglican Communion. The governing authority is the General Synod, which consists of the Church's seven bishops, the conveners of the provincial Standing Committee, the conveners of the boards, the Church's representatives on the Anglican Consultative Council and 124 elected members (62 from the clergy and 62 from the laity). The General Synod meets once a year. The bishop who convenes and presides at meetings of the General Synod is called the 'primus' and is elected by his fellow bishops.

There are 32,634 members of the Scottish Episcopal Church, seven bishops, around 500 serving clergy and 300 churches and places of worship.

**THE GENERAL SYNOD OF THE SCOTTISH EPISCOPAL CHURCH**, 21 Grosvenor Crescent, Edinburgh EH12 5EE **T** 0131-225 6357 **W** www.scotland.anglican.org
*Secretary-General*, John Stuart

**PRIMUS OF THE SCOTTISH EPISCOPAL CHURCH,** Most Revd David Chillingworth (Bishop of St Andrews, Dunkeld and Dunblane), *elected* 2009

**BISHOPS**
*Aberdeen and Orkney*, Rt. Revd Dr Bob Gillies, *b.* 1951, *cons.* 2007, *elected* 2007. *Clergy,* 55
*Argyll and the Isles*, Rt. Revd Kevin Pearson, *b.* 1954, *cons.* 2011, *elected* 2010. *Clergy,* 28
*Brechin*, Rt. Revd Dr Nigel Peyton, *b.* 1951, *cons.* 2011, *elected* 2011. *Clergy,* 34
*Edinburgh*, Rt. Revd Dr John Armes, *b.* 1955, *cons.* 2012, *elected* 2012. *Clergy,* 163
*Glasgow and Galloway*, Rt. Revd Dr Gregor Duncan, *b.* 1950, *cons.* 2010, *elected* 2010. *Clergy,* 116
*Moray, Ross and Caithness*, Rt. Revd Mark Strange, *b.* 1961, *cons.* 2007, *elected* 2007. *Clergy,* 61
*St Andrews, Dunkeld and Dunblane*, Most Revd David Chillingworth, *b.* 1951, *cons.* 2005, *elected* 2005. *Clergy,* 78

The minimum stipend of a diocesan bishop of the Scottish Episcopal Church for 2015 is £37,035 (ie 1.5 times the standard clergy stipend of £24,690).

## CHURCH OF IRELAND

The Anglican Church was the established church in Ireland from the 16th century but never secured the allegiance of the majority and was disestablished in 1871. The Church of Ireland is divided into the provinces of Armagh and Dublin, each under an archbishop. The provinces are subdivided into 12 dioceses.

The legislative body is the General Synod, which has 660 members in total, divided between the House of Bishops (12 members) and the House of Representatives (216 clergy and 432 laity). The Archbishop of Armagh is elected by the House of Bishops; other episcopal elections are made by an electoral college.

There are around 378,000 members of the Church of Ireland, 249, in Northern Ireland and 129,000 in the Republic of Ireland. There are two archbishops, ten bishops and 437 stipendiary clergy.

**CENTRAL OFFICE**, Church of Ireland House, Church Avenue, Rathmines, Dublin 6 **T** (+353) (1) 497 8422
*Chief Officer and Secretary of the Representative Church Body,* Adrian Clements

**PROVINCE OF ARMAGH**
*Archbishop of Armagh, Primate of all Ireland and Metropolitan,* Most Revd Richard Clarke, PHD, *b.* 1949, *cons.* 1996, *trans.* 2012. *Clergy,* 40

**BISHOPS**
*Clogher*, Rt. Revd John McDowell, *b.* 1956, *cons.* 2011, *apptd* 2011. *Clergy,* 26
*Connor*, Rt. Revd Alan Abernethy, *b.* 1957, *cons.* 2007, *apptd* 2007. *Clergy,* 72
*Derry and Raphoe*, Rt. Revd Kenneth Good, *b.* 1952, *cons.* 2002, *apptd* 2002. *Clergy,* 44
*Down and Dromore*, Rt. Revd Harold Miller, *b.* 1950, *cons.* 1997, *apptd* 1997. *Clergy,* 81

*Kilmore, Elphin and Ardagh*, Rt. Revd Ferran Glenfield, *b.* 1954, *cons.* 2013, *apptd* 2013. *Clergy,* 18
*Tuam, Killala and Achonry*, Rt. Revd Patrick Rooke, *b.* 1955, *cons.* 2011, *apptd* 2011. *Clergy,* 8

**PROVINCE OF DUBLIN**
*Archbishop of Dublin, Bishop of Glendalough, Primate of Ireland and Metropolitan,* Most Revd Michael Jackson, PHD, DPHIL, *b.* 1956, *cons.* 2002, *trans.* 2011. *Clergy,* 63

**BISHOPS**
*Cashel and Ossory*, Rt. Revd Michael Burrows, *b.* 1961, *cons.* 2006, *apptd* 2006. *Clergy,* 35
*Cork, Cloyne and Ross*, Rt. Revd Paul Colton, PHD, *b.* 1960, *cons.* 1999, *apptd* 1999. *Clergy,* 22
*Limerick and Killaloe*, Rt. Revd Kenneth Kearon, *b.* 1953, *cons.* 2015, *apptd* 2014. *Clergy,* 11
*Meath and Kildare*, Most Revd Patricia Storey, *b.* 1960, *cons.* 2013, *apptd* 2013. *Clergy,* 17

## OVERSEAS

**PRIMATES**
*Primate and Archbishop of Aotearoa, New Zealand and Polynesia,* Most Revd William Turei
*Primate of Australia,* Most Revd Phillip Freir
*Primate of Brazil,* Most Revd Francisco De Assis Da Silva
*Archbishop of the Province of Burundi,* Most Revd Bernard Ntahoturi
*Primate of Canada,* Most Revd Frederick Hiltz
*Archbishop of the Province of Central Africa,* Most Revd Albert Chama
*Primate of the Central Region of America,* Most Revd Sturdie Downs
*Archbishop of the Province of Congo,* Most Revd Kahwa Henri Isingoma
*Archbishop of Hong Kong Sheng Kung Hui,* Most Revd Dr Paul Kwong
*Archbishop of the Province of the Indian Ocean,* Most Revd Ian Ernest
*Primate of Japan (Nippon Sei Ko Kai),* Most Revd Nathaniel Makoto Uematsu
*Archbishop of Jerusalem and the Middle East,* Most Revd Dr Mouneer Anis
*Primate and Archbishop of All Kenya,* Most Revd Dr Eliud Wabukala
*Primate of Korea,* Most Revd Paul Kim
*Archbishop of Melanesia,* Most Revd David Vunagi
*Presiding Bishop of Mexico,* Most Revd Francisco Moreno
*Archbishop of the Province of Myanmar (Burma),* Most Revd Stephen Oo
*Metropolitan and Primate of All Nigeria,* Most Revd Nicholas Okoh
*Archbishop of Papua New Guinea,* Rt. Revd Clyde Igara
*Prime Bishop of the Philippines,* Most Revd Renato Mag-Gay Abibico
*Archbishop of the Province of Rwanda,* Most Revd Dr Onesphore Rwaje
*Archbishop of the Province of South East Asia,* Most Revd Bolly Lapok
*Primate of Southern Africa,* Most Revd Dr Thabo Makgoba
*Presiding Bishop of South America,* Most Revd Hector Zavala Muñoz
*Archbishop of the Province of South Sudan and Sudan,* Most Revd Dr Daniel Deng Bul Yak
*Archbishop of Tanzania,* Most Revd Jacob Chimeledya
*Archbishop of the Province of Uganda,* Most Revd Stanley Ntagali
*Presiding Bishop of the USA,* Most Revd Katharine Schori

*Primate and Metropolitan of the Province of West Africa,* Most Revd Dr Daniel Sarfo

*Archbishop of the Province of the West Indies,* Most Revd Dr John Holder

### OTHER CHURCHES AND EXTRA-PROVINCIAL DIOCESES

*Anglican Church of Bermuda, extra-provincial to Canterbury*
Bishop, Rt. Revd Nicholas Dill

*Church of Ceylon, extra-provincial to Canterbury*
Bishop of Colombo, Rt. Revd Dhiloraj Canagasabey
Bishop of Kurunagala, vacant

*Episcopal Church of Cuba,* Rt. Revd Griselda Del Carpio

*Falkland Islands, extra-provincial to Canterbury*
Bishop, Rt. Revd Nigel Stock (Bishop to the Forces)

*Lusitanian Church (Portuguese Episcopal Church), extra-provincial to Canterbury*
Bishop, Rt. Revd Jose Cabral

*Reformed Episcopal Church of Spain, extra-provincial to Canterbury*
Bishop, Rt. Revd Carlos López-Lozano

### MODERATION OF CHURCHES IN FULL COMMUNION WITH THE ANGLICAN COMMUNION

*Church of Bangladesh,* Most Revd Paul Sarkar
*Church of North India,* Most Revd Pradeep Samantaroy
*Church of South India,* Most Revd Govada Dyvasirvadam
*Church of Pakistan,* Most Revd Samuel Azariah

## CHURCH OF SCOTLAND

The Church of Scotland is the national church of Scotland. The church is reformed in doctrine, and presbyterian in constitution; ie based on a hierarchy of courts of ministers and elders and, since 1990, of members of a diaconate. At local level the Kirk Session consists of the parish minister and ruling elders. At district level the presbyteries, of which there are 44 in Britain, consist of all the ministers in the district, one ruling elder from each congregation, and those members of the diaconate who qualify for membership. The General Assembly is the supreme authority, and is presided over by a Moderator chosen annually by the Assembly. The sovereign, if not present in person, is represented by a Lord High Commissioner who is appointed each year by the Crown.

The Church of Scotland has around 400,000 members and 800 parish ministers. The majority of parishes are in Scotland, but there are also churches in England, Europe and overseas.

*Lord High Commissioner (2015–16),* Lord Hope of Craighead, KT, PC
*Moderator of the General Assembly (2015–16),* Rt. Revd Dr Angus Morrison
*Principal Clerk,* Revd John Chalmers
*Depute Clerk,* Revd George Whyte
*Procurator,* Laura Dunlop, QC
*Law Agent and Solicitor of the Church,* Janette Wilson
*Parliamentary Officer,* Chloe Clemmons
*General Treasurer,* Iain Grimmond
*Secretary, Church and Society Council,* Revd Ewan Aitken
CHURCH OFFICE, 121 George Street, Edinburgh EH2 4YN
T 0131-225 5722

### PRESBYTERIES AND CLERKS

*Aberdeen,* Revd George Cowie; Revd John Ferguson
*Abernethy,* Catherine Buchan
*Angus,* Revd Mike Goss
*Annandale and Eskdale,* Revd Bryan Haston
*Ardrossan,* Alan Saunderson

*Argyll,* Ian MacLagan
*Ayr,* Revd Kenneth Elliott
*Buchan,* George Berstan
*Caithness,* Revd Ronald Johnstone
*Dumbarton,* Revd David Clark
*Dumfries and Kirkcudbright,* Revd William Hogg
*Dundee,* Revd James Wilson
*Dunfermline,* Revd Elizabeth Kenny
*Dunkeld and Meigle,* Revd John Russell
*Duns,* Helen Longmuir
*Edinburgh,* Revd Dr George Whyte
*England,* Revd Dr Pete Mills
*Europe,* Revd Jim Sharp
*Falkirk,* Revd Robert Allan
*Glasgow,* Very Revd William Hewitt
*Gordon,* Revd Euan Glen
*Greenock and Paisley,* Revd Dr Peter McEnhill
*Hamilton,* Revd Shaw Paterson
*Inverness,* Revd Reginald Campbell
*Irvine and Kilmarnock,* Steuart Dey
*Jedburgh,* Revd W. Frank Campbell
*Kincardine and Deeside,* Revd Hugh Conkey
*Kirkcaldy,* Revd Rosemary Frew
*Lanark,* Revd Helen Jamieson
*Lewis,* Revd Thomas Sinclair
*Lochaber,* Ella Gill
*Lochcarron-Skye,* Revd Allan Macarthur
*Lothian,* John McCulloch
*Melrose and Peebles,* Revd Victoria Linford
*Moray,* Revd Robert Anderson
*Orkney,* David Baker
*Perth,* Revd Alan Reid
*Ross,* Ronald Gunstone
*St Andrews,* Revd James Redpath
*Shetland,* Revd Charles Greig
*Stirling,* Revd Alex Millar
*Sutherland,* Mary Stobo
*Uist,* Wilson McKinlay
*West Lothian,* Revd Duncan Shaw
*Wigtown and Stranraer,* vacant

The stipends for ministers in the Church of Scotland in 2015 range from £26,119–£32,098, depending on length of service.

## ROMAN CATHOLIC CHURCH

The Roman Catholic Church is a worldwide Christian church acknowledging as its head the Bishop of Rome, known as the Pope (father). Despite its widespread usage, 'Pope' is actually an unofficial term. The *Annuario Pontificio* (Pontifical Yearbook) lists eight official titles: Bishop of Rome, Vicar of Jesus Christ, Successor of the Prince of the Apostles, Supreme Pontiff of the Universal Church, Primate of Italy, Archbishop and Metropolitan of the Roman Province, Sovereign of the State of the Vatican City and Servant of the Servants of God.

The Pope leads a communion of followers of Christ, who believe they continue His presence in the world as servants of faith, hope and love to all society. The Pope is held to be the successor of St Peter and thus invested with the power which was entrusted to St Peter by Jesus Christ. A direct line of succession is therefore claimed from the earliest Christian communities. With the fall of the Roman Empire the Pope also became an important political leader. His territory is now limited to the 0.44 sq. km (0.17 sq. miles) of the Vatican City State, created to provide some independence to the Pope from Italy and other nations. The episcopal jurisdiction of the Roman Catholic Church is called the Holy See.

The Pope exercises spiritual authority over the church with the advice and assistance of the Sacred College of Cardinals, the supreme council of the church. The number of cardinals was fixed at 70 by Pope Sixtus V in 1586 but has increased steadily since the pontificate of John XXIII. On 28 February 2013, the date of Pope Benedict XVI's resignation, there were 207 cardinals.

Following the death or resignation of the Pope, the members of the College of Cardinals under the age of 80 are called to the Vatican to elect a successor. They are known as cardinal electors and form an assembly called the conclave. The conclave, which comprised 115 cardinal electors when it convened in March 2013, conducts a secret ballot in complete seclusion to elect the next Pope. A two-thirds majority is necessary before the vote can be accepted as final. When a cardinal receives the necessary number of votes, the Dean of the Sacred College formally asks him if he will accept election and the name by which he wishes to be known. On his acceptance of the office of Supreme Pontiff, the conclave is dissolved and the first Cardinal Deacon announces the election to the assembled crowd in St Peter's Square.

The Pope has full legislative, judicial and administrative power over the whole Roman Catholic Church. He is aided in his administration by the curia, which is made up of a number of departments. The Secretariat of State is the central office for carrying out the Pope's instructions and is presided over by the Cardinal Secretary of State. It maintains relations with the departments of the curia, with the episcopate, with the representatives of the Holy See in various countries, governments and private persons. The congregations and pontifical councils are the Pope's ministries and include departments such as the Congregation for the Doctrine of Faith, whose field of competence concerns faith and morals; the Congregation for the Clergy and the Congregation for the Evangelisation of Peoples, the Pontifical Council for the Family and the Pontifical Council for the Promotion of Christian Unity.

The Holy See, composed of the Pope and those who help him in his mission for the church, is recognised by the Conventions of Vienna as an international moral body. Apostolic nuncios are the Pope's diplomatic representatives; in countries where no formal diplomatic relations exist between the Holy See and that country, the papal representative is known as an apostolic delegate.

According to the 2014 Pontifical Yearbook the number of Roman Catholics worldwide was 1,229 million at the end of 2012; the number of bishops was 5,133 and there were 414,313 priests.

## SUPREME PONTIFF
**His Holiness Pope Francis** (Jorge Mario Bergoglio), *born* Buenos Aires, Argentina, 17 December 1936; *ordained priest* 13 December 1969; *appointed Archbishop* (of Buenos Aires), 28 February 1998; *created Cardinal* 21 February 2001; *assumed pontificate* 13 March 2013

## PONTIFF EMERITUS
**His Holiness Pope Benedict XVI** (Joseph Ratzinger), *born* Bavaria, Germany, 16 April 1927; *ordained priest* 29 June 1951; *appointed Archbishop* (of Munich), 24 March 1977; *created Cardinal* 27 June 1977; *assumed pontificate* 19 April 2005; *resigned pontificate* 28 February 2013

## SECRETARIAT OF STATE
*Secretary of State,* His Eminence Cardinal Pietro Parolin
*First Section (General Affairs),* Most Revd Giovanni Angelo Becciu (Titular Archbishop of Roselle)
*Second Section (Relations with Other States),* Most Revd Paul Gallagher (Titular Archbishop of Hodelm)

## BISHOPS' CONFERENCE
The Catholic Bishops' Conference of England and Wales is the permanent assembly of Catholic Bishops and Ordinaries in the two member countries. The membership of the Conference comprises the Archbishops, Bishops and Auxiliary Bishops of the 22 Dioceses within England and Wales, the Bishop of the Forces (Military Ordinariate), the Apostolic Eparch of the Ukrainian Church in Great Britain, the Ordinary of the Personal Ordinariate of Our Lady of Walsingham, and the Apostolic Prefect of the Falkland Islands. The Conference is headed by a president and vice-president. There are six departments, each with an episcopal chair: Education and Formation, Christian Life and Worship, Christian Responsibility and Citizenship, Dialogue and Unity, Evangelisation and Catechesis, and International Affairs.

The Bishops' Conference Standing Committee is made up of two directly elected bishops in addition to the Metropolitan Archbishops and chairs from each of the above departments. The committee has general responsibility for continuity of policy between the plenary sessions of the conference, preparing the conference agenda and implementing its decisions.

The administration of the Bishops' Conference is funded by a levy on each diocese, according to income. A general secretariat in London coordinates and supervises the Bishops' Conference administration activities. There are also other agencies and consultative bodies affiliated to the conference.

The Bishops' Conference of Scotland is the permanently constituted assembly of the eight bishops of Scotland. The conference is headed by the president (Most Revd Philip Tartaglia, Archbishop of Glasgow). The conference establishes various agencies which perform advisory functions in relation to the conference. The more important of these agencies are called commissions; each one is headed by a bishop president who, with the other members of the commissions, are appointed by the conference.

The Irish Catholic Bishops' Conference (also known as the Irish Episcopal Conference) has as its president the Most Revd Eamon Martin (Archbishop of Armagh). Its membership comprises all the archbishops and bishops of Ireland. It appoints various commissions and agencies to assist with the work of the Catholic Church in Ireland.

The Catholic Church in the UK has over 900,000 mass attendees, 5,500 priests and 4,550 churches.

Bishops' Conferences secretariats:
**ENGLAND AND WALES,** 39 Eccleston Square, London SW1V 1BX T 020-7630 8220 W www.cbcew.org.uk
*General Secretary,* Revd Christopher Thomas
**SCOTLAND,** 64 Aitken Street, Airdrie ML6 6LT T 01236-764061 W www.bcos.org.uk
*General Secretary,* Mgr Hugh Bradley
**IRELAND,** Columba Centre, Maynooth, County Kildare T (+353) (1) 505 3000 E columbacentre@iecon.ie W www.catholicbishops.ie
*Episcopal Secretary,* Most Revd Kieran O'Reilly (Archbishop of Cashel and Emly)
*Executive Secretary,* Mgr Gearóid Dullea

## GREAT BRITAIN
### APOSTOLIC NUNCIO TO GREAT BRITAIN
Most Revd Antonio Mennini, 54 Parkside, London SW19 5NE T 020-8944 7189

### ENGLAND AND WALES
THE MOST REVD ARCHBISHOPS
*Westminster,* Cardinal Vincent Nichols, *cons.* 1992, *apptd* 2009 *Archbishop Emeritus,* Cardinal Cormac Murphy-O'Connor, *cons.* 1977, *elevated* 2001 *Auxiliaries,* John Sherrington, *cons.* 2011; Nicholas

Hudson, *cons.* 2014. *Clergy,* 318. *Archbishop's House,* Ambrosden Avenue, London SW1P 1QJ **T** 020-7798 9033
*Birmingham,* Bernard Longley, *cons.* 2003, *apptd* 2009 *Auxiliaries,* William Kenney, *cons.* 1987; David McGough, *cons.* 2005; Robert Byrne, *cons.* 2014. *Clergy,* 430. *Archbishop's House,* 8 Shadwell Street, Birmingham B4 6EY **T** 0121-236 9090
*Cardiff,* George Stack, *cons.* 2001, *apptd* 2011. *Clergy,* 47. *Archbishop's House,* 43 Cathedral Road, Cardiff CF11 9HD **T** 029-2022 0411
*Liverpool,* Malcolm McMahon, *cons.* 2000, *apptd* 2014 *Auxiliary,* Thomas Williams, *cons.* 2003. *Clergy,* 402. *Liverpool Archdiocese Centre for Evangelisation,* Croxteth Drive, Sefton Park, Liverpool L17 1AA **T** 0151-522 1000
*Southwark,* Peter Smith, *cons.* 1995, *apptd* 2010 *Auxiliaries,* Patrick Lynch, *cons.* 2006; Paul Hendricks, *cons.* 2006. *Clergy,* 366. *Archbishop's House,* 150 St George's Road, London SE1 6HX **T** 020-7928 2495

THE RT. REVD BISHOPS
*Arundel and Brighton,* Michael Moth, *cons.* 2015, *apptd* 2015. *Clergy,* 95. *Bishop's House,* The Upper Drive, Hove, E. Sussex BN3 6NB **T** 01273-506387
*Brentwood,* Alan Williams, *cons.* 2014, *apptd* 2014. *Clergy,* 170. *Bishop's Office,* Cathedral House, Ingrave Road, Brentwood, Essex CM15 8AT **T** 01277-232266
*Clifton,* Declan Lang, *cons.* 2001, *apptd* 2001. *Clergy,* 153. *Bishop's House,* St Ambrose, North Road, Leigh Woods, Bristol BS8 3PW **T** 0117-973 3072
*East Anglia,* Alan Hopes, *cons.* 2003, *apptd* 2013. *Clergy,* 129. *Diocesan Curia,* The White House, 21 Upgate, Poringland, Norwich NR14 7SH **T** 01508-492202
*Hallam,* Ralph Heskett, *cons.* 2010, *apptd* 2014. *Clergy,* 71. *Bishop's House,* 75 Norfolk Road, Sheffield S2 2SZ **T** 0114-278 7988
*Hexham and Newcastle,* Seamus Cunningham, *cons.* 2009, *apptd* 2009. *Clergy,* 164. *Bishop's House,* East Denton Hall, 800 West Road, Newcastle upon Tyne NE5 2BJ **T** 0191-228 0003
*Lancaster,* Michael Campbell, *cons.* 2008, *apptd* 2009. *Clergy,* 97. *Bishop's Office,* The Pastoral Centre, Balmoral Road, Lancaster LA1 3BT **T** 01524-596050
*Leeds,* Marcus Stock. *Clergy,* 193. *Diocesan Curia,* Hinsley Hall, 62 Headingley Lane, Leeds LS6 2BX **T** 0113-230 4533
*Menevia (Wales),* Tom Burns, *cons.* 2002, *apptd* 2008. *Clergy,* 60. *Diocesan Office,* 27 Convent Street, Swansea SA1 2BX **T** 01792-644017
*Middlesbrough,* Terence Drainey, *cons.* 2008, *apptd* 2007. *Clergy,* 83. *Diocesan Curia,* 50A The Avenue, Linthorpe, Middlesbrough TS5 6QT **T** 01642-850505
*Northampton,* Peter Doyle, *cons.* 2005, *apptd* 2005. *Clergy,* 116. *Bishop's House,* Marriott Street, Northampton NN2 6AW **T** 01604-715635
*Nottingham,* vacant. *Clergy,* 166. *Bishop's House,* 27 Cavendish Road East, The Park, Nottingham NG7 1BB **T** 0115-947 4786
*Plymouth,* Mark O'Toole, *cons.* 2014, *apptd* 2013. *Clergy,* 50. *Bishop's House,* 45 Cecil Street, Plymouth PL1 5HW **T** 01752-224414
*Portsmouth,* Philip Egan, *cons.* 2012, *apptd* 2012. *Clergy,* 214. *Bishop's House,* Bishop Crispian Way, Portsmouth, Hants PO1 3HG **T** 023-9282 0894
*Salford,* John Arnold, *cons.* 2006, *trans.* 2014. *Clergy,* 218. *Diocesan Curia,* Wardley Hall, Worsley, Manchester M28 2ND **T** 0161-794 2825
*Shrewsbury,* Mark Davies, *cons.* 2010, *apptd* 2010. *Clergy* 112. *Diocesan Curia,* 2 Park Road South, Prenton, Wirral CH43 4UX **T** 0151-652 9855

*Wrexham (Wales),* Peter Brignall, *cons.* 2012, *apptd* 2012. *Clergy,* 16. *Bishop's House,* Sontley Road, Wrexham LL13 7EW **T** 01978-262726

SCOTLAND
THE MOST REVD ARCHBISHOPS
*St Andrews and Edinburgh,* Leo Cushley, *cons.* 2013, *apptd* 2013. *Archbishop Emeritus,* HE Cardinal Keith O'Brien, *cons.* 1985, *elevated* 2003. *Clergy,* 50. *Archdiocesan Offices,* 100 Strathearn Road, Edinburgh EH9 1BB **T** 0131-623 8900
*Glasgow,* Philip Tartaglia, *cons.* 2005, *elevated* 2012. *Clergy,* 198. *Diocesan Curia,* 196 Clyde Street, Glasgow G1 4JY **T** 0141-226 5898

THE RT. REVD BISHOPS
*Aberdeen,* Hugh Gilbert, *cons.* 2011, *apptd* 2011. *Clergy,* 47. *Bishop's House,* 3 Queen's Cross, Aberdeen AB15 4XU **T** 01224-319154
*Argyll and the Isles,* vacant. *Clergy,* 32. *Diocesan Office* Bishop's House, Esplanade, Oban, Argyll PA34 5AB **T** 01631-567436
*Dunkeld,* Stephen Robson, *cons.* 2012, *apptd* 2013. *Clergy,* 43. *Diocesan Curia,* 24–28 Lawside Road, Dundee DD3 6XY **T** 01382-225453
*Galloway,* William Nolan, *cons.* 2015, *apptd* 2014. *Clergy,* 19. *Diocesan Office,* 8 Corsehill Road, Ayr KA7 2ST **T** 01292-266750
*Motherwell,* Joseph Toal, *cons.* 2008, *trans.* 2014. *Clergy,* 123. *Diocesan Curia,* Coursington Road, Motherwell ML1 1PP **T** 01698-269114
*Paisley,* John Keenan, *cons.* 2014, *apptd* 2014. *Clergy,* 75. *Diocesan Curia,* Cathedral Precincts, Incle Street, Paisley PA1 1HR **T** 0141-847 6131

BISHOPRIC OF THE FORCES
vacant.
*Administration,* RC Bishopric of the Forces, Wellington House, St Omer Barracks, Thornhill Road, Aldershot, Hants GU11 2BG **T** 01252-348234

**IRELAND**
There is one hierarchy for the whole of Ireland. Several of the dioceses have territory partly in the Republic of Ireland and partly in Northern Ireland.

APOSTOLIC NUNCIO TO IRELAND
Most Revd Charles John Brown (Titular Archbishop of Aquileia), 183 Navan Road, Dublin 7 **T** (+353) (1) 838 0577

THE MOST REVD ARCHBISHOPS
*Armagh,* Eamon Martin (*also* Primate of all Ireland), *cons.* 2013, *apptd* 2014. *Clergy,* 135. *Bishop's Residence,* Ara Coeli, Cathedral Road, Armagh BT61 7QY **T** 028-3752 5103
*Cashel and Emly,* Kieran O'Reilly, *cons.* 2010, *trans.* 2015. *Clergy,* 83. *Archbishop's House,* Thurles, Co. Tipperary **T** (+353) (504) 21512
*Dublin,* Diarmuid Martin, *cons.* 1999, *apptd Coadjutor Archbishop* 2003, *succeeded as Archbishop* 2004. *Archbishop Emeritus,* HE Cardinal Desmond Connell, *cons.* 1988, *elevated* 2001. *Auxiliaries,* Eamonn Walsh, *cons.* 1990; Raymond Field, *cons.* 1997. *Clergy,* 389. *Archbishop's House,* Drumcondra, Dublin 9 **T** (+353) (1) 837 9253
*Tuam,* Dr Michael Neary, *cons.* 1992, *apptd* 1995. *Clergy,* 110. *Archbishop's House,* Tuam, Co. Galway **T** (+353) (93) 24166

THE MOST REVD BISHOPS

*Achonry,* Brendan Kelly, *cons.* 2008, *apptd* 2007. *Clergy,* 50.
*Bishop's House,* Edmondstown, Ballaghaderreen, Co.
Roscommon **T** (+353) (94) 986 0021

*Ardagh and Clonmacnois,* Francis Duffy, *cons.* 2013,
*apptd* 2013. *Clergy,* 60. *Diocesan Office,* St Michael's,
Ballinalee Road, Longford, Co. Longford **T** (+353) (43) 334 6432

*Clogher,* Liam MacDaid, *cons.* 2010, *apptd* 2010. *Clergy,* 74.
*Bishop's House,* Monaghan **T** (+353) (47) 81019

*Clonfert,* John Kirby, *cons.* 1988, *apptd* 1988. *Clergy,* 37.
*Bishop's House,* Coorheen, Loughrea, Co. Galway
**T** (+353) (91) 841560

*Cloyne,* William Crean, *cons.* 2013, *apptd* 2013. *Clergy,* 126.
*Diocesan Office,* Cobh, Co. Cork **T** (+353) (21) 481 1430

*Cork and Ross,* John Buckley, *cons.* 1984, *apptd* 1998.
*Clergy,* 133. *Diocesan Office,* Cork and Ross Offices,
Redemption Road, Cork **T** (+353) (21) 430 1717

*Derry,* Donal McKeown, *cons.* 2001, *apptd* 2014.
*Clergy,* 108. *Bishop's House,* St Eugene's Cathedral,
Derry BT48 9AP **T** 028-7126 2302

*Down and Connor,* Noel Treanor, *cons.* 2008, *apptd* 2008.
*Auxiliary,* Anthony Farquhar, *cons.* 1983. *Clergy,* 199.
*Bishop's Residence,* Lisbreen, 73 Somerton Road, Belfast,
Co. Antrim BT15 4DE **T** 028-9077 6185

*Dromore,* John McAreavey, *cons.* 1999, *apptd* 1999.
*Clergy,* 33. *Bishop's House,* 44 Armagh Road, Newry,
Co. Down BT35 6PN **T** 028-3026 2444

*Elphin,* Kevin Doran, *cons.* 2014, *apptd* 2014. *Clergy,* 66.
*Bishop's House,* Temple St, St Mary's, Sligo
**T** (+353) (71) 915 0106

*Ferns,* Denis Brennan, *cons.* 2006, *apptd* 2006. *Clergy,* 88.
*Bishop's House,* Summerhill, Wexford **T** (+353) (53) 912 2177

*Galway, Kilmacduagh and Kilfenora,* Martin Drennan,
*cons.* 1997, *apptd* 2005. *Clergy,* 57. *Diocesan Office,*
The Cathedral, Galway **T** (+353) (91) 563566

*Kerry,* Ray Browne, *cons.* 2013, *apptd* 2013. *Clergy,* 88.
*Bishop's House,* Killarney, Co. Kerry **T** (+353) (64) 663 1168

*Kildare and Leighlin,* Denis Nulty, *cons.* 2013, *apptd* 2013.
*Clergy,* 72. *Bishop's House,* Old Dublin Road, Carlow Town
**T** (+353) (59) 917 6725

*Killala,* John Fleming, *cons.* 2002, *apptd* 2002. *Clergy,* 40.
*Bishop's House,* Ballina, Co. Mayo **T** (+353) (96) 21518

*Killaloe,* vacant. *Clergy,* 95. *Diocesan Office,* Westbourne,
Ennis, Co. Clare **T** (+353) (65) 682 8638

*Kilmore,* Leo O'Reilly, *cons.* 1997, *apptd* 1998. *Clergy,* 67.
*Bishop's House,* Cullies, Cavan, Co. Cavan
**T** (+353) (49) 433 1496

*Limerick,* Brendan Leahy, *cons.* 2013, *apptd* 2013.
*Clergy,* 109. *Diocesan Office,* Social Service Centre,
Henry Street, Limerick **T** (+353) (61) 315856

*Meath,* Michael Smith, *cons.* 1984, *apptd* 1990. *Clergy,* 120.
*Bishop's House,* Dublin Road, Mullingar, Co. Westmeath
**T** (+353) (44) 934 8841

*Ossory,* Séamus Freeman, *cons.* 2007, *apptd* 2007. *Clergy,* 81.
*Diocesan Office,* James's Street, Kilkenny
**T** (+353) (56) 776 2448

*Raphoe,* Dr Philip Boyce, *cons.* 1995, *apptd* 1995. *Clergy,* 80.
*Bishop's House,* Ard Adhamhnáin, Letterkenny, Co. Donegal
**T** (+353) (74) 912 1208

*Waterford and Lismore,* Alphonsus Cullinan, *cons.* 2015,
*apptd* 2015. *Clergy,* 114. *Bishop's House,* John's Hill,
Waterford **T** (+353) (51) 874463

# OTHER CHURCHES IN THE UK

## ASSOCIATED PRESBYTERIAN CHURCHES OF SCOTLAND

The Associated Presbyterian Churches came into being in
1989 as a result of a division within the Free Presbyterian

Church of Scotland. The Associated Presbyterian Churches
is reformed and evangelistic in nature and emphasises the
importance of doctrine based primarily on the Bible and
secondly on the Westminster Confession of Faith. There
are an estimated 500 members, 8 ministers and 18
congregations in Scotland. There are also congregations in
Canada.

ASSOCIATED PRESBYTERIAN CHURCHES OF
SCOTLAND, 64 Roxburgh Road, Wick KW1 5HP
**T** 01955-928075 **W** www.apchurches.org
*Presbytery Clerk,* Revd Ross Macaskill

## BAPTIST CHURCH

Baptists trace their origins to John Smyth, who in 1609 in
Amsterdam reinstituted the baptism of conscious believers as
the basis of the fellowship of a gathered church. Members
of Smyth's church established the first Baptist church in
England in 1612. They came to be known as 'General'
Baptists and their theology was Arminian, whereas a later
group of Calvinists who adopted the baptism of believers
came to be known as 'Particular' Baptists. The two sections
of the Baptists were united into one body, the Baptist Union
of Great Britain and Ireland, in 1891. In 1988 the title was
changed to the Baptist Union of Great Britain.

Baptists emphasise the complete autonomy of the local
church, although individual churches are linked in various
kinds of associations. There are international bodies (such as
the Baptist World Alliance) and national bodies, but some
Baptist churches belong to neither. However, in Great Britain
the majority of churches and associations belong to the
Baptist Union of Great Britain. There are also Baptist Unions
in Wales, Scotland and Ireland, which are much smaller than
the Baptist Union of Great Britain, and there is some overlap
of membership.

There are currently around 135,000 members, 2,500
ministers and 2,084 churches associated with the Baptist
Union of Great Britain. The Baptist Union of Great Britain
is one of the founder members of the European Baptist
Federation (1948) and the Baptist World Alliance (1905); the
latter represents 42 million members worldwide.

In the Baptist Union of Wales (Undeb Bedyddwyr Cymru)
there are 11,355 members, 88 pastors and 386 churches,
including those in England.

In the Baptist Union of Scotland there are 11,500
members and 165 churches.

BAPTIST UNION OF GREAT BRITAIN, Baptist House,
PO Box 44, 129 Broadway, Didcot, Oxon OX11 8RT
**T** 01235-517700 **W** www.baptist.org.uk
*President (2015–16),* Revd Jenni Entrican
*General Secretary,* Revd Lynn Green

BAPTIST UNION OF WALES, Y Llwyfan, College Road,
Carmarthen SA31 3EQ **T** 01267-245660
**E** judith@bedyddwyrcymru.co.uk **W** www.buw.org.uk
*President of the English Assembly (2015–16),* Revd Peter
Thomas
*President of the Welsh Assembly (2015–16),* Revd I. Elfryn
Jones
*General Secretary of the Baptist Union of Wales,* Revd Judith
Morris

BAPTIST UNION OF SCOTLAND, 48 Speirs Wharf, Glasgow
G4 9TH **T** 0141-423 6169 **E** admin@scottishbaptist.org.uk
*General Director,* Revd A. Donaldson

## THE BRETHREN

The Brethren was founded in Dublin in 1827–8, basing
itself on the structures and practices of the early church and
rejecting denominationalism and clericalism. Many groups
sprang up; the group at Plymouth became the best known,
resulting in its designation by others as the 'Plymouth

Brethren'. Early worship had a prescribed form but quickly assumed an unstructured, non-liturgical format.

There are services devoted to worship, usually involving the breaking of bread, and separate preaching meetings. There is no salaried ministry.

A theological dispute led in 1848 to schism between the Open Brethren and the Closed or Exclusive Brethren, each branch later suffering further divisions.

Open Brethren churches are run by appointed elders and are completely independent, but freely cooperate with each other. Exclusive Brethren churches believe in a universal fellowship between congregations. They do not have appointed elders, but use respected members of their congregation to perform certain administrative functions.

The Brethren are established throughout the UK, Ireland, Europe, India, Africa and Australasia. In the UK there are over 70,000 members, 1,250 assembly halls and over 200 full-time Bible teachers, evangelists and administrators. There are a number of publishing houses that publish Brethren-related literature. Chapter Two is the main supplier of such literature in the UK; it also has a Brethren history archive which is available for use by appointment.

CHAPTER TWO, 3 Conduit Mews, London SE18 7AP
T 020-8316 5389 E info@chaptertwobooks.org.uk
W www.chaptertwobooks.org.uk

## CONGREGATIONAL FEDERATION

The Congregational Federation was founded by members of Congregational churches in England and Wales who did not join the United Reformed Church in 1972. There are also churches in Scotland and France affiliated to the federation. The federation exists to encourage congregations of believers to worship in free assembly, but it has no authority over them and emphasises their right to independence and self-governance.

The federation has 7,060 members, 187 accredited ministers and 265 churches in England, Wales and Scotland.

CONGREGATIONAL FEDERATION, 8 Castle Gate,
Nottingham NG1 7AS T 0115-911 1460
E admin@congregational.org.uk
W www.congregational.org.uk
*President of the Federation (2015–16)*, Betty Bentham
*General Secretary*, Yvonne Campbell

## FELLOWSHIP OF INDEPENDENT EVANGELICAL CHURCHES

The Fellowship of Independent Evangelical Churches (FIEC) was founded by Revd E. J. Poole-Connor (1872–1962) in 1922. In 1923 the fellowship published its first register of non-denominational pastors, evangelists and congregations who had accepted the doctrinal basis for the fellowship.

Members of the fellowship have two primary convictions: firstly to defend the evangelical faith, and secondly that evangelicalism is the bond that unites the fellowship, rather than forms of worship or church government.

The FIEC exists to promote the welfare of non-denominational Bible churches and to give expression to the fundamental doctrines of evangelical Christianity. It supports individual churches by gathering and disseminating information and resources and advising churches on current theological, moral, social and practical issues.

There are currently 516 churches affiliated to the fellowship.

FELLOWSHIP OF INDEPENDENT EVANGELICAL CHURCHES, 39 The Point, Market Harborough,
Leics LE16 7QU T 01858-434540 E admin@fiec.org.uk
W www.fiec.org.uk
*National Director*, John Stevens

## FREE CHURCH OF ENGLAND

The Free Church of England, otherwise called the Reformed Episcopal Church, is an independent episcopal church, constituted according to the historic faith, tradition and practice of the Church of England. Its roots lie in the 18th century, but it started to grow significantly from the 1840s onwards, as clergy and congregations joined it from the established church in protest against the Oxford Movement. The historic episcopate was conferred on the English church in 1876 through bishops of the Reformed Episcopal Church (which had broken away from the Protestant Episcopal Church in the USA in 1873). A branch of the Reformed Episcopal Church was founded in the UK and this merged with the Free Church of England in 1927 to create the present church. The Orders of the Free Church of England are recognised by the Church of England.

Worship is according to the *Book of Common Prayer* and some modern liturgy is permissable. Only men are ordained to the orders of deacon, presbyter and bishop.

The Free Church of England has two dioceses, 19 congregations and around 900 members in England. There is one congregation in St Petersburg, Russia and three congregations and six missions in Brazil.

THE FREE CHURCH OF ENGLAND, 329 Wolverhampton
Road West, Willenhall, W. Midlands WV13 2RL
T 01902-607335 W www.fcofe.org.uk
*Bishop Primus*, Rt. Revd Dr John Fenwick (Bishop of the Northern Diocese)
*General Secretary*, Rt. Revd Paul Hunt (Bishop of the Southern Diocese)

## FREE CHURCH OF SCOTLAND

The Free Church of Scotland was formed in 1843 when over 400 ministers withdrew from the Church of Scotland as a result of interference in the internal affairs of the church by the civil authorities. In 1900, all but 26 ministers joined with others to form the United Free Church (most of which rejoined the Church of Scotland in 1929). In 1904 the remaining 26 ministers were recognised by the House of Lords as continuing the Free Church of Scotland.

The church maintains strict adherence to the Westminster Confession of Faith (1648) and accepts the Bible as the sole rule of faith and conduct. Its general assembly meets annually. It also has links with reformed churches overseas. The Free Church of Scotland has about 12,000 members, 90 ministers and 100 congregations.

FREE CHURCH OF SCOTLAND, 15 North Bank Street,
The Mound, Edinburgh EH1 2LS T 0131-226 5286
E offices@freechurchofscotland.org.uk W www.freechurch.org
*Chief Administrative Officer*, Rod Morrison

## FREE PRESBYTERIAN CHURCH OF SCOTLAND

The Free Presbyterian Church of Scotland was formed in 1893 by two ministers of the Free Church of Scotland who refused to accept a Declaratory Act passed by the Free Church General Assembly in 1892. The Free Presbyterian Church of Scotland is Calvinistic in doctrine and emphasises observance of the Sabbath. It adheres strictly to the Westminster Confession of Faith (1648).

The church has about 700 members in Scotland. It has 17 ministers and 40 churches in the UK.

FREE PRESBYTERIAN CHURCH OF SCOTLAND,
133 Woodlands Road, Glasgow G3 6LE
E outreach@fpchurch.org.uk W www.fpchurch.org.uk
*Moderator (2015–16)*, Revd Keith Watkins
*Clerk of the Synod*, Revd John MacLeod

# HOLY APOSTOLIC CATHOLIC ASSYRIAN CHURCH OF THE EAST

The Holy Apostolic Catholic Assyrian Church of the East traces its beginnings to the middle of the first century. It spread from Upper Mesopotamia throughout the territories of the Persian Empire. The Assyrian Church of the East became theologically separated from the rest of the Christian community following the Council of Ephesus in 431. The church is headed by the Catholicos Patriarch and is episcopal in government. The liturgical language is Syriac (Aramaic). The Assyrian Church of the East and the Roman Catholic Church agreed a common Christological declaration in 1994, and a process of dialogue between the Assyrian Church of the East and the Chaldean Catholic Church, which is in communion with Rome but shares the Syriac liturgy, was instituted in 1996.

The church has around 325,000 members in the Middle East, India, Russia, Europe, North America and Australasia. In Great Britain there is one parish, which is situated in London. The church in Great Britain forms part of the Diocese of Europe under HG Mar Odisho Oraham.

HOLY APOSTOLIC CATHOLIC ASSYRIAN CHURCH OF THE EAST, St Mary's Church, Westminster Road, Hanwell, London W7 3TU T 020-8567 1814

# INDEPENDENT METHODIST CHURCHES

The Independent Methodist Churches were formed in 1805 and remained independent when the Methodist Church in Great Britain was formed in 1932. They are mainly concentrated in the industrial areas of the north of England.

The churches are Methodist in doctrine but their organisation is congregational. All the churches are members of the Independent Methodist Connexion of Churches. The controlling body of the Connexion is the Annual Meeting, to which churches send delegates. The Connexional President is elected every two years. Between annual meetings the affairs of the Connexion are handled by the Connexional Committee and departmental committees. Ministers are appointed by the churches and trained through the Connexion. The ministry is open to both men and women.

There are 1,600 members, 70 ministers and 74 churches in Great Britain.

INDEPENDENT METHODIST RESOURCE CENTRE, The Resource Centre, Fleet Street, Wigan WN5 0DS T 01942-223526 E resourcecentre@imcgb.org.uk W www.imcgb.org.uk
*President*, Ken McDermott
*General Secretary*, Brian Rowney

# LUTHERAN CHURCH

Lutheranism is based on the teachings of Martin Luther, the German leader of the Protestant Reformation. The authority of the scriptures is held to be supreme over church tradition. The teachings of Lutheranism are explained in detail in 16th-century confessional writings, particularly the Augsburg Confession. Lutheranism is one of the largest Protestant denominations and it is particularly strong in northern Europe and the USA. Some Lutheran churches are episcopal, while others have a synodal form of organisation; unity is based on doctrine rather than structure. Most Lutheran churches are members of the Lutheran World Federation, based in Geneva.

Lutheran services in Great Britain are held in 15 languages to serve members of different nationalities. Services usually follow ancient liturgies. English-language congregations are members either of the Lutheran Church in Great Britain or of the Evangelical Lutheran Church of England. The Lutheran Church in Great Britain and other Lutheran churches in Britain are members of the Lutheran Council of Great Britain, which represents them and coordinates their common work.

There are around 70 million Lutherans worldwide, with around 180,000 members in Great Britain.

THE LUTHERAN COUNCIL OF GREAT BRITAIN, 30 Thanet Street, London WC1H 9QH T 020-7388 4044 E enquiries@lutheran.org.uk W www.lutheran.org.uk
*Chair*, Revd Torbjorn Holt

# METHODIST CHURCH

The Methodist movement started in England in 1729 when the Revd John Wesley, an Anglican priest, and his brother Charles met with others in Oxford and resolved to conduct their lives by 'rule and method'. In 1739 the Wesleys began evangelistic preaching and the first Methodist chapel was founded in Bristol in the same year. In 1744 the first annual conference was held, at which the Articles of Religion were drawn up. Doctrinal emphases included repentance, faith, the assurance of salvation, social concern and the priesthood of all believers. After John Wesley's death in 1791 the Methodists withdrew from the established church to form the Methodist Church. Methodists gradually drifted into many groups, but in 1932 the Wesleyan Methodist Church, the United Methodist Church and the Primitive Methodist Church united to form the Methodist Church of Great Britain.

The governing body is the Conference. The Conference meets annually and consists of two parts: the ministerial and representative sessions. The Methodist Church is structured as a 'Connexion' of churches, circuits and districts. The local churches in a defined area form a circuit, and a number of these circuits make up each of the 31 districts. There are around 80 million Methodists worldwide. In Great Britain there are nearly 230,000 members, 3,680 presbyters, 171 Deacons and 5,023 churches.

THE METHODIST CHURCH OF GREAT BRITAIN, Methodist Church House, 25 Marylebone Road, London NW1 5JR T 020-7486 5502 E helpdesk@methodistchurch.org.uk W www.methodist.org.uk
*President of the Conference (2015–16)*, Revd Steve Wild
*General Secretary and Secretary of the Conference*, Revd Gareth Powell

THE METHODIST CHURCH IN IRELAND
The Methodist Church in Ireland is autonomous but has close links with British Methodism. It has a community roll of 47,401, members, 123 ministers, 280 lay preachers and 221 churches.

METHODIST CHURCH IN IRELAND, 1 Fountainville Avenue, Belfast BT9 6AN T 028-9032 4554 E secretary@irishmethodist.org W www.irishmethodist.org
*President (2015–16)*, Revd Brian Anderson
*Secretary*, Revd John Stephens

# ORTHODOX CHURCHES

EASTERN ORTHODOX CHURCH
The Eastern (or Byzantine) Orthodox Church is a communion of self-governing Christian churches that recognises the honorary primacy of the Ecumenical Patriarch of Constantinople.

The position of Orthodox Christians is that the faith was fully defined during the period of the Oecumenical Councils. In doctrine it is strongly trinitarian, and stresses the mystery and importance of the sacraments. It is episcopal in government. The structure of the Orthodox Christian year differs from that of western churches.

Orthodox Christians throughout the world are estimated to number about 300 million; there are around 300,000 in the UK.

## GREEK ORTHODOX CHURCH (PATRIARCHATE OF ANTIOCH)

The church is led by John X, Patriarch of Antioch, who was enthroned in February 2013. The UK forms part of the Archdiocese of the British Isles and Ireland. There are 15 parishes in the UK and the Republic of Ireland, including St George's Cathedral in London, and 27 clergy.

**ANTIOCHIAN ORTHODOX DEANERY OF THE UK AND IRELAND,** 29 Willis Road, Cale Green, Stockport, Cheshire SK3 8HQ **T** 0161-476 4847
**E** father.gregory@.gmail.com
**W** www.antiochian-orthodox.co.uk
*Dean,* Archpriest Fr. Gregory Hallam

## GREEK ORTHODOX CHURCH (PATRIARCHATE OF CONSTANTINOPLE)

The presence of Greek Orthodox Christians in Britain dates back at least to 1677 when Archbishop Joseph Geogirenes of Samos fled from Turkish persecution and came to London. The present Greek cathedral in Moscow Road, Bayswater, was opened for public worship in 1879, and the Diocese of Thyateira and Great Britain was established in 1922. There are now around 100 parishes and one monastery in the UK, served by one archbishop, three bishops and around 120 clergy.

**THE PATRIARCHATE OF CONSTANTINOPLE IN GREAT BRITAIN,** Archdiocese of Thyateira and Great Britain, Thyateira House, 5 Craven Hill, London W2 3EN **T** 020-7224 9301 **E** mail@thyateira.org.uk
**W** www.thyateira.org.uk
*Archbishop,* Gregorios of Thyateira and Great Britain

## THE RUSSIAN ORTHODOX CHURCH (PATRIARCHATE OF MOSCOW)

The records of Russian Orthodox Church activities in Britain date from the visit to England of Tsar Peter I in the early 18th century. Clergy were sent from Russia to serve the chapel established to minister to the staff of the Imperial Russian Embassy in London.

In 2007, after an 80-year division, the Russian Orthodox Church Outside Russia agreed to become an autonomous part of the Russian Orthodox Church, Patriarchate of Moscow. The reunification agreement was signed by Patriarch Alexy II, 15th Patriarch of Moscow and All Russia and Metropolitan Laurus, leader of the Russian Orthodox Church Outside Russia on 17 May at a ceremony at Christ the Saviour Cathedral in Moscow. Patriarch Alexy II died on 5 December 2008. Metropolitan Kirill of Smolensk and Kaliningrad was enthroned as the 16th Patriarch of Moscow and All Russia on 1 February 2009, having been elected by a secret ballot of clergy on 27 January 2009.

The diocese of Sourozh is the diocese of the Russian Orthodox Church in Great Britain and Ireland and is led by Archbishop Elisey of Sourozh.

**DIOCESE OF SOUROZH,** Diocesan Office, Cathedral of the Dormition of the Mother of God and All Saints, 67 Ennismore Gardens, London SW7 1NH **T** 020-7584 0096
**W** www.sourozh.org
*Diocesan Hierarch,* Archbishop Elisey of Sourozh

## SERBIAN ORTHODOX CHURCH (PATRIARCHATE OF SERBIA)

There are seven parishes in Great Britain and around 4,000 members. Great Britain is part of the Diocese of Great Britain and Scandinavia, which is led by Bishop Dositey. The church can be contacted via the church of St Sava in London.

**SERBIAN ORTHODOX CHURCH IN GREAT BRITAIN,** Church of Saint Sava, 89 Lancaster Road, London W11 1QQ
**T** 020-7727 8367 **E** crkva@spclondon.org
**W** www.spclondon.org
*Archpriest,* Very Revd Goran Spaic

## OTHER NATIONALITIES

The Patriarchates of Romania and Bulgaria (Diocese o Western Europe) have memberships estimated at 20,000 an 2,000 respectively, while the Georgian Orthodox Church ha around 500 members. The Belarusian (membership estimate at 2,400) and Latvian (membership of around 100).

## ORIENTAL ORTHODOX CHURCHES

The term 'Oriental Orthodox Churches' is now generall used to describe a group of six ancient eastern churche (Armenian, Coptic, Eritrean, Ethiopian, Indian (Malankara and Syrian) which rejected the Christological definitio of the Council of Chalcedon (AD 451). There are aroun 50 million members worldwide of the Oriental Orthodo Churches and over 20,000 in the UK.

## ARMENIAN ORTHODOX CHURCH (CATHOLICOSAT OF ETCHMIADZIN)

The Armenian Orthodox Church is led by HH Karekin I Catholicos of All Armenians.

**ARMENIAN CHURCH OF GREAT BRITAIN,** The Armenian Vicarage, Iverna Gardens, London W8 6TP **T** 020-7937 0152 **E** information@armenianchurch.org.uk
**W** www.armenianchurch.co.uk
*Primate,* vacant

## COPTIC ORTHODOX CHURCH

The Coptic Orthodox Church is headed by Pope Tawadro II, who was appointed in November 2012. There are thre dioceses in the UK: the Midlands, led by HG Bishop Missae Ireland, Scotland and north-east England, led by HG Bishop Antony; and the Papal Diocese which is led by HG Bishop Angaelos and covers all the remaining parishes in the UK.

**CATHEDRAL OF ST GEORGE AT THE COPTIC ORTHODOX CHURCH CENTRE,** Shephalbury Manor, Broadhall Way, Stevenage, Herts SG2 8NP **T** 020-7993 9001 **E** admin@copticcentre.com **W** www.copticcentre.com
*Bishop,* HG Bishop Angaelos

## BRITISH ORTHODOX CHURCH

The British Orthodox Church is canonically part of th Coptic Orthodox Patriarchate of Alexandria. As it minister to British people, all of its services are in English.

**THE BRITISH ORTHODOX CHURCH,** 10 Heathwood Gardens, Charlton, London SE7 8EP **T** 020-8854 3090 **E** info@britishorthodox.org **W** www.britishorthodox.org
*Metropolitan,* Abba Seraphim

## ERITREAN ORTHODOX TEWAHEDO CHURCH

The Eritrean Orthodox Church was granted independence i 1994 by Pope Shenouda III, following the declaration o Eritrea's independence from Ethiopia in 1993. In 2006, th Eritrean government removed the third patriarch, Abun Antonios, from office and imprisoned him; the governmen replaced him with Abune Dioskoros in 2007, although th Oriental Orthodox Churches continue to recognise Antonio as the rightful patriarch. The diocesan bishop for Nort America, Europe and the Middle East is HG Abune Makarios

## ETHIOPIAN ORTHODOX TEWAHEDO CHURCH

The Ethiopian Orthodox Church was administratively par of the Coptic Orthodox Church of Alexandria until 1959 when it was granted its own patriarch by the Copti Orthodox Pope of Alexandria and Patriarch of All Africa Cyril VI. The church in London was established in 1976.

**ETHIOPIAN ORTHODOX TAWAHEDO CHURCH,** Re'ese Adbarat Saint Mary of Debre Tsion, 1 St Philip Street, London SW8 3RT **T** 020-7819 9857
**E** info@debretsionlondon.org **W** www.debretsionlondon.org
*Priest-in-charge,* Archimandrite Aba Girma Kebede

## INDIAN ORTHODOX CHURCH

The Indian Orthodox Church, also known as the Malankara Orthodox Church, traces its origins to the first century. The head of the Malankara Orthodox Church is HH Baselios Mar Thoma Paulose II. The mother church of all the parishes in the UK and the Republic of Ireland is St Gregorios Church in London. The London parish has around 280 families as practising members.

**INDIAN ORTHODOX CHURCH**, St Gregorios Indian Orthodox Church, Cranfield Road, Brockley, London SE4 1UF
**T** 020-8691 9456 **E** ioclondon@gmail.com
**W** www.indian-orthodox.co.uk
*Diocesan Metropolitan,* HG Dr Mathews Mar Thimothios
*Vicar,* Revd Fr Thomas P. John

## SYRIAN ORTHODOX CHURCH

The Syrian (Syriac) Orthodox Church of Antioch is an Oriental Orthodox Church based in the Eastern Mediterranean headed by HH Moran Mor Ignatius Aphrem II. The Patriarchate Vicariate in the UK is represented by HE Archbishop Mor Athanasios Toma Dawood.

**SYRIAN ORTHODOX CHURCH IN THE UK**,
St Thomas Cathedral, 7–11 Armstrong Road, London W3 7JL
**T** 020-8749 5834 **E** enquiry-uk@syrianorthodoxchurch.net
**W** www.syrianorthodoxchurch.net
*Archbishop,* HE Mor Athanasius Toma Dawood

## PENTECOSTAL CHURCHES

Pentecostalism is inspired by the descent of the Holy Spirit upon the apostles at Pentecost. The movement began in Los Angeles, USA, in 1906 and is characterised by baptism with the Holy Spirit, divine healing, speaking in tongues (glossolalia) and a literal interpretation of the scriptures.

The Pentecostal movement in Britain dates from 1907. Initially, groups of Pentecostalists were led by laymen and did not organise formally. However, in 1915 the Elim Foursquare Gospel Alliance (more commonly called the Elim Pentecostal Church) was founded in Ireland by George Jeffreys and currently has about 550 churches, 68,500 adherents and 650 accredited ministers. In 1924 about 70 independent assemblies formed a fellowship called Assemblies of God in Great Britain and Ireland, which now incorporates around 570 churches, around 75,000 adherents and 1,015 ministers.

The Apostolic Church grew out of the 1904–5 Christian revivals in South Wales and was established in 1916. The Apostolic Church has around 110 churches, 7,180 adherents and 115 ministers in the UK. The New Testament Church of God was established in England in 1953 and has over 125 congregations, nearly 30,000 members and over 300 ministers across England and Wales.

In recent years many aspects of Pentecostalism have been adopted by the growing charismatic movement within the Roman Catholic, Protestant and Eastern Orthodox churches. There are about 105 million Pentecostalists worldwide, with over 350,000 adherents in the UK.

**THE APOSTOLIC CHURCH**, PO Box 51298, London SE11 9AJ **T** 020-7587 1802 **E** admin@apostolic-church.org
**W** www.apostolic-church.org
*National Leader,* Emmanuel Mbakwe

**ASSEMBLIES OF GOD**, National Ministry Centre, Mattersey, Doncaster DN10 5HD **T** 017-7781 7663 **E** info@aog.org.uk
**W** www.aog.org.uk
*National Leader,* John Partington

**THE ELIM PENTECOSTAL CHURCH**, Elim International Centre, De Walden Road, West Malvern, Worcestershire WR14 4DF **T** 0345-302 6750 **E** info@elimhq.net
**W** www.elim.org.uk
*General Superintendent,* Revd John Glass

**THE NEW TESTAMENT CHURCH OF GOD**, National Office, 3 Cheyne Walk, Northampton NN1 5PT
**T** 01604-824222 **W** www.ntcg.org.uk
*Administrative Bishop,* Donald Bolt

## PRESBYTERIAN CHURCH IN IRELAND

Irish Presbyterianism traces its origins back to the Plantation of Ulster in 1606, when English and Scottish Protestants began to settle on the land confiscated from the Irish chieftains. The first presbytery was established in Ulster in 1642 by chaplains of a Scottish army that had been sent to crush a Catholic rebellion in 1641.

The Presbyterian Church in Ireland is reformed in doctrine and belongs to the World Alliance of Reformed Churches. Structurally, the 545 congregations are grouped in 19 presbyteries under the General Assembly. This body meets annually and is presided over by a moderator who is elected for one year. The ongoing work of the church is undertaken by 12 boards under which there are specialist committees.

There are over 240,000 members of Irish presbyterian churches in Ireland and Northern Ireland.

**THE PRESBYTERIAN CHURCH IN IRELAND**, Assembly Buildings, 2–10 Fisherwick Place, Belfast BT1 6DW
**T** 028-9032 2284 **E** info@presbyterianireland.org
**W** www.presbyterianireland.org
*Moderator (2015–16),* Rt. Revd Ian McNie
*Clerk of Assembly and General Secretary,* Revd Trevor Gribben

## PRESBYTERIAN CHURCH OF WALES

The Presbyterian Church of Wales or Calvinistic Methodist Church of Wales is Calvinistic in doctrine and presbyterian in constitution. It was formed in 1811 when Welsh Calvinists severed the relationship with the established church by ordaining their own ministers. It secured its own confession of faith in 1823 and a Constitutional Deed in 1826, and since 1864 the General Assembly has met annually, presided over by a moderator elected for a year. The doctrine and constitutional structure of the Presbyterian Church of Wales was confirmed by act of parliament in 1931–2.

The Church has 25,000 members, 58 ministers and 653 congregations.

**THE PRESBYTERIAN CHURCH OF WALES**,
Tabernacle Chapel, 81 Merthyr Road, Whitchurch, Cardiff CF14 1DD **T** 029-2062 7465
**E** swyddfa.office@ebcpcw.org.uk **W** www.ebcpcw.org.uk
*Moderator (2014–15),* Revd Neil Kirkham
*General Secretary,* Revd Meirion Morris

## RELIGIOUS SOCIETY OF FRIENDS (QUAKERS)

Quakerism is a religious denomination which was founded in the 17th century by George Fox and others in an attempt to revive what they saw as the original 'primitive Christianity'. The movement, at first called Friends of the Truth, started in the Midlands, Yorkshire and north-west England, but there are now Quakers all over the UK and in 36 countries around the world. The colony of Pennsylvania, founded by William Penn, was originally a Quaker settlement.

Quakers place an emphasis on the experience of God in daily life rather than on sacraments or religious occasions. There is no church calendar. Worship is largely silent and there are no appointed ministers; the responsibility for conducting a meeting is shared equally among those present. Religious tolerance and social reform have always been important to Quakers, together with a commitment to peace and non-violence in resolving disputes.

There are more than 23,000 'friends' or Quakers in Great Britain. There are around 475 places where Quaker meetings are held, many of them Quaker-owned Friends Meeting Houses. The Britain Yearly Meeting is the name given to the central organisation of Quakers in Britain.

**THE RELIGIOUS SOCIETY OF FRIENDS (QUAKERS) IN BRITAIN**, Friends House, 173–177 Euston Road, London NW1 2BJ **T** 020-7663 1000 **E** enquiries@quaker.org.uk
**W** www.quaker.org.uk
*Recording Clerk,* Paul Parker

## SALVATION ARMY

The Salvation Army is an international Christian organisation working in 126 countries worldwide. As a church and registered charity, The Salvation Army is funded through donations from its members, the general public and, where appropriate, government grants. The Salvation Army was founded by Methodists William and Catherine Booth in the East End of London in 1865 and marked its 150th anniversary on 2 July 2015. It now has around 40,000 members and 1,067 Salvation Army Officers (full-time ministers) in the UK. There are over 700 local church and community centres, 62 residential support centres for homeless people, 16 care homes for older people and six substance-misuse centres. It also runs a clothing recycling programme, charity shops, foodbanks, a prison-visiting service and a family-tracing service. In 1878 it adopted a quasi-military command structure intended to inspire and regulate its endeavours and to reflect its view that the church was engaged in spiritual warfare.

**UK TERRITORIAL HEADQUARTERS**,
101 Newington Causeway, London SE1 6BN **T** 020-7367 4500 **E** info@salvationarmy.org.uk **W** www.salvationarmy.org.uk
*UK Territorial Commander,* Commissioner Clive Adams

## SEVENTH-DAY ADVENTIST CHURCH

The Seventh-day Adventist Church is a worldwide Christian church marked by its observance of Saturday as the Sabbath and by its emphasis on the imminent second coming of Jesus Christ. Adventists summarise their faith in '28 fundamental beliefs'. The church grew out of the Millerite movement in the USA during the mid-19th century and was formally established in 1863. The church has an ethnically and culturally diverse worldwide membership of over 17 million. In the UK and Ireland there are 34,048 members worshipping in around 300 churches and companies.

**BRITISH UNION CONFERENCE OF SEVENTH-DAY ADVENTISTS**, Stanborough Park, Watford WD25 9JZ
**T** 01923-672251 **E** info@adventist.org.uk
**W** www.adventist.org.uk
*President,* Pastor Ian Sweeney

## THE (SWEDENBORGIAN) NEW CHURCH

The New Church is based on the teachings of the 18th-century Swedish scientist and theologian Emanuel Swedenborg (1688–1772), who believed that Jesus Christ appeared to him and instructed him to reveal the spiritual meaning of the Bible. He claimed to have visions of the spiritual world, including heaven and hell, and conversations with angels and spirits. He published several theological works, including descriptions of the spiritual world and a Bible commentary.

Swedenborgians believe that the second coming of Jesus Christ is taking place, being not an actual physical reappearance of Christ, but rather his return in spirit. It is also believed that concurrent with our life on earth is life in a parallel spiritual world, of which we are usually unconscious until death. There are around 30,000 Swedenborgians

worldwide, with around 600 members, 18 churches and five ministers in the UK.

**THE GENERAL CONFERENCE OF THE NEW CHURCH**, Purley Chase Centre, Purley Chase Lane, Mancetter, Warwickshire CV9 2RQ **T** 01827-712370
**W** www.generalconference.org.uk
*Company Secretary,* Zoë Brooks

## UNDEB YR ANNIBYNWYR CYMRAEG

Undeb Yr Annibynwyr Cymraeg (the Union of Welsh Independents) was formed in 1872 and is a voluntary association of Welsh Congregational churches and personal members. It is mainly Welsh-speaking. Congregationalism in Wales dates back to 1639 when the first Welsh Congregational church was opened in Gwent. Member churches are traditionally congregationalist in organisation and Calvinistic in doctrine, although a wide range of interpretations are permitted. Each church has complete independence in the governance and administration of its affairs.

The Union has around 24,000 members, 80 ministers and 440 member churches.

**UNDEB YR ANNIBYNWYR CYMRAEG**, 5 Axis Court, Riverside Business Park, Swansea Vale, Swansea SA7 0AJ
**T** 01792-795888 **E** undeb@annibynwyr.org
**W** www.annibynwyr.org
*President of the Union (2014–16),* Revd Dr R. Alun Evans
*General Secretary,* Revd Dr Geraint Tudur

## UNITED REFORMED CHURCH

The United Reformed Church (URC) was first formed by the union of most of the Congregational churches in England and Wales with the Presbyterian Church of England in 1972. It is Calvinistic in doctrine, and its followers form independent self-governing congregations bound under God by covenant, a principle laid down in the writings of Robert Browne (1550–1633). From the late 16th century the movement was driven underground by persecution, but the cause was defended at the Westminster Assembly in 1643 and the Savoy Declaration of 1658 laid down its principles. Congregational churches formed county associations for mutual support and in 1832 these associations merged to form the Congregational Union of England and Wales.

In the 1960s there was close cooperation locally and nationally between congregational and presbyterian churches. This led to union negotiations and a Scheme of Union, supported by an act of parliament in 1972. In 1981 a further unification took place, with the Reformed Association of Churches of Christ becoming part of the URC. In 2000 a third union took place, with the Congregational Union of Scotland. At its basis the URC reflects local church initiative and responsibility with a conciliar pattern of oversight.

The URC is divided into 13 synods, each with a synod moderator. There are around 1,500 churches which serve around 58,000 adults and around 41,000 children and young people. There are around 550 ministers in active service.

The General Assembly is the central body, and comprises around 400 representatives, mainly appointed by the synods, of which half are lay persons and half are ministers. Since 2010 the General Assembly has met biennially to elect two moderators (one lay and one ordained), who then become the public representatives of the URC.

**UNITED REFORMED CHURCH**, 86 Tavistock Place, London WC1H 9RT **T** 020-7916 2020 **E** urc@urc.org.uk
**W** www.urc.org.uk
*Moderators of the General Assembly 2016–18,* Revd Kevin Watson; Alan Yates
*General Secretary,* Revd John Proctor

# WESLEYAN REFORM UNION

The Wesleyan Reform Union was founded by Methodists who left or were expelled from Wesleyan Methodism in 1849 following a period of internal conflict. Its doctrine is conservative evangelical and its organisation is congregational, each church having complete independence in the government and administration of its affairs. The union has around 1,540 members, 20 ministers and 96 churches.

THE WESLEYAN REFORM UNION,
Wesleyan Reform Church House, 123 Queen Street,
Sheffield S1 2DU T 0114-272 1938 E gen.sec@thewru.co.uk
W www.thewru.com
*President (2015–16)*, Andy Wilcock
*General Secretary*, Revd Colin Braithwaite

# NON-TRINITARIAN CHURCHES

## CHRISTADELPHIAN

Christadelphians believe that the Bible is the word of God and that it reveals both God's dealings with mankind in the past and his plans for the future. These plans centre on the work of Jesus Christ, who it is believed will return to earth to establish God's kingdom. The Christadelphian group was founded in the USA in the 1850s by the Englishman, Dr John Thomas.

THE CHRISTADELPHIAN MAGAZINE AND
PUBLISHING ASSOCIATION, 404 Shaftmoor Lane,
Hall Green, Birmingham B28 8SZ T 0121-777 6328
W www.thechristadelphian.com

## CHURCH OF CHRIST, SCIENTIST

The Church of Christ, Scientist was founded by Mary Baker Eddy in the USA in 1879 to 'reinstate primitive Christianity and its lost element of healing'. Christian Science teaches the need for spiritual regeneration and salvation from sin, but it is best known for its reliance on prayer alone in the healing of sickness. Adherents believe that such healing is the result of divine laws, or divine science, and is in direct line with that practised by Jesus Christ (revered, not as God, but as the son of God) and by the early Christian church.

The denomination consists of The First Church of Christ, Scientist, in Boston, Massachusetts, USA ('The Mother Church') and its branch churches in almost 80 countries worldwide. The Bible and Mary Baker Eddy's book, *Science and Health with Key to the Scriptures*, are used for daily spiritual guidance and healing by all members and are read at services. There are no clergy; those engaged in full-time healing are called Christian Science practitioners, of whom there are around 1,500 worldwide. The church also publishes *The Christian Science Monitor*.

No membership figures are available, since Mary Baker Eddy felt that numbers are no measure of spiritual vitality and ruled that such statistics should not be published. There are almost 2,000 branch churches worldwide.

CHRISTIAN SCIENCE COMMITTEE ON
PUBLICATION, 90 Long Acre, London WC2E 9RZ
T 020-8150 0245 E londoncs@csps.com
W www.christianscience.co.uk
*District Manager for the UK and Ireland*, Tony Lobl

## CHURCH OF JESUS CHRIST OF LATTER-DAY SAINTS

The Church of Jesus Christ of Latter-day Saints ('Mormons') was founded in New York State, USA, in 1830, and came to Britain in 1837. The oldest continuous congregation of the church is in Preston, Lancashire.

Mormons are Christians who claim to belong to the 'restored church' of Jesus Christ. They believe that true Christianity died when the last original apostle died, but that it was given back to the world by God and Jesus Christ through Joseph Smith, the church's founder and first president. They accept and use the Bible as scripture, but believe in continuing revelation from God; Mormons also use additional scriptures, including *The Book of Mormon: Another Testament of Jesus Christ*. The importance of the family is central to the church's beliefs and practices. Church members set aside Monday evenings as family home evenings when Christian family values are taught. Polygamy was formally discontinued in 1890.

The church has no paid ministry: local congregations are headed by a leader chosen from among their number. The world governing body, based in Utah, USA, is led by a president, believed to be the chosen prophet, and his two counsellors. There are over 15 million members worldwide, with 186,193 members and 335 congregations in the UK.

THE CHURCH OF JESUS CHRIST OF LATTER-DAY
SAINTS, UK Headquarters, 751 Warwick Road, Solihull,
W. Midlands B91 3DQ T 0121-712 1200
W www.mormonnewsroom.org.uk

## JEHOVAH'S WITNESSES

The movement now known as Jehovah's Witnesses grew from a Bible study group formed by Charles Taze Russell in 1872 in Pennsylvania, USA. In 1896 it adopted the name of the Watch Tower Bible and Tract Society, and in 1931 its members became known as Jehovah's Witnesses.

Jehovah's (God's) Witnesses believe in the Bible as the word of God, and consider it to be inspired and historically accurate. They take the scriptures literally, except where there are obvious indications that they are figurative or symbolic, and reject the doctrine of the Trinity. Witnesses also believe that all those approved of by Jehovah will have eternal life on a cleansed and beautified earth; only 144,000 will go to heaven to rule with Jesus Christ. They believe that the second coming of Christ began in 1914, that his thousand-year reign over the earth is imminent, and that armageddon (a final battle in which evil will be defeated) will precede Christ's rule of peace. Jehovah's Witnesses refuse to take part in military service and do not accept blood transfusions.

The eight-member world governing body is based in New York, USA. There is no paid ministry, but each congregation has elders assigned to look after various duties and every Witness takes part in the public ministry in their neighbourhood. There are 7.97 million Jehovah's Witnesses worldwide, with around 136,000 Witnesses in Great Britain organised into around 1,500 congregations.

BRITISH HEADQUARTERS, The Ridgeway,
London NW7 1RN T 020-8906 2211 W www.jw.org

## UNITARIAN AND FREE CHRISTIAN CHURCHES

Unitarian communities first became established in Poland and Transylvania in the 16th century. The first avowedly Unitarian place of worship in the British Isles opened in London in 1774. The General Assembly of Unitarian and Free Christian Churches came into existence in 1928 as the result of the amalgamation of two earlier organisations.

There are around 3,400 Unitarians in Great Britain in 170 self-governing congregations and fellowship groups.

GENERAL ASSEMBLY OF UNITARIAN AND FREE
CHRISTIAN CHURCHES, Essex Hall, 1–6 Essex Street,
London WC2R 3HY T 020-7240 2384 E info@unitarian.org.uk
W www.unitarian.org.uk
*President (2015–16)*, John Clifford

# COMMUNICATIONS

## POSTAL SERVICES

Royal Mail was privatised on 15 October 2013 when it was listed on the London Stock Exchange. Royal Mail Holdings plc owns Royal Mail Group Ltd – which operates Royal Mail, Parcelforce Worldwide and General Logistics Systems (GLS). The Post Office remains wholly state-owned.

Royal Mail is the sole provider of the 'universal service': postal products and associated minimum service standards that must be available to all addresses in the UK. In 2014 Royal Mail collected and delivered 1,068 million parcels and 13,342 million letters to 29 million addresses across the UK. Compared with 2013, the amount of parcels collected and delivered remained the same, but the amount of letters decreased slightly by 4 per cent.

Following the passing of the Postal Services Act 2011, the Office of Communications (OFCOM) assumed regulatory responsibility for postal services. OFCOM's primary responsibility is to secure the provision of a universal postal service with regard to its financial sustainability.

ROYAL MAIL GROUP LTD, 100 Victoria Embankment, London EC4Y 0HQ T 0345-774 0740
W www.royalmailgroup.com
OFCOM, Riverside House, 2A Southwark Bridge Road, London SE1 9HA T 0207-981 3000 W www.ofcom.org.uk

### PRICING IN PROPORTION
Since 2006 Royal Mail has priced mail according to its size as well as its weight. The system is intended to reflect the fact that larger, bulkier items cost more to handle than smaller, lighter ones. There are five basic categories of correspondence:

LETTER: *Length* up to 240mm, *width* up to 165mm, *thickness* up to 5mm, *weight* up to 100g; eg most cards and postcards
LARGE LETTER: *Length* up to 353mm, *width* up to 250mm, *thickness* up to 25mm, *weight* up to 750g; eg most A4 documents and magazines
SMALL PARCEL: *Length* up to 450mm, *width* up to 350mm, *thickness* up to 160mm, *weight* up to 2kg, eg books, clothes and gifts
MEDIUM PARCEL: *Length* up to 610mm, *width* up to 460mm, *thickness* up to 460mm, *weight* up to 20kg; eg gifts, shoes, heavy or bulky items
LARGE PARCEL (Parcelforce Worldwide): *Length* up to 150cm, with a combined length and width of less than 300cm, *weight* up to 30kg

For rolled and cylinder shaped parcels, eg posters and prints, the length of the item plus twice the diameter must not exceed 104cm, with the greatest dimension being no more than 90cm. Rolled and cylinder shaped parcels which measure up to 450mm in length and 80mm in diameter and which do not exceed 2kg can be sent as small parcels. Items larger than those listed above can only be sent via Parcelforce Worldwide as large parcels.

### INLAND POSTAL SERVICES
Following are details of a number of popular postal services along with prices correct as at April 2015. For a full list of prices *see* W www.royalmail.com

### FIRST AND SECOND CLASS

| Format | Maximum weight | First class | Second class |
| --- | --- | --- | --- |
| Letter/postcard | 100g | £0.63 | £0.54 |
| Large letter | 100g | £0.95 | £0.74 |
| | 250g | £1.26 | £1.19 |
| | 500g | £1.68 | £1.51 |
| | 750g | £2.42 | £2.05 |
| Small parcel | 1,000g | £3.30 | £2.80 |
| | 2,000g | £5.45 | £2.80 |
| Medium parcel | 1,000g | £5.65 | £4.89 |
| | 2,000g | £8.90 | £4.89 |
| | 5,000g | £15.85 | £13.75 |
| | 10,000g | £21.90 | £20.25 |
| | 20,000g | £33.40 | £28.55 |

First class post is normally delivered on the following working day and second class within three working days. Prices are exempt from VAT.

### LARGE PARCEL RATES (PARCELFORCE WORLDWIDE)

| Maximum weight | Lowest tariff* |
| --- | --- |
| 2kg | £11.99 |
| 5kg | £12.98 |
| 10kg | £16.40 |
| 15kg | £23.14 |
| 20kg | £28.51 |
| 25kg | £39.64 |
| 30kg | £43.78 |

* The rate listed includes VAT and is for delivery within two working days

### OVERSEAS POSTAL SERVICES
For charging purposes Royal Mail divides the world into four zones: UK, Europe, World Zone 1 and World Zone 2. There is a complete listing on the Royal Mail website (W www.royalmail.com/international-zones)

**Europe:** Albania, Andorra, Armenia, Austria, Azerbaijan, Azores, Balearic Islands, Belarus, Belgium, Bosnia and Hercegovina, Bulgaria, Canary Islands, Corsica, Croatia, Cyprus, Czech Rep., Denmark, Estonia, Finland, France, Georgia, Germany, Gibraltar, Greece, Greenland, Hungary, Iceland, Ireland, Italy, Kazakhstan, Kosovo, Kyrgyzstan, Latvia, Liechtenstein, Lithuania, Luxembourg, Macedonia, Malta, Moldova, Monaco, Montenegro, Netherlands, Norway, Poland, Portugal, Romania, Russia, San Marino, Serbia, Slovakia, Slovenia, Spain, Sweden, Switzerland, Tajikistan, Turkey, Turkmenistan, Ukraine, Uzbekistan

**World Zone 1:** N. America, S. America, Africa, the Middle East, the Far East and S. E. Asia

**World Zone 2:** Australia, British Indian Ocean Territory, Fiji, French Polynesia, Kiribati, Laos, Macau, Nauru, New Caledonia, New Zealand, Palau, Papua New Guinea, Pitcairn Islands, Singapore, Solomon Islands, Tonga, Tuvalu, Samoa

### INTERNATIONAL ECONOMY MAIL RATES*

| Maximum weight | Standard tariff |
| --- | --- |
| Letters up to 100g† | |
| 10g | £0.85 |
| 20g | £0.85 |
| 100g | £1.37 |

* Formerly Surface Mail
† Can only be sent by International Economy to destinations outside of Europe

| Maximum weight | Large letters | Small parcels and printed papers |
|---|---|---|
| 100g | £2.38 | £3.25 |
| 250g | £3.63 | £3.75 |
| 500g | £5.08 | £5.30 |
| 750g | £6.53 | £6.65 |
| 1,000g | – | £8.06 |
| 2,000g | – | £13.26 |

*Printed papers only* add £1.15 for each additional 250g, or part thereof, up to 5,000g

## INTERNATIONAL STANDARD MAIL RATES*

| Weight up to and including | Europe | World Zone 1 | World Zone 2 |
|---|---|---|---|
| Letters | | | |
| 10g | £1.00 | £1.00 | £1.00 |
| 20g | £1.00 | £1.33 | £1.33 |
| 100g | £1.52 | £2.25 | £2.25 |
| Large letters | | | |
| 100g | £2.45 | £3.15 | £3.30 |
| 250g | £3.70 | £4.75 | £5.05 |
| 500g | £5.15 | £7.45 | £7.90 |
| 750g | £6.60 | £10.15 | £10.75 |
| Small parcels and printed papers | | | |
| 100g | £3.45 | £4.10 | £4.45 |
| 250g | £3.95 | £5.00 | £5.45 |
| 500g | £5.50 | £7.70 | £8.45 |
| 750g | £6.85 | £10.30 | £11.15 |
| 1,000g | £8.26 | £12.95 | £13.90 |
| 2,000g | £13.46 | £19.75 | £21.50 |

*Printed papers only* add £1.15 for Europe, £1.70 for World Zone 1 or £1.90 for World Zone 2 for each additional 250g, or part thereof, up to 5,000g
* Formerly Airmail

## SPECIAL DELIVERY SERVICES

### INTERNATIONAL TRACKED AND SIGNED FOR SERVICES
There are various services available: *International Tracked & Signed* provides full end-to-end tracking, signature on delivery and online delivery confirmation to 53 destinations; *International Tracked* provides the same, but without a signature on delivery, to 39 destinations; and International Signed is tracked within the UK, a signature is taken on delivery and is available to 180 destinations. All Tracked and Signed For services deliver to Europe within 3–5 working days, and worldwide within 5–7 working days. Proof of posting and compensation up to £50 is provided as standard. Additional compensation up to £250 can be provided for an extra fee.
### SAME DAY
A courier service which provides same day delivery of urgent items in most places in the UK. With collection within the hour of booking, satellite tracking, delivery confirmation and automatic compensation up to £2,500, and for an additional fee, up to £20,000, the service is charged for on a loaded mile basis T 0330-088 5522
### SIGNED FOR
A service which offers proof of delivery including a signature from the receiver and compensation cover up to £50. The first class service is delivered the next working day and prices vary from £1.73 to £34.50 depending on the size and weight of the item. The second class service allows two to three working days for delivery with charges of £1.64 to £29.65.

### SPECIAL DELIVERY GUARANTEED
A guaranteed next working day delivery service by 9am or 1pm with a refund option guaranteed for late delivery. With many options available, Royal Mail offers a full list of prices online W www.royalmail.com/personal/uk-delivery/special-delivery

## OTHER SERVICES

### KEEPSAFE
Mail is held for up to two months while the addressee is away, and is delivered when the addressee returns. Prices start at £13.10 for 17 days up to £43.40 for 66 days.
### PASSPORT CHECK & SEND
For a fee of £9.75 passport applications are checked to ensure they meet the requirements set by HM Passport Office and are dispatched by special delivery. For further information *see* W www.postoffice.co.uk
### POST OFFICE BOX
A Post Office (PO) Box provides a short and memorable alternative address. Mail is held at a local delivery office until the addressee is ready to collect it, or delivered to a street address for an extra fee. Prices start at £144.00 for six months or £252.00 for a year.
### POSTCODE FINDER
Customers can search an online database to find UK postcodes and addresses. For more information *see* Royal Mail's postcode finder W www.royalmail.com/postcode-finder
### REDELIVERY
Customers can request a redelivery of an item for up to 18 days if it was unable to be delivered. A 48-hour notice period is required for redelivery or the item can be held at the recipient's local Post Office branch for a fee of £0.70 upon collection in addition to proof of identity and the original delivery notification card.
### REDIRECTION
Customers may arrange the redirection of their mail via post, at the Post Office or online, subject to verification of their identity. The service is available for 0–3 months, 3–6 months or 6–12 months at varying prices depending on the location of delivery. A full price list is available at W www.royalmail.com/personal/receiving-mail/redirection
### TRACK AND TRACE
An online service for customers to track the progress of items sent using any special delivery tracked and signed for service. It is accessible from W www.royalmail.com/track-your-item

## CONTACTS
Parcelforce Worldwide
　T 0344-800 4466 W www.parcelforce.com
Post Office enquiries T 0345-611 2970 W www.postoffice.co.uk
Postcode enquiry line T 0906-302 1222/ 0845-711 1222

# TELECOMMUNICATIONS

Mobile network technology has improved dramatically since the launch in 1985 of the first-generation global system for mobile communications (GSM), which offered little or no data capability. In 1992 Vodafone launched a new GSM network, usually referred to as 2G or second generation, which used digital encoding and allowed voice and low-speed data communications. This technology was extended, via the enhanced data transfer rate of 2.5G, to 3G – a family of mobile standards that provide high bandwidth support to applications such as voice- and video-calling, high-speed data transfer, television streaming and full internet access. Most recently, a 4G superfast mobile spectrum was rolled out, which delivers speeds of up to 100 megabits per second (Mbps), allowing for faster download speeds on a range of devices. In February 2015, OFCOM stated that 5G data connections could be available in the UK by 2020.

## FOURTH GENERATION (4G) AND WI-FI

In March 2011 OFCOM announced plans for the auction of additional spectrum (the airwaves on which all communications rely) to provide the necessary capacity for 4G technology in the UK. OFCOM originally aimed to begin the auction in early 2012, but following a consultation regarding the proposals in 2011, the auction did not take place until February 2013. The spectrum was auctioned in two bands – 800 MHz and 2.6 GHz – which lie within the 'sweetspot', the frequency in greatest demand. This combination of low and high frequencies provides the potential to cope with high demand of 4G services. The auction raised £2.34bn for HM Treasury, less than the £3.5bn that was forecast by the Office for Budget Responsibility, and considerably less than the 3G auction in 2000 which raised £22bn. The winning bidders for the distribution of 4G mobile broadband were Everything Everywhere (EE), Hutchison 3G UK (3), Niche Spectrum Ventures (a BT subsidiary), Telefonica (O2) and Vodafone.

4G coverage is expected to cover 98 per cent of the UK population indoors and above that when outdoors. The speeds offered by 4G are approximately five to ten times faster than 3G networks which allows for higher quality and faster streaming of media such as TV and films. The UK population in more rural areas, that was often outside 3G coverage, should also be able to access mobile broadband through the 4G spectrum.

EE was the first operator to launch 4G in late 2012 and by April 2013 the service was available in ten cities where the broadband speed was doubled to more than 20Mbps. O2 and Vodafone subsequently launched their 4G networks in late August 2013 while 3 began their service in December 2013. As at April 2015 EE, the largest network provider of 4G, had rolled out 4G coverage to around 510 towns and cities, covering over 80 per cent of the UK population.

The number of Wi-Fi hotspots around the world continued to increase in 2014 with 47.7 million public hotspots worldwide – the equivalent of one for every 150 people. France was ranked the most connected country with 13,096,824 hotspots, the USA second with 9,858,246, while the UK was third with 5,611,944 – one for every 11 people. There is Wi-Fi access at 150 London Underground stations, available in ticket halls, corridors and platforms. Additionally Wi-Fi is also available at 56 London Overground stations.

## FIXED-LINE SERVICES

Fixed-line services saw a slight increase in 2013 to 33.38 million connections in the UK from 33.20 million in 2012. However, fixed voice call minutes continued to decline, from 103 billion minutes in 2012 to 92 billion minutes in 2013, a steady decline from the 141 billion minutes recorded in 2008. Business customers continued to gravitate towards the use of mobile phones, emails and voice over internet protocol (VoIP) services such as Skype, with a decline of 0.4 million (6 per cent) to 8.3 million in the number of business lines in 2013.

The decrease in the number of business lines was offset slightly by a small increase in the number of residential lines which rose by 0.6 million (2.0 per cent) to 25.0 million in 2013. The increase is most likely due to the increasing number of households and the necessity of most UK households to have a fixed line in order to access fixed broadband services. The average cost of a residential fixed broadband connection increased in 2013 to £16.96 (3.7 per cent) due to the continued take-up of superfast broadband services. In turn, the average headline speed increased by 5.8Mbps to 17.8Mbps, while users who invested in higher speed packages, including superfast services received a headline speed of up to 30Mbps or more. Superfast broadband connections, of which there were none in 2009, increased to 5.6 million connections, from 3.2 million in 2012.

## MOBILE COMMUNICATIONS

OFCOM reported the first decrease in UK mobile subscriptions with 83.1 million active at the end of 2013, compared with 83.4 million at the end of 2012. There was a 20 per cent increase in smartphone ownership with 61 per cent of adults in the UK owning one at the start of 2014. There was a large reduction in the number of outgoing SMS messages sent in 2013, with 129.9 billion messages sent compared with 171.9 billion in 2012. The decline in text messaging is likely to be a result of the of the increasing number of smartphones being used for communication, with social media platforms and instant messaging services such as WhatsApp and iMessenger, often pre-installed, providing alternatives to SMS.

It was estimated that over 6 million 4G mobile subscriptions were active in the UK at the end of March 2014 which represented 8 per cent of active mobile subscriptions. This was a dramatic increase in 4G subscriptions of which there were only 318,000 at the start of 2013. At the end of 2013 there were an estimated 55 million UK mobile data connections, including machine-to-machine (M2M); the majority of this was due to an increase in the number of handsets used to access data services, up by 6.2 million (16.1 per cent) to 44.5 million as a result of increased smartphone ownership.

### MOBILE DATA USAGE

The proportion of adults who browsed the web, used email, downloaded apps and used instant messaging all increased

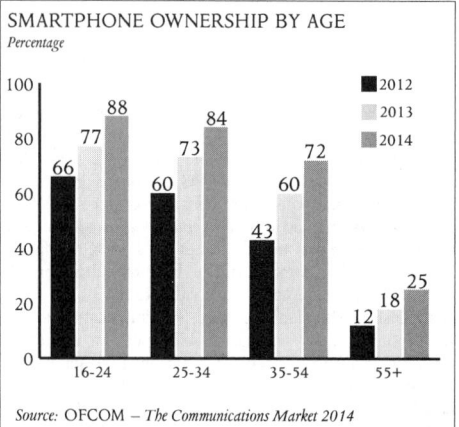

### SMARTPHONE OWNERSHIP BY AGE
*Percentage*

*Source: OFCOM – The Communications Market 2014*

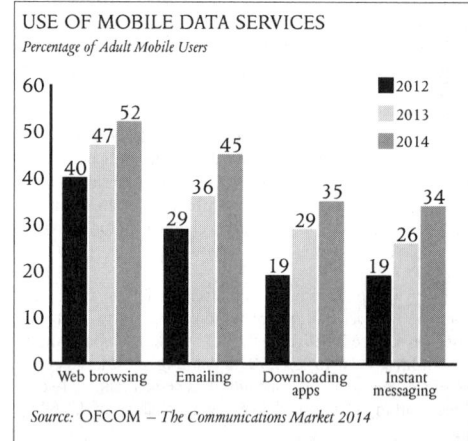

### USE OF MOBILE DATA SERVICES
*Percentage of Adult Mobile Users*

*Source: OFCOM – The Communications Market 2014*

t the start of 2014; 52 per cent of mobile users said they browsed the internet on their mobile phone in the first quarter of 2014, an 11 per cent increase compared to the same period in 2013. Between the 2013 and 2014 the number of mobile users who downloaded apps increased from 29 to 35 per cent while those using instant messaging increased from 26 to 34 per cent.

## HEALTH

In 1999 the Independent Expert Group on Mobile Phones (IEGMP) was established to examine the possible effects on health of mobile phones, base stations and transmitters. The main findings of the IEGMP's report *Mobile Phones and Health*, published in May 2000, were:

- exposure to radio frequency radiation below guideline levels did not cause adverse health effects to the general population
- the use of mobile phones by drivers of any vehicle can increase the chance of accidents
- the widespread use of mobile phones by children for non-essential calls should be discouraged because if there are unrecognised adverse health effects children may be more vulnerable
- there is no general risk to the health of people living near to base stations on the basis that exposures are expected to be much lower than guidelines set by the International Commission on Non-Ionising Radiation Protection

The government set up the Mobile Telecommunications Health and Research (MTHR) programme in 2001 to undertake independent research into the possible health risks from mobile telephone technology. The MTHR programme published its report in September 2007 concluding that, in the short term, neither mobile phones nor base stations have been found to be associated with any biological or adverse health effects. An international cohort study into the possible long-term health effects of mobile phone use was launched by the MTHR in April 2010. The study is known as COSMOS and aims to follow the health of 250,000 mobile phone users from five countries over 20 to 30 years. The full 2007 report and details of COSMOS can be found on the MTHR and COSMOS websites (W www.mthr.org.uk; www.ukcosmos.org).

A national measurement programme, to ensure that emissions from mobile phone base stations do not exceed the ICNIRP guideline levels, is overseen by OFCOM and annual audits of these levels can be found on the sitefinder part of its website. The Health Protection Agency (HPA), part of Public Health England from 1 April 2013, is responsible for providing information and advice in relation to the health effects of electromagnetic fields, including those emitted from mobile phones and base stations. In April 2012, the HPA's independent Advisory Group on Non-ionising Radiation published a report concluding that there was no convincing evidence that mobile phone technologies cause adverse effects on human health.

## SAFETY WHILE DRIVING

Under legislation that came into effect in December 2003 it is illegal for drivers to use a hand-held mobile phone while driving. Since February 2007, under the Road Safety Act 2006, the fixed penalty for using a hand-held mobile device while driving is £100 and three penalty points. The same fixed penalty can also be issued to a driver for not having proper control of a vehicle while using a hands-free device. If the police or driver chooses to take the case to court rather than issue or accept a fixed penalty notice, the driver may be disqualified from driving in addition to a maximum fine of £1,000 for car drivers and £2,500 for drivers of buses, coaches or heavy goods vehicles. The only exceptions for using a mobile phone while driving are to call the emergency services, or when the driver is safely parked.

## REGULATION

Under the Communications Act 2003, OFCOM is the independent regulator and competition authority for the UK communications industries, with responsibilities across television, radio, telecommunications and wireless communications services. Competition in the communications market is also regulated by the Office of Fair Trading, although OFCOM takes the lead in competition investigations in the UK market. The Competition Appeal Tribunal hears appeals against OFCOM's decisions, and price-related appeals are referred to the Competition Commission.

## CONTACTS

OFCOM, Riverside House, 2A Southwark Bridge Road, London SE1 9HA T 020-7981 3000 W www.ofcom.org.uk

## INTERNET

In 2014, 22 million households in Great Britain had internet access. This represented 84 per cent of households, up from 83 per cent in 2013. Of the households with internet access, 91 per cent used a fixed broadband connection.

In 2014 68 per cent of adults reported that they had used a device such as a mobile phone, portable computer (tablet or laptop) or other handheld device to access the internet 'on the go' (away from the home or workplace). Of these, 58 per cent used a mobile phone or smart phone, 43 per cent used a portable computer and 15 per cent used an ebook reader or other handheld device.

Over a four-year period between 2010–14, the number of adults who accessed the internet using a mobile phone more than doubled from 24 per cent to 58 per cent, with 96 per cent of those aged 16 to 24 reporting that they used their mobile phone to access the internet in 2014. The dramatic increase in these figures is predominantly due to the ownership of smartphones with enhanced technology to facilitate easier internet access.

In 2014, 54 per cent of all adults (aged 16+) used social networking sites such as Facebook and Twitter with 91 per cent of those aged 16 to 24 using these media platforms as a form of internet communication. For this age range, social networking has replaced sending emails as the most popular internet activity.

The youngest demographic represented, aged 16 to 24, were proportionally the largest users of many of the available internet activities, due to their familiarity with internet usage from an early age. This age group were most likely to engage in online activities including social networking, blogging, or downloading games, films or music. Those aged 25 to 34 engaged in more established activities such as personal banking and shopping – the latter saw a small increase in demand, with 74 per cent of adults buying goods or services online in 2014. A rise in internet shopping was also evident among those aged over 65, as 40 per cent made purchases online, over twice as many as in 2008.

There were 4 million households with no internet access in 2014, the majority (53 per cent) stating they did not need it. Of the households with no internet connection, 32 per cent indicated that this was due to a lack of computer skills, while other reasons included equipment costs (12 per cent) and access costs (11 per cent).

In 2014, 38 million adults (76 per cent) accessed the internet daily, 21 million more than in 2006, when directly comparable records began.

TOP TEN BROADBAND SUBSCRIBERS BY COUNTRY
*fixed lines*

| Country (2013 position) | Number of Subscribers 2014 |
|---|---|
| 1. China (all territories) (1) | 201,000,000 |
| 2. USA (2) | 97,000,000 |
| 3. Japan (3) | 36,000,000 |
| 4. Germany (4) | 29,000,000 |
| 5. France (6) | 26,000,000 |
| 6. Russia (5) | 25,000,000 |
| 7. UK (7) | 24,000,000 |
| 8. Brazil (8) | 23,000,000 |
| 9. South Korea (9) | 19,000,000 |
| 10. Mexico (*) | 17,000,000 |

\* Not in the 2013 Top Ten
*Sources:* Office for National Statistics – *Internet Access – Households and Individuals, 2014* (Crown Copyright); Point Topic

## GLOSSARY OF TERMS

*The following is a list of selected internet terms. It is by no means exhaustive but is intended to cover those that the average computer user might encounter.*

BANNER AD: An advertisement on a web page that links to a corresponding website when clicked.

BLOG: Short for 'web log' – an online personal journal that is frequently updated and intended to be read by the public. Blogs are kept by 'bloggers' and are commonly available as RSS feeds.

BOOKMARKS: A method of storing links or automatic pathways within web browsers which allow a user to quickly return to a webpage. Referred to as 'Favourites' in Internet Explorer.

BROWSER: Typically refers to a 'web browser' program that allows a computer user to view web page content on their computer, eg Firefox, Internet Explorer or Safari.

CLICK-THROUGH: The number of times a web user 'clicks through' a paid advertisement link to the corresponding website.

CLOUD COMPUTING: The use of IT resources as an on-demand service across a network; through cloud computing, software, advanced computation and archived information can be accessed remotely, without the user needing local dedicated hardware.

COOKIE: A piece of information placed on a user's hard disk by a web server. Cookies contain data about the user's activity on a website, and are returned to the server whenever a browser makes further requests. They are important for remembering information such as login and registration details, 'shopping cart' data, user preferences etc, and are often set to expire after a fixed period.

DOMAIN: A set of words or letters, separated by dots, used to identify an internet server, eg www.whitakers almanack.com, where 'www' denotes a web (http) server, 'whitakersalmanack' denotes the organisation name and 'com' denotes that the organisation is a company.

FIREWALL: A protection system designed to prevent unauthorised access to or from a private network.

FTP: File Transfer Protocol – a set of network rules enabling a user to exchange files with a remote server.

HACKER: A person who attempts to break or 'hack' into websites. Motives typically involve the desire to procure personal information such as addresses, passwords or credit card details. Hackers may also delete code or incorporate traces of malicious code to damage the functionality of a website.

HIT: A single request from a web browser for a single item from a web server. In order for a web browser to display a page that contains three graphics, four 'hits' would occur at the server: one for the HTML page and one for each of the three graphics. Therefore the number of hits on a website is not synonymous with the number of visitors.

HTML: HyperText Mark-up Language – a programming language used to denote or mark up how an internet page should be presented to a user from an HTTP server via a web browser.

HTTP: HyperText Transfer Protocol – an internet protocol whereby a web server sends web pages, images and files to a web browser.

HYPERLINK: A piece of specially coded text that users can click on to navigate to the web page, or element of a web page, associated with that link's code. Links are typically distinguished through the use of bold, underlined or differently coloured text.

JAVA: A programming language used widely on the internet.

MALWARE: A combination of the words 'malicious' and 'software'. Malware is software designed with the intention of infiltrating a computer and damaging its system.

OPEN-SOURCE: Describes a computer program that has its source code (the instructions that make up a program) freely available for viewing and modification.

PAGERANK: A link analysis algorithm used by search engines that assigns a numerical value based on a website's relevance and reputation. In general, a site with a higher pagerank has more traffic than a site with a lower one.

PHISHING: The fraudulent practice of sending emails to acquire personal information by masquerading as a legitimate company.

PODCAST: A form of audio and video broadcasting using the internet. Although the word is a portmanteau of 'iPod' and broadcasting, podcasting does not require the use of an iPod. A podcaster creates a list of files and makes it available in the RSS 2.0 format. The list can then be obtained using podcast 'retriever' software which makes the files available to digital devices (including iPods); users may then listen or watch at their convenience.

RSS FEED: Rich Site Summary or RDF Site Summary or Real Simple Syndication – a commonly used protocol for syndication and sharing of content, originally developed to facilitate the syndication of news articles, now widely used to share the content of blogs.

SEO: Search engine optimisation – the process of optimising the content of a web page to ensure that it is indexed by search engines.

SERVER: A node on a network that provides service to the terminals on the network. These computers have higher hardware specifications, ie more resources and greater speed, in order to handle large amounts of data.

SOCIAL NETWORKING: The practice of using a web-hosted service such as Facebook or Twitter to upload and share content and build friendship networks.

SPAM: A term used for unsolicited, generally junk, email.

TRAFFIC: The number of visitors to a website.

TWITTER: An online microblogging service that allows users to stay connected through the exchange of 140-character posts, known as 'tweets'.

URL: Uniform Resource Locator – address of a file accessible on the internet, eg http://www.whitakersalmanack.com

USER-GENERATED CONTENT (UGC): Refers to various media content produced or primarily influenced by end-users, as opposed to traditional media producers such as licensed broadcasters and production companies. These forms of media include digital video, blogging, podcasting, mobile phone photography and wikis.

# CONSERVATION AND HERITAGE

## NATIONAL PARKS

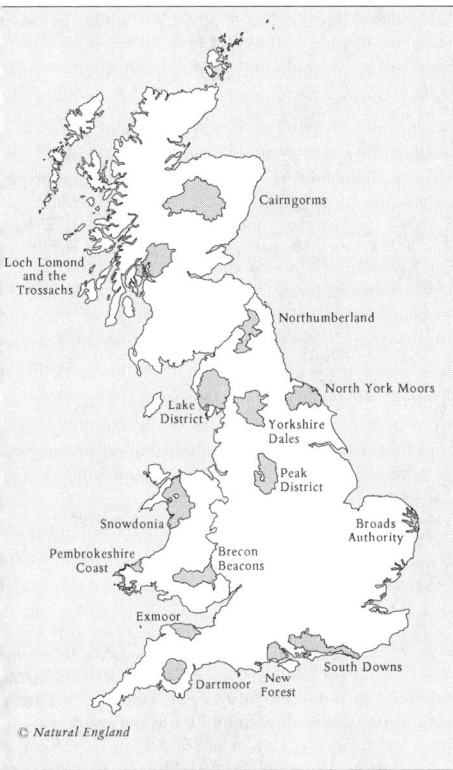

Cairngorms

Loch Lomond
and the
Trossachs

Northumberland

North York Moors

Lake
District

Yorkshire
Dales

Peak
District

Snowdonia

Broads
Authority

Pembrokeshire
Coast

Brecon
Beacons

Exmoor

South Downs

Dartmoor New
Forest

© *Natural England*

### ENGLAND AND WALES

There are nine national parks in England, and three in Wales. In addition, the Norfolk and Suffolk Broads are considered to have equivalent status to a national park. Under the National Parks and Access to the Countryside Act 1949, as clarified by the Natural Environment and Rural Communities Act 2006, the two purposes of the national parks are to conserve and enhance the parks' natural beauty, wildlife and cultural heritage, and to promote opportunities for the understanding and enjoyment of the special qualities of national parks by the public. If there is a conflict between the two purposes, then conservation takes precedence.

Natural England is the statutory body that has the power to designate national parks in England, and Natural Resources Wales (formerly Countryside Council for Wales) is responsible for national parks in Wales. Designations in England are confirmed by the Secretary of State for Environment, Food and Rural Affairs and those in Wales by the Welsh government. The designation of a national park does not affect the ownership of the land or remove the rights of the local community. The majority of the land in the national parks is owned by private landowners (around 75 per cent) or by bodies such as the National Trust and the Forestry Commission. The national park authorities own only a small percentage of the land themselves.

The Environment Act 1995 replaced the existing national park boards and committees with free-standing national park authorities (NPAs). NPAs are the sole local planning authorities for their areas and as such influence land use and development, and deal with planning applications. NPAs are responsible for carrying out the statutory purposes of national parks stated above.

In pursuing these purposes they have a statutory duty to seek to foster the economic and social well-being of the communities within national parks. The NPAs publish management plans setting out overarching policies for their area and appoint their own officers and staff.

The Broads Authority was established under the Norfolk and Suffolk Broads Act 1988 and meets the requirement for the authority to have a navigation function in addition to a regard for the needs of agriculture, forestry and the economic and social interests of those who live or work in the Broads.

### MEMBERSHIP

Membership of English NPAs comprises local authority appointees, members directly appointed by the Secretary of State for Environment, Food and Rural Affairs and members appointed by the secretary after consultation with local parishes. Under the Natural Environment and Rural Communities Act 2006 every district, county or unitary authority with land in a national park is entitled to appoint at least one member unless it chooses to opt out. The total number of local authority and parish members must exceed the number of national members.

Northumberland, Pembrokeshire Coast and Snowdonia NPAs have 18 members; Dartmoor has 19; the Lake District and North York Moors have 20; the Broads has 21; Exmoor, the New Forest and Yorkshire Dales have 22; Brecon Beacons 24; South Downs 27; and the Peak District 30.

In Wales, two-thirds of NPA members are appointed by the constituent local authorities and one-third by the Welsh government, advised by Natural Resources Wales.

### FUNDING

Core funding for the English NPAs and the Broads Authority is provided by central government through the Department for Environment, Food and Rural Affairs (DEFRA) National Park Grant. For 2015–16 a total of £44.7m was allocated.

In Wales, the three national parks are funded by the Welsh government and their constituent local authorities. Total budgeted revenue expenditure for 2015–16 was £14.5m.

All NPAs and the Broads Authority can take advantage of grants from other bodies including lottery and European grants.

The national parks (with date that designation was confirmed) are:

BRECON BEACONS (1957), Powys (66 per cent)/ Carmarthenshire/Rhondda, Cynon and Taff/Merthyr Tydfil/Blaenau Gwent/Monmouthshire, 1,344 sq. km/ 519 sq. miles – The park is centred on the Brecon Beacons mountain range, which includes the three highest mountains in southern Britain (Pen y Fan, Corn Du and Cribyn), but also includes the valleys of the rivers Usk and Wye, the Black Mountains to the east and the Black Mountain to the west. There are information centres at the visitor centre at Libanus (near Brecon), Abergavenny and Llandovery, as well as the Waterfalls Centre in Pontneddfechan.
*National Park Authority*, Plas y Ffynnon, Cambrian Way, Brecon, Powys LD3 7HP **T** 01874-624437 **W** www.beacons-npa.gov.uk
*Chief Executive*, John Cook

BROADS (1989), Norfolk/Suffolk, 303 sq. km/117 sq. miles – The Broads are located between Norwich and Great Yarmouth on the flood plains of the six rivers flowing through the area to the sea. The area is one of fens, winding waterways, woodland and marsh. The 60 or so broads are man-made, and many are connected to the rivers by dykes, providing over 200km (125 miles) of navigable waterways. There are information centres at Hoveton, Whitlingham Country Park and How Hill National Nature Reserve. There are yacht stations at Norwich, Reedham and Great Yarmouth.
*Broads Authority*, Yare House, 62–64 Thorpe Road, Norwich NR1 1RY T 01603-610734 W www.broads-authority.gov.uk
*Chief Executive*, Dr John Packman
DARTMOOR (1951), Devon, 953 sq. km/368 sq. miles – The park consists of moorland and rocky granite tors, and is rich in prehistoric remains. There are visitor centres at Haytor, Princetown (main visitor centre) and Postbridge.
*National Park Authority*, Parke, Bovey Tracey, Devon TQ13 9JQ T 01626-832093 E hq@dartmoor.gov.uk W www.dartmoor.gov.uk
*Chief Executive*, Kevin Bishop
EXMOOR (1954), Somerset (71 per cent)/Devon, 694 sq. km/268 sq. miles – Exmoor is a moorland plateau inhabited by wild Exmoor ponies and red deer. There are many ancient remains and burial mounds. There are national park centres at Dunster, Dulverton and Lynmouth.
*National Park Authority*, Exmoor House, Dulverton, Somerset TA22 9HL T 01398-323665 E info@exmoor-nationalpark.gov.uk W www.exmoor-nationalpark.gov.uk
*Chief Executive*, Dr Nigel Stone
LAKE DISTRICT (1951), Cumbria, 2,292 sq. km/885 sq. miles – The Lake District includes England's highest mountains (Scafell Pike, Helvellyn and Skiddaw) but it is most famous for its glaciated lakes. There are national park information centres at Bowness-on-Windermere, Keswick, Ullswater and a visitor centre at Brockhole, Windermere.
*National Park Authority*, Murley Moss, Oxenholme Road, Kendal, Cumbria LA9 7RL T 01539-724555 E hq@lakedistrict.gov.uk W www.lakedistrict.gov.uk
*Chief Executive*, Richard Leafe
NEW FOREST (2005), Hampshire, 570 sq. km/220 sq. miles – The forest has been protected since 1079 when it was declared a royal hunting forest. The area consists of forest, ancient woodland, heathland, farmland, coastal saltmarsh and mudflats. Much of the forest is managed by the Forestry Commission, which provides several campsites. There is a visitor centre at Lyndhurst.
*National Park Authority*, Town Hall, Avenue Road, Lymington, Hants SO41 9ZG T 01590-646600
E enquiries@newforestnpa.gov.uk W www.newforestnpa.gov.uk
*Chief Executive*, Alison Barnes
NORTH YORK MOORS (1952), North Yorkshire (96 per cent)/Redcar and Cleveland, 1,434 sq. km/554 sq. miles – The park consists of woodland, moorland and coast, and includes the Hambleton Hills and the Cleveland Way. There are visitor centres at Danby and Sutton Bank.
*National Park Authority*, The Old Vicarage, Bondgate, Helmsley, York YO62 5BP T 01439-772700
E general@northyorkmoors.org.uk W www.northyorkmoors.org.uk
*Chief Executive*, Andy Wilson
NORTHUMBERLAND (1956), Northumberland, 1,048 sq. km/404 sq. miles – The park is an area of hill country, comprising open moorland, blanket bogs and very small patches of ancient woodland, stretching from Hadrian's Wall to the Scottish border. There is an information centre at Once Brewed.
*National Park Authority*, Eastburn, South Park, Hexham, Northumberland NE46 1BS T 01434-605555
E enquiries@nnpa.org.uk
W www.northumberlandnationalpark.org.uk
*Chief Executive*, Tony Gates

PEAK DISTRICT (1951), Derbyshire (64 per cent)/ Staffordshire/South Yorkshire/Cheshire/West Yorkshire/ Greater Manchester, 1,437 sq. km/555 sq. miles – The Peak District includes the gritstone moors of the Dark Peak, the limestone dales of the White Peak and the crags and rolling farmland of the South West Peak. There are information centres at Bakewell, Castleton, Edale and Upper Derwent.
*National Park Authority*, Aldern House, Baslow Road, Bakewell, Derbyshire DE45 1AE T 01629-816200
E customer.service@peakdistrict.gov.uk
W www.peakdistrict.gov.uk
*Chief Executive*, Sarah Fowler
PEMBROKESHIRE COAST (1952 and 1995), Pembrokeshire, 621 sq. km/236 sq. miles – The park includes cliffs, moorland and a number of islands, including Skomer and Ramsey. There are information centres in Newport and Tenby and a gallery and visitor centre, Oriel y Parc, in St Davids. The park also manages Castell Henllys Iron Age Village and Carew Castle and Tidal Mill.
*National Park Authority*, Llanion Park, Pembroke Dock, Pembrokeshire SA72 6DY T 0845-345 7275
E info@pembrokeshirecoast.org.uk
W www.pembrokeshirecoast.org.uk
*Chief Executive*, Tegryn Jones
SNOWDONIA/ERYRI (1951), Gwynedd/Conwy, 2,176 sq. km/840 sq. miles – Snowdonia, which takes its name from Snowdon, is an area of deep valleys and rugged mountains. There are information centres at Aberdyfi, Beddgelert, Betws y Coed and Dolgellau.
*National Park Authority*, Penrhyndeudraeth, Gwynedd LL48 6LF T 01766-770274 E parc@snowdonia-npa.gov.uk
W www.snowdonia-npa.gov.uk
*Chief Executive*, Emyr Williams
THE SOUTH DOWNS (2010), West Sussex/Hampshire, 1,624 sq. km/627 sq. miles – The South Downs contains a diversity of natural habitats, including flower-studded chalk grassland, ancient woodland, flood meadow, lowland heath and rare chalk heathland. There are visitor centres at Beachy Head, Queen Elizabeth Country Park in Hampshire and Seven Sisters Country Park in East Sussex.
*National Park Authority*, North Street, Midhurst, W. Sussex GU29 9DH T 01730-814810 W www.southdowns.gov.uk
*Chief Executive*, Trevor Beattie
YORKSHIRE DALES (1954), North Yorkshire (88 per cent)/Cumbria, 1,769 sq. km/683 sq. miles – The Yorkshire Dales is composed primarily of limestone overlaid in places by millstone grit. The three peaks of Ingleborough, Whernside and Pen-y-ghent are within the park. There are information centres at Grassington, Hawes, Aysgarth Falls, Malham and Reeth.
*National Park Authority*, Yoredale, Bainbridge, Leyburn, N. Yorks DL8 3EL T 0300-456 0030 E info@yorkshiredales.org.uk
W www.yorkshiredales.org.uk
*Chief Executive*, David Butterworth

## SCOTLAND

On 9 August 2000 the national parks (Scotland) bill received royal assent, giving parliament the ability to create national parks in Scotland. The Act gives Scottish parks wider powers than in England and Wales, including statutory responsibilities for the local economy and rural communities. The board of the Cairngorms NPA comprises 19 members; seven appointed by the Scottish ministers, a further seven nominated to the board by the five local authorities in the park area and five locally elected members. The board of Loch Lomond and the Trossachs NPA comprises 17 members; six appointed by the Scottish ministers, a further six nominated by local authorities within the park boundaries and five elected via a postal ballot of the local electorate. In Scotland, the national parks are central government bodies and are wholly funded by the Scottish government. The draft budget for 2015–16 totalled £12.5m.

**CAIRNGORMS (2003)**, North-East Scotland, 4,528 sq. km/1,748 sq. miles – The Cairngorms national park is the largest in the UK, covering around 6 per cent of Scotland. It displays a vast collection of landforms, including five of the six highest mountains in the UK and contains 25 per cent of Britain's threatened species. The near natural woodlands contain remnants of the original ancient Caledonian pine forest. There are nine visitor centres within the park.
*National Park Authority,* 14 The Square, Grantown-on-Spey, Morayshire PH26 3HG **T** 01479-873535
**E** enquiries@cairngorms.co.uk **W** www.cairngorms.co.uk
*Chief Executive,* Grant Moir

**LOCH LOMOND AND THE TROSSACHS (2002)**, Argyll and Bute/Perth and Kinross/Stirling/West Dunbartonshire, 1,865 sq. km/720 sq. miles – The park boundaries encompass lochs, rivers, forests, 21 mountains above 914m (3,000ft) including Ben More and a further 19 mountains between 762m (2,500ft) and 914m (3,000ft). There is a national park centre in Balmaha. There are also seven visitor centres administered by VisitScotland.
*National Park Authority,* Carrochan, Carrochan Road, Balloch G83 8EG **T** 01389-722600 **E** info@lochlomond-trossachs.org
**W** www.lochlomond-trossachs.org
*Chief Executive,* Gordon Watson

## NORTHERN IRELAND
There is a power to designate national parks in Northern Ireland under the Nature Conservation and Amenity Lands Order (Northern Ireland) 1985, but there are currently no national parks in Northern Ireland.

# AREAS OF OUTSTANDING NATURAL BEAUTY

## ENGLAND AND WALES
Under the National Parks and Access to the Countryside Act 1949, provision was made for the designation of areas of outstanding natural beauty (AONBs). Natural England is responsible for AONBs in England and Natural Resources Wales for the Welsh AONBs. Designations in England are confirmed by the Secretary of State for Environment, Food and Rural Affairs and those in Wales by the Welsh government. The Countryside and Rights of Way (CROW) Act 2000 placed greater responsibility on local authorities to protect AONBs and made it a statutory duty for these authorities to produce a management plan for their AONB area. The CROW Act also provided for the creation of conservation boards for larger and more complex AONBs.

The primary objective of the AONB designation is to conserve and enhance the natural beauty of the area. Where an AONB has a conservation board, it has the additional purpose of increasing public understanding and enjoyment of the special qualities of the area; the board has greater weight should there be a conflict of interests between the two. In addition, the board is also required to foster the economic and social well-being of the local communities but without incurring significant expenditure in doing so. Overall responsibility for AONBs lies with the relevant local authorities or conservation board. To coordinate planning and management responsibilities between local authorities in whose area they fall, AONBs are overseen by a joint advisory committee (or similar body) which includes representatives from the local authorities, landowners, farmers, residents and conservation and recreation groups. Core funding for AONBs is provided by central government through DEFRA, local authorities and Natural Resources Wales.

The 38 AONBs (with date designation confirmed) are:

**ARNSIDE AND SILVERDALE (1972)**, Cumbria/Lancashire, 75 sq. km/29 sq. miles
**BLACKDOWN HILLS (1991)**, Devon/Somerset, 370 sq. km/143 sq. miles
**CANNOCK CHASE (1958)**, Staffordshire, 68 sq. km/26 sq. miles
**CHICHESTER HARBOUR (1964)**, Hampshire/West Sussex, 74 sq. km/29 sq. miles
**CHILTERNS (1965; extended 1990)**, Bedfordshire/Buckinghamshire/Herefordshire/Oxfordshire, 839 sq. km/324 sq. miles
**CLWYDIAN RANGE AND DEE VALLEY (1985; extended 2011)**, Denbighshire/Flintshire, 389 sq. km/150 sq. miles
**CORNWALL (1959; Camel Estuary 1983)**, 958 sq. km/370 sq. miles
**COTSWOLDS (1966; extended 1990)**, Gloucestershire/Oxfordshire/Warwickshire/Wiltshire/Worcestershire, 2,046 sq. km/790 sq. miles
**CRANBORNE CHASE AND WEST WILTSHIRE DOWNS (1983)**, Dorset/Hampshire/Somerset/Wiltshire, 983 sq. km/380 sq. miles
**DEDHAM VALE (1970; extended 1978, 1991)**, Essex/Suffolk, 90 sq. km/35 sq. miles
**DORSET (1959)**, Dorset/Somerset, 1,129 sq. km/436 sq. miles
**EAST DEVON (1963)**, 268 sq. km/103 sq. miles
**FOREST OF BOWLAND (1964)**, Lancashire/North Yorkshire, 803 sq. km/310 sq. miles
**GOWER (1956)**, Swansea, 188 sq. km/73 sq. miles
**HIGH WEALD (1983)**, East Sussex/Kent/Surrey/West Sussex, 1,461 sq. km/564 sq. miles
**HOWARDIAN HILLS (1987)**, North Yorkshire, 204 sq. km/79 sq. miles
**ISLE OF WIGHT (1963)**, 189 sq. km/73 sq. miles
**ISLES OF SCILLY (1976)**, 16 sq. km/6 sq. miles
**KENT DOWNS (1968)**, 878 sq. km/339 sq. miles
**LINCOLNSHIRE WOLDS (1973)**, 558 sq. km/215 sq. miles
**LLYN (1957)**, Gwynedd, 155 sq. km/60 sq. miles
**MALVERN HILLS (1959)**, Gloucestershire/Worcestershire, 105 sq. km/41 sq. miles
**MENDIP HILLS (1972; extended 1989)**, Somerset, 198 sq. km/76 sq. miles
**NIDDERDALE (1994)**, North Yorkshire, 603 sq. km/233 sq. miles
**NORFOLK COAST (1968)**, 451 sq. km/174 sq. miles
**NORTH DEVON (1960)**, 171 sq. km/66 sq. miles
**NORTH PENNINES (1988)**, Cumbria/Durham/North Yorkshire/Northumberland, 1,983 sq. km/766 sq. miles
**NORTH WESSEX DOWNS (1972)**, Hampshire/Oxfordshire/Wiltshire, 1,730 sq. km/668 sq. miles
**NORTHUMBERLAND COAST (1958)**, 138 sq. km/64 sq. miles
**QUANTOCK HILLS (1957)**, Somerset, 99 sq. km/38 sq. miles
**SHROPSHIRE HILLS (1959)**, 804 sq. km/310 sq. miles
**SOLWAY COAST (1964)**, Cumbria, 115 sq. km/44 sq. miles
**SOUTH DEVON (1960)**, 337 sq. km/130 sq. miles
**SUFFOLK COAST AND HEATHS (1970)**, 403 sq. km/156 sq. miles
**SURREY HILLS (1958)**, 419 sq. km/162 sq. miles
**TAMAR VALLEY (1995)**, Cornwall/Devon, 190 sq. km/73 sq. miles
**WYE VALLEY (1971)**, Gloucestershire/Herefordshire/Monmouthshire, 326 sq. km/126 sq. miles
**YNYS MON (ISLE OF ANGLESEY) (1967)**, 221 sq. km/85 sq. miles

## NORTHERN IRELAND

The Department of the Environment for Northern Ireland, with advice from the Council for Nature Conservation and the Countryside, designates AONBs in Northern Ireland. Dates given are those of designation.

ANTRIM COAST AND GLENS (1988), Co. Antrim, 725 sq. km/280 sq. miles
BINEVENAGH (2006), Co. Londonderry, 166 sq. km/ 64 sq. miles
CAUSEWAY COAST (1989), Co. Antrim, 42 sq. km/ 16 sq. miles
LAGAN VALLEY (1965), Co. Down, 39 sq. km/15 sq. miles
MOURNE (1986), Co. Down, 580 sq. km/224 sq. miles
RING OF GULLION (1991), Co. Armagh, 153 sq. km/ 59 sq. miles
SPERRIN (1968; extended 2008), Co. Tyrone/Co. Londonderry, 1,182 sq. km/456 sq. miles
STRANGFORD LOUGH AND LECALE (2010), Co. Down, 528 sq. km/204 sq. miles

## NATIONAL SCENIC AREAS

In Scotland, national scenic areas have a broadly equivalent status to AONBs. Scottish Natural Heritage recognises areas of national scenic significance. At the beginning of June 2015 there were 40, covering a land area of 1,021,600 hectares (2,524,400 acres) and a marine area of 359,500 hectares (888,300 acres).

Development within national scenic areas is dealt with by local authorities, who are required to consult Scottish Natural Heritage concerning certain categories of development. Disagreements between Scottish Natural Heritage and local authorities are referred to the Scottish government. Land management uses can also be modified in the interest of scenic conservation.

ASSYNT-COIGACH, Highland, 90,200ha/222,884 acres
BEN NEVIS AND GLEN COE, Highland, 101,600ha/ 251,053 acres
CAIRNGORM MOUNTAINS, Highland/Aberdeenshire/ Moray, 67,200ha/166,051 acres
CUILLIN HILLS, Highland, 21,900ha/54,115 acres
DEESIDE AND LOCHNAGAR, Aberdeenshire, 40,000ha/ 98,840 acres
DORNOCH FIRTH, Highland, 7,500ha/18,532 acres
EAST STEWARTRY COAST, Dumfries and Galloway, 4,500ha/11,119 acres
EILDON AND LEADERFOOT, Borders, 3,600ha/ 8,896 acres
FLEET VALLEY, Dumfries and Galloway, 5,300ha/ 13,096 acres
GLEN AFFRIC, Highland, 19,300ha/47,690 acres
GLEN STRATHFARRAR, Highland, 3,800ha/9,390 acres
HOY AND WEST MAINLAND, Orkney Islands, 14,800ha/ 36,571 acres
JURA, Argyll and Bute, 21,800ha/53,868 acres
KINTAIL, Highland, 15,500ha/38,300 acres
KNAPDALE, Argyll and Bute, 19,800ha/48,926 acres
KNOYDART, Highland, 39,500ha/97,604 acres
KYLE OF TONGUE, Highland, 18,500ha/45,713 acres
KYLES OF BUTE, Argyll and Bute, 4,400ha/10,872 acres
LOCH LOMOND, Argyll and Bute, 27,400ha/67,705 acres
LOCH NA KEAL, Mull, Argyll and Bute, 12,700ha/ 31,382 acres
LOCH RANNOCH AND GLEN LYON, Perthshire and Kinross, 48,400ha/119,596 acres
LOCH SHIEL, Highland, 13,400ha/33,111 acres
LOCH TUMMEL, Perthshire and Kinross, 9,200ha/ 22,733 acres

LYNN OF LORN, Argyll and Bute, 4,800ha/11,861 acres
MORAR, MOIDART AND ARDNAMURCHAN, Highland, 13,500ha/33,358 acres
NITH ESTUARY, Dumfries and Galloway, 9,300ha/ 22,980 acres
NORTH ARRAN, North Ayrshire, 23,800ha/58,810 acres
NORTH-WEST SUTHERLAND, Highland, 20,500ha/ 50,655 acres
RIVER EARN, Perthshire and Kinross, 3,000ha/7,413 acres
RIVER TAY, Perthshire and Kinross, 5,600ha/13,838 acres
ST KILDA, Eilean Siar (Western Isles), 900ha/2,224 acres
SCARBA, LUNGA AND THE GARVELLACHS, Argyll and Bute, 1,900ha/4,695 acres
SHETLAND, Shetland Isles, 11,600ha/28,664 acres
SMALL ISLANDS, Highland, 15,500ha/38,300 acres
SOUTH LEWIS, HARRIS AND NORTH UIST, Eilean Siar (Western Isles), 109,600ha/270,822 acres
SOUTH UIST MACHAIR, Eilean Siar (Western Isles), 6,100ha/15,073 acres
THE TROSSACHS, Stirling, 4,600ha/11,367 acres
TROTTERNISH, Highland, 5,000ha/12,355 acres
UPPER TWEEDDALE, Borders, 10,500ha/25,945 acres
WESTER ROSS, Highland, 145,300ha/359,036 acres

## THE NATIONAL FOREST

The National Forest is one of the UK's biggest environmental projects, creating a forest across 518.5 sq. km (200.2 sq. miles) of Derbyshire, Leicestershire and Staffordshire. Since the early 1990s, more than 8.5 million trees have been planted to create 7,000ha of new woodland landscapes. Forest cover has increased from 6 per cent to 20 per cent, with the aim of eventually covering approximately one-third of the designated area.

Since its establishment in 1995, the National Forest leads the project and is responsible for delivery of the government-approved National Forest Strategy, sponsored by DEFRA. Priorities include continued forest creation and management, economic development of the area for recreation and tourism, and engaging local communities in the forest to improve quality of life.

NATIONAL FOREST COMPANY, Bath Yard, Moira, Swadlincote, Derbyshire DE12 6BA T 01283-551211
E enquiries@nationalforest.org W www.nationalforest.org
*Chief Executive,* John Everitt

## SITES OF SPECIAL SCIENTIFIC INTEREST

Site of Special Scientific Interest (SSSI) is a legal notification applied to land in England, Scotland or Wales which Natural England (NE), Scottish Natural Heritage (SNH) or the Natural Resources Wales (NRW) identifies as being of special interest because of its flora, fauna, geological, geomorphological or physiographical features. In some cases, SSSIs are managed as nature reserves.

NE, SNH and NRW must notify the designation of an SSSI to the local planning authority, every owner/occupier of the land, and the environment secretary, the Scottish ministers or the National Assembly for Wales. Forestry and agricultural departments and a number of other interested parties are also formally notified.

Objections to the notification of an SSSI can be made and ultimately considered at a full meeting of the Council of NE or NRW. In Scotland an objection will be dealt with by the main board of SNH or an appropriate subgroup.

The protection of these sites depends on the cooperation of individual landowners and occupiers. Owner/occupiers must consult NE, SNH or NRW and gain written consent before they can undertake certain listed activities on the site. Funds are available through management agreements and grants to assist owners and occupiers in conserving sites' interests. Sites can also be protected by management schemes, management notices and other enforcement mechanisms. As a last resort a site can be purchased.

SSSIs in Britain as at June 2015:

| | Number | Hectares | Acres |
|---|---|---|---|
| England | 4,129 | 1,082,984 | 2,676,112 |
| Scotland | 1,423 | 1,022,350 | 2,526,282 |
| Wales | 1,062 | 261,902 | 647,173 |

## NORTHERN IRELAND
In Northern Ireland 360 areas of special scientific interest (ASSIs) have been declared by the Department of the Environment for Northern Ireland.

## NATIONAL NATURE RESERVES

National Nature Reserves are defined in the National Parks and Access to the Countryside Act 1949 as modified by the Natural Environment and Rural Communities Act 2006. National Nature Reserves may be managed solely for the purpose of conservation, or for both the purposes of conservation and recreation, providing this does not compromise the conservation purpose.

NE, SNH or NRW can declare as a national nature reserve land which is held and managed as a nature reserve under an agreement; land held and managed by NE, SNH or NRW; or land held and managed as a nature reserve by an approved body. NE, SNH or NRW can make by-laws to protect reserves from undesirable activities; these are subject to confirmation by the Secretary of State for Environment, Food and Rural Affairs, the National Assembly for Wales or the Scottish ministers.

National nature reserves in Britain as at June 2015:

| | Number | Hectares | Acres |
|---|---|---|---|
| England | 226 | 93,616 | 231,330 |
| Scotland | 51 | 128,202 | 316,793 |
| Wales | 76 | 25,561 | 63,162 |

## NORTHERN IRELAND
Nature reserves are established and managed by the Department of the Environment for Northern Ireland, with advice from the Council for Nature Conservation and the Countryside. Nature reserves are declared under the Nature Conservation and Amenity Lands (Northern Ireland) Order 1985; to date, 47 nature reserves have been declared.

## LOCAL NATURE RESERVES

Local Nature Reserves are defined in the National Parks and Access to the Countryside Act 1949 (as amended by the Natural Environment and Rural Communities Act 2006) as land designated for the study and preservation of flora and fauna, or of geological or physiographical features. Local Nature Reserves also have a statutory obligation to provide opportunities for the enjoyment of nature or open air recreation, providing this does not compromise the conservation purpose of the reserve. Local authorities in England, Scotland and Wales have the power to acquire, declare and manage reserves in consultation with NE, SNH and NRW. There is similar legislation in Northern Ireland, where the consulting organisation is the Environment Agency.

Any organisation, such as water companies, educational trusts, local amenity groups and charitable nature conservation bodies, such as wildlife trusts, may manage local nature reserves, provided that a local authority has a legal interest in the land. This means that the local authority must either own it, lease it or have a management agreement with the landowner.

Designated local nature reserves in Britain as at June 2015:

| | Number | Hectares | Acres |
|---|---|---|---|
| England | 1,574 | 38,967 | 96,287 |
| Scotland | 72 | 10,724 | 26,500 |
| Wales | 94 | 8,793 | 21,727 |

There are 24 local nature reserves in Northern Ireland.

## FOREST RESERVES

The Forestry Commission is the government department responsible for forestry policy throughout Great Britain. Forestry is a devolved matter, with the separate Forestry Commissions for England, Scotland and Wales reporting directly to their appropriate minister. The equivalent body in Northern Ireland is the Forest Service, an agency of the Department of Agriculture and Rural Development for Northern Ireland. The Forestry Commission in each country is led by a director who is also a member of the GB Board of Commissioners. As at March 2014, UK woodland certified by the Forestry Commission (including Forestry Commission-managed woodland) amounted to around 1,377,000ha (3,402,641 acres): 349,000ha (862,398 acres) in England, 141,000ha (348,419 acres) in Wales, 822,000ha (2,031,206 acres) in Scotland and 65,000ha (160,619 acres) in Northern Ireland. For more information, see W www.forestry.gov.uk

There are 35 forest nature reserves in Northern Ireland, covering 1,737 hectares (4,292 acres), designated and administered by the Forest Service. There are also 16 national nature reserves on Forest Service-owned property.

## MARINE NATURE RESERVES

Marine protected areas provide protection for marine flora and fauna, and geological and physiographical features on land covered by tidal waters or parts of the sea in or adjacent to the UK. These areas also provide opportunities for study and research.

### ENGLAND AND WALES
The Marine and Coastal Access Act 2009 created a new kind of statutory protection for marine protected areas in England and Wales, marine conservation zones (MCZs), which are designed to increase the protection of species and habitats deemed to be of national importance. The Secretary of State for Environment, Food and Rural Affairs and the National Assembly for Wales have the power to designate MCZs. Individual MCZs can have varying levels of protection: some include specific activities that are appropriately managed, while others prohibit all damaging and disturbing activities. The act converted the waters around Lundy Island, a former marine protected area, to MCZ status in 2010.

In 2009, Natural England and the Joint Nature Conservation Committee (JNCC) gave sea-users and stake-holders the ability to recommend potential MCZs to the UK government by establishing four regional projects. In September 2011, these projects recommended 127 MCZs, which were reviewed by Natural England and the JNCC. On 21 November 2013, the government announced the creation of 27 new MCZs, covering an area of around 9,700 sq. km, to protect wildlife including seahorses, coral reefs and oyster beds from dredging and bottom-trawling. A public consultation on the designation of an additional 23 MCZs, covering an area of 10,810 sq. km, closed in April 2015 with the results for the designations due in 2016. The 27 MCZs (with date designation confirmed) are:

*Inshore Sites*
ALN ESTUARY (2013), Northumberland, 0.39 sq. km
BLACKWATER, CROUCH, ROACH AND COLNE
    ESTUARIES (2013), Essex, 284 sq. km
BEACHY HEAD WEST (2013), E. Sussex, 24 sq. km
CHESIL BEACH AND STENNIS LEDGES (2013), Dorset,
    37 sq. km
CUMBRIA COAST (2013), Cumbria, 18 sq. km
FOLKESTONE POMERANIA (2013), Kent, 34 sq. km
FYLDE (2013), Lancs, 260 sq. km
ISLES OF SCILLY (2013), 30 sq. km
KINGMERE (2013), Sussex, 47 sq. km
LUNDY (2010 and 2013), Bristol Channel, 31 sq. km
THE MANACLES (2013), Cornwall, 3.5 sq. km
MEDWAY ESTUARY (2013), Kent, 60 sq. km
PADSTOW BAY AND SURROUNDS (2013), Cornwall,
    90 sq. km
PAGHAM HARBOUR (2013), Sussex, 3 sq. km
POOLE ROCKS (2013), Dorset, 4 sq. km
SKERRIES BANK AND SURROUNDS (2013), Devon,
    250 sq. km
SOUTH DORSET (2013), 193 sq. km
TAMAR ESTUARY, Devon/Cornwall (2013), 15 sq. km
THANET COAST (2013), Kent, 64 sq. km
TORBAY (2013), Devon, 20 sq. km
UPPER FOWEY AND PONT PILL (2013), Cornwall,
    2 sq. km
WHITSAND AND LOOE BAY (2013), Cornwall, 52 sq. km
*Offshore Sites*
THE CANYONS (2013), Cornwall, 661 sq. km
EAST OF HAIG FRAS (2013), Cornwall, 400 sq. km
NORTH EAST OF FARNES DEEP (2013),
    Northumberland, 492 sq. km
SOUTH-WEST DEEPS (WEST) (2013), Cornwall, 1,800
    sq. km
SWALLOW SAND (2013), Northumberland, 4,746 sq. km

## SCOTLAND
In July 2014, under the Marine (Scotland) Act 2010, the
Scottish government designated 17 marine protected
areas (MPAs) in Scottish inshore territorial waters (Clyde Sea Sill;
East Caithness Cliffs; Fetlar to Haroldswick; Loch Creran;
Loch Sunart; Loch Sunart to the Sound of Jura; Loch Sween;
Lochs Duich, Long and Alsh; Monarch Isles; Mousa to
Boddam; Noss Head; Papa Westray; Small Isles; South Arran;
Upper Loch Fyne and Loch Goil; Wester Ross; and Wyre
and Rousay Sounds). A further 13, also in July 2014, were
designated in offshore waters under the UK Marine and
Coastal Access Act 2009. These are: Central Fladen; East of
Gannet and Montrose Fields; Faroe–Shetland Sponge Belt;
Firth of Forth Banks Complex; Geikie Slide and Hebridean
Slope; Hatton–Rockall Basin; North-east Faroe Shetland
Channel; North-west Orkney; Norwegian Sediment
Boundary Plain; Rosemary Bank Seamount; Barra Fan and
Hebrides Terrace Seamount; Turbot Bank; and West
Shetland Shelf.

## NORTHERN IRELAND
The Marine Act (Northern Ireland) 2013 includes provisions
for establishing Marine Conservation Zones (MCZs), as well
as a system of marine planning, fisheries management and
marine licensing. MCZs may be designated for various
purposes including the conservation of marine species and
habitats, taking fully into account any economic, cultural or
social consequences of doing so. The Act also allows the NI
Department of the Environment to make byelaws to protect
MCZs from damage caused by unregulated activities such
as anchoring, kite surfing or jet skiing. It is an offence to

intentionally or recklessly destroy or damage a protected
feature of an MCZ.
    Strangford Lough was Northern Ireland's only marine
nature reserve, establised in 1995 under the Nature
Conservation and Amenity Lands Order (Northern Ireland)
1985, but it was redesignated as Northern Ireland's first
MCZ on the introduction of the Marine Act (Northern
Ireland) 2013.

## INTERNATIONAL CONVENTIONS

The UK is party to a number of international conventions.

### BERN CONVENTION
The 1979 Bern Convention on the Conservation of
European Wildlife and Natural Habitats came into force in
the UK in June 1982. There are 51 contracting parties and
a number of other states attend meetings as observers.
    The aims are to conserve wild flora and fauna and their
habitats, especially where this requires the cooperation of
several countries, and to promote such cooperation. The
convention imposes legal obligations on contracting parties,
protecting over 500 wild plant species and more than 1,000
wild animal species.
    All parties to the convention must promote national
conservation policies and take account of the conservation of
wild flora and fauna when setting planning and development
policies. Reports on contracting parties' conservation policies
must be submitted to the standing committee every four
years.
SECRETARIAT OF THE BERN CONVENTION
    STANDING COMMITTEE, Council of Europe,
    Avenue de L'Europe, 67075 Strasbourg-Cedex, France
    W www.coe.int/bernconvention

### BIOLOGICAL DIVERSITY
The UK ratified the Convention on Biological Diversity
(CBD) in June 1994. As at July 2015 there were 196 parties
to the convention.
    There are seven programmes addressing agricultural
biodiversity, marine and coastal biodiversity and the
biodiversity of inland waters, dry and sub-humid lands,
islands, mountains and forests. On 29 January 2000 the
Conference of the Parties adopted a supplementary
agreement to the convention known as the Cartagena
Protocol on Biosafety. The protocol seeks to protect
biological diversity from potential risks that may be posed by
introducing modified living organisms, resulting from
biotechnology, into the environment. As at July 2015, 170
countries were party to the protocol; the UK joined on 17
February 2004. The Nagoya Protocol on Access and Benefit-
sharing was adopted in October 2010 and entered into force
on 12 October 2014. It provides international rules and
procedure on liability and redress for damage to biodiversity
resulting from living modified organisms. As at July 2015,
59 countries were party to the protocol.
    The UK Biodiversity Action Plan (UKBAP), published in
1994, was the UK government's response to the CBD at the
1992 Rio Earth Summit. The UK Post-2010 Biodiversity
Framework replaced UKBAP when it was published in 2012
by DEFRA and the devolved administrations. The framework
covers the period 2011–20 and forms the UK government's
response to the strategic plan of the CBD. It includes five
internationally agreed strategic goals to be achieved by
2020: to address the underlying causes of biodiversity loss
by making biodiversity a mainstream issue across government
and society; to reduce the direct pressures on biodiversity and
promote sustainable use; to safeguard ecosystems, species and
genetic diversity; to enhance the benefits to all from

biodiversity and ecosystem services; and to enhance implementation through participatory planning, knowledge management and capacity building. The list of priority species and habitats under the biodiversity framework covers 1,150 species and 65 habitats.

Secretariat of the Convention on Biological Diversity, 413, Saint Jacques Street, Suite 800, Montreal, QC H2Y 1N9 Canada T +1514-288 2220 E secretariat@cbd.int W www.cbd.int

JNCC, Monkstone House, City Road, Peterborough PE1 1JY T 01733-555948 W www.jncc.defra.gov.uk

## BONN CONVENTION
The 1979 Convention on Conservation of Migratory Species of Wild Animals (also known as the CMS or Bonn Convention) came into force in the UK in October 1985. As at 1 July 2015, 120 countries were party to the convention.

It requires the protection of listed endangered migratory species and encourages international agreements covering these and other threatened species.

Seven agreements have been concluded to date under the convention. They aim to conserve seals in the Wadden Sea; bat populations in Europe; small cetaceans of the Baltic, north-east Atlantic, Irish and North Seas; cetaceans of the Mediterranean Sea, Black Sea and contiguous Atlantic area; African-Eurasian migratory waterbirds; albatrosses and petrels; and gorillas and their habitats. A further 19 memorandums of understanding have been agreed for the Siberian crane, slender-billed curlew, marine turtles of the Atlantic coast of Africa, Indian Ocean and South East Asia, the middle-European population of the great bustard, bukhara deer, aquatic warbler, West-African populations of the African elephant, saiga antelope, cetaceans of the Pacific Islands, dugongs (large marine mammals), eastern-Atlantic populations of the Mediterranean monk seals, ruddy-headed goose, grassland birds of southern South America, birds of prey of Africa and Eurasia, small cetaceans and manatees of West Africa, sharks, huemuls (Andean deer) and high Andean flamingoes. In addition, there are three special species initiatives: the central Asian flyway, the central Asian mammals initiative and Sahelo–Saharan megafauna plan.

UNEP/CMS SECRETARIAT, Platz der Vereinten Nationen 1, 53113 Bonn, Germany T (+49) (228) 815 2401 E secretariat@cms.int W www.cms.int

## CITES
The 1973 Convention on International Trade in Endangered Species of Wild Fauna and Flora (CITES), which entered into force in 1975, is an agreement between governments to ensure that international trade in specimens of wild animals and plants does not threaten their survival. The convention came into force in the UK in October 1976 and there are currently 181 member countries. Countries party to the convention ban commercial international trade in an agreed list of endangered species and regulate and monitor trade in other species that might become endangered. The convention accords varying degrees of protection to more than 35,000 species of animals and plants whether they are traded as live specimens or as products derived from them.

The Conference of the Parties to CITES meets every two to three years to review the convention's implementation. The Animal and Plant Health Agency at the Department for Environment, Food and Rural Affairs carries out the government's responsibilities under CITES.

CITES is implemented in the EU through a series of EC regulations known as the Wildlife Trade Regulations.

CITES SECRETARIAT, International Environment House, 11 Chemin des Anémones, CH-1219 Châtelaine, Geneva, Switzerland T (+41) (22) 917 8139/40 E info@cites.org W www.cites.org

## INTERNATIONAL WHALING COMMISSION
The International Convention for the Regulation of Whaling was signed in Washington DC in 1946 and currently has 88 member countries.

The measures in the convention provide for the complete protection of certain species; designate specified areas as whale sanctuaries; set limits on the numbers and size of whales which may be taken; prescribe open and closed seasons and areas for whaling; and prohibit the capture of suckling calves and female whales accompanied by calves. The International Whaling Commission meets annually to review and revise these measures.

THE INTERNATIONAL WHALING COMMISSION, The Red House, 135 Station Road, Impington, Cambridge, Cambridgeshire CB24 9NP T 01223-233 971 W www.iwc.int

## OSPAR
The Convention for the Protection of the Marine Environment of the North-East Atlantic (the OSPAR Convention) was adopted in Paris, France in September 1992 and entered into force in March 1998. The OSPAR Convention replaced both the Oslo Convention (1972) and the Paris Convention (1974), with the intention of providing a comprehensive approach to addressing all sources of pollution which may affect the maritime area, and matters relating to the protection of the maritime environment. An annex on biodiversity and ecosystems was adopted in 1998 to cover non-polluting human activities that can adversely affect the sea.

Fifteen countries plus the European Union are party to the convention; the UK ratified OSPAR in 1998. The OSPAR Commission makes decisions and recommendations and sets out actions to be taken by the contracting parties. The OSPAR Secretariat administers the work under the convention, coordinates the work of the contracting parties and runs the formal meeting schedule of OSPAR.

OSPAR SECRETARIAT, Victoria House, 37–63 Southampton Row, London WC1B 4DA T 020-7430 5200 E secretariat@ospar.org W www.ospar.org

## RAMSAR CONVENTION
The 1971 Convention on Wetlands of National Importance, called the Ramsar Convention, is an inter-governmental treaty that provides for the conservation and sustainable use of wetlands and their resources. The Convention entered into force in the UK in 1976.

Governments that are contracting parties to the convention must designate wetlands for inclusion in the List of Wetlands of International Importance (the 'Ramsar List') and include wetland conservation considerations in their land-use planning. As at May 2015, the Convention's 168 contracting parties had designated 2,208 wetland sites, covering 210,734,269 hectares. The UK currently has 170 designated sites covering 1,278,930 hectares.

The contracting parties meet every three years to assess progress. The 13th Meeting of the Conference of the Contracting Parties to the Ramsar Convention on Wetlands will take place in Dubai, UAE in 2018.

At the 12th meeting of the Convention, held in Uruguay in June 2015, a new Ramsar Strategic Plan was adopted for the years 2016–24. The four priorities central to the new plan are: to address the factors driving the loss and degradation of wetlands; to renew country commitment to conserve and protect the Ramsar site network; to promote wise use of wetlands and to restore wetlands that are relevant for biodiversity conservation, disaster risk reduction, livelihoods and climate change mitigation; and to improve the implementation of the Convention.

RAMSAR CONVENTION SECRETARIAT, Rue Mauverney 28, CH-1196 Gland, Switzerland T (+41) (22) 999 0170 E ramsar@ramsar.org W www.ramsar.org

# UK LEGISLATION

The Wildlife and Countryside Act 1981 gives legal protection to a wide range of wild animals and plants. Every five years the statutory nature conservation agencies (Natural England, Natural Resources Wales and Scottish Natural Heritage), working jointly through the JNCC, are required to review schedules 5 (animals, other than birds) and 8 (plants) of the Wildlife and Countryside Act 1981. They make recommendations to the Secretary of State for Environment, Food and Rural Affairs, the National Assembly for Wales and the Scottish government for changes to these schedules. The most recent variations of schedules 5 and 8 for England came into effect on 1 October 2011, following the fifth quinquennial review. The sixth review is currently underway.

Under section 9 of the act it is an offence to kill, injure, take, possess or sell (whether alive or dead) any wild animal included in schedule 5 of the act and to disturb its place of shelter and protection or to destroy that place. However certain species listed on schedule 5 are protected against some, but not all, of these activities.

Under section 13 of the act it is illegal without a licence to pick, uproot, sell or destroy plants listed in schedule 8. Since January 2001, under the Countryside and Rights of Way Act 2000, persons found guilty of an offence under part 1 of the Wildlife and Countryside Act 1981 face a maximum penalty of up to £5,000 and/or up to a six-month custodial sentence per specimen.

## BIRDS

The act lays down a close season for birds (listed on Schedule 2, part 1) from 1 February to 31 August inclusive, each year. Variations to these dates are made for:

Black grouse – 10 December to 20 August (10 December–1 September for Somerset, Devon and New Forest)
Capercaillie – 1 February to 30 September (England and Wales only)
Grey partridge – 1 February to 1 September
Pheasant – 1 February to 1 October
Ptarmigan and Red grouse – 10 December to 12 August
Red-legged partridge – 1 February to 1 September
Snipe – 1 February to 11 August
Woodcock – 1 February to 30 September (England and Wales); 1 February to 31 August (Scotland)
Birds listed on schedule 2, part 1 (below high water mark) (see below) – 21 February to 31 August
Wild duck and wild geese, in or over any area below the high-water mark of ordinary spring tides – 21 February to 31 August
Sundays and Christmas Day in Scotland, and Sundays for any area of England or Wales prescribed by the Secretary of State.

Birds listed on schedule 2, part 1, which may be killed or taken outside the close season are: capercaillie (England and Wales only); coot; certain wild duck (gadwall, goldeneye, mallard, Northern pintail, common pochard, Northern shoveler, teal, tufted duck, Eurasian wigeon); certain wild geese (Canada, greylag, pink-footed, white-fronted (in England and Wales only); golden plover; moorhen; snipe; and woodcock.

Section 16 of the 1981 act allows licences to be issued on either an individual or general basis, to allow the killing, taking and sale of certain birds for specified reasons such as public health and safety. All other wild birds are fully protected by law throughout the year.

## ANIMALS PROTECTED BY SCHEDULE 5

Adder *(Vipera berus)*
Anemone, Ivell's Sea *(Edwardsia ivelli)*
Anemone, Starlet Sea *(Nematostella vectensis)*
Bat, Horseshoe, all species *(Rhinolophidae)*
Bat, Typical, all species *(Vespertilionidae)*
Beetle *(Hypebaeus flavipes)*
Beetle, Bembridge Water *(Paracymus aeneus)*
Beetle, Lesser Silver Water *(Hydrochara caraboides)*
Beetle, Mire Pill *(Curimopsis nigrita)*
Beetle, Moccas *(Hypebaeus flavipes)*
Beetle, Rainbow Leaf *(Chrysolina cerealis)*
Beetle, Spangled Water *(Graphoderus zonatus)*
Beetle, Stag *(Lucanus cervus)*
Beetle, Violet Click *(Limoniscus violaceus)*
Beetle, Water *(Paracymus aeneus)*
Burbot *(Lota lota)*
Butterfly, Adonis Blue *(Lysandra bellargus)*
Butterfly, Black Hairstreak *(Strymonidia pruni)*
Butterfly, Brown Hairstreak *(Thecla betulae)*
Butterfly, Chalkhill Blue *(Lysandra coridon)*
Butterfly, Chequered Skipper *(Carterocephalus palaemon)*
Butterfly, Duke of Burgundy Fritillary *(Hamearis lucina)*
Butterfly, Glanville Fritillary *(Melitaea cinxia)*
Butterfly, Heath Fritillary *(Mellicta athalia or Melitaea athalia)*
Butterfly, High Brown Fritillary *(Argynnis adippe)*
Butterfly, Large Blue *(Maculinea arion)*
Butterfly, Large Copper *(Lycaena dispar)*
Butterfly, Large Heath *(Coenonympha tullia)*
Butterfly, Large Tortoiseshell *(Nymphalis polychloros)*
Butterfly, Lulworth Skipper *(Thymelicus acteon)*
Butterfly, Marsh Fritillary *(Eurodryas aurinia)*
Butterfly, Mountain Ringlet *(Erebia epiphron)*
Butterfly, Northern Brown Argus *(Aricia artaxerxes)*
Butterfly, Pearl-bordered Fritillary *(Boloria euphrosyne)*
Butterfly, Purple Emperor *(Apatura iris)*
Butterfly, Silver Spotted Skipper *(Hesperia comma)*
Butterfly, Silver-studded Blue *(Plebejus argus)*
Butterfly, Small Blue *(Cupido minimus)*
Butterfly, Swallowtail *(Papilio machaon)*
Butterfly, White Letter Hairstreak *(Stymonida w-album)*
Butterfly, Wood White *(Leptidea sinapis)*
Cat, Wild *(Felis silvestris)*
Cicada, New Forest *(Cicadetta montana)*
Crayfish, Atlantic Stream *(Austropotamobius pallipes)*
Cricket, Field *(Gryllus campestris)*
Cricket, Mole *(Gryllotalpa gryllotalpa)*
Cricket, Wart-biter *(Decticus verrucivorus)*
Damselfly, Southern *(Coenagrion mercuriale)*
Dolphin, all species *(Cetacea)*
Dormouse *(Muscardinus avellanarius)*
Dragonfly, Norfolk Aeshna *(Aeshna isosceles)*
Frog, Common *(Rana temporaria)*
Frog, Pool, Northern Clade *(Pelophylax lessonae)*
Goby, Couch's *(Gobius couchii)*
Goby, Giant *(Gobius cobitis)*
Hatchet Shell, Northern *(Thyasira gouldi)*
Hydroid, Marine *(Clavopsella navis)*
Lagoon Snail, De Folin's *(Caecum armoricum)*
Lagoon Worm, Tentacled *(Alkmaria romijni)*
Leech, Medicinal *(Hirudo medicinalis)*
Lizard, Sand *(Lacerta agilis)*
Lizard, Viviparous *(Lacerta vivipara)*
Marten, Pine *(Martes martes)*
Moth, Barberry Carpet *(Pareulype berberata)*
Moth, Black-veined *(Siona lineata or Idaea lineata)*
Moth, Fiery Clearwing *(Bembecia chrysidiformis)*
Moth, Fisher's Estuarine *(Gortyna borelii)*

Moth, New Forest Burnet *(Zygaena viciae)*
Moth, Reddish Buff *(Acosmetia caliginosa)*
Moth, Slender Scotch Burnet *(Zygaena loti)*
Moth, Sussex Emerald *(Thalera fimbrialis)*
Moth, Talisker Burnet *(Zygaena lonicerae)*
Mussel, Fan *(Atrina fragilis)*
Mussel, Freshwater Pearl *(Margaritifera margaritifera)*
Newt, Great Crested (or Warty) *(Triturus cristatus)*
Newt, Palmate *(Triturus helveticus)*
Newt, Smooth *(Triturus vulgaris)*
Otter, Common *(Lutra lutra)*
Porpoise, all species *(Cetacea)*
Sandworm, Lagoon *(Armandia cirrhosa)*
Sea Fan, Pink *(Eunicella verrucosa)*
Sea Slug, Lagoon *(Tenellia adspersa)*
Sea-mat, Trembling *(Victorella pavida)*
Seahorse, Short Snouted (England only) *(Hippocampus hippocampus)*
Seahorse, Spiny (England only) *(Hippocampus guttulatus)*
Shad, Allis *(Alosa alosa)*
Shad, Twaite *(Alosa fallax)*
Shark, Angel (England only) *(Squatina squatina)*
Shark, Basking *(Cetorhinus maximus)*
Shrimp, Fairy *(Chirocephalus diaphanus)*
Shrimp, Lagoon Sand *(Gammarus insensibilis)*
Shrimp, Tadpole (Apus) *(Triops cancriformis)*
Skate, White *(Rostroraja alba)*
Slow-worm *(Anguis fragilis)*
Snail, Glutinous *(Myxas glutinosa)*
Snail, Roman (England only) *(Helix pomatia)*
Snail, Sandbowl *(Catinella arenaria)*
Snake, Grass *(Natrix natrix or Natrix helvetica)*
Snake, Smooth *(Coronella austriaca)*
Spider, Fen Raft *(Dolomedes plantarius)*
Spider, Ladybird *(Eresus niger)*
Squirrel, Red *(Sciurus vulgaris)*
Sturgeon *(Acipenser sturio)*
Toad, Common *(Bufo bufo)*
Toad, Natterjack *(Bufo calamita)*
Turtle, Flatback *(Cheloniidae / Natator Depressus)*
Turtle, Green Sea *(Chelonia mydas)*
Turtle, Hawksbill *(Eretmochelys imbricate)*
Turtle, Kemp's Ridley Sea *(Lepidochelys kempii)*
Turtle, Leatherback Sea *(Dermochelys coriacea)*
Turtle, Loggerhead Sea *(Caretta caretta)*
Turtle, Olive Ridley *(Lepidochelys olivacea)*
Vendace *(Coregonus albula)*
Vole, Water *(Arvicola terrestris)*
Walrus *(Odobenus rosmarus)*
Whale, all species *(Cetacea)*
Whitefish *(Coregonus lavaretus)*

## PLANTS PROTECTED BY SCHEDULE 8

Adder's Tongue, Least *(Ophioglossum lusitanicum)*
Alison, Small *(Alyssum alyssoides)*
Anomodon, Long-leaved *(Anomodon longifolius)*
Beech-lichen, New Forest *(Enterographa elaborata)*
Blackwort *(Southbya nigrella)*
Bluebell *(Hyacinthoides non-scripta)*
Bolete, Royal *(Boletus regius)*
Broomrape, Bedstraw *(Orobanche caryophyllacea)*
Broomrape, Oxtongue *(Orobanche loricata)*
Broomrape, Thistle *(Orobanche reticulata)*
Cabbage, Lundy *(Rhynchosinapis wrightii)*
Calamint, Wood *(Calamintha sylvatica)*
Caloplaca, Snow *(Caloplaca nivalis)*
Catapyrenium, Tree *(Catapyrenium psoromoides)*
Catchfly, Alpine *(Lychnis alpina)*
Catillaria, Laurer's *(Catellaria laureri)*

Centaury, Slender *(Centaurium tenuiflorum)*
Cinquefoil, Rock *(Potentilla rupestris)*
Cladonia, Convoluted *(Cladonia convoluta)*
Cladonia, Upright Mountain *(Cladonia stricta)*
Clary, Meadow *(Salvia pratensis)*
Club-rush, Triangular *(Scirpus triquetrus)*
Colt's-foot, Purple *(Homogyne alpina)*
Cotoneaster, Wild *(Cotoneaster integerrimus)*
Cottongrass, Slender *(Eriophorum gracile)*
Cow-wheat, Field *(Melampyrum arvense)*
Crocus, Sand *(Romulea columnae)*
Crystalwort, Lizard *(Riccia bifurca)*
Cudweed, Broad-leaved *(Filago pyramidata)*
Cudweed, Jersey *(Gnaphalium luteoalbum)*
Cudweed, Red-tipped *(Filago lutescens)*
Cut-grass *(Leersia oryzoides)*
Diapensia *(Diapensia lapponica)*
Dock, Shore *(Rumex rupestris)*
Earwort, Marsh *(Jamesoniella undulifolia)*
Eryngo, Field *(Eryngium campestre)*
Fern, Dickie's Bladder *(Cystopteris dickieana)*
Fern, Killarney *(Trichomanes speciosum)*
Flapwort, Norfolk *(Leiocolea rutheana)*
Fleabane, Alpine *(Erigeron borealis)*
Fleabane, Small *(Pulicaria vulgaris)*
Fleawort, South Stack *(Tephroseris integrifolia ssp maritima)*
Frostwort, Pointed *(Gymnomitrion apiculatum)*
Fungus, Hedgehog *(Hericium erinaceum)*
Galingale, Brown *(Cyperus fuscus)*
Gentian, Alpine *(Gentiana nivalis)*
Gentian, Dune *(Gentianella uliginosa)*
Gentian, Early *(Gentianella anglica)*
Gentian, Fringed *(Gentianella ciliata)*
Gentian, Spring *(Gentiana verna)*
Germander, Cut-leaved *(Teucrium botrys)*
Germander, Water *(Teucrium scordium)*
Gladiolus, Wild *(Gladiolus illyricus)*
Goblin Lights *(Catolechia wahlenbergii)*
Goosefoot, Stinking *(Chenopodium vulvaria)*
Grass-poly *(Lythrum hyssopifolia)*
Grimmia, Blunt-leaved *(Grimmia unicolor)*
Gyalecta, Elm *(Gyalecta ulmi)*
Hare's-ear, Sickle-leaved *(Bupleurum falcatum)*
Hare's-ear, Small *(Bupleurum baldense)*
Hawk's-beard, Stinking *(Crepis foetida)*
Hawkweed, Northroe *(Hieracium northroense)*
Hawkweed, Shetland *(Hieracium zetlandicum)*
Hawkweed, Weak-leaved *(Hieracium attenuatifolium)*
Heath, Blue *(Phyllodoce caerulea)*
Helleborine, Red *(Cephalanthera rubra)*
Horsetail, Branched *(Equisetum ramosissimum)*
Hound's-tongue, Green *(Cynoglossum germanicum)*
Knawel, Perennial *(Scleranthus perennis)*
Knotgrass, Sea *(Polygonum maritimum)*
Lady's-slipper *(Cypripedium calceolus)*
Lecanora, Tarn *(Lecanora archariana)*
Lecidea, Copper *(Lecidea inops)*
Leek, Round-headed *(Allium sphaerocephalon)*
Lettuce, Least *(Lactuca saligna)*
Lichen, Arctic Kidney *(Nephroma arcticum)*
Lichen, Ciliate Strap *(Heterodermia leucomelos)*
Lichen, Coralloid Rosette *(Heterodermia propagulifera)*
Lichen, Ear-lobed Dog *(Peltigera lepidophora)*
Lichen, Forked Hair *(Bryoria furcellata)*
Lichen, Golden Hair *(Teloschistes flavicans)*
Lichen, Orange-fruited Elm *(Caloplaca luteoalba)*
Lichen, River Jelly *(Collema dichotomum)*
Lichen, Scaly Breck *(Squamarina lentigera)*
Lichen, Starry Breck *(Buellia asterella)*

Lily, Snowdon *(Lloydia serotina)*
Liverwort, Lindenberg's Leafy *(Adelanthus lindenbergianus)*
Lungwort, Tree *(Lobaria pulmonaria)*
Marsh-mallow, Rough *(Althaea hirsuta)*
Marshwort, Creeping *(Apium repens)*
Milk-parsley, Cambridge *(Selinum carvifolia)*
Moss *(Drepanocladius vernicosus)*
Moss, Alpine Copper *(Mielichoferia mielichoferi)*
Moss, Baltic Bog *(Sphagnum balticum)*
Moss, Blue Dew *(Saelania glaucescens)*
Moss, Blunt-leaved Bristle *(Orthotrichum obtusifolium)*
Moss, Bright Green Cave *(Cyclodictyon laetevirens)*
Moss, Cordate Beard *(Barbula cordata)*
Moss, Cornish Path *(Ditrichum cornubicum)*
Moss, Derbyshire Feather *(Thamnobryum angustifolium)*
Moss, Flamingo *(Desmatodon cernuus)*
Moss, Glaucous Beard *(Barbula glauca)*
Moss, Green Shield *(Buxbaumia viridis)*
Moss, Hair Silk *(Plagiothecium piliferum)*
Moss, Knothole *(Zygodon forsteri)*
Moss, Large Yellow Feather *(Scorpidium turgescens)*
Moss, Millimetre *(Micromitrium tenerum)*
Moss, Multi-fruited River *(Cryphaea lamyana)*
Moss, Nowell's Limestone *(Zygodon gracilis)*
Moss, Polar Feather *(Hygrohypnum polare)*
Moss, Rigid Apple *(Bartramia stricta)*
Moss, Round-leaved Feather *(Rhyncostegium rotundifolium)*
Moss, Schleicher's Thread *(Bryum schleicheri)*
Moss, Slender Green Feather *(Drepanocladus vernicosus)*
Moss, Triangular Pygmy *(Acaulon triquetrum)*
Moss, Vaucher's Feather *(Hypnum vaucheri)*
Mudwort, Welsh *(Limosella australis)*
Naiad, Holly-leaved *(Najas marina)*
Naiad, Slender *(Najas flexilis)*
Nail, Rock *(Calicium corynellum)*
Orache, Stalked *(Halimione pedunculata)*
Orchid, Early Spider *(Ophrys sphegodes)*
Orchid, Fen *(Liparis loeselii)*
Orchid, Ghost *(Epipogium aphyllum)*
Orchid, Lapland Marsh *(Dactylorhiza lapponica)*
Orchid, Late Spider *(Ophrys fuciflora)*
Orchid, Lizard *(Himantoglossum hircinum)*
Orchid, Military *(Orchis militaris)*
Orchid, Monkey *(Orchis simia)*
Pannaria, Caledonia *(Panneria ignobilis)*
Parmelia, New Forest *(Parmelia minarum)*
Parmentaria, Oil Stain *(Parmentaria chilensis)*
Pear, Plymouth *(Pyrus cordata)*
Penny-cress, Perfoliate *(Thlaspi perfoliatum)*
Pennyroyal *(Mentha pulegium)*
Pertusaria, Alpine Moss *(Pertusaria bryontha)*
Petalwort *(Petallophyllum ralfsi)*
Physcia, Southern Grey *(Physcia tribacioides)*
Pigmyweed *(Crassula aquatica)*
Pine, Ground *(Ajuga chamaepitys)*
Pink, Cheddar *(Dianthus gratianopolitanus)*
Pink, Childing *(Petroraghia nanteuilii)*
Pink, Deptford (England and Wales only) *(Dianthus armeria)*
Polypore, Oak *(Buglossoporus pulvinus)*
Pseudocyphellaria, Ragged *(Pseudocyphellaria lacerata)*
Psora, Rusty Alpine *(Psora rubiformis)*
Puffball, Sandy Stilt *(Battarraea phalloides)*
Ragwort, Fen *(Senecio paludosus)*
Ramping-fumitory, Martin's *(Fumaria martinii)*
Rampion, Spiked *(Phyteuma spicatum)*
Restharrow, Small *(Ononis reclinata)*
Rock-cress, Alpine *(Arabis alpina)*
Rock-cress, Bristol *(Arabis stricta)*
Rustwort, Western *(Marsupella profunda)*

Sandwort, Norwegian *(Arenaria norvegica)*
Sandwort, Teesdale *(Minuartia stricta)*
Saxifrage, Drooping *(Saxifraga cernua)*
Saxifrage, Tufted *(Saxifraga cespitosa)*
Saxifrage, Yellow Marsh *(Saxifrage hirulus)*
Solenopsora, Serpentine *(Solenopsora liparina)*
Solomon's-seal, Whorled *(Polygonatum verticillatum)*
Sow-thistle, Alpine *(Cicerbita alpina)*
Spearwort, Adder's-tongue *(Ranunculus ophioglossifolius)*
Speedwell, Fingered *(Veronica triphyllos)*
Speedwell, Spiked *(Veronica spicata)*
Spike-rush, Dwarf *(Eleocharis parvula)*
Star-of-Bethlehem, Early *(Gagea bohemica)*
Starfruit *(Damasonium alisma)*
Stonewort, Bearded *(Chara canescens)*
Stonewort, Foxtail *(Lamprothamnium papulosum)*
Strapwort *(Corrigiola litoralis)*
Sulphur-tresses, Alpine *(Alectoria ochroleuca)*
Turpswort *(Geocalyx graveolens)*
Violet, Fen *(Viola persicifolia)*
Viper's-grass *(Scorzonera humilis)*
Water-plantain, Floating *(Luronium natans)*
Water-plantain, Ribbon-leaved *(Alisma gramineum)*
Wood-sedge, Starved *(Carex depauperata)*
Woodsia, Alpine *(Woodsia alpina)*
Woodsia, Oblong *(Woodsia ilvenis)*
Wormwood, Field *(Artemisia campestris)*
Woundwort, Downy *(Stachys germanica)*
Woundwort, Limestone *(Stachys alpina)*
Yellow-rattle, Greater *(Rhinanthus serotinus)*

## WORLD HERITAGE SITES

The Convention Concerning the Protection of the World Cultural and Natural Heritage was adopted by the United Nations Educational, Scientific and Cultural Organization (UNESCO) in 1972 and ratified by the UK in 1984. As at July 2015, 191 states were party to the convention. The convention provides for the identification, protection and conservation of cultural and natural sites of outstanding universal value.

Cultural sites may be:
• an extraordinary exponent of human creative genius
• sites representing architectural and technological innovation or cultural interchange
• sites of artistic, historic, aesthetic, archaeological, scientific, ethnologic or anthropologic value
• 'cultural landscapes', ie sites whose characteristics are marked by significant interactions between human populations and their natural environment
• exceptional examples of a traditional settlement or land- or sea-use, especially those threatened by irreversible changes
• unique or exceptional examples of a cultural tradition or a civilisation either still present or extinct

Natural sites may be:
• those displaying critical periods of earth's history
• superlative examples of on-going ecological and biological processes in the evolution of ecosystems
• those exhibiting remarkable natural beauty and aesthetic significance or those where extraordinary natural phenomena are witnessed
• the habitat of threatened species and plants

Governments which are party to the convention nominate sites in their country for inclusion in the World Heritage List. Nominations are considered by the World Heritage Committee, an inter-governmental committee composed of 21 representatives of the parties to the convention. The committee is advised by the International Council on

Monuments and Sites (ICOMOS), the International Centre for the Study of the Preservation and Restoration of Cultural Property (ICCROM) and the International Union for the Conservation of Nature (IUCN). ICOMOS evaluates and reports on proposed cultural and mixed sites, ICCROM provides expert advice and training on how to conserve and restore cultural property and IUCN provides technical evaluations of natural heritage sites and reports on the state of conservation of listed sites.

A prerequisite for inclusion in the World Heritage List is the existence of an effective legal protection system in the country in which the site is situated and a detailed management plan to ensure the conservation of the site. Inclusion in the list does not confer any greater degree of protection on the site than that offered by the national protection framework.

If a site is considered to be in serious danger of decay or damage, the committee may add it to the World Heritage in Danger List. Sites on this list may benefit from particular attention or emergency measures to allay threats and allow them to retain their world heritage status, or in extreme cases of damage or neglect they may lose their world heritage status completely. As at July 2015, there were 48 sites on the World Heritage in Danger List, with the most recent additions including the Old City of Sana'a in Yemen and Hatra in Iraq.

Financial support for the conservation of sites on the World Heritage List is provided by the World Heritage Fund, administered by the World Heritage Committee. The fund's income is derived from compulsory and voluntary contributions from the states party to the convention and from private donations.

WORLD HERITAGE CENTRE, UNESCO, 7 Place de Fontenoy, 75352 Paris 07 SP, France E wh-info@unesco.org W whc.unesco.org

## DESIGNATED SITES

As at 8 July 2015, following the 39th session of the World Heritage Committee, 1,031 sites across 163 countries were on the World Heritage List. Of these, 26 are in the UK and three in British overseas territories; 24 are listed for their cultural significance (†), four for their natural significance (*) and one for both cultural and natural significance. Liverpool's Maritime Mercantile City is the only UK site on the List of World Heritage in Danger. The year in which sites were designated appears in the first set of parentheses. The number in the second set of parentheses denotes the position of each site on the map below.

UNITED KINGDOM

†Bath – the city (1987). (1)
†Blaenarvon industrial landscape, Wales (2000). (2)
†Blenheim Palace and Park, Oxfordshire (1987). (3)
†Canterbury Cathedral, St Augustine's Abbey, St Martin's Church, Kent (1988). (4)
†Castle and town walls of King Edward I, north Wales – Beaumaris, Caernarfon Castle, Conwy Castle, Harlech Castle (1986). (5)
†Cornwall and west Devon mining landscape (2006). (6)
†Derwent Valley Mills, Derbyshire (2001). (7)
*Dorset and east Devon coast (2001). (8)
†Durham Cathedral and Castle (1986). (9)
†Edinburgh old and new towns (1995). (10)
†Forth Bridge, Firth of Forth, Scotland (2015). (26)

†Frontiers of the Roman Empire– Hadrian's Wall, northern England; Antonine Wall, central Scotland (1987, 2005, 2008). (11)
*Giant's Causeway and Causeway coast, Co. Antrim (1986). (12)
†Greenwich, London – maritime Greenwich, including the Royal Naval College, Old Royal Observatory, Queen's House, town centre (1997). (13)
†Heart of Neolithic Orkney (1999). (14)
†Ironbridge Gorge, Shropshire – the world's first iron bridge and other early industrial sites (1986). (15)
†Liverpool – six areas of the maritime mercantile city (2004). (16)
†New Lanark, South Lanarkshire, Scotland (2001). (17)
†Pontcysyllte Aqueduct and Canal, Wrexham, Wales (2009). (18)
†Royal Botanic Gardens, Kew (2003). (19)
†*St Kilda, Eilean Siar (Western Isles) (1986). (20)
†Saltaire, West Yorkshire (2001). (21)
†Stonehenge, Avebury and related megalithic sites, Wiltshire (1986). (22)
†Studley Royal Park, Fountains Abbey, St Mary's Church, N. Yorkshire (1986). (23)
†Tower of London (1988). (24)
†Westminster Abbey, Palace of Westminster, St Margaret's Church, London (1987). (25)

BRITISH OVERSEAS TERRITORIES

*Henderson Island, Pitcairn Islands, South Pacific Ocean (1988)
*Gough Island and Inaccessible Island (part of Tristan da Cunha), South Atlantic Ocean (1995)
†Historic town of St George and related fortifications, Bermuda (2000)

WORLD HERITAGE SITES IN THE UK

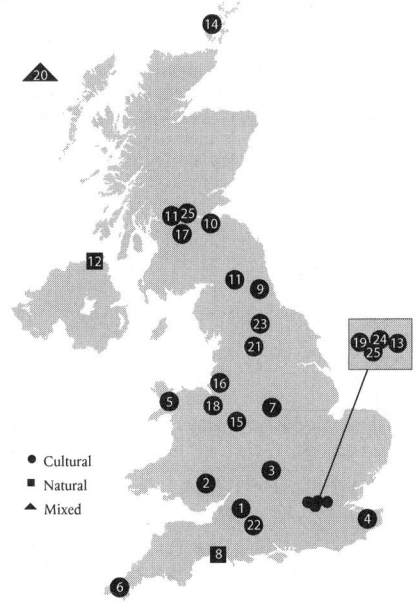

● Cultural
■ Natural
▲ Mixed

# HISTORIC BUILDINGS AND MONUMENTS

## ENGLAND

Under the Planning (Listed Buildings and Conservation Areas) Act 1990, the Secretary of State for Culture, Media and Sport has a statutory duty to approve lists of buildings or groups of buildings in England which are of special architectural or historic interest. In November 2009 responsibility for compiling the list of buildings was passed to English Heritage. Under the Ancient Monuments and Archaeological Areas Act 1979 as amended by the National Heritage Act 1983, the secretary of state is also responsible for compiling a schedule of ancient monuments. Decisions are taken on the advice of English Heritage. In April 2005 responsibility for the administration of the listing system was transferred from the secretary of state to English Heritage. In April 2011, English Heritage launched the National Heritage List for England, a searchable database of all nationally designated heritage assets (W www.historicengland.org.uk/listing/the-list).

## LISTED BUILDINGS

Listed buildings are classified into Grade I, Grade II* and Grade II. There are 376,099 listed buildings in England, of which approximately 90 per cent are Grade II listed. Almost all pre-1700 buildings are listed, as are most buildings of 1700 to 1840. English Heritage carries out thematic surveys of particular types of buildings with a view to making recommendations for listing. The main purpose of listing is to ensure that care is taken in deciding the future of a building. No changes which affect the architectural or historic character of a listed building can be made without listed building consent (in addition to planning permission where relevant). Applications for consent are normally dealt with by the local planning authority, although English Heritage is always consulted about proposals affecting Grade I and Grade II* properties. It is a criminal offence to demolish a listed building, or alter it in such a way as to affect its character, without consent.

| Area | No. of listed buildings as at July 2015 |
|---|---|
| 1. Devon | 20,856 |
| 2. Greater London | 19,331 |
| 3. Kent | 17,685 |
| 4. Somerset (inc. Bath) | 16,119 |
| 5. Essex | 14,294 |
| 6. North Yorkshire | 14,011 |
| 7. Cornwall | 13,946 |
| 8. Suffolk | 13,583 |
| 9. Hampshire (inc. Isle of Wight) | 13,562 |
| 10. Gloucestershire | 13,463 |

Source: National Heritage List for England

## SCHEDULED MONUMENTS

There are 19,717 scheduled monuments in England. All monuments proposed for scheduling are considered to be of national importance. Where buildings are both scheduled and listed, ancient monuments legislation takes precedence. The main purpose of scheduling a monument is to preserve it for the future and to protect it from damage, destruction or any unnecessary interference. Once a monument has been scheduled, scheduled monument consent is required before any works can be carried out. The scope of the control is more extensive and more detailed than that applied to listed buildings, but certain minor works, as detailed in the Ancient Monuments (Class Consents) Order 1994, may be carried out without consent. It is a criminal offence to carry out unauthorised work to scheduled monuments.

## WALES

Under the Planning (Listed Buildings and Conservation Areas) Act 1990 and the Ancient Monuments and Archaeological Areas Act 1979, the National Assembly for Wales is responsible for listing buildings and scheduling monuments in Wales on the advice of Cadw (the Welsh government's historic environment division) and the Royal Commission on the Ancient and Historical Monuments of Wales (RCAHMW). The criteria for evaluating buildings are similar to those in England and the same listing system is used. As at March 2015, there were 29,966 listed buildings and 4,182 scheduled monuments in Wales.

## SCOTLAND

Under the Planning (Listed Buildings and Conservation Areas) (Scotland) Act 1997 and the Ancient Monuments and Archaeological Areas Act 1979, Scottish ministers are responsible for listing buildings and scheduling monuments in Scotland on the advice of Historic Scotland and the Royal Commission on the Ancient and Historical Monuments of Scotland (RCAHMS). The criteria for evaluating buildings are similar to those in England but an A, B, C(S) categorisation is used. As at March 2015 there were 47,423 listed buildings and 8,183 scheduled monuments in Scotland.

## NORTHERN IRELAND

Under the Planning (Northern Ireland) Order 1991 and the Historic Monuments and Archaeological Objects (Northern Ireland) Order 1995, the Northern Ireland Environment Agency (part of the Department of the Environment of Northern Ireland) is responsible for listing buildings and scheduling monuments. The Historic Buildings Council for Northern Ireland and the relevant district council must be consulted on listing proposals, and the Historic Monuments Council for Northern Ireland must be consulted on scheduling proposals. The criteria for evaluating buildings are similar to those in England but an A, B+, B1 and B2 categorisation is used. As at March 2015 there were 8,621 listed buildings and 1,972 scheduled monuments in Northern Ireland.

## ENGLAND

For more information on English Heritage properties, including those listed below, the official website is W www.english-heritage.org.uk
For more information on National Trust properties in England, including those listed below, the official website is W www.nationaltrust.org.uk
KEY
(EH) English Heritage property
(NT) National Trust property
* UNESCO World Heritage Site (see also World Heritage Sites)

A LA RONDE (NT), Exmouth, Devon EX8 5BD T 01395-265514
Unique 16-sided house completed c.1796

ALNWICK CASTLE, Alnwick, Northumberland NE66 1NQ
T 01665-511100 W www.alnwickcastle.com
Seat of the Dukes of Northumberland since 1309; Italian
Renaissance-style interior; gardens with spectacular water
features

ALTHORP, Northants NN7 4HQ T 01604-770006
W www.spencerofalthorp.com
Spencer family seat; permanent Diana, Princess of Wales
exhibition

ANGLESEY ABBEY (NT), Lode, Cambs CB25 9EJ
T 01223-810080
Jacobean house (c.1600) with gardens and a working
watermill (Lode Mill) on the site of a 12th-century priory;
fine furnishings and a unique clock collection

APSLEY HOUSE (EH), London W1J 7NT T 020-7499 5676
Built by Robert Adam 1771–8, home of the Dukes of
Wellington since 1817 and known as 'No. 1 London';
collection of fine and decorative arts

ARUNDEL CASTLE, Arundel, W. Sussex BN18 9AB
T 01903-882173 W www.arundelcastle.org
Castle dating from the Norman Conquest; seat of the
Dukes of Norfolk

AVEBURY (EH/NT), Wilts SN8 1RF T 01672-539250
Remains of stone circles constructed 4,000 years ago
enclosing part of the later village of Avebury

BANQUETING HOUSE, Whitehall, London SW1A 2ER
T 0844-482 7777 W www.hrp.org.uk/banquetinghouse
Designed by Inigo Jones in 1619; ceiling paintings by
Rubens; site of the execution of Charles I

BASILDON PARK (NT), Reading, Berks RG8 9NR
T 01491-672382
Palladian mansion built in 1776–83 by John Carr

BATTLE ABBEY (EH), Battle, E. Sussex TN33 0AD
T 01424-775705
Remains of the abbey founded by William the Conqueror
on the site of the Battle of Hastings

BEESTON CASTLE (EH), Cheshire CW6 9TX
T 01829-260464
Built in the 13th century by Ranulf, sixth Earl of Chester
on the site of an Iron Age hillfort

BELVOIR CASTLE, Grantham, Lincs NG32 1PE
T 01476-871002 W www.belvoircastle.com
Seat of the Dukes of Rutland; 19th-century Gothic-style
castle; notable art collection

BERKELEY CASTLE, Glos GL13 9BQ T 01453-810303
W www.berkeley-castle.com
Completed late 12th century; site of the murder of
Edward II (1327)

BIRDOSWALD ROMAN FORT (EH), Brampton,
Cumbria CA8 7DD T 01697-747602
Stretch of Hadrian's Wall with Roman wall fort, turret and
milecastle

*BLENHEIM PALACE, Woodstock, Oxon OX20 1PP
T 01993-810530 W www.blenheimpalace.com
Seat of the Dukes of Marlborough and Winston
Churchill's birthplace; house designed by Vanbrugh;
landscaped parkland by Capability Brown

BLICKLING ESTATE (NT), Blickling, Norfolk NR11 6NF
T 01263-738030
Jacobean house with state rooms; extensive gardens,
temple and 18th-century orangery

BODIAM CASTLE (NT), Bodiam, E. Sussex TN32 5UA
T 01580-830196
Well-preserved medieval moated castle built in 1385

BOLSOVER CASTLE (EH), Bolsover, Derbys S44 6PR
T 01246-822844
17th-century castle on site of medieval fortress

BOSCOBEL HOUSE (EH), Bishops Wood, Shrops ST19 9AR
T 01902-850244
Timber-framed 17th-century hunting lodge; refuge of
fugitive Charles II from parliamentary troops

BOUGHTON HOUSE, Kettering, Northants NN14 1BJ
T 01536-515731 W www.boughtonhouse.org.uk
17th-century house with French-style additions; home of
the Dukes of Buccleuch and Queensbury

BOWOOD HOUSE, Calne, Wilts SN11 0LZ T 01249-812102
W www.bowood.org/bowood-house
18th-century house in Capability Brown park, featuring
Robert Adam orangery and renowned pinetum and
arboretum

BUCKFAST ABBEY, Buckfastleigh, Devon TQ11 0EE
T 01364-645500 W www.buckfast.org.uk
Benedictine monastery on medieval foundations

BUCKINGHAM PALACE, London SW1A 1AA
T 020-7766 7300 W www.royalcollection.org.uk
Purchased by George III in 1761, and the Sovereign's
official London residence since 1837; 19 state rooms,
including the Throne Room, and Queen's Gallery

BUCKLAND ABBEY (NT), Yelverton, Devon PL20 6EY
T 01822-853607
13th-century Cistercian monastery; home of Sir Francis
Drake

BURGHLEY HOUSE, Stamford, Lincs PE9 3JY T 01780-752451
W www.burghley.co.uk
Late Elizabethan house built by William Cecil, first Lord
Burghley

CARISBROOKE CASTLE (EH), Newport, Isle of Wight
PO30 1XY T 01983-523112
W www.carisbrookecastlemuseum.org.uk
Norman castle; museum; prison of Charles I 1647–8

CARLISLE CASTLE (EH), Carlisle, Cumbria CA3 8UR
T 01228-591922
Medieval castle; prison of Mary Queen of Scots

CASTLE ACRE PRIORY (EH), King's Lynn, Norfolk PE32 2XD
T 01760-755394
Remains include 12th-century church and prior's
lodgings

CASTLE DROGO (NT), Drewsteignton, Devon EX6 6PB
T 01647-433306
Granite castle designed by Lutyens in 1911

CASTLE HOWARD, N. Yorks YO60 7DA T 01653-648333
W www.castlehoward.co.uk
Designed by Vanbrugh 1699–1726; mausoleum designed
by Hawksmoor

CASTLE RISING CASTLE (EH), King's Lynn, Norfolk
PE31 6AH T 01553-631330 W www.castlerising.co.uk
12th-century keep with gatehouse and bridge, surrounded
by 20 acres of defensive earthworks

CHARLES DARWIN'S HOUSE (DOWN HOUSE) (EH),
Downe, Kent BR6 7JT T 01689-859119
The family home where Darwin wrote On the Origin of
Species

CHARTWELL (NT), Westerham, Kent TN16 1PS
T 01732-868381
Home and studio of Sir Winston Churchill

CHATSWORTH, Bakewell, Derbys DE45 1PP T 01246-565300
W www.chatsworth.org
Tudor mansion set in magnificent parkland; seat of the
Dukes of Devonshire

CHESTERS ROMAN FORT (EH), Chollerford,
Northumberland NE46 4EU T 01434-681379
Roman cavalry fort built to guard Hadrian's Wall

CHYSAUSTER ANCIENT VILLAGE (EH), Penzance,
Cornwall TR20 8XA T 07831-757934
Remains of nearly 2,000-year-old Celtic settlement; eight
stone-walled homesteads

CLANDON PARK (NT), West Clandon, Guildford, Surrey
GU4 7RQ T 01483-222502 W www.clandonpark.co.uk

18th-century Palladian mansion and gardens, which contain a Maori meeting house, brought back from New Zealand in 1892

CLIFFORD'S TOWER (EH), York YO1 9SA T 01904-646940
13th-century keep built on a mound; remains of a castle built by William the Conqueror

CORBRIDGE ROMAN SITE (EH), Corbridge, Northumberland NE45 5NT T 01434-632349
Excavated central area of a Roman garrison town

CORFE CASTLE (NT), Wareham, Dorset BH20 5EZ
T 01929-481294
Former royal castle dating from the 11th century and partially ruined during the English Civil War

CROFT CASTLE AND PARKLAND (NT), Yarpole, Herefordshire HR6 9PW T 01568-780246
17th-century quadrangular manor house with Georgian-Gothic interior; built close to ruin of pre-Conquest border castle

DEAL CASTLE (EH), Deal, Kent CT14 7BA T 01304-372762
Largest of the coastal defence forts built by Henry VIII; shaped like a rose with six inner and outer bastions

*DERWENT VALLEY MILLS, Belper, Derbyshire
T 01629-536831 W www.derwentvalleymills.org
Series of 18th- and 19th-century cotton mills; birthplace of the modern factory

DOVER CASTLE (EH), Dover, Kent CT16 1HU T 01304-211067
Castle with Roman, Saxon and Norman features; tunnels used as wartime operations rooms

DR JOHNSON'S HOUSE, Gough Square, London EC4A 3DE
T 020-7353 3745 W www.drjohnsonshouse.org
Home of Samuel Johnson 1748–59

DUNSTANBURGH CASTLE (EH/NT), Craster, nr Alnwick, Northumberland NE66 3TT T 01665-576231
14th-century castle ruins on a cliff with a substantial twin-towered gatehouse-keep

ELTHAM PALACE (EH), Eltham, London SE9 5QE
T 02082-94 2548
Art Deco house next to remains of medieval palace once occupied by Henry VIII; moated gardens

FARLEIGH HUNGERFORD CASTLE (EH), Bath, Somerset BA2 7RS T 01225-754026
Late 14th-century castle with inner and outer courts; chapel with rare medieval wall paintings

FARNHAM CASTLE KEEP (EH), Farnham, Surrey GU9 0AG
T 01252-721194 W www.farnhamcastle.com
Large 12th-century castle keep with motte and bailey wall

FISHBOURNE ROMAN PALACE, Fishbourne, Chichester, W. Sussex PO19 3QR T 01243-785859
W www.sussexpast.co.uk
Excavated Roman palace with largest collection of in-situ mosaics in Britain

*FOUNTAINS ABBEY (NT), nr Ripon, N. Yorks HG4 3DY
T 01765-608888
Ruined Cistercian monastery and corn mill; site includes Studley Royal, a Georgian water garden and deer park

FRAMLINGHAM CASTLE (EH), Framlingham, Suffolk
IP13 9BP T 0870-333 1181
Castle (c.1200) with high curtain walls enclosing an almshouse (1639); once the refuge of Mary Tudor

FURNESS ABBEY (EH), Barrow-in-Furness, Cumbria LA13 0PJ
T 01229-823420
Remains of church and cloister buildings founded in 1123

GLASTONBURY ABBEY, Glastonbury, Somerset BA6 9EL
T 01458-832267 W www.glastonburyabbey.com
12th-century abbey destroyed by fire in 1184 and later rebuilt; ruined in 1539 during dissolution of monasteries; site of an early Christian settlement

GOODRICH CASTLE (EH), Ross-on-Wye, Herefordshire
HR9 6HY T 01600-890538

Remains of 12th- and 13th-century castle; contains a famous mortar that ruined the castle in 1646

GREENWAY (NT), nr Brixham, Devon TQ5 0ES
T 01803-842382
Agatha Christie's holiday home which inspired several of the settings in her books, including the murder in *Dead Man's Folly*; large woodland; walled garden

GREENWICH, London SE10 9NF W www.visitgreenwich.org.uk
Former Royal Observatory (founded 1675) housing the time ball and zero meridian of longitude; the Queen's House, designed for Queen Anne, wife of James I, by Inigo Jones; Painted Hall and neoclassical Chapel (Old Royal Naval College)

GRIMES GRAVES (EH), Brandon, Norfolk IP26 5DE
T 01842-810656
Neolithic flint mines; one shaft can be descended

GUILDHALL, London EC2V 7HH T 020-7332 1313
W www.guildhall.cityoflondon.gov.uk
Centre of civic government of the City built c.1441; facade built 1788–9

HADDON HALL, Bakewell, Derbys DE45 1LA T 01629-812855
W www.haddonhall.co.uk
Well-preserved 12th-century manor house

HAILES ABBEY (EH), Cheltenham, Glos GL54 5PB
T 01242-602398
Ruins of a 13th-century Cistercian monastery

HAM HOUSE AND GARDEN (NT), Richmond-upon-Thames, Surrey TW10 7RS T 020-8940 1950
Stuart house with lavish interiors and formal gardens

HAMPTON COURT PALACE, East Molesey, Surrey KT8 9AU
T 0844-482 7777 W www.hrp.org.uk
16th-century palace originally built for Cardinal Wolsey with 17th- and 18th-century additions by Wren; Royal Tennis Court and world-renowned maze

HARDWICK HALL (NT), Chesterfield, Derbys S44 5QJ
T 01246-850430
Elizabethan house built for Bess of Hardwick

HARDY'S BIRTHPLACE (NT), Higher Bockhampton, Dorset
DT2 8QJ T 01305-262366
Birthplace and home of Thomas Hardy

HAREWOOD HOUSE, Harewood, W. Yorks LS17 9LG
T 0113-218 1010 W www.harewood.org
18th-century house designed by John Carr and Robert Adam; park by Capability Brown

HATFIELD HOUSE, Hatfield, Herts AL9 5NQ T 01707-287010
W www.hatfield-house.co.uk
Jacobean house built by Robert Cecil; features surviving wing of Royal Palace of Hatfield (c.1485), the childhood home of Elizabeth I

HELMSLEY CASTLE (EH), Helmsley, N. Yorks YO62 5AB
T 01439-770442
12th-century keep and curtain wall with 16th-century buildings; spectacular earthwork defences

HEVER CASTLE, nr Edenbridge, Kent TN8 7NG
T 01732-865224 W www.hevercastle.co.uk
13th-century double-moated castle; childhood home of Anne Boleyn

HIGH CROSS HOUSE (NT), nr Totnes, Devon TQ9 6ED
T 01803-842382
Celebrated Modernist house containing original Bauhaus furniture

HOLKHAM HALL, Wells-next-the-Sea, Norfolk NR23 1AB
T 01328-710227 W www.holkham.co.uk
Palladian mansion; notable fine art collection

HOUSESTEADS ROMAN FORT (EH), Hexham, Northumberland NE47 6NN T 01434-344363
Excavated Roman infantry fort on Hadrian's Wall with museum

*IRONBRIDGE GORGE, Ironbridge, Shropshire
W www.ironbridgeguide.info
Important Industrial Revolution site, featuring the world's
first iron bridge

KEDLESTON HALL (NT), Derbys DE22 5JH T 01332-842191
Palladian mansion built 1759–65; complete Robert Adam
interiors; museum of Asian artefacts

KELMSCOTT MANOR, nr Lechlade, Glos GL7 3HJ
T 01367-252486 W www.kelmscottmanor.org.uk
Built c.1600; summer home of William Morris, with
products of Morris and Co.

KENILWORTH CASTLE (EH), Kenilworth, Warks CV8 1NE
T 01926-852078
Largest castle ruin in England; Norman keep with
13th-century outer walls

KENSINGTON PALACE, Kensington Gardens, London W8 4PX
T 0844-482 7777 W www.hrp.org.uk
Built in 1605 and enlarged by Wren; birthplace of
Queen Victoria

KENWOOD HOUSE (EH), Hampstead Lane, London NW3 7JR
T 020-7973 3416
Neoclassical villa housing the Iveagh bequest of paintings
and furniture

KEW PALACE, Richmond-upon-Thames, Surrey TW9 3AB
T 0844-482 7777 W www.hrp.org.uk
Red-brick mansion (c.1631); includes Queen Charlotte's
Cottage, used by King George III and family as a
summerhouse

KINGSTON LACY (NT), Wimborne Minster, Dorset BH21 4EA
T 01202-883402
17th-century mansion with 19th-century alterations;
important art collection

KNEBWORTH HOUSE, Knebworth, Herts SG3 6PY
T 01438-812661 W www.knebworthhouse.com
Tudor manor house concealed by 19th-century Gothic
decoration; Lutyens gardens

KNOLE (NT), Sevenoaks, Kent TN15 0RP T 01732-462100
House built in 1456 set in 1,000-acre deer park; fine
art and furniture collection; birthplace of Vita
Sackville-West

LAMBETH PALACE, London SE1 7JU T 020-7898 1200
W www.archbishopofcanterbury.org
Official residence of the Archbishop of Canterbury since
the 13th century

LANERCOST PRIORY (EH), Brampton, Cumbria CA8 2HQ
T 01697-73030 W www.lanercostpriory.org.uk
The nave of the Augustinian priory's church, c.1166, is
still used; remains of other claustral buildings

LANHYDROCK (NT), Bodmin, Cornwall PL30 5AD
T 01208-265950
House dating from the 17th century; 50 rooms, including
kitchen and nursery

LEEDS CASTLE, nr Maidstone, Kent ME17 1PL
T 01622-765400 W www.leeds-castle.com
Castle dating from the 12th century, situated on two
islands in a lake; used as a royal palace by Henry VIII

LEVENS HALL, Kendal, Cumbria LA8 0PD T 01539-560321
W www.levenshall.co.uk
Elizabethan house with unique topiary garden (1694);
steam engine collection

LINCOLN CASTLE, Lincoln, Lincs LN1 3AA T 01522-782040
W www.lincolncastle.com
Built by William the Conqueror in 1068 on a Roman site;
one of only two double-motted castles in Britain

LINDISFARNE PRIORY (EH), Holy Island, Northumberland
TD15 2RX T 01289-389200
Founded in AD 635; re-established in the 12th century as
a Benedictine priory, now ruined

LITTLE MORETON HALL (NT), Congleton, Cheshire
CW12 4SD T 01260-272018
Iconic timber-framed moated Tudor manor house with
knot garden

LONGLEAT HOUSE, Warminster, Wilts BA12 7NW
T 01985-844400 W www.longleat.co.uk
Elizabethan house in Italian Renaissance style; Capability
Brown parkland with lakes; safari park

LULLINGSTONE ROMAN VILLA (EH), Eynsford, Kent
DA4 0JA T 01322-863467
Large villa occupied for much of the Roman period; fine
mosaics and unique Christian paintings

MIDDLEHAM CASTLE (EH), Middleham, N. Yorks DL8 4QG
T 01969-623899
12th-century keep within later fortifications; childhood
home of Richard III

MONTACUTE HOUSE (NT), Montacute, Somerset TA15 6XP
T 01935-823289
Elizabethan mansion with National Portrait Gallery
collection of portraits from the period

MOUNT GRACE PRIORY (EH), Northallerton, N. Yorks
DL6 3JG T 01609-883494
Carthusian priory with remains of monastic buildings

OLD SARUM (EH), Salisbury, Wilts SP1 3SD T 01722-335398
Iron Age hill fort enclosing remains of Norman castle and
cathedral

ORFORD CASTLE (EH), Orford, Suffolk IP12 2ND
T 01394-450472
Polygonal tower keep of c.1170 and remains of coastal
defence castle built by Henry II

OSBORNE HOUSE (EH), East Cowes, Isle of Wight PO32 6JX
T 01983-200022
Queen Victoria's seaside residence; built by Thomas Cubitt
in Italian Renaissance style; summer house, Swiss Cottage
and museum

OSTERLEY PARK (NT), Isleworth, Middx TW7 4RB
T 020-8232 5050
18th-century neoclassical mansion with Tudor stable
block

PENDENNIS CASTLE (EH), Falmouth, Cornwall TR11 4LP
Well-preserved 16th-century coastal defence castle

PENSHURST PLACE, Penshurst, Kent TN11 8DG
T 01892-870307 W www.penshurstplace.com
Medieval house featuring Baron's Hall (1341) and gardens
(1346); toy museum

PETWORTH HOUSE (NT), Petworth, W. Sussex GU28 0AE
T 01798-343929
Late 17th-century house set in Capability Brown
landscaped deer park; fine art collection

PEVENSEY CASTLE (EH), Pevensey, E. Sussex BN24 5LE
T 01323-762604
Walls of a fourth-century Roman fort; remains of an
11th-century castle

PEVERIL CASTLE (EH), Castleton, Derbys S33 8WQ
T 01433-620613
Remains of a 12th-century castle defended on two sides
by precipitous rocks

POLESDEN LACEY (NT), nr Dorking, Surrey RH5 6BD
T 01372-452048
Regency villa remodelled in the Edwardian era; fine
paintings and furnishings; walled rose garden

PORTCHESTER CASTLE (EH), Portchester, Hants PO16 9QW
T 02392-378291
Walls of a late Roman fort enclosing a Norman keep and
an Augustinian priory church

POWDERHAM CASTLE, Kenton, Devon EX6 8JQ
T 01626-890243 W www.powderham.co.uk
Medieval castle with 18th- and 19th-century alterations,
including James Wyatt music room

RABY CASTLE, Staindrop, Co. Durham DL2 3AH
T 01833-660202 W www.rabycastle.com
14th-century castle with walled gardens
RAGLEY HALL, Alcester, Warks B49 5NJ T 01789-762090
W www.ragleyhall.com
17th-century Palladian house with gardens and lake
RICHBOROUGH ROMAN FORT (EH), Richborough, Kent
CT13 9JW T 01304-612013
Remains of a Roman Saxon Shore fortress; landing-site of
the Claudian invasion in AD 43
RICHMOND CASTLE (EH), Richmond, N. Yorks DL10 4QW
T 01748-822493
12th-century keep with 11th-century curtain wall
RIEVAULX ABBEY (EH), nr Helmsley, N. Yorks YO62 5LB
T 01439-798228
Remains of a Cistercian abbey founded c.1132
ROCHESTER CASTLE (EH), Rochester, Kent ME1 1SW
T 01634-335882
11th-century castle partly on the Roman city wall, with a
well-preserved square keep of c.1127
ROCKINGHAM CASTLE, Market Harborough, Leics LE16 8TH
T 01536-770240 W www.rockinghamcastle.com
Built by William the Conqueror; formal gardens and
400-year-old 'elephant' hedge
ROMAN BATHS, Pump Room, Stall Street, Bath BA1 1LZ
T 01225-477785 W www.romanbaths.co.uk
Extensive remains of a Roman temple and bathing complex
which still flows with natural thermal water; museum
ROYAL PAVILION, Brighton BN1 1EE T 03000-290900
W www.brighton-hove-rpml.org.uk
Unique palace of George IV, in indo-gothic style with
chinoiserie interiors and Regency gardens
ST AUGUSTINE'S ABBEY (EH), Canterbury, Kent CT1 1PF
T 01227-767345
Remains of Benedictine monastery founded c.597
ST MAWES CASTLE (EH), St Mawes, Cornwall TR2 5DE
T 01326-270526
Coastal defence castle built by Henry VIII
ST MICHAEL'S MOUNT (NT), Marazion, Cornwall TR17 0HS
T 01736-710265 W www.stmichaelsmount.co.uk
12th-century church and castle with later additions,
situated on an iconic rocky island
*SALTAIRE VILLAGE, nr Shipley, W. Yorks
W www.saltairevillage.info
Victorian industrial village founded by mill owner Titus
Salt for his workers see also World Heritage Sites
SANDRINGHAM, Norfolk PE35 6EN T 01485-545400
W www.sandringhamestate.co.uk
The Queen's private residence; neo-Jacobean house built
in 1870 with gardens and country park
SCARBOROUGH CASTLE (EH), Scarborough, N. Yorks
YO11 1HY T 01723-372451
Remains of 12th-century keep and curtain walls
SHERBORNE CASTLE, Sherborne, Dorset DT9 5NR
T 01935-812072 W www.sherbornecastle.com
16th-century castle built by Sir Walter Raleigh set in
Capability Brown landscaped gardens
SHUGBOROUGH ESTATE (NT), Milford, Staffs ST17 0XB
T 0845-459 8900 W www.shugborough.org.uk
Late 17th century house in 18th-century park with
monuments, temples and pavilions in the Greek Revival
style; seat of the Earls of Lichfield
SKIPTON CASTLE, Skipton, N. Yorks BD23 1AW
T 01756-792442 W www.skiptoncastle.co.uk
Well-preserved D-shaped medieval castle with six round
towers and inner courtyard
SMALLHYTHE PLACE (NT), Tenterden, Kent TN30 7NG
T 01580-762334
Half-timbered 16th-century house

*STONEHENGE (EH), nr Amesbury, Wilts SP4 7DE
T 01722-343830
World-famous prehistoric monument comprising
concentric stone circles surrounded by a ditch and bank
STONOR PARK, Henley-on-Thames, Oxon RG9 6HF
T 01491-638587 W www.stonor.com
Medieval house with Georgian facade; refuge for Catholic
recusants after the Reformation
STOURHEAD (NT), Stourton, Wilts BA12 6QD
T 01747-841152
18th-century Palladian mansion with world-renowned
landscape gardens; King Alfred's Tower
STRATFIELD SAYE HOUSE, Hants RG7 2BT T 01256-882694
W www.stratfield-saye.co.uk
House built 1630–40; home of the Dukes of Wellington
since 1817
STRATFORD-UPON-AVON, Warks T 01789-868191
W www.stratford-upon-avon.co.uk
Shakespeare's Birthplace Trust with Shakespeare Centre;
Anne Hathaway's Cottage; Holy Trinity Church, where
Shakespeare is buried
SUDELEY CASTLE, Winchcombe, Glos GL54 5JD
T 01242-604244 W www.sudeleycastle.co.uk
Castle built in 1442; once owned by Richard III and
former home to Catherine Parr, sixth wife of Henry VIII;
restored in the 19th century
SULGRAVE MANOR, nr Banbury, Oxon OX17 2SD
T 01295-760205 W www.sulgravemanor.org.uk
Home of George Washington's family
SUTTON HOUSE (NT), Hackney, London E9 6JQ
T 020-8986 2264
Tudor house, built in 1535 by Sir Ralph Sadleir
SYON HOUSE, Brentford, Middx TW8 8JF T 020-8560 0882
W www.syonpark.co.uk
Built on the site of a former monastery; Robert Adam
interior; Capability Brown park
TINTAGEL CASTLE (EH), Tintagel, Cornwall PL34 0HE
T 01840-770328
13th-century cliff-top castle and 5th–6th-century Celtic
settlement; linked with Arthurian legend
TOWER OF LONDON, London EC3N 4AB T 0844-482 7777
W www.hrp.org.uk
Royal palace and fortress begun by William the Conqueror
in 1078; houses the Crown Jewels
TYNEMOUTH PRIORY AND CASTLE (EH), Tyne and Wear
NE30 4BZ T 0191-257 1090
Remains of a Benedictine priory, founded c.1090, moated
castle-towers, a gatehouse and keep on Saxon monastic
site
UPPARK (NT), South Harting, W. Sussex GU31 5QR
T 01730-825415
17th-century house, restored after fire; Fetherstonhaugh
art collection; 18th-century dolls' house
WALMER CASTLE (EH), Walmer, Kent CT14 7LJ
T 01304-364288
One of Henry VIII's coastal defence castles, now the
residence of the Lord Warden of the Cinque Ports
WARKWORTH CASTLE (EH), Warkworth, Northumberland
NE65 0UJ T 01665-711423
14th-century keep amid earlier ruins, with hermitage
upstream
WHITBY ABBEY (EH), Whitby, N. Yorks YO22 4JT
T 01947-603568
Remains of Norman church on the site of a monastery
founded in AD 657
WILTON HOUSE, nr Salisbury, Wilts SP2 0BJ T 01722-746714
W www.wiltonhouse.com
17th-century house on the site of a Tudor house and
ninth-century nunnery; Palladian bridge

WINDSOR CASTLE, Windsor, Berks SL4 1NJ T 020-7766 7304
W www.royalcollection.org.uk
Official residence of the Queen; oldest royal residence still
in regular use; largest inhabited castle in the world. Also St
George's Chapel; Queen Mary's Dolls' House

WOBURN ABBEY, Woburn, Beds MK17 9WA T 01525-290333
W www.woburn.co.uk
Built on the site of a Cistercian abbey; seat of the Dukes of
Bedford; art collection; antiques centre

WROXETER ROMAN CITY (EH), nr Shrewsbury, Shropshire
SY5 6PH T 01743-761330
Second-century public baths and part of the forum of the
Roman town of *Viroconium*

# WALES

For more information on Cadw properties, including those
listed below, the official website is W www.cadw.wales.gov.uk
For more information on National Trust properties in Wales,
including those listed below, the official website is
W www.nationaltrust.org.uk
KEY
(C) Property of Cadw: Welsh Historic Monuments
(NT) National Trust property
* UNESCO World Heritage Site (*see also* World Heritage
Sites)

*BEAUMARIS CASTLE (C), Anglesey LL58 8AP
T 01248-810361
Concentrically planned 13th-century castle, still virtually
intact

*BLAENAVON, Church Road, Blaenavon NP4 9AS T
01495-742333 W www.visitblaenavon.co.uk
18th- and 19th-century industrial landscape associated
with coal and iron production

CAERLEON ROMAN BATHS AND AMPHITHEATRE (C),
Newport NP18 1AE T 01633-422518
Rare example of a legionary bath-house and late
first-century arena surrounded by bank for spectators

*CAERNARFON CASTLE (C), Gwynedd LL55 2AY
T 01286-677617 W www.caernarfon-castle.co.uk
Huge fortress with polygonal towers built between 1283
and 1330, initially for King Edward I of England; setting
for the investiture of Prince Charles in 1969

CAERPHILLY CASTLE (C), Caerphilly CF83 1JD
T 029-2088 3143
Concentrically planned castle (*c.*1270) notable for its scale
and use of water defences

CARDIFF CASTLE, Cardiff CF10 3RB T 029-2087 8100
W www.cardiffcastle.com
Norman keep built on site of Roman fort; 'fairytale'
gothic-revival mansion added in the 19th century

CASTELL COCH (C), Tongwynlais, Cardiff CF15 7JS
T 029-2081 0101
'Fairytale'-style castle, rebuilt 1875–90 on medieval
foundations

CHEPSTOW CASTLE (C), Monmouthshire NP16 5EY
T 01291-624065
Rectangular keep amid extensive fortifications; developed
throughout the Middle Ages

*CONWY CASTLE (C), Gwynedd LL32 8AY T 01492-592358
Built for Edward I in 1283–7 on narrow rocky outcrop;
features eight towers and two barbicans

CRICCIETH CASTLE (C), Gwynedd LL52 0DP
T 01766-522227
Native Welsh 13th-century castle, taken and altered by
Edward I and Edward II

DENBIGH CASTLE (C), Denbighshire LL16 3NB
T 01745-813385

Remains of the castle (begun 1282), including
triple-towered gatehouses

DYFFRYN GARDENS (NT), St Nicholas, Cardiff CF5 6SU
T 029-2059 3328
Edwardian gardens designed by Thomas Mawson,
overlooked by a grand Edwardian mansion

*HARLECH CASTLE (C), Gwynedd LL46 2YH T 01766-780552
Well-preserved castle, constructed 1283–95, on an
outcrop above the former shoreline; withstood seven-year
siege 1461–8

PEMBROKE CASTLE, Pembrokeshire SA71 4LA
T 01646-684585 W www.pembroke-castle.co.uk
Castle founded in 1093; Great Tower built in late 12th
century; birthplace of King Henry VII

PENRHYN CASTLE (NT), Bangor, Gwynedd LL57 4HN
T 01248-353084
Neo-Norman castle built in the 19th century; railway and
dolls' museums; private art collection

*PONTCYSYLLTE AQUEDUCT AND CANAL, Trevor,
Wrexham LL20 7TG T 01978-292015
W www.pontcysyllte.co.uk
Longest and highest aqueduct in Great Britain; designed
by Thomas Telford and finished in 1805

POWIS CASTLE (NT), Welshpool, Powys SY21 8RF
T 01938-551944
Medieval castle with interior in variety of styles;
17th-century gardens; Clive of India museum

RAGLAN CASTLE (C), Monmouthshire NP15 2BT
T 01291-690228
Remains of 15th-century castle with moated hexagonal
keep

ST DAVIDS BISHOP'S PALACE (C), Pembrokeshire SA62 6PE
T 01437-720517
Remains of residence of Bishops of St Davids built
1328–47

TINTERN ABBEY (C), nr Chepstow, Monmouthshire NP16 6SE
T 01291-689251
Remains of 13th-century church and conventual buildings
of a 12th-century Cistercian monastery

TRETOWER COURT AND CASTLE (C), nr Crickhowell,
Powys NP8 1RD T 01874-730279
Medieval manor house rebuilt in the 15th century, with
remains of 12th-century castle near by

# SCOTLAND

For more information on Historic Scotland properties,
including those listed below, the official website is
W www.historic-scotland.gov.uk
For more information on National Trust for Scotland
properties, including those listed below, the official website is
W www.nts.org.uk
KEY
(HS) Historic Scotland property
(NTS) National Trust for Scotland property
* Part of the Heart of Neolithic Orkney UNESCO World
Heritage Site

ABBOTSFORD HOUSE, Melrose, Roxburghshire TD6 9BQ
T 01896-752043 W www.scottsabbotsford.co.uk
Home of Sir Walter Scott; features historic Scottish relics
and formal gardens

BALMORAL CASTLE, Ballater, Aberdeenshire AB35 5TB
T 01339-742534 W www.balmoralcastle.com
Baronial-style castle built for Victoria and Albert; the
Queen's private residence

BLACKHOUSE, ARNOL (HS), Lewis, Western Isles HS2 9DB
T 01851-710395
Traditional Lewis thatched house

BLAIR CASTLE, Blair Atholl, Perthshire PH18 5TL
T 01796-481207 W www.blair-castle.co.uk
Mid-18th-century mansion with 13th-century tower; seat
of the Dukes and Earls of Atholl
BOWHILL, Selkirk, Scottish Borders TD7 5ET T 01750-22204
W www.bowhillhouse.co.uk
Present house dates mainly from 1812; Seat of the Dukes
of Buccleuch and Queensberry; fine collection of
paintings
BROUGH OF BIRSAY (HS), Orkney KW17 2LX
T 01856-841815
Remains of Norse and Pictish village on the tidal island of
Birsay
CAERLAVEROCK CASTLE (HS), Glencaple, Dumfries and
Galloway DG1 4RU T 01387-770244
Unique triangular 13th-century moated castle with
classical Renaissance additions
CAIRNPAPPLE HILL (HS), Torphichen, West Lothian
T 01506-634622
Neolithic ceremonial site and Bronze Age burial chambers
CALANAIS STANDING STONES (HS), Lewis, Western Isles
HS2 9DY T 01851-621422
Standing stones in a cross-shaped setting, dating from
between 2900 and 2600 BC
CATERTHUNS (BROWN AND WHITE) (HS), Menmuir,
nr Brechin, Angus
Two large Iron Age hill forts
CAWDOR CASTLE, Nairn, Moray IV12 5RD T 01667-404401
W www.cawdorcastle.com
14th-century keep with 15th- and 17th-century additions
CLAVA CAIRNS (HS), nr Inverness, Inverness-shire IV2 5EU
T 01667-460232
Bronze Age cemetery complex of cairns and standing
stones
CRATHES CASTLE (NTS), nr Banchory, Aberdeenshire
AB31 5QJ T 0845-643 9215
16th-century baronial castle in woodland, fields and
gardens
CULZEAN CASTLE (NTS), Maybole, Ayrshire KA19 8LE
T 01655-884455
18th-century Robert Adam castle with oval staircase and
circular saloon
DRYBURGH ABBEY (HS), nr Melrose, Roxburghshire TD6 0RQ
T 01835-822381
12th-century abbey containing the tomb of Sir Walter
Scott
DUNVEGAN CASTLE, Skye IV55 8WF T 01470-521206
W www.dunvegancastle.com
13th-century castle with later additions; home of the
chiefs of the Clan MacLeod
EDINBURGH CASTLE (HS), EH1 2NG T 0131-225 9846
W www.edinburghcastle.gov.uk
Fortress perched on extinct volcano; includes the Scottish
Crown Jewels, Scottish National War Memorial, Scottish
United Services Museum
EDZELL CASTLE (HS), nr Brechin, Angus DD9 7UE
T 01356-648631
Ruined 16th-century tower house on medieval
foundations; early 17th-century walled garden
EILEAN DONAN CASTLE, Dornie, Ross and Cromarty
IV40 8DX T 01599-555202 W www.eileandonancastle.com
13th-century castle situated at the meeting point of three
sea lochs; Jacobite relics
ELGIN CATHEDRAL (HS), Moray IV30 1HU T 01343-547171
13th-century cathedral and octagonal chapterhouse
FLOORS CASTLE, Kelso, Roxburghshire TD5 7SF
T 01573-223333 W www.floorscastle.com
Largest inhabited castle in Scotland; seat of the Dukes of
Roxburghe; built in the 1720s by William Adam

FORT GEORGE (HS), Ardersier, Inverness-shire IV2 7TD
T 01667-460232
18th-century fort; still a working army barracks
GLAMIS CASTLE, Forfar, Angus DD8 1RJ T 01307-840393
W www.glamis-castle.co.uk
Seat of the Lyon family (later Earls of Strathmore and
Kinghorne) since 1372; the setting for Shakespeare's
*Macbeth*
GLASGOW CATHEDRAL (HS), Lanarkshire G4 0QZ
T 0141-552 8198 W www.glasgowcathedral.org.uk
Late 12th-century cathedral with vaulted crypt
GLENELG BROCHS (HS), Glenelg, Ross and Cromarty
T 01667-460232
Two broch towers (Dun Telve and Dun Troddan) with
well-preserved structural features
HOPETOUN HOUSE, South Queensferry, West Lothian
EH30 9SL T 0131-331 2451 W www.hopetoun.co.uk
Designed by Sir William Bruce in 1699 and enlarged by
William Adam 1721–48
HUNTLY CASTLE (HS), Aberdeenshire AB54 4SH
T 01466-793191
Ruin of a 16th- and 17th-century baronial residence
INVERARAY CASTLE, Argyll PA32 8XE T 01499-302203
W www.inveraray-castle.com
Gothic-style 18th-century castle designed by William
Adam and Roger Morris; seat of the Dukes of Argyll
IONA ABBEY (HS), Iona, Inner Hebrides PA76 6SQ
T 01681-700512
Monastery founded by St Columba in AD 563
JARLSHOF (HS), Sumburgh Head, Shetland ZE3 9JN
T 01950-460112
Prehistoric settlement with later ninth-century Norse
additions
JEDBURGH ABBEY (HS), Scottish Borders TD8 6JQ
T 01835-863925
Ruined Augustinian abbey founded c.1138
KISIMUL CASTLE (HS), Castlebay, Barra, Western Isles
HS9 5UZ T 01871-810313
Medieval island home of the Clan MacNeil
LINLITHGOW PALACE (HS), Kirkgate, Linlithgow, West
Lothian EH49 7AL T 01506-842896
Ruined royal palace, founded in 1424, set in park;
birthplace of James V and Mary, Queen of Scots
*MAESHOWE (HS), Stenness, Orkney KW16 3HH
T 01856-761606
Neolithic chambered tomb with Viking runes
MEIGLE SCULPTURED STONES (HS), Meigle, Perthshire
PH12 8SB T 01828-640612
Twenty-six carved Pictish stones dating from the late
8th to the late 10th centuries
MELROSE ABBEY (HS), Melrose, Roxburghshire TD6 9LG
T 01896-822562
Ruin of Cistercian abbey founded c.1136 by David I;
museum of medieval objects
MOUSA BROCH (HS), Island of Mousa, Shetland ZE2 9HP
Finest surviving Iron Age broch tower
NEW ABBEY CORN MILL (HS), Dumfriesshire DG2 8BX
T 01387-850260
Working water-powered mill built in the late 18th
century
*NEW LANARK, South Lanarkshire ML11 9DB
T 01555-661 345
18th-century village built around a cotton mill
PALACE OF HOLYROODHOUSE, Edinburgh EH8 8DX
T 0131-556 5100 W www.royalcollection.org.uk
The Queen's official Scottish residence; home to Mary,
Queen of Scots; main part of the palace built 1671–9
close to ruined 12th-century Augustinian abbey

\*RING O' BRODGAR (HS), Stenness, Orkney KW16
T 01856-841815
Neolithic circle of upright stones surrounded by circular ditch
ROSSLYN CHAPEL, Roslin, Midlothian EH25 9PU
T 0131-440 2159 W www.rosslynchapel.org.uk
Historic church built between 1446 and 1484 with unique stone carvings
ST ANDREWS CASTLE AND CATHEDRAL (HS), Fife
KY16 9AR (castle); 9QL (cathedral) T 01334-477196 (castle); 01334-472563 (cathedral)
Ruins of 13th-century castle, the former residence of bishops of St Andrews, and remains of the largest cathedral in Scotland; museum
SCONE PALACE, Perth, Perthshire PH2 6BD T 01738-552300
Georgian-Gothic house built 1802–12
\*SKARA BRAE (HS), nr Stromness, Orkney KW16 3LR
T 01856-841815
Neolithic village with adjacent replica house
SMAILHOLM TOWER (HS), nr Kelso, Roxburghshire TD5 7PG
T 01573-460365
Well-preserved 15th-century tower-house
STIRLING CASTLE (HS), Stirlingshire FK8 1EJ
T 01786-450000 W www.stirlingcastle.gov.uk
Great Hall and gatehouse built for James IV c.1500; palace built for James V in 1538; site of coronations including Mary, Queen of Scots
\*STONES OF STENNESS, Stenness, Orkney T 01856 841815
Four surviving Neolithic standing stones and the uprights of a three-stone dolmen
TANTALLON CASTLE (HS), North Berwick, East Lothian EH39 5PN T 01620-892727
Ruined 14th-century curtain wall with towers
THREAVE CASTLE (HS), Castle Douglas, Kirkcudbrightshire DG7 1TJ T 07711-223101
Ruined late 14th-century tower on an island; accessible only by boat
URQUHART CASTLE (HS), Drumnadrochit, Inverness-shire IV63 6XJ T 01456-450551
13th-century castle remains on the banks of Loch Ness

## NORTHERN IRELAND

For the Northern Ireland Environment Agency, the official website is W www.doeni.gov.uk/niea
For more information on National Trust properties in Northern Ireland, including those listed below, the official website is W www.nationaltrust.org.uk

KEY
(NIEA) Property in the care of the Northern Ireland Environment Agency
(NT) National Trust property

CARRICKFERGUS CASTLE (NIEA), Carrickfergus, Co. Antrim BT38 7BG T 028-9335 1273
Castle built in 1177 and taken by King John in 1210; garrisoned until 1928
CASTLE COOLE (NT), Enniskillen, Co. Fermanagh BT74 6JY
T 028-6632 2690
18th-century neoclassical mansion in parkland; designed by James Wyatt
CASTLE WARD (NT), Strangford, Co. Down BT30 7LS
T 028-4488 1204
18th-century house with Classical and Gothic facades
DEVENISH MONASTIC SITE (NIEA), nr Enniskillen, Co. Fermanagh T 028-6862 1588
Island monastery founded in the sixth century by St Molaise; church dating from 13th century
DOWNHILL DEMESNE AND HEZLETT HOUSE (NT), Castlerock, Co. Londonderry BT51 4RP T 028-7084 8728
Ruins of 18th-century mansion and a 17th century cottage in landscaped estate including Mussenden Temple
DUNLUCE CASTLE (NIEA), Bushmills, Co. Antrim BT57 8UY
T 028-2073 1938
Ruins of medieval stronghold of the McDonnells
FLORENCE COURT (NT), Enniskillen, Co. Fermanagh BT92 1DB T 028-6634 8249
Mid-18th-century house with Rococo decoration
GREY ABBEY (NIEA), Greyabbey, Co. Down BT22 2NQ
T 028-9181 1491
Substantial remains of a Cistercian abbey founded in 1193 set in landscaped parkland
MOUNT STEWART (NT), Newtownards, Co. Down BT22 2AD
T 028-4278 8387
18th-century house; octagonal Temple of the Winds
NENDRUM MONASTIC SITE (NIEA), Mahee Island, Co. Down T 028-9054 3037
Island monastery founded in the fifth century by St Machaoi
PATTERSON'S SPADE MILL (NT), Templepatrick, Co. Antrim BT39 0AP T 028-9443 3619
Last working water-driven spade mill in the UK
TULLY CASTLE (NIEA), Co. Fermanagh T 028-6862 1588
Fortified house and bawn built c.1619

# MUSEUMS AND GALLERIES

There are approximately 2,500 museums and galleries in the UK. As of February 2015, 1,581 of these were fully accredited by Arts Council England. Accreditation indicates that the museum or gallery has an appropriate constitution, is soundly financed, has adequate collection management standards and public services and has access to professional curatorial advice. A further 149 museums and galleries have applied for, or are in the process of obtaining accreditation, and these applications are assessed by either Arts Council England; CyMAL: Museums, Archives and Libraries Wales; Museums Galleries Scotland or the Northern Ireland Museums Council.

The following is a selection of museums and art galleries in the UK. Opening hours and admission charges vary. Further information about museums and galleries in the UK is available from the Museums Association (W www.museumsassociation.org T 020-7566 7800).

W www.culture24.org.uk includes a database of all the museums and galleries in the UK.

## ENGLAND

* England's national museums and galleries, which receive funding from a government department, such as the DCMS or MoD. These institutions are deemed to have collections of national importance, and the government is able to call upon their staff for expert advice

ALTON
*Jane Austen's House Museum*, Chawton, Hants GU34 1SD
T 01420-83262 W www.jane-austens-house-museum.org.uk
17th-century house which tells the author's story
BARNARD CASTLE
*The Bowes Museum*, Co. Durham DL12 8NP T 01833-690606
W www.bowesmuseum.org.uk
Public gallery in a French châteaux style featuring archaeology, fashion and ceramics. Houses one of the largest collections of Spanish art in the country
BATH
*American Museum*, Claverton Manor BA2 7BD T 01225-460503
W www.americanmuseum.org
American decorative arts from the 17th to 20th centuries; American heritage exhibition
*Fashion Museum*, Bennett Street BA1 2QH T 01225-477789
W www.museumofcostume.co.uk
Fashion from the 17th century to the present day
*Victoria Art Gallery*, Bridge Street BA2 4AT T 01225-477233
W www.victoriagal.org.uk
European Old Masters and British art since the 15th century
BEAMISH
*Beamish Museum*, Co. Durham DH9 0RG T 0191-370 4000
W www.beamish.org.uk
Living working museum of a northern town during Georgian, Victorian and Edwardian times
BEAULIEU
*National Motor Museum*, Hants SO42 7ZN T 01590-612345
W www.beaulieu.co.uk
National motor museum within the New Forest national park
BIRMINGHAM
*Aston Hall*, Trinity Road B6 6JD T 0121-675 4722
W www.birminghammuseums.org.uk/aston
Jacobean House containing paintings, furniture and tapestries from the 17th to 19th centuries

*Barber Institute of Fine Arts*, University of Birmingham, Edgbaston B15 2TS T 0121-414 7333 W www.barber.org.uk
Extensive coin collection; fine arts, including Old Masters
*Birmingham Museum and Art Gallery*, Chamberlain Square B3 3DH T 0121-303 1966 W www.bmag.org.uk
Includes notable collection of Pre-Raphaelite art
*Museum of the Jewellery Quarter*, Vyse Street, Hockley B18 6HA T 0121-554 3598
W www.birminghammuseums.org.uk/jewellery
Preserved jewellery workshop
*Thinktank*, Curzon Street B4 7XG T 0121-202 2222
W www.thinktank.ac
Science museum featuring over 200 hands-on displays and a Planetarium
BOURNEMOUTH
*Russell-Cotes Art Gallery and Museum*, East Cliff Promenade BH1 3AA T 01202-451858
W www.russell-cotes.bournemouth.gov.uk
Seaside villa housing 19th- and 20th-century art and sculptures from around the world
BOVINGTON
*Tank Museum*, Dorset BH20 6JG T 01929-405096
W www.tankmuseum.org
Collection of 200 tanks from their invention in 1915 to the modern conflict in Afghanistan
BRADFORD
*Bradford Industrial Museum*, Moorside Mills, Moorside Road, Eccleshill BD2 3HP T 01274-435900
W www.bradfordmuseums.org
Steam power, machinery and motor vehicle exhibits
*Cartwright Hall Art Gallery*, Lister Park BD9 4NS
T 01274-431212 W www.bradfordmuseums.org
British 19th- and 20th-century fine art, contemporary prints and south Asian art
*National Media Museum*, BD1 1NQ T 0844-856 3797
W www.nationalmediamuseum.org.uk
Photography, film and television interactive exhibits; features an IMAX cinema and the only permanent Cinerama screen in Europe
BRIGHTON
*Booth Museum of Natural History*, Dyke Road BN1 5AA
T 03000-290900
W www.brightonmuseums.org.uk/booth
Zoology, botany and geology collections; British birds in recreated habitats
*Brighton Museum and Art Gallery*, Royal Pavilion Gardens BN1 1EE T 03000-290900
W www.brightonmuseums.org.uk/brighton
Includes fine art and design, fashion, world art; Sussex history
BRISTOL
*Arnolfini*, Narrow Quay BS1 4QA T 0117-917 2300
W www.arnolfini.org.uk
Experimental contemporary visual arts, dance, performance, music; talks and workshops
*Blaise Castle House Museum*, Henbury Road BS10 7QS
T 0117-903 9818 W www.bristol.gov.uk/node/2869
18th-century mansion; social history collections
*Bristol Museum and Art Gallery*, Queen's Road BS8 1RL
T 0117-922 3571 W www.bristol.gov.uk/node/2904
Includes Victorian, Edwardian and French fine art; archaeology, local history and natural sciencies

*M Shed*, Prince's Wharf BS1 4RN **T** 0117-352 6600
**W** www.mshed.org
The story of Bristol's heritage of engineering, transport, music and industry
CAMBRIDGE
*Fitzwilliam Museum*, Trumpington Street CB2 1RB
**T** 01223-332900 **W** www.fitzmuseum.cam.ac.uk
Antiquities, fine and applied arts, clocks, ceramics, manuscripts, furniture, sculpture, coins and medals
*\*Imperial War Museum Duxford*, Duxford CB22 4QR
**T** 01223-835000 **W** duxford.iwm.org.uk
Displays of military and civil aircraft, tanks and naval exhibits
*Museum of Archaeology and Anthropology*, Downing Street CB2 3DZ **T** 01223-333516 **W** www.maa.cam.ac.uk
Global archaeological and anthropological collections; photography and modern art collections
*Sedgwick Museum of Earth Sciences*, Downing Street CB2 3EQ
**T** 01223-333456 **W** www.sedgwickmuseum.org
Extensive geological collection
*Whipple Museum of the History of Science*, Free School Lane CB2 3RH **T** 01223-330906 **W** www.hps.cam.ac.uk/whipple
Scientific instruments from the 14th century to the present
CARLISLE
*Tullie House Museum and Art Gallery*, Castle Street CA3 8TP
**T** 01228-618718 **W** www.tulliehouse.co.uk
Prehistoric archaeology, Hadrian's Wall; Viking and medieval Cumbria, and the social history of Carlisle
CHATHAM
*The Historic Dockyard*, ME4 4TE **T** 01634-823800
**W** www.thedockyard.co.uk
Maritime attractions including HMS *Cavalier*, the UK's last Second World War destroyer
*Royal Engineers Museum*, Prince Arthur Road, Gillingham ME4 4UG **T** 01634-822839 **W** www.re-museum.co.uk
Regimental history, ethnography, decorative art and photography
CHELTENHAM
*Art Gallery and Museum*, Clarence Street GL50 3JT
**T** 01242-237431 **W** www.cheltenhammuseum.org.uk
Arts and crafts, local heroes, fine art and natural history
CHESTER
*Grosvenor Museum*, Grosvenor Street CH1 2DD **T** 01244-972120
**W** www.grosvenormuseum.co.uk
Roman collections, natural history, art, Chester silver, local history and costume
CHICHESTER
*Weald and Downland Open Air Museum*, Singleton PO18 0EU
**T** 01243-811363 **W** www.wealddown.co.uk
Rebuilt vernacular buildings from south-east England; includes medieval houses and a working watermill; craft demonstrations, Tudor kitchen and cooking
COLCHESTER
*Colchester Castle Museum*, Castle Park CO1 1TJ **T** 01206-282939
**W** www.visitcolchester.com
Largest Norman keep in Europe standing on foundations of the Roman Temple of Claudius
COVENTRY
*Coventry Transport Museum*, Hales Street CV1 1JD
**T** 024-7623 4270 **W** www.transport-museum.com
Extensive collection of motor vehicles and bicycles; land speed record-holding car
*Herbert Art Gallery and Museum*, Jordan Well CV1 5QP
**T** 024-7623 7521 **W** www.theherbert.org
Local history, archaeology, industry and visual arts
DERBY
*Derby Museum and Art Gallery*, The Strand DE1 1BS
**T** 01332-641901
**W** www.derbymuseums.org/museumartgallery

Includes paintings by Joseph Wright of Derby, origins of Derby and military history
*Derby Silk Mill*, Silk Mill Lane DE1 3AF **T** 01332-255308
**W** www.derbymuseums.org/locations/the-silk-mill
Built on the site of the world's first factory; wildlife gallery, fine art, Bonnie Prince Charlie Room
*Pickford's House Museum*, Friar Gate DE1 1DA **T** 01332-715181
**W** www.derbymuseums.org/pickfords-house
Georgian town house designed by architect Joseph Pickford; museum of Georgian life and costume
DEVIZES
*Wiltshire Heritage Museum*, Long Street SN10 1NS
**T** 01380-727369 **W** www.wiltshiremuseum.org.uk
Natural and local history; art gallery; archaeological finds from prehistoric, Roman and Saxon sites
DORCHESTER
*Dorset County Museum*, High West Street DT1 1XA
**T** 01305-262735 **W** www.dorsetcountymuseum.org
Includes a collection of Thomas Hardy's manuscripts, books, notebooks and drawings; local history, geology and Roman mosaics
DOVER
*Dover Museum*, Market Square CT16 1PH **T** 01304-201066
**W** www.dovermuseum.co.uk
Contains the Dover Bronze Age Boat Gallery and archaeological finds from Bronze Age, Roman and Saxon sites
EXETER
*Royal Albert Memorial Museum and Art Gallery*, Queen Street EX4 3RX **T** 01392-265858 **W** www.rammuseum.org.uk
Natural history; archaeology; worldwide fine and decorative art including Exeter silver
GATESHEAD
*Baltic Centre for Contemporary Art*, South Shore Road NE8 3BA
**T** 0191-478 1810 **W** www.balticmill.com
Contemporary art exhibitions and events
*Shipley Art Gallery*, Prince Consort Road NE8 4JB
**T** 0191-477 1495 **W** www.twmuseums.org.uk/shipley
Contemporary crafts
GAYDON
*Heritage Motor Centre*, Banbury Road, Warks CV35 0BJ
**T** 01926-641188 **W** www.heritage-motor-centre.co.uk
The world's largest collection of British cars with nearly 300 vehicles spanning the classic, vintage and veteran eras
GLOUCESTER
*Gloucester Waterways Museum*, Gloucester Docks GL1 2EH
**T** 01452-318200
**W** www.canalrivertrust.org.uk/gloucester-waterways-museum
200-year history of Britain's canals and inland waterways
GOSPORT
*Royal Navy Submarine Museum*, Haslar Jetty Road, Hants PO12 2AS **T** 023-9251 0354 **W** www.submarine-museum.co.uk
Underwater warfare exhibition, including submarines HMS *Alliance* and HMS *Holland 1* – the Royal Navy's first submarine
GRASMERE
*Dove Cottage* and the *Wordsworth Museum*, Cumbria LA22 9SH
**T** 015394-35544 **W** www.wordsworth.org.uk
William Wordsworth's manuscripts, home and garden
HOVE
*Hove Museum and Art Gallery*, New Church Road BN3 4AB
**T** 03000-290900 **W** www.brightonmuseums.org.uk/hove
Toys, cinema, local history and fine art collections
HULL
*Ferens Art Gallery*, Queen Victoria Square HU1 3RA
**T** 01482-300300 **W** www.hullcc.gov.uk/ferens
European Old Masters, Victorian, Edwardian and contemporary British art

*Hull Maritime Museum,* Queen Victoria Square HU1 3DX
T 01482-300300 W www.hullcc.gov.uk
Hull's maritime heritage including whaling, fishing, navigation and merchant trade
HUNTINGDON
*The Cromwell Museum,* Grammar School Walk PE29 3LF
T 01480-375830 W www.cambridgeshire.gov.uk/info/20011/
archives_archaeology_and_museums/24/cromwell_museum
Portraits and memorabilia relating to Oliver Cromwell
IPSWICH
*Christchurch Mansion* and *Wolsey Art Gallery,* Christchurch
Park IP4 2BE T 01473-433554 W www.cimuseums.org.uk
Tudor house with paintings by Gainsborough, Constable and other Suffolk artists; furniture and 18th-century ceramics; temporary exhibitions
KEIGHLEY
*The Brontë Parsonage Museum,* Haworth, W. Yorks BD22 8DR
T 01535-642323 W www.bronte.org.uk
The former home of the literary Brontë sisters
KESWICK
*Pencil Museum,* Southey Works CA12 5NG T 01768-773626
W www.pencilmuseum.co.uk
500-year history of the pencil; demonstration events and workshops throughout the year
LEEDS
*Armley Mills, Leeds Industrial Museum,* Canal Road, Armley
LS12 2QF T 0113-263 7861 W www.leeds.gov.uk/armleymills
Once the world's largest woollen mill, now a museum for textiles and Leeds' industrial heritage
*Leeds Art Gallery,* The Headrow LS1 3AA T 0113-247 8256
W www.leeds.gov.uk/artgallery
Includes English watercolours, sculpture, contemporary art and prints from the region's artists
*Royal Armouries Museum,* Armouries Drive LS10 1LT
T 0113-220 1999 W www.royalarmouries.org
National collection of over 8,500 items of arms and armour from BC to present over five galleries: War, Tournament, Oriental, Self Defence and Hunting
LEICESTER
*Jewry Wall Museum,* St Nicholas Circle LE1 4LB T 0116-225 4971
W www.leicester.gov.uk
Archaeology; Roman Jewry Wall and baths; mosaics
*New Walk Museum and Art Gallery,* 53 New Walk LE1 7EA
T 0116-255 4900 W www.leicester.gov.uk
Natural and cultural history; ancient Egypt gallery; European art and decorative arts
LINCOLN
*The Collection,* Danes Terrace LN2 1LP T 01522-782040
W www.thecollectionmuseum.com
Artefacts from the Stone Age to the Roman, Viking and Medieval eras; adjacent art gallery; collections of contemporary art and craft, sculpture, porcelain, clocks and watches
*Museum of Lincolnshire Life,* Burton Road LN1 3LY
T 01522-782040
W www.lincolnshire.gov.uk/museumoflincolnshirelife
Social history; agricultural, industrial, military and commercial exhibits
LIVERPOOL
*\*International Slavery Museum,* Albert Dock L3 4AX
T 0151-478 4499 W www.liverpoolmuseums.org.uk/ism
Explores historical and contemporary aspects of slavery
*\*Lady Lever Art Gallery,* Wirral CH62 5EQ T 0151-478 4136
W www.liverpoolmuseums.org.uk/ladylever
Paintings, furniture and porcelain
*\*Merseyside Maritime Museum,* Albert Dock L3 4AQ
T 0151-478 4499 W www.liverpoolmuseums.org.uk/maritime
Floating exhibits, working displays and craft demonstrations; incorporates the *UK Border Agency National Museum*

*\*Museum of Liverpool,* Pier Head L3 1DG T 0151-478 4545
W www.liverpoolmuseums.org.uk/mol
Explores the significance of the city's geography, history and culture
*\*Sudley House,* Mossley Hill Road L18 8BX T 0151-478 4016
W www.liverpoolmuseums.org.uk/sudley
Late 18th- and 19th-century paintings in former shipowner's home
*\*Tate Liverpool,* Albert Dock L3 4BB T 0151-1702 7400
W www.tate.org.uk/liverpool
20th-century paintings and sculpture
*\*Walker Art Gallery,* William Brown Street L3 8EL
T 0151-478 4199 W www.liverpoolmuseums.org.uk/walker
Paintings from the 13th century to the present day
*\*World Museum Liverpool,* William Brown Street L3 8EN
T 0151-478 4393 W www.liverpoolmuseums.org.uk/wml
Includes Egyptian mummies, weapons and classical sculpture; planetarium, aquarium, vivarium and natural history centre
LONDON: GALLERIES
*Barbican Art Gallery,* Barbican Centre, Silk Street EC2Y 8DS
T 020-7638 4141 W www.barbican.org.uk
Art, music, theatre, dance and film exhibitions
*Courtauld Institute of Art Gallery,* Somerset House, Strand
WC2R 0RN T 020-7848 2526 W www.courtauld.ac.uk
Impressionist and post-impressionist paintings
*Dennis Severs' House,* 18 Folgate Street E1 6BX T 020-7247013
W www.dennissevershouse.co.uk
Candlelit recreation of a Huguenot silk weaver's home
*Dulwich Picture Gallery,* Gallery Road SE21 7AD
T 020-8693 5254 W www.dulwichpicturegallery.org.uk
England's first public art gallery; designed by Sir John Soane to house 17th- and 18th-century paintings
*Estorick Collection of Modern Italian Art,* Canonbury Square
N1 2AN T 020-7704 9522 W www.estorickcollection.com
Early 20th-century Italian drawings, paintings, sculptures and etchings, with an emphasis on Futurism
*Hayward Gallery,* Belvedere Road SE1 8XX T 020-7960 4200
W www.southbankcentre.co.uk
Temporary exhibitions
*\*National Gallery,* Trafalgar Square WC2N 5DN T 020-7747 2885
W www.nationalgallery.org.uk
Western painting from the 13th to 19th centuries; early Renaissance collection in the Sainsbury Wing
*\*National Portrait Gallery,* St Martin's Place WC2H 0HE
T 020-7306 0055 W www.npg.org.uk
Portraits of eminent people in British history
*Photographers' Gallery,* Ramillies Street W1F 7LW
T 020-7087 9300 W www.thephotographersgallery.org.uk
Temporary exhibitions; permanent camera obscura
*The Queen's Gallery,* Buckingham Palace SW1A 1AA
T 020-7766 7300 W www.royalcollection.org.uk
Art from the Royal Collection
*Royal Academy of Arts,* Burlington House, Piccadilly W1J 0BD
T 020-7300 8000 W www.royalacademy.org.uk
British art since 1750 and temporary exhibitions; annual Summer Exhibition
*Saatchi Gallery,* Duke of York's HQ, King's Road SW3 4RY
T 020-7823 2363 W www.saatchi-gallery.co.uk
Contemporary art including paintings, photographs, sculpture and installations
*Serpentine Gallery,* Kensington Gardens W2 3XA
T 020-7402 6075 W www.serpentinegallery.org
Temporary exhibitions of British and international contemporary art
*\*Tate Britain,* Millbank SW1P 4RG T 020-7887 8888
W www.tate.org.uk/britain
British art from the 16th century to the present; international modern art

*\* Tate Modern,* Bankside SE1 9TG **T** 020-7887 8888
  **W** www.tate.org.uk/modern
  International modern art from 1900 to the present
*\* Wallace Collection,* Manchester Square W1U 3BN
  **T** 020-7563 9500 **W** www.wallacecollection.org
  Old Masters; French 18th-century paintings, furniture,
  armour, porcelain, clocks and sculpture
*Whitechapel Art Gallery,* Whitechapel High Street E1 7QX
  **T** 020-7522 7888 **W** www.whitechapelgallery.org
  Temporary exhibitions of modern art
LONDON: MUSEUMS
*Bank of England Museum,* Threadneedle Street EC2R 8AH
  (entrance on Bartholomew Lane) **T** 020-7601 5545
  **W** www.bankofengland.co.uk/museum
  History of the Bank of England since 1694
*\* British Museum,* Great Russell Street WC1B 3DG
  **T** 020-7323 8299 **W** www.britishmuseum.org
  Collection of art and antiquities spanning 2 million years
  of human history; temporary exhibitions; houses the Elgin
  Marbles from the Parthenon
*Brunel Museum,* Rotherhithe SE16 4LF **T** 020-7231 3840
  **W** www.brunel-museum.org.uk
  Explores the engineering achievements of Isambard
  Kingdom Brunel and his father, Marc Brunel
*Cartoon Museum,* Little Russell Street WC1A 2HH
  **T** 020-7580 8155 **W** www.cartoonmuseum.org
  British cartoons, caricature and comic art from the 18th
  century to the present
*Charles Dickens Museum,* Doughty Street WC1N 2LX
  **T** 020-7405 2127 **W** www.dickensmuseum.com
  Dickens's home from 1837–9; manuscripts, personal items
  and paintings
*\* Churchill War Rooms,* King Charles Street SW1A 2AQ
  **T** 020-7930 6961 **W** cwr.iwm.org.uk
  Underground rooms used by Churchill and the
  government during the Second World War
*Cutty Sark,* King William Walk SE10 9HT **T** 020-8858 4422
  **W** www.rmg.co.uk/cuttysark
  The world's last remaining tea clipper; re-opened in April
  2012 following extensive restoration
*Design Museum,* Shad Thames SE1 2YD **T** 020-7403 6933
  **W** www.designmuseum.org
  The development of design and the mass-production of
  consumer objects
*Firepower, the Royal Artillery Museum,* Royal Arsenal, Woolwich
  SE18 6ST **T** 020-8855 7755 **W** www.firepower.org.uk
  The history and development of artillery over the last 700
  years including the collections of the Royal Regiment of
  Artillery
*Garden Museum,* Lambeth Palace Road SE1 7LB **T** 020-7401 8865
  **W** www.gardenmuseum.org.uk
  History and development of gardens and gardening;
  temporary exhibitions, symposia and events
*Geffrye Museum,* Kingsland Road E2 8EA **T** 020-7739 9893
  **W** www.geffrye-museum.org.uk
  English urban domestic interiors from 1600 to the present
  day; also paintings, furniture, decorative arts, walled herb
  garden and period garden rooms
*\* HMS Belfast,* The Queen's Walk SE1 2JH **T** 020-7940 6300
  **W** hmsbelfast.iwm.org.uk
  Life and work on board a Second World War cruiser
*\* Horniman Museum,* London Road SE23 3PQ **T** 020-8699 1872
  **W** www.horniman.ac.uk
  Museum of anthropology, musical instruments and natural
  history; aquarium; reference library; gardens
*\* Imperial War Museum,* Lambeth Road SE1 6HZ
  **T** 020-7416 5000 **W** www.iwm.org.ukc
  All aspects of the two World Wars and other military
  operations involving Britain and the Commonwealth since
  1914

*Jewish Museum,* Albert Street NW1 7NB **T** 020-7284 7384
  **W** www.jewishmuseum.org.uk
  Jewish life, history, art and religion
*London Metropolitan Archives,* Northampton Road EC1R 0HB
  **T** 020-7332 3820 **W** www.cityoflondon.gov.uk/lma
  Material on the history of London and its people dating
  from 1067 to the present day
*London Museum of Water and Steam,* Green Dragon Lane TW8
  0EN **T** 020-8568 4757 **W** www.waterandsteam.org.uk
  Large collection of steam engines; reopened in 2014 after
  refurbishment
*London Transport Museum,* Covent Garden Piazza WC2E 7BB
  **T** 020-7379 6344 **W** www.ltmuseum.co.uk
  Vehicles, photographs and graphic art relating to the
  history of transport in London
*MCC Museum,* Lord's Cricket Ground, St John's Wood NW8 8QN
  **T** 020-7616 8595 **W** www.lords.org/mcc
  Cricket exhibits including the Ashes, kits, paintings and
  W. G. Grace exhibit; guided tours by appointment
*\* Museum of Childhood (V&A),* Cambridge Heath Road E2 9PA
  **T** 020-8983 5200 **W** www.museumofchildhood.org.uk
  Toys, games and exhibits relating to the social history of
  childhood from the 17th century to the present
*\* Museum of London,* London Wall EC2Y 5HN **T** 020-7001 9844
  **W** www.museumoflondon.org.uk
  History of London from prehistoric times to the present
  day; Galleries of Modern London
*Museum of London Docklands,* West India Quay, Canary Wharf
  E14 4AL **T** 020-7001 9844
  **W** www.museumoflondon.org.uk/docklands
  Explores the story of London's river, port and people over
  2,000 years; includes the London Sugar Slavery Gallery
*National Archives Museum,* Kew TW9 4DU **T** 020-8876 3444
  **W** www.nationalarchives.gov.uk/museum
  Displays treasures from the archives, including the
  Domesday Book and Magna Carta
*\* National Army Museum,* Royal Hospital Road SW3 4HT
  **T** 020-7730 0717 **W** www.nam.ac.uk
  Five-hundred-year history of the British soldier; exhibits
  include model of the Battle of Waterloo and recreated First
  World War trench
*\* National Maritime Museum,* Romney Road SE10 9NF
  **T** 020-8858 4422
  **W** www.rmg.co.uk/national-maritime-museum
  Maritime history of Britain; collections include globes,
  clocks, telescopes and paintings; comprises the main
  building, the Royal Observatory and the Queen's House
*\* Natural History Museum,* Cromwell Road SW7 5BD
  **T** 020-7942 5000 **W** www.nhm.ac.uk
  Natural history collections and interactive Darwin Centre
*Petrie Museum of Egyptian Archaeology,* University College
  London, Malet Place WC1E 6BT **T** 020-7679 2884
  **W** www.ucl.ac.uk/museums/petrie
  Egyptian and Sudanese archaeology featuring around
  80,000 objects
*\* Royal Air Force Museum,* Hendon NW9 5LL **T** 020-8205 2266
  **W** www.rafmuseum.org.uk
  Aviation from before the Wright brothers to the present
*Royal Mews,* Buckingham Palace SW1W 1QH **T** 020-7766 7302
  **W** www.royalcollection.org.uk/visit/royalmews
  State vehicles, including the Queen's gold state coach;
  home to the Queen's horses; guided tours
*\* Science Museum,* Exhibition Road SW7 2DD **T** 0870 870 4868
  **W** www.sciencemuseum.org.uk
  Science, technology, industry and medicine exhibitions;
  children's interactive gallery; IMAX cinema
*Shakespeare's Globe Exhibition,* New Globe Walk, Bankside
  SE1 9DT **T** 020-7902 1400 **W** www.shakespearesglobe.com
  Recreation of Elizabethan theatre using 16th-century
  techniques; includes a tour of the theatre

*Sir John Soane's Museum,* Lincoln's Inn Fields WC2A 3BP
T 020-7405 2107 W www.soane.org
Art and antiquities collected by Soane throughout his
lifetime; authentic Georgian and Victorian interior
*Tower Bridge Exhibition,* SE1 2UP T 020-7403 3761
W www.towerbridge.org.uk
History of the bridge and display of Victorian steam
machinery; panoramic views from walkways
*Victoria and Albert Museum,* Cromwell Road SW7 2RL
T 020-7942 2000 W www.vam.ac.uk
Includes the National Art Library and the Gilbert
Collection; fine and applied art and design; furniture,
glass, textiles, theatre and dress collections; temporary
exhibitions
*Wellcome Collection,* Euston Road NW1 2BE T 020-7611 2222
W www.wellcomecollection.org
Contemporary and historic exhibitions and collections
including the Wellcome Library
*Wimbledon Lawn Tennis Museum,* Church Road SW19 5AE
T 020-8944 1066 W www.wimbledon.com/museum
Tennis trophies, fashion and memorabilia; view of Centre
Court
MALTON
*Eden Camp,* N. Yorks YO17 6RT T 01653-697777
W www.edencamp.co.uk
Restored POW camp and Second World War memorabilia
MANCHESTER
*Gallery of Costume,* Platt Hall, Rusholme M14 5LL
T 0161-245 7245 W www.manchestergalleries.org
Exhibits from the 17th century to the present day
*Imperial War Museum North,* Trafford Wharf Road M17 1TZ
T 0161-836 4000 W www.iwm.org.uk/north
History of war from the 20th century to the present
*Manchester Art Gallery,* Mosley Street M2 3JL T 0161-235 8888
W www.manchestergalleries.org
European fine and decorative art from the 17th to 20th
centuries
*Manchester Museum,* Oxford Road M13 9PL T 0161-275 2648
W www.museum.manchester.ac.uk
Collections include decorative arts, natural history and
zoology; three Ancient Worlds galleries
*Museum of Science and Industry,* Liverpool Road, Castlefield
M3 4FP T 0161-832 2244 W www.mosi.org.uk
On site of world's oldest passenger railway station;
galleries relating to space, energy, power, transport,
aviation, textiles and social history
*National Football Museum,* Cathedral Gardens M4 3BG
T 0161-605 8200 W www.nationalfootballmuseum.com
Home to the FIFA, FA and Football League collections
including the 1966 World Cup final ball
*People's History Museum,* Left Bank, Spinningfields M3 3ER
T 0161-838 9190 W www.phm.org.uk
History of British political and working life
*Whitworth Art Gallery,* Oxford Road M15 6ER T 0161-275 7450
W www.whitworth.manchester.ac.uk
Fine and modern art, wallpapers, prints, textiles and
sculptures
MILTON KEYNES
*Bletchley Park National Codes Centre,* Bucks MK3 6EB
T 01908-640404 W www.bletchleypark.org
Home of British codebreaking during the Second World
War; Enigma machine; computer museum and Alan Turing
gallery
MONKWEARMOUTH
*Monkwearmouth Station Museum,* North Bridge Street,
Sunderland SR5 1AP T 0191-567 7075
W www.seeitdoitsunderland.co.uk/monkwearmouth-station-
museum
Victorian train station; interactive galleries

NEWCASTLE UPON TYNE
*Discovery Museum,* Blandford Square NE1 4JA T 0191-232 6789
W www.twmuseums.org.uk/discovery
Science and industry, local history, fashion; Tyneside's
maritime history; digital jukebox of 2,000 film and TV
titles from the BFI National Archive
*Great North Museum: Hancock,* Barras Bridge NE2 4PT
T 0191-222 6765
W www.twmuseums.org.uk/greatnorthmuseum
Natural and ancient history; planetarium; Living Planet
display incorporates live animal tanks and aquaria
*Laing Art Gallery,* New Bridge Street NE1 8AG T 0191-232 7734
W www.twmuseums.org.uk/laing
19th and 20th century art including local painters;
ceramics, glass, Japanese decrotive arts and prints
NEWMARKET
*National Horseracing Museum,* High Street CB8 8JH
T 01638-667333 W www.nhrm.co.uk
The story of people and horses involved in racing;
temporary exhibitions
NORTH SHIELDS
*Stephenson Railway Museum,* Middle Engine Lane NE29 8DX
T 0191-200 7146 W www.twmuseums.org.uk/stephenson
Locomotive engines and rolling stock; open April through
November and school holidays outside this period
NOTTINGHAM
*Museum of Nottingham Life,* Brewhouse Yard, Castle Boulevard
NG7 1FB T 0115-876 1400 W www.nottinghamcity.gov.uk
Social history from the 17th to 20th centuries
*Natural History Museum,* Wollaton Hall, Wollaton NG8 2AE
T 0115-876 3100 W www.nottinghamcity.gov.uk
Geology, botany and zoology specimens housed in an
Elizabethan mansion
*Nottingham Castle and Art Gallery,* Lenton Road NG1 6EL
T 0115-876 1400
W www.mynottingham.gov.uk/nottinghamcastle
Paintings, ceramics, silver, glass and jewellery; history of
Nottingham
OXFORD
*Ashmolean Museum,* Beaumont Street OX1 2PH T 01865-278000
W www.ashmolean.org
Art and archaeology including Egyptian, Minoan,
Anglo-Saxon and Chinese exhibits; largest collection of
Raphael drawings in the world
*Modern Art Oxford,* Pembroke Street OX1 1BP T 01865-722733
W www.modernartoxford.org.uk
Temporary exhibitions
*Museum of the History of Science,* Broad Street OX1 3AZ
T 01865-277280 W www.mhs.ox.ac.uk
Displays include early scientific instruments, chemical
apparatus, clocks and watches
*Oxford University Museum of Natural History,* Parks Road
OX1 3PW T 01865-272950 W www.oum.ox.ac.uk
Entomology, geology, mineralogy and petrology, and
zoology
*Pitt Rivers Museum,* South Parks Road OX1 3PP T 01865-270927
W www.prm.ox.ac.uk
Anthropological and archaeological artefacts
PLYMOUTH
*City Museum and Art Gallery,* Drake Circus PL4 8AJ
T 01752-304774 W www.plymouthmuseum.gov.uk
Local and natural history; ceramics; silver; Old Masters;
world artefacts; temporary exhibitions
PORTSMOUTH
*Charles Dickens Birthplace,* Old Commercial Road PO1 4QL
T 023-9282 1879 W www.charlesdickensbirthplace.co.uk
Reproduction Regency house; Dickens memorabilia
*D-Day Museum,* Clarence Esplanade, Southsea PO5 3NT
T 023-9282 6722 W www.ddaymuseum.co.uk
Includes the Overlord embroidery

*Portsmouth Historic Dockyard*, HM Naval Base PO1 3LJ
T 023-9283 9766 W www.historicdockyard.co.uk
Incorporates the *National Museum of the Royal Navy*
(PO1 3NH T 023-9272 7574 W www.nmrn.org.uk), *HMS
Victory* – restoration work open to the public (PO1 3NH
T 023-9283 9766 W www.hms-victory.com), *HMS Warrior*
(PO1 3QX T 023-9277 8600 W www.hmswarrior.org), *Mary
Rose* (PO1 3LX T 023-9281 2931 W www.maryrose.org) and
*Action Stations* (PO1 3LJ T 023-9289 3338
W www.actionstations.org)
History of the Royal Navy and of the dockyard; warships
and technology spanning 500 years
PRESTON
*Harris Museum and Art Gallery*, Market Square PR1 2PP
T 01772-258248 W www.harrismuseum.org.uk
British art since the 18th century; ceramics, glass, costume
and local history; contemporary exhibitions
ST ALBANS
*Verulamium Museum*, St Michael's Street AL3 4SW
T 01727-751814 W www.stalbansmuseums.org.uk
Remains of Iron Age settlement and the third-largest city
in Roman Britain; moving to a new site in 2017
ST IVES
*Tate St Ives*, Porthmeor Beach, Cornwall TR26 1TG
T 01736-796226 W www.tate.org.uk/stives
Modern art, much by artists associated with St Ives;
includes the Barbara Hepworth Museum and Sculpture
Garden; open after 2014 part closure
SALISBURY
*Salisbury & South Wiltshire Museum*, The Close SP1 2EN
T 01722-332151 W www.salisburymuseum.org.uk
Local history and archaeology; Stonehenge exhibits
SHEFFIELD
*Graves Gallery*, Surrey Street S1 1XZ T 0114-278 2600
W www.museums-sheffield.org.uk
Twentieth-century British art; European art spanning four
centuries
*Millennium Galleries*, Arundel Gate S1 2PP T 0114-278 2600
W www.museums-sheffield.org.uk
Incorporates four different galleries: the Special
Exhibition Gallery, the Craft and Design Gallery, the
Metalwork Gallery and the Ruskin Gallery, which houses
John Ruskin's collection of paintings, drawings, books and
medieval manuscripts
*Weston Park Museum*, Western Bank S10 2TP T 0114-278 2600
W www.museums-sheffield.org.uk
World and local history; art and temporary exhibitions
SOUTHAMPTON
*City Art Gallery*, Commercial Road SO14 7LP T 023-8083 3007
W www.southampton.gov.uk/art
Western art from the Renaissance to the present
*SeaCity Museum*, Havelock Road SO14 7FY T 023-8083 3007
W www.seacitymuseum.co.uk
Opened in 2012, the museum tells the story of the city's
maritime past and present
SOUTH SHIELDS
*Arbeia Roman Fort*, Baring Street NE33 2BB T 0191-456 1369
W www.twmuseums.org.uk/arbeia
Excavated ruins; reconstructions of original buildings
*South Shields Museum and Art Gallery*, Ocean Road NE33 2JA
T 0191-456 8740 W www.twmuseums.org.uk/southshields
South Tyneside history; interactive art gallery
STOKE-ON-TRENT
*Etruria Industrial Museum*, Lower Bedford Street ST4 7AF
T 01782-233144 W www.etruriamuseum.org.uk
Britain's sole surviving steam-powered potter's mill
*Gladstone Pottery Museum*, Uttoxeter Road, Longton ST3 1PQ
T 01782-237777 W www.stokemuseums.org.uk/visit/gpm
The last complete Victorian pottery factory in Britain

*Potteries Museum and Art Gallery*, Bethesda Street ST1 3DW
T 01782-232323 W www.stokemuseums.org.uk/pmag
Pottery, china and porcelain collections and a Mark XVI
Spitfire
*The Wedgwood Museum*, Barlaston ST12 9ER T 01782-371902
W www.wedgwoodmuseum.org.uk
The story of Josiah Wedgwood and the company he
founded
SUNDERLAND
*Sunderland Museum and Winter Gardens*, Burdon Road SR1 1PP
T 0191-553 2323
W www.seeitdoitsunderland.co.uk/sunderland-museum-winter-
gardens
Fine and decorative art, local history and gardens
TELFORD
*Ironbridge Gorge Museums*, TF8 7DQ T 01952-433424
W www.ironbridge.org.uk
Ten museums including The Museum of the Gorge; The
Iron Bridge and Tollhouse; Blists Hill (late Victorian
working town); Brosely Pipeworks; Coalbrookdale
Museum of Iron; Coalport China Museum; Jackfield Tile
Museum; Tar Tunnel; Darby Houses
WAKEFIELD
*Hepworth Wakefield*, Gallery Walk WF1 5AW T 01924-247360
W www.hepworthwakefield.org
Historic and modern art; temporary exhibitions of
contemporary art
*National Coal Mining Museum for England*, New Road, Overton
WF4 4RH T 01924-848806 W www.ncm.org.uk
Includes underground tours of one of Britain's oldest
working mines
*Yorkshire Sculpture Park*, West Bretton WF4 4LG T 01924-832631
W www.ysp.co.uk
Open-air sculpture gallery including works by Henry
Moore, Barbara Hepworth and others in 500 acres of
parkland
WEYBRIDGE
*Brooklands Museum*, Brooklands Road KT13 0QN
T 01932-857381 W www.brooklandsmuseum.com
Birthplace of British motorsport; world's first
purpose-built motor racing circuit
WILMSLOW
*Quarry Bank Mill and Styal Estate*, Wilmslow SK9 4LA
T 01625-527468 W www.quarrybankmill.org.uk
Europe's most powerful working waterwheel owned
by the National Trust illustrating history of cotton
industry; costumed guides at restored Apprentice
House
WINCHESTER
*Winchester Science Centre and Planetarium*, Telegraph Way,
Hants SO21 1HZ T 01962-863791
W www.winchestersciencecentre.org
Interactive science centre and planetarium
WORCESTER
*City Art Gallery and Museum*, Foregate Street WR1 1DT
T 01905-25371
W www.whub.org.uk/cms/museums-worcestershire/mag.aspx
Includes the Regimental museum, 19th-century chemist
shop and changing art exhibitions
*Museum of Worcester Porcelain*, Severn Street WR1 2ND
T 01905-21247 W www.worcesterporcelainmuseum.org.uk
Worcester porcelain from 1751 to the present day
WROUGHTON
*Science Museum*, Wilts SN4 9LT T 01793-846200
W www.sciencemuseum.org.uk/wroughton
Object stores closed to the public due to redevelopment
work; Library and Archive are open to the public by
appointment

YEOVIL
*Fleet Air Arm Museum,* RNAS Yeovilton, Somerset BA22 8HT
  T 01935-840565 W www.fleetairarm.com
  History of naval aviation; historic aircraft, including
  Concorde 002
YORK
*Beningbrough Hall,* Beningbrough YO30 1DD
  T 01904-472027
  W www.nationaltrust.org.uk/beningbrough-hall
  18th-century house with portraits from the National
  Portrait Gallery; parklands and gardens
*JORVIK Viking Centre,* Coppergate YO1 9WT T 01904-615505
  W www.jorvik-viking-centre.co.uk
  Reconstruction of Viking York based on archaeological
  evidence
*National Railway Museum,* Leeman Road YO26 4XJ
  T 0844-815 3139 W www.nrm.org.uk
  Includes locomotives, rolling stock and carriages
*York Art Gallery,* Exhibition Square, YO1 7EW T 01904 687687
  W www.yorkartgallery.org
  600 years of British and European painting; ceramics
  and sculpture
*York Castle Museum,* Eye of York YO1 9RY T 01904-687687
  W www.yorkcastlemuseum.org.uk
  Includes Kirkgate, a reconstructed Victorian street;
  costume and military collections
*Yorkshire Museum,* Museum Gardens YO1 7FR T 01904-687687
  W www.yorkshiremuseum.org.uk
  Yorkshire life from Roman to medieval times; geology and
  biology; York observatory

# WALES

* Members of National Museum Wales, a public body that receives
its funding through grant-in-aid from the Welsh Assembly

ABERYSTWYTH
*Ceredigion Museum,* Terrace Road SY23 2AQ T 01970-633088
  W www.museum.ceredigion.gov.uk
  Local history, housed in a restored Edwardian theatre
*Silver Mountain Experience,* Ponterwyd SY23 3AB
  T 01970-890620 W www.silvermountainexperience.co.uk
  Tours of an 18th-century silver mine, with interactive
  challenges and games for children
BLAENAFON
**Big Pit National Coal Museum,* Torfaen NP4 9XP
  T 029-2057 3650 W www.museumwales.ac.uk/en/bigpit
  Colliery with an underground tour and exhibitions of
  modern mining equipment
BODELWYDDAN
*Bodelwyddan Castle,* Denbighshire LL18 5YA T 01745-584060
  W www.bodelwyddan-castle.co.uk
  Art gallery within an historic house; features temporary art
  exhibits
CAERLEON
**National Roman Legion Museum,* NP18 1AE T 029-2057 3550
  W www.museumwales.ac.uk/en/roman
  Features the oldest recorded piece of writing in Wales;
  pottery, Roman era gemstones
CARDIFF
**National Museum Cardiff,* Cathays Park CF10 3NP
  T 029-2057 3000 W www.museumwales.ac.uk/en/cardiff
  Houses Wales's national art, archaeology and natural
  history collections
**St Fagans: National History Museum,* St Fagans CF5 6XB
  T 029-2057 3500 W www.museumwales.ac.uk/en/stfagans
  Open-air museum with re-erected buildings, agricultural
  equipment and costume

*TECHNIQUEST,* Stuart Street CF10 5BW T 029-2047 5475
  W www.techniquest.org
  Interactive science exhibits, planetarium and science
  theatre
CRICCIETH
*Lloyd George Museum,* Llanystumdwy LL52 0SH T 01766-522071
  W www.gwynedd.gov.uk
  Childhood home of David Lloyd George
DRE-FACH FELINDRE
**National Wool Museum,* Llandysul SA44 5UP T 029-2057 3070
  W www.museumwales.ac.uk/en/wool
  Exhibitions, a working woollen mill and craft workshops
LLANBERIS
**National Slate Museum,* Gwynedd LL55 4TY T 029-2057 3700
  W www.museumwales.ac.uk/en/slate
  Former slate quarry with original machinery and plant;
  slate crafts demonstrations; working waterwheel
LLANDRINDOD WELLS
*National Cycle Collection,* Automobile Palace, Temple Street
  LD1 5DL T 01597-825531 W www.cyclemuseum.org.uk
  Approximately 250 bicycles on display, from 1819 to the
  present
PRESTEIGNE
*Judge's Lodging Museum,* Broad Street LD8 2AD T 01544-260650
  W www.judgeslodging.org.uk
  Restored apartments, courtroom, cells and servants'
  quarters
SWANSEA
**National Waterfront Museum,* Oystermouth Road SA1 3RD
  T 029-2057 3600 W www.museumwales.ac.uk/en/swansea
  Wales during the Industrial Revolution
*Swansea Museum,* Victoria Road SA1 1SN T 01792-653763
  W www.swansea.gov.uk/swanseamuseum
  Paintings, Egyptian artifacts, transport and nautical
  collections; war time Swansea
TENBY
*Tenby Museum and Art Gallery,* Castle Hill SA70 7BP
  T 01834-842809 W www.tenbymuseum.org.uk
  Local archaeology, history, geology and art

# SCOTLAND

* Members of National Museums of Scotland or National Galleries
of Scotland, which are non-departmental public bodies funded by,
and accountable to, the Scottish government

ABERDEEN
*Aberdeen Art Gallery,* Schoolhill AB10 1FQ T 01224-523700
  W www.aagm.co.uk
  Paintings, sculptures and graphics; temporary exhibitions
*Aberdeen Maritime Museum,* Shiprow AB11 5BY T 01224-337700
  W www.aagm.co.uk
  Maritime history, including shipbuilding and North Sea oil
AYR
*Robert Burns Birthplace Museum,* Murdoch's Lone,
  Alloway KA7 4PQ T 0844-493 2601
  W www.burnsmuseum.org.uk
  Comprises Burns Cottage, birthplace of the poet, gardens
  and a museum
EDINBURGH
*Britannia,* Leith EH6 6JJ T 0131-555 5566
  W www.royalyachtbritannia.co.uk
  Former royal yacht with royal barge and royal family
  picture gallery
*City Art Centre,* Market Street EH1 1DE T 0131-529 3993
  W www.edinburghmuseums.org.uk
  Rolling programme of exhibitions including historic and
  modern photography; contemporary art, design and
  architecture

*Museum of Childhood*, High Street EH1 1TG **T** 0131-529 4142
**W** www.edinburghmuseums.org.uk
Toys, games, clothes and exhibits relating to the social
history of childhood
*Museum of Edinburgh*, Canongate, Royal Mile EH8 8DD
**T** 0131-529 4143 **W** www.edinburghmuseums.org.uk
Local history, silver, glass and Scottish pottery
\**Museum of Flight*, East Fortune Airfield, East Lothian EH39 5LF
**T** 0300-123 6789 **W** www.nms.ac.uk/flight
Aviation from the early 20th century to the present
\**National Museum of Scotland*, Chambers Street EH1 1JF
**T** 0300-123 6789 **W** www.nms.ac.uk/scotland
Scottish history; world cultures; natural world; art and
design; science and technology
\**National War Museum of Scotland*, Edinburgh Castle EH1 2NG
**T** 0300-123 6789 **W** www.nms.ac.uk/war
Scotland's military history housed within Edinburgh
Castle
\**Scottish National Gallery*, The Mound EH2 2EL **T** 0131-624 6200
**W** www.nationalgalleries.org
Fine art from the early Renaissance to the end of the 19th
century
\**Scottish National Gallery of Modern Art*, Belford Road EH4 3DR
**T** 0131-624 6200 **W** www.nationalgalleries.org
Contemporary art featuring British, French and Russian
collections; outdoor sculpture park
\**Scottish National Portrait Gallery*, Queen Street EH2 1JD
**T** 0131-624 6200 **W** www.nationalgalleries.org/portraitgallery
Portraits of eminent people in Scottish history;
Photography Gallery; Victorian Library
*The Writers' Museum*, Lady Stair's Close EH1 2PA
**T** 0131-529 4901 **W** www.edinburghmuseums.org.uk
Exhibitions relating to Robert Burns, Sir Walter Scott and
Robert Louis Stevenson
FORT WILLIAM
*West Highland Museum*, Cameron Square PH33 6AJ
**T** 01397-702169 **W** www.westhighlandmuseum.org.uk
Highland life; Victorian and Jacobite collections
GLASGOW
*Burrell Collection*, Pollokshaws Road G43 1AT **T** 0141-287 2550
**W** www.glasgowlife.org.uk/museums
Paintings by major artists; medieval art, Chinese and
Islamic art
*Gallery of Modern Art*, Royal Exchange Square G1 3AH
**T** 0141-287 3050 **W** www.glasgowlife.org.uk/museums
Collection of contemporary Scottish and world art
*Hunterian*, University of Glasgow G12 8QQ **T** 0141-330 4221
**W** www.gla.ac.uk/hunterian
Rennie Mackintosh and Whistler collections; coins;
Scottish paintings; Pacific ethnographic collection;
archaeology; medicine
*Kelvingrove Art Gallery & Museum*, Argyle Street G3 8AG
**T** 0141-276 9599 **W** www.glasgowlife.org.uk/museums
Includes Old Masters; natural history; arms and armour
*Museum of Piping*, McPhater Street G4 0HW **T** 0141-353 0220
**W** www.thepipingcentre.co.uk
The history and origins of bagpiping
\**Museum of Rural Life*, Philipshill Road, East Kilbride G76 9HR
**T** 0300-123 6789 **W** www.nms.ac.uk/rural
History of rural life and work

*People's Palace and Winter Gardens*, Glasgow Green G40 1AT
**T** 0141-276 0788 **W** www.glasgowlife.org.uk/museums
Social history of Glasgow since 1750
*Riverside Museum*, 100 Pointhouse Place G3 8RS
**T** 0141-287 2720 **W** www.glasgowlife.org.uk/museums
Scotland's museum of transport and travel; the Tall Ship
*Glenlee*, a Clyde-built sailing ship, is berthed alongside
*St Mungo Museum of Religious Art and Life*, Castle Street G4 0RH
**T** 0141-276 1625 **W** www.glasgowlife.org.uk/museums
Exhibits detailing the world's major religions; oldest Zen
garden in Britain

## NORTHERN IRELAND

\*  Members of National Museums Northern Ireland, a non-
departmental public body of the Northern Ireland Office

ARMAGH
\**Armagh County Museum*, The Mall East BT61 9BE
**T** 028-3752 3070 **W** www.nmni.com/acm
Local history; fine art; archaeology; crafts
BANGOR
*North Down Museum*, Town Hall BT20 4BT **T** 028-9127 1200
**W** www.northdownmuseum.com
Presents the history of North Down, including its
early-Christian monastery and Plantation-era maps
BELFAST
*Titanic Belfast*, Queen's Road, Titanic Quarter BT3 9EP
**T** 028-9076 6386 **W** www.titanicbelfast.com
The story of RMS *Titanic* from her conception to demise;
Shipyard ride and ocean exploration centre
\**Ulster Museum*, Botanic Gardens BT9 5AB **T** 028-9044 0000
**W** www.nmni.com/um
Irish antiquities; natural and local history; fine and applied
arts
\**W5*, Odyssey, Queen's Quay BT3 9QQ **T** 028-9046 7700
**W** www.w5online.co.uk
Interactive science and technology centre
HOLYWOOD
\**Ulster Folk and Transport Museum*, Cultra BT18 0EU
**T** 028-9042 8428 **W** www.nmni.com/uftm
Open-air museum with original buildings from Ulster
town and rural life *c.*1900; indoor galleries including Irish
rail and road transport
LONDONDERRY
*The Tower Museum*, Union Hall Place BT48 6LU **T** 028-7137 2411
**W** www.derrycity.gov.uk/museums/tower-museum
Tells the story of Ireland through the history of
Londonderry
NEWTOWNARDS
*The Somme Heritage Centre*, Bangor Road BT23 7PH
**T** 028-9182 3202 **W** www.sommeassociation.com
Commemorates the part played by Irish forces in the First
World War
OMAGH
\**Ulster American Folk Park*, Castletown, Co. Tyrone BT78 5QU
**T** 028-8224 3292 **W** www.nmni.com/uafp
Open-air museum telling the story of Ulster's emigrants to
America; restored or recreated dwellings and workshops;
ship and dockside gallery

# SIGHTS OF LONDON

For historic buildings, museums and galleries in London, *see* the Historic Buildings and Monuments, and Museums and Galleries sections.

## BRIDGES

The bridges over the Thames in London, from east to west, are:

*Tower Bridge* (268m/880ft by 18m/60ft), architect: Horace Jones, engineer: John Wolfe Barry, opened 1894

*London Bridge* (262m/860ft by 32m/105ft), original 13th-century stone bridge rebuilt and opened 1831 (engineer: John Rennie), reconstructed in Arizona when current London Bridge opened 1973 (architect: Lord Holford, engineer: Mott, Hay and Anderson)

*Cannon Street Railway Bridge* (261m/855ft), engineers: John Hawkshaw and John Wolfe Barry, originally named Alexandra Bridge, opened 1866; renovated 1979–82

*Southwark Bridge* (244m/800ft by 17m/56ft), engineer: John Rennie, originally named Queen Street Bridge, opened 1819; rebuilt 1912–21 (architect: Ernest George, engineer: Mott, Hay and Anderson)

*Millennium Bridge* (325m/1,066ft by 4m/13ft), architect: Foster and Partners, engineer: Ove Arup and Partners, opened 2000; reopened after modification 2002

*Blackfriars Railway Bridge* (284m/933ft), engineers: John Wolfe Barry and Henri Marc Brunel, orginally named St Paul's Railway Bridge, opened 1886

*Blackfriars Bridge* (294m/963ft by 32m/105ft), engineer: Robert Mylne, opened 1769; rebuilt 1869 (engineer: Joseph Cubitt); widened 1909

*Waterloo Bridge* (366m/1,200ft by 24m/80ft), engineer: John Rennie, opened 1817; rebuilt 1945 (architect: Sir Giles Gilbert Scott, engineer: Rendel, Palmer and Triton)

*Golden Jubilee Bridges* (325m/1,066ft by 4.7m/15ft), architect: Lifschutz Davidson, engineer: WSP Group, opened 2002; commonly known as the Hungerford Footbridges

*Hungerford Railway Bridge* (366m/1,200ft), engineer: Isambard Kingdom Brunel, suspension bridge opened 1845; present railway bridge opened 1864 (engineer: John Hawkshaw); widened in 1886

*Westminster Bridge* (228m/748ft by 26m/85ft), engineer: Charles Labelye, opened 1750; rebuilt 1862 (architect: Charles Barry, engineer: Thomas Page)

*Lambeth Bridge* (237m/776ft by 18m/60ft), engineer: Peter W. Barlow, original suspension bridge opened 1862; current structure opened 1932 (architect: Reginald Blomfield, engineer: George W. Humphreys)

*Vauxhall Bridge* (231m/759ft by 24m/80ft), engineer: James Walker, opened 1816; redesigned and opened 1906 (architect: William Edward Riley, engineers: Alexander Binnie and Maurice Fitzmaurice)

*Grosvenor Railway Bridge* (213m/699ft), engineer: John Fowler, opened 1860; rebuilt 1965; also known as the Victoria Railway Bridge

*Chelsea Bridge* (213m/699ft by 25m/83ft), original suspension bridge opened 1858 (engineer: Thomas Page); rebuilt 1937 (architects: George Topham Forrest and E. P. Wheeler, engineer: Rendel, Palmer and Triton)

*Albert Bridge* (216m/710ft by 12m/40ft), engineer: Rowland M. Ordish, opened 1873; restructured 1884 (engineer: Joseph Bazalgette); strengthened 1971–3

*Battersea Bridge* (204m/670ft by 17m/56ft), engineer: Henry Holland, opened 1771; rebuilt 1890 (engineer: Joseph Bazalgette)

*Battersea Railway Bridge* (204m/670ft), engineer: William Baker, opened 1863; also known as Cremorne Bridge

*Wandsworth Bridge* (189m/619ft by 18m/60ft), engineer: Julian Tolmé, opened 1873; rebuilt 1940 (architect: E. P. Wheeler, engineer: T. Pierson Frank)

*Putney Railway Bridge* (229m/750ft), engineers: W. H. Thomas and William Jacomb, opened 1889; also known as the Fulham Railway Bridge or the Iron Bridge – it has no official name

*Putney Bridge* (213m/699ft by 23m/74ft), architect: Jacob Ackworth, original wooden bridge opened 1729; current granite structure completed in 1886 (engineer: Joseph Bazalgette). The starting point of the Boat Race.

*Hammersmith Bridge* (210m/688ft by 10m/33ft), engineer: William Tierney Clarke; the first suspension bridge in London, originally built 1827; rebuilt 1887 (engineer: Joseph Bazalgette)

*Barnes Railway Bridge* (also footbridge, 110m/360ft), engineer: Joseph Locke, opened 1849; rebuilt 1895 (engineers: London and South Western Railway); the original structure stands unused

*Chiswick Bridge* (137m/450ft by 21m/70ft), architect: Herbert Baker, engineer: Alfred Dryland, opened 1933. The bridge marks the end point of the Boat Race.

*Kew Railway Bridge* (175m/575ft), engineer: W. R. Galbraith, opened 1869

*Kew Bridge* (110m/360ft by 17m/56ft), engineer: Robert Tunstall, original timber bridge built 1759; replaced by a Portland stone structure in 1789 (engineer: James Paine); current granite bridge renamed King Edward VII Bridge in 1903, but still known as Kew Bridge (engineers: John Wolfe Barry and Cuthbert Brereton)

*Richmond Lock* (91m/300ft by 11m/36ft), engineer: F. G. M. Stoney, lock and footbridge opened 1894

*Twickenham Bridge* (85m/280ft by 21m/70ft), architect: Maxwell Ayrton, engineer: Alfred Dryland, opened 1933

*Richmond Railway Bridge* (91m/300ft), engineer: Joseph Locke, opened 1848; rebuilt 1906–8 (engineer: J. W. Jacomb-Hood)

*Richmond Bridge* (85m/280ft by 10m/33ft), architect: James Paine, engineer: Kenton Couse, built 1777; widened 1939

*Teddington Lock* (198m/650ft), engineer: G. Pooley, two footbridges opened 1889; marks the end of the tidal reach of the Thames

*Kingston Railway Bridge* architects: J. E. Errington and W. R. Galbraith, engineer: Thomas Brassey, opened 1863

*Kingston Bridge* (116m/382ft), engineer: Edward Lapidge, built 1825–8; widened 1911–14 (engineers: Basil Mott and David Hay) and 1999–2001

*Hampton Court Bridge*, engineers: Samuel Stevens and Benjamin Ludgator, built 1753; replaced by iron bridge 1865; present bridge opened 1933 (architect: Edwin Lutyens, engineer: W. P. Robinson)

## CEMETERIES

In 1832, in response to the overcrowding of burial grounds in London, the government authorised the establishment of seven non-denominational cemeteries that would encircle the city. These large cemeteries, known as the 'magnificent seven', were seen by many Victorian families as places in which to demonstrate their wealth and stature, and as a result there are some highly ornate graves and tombs.

## THE MAGNIFICENT SEVEN

*Abney Park,* Stoke Newington, N16 (13ha/32 acres), established 1840; tomb of William and Catherine Booth, founders of the Salvation Army, and memorials to many nonconformists and dissenters

*Brompton,* Old Brompton Road, SW10 (16.5ha/40 acres), established 1840; graves of Sir Henry Cole, Emmeline Pankhurst, John Wisden

*Highgate,* Swains Lane, N6 (15ha/38 acres), established 1839; graves of Douglas Adams, George Eliot, Eric Hobsbawm, Michael Faraday, Karl Marx, Ralph Miliband and Christina Rossetti

*Kensal Green,* Harrow Road, W10 (29ha/72 acres), established 1833; tombs of Charles Babbage, Isambard Kingdom Brunel, Wilkie Collins, George Cruikshank, Tom Hood, Leigh Hunt, Harold Pinter, William Makepeace Thackeray, Anthony Trollope

*Nunhead,* Linden Grove, SE15 (21ha/52 acres), established 1840; closed in 1969, restored and opened for burials

*Tower Hamlets,* Southern Grove, E3 (11ha/27 acres), established 1841, 350,000 interments; bombed heavily during the Second World War and closed to burials in 1966; now a nature reserve

*West Norwood Cemetery and Crematorium,* Norwood High Street, SE27 (17ha/42 acres), established 1837; tombs of C. W. Alcock, Mrs Beeton, Sir Henry Tate and Joseph Whitaker *(Whitaker's Almanack)*

## OTHER CEMETERIES

*Bunhill Fields,* City Road, EC1 (1.6ha/4 acres), 17th-century nonconformist burial ground containing the graves of William Blake, John Bunyan and Daniel Defoe

*City of London Cemetery and Crematorium,* Aldersbrook Road, E12 (81ha/200 acres), established 1856; grave of Bobby Moore

*Golders Green Crematorium,* Hoop Lane, NW11 (5ha/12 acres), established 1902; retains the ashes of Kingsley Amis, Lionel Bart, Enid Blyton, Marc Bolan, Sigmund Freud, Keith Moon, Ivor Novello, Bram Stoker and H. G. Wells

*Hampstead,* Fortune Green Road, NW6 (10.5ha/26 acres), established 1876; graves of Alan Coren, Kate Greenaway, Joseph Lister and Marie Lloyd

## MARKETS

*Billingsgate,* Trafalgar Way, E14 (fish), a market site for over 1,000 years, with the Lower Thames Street site dating from 1876; moved to the Isle of Dogs in 1982; owned and run by the City of London Corporation

*Borough,* Southwark Street, SE1 (vegetables, fruit, meat, dairy, bread), established on present site in 1756; privately owned and run

*Brick Lane,* E1 (jewellery, vintage clothes, bric-a-brac, food), open Sunday

*Brixton,* SW9 (African-Caribbean food, music, clothing), open Monday to Saturday

*Broadway,* E8 (food, fashion, crafts), re-established in 2004, open Saturday

*Camden Lock,* NW1 (second-hand clothing, jewellery, alternative fashion, crafts), established in 1973

*Columbia Road,* E2 (flowers), dates from 19th century; became dedicated flower market in the 20th century

*Covent Garden,* WC2 (antiques, handicrafts, jewellery, clothing, food), originally a fruit and vegetable market (*see* New Covent Garden market); it has been trading in its current form since 1980

*Grays,* Davies Street, W1K (antiques), indoor market in listed building, established 1977

*Greenwich,* SE10 (crafts, fashion, food), market revived in the 1980s

*Leadenhall,* Gracechurch Street, EC3V (meat, poultry, cheese, clothing), site of market since 14th century; present hall built 1881; owned and run by the City of London Corporation

*New Covent Garden,* SW8 (wholesale vegetables, fruit, flowers), established in 1670 under a charter of Charles II; relocated from central London in 1974

*New Spitalfields,* E10 (vegetables, fruit), established 1682, modernised 1928, moved out of the City to Leyton in 1991

*Old Spitalfields,* E1 (arts, crafts, books, clothes, organic food, antiques), continues to trade on the original Spitalfields site on Commercial Street

*Petticoat Lane,* Middlesex Street, E1, a market has existed on the site for over 500 years, now a Sunday morning market selling almost anything

*Portobello Road,* W11, originally for herbs and horse-trading from 1870; became famous for antiques after the closure of the Caledonian Market in 1948

*Smithfield,* EC1 (meat, poultry), built 1866–8, refurbished 1993–4; the site of St Bartholomew's Fair from 12th to 19th century; owned and run by the City of London Corporation

## MONUMENTS

### CENOTAPH

Whitehall, SW1. The Cenotaph (from the Greek meaning 'empty tomb') was built to commemorate 'The Glorious Dead' and is a memorial to all ranks of the sea, land and air forces who gave their lives in the service of the Empire during the First World War. Designed by Sir Edwin Lutyens and constructed in plaster as a temporary memorial in 1919, it was replaced by a permanent structure of Portland stone and unveiled by George V on 11 November 1920, Armistice Day. An additional inscription was made in 1946 to commemorate those who gave their lives in the Second World War

### FOURTH PLINTH

Trafalgar Square, WC2. The fourth plinth (1841) was designed for an equestrian statue that was never built due to lack of funds. From 1999 temporary works have been displayed on the plinth including *Ecce Homo* (Mark Wallinger), *Monument* (Rachel Whiteread), *Alison Lapper Pregnant* (Marc Quinn), *One & Other* (Antony Gormley) and *Hahn/Cock* (Katharina Fritsch). Since March 2015 *Gift Horse* (Hans Haacke), depicting a skeletal, riderless horse, has occupied the plinth. This will be followed in 2016 by *Really Good* (David Shrigley).

### LONDON MONUMENT

(Commonly called the Monument), Monument Street, EC3. Built to designs by Sir Christopher Wren and Robert Hooke between 1671 and 1677, the Monument commemorates the Great Fire of London, which broke out in Pudding Lane on 2 September 1666. The fluted Doric column is 36.6m (120ft) high, the moulded cylinder above the balcony supporting a flaming vase of gilt bronze is an additional 12.8m (42ft), and the column is based on a square plinth 12.2m (40ft) high (with fine carvings on the west face), making a total height of 61.6m (202ft) – the tallest isolated stone column in the world, with views of London from a gallery at the top (311 steps)

OTHER MONUMENTS

(sculptor's name in parentheses):

7 July Memorial (Carmody Groarke), Hyde Park
Viscount Alanbrooke (Roberts-Jones), Whitehall
Albert Memorial (Scott), Kensington Gore
Battle of Britain (Day), Victoria Embankment
Beatty (Wheeler), Trafalgar Square
Belgian Gratitude (setting by Blomfield, statue by Rousseau), Victoria Embankment
Boadicea (or Boudicca), Queen of the Iceni (Thornycroft), Westminster Bridge
Brunel (Marochetti), Victoria Embankment
Burghers of Calais (Rodin), Victoria Tower Gardens, Westminster
Burns (Steell), Embankment Gardens
Canada Memorial (Granche), Green Park
Carlyle (Boehm), Chelsea Embankment
Cavalry (Jones), Hyde Park
Edith Cavell (Frampton), St Martin's Place
Charles I (Le Sueur), Trafalgar Square
Charles II (Gibbons), Royal Hospital, Chelsea
Churchill (Roberts-Jones), Parliament Square
Cleopatra's Needle (20.9m/68.5ft high, c.1500 BC, erected in London in 1878; the sphinxes are Victorian), Thames Embankment
Clive (Tweed), King Charles Street
Captain Cook (Brock), The Mall
Oliver Cromwell (Thornycroft), outside Westminster Hall
Cunningham (Belsky), Trafalgar Square
Gen. Charles de Gaulle (Conner), Carlton Gardens
Diana, Princess of Wales Memorial Fountain (Gustafson Porter), Hyde Park
Disraeli, Earl of Beaconsfield (Raggi), Parliament Square
Lord Dowding (Winter), Strand
Duke of Cambridge (Jones), Whitehall
Duke of York (37.8m/124ft column, with statue by Westmacott), Carlton House Terrace
Edward VII (Mackennal), Waterloo Place
Elizabeth I (Kerwin, 1586, oldest outdoor statue in London; from Ludgate), Fleet Street
Eros (Shaftesbury Memorial) (Gilbert), Piccadilly Circus
Marechal/Marshall Foch (Mallisard, copy of one in Cassel, France), Grosvenor Gardens
Charles James Fox (Westmacott), Bloomsbury Square
Yuri Gagarin (Novikov, copy of Russian statue), The Mall
Mahatma Gandhi (Jackson), Parliament Square
George III (Cotes Wyatt), Cockspur Street
George IV (Chantrey), Trafalgar Square
George V (Reid Dick and Scott), Old Palace Yard
George VI (McMillan), Carlton Gardens
Gladstone (Thornycroft), Strand
Guards' (Crimea; Bell), Waterloo Place
Guards Division (Ledward, figures, Bradshaw, cenotaph), Horse Guards' Parade
Haig (Hardiman), Whitehall
Sir Arthur (Bomber) Harris (Winter), Strand
Gen. Henry Havelock (Behnes), Trafalgar Square
International Brigades Memorial (Spanish Civil War) (Ian Walters), Jubilee Gardens, South Bank
Irving (Brock), north side of National Portrait Gallery
Isis (Gudgeon), Hyde Park
James II (Gibbons), Trafalgar Square
Jellicoe (McMillan), Trafalgar Square
Samuel Johnson (Fitzgerald), opposite St Clement Danes
Kitchener (Tweed), Horse Guards' Parade
Abraham Lincoln (Saint-Gaudens, copy of one in Chicago), Parliament Square
Mandela (Walters), Parliament Square
Milton (Montford), St Giles, Cripplegate
Mountbatten (Belsky), Foreign Office Green

Gen. Charles James Napier (Adams), Trafalgar Square
Nelson (Railton), Trafalgar Square, with Landseer's lions (cast from guns recovered from the wreck of the Royal George)
Florence Nightingale (Walker), Waterloo Place
Palmerston (Woolner), Parliament Square
Sir Keith Park (Johnson), Waterloo Place
Peel (Noble), Parliament Square
Pitt (Chantrey), Hanover Square
Portal (Nemon), Embankment Gardens
Prince Albert (Bacon), Holborn Circus
Queen Elizabeth Gate (Lund and Wynne), Hyde Park Corner
Queen Mother (Jackson), Carlton Gardens
Raleigh (McMillan), Greenwich
Richard I (Coeur de Lion) (Marochetti), Old Palace Yard
Roberts (Bates), Horse Guards' Parade
Franklin D. Roosevelt (Reid Dick), Grosvenor Square
Royal Air Force (Blomfield), Victoria Embankment
Royal Air Force Bomber Command Memorial (O'Connor), Green Park
Royal Artillery (Great War) (Jagger and Pearson), Hyde Park Corner
Royal Artillery (South Africa) (Colton), The Mall
Captain Scott (Lady Scott), Waterloo Place
Shackleton (Jagger), Kensington Gore
Shakespeare (Fontana, copy of one by Scheemakers in Westminster Abbey), Leicester Square
Smuts (Epstein), Parliament Square
Sullivan (Goscombe John), Victoria Embankment
Trenchard (McMillan), Victoria Embankment
Victoria Memorial (Webb and Brock), in front of Buckingham Palace
Raoul Wallenberg (Jackson), Great Cumberland Place
George Washington (Houdon copy), Trafalgar Square
Wellington (Boehm), Hyde Park Corner
Wellington (Chantrey), outside Royal Exchange
John Wesley (Adams Acton), City Road
Westminster School (Crimea) (Scott), Broad Sanctuary
William III (Bacon), St James's Square
Wolseley (Goscombe John), Horse Guards' Parade

# PARKS, GARDENS AND OPEN SPACES

CITY OF LONDON CORPORATION OPEN SPACES

W www.cityoflondon.gov.uk

Ashtead Common (202ha/500 acres), Surrey
Burnham Beeches and Fleet Wood (220ha/540 acres), Bucks. Acquired by the City of London for the benefit of the public in 1880, Fleet Wood (26ha/65 acres) being presented in 1921
Coulsdon Common (51ha/127 acres), Surrey
Epping Forest (2,476ha/6,118 acres), Essex. Acquired by the City of London in 1878 and opened to the public in 1882. The Queen Elizabeth Hunting Lodge, built for Henry VIII in 1543, lies at the edge of the forest. The present forest is 19.3km (12 miles) long by around 3km (2 miles) wide, approximately one-tenth of its original area
*Epping Forest Buffer Land (718ha/1,774 acres), Waltham Abbey/Epping
Farthing Downs and New Hill (95ha/235 acres), Surrey
Hampstead Heath (275ha/680 acres), NW3. Including Golders Hill (15ha/36 acres) and Parliament Hill (110ha/271 acres)
Highgate Wood (28ha/70 acres), N6/N10
Kenley Common (56ha/139 acres), Surrey
Queen's Park (12ha/30 acres), NW6
Riddlesdown (43ha/104 acres), Surrey
Spring Park (20ha/50 acres), Kent
Stoke Common (80ha/198 acres), Bucks. Ownership was transferred to the City of London in 2007

*West Ham Park* (31ha/77 acres), E15
*West Wickham Common* (10ha/26 acres), Kent
Also over 150 smaller open spaces within the City of London, including *Finsbury Circus* and *St Dunstan-in-the-East*
\* Includes Copped Hall Park, Woodredon Estate and Warlies Park

## OTHER PARKS AND GARDENS

CHELSEA PHYSIC GARDEN, 66 Royal Hospital Road SW3 4HS T 020-7352 5646 W www.chelseaphysicgarden.co.uk
A garden of general botanical research and education, maintaining a wide range of rare and unusual plants; established in 1673 by the Society of Apothecaries
HAMPTON COURT PARK AND GARDENS (304ha/750 acres), Surrey KT8 9AU T 0844-482 7777 W www.hrp.org.uk
Also known as Home Park, the park lies beyond the palace's formal gardens. It contains a herd of deer and a 750-year-old oak tree from the original park
HOLLAND PARK (22ha/54 acres), Ilchester Place W8 T 020-7361 3000 W www.rbkc.gov.uk The largest park in the Royal Borough of Kensington and Chelsea, includes the Kyoto Garden
KEW, ROYAL BOTANIC GARDENS (120ha/300 acres), Richmond, Surrey TW9 3AB T 020-8332 5655 W www.kew.org
Founded in 1759 and declared a UNESCO World Heritage Site in 2003
THAMES BARRIER PARK (9ha/22acres), North Woolwich Road E16 2HP T 020-7476 3741 Opened in 2000, landscaped gardens with spectacular views of the Thames Barrier

## ROYAL PARKS

W www.royalparks.org.uk
*Bushy Park* (450ha/1,099 acres), Middx. Adjoins Hampton Court; contains an avenue of horse-chestnuts enclosed in a fourfold avenue of limes planted by William III
*Green Park* (19ha/47 acres), W1. Between Piccadilly and St James's Park, with Constitution Hill leading to Hyde Park Corner
*Greenwich Park* (74ha/183 acres), SE10. Enclosed by Humphrey, Duke of Gloucester, and laid out by Charles II from the designs of Le Nôtre. On a hill in Greenwich Park is the Royal Observatory (founded 1675). Its buildings are now managed by the National Maritime Museum (T 020-8858 4422 W www.rmg.co.uk) and the earliest building is named Flamsteed House, after John Flamsteed (1646–1719), the first astronomer royal
*Hyde Park* (142ha/350 acres), W1/W2. From Park Lane to Kensington Gardens and incorporating the Serpentine lake, Apsley House, the Achilles Statue, Rotten Row and the Ladies' Mile; fine gateway at Hyde Park Corner. To the north-east is Marble Arch, originally erected by George IV at the entrance to Buckingham Palace and re-erected in the present position in 1851. At Hyde Park Corner stands Wellington Arch, built in 1825–7, it opened to the public in 2012 following major renovation
*Kensington Gardens* (111ha/275 acres), W2/W8. From the western boundary of Hyde Park to Kensington Palace; contains the Albert Memorial, Serpentine Gallery and Peter Pan statue
*The Regent's Park* and *Primrose Hill* (197ha/487 acres), NW1. From Marylebone Road to Primrose Hill surrounded by the Outer Circle; divided by the Broad Walk leading to the Zoological Gardens
*Richmond Park* (1,000ha/2,500 acres), Surrey. Designated a National Nature Reserve, a Site of Special Scientific Interest and a Special Area of Conservation
*St James's Park* (23ha/58 acres), SW1. From Whitehall to Buckingham Palace; ornamental lake of 4.9ha (12 acres); the Mall leads from Admiralty Arch to Buckingham Palace

## PLACES OF HISTORICAL AND CULTURAL INTEREST

*1 Canada Square*
Canary Wharf E14 5AB T 020-7418 2000
W www.canarywharf.com
Also known as 'Canary Wharf', the steel and glass skyscraper is designed to sway 35cm in the strongest winds
*20 Fenchurch Street*
W www.20fenchurchstreet.co.uk
Designed by architect Rafael Viñoly the skyscraper was completed in March 2014 and is nicknamed the 'Walkie-Talkie' because of its shape. The top three floors include a large viewing platform and are open to the public
*30 St Mary Axe*
EC3A 8EP W www.30stmaryaxe.com
Completed in 2004 and commonly known as the 'Gherkin', each of the floors rotates five degrees from the one below
*122 Leadenhall Street*
EC3V 4AB W www.theleadenhallbuilding.com
The distinctive 225m (737ft) asymmetrical Leadenhall Building, designed by architects Rogers Stirk Harbour & Partners, was completed in 2014
*Alexandra Palace*
Alexandra Palace Way N22 7AY T 020-8365 2121
W www.alexandrapalace.com
The Victorian palace was severely damaged by fire in 1980 but was restored, and reopened in 1988. Alexandra Palace now provides modern facilities for exhibitions, conferences, banquets and leisure activities. There is a winter ice rink, a boating lake and a conservation area
*Barbican Centre*
Silk Street EC2Y 8DS T 020-7638 4141
W www.barbican.org.uk
Owned, funded and managed by the City of London Corporation, the Barbican Centre opened in 1982 and houses the Barbican Theatre, a studio theatre called The Pit and the Barbican Hall; it is also home to the London Symphony Orchestra. There are three cinemas, six conference rooms, two art galleries, a sculpture court, a lending library, trade and banqueting facilities and a conservatory
*British Library*
St Pancras, 96 Euston Road NW1 2DB T 0843-208 1144
W www.bl.uk ·
The largest building constructed in the UK in the 20th century with basements extending 24.5m underground. Holdings include the *Magna Carta*, the Gutenburg Bible, Shakespeare's First Folio, Beatles manuscripts and the first edition of *The Times* from 1788. Holds temporary exhibitions on a range of topics
*Central Criminal Court*
Old Bailey EC4M 7EH T 020-7248 3277
W www.cityoflondon.gov.uk
The highest criminal court in the UK, the 'Old Bailey' is located on the site of the old Newgate Prison. Trials held here have included those of Oscar Wilde, Dr Crippen and the Yorkshire Ripper. The courthouse has been rebuilt several times since 1674; Edward VII officially opened the current neo-baroque building in 1907
*Charterhouse*
Charterhouse Square EC1M 6AN T 020-7253 9503
W www.thecharterhouse.org
A Carthusian monastery from 1371 to 1538, purchased in 1611 by Thomas Sutton, who endowed it as a residence for aged men 'of gentle birth' and a school for poor scholars (removed to Godalming in 1872)

*Downing Street*
SW1 W www.number10.gov.uk
Number 10 Downing Street is the official town residence of the prime minister, number 11 of the Chancellor of the Exchequer and number 12 is the office of the government whips. The street was named after Sir George Downing, Bt., soldier and diplomat, who was MP for Morpeth 1660–84

*George Inn*
The George Inn Yard SE1 1NH T 020-7407 2056
W www.nationaltrust.org.uk/george-inn
The last galleried inn in London, built in 1677. Now owned by the National Trust and run as an ordinary public house

*Horse Guards*
Whitehall SW1
Archway and offices built about 1753. The changing of the guard takes place daily at 11am (10am on Sundays) and the inspection at 4pm. Only those with the Queen's permission may drive through the gates and archway into *Horse Guards Parade*, where the colour is 'trooped' on the Queen's official birthday

HOUSES OF PARLIAMENT W www.parliament.uk
*House of Commons*, Westminster SW1A 0AA T 020-7219 4272
*House of Lords*, Westminster SW1A 0PW T 020-7219 3107
The royal palace of Westminster, originally built by Edward the Confessor, was the normal meeting place of Parliament from about 1340. St Stephen's Chapel was used from about 1550 for the meetings of the House of Commons, which had previously been held in the Chapter House or Refectory of Westminster Abbey. The House of Lords met in an apartment of the royal palace. The fire of 1834 destroyed much of the palace, and the present Houses of Parliament were erected on the site from the designs of Sir Charles Barry and Augustus Welby Pugin between 1840 and 1867. The chamber of the House of Commons was destroyed by bombing in 1941, and a new chamber designed by Sir Giles Gilbert Scott was used for the first time in 1950. *Westminster Hall and the Crypt Chapel* was the only part of the old palace of Westminster to survive the fire of 1834. It was built by William II from 1097 to 1099 and altered by Richard II between 1394 and 1399. The hammerbeam roof of carved oak dates from 1396–8. The Hall was the scene of the trial of Charles I. The *Victoria Tower* of the House of Lords is 98.5m (323ft) high and *The Clock Tower* of the House of Commons is 96.3m (316ft) high and contains 'Big Ben', the hour bell said to be named after Sir Benjamin Hall, First Commissioner of Works when the original bell was cast in 1856. This bell, which weighed 16 tons 11 cwt, was found to be cracked in 1857. The present bell (13.5 tons) is a recasting of the original and was first brought into use in 1859. The dials of the clock are 7m (23ft) in diameter, the hands being 2.7m (9ft) and 4.3m (14ft) long (including balance piece).

During session, tours of the Houses of Parliament are only available to UK residents who have made advance arrangements through an MP or peer. Overseas visitors are no longer provided with permits to tour the Houses of Parliament during session, although they can tour on Saturdays and during the summer opening and attend debates for both houses in the Strangers' Galleries. During the summer recess, tickets for tours of the Houses of Parliament can be booked by telephone (T 0844-847 1672) or bought on site at the ticket office on Abingdon Green opposite Parliament and the Victoria Tower Gardens. The Strangers' Gallery of the House of Commons is open to the public when the house is sitting. To acquire tickets in advance, UK residents should write to their local MP and

overseas visitors should apply to their embassy or high commission in the UK for a permit. If none of these arrangements has been made, visitors should join the public queue outside St Stephen's Entrance, where there is also a queue for entry to the House of Lords Gallery

INNS OF COURT
The Inns of Court are ancient unincorporated bodies of lawyers which for more than five centuries have had the power to call to the Bar those of their members who have qualified for the rank or degree of Barrister-at-Law. There are four Inns of Court as well as many lesser inns:

*Lincoln's Inn*, WC2A 3TL T 020-7405 1393
W www.lincolnsinn.org.uk
The most ancient of the inns with records dating back to 1422. The hall and library buildings are from 1845, although the library is first mentioned in 1474; the old hall (late 15th century) and the chapel were rebuilt *c*.1619–23

*Inner Temple*, King's Bench Walk EC4Y 7HL T 020-7797 8250
W www.innertemple.org.uk
*Middle Temple*, Middle Temple Lane EC4Y 9BT
T 020-7427 4800 W www.middletemple.org.uk
Records for the Inner and Middle Temple date back to the beginning of the 16th century. The site was originally occupied by the Order of Knights Templar *c*.1160–1312. The two inns have separate halls thought to have been formed *c*.1350. The division between the two societies was formalised in 1732 with Temple Church and the Masters House remaining in common. The Inner Temple Garden is normally open to the public on weekdays between 12.30pm and 3pm

*Temple Church*, EC4Y 7BB T 020-7353 8559
W www.templechurch.com
The nave forms one of five remaining round churches in England

*Gray's Inn*, South Square WC1R 5ET T 020-7458 7800
W www.graysinn.info
Founded early 14th century; hall 1556–8
No other 'Inns' are active, but there are remains of *Staple Inn*, a gabled front on Holborn (opposite Gray's Inn Road). *Clement's Inn* (near St Clement Danes Church), *Clifford's Inn*, Fleet Street, and *Thavies Inn*, Holborn Circus, are all rebuilt. *Serjeants' Inn*, Fleet Street, and another (demolished 1910) of the same name in Chancery Lane, were composed of Serjeants-at-Law, the last of whom died in 1922

*Institute of Contemporary Arts*
The Mall SW1Y 5AH T 020-7930 3647 W www.ica.org.uk
Exhibitions of modern art in the fields of film, theatre, new media and the visual arts

*Lloyd's*
Lime Street EC3M 7HA T 020-7327 1000 W www.lloyds.com
International insurance market which evolved during the 17th century from Lloyd's Coffee House. The present building was opened for business in May 1986, and houses the Lutine Bell. Underwriting is on three floors with a total area of 10,591 sq. m (114,000 sq. ft). The Lloyd's building is not open to the general public

*London Central Mosque and the Islamic Cultural Centre*
Park Road NW8 7RG T 020-7724 3363 W www.iccuk.org
The focus for London's Muslims; established in 1944 but not completed until 1977, the mosque can accommodate about 5,000 worshippers; guided tours are available

*London Eye*
South Bank SE1 7PB T 0870-990 8883 W www.londoneye.com
Opened in March 2000 as London's millennium landmark, this 137m (450ft) observation wheel is the tallest cantilevered observation wheel in the world. The wheel provides a 30-minute ride offering panoramic views of the capital

*London Zoo*
Regent's Park NW1 4RY T 0844-225 1826 W www.zsl.org

*Madame Tussauds*
Marylebone Road NW1 5LR T 0871-894 3000
W www.madametussauds.com
Waxwork exhibition

*Mansion House*
Cannon Street EC4N 8BH T 020-7626 2500
W www.cityoflondon.gov.uk
The official residence of the Lord Mayor. Built in the 18th century in the Palladian style. Open to groups by appointment only

*Marlborough House*
Pall Mall SW1Y 5HX T 020-7747 6500
W www.thecommonwealth.org
Built by Wren for the first Duke of Marlborough and completed in 1711, the house reverted to the Crown in 1835. In 1863 it became the London house of the Prince of Wales and was the London home of Queen Mary until her death in 1953. In 1959 Marlborough House was given by the Queen as the headquarters for the Commonwealth Secretariat and it was opened as such in 1965. The Queen's Chapel, Marlborough Gate, was begun in 1623 from the designs of Inigo Jones for the Infanta Maria of Spain, and completed for Queen Henrietta Maria. Marlborough House is not open to the public

*Neasden Temple*
BAPS Shri Swaminarayan Mandir, Brentfield Road, Neasden NW10 8LD T 020-8965 2651 W http://londonmandir.baps.org
The first and largest traditional Hindu Mandir outside of India; opened in 1995

*Port of London*
Port of London Authority, Royal Pier Road, Kent DA12 2BG
T 01474-562200 W www.pla.co.uk
The Port of London covers the tidal section of the river Thames from Teddington to the seaward limit (the outer Tongue buoy and the Sunk light vessel), a distance of 150km (93 miles). The governing body is the Port of London Authority (PLA). Cargo is handled at privately operated riverside terminals between Fulham and Canvey Island, including the enclosed dock at Tilbury, 40km (25 miles) below London Bridge. Passenger vessels and cruise liners can be handled at moorings at Greenwich, Tower Bridge and Tilbury

*Queen Elizabeth Olympic Park*
Stratford E20 T 0800-072 2110
W www.queenelizabetholympicpark.co.uk
Built for the London 2012 Olympic and Paralympic Games, the park, which included the Olympic Stadium, Velodrome and Aquatics Centre has been redeveloped to provide 227ha (560 acres) of parkland with play areas, outside arts and theatre spaces, waterways and wetlands. The north of the park, which includes the Copper Box Arena sport venue, re-opened to the public in 2013. The south of the park, which re-opened in April 2014, incorporates three venues for arts and sports events and the *ArcelorMittal Orbit,* designed by Sir Anish Kapoor and Cecil Balmond; it is the UK's tallest sculpture (114.5m/376ft) and has two accessible observation floors

*Roman Remains*
The city wall of Roman *Londinium* was largely rebuilt during the medieval period but sections may be seen near the White Tower in the Tower of London; at Tower Hill; at Coopers' Row; at All Hallows, London Wall, its vestry being built on the remains of a semi-circular Roman bastion; at St Alphage, London Wall, showing a succession of building repairs from the Roman until the late medieval period; and at St Giles, Cripplegate. Sections of the great forum and basilica, more than 165 sq. m (1,776 sq. ft),

have been encountered during excavations in the area of Leadenhall, Gracechurch Street and Lombard Street. Traces of Roman activity along the river include a massive riverside wall built in the late Roman period, and a succession of Roman timber quays along Lower and Upper Thames Street. Finds from these sites can be seen at the Museum of London.

Other major buildings are the amphitheatre at Guildhall, remains of bath-buildings in Upper and Lower Thames Street, and the temple of Mithras in Walbrook

*Royal Albert Hall*
Kensington Gore SW7 2AP T 0845-401 5045
W www.royalalberthall.com
The elliptical hall, one of the largest in the world, was completed in 1871; since 1941 it has been the venue each summer for the Promenade Concerts founded in 1895 by Sir Henry Wood. Other events include pop and classical music concerts, dance, opera, sporting events, conferences and banquets

*Royal Courts of Justice*
Strand WC2A 2LL T 020-7947 7726 W www.justice.gov.uk
Victorian Gothic building that is home to the high court. Visitors are free to watch proceedings

*Royal Hospital, Chelsea*
Royal Hospital Road SW3 4SR T 020-7881 5200
W www.chelsea-pensioners.co.uk
Founded by Charles II in 1682, and built by Wren; opened in 1692 for old and disabled soldiers. The extensive grounds include the former Ranelagh Gardens and are the venue for the Chelsea Flower Show each May

*Royal Naval College*
Greenwich SE10 9NN T 020-8269 4747 W www.ornc.org
The building was the Greenwich Hospital until 1869. It was built by Charles II, largely from designs by John Webb, and by Queen Mary II and William III, from designs by Wren. It stands on the site of an ancient abbey, a royal house and Greenwich Palace, which was constructed by Henry VII. Henry VIII, Mary I and Elizabeth I were born in the royal palace and Edward VI died there

*Royal Opera House*
Covent Garden WC2E 9DD T 020-7240 1200
W www.roh.org.uk
Home of The Royal Ballet (1931) and The Royal Opera (1946). The Royal Opera House is the third theatre to be built on the site, opening 1858; the first was opened in 1732

*St James's Palace*
Pall Mall SW1A 1BQ W www.royal.gov.uk
Built by Henry VIII, only the Gatehouse and Presence Chamber remain; later alterations were made by Wren and Kent. Representatives of foreign powers are still accredited 'to the Court of St James's'. *Clarence House* (1825), the official London residence of the Prince of Wales and his sons, stands within the St James's Palace estate

*St Paul's Cathedral*
St Paul's Churchyard EC4M 8AD T 020-7246 8350
W www.stpauls.co.uk
Built 1675–1710. The cross on the dome is 111m (365ft) above ground level, the inner cupola 66.4m (218ft) above the floor. 'Great Paul' in the south-west tower weighs nearly 17 tons. The organ by Father Smith (enlarged by Willis and rebuilt by Mander) is in a case carved by Grinling Gibbons, who also carved the choir stalls

*Shakespeare's Globe*
New Globe Walk SE1 9DT T 020-7902 1400
W www.shakespearesglobe.com
Reconstructed in 1997, the open-air playhouse is a unique resource for the works of William Shakespeare through performance and education; a new indoor replica Jacobean theatre staged its first public performance in January 2014

*Shard*
London Bridge SE1 **T** 020-7493 5311 **W** www.the-shard.com
Completed in May 2012, the skyscraper stands at 310m
(1,016ft) and possesses a unique facade of 11,000 glass
panels and a 360-degree viewing gallery

*Somerset House*
Strand WC2R 1LA **T** 020-7845 4600
**W** www.somersethouse.org.uk
The river facade (183m/600ft long) was built in 1776–
1801 from the designs of Sir William Chambers; the
eastern extension, which houses part of King's College,
was built by Smirke in 1829–35. Somerset House was the
property of Lord Protector Somerset, at whose attainder
in 1552 the palace passed to the Crown, and it was a royal
residence until 1692. Somerset House has recently
undergone extensive renovation and is home to the
Embankment Galleries and the Courtauld Gallery. Open-
air concerts and ice-skating (Dec–Jan) are held in the
courtyard

SOUTH BANK, SE1
Arts complex on the south bank of the river Thames which
consists of:
*BFI Southbank* **T** 020-7928 3232 **W** www.bfi.org.uk
Opened in 1952 and administered by the British Film
Institute, has four auditoria of varying capacities. Venue
for the annual London Film Festival.
The *Royal Festival Hall* **T** 020-7960 4200
**W** www.southbankcentre.co.uk
Opened in 1951 for the Festival of Britain, adjacent are
the *Queen Elizabeth Hall,* the *Purcell Room* and the *Hayward
Gallery*
The *Royal National Theatre,* **T** 020-7452 3000
**W** www.nationaltheatre.org.uk
Opened in 1976; comprises the Olivier, the Lyttelton and
Dorfman theatres. The Cottesloe Theatre closed in
February 2013 and, following refurbishment reopened in
2014 as the Dorfman Theatre

*Southwark Cathedral*
London Bridge SE1 9DA **T** 020-7367 6700
**W** www.cathedral.southwark.anglican.org
Mainly 13th century, but the nave is largely rebuilt. The
tomb of John Gower (1330–1408) is between the Bunyan
and Chaucer memorial windows in the north aisle;
Shakespeare's effigy, backed by a view of Southwark and
the Globe Theatre, is in the south aisle; the tomb of
Bishop Andrewes (*d.*1626) is near the screen. The Lady
Chapel was the scene of the consistory courts of the reign
of Mary (Gardiner and Bonner) and is still used as a
consistory court. John Harvard, after whom Harvard
University is named, was baptised here in 1607, and the
chapel by the north choir aisle is his memorial chapel

*Thames Embankments*
Sir Joseph Bazalgette (1819–91) constructed the *Victoria
Embankment,* on the north side from Westminster to
Blackfriars for the Metropolitan Board of Works, 1864–

70; (the seats, of which the supports of some are a
kneeling camel, laden with spicery, and of others a winged
sphinx, were presented by the Grocers' Company and by
W. H. Smith, MP, in 1874); the *Albert Embankment,* on the
south side from Westminster Bridge to Vauxhall, 1866–9,
and the Chelsea Embankment, 1871–4. The total cost
exceeded £2m. Bazalgette also inaugurated the London
main drainage system, 1858–65. A medallion *(Flumini
vincula posuit)* has been placed on a pier of the *Victoria
Embankment* to commemorate the engineer

*Thames Flood Barrier*
**W** www.environment-agency.gov.uk
Officially opened in May 1984, though first used in
February 1983, the barrier consists of ten rising sector
gates which span approximately 520m from bank to bank
of the Thames at Woolwich Reach. When not in use the
gates lie horizontally, allowing shipping to navigate the
river normally; when the barrier is closed, the gates turn
through 90 degrees to stand vertically more than 50 feet
above the river bed. The barrier took eight years to
complete and can be raised within about 90 minutes

*Trafalgar Tavern*
Park Row, Greenwich SE10 9NW **T** 020-8858 2909
**W** www.trafalgartavern.co.uk
Regency-period riverside public house built in 1837.
Charles Dickens and William Gladstone were patrons

*Wembley Stadium*
Wembley HA9 0WS **T** 0844-980 8001
**W** www.wembleystadium.com
The second largest stadium in Europe; hosts major
sporting events and music concerts

*Westminster Abbey*
SW1P 3PA **T** 020-7222 5152 **W** www.westminster-abbey.org
Founded as a Benedictine monastery over 1,000 years ago,
the church was rebuilt by Edward the Confessor in 1065
and again by Henry III in the 13th century. The abbey is
the resting place for monarchs including Edward I, Henry
III, Henry V, Henry VII, Elizabeth I, Mary I and Mary,
Queen of Scots, and has been the setting of coronations
since that of William the Conqueror in 1066. In Poets'
Corner there are memorials to many literary figures, and
many scientists and musicians are also remembered here.
The grave of the Unknown Warrior is to be found in the
nave

*Westminster Cathedral*
Francis Street SW1P 1QW **T** 020-7798 9055
**W** www.westminstercathedral.org.uk
Roman Catholic cathedral built 1895–1903 from the
designs of John Francis Bentley. The campanile is 83m
(273ft) high

*Wimbledon All England Lawn Tennis Club*
Church Road SW19 5AE **T** 020-8944 1066
**W** www.wimbledon.com
Venue for the Wimbledon Championships. Includes the
Wimbledon Lawn Tennis Museum

# HALLMARKS

Hallmarks are the symbols stamped on gold, silver, palladium or platinum articles to indicate that they have been tested at an official Assay Office and that they conform to one of the legal standards. The marking of gold and silver articles to identify the maker was instituted in England in 1363 under a statute of Edward III. In 1478 the Assay Office in Goldsmiths' Hall was established and all gold and silversmiths were required to bring their wares to be date-marked by the Hall, hence the term 'hallmarked'.

With certain exceptions, all gold, silver, palladium or platinum articles are required by law to be hallmarked before they are offered for sale. Current hallmarking requirements come under the UK Hallmarking Act 1973 and subsequent amendments. The act is built around the principle of description, where it is an offence for any person to apply to an unhallmarked article a description indicating that it is wholly or partly made of gold, silver, palladium or platinum. There is an exemption by weight: compulsory hallmarks are not needed on gold and palladium under 1g, silver under 7.78g and platinum under 0.5g. Also, some descriptions, such as rolled gold and gold plate, are permissible. The British Hallmarking Council is a statutory body created as a result of the Hallmarking Act. It ensures adequate provision for assaying and hallmarking, supervises the assay offices and ensures the enforcement of hallmarking legislation. The four assay offices at London, Birmingham, Sheffield and Edinburgh operate under the act.

BRITISH HALLMARKING COUNCIL Secretariat, 1 Colmore Square, Birmingham B4 6AA T 0870-763 1455
W www.gov.uk/government/organisations/british-hallmarking-council

## COMPULSORY MARKS

Since January 1999 UK hallmarks have consisted of three compulsory symbols – the sponsor's mark, the millesimal fineness (purity) mark and the assay office mark. The distinction between UK and foreign articles has been removed, and more finenesses are now legal, reflecting the more common finenesses elsewhere in Europe.

### SPONSOR'S MARK
Formerly known as the maker's mark, the sponsor's mark was instituted in England in 1363. Originally a device such as a bird or fleur-de-lis, now it consists of a combination of at least two initials (usually a shortened form of the manufacturer's name) and a shield design. The London Assay Office offers 45 standard shield designs but other designs are possible by arrangement.

### MILLESIMAL FINENESS MARK
The millesimal fineness (purity) mark indicates the number of parts per thousand of pure metal in the alloy. The current finenesses allowed in the UK are:

| | |
|---|---|
| Gold | 999; 990; 916.6 (22 carat); 750 (18 carat); 585 (14 carat); 375 (9 carat) |
| Silver | 999; 958.4 (Britannia); 925 (sterling); 800 |
| Palladium | 999; 950; 500 |
| Platinum | 999; 950; 900; 850 |

### ASSAY OFFICE MARK
This mark identifies the particular assay office at which the article was tested and marked. The British assay offices are:

 LONDON, Goldsmiths' Hall, Gutter Lane, London EC2V 8AQ T 020-7606 8971
W www.thegoldsmiths.co.uk

 BIRMINGHAM, PO Box 151, Newhall Street, Birmingham B3 1SB T 0121-236 6951
W www.theassayoffice.co.uk

 SHEFFIELD, Guardians' Hall, Beulah Road, Hillsborough, Sheffield S6 2AN T 0114-231 2121
W www.assayoffice.co.uk

 EDINBURGH, Goldsmiths' Hall, 24 Broughton Street, Edinburgh EH1 3RH T 0131-556 1144
W www.edinburghassayoffice.co.uk

Assay offices formerly existed in other towns, eg Chester, Exeter, Glasgow, Newcastle, Norwich and York, each having its own distinguishing mark.

## OPTIONAL MARKS

Since 1999 traditional pictorial marks such as a crown for gold, the Britannia for 958 silver, the lion passant for 925 silver (lion rampant in Scotland) and the orb for 950 platinum may be added voluntarily to the millesimal mark. In 2010 a pictorial mark for 950 palladium was introduced.

 Gold – a crown

 Sterling silver (Scotland)

 Britannia silver

 Platinum – an orb

 Sterling silver (England)

 Palladium – the Greek goddess Pallas Athene

## OTHER MARKS

### FOREIGN GOODS
Foreign goods imported into the UK are required to be hallmarked before sale, unless they already bear a convention mark (see below) or a hallmark struck by an independent assay office in the European Economic Area which is deemed to be equivalent to a UK hallmark.

The following are the assay office marks used for gold imported articles until the end of 1998. For silver and platinum the symbols remain the same but the shields differ in shape.

 London

 Sheffield

 Birmingham

 Edinburgh

### CONVENTION HALLMARKS
The UK has been a signatory to the International Convention on Hallmarks since 1972. A convention hallmark struck by the UK assay offices is recognised by all member countries in the convention and, similarly, convention marks from member countries are legally recognised in the UK. There are currently 19 members of the hallmarking convention: Austria, Cyprus, Czech Republic, Denmark, Finland, Hungary, Ireland, Israel, Latvia, Lithuania, the

Netherlands, Norway, Poland, Portugal, Slovakia, Slovenia, Sweden, Switzerland, and the UK.

A convention hallmark comprises four marks: a sponsor's mark, a common control mark, a fineness mark, and an assay office mark.

Examples of common control marks (figures differ according to fineness, but the style of each mark remains the same for each article):

GOLD    SILVER    PALLADIUM    PLATINUM

## COMMEMORATIVE MARKS

There are other marks to commemorate special events: the silver jubilee of King George V and Queen Mary in 1935, the coronation of Queen Elizabeth II in 1953, her silver jubilee in 1977, and her golden jubilee in 2002. During 1999 and 2000 there was a voluntary additional Millennium Mark. A mark to commemorate the Queen's diamond jubilee in 2012 was available from July 2011 to October 2012:

    *Diamond Jubilee Hallmark*

## DATE LETTER

The date letter shows the year in which an article was assayed and hallmarked. Each alphabetical cycle has a distinctive style of lettering or shape of shield. The date letters were different at the various assay offices and the particular office must be established from the assay office mark before reference is made to tables of date letters. Date letter marks became voluntary from 1 January 1999.

The table which follows shows one specimen shield and letter used by the London Assay Office on silver articles for each alphabetical cycle from 1498. The same letters are found on gold articles but the surrounding shield may differ. Until 1 January 1975 two calendar years are given for each specimen date letter as the letter changed annually in May on St Dunstan's Day (the patron saint of silversmiths). Since 1 January 1975, each date letter has indicated a calendar year from January to December and each office has used the same style of date letter and shield for all articles:

### LONDON (GOLDSMITHS' HALL) DATE LETTERS FROM 1498

| | from | to | | from | to |
|---|---|---|---|---|---|
| | 1498–9 | 1517–18 | | 1756–7 | 1775–6 |
| | 1518–19 | 1537–8 | | 1776–7 | 1795–6 |
| | 1538–9 | 1557–8 | | 1796–7 | 1815–16 |
| | 1558–9 | 1577–8 | | 1816–17 | 1835–6 |
| | 1578–9 | 1597–8 | | 1836–7 | 1855–6 |
| | 1598–9 | 1617–18 | | 1856–7 | 1875–6 |
| | 1618–19 | 1637–8 | | 1876–7 (A to M square shield, N to Z as shown) | 1895–6 |
| | 1638–9 | 1657–8 | | 1896–7 | 1915–16 |
| | 1658–9 | 1677–8 | | 1916–17 | 1935–6 |
| | 1678–9 | 1696–7 | | 1936–7 | 1955–6 |
| | 1697 (from March, 1697 only) | 1715–16 | | 1956–7 | 1974 |
| | 1716–17 | 1735–6 | | 1975 | 1999 |
| | 1736–7 | 1738–9 | | 2000 | |
| | 1739–40 | 1755–6 | | | |

# BRITISH CURRENCY

The unit of currency is the pound sterling (£) of 100 pence. The decimal system was introduced on 15 February 1971.

## COIN

**Gold Coins**
One hundred pounds £100*
Fifty pounds £50*
Twenty-five pounds £25*
Ten pounds £10*
Five pounds £5
Two pounds £2
Sovereign £1
Half-sovereign 50p

**Silver Coins**
(Britannia coins*)
Two pounds £2
One pound £1
50 pence 50p
Twenty pence 20p

**Maundy Money†**
Fourpence 4p
Threepence 3p
Twopence 2p
Penny 1p

**Bi-colour Coins‡**
Two pounds £2

**Nickel-Brass Coins**
Two pounds £2 (pre-1997)§
One pound £1

**Cupro-Nickel Coins**
Crown £5 (since 1990)§
50 pence 50p
Crown 25p (pre-1990)§
20 pence 20p

**Nickel-plated Steel Coins ₵**
10 pence 10p
5 pence 5p

**Bronze Coins**
2 pence 2p
1 penny 1p

**Copper-plated Steel Coins***
2 pence 2p
1 penny 1p

\* Britannia coins: gold bullion introduced 1987; silver, 1997
† Ceremonial money given annually by the sovereign on Maundy Thursday to as many elderly men and women as there are years in the sovereign's age
‡ Cupro-nickel centre and nickel-brass outer ring
§ Commemorative coins; not intended for general circulation
₵ Pre-2012 the 10p and 5p coins were struck in cupro-nickel
** Since September 1992, although in 1998 the 2p was struck in both copper-plated steel and bronze

### GOLD COIN
Gold ceased to circulate during the First World War. Since then controls on buying, selling and holding gold coin have been imposed at various times but have subsequently been revoked. Under the Exchange Control (Gold Coins Exemption) Order 1979, gold coins may now be imported and exported without restriction, except gold coins which are more than 50 years old and valued at a sum in excess of £8,000; these cannot be exported without specific authorisation from the Department for Business, Innovation and Skills.

Value Added Taxation on the sale of gold coins was revoked in 2000.

### SILVER COIN
Prior to 1920 silver coins were struck from sterling silver, an alloy of which 925 parts in 1,000 were silver. In 1920 the proportion of silver was reduced to 500 parts. Since 1947 all 'silver' coins, except Maundy money, have been struck from cupro-nickel, an alloy of 75 parts copper and 25 parts nickel, except for the 20p, composed of 84 parts copper, 16 parts nickel. Maundy coins continue to be struck from sterling silver.

### BRONZE COIN
Bronze, introduced in 1860 to replace copper, is an alloy consisting mainly of copper with small amounts of zinc and tin. Bronze was replaced by copper-plated steel in September 1992 with the exception of 1998 when the 2p was made in both copper-plated steel and bronze.

### LEGAL TENDER AND VALUE IN CIRCULATION
*as at 31 March 2014*

| Denomination | Legal up to | Face value (£m est) |
| --- | --- | --- |
| Gold* | any amount | – |
| £2 | any amount | 832 |
| £1 | any amount | 1,553 |
| 50p | £10 | 474 |
| 20p | £10 | 553 |
| 10p | £5 | 163 |
| 5p | £5 | 192 |
| 2p | 20p | 131 |
| 1p | 20p | 113 |

\* Dated 1838 onwards, if not below least current weight

£5 (Crown since 1990) and 25p (Crown pre-1990) up to £10 are also legal tender but are only redeemable at the Post Office.

The following coins have ceased to be legal tender:

| | |
| --- | --- |
| Farthing | 31 Dec 1960 |
| Halfpenny (½d) | 31 Jul 1969 |
| Half-crown | 31 Dec 1969 |
| Threepence | 31 Aug 1971 |
| Penny (1d) | 31 Aug 1971 |
| Sixpence | 30 Jun 1980 |
| Halfpenny (½p) | 31 Dec 1984 |
| Old 5 pence | 31 Dec 1990 |
| Old 10 pence | 30 Jun 1993 |
| Old 50 pence | 28 Feb 1998 |

The Channel Islands and the Isle of Man issue their own coinage, which is legal tender only in the island of issue.

### COIN STANDARDS

| | Metal | Standard weight (g) | Standard diameter (mm) |
| --- | --- | --- | --- |
| 1p | bronze | 3.56 | 20.3 |
| 1p | copper-plated steel | 3.56 | 20.3 |
| 2p | bronze | 7.12 | 25.9 |
| 2p | copper-plated steel | 7.12 | 25.9 |
| 5p | nickel-plated steel | 3.25 | 18.0 |
| 10p | nickel-plated steel | 6.5 | 24.5 |
| 20p | cupro-nickel | 5.0 | 21.4 |
| 25p Crown | cupro-nickel | 28.28 | 38.6 |
| 50p | cupro-nickel | 8.00 | 27.3 |
| £1 | nickel-brass | 9.5 | 22.5 |
| £2 | nickel-brass | 15.98 | 28.4 |
| £2 | cupro-nickel, nickel-brass | 12.00 | 28.4 |
| £5 Crown | cupro-nickel | 28.28 | 38.6 |

The 'remedy' is the amount of variation from standard permitted in weight and fineness of coins when first issued from the Royal Mint.

## THE TRIAL OF THE PYX

The Trial of the Pyx is the examination by a jury to ascertain that coins made by the Royal Mint, which have been set aside in the pyx (or box), are of the proper weight, diameter and composition required by law. The trial is held annually, presided over by the Queen's Remembrancer, with a jury of freemen of the Company of Goldsmiths.

## BANKNOTES

Bank of England notes are issued in denominations of £5, £10, £20 and £50 for the amount of the fiduciary note issue, and are legal tender in England and Wales. No £1 notes have been issued since 1984 and in March 1998 the outstanding notes were written off in accordance with the provision of the Currency Act 1983.

The current E series of notes was introduced from June 1990, replacing the D series (*see* below). A new-style £20 note, the first in series F, was introduced in March 2007. A £50 note, the second in the F series, and the first banknote issued by the Bank of England to feature two portraits on the reverse, was issued in November 2011. The historical figures portrayed in these series are:

| | | |
|---|---|---|
| £5 | May 2002–date | Elizabeth Fry |
| £5 | Jun 1990–2003 | George Stephenson* |
| £10 | Nov 2000–date | Charles Darwin |
| £10 | Apr 1992–2003 | Charles Dickens* |
| £20 | Mar 2007–date | Adam Smith |
| £20 | Jun 1999–2010 | Sir Edward Elgar* |
| £20 | Jun 1991–2001 | Michael Faraday* |
| £50 | Nov 2011–date | Matthew Boulton and James Watt |
| £50 | Apr 1994–2014 | Sir John Houblon* |

* These notes have been withdrawn from circulation

## NOTE CIRCULATION

Note circulation is highest at the two peak spending periods of the year: around Christmas and during the summer holiday period.

The value of notes in circulation (£ million) at the end of February 2014 and 2015 was:

| | 2014 | 2015 |
|---|---|---|
| £5 | 1,540 | 1,601 |
| £10 | 7,182 | 7,371 |
| £20 | 36,483 | 38,912 |
| £50 | 11,025 | 11,788 |
| Other notes* | 3,967 | 4,118 |
| Total | 60,198 | 63,789 |

* Includes higher value notes used as backing for the note issues of authorised banks in Scotland and Northern Ireland

## LEGAL TENDER

Banknotes which are no longer legal tender are payable when presented at the head office of the Bank of England in London.

The white notes for £10, £20, £50, £100, £500 and £1,000, which were issued until April 1943, ceased to be legal tender in May 1945, and the white £5 note in March 1946.

The white £5 note issued between October 1945 and September 1956, the £5 notes issued between 1957 and 1963 (bearing a portrait of Britannia) and the first series to bear a portrait of the Queen, issued between 1963 and 1971, ceased to be legal tender in March 1961, June 1967 and September 1973 respectively.

The series of £1 notes issued during the years 1928 to 1960 and the 10 shilling notes issued from 1928 to 1961 (those without the royal portrait) ceased to be legal tender in May and October 1962 respectively. The £1 note first issued in March 1960 (bearing on the back a representation of Britannia) and the £10 note first issued in February 1964 (bearing a lion on the back), both bearing a portrait of the Queen on the front, ceased to be legal tender in June 1979. The £1 note first issued in 1978 ceased to be legal tender on 11 March 1988. The 10 shilling note was replaced by the 50p coin in October 1969, and ceased to be legal tender on 21 November 1970.

The D series of banknotes was introduced from 1970 and ceased to be legal tender from the dates shown below. The predominant identifying feature of each note was the portrayal on the back of a prominent figure from British history:

| | | |
|---|---|---|
| £1 | Feb 1978–Mar 1988 | Sir Isaac Newton |
| £5 | Nov 1971–Nov 1991 | Duke of Wellington |
| £10 | Feb 1975–May 1994 | Florence Nightingale |
| £20 | Jul 1970–Mar 1993 | William Shakespeare |
| £50 | Mar 1981–Sep 1996 | Sir Christopher Wren |

The £1 coin was introduced on 21 April 1983 to replace the £1 note.

## OTHER BANKNOTES

*Scotland* – Banknotes are issued by three Scottish banks. The Royal Bank of Scotland issues notes for £1, £5, £10, £20, £50 and £100. Bank of Scotland and the Clydesdale Bank issue notes for £5, £10, £20, £50 and £100. Scottish notes are not legal tender in the UK but they are an authorised currency.

*Northern Ireland* – Banknotes are issued by four banks in Northern Ireland. The Bank of Ireland and the Ulster Bank issue notes for £5, £10, £20, £50 and £100. The First Trust Bank issue notes for £10, £20, £50 and £100 and Danske Bank (formerly Northern Bank) issue notes for £10 and £20. Northern Ireland notes are not legal tender in the UK but they are an authorised currency.

*Channel Islands* – The States of Guernsey issues its own currency notes and coinage. The notes are for £1, £5, £10, £20 and £50, and the coins are for 1p, 2p, 5p, 10p, 50p, £1 and £2. The States of Jersey issues its own currency notes and coinage. The notes are for £1, £5, £10, £20, £50 and £100, and the coins are for 1p, 2p, 5p, 10p, 20p, 50p, £1 and £2.

*The Isle of Man* – The Isle of Man government issues notes for £1, £5, £10, £20 and £50. Although these notes are only legal tender in the Isle of Man, they may be exchanged at face value at certain UK banks at their discretion. The Isle of Man issues coins for 1p, 2p, 5p, 10p, 20p, 50p, £1, £2 and £5.

Although none of the series of notes specified above is legal tender in the UK, they are generally accepted by banks irrespective of their place of issue. At one time banks made a commission charge for handling Scottish and Irish notes but this was abolished some years ago.

# BANKING AND PERSONAL FINANCE

There are two main types of deposit-taking institutions: banks and building societies, although National Savings and Investments also provides savings products. Banks and building societies are regulated by the Prudential Regulation Authority, part of the Bank of England (*see* Financial Services Regulation), and National Savings and Investments is accountable to HM Treasury.

The main institutions within the British banking system are the Bank of England (the central bank), retail banks, investment banks and overseas banks. In its role as the central bank, the Bank of England acts as banker to the government and as a note-issuing authority; it also oversees the efficient functioning of payment and settlement systems.

Since May 1997, the Bank of England has had operational responsibility for monetary policy. At monthly meetings of its monetary policy committee the Bank sets the interest rate at which it will lend to the money markets.

## OFFICIAL INTEREST RATES 2005–15

| | |
|---|---|
| 4 August 2005 | 4.50% |
| 3 August 2006 | 4.75% |
| 9 November 2006 | 5.00% |
| 11 January 2007 | 5.25% |
| 10 May 2007 | 5.50% |
| 5 July 2007 | 5.75% |
| 6 December 2007 | 5.50% |
| 7 February 2008 | 5.25% |
| 10 April 2008 | 5.00% |
| 8 October 2008 | 4.50% |
| 6 November 2008 | 3.00% |
| 4 December 2008 | 2.00% |
| 8 January 2009 | 1.50% |
| 5 February 2009 | 1.00% |
| 5 March 2009 | 0.50% |

## RETAIL BANKING

Retail banks offer a wide variety of financial services to individuals and companies, including current and deposit accounts, loan and overdraft facilities, credit and debit cards, investment services, pensions, insurance and mortgages. All banks offer internet and telephone banking facilities and the majority also offer traditional branch services.

The Financial Ombudsman Service provides independent and impartial arbitration in disputes between banks and their customers (*see* Financial Services Regulation).

## PAYMENT CLEARINGS

The Payment Systems Regulator (PSR), a subsidiary of the Financial Conduct Authority (*see* Financial Services Regulation), is the economic regulator for the payment systems industry in the UK. Funded by an annual levy on the firms it regulates, it was established on 1 April 2015. The PSR's statutory objectives are:

• to ensure that payment systems are operated and developed in a way that considers and promotes the interests of all the businesses and consumers that use them
• to promote effective competition in the markets for payment systems and services – between operators, payment service providers and infrastructure providers
• to promote development and innovation in payment systems, in particular the infrastructure used to operate these systems

### DESIGNATED PAYMENT SYSTEMS
The PSR can only use its regulatory powers in relation to payment systems designated by HM Treasury, which regularly reviews this list. The current designated payment systems are: BACS, C&C (Cheque & Credit Clearing Company), CHAPS, Faster Payments Scheme (FPS), LINK, Northern Ireland Cheque Clearing (NICC), MasterCard, Visa Europe (Visa).

PSR, 25 The North Colonnade, Canary Wharf, London E14 5HS
T 020-7066 1000 E contactus@psr.org.uk W www.psr.org.uk

## GLOSSARY OF FINANCIAL TERMS

AER (ANNUAL EQUIVALENT RATE) – A notional rate quoted on savings and investment products which demonstrates the return on interest, when compounded and paid annually.

APR (ANNUAL PERCENTAGE RATE) – Calculates the total amount of interest payable over the whole term of a product (such as investment or loan), allowing consumers to compare rival products on a like-for-like basis. Companies offering loans, credit cards, mortgages or overdrafts are required by law to provide the APR rate. Where typical APR is shown, it refers to the company's typical borrower and so is given as a best example; rate and costs may vary depending on individual circumstances.

ANNUITY – A type of insurance policy that provides regular income in exchange for a lump sum. The annuity can be bought from a company other than the existing pension provider.

## MAJOR RETAIL BANKS' FINANCIAL RESULTS 2014

| Bank group | Profit/(loss) before taxation £ million | Profit/(loss) after taxation £ million | Total assets £ million |
|---|---|---|---|
| Barclays Bank | 2,309 | 854 | 1,358,693 |
| Cooperative Bank | (264) | (225) | 37,583 |
| HSBC Bank | 1,953 | 1,389 | 797,853 |
| Lloyds Banking Group | 1,762 | 1,499 | 854,896 |
| RBS Group | 2,643 | (2,711) | 1,050,763 |
| Santander UK | 1,399 | 1,110 | 275,977 |
| TSB Banking Group | 170 | 135 | 27,171 |
| Virgin Money Group | 34 | 9 | 26,537 |

ASU – Accident, sickness and unemployment insurance taken out by a borrower to protect against being unable to work for these reasons. The policy will usually pay a percentage of the normal monthly mortgage repayment if the borrower is unable to work.

ATM (AUTOMATED TELLER MACHINES) – Commonly referred to as cash machines. Users can access their bank accounts using a card for simple transactions such as withdrawing money and viewing an account balance. Some banks and independent ATM deployers charge for transactions.

BANKER'S DRAFT – A cheque drawn on a bank against a cash deposit. Considered to be a secure way of receiving money in instances where a cheque could 'bounce' or where it is not desirable to receive cash.

BASE RATE – The interest rate set by the Bank of England at which it will lend to financial institutions. This acts as a benchmark for all other interest rates.

BASIS POINT – Unit of measure (usually one-hundredth of a percentage point) used to express movements in interest rates, foreign rates or bond yields.

BUY-TO-LET – The purchase of a residential property for the sole purpose of letting to a tenant. Not all lenders provide mortgage finance for this purpose. Buy-to-let lenders assess projected rental income (typical expectations are between 125 and 130 per cent of the monthly interest payment) in addition to, or instead of, the borrower's income. Buy-to-let mortgages are available as either interest only or repayment.

CAPITAL GAIN/LOSS – Increase/decrease in the value of a capital asset when it is sold or transferred compared to its initial worth.

CAPPED RATE MORTGAGE – The interest rate applied to a loan is guaranteed not to rise above a certain rate for a set period of time; the rate can therefore fall but will not rise above the capped rate. The level at which the cap is fixed is usually higher than for a fixed rate mortgage for a comparable period of time. The lender normally imposes early redemption penalties within the first few years.

CASH CARD – Issued by banks and building societies for withdrawing cash from ATMs.

CHARGE CARD – Charge cards, eg American Express and Diners Club, can be used in a similar way to credit cards but the debt must be settled in full each month.

CHIP AND PIN CARD – A credit/debit card which incorporates an embedded chip containing unique owner details. When used with a PIN, such cards offer greater security as they are less prone to fraud. Since 14 February 2006, most card transactions in the UK have required the use of a chip and pin card.

CREDIT CARD – Normally issued with a credit limit, credit cards can be used for purchases until the limit is reached. There is normally an interest-free period on the outstanding balance of up to 56 days. Charges can be avoided if the balance is paid off in full within the interest-free period. Alternatively part of the balance can be paid and in most cases there is a minimum amount set by the issuer (normally a percentage of the outstanding balance) which must be paid on a monthly basis. Some card issuers charge an annual fee and most issuers belong to at least one major credit card network, eg Mastercard or Visa.

CREDIT RATING – Overall credit worthiness of a borrower based on information from a credit reference agency, such as Experian or Equifax, which holds details of credit agreements, payment records, county court judgements etc for all adults in the UK. This information is supplied to lenders who use it in their credit scoring or underwriting systems to calculate the risk of granting a loan to an individual and the probability that it will be repaid. Each lender sets their own criteria for credit worthiness and may accept or reject a credit application based on an individual's credit rating.

CRITICAL ILLNESS COVER – Insurance that covers borrowers against critical illnesses such as stroke, heart attack or cancer and is designed to protect mortgage or other loan payments.

DEBIT CARD – Debit cards were introduced on a large scale in the UK in the mid-1980s, replacing cash and cheques to purchase goods and services. They can be used to withdraw cash from ATMs in the UK and abroad and may also function as a cheque guarantee card. Funds are automatically withdrawn from an individual's bank account after making a purchase and no interest is charged.

DIRECT DEBIT – An instruction from a customer to their bank, which authorises the payee to charge costs to the customer's bank account.

DISCOUNTED MORTGAGE – Discounted mortgages guarantee an interest rate set at a margin below the standard variable rate for a period of time. The discounted rate will move up or down with the standard variable rate, but the payment rate will retain the agreed differential below the standard variable rate. The lender normally imposes early redemption penalties within the first few years.

EARLY REDEMPTION PENALTY – see Redemption Penalty

ENDOWMENT MORTGAGE – Only the interest on a property loan is paid back to the lender each month as long as an endowment life insurance policy is taken out for an agreed amount of time, typically 25 years. When the policy matures the lender will take repayment of the money owed on the property loan and any surplus goes to the policyholder. If the endowment policy shows a shortfall on projected returns, the policy holder must make further provision to pay off the mortgage.

EQUITY – When applied to real estate, equity is the difference between the value of a property and the amount outstanding on any loan secured against it. Negative equity occurs when the loan is greater than the market value of the property.

FIXED RATE MORTGAGE – A repayment mortgage where the interest rate on the loan is fixed for a set amount of time, normally a period of between one and ten years. The interest rate does not vary with changes to the base rate resulting in the monthly mortgage payment remaining the same for the duration of the fixed period. The lender normally imposes early redemption penalties within the first few years.

ISA (INDIVIDUAL SAVINGS ACCOUNT) – A means by which investors can save (in a cash ISA) and invest (in a stocks and shares ISA) without paying any tax on the proceeds. There are limits on the amount that can be invested during any given tax year (see Taxation).

INTEREST ONLY MORTGAGE – Only interest is paid by the borrower and capital remains constant for the term of the loan. The onus is on the borrower to make provision to repay the capital at the end of the term. This is usually achieved through an investment vehicle such as an endowment policy or pension.

LOAN TO VALUE (LTV) – This is the ratio between the size of a mortgage loan sought and the mortgage lender's valuation. On a loan of £55,000, for example, on a property valued at £100,000 the loan to value is 55 per cent. This means that there is sufficient equity in the property for the lender to be reassured that if interest or capital repayments were stopped, it could sell the property and recoup the money owed. Fewer options are available to borrowers requiring high LTV.

LONDON INTERBANK OFFERED RATE (LIBOR) – Is the interest rate that London banks charge when lending to one another on the wholesale money market. LIBOR is set by supply and demand of money as banks lend to each other in order to balance their books on a daily basis.

MIG (MORTGAGE INDEMNITY GUARANTEE) – An insurance for the lender paid by the borrower on high LTV mortgages (typically more than 90 per cent). It is a policy designed to protect the lender against loss in the event of the borrower defaulting or ceasing to repay a mortgage and is usually paid as a one-off premium or can be added to the value of the loan. It offers no protection to the borrower. Not all lenders charge MIG premiums.

OVERDRAFT – An 'authorised' overdraft is an arrangement made between customer and bank allowing the balance of the customer's account to go below zero; interest is normally charged at an agreed rate and sometimes an arrangement fee is charged. If the negative balance exceeds the agreed terms or a prior arrangement for an overdraft facility has not been made (an 'unauthorised' overdraft) then additional penalty fees may be charged and higher interest rates may apply. Interest-free overdrafts are available for customers in certain circumstances, such as full-time higher education students and recent graduates.

PERSONAL PENSION PLAN (PPP) – Designed for the self-employed or those in non-pensionable employment. Contributions made to a PPP are exempt from tax and the retirement age may be selected at any time from age 50 to 75. Up to 25 per cent of the pension fund may be taken as a tax-free cash sum on retirement.

PHISHING – A fraudulent attempt to obtain bank account details and security codes through an email. The email purports to come from a *bona fide* bank or building society and attempts to steer the recipient, usually under the pretext that the banking institution is updating its security arrangements, to a website which requests personal details.

PIN (PERSONAL IDENTIFICATION NUMBER) – A PIN is issued alongside a cash card to allow the user to access a bank account via an ATM. PINs are also issued with smart, credit and debit cards and, since 14 February 2006, have been compulsory as a security measure in the majority of purchases.

PORTABLE MORTGAGE – A mortgage product that can be transferred to a different property in the event of a house move. Preferable where early redemption penalties are charged.

REDEMPTION PENALTY – A charge levied for paying off a loan, debt balance or mortgage before a date agreed with the lender.

REPAYMENT MORTGAGE – In contrast to the interest only mortgage, the monthly repayment includes an element of the capital sum borrowed in addition to the interest charged.

SHARE – A share is a divided-up unit of the value of a company. If a company is worth £100m, and there are 50 million shares in issue, then each share is worth £2 (usually listed as pence). As the overall value of the company fluctuates so does the share price.

STANDING ORDER – An instruction made by the customer to their bank, which allows the transfer of a set amount to a payee at regular intervals.

UNIT TRUST – A 'pooled' fund of assets, usually shares, owned by a number of individuals. Managed by professional, authorised fund-management groups, unit trusts have traditionally delivered better returns than average cash deposits, but do rise and fall in value as their underlying investment varies in value.

VARIABLE RATE MORTGAGE – Repayment mortgages where the interest rate set by the lender increases or decreases in relation to the base interest rate which can result in fluctuating monthly repayments.

WITH-PROFITS – Usually applies to pensions, endowments, savings schemes or bonds. The intention is to smooth out the rises and falls in the stock market for the benefit of the investor. Actuaries working for the insurance company, or fund managers, hold back some profits in good years in order to make up the difference in years when shares perform badly.

# BANK FAMILY TREE

Includes the major retail banks operating in the UK as at
April 2015. Financial results for these banks are given on
page 485. Building societies are only included in
instances where they demutualised to become a bank.

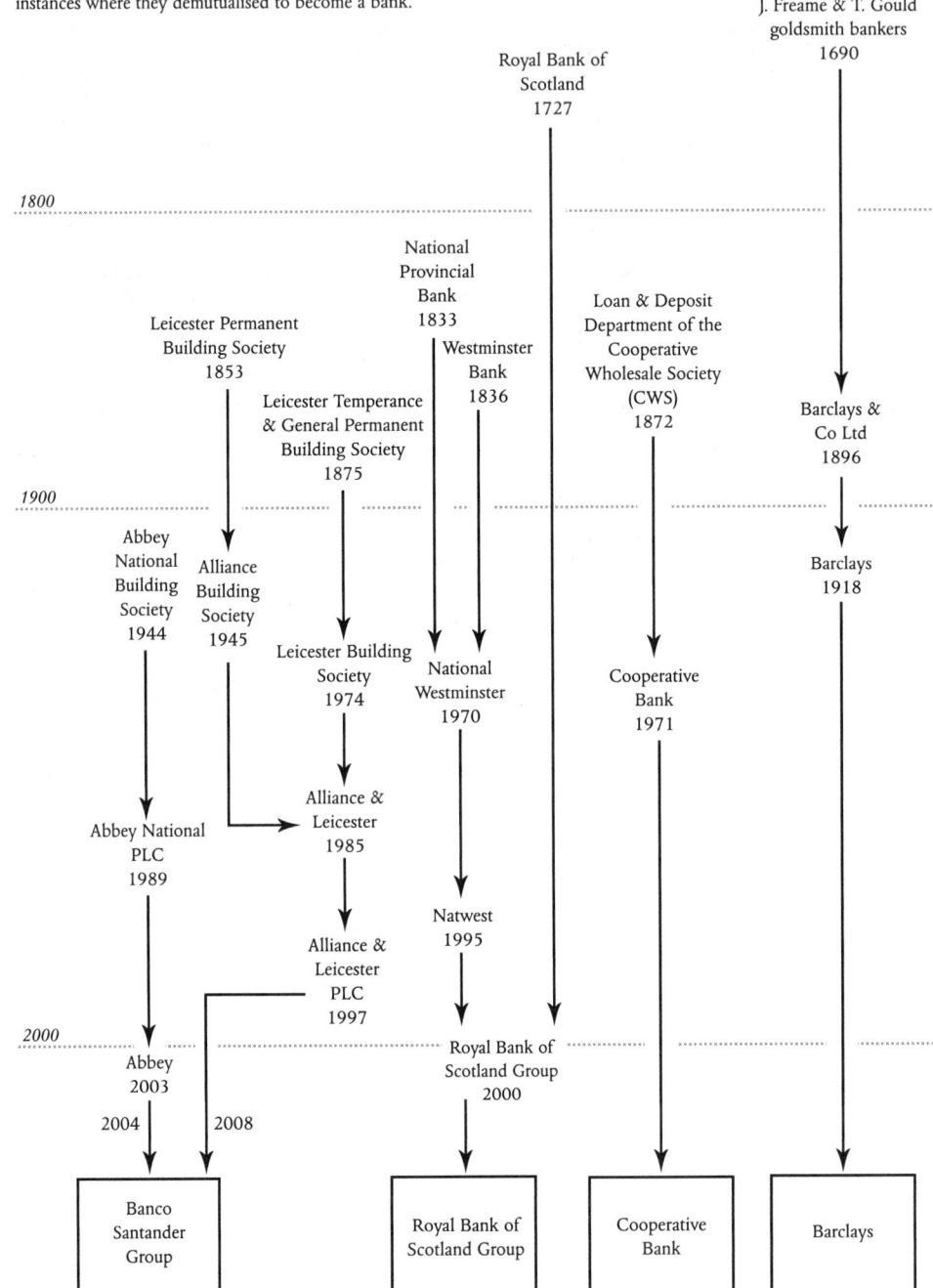

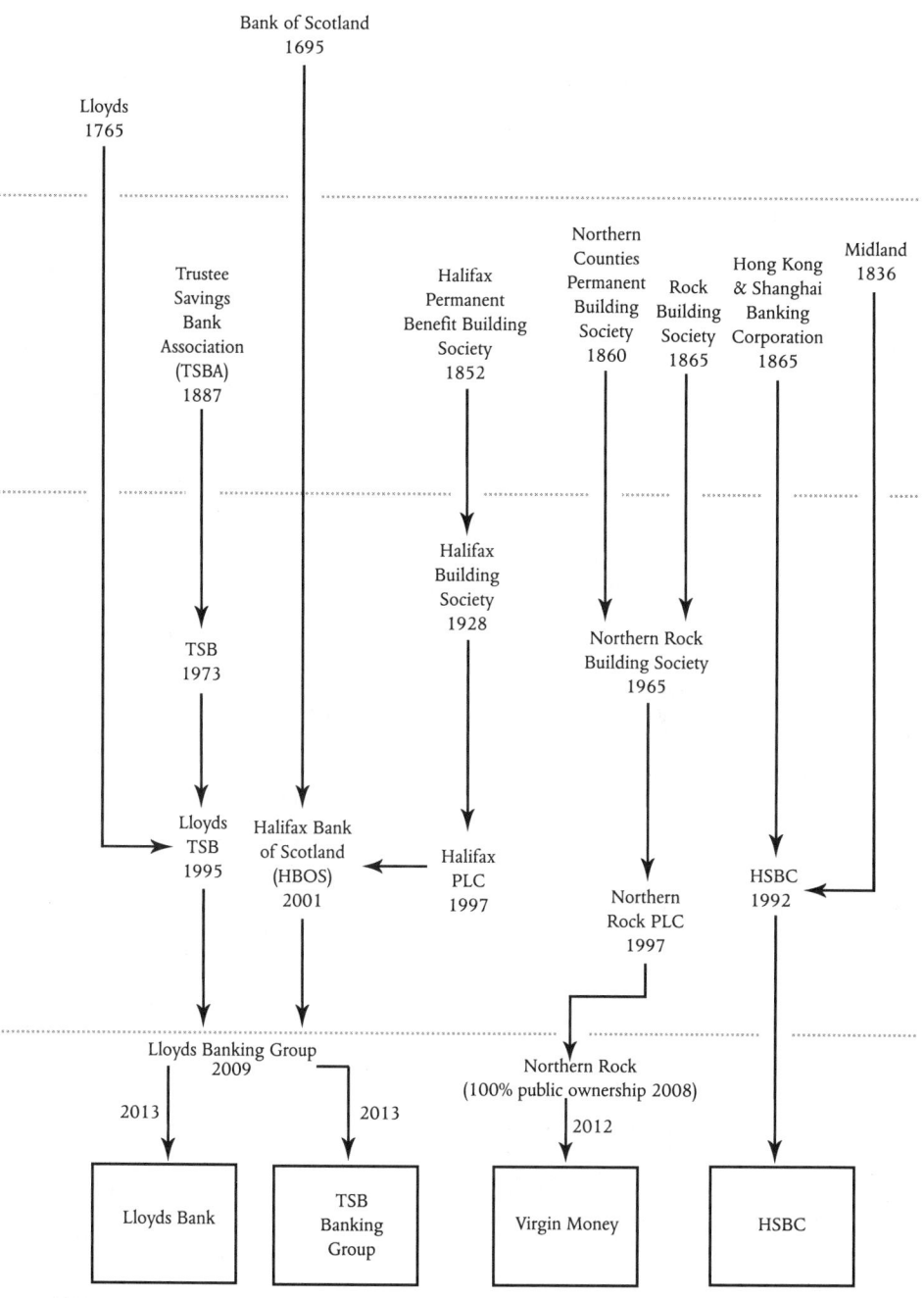

# FINANCIAL SERVICES REGULATION

Under the Financial Services and Markets Act 2000, as amended by the Financial Services Act (2012), the Financial Conduct Authority and the Prudential Regulation Authority are responsible for financial regulation in the UK.

## FINANCIAL CONDUCT AUTHORITY

The Financial Conduct Authority (FCA) is responsible for supervising the conduct of over 50,000 financial firms and for regulating the prudential standards of those firms not regulated by the Prudential Regulation authority. The FCA has three statutory objectives:

• to secure an appropriate degree of protection for consumers
• to protect and enhance the integrity of the UK financial system
• to promote effective market competition in the interests of consumers

ACCOUNTABILITY AND FUNDING
The FCA is accountable to HM Treasury and therefore to parliament, but is operationally independent of the government and is funded entirely by the firms which it regulates. The FCA is governed by a board appointed by HM Treasury, but day-to-day decisions and staff management are the responsibility of the executive committee.

The FCA's annual budget for 2015–16 is £479m.

THE FINANCIAL SERVICES REGISTER
The Financial Services Register lists financial services firms and individuals in the UK who are authorised by the FCA to do business and specifies which activity each firm or individual is regulated to undertake and what products or services each is approved to provide.

FINANCIAL CONDUCT AUTHORITY, 25 The North
Colonnade, Canary Wharf, London E14 5HS T 020-7066 1000
W www.fca.org.uk
*Chair,* John Griffith-Jones
*Chief Executive,* Martin Wheatley

## PRUDENTIAL REGULATION AUTHORITY

The Prudential Regulation Authority (PRA), part of the Bank of England, works alongside the FCA and is responsible for the prudential regulation and supervision of banks, building societies, credit unions, insurers and major investment firms. In total the PRA regulates around 1,700 financial firms.

The PRA has two statutory objectives: to promote safety and soundness of these firms and, specifically for insurers, to contribute to the securing of an appropriate degree of protection for policyholders.

The PRA's board includes the Governor of the Bank of England, the Deputy Governor for Financial Stability, the Deputy Governor for Prudential Regulation (also the chief executive of the PRA) and the chief executive of the FCA and is accountable to parliament.

PRUDENTIAL REGULATION AUTHORITY, 20 Moorgate,
London EC2R 6DA T 020-7601 4444
E enquiries@bankofengland.co.uk
W www.bankofengland.co.uk/pra
*Chief Executive,* Andrew Bailey

## COMPENSATION

Created under the Financial Services and Markets Act (2000), the Financial Services Compensation Scheme (FSCS) is the UK's statutory fund of last resort for customers of authorised financial services firms. It provides compensation if a firm authorised by the FCA or PRA is unable, or likely to be unable, to pay claims against it. In general this is when a firm has stopped trading and has insufficient assets to meet claims, or is in insolvency. The FSCS covers deposits, insurance policies, insurance broking, investment business and mortgage advice and arranging. The FSCS is independent of the UK regulators (FCA and PRA), separate staff and premises. However, the FCA and PRA appoint the directors. The chair's appointment (and removal) is subject to Treasury approval. The FSCS is funded by levies on authorised firms.

The Pension Protection Fund (PPF) is a statutory fund established under the Pensions Act 2004 and became operational on 6 April 2005. The fund was set up to pay compensation to members of eligible defined benefit pension schemes, where there is a qualifying insolvency event in relation to the employer and where there are insufficient assets in the pension scheme to cover PPF levels of compensation. Compulsory annual levies are charged on all eligible schemes to help fund the PPF, in addition to investment of PPF assets. The PPF is also responsible for the Fraud Compensation Fund – a fund that will provide compensation to occupational pension schemes that suffer a loss attributable to dishonesty.

FINANCIAL SERVICES COMPENSATION SCHEME,
10th Floor, Beaufort House, 15 St Botolph Street,
London EC3A 7QU T 020-7741 4100/0800-678 1100
W www.fscs.org.uk
*Chair,* Lawrence Churchill, CBE
*Chief Executive,* Mark Neale
PENSION PROTECTION FUND, Renaissance,
12 Dingwall Road, Croydon CR0 2NA T 0845-600 2541
E information@ppf.gsi.gov.uk
W www.pensionprotectionfund.org.uk
*Chair,* Lady Judge, CBE
*Chief Executive,* Alan Rubenstein

## DESIGNATED PROFESSIONAL BODIES

Professional firms are exempt from requiring direct regulation by the FCA if they carry out only certain restricted activities that arise out of, or are complementary to, the provision of professional services, such as arranging the sale of shares on the instructions of executors or trustees, or providing services to small, private companies. These firms are, however, supervised by designated professional bodies (DPBs). There are a number of safeguards to protect consumers dealing with firms that do not require direct regulation. These arrangements include:

• the FCA's power to ban a specific firm from taking advantage of the exemption and to restrict the regulated activities permitted to the firms
• rules which require professional firms to ensure that their clients are aware that they are not authorised persons

• a requirement for the Dpbs to supervise and regulate the firms and inform the FCA on how the professional firms carry on their regulated activities

*See* Professional Education section for contact details of the following Dpbs:

*Association of Chartered Certified Accountants*
*Council for Licensed Conveyancers*
*Institute of Actuaries*
*Institute of Chartered Accountants in England and Wales*
*Institute of Chartered Accountants in Ireland*
*Institute of Chartered Accountants of Scotland*
*Law Society of England and Wales*
*Law Society of Northern Ireland*
*Law Society of Scotland*
*Royal Institution of Chartered Surveyors*

## RECOGNISED INVESTMENT EXCHANGES

The FCA currently supervises eight recognised investment exchanges (RIEs) in the UK; recognition confers an exemption from the need to be authorised to carry out regulated activities in the UK. The RIEs are organised markets on which member firms can trade investments such as equities and derivatives. The RIEs are listed with their year of recognition in parentheses:

**BATS TRADING (2013)**, 6th Floor 10 Lower Street, London EC3R 6AF **T** 020-7012 8900 **W** www.batstrading.co.uk
**CME EUROPE LTD (2014)**, 1 New Change, London EC4M 9AF **T** 020-3379 3700 **W** www.cmegroup.com/europe
**EURONEXT LONDON LTD (2014)**, Juxon House, 100 St. Paul's Churchyard, London EC4M 8BU **T** 020-7280 6850 **W** www.euronext.com
**ICAP SECURITIES & DERIVATIVES EXCHANGE LTD (2007)**, 2 Broadgate, London EC2M 7UR **T** 020-7050 7650 **W** www.isdx.com
**ICE FUTURES EUROPE (2015)**, 5th Floor Milton Gate, 60 Chiswell Street, London EC1Y 4SA **T** 020-7065 7700 **W** www.theice.com
**LIFFE ADMINISTRATION AND MANAGEMENT (2001)**, Milton Gate, 60 Chiswell Street, London EC1Y 4SA **T** 020-7065 7700 **W** www.intercontinentalexchange.com
**LONDON METAL EXCHANGE (2001)**, 56 Leadenhall Street, London EC3A 2BJ **T** 020-7264 5555 **W** www.lme.co.uk
**LONDON STOCK EXCHANGE (2001)**, 10 Paternoster Square, London EC4M 7LS **T** 020-7797 1000 **W** www.londonstockexchange.com

## RECOGNISED CLEARING HOUSES

The Bank of England is responsible for recognising and supervising recognised clearing houses (RCHs), which organise the settlement of transactions on recognised investment exchanges. There are currently five RCHs in the UK:

**CME CLEARING EUROPE (2010)**, 1 New Change, London EC4M 9AF **T** 020-3379 3700 **W** www.cmeclearingeurope.co.uk
**EUROCLEAR UK AND IRELAND (2001)**, 33 Cannon Street, London EC4M 5SB **T** 020-7849 0000 **W** www.euroclear.com/en.html
**ICE CLEAR EUROPE (2008)**, 5th Floor, Milton Gate, 60 Chiswell Street, London EC1Y 4SA **T** 020-7065 7600 **W** www.theice.com/clear_europe

**LCH (LONDON CLEARING HOUSE) CLEARNET (2001)**, Aldgate House, 33 Aldgate High Street, London EC3N 1EA **T** 020-7426 7000 **W** www.lchclearnet.com
**LME (LONDON METAL EXCHANGE) CLEAR (2014)**, 56 Leadenhall Street, London EC3A 2BJ **T** 020-7264 5555 **W** www.lme.co.uk

## OMBUDSMAN SCHEMES

The Financial Ombudsman Service was set up by the Financial Services and Markets Act 2000 to provide consumers with a free, independent service for resolving disputes with authorised financial firms. The Financial Ombudsman Service can consider complaints about most financial matters including: banking; credit cards and store cards; financial advice; hire purchase and pawnbroking; insurance; loans and credit; money transfer; mortgages; payday lending and debt collecting; payment protection insurance; pensions; savings and investments; stocks, shares, unit trusts and bonds.

Complainants must first complain to the firm involved. They do not have to accept the ombudsman's decision and are free to go to court if they wish, but if a decision is accepted, it is binding for both the complainant and the firm.

The Pensions Ombudsman can investigate and decide complaints and disputes regarding the way occupational and personal pension schemes are administered and managed. The Pensions Ombudsman is also the Ombudsman for the Pension Protection Fund (PPF) and the Financial Assistance Scheme (which offers help to those who were a member of an under-funded defined benefit pension scheme that started to wind-up in specific financial circumstances between 1 January 1997 and 5 April 2005).

**FINANCIAL OMBUDSMAN SERVICE**, Exchange Tower, London E14 9SR **Helpline** 0800-023 4567 **T** 020-7964 1000 **E** complaint.info@financial-ombudsman.org.uk **W** www.financial-ombudsman.org.uk
*Chief Executive and Chief Ombudsman,* Caroline Wayman
**PENSIONS OMBUDSMAN**, 11 Belgrave Road, London SW1V 1RB **T** 020-7630 2200 **E** enquiries@pensions-ombudsman.org.uk **W** www.pensions-ombudsman.org.uk
*Pensions Ombudsman,* Tony King
*Deputy Pensions Ombudsman,* Jane Irvine

## PANEL ON TAKEOVERS AND MERGERS

The Panel on Takeovers and Mergers is an independent body, established in 1968, whose main functions are to issue and administer the City code and to ensure equality of treatment and opportunity for all shareholders in takeover bids and mergers. The panel's statutory functions are set out in the Companies Act 2006.

The panel comprises up to 35 members drawn from major financial and business institutions. The chair, deputy chair and up to 20 other members are nominated by the panel's own nomination committee. The remaining members are nominated by professional bodies representing the banking, insurance, investment, pension and accountancy industries, the Association for Financial Markets in Europe and the CBI.

**PANEL ON TAKEOVERS AND MERGERS**, 10 Paternoster Square, London EC4M 7DY **T** 020-7382 9026 **E** info@thetakeoverpanel.org.uk **W** www.thetakeoverpanel.org.uk
*Chair,* Sir Gordon Langley

# NATIONAL SAVINGS AND INVESTMENTS

NS&I (National Savings and Investments) is an executive agency of HM Treasury and one of the UK's largest financial providers, with over 25 million customers and over £100bn invested. NS&I offers savings and investment products to personal savers and investors and the money is used to manage the national debt. When people invest in NS&I they are lending money to the government which pays them interest or prizes in return. All products are financially secure because they are guaranteed by HM Treasury.

## TAX-FREE PRODUCTS

### SAVINGS CERTIFICATES

*Index-linked Saving Certificates*
Otherwise known as inflation-beating savings, index-linked saving certificates are fixed rate investments that pay tax-free returns guaranteed to be above inflation. They are sold in limited issues with a minimum and maximum investment.

*Fixed Interest Saving Certificates*
Fixed interest saving certificates are fixed rate investments that pay tax-free returns. They are sold in limited issues with a minimum and maximum investment.

### PREMIUM BONDS
Introduced in 1956, premium bonds enable savers to enter a regular draw for tax-free prizes, while retaining the right to get their money back. A sum equivalent to interest on each bond is put into a prize fund and distributed by monthly prize draws. The prizes are drawn by ERNIE (electronic random number indicator equipment) and are free of all UK income tax and capital gains tax. Two £1m jackpots are drawn each month in addition to other tax-free prizes ranging in value from £25 to £100,000.

Bonds are in units of £1, with a minimum purchase of £100 (£50 if the purchase is by standing order), up to a maximum holding limit of £40,000 per person. Bonds become eligible for prizes once they have been held for one clear calendar month following the month of purchase. Each £1 unit can win only one prize per draw, but it will be awarded the highest for which it is drawn. Bonds remain eligible for prizes until they are repaid.

The scheme offers a facility to reinvest prize wins automatically. Upon completion of an automatic prize reinvestment mandate, holders receive new bonds which are immediately eligible for future prize draws. Bonds can only be held in the name of an individual and not by organisations.

### CHILDREN'S BONDS
Children's bonus bonds were introduced in 1991. In September 2012 changes were made to the product; including a change in name to Children's Bonds, which reflects the way interest is paid. Any amount between £25 and £3,000 can be invested and interest is added at a fixed rate each year for five years. The minimum holding is £25 and the maximum holding is £3,000 per child per issue. They can be bought by parents, guardians and grandparents (including great grandparents) for any child under 16, but the investment must be managed by a parent or guardian. All returns are totally exempt from UK income tax.

### INDIVIDUAL SAVINGS ACCOUNTS
Since April 1999 NS&I has offered cash individual savings accounts (ISAs). Its Direct ISA, launched in April 2006, can be opened and managed online and by telephone with a minimum investment of £1 and a maximum investment of £15,240 in the 2015–16 tax year. Interest for the Direct ISA is calculated daily and is free of tax.

## OTHER PRODUCTS

### GUARANTEED EQUITY BONDS
Guaranteed equity bonds are five-year investments where the returns are linked to the performance of the FTSE-100 index with a guarantee that the original capital invested will be returned even if the FTSE-100 index falls over the five years. They are sold in limited issues with a minimum investment of £1,000 and a maximum of £1m. The returns are subject to income tax on maturity, unless they are held in a self-invested pension plan (SIPP).

### SAVINGS AND INVESTMENT ACCOUNTS
The direct saver account was launched in March 2010. Customers are able to invest between £1 and £2m per person. The account can be managed online or by telephone. Interest is paid without deduction of tax at source.

The investment account is a postal-only account which pays tiered rates of interest. It can be opened with a minimum balance of £20 and has a maximum limit of £1m. The interest is paid without deduction of tax at source.

### INCOME BONDS
NS&I income bonds were introduced in 1982. They are suitable for those who want to receive regular monthly payments of interest while preserving the full cash value of their capital. The minimum holding for each investment is £500 and the maximum £1m per person. A variable rate of interest is calculated on a day-to-day basis and paid monthly. Interest is taxable but is paid without deduction of tax at source.

### GUARANTEED INCOME BONDS
Guaranteed income bonds were introduced in February 2008 and changes were made to the product in September 2012. They are designed for those who want to receive regular monthly payments of interest while preserving the full cash value of their capital. There is a minimum and maximum holding per person, per issue. Joint investors can combine their allowance to invest up to double the maximum individual holding per issue. A fixed rate of interest is calculated on a day-to-day basis and paid monthly. Interest is taxable and tax is deducted at source. They are sold in limited issues.

### GUARANTEED GROWTH BONDS
Guaranteed growth bonds were introduced in February 2008 and changes were made to the product in September 2012. As for Guaranteed income bonds, there is a minimum and maximum holding per person, per issue and joint investors can combine their allowance to invest up to double the maximum individual holding per issue. A fixed rate of interest is calculated on a day-to-day basis and is paid annually on the anniversary of the date of investment. Interest is taxable and tax is deducted at source. They are sold in limited issues.

### FURTHER INFORMATION
Further information regarding products and their current availability can be obtained online (W www.nsandi.com) and by telephone (T 0500-007007).

# THE NATIONAL DEBT

## HISTORY

The early 1700s saw the meteoric rise of the banking and financial markets in Great Britain, with the emerging stock market revolving around government funds. The ability to raise money by means of creating debt through the issue of bills and bonds heralded the beginning of the national debt.

The war years of 1914–18 saw an increase in the national debt from £650m at the start of the war to £7,500m by 1919. The Treasury developed new expertise in foreign exchange, currency, credit and price control in order to manage the post-war economy. The slump of the 1930s necessitated the restructuring of the UK economy following the Second World War (the national debt stood at £21bn by its end) and the emphasis was placed on economic planning and financial relations.

The relatively high period of inflation in the 1970s and 1980s led to the rise of the national debt in nominal terms from £36bn in 1972 to £197bn in 1987 and then to £419bn in March 1998. Although in nominal terms the national debt has risen sharply in recent years, as a percentage of GDP it has decreased dramatically since the end of the Second World War, when it stood at 250 per cent of GDP (for current figures, *see* table below).

## THE UK DEBT MANAGEMENT OFFICE

The decision in 1997 to transfer monetary policy to the Bank of England, while the Treasury retained control of fiscal policy, led to the creation of the UK Debt Management Office (DMO) as an executive agency of HM Treasury in April 1998. Initially the DMO was responsible only for the management of government marketable debt and for issuing gilts. In April 2000 responsibility for exchequer cash management and for issuing Treasury bills (short-dated securities with maturities of less than one year) was transferred from the Bank of England to the DMO. The national debt also includes the (non-marketable) liabilities of National Savings and Investments and other public sector and foreign currency debt.

In 2002 the operations of the long-standing statutory functions of the Public Works Loan Board, which lends capital to local authorities, and the Commissioners for the Reduction of the National Debt, which manages the investment portfolios of certain public funds, were integrated within the DMO (*see also* Government Departments).

## UK PUBLIC SECTOR NET DEBT

|                    | £ billion | per cent of GDP |
|--------------------|-----------|-----------------|
| 2013–14 (outturn)  | 1,402     | 79.1            |
| 2014–15 (forecast) | 1,479     | 80.4            |
| 2015–16 (forecast) | 1,533     | 80.2            |

*Source:* HM Treasury: *Budget 2015* (Crown copyright)

# THE LONDON STOCK EXCHANGE

The London Stock Exchange Group (LSEG) serves the needs of companies by providing facilities for raising capital. It also operates marketplaces for members to trade financial instruments, including equities, bonds and derivatives, on behalf of investors and institutions such as pension funds and insurers.

LSEG's key subsidiary companies are the London Stock Exchange, Borsa Italiana, MTS (an electronic platform for the trading of European government and corporate bonds), Turquoise (a trading platform for European equities) and FTSE (a global index provider).

Headquartered in London, with significant operations in Italy, France, North America and Sri Lanka, the group employs around 2,800 people.

## HISTORY

The London Stock Exchange is one of the world's oldest stock exchanges, dating back more than 300 years to its origins in the coffee houses of 17th-century London. It was formally established as a membership organisation in 1801.

### MAJOR DEVELOPMENTS

'BIG BANG'
In 1986 a package of reforms which are now known as 'Big Bang' transformed the London Stock Exchange and the City of London, liberalising the way in which banks and stock-broking firms operated and facilitating greater foreign investment. The London Stock Exchange ceased granting voting rights to individual members and became a private company. The 'Big Bang' also saw the start of a move towards fully electronic trading and the closure of the trading floor.

INTRODUCTION OF SETS
In October 1997, the Exchange introduced SETS, its electronic order book. The system enhanced the efficiency and transparency of trading on the Exchange, allowing trades to be executed automatically and anonymously rather than negotiated by telephone.

DEMUTUALISATION AND LISTING
The London Stock Exchange demutualised in 2000 and listed on its own main market in 2001.

MERGER WITH BORSA ITALIANA
In October 2007 the London Stock Exchange merged with the Italian stock exchange, Borsa Italiana, creating London Stock Exchange Group (LSEG).

DIVERSIFICATION
Since 2009 LSEG has diversified its business beyond the listing and trading of UK and Italian equities:

- In 2009 LSEG purchased Sri Lankan technology company MillenniumIT which provides technology to stock exchanges, brokerages and regulators around the world. It also supplies the trading technology to LSEG's own markets
- In 2010 LSEG acquired a majority stake in Turquoise, a platform facilitating the trading of stocks listed in 18 European countries and the USA
- In 2011 LSEG became the owner of FTSE, the international business which creates and manages over 200,000 financial indices
- In 2013 LSEG purchased a majority stake in LCH (London Clearing House) Clearnet (*see also* Financial Services Regulation, Recognised Clearing Houses)

## UK EQUITY MARKETS

LSEG offers a range of listing options for companies, according to their size, history and requirements:

- The Main Market has the highest standards of regulation and disclosure obligations and is overseen by the UK Listing Authority (UKLA), a division of the Financial Conduct Authority (FCA). A Main Market listing enables established companies to raise capital, widen their investor base and have their shares traded alongside global peers. They are also eligible for inclusion in key indices, such as the FTSE 100 and the FTSE 250
- The Alternative Investment Market (AIM), established in June 1995, is specially designed to meet the needs of small and growing companies. It enables them to raise capital and broaden their investor base in a more flexible regulatory environment, while still being traded on an internationally recognised market. AIM companies retain an experienced Nominated Adviser (or 'Nomad') firm, which is responsible for ensuring the company's suitability for the market
- The Professional Securities Market (PSM), established in July 2005, allows companies to target professional investors only, on a market that offers greater flexibility in accounting standards
- The Specialist Fund Market (SFM), established in November 2007, is a market for highly specialised investment entities, such as hedge funds or private equity funds, that wish to target institutional investors only

As at April 2015 there were 5,191 companies listed on LSEG's primary markets, with a combined market value of £1,891,386m: 1,557 on the Main Market (1,218 on the UK main market and 339 on the international main market), 3,591 on the AIM, 15 on the PSM and 28 entities on the SFM.

LONDON STOCK EXCHANGE, 10 Paternoster Square, London EC4M 7LS **T** 020-7797 1000
**W** www.lseg.com
*Chair*, Chris Gibson-Smith, PHD
*Chief Executive*, Xavier Rolet

# ECONOMIC STATISTICS

## THE BUDGET (SUMMER 2015)

### GOVERNMENT EXPENDITURE

DEPARTMENTAL EXPENDITURE LIMITS £ billion

|  | Plans 2015–16 |
|---|---|
| *Resource DEL* |  |
| Education | 53.5 |
| NHS (Health) | 111.9 |
| Transport | 2.3 |
| Business, Innovation and Skills | 13.1 |
| CLG Communities | 2.5 |
| CLG Local Government | 10.6 |
| Home Office | 10.2 |
| Justice | 6.3 |
| Law Officers' Departments | 0.5 |
| Defence | 28.1 |
| Foreign and Commonwealth Office | 1.8 |
| International Development | 7.4 |
| Energy and Climate Change | 1.4 |
| Environment, Food and Rural Affairs | 1.6 |
| Culture, Media and Sport | 1.1 |
| Work and Pensions | 6.3 |
| Scotland | 25.5 |
| Wales | 12.9 |
| Northern Ireland | 9.6 |
| Chancellor's departments | 3.5 |
| Cabinet Office | 2.5 |
| Small and Independent bodies | 1.6 |
| Reserve | 2.0 |
| Special reserve | 0.2 |
| Adjustment for budget exchange | (0.5) |
| TOTAL RESOURCE DEL | 316.1 |
| OBR Allowance for shortfall | (1.0) |
| *OBR Resource DEL* | 315.1 |
| *Capital DEL* |  |
| Education | 4.7 |
| NHS (Health) | 4.6 |
| Transport | 6.1 |
| Business, Innovation and Skills | 3.8 |
| CLG Communities | 5.3 |
| CLG Local Government | 0.0 |
| Home Office | 0.4 |
| Justice | 0.3 |
| Law Officers' Departments | 0.0 |
| Defence | 6.8 |
| Foreign and Commonwealth Office | 0.1 |
| International Development | 2.6 |
| Energy and Climate Change | 2.5 |
| Environment, Food and Rural Affairs | 0.5 |
| Culture, Media and Sport | 0.4 |
| Work and Pensions | 0.2 |
| Scotland | 3.1 |
| Wales | 1.5 |
| Northern Ireland | 1.1 |
| Chancellor's departments | 0.3 |
| Cabinet Office | 0.4 |
| Small and Independent bodies | 0.1 |
| Reserve | 0.9 |
| Special reserve | 0.1 |
| Adjustment for budget exchange | (1.6) |
| TOTAL CAPITAL DEL | 44.4 |
| OBR Allowance for shortfall | (2.0) |
| *OBR Capital DEL* | 42.4 |
| TOTAL DEL | 360.5 |

* OBR = Office for Budget Responsibility

Source: HM Treasury – *Summer Budget 2015* (Crown copyright)

### TOTAL MANAGED EXPENDITURE £ billion

|  | Plans 2015–16 | Plans 2016–17 | Plans 2017–18 |
|---|---|---|---|
| *Current Expenditure* |  |  |  |
| Resource Annually Managed Expenditure (AME) | 337.9 | 344.3 | 358.6 |
| Resource DEL | 315.1 | – | – |
| Ring-fenced depreciation | 22.3 | – | – |
| Resource DEL, including depreciation | – | 341.4 | 339.7 |
| *Capital Expenditure* |  |  |  |
| Capital AME | 24.7 | 26.0 | 26.3 |
| Capital DEL | 42.4 | 42.6 | 43.3 |
| TOTAL MANAGED EXPENDITURE | 742.3 | 754.3 | 768.0 |
| *Total Managed Expenditure (% GDP)* | 39.6% | 38.7% | 37.8% |

Source: HM Treasury – *Summer Budget 2015* (Crown copyright)

### GOVERNMENT RECEIPTS £ billion

|  | Outturn 2014–15 | Forecast 2015–16 | Forecast 2016–17 |
|---|---|---|---|
| Income tax (gross of tax credits)[1] | 163.7 | 170.2 | 184.8 |
| Pay as you earn | 140.0 | 145.2 | 155.1 |
| Self assessment | 23.6 | 25.3 | 31.3 |
| National insurance contributions (NICs) | 110.3 | 114.8 | 125.8 |
| Value added tax | 111.3 | 115.9 | 119.2 |
| Corporation tax | 42.9 | 43.1 | 43.4 |
| Petroleum revenue tax | 0.1 | 0.0 | (0.1) |
| Fuel duties | 27.2 | 27.1 | 27.3 |
| Business rates | 27.3 | 28.0 | 29.0 |
| Council tax | 27.9 | 28.4 | 29.0 |
| VAT refunds | 13.7 | 13.6 | 13.8 |
| Capital gains tax | 5.6 | 6.4 | 7.4 |
| Inheritance tax | 3.8 | 4.2 | 4.6 |
| Stamp duty land tax | 10.9 | 11.5 | 12.6 |
| Stamp taxes on shares | 2.9 | 3.2 | 3.3 |
| Tobacco duties | 9.3 | 9.1 | 9.0 |
| Spirits duties | 3.0 | 3.2 | 3.2 |
| Wine duties | 3.8 | 4.0 | 4.1 |
| Beer and cider duties | 3.6 | 3.5 | 3.4 |
| Air passenger duty | 3.2 | 3.1 | 3.2 |
| Insurance premium tax | 3.0 | 3.5 | 4.5 |
| Climate change levy | 1.6 | 2.3 | 2.4 |
| Other HMRC taxes[2] | 6.6 | 6.9 | 6.9 |
| Vehicle excise duties | 5.9 | 5.6 | 5.5 |
| Bank levy | 2.8 | 3.7 | 3.1 |
| Bank surcharge | 0.0 | 0.0 | 0.9 |
| Licence fee receipts | 3.1 | 3.1 | 3.2 |
| Enviromental levies | 3.6 | 6.0 | 7.3 |
| EU ETS* Auction recipts | 0.4 | 0.3 | 0.3 |
| Scottish taxes | 0.0 | 0.6 | 0.7 |
| Diverted profits tax | 0.0 | 0.0 | 0.3 |
| Other taxes | 6.2 | 7.1 | 7.1 |
| *Total Taxes* | 603.6 | 628.9 | 665.2 |

*Less* own resources

| | | | |
|---|---|---|---|
| contribution to EU | (3.0) | (3.1) | (3.2) |
| Interest and dividends | 5.8 | 5.8 | 6.6 |
| Gross operating surplus | 36.9 | 39.2 | 41.1 |
| Other receipts | 3.0 | 2.0 | 1.5 |
| CURRENT RECEIPTS | 646.4 | 672.8 | 711.2 |
| UK oil and gas revenues[3] | 2.2 | 0.7 | 0.5 |

\* ETS = Emissions Trading System

[1] Income tax includes PAYE and Self Assessment receipts, and also includes tax on savings income and other minor income tax components

[2] Consists of landfill tax (excluding Scotland from 2015–16), aggregates levy, betting and gaming duties, and customs duties and levies

[3] Consists of offshore corporation tax and petroleum revenue tax

*Source:* HM Treasury – *Summer Budget 2015* (Crown copyright)

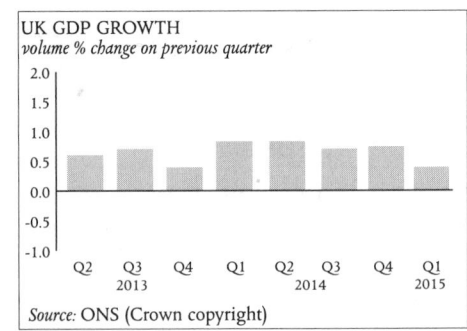

**UK GDP GROWTH**
*volume % change on previous quarter*

*Source:* ONS (Crown copyright)

# TRADE

### TRADE IN GOODS £ million

| | Exports | Imports | Balance |
|---|---|---|---|
| 2008 | 251,565 | 345,826 | (94,261) |
| 2009 | 227,727 | 310,660 | (82,933) |
| 2010 | 265,243 | 363,828 | (98,585) |
| 2011 | 298,421 | 398,513 | (100,092) |
| 2012 | 300,457 | 409,157 | (108,700) |
| 2013 | 304,756 | 412,646 | (107,890) |
| 2014 | 292,867 | 412,472 | (119,605) |

*Source:* ONS (Crown copyright)

### BALANCE OF PAYMENTS, 2014

| Current Account | £ million |
|---|---|
| Trade in goods and services | |
|   Trade in goods | (119,605) |
|   Trade in services | 85,863 |
| *Total trade in goods and services* | (33,742) |
| Income | |
|   Compensation of employees | (440) |
|   Investment income | (37,747) |
|   Other | (567) |
| *Total income* | (38,754) |
| *Total secondary income* | (25,424) |
| TOTAL (CURRENT BALANCE) | (97,920) |

*Source:* ONS (Crown copyright)

# UK EMPLOYMENT

### DISTRIBUTION OF THE WORKFORCE

| | Mar 2014 | Mar 2015 |
|---|---|---|
| Workforce jobs | 33,051,000 | 33,673,000 |
| HM forces | 167,000 | 161,000 |
| Self-employment jobs | 4,529,000 | 4,370,000 |
| Employees jobs | 28,334,000 | 29,124,000 |
| Government-supported trainees | 21,000 | 19,000 |

*Source:* ONS – *Labour Market Statistics 2015* (Crown copyright)

### EMPLOYED AND UNEMPLOYED BY GENDER
*thousands*

| | Apr–Jun 2014 | | Apr–Jun 2015 | |
|---|---|---|---|---|
| | *Male* | *Female* | *Male* | *Female* |
| EMPLOYED | | | | |
| All aged 16+ | 16,326 | 14,355 | 16,499 | 14,535 |
| UNEMPLOYED | | | | |
| All aged 16+ | 2,074 | 930 | 1,852 | 838 |

*Source:* ONS – *Labour Market Statistics 2015* (Crown copyright)

### DURATION OF UNEMPLOYMENT, APR–JUN 2015

| | |
|---|---|
| All unemployed | 1,852,000 |
|   Less than 6 months | 971,000 |
|   6 months–1 year | 305,000 |
|   1 year + | 575,000 (31.1% of total) |

*Source:* ONS – *Labour Market Statistics 2015* (Crown copyright)

### MEDIAN EARNINGS, 2014

| | All | Male | Female |
|---|---|---|---|
| Median gross annual earnings\* | 27.2 | 29.4 | 23.9 |
| *(£, thousands)* | | | |
| Median gross weekly earnings *(£)* | 518.0 | 557.08 | 461.90 |
| Median hourly earnings, excluding overtime *(£)* | 13.08 | 13.59 | 12.31 |

\* Full-time

*Source:* ONS (Crown copyright)

### LABOUR STOPPAGES BY DURATION, 2014

| | |
|---|---|
| Under 5 days | 92 |
| 5–10 days | 6 |
| 11–20 days | 0 |
| 21–30 days | 0 |
| 31–50 | 0 |
| 50+ | 0 |
| All stoppages | 98 |

*Source:* ONS (Crown copyright)

### LABOUR DISPUTES BY INDUSTRY, 2014

| Industry Group | Working Days Lost |
|---|---|
| Manufacturing | 7,600 |
| Sewage, waste and water supply | 400 |
| Construction | 2,800 |
| Transport, storage and communication | 24,900 |
| Financial, insurance and administration | 6,500 |
| Public administration and defence | 390,300 |
| Education | 312,800 |
| Human health and social work | 36,300 |
| Arts entertainment | 800 |

*Source:* ONS (Crown copyright)

### TRADE UNIONS

| Year | No. of unions | Total membership |
|---|---|---|
| 2011–12 | 172 | 7,261,210 |
| 2012–13 | 166 | 7,197,415 |
| 2013–14 | 166 | 7,086,116 |
| 2014–15 | 160 | 7,010,527 |

*Source: Annual Report of the Certification Officer 2014–15*

# COST OF LIVING AND INFLATION RATES

The first cost of living index to be calculated took July 1914 as 100 and was based on the pattern of expenditure of working-class families in 1914. The cost of living index was superseded in 1947 by the general index of retail prices (RPI), although the older term is still popularly applied.

The Harmonised Index of Consumer Prices (HICP) was introduced in 1997 to enable comparisons within the European Union using an agreed methodology. In 2003 the National Statistician renamed the HICP the Consumer Prices Index (CPI) to reflect its role as the main target measure of inflation for macroeconomic purposes. In March 2013 CPIH, an additional index which includes owner-occupiers' housing costs, was introduced.

The RPI and indices based on it continue to be published alongside the CPI. Private-sector pensions and index-linked gilts continue to be calculated with reference to RPI or its derivatives.

## CPI AND RPI

The CPI and RPI measure the changes month by month in the average level of prices of goods and services purchased by households in the UK. The indices are compiled using a selection of around 700 goods and services, and the prices charged for these items are collected at regular intervals at about 140 locations throughout the country. The Office for National Statistics (ONS) reviews the components of the indices once a year to reflect changes in consumer preferences and the establishment of new products. The table below shows changes made by the ONS to the CPI shopping basket' in 2015.

The CPI excludes a number of items that are included in the RPI, mainly related to housing, such as council tax, and a range of owner-occupier housing costs, such as mortgage payments. The CPI covers all private households, whereas the RPI excludes the top 4 per cent by income and pensioner households which derive at least three-quarters of their income from state benefits. The two indices use different methodologies to combine the prices of goods and services, which means that since 1996 the CPI inflation measure is less than the RPI inflation measure.

## INFLATION RATE

The 12-monthly percentage change in the 'all items' index of the RPI or CPI is referred to as the rate of inflation. As the most familiar measure of inflation, the RPI is often referred to as the 'headline rate of inflation'. The CPI is the main measure of inflation for macroeconomic purposes and forms the basis of the government's inflation target, which is currently 2 per cent. The percentage change in prices between any two months/years can be obtained using this formula:

$$\frac{\text{Later date RPI/CPI} - \text{Earlier date RPI/CPI}}{\text{Earlier date RPI/CPI}} \times 100$$

For example, to find the CPI rate of inflation for 2006, using the annual averages for 2005 and 2006:

$$\frac{102.3 - 100.0}{100.0} \times 100 = 2.3$$

From 14 February 2006 the reference year for the CPI was re-based to 2005=100 to improve price comparison clarity across the EU. None of the underlying data, from which the re-referenced series was calculated, was revised. Historical

## CHANGES TO THE 'SHOPPING BASKET' OF GOODS AND SERVICES IN 2015

The table below shows changes to the CPI* basket of goods and services made by the ONS in 2015 in order to reflect changes in consumer preferences and the establishment of new products.

| Goods and services group | Removed items | New items |
| --- | --- | --- |
| Alcoholic beverage | – | bottled speciality beer/ale |
| Audio-visual equipment | – | headphones |
| Cultural services | – | games consoles online subscription services; music streaming subscription services |
| Financial services | foreign exchange commission | |
| Food | frozen pizza; home killed beef (braising steak); oven-ready joint; yoghurt drink | chilled pizza; liver; melon; oven-ready gammon or pork joint; protein powder; sweet potato |
| Gardens & pets | cut flowers (lilies) | – |
| Maintenance of dwelling | white emulsion paint | non-white emulsion paint |
| Operation of personal transport equipment | satellite navigation device | |
| Telephone equipment | – | mobile phone accessory |
| Tobacco | – | electronic cigarette refills/liquid |

* RPI goods and services are grouped together under different classifications

rates of change (such as annual inflation figures), calculated from the re-based rounded index levels, were revised due to the effect of rounding. The CPI rate of inflation figure given in the table below may differ by plus or minus 0.1 percentage points from the figure calculated by the above equation. The change of reference period and revision due to rounding does not apply to the RPI, which remains unchanged.

The RPI and CPI figures are published on either the second or third Tuesday of each month in an indices bulletin on the ONS website (W www.ons.gov.uk).

## PURCHASING POWER OF THE POUND

Changes in the internal purchasing power of the pound may be defined as the 'inverse' of changes in the level of prices:

when prices go up, the amount which can be purchased with a given sum of money goes down. To find the purchasing power of the pound in one month or year, given that it was 100p in a previous month or year, the calculation would be:

$$100p \times \frac{\text{Earlier month/year RPI}}{\text{Later month/year RPI}}$$

Thus, if the purchasing power of the pound is taken to be 100p in 1975, the comparable purchasing power in 2000 would be:

$$100p \times \frac{34.2}{170.3} = 20.1p$$

For longer term comparisons, it has been the practice to use an index which has been constructed by linking together the RPI for the period 1962 to date; an index derived from the consumers' expenditure deflator for the period from 1938 to 1962; and the pre-war 'cost of living' index for the period 1914 to 1938. This long-term index enables the internal purchasing power of the pound to be calculated for any year from 1914 onwards. It should be noted that these figures can only be approximate.

| | Annual average RPI (1987 = 100) | Purchasing power of £ (1998 = 1.00) | Annual average CPI (2005 = 100)* | Annual average CPIH (2005=100) | Rate of inflation (RPI/CPI/CPIH) |
|---|---|---|---|---|---|
| 1914 | 2.8 | 58.18 | | | |
| 1915 | 3.5 | 46.54 | | | |
| 1920 | 7.0 | 23.27 | | | |
| 1925 | 5.0 | 32.58 | | | |
| 1930 | 4.5 | 36.20 | | | |
| 1935 | 4.0 | 40.72 | | | |
| 1938 | 4.4 | 37.02 | | | |
| *There are no official figures for 1939–45* | | | | | |
| 1946 | 7.4 | 22.01 | | | |
| 1950 | 9.0 | 18.10 | | | |
| 1955 | 11.2 | 14.54 | | | |
| 1960 | 12.6 | 12.93 | | | |
| 1965 | 14.8 | 11.00 | | | |
| 1970 | 18.5 | 8.80 | | | |
| 1975 | 34.2 | 4.76 | | | |
| 1980 | 66.8 | 2.44 | 18.0 | | |
| 1985 | 94.6 | 1.72 | 6.1 | | |
| 1990 | 126.1 | 1.29 | 71.5 | | 9.5/7.0 |
| 1995 | 149.1 | 1.09 | 86.0 | | 3.5/2.6 |
| 1998 | 162.9 | 1.00 | 91.1 | | 3.4/1.6 |
| 2000 | 170.3 | 0.96 | 93.1 | | 3.0/0.8 |
| 2005 | 192.0 | 0.85 | 100.0 | 100.0 | 2.8/2.1 |
| 2006 | 198.1 | 0.82 | 102.3 | 102.3 | 3.2/2.3/2.3 |
| 2007 | 206.6 | 0.79 | 104.7 | 104.6 | 4.3/2.3/2.2 |
| 2008 | 214.8 | 0.76 | 108.5 | 108.1 | 4.0/3.6/3.4 |
| 2009 | 213.7 | 0.76 | 110.8 | 110.3 | −0.5/2.2/2.0 |
| 2010 | 223.6 | 0.73 | 114.5 | 113.4 | 4.6/3.3/2.9 |
| 2011 | 235.2 | 0.69 | 119.6 | 118.0 | 5.2/4.5/4.1 |
| 2012 | 242.7 | 0.67 | 123.0 | 121.2 | 3.2/2.8/2.7 |
| 2013 | 250.1 | 0.65 | 126.1 | 124.1 | 3.0/2.6/2.4 |
| 2014 | 256.0 | 0.64 | 128.0 | 125.8 | 2.4/1.5/1.4 |

* In accordance with an EU Commission regulation, all published CPI figures were re-based to 2005=100 with effect from 14 February 2006, replacing the 1996=100 series

# INSURANCE

## AUTHORISATION AND REGULATION OF INSURANCE COMPANIES

Since April 2013, under the Financial Services Act 2012, the prudential supervision of banks and insurers is the responsibility of the Prudential Regulation Authority (PRA), an operationally independent subsidiary of the Bank of England. The Financial Conduct Authority (FCA) is responsible for consumer protection and markets oversight. All life insurers, general insurers, reinsurers, insurance and reinsurance brokers, financial advisers and composite firms are statutorily regulated. See also Financial Services Regulation.

Firms wishing to effect or carry out contracts of insurance must apply for authorisation to do so. The PRA assesses applicant insurers from a prudential perspective, using the same framework that is employed for supervision of existing insurers. The FCA then assesses applicants from a conduct perspective. Although the PRA manages the authorisation process, an insurer will be granted authorisation only where both the FCA and the PRA are satisfied that an insurer meets the relevant requirements.

As at July 2014 there were over 1,300 insurance organisations and friendly societies with authorisation to transact one or more classes of insurance business in the UK. However, the single European insurance market, established in 1994, gave insurers authorised in any other European Union country automatic UK authorisation without further formality. The number of insurers operating within the single European market has been decreasing since 2010 and currently stands at around 5,300.

## COMPLAINTS

Disputes between consumers and financial businesses can be referred to the Financial Ombudsman Service (FOS). Consumers with a complaint about any form of money matter, including insurance, mortgages, savings and credit, must firstly take the matter to the highest level within the provider. If it remains unresolved and it involves an amount below £150,000 (£100,000 for complaints received before 1 January 2012), it can be referred, free of charge, to the FOS, which examines the facts of a complaint and delivers a decision binding on the provider (but not the consumer). Small businesses with a turnover of up to €2m (£1.7m) and fewer than ten employees also have access to the scheme. In 2013, 74 per cent of new complaints about financial serivces companies related to payment protection insurance. Other types of insurance, such as motor, buildings and life insurance, accounted for just 7 per cent of the complaints received. See also Financial Services Regulation.

## ASSOCIATION OF BRITISH INSURERS

Over 90 per cent of the domestic business of UK insurance companies is transacted by the 250 members of the Association of British Insurers (ABI). The ABI is a trade association which protects and promotes the interests of all its insurance company members. Only insurers authorised in the EU are eligible for membership. Brokers, intermediaries, financial advisers and claims handlers may not join the ABI but may have their own trade associations.

**ASSOCIATION OF BRITISH INSURERS (ABI),**
51 Gresham Street, London EC2V 7HQ T 020-7600 3333
W www.abi.org.uk
*Chair,* Paul Evans
*Director-General,* Huw Evans

## BALANCE OF PAYMENTS

The financial services industry contributes 8 per cent to the UK's gross domestic product (GDP). In 2013 insurance sector net exports totalled £10.2bn.

## WORLDWIDE MARKET

The UK insurance industry is the largest in Europe and currently the third largest in the world behind the USA and Japan. China has the fastest growing insurance market and is expected to overtake the UK in the next few years.

| Market | Premium income ($bn) | Percentage of total |
|--------|--------|--------|
| USA | 1,787 | 34.6 |
| Japan | 532 | 10.3 |
| UK | 330 | 6.4 |

## TAKEOVERS AND MERGERS

As predicted, 2014 saw an increase in mergers and acquisitions as excess capital and pressure to sell non-core assets drove an upsurge in activity.

In January 2014 Co-operative Insurance ended speculation that it would sell its general business arm by confirming that it was no longer for sale.

In April new RSA (Royal Insurance and Sun Alliance) chief executive Stephen Hester began a series of disposals designed to focus RSA's operations on UK, Ireland, Scandinavia and Latin America. It began with the sale of RSA's Baltic and Polish operations and was followed by sales of businesses in Canada, China, Hong Kong, India, Italy and Singapore. By the end of the year sales had topped £500m.

Standard Life also disposed of an overseas operation when it sold its Canadian unit to Canada's largest life insurer, Manulife Financial for £2.2bn in cash.

December 2014 saw the largest deal involving UK companies in six years when AVIVA took over Friends Life in a £5.6bn deal. The combined group will have around 16 million UK customers and assets of over £330bn.

## INDUSTRY ISSUES

Since 2002 the European Commission (EC) has been formulating plans for Solvency II, which aims to establish an EU-wide set of requirements for capital adequacy and management standards, modernising and consolidating a large number of EU directives known as Solvency I which was established in the 1970s. Solvency II will codify 14 EU insurance directives. Agreement was finally reached in November 2014 and the agreed implementation date of 1 January 2016 looks very likely. However there are a number of objections and concerns to be ironed out, particularly the effect on American subsidiaries of UK companies, who may find themselves at a disadvantage with local competitors because of the 'equivalency' requirements.

## GENERAL INSURANCE

The period of extreme weather and serious flooding between 23 December 2013 and 28 February 2014 brought the subject of flooding, flood protection and the continuance of cover for homes in high flood risk areas back to the top of the agenda. This period saw nearly 19,000 flood claims totalling £451m and over 448,000 storm damage claims costing nearly £650m.

Even before these events, agreement had been reached between the UK government and insurers for a not-for-profit flood reinsurance fund ('Flood Re') owned and managed by the insurance industry to ensure domestic properties in high risk areas continued to receive affordable cover for flooding. During 2014 the industry and government continued work on the finer details, and the Water Act 2014 received royal assent on 24 May 2014.

In August 2014, insurers voiced serious concerns about the government's proposals to reform the Riot (Damages) Act 1886. At present, under the act, compensation is paid by the police to homeowners and businesses who suffer riot damage to their property or possessions if they have no insurance or are under insured. There is no limit on the amount of compensation payable. Insurers are also able to claim under the act for any payments made to customers – this has meant that they have not needed to charge policyholders for riot cover. Under the new proposals businesses with a turnover over £2m and most car owners would be excluded from claiming which would mean premium increases for those people who buy insurance and no compensation at all for the uninsured.

The fight against general insurance fraud continued with several motor insurance initiatives. In December 2014 a new service called My Licence was launched by the Motor Insurers' Bureau and the Driver and Vehicle Licensing Agency. The initiative was developed in partnership with the Association of British Insurers and the Department for Transport. The scheme allows motor insurers to ask applicants for their driving licence number, which will then allow them to access the DVLA's driver database to acquire a complete and accurate record of the applicants' entitlements, endorsements and any convictions. This will eliminate withholding of information on motoring convictions. A survey during the year highlighted that over 3,500 motor insurance applications a week contain incorrect details on endorsements and convictions. Motor insurance was the biggest area for fraud in 2013, with nearly 60,000 fraudulent claims discovered, an increase of 34 per cent on 2012.

Another area of concern for motor insurers was the increase in claims for 'whiplash' (soft tissue injury). An estimated £2bn a year is paid in claims of this nature; it is very difficult to verify the extent of a claimant's injury which makes these claims open to exploitation by fraudsters. To combat this, the Ministry of Justice have established a new body, MedCo, which runs an IT system that provides an independently and randomly selected choice of appropriately accredited medical experts or medical reporting organisations from which a solicitor can choose who to instruct to examine a claim. The MedCo system launched on 6 April 2015 ending the practice of lawyers and claimants using their own experts and ensuring that it is no longer possible for claimant lawyers to source reports from an individual or organisation with which they have a financial link. It is hoped that the system will deter those aiming to cheat the system.

Overall, insurance frauds totalling £1.3bn were detected in 2014, an increase of 18 per cent.

Despite the rise in fraud, the cost of motor insurance decreased in 2014 by around 4 per cent. An average motorist is now paying £372 a year for motor cover. Home buildings and contents policies also saw decreases with an average buildings policy reduced by 6 per cent to £230 a year and an average home contents policy decreasing by 5 per cent to £124 a year.

With the notable exception of weather related and business interruption claims, most other classes of business saw claims payments decrease in 2014. Fire and theft claims reduced by 9 per cent and 4.2 per cent respectively and subsidence claims decreased by around 2 per cent.

## LONDON INSURANCE MARKET

The London Insurance Market is a unique wholesale marketplace and a distinct, separate sector of the UK insurance and reinsurance industry. It is the world's leading market for internationally traded insurance and reinsurance, its business comprising mainly overseas non-life large and high-exposure risks. It is the only place in the world where all 20 of the world's largest insurance companies have an office. The market is centred on the square mile of the City of London, which provides the required financial, banking, legal and other support services. Around 58 per cent of London market business is transacted at Lloyd's of London, the remainder through insurance companies and protection and indemnity clubs. In 2013 the market had a written gross premium income of around £60bn. Around 200 Lloyd's brokers service the market.

The trade association for the international insurers and reinsurers writing primarily non-marine insurance and all classes of reinsurance business in the London market is the International Underwriting Association (IUA).

INTERNATIONAL UNDERWRITING ASSOCIATION, London Underwriting Centre, 3 Minster Court, Mincing Lane, London EC3R 7DD T 020-7617 4444 W www.iua.co.uk
*Chair*, Malcolm Newman
*Chief Executive*, Dave Matcham

## BRITISH INSURANCE COMPANIES

The following insurance company figures refer to members and certain non-members of the ABI.

CLAIMS STATISTICS *(£m)*

|  | 2010 | 2011 | 2012 | 2013 | 2014 |
|---|---|---|---|---|---|
| Theft | 529 | 603 | 554 | 472 | 452 |
| Fire | 1,072 | 1,156 | 995 | 1,051 | 952 |
| Weather | 707 | 618 | 1,087 | 703 | 1,029 |
| Domestic subsidence | 171 | 158 | 114 | 101 | 99 |
| Business interruption | 180 | 161 | 161 | 100 | 127 |
| *Total* | 2,659 | 2,696 | 2,911 | 2,427 | 2,659 |

WORLDWIDE GENERAL BUSINESS TRADING RESULTS *(£m)*

|  | 2012 | 2013 |
|---|---|---|
| Net written premiums | 46,825 | 50,154 |
| Underwriting results | 778 | 1,444 |
| Investment income | 2,822 | 1,219 |
| Overall trading profit | 3,600 | 2,663 |
| Profit as percentage of premium income | 7.7 | 5.3 |

WORLDWIDE GENERAL BUSINESS UNDERWRITING RESULTS *(£m)*

| | 2012 UK | Overseas | Total | 2013 UK | Overseas | Total |
|---|---|---|---|---|---|---|
| *Motor* | | | | | | |
| Premiums | 11,569 | 4,837 | 16,406 | 10,960 | 5,260 | 16,220 |
| Profit (loss) | (301) | 204 | (97) | (53) | 194 | 141 |
| Percentage of premiums | (2.6) | 4.2 | (0.6) | (0.5) | 3.7 | 0.9 |
| *Non-motor* | | | | | | |
| Premiums | 19,507 | 7,947 | 27,454 | 19,845 | 10,976 | 30,821 |
| Profit (loss) | 159 | 468 | 627 | 866 | 196 | 1,062 |
| Percentage of premiums | 0.8 | 5.9 | 2.3 | 4.4 | 1.8 | 3.4 |

NET PREMIUM INCOME BY SECTOR *(£m)*

| | 2012 UK | Overseas | 2013 UK | Overseas |
|---|---|---|---|---|
| Motor | 11,556 | 4,837 | 10,960 | 5,260 |
| Non-motor | 19,504 | 7,947 | 19,845 | 10,976 |
| Marine, aviation and transport | 1,187 | 495 | 1,130 | 762 |
| Reinsurance | 848 | 355 | 830 | 387 |
| *Total general business* | 33,095 | 13,634 | 32,765 | 17,385 |
| Ordinary long-term | 121,056 | 38,122 | 119,678 | 43,423 |
| TOTAL | 154,151 | 51,756 | 152,443 | 60,808 |

## LLOYD'S OF LONDON

Lloyd's of London is an international market for almost all types of general insurance. Lloyd's currently has the capacity to accept insurance premiums of around £26bn. Much of this business comes from outside the UK and makes a valuable contribution to the balance of payments.

A policy is underwritten at Lloyd's by a mixture of private and corporate members. Specialist underwriters accept insurance risks at Lloyd's on behalf of members (referred to as 'Names') grouped in syndicates. There are currently 94 syndicates of varying sizes, each managed by one of the 59 underwriting agents approved by the Council of Lloyd's.

Members divide into three categories: corporate organisations, individuals who have no limit to their liability for losses, and those who have an agreed limit (known as NameCos).

Lloyd's is incorporated by an act of parliament (Lloyd's Acts 1871 onwards) and is governed by an 18-person council, made up of six working, six external and six nominated members. The structure immediately below this changed when, in 2002, Lloyd's members voted at an extraordinary general meeting to implement a new franchise system for the market with the aim of improving profitability. The first move was the introduction of a new governance structure, replacing the Lloyd's Market Board and the Lloyd's Regulatory Board with an 11-person Lloyd's Franchise Board. Four main committees report to this board.

The corporation is a non-profit making body chiefly financed by its members' subscriptions. It provides the financed, administrative staff and services for Lloyd's premises, administrative staff and services for Lloyd's underwriting syndicates. It does not, however, assume corporate liability for the risks accepted by its members. Individual members are responsible to the full extent of their personal means for their underwriting affairs unless they have converted to limited liability companies.

Lloyd's syndicates have no direct contact with the public. All business is transacted through insurance brokers accredited by the Corporation of Lloyd's. In addition, non-Lloyd's brokers in the UK, when guaranteed by Lloyd's brokers, are able to deal directly with Lloyd's motor syndicates, a facility that has made the Lloyd's market more accessible to the insuring public.

Under the Financial Services and Markets Act 2000, Lloyds is regulated by the FCA and the PRA. However, in situations where Lloyd's internal regulatory and compensation arrangements are more far-reaching – as for example with the Lloyd's Central Fund which safeguards claim payments to policyholders – the regulatory role is delegated to the Council of Lloyd's.

### DEVELOPMENTS IN 2014

Despite predictions of a softening market and the possible impact of low interest rates, Lloyd's recorded another outstanding year with profits of £3.2bn, matching the figure for 2013. The combined ratio – the sum of losses incurred plus operating expenses expressed as a percentage of earned premium – was 88.1 per cent and the return on capital was 14.7 per cent. Gross written premiums decreased very slightly over 2013 to £25.28bn.

A major factor in the results for the past two years has been the absence of serious catastrophes, particularly no major hurricane damage. This situation cannot continue indefinitely and with premium levels under pressure and low investment returns the possibility of price rises remain. However, there is also intense competition, which may reduce their effect.

Only the motor and aviation accounts recorded losses during the year although the aviation figure was small (£8m) and the motor loss was reduced to £69m from £87m in 2013.

LLOYD'S OF LONDON, One Lime Street, London EC3M 7HA T 020-7327 1000 W www.lloyds.com
*Chair,* John Nelson
*Chief Executive,* Inga Beale

### LLOYD'S MEMBERSHIP

| | 2013 | 2014 |
|---|---|---|
| Individual | 529 | 447 |
| Corporate | 1,623 | 1,686 |

### LLOYD'S SEGMENTAL RESULTS 2014 *(£m)*

| | Gross premiums written | Net earned premium | Result |
|---|---|---|---|
| Reinsurance | 8,497 | 6,680 | 1,250 |
| Casualty | 4,963 | 3,939 | 81 |
| Property | 6,281 | 4,572 | 577 |
| Marine | 2,142 | 1,759 | 85 |
| Motor | 1,213 | 1,082 | (69) |
| Energy | 1,533 | 1,093 | 189 |
| Aviation | 582 | 377 | (8) |
| Life | 72 | 73 | 5 |
| *Total from syndicate operations* | 25,283 | 19,575 | 2,110 |

# LIFE AND LONG-TERM INSURANCE AND PENSIONS

At the end of 2013 life and pensions providers may have expected that the year ahead would bring a period of relative calm and consolidation entering into the second year of auto-enrolment into workplace pensions and the second year of the new 'twin peaks' regulatory system, despite the inevitable review of fees charged and further internal preparations for the start of Solvency II (*see* Industry Issues). The period before a General Election often sees a reduction in the number of new government initiatives but the spring of 2014 proved to be far from quiet.

In March, the UK life insurance industry was rocked by three regulatory announcements that temporarily knocked billions off the market value of insurers. These developments may have long-term consequences for the industry and for some types of business.

Firstly, the UK government announced a cap on the charges that companies can impose on workplace pensions (auto-enrolment). The proposed cap was lower than many companies were already charging, and it was thought that some companies would struggle to operate profitably with charges at the proposed level. Secondly, the media reportage of an FCA review into legacy products or 'zombie funds'. These are products like personal pensions, endowments and whole life insurance policies, that are in funds that are now closed. The policies date from the 1970s to 2000 and the review will examine whether or not customers are getting a fair deal, particularly on exit fees.

Initially, the announcement caused serious concern in the markets, especially for the insurers who specialise in closed-book business. Following criticism from the ABI and the Chancellor of the Exchequer, the FCA clarified that the review was much less intrusive than had been reported and ordered an enquiry into the way the announcement had been handled. The markets subsequently recovered.

The most far-reaching of the three developments came in the Budget when the chancellor announced that anyone aged 55 or over, who held a pension based on how much had been paid in, a defined contribution (DC) scheme, would no longer be forced to buy an annuity with their pension pot. Instead savers would be free to take the proceeds and invest or spend them as they see fit. This change represented one of the biggest adjustments to the UK pension regime for almost a century and posed a significant challenge to major players in the annuity field.

As the year went on concerns emerged about whether consumers would use the government's free advice service or take adequate advice elsewhere, before making a decision on what to do with their pension pot. There is also a potential problem with fraudsters offering dubious investment vehicles or advice. The new rules came into effect on 6 April 2015 and the industry faces challenges in making annuities an attractive option and developing new products for the released funds.

## PAYMENTS TO POLICYHOLDERS *(£m)*

|  | 2012 | 2013 |
|---|---|---|
| Payments to UK policyholders | 152,177 | 160,615 |
| Payments to overseas policyholders | 30,034 | 30,551 |
| *Total* | 182,211 | 191,166 |

## WORLDWIDE LONG-TERM PREMIUM INCOME *(£m)*

|  | 2009 | 2010 | 2011 | 2012 | 2013 |
|---|---|---|---|---|---|
| UK Life Insurance |  |  |  |  |  |
| Regular Premium | 7,990 | 7,455 | 6,717 | 6,058 | 5,419 |
| Single Premium | 12,346 | 11,786 | 9,290 | 8,622 | 4,525 |
| *Total* | 20,336 | 19,241 | 16,007 | 14,680 | 9,944 |
| Individual Pensions |  |  |  |  |  |
| Regular Premium | 9,629 | 10,651 | 11,155 | 12,554 | 11,199 |
| Single Premium | 18,095 | 17,567 | 16,123 | 16,392 | 12,936 |
| *Total* | 27,724 | 28,218 | 27,278 | 28,946 | 24,135 |
| Occupational Pensions |  |  |  |  |  |
| Regular Premium | 5,599 | 4,340 | 3,809 | 3,270 | 4,744 |
| Single Premium | 63,388 | 59,693 | 67,995 | 67,566 | 75,827 |
| *Total* | 68,987 | 64,033 | 71,804 | 70,836 | 80,571 |
| Other (eg income protection, long-term care) | 1,473 | 1,482 | 1,456 | 1,764 | 1,457 |
| TOTAL UK PREMIUM INCOME | 118,520 | 112,974 | 116,545 | 116,226 | 116,107 |
| Overseas Premium Income |  |  |  |  |  |
| Regular Premium | 11,240 | 11,971 | 11,654 | 11,881 | 12,782 |
| Single Premium | 29,212 | 29,885 | 26,873 | 28,857 | 31,425 |
| *Total* | 40,452 | 41,856 | 38,527 | 40,738 | 44,207 |
| TOTAL WORLDWIDE PREMIUM INCOME | 158,972 | 154,830 | 155,072 | 156,964 | 160,314 |

## PRIVATE MEDICAL INSURANCE

|  | 2009 | 2010 | 2011 | 2012 | 2013 |
|---|---|---|---|---|---|
| Number of people covered *(thousand)* | 5,938 | 5,841 | 5,668 | 5,611 | 5,143 |
| Corporate | 4,384 | 4,305 | 4,232 | 4,210 | 3,787 |
| Personal | 1,554 | 1,536 | 1,436 | 1,401 | 1,356 |
| Gross Earned Premiums *(£m)* | 3,444 | 3,614 | 3,548 | 3,625 | 3,597 |
| Corporate | 1,838 | 1,982 | 1,929 | 2,010 | 1,982 |
| Personal | 1,606 | 1,632 | 1,619 | 1,615 | 1,615 |
| Gross Claims Incurred *(£m)* | 2,679 | 2,858 | 2,727 | 2,770 | 2,674 |

# TAXATION

The government raises money to pay for public services such as education, health and the social security system through tax. Each year the Chancellor of the Exchequer's budget sets out how much it will cost to provide these services and how much tax is therefore needed to pay for them. HM Revenue and Customs (HMRC) is the government department that collects it. There are several different types of tax. The varieties that individuals may have to pay include income tax payable on earnings, pensions, state benefits, savings and investments; capital gains tax (CGT) payable on the disposal of certain assets; inheritance tax (IHT) payable on estates upon death and certain lifetime gifts; stamp duty payable when purchasing property and shares; and value added tax (VAT) payable on goods and services, plus certain other duties such as fuel duty on petrol and excise duty on alcohol and tobacco. Government funds are also raised from companies and small businesses through corporation tax.

New taxation measures and changes to the administration of the taxation system are normally announced by the incumbent Chancellor of the Exchequer in either the government's autumn statement or its annual Budget which is delivered in the Spring.

The government has a stated policy of investing manpower and funding into reducing tax evasion and avoidance by both individuals and companies. Information and updates on the latest measures can be found on the government's website (W www.gov.uk/government/policies/reducing-tax-evasion-and-avoidance).

The government also has an ongoing drive to simplify the UK tax system via the Office of Tax Simplification (OTS). Details of the OTS and its work can also be found on the government's website (W www.gov.uk/government/organisations/office-of-tax-simplification). The OTS welcomes views from individuals and can be contacted via email (E ots@ots.gsi.gov.uk).

## HELP AND INFORMATION ON TAXATION

For information and help on any aspect of personal taxation individuals may contact their local tax office or call the HMRC helpline (T 0300-200 3300).

HMRC closed its network of enquiry centres in the first half of 2014 because visitor numbers had dropped dramatically. To help the estimated 1.5 million customers identified as needing extra help to get their taxes and entitlements right, HMRC introduced a new service offering more in-depth support on the phone and a mobile advisory service if a face-to-face appointment is required.

The HMRC website (W www.gov.uk/government/organisations/hm-revenue-customs) provides wide-ranging information online. All HMRC forms, leaflets and guides are listed on, and can be downloaded from, the website or ordered by telephone. A list of all HMRC telephone helplines and order lines is also on the website. Those most relevant to topics covered in this section on taxation are included at pertinent points throughout.

## INCOME TAX

Income tax is levied on different sorts of income. Not all types of income are taxable, however, and individuals are only taxed on their 'taxable income' above a certain level. Reliefs and allowances can also reduce or, in some cases, cancel out an individual's income tax bill.

An individual's taxable income is assessed each tax year, starting on 6 April and ending on 5 April the following year.

The information below relates specifically to the year of assessment 2015–16, ending on 5 April 2016, and has only limited application to earlier years. Changes due to come into operation at a later date are briefly mentioned where information is available. Types of income that are taxable include:

- earnings from employment or self-employment
- most pensions income including state, company and personal pensions
- interest on most savings
- income (dividends) from shares
- income from property
- income received from a trust
- certain state benefits
- an individual's share of any joint income

There are certain sorts of income on which individuals never pay tax. These are ignored altogether when working out how much income tax an individual may need to pay. Types of income that are not taxable include:

- certain state benefits and tax credits such as child benefit, working tax credit, child tax credit, pension credit, attendance allowance, personal independence payment, housing benefit and maternity allowance
- winter fuel payments
- income from National Savings and Investments savings certificates
- interest, dividends and other income from various tax-free investments, notably individual savings accounts (ISAs)
- premium bond and national lottery prizes

### PERSONAL ALLOWANCE

Every individual resident in the UK has a 'personal allowance' for tax purposes. This is the amount of taxable income that an individual can earn or receive each year tax-free. This tax year (2015–16) the basic personal allowance or tax-free amount is £10,600, an increase of £600 from the 2014–15 figure of £10,000. Individuals may be entitled to a higher personal allowance if they were born before 6 April 1938. As previously announced, the cash value of date-of-birth related allowances are now frozen until they eventually align with the basic personal allowance. The government's plan, as announced in the 2015 Budget, is to have a single personal allowance for all taxpayers regardless of age from 2016–17.

Income tax is only due on an individual's taxable income that is above his or her tax-free allowance. Husbands and wives are taxed separately, with each entitled to his or her personal allowance. Each spouse may obtain other allowances and reliefs where the required conditions are satisfied.

Since 2013–14, the amount of an individual's personal allowance has depended on their date of birth and their total income received from all taxable sources for the tax year. For 2015–16, there are two date-of-birth related levels of personal allowance. Everyone born after 6 April 1938 receives an allowance of £10,600 a year while those born before this date receive £10,660.

If an individual born before 5 April 1948 has an income over the £27,700 'income limit' for age-related allowances but not more than £100,000, their age-related allowance reduces by half the amount (£1 for every £2) he or she has over the £27,700 limit, until the basic rate allowance for those born after 5 April 1948 is reached.

Since April 2010 all three levels of personal allowance have been subject to a single income limit of £100,000, meaning that the personal allowance is reduced for individuals with an 'adjusted net income' (*see* below) over £100,000. Those individuals with an 'adjusted net income' below or equal to the £100,000 limit are entitled to the full amount of personal allowance. However, where an individual's adjusted net income is above the £100,000 limit, their personal allowance is reduced by half the amount (£1 for every £2) they have over that limit, irrespective of their age or date of birth, until their personal allowance is reduced to nil.

An individual's 'adjusted net income' is calculated in a series of steps. The starting point is 'net income', which is the total of the individual's income subject to income tax less specified deductions such as payments made gross to pension schemes. This net income is then reduced by the grossed-up amount of the individual's Gift Aid contributions to charities and the grossed-up amount of the individual's pension contributions that have received tax relief at source. The final step is to add back any relief for payments to trade unions or police organisations deducted in arriving at the individual's net income. The result is the individual's adjusted net income.

From April 2015 some married couples and civil partners, made up of one non-taxpayer and one basic-rate taxpayer, became eligible for the new marriage allowance, which allows them to share some of the non-taxpayer's unused annual income tax allowance. In the 2015–16 tax year, the new allowance allows a spouse or civil partner with an income less than £10,600 to transfer up to £1,060 of their unused personal allowance to their higher-income partner. So long as the person receiving the transfer is a basic-rate taxpayer, which, in most cases, means having an income of between £10,601 and £42,385, this transferable tax allowance is worth up to £212 in 2015–16.

## INCOME TAX ALLOWANCES

| | 2014–15 | 2015–16 |
|---|---|---|
| Personal Allowance | | |
| Those born after 5 April 1948 | £10,000 | £10,600 |
| Those born between 6 April 1938 and 5 April 1948 | £10,500 | £10,600 |
| Those born before 6 April 1938 | £10,660 | £10,660 |
| Income limit for personal allowance | £100,000 | £100,000 |
| Income limit for personal allowances (born before 6 April 1948) | £27,000 | £27,000 |
| Transferable tax allowance for married couples and civil partners | — | £1,060 |

## BLIND PERSON'S ALLOWANCE

If an individual is registered blind or is unable to perform any work for which eyesight is essential, he or she can claim blind person's allowance, an extra amount of tax-free income added to the personal allowance. In 2015–16 the blind person's allowance is £2,290. It is the same for everyone who can claim it, whatever his or her age or level of income. If an individual is married or in a civil partnership and cannot use all of his or her blind person's allowance because of insufficient income, the unused part of the allowance can be passed to the spouse or civil partner.

## CALCULATING INCOME TAX DUE

Individuals' liability to pay income tax is determined by establishing their level of taxable income for the year. For married couples and civil partners, income must be allocated between the couple by reference to the individual who is beneficially entitled to that income. Where income arises from jointly held assets, it is normally apportioned equally between the partners. If, however, the beneficial interests in jointly held assets are not equal, in most cases couples can make a special declaration to have income apportioned by reference to the actual interests in that income.

To work out an individual's liability for tax, his or her taxable income must be allocated between three different types: earned income (excluding income from savings and dividends); income from savings; and company dividends from shares and other equity-based investments.

After the tax-free personal allowance plus any deductible allowances and reliefs have been taken into account, the amount of tax an individual pays is calculated using different tax rates and a series of tax bands. The tax band applies to an individual's income after tax allowances and any reliefs have been taken into account. Individuals are not taxed on all of their income.

For the tax year 2015–16, the basic rate of income tax is 20 per cent (20 pence in the pound) and the higher rate is 40 per cent (40 pence in the pound). The additional rate is 45 per cent (45 pence in the pound).

The starting rate of tax for savings income such as bank or building society interest was reduced from 10 per cent to nil from April 2015 and the maximum amount of taxable savings income that can be eligible for this starting rate was increased from £2,880 to £5,000. If an individual's taxable non-savings income is above £5,000, the zero per cent starting rate for savings is not available for their savings income.

For 2015–16 the basic rate limit above which tax is payable at the higher rate of 40 per cent is £31,785 and the higher rate limit, above which tax is payable at the additional rate of 45 per cent, remains at £150,000.

## INCOME TAX RATES (PER CENT) AND TAX BANDS FOR 2015–16

| Band | Earned income | Band | Savings | Dividends |
|---|---|---|---|---|
| £0–£31,785 | 20% | £0–£5,000* | 0% | 10% |
| £31,785+ | 40% | £5,000–£31,785 | 20% | 10% |
| £150,000+ | 45% | £31,785+ | 40% | 32.5% |
| | | £150,000+ | 45% | 37.5% |

* If an individual's taxable non-savings income is above £5,000 the 20 per cent tax band applies to savings income from £0–£31,785

The first calculation is applied to earned income which includes income from employment or self-employment, most pension income and rental income plus the value of a wide range of employee fringe benefits such as company cars, living accommodation and private medical insurance (for more information on fringe benefits, *see* later section on payment of income tax). In working out the amount of an individual's net taxable earnings, all expenses incurred 'wholly, exclusively and necessarily' in the performance of his or her work duties, together with the cost of business travel, may be deducted. Fees and subscriptions to certain professional bodies may also be deducted. Redundancy payments and other sums paid on the termination of an employment are assessable income, but the first £30,000 is normally tax-free provided the payment is not linked with the recipient's retirement or performance.

The first £31,785 of taxable income remaining after the tax-free allowance plus any deductible allowances and reliefs have been taken into account, is taxed at the basic rate of 20 per cent. Taxable income between £31,785 and £150,000 is taxed at the higher rate of 40 per cent. Taxable income above £150,000 is taxed at the additional rate of 45 per cent.

Savings and dividends income is added to an individual's other taxable income and taxed last. This means that tax on such sorts of income is based on an individual's highest income tax band.

It was announced in the 2015 Budget that the basic rate limit will be increased to £31,900 for 2016–17 amd £32,300 for 2017–18.

## SAVINGS INCOME

The second calculation is applied to any income from savings received by an individual. The appropriate rate at which it must be taxed is determined by adding income from savings to an individual's other taxable income, excluding dividends.

There is a zero per cent starting rate for savings income only, with a limit of £5,000. If an individual's taxable non-savings income exceeds this limit, the zero per cent savings rate is not applicable. Savings income above £5,000 and below the £31,785 basic rate limit is taxable at 20 per cent. Savings income between £31,785 and £150,000 is taxable at 40 per cent. Savings income over £150,000 is taxed at 45 per cent. If savings income falls on both sides of a tax band, the relevant amounts are taxed at the rates for each tax band.

Most savings income, such as interest paid on bank and building society accounts, already has tax at a rate of 20 per cent deducted from it 'at source' – that is, before it is paid out to individuals. This is confirmed by the entry 'net interest' on bank and building society statements.

Higher rate taxpayers whose income is sufficient to pay 40 or 45 per cent tax on their savings income must let their tax office know what savings income they have received so that the extra tax they owe can be collected.

Non-taxpayers – ie individuals, including most children, whose taxable income is less than their tax allowances – can register to have their savings interest paid 'gross' without any tax being deducted from it at source. To do this, they must complete form R85, available at all banks and building societies. Parents or guardians need to fill in this form on behalf of those under 16.

The eligibility rules for completing a form R85 changed from April 2015. Previously an R85 could be completed only by a saver whose total taxable income for the tax year was below their tax-free personal allowance. From 6 April 2015, a saver who is unlikely to be liable for tax on any of their savings income in the tax year can complete an R85 and register to receive interest without tax deducted even if they pay tax on other (non-savings) income. In practice, this means that if a saver's total taxable income is expected to be below the total of their tax-free personal allowance plus the £5,000 starting rate for savings, they can register to have interest paid on their accounts without tax deducted using form R85. For individuals who are unsure whether they are eligible to register to have their savings interest paid gross, HMRC offers an 'R85 checker' on its website (W www.hmrc.gov.uk/tools/r85/r85-2015.htm).

Non-taxpayers who have already had tax deducted from their savings interest can claim it back from HMRC by filling in form R40. For help or information about registering to get interest paid tax-free or to claim tax back on savings interest, individuals may visit W www.gov.uk/apply-tax-free-interest-on-savings or call a dedicated helpline on T 0300-200 3312.

It was announced in the 2015 Budget that from April 2016, a new tax-free personal savings allowance of £1,000 (or £500 for higher rate taxpayers) would be introduced on the interest individuals earn on savings. The result will be that 95 per cent of individuals will not have to pay tax on the first £1,000 (£500 for higher rate taxpayers) of interest they earn on their savings. A basic rate taxpayer with a total income up to £42,700 a year will be eligible for the £1,000 tax-free savings allowance. A higher rate taxpayer earning from £42,701 to £150,000 will be eligible for a £500 tax-free savings allowance. From April 2016 banks and building societies will stop automatically taking 20 per cent in income tax from the interest earned on standard savings accounts and will pay gross interest instead. This means that non-taxpayers, including most children and many pensioners, will no longer have to fill out form R85 (described above) in order to get their savings interest paid tax free.

## DIVIDEND INCOME

The third and final income tax calculation is on UK dividends, which means income from shares in UK companies and other share-based investments including unit trusts and open-ended investment companies (OEICs).

Dividend tax rates differ from those on savings income. The rate that an individual pays on his or her dividends depends on the amount of his or her overall taxable income (after allowances). Dividend income at or below the £31,785 basic rate tax limit is taxable at 10 per cent, between £31,785 and £150,000 at 32.5 per cent, and above £150,000 at 37.5 per cent.

When dividends are paid, a voucher is sent that shows the dividend paid and the amount of associated 'tax credit'. Companies pay dividends out of profits on which they have already paid or are due to pay tax. The tax credit takes account of this and is available to the shareholder to offset against any income tax that may be due on their dividend income. The dividend paid represents 90 per cent of their dividend income. The remaining 10 per cent is made up of the tax credit. In other words the tax credit represents 10 per cent of the dividend income.

Individuals who pay tax at the basic rate have no tax to pay on their dividend income because the tax liability is 10 per cent – the same amount as the tax credit. Higher rate taxpayers pay a total of 32.5 per cent tax on dividend income above the £31,865 basic rate income tax limit, but because the first 10 per cent of the tax due on their dividend income is already covered by the tax credit, in practice they owe only 22.5 per cent. For the same reason, additional rate taxpayers who pay a total of 37.5 per cent on dividend income above the £150,000 additional rate tax limit, owe only 27.5 per cent in practice.

Non-taxpayers cannot claim the 10 per cent tax credit. This is because income tax has not been deducted from the dividends paid to them. The view is that they have simply been given a 10 per cent credit against any income tax due.

If there is significant change to an individual's savings or other income, whatever his or her current tax bracket, it is the individual's responsibility to contact the relevant tax office immediately, even if he or she does not normally complete a tax return. This enables the tax office to work out whether extra or less tax should be paid.

## INDIVIDUAL SAVINGS ACCOUNTS

There is a small selection of savings and investment products that are tax-free. This means that there is no tax to pay on any income generated in the form of interest or dividends, nor on any increase in the value of the capital invested. Their tax-efficient status has been granted by the government in order to give people an incentive to save more. For this reason there are usually limits and restrictions on the amount of money an individual may invest in such savings and investments. Individual savings accounts (ISAs) are the best known among tax-efficient savings and investments. Individuals can use an ISA to save cash, or invest in stocks and shares.

To be eligible to invest in ISAs and receive all profits free of tax, individuals must be UK residents and be aged 18 or over (over 16 for cash ISAs). An ISA must be in an individual's name and cannot be held jointly with another person.

Major changes to ISAs announced in the 2014 Budget, took effect from 1 July 2014. For the 2014–15 tax year individuals could save up to £11,880 each tax year in an adult ISA and could invest in two separate ISAs each tax year: a cash ISA and a stocks and shares ISA (an umbrella term covering investments in unit trusts, company shares, bonds, investment-type life insurance etc). Up to £5,940 of an individual's ISA allowance could be saved in one cash ISA with one provider. The remainder of the £11,880 could be invested in one stocks and shares ISA with either the same or a different provider. Alternatively an individual could open a single stocks and shares ISA and invest the full £11,880.

ISA savers had the option to transfer some or all of the money they had saved in previous tax years in cash ISAs to their stocks and shares ISA without affecting their annual ISA investment allowance. They could also choose to transfer all the money they had saved to date in a cash ISA in the current tax year to a stocks and shares ISA. However, the rules did not allow the reverse; that is, the transfer of monies saved in a stocks and shares ISA to a cash ISA.

On 1 July 2014 ISAs were reformed into a simpler product and overall annual subscription limit for these accounts was increased to £15,000 for 2014–15 and it was raised again to £15,240 for 2015–16. Since July 2014 individuals aged 18 or over can hold any combination of cash or stocks and shares in an ISA. Individuals aged 16 to 18 also have a full ISA allowance, £15,240 for 2015–16, but are restricted to cash-only ISAs.

ISA savers can now choose to subscribe their full allowance to a cash account where previously only 50 per cent of the allowance could be saved in cash. Investors also now have the right to transfer their investments from a stocks and shares to a cash account if they wish. There have also been consequential changes to the rules on the investments that can be held in a ISA, so that a wider range of securities, including certain retail bonds with less than five years before maturity, can be invested.

Further flexibility for ISAs was announced in the 2015 Budget. Instead of only being able to make deposits totalling £15,240, in the 2015–16 tax year, individuals can now take out their money from an ISA and put it back in without losing their ISA tax benefits as long as the repayment is made in the same tax year as the withdrawal.

From December 2014 there was a change in the law to allow spouses and civil partners to inherit their partner's ISA benefits after death. It had previously been the case that when an ISA saver died, their ISA tax advantages died with them, even if they were saving as a couple. Since April 2015, surviving spouses and civil partners are now able to invest as much into their own ISA as their spouse or civil partner used to have, in addition to their normal annual ISA limit.

There are also annual savings limits on the amount that can be invested in long-term, tax-free savings accounts for children called Junior ISAs. Parents or guardians with parental responsibility can open Junior ISAs for children aged under 18 who live in the UK. The Junior ISA investment limit for 2015–16 is £4,080 per child. However, while parents can open and manage Junior ISAs for their children, the invested money belongs to the child who can take control of their account when they are 16 and withdraw the money when they are 18. Children aged 16 and 17 can open their own Junior ISA as well as an adult cash ISA. Junior ISAs automatically turn into an adult ISA when the child turns 18.

It was announced in the 2015 Budget that with effect from 1 July 2015 the list of qualifying investments for ISAs would be extended to include listed bonds issued by cooperative societies, community benefit societies and SME (small and medium-sized enterprise) securities that are admitted to trading on a recognised stock exchange. The government is also consulting on further extending this list of qualifying investments to include debt securities and equity securities offered via crowd funding platforms.

It was also announced in the 2015 Budget that new Help to Buy ISAs would be introduced to help individuals save a deposit towards buying their first home. From autumn 2015, aspiring first-time buyers aged 16 or over may save up to £200 a month in a Help to Buy ISA and the government will boost their savings by 25 per cent; £50 for every £200 saved, up to a maximum bonus of £3,000 per person. If, therefore, an individual saves £12,000, the government bonus will boost their total savings to £15,000. Savers can start an account with a lump-sum deposit of up to £1,000. The minimum savings to qualify for the scheme are £1,600, but there is no monthly minimum investment. Savings held in a Help to Buy ISA can be accessed at any time but the government payment is only added if and when the savings are used as a deposit on a home in the UK. The bonus is available on home purchases of up to £450,000 in London and up to £250,000 outside London.

Further details about ISAs are available via the HMRC's savings helpline (T 0300-200 3312).

## DEDUCTIBLE ALLOWANCES AND RELIEF

Income taxpayers may be entitled to certain tax-deductible allowances and reliefs as well as their personal allowances. Examples include the married couple's allowance and maintenance payments relief, (*see* below). Unlike the tax-free allowances, these are not amounts of income that an individual can receive tax-free but amounts by which their tax bill can be reduced.

### MARRIED COUPLE'S ALLOWANCE

A married couple's allowance (MCA) is available to taxpayers who are married or are in a civil partnership only where one or other partner was born before 6 April 1935. Eligible couples can start to claim the MCA from the year of marriage or civil partnership registration.

The MCA is restricted to give relief at a fixed rate of 10 per cent, which means that – unlike the personal allowance – it is not income that can be received without paying tax. Instead, it reduces an individual's tax bill by up to a fixed amount calculated as 10 per cent of the amount of the allowance to which they are entitled.

In 2015–16, the MCA is £8,355 at 10 per cent, worth up to £835.50 off a couple's tax bill. The MCA is made up of two parts. There is a minimum amount (£3,220 in 2015–16) which will always be due. The remaining amount (£8,355 in 2015–16) can be reduced if the husband's income exceeds certain limits.

The husband will normally receive the allowance, but the couple can jointly decide which of them will get the minimum amount of the allowance. Alternatively, they can decide to have the minimum amount of the allowance split equally between them. They must inform their tax office of their decision before the start of the new tax year in which they want the decision to take effect. Once this is done, the change will apply until the couple decides to alter it. The remaining part of the allowance must go to the husband unless he lacks sufficient income to use it.

If an individual does not have enough income to use all of his or her share of the MCA, the tax office can transfer the unused part of it to his or her spouse or civil partner.

Like the personal allowance, the MCA can be gradually reduced at the rate of £1 of the allowance for every £2 of income above the income limit (£27,700 in 2015–16). The amount of MCA can only be affected by the husband's income, and it only starts to be affected if his personal allowance has already been reduced back to the basic level for people born after 5 April 1948. The wife's income never affects the amount of MCA. Whatever the level of the husband's income, the MCA can never be reduced below the minimum amount: in 2015–16 this is £3,220 at 10 per cent.

The same system of allowance allocation applies to civil partners based on the income of the highest earner.

MAINTENANCE PAYMENTS RELIEF
An allowance is available to reduce an individual's tax bill for maintenance payments he or she makes to his or her ex-spouse or former civil partner in certain circumstances. To be eligible one or other partner must have been born before 6 April 1935; the couple must be legally separated or divorced; the maintenance payments being made must be under a court order; and the payments must be for the maintenance of an ex spouse or former civil partner (provided he or she is not now remarried or in a new civil partnership) or for children who are under 21. For the tax year 2015–16, this allowance can reduce an individual's tax bill by:

- 10 per cent of £3,220 (maximum £322) – this applies where an individual makes maintenance payments of £3,220 or more a year
- 10 per cent of the amount the individual has actually paid – this applies where an individual makes maintenance payments of less than £3,220 a year

An individual cannot claim a tax reduction for any voluntary payments he or she makes for a child, ex-spouse or former civil partner. To claim maintenance payments relief, individuals should contact their tax office.

CHARITABLE DONATION
A number of charitable donations qualify for tax relief. Individuals can increase the value of regular or one-off charitable gifts of money, however small, by using the Gift Aid scheme that allows charities or community amateur sports clubs (CASCs) to reclaim 20 per cent basic rate tax relief on donations they receive. If a taxpayer gives £10 using Gift Aid, for example, the donation is worth £12.50 to the charity or CASC.

Individuals who pay 40 per cent higher rate income tax can claim back the difference between the 40 per cent and the 20 per cent basic rate of income tax on the total (gross) value of their donations. For example, a 40 per cent tax payer donates £100; the total value of this donation to the charity or CASC is £125, of which the individual can claim back 20 per cent (£25) for themselves. Similarly, those who pay 45 per cent additional rate income tax can claim back the difference between the 45 per cent and the 20 per cent basic rate on the total (gross) value of their donations. On a £100 donation, this means they can claim back £31.25.

In order to make a Gift Aid donation, individuals need to make a Gift Aid declaration. The charity or CASC will normally ask an individual to complete a simple form. One form can cover every gift made to the same charity or CASC for whatever period chosen, including both gifts made in the past and in the future. In April 2013 the government introduced a new scheme where charities are able to claim a Gift Aid-type tax refund on small, ad-hoc donations up to a total of £5,000 a year per charity, without the need for donors to fill in any forms at all. This means Gift Aid can be claimed on the contents of collecting tins, for example. If a charity collects the full £5,000, it will get £1,250 back.

Individuals can use Gift Aid provided the amount of income tax and/or capital gains tax they have paid in the tax year in which their donations are made is at least equal to the amount of basic rate tax the charity or CASC is reclaiming on their gifts. It is the responsibility of the individual to make sure this is the case. If an individual makes Gift Aid donations and has not paid sufficient tax, they may have to pay the shortfall to HMRC. The Gift Aid scheme is not suitable for non-taxpayers.

Individuals who complete a tax return and are due a tax refund can ask HMRC to treat all or part of it as a Gift Aid donation.

For employees or those in receipt of an occupational pension, a tax-efficient way of making regular donations to charities is to use the payroll giving scheme. It allows the donations to be paid from a salary or pension before income tax is deducted. This effectively reduces the cost of giving for donors, which may allow them to give more.

For example, it costs a basic-rate taxpayer only £8 in take-home pay to give £10 to charity from their pre-tax pay. Where a donor pays 40 per cent higher rate tax, that same £10 donation costs the taxpayer £6 and for donors who pay the additional 45 per cent rate tax, it costs £5.50.

Anyone who pays tax through the pay as you earn (PAYE) system (*see* Payment of Income Tax) can give to any charity of their choosing in this way, providing their employer or pension provider offers the payroll giving scheme. There is no limit to the amount individuals can donate.

A reduced rate of inheritance tax (IHT) applies where an individual, in their will, leaves 10 per cent or more of their net estate to charity. In such cases the current IHT 40 per cent rate is reduced to 36 per cent. The reduced rate applies where death occurred on or after 6 April 2012.

Details of tax-efficient charitable giving methods can be found at W www.gov.uk/donating-to-charity

TAX RELIEF ON PENSION CONTRIBUTIONS
Pensions are long-term investments designed to help ensure that people have enough income in retirement. The government encourages individuals to save towards a pension by offering tax relief on their contributions. Tax relief reduces an individual's tax bill or increases their pension fund.

The way tax relief is given on pension contributions depends on whether an individual pays into a company, public service or personal pension scheme.

For employees who pay into a company or public service pension scheme, most employers take the pension contributions from the employee's pay before deducting tax, which means that the individual – whether they pay income tax at the basic or higher rate – gets full tax relief straight away. Some employers, however, use the same method of paying pension contributions as that used by personal pension scheme payers described below.

Individuals who pay into a personal pension scheme make contributions from their net salary; that is, after tax has been deducted. For each pound that individuals contribute to their pension from net salary, the pension provider claims tax back from the government at the basic rate of 20 per cent and reinvests it on behalf of the individual into the scheme. In practice this means that for every £80 an individual pays into their pension, they receive £100 in their pension fund.

Higher rate taxpayers currently get 40 per cent tax relief on money they put into a pension. On contributions made from net salary, the first 20 per cent is claimed back from HMRC by the pension scheme in the same way as for a lower rate taxpayer. It is then up to individuals to claim back the other 20 per cent from their tax office, either when they fill in their annual tax return or by telephone or letter. In a similar fashion, individuals subject to the 45 per cent additional rate of income tax can get 45 per cent tax relief on their pension contributions.

Most providers of retirement annuities, which are a type of personal pension scheme set up before July 1988, do not offer a 'tax relief at source' scheme whereby they claim back tax at the basic rate, as is the case with more modern personal pensions. In such cases, contributing individuals need to claim the tax relief they are due through their tax return or by telephoning or writing to HMRC.

Non-taxpayers can still pay into a personal pension scheme and benefit from 20 per cent basic rate relief on the first £2,880 a year they contribute. In practice this means that the government tops up their £2,880 contribution to make it £3,600 which is the current universal pension allowance. Such pension contributions may be made on behalf of a non-taxpayer by another individual. An individual may, for example, contribute to a pension on behalf of a husband, wife, civil partner, child or grandchild. Tax relief will be added to their contribution at the basic rate, again on up to £2,880 a year benefiting the recipient, but their own tax bill will not be affected.

In any one tax year, individuals can get tax relief on pension contributions made into any number and type of registered pension schemes of 100 per cent of their annual earnings, irrespective of age, up to a maximum 'annual allowance'. For the tax year 2015–16 the annual allowance is £40,000. Individuals pay tax at 40 per cent on any contributions they make above the annual allowance. Everyone also has a 'lifetime allowance' (£1.25m in 2015–16) which means taxpayers can save up to a total of £1.25m in their pension fund and still get tax relief at their highest income tax rate on all of their contributions.

It was announced in the 2015 Budget that the pensions lifetime allowance would be reduced from £1.25m to £1m from April 2016. A protection regime will be introduced alongside the reduction to protect pension savers who think they may be affected by this change.

For information on pensions and tax relief visit W www. gov.uk/browse/working. Another useful source of information and advice is The Pensions Advisory Service (TPAS), an independent voluntary organisation grant-aided by the Department for Work and Pensions at W www.pensions advisoryservice.org.uk; its Pensions Helpline is on T 0300-123 1047.

## PAYMENT OF INCOME TAX
Employees have their income tax deducted from their wages throughout the year by their employer who sends it on to HMRC. Those in receipt of a company pension have their due tax deducted in the same way by their pension provider. This system of collecting income tax is known as 'pay as you earn' (PAYE).

### BENEFITS IN KIND
The PAYE system is also used to collect tax on certain fringe benefits or 'benefits in kind' that employees or directors receive from their employer, but are not included in their salary. These include company cars, private medical insurance paid for by the employer or cheap or free loans from the employer. Some fringe benefits are tax-free, including employer-paid contributions into an employee's pension fund, cheap or free canteen meals, works buses, in-house sports facilities, reasonable relocation expenses, provision of a mobile phone and workplace nursery places provided for the children of employees. For taxable fringe benefits, tax is paid on the 'taxable value' of the benefit.

Employers submit returns for individual employees earning at or above the £8,500 per annum threshold (including the value of expenses and benefits) to the tax office on the form P11D, with details of any fringe benefits they have been given. For those earning less than the £8,500 threshold (part-time employees) a P9D form is submitted. Employees should get a copy of this form by 6 July following the end of the tax year and must enter the value of the fringe benefits they have received on their tax return for the relevant year, even if tax has already been paid on them under PAYE. Fringe benefits may be taxed under PAYE by being offset against personal tax allowances in an individual's PAYE code. Otherwise tax will be collected after the end of the tax year by the issue of an assessment on the fringe benefits.

### SELF-ASSESSMENT
Individuals who are not on PAYE, notably the self-employed, need to complete a self-assessment tax return each year, in paper form or online (W www.gov.uk/log-in-file-self-assessment-tax-return), and pay any income tax owed in twice-yearly instalments. Some individuals with more complex tax affairs such as those who earn money from rents or investments above a certain level may also need to fill out a self-assessment return, even if they are on PAYE. HMRC uses the figures supplied on the tax return to work out the individual's tax bill, or they can choose to work it out themselves. It is called 'self-assessment' because individuals are responsible for making sure the details they provide are correct.

Tax returns are usually sent out in early April, following the end of the tax year to which they apply. They may also go out at other times, for example if an individual wants to claim an allowance or repayment or to register for self-assessment for the first time.

Individuals with simple tax affairs may receive a short four-page return. Those with more complex affairs must fill out a full return that has 12 core pages plus extra pages, depending on the sorts of income received.

Central to the self-assessment system is the requirement for individuals to contact their tax office if they do not receive a self-assessment return but think they should or if their financial circumstances change. Individuals have six months from when the tax year ends to report any new income, for example. If an individual becomes self-employed, they have three months after the calendar month in which they began self-employed work to let HMRC know. This can be done by telephoning the helpline number for the newly self-employed on T 0300-200 3504.

### TAX RETURN FILING AND PAYMENT DEADLINES
There are also key deadlines for filing (sending in) completed tax returns and paying the tax due. Failure to do so can incur penalties, interest charges and surcharges.

### KEY FILING DATES FOR SELF-ASSESSMENT RETURNS

| Date | Why the date is important |
|---|---|
| 31 Oct* | Deadline for filing paper returns* for tax year ending the previous 5 April |
| 30 Dec | Deadline for online filing where the amount owed for tax year ending the previous 5 April is less than £3,000 and the taxpayer wants HMRC to collect any tax due through their PAYE tax code |
| 31 Jan† | Deadline for online filing of returns for tax year ending the previous 5 April |

\* Or three months from the date the return was requested if this was after 31 July

† Or three months from the date the return was requested if this was after 31 October

KEY SELF-ASSESSMENT PAYMENT DATES

| Date | What payment is due? |
|---|---|
| 31 Jan | Deadline for paying the balance of any tax owed – the 'balancing payment' – for the tax year ending the previous 5 April. It is also the date by which a taxpayer must make any first 'payment on account' (advance payment) for the current tax year. For example, on 31 January 2016 a taxpayer may have to pay both the balancing payment for the year 2015–16 and the first payment on account for 2016–17. |
| 31 Jul | Deadline for making a second payment on account for the current tax year |

LATE FILING AND PAYMENT PENALTIES

Late filing of tax returns incurs an automatic £100 penalty although individuals may appeal against the penalty if they have a reasonable excuse. For late filing of 2014–15 tax returns the following penalties also apply:

• Over three months late – £10 each day, up to a maximum of £900, in addition to the penalty above
• Over six months late – an additional £300 or 5 per cent of the tax due, whichever is the higher, in addition to the penalty above
• Over 12 months late – a further £300 or 5 per cent of the tax due, whichever is the higher. In serious cases HMRC reserve the right to ask for 100 per cent of the tax due instead. In both instances this is in addition to the penalty above

Late payment of tax owing for 2014–15 incurs the following penalties:

• Over 30 days – 5 per cent of the tax unpaid at that date
• Over six months – an additional 5 per cent of the tax unpaid at that date
• Over 12 months – a further 5 per cent of the tax unpaid at that date

Interest is due on all outstanding amounts, including any unpaid penalties, until payment is received in full.

It was announced in the 2015 Budget that the government intends to abolish the annual tax return for millions of individuals and small businesses through the introduction of digital tax accounts as part of its aim to modernise and simplify the taxation system. The government says that by early 2016, 10 million individuals (and 5 million small businesses) will have access to their own digital tax account which will bring together all of a taxpayer's details in one secure place akin to an online bank account. By the end of this parliament, the expectation is that every individual and small business in the UK will have one. Individuals will be able to register, file, pay and update their information at any time of the year using a digital device of their choice.

TAX CREDITS

Child tax credit, working tax credit and the new universal credit are paid to qualifying individuals. Although the titles of these credits incorporates the word 'tax', they do not affect the amount of income tax payable or repayable. They are forms of social security benefits. See Social Welfare.

# CAPITAL GAINS TAX

Capital gains tax (CGT) is a tax on the gain or profit that an individual makes when they sell, give away or otherwise dispose of an asset – that is, something they own such as shares, land or buildings. An individual potentially has to pay CGT on gains they make from any disposal of assets during a tax year. There is, however, a tax-free allowance and some additional reliefs that may reduce an individual's CGT bill. The following information relates to the tax year 2015–16 ending on 5 April 2016.

CGT is paid by individuals who are either resident or ordinarily resident in the UK for the tax year, executors or administrators – 'personal representatives' – responsible for a deceased person's financial affairs and trustees of a settlement. Non-residents are not usually liable to CGT unless they carry on a business in the UK through a branch or agency. However, from April 2015, the government introduced a CGT charge on future gains made by non-residents disposing of UK residential property. Special CGT rules apply to individuals who used to live and work in the UK but have since left the country.

CAPITAL GAINS CHARGEABLE TO CGT

Typically, individuals have made a gain if they sell an asset for more than they paid for it. It is the gain that is taxed, not the amount the individual receives for the asset. For example, a man buys shares for £1,000 and later sells them for £3,000. He has made a gain of £2,000 (£3,000 less £1,000). If someone gives an asset away, the gain will be based on the difference between what the asset was worth when originally acquired compared with its worth at the time of disposal. The same is true when an asset is sold for less than its full worth in order to give away part of the value. For example, a woman buys a property for £120,000 and three years later, when the property's market value has risen to £180,000, she gives it to her son. The son may pay nothing for the property or pay less than its true worth, eg £100,000. Either way, she has made a gain of £60,000 (£180,000 less £120,000).

If an individual disposes of an asset he or she received as a gift, the gain is worked out according to the market value of the asset when it was received. For example, a man gives his sister a painting worth £8,000. She pays nothing for it. Later she sells the painting for £10,000. For CGT purposes, she is treated as making a gain of £2,000 (£10,000 less £8,000). If an individual inherits an asset, the estate of the person who died does not pay CGT at the time. If the inheritor later disposes of the asset, the gain is worked out by looking at the market value at the time of the death. For example, a woman acquires some shares for £5,000 and leaves them to her niece when she dies. No CGT is payable at the time of death when the shares are worth £8,000. Later the niece sells the shares for £10,000. She has made a gain of £2,000 (£10,000 less £8,000).

Individuals may also have to pay CGT if they dispose of part of an asset or exchange one asset for another. Similarly, CGT may be payable if an individual receives a capital sum of money from an asset without disposing of it, for example where he or she receives compensation when an asset is damaged.

Assets that may lead to a CGT charge when they are disposed of include:

• shares in a company
• units in a unit trust
• land and buildings (though not normally an individual's main home – see 'disposal of a home' section for details)
• higher value jewellery, paintings, antiques and other personal effects assets used in business such as goodwill

EXEMPT GAINS

Certain kinds of assets do not give rise to a chargeable gain when they are disposed of. Assets exempt from CGT include:

• an individual's private car
• an individual's main home, if certain conditions are met
• tax-free investments such as assets held in an ISA
• UK government gilts or 'bonds'

- personal belongings including jewellery, paintings and antiques individually worth £6,000 or less
- cash in sterling or foreign currency held for an individual for his/her family's own personal use
- betting, lottery or pools winnings
- personal injury compensation

## DISPOSAL OF A HOME: PRIVATE RESIDENCE RELIEF

When an individual sells their own home they automatically qualify for private residence relief which means they do not have to pay any CGT provided that:

- the property has been their only home or main residence since they bought it, and
- they have used it as their home and for no other purpose

Even if an individual has not lived in the property for all of the time that they owned it, they may still be entitled to the full relief.

Under the relief rules, the final 18 months of ownership are always treated as if the individual lived in the property even if they did not. This means that if an individual moves out of one home and into a new one, they have up to 18 months in which to sell their former home without incurring any CGT on the sale proceeds. This 'final period of exemption' was halved from 36 months to the current 18 months in April 2014.

Full relief is granted to individuals when they sell their home if they could not live in it for periods because they were working abroad. Full relief is also granted if an individual is prevented from living in the home for periods totalling a maximum of four years because their job requires them to work elsewhere in the UK. In both cases however, for the property to qualify for full relief, the general rule is that it must have been the individual's only or main home both before and after they worked away.

Individuals can also get full relief when they sell their home if they have lived away from it for reasons other than working away provided all of the following apply:

- they were not living away from the home for more than three years in total during the time they owned the property
- they were not entitled to private residence relief on any other property during that time
- the property was their only or main home both before and after they lived elsewhere

There are instances when individuals may not get the full amount of private residence relief when they sell their home. These include if:

- the garden or grounds, including the site of the house, are larger than 5,000 square metres
- any part of the home has been used exclusively for business purposes
- all or part of the home has been let out (or more than one lodger has been taken in at a time). The owner may, however, be entitled to another form of CGT relief – letting relief – instead
- the main reason the property was bought was to make a profit from a quick sale

If an individual lives in – not just owns – more than one property, they can 'nominate' which should be treated as their main home for private residence relief purposes. Married couples or those in a civil partnership must make such a nomination jointly as they are only entitled to private residence relief on one house between them.

It was announced in the 2014 Budget that, from April 2015, this ability to nominate which home should qualify for private residence relief will cease. Instead it will be decided on objective grounds which of an individual's two or more homes is indeed their main or primary residence.

Certain other kinds of disposal similarly do not give rise to a chargeable gain. For example, individuals who are married or in a civil partnership and who live together may sell or give assets to their spouse or civil partner without having to pay CGT. Individuals may not, however, give or sell assets cheaply to their children without having to consider CGT. There is no CGT to pay on assets given to a registered charity.

## CALCULATING CGT

CGT is worked out for each tax year and is charged on the total of an individual's taxable gains after taking into account certain costs and reliefs that can reduce or defer chargeable gains, allowable losses made on assets to which CGT normally applies and an annual exempt (tax-free) amount that applies to every individual. If the total of an individual's net gains in a tax year is less than the annual exempt amount (AEA), the individual will not have to pay CGT. For the tax year 2015–16 the AEA is £11,100. If an individual's net gains are more than the AEA, they pay CGT on the excess. Should any part of the exemption remain unused, this cannot be carried forward to a future year.

There are certain reliefs available that may eliminate, reduce or defer CGT. Some reliefs are available to many people while others are available only in special circumstances. Some reliefs are given automatically while others are given only if they are claimed. Some of the costs of buying, selling and improving assets may be deducted from total gains when working out an individual's chargeable gain.

## RATES OF TAX

The net gains remaining, if any, calculated after subtracting the AEA, deducting costs and taking into account all CGT reliefs, incur liability to capital gains tax. Individuals pay CGT at a rate of 18 per cent on gains up to the unused amount of the basic rate income tax band (if any) and at 28 per cent on gains above that amount. The CGT rate charged to trustees and personal representatives is 28 per cent.

CGT for 2015–16 is due for payment in full on 31 January 2017. If payment is delayed, interest or surcharges may be imposed. A husband and wife or registered civil partners who live together are separately assessed for CGT. Each partner must independently calculate his or her gains and losses with each entitled to the AEA of £11,100 for 2015–16.

## VALUATION OF ASSETS

The disposal proceeds – ie the amount received as consideration for the disposal of an asset – are the sum used to establish the gain or loss once certain allowable costs have been deducted. In most cases this is straightforward because the disposal proceeds are the amount actually received for disposing of the asset. This may include cash payable now or in the future and the value of any asset received in exchange for the asset disposed of. However, in certain circumstances, the disposal proceeds may not accurately reflect the value of the asset and the individual may be treated as disposing of an asset for an amount other than the actual amount (if any) that they received. This applies, in particular, where an asset is transferred as a gift or sold for a price known to be below market value. Disposal proceeds in such transactions are deemed to be equal to the market value of the asset at the time it was disposed of rather than the actual amount (if any) received for it.

Market value represents the price that an asset might reasonably be expected to fetch upon sale in the open market.

In the case of unquoted shares or securities, it is to be assumed that the hypothetical purchaser in the open market would have available all the information that a prudent prospective purchaser of shares or securities might reasonably require if that person were proposing to purchase them from a willing vendor by private treaty and at arm's length. The market value of unquoted shares or securities will often be established following negotiations with the specialist HMRC Shares and Assets Valuation department. The valuation of land and interests in land in the UK is dealt with by the Valuation Office Agency. Special rules apply to determine the market value of shares quoted on the London Stock Exchange.

## ALLOWABLE COSTS

When working out a chargeable gain, once the actual or notional disposal proceeds have been determined, certain allowable costs may be deducted. There is a general rule that no costs that could be taken into account when working out income or losses for income tax purposes may be deducted. Subject to this, allowable costs are:

• acquisition costs – the actual amount spent on acquiring the asset or, in certain circumstances, the equivalent market value
• incidental costs of acquiring the asset such as fees paid for professional advice, valuation costs, stamp duty and advertising costs to find a seller
• enhancement costs – incurred for the purpose of enhancing the value of the asset (not including normal maintenance and repair costs)
• expenditure on defending or establishing a person's rights over the asset
• incidental costs of disposing of the asset such as fees paid for professional advice, valuation costs, stamp duty and advertising costs to find a buyer

If an individual disposes of part of his or her interest in an asset, or part of a holding of shares of the same class in the same company, or part of a holding of units in the same unit trust, he or she can deduct part of the allowable costs of the asset or holding when working out the chargeable gain. Allowable costs may also be reduced by some reliefs.

## ENTREPRENEURS' RELIEF

Entrepreneurs' Relief allows individuals in business and some trustees to claim relief on the first £10m of gains made on the disposal of any of the following: all or part of a business; the assets of a business after it has ceased; and shares in a company. The relief is available to taxpayers as individuals if they are in business, for example as a sole trader or as a partner in a trading business, or if they hold shares in their own personal trading company. This relief is not available for companies.

Depending on the type of disposal, certain qualifying conditions need to be met throughout a qualifying one-year period. For example, if an individual is selling all or part of their business, they must have owned the business during a one-year period that ends on the date of the disposal.

Recent changes include a condition announced at Budget 2015 which prevents claims to entrepreneurs' relief in respect of gains on disposals of privately-held assets used in business unless they are associated with a significant material disposal, that is to say a disposal of at least a 5 per cent shareholding in the company or of at least a 5 per cent share in the assets of the partnership carrying the business. This condition has effect for disposals on or after 18 March 2015.

Where Entrepreneurs' Relief applies, qualifying gains liable to CGT are charged at 10 per cent. An individual can make claims for this relief on more than one occasion as long as the lifetime total of all their claims does not exceed £10m of gains qualifying for relief.

## BUSINESS ASSET ROLL-OVER RELIEF

When certain types of business asset are sold or disposed of and the proceeds reinvested in new qualifying trading assets, business asset roll-over relief makes it possible to 'roll-over' or postpone the payment of any CGT that would normally be due. The gain is deducted from the base cost of the new asset and only becomes chargeable to CGT on the eventual disposal of that replacement asset unless a further roll-over situation then develops. Full relief is available if all the proceeds from the original asset are reinvested in the qualifying replacement asset.

For example, a trader sells a freehold office for £75,000 and makes a gain of £30,000. All of the proceeds are reinvested in a new freehold business premises costing £90,000. The trader can postpone the whole of the £30,000 gain made on the sale of the old office, as all of the proceeds have been reinvested. When the trader eventually sells the new business premises and the CGT bill becomes payable, the cost of the new premises will be treated as £60,000 (£90,000 less the £30,000 gain).

If only part of the proceeds from the disposal of an old asset is reinvested in a new one, it may still be possible to postpone paying tax on part of the gain until the eventual disposal of the new asset.

Relief is only available if the acquisition of the new asset takes place within a period between 12 months before, and 36 months after, the disposal of the old asset. However, HMRC may extend this time limit at their discretion where there is a clear intention to acquire a replacement asset. The most common types of business assets that qualify for roll-over relief are land, buildings occupied and used for the purposes of trade, and fixed plant and machinery. Assets used for the commercial letting of furnished holiday accommodation qualify if certain conditions are satisfied.

## GIFTS HOLD-OVER RELIEF

The gift of an asset is treated as a disposal made for a consideration equal to market value, with a corresponding acquisition by the transferee at an identical value. In the case of gifts of business assets made by individuals and a limited range of trustees, a form of hold-over relief may be available. This relief, which must be claimed, in effect enables liability for CGT to be deferred and passed to the person to whom the gift is made. Relief is limited to the transfer of certain assets including the following:

• gifts of assets used for the purposes of a business carried on by the donor or his or her personal company
• gifts of shares in trading companies that are not listed on a stock exchange
• gifts of shares or securities in the donor's personal trading company
• gifts of agricultural land and buildings that would qualify for inheritance tax agricultural property relief
• gifts that are chargeable transfers for inheritance tax purposes
• certain types of gifts that are specifically exempt from inheritance tax

Hold-over relief is automatically due on certain sorts of gifts including gifts to charities and community amateur sports clubs, and gifts of works of art where certain undertakings have been given. There are certain rules to prevent gifts hold-over relief being used for tax-avoidance purposes. For example, restrictions may apply where an individual gifts assets to trustees administering a trust in which the individual retains an interest or the assets transferred comprise a dwelling-house. Subject to these exceptions, the effect of a valid claim for hold-over relief is similar to a claim for roll-over relief on the disposal of business assets.

## OTHER CGT RELIEFS
There are certain other CGT reliefs available on the disposal of property, shares and business assets. For detailed information on all CGT reliefs and for more general guidance on CGT visit W www.gov.uk/personal-tax/capital-gains-tax

## REPORTING AND PAYING CGT
Individuals are responsible for telling HMRC about capital gains on which they have to pay tax. Individuals who receive a self-assessment tax return may report capital gains by filling in the capital gains supplementary pages – the return explains how to obtain these pages if needed.

Individuals who do not normally complete a tax return but who need to report capital gains or losses should contact their local tax office.

There is a time limit for claiming capital losses. The deadline is four years from 31 January after the end of the tax year in which the loss was made.

# INHERITANCE TAX

Inheritance tax (IHT) is a tax on the value of a person's estate on death and on certain gifts made by an individual during his or her lifetime, usually payable within six months of death. Broadly speaking, a person's estate is everything he or she owned at the time of death including property, possessions, money and investments, less his or her debts. Not everyone pays IHT. It only applies if the taxable value of an estate is above the current IHT threshold. If an estate, including any assets held in trust and gifts made within seven years of death, is less than the threshold, no IHT will be due.

The nil-rate band for 2015–16 is £329,000, the first increase since the nil-rate band was frozen at £325,000 in 2010.

A claim can be made to transfer any unused IHT nil-rate band on a person's death to the estate of their surviving spouse or civil partner. This applies where the IHT nil-rate band of the first deceased spouse or civil partner was not fully used in calculating the IHT liability of their estate. When the surviving spouse or civil partner dies, the unused amount may be added to their own nil-rate band (*see* below for details).

IHT used to be something only very wealthy individuals needed to consider. This is no longer the case. The fact that the IHT threshold has not kept pace with house price inflation in recent years means that the estates of some 'ordinary' taxpayers are now liable for IHT purely because of the value of their home. However, there are a number of ways that individuals – while still alive – can legally reduce the IHT bill that will apply to their estates on death. Several valuable IHT exemptions are available (explained further below) which allow individuals to pass on assets during their lifetime or in their will without any IHT being due. Detailed information on IHT is available at W www.gov.uk/inheritance-tax Further help is also available from the Probate and Inheritance Helpline (T 0300-123 1072).

## DOMICILE
Liability to IHT depends on an individual's domicile at the time of any gift or on death. Domicile is a complex legal concept and what follows explains some of the main issues. An individual is domiciled in the country where he or she has a permanent home. Domicile is different from nationality or residence, and an individual can only have one domicile at any given time.

A 'domicile of origin' is normally acquired from the individual's father on birth, though this may not be the country in which he or she is born. For example, a child born in Germany while his or her father is working there, but whose permanent home is in the UK, will have the UK as his or her domicile of origin. Until a person legally changes his or her domicile, it will be the same as that of the person on whom they are legally dependent.

Individuals can legally acquire a new domicile – a 'domicile of choice' – from the age of 16 by leaving the current country of domicile and settling in another country and providing strong evidence of intention to live there permanently or indefinitely. Women who were married before 1974 acquired their husband's domicile and still retain it until they legally acquire a new domicile.

For IHT purposes, there is a concept of 'deemed domicile'. This means that even if a person is not domiciled in the UK under general law, he or she is treated as domiciled in the UK at the time of a transfer (ie at the time of a lifetime gift or on death) if he or she (a) was domiciled in the UK within the three years immediately before the transfer, or (b) was 'resident' in the UK in at least 17 of the 20 income tax years of assessment ending with the year in which a transfer is made. Where a person is domiciled, or treated as domiciled, in the UK at the time of a gift or on death, the location of assets is immaterial and full liability to IHT arises. A non-UK domiciled individual is also liable to IHT but only on chargeable property in the UK.

The assets of husband and wife and registered civil partners are not merged for IHT purposes, except that the IHT value of assets owned by one spouse or civil partner may be affected if the other also owns similar assets (eg shares in the same company or a share in their jointly owned house). Each spouse or partner is treated as a separate individual entitled to receive the benefit of his or her exemptions, reliefs and rates of tax.

## IHT EXEMPTIONS
There are some important exemptions that allow individuals to legally pass assets on to others, both before and after their death – without being subject to IHT.

*Exempt Beneficiaries*
Assets can be given away to certain people and organisations without any IHT having to be paid. These gifts, which are exempt whether individuals make them during their lifetime or in their will, include gifts to:

- a husband, wife or civil partner, even if the couple is legally separated (but not if they are divorced or the civil partnership has dissolved). Note that gifts to an unmarried partner or a partner with whom the donor has not formed a civil partnership are not exempt
- a 'qualifying' charity established in the EU or another specified country
- some national institutions, including national museums, universities and the National Trust
- UK political parties

*Annual Exemption*
The first £3,000 of gifts made each tax year by each individual is exempt from IHT. If this exemption is not used, or not wholly used in any year, the balance may be carried forward to the following year only. A couple, therefore, may give away a total of £6,000 per tax year between them or £12,000 if they have not used their previous year's annual exemptions.

*Wedding Gifts/Civil Partnership Ceremony Gifts*
Some gifts are exempt from IHT because of the type of gift or reason for making it. Wedding or civil partnership

ceremony gifts made to either of the couple are exempt from HT up to certain amounts:

• gifts by a parent, £5,000
• gifts by a grandparent or other relative, £2,500
• gifts by anyone else, £1,000

The gift must be made on or shortly before the date of the wedding or civil partnership ceremony. If the ceremony is called off but the gift is made, this exemption will not apply.

*Small Gifts*
An individual can make small gifts, up to the value of £250, to any number of people in any one tax year without them being liable for IHT. However, a larger sum such as £500 cannot be given and exemption claimed for the first £250. In addition, this exemption cannot be used with any other exemption when giving to the same person. For example, a parent cannot combine a 'small gifts exemption' with a 'wedding/civil partnership ceremony gift exemption' to give a child £5,250 when he or she gets married or forms a civil partnership. Neither may an individual combine a 'small gifts exemption' with the 'annual exemption' to give someone £3,250. Note that it is possible to use the 'annual exemption' with any other exemption, such as the 'wedding/civil partnership ceremony gift exemption'. For example, if a child marries or forms a civil partnership, the parent can give him or her a total IHT-free gift of £8,000 by combining £5,000 under the wedding/civil partnership gift exemption and £3,000 under the annual exemption.

*Normal Expenditure*
Any gifts made out of individuals' after-tax income (not capital) are exempt from IHT if they are part of their normal expenditure and do not result in a fall in their standard of living. These can include regular payments to someone, such as an allowance or gifts for Christmas or a birthday and regular premiums paid on a life insurance policy for someone else.

*Maintenance Gifts*
An individual can make IHT-free maintenance payments to his or her spouse or registered civil partner, ex-spouse or former civil partner, relatives dependent because of old age or infirmity, and children (including adopted children and step-children) who are under 18 or in full-time education.

## POTENTIALLY EXEMPT TRANSFERS
If an individual makes a gift to either another individual or certain types of trust and it is not covered by one of the above exemptions, it is known as a 'potentially exempt transfer' (PET). A PET is only free of IHT on two strict conditions: (a) the gift must be made at least seven years before the donor's death. If the donor does not survive seven years after making the gift, it will be liable for IHT and (b) the gift must be made as a true gift with no strings attached (technically known as a 'gift with reservation of benefit'). This means that the donor must give up all rights to the gift and stop benefiting from it in any way.

If a gift is made and the donor does retain some benefit from it then it will still count as part of his or her estate no matter how long he or she lives after making it. For example, a father could make a lifetime gift of his home to his child. However, HMRC would not accept this as a true gift if the father continued to live in the home (unless he paid his child a full commercial rent to do so) because he would be considered to still have a material interest in the gifted home. Its value, therefore, would still be liable for IHT.

In some circumstances a gift with strings attached might give rise to an income tax charge on the donor based on the value of the benefit he or she retains. In this case the donor

can choose whether to pay the income tax or have the gift treated as a gift with reservation.

## CHARGEABLE TRANSFERS
Any remaining lifetime gifts that are not (potentially or otherwise) exempt transfers are chargeable transfers or 'chargeable gifts', meaning that they incur liability to IHT. Chargeable transfers comprise mainly gifts to or from companies and gifts to particular types of trust. There is an immediate claim for IHT on chargeable gifts, and additional tax may be payable if the donor dies within seven years of making a chargeable gift.

## DEATH
Immediately before the time of death an individual is deemed to make a transfer of value. This transfer will comprise the value of assets forming part of the deceased's estate after subtracting most liabilities. Any exempt transfers may be excluded such as transfers for the benefit of a surviving spouse or civil partner, and charities. Death may also trigger three additional liabilities:

• a PET made within the seven years before the death loses its potential status and becomes chargeable to IHT
• the value of gifts made with reservation may incur liability if any benefit was enjoyed within the seven years before the death
• additional tax may become payable for chargeable lifetime transfers made within the seven years before the death

The 'personal representative' (the person nominated to handle the affairs of the deceased person) arranges to value the estate and pay any IHT that is due. One or more personal representatives can be nominated in a person's will, in which case they are known as the 'executors'. If a person dies without leaving a will a court can nominate the personal representative, who is then known as the 'administrator'. Valuing the deceased person's estate is one of the first things his or her personal representative needs to do. The representative will not normally be able to take over management of the estate (called 'applying for probate') until all or some of any IHT that is due has been paid.

## VALUATIONS
When valuing a deceased person's estate all assets (property, possessions and money) owned at the time of death and certain assets given away during the seven years before death must be included. The valuation must accurately reflect what those assets would reasonably fetch in the open market at the date of death. The value of all of the assets that the deceased owned should include:

• his or her share of any assets owned jointly with someone else, for example a house owned with a partner
• any assets that are held in a trust, from which the deceased had the right to benefit
• any assets given away, but in which he or she kept an interest (gifts with reservation)
• PETs given away within the last seven years

Most estate assets can be valued quite easily, for example money in bank accounts or stocks and shares. In other instances the help of a professional valuer may be needed. Advice on how to value different assets including joint or trust assets is available at W www.gov.uk/valuing-estate-of-someone-who-died When valuing an estate, special relief is made available for certain assets. The two main reliefs are business relief and agricultural property relief, outlined below. Once all assets have been valued, the next step is to deduct from the total assets everything that the deceased person owed such as unpaid bills, outstanding mortgages and other loans plus their funeral expenses.

The value of all of the assets, less the deductible debts, is their estate. IHT is only payable on any value above £329,000 for the tax year 2015–16 at the current rate of 40 per cent.

A new reduced rate of IHT was introduced at the beginning of the 2012–13 tax year to encourage individuals to pledge part of their estate to charity on death. Where 10 per cent or more of a deceased's net estate (after deducting IHT exemptions, reliefs and the nil-rate band) is left to charity, the 40 per cent rate is reduced to 36 per cent.

## RELIEF FOR SELECTED ASSETS

*Agricultural Property*

If an individual owns agricultural property and it is part of a working farm, it is possible to pass on some of this property free of IHT, either during that individual's lifetime or on their death. Agricultural property generally includes land or pasture used in the growing of crops or intensive rearing of animals for food consumption. It can also include farmhouses and farm cottages. The agricultural property can be owner-occupied or let. Relief is only due if the transferor has owned the property and it has been occupied for agricultural purposes for a minimum period.

The chargeable value transferred, either on a lifetime gift or on death, must be determined. This value may then be reduced by a percentage. Depending on the type of property, it will normally qualify for relief of 100 per cent.

*Business Relief*

Business relief is available on transfers of certain types of business and of business assets if they qualify as relevant business property and the transferor has owned them for a minimum period. The relief can be claimed for transfers made during the person's lifetime or on their death. Where the chargeable value transferred is attributable to relevant business property, the business relief reduces that value by a percentage of either 50 or 100 per cent, depending on the type of asset. Business relief may be claimed on relevant business property including property and buildings or assets such as unlisted shares or machinery.

It is a general requirement that the property must have been retained for a period of two years before the transfer or death, and restrictions may be necessary if the property has not been used wholly for business purposes. The same property cannot obtain both business property relief and the relief available for agricultural property.

## CALCULATION OF TAX PAYABLE

The calculation of IHT payable adopts the use of a cumulative or 'running' total. Looking back seven years from the death the chargeable value of gifts in that period is added to the total value of the estate at death. The gifts will use up all or part of the inheritance tax threshold (the 'nil-rate band' above which IHT becomes payable) first.

*Lifetime Chargeable Transfers*

The value transferred by lifetime chargeable transfers must be added to the seven-year running total to calculate whether any IHT is due. If the nil-rate band is exceeded, tax will be imposed on the excess at the rate of 20 per cent. However, if the donor dies within a period of seven years from the date of the chargeable lifetime transfer, additional tax may be due. This is calculated by applying tax at the full rate of 40 per cent in substitution for the rate of 20 per cent previously used. The amount of tax is then reduced to a percentage by applying tapering relief. This percentage is governed by the number of years from the date of the lifetime gift to the date of death, as follows:

| PERIOD OF YEARS BEFORE DEATH | |
| --- | --- |
| Not more than 3 | 100% |
| More than 3 but not more than 4 | 80% |
| More than 4 but not more than 5 | 60% |
| More than 5 but not more than 6 | 40% |
| More than 6 but not more than 7 | 20% |

Should this exercise produce liability greater than that previously paid at the 20 per cent rate on the lifetime transfer, additional tax, representing the difference, must be paid. Where the calculation shows an amount falling below tax paid on the lifetime transfer, no additional liability can arise nor will the shortfall become repayable.

Tapering relief is, of course, only available if the calculation discloses a liability to IHT. There is no liability if the lifetime transfer falls within the nil-rate band.

*Potentially Exempt Transfers*

Where a PET loses immunity from liability to IHT because the donor dies within seven years of making the transfer, the value transferred enters into the running total. Any liability to IHT will be calculated by applying the full rate of 40 per cent, reduced to the percentage governed by tapering relief if the original transfer occurred more than three years before death. Again, liability to IHT can only arise if the nil-rate band is exceeded.

*Death*

On death, IHT is due on the value of the deceased's estate plus the running total of gifts made in the seven years before death if they come to more than the nil-rate band. IHT is then charged at the full rate of 40 per cent on the amount in excess of the nil-rate band.

*Settled Property and Trusts*

Trusts are special legal arrangements that can be used by individuals to control how their assets are distributed to their beneficiaries and minimise their IHT liability. Complex rules apply to establish IHT liability on settled property which includes property held in trust, and individuals are advised to take expert legal advice when setting up trusts.

RATES OF TAX

There are four rates:

- a nil-rate
- a lifetime rate of 20 per cent
- a full rate of 40 per cent
- a reduced rate of 36 per cent applicable to taxable estates where 10 per cent of the net estate has been left to charity (*see* above)

After being frozen for several years the nil-rate band has increased by 1 per cent to £329,000 for 2015–16. Any excess over this level is taxable at 20 per cent, 40 per cent or 36 per cent as the case may be.

TRANSFER OF NIL-RATE BAND

Transfers of property between spouses or civil partners are generally exempt from IHT. This means that someone who dies leaving some or all of their property to their spouse or civil partner may not have fully used up their nil-rate band. Under rules introduced in autumn 2007, any nil-rate band unused on the first death can be used when the surviving spouse or civil partner dies. A transfer of unused nil-rate band from a deceased spouse or civil partner (no matter what the date of their death) may be made to the estate of their surviving spouse or civil partner.

Where a valid claim to transfer unused nil-rate band is made, the nil-rate band that is available when the surviving spouse or civil partner dies is increased by the proportion of the nil-rate band unused on the first death. For example, if on the first death the chargeable estate is £150,000 and the nil-rate band is £300,000, 50 per cent of the nil-rate band would be unused. If the nil-rate band when the survivor dies is £329,000, then that would be increased by 50 per cent to £493,500. The amount of the nil-rate band that can be transferred does not depend on the value of the first spouse or civil partner's estate. Whatever proportion of the nil-rate band is unused on the first death is available for transfer to the survivor.

The amount of additional nil-rate band that can be accumulated by any one surviving spouse or civil partner is limited to the value of the nil-rate band in force at the time of their death. This may be relevant where a person dies having survived more than one spouse or civil partner.

Where these rules have effect, personal representatives do not have to claim for the unused nil-rate band to be transferred at the time of the first death. Any claims for transfer of unused nil-rate band amounts are made by the personal representatives of the estate of the second spouse or civil partner to die when they make an IHT return.

Guidance on how to transfer the nil-rate band can be found at  W www.gov.uk/inheritance-tax/leaving-assets-spouse-civil-partner

## PAYMENT OF TAX

IHT is normally due six months after the end of the month in which the death occurs or the chargeable transaction takes place. This is referred to as the 'due date'. Tax on some assets such as business property, certain shares and securities and land and buildings (including the deceased person's home) can be deferred and paid in equal instalments over ten years, though interest will be charged in most cases. If IHT is due on lifetime gifts and transfers, the person or transferee who received the gift or assets is normally liable to pay the IHT, though any IHT already paid at the time of a transfer into a trust or company will be taken into account. If tax owed is not paid by the due date, interest is charged on any unpaid IHT, no matter what caused the delay in payment.

It has been announced that HMRC will be investing in a new online service to support the administration of IHT. This will do away with the need to complete paper forms and enable individuals to proceed with their application for probate and submit IHT accounts online. It is anticipated that the new online service will become available in 2016.

## CORPORATION TAX

Corporation tax is a tax on a company's profits, including all its income and gains. This tax is payable by UK resident companies and by non-resident companies carrying on a trade in the UK through a permanent establishment. The following comments are confined to companies resident in the UK. The word 'company' is also used to include:

• members' clubs, societies and associations
• trade associations
• housing associations
• groups of individuals carrying on a business but not as a partnership (for example, cooperatives)

A company's taxable income is charged by reference to income or gains arising in its 'accounting period', which is normally 12 months long. In some circumstances accounting periods can be shorter than 12 months, but never longer. The accounting period is also normally the period for which a company's accounts are drawn up, but the two periods do not have to coincide.

If a company is liable to pay corporation tax on its profits, several things must be done. HMRC must be informed that the company exists and is liable for tax. A self-assessment company tax return plus full accounts and calculation of tax liability must be filed by the statutory filing date, normally 12 months after the end of the accounting period. Companies have to work out their own tax liability and have to pay their tax without prior assessment by HMRC. Records of all company expenditure and income must be kept in order to work out the tax liability correctly. Companies are liable to penalties if they fail to carry out these obligations.

A radically simpler way for small self-employed businesses, such as sole traders and partnerships, to calculate their tax was introduced with effect from the 2013–14 tax year. Such businesses with receipts of up to £81,000 are able to work out their income on a cash basis and use simplified expenses rules, rather than having to follow the rules for larger businesses. Limited companies and limited liability partnerships can not use cash basis. If a small business uses cash basis accounting and the business grows during the tax year, it can stay in the scheme up to a total business income of £162,000 a year.

Corporation tax information is available at W www.gov.uk/browse/business/business-tax and companies may file their company tax returns online (W www.gov.uk/file-your-company-accounts-and-tax-return).

### RATE OF TAX

The rate of corporation tax is fixed for a financial year starting on 1 April and ending on the following 31 March. If a company's accounting period does not coincide with the financial year, its profits must be apportioned between the financial years and the tax rates for each financial year applied to those profits. The corporation tax liability is the total tax for both financial years.

A major change to corporation tax rates, first announced in the 2013 Budget, was brought in for the tax year 2015–16. For many years previously, corporation tax rates were based on three thresholds. Small companies with taxable profits up to £300,000 were taxed at the small profits rate: 20 per cent for 2014–15 and 2013–14. Companies with taxable profits between £300,000 and £1,500,000 were taxed at the marginal rate: 21.25 per cent in 2014–15 and 23.75 per cent in 2013–14. Companies with taxable profits over £1,500,000 were taxed at the main rate of corporation tax: 21 per cent for 2014–15 and 23 per cent for 2013–14.

From 1 April 2015, the main rate of corporation tax was reduced to 20 per cent, thereby unifying the small profits rate and the main rate, eliminating marginal relief and giving UK companies a single 20 per cent rate of corporation tax.

### CORPORATION TAX ON PROFITS

| £ per year | 2015–16 | 2014–15 |
|---|---|---|
| £0–£300,000 | 20% | 20% |
| £300,001–£1,500,000 | 20% | Marginal relief |
| £1,500,001 or more | 20% | 21% |

### CAPITAL ALLOWANCES

Businesses can claim tax allowances, called capital allowances, on certain purchases or investments. This means that a proportion of these costs can be deducted from a business' taxable profits and reduce its tax bill. Capital allowances are currently available on plant and machinery, buildings, and research and development. The amount of the allowance depends on what is being claimed for.

Detailed information on capital allowances is available at W www.gov.uk/capital-allowances/overview

## PAYMENT OF TAX

Corporation tax liabilities are normally due and payable in a single lump sum not later than nine months and one day after the end of the accounting period. For 'large' companies – those with profits over £1.5m – there is a requirement to pay corporation tax in four quarterly instalments. Where a company is a member of a group, the profits of the entire group must be merged to establish whether the company is 'large'.

HMRC runs a Business Payment Support Service (BPSS) which allows businesses facing temporary financial difficulties more time to pay their tax bills. Traders concerned about their ability to meet corporation tax, VAT or other payments owed to HMRC can call the Business Payment Support Line (T 0300-200 3835) seven days a week. This helpline is for new enquiries only, not for traders who have already been contacted by HMRC about an overdue payment. For details of the service visit W www.gov.uk/government/organisations/hm-revenue-customs/contact/business-payment-support-service

## CAPITAL GAINS

Chargeable gains arising to a company are calculated in a manner similar to that used for individuals. However, companies are not entitled to the CGT annual exemption. Companies do not suffer CGT on chargeable gains but incur liability to corporation tax instead. Tax is due on the full chargeable gain of an accounting period after subtracting relief for any losses.

## GROUPS OF COMPANIES

Each company within a group is separately charged corporation tax on profits, gains and income. However, where one group member realises a loss for which special rules apply, other than a capital loss, a claim may be made to offset the deficiency against profits of some other member of the same group. The transfer of capital assets from one member of a group to a fellow member will usually incur no liability to tax on chargeable gains.

## SPORTS CLUBS

Though corporation tax is payable by unincorporated associations, including most sports clubs on their profits, a substantial exemption from liability to corporation tax is available to qualifying registered community amateur sports clubs (CASCs). Sports clubs that are registered as CASCs are exempt from liability to corporation tax on:

- profits from trading where the turnover of the trade is less than £30,000 in a 12-month period
- income from letting property where the gross rental income is less than £20,000 in a 12-month period
- bank and building society interest received
- chargeable gains
- any Gift Aid donations

All of the exemptions depend upon the club having been a registered CASC for the whole of the relevant accounting period and the income or gains being used only for qualifying purposes. If the club has only been a registered CASC for part of an accounting period the exemption amounts of £50,000 (for trading) and £30,000 (for income from property) are reduced proportionately. Only interest and gains received after the club is registered are exempted.

Some of the rules for CASCs changed on 1 April 2015. Full details can be found at W www.gov.uk/government/publications/community-amateur-sports-clubs-detailed-guidance-notes

Charities are also generally exempt from corporation tax where they operate through a company structure.

## VALUE ADDED TAX

Value added tax (VAT) is a tax on consumer expenditure charged when an individual buys goods and services in the European Union, including the UK. It is normally included in the sale price of goods and services and paid at the point of purchase. Each EU country has its own rate of VAT. From a business point of view, VAT is charged on most business transactions involving the supply of goods and services by a registered trader in the UK and Isle of Man. It is also charged on goods and some services imported from places outside the EU and on goods and some services coming into the UK from the other EU countries. VAT is administered by HMRC. A wide range of information on VAT, including VAT forms, is available online (W www.gov.uk/business-tax/vat). HMRC also runs a VAT Enquiries helpline (T 0300-200 3700).

## RATES OF TAX

There are three rates of VAT in the UK. The standard rate, payable on most goods and services in the UK, is 20 per cent.

The reduced rate – currently 5 per cent – is payable on certain goods and services including, for example, domestic fuel and power, children's car seats, women's sanitary products, contraceptive products, smoking cessation products and the installation of energy-saving materials such as wall insulation and solar panels.

A zero, or nil, rate applies to certain items including, for example, children's clothes, books, newspapers, most food and drink, and drugs and aids for disabled people. There are numerous exceptions to the zero-rated categories, however. While most food and drink is zero-rated, items including ice creams, chocolates, sweets, potato crisps and alcoholic drinks are not. Neither are drinks or items sold for consumption in a restaurant or cafe. Takeaway cold items such as sandwiches are zero-rated, while takeaway hot foods like fish and chips are not.

## REGISTRATION

All traders, including professional persons and companies, must register for VAT if they are making 'taxable supplies' of a value exceeding stated limits. All goods and services that are VAT-rated are defined as 'taxable supplies' including zero-rated items which must be included when calculating the total value of a trader's taxable supplies – his or her 'taxable turnover'. The limits that govern mandatory registration are amended periodically.

An unregistered trader must register for VAT if:

- at the end of any month the total value of his or her taxable turnover (not just profit) for the past 12 months or less is more than the current VAT threshold of £82,000
*and*
- at any time he or she has reasonable grounds to expect that his or her taxable turnover will be more than the current registration threshold of £82,000 in the next 30 days alone

To register for VAT, one or more forms must be completed and sent to HMRC within 30 days of any of the above. Basic VAT registration can currently be completed online (W https://online.hmrc.gov.uk/registration/). Traders who do not register at the correct time can be fined. Traders must charge VAT on their taxable supplies from the date they first need to be registered. Traders who only supply zero-rated goods may ot have to register for VAT even if their taxable turnover goes above the registration threshold. However, a trader in this position must inform HMRC first and apply to be exempt from registration'. A trader whose taxable turnover does not reach the mandatory registration limit may choose to register for VAT voluntarily if what he or she does counts as a business for VAT purposes. This step may be thought advisable to recover input tax (*see* below) or to compete with other registered traders. Registered traders may submit an application for deregistration if their taxable turnover subsequently falls. An application for deregistration can be made if the taxable turnover for the year beginning on the application date is not expected to exceed £80,000.

## INPUT TAX

Registered traders suffer input tax when buying in goods or services for the purposes of their business. It is the VAT that traders pay out to their suppliers on goods and services coming *in* to their business. Relief can usually be obtained for input tax suffered, either by setting that tax against output tax due or by repayment. Most items of input tax can be relieved in this manner. Where a registered trader makes both exempt supplies and taxable supplies to his customers or clients, there may be some restriction in the amount of input tax that can be recovered.

## OUTPUT TAX

When making a taxable supply of goods or services, registered traders must account for output tax, if any, on the value of that supply. Output tax is the term used to describe the VAT on the goods and services that they supply or sell – the VAT on supplies going *out* of the business and collected from customers on each sale made. Usually the price charged by the registered trader will be increased by adding VAT, but failure to make the required addition will not remove liability to account for output tax. The liability to account for output tax, and also relief for input tax, may be affected where a trader is using a special secondhand goods scheme.

## EXEMPT SUPPLIES

VAT is not chargeable on certain goods and services because the law deems them 'exempt' from VAT. These include the provision of burial and cremation facilities, insurance, loans of money, certain types of education and training and some property transactions. The granting of a lease to occupy land or the sale of land will usually comprise an exempt supply, for example, but there are numerous exceptions. Exempt supplies do not enter into the calculation of taxable turnover that governs liability to mandatory registration (*see* above). Such supplies made by a registered trader may, however, limit the amount of input tax that can be relieved. It is for this reason that the exemption may be useful.

## COLLECTION OF TAX

Registered traders submit VAT returns for accounting periods usually of three months in duration, but arrangements can be made to submit returns on a monthly basis. Very large traders must account for tax on a monthly basis, but this does not affect the three-monthly return. The return will show both the output tax for supplies made by the trader in the accounting period and also the input tax for which relief is claimed. If the output tax exceeds input tax the balance must be remitted with the VAT return. Where input tax suffered exceeds the output tax due, the registered trader may claim the excess from HMRC.

This basis for collecting tax explains the structure of VAT. Where supplies are made between registered traders the supplier will account for an amount of tax that will usually be identical to the tax recovered by the person to whom

the supply is made. However, where the supply is made to a person who is not a registered trader there can be no recovery of input tax and it is on this person that the final burden of VAT eventually falls. Where goods are acquired by a UK trader from a supplier within the EU, the trader must also account for the tax due on acquisition. There are a number of simplified arrangements to make VAT accounting easier for businesses, particularly small businesses, and there is advice on the HMRC website about how to choose the most appropriate scheme for a business:

### Cash Accounting
This scheme allows businesses to only pay VAT on the basis of payments received from their customers rather than on invoice dates or time of supply. It can therefore be useful for businesses with cash flow problems that cannot pay their VAT as a result. Businesses may use the cash accounting scheme if taxable turnover is under £1.35m. There is no need to apply for the scheme – eligible businesses may start using it at the beginning of a new tax period. If a trader opts to use this scheme, he or she can do so until the taxable turnover reaches £1.6m.

### Annual Accounting
If taxable turnover is under £1.35m a year, the trader may join the annual accounting scheme which allows them to make nine monthly or three quarterly instalments during the year based on an estimate of their total annual VAT bill. At the end of the year they submit a single return and any balance due. The advantages of this scheme for businesses are easier budgeting and cash flow planning because fixed payments are spread regularly throughout the year. Once a trader has joined the annual accounting scheme, membership may continue until the annual taxable turnover reaches £1.6m.

### Flat Rate Scheme
This scheme allows small businesses with an annual taxable turnover of less than £150,000 to save on administration by paying VAT as a set flat percentage of their annual turnover instead of accounting internally for VAT on each individual 'in and out'. The percentage rate used is governed by the trade sector into which the business falls. The scheme can no longer be used once annual income exceeds £230,000.

### Retail Schemes
There are special schemes that offer retailers an alternative if it is impractical for them to issue invoices for a large number of supplies direct to the public. These schemes include a provision to claim relief from VAT on bad debts where goods or services are supplied to a customer who does not pay for them.

VAT FACT SUMMARY
*from 1 April 2015*

| | |
|---|---|
| Standard rate | 20% |
| Reduced rate | 5% |
| Registration (last 12 months or next 30 days) | £82,000 |
| Deregistration (next 12 months under) | £80,000 |
| Cash accounting scheme – up to | £1,350,000 |
| Flat rate scheme – up to | £150,000 |
| Annual accounting scheme – up to | £1,350,000 |

## STAMP DUTY

For the majority of people, contact with stamp duty arises when they buy a property. Stamp duty is payable by the buyer as a way of raising revenue for the government based on the purchase price of a property, stocks and shares. This section aims to provide a broad overview of stamp duty as it may affect the average person.

## STAMP DUTY LAND TAX

Stamp duty land tax was introduced on 1 December 2003 and covers the purchase of houses, flats and other land, buildings and certain leases in the UK.

Before 1 December 2003 property purchasers had to submit documents providing all details of the purchase to the Stamp Office for 'stamping'. The purchaser's solicitor or licensed conveyancer would then send the stamped documentation to the appropriate land registry to register ownership of the property. Under stamp duty land tax, purchasers do not have to send documents for stamping. Instead, a land transaction return form SDLT1, which contains all information regarding the purchase that is relevant to HMRC, is signed by the purchaser. Buyers of property are responsible for completing the land transaction return and payment of stamp duty, though the solicitor or licensed conveyancer acting for them in a land transaction will normally complete the relevant paperwork. Once HMRC has received the completed land transaction return and the payment of any stamp duty due, a certificate will be issued that enables a solicitor or licensed conveyancer to register the property in the new owner's name at the Land Registry.

The threshold for notification of residential property is currently £40,000. This means that taxpayers entering into a transaction involving residential or non-residential property where the chargeable consideration is less than £40,000 do not need to notify HMRC about the transaction.

Since 1 April 2015 stamp duty has no longer applied to land transactions in Scotland. These are now subject to land and buildings transaction tax, details of which can be found online (W www.gov.uk/sdlt-scottish-transactions).

### RATES OF STAMP DUTY LAND TAX

Stamp duty is charged at different rates and has thresholds for different types of property and different values of transaction. The tax rate and payment threshold can vary according to whether the property is in residential or non-residential use and whether it is freehold or leasehold.

The government amended the rates and changed the calculation of stamp duty on purchases of residential property on 4 December 2014.

Previously, stamp duty was charged at a single rate for the entire price of a property. When assessing how much stamp duty was payable, the entire purchase price had to be taken into account so that the relevant stamp duty rate was paid on the whole sum, not just on the amount over each tax threshold. For example, on a property bought for £250,000, 1 per cent (£2,500) was payable in stamp duty. On a property bought for £250,001, however, 3 per cent of the whole price (£7,500) was payable.

Since 4 December 2014, however, stamp duty on purchases of residential property has been charged at increasing rates for each portion of the price.

For 2015–16, stamp duty is payable at the following rates on a residential property purchase: nothing on the first £125,000 of the property price; 2 per cent on the next £125,000; 5 per cent on the next £675,000; 10 per cent on the next £575,000 and 12 per cent on the rest.

For example, on a property bought for £275,000, a total of £3,750 is payable in stamp duty. This is made up of: nothing on the first £125,000, £2,500 (2 per cent) on the next £125,000 and £1,250 (5 per cent) on the remaining £25,000.

Stamp duty on residential property purchases 2015–16:

| Portion of the transaction value | Stamp duty is charged at |
|---|---|
| Up to £125,000 | zero |
| Between £125,001 and £250,000 | 2 per cent |
| Between £250,001 and £925,000 | 5 per cent |
| Between £925,001 and £1,500,000 | 10 per cent |
| Over £150,000,000 | 12 per cent |

Stamp duty is charged at 15 per cent on residential properties costing more than £500,000 bought by bodies such as companies and collective investment schemes, though there are some exceptions. For example, stamp duty is payable based on the new rates and bands in the table above where the property is used for a property rental business.

On purchases of non-residential and mixed-use properties, stamp duty is payable at the following rates:

- nothing on the property price, premium or value up to £150,000 (annual rent less than £1,000)
- 1 per cent on properties up to £150,000 (annual rent £1,000 or more)
- 1 per cent on properties between £150,001 and £250,000 (rent £1,000 or more)
- 3 per cent on properties between £250,001 and £500,000 (rent £1,000 or more)
- 4 per cent on properties over £500,000 (rent £1,000 or more)

To work out the amount of stamp duty payable on residential or non-residential property, a stamp duty land tax calculator is available online (W www.hmrc.gov.uk/tools/sdlt/land-and-property.htm).

## STAMP DUTY RESERVE TAX

Stamp duty or stamp duty reserve tax (SDRT) is payable at the rate of 0.5 per cent when shares are purchased. Stamp duty is payable when the shares are transferred using a stock transfer form, whereas SDRT is payable on 'paperless' share transactions where the shares are transferred electronically without using a stock transfer form. Most share transactions nowadays are paperless and settled by stockbrokers through CREST (the electronic settlement and registration system). SDRT therefore now accounts for the majority of taxation collected on share transactions effected through the London Stock Exchange.

The flat rate of 0.5 per cent is based on the amount paid for the shares, not what they are worth. If, for example, shares are bought for £2,000, £10 SDRT is payable, whatever the value of the shares themselves. If shares are transferred for free, no SDRT is payable.

A higher rate of 1.5 per cent is payable where shares are transferred into a 'depository receipt scheme' or a 'clearance service'. These are special arrangements where the shares are held by a third party.

CREST automatically deducts the SDRT and sends it to HMRC. A stockbroker will settle up with CREST for the cost of the shares and the SDRT and then bill the purchaser for these and the broker's fees. If shares are not purchased through CREST, the stamp duty must be paid by the purchaser to HMRC.

UK stamp duty or SDRT is not payable on the purchase of foreign shares, though there may be foreign taxes to pay. SDRT is already accounted for in the price paid for units in unit trusts or shares in open-ended investment companies.

### HELP AND INFORMATION

Further information on stamp duty land tax and SDRT is available via the stamp taxes helpline on T 0300-200 3510 or the government information website (W www.gov.uk).

# LEGAL NOTES

These notes outline certain aspects of the law as they might affect the average person. They are intended only as a broad guideline and are by no means definitive. The law is constantly changing so expert advice should always be taken. In some cases, sources of further information are given in these notes.

It is always advisable to consult a solicitor without delay. Anyone who does not have a solicitor can contact the following for assistance in finding one: Citizens Advice (W www.citizensadvice.org.uk), the Community Legal Service (W www.gov.uk) or the Law Society of England and Wales. For assistance in Scotland, contact Citizens Advice Scotland (W www.cas.org.uk) or the Law Society of Scotland.

Legal aid schemes exist to make the help of a lawyer available to those who would not otherwise be able to afford one. Entitlement for most types of legal aid depends on an individual's means but a solicitor or Citizens Advice will be able to advise on this.

LAW SOCIETY OF ENGLAND AND WALES,
113 Chancery Lane, London WC2A 1PL T 020-7242 1222
W www.lawsociety.org.uk
LAW SOCIETY OF SCOTLAND, 26 Drumsheugh Gardens,
Edinburgh EH3 7YR T 0131-226 7411 W www.lawscot.org.uk

## ABORTION

Abortion is governed by the Abortion Act 1967. Under its provisions, a legally induced abortion must be:
* performed by a registered medical practitioner
* carried out in an NHS hospital or other approved premises
* certified by two registered medical practitioners as justified on one or more of the following grounds:
(a) that the pregnancy has not exceeded its 24th week and that the continuance of the pregnancy would involve risk, greater than if the pregnancy were terminated, of injury to the physical or mental health of the pregnant woman or any existing children of her family
(b) that the termination is necessary to prevent grave permanent injury to the physical or mental health of the pregnant woman
(c) that the continuance of the pregnancy would involve risk to the life of the pregnant woman, greater than if the pregnancy were terminated
(d) that there is a substantial risk that if the child were born it would suffer from such physical or mental abnormalities as to be seriously handicapped.

In determining whether the continuance of a pregnancy would involve such risk of injury to health as is mentioned in grounds (a) or (b), account may be taken of the pregnant woman's actual or reasonably foreseeable environment.

The requirements relating to the opinion of two registered medical practitioners and to the performance of the abortion at an NHS hospital or other approved place cease to apply in circumstances where a registered medical practitioner is of the opinion, formed in good faith, that a termination is immediately necessary to save the life, or to prevent grave permanent injury to the physical or mental health, of the pregnant woman.

The Abortion Act 1967 does not apply to Northern Ireland, where abortion is not legal.

FAMILY PLANNING ASSOCIATION (UK),
23–28 Penn Street, London N1 5DL T 020-7608 5240
W www.fpa.org.uk

BRITISH PREGNANCY ADVISORY SERVICE (BPAS),
20 Timothys Bridge Road, Stratford-upon-Avon CV37 9BF
T 0345-365 5050 W www.bpas.org

## ADOPTION OF CHILDREN

The Adoption and Children Act 2002 reformed the framework for domestic and intercountry adoption in England and Wales and some parts of it extend to Scotland and Northern Ireland. The Children and Adoption Act 2006, recently amended by the Children and Families Act 2014, introduced further provisions for adoptions involving a foreign element.

### WHO MAY APPLY FOR AN ADOPTION ORDER
A couple (whether married or two people living as partners in an enduring family relationship) may apply for an adoption order where both of them are over 21 or where one is only 18 but the natural parent and the other is 21. An adoption order may be made for one applicant where that person is 21 and: a) the court is satisfied that person is the partner of a parent of the person to be adopted; or b) they are not married and are not civil partners; or c) married or in a civil partnership but they are separated from their spouse or civil partner and living apart with the separation likely to be permanent; or d) their spouse/civil partner is either unable to be found, or their spouse/civil partner is incapable by reason of ill-health of making an application. There are certain qualifying conditions an applicant must meet, eg residency in the British Isles.

### ARRANGING AN ADOPTION
Adoptions may generally only be arranged by an adoption agency or by way of an order from the high court; breach of the restrictions on who may arrange an adoption would constitute a criminal offence. When deciding whether a child should be placed for adoption, the court or adoption agency must consider all the factors set out in the 'welfare checklist' – the paramount consideration being the child's welfare, throughout his or her life. These factors include the child's wishes, needs, age, sex, background and any harm which the child has suffered or is likely to suffer. At all times, the court or adoption agency must bear in mind that delay is likely to prejudice a child's welfare.

### ADOPTION ORDER
Once an adoption has been arranged, a court order is necessary to make it legal; this may be obtained from the high court, county court or magistrates' court (including the family proceedings court). An adoption order may not be given unless the court is satisfied that the consent of the child's natural parents (or guardians) has been given correctly. Consent can be dispensed with on two grounds: where the parent or guardian cannot be found or is incapable of giving consent, or where the welfare of the child so demands.

An adoption order extinguishes the parental responsibility that a person other than the adopters (or adopter) has for the child. Where an order is made on the application of the partner of the parent, that parent keeps parental responsibility. Once adopted, the child has the same status as a child born to the adoptive parents, but may lose rights to the estates of those losing their parental responsibility.

### REGISTRATION AND CERTIFICATES
All adoption orders made in England and Wales are required to be registered in the Adopted Children Register which also

contains particulars of children adopted under registrable foreign adoptions. The General Register Office keeps this register from which certificates may be obtained in a similar way to birth certificates. The General Register Office also has equivalents in Scotland and Northern Ireland.

## TRACING NATURAL PARENTS OR CHILDREN WHO HAVE BEEN ADOPTED

An adult adopted person may apply to the Registrar-General to obtain a certified copy of his/her birth certificate. Adoption agencies and adoption support agencies should provide services to adopted persons to assist them in obtaining information about their adoption and facilitate contact with their relatives. There is an Adoption Contact Register which provides a safe and confidential way for birth parents and other relatives to assure an adopted person that contact would be welcome. The BAAF (*see* below) can provide addresses of organisations which offer advice, information and counselling to adopted people, adoptive parents and people who have had their children adopted.

**BRITISH ASSOCIATION FOR ADOPTION AND**
FOSTERING (BAAF), Saffron House, 6–10 Kirby Street, London EC1N 8TS T 020-7421 2600 W www.baaf.org.uk

## SCOTLAND

The relevant legislation is the Adoption and Children (Scotland) Act 2007 which came into force on 28 September 2009. In addition, adoptions with a foreign element are governed by the Adoptions with a Foreign Element (Scotland) Regulations 2009. Pre-2009 adoptions are governed by Part IV of the Adoption (Scotland) Act 1978. The provisions of the 2007 act are similar to those described above. In Scotland, petitions for adoption are made to the sheriff court or the court of session.

**BRITISH ASSOCIATION FOR ADOPTION AND**
FOSTERING (BAAF), BAAF Scottish Centre, 113 Rose Street, Edinburgh EH2 3DT T 0131-226 9270

## BIRTHS (REGISTRATION)

It is the duty of the parents of a child born in England or Wales to register the birth within 42 days of the date of birth at the register office in the district in which the baby was born. If it is inconvenient to go to the district where the birth took place, the information for the registration may be given to a registrar in another district, who will send your details to the appropriate register office. Failure to register the birth within 42 days without reasonable cause may leave the parents liable to a penalty. If a birth has not been registered within 12 months of its occurrence it is possible for the late registration of the birth to be authorised by the Registrar-General, provided documentary evidence of the precise date and place of birth are satisfactory.

Births that take place in England may only be registered in English, but births that take place in Wales may be registered bilingually in Welsh and English. In order to do this, the details must be given in Welsh and the registrar must be able to understand and write in Welsh.

If the parents of the child were married to each other at the time of the birth (or conception), either the mother or the father may register the birth alone. If the parents were not married to each other at the time of the child's birth (or conception), the father's particulars may be entered in the register only where he attends the register office with the mother and they sign the birth register together. Where an unmarried parent is unable to attend the register office, either parent may submit to the registrar a statutory declaration on Form 16 (or Form 16W for births which took place in Wales) acknowledging the father's paternity (this form may be obtained from any registrar in England or Wales or online at W www.gro.gov.uk); alternatively a parental responsibility agreement or appropriate court order may be produced to the registrar.

If the father's details are not included in the birth register, it may be possible to re-register the birth at a later date. If the parents do not register the birth of their child the following people may do so:
• an occupier of the house or an administrative member of staff of the hospital where the child was born
• a person who was present at the birth
• a person who is responsible for the child
Upon registration of the birth a short certificate is issued. It may be possible to register the birth while still at hospital. Hospitals will advise individually whether this is possible.

## SAME-SEX COUPLES

Male couples must get a parental order from the court before they can be registered as parents. Female couples can include both of their names on the child's birth certificate when registering the birth; however the rules differ depending on whether or not they are in a civil partnership.

In the case of female civil partners, either woman can register the birth on her own if all of the following are true:
• the mother had the child by donor insemination or fertility treatment
• she was in a civil partnership at the time of the treatment
• her civil partner is the child's legal parent
When a mother is not in a civil partnership, her partner can be seen as the child's second parent if both women:
• are treated together in the UK by a licensed clinic
• have made a 'parenthood agreement'
However, for both parents' details to be recorded on the birth certificate, the parents must do one of the following:
• register the birth jointly
• complete a 'statutory declaration of acknowledgement of parentage' form and one parents takes the signed form when she registers the birth
• get a document from the court (eg a court order) giving the second female parent parental responsibility and one parent shows the document when she registers the birth

## BIRTHS ABROAD

There are certain countries where birth registrations may be made for British citizens overseas (for more details on British citizenship *see* below). The British consul or high commission may register the births and issue certificates which are then sent to the General Register Office. If a birth is registered by the British consul or high commission, the registration would show the person's claim to British citizenship, British overseas territories citizenship or British overseas citizenship. All consular birth registrations are now performed at the Foreign and Commonwealth Office's facility.

## SCOTLAND

In Scotland the birth of a child must be registered within 21 days at the registration office of any registration district in Scotland.

If the child is born, either in or out of Scotland, on a ship, aircraft or land vehicle that ends its journey at any place in Scotland, the child, in most cases, will be registered as if born in that place.

## CERTIFICATES OF BIRTHS, DEATHS OR MARRIAGES

Certificates of births, marriages and deaths that have taken place in England and Wales since 1837 can be obtained from the General Register Office (GRO).

Marriage or death certificates may also be obtained from the minister of the church in which the marriage or funeral took place. Any register office can advise about the best way to obtain certificates.

The fees for certificates are:

*Online application:*
- full certificate of birth, marriage, death or adoption, £9.25
- full certificate of birth, marriage, death or adoption with GRO reference supplied, £9.25

*By postal/phone/fax application:*
- full certificate of birth, marriage, death or adoption, £9.25
- full certificate of birth, marriage, death or adoption with GRO reference supplied, £9.25
- extra copies of the same birth, marriage or death certificate issued at the same time, £9.25

A priority service is available for an additional fee.

A complete set of the GRO indexes including births, deaths and marriages, civil partnerships, adoptions and provisional indexes for births and deaths up to March 2015 are available at the British Library, City of Westminster Archives Centre, Manchester Central Library, Newcastle City Library, Library of Birmingham, Bridgend Reference and Information Library and Plymouth Central Library. Copies of GRO indexes may also be held at some libraries, family history societies, local records offices and The Church of Jesus Christ of Latter Day Saints family history centres. Some organisations may not hold a complete record of indexes and a small fee may be charged by some of them. GRO indexes are also available online.

The Society of Genealogists has many records of baptisms, marriages and deaths prior to 1837.

## SCOTLAND

Certificates of births, deaths or marriages that have taken place in Scotland since 1855 can be obtained from the National Records of Scotland (formerly the General Register Office for Scotland) or from the appropriate local registrar.

*Applicable fees – local registrar:*
- each extract or abbreviated certificate of birth, death, marriage, civil partnership or adoption within a month of registration, £10.00
- each extract or abbreviated certificate of birth, death, marriage, civil partnership or adoption outwith a month of registration, £15.00

A priority service is available for an additional fee.

The National Records of Scotland also keeps the Register of Divorces (including decrees of declaration of nullity of marriage), and holds parish registers dating from before 1855.

*Applicable fees – National Records of Scotland:*
- personal application, or postal, telephone or fax order: £15.00

A priority service for a response within 24 hours is available for an additional fee of £15.00.

A search of birth, death and marriage records including records of Church of Scotland parishes and other statutory records can be done at the Scotland's People Centre. There are also indexes to some of the old parish registers death and burial records in the library at the centre and indexes and images of census records from 1841–1911 are available. The charges for such searches are as follows:
- full or part-day search pass, £15.00
- Quarterly search pass, £490.00
- annual search pass, £1,450.00

Online searching is also available. For more information, visit W www.scotlandspeople.gov.uk.

THE GENERAL REGISTER OFFICE, General Register Office, Certificate Services Section, PO Box 2, Southport PR8 2JD
T 0300-123 1837 W www.gro.gov.uk/gro/content/certificates

THE NATIONAL RECORDS OF SCOTLAND, New Register House, 3 West Register Street, Edinburgh EH1 3YT
T 0131-334 0380 W www.nrscotland.gov.uk

SCOTLAND'S PEOPLE CENTRE, General Register House, 2 Princes Street, Edinburgh EH1 3YY T 0131-314 4300
W www.scotlandspeoplehub.gov.uk

THE SOCIETY OF GENEALOGISTS, 14 Charterhouse Buildings, Goswell Road, London EC1M 7BA T 020-7251 8799
W www.sog.org.uk

## BRITISH NATIONALITY

There are different types of British nationality status: British citizenship; British overseas citizenship; British national (overseas); British overseas territories citizenship; British protected persons; and British subjects. The most widely held of these is British citizenship. Everyone born in the UK before 1 January 1983 became a British citizen when the British Nationality Act 1981 came into force, with the exception of children born to certain diplomatic staff working in the UK at the time. Individuals born outside the UK before 1 January 1983 but who at that date were citizens of the UK and colonies and had a right of abode in the UK also became British citizens. British citizens have the right to live permanently in the UK and are free to leave and re-enter the UK at any time.

A person born on or after 1 January 1983 in the UK (including, for this purpose, the Channel Islands and the Isle of Man) is entitled to British citizenship if he/she falls into one of the following categories:
- he/she has a parent who is a British citizen
- he/she has a parent who is settled in the UK
- he/she is a newborn infant found abandoned in the UK
- his/her parents subsequently settle in the UK or become British citizens and an application is made before he/she is 18
- he/she lives in the UK for the first ten years of his/her life and is not absent for more than 90 days in each of those years
- he/she is adopted in the UK and one of the adopters is a British citizen
- the home secretary consents to his/her registration while he/she is a minor
- if he/she has always been stateless and lives in the UK for a period of five years before his/her 22nd birthday
- if he/she has been born on or after 13 January 2010 to a parent who is a member of the UK armed forces
- if he/she has been born on or after 13 January 2010 and a parent becomes a member of the UK armed forces, and an application is made before he/she is 18

A person born outside the UK may acquire British citizenship if he/she falls into one of the following categories:
- he/she has a parent who is a British citizen otherwise than by descent, eg a parent who was born in the UK
- he/she has a parent who is a British citizen serving the crown or a European community institution overseas and was recruited to that service in the UK (including qualifying territories for those born on or after 21 May 2002) or in the European Community (for services within an EU institution); or if the applicant himself/herself has at any time been in crown, or similar, service under the government of a British overseas territory
- if he/she has been born on or after 13 January 2010 to a parent who is a member of the UK armed forces serving outside the UK and qualifying territories, is of good character and (if he/she is a minor at the time of application) all parents then alive consent in signed writing
- the home secretary consents to his/her registration while he/she is a minor

• he/she is a British overseas territories citizen, a British overseas citizen, a British subject or a British protected person and has been lawfully resident in the UK for five years
• he/she is a British overseas territories citizen who acquired that citizenship from a connection with Gibraltar
• he/she is adopted or naturalised
Where parents are married, the status of either may confer citizenship on their child. Since July 2006, both parents are able to pass on nationality even if they are not married, provided that there is satisfactory evidence of paternity. For children born before July 2006, it must be shown that there is parental consent and that the child would have an automatic claim to citizenship or entitlement to registration had the parents been married. Where parents are not married, the status of the mother determines the child's citizenship.

Under the 1981 act, Commonwealth citizens and citizens of the Republic of Ireland were entitled to registration as British citizens before 1 January 1983. In 1983, citizens of the Falkland Islands were granted British citizenship.

Renunciation of British citizenship must be registered with the home secretary and will be revoked if no new citizenship or nationality is acquired within six months. If the renunciation was required in order to retain or acquire another citizenship or nationality, the citizenship may be reacquired only once. If the renunciation was for another reason, the home secretary may allow reacquisition more than once, depending on the circumstances. The secretary of state may deprive a person of a citizenship status if he or she is satisfied that the person has done anything seriously prejudicial to the vital interests of the UK, or a British overseas territory, unless making the order would have the effect of rendering such a person stateless. A person may also be deprived of a citizenship status which results from his registration or naturalisation if the secretary of state is satisfied that the registration or naturalisation was obtained by fraud, false representation or concealment of a material fact.

### BRITISH DEPENDENT TERRITORIES CITIZENSHIP
Since 26 February 2002, this category of nationality no longer exists and has been replaced by British overseas territory citizenship.

If a person had this class of nationality only by reason of a connection to the territory of Hong Kong, they lost it automatically when Hong Kong was returned to the People's Republic of China. However, if after 30 June 1997, they had no other nationality and would have become stateless, or were born after 30 June 1997 and would have been born stateless (but had a parent who was a British national (overseas) or a British overseas citizen), they became a British overseas citizen.

### BRITISH OVERSEAS CITIZENSHIP
Under the 1981 act, as amended by the British Overseas Territories Act 2002, this type of citizenship was conferred on any UK and colonies citizens who did not become either a British citizen or a British overseas territories citizen on 1 January 1983 and as such is now, for most purposes, only acquired by persons who would otherwise be stateless.

### BRITISH OVERSEAS TERRITORIES CITIZENSHIP
This category of nationality replaced British dependent territories citizenship. Most commonly, this form of nationality is acquired where, after 31 December 1982, a person was a citizen of the UK and colonies and did not become a British citizen, and that person, or their parents or grandparents, were born, registered or naturalised in the specified British overseas territory. However, on 21 May 2002, people became British citizens if they had British

overseas territories citizenship by connection with any British overseas territory, except for the sovereign base areas of Akrotiri and Dhekelia in Cyprus.

### RESIDUAL CATEGORIES
British subjects, British protected persons and British nationals (overseas) may be entitled to registration as British citizens on completion of five years' legal residence in the UK.

Citizens of the Republic of Ireland who were also British subjects before 1 January 1949 can retain that status if they fulfil certain conditions.

### EUROPEAN UNION CITIZENSHIP
British citizens (including Gibraltarians who are registered for this purpose) are also EU citizens and are entitled to travel freely to other EU countries to work, study, reside and set up a business. EU citizens have the same rights with respect to the UK.

### NATURALISATION
Naturalisation is granted at the discretion of the home secretary. The basic requirements are lawful residence in the UK in the five years immediately preceding application (three years if the applicant is married to, or is the civil partner of a British citizen), good character, adequate knowledge of the English, Welsh or Scottish Gaelic language, passing the UK citizenship test and an intention to reside permanently in the UK.

### STATUS OF ALIENS
Aliens, being persons without any of the above forms of British nationality, may not hold public office or vote in Britain and they may not own a British ship or aircraft. Citizens of the Republic of Ireland and Commonwealth citizens are not deemed to be aliens. Certain provisions of the Immigration and Asylum Act 1999 make provision about immigration and asylum and about procedures in connection with marriage by superintendent registrar's certificate.

## CONSUMER LAW

### SALE OF GOODS
A sale of goods contract is the most common type of contract. It is governed by the Sale of Goods Act 1979 (as amended by the Sale and Supply of Goods Act 1994). The act provides protection for buyers by implying terms into every sale of goods contract. These terms include:
• where the seller sells goods by reference to a description, an implied term that the goods will match that description and, where the sale is by sample and description, it will not be sufficient that the bulk of the goods correspond with the sample if the goods do not also correspond with the description
• where goods are sold by a business seller, an implied term that the goods will be of satisfactory quality ie they meet the standard that a reasonable person would regard as satisfactory, taking into account any description of the goods, the price, and all other relevant circumstances. The quality of the goods includes their state and condition, relevant aspects being whether they are fit for all the purposes for which such goods are commonly supplied, their appearance and finish, freedom from minor defects and their safety and durability. This term will not be implied, however, if a buyer has examined the goods (including in a sale by sample) and should have noticed the defect or if the seller specifically drew the buyer's attention to the defect

- where goods are sold by a business seller, an implied term that the goods are reasonably fit for any purpose made known to the seller by the buyer (either expressly or by implication), unless it is shown that the buyer does not rely on the seller's judgment, or it is not reasonable for him/her to do so

Some of the above terms can be excluded from contracts by the seller. The seller's right to do this is, however, restricted by the Unfair Contract Terms Act 1977. The act offers more protection to a buyer who 'deals as a consumer' (that is where the seller is selling in the course of a business, the goods are of a type ordinarily bought for private use and the goods are bought by a buyer who is not a business buyer) and does not allow for the implied terms described above to be excluded. In a sale of second-hand goods by auction (at which individuals have the opportunity of attending the sale in person), a buyer does not deal as a consumer.

## HIRE-PURCHASE AGREEMENTS
Terms similar to those implied in contracts of sales of goods are implied into contracts of hire-purchase, under the Supply of Goods (Implied Terms) Act 1973. The 1977 act limits the exclusion of these implied terms as before.

## SUPPLY OF GOODS AND SERVICES
Under the Supply of Goods and Services Act 1982, similar terms are also implied in other types of contract under which ownership of goods passes, and contracts for the hire of goods (though not hire-purchase agreements). These types of contracts have additional implied terms:
- that the supplier will use reasonable care and skill in carrying out the service
- that the supplier will carry out the service in a reasonable time (unless the time has been agreed)
- that the supplier will make a reasonable charge (unless the charge has already been agreed)

The 1977 act limits the exclusion of these implied terms in a similar manner as before.

## UNFAIR TERMS
The Unfair Terms in Consumer Contracts Regulations 1999 apply to contracts between business sellers (or suppliers of goods and services) and consumers. Where the terms have not been individually negotiated (ie where the terms were drafted in advance so that the consumer was unable to influence those terms), a term will be deemed unfair if it operates to the detriment of the consumer (ie causes a significant imbalance in the parties' rights and obligations arising under the contract). An unfair term does not bind the consumer but the contract may continue to bind the parties if it is capable of existing without the unfair term. The regulations contain a non-exhaustive list of terms that are regarded as potentially unfair. When a term does not fall into such a category, whether it will be regarded as fair or not will depend on many factors, including the nature of the goods or services, the surrounding circumstances (such as the bargaining strength of both parties) and the other terms in the contract. The Consumer Rights Act 2015 (see below) replaces the 1999 regulations.

## CONSUMER PROTECTION
The Consumer Protection from Unfair Trading Regulations 2008 (CPRs) replaced much previous consumer protection regulation, including the majority of the Trade Descriptions Act 1968. The CPRs prohibit 31 specific practices, including pyramid schemes. In addition the CPRs prohibit business sellers from making misleading actions and misleading omissions, which cause, or are likely to cause, the average consumer to take a different transactional decision. There is also a general duty not to trade unfairly. The CPRs were amended by the Consumer Protection (Amendment) Regulations 2014, which entered into force on 1 October 2014 and introduced a new direct civil right of redress for consumers against businesses for misleading and aggressive practices, as well as extending the CPRs to cover misleading and aggressive demands for payment.

Under the Consumer Protection Act 1987, producers of goods are liable for any injury, death or damage to any property exceeding £275 caused by a defect in their product (subject to certain defences).

Consumers are also afforded protection under the Consumer Contracts (Information, Cancellation and Additional Charges) Regulations 2013, which came into force on 13 June 2014.

The Consumer Rights Act 2015, which received royal assent on 26 March 2015, consolidates many of the key provisions within existing consumer rights legislation, including the Sale of Goods Act 1979, the Supply of Goods (Implied Terms) Act 1973 and the Supply of Goods and Services Act 1982. The Act also revokes the Unfair Terms in Consumer Contracts Regulations 1999, whose relevant provisions now form part of the 2015 Act. The Act also provides a new section on digital goods. The main provisions of the Consumer Rights Act came into force in October 2015.

## CONSUMER CREDIT
In matters relating to the provision of credit (or the supply of goods on hire or hire-purchase), consumers are also protected by the Consumer Credit Act 1974 (as amended by the Consumer Credit Act 2006). The act was most recently amended by a number of statutory instruments made under the Financial Services and Markets Act 2000. These came into force on 1 April 2014 and represent a major overhaul of the consumer credit regime which was carried out in order to implement the recent EU Consumer Credit Directive. Under the new regime, responsibility for consumer credit regulation has been transferred from the Office of Fair Trading (OFT), which has ceased to exist, to the Financial Conduct Authority (FCA). Previously, a licence issued by the OFT was required in order to conduct a consumer credit, consumer hire or an ancillary credit business, subject to certain exemptions. The requirement to obtain a licence from the OFT has been replaced by the need to obtain authorisation from the FCA to carry out a consumer credit 'regulated' activity, likewise subject to certain exemptions. Provisions of the 1974 Act as amended include:
- in order for a creditor to enforce a regulated agreement, the agreement must comply with certain formalities and must be properly executed. An improperly executed regulated agreement is enforceable only on an order of the court. The debtor must also be given specified information by the creditor or his/her broker or agent during the negotiations which take place before the signing of the agreement. The agreement must also state certain information to ensure that the debtor or hirer is aware of the rights and duties conferred or imposed on him/her and the protection and remedies available to him/her under the act
- the right to withdraw from or cancel some contracts depending on the circumstances. For example, subject to certain exceptions, a borrower may withdraw from a regulated credit agreement within 14 days without giving any reason. The exceptions include agreements for credit exceeding £60,260 and agreements secured on land. The right to withdraw applies only to the credit agreement itself and not to goods or services purchased with it. The borrower must also repay the credit and any interest

• if the debtor is in breach of the agreement, the creditor must serve a default notice before taking any action such as repossessing the goods
• if the agreement is a hire purchase or conditional sale agreement, the creditor cannot repossess the goods without a court order if the debtor has paid one third of the total price of the goods
• in agreements where the relationship between the creditor and the debtor is unfair to the debtor, the court may alter or set aside some of the terms of the agreement

It is intended that the statutory basis of consumer credit regulation, under the 1974 Act, will be replaced by a rules-based approach under the new regime. The FCA will be reviewing the stautory framework over the next few years and will develop rule-based alternatives where possible.

## SCOTLAND

The legislation governing the sale and supply of goods applies to Scotland as follows:
• the Sale of Goods Act 1979 applies with some modifications and it has been amended by the Sale and Supply of Goods Act 1994
• the Supply of Goods (Implied Terms) Act 1973 applies
• the Supply of Goods and Services Act 1982 does not extend to Scotland but some of its provisions were introduced by the Sale and Supply of Goods Act 1994
• only Parts II and III of the Unfair Contract Terms Act 1977 apply
• the Trade Descriptions Act 1968 applies with minor modifications
• the Consumer Credit Act 1974 applies
• the Consumer Credit Act 2006 applies
• the Consumer Protection Act 1987 applies
• the General Product Safety Regulations 2005 apply
• the Unfair Terms in Consumer Contracts Regulations 1999 apply
• the Unfair Terms in Consumer Contracts (Amendment) Regulations 2001 apply
• the Consumer Protection (Distance Selling) Regulations 2000 apply
• the Sale and Supply of Goods to Consumers Regulations 2002 apply
• the Consumer Protection from Unfair Trading Regulations 2008 apply

## PROCEEDINGS AGAINST THE CROWN

Until 1947, proceedings against the Crown were generally possible only by a procedure known as a petition of right, which put the private litigant at a considerable disadvantage. The Crown Proceedings Act 1947 placed the Crown (not the sovereign in his/her private capacity, but as the embodiment of the state) largely in the same position as a private individual and made proceedings in the high court involving the Crown subject to the same rules as any other case. The act did not, however, extinguish or limit the Crown's prerogative or statutory powers, and it continued the immunity of HM ships and aircraft. It also left certain Crown privileges unaffected. The act largely abolished the special procedures which previously applied to civil proceedings by and against the Crown. Civil proceedings may be initiated against the appropriate government department or, if there is doubt regarding which is the appropriate department, against the attorney-general.

In Scotland proceedings against the Crown founded on breach of contract could be taken before the 1947 act and no special procedures applied. The Crown could, however, claim certain special pleas. The 1947 act applies in part to Scotland and brings the practice of the two countries as closely together as the different legal systems permit. As a result of the Scotland Act 1998, actions against government departments should be raised against the Lord Advocate or the advocate-general. Actions should be raised against the Lord Advocate where the department involved administers a devolved matter. Devolved matters include agriculture, education, housing, local government, health and justice. Actions should be raised against the advocate-general where the department is dealing with a reserved matter. Reserved matters include defence, foreign affairs and social security.

## DEATHS

### WHEN A DEATH OCCURS

If the death (including stillbirth) was expected, the doctor who attended the deceased during their final illness should be contacted. If the death was sudden or unexpected, the family doctor (if known) and police should be contacted. If the cause of death is quite clear, the doctor will provide:
• a medical certificate that shows the cause of death
• a formal notice that states that the doctor has signed the medical certificate and that explains how to get the death registered
• if the death was known to be caused by a natural illness but the doctor wishes to know more about the cause of death, he/she may ask the relatives for permission to carry out a post-mortem examination

In England and Wales a coroner is responsible for investigating deaths occurring:
• when there is no doctor who can issue a medical certificate of cause of death
• no doctor has treated the deceased during his or her last illness or when the doctor attending the patient did not see him or her within 14 days before death, or after death
• the death occurred during an operation or before recovery from the effect of an anaesthetic
• the death was sudden and unexplained or attended by suspicious circumstances
• the death might be due to an industrial injury or disease, or to accident, violence, neglect or abortion
• the death occurred in prison or in police custody

The doctor will write on the formal notice that the death has been referred to the coroner; if the post-mortem shows that death was due to natural causes, the coroner may issue a notification which gives the cause of death so that the death can be registered. If the cause of death was violent or unnatural, is still undetermined after a post-mortem, or took place in prison or police custody, the coroner must hold an inquest. The coroner must hold an inquest in these circumstances even if the death occurred abroad (and the body has been returned to England or Wales).

In Scotland the office of coroner does not exist. The local procurator fiscal inquires into sudden or suspicious deaths. A fatal accident inquiry will be held before the sheriff where the death has resulted from an accident during the course of the employment of the person who has died, or where the person who has died was in legal custody, or where the Lord Advocate deems it in the public interest that an inquiry be held.

### REGISTERING A DEATH

In England and Wales the death can be registered at any register office, although if it is registered by the registrar of births and deaths for the district in which it occurred, the necessary documents can be obtained on the same day. A death which occurs in Scotland can be registered in any registration district in Scotland. Information concerning a death can be given before any registrar of births and deaths in England and Wales. The registrar will pass the relevant details to the registrar for the district where the death occurred, who will then register the death.

In England and Wales the death must normally be registered within five days (unless the registrar says this period can be extended); in Scotland within eight days. If the death has been referred to the coroner/local procurator fiscal it cannot be registered until the registrar has received authority from the coroner/local procurator fiscal to do so. Failure to register a death involves a penalty in England and Wales and may lead to a court decree being granted by a sheriff in Scotland. A stillbirth normally needs to be registered within 42 days, and at the latest within three months. In many cases this can be done at the hospital or at the local register office. In Scotland this must be done within 21 days.

If the death occurred at a house or hospital, the death may be registered by:

• any relative of the deceased
• any person present at the death
• the owner or occupier of the house or hospital if he/she knew of the occurrence of the death
• any person making the funeral arrangements with the funeral director
• an administrator from the hospital
• in Scotland, the deceased's executor or legal representative

For deaths that took place elsewhere, the death may be registered by:

• any relative of the deceased
• someone present at the death
• someone who found the body
• a person in charge of the body
• any person making the funeral arrangements with the funeral director

The majority of deaths are registered by a relative of the deceased. The registrar would normally allow one of the other listed persons to register the death only if there were no relatives available.

The person registering the death should take the medical certificate of the cause of death (signed by a doctor) with them; it is also useful, though not essential, to take the deceased's birth and marriage/civil partnership certificates, council tax bill, driving licence, passport, NHS medical card, pension documentation and life assurance details. The details given to the registrar must be absolutely correct, otherwise it may be difficult to change them later. The person registering the death should check the entry carefully before it is signed. The registrar will issue a certificate for burial or cremation, and a certificate of registration of death (commonly known as a 'death certificate' which is issued for social security purposes if the deceased received a state pension or benefits) – both free of charge. A death certificate is a certified copy of the entry in the death register; copies can be provided on payment of a fee and may be required for the following purposes, in particular by the executor or administrator when sorting out the deceased's affairs:

• the will
• bank and building society accounts
• savings bank certificates and premium bonds
• insurance policies
• pension claims

If the death occurred abroad or on a foreign ship or aircraft, the death should be registered according to the local regulations of the relevant country and a death certificate should be obtained. In many countries the death can also be registered with the British consulate in that country and a record will be kept at the General Register Office. This avoids the expense of bringing the body back.

After 12 months (three months in Scotland) of death or the finding of a dead body, no death can be registered without the written authority of the registrar-general.

## BURIAL AND CREMATION

In most circumstances in England and Wales a certificate for burial or cremation must be obtained from the registrar before the burial or cremation can take place. If the death has been referred to the coroner, an order for burial or a certificate for cremation must be obtained. In Scotland a body may be buried (but not cremated) before the death is registered.

Funeral costs can normally be repaid out of the deceased's estate and should be given priority over any other claims. If the deceased has left a will it may contain directions concerning the funeral; however, these directions need not be followed by the executor.

The deceased's papers should also indicate whether a grave space had already been arranged. This information will be contained in a document known as a 'Deed of Grant'. Most town churchyards and many suburban churchyards are no longer open for burial because they are full. Most cemeteries are non-denominational and may be owned by local authorities or private companies; fees vary.

If the body is to be cremated, an application form, two cremation certificates (for which there is a charge) or a certificate for cremation if the death was referred to the coroner, and a certificate signed by the medical referee must be completed in addition to the certificate for burial or cremation (the form is not required if the coroner has issued a certificate for cremation). All the forms are available from the funeral director or crematorium. Most crematoria are run by local authorities; the fees can include the medical referee's fee and the use of the chapel. Ashes may be scattered, buried in a churchyard or cemetery, or kept.

The registrar must be notified of the date, place and means of disposal of the body within 96 hours (England and Wales) or three days (Scotland).

If the death occurred abroad or on a foreign ship or aircraft, a local burial or cremation may be arranged. If the body is to be brought back to England or Wales, a death certificate from the relevant country or an authorisation for the removal of the body from the country of death from the coroner or relevant authority, together with a certificate of embalming, will be required. The British consulate can help to arrange this documentation. To arrange a funeral in England or Wales, an authenticated translation of a foreign death certificate or a death certificate issued in Scotland or Northern Ireland which must show the cause of death, is needed, together with a certificate of no liability to register from the registrar in England and Wales in whose sub-district it is intended to bury or cremate the body. If it is intended to cremate the body, a cremation order will be required from the Home Office or a certificate for cremation. If the body is to be cremated in Scotland, an order from the Scottish government Health Department must be obtained.

THE GENERAL REGISTER OFFICE, General Register Office, PO Box 2, Southport PR8 2JD T 0300-123 1837 W www.gro.gov.uk/gro/content/certificates
THE NATIONAL RECORDS OF SCOTLAND, New Register House, 3 West Register Street, Edinburgh EH1 3YT T 0131-334 0380 W www.nrscotland.gov.uk

# DIVORCE, DISSOLUTION AND RELATED MATTERS

Divorce is the legal process which ends a marriage. The process is the same whether the parties are of the opposite or same sex pursuant to the Marriage (Same Sex Couples) Act 2013. Dissolution is a similar process which ends a civil partnership. Divorce and dissolution should be distinguished from judicial separation which does not legally dissolve the marriage/civil partnership but removes the legal requirement for a married couple to live together.

## DIVORCE

An application for a matrimonial order for divorce may only be presented to the court after one year of marriage and it must be based on matters which occurred within that time. The spouse who lodges this document is known as the 'petitioner' throughout the divorce proceedings and the other spouse is the 'respondent'.

Whether the English court may or may not have jurisdiction to deal with any divorce will depend on where the parties spent their married life and whether or not one party has retained the residence in Engalnd (and Wales). If there is a dispute as to which of two jurisdictions should host the divorce, where the two jurisdictions likely to be relevant are EU countries then the usual rule is that the divocrce takes place in the country where the petition is filed first. The exception to this rule is Denmark, which opted out of the EU regulation which determines forums in this way.

If the two countries are not within the EU, or one of them is Denmark, then the forum of divorce may be determined by which is the more appropriate or convenient. An election of a country in a pre-nuptial agreement can be very important in resolving that dispute, although it cannot override the 'first in time' rule between EU countries (except Denmark) referred to above (save in the case of maintenance claims).

Some EU countries have signed up to a convention which would allow a couple to elect a choice of law even in EU countries whereby one country would be required to apply the law of another. For the time being, England has not signed up to that convention, and would apply English law only, though that may change in time.

There is only one ground for divorce, namely that the marriage has broken down irretrievably. This ground must be 'proved' by one of the following facts:
- the respondent has committed adultery and the petitioner finds it intolerable to live with him/her
- the respondent has behaved in such a way that the petitioner cannot reasonably be expected to live with him/her
- the respondent has deserted the petitioner for a continuous period of at least two years
- the two spouses have lived apart for at least two years and the respondent agrees to a divorce
- the two spouses have lived apart for at least five years

If the court is satisfied that the petitioner has proved one of those facts then it must grant a decree nisi (see below) unless it is satisfied that the marriage has not broken down.

## DECREE NISI

If the judge is satisfied that the petitioner has proved the contents of the divorce petition, a date will be set for the pronouncement of the decree nisi in open court. The decree nisi is a preliminary decree of divorce; the marriage will not be legally dissolved until the decree absolute. Neither party needs to attend and all the proceedings up to this point are usually carried out on paper.

## DECREE ABSOLUTE

The final step in the divorce procedure is to obtain a decree absolute which formally ends the marriage. The petitioner can apply for this six weeks and one day after the date of the decree nisi. If the petitioner does not apply the respondent can apply, but only after three months from the earliest date on which the petitioner could have applied.

A decree absolute will not usually be granted until the parties have agreed, or the court has dealt with, the parties' financial situation (see below for details of financial provision).

## DISSOLUTION OF CIVIL PARTNERSHIPS

The legal process for dissolution of a civil partnership follows a model closely based on divorce. Irretrievable breakdown of the partnership is the sole ground for dissolution. The facts to be proved to establish this are the same as for divorce, with the exception of adultery which, due to its legal definition, can only apply to opposite sex couples. Adultery can, however, be used as an example of unreasonable behaviour.

## FINANCIAL RELIEF ANCILLARY TO DIVORCE, NULLITY AND JUDICIAL SEPARATION

Following a petition for divorce, nullity or judicial separation, it is open to either spouse or former spouse to make a claim for financial provision provided they have not remarried. It is common practice for such an application to be made at the same time, or shortly after, a divorce petition has been issued. The courts have wide powers to make financial provision where a marriage breaks down. Orders can be made for:
- spousal maintenance (periodical payments) which can be capitalised into a lump sum
- lump sum payments
- adjustment or transfer of interests in property
- adjustment of interests in trusts and settlements
- orders relating to pensions

## EXERCISE OF THE COURT'S POWERS TO ORDER FINANCIAL PROVISION

The court must exercise its powers so as to achieve an outcome which is fair between the parties, although it has a wide discretion in determining what is a fair financial outcome. It will consider the worldwide assets of both parties, whether liquid or illiquid. In exercising its discretion, the court has to consider a range of statutory factors including:
- the income, earning capacity, property and other financial resources which either party has or is likely to have in the foreseeable future, including, in the case of earning capacity, any increase in that capacity which it would in the opinion of the court be reasonable to expect a party to the marriage to take steps to acquire
- the financial needs, obligations and responsibilities which each of the parties to the marriage has or is likely to have in the foreseeable future
- the standard of living enjoyed by the family before the breakdown of the marriage
- the age of each party to the marriage and the duration of the marriage
- any physical or mental disability of either of the parties to the marriage
- the contribution which each of the parties has made or is likely to make in the foreseeable future to the welfare of the family, including any contribution by looking after the home or caring for the family
- the conduct of each of the parties, if that conduct is such that it would in the opinion of the court be inequitable to disregard it
- the value to each of the parties to the marriage of any benefit which, by reason of the dissolution of that marriage, that party will lose the chance of acquiring

When considering the above factors, the court must give paramount consideration to the welfare of any child of the family.

The court has a wide discretion in considering these factors in order to achieve an outcome it considers to be fair. The court's approach changed dramatically following the House of Lords decision of White v White in October 2000 where it was said that, after providing for the parties' reasonable ideas the remaining assets should be shared.

In the House of Lords cases of Miller and McFarlane the court refined the thinking in the White case to say that the court should strive to achieve a fair result by considering three strands:

- the needs of the parties going forward
- compensation for any economic disparity between the parties (such as where one party has sacrificed their career to become a full-time parent)
- sharing

In October 2010, the supreme court gave judgment in *Radmacher v Granatino* which made it clear that a person now entering into a pre-nuptial agreement will be considered to have intended to be held to that agreement. However, the court will still be able to decide as to whether the agreement is fair and whether the terms setting out the financial provision on divorce should be enforced in whole or in part. The supreme court gave some guidelines on when a pre-nuptial agreement would be considered 'fair', but ultimately it depends on the facts of the individual case.

The Law Commission's Marital Property, Needs and Agreements Report, published in February 2014, proposed the introduction of 'qualifying nuptial agreements' which would be enforceable contracts allowing couples to make binding agreements concerning the financial consequences of divorce or dissolution. In order for an agreement to qualify, certain procedural safeguards would need to be met. Agreements could not be used by parties to contract out of meeting the financial needs of the other or of any children. The report is currently awaiting the government's response.

## FINANCIAL PROVISION ON DISSOLUTION OF A CIVIL PARTNERSHIP

The Civil Partnership Act 2004 makes provisions for financial relief for civil partners generally and extends the same rights and responsibilities invoked by marriage. Again the court must consider a number of factors when exercising its discretion and must take into account all of the circumstances of the case while giving first consideration to the welfare of any child of the family who is under 18. The list of statutory factors the court must consider resemble those for marriage and it is likely that the interpretation of these factors will be based on the courts' interpretation of the factors relating to marriage.

## COHABITING COUPLES

There is no such thing as a common law spouse.Unmarried couples do not benefit from the same statutory protection afforded to married couples. Instead, the rights of cohabitees are based on property law and trust interests. Therefore, it is advisable to consider entering into a contract, or 'cohabitation agreement', which establishes how money and property should be divided in the event of a relationship breakdown.

The cohabitation rights bill 2013–14, which sought to introduce certain protections for cohabitees during their lifetime and on death, was introduced in October 2013 but made no progress. Thus, cohabitation agreements continue to be governed by the same general principles of property, trust, and contract law.

## FINANCIAL PROVISION FOR CHILDREN

All parents are under a legal obligation to support their children financially.A parent who does not have day-to-day care of a child is under a duty to pay child maintenance to the parent who does.

Parents can arrange child maintenance themselvesor through theChild Maintenance Service (CMS), (formerly the Child Support Agency (CSA)).

There are three different methods of calculating child support under the child Maintenance schemes:

- the 'old' scheme (for all applications up until March 2003)
- the net income scheme (for post-March 2003 applications)
- the gross income scheme for all new applications since 25 November 2013

By 2017, all child maintenance calculations will be dealt with under the gross income scheme. CMS uses the paying parent's gross annual income from the latest available tax year as a starting point to work out child maintencance with reference to the gross income maximum of £156,000. Once the gross income information is received, the CMS applies a specific formula to work out the level of child maintenance payable.

Under the gross income scheme, it is mandatory for parents to have a conversation with the Child Maintenance Options (CMO) team to discuss their choices and consider alternatives before they proceed with their application. The CMO will discuss the various options available to parents if they cannot agree a so-called 'family-based arrangement' between themselves:

- 'Direct Pay' (known as 'Maintenance Direct' under a CSA arrangement) which enables parents to keep control of making and receiving payments. The statutory service works out the payment amounts for parents but will not be involved in other areas, such as collection and enforcement
- 'Collect and Pay' (known as the 'calculation and collection services' under a CSA arrangement) whereby the CSA or CMS calculates how much maintenance the paying parent owes. If payments aren't made on time, a range of enforcement actions can be taken

Within 72 hours of a payment being missed, the CMS will contact the paying parent to seek continuing payments. Where there is persistent non-payment, the CMS is able to take money directly from the paying parent, either from their earnings or bank account, or to take court action.

Provision is also made under Schedule 1 of the Children Act 1989 for unmarried parents to apply to the court for lump sum and property adjustment orders and, in limited circumstances, orders for child maintenance.

## SCOTLAND

Although some provisions are similar to those for England and Wales, there is separate legislation for Scotland covering nullity of marriage, judicial separation, divorce and ancillary matters. The principal legislation in relation to family law in Scotland is the Family Law (Scotland) Act 1985. The Family Law (Scotland) Act 2006 came in to force on 4 May 2006, and introduced reforms to various aspects of Scottish family law. The following is confined to major points on which the law in Scotland differs from that of England and Wales.

An action for judicial separation or divorce may be raised in the court of session; it may also be raised in the sheriff court if either party was resident in the sheriffdom for 40 days immediately before the date of the action or for 40 days ending not more than 40 days before the date of the action and has no known residence in Scotland at that date. The fee for starting a divorce petition in the sheriff court is £141.

The grounds for raising an action of divorce in Scotland are set down in The Divorce (Scotland) Act 1976 and have been subject to reform in terms of the 2006 act. The current grounds for divorce are:

- the defender has committed adultery. When adultery is cited as proof that the marriage has broken down irretrievably, it is not necessary in Scotland to prove that it is also intolerable for the pursuer to live with the defender
- the defender's behaviour is such that the pursuer cannot reasonably be expected to cohabit with the defender

- there has been no cohabitation between the parties for one year prior to the raising of the action for divorce, and the defender consents to the granting of decree of divorce
- there has been no cohabitation between the parties for two years prior to the raising of the action for divorce
- an interim gender recognition certificate under the Gender Recognition Act 2004 has, after the date of marriage, been issued to either party to the marriage. However, as a result of changes under the Marriage and Civil Partnership (Scotland) Act 2014, this ground of divorce will sometimes not be available where a full gender recognition certificate has been issued under the 2004 Act.

The previously available ground of desertion was abolished by the 2006 Act.

A simplified procedure for 'do-it-yourself divorce' was introduced in 1983 for certain divorces. If the action is based on one or two years' separation and will not be opposed or because a gender recognition certificate has been issued; there are no children under 16; no financial claims; there is no sign that the applicant's spouse is unable to manage his or her affairs through mental illness or handicap; and there are no other court proceedings underway which might result in the end of the marriage, the applicant can access the appropriate forms to enable him or her to proceed on the Scottish Courts website. The fee is £107 as at 1 April 2014, however the applicant may be exempt from paying the fee if they are in receipt of certain benefits; or if legal advice and assistance is being provided him or her by a solicitor in terms of the Legal Aid (Scotland) Act 1986.

Where a divorce action has been raised, it may be put on hold for a variety of reasons. In all actions for divorce an extract decree, which brings the marriage to an end, will be made available 14 days after the divorce has been granted. Unlike in England, there is no decree nisi, only a final decree of divorce. Parties must ensure that all financial issues have been resolved prior to divorce, as it is not possible to seek further financial provision after divorce has been granted.

### FINANCIAL PROVISION

In relation to financial provision on divorce, the first, and most important, principle is fair sharing of the matrimonial property. There is a presumption that fair share means an equal share of the matrimonial property, which can be departed from if justified by special circumstances. In terms of Scots law matrimonial property is defined as all property acquired by either spouse from the date of marriage up to the date of separation. Property acquired before the marriage is not deemed to be matrimonial unless it was acquired for use by the parties as a family home or as furniture for that home. Property acquired after the date of separation is not matrimonial property. Any property acquired by either of the parties by way of gift or inheritance during the marriage is excluded and does not form part of the matrimonial property.

When considering whether to make an award of financial provision a court shall also take account of any economic advantage derived by either party to the marriage as a result of contributions, financial or otherwise, by the other, and of any economic disadvantage suffered by either party for the benefit of the other party. The court must also ensure that the economic burden of caring for a child under the age of 16 is shared fairly between the parties.

A court can also consider making an order requiring one party to pay the other party a periodical allowance for a certain period of time following divorce. Such an order may be appropriate in cases where there is insufficient capital to effect a fair sharing of the matrimonial property. Orders for periodical allowance are uncommon, as courts will favour a 'clean break' where possible.

### CHILDREN

The court has the power to award a residence order in respect of any children of the marriage or to make an order regulating the child's contact with the non-resident parent. The court will only make such orders if it is deemed better for the child to do so than to make no order at all, and the welfare of the children is of paramount importance. The fact that a spouse has caused the breakdown of the marriage does not in itself preclude him/her from being awarded residence.

### NULLITY

An action for 'declaration of nullity' can be brought if someone with a legitimate interest is able to show that the marriage is void or voidable. The action can only be brought in the court of session. Although the grounds on which a marriage may be void or voidable are similar to those on which a marriage can be declared invalid in England, there are some differences. Where a spouse is capable of sexual intercourse but refuses to consummate the marriage, this is not a ground for nullity in Scots law, though it could be a ground for divorce. Where a spouse was suffering from venereal disease at the time of marriage and the other spouse did not know, this is not a ground for nullity in Scots law, neither is the fact that a wife was pregnant by another man at the time of marriage without the knowledge of her husband.

### COHABITING COUPLES

The law in Scotland now provides certain financial and property rights for cohabiting couples in terms of the Family Law (Scotland) Act 2006, or 'the 2006 Act'. The relevant 2006 Act provisions do not place cohabitants in Scotland on an equal footing with married couples or civil partners, but provide some rights for cohabitants in the event that the relationship is terminated by separation or death. The provisions relate to couples who cease to cohabit after 4 May 2006.

The legislation provides for a presumption that most contents of the home shared by the cohabitants are owned in equal shares. A former cohabitant can also seek financial provision on termination of the relationship in the form of a capital payment if they can successfully demonstrate that they have been financially disadvantaged, and that conversely the other cohabitant has been financially advantaged, as a consequence of contributions made (financial or otherwise). An order can also be made in respect of the economic burden of caring for a child of whom the cohabitants are the parents. Such a claim must be made no later than one year after the day on which the cohabitants cease to cohabit.

The 2006 Act also provides that a cohabitant may make a claim on their partner's estate in the event of that partner's death, providing that there is no will. A claim of this nature must be made no later than six months after the date of the partner's death.

THE CENTRAL FAMILY COURT, First Avenue House,
42–49 High Holborn, London WC1 6NP T 0207-421 8594
THE COURT OF SESSION, Parliament House, Parliament
Square, Edinburgh EH1 1RQ T 0131-225 2595
W www.scotcourts.gov.uk
THE CHILD SUPPORT AGENCY, T 0345-713 3133
W www.csa.gov.uk

# EMPLOYMENT LAW

### EMPLOYEES

A fundamental distinction in UK employment law is that drawn between an employee and someone who is self-employed. Further, there is an important, intermediate category introduced by legislation: 'workers' covers all employees but also catches others who do not have full employment status. An 'employee' is someone who has entered into or works under a contract of employment, while a 'worker' has entered into or works under a contract whereby he undertakes to do or perform personally any work or services for another party whose status is not that of a client or customer. Whether or not someone is an employee or a worker as opposed to being genuinely self-employed is an important and complex question, for it determines that person's statutory rights and protections. For certain purposes, such as protection against discrimination, protection extends to some genuinely self-employed people as well as workers and employees.

The greater the level of control that the employer has over the work carried out, the greater the depth of integration of the employee in the employer's business, and the closer the obligations to provide and perform work between the parties, the more likely it is that the parties will be employer and employee.

## PAY AND CONDITIONS

The Employment Rights Act 1996 consolidated the statutory provisions relating to employees' rights. Employers must give each employee employed for one month or more a written statement containing the following information:

* names of employer and employee
* date when employment began and the date on which the employee's period of *continuous* employment began (taking into account any employment with a previous employer which counts towards that period)
* the scale, rate or other method of calculating remuneration and intervals at which it will be paid
* job title or description of job
* hours and the permitted place(s) of work and, where there are several such places, the address of the employer
* holiday entitlement and holiday pay
* provisions concerning incapacity for work due to sickness and injury, including provisions for sick pay
* details of pension scheme(s)
* length of notice the employee is obliged to give and entitled to receive in order to terminate the contract of employment
* if the employment is not intended to be permanent, the period for which it is expected to continue or, if it is for a fixed term, the end date of the contract
* details of any collective agreement (including the parties to the agreement) which directly affects the terms of employment
* details of disciplinary and grievance procedures (including the individual to whom a complaint should be made and the process of making that complaint)
* if the employee is to work outside the UK for more than one month, the period of such work and the currency in which payment is made and any additional remuneration or benefits payable to them
* a note stating whether a contracting-out certificate is in force

This must be given to the employee within two months of the start of their employment.

If the employer does not provide the written statement within two months (or a statement of any changes to these particulars within one month of the changes being made) then the employee can complain to an employment tribunal, which can specify the information that the employer should have given. When, in the context of an employee's successful tribunal claim, the employer is also found to have been in breach of the duty to provide the written statement at the time proceedings were commenced, the tribunal must award the employee two weeks' pay, and may award four weeks' pay, subject to the statutory cap, unless it would be unjust or inequitable to do so.

The Working Time Regulations 1998, the National Minimum Wage Act 1998, Employment Relations Act 1999, the Employment Act 2002 and the Employment Act 2008 now supplement the 1996 act.

## FLEXIBLE WORKING

The Flexible Working Regulations 2014 gives all employees, from 30 June 2014, the right to apply for flexible working after working for the same employer for at least 26 weeks. An employer must consider and decide upon a request within three months and must have a sound business reason for rejecting any request. If an application under the act is not dealt with in accordance with a prescribed procedure, or is rejected on other than specific grounds, the employee may complain to an employment tribunal.

## SICK PAY

Employees absent from work through illness or injury are entitled to receive Statutory Sick Pay (SSP) from the employer from the fourth day of absence for a maximum period of 28 weeks. The right to SSP will cease where an employee has had linked periods of sickness that have spanned a period of three years.

## MATERNITY AND PARENTAL RIGHTS

Under the Employment Relations Act 1999, the Employment Act 2002, the Maternity and Parental Leave Regulations 1999 (as amended in 2002 and 2006), the Paternity and Adoption Leave Regulations 2002 and 2003, the Additional Paternity Leave Regulations 2010 and the Shared Parental Leave Regulations 2014, both men and women are entitled to take leave when they become a parent (including by adoption). Women are protected from discrimination, detriment or dismissal by reason of their pregnancy or maternity, including discrimination by association and by perception. Men and adoptive parents are protected from suffering a detriment or dismissal for taking paternity, adoption or parental leave.

Any woman who needs to attend an antenatal appointment on the advice of a registered medical professional is entitled to paid leave from work to attend. All pregnant women are entitled to a maximum period of maternity leave of 52 weeks. This comprises 26 weeks' ordinary maternity leave, followed immediately by 26 weeks' additional maternity leave. A woman who takes ordinary maternity leave normally has the right to return to the job in which she was employed before her absence. If she takes additional maternity leave, she is entitled to return to the same job or, if that is not reasonably practicable, to another job that is suitable and appropriate for her to do. There is a two-week period of compulsory maternity leave, immediately following the birth of the child, wherein the employer is not permitted to allow the mother to work.

A woman will qualify for Statutory Maternity Pay (SMP), which is payable for up to 39 weeks, if she has been continuously employed for not less than 26 weeks prior to the 15th week before the expected week of childbirth. For further information *see* Social Welfare, Employer Payments.

Employees are entitled to adoption leave and adoption pay (at the same rates as SMP) subject to fulfilment of similar criteria to those in relation to maternity leave and pay, but note that there is a 26-week qualifying period for adoption leave. Where a couple is adopting a child, either one (but not both) of the parents may take adoption leave, and the other may take paternity leave.

Certain employees are entitled to paternity leave on the birth or adoption of a child. To be eligible, the employee must be the child's father, or the partner of the mother or adopter, and meet other conditions. These conditions are, firstly, that they must have been continuously employed for not less than 26 weeks prior to the 15th week before the expected week of childbirth (or, in the case of adoptions, 26 weeks ending with the week in which notification of the adoption match is given) and, secondly, that the employee must have or expect to have responsibility for the upbringing of the child. The employee may take either one week's leave, or two consecutive weeks' leave. This leave may be taken at any time between the date of the child's birth (or placement for adoption) and 56 days later. A statutory payment is available during this period.

For births and adoptions from 3 April 2011 but before 5 April 2015, an eligible employee has been able to take additional paternity leave at the end of the mother's or adopter's leave period provided the child is at least 20 weeks old or was placed for adoption at least 20 weeks previously. The maximum period of leave is 26 weeks and leave cannot extend beyond the child's first birthday.

For births on or after 5 April 2015, eligible parents are entitled to shared parental leave (SPL) whereby they will be able to share a pot of leave of up to 50 weeks and 27 weeks of pay, after the initial two weeks of maternity leave that is compulsory for the mother. During that 50 week period, parents can decide to be off work at the same time and/or take it in turns to have periods of leave to look after their child. To be eligible, the employee must be the child's mother, father, partner of the mother or adopter, and must have worked for the same employer for not less than 26 weeks prior to the 15th week before the expected week of childbirth (or, in case of adoptions, 26 weeks ending with the week in which notification of the adoption match is given). The amount of leave available is calculated using the mother's entitlement to maternity leave. If a mother reduces maternity leave she and/or her partner may opt to take SPL for the remaining weeks. On taking SPL, a woman will be entitled to statutory shared parental pay at the same rate as SMP.

For more information *see* Social Welfare, Employer Payments.

Any employee with one year's service who has, or expects to have, responsibility for a child may take parental leave to care for the child. Each parent is entitled to a total of 18 weeks parental leave for each child or adopted child. This leave must be taken (at the rate of no more than four weeks a year, and in blocks of whole weeks only) before the child's 18th birthday.

## SUNDAY TRADING

The Sunday Trading Act 1994 allows shops to open on Sunday. The Employment Rights Act 1996 gives shop workers and betting workers the right not to be dismissed, selected for redundancy or to suffer any detriment (such as the denial of overtime, promotion or training) if they refuse to work on Sundays. This does not apply to those who, under their contracts, are employed to work on Sundays.

## TERMINATION OF EMPLOYMENT

An employee may be dismissed without notice if guilty of gross misconduct but in other cases a period of notice must be given by the employer. The minimum periods of notice specified in the Employment Rights Act 1996 are:
- one week if the employee has been continuously employed for one month or more but for less than two years
- one week for each complete year of continuous employment, if the employee has been employed for two years or more, up to a maximum of 12 weeks' notice
- longer periods apply if these are specified in the contract of employment

If an employee is dismissed with less notice than he/she is entitled to by statute, or under their contract if longer, he/she

will have a wrongful dismissal claim (unless the employer paid the employee in lieu of notice in accordance with a contractual provision entitling it to do so). This claim for wrongful dismissal can be brought by the employee either in the civil courts or the employment tribunal, but if brought in the tribunal the maximum amount that can be awarded is £25,000.

## REDUNDANCY

An employee dismissed because of redundancy may be entitled to redundancy pay. This applies if:
- the employment commenced before 6 April 2012 and the employee has at least one year's continuous service or the employment commenced on or after 6 April 2012 and the employee has at least two years' continuous service
- the employee is dismissed by the employer by reason of redundancy (this can include cases of voluntary redundancy)

Redundancy can mean closure of the entire business, closure of a particular site of the business, or a reduction in the need for employees to carry out work of a particular kind.

An employee may not be entitled to a redundancy payment if offered a suitable alternative job by the same employer. The amount of statutory redundancy pay depends on the length of service, age, and their earnings, subject to a weekly maximum of (currently) £475. The maximum payment that can be awarded is £14,250. The redundancy payment is guaranteed by the government in cases where the employer becomes insolvent.

## UNFAIR DISMISSAL

Complaints of unfair dismissal are dealt with by an employment tribunal. Any employee whose employment commenced before 6 April 2012 with at least one year's continuous service or any employee whose employment commenced on or after 6 April 2012 with at least two year's continuous service (subject to exceptions, including in relation to whistleblowers – *see* below) can make a complaint to the tribunal. At the tribunal, it is for the employee to show that the employer dismissed them either expressly or constructively and it is for the employer to prove that the dismissal was due to one or more potentially fair reasons: a statutory restriction preventing the continuation of the employee's contract; the employee's capability or qualifications for the job he/she was employed to do; the employee's conduct; redundancy; or some other substantial reason.

If the employer succeeds in showing this, the tribunal must then decide whether the employer acted reasonably in dismissing the employee for that reason. If the employee is found to have been unfairly dismissed, the tribunal can order that he/she be reinstated, re-engaged or compensated. Any person believing that they may have been unfairly dismissed should contact their local Citizens Advice bureau or seek legal advice. A claim must be brought within three months of the date of effective termination of employment.

The normal maximum compensatory award for unfair dismissal is £78,335 (as at April 2015). If the dismissal occurred after 6 April 2009 and the employer unreasonably failed to follow the ACAS Code of Practice on Disciplinary and Grievance Procedures in carrying out the dismissal, the tribunal may increase the employee's compensation by up to 25 per cent.

## WHISTLEBLOWING

Under the whistleblowing legislation (Public Interest Disclosure Act 1998, which inserted provisions into the Employment Rights Act 1996) dismissal of an employee is automatically unfair if the reason or principal reason for he dismissal is that the employee has made a protected disclosure. The legislation also makes it unlawful to subject workers (a broad category that includes employees and certain other individuals, such as agency workers) who have made a protected disclosure to any detriment on the ground that they have done so.

For a disclosure to qualify for protection, the claimant must show that he or she has disclosed information, which in his or her reasonable belief tends to show one or more of the following six categories of wrongdoing: criminal offences; breach of any legal obligation; miscarriages of justice; danger to the health and safety of any individual; damage to the environment; or the deliberate concealing of information about any of the other categories. The malpractices can be past, present, prospective or merely alleged.

A qualifying disclosure will only be protected if the manner of the disclosure fulfils certain conditions, which varies according to the type of disclosure. With effect from 25 June 2013, there is no requirement for the disclosure to have been made in 'good faith', although where it appears to the tribunal that the protected disclosure was not made in good faith, the tribunal may reduce any compensatory award it makes by up to 25 per cent if it considers that it is just and equitable to do so in all the circumstances.

Any whistleblower claim in the employment tribunal must normally be brought within three months of the date of dismissal or other act leading to a detriment.

An individual does not need to have been working with the employer for any particular period of time to be able to bring such a claim and compensation is uncapped (and can include an amount for injury to feelings).

## DISCRIMINATION

Discrimination in employment on the grounds of sex (including gender reassignment), sexual orientation, being pregnant or on maternity leave, race, colour, nationality, ethnic or national origins, religion or belief, marital or civil partnership status, age or disability is unlawful. Discrimination legislation generally covers direct discrimination, indirect discrimination, harassment and victimisation. Only in limited circumstances can such discrimination be justified (rendering it lawful).

An individual does not need to be employed for any particular period of time to be able to claim discrimination (discrimination can be alleged at the recruitment phase), and discrimination compensation is uncapped (and can include an amount for injury to feelings). These features distinguish the discrimination laws from, for example, the unfair dismissal laws.

The Equality Act 2010 was passed on 8 April 2010 and the main provisions came into force on 1 October 2010. The Act unifies several pieces of discrimination legislation, providing one definition of direct discrimination, indirect discrimination, harassment and victimisation. The Equality Act applies to those employed in Great Britain but not to employees in Northern Ireland or (subject to EC exceptions) to those who work mainly abroad, and provides that:

• it is unlawful to discriminate on the grounds of sex, gender reassignment or marital/civil partner status, being pregnant or on maternity leave, including discrimination by association and by perception. This covers all aspects of employment (including advertising for jobs), but there are some limited exceptions, such as where the essential nature of the job requires it to be given to someone of a particular sex, or where decency and privacy requires it. The act entitles men and women to equality of remuneration for equivalent work or work of the same value

• individuals have the right not to be discriminated against on the grounds of race, colour, nationality, or ethnic or national origins and this applies to all aspects of employment. Employers may also take lawful positive action, including in relation to recruitment and promotion

• discrimination against a disabled person in all aspects of employment is unlawful. This includes protecting carers from discrimination by association with the disabled persons that they look after. In certain circumstances, the employer may show that the less favourable treatment is justified and so does not constitute discrimination. The act also imposes a duty on employers to make 'reasonable adjustments' to the arrangements and physical features of the workplace if these place disabled people at a substantial disadvantage compared with those who are not disabled. The definition of a 'disabled person' is wide and includes people diagnosed with HIV, cancer and multiple sclerosis

• discrimination against a person on the grounds of religion or belief (or lack of belief) including discrimination by association and by perception, in all aspects of employment, is unlawful

• discrimination against an individual on the grounds of sexual orientation, including discrimination by association and by perception, in all aspects of employment, is unlawful

• age discrimination in the workplace is unlawful, and an employer may no longer dismiss an employee by reason of retirement once they have reached a certain age. However, it is lawful to discriminate because of age in relation to benefits based on length of service, redundancy pay, national minimum wage and insurance benefits.

The responsibility for monitoring equality in society rests with the Equality and Human Rights Commission.

In Northern Ireland similar provisions exist to those that were in force in Great Britain prior to the coming into force of the Equality Act but are contained in separate legislation (although the Disability Discrimination Act does extend to Northern Ireland).

In Northern Ireland there is one combined body working towards equality and eliminating discrimination, the Equality Commission for Northern Ireland.

## WORKING TIME

The Working Time Regulations 1998 impose rules that limit working hours and provide for rest breaks and holidays. The regulations apply to workers and so cover not only employees but also other individuals who undertake to perform personally any work or services (eg freelancers). The regulations are complex and subject to various exceptions and qualifications but the basic provisions relating to adult day workers are as follows:

• No worker is permitted to work more than an average of 48 hours per week (unless they have made a genuine voluntary opt-out of this limit – it is not sufficient to make it a term of the contract that the worker opts out), and a worker is entitled to, but is not required to take, the following breaks:

• 11 consecutive hours' uninterrupted rest in every 24-hour period

• an uninterrupted rest period of 24 hours in each 7-day period or 48 hours in each fortnight (in addition to the daily rest period)

• 20 minutes' rest break provided that the working day is longer than 6 hours

• 5.6 weeks' paid annual leave (28 days full-time). This equates to 4 weeks plus public holidays

There are specific provisions relating to night work, young workers (ie those over school leaving age but under 18) and a variety of workers in specialised sectors (such as off-shore oil rig workers).

# HUMAN RIGHTS

On 2 October 2000 the Human Rights Act 1998 came into force in the UK. This act incorporates the European Convention on Human Rights into the law of the UK. The main principles of the act are as follows:
• all legislation must be interpreted and given effect by the courts as compatible with the Convention so far as it is possible to do so. Before the second reading of a new bill the minister responsible for the bill must provide a statement regarding its compatibility with the Human Rights Act
• subordinate legislation (eg statutory instruments) which is incompatible with the Convention can be struck down by the courts
• primary legislation (eg an act of parliament) which is incompatible with the Convention cannot be struck down by a court, but the higher courts can make a declaration of incompatibility which is a signal to parliament to change the law
• all public authorities (including courts and tribunals) must not act in a way which is incompatible with the Convention
• individuals whose Convention rights have been infringed by a public authority may bring proceedings against that authority, but the act is not intended to create new rights as between individuals

The main human rights protected by the Convention are the right to life (article 2); protection from torture and inhuman or degrading treatment (article 3); protection from slavery or forced labour (article 4); the right to liberty and security of the person (article 5); the right to a fair trial (article 6); the right not to be subject to retrospective criminal offences (article 7); the right to respect for private and family life (article 8); freedom of thought, conscience and religion (article 9); freedom of expression (article 10); freedom of peaceful association and assembly (article 11); the right to marry and found a family (article 12); protection from discrimination (article 14); the right to property (article 1 protocol No.1); the right to education (article 2 protocol No.1); and the right to free elections (article 3 protocol No.1). Most of the Convention rights are subject to limitations which deem the breach of the right acceptable on the basis it is 'necessary in a democratic society'.

Human rights are also enshrined in the common law (of tort). Although this is of historical significance, the common law (for example the duty of confidentiality) remains especially important regarding violations of human rights that occur between private parties, where the Human Rights Act 1998 does not apply.

# PARENTAL RESPONSIBILITY

The Children Act 1989 (as amended by the Children and Families Act 2014) gives both the mother and father parental responsibility for the child if the parents are married to each other at the time of the child's birth. If the parents are not married, only the mother has parental responsibility. The father may acquire it in accordance with the provisions of section 4 of the Children Act 1989. He can do this in one of several ways, including: by being registered as the father on the child's birth certificate with the consent of the mother (only for fathers of children born after 1 December 2003, following changes to the Adoption and Children Act 2002); by applying to the court for a parental responsibility order; by entering into a parental responsibility agreement with the mother which must be in the prescribed form; or by marrying the mother of the child.

Following changes to the Children Act 1989 (introduced by the Children and Families Act 2014), if a court makes a child arrangements order in favour of a father, providing that the child lives with that father, the court must make a parental responsibility order in his favour. If the child arrangements order provides that the child spend time or otherwise have contact with the father, the court must consider whether to make a parental responsibility order (residence orders were replaced by child arrangement orders under the Children and Families Act 2014, but if obtained prior to 22 April 2014 are still valid).

Where a child's parent, who has parental responsibility, marries or enters into a civil partnership with a person who is not the child's parent, the child's parent(s) with parental responsibility can agree for the step-parent to have parental responsibility, or the step-parent may acquire parental responsibility by order of the court (section 4A(1) Children Act 1989).

If a child is born to female civil partners or female same-sex spouses as a result of IVF or AID treatment received after 5 April 2009, both individuals will have parental responsibility for that child. From 1 September 2009 a female, who is not in a civil partnership or same-sex marriage with the mother at the date of the child's birth, but is the child's other parent (under the Human Fertilisation and Embryology Act 2008), can acquire parental responsibility in the same way as set out above in relation to a father. Parental responsibility will also be acquired if the mother and the child's other parent enter into a civil partnership or (from 13 March 2014) a same-sex marriage after the child's date of birth.

Since 6 April 2010, following surrogacy arrangements, the court can order that a parental order is made in favour of the surrogate couple if at least one of them is a biological parent. Where the court makes a child arrangements order and a person (who is not the parent or guardian of the child) is named in the order as a person with whom the child is to spend time or otherwise have contact (but not named as a person with whom the child is to live), the court may provide in the order for that person to have parental responsibility for the child.

An adoption order gives parental responsibility for the child to the adopters. It extinguishes parental responsibility that any person had for the child immediately before the making of the order.

In Scotland, the relevant legislation is the Children (Scotland) Act 1995, which gives the mother parental rights and responsibilities for her child whether or not she is married to the child's father. A father who is married to the mother, either at the time of the child's conception or subsequently, will also have automatic parental rights and responsibilities. Section 23 of the 2006 act provides that an unmarried father will obtain automatic parental responsibilities and rights if he is registered as the father on the child's birth certificate. For unmarried fathers who are not named on the birth certificate, or whose children were born before the 2006 act came into force, it is possible to acquire parental responsibilities and rights by applying to the court or by entering into a parental responsibilities and rights agreement with the mother. The father of any child, regardless of parental rights, has a duty to aliment that child until he/she is 18 (or under 25 if the child is still at an educational establishment or training for employment or for a trade, profession or vocation).

### LEGITIMATION
Under the Legitimacy Act 1976, an illegitimate person automatically becomes legitimate when his/her parents marry. This applies even where one of the parents was married to a third person at the time of the birth. In such cases it is necessary to re-register the birth of the child.

In Scotland, the status of illegitimacy has been abolished by section 21 of the 2006 act. The Law Reform Act 1987 reformed the law so as to remove so far as possible the legal disadvantages of illegitimacy.

## JURY SERVICE

In England and Wales, the law concerning juries is largely consolidated in the Juries Act 1974 (as amended by the Criminal Justice and Courts Act 2015). In England and Wales, a person charged with a serious criminal offence is entitled to have their trial heard by a jury in a crown court, except in cases where there is a danger of jury tampering or where jury tampering has taken place.

In civil cases, there is a right to a jury in the Queen's Bench Division of the high court in cases where the person applying for a jury has been accused of fraud, as well as in cases of malicious prosecution or false imprisonment. The same applies to the county court. In all other cases in the Queen's Bench Division only the judge has discretion to order trial with a jury, though such an order is seldom made. In the chancery division of the high court a jury is never used. The same is true in the family division of the high court.

No right to a jury trial exists in Scotland, although more serious offences are heard before a jury. In England and Wales criminal cases and civil cases in the high court are generally heard by a jury of 12 members, but in the county court the jury is smaller, normally consisting of eight members. In the event that a juror is excused the trial can proceed so long as there are at least seven remaining jurors in the county court and nine in the case of the high court or crown court. At an inquest, there must be at least seven and no more than 11 members. In Scotland there are 12 members of a jury in a civil case in the court of session and certain sheriff court cases, and 15 in a criminal trial in the high court of justiciary. Jurors are normally asked to serve for ten working days, during which time they could sit on more than one case. Jurors selected for longer cases are expected to sit for the duration of the trial.

In England and Wales, every 'registered' parliamentary or local government elector between the ages of 18 and 70 (the Criminal Justice and Courts Act has amended the maximum age to 75, although this provision is not in force at the time of writing) who has lived in the UK (including, for this purpose, the Channel Islands and the Isle of Man) for any period of at least five years since reaching the age of 13 is qualified to serve on a jury unless he/she is 'mentally disordered' or disqualified.

Those disqualified from jury service include:

- those who have at any time been sentenced by a court in the UK (including, for this purpose, the Channel Islands and the Isle of Man) to a term of imprisonment or youth custody of five years or more
- those who have within the previous ten years served any part of a sentence of imprisonment, youth custody or detention, been detained in a young offenders' institution, received a suspended sentence of imprisonment or order for detention, or received a community order
- those who are on bail in criminal proceedings
- those who have been convicted of a jury misconduct offence

The court has the discretion to excuse a juror from service, or defer the date of service, if the juror can show there is good reason why he/she should be excused from attending or good reason why his/her attendance should be deferred. It is an offence (punishable by a fine) to fail to attend when summoned, to serve knowing that you are disqualified from service, or to make false representations in an attempt to evade service. If a juror fails to turn up for service, or attends but cannot serve due to being under the influence of drink or drugs, this is punishable as contempt of court. Any party can object to any juror if he/she can show cause to the trial judge.

It may be appropriate for a judge to excuse a juror from a particular case if he is personally concerned in the facts of the particular case, or closely connected with a party to the proceedings or with a prospective witness. The judge may also discharge any juror who, from a mental or physical incapacity, temporary or permanent, or alternatively due to linguistic difficulties, cannot pay proper attention to the evidence.

An individual juror (or the entire jury) can be discharged if it is shown that they or any of their number have, among other things, separated from the rest of the jury without the leave of the court; talked to any person out of court who is not a member of the jury; determined the verdict of the trial by drawing lots; come to a compromise on the verdict; been drunk, or otherwise incapacitated, while carrying out their duties as a juror; exerted improper pressure on the other members of the jury (eg harassment or bullying); declined to take part in the jury's functions; displayed actual or apparent bias (eg racism, sexism or other discriminatory or deliberate hostility); or inadvertently possessed knowledge of the bad character of a party to the proceedings which has not been adduced as evidence in the proceedings. The factual situations that arise are many, and include falling asleep during the trial, asking friends on Facebook for help in making a decision, consulting an ouija board in the course of deliberations, making telephone calls after retirement, and lunching with a barrister not connected with the proceedings.

The Criminal Justice and Courts Act 2015 has introduced four new offences of juror misconduct with a penalty of up to two years in prison. A juror commits an offence if he: (a) intentionally seeks information during a trial where he knows, or ought to reasonably know, that the information sought is or may be relevant to the case; (b) passes on to another juror information obtained through such research; (c) engages in conduct from which it may reasonably be concluded that he intends to try the issue otherwise than on the basis of the evidence presented in the proceedings on the issue; and (d) discloses information about the jury's deliberations, subject to specified exceptions. A person who has been convicted of one of the above offences within the last 10 years will be disqualified from jury duty. A judge now has a discretionary power to order members of a jury to surrender their electronic communication devices for a period of time, and a court security officer is authorised to search a juror for a device that a judge has ordered be surrendered.

In England and Wales, the jury's verdict need not be unanimous. In criminal proceedings, and civil proceedings in the high court, the agreement of 10 jurors will suffice when there are not fewer than 11 people on the jury (or 9 in a jury of 10). In civil proceedings in the county court the agreement of seven or eight jurors will suffice. Where a majority verdict is given, the court must be satisfied that the jury had reasonable time to consider its verdict based on the nature and complexity of the case. In criminal proceedings this must be no less than two hours and ten minutes (allowing time for the jury to settle after retiring).

A juror is immune from prosecution or civil claim in respect of anything said or done by him or her in the discharge of their office. It is an offence for a juror to disclose what happened in the jury room even after the trial is over. A juror may claim travelling expenses, a subsistence allowance and an allowance for other financial loss (eg loss of earnings or benefits, fees paid to carers or child-minders) up to a stated limit. For more information on jury service, visit **W** www.gov.uk/jury-service/overview

## SCOTLAND

Qualification criteria for jury service in Scotland are similar to those in England and Wales, except that members of the judiciary are ineligible for ten years after ceasing to hold their post, and others concerned with the administration of justice are only eligible for service five years after ceasing to hold office. Certain persons have the right to apply to be excused – full-time members of the medical, dental, nursing, veterinary and pharmaceutical professions, full-time members of the armed forces, ministers of religion, persons who have served on a jury within the previous five years, members of the Scottish parliament, members of the Scottish government, junior Scottish ministers and those aged 71 years or over. Those who are incapable by reason of a mental disorder may also be excused. Such an application will be accepted if the application is made within 7 days of the person being notified that they may have to serve. For civil trials there is an age limit of 65 years. Those convicted of a crime and sentenced to a period of imprisonment of 5 years or more are automatically disqualified. The maximum fine for a person serving on a jury while knowing himself/herself to be ineligible is £1,000. The maximum fine for failing to attend without good cause in criminal trials is also £1,000, however in civil proceedings the maximum fine is £200.

HER MAJESTY'S COURTS AND TRIBUNALS SERVICE,
102 Petty France, London SW1H 9AJ T 0845-456 8770
JURY CENTRAL SUMMONING BUREAU,
Freepost LON 19669, Pocock Street, London SE1 0YG
T 0845-803 8003 E jurysummoning@hmcts.gsi.gov.uk
SCOTTISH COURTS SERVICE, Saughton House,
Broomhouse Drive, Edinburgh EH11 3XD T 0131-444 3300
W www.scotcourts.gov.uk
THE CLERK OF JUSTICIARY, High Court of Justiciary,
Lawnmarket, Edinburgh EH2 2NS T 0131-240 6900

# LANDLORD AND TENANT

## RESIDENTIAL LETTINGS

The provisions outlined here apply only where the tenant lives in a separate dwelling from the landlord and where the dwelling is the tenant's only or main home. It does not apply to licensees such as lodgers, guests or service occupiers.

The 1996 Housing Act radically changed certain aspects of the legislation referred to below; in particular, the grant of assured and assured shorthold tenancies under the Housing Act 1988.

## ASSURED SHORTHOLD TENANCIES

If a tenancy was granted on or after 15 January 1989 and before 28 February 1997, the tenant would have an assured tenancy unless the landlord served notice under section 20 in the prescribed form prior to the commencement of the tenancy, stating that the tenancy is to be an assured shorthold tenancy and the tenancy is for a minimum fixed term period of six months (see below). An assured tenancy gives that tenant greater security. The tenant could, for example, stay in possession of the dwelling for as long as the tenant observed the terms of the tenancy. The landlord cannot obtain possession from such a tenant unless the landlord can establish a specific ground for possession (set out in the Housing Act 1988) and obtains a court order. The rent payable is that agreed with the landlord at the start of the tenancy. The landlord has the right to increase the rent annually by serving a notice. If that happens the tenant can apply to have the rent fixed by the rent assessment committee of the local authority. The tenant or the landlord may request that the committee sets the rent in line with open market rents for that type of property.

Under the Housing Act 1996, all new lettings (below an annual rent threshold of £100,000 since October 2010) entered into on or after 28 February 1997 (for whatever term) will be assured shorthold tenancies unless the landlord serves a notice stating that the tenancy is not to be an assured shorthold tenancy. This means that the landlord is entitled to possession at the end of the tenancy provided he serves a notice under section 21 Housing Act 1988 and commences the proceedings in accordance with the correct procedure. The landlord must obtain a court order, however, to obtain possession if the tenant refuses to vacate at the end of the tenancy. If the tenancy is an assured shorthold tenancy, the court must grant the order.

## REGULATED TENANCIES

Before the Housing Act 1988 came into force on 15 January 1989 there were regulated tenancies; some are still in existence and are protected by the Rent Act 1977. Under this act it is possible for the landlord or the tenant to apply to the local rent officer to have a 'fair' rent registered. The fair rent is then the maximum rent payable.

## SECURE TENANCIES

Secure tenancies are generally given to tenants of local authorities, housing associations (before 15 January 1989) and certain other bodies. This gives the tenant security of tenure unless the terms of the agreement are broken by the tenant and it is reasonable to make an order for possession. Those with secure tenancies may have the right to buy their property. In practice this right is generally only available to council tenants.

The Prevention of Social Housing Fraud Act came into force in October 2013. It creates criminal offences for unlawful sub-letting by secure and assured tenants of social housing.

## AGRICULTURAL PROPERTY

Tenancies in agricultural properties are governed by the Agricultural Holdings Act 1986, the Agricultural Tenancies Act 1995 (both amended by the Regulatory Reform (Agricultural Tenancies) (England and Wales) Order 2006), the Tribunals, Courts and Enforcement Act 2007, the Legal Services Act 2007 and the Rent (Agriculture) Act 1976, which give similar protections to those described above, eg security of tenure, right to compensation for disturbance, etc. Similar provisions are applied to Scotland by the Agricultural Holdings (Scotland) Act 2003 for those leases entered into on or after 27 November 2003. The Agricultural Holdings (Scotland) Act 1991 continues to apply to those leases in Scotland entered into prior to this date and in certain other circumstances outlined by the 2003 act. However, one distinction to note between the 1991 act and the 2003 act is that those leases governed by the former have full security of tenure, subject to certain exceptions, whereas leases under the 2003 act are fixed term arrangements of various durations.

## EVICTION

The Protection from Eviction Act 1977 (as amended by the Housing Act 1988 and Nationality, Immigration and Asylum Act 2002) sets out the procedure a landlord must follow in order to obtain possession of property. It is unlawful for a landlord to evict a tenant otherwise than in accordance with the law. For common law tenancies and for Rent Act tenants a notice to quit in the prescribed form giving 28 days notice is required. For secure and assured tenancies a notice seeking possession must be served. It is unlawful for the landlord to evict a person by putting their belongings on to the street, by changing the locks and so on. It is also unlawful for a landlord to harass a tenant in any way in order to persuade him/her to give up the tenancy. The tenant may be able to obtain an injunction to restrain the actions of the landlord and get back into the property and be awarded damages.

## LANDLORD RESPONSIBILITIES
Under the Landlord and Tenant Act 1985, where the term of the lease is less than seven years, the landlord is responsible for maintaining the structure and exterior of the property, for sanitation, for heating and hot water, and all installations for the supply of water, gas and electricity.

While the responsibility of maintaining the premises remains intact, since July 2012 landlords are no longer permitted to enter the rental premises for the purpose of viewing their state and condition. This power of entry was revoked by the Protection of Freedoms Act 2012.

## LEASEHOLDERS
Strictly speaking, leaseholders have bought a long lease rather than a property and in certain limited circumstances the landlord can end the tenancy. Under the Leasehold Reform Act 1967 (as amended by the Housing Acts 1969, 1974, 1980 and 1985), leaseholders of houses may have the right to buy the freehold or to take an extended lease for a term of 50 years. This applies to leases where the term of the lease is over 21 years, at a low rent, and where the leaseholder has occupied the house as his/her only or main residence for the last two years, or for a total of two years over the last ten. The tenant must give the landlord written notice of his desire to acquire the freehold or extend the leasehold.

The Leasehold Reform, Housing and Urban Development Act came into force in 1993 and allows the leaseholders of flats in certain circumstances to buy the freehold of the building in which they live.

Responsibility for maintenance of the structure, exterior and interior of the building should be set out in the lease. Usually the upkeep of the interior of his/her part of the property is the responsibility of the leaseholder, and responsibility for the structure, exterior and common interior areas is shared between the freeholder and the leaseholder(s).

If leaseholders are dissatisfied with charges made in respect of lease extensions, they are entitled to have their situation evaluated by the Leasehold Valuation Tribunal.

The Commonhold and Leasehold Reform Act 2002 makes provision for the freehold estate in land to be registered as commonhold land and for the legal interest in the land to be vested in a 'commonhold association' ie a private limited company.

## BUSINESS LETTINGS
The Landlord and Tenant Acts 1927 and 1954 (as amended) give security of tenure to the tenants of most business premises. The landlord can only evict the tenant on one of the grounds laid down in the 1954 act, and in some cases where the landlord repossesses the property the tenant may be entitled to compensation.

## SCOTLAND
In Scotland assured and short assured tenancies exist for residential lettings entered into after 2 January 1989 and are similar to assured shorthold tenancies in England and Wales. The relevant legislation is the Housing (Scotland) Act 1988.

Most tenancies created before 2 January 1989 were regulated tenancies and the Rent (Scotland) Act 1984 still applies where these exist. The act defines, among other things, the circumstances in which a landlord can increase the rent when improvements are made to the property. The provisions of the Rent Act do not apply to tenancies where the landlord is the Crown, a local authority or a housing corporation.

The Antisocial Behaviour etc (Scotland) Act 2004 provides that all private landlords letting property in Scotland must register with the local authority in which the let property is situated, unless the landlord is a local authority, or a registered social landlord. Exceptions also apply to holiday lets, owner-occupied accommodation and agricultural holdings. The act applies to partnerships, trusts and companies as well as to individuals.

Tenancy Deposit Schemes (Scotland) Regulations 2011 require that a landlord must pay deposits taken from tenants into an approved scheme and ensure that the money is held by an approved scheme for the duration of the tenancy. Evidence of registration with the relevant local authority in terms of the 2004 act must be provided when the deposit is paid over.

Landlords who provide an assured or short assured tenancy must provide new tenants with a Tenant Information Pack. The tenant Information pack includes information on the Repairing Standard, and its provision satisfies the separate obligation of a landlord to provide a tenant with written information about the landlord's duty to repair and maintain in terms of the Housing (Scotland) Act 2006.

The Housing (Scotland) Acts of 1987 and 2001 relate to local authority and registered social landlord responsibilities for housing, the right to buy, and local authority secured tenancies. The provisions are broadly similar to England and Wales. The Housing (Scotland) Act 2010 is now in force. This reforms right-to-buy provisions, modernises social housing regulation, introduces the Scottish social housing charter and replaces the regulatory framework established by the 2001 act.

In Scotland, business premises are not controlled by statute to the same extent as in England and Wales, although the Tenancy of Shops (Scotland) Act 1949 gives some security to tenants of shops. Tenants of shops can apply to the sheriff, within 21 days of being served a notice to quit, for a renewal of tenancy if threatened with eviction. This application may be dismissed on various grounds, including where the landlord has offered to sell the property to the tenant at an agreed price or, in the absence of agreement as to price, at a price fixed by a single arbiter appointed by the parties or the sheriff. The act extends to properties where the Crown or government departments are the landlords or the tenants.

Under the Leases Act 1449 the landlord's successors (either purchasers or creditors) are bound by the agreement made with any tenants so long as the following conditions are met:
• the lease, if for more than one year, must be in writing
• there must be a rent
• there must be a term of expiry
• the tenant must have entered into possession
• the subjects of the lease must be land
• the landlord, if owner, must be the proprietor with a recorded title, ie the title deeds recorded in the Register of Sasines or registered in the Land Register

On 28 November 2015 certain leases which were granted for more than 175 years and under which the rent does not exceed £100 a year, will convert to heritable titles. Therefore the tenants under these leases will become the owners of the property. Conversion of the lease will be automatic, provided certain conditions are met, unless the tenant opts out. It is possible for the landlord to claim compensation for their loss of income.

## LEGAL AID

The Access to Justice Act 1999 transformed what used to be known as the Legal Aid system. The Legal Aid Board was replaced by the Legal Services Commission, which was responsible for the development and administration of two legal funding schemes in England and Wales, namely the Criminal Defence Service and the Community Legal Service. The Criminal Defence Service assisted people who were under police investigation or facing criminal charges. The Community Legal Service was designed to increase access to legal information and advice by involving a much wider network of funders and providers in giving publicly funded legal services. In Scotland, provision of legal aid is governed by the Legal Aid (Scotland) Act 1986, the Legal Profession and Legal Aid (Scotland) Act 2007 and the Scottish Civil Justice Council and Criminal Legal Assistance Act 2013, and administered by the Scottish Legal Aid Board.

Under the Legal Aid, Sentencing and Punishment of Offenders Act 2012 (LASPO), which came into force on 1 April 2013, the Legal Services Commission was abolished and replaced by the newly created Legal Aid Agency. The act has also limited the areas of law that fall within the scope of legal aid funding, especially those related to civil legal services. However, the act does include provisions for funding in exceptional cases, such as where failure to provide legal aid would result in a violation of an individual's human rights or where providing legal aid would serve a wider public interest. Further, the act allows for areas of law to be added or omitted from the scope of legal aid independently, without subsequent legislation.

LASPO took whole areas of law out of scope for legal aid; some areas only qualify if they meet certain criteria. Broadly, the following categories of cases are now out of such scope: (a) family cases where there is no proof of domestic violence, forced marriage or child abduction; (b) immigration cases that do not involve asylum or detention; (c) housing and debt matters unless they constitute an immediate risk to the home; (d) welfare benefit cases except appeals to the upper tribunal or high court; (e) almost all clinical negligence cases; and (f) employment cases that do not involve human trafficking or a contravention of the Equality Act 2010.

LEGAL AID AGENCY,
W www.gov.uk/government/organisations/legal-aid-agency

## CIVIL LEGAL AID

From 1 January 2000, only organisations (such as solicitors or Citizens Advice) with a contract with the Legal Services Commission (now Legal Aid Agency) have been able to give initial help in any civil matter. Moreover, from that date decisions about funding were devolved from the Legal Services Commission to contracted organisations in relation to any level of publicly funded service in family and immigration cases. For other types of case, applications for public funding are made through a solicitor (or other contracted legal services providers) in much the same way as the former Legal Aid.

Under the civil funding scheme there are broadly six levels of service available:
• legal help
• help at court
• family help – either family help (lower) or family help (higher)
• legal representation – either investigative help or full representation
• family mediation
• such other services as authorised by specific orders

### ELIGIBILITY

Eligibility for funding from the Legal Aid Agency depends broadly on five factors:
• the level of service sought (see above)
• whether the applicant qualifies financially

• the merits of the applicant's case
• a costs-benefits analysis (if the costs are likely to outweigh any benefit that might be gained from the proceedings, funding may be refused)
• whether there is any public interest in the case being litigated (ie whether the case has a wider public interest beyond that of the parties involved, eg a human rights case)

The limits on capital and income above which a person is not entitled to public funding vary with the type of service sought.

LASPO has abolished capital passporting, meaning that all applicants are subject to the same capital test regardless of whether or not they are receiving benefits. The 2012 act also amended the merits criteria so that legal aid may be refused where the case is suitable for alternative funding, such as Conditional Fee Agreements.

### CONTRIBUTIONS

Some of those who qualify for Legal Aid Agency funding will have to contribute towards their legal costs. Contributions must be paid by anyone who has a disposable income or disposable capital exceeding a prescribed amount. The rules relating to applicable contributions are complex and detailed information can be obtained from the Legal Aid Agency.

### STATUTORY CHARGE

A statutory charge is made if a person keeps or gains money or property in a case for which they have received legal aid. This means that the amount paid by the Legal Aid Agency fund on their behalf is deducted from the amount that the person receives. This does not apply if the court has ordered that the costs be paid by the other party (unless the amount paid by the other party does not cover all of the costs). In certain circumstances, the Legal Aid Agency may waive or postpone payment.

### CONTINGENCY OR CONDITIONAL FEES

This system was introduced by the Courts and Legal Services Act 1990. It can offer legal representation on a 'no win, no fee' basis. It provides an alternative form of assistance, especially for those cases which are ineligible for funding by the Legal Aid Agency. The main area for such work is in the field of personal injuries.

Not all solicitors offer such a scheme and different solicitors may well have different terms. The effect of the agreement is that solicitors may not make any charges, or may waive some of their charges, until the case is concluded successfully. If a case is won then the losing party will usually have to pay towards costs, with the winning party contributing around one third.

## SCOTLAND

Civil legal aid is available for cases in the following:
• the sheriff courts
• the court of session
• the supreme court
• the lands valuation appeal court
• the Scottish land court
• the Lands Tribunal for Scotland
• the Employment Appeal Tribunals
• the Proscribed Organisations Appeal Commission
• certain appeals before the Social Security Commissioners

Civil legal aid is not available for election petitions, small claims, simplified divorce procedures or petitions by a debtor for his own sequestration. In defamation actions additional criteria must be met in order for legal aid to be available.

Eligibility for civil legal aid is assessed in a similar way to that in England and Wales, though the financial limits differ in some respects. A person shall be eligible for civil legal aid if their disposable income does not exceed £26,239 a year. A person may be refused civil aid if their disposable capital

exceeds £13,017 and it appears to the Legal Aid board that they can afford to pay without legal aid. Additionally:
- if disposable capital is between £7,853 and £13,017, the applicant will be required to pay a contribution which will be equal to the difference between £7,853 and their disposable capital
- if disposable income is between £3,522 and £11,540, a contribution of one third of the difference between £3,522 and the disposable income may be payable
- if disposable income is between £11,541 and £15,743, one third of the difference between £3,522 and £11,540 plus half the difference between £11,541 and the disposable income may be payable
- if disposable income is between £15,744 and £26,239, a contribution of the following: one third of the difference between £3,522 and £11,540, plus half the difference between £11,541 and £15,743, plus all the remaining disposable income between £15,744 and £26,239 – will be payable

## CRIMINAL LEGAL AID
The Legal Aid Agency provides defendants facing criminal charges with free legal representation if they pass a merits test and a means test.

Criminal legal aid covers the cost of preparing a case and legal representation in criminal proceedings. It is also available for appeals against verdicts or sentences in magistrates' courts, the crown court or the court of appeal. It is not available for bringing a private prosecution in a criminal court.

If granted criminal legal aid, either the person may choose their own solicitor or the court will assign one. Contributions to the legal costs may be required. The rules relating to applicable contributions are complex and detailed information can be obtained from the Legal Aid Agency.

### DUTY SOLICITORS
LASPO also provides for free initial advice and initial assistance to anyone questioned by the police (whether under arrest or helping the police with their enquiries). No means test or contributions are required for this.

## SCOTLAND
Legal advice and assistance operates in a similar way in Scotland. A person is eligible:
- if disposable income does not exceed £245 a week. If disposable income is between £105 and £245 a week, contributions are payable
- if disposable capital does not exceed £1,716 (if the person has dependent relatives, the savings allowance is higher)
- if receiving income support or income-related job seeker's allowance they qualify automatically provided their disposable capital is not over the limit

The procedure for application for criminal legal aid depends on the circumstances of each case. In solemn cases (more serious cases, such as murder) heard before a jury, a person is automatically entitled to criminal legal aid until they are given bail or placed in custody. Thereafter, it is for the court to decide whether to grant legal aid. The court will do this if the person accused cannot meet the expenses of the case without undue hardship on him or his dependants. In less serious cases the procedure depends on whether the person is in custody:
- anyone taken into custody has the right to free legal aid from the duty solicitor up to and including the first court appearance
- if the person is not in custody and wishes to plead guilty, they are not entitled to criminal legal aid but may be entitled to legal advice and assistance, including assistance by way of representation

However, regardless of whether the person is in custody if they wish to plead not guilty, they can apply for criminal legal aid. This must be done within 14 days of the first court appearance at which they made the plea

The criteria used to assess whether or not criminal legal aid should be granted is similar to the criteria for England and Wales. When meeting with your solicitor, take evidence of your financial position such as details of savings, bank statements, pay slips, pension book or benefits book.

Under the relevant provisions of the Scottish Civil Justice Council and Criminal Legal Assistance Act 2013, a person in receipt of criminal legal aid or criminal assistance by way of representation, will be required, in most circumstances, to make contributions where their weekly disposable income is £82 or above or if their disposable capital is £750 or more. The Scottish government has delayed the implementation of these provisions and no timetable has yet been proposed.

THE SCOTTISH LEGAL AID BOARD, Thistle House, 91 Haymarket Terrace, Edinburgh EH12 5HE T 0131-226 7061 W www.slab.org.uk

# MARRIAGE

Any two persons may marry provided that:
- they are at least 16 years old on the day of the marriage (in England and Wales persons under the age of 18 must generally obtain the consent of their parents or guardian; if consent is refused an appeal may be made to the high court, the county court or a court of summary jurisdiction)
- they are not related to one another in a way which would prevent their marrying
- they are unmarried (a person who has already been married must produce documentary evidence that the previous marriage has been ended by death, divorce or annulment)
- they are capable of understanding the nature of a marriage ceremony and of consenting to marriage

It is now lawful for same sex couples to marry by way of civil or religious ceremony following the passing of the Marriage (Same Sex Couples) Act 2013, which came into force in March 2014. In addition, an existing marriage will now be able to continue where one or both parties change their legal gender and both parties wish to remain married. The Act also makes provision for civil partners to convert their civil partnership into a marriage if they wish to do so.

The parties should check the marriage will be recognised as valid in their home country if either is not a British citizen.

### DEGREES OF RELATIONSHIP
A marriage between persons within the prohibited degrees of consanguinity, affinity or adoption is void.

Neither party may marry his or her parent, child, grandparent, grandchild, sibling, parent's sibling, sibling's child, adoptive parent, former adoptive parent, adoptive child or former adoptive child. All references to siblings include half-brothers/sisters.

Under the Marriage (Prohibited Degrees of Relationship) Act 1986, some exceptions to the law permit a personto marry certain step-relatives or in-laws.

In addition to the above, a person may not marry a child of their former civil partner, a child of a former spouse, the former civil partner of a grandparent, the former civil partner of a parent, the former spouse of a grandparent, the former spouse of a parent, the grandchild of a former civil partner or the grandchild of a former spouse, unless that relationship is the only reason they cannot marry and both persons are over 21 and the younger party has not at any time before attaining the age of 18 been a child of the family in relation to the other party.

## ENGLAND AND WALES
### TYPES OF MARRIAGE CEREMONY
It is possible to marry by either religious or civil ceremony. A religious ceremony can take place at a church or chapel of the Church of England or the Church in Wales, or at any other place of worship which has been formally registered by the Registrar-General. Same-sex marriages can also take place in a religious building, provided that the premises have been registered for the marriage of same-sex couples and the relevant governing authority in relation to the building has provided written consent. It is not possible, however, for same-sex marriages to take place in an Anglican church.

A civil ceremony can take place at a register office, a venue approved by the local authority or any religious premises where permission has been given by the relevant organisation and is approved by the local authority.

An application for an approved premises licence must be made by the owners or trustees of the building concerned; it cannot be made by the prospective marriage couple. Approved premises must be regularly open to the public so that the marriage can be witnessed; the venue must be deemed to be a permanent and immovable structure. Open-air ceremonies are prohibited.

Non-Anglican marriages may also be solemnised following the issue of a Registrar-General's licence in unregistered premises where one of the parties is seriously ill, is not expected to recover, and cannot be moved to registered premises. Detained and housebound persons may be married at their place of residence.

### MARRIAGE IN THE CHURCH OF ENGLAND OR THE CHURCH IN WALES
*Marriage by banns*
The marriage can take place in a parish in which one of the parties lives, or in a church in another parish if it is the usual place of worship of either or both of the parties. Further to regulations introduced in October 2008 also, marriages can also take place in a parish where one of the parties was baptised or prepared for confirmation (but not if combined rite); a parish where one of the parties lived or attended worship for six months or more; a parish where one of the parents of either of the parties lived for six months or more; a parish where one of the parents of either of the parties attended public worship for six months or more in the child's lifetime; or a parish where the parents or grandparents of either of the parties were married. The banns (ie the announcement of the marriage ceremony) must be called in the parish in which the marriage is to take place on three Sundays before the day of the ceremony; if either or both of the parties lives in a different parish the banns must also be called there. After three months the banns are no longer valid. The minister will not perform the marriage unless satisfied that the banns have been properly called.

*Marriage by common licence*
The vicar who is to conduct the marriage will arrange for a common licence to be issued by the diocesan bishop; this dispenses with the necessity for banns. One of the parties must have lived in the parish for 15 days immediately before the grant of the licence or must usually worship at the parish church or authorised chapel of that parish. Eligibility requirements vary from diocese to diocese, but it is not normally required that the parties should have been baptised. The licence is valid for three months.

*Marriage by special licence*
A special licence is granted by the Archbishop of Canterbury where a party has a genuine connection to a particular church or chapel but does not satisfy the legal requirements to marry

there. The parties are usually required to demonstrate that they have a worshipping connection to the church or chapel. The special licence will expire after three months. Application must be made to the registrar of the Faculty Office: 1 The Sanctuary, London SW1P 3JT **T** 020-7222 5381.

*Marriage by certificate*
The marriage can be conducted on the authority of a superintendent registrar's certificates, provided that the consent of the minister of the church or chapel where the marriage is to take place is obtained. One of the parties must live in the parish or must usually worship at the church/chapel.

### MARRIAGE BY OTHER RELIGIOUS CEREMONY
One of the parties must normally live in the registration district where the marriage is to take place. If the building where the parties wish to be married has not been registered, the couple can still have a religious ceremony there, but will also need to have a separate civil ceremony for the marriage to be valid. If the building is registered, in addition to giving notice to the superintendent registrar it may also be necessary to book a registrar, or authorised person to be present at the ceremony.

### CIVIL MARRIAGE
A marriage may be solemnised at any register office, registered building or approved premises in England and Wales, without either of the parties being resident in the same district. The superintendent registrar of the district should be contacted, and, if the marriage is to take place at approved premises, the necessary arrangements at the venue must also be made.

### NOTICE OF MARRIAGE
Where a marriage is intended to take place on the authority of a superintendent registrar's certificates, a notice of the marriage must be given in person to the superintendent registrar of the relevant district.

Both parties must have lived in a registration district in England or Wales for at least seven days immediately before giving notice personally at the local register office. If they live in different registration districts, notice must be given in both districts by the respective party in person. The marriage can take place in any register office or other approved premises in England and Wales no sooner than 28 days after notice has been given, when the superintendent registrar issues a certificate

A notice of marriage is valid for 12 months, unless it is for the marriage of a detained or housebound person, when it will usually only be accepted within three months of publication. Notice for marriages taking place within the Church of England or Church of Wales are also only valid for three months following publication. It should be possible to make an advance (provisional) booking 12 months before the ceremony. In this case it is still necessary to give formal notice three months before the marriage. When giving notice of the marriage it is necessary to produce official proof, if relevant, that any previous marriage has ended in divorce or death by producing a certified copy of the decree absolute or death certificate; it is also necessary for each of the parties to provide evidence of name and surname, date of birth, place of residence and nationality, for example, with a passport or birth certificate. If either party is under 18 years old, evidence of consent by their parent or guardian is required. There are special procedures for those wishing to get married in the UK that are subject to immigration control; the register office will be able to advise on these.

## SOLEMNISATION OF THE MARRIAGE

On the day of the wedding there must be at least two other people present who are prepared to act as witnesses and sign the marriage register. A registrar of marriages must be present at a marriage in a register office or at approved premises, but an authorised person may act in the capacity of registrar in a registered building.

If the marriage takes place at approved premises, the room must be separate from any other activity on the premises at the time of the ceremony, and no food or drink can be sold or consumed in the room during the ceremony or for one hour beforehand.

The marriage must be solemnised with open doors. At some time during the ceremony the parties must make a declaration that they know of no legal impediment to the marriage and they must also say the contracting words; the declaratory and contracting words may vary according to the form of service. A civil marriage cannot contain any religious aspects, but it may be possible for non-religious music and/or readings to be included. It may also be possible to embellish the marriage vows taken by the couple.

## CIVIL FEES

*Notice and registration of Marriage at a Register Office*
By superintendent registrar's certificate, £35 per person for the notice of the marriage (which is not refundable if the marriage does not in fact take place) and £46 for the registration of the marriage.

*Marriage at a Register Office/Approved Premises*
Fees for marriage at a register office are set by the local authority responsible. An additional fee will also be payable for the registrar's attendance at the marriage on an approved premises. This is also set locally by the local authority responsible. A further charge is likely to be made by the owners of the building for the use of the premises. For marriages taking place in a religious building other than the Church of England or Church of Wales, an additional fee of £84 is payable for the registrar's attendance at the marriage unless an 'Authorised Person' appointed by the trustees of the building has agreed to register the marriage. Additional fees may be charged by the trustees of the building for the wedding and by the person who performs the ceremony.

## ECCLESIASTICAL FEES

(Church of England and Church in Wales)
*Marriage by banns*
For publication of banns, £28*
For certificate of banns issued at time of publication, £13*
For marriage service, £413*
For marriage certificate at time of registration £4 and £10 thereafter
* These fees are revised from 1 January each calendar year. Some may not apply to the Church in Wales

## SCOTLAND

### REGULAR MARRIAGES

A regular marriage is one which is celebrated by a minister of religion or authorised registrar or other celebrant. Each of the parties must complete a marriage notice form and return it to the district registrar for the area in which they are to be married, irrespective of where they live, within the three month period prior to the date of the marriage and not later than 29 days prior to that date. The district registrar must then enter the date of receipt and certain details in a marriage book kept for this purpose, and must also enter the names of the parties and the proposed date of marriage in a list which is displayed in a conspicuous place at the registration office until the date of the marriage has passed. All persons wishing to enter into a regular marriage in Scotland must follow the same preliminary procedure regardless of whether they intend to have a religious or civil ceremony. Before the marriage ceremony takes place any person may submit an objection in writing to the district registrar.

A marriage schedule, which is prepared by the registrar, will be issued to one or both of the parties in person up to seven days before a religious marriage; for a civil marriage the schedule will be available at the ceremony. The schedule must be handed to the celebrant before the ceremony starts and it must be signed immediately after the wedding. For religious marriages the schedule must be sent within three days by the parties to the district registrar who must register the marriage as soon as possible thereafter. In civil marriages, the district registrar must register the marriage as soon as possible.

The authority to conduct a religious marriage is deemed to be vested in the authorised celebrant rather than the building in which it takes place; open-air religious ceremonies are therefore permissible in Scotland.

From 10 June 2002 it has been possible, under the Marriage (Scotland) Act 2002, for venues or couples to apply to the local council for a licence to allow a civil ceremony to take place at a venue other than a registration office. To obtain further information, a venue or couple should contact the district registrar in the area they wish to marry.

### MARRIAGE BY COHABITATION WITH HABIT AND REPUTE

Prior to the enactment of the Family Law (Scotland) Act 2006, if two people had lived together constantly as husband and wife and were generally held to be such by the neighbourhood and among their friends and relations, a presumption could arise from which marriage could be inferred. Before such a marriage could be registered, however, a decree of declarator of marriage had to be obtained from the court of session. Section 3 of the 2006 act provides that it will no longer be possible for a marriage to be constituted by cohabitation with habit and repute, but it will still be possible for couples whose period of cohabitation began before commencement of the 2006 act to seek a declarator under the old rule of law.

### SAME-SEX MARRIAGES

On 12 March 2014 the Scottish government passed the Marriage and Civil Partnership (Scotland) Act 2014. This permits same-sex couples to get married, either in a civil ceremony or a 'religious or belief' ceremony where the religious or belief body has opted-in to solemnising same-sex marriage. Also, certain same-sex couples who have entered into a civil partnership have the option under the Act to change their civil partnership to a marriage.

It is still possible for same-sex couples to enter into a civil partnership and this may be a 'religious or belief' civil partnership if the religious or belief body has agreed to perform these.

### CIVIL FEES

The fee for submitting a notice of marriage to the district registrar is £30.00 per person. Solemnisation of a civil marriage costs £55.00, while the extract of the entry in the register of marriages attracts a fee of £10.00. The costs of religious marriage ceremonies can vary.

THE GENERAL REGISTER OFFICE, PO Box 2,
Southport PR8 2JD **T** 0845-603 7788
**W** www.gro.gov.uk/gro/content/certificates
THE NATIONAL RECORDS OF SCOTLAND,
New Register House, 2 Princes Street, Edinburgh EH1 3YY
**T** 0131-314 0380 **W** www.nrsscotland.gov.uk

# TOWN AND COUNTRY PLANNING

There are a number of acts governing the development of land and buildings in England and Wales and advice should always be sought from Citizens Advice or the local planning authority before undertaking building works on any land or property. If development takes place which requires planning permission without permission being given, enforcement action may take place and the situation may need to be rectified. Planning law in Scotland is similar but certain Scotland-specific legislation applies so advice should always be sought.

## PLANNING PERMISSION
Planning permission is needed if the work involves:
- making a material change in use, such as dividing off part of the house or garden so that it can be used as a separate home or dividing off part of the house for commercial use, eg for a workshop
- going against the terms of the original planning permission, eg there may be a restriction on fences in front gardens on an open-plan estate
- building, engineering or mining, except for the permitted developments below
- new or wider access to a main road
- additions or extensions to flats or maisonettes
- work which might obstruct the view of road users

Planning permission is not needed to carry out internal alterations or work which does not affect the external appearance of the building, and are not works for making good war damage or works begun after 5 December 1968 for the alteration of a building by providing additional space in it underground.

Under regulations which came into effect on 1 October 2008, there are certain types of development for which the Secretary of State for the Environment, Food and Rural Affairs has granted general permissions (permitted development rights). These include house extensions and additions, outbuildings and garages, other ancillary garden buildings such as swimming pools or ponds, and laying patios, paths or driveways for domestic use. All developments are subject to a number of conditions.

Before carrying out any of the above permitted developments you should contact your local planning authority to find out whether the general permission has been modified in your area. For more information, visit W www.planningportal.gov.uk

## OTHER RESTRICTIONS
It may be necessary to obtain other types of permissions before carrying out any development. These permissions are separate from planning permission and apply regardless of whether or not planning permission is needed, eg:
- building regulations will probably apply if a new building is to be erected, if an existing one is to be altered or extended, or if the work involves building over a drain or sewer. The building control department of the local authority will advise on this
- any alterations to a listed building or the grounds of a listed building must be approved by the local authority. Listing will include not only the main building but everything in the curtilage of the building
- local authority approval is necessary if a building (or, in some circumstances, gates, walls, fences or railings) in a conservation area is to be demolished; each local authority keeps a register of all local buildings that are in conservation areas
- many trees are protected by tree preservation orders and must not be pruned or taken down without local authority consent

- bats and many other species are protected, and Natural England, Natural Resources Wales or Scottish Natural Heritage must be notified before any work is carried out that will affect the habitat of protected species, eg timber treatment, renovation or extensions of lofts
- developments in areas with special designations, such as National Parks, Areas of Outstanding Natural Beauty, National Scenic Areas or in the Norfolk or Suffolk Broads, are subject to greater restrictions. The local planning authority will advise or refer enquirers to the relevant authority

There may also be restrictions contained in the title to the property which require you to get someone else's agreement before carrying out certain developments, and which should be considered when works are planned.

# VOTERS' QUALIFICATIONS

Those entitled to vote at parliamentary, and local government elections are those who, at the date of taking the poll, are:
- on the electoral roll
- aged 18 years or older
- British citizens, Commonwealth citizens or citizens of the Irish Republic who are resident in the UK
- those who suffer from no other legal bar to voting (eg prisoners). It should be noted that there is some uncertainty regarding the future of the legal bar on prisoners' voting following a decision taken by the European Court of Human Rights
- in Northern Ireland electors must have been resident in Northern Ireland during the whole of the three-month period prior to the relevant date
- citizens of any EU member state may vote in local elections if they meet the criteria listed above (save for the nationality requirements)

British citizens resident abroad are entitled to vote, provided they have been registered to vote in the UK within the last 15 years, as overseas electors in domestic parliamentary elections in the constituency in which they were last resident if they are on the electoral roll of the relevant constituency. Members of the armed forces and their spouses or civil partners, Crown servants and employees of the British Council who are overseas, along with their spouses and civil partners, are entitled to vote regardless of how long they have been abroad. British citizens who had never been registered as an elector in the UK are not eligible to register as an overseas voter unless they left the UK before they were 18, providing they left the country no more than 15 years ago. Overseas electors may opt to vote by proxy or by postal vote. Overseas voters may not vote in local government elections.

The main categories of people who are not entitled to vote at general elections are:
- sitting peers in the House of Lords
- convicted persons detained in pursuance of their sentences (though remand prisoners, unconvicted prisoners and civil prisoners can vote if on the electoral register). This is currently subject to review, as detailed above
- those convicted within the previous five years of corrupt or illegal election practices
- EU citizens (who may only vote in EU and local government elections)

Under the Representation of the Peoples Act 2000, several new groups of people are permitted to vote for the first time. These include: people who live on barges; people in mental health hospitals (other than those with criminal convictions) and homeless people who have made a 'declaration of local connection'.

## REGISTERING TO VOTE

Voters must be entered on an electoral register. The Electoral Registration Officer (ERO) for each council area is responsible for preparing and publishing the register for his area by 1 December each year. Names may be added to the register to reflect changes in people's circumstances as they occur and each month during December to August, the ERO publishes a list of alterations to the published register.

On 10 May 2012, the government introduced the electoral registration and administration bill, which received royal assent on 31 January 2013. The act replaced household registration with individual elector registration, meaning each elector must apply individually to be registered to vote. Individuals will also be asked for identifying information such as date of birth and national insurance number. The act also introduced a number of changes relating to electoral administration and the conduct of elections. Anyone failing to supply information to the ERO when requested, or supplying false information, may be fined by up to £1,000. Further, the ERO may impose a civil penalty on those who fail to make an application for registration when required to do so by the ERO. Application forms and more information are available from the Electoral Commission (W www.aboutmyvote.co.uk).

## VOTING

Voting is not compulsory in the UK. Those who wish to vote do so in person at the allotted polling station. Postal votes are now available to anyone on request and you do not need to give a reason for using a postal vote.

A proxy (whereby the voter nominates someone to vote in person on their behalf) can be appointed to act in a specific election, for a specified period of time or indefinitely. For the appointment of an indefinite or long-term proxy, the voter needs to specify physical employment, study reasons or a disability to explain why they are making an application. With proxy votes where a particular election is specified, the voter needs to provide details of the circumstances by which they cannot reasonably be expected to go to the polling station. Applications for a proxy are normally available up to six working days before an election, but should the voter fall ill on election day, it is possible to appoint a proxy up until polling day.

## WILLS

A will is used to appoint executors (who will administer the estate), give directions as to the disposal of the body, appoint guardians for children and determine how and to whom property is to be passed. A well-drafted will can operate to reduce the level of inheritance tax which the estate pays. It is best to have a will drawn up by a solicitor, but if a solicitor is not employed the following points must be taken into account:

- if possible the will must not be prepared on behalf of another person by someone who is to benefit from it or who is a close relative of a major beneficiary
- the language used must be clear and unambiguous and it is better to avoid the use of legal terms where the same thing can be expressed in plain language
- it is better to rewrite the whole document if a mistake is made. If necessary, alterations can be made by striking through the words with a pen, and the signature or initials of the testator and the witnesses must be put in the margin opposite the alteration. No alteration of any kind should be made after the will has been executed
- if the person later wishes to change the will or part of it, it is better to write a new will revoking the old. The use of

codicils (documents written as supplements or containing modifications to the will) should be left to a solicitor
- the will should be typed or printed, or if handwritten be legible and preferably in ink

The form of a will varies to suit different cases – a solicitor will be able to advise as to wording, however, 'DIY' will-writing kits can be purchased from good stationery shops and many banks offer a will-writing service.

## LAPSED LEGATEES

If a person who has been left property in a will dies before the person who made the will, the gift fails and will pass to the person entitled to everything not otherwise disposed of (the residuary estate). If the beneficiary of the residuary estate dies before the person who made the will, the gift of the residuary estate also fails and passes to the closest relative(s) of the testator in accordance with the intestacy rules.

It is always better to draw up a new will if a beneficiary predeceases the person who made the will.

## EXECUTORS

It is usual to appoint two executors, although one is sufficient. No more than four persons can deal with the estate of the person who has died. The name and address of each executor should be given in full (the addresses are not essential but including them adds clarity to the document). Executors should be 18 years of age or over. An executor may be a beneficiary of the will.

## WITNESSES

A person who is a beneficiary of a will, or the spouse or civil partner of a beneficiary at the time the will is signed, must not act as a witness or else he/she will be unable to take his/her gift. There is nothing preventing the spouse or civil partner of the person making the will from acting as a witness, but as it is rare for a spouse or civil partner not to benefit from the will of his/her spouse or civil partner, an independent witness is usually better.

It is also better that a person does not act as an executor and as a witness, as he/she can take no benefit (including remuneration) under a will to which he/she is witness. In relation to deaths on or after 1 February 2001, however, a professional executor who is also a witness can receive payments due to him or her under a term in the will for services provided as executor.

The identity of the witnesses should be made as explicit as possible, such as by stating their names, addresses, and occupations.

## EXECUTION OF A WILL

The person making the will should sign his/her name in the presence of the two witnesses. It is advisable to sign at the foot of the document, so as to avoid uncertainty about the testator's intention. The witnesses must then sign their names while the person making the will looks on. If this procedure is not adhered to, the will may be considered invalid. There are certain exceptional circumstances where these rules are relaxed, eg where the person may be too ill to sign.

## CAPACITY TO MAKE A WILL

Anyone aged 18 or over can make a will. However, if there is any suspicion that the person making the will is not, through reasons of infirmity or age, fully in command of his/her faculties, it is advisable to arrange for a medical practitioner to examine the person making the will at the time it is to be executed (to verify his/her mental capacity and to record that medical opinion in writing), and to ask the examining practitioner to act as a witness. If a person is not mentally able to make a will, the court may do this for him/her by virtue of the Mental Capacity Act 2005.

## REVOCATION

A will may be revoked or cancelled in a number of ways:
• a later will revokes an earlier one if it says so; otherwise the earlier will is by implication revoked by the later one to the extent that it contradicts or repeats the earlier one
• a will is revoked if the physical document on which it is written is destroyed by the person whose will it is. There must be an intention to revoke the will and an act of destruction. It may not be sufficient to obliterate the will with a pen
• a will is revoked by the testator making a written declaration to this effect executed in the same way as a will
• a will is also revoked when the person marries or forms a civil partnership, unless it is clear from the will that the person intended the will to stand after that particular marriage or civil partnership. A will is not revoked, however, by the conversion of a civil partnership to a marriage
• where a marriage or civil partnership ends in divorce or dissolution or is annulled or declared void, gifts to the spouse or civil partner and the appointment of the spouse or civil partner as executor fail unless the will says that this is not to happen. A former spouse or civil partner is treated as having predeceased the testator. A separation does not change the effect of a married person or civil partner's will.

## PROBATE AND LETTERS OF ADMINISTRATION

Probate is granted to the executors named in a will and once granted, the executors are obliged to carry out the instructions of the will. Letters of administration are granted where no executor is named in a will or is willing or able to act or where there is no will or no valid will; this gives a person, often the next of kin, similar powers and duties to those of an executor.

Applications for probate or for letters of administration can be made to the Principal Registry of the Family Division, to a district probate registry or to a probate sub-registry. Applicants will need the following documents: the Probate Application Form; the original will and codicils (if any) and three copies; a certificate of death; oath for executors or administrators; and the appropriate tax form (an 'IHT 205' if no inheritance tax is owed; otherwise an 'IHT 400' and 'IHT 421'), in addition to a cheque for the relevant probate fee. Certain property, up to the value of £5,000, may be disposed of without a grant of probate or letters of administration, as can assets that do not pass under the will such as jointly owned assets which pass automatically on the death of one of the joint holders to the survivor.

## WHERE TO FIND A PROVED WILL

Since 1858 wills which have been proved, that is wills on which probate or letters of administration have been granted, must have been proved at the Principal Registry of the Family Division or at a district probate registry. The Lord Chancellor has power to direct where the original documents are kept but most are filed where they were proved and may be inspected there and a copy obtained. The Principal Registry also holds copies of all wills proved at district probate registries and these may be inspected at First Avenue House, High Holborn, London. An index of all grants, both of probate and of letters of administration, is compiled by the Principal Registry and may be seen either at the Principal Registry or at a district probate registry.

It is also possible to discover when a grant of probate or letters of administration is issued by requesting a standing search. In response to a request and for a small fee, a district probate registry will supply the names and addresses of executors or administrators and the registry in which the grant was made, of any grant in the estate of a specified person made in the previous 12 months or following six months.

## PRINCIPAL REGISTRY (FAMILY DIVISION),

First Avenue House, 42–49 High Holborn, London WC1 6NP
T 020-7947 6000

## INTESTACY

Intestacy occurs when someone dies without leaving a will or leaves a will which is invalid or which does not take effect for some reason. Intestacy can be partial, for instance, if there is a will which disposes of some but not all of the testator's property. In such cases the person's estate (property, possessions, other assets following the payment of debts) passes to certain members of the family. If a will has been written that disposes of only part of a person's property, these rules apply to the part which is undisposed of.

Some types of property do not follow the intestacy rules, for example, property held as joint tenants, insurance policies taken out for specified individuals or assigned into trust during the testator's lifetime and death benefits under a pension scheme.

Following a lengthy review by the Law Commission, the intestacy rules changed on 1 October 2014.

If the person (intestate) leaves a spouse or a civil partner who survives for 28 days and children (legitimate, illegitimate and adopted children and other descendants), the estate is divided as follows:
• if the estate is worth more than £250,000, the spouse or civil partner takes the 'personal chattels' (household articles, including cars, but nothing used for business purposes), £250,000 and half of the rest of the estate absolutely
• the rest of the estate goes to the children*

If the intestate leaves a spouse or civil partner who survives for 28 days but no children, the spouse or civil partner will take the estate in its entirety, regardless of its value.

If there is no surviving spouse or civil partner, the estate is distributed among those who survive the intestate as follows (these provisions remained unchanged at 1 October 2014):
• to surviving children*, but if none to
• parents (equally, if both alive), but if none to
• brothers and sisters of the whole blood* (including issue of deceased ones), but if none to
• brothers and sisters of the half blood* (including issue of deceased ones), but if none to
• grandparents (equally, if more than one), but if none to
• aunts and uncles of the whole blood*, but if none to
• aunts and uncles of the half blood*, but if none to
• the Crown, Duchy of Lancaster or the Duke of Cornwall *(bona vacantia)*

* To inherit, a member of these groups must survive the intestate and attain the age of 18, or marry under that age. If they die under the age of 18 (unless married under that age), their share goes to others, if any, in the same group. If any member of these groups predeceases the intestate leaving children, their share is divided equally among their children.

In England and Wales the provisions of the Inheritance (Provision for Family and Dependants) Act 1975 may allow other people to claim provision from the deceased's assets. This act also applies to cases where a will has been made and allows a person to apply to the court if they feel that the will or rules of intestacy (or both) do not make adequate

provision for them. The court can order payment from the deceased's assets or the transfer of property from them if the applicant's claim is accepted. The application must be made within six months of the grant of probate or letters of administration and the following people can make an application:
• the spouse or civil partner
• a former spouse or civil partner who has not remarried or formed a subsequent civil partnership
• a child of the deceased
• someone treated as a child of the deceased's family where the deceased stood in the role of a parent to the applicant
• someone maintained by the deceased
• someone who has cohabited for two years before the death in the same household as the deceased and as the husband or wife or civil partner of the deceased

## SCOTLAND
In Scotland any person over 12 and of sound mind can make a will. The person making the will can only freely dispose of the heritage and what is known as the 'dead's part' of the estate because:
• the spouse or civil partner has the right to inherit one-third of the moveable estate if there are children or other descendants, and one-half of it if there are not
• children are entitled to one-third of the moveable estate if there is a surviving spouse or civil partner, and one-half of it if there is not
The remaining portion of the moveable estate is the dead's part, and legacies and bequests are payable from this. Debts are payable out of the whole estate before any division.

From August 1995, wills no longer needed to be 'holographed' and it is now only necessary to have one witness. The person making the will still needs to sign each page. It is better that the will is not witnessed by a beneficiary although the attestation would still be sound and the beneficiary would not have to relinquish the gift.

Subsequent marriage or civil partnership does not revoke a will but the birth of a child who is not provided for may do so. A will may be revoked by a subsequent will, either expressly or by implication, but in so far as the two can be read together both have effect. If a subsequent will is revoked, the earlier will may be revived provided it wasn't physically destroyed. However, the Scottish government has proposed changes to this in the succession (Scotland) bill which was introduced into the Scottish parliament in June 2015.

Wills may be registered in the sheriff court Books of the Sheriffdom in which the deceased lived or in the Books of Council and Session at the Registers of Scotland.

## CONFIRMATION
Confirmation (the Scottish equivalent of probate) is obtained in the sheriff court of the sheriffdom in which the deceased was domiciled at the time of death. Executors are either 'nominate' (named by the deceased in the will) or 'dative' (appointed by the court in cases where no executor is named in a will or in cases of intestacy). Applicants for confirmation must first provide an inventory of the deceased's estate and a schedule of debts, with an affidavit. In estates under £36,000 gross, confirmation can be obtained under a simplified procedure at reduced fees, with no need for a solicitor. The local sheriff clerk's office can provide assistance.

PRINCIPAL REGISTRY (FAMILY DIVISION),
First Avenue House, 42–49 High Holborn, London WC1 6NP
T 020-7947 6000
REGISTERS OF SCOTLAND, Meadowbank House,
153 London Road, Edinburgh EH8 7AU T 0845-607 0161

## INTESTACY
The rules of distribution are contained in the Succession (Scotland) Act 1964 and are extended to include civil partners by the Civil Partnership Act 2004.

A surviving spouse or civil partner is entitled to 'prior rights'. Once the provisions of the Marriage and Civil Partnership Act 2014 come into force references to people who are or were married are to be read as referring to both opposite and same-sex marriage. Prior rights mean that if certain conditions are met the spouse or civil partner has the right to inherit:
• the matrimonial or family home up to a value of £473,000, or one matrimonial or family home if there is more than one, or, in certain circumstances, the value of the home
• the furnishings and contents of that home, up to the value of £29,000
• a cash sum of £50,000 if the deceased left children or other descendants, or £89,000 if not
These figures are increased from time to time by regulations.

Once prior rights have been satisfied legal rights are settled. Legal rights are:
• *Jus relicti(ae) and rights under the section 131 of the Civil Partnership Act 2004* – the right of a surviving spouse or civil partner to one-half of the net moveable estate, after satisfaction of prior rights, if there are no surviving children; if there are surviving children, the spouse or civil partner is entitled to one-third of the net moveable estate
• *Legitim and rights under the section 131 of the Civil Partnership Act 2004* – the right of surviving children to one-half of the net moveable estate if there is no surviving spouse or civil partner; if there is a surviving spouse or civil partner, the children are entitled to one-third of the net moveable estate after the satisfaction of prior rights
Once prior and legal rights have been satisfied, the remaining estate will be distributed in the following order:
• to descendants
• if no descendants, then to collaterals (ie brothers and sisters) and parents with each being entitled to half of the estate, or if only either parents or collaterals survive, the whole of the estate
• surviving spouse or civil partner
• if no collaterals, parents, spouse or civil partner, then to ascendants collaterals (ie aunts and uncles), and so on in an ascending scale
• if all lines of succession fail, the estate passes to the Crown
Relatives of the whole blood are preferred to relatives of the half blood. Also the right of representation, ie the right of the issue of a person who would have succeeded if he/she had survived the intestate applies.

The Family Law (Scotland) Act 2006 makes provision to allow an unmarried cohabitant to make a financial claim against the estate of a cohabitant who dies intestate. In general a claim must be made within six months of the deceased's death. The court must take into account certain factors when considering such a claim. If the claim is successful the court has the power to order payment of a capital sum and transfer of property.

# INTELLECTUAL PROPERTY

Intellectual property is a broad term covering a number of legal rights provided by the government to help people protect their creative works and encourage further innovation. By using these legal rights people can own the things they create and control the way in which others use their innovations. Intellectual property owners can take legal action to stop others using their intellectual property, they can license their intellectual property to others or they can sell it on. Different types of intellectual property utilise different forms of protection including copyright, designs, patents and trade marks, which are all covered below in more detail.

CHANGES TO INTELLECTUAL PROPERTY LAW
• Reforms to the Copyright, Designs and Patents Act 1988 came into force on 1 June 2014 giving a number of sectors a legal framework suitable for the digital age, removing unnecessary regulations and enabling these sectors to better preserve and use copyright material. Under the reforms, disabled people and disability groups can make accessible copies of copyright material (eg music, film, books) when no commercial alternative exists, researchers benefit from the introduction of a new text and data mining exception for non-commercial research and schools, colleges and universities can obtain a licence to use copyright material on interactive whiteboards and in presentations without accidentally infringing copyright. An existing preservation exception was expanded to cover all types of copyright work, and now applies to museums and galleries as well as libraries and archives.
• A new online patent renewal service (W www.gov.uk/renew-patent) was launched on 1 July 2014; designed to make renewing over 400,000 patents each year simpler, quicker and cheaper for businesses and inventors
• The Intellectual Property Act 2014 came into effect on 1 October 2014. The Act modernised intellectual property law to help UK businesses better protect their rights. The Act also implemented reforms to design legislation and introduced a number of changes to patent law making it cheaper and easier to use and defend patents.

## COPYRIGHT

Copyright protects all original literary, dramatic, musical and artistic works, as well as sound and film recordings and broadcasts. Among the works covered by copyright are novels, computer programs, newspaper articles, sculptures, technical drawings, websites, maps and photographs. Under copyright the creators of these works can control the various ways in which their material may be exploited, the rights broadly covering copying, adapting, issuing (including renting and lending) copies to the public, performing in public, and broadcasting the material. The transfer of copyright works to formats accessible to visually impaired persons without infringement of copyright was enacted in 2002.

Copyright protection in the UK is automatic and there is no official registration system. The creator of a work can help to protect it by including the copyright symbol ©, the name of the copyright owner, and the year in which the work was created. In addition, steps can be taken by the work's creator to provide evidence that he/she had the work at a particular time (eg by depositing a copy with a bank or solicitor). The main legislation is the Copyright, Designs and Patents Act 1988 (as amended). As a result of an EU directive effective from January 1996, the term of copyright protection for

literary, dramatic, musical (including song lyrics and musical compositions) and artistic works lasts for 70 years after the death of the creator. For film, copyright lasts for 70 years after the director, authors of the screenplay and dialogue, or the composer of any music specially created for the film have all died. Sound recordings are protected for 50 years after their publication (or their first performance if they are not published), and broadcasts for 50 years from the end of the year in which the broadcast/transmission was made. The typographical arrangement of published editions remains under copyright protection for 25 years from the end of the year in which the particular edition was published.

The main international treaties protecting copyright are the Berne Convention for the Protection of Literary and Artistic Works (administered by the World Intellectual Property Organisation (WIPO)), the Rome Convention for the Protection of Performers, Producers of Phonograms and Broadcasting Organisations (administered by the United Nations Educational, Scientific and Cultural Organization (UNESCO), the International Labour Organisation and WIPO), the Geneva Phonograms Convention (administered by WIPO), and the Universal Copyright Convention (developed by UNESCO); the UK is a signatory to these conventions. Copyright material created by UK nationals or residents is protected in the countries that have signed one of the above-named conventions by the national law of that country. A list of participating countries may be obtained from the UK Intellectual Property Office. The World Trade Organisation's Trade-Related Aspects of Intellectual Property Rights (TRIPS) agreement, signed in 1995, may also provide copyright protection abroad.

Two treaties which strengthen and update international standards of protection, particularly in relation to new technologies, were agreed in December 1996: the WIPO Copyright Treaty, and the WIPO Performances and Phonograms Treaty. In May 2001 the European Union passed a new directive (which in 2003 became law in the UK) aimed at harmonising copyright law throughout the EU to take account of the internet and other technologies. More information can be found online (W www.ipo.gov.uk).

LICENSING
Use of copyright material without seeking permission in each instance may be permitted under 'blanket' licences available from national copyright licensing agencies. The International Federation of Reproduction Rights Organisations facilitates agreements between its member licensing agencies and on behalf of its members with organisations such as WIPO, UNESCO, the European Union and the Council of Europe. More information can be found online (W www.ifrro.org).

## DESIGN PROTECTION

Design protection covers the outward appearance of an article and in the UK takes two forms: registered design and design right, which are not mutually exclusive. Registered design protects the aesthetic appearance of an article, including shape, configuration, pattern or ornament; artistic works such as sculptures are excluded, being generally protected by copyright. To achieve design protection the owner of the design must apply to the Intellectual Property Office. In order to qualify for protection, a design must be new and materially different from earlier UK published designs. Initial registration lasts for five years and can be extended in five-year increments to a maximum of 25 years.

The current legislation is the Registered Designs Act 1949 which has been amended several times, most recently by the Regulatory Reform Order 2006.

UK applicants wishing to protect their designs in the EU can do so by applying for a Registered Community Design with the Office for Harmonization in the Internal Market. Outside the EU separate applications must be made in each country in which protection is sought.

Design right is an automatic right which applies to the shape or configuration of articles and does not require registration. Unlike registered design, two-dimensional designs do not qualify for protection but designs of electronic circuits are protected by design right. Designs must be original and non-commonplace. The term of design right is ten years from first marketing of the design, or 15 years after the creation of the design, whichever is earlier. This right is effective only in the UK. After five years anyone is entitled to apply for a licence of right, which allows others to make and sell products copying the design. The current legislation is Part 3 of the Copyright, Designs and Patents Act 1988.

## PATENTS

A patent is a document issued by the UK Intellectual Property Office relating to an invention. It gives the proprietor the right for a limited period to stop others from making, using, importing or selling the invention without the inventor's permission. In return the patentee pays a fee to cover the costs of processing the patent and publicly discloses details of the invention.

To qualify for a patent an invention must be new, must be functional or technical, must exhibit an inventive step, and must be capable of industrial application. The patent is valid for a maximum of 20 years from the date on which the application was filed, subject to payment of annual fees from the end of the fifth year.

The UK Intellectual Property Office, established in 1852, is responsible for ensuring that all stages of an application comply with the Patents Act 1977, and that the invention meets the criteria for a patent.

WIPO is responsible for administering many of the international conventions on intellectual property. The Patent Cooperation Treaty allows inventors to file a single application for patent rights in some or all of the contracting states. This application is searched by an International Searching Authority to confirm the invention is novel and that the same concept has not already been made publicly available. The application and search report are then published by the International Bureau of WIPO. It may also be the subject of an (optional) international preliminary examination. Applicants must then deal directly with the patent offices in the countries where they are seeking patent rights. The European Patent Convention allows inventors to obtain patent rights in all the contracting states by filing a single application with the European Patent Office. More information can be found online (W www.ipo.gov.uk).

## RESEARCH DISCLOSURES

Research disclosures are publicly disclosed details of inventions. Once published, an invention is considered no longer novel and becomes 'prior art'. Publishing a disclosure is significantly cheaper than applying for a patent; however, unlike a patent, it does not entitle the author to exclusive rights to use or license the invention. Instead, research disclosures are primarily published to ensure the inventor the freedom to use the invention. This works because publishing legally prevents other parties from patenting the disclosed innovation and in the UK, patent law dictates that by disclosing details of an invention, even the inventor relinquishes their right to a patent.

In theory, publishing details of an invention anywhere should be enough to constitute a research disclosure. However, to be effective, a research disclosure needs to be published in a location which patent examiners will include in their prior art searches. To ensure global legal precedent it must be included in a publication with a recognised date stamp and made publicly available throughout the world.

*Research Disclosure,* established in 1960 and operated by Questel Ireland Ltd, is the primary publisher of research disclosures. It is the only disclosure service recognised by the Patent Cooperation Treaty as a mandatory search resource which must be consulted by the international search authorities. More information can be found online (W www.researchdisclosure.com).

## TRADE MARKS

Trade marks are a means of identification, enabling traders to make their goods and services readily distinguishable from those supplied by others. Trade marks can take the form of words, a logo or a combination of both. Registration prevents other traders using the same or similar trade marks for similar products or services.

In the UK trade marks are registered at the UK Intellectual Property Office. In order to qualify for registration a trade mark must be capable of distinguishing its proprietor's goods or services from those of other undertakings; it should be non-deceptive, should not describe the goods and services or any characteristics of them, should not be contrary to law or morality and should not be similar or identical to any earlier trade marks for the same or similar goods or services. The owner of a registered trade mark may include an fi symbol next to it, and must renew their registration every ten years to keep it in force. The relevant current legislation is the Trade Marks Act 1994 (as amended).

It is possible to obtain an international trade mark registration, effective in 92 countries, under the Madrid system for the international registration of marks, to which the UK is party. British companies can obtain international trade mark registration in those countries party to the system through a single application to WIPO.

EU trade mark regulation is administered by the Office for Harmonization in the Internal Market (Trade Marks and Designs) in Alicante, Spain. The office registers Community trade marks, which are valid throughout the European Union. The registration of trade marks in individual member states continues in parallel with EU trade mark standards.

### DOMAIN NAMES

An internet domain name (eg www.bloomsbury.com) has to be registered separately from a trade mark, and this can be done through a number of registrars which charge varying rates and compete for business. For each top-level domain name (eg uk.com), there is a central registry to store the unique internet names and addresses using that suffix. A list of accredited registrars can be found online (W www.icann.org).

### CONTACTS

COPYRIGHT LICENSING AGENCY LTD, Saffron House, 6–10 Kirby Street, London EC1N 8TS T 020-7400 3100 W www.cla.co.uk

EUROPEAN PATENT OFFICE, 80298 Munich, Germany T (+49) 89 2399-0 W www.epo.org

INTELLECTUAL PROPERTY OFFICE, Concept House, Cardiff Road, Newport NP10 8QQ T 0300-300 2000 W www.ipo.gov.uk

WORLD INTELLECTUAL PROPERTY ORGANIZATION, 34 chemin des Colombettes, CH-1211 Geneva 20, Switzerland T (+41) 22 338 9111 W www.wipo.int

# THE MEDIA

## CROSS-MEDIA OWNERSHIP

The rules surrounding cross-media ownership were overhauled as part of the 2003 Communications Act. The act simplified and relaxed existing rules to encourage dispersion of ownership and new market entry while preventing the most influential media in any community being controlled by too narrow a range of interests. However, transfers and mergers are not solely subject to examination on competition grounds by the competition authorities. The Secretary of State for Culture, Media and Sport has a broad remit to decide if a transaction is permissible and can intervene on public interest grounds (relating both to newspapers and cross-media criteria, if broadcasting interests are also involved); the Secretary of State for Business, Innovation and Skills may also intervene in a media merger if it raises public interest considerations. The Office of Communications (OFCOM) has an advisory role in this context. Government and parliamentary assurances were given that any intervention into local newspaper transfers would be rare and exceptional. Following a request from the Secretary of State for Culture, Media and Sport in June 2010 for a removal of all restrictions from the ownership of local media, OFCOM recommended the liberalisation of local cross-media regulations to enable a single owner to control newspapers, a TV licence and radio stations in one area.

## REGULATION

OFCOM is the regulator for the communication industries in the UK and has responsibility for television, radio, telecommunications and wireless communications services. OFCOM is required to report annually to parliament and exists to further the interests of consumers by balancing choice and competition with the duty to foster plurality; protect viewers and listeners and promote cultural diversity in the media; and to ensure full and fair competition between communications providers.

OFFICE OF COMMUNICATIONS (OFCOM)
Riverside House, 2A Southwark Bridge Road, London SE1 9HA
T 020-7981 3000 W www.ofcom.org.uk
*Chief Executive,* Sharon White

## COMPLAINTS

Under the Communications Act 2003 OFCOM's licensees are obliged to adhere to the provisions of its codes (including advertising, programme standards, fairness, privacy and sponsorship). Complainants should contact the broadcaster in the first instance (details can be found on OFCOM's website); however, if the complainant wishes the complaint to be considered by OFCOM, it will do so. Complaints should be made within a reasonable time, as broadcasters are only required to keep recordings for the following periods: radio, 42 days; television, 90 days; and cable and satellite, 60 days. OFCOM can fine a broadcaster, revoke a licence or take programmes off the air. Since November 2004 complaints relating to individual advertisements on TV or radio have been dealt with by the Advertising Standards Authority.

ADVERTISING STANDARDS AUTHORITY
Mid City Place, 71 High Holborn, London WC1V 6QT
T 020-7492 2222 W www.asa.org.uk
*Chief Executive,* Guy Parker

## TELEVISION

There are six major television broadcasters operating in the UK. Four of these – the BBC, ITV, Channel 4 and Channel 5 – launched as free-to-air analogue terrestrial networks. BSkyB and Virgin Media Television provide satellite television services.

Beginning as a radio station in 1922, the BBC is the oldest broadcaster in the world. The corporation began a London-only television service from Alexandra Palace in 1936 and achieved nationwide coverage 15 years later. A second station, BBC Two, was launched in 1964. The BBC's other free-to-air channels available in the UK comprise BBC Three, BBC Four, BBC One HD, BBC Two HD, BBC News, BBC Parliament and the children's channels, CBeebies and CBBC. BBC's iPlayer service was launced Christmas Day 2007 and allows users to view and listen to programmes from the last seven days instantly, stream live television and download programmes on to a computer or mobile device for up to 30 days. An integrated service for radio was launched in June 2008. In 2009, iPlayer was extended to more than 20 devices, including mobile phones and games consoles, and a HD service was launched. The BBC services are funded by the licence fee. The corporation also has a commercial arm, BBC Worldwide, which was formed in 1994 and exists to maximise the value of the BBC's programme and publishing assets for the benefit of the licence payer. Its businesses include international programming distribution, magazines, other licensed products, live events and media monitoring.

The ITV (Independent Television) network began broadcasting in 1955 on Channel 3 in the London area, under the Television Act 1954 which made provision for commercial television in the UK. The ITV network originally comprised a number of independent licensees, the majority of which have now merged to form ITV plc. The network generates funds through broadcasting television advertisements. The ITV network channels now include ITV2, ITV3, ITV4, ITVBe and CiTV. ITV Player, similar to iPlayer, was launched December 2008. ITV Network Centre is wholly owned by the ITV companies and undertakes commissioning and scheduling of programmes shown across the ITV network and, as with the other terrestrial channels, 25 per cent of programmes must come from independent producers.

Channel 4 and S4C (Sianel Pedwar Cymru – Channel Four Wales) were launched in 1982 to provide programmes with a distinctive character that appeal to interests not catered for by ITV. Channel 4 has a remit to be innovative, experimental and distinctive. Although publicly owned, Channel 4 receives no public funding and is financed predominantly through advertising, but unlike ITV, Channel 4 is not shareholder-owned. It has expanded to create the stations E4, More4, Film4, 4Music and, in July 2012, catchup channel 4seven. All 4 is Channel 4's online service which enables viewers to download and revisit programmes from the last 30 days as well as access an older archive of footage. All 4 replaced Channel 4's first online platform 4oD (launched in 2006) in March 2015. S4/C, the Welsh language public service broadcaster, received annual funding from the Department for Culture, Media and Sport (DCMS), which was reduced by 93 per cent between 2010 and 2014; it now receives just under £7m a year. Amid funding concerns for the future of S4C, it was agreed that the BBC would fund most of S4C's activities from the licence fee, contributing £75.25m in 2015–16. S4C will remain independent and be entitled to receive UK government funding and generate its own revenue. The on-demand service is called S4C Clic.

Channel 5 began broadcasting in 1997. It was rebranded Five in 2002 but reverted to its original name, Channel 5, after the station was acquired by Northern & Shell in July 2010. Digital stations 5USA and 5* (formerly Five Life, then Fiver) were launched in October 2006. Demand Five is an online service, launched in June 2008, where viewers can watch and download content from the last 30 days.

BSkyB was formed after the merger in 1990 of Sky Television and British Sky Broadcasting. 21st Century Fox has a 39.14 per cent controlling stake in the company, which operates a satellite television service with 900 television channels, including Sky One and the Sky Sports and Sky Movies ranges. Sky Digital was launched on 1 October 1998. Its key selling points were the improvement in sound and picture quality and an increased number of channels, some of which were exclusive to Sky Digital. In 2001, Sky Digitial was rebranded to just 'Sky'. With the 2005 acquisition of Easynet, an internet access provider and network operator, BSkyB now offers voice over IP (VoIP) telephony, video on demand and internet-based TV. With a free box, Sky+ and Sky+ HD customers are able to pause and rewind live TV and record favourite programmes both at home or with a compatible device while on the move. In July 2010 BSkyB acquired Virgin Media Television, including its portfolio of channels such as Bravo and Challenge. On 13 November 2014 BSkyB paid 21st Century Fox £2.45bn and a 21 per cent stake in the National Geographic Channel to buy out Sky Italia; an 89.71 per cent stake in Sky Deutschland was also acquired for £4.44bn. The transaction will give BSkyB 20 million pay-TV customers across Europe. As at 30 July 2015, there were just over 12 million Sky customers in the UK.

In February 2011, a new version of OFCOM's Broadcasting Code came into force, permitting product placement for the first time in UK-produced television programmes. A large 'P' logo designed by OFCOM and broadcasters is displayed at the beginning and end of each programme containing product placement. The first instance of product placement occurred on 28 February 2011.

## THE TELEVISION LICENCE

In the UK and its dependencies, a television licence is required to receive any publicly broadcast television service, regardless of its source, including commercial, satellite and cable programming. A TV licence registered to a home address allows the viewer to watch television on laptops, tablets and mobile phones outside the place of residence. If a viewer only watches catch-up TV, not live TV, using services such as BBC iPlayer, and this is the only means by which the viewer watches broadcasts, a television licence is not required.

The TV licence is classified as a tax, therefore non-payment is a criminal offence. A fine of up to £1,000 can be imposed on those successfully prosecuted. The TV licence is issued on behalf of the BBC as the licensing authority under the Communications Act 2003. In 2014–15 income from licence fees totalled £3,735m, a £9m increase on 2013–14. A six-year licence fee settlement was agreed in 2010 which froze the annual colour television licence fee at £145.50 until 2017. A black and white licence costs £49. Concessions are available for the elderly and people with disabilities. Further details can be found at W www.tvlicensing.co.uk/information

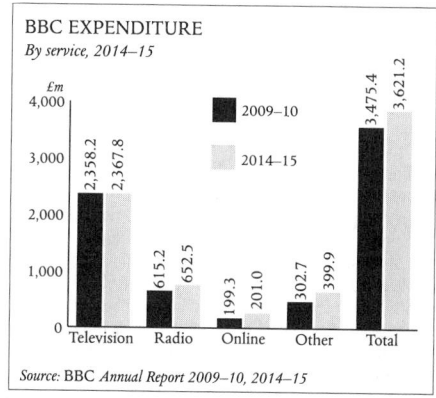

BBC EXPENDITURE
By service, 2014–15

Source: BBC Annual Report 2009–10, 2014–15

## DIGITAL TELEVISION

The Broadcasting Act 1996 provided for the licensing of 20 or more digital terrestrial television (DTT) channels (on six frequency channels or 'multiplexes'). The first digital services went on air in autumn 1998.

In June 2002, following the collapse of ITV Digital, the digital terrestrial television licence was awarded to a consortium made up of the BBC, BSkyB and transmitter company Crown Castle by the Independent Television Commission. Freeview was launched on 30 October 2002: it now offers around 70 digital channels and 30 radio stations and requires the one-off purchase of a set-top box, but is subsequently free of charge with no subscription. In Autumn 2005 ITV and Channel 4 officially became shareholders, each taking a 20 per cent stake. As at July 2014, more than 20 million homes use Freeview on at least one set, amounting to around 30 per cent of UK households. Freeview additionally offers the UK's top six channels in HD, with a further 54 channels and 25 radio stations, including BBC News and Aljazeera, available to 70 per cent of UK homes since June 2014. There is an additional Freeview+ service which works in a similar fashion to Sky+. As at July 2014, 97 per cent of British homes had access to digital TV.

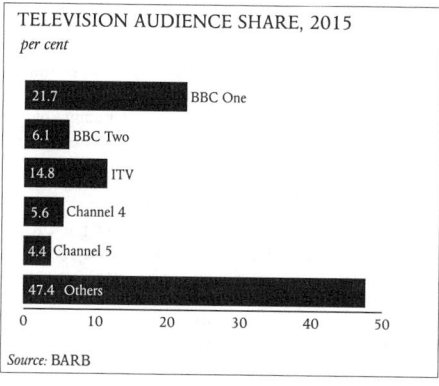

TELEVISION AUDIENCE SHARE, 2015
per cent

Source: BARB

## RECENT DEVELOPMENTS

The internet has now firmly established itself as an alternative to live and programmed TV, particularly for those aged 16 to 34. Since the launch of 4oD in 2006 and BBC iPlayer in 2007, there has been a noticeable shift in the way viewers can watch their favourite programmes. Technological advancements have also contributed to this new phenomenon; more than half of the UK population e uses a tablet, nearly 75 per cent of UK homes have access to superfast broadband and the number of public Wi-Fi spots reached 41,798 in 2014. There is now a much bigger emphasis on catch-up, on-demand and streaming services than previously, with 3.5 billion requests on BBC iPlayer in 2014, up 12.9 per cent on 2013. Tablet requests alone increased by 51 per cent from 2013 and download requests of the BBC iPlayer mobile app totalled 662 million in 2014. Streaming services such as Netflix have experienced a surge in popularity, with subscribers able to stream programmes through computers, mobiles, tablets and games consoles on up to four devices at a time for a monthly subscription fee. Netflix also commissions and distributes its own programmes, available exclusively to their subscribers, contributing to their popularity; as at 2014, Netflix had an estimated 2.8 million subscribers in the UK. The BBC has provided exclusive content and programmes on the iPlayer since 2014 and has announced plans to move BBC Three to an exclusive online service from early 2016. These transitions indicate that online catch-up and streaming services are now becoming competitive TV destinations in their own right.

Set-top boxes have also adapted to this viewing shift. YouView, in partnership with BBC, ITV, Channel Four, Channel Five, BT, Talk Talk and Arqiva, launched in July 2012. Subscribers are able to watch programmes (including on-demand), pause and rewind live TV and listen to digital radio via a hybrid set-top box connected to broadband. Originally envisaged as free-to-air, it has drawn criticism for tying customers into broadband services and subscriptions with BT and Talk Talk, with the one-off payment for the YouView box more expensive than the Freeview box. In June 2014, Freeview announced plans for a Freeview Connect service, which would provide catch-up services including iPlayer and 4oD as standard on smart TVs with broadband connections. It is seen as a free alternative to YouView, whereby viewers would still require a broadband connection but would not be tied to a specific provider. BBC, ITV and Channel Four announced they will substantially decrease their investment in YouView and instead invest a total of around £100m in the development of Freeview Connect.

Despite the rise in the popularity of tablets, traditional TV sets are still the most popular way to watch television. HD TV provides more vibrant colours and greater detail and picture clarity, along with improved sound quality. An HD television screen uses 1,280 by 720 pixels up to 1,920 by 1,080 pixels. HD Ready TVs operate at 720p while full HD TVs tend to operate on 1080p or 1080i; the differences between these three settings are down to the number of lines in the resolution and the type of scanning technology. 'HD Ready' simply means the TV will only operate a higher definition once plugged into a decoder, whereas full HD has this built in. Up to 12 channels are available in HD through Freeview. In 2014, the average screen size in the UK was 34.5 inches wide, indicating a trend towards bigger screens. Sales of Smart TVs, which can access apps, browse the internet and stream video, reached nearly 1.5 million in 2013 – a 211 per cent increase since 2011.

In April 2010, Samsung released the first consumer 3D TV; in the same month Sky launched the UK's first dedicated 3D channel. Several sporting events have been broadcast in 3D including the Wimbledon Championships. The BBC began a two-year 3D trial in 2011 but announced in July 2013 it would suspend 3D programming for an indefinite period of time due to a lack of public appetite for the technology. Of the estimated 1.5 million 3D TV sets in the UK, just 5 per cent used 3D to watch the Queen's Christmas Speech 2013.

In September 2012 OFCOM awarded its first local TV licences after announcing plans to broadcast 19 channels in total. In November 2013, Estuary TV, based in Grimsby, was the first to be launched. The government has backed the local TV initiative and the channels broadcast on channel 8 on Freeview in England and Northern Ireland and channel 26 in Scotland and Wales.

## CONTACTS

### THE BRITISH BROADCASTING CORPORATION
*BBC Broadcasting House,* Portland Place, London W1A 1AA
**W** www.bbc.co.uk
*BBC North,* Media City UK, Bridge House, Salford Quays, Manchester M50 2BH
*Chair,* Rona Fairhead
*Director-General,* Baron Hall of Birkenhead
*BBC Worldwide,* Television Centre, 101 Wood Lane, London W12 7FA **W** www.bbcworldwide.com

### INDEPENDENT TELEVISION NETWORK
*ITV Network Centre,* 200 Gray's Inn Road, London WC1X 8HF
**T** 020-7156 6000 **W** www.itv.com
*Chair,* Archie Norman

### INDEPENDENT TELEVISION NETWORK REGIONS
*Anglia (eastern England),* **W** www.itv.com/anglia
*Border (Borders and the Isle of Man),* **W** www.itv.com/border
*Calendar (Yorkshire),* **W** www.itv.com/calendar
*Central (east, west and south Midlands),* **W** www.itv.com/central
*Channel (Channel Islands),* **W** www.itv.com/channel
*Granada (north-west England),* **W** www.itv.com/granada
*London* **W** www.itv.com/london
*Meridian (south and south-east England),* **W** www.itv.com/meridian
*STV (Scotland),* **W** www.stv.tv
*Tyne Tees (north-east England),* **W** www.itv.com/tynetees
*Ulster (Northern Ireland),* **W** www.u.tv
*Wales,* **W** www.itv.com/wales
*West,* **W** www.itv.com/west

### OTHER TELEVISION COMPANIES
*Channel 4 Television,* 124 Horseferry Road, London SW1P 2TX
**T** 020-7396 4444 **W** www.channel4.com
*Channel 5 Broadcasting Ltd,* 10 Lower Thames Street, London EC3R 6EN **T** 020-8612 7700 **W** www.channel5.com
*Independent Television News (ITN),* 200 Gray's Inn Road, London WC1X 8XZ **T** 020-7833 3000 **W** www.itn.co.uk
Provides news programming for ITV and Channel 4.
*Sianel Pedwar Cymru (S4/C),* Parc Ty Glas, Llanishen, Cardiff CF14 5DU **T** 0870-600 4141 **W** www.s4c.co.uk

### DIRECT BROADCASTING BY SATELLITE TELEVISION
*British Sky Broadcasting Group PLC,* Grant Way, Isleworth, Isleworth TW7 5QD **T** 033-3100 0333 **W** www.sky.com
*Chair,* Nicholas Ferguson, CBE

## RADIO

UK domestic radio services are broadcast across three wavebands: FM, medium wave and long wave (used by BBC Radio 4). In the UK the FM waveband extends in frequency from 87.5MHz to 108MHz and the medium waveband from 531kHz to 1602kHz. A number of radio stations are broadcast in both analogue and digital as well as a growing number in digital alone. As at June 2014, the BBC Radio network controlled around 53.0 per cent of the listening market (*see* BBC Radio section), and the independent sector (*see* Independent Radio section) 44.4 per cent. As at June 2015, a listener tunes into an average of 21.7 hours of radio per week.

ESTIMATED RADIO AUDIENCE SHARE

| | Apr–Jun 2013 | Apr–Jun 2014 | Percentage Apr–Jun 2015 |
|---|---|---|---|
| BBC Radio 1 | 6.8 | 6.8 | 6.4 |
| BBC Radio 2 | 17.2 | 17.7 | 17.6 |
| BBC Radio 3 | 1.2 | 1.0 | 1.3 |
| BBC Radio 4 | 12.1 | 11.6 | 11.7 |
| BBC Radio Five Live | 4.1 | 4.1 | 3.5 |
| Five Live Sports Extra | 0.3 | 0.3 | 0.6 |
| BBC 6 Music | 1.5 | 1.6 | 1.8 |
| BBC Asian Network UK | 0.3 | 0.3 | 0.4 |
| 1Xtra | 0.5 | 0.5 | 0.5 |
| BBC Local/Regional | 8.3 | 7.7 | 7.5 |
| BBC World Service | 0.6 | 0.7 | 0.7 |
| All BBC | 53.9 | 53.3 | 53.0 |
| All independent | 43.7 | 43.2 | 44.4 |
| All national independent | 13.3 | 12.9 | 14.5 |
| All local independent | 30.4 | 30.3 | 29.8 |
| Other | 2.4 | 3.5 | 2.6 |

*Source: RAJAR*

## DIGITAL RADIO

DAB (digital audio broadcasting) allows more services to be broadcast to a higher technical quality and provides the data facility for text and pictures. It was developed in a collaborative research project under the pan-European Eureka 147 initiative and has been adopted as a world standard by the International Telecommunication Union for new digital radio systems. The frequencies allocated for terrestrial digital radio in the UK are 174 to 239MHz. Additional spectrum (in the 'L-Band' range: 1452–1478MHz) was introduced in 2007.

Digital radio is available through digital radio sets, car radios, online, on games consoles and on mobile devices such as phones and tablets. An alternative method is to listen to digital radio through television sets via Freeview, cable or satellite.

The listening share via all digital platforms at the end of June 2014 was 37 per cent, the same as in June 2014. DAB accounts for 65 per cent of total digital listening, 17 per cent is online and 12 per cent on digital TV (DTV). In June 2009 the government published the white paper *Digital Britain*, which recommended that most services carried on the national and local DAB multiplexes should cease broadcasting on analogue radio by 2015, though the switch-off is now expected to take place between 2018 and 2020. Ultra-local radio, consisting of small independent and community stations, would continue to broadcast on FM. There are two criteria that must be met for digital migration to occur:

• at least 50 per cent of radio listening is digital
• national DAB coverage is comparable to FM coverage, and local DAB reaches 90 per cent of the population and all major roads

## LICENSING

The Broadcasting Act 1996 provided for the licensing of digital radio services (on multiplexes, where a number of stations share one frequency to transmit their services). To allocate the multiplexes, OFCOM advertises licences for which interested parties can bid. Once the licence has been awarded, the new owner seeks out services to broadcast on the multiplex. The BBC has a separate national multiplex for its services. There are local multiplexes around the country, each broadcasting an average of seven services, plus the local BBC station.

## INNOVATIONS

The internet offers a number of advantages compared to other digital platforms such as DAB including higher sound quality, a greater range of channel availability and flexibility in listening opportunity. Listeners can tune in to the majority of radio stations live on the internet or listen again online generally up to seven days after broadcast. DAB radio does not allow the same interactivity: the data is only able to travel one-way from broadcaster to listener whereas the internet allows a two-way flow of information.

Increase in WiFi hotspots also means listening to radio, podcasts and catch-up programmes is easy to do through tablets and mobile phones; 22 per cent of adults claim to listen to the radio via a mobile phone or tablet at least once a month, while the percentage for those aged 15 to 24 is noticeably higher at 34 per cent. The increase in music streaming services and radio-related apps has had a major effect on music discovery and sharing. In the UK in 2014 the number of streams a week averaged 285 million. Since 6 July 2014 the UK Official Charts Company has included streaming services in its compilation, with 100 streams the equivalent to one purchase.

Since 2005 most radio stations offer all or part of their programmes as downloadable files, known as podcasts, to listen to on computers, mobiles or tablets. Podcasting technology allows listeners to subscribe in order to receive automatically the latest episodes of regularly transmitted programmes as soon as they become available.

The relationship between radio stations and their audiences is also undergoing change. The quantity and availability of music on the internet has led to the creation of shows dedicated entirely to music sent in by listeners. Another new development in internet-based radio has been personalised radio stations, such as last.fm and Spotify. Last.fm 'recommends' songs based on the favourite artists and previous choices of the user. Spotify, available as an app on most smart phones and tablets as well as online, allows listeners access to the track, artist or genre of their choice, or to share and create playlists. It has seen steady growth in popularity since its launch in 2008, with over 20 million paying subscribers and over 75 million active users globally, as at June 2015. Spotify 'learns as you listen' and makes associated recommendations based on user choices. SoundCloud, founded in 2007, is an innovative 'sound platform' which enables users to upload their own music and recordings to share privately or publicly. Artists who upload their music are given a URL, allowing their music to be embedded anywhere, making it easier to share through social media platforms such as Twitter and Facebook. Users can also create their own playlists and link them to social media platforms. Radioplayer (W www.radioplayer.co.uk), a not-for-profit company backed by the BBC, Global Radio, Bauer Media and RadioCentre, allows audiences to listen to live and catch-up radio from one place. There are around 400 stations available and a 'recommended' service which offers station suggestions depending on location, what is trending and the type of music the user likes. Radioplayer launched as a mobile app in 2012 and a tablet app in 2013. Through the tablet app, users sample an average of 4.6 stations a week in comparison with just 2.1 for analogue users.

## BBC RADIO

BBC Radio broadcasts network services to the UK, Isle of Man and the Channel Islands, with over 35 million listeners each week. There is also a tier of national services in Wales, Scotland and Northern Ireland and around 40 local radio stations in England and the Channel Islands. In Wales and Scotland there are also dedicated language services in Welsh

and Gaelic respectively. The frequency allocated for digital BBC broadcasts is 225.648MHz.
BBC Radio, Broadcasting House, Portland Place, London W1A 1AA **W** www.bbc.co.uk/radio

## BBC NETWORK RADIO STATIONS

*Radio 1* (contemporary pop music and entertainment news) – 24 hours a day, *Frequencies:* 97–99 FM and digital
*Radio 2* (popular music, entertainment, comedy and the arts) – 24 hours a day, *Frequencies:* 88–91 FM and digital
*Radio 3* (classical music, classic drama, documentaries and features) – 24 hours a day, *Frequencies:* 90–93 FM and digital
*Radio 4* (news, documentaries, drama, entertainment and cricket on long wave in season) – 5.20am–1am daily, with BBC World Service overnight, *Frequencies:* 92–95 FM/103–105 FM and 198 LW and digital
*Radio Five Live* (news and sport) – 24 hours a day, *Frequencies:* 909/693 MW and digital
*Five Live Sports Extra* (live sport) – schedule varies, digital only
*6 Music* (contemporary and classic pop and rock music) – 24 hours a day, digital only
*Asian Network* (news, music and sport) – 5am–1am, with Radio Five Live overnight, *Frequencies:* various MW frequencies in Midlands and digital
*1Xtra* (urban music: drum & bass, garage, hip hop, R&B) – 24 hours a day, digital only

## BBC NATIONAL RADIO STATIONS

*Radio Cymru* (Welsh-language), *Frequencies:* 92–105 FM and digital
*Radio Foyle*, *Frequencies:* 93.1 FM and 792 MW and digital
*Radio nan Gaidheal* (Gaelic service), *Frequencies:* 103–105 FM and digital
*Radio Scotland*, *Frequencies:* 92–95 FM and 810 MW and digital. Local programmes for Orkney, Shetland and Highlands and Islands
*Radio Ulster*, *Frequencies:* 1341 MW and 92–95 FM and digital. Local programmes on Radio Foyle
*Radio Wales*, *Frequencies:* 657/882 MW and 93–104 FM and digital

## BBC WORLD SERVICE

The BBC World Service broadcasts to an estimated weekly audience of 1.3 million people in the UK and 210 million worldwide, in 28 languages including English, and is now available in around 150 capital cities. It no longer broadcasts in Dutch, French for Europe, German, Hebrew, Italian, Japanese or Malay because it was found that most speakers of these languages preferred to listen to the English broadcasts. In 2006 services in ten languages (Bulgarian, Croatian, Czech, Greek, Hungarian, Kazakh, Polish, Slovak, Slovene and Thai) were terminated to provide funding for a new Arabic television channel, which was launched in March 2008. In August 2008 the BBC's Romanian World Service broadcasts were discontinued after 68 years. In January 2011 the BBC announced five more language services would be terminated: Albanian, Caribbean English, Macedonian, Portuguese for Africa and Serbian. The BBC World Service website offers interactive news services in 28 languages including English, Arabic, Chinese, Hindi, Persian, Portuguese for Brazil, Russian, Spanish and Urdu with audiostreaming available.

LANGUAGES
Arabic, Azeri, Bangla, Burmese, Cantonese, English, French, Hausa, Hindi, Indonesian, Kinyarwanda, Kirundi, Kyrgyz, Nepali, Pashto, Persian, Portuguese, Russian, Sinhala, Somali, Spanish, Swahili, Tamil, Turkish, Ukrainian, Urdu, Uzbek and Vietnamese.
*UK frequencies:* digital; overnight on BBC Radio 4.
*BBC Learning English* teaches English worldwide through radio, television and a wide range of published and online courses.
*BBC Media Action* is a registered charity established in 1999 by BBC World Service, known as the BBC World Service Trust until December 2011. It promotes development through the innovative use of the media in the developing world.
*BBC Monitoring* tracks the global media for the latest news reports emerging around the world.
BBC WORLD SERVICE, 1st Floor Brock House, 19 Langham Street, London W1A 1AA **W** www.bbc.co.uk/worldservice

## INDEPENDENT RADIO

Until 1973, the BBC had a legal monopoly on radio broadcasting in the UK. During this time, the corporation's only competition came from pirate stations located abroad, such as Radio Luxembourg. Christopher Chataway, Minister for Post and Telecommunications, changed this by creating the first licences for commercial radio stations. The Independent Broadcasting Authority (IBA) awarded the first of these licences to the London Broadcasting Company (LBC) to provide London's news and information service. LBC was followed by Capital Radio, to offer the city's entertainment service, Radio Clyde in Glasgow and BRMB in Birmingham.

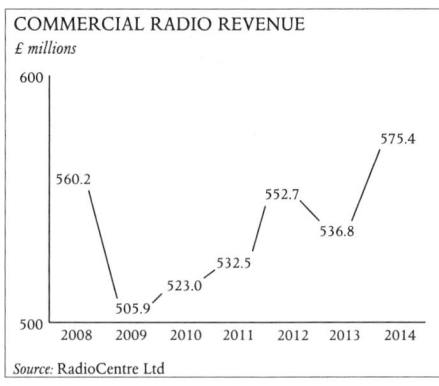

COMMERCIAL RADIO REVENUE
£ millions

*Source:* RadioCentre Ltd

The IBA was dissolved when the Broadcasting Act of 1990 de-regulated broadcasting, to be succeeded by the less rigid Radio Authority (RA). The RA began advertising new licences for the development of independent radio in January 1991. It awarded national and local radio, satellite and cable services licences, and long-term restricted service licences for stations serving non-commercial establishments such as hospitals and universities. The first national commercial digital multiplex licence was awarded in October 1998 and a number of local digital multiplex licences followed. At the end of 2003 the RA was replaced by OFCOM, which now carries out the licensing administration.

RadioCentre was formed in July 2006 as a result of the merger between the Radio Advertising Bureau (RAB) and the Commercial Radio Companies Association (CRCA), the former non-profit trade body for commercial radio companies in the UK, to operate essentially as a union for commercial radio stations.
*RadioCentre*, 6th Floor, 55 New Oxford Street, London WC1A 1BS **T** 020-7010 0600 **W** www.radiocentre.org
*Chief Executive*, Siobhan Kenny

# THE PRESS

The newspaper and periodical press in the UK is large and diverse, catering for a wide variety of views and interests. There is no state control or censorship of the press; however, it is subject to the laws on publication.

The press is not state-subsidised and receives few tax concessions. The income of most newspapers and periodicals is derived largely from sales and from advertising. The Advertising Association reported that advertising revenue would return to growth in 2015 – only the second annual increase since 2007 – with UK national newspapers expecting to receive £1.42bn in advertising, reflecting a 1 per cent increase on 2014.

## LEVESON REPORT

The Leveson Inquiry, established under the Inquiries Act 2005, was announced by the prime minister on 13 July 2011 to investigate the role of press and police in the *News of the World* phone-hacking scandal. Lord Justice Leveson was appointed as chair of the inquiry. The hearings began on 14 November 2011 and ended on 24 July 2012 following the testimonies of 650 witnesses.

The Leveson Report was published in late November 2012 and featured several broad and complex recommendations as to how the press should be regulated. The report generally recommended that the press should continue to be self-regulated, with the government allowed no direct power over what is published, and that a new press standards body, with a new code of conduct, should be established by legislation in order to ensure regulation is independent and effective. Lord Justice Leveson concluded that this arrangement should give the public confidence that their complaints would be dealt with seriously and ensure the press would be protected from interference.

## SELF-REGULATION

Following the publication of the Leveson Report the Press Complaints Commission (PCC), which had been established in January 1991 as a non-statutory body to operate the press's self-regulation, was closed and replaced by the Independent Press Standards Organisation (IPSO) on 8 September 2014. While the majority of newspapers have signed up to the new regulator, several have not, including *The Guardian*, the *Financial Times*, *The Independent* and the *London Evening Standard*.

In 2013 a royal charter on press regulation was granted by the Privy Council to create a watchdog to oversee a new regulator. On 3 November 2014, a fully independent body, the Press Recognition Panel (PRP) was established to consider whether press regulators meet the criteria recommended in the Leveson Report and, if so, to afford these regulators official recognition.

IPSO has not sought recognition from the PRP, but another regulator, IMPRESS, established by a group of free speech campaigners, is aiming to become compliant with the requirements of the Leveson Report and announced in May 2015 its intention to seek recognition from the PRP.

INDEPENDENT PRESS STANDARDS ORGANISATION,
Gate House, 1 Farringdon Street, London EC4M 7LH
T 0300-123 2220 E inquiries@ipso.co.uk W www.ipso.co.uk
*Chair,* Sir Alan Moses

PRESS RECOGNITION PANEL, 88 Wood Street, London
EC2V 7RS W contact@pressrecognitionpanel.org.uk
W www.pressrecognitionpanel.org.uk
*Chair,* Dr David Wolfe, QC

## NEWSPAPERS

Newspapers are mostly financially independent of any political party, though most adopt a political stance in their editorial comments, usually reflecting proprietorial influence. Ownership of the national and regional daily newspapers is concentrated in the hands of large corporations whose interests cover publishing and communications, although *The Guardian* and *The Observer* are owned by the Scott Trust, formed in 1936 to protect the financial and editorial independence of *The Guardian* in perpetuity. The rules on cross-media ownership, as amended by the Broadcasting Act 1996, which limited the extent to which newspaper organisations may become involved in broadcasting, have been relaxed by the Communications Act 2003: newspapers with over a 20 per cent share of national circulation may own national and/or local radio licences.

In October 2010, *The Independent* launched a concise newspaper, *i*, the first new daily newspaper since 1986. In July 2011, *News of the World* was closed by its parent company, News International, following accusations of phone-hacking. In February 2012 News International printed the first edition of *The Sun on Sunday*, a Sunday format of the daily tabloid paper *The Sun*. There are 14 daily and Sunday national papers and several hundred local papers that are published daily, weekly or twice-weekly. Scotland, Wales and Northern Ireland all have at least one daily and one Sunday national paper.

### UK CIRCULATION

| National Daily Newspapers | June 2014 | June 2015 | % +/− |
| --- | --- | --- | --- |
| The Sun | 2,033,606 | 1,818,935 | −10.56 |
| Daily Mail | 1,673,580 | 1,626,846 | −2.79 |
| Daily Mirror | 958,675 | 855,987 | −10.71 |
| The Daily Telegraph | 514,591 | 489,739 | −4.83 |
| Daily Express | 479,703 | 432,565 | −9.83 |
| Daily Star | 466,934 | 416,379 | −10.83 |
| The Times | 393,531 | 389,409 | −1.05 |
| i | 286,357 | 274,556 | −4.12 |
| Financial Times | 220,532 | 214,256 | −2.85 |
| Daily Record | 213,895 | 191,042 | −10.68 |
| The Guardian | 185,312 | 171,218 | −7.61 |
| The Independent | 63,506 | 57,930 | −8.78 |

| National Sunday Newspapers | June 2014 | June 2015 | % +/− |
| --- | --- | --- | --- |
| The Sun on Sunday | 1,635,068 | 1,466,439 | −10.31 |
| The Mail on Sunday | 1,528,562 | 1,434,018 | −6.19 |
| Sunday Mirror | 922,491 | 815,766 | −11.57 |
| The Sunday Times | 815,760 | 764,562 | −6.28 |
| Sunday Express | 418,131 | 376,509 | −9.95 |
| The Sunday Telegraph | 406,200 | 374,617 | −7.78 |
| The Sunday People | 369,312 | 316,320 | −14.35 |
| Daily Star Sunday | 294,944 | 257,859 | −12.57 |
| Sunday Mail | 237,636 | 207,628 | −12.61 |
| Sunday Post | 216,694 | 191,140 | −11.79 |
| The Observer | 207,005 | 189,279 | −8.56 |
| The Independent on Sunday | 100,102 | 97,218 | −2.88 |

*Source:* Audit Bureau of Circulations Ltd

Newspapers are usually published in either broadsheet or smaller, tabloid format. The 'quality' daily papers – ie those providing detailed coverage of a wide range of public matters – have traditionally been broadsheets, the more populist newspapers tabloid. In 2004 this correlation between format and content was redefined when two traditionally broadsheet newspapers, *The Times* and *The Independent*, switched to tabloid-sized editions, while *The Guardian* launched a 'Berliner' format in September 2005. In October 2005 *The Independent on Sunday* became the first Sunday broadsheet to be published in the tabloid (or 'compact') size, and *The Observer*, like its daily counterpart *The Guardian*, began publishing in the Berliner format in January 2006.

## NEWSPAPERS ONLINE

The demand to read news instantly and while on the move has increased the popularity of newspaper websites. Most newspapers now operate their own websites in line with their print editions, often including the same material as seen in daily printed editions but can also include video and audio features. Many articles and columns additionally have the option of reader contributions and debate. Certain newspapers charge a subscription fee to access their websites but the majority are free to browse.

### NATIONAL PRESS WEBSITE DAILY AVERAGE BROWSERS

| National Press Website | June 2014 | June 2015 | % +/− |
|---|---|---|---|
| MailOnline | 10,912,083 | 13,635,561 | 24.96 |
| theguardian.com | 5,718,502 | 7,771,486 | 35.90 |
| Mirror Group Nationals | 2,680,547 | 4,265,187 | 59.12 |
| Telegraph | 3,901,515 | 4,097,915 | 5.03 |
| The Independent | 1,856,894 | 2,551,686 | 37.42 |
| express.co.uk | 705,976 | 1,028,026 | 45.62 |
| dailystar.co.uk | 524,986 | 769,101 | 46.50 |

*Source:* Audit Bureau of Circulations Ltd

### NATIONAL DAILY NEWSPAPERS

DAILY EXPRESS
Northern & Shell Building, 10 Lower Thames Street,
London EC3R 6EN **T** 020-8612 7000 **W** www.express.co.uk
*Editor,* Hugh Whittow
DAILY MAIL
Northcliffe House, 2 Derry Street, London W8 5TT
**T** 020-7938 6000 **W** www.dailymail.co.uk
*Editor,* Paul Dacre
DAILY MIRROR
1 Canada Square, Canary Wharf, London E14 5AP
**T** 020-7293 3000 **W** www.mirror.co.uk
*Editor,* Lloyd Embley
DAILY RECORD
1 Central Quay, Glasgow G3 8DA **T** 0141-309 3000
**W** www.dailyrecord.co.uk
*Editor,* Murray Foote
DAILY STAR
Northern & Shell Building, 10 Lower Thames Street,
London EC3R 6EN **T** 020-8612 7000 **W** www.dailystar.co.uk
*Editor,* Dawn Neesom
THE DAILY TELEGRAPH
111 Buckingham Palace Road, London SW1W 0DT
**T** 020-7931 2000 **W** www.telegraph.co.uk
*Editor,* Chris Evans
FINANCIAL TIMES
1 Southwark Bridge, London SE1 9HL **T** 020-7873 3000
**W** www.ft.com
*Editor,* Lionel Barber

THE GUARDIAN
King's Place, 90 York Way, London N1 9GU **T** 020-3353 2000
**W** www.theguardian.com
*Editor,* Katharine Viner
THE HERALD
200 Renfield Street, Glasgow G2 3QB **T** 0141-302 7000
**W** www.heraldscotland.com
*Editor,* Magnus Llewellin
THE INDEPENDENT *AND* i
Northcliffe House, 2 Derry Street, London W8 5HF
**T** 020-7005 2000 **W** www.independent.co.uk
*Editor,* Amol Rajan and Oliver Duff
THE SCOTSMAN
152 Morrison Street, Edinburgh EH3 8EB **T** 0131-620 8620
**W** www.scotsman.com
*Editor,* Ian Stewart
THE SUN
3 Thomas More Square, London E98 1XY **T** 020-7782 4000
**W** www.thesun.co.uk
*Editor,* Tony Gallagher
THE TIMES
1 Pennington Street, London E98 1TT **T** 020-7782 5000
**W** www.thetimes.co.uk
*Editor,* John Witherow

### WEEKLY NEWSPAPERS

DAILY STAR SUNDAY
Northern and Shell Building, 10 Lower Thames Street,
London EC3R 6EN **T** 020-8612 7000
**W** www.dailystar.co.uk/sunday
*Editor,* Stuart James
INDEPENDENT ON SUNDAY
Northcliffe House, 2 Derry Street, London W8 5TT
**T** 020-7005 2000 **W** www.independent.co.uk
*Editor,* Lisa Markwell
MAIL ON SUNDAY
2 Derry Street, London W8 HFT **T** 020-7938 6000
**W** www.mailonsunday.co.uk
*Editor,* Geordie Greig
THE OBSERVER
Kings Place, 90 York Way, London N1 9GU **T** 020-3353 2000
**W** www.observer.theguardian.com
*Editor,* John Mulholland
THE SUNDAY PEOPLE
1 Canada Square, Canary Wharf, London E14 5AP
**T** 020-7293 3000 **W** www.people.co.uk
*Editor,* James Scott
SCOTLAND ON SUNDAY
Barclay House, 108 Holyrood Road, Edinburgh EH8 8AS
**T** 0131-620 8620 **W** www.scotlandonsunday.com
*Editor,* Ian Stewart
THE SUN ON SUNDAY
3 Thomas More Square, London E98 1XY **T** 020-7782 4000
**W** www.thesun.co.uk
*Editor,* Victoria Newton
SUNDAY EXPRESS
Northern & Shell Building, 10 Lower Thames Street,
London EC4R 6EN **T** 020-8612 7000
**W** www.sundayexpress.co.uk
*Editor,* Martin Townsend
SUNDAY HERALD
200 Renfield Street, Glasgow G2 3QB **T** 0141-302 7000
**W** www.sundayherald.com
*Editor,* Richard Walker
SUNDAY MAIL
1 Central Quay, Glasgow G3 8DA **T** 0141-309 3000
**W** www.sundaymail.com
*Editor,* Jim Wilson

SUNDAY MIRROR
1 Canada Square, Canary Wharf, London E14 5AP
T 020-7293 3000 **W** www.sundaymirror.co.uk
*Editor,* Lloyd Embley
SUNDAY POST
144 Port Dundas Road, Glasgow G4 0HZ **T** 0141-332 9933
**W** www.sundaypost.com
*Editor,* Donald Martin
SUNDAY TELEGRAPH
111 Buckingham Palace Road, London SW1W 0DT
T 020-7931 2000 **W** www.telegraph.co.uk
*Editor,* Ian MacGregor
THE SUNDAY TIMES
3 Thomas More Square, London E98 1XY **T** 020-7782 5000
**W** www.thesundaytimes.co.uk
*Editor,* Martin Ivens

## REGIONAL DAILY NEWSPAPERS
### EAST ANGLIA
CAMBRIDGE NEWS
Winship Road, Milton, Cambs. CB24 6PP **T** 01223-434434
**W** www.cambridge-news.co.uk
*Editor,* Paul Brackley
EAST ANGLIAN DAILY TIMES
Lower Brook Street, Ipswich IP4 1AN **T** 01473-230023
**W** www.eadt.co.uk
*Editor,* Terry Hunt
EASTERN DAILY PRESS
Prospect House, Rouen Road, Norwich NR1 1RE **T** 01603-628311
**W** www.edp24.co.uk
*Editor,* Nigel Pickover
IPSWICH STAR
Lower Brook Street, Ipswich, Suffolk IP4 1AN **T** 01473-230023
**W** www.ipswichstar.co.uk
*Editor,* Terry Hunt
NORWICH EVENING NEWS
Prospect House, Rouen Road, Norwich NR1 1RE **T** 01603-628311
**W** www.eveningnews24.co.uk
*Editor,* Nigel Pickover

### EAST MIDLANDS
BURTON MAIL
65–68 High Street, Burton upon Trent DE14 1LE **T** 01283-512345
**W** www.burtonmail.co.uk
*Editor,* Emma Turton
DERBY TELEGRAPH
Northcliffe House, Meadow Road, Derby DE1 2BH
T 01332-291111 **W** www.derbytelegraph.co.uk
*Editor,* Neil White
THE LEICESTER MERCURY
St George Street, Leicester LE1 9FQ **T** 0116-251 2512
**W** www.leicestermercury.co.uk
*Editor,* Kevin Booth
LINCOLNSHIRE ECHO
Witham Wharf, Brayford Wharf East, Lincoln LN5 7HY
T 01522-820000 **W** www.lincolnshireecho.co.uk
*Editor,* Mel West
NORTHAMPTON CHRONICLE & ECHO
Albert House, Victoria Street, Northants NN1 3NR
T 01604-467000 **W** www.northamptonchron.co.uk
*Editor,* David Summers
NOTTINGHAM POST
City Gate, Tollhouse Hill, Notts NG1 5FS **T** 0115-948 2000
**W** www.nottinghampost.com
*Editor,* Mike Sassi

### LONDON
EVENING STANDARD
Northcliffe House, 2 Derry Street, London W8 5TT
T 020-3367 7000 **W** www.standard.co.uk
*Editor,* Sarah Sands

METRO
Northcliffe House, 2 Derry Street, London W8 5TT
T 020-3615 3480 **W** www.metro.co.uk
*Editor,* Ted Young

### NORTH EAST
EVENING CHRONICLE
Groat Market, Newcastle upon Tyne NE1 1ED **T** 0191-232 7500
**W** www.chroniclelive.co.uk
*Editor,* Darren Thwaites
HARTLEPOOL MAIL
New Clarence House, Wesley Square, Hartlepool TS24 8BX
T 01429-239333 **W** www.hartlepoolmail.co.uk
*Editor,* Joy Yates
THE JOURNAL
Groat Market, Newcastle upon Tyne NE1 1ED **T** 0191-201 6491
**W** www.thejournal.co.uk
*Editor,* Brian Aitken
THE NORTHERN ECHO
PO Box 14, Priestgate, Darlington, Co. Durham DL1 1NF
T 01325-381313 **W** www.thenorthernecho.co.uk
*Editor,* Peter Barron
THE SHIELDS GAZETTE
Chapter Row, South Shields, Tyne & Wear NE33 1BL
T 0191-427 4800 **W** www.shieldsgazette.com
*Editor,* Joy Yates
THE SUNDAY SUN
Groat Market, Newcastle upon Tyne NE1 1ED **T** 0191-232 7500
**W** www.sundaysun.co.uk
*Editor,* Matt McKenzie
SUNDERLAND ECHO
Echo House, Pennywell, Sunderland SR4 9ER **T** 0191-501 5800
**W** www.sunderlandecho.com
*Editor,* John Szymanski
TEESIDE GAZETTE
Borough Road, Middlesbrough TS1 3AZ **T** 01642-345401
**W** www.gazettelive.co.uk
*Editor,* Chris Styles

### NORTH WEST
THE BLACKPOOL GAZETTE
Avroe House, Avroe Crescent, Blackpool FY4 2DP **T** 01253-400888
**W** www.blackpoolgazette.co.uk
*Editor,* Jon Rhodes
THE BOLTON NEWS
The Wellsprings, Victoria Square, Bolton BL1 1AR **T** 01204-522345
**W** www.theboltonnews.co.uk
*Editor,* Ian Savage
CARLISLE NEWS AND STAR
Newspaper House, Dalston Road, Carlisle CA2 5UA
T 01228-612600 **W** www.newsandstar.co.uk
*Editor,* David Helliwell
LANCASHIRE EVENING POST
Oliver's Place, Preston PR2 9ZA **T** 01772-254841 **W** www.lep.co.uk
*Editor,* Gillian Gray
LANCASHIRE TELEGRAPH
1 High Street, Newspaper House, Blackburn, Lancs. BB1 1HT
T 01254 678678 **W** www.lancashiretelegraph.co.uk
*Editor,* Kevin Young
LIVERPOOL ECHO
PO Box 48, Old Hall Street, Liverpool L69 3EB **T** 0151-227 2000
**W** www.liverpoolecho.co.uk
*Editor,* Alastair Machray
MANCHESTER EVENING NEWS
Mitchell Henry House, Hollinwood Avenue, Chadderton OL9 8EF
T 0161-832 7200 **W** www.manchestereveningnews.co.uk
*Editor,* Rob Irvine
NORTH-WEST EVENING MAIL
Abbey Road, Barrow-in-Furness, Cumbria LA14 5QS
T 01229-840100 **W** www.nwemail.co.uk
*Editor,* Jonathan Lee

OLDHAM EVENING CHRONICLE
PO Box 47, 172 Union Street, Oldham, Lancs. OL1 1EQ
T 0161-633 2121 W www.oldham-chronicle.co.uk
*Editor,* Dave Whaley

SOUTH EAST
THE ARGUS
Argus House, Crowhurst Road, Hollingbury, Brighton BN1 8AR
T 01273-544544 W www.theargus.co.uk
*Editor,* Mike Gilson
ECHO
Newspaper House, Chester Hall Lane, Basildon, Essex SS14 3BL
T 01268-522792 W www.echo-news.co.uk
*Editor,* Chris Hatton
MEDWAY MESSENGER
Medway House, Ginsbury Close, Sir Thomas Longley Road, Strood,
Kent ME2 4DU T 01634-227800
W www.kentonline.co.uk/medway
*Editor,* Bob Bounds
THE NEWS, PORTSMOUTH
1000 Lakeside, North Harbour, Portsmouth PO6 3EN
T 023-9266 4488 W www.portsmouth.co.uk
*Editor,* Mark Waldron
OXFORD MAIL
Osney Mead, Oxford OX2 0EJ T 01865-425262
W www.oxfordmail.co.uk
*Editor,* Simon O'Neill
READING EVENING POST
8 Tessa Road, Reading, Berks. RG1 8NS T 0118-918 3000
W www.getreading.co.uk
*Editor,* Andy Murrill
THE SOUTHERN DAILY ECHO
Newspaper House, Test Lane, Redbridge, Southampton SO16 9JX
T 023-8042 4777 W www.dailyecho.co.uk
*Editor,* Ian Murray

SOUTH WEST
BRISTOL POST
Temple Way, Bristol BS2 0BY T 0117-934 3000
W www.bristolpost.co.uk
*Editor,* Mike Norton
DAILY ECHO
Richmond Hill, Bournemouth BH2 6HH T 01202-554601
W www.bournemouthecho.co.uk
*Editor,* Toby Granville
DORSET ECHO
Fleet House, Hampshire Road, Weymouth, Dorset DT4 9XD
T 01305-830930 W www.dorsetecho.co.uk
*Editor,* Toby Granville
EXETER EXPRESS & ECHO
Heron Road, Sowton, Exeter EX2 7NF T 01392-442220
W www.exeterexpressandecho.co.uk
*Editor,* Jon-Paul Hedge
GLOUCESTER CITIZEN
6–8 The Oxebode, Gloucester GL1 2RZ T 01242-278000
W www.gloucestercitizen.co.uk
*Editor,* Jenny Eastwood
GLOUCESTERSHIRE ECHO
St James's Square, Cheltenham GL50 3PR T 01242-278000
W www.gloucestershireecho.co.uk
*Editor,* Matt Holmes
THE HERALD
3rd Floor, Millbay Road, Plymouth PL1 3LF T 01752-293000
W www.plymouthherald.co.uk
*Editor,* Paul Burton
SUNDAY INDEPENDENT
Sunday Independent Ltd, Tindle Suite, Webbs House, Cornwall
PL14 6AH T 01579-342174 W www.sundayindependent.co.uk
*Editor,* John Collings

SWINDON ADVERTISER
100 Victoria Road, Old Town, Swindon SN1 3BE T 01793-528144
W www.swindonadvertiser.co.uk
*Editor,* Gary Lawrence
TORQUAY HERALD EXPRESS
Barton Hill Road, Torquay, Devon TQ2 8JN T 01803-676000
W www.torquayheraldexpress.co.uk
*Editor,* Jim Parker
WESTERN DAILY PRESS
Temple Way, Bristol BS99 7HD T 0117-934 3000
W www.westerndailypress.co.uk
*Editor,* Rob Stokes
THE WESTERN MORNING NEWS
3rd Floor, Millbay Road, Plymouth PL1 3LF T 01752-293000
W www.westernmorningnews.co.uk
*Editor,* Bill Martin

WEST MIDLANDS
BIRMINGHAM MAIL
6th Floor, Fort Dunlop, Fort Parkway, Birmingham B24 9FF
T 0121-234 5536 W www.birminghammail.co.uk
*Editor,* David Brookes
THE BIRMINGHAM POST
6th Floor, Fort Dunlop, Fort Parkway, Birmingham B24 9FF
T 0121-236 3366 W www.birminghampost.co.uk
*Editor,* Stacey Barnfield
COVENTRY TELEGRAPH
Corporation Street, Coventry CV1 1FP T 024-7663 3633
W www.coventrytelegraph.net
*Editor,* Keith Perry
EXPRESS & STAR
51–53 Queen Street, Wolverhampton WV1 1ES T 01902-313131
W www.expressandstar.com
*Editor,* Keith Harrison
THE SENTINEL
Sentinel House, Bethesda Street, Stoke-on-Trent ST1 3GN
T 01782-864100 W www.stokesentinel.co.uk
*Editor,* Martin Tideswell
SHROPSHIRE STAR
Waterloo Road, Ketley, Telford TF1 5HU T 01952-242424
W www.shropshirestar.com
*Editor,* Martin Wright
WORCESTER NEWS
Berrows House, Hylton Road, Worcester WR2 5JX
T 01905-748200 W www.worcesternews.co.uk
*Editor,* Peter John

YORKSHIRE AND HUMBERSIDE
GRIMSBY TELEGRAPH
80 Cleethorpe Road, Grimsby, Lincs DN31 3EH T 01472-360360
W www.grimsbytelegraph.co.uk
*Editor,* Michelle Lalor
HALIFAX COURIER
PO Box 19, King Cross Street, Halifax HX1 2SF T 01422-260200
W www.halifaxcourier.co.uk
*Editor,* John Kenealy
THE HUDDERSFIELD DAILY EXAMINER
Pennine Business Park, Longbow Close, Bradley Road, Huddersfield
HD2 1GQ T 01484-430000 W www.examiner.co.uk
*Editor,* Roy Wright
HULL DAILY MAIL
Blundell's Corner, Beverley Road, Hull HU3 1XS T 01482-327111
W www.hulldailymail.co.uk
*Editor,* Neil Hodgkinson
THE PRESS
PO Box 29, 76–86 Walmgate, York YO1 9YN T 01904-567131
W www.yorkpress.co.uk
*Editor,* Perry Austin-Clarke

SCARBOROUGH NEWS
17–23 Aberdeen Walk, Scarborough, N. Yorks YO11 1BB
 T 01723-363636 W www.thescarboroughnews.co.uk
 *Editor,* Ed Asquith
SHEFFIELD STAR
York Street, Sheffield S1 1PU T 0114-276 7676
 W www.thestar.co.uk
 *Editor,* James Mitchinson
TELEGRAPH & ARGUS
Hall Ings, Bradford BD1 1JR T 01274-729511
 W www.telegraphandargus.co.uk
 *Editor,* Perry Austin-Clarke
YORKSHIRE EVENING POST
26 Whitehall Road, Leeds LS12 1BE T 0113-243 2701
 W www.yorkshireeveningpost.co.uk
 *Editor,* Jeremy Clifford
YORKSHIRE POST
26 Whitehall Road, Leeds LS12 1BE T 0113-243 2701
 W www.yorkshirepost.co.uk
 *Editor,* Jeremy Clifford

SCOTLAND
THE COURIER
80 Kingsway East, Dundee DD4 8SL T 01382-223131
 W www.thecourier.co.uk
 *Editor,* Richard Neville
DUNDEE EVENING TELEGRAPH
80 Kingsway East, Dundee DD4 8SL T 01382-575331
 W www.eveningtelegraph.co.uk
 *Editor,* Richard Prest
EDINBURGH EVENING NEWS
Barclay House, 108 Holyrood Road, Edinburgh EH8 8AS
 T 0131-620 8620 W www.edinburghnews.scotsman.com
 *Editor,* Frank O'Donnell
EVENING EXPRESS
Aberdeen Journals Ltd, Lang Stracht, Mastrick, Aberdeen
 AB15 6DF T 01224-691212 W www.eveningexpress.co.uk
 *Editor,* Alan McCabe
GLASGOW EVENING TIMES
200 Renfield Street, Glasgow G2 3QB T 0141-302 7000
 W www.eveningtimes.co.uk
 *Editor,* Tony Carlin
INVERNESS COURIER
New Century House, Stadium Road, Inverness IV1 1FF
 T 01463-233059 W www.inverness-courier.co.uk
 *Editor,* Robert Taylor
PAISLEY DAILY EXPRESS
1 Central Quay, Glasgow G3 8DA T 0141-887 7911
 W www.paisleydailyexpress.co.uk
 *Editor,* John Hutcheson
THE PRESS AND JOURNAL
Lang Stracht, Aberdeen AB15 6DF T 01224-690222
 W www.pressandjournal.co.uk
 *Editor,* Damian Bates

WALES
THE LEADER
Mold Business Park, Mold, Flintshire CH7 1XY T 01352-707707
 W www.leaderlive.co.uk
 *Editor,* Barrie Jones
SOUTH WALES ARGUS
Cardiff Road, Maesglas, Newport NP20 3QN T 01633-810000
 W www.southwalesargus.co.uk
 *Editor,* Kevin Ward
SOUTH WALES ECHO
6 Park Street, Cardiff CF10 1XR T 029-2024 3630
 W www.walesonline.co.uk
 *Editor,* Catrin Pascoe

SOUTH WALES EVENING POST
Urban Village, High Street, Swansea SA1 1NW T 01792-545500
 W www.southwales-eveningpost.co.uk
 *Editor,* Jonathan Roberts
WESTERN MAIL
6 Park Street, Cardiff CF10 1XR T 029-2024 3630
 W www.walesonline.co.uk
 *Editor,* Alan Edmunds

NORTHERN IRELAND
BELFAST TELEGRAPH
124–144 Royal Avenue, Belfast BT1 1DN T 028-9026 4000
 W www.belfasttelegraph.co.uk
 *Editor,* Mike Gilson
IRISH NEWS
113–117 Donegall Street, Belfast BT1 2GE T 028-9032 2226
 W www.irishnews.com
 *Editor,* Noel Doran
NEWS LETTER
Ground Floor, Metro Building, 6–9 Donegall Sq. South,
 Belfast BT1 5JA T 028-9089 7700 W www.newsletter.co.uk
 *Editor,* Rankin Armstrong
SUNDAY LIFE
124–144 Royal Avenue, Belfast BT1 1EB T 028-9026 4000
 W www.sundaylife.co.uk
 *Editor,* Martin Breen

CHANNEL ISLANDS
GUERNSEY PRESS
PO Box 57, Braye Road, Vale, Guernsey GY1 3BW
 T 01481-240240 W www.guernseypress.com
 *Editor,* Shaun Green
JERSEY EVENING POST
Guiton House, Five Oaks, St Saviour, Jersey JE4 8XQ
 T 01534-611611 W www.jerseyeveningpost.com
 *Editor,* Andy Sibcy

## PERIODICALS

ART
AESTHETICA
PO Box 371, York YO23 1WL T 01904-629137
 W www.aestheticamagazine.com
 *Editor,* Cherie Federico
APOLLO
22 Old Queen Street, London SW1H 9HP T 020-7961 0150
 W www.apollo-magazine.com
 *Editor,* Thomas Marks
ART MONTHLY
28 Charing Cross Road, London WC2H 0DB T 020-7240 0389
 W www.artmonthly.co.uk
 *Editor,* Patricia Bickers
ARTREVIEW
1 Honduras Street, London EC1Y 0TH T 020-7490 8138
 W www.artreview.com
 *Editor,* Mark Rappolt
TATE ETC.
Tate, Millbank, London SW1P 4RG T 020-7887 8724
 W www.tate.org.uk
 *Editor,* Simon Grant

BUSINESS AND FINANCE
THE ECONOMIST
25 St James's Street, London SW1A 1HG T 020-7830 7000
 W www.economist.com
 *Editor,* Zanny Minton Beddoes
MANAGEMENT TODAY
Haymarket, Teddington Studios, Broom Road, Teddington
 TW11 9BE T 01604-828702 W www.managementtoday.co.uk
 *Editor,* Matthew Gwyther

**MARKETING WEEK**
79 Wells Street, London W1T 3QN **T** 020-7292 3711
**W** www.marketingweek.co.uk
*Editor,* Russell Parsons

**MONEYWEEK**
8th Floor, Friars Bridge Court, 41-45 Blackfriars Road, London
SE1 8NZ **T** 020-7633 3780 **W** www.moneyweek.com
*Editor,* Merryn Somerset Webb

**PUBLIC FINANCE**
17 Britton Street, London EC1M 5TP **T** 020-8950 9117
**W** www.publicfinance.co.uk
*Editor,* Vivienne Russell

**CELEBRITY**

**CLOSER**
Endeavour House, 189 Shaftesbury Avenue, London WC2H 8JG
**T** 020-7859 8463 **W** www.closeronline.co.uk
*Editor,* Lisa Burrow

**HEAT**
Endeavour House, 189 Shaftesbury Avenue, London WC2H 8JG
**T** 020-7437 9011 **W** www.heatworld.com
*Editor,* Lucie Cave

**HELLO!**
Wellington House, 69–71 Upper Ground, London SE1 9PQ
**T** 020-7667 8901 **W** www.hellomagazine.com
*Editor,* Rosie Nixon

**OK!**
10 Lower Thames Street, London EC3R 6EN **T** 020-8612 7000
**W** www.ok.co.uk
*Editor,* Kirsty Tyler

**CHILDREN'S AND FAMILY**

**THE BEANO**
185 Fleet Street, London EC4A 2HS **W** www.beano.com
*Editor,* Craig Graham

**MOTHER & BABY**
Endeavour House, 189 Shaftesbury Avenue, London WC2H 8JG
**T** 020-7437 9011 **W** www.motherandbaby.co.uk
*Editor,* Claire Irvin

**YOUR CAT**
BPG Stamford Ltd, 1-6 Buckminster Yard, Main Street,
Buckminster, Grantham, Lincs NG33 5SA **T** 0844-848-8257
**W** www.yourcat.co.uk
*Editor,* Chloë Hukin

**YOUR DOG**
BPG Stamford Ltd, 1-6 Buckminster Yard, Main Street,
Buckminster, Grantham, Lincs NG33 5SA **T** 0844-848 8257
**W** www.yourdog.co.uk
*Editor,* Sarah Wright

**YOUR HORSE**
Media House, Peterborough Business Park, Lynch Wood,
Peterborough PE2 6EA **T** 01733-468000
**W** www.yourhorse.co.uk
*Editor,* Imogen Johnson

**CLASSICAL AND OPERA MUSIC**

**BBC MUSIC**
Immediate Media Company Bristol Ltd, Tower House,
Fairfax Street, Bristol BS1 3BN **T** 0117-927 9009
**W** www.classical-music.com
*Editor,* Oliver Condy

**CLASSICAL MUSIC**
Rhinegold House, 20 Rugby Street, London WC1N 3QZ
**T** 020-7333 1729 **W** www.classicalmusicmagazine.org
*Editor,* Kimon Daltas

**GRAMOPHONE**
Haymarket, Teddington Studios, Broom Road, Teddington,
Middlesex TW11 9BE **T** 020-8267 5000
**W** www.gramophone.co.uk
*Editor,* Martin Cullingford

**OPERA**
36 Black Lion Lane, London W6 9BE **T** 020-8563 8893
**W** www.opera.co.uk
*Editor,* John Allison

**COMPUTERS AND TECHNOLOGY**

**ANDROID**
Imagine Publishing, Richmond House, 33 Richmond Hill,
Bournemouth BH2 6EZ **T** 01202-586200
**W** www.littlegreenrobot.co.uk
*Deputy Editor,* Jack Parsons

**EDGE**
Future Publishing Ltd, 2 Balcombe Street, London NW1 6NW
**T** 01225-442244 **W** www.edge-online.com
*Editor,* Tony Mott

**PC PRO**
Dennis Technology, 30 Cleveland Street, London W1T 4JD
**T** 020-7907 6000 **W** www.alphr.com
*Editor,* Tim Danton

**STUFF**
Haymarket, Teddington Studios, Broom Road, Teddington,
Middlesex TW11 9BE **T** 020-8267 5036 **W** www.stuff.tv
*Editor,* Will Findlater

**T3**
Future Publishing, 2 Balcombe Street, London NW1 6NW
**T** 020-7042 4000 **W** www.t3.com
*Editor,* Dan Grabham

**WEB USER**
Dennis Publishing, 30 Cleveland Street, London W1T 4JD
**T** 020-7907 6000 **W** www.webuser.co.uk
*Editor,* Daniel Booth

**WIRED**
Condé Nast, Vogue House, Hanover Square, London W1S 1JU
**T** 0844-848 5202 **W** www.wired.co.uk
*Editor,* Scott Dadich

**CRAFT**

**CARDMAKING & PAPERCRAFT**
Immediate Media, Tower House, Fairfax Street, Bristol BS1 3BN
**T** 0117-933 8081 **W** www.cardmakingandpapercraft.com
*Editor,* Kirstie Sleight

**SIMPLY KNITTING**
Future Publishing Ltd, 30 Monmouth Street, Bath BA1 2BW
**T** 01225-442244 **W** www.simplyknitting.co.uk
*Editor,* Kirstie McLeod

**THE WORLD OF CROSS STITCHING**
Immediate Media, Tower House, Fairfax Street, Bristol BS1 3BN
**T** 0117-314 8351 **W** www.cross-stitching.com
*Editor,* Ruth Southorn

**ENTERTAINMENT**

**EMPIRE**
Endeavour House, 189 Shaftesbury Avenue, London WC2H 8JG
**T** 020-7437 9011 **W** www.empireonline.com
*Editor (acting),* Ian Nathan

**RADIO TIMES**
Vineyard House, 44 Brook Green, London W6 7BT
**T** 020-7150 5800 **W** www.radiotimes.com
*Editor,* Ben Preston

**SIGHT & SOUND**
3rd Floor Chancery Exchange, 10 Furnival Street, London
EC4A 1AB **T** 020-8955 7070 **W** www.bfi.org.uk/sightandsound
*Editor,* Nick James

**TIME OUT**
4th Floor, 125 Shaftesbury Avenue, London WC2H 8AD
**T** 020-7813 3000 **W** www.timeout.com
*Editor,* Caroline McGinn

TOTAL FILM
2 Balcombe Street, London NW1 6NW **T** 020-7042 4000
  **W** www.gamesradar.com/totalfilm
  *Editor,* Jane Crowther

FASHION AND BEAUTY
COSMOPOLITAN
Hearst Magazines, 33 Broadwick Street, London W1F 0DQ
  **T** 020-7439 5000 **W** www.cosmopolitan.co.uk
  *Editor,* Louise Court
ELLE
Hearst Magazines, 72 Broadwick Street, London W1F 9EP
  **T** 020-7150 7000 **W** www.elleuk.com
  *Editor,* Lorraine Candy
GLAMOUR
Condé Nast, Vogue House, Hanover Square, London W1S 1JU
  **T** 020-7499 9080 **W** www.glamourmagazine.co.uk
  *Editor,* Cindi Leive
GRAZIA
Endeavour House, 189 Shaftesbury Avenue, London WC2H 8JG
  **T** 0845-601 1356 **W** www.graziadaily.co.uk
  *Editor,* Angela Buttolph
HARPER'S BAZAAR
Hearst Magazines, 72 Broadwick Street, London W1F 9EP
  **T** 0844-848 5203 **W** www.harpersbazaar.co.uk
  *Editor,* Justine Picardie
MARIE CLAIRE
Blue Fin Building, 110 Southwark Street, London SE1 4SU
  **T** 020-3148 5000 **W** www.marieclaire.co.uk
  *Editor,* Trish Halpin
VOGUE
Condé Nast, Vogue House, Hanover Square, London W1S 1JU
  **T** 0844-848 5202 **W** www.vogue.co.uk
  *Editor,* Alexandra Shulman

FOOD AND DRINK
FOOD AND TRAVEL
Suite 51, The Business Centre, Ingate Place, London SW8 3NS
  **T** 020-7501 0511 **W** www.foodandtravel.com
  *Editor,* Renate Ruge
GOOD FOOD
44 Vineyard House, Brook Green, London W6 7BT
  **T** 020-7150 5022 **W** www.bbcgoodfood.com
  *Editor,* Gillian Carter
JAMIE
800 Guillat Avenue, Kent Science Park, Sittingbourne ME9 8GU
  **T** 0844-249 0478 **W** www.jamieoliver.com/magazine
  *Editor,* Andy Harris
OLIVE
Vineyard House, 44 Brook Green, London W6 7BT
  **T** 020-7150 5024 **W** www.olivemagazine.com
  *Editor,* Christine Hayes
WHISKY
St Faiths House, Mountergate, Norwich NR1 1PY
  **T** 01603-633 808 **W** www.whiskymag.com
  *Editor,* Rupert Wheeler

GENERAL INTEREST
BBC HISTORY
Tower House, Fairfax Street, Bristol BS1 3BN **T** 0117-927 9009
  **W** www.historyextra.com
  *Editor,* Rob Attar
BOOKSELLER
Crowne House, 56-58 Southwark Street, London SE1 1UN
  **T** 01604-251040 **W** www.thebookseller.com
  *Editor,* Philip Jones
HISTORY TODAY
25 Bedford Avenue, London WC1B 3AT **T** 020-3219 7810
  **W** www.historytoday.com
  *Editor,* Paul Lay

LITERARY REVIEW
44 Lexington Street, London W1F OLW **T** 020-7437 9392
  **W** www.literaryreview.co.uk
  *Editor,* Nancy Sladek
NEW STATESMAN
John Carpenter House, 7 Carmelite Street, Blackfriars, London
  EC4Y 0AN **T** 020-7936 6400 **W** www.newstatesman.com
  *Editor,* Jason Cowley
PRIVATE EYE
6 Carlisle Street, London W1D 3BN **T** 020-7437 4017
  **W** www.private-eye.co.uk
  *Editor,* Ian Hislop
PROSPECT
25 Sackville Street, London W1S 3HQ **T** 020-7255 1281
  **W** www.prospectmagazine.co.uk
  *Editor,* Bronwen Maddox
RAILWAY
Mortons Media Ltd, Horncastle, Lincs LN9 6JR **T** 01507-529529
  **W** www.railwaymagazine.co.uk
  *Editor,* Nick Pigott
READER'S DIGEST
PO Box 7853, Ringwood BH24 9FH **T** 0844-332 4994
  **W** www.readersdigest.co.uk
  *Editor,* Liz Vaccariello
SAGA
Saga Publishing Ltd, Enbrook Park, Folkestone, Kent CT20 3SE
  **T** 01303-771111 **W** www.saga.co.uk
  *Editor,* Katy Bravery
THE SPECTATOR
22 Old Queen Street, London SW1H 9HP **T** 020-7961 0200
  **W** www.spectator.co.uk
  *Editor,* Fraser Nelson
TLS (THE TIMES LITERARY SUPPLEMENT)
1 London Bridge Street, London SE1 9GF **T** 020-7782 5000
  **W** www.the-tls.co.uk
  *Editor,* Peter Stothard
THE WEEK
30 Cleveland Street, London W1T 4JD **T** 020-7907 6000
  **W** www.theweek.co.uk
  *Editor,* Holden Frith
WHO DO YOU THINK YOU ARE?
Tower House, Fairfax Street, Bristol BS1 3BN **T** 0117-314 7400
  **W** www.whodoyouthinkyouaremagazine.com
  *Editor,* Sarah Williams

HEALTH AND FITNESS
HEALTH & FITNESS
30 Cleveland Street, London W1T 4JD **T** 020-7907 6000
  **W** www.womensfitness.co.uk
  *Editor,* Mary Comber
MEN'S FITNESS
Dennis Publishing, 30 Cleveland Street, London W1T 4JD
  **T** 020-7907 6000 **W** www.mensfitness.co.uk
  *Editor,* Max Anderton
MEN'S HEALTH
Hearst Magazines, 72 Broadwick Street, London W1F 9EP
  **T** 01858-438851 **W** www.menshealth.co.uk
  *Editor,* Toby Wiseman
RUNNER'S WORLD
33 Broadwick Street, London W1F 9EP **T** 020-7339 4409
  **W** www.runnersworld.co.uk
  *Editor,* David Wiley
WEIGHT WATCHERS
Millennium House, Ludlow Road, Maidenhead, Berkshire SL6 2SL
  **T** 07900-494 736 **W** www.weightwatchers.co.uk
  *Editor,* Julie Lee
WOMEN'S FITNESS
30 Cleveland Street, London W1T 4JD **T** 020-7907 6000
  **W** www.womensfitness.co.uk
  *Editor,* Joanna Knight

## HOBBIES AND GAMES
### AIRFIX MODEL WORLD
Key Publishing Ltd, PO Box 100, Stamford PE9 1XQ
T 01780-755131 W www.airfixmodelworld.com
*Editor*, Chris Clifford
### ANGLING TIMES
Bauer Consumer Media Ltd, 1 Lincoln Court, Lincoln Road,
Peterborough PE1 2RF T 01733-395097
W www.gofishing.co.uk
*Editor*, Steve Fitzpatrick
### BRITISH RAILWAY MODELLING
Warners Group Publications, The Maltings, West Street,
Bourne, Lincs PE10 9PH T 01778-391000
W www.model-railways-live.co.uk
*Editor*, Ben Jones
### CHESS
Chess & Bridge Ltd, 44 Baker Street, London W1U 7RT
T 020-7486 7015 W www.chess.co.uk
*Editor*, John Saunders
### COIN NEWS
Token Publishing Ltd, Orchard House, Duchy Road, Heathpark,
Honiton, Devon EX14 1YD T 01404-46972
W www.tokenpublishing.com
*Editor*, John Mussell
### HORNBY
Key Publishing Ltd, PO Box 100, Stamford PE9 1XQ
T 01780-755131 W www.hornbymagazine.com
*Editor*, Mike Wild

## HOME AND GARDEN
### GARDENERS' WORLD
Immediate Media, 5th Floor, Vineyard House, 44 Brook Green,
London W6 7BT T 020-7150 5700
W www.gardenersworld.com
*Editor*, Lucy Hall
### GOOD HOUSEKEEPING
Hearst Magazines, 72 Broadwick Street, London W1F 9EP
T 020-7439 5000 W www.goodhousekeeping.co.uk
*Editor*, Jane Francisco
### HOUSE & GARDEN
Condé Nast Publications, Vogue House, Hanover Square,
London W1S 1JU T 020-7499 9080
W www.houseandgarden.co.uk
*Editor*, Susan Crew
### LIVING ETC
IPC Media, Blue Fin Building, 110 Southwark Street, London
SE1 0SU T 020-3148 7443
W www.housetohome.co.uk/livingetc
*Editor*, Sarah Baldwin

## MEN'S LIFESTYLE
### ATTITUDE
Vitality Publishing Ltd, 3rd Floor, 207 Old Street, London EC1V 9NR
T 020-7608 6300 W www.attitude.co.uk
*Editor*, Matthew Todd
### ESQUIRE
Hearst Magazines, 72 Broadwick Street, London W1F 9EP
T 020-7439 5000 W www.esquire.co.uk
*Editor*, Alex Bilmes
### FHM
Endeavour House, 189 Shaftesbury Avenue, London WC2H 8JG
T 020-7295 8534 W www.fhm.com
*Editor*, Joe Barnes
### GAY TIMES
Millivres Prowler Group, Spectrum House, 32-34 Gordon House
Road, London NW5 1LP T 020-7424 7400
W www.gaytimes.co.uk
*Editor*, Darren Scott

### GQ
Vogue House, 1 Hanover Square, London W1S 1JU
T 020-7499 9080 W www.gq-magazine.co.uk
*Editor*, Dylan Jones
### LOADED
Clarenden House, Shenley Road, Borehamwood, Herts WD6 1AG
T 020-7580 6419 W www.loaded.co.uk
*Editor*, Aaron Tinney

## MOTORING
### BIKE
Bauer Media, Media House, Lynchwood, Peterborough PE2 6EA
T 01733-468000 W www.bikemagazine.co.uk
*Editor*, Brice Minnigh
### CARAVAN
Warners Group Publications, The Maltings, West Street,
Bourne, Lincs PE10 9PH T 01778-392450
W www.outandaboutlive.co.uk
*Editor*, John Sootheran
### F1 RACING
Haymarket, Teddington Studios, Broom Road, Teddington
TW11 9BE T 020-8267 5806 W www.f1racing.co.uk
*Editor*, Anthony Rowlinson
### OCTANE
Dennis Publishing Ltd, 30 Cleveland Street, London W1T 4JD
T 020-7907 6000 W www.classicandperformancecar.com
*Editor*, David Lillywhite
### PRACTICAL CARAVAN
Haymarket, Teddington Studios, Teddington Lock, Broom Road,
Teddington TW11 9BE T 020-8267 5629
W www.practicalcaravan.com
*Editor*, Nigel Donnelly
### TOP GEAR
Energy Centre, Media Centre, 201 Wood Lane, London W12 7TQ
T 020-8433 3598 W www.topgear.com
*Editor*, Charlie Turner

## PHOTOGRAPHY
### AMATEUR PHOTOGRAPHER
Blue Fin Building, 110 Southwark Street, London SE1 0SU
T 020-3148 4138 W www.amateurphotographer.co.uk
*Editor*, Nigel Atherton
### DIGITAL PHOTOGRAPHER
Imagine Publishing, Richmond House, 33 Richmond Hill,
Bournemouth BH2 6EZ T 01202-586200
W www.dphotographer.co.uk
*Editor*, Amy Squibb
### PHOTOGRAPHY MONTHLY
Archant House, Oriel Road, Cheltenham GL50 1BB
T 01242-211080 W www.photographymonthly.com
*Editor*, Jeff Meyer
### PROFESSIONAL PHOTOGRAPHER
Archant House, Oriel Road, Cheltenham GL50 1BB
T 0844-848 5232 W www.professionalphotographer.co.uk
*Editor*, Adam Scorey

## POPULAR MUSIC
### CLASH
194 Hercules Road, London SE1 7LD T 020-7628 2312
W www.clashmusic.com
*Editor*, Simon Harper
### CLASSIC ROCK
Prospect Business Centre, 3 Stanley Boulevard, Blantyre G72 0BN
T 01604-251040 W www.classicrock.teamrock.com
*Editor*, Scott Rowley
### DIY
Arch 462, Kingsland Viaduct, 83 Rivington Street, London
EC2A 3AY W www.diymag.com
*Editor*, Stephen Ackroyd

GUITARIST
Future Publishing Ltd, Beauford Court, 30 Monmouth Street,
Bath BA1 2BW **T** 01225-442244
**W** www.musicradar.com/guitarist
*Editor,* Mick Taylor
KERRANG!
Bauer Media, Media House, Lynchwood, Peterborough PE2 6EA
**T** 01733-468000 **W** www.kerrang.com
*Editor,* James McMahon
MOJO
Endeavour House, 189 Shaftesbury Avenue, London WC2H 8JG
**T** 020-7208 3443 **W** www.mojo4music.com
*Editor,* Phil Alexander
NME
9th Floor, Blue Fin Building, 110 Southwark Street, London
SE1 0SU **T** 0845-676 7778 **W** www.nme.com
*Editor,* Mike Williams
Q
Endeavour House, 189 Shaftesbury Avenue, London WC2H 8JG
**T** 020-7295 5000 **W** www.qthemusic.com
*Editor,* Phil Alexander
UNCUT
Blue Fin Building, 110 Southwark Street, London SE1 0SU
**T** 020-3148 5000 **W** www.uncut.co.uk
*Editor,* John Mulvey

SCIENCE AND NATURE
BBC WILDLIFE
4th Floor, Tower House, Fairfax Street, Bristol BS1 3BN
**T** 0117-314 7366 **W** www.discoverwildlife.com
*Editor,* Matt Swaine
BIRD WATCHING
Bauer Media, Media House, Lynch Wood, Peterborough PE2 6EA
**T** 01733-468000 **W** www.birdwatching.co.uk
*Editor,* Matthew Merritt
COUNTRYFILE
9th Floor, Tower House, Fairfax Street, Bristol BS1 3BN
**T** 0117-927 9009 **W** www.countryfile.com
*Editor,* Fergus Collins
FOCUS
Bristol Magazines Ltd, Tower House, Fairfax Street, Bristol BS1 3BN
**T** 0117-314 7388 **W** www.sciencefocus.com
*Editor,* Graham Southorn
HOW IT WORKS
Imagine Publishing Ltd, Richmond House, 33 Richmond Hill,
Bournemouth BH2 6EZ **T** 01202-586200
**W** www.howitworksdaily.com
*Editor,* Dave Farfield
NEW SCIENTIST
Lacon House, 84 Theobalds Road, London WC1X 8NS
**T** 020-7611 1206 **W** www.newscientist.com
*Editor,* Sumit Paul-Choudhury
SKY AT NIGHT
Immediate Media Company Bristol Ltd, Tower House, Fairfax
Street, Bristol BS1 3BN **T** 0844 844 0254
**W** www.skyatnightmagazine.com
*Editor,* Chris Bramley

SPORT
ALL OUT CRICKET
TriNorth Ltd, Unit 3.40 Canterbury Court, 1–3 Brixton Road,
London SW9 6DE **T** 020-3176 0187 **W** www.alloutcricket.com
*Editor,* Phil Walker
BOXING MONTHLY
Topwave Ltd, 40 Morpeth Road, London E9 7LD **T** 020-8986 4141
**W** www.boxing-monthly.co.uk
*Editor,* Graham Houston

COUNTRY WALKING
Bauer Media, 1 Lincoln Court, Lincoln Road, Peterborough,
PE1 2RF **T** 01733-468205 **W** www.livefortheoutdoors.com
*Editor,* Mark Sutcliffe
THE CRICKETER
The Cricketer Publishing Ltd, 70 Great Portland Street,
London W1W 7UW **T** 020-7460 5200
**W** www.thecricketer-magazine.com
*Editor,* Simon Hughes
FOURFOURTWO
Haymarket, Teddington Studios, Broom Road, Teddington,
Middlesex TW11 9BE **T** 020-8267 5661
**W** www.fourfourtwo.com
*Editor,* Hitesh Ratna
GOLF MONTHLY
9th Floor, Blue Fin Building, 110 Southwark Street,
London SE1 0SU **T** 020-3148 4527
**W** www.golf-monthly.co.uk
*Editor,* Michael Harris
HORSE & HOUND
Blue Fin Building, 110 Southwark Street, London SE1 0SU
**T** 020-3148 4562 **W** www.horseandhound.co.uk
*Editor,* Sarah Jenkins
MATCH
Media House, Lynchwood, Peterborough PE2 6EA
**T** 01733-468008 **W** www.matchmag.co.uk
*Editor,* James Bandy
RUGBY WORLD
Blue Fin Building, 110 Southwark Street, London SE1 0SU
**T** 0844-848 0848 **W** www.rugbyworld.com
*Editor,* Owain Jones
SPORT
Third Floor, Courtyard Building, 11 Curtain Road, London
EC2A 3LT **T** 020-7959 7942 **W** www.sport-magazine.co.uk
*Editor,* Simon Caney
SUPERBIKE
Blaze Publishing, Lawrence House, Morrell Street,
Leamington Spa CV37 5SZ **T** 020-8873 4454
**W** www.superbike.co.uk
*Editor,* John Hogan
TENNISHEAD
PO Box 70948, London SW19 9GL **T** 020-8408 7148
**W** www.tennishead.net
*Editor,* Lee Goodall
WORLD SOCCER
Blue Fin Building, 110 Southwark Street, London SE1 0SU
**T** 020-3148 4817 **W** www.worldsoccer.com
*Editor,* Gavin Hamilton

TRAVEL
CONDÉ NAST TRAVELLER
Vogue House, Hanover Square, London W1S 1JU
**T** 0844-848 2851 **W** www.cntraveller.com
*Editor,* Melinda Stevens
FRANCE
Archant House, 3 Oriel Road, Cheltenham GL50 1BB
**T** 01242-216050 **W** www.completefrance.com
*Editor,* Carolyn Boyd
LONELY PLANET
Media Centre (GH0S), 201 Wood Lane, London W12 7TQ
**T** 020-8433 1333 **W** www.lonelyplanet.com
*Editor,* Peter Grunert
NATIONAL GEOGRAPHIC TRAVELLER
Absolute Publishing Ltd, 197-199 City Road,
London EC1V 1JN **T** 020-7253 9906
**W** www.natgeotraveller.co.uk
*Editor,* Pat Riddell

# TRADE AND PROFESSIONAL BODIES

The following is a list of employers' and trade associations and other professional bodies in the UK. It does not represent a comprehensive list. For further professional bodies *see* Professional Education.

## ASSOCIATIONS

ABTA – THE TRAVEL ASSOCIATION, 30 Park Street, London SE1 9EQ T 020-3117 0500 E abta@abta.co.uk
W www.abta.com
*Chief Executive*, Mark Tanzer
ADVERTISING ASSOCIATION, 7th Floor North, Artillery House, 11–19 Artillery Row, London SW1P 1RT T 020-7340 1100
E aa@adassoc.org.uk W www.adassoc.org.uk
*Chief Executive*, Tim Lefroy
AEROSPACE DEFENCE SECURITY, Salamanca Square, 9 Albert Embankment, London SE1 7SP T 020-7091 4500
E enquiries@adsgroup.org.uk W www.adsgroup.org.uk
*Chief Executive*, Paul Everitt
AGRICULTURAL ENGINEERS ASSOCIATION, Samuelson House, 62 Forder Way, Hampton, Peterborough PE7 8JB T 0845-644 8748 E ab@aea.uk.com
W www.aea.uk.com
*Chief Executive*, Ruth Bailey
ASBESTOS REMOVAL CONTRACTORS ASSOCIATION, Unit 1, Stretton Business Park 2, Brunel Drive, Stretton DE13 0BY T 01283-566467 E info@arca.org.uk
W www.arca.org.uk
*Chief Executive*, Steve Sadley
ASSOCIATION FOR CONSULTANCY AND ENGINEERING, Alliance House, 12 Caxton Street, London SW1H 0QL T 020-7222 6557 E consult@acenet.co.uk
W www.acenet.co.uk
*Chief Executive*, Dr Nelson Ogunshakin, OBE
ASSOCIATION OF ACCOUNTING TECHNICIANS, 140 Aldersgate Street, London EC1A 4HY T 020-7397 3000
E aat@aat.org.uk W www.aat.org.uk
*Chief Executive*, Mark Farrar
ASSOCIATION OF ANAESTHETISTS OF GREAT BRITAIN AND IRELAND, 21 Portland Place, London W1B 1PY T 020-7631 1650 E info@aagbi.org
W www.aagbi.org
*President*, Dr Andrew Hartle
ASSOCIATION OF BRITISH INSURERS, 51 Gresham Street, London EC2V 7HQ T 020-7600 3333 E info@abi.org.uk
W www.abi.org.uk
*Director-General*, Huw Evans
ASSOCIATION OF BUSINESS RECOVERY PROFESSIONALS, 8th Floor, 120 Aldersgate Street, London EC1A 4JQ T 020-7566 4200 E association@r3.org.uk
W www.r3.org.uk
*Chief Executive*, Graham Rumney
ASSOCIATION OF CONSULTING SCIENTISTS, 5 Willow Heights, Cradley Heath B64 7PL T 0121-602 3515
E secretary@consultingscientists.co.uk
*Secretary*, Dr Stuart Guy
ASSOCIATION OF CONVENIENCE STORES LTD, Federation House, 17 Farnborough Street, Farnborough GU14 8AG T 01252-515001 E acs@acs.org.uk
W www.acs.org.uk
*Chief Executive*, James Lowman
ASSOCIATION OF CORPORATE TREASURERS, 51 Moorgate, London EC2R 6BH T 020-7847 2540
E enquiries@treasurers.org W www.treasurers.org
*Chief Executive*, Colin Tyler

ASSOCIATION OF DRAINAGE AUTHORITIES, 6 Electric Parade, Surbiton KT6 5NT T 020-8399 7350
E admin@ada.org.uk W www.ada.org.uk
*Chief Executive*, Jean Venables, CBE, FRENG
BOOKSELLERS ASSOCIATION, 6 Bell Yard, London WC2A 2JR T 020-7421 4640 E mail@booksellers.org.uk
W www.booksellers.org.uk
*Chief Executive*, T. E. Godfray
BPI (BRITISH PHONOGRAPHIC INDUSTRY), Riverside Building, County Hall, Westminster Bridge Road, London SE1 7JA T 020-7803 1300 E general@bpi.co.uk
W www.bpi.co.uk
*Chief Executive*, Geoff Taylor
BRITISH ANTIQUE DEALERS' ASSOCIATION, 20 Rutland Gate, London SW7 1BD T 020-7589 4128
E info@bada.org W www.bada.org
*Secretary-General*, Mark Dodgson
BRITISH ASSOCIATION OF SOCIAL WORKERS, 16 Kent Street, Birmingham B5 6RD T 0121-622 3911
E online@basw.co.uk W www.basw.co.uk
*Chief Executive*, Bridget Robb
BRITISH BANKERS' ASSOCIATION, Pinners Hall, 105–108 Old Broad Street, London EC2N 1EX
T 020-7216 8800 E info@bba.org.uk W www.bba.org.uk
*Chief Executive*, Anthony Browne
BRITISH BEER & PUB ASSOCIATION, Ground Floor, Brewers' Hall, Aldermanbury Square, London EC2V 7HR
T 020-7627 9191 E contact@beerandpub.com
W www.beerandpub.com
*Chief Executive*, Brigid Simmonds, OBE
BRITISH CHAMBERS OF COMMERCE, 65 Petty France, London SW1H 9EU T 020-7654 5800
W www.britishchambers.org.uk
*Director-General*, John Longworth
BRITISH ELECTROTECHNICAL AND ALLIED MANUFACTURERS ASSOCIATION (BEAMA), Westminster Tower, 3 Albert Embankment, London SE1 7SL
T 020-7793 3000 E info@beama.org.uk W www.beama.org.uk
*Chief Executive*, Dr Howard Porter
BRITISH HOROLOGICAL INSTITUTE, Upton Hall, Upton, Newark NG23 5TE T 01636-813795
E clocks@bhi.co.uk W www.bhi.co.uk
*Chief Executive*, Dudley Giles
BRITISH HOSPITALITY ASSOCIATION, Queens House, 55–56 Lincoln's Inn Fields, London WC2A 3BH
T 020-7404 7744 E bha@bha.org.uk W www.bha.org.uk
*Chief Executive*, Ufi Ibrahim
BRITISH INSTITUTE OF PROFESSIONAL PHOTOGRAPHY, The Coach House, The Firs, High Street, Whitchurch, Aylesbury HP22 4SJ T 01296-642020
E info@bipp.com W www.bipp.com
*Chief Executive*, Chris Harper
BRITISH INSURANCE BROKERS' ASSOCIATION, 8th Floor, John Stow House, 18 Bevis Marks, London EC3A 7JB T 0870-950 1790 E enquiries@biba.org.uk
W www.biba.org.uk
*Chief Executive*, Steve White
BRITISH MARINE FEDERATION, Marine House, Thorpe Lea Road, Egham TW20 8BF T 01784-473377
E info@britishmarine.co.uk W www.britishmarine.co.uk
*Chief Executive*, Howard Pridding
BRITISH MEDICAL ASSOCIATION, BMA House, Tavistock Square, London WC1H 9JP T 020-7387 4499
W www.bma.org.uk
*Chief Executive*, Keith Ward

BRITISH OFFICE SUPPLIES AND SERVICES (BOSS) FEDERATION, c/o British Printing Industries Federation, 2 Villiers Court, Meriden Business Park, Copse Drive, Coventry CV5 9RN T 01676-526030 E info@bossfederation.co.uk W www.bossfederation.co.uk *Chief Executive*, Michael Gardner

BRITISH PLASTICS FEDERATION, 6 Bath Place, Rivington Street, London EC2A 3JE T 020-7457 5000 E reception@bpf.co.uk W www.bpf.co.uk *Director-General*, Philip Law

BRITISH PORTS ASSOCIATION, 1st Floor, 30 Park Street, London SE1 9EQ T 020-7260 1780 E info@britishports.org.uk W www.britishports.org.uk *Director*, David Whitehead

BRITISH PRINTING INDUSTRIES FEDERATION, 2 Villiers Court, Meriden Business Park, Copse Drive, Coventry CV5 9RN T 0845-250 7050 W www.britishprint.com *Chief Executive*, Charles Jarrold

BRITISH PROPERTY FEDERATION, 5th Floor, St Albans House, 57–59 Haymarket, London SW1Y 4QX T 020-7828 0111 E info@bpf.org.uk W www.bpf.org.uk *Chief Executive*, Melanie Leech

BRITISH RETAIL CONSORTIUM, 21 Dartmouth Street, London SW1H 9BP T 020-7854 8900 E info@brc.org.uk W www.brc.org.uk *Director-General*, Helen Dickinson

BRITISH TYRE MANUFACTURERS' ASSOCIATION LTD, 5 Berewyk Hall Court, White Colne, Colchester CO6 2QB T 01787-226995 E mail@btmauk.com W www.btmauk.com *Chief Executive*, Graham Willson

BUILDING SOCIETIES ASSOCIATION, York House, 23 Kingsway, London WC2B 6UJ T 020-7520 5900 E simon.rex@bsa.org.uk W www.bsa.org.uk *Chief Executive*, Robin Fieth

CHARTERED ASSOCIATION OF BUILDING ENGINEERS, Lutyens House, Billing Brook Road, Weston Favell, Northampton NN3 8NW T 01604-404121 W www.cbuilde.com *Chief Executive*, Dr John Hooper

CHARTERED INSTITUTE FOR ARCHAEOLOGISTS, Miller Building, University of Reading RG6 6AB T 0118-378 6446 E admin@archaeologists.net W www.archaeologists.net *Chief Executive*, Peter Hinton

CHARTERED INSTITUTE OF ENVIRONMENTAL HEALTH, Chadwick Court, 15 Hatfields, London SE1 8DJ T 020-7928 6006 E information@cieh.org W www.cieh.org *Chief Executive*, Graham Jukes

CHARTERED INSTITUTE OF JOURNALISTS, 2 Dock Offices, Surrey Quays Road, London SE16 2XU T 020-7252 1187 E memberservices@cioj.co.uk W www.cioj.co.uk *General Secretary*, Dominic Cooper

CHARTERED INSTITUTE OF PURCHASING AND SUPPLY, Easton House, Church Street, Easton on the Hill, Stamford PE9 3NZ T 01780-756777 W www.cips.org *Chief Executive*, David Noble

CHARTERED INSTITUTE OF TAXATION, 1st Floor Artillery House, 11–19 Artillery Row, London SW1Y 1RT T 020-7340 0550 W www.tax.org.uk *Chief Executive*, Peter Fanning

CHARTERED INSURANCE INSTITUTE, 42–48 High Road, South Woodford, London E18 2JP T 020-8989 8464 E customer.serv@cii.co.uk W www.cii.co.uk *Chief Executive*, Dr Sandy Scott

CHARTERED MANAGEMENT INSTITUTE, Management House, Cottingham Road, Corby NN17 1TT T 01536-204222 E enquiries@managers.org.uk W www.managers.org.uk *Chief Executive*, Anne Francke

CHARTERED QUALITY INSTITUTE, 2nd Floor North, Chancery Exchange, 10 Furnival Street, London EC4A 1AB T 020-7245 6722 E membership@thecqi.org W www.thecqi.org *Chief Executive*, Simon Feary

CHEMICAL INDUSTRIES ASSOCIATION, Kings Buildings, Smith Square, London SW1P 3JJ T 020-7834 3399 E enquiries@cia.org.uk W www.cia.org.uk *Chief Executive*, Steve Elliott

CONFEDERATION OF PAPER INDUSTRIES, 1 Rivenhall Road, Swindon SN5 7BD T 01793-889600 E cpi@paper.org.uk W www.paper.org.uk *Director-General*, David Workman

CONFEDERATION OF PASSENGER TRANSPORT UK, Drury House, 34–43 Russell Street, London WC2B 5HA T 020-7240 3131 E admin@cpt-uk.org W www.cpt-uk.org *Chief Executive*, Simon Posner

CONSTRUCTION PRODUCTS ASSOCIATION, 26 Store Street, London WC1E 7BT T 020-7323 3770 W www.constructionproducts.org.uk *Chief Executive*, Diana Montgomery

DAIRY UK, 6th floor, 210 High Holborn, London WC1V 7EP T 020-7405 1484 E info@dairyuk.org W www.dairyuk.org *Chief Executive*, Dr Judith Bryans

EEF, THE MANUFACTURERS' ORGANISATION, Broadway House, Tothill Street, London SW1H 9NQ T 020-7222 7777 E enquiries@eef.org.uk W www.eef.org.uk *Chief Executive*, Terry Scuoler

ENERGY UK, Charles House, 5–11 Regent Street, London SW1Y 4LR T 020-7930 9390 W www.energy-uk.org.uk *Chief Executive (interim)*, Lawrence Slade

FEDERATION OF BAKERS, 6 Catherine Street, London WC2B 5JW T 020-7420 7190 E info@bakersfederation.org.uk W www.bakersfederation.org.uk *Director*, Gordon Polson

FEDERATION OF MASTER BUILDERS, David Croft House, 25 Ely Place, London EC1N 6TD T 020-7025 2900 W www.fmb.org.uk *Chief Executive*, Brian Berry

FEDERATION OF SPORTS AND PLAY ASSOCIATIONS, Office 8, Rural Innovation Centre, Unit 169 – Avenue H, Stoneleigh Park, Kenilworth CV8 2LG T 024-7641 4999 E info@sportsandplay.com W www.sportsandplay.com *Managing Director*, Jane Montgomery

FINANCE AND LEASING ASSOCIATION, 2nd Floor, Imperial House, 15–19 Kingsway, London WC2B 6UN T 020-7836 6511 E info@fla.org.uk W www.fla.org.uk *Director-General*, Stephen Sklaroff

FOOD AND DRINK FEDERATION, 6 Catherine Street, London WC2B 5JJ T 020-7836 2460 W www.fdf.org.uk *Director-General*, Ian Wright

FREIGHT TRANSPORT ASSOCIATION LTD, Hermes House, St John's Road, Tunbridge Wells TN4 9UZ T 01892-526171 E enquiry@fta.co.uk W www.fta.co.uk *Chief Executive*, David Wells

GLASGOW CHAMBER OF COMMERCE, 30 George Square, Glasgow G2 1EQ T 0141-204 2121 E chamber@glasgowchamberofcommerce.com W www.glasgowchamberofcommerce.com *Chief Executive*, Stuart Patrick

INSTITUTE OF BREWING & DISTILLING, 44A Curlew Street, Butler's Wharf, London SE1 2ND T 020-7499 8144 E enquiries@ibd.org.uk W www.ibd.org.uk *Executive Director*, Simon Jackson

INSTITUTE OF BRITISH ORGAN BUILDING, 13 Ryefields, Thurston, Bury St Edmunds IP31 3TD T 01359-233433 E administrator@ibo.co.uk W www.ibo.co.uk *President*, Dr Christopher Batchelor

INSTITUTE OF CHARTERED FORESTERS,
59 George Street, Edinburgh EH2 2JG **T** 0131-240 1425
**E** icf@charteredforesters.org **W** www.charteredforesters.org
*Executive Director,* Shireen Chambers
INSTITUTE OF CHARTERED SECRETARIES AND
ADMINISTRATORS, Saffron House, 6–10 Kirby Street,
London EC1N 8TS **T** 020-7580 4741 **E** info@icsa.org.uk
**W** www.icsa.org.uk
*Chief Executive,* Simon Osborne
INSTITUTE OF CHARTERED SHIPBROKERS,
85 Gracechurch Street, London EC3V 0AA **T** 020-7623 1111
**E** enquiries@ics.org.uk **W** www.ics.org.uk
*Director,* Julie Lithgow
INSTITUTE OF DIRECTORS, 116 Pall Mall, London
SW1Y 5ED **T** 020-7766 8888 **E** enquiries@iod.com
**W** www.iod.com
*Director-General,* Simon Walker
INSTITUTE OF EXPORT, Export House, Minerva Business
Park, Lynch Wood, Peterborough PE2 6FT **T** 01733-404400
**W** www.export.org.uk
*Director-General,* Lesley Batchelor, OBE
INSTITUTE OF FINANCIAL ACCOUNTANTS,
The Podium, 1 Eversholt Street, London NW1 2DN
**T** 020-7554 0730 **E** mail@ifa.org.uk **W** www.ifa.org.uk
*Chief Executive,* David Woodgate
INSTITUTE OF HEALTHCARE MANAGEMENT,
John Snow House, 59 Mansell Street, London E1 8AN
**T** 020-7265 7321 **E** enquiries@ihm.org.uk **W** www.ihm.org.uk
*Chief Executive,* Shirley Cramer, CBE
INSTITUTE OF HOSPITALITY, Trinity Court, 34 West Street,
Sutton, Surrey SM1 1SH **T** 020-8661 4900
**W** www.instituteofhospitality.org
*Chief Executive,* Peter Ducker
INSTITUTE OF INTERNAL COMMUNICATION,
Suite G10, Gemini House, Sunrise Parkway, Linford Wood,
MK14 6PW **T** 01908-232168 **E** enquiries@ioic.org.uk
**W** www.ioic.org.uk
*Chief Executive,* Steve Doswell
INSTITUTE OF MANAGEMENT SERVICES,
Brooke House, 24 Dam Street, Lichfield WS13 6AA
**T** 01543-266909 **E** admin@ims-stowe.fsnet.co.uk
**W** www.ims-productivity.com
*Chair,* Dr Andrew Muir
INSTITUTE OF QUARRYING, McPherson House,
8A Regan Way, Chetwynd Business Park, Chilwell, Nottingham
NG9 6RZ **T** 0115-972 9995 **E** mail@quarrying.org
**W** www.quarrying.org
*Executive Director,* Phil James
INSTITUTE OF THE MOTOR INDUSTRY, Fanshaws,
Brickendon, Hertford SG13 8PQ **T** 01992-511521
**E** comms@theimi.org.uk **W** www.theimi.org.uk
*Chief Executive,* Steve Nash
INSTITUTION OF OCCUPATIONAL SAFETY AND
HEALTH, The Grange, Highfield Drive, Wigston LE18 1NN
**T** 0116-257 3100 **E** reception@iosh.co.uk **W** www.iosh.co.uk
*Chief Executive,* Jan Chmiel
IP FEDERATION, 5th Floor, 63–66 Hatton Garden,
London EC1N 8LE **T** 020-7242 3923 **E** admin@ipfederation.com
**W** www.ipfederation.com
*President,* Carol Arnold
MAGISTRATES' ASSOCIATION, 28 Fitzroy Square,
London W1T 6DD **T** 020-7387 2353
**E** information@magistrates-association.org.uk
**W** www.magistrates-association.org.uk
*Chief Executive,* Chris Brace
MANAGEMENT CONSULTANCIES ASSOCIATION,
5th Floor, 36–38 Cornhill, London EC3V 3NG **T** 020-7645 7950
**E** info@mca.org.uk **W** www.mca.org.uk
*Chief Executive,* Alan Leaman, OBE

MASTER LOCKSMITHS ASSOCIATION, 5D Great
Central Way, Woodford Halse, Daventry NN11 3PZ
**T** 01327-262 255 **E** enquiries@locksmiths.co.uk
**W** www.locksmiths.co.uk
*Director of Development,* Dr Steffan George
NATIONAL ASSOCIATION OF BRITISH MARKET
AUTHORITIES, The Guildhall, Oswestry,
Shrops SY11 1PZ **T** 01691-680713
**E** nabma@nabma.com **W** www.nabma.com
*Chief Executive,* Graham Wilson, OBE
NATIONAL ASSOCIATION OF ESTATE AGENTS,
Arbon House, 6 Tournament Court, Edgehill Drive, Warwick
CV34 6LG **T** 0845-250 6001 **W** www.naea.co.uk
*President,* Simon Gerrard
NATIONAL CATTLE ASSOCIATION (DAIRY), Brick House,
Risbury, Leominster HR6 0NQ **T** 01568-760632
**E** timbrigstocke@hotmail.com
*Executive Secretary,* Tim Brigstocke, MBE
NATIONAL FARMERS' UNION (NFU), Agriculture
House, Stoneleigh Park, Stoneleigh CV8 2LZ **T** 024-7685 8500
**W** www.nfuonline.com
*Director-General,* Andy Robertson
NATIONAL FEDERATION OF RETAIL NEWSAGENTS,
Yeoman House, Sekforde Street, London EC1R 0HF
**T** 020-7253 4225 **E** service@nfrnonline.com
**W** www.nfrnonline.com
*Chief Executive,* Paul Baxter
NATIONAL LANDLORDS ASSOCIATION, 2nd Floor,
200 Union Street, London SE1 0LX **T** 020-7840 8900
**E** info@landlords.org.uk **W** www.landlords.org.uk
*Chief Executive,* Richard Lambert
NATIONAL MARKET TRADERS FEDERATION,
Hampton House, Hawshaw Lane, Hoyland, Barnsley S74 0HA
**T** 01226-749021 **E** genoffice@nmtf.co.uk **W** www.nmtf.co.uk
*Chief Executive,* Joe Harrison
NATIONAL PHARMACY ASSOCIATION, Mallinson House,
38–42 St Peter's Street, St Albans, Herts AL1 3NP
**T** 01727-858687 **E** npa@npa.co.uk **W** www.npa.co.uk
*Chief Executive,* vacant
NEWS MEDIA ASSOCIATION, 292 Vauxhall Bridge Road,
London SW1V 1AE **T** 020-7963 7480 **E** nma@newsmediauk.org
**W** www.newsmediauk.org
*Chief Executive,* David Newell
OIL AND GAS UK, 6th Floor East, Portland House,
Bressenden Place, London SW1E 5BH **T** 020-7802 2400
**E** info@oilandgasuk.co.uk **W** www.oilandgasuk.co.uk
*Chief Executive,* Malcolm Webb
PROPERTY CARE ASSOCIATION, 11 Ramsay Court,
Kingfisher Way, Hinchingbrooke Business Park, Huntingdon
PE29 6FY **T** 0844-375 4301 **E** pca@property-care.org
**W** www.property-care.org
*Chief Executive,* Stephen Hodgson
PUBLISHERS ASSOCIATION, 29B Montague Street,
London WC1B 5BW **T** 020-7691 9191
**E** mail@publishers.org.uk **W** www.publishers.org.uk
*Chief Executive,* Richard Mollet
RADIOCENTRE, 6th Floor, 55 New Oxford Street,
London WC1A 1BS **T** 020-7010 0600 **E** info@radiocentre.org
**W** www.radiocentre.org
*Chief Executive,* Siobhan Kenny
ROAD HAULAGE ASSOCIATION LTD, Roadway House,
Bretton PE3 8DD **T** 01274-863100 **W** www.rha.uk.net
*Chief Executive,* Richard Burnett
ROYAL ASSOCIATION OF BRITISH DAIRY FARMERS,
Dairy House, Unit 31, Abbey Park, Stareton, Kenilworth
CV8 2LY **T** 0845-458 2711 **E** office@rabdf.co.uk
**W** www.rabdf.co.uk
*Chief Executive,* Nick Everington

ROYAL FACULTY OF PROCURATORS IN GLASGOW,
12 Nelson Mandela Place, Glasgow G2 1BT T 0141-332 3593
E library@rfpg.org W www.rfpg.org
*Chief Executive,* John McKenzie
SHELLFISH ASSOCIATION OF GREAT BRITAIN,
Fishmongers' Hall, London Bridge, London EC4R 9EL
T 020-7283 8305 W www.shellfish.org.uk
*Director,* David Jarrad
SOCIETY OF LOCAL AUTHORITY CHIEF EXECUTIVES
AND SENIOR MANAGERS (SOLACE), Suite 1.3A,
1st Floor, 21–24 Millbank Tower, Millbank, London SW1P 4QP
T 0845-652 4010 E debbie.wood@solace.org.uk
W www.solace.org.uk
*Directors,* Graeme McDonald; Terry McDougal;
Debbie Wood
SOCIETY OF MOTOR MANUFACTURERS AND
TRADERS LTD, 71 Great Peter Street, London SW1P 2BN
T 020-7235 7000 E communications@smmt.co.uk
W www.smmt.co.uk
*Chief Executive,* Mike Hawes
TIMBER TRADE FEDERATION, The Building Centre,
26 Store Street, London WC1E 7BT T 020-3205 0067
E ttf@ttf.co.uk W www.ttf.co.uk
*Chief Executive,* vacant
TRADING STANDARDS INSTITUTE, 1 Sylvan Court,
Sylvan Way, Southfields Business Park, Basildon SS15 6TH
T 01268-582200 E institute@tsi.org.uk
W www.tradingstandards.gov.uk
*Chief Executive,* Leon Livermore
UK CHAMBER OF SHIPPING, 30 Park Street, London SE1 9EQ
T 020-7417 2800 E query@ukchamberofshipping.com
W www.ukchamberofshipping.com
*Chief Executive,* Guy Platten
UK FASHION AND TEXTILE ASSOCIATION, 3 Queen
Square, London WC1N 3AR T 020-7843 9460 E info@ukft.org
W www.ukft.org
*Chief Executive,* John Miln
UK LEATHER FEDERATION, Leather Trade House,
Kings Park Road, Moulton Park, Northampton NN3 6JD
T 01604-679999 E info@uklf.org W www.ukleather.org
*Director,* Dr Kerry Senior
UK PETROLEUM INDUSTRY ASSOCIATION LTD,
Quality House, Quality Court, Chancery Lane,
London WC2A 1HP T 020-7269 7600 E info@ukpia.com
W www.ukpia.com
*Director-General,* Chris Hunt

ULSTER FARMERS' UNION, 475 Antrim Road,
Belfast BT15 3DA T 028-9037 0222 E info@ufuhq.com
W www.ufuni.org
*Chief Executive,* Wesley Aston
WINE AND SPIRIT TRADE ASSOCIATION,
International Wine and Spirit Centre, 39–45 Bermondsey Street,
London SE1 3XF T 020-7089 3877 E info@wsta.co.uk
W www.wsta.co.uk
*Chief Executive,* Miles Beale

## CBI

Cannon Place, 78 Cannon Street, London EC4N 6HN
T 020-7379 7400 E enquiries@cbi.org.uk W www.cbi.org.uk

The CBI was founded in 1965 and is an independent non-party political body financed by industry and commerce. It works with the UK government, international legislators and policymakers to help UK businesses compete effectively. It is the recognised spokesman for the business viewpoint and is consulted as such by the government.

The CBI speaks for some 190,000 businesses that together employ approximately one-third of the private sector workforce. Member companies, which decide all policy positions, include FTSE 100 index listed companies, small- and medium-size firms, micro businesses, private and family owned businesses, start-ups and trade associations.

The CBI board is chaired by the president and meets four times a year. It is assisted by 14 expert standing committees which advise on the main aspects of policy. There are 13 regional councils and offices, covering the administrative regions of England, Wales, Scotland and Northern Ireland. There are also offices in Beijing, Brussels, New Delhi and Washington DC.

*Director-General,* John Cridland, CBE

WALES, 2 Caspian Point, Caspian Way, Cardiff Bay, Cardiff
CF10 4DQ T 029-2097 7600 E wales.mail@cbi.org.uk
*Regional Director,* Emma Watkins
SCOTLAND, 160 West George Street, Glasgow G2 2HQ
T 0141-222 2184 E scot.mail@cbi.org.uk
*Regional Director,* Hugh Aitken
NORTHERN IRELAND, Hamilton House, 3 Joy Street,
Belfast BT2 8LE T 028-9010 1100 E ni.mail@cbi.org.uk
*Regional Director,* Nigel Smyth

# TRADE UNIONS

A trade union is an organisation of workers formed for the purpose of collective bargaining over pay and working conditions. Trade unions may also provide legal and financial advice, sickness benefits and education facilities to their members. Legally any employee has the right to join a trade union, but not all employers recognise all or any trade unions. Conversely an employee also has the right not to join a trade union, in particular since the practice of a 'closed shop' system, where all employees have to join the employer's preferred union, is no longer permitted. Below is a list of key dates in the development of the British trade unionist movement.

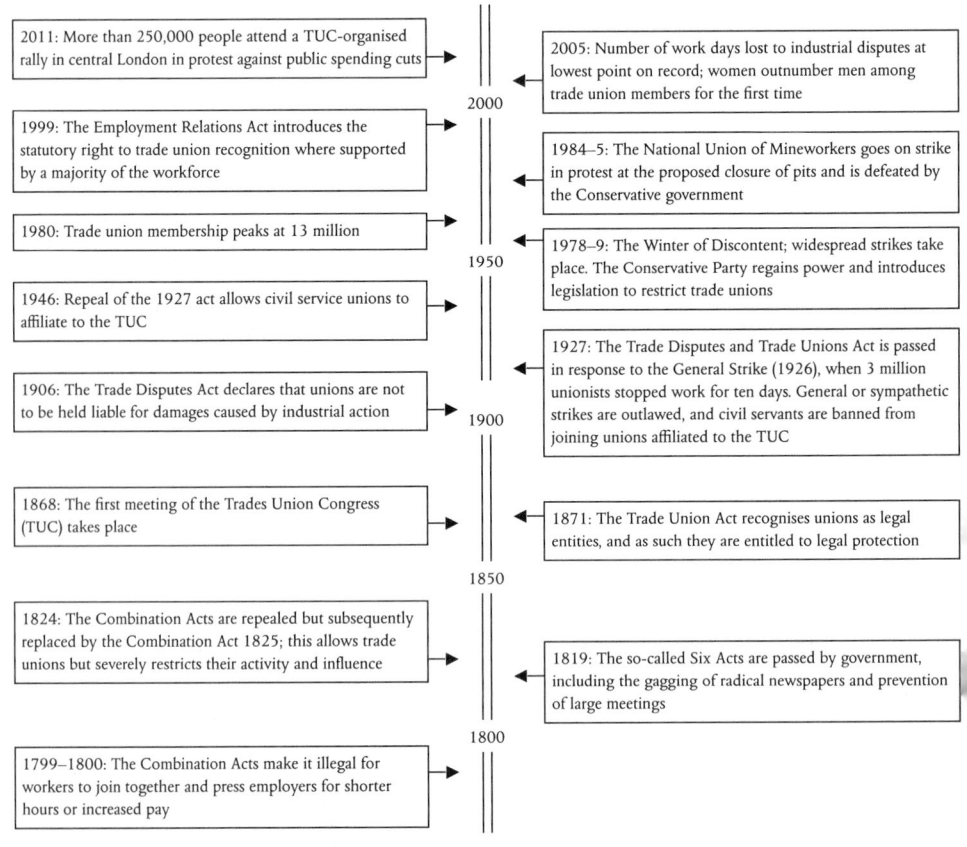

2011: More than 250,000 people attend a TUC-organised rally in central London in protest against public spending cuts

2005: Number of work days lost to industrial disputes at lowest point on record; women outnumber men among trade union members for the first time

2000

1999: The Employment Relations Act introduces the statutory right to trade union recognition where supported by a majority of the workforce

1984–5: The National Union of Mineworkers goes on strike in protest at the proposed closure of pits and is defeated by the Conservative government

1980: Trade union membership peaks at 13 million

1978–9: The Winter of Discontent; widespread strikes take place. The Conservative Party regains power and introduces legislation to restrict trade unions

1950

1946: Repeal of the 1927 act allows civil service unions to affiliate to the TUC

1927: The Trade Disputes and Trade Unions Act is passed in response to the General Strike (1926), when 3 million unionists stopped work for ten days. General or sympathetic strikes are outlawed, and civil servants are banned from joining unions affiliated to the TUC

1906: The Trade Disputes Act declares that unions are not to be held liable for damages caused by industrial action

1900

1868: The first meeting of the Trades Union Congress (TUC) takes place

1871: The Trade Union Act recognises unions as legal entities, and as such they are entitled to legal protection

1850

1824: The Combination Acts are repealed but subsequently replaced by the Combination Act 1825; this allows trade unions but severely restricts their activity and influence

1819: The so-called Six Acts are passed by government, including the gagging of radical newspapers and prevention of large meetings

1800

1799–1800: The Combination Acts make it illegal for workers to join together and press employers for shorter hours or increased pay

## THE CENTRAL ARBITRATION COMMITTEE

22nd Floor, Euston Tower, 286 Euston Road, London NW1 3JJ
T 020-7904 2300 E enquiries@cac.gov.uk
W www.gov.uk/government/organisations/central-arbitration-committee

The Central Arbitration Committee's main role is concerned with requests for trade union recognition and de-recognition under the statutory procedures of Schedule A1 of the Employment Rights Act 1999. It also determines disclosure of information complaints under the Trade Union and Labour Relations (Consolidation) Act 1992, considers applications and complaints under the Information and Consultation Regulations 2004, and performs a similar role in relation to European works councils, companies, cooperative societies and cross-border mergers.
*Chair,* Sir Michael Burton
*Chief Executive,* Simon Gouldstone

## TRADES UNION CONGRESS (TUC)

Congress House, 23–28 Great Russell Street, London WC1B 3LS
T 020-7636 4030
E info@tuc.org.uk W www.tuc.org.uk

The Trades Union Congress (TUC), founded in 1868, is an independent association of trade unions. The TUC promotes the rights and welfare of those in work and helps the unemployed. The TUC brings Britain's unions together to draw up common polices; lobbies the government to implement policies that will benefit people at work; campaigns on economic and social issues; represents working people on public bodies, in the European Union and at the UN employment body – the International Labour Organisation; carries out research on employment-related issues; runs training and education programmes for union representatives; helps unions to develop new services for their members and negotiate with each other; and builds links with other trade union bodies worldwide.

The governing body of the TUC is the annual congress which sets policy. Between congresses, business is conducted by a 56-member general council, which meets every two months to oversee the TUC's work programme and sanction new policy initiatives. Each year, at its first post-congress meeting, the general council appoints an executive committee and the TUC president for that congress year. The executive committee meets monthly to implement and develop policy, manage TUC financial affairs and deal with any urgent business. The president chairs general council and executive meetings and is consulted by the General Secretary on all major issues.

There are 51 affiliated unions, with a total membership of 5.8 million.

*President (2015–16)*, Liz Snape
*General Secretary*, Frances O'Grady

## SCOTTISH TRADES UNION CONGRESS (STUC)

333 Woodlands Road, Glasgow G3 6NG T 0141-337 8100
E info@stuc.org.uk W www.stuc.org.uk

The congress was formed in 1897 and acts as a national centre for the trade union movement in Scotland. The STUC promotes the rights to welfare of those in work and helps the unemployed. It helps its member unions to promote membership in new areas and industries, and campaigns for rights at work for all employees, including part-time and temporary workers, whether union members or not. It also makes representations to government and employers. In April 2015 the STUC had around 620,000 members from 39 affiliated unions and 20 trade union councils.

The annual congress in April elects a 36-member general council on the basis of six sections.

*President (2015–16)*, Lawrence Wason
*General Secretary*, Grahame Smith

## WALES TUC

Transport House, 1 Cathedral Road, Cardiff CF11 9SD
T 029-2034 7010
E wtuc@tuc.org.uk W www.tuc.org.uk/wales

The Wales TUC was established in 1974 to ensure that the role of the TUC was effectively undertaken in Wales. Its structure reflects the four economic regions of Wales and matches the regional committee areas of the National Assembly of Wales. The regional committees oversee the implementation of Wales TUC policy and campaigns in the relevant regions, and liaise with local government, training organisations and regional economic development bodies. The Wales TUC seeks to reduce unemployment, increase the levels of skill and pay, and eliminate discrimination.

The governing body of Wales TUC is the conference, which meets annually in May and elects a general council (usually of around 50 people) that oversees the work of the TUC throughout the year.

There are around 50 affiliated unions representing around 500,000 workers.

*President (2015–16)*, Margaret Thomas
*General Secretary*, Martin Mansfield

## TUC-AFFILIATED UNIONS

*As at April 2015*

ACCORD, Simmons House, 46 Old Bath Road, Charvil RG10 9QR
T 0118-934 1808 E info@accordhq.org
W www.accord-myunion.org
*General Secretary*, Ged Nichols *Membership:* 24,177

ADVANCE, 2nd Floor, 16–17 High Street, Tring HP23 5AH
T 01442-891122 E info@advance-union.org
W www.advance-union.org
*General Secretary*, Linda Rolph *Membership:* 6,784

AEGIS THE UNION, 1–3 Lochside Crescent, Edinburgh Park, Edinburgh EH12 9SE T 0131-549 5474
E members@aegistheunion.co.uk W www.aegistheunion.co.uk
*General Secretary*, Brian Linn *Membership:* 4,602

AEP (ASSOCIATION OF EDUCATIONAL PSYCHOLOGISTS), 4 The Riverside Centre, Frankland Lane, Durham DH1 5TA T 0191-384 9512 E enquiries@aep.org.uk
W www.aep.org.uk
*General Secretary*, Kate Fallon *Membership:* 3,297

AFA (ASSOCIATION OF FLIGHT ATTENDANTS), c/o 32 Wingfield Road, London SW2 4DS
T 0208-276 6723 E afalhr@unitedafa.org
W www.afacwa.org
*President*, Anthony King *Membership:* 500

ASLEF (ASSOCIATED SOCIETY OF LOCOMOTIVE ENGINEERS AND FIREMEN), 75–77 St John Street, Clerkenwell, London EC1M 4NN T 020-7324 2400
E info@aslef.org.uk W www.aslef.org.uk
*General Secretary*, Mick Whelan *Membership:* 20,054

ATL (ASSOCIATION OF TEACHERS AND LECTURERS), 7 Northumberland Street, London WC2N 5RD
T 020-7930 6441 E info@atl.org.uk W www.atl.org.uk
*General Secretary*, Dr Mary Bousted
*Membership:* 127,899

BALPA (BRITISH AIRLINE PILOTS ASSOCIATION), BALPA House, 5 Heathrow Boulevard, 278 Bath Road, West Drayton UB7 0DQ T 020-8476 4000
E balpa@balpa.org W www.balpa.org
*General Secretary*, Jim McAuslan *Membership:* 7,900

BDA (BRITISH DIETETIC ASSOCIATION), 5th Floor, Charles House, 148–149 Great Charles Street, Queensway, Birmingham B3 3HT T 0121-200 8080 E info@bda.uk.com
W www.bda.uk.com
*Chief Executive*, Andy Burman *Membership:* 7,609

BECTU (BROADCASTING, ENTERTAINMENT, CINEMATOGRAPH AND THEATRE UNION), 373–377 Clapham Road, London SW9 9BT T 020-7346 0900
E info@bectu.org.uk W www.bectu.org.uk
*General Secretary*, Gerry Morrissey *Membership:* 24,753

BFAWU (BAKERS, FOOD AND ALLIED WORKERS' UNION), Stanborough House, Great North Road, Stanborough, Welwyn Garden City AL8 7TA T 01707-260150
E info@bfawu.org W www.bfawu.org
*General Secretary*, Ronnie Draper *Membership:* 20,216

BOS TU (BRITISH ORTHOPTIC SOCIETY TRADE UNION), Salisbury House, Station Road, Ely, Cambridge CB1 2LA T 01353-665541 E bios@orthoptics.org.uk
W www.orthoptics.org.uk
*Chair*, Lesley-Anne Baxter *Membership:* 1,019

BSU (BRITANNIA STAFF UNION), Court Lodge, Leonard Street, Leek ST13 5JP T 01538-399627
E bsu@themail.co.uk W www.britanniasu.org.uk
*General Secretary*, John Stoddard *Membership:* 2,373

COMMUNITY, 465C Caledonian Road, London N7 9GX
T 020-7420 4000 E info@community-tu.org
W www.community-tu.org
*General Secretary*, Roy Rickhuss *Membership:* 31,886

CSP (CHARTERED SOCIETY OF PHYSIOTHERAPY), 14 Bedford Row, London WC1R 4ED T 020-7306 6666
E enquiries@csp.org.uk W www.csp.org.uk
*Chief Executive*, Karen Middleton, CBE
*Membership:* 39,750

CWU (COMMUNICATION WORKERS UNION), 150 The Broadway, Wimbledon, London SW19 1RX
T 020-8971 7200 E info@cwu.org W www.cwu.org
*General Secretary*, Billy Hayes *Membership:* 201,729

EIS (EDUCATIONAL INSTITUTE OF SCOTLAND), 46 Moray Place, Edinburgh EH3 6BH T 0131-225 6244
E enquiries@eis.org.uk W www.eis.org.uk
*General Secretary*, Larry Flanagan *Membership:* 54,780

EQUITY, Guild House, Upper St Martin's Lane, London WC2H 9EG **T** 020-7379 6000 **E** info@equity.org.uk **W** www.equity.org.uk
*General Secretary,* Christine Payne *Membership:* 40,160
FBU (FIRE BRIGADES UNION), Bradley House, 68 Coombe Road, Kingston upon Thames KT2 7AE **T** 020-8541 1765 **E** office@fbu.org.uk **W** www.fbu.org.uk
*General Secretary,* Matt Wrack *Membership:* 39,983
FDA, 8 Leake Street, London SE1 7NN **T** 020-7401 5555 **E** info@fda.org.uk **W** www.fda.org.uk
*General Secretary,* Dave Penman *Membership:* 16,966
GMB, 22 Stephenson Way, London NW1 2HD **T** 020-7391 6700 **E** info@gmb.org.uk **W** www.gmb.org.uk
*General Secretary,* Sir Paul Kenny *Membership:* 620,970
HCSA (HOSPITAL CONSULTANTS' AND SPECIALISTS' ASSOCIATION), 1 Kingsclere Road, Overton, Basingstoke RG25 3JA **T** 01256-771777 **E** conspec@hcsa.com **W** www.hcsa.com
*Chief Executive,* Eddie Saville *Membership:* 3,228
MU (MUSICIANS' UNION), 60–62 Clapham Road, London SW9 0JJ **T** 020-7582 5566 **E** info@theMU.org **W** www.theMU.org
*General Secretary,* John F. Smith *Membership:* 30,710
NACO (NATIONAL ASSOCIATION OF COOPERATIVE OFFICIALS), 6A Clarendon Place, Hyde SK14 2QZ **T** 0161-351 7900 **E** info@naco.coop **W** www.naco.coop
*General Secretary,* Neil Buist *Membership:* 1,819
NACODS (NATIONAL ASSOCIATION OF COLLIERY OVERMEN, DEPUTIES AND SHOTFIRERS), Wadsworth House, 130–132 Doncaster Road, Barnsley S70 1TP **T** 01226-203743 **E** natnacods@googlemail.com **W** www.nacods.org.uk
*General Secretary,* Rowland Soar *Membership:* 233
NAHT (NATIONAL ASSOCIATION OF HEAD TEACHERS), 1 Heath Square, Boltro Road, Haywards Heath RH16 1BL **T** 01444-472472 **E** info@naht.org.uk **W** www.naht.org.uk
*General Secretary,* Russell Hobby *Membership:* 28,102
NAPO (TRADE UNION AND PROFESSIONAL ASSOCIATION FOR FAMILY COURT AND PROBATION STAFF), 4 Chivalry Road, London SW11 1HT **T** 020-7223 4887 **E** info@napo.org.uk **W** www.napo.org.uk
*General Secretary,* Ian Lawrence *Membership:* 8,123
NASS (NATIONAL ASSOCIATION OF STABLE STAFF), The New Astley Club, Fred Archer Way, Newmarket CB8 8NT **T** 01638-663411 **E** admin@naoss.co.uk **W** www.naoss.co.uk
*Chief Executive,* George McGrath *Membership:* 1,782
NASUWT (NATIONAL ASSOCIATION OF SCHOOLMASTERS/UNION OF WOMEN TEACHERS), Hillscourt Education Centre, Rose Hill, Rednal, Birmingham B45 8RS **T** 0121-453 6150 **E** nasuwt@mail.nasuwt.org.uk **W** www.nasuwt.org.uk
*General Secretary,* Ms Chris Keates *Membership:* 295,565
NAUTILUS INTERNATIONAL, 1–2 The Shrubberies, George Lane, South Woodford, London E18 1BD **T** 020-8989 6677 **E** enquiries@nautilusint.org **W** www.nautilusint.org
*General Secretary,* Mark Dickinson *Membership:* 15,800
NGSU (NATIONWIDE GROUP STAFF UNION), Middleton Farmhouse, 37 Main Road, Middleton Cheney OX17 2QT **T** 01295-710767 **E** ngsu@ngsu.org.uk **W** www.ngsu.co.uk
*General Secretary,* Tim Poil *Membership:* 11,852
NUJ (NATIONAL UNION OF JOURNALISTS), Headland House, 308–312 Gray's Inn Road, London WC1X 8DP **T** 020-7843 3700 **E** info@nuj.org.uk **W** www.nuj.org.uk
*General Secretary,* Michelle Stanistreet
*Membership:* 30,434

NUM (NATIONAL UNION OF MINEWORKERS), Miners' Offices, 2 Huddersfield Road, Barnsley S70 2LS **T** 01226-215555 **E** chris.kitchen@num.org.uk **W** www.num.org.uk
*National Secretary,* Chris Kitchen *Membership:* 1,283
NUT (NATIONAL UNION OF TEACHERS), Hamilton House, Mabledon Place, London WC1H 9BD **T** 020-7388 6191 **E** enquiries@nut.org.uk **W** www.teachers.org.uk
*General Secretary,* Christine Blower
*Membership:* 330,719
PCS (PUBLIC AND COMMERCIAL SERVICES UNION), 160 Falcon Road, London SW11 2LN **T** 020-7924 2727 **W** www.pcs.org.uk
*General Secretary,* Mark Serwotka *Membership:* 247,345
PFA (PROFESSIONAL FOOTBALLERS' ASSOCIATION), 20 Oxford Court, Bishopsgate, Manchester M2 3WQ **T** 0161-236 0575 **E** info@thepfa.co.uk **W** www.thepfa.com
*Chief Executive,* Gordon Taylor, OBE
*Membership:* 2,942
POA (PROFESSIONAL TRADE UNION FOR PRISON, CORRECTIONAL AND SECURE PSYCHIATRIC WORKERS), Cronin House, 245 Church Street, London N9 9HW **T** 020-8803 0255 **E** general@poauk.org.uk **W** www.poauk.org.uk
*General Secretary,* Steve Gillan *Membership:* 31,130
PROSPECT, New Prospect House, 8 Leake Street, London SE1 7NN **T** 020-7902 6600 **E** enquiries@prospect.org.uk **W** www.prospect.org.uk
*General Secretary,* Mike Clancy *Membership:* 118,761
RMT (NATIONAL UNION OF RAIL, MARITIME AND TRANSPORT WORKERS), Unity House, 39 Chalton Street, London NW1 1JD **T** 020-7387 4771 **E** info@rmt.org.uk **W** www.rmt.org.uk
*General Secretary,* Mick Cash *Membership:* 80,105
SCP (SOCIETY OF CHIROPODISTS AND PODIATRISTS), 1 Fellmonger's Path, Tower Bridge Road, London SE1 3LY **T** 020-7234 8620 **E** reception@scpod.org **W** www.scpod.org
*General Secretary,* Joanna Brown *Membership:* 9,298
SOR (SOCIETY OF RADIOGRAPHERS), 207 Providence Square, Mill Street, London SE1 2EW **T** 020-7740 7200 **W** www.sor.org
*Chief Executive,* Richard Evans *Membership:* 26,485
STAFF UNION WEST BROMWICH BUILDING SOCIETY, 374 High Street, West Bromwich B70 8LR **T** 0870-220 7720 **E** staffunion@westbrom.co.uk
*General Secretary,* Julie Holton *Membership:* 523
TSSA (TRANSPORT SALARIED STAFFS' ASSOCIATION), Walkden House, 10 Melton Street, London NW1 2EJ **T** 020-7387 2101 **E** enquiries@tssa.org.uk **W** www.tssa.org.uk
*General Secretary,* Manuel Cortes *Membership:* 21,726
UCAC (UNDEB CENEDLAETHOL ATHRAWON CYMRU) (NATIONAL UNION OF THE TEACHERS OF WALES), Prif Swyddfa UCAC, Ffordd Penglais, Aberystwyth SY23 2EU **T** 01970-639950 **E** ucac@athrawon.com **W** www.athrawon.com
*General Secretary,* Elaine Edwards *Membership:* 4,222
UCATT (UNION OF CONSTRUCTION, ALLIED TRADES AND TECHNICIANS), UCATT House, 177 Abbeville Road, London SW4 9RL **T** 020-7622 2442 **E** info@ucatt.org.uk **W** www.ucatt.org.uk
*General Secretary,* Steve Murphy *Membership:* 86,983
UCU (UNIVERSITY AND COLLEGE UNION), Carlow Street, London NW1 7LH **T** 020-7756 2500 **E** hq@ucu.org.uk **W** www.ucu.org.uk
*General Secretary,* Sally Hunt *Membership:* 113,227

UNISON, 130 Euston Road, London NW1 2AY
T 0800-085 7857 W www.unison.org.uk
*General Secretary,* Dave Prentis *Membership:* 1,266,711
UNITE, 128 Theobald's Road, London WC1X 8TN
T 020-7611 2500 W www.unitetheunion.org
*General Secretary,* Len McCluskey
*Membership:* 1,310,649
URTU (UNITED ROAD TRANSPORT UNION),
Almond House, Oak Green, Stanley Green Business Park,
Cheadle Hulme SK8 6QL T 0800-526639 E info@urtu.com
W www.urtu.com
*General Secretary,* Robert Monks *Membership:* 12,200
USDAW (UNION OF SHOP, DISTRIBUTIVE AND
ALLIED WORKERS), 188 Wilmslow Road,
Manchester M14 6LJ T 0161-224 2804
E enquiries@usdaw.org.uk W www.usdaw.org.uk
*General Secretary,* John Hannett *Membership:* 433,402
WGGB (WRITERS' GUILD OF GREAT BRITAIN),
134 Tooley Street, London SE1 2TU T 020-7833 0777
E admin@writersguild.org.uk W www.writersguild.org.uk
*General Secretary,* Bernie Corbett *Membership:* 1,126

# NON-AFFILIATED UNIONS

*As at April 2015*
ASCL (ASSOCIATION OF SCHOOL AND COLLEGE
LEADERS), 130 Regent Road, Leicester LE1 7PG
T 0116-299 1122 E info@ascl.org.uk W www.ascl.org.uk
*General Secretary,* Brian Lightman
*Membership:* around 18,000

BDA (BRITISH DENTAL ASSOCIATION),
64 Wimpole Street, London W1G 8YS T 020-7935 0875
E enquiries@bda.org W www.bda.org
*Chief Executive,* Peter Ward *Membership:* 19,201
CIOJ (CHARTERED INSTITUTE OF JOURNALISTS),
2 Dock Offices, Surrey Quays Road, London SE16 2XU
T 020-7252 1187 E memberservices@cioj.co.uk
W www.cioj.co.uk
*General Secretary,* Dominic Cooper
*Membership:* around 2,000
NSEAD (NATIONAL SOCIETY FOR EDUCATION IN
ART AND DESIGN), 3 Mason's Wharf, Potley Lane,
Corsham SN13 9FY T 01225-810134 E info@nsead.org
W www.nsead.org
*General Secretary,* Mrs Lesley Butterworth
*Membership:* 2,000
RCM (ROYAL COLLEGE OF MIDWIVES), 15 Mansfield
Street, London W1G 9NH T 030-0303 0444 E info@rcm.org.uk
W www.rcm.org.uk
*General Secretary,* Prof. Cathy Warwick, CBE
*Membership:* around 42,000
SOCIETY OF AUTHORS, 84 Drayton Gardens, London
SW10 9SB T 020-7373 6642 E info@societyofauthors.org
W www.societyofauthors.org
*Chief Executive,* Nicola Solomon *Membership:* 9,350
SSTA (SCOTTISH SECONDARY TEACHERS'
ASSOCIATION), West End House, 14 West End Place,
Edinburgh EH11 2ED T 0131-313 7300 E info@ssta.org.uk
W www.ssta.org.uk
*General Secretary,* Seamus Searson
*Membership:* around 8,500

# SPORTS BODIES

## SPORTS COUNCILS

SPORT AND RECREATION ALLIANCE,
Burwood House, 14 Caxton Street, London SW1H 0QT
T 020-7976 3900 E info@sportandrecreation.org.uk
W www.sportandrecreation.org.uk
*Chief Executive,* Emma Borgis
SPORT ENGLAND, 1st Floor, 21 Bloomsbury Street,
London WC1B 3HF T 0845-850 8508
E info@sportengland.org W www.sportengland.org
*Chief Executive,* Jennie Price
SPORT NORTHERN IRELAND, House of Sport,
2A Upper Malone Road, Belfast BT9 5LA T 028-9038 1222
E info@sportni.net W www.sportni.net
*Chief Executive,* Antoinette McKeown
SPORTSCOTLAND, Doges, Templeton on the Green,
62 Templeton Street, Glasgow G40 1DA T 0141-534 6500
E website@sportscotland.org.uk W www.sportscotland.org.uk
*Chief Executive,* Stewart Harris
SPORT WALES, Sophia Gardens, Cardiff CF11 9SW
T 0300-300 3111 E info@sportwales.org.uk
W www.sportwales.org.uk
*Chief Executive,* Sarah Powell
UK SPORT, Ground Floor, 21 Bloomsbury Street,
London WC1B 3HF T 020-7211 5100 E info@uksport.gov.uk
W www.uksport.gov.uk
*Chief Executive,* Liz Nicholl, OBE

## AMERICAN FOOTBALL

BRITISH AMERICAN FOOTBALL ASSOCIATION,
West House, Hedley on the Hill, Stocksfield NE43 7SW
T 01661-843179 E bafachairman@gmail.com
W www.britishamericanfootball.org
*Chair,* Charles Macnamara

## ANGLING

ANGLING TRUST, Eastwood House, 6 Rainbow Street,
Leominster, Herefordshire HR6 8DQ T 0844-770 0616
E admin@anglingtrust.net W www.anglingtrust.net
*Chief Executive,* Mark Lloyd

## ARCHERY

ARCHERY GB, Lilleshall National Sports Centre,
Newport TF10 9AT T 01952-677888
E enquiries@archerygb.org W www.archerygb.org
*Chief Executive,* David Sherratt

## ASSOCIATION FOOTBALL

FOOTBALL ASSOCIATION, Wembley Stadium,
PO Box 1966, SW1P 9EQ T 0844-980 8200 E info@thefa.com
W www.thefa.com
*Chair,* Greg Dyke
FOOTBALL ASSOCIATION OF WALES, 11–12 Neptune
Court, Vanguard Way, Cardiff CF24 5PJ T 029-2043 5830
E info@faw.co.uk W www.faw.org.uk
*Chief Executive,* Jonathan Ford
FOOTBALL LEAGUE, Edward VII Quay, Navigation Way,
Preston PR2 2YF T 0844-463 1888
E enquiries@football-league.co.uk
W www.football-league.co.uk
*Chief Executive,* Shaun Harvey
IRISH FOOTBALL ASSOCIATION, 20 Windsor Avenue,
Belfast BT9 6EG T 028-9066 9458 E info@irishfa.com
W www.irishfa.com
*Chief Executive,* Patrick Nelson

PREMIER LEAGUE, 30 Gloucester Place, London W1U 8PL
T 020-7864 9000 E info@premierleague.com
W www.premierleague.com
*Chief Executive,* Richard Scudamore
SCOTTISH FOOTBALL ASSOCIATION, Hampden Park,
Glasgow G42 9AY T 0141-616 6000 E info@scottishfa.co.uk
W www.scottishfa.co.uk
*Chief Executive,* Stewart Regan
SCOTTISH PROFESSIONAL FOOTBALL LEAGUE,
The National Stadium, Hampden Park, Glasgow G42 9DE
T 0141-620 4160 E info@spfl.co.uk W www.spfl.co.uk
*Chief Executive,* Neil Doncaster

## ATHLETICS

ATHLETICS NORTHERN IRELAND, Athletics House,
Old Coach Road, Belfast BT9 5PR T 028-9060 2707
E info@athleticsni.org W www.athleticsni.org
*General Secretary,* John Allen
SCOTTISH ATHLETICS, Caledonia House, South Gyle,
Edinburgh EH12 9DQ T 0131-539 7320
E admin@scottishathletics.org.uk
W www.scottishathletics.org.uk
*Chief Executive,* Nigel Holl
UK ATHLETICS, Athletics House, Alexander Stadium,
Walsall Road, Birmingham B42 2BE T 0121-713 8400
E enquiries@englandathletics.org
W www.britishathletics.org.uk
*Chief Executive,* Niels de Vos
WELSH ATHLETICS, Cardiff International Sports Stadium,
Leckwith Road, Cardiff CF11 8AZ T 029-2064 4870
E office@welshathletics.org W www.welshathletics.org
*Chief Executive,* Matt Newman

## BADMINTON

BADMINTON ENGLAND, National Badminton Centre,
Bradwell Road, Milton Keynes MK8 9LA T 01908-268400
E enquiries@badmintonengland.co.uk
W www.badmintonengland.co.uk
*Chief Executive,* Adrian Christy
BADMINTON SCOTLAND, Cockburn Centre,
40 Bogmoor Place, Glasgow G51 4TQ T 0141-445 1218
E enquiries@badmintonscotland.org.uk
W www.badmintonscotland.org.uk
*Chief Executive,* Anne Smillie
BADMINTON WALES, Sport Wales National Centre,
Sophia Gardens, Cardiff CF11 9SW T 0300-300 3124
E wbu@badmintonwales.net W www.badmintonwales.net
*Chief Executive,* Eddie O'Neill

## BASEBALL

BASEBALLSOFTBALL UK, Ariel House,
74A Charlotte Street, London W1T 4QJ T 020-7453 7055
W www.baseballsoftballuk.com
*Chief Executive,* Jenny Fromer

## BASKETBALL

BASKETBALL ENGLAND, English Institute of Sport, Sheffield
S9 5DA T 0114-284 1060 E info@basketballengland.co.uk
W www.basketballengland.co.uk
*Chief Executive,* Mark Clark
BASKETBALL SCOTLAND, Caledonia House, South Gyle,
Edinburgh EH12 9DQ T 0131-317 7260
E enquiries@basketball-scotland.com
W www.basketballscotland.co.uk
*Chief Executive,* Kevin Pringle

# BILLIARDS AND SNOOKER
**WORLD SNOOKER**, 75 Whiteladies Road, Clifton,
Bristol BS8 2NT **T** 0117-317 8200 **E** info@worldsnooker.com
**W** www.worldsnooker.com
*Chair,* Jason Ferguson

# BOBSLEIGH
**BRITISH BOBSLEIGH AND SKELETON ASSOCIATION**,
Sports Training Village, University of Bath, Bath BA2 7AY
**T** 01225-383696 **E** office@britishskeleton.co.uk
**W** www.britishskeleton.co.uk
*Chair,* Lord Clifton Wrottesley

# BOWLS
**BOWLS ENGLAND**, Riverside House, Milverton Hill,
Royal Leamington Spa CV32 5HZ **T** 01926-334609
**E** enquiries@bowlsengland.com **W** www.bowlsengland.com
*Chief Executive,* Tony Allcock, MBE
**BRITISH ISLES BOWLS COUNCIL**, 12/1 Oxgangs Avenue,
Edinburgh EH13 9JB **T** 01314-455838
**E** bibcsecretary@aol.co.uk **W** www.britishislesbowls.com
*Hon. Secretary,* Duncan McLaren
**ENGLISH INDOOR BOWLING ASSOCIATION**,
David Cornwell House, Bowling Green, Melton Mowbray
LE13 0FA **T** 01664-481900 **E** enquiries@eiba.co.uk
**W** www.eiba.co.uk
*Chief Executive,* Peter Thompson

# BOXING
**AMATEUR BOXING ASSOCIATION OF ENGLAND**,
English Institute of Sport, Coleridge Road, Sheffield S9 5DA
**T** 0114-223 5654 **W** www.abae.co.uk
*Chief Executive,* Mark Abberley
**BRITISH BOXING BOARD OF CONTROL**, 14 North Road,
Cardiff CF10 3DY **T** 029-2036 7000 **E** admin@bbbofc.com
**W** www.bbbofc.com
*General Secretary,* Robert Smith

# CANOEING
**BRITISH CANOE UNION**, National Water Sport Centre,
Adbolton Lane, Nottingham NG12 2LU **T** 0845-370 9500
**E** info@britishcanoeing.org.uk
**W** www.britishcanoeunion.org.uk
*Chief Executive,* Paul Owen

# CHESS
**ENGLISH CHESS FEDERATION**, The Watch Oak,
Chain Lane, Battle TN33 0YD **T** 01424-775222
**E** office@englishchess.org.uk **W** www.englishchess.org.uk
*Chief Executive,* Phil Ehr

# CRICKET
**ENGLAND AND WALES CRICKET BOARD**,
Lord's Cricket Ground, London NW8 8QZ **T** 020-7432 1200
**E** feedback@ecb.co.uk **W** www.ecb.co.uk
*Chief Executive,* Tom Harrison
**MCC**, Lord's Cricket Ground, St John's Wood, London NW8 8QN
**T** 020-7616 8500 **E** reception@mcc.org.uk **W** www.lords.org
*Chief Executive and Secretary,* Derek Brewer

# CROQUET
**CROQUET ASSOCIATION**, Old Bath Road, Cheltenham
GL53 7DF **T** 01242-242318 **E** caoffice@croquet.org.uk
**W** www.croquet.org.uk
*Manager,* Elizabeth Larsson

# CURLING
**BRITISH CURLING**, Cairnie House, Ingleston EH28 8NB
**T** 0131-333 3003 **E** info@britishcurling.com
**W** www.britishcurling.org.uk
*Chief Operating Officer,* Bruce Crawford

**ROYAL CALEDONIAN CURLING CLUB**, Cairnie House,
Ingliston, Newbridge EH28 8NB **T** 0131-333 3003
**E** office@royalcaledoniancurlingclub.org
**W** www.royalcaledoniancurlingclub.org
*Chief Executive,* Bruce Crawford

# CYCLING
**BRITISH CYCLING FEDERATION**, Stuart Street,
Manchester M11 4DQ **T** 0161-274 2000
**E** info@britishcycling.org.uk **W** www.britishcycling.org.uk
*Chief Executive,* Ian Drake

# DARTS
**BRITISH DARTS ORGANISATION**, Unit 4,
Glan-y-Llyn Industrial Estate, Taffs Well, Cardiff CF15 7JD
**T** 02920-811815 **E** britishdartsorg@btconnect.com
**W** www.bdodarts.com
*Director,* Wayne Williams

# EQUESTRIANISM
**BRITISH EQUESTRIAN FEDERATION**, Abbey Park,
Kenilworth CV8 2RH **T** 02476-698871 **E** info@bef.co.uk
**W** www.bef.co.uk
*Chief Executive,* Andrew Finding, OBE
**BRITISH EVENTING**, Abbey Park, Kenilworth CV8 2RN
**T** 024-7669 8856 **E** info@britisheventing.com
**W** www.britisheventing.com
*Chief Executive,* Mike Etherington-Smith

# ETON FIVES
**ETON FIVES ASSOCIATION**, 45 Sandhills Crescent,
Hillfield, Solihull B91 3UE **T** 07833-600230
**E** efa@etonfives.co.uk **W** www.fivesonline.net
*Chair,* Richard Black

# FENCING
**BRITISH FENCING**, 1 Baron's Gate, 33 Rothschild Road,
London W4 5HT **T** 020-8742 3032
**E** headoffice@britishfencing.com **W** www.britishfencing.com
*Chief Executive,* Georgina Usher

# GLIDING
**BRITISH GLIDING ASSOCIATION**, 8 Merus Court,
Meridian Business Park, Leicester LE19 1RJ
**T** 0116-289 2956 **E** office@gliding.co.uk
**W** www.gliding.co.uk
*Chief Executive,* Pete Stratten

# GOLF
**ENGLAND GOLF**, The National Golf Centre, Woodhall Spa
LN10 6PU **T** 01526-354500 **E** info@englandgolf.org
**W** www.englandgolf.org
*Chief Executive,* David Joy
**LADIES' GOLF UNION**, The Scores, St Andrews KY16 9AT
**T** 01334-475811 **E** info@lgu.org **W** www.lgu.org
*Chief Executive,* vacant
**THE ROYAL AND ANCIENT GOLF CLUB**, Golf Place,
St Andrews KY16 9JD **T** 01334-460000
**E** thesecretary@randagc.org **W** www.randa.org
*Secretary,* Martin Slumbers

# GYMNASTICS
**BRITISH GYMNASTICS**, Ford Hall, Lilleshall National Sports
Centre, Newport TF10 9NB **T** 0845-129 7129
**E** information@british-gymnastics.org
**W** www.british-gymnastics.org
*Chief Executive,* Jane Allen

## HANDBALL

ENGLAND HANDBALL, The Halliwell Jones Stadium,
Winwick Road, Warrington WA2 7NE T 01925 246482
E handball@englandhandball.com
W www.englandhandball.com
*Chief Executive,* David Meli

## HOCKEY

ENGLAND HOCKEY, Bisham Abbey National Sports Centre,
Marlow SL7 1RR T 01628-897500 E info@englandhockey.co.uk
W www.englandhockey.co.uk
*Chief Executive,* Sally Munday
HOCKEY WALES, Sport Wales National Centre, Sophie
Gardens, Cardiff CF11 9SW T 0300-300 3126
E info@hockeywales.org.uk W www.hockeywales.org.uk
*Chief Executive,* Helen Bushell
SCOTTISH HOCKEY UNION, Glasgow National Hockey
Centre, 8 King's Drive, Glasgow G40 1HB T 0141-550 5999
W www.scottish-hockey.org.uk
*Chief Executive,* David Sweetman

## HORSERACING

BRITISH HORSERACING AUTHORITY,
75 High Holborn, London WC1V 6LS T 020-7152 0000
E info@britishhorseracing.com W www.britishhorseracing.com
*Chief Executive,* Nick Rust
THE JOCKEY CLUB, 75 High Holborn, London WC1V 6LS
T 020-7611 1800 E info@thejockeyclub.co.uk
W www.thejockeyclub.co.uk
*Chief Executive,* Simon Bazalgette

## ICE SKATING

NATIONAL ICE SKATING ASSOCIATION, Grains Building,
High Cross Street, Hockley, Nottingham NG1 3AX T 0115-988
8060 E info@iceskating.org.uk W www.iceskating.org.uk
*Chief Executive,* Nick Sellwood

## LACROSSE

ENGLISH LACROSSE ASSOCIATION, Wenlock Way
Offices, Wenlock Way, Manchester M12 5DH T 0843-658 5006
E info@englishlacrosse.co.uk W www.englishlacrosse.co.uk
*Chief Executive,* Mark Coups

## LAWN TENNIS

LAWN TENNIS ASSOCIATION, National Tennis Centre,
100 Priory Lane, London SW15 5JQ T 020-8487 7000
E info@lta.org.uk W www.lta.org.uk
*Chief Executive,* Michael Downey

## MARTIAL ARTS

BRITISH JUDO ASSOCIATION, Suite B, Loughborough
Technology Centre, Epinal Way, Loughborough LE11 3GE
T 01509-631670 E bja@britishjudo.org.uk
W www.britishjudo.org.uk
*Chief Executive,* Andrew Scoular
BRITISH JU JITSU ASSOCIATION, 5 Avenue Parade,
Accrington BB5 6PN T 03333-202039 E bjjagb@icloud.com
W www.bjjagb.com
*Chair,* Prof. Martin Dixon
BRITISH TAEKWONDO, 4 Tinshill Lane, Leeds Ls16 7AP
E admin@britishtaekwondo.org
W www.britishtaekwondo.org.uk
*Chair,* Adrian Tranter

## MODERN PENTATHLON

PENTATHLON GB, 22/23 Eastwood, University of Bath,
Claverton Down, Bath BA2 7AY T 01225-386808
E admin@pentathlongb.org W www.pentathlongb.org
*Chief Executive,* Nigel Laughton

## MOTOR SPORTS

AUTO-CYCLE UNION, ACU House, Wood Street,
Rugby CV21 2YX T 01788-566400 E admin@acu.org.uk
W www.acu.org.uk
*General Secretary,* Gary Thompson, MBE
MOTOR SPORTS ASSOCIATION, Motor Sports House,
Riverside Park, Colnbrook, SL3 0HG T 01753-765000
W www.msauk.org
*Chief Executive,* Rob Jones
SCOTTISH AUTO CYCLE UNION, 28 West Main Street,
Uphall EH52 5DW T 01506-858354 E office@sacu.co.uk
W www.sacu.co.uk
*President,* Ian Barnes

## MOUNTAINEERING

BRITISH MOUNTAINEERING COUNCIL,
The Old Church, 177–179 Burton Road, Manchester M20 2BB
T 0161-445 6111 E office@thebmc.co.uk
W www.thebmc.co.uk
*Chief Executive,* Dave Turnbull

## MULTI-SPORTS BODIES

BRITISH OLYMPIC ASSOCIATION, 60 Charlotte Street,
London W1T 2NU T 020-7842 5700 E boa@boa.org.uk
W www.teamgb.com
*Chief Executive,* Bill Sweeney
BRITISH PARALYMPIC ASSOCIATION,
60 Charlotte Street, London W1T 2NU T 020-7842 5789
E info@paralympics.org.uk W www.paralympics.org.uk
*Chief Executive,* Tim Hollingsworth
BRITISH UNIVERSITIES AND COLLEGES SPORT,
20–24 Kings Bench Street, London SE1 0QX
T 020-7633 5080 W www.bucs.org.uk
*Chief Executive,* Karen Rothery
COMMONWEALTH GAMES ENGLAND,
307–308 High Holborn, National Sports Centre,
London WC1V 7LL T 020-7831 3444 E info@weareengland.org
W www.weareengland.org
*Chief Executive,* Paul Blanchard
COMMONWEALTH GAMES FEDERATION,
CAN Mezzanine, 49–51 East Road, London N1 6AH
T 020-7250 8118 E info@thecgf.com W www.thecgf.com
*Chief Executive,* David Grevemberg
ENGLISH FEDERATION OF DISABILITY SPORT,
Loughborough University, 3 Oakwood Drive,
Loughborough LE11 3QF T 01509-227750 W www.efds.co.uk
*Chief Executive,* Barry Horne

## NETBALL

ENGLAND NETBALL, Netball House, 1–12 Old Park Road,
Hitchin SG5 2JR T 01462-442344 E info@englandnetball.co.uk
W www.englandnetball.co.uk
*Chief Executive,* Joanna Adams
NETBALL NI, Unit F, Curley Pavilion, Portside Business Park,
189 Airport Road West, Belfast BT3 9ED T 028-9073 6320
W www.netballni.org
*Hon. President,* Lorraine Lindsay
NETBALL SCOTLAND, Emirates Arena, 1000 London Road,
Glasgow G40 3HY T 0141-428 3460
E membership@netballscotland.com
W www.netballscotland.com
*Chief Executive,* Maggie Murray
WELSH NETBALL ASSOCIATION, Sport Wales National
Centre, Sophia Gardens, Cardiff CF11 9SW
T 0845-045 4302 E welshnetball@welshnetball.com
W www.welshnetball.co.uk
*Chief Executive,* Alun Davies

## ORIENTEERING

BRITISH ORIENTEERING, Scholes Mill, Old Coach Road, Darley Dale, Matlock DE4 5FY T 01629-583037 E info@britishorienteering.org.uk W www.britishorienteering.org.uk
*Chief Executive*, Mike Hamilton

## POLO

THE HURLINGHAM POLO ASSOCIATION, Manor Farm, Little Coxwell, Faringdon SN7 7LW T 01367-242828 E enquiries@hpa-polo.co.uk W www.hpa-polo.co.uk
*Chief Executive*, David Woodd

## RACKETS AND REAL TENNIS

TENNIS AND RACKETS ASSOCIATION, c/o The Queen's Club, Palliser Road, London W14 9EQ T 020-7835 6937 E office@tennisandrackets.com W www.tennisandrackets.com
*Chief Executive*, C. S. Davies

## ROWING

BRITISH ROWING, 6 Lower Mall, Hammersmith, London W6 9DJ T 020-8237 6700 E info@gbrowningteam.org.uk W www.britishrowing.org
*Chief Executive*, Andy Parkinson
HENLEY ROYAL REGATTA, Regatta Headquarters, Henley-on-Thames RG9 2LY T 01491-572153 W www.hrr.co.uk
*Secretary*, D. G. M. Grist

## RUGBY LEAGUE

BRITISH AMATEUR RUGBY LEAGUE ASSOCIATION, West Yorkshire House, 4 New North Parade, Huddersfield HD1 5JP T 01484-599113 E secretary@barla.org.uk W www.barla.org.uk
*Chair*, Sue Taylor
RUGBY FOOTBALL LEAGUE, Red Hall, Red Hall Lane, Leeds LS17 8NB T 0844-477 7113 E enquiries@rfl.uk.com W www.therfl.co.uk
*Chief Executive*, Nigel Wood

## RUGBY UNION

IRISH RUGBY FOOTBALL UNION, 10–12 Lansdowne Road, Ballsbridge, Dublin 4 T (+353) 1647 3800 E info@irishrugby.ie W www.irishrugby.ie
*Chief Executive*, Philip Browne
RUGBY FOOTBALL UNION, Rugby House, Twickenham Stadium, 200 Whitton Road, Twickenham TW2 7BA T 0871-222 2120 E enquiries@therfu.com W www.rfu.com
*Chief Executive*, Ian Ritchie
RUGBY FOOTBALL UNION FOR WOMEN, Rugby House, Twickenham Stadium, 200 Whitton Road, Twickenham, TW2 7BA T 0871-222 2120 E enquiries@therfu.com W www.rfu.com
*Managing Director*, Rosie Williams
SCOTTISH RUGBY UNION, Murrayfield, Edinburgh EH12 5PJ T 0131-346 5000 E feedback@sru.org.uk W www.scottishrugby.org
*Chief Executive*, Mark Dodson
SCOTTISH WOMEN'S RUGBY UNION, Scottish Rugby Union, Murrayfield, Edinburgh EH12 5PJ T 0131-346 5000 E feedback@sru.org.uk W www.scottishrugby.org
*Chief Executive*, Mark Dodson
WELSH RUGBY UNION, Millennium Stadium, Westgate Street, Cardiff CF10 1NS T 0844-249 1999 E info@wru.co.uk W www.wru.co.uk
*Chief Executive*, Roger Lewis

## SHOOTING

BRITISH SHOOTING, Bisham Abbey National Sports Centre, Marlow Road, Bisham, Marlow SL7 1RR T 01628-488800 E admin@britishshooting.org.uk W www.britishshooting.org.uk
*Chief Executive*, Hamish McInnes
CLAY PIGEON SHOOTING ASSOCIATION, Edmonton House, National Shooting Centre, Brookwood, Woking GU24 0NP T 01483-485400 E info@cpsa.co.uk W www.cpsa.co.uk
*Chief Executive*, Nick Fellows
NATIONAL RIFLE ASSOCIATION, Bisley, Brookwood, GU24 0PB T 01483-797777 E info@nra.org.uk W www.nra.org.uk
*Chief Executive*, Andrew Mercer
NATIONAL SMALL-BORE RIFLE ASSOCIATION, Lord Roberts Centre, Bisley Camp, Brookwood, Woking GU24 0NP T 01483-485505 W www.nsra.co.uk
*Chair*, Robert Newman

## SNOWBOARDING

BRITISH SKI AND SNOWBOARD, 60 Charlotte Street, London W1T 2NU T 020-7842 5764 E bss@teambss.org.uk W www.teambss.org.uk
*Chief Executive*, Dave Edwards

## SPEEDWAY

BRITISH SPEEDWAY, ACU Headquarters, Wood Street, Rugby CV21 2YX T 01788-560648 E office@speedwaygb.co W www.speedwaygb.co
*Chair*, Alex Harkess

## SQUASH

ENGLAND SQUASH AND RACKETBALL, National Squash Centre, Sportcity, Manchester M11 3FF T 0161-231 4499 E enquiries@englandsquashandracketball.com W www.englandsquashandracketball.com
*Chief Executive*, Keir Worth
SCOTTISH SQUASH AND RACKETBALL LIMITED, Caledonia House, 1 Redheughs Rigg, South Gyle, Edinburgh EH12 9DQ T 0131-625 4425 E info@scottishsquash.org W www.scottishsquash.org
*Chief Executive*, Shonagh MacVicar
WALES SQUASH AND RACKETBALL, Sport Wales National Centre, Sophia Close, Cardiff CF11 9SW T 0845-045 0902 W www.walessquashandracketball.co.uk
*Chair*, Phil Brailey

## SUB-AQUA

BRITISH SUB-AQUA CLUB, Telford's Quay, South Pier Road, Ellesmere Port CH65 4FL T 0151-350 6200 E info@bsac.com W www.bsac.com
*Chief Executive*, Mary Tetley

## SWIMMING

AMATEUR SWIMMING ASSOCIATION, Pavilion 3, Sport Park, 3 Oakwood Drive, Loughborough LE11 3QF T 01509-618700 E customerservices@swimming.org W www.swimming.org
*Chief Executive*, A. Paker
SCOTTISH SWIMMING, National Swimming Academy, University of Stirling, Stirling, FK9 4LA T 01786-466520 E info@scottishswimming.com W www.scottishswimming.com
*Chief Executive*, Forbes Dunlop
SWIM WALES, WNPS, Sketty Lane, Swansea SA2 8QG T 01792-513636 W www.swimwales.org
*Chief Executive*, Robert James

## TABLE TENNIS

ENGLISH TABLE TENNIS ASSOCIATION, Norfolk House,
88 Saxon Gate West, Milton Keynes MK9 2DL
T 01908-208860 E help@tabletennisengland.co.uk
W www.tabletennisengland.co.uk
*Chief Executive,* Sara Sutcliffe
TABLE TENNIS SCOTLAND, Caledonia House, South Gyle,
Edinburgh EH12 9DQ T 0131-317 8077
E ttsadmin@btconnect.com W www.tabletennisscotland.com
*Chair,* Terry McLernon
TABLE TENNIS WALES, Glanrhyd, Ebbw View, Beaufort,
Ebbw Vale NP23 5NU T 01244-571335 W www.ttaw.co.uk
*Chair,* Bernard Carter

## TRIATHLON

BRITISH TRIATHLON, PO Box 25, Loughborough LE11 3WX
T 01509-226161 E info@britishtriathlon.org
W www.britishtriathlon.org
*Chief Executive,* Jack Buckner

## VOLLEYBALL

NORTHERN IRELAND VOLLEYBALL ASSOCIATION,
21 Broughton Park, Belfast BT6 0BD W www.nivolleyball.com
*General Secretary,* Johnny McClenaghan
SCOTTISH VOLLEYBALL ASSOCIATION,
48 The Pleasance, Edinburgh EH8 9TJ T 0131-556 4633
W www.scottishvolleyball.org
*Chief Executive,* Margaret Ann Fleming
VOLLEYBALL ENGLAND, SportPark,
Loughborough University, 3 Oakwood Drive,
Loughborough LE11 3QF T 01509-227722
E info@volleyballengland.org W www.volleyballengland.org
*Chief Executive,* Lisa Wainwright
VOLLEYBALL WALES, 13 Beckgrove Close, Pengam Green,
Cardiff CF24 2SE T 029-2041 6537
E ysaker@volleyballwales.org W www.volleyballwales.org
*Chair,* Yvonne Saker

## WALKING

RACE WALKING ASSOCIATION, Hufflers, Heard's Lane,
Shenfield, Brentwood CM15 0SF T 01277-220687
E racewalkingassociation@btinternet.com
W www.racewalkingassociation.org.uk
*Hon. General Secretary,* Peter Cassidy

## WATER SKIING

BRITISH WATER SKI AND WAKEBOARD, The Forum,
Hanworth Lane, Chertsey, KT16 9JX T 01932-560007
E info@bwsf.co.uk W www.bwsw.org.uk
*Chief Executive,* Patrick Donovan

## WEIGHTLIFTING

BRITISH WEIGHT LIFTING, Belmont House, 20 Wood Lane,
Leeds LS6 2AE T 0113-224 9402
E enquiries@britishweightlifting.org
W www.britishweightlifting.org
*Chief Executive,* Ashley Metcalfe

## WRESTLING

BRITISH WRESTLING ASSOCIATION, 12 Westwood Lane,
Chesterfield S43 1PA T 01246-236443
E admin@britishwrestling.org W www.britishwrestling.org
*Chief Executive,* Colin Nicholson

## YACHTING

ROYAL YACHTING ASSOCIATION, RYA House,
Ensign Way, Hamble, Southampton SO31 4YA
T 023-8060 4100 W www.rya.org.uk
*Chief Executive,* Sarah Treseder

# CLUBS

Originally called gentlemen's clubs, these organisations are permanent institutions with a fixed clubhouse, which usually includes restaurants, bars, a library and overnight accommodation. Members are fee-paying and typically vetted for their suitability.

Gentlemen's clubs were created for males of the English upper class and grew out of the 17th-century fashion for coffee houses which enjoyed enormous popularity, despite opposition from Charles II, who believed they encouraged the spreading of royal disaffection. The first of the London clubs – White's – was founded in 1693 by Francesco Bianco in St James's Street, in the area that quickly became known as 'clubland'. Membership to the first of the clubs was a matter of hereditary privilege or special favour, a deliberately exclusionary measure which prompted an enormous growth in the number of clubs throughout the 19th century, fed by a burgeoning and aspirational middle class.

At the turn of the 20th century, there were more than 200 gentlemen's clubs in London alone, half of which had been founded since 1870. Inevitably, this level of competition could not be sustained, particularly given the number of men killed in two world wars. Financial restrictions necessitated greater provision for women and the relaxation of the social qualifications needed for membership. Nevertheless, waiting lists still exist for the leading clubs and a recommendation from at least one current member is almost always required to join.

ARMY AND NAVY CLUB (1837), 36 Pall Mall, London SW1Y 5JN T 020-7930 9721 E secretary@therag.co.uk W www.armynavyclub.co.uk
*Chief Executive and Secretary,* Ayres de Souza
*Former member:* The Duke of Wellington
ARTS CLUB (1863), 40 Dover Street, London W1S 4NP T 020-7499 8581 E reservations@theartsclub.co.uk W www.theartsclub.co.uk
*Secretary,* Rémy Lysé
*Former members:* Charles Dickens, Algernon Charles Swinburne, Ivan Turgenev
ATHENAEUM (1824), 107 Pall Mall, London SW1Y 5ER T 020-7930 4843 E library@hellenist.org.uk W www.athenaeumclub.co.uk
*Secretary,* J. H. Ford
*Former members:* Matthew Arnold, Michael Faraday, Anthony Trollope
ATHENAEUM (1797), Church Alley, Liverpool L1 3DD T 0151-709 7770 E reception@theathenaeum.org.uk W www.theathenaeum.org.uk
*Hon. Secretary,* David Honour
*Former members:* William H. Duncan, William Roscoe
AUTHORS' CLUB (1891), c/o National Liberal Club, Whitehall Place, London SW1A 2HE T 020-7287 3381 E info@authorsclub.co.uk
*Honorary Secretary,* Victoria Carew Hunt
*Former members:* Arthur Conan Doyle, Graham Greene, Thomas Hardy, H. G. Wells, Oscar Wilde
BEEFSTEAK CLUB* (1876), 9 Irving Street, London WC2H 7AH T 020-7930 5722 E office@thebeefsteakclub.co.uk
*Secretary,* Maria Hibbert
*Former members:* John Betjeman, Rudyard Kipling, Harold Macmillan
BOODLE'S* (1762), 28 St James's Street, London SW1A 1HJ T 020-7930 7166 E secretary@boodles.org
*Secretary,* Andrew Phillips
*Former members:* Winston Churchill, Ian Fleming

BROOKS'S* (1764), St James's Street, London SW1A 1LN T 020-7493 4411 E secretary@brooksclub.org
*Secretary,* Ian Faul
*Former members:* Edward Gibbon, Roy Jenkins, William Pitt
BUCK'S CLUB* (1919), 18 Clifford Street, London W1S 3RF T 020-7734 2337 E secretary@bucksclub.co.uk
*Secretary,* Maj. Rupert Lendrum
CALEDONIAN CLUB (1891), 9 Halkin Street, London SW1X 7DR T 020-7235 5162 E admin@caledonianclub.com W www.caledonianclub.com
*Secretary,* Ian Campbell
CANNING CLUB (1910), 4 St James's Square, London SW1Y 4JU T 020-7827 5768 E canningclub@theinandout.co.uk W www.theinandout.co.uk
*Secretary,* Sarah Sinclair
CARLTON CLUB (1832), 69 St James's Street, London SW1A 1PJ T 020-7493 1164 E info@carltonclub.co.uk W www.carltonclub.co.uk
*Secretary,* Sandra Boffa
*Former members:* Stanley Baldwin, Benjamin Disraeli, Harold Macmillan, John Major, Margaret Thatcher
CAVALRY AND GUARDS CLUB (1890), 127 Piccadilly, London W1J 7PX T 020-7499 1261 E secretary@cavgds.co.uk W www.cavgds.co.uk
*Secretary,* David Cowdery
*Former member:* Lawrence Oates
CHELSEA ARTS CLUB (1891), 143 Old Church Street, London SW3 6EB T 020-7376 3311 E office@chelseaartsclub.com W www.chelseaartsclub.com
*Secretary,* David Cowdery
*Former members:* Laurie Lee, John Singer Sargent, Walter Sickert, James McNeill Whistler
CITY LIVERY CLUB (1914), Bell Wharf Lane, Upper Thames Street, London EC4R 3TB T 020-7248 0620 E clerk@cityliveryclub.com W www.cityliveryclub.com
*Hon. Secretary,* Dr Trevor Brignall
CITY OF LONDON CLUB (1832), 19 Old Broad Street, London EC2N 1DS T 020-7588 7991 E secretary@cityoflondonclub.com W www.cityoflondonclub.com
*Secretary,* Edward James
*Former members:* Robert Peel, Duke of Wellington
CITY UNIVERSITY CLUB (1895), 50 Cornhill, London EC3V 3PD T 020-7626 8571 E secretary@cityuniversityclub.co.uk W www.cityuniversityclub.co.uk
*Secretary,* Mary Anne Salisbury
EAST INDIA CLUB* (1849), 16 St James's Square, London SW1Y 4LH T 020-7930 1000 E secretary@eastindiaclub.co.uk W www.eastindiaclub.co.uk
*Secretary,* Alex Bray
FARMERS CLUB (1842), 3 Whitehall Court, London SW1A 2EL T 020-7930 3557 E reception@thefarmersclub.com W www.thefarmersclub.com
*Secretary,* Air Cdre Stephen Skinner
FOX CLUB (2003), 46 Clarges Street, London W1J 7ER T 020-7495 3656 E essi@foxclublondon.com W www.foxclublondon.com
*General Manager,* Bethan Seaton
GARRICK CLUB* (1831), 15 Garrick Street, London WC2E 9AY T 020-7379 6478 E hallporters@garrickclub.co.uk W www.garrickclub.co.uk
*Secretary,* Ann Robbie
*Former members:* Charles Dickens, William Thackeray

GROUCHO CLUB (1985), 45 Dean Street, London W1D 4QB
T 020-7439 4685 E reception@thegrouchoclub.com
W www.thegrouchoclub.com
*Manager,* Bernie Katz
HURLINGHAM CLUB (1869), Ranelagh Gardens,
London SW6 3PR T 020-7610 7400
E main.reception@hurlinghamclub.org.uk
W www.hurlinghamclub.org.uk
*Chief Executive,* Rear-Adm. Niall Kilgour, CB
IN & OUT (NAVAL AND MILITARY CLUB) (1862),
4 St James's Square, London SW1Y 4JU T 020-7827 5757
E club@theinandout.co.uk W www.theinandout.co.uk
*Secretary,* Lt. Col. Christopher Hogan
*Former member:* Robert Falcon Scott
LANSDOWNE CLUB (1935), 9 Fitzmaurice Place,
London W1J 5JD T 020-7629 7200
E secretary@LansdowneClub.com W www.lansdowneclub.com
*Secretary,* Tim Cagney
LONDON PRESS CLUB (1882), 7–10 Adam Street,
The Strand, London WC2N 6AA T 020-7520 9082
E info@londonpressclub.co.uk W www.londonpressclub.co.uk
*Secretary,* Brooke Jacobs
*Former members:* Lord Astor, Lord Rothermere
NATIONAL LIBERAL CLUB (1882), Whitehall Place,
London SW1A 2HE T 020-7930 9871 E secretary@nlc.org.uk
W www.nlc.org.uk
*Secretary,* Simon Roberts
*Former members:* Winston Churchill, William Gladstone,
Ramsay MacDonald, George Bernard Shaw, H. G. Wells
NEW CAVENDISH CLUB (1920), 44 Great Cumberland Place,
London W1H 7BS T 075-0350 4639
E info@newcavendishclub.co.uk
W www.newcavendishclub.co.uk
*Club Manager,* Alex Maitland
*Former member:* Lady Bonham-Carter
NEW CLUB (1787), 86 Princes Street, Edinburgh EH2 2BB
T 0131-226 4881 E info@newclub.co.uk
W www.newclub.co.uk
*Secretary,* Col. A. P. W. Campbell
*Former members:* Alec Douglas-Home, Walter Scott
NEW CLUB (1874), 2 Montpellier Parade, Cheltenham
GL50 1UD T 01242-541121 E secretary@thenewclub.co.uk
W www.thenewclub.co.uk
*Hon. Secretary,* Peter Walsh
NORFOLK CLUB (1770), 17 Upper King Street,
Norwich NR3 1RB T 01603-626767
E generalmanager@thenorfolkclub.co.uk
W www.thenorfolkclub.co.uk
*General Manager,* Lukasz Stachowicz
NORTHERN COUNTIES CLUB (1829), 11 Hood Street,
Newcastle upon Tyne NE1 6LH T 0191-232 2744
E secretary@northerncountiesclub.co.uk
W www.northerncountiesclub.co.uk
ORIENTAL CLUB (1824), Stratford House, Stratford Place,
London W1C 1ES T 020-7629 5126 E sec@orientalclub.org.uk
W www.orientalclub.org.uk
*Secretary,* M. Rivett
OXFORD AND CAMBRIDGE CLUB (1830), 71 Pall Mall,
London SW1Y 5HD T 020-7930 5151 E club@oandc.uk.com
W www.oxfordandcambridgeclub.co.uk
*Secretary,* Alistair Telfer
*Former members:* Clement Attlee, William Gladstone
PORTLAND CLUB (1816), 36 Pall Mall, London SW1Y 4ER
T 020-7930 0444
*Secretary,* John Burns, CBE
PRATT'S CLUB* (1841), 14 Park Place, London SW1A 1LP
T 020-7493 0397 E secretary@prattsclub.org
*Secretary,* Lt. Col. O. R. StJ. Breakwell, MBE
*Former member:* Winston Churchill

REFORM CLUB (1836), 104–105 Pall Mall, London SW1Y 5EW
T 020-7930 9374 E generaloffice@reformclub.com
W www.reformclub.com
*Secretary,* Crispin Morton
*Former members:* Isambard Kingdom Brunel, Guy Burgess,
Arthur Conan Doyle, Henry James, David Lloyd George
ROYAL AIR FORCE CLUB (1918), 128 Piccadilly,
London W1J 7PY T 020-7399 1000 E admin@rafclub.org.uk
W www.rafclub.org.uk
*Secretary,* Miles Pooley
ROYAL AUTOMOBILE CLUB (1897), 89 Pall Mall,
London SW1Y 5HS T 020-7930 2345
E secretary@royalautomobileclub.co.uk
W www.royalautomobileclub.co.uk
*Secretary,* Miles Wade, CBE
*Former members:* Winston Churchill, Rudyard Kipling,
Charles Rolls
ROYAL NORTHERN & UNIVERSITY CLUB* (1854),
9 Albyn Place, Aberdeen AB10 1YE T 01224-583292
E secretary@rnuc.org.uk W www.rnuc.org.uk
*Manager,* Ron Esslemont
ROYAL OVER-SEAS LEAGUE (1910), Over-Seas House,
Park Place, St James's Street, London SW1A 1LR
T 020-7408 0214 E info@rosl.org.uk W www.rosl.org.uk
*Director-General,* Maj.-Gen. Roddy Porter, MBE
SAVILE CLUB* (1868), 69 Brook Street, London W1K 4ER
T 020-7629 5462 W www.savileclub.co.uk
*Secretary,* Julian Malone-Lee
*Former members:* Max Beerbohm, Thomas Hardy,
Robert Louis Stevenson
SCOTTISH ARTS CLUB (1872), 24 Rutland Square,
Edinburgh EH1 2BW T 0131-229 8157
E office@scottishartsclub.co.uk W www.scottishartsclub.co.uk
*President,* Diana Allen
SLOANE CLUB (1976), Lower Sloane Street, London
SW1W 8BS T 020-7730 9131 E reservations@sloaneclub.co.uk
W www.sloaneclub.co.uk
*Membership Secretary,* Fran Bremner
TRAVELLERS CLUB* (1819), 106 Pall Mall, London SW1Y 5EP
T 020-7930 8688 E secretary@thetravellersclub.org.uk
W www.thetravellersclub.org.uk
*Secretary,* David Broadhead
*Former members:* Arthur Balfour, Alec Douglas-Home,
Anthony Powell, Sir Patrick Leigh-Fermor
TURF CLUB (1868), 5 Carlton House Terrace,
London SW1Y 5AQ T 020-7930 8555 E mail@turfclub.co.uk
*Secretary,* Col. A. J. E. Malcolm, OBE
ULSTER REFORM CLUB (1885), 4 Royal Avenue,
Belfast BT1 1DA T 028-9032 3411
E info@ulsterreformclub.com W www.ulsterreformclub.com
*Chief Executive,* A. W. Graham
UNIVERSITY WOMEN'S CLUB† (1886), 2 Audley Square,
London W1K 1DB T 020-7499 2268
E reservations@uwc-london.com
W www.universitywomensclub.com
*Chief Executive,* Cdr Rod Craig, RN
VINCENT'S* (1863), 1A King Edward Street, Oxford OX1 4HS
T 01865-722984 E bursar@vincents.org W www.vincents.org
*Bursar,* Stephen Eeley
*Former members:* Roger Bannister, King Edward VIII
WESTERN CLUB (1825), 32 Royal Exchange Square,
Glasgow G1 3AB T 0141-221 2016
E secretary@westernclub.co.uk W www.westernclub.co.uk
*Secretary,* Douglas Gifford
WHITE'S* (1693), 37–38 St James's Street, London SW1A 1JG
T 020-7493 6671
*Secretary,* D. A. Anderson
*Former members:* David Cameron, Evelyn Waugh

* Men only          † Women only

# CHARITIES AND SOCIETIES

The following is a selection of charities, societies and non-profit organisations in the UK and does not represent a comprehensive list. For professional and employment-related organisations, *see* Professional Education and Trade and Professional Bodies.

ACE CULTURAL TOURS (1958), Stapleford Granary, Bury Road, Stapleford, Cambridge CB22 5BP **T** 01223-841055 **E** ace@aceculturaltours.co.uk **W** www.aceculturaltours.co.uk
*General Secretary,* Paul Barnes
ACTIONAID (1972), 33–39 Bowling Green Lane, London EC1R 0BJ **T** 020-3122 0561 **E** mail@actionaid.org **W** www.actionaid.org
*Chief Executive,* Girish Menon
ACTION FOR BLIND PEOPLE (1857), 53 Sandgate Street, London SE15 1LE **T** 020-7635 4800 **E** helpline@rnib.org.uk **W** www.actionforblindpeople.org.uk
*Chief Executive,* Miriam Martin
ACTION FOR CHILDREN (1869), 3 The Boulevard, Watford WD18 8AG **T** 0300-123 2112 **E** ask.us@actionforchildren.org.uk **W** www.actionforchildren.org.uk
*Chief Executive,* Sir Tony Hawkhead
ACTION MEDICAL RESEARCH (1952), Vincent House, Horsham RH12 2DP **T** 01403-210406 **E** info@action.org.uk **W** www.action.org.uk
*Chief Executive,* Julie Buckler
ACTION ON HEARING LOSS (1911), 19–23 Featherstone Street, London EC1Y 8SL **T** 0808-808 0123, **Textphone** 0808-808 9000 **E** informationline@hearingloss.org.uk **W** www.actiononhearingloss.org.uk
*Chief Executive,* Paul Breckell
ACTORS' BENEVOLENT FUND (1882), 6 Adam Street, London WC2N 6AD **T** 020-7836 6378 **E** office@abf.org.uk **W** www.actorsbenevolentfund.co.uk
*General Secretary,* Stuart Crozier
ACTORS' CHILDREN'S TRUST (1896), 58 Bloomsbury Street, London WC1B 3QT **T** 020-7636 7868 **E** robert@tactactors.org **W** www.tactactors.org
*General Secretary,* Robert Ashby
ADAM SMITH INSTITUTE (1977), 23 Great Smith Street, London SW1P 3BL **T** 020-7222 4995 **W** www.adamsmith.org
*Director,* Dr Eamonn Butler
ADDACTION (1967), 67–69 Cowcross Street, London EC1M 6PU **T** 020-7251 5860 **E** info@addaction.org.uk **W** www.addaction.org.uk
*Chief Executive,* Simon Antrobus
ADVERTISING STANDARDS AUTHORITY (1962), Mid City Place, 71 High Holborn, London WC1V 6QT **T** 020-7492 2222 **W** www.asa.org.uk
*Chief Executive,* Guy Parker
AFASIC (1968), 1st Floor, Olive House, 20 Bowling Green Lane, London EC1R 0BD **T** 020-7490 9410 **E** info@afasic.org.uk **W** www.afasic.org.uk
*Chief Executive,* Linda Lascelles
AGE CYMRU (2010), Ty John Pathy, 13–14 Neptune Court, Vanguard Way, Cardiff CF24 5PJ **T** 029-2043 1555 **E** enquiries@agecymru.org.uk **W** www.agecymru.org.uk
*Chief Executive,* Robert Taylor
AGE SCOTLAND (1943), Causewayside House, 160 Causewayside, Edinburgh EH9 1PR **T** 0845-833 0200 **E** info@agescotland.org.uk **W** www.agescotland.org.uk
*Chief Executive,* Brian Sloan
AGE UK (2010), Tavis House, 1–6 Tavistock Square, London WC1H 9NA **T** 0800-169 6565 **E** contact@ageuk.org.uk **W** www.ageuk.org.uk
*Chief Executive,* Tom Wright, CBE

ALCOHOLICS ANONYMOUS (1947), PO Box 1, 10 Toft Green, York YO1 7NJ **T** 01904-644026, Helpline 0845-769 7555 **E** help@alcoholics-anonymous.org.uk **W** www.alcoholics-anonymous.org.uk
*General Secretary,* Roger Booth
ALEXANDRA ROSE CHARITIES (1912), 5 Mead Lane, Farnham GU9 7DY **T** 01252-726171 **W** www.alexandrarosecharities.org.uk
*National Director,* Margaret Stock
ALZHEIMER'S SOCIETY (1979), Devon House, 58 St Katharine's Way, London E1W 1LB **T** 020-7423 3500 **E** enquiries@alzheimers.org.uk **W** www.alzheimers.org.uk
*Chief Executive,* Jeremy Hughes
AMBITION (1925), 371 Kennington Lane, London SE11 5QY **T** 020-7793 0787 **E** info@ambitionuk.org **W** www.ambitionuk.org
*Chief Executive,* Helen Marshall
AMNESTY INTERNATIONAL UK (1961), The Human Rights Action Centre, 17–25 New Inn Yard, London EC2A 3EA **T** 020-7033 1500 **E** sct@amnesty.org.uk **W** www.amnesty.org.uk
*UK Director,* Kate Allen
AMREF UK (1957), 15–18 White Lion Street, London N1 9PD **T** 020-7269 5520 **E** info@amref.org **W** www.amrefuk.org
*Chief Executive,* Miranda Harington
ANCIENT MONUMENTS SOCIETY (1924), St Ann's Vestry Hall, 2 Church Entry, London EC4V 5HB **T** 020-7236 3934 **E** office@ancientmonumentssociety.org.uk **W** www.ancientmonumentssociety.org.uk
*Secretary,* M. J. Saunders, MBE
ANGLO-BELGIAN SOCIETY (1982), 8 Northumberland Avenue, London WC2N 5BY **E** secretary@anglo-belgiansoc.co.uk **W** www.anglobelgiansociety.com
*Chairman,* Caroline Colvin, OBE
ANGLO-DANISH SOCIETY (1924), 43 Maresfield Gardens, London NW3 5TF **T** 020-7794 8781 **E** info@anglo-danishsociety.org.uk **W** www.anglo-danishsociety.org.uk
*Chair,* Christian Williams
ANGLO-NORSE SOCIETY (1918), 25 Belgrave Square, London SW1X 8QD **T** 020-8452 4843 **E** secretariat@anglo-norse.org.uk **W** www.anglo-norse.org.uk
*Chair,* Sir Richard Dales, KCVO, CMG
ANIMAL CONCERN (1876), PO Box 5178, Dumbarton G82 5YJ **T** 01389-841639 **E** animals@jfrobins.force9.co.uk **W** www.animalconcern.org
*Secretary,* John F. Robins
ANIMAL HEALTH TRUST (1942), Lanwades Park, Kentford, Newmarket CB8 7UU **T** 01638-751000 **E** info@aht.org.uk **W** www.aht.org.uk
*Chief Executive,* Dr Mark Vaudin
ANTHONY NOLAN (1974), 2–3 Heathgate Place, 75–87 Agincourt Road, London NW3 2NU **T** 0303-303 0303 **E** info@anthonynolan.org **W** www.anthonynolan.org
*Chief Executive,* Henny Braund
ANTHROPOSOPHICAL SOCIETY IN GREAT BRITAIN (1923), Rudolf Steiner House, 35 Park Road, London NW1 6XT **T** 020-7723 4400 **E** rsh-office@anth.org.uk **W** www.rsh.anth.org.uk
*General Secretary,* Philip Martyn

ANTI-SLAVERY INTERNATIONAL (1839),
Thomas Clarkson House, The Stableyard, Broomgrove Road,
London SW9 9TL T 020-7501 8920 E info@antislavery.org
W www.antislavery.org
*Director,* Aidan McQuade

ARCHITECTS BENEVOLENT SOCIETY (1850),
43 Portland Place, London W1B 1QH T 020-7580 2823
E help@absnet.org.uk W www.absnet.org.uk
*CEO,* Robert Ball

ARCHITECTURAL HERITAGE FUND (1976),
15 Whitehall, London SW1A 2DD T 020-7925 0199
E ahf@ahfund.org.uk W www.ahfund.org.uk
*Chief Executive,* Ian Morrison

ARLIS/UK AND IRELAND (1969), The National Art Library,
Word & Image Department, Victoria & Albert Museum,
Cromwell Road, London SW7 2RL T 020-7942 2317
E arlis@vam.ac.uk W www.arlis.org.uk
*Chair,* Chris Fowler

ART FUND (1903), 2 Granary Square, King's Cross,
London N1C 4BH T 020-7225 4800 W www.artfund.org
*Director,* Dr Stephen Deuchar

ARTHRITIS CARE (1947), Linen Court, 10 East Road,
London N1 6AD T 020-7380 6500 E info@arthritiscare.org.uk
W www.arthritiscare.org.uk
*Chief Executive,* Judi Rhys

ASSOCIATION FOR LANGUAGE LEARNING (1990),
University of Leicester, University Road, Leicester LE1 7RH
T 0116-229 7602 E info@all-languages.org.uk
W www.all-languages.org.uk
*Director,* Rachel Middleton

ASSOCIATION FOR SCIENCE EDUCATION (1901),
College Lane, Hatfield AL10 9AA T 01707-283000
E info@ase.org.uk W www.ase.org.uk
*Chief Executive,* Shaun Reason

ASSOCIATION FOR THE PROTECTION OF RURAL
SCOTLAND (1926), 3rd Floor, Gladstone's Land,
483 Lawnmarket, Edinburgh EH1 2NT T 0131-225 7012
E info@ruralscotland.org W www.ruralscotland.btck.co.uk
*Director,* John Mayhew

ASSOCIATION OF FINANCIAL MUTUALS (1995),
7 Castle Hill, Caistor, LN7 6QL T 0844-879 7863
E martin@financialmutuals.org W www.financialmutuals.org
*Chief Executive,* Martin Shaw

ASSOCIATION OF GENEALOGISTS AND
RESEARCHERS IN ARCHIVES (1968), Box A,
14 Charterhouse Buildings, Goswell Road, London EC1M 7BA
E info@agra.org.uk W www.agra.org.uk
*Chairman,* Ian Waller

ASSOCIATION OF ROYAL NAVY OFFICERS (1920),
70 Porchester Terrace, London W2 3TP T 020-7402 5231
E asec@arno.org.uk W www.arno.org.uk
*Director,* Cdr Mike Goldthorpe

ASSOCIATION OF SPEAKERS CLUBS (1971),
40 Brougham Street, Greenock PA16 8AH
T 01475-806214 E national.secretary@the-asc.org.uk
W www.the-asc.org.uk
*National President,* Graham McLachlan

ASTHMA UK (1927), 18 Mansell Street, London E1 8AA
T 020-7786 4900 E info@asthma.org.uk
W www.asthma.org.uk
*Chief Executive,* Kay Boycott

AUDIT BUREAU OF CIRCULATIONS LTD (1931),
Saxon House, 211 High Street, Berkhamsted HP4 1AD
T 01442-870800 E comms@abc.org.uk W www.abc.org.uk
*Chair,* Sally Cartwright, OBE

AUTISM INITIATIVES (1971), 7 Chesterfield Road,
Liverpool L23 9XL T 0151-330 9500
E info@autisminitiatives.org W www.autisminitiatives.org
*Chair,* Brian Williams

AUTOMOBILE ASSOCIATION (1905), Fanum House,
Basing View, Basingstoke RG21 4EA T 0845-607 6727
E customer.services@theaa.com W www.theaa.com
*Executive Chairman,* Bob Mackenzie

BALTIC EXCHANGE (1744), 38 St Mary Axe,
London EC3A 8BH T 020-7283 9300
E enquiries@balticexchange.com
W www.balticexchange.com
*Chief Executive,* Jeremy Penn

BALTIC EXCHANGE CHARITABLE SOCIETY (1978),
38 St Mary Axe, London EC3A 8BH T 020-7283 6090
E enquiries@balticexchange.com W www.balticexchange.com
*Secretary,* R. J. M. Butler

BARNARDO'S (1866), Tanners Lane, Barkingside,
Ilford IG6 1QG T 020-8550 8822 W www.barnardos.org.uk
*Chief Executive,* Javed Khan

BARRISTERS' BENEVOLENT ASSOCIATION (1873),
14 Gray's Inn Square, London WC1R 5JP T 020-7242 4761
E enquiries@the-bba.com W www.the-bba.com
*Chair,* Terence Mowschenson, QC

BBC MEDIA ACTION (1999), New Broadcasting House,
Portland Place, London W1A 1AA T 020-8743 8000
E media.action@bbc.co.uk W www.bbc.co.uk/mediaaction
*Executive Director,* Caroline Nursey

BCS, THE CHARTERED INSTITUTE FOR IT (1957),
1st Floor, Block D, North Star House, North Star Avenue
SN2 1FA T 01793-417417 W www.bcs.org
*Chief Executive,* Paul Fletcher

BEAT (1989), Wensum House, 103 Prince of Wales Road,
Norwich NR1 1DW T 0300-123 3355,
**Helpline** 0845-634 1414, **Youthline** 0845-634 7650
E info@b-eat.co.uk W www.b-eat.co.uk
*Chief Executive,* Susan Ringwood

BEVIN BOY VETERANS (1989), 23 Great Cranford Street,
Poundbury, Dorchester DT1 3SQ T 01305-261269
E warwicktaylor@btinternet.com
W www.theforgottenconscript.co.uk
*President,* Warwick Taylor, MBE

BIBLE SOCIETY (1804), Stonehill Green, Westlea,
Swindon SN5 7DG T 01793-418222
E contactus@biblesociety.org.uk
W www.biblesociety.org.uk
*Chief Executive,* James Catford

BIBLIOGRAPHICAL SOCIETY (1892), c/o University of
London, Institute of English Studies, Senate House,
Malet Street, London WC1E 7HU T 020-7862 8679
E secretary@bibsoc.org.uk W www.bibsoc.org.uk
*Hon. Secretary,* Margaret Ford

BIPOLAR UK (1983), 11 Belgrave Road, London SW1V 1RB
T 020-7931 6480 E info@bipolaruk.org.uk
W www.bipolaruk.org.uk
*Chief Executive,* Suzanne Hudson

BIRMINGHAM AND WARWICKSHIRE
ARCHAEOLOGICAL SOCIETY (1870),
c/o Birmingham and Midland Institute, 9 Margaret Street,
Birmingham B3 3BS W www.bwas-online.co.uk
*President,* Stephanie Ratkai

BLISS (1979), Chapter House, London SE1 3JW
T 020-7378 1122, **Helpline** 0500-618140
E information@bliss.org.uk W www.bliss.org.uk
*Chief Executive,* Caroline Davey

BLUE CROSS (1897), Shilton Road, Burford OX18 4PF
T 0300-077 1897 E info@bluecross.org.uk
W www.bluecross.org.uk
*Chief Executive,* Sally de la Bedoyere

BOOK AID INTERNATIONAL (1954), 39–41 Coldharbour
Lane, London SE5 9NR T 020-7733 3577 E info@bookaid.org
W www.bookaid.org
*Director,* Alison Hubert

BOOK TRADE CHARITY (BTBS) (1837), The Foyle Centre, The Retreat, Kings Langley WD4 8LT **T** 01923-263128 **E** info@booktradecharity.org **W** www.booktradecharity.org
*Chief Executive,* David Hicks

BOOKTRUST (1926), G8 Battersea Studios, 80 Silverthorne Road, London SW8 3HE **T** 020-7801 8800 **E** queries@booktrust.org.uk **W** www.booktrust.org.uk
*Chief Executive,* Diana Gerald

BOTANICAL SOCIETY OF BRITAIN AND IRELAND (1836), 57 Walton Road, Shirehampton, Bristol BS11 9TA **E** info@bsbi.org.uk **W** www.bsbi.org.uk
*President,* Ian Denholm

BOTANICAL SOCIETY OF SCOTLAND (1836), c/o Royal Botanic Garden Edinburgh, 20A Inverleith Row, Edinburgh EH3 5LR **T** 0131-552 7171 **W** www.botanical-society-scotland.org.uk
*General Secretary,* Trudi Dorr

BOYS' BRIGADE (1883), Felden Lodge, Felden, Hemel Hempstead HP3 0BL **T** 01442-231681 **E** enquiries@boys-brigade.org.uk **W** www.boys-brigade.org.uk
*Brigade Secretary,* Steve Dickinson

BRISTOL AND GLOUCESTERSHIRE ARCHAEOLOGICAL SOCIETY (1876), 87 Brookfield Road, Hucclecote GL3 3HH **T** 01452-616387 **E** jan@xmera.co.uk **W** www.bgas.org.uk
*Hon. General Secretary,* Dr Jan Broadway

BRITISH ACADEMY OF FORENSIC SCIENCES (1960), Franklin-Wilkins Building, 150 Stamford Street, King's College London, London SE1 9NH **T** 020-7848 4130 **E** denise.syndercombe-court@kcl.ac.uk **W** www.bafs.org.uk
*Secretary-General,* Dr Denise Syndercombe Court

BRITISH ASSOCIATION FOR EARLY CHILDHOOD EDUCATION (1923), 136 Cavell Street, London E1 2JA **T** 020-7539 5400 **E** office@early-education.org.uk **W** www.early-education.org.uk
*Chief Executive,* Beatrice Merrick

BRITISH ASSOCIATION FOR LOCAL HISTORY (1982), PO Box 6549, Somersal Herbert DE6 5WH **T** 01283-585947 **E** mail@balh.org.uk **W** www.balh.org.uk
*Business Manager,* Annmarie Jones

BRITISH ASTRONOMICAL ASSOCIATION (1890), Burlington House, Piccadilly, London W1J 0DU **T** 020-7734 4145 **W** www.britastro.org
*President,* Hazel McGee

BRITISH BEEKEEPERS' ASSOCIATION (1874), National Beekeeping Centre, Stoneleigh Park, Kenilworth CV8 2LG **T** 0871-811 2282 **E** bbka@britishbeekeepers.com **W** www.bbka.org.uk
*General Secretary,* Jane Moseley

BRITISH BOARD OF FILM CLASSIFICATION (1912), 3 Soho Square, London W1D 3HD **T** 020-7440 1570 **E** feedback@bbfc.co.uk **W** www.bbfc.co.uk
*Director,* David Cooke

BRITISH CATTLE BREEDERS CLUB (1946), Underhill Farm, Glutton Bridge, Earl Sterndale, Buxton SK17 0RN **T** 07966-032079 **E** heidi.bradbury@cattlebreeders.org.uk **W** www.cattlebreeders.org.uk
*Chair,* Roger Trewhella

BRITISH COPYRIGHT COUNCIL (1965), 2 Pancras Square, London N1C 4AG **T** 01986-788122 **E** info@britishcopyright.org **W** www.britishcopyright.org
*Chief Executive,* Janet Ibbotson

BRITISH DEAF ASSOCIATION (1890), 3rd Floor, 356 Holloway Road, London N7 6PA **T** 020-7697 4140 **E** bda@bda.org.uk **W** www.bda.org.uk
*Chief Executive,* David Buxton

BRITISH DRIVING SOCIETY LTD (1957), Church Road, Endersley, Wingfield Eye IP21 5QZ **T** 01379 384612 **E** email@britishdrivingsociety.co.uk **W** www.britishdrivingsociety.co.uk
*President,* John Parker

BRITISH ECOLOGICAL SOCIETY (1913), Charles Darwin House, 12 Roger Street, London WC1N 2JU **T** 020-7685 2500 **E** info@britishecologicalsociety.org **W** www.britishecologicalsociety.org
*Executive Director,* Dr Hazel Norman

BRITISH FALSE MEMORY SOCIETY (1993), PO Box 172, Stockport SK6 9BP **T** 01225-333654 **E** bfms@bfms.org.uk **W** www.bfms.org.uk
*Director,* Madeline Greenhalgh

BRITISH HEALTH CARE ASSOCIATION (1930), PO Box 6752, Elgin IV30 9BN **T** 01343-830148 **E** info@bhca.org.uk **W** www.bhca.org.uk
*National Secretary,* Liz Price

BRITISH HEART FOUNDATION (1961), Greater London House, 180 Hampstead Road, London NW1 7AW **T** 020-7554 0000 **W** www.bhf.org.uk
*Chief Executive,* Simon Gillespie

BRITISH HUMANIST ASSOCIATION (1896), 39 Moreland Street, London EC1V 8BB **T** 020-7324 3060 **E** info@humanism.org.uk **W** www.humanism.org.uk
*Chief Executive,* Andrew Copson

BRITISH INSTITUTE IN EASTERN AFRICA (1959), 10 Carlton House Terrace, London SW1Y 5AH **T** 020-7969 5201 **E** biea@britac.ac.uk **W** www.biea.ac.uk
*Director,* Dr Joost Fontein

BRITISH INTERPLANETARY SOCIETY (1933), 27–29 South Lambeth Road, London SW8 1SZ **T** 020-7735 3160 **E** info@bis-space.com **W** www.bis-space.com
*Executive Secretary,* Suszann Parry

BRITISH-ISRAEL-WORLD FEDERATION (1919), 121 Low Etherley, Bishop Auckland, Co. Durham DL14 0HA **T** 01388-834395 **E** admin@britishisrael.co.uk **W** www.britishisrael.co.uk
*President,* M. A. Clark

BRITISH NUTRITION FOUNDATION (1967), 6th Floor, Imperial House, 15–19 Kingsway, London WC2B 6UN **T** 020-7557 7930 **E** postbox@nutrition.org.uk **W** www.nutrition.org.uk
*Director-General,* Prof. Judith Buttriss, PHD

BRITISH ORNITHOLOGISTS' UNION (1858), PO Box 417, Peterborough PE7 3FX **T** 01733-844820 **E** bou@bou.org.uk **W** www.bou.org.uk
*Senior Administrator,* S. P. Dudley

BRITISH RED CROSS (1870), 44 Moorfields, London EC2Y 9AL **T** 0844-871 1111, **Textphone** 020-7562 2000 **E** information@redcross.org.uk **W** www.redcross.org.uk
*Chief Executive,* Mike Adamson

BRITISH SUNDIAL SOCIETY (1989), c/o The Royal Astronomical Society, Burlington House, London W1J 0BQ **T** 01233-712550 **E** secretary@sundialsoc.org.uk **W** www.sundialsoc.org.uk
*Chairman,* Dr Frank King

BRITISH TRUST FOR ORNITHOLOGY (1933), The Nunnery, Thetford IP24 2PU **T** 01842-750050 **E** info@bto.org **W** www.bto.org
*Director,* Dr Andy Clements

BUCKINGHAMSHIRE ARCHAEOLOGICAL SOCIETY (1847), County Museum, Church Street, Aylesbury HP20 2QP **T** 01296 397200 **E** help@buckscc.gov.uk **W** www.bucksas.org.uk
*Chairman,* Peter Marsden

BUSINESS AND PROFESSIONAL WOMEN UK LTD (1938), 74 Fairfield Rise, Billericay CM12 9NU **T** 01277-623867 **E** hq@bpwuk.org.uk **W** www.bpwuk.org.uk
*President,* Lynn Everson

CALOUSTE GULBENKIAN FOUNDATION (1956),
50 Hoxton Square, Hoxton, London N1 6PB T 020-7012 1400
E info@gulbenkian.org.uk W www.gulbenkian.org.uk
*Director,* Andrew Barnett
CAMPAIGN FOR NUCLEAR DISARMAMENT (1958),
162 Holloway Road, London N7 8DQ T 020-7700 2393
E enquiries@cnduk.org W www.cnduk.org
*General Secretary,* Kate Hudson
CANCER RESEARCH UK (2002), Angel Building,
407 St John Street, London EC1V 4AD T 0300-123 1022
W www.cancerresearchuk.org
*Chief Executive,* Harpal Kumar
CAREERS RESEARCH AND ADVISORY CENTRE
(1964), 2nd Floor, Sheraton House, Castle Park,
Cambridge CB3 0AX T 01223-460277 E enquiries@crac.org.uk
W www.crac.org.uk
*Chief Executive,* Ellen Pearce
CARERS TRUST (2012), 32–36 Loman Street, London
SE1 0EH T 0844-800 4361 E info@carers.org
W www.carers.org
*Chief Executive,* Gail Scott-Spicer
CARERS UK (1965), 20 Great Dover Street, London SE1 4LX
T 020-7378 4999 W www.carersuk.org
*Chief Executive,* Helena Herklots
CARNEGIE UNITED KINGDOM TRUST (1913),
Andrew Carnegie House, Pittencrieff Street,
Dunfermline KY12 8AW T 01383-721445
E info@carnegieuk.org W www.carnegieuktrust.org.uk
*Chief Executive,* Martyn Evans
CATHEDRALS FABRIC COMMISSION FOR ENGLAND
(1991), Church House, Great Smith Street, London SW1P 3NZ
T 020-7898 1863 E enquiries@churchofengland.org
W www.churchcare.co.uk
*Secretary,* Janet Gough
CAVELL NURSES' TRUST (1917), Grosvenor House,
Prospect Hill, Worcestershire, B97 4DL T 01527-595999
E admin@cavellnursestrust.org W www.cavellnursestrust.org
*Chief Executive,* Stephen Charlton
CENTRAL COUNCIL OF CHURCH BELL RINGERS
(1891), 11 Bullfields, Sawbridgeworth, CM21 9DB
T 01279-726159 E secretary@cccbr.org.uk
W www.cccbr.org.uk
*Hon. Secretary,* Mary Bone
CENTREPOINT (1969), Central House,
25 Camperdown Street, London E1 8DZ T 0845-466 3400
W www.centrepoint.org.uk
*Chief Executive,* Seyi Obakin
CEREDIGION HISTORICAL SOCIETY (1909),
Abermagwr, Aberystwyth, SY23 4AR T 01974-261222
E ymholiadau@cymdeithashanesceredigion.org
W www.ceredigionhistoricalsociety.org
*Hon. Secretary,* Mrs E. Baskerville
CHATHAM HOUSE (1920), Chatham House,
10 St James's Square, London SW1Y 4LE T 020-7957 5700
E contact@chathamhouse.org W www.chathamhouse.org
*Director,* Dr Robin Niblett
CHILD POVERTY ACTION GROUP (1965),
30 Micawber Street, London N1 7TB T 020-7837 7979
E info@cpag.org.uk W www.cpag.org.uk
*Chief Executive,* Alison Garnham
CHILDREN 1ST (1884), 83 Whitehouse Loan,
Edinburgh EH9 1AT T 0131-446 2300
E info@children1st.org.uk W www.children1st.org.uk
*Chief Executive,* Alison Todd
CHILDREN'S SOCIETY (1881), Edward Rudolf House,
Margery Street, London WC1X 0JL T 020-7841 4400
E supportercare@childrenssociety.org.uk
W www.childrenssociety.org.uk
*Chief Executive,* Matthew Reed

CHURCH BUILDINGS COUNCIL (1921), Church House,
Great Smith Street, London SW1P 3NZ T 020-7898 1863
E churchcare@churchofengland.org W www.churchcare.co.uk
*Secretary,* Janet Gough
CHURCH MISSION SOCIETY (1799), Watlington Road,
Oxford OX4 6BZ T 01865-787400 E info@cms-uk.org
W www.cms-uk.org
*Executive Leader,* Rev. Philip Mounstephen
CHURCH MONUMENTS SOCIETY (1979), Moor View,
Exbourne EX20 3SA T 01837-851483
E churchmonuments@aol.com
W www.churchmonumentssociety.org
*Hon. Secretary,* Barbara Tomlinson
CITIZENS ADVICE (1939), 3rd Floor North, 200 Aldersgate,
London EC1A 4HD T 03000-231231
W www.citizensadvice.org.uk
*Chief Executive,* Gillian Guy, CBE
CITY BUSINESS LIBRARY (1970), City Business Library,
Aldermanbury, London EC2V 7HH T 020-7332 1812
E cbl@cityoflondon.gov.uk
W www.cityoflondon.gov.uk/citybusinesslibrary
*Head of Guildhall and City Business Libraries,* Sara Pink
CITY OF STOKE-ON-TRENT MUSEUM
ARCHAEOLOGICAL SOCIETY (1959), c/o The Potteries
Museum and Art Gallery, Hanley, Stoke-on-Trent ST1 3DW
T 01782-564753 E info@stokearchaeologysociety.org.uk
W www.stokearchaeologysociety.org.uk
*Chair,* Janet Cairns
CLASSICAL ASSOCIATION (1903), Park House,
15-23 Greenhill Crescent, Watford WD18 8PH
T 01923 239 300 E office@classicalassociation.org
W www.classicalassociation.org
*Secretary,* Claire Davenport
COMMONWEALTH SOCIETY FOR THE DEAF
'SOUND SEEKERS' (1959), c/o UCL Ear Institute,
332–336 Gray's Inn Road, London WX1X 8EE T 020-7833 0035
E help@sound-seekers.org.uk W www.sound-seekers.org.uk
*Chief Executive,* Lucy Carter
CONTEMPORARY APPLIED ARTS (1948),
89 Southwark Street, London SE1 0HX T 020 7620 0086
E sales@caa.org.uk W www.caa.org.uk
*Executive Director,* Christine Lalumia
CO-OPERATIVE PARTY (1917), 65 St John Street,
London EC1M 4AN T 020-7367 4150 E mail@party.coop
W www.party.coop
*General Secretary,* Karin Christiansen
CO-OPERATIVES UK (1869), Holyoake House,
Hanover Street, Manchester M60 0AS T 0161-214 1750
E info@uk.coop W www.uk.coop
*Secretary-General,* Ed Mayo
COUNCIL FOR AWARDS OF ROYAL AGRICULTURAL
SOCIETIES (1970), Springvale, Orchard Close,
Shaldon, TQ14 0HF T 01626-873159
E ejwibberley@btinternet.com
*Hon. Secretary,* Prof. John Wibberley
COUNCIL OF UNIVERSITY CLASSICAL
DEPARTMENTS (1972), Institute of Classical Studies,
Senate House, Malet Street, London WC1E 7HU
T 020 7862 8702 E greg.woolf@sas.ac.uk
W http://cucd.blogs.sas.ac.uk/
*Chair,* Prof. G. Woolf
COUNTRY HOUSES FOUNDATION (2005),
Steephouse Farm, Uley Road, Dursley GL11 5AD
T 0845-402 4102 E info@countryhousesfoundation.org.uk
W www.countryhousesfoundation.org.uk
*Chief Executive,* David Price
COUNTRY LAND & BUSINESS ASSOCIATION (1907),
16 Belgrave Square, London SW1X 8PQ T 020-7235 0511
E mail@cla.org.uk W www.cla.org.uk
*President,* Harry Cotterell

COUNTRYSIDE ALLIANCE (1997), Old Town Hall, 367 Kennington Road, London SE11 4PT **T** 020-7840 9200 **W** www.countryside-alliance.org.uk
*Executive Chair,* Barney White-Spunner

CRISIS UK (1967), 66 Commercial Street, London E1 6LT **T** 0300-636 1967 **E** enquiries@crisis.org.uk **W** www.crisis.org.uk
*Chief Executive,* Jon Sparkes

CROHN'S AND COLITIS UK (1979), 4 Beaumont House, Sutton Road, St Albans AL1 5HH **T** 01727-830038 **E** info@chronsandcolitis.org.uk **W** www.chronsandcolitis.org.uk
*Chief Executive,* David Barker

CRUSE BEREAVEMENT CARE (1959), Unit 01, One Victoria Villas, Richmond TW9 2GW **T** 020-8939 9530, **Helpline** 0844-477 9400 **E** info@cruse.org.uk **W** www.cruse.org.uk
*Chief Executive,* Debbie Kerslake

CTC (THE UK'S NATIONAL CYCLISTS' ORGANISATION) (1878), Parklands, Railton Road, Guildford GU2 9JX **T** 01483-238337 **E** cycling@ctc.org.uk **W** www.ctc.org.uk
*Director,* Paul Tuohy

CUMBERLAND AND WESTMORLAND ANTIQUARIAN AND ARCHAEOLOGICAL SOCIETY (1866), Westlands, Westbourne Drive, Lancaster LA1 5EE **T** 01524-67523 **E** info@cwaas.org.uk **W** www.cwaas.org.uk
*General Secretary,* Marion E. M. McClintock

CYSTIC FIBROSIS TRUST (1964), 11 London Road, Bromley BR1 1BY **T** 020-8464 7211 **W** www.cysticfibrosis.org.uk
*Chief Executive,* Ed Owen

DEMOS (1994), Third Floor, Magdalen House, 136 Tooley Street, London SE1 2TU **T** 0845-458 5949 **E** hello@demos.co.uk **W** www.demos.co.uk
*Chair,* Claudia Wood

DIABETES UK (1934), Macleod House, 10 Parkway, London NW1 7AA **T** 034-5123 2399 **E** info@diabetes.org.uk **W** www.diabetes.org.uk
*Chief Executive,* Barbara Young

DISABILITY RIGHTS UK (1977), Ground Floor, 49–51 East Road, London N1 6AH **T** 020-7250 8181 **E** enquiries@disabilityrightsuk.org **W** www.disabilityrightsuk.org
*Chief Executive,* Liz Sayce

DITCHLEY FOUNDATION (1958), Ditchley Park, Enstone, Chipping Norton OX7 4ER **T** 01608-677346 **E** info@ditchley.co.uk **W** www.ditchley.co.uk
*Director,* Sir John Holmes, GCVO, KBE, CMG

DOWN'S SYNDROME ASSOCIATION (1970), Langdon Down Centre, 2A Langdon Park, Teddington TW11 9PS **T** 0333-121 2300 **E** info@downs-syndrome.org.uk **W** www.downs-syndrome.org.uk
*Chief Executive,* Carol Boys

DUKE OF EDINBURGH'S AWARD (1956), Gulliver House, Madeira Walk, Windsor SL4 1EU **T** 01753-727400 **E** info@dofe.org **W** www.dofe.org
*Chief Executive,* Peter Westgarth

DYSLEXIA ACTION (2006), Dyslexia Action House, 10 High Street, Egham TW20 9EA **T** 0300-3038357 **E** info@dyslexiaaction.org.uk **W** www.dyslexiaaction.org.uk
*Chief Executive,* Kevin Geeson

EAST OF ENGLAND AGRICULTURAL SOCIETY (1797), East of England Showground, Peterborough PE2 6XE **T** 01733-234451 **E** info@eastofengland.org.uk **W** www.eastofengland.org.uk
*Chief Executive,* Jeremy Staples

ECCLESIOLOGICAL SOCIETY (1879), 68 Scholars Road, Balham SW12 0PG **E** info@ecclsoc.org **W** www.ecclsoc.org
*Chairman,* Trevor Cooper

EGYPT EXPLORATION SOCIETY (1882), 3 Doughty Mews, London WC1N 2PG **T** 020-7242 1880 **E** contact@ees.ac.uk **W** www.ees.ac.uk
*Director,* Chris Naunton

ELECTORAL REFORM SOCIETY (1884), 2–6 Boundary Row, London SE1 8HP **T** 020-3714 4070 **E** ers@electoral-reform.org.uk **W** www.electoral-reform.org.uk
*Chief Executive,* Katie Ghose

ELGAR SOCIETY (1951), 6 Carriage Close, St Johns, Worcester WR2 6AE **T** 01905-339371 **E** vice.chair@elgar.org **W** www.elgar.org
*Chairman,* Steven Halls

EMERGENCY PLANNING SOCIETY (1993), The Hawkhills, Easingwold, York YO61 3EG **T** 0845-600 9587 **E** info@the-eps.org **W** www.the-eps.org
*Chair,* Tony Thompson

ENGLISH ASSOCIATION (1906), University of Leicester, University Road, Leicester LE1 7RH **T** 0116-229 7622 **E** engassoc@le.ac.uk **W** www.le.ac.uk/engassoc
*Chief Executive,* Helen Lucas

ENGLISH CHESS FEDERATION (1904), The Watch Oak, Chain Lane, Battle TN33 0YD **T** 01424-775222 **E** office@englishchess.org.uk **W** www.englishchess.org.uk
*Chief Executive,* Phil Ehr

ENGLISH FOLK DANCE AND SONG SOCIETY (1932), Cecil Sharp House, 2 Regent's Park Road, London NW1 7AY **T** 020-7485 2206 **E** info@efdss.org **W** www.efdss.org
*Chief Executive,* Katy Spicer

ENGLISH SPELLING SOCIETY (1908), 74 Millfield Road, West Kingsdown, Sevenoaks TN15 6BU **T** 07746 796 989 **E** enquiries@spellingsociety.org **W** www.spellingsociety.org
*Chairman,* Stephen Linstead

EPILEPSY SOCIETY (1892), Chesham Lane, Chalfont St Peter SL9 0RJ **T** 01494-601300, **Helpline** 01494-601400 **W** www.epilepsysociety.org.uk
*Chief Executive,* Angela Geer

ESPERANTO ASSOCIATION OF BRITAIN (1976), Esperanto House, Station Road, Barlaston, Stoke-on-Trent ST12 9DE **T** 0845-230 1887 **E** eab@esperanto.org.uk **W** www.esperanto.org.uk
*President,* Paul Gubbins

EVANGELICAL LIBRARY Units 5 & 6 Gateway Mews, Ring Way, Bounds Green, London N11 2UT **T** 020-8362 0868 **E** elenquire@gmail.com **W** www.evangelical-library.org.uk
*Librarian,* S. J. Taylor

FABIAN SOCIETY (1884), 61 Petty France, London SW1H 9EU **T** 020-7227 4900 **E** info@fabian-society.org.uk **W** www.fabians.org.uk
*General Secretary,* Andrew Harrop

FAITH AND THOUGHT (1865), 15 The Drive, Harlow CM20 3QD **E** revjdbuxton@sky.com **W** www.faithandthought.org.uk
*President,* Prof. Colin J. Humphreys

FAUNA & FLORA INTERNATIONAL (1903), Jupiter House, Station Road, Cambridge CB1 2JD **T** 01223-571000 **E** info@fauna-flora.org **W** www.fauna-flora.org
*Chief Executive,* Mark Rose

FEDERATION OF BRITISH ARTISTS (1961), 17 Carlton House Terrace, London SW1Y 5BD **T** 020-7930 6844 **E** info@mallgalleries.com **W** www.mallgalleries.org.uk
*Director,* Lewis McNaught

FIELDS IN TRUST (1925), 2nd Floor, 15 Crinan Street, London N1 9SQ **T** 020-7427 2110 **E** info@fieldsintrust.org **W** www.fieldsintrust.org
*Chief Executive,* Helen Griffiths

FIELD STUDIES COUNCIL (1943), Preston Montford, Montford Bridge, Shrewsbury SY4 1HW **T** 0845-345 4071 **E** enquiries@field-studies-council.org **W** www.field-studies-council.org
*Chief Executive,* Rob Lucas

FIGHT FOR SIGHT (1965), 5th Floor, 9–13 Fenchurch
Buildings, Fenchurch Street, London EC3M 5HR
T 020-7264 3900 E info@fightforsight.org.uk
W www.fightforsight.org.uk
*Chief Executive*, Michele Acton
FLEET AIR ARM OFFICERS' ASSOCIATION (1957),
4 St James's Square, London SW1Y 4JU T 020-7930 7722
E admin@fleetairarmoa.org W www.fleetairarmoa.org
*President*, Vice-Adm. Sir Adrian Johns, KCB, CBE
FORENSIC SCIENCE SOCIETY (1959), Clarke House,
18A Mount Parade, Harrogate HG1 1BX T 01423-506068
E info@csofs.org
W www.charteredsocietyofforensicsciences.org
*Chief Executive*, Dr Anya Hunt
FRANCO-BRITISH SOCIETY (1924), 3 Dovedale Studios,
465 Battersea Park Road, London SW11 4LR
E francobritsoc@gmail.com W www.franco-british-society.org
*Executive Secretary*, Isabelle Gault
FRIENDS OF FRIENDLESS CHURCHES (1957),
St Ann's Vestry Hall, 2 Church Entry, London EC4V 5HB
T 020-7236 3934 E office@friendsoffriendlesschurches.org.uk
W www.friendsoffriendlesschurches.org.uk
*Director*, Matthew Saunders, MBE
FRIENDS OF THE BODLEIAN (1925), Bodleian Library,
Broad Street, Oxford OX1 3BG T 01865-277234
E fob@bodleian.ox.ac.uk
W www.bodleian.ox.ac.uk/bodley/friends
*Chair*, Prof. Richard McCabe
FRIENDS OF THE EARTH SCOTLAND (1978),
Thorn House, 5 Rose Street, Edinburgh EH2 2PR
T 0131-243 2700 E info@foe-scotland.org.uk
W www.foe-scotland.org.uk
*Director*, Dr Richard Dixon
FURNITURE HISTORY SOCIETY (1964), 1 Mercedes
Cottages, St John's Road, Haywards Heath RH16 4EH
T 01444-413845 E furniturehistorysociety@hotmail.com
W www.furniturehistorysociety.org
*President*, Sir Nicholas Goodison
GALLIPOLI ASSOCIATION (1969), Box 630 Wey House,
15 Church Street, Weybridge KT138NA T 01784-479148
E webmaster@gallipoli-association.org
W www.gallipoli-association.org
*Hon. Secretary*, J. C. Watson Smith
GAME AND WILDLIFE CONSERVATION TRUST
(1969), Burgate Manor, Fordingbridge SP6 1EF
T 01425-652381 E info@gwct.org.uk W www.gwct.org.uk
*Chief Executive*, Teresa Dent
GARDEN HISTORY SOCIETY (1965), 70 Cowcross Street,
London EC1M 6EJ T 020-7608 2409
E enquiries@gardenhistorysociety.org
W www.gardenhistorysociety.org
*Chairman*, Dominic Cole
GEMMOLOGICAL ASSOCIATION OF GREAT BRITAIN
(GEM-A) (1931), 21 Ely Place, London EC1N 6TD
T 020-7404 3334 E information@gem-a.com
W www.gem-a.com
*Chief Executive*, James Riley, FGA, DGA
GENERAL MEDICAL COUNCIL (1858), 3 Hardman Street,
Manchester M3 3AW T 0161-923 6602 E gmc@gmc-uk.org
W www.gmc-uk.org
*Chief Executive*, Niall Dickson
GENERAL OPTICAL COUNCIL (1958), 41 Harley Street,
London W1G 8DJ T 020-7580 3898 E goc@optical.org
W www.optical.org
*Chief Executive / Registrar*, Samantha Peters
GEOGRAPHICAL ASSOCIATION (1893), 160 Solly Street,
Sheffield S1 4BF T 0114-296 0088 E info@geography.org.uk
W www.geography.org.uk
*Chief Executive*, Alan Kinder

GEOLOGICAL SOCIETY OF LONDON (1807),
Burlington House, Piccadilly, London W1J 0BG
T 020-7434 9944 E enquiries@geolsoc.org.uk
W www.geolsoc.org.uk
*Executive Secretary*, E. Nickless
GEORGIAN GROUP (1937), 6 Fitzroy Square,
London W1T 5DX T 0871-750 2936
E info@georgiangroup.org.uk W www.georgiangroup.org.uk
*Secretary*, Robert Bargery
GIRLGUIDING UK (1910), 17–19 Buckingham Palace Road,
London SW1W 0PT T 020-7834 6242 E info@girlguiding.org.uk
W www.girlguiding.org.uk
*Chief Guide*, Gill Slocombe
GIRLS' BRIGADE ENGLAND AND WALES (1965),
Cliff College, Calver, Hope Valley S32 3XG T 01246-582322
E gbco@girlsbrigadeew.org.uk W www.girlsb.org.uk
*National Director*, Ruth Gilson
GLADSTONE'S LIBRARY (1894), Church Lane,
Hawarden CH5 3DF T 01244-532350 E enquiries@gladlib.org
W www.gladstoneslibrary.org
*Warden*, Revd Peter Francis
GREEK INSTITUTE (1969), 29 Onslow Gardens,
London N21 1DY T 020-8360 7968 E info@greekinstitute.co.uk
W www.greekinstitute.co.uk
*Director*, Dr K. Tofallis
GREENPEACE UK (1979), Canonbury Villas, London N1 2PN
T 020-7865 8100 E info.uk@greenpeace.org
W www.greenpeace.org.uk
*Executive Director*, John Sauven
GUIDE DOGS (1934), Hillfields, Burghfield Common,
Reading RG7 3YG T 0118-983 5555
E guidedogs@guidedogs.org.uk W www.guidedogs.org.uk
*Chief Executive*, Richard Leaman
GUILD OF GLASS ENGRAVERS (1975), c/o Broadfield
House Glass Museum, Compton Drive, Kingswinford,
West Midlands DY6 9NS T 07834-549925
E enquiries@gge.org.uk W www.gge.org.uk
*President*, Tracey Sheppard
GUY'S AND ST THOMAS' CHARITY (1553), Second Floor,
Francis House, 9 King's Head Yard, London SE1 1NA
T 020-7089 4550 E info@gsttcharity.org.uk
W www.gsttcharity.org.uk
*Chief Executive*, Peter Hewitt
HALIFAX ANTIQUARIAN SOCIETY (1900),
356 Oldham Road, Sowerby Bridge HX6 4QU T 01422-823966
E halifaxantiquarian@gmail.com W www.halifaxhistory.org.uk
*Hon. Secretary*, Anne Kirker
HARVEIAN SOCIETY OF LONDON (1831),
Lettsom House, 11 Chandos Street, London W1G 9EB
T 020-7580 1043 E harveiansoclondon@btconnect.com
W www.harveiansocietyoflondon.btck.co.uk
*Executive Secretary*, Cdr Mike Flynn, FCMI MCPID
HAWICK ARCHAEOLOGICAL SOCIETY (1856),
8 Melgund Place, Hawick TD9 9HY T 01450-376220
E iain@croftangry.com
*President*, Iain Scott
HEARING LINK (1947), 27–28 The Waterfront,
Eastbourne BN23 5UZ T 0300-111 1113
E enquiries@hearinglink.org W www.hearinglink.org
*Chief Executive*, Dr Lorraine Gailey
HISPANIC AND LUSO BRAZILIAN COUNCIL (1943),
Canning House, 14/15 Belgrave Square, London SW1X 8PS
T 020-7811 5600 E enquiries@canninghouse.org
W www.canninghouse.org
*Chief Executive*, Robert Capurro
HONG KONG ASSOCIATION (1961), Swire House,
59 Buckingham Gate, London SW1E 6AJ T 020-7963 9447
E communications@hkas.org.uk W www.hkas.org.uk
*Executive Director*, Robert Guy

HOUSING JUSTICE (2003), 256 Bermondsey Street,
London SE1 3UJ **T** 020-3544 8094
**E** info@housingjustice.org.uk **W** www.housingjustice.org.uk
*Chief Executive,* Alison Gelder
HUGUENOT SOCIETY OF GREAT BRITAIN AND
IRELAND (1885), PO Box 444, Ruislip, HA4 4GU
**T** 020-7679 2046 **E** secretary@huguenotsociety.org.uk
**W** www.huguenotsociety.org.uk
*Hon. Secretary,* Anne Nugent
HUMANE RESEARCH TRUST (1962), Brook House,
29 Bramhall Lane South, Bramhall, Stockport SK7 2DN
**T** 0161-439 8041 **E** info@humaneresearch.org.uk
**W** www.humaneresearch.org.uk
*Chair,* L. M. Rhoades
HYMN SOCIETY OF GREAT BRITAIN AND
IRELAND (1936), Windrush, Braithwaite CA12 5SZ
**T** 01768-778054 **E** robcanham.causeypike@gmail.com
**W** www.hymnsocietygbi.org.uk
*Hon. Secretary,* Revd Robert A. Canham
IFS SCHOOL OF FINANCE (1879), 8th Floor,
Peninsular House, 36 Monument Street, London, EC3R 8LJ
**T** 01227-818609 **E** customerservices@ifslearning.ac.uk
**W** www.ifslearning.ac.uk
*Principal,* Alex Fraser
INCORPORATED COUNCIL OF LAW REPORTING
FOR ENGLAND AND WALES (1865), Megarry House,
119 Chancery Lane, London WC2A 1PP **T** 020-7242 6471
**E** enquiries@iclr.co.uk **W** www.iclr.co.uk
*Chief Executive,* Kevin Laws
INDEPENDENT AGE (1863), 18 Avonmore Road,
London W14 8RR **T** 020-7605 4200
**E** charity@independentage.org.uk
**W** www.independentage.org
*Chief Executive,* Janet Morrison
INDUSTRY AND PARLIAMENT TRUST (1977), Suite 101,
3 Whitehall Court, London SW1A 2EL **T** 020-7839 9400
**E** industryandparliamenttrust@ipt.org.uk **W** www.ipt.org.uk
*Chief Executive,* Nick Maher
INSTITUTE OF HEALTH PROMOTION AND
EDUCATION (1962), c/o 20 Mardley Avenue,
Welwyn, Herts AL6 0UD **T** c/o 01438-840040
**E** honsec@ihpe.org.uk **W** www.ihpe.org.uk
*President,* Dr Mark Forshaw
INSTITUTION OF ENGINEERING AND
TECHNOLOGY (1871), Michael Faraday House,
Six Hills Way, Stevenage SG1 2AY **T** 01438-313311
**E** postmaster@theiet.org **W** www.theiet.org
*Chief Executive & Secretary,* Nigel Fine
INTERCONTINENTAL CHURCH SOCIETY (1823),
Unit 11, Ensign Business Centre, Westwood Way,
Westwood Business Park, Coventry CV4 8JA **T** 024-7646 3940
**E** enquiries@ics-uk.org **W** www.ics-uk.org
*Mission Director,* Revd Richard Bromley
INTERNATIONAL AFRICAN INSTITUTE (1926),
SOAS, Thornhaugh Street, Russell Square, London WC1H 0XG
**T** 020-7898 4420 **E** iai@soas.ac.uk
**W** www.internationalafricaninstitute.org
*Hon. Director,* Prof. Philip Burnham
INTERNATIONAL INSTITUTE FOR CONSERVATION
OF HISTORIC AND ARTISTIC WORKS (1950),
3 Birdcage Walk, London SW1H 9JJ **T** 020-7799 5500
**E** iic@iiconservation.org **W** www.iiconservation.org
*Secretary-General,* Josephine Kirby Atkinson
INTERNATIONAL POLICE ASSOCIATION (BRITISH
SECTION) (1950), IPA HQ, 1 Fox Road, West Bridgford,
Nottingham NG2 6AJ **T** 0115-981 3638 **E** mail@ipa-uk.org
**W** www.ipa-uk.org
*Secretary General,* Dave Taylor

IRAN SOCIETY (1911), 25 Eccleston Place,
London SW1W 9NF **T** 020-7235 5122 **E** info@iransociety.org
**W** www.iransociety.org
*President,* Sir Richard Dalton, KCMG
ISLE OF WIGHT NATURAL HISTORY AND
ARCHAEOLOGICAL SOCIETY (1919), Unit 16,
Prospect Business Centre, Prospect Road, Cowes PO31 7AD
**T** 01983-282596 **E** iwnhas@btconnect.com
**W** www.iwnhas.org
*President,* Dr Colin Pope
JAPAN SOCIETY (1891), 13/14 Cornwall Terrace,
London NW1 4QP **T** 020-7935 0475
**E** info@japansociety.org.uk **W** www.japansociety.org.uk
*Chief Executive,* Heidi Potter
JERUSALEM AND THE MIDDLE EAST CHURCH
ASSOCIATION (1929), 1 Hart House, The Hart,
Farnham GU9 7HJ **T** 01252-726994
**E** secretary@jmeca.eclipse.co.uk **W** www.jmeca.org.uk
*Chair,* John Clark
JOHN STUART MILL INSTITUTE (1992), 1 Whitehall Place,
London SW1A 2HE **T** 07973-752473 **E** jsmi@cyberstar.uk.com
**W** www.jsmillinstitute.org.uk
*Convenor,* Dr Alan Butt Philip
JUSTICE (1957), 59 Carter Lane, London EC4V 5AQ
**T** 020-7329 5100 **E** admin@justice.org.uk
**W** www.justice.org.uk
*Director,* Andrea Coomber
KENT ARCHAEOLOGICAL SOCIETY (1857),
Maidstone Museum, St Faiths Street, Maidstone ME14 1LH
**T** 07792-601328 **E** secretary@kentarchaeology.org.uk
**W** www.kentarchaeology.org.uk
*Hon. General Secretary,* Dr P. Stutchbury
KING'S FUND (1897), 11–13 Cavendish Square,
London W1G 0AN **T** 020-7307 2400
**E** enquiry@kingsfund.org.uk **W** www.kingsfund.org.uk
*Chief Executive,* Chris Ham
KIPLING SOCIETY (1927), 31 Brookside, Billericay,
Essex CM11 1DT **T** 077-1432 6532
**E** john.lambert1@btinternet.com **W** www.kipling.org.uk
*Hon. Secretary,* John Lambert
LEAGUE OF THE HELPING HAND (1908), PO Box 342,
Burgess Hill, RH15 5AQ **T** 01444-236099
**E** secretary@lhh.org.uk **W** www.lhh.org.uk
*Executive Secretary,* Yee Ling Hughes
LEPROSY MISSION, ENGLAND, WALES, THE
CHANNEL ISLANDS AND THE ISLE OF MAN (1874),
Goldhay Way, Orton Goldhay, Peterborough PE2 5GZ
**T** 01733-370505 **E** post@tlmew.org.uk
**W** www.leprosymission.org.uk
*National Director,* Peter A. Walker
LINNEAN SOCIETY OF LONDON (1788),
Burlington House, Piccadilly, London W1J 0BF **T** 020-7434 4479
**E** info@linnean.org **W** www.linnean.org
*Executive Secretary,* Dr Elizabeth Rollinson
LIONS CLUBS INTERNATIONAL (BRITISH ISLES
AND IRELAND) (1950), 257 Alcester Road South,
Kings Heath, Birmingham B14 6DT **T** 0845-833 9502
**W** www.lionsclubs.co
*Office Manager,* Brigitte Waterfield
LOCAL GOVERNMENT ASSOCIATION (1997),
Local Government House, Smith Square, London SW1P 3HZ
**T** 020-7664 3000 **E** info@local.gov.uk **W** www.local.gov.uk
*Chief Executive,* Carolyn Downs
LONDON CATALYST (1873), 45 Westminster Bridge Road,
London SE1 7JB **T** 020-7021 4204
**E** london.catalyst@peabody.org.uk
**W** www.londoncatalyst.org.uk
*Director,* Victor Willmott

LONDON COUNCILS (2000), 59½ Southwark Street, London SE1 0AL T 020-7934 9999
E info@londoncouncils.gov.uk W www.londoncouncils.gov.uk
*Chief Executive*, John O'Brien

LONDON SOCIETY (1912), Mortimer Wheeler House, 46 Eagle Wharf Road, London N1 7ED T 020-7253 9400
E info@londonsociety.org.uk W www.londonsociety.org.uk
*Chair*, Peter Murray

MACMILLAN CANCER SUPPORT (1911), 89 Albert Embankment, London SE1 7UQ T 020-7840 7840
W www.macmillan.org.uk
*Chief Executive*, Lynda Thomas

MARIE CURIE CANCER CARE (1948), 89 Albert Embankment, London SE1 7TP T 0800-716146
E supporter.services@mariecurie.org.uk
W www.mariecurie.org.uk
*Chief Executive*, Dr Jane Collins

MARINE BIOLOGICAL ASSOCIATION OF THE UK (1884), Citadel Hill, Plymouth PL1 2BP T 01752-633207
E sec@mba.ac.uk W www.mba.ac.uk
*President*, Prof. Sir John Beddington, CMG FRS

MARINE SOCIETY AND SEA CADETS (1756), 202 Lambeth Road, London SE1 7JW T 020-7654 7000
E info@ms-sc.org W www.ms-sc.org
*Chief Executive*, Martin Coles

MARRIAGE CARE (1946), Bishops' Park House, 25-29 Fulham High Street, London SW6 3JH T 080-0389 3801
E info@marriagecare.org.uk W www.marriagecare.org.uk
*Chief Executive*, Mark Molden

ME ASSOCIATION (1976), 7 Apollo Office Court, Radclive Road, Gawcott MK18 4DF T 0844-576 5326
E meconnect@meassociation.org.uk
W www.meassociation.org.uk
*Chair*, Neil Riley

MEDIAWATCH-UK (1965), 3 Willow House, Kennington Road, Ashford TN24 0NR T 01233-633936
E info@mediawatchuk.org W www.mediawatchuk.org
*Director*, Vivienne Pattison

MEDICAL SOCIETY OF LONDON (1773), Lettsom House, 11 Chandos Street, London W1G 9EB T 020-7580 1043
E medicalsoclondon@btconnect.com
W www.medsoclondon.org
*Registrar / CEO*, Cdr Mike Flynn, FCMI MCPID

MEDICAL WOMEN'S FEDERATION (1917), Tavistock House North, Tavistock Square, London WC1H 9HX
T 020-7387 7765 E admin.mwf@btconnect.com
W www.medicalwomensfederation.org.uk
*President*, Dr Sally Davies

MENCAP (ROYAL MENCAP SOCIETY) (1946), 123 Golden Lane, London EC1Y 0RT T 020-7454 0454
E information@mencap.org.uk W www.mencap.org.uk
*Chief Executive*, Jan Tregelles

MIDDLE EAST ASSOCIATION (1961), Floor 6, 27 St James's Street, London SW1A 1HA T 020-7839 2137
E info@the-mea.co.uk W www.the-mea.co.uk
*Chief Executive*, Peter Meyer

MIGRAINE ACTION (1958), 27 East Street, LE1 6NB T 08456-011033 E info@migraine.org.uk
W www.migraine.org.uk
*Chief Executive*, Simon Evans

MIND (NATIONAL ASSOCIATION FOR MENTAL HEALTH) (1946), 15–19 Broadway, London E15 4BQ
T 020-8519 2122, **Infoline** 0300-123 3393
E contact@mind.org.uk W www.mind.org.uk
*Chief Executive*, Paul Farmer

MINERALOGICAL SOCIETY (1876), 12 Baylis Mews, Amyand Park Road, Twickenham TW1 3HQ T 020-8891 6600
E info@minersoc.org W www.minersoc.org
*Executive Director*, Kevin Murphy

MISSING PEOPLE (1993), 284 Upper Richmond Road West, London SW14 7JE T 020-8392 4590
E info@missingpeople.org.uk W www.missingpeople.org.uk
*Chief Executive*, Jo Youle

MULTIPLE SCLEROSIS SOCIETY (1953), MS National Centre, 372 Edgware Road, London NW2 6ND
T 020-8438 0700 W www.mssociety.org.uk
*Chief Executive*, Michelle Mitchell

MUSEUMS ASSOCIATION (1889), 42 Clerkenwell Close, London EC1R 0AZ T 020-7566 7800
E www.museumsassociation.org
*Director*, Sharon Heal

NABS (1916), 6th Floor, 388 Oxford Street, London W1C 1JT
T 020-7290 7070 E nabs@nabs.org.uk W www.nabs.org.uk
*Chief Executive*, Diana Tickell

NACRO, THE CRIME REDUCTION CHARITY (1966), 1st Floor, 46 Loman Street, London SE1 0EH T 020-7840 7200
E debbie.mcintosh@nacro.org.uk W www.nacro.org.uk
*Chief Executive*, Jacob Tas

NATIONAL ASSOCIATION OF OFFICIAL PRISON VISITORS (1924), 27 Collier Lane, BaildonShipley, BD17 5LN
E info@naopv.com W www.naopv.com
*National Chairman*, Ian Allred

NATIONAL BENEVOLENT CHARITY (1812), Peter Herve House, Eccles Court, Tetbury GL8 8EH
T 01666-505500 E office@thenbc.org.uk
W www.thenbc.org.uk
*Chief Executive*, Paul Rossi

NATIONAL COUNCIL OF WOMEN OF GREAT BRITAIN (1895), 72 Victoria Road, Darlington DL1 5JG
T 01325-367375 E info@ncwgb.org W www.ncwgb.org
*President*, Gwenda Nicholas

NATIONAL FEDERATION OF WOMEN'S INSTITUTES (1915), 104 New Kings Road, London SW6 4LY
T 020-7371 9300 W www.thewi.org.uk
*General Secretary*, Jana Osborne

NATIONAL FOUNDATION FOR EDUCATIONAL RESEARCH IN ENGLAND AND WALES (1946), The Mere, Upton Park, Slough SL1 2DQ T 01753-574123
E enquiries@nfer.ac.uk W www.nfer.ac.uk
*Chief Executive*, Carole Willis

NATIONAL OSTEOPOROSIS SOCIETY (1986), Camerton, Bath BA2 0PJ T 01761-471771,
**Helpline** 0845-450 0230 E info@nos.org.uk
W www.nos.org.uk
*Chief Executive*, Claire Severgnini

NATIONAL TRUST (1895), Heelis, Kemble Drive, Swindon SN2 2NA T 0844-800 1895
E enquiries@thenationaltrust.org.uk
W www.nationaltrust.org.uk
*Director-General*, Dame Helen Ghosh

NATIONAL TRUST FOR SCOTLAND (1931), Hermiston Quay, 5 Cultins Road, Edinburgh EH11 4DF
T 0131-458 0200 E information@nts.org.uk W www.nts.org.uk
*Chief Executive*, Simon Skinner

NATIONAL UNION OF STUDENTS (NUS) (1922), Macadam House, 275 Gray's Inn Road, London WC1X 8QB
T 0845-521 0262 W www.nus.org.uk
*President*, Toni Pearce

NAT (NATIONAL AIDS TRUST) (1987), New City Cloisters, 196 Old Street, London EC1V 9FR T 020-7814 6767
E info@nat.org.uk W www.nat.org.uk
*Chief Executive*, Deborah Gold

NAVY RECORDS SOCIETY (1893), The Mill, Stanford Dingley, Reading RG7 6LS T 01189-744789
E honsec@navyrecords.org.uk W www.navyrecords.org.uk
*Hon. Secretary*, Robin Brodhurst

NEWCOMEN SOCIETY (1920), The Science Museum, London SW7 2DD T 020-7371 4445 W www.newcomen.com
*President*, Michael Grace

NORFOLK AND NORWICH ARCHAEOLOGICAL
SOCIETY (1846), 64 The Close, Cathedral,
Norwich NR1 4DH E secretary@nnas.info W www.nnas.info
*Hon. Secretary,* Alice Cattermole

NSPCC (1884), Weston House, 42 Curtain Road,
London EC2A 3NH T 020-7825 2500 E help@nspcc.org.uk
W www.nspcc.org.uk
*Chief Executive,* Peter Wanless

NUFFIELD FOUNDATION (1943), 28 Bedford Square,
London WC1B 3JS T 020-7631 0566
E info@nuffieldfoundation.org W www.nuffieldfoundation.org
*Director,* Sharon Witherspoon, MBE

NUTRITION SOCIETY (1941), 10 Cambridge Court,
210 Shepherds Bush Road, London W6 7NJ T 020-7602 0228
E office@nutritionsociety.org W www.nutritionsociety.org
*Chief Executive,* Mark Hollingsworth, MBA FINSTLM

OPEN-AIR MISSION (1853), 4 Harrier Court,
Woodside Road, Slip End, Luton LU1 4DQ T 01582-841141
E oamission@btinternet.com W www.oamission.com
*General Secretary,* Andy Banton

OPEN SPACES SOCIETY (1865), 25A Bell Street,
Henley-on-Thames RG9 2BA T 01491-573535 E hq@oss.org.uk
W www.oss.org.uk
*General Secretary,* Kate Ashbrook

ORDER OF SAINT LAZARUS OF JERUSALEM (1098),
Centre for Evangelisation, Croxteth Drive, Sefton Park L17 1AA
E grand-secretary@oslj.org W www.oslj.org
*Magistral Delegate,* Aaron Kiely

ORDERS AND MEDALS RESEARCH SOCIETY (1942),
PO Box 6195, Royal Leamington Spa CV31 9JU
T 01926-312176 E generalsecretary@omrs.org
W www.omrs.org
*General Secretary,* Dahlia Harrison, OMRS

OXFAM GREAT BRITAIN (1942), Oxfam House,
John Smith Drive, Cowley, Oxford OX4 2JY T 0300-200 1292
E enquiries@oxfam.org.uk W www.oxfam.org.uk
*Chief Executive,* Max Goldring

OXFORD UNIVERSITY SOCIETY (1932),
University Alumni Office, Wellington Square, Oxford OX1 2JD
T 01865-611610 E enquiries@alumni.ox.ac.uk
W www.alumni.ox.ac.uk
*Director of Alumni Relations,* Christine Fairchild

PARKINSON'S UK (1969), 215 Vauxhall Bridge Road,
London SW1V 1EJ T 020-7931 8080 E hello@parkinsons.org.uk
W www.parkinsons.org.uk
*Chief Executive,* Steve Ford

PARLIAMENTARY AND SCIENTIFIC COMMITTEE
(1939), 3 Birdcage Walk, Westminster, London SW1H 9JJ
T 020-7222 7085 E office@scienceinparliament.org.uk
W www.scienceinparliament.org.uk
*Executive Secretary,* Prof. Alan Malcolm

PATIENTS ASSOCIATION (1963), PO Box 935,
Harrow HA1 3YJ T 020-8423 9111, Helpline 0845-608 4455
E helpline@patients-association.com
W www.patients-association.com
*CEO,* Katherine Murphy

PEABODY TRUST (1862), Minster Court,
45 Westminster Bridge Road, London SE1 7JB T 020-7021 4444
E peabody.direct@peabody.org.uk W www.peabody.org.uk
*Chief Executive,* Stephen Howlett

PEN INTERNATIONAL (1921), Brownlow House,
50–51 High Holborn, London WC1V 6ER T 020-7405 0338
E info@pen-international.org W www.pen-international.org
*Executive Director,* Carles Torner

PERENNIAL (1839), 115–117 Kingston Road,
Leatherhead KT22 7SU T 01372-373962
E info@perennial.org.uk W www.perennial.org.uk
*Chief Executive,* Richard Capewell

PILGRIMS OF GREAT BRITAIN (1902), PO Box 1289,
Maidstone ME18 5WQ T 01622-817780
E sec@pilgrimsociety.org W www.pilgrimsociety.org
*Chair,* Ronald M. Freeman

PLAIN ENGLISH CAMPAIGN (1979), PO Box 3, New Mills,
High Peak SK22 4QP T 01663-744409
E info@plainenglish.co.uk W www.plainenglish.co.uk
*Director,* Ms C. Maher

POLICE HISTORY SOCIETY (1985), 68 High Garrett,
Braintree CM7 5NT T 01376-551819
E info@policehistorysociety.co.uk
W www.policehistorysociety.co.uk
*Hon. Secretary,* Martin Stallion

POWYSLAND CLUB (1867), Triangle House, Union Street,
Welshpool SY21 7PG E info@powyslandclub.co.uk
W www.powyslandclub.co.uk
*Hon. Secretary,* Dr Roger L. Brown

PRAYER BOOK SOCIETY (1975), The Studio,
Copyhold Farm, Goring Heath, Reading RG8 7RT
T 0118-984 2582 E pbs.admin@pbs.org.uk W www.pbs.org.uk
*Chairman,* Prudence Dailey

PRE-SCHOOL LEARNING ALLIANCE (1961),
The Fitzpatrick Building, 188 York Way, London N7 9AD
T 020-7697 2595 E info@pre-school.org.uk
W www.pre-school.org.uk
*Chief Executive,* Neil Leitch

PRINCE'S TRUST (1976), 9 Eldon Street, London EC2M 7LS
T 0800-842 842 E info@princes-trust.org.uk
W www.princes-trust.org.uk
*Chief Executive,* Martina Milburn, CBE

PRIVATE LIBRARIES ASSOCIATION (1956),
Ravelston, South View Road, Pinner HA5 3YD
E maslen@maslen.karoo.co.uk W www.plabooks.org
*Hon. Secretary,* Jim Maslen

PROFESSIONAL ASSOCIATION FOR CHILDCARE AND
EARLY YEARS (1971), Royal Court, 81 Tweedy Road,
Bromley BR1 1TG T 0300-003 0005 E info@pacey.org.uk
W www.pacey.org.uk
*Chief Executive,* Liz Bayram

QUEEN'S NURSING INSTITUTE (1887),
1A Henrietta Place, London W1G 0LZ T 020-7549 1400
E mail@qni.org.uk W www.qni.org.uk
*Director,* Dr Crystal Oldman

RAILWAY AND CANAL HISTORICAL SOCIETY (1954),
17 Lovelace Road, Oxford OX2 8LP T 01865-513063
E secretary@rchs.org.uk W www.rchs.org.uk
*Hon. Secretary,* M. Searle

RARE BREEDS SURVIVAL TRUST (1973), Stoneleigh Park,
Nr. Kenilworth CV8 2LG T 024-7669 6551
E enquiries@rbst.org.uk W www.rbst.org.uk
*CEO,* Tom Beeston

REFUGEE COUNCIL (1951), PO Box 68614,
London E15 9DQ T 020-7346 6700
E info@refugeecouncil.org.uk W www.refugeecouncil.org.uk
*Chief Executive,* Maurice Wren

REGULAR FORCES EMPLOYMENT ASSOCIATION LTD
(1885), 1st Floor, Mountbarrow House, 12 Elizabeth Street,
London SW1W 9RB T 01212-360058 E headoffice@ctp.org.uk
W www.rfea.org.uk
*Chief Executive,* Brig. Stephen Gledhill

RETHINK (1972), 15th Floor, 89 Albert Embankment,
London SE1 7TP T 0121 522 7007 E info@rethink.org
W www.rethink.org
*Chief Executive,* Mark Winstanley

ROYAL AERONAUTICAL SOCIETY (1866),
4 Hamilton Place, London W1J 7BQ T 020-7670 4300
E raes@aerosociety.com W www.aerosociety.com
*Chief Executive,* Simon Luxmoore

ROYAL ASTRONOMICAL SOCIETY (1820),
Burlington House, Piccadilly, London W1J 0BQ **T** 020-7734
4582 **E** info@ras.org.uk **W** www.ras.org.uk
*Executive Secretary,* Pamela Mortimer
ROYAL BIRMINGHAM SOCIETY OF ARTISTS (1814),
4 Brook Street, Birmingham B3 1SA **T** 0121-236 4353
**E** rbsagallery@rbsa.org.uk **W** www.rbsa.org.uk
*Gallery Director,* Marie Considine
ROYAL BRITISH LEGION (1921), 199 Borough High Street,
London SE1 1AA **T** 0808-802 8080 **E** info@britishlegion.org.uk
**W** www.britishlegion.org.uk
*Director-General,* Chris Simpkins
ROYAL BRITISH LEGION SCOTLAND (1921),
New Haig House, Logie Green Road, Edinburgh EH7 4HQ
**E** info@legionscotland.org.uk **W** www.legionscotland.org.uk
*Chief Executive,* Kevin Gray, MM
ROYAL CELTIC SOCIETY (1820), 25 Rutland Street,
Edinburgh EH1 2RN **T** 0131-228 6449
**E** gcameron@stuartandstuart.co.uk
**W** www.royalcelticsociety.org.uk
*Secretary,* J. Gordon Cameron, WS
ROYAL CHORAL SOCIETY (1872), Studio 9, 92 Lots Road,
London SW10 0QD **T** 020-7376 3718
**E** administrator@royalchoralsociety.co.uk
**W** www.royalchoralsociety.co.uk
*Administrator,* Janet Jalfon
ROYAL COMMISSION FOR THE EXHIBITION
OF 1851 (1850), 453 Sherfield Building,
Imperial College SW7 2AZ **T** 020-7594 8790
**E** royalcom1851@imperial.ac.uk
**W** www.royalcommission1851.org.uk
*Secretary,* Nigel Williams, CENG
ROYAL COMMONWEALTH EX-SERVICES LEAGUE
(1921), Haig House, 199 Borough High Street,
London SE1 1AA **T** 020-3207 2413
**E** mgordon-roe@commonwealthveterans.org.uk
**W** www.commonwealthveterans.org.uk
*Secretary General,* Lt.-Col. C. F. Warren
ROYAL HORTICULTURAL SOCIETY (1804),
80 Vincent Square, London SW1P 2PE **T** 0845-260 5000
**W** www.rhs.org.uk
*Director-General,* Sue Biggs
ROYAL HUMANE SOCIETY (1774), 50/51 Temple
Chambers, 3–7 Temple Avenue, London EC4Y 0HP
**T** 020-7936 2942 **E** info@royalhumanesociety.org.uk
**W** www.royalhumanesociety.org.uk
*Secretary,* Dick Wilkinson, TD
ROYAL INSTITUTE OF NAVIGATION (1947),
1 Kensington Gore, London SW7 2AT **T** 020-7591 3130
**E** admin@rin.org.uk **W** www.rin.org.uk
*Director,* Capt. P. Chapman-Andrews, LVO, MBE, RN
ROYAL INSTITUTE OF OIL PAINTERS (1882),
17 Carlton House Terrace, London SW1Y 5BD **T** 020-7930 6844
**E** enquiries@theroi.org.uk **W** www.theroi.co.uk
*President,* Ian Cryer
ROYAL INSTITUTE OF PAINTERS IN WATER
COLOURS (1831), 17 Carlton House Terrace,
London SW1Y 5BD **T** 020-7930 6844 **E** info@mallgalleries.com
**W** www.royalinstituteofpaintersinwatercolours.org
*President,* Andy Wood
ROYAL INSTITUTION OF GREAT BRITAIN (1799),
21 Albemarle Street, London W1S 4BS **T** 020-7409 2992
**E** ri@ri.ac.uk **W** www.rigb.org
*Chief Executive,* Chris Rofe
ROYAL LIFE SAVING SOCIETY UK (1891), River House,
High Street, Broom B50 4HN **T** 01789-773994
**E** info@rlss.org.uk **W** www.rlss.org.uk
*President,* P. Moyes

ROYAL MASONIC TRUST FOR GIRLS AND BOYS
(1982), 60 Great Queen Street, London WC2B 5AZ
**T** 020-7405 2644 **E** info@rmtgb.org **W** www.rmtgb.org
*Chief Executive,* Les Hutchinson
ROYAL MEDICAL BENEVOLENT FUND (1836),
24 Kings Road, London SW19 8QN **T** 020-8540 9194
**E** info@rmbf.org **W** www.rmbf.org
*Chief Executive,* Steve Crone
ROYAL MICROSCOPICAL SOCIETY (1839),
37–38 St Clements, Oxford OX4 1AJ **T** 01865-254760
**E** info@rms.org.uk **W** www.rms.org.uk
*Administrator,* Karen Collins
ROYAL MUSICAL ASSOCIATION (1874), 4 Chandos Road,
Chorlton-cum-Hardy M21 0ST **T** 0161-861 7542
**E** exec@rma.ac.uk **W** www.rma.ac.uk
*President,* Prof. Mark Everist
ROYAL NATIONAL COLLEGE FOR THE BLIND (1872),
Venns Lane, Hereford HR1 1DT **T** 01432-376621
**E** info@rnc.ac.uk **W** www.rnc.ac.uk
*Principal,* Sheila Tallon
ROYAL NATIONAL INSTITUTE OF BLIND PEOPLE
(1868), 105 Judd Street, London WC1H 9NE
**T** 030-3123 9999 **E** helpline@rnib.org.uk
**W** www.rnib.org.uk
*Chief Executive,* Lesley-Anne Alexander, CBE
ROYAL NATIONAL LIFEBOAT INSTITUTION (1824),
West Quay Road, Poole BH15 1HZ **T** 0845-122 6999
**W** www.rnli.org
*Chief Executive,* Paul Boissier, CB MA
ROYAL NAVAL BENEVOLENT TRUST (1922),
Castaway House, 311 Twyford Avenue, Portsmouth PO2 8RN
**T** 023-9269 0112 **E** rnbt@rnbt.org.uk **W** www.rnbt.org.uk
*Chief Executive,* Cdr Stephen Farrington, QGM, RN
ROYAL NAVY OFFICERS' CHARITY (1739),
70 Porchester Terrace, London W2 3TP **T** 020-7402 5231
**E** rnoc@rnoc.org.uk
*Chief Executive,* Cdr M. Goldthorpe, RN
ROYAL PHILATELIC SOCIETY LONDON (1869),
41 Devonshire Place, London W1G 6JY **T** 020-7486 1044
**E** secretary@rpsl.org.uk **W** www.rpsl.org.uk
*President,* Christopher King
ROYAL PHOTOGRAPHIC SOCIETY (1853), Fenton House,
122 Wells Road, Bath BA2 3AH **T** 01225-325733
**E** reception@rps.org **W** www.rps.org
*Director-General,* Dr Michael Pritchard
ROYAL SCHOOL OF CHURCH MUSIC (1927),
19 The Close, Salisbury SP1 2EB **T** 01722-424848
**E** enquiries@rscm.com **W** www.rscm.com
*Director,* Andrew Reid
ROYAL SCHOOL OF NEEDLEWORK (1872),
Apartment 12A, Hampton Court Palace KT8 9AU
**T** 020-3166 6932 **E** enquiries@royal-needlework.org.uk
**W** www.royal-needlework.org.uk
*Chief Executive,* Dr Susan Kay-Williams
ROYAL SOCIETY FOR ASIAN AFFAIRS (1901),
25 Eccleston Place, London SW1W 9NF **T** 020-7235 5122
**E** sec@rsaa.org.uk **W** www.rsaa.org.uk
*Chair,* Sir David John, KCMG
ROYAL SOCIETY FOR THE PREVENTION OF
ACCIDENTS (1917), 28 Calthorpe Road, Edgbaston,
Birmingham B15 1RP **T** 0121-248 2000 **E** help@rospa.com
**W** www.rospa.com
*Chief Executive,* Tom Mullarkey, MBE
ROYAL SOCIETY FOR THE PREVENTION OF
CRUELTY TO ANIMALS (1824), Wilberforce Way,
Southwater, Horsham RH13 9RS **T** 0300-123 0100
**W** www.rspca.org.uk
*Chief Executive,* vacant

ROYAL SOCIETY FOR THE PROTECTION OF BIRDS (1889), The Lodge, Sandy SG19 2DL T 01767-680551 W www.rspb.org.uk
*Chief Executive*, Mike Clarke

ROYAL SOCIETY OF LITERATURE (1820), Somerset House, Strand, London WC2R 1LA T 020-7845 4678 E info@rsliterature.org W www.rsliterature.org
*President*, Colin Thubron

ROYAL SOCIETY OF MARINE ARTISTS (1939), 17 Carlton House Terrace, London SW1Y 5BD T 020-7930 6844 E info@rsma-web.co.uk W www.rsma-web.co.uk
*President*, Elizabeth Smith

ROYAL SOCIETY OF MEDICINE (1805), 1 Wimpole Street, London W1G 0AE T 020-7290 2900 E membership@rsm.ac.uk W www.rsm.ac.uk
*Chief Executive*, Ian Balmer

ROYAL SOCIETY OF MINIATURE PAINTERS, SCULPTORS AND GRAVERS (1895), 89 Roseberry Road, Dursley GL11 4PU T 01454-269268 E info@royal-miniature-society.org.uk W www.royal-miniature-society.org.uk
*President*, Rosalind Pierson

ROYAL SOCIETY OF MUSICIANS OF GREAT BRITAIN (1738), 10 Stratford Place, London W1C 1BA T 020-7629 6137 E enquiries@royalsocietyofmusicians.co.uk W www.royalsocietyofmusicians.co.uk
*Secretary*, Charlotte Penton-Smith

ROYAL SOCIETY OF PORTRAIT PAINTERS (1891), 17 Carlton House Terrace, London SW1Y 5BD T 020-7930 6844 E enquiries@therp.co.uk W www.therp.co.uk
*President*, Robin-Lee Hall

ROYAL SOCIETY OF ST GEORGE (1894), Enterprise House, 10 Church Hill, Loughton IG10 1LA T 020-3225 5011 E info@royalsocietyofstgeorge.com W www.royalsocietyofstgeorge.com
*Chairman*, Joanna M. Cadman

ROYAL STAR AND GARTER HOMES (1916), 15 Castle Mews, Hampton TW12 2NP T 020-8481 7676 E general.enquiries@starandgarter.org W www.starandgarter.org
*Chief Executive*, Mike Barter

ROYAL WATERCOLOUR SOCIETY (1804), Bankside Gallery, 48 Hopton Street, London SE1 9JH T 020-7928 7521 E info@banksidegallery.com W www.royalwatercoloursociety.co.uk
*President*, Thomas Plunkett

ROYAL ZOOLOGICAL SOCIETY OF SCOTLAND (1909), Edinburgh Zoo, 134 Corstorphine Road, Edinburgh EH12 6TS T 0131-334 9171 E info@rzss.org.uk W www.edinburghzoo.org.uk
*Chief Executive*, Chris West

ST ALBANS AND HERTFORDSHIRE ARCHITECTURAL AND ARCHAEOLOGICAL SOCIETY (1845), 24 Monks Horton Way, St Albans AL1 4HA T 01727-851734 E admin@stalbanshistory.org W www.stalbanshistory.org
*Secretary*, B. R. Hanlon

ST JOHN AMBULANCE (1877), 27 St John's Lane, London EC1M 4BU T 0870-010 4950 W www.sja.org.uk
*Chief Executive*, Sue Killen

SALTIRE SOCIETY (1936), 9 Fountain Close, 22 High Street, Edinburgh EH1 1TF T 0131-556 1836 E saltire@saltiresociety.org.uk W www.saltiresociety.org.uk
*Executive Director*, Jim Tough

SAMARITANS (1953), The Upper Mill, Kingston Road, Ewell KT17 2AF T 020-8394 8300, **Helpline** 0845-790 9090 E admin@samaritans.org W www.samaritans.org
*Chief Executive*, Catherine Johnstone

SANE (1986), 1st Floor, Cityside House, 40 Adler Street, London E1 1EE T 020-7375 1002, **Helpline** 0845-767 8000 E info@sane.org.uk W www.sane.org.uk
*Chief Executive*, Ms M. Wallace, MBE

SAVE BRITAIN'S HERITAGE (1975), 70 Cowcross Street, London EC1M 6EJ T 020-7253 3500 E office@savebritainsheritage.org W www.savebritainsheritage.org
*President*, Marcus Binney, CBE

SAVE THE CHILDREN (1919), 1 St John's Lane, London EC1M 4AR T 020-7012 6400 E supporter.care@savethechildren.org.uk W www.savethechildren.org.uk
*Chief Executive*, Justin Forsyth

SCHOOL LIBRARY ASSOCIATION (1937), 1 Pine Court, Kembrey Park, Swindon SN2 8AD T 01793-530166 E info@sla.org.uk W www.sla.org.uk
*Chief Executive*, Mrs T. Adams

SCOPE (1952), 6 Market Road, London N7 9PW T 020-7619 7100, **Helpline** 0808-800 3333 E supportercare@scope.org.uk W www.scope.org.uk
*Chief Executive*, Richard Hawkes

SCOTTISH ASSOCIATION FOR MARINE SCIENCE (1884), Scottish Marine Institute, Oban, Argyll PA37 1QA T 01631-559000 E info@sams.ac.uk W www.sams.ac.uk
*Acting Director*, Prof. Axel Miller

SCOTTISH COUNCIL FOR VOLUNTARY ORGANISATIONS (1943), Mansfield Traquair Centre, 15 Mansfield Place, Edinburgh EH3 6BB T 0131-474 8000 E enquiries@scvo.org.uk W www.scvo.org.uk
*Chief Executive*, M. Sime

SCOTTISH GENEALOGY SOCIETY (1953), Library and Family History Centre, 15 Victoria Terrace, Edinburgh EH1 2JL T 0131-220 3677 E info@scotsgenealogy.com W www.scotsgenealogy.com
*Hon. Chairman*, Gregory Lauder-Frost

SCOTTISH LAND AND ESTATES (1906), Stuart House, Eskmills Business Park, Musselburgh EH21 7PB T 0131-653 5400 E info@scottishlandandestates.co.uk W www.scottishlandandestates.co.uk
*Chief Executive*, Douglas McAdam

SCOTTISH NATIONAL WAR MEMORIAL (1927), The Castle, Edinburgh EH1 2YT T 0131-226 7393 E info@snwm.org W www.snwm.org
*Secretary to the Trustees*, Lt.-Col. R. J. Binks

SCOTTISH SOCIETY FOR THE PREVENTION OF CRUELTY TO ANIMALS (1839), Kingseat Road, Halbeath, Dunfermline KY11 8RY T 03000-999999 E info@scottishspca.org W www.scottishspca.org
*Chief Executive*, Stuart Earley

SCOTTISH WILDLIFE TRUST (1964), Harbourside House, 110 Commercial Street, Edinburgh EH6 6NF T 0131-312 7765 E enquiries@scottishwildlifetrust.org.uk W www.scottishwildlifetrust.org.uk
*Chief Executive*, Jonathan Hughes

SCOUT ASSOCIATION (1907), Gilwell Park, Chingford, London E4 7QW T 020-8443 7100 E info.centre@scouts.org.uk W www.scouts.org.uk
*Chief Executive*, Matt Hyde

SEEABILITY (1799), Newplan House, 41 East Street, Epsom KT17 1BL T 01372-755000 E enquiries@seeability.org W www.seeability.org
*Chief Executive*, D. Scott-Ralphs

SELDEN SOCIETY (1887), School of Law, Queen Mary, Mile End Road, London E1 4NS T 020-7882 3968 E selden-society@qmul.ac.uk W www.selden-society.qmul.ac.uk
*Secretary*, V. Tunkel

SENSE (THE NATIONAL DEAFBLIND AND RUBELLA ASSOCIATION) (1955), 101 Pentonville Road, London N1 9LG T 0300-330 9250 E info@sense.org.uk
W www.sense.org.uk
*Chief Executive,* Gill Morbey, OBE

SHELTER (NATIONAL CAMPAIGN FOR HOMELESS PEOPLE) (1966), 88 Old Street, London EC1V 9HU
T 0300-330 1234, **Helpline** 0808-800 4444
E info@shelter.org.uk W www.shelter.org.uk
*Chief Executive,* Campbell Robb

SOCIÉTÉ JERSIAISE (1873), 7 Pier Road, St Helier JE2 4XW
T 01534-758314 E societe@societe-jersiaise.org
W www.societe-jersiaise.org
*Administrative Secretary,* Ms C. Cornick

SOCIETY FOR NAUTICAL RESEARCH (1910), 14 Milton Place, Gravesend DA12 2BT T 01482-465183
E honsec@snr.org.uk W www.snr.org.uk
*Hon. Secretary,* Dr Byrne Mcleod

SOCIETY FOR PROMOTING CHRISTIAN KNOWLEDGE (1698), 36 Causton Street, London SW1P 4ST T 020-7592 3900 E spck@spck.org.uk
W www.spck.org.uk
*CEO,* Sam Richardson

SOCIETY FOR THE PROMOTION OF ROMAN STUDIES (1910), Senate House, Malet Street, London WC1E 7HU T 020-7862 8727
E office@romansociety.org W www.romansociety.org
*Secretary,* Dr Fiona Haarer

SOCIETY OF ANTIQUARIES OF NEWCASTLE UPON TYNE (1813), Great North Museum: Hancock, Barras Bridge, Newcastle upon Tyne NE2 4PT T 0191-231 2700
E admin@newcastle-antiquaries.org.uk
W www.newcastle-antiquaries.org.uk
*President,* Derek Cutts

SOCIETY OF ANTIQUARIES OF SCOTLAND (1780), National Museums Scotland, Chambers Street, Edinburgh EH1 1JF T 0131-247 4133 E info@socantscot.org
W www.socantscot.org
*Director,* Dr Simon Gilmour, FSA, FSA SCOT, MIFA

SOCIETY OF BOTANICAL ARTISTS (1985), 1 Knapp Cottages, Wyke, Gillingham SP8 4NQ
T 01747-825718 E pam@soc-botanical-artists.org
W www.soc-botanical-artists.org
*Executive Secretary,* Pam Henderson

SOCIETY OF EDITORS (1999), University Centre, Granta Place, Mill Lane, Cambridge CB2 1RU
T 01223-304080 E office@societyofeditors.org
W www.societyofeditors.co.uk
*Executive Director,* Bob Satchwell

SOCIETY OF GLASS TECHNOLOGY (1917), 9 Churchill Way, Chapeltown S35 2PY T 0114-263 4455
E info@sgt.org W www.sgt.org
*Managing Editor,* David Moore

SOCIETY OF INDEXERS (1957), Woodbourn Business Centre, 10 Jessell Street, Sheffield S9 3HY T 0114-244 9561
E admin@indexers.org.uk W www.indexers.org.uk
*Chair,* Cathryn Pritchard

SOCIETY OF LEGAL SCHOLARS (1908), School of Law, Southampton University, Southampton SO17 1BJ
T 023-8059 4039 E admin@legalscholars.ac.uk
W www.legalscholars.ac.uk
*Hon. Secretary,* Richard Taylor

SOCIETY OF SOLICITORS IN THE SUPREME COURT OF SCOTLAND (1784), SSC Library, Parliament House, 11 Parliament Square, Edinburgh EH1 1RF
T 0131-225 6268 E enquiries@ssclibrary.co.uk
W www.ssclibrary.co.uk
*Secretary,* David Lamb

SOCIETY OF WOMEN ARTISTS (1855), Foxcote Cottage, Foxcote, Cheltenham, Andoversford GL54 4LP T 07528-477002
E rebeccacottonswa@gmail.com
W www.society-women-artists.org.uk
*Executive Secretary,* Rebecca Cotton

SOCIETY OF WRITERS TO HM SIGNET (1594), The Signet Library, Parliament Square, Edinburgh EH1 1RF
T 0131-220 3249 E reception@wssociety.co.uk
W www.wssociety.co.uk
*Chief Executive,* Robert Pirrie

STANDING COUNCIL OF SCOTTISH CHIEFS, 38/3 Moray Place, Edinburgh EH3 6BT T 01506-412289
E frank.wherrett1@talktalk.net W www.clanchiefs.org
*Hon. Secretary,* Frank J. Wherrett, FSA (SCOT)

STANDING COUNCIL OF THE BARONETAGE (1903), Forestside, Martin's Corner, Hambledon, Waterlooville PO7 4RA
T 023-9263 2672 E secretary@baronetage.org
W www.baronetage.org
*Chair,* Sir Simon Watson, BT.

SUFFOLK INSTITUTE OF ARCHAEOLOGY AND HISTORY (1848), 116 Hardwick Lane, Bury St Edmunds IP33 2LE T 01284-753228
E generalsecretary@suffolkinstitute.org.uk
W www.suffolkinstitute.org.uk
*Hon. Secretary,* Jane Carr

SUSTRANS (1977), 2 Cathedral Square, College Green, Bristol BS1 5DD T 0117-926 8893 E reception@sustrans.org.uk
W www.sustrans.org.uk
*Chief Executive,* Malcolm Shepherd

SWEDENBORG SOCIETY (1810), 20–21 Bloomsbury Way, London WC1A 2TH T 020-7405 7986
E admin@swedenborg.org.uk W www.swedenborg.org.uk
*Secretary,* Richard Lines

TEACHER SUPPORT NETWORK (1877), 40A Drayton Park, London N5 1EW T 020-7697 2750,
**Helpline** 0800-056 2561 E enquiries@teachersupport.info
W www.teachersupport.info
*Chief Executive,* Julian Stanley

TERRENCE HIGGINS TRUST (1982), 314–320 Gray's Inn Road, London WC1X 8DP
T 020-7812 1600 E info@tht.org.uk W www.tht.org.uk
*Chief Executive,* Dr Rosemary Gillespie

THEATRES TRUST (1976), 22 Charing Cross Road, London WC2H 0QL T 020-7836 8591
E info@theatrestrust.org.uk W www.theatrestrust.org.uk
*Director,* Mhora Samuel

TREE COUNCIL (1974), 4 Docks Offices, Surrey Quays Road, London SE16 2XU T 020-7407 9992 E info@treecouncil.org.uk
W www.treecouncil.org.uk
*Director-General,* Pauline Buchanan Black

TURNER SOCIETY (1975), BCM Box Turner, London WC1N 3XX W www.turnersociety.org.uk
*Chair,* Andrew Wilton

UNDERSTANDING ANIMAL RESEARCH (2008), Hodgkin Huxley House, 30 Farringdon Lane, London EC1R 3AW
T 020-3670 1230 E office@uar.org.uk W www.uar.org.uk
*Chief Executive,* Wendy Jarrett

UNITED GRAND LODGE OF ENGLAND (1717), Freemasons' Hall, Great Queen Street, London WC2B 5AZ
T 020-7831 9811 E enquiries@ugle.org.uk W www.ugle.org.uk
*Grand Master,* HRH the Duke of Kent, KG, GCMG, GCVO

UNITED NATIONS ASSOCIATION - UK (1945), 3 Whitehall Court, London SW1A 2EL T 020-7766 3454
E info@una.org.uk W www.una.org.uk
*Executive Director,* Natalie Samarasinghe

UNITED REFORMED CHURCH HISTORY SOCIETY (1972), Westminster College, Madingley Road, Cambridge CB3 0AA T 01223-330620 E hw374@cam.ac.uk
*Hon. Secretary,* Mrs M. Thompson

UNIVERSITIES FEDERATION FOR ANIMAL WELFARE (1926), The Old School, Brewhouse Hill, Wheathampstead AL4 8AN T 01582-831818 E ufaw@ufaw.org.uk W www.ufaw.org.uk
*Chief Executive & Scientific Director,* Dr R. C. Hubrecht
VEGAN SOCIETY (1944), Donald Watson House, 21 Hylton Street, Hockley B18 6HJ T 0121-523 1739 E info@vegansociety.com W www.vegansociety.com
*Chief Executive,* Jasmijn de Boo
VERNACULAR ARCHITECTURE GROUP (1952), Sunnyfield, 3 Church Row, Redwick NP26 3DE T 01633-889019 E lindajhall@googlemail.com W www.vag.org.uk
*President,* Martin Cherry
VICTIM SUPPORT (1979), Hallam House, 56–60 Hallam Street, London W1W 6JL T 020-7268 0200, Helpline 08 08 16 89 111 E reception@victimsupport.org.uk W www.victimsupport.org.uk
*Chief Executive,* Mark Castle, OBE
VICTIM SUPPORT SCOTLAND (1985), 15–23 Hardwell Close, Edinburgh EH8 9RX T 0131-668 4486 E info@victimsupportsco.org.uk W www.victimsupportsco.org.uk
*Chief Executive,* D. McKenna
VICTORIAN SOCIETY (1958), 1 Priory Gardens, Bedford Park, London W4 1TT T 020-8994 1019 E admin@victoriansociety.org.uk W www.victoriansociety.org.uk
*Director,* Christopher Costelloe
VIKING SOCIETY FOR NORTHERN RESEARCH (1892), Department of Scandinavian Studies, University College, Gower Street, London WC1E 6BT T 020-7679 7176 E vsnr@ucl.ac.uk W www.vsnr.org
*Hon. Secretary Dr,* Haki Antonsson
WAR WIDOWS' ASSOCIATION OF GREAT BRITAIN (1971), 199 Borough High Street, SE1 1AA T 0845-241 2189 E info@warwidows.org.uk W www.warwidows.org.uk
*Chair,* Irene Wills
WESLEY HISTORICAL SOCIETY (1893), 7 Haugh Shaw Road, Halifax, W. Yorks HX1 3AH T 01422-250780 E johnahargreaves@blueyonder.co.uk W www.wesleyhistoricalsociety.org.uk
*General Secretary,* Dr John A. Hargreaves, FSA, FHA, FRHISTS

WOMEN'S ENGINEERING SOCIETY (1919), c/o The IET, Michael Faraday House, Six Hills Way, Stevenage SG1 2AY T 01438-765506 E info@wes.org.uk W www.wes.org.uk
*Office Manager,* Cath Heslop
WOODLAND TRUST (1972), Kempton Way, Grantham NG31 6LL T 01476-581111 E enquiries@woodlandtrust.org.uk W www.woodlandtrust.org.uk
*Chief Executive,* Beccy Speight
WORCESTERSHIRE ARCHAEOLOGICAL SOCIETY (1854), 26 Albert Park Road, Malvern WR14 1HN T 01684 565190 E secretary@worcestershirearchaeologicalsociety.org.uk W www.worcestershirearchaeologicalsociety.org.uk
*Hon. Secretary,* Dr J. W. Dunleavey
WORLD SHIP SOCIETY LTD (1946), 49 Mount Road, Mitcham CR4 3EZ T 07709-028384 E jimmy.poole@worldshipsociety.org W www.worldshipsociety.org
*Secretary,* Jimmy Poole
YMCA (1844), 29–35 Farringdon Road, London EC1M 3JF T 020-7186 9500 E enquiries@ymca.org.uk W www.ymca.org.uk
*Chief Executive,* Denise Hatton
YOUNG WOMEN'S TRUST (1855), 7-8 Newbury Street, London EC1A 7HU T 020-7600 7451 E info@youngwomenstrust.org W www.youngwomenstrust.org
*Chief Executive,* Dr Carole Easton
YOUTH HOSTELS ASSOCIATION (ENGLAND & WALES) (1930), Trevelyan House, Dimple Road, Matlock DE4 3YH T 01629-592600 E customerservices@yha.org.uk W www.yha.org.uk
*Chief Executive,* Caroline White
ZOOLOGICAL SOCIETY OF LONDON (1826), Regent's Park, London NW1 4RY T 0344 225 1826 E info@zsl.org W www.zsl.org
*Director-General,* Ralph Armond

# THE WORLD

# THE WORLD IN FIGURES

## THE EARTH

The shape of the Earth is that of an oblate spheroid or solid of revolution whose meridian sections are ellipses, while the sections at right angles are circles.

### DIMENSIONS

Equatorial diameter = 12,742.01km (7,917.51 miles)
Polar diameter = 12,713.50km (7,899.80 miles)
Equatorial circumference = 40,030.20km
  (24,873.6 miles)
Polar circumference = 40,007.86km (24,859.73 miles)
Mass = 5,972,190,000,000,000,000,000,000kg
  ($5.972 \times 10^{24}$kg)

The equatorial circumference is divided into 360 degrees of longitude, which is measured in degrees, minutes and seconds east or west of the Greenwich (or 'prime') meridian (0°) to 180°; the meridian 180° E coinciding with 180° W. This was internationally ratified in 1884.

Distance north and south of the equator is measured in degrees, minutes and seconds of latitude. The equator is 0°, the North Pole is 90°N. and the South Pole is 90°S. The tropics lie at 23° 27′ N. (tropic of cancer) and 23° 27′ S. (tropic of capricorn). The Arctic Circle lies at 66° 33′ N. and the Antarctic Circle at 66° 33′ S. (Note the tropics and the Arctic and Antarctic circles are affected by the slow decrease in obliquity of the ecliptic, of about 0.47 arcseconds per year. The effect of this is that the Arctic and Antarctic circles are currently moving towards their respective poles by about 14m per annum, while the tropics move towards the equator by the same amount.)

### AREA ETC

The surface area of the Earth is 510,064,472km² (196,936,994 miles²), of which the water area is 70.92 per cent and the land area is 29.08 per cent.

The radial velocity on the Earth's surface at the equator is 1,669.79km per hour (1,037.56mph). The Earth's mean velocity in its orbit around the Sun is 107,218km per hour (66,622mph). The Earth's mean distance from the Sun is 149,598,262km (92,956,050 miles).

## OCEANS

### LARGEST BY AREA

|          | $km^2$      | $miles^2$  |
|----------|-------------|------------|
| Pacific  | 165,250,000 | 63,800,000 |
| Atlantic | 82,440,000  | 31,830,000 |
| Indian   | 73,440,000  | 28,360,000 |
| Southern | 20,327,000  | 7,848,300  |
| Arctic   | 14,090,000  | 5,440,000  |

The equator divides the Pacific into the North and South Pacific and the Atlantic into the North and South Atlantic. In 2000 the International Hydrographic Organisation approved the description of the 20,327,000km² (7,848,300 miles²) of circum-Antarctic waters up to 60°S. as the Southern Ocean.

### GREATEST KNOWN OCEAN DEPTHS

| Greatest depth       | Location | metres | feet   |
|----------------------|----------|--------|--------|
| Mariana Trench*      | Pacific  | 10,994 | 36,070 |
| Puerto Rico Trench   | Atlantic | 8,380  | 27,493 |
| Diamantina Trench    | Indian   | 8,047  | 26,401 |
| South Sandwich Trench| Southern | 7,235  | 23,737 |
| Molloy Deep          | Arctic   | 5,607  | 18,397 |

* On 23 January 1960, Jacques Piccard (Switzerland) and Don Walsh (USA) descended in the bathyscaphe *Trieste* to the floor of the Mariana Trench, a depth later calculated as 10,916m (35,814ft). The current depth was calculated by the Japanese remote-controlled probe *Kaiko* on 24 March 1995. On 1 June 2009, sonar mapping of the Challenger Deep in the Mariana Trench by the US oceanographic research vessel *Kilo Moana* indicated a possible depth of 10,971m (35,994ft)

## SEAS

### LARGEST BY AREA

|                | $km^2$    | $miles^2$ |
|----------------|-----------|-----------|
| South China    | 3,685,000 | 1,423,000 |
| Caribbean      | 2,753,000 | 1,063,000 |
| Mediterranean  | 2,509,900 | 969,100   |
| Bering         | 2,304,000 | 890,000   |
| Okhotsk        | 1,582,000 | 611,000   |
| Gulf of Mexico | 1,550,000 | 600,000   |
| Japan          | 978,000   | 377,600   |
| Hudson Bay     | 819,000   | 316,000   |
| Andaman        | 798,000   | 308,000   |
| East China     | 750,000   | 290,000   |
| North Sea      | 570,000   | 220,000   |
| Red Sea        | 453,000   | 174,900   |
| Black Sea      | 422,000   | 163,000   |

### GREATEST KNOWN SEA DEPTHS

| Greatest depth                  | metres | feet   |
|---------------------------------|--------|--------|
| Caribbean (Cayman Trench)       | 7,686  | 25,216 |
| Philippine Sea (Ryukyu Trench)  | 7,507  | 24,629 |
| Mediterranean (Calypso Deep)    | 5,267  | 17,280 |
| Gulf of Mexico (Sigsbee Deep)   | 5,203  | 17,070 |
| South China                     | 5,016  | 16,457 |
| Andaman                         | 4,400  | 14,500 |
| Bering (Bowers Basin)           | 4,097  | 13,442 |
| Japan                           | 3,742  | 12,276 |
| Okhotsk                         | 3,372  | 11,063 |
| Red Sea                         | 3,040  | 9,974  |
| Black Sea                       | 2,212  | 7,257  |
| North Sea                       | 700    | 2,300  |

## THE CONTINENTS

There are generally considered to be seven continents: Africa, North America, South America, Antarctica, Asia, Australia and Europe. Europe and Asia are sometimes considered a single continent: Eurasia, and North and South America are sometimes referred to together as the Americas.

AFRICA is surrounded by sea except for the narrow isthmus of Suez in the north-east, through which was cut the Suez Canal (opened 17 November 1869). Its extreme longitudes are 17° 20′ W. at Cabo Verde, Senegal, and 51° 24′ E. at Raas Xaafuun, Somalia. The extreme latitudes are 37° 20′ N. at Cape Blanc, Tunisia, and 34° 50′ S. at Cape

Agulhas, South Africa, about 7,081km (4,400 miles) apart. The equator passes across Gabon, Republic of the Congo, Uganda, Kenya and Somalia in the middle of the continent.

NORTH AMERICA, including Mexico, is surrounded by ocean except in the south, where the isthmian states of Central America link North America with South America. Its extreme longitudes are 168° 5′ W. at Cape Prince of Wales, Alaska, and 55° 40′ W. at Cape Charles, Newfoundland. The extreme continental latitudes are the tip of the Boothia peninsula, NW Territories, Canada (71° 51′ N.) and 14° 22′ N. in southern Mexico near La Victoria, Guatemala.

SOUTH AMERICA lies mostly in the southern hemisphere, the equator passing across Ecuador, Colombia and Brazil in the north of the continent. It is surrounded by ocean except where it is joined to Central America in the north by the narrow isthmus through which was cut the Panama Canal (opened 15 August 1914). Its extreme longitudes are 34° 47′ W. at Cape Branco in Brazil and 81° 20′ W. at Punta Pariña, Peru. The extreme continental latitudes are 12° 25′ N. at Punta Gallinas, Colombia, and 53° 54′ S. at the southernmost tip of Peninsula de Brunswick, Chile. Cape Horn, on Cape Island, Chile, lies in 55° 59′ S.

ANTARCTICA lies almost entirely within the Antarctic Circle (66° 33′ S.) and is the largest of the world's glaciated areas. Ninety-eight per cent of the continent is permanently covered in ice. The ice amounts to some 29 million km³ (7 million miles³) and represents more than 70 per cent of the world's fresh water. The ice sheet is on average 2.45km (1.5 miles) thick; if it were to melt, the world's seas would rise by more than 60m (197ft). The environment is too hostile for unsupported human habitation.

ASIA is the largest continent and occupies 29.6 per cent of the world's land surface. The extreme longitudes are 26° 05′ E. at Baba Buran, Turkey, and 169° 40′ W. at Mys Dezhneva, Russia, a distance of about 9,656km (6,000 miles). Its extreme northern latitude is 77° 45′ N. at Mys Chelyuskin, Russia, and it extends over 8,046km (5,000 miles) south to Tanjong Piai, Malaysia.

AUSTRALIA is the smallest of the continents and lies in the southern hemisphere. It is entirely surrounded by ocean. Its extreme longitudes are 113° 11′ E. at Steep Point, Western Australia, and 153° 11′ E. at Cape Byron, New South Wales. The extreme latitudes are 10° 42′ S. at Cape York, Queensland, and 39°S. at South East Point, Tasmania. Australia, together with New Zealand (Australasia), Papua New Guinea and the Pacific Islands, comprises Oceania.

EUROPE, including European Russia, is the smallest continent in the northern hemisphere. Its extreme latitudes are 71° 11′ N. at Nord Kapp in Norway, and 36° 23′ N. at Akra Tainaron (Matapas) in southern Greece, a distance of about 3,862km (2,400 miles). Its breadth from Cabo Carvoeiro in Portugal (9° 34′ W.) in the west to the Kara River, north of the Urals (66° 30′ E.) in the east is about 5,310km (3,300 miles). The division between Europe and Asia is generally regarded as the watershed of the Ural Mountains; down the Ural river to Atyrau, Kazakhstan; across the Caspian Sea to Apsheronskiy Poluostrov, near Baku; along the watershed of the Caucasus Mountains to Anapa and then across the Black Sea to the Bosporus in Turkey; across the Sea of Marmara to Canakkale Bogazi (Dardanelles).

| Continent | Area | |
|---|---|---|
| | km² | miles² |
| Asia | 44,614,000 | 17,226,000 |
| Africa | 30,365,000 | 11,724,000 |
| North America | 24,230,000 | 9,355,000 |
| South America | 17,814,000 | 6,878,000 |
| Antarctica | 14,200,000 | 5,500,000 |
| Europe* | 9,699,000 | 3,745,000 |
| Australia | 7,702,501 | 2,973,952 |

* Includes 5,571,000km² (2,151,000 miles²) of former USSR territory, including the Baltic states, Belarus, Moldova, Ukraine and the part of Russia west of the Ural Mountains and Kazakhstan west of the Ural river. European Turkey (24,378km²/9,412 miles²) comprises territory to the west and north of the Bosporus and the Dardanelles

## GLACIATED AREAS

It is estimated that around 14,800,000km² (5,712,800 miles²) or 10 per cent of the world's land surface is permanently covered with ice. Glacial retreat and thinning occurs where glaciers melt faster than they are created. The phenomenon has been observed since the mid-19th century but has accelerated since about 1980 as a result of global warming. It is most notable in the Antarctic: a 2005 report by the American Association for the Advancement of Science indicated that 87 per cent of the continent's 244 marine glaciers have retreated over the past 50 years. The largest glacier is the 515km (320 miles) long Lambert-Fisher Ice Passage, Mac Robertson Land, Eastern Antarctica.

| Location | Area | |
|---|---|---|
| | km² | miles² |
| South Polar regions | 13,829,000 | 5,340,000 |
| North Polar regions (incl. Greenland) | 1,965,000 | 758,500 |

## LARGEST ISLANDS

| Island and ocean | Area | |
|---|---|---|
| | km² | miles² |
| Greenland (Kalaallit Nunaat), Arctic | 2,166,086 | 836,330 |
| New Guinea, Pacific | 785,753 | 303,381 |
| Borneo, Pacific | 743,330 | 287,000 |
| Madagascar, Indian | 587,041 | 226,657 |
| Baffin Island, Arctic | 507,451 | 195,928 |
| Sumatra, Indian | 473,606 | 182,860 |
| Honshu, Pacific | 227,898 | 87,992 |
| Great Britain, Atlantic | 218,077 | 84,200 |
| Victoria Island, Arctic | 217,291 | 83,896 |
| Ellesmere Island, Arctic | 196,236 | 75,767 |

## LARGEST DESERTS

| Desert and location | Area (approx) | |
|---|---|---|
| | km² | miles² |
| Antarctica | 14,200,000 | 5,500,000 |
| Sahara, N. Africa | 8,600,000 | 3,320,000 |
| Arabian, Middle East | 2,330,000 | 900,000 |
| Gobi, Mongolia/China | 1,300,000 | 500,000 |
| Kalahari, Botswana/Namibia/ S. Africa | 930,000 | 360,000 |
| Patagonian, Argentina/Chile | 670,000 | 260,000 |
| Great Victoria, Australia | 424,400 | 163,900 |
| Syrian, Middle East | 518,000 | 200,000 |

| Desert and location | Area (approx) | |
|---|---|---|
| | km² | miles² |
| Great Basin, USA | 492,000 | 190,000 |
| Chihuahuan, USA/Mexico | 450,000 | 175,000 |

## DEEPEST DEPRESSIONS

| Depression and location | Maximum depth below sea level | |
|---|---|---|
| | metres | feet |
| Dead Sea, Jordan/Israel | 413 | 1,354 |
| Lake Assal, Djibouti | 157 | 515 |
| Turfan Depression, Sinkiang, China | 155 | 508 |
| Qattara Depression, Egypt | 133 | 435 |
| Batyr Depression, Kazakhstan | 130 | 425 |
| Kobar Sink, Ethiopia | 116 | 381 |
| Death Valley, California, USA | 86 | 282 |
| Salton Sea, California, USA | 69 | 227 |
| Caspian Depression, Russia/Kazakhstan | 27 | 90 |

The world's largest exposed depression is the Caspian Depression covering the hinterland of the northern third of the Caspian Sea, which is itself 27m (90ft) below sea level.

Western Antarctica and central Greenland largely comprise crypto-depressions under ice burdens. The Antarctic Bentley subglacial trench has a bedrock 2,538m (8,326ft) below sea level. In Greenland (lat. 73° N., long. 39° W.) the bedrock is 365m (1,197ft) below sea level.

Around 26 per cent of the area of the Netherlands lies marginally below sea level, an area of more than 10,000km² (3,860 miles²).

## CAVES

### DEEPEST CAVES
The world's deepest cave was discovered in January 2001 by a team of Ukrainian cave explorers in the Arabikskaya system in the western Caucasus mountains of Georgia. It is a branch of the Voronya or 'Crow's Cave'.

| Cave system/location | Depth | |
|---|---|---|
| | metres | feet |
| Krubera (Voronya), Georgia | 2,191 | 7,188 |
| Illyuzia-Mezhonnogo-Snezhnaya, Georgia | 1,753 | 5,751 |
| Lamprechtsofen Vogelschacht, Austria | 1,632 | 5,354 |
| Gouffre Mirolda, France | 1,626 | 5,335 |
| Réseau Jean Bernard, France | 1,602 | 5,256 |
| Torca del Cerro del Cuevon/Torca de las Saxifragas, Spain | 1,589 | 5,213 |
| Sarma, Georgia | 1,543 | 5,062 |
| Shakta Vyacheslav, Georgia | 1,508 | 4,947 |
| Sima de la Cornisa (Torca Magali), Spain | 1,507 | 4,944 |
| Cehi 2, Slovenia | 1,502 | 4,928 |
| Sistema Cheve (Cuicateco), Mexico | 1,484 | 4,868 |
| Sistema Huautla, Mexico | 1,475 | 4,839 |

### LONGEST CAVE SYSTEMS

| Cave system/location | Total known length | |
|---|---|---|
| | km | miles |
| Mammoth Cave System, Kentucky, USA | 643.7 | 400 |
| Jewel Cave, South Dakota, USA | 241.6 | 150 |
| Optimistychna, Ukraine | 232.0 | 144 |
| Wind Cave, South Dakota, USA | 218.4 | 136 |
| Sistema Sac Actun, Mexico (submerged, but dry) | 217.4 | 135 |
| Lechuguilla Cave, New Mexico, USA | 209.6 | 130 |
| Hölloch, Switzerland | 195.9 | 122 |
| Fisher Ridge System, Kentucky, USA | 183.6 | 114 |
| Sistema Ox Bel Ha, Mexico (submerged) | 182.2 | 113 |
| Gua Air Jernih, Malaysia | 175.7 | 109 |
| Siebenhengste-hohgant, Switzerland | 156.0 | 97 |
| Schoenbergsystem, Austria | 130.2 | 81 |

## LONGEST MOUNTAIN RANGES

| Range and location | Length | |
|---|---|---|
| | km | miles |
| Cordillera de Los Andes, South America | 8,850 | 5,500 |
| Rocky Mountains, North America | 4,800 | 3,000 |
| Great Dividing Range, Australia | 3,700 | 2,300 |
| Transantarctic Mountains, Antarctica | 3,200 | 2,000 |
| West Sumatran-Javan Range, Indonesia | 2,900 | 1,800 |
| Serra do Mar, Brazil | 2,600 | 1,600 |
| Himalaya, Central Asia | 2,500 | 1,550 |
| Tien Shan, Central Asia | 2,400 | 1,500 |
| New Guinea Highlands, New Guinea | 2,010 | 1,250 |

## HIGHEST MOUNTAINS

| Mountain (first ascent) | Height | |
|---|---|---|
| | metres | feet |
| Mt Everest* [Qomolangma] (29 May 1953) | 8,850 | 29,035 |
| K2 [Qogir]† (31 July 1954) | 8,611 | 28,251 |
| Kangchenjunga (25 May 1955) | 8,586 | 28,169 |
| Lhotse (18 May 1956) | 8,516 | 27,940 |
| Makalu (15 May 1955) | 8,463 | 27,766 |
| Cho Oyu (19 October 1954) | 8,201 | 26,906 |
| Dhaulagiri I (13 May 1960) | 8,167 | 26,795 |
| Manaslu I [Kutang I] (9 May 1956) | 8,163 | 26,781 |
| Nanga Parbat [Diamir] (3 July 1953) | 8,126 | 26,660 |
| Annapurna I (3 June 1950) | 8,091 | 26,545 |

* Named after Sir George Everest (1790–1866), Surveyor-General of India 1830–43, in 1863. He pronounced his name 'Eve-rest'.

† Formerly named after Col. Henry Haversham Godwin-Austen (1834–1923), who worked on the Trigonometrical Survey of India, which established the heights of the Himalayan peaks, including Everest

The culminating summits in the other major mountain ranges are:

| Mountain, by range or country | Height | |
|---|---|---|
| | metres | feet |
| Victory Peak [Pik Pobedy], Tien Shan | 7,439 | 24,406 |
| Mt Aconcagua, Cordillera de Los Andes | 6,959 | 22,831 |
| Mt McKinley (S. Peak), Alaska Range | 6,194 | 20,320 |
| Kilimanjaro (Kibo), Tanzania | 5,895 | 19,340 |
| Hkakabo Razi, Myanmar | 5,881 | 19,296 |
| Mt Elbrus, (W. Peak), Caucasus | 5,642 | 18,510 |
| Citlaltépetl [Orizaba], Mexico | 5,610 | 18,406 |
| Jaya Peak, Central New Guinea Range | 5,030 | 16,500 |
| Vinson Massif, Antarctica | 4,892 | 16,050 |
| Mt Blanc, Alps | 4,807 | 15,771 |

## HIGHEST ACTIVE VOLCANOES

Although it displays fumarolic activity, emitting steam and gas, no major eruption has ever been observed of the world's highest volcano and second highest peak in the western hemisphere, the 6,893m (22,615ft) Ojos del Salado, in the Andes on the

Argentina/Chile border. For comparison, Eyjafjallajokull, the Icelandic volcano which erupted in 2010 causing air transport chaos, has an elevation of 1,666m (5,466ft).

The volcanoes listed below include only those that have had activity recorded since 1960.

| Volcano and location (most recent activity) | Height | |
|---|---|---|
| | metres | feet |
| San Pedro, Andes, Chile (1960) | 6,145 | 20,161 |
| Aracar, Andes, Argentina (1993) | 6,082 | 19,954 |
| Volcan Guallatiri, Andes, Chile (1960) | 6,071 | 19,918 |
| Tupungatito, Andes, Chile (1987) | 6,000 | 19,685 |
| Sabancaya, Andes, Peru (ongoing) | 5,967 | 19,577 |
| San José, Andes, Argentina/Chile (1960) | 5,856 | 19,213 |
| Lascar, Andes, Chile (2013) | 5,592 | 18,346 |
| Popocatepetl, Mexico (ongoing) | 5,426 | 17,802 |
| Nevado del Ruiz, Colombia (2015) | 5,321 | 17,457 |
| Sangay, Andes, Ecuador (ongoing) | 5,230 | 17,159 |
| Irruputuncu, Chile (1995) | 5,163 | 16,939 |
| Tungurahua, Ecuador (ongoing) | 5,023 | 16,479 |

# LAKES

## LARGEST LAKES

The areas of some of the lakes listed are subject to seasonal variation. The most voluminous lakes are the Caspian Sea (saline) with 78,200km$^3$ (18,800 miles$^3$) and Baikal (fresh water) with 23,000km$^3$ (5,518 miles$^3$). Baikal is also the world's deepest lake (see below). It is estimated that it contains as much water as the entire Great Lakes system in North America – more than 20 per cent of the world's fresh water and some 90 per cent of all the fresh water in Russia.

The Aral was once the fifth largest in the world, with an area of 68,000km$^2$ (26,255 miles$^2$), but since the 1960s many of its feeder rivers have been diverted for irrigation, as a result of which its area shrank to 17,160km$^2$ (6,626 miles$^2$). Its salinity was almost three times that of seawater, and pollution led to the extinction of many aquatic species. Since the construction of the Kok-Aral dam (2005), water levels are rising again, especially in the north.

| Lake and location | Area | | Length | |
|---|---|---|---|---|
| | km$^2$ | miles$^2$ | km | miles |
| Caspian Sea, Iran/ Azerbaijan/Russia/ Turkmenistan/ Kazakhstan | 386,400 | 149,200 | 1,200 | 750 |
| Michigan–Huron, USA/Canada* | 117,610 | 45,300 | 1,010 | 627 |
| Superior, Canada/USA | 82,100 | 31,700 | 563 | 350 |
| Victoria, Uganda/ Tanzania/Kenya | 69,484 | 26,828 | 337 | 210 |
| Tanganyika, Dem. Rep. of Congo/Tanzania/ Zambia/Burundi | 32,900 | 12,700 | 660 | 410 |
| Baikal, Russia | 31,500 | 12,200 | 636 | 395 |
| Great Bear, Canada | 31,328 | 12,096 | 320 | 200 |
| Malawi [Nyasa], Tanzania/Malawi/ Mozambique | 29,604 | 11,430 | 584 | 363 |
| Great Slave, Canada | 28,568 | 11,030 | 480 | 298 |
| Erie, Canada/USA | 25,670 | 9,910 | 388 | 241 |

* Lakes Michigan and Huron may be regarded as lobes of the same lake. The Michigan lobe has an area of 57,750km$^2$ (22,300 miles$^2$) and the Huron lobe an area of 59,570km$^2$ (23,000 miles$^2$)

## UNITED KINGDOM (BY COUNTRY)

| Lake and location | Area | | Length | |
|---|---|---|---|---|
| | km$^2$ | miles$^2$ | km | miles |
| Lough Neagh, Northern Ireland | 396.00 | 153.00 | 28.90 | 18.00 |
| Loch Lomond, Scotland | 71.12 | 27.46 | 36.44 | 22.64 |
| Windermere, England | 14.74 | 5.69 | 16.90 | 10.50 |
| Lake Vyrnwy, Wales (artificial) | 4.53 | 1.75 | 7.56 | 4.70 |
| Llyn Tegid [Bala], Wales | 4.38 | 1.69 | 5.80 | 3.65 |

## LARGEST MANMADE LAKES

| Dam/lake* (year of completion) | Volume | |
|---|---|---|
| | km$^3$ | miles$^3$ |
| Nalubaale dam [Owen Falls], Uganda/Kenya/Tanzania (1954) | 204.80 | 49.13 |
| Kariba, Zimbabwe/Zambia (1959) | 180.60 | 43.33 |
| Bratsk, Russia (1967) | 169.27 | 40.61 |
| Nasser, Egypt (1970) | 168.90 | 40.52 |
| Volta, Ghana (1965) | 153.00 | 36.71 |
| Manicouagan [Daniel Johnson dam], Canada (1968) | 141.85 | 34.03 |
| Guri [Raul Leoni], Venezuela (1986) | 138.00 | 33.11 |
| Krasnoyarskoye, Russia (1967) | 73.30 | 17.58 |
| Wadi-Tatar, Iraq (1967) | 72.80 | 17.46 |
| Williston (W. A. C. Bennett dam), Canada (1967) | 70.31 | 16.87 |

* Formed as a result of dam construction
The UK's largest reservoir is Kielder Water, Northumberland (1982) with a volume of 0.2km$^3$ (0.048 miles$^3$)

## DEEPEST LAKES

| Lake and location | Greatest depth | |
|---|---|---|
| | metres | feet |
| Baikal, Russia | 1,637 | 5,371 |
| Tanganyika, Burundi/Tanzania/Dem. Rep. of Congo/Zambia | 1,470 | 4,823 |
| Caspian Sea, Azerbaijan/Iran/ Kazakhstan/Russia/Turkmenistan | 1,025 | 3,363 |
| O'Higgins [San Martin], Chile/Argentina | 836 | 2,743 |
| Malawi [Nyasa], Malawi/Mozambique/ Tanzania | 706 | 2,316 |
| Ysyk, Kyrgyzstan | 668 | 2,192 |
| Great Slave, Canada | 614 | 2,015 |
| Crater, Oregon, USA | 594 | 1,949 |
| Matano, South Sulawesi, Indonesia | 590 | 1,936 |
| Buenos Aires [General Carrera], Argentina/Chile | 586 | 1,923 |
| Hornindalsvastnet, Norway | 514 | 1,686 |
| Sarez, Tajikistan | 505 | 1,657 |
| Toba, Sumatra, Indonesia | 505 | 1,657 |
| Argentino, Argentina | 500 | 1,640 |
| Tahoe, California/Nevada, USA | 500 | 1,640 |

Loch Morar, Highland, Scotland is the UK's deepest lake at 310m (1,017ft).

# LONGEST RIVERS

| River, source–outflow | Length | |
|---|---|---|
| | km | miles |
| Nile [Bahr-el-Nil], R. Luvironza, Burundi–E. Mediterranean Sea | 6,650 | 4,132 |
| Amazon [Amazonas], Lago Villafro, Peru–S. Atlantic Ocean | 6,448 | 4,007 |
| Yangtze [Chang Jiang], Kunlun Mts, W. China–Yellow Sea | 6,300 | 3,915 |

| River, source–outflow | Length | |
|---|---|---|
| | km | miles |
| Mississippi-Missouri-Red Rock, Montana–Gulf of Mexico | 5,971 | 3,710 |
| Yenisey-Selenga, W. Mongolia–Kara Sea | 5,539 | 3,442 |
| Huang He [Yellow River], Bayan Har Shan range, Central China–Yellow Sea | 5,464 | 3,395 |
| Ob-Irtysh, W. Mongolia–Kara Sea | 5,410 | 3,362 |
| Congo [Zambia], R. Lualaba, Dem. Rep. of Congo-Zambia–S. Atlantic Ocean | 4,665 | 2,900 |
| Amur-Argun, R. Argun, Khingan Mts, N. China–Sea of Okhotsk | 4,416 | 2,744 |
| Lena, R. Kirenga, W. of Lake Baikal–Laptev Sea, Arctic Ocean | 4,400 | 2,734 |

### BRITISH ISLES

| River, source–outflow | Length | |
|---|---|---|
| | km | miles |
| Shannon, Co. Cavan, Rep. of Ireland–Atlantic Ocean | 372 | 231 |
| Severn, Powys, Wales–Bristol Channel | 354 | 220 |
| Thames, Gloucestershire, England–North Sea | 346 | 215 |
| Tay, Perthshire, Scotland–North Sea | 193 | 120 |
| Clyde, Lanarkshire, Scotland–Firth of Clyde | 170 | 106 |
| Tweed, Scottish Borders–North Sea | 155 | 96.5 |
| Bann (Upper and Lower), Co. Down, N. Ireland–Atlantic Ocean | 129 | 80 |

## WATERFALLS

### GREATEST BY HEIGHT

| Waterfall, river and location | Total drop | | Greatest single leap | |
|---|---|---|---|---|
| | metres | feet | metres | feet |
| Angel, Carrao Auyan Tepui, Venezuela | 979 | 3,212 | 807 | 2,648 |
| Tugela, Tugela, S. Africa (5 leaps) | 947 | 3,110 | 411 | 1,350 |
| Ramnefjellsfossen, Jostedal Glacier, Norway | 800 | 2,625 | 600 | 1,970 |
| Mongefossen, Monge, Norway | 773 | 2,535 | – | – |
| Gocta, Cocahuayco, Peru | 771 | 2,531 | – | – |
| Mutarazi, Mutarazi, Zimbabwe | 762 | 2,499 | 479 | 1,572 |
| Yosemite, Yosemite Creek, USA | 740 | 2,425 | 436 | 1,430 |
| Ostre Mardola Foss, Mardals, Norway* | 655 | 2,149 | 296 | 974 |
| Tyssestrengene, Tysso, Norway* | 646 | 2,120 | 289 | 948 |
| Kukenaam, Arabopo, Venezuela | 610 | 2,000 | – | – |

* Volume much affected by hydroelectric harnessing

## POPULATIONS

### MOST POPULOUS COUNTRIES IN THE WORLD

| Country | Population* | Area (sq. km) | World Comparison |
|---|---|---|---|
| China | 1,367,485,388 | 9,596,961 | 4 |
| India | 1,251,695,584 | 3,287,263 | 7 |
| USA | 321,368,864 | 9,826,675 | 3 |
| Indonesia | 255,993,674 | 1,904,569 | 15 |
| Brazil | 204,259,812 | 8,514,877 | 5 |
| Pakistan | 199,085,847 | 796,095 | 36 |
| Nigeria | 181,562,055 | 923,768 | 32 |
| Bangladesh | 168,957,745 | 143,998 | 95 |
| Russia | 142,423,773 | 17,098,242 | 1 |
| Japan | 126,919,659 | 377,915 | 62 |

*July 2015 estimate

### POPULATION GROWTH RATE

| Top 10 | | Bottom 10 | |
|---|---|---|---|
| Country | Growth Rate (%) | Country | Growth Rate (%) |
| Lebanon | 9.37 | Syria | −9.73 |
| Zimbabwe | 4.36 | Moldova | −1.02 |
| South Sudan | 4.12 | Bulgaria | −0.83 |
| Jordan | 3.86 | Estonia | −0.68 |
| Qatar | 3.58 | Ukraine | −0.64 |
| Malawi | 3.33 | Latvia | −0.62 |
| Niger | 3.28 | Montenegro | −0.49 |
| Burundi | 3.28 | South Africa | −0.48 |
| Uganda | 3.24 | Serbia | −0.46 |
| Libya | 3.08 | Fed. States of Micronesia | −0.42 |

## DAMS

### TALLEST DAMS

| Dam and location (year of completion) | Height | |
|---|---|---|
| | metres | feet |
| Jinping-I, China (2014) | 305 | 1,001 |
| Nurek, Tajikistan (1980) | 300 | 984 |
| Xiaowan, China (2010) | 292 | 958 |
| Grande Dixence, Switzerland (1961) | 285 | 935 |
| Xiluodu, China (2014) | 278 | 912 |
| Inguri, Georgia (1980) | 272 | 892 |
| Vajont, Italy (1961)* | 262 | 859 |
| Nuozhadu, China (2013) | 262 | 858 |
| Manuel Moreno Torres, Mexico (1981) | 261 | 856 |

* Disused

## TALLEST

All heights are in accordance with the Council on Tall Buildings and Urban Habitat's regulations, which measure from the ground level of the main entrance to the architectural tip of the building and include spires but not antennae, signage or flag poles.

### INHABITED BUILDINGS

| Building and location (year of completion) | Height | |
|---|---|---|
| | metres | feet |
| Burj Khalifa, Dubai, UAE (2010) | 828 | 2,717 |
| Shanghai Tower, Shanghai, China (2015*) | 632 | 2,073 |
| Abraj Al-Bait, Mecca, Saudi Arabia (2012) | 601 | 1,972 |
| One World Trade Center, New York, USA (2014) | 541 | 1,776 |
| Taipei 101, Taipei, Taiwan (2004) | 508 | 1,667 |
| Shanghai World Finance Centre, Shanghai, China (2008) | 492 | 1,614 |
| International Commerce Centre, Hong Kong, China (2010) | 484 | 1,588 |

| Building and location (year of completion) | Height | |
| --- | --- | --- |
| | metres | feet |
| Petronas Towers I and II, Kuala Lumpur, Malaysia (1998) | 452 | 1,482 |
| Zifeng Tower, Nanjing, China (2010) | 450 | 1,476 |
| KK100, Shenzhen, China (2011) | 442 | 1,450 |
| Willis Tower, Chicago, USA (1974)† | 442 | 1,450 |
| Guangzhou International Finance Centre, China (2010) | 439 | 1,440 |
| Trump International Hotel and Tower, Chicago, USA (2009) | 423 | 1,389 |
| Jin Mao Tower, Shanghai, China (1999) | 421 | 1,380 |
| Princess Tower, Dubai, UAE (2012) | 413 | 1,356 |
| Al Hamra Tower, Kuwait (2011) | 412 | 1,354 |
| Two International Finance Centre, Hong Kong, China (2003) | 412 | 1,354 |

* Scheduled completion date
† With TV antennae, 520m (1,707ft)

## STRUCTURES

| Structure and location (year of completion) | | |
| --- | --- | --- |
| Tokyo Skytree, Tokyo, Japan (2012) | 634 | 2,080 |
| KVLY (formerly KTHI)-TV Mast, North Dakota (guyed), USA (1963)* | 629 | 2,063 |
| Canton, Guangzhou, China (2010) | 600 | 1,968 |
| CN Tower, Toronto, Canada (1976) | 553 | 1,815 |
| Ostankino Tower, Moscow, Russia (1967) | 540 | 1,774 |

* The USA has numerous other guyed TV towers above 600m (1,969ft)

## TWIN TOWERS

| Structure and location (year of completion) | Floors | Height | |
| --- | --- | --- | --- |
| | | metres | feet |
| Petronas Towers, Kuala Lumpur, Malaysia (1998) | 88 | 452 | 1,483 |
| Emirates Park Towers, Dubai, UAE (2012) | 82 | 355 | 1,166 |
| SPG Globel Twin Towers, Suzhou, China (2010) | 54 | 282 | 925 |
| The Cullinan, Hong Kong, China (2008) | 68 | 270 | 886 |
| Al Kazim Towers, Dubai, UAE (2008) | 53 | 265 | 869 |
| Grand Gateway, Shanghai, China (2005) | 54 | 262 | 859 |
| Dual Towers, Manama, Bahrain (2007) | 53 | 260 | 853 |
| The Imperial, Mumbai, India (2009) | 60 | 256 | 840 |
| Al Fattan Towers, Dubai, UAE (2006) | 51 | 245 | 804 |
| Abraj Al Bait Towers, Mecca, Saudi Arabia (2012) | 42 | 240 | 787 |

*Destroyed 2001*

| | | | |
| --- | --- | --- | --- |
| World Trade Center One, New York City, USA (1972) | 110 | 417 | 1,368 |
| World Trade Center Two, New York City, USA (1973) | 110 | 415 | 1,362 |

## CHURCHES

| Structure and location (year of completion) | Height | |
| --- | --- | --- |
| | metres | feet |
| Sagrada Família, Barcelona, Spain (2026*) | 170 | 560 |
| Ulm Minster, Ulm, Germany (1890) | 162 | 530 |
| Our Lady of Peace Basilica, Yamoussoukro, Côte d'Ivoire (1990) | 158 | 518 |
| Cologne Cathedral, Cologne, Germany (1880) | 157 | 515 |
| Notre-Dame Cathedral, Rouen, France (1876) | 151 | 495 |

| | | |
| --- | --- | --- |
| St Nicholas Church, Hamburg, Germany (1874) | 148 | 485 |
| Notre-Dame Cathedral, Strasbourg, France (1439) | 144 | 472 |
| Queen of Peace Shrine and Basilica, Lichen, Poland (2004) | 140 | 459 |
| Basilica of St Peter, Rome, Italy (1626) | 138 | 452 |
| St Stephen's Cathedral, Vienna, Austria (1433) | 137 | 448 |

* Scheduled completion date, the 100th anniversary of the death of its architect, Antoni Gaudí; open for worship following its consecration by Pope Benedict XVI in 2010

The Chicago Methodist Temple, Chicago, USA (completed 1924) is 173m (568ft) high, but is sited atop a 25-storey, 100m (328ft) building. Salisbury Cathedral (1521), at 123m (404ft), is the UK's tallest religious building. St Paul's Cathedral, London, and Liverpool Anglican Cathedral are the only others in the UK over 100m (328ft) tall. At 94m (309ft) the Church of St Walburge, Preston, Lancashire is the tallest church in Britain that is not a cathedral.

## TALLEST STRUCTURES – A CHRONOLOGY

| Structure and location | Year | Height | |
| --- | --- | --- | --- |
| | | metres | feet |
| Djoser's Step Pyramid, Saqqara, Egypt | c.2650 BC | 62 | 204 |
| Pyramid of Meidum, Egypt | c.2600 BC | 92 | 302 |
| Snefru's Bent Pyramid, Dahshur, Egypt | c.2600 BC | 102 | 336 |
| Red Pyramid, Dahshur, Egypt | c.2590 BC | 104 | 341 |
| Great Pyramid, Giza, Egypt* | c.2580 BC | 147 | 481 |
| Liuhe (Six Harmonies) Pagoda, Hangzhou, China† | AD 970 | 150 | 492 |
| Lincoln Cathedral, Lincoln, England‡ | 1311–1400 | 160 | 525 |
| St Paul's Cathedral, London, England§ | 1315 | 149 | 489 |
| St Mary's Church, Stralsund, Germany | 1384–1478 | 151 | 495 |
| St Olaf's Church, Tallinn, Estonia¶ | 1438–1519 | 159 | 522 |
| Notre-Dame Cathedral, Strasbourg, France | 1439 | 142 | 466 |
| St Nicholas Church, Hamburg, Germany | 1874 | 147 | 482 |
| Notre-Dame Cathedral, Rouen, France | 1876 | 151 | 495 |
| Cologne Cathedral, Cologne, Germany | 1880 | 157 | 515 |
| Washington Monument, Washington DC, USA | 1884 | 169 | 555 |
| Eiffel Tower, Paris, France | 1889 | 300 | 984 |
| Chrysler Building, New York, USA | 1930 | 319 | 1,046 |
| Empire State Building, New York, USA | 1931 | 381 | 1,250 |
| KWTV Mast, Oklahoma City, USA | 1954 | 481 | 1,577 |
| KOBR-TV Tower, Caprock, USA | 1960 | 490 | 1,608 |
| KFVS TV Mast, Egypt Mills, USA | 1960 | 511 | 1,677 |
| KVLY (formerly KTHI)-TV Mast, Blanchard, USA | 1963 | 629 | 2,063 |

| Structure and location | Year | Height | |
|---|---|---|---|
| | | metres | feet |
| Warszawa Radio Mast, Konstantynow, Poland** | 1974 | 646 | 2,120 |
| Burj Khalifa, Dubai, UAE | 2010 | 828 | 2,717 |

\* Later reduced through loss of topstone to 137m (449ft)
† Destroyed in 1121
‡ Destroyed in 1549
§ Destroyed in 1561
⁕ Spire burned down in 1625; renovated in 1931 to present height of 123m (403ft)
** Collapsed in 1991 during renovation

# BRIDGES

The longest stretch of bridging of any kind is the Danyang–Kunshan Grand Bridge (2010) in China at 164km (102 miles). The 'floating' bridging at Evergreen Point, Seattle, Washington, USA (1963), is 3,839m (12,596ft) long, of which 2,310m (7,578ft) floats.

## LONGEST SUSPENSION SPANS

| Bridge and location (year of completion) | Length | |
|---|---|---|
| | metres | feet |
| Akashi-Kaikyo, Japan (1998) | 1,991 | 6,532 |
| Xihoumen, China (2009) | 1,650 | 5,413 |
| Great Belt Bridge, Denmark (1998) | 1,624 | 5,328 |
| Yi Sun-sin, South Korea (2012) | 1,545 | 5,069 |
| Runyang, China (2005) | 1,490 | 4,888 |
| Nanjing Fourth Yangtze, China (2012) | 1,418 | 4,652 |
| Humber, England (1981) | 1,410 | 4,626 |
| Jiangyin, China (1999) | 1,385 | 4,544 |
| Tsing Ma, Hong Kong, China (1997) | 1,377 | 4,518 |
| Hardanger, Norway (2013) | 1,310 | 4,298 |

## LONGEST CANTILEVER SPANS

| Bridge and location (year of completion) | Length | |
|---|---|---|
| | metres | feet |
| Pont de Québec, St Lawrence, Canada (1917) | 548.6 | 1,800 |
| Forth, Scotland (two spans of 1,710ft each) (1890) | 521.2 | 1,710 |
| Minato, Japan (1974) | 510.0 | 1,673 |
| Commodore Barry, New Jersey/Pennsylvania, USA (1974) | 501.1 | 1,644 |
| Crescent City Connection, Louisiana, USA (I 1958, II 1988) | 480.0 | 1,575 |
| Howrah, India (1943) | 457.2 | 1,500 |
| Veterans Memorial, Louisiana, USA (1995) | 445.0 | 1,460 |
| Tokyo Gate, Japan (2012) | 440.0 | 1,443 |
| San Francisco Oakland Bay, California, USA (1936) | 426.7 | 1,400 |
| J. C. Van Horne, New Brunswick, Canada (1961) | 380.0 | 1,247 |

## LONGEST STEEL ARCH SPANS

| Bridge and location (year of completion) | Length | |
|---|---|---|
| | metres | feet |
| Sheikh Rashid bin Saeed Crossing, Dubai, UAE (2015*) | 667.0 | 2,188 |
| Chaotianmen, China (2009) | 552.0 | 1,811 |
| Lupu, China (2003) | 550.0 | 1,804 |
| New River Gorge, West Virginia, USA (1977) | 518.0 | 1,700 |
| Bayonne [Kill van Kull], New Jersey/ New York, USA (1931) | 510.0 | 1,675 |
| Sydney Harbour, Australia (1932) | 502.9 | 1,650 |
| Chenab, India (2017*) | 460.0 | 1,509 |
| Wushan, China (2005) | 460.0 | 1,509 |
| Zhaoqing, China (2014) | 450.0 | 1,476 |

\* Scheduled completion date

## LONGEST SHIP CANALS

| Canal | Length | | Min. depth | |
|---|---|---|---|---|
| | km | miles | metres | feet |
| White Sea–Baltic [formerly Stalin] (1933), of which canalised river 51.5km (32 miles) | 227 | 141.00 | 5.0 | 16.5 |
| Rhine–Main–Danube, Germany (1992) | 171 | 106.25 | 4.0 | 13.1 |
| *Suez (1869), links Red and Mediterranean Seas | 162 | 100.60 | 12.9 | 42.3 |
| V. I. Lenin Volga–Don, Russia (1952), links Black and Caspian Seas | 100 | 62.20 | 3.6 | 11.8 |
| Kiel (or North Sea), Germany (1895), links North and Baltic Seas | 98 | 60.90 | 11.0 | 37.0 |
| Alphonse XIII, Spain (1926), gives Seville access to Atlantic Ocean | 85 | 53.00 | 7.6 | 25.0 |
| Panama (1914), links Pacific Ocean and Caribbean Sea; lake chain, 78.9km (49 miles) dug | 82 | 50.71 | 13.0 | 43.0 |
| *Houston, USA (1940), links inland city with Gulf of Mexico | 81 | 50.50 | 11.0 | 36.0 |
| Danube–Black Sea, Romania (1984) | 64.4 | 40.02 | 7.0 | 23.0 |
| Manchester Ship, UK (1894), links city with Irish Channel | 58 | 36.00 | 8.5 | 28.0 |

\* Has no locks

The first section of China's Grand Canal, running 1,782km (1,107 miles) from Beijing to Hangzhou, was opened in AD 610 and completed in 1283. Today it is limited to 2,000-tonne vessels.

The St Lawrence Seaway comprises the Beauharnois, Welland and Welland Bypass and Seaway 54–59 canals, and allows access to Duluth, Minnesota, USA via the Great Lakes from the Atlantic end of Canada's Gulf of St Lawrence, a distance of 3,769km (2,342 miles). The St Lawrence Canal, completed in 1959, is 293km (182 miles) long.

# AIR DISTANCES

| | London (LHR) | Paris (CDG) | Madrid (MAD) | Rome (FCO) | Moscow (DME) | Dubai (DXB) | New York (JFK) | Delhi (DEL) | Beijing (PEK) | Los Angeles (LAX) | Durban (DUR) | Bangkok (BKK) | Tokyo (HND) | Hong Kong (HKG) | Singapore (SIN) | Buenos Aires (BHI) | Sydney (SYD) |
|---|---|---|---|---|---|---|---|---|---|---|---|---|---|---|---|---|---|
| London (LHR) | | 216 / 348km | 773 / 1,244km | 899 / 1,446km | 1,587 / 2,553km | 3,421 / 5,505km | 3,452 / 5,554km | 4,191 / 6,744km | 5,081 / 8,175km | 5,457 / 8,780km | 5,904 / 9,499km | 5,959 / 9,588km | 5,975 / 9,614km | 5,996 / 9,647km | 6,767 / 10,888km | 7,241 / 11,651km | 10,575 / 17,016km |
| Paris (CDG) | 216 / 348km | | 660 / 1,063km | 685 / 1,102km | 1,547 / 2,489km | 3,260 / 5,245km | 3,635 / 5,849km | 4,088 / 6,578km | 5,103 / 8,211km | 5,671 / 9,124km | 5,692 / 9,159km | 5,879 / 9,459km | 6,047 / 9,730km | 5,971 / 9,607km | 6,668 / 10,729km | 7,220 / 11,617km | 10,529 / 16,941km |
| Madrid (MAD) | 773 / 1,244km | 660 / 1,063km | | 829 / 1,334km | 2,140 / 3,444km | 3,517 / 5,659km | 3,589 / 5,775km | 4,518 / 7,269km | 5,734 / 9,226km | 5,846 / 9,406km | 5,312 / 8,546km | 6,343 / 10,206km | 6,706 / 10,790km | 6,541 / 10,524km | 7,079 / 11,390km | 6,589 / 10,602km | 10,986 / 17,676km |
| Rome (FCO) | 899 / 1,446km | 685 / 1,102km | 829 / 1,334km | | 1,491 / 2,398km | 2,703 / 4,349km | 4,278 / 6,884km | 3,694 / 5,944km | 5,076 / 8,167km | 6,356 / 10,226km | 5,059 / 8,140km | 5,523 / 8,886km | 6,162 / 9,915km | 5,779 / 9,298km | 6,250 / 10,057km | 7,252 / 11,668km | 10,157 / 16,342km |
| Moscow (DME) | 1,587 / 2,553km | 1,547 / 2,489km | 2,140 / 3,444km | 1,491 / 2,398km | | 2,262 / 3,639km | 4,702 / 7,566km | 2,679 / 4,311km | 3,605 / 5,800km | 6,122 / 9,851km | 5,868 / 9,441km | 4,388 / 7,060km | 4,672 / 7,518km | 4,424 / 7,118km | 5,218 / 8,396km | 8,720 / 14,031km | 8,992 / 14,468km |
| Dubai (DXB) | 3,421 / 5,505km | 3,260 / 5,245km | 3,517 / 5,659km | 2,703 / 4,349km | 2,262 / 3,639km | | 6,850 / 11,022km | 1,359 / 2,187km | 3,639 / 5,855km | 8,340 / 13,420km | 4,102 / 6,600km | 3,051 / 4,909km | 4,941 / 7,949km | 3,685 / 5,929km | 3,634 / 5,847km | 8,733 / 14,051km | 7,482 / 12,039km |
| New York (JFK) | 3,452 / 5,554km | 3,635 / 5,849km | 3,589 / 5,775km | 4,278 / 6,884km | 4,702 / 7,566km | 6,850 / 11,022km | | 7,319 / 11,777km | 6,839 / 11,004km | 2,475 / 3,983km | 8,249 / 13,273km | 8,678 / 13,963km | 6,774 / 10,899km | 8,074 / 12,990km | 9,539 / 15,349km | 5,511 / 8,868km | 9,952 / 16,013km |
| Delhi (DEL) | 4,191 / 6,744km | 4,088 / 6,578km | 4,518 / 7,269km | 3,694 / 5,944km | 2,679 / 4,311km | 1,359 / 2,187km | 7,319 / 11,777km | | 2,371 / 3,815km | 8,015 / 12,896km | 5,024 / 8,083km | 1,831 / 2,947km | 3,649 / 5,871km | 2,332 / 3,752km | 2,580 / 4,152km | 10,017 / 16,117km | 6,477 / 10,422km |
| Beijing (PEK) | 5,081 / 8,175km | 5,103 / 8,211km | 5,734 / 9,226km | 5,076 / 8,167km | 3,605 / 5,800km | 3,639 / 5,855km | 6,839 / 11,004km | 2,371 / 3,815km | | 6,252 / 10,059km | 7,276 / 11,707km | 2,057 / 3,309km | 1,303 / 2,097km | 1,235 / 1,987km | 2,781 / 4,474km | 12,321 / 19,825km | 5,553 / 8,934km |
| Los Angeles (LAX) | 5,457 / 8,780km | 5,671 / 9,124km | 5,846 / 9,406km | 6,356 / 10,226km | 6,122 / 9,851km | 8,340 / 13,420km | 2,475 / 3,983km | 8,015 / 12,896km | 6,252 / 10,059km | | 10,635 / 17,111km | 8,271 / 13,308km | 5,489 / 8,831km | 7,261 / 11,684km | 8,772 / 14,114km | 6,164 / 9,918km | 7,490 / 12,051km |
| Durban (DUR) | 5,904 / 9,499km | 5,692 / 9,159km | 5,312 / 8,546km | 5,059 / 8,140km | 5,868 / 9,441km | 4,102 / 6,600km | 8,249 / 13,273km | 5,024 / 8,083km | 7,276 / 11,707km | 10,635 / 17,111km | | 5,511 / 8,868km | 8,353 / 13,440km | 6,560 / 10,555km | 5,244 / 8,438km | 5,147 / 8,282km | 6,571 / 10,573km |
| Bangkok (BKK) | 5,959 / 9,588km | 5,879 / 9,459km | 6,343 / 10,206km | 5,523 / 8,886km | 4,388 / 7,060km | 3,051 / 4,909km | 8,678 / 13,963km | 1,831 / 2,947km | 2,057 / 3,309km | 8,271 / 13,308km | 5,511 / 8,868km | | 2,853 / 4,590km | 1,049 / 1,688km | 877 / 1,411km | 10,420 / 16,766km | 4,663 / 7,503km |
| Tokyo (HND) | 5,975 / 9,614km | 6,047 / 9,730km | 6,706 / 10,790km | 6,162 / 9,915km | 4,672 / 7,518km | 4,941 / 7,949km | 6,774 / 10,899km | 3,649 / 5,871km | 1,303 / 2,097km | 5,489 / 8,831km | 8,353 / 13,440km | 2,853 / 4,590km | | 1,805 / 2,904km | 3,289 / 5,292km | 11,217 / 18,048km | 4,838 / 7,785km |
| Hong Kong (HKG) | 5,996 / 9,647km | 5,971 / 9,607km | 6,541 / 10,524km | 5,779 / 9,298km | 4,424 / 7,118km | 3,685 / 5,929km | 8,074 / 12,990km | 2,332 / 3,752km | 1,235 / 1,987km | 7,261 / 11,684km | 6,560 / 10,555km | 1,049 / 1,688km | 1,805 / 2,904km | | 1,588 / 2,555km | 11,278 / 18,147km | 4,582 / 7,372km |
| Singapore (SIN) | 6,767 / 10,888km | 6,668 / 10,729km | 7,079 / 11,390km | 6,250 / 10,057km | 5,218 / 8,396km | 3,634 / 5,847km | 9,539 / 15,349km | 2,580 / 4,152km | 2,781 / 4,474km | 8,772 / 14,114km | 5,244 / 8,438km | 877 / 1,411km | 3,289 / 5,292km | 1,588 / 2,555km | | 9,717 / 15,634km | 3,908 / 6,288km |
| Buenos Aires (BHI) | 7,241 / 11,651km | 7,220 / 11,617km | 6,589 / 10,602km | 7,252 / 11,668km | 8,720 / 14,031km | 8,733 / 14,051km | 5,511 / 8,868km | 10,017 / 16,117km | 12,321 / 19,825km | 6,164 / 9,918km | 5,147 / 8,282km | 10,420 / 16,766km | 11,217 / 18,048km | 11,278 / 18,147km | 9,717 / 15,634km | | 6,996 / 11,257km |
| Sydney (SYD) | 10,575 / 17,016km | 10,529 / 16,941km | 10,986 / 17,676km | 10,157 / 16,342km | 8,992 / 14,468km | 7,482 / 12,039km | 9,952 / 16,013km | 6,477 / 10,422km | 5,553 / 8,934km | 7,490 / 12,051km | 6,571 / 10,573km | 4,663 / 7,503km | 4,838 / 7,785km | 4,582 / 7,372km | 3,908 / 6,288km | 6,996 / 11,257km | |

Figures are in miles, and represent the great circle distance (the shortest distance between two points on the surface of the earth)

# TRAVEL OVERSEAS

## PASSPORT REGULATIONS

Application forms for UK passports can be obtained from Her Majesty's Passport Office's telephone advice line or website, regional passport offices or from main post offices.
HM PASSPORT OFFICE, T 0300-222 0000
W www.gov.uk/government/organisations/hm-passport-office

*Regional Passport Offices*
BELFAST, Law Society House, Ground Floor, 90–106 Victoria Street, Belfast BT1 3GN
DURHAM, Millburngate House, Durham DH97 1PA
GLASGOW, 3 Northgate, 96 Milton Street, Cowcaddens, Glasgow G4 0BT
LIVERPOOL, 101 Old Hall Street, Liverpool L3 9BD
LONDON, Globe House, 89 Eccleston Square, London SW1V 1PN
NEWPORT, Nexus House, Mission Court, Newport NP20 2DW
PETERBOROUGH, Aragon Court, Northminster Road, Peterborough PE1 1QG

Passport offices are open Monday to Saturday on an appointment-only basis (appointments should be arranged by calling the central telephone number listed above). For an additional fee, passport offices provide either a premium one-day service (not available for a first adult or child passport, extending a limited passport, replacing a lost, stolen or damaged passport or for complex amendments) or a one-week fast track service (except for first adult passports).

Standard postal applications take at least three weeks to be processed. The completed application form should be posted, with the appropriate supporting documents and fee, to the regional passport office indicated on the addressed envelope which is provided with each application form. Accompanying cheques should be made payable to 'Her Majesty's Passport Office', or to 'Post Office Ltd' when using the Check & Send service. For online applications, the completed online form will be printed out by the applicant, signed and posted to the Passport Office. After the paper copy has been received, online applications are returned within three weeks.

Applications can also be submitted through Check & Send outlets at selected main post offices, who, for a handling charge of £9.75, will forward the application form to the relevant regional passport office after having checked that it has been completed correctly and has the appropriate documents attached. These applications take a minimum of two weeks (first adult passport applications may take six weeks including a passport interview).

A passport cannot be issued or extended on behalf of a person already abroad; such persons should apply online (W https://passportapplication.service.gov.uk) or to the nearest local embassy, British High Commission or Consulate.

UK passports are granted to British citizens, British nationals (overseas), British overseas territories citizens, British overseas citizens, British subjects and British protected persons, and are generally available for travel to all countries. The possession of a passport does not exempt the holder from compliance with any immigration regulations in force in British or foreign countries, or from the necessity of obtaining a visa where required (*see* below for a list of countries for which UK citizens do not require a visa).

Biometric passports were introduced in 2006. The design and security features, including a chip containing the biometrics (the facial image and biographical data of the holder), render the passport more secure against forgery and aid border controls.

### ADULTS
A passport granted to a person over 16 will normally be valid for ten years. Thereafter, or if at any time the passport contains no further space for visas, a new passport must be obtained.

British nationals born on or before 2 September 1929 are eligible for a free standard passport.

### CHILDREN
Since 5 October 1998 all children under the age of 16 travelling abroad are required to have their own passport. This is primarily to help prevent child abductions. The passports are initially valid for five years, but can be renewed for a further five years at the end of this period.

### COUNTERSIGNATURES
A countersignature is needed if the application is for a first passport, to replace a lost, stolen or damaged passport, or to renew a passport for a child aged 11 or under. A countersignature is also needed for renewals if the applicant's appearance has significantly changed and the photograph in their previous passport is unrecognisable. The signatory must be willing to enter their own passport number on to the form. The list of acceptable countersignatories includes: MP; justice of the peace; minister of religion; a professionally qualified person (eg doctor, engineer, lawyer, teacher); bank officer; military officer; airline pilot; police officer; or a person of similar standing who has known the applicant for at least two years, who lives in the UK and who holds a British or Irish passport. A relative or partner, someone living at the same address as the applicant, or an employee of HM Passport Office must not countersign the application.

### PHOTOGRAPHS
Two identical, unmounted, recent colour photographs of the applicant must be sent. These photographs should measure 45mm by 35mm, be printed on plain white photographic paper and should be taken full face against a plain cream or light grey background. The photo must show the applicant's full face, looking straight at the camera, with a neutral expression and with their mouth closed. If a countersignature is required for the application, the person who countersigned the form should also certify one photograph as a true likeness of the applicant.

### DOCUMENTATION
In addition to two photographs, the applicant's current or previous British passport, and other documents in support of the statements made in the application, must be produced at the time of applying. Details of which documents are required are set out in the notes accompanying the application form.

If the passport applicant is a British national by naturalisation or registration, the certificate proving this must be produced with the application, unless the applicant holds a previous British passport issued after registration or naturalisation.

### INTERVIEWS
Interviews for adults applying for their first passport (not including those who held their own passport as a child) were introduced on 1 June 2007 to combat passport fraud and forgery. After applying for a passport, applicants will be sent a letter asking them to book an interview at one of the offices in the UK. Interviews last for approximately 30 minutes and applicants are asked to confirm facts about themselves that someone attempting to steal their identity would not know.

HM Passport Office recommends that new applicants now allow six weeks to receive their passport. There is no one-week fast-track service for first adult passports.

## 48-PAGE PASSPORTS

The 48-page 'jumbo' passport is intended to meet the needs of frequent travellers who fill standard passports well before the validity has expired. It is valid for ten years but is not available for children.

| PASSPORT FEES* | |
| --- | --- |
| Adult passport† | £72.50 |
| Child passport† | £46.00 |
| 48-page passport | £85.50 |
| People born on or before 2 Sep 1929 | Free |

* Standard postal applications only. Applications made at UK regional offices have a higher fee

† New passports and renewal or amendment of a passport are priced at the same rate

## HEALTH ADVICE

The NHS Choices website provides health advice for those travelling abroad, including information on immunisations and reciprocal health agreements with other countries. *See* W www.nhs.uk/livewell/travelhealth

*See also* National Health Service, Health Advice and Medical Treatment Abroad.

## VISA REQUIREMENTS

The countries listed below do not require British citizens to hold a valid visa or tourist card before arrival on short visits. For longer visits – or for countries not listed – it is advisable to check specific visa requirements with the appropriate embassy before making final travel arrangements (*see* Countries of the World section for foreign embassy contact details or W www.gov.uk/browse/abroad).

All EU member states and their overseas territories (*see* The European Union) except Ascension Island and Tristan da Cunha; Albania, Andorra, Antigua and Barbuda, Argentina, Armenia, Bahamas, Barbados, Belize, Bolivia, Bosnia and Hercegovina, Botswana, Brazil, Brunei, Canada, Chile, Colombia, Costa Rica, Dominica, Ecuador, El Salvador, Fiji, Gambia, Georgia, Grenada, Guatemala, Guyana, Haiti, Honduras*, Hong Kong, Iceland, Indonesia, Israel, Jamaica, Japan, Kazakhstan, Kiribati, Kosovo, Kuwait‡, Republic of Korea (South Korea), Kyrgyzstan, Lebanon*, Lesotho*, Liechtenstein, Macau, Macedonia, Madagascar*, Malawi*, Malaysia, Maldives*, Mauritius, Mexico*, Micronesia (Federated States of)*, Moldova, Monaco, Mongolia, Montenegro, Morocco, Namibia, New Zealand, Nicaragua, Norway, Palau, Panama‡, Paraguay, Peru, the Philippines, Samoa, San Marino, Senegal, Serbia, Seychelles, Singapore, Solomon Islands, South Africa, St Kitts and Nevis, St Lucia, St Vincent and the Grenadines, Swaziland, Switzerland, Taiwan, Thailand, Tonga, Trinidad and Tobago, Tunisia, Tuvalu, Ukraine, United Arab Emirates*, Uruguay, USA†, Vanuatu, Venezuela‡, Vietnam, Western Sahara.

* Upon entry to these countries a visa or tourist card will be issued at no extra charge

† Those travelling to the USA under the Visa Waiver Programme must provide details online (the Electronic System for Travel Authorisation) at least 72 hours in advance of travel

‡ Only applicable when arriving by air, those arriving at overland crossings or by sea should arrange documentation in advance

Brunei, Iraq, Solomon Islands, Sudan and Yemen bar entry to travellers with HIV/AIDS. Jordan, Papua New Guinea, Qatar, Russia and UAE have some entry restrictions for visitors with HIV/AIDS.

Residents of the following countries must hold a valid visa for every entry to the UK:

Afghanistan, Albania, Algeria, Angola, Armenia, Azerbaijan, Bahrain, Bangladesh, Belarus, Benin, Bhutan, Bolivia, Bosnia and Hercegovina, Burkina Faso, Burundi, Cabo Verde, Cambodia, Cameroon, Central African Republic, Chad, China, Colombia, Comoros, Dem. Rep. of Congo, Rep. of Congo, Côte d'Ivoire, Cuba, Djibouti, Dominican Republic, Ecuador, Egypt, Equatorial Guinea, Eritrea, Ethiopia, Fiji, Gabon, Gambia, Georgia, Ghana, Guinea, Guinea-Bissau, Guyana, Haiti, India, Indonesia, Iran, Iraq, Jamaica, Jordan, Kazakhstan, Kenya, Dem. People's Republic of Korea (North Korea), Kosovo, Kuwait, Kyrgyzstan, Laos, Lebanon, Lesotho, Liberia, Libya, Macedonia, Madagascar, Malawi, Mali, Mauritania, Moldova, Mongolia, Montenegro, Morocco, Mozambique, Myanmar, Nepal, Niger, Nigeria, Oman*, Pakistan, Palestinian Authority, Peru, Philippines, Qatar*, Russian Federation, Rwanda, Sao Tome and Príncipe, Saudi Arabia, Senegal, Serbia, Sierra Leone, Somalia, South Africa, South Sudan, Sri Lanka, Sudan, Suriname, Swaziland, Syria, Taiwan†, Tajikistan, Tanzania, Thailand, Togo, Tunisia, Turkey, Turkmenistan, Uganda, Ukraine, United Arab Emirates*, Uzbekistan, Venezuela, Vietnam, Yemen, Zambia, Zimbabwe.

* An electronic visa waiver should be obtained online prior to travel

† Passports containing personal ID numbers do not require visas

## BAGGAGE RESTRICTIONS

Individual airlines may set their own limits for hand luggage sizes, and travellers should check these before arriving at the airport: oversized baggage may have to be checked in as hold luggage, which often incurs a fee. Since January 2008, some airports have allowed passengers to take more than one item into the aircraft cabin. Other airports in the UK still have a one-bag restriction in place, and individual airlines may operate their own policies.

Passengers are allowed to carry small amounts of liquids as cabin luggage. These must be in containers not greater than 100ml, and placed in a single, transparent resealable bag which must not exceed 1 litre in capacity. Liquids are classified as drinks, make-up such as mascara or lipstick, sprays, pastes and gels. Medicines that are larger than 100ml must be accompanied by relevant documentation, such as a doctor's letter, and prior approval should be sought from the airline and departure airport. When travelling with a baby, enough liquid baby food, milk and sterilised water for the journey can be taken on board but containers may be opened and screened by security. One lighter is permitted as cabin luggage; this must be carried separately in a clear bag for the duration of the flight and not placed in the main hand luggage bag.

Sharp items must not be carried in hand luggage; any essential items should be placed in a bag in the hold. Prohibited sharp items include knives, large scissors, razor blades, tools, hiking poles and corkscrews. Other prohibited items include ammunition, chemical and toxic substances, work tools, sporting equipment, fireworks, party poppers and non-safety matches.

Electrical equipment such as laptops, MP3 players, mobile phones and cameras are allowed in hand luggage but they must be removed and screened seperately prior to boarding. Some electronic equipment is prohibited from use at certain times during a flight.

The amount passengers can check-in to the hold is determined by each airline. The airline will usually set a 'free' baggage allowance' according to the number of items and the weight of each item; if this is exceeded there is normally an excess charge. *See* W www.gov.uk/hand-luggage-restrictions overview for more information on baggage restrictions.

# THE EUROPEAN UNION

| MEMBER STATE | ACCESSION DATE | POPULATION* | COUNCIL VOTES | EP SEATS† |
|---|---|---|---|---|
| Austria | 1 Jan 1995 | 8,665,550 | 10 | 18 |
| Belgium | 1 Jan 1958 | 11,323,973 | 12 | 21 |
| Bulgaria | 1 Jan 2007 | 7,186,893 | 10 | 17 |
| Croatia | 1 July 2013 | 4,464,844 | 7 | 11 |
| Cyprus | 1 May 2004 | 1,189,197 | 4 | 6 |
| Czech Republic | 1 May 2004 | 10,644,842 | 12 | 21 |
| Denmark | 1 Jan 1973 | 5,581,503 | 7 | 13 |
| Estonia | 1 May 2004 | 1,265,420 | 4 | 6 |
| Finland | 1 Jan 1995 | 5,476,922 | 7 | 13 |
| France | 1 Jan 1958 | 66,553,766 | 29 | 74 |
| Germany | 1 Jan 1958 | 80,854,408 | 29 | 96 |
| Greece | 1 Jan 1981 | 10,775,643 | 12 | 21 |
| Hungary | 1 May 2004 | 9,897,541 | 12 | 21 |
| Ireland | 1 Jan 1973 | 4,892,305 | 7 | 11 |
| Italy | 1 Jan 1958 | 61,855,120 | 29 | 73 |
| Latvia | 1 May 2004 | 1,986,705 | 4 | 8 |
| Lithuania | 1 May 2004 | 2,884,433 | 7 | 11 |
| Luxembourg | 1 Jan 1958 | 570,252 | 4 | 6 |
| Malta | 1 May 2004 | 413,965 | 3 | 6 |
| The Netherlands | 1 Jan 1958 | 16,947,904 | 13 | 26 |
| Poland | 1 May 2004 | 38,562,189 | 27 | 51 |
| Portugal | 1 Jan 1986 | 10,825,309 | 12 | 21 |
| Romania | 1 Jan 2007 | 21,666,350 | 14 | 32 |
| Slovakia | 1 May 2004 | 5,445,027 | 7 | 13 |
| Slovenia | 1 May 2004 | 1,983,412 | 4 | 8 |
| Spain | 1 Jan 1986 | 48,146,134 | 27 | 54 |
| Sweden | 1 Jan 1995 | 9,801,616 | 10 | 20 |
| United Kingdom | 1 Jan 1973 | 64,088,222 | 29 | 73 |

* July 2015 estimate

† Under the Lisbon Treaty the total number of MEPs was set at 751 from the 2014 election onwards

*Sources:* CIA World Factbook; www.europa.eu

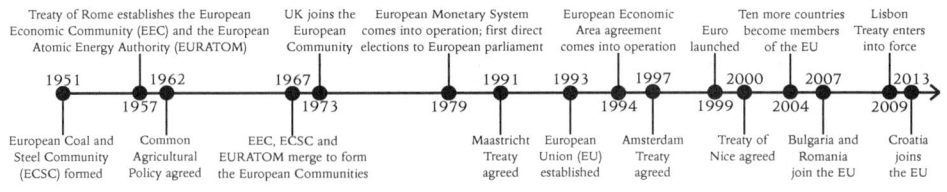

## LEGISLATION

The core of the European Union (EU) policy-making process is a dialogue between the European Commission (EC), which initiates and implements policy, and the Council of the European Union and the European parliament, which take policy decisions.

The original legislative process is known as the consultation procedure. The commission drafts a proposal which it submits to the council and to the parliament. The council then consults the Economic and Social Committee, the parliament and the Committee of the Regions; the parliament may request that amendments are made. With or without these amendments, the proposal is then adopted by the council and becomes law. The consultation procedure now only applies to cases not specifically subject to one of the other procedures.

The Single European Act introduced the assent procedure (now the consent procedure), whereby an absolute majority of the parliament must vote to approve laws in certain fields before they are passed. Issues covered by the procedure include uniform procedure for elections, some international agreements, violation of human rights and the accession of new member states.

The Maastricht Treaty introduced the co-decision procedure as an extension of the cooperation procedure; if, after the parliament's second reading of a proposal, the council and parliament fail to agree, a conciliation committee of the two will aim to reach a compromise. If a compromise is not reached, the parliament can reject the legislation by the vote of an absolute majority of its members. The Amsterdam Treaty extended the co-decision procedure to all areas covered by qualified majority voting, with the exception of measures related to the European Monetary Union.

The Lisbon Treaty extended the use of the co-decision procedure to several new fields, and renamed it the ordinary legislative procedure. The treaty strengthens the role of the European parliament so that it is involved in almost all new legislation. The changes give the European parliament equal powers in areas such as legal immigration, crime prevention and police cooperation. As a result of the Lisbon Treaty, the Council of the European Union must now vote in public on any new legislation, and if one-third of national parliaments disagree with a proposal then it can be sent back to be reviewed.

The council, commission and parliament can issue the following legislation:

• regulations, which are binding in their entirety and directly applicable to all member states; they do not need to be incorporated into national law to come into effect
• directives, which are less specific, binding as to the result to be achieved but leaving the method of implementation open to member states; a directive thus has no force until it is incorporated into national law
• decisions, which are also binding but are addressed solely to one or more member states or individuals in a member state
• recommendations or opinions, which are merely persuasive.

The council and parliament also have certain budgetary powers and determine all expenditure together. The final decision on whether the budget should be adopted or rejected lies with the parliament.

The European Central Bank (ECB) has legislative powers within its field of competence. The commission also has limited legislative powers, where it has been delegated the power to implement or revise legislation by the council.

## SCHENGEN AGREEMENT

The Schengen agreement was signed by France, Germany, Belgium, Luxembourg and the Netherlands in 1985. The agreement committed the five states to abolishing internal border controls, erecting external frontiers against illegal immigrants, drug traffickers, terrorists and organised crime, and it implemented the Schengen Information System which enables national border control, customs and police authorities from Schengen member states to share and access data on specific individuals, such as a person who may have been involved in a serious crime, or vehicles, documents or objects which may have been stolen, lost or misappropriated. The second-generation Schengen Information System (SIS II) entered into operation in April 2013. SIS II has improved functionalities such as new types of alerts and the potential to enter biometrics. It also contains copies of European arrest warrants, facilitating the detention of persons wanted for arrest, surrender or extradition.

Subsequently signed by Portugal and Spain, the agreement was ratified by the seven signatory states and entered into force in March 1995 with the removal of internal frontier, passport, customs and immigration controls. Austria and Italy became full members of the agreement in 1997; Greece in 2000; and Denmark, Finland and Sweden in 2001. The Czech Republic, Estonia, Hungary, Latvia, Lithuania, Malta, Poland, Slovakia and Slovenia joined in 2007. Although not members of the EU, Iceland and Norway joined the agreement in 2001 and Switzerland in 2008. The European Council granted Liechtenstein membership in 2011. There is no date set for Bulgaria, Croatia, Cyprus or Romania to join. The UK and the Republic of Ireland have not signed the agreement and are only partial participants, since their border controls have been maintained.

The Schengen agreement originated as an inter-governmental agreement and was adopted by the EU following the signing of the Amsterdam Treaty.

## MAASTRICHT TREATY

Agreed at Maastricht, the Netherlands, in 1991, the treaty came into effect in November 1993 following ratification by the member states. Three pillars formed its basis:

• the European Community (removing Economic from its name) with its established institutions and decision-making processes
• a common foreign and security policy charged with providing a forum for member states and EU institutions to consult on foreign affairs

cooperation in justice and home affairs, with the Council of the European Union coordinating policies on asylum, immigration, conditions of entry, cross-border crime, drug trafficking and terrorism

The treaty established a common European citizenship for nationals of all member states and introduced the principle of subsidiarity, whereby decisions are taken at the most appropriate level (national, regional or local). It extended European Community competency into the areas of environmental and industrial policies, consumer affairs, health, and education and training, and extended qualified majority voting in the Council of the European Union to some areas which had previously required a unanimous vote. The powers of the European parliament over the budget and over the EC were also enhanced, and a co-decision procedure enabled the parliament to override decisions made by the council in certain policy areas. A separate protocol to the Maastricht Treaty on social policy was agreed by 11 states and was incorporated into the Amsterdam Treaty in 1997 following adoption by the UK.

## AMSTERDAM TREATY

The treaties of Rome and Maastricht were amended through the Amsterdam Treaty, which was signed in 1997 and came into effect on 1 May 1999. It extended the scope of qualified majority voting and the powers of the European parliament. It also included a formal commitment to fundamental human rights, gave additional powers to the European Court of Justice and provided for the reform of common foreign and security policy.

## LISBON TREATY

The Lisbon Treaty was drawn up to replace the original European constitution, which was rejected in referendums in France and the Netherlands in 2005. It amends, rather than replaces, existing EU and European Community treaties. Ireland, the only country to hold a referendum on the Lisbon Treaty, voted against ratification on 12 June 2008. It held a second referendum on 2 October 2009 in which 67 per cent voted in favour, and – as a result of all EU countries approving the treaty – it came into force on 1 December 2009.

The Lisbon Treaty granted 'legal personality' (the right under international law to adopt laws and treaties) to the EU. The three pillars created by the Maastricht Treaty (see above) merged to make the EU a single legal entity, replacing the European Community. The Lisbon Treaty introduced a number of changes to the EU: a new president was appointed to the European Council for a two-and-a-half year term to replace the previous system of a six-month rotating presidency (this still exists in a reduced capacity for the Council of the European Union). The position of High Representative of the Union for Foreign Affairs and Security Policy was created, to enhance the EU's relations with other countries. The European parliament was strengthened and given more legislative and budgetary powers, and the number of MEPs was set at 751 from the 2014 election onwards. The system of qualified majority voting was extended to new policy areas and since 2014 has been based on a double majority of member states and people; a decision must be agreed by 55 per cent of member states representing at least 65 per cent of the EU population. The treaty establishes the principle of 'mutual recognition', whereby each member state acknowledges that legal decisions by other member states are valid; the UK has an opt-out clause with regard to some policies, such as external borders, asylum and immigration.

# ENLARGEMENT AND EXTERNAL RELATIONS

The procedure for accession to the EU is laid down in the Treaty of Rome; states must be stable European democracies governed by the rule of law with free-market economies. A membership application is studied by the EC, which produces an 'opinion'. If the opinion is positive, negotiations may be opened leading to an accession treaty that must be approved by all member state governments and parliaments, the European parliament, and the applicant state's government and parliament.

Cyprus, the Czech Republic, Estonia, Hungary, Latvia, Lithuania, Malta, Poland, Slovakia and Slovenia became full members of the EU on 1 May 2004. Bulgaria and Romania joined the EU on 1 January 2007, and Croatia on 1 July 2013. The Council of the EU recalled the offer of an accession partnership to Turkey in 2002, following the commission's conclusion that Turkey did not yet fully meet the required political criteria. However, at its December 2004 meeting in Brussels, the council decided that Turkey sufficiently met the Copenhagen political criteria, and accession negotiations began in October 2005. Montenegro was granted candidate status in December 2005 and accession negotiations began on 29 June 2012. Macedonia was granted candidate status in December 2005, but accession negotiations have not yet begun. Iceland applied for membership in July 2009 and accession negotiations started in June 2010, but were put on hold by the Icelandic government in May 2013. Serbia applied for membership in December 2009 and accession negotiations commenced in January 2014 while Albania was granted candidate status in June 2014. There are currently two potential candidates for membership of the EU: Bosnia and Hercegovina, and Kosovo.

The EU has several types of agreements with other European and non-European states. Association agreements (AAs), which must be ratified by all EU member states, can include commitments to reforming the country's trade, human rights, economy or political system in exchange for financial assistance or trade agreements. Partnership and cooperation agreements (PCAs) are legal frameworks, based on respect for democratic principles and human rights, setting out the political, economic and trade relationship between the EU and its partner countries. Each PCA is a ten-year bilateral treaty signed and ratified by the EU and the individual state. After the ten-year period expires the agreements are automatically renewed annually unless one of the parties objects. Agreements have been implemented (date when PCA entered into force in parentheses) with Russia (1997), Moldova and Ukraine (1998), Armenia, Azerbaijan, Georgia, Kazakhstan, Kyrgyzstan and Uzbekistan (1999), Tajikistan (2010), Indonesia (2014) and the Philippines and Vietnam (2015). In 2003 the PCA council summit strengthened EU cooperation with the Russian Federation by establishing a permanent partnership council (PPC). Negotiations for a new agreement to replace and update the existing PCA between the EU and Russia began in 2008 but have not been concluded.

Trade and cooperation agreements are intended to foster trade and economic relations, and include a commitment to respect the human rights and democratic principles of both parties. The EC has negotiated around 120 agreements worldwide.

The European neighbourhood policy was developed in 2004 and applies to the enlarged EU's immediate neighbours. It aims to strengthen stability and security through economic integration and deeper political relationships based on a mutual commitment to common values (democracy, human rights, rule of law, good governance and market economy).

A stabilisation and association agreement (SAA) – which is tailored to the western Balkan states – provides the contractual framework for relations to enable accession to the EU. Candidate or potential candidate countries with SAAs in force are Macedonia (2004), Albania (2009), Montenegro (2010), Serbia (2013) and most recently Bosnia and Hercegovina (1 June 2015). The EC adopted the SAA proposal for Kosovo on 30 April 2015, which is expected to enter into force in 2016 once the Council of the EU and the European parliament have also reached agreement on the proposal.

## TREATY OF NICE

The Treaty of Nice was signed in 2001 and came into effect in 2003. It enabled the EU to accommodate up to 13 new member states, and extended qualified majority voting to 30 further articles of the treaties that previously required unanimity. The weighting of votes in the European Council was altered from 1 January 2005 for the new member states. To obtain a qualified majority, a decision requires a specified number of votes (to be reviewed following each accession); the decision has to be approved by a majority of member states and represent at least 62 per cent of the total population of the EU. The treaty also set the number of MEPs that both existing and new member states would have following enlargement.

The Maastricht Treaty established the right of groups of member states to work together without requiring the participation of all members (enhanced cooperation); the Treaty of Nice removed the right of individual member states to veto the launch of enhanced cooperation.

# ECONOMY

## BUDGET OF THE EUROPEAN UNION

The principles of funding the European Union budget (formerly known as the European Community budget) were established by the Treaty of Rome and remain, with modifications, to this day. There is a legally binding limit on the overall level of resources (known as 'own resources') that the EU can raise from its member states; this limit is defined as a percentage of gross national income (GNI). Budget revenue and expenditure must balance, and there is therefore no deficit financing. The 'own resources' decision, which came into effect in 1975 and has been regularly updated, states that there are four sources of funding under which each member state makes contributions: duties charged on agricultural imports into the EU from non-member states; customs duties on imports from non-member states; contributions based on member states' shares of a notional EU-harmonised VAT base; and contributions based on member states' shares of total GNI. The latter is the budget-balancing item and covers the difference between total expenditure and the revenue from the other three sources. On 3 July 2013 the European parliament voted in favour of a budget for 2014–20; the budget was officially adopted following a vote on the legislation in November 2013. The overall budget for the seven-year period is €960bn in commitments and €908bn in payments (at 2011 prices). The EU's multiannual financial framework (MFF) for 2014–20 is 3.5 per cent less than the commitment appropriations under the MFF 2007–13 and 3.7 per cent less than the payment appropriations for the same period. In line with the political priorities of the EU, a strong emphasis was put on expenditure aimed at boosting growth and creating jobs, with an increase of 37 per cent over the 2007–13 model dedicated to 'competitiveness for growth and jobs'.

## EU BUDGET 2015

| | CA | PA |
|---|---|---|
| Smart and inclusive growth* | 66,782 | 66,923 |
| Sustainable growth: natural resources | 58,809 | 55,999 |
| Security and citizenship | 2,147 | 1,860 |
| Global Europe | 8,408 | 7,422 |
| Administration | 8,660 | 8,659 |
| Special Instruments | 515 | 352 |
| Total | €145,322m | €141,214m |

(1 euro = £0.72 as at 1 June 2015)
* Includes 'competitiveness for growth and jobs' and 'economic, social and territorial cohesion'
CA: commitment appropriations (maximum value of commitments to pay future bills)
PA: payment appropriations (actual amounts to pay for previous commitments)
Source: www.ec.europa.eu

## SINGLE MARKET

Even after the removal of tariffs and quotas between member states in the 1970s and 1980s, the European Community was still separated into a number of national markets by a series of non-tariff barriers. It was to overcome these internal barriers to trade that the concept of the single market was developed. The measures to be undertaken were codified in the commission's 1985 white paper on completing the internal market.

The white paper included articles removing obstacles distorting the internal market: the elimination of frontier controls; the mutual recognition of professional qualifications; the harmonisation of product specifications, largely by the mutual recognition of national standards; open tendering for public procurement contracts; the free movement of capital; the harmonisation of VAT and excise duties; and the reduction of state aid to particular industries. The Single European Act (SEA) aided the completion of the single market by changing the legislative process within the European Community, particularly with the introduction of qualified majority voting in the Council of the European Union for some policy areas, and the introduction of the assent procedure in the European parliament. The Single European Act also extended European Community competence into the fields of technology, the environment, regional policy, monetary policy and external policy. The single market came into effect on 1 January 1993, though full implementation of the elimination of frontier controls and the harmonisation of taxes have been repeatedly delayed. A fundamental review of the single market was completed in 2007, which resulted in an operational set of initiatives intended to modernise single market policy. Following the abolition of the European Community in 2009 as a result of the Lisbon Treaty, the single market policy now applies to the EU.

## EUROPEAN ECONOMIC AREA

The single market programme spurred European non-member states to open negotiations with the European Community on preferential access for their goods, services, labour and capital to the single market. Principal among these states were European Free Trade Association (EFTA) members who opened negotiations on extending the single market to EFTA by the formation of the European Economic Area (EEA), encompassing all 19 European Community and EFTA states. Agreement was reached in 1992, but the operation of the EEA was delayed by its rejection in a Swiss referendum, necessitating an additional protocol agreed by he remaining 18 states. The EEA came into effect in 1994 after ratification by 17 member states (Liechtenstein joined in 1995 after adapting its customs union with Switzerland).

Austria, Finland and Sweden joined the EU on 1 January 1995, leaving only Iceland, Liechtenstein and Norway as the non-EU EEA members. Under the EEA agreement, the three states are to adopt the EU's *acquis communautaire,* apart from in the fields of agriculture, fisheries, and coal and steel.

The EEA is controlled by regular ministerial meetings and by a joint EU-EFTA committee which extends relevant EU legislation to EEA states. Apart from single market measures, there is cooperation in several areas, including education, civil protection, research and development, consumer policy and tourism. An EFTA court has been established in Luxembourg and an EFTA surveillance authority in Brussels to supervise the implementation of the EEA Agreement.

The EEA Enlargement Agreement came into force on 1 May 2004, which allowed the simultaneous expansion of both the EU and the EEA without disruption of the internal market. A similar process took place to ensure that Bulgaria and Romania could become contracting parties to the EEA upon joining the EU in 2007 and Croatia in 2013.

## EUROPEAN MONETARY SYSTEM AND THE SINGLE CURRENCY

The European Monetary System (EMS) began operation in March 1979 with three main purposes. The first was to establish monetary stability in Europe, initially in exchange rates between European Community member state currencies through the Exchange Rate Mechanism (ERM), and in the longer term as part of a wider stabilisation process, overcoming inflation and budget and trade deficits. The second purpose was to overcome the constraints resulting from the interdependence of European Community economies, and the third was to aid the long-term process of European monetary integration.

The Maastricht Treaty set in motion timetables for achieving economic and monetary union (EMU) and a single currency (the euro). In May 1998, 11 member states were judged to fulfil or be close to fulfilling the necessary convergence criteria for participation in the first stage of EMU: Austria, Belgium, Finland, France, Germany, Ireland, Italy, Luxembourg, the Netherlands, Portugal and Spain. The criteria were that:

- the budget deficit should be 3 per cent or less of gross domestic product (GDP)
- total national debt must not exceed 60 per cent of GDP
- inflation should be no more than 1.5 per cent above the average rate of the three best performing economies in the EU
- long-term interest rates should be no more than 2 per cent above the average of the three best-performing economies in the EU in the previous 12 months
- applicants must have been members of the ERM for two years without having realigned or devalued their currency

Under the terms of a stability and growth pact agreed in December 1996 and revised in 2005, penalties may be imposed on EMU members with high budget deficits. Governments with deficits exceeding 3 per cent of GDP will receive a warning and will be obliged to pay up to 0.5 per cent of their GDP into a fund after ten months. This will become a fine if the budget deficit is not rectified within two years. A member state with negative growth will be allowed to apply for an exemption from the fine by referring to a number of relevant factors outlined in the pact.

As a result of the global economic downturn, by May 2010, 24 out of 27 countries in the EU had a deficit exceeding 3 per cent of GDP. The EC revised its existing recommendations in November 2009 and proposed extended deadlines for each country to correct its budget deficit. In the case of the UK, a deadline of 2014–15 was proposed, the longest deadline given to any of the EMU nations.

On 1 January 1999 the 11 qualifying member states adopted the euro at irrevocably fixed exchange rates, the European Central Bank (ECB) took charge of the single monetary policy, and the euro replaced the ECU (an artificial currency adopted by European Community member states in 1979 as an internal accounting unit for the EMS) on a one-for-one basis.

Subsequent member states who have fulfilled the criteria for participation and adopted the euro includes Greece on 1 January 2001, Slovenia on 1 January 2007, Cyprus and Malta on 1 January 2008, Slovakia on 1 January 2009, Estonia on 1 January 2011, Latvia on 1 January 2014 and Lithuania on 1 January 2015. Referendums on the adoption of the euro have been held in Denmark and Sweden, but participation was rejected. In June 2003 the UK announced that the euro would not be adopted at present on the grounds that the country was not economically ready to join the single currency, though a future joining of the eurozone was not ruled out.

The euro is now the legal currency in 19 participating states and is used by around 337.5 million people. Euro notes and coins were introduced on 1 January 2002 and circulated alongside national currencies for a period of up to two months, after which time national notes and coins ceased to be legal tender.

The ECB meets twice a month in Frankfurt to set the following month's monetary policy applicable to the countries participating in the euro. Its governing council has 25 members: the six members of the ECB's executive board and the 19 governors of the national central banks of the participating states.

### THE EURO CRISIS

*Greece*

Early in 2010, Greece's soaring budget deficit and the escalating cost of servicing the country's debt brought it to the verge of economic meltdown. In May 2010 the EC, ECB and IMF agreed a rescue package totalling €110bn (£95bn) and in February 2012 a further bailout package worth €130bn (£110bn). In November 2012, faced with the possibility of defaulting on its repayments, the Greek parliament passed a number of austerity measures. In June–July 2015 Greece defaulted on an IMF repayment, the ECB withdrew emergency funding and the government had to impose capital controls and close banks. International creditors offered a further bailout plan on the basis of the introduction of additional austerity measures; the rescue package was rejected by 60 per cent of the population in a referendum held on 5 July. Subsequently, a third bailout package totalling €86bn (£62bn), with different, but equally stringent, austerity measures was secured in August 2015, essentially to avoid Greece's departure from the eurozone. *See also* The Year 2014–15, Business and Finance.

*Other Countries*

In November 2010 the near collapse of the banking system in Ireland led to the approval of a €85bn (£72bn) rescue package by the EU and the IMF. In April 2011 Portugal requested financial assistance from the EU after rising borrowing costs left the government unable to pay its debts, and in May 2011 European finance ministers finalised the terms of a three-year bailout agreement worth €78bn

(£69bn). The Spanish government requested a eurozone rescue loan of around €100bn (£77bn) on 10 June 2012; eurozone finance ministers approved the loan on the same day. On 25 June, Cyprus became the fifth eurozone member to ask for financial assistance, citing significant exposure to the crippled Greek economy. A €10bn support package was agreed on 25 March 2013.

## COMMON AGRICULTURAL POLICY

The Common Agricultural Policy (CAP) was established to increase agricultural production, provide a fair standard of living for farmers and ensure the availability of food at reasonable prices. This aim was achieved by a number of mechanisms, including import levies, intervention purchase and export subsidies.

These measures stimulated production but also placed increasing demands on the budget, which was exacerbated by the increase in EC members and yields enlarged by technological innovation; the CAP now accounts for over 40 per cent of EU expenditure. To surmount these problems reforms were agreed in 1984, 1988, 1992, 1997, 1999, 2003, 2008 and 2013.

### REFORMS

The 1984 reforms created the system of co-responsibility levies: farm payments to the EC by volume of product sold. This system was supplemented by national quotas for particular products, such as milk. The 1988 reforms emphasised 'set-aside', whereby farmers are given direct grants to take land out of production as a means of reducing surpluses. The set-aside reforms were extended in 1993 for another five years and to every farm in the EC. The 1999 reforms further reduced surpluses of cereals, beef and milk by cutting the intervention prices by up to 20 per cent and compensating producers by making area payments. Under the reforms, CAP rules were also simplified, eliminating inconsistencies between policies.

In 2003, EU farm ministers adopted a fundamental reform of the CAP, which included the following provisions:

- a single farm payment for EU farmers, independent of production (begun in 2005)
- payment to be linked to meeting environmental, food safety, animal and plant health and animal welfare standards, and the requirement to keep all farmland in good condition
- a strengthened rural development policy with more EU money to help farmers meet EU production standards (begun in 2005)
- a reduction in direct payments for bigger farms
- a mechanism for financial discipline to ensure that the farm budget fixed until 2013 is not exceeded

The ten EU members that joined in 2004 were also given access to a special €5.8bn (£3.9bn) three-year funding package. The 2007–13 EU budget stipulated that no extra money would be made available to pay farm subsidies to Bulgaria and Romania.

A CAP 'health check' was carried out in 2008 and resulted in proposals intended to further modernise and streamline EU agricultural policy, and to allow farmers to follow market signals by breaking the link between direct payments and production. These include abolishing the requirement for farmers to leave 10 per cent of their arable land fallow, a gradual increase in milk quotas before their abolition in 2015 and a general reduction in market intervention.

On 13 March 2013, MEPs voted to adopt a controversial package of legislation, including approving both the extension of quotas and the rural development programme

that involves shared financing with national governments. The stated aim of the CAP reform was to strengthen the competitiveness and sustainability of agriculture and maintain its presence in all regions, to guarantee European citizens healthy and quality food production, and to preserve the environment and develop rural areas. On 26 June 2013, a political agreement on the CAP 2014–20 reforms was reached between the European Commission, parliament and council and on 16 December 2013, the council of EU agriculture ministers formally adopted the four basic regulations for the reformed CAP in addition to the transition rules for 2014. On 1 March 2014, the EC adopted the first package of delegated acts.

# INSTITUTIONS

## EUROPEAN PARLIAMENT

E eplondon@europarl.europa.eu W www.europarl.europa.eu; www.europarl.org.uk

The European parliament (EP) originated as the common assembly of the ECSC, acquiring its present name in 1962. The parliament now comprises 751 seats representing citizens of the 28 countries in the EU. Members (MEPs), initially appointed from the membership of national parliaments, have been directly elected at five-year intervals since 1979. Elections to the parliament are held on differing bases throughout the EU; British MEPs have been elected by a regional list system of proportional representation since June 1999. The most recent elections were held in May 2014.

MEPs serve on committees which scrutinise draft EU legislation and the activities of the EC. A minimum of 12 plenary sessions a year are held in Strasbourg and six additional shorter plenary sessions a year are held in Brussels; committees meet in Brussels, and the secretariat's headquarters is in Luxembourg.

The influence of the EP has gradually expanded within the EU since the Single European Act 1985, which introduced the cooperation procedure; the Maastricht Treaty, which extended the cooperation procedure and introduced the co-decision (now ordinary legislative) procedure (see Legislation); the Amsterdam Treaty, which effectively extended the ordinary legislative procedure to all areas except economic and monetary union, and taxation; and the Lisbon Treaty, which gave parliament legislative powers comparable with the Council of the European Union. The EP has general powers of supervision over the EC, and powers of consultation and co-decision with the Council of the European Union; it votes to approve a newly appointed commission and can dismiss it at any time by a two-thirds majority. Under the Maastricht Treaty it has the right to be consulted on the appointment of the new commission, and can also veto its appointment. Under the Lisbon Treaty, the parliament elects the president of the commission on the proposal of the European Council. The EP has an equal right to decide on budgetary matters as the Council of the European Union, and they work together to approve and adopt the entire annual budget. In accordance with the Maastricht Treaty, the EP appoints the European Ombudsman to provide citizens with redress against maladministration by EU institutions.

The EP's organisation is deliberately biased in favour of multinational political groupings; recognition of a political grouping in the parliament entitles it to offices, funding, representation on committees and influence in debates and legislation. A political group must be composed of a minimum of 25 MEPs elected in at least seven member states. For a list of UK MEPs, see European Parliament.

PARLIAMENT, allée du Printemps, F-67070 Strasbourg Cedex, France
E epstrasbourg@europarl.europa.eu
Wiertzstraat 60, B-1047 Brussels, Belgium
E parlamentarium@europarleuropa.eu
SECRETARIAT, Centre Européen, Plateau du Kirchberg, BP 1601, L-2929 Luxembourg
T (+352) 43001
*President,* Martin Schulz (Germany)
OMBUDSMAN, 1 avenue du Président Robert Schuman, CS 30403, F-67001 Strasbourg Cedex, France
W www.ombudsman.europa.eu
*Ombudsman,* Emily O'Reilly (Ireland)

EUROPEAN PARLIAMENT UK OFFICE
Europe House, 32 Smith Square, London SW1P 3EU
eplondon@europarl.europa.eu W www.europarl.org.uk

EUROPEAN PARLIAMENT OFFICE IN SCOTLAND
The Tun, 4 Jackson's Entry, Holyrood Road, Edinburgh EH8 8PJ
epedinburgh@europarl.europa.eu W www.europarl.org.uk

## COUNCIL OF THE EUROPEAN UNION
Wetstraat 175, Rue de la Loi, B-1048 Brussels, Belgium
W www.consilium.europa.eu

The Council of the European Union (Council of Ministers) is the main decision-making body of the EU, and formally comprises the ministers of the member states. Depending on the issue on the agenda, each country will be represented by the minister responsible for that subject. It passes laws, usually legislating jointly with the European parliament; coordinates the broad economic policies of the member states; approves the EU's budget jointly with the European parliament; defines and implements the EU's common foreign and security policy; concludes agreements between the EU and other states or international organisations; and coordinates the actions of member states and adopts measures in the area of police and judicial cooperation.

Council decisions are taken using one of three methods: by qualified majority vote, by a simple majority, or by unanimity. The treaties define which one of the three methods should be used in each subject area. Unanimity votes are taken on sensitive issues such as taxation and defence, but the qualified majority vote (QMV) is now used for the majority of council decisions. Under the provisions of the Lisbon Treaty, a new system of QMV began on 1 November 2014 although, until 31 March 2017, any member state may request that a decision be taken in accordance with the old QMV rules outlined below. Under the new system a qualified majority is achieved if:

• at least 55 per cent of member states approve (72 per cent where the council does not act on a proposal from the commission) *and*
• these member states represent at least 65 per cent of the EU's population

This system therefore assigns a vote to each member state while taking account of their demographic weight.

Under the old QMV system, member states had weighted votes in the council loosely proportional to their relative population sizes (*see* introductory table), with a total of 345 votes. Under this system a qualified majority was reached if a majority of member states approved (in some cases a two-thirds majority) *and* a minimum of 255 votes were cast in favour of the proposal (ie 73.9 per cent of the total). In addition, a member state could ask for confirmation that the votes in favour represented at least 62 per cent of the total population of the EU. If this was found not to be the case, the decision was not adopted.

The presidency of the Council of the European Union is held in rotation for six-month periods, setting the agenda for and chairing council meetings in all policy areas except foreign affairs. The holders of the presidency for the years 2015–16 are:

2015 Jan–Jun, Latvia     2016 Jan–Jun, Netherlands
2015 Jul–Dec, Luxembourg     2016 Jul–Dec, Slovakia

In the area of foreign affairs, council meetings are chaired by the High Representative of the Union for Foreign Affairs and Security Policy.
*High Representative of the Union for Foreign Affairs and Security Policy,* Federica Mogherini (Italy)

GENERAL SECRETARIAT OF THE COUNCIL OF THE EUROPEAN UNION
Wetstraat 175, rue de la Loi, B-1048 Brussels, Belgium
W www.consilium.europa.eu
*Secretary-General of the Council of the European Union,* Uwe Corsepius (Germany)

### EUROPEAN COUNCIL
The European Council, formed in 1974, was given formal recognition by the Single European Act in 1987; on 1 December 2009, under the Lisbon Treaty it has become a fully fledged institution of the EU with a permanent president. It normally meets four times a year, unless a special meeting is convened by the president, and comprises the heads of state or government of each EU member state and the president of the EC. Meetings are chaired by the president of the council.

The primary function of the European Council is to give political guidance in all areas of EU activity at both European and national levels. The European Council can issue declarations and resolutions expressing the opinions of the heads of state and governments, but its decisions are not legally binding.
*President of the European Council,* Donald Tusk (Poland)

## EUROPEAN COMMISSION
Wetstraat 200, rue de la Loi, B-1049 Brussels, Belgium

The European Commission (EC) consists of 28 commissioners, one per member state. The members of the commission are appointed for five-year renewable terms by the agreement of the member states; the terms run concurrently with the terms of the European parliament. The president and the other commissioners are nominated by the governments of the member states, and, under the terms of the Lisbon Treaty, the appointments are approved by the European parliament. The commissioners pledge sole allegiance to the EU. The commission initiates and implements EU legislation and is the guardian of the EU treaties. It is the exponent of community-wide interests rather than national preoccupations of the council. Each commissioner is supported by advisers and oversees the departments assigned to them, known as directorates-general and services.

President Jean-Claude Juncker was elected for a first mandate by the European parliament on 15 July 2014. He received 422 votes from a total of 729 and he took office in November 2014.

The commission has a total staff of around 33,000 permanent civil servants and temporary agents.

COMMISSIONERS *as at June 2015*
*President,* Jean-Claude Juncker (Luxembourg)
*First Vice-President, Better Regulation, Inter-Institutional Relations, the Rule of Law and the Charter of Fundamental Rights,* Frans Timmermans (Netherlands)
*Vice-President, High Representative of the Union for Foreign Affairs and Security Policy,* Federica Mogherini (Italy)

*Vice-President, Budget and Human Resources,* Kristalina Georgieva (Bulgaria)
*Vice-President, Digital Single Market,* Andrus Ansip (Estonia)
*Vice-President, Energy Union,* Maros Sefcovic (Slovakia)
*Vice-President, Euro amd Social Dialogue,* Valdis Dombrovskis (Latvia)
*Vice-President, Jobs, Growth, Investment and Competitiveness,* Jyrki Katainen (Finland)
*Transport and Space,* Violeta Bulc (Slovenia)
*Digital Economy and Society,* Gunther Oettinger (Germany)
*European Neighbourhood Policy and Enlargement Negotiations,* Johannes Hahn (Austria)
*Trade,* Cecilia Malmstrom (Sweden)
*International Cooperation and Development,* Neven Mimica (Croatia)
*Climate Action and Energy,* Miguel Arias Canete (Spain)
*Environment, Maritime Affairs and Fisheries,* Karmenu Vella (Malta)
*Health and Food Safety,* Vytenis Andriukaitis (Lithuania)
*Migration and Home Affairs,* Dimitris Avramopoulos (Greece)
*Employment, Social Affairs, Skills and Labour Mobility,* Marianne Thyssen (Belgium)
*Economic and Financial Affairs, Taxation and Customs,* Pierre Moscovici (France)
*Humanitarian Aid and Crisis Management,* Christos Stylianides (Cyprus)
*Agriculture and Rural Development,* Phil Hogan (Ireland)
*Financial Stability, Financial Services and Capital Markets Union,* Jonathan Hill (UK)
*Internal Markets., Industry, Entrepreneurship and SMEs,* Elzbieta Bienkowska (Poland)
*Justice, Consumers and Gender Equality,* Vera Jourova (Czech Republic)
*Education, Culture, Youth and Citizenship,* Tibor Navracsics (Hungary)
*Regional Policy,* Corina Cretu (Romania)
*Competition,* Margrethe Vestager (Denmark)
*Research, Innovation and Science,* Carlos Moedas (Portugal)

EC REPRESENTATION OFFICES
UK, Europe House, 32 Smith Square, London SW1P 3EU
    T 020-7973 1992
WALES, 2 Caspian Point, Caspian Way, Cardiff CF10 4QQ
    T 029-2089 5020
SCOTLAND, 9 Alva Street, Edinburgh EH2 4PH
    T 0131-225 2058
NORTHERN IRELAND, 74–76 Dublin Road, Belfast BT2 7HP
    T 028-9024 0708

## COURT OF JUSTICE OF THE EUROPEAN UNION

Palais de la Cour de Justice, boulevard Konrad Adenauer, Kirchberg, L-2925 Luxembourg
W www.curia.europa.eu

The Lisbon Treaty gave a new framework to the EU court system. The court of justice of the European Union is now composed of three courts: the court of justice, the general court and the civil service tribunal.

### COURT OF JUSTICE
The court of justice exists to safeguard the law in the interpretation and application of EU treaties, to decide on the legality of EU legislation, and to determine infringements of the treaties. Cases may be brought to it directly by the member states and EU institutions. Questions on EU law may be referred to the court of justice by national courts. The decisions of the court are directly binding in the member states. The court's powers were extended by the Maastricht

Treaty, allowing it to impose fines on member states who breach EU law. The court comprises 28 judges – one from each member state – and nine advocates-general. These positions are appointed for renewable six-year terms by the member governments.
*President,* Vassilios Skouris (Greece)

### GENERAL COURT
Established under powers conferred by the Single European Act, the general court (known as the Court of First Instance until 1 December 2009) has jurisdiction to hear and determine direct actions brought by natural persons (ie human beings) or legal persons (ie an entity with a legal personality, such as a company, association etc) against any of the institutions, bodies, agencies or offices of the EU, except those cases reserved for the court of justice. Additionally, the general court hears actions seeking compensation for damage caused by the institutions of the EU or their staff. It also has jurisdiction to hear actions brought by member states against the EC and actions relating to community trade marks. The court is composed of 28 judges, one from each member state, appointed for renewable six-year terms by the individual national governments.
*President,* Marc Jaeger (Luxembourg)

### CIVIL SERVICE TRIBUNAL
Established in 2005, the civil service tribunal has jurisdiction to hear disputes between civil servants and the EU in matters such as pay, disciplinary measures and accidents at work. It does not deal with disputes between national governments and their employees. There are seven judges, appointed for renewable six-year terms.
*President,* Sean Van Raepenbusch (Belgium)

## EUROPEAN COURT OF AUDITORS
12 rue Alcide de Gasperi, L-1615 Luxembourg
E eca-info@eca.europa.eu  W www.eca.europa.eu

The European Court of Auditors, established in 1977, examines the accounts of all revenue and expenditure of the EU. It evaluates whether all revenue has been received and all expenditure incurred in a lawful and regular manner and in accordance with the principles of sound financial management. The court issues an annual report and a statement of assurance as to the reliability of the accounts and the legality and regularity of the underlying transactions. It also publishes special reports on specific topics and delivers opinions on financial matters. The court has one member from each member state, appointed for a renewable six-year term by the Council of the European Union following consultation with the European parliament.
*President,* Vitor Caldeira (Portugal)

## FINANCIAL BODIES

## EUROPEAN CENTRAL BANK
Kaiserstrasse 29, D-60311 Frankfurt am Main, Germany
E info@ecb.europa.eu  W www.ecb.europa.eu

The ECB, which superseded the European Monetary Institute, became fully operational on 1 January 1999 and defines and implements the single monetary policy for the euro area. The ECB's main task is to maintain the euro's purchasing power and price stability in the 18 EU countries that have introduced the currency since 1999. Its decision-making bodies are the executive board, the governing council and the general council. The executive board consists of the president, the vice-president and four other members. All members are appointed by the governments of the states participating in the single currency, at the level of heads of state and government. The governing council, the main decision-making body of the ECB, comprises the six members of the executive board and the governors of the national central banks of the 19 euro area states. The general council comprises the president and vice-president and the 28 governors of the national central banks of all the member states of the EU, the other members of the executive board being entitled to participate but not to vote. The ECB is independent of national governments and of all other EU institutions.

*President,* Mario Draghi (Italy)
*Vice-President,* Vitor Constancio (Portugal)

## EUROPEAN INVESTMENT BANK
100 boulevard Konrad Adenauer, L-2950 Luxembourg
**E** info@eib.org **W** www.eib.europa.eu

The European Investment Bank (EIB) was set up in 1958 under the terms of the Treaty of Rome and is the financing arm of the EU. The EIB's main activity is to provide long-term loans in support of investments undertaken by private or public promoters, for projects furthering European integration.

The EIB also operates outside the EU, in support of EU development and cooperation policies in partner countries including the enlargement area of Europe (both candidate and potential candidate countries), the Mediterranean, Russia and the southern Caucasus, Africa, the Caribbean, the Pacific, Asia and Latin America.

The EIB assesses and selects the projects it finances independently and usually only finances up to 50 per cent of the total cost of a project.

The bank is not dependent on the EU budget, and raises its own resources on the capital markets. It is the biggest supranational bond issuer and lender in the world with an AAA credit rating. In 2014 it lent a total of €77bn (£55bn), of which €69bn (£49bn) went to projects in EU member states.

The shareholders of the EIB are the 28 member states, whose ministers of economy and finance constitute its board of governors. This body lays down general directives on the credit policy of the bank and appoints members to the board of directors. The board of directors consists of 28 members nominated by the member states, and one by the European Commission. It takes decisions on the granting and raising of loans and the fixing of interest rates. The management committee, composed of the bank's president and eight vice-presidents and also appointed by the board of governors, is responsible for the day-to-day operations of the bank.

*President,* Werner Hoyer (Germany)

## ADVISORY BODIES

### COMMITTEE OF THE REGIONS
Bâtiment Jacques Delors, rue Belliard 99–101, B-1040 Brussels, Belgium
**W** www.cor.europa.eu

The Committee of the Regions (CoR) was established in 1994 and is the political assembly which provides local and regional authorities with a voice within the EU. The Lisbon Treaty obliges the EC, the Council of the European Union and the European parliament to consult the CoR whenever new legislative proposals are made in areas which have repercussions at regional or local level. The CoR then issues opinions on these proposals for EU laws, and also has the right to comment on any amendments to proposed legislation by MEPs. The CoR has the right to challenge new EU laws in the European court of justice if it believes it has

not been correctly consulted by the commission, parliament or council or for any infringement of the subsidiarity principle.

The committee has 350 full members; the proportion of members from each of the 28 member states of the EU approximately reflects the size of the individual country's population. Committee members are proposed by the member states to the Council of the European Union, which appoints them for a five-year renewable term of office. Members must hold a regional or local authority electoral mandate or be politically accountable to an elected assembly. They participate in the work of seven specialist commissions which are responsible for drafting the CoR's opinions and resolutions on a wide range of topics.

*President,* Markku Markkula (Finland)
*Secretary-General,* Jiri Burianek (Czech Republic/Germany)

### EUROPEAN ECONOMIC AND SOCIAL COMMITTEE
rue Belliard 99, B-1040 Brussels, Belgium **W** www.eesc.europa.eu

The European Economic and Social Committee (EESC) is a consultative body of the EU. It comprises 353 members drawn from economic and social interest groups in Europe; these members are appointed by the governments of the 28 member states for a five-year renewable term. The last renewal occurred in October 2010 for the 2010–15 mandate. The EESC is divided into three groups: employers, workers, and other interest groups such as consumers, farmers and the self-employed. Every two-and-a-half years the EESC elects a bureau made up of 40 members, including a president and two vice-presidents chosen from each of the three groups in rotation. The EESC issues opinions on draft EU legislation, which are forwarded to the commission, council and parliament. The EESC's competencies have increased as a result of revisions to the Treaty of Rome, and the Lisbon Treaty strengthens the committee's role.

*President,* Henri Malosse (France)
*Secretary-General,* Luis Planas Puchades (Spain)

## AGENCIES

### EUROPEAN ENVIRONMENT AGENCY
Kongens Nytorv 6, DK-1050 Copenhagen K, Denmark
**T** (+45) 3336 7100 **W** www.eea.europa.eu

The European Environment Agency (EEA) aims to support sustainable development and to help achieve significant and measurable improvement in Europe's environment, through the provision of information to policy-making agents and the public. The EEA has been operational since 1994, and now has 33 member countries. It is an EU body but is open to non-EU countries that share its objectives. The management board consists of representatives of the member countries, two representatives of the EC and two representatives designated by the European parliament.

*Chair,* Elisabeth Freytag-Rigler (Austria)

### EUROPEAN JUDICIAL COOPERATION UNIT (EUROJUST)
Maanweg 174, 2516 AB The Hague, The Netherlands
**E** info@eurojust.europa.eu **W** www.eurojust.europa.eu

The European Union's Judicial Cooperation Unit (Eurojust) was established in 2002 with the aim of developing Europe-wide cooperation in cases involving serious crime committed across more than one member state's jurisdiction. Eurojust also facilitates the provision of international mutual legal assistance and helps to implement extradition requests. It is a key interlocutor with the European parliament, the Council of the European Union and the EC.

The college of Eurojust is composed of 28 national members, one nominated by each member state. These members are experienced prosecutors, judges or police officers. *President of the College,* Michèle Coninsx (Belgium)

## EUROPEAN POLICE OFFICE (EUROPOL)

Eisenhowelaan 73, 2517 KK The Hague, The Netherlands
W www.europol.europa.eu

The European Police Office (Europol) came into being on 1 October 1998 and assumed its full powers on 1 July 1999. It superseded the Europol Drugs Unit and exists to improve police cooperation between member states and to combat terrorism, illicit traffic in drugs and other serious forms of organised international crime. It is ultimately responsible to the Council of the European Union. Each member state has a national unit to liaise with Europol, and the units send at least one liaison officer to represent its interests at Europol headquarters. Europol employs around 800 staff at its headquarters and handles around 9,000 cases a year. It works closely with law enforcement agencies in the 28 EU member states and non-EU partner states, including Australia, the USA and Canada.

On 11 January 2013, the European Cybercrime Centre (EC3), located at Europol headquarters, was launched to combat illegal online activities carried out by organised crime groups.

*Director,* Rob Wainwright (UK)

# EUROPEAN PARLIAMENT POLITICAL GROUPINGS

*as at September 2015*

|  | EPP | S&D | ALDE | Greens/EFA | ECR | GUE/NGL | EFD | ENF | Others | Total |
|---|---|---|---|---|---|---|---|---|---|---|
| Austria | 5 | 5 | 1 | 3 | – | – | – | 4 | – | 18 |
| Belgium | 4 | 4 | 6 | 2 | 4 | – | – | 1 | – | 21 |
| Bulgaria | 7 | 4 | 4 | – | 2 | – | – | – | – | 17 |
| Croatia | 5 | 2 | 2 | 1 | 1 | – | – | – | – | 11 |
| Cyprus | 2 | 2 | – | – | – | 2 | – | – | – | 6 |
| Czech Republic | 7 | 4 | 4 | – | 2 | 3 | 1 | – | – | 21 |
| Denmark | 1 | 3 | 3 | 1 | 4 | 1 | – | – | – | 13 |
| Estonia | 1 | 1 | 3 | 1 | – | – | – | – | – | 6 |
| Finland | 3 | 2 | 4 | 1 | 2 | 1 | – | – | – | 13 |
| France | 20 | 13 | 7 | 6 | – | 4 | 1 | 21 | 2 | 74 |
| Germany | 34 | 27 | 4 | 13 | 8 | 8 | – | – | 2 | 96 |
| Greece | 5 | 4 | – | – | 1 | 6 | – | – | 5 | 21 |
| Hungary | 12 | 4 | – | 2 | – | – | – | – | 3 | 21 |
| Ireland | 4 | 1 | 1 | – | 1 | 4 | – | – | – | 11 |
| Italy | 15 | 31 | – | – | 2 | 3 | 17 | 5 | – | 73 |
| Latvia | 4 | 1 | 2 | 1 | 1 | – | 1 | – | – | 8 |
| Lithuania | 2 | 2 | 4 | 1 | 1 | – | 1 | – | – | 11 |
| Luxembourg | 3 | 1 | 1 | 1 | – | – | – | – | – | 6 |
| Malta | 3 | 3 | – | – | – | – | – | – | – | 6 |
| The Netherlands | 5 | 3 | 7 | 2 | 2 | 3 | – | 4 | – | 26 |
| Poland | 23 | 5 | – | – | 19 | – | 1 | 2 | 1 | 51 |
| Portugal | 7 | 8 | 2 | – | – | 4 | – | – | – | 21 |
| Romania | 13 | 15 | 3 | – | – | – | – | 1 | – | 32 |
| Slovakia | 6 | 4 | – | – | 3 | – | – | – | – | 13 |
| Slovenia | 5 | 1 | 1 | 1 | – | – | – | – | – | 8 |
| Spain | 17 | 14 | 8 | 4 | – | 11 | – | – | – | 54 |
| Sweden | 4 | 6 | 3 | 4 | – | 1 | 2 | – | – | 20 |
| UK | – | 20 | 1 | 6 | 20 | 1 | 24 | 1 | 1 | 73 |
| *Total* | 217 | 190 | 70 | 50 | 74 | 52 | 45 | 39 | 14 | 751 |

EPP – European People's Party (Christian Democrats)
W www.eppgroup.eu
S&D – Progressive Alliance of Socialists and Democrats in the European Parliament
W www.socialistsanddemocrats.eu
ALDE – Alliance of Liberals and Democrats for Europe
W www.alde.eu
Greens/EFA – Greens/European Free Alliance
W www.greens-efa.eu

ECR – European Conservatives and Reformists
W www.ecrgroup.eu
GUE/NGL – European United Left/Nordic Green Left
W www.guengl.eu
EFD – Europe of Freedom and Democracy Group
W www.efdgroup.eu
ENF – Europe of Nations and Freedom Group

# INTERNATIONAL ORGANISATIONS

International organisations are intergovernmental organisations, whose membership can only include either sovereign states or other international organisations. They are subject to international law and are capable of entering into agreements among themselves or with states. They do not include private non-governmental organisations with an international scope. International organisations are usually established by a treaty providing them with legal recognition, which distinguishes them from collections of states such as the G8.

## AFRICAN UNION
PO Box 3243, Addis Ababa, Ethiopia
T (+251) (1) 1551 7700 E webmaster@africa-union.org
W www.au.int

The African Union (AU) was launched in 2002 as a successor to the amalgamated Organisation of African Unity (OAU) and the African Economic Community. It currently has 54 members, representing every African country except Morocco. Morocco left the OAU in 1984 in protest at the admission of Saharan Arab Democratic Republic (representing Western Sahara). The AU aims to further African unity, solidarity and democracy, to coordinate political, economic, social and defence policies, and to intervene in regional conflicts on a humanitarian basis.

Chief AU governing organs include the assembly of heads of state or government, the ultimate decision-making body; the executive council, composed of foreign ministers from member states and which advises the assembly; the African Commission, which is the AU secretariat and consists of one chair, one deputy chair and eight commissioners, each with a separate portfolio, who elect a chair to a four-year term; the peace and security council, modelled on that of the UN and capable of military intervention; and the pan-African parliament, established in 2004 to advise heads of state.

Substantial budgetary arrears due to delays in the payment of national contributions have presented the AU with difficulties in achieving its objectives. Currently the AU has a joint peace keeping force with the United Nations (UNAMID) that has been deployed in the Darfur region of Sudan since 2007 (*see also* United Nations, Peacekeeping Forces). The AU mission in Somalia, AMISOM, was mandated in 2007 by the AU peace and security council and as at November 2015 had deployed 22,126 military personnel to the country.

*Chair,* Dr Nkosazana Dlamini Zuma (South Africa)

## ANDEAN COMMUNITY
General Secretariat, Paseo de la República 3895, San Isidro, Lima 27, Peru
T (+51) (1) 710 6400 E correspondencia@comunidadandina.org
W www.comunidadandina.org

The Andean Community (CAN), known as the Andean Pact until 1996, began operating formally on 21 November 1969 when its commission was established. It comprises four member states – Bolivia, Colombia, Ecuador and Peru – and the organisations and institutions of the Andean Integration System (AIS). Argentina, Brazil, Chile, Paraguay and Uruguay are associated states.

The community's objectives are to facilitate economic growth, create jobs and facilitate regional integration towards the goal of a Latin American common market. It also aims to reduce the inequalities in development between member states. It pursues its objectives through a programme of trade liberalisation, a common external tariff, the relaxation of border controls, coordination between national legislatures and the promotion of industrial, agricultural and technological development. The community also promotes democratic practices, respect for human rights and environmental sustainability. Additionally, CAN supports cultural integration by providing media platforms for sharing documentaries, news and other cultural programming.

The general secretariat of the Andean Community is its executive body, responsible for administration and dispute resolution. The general secretariat operates under the direction of the secretary-general, who is elected by the Andean Council of Foreign Ministers (ACFM). It can propose decisions or suggestions to the ACFM; it also manages the integration process, ensures that community commitments are fulfilled and maintains relations with the member countries and the executive bodies of other international organisations.

The Andean presidential council is the highest-level body of the AIS and comprises the presidents of the member states. Its responsibilities include setting new policies, evaluating the integration process and communicating with other bodies. The chairmanship is rotated among the members of the council each calendar year.

Since 2005, a policy of free flow of persons has enabled citizens to travel, work and study throughout the area without a visa.

*Secretary-General,* Pablo Guzmán Laugier (Bolivia)

## ARAB MAGHREB UNION
73 rue Tensift, Agdal, Rabat, Morocco
T (+212) (5) 376 81371 E sg.uma@maghrebarabe.org
W www.maghrebarabe.org

The Treaty establishing the Arab Maghreb Union (AMU) was signed on 17 February 1989 by the heads of state of the five member states: Algeria, Libya, Mauritania, Morocco and Tunisia. The AMU aims to strengthen ties between the member countries by developing agriculture and commerce, working towards a customs union and economic common market.

Decisions must be unanimous and are made by a council of heads of state, which is briefed by a council of foreign affairs ministers. The council of heads of state has not assembled since 1994 because of a dispute over the status of Western Sahara. A consultative assembly – consisting of 30 representatives from each member state – is based in Algiers; the secretariat is in Rabat; and the court of justice, with two judges from each country, operates in Nouakchott, Mauritania.

*Secretary-General,* Habib Ben Yahia (Tunisia)

## ARCTIC COUNCIL
Fram Centre, 9296Troms, Norway
T (+47) 7775 0140 E acs@arctic-council.org
W www.arctic-council.org

The Arctic Council was founded in 1996 in Ottawa, Canada, and is a regional forum for socio-economic development and scientific research within the Arctic region, with particular emphasis on environmental conservation and sustainable developments. It comprises eight states: Canada, Denmark (including Greenland and the Faroe Islands), Finland, Iceland, Norway, Russia, Sweden and the USA. A further six organisations representing indigenous peoples are granted permanent participatory status and include the Saami Council, Inuit Circumpolar Conference and the Arctic Athabaskan Council. 12 states (China, France, Germany, India, Italy, Japan, the Netherlands, Poland, Singapore, South Korea, Spain and the UK) have observer status.

Decisions within the Arctic Council are made at biennial ministerial meetings attended by foreign ministers or designates of the member states. The chairmanship of the council and secretariat also rotate on a biennial basis. Between these meetings, the operation of the council is administered by the Committee of Senior Arctic Officials, which meets biannually.

Arctic Council initiatives are carried out by six working groups, each focusing on specific issues such as the monitoring and prevention of pollution; climate change; biodiversity; and public health.

*Chair 2015–17,* John Kerry (USA)
*Director of the Secretariat,* Magnus Johannesson (Iceland)

## ASIA COOPERATION DIALOGUE

E acd@mfa.go.th W www.acddialogue.com

The Asia Cooperation Dialogue (ACD) was initiated by the former prime minister of Thailand, Thaksin Shinawatra, and inaugurated in June 2002. It currently has 32 members, with Morocco granted development partner status.

Its purpose is to provide a continent-wide forum to assist development in countries in Asia, with the ultimate goal of creating a consolidated Asian trade community to enhance competitiveness in the global market and to reduce poverty. It aims to achieve these objectives through promoting interdependence among Asian countries, improving quality of life and expanding the continent's trade and financial markets.

Representatives from each of the member states (typically foreign ministers) meet annually to discuss ACD developments, issues of regional cooperation and methods of enhancing Asian unity. In addition, ministers also meet during the annual UN general assembly to discuss the implementation of policy and a common approach to international issues.

## ASIAN-AFRICAN LEGAL CONSULTATIVE ORGANISATION

29 C, Rizal Marg, Diplomatic Enclave, Chanakyapuri, New Delhi 110021, India
T (+91) (11) 2419 7000 E mail@aalco.int W www.aalco.int

The Asian-African Legal Consultative Organisation (AALCO), founded as a result of the Bandung Conference of 1955, was previously known as both the Asian Legal Consultative Committee and the Asian-African Legal Consultative Committee before its name was changed again in 2001. It was initially established as a non-permanent committee for a five-year term which was repeatedly extended until 1981, when it was granted permanent status. It has 47 member states.

The functions of the AALCO include serving as an advisory body to its member states in the field of international law, operating as a forum for common concerns among its members and making recommendations to governments and other international organisations. Representatives from member states meet for the annual session which is hosted on a rotational basis and is attended by members of government, observers from other organisations and members of the International Court of Justice and International Law Commission.

The secretariat is located in New Delhi and is responsible for the day-to-day functioning of the organisation. It is headed by a secretary-general, who is elected to a four-year term that can be renewed once. Other infrastructure includes four regional arbitration centres, located in Egypt, Iran, Malaysia and Nigeria.
*Secretary-General,* Dr Rahmat Mohamad (Malaysia)

## ASIAN DEVELOPMENT BANK

6 ADB Avenue, Mandaluyong City 1550, Metro Manila, The Philippines
T (+63) 632 4444 W www.adb.org

The Asian Development Bank (ADB), founded in 1966, is a multilateral financial institution dedicated to reducing poverty in Asia and the Pacific. It has 67 member countries from across the world. The ADB extends loans, equity investments and technical assistance to governments and public and private enterprises in its member countries, and promotes the investment of public and private capital for development. The bank's programmes prioritise economic growth, human development, good governance, environmental protection, private sector growth and regional cooperation.

The ADB is controlled by its board of governors, which meets annually and consists of a representative from each of the member states. It elects and delegates its powers to a board of directors which is responsible for administration and policy review.

The ADB raises funds through members' contributions and issuing bonds on the world's capital markets. In 2014, the ADB provided loans totalling US$11,200m (£7,277m), grants amounting to US$405m (£263m), and US$148m (£96m) in technical assistance.
*President,* Takehiko Nakao (Japan)

## ASIA-PACIFIC ECONOMIC COOPERATION

35 Heng Mui Keng Terrace, Singapore 119616
T (+65) 6891 9600 E info@apec.org W www.apec.org

The Asia-Pacific Economic Cooperation (APEC) is an economic forum for Pacific Rim countries to discuss regional economy, cooperation, trade and investment. APEC was founded in 1989 in response to the growing interdependence among Asia-Pacific economies. The 1994 Declaration of Common Resolve envisaged free and open trade between member states with industrialised economies by 2010, extending to members with developing economies by 2020. At the 2014 summit in Beijing, China APEC leaders issued the twenty-second APEC economic leaders' declaration in which they committed to increased regional economic integration, innovative development, economic reform and growth and strengthened connectivity and infrastructure. Its 21 members define and fund work programmes for APEC's four committees, 15 working groups and other special task groups.

APEC's chairmanship rotates annually among member states and the chair is responsible for hosting the annual leaders' meeting, as well as meetings of foreign affairs and trade ministers. The permanent secretariat, based in Singapore, is responsible for implementing policy, and is headed by an executive director selected by member states to serve a three-year term.
*Executive Director,* Dr Alan Bollard (New Zealand)

## ASSOCIATION OF SOUTH-EAST ASIAN NATIONS

Jalan Sisingamangaraja 70a, Jakarta 12110, Indonesia
T (+62) (21) 726 2991/724 3372 E public@aseansec.org
W www.asean.org

The Association of South-East Asian Nations (ASEAN) is a geo-political and economic organisation formed in 1967 with the aim of accelerating economic growth, social progress and cultural development, and ensuring regional stability. It currently has ten member states.

The ASEAN summit, a biannual meeting of the heads of government, is the organisation's highest authority. The biannual ASEAN foreign ministers' meeting (ASEAN Coordinating Council) is responsible for preparing summit meetings, implementing their policies, and coordinating ASEAN's activities. The ASEAN economic ministers meet annually to coordinate economic policy.

An ASEAN free trade area was implemented in 2003, while a common preferential tariff was introduced in 1993. At the ASEAN summit in 1995, a South East Asia nuclear-weapon-free zone was declared. In December 2008 a new charter came into force which gave ASEAN legal status and a new institutional framework, committed it to the promotion of democracy, and provided for the establishment of the intergovernmental commission on human rights. By the end of 2015 ASEAN members were set to form a common market.

The secretary-general of ASEAN is appointed by rotation and can initiate, advise on, coordinate and implement ASEAN activities. In addition to the ASEAN secretariat based in Jakarta, each member state has a national secretariat in its foreign ministry which organises and implements activities at a national level.

*Secretary-General,* Le Luong Minh (Vietnam)

## BALTIC ASSEMBLY

Citadeles Street 2 – 616, Riga, LV-1010, Latvia
T (+371) 6722 5178 E baltasam@baltasam.org
W www.baltasam.org

Established in November 1991, the Baltic Assembly (BA) is an international organisation for cooperation between the parliaments of Estonia, Latvia and Lithuania. Each member state appoints between 12 and 16 parliamentarians to the assembly, including a chair and vice-chair of the national delegation. The political allegiances of the appointees reflect party proportions in each of the domestic parliaments. The BA holds an annual session in each of the member states in rotation. Several permanent and *ad hoc* committees also meet up to three times a year. The Baltic council of ministers, which comprises the heads of government and ministers of the member states, meets with the BA once a year and promotes intergovernmental and regional cooperation between the Baltic states; the joint sessions are known as the Baltic council.

*President,* Giedre Purvaneckiene (Lithuania, 2015)

## CAB INTERNATIONAL

Nosworthy Way, Wallingford, Oxon OX10 8DE
T 01491-832111 E enquiries@cabi.org W www.cabi.org

Founded in 1910, CAB International (CABI) (formerly the Commonwealth Agricultural Bureau) is a non-profit organisation that provides scientific expertise to assist sustainable development and environmental protection. The organisation consists of 42 countries, five British overseas territories and one associate member (the Netherlands); each is represented on both the executive council, which meets biannually, and the review conference, held every five years to appraise policy and set future goals. A governing board provides guidance on policy issues.

CABI has three divisions: publishing, development projects and research, and microbial services. Each division undertakes research and provides consultancy aimed at raising agricultural productivity, conserving biological resources, protecting the environment and controlling disease. Any country is eligible to apply for membership.

*Chief Executive,* Dr Trevor Nicholls (UK)

## CARIBBEAN COMMUNITY

PO Box 10827, Turkeyen, Greater Georgetown, Guyana
T (+592) 222 0001/0075 E registry@caricom.org
W www.caricom.org

The Caribbean Community (CARICOM) was established as the Caribbean Community and Common Market in 1973 with the signing of the Treaty of Chaguaramas. The objectives of CARICOM is to improve member states' working and living standards, boost employment levels, promote economic development and competitiveness, coordinate foreign and economic policies and enhance cooperation in the delivery of services such as health and education.

The supreme organ is the Conference of Heads of Government, which determines policy and resolves conflict. The Community Council of Ministers consists of ministers of government assigned to CARICOM affairs and is responsible for economic and strategic planning. The principal administrative arm is the secretariat, based in Guyana. The Bureau of the Conference of Heads of Government is the executive body; it comprises the chair of the conference, the outgoing chair and the secretary-general, who are all authorised to initiate proposals and to secure the implementation of decisions. In addition, there are five ministerial councils dealing with trade and economic development, foreign and community relations, human and social development, finance and planning, and national security and law enforcement.

There are 15 member states of CARICOM plus five associate members, 13 of which are party to the Revised Treaty of Chaguaramas, which established the Caribbean Community including the CARICOM single market and economy (CSME) in 2006.

*Secretary-General,* Irwin LaRocque (Dominica)

## THE COMMONWEALTH

The Commonwealth is a voluntary association of 53 sovereign and independent states together with their associated states and dependencies. All of the states were formerly parts of the British Empire or League of Nations (later the UN) mandated territories, except for Mozambique and Rwanda which were admitted because of their history of cooperation with neighbouring Commonwealth nations.

The status and relationship of member nations were first defined by the inter-imperial relations committee of the 1926 Imperial Conference, when the six existing dominions (Australia, Canada, the Irish Free State, Newfoundland, New Zealand and South Africa) were described as 'autonomous communities within the British Empire, equal in status, in no way subordinate one to another in any aspect of their domestic or external affairs, though united by a common allegiance to the Crown and freely associated as members of the British Commonwealth of Nations'. This formula was given legal substance by the statute of Westminster in 1931.

This concept of a group of countries owing allegiance to a single crown changed in 1949 when India became a republic. India's continued membership of the Commonwealth was agreed by the other members on the basis of its 'acceptance of the monarch as the symbol of the free association of its independent member nations and as such the head of the Commonwealth'. This enabled subsequent new republics to join the association. Member nations agreed at the time of the accession of Queen Elizabeth II to recognise Her Majesty as the new head of the Commonwealth. However, the position is not vested in the British Crown.

### THE MODERN COMMONWEALTH

As the UK's former colonies joined, after India and Pakistan in 1947, the Commonwealth was transformed into a multiracial association of equal nations, increasingly focused on promoting development and racial equality. South Africa withdrew in 1961 when it became clear that its reapplication for membership on becoming a republic would be rejected over its policy of apartheid.

The new goals of advocating democracy, the rule of law, good government and social justice were enshrined in the Harare Commonwealth Declaration (1991), which formed the basis of new membership guidelines agreed in Cyprus in 1993. Following the adoption of measures at the New Zealand summit in 1995 against serious or persistent violations of these principles, Nigeria was suspended in 1995 and Sierra Leone was suspended in 1997 for anti-democratic behaviour. Sierra Leone's suspension was revoked the following year when a legitimate government was returned to power. Similarly, Nigeria's suspension was lifted in 1999, the day a newly elected civilian president took office. The Edinbugh Commonwealth Economic Declaration (1997) established a set of economic principles for the Commonwealth, promoting economic growth while protecting smaller member states from the negative effects of globalisation. Zimbabwe was suspended from the councils of the Commonwealth in March 2002, and in 2003 the Zimbabwean government officially confirmed its departure from the association. Following the bloodless coup led by General Pervez Musharraf in 1999, Pakistan faced its first suspension from the Commonwealth. It was readmitted in 2004 only to be suspended again in 2007 after the imposition of emergency rule. The suspension was lifted after successful democratic elections in February 2008. Fiji's Commonwealth membership was suspended in September 2009 after its military government refused to commit to elections in 2010, but was reinstated in September 2014 following democratically held elections that took place earlier in the same month.

## MEMBERSHIP
Membership of the Commonwealth involves acceptance of the association's basic principles and is subject to the approval of existing members. There are 53 members at present, of which 16 have Queen Elizabeth II as head of state, 32 are republics and five have national monarchies. (The date of joining the Commonwealth is shown in parentheses.)

*Antigua and Barbuda (1981)
*Australia (1931)
*The Bahamas (1973)
Bangladesh (1972)
*Barbados (1966)
Belize (1981)
Botswana (1966)
Brunei (1984)
Cameroon (1995)
*Canada (1931)
Cyprus (1961)
Dominica (1978)
Fiji (1970)
Ghana (1957)
*Grenada (1974)
Guyana (1966)
India (1947)
*Jamaica (1962)
Kenya (1963)
Kiribati (1979)
Lesotho (1966)
Malawi (1964)
Malaysia (1957)
Maldives (1982)
Malta (1964)
Mauritius (1968)
Mozambique (1995)

Namibia (1990)
Nauru (1968)
*New Zealand (1931)
Nigeria (1960)
Pakistan (1947)
*Papua New Guinea (1975)
Rwanda (2009)
*St Kitts and Nevis (1983)
*St Lucia (1979)
*St Vincent and the
    Grenadines (1979)
Samoa (1970)
Seychelles (1976)
Sierra Leone (1961)
Singapore (1965)
*Solomon Islands (1978)
South Africa (1931)
Sri Lanka (1948)
Swaziland (1968)
Tanzania (1961)
Tonga (1970)
Trinidad and Tobago (1962)
*Tuvalu (1978)
Uganda (1962)
*United Kingdom
Vanuatu (1980)
Zambia (1964)

* Realms of Queen Elizabeth II

## COUNTRIES THAT HAVE LEFT THE COMMONWEALTH
Republic of Ireland (1949)
South Africa (1961, rejoined 1994)
Pakistan (1972, rejoined 1989; suspended 1999, suspension lifted 2004; suspended 2007, suspension lifted 2008)
Zimbabwe (2003)
The Gambia (2013)

In each of the realms where Queen Elizabeth II is head of state (except for the UK), she is personally represented by a governor-general, who holds in all essential respects the same position in relation to the administration of public affairs in the realm as is held by Her Majesty in the UK. The governor-general is appointed by the Queen on the advice of the government of the state concerned.

## INTERGOVERNMENTAL AND OTHER LINKS
The main forum for consultation is the Commonwealth Heads of Government Meetings, held biennially to discuss international developments and to consider cooperation among members. Decisions are reached by consensus and the views of the meeting are set out in a communiqué. There are also annual meetings of finance ministers and frequent meetings of ministers and officials in other fields, such as education, health, gender and youth affairs. Inter-governmental links are complemented by the activities of some 80 Commonwealth non-governmental organisations linking professionals, sportsmen and sportswomen, and interest groups. The Commonwealth Games take place every four years.

## COMMONWEALTH SECRETARIAT
The Commonwealth has a secretariat, established in 1965 in London, which is funded by member governments. This is the main agency for multilateral communication between member governments on issues relating to the Commonwealth as a whole. It promotes consultation and cooperation, disseminates information on matters of common concern, organises meetings including the biennial summits, coordinates Commonwealth activities and provides technical assistance for economic and social development through the Commonwealth fund for technical cooperation.

The Commonwealth Foundation was established by Commonwealth governments in 1965 as an autonomous body with a board of governors representing Common-wealth governments that fund the foundation. It promotes and funds exchanges and other activities aimed at strengthening the skills and effectiveness of professionals and non-governmental organisations. It also promotes culture, rural development, social welfare, human rights and gender equality.

COMMONWEALTH SECRETARIAT, Marlborough House, Pall Mall, London SW1Y 5HX T 020-7747 6500
E info@commonwealth.int W www.thecommonwealth.org
*Secretary-General,* Kamalesh Sharma (India)
COMMONWEALTH FOUNDATION, Marlborough House, Pall Mall, London SW1Y 5HY T 020-7930 3783
E foundation@commonwealth.int
W www.commonwealthfoundation.com
*Chair,* Anand Satyanand (New Zealand)
COMMONWEALTH EDUCATION TRUST, New Zealand House, 80 Haymarket, London SW1Y 4TE T 020-7024 9822
E info@cet1886.org W www.cet1886.org
*Chair,* Judith Hanratty (New Zealand)

## COMMONWEALTH OF INDEPENDENT STATES

Jlitsa Kirova 17, Minsk 220030, Belarus
T (+375) (17) 222 35 17 E cr@cis.minsk.by W www.cis.minsk.by

The Commonwealth of Independent States (CIS) is a multi-lateral grouping of 11 former Soviet republics, including nine full members; Ukraine, a participating member; and Turkmenistan, an associate member. It was formed in 1991 and its charter was signed by ten states in 1993–4. The CIS acts as a coordinating mechanism for foreign, defence and economic policies and as a forum for addressing problems common to former members of the USSR. These matters are addressed in more than 70 inter-state, intergovernmental coordinating and consultative statutory bodies.

The two supreme CIS organs are the council of heads of state, which meets twice a year, and the council of heads of government. The executive committee, based in Minsk and Moscow, provides administrative support. There are also numerous ministerial, parliamentary, economic and security councils.

On becoming members of the CIS, the member states agreed to recognise their existing borders, respect one another's territorial integrity and reject the use of military force or coercion to settle disputes. A treaty on collective security was signed in 1992 by six states, and a joint peacemaking force, to intervene in CIS conflicts, was agreed upon by nine states. Russia concluded bilateral and multilateral agreements with other CIS states under the supervision of the council of heads of collective security (established 1993). These agreements became the Collective Security Treaty, enabling Russia to station troops in eight of the CIS states, and giving Russian forces de facto control of virtually all of the former USSR's external borders. Only Ukraine and Moldova remained outside the defence cooperation framework and did not sign the treaty. In 1999, Azerbaijan, Georgia and Uzbekistan withdrew from the treaty and formed a new defensive (GUAM) with Moldova and Ukraine. Georgia withdrew from the organisation entirely in August 2009, following the country's war with Russia in 2008. In May 2014, Ukraine announced that it would begin the process of withdrawing from the CIS.

In 1991, 11 republics signed a treaty forming an economic community. Members agreed to refrain from economic actions that would damage each other and to coordinate economic and monetary policies. A coordinating consultative committee, an economic arbitration court and an inter-state bank were established. Members also affirmed the principles of private ownership, free enterprise and competition as the basis for economic recovery.

The 11 CIS members who signed the Establishment of an Economic Union Treaty in September 1993 committed themselves to a common economic space with free movement of goods, services, capital and labour. In 2000 the presidents of the five countries approved a treaty establishing the Eurasian Economic Community, and in 2010 Russia, Belarus and Kazakhstan formed a customs union, which Kyrgyzstan and Armenia joined in 2015. In April 2011 the economic council approved a draft agreement for the development of a free trade zone that would include all of the CIS member states: the agreement was signed by the CIS states with the exception of Azerbaijan, Uzbekistan and Turkmenistan in October 2011. On 1 January 2012 the customs union of Russia, Belarus and Kazakhstan transformed into an single economic space (SES), a higher form of economic integration, ensuring freedom of movement of goods, services, capital, labour, and equal treatment of economic entities within the three countries. Kazakhstan assumed the presidency of the Commonwealth on 1 January 2015.

*Executive Secretary,* Sergey Lebedev (Russia)

## COOPERATION COUNCIL FOR THE ARAB STATES OF THE GULF

PO Box 7153, Riyadh 11-462, Saudi Arabia
T (+966) (1) 482 7777 W www.gcc-sg.org

The Cooperation Council for the Arab States of the Gulf, or Gulf Cooperation Council (GCC), was established on 25 May 1981. Its main objectives are increasing coordination and integration, harmonising economic, commercial, educational and social policies and promoting scientific and technical innovation among its member states. It established a common market in 2008, and set up a customs union in 2003 which was due to be operational in 2015 but is yet to be fully enforced. The GCC has six members: Oman, the United Arab Emirates, Bahrain, Kuwait, Qatar and Saudi Arabia

The highest authority of the GCC is the supreme council, whose presidency rotates among members' heads of states. It holds one regular session every year, but extraordinary sessions may be convened if necessary.

The ministerial council, which ordinarily meets every three months, consists of the foreign ministers of the member states or other delegated ministers. It is authorised to propose policies and recommendations.

*Secretary-General,* Abdul Latif bin Rashid Al Zayani (Bahrain)

## COUNCIL OF EUROPE

Avenue de l'Europe, F-67075 Strasbourg-Cedex, France
T (+33) (3) 8841 2000 W www.coe.int

The Council of Europe was founded in 1949. Its aim is to achieve greater unity between its members, to safeguard their European heritage and to facilitate their progress in economic, social, cultural, educational, scientific, legal and administrative matters, and to further pluralist democracy, human rights and fundamental freedoms. It has 47 member states, including the 28 members of the European Union.

The organs are the committee of ministers, consisting of the foreign ministers of member countries, and the parliamentary assembly of 318 members (and 318 substitutes), elected or chosen by the national parliaments of member countries in proportion to the relative strength of political parties.

The committee of ministers is the executive organ. The majority of its conclusions take the form of international agreements (known as European conventions) or recommendations to governments. Decisions of the ministers may also be embodied in partial agreements to which a limited number of member governments are party.

One of the principal achievements of the Council of Europe is the European Convention on Human Rights (1950), which entered into force on 3 September 1953, and under which the European Court of Human Rights was established in 1959. The court oversees the implementation of the convention in the member states. It sits in chambers of seven judges or, exceptionally, as a grand chamber of 17 judges. Litigants must exhaust legal processes in their own country prior to bringing cases before the court.

Among other conventions and agreements are the European Convention for the Prevention of Torture, the European Social Charter, the Framework Convention for the protection of national minorities, the Istanbul Convention which combats violence against women, the Lanzarote Convention to protect children against sexual abuse and the Convention on Cyber Crime

In 1990 the Venice Commission, an independent legal advisory body, was set up to assist in developing legislative, administrative and constitutional reforms in both European and non-European countries; it currently has 60 member states, one associate member and five observers.

Non-member states take part in certain Council of Europe activities, such as educational, cultural and sports activities on a regular or *ad hoc* basis.

The council's ordinary budget for 2015 totals €417m (£304m).

*Secretary-General,* Thorbjorn Jagland (Norway)

## COUNCIL OF THE BALTIC SEA STATES
Slussplan 9, PO Box 2010, 103 11 Stockholm, Sweden
T (+46) 8440 1920 E cbss@cbss.org W www.cbss.org

The Council of the Baltic Sea States was established in 1992 with the aim of creating a regional forum to increase cooperation and coordination among the countries that border the Baltic Sea. The organisation focuses mainly on the environment, economic development, energy, education and culture, civil security and humanitarian issues. It currently has 12 members (the 11 countries of the Baltic Sea region and the European Commission) while a further ten countries (including the UK and the USA) hold observer status.

The council consists of the foreign ministers of each member state and a member of the European Commission. The presidency of the council rotates among the member states on an annual basis, and the annual session is held in the presiding country. The foreign minister of the presiding country is responsible for coordinating the council's activities and is assisted by the committee of senior officials; a permanent international secretariat established in Stockholm, Sweden in 1998 and financed jointly by the member states. The council does not have a general budget or project fund; member countries are responsible for funding common activities and/or for seeking and coordinating financing from other sources.

*President,* Poland (2015–16)

## ECONOMIC COMMUNITY OF WEST AFRICAN STATES
101 Yakubu Gowon Crescent, Asokoro District, PMB 401, Abuja, Nigeria
T (+234) (9) 314 76479 E info@ecowas.int W www.ecowas.int

The Economic Community of West African States (ECOWAS) was founded in 1975 and came into operation in 1977. It aims to promote the economic, social and cultural development of West Africa through mutual cooperation, and to prevent and control regional conflicts.

The supreme authority of ECOWAS is vested in the annual summit of heads of government of all 15 member states. A council of ministers meets biannually to monitor the organisation and make recommendations to the summit. Since restructuring in 2007, ECOWAS has been managed by a commission, headed by the president. The ECOWAS parliament was inaugurated in November 2000 and judges for the court of justice were appointed in January 2001. Chad currently holds observer status.

Five member states of ECOWAS (The Gambia, Ghana, Guinea, Nigeria and Sierra Leone) plan.to introduce the eco as a single common currency in 2020. Eight other states currently use the CFA franc – it is planned eventually to amalgamate the two currencies. An ECOWAS travel certificate is issued allowing free movement within the community, and nine countries have a common passport.

An ECOWAS peacekeeping force has been involved in attempts to restore peace in Liberia (1990–6), Sierra Leone (1997–9) and in Guinea-Bissau (1998–9). In December 2010 the Côte d'Ivoire was suspended from ECOWAS following the failure of its *de facto* president, Laurent Gbagbo, to step down after a presidential election; the country was reinstated the following year following Mr Gbagbo's arrest. In March 2011 both Guinea and Niger were reinstated to the organisation; their memberships had been suspended, for failure to hold satisfactory democratic elections in 2009. ECOWAS suspended Mali in March 2012 and, a few weeks later, in April, Guinea-Bissau, demanding the immediate restoration of constitutional order in both states following military coups in both countries.

*President,* Kadré Désiré Ouédraogo (Burkina Faso)

## EUROPEAN BANK FOR RECONSTRUCTION AND DEVELOPMENT
One Exchange Square, London EC2A 2JN
T 020-7338 6000 W www.ebrd.com

Since its establishment in 1991, the European Bank for Reconstruction and Development (EBRD) has become the largest financial investor in a region that stretches from central Europe and the Western Balkans to central Asia. Since 2011 the Bank – owned by 64 countries, the EU and the European Investment Bank – has been laying the foundations for the expansion of its operations to the southern and eastern Mediterranean region.

The main forms of EBRD financing are loans, equity investments and guarantees. EBRD's charter stipulates that at least 60 per cent of lending must go to the private sector, reflecting its particular interest in strengthening the financial sector and to promoting small and medium-sized businesses. It works in cooperation with national governments, private companies and international organisations such as the OECD, the IMF, the World Bank and the UN specialised agencies. The EBRD is also able to borrow on world capital markets.

The EBRD's highest authority is the board of governors; each member appoints one governor and one alternate. The governors delegate most powers to a 23-member board of directors; the directors are responsible for the EBRD's operations and budget, and are elected by the governors for three-year terms. The governors also elect the president of the board of directors, who acts as the bank's president for a four-year term.

The EBRD sustained a business volume of €8.9bn (£6.5bn) in 2014 and its portfolio of investments increased from €37.8bn (£27.6bn) at the end of 2013 to €38.7bn (£28.3bn) at the end of 2014.

*President,* Sir Suma Chakrabarti (India)

## EUROPEAN FREE TRADE ASSOCIATION
9–11 rue de Varembé, CH-1211 Geneva 20, Switzerland
T (+41) (22) 332 2600 E mail.gva@efta.int W www.efta.int

The European Free Trade Association (EFTA) was founded in 1960 on the premise of free trade as a means of achieving growth and prosperity among its member states as well as promoting closer economic cooperation between the Western European countries. The immediate aim of the Association was to provide a framework for the liberalisation of trade in goods among its member states.

EFTA was founded by seven countries: Austria, Denmark, Norway, Portugal, Sweden, Switzerland and the UK. Finland joined in 1961, Iceland in 1970 and Liechtenstein in 1991. In 1973, the UK and Denmark left EFTA to join the European Community. They were followed by Portugal in 1986 and by Austria, Finland and Sweden in 1995. Today the four EFTA member states are Iceland, Liechtenstein, Norway and Switzerland.

The Agreement on the European Economic Area (EEA) was signed in 1992 and entered into force in January 1994. The agreement brings together the 27 EU (European Union) member states and the three EEA EFTA states – Iceland, Liechtenstein and Norway – in a single market, referred to as the 'internal market'. Switzerland is not a member of the

EEA, but has a series of bilateral agreements with the EU. The secretariat in Brussels provides support for the mangement of the EEA agreement, including the preparation of new legislation.

Currently, the EFTA states have free trade agreements with the following partners: Albania; Bosnia and Hercegovina; Canada; Central American States (Costa Rica, Guatemala and Panama); Chile; Colombia; Egypt; the Cooperation Council for Arab States of the Gulf; Hong Kong, China; Israel; Jordan; the Rep. of Korea; Lebanon; Macedonia; Mexico; Montenegro; Morocco; the Palestinian Authority; Peru; Serbia; Singapore; Southern African Customs Union; Tunisia; Turkey; and Ukraine. Negotiations on free trade agreements are ongoing with Algeria; Honduras; India; Indonesia; Malaysia; the Philippines; the customs union of Russia, Belarus and Kazakhstan; Thailand; and Vietnam.

The EFTA Council is the highest governing body in the EFTA. Member states usually meet eight times a year at ambassadorial level in Geneva.

*Secretary-General,* Kristinn Arnason (Iceland)

## EUROPEAN ORGANISATION FOR NUCLEAR RESEARCH (CERN)

CH-1211 Geneva 23, Switzerland
T (+41) (22) 767 8484 E cern.reception@cern.ch W www.cern.ch

The convention establishing the European Organisation for Nuclear Research (CERN) came into force in 1954. CERN promotes European collaboration in high-energy physics with scientific goals and no military implication. It has 21 member states, one candidate for accession, one associate member state, one associate member state in the pre-stage to membership, and six members with observer status, including the European Commission and UNESCO.

The council, which is the highest policy-making body, comprises two delegates from each member state and is chaired by the president, who is elected by the council in session. The council also appoints a director-general, who is responsible for the internal organisation of CERN. The director-general heads a workforce of approximately 2,400, including physicists, craftsmen, technicians and administrative staff. At present more than 10,000 scientists use CERN's facilities.

Tim Berners-Lee developed the World Wide Web while working at CERN in 1989, and in 2008 CERN completed construction work on the Large Hadron Collider, the world's largest and most powerful particle accelerator.

*Director-General,* Dr Rolf-Dieter Heuer (Germany)

## EUROPEAN SPACE AGENCY

8–10 rue Mario Nikis, 75738 Paris Cedex 15, France
T (+33) (1) 5369 7654 E contactesa@esa.int W www.esa.int

The European Space Agency (ESA) was created in 1975 by the merger of the European Space Research Organisation and the European Launcher Development Organisation. Its aims include the advancement of space research and technology and the implementation of European space policy. ESA has 22 member states and one cooperating state, with five other nations participating in the Plan for European Cooperating States. ESA's mandatory activities are funded by contributions from all member states and calculated in accordance with each country's gross national income. In 2015, ESA's budget amounted to €4,433m (£3,237m).

The agency is directed by a council composed of representatives of its member states; its chief officer is the director-general who is elected by the council every four years. ESA has liaison offices in Belgium (for the EU), the USA and Russia, while a launch base is stationed in French Guiana.

*Director-General,* Jean-Jacques Dordain (France)

## EUROPEAN UNION

*See* European Union section

## FOOD AND AGRICULTURE ORGANISATION OF THE UNITED NATIONS

Viale delle Terme di Caracalla, 00153 Rome, Italy
T (+39) (06) 57051 E fao-hq@fao.org W www.fao.org

The Food and Agriculture Organisation (FAO) is a specialised UN agency, established in 1945. It assists rural populations by raising levels of nutrition and living standards, and by encouraging greater efficiency in food production and distribution. It analyses and publishes information on agriculture and natural resources. The FAO also advises governments on national agricultural policy and planning through its investment centre and collaboration with the World Bank and other financial institutions. The FAO's field programme covers a range of activities, including strengthening crop yields, rural development and livestock heath and productivity.

The FAO's priorities are sustainable agriculture, rural development and food security. The organisation monitors potential famine areas, channels emergency aid from governments and other agencies, assists in rehabilitation and responds to urgent or unforeseen requests for technical assistance.

The FAO has 195 members (194 states plus the European Union), and two associate members (the Faroe Islands and Tokelau). It is governed by a biennial conference of its members which sets a programme and budget. The budget for 2016–17 is US$2,562m (£1,668m) funded by member countries in proportion to their gross national income. The FAO is also funded by donor governments and other institutions.

The conference elects a director-general and a 49-member council which governs between conferences. The regular and field programmes are administered by a secretariat, headed by the director-general. Five regional, ten sub-regional and 74 national offices help administer the field programme.

*Director-General,* Jose Graziano da Silva (Brazil)

## INTERNATIONAL ATOMIC ENERGY AGENCY

PO Box 100, Wagramer Strasse 5, A-1400 Vienna, Austria
T (+43) (1) 26000 E official.mail@iaea.org W www.iaea.org

The International Atomic Energy Agency (IAEA) was established in 1957. It is an intergovernmental organisation that reports to, but is not a specialised agency of, the UN.

The IAEA aims to enhance the contribution of atomic energy to peace, health and prosperity. It does not advocate the use of atomic energy for military purposes. It establishes atomic energy safety standards and offers services to its member states to upgrade safety and security measures for their nuclear installations and material, and for radioactive sources, material and waste. It is the focal point for international conventions on the early notification of a nuclear accident, accident assistance, civil liability for nuclear damage, physical protection of nuclear material and the safety of spent fuel and radioactive waste management. The IAEA also encourages research and training in nuclear power. It is additionally charged with drawing up safeguards and verifying their enforcement in accordance with several international nuclear weapons treaties.

The IAEA has 164 members that meet annually in a general conference. The conference decides policy, a programme and a budget – €348.2m (£254.4m) in 2015 – as well as electing a director-general and a 35-member board of governors. The board meets five times a year to review and formulate policy, address budgetary concerns and consider applications for membership. Project and policy changes are implemented by the secretariat.

*Director-General,* Yukiya Amano (Japan)

## INTERNATIONAL CIVIL AVIATION ORGANISATION

999 Robert-Bourassa Boulevard, Montréal, Québec, Canada H3C 5H7

T (+1) (514) 954 8219 E icaohq@icao.int W www.icao.int

The International Civil Aviation Organisation (ICAO) was founded with the signing of the Chicago Convention on International Civil Aviation in 1944 and became a specialised agency of the UN in 1947. It sets international technical standards and regulations for aviation safety, security and efficiency, as well as environmental protection. ICAO has 191 members and is governed by an assembly, which convenes triennially. A council of 36 members is elected, which represents leading air transport nations as well as less developed countries. The council elects the president, appoints the secretary-general and supervises the organisation through subsidiary committees, serviced by a secretariat.

*President of the Council,* Dr Olumuyiwa Bernard Aliu (Nigeria)

## INTERNATIONAL CRIMINAL POLICE ORGANISATION (INTERPOL)

200 Quai Charles de Gaulle, F-69006 Lyon, France

W www.interpol.int

Interpol was set up in 1923 to establish an international criminal records office and to harmonise extradition procedures. The organisation has a global membership of 190 countries. Interpol's aims are to promote cooperation between criminal police authorities and to support government agencies concerned with combating crime, while respecting national sovereignty. It is financed largely by annual contributions from the governments of the member countries and supplementary funding from private and commercial sources.

Interpol policy is formulated by the general assembly which meets annually and is composed of delegates appointed by the member countries. The 13-member executive committee is elected by the general assembly from the member countries' delegates and is chaired by the president, who serves a four-year term of office. The permanent administrative organ is the general secretariat, headed by the secretary-general, who is appointed by the general assembly.

The UK Interpol National Central Bureau is operated by the National Crime Agency (NCA).

*Secretary-General,* Jürgen Stock (Germany)

## INTERNATIONAL ENERGY AGENCY

9 rue de la Fédération, F-75739 Paris Cedex 15, France

T (+33) (1) 4057 6500/01 E info@iea.org W www.iea.org

The International Energy Agency (IEA), founded in 1974, is an autonomous agency within the framework of the Organisation for Economic Cooperation and Development (OECD). The IEA's objectives include the improvement of energy cooperation worldwide, development of alternative energy sources and the promotion of relations between oil-producing and oil-consuming countries. The IEA also maintains an emergency system to alleviate the effects of severe oil supply disruptions.

The main decision-making body is the governing board, composed of senior energy officials from member countries. The IEA secretariat, with a staff of energy experts, carries out the work of the governing board and its subordinate

bodies. The executive director is appointed by the board. The IEA has 29 member states; the European Commission also participates in its work.

*Executive Director,* Maria van der Hoeven (the Netherlands)

## INTERNATIONAL FRANCOPHONE ORGANISATION

Cabinet du Secrétaire général, 19–21 avenue Bosquet, 75007 Paris, France

T (+33) (1) 4437 3300 W www.francophonie.org

The International Francophone Organisation *(International Organisation of La Francophonie* – IOF) is an inter-governmental organisation founded in 1970 by 21 French-speaking countries. Its 77 member states and governments, 57 members and 23 observers, together represent over 890 million people; 220 million of which speak French regularly, with varying degrees of fluency. The IOF organises political activities and actions multilateral cooperation that benefits French-speaking populations. It represents its member states internationally, promotes French language and francophone cultural industries with the aim of preventing conflict and promoting development.

The conference of heads of state and government of countries with French as a common language – also known as La Francophonie summit – takes place biennially. Other institutions include the permanent ministerial conference and the permanent council.

*Secretary-General,* Michaëlle Jean (Canada)

## INTERNATIONAL FUND FOR AGRICULTURAL DEVELOPMENT

44 Via Paolo di Dono, 00142 Rome, Italy

T (+39) (06) 54591 E ifad@ifad.org W www.ifad.org

The International Fund for Agricultural Development (IFAD) began operations as a UN specialised agency in 1977. It develops and finances agricultural and rural projects in developing countries and aims to promote employment and additional income for poor farmers, reduce malnutrition and improve food security systems.

IFAD has 176 member states divided into three lists: List A (primarily OECD countries), List B (primarily OPEC countries), and List C (developing countries) which is subdivided into C1 (Africa), C2 (Europe, Asia and the Pacific) and C3 (Latin America and the Caribbean). All powers are vested in a governing council of all member states, which meets annually. It elects an executive board which is composed of 18 members and 18 alternate members and is chaired by the president of the IFAD. The president serves a four-year term that can be renewed once.

*President,* Kanayo F. Nwanze (Nigeria)

## INTERNATIONAL HYDROGRAPHIC ORGANISATION

4b quai Antoine 1er, B.P. 445, MC 98011, Monaco

T (+377) 9310 8100 E info@iho.int W www.iho.int

The International Hydrographic Organisation (IHO) began operating in 1921 with 19 member states and headquarters in the Principality of Monaco. In 1970 its name was changed from the International Hydrographic Bureau. The IHO is an intergovernmental organisation that has a purely consultative role and aims to support safety in international navigation, set policy for marine conservation and improve coordination between national hydrographic institutions. The IHO has a membership of 82 states that meet at five-yearly conferences to set policy, approve budget, review progress and adopt programmes of work. Each member is represented at these conferences by their most senior hydrographer. All member states have an opportunity to initiate new proposals for IHO

consideration. Outside of its membership, the IHO acts to promote hydrography and facilitate the exchange of technology with developing countries. It is also the source that defines the boundaries between seas and oceans.
*President*, Robert Ward (Australia)

# INTERNATIONAL LABOUR ORGANISATION
4 route des Morillons, CH-1211, Genève 22, Switzerland
T (+41) (22) 799 6111 E ilo@ilo.org W www.ilo.org

The International Labour Organisation (ILO) was established in 1919 as an autonomous body of the League of Nations and became the UN's first specialised agency in 1946. The ILO aims to promote employment, improve working conditions, extend social protection and promote dialogue between government, workers' and employers' organisations.

It sets minimum international labour standards through the drafting of international conventions. Member countries are obliged to submit these to their domestic authorities for ratification, and thus undertake to bring their domestic legislation in line with the conventions. Members must report to the ILO periodically on how these regulations are being implemented. The ILO is also a principal resource centre for information, analysis and guidance on labour and employment.

The ILO has 186 member states and is composed of the International Labour Conference, the governing body and the International Labour Office. The conference of members meets annually and is attended by national delegations. It adopts international labour conventions and recommendations, provides a forum for discussion of economic and social issues and approves the ILO's programme and budget.

The 56-member governing body is composed of 28 government, 14 worker and 14 employer members and acts as the ILO's executive council. It convenes triannually. Ten governments, including the UK, hold permanent seats on the governing body because of their industrial importance. There are also various regional conferences and advisory committees. The ILO acts as a secretariat and as a centre for operations, publishing and research.
*Director-General*, Guy Ryder (UK)

# INTERNATIONAL MARITIME ORGANISATION
4 Albert Embankment, London SE1 7SR
T 020-7735 7611 E info@imo.org W www.imo.org

Originally named the Inter-Governmental Maritime Consultative Organisation, the International Maritime Organisation (IMO) was established as a UN specialised agency in 1948. Owing to delays in treaty ratification it did not commence operations until 1958.

The IMO fosters intergovernmental cooperation in technical matters relating to international shipping, particularly regarding safety and security at sea, efficiency in navigation and protecting the marine environment from pollution caused by shipping. The IMO is responsible for convening maritime conferences and drafting marine conventions. It also provides technical aid to countries wishing to develop their activities at sea.

The IMO has 171 members and three associate members. It is governed by an assembly comprising delegates of all its members. It meets biennially to formulate policy, set a budget (£32.6m for 2015), to vote on specific recommendations on pollution, maritime safety and security, and to elect the council. The council, which meets twice a year, fulfils the functions of the assembly between sessions and appoints a secretary-general. It consists of 40 members: ten from the world's largest shipping nations, ten from the nations most

dependent on seaborne trade and 20 other members to ensure a fair geographical representation. The IMO acts as the secretariat for the London Convention (1972) and its 1996 protocol which regulates the disposal of land-generated waste at sea.
*Secretary-General*, Koji Sekimizu (Japan)

# INTERNATIONAL MONETARY FUND
700 19th Street NW, Washington DC 20431, USA
T (+1) (202) 623 7000 E publicaffairs@imf.org W www.imf.org

The International Monetary Fund (IMF) was established at the UN Monetary and Financial Conference at Bretton Woods, New Hampshire, in 1944. Its articles of agreement entered into force in 1945 and it began operations in 1947.

The IMF exists to promote international monetary cooperation and the expansion of world trade to ensure international economic stability. It advises members on their economic and financial policies; promotes policy coordination among the major industrial countries; gives technical assistance in central banking, balance of payments accounting, taxation and other financial matters; and provides loans to states with weak economies. The IMF serves as a forum for members to discuss monetary policy issues and seeks the balanced growth of international trade. It has 188 members; Tuvalu joined in June 2010 and South Sudan in April 2012.

Upon joining the IMF, a member is assigned a quota based on that member's relative standing in the world economy and its balance of payments. The quota determines the maximum size of the member's capital subscription to the fund, access to IMF resources, voting power and share in the allocation of special drawing rights (SDRs). Quotas are reviewed at regular intervals (usually every five years) and adjusted accordingly. After the 13th general review in 2008 the IMF board of governors adopted a reform package which would grant *ad hoc* quota increases to 54 countries found to be under-represented, and triple the number of basic votes to all members, thereby enhancing the representation of emerging and low-income countries. These reforms became effective in March 2011. In December 2010 the board of governors approved recommendations of the 14th general review – namely the doubling of all available quotas, a shift in 6 per cent of quotas from over-to under-represented countries, and an overall realignment in quota shares to reflect emerging markets and developing countries (EDMCs). Under these reforms, China will become the third largest member country and three further EDMCs (Brazil, India and Russia) will be among the top ten shareholders. These reforms will become effective upon their acceptance by three-fifths of members having 85 per cent of total voting power. Work on the 15th general review has been delayed, pending implementation of the 2010 reforms. In February 2015, the board of governors adopted a resolution calling for the completion of the 15th review by 15 December 2015.

The SDR (special drawing rights), the reserve currency created by the IMF in 1969, is calculated daily on a basket of usable currencies and is the IMF's unit of account; as at 31 July 2015, 1 SDR equalled US$1.40 (£0.90). SDRs are allocated at intervals to supplement members' reserves and thereby improve international financial liquidity. Total quotas currently stand at SDR238.2bn.

The IMF is not a bank and does not lend money; it provides temporary financial assistance by selling a member's SDRs or other members' currencies in exchange for the member's own currency. The member can then use the purchased currency to alleviate its balance of payments difficulties. IMF financial resources derive primarily from members' capital subscriptions, which are proportionally related to their quotas. In addition, the IMF is authorised to borrow from official lenders. It may also draw on a line of credit from 38 member countries and institutions under the new arrangements to borrow (NAB). Once activated, NAB can provide supplementary resources of up to SDR370bn to the IMF. In limited cases the IMF can also access a potential amount totalling SDR17bn from 11 countries under the so-called general arrangements to borrow (GAB), with an additional SDR1.5bn available under an associated arrangement with Saudi Arabia.

Benign market conditions between 2004 and 2008 prompted many countries to start repaying their outstanding loans and demand for the fund's resources dropped dramatically; however, in 2008 the IMF increased its lending in response to the global financial crisis. In March 2009 the IMF announced a number of reforms to its lending framework, intended to provide greater speed and flexibility in lending arrangements, doubled access limits on loans and more closely tailor the conditionality of loans to fit the recipient state's requirements. In February 2010 a defined poverty line was introduced under which countries would qualify to access low-cost concessional loans under the poverty reduction and growth trust. In 2011 the IMF further refined its lending options to better meet the needs of its member countries as global growth continued to weaken in response to the ongoing crisis in the euro area. The 2011 measures included the introduction of a precautionary credit line to enable the IMF to provide upfront liquidity, including for countries with sound policies that had been affected by economic shocks beyond their control, and a rapid financing instrument for emergency assistance to support member countries experiencing a range of urgent balance of payments needs, without the need for a fully fledged programme. On total outstanding IMF credits amounted to SDR57.3bn, or US$80.2bn (£51.6bn).

The IMF supports long-term efforts at economic reform and transformation as well as medium-term programmes under the extended fund facility, which runs for three to four years and is aimed at overcoming balance of payments difficulties stemming from macroeconomic and structural problems. Typically, measures are introduced to reform taxation and the financial sector, to privatise state-owned enterprises and to make labour markets more flexible.

The IMF is headed by a board of governors, comprising one representative and one alternate representative of each member state, which meets annually. The governors delegate powers to 24 executive directors, who are appointed by elected by member countries. The executive directors are responsible for the daily operation of the fund and the election of the managing director.

*Managing Director,* Christine Lagarde (France)

## INTERNATIONAL ORGANISATION FOR MIGRATION

17 Route des Morillons, CH-1211 Geneva 19, Switzerland
T (+41) 22717 9111 E hq@iom.int W www.iom.int

The International Organisation for Migration (IOM) was founded in 1951 to resettle European displaced persons and refugees. During the 1960s and 1970s the IOM developed links with the United Nations High Commissioner for Refugees and began a programme of assistance and reintegration outside of Europe.

The role of the IOM is to help ensure the orderly and humane management of migration; its remit includes migration health services, international migration law, counter-trafficking measures, emergency and post-crisis management and assisted voluntary returns. It employs more

than 8,400 staff and is present in over 480 field locations. There are 157 member states and ten states with observer status.

The IOM is led by a director-general who is elected for a five-year term. The director-general's office has the constitutional authority to manage the organisation, carry out the activities within its mandate and develop current policies, procedures and strategies. The office of the inspector-general (OIG) incorporates the functions of evaluation, internal audit and assessment of projects.

*Director-General,* William Lacy Swing (USA)

## INTERNATIONAL RED CROSS AND RED CRESCENT MOVEMENT

19 Avenue de la paix, CH-1202 Geneva, Switzerland
T (+41) 2273 46001 W www.icrc.org

The International Red Cross and Red Crescent Movement is composed of three elements – the International Committee of the Red Cross, the International Federation of Red Cross and Red Crescent Societies, and the National Red Cross and Red Crescent Societies.

The International Committee of the Red Cross (ICRC), the organisation's founding body, was formed in 1863. It aims to protect and assist victims of armed conflict. It also seeks to ensure the application of the Geneva Conventions regarding prisoners of war and detainees.

The International Federation of Red Cross and Red Crescent Societies (IFRC) was founded in 1919 to assist the humanitarian activities of national societies, coordinate their relief operations for victims of natural disasters and care for refugees outside areas of conflict. There are Red Cross and Red Crescent societies in 189 countries and it has more than 60 field delegations internationally.

The international conference of the Red Cross and Red Crescent meets every four years, bringing together delegates of the ICRC, the International Federation and the national societies, as well as representatives of all states party to the Geneva Conventions.

*Director-General of the ICRC,* Yves Daccord (Switzerland)
*President of the IFRC,* Tadateru Konoe (Japan)

## INTERNATIONAL TELECOMMUNICATION UNION

Place des Nations, CH-1211 Geneva 20, Switzerland
T (+41) (22) 730 5111 E itumail@itu.int W www.itu.int

The International Telecommunication Union (ITU) was founded in Paris in 1865 as the International Telegraph Union and became a UN specialised agency in 1947.

ITU is an intergovernmental organisation for the development of telecommunications and the harmonisation of national telecommunication policies. It comprises 193 member states, more than 700 sector members and associates who represent public and private organisations involved in telecommunications. Its mission is to promote the development of information and communication technologies and to offer assistance to developing countries.

For nearly 150 years, ITU has coordinated the shared global use of the radio spectrum, promoted international cooperation in assigning satellite orbits, worked to improve communication infrastructure in the developing world and established the worldwide standards for the interconnection of a vast range of communications systems: from broadband networks to new-generation wireless technologies, aeronautical and maritime navigation, radio astronomy, satellite-based meteorology and converging fixed-line and mobile telephone, internet and broadcasting technologies.

*Secretary-General,* Houlin Zhao (China)

## INTERNATIONAL TRADE UNION CONFEDERATION

Boulevard du Roi Albert II, 5 B 1, B-1210 Brussels, Belgium
T (+32) (2) 224 0211 E info@ituc-csi.org W www.ituc-csi.org

The International Trade Union Confederation (ITUC) was created in 2006 by the merger between the International Confederation of Free Trade Unions (ICFTU), the World Confederation of Labour (WCL) and other independent unions. Through public and industrial advocacy work it seeks to assert and defend the rights and interests of workers, and to foster international cooperation between trade unions. In June 2015 the ITUC represented 176 million workers in 162 countries and territories and had 328 national affiliates.

The congress, the supreme authority of the ITUC, meets once every four years to review and propose policy and to elect the 78-member general council. Council members are elected according to population-weighted geographical regions, with six seats reserved for nomination by the women's committee, and two by the youth committee. The council, and the general secretary elected at each congress, govern the organisation. It also elects a 25-member executive bureau from among its members which deals with urgent issues and those delegated to it by the council; it also makes decisions on finances and formulates the annual budget for council approval.

The ITUC has regional organisations for Asia-Pacific (ITUC-AP), Africa (ITUC-AF), the Americas (TUCA) and Europe (the pan-European regional council, or PERC). It also cooperates closely with the Global Union Federations, the Trade Union Advisory Committee to the Organisation for Economic Cooperation and Development (OECD), the European Trade Union Confederation, the International Labour Organisation, a number of other UN specialised agencies and national and regional unions and organisations.
*General Secretary*, Sharan Burrow (Australia)

## INTERNATIONAL WHALING COMMISSION

The Red House, 135 Station Road, Cambridge CB24 9NP
T 01223-233971 W www.iwc.int

The International Whaling Commission (IWC) was set up under the International Convention for the Regulation of Whaling, signed in Washington DC in 1946. It has 88 member states. The purpose of the IWC is to provide for the conservation of whale stocks, enabling the development of the whaling industry. The organisation reviews and revises the schedule to the convention that decrees the complete protection of certain species, sets limits for when and where whaling can take place, coordinates and funds whale research and publishes and promotes scientific studies.

The IWC has four main committees, responsible for scientific, technical, conservation and finance matters. There are further sub-committees and working groups concerned with aboriginal subsistence whaling, infractions, small cetaceans, whalewatching, whale-killing methods and animal welfare issues.
*Executive Secretary*, Simon Brockington (UK)

## LEAGUE OF ARAB STATES

Al-Tahrir Square, PO Box 11642, Cairo, Egypt
T (+20) (2) 2575 0511 W www.lasportal.org

The League of Arab States was founded in 1945 to protect the independence and sovereignty of its member states, supervise the affairs and interests of Arab countries and promote coordination among them. The organisation has 22 members, including Palestine. The League itself has observer status at the United Nations.

The heads of member states meet annually at the Arab League summit, while foreign ministers convene every six months as part of the Arab League council. Member states participate in various specialised agencies which develop specific areas of cooperation between Arab states. These include the Arab Monetary Fund; the Arab Satellite Communications Organisation; the Arab Academy for Science, Technology and Maritime Transport; the Arab Bank for Economic Development in Africa; the Arab League Educational, Cultural and Scientific Organisation; and the Council of Arab Economic Unity.
*Secretary-General*, Nabil El Araby (Egypt)

## MERCOSUR

Luis Piera 1992, Piso 1, 11200-Montevideo, Uruguay
T (+598) (2) 412 9024 W www.mercosur.int

MERCOSUR (the Southern Common Market) was created by the Treaty of Asunción, signed by Argentina, Brazil, Paraguay and Uruguay on 26 March 1991. Venezuela signed an adhesion protocol in 2006 and became a full member in 2012. Bolivia, which had been an associate member since 1997, became a full member on 17 July 2015. Six other countries (Chile, Colombia, Ecuador, Guyana, Peru and Suriname) have associate member status.

The Common Market Council (CMC) is the highest-level agency of MERCOSUR, with authority to formulate policy and enforce member states' compliance with the Treaty of Asunción. The CMC comprises ministers of foreign affairs and economic ministers of the member states; it meets at least once a year.

The Common Market Group is the executive body of MERCOSUR and is coordinated by the foreign ministries of the member states. Its function is to implement decisions made by the CMC and resolve disputes, and if necessary, establish subgroups to work on particular issues. Other bodies include a joint parliamentary committee, a trade commission and a socio-economic advisory forum. The presidency of MERCOSUR rotates between member states every six months.

In 2005, Argentina, Brazil, Paraguay and Uruguay became associate members of the Andean Community, reciprocating MERCOSUR's action to grant associate membership to all Andean Community nations. In December 2005, the Colombian president ratified a free trade agreement (FTA) with MERCOSUR giving Colombian products preferential access to MERCOSUR countries. MERCOSUR signed an FTA with Israel in December 2007, the bloc's first such agreement outside Latin America. After stalling in 2004, negotiations with the EU over a possible FTA were relaunched in May 2010 and an exchange of formal offers on tarrifs is expected by the end of 2015.
*Presidency*, Paraguay (Jul–Dec 2015)

## NORDIC COUNCIL

Ved Stranden 18, 1061 Copenhagen K, Denmark
T (+45) 3396 0400 E nordisk-rad@norden.org W www.norden.org

The Nordic Council was established in March 1952 as an advisory body on economic and social cooperation, comprising parliamentary delegates from Denmark, Iceland, Norway and Sweden. It was subsequently joined by Finland (1955), and representatives from the Faroes (1970), the Aland Islands (1970) and Greenland (1984).

Cooperation is regulated by the Helsinki Treaty, signed in 1962. This was amended in 1971 to create a Nordic council of ministers, which discusses all matters except defence and foreign affairs. Decisions of the council of ministers, which are taken by consensus, are binding, although if ratification by member parliaments is required, decisions only become effective following parliamentary approval. The council of ministers is advised by the Nordic Council, to which it reports annually. There are ministers for Nordic cooperation in every member government.

The Nordic Council comprises 87 voting delegates nominated from member parliaments and numerous non-voting government representatives. It meets at least once a year in plenary sessions. The full council chooses a 13-member presidium, which conducts business between sessions. A secretariat, headed by a secretary-general, provides administrative support. The presidency of the Nordic Council rotates between the five countries, and the presiding country always hosts the annual council session.

*President,* Hoskuldur Porhallsson (Iceland, 2015)

## NORTH AMERICAN FREE TRADE AGREEMENT

NAFTA SECRETARIAT, CANADIAN SECTION,
111 Sussex Drive, 5th Floor, Ottawa, Ontario K1N 1J1, Canada
T (+1) (343) 203 4274 E canada@nafta-sec-alena.org

NAFTA SECRETARIAT, MEXICAN SECTION, Blvd. Adolfo López Mateos 3025, 2o Piso, Col. Héroes de Padierna, C.P. 10700, Mexico, D.F.
T (+52) (55) 5629 9630 E naftamexico@nafta-sec-alena.org

NAFTA SECRETARIAT, US SECTION, Room 2061, 14th Street and Constitution Avenue, NW, Washington DC, 20230, USA
T (+1) (202) 482 5438 E usa@nafta-sec-alena.org
W www.nafta-sec-alena.org

The leaders of Canada, Mexico and the USA signed the North American Free Trade Agreement (NAFTA) on 17 December 1992 in their respective capitals; it came into force in January 1994 after being ratified by the legislatures of the three member states.

NAFTA aims to eliminate barriers to trade in goods and services, promote fair competition within the free trade area, protect and enforce intellectual property rights and create a framework for further cooperation. To achieve these aims, import tariffs, quotas and limits on cross-border investment have been removed.

The NAFTA secretariat is composed of Canadian, Mexican and US sections. It is responsible for administering the dispute-settlement provisions of the agreement, providing assistance to the Free Trade Commission and support for various committees and working groups, and facilitating the operation of the agreement.

## NORTH ATLANTIC TREATY ORGANISATION

Bvld Leopold III, Brussels B-1110, Belgium
T (+32) (2) 707 4111 E natodoc@hq.nato.int W www.nato.int

The North Atlantic Treaty Organisation (NATO) is a political and military alliance designed to provide common security for its members through cooperation and consultation in political, military and economic as well as scientific and other non-military fields.

The North Atlantic Treaty (Treaty of Washington) was signed in 1949 by Belgium, Canada, Denmark, France, Iceland, Italy, Luxembourg, the Netherlands, Norway, Portugal, the UK and the USA. Greece and Turkey acceded to the treaty in 1952, the Federal Republic of Germany in 1955 (the reunited Germany acceded in October 1990), Spain in 1982, and the Czech Republic, Hungary and Poland in 1999. Bulgaria, Estonia, Latvia, Lithuania, Romania, Slovakia and Slovenia signed membership protocols in March 2003 and officially joined NATO in March 2004. Albania and Croatia became official members in April 2009, having signed membership accords in September 2008.

## STRUCTURE

The North Atlantic council (NAC), chaired by the secretary-general, is the highest authority of the alliance and is composed of permanent representatives of the 28 member countries. It meets weekly, but also holds meetings at higher levels involving foreign and defence ministers and heads of government. The permanent representatives (ambassadors) head national delegations of advisers and experts. The nuclear planning group (NPG) is composed of all member countries, with the exception of France, and meets at ministerial level at least once a year. The NATO secretary-general chairs the council and the NPG. Much of the NAC policy is prepared and drafted by the senior political committee, a group of deputy permanent representatives and policy advisers.

The senior military authority in NATO, which advises the council, is the military committee, composed of the chief of defence staffs of each member country except Iceland, which has no military forces and is represented by a civilian. The military committee, which is assisted by an integrated international military staff, also meets in permanent session with permanent military representatives and is responsible for making recommendations to the council on measures considered necessary for the common defence of the NATO area and for supplying guidance on military matters to the NATO strategic commanders. The chair of the military committee, elected for a period of two to three years, represents the committee on the council.

The alliance's military command structure is divided between two functional strategic commands: Allied Command Operations (ACO) is responsible for all NATO military operations, whereas Allied Command Transformation (ACT) is charged with training and restructuring NATO military forces and capabilities. The headquarters of ACO is at the Supreme Headquarters of the Allied Powers Europe (SHAPE) at Mons, Belgium, and comes under the command of the Supreme Allied Commander Europe (SACEUR). The headquarters of ACT is at Norfolk, Virginia, USA, and is under the command of the Supreme Allied Commander Transformation (SACT). There is also a regional planning group for Canada and the USA. At the Lisbon summit in November 2010, NATO leaders approved a plan to streamline the ACO while maintaining its military capability; the plans will result in a reduction of personnel within the military command structure from 13,000 to 8,800 and is expected to be fully implemented by the end of 2015.

## POST COLD WAR DEVELOPMENTS

The Euro-Atlantic partnership council (EAPC) was established in 1997 to develop closer security links with Eastern European and former Soviet states. Replacing the North Atlantic cooperation council (NACC) as the first institutional framework for cooperation between NATO member countries and former adversaries from Central and Eastern Europe, the EAPC focuses on defence planning, defence industry conversion, defence management and force structuring. Its membership comprises the 28 NATO members and Armenia, Austria, Azerbaijan, Belarus, Bosnia and Hercegovina, Finland, Georgia, Ireland, Kazakhstan, Kyrgyzstan, Macedonia, Malta, Moldova, Montenegro, Russia, Serbia, Sweden, Switzerland, Tajikistan, Turkmenistan, Ukraine and Uzbekistan. The EAPC provides the multilateral, political framework for the partnership for peace programme (PFP). The PFP is the basis for practical, bilateral security cooperation between NATO and all partner countries in the fields of defence planning and budgeting, military exercises and civil emergency operations. It also works to improve the interoperability between the forces of partner and member countries to enable them to undertake joint operations and has provided the context for cooperation by many of the partner countries in NATO-led peacekeeping and peace-support operations in Bosnia and Hercegovina, Kosovo and Afghanistan.

NATO and Russia committed themselves to helping build a stable and secure partnership based on mutual interest when they signed the 1997 Founding Act on mutual relations, cooperation and security, which provided for the creation of a NATO-Russia permanent joint council (PJC). In 2002 it was replaced by the NATO-Russia council (NRC). The NRC usually meets every month at ambassadorial level and twice each year at ministerial level to address issues of joint concern such as terrorist threats and the narcotics trade, and to pursue bilateral programmes in defence reform, search and rescue, and civil emergency planning. Since April 2014, following Russia's military intervention in Ukraine, NATO has suspended all practical cooperation with Russia, including the NRC, save for high level communications at ambassadorial level and above. NATO previously suspended formal NRC meetings and cooperation with Russia in response to Russia's military action in Georgia in 2008.

The establishment of the NATO-Ukraine commission (NUC) in 1997 committed both parties to developing their relationship under a programme of consultation and co-operation on political and security issues. The NATO-Georgia commission (NGC), created in 2008, is pursuing political dialogue between NATO and Georgia, and helping to supervise Georgia's progress towards membership of NATO. The NGC is also co-ordinating support to help the country recover from the summer 2008 conflict.

NATO's Mediterranean dialogue, launched in 1994, aims to improve trust and understanding of NATO's goals and objectives among the countries of the southern Mediterranean area: Algeria, Egypt, Israel, Jordan, Mauritania, Morocco and Tunisia. At its summit meeting in 2004, the alliance launched the Istanbul cooperation initiative (ICI), promoting practical cooperation with the Gulf cooperation council (GCC) and other interested countries in the Middle East. To date Bahrain, Qatar, Kuwait and the United Arab Emirates have joined the ICI.

The development of a European security and defence identity, which would strengthen NATO's European pillar, was agreed at the 1999 NATO summit meeting in Washington. Subsequent developments have served to strengthen cooperation between NATO and the European Union and to establish a strategic partnership.

At the 2002 Prague summit, further measures to improve defence capabilities were taken on the basis of a new capabilities commitment, in which member countries agreed to specific targets and time frames for improvements. A military concept for defence against terrorism was also agreed, and additional initiatives taken in the areas of nuclear, biological and chemical weapons defence and protection against cyber attacks. The NATO response force, a rapid-reaction unit comprising land, sea and air special forces, was officially launched at the Prague summit and became fully operational in 2006. The Lisbon summit in 2010 saw the publication of NATO's strategic concept, a statement of core principles that emphasized the importance of international cooperation in defence, security and crisis management, with particular reference to strengthening NATO's relationships with the EU and UN. At the 2014 Wales summit, it was decided to enhance the NATO response force by establishing a very high readiness joint task force (VJTF) to deploy within just a few days to challenges that arise. The VJTF was deployed for exercises for the first time in June 2015 and is expected to be operationally capable by the 2016 Warsaw summit.

## AFGHANISTAN

From January 2001, following the establishment of the Afghan Transitional Authority, an international security assistance force (ISAF) was created on the basis of a UN mandate to provide the security required to allow infrastructure reconstruction and create a stable democratic government. In 2002, NATO began providing support for ISAF at the request of the lead nations and, in August 2003, assumed full responsibility for the leadership of ISAF. In accordance with an October 2003 UN security council mandate, ISAF gradually extended its authority from the capital, Kabul, to assume responsibility for the security, reconstruction and development of the entire country in October 2006. The gradual transition of security responsibility from ISAF to the Afghan national security forces commenced in 2010 and was completed at the end of 2014. In January 2015, a new non-combat resolute support mission was launched to train, assist and advise Afghan security forces. NATO officials have committed to providing financial support to the region until the end of 2017.

## KOSOVO

NATO has been leading a peace-support operation in Kosovo since June 1999 in support of wider international efforts to build peace and stability in the area. Approximately 4,500 troops from the NATO-led Kosovo Force (KFOR), provided by 31 countries, are currently deployed in the region.

## TURKEY

In December 2012, the Turkish government requested support for its air defence system in the wake of the escalating conflict in Syria. The request was prompted by several incidents of cross-border fire and resulting civilian casualties. Germany, The Netherlands and the USA agreed to provide patriot air defence systems for purely defensive deployment in Adana, Gaziantep and Kahramanmaras. All defence systems have been operational under NATO command and control since February 2013. In January 2015, Spanish troops replaced the Dutch unit stationed in Adana.

## AFRICA

NATO counter-piracy operations were active between October and December 2008, and again between March and July 2009, in response to the growing threat presented by piracy in the Horn of Africa region. Currently, Operation Ocean Shield – approved by the North Atlantic council in August 2009 and extended until the end of 2016 – is focused on at-sea operations, but also offers assistance to regional states in developing their capacity to combat piracy.

Since 2007 NATO has provided specialist support to the African Union in their ongoing deployment to Somalia (AMISOM) and is also assisting in the establishment of a continental on-call security force (African Standby Force) which is expected to reach its full operational capability by the end of 2015.

*Secretary-General and Chair of the North Atlantic Council, of the DPC and of the NPG,* Jens Stoltenberg (Norway)

# ORGANISATION FOR ECONOMIC COOPERATION AND DEVELOPMENT

2 rue André Pascal, 75775 Paris Cedex 16, France
T (+33) (1) 4524 8200 E webmaster@oecd.org W www.oecd.org

The Organisation for Economic Cooperation and Development (OECD) was formed in 1961 to replace the Organisation for European Economic Cooperation. It is the instrument for international cooperation among industrialised member countries on economic and social policies. Its objectives are to assist its member governments in creating policies designed to achieve high, sustained economic growth and maintain financial stability, to contribute to world trade on a multilateral basis and to stimulate members' aid to developing countries. The OECD has 34 member countries, most of which have developed, high-income economies. The European Commission is involved in the work of the OECD but is not a member of the organisation.

The council is the supreme body of the organisation. It is composed of one representative for each member country plus one representative of the European Commission (the European Commission does not have the right to vote) and meets at permanent representative level under the chairmanship of the secretary-general, and at ministerial level (usually once a year) under the chair of a minister. Decisions and recommendations are adopted by consensus. Most of the OECD's work is undertaken by around 250 specialised committees and working parties. These are serviced by an international secretariat headed by a secretary-general.

In 2010 Chile, Estonia, Israel and Slovenia acceded to the OECD; Columbia, Costa Rica, Latvia, Lithuania and the Russian Federation are candidates for accession. The organisation has links to many other non-member states and in 2007 launched a programme of enhanced engagement with Brazil, China, India, Indonesia and South Africa. The funding of the OECD is divided according to a member state's economy and population size; the USA, the largest contributor, supplies almost 22 per cent of the organisation's budget.

*Secretary-General,* Angel Gurría (Mexico)

## ORGANISATION FOR SECURITY AND COOPERATION IN EUROPE

6 Wallnerstrasse, 1010 Vienna, Austria
T (+43) (1) 514360 E pm@osce.org W www.osce.org

The Organisation for Security and Cooperation in Europe (OSCE) was launched in 1975 as the Conference on Security and Cooperation in Europe (CSCE) under the Helsinki Final Act. This established agreements between NATO members, Warsaw Pact members, and neutral and non-aligned European countries covering security, cooperation and human rights. It was renamed in 1994.

The Charter of Paris for a New Europe, signed in November 1990, committed members to support multiparty democracy, free-market economics, the rule of law and human rights. The signatories also agreed to regular meetings of heads of government, ministers and officials. The first CSCE summit was held in Helsinki in July 1992, at which the Helsinki Document was adopted. This declared the CSCE to be a regional organisation under the UN charter and defined the structures of the organisation.

Three structures have been established: the ministerial council, which comprises the foreign ministers of participating states and meets at least once a year; the permanent council, which is the main regular body for political consulation, meeting weekly in Vienna; and the forum for security cooperation, also meeting weekly. The chairmanship of the OSCE rotates annually and the post of chair-in-office is held by the foreign minister of a participating state.

The OSCE is also underpinned by four permanent institutions: a secretariat (Vienna); an office for democratic institutions and human rights (Warsaw), which is charged with furthering human rights, democracy and the rule of law; an office of the high commissioner on national minorities (The Hague), which identifies ethnic tensions that might endanger peace and promotes their resolution; and a representative on freedom of the media (Vienna), which is responsible for assisting governments in the furthering of free, independent and pluralistic media.

The OSCE has 17 field operations in Europe, the Caucasus and Central Asia. Since 1996, the OSCE has observed more than 150 elections and supervised all elections in Bosnia and Hercegovina between 1996 and 2000 and in Kosovo between 2000 and 2004. In 1999, the charter on European security committed the OSCE to cooperating with other organisations and institutions concerned with the promotion of security within the OSCE area. The OSCE has 57 participating states and in 2015 its budget was €141.1m (£103.6m).

*Chair,* Ivica Dacic (Serbia, 2015)

## ORGANISATION OF AMERICAN STATES

17th Street and Constitution Avenue, NW, Washington DC 20006–4499, USA
T (+1) (202) 370 5000 W www.oas.org

Originally founded in 1890 for largely commercial purposes, the Organisation of American States (OAS) adopted its present name and charter in 1948. The charter entered into force in 1951 and was amended in 1970, 1988, 1996 and 1997. OAS has 35 member states, though the membership of Honduras was suspended in July 2009 following a coup against President Jose Zelaya; its suspension was lifted in June 2011. The European Union and 69 non-American states have permanent observer status.

The OAS aims to strengthen the peace and security of the Americas; to promote and consolidate representative democracy; to prevent or resolve any political, judicial or economic issues which may arise among member states; to promote their economic, social and cultural development; and to achieve an effective limitation of conventional weapons.

Policy is determined by the annual general assembly, the organisation's supreme authority, which elects the secretary-general for a five-year term. The meeting of consultation of ministers of foreign affairs considers urgent problems on an *ad hoc* basis. The permanent council, comprising one ambassador from each member state, implements the policies approved by the general assembly, acts as an intermediary in cases of disputes arising between states and oversees the general secretariat, the main administrative body. The inter-American council for integral development was created in 1996 by the ratification of the protocol of Managua to promote sustainable development and eliminate poverty.

*Secretary-General,* Luis Almagro Lemes (Uruguay)

## ORGANISATION OF ARAB PETROLEUM EXPORTING COUNTRIES

PO Box 20501, Safat 13066, Kuwait
T (+965) 2495 9000 E oapec@oapecorg.org W www.oapecorg.org

The Organisation of Arab Petroleum Exporting Countries (OAPEC) was founded in 1968. Its objectives are to promote cooperation in economic activities, unite efforts to ensure the flow of oil to consumer markets and create a favourable climate for capital investment and the development of the petroleum industry. OAPEC has 11 member states, although Tunisia's membership has been inactive since 1986.

The ministerial council is composed of oil ministers from the member countries and meets twice a year to determine policy and approve the budgets and accounts of the general secretariat and the judicial tribunal. The judicial tribunal is composed of between seven and 11 judges who rule on disputes between member countries and between countries and oil companies. The executive organ of OAPEC is the general secretariat.

The active members are Algeria, Bahrain, Egypt, Iraq, Kuwait, Libya, Qatar, Saudi Arabia, Syria and the United Arab Emirates.

*Secretary-General,* Abbas Ali Naqi (Kuwait)

## ORGANISATION OF THE BLACK SEA ECONOMIC COOPERATION

Sakip Sabanci Caddesi, Musir Fuad Pasa Yalisi, Eski Tersane, 34467-Emirgan, Istanbul, Turkey
T (+90) (212) 229 6330/6335 E info@bsec-organization.org
W www.bsec-organization.org

The Black Sea Economic Cooperation (BSEC) resulted from the Istanbul Summit Declaration and the adoption of the Bosphorus statement on 25 June 1992; it acquired a permanent secretariat in 1994. A charter was inaugurated to found the Organisation of the Black Sea Economic Cooperation in May 1999 following the Yalta Summit of the heads of state or government in June 1998. It has 12 member states.

The organisation aims to promote closer political and economic cooperation between the countries in the Black Sea region and to foster greater security, foreign investment and good governance.

The council of the ministers of foreign affairs is the highest decision-making authority; it elects the organisation's secretary-general and meets twice-yearly. The meetings rotate among the member states and the chair is the foreign minister of the state in which the meeting is held. There is also a committee of senior officials, and a number of working groups which deal with specific areas of cooperation. BSEC has a permanent secretariat based in Istanbul.

*Secretary-General,* Victor Tvircun (Moldova)

## ORGANISATION OF THE ISLAMIC CONFERENCE

PO Box 178, Jeddah 21411, Saudi Arabia
T (+966) (12) 651 5222 W www.oic-oci.org

The Organisation of the Islamic Conference (OIC) was established in 1969 with the purpose of promoting solidarity and cooperation between its member states. It also has the specific aims of supporting the formation of a Palestinian state, coordinating the views of member states in international forums such as the UN, and improving cooperation in the fields of economics, culture and science.

The OIC has three main bodies: the Islamic summit, the organisation's supreme authority composed of the heads of member states, which meets triennially; the annual conference of foreign ministers; and the general secretariat, which implements policy and is headed by a secretary-general elected by the conference of foreign ministers for a once-renewable five-year term.

In addition to this structure, the OIC has several subsidiary bodies, institutions and standing committees. These include the Islamic Solidarity Fund, to aid Islamic institutions in member countries; the Islamic Development Bank, to finance development projects in member states and the Islamic Educational, Scientific and Cultural Organisation.

Since 1991, the OIC has spoken out in protest of violence against Muslims in India, the Occupied Territories and Bosnia-Hercegovina. From 1993 to 1995 the OIC coordinated the offering of troops to the UN by Muslim states to protect Muslim areas of Bosnia-Hercegovina.

The organisation has 57 members (27 states in Africa; 24 in the Middle East, central and South East Asia plus the Palestinian Authority; three in Europe, and two in South America) and five observer states.

*Secretary-General,* Iyad Ameen Madani (Saudi Arabia)

## ORGANISATION OF THE PETROLEUM EXPORTING COUNTRIES

Helferstorferstrasse 17, A-1010 Vienna, Austria
T (+43) (1) 2111 20 W www.opec.org

The Organisation of the Petroleum Exporting Countries (OPEC) was created in 1960 as a permanent inter-governmental organisation with the principal aims of unifying and coordinating the petroleum policies of its 12 member countries, and stabilising prices and supply in international oil markets.

The supreme authority is the conference of ministers, which generally comprises the oil and energy ministers of the member countries. The conference meets in formal session twice a year to discuss oil policy, energy and administrative matters. The board of governors implements conference resolutions and oversees the running of the OPEC secretariat located in Vienna, Austria.

According to OPEC's annual statistical review, OPEC's 12 member countries held 80.8 per cent of the world's crude oil reserves at the end of 2014, and that year accounted for 41.8 per cent of the world's oil production.

*Secretary-General,* Abdalla Salem El-Badri (Libya)

## PACIFIC ISLANDS FORUM

Secretariat, Private Mail Bag, Suva, Fiji
T (+679) 331 2600 E info@forumsec.org W www.forumsec.org

The Pacific Islands Forum (PIF), formerly the South Pacific Forum, was established in 1971 and represents heads of governments of 16 independent and self-governing Pacific island countries. It aims to foster cooperation between its governments and to represent the interests of the region in international organisations. The PIF meets annually, after which a dialogue is conducted at ministerial level with 14 forum partner states and the European Union.

The PIF secretariat is governed by the forum officials committee (FOC), composed of senior figures from each member country. It comprises divisions dealing with development and economic policy, trade and investment, political and international affairs and services, and is responsible for implementing the forum's decisions.

French Polynesia and New Caledonia became associate members in 2006, and Tokelau in 2014. The African, Caribbean and Pacific Group of States, American Samoa, The Asian Development Bank, the Commonwealth, Commonwealth of the Northern Marianas, Guam, the International Organisation for Migration, Timor-Leste, the United Nations, Wallis and Futuna, Western and Central Pacific Fisheries Commission and the World Bank currently hold special observer status. Fiji's membership was suspended in May 2009 over the failure of its military government to commit to a timeframe for a return to democratic government; the suspension was lifted in 2014.

*Secretary-General,* Dame Meg Taylor, DBE (Papua New Guinea)

## PARTNERS IN POPULATION AND DEVELOPMENT

IPH Building, Mohakhali, Dhaka-1212, Bangladesh
T (+88) (2) 988 1882 E partners@ppdsec.org
W www.partners-popdev.org

Partners in Population and Development (PPD) is an inter-governmental organisation launched at the UN International Conference on Population and Development in Cairo in 1994. It has 25 member states. PPD is dedicated to forming partnerships between and among individuals, organisations and the governments of developing countries. It provides a platform for its members to share successful experiences in education, migration, sexual health and combating infant mortality.

PPD is controlled by a board of directors consisting of ministers or other high-ranking officials in the field of population and development from member countries. The responsibilities of the board include setting policy, promoting cooperation among members and providing advice to the secretariat. The secretariat is based in Dhaka, Bangladesh, and is mandated to serve as the administrative centre of the organisation. It ensures policies are implemented and identifies new areas for collaboration. PPD also has an international programme advisory committee consisting of specialists who advise the board and secretariat on current trends in population, development and reproductive health.

PPD is a permanent observer at the United Nations.

*Chair,* Dr Li Bin (China)

## SECRETARIAT OF THE PACIFIC COMMUNITY

BP D5, Nouméa, 98848, New Caledonia
T (+687) 262 000 E spc@spc.int W www.spc.int

The Secretariat of the Pacific Community (SPC) (formerly the South Pacific Commission) was established in 1947 by Australia, France, the Netherlands, New Zealand, the UK and the USA with the aim of promoting the economic and social stability of the islands in the region. The community now numbers 26 member states and territories: the four remaining founder states (the Netherlands and the UK have withdrawn) and the other 22 states and territories of Melanesia, Micronesia and Polynesia.

The SPC is a technical assistance agency with programmes in marine and land development and health and social policy. The governing body is the conference of the Pacific community, which meets every two years.

*Director-General,* Dr Colin Tukuitonga (Niue)

## SHANGHAI COOPERATION ORGANISATION

7 Ritan Road, Chaoyang District, 100600 Beijing, China
T (+86) (10) 6532 9807 E sco@sectsco.org W www.sectsco.org

The Shanghai Cooperation Organisation (SCO) is a permanent intergovernmental organisation. It was established in 1996 as the Shanghai Five, when China, Kazakhstan, Kyrgyzstan, Russia and Tajikistan signed an agreement on cooperating to resolve disputes along the former Sino-Soviet border. It was renamed in 2001 when Uzbekistan became an official member.

The main principle of the SCO is strengthening co-operation among member states across a range of fields, including politics, economics, science, culture, energy, transport, environmental protection and tourism.

The heads of state council is the organisation's supreme body and meets annually to formulate SCO policy. The heads of government council also holds annual meetings to discuss cooperation strategies and approve budgets. The SCO has two permanent bodies: a secretariat based in Beijing and a regional anti-terrorist structure in Tashkent. The secretary-general and the director of the executive committee are appointed by the council of heads of state for a period of three years.

*Secretary-General,* Dmitry F. Mezentsev (Russia)

## SOUTH ASIAN ASSOCIATION FOR REGIONAL COOPERATION

PO Box 4222, Tridevi Marg, Kathmandu, Nepal
T (+977) (1) 422 1785/ 6350 E saarc@saarc-sec.org
W www.saarc-sec.org

The South Asian Association for Regional Cooperation (SAARC) was established in 1985 by Bangladesh, Bhutan, India, the Maldives, Nepal, Pakistan and Sri Lanka; Afghanistan was admitted as its eighth member in 2007. Its primary objective is the acceleration of economic and social development in member states through collective action in agreed areas of cooperation. These include agricultural development, climate change, science and technology, health, education and communications.

A SAARC preferential trading arrangement, designed to reduce tariffs on trade between SAARC member states, was signed in 1993 and entered into force in 1995. The South Asian free trade area (SAFTA) was agreed in 2004 and came into effect in 2006, with the aim of greatly reducing trade tarriffs by the end of 2016.

The highest authority rests with the heads of state or government of each member state. The council of ministers, which meets twice a year, is made up of the foreign ministers of the member states and is responsible for formulating policy. The standing committee is composed of the foreign secretaries of the member states and monitors and coordinates SAARC programmes; it meets as often as is necessary. Technical committees are assigned to individual areas of SAARC's activities. Its secretariat monitors, facilitates and promotes SAARC's activities and serves as a channel of communication between the association and other regional and intergovernmental institutions.

In 2005, as the only country in South Asia not to be a member of SAARC, Iran declared its wish to join and has since become an observer member, along with seven other states and the European Union.

*Secretary-General,* Arjun Bahadur Thapa (Nepal)

## SOUTHERN AFRICAN DEVELOPMENT COMMUNITY

Plot No. 54385, Private Bag 0095, Gaborone, Botswana
T (+267) 395 1863 E registry@sadc.int W www.sadc.int

The Southern African Development Community (SADC) was formed in 1992 by the members of its predecessor, the Southern African Development Coordination Conference. The latter was founded in 1980 to harmonise economic development among southern Africa's 'majority ruled' countries and reduce their dependence on then apartheid South Africa. The SADC now comprises 15 countries, including South Africa. Madagascar's membership was reactivated in January 2014 after years of suspension following a coup in March 2009.

The SADC aims to evolve common political values, promote economic growth, regional security, sustainable development and the interdependence of member states. An annual summit attended by members' heads of state is the SADC's supreme authority, and its policies are implemented by a secretariat.

*Executive Secretary,* Stergomena Lawrence Tax (Tanzania)

## UNITED NATIONS

*Headquarters,* 405 East 42nd Street, New York, NY 10017, USA
T (+1) (212) 963 1234 W www.un.org
*Regional Information Centre,* rue de la Loi 155, Block C2, 7th Floor, Brussels 1040, Belgium
T (+32) (2) 788 8484 E info@unric.org W www.unric.org

The United Nations (UN) is an intergovernmental organisation dedicated, through signature of the UN charter, to the maintenance of international peace and security and the solution of economic, social and political problems through international cooperation.

The UN was founded as a successor to the League of Nations and inherited many of its procedures and institutions. The name United Nations was first used in the Washington Declaration of 1942 to describe the 26 states that had allied to fight the Axis powers. The UN charter developed from discussions at the Moscow conference of the foreign ministers of China, the Soviet Union, the UK and the USA in 1943. Further progress was made at Dumbarton Oaks, Washington, in 1944 during talks involving the same states. The role of the security council was formulated at the Yalta conference in 1945. The charter was formally drawn up by 50 allied nations at the San Francisco conference between April and June 1945, when it was signed. Following ratification, the UN came into effect on 24 October 1945, which is celebrated annually as United Nations Day. The UN flag is light blue with the UN emblem centred in white.

The principal organs of the UN are the general assembly, the security council, the economic and social council, the secretariat and the international court of justice. The economic and social council is an auxiliary, charged with assisting and advising the general assembly, security council and member states, and coordinating the economic and social aspects of the work of UN agencies and commissions. The official languages used are Arabic, Chinese, English, French, Russian and Spanish; the working languages of the secretariat and the international court of justice are English and French.

MEMBERSHIP

Membership is open to all countries that accept the charter and its principle of peaceful co-existence. New members are admitted by the general assembly on the recommendation of the security council. The original membership of 51 states has grown to 193 *(see* below).

*Members of the UN*

| | | | |
|---|---|---|---|
| Afghanistan | Dominican Republic* | Libya | St Vincent and the |
| Albania | Ecuador* | Liechtenstein | Grenadines |
| Algeria | Egypt* | Lithuania | Samoa |
| Andorra | El Salvador* | Luxembourg* | San Marino |
| Angola | Equatorial Guinea | Macedonia, Former | São Tomé and Princpe |
| Antigua and Barbuda | Eritrea | Yugoslav Republic of | Saudi Arabia* |
| Argentina* | Estonia | Madagascar | Senegal |
| Armenia | Ethiopia* | Malawi | Serbia |
| Australia* | Fiji | Malaysia | Seychelles |
| Austria | Finland | Maldives | Sierra Leone |
| Azerbaijan | France* | Mali | Singapore |
| Bahamas | FYR Macedonia | Malta | Slovakia |
| Bahrain | Gabon | Marshall Islands | Slovenia |
| Bangladesh | The Gambia | Mauritania | Solomon Islands |
| Barbados | Georgia | Mauritius | Somalia |
| Belarus* | Germany | Mexico* | South Africa* |
| Belgium* | Ghana | Micronesia, Federated | South Sudan |
| Belize | Greece* | States of | Spain |
| Benin | Grenada | Moldova | Sri Lanka |
| Bhutan | Guatemala* | Monaco | Sudan |
| Bolivia* | Guinea | Mongolia | Suriname |
| Bosnia and Hercegovina | Guinea-Bissau | Montenegro | Swaziland |
| Botswana | Guyana | Morocco | Sweden |
| Brazil* | Haiti* | Mozambique | Switzerland |
| Brunei | Honduras* | Myanmar | Syria* |
| Bulgaria | Hungary | Namibia | Tajikistan |
| Burkina Faso | Iceland | Nauru | Tanzania |
| Burundi | India* | Nepal | Thailand |
| Cabo Verde | Indonesia | The Netherlands* | Timor-Leste |
| Cambodia | Iran* | New Zealand* | Togo |
| Cameroon | Iraq* | Nicaragua* | Tonga |
| Canada* | Ireland | Niger | Trinidad and Tobago |
| Central African | Israel | Nigeria | Tunisia |
| Republic | Italy | Norway* | Turkey* |
| Chad | Jamaica | Oman | Turkmenistan |
| Chile* | Japan | Pakistan | Tuvalu |
| China* | Jordan | Palau | Uganda |
| Colombia* | Kazakhstan | Panama* | Ukraine* |
| Comoros | Kenya | Papua New Guinea | United Arab Emirates |
| Congo, Dem. Rep of the | Kiribati | Paraguay* | United Kingdom* |
| Congo, Republic of the | Korea, Dem. People's | Peru* | United States of |
| Costa Rica* | Rep. of | The Philippines* | America* |
| Côte d'Ivoire | Korea, Rep. of | Poland* | Uruguay* |
| Croatia | Kuwait | Portugal | Uzbekistan |
| Cuba* | Kyrgyzstan | Qatar | Vanuatu |
| Cyprus | Laos | Romania | Venezuela* |
| Czech Republic | Latvia | Russian Federation* | Vietnam |
| Denmark* | Lebanon* | Rwanda | Yemen |
| Djibouti | Lesotho | St Kitts and Nevis | Zambia |
| Dominica | Liberia* | St Lucia | Zimbabwe |

* Original member (ie from 1945). Czechoslovakia, Yugoslavia and the USSR were all original members until their dissolution.

OBSERVERS

Permanent observer status is held by the Holy See. The Palestinian Authority has special observer status.

*THE GENERAL ASSEMBLY*

UN Plaza, New York, NY 10017, USA

The general assembly is the main deliberative organ of the UN. It consists of all members, each entitled to five representatives but having only one vote. The annual session begins on the third Tuesday of September, when the president is elected, and usually continues until mid-December. Special sessions are held on specific issues and emergency special sessions can be called within 24 hours.

The assembly is empowered to discuss any matter within the scope of the charter – except when it is under consideration by the security council – and to make recommendations. Under the peace resolution, adopted in 1950, the assembly may also take action to maintain international peace and security when the security council fails to do so because of a lack of unanimity of its permanent members. Important decisions (such as those on peace and security, the election of officers, the budget, etc) need a two-thirds majority. Others need a simple majority. The assembly has effective power only over the internal operations of the UN itself; external recommendations are not legally binding.

The work of the general assembly is divided among a number of committees, on each of which every member has the right to be represented. Subjects include human rights, the use of torture, peacekeeping, assistance to developing countries and discrimination. In addition, the general assembly appoints *ad hoc* committees to consider more specific issues. All committees consider items referred to them by the assembly and recommend draft resolutions to its plenary meeting.

The assembly is assisted by a number of functional committees. The general committee coordinates its proceedings and operations, while the credentials committee verifies the representatives.

*President of the General Assembly,* Sam Kutesa (Uganda)

SPECIALISED BODIES

The assembly has created a large number of specialised bodies, some of which are supervised jointly with the economic and social council. They are supported by UN and voluntary contributions from governments, non-governmental organisations and individuals. These organisations include:

CONFERENCE ON DISARMAMENT

Palais des Nations, CH-1211 Geneva 10, Switzerland

The Conference on Disarmament (CD) was established in 1979 as the international community's multilateral disarmament negotiating forum. Originally comprising 40 member states, the CD has expanded to 65 members. The Non-Proliferation of Nuclear Weapons Treaty entered into force on 5 March 1970 and has so far been ratified by 190 states. A chemical weapons convention was agreed in Paris in 1993 and came into force in April 1997 after being ratified by 87 countries. Currently 189 states participate in the convention, which bans the use, production, stockpiling and transfer of all chemical weapons. A convention prohibiting the use of cluster munitions, agreed in Dublin in 2008 and currently ratified by 92 states, entered into force on 1 August 2010.

UNITED NATIONS CHILDREN'S FUND (UNICEF)

3 UN Plaza, New York, NY 10017, USA T (+1) 212 326 7000
W www.unicef.org
UNICEF House, 30A Great Sutton St, London EC1V 0DU
T 020-7490 2388

Established in 1946 to assist children and mothers in the immediate post-war period, UNICEF now concentrates on developing countries. It provides primary healthcare and health education, and conducts programmes in oral hydration, immunisation against common diseases, HIV/AIDS treatment and prevention and child growth monitoring. It also works to provide children with equal access to quality education.

UNITED NATIONS DEVELOPMENT PROGRAMME (UNDP)

1 UN Plaza, New York, NY 10017, USA T (+1) 212 906 5000
W www.undp.org

Established in 1965 from the merger of the UN expanded programme of technical assistance and the UN special fund, UNDP is the central funding agency for economic and social development projects around the world. Much of its annual expenditure is channelled through UN specialised agencies, governments and non-governmental organisations.

UNITED NATIONS HIGH COMMISSIONER FOR REFUGEES (UNHCR)

Case Postale 2500, CH-1211 Geneva 2 Depot, Switzerland
T (+41) 22 739 8111 W www.unhcr.org

Established in 1950 to protect the rights and interests of refugees, UNHCR organises emergency relief and longer-term solutions, such as voluntary repatriation, local integration or resettlement. UNHCR is also mandated to assist stateless people.

UNITED NATIONS RELIEF AND WORKS AGENCY FOR PALESTINE REFUGEES IN THE NEAR EAST (UNRWA)

HQ Gaza, PO Box 371, Gaza City
T (+972) 8 288 7701 W www.unrwa.org

The UNRWA was established in 1949 to bring relief to the Palestinians displaced by the Arab-Israeli conflict. The UN general assembly has repeatedly voted every three years to extend its mandate, most recently until June 2017.

UNITED NATIONS HUMAN RIGHTS COUNCIL (UNHRC)

Palais des Nations, CH-1211 Geneva 10, Switzerland
T (+41) (22) 917 9220 E infodesk@ohchr.org W www.ohchr.org

The UNHRC is a 47-member council, established in 2006, replacing the United Nations Commission on Human Rights (UNCHR). The UNHRC has a mandate to promote (and prevent violations of) human rights by engaging in dialogue with governments and international organisations. It is also responsible for the coordination of all UN human rights activities and reports to, and is directly elected by, the general assembly.

*THE SECURITY COUNCIL*

UN Plaza, New York, NY 10017, USA
W www.un.org/en/sc

The security council is the senior arm of the UN and has the primary responsibility for maintaining world peace and security. It consists of 15 members, each with one representative and one vote. There are five permanent members – China, France, Russia, the UK and the USA – and ten non-permanent members. Each of the non-permanent members is elected for a two-year term by a two-thirds majority of the general assembly and is ineligible for immediate re-election. Five of the elective seats are allocated to Africa and Asia, one to eastern Europe, two to Latin America and two to western Europe and remaining countries.

Decisions on procedural matters require affirmative votes from at least nine of the 15 members. Other matters require the same, but must include the affirmative votes of the permanent members; they thus have a right of veto. The abstention of a permanent member does not constitute a veto. The presidency rotates each month by state in (English) alphabetical order. Parties in a dispute, other non-members and individuals can be invited to participate in security council debates but are not permitted to vote.

The security council is empowered to settle or adjudicate in disputes or situations which threaten international peace and security. It can adopt political, economic and military measures to achieve this end. Any matter considered to be a threat to or breach of the peace or an act of aggression can be brought to the security council's attention by any member state or by the secretary-general. The charter envisaged members placing at the disposal of the security council armed forces and other facilities which would be coordinated by the military staff committee, composed of military representatives of the five permanent members. The security council is also supported by a committee of experts, to advise on procedural and technical matters, and a committee on admission of new members.

Owing to superpower disunity, the security council has rarely played the decisive role set out in the charter; the military staff committee was effectively suspended from 1948 until 1990, when a meeting was convened during the Gulf crisis on the formation and control of UN-supervised armed forces. In 1992, heads of government laid plans to transform the UN in light of the changed post-Cold War world. The secretary-general produced *An Agenda for Peace*, a report which centred on the establishment of a UN army composed of national contingents on permanent standby, as envisaged at the time of the UN's formation. However, enthusiasm for UN intervention waned during the rest of the decade after a problematic mission in Somalia during which 42 UN personnel were killed. The security council has since been criticised for its failure to intervene in subsequent conflicts, including the genocide in Rwanda and the ongoing situation in Darfur. More recently it has applied sanctions to Iran, North Korea, the Pakistani militant group Lashkar-e-Taiba, and figures within Libya,the Côte d'Ivoire and South Sudan.

The security council also has the power to elect judges to the international court of justice and to recommend to the general assembly the election of a secretary-general.

## PEACEKEEPING FORCES

The security council has established a number of peace-keeping forces since its foundation, comprising contingents provided mainly by neutral and non-aligned UN members. As at 31 March 2015, current operations were:

| Continent | UN Code | Year implemented | Uniformed personnel deployed |
|---|---|---|---|
| **Africa** | | | |
| Western Sahara | MINURSO | 1991 | 216 |
| Liberia | UNMIL | 2003 | 5,869 |
| Côte d'Ivoire | UNOCI | 2004 | 7,511 |
| Darfur, Sudan | UNAMID | 2007 | 16,815 |
| Dem. Rep. of the Congo | MONUSCO | 2010 | 20,878 |
| South Sudan | UNMISS | 2011 | 11,734 |
| Sudan | UNISFA | 2011 | 4,090 |
| Mali | MINUSMA | 2013 | 11,510 |
| Central African Rep. | MINUSCA | 2014 | 9,902 |
| **The Americas** | | | |
| Haiti | MINUSTAH | 2004 | 7,125 |

| | | | |
|---|---|---|---|
| **Asia** | | | |
| India and Pakistan | UNMOGIP | 1949 | 42 |
| **Europe** | | | |
| Cyprus | UNFICYP | 1964 | 1,072 |
| Kosovo | UNMIK | 1999 | 15 |
| **Middle East** | UNTSO | 1948 | 143 |
| Syria | UNDOF | 1974 | 785 |
| Lebanon | UNIFIL | 1978 | 11,430 |

| TOP FIVE CONTRIBUTORS TO UN PEACEKEEPING MISSIONS (*as at* 31 May 2015) | |
|---|---|
| *Country* | *Number of Troops* |
| Pakistan | 8,234 |
| Bangladesh | 8,078 |
| Ethiopia | 7,712 |
| India | 7,050 |
| Rwanda | 5,077 |

*Source:* www.un.org/en/peacekeeping

## INTERNATIONAL CRIMINAL TRIBUNAL FOR THE FORMER YUGOSLAVIA

Churchillplein 1, 2517 JW The Hague, The Netherlands
T (+31) 7051 28752 W www.icty.org

In February 1993, the security council voted to establish the International Criminal Tribunal for the Former Yugoslavia (ICTY), a war crimes tribunal to hear cases covering breaches of the Geneva Conventions and crimes against humanity during the Balkans conflict of the 1990s. In December 2010 the UN security council approved the creation of the Inter-national Residual Mechanism for Criminal Tribunals (IRMCT), which took over the functions of the ICTY on 1 July 2013 and can not raise new indictments. The IRMCT will oversee the completion of the ICTY and ICTR (*see* below).
*President,* Theodor Meron (USA)

## INTERNATIONAL CRIMINAL TRIBUNAL FOR RWANDA

Churchillplein 1, 2517 JW The Hague, The Netherlands
T (+31) 7051 25027 E ictr-press@un.org W www.unictr.org

Following serious violations of humanitarian law in Rwanda, the UN security council created the International Criminal Tribunal for Rwanda on 8 November 1994 in order to contribute to the process of national reconciliation and the maintenance of peace in the region. Its remit was to prosecute persons responsible for genocide and other serious international humanitarian law violations committed in the territory of Rwanda between 1 January 1994 and 31 December 1994, and by Rwandan citizens in the territory of neighbouring states during the same period. The IRMCT (*see* above) took over the functions of the ICTR on 1 July 2012 and can not raise new indictments.
*President,* Vagn Joensen (Denmark)

## THE ECONOMIC AND SOCIAL COUNCIL

UN Plaza, New York, NY 10017, USA
E ecosocinfo@un.org W www.un.org/ecosoc

The economic and social council is responsible under the general assembly for the economic and social work of the UN and for the coordination of the activities of the 14 specialised agencies and other UN bodies. It makes reports and recommendations on economic, social, cultural, educational, health and related matters, often in consultation with non-governmental organisations, passing the reports to the general assembly and other UN bodies. It also drafts conventions for submission to the assembly and calls conferences on matters within its remit.

The council consists of 54 members, who are elected by the general assembly for overlapping three-year terms. Each member has one vote and can be immediately re-elected. The council elects a president and four vice-presidents each year: this five-member bureau proposes the council's agenda, draws up a programme of work and organises the substantive session. This session is held each July, and decisions are reached by a simple majority vote of those present.

The council has established a number of functional commissions and standing committees on particular issues. These include commissions on social development, sustainable development, population and development, the status of women, crime prevention and criminal justice, narcotic drugs, and science and technology for development, as well as five regional economic commissions.

*President,* Martin Sajdik (Austria)

### THE SECRETARIAT

UN Plaza, New York, NY 10017, USA

The secretariat services the other principle UN organs and administers their programmes and policies. It is headed by a secretary-general elected by a majority vote of the general assembly on the recommendation of the security council. He is assisted by some 44,000 staff worldwide. The secretary-general is charged with bringing to the attention of the security council any matter which he considers poses a threat to international peace and security. He may also bring other matters to the attention of the general assembly and other UN bodies and may be entrusted by them with additional duties. As chief administrator to the UN, the secretary-general is present in person or via representatives at all meetings of the other five main organs of the UN. He may also act as a mediator in disputes between member states.

The power and influence of the secretary-general has been determined largely by the character of the office-holder and by the state of relations between the superpowers. The improvement of these relations since the mid-1980s has increased the effectiveness of the UN, particularly in its attempts to intervene in international disputes. Good collaboration betweeen the Secretary-General and super-powers helped to end the Iran-Iraq War and sponsored peace in Central America. Following Iraq's invasion of Kuwait in 1990, the UN took its first collective security action since the Korean War. Conflicts in Cyprus, Timor–Leste, Libya, Nigeria and Western Sahara were successfully prevented from escalating or spreading during the administration of Kofi Annan. However, the UN was heavily criticised for its failure to act in the Rwandan genocide of 1994 and its inability to halt the conflict in Darfur, while the invasion of Iraq by the USA and UK in 2003 without a UN mandate, illegal under the organisation's charter, seriously undermined its authority.

*Secretary-General,* Ban Ki-moon (South Korea)
*Deputy Secretary-General,* Jan Eliasson (Sweden)

| FORMER SECRETARIES-GENERAL | |
|---|---|
| 1946–52 | Trygve Lie (Norway) |
| 1953–61 | Dag Hammarskjold (Sweden) |
| 1961–71 | U Thant (Myanmar) |
| 1972–81 | Kurt Waldheim (Austria) |
| 1982–91 | Javier Pérez de Cuéllar (Peru) |
| 1992–96 | Boutros Boutros-Ghali (Egypt) |
| 1997–2006 | Kofi Annan (Ghana) |

### UK MISSION TO THE UN

1 Dag Hammarskjold Plaza, 885 Second Avenue, New York, NY 10017, USA

T (+1) (212) 745 9200 E uk@un.int W www.ukun.fco.gov.uk

*Permanent Representative to the UN and Representative on the Security Council,* HE Matthew Rycroft, CBE, *apptd* 2015

### UK MISSION TO THE UN AND OTHER INTERNATIONAL ORGANISATIONS IN GENEVA

58 Avenue Louis Casai, 1216 Cointrin GE Geneva, Switzerland

T (+41) (22) 918 2300 E geneva_un@fco.gov.uk

*Permanent UK Representative,* HE Julian Braithwaite, *apptd* 2015

### UK MISSION TO THE UN IN VIENNA

Jaurèsgasse 12, A-1030 Vienna, Austria

T (+43) (1) 716 130 E ukmis.vienna@fco.gov.uk

W ukinaustria.fco.gov.uk

*Permanent UK Representative,* HE Susan le Jeune d'Allegeershecque, CMG, *apptd* 2012

### REGIONAL UN INFORMATION CENTRE

Block C2, Level 7, 155 rue de la Loi, Brussels 1040, Belgium

T (+32) 2788 8484 E info@unric.org W www.unric.org

### THE INTERNATIONAL COURT OF JUSTICE

Peace Palace, Carnegieplein 2, 2517 KJ, The Hague, The Netherlands

T (+31) (70) 302 2323 W www.icj-cij.org

The international court of justice is the principal judicial organ of the UN, and its statute is an integral part of the UN charter; all members of the UN are *ipso facto* parties to it. The court is composed of 15 judges, elected by both the general assembly and the security council for nine-year terms, which are renewable. Judges may deliberate over cases in which their country is involved. If no judge on the bench is from a country that is a party to a dispute under consideration, that party may designate a judge to participate *ad hoc* in that particular deliberation. If any party to a case fails to adhere to the judgment of the court, the other party may have recourse to the security council.

*President,* Ronny Abraham (France)
*Vice-President,* Abdulqawi Ahmed Yusuf (Somalia)
*Judges,* James Crawford (Australia); Antonio A. Cancado Trindade (Brazil); Xue Hanqin (China); Ronny Abraham (France); Dalveer Bhandari (India); Giorgio Gaja (Italy); Patrick Robinson (Jamaica); Hisashi Owada (Japan); Mohamed Bennouna (Morocco); Giorgio Gaja (Russia); Peter Tomka (Slovakia); Abdulqawi Ahmed Yusuf (Somalia); Julia Sebutinde (Uganda); Christopher Greenwood (UK); Joan Donoghue (USA)

### UNITED NATIONS EDUCATIONAL, SCIENTIFIC AND CULTURAL ORGANISATION

7 place de Fontenoy, F-75352 Paris, France

T (+33) (01) 4568 1000 W www.unesco.org

The United Nations Educational, Scientific and Cultural Organisation (UNESCO) was established in 1945. It promotes collaboration among its member states in education, science, culture and communication. It aims to promote a universal respect for human rights, justice and the rule of law, without distinction of race, sex, language or religion, in accordance with the UN charter.

UNESCO runs a number of programmes to improve education and extend access to it. It provides assistance to ensure the free flow of information and its wider dissemination without any barriers to freedom of expression, to safeguard cultural heritages and encourage sustainable development. It fosters research and study in the social and environmental sciences. The UNESCO world heritage list, decided upon by a 21-member committee of state representatives, includes 1007 cultural and natural sites of 'outstanding universal value'.

UNESCO has 195 member states and nine associate members. The general conference, consisting of representatives of all the members, meets biennially to decide the programme and the budget. It elects the 58-member executive board, which supervises operations, and appoints a director-general who heads a secretariat responsible for carrying out the organisation's programmes. In most member states national commissions liaise with UNESCO to execute its policies.

*Director-General,* Irina Bokova (Bulgaria)

## UNITED NATIONS INDUSTRIAL DEVELOPMENT ORGANISATION

Vienna International Centre, Wagramerstrasse 5, PO Box 300, A-1400 Vienna, Austria
T (+43) (1) 260 260 E unido@unido.org W www.unido.org

The United Nations Industrial Development Organisation (UNIDO) was established in 1966 by the UN general assembly to act as the central coordinating body for industrial activities within the UN. It became a UN specialised agency in 1979. UNIDO aims to help countries with developing and transitional economies by increasing the productivity and competitiveness of their agricultural, technological and energy industries.

As at March 2015, 170 states were members of UNIDO . It is funded by regular and operational budgets, together with contributions for technical cooperation activities. The regular budget is derived from member states' contributions. Technical cooperation is funded mainly through voluntary contributions from donor countries and institutions and by intergovernmental and non-governmental organisations. A general conference of all the members meets biennially to discuss strategy and policy, approve the budget – €175.9m (£129m) for the biennium 2016–17 – and elect the director-general. The industrial development board is composed of representatives from 53 member states and reviews the work programme and the budget, which is prepared by the programme and budget committee of 27 member states.

*Director-General,* Li Yong (China)

## UNIVERSAL POSTAL UNION

4 Weltpoststrasse, CH-3000 Bern 15, Switzerland
T (+41) (31) 350 3111 E info@upu.int W www.upu.int

The Universal Postal Union (UPU) was established by the Treaty of Bern 1874, taking effect from 1875, and became a UN specialised agency in 1948. The UPU exists to form and regulate a single postal territory of all member countries for the reciprocal exchange of correspondence without discrimination. With a total of 192 members, it also assists and advises on the improvement of postal services.

The universal postal congress is the UPU's supreme authority and meets every four years. The council of administration meets annually to supervise the union's work between congresses, to investigate regulatory developments and policy issues, to approve the budget and to examine proposed treaty changes. The consultative committee was set up in 2004 to further the interests of the wider postal sector. It brings together representative bodies of customers, service providers, manufacturers and suppliers, and provides a forum for dialogue between postal industry stakeholders. The three UPU bodies are served by the international bureau, a secretariat headed by a director-general.

Funding is provided by members according to a scale of contributions drawn up by the congress. The council of administration sets the budget which amounts to approximately SFr37m (£25m) a year.

*Director-General,* Bishar Abdirahman Hussein (Kenya)

## UNREPRESENTED NATIONS AND PEOPLES ORGANISATION

Laan van Meerdervoort 70, 2517 AN, The Hague, The Netherlands
T (+31) (0) 70 364 6504 E unpo@unpo.org W www.unpo.org

The Unrepresented Nations and Peoples Organisation (UNPO) was founded in 1991 to offer an international forum for occupied nations, indigenous peoples and national minorities who are not represented in other international organisations.

The UNPO does not aim to represent these nations and peoples, but rather to assist and empower them to represent themselves more effectively, and provides professional services and facilities as well as education and training in the fields of diplomacy, international and human rights law, democratic processes, institution building, conflict management and resolution, and environmental protection.

Participation is open to all nations and peoples who are inadequately represented at the UN and who declare allegiance to five principles relating to the right of self-determination of all peoples: human rights, democracy, tolerance, non-violence and respect for the rights of minorities. Applicants must show that they constitute a nation or people and that the organisation applying for membership is representative of that nation or people.

As at June 2015, UNPO had 46 full members.

*General Secretary,* Marino Busdachin (Italy)

## WORLD BANK GROUP

1818 H Street NW, Washington DC 20433, USA
T (+1) (202) 473 1000 W www.worldbank.org

The World Bank Group was founded in 1944 from the consolidation of five major development organisations and is one of the world's largest sources of development assistance. It has 188 member states. Originally directed towards post-war reconstruction in Europe, the bank subsequently turned towards assisting less-developed countries worldwide, and in 2014 provided US$65.6bn (£42.8bn) for 12,338 projects across the developing world. It works with government agencies, non-governmental organisations and the private sector to formulate assistance strategies. Its local offices implement the bank's programme in each country.

The World Bank is owned by the governments of member countries and its capital is subscribed by its members. It finances its lending primarily from borrowing in world capital markets, and derives a substantial contribution to its resources from its retained earnings and the repayment of loans.

The World Bank Group consists of two institutions and three affiliates. The International Bank for Reconstruction and Development (IBRD) provides loans and development assistance to middle-income countries and credit-worthy poorer countries (total loans for 2014 US$18.6bn (£12.1bn)). The International Development Association (IDA) performs the same function as the IBRD but primarily to less-developed countries and on terms that bear less heavily on their balance of payments than IBRD loans (total loans for 2014 US$22.2bn (£14.5bn)).

The three affiliates are the International Finance Corporation (IFC), which has 184 members and promotes private sector investment in developing countries by mobilising domestic and foreign capital; the Multilateral Investment Guarantee Agency (MIGA), which has 181 members and promotes foreign direct investment in developing states by insuring investors against political risk and helping member countries to improve their investment climates; and the International Centre for Settlement of Investment Disputes, which has 159 full members (known as contracting states) and provides facilities for resolving disputes between foreign investors and their host countries.

The IBRD, IDA and the affiliates are financially and legally distinct but share headquarters. The IBRD is headed by a board of governors, which meets annually and consists of one governor and one alternate governor appointed by each member country; most IBRD governors also serve on the separate boards of the IDA, IFC and MIGA. Twenty-five executive directors exercise all powers of the World Bank (except those reserved to the board of governors). The president, elected by the board of executive directors, conducts the business of the bank, assisted by an international staff. Membership in both the IFC and the IDA is open to all IBRD countries. The IDA is administered by the same staff as the bank; the IFC has its own personnel but can draw on the IBRD for administrative and other support. All share the same president.

*President,* Jim Yong Kim (USA)

## WORLD CUSTOMS ORGANISATION

30 rue de Marché, B-1210, Brussels, Belgium
T (+32) 2209 9211 W www.wcoomd.org

Established in 1952 as the Customs Cooperation Council, the World Customs Organisation (WCO) is an independent intergovernmental organisation whose primary mission is to enhance the effectiveness and efficiency of customs administrations worldwide. It is the only international body specialised in customs matters, and is recognised as the voice of the global customs community and a centre of customs expertise.

Comprising 180 member customs administrations that process approximately 98 per cent of international trade, the WCO is governed by a council which meets annually and in which each member has one vote. The council is supported by a policy commission, a finance committee, an audit committee, various technical committees, and a permanent secretariat charged with implementing council decisions.

*Secretary-General,* Kunio Mikuriya (Japan)

## WORLD HEALTH ORGANISATION

Avenue Appia 20, 1211 Geneva 27, Switzerland
T (+41) (22) 791 2111 W www.who.int

The UN International Health Conference, held in 1946, established the World Health Organisation (WHO) as a UN specialised agency, with effect from 1948. It is dedicated to attaining the highest possible level of health for all. It collaborates with member governments, UN agencies and other bodies to improve health standards, control communicable diseases and promote all aspects of family and environmental health. It seeks to raise the standards of health teaching and training, and promotes research through collaboration with research centres worldwide.

WHO has 194 members and is governed by an annual assembly of members. This sets policy, approves the budget, appoints a director-general, and adopts health conventions and regulations. It also elects 34 member states to designate one expert each to serve on the executive board. The board sets the assembly's agenda and implements its policies, suggests initiatives, and is empowered to deal with emergencies. A secretariat, headed by the director-general, supervises the activities of six regional offices.

*Director-General,* Dr Margaret Chan (China)

## WORLD INTELLECTUAL PROPERTY ORGANISATION

34 chemin des Colombettes, CH-1211, Geneva 20, Switzerland
T (+41) (22) 338 9111 W www.wipo.int

The World Intellectual Property Organisation (WIPO) was established in Stockholm in 1967 by the signing of the WIPO Convention, which entered into force in 1970. WIPO administers 26 treaties that deal with different legal and administrative aspects of intellectual property, notably the Paris Convention for the protection of industrial property and the Bern Convention for the protection of literary and artistic works. WIPO became a UN specialised agency in 1974.

Intellectual property falls into two main branches: industrial property (inventions, trademarks, industrial designs and geographical indications) and copyright (literary, musical, photographic, audiovisual and artistic works, etc). WIPO helps ensure that creative intellectual activity is rewarded, and facilitates technology transfer, particularly to developing countries.

WIPO's mission is to promote the protection of intellectual property rights worldwide. The organisation's activities fall into three broad categories: the progressive development of international intellectual property law, assistance to developing countries, and the provision of services which facilitate the process of obtaining intellectual property rights in multiple countries.

WIPO had 188 members as at June 2015. The biennial session of the general assembly, the conference and the coordination committee set policy, a programme and a budget. A separate agency, the International Union for the Protection of New Varieties of Plants (UPOV), established by convention in 1961, is linked to WIPO and has 72 members.

*Director-General,* Francis Gurry (Australia)

## WORLD METEOROLOGICAL ORGANISATION

7 bis, avenue de la Paix, PO Box 2300, CH-1211 Geneva 2, Switzerland
T (+41) (22) 730 8111 W www.wmo.int

The World Meteorological Organisation (WMO) was established in 1950 and became a UN specialised agency in 1951, succeeding the International Meteorological Organisation founded in 1873. It facilitates cooperation in the establishment of networks for making, processing and exchanging meteorological, climatological, hydrological and geophysical observations. It also fosters collaboration between meteorological and hydrological services, and furthers the application of meteorology to aviation, shipping, environment, water problems, agriculture and the mitigation of natural disasters.

In June 2015, the WMO had 185 member states and six member territories. Six regional associations are responsible for the coordination of activities within their own regions. There are also eight technical commissions, which study meteorological and hydrological problems, establish methodology and procedures, and make recommendations to the executive council and the congress. The supreme authority is the world meteorological congress, which meets every four years to determine general policy and set the budget (SFr266.2m (£179.9m) for the four-year period 2016–19). It also elects 31 members of the 37-member executive council which supervises the implementation of congress decisions, initiates studies and makes recommendations on matters requiring international action. The secretariat is headed by a secretary-general, appointed by the congress.

*Secretary-General (2012–15),* Michel Jarraud (France)
*Secretary-General (2016–19),* Petteri Taalas (Finland)

## WORLD TOURISM ORGANISATION

Capitán Haya 42, 28020 Madrid, Spain
T (+34) 9156 78100 E omt@unwto.org W www2.unwto.org

The World Tourism Organisation (UNWTO) was officially launched in 1975 to act as an executing agency of the United Nations Development Programme. Primarily concerned with developing public and private sector partnerships, the UNWTO also promotes the global code of ethics for tourism, a framework of policy aimed at tour operators, governments, labour organisations and travellers. There are 156 member states and six associate member states.

The general assembly is the principal gathering of the UNWTO and meets every two years in order to approve policy and budget. Every four years, the assembly elects a secretary-general. The executive council is UNWTO's governing board and meets at least twice a year to ensure the organisation adheres to policy and budget. It is composed of 32 members of the general assembly. As host country of UNWTO's headquarters, Spain has a permanent seat on the executive council.

*Secretary-General,* Taleb Rifai (Jordan)

## WORLD TRADE ORGANISATION

Centre William Rappard, 154 rue de Lausanne,
CH-1211 Geneva 21, Switzerland
T (+41) (22) 739 5111 E enquiries@wto.org W www.wto.org

The World Trade Organisation was established on 1 January 1995 as the successor to the General Agreement on Tariffs and Trade (GATT).

The GATT was dedicated to the expansion of non-discriminatory international trade and progressively extended free trade via 'rounds' of multilateral negotiations. The final act of the comprehensive Uruguay round of negotiations was signed by trade ministers from the 123 GATT negotiating states and the EU in Marrakesh, Morocco, in 1994. New talks on agriculture and services began in 2000 and were incorporated into a broader agenda launched at the 2001 ministerial conference in Doha, Qatar.

The WTO is the legal and institutional foundation of the multilateral trading system. It provides the contractual obligations determining how governments frame and implement trade policy, and provides the forum for the debate, negotiation and adjudication of trade issues. The WTO's principal aims are to liberalise world trade and place it on a secure basis; it seeks to achieve this through the combination of an agreed set of trade rules and market-access agreements and further trade liberalisation negotiations. The WTO also administers and implements multilateral agreements in fields such as agriculture, industrial goods, services, government procurement, rules of origin and intellectual property.

The highest authority of the WTO is the ministerial conference composed of all members, which usually meets once every two years. The general council meets as required and acts on behalf of the ministerial conference in regard to the regular working of the WTO. The general council also convenes in two particular forms: as the dispute-settlement body, dealing with disagreements between members arising from WTO agreements or commitments; and as the trade policy review body, conducting regular reviews of the trade policies of members. A secretariat of 640 staff, headed by a director-general, services WTO bodies and provides trade performance and trade policy analysis.

As of June 2015, the WTO has 161 members and 23 observer governments. The most recent member – Seychelles – joined the WTO in 2015. The WTO budget for 2015 is SFr197.2m (£133.5m), with members' contributions calculated on the basis of their share of international trade. The official languages of the WTO are English, French and Spanish.

*Director-General,* Roberto Azevedo (Brazil)

# COUNTRIES OF THE WORLD A–Z

## DEFINITIONS AND ABBREVIATIONS

est = estimate
IDD = International direct dialling

AIRPORTS – figures reference airports with paved runways only, unless otherwise specified
BIRTH RATE – figures are per 1,000 population
CORRUPTION PERCEPTIONS INDEX (CPI) SCORE – the perception of the degree of public sector corruption as seen by business people and country analysts; ranging from 0 (highly corrupt) to 100 (very clean). Overall position given in parentheses. © Transparency International
DEATH PENALTY:
Retained (not used) – countries that retain the death penalty for ordinary crimes such as murder but can be considered to have abolished it in practice
Retained for certain crimes – countries whose laws provide for the death penalty only for exceptional crimes ('Last used' = date of last execution)
Retained – countries that retain the death penalty for ordinary crimes
GROSS ENROLMENT RATIO – the ratio of total enrolment, regardless of age, to the total population of the relevant age group expressed as a percentage; this figure can be above 100 per cent where, for example, a greater number of children are attending classes designed for six-year-olds than there are six-year-olds in the country, owing to some children starting school late or skipping a year
GROSS NATIONAL INCOME (GNI) – the total income earned by a country's residents; the second figure is GNI divided by the population to give a per capita figure
HIV/AIDS ADULT PREVALENCE – estimate of the percentage of the total adult population (aged 15–49) infected with HIV/AIDS
INFANT MORTALITY RATE – averages for male and female infants under one year old and per 1,000 live births
LIFE EXPECTANCY – averages, at birth, for males and females
LITERACY (ADULT) – the World Bank defines literacy as the percentage of the population aged 15 and above that can read and write a short statement on their everyday life. Where the World Bank figure is not available the statistic provided is that given by the government of that country. This figure is not always comparable due to differing definitions of what constitutes adult literacy.
MILITARY EXPENDITURE – figures are the most recent available at constant 2011 prices and exchange rates
MORTALITY RATE – figures are per 1,000 population. This indicator is significantly affected by age distribution, and most countries will eventually show a rise in the overall death rate, in spite of continued decline in mortality at all ages, as declining fertility results in an ageing population
POPULATION BELOW POVERTY LINE – although strict definitions of poverty vary considerably between nations, this figure most commonly represents the percentage of the adult population whose income is less than US$1 per day
TOTAL EXTERNAL DEBT – the total public and private debt owed to non-residents repayable in foreign currency, goods or services
WORLD PRESS FREEDOM INDEX (WPFI) SCORE – the perception of press freedom based on assessments carried out by journalists and human rights activists; two scores ranging between 0 (low censorship) and 100 (high censorship) are given. The first is based on six criteria – pluralism, media independence, environment and self-censorship, legislative framework, transparency and infrastructure – the second score measures the treatment of journalists. The overall position is given in parentheses. © Reporters Without Borders

## AFGHANISTAN

*Jamhuri-ye Eslami-ye Afghanestan – Islamic Republic of Afghanistan*

*Area* – 652,230 sq. km
*Capital* – Kabul; population, 4,635,000 (2015 est)
*Major cities* – Herat, Jalalabad, Kandahar, Mazar-e-Sharif
*Currency* – Afghani (Af) of 100 puls
*Population* – 32,564,342 rising at 2.32 per cent a year (2015 est); Pashtun (42 per cent), Tajik (27 per cent), Hazara (9 per cent), Uzbek (9 per cent), Aimak (4 per cent), Turkmen (3 per cent), Baloch (2 per cent) (est)
*Religion* – Muslim (Sunni 80 per cent, Shia 19 per cent) (est); Islam is the state religion
*Language* – Dari (a dialect of Persian), Pashto (both official); Balochi, Nuristani, Pamiri, Pashai, Turkmen and Uzbek are official in some areas
*Population density* – 47 per sq. km (2013 est)
*Urban population* – 24.1 per cent (2013 est)
*Median age (years)* – 18.1 (2014 est)
*National anthem* – 'Milli Surud' ['National Anthem']
*National day* – 19 August (Independence Day)
*Death penalty* – Retained
*CPI score* – 12 (172)

### CLIMATE AND TERRAIN
Mountains, chief among which are the Hindu Kush, cover three-quarters of the country, with plains in the north and south-west. Elevation extremes range from 7,485m (Noshak, a peak in the Hindu Kush) to 258m (Amu Darya). There are three great river basins: the Amu Dar'ya (Oxus), Helmand and Kabul. Natural hazards are flooding, drought and earthquakes. Average annual rainfall is around 247mm per year. Temperatures in Afghanistan average 0.7°C in January and 25.7°C in July.

### POLITICS
Under the 2004 constitution, the executive president, who is directly elected for a five-year term, appoints the government, subject to the approval of the lower house of the legislature. The bicameral National Assembly, the *Jirga*, comprises the House of the People *(Wolesi Jirga)*, the lower house and the House of Elders *(Meshrano Jirga)*. The House of the People

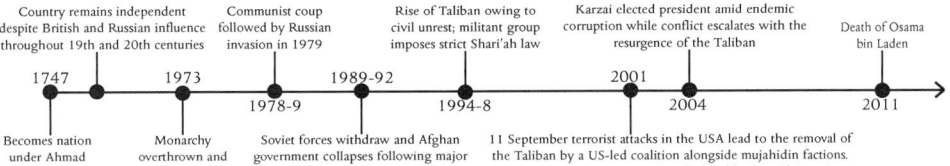

Country remains independent despite British and Russian influence throughout 19th and 20th centuries — 1747

Becomes nation under Ahmad Shah Durrani

1973 — Communist coup followed by Russian invasion in 1979

1978-9 — Monarchy overthrown and republic declared

1989-92 — Rise of Taliban owing to civil unrest; militant group imposes strict Shari'ah law

1994-8 — Soviet forces withdraw and Afghan government collapses following major resistance from guerrilla (Mujahidin) forces

2001 — Karzai elected president amid endemic corruption while conflict escalates with the resurgence of the Taliban

2004 — 11 September terrorist attacks in the USA lead to the removal of the Taliban by a US-led coalition alongside mujahidin factions. An interim government is installed, led by Hamid Karzai

Death of Osama bin Laden — 2011

has 249 members directly elected for a five-year term; ten seats are reserved for the Kuchi ethnic group and at least 65 seats for women. The House of Elders has 102 members: 34 elected by provincial councils for a three-year term, 34 elected by district councils for a four-year term and 34 appointed by the president for a five-year term. Political parties have not been legally recognised since the 2005 parliamentary elections and candidates must run as independents.

Hamid Karzai was elected president in 2004, and was re-elected in 2009; he stepped down when his second term concluded in 2014, after NATO handed control to the Afghan state. Following the disputed June 2014 presidential elections, it was declared on 21 September that Ashraf Ghani would become president, ending months of political deadlock.

## HEAD OF STATE

*President,* Ashraf Ghani Ahmadzai, *sworn in* 7 December 2004, *re-elected* 2009
*First Vice-President,* Abdul Rashid Dustom
*Second Vice-President,* Sarwar Danish

## SELECTED GOVERNMENT MEMBERS *as at April 2015*

*Chief Executive Officer,* Abdullah Abdullah
*Defence (acting),* Enayatullah Nazari
*Finance,* Eklil Ahmad Hakimi
*Foreign Affairs,* Salahuddin Rabbani

## EMBASSY OF THE ISLAMIC REPUBLIC OF AFGHANISTAN

31 Princes Gate, London SW7 1QQ
T 020-7589 8891 E consulate@afganistanembassy.org.uk
*Ambassador Extraordinary and Plenipotentiary,* HE Dr Mohammad Daud Yaar, *apptd* 2012

## BRITISH EMBASSY

PO Box 334, 15th Street, Roundabout Wazir Akbar Khan, Kabul
T (+93) (0) 700 102 000 E britishembassy.kabul@fco.gov.uk
W www.gov.uk/government/world/afghanistan
*Ambassador Extraordinary and Plenipotentiary (acting),* HE Robert Chatterton Dickson, *apptd* 2015

## DEFENCE

As of February 2015, 13,195 NATO troops remained in Afghanistan as part of the Resolute Support Mission.

| Aged 16–49, 2010 est | Males | Females |
|---|---|---|
| Available for military service | 7,056,339 | 6,653,419 |
| Fit for military service | 4,050,222 | 3,797,087 |

*Military expenditure –* US$268m (2014)

## ECONOMY AND TRADE

The economy, devastated by over 30 years of conflict, has improved significantly since 2001. Economic growth has been sustained over the decade, although security problems, weak governance, poor infrastructure and corruption continue to hamper reconstruction. Poverty is being reduced through substantial civilian aid donations, including an additional US$16bn (£10.5bn) pledged in July 2012. Eradication of the opium trade (which constitutes about 60 per cent of the economy) and exploration for oil and gas in the north are two major long-term policy objectives. Since 2011, the Afghan and US governments have pursued a policy of turning Afghanistan into a regional trade hub for central Asian commodities, such as gas and cotton.

Around 79 per cent of the workforce is engaged in agriculture, both subsistence and commercial, which accounts for some 20 per cent of GDP. The main agricultural products are opium, wheat, fruit, nuts, wool, meat, sheepskins and lambskins. Natural gas, coal, copper and semi-gemstones are extracted. The main trading partners are the USA, Pakistan and India. Principal exports are agricultural products, handwoven carpets and gemstones. Imports are chiefly machinery and other capital goods, food, textiles and petroleum products.

*GNI –* US$21,043m; US$690 per capita (2013)
*Annual average growth of GDP –* 3.2 per cent (2014 est)
*Inflation rate –* 7.6 per cent (2013 est)
*Population below poverty line –* 35.8 per cent (2011 est)
*Unemployment –* 8.6 per cent (2015 est)
*Total external debt –* US$1,280m (2010–11 est)
*Imports –* US$5,400m (2013 est)
*Exports –* US$500m (2013 est)

## BALANCE OF PAYMENTS

*Trade –* US$4,900m deficit (2013)
*Current Account –* US$1,158m surplus (2014 est)

| Trade with UK | 2013 | 2014 |
|---|---|---|
| Imports from UK | £66,275,962 | £29,647,442 |
| Exports to UK | £2,362,667 | £1,810,624 |

## COMMUNICATIONS

*Airports –* 23; two international, including Kabul and Kandahar
*Waterways –* The Amu Dar'ya river makes up most of the 1,200km of inland waterways; the main river ports are Kheyrabad and Shir Khan
*Roadways –* Much of the road system is in disrepair, although major highways between Kabul, Kandahar and Herat have been reconstructed; there are 12,350km of paved roadways
*Telecommunications –* 13,500 fixed lines and 18 million mobile subscriptions (2012); there were 1 million internet users in 2009
*Internet code and IDD –* af; 93 (from UK), 44 (to UK)
*Major broadcasters –* The principal and state-owned broadcaster is National Radio-TV Afghanistan (NRTA), alongside 68 private television stations and 174 radio stations
*Press –* There are nine daily newspapers, including the privately owned *Hasht-e Sobh* and *Mandegar,* and the government sponsored *Hewad*
*WPFI score –* 37,44 (122)

## EDUCATION AND HEALTH

Education is free and nominally compulsory; elementary schools having been established in most centres.

*Literacy rate* – 58.2 per cent (2015 est)
*Gross enrolment ratio (percentage of relevant age group)* –
  primary 104 per cent; secondary 54 per cent (2012 est);
  tertiary 4 per cent (2011 est)
*Health expenditure (per capita)* – US$49 (2013)
*Hospital beds (per 1,000 people)* – 0.5 (2012)
*Life expectancy (years)* – 50.49 (2014 est)
*Mortality rate* – 14.12 (2014 est)
*Birth rate* – 38.84 (2014 est)
*Infant mortality rate* – 117.23 (2014 est)

# ALBANIA

*Republika e Shqiperise* – Republic of Albania

*Area* – 28,748 sq. km
*Capital* – Tirana; population, 620,000 (2015 est)
*Major towns* – Durres, Elbasan, Shkoder, Vlore
*Currency* – Lek (Lk) of 100 qindarka
*Population* – 3,029,278 rising at 0.3 per cent a year
  (2015 est); Albanian (82.6 per cent), Greek (0.9 per cent)
  (est)
*Religion* – Muslim 59 per cent (Sunni, and Bektashi form of
  Shia Sufism), Christian (Roman Catholic 10 per cent,
  Orthodox 7 per cent) (est). Religious observance was
  banned in 1967; private religious practice has been
  permitted since 1990
*Language* – Albanian (official), Macedonian, Greek, Vlach,
  Romani, Turkish, Italian, Serbo-Croatian
*Population density* – 101 per sq. km (2013)
*Urban population* – 55.6 per cent (2013 est)
*Median age (years)* – 31.6 (2014 est)
*National anthem* – 'Himni i Flamurit' ['Hymn to the Flag']
*National day* – 28 November (Independence Day)
*Death penalty* – Abolished for all crimes (since 2007)
*CPI score* – 33 (110)

## CLIMATE AND TERRAIN
About two-thirds of the country is mountainous, and 36
per cent is covered by forest. Elevation extremes range from
2,764m (Maja e Korabit, a peak on the Macedonian border)
to 0m (Adriatic Sea). The climate is Mediterranean on the
coast and continental in the interior. The average daily

temperature ranges between 2.1°C in January and 21.8°C in
July and August.

## POLITICS
Under the 1998 constitution, the president is elected by
the legislature for a five-year term, renewable once. The
unicameral legislature, the People's Assembly, has 140
members directly elected for four-year terms. The president
appoints the prime minister, who must be approved by the
People's Assembly. The assembly elects the council of
ministers.

Bujar Nishani, of the Democratic Party (PD), was elected
president in 2012 in the fourth round of voting. Legislative
elections were held in June 2013 and won by the Alliance for
a European Albania, a coalition led by the Socialist Party of
Albania (PS), who secured a landslide victory against the
incumbent PD, taking a total of 84 seats to their 56.

Albania applied to join the EU in 2009 and obtained
candidate status in 2014.

### HEAD OF STATE
*President*, Bujar Nishani, *elected* 11 June 2012, *took office*
  24 July 2012

### SELECTED GOVERNMENT MEMBERS *as at April 2015*
*Prime Minister*, Edi Rama
*Deputy Prime Minister*, Niko Peleshi
*Defence*, Mimi Kodheli
*Finance*, Shkelgim Cani

### EMBASSY OF THE REPUBLIC OF ALBANIA
33 St George's Drive, London SW1V 4DG
T 020-7828 8897 E embassy.london@mfa.gov.al
W www.albanianembassy.co.uk
*Ambassador Extraordinary and Plenipotentiary*, HE Mal
  Berisha, *apptd* 2013

### BRITISH EMBASSY
Rruga Skenderbeg 12, Tirana
T (+355) (4) 223 4973 W www.gov.uk/government/world/albania
*Ambassador Extraordinary and Plenipotentiary*, Nicholas
  Cannon, OBE, *apptd* 2012

### DEFENCE
The Albanian Armed Forces (AAF) is a joint force.

| Aged 16–49, 2010 est | Males | Females |
| --- | --- | --- |
| Available for military service | 731,111 | 780,216 |
| Fit for military service | 622,379 | 660,715 |

*Military expenditure* – US$135m (2014)*

* Does not include spending on pensions

### ECONOMY AND TRADE
Albania is one of the poorest countries in Europe, although
liberalisation measures have resulted in gradual growth since
1993. The economy is still heavily dependent on overseas

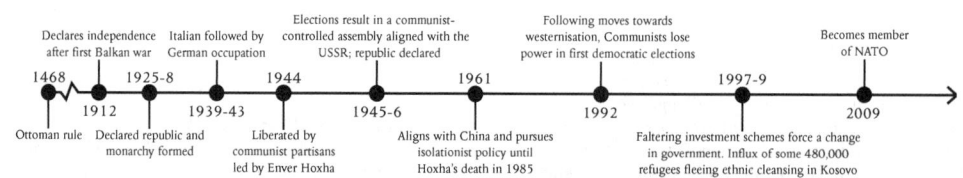

| 1468 | 1925-8 | 1944 | 1961 | 1997-9 | |
| --- | --- | --- | --- | --- | --- |

Declares independence after first Balkan war | Italian followed by German occupation | Elections result in a communist-controlled assembly aligned with the USSR; republic declared | Following moves towards westernisation, Communists lose power in first democratic elections | Becomes member of NATO

1912 | 1939-43 | 1945-6 | 1992 | 2009

Ottoman rule | Declared republic and monarchy formed | Liberated by communist partisans led by Enver Hoxha | Aligns with China and pursues isolationist policy until Hoxha's death in 1985 | Faltering investment schemes force a change in government. Influx of some 480,000 refugees fleeing ethnic cleansing in Kosovo

aid, primarily from the EU, and remittances from expatriate workers, which fell from between 12 and 15 per cent of GDP to 7 per cent following the global financial crisis in 2008. Trade and banking sector ties with the fragile economies of Greece and Italy, high levels of public debt, corruption and organised crime remain significant economic challenges. The inefficient energy and transport sectors have been improved by investment, although they remain underdeveloped by European standards.

Agriculture accounts for 54.6 per cent of employment but only 18.4 per cent of GDP. The main crops are wheat, corn, vegetables, fruit, sugar beet and livestock products. The principal industries are food processing, perfumes and cosmetic products, textiles and clothing, timber, oil, cement, chemicals, mining (base metals) and hydro-electric power.

Trade is mainly with Italy, Spain, Greece and Italy. Exports include textiles and footwear, asphalt, metals and metal ores, crude oil, tobacco, fruit and vegetables. Imports include machinery and equipment, foodstuffs, textiles and chemicals.

*GNI* – US$13,064m; US$4,710 per capita (2013)
*Annual average growth of GDP* – 2.1 per cent (2014 est)
*Inflation rate* – 1.9 per cent (2013 est)
*Population below poverty line* – 14.3 per cent (2012 est)
*Unemployment* – 17.2 per cent (2015 est)
*Total external debt* – US$7,854m (2014 est)
*Imports* – US$4,902m (2013)
*Exports* – US$2,332m (2013)

BALANCE OF PAYMENTS
*Trade* – US$2,570m deficit (2013)
*Current Account* – US$1,841m deficit (2014 est)

| Trade with UK | 2013 | 2014 |
| --- | --- | --- |
| Imports from UK | £19,284,249 | £20,287,685 |
| Exports to UK | £9,766,564 | £8,726,388 |

## COMMUNICATIONS
*Airport* – There is an international airport in Tirana
*Roadways and railways* – 7,020km; 339km
*Telecommunications* – 312,000 fixed lines and 3.5 million mobile subscriptions (2012); there were 1.3 million internet users in 2009
*Internet code and IDD* – al; 355 (from UK), 44 (to UK)
*Major broadcasters* – Albanian Radio and TV (RTSh), Top Channel and TV Klan
*Press* – There are 25 daily newspapers, including *Shekulli*, *Gazeta Shqiptare* and the *Tirana Times*
*WPFI score* – 28,77 (82)

## EDUCATION AND HEALTH
*Literacy rate* – 99 per cent (2015 est)
*Gross enrolment ratio (percentage of relevant age group)* – primary 110 per cent; secondary 78 per cent (2010 est); tertiary 56 per cent (2012 est)
*Health expenditure (per capita)* – US$240 (2013)
*Hospital beds (per 1,000 people)* – 2.6 (2012)
*Life expectancy (years)* – 77.96 (2014 est)
*Mortality rate* – 6.47 (2014 est)
*Birth rate* – 12.73 (2014 est)
*Infant mortality rate* – 13.19 (2014 est)

# ALGERIA

*Al-Jumhuriyah al-Jaza'iriyah ad Dimuqratiyah ash Sha'biyah* – *People's Democratic Republic of Algeria*

*Area* – 2,381,741 sq. km
*Capital* – Algiers (El Djazair, Al Jaza'ir); population, 2,590,000 (2015 est)
*Major cities* – Annaba, Blida, Constantine (Qacentina), Oran (Wahran)
*Currency* – Algerian dinar (DA) of 100 centimes
*Population* – 39,542,166 rising at 1.84 per cent a year (2015 est); Arab-Berber (99 per cent) (est)
*Religion* – Muslim (Sunni 99 per cent), Christian and Jewish (less than 1 per cent) (est)
*Language* – Arabic (official), French, Berber dialects
*Population density* – 16 per sq. km (2013)
*Urban population* – 74.7 per cent (2013 est)
*Median age (years)* – 27.3 (2014 est)
*National anthem* – 'Kassaman' ['We Pledge']
*National day* – 1 November (Revolution Day)
*Death penalty* – Retained (last used 1993)
*CPI score* – 36 (100)

## CLIMATE AND TERRAIN
Algeria, the largest country in Africa, is dominated by the Sahara desert, which covers more than 80 per cent of its territory. Elevation extremes range from 3,003m (Mt Tahat) to –40m (Chott Melrhir, a salt lake). The mountains are subject to earthquakes, and to flooding during the rainy season (November–March). The temperate northern coastal areas receive the greatest and most frequent rainfall, whereas the interior plateaux are drier and experience cold winters and hot summers.

## POLITICS
Algeria's 1976 constitution was amended in 1989 to reintroduce political pluralism, and was revised in 2008, most notably to remove the limit on presidential terms. The president is directly elected for a five-year term, which may be renewed. The bicameral *Barlaman* comprises the National People's Assembly, the lower house and the National Council. The assembly has 389 members, directly elected for a five-year term. The National Council has 144 members; 48 are appointed by the president, and 96 are indirectly elected for a six-year term by electoral colleges formed by local councils; half of these elected members are re-elected every three years. Although Algeria is no longer a one-party state, parties based on religion or on race, language, gender or region are banned under the constitution.

In the 2012 legislative election, the ruling National Liberation Front-led coalition won the most seats and retained control in both houses. In April 2014, President Bouteflika was re-elected for a fourth term despite not campaigning due to ill health and Abdelmalek Sellal was appointed prime minister.

| | Gains independence following | Elected president Abdelaziz | Second amnesty between militants approved |
| Conquered by the | guerrilla war with socialist | Bouteflika's 'civil concord' with | but broken by bombings carried out by a |
| Ottoman Empire | *Front de Libération Nationale* | Islamists approved by referendum | group aligning itself with al-Qaida |

c.600 — 1830 — 1989-92 — 2005 — 2011

c.1525 — 1962 — 1999 — 2006

| A Berber-populated Roman | Annexed by | A ban on the Islamic Salvation | Agreement reached with Berber-populated | Major demonstrations cause |
| province, Algeria is conquered | France | Front triggers civil unrest and | Kabylie for increased investment in the region | government to cut food prices and |
| by Arabs and converted to Islam | | a state of emergency | and greater recognition of the Berber language | lift the 19-year state of emergency |

## HEAD OF STATE
President, *Defence*, Abdelaziz Bouteflika, *elected* 15 April 1999, *re-elected* 2004, 2009, 2014

## SELECTED GOVERMENT MEMBERS *as at April 2015*
Prime Minister, Abdelmalek Sellal
Finance, Mohamed Djellab
Foreign Affairs, Ramtane Lamamra

## ALGERIAN EMBASSY
6 Hyde Park Gate, London SW7 5EW
T 020-7589 6885 E info@algerian-consulate.org.uk
W www.algerian-consulate.org.uk
*Ambassador Extraordinary and Plenipotentiary,* HE Amar Abba, *apptd* 2010

## BRITISH EMBASSY
3 Chemin Capitaine Hocine Slimane, Hydra, Algiers
T (+213) (770) 085 000 E britishembassy.algiers@fco.gov.uk
W www.gov.uk/government/world/algeria
*Ambassador Extraordinary and Plenipotentiary,* HE Andrew Noble, LVO, *apptd* 2014

## DEFENCE

| Aged 16–49, 2010 est | Males | Females |
| --- | --- | --- |
| Available for military service | 10,273,129 | 10,114,552 |
| Fit for military service | 8,622,897 | 8,626,222 |

*Military expenditure* – US$11,862m (2014)
*Conscription* – 19–30 years of age; 18 months

## ECONOMY AND TRADE
After independence, Algeria's economy was dominated by the state until a privatisation programme was introduced in 1997. Reform, combined with high oil prices, resulted in trade surpluses, record foreign exchange reserves and the reduction of foreign debt, despite recent blocks on the privatisation process. Diversification away from the energy sector and development of the financial system has been hampered by a lack of foreign investment. The payment of large government subsidies, predicted to reach approximately 13 per cent of GDP in 2014, have put a strain on government finances.

Algeria has substantial oil and gas reserves and the hydrocarbon industry accounts for 30 per cent of GDP, nearly 60 per cent of government revenue and over 95 per cent of export earnings. Services provide 43.1 per cent of GDP, industry 48.3 per cent and agriculture 8.6 per cent. Industries other than oil and gas production and processing include mining, electrical goods, food processing and light industries.

Algeria's main trading partners are the USA, France, Italy, other EU countries and China. The chief imports are capital goods, foodstuffs and consumer goods.
*GNI* – US$208,795m; US$5,330 per capita (2013)
*Annual average growth of GDP* – 4 per cent (2014 est)
*Inflation rate* – 3.3 per cent (2013 est)
*Population below poverty line* – 23 per cent (2006 est)
*Unemployment* – 9.6 per cent (2015 est)
*Total external debt* – US$4,872m (2014 est)
*Imports* – US$54,965m (2013)
*Exports* – US$65,555m (2013)

## BALANCE OF PAYMENTS
*Trade* – US$10,590m surplus (2013)
*Current Account* – US$9,289m deficit (2014)

| Trade with UK | 2013 | 2014 |
| --- | --- | --- |
| Imports from UK | £529,997,028 | £479,591,455 |
| Exports to UK | £3,310,758,321 | £3,331,992,900 |

## COMMUNICATIONS
*Airports and waterways* – 64, including Algiers and Constantine; major ports are at Algiers and Bejaia
*Roadways and railways* – 87,605km, including 645km of motorways; 3,973km
*Telecommunications* – 3.2 million fixed lines and 37.69 million mobile subscriptions (2012); there were 4.7 million internet users in 2009
*Internet code and IDD* – dz; 213 (from UK), 44 (to UK)
*Major broadcaster* – Enterprise Nationale de Télévision (ENTV) is the state broadcaster
*Press* – There are more than 80 newspapers available in Algiers, including *El Khabar, Ech Chourouk* and *Le Quotidien d'Oran*
*WPFI score* – 36,63 (119)

## EDUCATION AND HEALTH
*Literacy rate* – 95.6 per cent (2015 est)
*Gross enrolment ratio (percentage of relevant age group)* – primary 117 per cent (2012 est); secondary 98 per cent (2011 est); tertiary 31 per cent (2012 est)
*Health expenditure (per capita)* – US$314 (2013)
*Life expectancy (years)* – 76.39 (2014 est)
*Mortality rate* – 4.31 (2014 est)
*Birth rate* – 23.99 (2014 est)
*Infant mortality rate* – 21.76 (2014 est)

# ANDORRA

*Principat d'Andorra – Principality of Andorra*

*Area* – 468 sq. km
*Capital* – Andorra la Vella; population, 23,000 (2011 est)
*Major cities* – Encamp, Les Escaldes, Sant Julià de Lòria
*Currency* – Euro (€) of 100 cents

*Population* – 85,580 rising at 0.12 per cent a year (2015 est);
Spanish (43 per cent), Andorran (33 per cent), Portuguese
(11 per cent), French (7 per cent) (est)
*Religion* – Christian (predominantly Roman Catholic)
*Language* – Catalan (official), French, Spanish (Castilian),
Portuguese
*Population density* – 169 per sq. km (2013)
*Urban population* – 86.2 per cent (2013 est)
*Median age (years)* – 42.4 (2014 est)
*National anthem* – 'El Gran Carlemany' ['The Great
Charlemagne']
*National day* – 8 September (Our Lady of Meritxell Day)
*Death penalty* – Abolished for all crimes (since 1990)
*Life expectancy (years)* – 82.65 (2014 est)
*Mortality rate* – 6.82 (2014 est)
*Birth rate* – 8.48 (2014 est)
*Infant mortality rate* – 3.69 (2014 est)

## CLIMATE AND TERRAIN
Andorra is a country of dramatic mountains interspersed by
narrow valleys; over a third of the country is forested.
Elevation extremes range from 2,946m (Pic de Coma Pedrosa)
to 840m (Riu Runer). The climate is alpine, with heavy
snowfall in winter and warm summers. Average temperature
ranges from 1.6°C in January to 18.3°C in August.

## HISTORY AND POLITICS
Liberated from Moorish rule by Charlemagne in 803,
Andorra is a neutral principality that was formed by a *paréage*
(a type of feudal treaty) in 1278 and since then has owed
dual allegiance to two co-princes, the Spanish Bishop of
Urgell and the head of state of France. Andorra became an
independent democratic parliamentary co-principality in
1993. The country subsequently formalised its links with the
EU, and joined the UN and the Council of Europe.

Andorra has a unicameral legislature, the General Council
of the Valleys *(Consell General de las Valls)*, whose 28 members
are directly elected for a four-year term by proportional
representation. The council appoints the president of the
executive council, who nominates government members.

Under the 1993 constitution, the heads of state are two
co-princes, the President of France and the Bishop of Urgel,
Spain. They are represented in Andorra by the permanent
delegates (the Spanish vicar-general of the diocese of Urgel
and the French prefect of the Pyrenees Orientales
department), but their powers now relate solely to relations
with France and Spain. The constitution established an
independent judiciary and allows Andorra to conduct its
own foreign policy, while its people may now join political
parties and trade unions.

In the March 2015 legislative election, the Democrats for
Andorra party remained in power despite losing five seats,
winning 15 of the 28 seats in the general council.

HEADS OF STATE
*The President of France*, François Hollande
*The Bishop of Urgell*, Joan Enric Vives i Sicilia
*Permanent French Delegate*, Sylvie Hubac
*Permanent Episcopal Delegate*, Josep Maria Mauri i Prior

SELECTED GOVERNMENT MEMBERS *as at April 2015*
*President of the Executive Council, Culture*, Antoni Martí
*Economy and Territory*, Jordi Alcobe
*Foreign Affairs*, Gilbert Saboya
*Interior and Justice*, Xavier Espot Zamora

BRITISH CONSULATE-GENERAL
*Ambassador*, HE Simon Manley, CMG, *apptd* 2013, resident
at Madrid, Spain

## ECONOMY AND TRADE
The economy is largely based on tourism, banking and
commerce, which together account for over 75 per cent of
GDP. A recent drop in tourism, caused by the economic
downturn in neighbouring countries, contributed to a dip
in GDP and a deterioration in public finances, forcing the
government to implement several austerity measures.
Following pressure from the EU, controversial bank secrecy
laws were reformed in 2009 and the country's low tax
economy modified in January 2015 by the introduction of
corporation tax in 2012 and the nation's first income tax, a
flat rate of 10 per cent. Other activities include manufacturing
tobacco products, forestry, furniture-making and sheep-
farming. Andorra is a member of the EU Customs Union and
is treated as an EU member for trade in manufactured goods
and as a non-EU member for agricultural products.
*GNI* – US$3,447m (2008); US$43,110 per capita (2008)
*Annual average growth of GDP* – –1.6 per cent (2012 est)
*Inflation rate* – 1.1 per cent (2012 est)
*Unemployment* – 4 per cent (2012 est)
*Imports* – US$1,455m (2013)
*Exports* – US$99m (2013)

BALANCE OF PAYMENTS
*Trade* – US$1,356m deficit (2013)

| Trade with UK | 2013 | 2014 |
| --- | --- | --- |
| Imports from UK | £8,833,612 | £6,924,890 |
| Exports to UK | £178,651 | £446,454 |

## COMMUNICATIONS
*Roadways* – 320km
*Telecommunications* – 39,000 fixed lines and 65,000 mobile
subscriptions (2012); there were 67,100 internet users in 2009
*Internet code and IDD* – ad; 376 (from UK), 44 (to UK)
*Major broadcaster* – Radio i Televisio d'Andorra
*Press* – Major newspapers include *Diari d'Andorra* and *El
Periodic d'Andorra*
*WPFI score* – 19,87 (32)

# ANGOLA

*Republica de Angola – Republic of Angola*

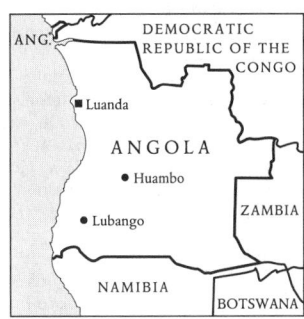

*Area* – 1,246,700 sq. km; includes the exclave of Cabinda
*Capital* – Luanda; population, 5,899,000 (2015 est)
*Major cities* – Benguela, Huambo, Lubango
*Currency* – Kwanza (Kzrl) of 100 centimos
*Population* – 19,625,353 rising at 2.78 per cent a year
(2015 est); Ovimbundu (37 per cent), Kimbundu
(25 per cent), Bakongo (13 per cent), Mestizo (2 per
cent), other African, including Lunda-Chokwe and
Ngangela (22 per cent) (est)

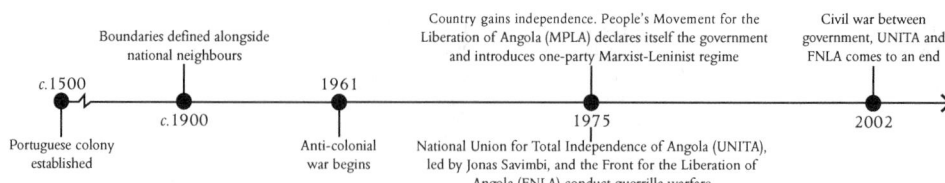

Portuguese colony established — *c.*1500

Boundaries defined alongside national neighbours — *c.*1900

Anti-colonial war begins — 1961

Country gains independence. People's Movement for the Liberation of Angola (MPLA) declares itself the government and introduces one-party Marxist-Leninist regime — 1975

National Union for Total Independence of Angola (UNITA), led by Jonas Savimbi, and the Front for the Liberation of Angola (FNLA) conduct guerrilla warfare

Civil war between government, UNITA and FNLA comes to an end — 2002

*Religion* – Christian (Roman Catholic 50 per cent, Protestant 33 per cent); a small portion of the rural population practises indigenous beliefs (est)
*Language* – Portuguese (official), Bantu
*Population density* – 17 per sq. km (2013)
*Urban population* – 60.7 per cent (2013 est)
*Median age (years)* – 17.9 (2014 est)
*National anthem* – 'Angola Avante' ['Forward Angola']
*National day* – 11 November (Independence Day)
*Death penalty* – Abolished for all crimes (since 1992)
*CPI score* – 19 (161)
*Literacy rate* – 72.9 per cent (2015 est)
*Gross enrolment ratio (percentage of relevant age group)* – primary 140 per cent; secondary 32 per cent; tertiary 7 per cent (2011 est)
*Health expenditure (per capita)* – US$267 (2013)
*Hospital beds (per 1,000 people)* – 0.8 (2005)
*Life expectancy (years)* – 55.29 (2014 est)
*Mortality rate* – 11.67 (2014 est)
*Birth rate* – 38.97 (2013 est)
*Infant mortality rate* – 79.99 (2014 est)
*HIV/AIDS adult prevalence* – 2.4 per cent (2013 est)

## CLIMATE AND TERRAIN

The land rises from a narrow coastal plain to a vast interior plateau, with desert to the south. The highest point of elevation is 2,620m (Morro do Moco) and the lowest is 0m (Atlantic Ocean). The climate is tropical in the north – with a cool, dry season from April to September and a hot, rainy season from October to March – and sub-tropical in the south and along the coast to Luanda.

## POLITICS

Under the 2010 constitution, the president is the head of the party with the largest number of seats in the legislature. The unicameral National Assembly has 223 members, elected by proportional representation for a five-year term.

Political pluralism was introduced under the 1991 peace agreement and multiparty elections were held in 1992, though the National Union for Total Independence of Angola (UNITA) refused to accept the results. The first legislative elections since 1992, held in 2008, were won by the People's Movement for the Liberation of Angola (MPLA); it retained its majority in the 2012 legislative election, with 175 seats to UNITA's 32. The new constitution introduced in 2010 ended direct election of the president, created the office of vice-president and abolished the post of prime minister; as leader of the MPLA, Jose Eduardo dos Santos remained president following the 2012 legislative election. Local elections were scheduled to take place in 2014, but have been delayed by the government.

HEAD OF STATE
*President,* Jose Eduardo dos Santos, *took office* 21 September 1979, *re-elected* 30 September 1992, 2008, 2012
*Vice-President,* Manuel Domingos Vicente

SELECTED GOVERNMENT MEMBERS *as at April 2015*
*Defence,* Joao Manuel Goncalves Lourenco
*Finance,* Armando Manuel

*Foreign Affairs,* George Rebelo Pinto Chicoti
*Interior,* Angelo de Barros Veiga Tavares

EMBASSY OF THE REPUBLIC OF ANGOLA
22 Dorset Street, London W1U 6QY
T 020-7299 9850 E embassy@angola.org.uk
W www.angola.org.uk
*Ambassador Extraordinary and Plenipotentiary,* HE Miguel Gaspar Fernandes Neto, *apptd* 2012

BRITISH EMBASSY
Rua 17 de Setembro 4, Caixa, Luanda 1244
T (+244) (22) 233 4583 E postmaster.luand@fco.gov.uk
W www.gov.uk/government/world/angola
*Ambassador Extraordinary and Plenipotentiary,* HE John Dennis, *apptd* 2014

SECESSION
In the oil-rich northern exclave of Cabinda, separatists have conducted a low-level guerrilla war since the mid-1970s. The government has been unable to end the fighting either through negotiation or by military means. A ceasefire and peace agreement reached in 2006 has not been observed by all parties.

## DEFENCE

| Aged 16–49, 2010 est | Males | Females |
| --- | --- | --- |
| Available for military service | 3,062,438 | 2,964,262 |
| Fit for military service | 1,546,781 | 1,492,308 |

*Military expenditure* – US$6,842m (2014)
*Conscription* – 20–45 years of age, male only; 2 years

## ECONOMY AND TRADE

The economy is still recovering from decades of corruption, mismanagement and civil war, but liberalisation and stabilisation are being achieved. Post-war increases in oil, diamond and agricultural production have driven strong economic growth, although the economy contracted in 2009 as the global downturn reduced demand for exports. The extractive industries and infrastructure projects have attracted foreign investment despite the corruption and stifling bureaucracy that have deterred investors in other sectors.

Angola, especially Cabinda, is rich in natural resources. The main industries involve extracting and processing oil (Angola is Africa's second largest producer of oil, with production and related activities accounting for around 85 per cent of GDP), diamonds, metals and other minerals, forestry, fishing, food processing and the manufacture of cement, metal products, tobacco products and textiles, and ship repair. Angola has large areas of good farmland, but the prevalence of unexploded landmines has reduced the area under cultivation and forced many areas back to subsistence agriculture, although coffee, sisal and cotton are produced for export. A dependence on imported consumable goods (Angola imports around 80 per cent of its food), poor infrastructure and high property prices have caused Luanda to become the world's most expensive city.

The main trading partners are China, the USA, India and Portugal. The principal exports are crude oil, diamonds, refined petroleum products, coffee, sisal, fish, timber and cotton. The main imports are machinery and electrical equipment, vehicles and spare parts, medicines, food, textiles and military goods.

*GNI* – US$110,907m; US$5,170 per capita (2013)
*Annual average growth of GDP* – 3.9 per cent (2014 est)
*Inflation rate* – 8.8 per cent (2013 est)
*Population below poverty line* – 40.5 per cent (2006 est)
*Unemployment* – 8.2 per cent (2015 est)
*Total external debt* – US$22,930m (2014 est)
*Imports* – US$22,670m (2013)
*Exports* – US$67,438m (2013)

**BALANCE OF PAYMENTS**
*Trade* – US$44,768m surplus (2013)
*Current Account* – US$109m deficit (2014 est)

| Trade with UK | 2013 | 2014 |
|---|---|---|
| Imports from UK | £548,232,630 | £604,721,279 |
| Exports to UK | £660,427,462 | £414,927,446 |

## COMMUNICATIONS
*Airports and waterways* – 31; main ports include Cabinda, Lobito, Luanda and Namibe
*Roadways and railways* – 5,349km; 2,764km
*Telecommunications* – 303,000 fixed lines and 9.8 million mobile subscriptions (2012); there were 606,700 internet users in 2009
*Internet code and IDD* – ao; 244 (from UK), 44 (to UK)
*Major broadcasters* – Only the government-owned Televisao Publica de Angola (TPA) and Radio National de Angola (RNA) have national coverage
*Press* – The government owned *Jornal de Angola* is the only daily newspaper
*WPFI score* – 37,84 (123)

# ANTIGUA AND BARBUDA

*Antigua and Barbuda*

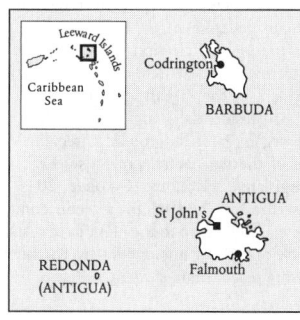

*Area* – 442.6 sq. km: Antigua 280 sq. km; Barbuda 161 sq. km; Redonda 1.6 sq. km
*Capital* – St John's; population, 27,000 (2011 est)
*Currency* – East Caribbean dollar (EC$) of 100 cents
*Population* – 92,436; rising at 1.24 per cent a year (2015 est)
*Religion* – Christian (Protestant 76.4 per cent, Roman Catholic 10.4 per cent), other 12.2 per cent (est)
*Language* – English (official), local dialects
*Population density* – 205 per sq. km (2013)
*Urban population* – 29.8 per cent (2013 est)
*Median age (years)* – 31.1 (2014 est)
*National anthem* – 'Fair Antigua, We Salute Thee'

*National day* – 1 November (Independence Day)
*Death penalty* – Retained (last used 1991)
*Literacy rate* – 99 per cent (2011 est)
*Gross enrolment ratio (percentage of relevant age group)* – primary 98 per cent; secondary 105 per cent; tertiary 23 per cent (2012 est)
*Life expectancy (years)* – 76.12 (2014 est)
*Mortality rate* – 5.7 (2014 est)
*Birth rate* – 15.947 (2014 est)
*Infant mortality rate* – 13.29 (2014 est)

## CLIMATE AND TERRAIN
Unlike most other Leeward Islands, Antigua has few high hills and little forest cover. Its elevation extremes range from 402m (Boggy Peak) to 0m (Caribbean Sea). Barbuda, 48km north of Antigua, is a flat coral island with a large lagoon. Both islands are tropical, but drier than most of the West Indies. They lie within the hurricane belt and are subject to tropical storms and hurricanes between August and October.

## HISTORY AND POLITICS
Prehistoric settlers were succeeded by the Arawaks, then the Caribs. Although the islands were discovered by Columbus in 1493, the European (English) settlement of Antigua began only in 1632. Barbuda was colonised from Antigua in 1661. Administered as part of the Leeward Islands Federation from 1871 to 1956, it became internally self-governing in 1967 and fully independent on 1 November 1981.

The head of state is Queen Elizabeth II, represented by the governor-general. The bicameral parliament comprises a senate of 17 members, appointed by the governor-general on the advice of the prime minister and opposition leader, and a House of Representatives of 17 directly elected members; both chambers serve a five-year term.

The Antigua Labour Party defeated the United Progressive Party in the 2014 legislative elections.

*Governor-General,* HE Dr Sir Rodney Williams, GCMG, apptd 2014

SELECTED GOVERNMENT MEMBERS *as at April 2015*
*Prime Minister,* Gaston Browne
*Minister of Foreign Affairs,* Charles Fernandez
*Tourism,* Asot Michael

HIGH COMMISSION FOR ANTIGUA AND BARBUDA
2nd Floor, 45 Crawford Place, London W1H 4LP
T 020-7258 0070 E enquiries@antigua-barbuda.com
W www.antigua-barbuda.com
*High Commissioner,* HE Sir Ronald Michael Sanders, KCMG, apptd 2014

BRITISH HIGH COMMISSION
*High Commissioner,* HE Victoria Glynis Dean, apptd 2013, resident at Bridgetown, Barbados

## DEFENCE

| Aged 16–49, 2010 est | Males | Females |
|---|---|---|
| Available for military service | 21,141 | 24,056 |
| Fit for military service | 17,676 | 19,960 |

*Military expenditure* – not available

## ECONOMY AND TRADE
The economy is largely based on tourism and related services (contributing nearly 60 per cent of GDP), with light manufacturing (bedding, handicrafts, electronic components) for export, and agriculture (livestock, sea island cotton, market gardening, fishing) for local consumption. Economic

growth and fiscal reform between 2004 and 2007 enabled the government to reduce public debt. However, from 2008, a severe decline in tourism caused by the global economic downturn and the collapse of Allen Stanford's Antigua-based financial group (which included Antigua's major financial institution) hit the economy badly. The islands' finances are also vulnerable to natural disasters and international oil prices. The economy grew in 2012 by 2.8 per cent and 2 per cent in 2013.

*GNI* – US$1,174m; US$13,050 per capita (2013)
*Annual average growth of GDP* – 1.9 per cent (2014 est)
*Inflation rate* – 1.1 per cent (2013 est)
*Total external debt* – US$441.2m (2012 est)
*Imports* – US$515m (2013)
*Exports* – US$32m (2013)

BALANCE OF PAYMENTS
*Trade* – US$483m deficit (2013)
*Current Account* – US$181m deficit (2014 est)

| Trade with UK | 2013 | 2014 |
|---|---|---|
| Imports from UK | £13,698,715 | £14,272,976 |
| Exports to UK | £5,496,973 | £762,507 |

## COMMUNICATIONS
*Airports and waterways* – Two; the main port is at St John's
*Roadways* – 386km
*Telecommunications* – 35,000 fixed lines and 179,800 mobile subscriptions (2012); there were 65,000 internet users in 2009
*Internet code and IDD* – ag; 1 268 (from UK), 011 44 (to UK)
*Major broadcasters* – The Antigua and Barbuda Broadcasting Service (ABS) is the state broadcaster; private and public TV and radio stations are affiliated with political parties
*Press* – *The Antigua Sun* is the only daily newspaper
*WPFI score* – 20,81 (36)

# ARGENTINA

*República Argentina – Argentine Republic*

*Area* – 2,780,400 sq. km
*Capital* – Buenos Aires; population, 14,122,000 (2015 est)
*Major cities* – Córdoba, La Plata, Mar del Plata, Mendoza, Rosario, Salta, San Miguel de Tucumán, Santa Fé

*Currency* – Argentine Peso of 100 centavos
*Population* – 43,431,886 rising at 0.93 per cent a year (2015 est)
*Religion* – Christian (Roman Catholic 92 per cent, Protestant 2 per cent), Jewish (2 per cent) (est)
*Language* – Spanish (official), Italian, English, German, French; Mapudungun and Quechua (both indigenous)
*Population density* – 15 per sq. km (2013)
*Urban population* – 92.8 per cent (2013 est)
*Median age (years)* – 31.2 (2014 est)
*National anthem* – 'Himno Nacional Argentina' ['Argentine National Anthem']
*National day* – 25 May (Revolution Day)
*Death penalty* – Abolished for all crimes (since 2008)
*CPI score* – 34 (107)

## CLIMATE AND TERRAIN
The Andes mountain range runs the full length of the country, along its western border with Chile, and the area is prone to earthquakes. East of the Andes, the north is mostly subtropical rainforest, the centre contains the vast grasslands of the pampas, and the southern Patagonian plateau is arid and desolate, with glaciers in the far south. The highest point of elevation is 6,960m (Cerro Aconcagua) and the lowest is −105m (Laguna del Carbon). Temperatures range from subtropical in the north to subantarctic in the south. Average temperatures range from 20.5°C in January to 7.3°C in July.

## POLITICS
Following constitutional amendments agreed in 1994, the executive president is directly elected for a four-year term, renewable once. The bicameral National Congress consists of a 72-member senate (three members for each province and three for Buenos Aires) and a 257-member Chamber of Deputies. Deputies are directly elected for a four-year term, with half of the seats renewable every two years. Senators are directly elected for a six-year term, with one-third of seats renewable every two years.

The Argentine Republic is a federation of 23 provinces, each with an elected governor and legislature, plus the federal district of Buenos Aires, which has an elected mayor and autonomous government.

The 2011 presidential election was won in the first round by Cristina Fernández de Kirchner, who gained re-election with 54 per cent of the overall vote. The Front for Victory (FpV), the pro-presidential wing of the internally divided Judicialist Party, a Peronist grouping, regained control of both houses of the legislature, previously lost in the 2009 mid-term legislative elections. October 2013 legislative elections saw the FpV and its allies retain control of both houses despite a slight drop in the number of seats, blamed in part on a lack of active campaigning by Kirchner who was recovering from recent brain surgery.

HEAD OF STATE
*President,* Cristina Fernández de Kirchner, *sworn in* 10 December 2007, *re-elected* 10 December 2011
*Vice-President,* Amado Boudou

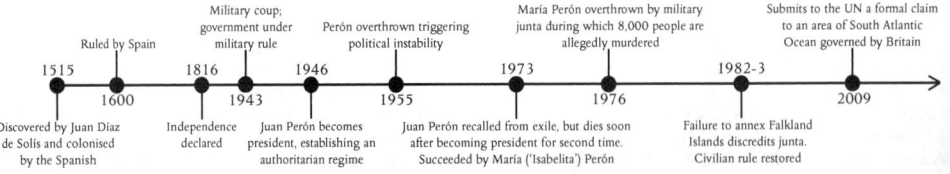

| | Military coup; government under military rule | | Perón overthrown triggering political instability | | María Perón overthrown by military junta during which 8,000 people are allegedly murdered | | Submits to the UN a formal claim to an area of South Atlantic Ocean governed by Britain |
|---|---|---|---|---|---|---|---|
| Ruled by Spain | | | | | | | |
| 1515 | 1816 | 1946 | | 1973 | | 1982-3 | |
| 1600 | 1943 | | 1955 | | 1976 | | 2009 |
| Discovered by Juan Díaz de Solís and colonised by the Spanish | Independence declared | Juan Perón becomes president, establishing an authoritarian regime | | Juan Perón recalled from exile, but dies soon after becoming president for second time. Succeeded by María ('Isabelita') Perón | | Failure to annex Falkland Islands discredits junta. Civilian rule restored | |

SELECTED GOVERNMENT MEMBERS *as at April 2015*
*Defence,* Agustin Rossi
*Economy,* Axel Kicillof
*Foreign Relations,* Héctor Timerman
*Interior,* Anibal Randazzo

## EMBASSY OF THE ARGENTINE REPUBLIC
65 Brook Street, London W1K 4AH
T 020-7318 1300 E info@argentine-embassy-uk.org
W www.argentine-embassy-uk.org
*Ambassador Extraordinary and Plenipotentiary,* HE Alicia Castro, *apptd* 2012

## BRITISH EMBASSY
Dr Luis Agote 2412, 1425 Buenos Aires
T (+54) (11) 4808 2200
W www.gov.uk/government/world/argentina
*Ambassador Extraordinary and Plenipotentiary,* HE Dr John Freeman, *apptd* 2012

## DEFENCE

| *Aged 16–49, 2010 est* | *Males* | *Females* |
|---|---|---|
| Available for military service | 10,038,967 | 9,959,134 |
| Fit for military service | 8,458,362 | 8,414,460 |

*Military expenditure* – US$4,347m (2017)

## ECONOMY AND TRADE
The economy recovered rapidly from the economic collapse of 2001–2, experiencing strong growth from 2003. Argentina restructured its defaulted debt in 2005 and repaid its IMF loan in 2006, but experienced a recession in 2008–9 caused by the global downturn. A shortfall in energy supplies remains a problem as does the vast depletion of hard currency reserves and the continuing devaluation of the peso, which in January 2014 saw its sharpest one-day fall against the dollar since the 2002 crisis. Following a US court ruling in July 2014 in favour of bond holders who had not accepted previous debt restructuring – mainly US hedge funds – the government chose to default on its debt for the eighth time in Argentinian history. The default has cut the country adrift from the international markets and dramatically reduced foreign investment. Demand from Asia for Argentina's agricultural products has helped to prop up the ailing economy.

The country is rich in natural resources, particularly lead, zinc, tin, copper, iron ore, manganese, uranium, oil and coal. The fertile pampas supports a strong and export-orientated agricultural sector; the main crops are cereals, oil-bearing seeds, fruit, tea, tobacco and livestock products, especially beef, mutton and wool.

The main industrial activities are food processing (meat-packing, flour-milling, sugar-refining, wine production) and the production of motor vehicles, consumer durables, textiles, chemicals, petrochemicals, printing, metallurgy and steel.

The main trading partners are Brazil, China and the USA. The principal exports include soya beans and derivatives, petroleum and gas, motor vehicles and cereals. The major imports are machinery, motor vehicles, petroleum and natural gas, organic chemicals and plastics.

*GNI* – US$435,223m; US$9,740 per capita (2011)
*Annual average growth of GDP* – 1.7 per cent (2014 est)
*Inflation rate* – 20.8 per cent (2013 est)
*Population below poverty line* – 30 per cent (2010 est)
*Unemployment* – 7.4 per cent (2015 est)
*Total external debt* – US$115,700m (2014 est)
*Imports* – US$74,002m (2013)
*Exports* – US$83,026m (2013)

## BALANCE OF PAYMENTS
*Trade* – US$9,024m surplus (2013)
*Current Account* – US$468m deficit (2014 est)

| *Trade with UK* | *2013* | *2014* |
|---|---|---|
| Imports from UK | £343,382,547 | £298,807,079 |
| Exports to UK | £619,267,587 | £563,944,956 |

## COMMUNICATIONS
*Airports and waterways* – 161, major airports include Buenos Aires, Córdoba, Rio Gallegos and Salta; 11,000km of waterways
*Roadways and railways* – 69,412km, including 734km of motorway; 36,966km
*Telecommunications* – 10 million fixed lines and 58.6 million mobile subscriptions (2012); there were 13.69 million internet subscribers in 2009
*Internet code and IDD* – ar; 54 (from UK), 44 (to UK)
*Major broadcasters* – The privately owned Telefe and Canal 13 are the leading television broadcasters; Radio Nacional is the state-run radio broadcaster
*Press* – There are over 150 daily newspapers, including *Clarin, La Nación* and *Cronica*
*WPFI score* – 26,11 (57)

## EDUCATION AND HEALTH
Education is compulsory until the age of 14.
*Literacy rate* – 99.3 per cent (2015 est)
*Gross enrolment ratio (percentage of relevant age group)* – primary 118 per cent; secondary 92 per cent; tertiary 79 per cent (2011 est)
*Health expenditure (per capita)* – US$1,074 (2013)
*Hospital beds (per 1,000 people)* – 4.7 (2012)
*Life expectancy (years)* – 77.51 (2014 est)
*Mortality rate* – 7.34 (2014 est)
*Birth rate* – 16.88 (2014 est)
*Infant mortality rate* – 9.96 (2014 est)

## ARGENTINE ANTARCTIC TERRITORY

The Argentine Antarctic Territory consists of the Antarctic Peninsula and a triangular section extending to the South Pole, defined as the area between 25°W. and 74°W. and 60°S. This overlaps with both Britain's and Chile's claimed areas (*see also* The North and South Poles). Administratively, the territory is a department of the province of Tierra del Fuego, Antarctica and South Atlantic Islands. The population varies seasonally between approximately 150 and 660 people, all of whom are scientific researchers and their dependants.

## ARMENIA

*Hayastani Hanrapetut'yun – Republic of Armenia*

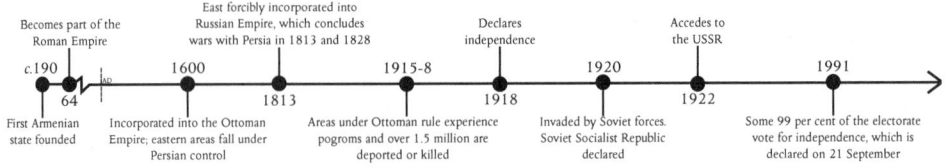

| Becomes part of the Roman Empire | East forcibly incorporated into Russian Empire, which concludes wars with Persia in 1813 and 1828 | Declares independence | Accedes to the USSR |

*c.*190 ... 1600 ... 1915-8 ... 1920 ... 1991

64 ... 1813 ... 1918 ... 1922

| First Armenian state founded | Incorporated into the Ottoman Empire; eastern areas fall under Persian control | Areas under Ottoman rule experience pogroms and over 1.5 million are deported or killed | Invaded by Soviet forces. Soviet Socialist Republic declared | Some 99 per cent of the electorate vote for independence, which is declared on 21 September |

*Area* – 29,743 sq. km
*Capital* – Yerevan; population, 1,274,000 (2015 est)
*Major cities* – Gyumri, Vanadzor
*Currency* – Dram of 100 luma
*Population* – 3,056,382 falling at 0.15 per cent a year (2015 est); Armenian (98.1 per cent), Yezidi (1.1 per cent) (2011). The Armenian diaspora numbers at least 4,700,000
*Religion* – Christian (Armenian Apostolic 92.6 per cent, other Christian 3.4 per cent) (est). The kingdom of Armenia was the first state to adopt Christianity as its official religion, in AD 301
*Language* – Armenian, Kurdish
*Population density* – 105 per sq. km (2013)
*Urban population* – 64.2 per cent (2013 est)
*Median age (years)* – 33.7 (2014 est)
*National anthem* – 'Mer Hayrenik' ['Our Fatherland']
*National day* – 21 September (Independence Day)
*Death penalty* – Abolished for all crimes (since 2003)
*CPI score* – 37 (94)

## CLIMATE AND TERRAIN
Landlocked Armenia is situated in the south-western part of the Caucasus region. It lies at a high altitude and consists of vast plateaux surrounded by mountain ranges. The elevation extremes range from 4,090m (Mt Aragats) to 400m (Debed river). The climate is continental, with hot summers, cold winters and low rainfall. Armenia experiences occasional droughts and severe earthquakes.

## POLITICS
The 1995 constitution was amended by referendum in 2005. The president is directly elected for a five-year term, renewable only once. The unicameral National Assembly *(Azgayin Joghov)* has 131 members who are directly elected for a five-year term.

In the 2012 legislative election, the Republican Party of Armenia (RPA) remained the largest party in the legislature, with 69 seats, and its leader, Serzh Sargsyan, continued in office at the head of a four-party coalition government. Sargsyan was re-elected in the 2013 presidential election in the first round with 52.8 per cent of the vote. Hovik Abrahamyan was appointed prime minister in April 2014 following Armen Gevorgyan's resignation in protest at President Sargsyan's proposals to reform the pension system.

### HEAD OF STATE
*President*, Serzh Sargsyan, *elected* 19 February 2008, *re-elected* 13 February 2013

SELECTED GOVERNMENT MEMBERS *as at April 2015*
*Prime Minister*, Hovik Abrahamyan
*Deputy Prime Minister*, Vache Gabrielyan
*Defence*, Seyran Ohanyan
*Economy*, Karen Chshmarityan

EMBASSY OF THE REPUBLIC OF ARMENIA
25A Cheniston Gardens, London W8 6TG
T 020-7938 5435 E armembassyuk@mfa.am
W http://uk.mfa.am/en

*Ambassador Extraordinary and Plenipotentiary*, HE Dr Armen Sarkissian, *apptd* 2013

BRITISH EMBASSY
34 Baghramyan Avenue, Yerevan 0019
T (+374) (10) 264 301 E enquiries.yerevan@fco.gov.uk
W www.gov.uk/government/world/armenia
*Ambassador Extraordinary and Plenipotentiary*, HE Jonathan Aves and HE Katherine Leach, *apptd* 2012

## FOREIGN RELATIONS
There is a longstanding dispute with Azerbaijan over the predominantly Armenian-populated Azeri region of Nagorny-Karabakh; Armenia claims this territory as historically native land arbitrarily granted to Soviet Azerbaijan by Stalin in 1921–2. The territory's government voted to transfer to Armenia in 1988 but this was rejected by the USSR. When the USSR collapsed in 1991, the territory declared independence. Azeri attempts to reassert control were met with resistance which escalated into a war that lasted from 1992 until a ceasefire was agreed between Armenia, Azerbaijan and Nagorny-Karabakh in 1994. By this time, Nagorno-Karabakh forces, supported by Armenia, had captured all of Nagorny-Karabakh, all Azeri territory that separated Nagorny-Karabakh from Armenia and all mountainous Azeri territory around the enclave. Talks mediated by the Organisation for Security and Cooperation in Europe failed to make any progress towards a peaceful resolution until 2008, when Armenia and Azerbaijan agreed to intensify efforts, although recent years have seen stalled negotiations and regular ceasefire breaches – including the deaths in July 2014 of 14 Azeri soldiers, the highest number of fatalities incurred during the dispute since 1994.

## DEFENCE
Russia maintains around 5,000 army personnel in Armenia, and in 2010 its lease on a military base was extended to 2044.

| Aged 16–49, 2010 est | Males | Females |
| --- | --- | --- |
| Available for military service | 805,847 | 854,296 |
| Fit for military service | 644,372 | 717,272 |

*Military expenditure* – US$471m (2014 est)
*Conscription* – 18–27 years of age; 2 years

## ECONOMY AND TRADE
The economy experienced a severe decline following the break-up of the USSR in 1991, adding to existing problems arising from the 1988 earthquake and subsequently exacerbated by the Nagorny-Karabakh conflict and the consequent trade embargos imposed by Azerbaijan and Turkey, both of which are still in place. Economic liberalisation from 1994 brought sustained high growth and falls in inflation and poverty levels until the global economic crisis. This triggered a severe recession in 2009, largely owing to declines in construction and remittances, despite loans from Russia and international institutions; a recovery began in 2010 and continued into 2013. The poor

performance of the Eurozone and Russian economies remains a long-term threat to growth. Armenia became a founding member of the Eurasian Economic Union (EEU) on 1 January 2015 (*see* Events).

The agricultural sector produces fruit, vegetables and livestock as cash crops, and grain; it contributes 21.9 per cent of GDP and employs 44.2 per cent of the workforce. There are large mineral deposits, including iron and copper ore and non-ferrous metals. Industry, which contributes 37.3 per cent of GDP, is diversified and most small- and medium-sized enterprises are now privatised. The main activities are diamond-processing, the production of industrial machinery, vehicles and parts, textiles and clothing, chemicals, instruments, microelectronics, jewellery, software development and food processing.

The main trading partners are Russia, EU countries, Iran, other former Soviet bloc states, China and the USA. Principal exports are pig iron, copper, non-ferrous metals, diamonds, mineral products, food and energy. The main imports are natural gas, petrol, tobacco products, foodstuffs and diamonds.

*GNI* – US$11,314m; US$3,800 per capita (2013)
*Annual average growth of GDP* – 3.2 per cent (2014 est)
*Inflation rate* – 5.8 per cent (2013 est)
*Population below poverty line* – 32 per cent (2013 est)
*Unemployment* – 16.7 per cent (2015 est)
*Total external debt* – US$7,943m (2014 est)
*Imports* – US$4,386m (2013)
*Exports* – US$1,479m (2013)

BALANCE OF PAYMENTS
*Trade* – US$2,907m deficit (2013)
*Current Account* – US$9,495m deficit (2014 est)

| Trade with UK | 2013 | 2014 |
| --- | --- | --- |
| Imports from UK | £19,450,400 | £14,266,004 |
| Exports to UK | £2,321,823 | £515,652 |

## COMMUNICATIONS
*Airports* – Ten
*Roadways and railways* – 7,705km; 869km
*Telecommunications* – 584,000 fixed lines and 3.22 million mobile subscriptions (2012); there were 208,200 internet users in 2009
*Internet code and IDD* – am; 374 (from UK), 44 (to UK)
*Major broadcasters* – Public TV of Armenia (state-run) and Armenia TV (commercial), alongside 24 private television stations
*Press* – Daily newspapers include *Aravot*, *Aykakan Zhanamak* and the state-operated *Ayastani Anrapetutyun*
*WPFI score* – 28,43 (78)

## EDUCATION AND HEALTH
State education is free and compulsory for all children aged seven to 14. Senior secondary school may be attended from the ages of 14 to 16.
*Literacy rate* – 99.7 per cent (2015 est)
*Gross enrolment ratio (percentage of relevant age group)* – primary 102 per cent (2011 est); secondary 96 per cent; tertiary 46 per cent (2012 est)
*Health expenditure (per capita)* – US$159 (2013)
*Hospital beds (per 1,000 people)* – 3.9 (2012)
*Life expectancy (years)* – 74.12 (2014 est)
*Mortality rate* – 9.3 (2014 est)
*Birth rate* – 13.92 (2014 est)
*Infant mortality rate* – 13.97 (2014 est)

# AUSTRALIA

*Commonwealth of Australia*

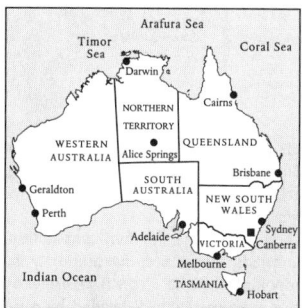

*Area* – 7,691,951 sq. km (excluding overseas territories)
*Capital* – Canberra; population, 412,000 (2015 est)
*Major cities* – Adelaide, Brisbane, Melbourne, Perth, Sydney
*Currency* – Australian dollar ($A) of 100 cents
*Population* – 22,751,014 rising at 1.07 per cent a year (2015 est)
*Religion* – Christian (Protestant 28.8 per cent, Roman Catholic 25.3 per cent), Buddhist 2.5 per cent, Muslim 2.2 per cent, Hindu 1.3 per cent (est)
*Language* – English, Mandarin, Italian, Arabic, Greek, Cantonese, Vietnamese, Aboriginal languages
*Population density* – 3 per sq. km (2013)
*Urban population* – 89.5 per cent (2013 est)
*Median age (years)* – 38.3 (2014 est)
*National anthem* – 'Advance Australia Fair'
*National day* – 26 January (Australia Day)
*Death penalty* – Abolished for all crimes (since 1985)
*CPI score* – 80 (11)

## CLIMATE AND TERRAIN
The majority of Australia is a plateau, with hills, low mountain ranges and sparsely populated deserts in the interior, and tropical wetlands and rainforest in the north-east. Mountain ranges running down the east coast are the source of the Murray and Darling river systems, which flow across the densely populated fertile plain in the south-east. Off the north-east coast is the Great Barrier Reef, the world's largest coral reef. Elevation ranges from 2,229m (Mt Kosciuszko) to −15m (Lake Eyre). The climate is arid or semi-arid in the interior, tropical in the north and temperate in the south and east.

## POLITICS
Under the 1901 constitution, the Commonwealth of Australia is a federation of six states. The constitution defines the powers of the federal government, and residuary legislative power remains with the states.

The head of state is Queen Elizabeth II, represented by the governor-general, who is appointed on the advice of the Australian prime minister. The bicameral parliament consists of the senate and the House of Representatives. The constitution provides that the number of members of the House of Representatives shall be proportionate to the population of each state, with a minimum of five members for each state, and that the number of senators shall be, as nearly as is practicable, half the number of representatives. There are currently 150 members, including two members for the Northern Territory and two for the Australian Capital Territory; they are directly elected for a three-year term. There are 76 senators; each state returns 12 senators, who are

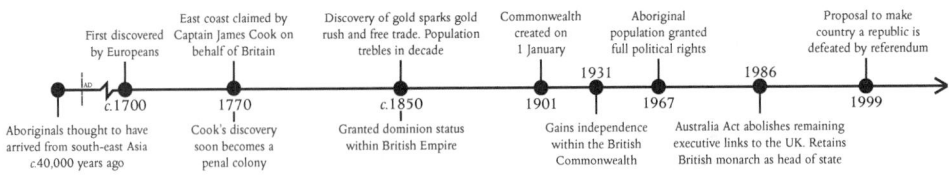

| | East coast claimed by | Discovery of gold sparks gold | Commonwealth | Aboriginal | Proposal to make |
| First discovered | Captain James Cook on | rush and free trade. Population | created on | population granted | country a republic is |
| by Europeans | behalf of Britain | trebles in decade | 1 January | full political rights | defeated by referendum |

directly elected for a six-year term, with half retiring every third year. The Australian Capital Territory and the Northern Territory each return two senators, who are directly elected for a three-year term.

Each of the six states has its own constitution, executive, legislature and judicature. Executive authority is vested in a governor (appointed by the Crown), assisted by a council of ministers or executive council headed by a state premier. There are ten territories, and three – the Australian Capital Territory, Northern Territory and Norfolk Island – have limited self-government, with an executive authority headed by an administrator (appointed by the governor-general), and legislative assembly led by a chief minister. The other territories are directly administered by the federal government.

The Liberal–National Coalition, led by Tony Abbott of the Liberal Party of Australia, defeated the incumbent Australian Labor Party (ALP) in the September 2013 federal elections, winning a significant overall majority in the House of Representatives, but not in the Senate. His victory ended seven years of government by the ALP and followed a divisive leadership battle within the party that saw deputy prime minister Julia Gillard challenge Kevin Rudd and become Australia's first female prime minister in June 2010 and then relinquish the premiership back to him exactly three years later, following plummeting opinion polls. In September 2015, Malcolm Turnbull replaced Tony Abbot as prime minister after the Liberal Party carried out a leadership ballot following plummeting opinion polls.
*Governor-General,* HE Sir Peter Cosgrove, *apptd* 2014

SELECTED GOVERNMENT MEMBERS *as at September 2015*
*Prime Minister,* Malcolm Turnbull
*Deputy Prime Minister, Infrastructure and Regional Development,* Warren Truss
*Defence,* Kevin Andrews
*Finance,* Mathias Cormann
*Foreign Affairs and Trade,* Julie Bishop

AUSTRALIAN HIGH COMMISSION
Australia House, Strand, London WC2B 4LA
T 020-7379 4334 W www.uk.embassy.gov.au
*High Commissioner,* HE Alexander Downer *apptd* 2014

BRITISH HIGH COMMISSION
Commonwealth Avenue, Yarralumla, Canberra, ACT 2600
T (+61) (2) 6270 6666 E canberra.enquiries@fconet.fco.gov.uk
W www.gov.uk/government/world/australia
*High Commissioner,* HE Paul Madden, CMG, *apptd* 2011

## DEFENCE

| *Aged 16–49, 2010 est* | *Males* | *Females* |
| --- | --- | --- |
| Available for military service | 5,316,464 | 5,116,722 |
| Fit for military service | 4,411,958 | 4,239,985 |

*Military expenditure* – US$25,411m (2014)

## ECONOMY AND TRADE

Australia has a highly diversified and internationally competitive market economy that saw sustained strong growth from 1992 to 2014. It weathered the global downturn better than most developed countries, avoiding recession through a government fiscal stimulus package and low interest rates. Recent problems have been climate related, with floods, droughts and extensive bush fires all affecting agriculture, mining and infrastructure. The service sector contributes 67.4 per cent of GDP and employs 75 per cent of the workforce, industry accounts for 28.9 per cent of GDP and 21.1 per cent of labour, and agriculture contributes 3.7 per cent of GDP and employs 3.6 per cent of the workforce.

The diversity of Australia's climate and soil conditions means that a wide range of crops can be grown, although most are confined to specific regions. Scant or erratic rainfall, limited scope for irrigation and unsuitable soils or topography have restricted intensive agriculture, although wheat is a major export, and sugar cane and fruit are important crops. Cattle and sheep ranching is widespread, providing meat, meat derivatives, wool and dairy products.

Significant natural resources include bauxite, coal, copper, diamonds, gold, iron ore, lead, mineral salts, nickel, silver, tin, tungsten, uranium, zinc, oil and natural gas. The main industrial activities are mining, the production of industrial and transport equipment, chemicals and steel, and food processing. Production and processing of hydrocarbons expected to increase once the oil and gas fields in the Timor Sea begin full production.

## STATES AND TERRITORIES

| | Area (sq. km) | Population (2014 est) | Capital | Premier (2015) |
| --- | --- | --- | --- | --- |
| Australian Capital Territory (ACT) | 2,358 | 386,000 | Canberra | Andrew Barr† |
| New South Wales (NSW) | 800,642 | 7,518,500 | Sydney | Michael Baird |
| Northern Territory (NT) | 1,349,129 | 245,100 | Darwin* | Adam Giles† |
| Queensland (Qld) | 1,730,648 | 4,722,400 | Brisbane | Annastacia Palaszczuk |
| South Australia (SA) | 983,482 | 1,685,700 | Adelaide | Jay Weatherill |
| Tasmania (Tas.) | 68,401 | 514,800 | Hobart | William Hodgman |
| Victoria (Vic.) | 227,416 | 5,841,700 | Melbourne | Daniel Andrews |
| Western Australia (WA) | 2,529,875 | 2,573,400 | Perth | Colin Barnett |

* Seat of administration   † Chief Minister

Over the past 20 years, the focus of Australia's trade, like its foreign policy, has shifted from Europe to Asia and the Pacific region. It is a leading member of the Asia-Pacific Economic Cooperation forum, and a free-trade agreement (FTA) between Australia and the Association of Southeast Asian Nations (ASEAN) countries entered into force in 2010; it is also negotiating for FTAs with China, Japan, India, South Korea and Malaysia. Major trading partners include China, Japan, South Korea, India, the USA, Singapore and Germany. The chief exports are coal, iron ore, gold, meat, wool, alumina, wheat, machinery and transport equipment. The main imports are machinery and transport equipment, computers, office and telecoms equipment, crude oil and petroleum products.

*GNI* – US$1,512,604m; US$65,390 per capita (2013)
*Annual average growth of GDP* – 2.8 per cent (2014 est)
*Inflation rate* – 2.4 per cent (2013 est)
*Unemployment* – 5.7 per cent (2015 est)
*Total external debt* – US$1,480,000m (2014 est)
*Imports* – US$242,133m (2013)
*Exports* – US$252,968m (2013)

BALANCE OF PAYMENTS
*Trade* – US$10,836m deficit (2013)
*Current Account* – US$39,875m deficit (2014 est)

| Trade with UK | 2013 | 2014 |
| --- | --- | --- |
| Imports from UK | £4,050,917,476 | £3,677,695,142 |
| Exports to UK | £2,593,347,328 | £2,153,990,084 |

## COMMUNICATIONS

*Airports* – 349; there are international airports in each of the eight territories
*Waterways* – 2,000km; major ports in all of the state capitals except Hobart
*Roadways and railways* – 356,343km; 38,445km
*Telecommunications* – 10.47 million fixed lines and 24.4 million mobile subscriptions (2012); there were 15.81 million internet subscribers in 2009
*Internet country code and IDD* – au; 61 (from UK), 11 41 (to UK)
*Major broadcasters* – The Australian Broadcasting Corporation (ABC) and Special Broadcasting Service (SBS), both public, provide radio and TV coverage; other major television networks include Australia Network and Foxtel (owned by News Corporation)
*Press* – Two major media groups – News Corp Australia and Fairfax Media – account for 85 per cent of newspaper sales; major titles include *The Sydney Morning Herald, The Australian* and *The Daily Telegraph*
*WPFI score* – 17,03 (25)

## EDUCATION AND HEALTH

Education is administered by each state and territory, and is compulsory between the ages of five and 17.
*Gross enrolment ratio (percentage of relevant age group)* – primary 105 per cent; secondary 136 per cent; tertiary 86 per cent (2012 est)
*Health expenditure (per capita)* – US$5,827 (2013)
*Hospital beds (per 1,000 people)* – 3.9 (2010)
*Life expectancy (years)* – 82.07 (2014 est)
*Mortality rate* – 7.07 (2014 est)
*Birth rate* – 12.19 (2014 est)
*Infant mortality rate* – 4.43 (2014 est)

## EXTERNAL TERRITORIES

Most of the territories are administered by the federal government through the Department of Regional Australia,

Regional Development and Local Government; the Australian Antarctic Territory and the Territory of Heard Island and McDonald Islands are administered through the Australian Antarctic Division of the Department of Sustainability, Environment, Water, Population and Communities.

## ASHMORE AND CARTIER ISLANDS

The Ashmore Islands (comprising Middle, East and West Islands) and Cartier Island are situated in the Indian Ocean 320km off Australia's north-west coast. The islands became an Australian territory in 1933. A nature reserve was established on Ashmore Reef in 1983 and a marine reserve around Cartier Island in 2000.

## AUSTRALIAN ANTARCTIC TERRITORY

The Australian Antarctic Territory was established in 1933 and is 5,896,500 sq. km. It comprises all the islands and territories, other than Adélie Land, that are situated south of latitude 60°S. and lying between 160°E. longitude and 45°E. longitude. (*See also* The North and South Poles.)

## CHRISTMAS ISLAND

*Area* – 135 sq. km
*Population* – 1,530 rising at 1.11 per cent a year (2014 est)

Christmas Island is situated in the Indian Ocean about 1,565km north-west of Northwest Cape in Western Australia. The island was annexed by Britain in 1888. Sovereignty was transferred to Australia in 1958. The Shire of Christmas Island (SOCI) is responsible for local government services on the island; its council has nine members directly elected for a four-year term. The main activities are phosphate mining, tourism and the government sector.
*Administrator,* Barry Haase, *apptd* 2014

## COCOS (KEELING) ISLANDS

*Area* – 14 sq. km
*Population* – 596 (2014 est)

The Cocos (Keeling) Islands are two separate atolls (North Keeling Island and, 24km to the south, the main atoll) comprising 27 small coral islands, situated in the Indian Ocean, about 2,950km north-west of Perth. The two inhabited islands of the southern atoll are West Island and Home Island, where around 80 per cent of the population lives, including most of the Cocos Malay community.

The islands were declared a British possession in 1857. In 1886 Queen Victoria granted all land in the islands to George Clunies-Ross and his heirs, who established coconut plantations worked by imported Malay labour. Sovereignty was transferred to Australia in 1955, and the government purchased the Clunies-Ross land and property in 1978, 1984 and 1993. The land is held in trust for the residents, with the local government body, the Shire of the Cocos (Keeling) Islands, as trustee. In 1984 the Cocos community, in a UN-supervised Act of Self-Determination, voted to integrate with Australia. The seven-member Shire Council of Cocos (Keeling) Islands is responsible for local government services. The public sector is the main employer and there is a little tourism; coconuts are the only cash crop.
*Administrator,* Barry Haase, *apptd* 2014

## CORAL SEA ISLANDS TERRITORY

The Coral Sea Islands Territory lies east of Queensland between the Great Barrier Reef and longitude 156° 06′ E., and between latitudes 12°S. and 24°S. It comprises scattered islands, spread over a sea area of 780,000 sq. km. There is a manned meteorological station on Willis Island but otherwise the islands are uninhabited. Established in 1969, the territory is now a nature reserve, administered jointly by the Department of Sustainability, Environment, Water, Population and Communities, and the Department of Agriculture, Fisheries and Forestry.

## HEARD ISLAND AND MCDONALD ISLANDS
The Territory of Heard Island and the McDonald Islands, about 4,100km south-west of Perth, comprises all the islands and rocks lying between 52° 30′ and 53° 30′ S. latitude and 72° and 74° 30′ E. longitude. The subantarctic islands, which have active volcanoes, were discovered in the 1850s and sovereignty was transferred from Britain to Australia in 1947. The islands are now part of a marine reserve established in 2002.

## JERVIS BAY TERRITORY
*Area* – 76 sq. km
*Population* – 377 (2011 census)

The territory consists of 66 sq. km of land on the southern shore of Jervis Bay, 9 sq. km of marine waters and Bowen Island (0.5 sq. km), and lies about 200km south of Sydney. Originally part of New South Wales, the territory was acquired by the federal government in 1915 to provide Canberra with access to the sea. Much of the land and water now comprises Booderee National Park, leased from the Wreck Bay Aboriginal Community who since the 1980s have been granted 90 per cent of the land. The main economic activity is tourism.

## NORFOLK ISLAND
*Area* – 36 sq. km
*Population* – 2,210 rising at 0.01 per cent a year (2014 est)
*Seat of government* – Kingston
*National day* – 8 June (Bounty Day)

Discovered by Captain Cook in 1774, Norfolk Island is situated in the South Pacific Ocean, about 1,600km north-east of Sydney. In 1856, 194 descendants of the *Bounty* mutineers accepted an invitation to leave Pitcairn and settle on Norfolk Island, which had served as a penal colony.

The island became a territory in 1914 and has been internally self-governing since 1979. The nine-member legislative assembly is directly elected for a three-year term, and elects the five-member executive council. This advises the administrator, who represents the federal government. The economy is dependent on tourism; other economic activities include the sale of postage stamps and pine and palm seeds, livestock-rearing and agriculture.
*Administrator,* Gary Hardgrave, *apptd* 2014

# AUSTRIA

*Republik Österreich – Republic of Austria*

*Area* – 83,871 sq. km
*Capital* – Vienna (Wien); population, 1,763,000 (2015 est)
*Major cities* – Graz, Innsbruck, Klagenfurt, Linz, Salzburg
*Currency* – Euro (€) of 100 cents
*Population* – 8,665,550 rising at 0.55 per cent a year (2015 est); Austrian (91.1 per cent), former Yugoslav (4 per cent), Turkish (1.6 per cent) (2001 est)
*Religion* – Christian (Roman Catholic 66 per cent, Protestant 4 per cent, Eastern Orthodox 2 per cent), Muslim 4 per cent (est)
*Language* – German (official), Croatian and Hungarian (official in Burgenland), Slovene (official in Carinthia), Turkish, Serbian
*Population density* – 103 per sq. km (2013)
*Urban population* – 68.1 per cent (2013 est)
*Median age (years)* – 44.3 (2014 est)
*National anthem* – 'Land der Berge, Land am Strome' ['Land of Mountains, Land on the River']
*National day* – 26 October (date law of neutrality passed, 1955)
*Death penalty* – Abolished for all crimes (since 1968)
*CPI score* – 72 (23)

## CLIMATE AND TERRAIN
The north and east of the country feature rolling hills in the river Danube basin, while the west and south contain the eastern Alps, which cover nearly two-thirds of the country. The highest point of elevation is 3,798m (Grossglockner) and the lowest is 115m (Neusiedler See). The climate is continental in the lowlands and alpine in the mountains, with average temperatures in Vienna ranging from −2.1°C in January to 16.4°C in July and August.

## POLITICS
Under the 1955 constitution, the federal president is directly elected for a six-year term, renewable once. There is a bicameral legislature, the *Parlament*, consisting of the National Council *(Nationalrat)*, which has 183 members directly elected for a four-year term, and the Federal Council *(Bundesrat)*, which has 62 members elected for terms of five to six years by the provincial assemblies. Some powers may only be exercised by both houses acting together as the Federal Assembly *(Bundesversammlung)*. The executive is headed by the federal chancellor, who is appointed by the president.

The 2004 presidential election was won by Heinz Fischer of the Social Democrats (SPÖ), who was re-elected in 2010. Following the 2013 legislative election, the SPÖ and the Austrian People's Party (ÖVP) remained the largest parties but both lost ground to the right-wing Freedom Party of Austria (FPÖ); the SPÖ–ÖVP coalition continued under SPÖ leader, Werner Faymann.

HEAD OF STATE
*Federal President,* Heinz Fischer, *took office* 8 July 2004, *re-elected* 2010

SELECTED GOVERNMENT MEMBERS *as at April 2015*
*Chancellor,* Werner Faymann
*Vice-Chancellor, Economy,* Reinhold Mitterlehner
*Defence, Sports,* Gerald Klug

EMBASSY OF AUSTRIA
18 Belgrave Mews West, London SW1X 8HU
T 020-7344 3250 E london-ob@bmeia.gv.at
W www.bmeia.gv.at/london
*Ambassador Extraordinary and Plenipotentiary,* HE Dr Emil Brix, *apptd* 2010

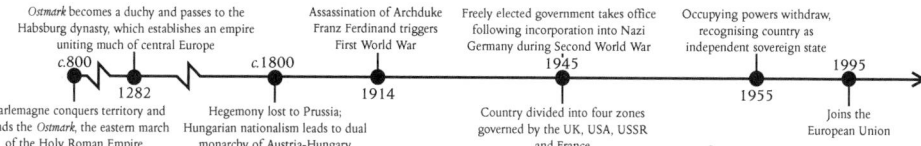

Ostmark becomes a duchy and passes to the Habsburg dynasty, which establishes an empire uniting much of central Europe
*c.*800

Charlemagne conquers territory and founds the *Ostmark*, the eastern march of the Holy Roman Empire
1282

Hegemony lost to Prussia; Hungarian nationalism leads to dual monarchy of Austria-Hungary
*c.*1800

Assassination of Archduke Franz Ferdinand triggers First World War
1914

Freely elected government takes office following incorporation into Nazi Germany during Second World War
1945

Country divided into four zones governed by the UK, USA, USSR and France
1955

Occupying powers withdraw, recognising country as independent sovereign state
1995

Joins the European Union

## BRITISH EMBASSY
Jaurèsgasse 12, 1030 Vienna
**T** (+43) (1) 716 130 **E** viennaconsularenquiries@fco.gov.uk
**W** www.gov.uk/government/world/austria
*Ambassador Extraordinary and Plenipotentiary,* HE Susan le Jeune d'Allegeershecque, *apptd* 2011

## FEDERAL STRUCTURE
There are nine provinces *(Bundesländer)*: Burgenland, Carinthia, Lower Austria, Salzburg, Styria, Tyrol, Upper Austria, Vienna and Vorarlberg. Each has its own assembly and government.

## DEFENCE

| *Aged 16–49, 2010 est* | *Males* | *Females* |
|---|---|---|
| Available for military service | 1,941,110 | 1,910,434 |
| Fit for military service | 1,579,862 | 1,554,130 |

*Military expenditure* – US$3,257m (2014)
*Conscription* – 18–35 years of age, male only; 6 months

## ECONOMY AND TRADE
Austria has a well-developed market economy which is closely linked to other EU states. Its strong commercial links with central, eastern and south-eastern Europe, an attraction for foreign investors in the past, increased its vulnerability in the global economic downturn, and its financial sector required state support. The economy went into recession in 2008 but started to recover throughout 2010 and 2011 before contracting in 2012; the Austrian parliament agreed an austerity budget in March 2012 that aims to bring the public finances into balance by 2016.

The services sector contributes most to GDP (69.8 per cent in 2014), followed by industry (28.6 per cent) and the small but highly developed agricultural sector (1.5 per cent). The main industries include tourism, construction, manufacturing of machinery, vehicles and parts, food processing, timber and wood processing, production of metals and metal goods, chemicals, paper and cardboard, and communications equipment.

Austria's main trading partners are Germany, France, Italy and Switzerland. Principal exports include the goods produced by the main industries, iron and steel, and textiles. The main imports are machinery and equipment, vehicles, chemical products, metal goods, oil and oil products, and foodstuffs.
*GNI* – US$427,321m; US$50,430 per capita (2013)
*Annual average growth of GDP* – 1 per cent (2014 est)
*Inflation rate* – 2 per cent (2013 est)
*Population below poverty line* – 6.2 per cent (2012 est)
*Unemployment* – 4.8 per cent (2015 est)
*Total external debt* – US$812,000m (2012 est)
*Imports* – US$172,596m (2013)
*Exports* – US$166,546m (2013)

### BALANCE OF PAYMENTS
*Trade* – US$6,050m deficit (2013)
*Current Account* – US$7,967 surplus (2014 est)

| Trade with UK | 2013 | 2014 |
|---|---|---|
| Imports from UK | £1,607,005,257 | £1,617,705,162 |
| Exports to UK | £2,868,443,669 | £3,128,685,633 |

## COMMUNICATIONS
*Airports* – 24; principal airports include Vienna, Salzburg and Innsbruck
*Waterways* – 358km of navigable waterways; considerable trade through Danube ports (Vienna, Krems, Enns, Linz)
*Roadways and railways* – 124,508km, including 1,719km of motorways; 6,399km
*Telecommunications* – 3.34 million fixed lines and 13.59 million mobile subscriptions (2012); there were 6.14 million internet subscribers in 2009
*Internet code and IDD* – at; 43 (from UK), 44 (to UK)
*Major broadcasters* – Österreichischer Rundfunk (ÖRF) (public) and ATV (commercial)
*Press* – Regional newspapers compete effectively against national publications. Leading titles include *Die Presse, Kleine Zeitung* (Graz), *Wiener Zeitung* (Vienna), *Der Standard* and *Der Kurier*
*WPFI score* – 10,85 (7)

## EDUCATION AND HEALTH
Education is free and compulsory from six to 15.
*Gross enrolment ratio (percentage of relevant age group)* – primary 101 per cent; secondary 98 per cent; tertiary 72 per cent (2012 est)
*Health expenditure (per capita)* – US$5,427 (2013)
*Hospital beds (per 1,000 people)* – 7.6 (2011)
*Life expectancy (years)* – 80.17 (2014 est)
*Mortality rate* – 10.38 (2014 est)
*Birth rate* – 8.76 (2014 est)
*Infant mortality rate* – 4.16 (2014 est)

# AZERBAIJAN

*Azarbaycan Respublikasi – Republic of Azerbaijan*

*Area* – 86,600 sq. km
*Capital* – Baku (Baki); population, 2,661,000 (2015 est)
*Major cities* – Ganca, Sumqayit
*Currency* – New Manat of 100 gopik
*Population* – 9,780,780 rising at 0.96 per cent a year (2015 est); Azeri (91.6 per cent), Lezgian (2 per cent), Armenian (1.3 per cent), Russian (1.3 per cent), Talysh (1.3 per cent) (2009). There are more Azeris in Iran than in Azerbaijan. Almost all of the Armenian population lives in the Nagorny-Karabakh enclave
*Religion* – Muslim 96 per cent (Shia 65 per cent, Sunni 35 per cent) (est)

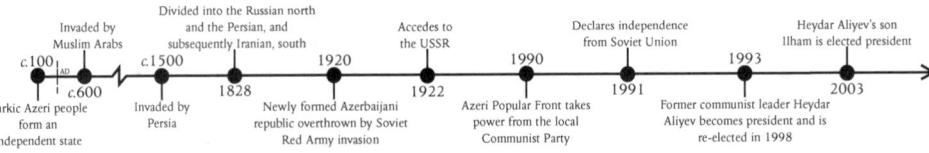

Invaded by Muslim Arabs | Divided into the Russian north and the Persian, and subsequently Iranian, south | Accedes to the USSR | Declares independence from Soviet Union | Heydar Aliyev's son Ilham is elected president

c.100 AD — c.1500 — 1920 — 1990 — 1993

c.600 — 1828 — 1922 — 1991 — 2003

Turkic Azeri people form an independent state | Invaded by Persia | Newly formed Azerbaijani republic overthrown by Soviet Red Army invasion | Azeri Popular Front takes power from the local Communist Party | Former communist leader Heydar Aliyev becomes president and is re-elected in 1998

*Language* – Azeri (official), Russian, Armenian
*Population density* – 114 per sq. km (2013)
*Urban population* – 54.1 per cent (2013 est)
*Median age (years)* – 30.1 (2014 est)
*National anthem* – 'Azerbaijan Marsi' ['March of Azerbaijan']
*National day* – 28 May (founding of the republic, 1918)
*Death penalty* – Abolished for all crimes (since 1998)
*CPI score* – 29 (126)

## CLIMATE AND TERRAIN
Azerbaijan lies on the western shore of the Caspian Sea, in the eastern part of the Caucasus region. It includes the exclave of Nakhichevana, separated from it by Armenia. The north-east of Azerbaijan rises to the south-eastern end of the main Great Caucasus mountain range; to the country's south-west lie the lower Caucasus hills, and in its south-eastern corner the spurs of the Talysh Ridge. Central Azerbaijan lies in a low plain irrigated by the river Kura and the lower reaches of its tributary the Araks. Elevation ranges from 4,485m (Bazarduzu Dagi) to −28m (Caspian Sea). Climate and landscape vary greatly, but rainfall is generally low.

## POLITICS
The 1995 constitution was amended in 2002 and 2009, when the limit on presidential terms was amended to two terms (2002) and then abolished (2009). The executive president is directly elected for a five-year term, which is renewable. The unicameral National Assembly *(Milli Majlis)* has 125 members directly elected for a five-year term. The president appoints the prime minister and the cabinet.

Ilham Aliyev was re-elected for a third term in 2013. In the 2010 legislative election, the New Azerbaijan Party, which is aligned with President Aliyev, increased its number of seats, achieving an overall majority. For dispute with Armenia over the Nagorny-Karabakh region *see* Armenia, Foreign Relations.

HEAD OF STATE
*President,* Ilham Aliyev, *sworn in* 31 October 2003, *re-elected* 2008, 2013

SELECTED GOVERNMENT MEMBERS *as at April 2015*
*Prime Minister,* Artur Rasizade
*First Deputy Prime Minister,* Yagub Abdulla Eyyubov
*Deputy Prime Ministers,* Ismat Abbasov; Ali Ahmadov; Elchin Efendiyev; Ali Hasanov; Abid Sharifov
*Defence,* Lt.-Gen. Zakir Hasanov

EMBASSY OF THE REPUBLIC OF AZERBAIJAN
4 Kensington Court, London W8 5DL
T 020-7938 3412 E london@mission.mfa.gov.az
W www.azembassy.org.uk
*Ambassador Extraordinary and Plenipotentiary,* HE Tahir Taghizade, *apptd* 2014

BRITISH EMBASSY
45 Khagani Street, Baku AZ 1010
T (+994) (12) 437 7878 E generalenquiries.baku@fco.gov.uk
W www.gov.uk/government/world/azerbaijan
*Ambassador Extraordinary and Plenipotentiary,* HE Irfan Siddiq, OBE, *apptd* 2013

## DEFENCE

| | Males | Females |
| --- | --- | --- |
| *Aged 16–49, 2010 est* | | |
| Available for military service | 2,354,249 | 2,334,632 |
| Fit for military service | 1,773,993 | 1,964,012 |

*Military expenditure* – US$3,583m (2014)
*Conscription* – 18–35 years of age, male only; 18 months, or 12 months for university graduates

## ECONOMY AND TRADE
Despite high economic growth in recent years, Azerbaijan's transition from a command to a market economy is slow. This has been exacerbated by its failure to attract foreign investment in sectors other than energy, widespread corruption and systemic inefficiencies. The economy is dominated by oil and natural gas extraction and related industries, centred in Baku and Sumqayit, and exploited through co-production deals with foreign companies. Oil pipelines (1,424km) link the Azeri oilfields to Black Sea ports in Russia, Georgia and Turkey. Though economic performance in 2015 was expected to be constrained by low global oil prices, the country's sovereign oil fund remains one of the wealthiest in the world at US$37.3bn and public debt remains low.

Although agriculture contributes only 5.7 per cent of GDP, it employs nearly 40 per cent of the workforce. The main crops are cotton, cereals, rice, fruit, vegetables, tea, tobacco and livestock. Industry, which contributes 61.2 per cent of GDP, produces oil, natural gas, petroleum products, oilfield equipment, steel, iron ore, cement, chemicals, petrochemicals and textiles.

Russia and other former Soviet republics are increasingly being replaced as trade partners by Turkey, India, the USA and various European countries. Oil and gas constitute around 90 per cent of exports, which also include machinery, cotton and foodstuffs. Principal imports are machinery and equipment, oil products, foodstuffs, metals and chemicals.
*GNI* – US$69,184m; US$7,350 per capita (2013)
*Annual average growth of GDP* – 4.5 per cent (2014 est)
*Inflation rate* – 2.4 per cent (2013 est)
*Population below poverty line* – 5.3 per cent (2013 est)
*Unemployment* – 5.9 per cent (2015 est)
*Total external debt* – US$12,910m (2014 est)
*Imports* – US$10,713m (2013)
*Exports* – US$23,975m (2013)

BALANCE OF PAYMENTS
*Trade* – US$13,263m surplus (2013)
*Current Account* – US$11,357m surplus (2014)

| Trade with UK | 2013 | 2014 |
| --- | --- | --- |
| Imports from UK | £917,219,383 | £578,582,524 |
| Exports to UK | £228,258,472 | £122,085,354 |

## COMMUNICATIONS
*Airports* – 30; international airports at Baku, Ganca, Lankaran and Nakhichevan
*Waterways* – The Baku International Sea Trade port provides links to Turkmenistan and other trade and passenger routes
*Roadways and railways* – 26,789km; 2,918km

*Telecommunications* – 1.73 million fixed lines and 10.12 million mobile telephone subscriptions (2012); there were 2.42 million internet users in 2009
*Internet* – az; 994 (from UK), 44 (to UK)
*Major broadcasters* – AzTV, Azerbaijan Radio (state-run), iTV and ANS TV
*Press* – Printing presses are generally reserved for pro-government titles such as *Azarbaycan*; opposition newspapers include *Azadliq* and *Yeni* Musavat
*WPFI score* – 58,41 (162)

## EDUCATION AND HEALTH

Education up to university level is free.
*Literacy rate* – 99.9 per cent (2015 est)
*Gross enrolment ratio (percentage of relevant age group)* – primary 98 per cent; secondary 100 per cent; tertiary 20 per cent (2012 est)
*Health expenditure (per capita)* – US$436 (2013)
*Hospital beds (per 1,000 people)* – 4.7 (2012)
*Life expectancy* – 71.91 (2014 est)
*Mortality rate* – 7.09 (2014 est)
*Birth rate* – 16.96 (2014 est)
*Infant mortality rate* – 26.67 (2014 est)

# THE BAHAMAS

*Commonwealth of the Bahamas*

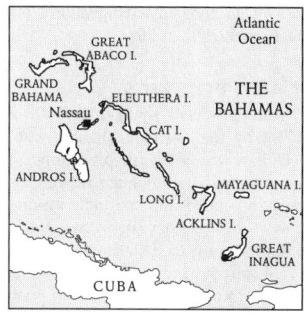

*Area* – 13,880 sq. km
*Capital* – Nassau, on New Providence; population, 254,000 (2011 est)
*Major city* – Freeport, on Grand Bahama
*Currency* – Bahamian dollar (B$) of 100 cents
*Population* – 324,597 rising at 0.85 per cent a year (2015 est)
*Religion* – Christian (Protestant 69.9 per cent, Roman Catholic 12 per cent, other 13 per cent) (est)
*Language* – English (official), Creole
*Population density* – 38 per sq. km (2013)
*Urban population* – 84.6 per cent (2013 est)
*Median age (years)* – 31.2 (2014 est)
*National anthem* – 'March on, Bahamaland'
*National day* – 10 July (Independence Day)
*Death penalty* – Retained (last used 2000)
*CPI score* – 71 (24)
*Life expectancy (years)* – 71.93 (2014 est)
*Mortality rate* – 7 (2014 est)
*Birth rate* – 15.65 (2014 est)
*Infant mortality rate* – 12.5 (2014 est)
*HIV/AIDS adult prevalence* – 0.5 per cent (2013 est)

## CLIMATE AND TERRAIN

The Bahamas consist of more than 700 islands and 2,400 cays, all low-lying. The highest point is 63m (Mt Alvernia,

on Cat Island) and the lowest 0m (Atlantic Ocean). The principal islands include: Abaco Islands, Acklins, Andros, Berry Islands, Bimini, Cat Island, Crooked Island, Eleuthera, Exuma, Grand Bahama, Great Inagua, Harbour Island, Long Island, Mayaguana, New Providence, Ragged Island, Rum Cay, San Salvador and Spanish Wells. The 14 major islands are inhabited, as are a few of the smaller islands. The climate is semitropical. The hurricane season is June to November.

## HISTORY AND POLITICS

The islands were discovered by Columbus in 1492, settled by the British from the 17th century and became a crown colony in 1717. The Bahamas became internally self-governing in 1964 and gained independence on 10 July 1973.

The Progressive Liberal Party (PLP) held power for 25 years until the Free National Movement (FNM) won an absolute majority in the 1992 general election. Power has subsequently alternated between the two parties. The PLP regained its majority in the 2012 legislative election, winning 29 of the 38 seats.

The head of state is Queen Elizabeth II, who is represented by a governor-general. The bicameral parliament has a senate of 16 appointed members and a House of Assembly of 41 members; both chambers serve a five-year term.
*Governor-General,* HE Dame Marguerite Pindling, GCMG, apptd 2014

SELECTED GOVERNMENT MEMBERS *as at April 2015*
*Prime Minister, Finance,* Perry Christie
*Deputy Prime Minister,* Philip Davies
*National Security,* Bernard Nottage

HIGH COMMISSION OF THE COMMONWEALTH OF THE BAHAMAS
10 Chesterfield Street, London W1J 5JL
T 020-7408 4488 E information@bahamashclondon.net
W www.bahamashclondon.net
*High Commissioner,* HE Eldred Edison Bethel, apptd 2012

BRITISH HIGH COMMISSION
*High Commissioner,* David Fitton, CMG, apptd 2013, resident in Kingston, Jamaica

## DEFENCE

| *Aged 16–49, 2010 est* | *Males* | *Females* |
|---|---|---|
| Available for military service | 85,568 | – |
| Fit for military service | 63,429 | 64,645 |

*Military expenditure* – US$68.9m (2013)

## ECONOMY AND TRADE

The economy, the wealthiest in the Caribbean, is dominated by tourism and offshore financial services, which together contribute over 90.8 per cent of GDP. The economy entered recession in 2007–11 when the service industry was disrupted by the global financial crisis and the number of tourists from the USA (over 75 per cent of all visitors) declined. The economy grew modestly from 2011–14. The country remains a low tax state, charging neither corporation or income tax, though a sales tax was introduced for the first time on 15 January 2015.

Manufacturing and agriculture account for 2.1 per cent of GDP and 14 per cent of employment. Agriculture centres mainly on fresh vegetables, fruit, meat and eggs. Mineral reserves produce aragonite and salt for export. Other industries include cement, rum, pharmaceuticals and steel pipe production, and the provision of oil trans-shipment services.

The main trading partners are the USA, Singapore, South Korea, India and China. The chief exports are mineral products and salt, animal products, fruit and vegetables, and polystyrene products. Imports are chiefly machinery and transport equipment, manufactured articles, chemicals, fuel, foodstuffs and livestock.

*GNI* – US$8,138m; US$21,570 per capita (2013)
*Annual average growth of GDP* – 1.2 per cent (2014 est)
*Inflation rate* – 0.4 per cent (2013 est)
*Population below poverty line* – 9.3 per cent (2010 est)
*Unemployment* – 12.2 per cent (2015 est)
*Total external debt* – US$17,560m (2013 est)
*Imports* – US$3,276m (2013)
*Exports* – US$715m (2013)

BALANCE OF PAYMENTS
*Trade* – US$2,561m deficit (2013)
*Current Account* – US$1,871m deficit (2014)

| Trade with UK | 2013 | 2014 |
| --- | --- | --- |
| Imports from UK | £15,899,753 | £20,663,683 |
| Exports to UK | £4,317,450 | £5,855,549 |

## COMMUNICATIONS

*Airports* – 24; international airports are operated from Andros, Chubb Cay, Eleuthera, Exuma, Grand Bahama and New Providence

*Waterways* – The main ports are Nassau (New Providence), Freeport and South Riding Point (Grand Bahama); the Bahamas is a major ship registry, and 1,063 of the 1,160 ships registered in 2010 were foreign-owned

*Roadways* – 1,620km

*Telecommunications* – 137,000 fixed lines (2011) and 254,000 mobile phone subscriptions (2012); there were 115,800 internet users in 2009

*Internet code and IDD* – bs; 1 242 (from UK), 011 44 (to UK)

*Major broadcasters* – The public Broadcasting Corporation of the Bahamas (BCB) operates ZNS TV and ZNS Bahamas (radio)

*Press* – Daily newspapers include *The Nassau Guardian*, *The Tribune* and *The Freeport News*

## BAHRAIN

*Mamlakat al-Bahrayn – Kingdom of Bahrain*

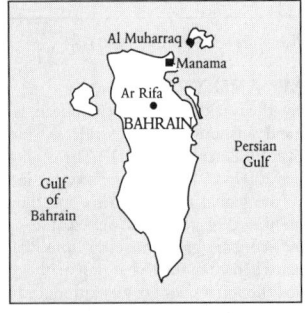

*Area* – 760 sq. km
*Capital* – Manama; population, 262,000 (2015 est)
*Major towns* – Al Muharraq, Ar Rifa, Madinat Hamad
*Currency* – Bahraini dinar (BD) of 1,000 fils

*Population* – 1,346,613 rising at 2.41 per cent a year (2015 est); the non-Bahraini population includes large numbers of Europeans and South Asians (almost 55 per cent of the population)
*Religion* – Muslim 99.8 per cent (est); Islam is the state religion
*Language* – Arabic (official), English, Farsi, Urdu
*Population density* – 1,753 per sq. km (2013)
*Urban population* – 88.8 per cent (2013 est)
*Median age (years)* – 31.6 (2014 est)
*National anthem* – 'Bahrainona' ['Our Bahrain']
*National day* – 16 December (date of independence from British protection, 1971)
*Death penalty* – Retained
*CPI score* – 49 (55)
*Literacy rate* – 99.8 per cent (2015 est)
*Life expectancy (years)* – 78.58 (2014 est)
*Mortality rate* – 2.67 (2014 est)
*Birth rate* – 13.92 (2013 est)
*Infant mortality rate* – 9.68 (2014 est)

## CLIMATE AND TERRAIN

Bahrain consists of an archipelago of 36 low-lying islands situated approximately halfway down the Persian Gulf, some 32km off the east coast of Saudi Arabia. The largest of these, Bahrain Island, is about 48km long and 16km wide at its broadest. Elevation extremes range from 122m (Jabal ad Dukhan) to 0m at sea level. The climate is arid, hot and humid, with average maximum temperatures ranging from 16°C in January to 37.1°C in July.

## HISTORY AND POLITICS

Bahrain was ruled by Persia (Iran) from 1602 until it was ousted in 1783 by the al-Khalifa family, who remain in power. The emirate was a British protectorate from 1820 until 1971, when it became independent. In 1975 the legislature was suspended and the emir assumed virtually absolute power after clashes between Sunni and Shia factions. Moves to return to democratic rule were made in response to civil agitation in the 1990s, until Sheikh Hamad succeeded to the throne and initiated the transition to a constitutional monarchy. The 2002 constitution established Bahrain as a kingdom and a constitutional monarchy, and legalised elections. There has been ongoing agitation for further democratisation, particularly by the Shia majority against the predominantly Sunni authorities.

In February 2011 this flared up into mass demonstrations that were repressed brutally by the government from March, when martial law was declared and the Pearl monument, the focal point of the demonstrations in Manama, was demolished. A report into the unrest, commissioned by Sheikh Hamad, was released in November 2011 and confirmed the practice of torture and infringements of human rights; in response, the ruler vowed to 'learn lessons' from the unrest and promised to reform the country's laws to make them compatible with international standards. Despite national talks beginning in February 2013 and the appointment of the moderate Sheikh Salman bin Hamad al-Khalifa as First Deputy Prime Minister in March of that year, there has yet to be a resolution to the unrest. In October 2014, one month before legislative elections, al-Wefaq, the main Shia political organisation, was banned from operating for three months, although it had previously announced it would boycott the vote maintaining the current electoral system fails to represent the country's Shia majority.

In the 2014 legislative election, independents won 37 of the 40 contested seats; al-Wefaq lost all 18 of the seats it had won in 2011. The number of seats held by Sunni Islamist groups declined by two. Voter turnout was poor – the government estimated that around 51.5 per cent of the population voted, while opposition parties claimed turnout was as low as 30 per cent.

Under the 2002 constitution, the country is a hereditary constitutional monarchy with the king as head of state. The king appoints the cabinet. The bicameral National Assembly consists of a lower house, the Council of Representatives, and an upper house, the Consultative Council. The lower house has 40 members directly elected for a four-year term, and the upper house has 40 members appointed by the king for a four-year term. The 2002 constitution granted women the right to vote and to stand for election.

### HEAD OF STATE

*HH The King of Bahrain*, Sheikh Hamad bin Isa al-Khalifa, KCMG, *Commander-in-Chief of the Armed Forces, succeeded as emir* 6 March 1999, *proclaimed king* 14 February 2002
*Crown Prince, First Deputy Prime Minister, Chair of the Economic Development Board,* Sheikh Salman bin Hamad al-Khalifa

SELECTED GOVERNMENT MEMBERS *as at April 2015*
*Prime Minister,* HH Sheikh Khalifa bin Salman al-Khalifa
*First Deputy Prime Minister,* HH Salman bin Hamad bin Isa al-Khalifa
*Deputy Prime Ministers,* Sheikh Khalid bin Abdulla al-Khalifa; Sheikh Ali bin Khalifa al-Khalifa; Sheikh Mohammad bin Mubarak al-Khalifa; Sheikh Jawad bin Salim al-Arrayedh
*Defence,* Maj.-Gen. Yusuf bin Ahmed bin Hussain Al-Jalahma
*Finance,* Sheikh Ahmed bin Mohammed al-Khalifa
*Foreign Affairs,* Sheikh Khalid bin Ahmed bin Mohammed al-Khalifa

### EMBASSY OF THE KINGDOM OF BAHRAIN
30 Belgrave Square, London SW1X 8QB
T 020-7201 9170 E information@bahrainembassy.co.uk
W www.bahrainembassy.co.uk
*Ambassador Extraordinary and Plenipotentiary,* HE Alice Thomas Samaan, *apptd* 2011

### BRITISH EMBASSY
PO Box 114, 21 Government Avenue, Manama 306
T (+973) 1757 4100 W www.gov.uk/government/world/bahrain
*Ambassador Extraordinary and Plenipotentiary,* HE Iain Lindsay, OBE, *apptd* 2011

### DEFENCE

| Aged 16–49, 2010 est | Males | Females |
| --- | --- | --- |
| Available for military service | 508,863 | 290,801 |
| Fit for military service | 423,757 | 245,302 |

*Military expenditure* – US$1,433m (2014)

### ECONOMY AND TRADE
Bahrain was one of the first Gulf states to discover oil, in the 1930s, but reserves and production are lower than in neighbouring countries. It has diversified its economy, developing particularly as a regional financial and business centre, and as a tourist destination. Petroleum production and refining still accounts for an estimated 19 per cent of GDP, 87 per cent of government revenue and 77 per cent of total export receipts. Other industries include petrochemicals, aluminium smelting, and shipbuilding and repair. Bahrain's main trading partners are Saudi Arabia, the EU, Far Eastern countries and the USA, with whom a Free Trade Agreement was agreed in 2006.

*GNI* – US$25,958m; US$19,700 per capita (2012)
*Annual average growth of GDP* – 3.9 per cent (2014 est)
*Inflation rate* – 3.2 per cent (2013 est)
*Unemployment* – 7.6 per cent (2015 est)
*Total external debt* – US$18,720m (2014 est)
*Imports* – US$13,000m (2013)
*Exports* – US$17,500m (2013)

BALANCE OF PAYMENTS
*Trade* – US$4,500m surplus (2013)
*Current Account* – US$1,801m surplus (2014)

| Trade with UK | 2013 | 2014 |
| --- | --- | --- |
| Imports from UK | £269,849,344 | £295,479,981 |
| Exports to UK | £173,416,783 | £155,924,735 |

### COMMUNICATIONS
*Airports* – Four; Bahrain International Airport is a major air traffic centre in the Gulf
*Waterways* – The main ports are Khalifa bin Salman and Mina Salman
*Roadways* – There are 3,392km of paved roadways; the four main islands are connected by causeways, and a 25km causeway links Bahrain to Saudi Arabia
*Telecommunications* – 290,000 main lines and 2.125 million mobile phone subscriptions (2012); there were 419,500 internet users in 2009
*Internet code and IDD* – bh; 973 (from UK), 44 (to UK)
*Major broadcasters* – State-run Bahrain Radio and Television Corporation (BRTC) operates radio networks and five terrestrial TV networks. Bahrain suspended the Saudi-financed al-Arab satellite news TV channel from operating in February 2015 (*see* Events)
*Press* – Six daily newspapers are published, including *Akhbar al-Khaleej, al-Ayam* and *al-Wasat*
*WPFI score* – 58,69 (163)

## BANGLADESH

*Gana Prajatantri Bangladesh – People's Republic of Bangladesh*

*Area* – 143,998 sq. km
*Capital* – Dhaka; population, 15,669,000 (2015 est)
*Major cities* – Chittagong, Gazipur, Khulna, Narayanganj
*Currency* – Taka (Tk) of 100 paisa
*Population* – 168,957,745 rising at 1.6 per cent a year (2015 est); Bengali (98 per cent) (1998 est)
*Religion* – Muslim 90 per cent (the vast majority are Sunni), Hindu 9.5 per cent (est); Islam is the state religion
*Language* – Bangla (official), English
*Population density* – 1,203 per sq. km (2013)
*Urban population* – 29.4 per cent (2013 est)
*Median age (years)* – 24.3 (2014 est)

*National anthem* – 'Amar Shonar Bangla' ['My Golden Bengal']
*National day* – 26 March (Independence Day)
*Death penalty* – Retained
*CPI score* – 25 (145)

## CLIMATE AND TERRAIN

Although hilly in the south-east and north-east, over 75 per cent of the country is less than 3m above sea level, situated on the alluvial plain and delta of the Ganges (Padma)–Brahmaputra (Jamuna)–Meghna river system, which empties into the Bay of Bengal, the largest estuarine delta in the world. The highest elevation is 1,230m (Keokradong) and the lowest 0m at the Indian Ocean. The climate is tropical, with a monsoon season (June–September) during which heavy rainfall causes flooding in around one-third of the country each year; annual average rainfall is up to 2,339mm.

## HISTORY AND POLITICS

Bangladesh consists of what was the eastern part of Bengal province and the Sylhet district of Assam province in British India. On independence in 1947, these territories acceded to Pakistan, forming the province of East Bengal (renamed East Pakistan in 1955). Tensions between East and West Pakistan (separated by over 1,600km) caused the East to secede in 1971. After months of civil war, and following the intervention of India, Bangladesh achieved independence from Pakistan on 16 December 1971.

Since independence, Bangladesh has experienced periods of political instability, with a number of coups and attempted coups, the assassinations of President Mujibar Rahman (1975) and President Zia (1981), and periods of government under martial law (1975–8, 1982–6) or a state of emergency (1987–8, 2007–8).

Parliamentary government has remained in place since 1991, despite occasional boycotts of parliament. Governments have been formed, or coalition governments led, by one of the two main parties: the Bangladesh Nationalist Party (BNP), led by Khaleda Zia (widow of President Zia), in 1991–6 and 2001–6; and the Awami League, led by Sheikh Hasina Wajed (daughter of President Mujibar Rahman), in 1996–2001 and since January 2009.

The run-up to legislative elections in January 2014 was marred by widespread violent protests throughout the country after the BNP's Khaleda Zia declared a boycott of the election in response to Sheikh Hasina's refusal to hand over to a neutral caretaker government – a constitutional requirement overturned in 2011 – for the duration of the proceedings. The boycott resulted in a default win and overwhelming majority for the Awami League, with the party gaining 234 seats to the BNP's 34. Following the death of Zillur Rahman in March 2013, Abdul Hamid was elected president unopposed.

In January 2015 Khaleda Zia called for a general strike in order to bring about early elections; at least 50 people died and 1,000 were injured in the ensuing violence, with the BNP leader herself charged with instigating an arson attack that killed seven people.

The head of state is the president, elected by the legislature for a five-year term. The unicameral parliament, *Jatiya Sangsad*, has 345 members directly elected for a five-year term; under a 2004 constitutional amendment, 45 seats are reserved for women. The president appoints the prime minister, and the cabinet on the advice of the prime minister.

HEAD OF STATE
*President*, Abdul Hamid, *elected* 22 April 2013

SELECTED GOVERNMENT MEMBERS *as at April 2015*
*Prime Minister, Defence*, Sheikh Hasina Wajed
*Education*, Nurul Islam Nahid
*Finance*, Abu Maal Abdul Muhith

HIGH COMMISSION FOR THE PEOPLE'S REPUBLIC OF BANGLADESH
28 Queen's Gate, London SW7 5JA
T 020-7584 0081 E info@bhclondon.org.uk
W www.bhclondon.org.uk
*High Commissioner,* HE Abdul Hannan, *apptd* 2014

BRITISH HIGH COMMISSION
PO Box 6079, United Nations Road, Baridhara, Dhaka 1212
T (+880) (2) 882 2705 E press.dhaka@fco.gov.uk
W www.gov.uk/government/world/bangladesh
*High Commissioner,* HE Robert Gibson, CMG, *apptd* 2011

## DEFENCE

| *Aged 16–49, 2010 est* | *Males* | *Females* |
| --- | --- | --- |
| Available for military service | 36,520,491 | – |
| Fit for military service | 30,486,086 | 35,616,093 |

*Military expenditure* – US$2,010m (2014)

## ECONOMY AND TRADE

Bangladesh is a poor country, highly dependent on foreign aid. Nearly a third of the population lives below the poverty line. Many migrate to the Gulf states and South East Asia to find work, and their remittances, which total around 15 per cent of GDP, and garment manufacturing are the mainstay of the economy. These have fuelled the steady growth of 6 per cent a year since the mid-1990s, which has continued throughout the global downturn. However, inefficient state-owned enterprises, slow implementation of economic reforms, corruption, inflation and unreliable power supplies are obstacles to greater growth.

The service and industrial sectors account for 58.3 per cent and 26.5 per cent of GDP respectively. Although the smallest contributor to GDP (15.1 per cent), agriculture is the primary occupation of 45 per cent of the workforce. The chief industries are based on processing agricultural and fisheries products such as cotton, jute, tea, sugar, fish and seafood, the manufacture of textiles, garments, newsprint, cement and fertiliser, and light engineering. Most exports are to the USA and EU countries; imports come mainly from China, India and other Asian countries.

*GNI* – US$158,833m; US$1,010 per capita (2013)
*Annual average growth of GDP* – 6.2 per cent (2014 est)
*Inflation rate* – 7.5 per cent (2013 est)
*Population below poverty line* – 31.5 per cent (2010 est)
*Unemployment* – 4.2 per cent (2015 est)
*Total external debt* – US$33,200m (2014 est)
*Imports* – US$33,576m (2013)
*Exports* – US$27,033m (2013)

BALANCE OF PAYMENTS
*Trade* – US$6,543m deficit (2013)
*Current Account* – US$132m deficit (2014)

| Trade with UK | 2013 | 2014 |
| --- | --- | --- |
| Imports from UK | £140,821,633 | £130,873,537 |
| Exports to UK | £1,796,616,521 | £1,666,774,146 |

## COMMUNICATIONS

*Airports* – 16, including international airports at Dhaka, Cittagong and Sylhet

*Waterways* – Principal seaports are Chittagong and Mongla, and there are smaller ports in Chalna and Khulna; the 8,370km of waterways are a key element of the transport infrastructure, although reduced to 5,200km in dry season
*Roadways and railways* – 1,063km; 2,622km
*Telecommunications* – 962,000 fixed lines (2012) and 97.18 million mobile phone subscriptions (2011); there were 617,300 internet users in 2009
*Internet country code and IDD* – bd; 880 (from UK), 44 (to UK)
*Major broadcasters* – The government-run Bangladesh Television (BTV) and Radio Bangladesh are the principal channels; private broadcasters include ATN Bangla, Channel i and NTV
*Press* – Leading titles include English-language dailies *New Age*, *The New Nation* and *The Independent*, and the Bangla *Daily Prothom Alo*, *Dainik Ittefaq* and *Dainik Jugantor*
*WPFI score* – 42,95 (146)

## EDUCATION AND HEALTH

Education is compulsory and free for children aged 6 to 10, but drop-out rates are high.
*Literacy rate* – 83.2 per cent (2015 est)
*Gross enrolment ratio (percentage of relevant age group)* – primary 114 per cent (2011 est); secondary 54 per cent (2012 est); tertiary 13 per cent (2011 est)
*Health expenditure (per capita)* – US$32 (2013)
*Hospital beds (per 1,000 people)* – 0.6 (2011)
*Life expectancy (years)* – 70.65 (2014 est)
*Mortality rate* – 5.64 (2014 est)
*Birth rate* – 21.61 (201 est)
*Infant mortality rate* – 45.67 (2014 est)

# BARBADOS

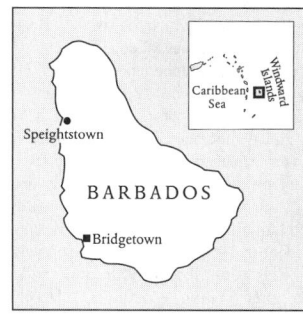

*Area* – 430 sq. km
*Capital* – Bridgetown, in the parish of St Michael; population, 122,000 (2011 est)
*Currency* – Barbados dollar (BD$) of 100 cents
*Population* – 290,604 rising at 0.31 per cent a year (2015 est)
*Religion* – Christian 75.5 per cent (Protestant 66.3 per cent, of which the largest denomination is Anglican), Rastafarian 1 per cent (est)
*Language* – English (official), Bajan
*Population density* – 662 per sq. km (2013)
*Urban population* – 45.4 per cent (2013)
*Median age (years)* – 37.6 (2014 est)
*National anthem* – 'In Plenty and in Time of Need'
*National day* – 30 November (Independence Day)
*Death penalty* – Retained (last used 1984)
*CPI score* – 74 (17)

## CLIMATE AND TERRAIN

Barbados is the most easterly of the Caribbean islands. The land rises gently to central highlands, and elevation extremes range from 336m (Mt Hillaby) to 0m (Atlantic Ocean). The climate is tropical with a wet season from July to November, when the island is subject to occasional hurricanes.

## HISTORY AND POLITICS

Early settlers were succeeded by the Arawaks and then the Caribs. The island was uninhabited when settled by the English in 1627 and was a crown colony from 1652, achieving self-government in 1961. It became an independent state on 30 November 1966.

Since independence, power has alternated between the two main political parties, the Barbados Labour Party (BLP) and the Democratic Labour Party (DLP). In the 2008 general election the DLP defeated the BLP and took office under David Thompson. He died in October 2010 and was succeeded as prime minister by his deputy, Freundel Stuart. In February 2013, the DLP and Stuart narrowly retained power, winning 16 of the 30 seats in the parliamentary elections.

The head of state is Queen Elizabeth II, represented by the governor-general. The bicameral parliament consists of a senate of 21 appointed members and a House of Assembly of 30 directly elected members; both chambers serve a five-year term.

There are 11 administrative areas (parishes): Christ Church, St Andrew, St George, St James, St John, St Joseph, St Lucy, St Michael, St Peter, St Philip and St Thomas.

*Governor-General,* HE Sir Elliott Belgrave, GCMG, *apptd* June 2012

SELECTED GOVERNMENT MEMBERS *as at April 2015*
*Prime Minister,* Freundel Stuart
*Attorney-General, Home Affairs,* Adriel Brathwaite
*Finance,* Christopher Sinckler
*Foreign Affairs,* Maxine McClean

BARBADOS HIGH COMMISSION
1 Great Russell Street, London WC1B 3ND
T 020-7299 7150 E london@foreign.gov.bb
*High Commissioner,* HE Guy Arlington Hewitt, *apptd* 2014

BRITISH HIGH COMMISSION
PO Box 676, Lower Collymore Rock, Bridgetown
T (+1) (246) 430 7800 E ukinbarbados@fco.gov.uk
W www.gov.uk/government/world/barbados
*High Commissioner,* HE Victoria Dean, *apptd* 2013

## DEFENCE

| *Aged 16–49, 2010 est* | *Males* | *Females* |
| --- | --- | --- |
| Available for military service | 73,820 | 73,835 |
| Fit for military service | 58,125 | 58,016 |

*Military expenditure* – US$20.9m (2013)

## ECONOMY AND TRADE

Historically, Barbados' chief products were sugar, rum and molasses. Since independence, tourism, offshore finance and information services, and light industry have become more significant. The global economic downturn affected tourism in particular, causing the economy to enter recession in 2009. After achieving slow growth between 2010 and 2012, the economy contracted in 2013 and 2014.

The main trading partners are Trinidad and Tobago, the USA and Saint Lucia. Chief exports are manufactured goods, sugar and molasses, rum, other food and beverages, chemicals and electronic components.

*GNI* – US$4,270m; US$15,080 per capita (2012)
*Annual average growth of GDP* – –0.6 per cent (2014 est)
*Inflation rate* – 1.8 per cent (2013 est)
*Unemployment* – 13.1 per cent (2015 est)
*Total external debt* – US$4,490m (2012 est)
*Imports* – US$1,759m (2013)
*Exports* – US$463m (2013)

BALANCE OF PAYMENTS
*Trade* – US$1,296m deficit (2013)
*Current Account* – US$394m deficit (2014 est)

| Trade with UK | 2013 | 2014 |
| --- | --- | --- |
| Imports from UK | £42,721,556 | £33,954,206 |
| Exports to UK | £11,026,618 | £6,043,843 |

## COMMUNICATIONS
*Airports* – The Grantley Adams International near Bridgetown is the only international airport on the island
*Waterways* – Bridgetown, the only port of entry, has a deep-water harbour
*Roadways* – There are 1,600km of roadways, all of which are surfaced
*Telecommunications* – 144,000 fixed lines and 347,000 mobile phone subscriptions (2012); there were 188,000 internet users in 2008
*Internet country code and IDD* – bb; 1 246 (from UK), 011 44 (to UK)
*Major broadcasters* – Caribbean Broadcasting Corporation (CBC) is the sole TV station and operates a number of public and commercial channels
*Press* – Major newspapers include *The Barbados Advocate* and *The Nation*

## EDUCATION AND HEALTH
Education is free in government schools at primary (ages four to 11), secondary (ages 11 to 18) and tertiary levels, and is compulsory until the age of 16.
*Literacy rate* – 99.7 per cent (2004 est)
*Gross enrolment ratio (percentage of relevant age group)* – primary 105 per cent; secondary 105 per cent; tertiary 61 per cent (2011 est)
*Health expenditure (per capita)* – US$1,007 (2015)
*Hospital beds (per 1,000 people)* – 6.2 (2012)
*Life expectancy (years)* – 74.99 (2014 est)
*Mortality rate* – 8.41 (2014 est)
*Birth rate* – 11.97 (2014 est)
*Infant mortality rate* – 10.93 (2014 est)
*HIV/AIDS adult prevalence* – 0.1 per cent (2013 est)

# BELARUS

*Respublika Byelarus'* – *Republic of Belarus*

*Area* – 207,600 sq. km
*Capital* – Minsk (the administrative centre of the CIS); population, 1,910,000 (2015 est)
*Major cities* – Brest, Homyel, Hrodna, Mahilyow, Vitsyebsk
*Currency* – Belarusian rouble (Br) of 100 kopeks
*Population* – 9,589,689 falling at 0.2 per cent a year (2015 est); Belarusian (83.7 per cent), Russian (8.3 per cent), Polish (3.1 per cent), Ukrainian (1.7 per cent) (2009)
*Religion* – Christian (Belarusian Orthodox 68 per cent, Roman Catholic 14 per cent) (est)
*Language* – Belarusian, Russian (both official), Polish, Ukrainian
*Population density* – 47 per sq. km (2013)
*Urban population* – 75.9 per cent (2013 est)
*Median age (years)* – 39.4 (2014 est)
*National anthem* – 'My Belarusy' ['We, the Belarusians']
*National day* – 3 July (Independence Day)
*Death penalty* – Retained
*CPI score* – 31 (119)

## CLIMATE AND TERRAIN
Much of Belarus is a plain, with many lakes, swamps and marshes, and forest cover is around 43 per cent. Its main rivers are the upper reaches of the Dnieper, the Nyoman and the Western Dvina. Elevation extremes range from 346m (Dzyarzhynskaya Hara) to 90m (Nyoman river). The climate is continental, with cold winters and warm, humid summers.

## HISTORY AND POLITICS
In the 13th century the area was absorbed into the grand duchy of Lithuania, which entered into the Polish Commonwealth from the 16th until the 18th centuries. Following the partitions of Poland in the late 18th century it became part of the expanding Russian Empire. It was the site of fierce fighting during the First World War, but its brief period of independence in 1918 ended, after a war over the territory, in partition between Poland and the USSR. The Polish territory was largely regained by the USSR after the Second World War, which devastated Belarus; over a quarter of the population was killed.

Belarus declared its independence from the USSR after a failed coup in Moscow in 1991. Stanislav Shuskevich became Belarusian leader at the head of a coalition of communists and democrats, but he was forced to resign in 1994. He was replaced by Gen. Mecheslav Grib, who pursued closer political, economic and trade relations with Russia.

Alexander Lukashenko was elected to the newly created post of president in 1994. Since coming to power, President Lukashenko has opposed privatisation and economic liberalisation (precipitating economic collapse), subverted political processes and repressed opposition and the media, creating what Condoleezza Rice, the former US Secretary of State, referred to in 2005 as the 'last dictatorship in Europe'. The EU and USA have imposed sanctions several times because of the regime's poor human rights record and obstructiveness towards international election monitors. In the 2010 presidential election, President Lukashenko was returned with 79.7 per cent of the vote. In the 2010 legislative elections, all the seats were won by the president's supporters. The result prompted mass protests and arrests amid claims the election had been rigged. In September, opposition parties boycotted the parliamentary elections, asserting the elections were undemocratic. In December 2014, President Lukashenko dismissed Prime Minister Mikhail Myasnikovich and instigated the biggest cabinet reshuffle since 2010 after the government failed to meet economic targets, appointing a new prime minister, Andrey Kabyakow, later the same month.

Under the 1994 constitution, the president is directly elected for a five-year term; this was renewable only once until a 2004 constitutional amendment removed the two-term limit. The legislature is the bicameral National Assembly, comprising a 110-member House of Representatives (lower chamber), directly elected for a four-year term, and a Council of the Republic, with 56 members elected by regional *soviets* (councils) and eight members appointed by the president, for a four-year term.

The president may appoint half the members of the constitutional court and the electoral commission.

## HEAD OF STATE

*President,* Alexander Lukashenko, *elected* 10 July 1994, *re-elected* 2001, 2006, 2010

## SELECTED GOVERNMENT MEMBERS *as at April 2015*

*Prime Minister,* Andrey Kabyakow
*First Deputy Prime Minister,* Vasily Matyushevsky
*Deputy Prime Ministers,* Natalya Kachanova; Anatoly Kalinin; Mikhail Rusyy; Vladimir Semashko
*Foreign Affairs,* Vladimir Makey

## EMBASSY OF THE REPUBLIC OF BELARUS

6 Kensington Court, London W8 5DL
T 020-7937 3288 E uk.london@mfa.gov.by
W http://uk.mfa.gov.by/en
*Ambassador Extraordinary and Plenipotentiary,* HE Sergei Aleinik, *apptd* 2013

## BRITISH EMBASSY

37 Karl Marx Street, 220030 Minsk
T (+375) (172) 298 200 E ukin.belarus@fconet.fco.gov.uk
W www.gov.uk/government/world/belarus
*Ambassador Extraordinary and Plenipotentiary,* HE Bruce Bucknell, *apptd* 2012

## FOREIGN RELATIONS

Belarus was a founder member of the Commonwealth of Independent States (CIS) in 1991. President Lukashenko, who opposed the break-up of the Soviet Union, has sought closer relations with Russia. In 1997 a treaty was signed with Russia providing for closer political and economic integration, and in 1999 the two countries signed a treaty that committed them to becoming a confederal state. In 2011 Belarus formed an economic union with Kazakhstan and Russia, removing tariffs and customs control along their shared borders. In January 2015, Belarus and Russia became founding members of the Eurasian Economic Union (EEU), establishing a common market, commission, bank and supranational court between the two countries, Armenia and Kazakhstan (*see* Events).

## DEFENCE

| Aged 16–49, 2010 est | Males | Females |
|---|---|---|
| Available for military service | 2,401,785 | 2,429,653 |
| Fit for military service | 1,693,626 | 2,012,401 |

*Military expenditure* – US$979m (2014)
*Conscription* – 18–27 years of age; 12–18 months, dependent on level of education

## ECONOMY AND TRADE

Although prosperous under the Soviet regime, the country experienced a dramatic decline after independence. Since 1994 President Lukashenko has resisted structural reform of the economy and reimposed state control of prices and currency exchange rates. Some privatised businesses have been renationalised, and the small private sector is subject to pressure and intervention by the state, circumstances that continue to discourage foreign investment. The country is highly dependent on Russia for its energy needs, and economic growth in recent years was largely based on the re-export at market prices of heavily discounted oil and natural gas from Russia. Russian economic dominance over Belarus further increased in November 2011 in a deal which agreed the sale of oil to Belarus at a discount of 60 per cent below other European states in exchange for Russian ownership of Belarusian oil pipeline firm Beltransgaz, and again in January 2013 when a US$2 billion loan was announced. In January 2014, Russia agreed to provide Belarus with a further loan of US$2bn (£1.36bn) in order to help Belarus make debt service payments of US$3.1bn (£2.11bn), due that year.

The main economic activities are oil-refining and the manufacture of heavy machinery and equipment, vehicles, domestic appliances, chemicals and textiles. These commodities, along with oil, mineral products, metals and foodstuffs, constitute the main exports and the main imports. The main trading partner is Russia.

*GNI* – US$63,678m; US$6,730 per capita (2013)
*Average annual growth of GDP* – 0.9 per cent (2014 est)
*Inflation rate* – 18.3 per cent (2013 est)
*Population below poverty line* – 5.5 per cent (2013 est)
*Unemployment* – 5.8 per cent (2015 est)
*Total external debt* – US$40,330m (2014 est)
*Imports* – US$42,999m (2013)
*Exports* – US$37,232m (2013)

## BALANCE OF PAYMENTS

*Trade* – US$5,766m deficit (2013)
*Current Account* – US$4,644m deficit (2014 est)

| Trade with UK | 2013 | 2014 |
|---|---|---|
| Imports from UK | £92,845,271 | £84,047,346 |
| Exports to UK | £73,977,067 | £53,534,056 |

## COMMUNICATIONS

*Airports* – 33, including an international airport in Minsk plus six other major domestic airports
*Waterways* – Belarus has an extensive 2,500km canal and river system, but its use is limited by shallowness or remoteness
*Roadways and railways* – 74,651km; 5,537km
*Telecommunications* – 4.41 million fixed lines and 10.67 million mobile phone subscriptions (2012); there were 2.64 million internet users in 2009
*Internet code and IDD* – by; 375 (from UK), 810 44 (to UK)
*Major broadcasters* – The four national TV channels, including Belarussian TV, are state-run; the government-owned Belarussian Radio is the principal radio broadcaster. Exile groups operate radio stations and TV channels from Poland, such as Belsat (TV) and Radio Racja
*Press* – Major government newspapers include *Sovetskaya Belorussiya* (Russian-language daily) and *Zvyazda* (Belarussian-language daily); independent titles, such as *Narodnaya Volya,* operate but face harassment
*WPFI score* – 47,98 (157)

## EDUCATION AND HEALTH

Education is compulsory between the ages of six and 15.
*Literacy rate* – 99.8 per cent (2015 est)
*Gross enrolment ratio (percentage of relevant age group)* – primary 99 per cent; secondary 106 per cent; tertiary 91 per cent (2012 est)
*Health expenditure (per capita)* – US$3,463 (2013)

*Hospital beds (per 1,000 people)* – 11.3 (2011)
*Life expectancy (years)* – 72.15 (2014 est)
*Mortality rate* – 13.51 (2014 est)
*Birth rate* – 10.86 (2014 est)
*Infant mortality rate* – 3.64 (2014 est)

# BELGIUM

*Koninkrijk Belgie/Royaume de Belgique/Königreich Belgien –*
*Kingdom of Belgium*

*Area* – 30,528 sq. km
*Capital* – Brussels; population, 2,089,000 (2015 est)
*Major cities* – Antwerp, Bruges, Charleroi, Ghent, Liège
*Currency* – Euro (€) of 100 cents
*Population* – 11,323,973 rising at 0.76 per cent a year
   (2015 est); Fleming (58 per cent), Walloon (31 per cent)
   (est)
*Religion* – Christian (Roman Catholic 50 per cent) (est)
*Language* – Dutch (Flemish), French, German (all official)
*Population density* – 370 per sq. km (2013)
*Urban population* – 97.5 per cent (2013 est)
*Median age (years)* – 43.1 (2014 est)
*National anthem* – 'La Brabançonne' ['The Song of Brabant']
*National day* – 21 July (Accession of King Leopold I, 1831)
*Death penalty* – Abolished for all crimes (since 1996)
*CPI score* – 76 (15)

## CLIMATE AND TERRAIN

There are two distinct regions: the west is generally low-lying and fertile, while in the east the forested hills of the Ardennes are more rugged with poorer soil. Elevation extremes range from 694m (Signal de Botrange) to 0m on the North Sea coast. The polders near the coast, which are protected against floods by dykes, cover an area of around 500 sq. km. Average temperatures range from 3.2°C in January to 18.3°C in July and August.

## POLITICS

Belgium is a constitutional monarchy with a hereditary monarch as head of state. Amendments to the constitution since 1968 have devolved power to the regions. The national government retains competence only in foreign and defence policies, the national budget and monetary policy, social security, and the judicial, legal and penal systems. The bicameral legislature, the Federal Chambers, consists of a senate and a Chamber of Representatives. The latter has 150 members, directly elected by proportional representation for a four-year term. From 2014 the senate had 60 members, indirectly elected by Parliament and the regions.

There are three language communities: Flemish, Francophone and Germanophone. Each community has its own assembly, which elects the community government. At this level, Flanders is covered by the Flemish community assembly; most of Wallonia is covered by the Francophone community assembly, and areas of Wallonia lying in the German-speaking communities of Eupen and Malmédy are covered by the Germanophone community assembly; Brussels is covered by a joint community commission of the Flemish and Francophone community assemblies.

At regional level, Belgium is divided into three: Brussels capital region, the Flemish region and the Walloon region. Each region has its own directly elected assembly and government.

The ten provinces of Belgium are: Antwerp, East Flanders, Flemish Brabant, Hainaut, Liège, Limburg, Luxembourg, Namur, Walloon Brabant and West Flanders. In addition, 589 communes form the lowest level of local government.

Prince Philippe ascended the throne in July 2013 following the abdication of his father, King Albert, due to ill health. In the May 2014 legislative elections, the New Flemish Alliance emerged as the largest party, as it had done in the 2010 elections, and was nominated to form a ruling coalition. In October, following months of negotiations, Charles Michel of the centre-right Francophone Reform Movement party formed a coalition government with the Flemish nationalist New Flemish Alliance.

*Minister-President of the Brussels Capital Government,* Rudi
   Vervoort
*Minister-President of the Flemish Community and Flemish
   Region,* Geert Bourgeois
*Minister-President of the French Community and Walloon
   Region,* Paul Magnette
*Minister-President of the German-speaking Community,* Oliver
   Paasch

HEAD OF STATE
*HM The King of the Belgians,* King Philippe, *born* 15 April
   1960, *acceded* 21 July 2013
*Heir,* HRH Princess Elisabeth, *born* 25 October 2001

SELECTED GOVERNMENT MEMBERS *as at April 2015*
*Prime Minister,* Charles Michel
*Deputy Prime Ministers,* Alexander De Croo *(Development)*;
   Kris Peeters *(Economy)*; Jan Jambon *(Interior)*; Didier
   Reynders *(Foreign Affairs)*

EMBASSY OF BELGIUM
17 Grosvenor Crescent, London SW1X 7EE
T 020-7470 3700 E london@diplobel.fed.be
W www.diplomatie.be/london
*Ambassador Extraordinary and Plenipotentiary,* HE Guy
   Trouveroy, *apptd* 2014

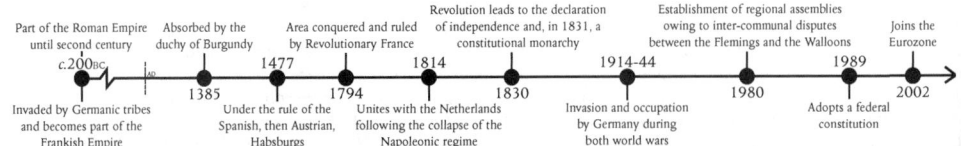

Revolution leads to the declaration
Part of the Roman Empire   Absorbed by the   Area conquered and ruled   of independence and, in 1831, a        Establishment of regional assemblies
until second century        duchy of Burgundy   by Revolutionary France   constitutional monarchy        owing to inter-communal disputes        Joins the
                                                                                          between the Flemings and the Walloons    Eurozone
   c.200BC                           1477                 1814              1914-44                            1989
              AD
                   1385                 1794                  1830                          1980                            2002
Invaded by Germanic tribes   Under the rule of the   Unites with the Netherlands   Invasion and occupation   Adopts a federal
and becomes part of the      Spanish, then Austrian,   following the collapse of the   by Germany during        constitution
Frankish Empire              Habsburgs               Napoleonic regime           both world wars

BRITISH EMBASSY
Avenue d'Auderghem 10, 1040 Brussels
T (+32) (2) 287 6211 E public.brussels@fco.gov.uk
W www.gov.uk/government/world/belgium
*Ambassador Extraordinary and Plenipotentiary,* HE Alison
Rose, *apptd* 2014

## DEFENCE
The headquarters of NATO, and of its Supreme Headquarters
Allied Powers Europe, are in Belgium.

| Aged 16–49, 2010 est | Males | Females |
| --- | --- | --- |
| Available for military service | 2,359,232 | 2,291,689 |
| Fit for military service | 1,934,957 | 1,877,268 |

*Military expenditure* – US$5,190m (2014)

## ECONOMY AND TRADE
Belgium has a free-market economy with highly diversified
industrial and commercial sectors. With few natural
resources, industry is based largely on processing imported
raw materials for export. This makes the economy dependent
on the state of world markets; public debt was predicted to
reach around 106 per cent of GDP in 2015. Though the
economy grew 0.9 per cent in 2014, the fastest rate for three
years, Belgium's high level of integration into the struggling
Eurozone, spiralling labour costs and low productivity
represent significant threats to future growth. The country's
regional and political divide is reflected in the Belgian
economy. Flanders, including the major ports of Antwerp,
Brussels and Ghent, contributes 57 per cent of GDP and has
higher levels of employment and productivity. Wallonia, the
richer portion of the country in the 19th century, has become
poorer due to the declining importance of its heavy industry,
although Liège and Charleroi remain important industrial
centres.

Principal industries are engineering and metal products,
vehicle assembly, transport equipment, scientific instruments,
food processing and beverages, chemicals, base metals,
textiles, glass, petroleum and diamonds. Industry accounts
for 21.1 per cent of GDP and 25 per cent of employment.
There is a large service sector, partly owing to the location
in Brussels of EU institutions, NATO headquarters and a
number of other international organisations. The service
sector accounts for 78.1 per cent of GDP. There is a small
agricultural sector (0.8 per cent of GDP).

Around three-quarters of trade is with other EU states,
especially Germany, France and the Netherlands. External
trade statistics relate to Luxembourg as well as Belgium, as
the two countries formed an economic union in 1921.

*GNI* – US$518,241m; US$46,290 per capita (2013)
*Annual average growth of GDP* – 1 per cent (2014 est)
*Inflation rate* – 1.1 per cent (2013 est)
*Population below poverty line* – 15.2 per cent (2007 est)
*Unemployment* – 8.7 per cent (2015 est)
*Total external debt* – US$1,424,000m (2012 est)
*Imports* – US$451,921m (2013)
*Exports* – US$467,831m (2013)

BALANCE OF PAYMENTS
*Trade* – US$15,910,145m surplus (2013)
*Current Account* – US$8,714m surplus (2014)

| Trade with UK | 2013 | 2014 |
| --- | --- | --- |
| Imports from UK | £13,606,471,539 | £12,608,646,464 |
| Exports to UK | £20,126,790,706 | £20,613,278,124 |

## COMMUNICATIONS
*Airports* – 26; the main airports are at Antwerp, Brussels,
Liège and Ostend-Bruges

*Waterways* – There are 2,043km of inland waterways, of
which 1,528km are in regular commercial use; ship canals
and the Meuse (Maas), Sambre and Schelde rivers form an
integral part of the network. The major inland ports are
located in Brussels, Ghent and Antwerp
*Roadways* – 120,514km, including 1,756km of motorways
*Railways* – The rail system is run by Belgian National
Railways (NMBS/SNCB) and, at 3,233km, the network is
one of the densest in the world
*Telecommunications* – 4.631 million main lines and 12.88
million mobile phone subscriptions (2012); there were 8.113
million internet users in 2009
*Internet code and IDD* – be; 32 (from UK), 44 (to UK)
*Major broadcasters* – Television and radio broadcasters
include French-language RTBF and Dutch-language VRT
*Press* – Major newspapers include Dutch-language daily *Het
Nieuwsblad* and French-language daily *Le Soir*
*WPFI score* – 11,98 (15)

## EDUCATION AND HEALTH
Nursery schools provide free education for children from
two-and-a-half to six years of age. The official school-
leaving age is 18.
*Gross enrolment ratio (percentage of relevant age group)* –
primary 103 per cent; secondary 107 per cent; tertiary
71 per cent (2012 est)
*Health expenditure (per capita)* – US$5,093 (2013)
*Hospital beds (per 1,000 people)* – 6.5 (2012)
*Life expectancy (years)* – 79.92 (2014 est)
*Mortality rate* – 10.76 (2014 est)
*Birth rate* – 9.99 (2014 est)
*Infant mortality rate* – 4.18 (2014 est)

# BELIZE

*Area* – 22,966 sq. km
*Capital* – Belmopan; population, 14,000 (2011 est)
*Major towns* – Belize City (the former capital), Orange Walk,
San Ignacio
*Currency* – Belize dollar (BZ$) of 100 cents; the Belize dollar
is tied to the US dollar
*Population* – 347,369 rising at 0.87 per cent a year
(2015 est); mestizo (48.7 per cent), Creole (24.9 per cent),
Maya (10.6 per cent), Garifuna (6.1 per cent) (2000)
*Religion* – Christian 71.8 per cent (of which Roman Catholic
39.3 per cent) (est)
*Language* – English (official), Spanish, Creole, Mayan
dialects, Garifuna, German
*Population density* – 15 per sq. km (2013)
*Urban population* – 44.3 per cent (2013 est)
*Median age (years)* – 21.8 (2014 est)
*National anthem* – 'Land of the Free'

*National day* – 21 September (Independence Day)
*Death penalty* – Retained (last used 1985)

## CLIMATE AND TERRAIN

Belize comprises a large coastal plain, swamps in the north, fertile land in the south and the Maya Mountains in the south-west. The highest point of elevation is 1,160m (Doyle's Delight), the lowest is 0m (Caribbean Sea). Part of the Mesoamerican barrier reef system, the western hemisphere's longest, runs nearly the entire length of the coastline. The climate is subtropical but is cooled by trade winds. The hurricane season is from May to November.

## HISTORY AND POLITICS

Numerous ruins in the area indicate that Belize was heavily populated by the Maya. The first British settlement was established in 1638 but was subject to repeated attacks by the Spanish, who claimed sovereignty until their defeat by the British navy and settlers in 1798. In 1862 the settlement was given colonial status as British Honduras. The colony became self-governing in 1964. In 1973 it was renamed Belize and it was granted independence on 21 September 1981.

Since independence, power has alternated between two main political parties, the People's United Party (PUP) and the United Democratic Party (UDP). The UDP lost seats to the PUP in the 2012 legislative elections, but retained its overall majority under prime minister Dean Barrow.

Under the 1981 constitution, the head of state is Queen Elizabeth II, represented by a governor-general. There is a bicameral National Assembly, comprising a House of Representatives with 31 members directly elected for a five-year term, and a senate of 13 members appointed by the governor-general, including six on the advice of the prime minister, three on the advice of the opposition leader and three representing various sectors of society; a referendum in 2008 approved the reform of the senate into an elected chamber, effective from the next elections. The prime minister is appointed by the governor-general and is responsible to the legislature.

*Governor-General*, HE Sir Colville Young, GCMG, *apptd* 17 November 1993

SELECTED GOVERNMENT MEMBERS *as at April 2015*
*Prime Minister, Finance*, Dean Barrow
*Deputy Prime Minister*, Gaspar Vega
*Foreign Affairs, Attorney General*, Wilfred Elrington

BELIZE HIGH COMMISSION
3rd Floor, 45 Crawford Place, London W1H 4LP
T 020-7723 3603 E info@belizehighcommission.co.uk
W www.belizehighcommission.co.uk
*High Commissioner*, HE Perla Maria Perdomo, *apptd* 2012

BRITISH HIGH COMMISSION
North Ring Road, Melhado Parade, PO Box 91, Belmopan
T (+501) 822 2981 E brithicom@btl.net
W www.gov.uk/government/world/belize
*High Commissioner*, HE Peter Hughes, OBE, *apptd* 2013

FOREIGN RELATIONS
There is a longstanding territorial dispute with Guatemala, which claims the southern part of Belize. Following years of negotiations, both countries were due to hold simultaneous referenda in October 2013 as to whether the dispute should be presented to the International Court of Justice, but the referenda were later suspended and were due to be carried

out in 2015. In February 2015, 37 Belizeans were arrested by Guatemalan authorities after they took part in an excursion into the disputed territory.

## DEFENCE

| Aged 16–49, 2010 est | Males | Females |
| --- | --- | --- |
| Available for military service | 81,284 | 79,185 |
| Fit for military service | 59,431 | 57,221 |

*Military expenditure* – US$17.6m (2014)

## ECONOMY AND TRADE

The economy grew steadily from 1999 to 2007, bolstered from 2006 by commercial exploitation of oil reserves. It contracted sharply in 2009 owing to the global downturn, natural disasters and the drop in international oil prices but started to recover in 2010. From 2010–12 the economy grew at a rate of 2 per cent per year and then by 2.5 per cent in 2013. In January 2013 the government announced the restructure of its US$544m commercial external debt, or 'superbond', on which it defaulted in 2012. Oil output has declined since 2011 and is expected to negatively affect future growth.

The services sector has grown as tourism has developed, and accounts for around 70.9 per cent of GDP; industry contributes around 16 per cent, and agriculture and fisheries around 13.1 per cent. The main industries apart from tourism are garment manufacturing, food processing, construction and oil production. The chief trading partners are the USA, the UK and Germany. The major exports are sugar, bananas, citrus fruits and juice, garments, shrimp, fish products, molasses, timber and crude oil. Imports are primarily machinery and transport equipment, manufactured goods, fuel, chemicals, pharmaceuticals, food, beverages and tobacco.
*GNI* – US$1,496m; US$4,510 per capita (2013)
*Annual average growth of GDP* – 2 per cent (2014 est)
*Inflation rate* – 0.7 per cent (2013 est)
*Population below poverty line* – 41 per cent (2013 est)
*Unemployment* – 8.2 per cent (2015 est)
*Total external debt* – US$1,240m (2014 est)
*Imports* – US$930m (2013)
*Exports* – US$315m (2013)

BALANCE OF PAYMENTS
*Trade* – US$616m deficit (2013)
*Current Account* – US$97m deficit (2014 est)

| Trade with UK | 2013 | 2014 |
| --- | --- | --- |
| Imports from UK | £8,618,556 | £7,682,887 |
| Exports to UK | £72,223,351 | £57,991,549 |

## COMMUNICATIONS

*Airports* – Six, including the international airport at Belize City
*Waterways* – Although there are 825km of waterways, these are only accessible by small craft
*Roadways* – There are 488km of surfaced roads
*Telecommunications* – 25,400 fixed lines and 164,200 mobile phone subscriptions (2012); there were 36,000 internet users in 2009
*Internet code and IDD* – bz; 501 (from UK), 44 (to UK)
*Major broadcasters* – Commercial broadcasters include Channels 5 and 7 (TV), Love FM and Krem FM (radio); in 2014, a court approved the nationalisation of Belize Telemedia, the country's largest telecoms provider
*Press* – The country has no daily newspapers
*WPFI score* – 18,54 (30)

# EDUCATION AND HEALTH
Education is free and compulsory for eight years.
*Gross enrolment ratio (percentage of relevant age group)* –
primary 121 per cent; secondary 84 per cent; tertiary
26 per cent (2012 est)
*Hospital beds (per 1,000 people)* – 1.1 (2012)
*Life expectancy (years)* – 68.49 (2014 est)
*Mortality rate* – 5.95 (2014 est)
*Birth rate* – 25.14 (2014 est)
*Infant mortality rate* – 20.31 (2014 est)
*HIV/AIDS adult prevalence rate* – 0.3 per cent (2013 est)

# BENIN

*République du Bénin – Republic of Benin*

*Area* – 112,622 sq. km
*Capital* – Porto-Novo; population, 314,000 (2011 est);
Cotonou, the seat of government, population, 871,000
(2015 est)
*Major cities* – Abomey-Calavi, Bohicon, Djougou, Parakou
*Currency* – Franc CFA of 100 centimes
*Population* – 10,448,647 rising at 2.78 per cent a year
(2015 est); Fon (39.2 per cent), Adja (15.2 per cent),
Yoruba (12.3 per cent), Bariba (9.2 per cent), Peulh
(7 per cent), Ottamari (6.1 per cent), Yoa-Lokpa (4 per
cent), Dendi (2.5 per cent) (2002)
*Religion* – Christian 43 per cent (Roman Catholic
27 per cent, Protestant 10.4 per cent), Muslim 24 per cent
(predominantly Sunni), Vodun (voodoo) 17 per cent, other
indigenous religions 6 per cent. Many Christians and
Muslims also practise voodoo, which originated in this
region of Africa, or other indigenous religions
*Language* – French (official), Fon, Yoruba and other African
languages
*Population density* – 92 per sq. km (2013)
*Urban population* – 46.2 per cent (2013 est)
*Median age (years)* – 17.7 (2014 est)
*National anthem* – 'L'Aube Nouvelle' ['The Dawn of a New
Day']
*National day* – 1 August (Independence Day)
*Death penalty* – Abolished for all crimes (since 2012)
*CPI score* – 39 (80)
*Literacy rate* – 52.5 per cent (2015 est)

*Gross enrolment ratio (percentage of relevant age group)* –
primary 123 per cent (2012 est); secondary 48 per cent;
tertiary 12 per cent (2011 est)
*Health expenditure (per capita)* – US$37 (2013)
*Hospital beds (per 1,000 people)* – 0.5 (2010)
*Life expectancy (years)* – 61.07 (2014 est)
*Mortality rate* – 8.39 (2014 est)
*Birth rate* – 36.51 (2014 est)
*Infant mortality rate* – 57.09 (2014 est)
*HIV/AIDS adult prevalence* – 0.1 per cent (2013 est)

## CLIMATE AND TERRAIN
Benin has a short coastline of 121km on the Gulf of Guinea,
but extends northwards inland for over 700km. The coast is
a sandbar backed by lagoons that are fed by rivers. The land
rises to a central plateau with the Atacora massif in the north-
west, and falls to plains in the Niger basin in the north-east.
Elevation extremes range from 658m (Mt Sokbaro) to 0m
(Atlantic Ocean) at the lowest. The climate is tropical in the
south and semi-arid in the north.

## POLITICS
Under the 1990 constitution, the executive president is
directly elected for a five-year term, renewable only once.
The unicameral National Assembly has 83 members, directly
elected for a four-year term. The president appoints and
chairs the council of ministers.

The 2006 presidential election was won in the second
round by Thomas Yayi Boni, an independent candidate, and
he was re-elected in March 2011. In the 2011 legislative
election, the Cauri Forces for an Emerging Benin (FCBE),
which supports the president, remained the largest group
in the National Assembly, winning 41 seats. In August 2013
the president removed the post of prime minister from the
cabinet. The FCBE remained the largest party in the National
Assembly following legislative elections in April 2015.

### HEAD OF STATE
*President and Head of the Armed Forces,* Thomas Yayi Boni,
elected 19 March 2006, re-elected 2011

### SELECTED GOVERNMENT MEMBERS *as at
September 2015*
*Foreign Affairs,* Saliou Akadiri
*Defence,* Robert Théophile Yarou
*Economy, Finance,* Komi Koutché
*Interior, Security,* Placide Azande

### EMBASSY OF THE REPUBLIC OF BENIN
87 Avenue Victor Hugo, 75116 Paris, France
T (+33) 1 4500 9882 E ambassade.benin@gofornet.com
*Ambassador Extraordinary and Plenipotentiary,* HE
Jules-Armand Aniambossou, *apptd* 2014

### BRITISH HIGH COMMISSION
HE Peter Jones, *apptd* 2011, resident at Accra, Ghana

## DEFENCE

| Aged 16–49, 2010 est | Males | Females |
| --- | --- | --- |
| Available for military service | 2,095,373 | 2,038,351 |
| Fit for military service | 1,385,065 | 1,400,045 |

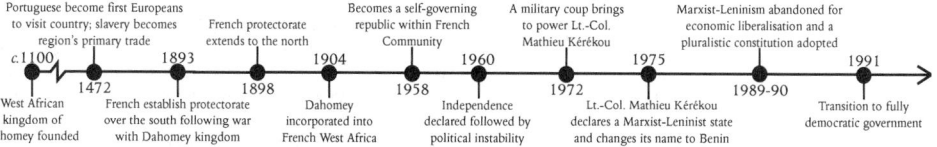

| | Portuguese become first Europeans to visit country; slavery becomes region's primary trade | French protectorate extends to the north | Becomes a self-governing republic within French Community | A military coup brings to power Lt.-Col. Mathieu Kérékou | Marxist-Leninism abandoned for economic liberalisation and a pluralistic constitution adopted | |
| --- | --- | --- | --- | --- | --- | --- |
| c.1100 | 1893 | | 1904 | 1960 | 1975 | 1991 |
| 1472 | 1898 | | 1958 | 1972 | 1989–90 | |
| West African kingdom of Dahomey founded | French establish protectorate over the south following war with Dahomey kingdom | Dahomey incorporated into French West Africa | Independence declared followed by political instability | Lt.-Col. Mathieu Kérékou declares a Marxist-Leninist state and changes its name to Benin | Transition to fully democratic government | |

*Military expenditure* – US$93m (2014)
*Conscription* – 18–35 years of age; 18 months (selective)

## ECONOMY AND TRADE

Although the economy is underdeveloped and still burdened by foreign debt, Benin has benefited from increased competitiveness and debt reduction or relief since its economic restructuring commenced. Privatisation of industries, including utilities, began in 2001 and economic growth has been steady since 2000. However, this has been outweighed by rapid population growth, and over a third of the population remains below the poverty line. The economy is based on agriculture, particularly cotton production, and re-export trade with neighbouring countries; customs receipts provide about half of government revenue, but much of the re-export trade operates outside the official economy and is unrecorded. Growth in the agricultural sector and revenue generated by the country's ports is expected to allow the economy to grow by 4.9 per cent in 2014 and 5.3 per cent in 2015.

Agriculture is mostly at subsistence level and contributes 31.8 per cent to GDP, declining recently as industry (12.3 per cent) and services (55.9 per cent) have developed. The main cash crops are cotton, cashew nuts, shea butter, palm products and seafood, and the principal industrial activities are textiles and food processing. The main trading partners are China (25 per cent of exports; 37.2 per cent of imports) and India, to which textiles and some of the cash crops are exported. The principal imports are food, capital goods and fuel.

*GNI* – US$8,155m; US$790 per capita (2013)
*Annual average growth of GDP* – 5.5 per cent (2014 est)
*Inflation rate* – 1 per cent (2013 est)
*Population below poverty line* – 36.2 per cent (2011 est)
*Total external debt* – US$2,458m (2014 est)
*Imports* – US$2,148m (2013)
*Exports* – US$1,154m (2013)

BALANCE OF PAYMENTS
*Trade* – US$995m deficit (2013)
*Current Account* – US$738m deficit (2014 est)

| Trade with UK | 2013 | 2014 |
| --- | --- | --- |
| Imports from UK | £70,180,970 | £63,223,674 |
| Exports to UK | £60,618 | £183,301 |

## COMMUNICATIONS

*Airports and waterways* – One, serving Cotonou, which is also the major seaport
*Roadways and railways* – 1,400km; 438km
*Telecommunications* – 156,700 fixed lines and 8.408 million mobile telephones in use (2012); there were 200,100 internet users in 2009
*Internet code and IDD* – bj; 229 (from UK), 44 (to UK)
*Major broadcasters* – Television Nationale and Radio Nationale are the official state broadcasters
*Press* – Dozens of newspapers and periodicals are published, including *Le Matinal*, *Fraternite* and *La Nation*; the International Press Institute had rated Benin as having one of West Africa's freest medias, though its ranking has decreased since the election of President Yayi in 2006
*WPFI score* – 29,24 (84)

# BHUTAN

*Druk Gyalkhap – Kingdom of Bhutan*

*Area* – 38,394 sq. km
*Capital* – Thimphu; population, 99,000 (2011 est)
*Major towns* – Geylegphug, Phodrang, Phuentsholing, Wangdue
*Currency* – Ngultrum (Nu) of 100 chetrum (Indian currency is also legal tender)
*Population* – 741,919 rising at 1.11 per cent a year (2015 est); Ngalop (Bhote) (50 per cent), ethnic Nepalese (35 per cent), indigenous or migrant tribes (15 per cent) (est)
*Religion* – Lamaistic Buddhist 75.3 per cent, Hindu 22.1 per cent (est)
*Language* – Dzongkha (official), Sharchhopka, Lhotshamkha
*Population density* – 20 per sq. km (2013)
*Urban population* – 37.1 per cent (2013 est)
*Median age (years)* – 26.2 (2014 est)
*National anthem* – 'Druk Tsendhen' ['The Thunder Dragon Kingdom']
*National day* – 17 December (inauguration of first hereditary monarch, 1907)
*Death penalty* – Abolished for all crimes (since 2004)
*CPI score* – 65 (30)
*Literacy rate* – 88.6 per cent (2015 est)
*Gross enrolment ratio (percentage of relevant age group)* – primary 112 per cent; secondary 74 per cent; tertiary 9 per cent (2012 est)
*Life expectancy (years)* – 68.98 (2014 est)
*Mortality rate* – 6.78 (2014 est)
*Birth rate* – 18.12 (2014 est)
*Infant mortality rate* – 37.89 (2014 est)

## CLIMATE AND TERRAIN

Bhutan is crossed by numerous rivers, and most of the population and cultivated land is found in the deep, fertile valleys of the highlands. There is a mountainous northern region that is infertile and sparsely populated, central highlands, and densely forested foothills in the south, which are mainly inhabited by Nepalese settlers and indigenous tribespeople. Extremes of elevation range from 7,570m (Gangkar Puensum) to 97m (Drangeme Chhu). The climate is determined by altitude, varying from subtropical in the south to alpine in the north. There is heavy annual rainfall of up to 1,000mm in the central valleys and 5,000mm in the south, which experiences monsoons from June to September.

## HISTORY AND POLITICS

Bhutan's external relations were under the guidance of Britain from the 19th century until 1947, and of India from 1947 until 2007; a 2007 revision of the friendship treaty between the two countries left Bhutan free to manage its external relations without India's advice.

Although the country has opened up since the 1970s, the monarchy has taken measures to preserve its indigenous culture and the environment, including the compulsory wearing of national dress and restrictions on tourism. The emphasis on the majority culture has caused tension with the sizeable Nepali minority. Many were denied citizenship in the 1990s and obliged to leave, which resulted in over 100,000 becoming refugees in Nepal, where most remain, living in refugee camps.

Bhutan's transition from an absolute monarchy to a democracy began in the 1950s, with the establishment of an elected legislature in 1953, and the transfer of powers from the king to the legislature in 1969 and 1989. The 2008 constitution formally established Bhutan as a parliamentary democracy with a constitutional monarchy, and provided for universal suffrage. King Jigme Singye Wangchuk abdicated in 2006 in favour of the Crown Prince.

In July 2013, elections to the National Assembly resulted in an unexpected win for the People's Democratic Party (PDP), which overtook the ruling Bhutan Peace and Prosperity Party (DPT) with a total of 32 seats to the DPT's 15. Tshering Tobgay, leader of the PDP, was appointed prime minister and formed a government.

Under the 2008 constitution, the head of state is a hereditary constitutional monarch, who must retire at the age of 65 and who may be required to abdicate by a two-thirds majority of the legislature. The bicameral parliament comprises a National Assembly with 47 directly elected members and a National Council with 25 members: 20 directly elected and five appointed by the king. Both chambers serve a fixed five-year term. The cabinet is appointed by the king on the recommendation of the prime minister, who may serve two parliamentary terms. In April 2013 a new National Council was elected.

### HEAD OF STATE

HM The King of Bhutan, Jigme Khesar Namgyal Wangchuk, born 21 February 1980, acceded 14 December 2006, crowned 6 November 2008

SELECTED GOVERNMENT MEMBERS as at April 2015
Prime Minister, Tshering Tobgay
Finance, Namgay Dorji
Foreign Affairs, Rinzin Dorje
Home and Cultural Affairs, Damcho Dorji

### BRITISH DEPUTY HIGH COMMISSION

British Deputy High Commissioner, Scott Furssedonn-Wood, apptd 2013, resident at Kolkata, India

### ECONOMY AND TRADE

The economy is being cautiously modernised but is still based on agriculture (14.4 per cent of GDP in 2014) in what is largely a self-sufficient rural society. Industry (41.6 per cent of GDP) is on a small scale, and the growing services sector (44 per cent of GDP) is mostly the result of increased tourism. Agriculture and animal husbandry, much at subsistence level, engage over 43 per cent of the workforce, although the mountainous terrain and heavy forest cover limit the area under cultivation. The construction of hydro-power dams designed to export electricity to India was expected to help increase growth from 5.2 per cent in 2014 to 7.5 per cent in 2015. The principal food crops are rice, cereals, vegetables and fruit, especially oranges. Industries include forestry, mining (limestone, gypsum, dolomite, graphite, coal), cement and calcium carbide production, food processing, distilling, hydro-electric power generation and tourism.

The main trading partners are India, China and South Korea. The principal exports are electricity (to India), ferrosilicon, cement, calcium carbide, copper wire, manganese and vegetable oil. The main imports are fuel and lubricants, passenger vehicles, machinery and parts, fabrics and rice.

GNI – US$1,758m; US$2,330 per capita (2013)
Annual average growth of GDP – 6.4 per cent (2014 est)
Inflation rate – 7 per cent (2013 est)
Population below poverty line – 12 per cent (2012 est)
Unemployment – 2.2 per cent (2015 est)
Total external debt – US$1,707m (2014 est)
Imports – US$1,038m (2013)
Exports – US$528m (2013)

BALANCE OF PAYMENTS
Trade – US$510m deficit (2013)
Current Account – US$459m deficit (2014 est)

| Trade with UK | 2013 | 2014 |
| --- | --- | --- |
| Imports from UK | £1,346,698 | £1,018,282 |
| Exports to UK | £35,711 | £262,776 |

### COMMUNICATIONS

Airports – Two, including an international airport in Paro
Roadways – 4,991km, including 622km of motorways
Telecommunications – 27,000 fixed lines and 560,000 mobile subscriptions (2012); there were 50,000 internet users in 2009
Internet code and IDD – bt; 975 (from UK), 44 (to UK)
Major broadcasters – Fear that outside influences would undermine Bhutanese culture meant that radio broadcasting began only in 1973, and television broadcasting and internet access in 1999; radio and television services are provided by the state-owned Bhutan Broadcasting Services (BBS)
Press – The country's two daily newspapers are Kuensel and Bhutan Today, which was launched in English in 2008
WPFI score – 32,65 (104)

# BOLIVIA

Estado Plurinacional de Bolivia – Plurinational State of Bolivia

Area – 1,098,581 sq. km
Capital – La Paz, the seat of government; population, 1,907,000 (2015 est); Sucre, the legal capital and seat of the judiciary; population, 397,000 (2015 est)
Major cities – Cochabamba, El Alto, Oruro, Santa Cruz
Currency – Boliviano ($b) of 100 centavos
Population – 10,800,882 rising at 1.56 per cent a year (2015 est); Quechua (30 per cent), mestizo (30 per cent), Aymara (25 per cent) (est)
Religion – Christian (Roman Catholic 95 per cent, Protestant 5 per cent) (est)

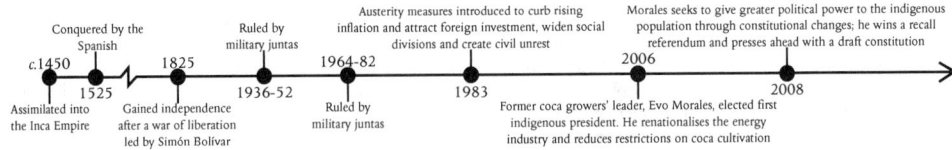

Conquered by the Spanish

*c.*1450

1525

Assimilated into the Inca Empire

Ruled by military juntas

1825

Gained independence after a war of liberation led by Simón Bolívar

1936-52

Austerity measures introduced to curb rising inflation and attract foreign investment, widen social divisions and create civil unrest

1964-82

Ruled by military juntas

1983

Former coca growers' leader, Evo Morales, elected first indigenous president. He renationalises the energy industry and reduces restrictions on coca cultivation

Morales seeks to give greater political power to the indigenous population through constitutional changes; he wins a recall referendum and presses ahead with a draft constitution

2006

2008

*Language* – Spanish, 36 indigenous languages (all official); Quechua and Aymara are the main indigenous languages
*Population density* – 10 per sq. km (2013)
*Urban population* – 67.7 per cent (2013 est)
*Median age (years)* – 23.4 (2014 est)
*National anthem* – 'Himno Nacional de Bolivia' ['National Anthem of Bolivia']
*National day* – 6 August (Independence Day)
*Death penalty* – Abolished for all crimes (since 2013)
*CPI score* – 35 (103)

## CLIMATE AND TERRAIN
Landlocked Bolivia's main topographical feature is its great central plateau, the Altiplano. Over 800km in length and at an average altitude of 3,750m above sea level, this plateau lies between two great chains of the Andes that traverse the country from north to south. Lake Titicaca, shared with Peru, lies on the Altiplano. Elevation extremes range from 6,542m (Nevado Sajama) to 90m (Rio Paraguay). The low-lying north and eastern plains are drained by the principal rivers, the Beni, Itenez, Madre de Dios and Mamoré. The climate varies dramatically between regions: on the lowlands of the Amazon basin, temperatures average around 25°C; above 500m on the Altiplano, conditions are subpolar. The south is prone to droughts. The wet season is October to April.

## POLITICS
The 1967 constitution was revised in 1994 and 2009. It provides for an executive president who is directly elected for a five-year term, which may be renewed once. The bicameral Plurinational Legislative Assembly, or National Congress, consists of a 36-member Chamber of Senators and a 130-member Chamber of Deputies; members of both chambers are directly elected for a five-year term.

President Morales, leader of the Movement Towards Socialism (MAS), took office in 2006 after winning the 2005 presidential elections, and was re-elected in 2009. After the Constitutional Court ruled that Morales could stand for a third term, the president ran in and subsequently won the October 2014 presidential elections. In the simultaneous legislative elections, MAS won large majorities in both houses, winning 84 out of 130 seats in the Chamber of Deputies and 25 out of 36 seats in the Chamber of Senators.

### HEAD OF STATE
*President,* Juan Evo Morales Ayma, *elected* 18 December 2005, *sworn in* 22 January 2006, *re-elected* 2009, *re-elected* 20 October 2015, *sworn in* 22 January 2015
*President of the Senate, Vice-President,* Alvaro Garcia Linera

### SELECTED GOVERNMENT MEMBERS *as at April 2015*
*Defence,* Reymi Ferreira
*Economy and Public Finance,* Luis Alberto Arce Catacora
*Foreign Affairs,* David Choquehuanca Cespedes

### BOLIVIAN EMBASSY
106 Eaton Square, London SW1W 9AD
**T** 020-7235 4248 **E** embol@bolivianembassy.co.uk
**W** www.bolivianembassy.co.uk
*Ambassador Extraordinary and Plenipotentiary,* HE Roberto Calzadilla, *apptd* 2014

### BRITISH EMBASSY
Avenida Arce 2732, La Paz
**T** (+591) (2) 243 3424 **E** BELaPaz@fco.gov.uk
**W** www.gov.uk/government/world/bolivia
*Ambassador Extraordinary and Plenipotentiary,* HE Ross Denny, *apptd* 2011

## DEFENCE

| Aged 16–49, 2010 est | Males | Females |
| --- | --- | --- |
| Available for military service | 2,472,490 | 2,535,768 |
| Fit for military service | 1,762,260 | 2,013,281 |

*Military expenditure* – US$487m (2014)
*Conscription* – 18–49 years of age; 12 months

## ECONOMY AND TRADE
The country is one of the most underdeveloped and least affluent in South America, although steady growth since the 1990s has lowered the proportion of the population living below the poverty line to less than half. The government of Evo Morales has implemented a wide-reaching socialist agenda since gaining power, nationalising 20 companies since 2006, including the oil and gas sectors. Economic performance has also improved, with the 6.5 per cent growth in GDP in 2013 the country's best performance in 30 years. Poverty has fallen from 38 per cent in 2005 to 24 per cent in 2011, and the country has amassed a large sovereign debt fund. The performance of the economy has drawn praise from some international organisations, including the IMF, despite Morales' criticism of mainstream financial institutions. The economy remains vulnerable to falling commodity prices, integration with the struggling Argentinian and Brazilian economies and a shortage in international investment caused by the country's nationalisation program.

Mining (principally for zinc, tin and gold) and smelting, natural gas and oil production, agriculture and textiles are the principal industries. Industry contributes 38.9 per cent of GDP, agriculture 13.1 per cent and services 48 per cent.

The main trading partners are Brazil, the USA, Argentina and Chile. Principal exports are natural gas, soya beans and soya products, crude oil, zinc ore and tin. The main imports are petroleum products, plastics, paper, aircraft and aircraft parts, processed food, vehicles and insecticides.
*GNI* – US$27,214m; US$2,550 per capita (2013)
*Annual average growth of GDP* – 5.8 per cent (2014 est)
*Inflation rate* – 5.7 per cent (2013 est)
*Population below poverty line* – 45 per cent (2011 est)
*Unemployment* – 3.2 per cent (2015 est)
*Total external debt* – US$8,073m (2014 est)
*Imports* – US$9,221m (2013)
*Exports* – US$11,189m (2013)

### BALANCE OF PAYMENTS
*Trade* – US$1,967m surplus (2013)
*Current Account* – US$252m surplus (2014 est)

| Trade with UK | 2013 | 2014 |
| --- | --- | --- |
| Imports from UK | £23,241,330 | £19,899,341 |
| Exports to UK | £15,953,636 | £31,969,354 |

## COMMUNICATIONS

*Airports* – 21, including four international airports serving the major cities

*Waterways* – There are 10,000km of commercially navigable waterways, with an inland port on the river Paraguay at the border with Brazil; Bolivia has free port privileges at seaports in Argentina, Brazil, Chile and Paraguay, and a lease on a free-trade zone at the Peruvian port of Ilo

*Roadways and railways* – 11,993km; the 3,652km of railways form an eastern network and an Andean network

*Telecommunications* – 880,600 fixed lines and 9.494 million mobile subscriptions (2012); there were 1.103 million internet users in 2009

*Internet code and IDD* – bo; 591 (from UK), 10/11/12/13 44 (to UK; depends on area and/or carrier)

*Major broadcasters* – Since the election of Evo Morales, the government has acquired a growing number of media outlets; the leading state-run broadcasters are Bolivia TV and Radio Patria Nueva. In 2013, a law was passed requiring that private media companies publish government messages, damaging the finances of many by limiting commercial advertising space

*Press* – Daily newspapers are published on a regional basis; leading titles include *La Razon* (La Paz), *Los Tiempos* (Cochabamba) and *El Deber* (Santa Cruz)

*WPFI score* – 31,29 (94)

## EDUCATION AND HEALTH

Elementary education is free and officially, though often not in practice, compulsory from the ages of six to 13.

*Literacy rate* – 99 per cent (2015 est)

*Gross enrolment ratio (percentage of relevant age group)* – primary 94 per cent; secondary 77 per cent (2011 est)

*Health expenditure (per capita)* – US$174 (2013)

*Hospital beds (per 1,000 people)* – 1.1 (2012)

*Life expectancy (years)* – 68.55 (2014 est)

*Mortality rate* – 6.59 (2014 est)

*Birth rate* – 23.28 (2014 est)

*Infant mortality rate* – 38.61 (2014 est)

# BOSNIA AND HERCEGOVINA

*Bosna i Hercegovina – Bosnia and Hercegovina*

*Area* – 51,197 sq. km

*Capital* – Sarajevo; population, 419,000 (2015 est)

*Major towns* – Banja Luka, Bijeljina, Mostar, Tuzla, Zenica

*Currency* – Convertible mark (KM) of 100 fenings

*Population* – 3,867,055 falling at 0.13 per cent a year (2015 est); Bosniak (48 per cent), Serb (37.1 per cent), Croat (14.3 per cent) (2000 est)

*Religion* – Muslim 40 per cent (predominantly Sunni), Christian (Serb Orthodox 31 per cent, Roman Catholic 15 per cent) (est)

*Language* – Bosnian, Croatian, Serbian (all official)

*Population density* – 75 per sq. km (2013)

*Urban population* – 49.3 per cent (2012 est)

*Median age (years)* – 40.8 (2014 est)

*National anthem* – 'Drzavna Himna Bosne i Hercegovine' ['National Anthem of Bosnia and Hercegovina']

*National day* – 25 November (formation of the anti-fascist resistance council, 1943)

*Death penalty* – Abolished for all crimes (since 2001)

*CPI score* – 39 (80)

*Literacy rate* – 99.7 per cent (2015 est)

*Gross enrolment ratio (percentage of relevant age group)* – primary 88 per cent; secondary 90 per cent (2010 est); tertiary 38 per cent (2012 est)

*Health expenditure (per capita)* – US$449 (2013)

*Hospital beds (per 1,000 people)* – 3.5 (2010)

*Life expectancy (years)* – 76.33 (2014 est)

*Mortality rate* – 9.64 (2014 est)

*Birth rate* – 8.89 (2014 est)

*Infant mortality rate* – 5.84 (2014 est)

## CLIMATE AND TERRAIN

The mountainous centre of the country is split by deep valleys, while the north is lower-lying, falling to the basin of the river Sava, which forms the northern border with Croatia. The Dinaric Alps lie along the western border. The highest point of elevation is 2,386m (Maglic), the lowest point is 0m (Adriatic Sea). Average temperatures range from 0°C in January to 20.3°C in July and August.

## POLITICS

Under the Dayton Peace Accord, the Bosnian republican (national) government is responsible for foreign affairs, currency, citizenship and immigration. The head of state is a collective presidency comprising a representative from each of the three main ethnic groups, all directly elected for a four-year term; the chair of the presidency rotates among its members every eight months. Legislative authority is vested in the bicameral Parliamentary Assembly, comprising a House of Peoples and a House of Representatives. Both houses have four-year terms. The House of Peoples has 15 members – ten from the Federation and five from the Republika Srpska – who are appointed from the House of Representatives. The House of Representatives has 42 members who are directly elected to the two constituent chambers: the Chamber of Deputies of the Federation, which has 28 members, and the Chamber of Deputies of the Republika Srpska, which has 14 members.

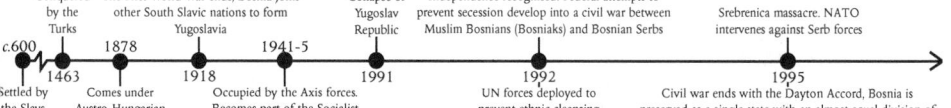

In the Bosniak–Croat Federation, the president and vice-president are elected by the Bosniak and Croat members of the House of Peoples for a four-year term; a second vice-president is elected to represent the Serb population. There is a bicameral Assembly comprising a 58-member House of Peoples elected on an ethnic basis and a House of Representatives with 98 directly elected members.

In the Republika Srpska, the president is directly elected for a four-year term. There is a unicameral People's Assembly with 83 members directly elected for a four-year term.

There is a national council of ministers and each of the entities also has its own executive. All appointments to the executives are in consultation with the UN High Representative, who has the power of veto.

The latest legislative elections were held in October 2010. In the federal legislature, the Bosniak-dominated Social Democratic Party (SDP) and the Serb-dominated Party of Independent Social Democrats (SNSD) won an equal number of seats, eventually leading to the formation of a coalition government led by Vjekoslav Bevanda, the Bosnian-Croat leader of the Croatian Democratic Union at the end of 2011. The SDP won a narrow majority in the Bosniak–Croat legislature and formed a coalition government under Nermin Niksic. In the Republika Srpska, the SNSD retained its majority and formed a new coalition government under Aleksandar Dzombic.

In the presidential elections in October 2014, Mladen Ivanic (Serb) and Dragan Covic (Croat) were elected to the collective federal presidency, and Bakir Izetbegovic was re-elected as the Bosniak member. Milorad Dodik was re-elected president of Republika Srpska. The presidential election in the Bosniak–Croat Federation in February 2015 was won by Marinko Cavara.

*REPUBLIC OF BOSNIA AND HERCEGOVINA*
HEADS OF STATE
*Presidency Members,* Dragan Covic *(Croat),* Mladen Ivanic *(Serb),* Bakir Izetbegovic *(Bosniak)*

SELECTED GOVERNMENT MEMBERS *as at April 2015*
*Chair of the Council of Ministers,* Denis Zvizdic
*Defence,* Marina Pendes
*Finance,* Vjekoslav Bevanda
*Foreign Affairs,* Igor Crnadak

*FEDERATION OF BOSNIA AND HERCEGOVINA*
*President,* Marinko Cavara
*Vice-Presidents,* Milan Dunovic; Melika Mahmutbegovic

SELECTED GOVERNMENT MEMBERS *as at April 2015*
*Prime Minister,* Fadil Novalic
*Deputy Prime Ministers,* Jelka Milicevic; Aleksander Remetic
*Interior,* Aljosa Campara

*REPUBLIKA SRPSKA*
*President,* Milorad Dodik
*Vice-Presidents,* Josip Jerkovic; Ramiz Salkic

SELECTED GOVERNMENT MEMBERS *as at April 2015*
*Prime Minister,* Zeljka Cvijanovic
*Finance,* Zoran Tegeltija
*Interior,* Dragan Lukac

OFFICE OF THE UN HIGH REPRESENTATIVE/EU SPECIAL REPRESENTATIVE
*UN High Representative,* Dr Valentin Inzko, *apptd* 2009
*EU Special Representative,* Lars-Gunnar Wigemark, *apptd* 2015

EMBASSY OF BOSNIA AND HERCEGOVINA
5–7 Lexham Gardens, London W8 5JJ
T 020-7373 0867 E embassy@bhembassy.co.uk
W www.bhembassy.co.uk
*Ambassador Extraordinary and Plenipotentiary,* HE Mustafa Mujezinovic, *apptd* 2012

BRITISH EMBASSY
39a Hamdije Cemerlica Street, 71000 Sarajevo
T (+387) (0) 33 282 200 E britemb@bih.net.ba
W www.gov.uk/government/world/bosnia-and-herzegovina
*Ambassador Extraordinary and Plenipotentiary,* HE Edward Ferguson, *apptd* 2014

## DEFENCE

A reform process completed in 2006 united the separate armies of the Republika Sprska and the Federation of Bosnia and Hercegovina into a single entity.

| Aged 16–49, 2010 est | Males | Females |
|---|---|---|
| Available for military service | 1,180,829 | 1,143,919 |
| Fit for military service | 968,242 | 937,327 |

*Military expenditure –* US$200m (2014)*

* Does not include spending on arms imports

## ECONOMY AND TRADE

When the civil war broke out, the structure of the economy – dominated by state-owned industries, mainly of a military nature – still reflected the central planning of the communist era. Economic restructuring, such as privatisation, has been slow and uneven, although the financial sector is now largely privatised and stable. The difficulties inherent in tackling problems such as the large public sector, large deficits and high unemployment are exacerbated by the duplication of administrative functions and reluctant cooperation between the different national and local political and administrative entities. There is a large unofficial economy, but undeclared activity has declined since the introduction of VAT in 2006. Since the 2008 global economic crisis GDP has been sluggish and government spending accounts for about half of the total. In October 2012 the IMF agreed a new stand-by arrangement with Bosnia and Hercegovina to ease fiscal problems brought about by social spending and the global downturn. The economy is expected to grow by 3.1 per cent between 2015 and 2019.

Most agricultural products are for domestic consumption and foodstuffs also have to be imported. The main industrial activities include mining (metals, minerals and coal), production of steel, textiles, tobacco products, wooden furniture, ammunition and domestic appliances, assembly of vehicles, tanks and aircraft, and oil refining. The country produces enough hydroelectric power for its needs and exports electricity. The main trading partners are Croatia, Slovenia, Germany, Austria and Italy. Principal exports are metals, clothing and wood products, and the main imports are machinery and equipment, chemicals, fuels and foodstuffs.

*GNI –* US$18,309m; US$4,780 per capita (2013)
*Annual average growth of GDP –* 1 per cent (2014 est)
*Inflation rate –* −0.1 per cent (2013 est)
*Population below poverty line –* 17.9 per cent (2011 est)
*Unemployment –* 44.1 per cent (2012 est)
*Total external debt –* US$11,370m (2014 est)
*Imports –* US$10,303m (2013)
*Exports –* US$5,688m (2013)

BALANCE OF PAYMENTS
*Trade –* US$4,615m deficit (2013)
*Current Account –* US$1,268m deficit (2014 est)

| Trade with UK | 2013 | 2014 |
|---|---|---|
| Imports from UK | £21,261,849 | £22,366,940 |
| Exports to UK | £22,244,549 | £18,872,747 |

## COMMUNICATIONS

*Airports* – Seven, including international airports in Sarajevo, Banja Luka, Mostar and Tuzla

*Waterways* – Although the country has 20km of coastline on the Adriatic Sea, there are no seaports

*Roadways and railways* – 19,426km, including 4,652km of motorways; 601km

*Telecommunications* – 878,000 fixed lines and 3.35 million mobile subscriptions (2012); there were 1.422 million internet users in 2009

*Internet code and IDD* – ba; 387 (from UK), 44 (to UK)

*Major broadcasters* – More than 200 commercial TV and radio stations are on the air in Bosnia; national broadcaster BHTV1 operates alongside two separate-entity broadcasters. Major radio broadcasters include the Bosniak-Croat Radio FBiH and the Bosnian Serb station RTRS

*Press* – There are five major daily newspapers, including *Oslobodjenje, Nezavisne Novine* and *Dnevni List*

*WPFI score* – 27,51 (66)

# BOTSWANA

*Republic of Botswana*

*Area* – 581,730 sq. km

*Capital* – Gaborone; population, 422,000 (2015 est)

*Major cities* – Francistown, Maun, Molepolole

*Currency* – Pula (P) of 100 thebe

*Population* – 2,182,719 rising at 1.21 per cent a year (2015 est); Tswana (79 per cent), Kalanga (11 per cent), Basarwa (3 per cent) (est)

*Religion* – Christian 71.6 per cent (predominantly Protestant), Badimo 6 per cent (est)

*Language* – English (official), Setswana, Kalanga, Sekgalagadi

*Population density* – 4 per sq. km (2013)

*Urban population* – 62.9 per cent (2013 est)

*Median age (years)* – 22.9 (2014 est)

*National anthem* – 'Fatshe Leno La Rona' ['Blessed Be This Noble Land']

*National day* – 30 September (Botswana Day)

*Death penalty* – Retained

*CPI score* – 63 (31)

## CLIMATE AND TERRAIN

Botswana lies on an undulating plateau and is covered by the Kalahari desert in the south and west. To the east, streams run into the Marico, Notwani and Limpopo rivers. In the north lies a flat region comprising the Makgadikgadi salt pans and the swampland of the Okavango delta. Elevation extremes range from 1,489m (Tsodilo Hills) to 513m (junction of the Limpopo and Shashe rivers). The climate is subtropical in the north, arid in the south and west, and more temperate in the east, which has regular rain. Average temperatures range from 15°C in July to 26.7°C in January.

## HISTORY AND POLITICS

The Tswana people were predominant in the area from the 17th century. In 1885, at the request of indigenous chiefs fearing invasion by the Boers, Britain formally took control of Bechuanaland, and the northern part of the territory was declared the Bechuanaland Protectorate, while land to the south of the Molopo river became British Bechuanaland, which was later incorporated into the Cape Colony and eventually South Africa. In 1964, the Bechuanaland Protectorate became self-governing, and on 30 September 1966 it became an independent republic under the name Botswana. Since independence, Botswana has been stable and relatively prosperous, owing to the diamond mining industry. There is a high level of HIV/AIDS among the population, and although an advanced treatment programme in place since 2001 is reducing the level of infection, the country faces serious demographic and social problems.

President Festus Mogae stood down in 2008, having completed two terms of office, and was succeeded by the vice-president, Lt.-Gen. Ian Khama, son of the country's first president. The Botswana Democratic Party (BDP) was re-elected to power in the October 2014 legislative elections, winning 33 of 57 seats. President Khama was re-elected by parliament on 26 October 2014.

Under the 1966 constitution, the executive president is elected by the legislature for a five-year term, renewable once. He appoints the vice-president and the cabinet. The unicameral National Assembly has 57 members directly elected for a five-year term, plus a variable number of members (currently four) nominated by the president and elected by the assembly. A 15-member House of Chiefs advises on tribal matters and constitutional changes.

HEAD OF STATE

*President,* Lt.-Gen. (retd) Ian Khama, *sworn in* 1 April 2008, *elected* 18 October 2009, *re-elected* 26 October 2014, *sworn in* 28 October 2014

*Vice-President,* Mokgweetsi Masisi

SELECTED GOVERNMENT MEMBERS *as at April 2015*

*Finance and Development Planning,* Ontefetse Kenneth Matambo

*Defence,* Shaw Kgathi

*Foreign Affairs,* Pelonomi Venson-Moitoi

BOTSWANA HIGH COMMISSION
6 Stratford Place, London W1C 1AY
T 020-7499 0031 E bohico@govbw.com
*High Commissioner,* HE Roy Blackbeard, *apptd* 1998

BRITISH HIGH COMMISSION
Plot 1079–1084, Main Mall, off Queens Road, Gaborone
T (+267) 395 2841 E bhc@botsnet.bw
W www.gov.uk/government/world/botswana
*High Commissioner,* HE Nicholas Pyle OBE, MBE, *apptd* 2013

## DEFENCE

| Aged 16–49, 2010 est | Males | Females |
|---|---|---|
| Available for military service | 557,647 | 531,095 |
| Fit for military service | 340,949 | 302,332 |

*Military expenditure* – US$304m (2014 est)

## ECONOMY AND TRADE

Botswana has been relatively prosperous since independence because of its mining industry, political stability and sound economic management. Despite this, about 30 per cent of the population lives below the poverty line. Longer-term problems are the impact of the high levels of HIV/AIDS among the workforce and the levelling off of diamond production, which usually accounts for 70 to 80 per cent of export earnings; diamond exports declined owing to the global downturn, causing the economy to contract sharply in 2009. The government has sought to reduce the economy's dependence on the diamond industry by diversifying. A major drought and power shortages restricted economic growth in 2012 and 2013. Safari tourism and financial services have grown in recent years, and the services sector now contributes 69.4 per cent of GDP. The industrial sector contributes 28.7 per cent of GDP, mainly from mining diamonds, copper, nickel, salt, soda ash, potash, coal, iron ore and silver. Agriculture is mostly pastoral and accounts for 1.9 per cent of GDP.

The main trading partners are the EU, southern African countries and Israel. Principal exports are diamonds, copper, nickel, soda ash, meat and textiles. The main imports are foodstuffs, machinery, electrical goods, transport equipment, textiles, fuel and petroleum products.

*GNI* – US$15,702m; US$7,770 per capita (2013)
*Annual average growth of GDP* – 4.4 per cent (2014 est)
*Inflation rate* – 5.9 per cent (2013 est)
*Unemployment* – 19.3 per cent (2015 est)
*Total external debt* – US$2,505m (2014 est)
*Imports* – US$7,007m (2013)
*Exports* – US$7,765m (2013)

BALANCE OF PAYMENTS
*Trade* – US$758m surplus (2013)
*Current Account* – US$2,703m surplus (2014 est)

| Trade with UK | 2013 | 2014 |
| --- | --- | --- |
| Imports from UK | £668,442,149 | £25,712,294 |
| Exports to UK | £2,352,809,830 | £25,409,708 |

## COMMUNICATIONS

*Airports* – Ten, including the international airport in Gaborone
*Roadways* – 17,916km, of which 6,116km are paved
*Railways* – The only railway is the 888km line from Zimbabwe to South Africa, which passes through eastern Botswana
*Telecommunications* – 160,500 fixed lines and 3.08 million mobile subscriptions (2012); there were 120,000 internet users in 2009
*Internet code and IDD* – bw; 267 (from UK), 44 (to UK)
*Major broadcasters* – State-run television broadcaster Botswana TV was established in 2000 and a private station is hosted by eBotswana; state-run Radio Botswana operates a commercial FM station from Gaborone, while other stations such as Yarona FM operate a private service
*Press* – Major daily newspapers include the state-run *Daily News* and the privately owned *Mmegi*
*WPFI score* – 22,91 (42)

## EDUCATION AND HEALTH

Botswana does not have a compulsory education policy, although many children receive 12 years of education (seven years of primary education, three years of junior secondary and two years of senior secondary). In 2006 fees were reintroduced for state secondary schools, which had been free of charge for over 20 years.

*Literacy rate* – 97.9 per cent (2015 est)
*Gross enrolment ratio (percentage of relevant age group)* – primary 108 per cent; secondary 80 per cent (2011 est)
*Health expenditure (per capita)* – US$397 (2013)
*Hospital beds (per 1,000 people)* – 1.8 (2010)
*Life expectancy (years)* – 54.06 (2014 est)
*Mortality rate* – 13.32 (2014 est)
*Birth rate* – 21.34 (2014 est)
*Infant mortality rate* – 9.38 (2014 est)
*HIV/AIDS adult prevalence* – 23 per cent (2012)

# BRAZIL

*Republica Federativa do Brasil – Federative Republic of Brazil*

*Area* – 8,514,877 sq. km
*Capital* – Brasilia; population, 2,536,000 (2015 est)
*Major cities* – Belo Horizonte, Fortaleza, Porto Alegre, Recife, Rio de Janeiro (the former capital), Salvador, Sao Paulo
*Currency* – Real (R$) of 100 centavos
*Population* – 204,259,812 rising at 0.77 per cent a year (2015 est)
*Religion* – Christian (Roman Catholic 64.6 per cent, Protestant 22.2 per cent), Spiritist 2.2 per cent (est)
*Language* – Portuguese (official), Spanish, German, Italian, Japanese, English, Amerindian languages
*Population density* – 24 per sq. km (2013)
*Urban population* – 85.2 per cent (2012 est)
*Median age (years)* – 30.7 (2014 est)
*National anthem* – 'Hino Nacional Brasileiro' ['Brazilian National Anthem']
*National day* – 7 September (Independence Day)
*Death penalty* – Retained for certain crimes (last used 1855)
*CPI score* – 43 (69)

## CLIMATE AND TERRAIN

Brazil has six distinct topographical areas: the Amazon basin (north and west of the country), the Parana-Paraguay river basin (south; the Parana drains the Pantanal, the world's largest freshwater wetland), the Guiana Highlands (north of the Amazon), the Mato Grosso plateau (centre), the Brazilian Highlands (south of the Amazon) and the coastal strip. Elevation extremes range from 2,994m (Pico da Neblina) to 0m (Atlantic Ocean). Brazil has the world's largest rainforest, as well as large expanses of savannah *(cerrado)*. The climate is mostly tropical, with the equator passing through the north and the Tropic of Capricorn through the south-east. The Amazon basin sees annual rainfall of up to 2,300mm a year and there is no dry season. The north-east is the driest area of the country and can experience long periods of drought. The southern states have a seasonal temperate climate.

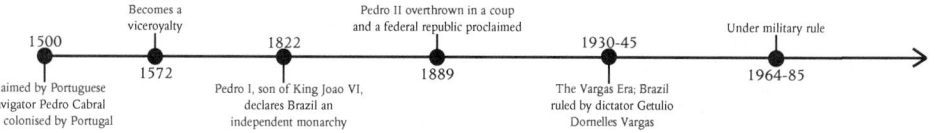

Becomes a viceroyalty

1500 | 1572 | 1822 | 1889 | 1930–45 | 1964–85

Pedro II overthrown in a coup and a federal republic proclaimed

Under military rule

Claimed by Portuguese navigator Pedro Cabral nd colonised by Portugal

Pedro I, son of King Joao VI, declares Brazil an independent monarchy

The Vargas Era; Brazil ruled by dictator Getulio Dornelles Vargas

## POLITICS

The Federative Republic of Brazil is composed of the Federal District of Brasilia, in which the capital lies, and 26 states: Acre, Alagoas, Amapa, Amazonas, Bahia, Ceara, Espirito Santo, Goias, Maranhao, Mato Grosso, Mato Grosso do Sul, Minas Gerais, Para, Paraiba, Parana, Pernambuco, Piaui, Rio de Janeiro, Rio Grande do Norte, Rio Grande do Sul, Rondonia, Roraima, Santa Catarina, Sao Paulo, Sergipe and Tocantins. Each state has its own governor and legislative assembly.

Under the 1988 constitution (amended in 1997), the executive president is directly elected for a four-year term, which is renewable once. The National Congress consists of an 81-member federal senate (three senators per state, directly elected for an eight-year term) and a 513-member Chamber of Deputies which is directly elected every four years; the number of deputies per state depends upon the state's population.

In the October 2014 presidential election Dilma Rousseff of the Workers' Party (PT) was re-elected following a second round of voting. In the simultaneous legislative election, With the Strength of the People, a centre-left grouping ed by the PT, won a majority in both houses of Congress. Her government has been dogged by corruption allegations while a number of protests took place in early 2015 over the country's poor economic performance and the cost of hosting the 2016 Olympic Games, mirroring demonstrations that took place before and during the 2014 World Cup.

HEAD OF STATE
*President,* Dilma Rousseff, *sworn in* 1 January 2011
*Vice-President,* Michel Temer

SELECTED GOVERNMENT MEMBERS *as at April 2015*
*Attorney-General,* Luis Inacio Lucena Adams
*Defence,* Jaques Wagner
*Finance,* Joaquim Levy
*Foreign Affairs,* Mauro Luiz Lecker Viera

EMBASSY OF BRAZIL
14/16 Cockspur Street, London SW1Y 5BL
T 020-7747 4500 E info.london@itamaraty.gov.br
W www.brazil.org.uk
*Ambassador Extraordinary and Plenipotentiary,* vacant

BRITISH EMBASSY
etor de Embaixadas Sul, Quadra 801, Lote 8, CEP 70408-900, Brasilia DF
T (+55) (61) 3329 2300 W www.gov.uk/government/world/brazil
*Ambassador Extraordinary and Plenipotentiary,* HE Alex Ellis, CMG, *apptd* 2013

## DEFENCE

| Aged 16–49, 2010 est | Males | Females |
| --- | --- | --- |
| Available for military service | 53,350,703 | 53,433,918 |
| Fit for military service | 38,993,989 | 44,841,661 |

*Military expenditure* – US$31,744m (2014)
*Conscription* – 18–45 years of age; 9–12 months

## ECONOMY AND TRADE

Historically subject to boom and bust cycles, the economy was stabilised by reforms in the 1990s. Tight fiscal management, IMF programmes, a growth in output and an expanding export base have produced steady growth since 2003. Unemployment and income inequality have decreased steadily in the past 15 years, although poverty is still widespread. Brazil's economy is based on well-developed agriculture, mining, manufacturing and service sectors, and in 2011, became the seventh largest economy in the world, ahead of the UK. In 2014, Brazil's economy entered recession for the first time in five years, due to rising inflation and decreasing demand from China. The state-run oil producer Petrobas, Brazil's largest company, has been plagued by corruption charges in the last year (*see* Events).

The country is rich in mineral deposits, including iron ore (haematite), bauxite, gold, manganese, nickel, platinum and uranium. It produces oil, gas and hydroelectricity, and is close to self-sufficiency in oil. Brazil is the world's largest producer of coffee; the other main agricultural products are soya beans, wheat, rice, maize, sugar cane, cocoa, citrus fruit and beef. The expansion of agriculture and forestry threaten the rainforest, although recent governments' attempts to prevent further depredations by loggers and farmers have slowed the rate of deforestation considerably. Tourism is a growing industry. In 2014, services generated 70.4 per cent of GDP, industry 23.8 per cent and agriculture 5.8 per cent.

Brazil's main trading partners are the USA, China, Argentina and Germany. Principal exports are transport equipment, iron ore, soya beans, footwear, coffee and vehicles. The main imports are machinery, electrical and transport equipment, chemical products, oil, vehicle parts and electronics.
*GNI* – US$2,342,551m; US$11,690 per capita (2013)
*Annual average growth of GDP* – 0.3 per cent (2014 est)
*Inflation rate* – 6.2 per cent (2013 est)
*Population below poverty line* – 8.9 per cent (2013 est)
*Unemployment* – 6.5 per cent (2015 est)
*Total external debt* – US$535,400m (2014 est)
*Imports* – US$244,677m (2013)
*Exports* – US$242,179m (2013)

BALANCE OF PAYMENTS
*Trade* – US$2,498m deficit (2013)
*Current Account* – US$91,289m deficit (2014)

| Trade with UK | 2013 | 2014 |
| --- | --- | --- |
| Imports from UK | £2,573,912,651 | £2,306,692,220 |
| Exports to UK | £2,960,324,040 | £2,645,852,463 |

## COMMUNICATIONS

*Airports* – 698; international flights operate to the major cities
*Waterways* – In remote regions, transport is primarily by air or water, utilising the 50,000km of navigable waterways
*Roadways and railways* – 212,798km; the Trans-Amazonian Highway connects the Amazon region with the rest of the country, although it is mostly unpaved and often becomes impassable in the rainy season; 28,538km
*Telecommunications* – 44.3 million fixed lines and 248.324 million mobile subscriptions (2012); there were 75.98 million internet users in 2009

*Internet code and IDD* – br; 55 (from UK), 14/15/21/23/31 44 (to UK, varies depending on area and/or carrier)
*Major broadcasters* – Domestic conglomerates – most notably Globo – dominate the market and run television and radio networks, newspapers and subscription television stations
*Press* – There are six major daily newspapers, including *O Dia, O Correio Brazilinese* and *Jornal do Brasil*
*WPFI score* – 31,93 (99)

## EDUCATION AND HEALTH
Public education is free at all levels, and is compulsory between the ages of seven and 14.
*Literacy rate* – 98.9 per cent (2015 est)
*Gross enrolment ratio (percentage of relevant age group)* – primary 127 per cent; secondary 101 per cent; tertiary 36.1 per cent (2011 est)
*Health expenditure (per capita)* – US$1,083 (2013)
*Hospital beds (per 1,000 people)* – 2.3 (2012)
*Life expectancy (years)* – 73.28 (2014 est)
*Mortality rate* – 6.54 (2014 est)
*Birth rate* – 14.72 (2014 est)
*Infant mortality rate* – 19.21 (2014 est)

# BRUNEI

*Negara Brunei Darussalam – Brunei Darussalam*

*Area* – 5,765 sq. km
*Capital* – Bandar Seri Begawan; population, 241,000 (2011 est)
*Major towns* – Kampong Ayer, Kuala Belait, Seria
*Currency* – Brunei dollar (B$) of 100 sen (fully interchangeable with Singapore currency)
*Population* – 429,646 rising at 1.62 per cent a year (2015 est); Malay (65.7 per cent), Chinese (10.3 per cent), indigenous (3.4 per cent) (2011 est)
*Religion* – Muslim 78.8 per cent (predominantly Sunni), Christian 8.7 per cent, Buddhist 7.8 per cent (est); Islam is the state religion
*Language* – Malay (official), English, Chinese languages
*Population density* – 79 per sq. km (2013)
*Urban population* – 76.7 per cent (2013 est)
*Median age (years)* – 29.3 (2014 est)
*National anthem* – 'Allah Peliharakan Sultan' ['God Bless the Sultan']
*National day* – 23 February (date of independence from British protection, 1984)
*Death penalty* – Retained (no known use since 1957)
*CPI score* – Not included in 2014

## CLIMATE AND TERRAIN
The country lies on the north-west coast of the island of Borneo. It is surrounded and divided in two by the Malaysian

state of Sarawak. The terrain is estimated to be around 70 per cent rainforest, with extensive mangrove swamps along the coastal plain. There are mountains on the border with Sarawak. Elevation extremes range from 1,850m (Bukit Pagon) to 0m (South China Sea). The climate is tropical, with high humidity, and an annual average daily temperature of 26.3°C.

## HISTORY AND POLITICS
Formerly a powerful Muslim sultanate that controlled Borneo and parts of the Philippines, Brunei was reduced to its present size by the mid-19th century and came under British protection in 1889. It chose to remain a British dependency in 1963 rather than joining the Federation of Malaysia. Internally self-governing from 1959, Brunei gained full independence on 1 January 1984.

In 1962 the legislative election was annulled after it was won by a party that sought to remove the sultan; a state of emergency was declared and the sultan has ruled by decree ever since. A ministerial system of government was introduced in 1984. Some political liberalisation and modernisation has taken place since 2004, when the legislature was reconvened after 20 years. In April 2014 Brunei became the first East Asian country to adopt sharia law.

Parts of the 1959 constitution have been suspended since the state of emergency began in 1962. Supreme executive authority is vested in the sultan, a hereditary monarch who presides over and is advised by a privy council, a religious council and the council of cabinet ministers. The legislative council was reconvened in 2004 with 21 members appointed by the sultan; it has passed constitutional amendments to increase its size to 45 members, 15 of whom will be directly elected. No date has been set for an election.

### HEAD OF STATE
*HM The Sultan of Brunei, Prime Minister, Defence, Finance,*
HM Hassanal Bolkiah, GCB, *acceded* 5 October 1967, *crowned* 1 August 1968
*HM Crown Prince, Senior Minister in the Prime Minister's Office,* Prince Al-Muhtadee Billah

SELECTED GOVERNMENT MEMBERS *as at April 2015*
*Foreign Affairs,* Prince Mohamed Bolkiah
*Home Affairs,* Pehin Dato Ustaz Badaruddin bin Pengarah Othman

BRUNEI DARUSSALAM HIGH COMMISSION
19–20 Belgrave Square, London SW1X 8PG
T 020-7581 0521 E info@bdhcl.co.uk
*High Commissioner,* HE Maj.-Gen. Dato Haji Aminuddin Ihsan

BRITISH HIGH COMMISSION
2.01, 2nd Floor, Block D, Kompleks Yayasan Sultan Haji Hassanal Bolkiah, Jalan Pretty, PO Box 2197, Brunei
T (+673) (2) 222 231 E ukinbrunei@fco.gov.uk
W www.gov.uk/government/world/brunei
*High Commissioner,* David Campbell, *apptd* 2013

### DEFENCE

| Aged 16–49, 2010 est | Males | Females |
| --- | --- | --- |
| Available for military service | 112,688 | 117,536 |
| Fit for military service | 95,141 | 99,386 |

*Military expenditure* – US$528m (2014)

# ECONOMY AND TRADE

The economy is based on the production of oil and natural gas and the income from overseas investments. Royalties and taxes from these operations form the bulk of government revenue and have enabled the construction of free health, education and welfare services; Brunei's GDP per capita is one of the highest in Asia, however, oil and gas reserves, which make up 60 per cent of GDP, are declining and Brunei is now trying to diversify its economy, developing Islamic financial services and tourism. Declining global oil prices are expected to wipe out the country's fiscal surplus by 2016 and significantly reduce the country's trade surplus.

Agriculture accounts for 0.8 per cent of GDP, industry 66.5 per cent and services 32.8 per cent. The main trading partners are Japan, Singapore, Indonesia, South Korea and the UK. Principal exports are crude oil, natural gas and clothing. The main imports are machinery and transport equipment, manufactured goods, food (over 80 per cent of domestic requirements are imported) and chemicals.
*GNI* – US$12,460m; US$31,590 per capita (2009)
*Annual average growth of GDP* – 5.3 per cent (2014 est)
*Inflation rate* – 0.4 per cent (2013 est)
*Unemployment* – 3.3 per cent (2015 est)
*Imports* – US$3,365m (2010)
*Exports* – US$9,172m (2010)

BALANCE OF PAYMENTS
*Trade* – US$6,448m surplus (2010)
*Current Account* – US$3,558m surplus (2014 est)

| Trade with UK | 2013 | 2014 |
| --- | --- | --- |
| Imports from UK | £954,197,371 | £182,904,190 |
| Exports to UK | £51,967,370 | £78,086,143 |

# COMMUNICATIONS

*Airports and waterways* – There is one international airport; the largest port is at Muara and the 209km of internal waterways are navigable only by shallow craft
*Roadways* – 2,425km
*Telecommunications* – 70,933 fixed lines and 469,700 mobile subscriptions (2012); there were 319,000 internet users in 2009
*Internet code and IDD* – bn; 673 (from UK), 44 (to UK)
*Major broadcasters* – The only broadcast media organisation, Radio Television Brunei (RTB), is state-owned; it broadcasts in Malay and English
*Press* – Daily newspapers include the English-language *Borneo Bulletin* and *Brunei Times* and Malay *Media Permata*
*WPFI score* – 36,76 (121)

# EDUCATION AND HEALTH

All levels of education are free but not compulsory, most children receive a minimum of 12 years of schooling.
*Literacy rate* – 99.9 per cent (2015 est)
*Gross enrolment ratio (percentage of relevant age group)* – primary 95 per cent; secondary 108 per cent; tertiary 24 per cent (2012 est)
*Hospital beds (per 1,000 people)* – 2.8 (2012)
*Life expectancy (years)* – 76.77 (2014 est)
*Mortality rate* – 3.47 (2014 est)
*Birth rate* – 17.49 (2014 est)
*Infant mortality rate* – 10.48 (2014 est)

# BULGARIA

*Republika Balgariya – Republic of Bulgaria*

*Area* – 110,879 sq. km
*Capital* – Sofia; population, 1,195,000 (2015 est)
*Major cities* – Burgas, Plovdiv, Varna
*Currency* – Lev of 100 stotinki
*Population* – 7,186,893 falling at 0.58 per cent a year (2015 est); Bulgarian (76.9 per cent), Turkish (8 per cent), Roma (4.4 per cent) (2011)
*Religion* – Eastern Orthodox 59.4 per cent, Muslim 7.8 per cent (predominantly Sunni) (est)
*Language* – Bulgarian (official), Turkish, Romani
*Population density* – 67 per sq. km (2013)
*Urban population* – 74.3 per cent (2013 est)
*Median age (years)* – 42.6 (2014 est)
*National anthem* – 'Mila Rodino' ['Dear Motherland']
*National day* – 3 March (Liberation Day)
*Death penalty* – Abolished for all crimes (since 1998)
*CPI score* – 43 (69)

## CLIMATE AND TERRAIN

The Balkan Mountains cross the country from west to east, averaging 2,000m in height, and the Rhodope Mountains in the south-west climb to almost 3,000m. Elevation extremes range from 2,925m (Musala) to 0m (Black Sea). The lowland plains of the north and south-east are in the basins of the main rivers: the Danube in the north, which forms much of the border with Romania, and the Maritsa, which divides the Balkan and Rhodope ranges. The climate is temperate, with cold, damp winters and hot, dry summers. Average temperatures in Sofia range from 0°C in January to 22.3°C in July.

## POLITICS

Under the 1991 constitution, the president is directly elected for a five-year term, renewable once. The head of government is the prime minister, who is appointed by the president, and is usually the leader of the largest party in the legislature. There is a unicameral National Assembly of 240 members who are directly elected for a four-year term.

In the 2009 legislative election, the new centre-right party Citizens for European Development of Bulgaria (GERB) won the most seats, but without an overall majority, and formed a minority government with support from small right-wing parties. Rosen Plevneliev of the GERB won the 2011 presidential election, picking up 40 per cent of the vote; he was inaugurated on 21 January 2012.

In July 2014, the Socialist government of Prime Minister Plamen Oresharski resigned, following his party's poor performance in European elections and pressure from the EU over his support for the Russian South Stream gas pipeline (*see* Events). Early legislative elections were arranged for October and saw eight parties win seats in an election with a turnout as low as 50 per cent. In November, former

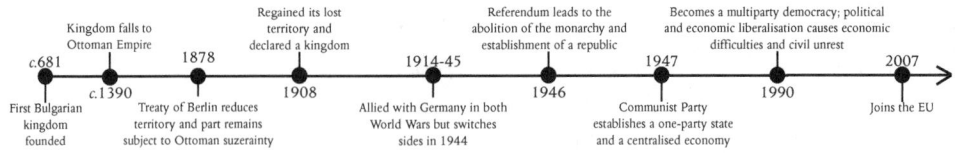

Kingdom falls to Ottoman Empire — c.681

First Bulgarian kingdom founded — c.1390

1878 — Treaty of Berlin reduces territory and part remains subject to Ottoman suzerainty

Regained its lost territory and declared a kingdom — 1908

1914-45 — Allied with Germany in both World Wars but switches sides in 1944

Referendum leads to the abolition of the monarchy and establishment of a republic — 1946

1947 — Communist Party establishes a one-party state and a centralised economy

Becomes a multiparty democracy; political and economic liberalisation causes economic difficulties and civil unrest — 1990

2007 — Joins the EU

prime minister Boyko Borissov of the centre-right Citizens for European Development of Bulgaria (GERB) party formed a minority government in coalition with three other parties.

## HEAD OF STATE
*President,* Rosen Plevneliev, *elected* 30 October 2011
*Vice-President,* Margarita Popova

SELECTED GOVERNMENT MEMBERS *as at July 2015*
*Prime Minister,* Boyko Borissov
*Deputy Prime Ministers,* Rumiana Bachvarova *(Interior),*
Tomislav Donchev *(EU Funds and Economic Policy),*
Ivailo Kalfin *(Labour),* Meglena Kuneva *(Europe)*

## EMBASSY OF THE REPUBLIC OF BULGARIA
186–188 Queen's Gate, London SW7 5HL
T 020-7584 9400 E info@bulgarianembassy.org.uk
W www.bulgarianembassy-london.org
*Ambassador Extraordinary and Plenipotentiary,* HE Konstantin Stefanov Dimitrov, *apptd* 2012

## BRITISH EMBASSY
9 Moskovska Street, Sofia 1000
T (+359) (2) 933 9222 E britishembassysofia@fco.gov.uk
W www.gov.uk/government/world/bulgaria
*Ambassador Extraordinary and Plenipotentiary,* HE Sarah Riley, *apptd* 2014

## DEFENCE

| Aged 16–49, 2010 est | Males | Females |
| --- | --- | --- |
| Available for military service | 1,637,470 | 1,621,352 |
| Fit for military service | 1,320,955 | 1,337,616 |

*Military expenditure* – US$837m (2014)

## ECONOMY AND TRADE
The government adopted radical economic reforms in 1996 and the economy achieved stability and attracted significant foreign investment, although administrative corruption, a weak judiciary and organised crime remain potential deterrents. Despite steady economic growth in 2004–8 and responsible fiscal management, the economy contracted in the global economic downturn as industrial production and exports declined. Recovery has been slow, with growth at 1.5 per cent in 2014.

Natural resources include copper, lead, zinc, other minerals, coal and timber. Fertile arable land produces vegetables, fruit, tobacco, wine, wheat, barley, sunflowers and livestock. Agriculture employs 7.1 per cent of the workforce and accounts for 4.9 per cent of GDP. Industries include energy generation, food processing, beverages, tobacco, machinery and equipment, base metals, chemicals, mining and oil refining. Tourism is growing, with a 4.8 per cent increase in visitors reported for 2014.

The main trading partners are EU countries, Russia and Turkey. Principal exports are clothing and footwear, iron and steel, machinery and equipment, and fuels. The main imports are predominantly machinery and raw materials for the industrial sector.
*GNI* – US$53,456m; US$7,360 per capita (2013)
*Annual average growth of GDP* – 1.4 per cent (2014 est)

*Inflation rate* – 0.9 per cent (2013 est)
*Population below poverty line* – 21 per cent (2013 est)
*Unemployment* – 13.8 per cent (2015 est)
*Total external debt* – US$54,040m (2014 est)
*Imports* – US$34,350m (2013)
*Exports* – US$29,492m (2013)

BALANCE OF PAYMENTS
*Trade* – US$4,858m deficit (2013)
*Current Account* – US$25m surplus (2014)

| Trade with UK | 2013 | 2014 |
| --- | --- | --- |
| Imports from UK | £389,714,638 | £441,572,513 |
| Exports to UK | £368,466,696 | £350,231,756 |

## COMMUNICATIONS
*Airports and waterways* – 57, the main airports are at Sofia, Plovdiv, Burgas and Varna; the main ports are Burgas and Varni on the Black Sea, and there are 470km of waterways
*Roadways and railways* – 19,235km, including 458km of motorways; 4,152km
*Telecommunications* – 2.253 million fixed lines and 10.78 million mobile telephone subscriptions (2012); there were 3.395 million internet users in 2009
*Internet code and IDD* – bg; 359 (from UK), 44 (to UK)
*Major broadcasters* – Public service broadcasters Bulgarian National Radio and Bulgarian National Television share the radio and TV markets with a vigorous commercial sector that provides national and regional broadcasting
*Press* – Major daily newspapers include *Dnevnik, Trud* and *24 Chasa*
*WPFI score* – 32,91 (106)

## EDUCATION AND HEALTH
Education is free and compulsory from seven to 16 years.
*Literacy rate* – 98 per cent (2015 est)
*Gross enrolment ratio (percentage of relevant age group)* – primary 100 per cent; secondary 93 per cent; tertiary 63 per cent (2012 est)
*Health expenditure (per capita)* – US$555 (2013)
*Hospital beds (per 1,000 people)* – 6.4 (2011)
*Life expectancy (years)* – 74.33 (2014 est)
*Mortality rate* – 14.3 (2014 est)
*Birth rate* – 8.92 (2014 est)
*Infant mortality rate* – 15.08 (2014 est)

# BURKINA FASO

*Area* – 274,200 sq. km
*Capital* – Ouagadougou; population, 2,700,000 (2015 est)
*Major city* – Bobo-Dioulasso
*Currency* – Franc CFA of 100 centimes
*Population* – 18,931,686 rising at 3.03 per cent a year (2015 st); 63 ethnic groups, of which Mossi (40 per cent) (est) is the largest
*Religion* – Muslim 60.5 per cent (predominantly Sunni), Christian (Roman Catholic 19 per cent, Protestant denominations 4.2 per cent)
*Language* – French (official), various African languages (spoken by 90 per cent of the population)
*Population density* – 62 per sq. km (2013)
*Urban population* – 28.2 per cent (2013 est)
*Median age (years)* – 17 (2014 est)
*National anthem* – 'Ditanye' ['Anthem of Victory']
*National day* – 11 December (Republic Day)
*Death penalty* – Retained (not used since 1988)
*CPI score* – 38 (85)

## CLIMATE AND TERRAIN

The landlocked state occupies a plateau dissected by the White, Black and Red Volta rivers. There are tropical savannahs in the south and the north is semi-desert. Elevation extremes range from 749m (Tena Kourou) to 200m (Mouhoun, or Black Volta, river). The climate is tropical, with a wet season from May to September; there are recurring droughts. Average temperatures range from 25.2°C in January to to 32.7°C in April.

## HISTORY AND POLITICS

Burkina Faso (Upper Volta until 1983) was part of the Mossi Empire in the 18th and 19th centuries. It was administered as part of other French colonies between 1932 and 1947, and in 1958 it became autonomous within the French Community; independence was achieved on 5 August 1960.

In the three decades after independence there was a succession of military regimes; the last military coup, in 1987, brought to power Captain Blaise Compaoré. Military rule ended in 1991 when a new constitution was adopted and multiparty elections were held in 1992. Despite the constitutional restriction on the number of terms that a president may serve, President Compaoré was re-elected for a fourth term in 2010. In January 2014, protests took place across the country after President Compaoré announced that he would look to alter the constitution in order to stand in the 2015 elections. In October, demonstrators stormed the presidential palace, causing the president to resign and flee to the Côte d'Ivoire. In November, military and political leaders appointed former foreign secretary Michel Kafando as interim president of a mixed civilian and military government. New legislative elections were due to be held in October 2015.

The 1991 constitution was amended in 2000 to reduce the presidential term from seven years. The president is directly elected for a five-year term, renewable once, although this limit has been ignored by President Compaoré. The unicameral National Assembly has 111 deputies, who are directly elected for a five-year term. Executive power is vested jointly in the president and the council of ministers, both responsible to the legislature.

## HEAD OF STATE

*Transitional President, Foreign Affairs,* Michel Kafando, *sworn in* 18 November 2014

## SELECTED GOVERNMENT MEMBERS *as at April 2015*

*Prime Minister, Defence,* Isaac Zida
*Economy and Finance,* Jean Gustave Sanon

## EMBASSY OF THE REPUBLIC OF BURKINA FASO

16 Place Guy d'Arezzo, 1180 Brussels, Belgium
T (00) (+32) (2) 345 9912 E ambassade.burkina@skynet.be
W www.ambassadeduburkina.be
*Ambassador Extraordinary and Plenipotentiary,* HE Frédéric Assomption Korsaga, *apptd* 2013

## BRITISH AMBASSADOR

HE Jon Benjamin, *apptd* 2014, resident at Accra, Ghana

## DEFENCE

| *Aged 16–49, 2010 est* | *Males* | *Females* |
|---|---|---|
| Available for military service | 3,735,735 | – |
| Fit for military service | 2,366,168 | 2,367,673 |

*Military expenditure* – US$166m (2014)

## ECONOMY AND TRADE

The country is one of the poorest in the world, with around 90 per cent of the population engaged in subsistence agriculture and animal husbandry, which are vulnerable to periodic droughts. The economy is heavily dependent on cotton and gold exports and therefore also exposed to the vagaries of global price fluctuations. Civil war in neighbouring Côte d'Ivoire harmed trade by cutting off transport routes, and caused many expatriate Burkinabes to return home, adding to the unemployment problem and depriving the economy of their remittances. During 2013, unrest in Mali caused similar problems and a number of public protests were held about socio-economic issues; the government reduced income taxes and price controls to alleviate discontent. Despite these difficulties, the economy has continued to grow rapidly, achieving growth of 6.9 per cent in 2013 and 7 per cent in 2014. Major infrastructure projects, including road building and the construction of a new airport in Ouagadougou, began in 2014.

Agriculture contributes 38 per cent of GDP; the main product apart from cotton is livestock. Although there are few natural resources, a growing quantity of gold is mined and exploration for other minerals has begun. The processing of cotton and other agricultural products, gold mining and the manufacturing of beverages, soap, cigarettes and textiles are the main industries, contributing 22 per cent to GDP. Services account for 40 per cent of GDP.

The main export markets are China, Turkey and Belgium. Principal exports are cotton, livestock and gold. The chief import providers are Côte d'Ivoire and France, supplying capital goods, foodstuffs and fuel.

*GNI* – US$12,715,453m; US$670 per capita (2013)
*Annual average growth of GDP* – 6.7 per cent (2014 est)
*Inflation rate* – 0.5 per cent (2013 est)
*Population below poverty line* – 46.7 per cent (2009 est)
*Unemployment* – 2.9 per cent (2015 est)
*Total external debt* – US$2,974m (2014 est)
*Imports* – US$3,499m (2013)
*Exports* – US$2,161m (2013)

## BALANCE OF PAYMENTS

*Trade* – US$1,338m deficit (2013)
*Current Account* – US$767m deficit (2014 est)

| Trade with UK | 2013 | 2014 |
|---|---|---|
| Imports from UK | £13,092,256 | £8,180,917 |
| Exports to UK | £351,725 | £2,469,817 |

## COMMUNICATIONS

*Airports* – Two; the main international airport is at Ouagadougou

*Roadways and railways* – 15,272km; 622km

*Telecommunications* – 141,400 fixed lines and 9.98 million mobile subscriptions (2012); there were 178,100 internet users in 2009

*Internet code and IDD* – bf; 226 (to UK), 44 (from UK)

*Major broadcasters* – Radio is the most popular medium with the state-run Radio Burkina the largest broadcaster; state-run Television Nationale du Burkina is one of the largest television broadcasters

*Press* – There are five daily national newspapers, including the government-run *Sidwaya*, *L'Observateur Paalga* and *Le Pays*

*WPFI score* – 23,79 (46)

## EDUCATION AND HEALTH

Education is nominally compulsory from ages six to 16 but the prohibitive cost of school supplies and a lack of resources prevent many children from attending.

*Literacy rate* – 45.4 per cent (2015)

*Gross enrolment ratio (percentage of relevant age group)* – primary 85 per cent; secondary 26 per cent; tertiary 5 per cent (2012 est)

*Health expenditure (per capita)* – US$36 (2013)

*Hospital beds (per 1,000 people)* – 0.4 (2010)

*Life expectancy (years)* – 54.78 (2014 est)

*Mortality rate* – 11.96 (2014 est)

*Birth rate* – 42.42 (2014 est)

*Infant mortality rate* – 76.8 (2014 est)

*HIV/AIDS adult prevalence* – 1 per cent (2012 est)

# BURUNDI

*Republika y'u Burundi/République du Burundi* – Republic of Burundi

*Area* – 27,830 sq. km

*Capital* – Bujumbura; population, 750,000 (2015 est)

*Major towns* – Bubanza, Gitega, Muyinga, Ngozi

*Currency* – Burundi franc (FBu) of 100 centimes

*Population* – 10,742,276 rising at 3.28 per cent a year (2015 est); Hutu (85 per cent), Tutsi (14 per cent), Twa (1 per cent) (est)

*Religion* – Christian (Roman Catholic 62.1 per cent, Protestant denominations 23.9 per cent), Muslim 2.5 per cent

*Language* – Kirundi, French (both official), Swahili, English

*Population density* – 396 per sq. km (2013)

*Urban population* – 11.5 per cent (2013 est)

*Median age (years)* – 17 (2014 est)

*National anthem* – 'Burundi Bwacu' ['Our Burundi']

*National day* – 1 July (Independence Day)

*Death penalty* – Abolished for all crimes (since 2009)

*CPI score* – 20 (159)

*Literacy rate* – 87.6 per cent (2015 est)

*Gross enrolment ratio (percentage of relevant age group)* – primary 137 per cent; secondary 28 per cent (2012 est); tertiary 3 per cent (2010 est)

*Health expenditure (per capita)* – US$21 (2013)

*Hospital beds (per 1,000 people)* – 1.9 (2011)

*Life expectancy (years)* – 59.55 (2014 est)

*Mortality rate* – 9.54 (2014 est)

*Birth rate* – 42.33 (2014 est)

*Infant mortality rate* – 63.44 (2014 est)

*HIV/AIDS adult prevalence* – 1.1 per cent (2013 est)

## CLIMATE AND TERRAIN

Burundi lies across the Nile–Congo watershed in central Africa. A hilly interior rises from an average altitude of 1,700m to the country's highest point at 2,670m (Heha) and falls to a plateau in the east. The river Ruzizi forms part of the north-western border with the Democratic Republic of the Congo, along with Lake Tanganyika (the lowest elevation in the country at 772m) in the south-west. The climate is equatorial, moderated by altitude; the average temperature in the lower regions is 29°C, and in the higher regions is 20°C. There are two rainy seasons: February to April and October to December.

## POLITICS

Under the 2005 constitution, the executive president is directly elected for a five-year term, renewable once. The bicameral *Parlement* comprises the National Assembly and the senate; members of both serve a five-year term. The National Assembly has 100 directly elected members, three co-opted members from the Twa ethnic group, and up to 21 members (currently 15) co-opted to ensure a 60 per cent Hutu and 40 per cent Tutsi split and that 30 per cent of the total are women. The senate has 49 members: 34 directly elected members (one Hutu and one Tutsi from each province); three co-opted Twa members; all former presidents; and enough women to make the number of women senators up to 30 per cent of the total. The constitution also specifies the proportion of Hutu, Tutsi and female members of the council of ministers.

Pierre Nkurunziza of the National Council for the Defence of Democracy–Forces for the Defence of Democracy (CNDD-FDD), a Hutu party, was elected president by the newly elected legislature in 2005 and by direct presidential elections in June 2010. The CNDD-FDD retained large majorities in both houses following the 2010 legislative elections.

In May 2015, Burundi's constitutional court ruled that President Nkurunziza could stand for a third term of office, despite the fact that the constitution limited incumbents to two terms. The decision sparked protests across Burundi, which killed dozens of people and caused over 150,000

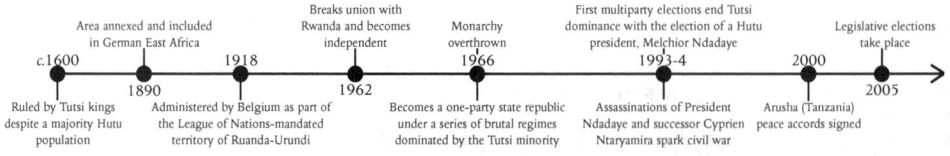

| Area annexed and included in German East Africa | Breaks union with Rwanda and becomes independent | Monarchy overthrown | First multiparty elections end Tutsi dominance with the election of a Hutu president, Melchior Ndadaye | Legislative elections take place |
|---|---|---|---|---|
| *c.*1600 | 1918 | 1966 | 1993-4 | 2000 |
| 1890 | 1962 | | | 2005 |
| Ruled by Tutsi kings despite a majority Hutu population | Administered by Belgium as part of the League of Nations-mandated territory of Ruanda-Urundi | Becomes a one-party state republic under a series of brutal regimes dominated by the Tutsi minority | Assassinations of President Ndadaye and successor Cyprien Ntaryamira spark civil war | Arusha (Tanzania) peace accords signed |

o flee to neighbouring states, and a failed military coup attempt. The CNDD-FDD remained the largest party in both chambers following the June legislative elections, while President Nkurunziza was re-elected in the July presidential elections. Both polls were boycotted by a number of opposition groups.

## HEAD OF STATE

*President,* Pierre Nkurunziza, *sworn in* 26 August 2005, re-elected 2010, 2015
*First Vice-President,* Gaston Sindimwo
*Second Vice-President,* Joseph Butore

SELECTED GOVERNMENT MEMBERS *as at September 2015*
*Defence,* Emmanuel Ntahonvukiye
*Finance,* Tabu Abdallah Manirakiza
*Interior,* Pascal Barandagiye

## EMBASSY OF THE REPUBLIC OF BURUNDI

Uganda House, 2nd Floor, 58-59 Trafalgar Square, London WC2N 5DX **T** 020-7930 4958
**E** info@burundiembassy.org.uk
**W** www.burundiembassy.org.uk
*Ambassador Extraordinary and Plenipotentiary,* HE Deo Sindayihebura, *apptd* 2014

## BRITISH AMBASSADOR

HE William Gelling, OBE, *apptd* 2014, resident at Kigali, Rwanda

## DEFENCE

| Aged 16–49, 2010 est | Males | Females |
| --- | --- | --- |
| Available for military service | 2,182,327 | 2,202,125 |
| Fit for military service | 1,398,769 | 1,481,417 |

*Military expenditure –* US$62.2m (2014)

## ECONOMY AND TRADE

Economic activity has increased since the civil war ended, but reform and reconstruction are hampered by a lack of administrative capacity, a poorly educated workforce, corruption and poor law enforcement. Agriculture is the mainstay of the economy, contributing 40.3 per cent of GDP. Subsistence agriculture has contracted recently owing to continued insecurity, population growth and soil erosion. Exports of coffee and tea account for around 90 per cent of foreign exchange earnings, leaving the economy vulnerable to the effects of global price fluctuations and weather conditions. Industry is relatively small-scale and employs around 2.3 per cent of the workforce but contributes 171 per cent of GDP. The main activities are light manufacturing, food processing, the assembly of imported components and public sector construction. Since 2013 there has been major investment in infrastructure projects, which are expected to help the economy grow by 4.7 per cent in 2015.

Most trade is with Switzerland, Belgium, Saudi Arabia, the UK and China, but it is constrained by the poor transport infrastructure and landlocked location. The main exports are coffee, tea, sugar, cotton and hides. The principal imports are capital goods, petroleum products and food.
*GNI –* US$2,646m; US$260 per capita (2013)
*Annual average growth of GDP –* 4.7 per cent (2014 est)
*Inflation rate –* 8.1 per cent (2013 est)
*Population below poverty line –* 68 per cent (2002 est)
*Total external debt –* US$742,100m (2014 est)
*Imports –* US$811m (2013)
*Exports –* US$99m (2013)

## BALANCE OF PAYMENTS

*Trade –* US$712m deficit (2013)
*Current Account –* US$544m deficit (2014 est)

| Trade with UK | 2013 | 2014 |
| --- | --- | --- |
| Imports from UK | £2,119,724 | £3,188,075 |
| Exports to UK | £68,492 | £311,629 |

## COMMUNICATIONS

*Airports and waterways –* Bujumbura has the only airport with a surfaced runway and the only port, while movement around Lake Tanganyika is by water
*Roadways –* A limited road network, of which only 1,286km is paved, is concentrated around Bujumbura
*Railways –* There are no railways at present but the East African railways master plan, a project designed to expand the rail network in this region of Africa, is in its planning stage
*Telecommunications –* 17,400 fixed lines and 2.247 million mobile subscriptions (2012); there were 157,800 internet users in 2009
*Internet code and IDD –* bi; 257 (from UK), 44 (to UK)
*Major broadcasters –* The government-controlled Radio Télévision Nationale du Burundi (RTNB) runs the main national television and radio stations
*Press –* The only regularly published newspaper is the government-owned *Le Renouveau*
*WPFI score –* 42,93 (145)

## CABO VERDE

*Republica de Cabo Verde – Republic of Cabo Verde*

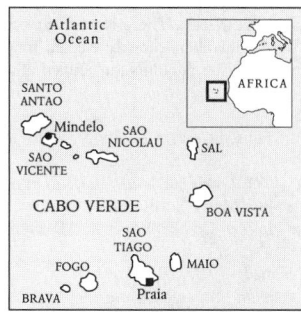

*Area –* 4,033 sq. km; comprises the Windward Islands (Sao Vicente, Santa Luzia, Santo Antao, Sao Nicolau, Boa Vista and Sal) and Leeward Islands (Brava, Fogo, Maio and Sao Tiago)
*Capital –* Praia, on Sao Tiago; population, 132,000 (2011 est)
*Major town –* Mindelo
*Currency –* Escudo Caboverdiano ($) of 100 centavos
*Population –* 545,993 rising at 1.36 per cent a year (2015 est)
*Religion –* Christian (Roman Catholic 77.3 per cent, Protestant 3.7 per cent), Muslim 1.8 per cent (est)
*Language –* Portuguese (official), Creole
*Population density –* 124 per sq. km (2013)
*Urban population –* 64.1 per cent (2013 est)
*Median age (years) –* 24 (2014 est)
*National anthem –* 'Cantico da Liberdade' ['Song of Freedom']
*National day –* 5 July (Independence Day)
*Death penalty –* Abolished for all crimes (since 1981)
*CPI score –* 57 (42)

*Literacy rate* – 98.3 per cent (2015 est)
*Gross enrolment ratio (percentage of relevant age group)* – primary 112 per cent; secondary 93 per cent; tertiary 21 per cent (2012 est)
*Health expenditure (per capita)* – US$165 (2013)
*Life expectancy (years)* – 71.57 (2014 est)
*Mortality rate* – 6.17 (2014 est)
*Birth rate* – 20.72 (2014 est)
*Infant mortality rate* – 24.28 (2014 est)

## CLIMATE AND TERRAIN
The archipelago of ten islands of volcanic origin lies 600km off the west African coast. Elevation extremes range from 2,829m (Mt Fogo, an active volcano on Fogo island) to 0m (Atlantic Ocean). The climate is hot and dry, with periodic droughts.

## HISTORY AND POLITICS
The islands were first discovered and colonised *c.*1460 by Portugal. Administered with Portuguese Guinea until 1879, they became an overseas province in 1951. The country achieved independence on 5 July 1975 after a campaign by the African Party for the Independence of Guinea Bissau and Cape Verde (PAIGC).

The republic was a one-party state under the African Party for the Independence of Cape Verde (PAICV) until 1990. Multiparty elections in 1991 were won by the opposition Movement for Democracy (MPD), and the MPD candidate was elected president. The 2001 legislative elections returned the PAICV to power and the party retained its overall majority in the 2006 and 2011 legislative elections. MPD leader Jorge Fonseca won the 2011 presidential election, taking office in September of that year.

Under the 1992 constitution, the president is directly elected for a five-year term. There is a unicameral National Assembly with 72 members directly elected for a five-year term. The prime minister appoints the council of ministers.

### HEAD OF STATE
*President,* Jorge Fonseca, *elected* 21 August 2011

SELECTED GOVERNMENT MEMBERS *as at April 2015*
*Prime Minister,* Jose Maria Neves
*Deputy Prime Minister,* Cristina Lopes de Almeida Fontes Lima
*Defence,* Rui Semedo
*Finance and Planning,* Cristina Duarte
*Foreign Relations,* Jorge Tolentino

### EMBASSY OF THE REPUBLIC OF CABO VERDE
Avenue Jeanne 29, 1050 Brussels, Belgium
T (+32) (2) 643 6270
*Ambassador Extraordinary and Plenipotentiary,* vacant

### BRITISH AMBASSADOR
HE John Marshall, *apptd* 2011, resident at Dakar, Senegal

## DEFENCE

| Aged 16–49, 2010 est | Males | Females |
|---|---|---|
| Available for military service | 132,087 | 136,956 |
| Fit for military service | 106,864 | 117,518 |

*Military expenditure* – US$10.8m (2014)
*Conscription* – 18–35 years of age; 24 months (selective)

## ECONOMY AND TRADE
The islands have few natural resources, little fresh water and are subject to periods of prolonged drought. A well-managed economy has produced steady growth, and further reforms are intended to attract foreign investment to aid diversification and development of the private sector. The government is dependent on foreign aid and remittances; owing to large-scale emigration the expatriate population is larger than the resident one, and remittances are equivalent to over 20 per cent of GDP. The service sector dominates, with commerce, tourism, transport and public services accounting for 71.4 per cent of GDP. Industry contributes 18.6 per cent and agriculture 10 per cent; fishing resources are not fully exploited. The main industries are the production of food, beverages, garments and footwear, fishing and fish processing, salt mining and ship repair. The economy is expected to grow by 3.1 per cent in 2014, thanks to the ongoing recovery of the Eurozone and continued public sector demand.

The main trading partners are Portugal, Spain and the Netherlands. Exports are fuel, footwear, garments, fish and hides. Imports include foodstuffs (over 80 per cent of food is imported), industrial products, transport equipment and fuel.
*GNI* – US$1,804m; US$3,620 per capita (2013)
*Annual average growth of GDP* – 1 per cent (2014 est)
*Inflation rate* – 1.5 per cent (2013 est)
*Population below poverty line* – 30 per cent (2000 est)
*Unemployment* – 8.6 per cent (2015 est)
*Total external debt* – US$1,559m (2014 est)
*Imports* – US$727m (2013)
*Exports* – US$69m (2013)

BALANCE OF PAYMENTS
*Trade* – US$658m deficit (2013)
*Current Account* – US$173m deficit (2014 est)

| Trade with UK | 2013 | 2014 |
|---|---|---|
| Imports from UK | £13,234,597 | £22,990,127 |
| Exports to UK | £391,947 | £19,652,509 |

## COMMUNICATIONS
*Airports and waterways* – Nine, including airports at Praia and on Sal; the main ports are Praia and Mindelo
*Roadways* – 932km
*Telecommunications* – 70,200 fixed lines and 425,300 mobile subscriptions (2012); there were 150,000 internet users in 2009
*Internet code and IDD* – cv; 238 (from UK), 44 (to UK)
*Major broadcasters* – Radio and television services are operated by the state-run Radiotelevisao Caboverdiana
*WPFI score* – 20,69 (36)

# CAMBODIA

*Preahreacheanachakr Kampuchea – Kingdom of Cambodia*

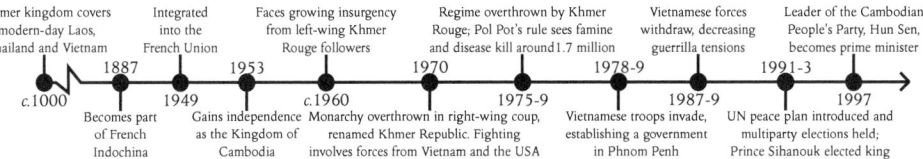

| Khmer kingdom covers modern-day Laos, Thailand and Vietnam | Integrated into the French Union | Faces growing insurgency from left-wing Khmer Rouge followers | Regime overthrown by Khmer Rouge; Pol Pot's rule sees famine and disease kill around 1.7 million | Vietnamese forces withdraw, decreasing guerrilla tensions | Leader of the Cambodian People's Party, Hun Sen, becomes prime minister |
| 1887 | 1953 | 1970 | 1978-9 | 1991-3 |

c.1000 — 1949 — c.1960 — 1975-9 — 1987-9 — 1997

| Becomes part of French Indochina | Gains independence as the Kingdom of Cambodia | Monarchy overthrown in right-wing coup, renamed Khmer Republic. Fighting involves forces from Vietnam and the USA | Vietnamese troops invade, establishing a government in Phnom Penh | UN peace plan introduced and multiparty elections held; Prince Sihanouk elected king |

*Area* – 181,035 sq. km

*Capital* – Phnom Penh; population, 1,729,000 (2015 est)

*Major towns* – Battambang, Siem Reap, Poipet

*Currency* – Riel of 100 sen; the US dollar is widely used

*Population* – 15,708,756 rising at 1.58 per cent a year (2015 est); Khmer (90 per cent), Vietnamese (5 per cent), Chinese (1 per cent) (est)

*Religion* – Buddhist (Theravada) 96.9 per cent, Muslim 1.9 per cent (predominantly Sunni) (est)

*Language* – Khmer (official)

*Population density* – 86 per sq. km (2013)

*Urban population* – 20.3 per cent (2013 est)

*Median age (years)* – 24.1 (2014 est)

*National anthem* – 'Nokoreach' ['Royal Kingdom']

*National day* – 9 November (Independence Day)

*Death penalty* – Abolished for all crimes (since 1989)

*CPI score* – 21 (156)

*Literacy rate* – 91.5 per cent (2015 est)

*Gross enrolment ratio (percentage of relevant age group)* – primary 124 per cent

*Health expenditure (per capita)* – US$51 (2012)

*Hospital beds (per 1,000 people)* – 0.7 (2011)

*Life expectancy (years)* – 63.78 (2014 est)

*Mortality rate* – 7.78 (2014 est)

*Birth rate* – 24.4 (2014 est)

*Infant mortality rate* – 51.36 (2014 est)

## CLIMATE AND TERRAIN

Cambodia is a mostly flat country, apart from the Cardamom Mountains in the south-west and the uplands of the north-east. The fertile central plains are drained by rivers that run into Tonle Sap, the largest lake in South East Asia, and into the Mekong river, which flows through the country from north to south. The highest point of elevation is 1,810m (Phnum Aoral) while the lowest is 0m (Gulf of Thailand). The climate is tropical, with a monsoon season from May to November.

## POLITICS

Under the 1993 constitution, Cambodia is a pluralist liberal democracy with a hereditary constitutional monarchy. The monarch is chosen from eligible royal males by a Council of the Throne elected by parliament. Executive power rests with the government, which is responsible to parliament. The bicameral parliament comprises the National Assembly, which has 123 members directly elected for a five-year term, and the senate, which has 61 members, 57 of whom are elected for a six-year term by the National Assembly and commune councils, with two members appointed by the king and two appointed by the National Assembly.

King Sihanouk abdicated in 2004 and was succeeded by his son, Prince Norodom Sihamoni. In the 2013 election the Cambodian People's Party won 68 seats in the National Assembly – losing the large majority that, in the 2008 elections, had allowed them to form a government without a coalition for the first time. Prime Minister Hun Sen, who has been in office since 1985, was sworn in for a further five-year term in September 2013.

## HEAD OF STATE

HM *The King of Cambodia,* Norodom Sihamoni, *crowned* 29 October 2004

*President of the National Assembly,* Heng Samrin

## SELECTED GOVERNMENT MEMBERS *as at April 2015*

*Prime Minister,* Hun Sen

*Deputy Prime Ministers,* Gen. Tea Banh *(Defence)*; Keat Chhon; Hor Namhong *(Foreign Affairs)*; Sar Kheng *(Interior)*; Sok An; Yim Chhai Ly; Ben Chhin; Ke Kim Yan; Men Sam An

## ROYAL EMBASSY OF CAMBODIA

64 Brondesbury Park, London NW6 7AT

T 020-8451 7997 E cambodianembassy@btconnect.com

W www.cambodianembassy.org.uk

*Ambassador Extraordinary and Plenipotentiary,* HE Meas Kim Heng, *apptd* 2014

## BRITISH EMBASSY

27–29 Street 75, Sangat Srah Chak, Khan Daun Penh, Phnom Penh 12201

T (+855) (0) 23 427 124

W www.gov.uk/government/world/cambodia

*Ambassador Extraordinary and Plenipotentiary,* HE William Longhurst, *apptd* 2014

## SECURITY PROBLEMS

The Khmer Rouge continued to fight a guerrilla war until 1996, when it was weakened by internal divisions. Pol Pot was tried by the Khmer Rouge in 1997 and died in captivity in 1998. The remaining Khmer Rouge soldiers surrendered in 1999. A UN-backed tribunal was established in 2007 to try former leaders of the Khmer Rouge regime for atrocities committed during its rule.

Relations with Thailand deteriorated after 2008 because of a long-running dispute over the border in the area of the Preah Vihear temple, with sporadic exchanges of fire and occasional fighting between the two countries' forces. In November 2013 the International Court of Justice ruled that Thailand must withdraw its troops from the temple and granted most of the territory to Cambodia.

## DEFENCE

| Aged 16–49, 2010 est | Males | Females |
| --- | --- | --- |
| Available for military service | 3,883,724 | 4,003,585 |
| Fit for military service | 2,638,167 | 2,965,328 |

*Military expenditure* – US$278m (2014 est)

## ECONOMY AND TRADE

Since 1999 the government has made progress with economic reform and development but the country remains very poor. The demographic imbalance (over half the population is under 25), lack of education and skills, deeply ingrained corruption and an absence of basic infrastructure also pose serious problems. Nevertheless, the economy grew strongly by 7 per cent in 2014 and was expected to accelerate to 7.3 per cent in 2015. Economic growth has been driven by the expansion of garment manufacturing, construction, agriculture, tourism and mining, which is attracting foreign investment, but the benefits are largely limited to urban areas. The discovery of oil and gas deposits in territorial waters promises additional revenue once exploitation begins. Around 180,000 migrants returned from

Thailand in 2014, following fears that they would be persecuted by Thailand's military government.

The service sector contributes 41.8 per cent of GDP, agriculture 32.7 per cent and industry 25.5 per cent. Agriculture engages 55.8 per cent of the workforce; the main crops are rice, rubber, maize, vegetables, cashew nuts and tapioca. The main industrial activities are tourism, garment and textiles manufacturing, processing of agricultural and forestry products, fishing, and mining gemstones. The main trading partners are the USA (32.6 per cent of exports), Thailand (27.1 per cent of imports), Vietnam, the UK and China.
*GNI* – US$13,326m; US$950 per capita (2013)
*Annual average growth of GDP* – 7.2 per cent (2014 est)
*Inflation rate* – 2.9 per cent (2013 est)
*Population below poverty line* – 20 per cent (2012 est)
*Unemployment* – 0.4 per cent (2015 est)
*Total external debt* – US$7,377m (2014 est)
*Imports* – US$13,000m (2013)
*Exports* – US$9,100m (2013)

BALANCE OF PAYMENTS
*Trade* – US$3,900m deficit (2013)
*Current Account* – US$1,987m deficit (2014 est)

| Trade with UK | 2013 | 2014 |
| --- | --- | --- |
| Imports from UK | £17,782,635 | £11,157,140 |
| Exports to UK | £589,391,949 | £680,393,318 |

## COMMUNICATIONS
*Airports* – Six, the main airports are at Phnom Penh, Siem Reap and Sihanoukville
*Waterways* – There are 3,700km of navigable waterways, mostly on the Mekong river, and ships of up to 2,500 tonnes can sail as far as Phnom Penh all year round
*Roadways and railways* – 2,492km; 690km
*Telecommunications* – 584,000 fixed lines and 19.1 million mobile phone subscriptions (2012); there were 78,500 internet users in 2009
*Internet code and IDD* – kh; 855 (from UK), 1 44 (to UK)
*Major broadcasters* – There are 11 TV broadcasters, including the government-run National Television of Cambodia (TVK); there are roughly 160 radio broadcasters
*Press* – Daily newspapers include the pro-government *Reaksmei Kampuchea* (Khmer), and the English-language *Cambodia Daily* and *Phnom Penh Post*
*WPFI score* – 40,99 (139)

# CAMEROON

*République du Cameroun – Republic of Cameroon*

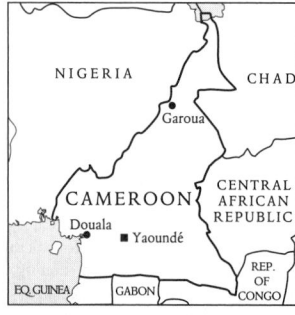

*Area* – 475,440 sq. km
*Capital* – Yaoundé; population, 3,060,000 (2015 est)

*Major cities* – Bafoussam, Bamenda, Douala, Garoua
*Currency* – Franc CFA of 100 centimes
*Population* – 23,739,218 rising at 2.59 per cent a year (2015 est); Cameroon Highlanders (31 per cent), Equatorial Bantu (19 per cent), Kirdi (11 per cent), Fulani (10 per cent), Northwestern Bantu (8 per cent), Eastern Nigritic (7 per cent) (est)
*Religion* – Christian 69 per cent (Roman Catholic 38 per cent, Protestant 26 per cent), Muslim 21 per cent, indigenous beliefs 6 per cent (est)
*Language* – English, French (both official), about 24 African languages
*Population density* – 47 per sq. km (2013)
*Urban population* – 53.2 per cent (2013 est)
*Median age (years)* – 18.3 (2014 est)
*National anthem* – 'O Cameroun, Berceau de nos Ancetres' ['O Cameroon, Cradle of Our Forefathers']
*National day* – 20 May (Republic Day)
*Death penalty* – Retained (last used 1997)
*CPI score* – 27 (136)
*Literacy rate* – 83.8 per cent (2015 est)
*Gross enrolment ratio (percentage of relevant age group)* – primary 111 per cent; secondary 50 per cent (2012 est); tertiary 12 per cent (2011 est)
*Health expenditure (per capita)* – US$67 (2013)
*Hospital beds (per 1,000 people)* – 1.3 (2010)
*Life expectancy (years)* – 57.35 (2014 est)
*Mortality rate* – 10.4 (2014 est)
*Birth rate* – 36.58 (2014 est)
*Infant mortality rate* – 55.1 (2014 est)
*HIV/AIDS adult prevalence* – 0.5. per cent (2013)

## CLIMATE AND TERRAIN
There are three main geographic zones: desert plains and savannah in the north (the Lake Chad basin), mountains and plateaux in the central region and tropical rainforests in the south and east. Elevation extremes range from 4,095m (Fako on Mt Cameroon, an active volcano) to 0m (Atlantic Ocean). The climate varies from tropical in the south to arid in the north. There is a wet season from April to September in the north, while there is low rain from March to June and heavy rain from September to November in the south.

## POLITICS
The 1972 constitution was amended in 1990 to enable a return to multiparty rule, in 1996 to extend the presidential term and to provide for the establishment of a second legislative chamber (yet to be implemented), and in 2008 to remove the limit on the number of presidential terms.

The president is directly elected for a seven-year term and appoints the prime minister and cabinet. The unicameral National Assembly has 180 members, directly elected for a five-year term.

In the 2013 legislative election, the Cameroon People's Democratic Movement (RDPC) retained its overwhelming majority in the legislature, winning 148 of the available 180 seats. Incumbent president Paul Biya retained the presidency in 2011, picking up 78 per cent of the vote.

Cameroon has experienced an increasing number of cross-border raids by the Nigeria based Islamist group Boko Haram since 2014. In response, a multinational task force consisting of troops from Cameroon and Chad has carried out attacks on Boko Haram bases in northern Nigeria.

HEAD OF STATE
*President,* Paul Biya, *took power* 6 November 1982, *elected* 14 January 1984, *re-elected* 1988, 1992, 1997, 2004, 2011

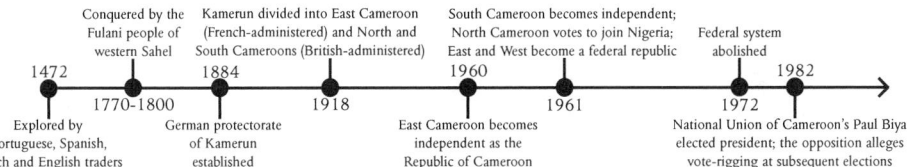

| | | | |
|---|---|---|---|
| Conquered by the Fulani people of western Sahel | Kamerun divided into East Cameroon (French-administered) and North and South Cameroons (British-administered) | South Cameroon becomes independent; North Cameroon votes to join Nigeria; East and West become a federal republic | Federal system abolished |
| 1472 | 1884 | 1960 | 1982 |
| 1770–1800 | 1918 | 1961 | 1972 |
| Explored by Portuguese, Spanish, Dutch and English traders | German protectorate of Kamerun established | East Cameroon becomes independent as the Republic of Cameroon | National Union of Cameroon's Paul Biya elected president; the opposition alleges vote-rigging at subsequent elections |

**SELECTED GOVERNMENT MEMBERS** *as at April 2015*
*Prime Minister,* Philemon Yang
*Deputy Prime Minister,* Amadou Ali
*Economy,* Emmanuel Nganou Djoumessi
*Foreign Affairs,* Pierre Mbonjo

**HIGH COMMISSION FOR THE REPUBLIC OF CAMEROON**
84 Holland Park, London W11 3SB
☎ 020-7727 0771 **E** info@cameroonhighcommission.co.uk
⊕ www.cameroonhighcommission.co.uk
*High Commissioner,* HE Nkwelle Ekaney, *apptd* 2008

**BRITISH HIGH COMMISSION**
PO Box 547, Avenue Winston Churchill, Yaoundé, Centre Region 547
☎ (+237) 2222 0796 **E** bhc.yaounde@fco.gov.uk
⊕ www.gov.uk/government/world/cameroon
*High Commissioner,* HE Brian Olley, *apptd* 2013

## DEFENCE

| *Aged 16–49, 2010 est* | *Males* | *Females* |
|---|---|---|
| Available for military service | 4,667,251 | 4,548,909 |
| Fit for military service | 2,794,998 | 2,718,110 |

*Military expenditure* – US$401m (2014)

## ECONOMY AND TRADE

Political stability and natural resources such as oil and timber have enabled agricultural, industrial and infrastructure development. Coupled with the growth of domestic demand and implementation of large-scale infrastructure projects, this has helped to counteract the effects of the global downturn. Cameroon also has a large and top-heavy public sector and endemic corruption, and recent IMF funding and debt relief have been conditional on progress towards privatisation and greater financial transparency. The emergence of Boko Haram in Nigeria presents a long-term threat to tourist revenue and international investment.

Industry contributes 27.6 per cent to GDP, agriculture 19.9 per cent and services 52.5 per cent. Around 70 per cent of the workforce is engaged in agriculture. The main industrial activity is oil production and refining. Revenue is also earned from the oil pipeline passing through the country from Chad. Despite starting several large-scale energy projects, Cameroon struggles to appeal to foreign investors due to the structure of its public sector and corruption.

The main trading partners are EU countries, China, Nigeria, India and the USA. Principal exports are crude oil and petroleum products, timber, cocoa, aluminium, coffee and cotton. Imports are chiefly machinery, electrical and transport equipment, fuel and food.

*GNI* – US$28,630m; US$1,290 per capita (2013)
*Annual average growth of GDP* – 5.1 per cent (2014 est)
*Inflation rate* – 1.9 per cent (2013 est)
*Population below poverty line* – 48 per cent (2000 est)
*Unemployment* – 4.3 per cent (2015 est)
*Total external debt* – US$5,006m (2014 est)
*Imports* – US$7,006m (2013)
*Exports* – US$4,204m (2013)

**BALANCE OF PAYMENTS**
*Trade* – US$2,802m deficit (2013)
*Current Account* – US$1,333m deficit (2014 est)

| *Trade with UK* | *2013* | *2014* |
|---|---|---|
| Imports from UK | £65,709,955 | £46,529,014 |
| Exports to UK | £99,709,343 | £151,219,996 |

## COMMUNICATIONS

*Airports* – 11; the main airports are at Douala, Garoua and Yaoundé
*Waterways* – The main seaports are at Douala and the Limboh terminal. The river Benue is navigable up to Garoua in the rainy season
*Roadways and railways* – 4,108km; 1,245km
*Telecommunications* – There are 737,400 fixed lines and 13.1 million mobile subscriptions (2012); there were 749,600 internet users in 2009
*Internet code and IDD* – cm; 237 (from UK), 44 (to UK)
*Major broadcasters* – The state-run Cameroon Radio-Television Corporation (CRTV) held a monopoly on broadcast media until liberalisation in 2001 allowed commercial television and radio stations to be established; other major broadcasters include Canal 2 and Radio Siantou
*Press* – The government-owned *Cameroon Tribune* is the main, daily national newspaper
*WPFI score* – 39,63 (133)

# CANADA

*Area* – 9,984,670 sq. km
*Capital* – Ottawa; population, 994,000 (2015 est)
*Major cities* – Calgary, Edmonton, Hamilton, Montréal, Québec, Toronto, Vancouver, Winnipeg
*Currency* – Canadian dollar (C$) of 100 cents
*Population* – 35,099,836 rising at 0.75 per cent a year (2015 est)
*Religion* – Christian (Catholic 40.5 per cent, Protestant 20.3 per cent, other 6.3 per cent), Muslim 3.2 per cent, Hindu 1.5 per cent, Sikh 1.4 per cent, Buddhist 1.1 per cent, Jewish 1 per cent (est)
*Language* – English, French (both official), Punjabi, Italian, Spanish, German, Cantonese, Tagalog, Arabic
*Population density* – 4 per sq. km (2013)
*Urban population* – 80.9 per cent (2013 est)
*Median age (years)* – 41.7 (2014 est)
*National anthem* – 'O Canada'

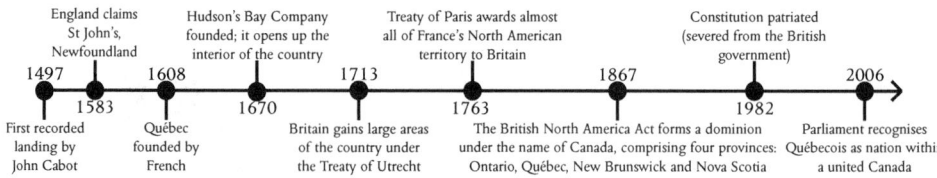

England claims St John's, Newfoundland — 1497

First recorded landing by John Cabot — 1583

Québec founded by French — 1670

Hudson's Bay Company founded; it opens up the interior of the country — 1608

Britain gains large areas of the country under the Treaty of Utrecht — 1713

Treaty of Paris awards almost all of France's North American territory to Britain — 1763

The British North America Act forms a dominion under the name of Canada, comprising four provinces: Ontario, Québec, New Brunswick and Nova Scotia — 1867

Constitution patriated (severed from the British government) — 1982

Parliament recognises Québecois as nation within a united Canada — 2006

*National day* – 1 July (Canada Day)
*Death penalty* – Abolished for all crimes (since 1998)
*CPI score* – 81 (10)

## CLIMATE AND TERRAIN

The six main geographic divisions of Canada are: the Appalachian–Acadian region; the Canadian Shield, which comprises more than half the country; the St Lawrence–Great Lakes lowland; the interior plains; the Cordilleran region; and the Arctic archipelago, which lies under continuous permafrost. The most southerly point is Middle Island in Lake Erie. Elevation extremes range from 5,959m (Mt Logan) to 0m (Atlantic Ocean). The climate varies from temperate in the south to subarctic and arctic in the north. The east and centre experience greater extremes than in corresponding latitudes in Europe, but the climate is milder in the south-western part of the prairie region and the southern parts of the Pacific slope. The tornado season is April to September, peaking in June and early July in southern Ontario, Alberta, Québec, Saskatchewan and Manitoba through to Thunder Bay. The interior of British Columbia and western New Brunswick are also tornado zones.

## POLITICS

Under the 1982 constitution, the head of state is Queen Elizabeth II, represented by a governor-general appointed on the advice of the Canadian prime minister.

The bicameral parliament consists of a senate and a House of Commons. The senate comprises 105 members, who serve until the age of 75, appointed by the governor-general on the recommendation of the prime minister; seats are assigned on a regional basis. A reform bill introduced in 2011 proposed nine-year non-renewable terms for senators. The House of Commons has 308 members, directly elected for a four-year term. Representation is proportional to the population of each province. Each province is largely self-governing, with its own lieutenant-governor and unicameral legislative assembly. The territories are administered by the federal government.

A parliamentary vote of no confidence ended 12 years of Liberal government in 2005. In snap general elections in 2006 and 2008, the Conservative Party won the most seats, but not a majority, and formed minority governments under Stephen Harper. His government won a snap general election in May 2011, increasing its seats to achieve an overall majority. The next legislative election is scheduled to take place on 19 October 2015.

GOVERNOR-GENERAL
*Governor-General*, HE David Johnston, *apptd* 2010

SELECTED GOVERNMENT MEMBERS *as at April 2015*
*Prime Minister*, Stephen Harper
*Defence*, Jason Kenney
*Finance*, Joe Oliver
*Foreign Affairs*, Robert Nicholson

CANADIAN HIGH COMMISSION
Macdonald House, 1 Grosvenor Square, London W1K 4AB
T 020-7258 6600 W www.unitedkingdom.gc.ca
*High Commissioner*, HE Gordon Campbell, *apptd* 2011

BRITISH HIGH COMMISSION
80 Elgin Street, Ottawa, Ontario K1P 5K7
T (+1) (613) 237 1530 E ukincanada@fco.gov.uk
W www.gov.uk/government/world/canada
*High Commissioner*, HE Howard Drake, OBE, *apptd* 2013

DEFENCE
The Canadian armed forces are unified and organised into three functional commands: land force command, maritime command and air command.

| *Aged 16–49, 2010 est* | *Males* | *Females* |
|---|---|---|
| Available for military service | 8,031,266 | 7,755,550 |
| Fit for military service | 6,633,472 | 6,389,669 |

*Military expenditure* – US$17,452m (2014)

## FEDERAL STRUCTURE

| *Provinces or Territories* (with official contractions) | *Population* (2014) | *Area (sq. km)* | *Capital* | *Premier* |
|---|---|---|---|---|
| Alberta (AB) | 4,121,692,400 | 661,848 | Edmonton | Jim Prentice |
| British Columbia (BC) | 4,631,302 | 944,735 | Victoria | Christy Clark |
| Manitoba (MB) | 1,282,043 | 647,797 | Winnipeg | Greg Selinger |
| New Brunswick (NB) | 753,914 | 72,908 | Fredericton | Brian Gallant |
| Newfoundland and Labrador (NL) | 526,977 | 405,212 | St John's | Paul Davis |
| Northwest Territories (NT) | 43,623 | 1,346,106 | Yellowknife | Bob McLeod* |
| Nova Scotia (NS) | 942,668 | 55,284 | Halifax | Stephen McNeil |
| Nunavut (NU) | 36,585 | 2,093,190 | Iqaluit | Peter Taptuna* |
| Ontario (ON) | 13,678,740 | 1,076,395 | Toronto | Kathleen Wynne |
| Prince Edward Island (PE) | 146,283 | 5,660 | Charlottetown | Wade MacLauchlan |
| Québec (QC) | 8,214,672 | 1,542,056 | Québec City | Philippe Couillard |
| Saskatchewan (SK) | 1,125,410 | 651,036 | Regina | Brad Wall |
| Yukon Territory (YT) | 36,510 | 482,443 | Whitehorse | Darrell Pasloski* |

* Territorial government leader

## ECONOMY AND TRADE

Canada has a highly developed, industrialised and diversified market economy, which was transformed from a pre-dominantly rural to an industrial economy in the second half of the 20th century by the growth of mining, manufacturing and services. Tight management of government finances resulted in balanced budgets from the late 1990s until 2007, and free-trade agreements with the USA in 1989 and 1994 (NAFTA) stimulated trade. The economy went into recession in 2008 owing to the global downturn; recovery began in 2010 and marginal growth was achieved in 2012–14. Growth in 2015 is expected to be negatively impacted by the global decline in crude oil prices, though other exports will be helped by the low value of the Canadian dollar.

Canada's wealth of natural resources make it the world's largest exporter of timber, pulp and newsprint (over half the land is tree-covered), and it is one of the world's largest exporters of minerals, particularly uranium (of which it is the world's second largest single producer) and diamonds. As of 2012, around 7.2 per cent of the land area is farmed, of which 4.6 per cent is under cultivation, mostly in the prairie region of western Canada. The country is one of the world's leading food producers, particularly of wheat, barley, oilseed, tobacco, fruit, vegetables and dairy products. The fishing industry is also significant but has declined in recent years because of restrictions introduced to protect stocks after decades of overfishing. Oil, natural gas and hydroelectricity production is high enough for Canada to be a net exporter of energy; oil production, in particular, has become a significant economic driver, and Canada's oil reserves are ranked third in the world behind Saudi Arabia and Venezuela. The government has plans to develop the oil and gas-rich Arctic area and the assertion of its sovereignty has attracted criticism from other Arctic countries and is complicated by the lack of international agreement on countries' territorial claims.

In 2013, the services sector contributed 70.1 per cent of GDP, industry 28.2 per cent and agriculture 1.7 per cent.

The USA is Canada's main trading partner, taking 74.5 per cent of exports and providing 50.6 per cent of imports. The main exports are motor vehicles and parts, industrial machinery, aircraft, telecommunications equipment, chemicals, plastics, fertilisers, forestry products, energy products (including crude oil, natural gas and electricity) and aluminium.

*GNI* – US$1,835,382m; US$52,200 per capita (2013)
*Annual average growth of GDP* – 2.3 per cent (2014 est)
*Inflation rate* – 0.9 per cent (2013 est)
*Population below poverty line* – 9.4 per cent (2008 est)
*Unemployment* – 7 per cent (2015 est)
*Total external debt* – US$1,331,000m (2012 est)
*Imports* – US$461,925m (2013)
*Exports* – US$458,397m (2013)

BALANCE OF PAYMENTS
*Trade* – US$3,528m deficit (2013)
*Current Account* – US$39,372m deficit (2014)

| Trade with UK | 2013 | 2014 |
| --- | --- | --- |
| Imports from UK | £4,501,543,537 | £4,090,916,990 |
| Exports to UK | £10,589,799,391 | £9,887,897,753 |

## COMMUNICATIONS

*Airports* – There are 523 paved airports and airstrips, of which 26 serve major cities
*Waterways* – There are 636km of waterways and over 300 ports, the most significant of which are Vancouver and Prince Rupert on the Pacific coast and Montréal, Halifax, Port Cartier, Sept-Iles/Pointe Noire, Saint John and Québec in the east. Most deep-water ports are open all year, and

Churchill, on Hudson's Bay, is ice-free for longer periods as a result of climate change. In addition, the Great Lakes/St Lawrence Seaway system, the world's longest inland waterway for ocean-going shipping, provides access to the North American interior
*Roadways and railways* – 415,600km, including 17,000km of motorways; the 46,552km railway network transports more than 340 million tonnes of freight each year
*Telecommunications* – There are 18.01 million fixed lines and 26.263 million mobile telephones subscriptions (2012); there were 26.96 million internet users in 2009
*Internet code and IDD* – ca; 1 (from UK), 011 44 (to UK)
*Major broadcasters* – The public broadcaster, the Canadian Broadcasting Corporation (CBC), transmits programmes in English and French, and provides services for indigenous peoples in the north of the country. Société Radio-Canada is the French-language public broadcasting service
*Press* – Major newspapers include *The Toronto Sun*, *National Post* and *Le Journal de Montréal* (French-language)
*WPFI score* – 10,99 (8)

## EDUCATION AND HEALTH

Education is compulsory from ages six to 16 (18 in Ontario and New Brunswick).
*Gross enrolment ratio (percentage of relevant age group)* – primary 98 per cent; secondary 103 per cent (2011 est)
*Health expenditure (per capita)* – US$5,718 (2013)
*Hospital beds (per 1,000 people)* – 2.7 (2010)
*Life expectancy (years)* – 81.67 (2014 est)
*Mortality rate* – 8.31 (2014 est)
*Birth rate* – 10.29 (2014 est)
*Infant mortality rate* – 4.71 (2014 est)

# CENTRAL AFRICAN REPUBLIC

*République Centrafricaine – Central African Republic*

*Area* – 622,984 sq. km
*Capital* – Bangui; population, 790,000 (2015 est)
*Major cities* – Berbérati, Bimbo, Carnot
*Currency* – Franc CFA of 100 centimes
*Population* – 5,391,539 rising at 2.13 per cent a year (2015 est); Baya (33 per cent), Banda (27 per cent), Mandja (13 per cent), Sara (10 per cent), Mboum (7 per cent), M'Baka (4 per cent), Yakoma (4 per cent) (est)
*Religion* – Christian (Protestant denominations 51 per cent, Roman Catholic 29 per cent), Muslim 10 per cent (est). Some also practise animism, although these beliefs are often integrated into Christian and Muslim worship
*Language* – French (official), Sangho, other African languages
*Population density* – 7 per sq. km (2013)
*Urban population* – 39.5 per cent (2013 est)
*Median age (years)* – 19.4 (2014 est)

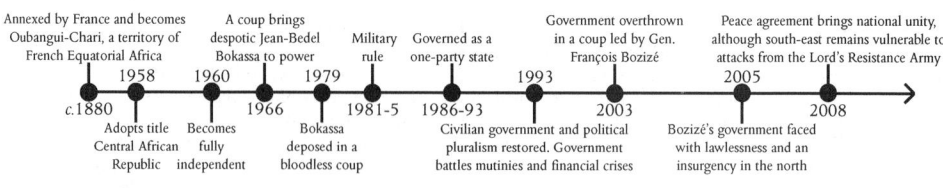

Annexed by France and becomes Oubangui-Chari, a territory of French Equatorial Africa — **1958**

A coup brings despotic Jean-Bedel Bokassa to power — **1960**

Military rule — **1979**

Governed as a one-party state — **1981-5**

Government overthrown in a coup led by Gen. François Bozizé — **1993**

Peace agreement brings national unity, although south-east remains vulnerable to attacks from the Lord's Resistance Army — **2005**

*c.*1880 — Adopts title Central African Republic

**1966** — Becomes fully independent

**1986-93** — Bokassa deposed in a bloodless coup

**2003** — Civilian government and political pluralism restored. Government battles mutinies and financial crises

**2008** — Bozizé's government faced with lawlessness and an insurgency in the north

*National anthem* – 'La Renaissance' ['The Rebirth']
*National day* – 1 December (Republic Day)
*Death penalty* – Retained (last used 1981)
*CPI score* – 24 (150)
*Literacy rate* – 36.4 per cent (2015 est)
*Gross enrolment ratio (percentage of relevant age group)* – primary 95 per cent; secondary 18 per cent; tertiary 3 per cent (2012 est)
*Health expenditure (per capita)* – US$13 (2013)
*Hospital beds (per 1,000 people)* – 1 (2011)
*Life expectancy (years)* – 51.35 (2014 est)
*Mortality rate* – 14.11 (2014 est)
*Birth rate* – 35.45 (2014 est)
*Infant mortality rate* – 92.86 (2014 est)
*HIV/AIDS adult prevalence* – 4.7 per cent (2009 est)

## CLIMATE AND TERRAIN
This landlocked state lies on a plateau between the Chad and Congo river basins, with mostly savannah in the north and rainforest in the south. The main river is the Oubangui, which is the lowest point of elevation (335m). The highest point is Mt Ngaoui (1,420m). The climate is tropical, with a wet season in the north from May to September and in the south from May to October. The north can experience average temperatures of up to 34°C between January and April, and the humidity can be extreme. Seasonal temperatures vary slightly, ranging from 24.3°C in August to 27.7°C in March.

## POLITICS
Under the 2004 constitution, the president is elected for a five-year term, renewable once. The unicameral National Assembly has 105 members, directly elected for a five-year term. The prime minister is appointed by the president and appoints the ministers.

Legislative elections in January and March 2011 were won by the Kwa Na Kwa (KNK) coalition, a group loyal to President Francois Bozizé. In March 2013 President Bozizé, who initially seized power in 2003 and won presidential elections in 2005 and 2011, fled the country after the New Seleka rebel coalition took the capital by force; the rebel leader Michel Djotodia suspended the constitution and dissolved parliament. Djotodia was forced to resign in January 2014 after he failed to stop sectarian violence between Seleka and Christian militias. On 20 January Catherine Samba Panza was elected to interim president. Continued violence in 2015 caused fresh elections to be delayed until October 2015 when a referendum on a new constitution will also be held.

HEAD OF STATE
*Interim President,* Catherine Samba-Panza, *took office* January 2014

SELECTED GOVERNMENT MEMBERS *as at* September 2015
*Prime Minister,* Mahamat Kamoun
*Defence,* Marie Koyara
*Finance,* Assane Kadre
*Foreign Affairs,* Samuel Ranba

EMBASSY OF THE CENTRAL AFRICAN REPUBLIC
30 Rue des Perchamps, 75016 Paris, France
**T** (+33) (1) 4224 4256
*Ambassador Extraordinary and Plenipotentiary,* vacant

BRITISH AMBASSADOR
HE Brian Olley, *apptd* 2013, resident at Yaoundé, Cameroon

## DEFENCE

| Aged 16–49, 2010 est | Males | Females |
| --- | --- | --- |
| Available for military service | 1,149,856 | 1,145,897 |
| Fit for military service | 655,875 | 661,308 |

*Military expenditure* – US$51.6m (2010)
*Conscription* – 18 years of age; 24 months (selective)

## ECONOMY AND TRADE
The economy is largely undeveloped owing to decades of instability and misrule. Development is still hindered by political factionalism, a landlocked position and poor transport infrastructure, an unskilled workforce, massively unequal income distribution, and corruption. The country is dependent on international aid and the amount received only partially meets humanitarian needs. Sectarian fighting in 2013 caused a 34.2 per cent drop in GDP growth. The economy recovered slightly in 2014, growing by 1.5 per cent in 2014 and is expected to grow by 5.7 per cent in 2015, still lower than the pre-civil war rate.

Natural resources include diamonds, gold, uranium and timber; diamond and gold mining, and forestry are among the main industrial activities but the economy still depends mostly on agriculture, which accounts for 56.6 per cent of GDP. Most production is at subsistence level but cotton, coffee and tobacco form the main exports along with diamonds and timber. The main imports are food, textiles, fuels and machinery. Trade is mainly with Belgium, the Netherlands, France and China.
*GNI* – US$1,475m; US$320 per capita (2013)
*Annual average growth of GDP* – 1 per cent (2014 est)
*Inflation rate* – 1.5 per cent (2013 est)
*Unemployment* – 9.0 per cent (2015 est)
*Total external debt* – US$560.6m (2014 est)
*Imports* – US$250m (2013)
*Exports* – US$140m (2013)

BALANCE OF PAYMENTS
*Trade* – US$111m deficit (2013)
*Current Account* – US$11m deficit (2014 est)

| Trade with UK | 2013 | 2014 |
| --- | --- | --- |
| Imports from UK | £659,685 | £1,399,234 |
| Exports to UK | £214,270 | £129,750 |

## COMMUNICATIONS
*Airports* – Two, the principal airport is at Bangui
*Waterways* – There are 2,800km of waterways, mostly on the Oubangui and Sangha rivers, that are navigable all year and are important passenger and freight transport routes
*Roadways* – 20,278km

*Telecommunications* – There are 5,600 fixed lines and 1.07 million mobile telephone subcriptions (2012); there were 22,600 internet users in 2009
*Internet code and IDD* – cf; 236 (from UK), 44 (to UK)
*Major broadcasters* – Major broadcasters include the state-run Télévision Centrafricaine and Radio Centrafique; Radio Ndeke Luka operates nationally and is funded by the UN and foreign NGOs
*Press* – There are five privately owned daily newspapers, including *Le Citoyen*, *Le Confident* and *L'Hirondelle*
*WPFI score* – 33,84 (110)

# CHAD

*République du Tchad/Jumhuriyat Tshad* – *Republic of Chad*

*Area* – 1,284,000 sq. km
*Capital* – N'Djamena; population, 1,260,000 (2015 est)
*Major cities* – Abéché, Moundou, Sarh
*Currency* – Franc CFA of 100 centimes
*Population* – 11,631,456 rising at 1.89 per cent a year (2015 est); the population is made up of around 200 ethnic groups of which Sara, Mayo-Kebbi, Kanem-Bornou, Ouaddai, Hadjarai and Arab are the largest
*Religion* – Muslim 58 per cent, Christian (Roman Catholic 18 per cent, Protestant 16 per cent), indigenous beliefs are practised in the south
*Language* – French, Arabic (both official), Sara (in the south)
*Population density* – 10 per sq. km (2013)
*Urban population* – 22 per cent (2013 est)
*Median age (years)* – 17.2 (2014 est)
*National anthem* – 'La Tchadienne' ['People of Chad']
*National day* – 11 August (Independence Day)
*Death penalty* – Retained (last used 2003)
*CPI score* – 22 (154)
*Literacy rate* – 52.7 per cent (2015 est)
*Gross enrolment ratio (percentage of relevant age group)* – primary 95 per cent; secondary 23 per cent (2012 est); tertiary 2 per cent (2011 est)
*Health expenditure (per capita)* – US$25 (2012)
*Life expectancy (years)* – 49.44 (2014 est)
*Mortality rate* – 14.56 (2014 est)
*Birth rate* – 37.29 (2014 est)
*Infant mortality rate* – 90.3 (2014 est)
*HIV/AIDS adult prevalence* – 2.7 per cent (2012 est)

## CLIMATE AND TERRAIN

The population is concentrated in the fertile lowlands of the south, away from the arid central and northern desert areas. The highest point of elevation is 3,415m (Emi Koussi) and the lowest is 160m (the Djourab depression). The climate is desert in the north and tropical in the south, with a wet season from July to September.

## HISTORY AND POLITICS

Chad was colonised by France from the 1890s, becoming part of French Equatorial Africa. It became self-governing after the Second World War and independent on 11 August 1960. A one-party state was declared in 1963 by the president, a southerner, which in 1965 prompted a rebellion in the north against a perceived pro-southern bias in the government. Regional and ethnic tensions, most notably between the Muslim Arab north and the Christian and animist African south have made the country politically unstable since independence. Chad's instability was exacerbated from the 1970s to the 1990s by Libya's support for some rebels and its annexation of territory in northern Chad, and since 2004 by the overspill of the Darfur conflict in Sudan.

Idriss Déby seized power in 1990 after leading a rebellion in eastern Chad, and initiated a transition to democracy. A new constitution was introduced in 1996, and the first multiparty elections were held.

Déby won the first multiparty presidential election in 1996 and was re-elected in 2001, 2006 and 2011, despite doubts over the integrity of the polls. The 2011 legislative election was won by Déby's Patriotic Salvation Movement (MPS) and its allies, with 133 seats. New legislative elections are due before the end of 2015.

The 1996 constitution was amended in 2005 to remove the limit on the number of terms a president may serve. The president is directly elected for a five-year term. The unicameral National Assembly of 188 members is directly elected for a four-year term. The prime minister is appointed by the president.

HEAD OF STATE
*President,* Idriss Déby, *took power* December 1990, *elected* 3 July 1996, *re-elected* 2001, 2006, 2011

SELECTED GOVERNMENT MEMBERS *as at September 2015*
*Prime Minister,* Kalzeubet Pahimi Deubet
*Defence,* Benaindo Tatola
*Economy,* Aziz Mahamat
*Finance,* Ngarlenan Docdjengar
*Foreign Affairs,* Moussa Faki Mahamat

EMBASSY OF THE REPUBLIC OF CHAD
Boulevard Lambermont 52, 1030 Brussels, Belgium
T (+32) (2) 215 1975 E ambassade.tchad@chello.be
W www.ambassadedutchad.be
*Ambassador Extraordinary and Plenipotentiary,* HE Ousmane Matar Breme, *apptd* 2013

BRITISH AMBASSADOR
HE Brian Olley, *apptd* 2013, resident at Yaoundé, Cameroon

INSURGENCIES
The series of insurgencies over the decades since independence means that no government has ever controlled the whole of the country. Rebel offensives reached the capital in 2006 and 2008 before being repulsed. In 2009, eight rebel groups united to form the Union of Resistance Forces alliance.

From 2004, the east and south-east were further destabilised by the overspill of fighting from Sudan's Darfur region. The EU/UN mission deployed in 2008 to protect Sudanese refugees in Chad was withdrawn in 2010, and relations with Sudan have now been normalised and the border reopened. In 2012, the leader of rebel group FPR (Popular Front for Recovery), Abdel Kader Baba Ladde, surrendered to military forces in the Central African Republic and returned to Chad. In 2013, following a coup in the Central African Republic, a regional summit in Chad agreed that neighbouring countries should send troops to restore security to the region.

In July 2014, France announced it would set up a new military operation in the Sahel region in an effort to stop the emergence of jihadist groups. The operation, based in the Chadian capital N'Djamena, will involve around 3,000 French troops, along with troops from Burkina Faso, Chad, Mali and Mauritania.

## DEFENCE

| Aged 16–49, 2010 est | Males | Females |
|---|---|---|
| Available for military service | 2,090,244 | 2,441,321 |
| Fit for military service | 1,183,242 | 1,395,811 |

*Military expenditure* – US$610m (2011 est)
*Conscription* – 20 years of age, male only; 36 months
 (women are subject to 12 months of service at age 21)

## ECONOMY AND TRADE

Economic development has been limited by political instability, corruption, the landlocked location and poor transport infrastructure. About 80 per cent of the workforce is occupied in subsistence agriculture, herding and fishing, which contributes over 54.3 per cent of GDP, and the remaining 20 per cent are practically all employed in services, which contribute 32.4 per cent of GDP. The main focus of development, funded by foreign investment and international aid, is the exploitation of oil deposits in the Doba basin in the south, which came into production in 2003; the oil is exported via a pipeline through Cameroon. An oil refinery was constructed in N'jamena in 2011. Other industries include processing cotton (the main industry before oil) and other agricultural products, and light manufacturing. Industry generates 9.9 per cent of GDP.

Production from new oil wells allowed growth to reach double digits in 2014. In October 2014 the government also received compensation from the China National Petroleum Corporation (CNPC) after the company was found to have dumped crude oil in the Koudalwa region in 2013, a decision which is expected to improve economic ties with China. Chad's top band of income tax, 60 per cent, is the highest in the world.

Chad's main trading partners are the USA (81.9 per cent of exports), France, China and Cameroon. Principal exports are oil, cattle, cotton and gum arabic. The main imports are machinery and transport equipment, industrial goods, food and textiles.

*GNI* – US$9,751m; US$1,020 per capita (2013)
*Annual average growth of GDP* – 9.6 per cent (2014 est)
*Inflation rate* – 0.1 per cent (2013 est)
*Population below poverty line* – 46.7 per cent (2011 est)
*Unemployment* – 8.4 per cent (2015 est)
*Total external debt* – US$3,222m (2014 est)
*Imports* – US$2,997m (2013)
*Exports* – US$4,496m (2013)

BALANCE OF PAYMENTS
*Trade* – US$1,498m surplus (2013)
*Current Account* – US$1,219m deficit (2014 est)

| Trade with UK | 2013 | 2014 |
|---|---|---|
| Imports from UK | £11,154,871 | £8,281,707 |
| Exports to UK | £407,048 | £59,007 |

## COMMUNICATIONS

*Airports and waterways* – Nine, the principal airport is at N'Djamena; the Chari and Legone rivers are navigable only in the wet season

*Roadways* – Only 206km are surfaced
*Telecommunications* – There are 29,900 fixed lines and 4.2 million mobile subscriptions (2012); there were 168,100 internet users in 2009
*Internet code and IDD* – td; 235 (from UK), 15 44 (to UK)
*Major broadcasters* – Al-Nassour and the state-owned Télé-Tchad are the only two TV stations; Radiodiffusion Nationale Tchadienne is the state-controlled radio station
*Press* – *Le Progres* is the country's only daily newspaper; other privately owned periodicals include *N'Djamena Bi-Hebdo* and *Abba Garde*
*WPFI score* – 40,17 (135)

# CHILE

*República de Chile – Republic of Chile*

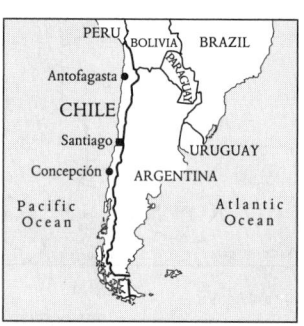

*Area* – 756,102 sq. km
*Capital* – Santiago; population, 6,225,000 (2015 est)
*Major cities* – Antofagasta, Concepción, Puente Alto, San Bernardo, Temuco, Valparaíso, Viña del Mar
*Currency* – Chilean peso ($) of 100 centavos
*Population* – 17,508,260 rising at 0.82 per cent a year (2015 est)
*Religion* – Christian (Roman Catholic 66.7 per cent, Protestant 16.4 per cent) (est)
*Language* – Spanish (official), English, Mapudungun and other indigenous languages
*Population density* – 24 per sq. km (2013)
*Urban population* – 89.6 per cent (2013 est)
*Median age (years)* – 33.3 (2014 est)
*National anthem* – 'Himno Nacional de Chile' ['National Anthem of Chile']
*National day* – 18 September (Independence Day)
*Death penalty* – Retained for certain crimes (last used 1985)
*CPI score* – 73 (21)

## CLIMATE AND TERRAIN

Chile extends over 4,600km from the arid north around Arica to Cape Horn, with an average breadth of 180km. The Atacama desert lies in the north. In the central zone there is a fertile valley between the Andes and the low coastal range of mountains, with a Mediterranean climate; two-thirds of the population live here. Chilean Patagonia, in the south, extends into subantarctic terrain, with glaciers and icefields; the climate is cool with high precipitation. Elevation extremes range from 6,880m (Nevado Ojos del Salado) to 0m (Pacific Ocean). Its Pacific island possessions include the Juan Fernández group and Easter Island, and the Chilean Antarctic Territory covers the Antarctic peninsula and an area of the landmass that extends from 53°W. to 90°W. along a latitude of 60°S.

# HISTORY AND POLITICS

Chile was conquered in the 16th century by the Spanish, who subjugated the indigenous population. It remained under Spanish rule until 1810, when the first autonomous government was established. Independence was achieved in 1818 after a revolutionary war.

A military coup in 1973 overthrew the Marxist president Salvador Allende. General Augusto Pinochet, the coup leader, assumed the presidency and retained the office until elections were held in 1989, beginning the transition to full democracy. Between 1998 and his death in 2006, a number of unsuccessful attempts were made to bring Gen. Pinochet to trial for human rights atrocities committed during his time in office.

In the 2013 legislative elections, the centre-left New Majority coalition won 67 seats, 18 more than the incumbent Alliance for Chile, in the lower chamber, and 21 of the 38 seats in the senate. Michelle Bachelet, the former president and the candidate of the Socialist Party of Chile (part of the New Majority), won the 2013 presidential election.

The 1981 constitution was amended in 1989 and 2005. The executive president is directly elected for a four-year term that is not renewable. The bicameral National Congress comprises a senate of 38 members elected for an eight-year term (half renewed every four years) and a Chamber of Deputies of 118 members directly elected for a four-year term. On 15 January 2015, the Senate voted to abolish Chile's unique binominal electoral system, in which two MPs were elected to each constituency, introducing a system of proportional representation.

## HEAD OF STATE

*President,* Michelle Bachelet, *elected* 15 December 2013, *sworn in* 11 March 2014

## SELECTED GOVERNMENT MEMBERS *as at April 2015*

*Defence, Interior,* Rodrigo Peñailillo Briceño
*Economy,* Luis Felipe Céspedes
*Finance,* Alberto Arenas de Mesa

## EMBASSY OF CHILE

37–41 Old Queen Street, London SW1H 9JA
T 020-7222 2361 E embachile@embachile.co.uk
W www.chileabroad.gov.cl/reino-unido
*Ambassador Extraordinary and Plenipotentiary,* HE Rolando Drago, *apptd* 2014

## BRITISH EMBASSY

Avda. El Bosque Norte 0125, Las Condes, Santiago
T (+56) (2) 370 4100 E embsan@britemb.cl
W www.gov.uk/government/world/chile
*Ambassador Extraordinary and Plenipotentiary,* HE Fiona Clouder, *apptd* 2014

## DEFENCE

| Aged 16–49, 2010 est | Males | Females |
| --- | --- | --- |
| Available for military service | 4,324,732 | 4,251,954 |
| Fit for military service | 3,621,475 | 3,561,099 |

*Military expenditure* – US$5,149m (2014)

## ECONOMY AND TRADE

Economic reforms in the late 1970s and the 1980s, and sound financial management, have made Chile one of the most successful economies in Latin America; in 2010 it became the first South American country to join the OECD. Growth is based on high copper prices, a strong export base and growing domestic demand. In 2012, foreign investment

reached a record US$28.2bn, a 63 per cent increase on the previous record in 2011. In 2015, the government announced the introduction of a US$5.5bn (£3.68bn) economic stimulus package aimed at increasing growth. Despite increasing inflation, the new stimulus package is expected to help the economy grow by 2.9 per cent in 2015 and 3.9 per cent in 2016.

Chile is the world's largest producer of copper, and the world's only commercial producer of nitrate of soda (Chile saltpetre) from natural resources. The chief industries are mining, forestry, fishing, food and fish processing, and winemaking.

The main trading partners are the USA, China, Brazil, Argentina and Japan. Principal exports are copper, fruit, fish products, paper and pulp, chemicals and wine. The main imports are petrol and petroleum products, chemicals, electrical and telecommunications equipment, industrial machinery, vehicles and natural gas.

*GNI* – US$268,296m; US$15,230 per capita (2013)
*Annual average growth of GDP* – 2 per cent (2014 est)
*Inflation rate* – 1.8 per cent (2013 est)
*Population living below poverty line* – 14.4 per cent (2011 est)
*Unemployment* – 5.8 per cent (2015 est)
*Total external debt* – US$140,000m (2014 est)
*Imports* – US$80,443m (2013)
*Exports* – US$77,877m (2013)

BALANCE OF PAYMENTS
*Trade* – US$2,566m deficit (2013)
*Current Account* – US$2,993m deficit (2014 est)

| Trade with UK | 2013 | 2014 |
| --- | --- | --- |
| Imports from UK | £1,076,833,410 | £474,672,279 |
| Exports to UK | £610,752,462 | £598,326,794 |

## COMMUNICATIONS

*Airports and waterways* – 90, the principal airport is at Santiago; the main ports are Arica, Antofagasta, Coquimbo, San Antonio, Talcahuano and Valparaíso
*Roadways and railways* – 18,119km, including 2,387km of motorways; 7,082km of railways
*Telecommunications* – 3.276 million fixed lines and 24.13 million mobile subscriptions (2012); there were around 7 million internet users in 2009
*Internet code and IDD* – cl; 56 (from UK), 44 (to UK)
*Major broadcasters* – The National Television of Chile is state-owned but not under direct government control; Radio Cooperativa is a news-based private network which broadcasts alongside numerous other private radio stations
*Press* – Major newspaper publications include *El Mercurio* and *La Tercera*; the government-owned *La Nación* was privatised in January 2014
*WPFI score* – 23 (43)

## EDUCATION AND HEALTH

Education is free and compulsory from ages six to 17, although the education system has suffered from underinvestment and mismanagement resulting in ongoing student protests.
*Literacy rate* – 98.7 per cent (2015 est)
*Gross enrolment ratio (percentage of relevant age group)* – primary 101 per cent; secondary 89 per cent; tertiary 74 per cent (2012 est)
*Health expenditure (per capita)* – US$1,204 (2013)
*Hospital beds (per 1,000 people)* – 2.1 (2011)
*Life expectancy (years)* – 78.44 (2014 est)
*Mortality rate* – 5.93 (2014 est)
*Birth rate* – 13.97 (2014 est)
*Infant mortality rate* – 7.02 (2014 est)

# CHINA

*Zhonghua Renmin Gongheguo – People's Republic of China*

*Area* – 9,596,960 sq. km
*Capital* – Beijing; population, 21,009,000 (2015 est)
*Major cities* – Chengdu, Chongqing, Dongguan, Foshan, Guangzhou, Nanjing, Shanghai, Shenyang, Shenzhen, Tianjin, Wuhan, Xi'an
*Currency* – Renminbi (RMB) or yuan (Y) of ten jiao or 100 fen
*Population* – 1,367,485,388 rising at 0.45 per cent a year (2015 est); Han Chinese (91.56 per cent), around 55 ethnic minorities (8.5 per cent) (2000)
*Religion* – officially atheist, but permits four state-registered religions: Buddhism, Taoism, Islam, and Catholic and Protestant Christianity. It is difficult to estimate numbers, as many congregations worship in private; Mahayana Buddhism and Taoism are the predominant faiths but Christianity is growing rapidly
*Language* – Mandarin (official), Cantonese, Shanghainese, Fuzhou, Xiang, Gan, Taiwanese; common speech, or *putonghua* (often referred to as Mandarin), is based on the northern dialect and is promoted throughout the country
*Population density* – 145 per sq. km (2013)
*Urban population* – 53.2 per cent (2012 est)
*Median age (years)* – 36.7 (2014 est)
*National anthem* – 'Yiyongjun Jinxingqu' ['The March of the Volunteers']
*National day* – 1 October (Founding of People's Republic)
*Death penalty* – Retained
*CPI score* – 36 (100)

## CLIMATE AND TERRAIN

China is twice the size of western Europe and contains a vast range of landscapes and climates. The highest mountains are on the Tibetan plateau, in the west of the country, where the highest elevation is 8,850m (Mt Everest). To the north of the Tibetan plateau, the land drops to the arid, semi-desert steppes bisected by the Tian Shan mountains; the country's lowest elevation is –154m at Turpan Pendi. The southern plains and east coast have the most fertile land, irrigated by the Huang He (Yellow), Chang Jiang (Yangtze) and Xi Jiang (West) rivers, and are the most heavily populated areas.

There are seven climate zones. The north-east has cold winters, fierce winds, warm and humid summers, and erratic rainfall. The mountainous south-west has mild winters and warm summers. Inner Mongolia has cold winters and hot summers. Central China has warm and humid summers with occasional tropical cyclones. South China is partly tropical with heavy rainfall. The high Tibet plateau is subject to harsh winters. Xinjiang and the west have a desert climate, with cold winters and little rain.

## POLITICS

The Communist Party of China is the dominant political party, and all elements of the political system are subordinate to it. A party congress is held every five years and elects the Politburo and its standing committee. This standing committee is the policy- and decision-making body and the *de facto* government.

Under the 1982 constitution, the National People's Congress (NPC) is the highest organ of state power. It has 2,987 members, indirectly elected for a five-year term, and holds only one full session a year; between sessions, its work is delegated to its standing committee. The congress elects the premier and, on his nomination, the State Council. The head of state is the president, also elected by the congress, who serves a five-year term, renewable once.

Deputies to people's congresses at the primary level are directly elected by the voters from a list of approved candidates. These congresses elect the deputies to the congress at the next highest level. Deputies to the NPC are elected by the provincial and municipal people's congresses, and by the armed forces.

Local government is conducted through people's governments at provincial/municipal, prefecture/city, county/district, township and village levels. There are 22 provinces (Taiwan is claimed as a 23rd province), four municipalities directly under the central government, five autonomous regions, and two special administrative areas; provinces may contain autonomous counties or towns for ethnic minorities.

In 2012 Xi Jinping took over as General Secretary of the Communist Party of China, becoming president in 2013. He stated that he aimed to make corruption-free governance and economic growth key elements of his administration, the former of which has resulted in several high-profile purges of senior officials. Li Keqiang was elected premier by the 12th National People's Congress in 2013.

HEAD OF STATE
*President,* Xi Jinping, *elected* 14 March 2013
*Vice-President,* Li Yuanchao

STATE COUNCIL *as at April 2015*
*Premier,* Li Keqiang
*Vice-Premiers,* Zhang Gaoli; Ma Kai; Liu Yandong; Wang Yang
*State Councillors,* Yang Jiechi; Yang Jing; Guo Shengkun; Wang Yong; Chang Wanquan

| | | | | | | |
|---|---|---|---|---|---|---|
| Last emperor of the Qing dynasty abdicates. Revolution spreads | Japan occupies Manchuria and other areas | Internal disagreements result in Japan's occupation of most northern and coastal areas | CCP victors of civil war. The party inaugurates the People's Republic of China and the KMT goes into exile in Taiwan | | Pro-democracy demonstrations, centred on Tiananmen Square in Beijing, lead to the deaths of over 3,000 protestors | |

2000   1927   1934-5   1945   1958-61   1966-70   2003
1912   1932   1939   1946-9   1989

| | | | | | | |
|---|---|---|---|---|---|---|
| Ruled by imperial dynasties | The KMT forms a government in Nanjing | The Chinese Communist Party breaks and retreats in the 'Long March' | Japanese occupation ended by the Allies. CCP seizes control over territory | Millions die from famine after Mao Zedong's 'Great Leap Forward'; an attempt to industrialise rural areas | Cultural Revolution | Hu Jintao is elected president |

SELECTED GOVERNMENT MEMBERS *as at April 2015*
*Civil Affairs,* Li Liguo
*Finance,* Lou Jiwei
*Foreign Affairs,* Wang Yi

EMBASSY OF THE PEOPLE'S REPUBLIC OF CHINA
49–51 Portland Place, London W1B 1JL
T 020-7299 4049 W www.chinese-embassy.org.uk
*Ambassador Extraordinary and Plenipotentiary,* HE Liu
Xiaoming, *apptd* 2010

BRITISH EMBASSY
11 Guang Hua Lu, Jian Guo Men Wai, 100600, Beijing, China
T (+86) 0(10) 5192 4000 W www.gov.uk/government/world/china
*Ambassador,* HE Barbara Woodward, CMG, OBE,
*apptd* 2015

HUMAN RIGHTS
China's political system has become more liberal since 1978, when economic reforms allowing for greater amounts of personal freedom were introduced, with further liberalisation taking place during the regime of Deng Xiaoping from 1981–7. The constitution was amended to officially recognise human rights in 2004, and National Human Rights Action Plans, issued by the State Council, were released in 2009 and 2012. The practice of sending prisoners to labour camps for 're-education' was officially abolished in 2007; the majority of camps were independently confirmed to have been closed in 2014. Despite reform, the state continues to tightly control freedom of expression, religion, association and reproduction rights. Ethnic minorities in Tibet, Inner Mongolia and Xinjiang, home to the Uygur Muslim separatist movement, experience widespread discrimination. The country is thought to have executed approximately 4,000 people in 2014, more than every other country in the world combined, and applies the death sentence to a variety of non-violent crimes, including corruption. Prominent critics of the regime are frequently subjected to house arrest and torture. Notable dissidents include: Chen Guangcheng, a blind human rights lawyer who fled to the USA in 2012; Liu Xiaobo, winner of the Nobel Peace prize in 2010; and the artist Ai Weiwei. In April 2014, President Xi Jinping stated that China would never develop into a pluralist, Western-style democracy.

DEFENCE
All three military arms are part of the People's Liberation Army (PLA).

| *Aged 16–49, 2010 est* | *Males* | *Females* |
| --- | --- | --- |
| Available for military service | 385,821,101 | 363,789,674 |
| Fit for military service | 318,265,016 | 300,323,611 |

*Military expenditure* – US$216,371m (2014 est)
*Conscription* – 18–24 years of age; 24 months (selective)

## ECONOMY AND TRADE
Liberalisation since the 1980s has transformed the economy, developing a more autonomous state sector, a rapidly growing private sector and a leading presence in global trade and investment. A massive industrial base and transport infrastructure have been constructed, especially in the coastal regions, and the economy has become a free market in all but name, with several stock markets and Shanghai's emergence as a financial centre. China attracts considerable foreign investment and has become a major investor overseas. GDP has grown more than ten-fold since 1978,

and China's economy is now the second-largest in the world after the US.

Although some 250 million people who migrated to urban areas have been lifted out of poverty in the past two decades, the effects of the rapid transformation have been unevenly distributed. In 2012 it was reported China's city dwellers outnumber China's rural population for the first time; there are wide income differences between urban and rural areas, poor healthcare provision, lack of access to public services for migrant workers, rampant official corruption and environmental degradation of land, water and air. The government is also keen to increase domestic consumption (a priority of the 2011–16 five-year plan), and so reduce the economy's reliance on exports for growth. The economy grew by 7.4 per cent in 2014, the slowest growth rate since 1990. Growth is expected to remain relatively modest as China gradually transitions from a heavy manufacturing focus to a service economy. Falling world oil prices, and a stabilising property market is expected to help the economy grow by 7 per cent in 2015.

China's expansion boosted its need for oil and coal, met initially by imports but increasingly by domestic production. However, to achieve its aim of reducing environmental degradation, China is looking more to nuclear power (although nuclear approval has been suspended indefinitely owing to safety concerns following the Fukushima Daiichi plant disaster in Japan) and alternative energy generation, such as hydroelectric power from the Three Gorges Dam.

Although rural areas have seen few benefits from the economic transformation and are suffering the effects of rural depopulation and pollution, agriculture remains important; it contributes 9.7 per cent of GDP but employs 34.8 per cent of the workforce. The main crops are rice, cereals, vegetables, peanuts, tea, fruit, cotton and oilseed crops. Livestock is raised in large numbers. Silk farming is one of the oldest industries. Cotton, woollen and silk textiles are manufactured in large quantities.

The highly diversified industrial sector, encompassing heavy industry, manufacturing and construction, contributes 43.9 per cent of GDP and employs 30.3 per cent of the workforce. The services sector accounts for 46.4 per cent of GDP and 36.1 per cent of employment. Tourism is now a major industry.

Exports include machinery, electrical equipment, data processing equipment, garments, textiles, iron and steel, and optical and medical equipment. The principal imports are electrical and other machinery, oil and mineral fuels, optical and medical equipment, metal ores, plastics and organic chemicals. The main trading partners are the USA, Hong Kong, Taiwan, Japan and South Korea, although trade with Latin America and Africa is growing.

*GNI* – US$8,905,335m; US$6,560 per capita (2013)
*Annual average growth of GDP* – 7.4 per cent (2014 est)
*Inflation rate* – 2.6 per cent (2013 est)
*Population below poverty line* – 6.1 per cent (2011 est)
*Unemployment* – 4.8 per cent (2015 est)
*Total external debt* – US$894,900m (2014 est)
*Imports* – US$1,950,380m (2013)
*Exports* – US$2,210,250m (2013)

BALANCE OF PAYMENTS
*Trade* – US$259,870m surplus (2013)
*Current Account* – US$209,819m surplus (2014)

| *Trade with UK* | *2013* | *2014* |
| --- | --- | --- |
| Imports from UK | £11,584,770,244 | £15,933,536,838 |
| Exports to UK | £31,578,991,587 | £33,890,620,938 |

## COMMUNICATIONS

*Airports* – There are 463 airports and airfields and several national air carriers

*Waterways* – The main seaports are Shanghai and Dalian in the north, and Guangzhou in the south; there are 110,000km of navigable waterways, Nanjing is the largest river port, and the Huang He (Yellow), Chang Jiang (Yangtze) and Xi Jiang (West) are the most significant river routes

*Roadways* – The 3,453,890km road network allows access to all towns and villages, and the major cities are linked by 84,946km of modern highways

*Railways* – The rail system has 86,000km of track, although only 36,000km is electrified; extension of the Qinghai–Tibet railway has opened up the remote western province

*Telecommunications* – 278.86 million fixed lines and 1.1 billion mobile subscriptions (2012); there were 618 million internet users in 2013

*Internet code and IDD* – cn; 86 (from UK), 44 (to UK)

*Major broadcasters* – The Communist Party maintains a firm grip on media and the internet. Television, provided by Chinese Central TV (CCTV), is the most popular medium; there are around 3,300 channels and 418 million households have access to television. All of China's 2,600 radio stations are state-owned

*Press* – Every city has its own newspaper – approximately 1,900 newspapers are published every week; national dailies include *Renmin Ribao* (Communist Party newspaper), *Zhongguo Qingnian Bao* and *China Daily* (English-language)

*WPFI score* – 73,55 (176)

## EDUCATION AND HEALTH

Primary education lasts six years and secondary education six years (three years in junior middle school and three optional years in senior middle school).

*Literacy rate* – 99.7 per cent (2015 est)

*Gross enrolment ratio (percentage of relevant age group)* – primary 128 per cent; secondary 89 per cent; tertiary 27 per cent (2012 est)

*Health expenditure (per capita)* – US$367 (2013)

*Hospital beds (per 1,000 people)* – 3.8 (2011)

*Life expectancy (years)* – 75.15 (2014 est)

*Mortality rate* – 7.44 (2014 est)

*Birth rate* – 12.17 (2014 est)

*Infant mortality rate* – 14.79 (2014 est)

## TIBET

*Area* – 1,199,164 sq. km

*Population* – 3,002,166 (2011 est)

*Capital* – Lhasa

Tibet is a plateau, seldom lower than 3,000m, in south-west China. It forms the frontier with India (boundary imperfectly demarcated), from which it is separated by the Himalayas from Kashmir to Myanmar; Nepal also and Bhutan also border it to the south. The Indus, Brahmaputra, Mekong and Yangtze rivers all rise on the Tibet plateau.

Tibet was under Mongol rule almost continuously from the 13th to the 17th centuries. Chinese control grew from the 18th century and direct rule began in 1910, but with the collapse of the Chinese Empire in 1911, Tibet declared its independence and the Dalai Lama ruled undisturbed until Communist rule was established in China. In 1950 Chinese Communist forces invaded Tibet, and in 1951 the Tibetan authorities signed a treaty agreeing joint Chinese–Tibetan rule. A series of revolts against Chinese rule culminated in a 1959 uprising in the capital, which was crushed following several days of fighting after which military rule was imposed. The Dalai Lama fled to India where he and his followers were granted political asylum and established a government in exile. Tibet became an Autonomous Region of China in 1965. Martial law was declared in Tibet in 1989.

The Panchen Lama, the second-highest Lama, remained in Lhasa after 1959; when he died in 1989, China rejected the Dalai Lama's choice of successor and enthroned its own candidate. Subsequent appointments have been handled in a similar manner. Despite occasional talks between the Chinese government and representatives of the Dalai Lama, relations remain poor. In March 2011, the Dalai Lama announced his intention to withdraw from political life, transferring leadership to Lobsang Sangay, prime minister of the Tibetan parliament. In September 2012 his title was amended to political leader *(Sikyong)*.

Another source of tension is the large number of Chinese migrants who have settled in Tibet since the 1970s, a development that the Tibetan government-in-exile regards as an attempt to eradicate the culture of the Tibetan people. Chinese now considerably outnumber Tibetans and have benefited disproportionately from the economic development of recent years.

Peaceful anti-Chinese demonstrations in Tibet increased in early 2008 as the imminence of the Beijing Olympics put China's human rights record under greater international scrutiny. The violence of the Chinese crackdown was condemned worldwide, and pro-Tibet activists abroad disrupted the Olympic torch relay in several countries. Resistance and unrest continue: in 2009, in a show of passive resistance, farmers in Tibet and neighbouring provinces refused to till the fields or plant crops; in 2011, demonstrations sparked by the self-immolation of a Tibetan monk in the Sechuan province led to hundreds of arrests. More than 130 other self-immolations have taken place since.

## SPECIAL ADMINISTRATIVE REGIONS

### HONG KONG

*Xianggang Tebie Xingzhengqu – Hong Kong Special Administrative Region*

*Area* – 1,104 sq. km

*Currency* – Hong Kong dollar (HK$) of 100 cents

*Population* – 7,112,688 rising at 0.41 per cent a year (2014 est)

*Population density* – 6,845 per sq. km (2013)

*Flag* – Red, with a white bauhinia flower of five petals each containing a red star

*National day* – 1 July (Establishment Day)

*Death penalty* – Abolished for all crimes (since 2003)

*CPI score* – 75 (15)

### CLIMATE AND TERRAIN

Hong Kong consists of Hong Kong Island, Kowloon and the New Territories (on a peninsula of the mainland in Guangdong province) and over 260 islands, including Lantau Island. Hong Kong Island is about 18km long and 3–8km wide. It is separated from the mainland by a narrow strait. The highest point is Tai Mo Shan (958m). The climate is subtropical, with hot, wet summers and cool, dry winters. Mean monthly temperatures range from 16°C to 29°C. Tropical cyclones occur between May and November, and over 75 per cent of the average annual rainfall of 2,180mm falls between May and September.

### HISTORY AND POLITICS

Hong Kong developed as a major regional trading port because of its location on the main Far Eastern trade routes. Hong Kong Island was first occupied by Britain in 1841 and formally ceded to Britain in 1842. Kowloon was acquired in 1860, and the New Territories by a 99-year lease signed in 1898.

In 1984, the UK and China agreed that China would resume sovereignty over Hong Kong in 1997, and on 1 July 1997, Hong Kong became a Special Administrative Region (SAR) of the People's Republic of China. The 1984 joint declaration and the Basic Law (1990) guarantee that the SAR's social and economic systems will remain unchanged for 50 years and grant it a high degree of autonomy.

Although the Basic Law provides for the development of democratic processes, political reform has been slow, prompting frequent demonstrations to demand full democracy or to oppose measures perceived to be repressive. In 2007 the Chinese government said that the chief executive could be directly elected from 2017 and the legislature members from 2020.

The Basic Law, approved in 1990, has served as Hong Kong's constitution since 1997. Its government is headed by the chief executive, who is elected by a 1,200-member electoral committee and serves a five-year term. The chief executive is aided by an executive council consisting of 15 principal officials, who are the heads of administrative departments, and 14 non-official members. The legislative council consists of 70 members, 35 directly elected by geographic constituencies, and 30 elected by functional, occupation-based constituencies; they serve a four-year term.

Leung Chun-ying was elected chief executive in March 2012, replacing Donald Tsang, who served two terms between 2005 and 2012. In the 2012 legislative elections, pro-China parties won 43 seats while pro-democracy parties won 27.

*Chief Executive,* Leung Chun-ying, *elected* 25 March 2012, *sworn in* 1 July 2012

SELECTED GOVERNMENT MEMBERS *as at April 2015*
*Chief Secretary for Administration,* Carrie Lam Cheng
   Yuet-ngor
*Financial Secretary,* John Tsang Chun-wah
*Secretary for Justice,* Rimsky Yuen Kwok-keung

BRITISH CONSULATE-GENERAL
PO Box 528, 1 Supreme Court Road, Central Hong Kong
T (+852) 2901 3000 E hongkong.consular@fco.gov.uk
W www.gov.uk/government/world/hong-kong
*Consul-General,* Caroline Wilson, *apptd* 2012

ECONOMY AND TRADE
The economy has moved away from manufacturing (which has mostly relocated to mainland China) and is now service-based, with a high reliance on international trade and re-exports. It has developed into a regional corporate and banking centre, and has benefited in recent years from closer integration with China through increased trade, tourism and financial links. Although badly affected by the global economic downturn in 2008–9, and vulnerable to future volatility, the strength of the Chinese economy helped it to recover quickly. In 2014, Hong Kong signed the Closer Economic Partnership Arrangement with China which aims to eliminate trade barriers and liberalise trade between the two economies.

The economy is dominated by the service sector, which accounted for 93 per cent of GDP in 2013. The main contributors to this are tourism, financial services and shipping. Industry contributes 6.9 per cent of GDP. Principal products are textiles, clothing, electronics, plastics, toys, clocks and watches.

The principal export markets are China (57.7 per cent), the USA and Japan. China is also Hong Kong's principal supplier of imported goods (44.5 per cent).

*GNI* – US$268,865m; US$36,560 per capita (2012)
*Annual average growth of GDP* – 3 per cent (2013 est)
*Inflation rate* – 4.3 per cent (2013 est)
*Unemployment* – 3.1 per cent (2013 est)
*Imports* – US$523,558m (2013)
*Exports* – US$458,959m (2013)

BALANCE OF PAYMENTS
*Trade* – US$64,599m deficit (2013)
*Current Account* – US$12,908m surplus (2011)

| Trade with UK | 2013 | 2014 |
| --- | --- | --- |
| Imports from UK | £9,024,243,908 | £459,025,353 |
| Exports to UK | £7,012,230,707 | £598,897,198 |

COMMUNICATIONS
*Airports* – There are two airports, one accommodating international flights
*Waterways* – Hong Kong has one of the world's finest natural harbours, and is the third-busiest container port in the world
*Roadways* – 2,090km (2012)
*Telecommunications* – 4.346 million fixed lines and 16.403 million mobile subscriptions (2012); there were 4.873 million internet users in 2009
*Internet code and IDD* – hk; 852 (from UK), 1 44 (to UK)
*WPFI score* – 27,76 (70)

EDUCATION AND HEALTH
Education is free and compulsory for children up to age 15.
*Literacy rate* – 99.2 per cent (2012 est)
*Gross enrolment ratio (percentage of age group)* – primary 98 per cent; secondary 86 per cent; tertiary 60 per cent (2011 est)
*Life expectancy (years)* – 82.78 (2014 est)
*Mortality rate* – 6.93 (2014 est)
*Birth rate* – 9.38 (2014 est)
*Infant mortality rate* – 2.73 (2014 est)

MACAU (AOMEN)
*Aomen Tebie Xingzhengqu* – Macau Special Administrative Region
*Area* – 28.2 sq. km
*Currency* – Pataca (MOP$) of 100 avos
*Population* – 587,914 rising at 0.83 per cent a year (2014 est)
*Population density* – 18,942 per sq. km (2013)
*Flag* – Green, with a white lotus flower above a white stylised bridge and water, under a large gold five-point star and four gold stars in crescent
*National day* – 20 December (Establishment Day)
*Internet code and IDD* – mo; 853 (from UK), 44 (to UK)

CLIMATE AND TERRAIN
Macau consists of the Macau peninsula and the islands of Coloane and Taipa. It is situated at the western side of the mouth of the Pearl river, bordering Guangdong province in south-east China. It is 64km from Hong Kong. Its area has nearly doubled since the 19th century due to land reclamation. The highest point is Coloane Alto (172m). The climate is subtropical.

HISTORY AND POLITICS
The first Portuguese ship arrived at Macau in 1513 and trade with China commenced in 1553. Macau became a Portuguese colony in 1557; China recognised Portugal's sovereignty over Macau by treaty in 1887. An agreement to transfer the administration of Macau to China was signed in 1987, and Macau became the Macau Special Administrative Region (MSAR) of China on 20 December 1999. Fernando

Chui was elected unopposed as chief executive in 2009, and the most recent legislative election was held in September 2009.

The Basic Law (1993) has served as Macao's constitution since 1999. The chief executive is elected by a 300-member election committee and serves a five-year term of office, which may be renewed once. The chief executive is assisted by the ten-member executive council. The legislative assembly has 29 members, who serve for four years; 12 are directly elected in geographic constituencies, ten are indirectly elected in functional constituencies and seven are appointed by the chief executive.

*Chief Executive,* Fernando Chui Sai On, *elected* July 2009, *sworn in* 20 December 2009

SELECTED GOVERNMENT MEMBERS *as at April 2015*
*Economy and Finance,* Leong Vai Tac
*Secretary for Administration and Justice,* Chan Hoi Fan

CONSUL-GENERAL
Caroline Wilson, *apptd* 2012, resident at Hong Kong

ECONOMY AND TRADE
The economy is based on tourism and gambling, which have grown rapidly since 2001, and garment and textile manufacturing, which is in decline. Visitors totalled 29.3 million in 2013, the majority coming from mainland China, where gambling is illegal. The service sector contributes about 93.5 per cent of GDP and industry 6.5 per cent. The principal products and exports are clothing, textiles, footwear, toys, electronics, machinery and parts. The main trading partners are Hong Kong, China – with whom a Comprehensive Economic Partnership Agreement was signed in 2013 – and the USA.

*GNI* – US$31,809m; US$55,720 per capita (2011)
*Annual average growth of GDP* – 10 per cent (2012 est)
*Inflation rate* – 5.4 per cent (2013 est)
*Unemployment* – 1.9 per cent (2012 est)
*Imports* – US$10,141m (2013)
*Exports* – US$1,138m (2013)

BALANCE OF PAYMENTS
*Trade* – US$9,002m deficit (2013)
*Current Account* – US$6,238m surplus (2009)

| Trade with UK | 2013 | 2014 |
| --- | --- | --- |
| Imports from UK | £64,996,812 | £10,159,105 |
| Exports to UK | £17,463,801 | £711,719 |

# COLOMBIA

*República de Colombia – Republic of Colombia*

*Area* – 1,138,910 sq. km
*Capital* – Bogotá; population, 8,991,000 (2015 est)
*Major cities* – Barranquilla, Cali, Cartagena, Medellín
*Currency* – Colombian peso ($) of 100 centavos
*Population* – 46,736,728 rising at 1.04 per cent a year (2015 est)
*Religion* – Christian (predominantly Roman Catholic) (est)
*Language* – Spanish (official)
*Population density* – 44 per sq. km (2013)
*Urban population* – 75.8 per cent (2013 est)
*Median age (years)* – 28.9 (2014 est)
*National anthem* – 'Himno Nacional de la República de Colombia' ['National Anthem of the Republic of Colombia']
*National day* – 20 July (Independence Day)
*Death penalty* – Abolished for all crimes (since 1910)
*CPI score* – 37 (94)

CLIMATE AND TERRAIN
The western, central and eastern ranges of the Andes run from the south-west to north-east of Colombia, separating the arid north-eastern peninsula and the tropical coastal regions in the north and west from the densely forested south-eastern lowlands and the vast tablelands in the east. This last region, having a temperate climate, is the most densely populated part of the country. Elevation extremes range from 5,775m (Pico Simon Bolivar and Pico Cristobal Colon) to 0m (Pacific Ocean). The principal rivers are the Magdalena, which flows into the Caribbean; the Guaviare and Meta, tributaries of the Orinocco; and the Caquetá and Putumayo, which drain into the Amazon basin. The predominantly tropical climate is moderated by altitude in the interior.

HISTORY AND POLITICS
Spanish settlement of the region began in 1525, and Colombia was ruled as part of a viceroyalty until 1810, when independence was declared. In 1819, Simón Bolivar established the Republic of Gran Colombia, consisting of the territories now known as Colombia, Panama, Venezuela and Ecuador, after finally defeating the Spanish. In 1829–30 Venezuela and Ecuador withdrew, and in 1831 the remaining territories formed a separate state, which adopted the name of Colombia in 1866; Panama seceded in 1903.

Power alternated between the Conservative and Liberal parties from the mid-19th century. In 1949, a civil war broke out which lasted until 1957, when the Conservative and Liberal parties formed a coalition government known as the National Front. This arrangement continued until 1974 and was revived in 1978 in an attempt to maintain the rule of law in the face of violence by drugs cartels, a left-wing insurgency and counter-attacks by right-wing paramilitaries. Despite foreign assistance and increased military spending, drug trafficking continues to be widespread, although it has become less of a threat to civil order.

In the 2014 legislative elections, parties that supported President Calderón won the majority of seats in both chambers. The 2014 presidential election was won by President Calderón after a second round of voting.

Under the 1991 constitution, amended in 2005, the executive president is directly elected for a four-year term, which is renewable once. The bicameral congress comprises the 166-member House of Representatives, and the 102-member senate. All members are directly elected for a four-year term. Two senate seats are reserved for representatives of indigenous people.

HEAD OF STATE
*President,* Juan Manuel Santos Calderón, *elected* 20 June 2010, *sworn in* 7 August 2010
*Vice-President,* German Vargas Lleras

SELECTED GOVERNMENT MEMBERS *as at April 2015*
*Defence,* Juan Carlos Pinzon
*Finance,* Mauricio Cardenas Santa Maria
*Foreign Affairs,* Maria Angela Holguin
*Justice,* Yesid Reyes Alvarado

EMBASSY OF COLOMBIA
3 Hans Crescent, London SW1X 0LN
T 020-7589 9177 E egranbretana@cancilleria.gov.co
W www.colombianembassy.co.uk
*Ambassador Extraordinary and Plenipotentiary,* HE Nestor Osorio, *apptd* 2014

BRITISH EMBASSY
Carrera 9, No 76–49, Piso 8, Edificio ING Barings, Bogotá
T (+57) (1) 326 8300 E embajadabritanica.bogota@fco.gov.uk
W www.gov.uk/government/world/colombia
*Ambassador Extraordinary and Plenipotentiary,* HE Lindsay Croisdale-Appleby, *apptd* 2013

INSURGENCIES
Colombia has been dogged by violence since the 1960s, initially from insurgency by left-wing guerrilla groups, mainly the Revolutionary Armed Forces of Colombia (FARC) and the National Liberation Army (ELN), countered by right-wing paramilitaries affiliated with the United Self-Defence Forces of Colombia (AUC), which was suspected of having links with the security forces. In the 1980s, lawlessness increased with the rise of drug-producing and drug-trafficking cartels. An estimated 220,000 people, mainly civilians, have been killed during the conflict.

Action against the insurgents and drug cartels since 2002 has extended state control to the extent that the government now has a presence in every municipality. Talks with the AUC from 2004 led to demobilisation of most units in 2006, and in November 2012, FARC rebels declared a two-month ceasefire and began talks in Havana, Cuba. President Santos suspended the talks in November 2014 after the FARC kidnapped a Colombian general (*see* Events). They resumed in January 2015 after FARC declared an indefinite ceasefire.

Neighbouring countries are affected by the overspill from the violence in Colombia, and cross-border incursions by Colombian forces in pursuit of the FARC, ELN or AUC have affected relations with both Ecuador and Venezuela in recent years. Venezuela also strongly opposes the USA's military presence in Colombia to counter drug-trafficking.

DEFENCE

| Aged 16–49, 2010 est | Males | Females |
|---|---|---|
| Available for military service | 11,692,647 | 11,727,625 |
| Fit for military service | 9,150,400 | 9,861,760 |

*Military expenditure* – US$13,054m (2014)
*Conscription* – 18–24 years of age; 18 months

ECONOMY AND TRADE
An improving security situation, economic liberalisation and international investment aided economic growth from 2002 to 2008. Although the economy contracted in 2009 owing to the global downturn, real GDP has grown at an average rate of over 4 per cent for the past four years. High global coffee prices allowed the government to abolish expensive farming subsidies in 2014 while falling global oil prices present a risk to future growth.

Services account for around 56.6 per cent of GDP, industry 37.3 per cent and agriculture 6.1 per cent. Coal, oil, natural gas and hydroelectricity resources are exploited, and coal accounts for about 88 per cent of mining output; iron ore, nickel, gold, emeralds, copper and other minerals account for the remainder. Major cash crops are coffee, bananas and cut flowers. Cattle are raised in large numbers, and forestry is also important.

The principal trading partners are the USA, China, Mexico and the EU. Main exports are oil, coffee, coal, nickel, emeralds, garments, bananas and cut flowers. Imports include industrial and transport equipment, consumer goods, chemicals, paper products and fuels.

*GNI* – US$366,638m; US$7,590 per capita (2013)
*Annual average growth of GDP* – 5 per cent (2014 est)
*Inflation rate* – 2 per cent (2013 est)
*Population below poverty line* – 30.6 per cent (2013 est)
*Unemployment* – 10.3 per cent (2015 est)
*Total external debt* – US$84,000m (2014 est)
*Imports* – US$59,397m (2013)
*Exports* – US$58,657m (2013)

BALANCE OF PAYMENTS
*Trade* – US$740m surplus (2013)
*Current Account* – US$19,291m deficit (2014 est)

| Trade with UK | 2013 | 2014 |
|---|---|---|
| Imports from UK | £338,058,885 | £333,867,993 |
| Exports to UK | £781,087,651 | £646,322,016 |

COMMUNICATIONS
*Airports* – 121, the principal airports are at Bogotá, Barranquilla and Cali
*Waterways* – 18,300km of navigable waterways; the main seaports are Barranquilla and Cartagena on the Caribbean Sea and Buenaventura on the Pacific coast
*Roadways and railways* – 141,374km; 874km
*Telecommunications* – 6.29 million fixed lines and 49.07 million mobile subscriptions (2012); there were 22.54 million internet users in 2009
*Internet code and IDD* – co; 57 (from UK), 5/7/9 44 (to UK)
*Major broadcasters* – The state-run Senal Columbia is one of the largest television broadcasters in the country; Caracol runs several radio networks across the country alongside the state-run Radio Nacional de Columbia
*Press* – Daily newspapers include *El Tiempo, El Nuevo Siglo* and *El Espacio*
*WPFI score* – 39,08 (128)

EDUCATION AND HEALTH
Elementary education is free and compulsory from age six to 15. Healthcare is provided through a mixture of contributory and subsidised health schemes by both the private and the public sector.
*Literacy rate* – 98.7 per cent (2015 est)
*Gross enrolment ratio (percentage of relevant age group)* – primary 107 per cent; secondary 93 per cent; tertiary 45 per cent (2012 est)
*Health expenditure (per capita)* – US$533 (2013)
*Hospital beds (per 1,000 people)* – 1.5 (2012)
*Life expectancy (years)* – 75.25 (2014 est)
*Mortality rate* – 5.36 (2014 est)
*Birth rate* – 16.73 (2014 est)
*Infant mortality rate* – 15.02 (2014 est)

# THE COMOROS

*Udzima wa Komori/Jumhuriyat al-Qamar al-Muttahidah/
Union des Comores – Union of the Comoros*

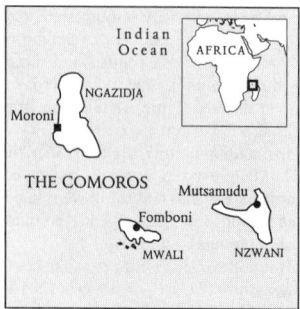

*Area* – 2,235 sq. km (excluding Mayotte). The Comoros
includes the islands of Ngazidja (formerly Grande
Comore), Nzwani (Anjouan), Mwali (Moheli) and certain
islets in the Indian Ocean. Mayotte, the easternmost island
of the archipelago, is a French dependency
*Capital* – Moroni, on Ngazidja; population, 55,000
(2015 est)
*Major towns* – Domoni, Fomboni, Mutsamudu
*Currency* – Comoran franc (KMF) of 100 centimes. The Franc
CFA of 100 centimes is also used
*Population* – 780,971 rising at 1.77 per cent a year
(2015 est)
*Religion* – Muslim (Sunni 99 per cent) (est); Islam is the state
religion
*Language* – Arabic, French (both official), Shikomoro (a blend
of Swahili and Arabic)
*Population density* – 395 per sq. km (2013)
*Urban population* – 28.2 per cent (2013 est)
*Median age (years)* – 19.2 (2014 est)
*National anthem* – 'Udzima wa ya Masiwa' ['The Union of the
Great Islands']
*National day* – 6 July (Independence Day)
*Death penalty* – Retained (last used 1997)
*CPI score* – 26 (142)
*Literacy rate* – 87.6 per cent (2015 est)
*Gross enrolment ratio (percentage of relevant age group)* –
primary 117 per cent; secondary 73 per cent; tertiary
11 per cent (2012 est)
*Life expectancy (years)* – 63.48 (2014 est)
*Mortality rate* – 7.76 (2014 est)
*Birth rate* – 29.05 (2014 est)
*Infant mortality rate* – 65.31 (2014 est)
*HIV/AIDS adult prevalence* – 0.2 per cent (2013 est)

## CLIMATE AND TERRAIN

Located in the Mozambique Channel between Africa and
Madagascar, Ngazidja, Nzwani and Mwali are mountainous
volcanic islands in the Comoros archipelago. The highest
point is Karthala (2,360m) on Ngazidja, an active volcano
that last erupted in 2007, and the lowest is 0m (Indian
Ocean). The climate is tropical, with a hot, rainy season from
October to April; the islands are prone to cyclones during the
rainy season.

## HISTORY AND POLITICS

The islands were settled by a variety of peoples before
becoming part of the trading empire of the Shirazis of Persia,
who established sultanates in the 15th to 16th centuries. In
1886, France established protectorates over the islands,

making them a colony in 1912. They achieved internal
self-government in 1961. In a 1974 referendum, the
residents of three of the main islands voted in favour of
independence, which was declared on 6 July 1975; Mayotte
voted to remain part of France.

The republic experienced about 18 coups or attempted
coups between 1975 and 1999. Nzwani and Mwali seceded
in 1997 but, after a coup in 1999, the military took control
of all the islands' governments and reunited the state. Talks
on the secessionist crisis produced a new constitution,
introducing a federal structure with greater autonomy for the
individual islands. Another constitutional crisis arose in June
2007 when the incumbent president of Nzwani, Mohamed
Bacar, refused to stand down and then held elections which
he claimed to have won. The federal government declared the
elections null and void, and in March 2008 federal troops,
supported by African Union forces, ousted Bacar.

The federal president and island governors were elected in
December 2010 and took office in May 2011; the federal
presidency election was won by Ikililou Dhoinine, of
Mwali. In the 2015 legislative elections, the Union for
the Development of the Comoro (UPDC), supporters of
President Dhoinine, became the largest party, winning eight
of the 24 directly elected seats.

The 2002 constitution created a federal structure.
Constitutional amendments approved in 2009 downgraded
the islands' presidents to governors, ended the rotation of the
federal presidency among the islands, and harmonised
presidential and legislative terms by extending those of the
president and governors.

Under the amended constitution, the union president is
elected for a five-year term. The executive president appoints
the union ministers. The unicameral Assembly of the Union
has 33 members; three are appointed by each of the three
island parliaments and 24 are directly elected for a five-year
term.

Each island has its own governor and legislative assembly,
and each governor may appoint eight ministers to form a
government. Governors serve a five-year term. The islands'
governments deal with local issues; foreign affairs, finance,
defence, judicial and religious matters remain the responsibility of the union government. There are still areas of dispute,
principally over security, budget control and customs revenue.

HEAD OF STATE
*President of the Union,* Ikililou Dhoinine, *elected* 26 December
2010, *sworn in* 26 May 2011

SELECTED GOVERNMENT MEMBERS *as at April 2015*
*Vice-Presidents,* Nourdine Bourhane; Fouad Ben Mohadji;
Mohamed Ali Soilihi *(Finance, Economy)*
*Foreign Relations,* Elarif Said Hassane
*Interior,* Housseine Hassan Ibrahim

BRITISH AMBASSADOR
HE Jonathan Drew, MBE, *apptd* 2013, resident at Port Louis,
Mauritius

## ECONOMY AND TRADE

The Comoros is very poor and heavily dependent on foreign
aid and technical assistance. It has few natural resources, an
uneducated workforce and poor transport infrastructure.
Unemployment is high and remittances from 150,000
Comorans living abroad are a valuable contribution to the
economy. In December 2012 the IMF and World Bank
supported US$176 million in debt relief for the Comoros,
allowing a 59 per cent decrease in future external debt over a
period of 40 years. In 2015 the country is predicted to
achieve a fourth year of consecutive growth driven by

increasing external investment, particularly from Arab nations. The country has been able to run a fiscal surplus since 2011. Agriculture, fishing and forestry account for 50.4 per cent of GDP and employ around 80 per cent of the population; service industries account for about 35.9 per cent and the manufacturing industry 13.7 per cent. The main industries are fishing, tourism and perfume distillation. The main trading partners are the Netherlands, France, Pakistan and Singapore. Principal exports are vanilla, perfume essence, copra and cloves; coconuts, bananas and cassava are also cultivated.

*GNI* – US$614m; US$840 per capita (2013)
*Annual average growth of GDP* – 3.9 per cent (2014 est)
*Inflation rate* – 2.3 per cent (2013 est)
*Population below poverty line* – 60 per cent (2002 est)
*Unemployment* – 8.0 per cent (2015 est)
*Total external debt* – US$251,600m (2014 est)
*Imports* – US$285m (2013)
*Exports* – US$25m (2013)

BALANCE OF PAYMENTS
*Trade* – US$260m deficit (2013)
*Current Account* – US$76m deficit (2014 est)

| Trade with UK | 2013 | 2014 |
| --- | --- | --- |
| Imports from UK | £381,037 | £304,841 |
| Exports to UK | £147,115 | £159,155 |

## COMMUNICATIONS
*Airports and waterways* – Four, the main international airport is based on Moroni; the principal ports are based at Moroni and Mutsamudu
*Roadways* – 673km
*Telecommunications* – 24,000 fixed lines and 250,000 mobile subscriptions (2012); there were 24,300 internet users in 2009
*Internet code and IDD* – km; 269 (from UK), 44 (to UK)
*Major broadcasters* – National radio and television broadcasting is provided by state-run networks and some island governments run radio and television stations
*Press* – No daily newspapers are published; the state-owned al-Watwan is published weekly
*WPFI score* – 24,52 (50)

# DEMOCRATIC REPUBLIC OF THE CONGO

*République Démocratique du Congo* – Democratic Republic of the Congo

*Area* – 2,344,858 sq. km
*Capital* – Kinshasa; population, 11,587,000 (2015 est)
*Major cities* – Bukavu, Kananga, Kisangani, Kolwezi, Likasi, Lubumbashi, Mbuji-Mayi

*Currency* – Congolese franc (FC) of 100 centimes
*Population* – 79,375,136 rising at 2.45 per cent a year (2015 est). The population is composed of over 200 ethnic groups, including Bantu, Hamitic, Nilotic, Sudanese and Pygmoid; the four largest tribes, Mongo, Luba, Kongo (all Bantu) and Mangbtu-Azande (Hamitic), make up around 45 per cent of the population
*Religion* – Christian (Roman Catholic 50 per cent, Protestant 20 per cent), Kimbanguist 10 per cent, Muslim 10 per cent (est)
*Language* – French (official), Lingala, Kingwana (a Swahili dialect), Kikongo, Tshiluba
*Population density* – 30 per sq. km (2013)
*Urban population* – 35.4 per cent (2013 est)
*Median age (years)* – 17.9 (2014 est)
*National anthem* – 'Debout Congolais' ['Arise, Congolese']
*National day* – 30 June (Independence Day)
*Death penalty* – Retained
*CPI score* – 22 (154)
*Literacy rate* – 81 per cent (2015 est)
*Gross enrolment ratio (percentage of relevant age group)* – primary 111 per cent; secondary 43 per cent; tertiary 8 per cent (2012 est)
*Health expenditure (per capita)* – US$15 (2012)
*Life expectancy (years)* – 56.54 (2014 est)
*Mortality rate* – 10.3 (2014 est)
*Birth rate* – 35.62 (2014 est)
*Infant mortality rate* – 73.15 (2014 est)
*HIV/AIDS adult prevalence* – 1.1 per cent (2012 est)

## CLIMATE AND TERRAIN
Africa's second-largest country lies on the equator, most of it in the basin of the river Congo and its principal tributaries, the Lualaba and the Kasai. A chain of mountains and lakes (Albert, Edward, Kivu and Tanganyika) runs along the eastern border. Elevation extremes range from 5,110m (Mt Ngaliema, also known as Mt Stanley) to 0m (Atlantic Ocean). The climate is tropical, though cooler in the eastern and southern highlands. There are different climatic cycles either side of the equator, which passes through the north of the country, with a wet season in the north from April to November and in the south from October to May.

## POLITICS
Under the 2006 constitution, the executive president is directly elected for a five-year term, renewable once. The bicameral *Parlement* consists of the National Assembly, which has 500 members directly elected for a five-year term, and the senate, which has 108 members elected by the provincial assemblies to serve a five-year term, plus former elected presidents, who are senators for life.

Joseph Kabila succeeded his father Laurent (assassinated in 2001) as president. After a period of transitional government, a new constitution came into effect in 2006 and presidential and legislative elections were held. The presidential election was won in the second round by Joseph Kabila, who went on to win re-election in November 2011, picking up nearly 49 per cent of the vote; his People's Party for Reconstruction and Development lost a large number of seats in the 2011 legislative election. Violent protests broke out in Kinshasa in January 2015 after President Kabila suggested he would consider changing the constitution in order to allow him to seek a third term of office. New legislative elections are expected to be held in 2016.

HEAD OF STATE
*President,* Maj.-Gen. Joseph Kabila, *sworn in* 26 January 2001, *sworn in as president of the transitional government* 7 April 2003, *elected* 29 October 2006, *re-elected* 2011

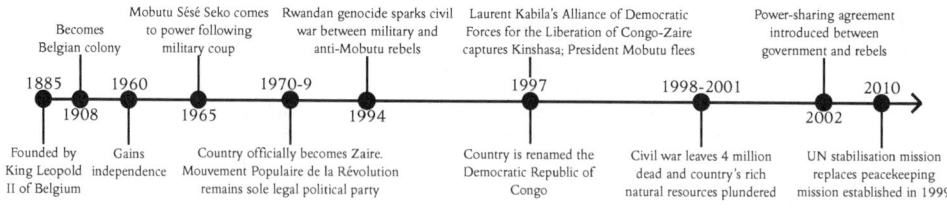

| | Mobutu Sésé Seko comes | Rwandan genocide sparks civil | Laurent Kabila's Alliance of Democratic | Power-sharing agreement |
| Becomes | to power following | war between military and | Forces for the Liberation of Congo-Zaire | introduced between |
| Belgian colony | military coup | anti-Mobutu rebels | captures Kinshasa; President Mobutu flees | government and rebels |

1885 ... 1960 ... 1970-9 ... 1997 ... 1998-2001 ... 2010
1908 ... 1965 ... 1994 ... 2002

| Founded by | Gains | Country officially becomes Zaire. | Country is renamed the | Civil war leaves 4 million | UN stabilisation mission |
| King Leopold | independence | Mouvement Populaire de la Révolution | Democratic Republic of | dead and country's rich | replaces peacekeeping |
| II of Belgium | | remains sole legal political party | Congo | natural resources plundered | mission established in 1999 |

SELECTED GOVERNMENT MEMBERS *as at April 2015*
*Prime Minister,* Augustin Matata Ponyo Mapon
*Deputy Prime Ministers,* Evariste Boshab Mabudj *(Interior)*;
   Thomas Luhaka Losenjola; Willy Makiashi
*Economy,* Modeste Bahati Lukwebo
*Foreign Affairs,* Raymond Tshibanda N'tunga Mulongo

EMBASSY OF THE DEMOCRATIC REPUBLIC OF THE
CONGO
45–49 Great Portland Street, London W1W 7LD
T 020-7580 3931 E missionrdclondres@gmail.com
W http://ambardc-londres.gouv.cd
*Ambassador Extraordinary and Plenipotentiary,* vacant

BRITISH EMBASSY
83 Avenue du Roi Baudouin, Gombe, Kinshasa
T (+243) 81 556 6200 E ambassade.britannique@fco.gov.uk
W www.gov.uk/government/world/democratic-republic-of-congo
*Ambassador Extraordinary and Plenipotentiary,* HE Diane
   Corner, *apptd* 2013

DEFENCE

| *Aged 16–49, 2010 est* | *Males* | *Females* |
| Available for military service | 15,980,106 | – |
| Fit for military service | 10,168,258 | 10,331,693 |

*Military expenditure* – US$456m (2014)
*Conscription* – 18–45 years of age

ECONOMY AND TRADE
A decade of civil war left the country with huge external debt, little infrastructure, widespread corruption and an environment that discourages foreign investment. Improved stability since 2003 has allowed some economic growth, although the global downturn caused the economy to contract in 2008–9. Growth returned in 2010–11, and government reforms, international aid and debt relief are helping the economy in its continuing recovery. The economy averaged strong growth of 8 per cent between 2012 and 2015, but average wages have not grown and poverty remains high, with just under half of all children suffering from malnutrition. The east of the country was disproportionately affected by the civil war and remains particularly underdeveloped.
   The country has great potential wealth in the form of immense natural resources, including copper, cobalt, diamonds, gold, silver, uranium, other minerals, coal, oil, timber and hydroelectric power; mining is the largest source of export income. Agriculture contributes 40.4 per cent of GDP, the services sector 36.6 per cent and industry 23 per cent. Apart from mining and mineral processing, the main industrial activities are the production of textiles, plastics, footwear, cigarettes, metal products, processed food, beverages, timber and cement, and ship repair. Oil deposits are exploited off the Congo estuary, and hydroelectric schemes on the river Congo supply power to the major cities.
   The main trading partners are China, South Africa, Belgium, Zambia and Zimbabwe. Principal exports are diamonds, gold, copper, cobalt, wood products, crude oil and coffee. The main imports are foodstuffs, industrial machinery, transport equipment and fuels.
*GNI* – US$29,066m; US$430 per capita (2013)
*Annual average growth of GDP* – 8.6 per cent (2014 est)
*Inflation rate* – 1.6 per cent (2013 est)
*Population below poverty line* – 71 per cent (2006 est)
*Unemployment* – 7.8 per cent (2015 est)
*Total external debt* – US$6,955m (2014 est)
*Imports* – US$6,300m (2013 est)
*Exports* – US$6,300m (2013 est)

BALANCE OF PAYMENTS
*Trade* – US$0m surplus (2013)
*Current Account* – US$3,312m deficit (2014 est)

| *Trade with UK* | *2013* | *2014* |
| Imports from UK | £33,247,902 | £32,543,301 |
| Exports to UK | £2,947,661 | £1,626,166 |

COMMUNICATIONS
*Airport* – 26, the principal airports being at Kinshasa, Kananga, Goma, Gemena and Mbandaka
*Waterways* – The river Congo and its main tributaries provide 15,000km of waterways, with the principal ports in Banana, Boma and Matadi
*Roadways and railways* – There are 2,794km of surfaced roads; the 4,007km rail system links the interior to the rivers and to the great lakes in the east
*Telecommunications* – 58,200 fixed lines in use and 19.487 million mobile subscriptions (2012); there were 290,000 internet users in 2008
*Internet code and IDD* – cd; 243 (from UK), 44 (to UK)
*Major broadcasters* – The state-controlled Radio-Télévision Nationale Congolaise (RTNC) and the popular radio station La Voix du Congo approach national coverage; the UN and foreign NGOs sponsor Radio Okapi
*Press* – Major dailies include *Le Potentiel, La Reference Plus* and *L'Avenir*
*WPFI score* – 44,31 (150)

REPUBLIC OF THE CONGO

*République du Congo – Republic of the Congo*

*Area* – 342,000 sq. km
*Capital* – Brazzaville; population, 1,850,000 (2015 est)
*Major cities* – Loubomo, Pointe-Noire
*Currency* – Franc CFA of 100 centimes
*Population* – 4,755,097 rising at 2 per cent a year (2015 est); Kongo (48 per cent), Sangha (20 per cent), Teke (17 per cent) and M'Bochi (12 per cent) (est) are the largest of the 15 main Bantu groups
*Religion* – Christian (Roman Catholic 33.1 per cent, Awakening Churches 22.3 per cent, Protestant 19.9 per cent), Muslim 1.6 per cent, Kimbanguist 1.5 per cent (est)
*Language* – French (official), Lingala, Monokutuba, Kikongo
*Population density* – 13 per sq. km (2013)
*Urban population* – 64.5 per cent (2013 est)
*Median age (years)* – 19.8 (2014 est)
*National anthem* – 'La Congolaise' ['The Congolese']
*National day* – 15 August (Independence Day)
*Death penalty* – Retained (last used 1982)
*CPI score* – 23 (152)

## CLIMATE AND TERRAIN
The republic, which lies on the equator, is covered by grassland, mangrove and dense rainforest. The land rises from the narrow Atlantic coastal plain to a central plateau; in the north and east it falls to the northern part of the basin of the river Congo, which forms part of the border with the Democratic Republic of the Congo, and to the valleys of the Sangha and Alima rivers in the north. Elevation extremes range from 903m (Mt Berongou) to 0m (Atlantic Ocean). The climate is tropical. Average temperatures range from 23.5°C in July to 26°C in March. Outside the main dry season between June and September, the country is prone to flooding.

## HISTORY AND POLITICS
The first European visitors to the area were the Portuguese, who established slave trading in the 16th century. The French established a colonial presence in the area in the 1880s and, as Middle Congo, it was part of French Equatorial Africa from 1910. It became independent as the Republic of the Congo on 17 August 1960.

One-party socialism was introduced in 1964; the Congolese Labour Party (PCT) was set up shortly after a military coup in 1968 and continued to rule until 1990, when Marxism was renounced and the PCT abandoned its monopoly of power. Elections in 1993 left the PCT a minority party, and the power shift destabilised the country, with factional fighting after the 1993 election, a civil war between 1997 and 1999 following Denis Sassou-Nguesso's deposition of the elected president, and a renewed insurgency by opponents of the PCT over the manipulation of the 2002 elections. A peace accord ended the insurgency in 2003 but the peace remains fragile and remnants of the rebel militias are still active in the south of the country.

Sassou-Nguesso was elected president in 2002, and was re-elected in 2009; the legitimacy of both victories was suspect after the barring or withdrawal of opponents, fraud and other irregularities. In the 2012 legislative election the PCT expanded upon its large majority, taking 89 of the 139 seats available. In March 2015, President Sassou-Nguesso announced that he would seek to hold a national referendum on changing the country's constitution in order to allow him to serve a third term and contest the 2016 presidential elections.

Under the 2002 constitution, parties organised on regional, ethnic or religious lines are banned. The executive president is directly elected for a seven-year term, renewable once, and appoints the cabinet. The bicameral *Parlement* comprises the National Assembly, with 137 members directly elected for a five-year term, and the senate, which has 72 members indirectly elected for a six-year term, half of the members retiring every three years.

HEAD OF STATE
*President*, Denis Sassou-Nguesso, *took power* October 1997, *elected* 10 March 2002, *re-elected* 2009

SELECTED GOVERNMENT MEMBERS *as at April 2015*
*Defence*, Charles Richard Mondjo
*Economy, Finance and Planning*, Gilbert Ondongo
*Foreign Affairs*, Basile Ikouébé

EMBASSY OF THE REPUBLIC OF THE CONGO
37 bis Rue Paul Valéry, 75116 Paris, France
T (+33) (1) 4500 6057
*Ambassador Extraordinary and Plenipotentiary*, HE Henri Marie Joseph Lopes, *apptd* 1999

BRITISH AMBASSADOR
HE Diane Corner, *apptd* 2013, resident at Kinshasa, DR of the Congo

## DEFENCE

| Aged 16–49, 2010 est | Males | Females |
| --- | --- | --- |
| Available for military service | 928,664 | 914,265 |
| Fit for military service | 577,944 | 566,587 |

*Military expenditure* – US$218m (2010)

## ECONOMY AND TRADE
A decade of civil conflict left the country with a high external debt, a devastated infrastructure and widespread poverty. Since 2003 the government has made efforts to address these problems and has benefited from debt relief in 2006, 2007 and 2010. GDP growth has averaged 5 per cent in the past four years.

Oil production is the backbone of the economy and declining production and falling global commodity prices represent a major threat to the economy. Mining (particularly of diamonds), forestry, brewing, agricultural processing and cement production are the other main industries; new projects, notably the mining of iron ore, are expected to add around US$1 billion to annual revenue. Industry accounts for 74.4 per cent of GDP, services for 22.3 per cent and agriculture, which is mostly at subsistence level, for 3.3 per cent.

The main trading partners are China, the USA and France. Principal exports are oil, timber, plywood, sugar, cocoa, coffee and diamonds. Imports are mainly capital equipment, construction materials and foodstuffs.
*GNI* – US$11,527m; US$2,590 per capita (2013)
*Annual average growth of GDP* – 6 per cent (2014 est)
*Inflation rate* – 6 per cent (2013 est)
*Population below poverty line* – 22.4 per cent (2014 est)
*Unemployment* – 7.8 per cent (2015 est)
*Total external debt* – US$3,956m (2014 est)
*Imports* – US$5,500m (2013)
*Exports* – US$9,800m (2013)

BALANCE OF PAYMENTS
*Trade* – US$4,300m surplus (2013)
*Current Account* – US$839m deficit (2014 est)

| Trade with UK | 2013 | 2014 |
| --- | --- | --- |
| Imports from UK | £64,859,649 | £78,263,581 |
| Exports to UK | £222,360,453 | £79,185,576 |

## COMMUNICATIONS

*Airports* – Eight, including an international airport at Brazzaville
*Waterways* – Pointe-Noire is the main seaport and also the centre of the offshore oil industry. Brazzaville is the main river port, lying on the river Congo which, with the river Oubangui, provides 1,120km of commercially navigable waterways
*Roadways and railways* – 864km; 886km
*Telecommunications* – 14,900 fixed lines and 4.283 million mobile subscriptions (2012); there were 245,200 internet users in 2009
*Internet code and IDD* – cg; 242 (from UK), 44 (to UK)
*Major broadcasters* – TV Congo is the only television station and is controlled by the state. Two government radio stations, Radio Congo and Radio Brazzaville, exist alongside commercial and community stations
*Press* – The government-run *La Nouvelle République* is the country's only daily newspaper
*WPFI score* – 33 (107)

## EDUCATION AND HEALTH

Schooling is free and compulsory between ages six and 16.
*Literacy rate* – 81 per cent (2015 est)
*Gross enrolment ratio (percentage of relevant age group)* –
primary 109 per cent; secondary 54 per cent; tertiary 10 per cent (2012 est)
*Health expenditure (per capita)* – US$131 (2013)
*Life expectancy (years)* – 58.52 (2014 est)
*Mortality rate* – 10.17 (2014 est)
*Birth rate* – 36.59 (2014 est)
*Infant mortality rate* – 59.34 (2014 est)
*HIV/AIDS adult prevalence* – 2.8 per cent (2012 est)

## COSTA RICA

*República de Costa Rica – Republic of Costa Rica*

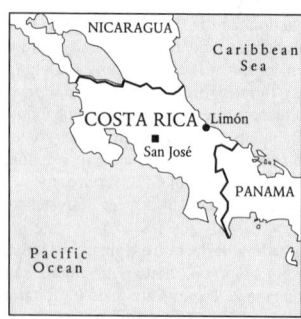

*Area* – 51,100 sq. km
*Capital* – San José; population, 1,170,000 (2015 est)
*Major towns* – Alajuela, Liberia, Limón, Paraíso, San Francisco
*Currency* – Costa Rican colón of 100 céntimos
*Population* – 4,814,144 rising at 1.22 per cent a year (2015 est)
*Religion* – Christian (Roman Catholic 63 per cent, Protestant 23 per cent) (est)
*Language* – Spanish (official), English
*Population density* – 95 per sq. km (2013)
*Urban population* – 65.6 per cent (2013 est)
*Median age (years)* – 30 (2014 est)
*National anthem* – 'Noble Patria, Tu Hermosa Bandera' ['Noble Fatherland, Your Beautiful Flag']
*National day* – 15 September (Independence Day)

*Death penalty* – Abolished for all crimes (since 1877)
*CPI score* – 32 (115)
*Literacy rate* – 99.3 per cent (2015 est)
*Gross enrolment ratio (percentage of relevant age group)* –
primary 105 per cent; secondary 104 per cent; tertiary 47 per cent (2012 est)
*Health expenditure (per capita)* – US$1,005 (2013)
*Hospital beds (per 1,000 people)* – 1.2 (2012)
*Life expectancy (years)* – 78.23 (2014 est)
*Mortality rate* – 4.49 (2014 est)
*Birth rate* – 16.08 (2014 est)
*Infant mortality rate* – 8.7 (2014 est)

## CLIMATE AND TERRAIN

The Cordillera de Guanacaste (north-west), Cordillera de Talamanca and Cordillera Central (south-east) form a chain of volcanic mountain ranges that traverse the country from north to south. A central valley lies between the ranges, and the land slopes to plains on the Pacific and Caribbean coasts. Elevation extremes range from 3,810m (Cerro Chirripó Grande) to 0m (Pacific Ocean). The climate is tropical, with average temperatures ranging from 24.3°C in November to 26.8°C in April, and a wet season from May to November. The area is subject to occasional earthquakes, hurricanes, flooding and landslides.

## HISTORY AND POLITICS

Visited by Columbus in 1502, Costa Rica was colonised by the Spanish from the 1560s and remained under Spanish rule until Central America gained its independence in 1821. Costa Rica was part of a Central American federation of former Spanish provinces from 1823 until its secession in 1838. Political unrest in the mid-20th century led to a brief civil war in 1948, after which the army was abolished and replaced with a national guard. Subsequently power alternated between the two main political parties, the National Liberation Party (PLN) and the Social Christian Unity Party (PUSC), but in recent years the scandal-ridden PUSC has lost ground to emerging new parties.

In the 2014 legislative elections, the PLN remained the largest party despite losing seats for the second consecutive election. The simultaneous presidential election was won by the Citizen's Action Party candidate Luis Guillermo Solís.

Under the 1949 constitution, the executive president is directly elected for a four-year term. The unicameral legislative assembly has 57 members directly elected for a four-year term.

HEAD OF STATE
*President*, Luis Guillermo Solís, *elected* 7 April 2014, *sworn in* 8 May 2010
*First Vice-President, Finance*, Helio Fallas Venegas
*Second Vice-President*, Ana Helena Chacón Echeverria

SELECTED GOVERNMENT MEMBERS *as at April 2015*
*Economy*, Welmer Ramos González
*Foreign Affairs*, Manuel González Sanz

EMBASSY OF COSTA RICA
14 Lancaster Gate, London W2 3LH
T 020-7706 8844 E info@costaricanembassy.co.uk
*Ambassador Extraordinary and Plenipotentiary*, vacant

BRITISH EMBASSY
Edificio Centro Colón, Paseo Colón and Streets 38 and 40, San Jose, Apartado 815–1007
T (+506) 2258 2025 E ukin.costarica@fco.gov.uk
W www.gov.uk/government/world/costa-rica
*Ambassadors Extraordinary and Plenipotentiary*, HE Sharon Campbell, *apptd* 2011

# DEFENCE

| Aged 16–49, 2010 est | Males | Females |
|---|---|---|
| Available for military service | 1,255,798 | 1,230,202 |
| Fit for military service | 1,058,419 | 1,037,053 |

## ECONOMY AND TRADE

Sixty years of political stability have allowed steady economic growth, the creation of a social welfare system, the highest levels of foreign direct investment in Latin America and a reduction in poverty to less than 25 per cent of the population, though the social benefit system is becoming increasingly strained due to restrictions on government spending and increased immigration. The economy grew by approximately 4.3 per cent from 2012–13. Costa Rica introduced a floating exchange rate regime for the Costa Rican colón on 2 February 2015 in order to create more flexible exchange rates and to manage inflation.

Tourism is the largest single industry, and with one-third of the country now national parkland or nature reserve, eco-tourism is on the increase. Services account for about 73.4 per cent of GDP while the manufacturing industry accounts for 20.5 per cent, the principal products being microprocessors, foodstuffs, medical equipment, textiles, clothing, construction materials, fertiliser and plastic goods. The agricultural sector contributes 6 per cent of GDP; the principal products are tropical fruit, coffee, ornamental plants, sugar, rice, vegetables, meat and timber.

The main trading partners are the USA, China, the Netherlands and Mexico. The chief exports are tropical fruit, coffee, plants, sugar, beef, seafood, electrical components and medical equipment. The chief imports are raw materials, consumer goods, capital equipment, petrol and construction materials.

GNI – US$46,534m; US$9,550 per capita (2013)
Annual average growth of GDP – 3.6 per cent (2014 est)
Inflation rate – 5.2 per cent (2013 est)
Population below poverty line – 22.4 per cent (2014 est)
Unemployment – 7.5 per cent (2015 est)
Total external debt – US$18,370m (2014 est)
Imports – US$17,923m (2013)
Exports – US$11,542m (2013)

BALANCE OF PAYMENTS
Trade – US$6,381m deficit (2013)
Current Account – US$2,151m deficit (2014 est)

| Trade with UK | 2013 | 2014 |
|---|---|---|
| Imports from UK | £52,975,571 | £58,717,917 |
| Exports to UK | £182,484,662 | £207,639,835 |

## COMMUNICATIONS

Airports and waterways – 47, the principal airports are at San José and Limón; the chief seaports are Limón on the Atlantic coast, and Puntarenas and de Caldera on the Pacific coast
Roadways and railways – There are 10,133km of paved roads; 278km of unused railways
Telecommunications – 1.018 million fixed lines and 6.151 million mobile subscriptions (2012); there were 1.485 million internet users in 2009
Major broadcasters – Public broadcasting is provided by Canal 13 (TV) and Radio Nacional; cable television is widely available
Press – Media are generally free from state interference; daily newspapers include Al Dia, Diario Extra and La Nacion
Internet code and IDD – cr; 506 (from UK), 44 (to UK)
WPFI score – 12,26 (16)

# CÔTE D'IVOIRE

République de Côte d'Ivoire – the Ivory Coast

Area – 322,463 sq. km
Capital – Yamoussoukro (since 1983); population, 966,000 (2011 est); slow progress in transferring functions means that the former capital, Abidjan (population, 4,800,000; 2015 est), remains the seat of government at present
Major cities – Abidjan, Bouaké, Daloa, Korhogo
Currency – Franc CFA of 100 centimes
Population – 23,295,302 rising at 1.91 per cent a year (2015 est); over 60 ethnic groups, including the Akan (42.1 per cent), Voltaiques or Gur (17.6 per cent), Northern Mandes (16.5 per cent), Krous (11 per cent), Southern Mandes (10 per cent) (est)
Religion – Muslim 38.6 per cent, Christian 32.8 per cent, indigenous religions 11.9 per cent (est); many Christians and Muslims incorporate indigenous beliefs into their worship
Language – French (official), around 60 native dialects of which Dioula is the most widely spoken
Population density – 64 per sq. km (2013)
Urban population – 52.8 per cent (2013 est)
Median age (years) – 20.3 (2014 est)
National anthem – 'L'Abidjanaise' ['Song of Abidjan']
National day – 7 August (Independence Day)
Death penalty – Abolished for all crimes (since 2000)
CPI score – 32 (115)
Literacy rate – 50.2 per cent (2015 est)
Gross enrolment ratio (percentage of relevant age group) – primary 94 per cent; secondary 27 per cent; tertiary 4 per cent (2012 est)
Health expenditure (per capita) – US$87 (2013)
Life expectancy (years) – 58.01 (2014 est)
Mortality rate – 9.67 (2014 est)
Birth rate – 29.25 (2014 est)
Infant mortality rate – 60.16 (2014 est)
HIV/AIDS adult prevalence – 2.5 per cent (2013 est)

## CLIMATE AND TERRAIN

The land rises from a coastal plain to a large interior plateau with mountains in the north and west. Coastal lagoons give way to tropical rainforest in the centre and savannah in the north; deforestation means that the area of savannah is increasing. The country is dissected by the Sassandra, Bandama and Komoé rivers, the first two forming large central lakes. Elevation extremes range from 1,752m (Mt Nimba) to 0m (Gulf of Guinea). The climate is tropical in the south and semi-arid in the north. The south has two rainy seasons (May to July, October to November) and the north has one (June to September). The average annual temperature is 26.8°C.

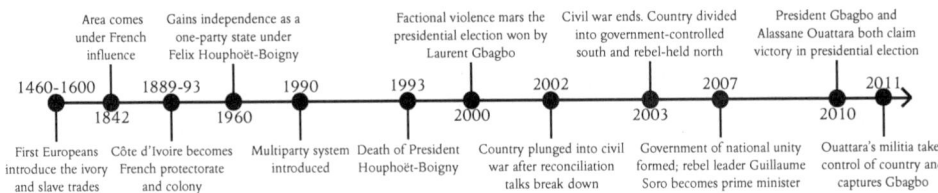

Area comes under French influence | Gains independence as a one-party state under Felix Houphoët-Boigny | | Factional violence mars the presidential election won by Laurent Gbagbo | Civil war ends. Country divided into government-controlled south and rebel-held north | President Gbagbo and Alassane Ouattara both claim victory in presidential election

1460–1600 | 1889–93 | 1990 | 1993 | 2002 | 2007 | 2011

1842 | 1960 | | 2000 | 2003 | 2010

First Europeans introduce the ivory and slave trades | Côte d'Ivoire becomes French protectorate and colony | Multiparty system introduced | Death of President Houphoët-Boigny | Country plunged into civil war after reconciliation talks break down | Government of national unity formed; rebel leader Guillaume Soro becomes prime minister | Ouattara's militia takes control of country and captures Gbagbo

## POLITICS

Since the turn of the century Côte d'Ivoire has seen increased civil unrest and ethnic tensions. Following an election in 2010 the incumbent president Laurent Gbagbo refused to concede to the internationally acknowledged victor, Alassane Ouattara; following a four-month stalemate Ouattara took office by force. In the 2011 parliamentary elections, President Ouattara and his allies obtained a majority, however, in 2012 Ouattara sacked his government in a row over changes in marriage laws. New presidential elections are scheduled to take place in October 2015.

Under the 2000 constitution, the executive president is directly elected for a five-year term, renewable once. The president appoints the prime minister and the other ministers, who are nominated by the prime minister. The unicameral National Assembly has 225 members, directly elected for a five-year term.

### HEAD OF STATE

*President,* Alassane Ouattara, *elected* 28 November 2010, *sworn in* 6 May 2011

SELECTED GOVERNMENT MEMBERS *as at April 2015*
*Prime Minister, Finance and Economy,* Daniel Kablan Duncan
*Foreign Affairs,* Charles Koffi Diby
*Interior,* Hamed Bakayoko

### EMBASSY OF THE REPUBLIC OF CÔTE D'IVOIRE

2 Upper Belgrave Street, London SW1X 8BJ
T 020-7235 6991
*Ambassador Extraordinary and Plenipotentiary,* HE Claude Stanislaus Bouah-Kamon, *apptd* 2011

### BRITISH EMBASSY

Cocody, Quartier Ambassades, Rue l'Impasse du Belier, Rue A 58, 01 BP 2581, Abidjan 01
T (+225) 2244 2669 E uk_abidjan@yahoo.fr
W www.gov.uk/government/world/cote-d-ivoire
*Ambassador Extraordinary and Plenipotentiary,* HE Mark Bensberg, *apptd* 2014

### DEFENCE

| Aged 16–49, 2010 est | Males | Females |
| --- | --- | --- |
| Available for military service | 5,247,522 | 5,047,901 |
| Fit for military service | 3,360,087 | 3,196,033 |

*Military expenditure –* US$407m (2012 est)

### ECONOMY AND TRADE

The country was one of the most prosperous in the region, attracting large numbers of migrant workers from neighbouring countries, until the political turbulence of the late 1990s caused many to return home. The civil war particularly damaged the economy in the cotton-growing north, although recovery is beginning, and continuing political instability has hampered diversification away from agriculture, which makes the economy vulnerable to price fluctuations in its key exports. However, since 2006, revenue from oil, gas and refined products has outstripped earnings from cocoa, and offshore exploration for other deposits continues. The economy grew by 8.8 per cent in 2013 and is expected to grow by 9 per cent in 2014 and 2015. In 2014 the UN overturned a ban on the export on the country's diamonds which had been put in place in 2005 in order to stop the trade funding armed rebel groups. Improved political stability allowed the African Development Bank to return to Abidjan in 2014, having relocated to Tunisia for 11 years during the civil war. Poor infrastructure and business practices are a barrier to future growth, with Côte d'Ivoire having one of the most complex tax codes in Africa.

Services account for 52.1 per cent of GDP, agriculture for 25.9 per cent and industry for 21.9 per cent. Agriculture employs around 68 per cent of the workforce, producing cocoa (of which Côte d'Ivoire is the world's largest producer and exporter), coffee, cotton, bananas, pineapples and palm oil for export. The principal industries are food processing, forestry, oil refining, vehicle assembly, gold mining, textiles, fishing and the production of oil, natural gas and hydro-electric power; the country is a net exporter of electricity. The main trading partners are Nigeria, France, other EU and west African states, and China.

*GNI –* US$29,492m; US$1,450 per capita (2013)
*Annual average growth of GDP –* 8.5 per cent (2014 est)
*Inflation rate –* 2.6 per cent (2013 est)
*Population below poverty line –* 42 per cent (2006 est)
*Unemployment –* 3.8 per cent (2015 est)
*Total external debt –* US$11,500m (2014 est)
*Imports –* US$12,898m (2013)
*Exports –* US$13,748m (2013)

### BALANCE OF PAYMENTS

*Trade –* US$1,087m surplus (2012)
*Current Account –* US$1,113m surplus (2014 est)

| Trade | 2013 | 2014 |
| --- | --- | --- |
| Imports from UK | £101,161,599 | £8,297,146 |
| Exports to UK | £125,906,878 | £14,661,600 |

### COMMUNICATIONS

*Airports –* Seven, the principal international airport being at Abidjan
*Waterways –* There are 980km of navigable rivers, canals and lagoons; the main seaports are Abidjan and San Pedro
*Roadways and railways –* 6,502km; 660km
*Telecommunications –* 268,000 fixed lines and 19.827 million mobile telephone subscriptions (2012); there were 967,300 internet users in 2009
*Internet code and IDD –* ci; 225 (from UK), 44 (to UK)
*Major broadcasters –* The state broadcaster, Radiodiffusion Télévision Ivoirienne (RTI), operates two national radio stations and two television channels; in 2012 the government allowed private companies to enter the radio and TV markets for the first time

*Press* – Nine newspapers are published daily, including the state-owned *Fraternité Matin* and the privately owned *Le Nouveau Reveil*
*WPFI score* – 30,45 (86)

# CROATIA

*Republika Hrvatska – Republic of Croatia*

*Area* – 56,594 sq. km
*Capital* – Zagreb; population, 704,000 (2015 est)
*Major cities* – Osijek, Rijeka (Fiume), Split, Zadar
*Currency* – Kuna of 100 lipa
*Population* – 4,464,844 falling at 0.13 per cent a year (2015 est); Croat (90.4 per cent), Serb (4.4 per cent) (2011)
*Religion* – Christian (Roman Catholic 86.3 per cent, Serbian Orthodox 4.4 per cent), Muslim 1.5 per cent (est)
*Language* – Croatian (official), Serbian
*Population density* – 76 per sq. km (2013)
*Urban population* – 58.4 per cent (2013 est)
*Median age (years)* – 42.1 (2014 est)
*National anthem* – 'Lijepa Nasa Domovino' ['Our Beautiful Homeland']
*National day* – 8 October (Independence Day)
*Death penalty* – Abolished for all crimes (since 1990)
*CPI score* – 48 (61)

## CLIMATE AND TERRAIN

There are three major geographic areas: the plains of the Pannonian region in the north, the central mountain belt, and the Adriatic coast region of Istria and Dalmatia, which has 1,185 islands and islets and 1,777km of coastline. Elevation extremes range from 1,831m (Dinara) to 0m (Adriatic Sea). The climate varies significantly between the Dalmatian coast, where the winters are mild and the summers hot, and inland areas, which have colder temperatures and rain in the summer. Average temperatures range from 1.8°C in January to 28°C in July.

## POLITICS

The 1990 constitution was amended in 2000 to increase the powers of the legislature, making the presidency a largely ceremonial role, and in 2001 to abolish the upper house of the legislature. The head of state is a president, who is directly elected for a five-year term. The legislature, the Croatian Assembly, has one chamber, the House of Representatives, which has 151 members directly elected for a four-year term. The prime minister is appointed by the legislature and appoints the cabinet.

In the 2011 legislative election, a coalition consisting of the Social Democratic Party of Croatia (SDP), the Croatian People's Party and two smaller parties (the Kukuriku coalition) overtook the Croatian Democratic Union (HDZ) to secure an overall majority in the parliament. SDP leader Zoran Milanovic was named prime minister in December 2011 and set about forming a government based on the Kukuriku coalition. The 2015 presidential elections were narrowly won by Kolinda Grabar-Kitarovic of the HDZ after a second round of voting. Croatia became a member of the EU in July 2013.

### HEAD OF STATE

*President*, Kolinda Grabar-Kitarovic, *elected* 12 January 2015, *sworn in* 18 February 2015

### SELECTED GOVERNMENT MEMBERS *as at April 2014*

*Prime Minister*, Zoran Milanovic
*First Deputy Prime Minister, Foreign Affairs*, Vesna Pusic
*Deputy Prime Ministers*, Branko Grcic; Ranko Ostojic
*(Interior)*; Milanka Opacic
*Defence*, Ante Kotromanovic
*Finance*, Boris Lalovac

### EMBASSY OF THE REPUBLIC OF CROATIA

21 Conway Street, London W1T 6BN
T 020-7387 2022 E vrhlon@mvep.hr W http://uk.mvp.hr
*Ambassador Extraordinary and Plenipotentiary*, HE Dr Ivan Grdesic, *apptd* 2012

### BRITISH EMBASSY

Ivana Lucica 4, 10000 Zagreb
T (+385) 600 9100 E british.embassyzagreb@fco.gov.uk
W www.gov.uk/government/world/croatia
*Ambassador*, HE Ian Cameron Cliff, *apptd* 2015

### DEFENCE

| *Aged 16–49, 2010 est* | *Males* | *Females* |
| --- | --- | --- |
| Available for military service | 1,016,234 | 1,017,355 |
| Fit for military service | 770,710 | 839,732 |

*Military expenditure* – US$875m (2014 est)

### ECONOMY AND TRADE

As part of Yugoslavia, Croatia was a prosperous and industrialised area, but the conflict in 1991–5 damaged its infrastructure, large areas of farmland, industrial productivity and the tourist industry. From 2000 to 2007 there was steady economic growth, led by a recovery in tourism, banking and public investment. However, a growing trade deficit, high unemployment, the size of the public sector and the economy's over-reliance on tourism are longer-term

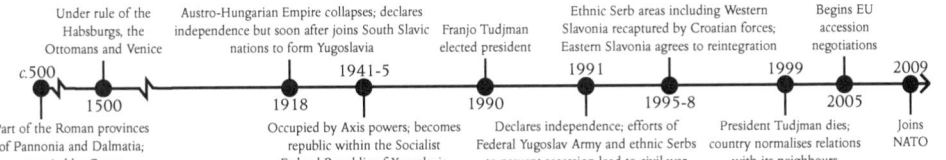

Under rule of the Habsburgs, the Ottomans and Venice — Austro-Hungarian Empire collapses; declares independence but soon after joins South Slavic nations to form Yugoslavia — Franjo Tudjman elected president — Ethnic Serb areas including Western Slavonia recaptured by Croatian forces; Eastern Slavonia agrees to reintegration — Begins EU accession negotiations

c.500 — 1941-5 — 1991 — 1999 — 2009

1500 — 1918 — 1990 — 1995-8 — 2005

Part of the Roman provinces of Pannonia and Dalmatia; occupied by Croats — Occupied by Axis powers; becomes republic within the Socialist Federal Republic of Yugoslavia — Declares independence; efforts of Federal Yugoslav Army and ethnic Serbs to prevent secession lead to civil war — President Tudjman dies; country normalises relations with its neighbours — Joins NATO

problems that left the economy vulnerable in the global economic downturn in 2008. The country joined the EU in 2013 but does not yet qualify to join the Economic and Monetary Union. Croatia entered its sixth successive year of recession in 2014, becoming one of the EU's worst performing economies, having lost 13 per cent of GDP during its economic downturn. Privatisation projects have stalled and unemployment among young people is close to 50 per cent.

The service sector accounts for 68.9 per cent of GDP, industry for 26.6 per cent and agriculture for 4.5 per cent. Tourism is a major contributor to GDP. Industry produces chemicals and plastics, machine tools, metals and metal products, electronics, wood products, construction materials and textiles, and includes food processing, shipbuilding and oil refining. Agricultural production includes cereals, pulses, fruit and vegetables, livestock and dairy products. Most trade is with EU and neighbouring countries.

*GNI –* US$57,081m; US$13,430 per capita (2013)
*Annual average growth of GDP –* −0.8 per cent (2014 est)
*Inflation rate –* 2.2 per cent (2013 est)
*Population below poverty line –* 20.5 per cent (2011 est)
*Unemployment –* 16.7 per cent (2015 est)
*Total external debt –* US$61,040m (2014 est)
*Imports –* US$20,961m (2013)
*Exports –* US$11,928m (2013)

BALANCE OF PAYMENTS
*Trade –* US$9,033m deficit (2013)
*Current Account –* US$38m surplus (2014 est)

| Trade with UK | 2013 | 2014 |
| --- | --- | --- |
| Imports from UK | £65,144,274 | £141,920,695 |
| Exports to UK | £74,098,971 | £67,404,565 |

## COMMUNICATIONS
*Airports and waterways* – 24; there are 785km of inland waterways and frequent ferry services to the many Adriatic islands
*Roadways and railways* – 29,410km, including 1,254km of motorways; 2,722km
*Telecommunications* – 1.64 million fixed lines and 4.97 million mobile subscriptions (2012); there were 2.234 million internet users in 2009
*Internet code and IDD* – hr; 385 (from UK), 44 (to UK)
*Major broadcasters* – Croatian Radio-Television (HRT) is the national state-owned public service broadcaster
*Press* – Leading daily newspapers include *Vecernji List, Jutarnji List* and *Slobodna Dalmacija*
*WPFI score* – 26,12 (58)

## EDUCATION AND HEALTH
Education is free and compulsory for all children from ages six to 15.
*Literacy rate* – 99.7 per cent (2015 est)
*Gross enrolment ratio (percentage of relevant age group)* – primary 97 per cent; secondary 98 per cent; tertiary 62 per cent (2012 est)
*Health expenditure (per capita)* – US$908 (2012)
*Hospital beds (per 1,000 people)* – 5.9 (2012)
*Life expectancy (years)* – 76.41 (2014 est)
*Mortality rate* – 12.13 (2014 est)
*Birth rate* – 9.49 (2014 est)
*Infant mortality rate* – 5.87 (2014 est)

# CUBA

*República de Cuba – Republic of Cuba*

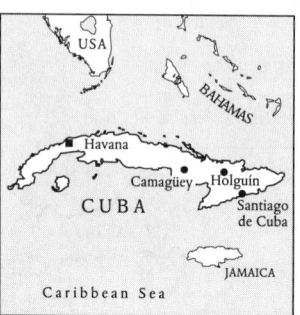

*Area* – 110,860 sq. km
*Capital* – Havana; population, 2,130,000 (2015 est)
*Major cities* – Camagüey, Guantánamo, Holguín, Santa Clara, Santiago de Cuba
*Currency* – Cuban peso ($) of 100 centavos
*Population* – 11,031,433 falling at 0.15 per cent a year (2015 est)
*Religion* – Christian (Roman Catholic 60 per cent, Protestant 5 per cent) (est); many practise Santería (African religions syncretised with Christianity). Religious activity is tightly controlled; house churches must be state-registered
*Language* – Spanish (official)
*Population density* – 106 per sq. km (2013)
*Urban population* – 75.1 per cent (2013 est)
*Median age (years)* – 39.9 (2014 est)
*National anthem* – 'El Himno de Bayamo' ['The Anthem of Bayamo']
*National day* – 1 January (Triumph of the Revolution)
*Death penalty* – Retained
*CPI score* – 46 (63)

## CLIMATE AND TERRAIN
The largest island in the Caribbean, Cuba is part of an archipelago that also includes Isla de la Juventud and around 1,600 other islets and cays. The island of Cuba has three mountainous ranges running from east to west. Elevation extremes range from 2,005m (Pico Turquino) to 0m (Caribbean Sea). The climate is subtropical, with an average annual temperature of 25.5°C.

## POLITICS
The Communist Party of Cuba (PCC) is the only authorised political party. The 1976 constitution was amended in 1991 to allow direct election of the National Assembly by secret ballot, and in 2002 to enshrine socialism in the constitution. The president is elected by the legislature for a five-year term. The unicameral National Assembly of the People's Power has 614 members directly elected for a five-year term; all candidates are approved by the PCC and stand unopposed. Between its sessions, the assembly is represented by the Council of State, whose members are elected by the assembly.

Fidel Castro, who had been president since 1959, announced in February 2008 that he would not accept another term in office due to ill health. His brother, Raúl Castro, who had been acting president since July 2006, was elected head of state and head of government later that month by the National Assembly; he was re-elected in February 2013 and announced that he would step down at the end of his second term.

Settled by Spanish — 1492 — Visited by Columbus

Becomes independent; USA retains naval bases on the island — 1898 — 1600 — War of independence won; Spain cedes Cuba to the USA — 1902 — Dictator Gen. Fulgencio Batista overthrown by Fidel Castro

Communist state established, allied with USSR; USA begins economic and trade embargo — 1959 — 1961 — Cuban missile crisis; the USA and USSR almost engage in nuclear conflict due to missile site construction on Cuba

Collapse of the USSR; Cuban government relaxes state economic controls — 1962 — 1991 — Fidel Castro steps down as president owing to ill-health; he is replaced by his brother Raúl

After 53 years Cuba and the USA restore diplomatic relations — 2008 — 2014

## HEAD OF STATE

*President of Council of State and Council of Ministers,* Gen. Raúl Castro Ruz, *elected* 24 February 2008, re-elected February 2013

*First Vice-President of Council of State,* Miguel Diaz-Canel Bermudez

SELECTED GOVERNMENT MEMBERS *as at April 2015*
*Vice Presidents of Council of Ministers,* Gen. Antonio Enrique Lusson Batlle; Marino Murillo Jorge; Ramiro Valdes Menendez; Adel Izquierdo Rodriguez; Ricardo Cabrisas Ruiz; Ulises Rosales del Toro; Jose Ramon Machado Ventura

*Finance and Prices,* Lina Pedraza Rodriguez
*Foreign Relations,* Bruno Rodriguez Parrilla

## EMBASSY OF THE REPUBLIC OF CUBA

167 High Holborn, London WC1 6PA
T 020-7240 2488 E secembajador@uk.embacuba.cu
W www.cubadiplomatica.cu/reinounido
*Ambassador Extraordinary and Plenipotentiary,* vacant

## BRITISH EMBASSY

Calle 34, No 702, Miramar, Playa, Havana
T (+53) (0) 7214 2200 E embrit@enet.cu
W www.gov.uk/government/world/cuba
*Ambassador Extraordinary and Plenipotentiary,* HE Timothy Cole, *apptd* 2012

## DEFENCE

| *Aged 16–49, 2010 est* | *Males* | *Females* |
| --- | --- | --- |
| Available for military service | 2,998,201 | 2,919,107 |
| Fit for military service | 2,446,131 | 2,375,590 |

*Military expenditure* – US$119m (2013)
*Conscription* – 17–28 years of age; 24 months for men and women

## ECONOMY AND TRADE

After the revolution virtually all land and industrial and commercial enterprises were nationalised. With the collapse of communism in Europe in 1989–91, the economy deteriorated sharply, necessitating rationing of energy, food and consumer goods, and obliging the government to introduce reforms. Since 1993, liberalisation has gradually opened up the economy to limited private enterprise and foreign ownership of property and business enterprises, and introduced price rises for some goods and services and income tax. The reforms resulted in steady growth, in particular stimulating tourism and the oil and mining industries, but the standard of living for most Cubans is still below the pre-1991 level. Further economic difficulties arising from the global economic downturn, which precipitated a marked fall in tourism and nickel prices, led to a further easing of restrictions on private enterprise in 2010 and plans to reduce public sector employment.

In 2014, the Obama administration announced that it would re-establish communications with Cuba, paving the way for greater foreign travel and business interaction between the two countries. In January 2015, the two governments began talks to remove the embargo entirely and the US ended its ban on the importation of Cuban cigars, first introduced in 1962.

Agriculture contributes 3.9 per cent of GDP and employs around 19.7 per cent of the workforce. Industrial activities include sugar refining, oil production, tobacco processing, construction, nickel mining and production of steel, cement, agricultural machinery and pharmaceuticals. Industry contributes 22.3 per cent of GDP, and the service sector 73.7 per cent. The state sector employs 72.3 per cent of the workforce.

The main trading partners are China, Canada, Venezuela and Spain; Venezuela provides Cuba with 100,000 subsidised barrels of oil a day, although economic problems in Venezuela may soon end this arrangement. Principal exports are sugar, nickel, tobacco, fish, medical products, citrus fruits and coffee. The main imports are oil, food, machinery and equipment, and chemicals.

*GNI* – US$66,3970m; US$5,890 per capita (2011)
*Annual average growth of GDP* – 1.3 per cent (2014 est)
*Inflation rate* – 6 per cent (2013 est)
*Unemployment* – 3.3 per cent (2015 est)
*Total external debt* – US$25,230m (2014 est)

BALANCE OF PAYMENTS
Trade – US$6,573m deficit (2010)

| *Trade with UK* | *2013* | *2014* |
| --- | --- | --- |
| Imports from UK | £24,092,004 | £19,129,355 |
| Exports to UK | £114,169,535 | £43,278,320 |

## COMMUNICATIONS

*Airports* – 64; the main international airport is at Havana
*Waterways* – There are 240km of navigable waterways; the main ports are Havana, Cienfuegos and Matanzas
*Roadways and railways* – 29,820km; 8,203km, 4,533km of which are used exclusively by sugar plantations
*Telecommunications* – 1.217 million fixed line users and 1.682 million mobile subscriptions (2012); there were 1.6 million internet users in 2009
*Internet code and IDD* – cu; 53 (from UK), 44 (to UK)
*Major broadcasters* – The government operates four television channels and six radio stations including Cubavision (TV) and Radio Rebelde; Radio-TV Marti, a US government-backed station, transmits from Florida
*Press* – Cuba is the only country in the Americas not to have an independent press; the official Communist Party newspaper is *Granma*
*WPFI score* – 70,21 (169)

## EDUCATION AND HEALTH

Education is free of charge and compulsory between ages six and 15. Healthcare is free.
*Literacy rate* – 100 per cent (2015 est)
*Gross enrolment ratio (percentage of relevant age group)* – primary 99 per cent; secondary 90 per cent; tertiary 62 per cent (2012 est)

*Health expenditure (per capita)* – US$603 (2013)
*Hospital beds (per 1,000 people)* – 5.3 (2012)
*Life expectancy (years)* – 78.22 (2014 est)
*Mortality rate* – 7.64 (2014 est)
*Birth rate* – 9.90 (2014 est)
*Infant mortality rate* – 4.7 (2014 est)

# CYPRUS

*Kypriaki Dimokratia/Kibris Cumhuriyeti – Republic of Cyprus*

*Area* – 9,251 sq. km, of which 3,355 sq. km are in the Turkish Cypriot-administered area
*Capital* – Nicosia, population, 300,000 (2011 est)
*Major cities* – Larnaca, Limassol, Strovolos (south of the partition); Famagusta, Kyrenia (north)
*Currency* – Euro (€) of 100 cents (south), Turkish lira (north)
*Population* – 1,189,197 rising at 1.43 per cent a year (2015 est); Greek (77 per cent), Turkish (18 per cent) (2001 est)
*Religion* – Christian (Greek Orthodox 95 per cent) south of the partition; Muslim 98 per cent (mainly Sunni) in the north
*Language* – Greek, Turkish (both official), English, Romanian, Russian, Bulgarian, Arabic, Filipino
*Population density* – 124 per sq. km (2013)
*Urban population* – 70.9 per cent (2013 est)
*Median age (years)* – 35.7 (2014 est)
*National anthem* – 'Ymnos eis tin Eleutherian' ['Hymn to Liberty']
*National day* – 1 October (Independence Day); Turkish Cypriots celebrate on 15 November
*Death penalty* – Abolished for all crimes (since 2002)
*CPI score* – 63 (31)
*Literacy rate* – 99.9 per cent (2015 est)
*Life expectancy (years)* – 78.34 (2013 est)
*Mortality rate* – 6.57 (2014 est)
*Birth rate* – 11.44 (2014 est)
*Infant mortality rate* – 8.54 (2014 est)

## CLIMATE AND TERRAIN
Cyprus is the third-largest island in the Mediterranean. It has two mountain ranges, the Pentadaktylos along the north coast, and the Troodos in the centre and west. Plains lie between the two ranges and on parts of the south coast. Elevation extremes range from 1,951m (Mt Olympus, Troodos range) to 0m (Mediterranean Sea). The climate is Mediterranean, with very warm summers.

## POLITICS
The 1960 constitution provides for power-sharing between the Greek and Turkish Cypriots but some of these provisions have been in abeyance since 1963, when the Turkish Cypriots withdrew from the power-sharing arrangements. The executive president is directly elected for a five-year term. The unicameral legislature, the House of Representatives, has 80 members, directly elected for a five-year term; elections to the 24 seats reserved for Turkish Cypriots have not taken place since 1963.

Legislative elections held in May 2011 resulted in gains for the Progressive Party of the Working People (AKEL) and the opposition Democratic Rally (DISY) party; AKEL maintained its majority in the House of Representatives through a coalition with the Democratic Party (DIKO). DISY's Nikos Anastasiades was elected president in February 2013. In February 2014, the DIKO announced it would leave the coalition following the government's decision to resume talks with Northern Cyprus. Peace talks were suspended in October after Cyprus claimed that Turkey had prevented it from exploring for potential gas fields off the south coast of the island.

### HEAD OF STATE
*President,* Nikos Anastasiades, *elected* 24 February 2013, *sworn in* 28 February 2013

SELECTED GOVERNMENT MEMBERS *as at April 2015*
*Defence,* Christoforos Fokaides
*Finance,* Charis Georgiadis
*Foreign Affairs,* Ioannis Kasoulidis

HIGH COMMISSION FOR THE REPUBLIC OF CYPRUS
13 St James's Square, London SW1Y 4LB
T 020-7321 4100 E cyphclondon@btconnect.com
*High Commissioner,* HE Euripides L. Evriviades, *apptd* 2013

BRITISH HIGH COMMISSION
PO Box 21978, Alexander Pallis Street, 1587 Nicosia
T (+357) 2286 1100 E brithc.2@cytanet.com.cy
W www.gov.uk/government/world/cyprus
*High Commissioner,* HE Ric Todd, *apptd* 2014

BRITISH SOVEREIGN BASE AREAS
The Sovereign Base Areas (SBAs) of Akrotiri and Dhekelia are those parts of Cyprus that remained under British sovereignty and jurisdiction after independence, and have the status of a UK overseas territory. They are around 231 sq. km in size. There are approximately 15,700 residents: 7,700 Cypriots, and 8,000 military and UK-based civilian personnel and their dependants.
*Administrator of the British Sovereign Base Areas,* Maj.-Gen. Richard J. Cripwell, *apptd* 2013

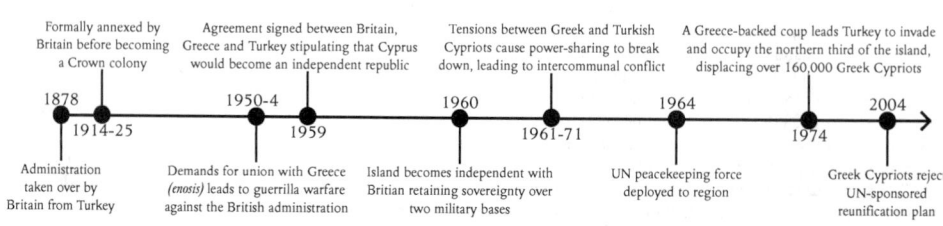

| Formally annexed by Britain before becoming a Crown colony | Agreement signed between Britain, Greece and Turkey stipulating that Cyprus would become an independent republic | Tensions between Greek and Turkish Cypriots cause power-sharing to break down, leading to intercommunal conflict | A Greece-backed coup leads Turkey to invade and occupy the northern third of the island, displacing over 160,000 Greek Cypriots |
|---|---|---|---|
| 1878 | 1950-4 | 1960 | 1964 | 2004 |
| 1914-25 | 1959 | 1961-71 | 1974 | |
| Administration taken over by Britain from Turkey | Demands for union with Greece (*enosis*) leads to guerrilla warfare against the British administration | Island becomes independent with Britian retaining sovereignty over two military bases | UN peacekeeping force deployed to region | Greek Cypriots reject UN-sponsored reunification plan |

# TURKISH REPUBLIC OF NORTHERN CYPRUS

In 1974, a Greece-backed coup against the Cypriot government led Turkey, fearing the coup was a precursor to the union of Cyprus with Greece, to invade northern Cyprus and occupy over a third of the island. The following year, a Turkish Federated State of Cyprus was declared, and in 1983 a declaration of statehood was issued which purported to establish the Turkish Republic of Northern Cyprus. The declaration was condemned by the UN Security Council and only Turkey has recognised the republic. A constitution was adopted in 1985, and elections have been held at regular intervals since.

Reunification talks were unsuccessful in the 1980s and 1990s, and although Turkish Cypriots approved a UN-sponsored reunification plan put to simultaneous referendums in 2004, it was rejected by Greek Cypriots. Since 2004, the EU has given aid to the area to promote and ease reunification, and UN-facilitated talks began in 2008.

The 2013 legislative election was won by the Republican Turkish Party, which favours a unified Cyprus. Mustafa Akinci won the 2015 presidential election, replacing Dervis Eroglu.

## DE FACTO HEAD OF STATE
*President,* Mustafa Akinci, *elected* 24 April 2015, *sworn in* 30 April 2015
*Prime Minister,* Ozkan Yorgancioglu

## DEFENCE
A military airfield in Paphos provides a base for Greek military aircraft, as Cyprus does not possess its own air force.

| Aged 16–49, 2010 est | Males | Females |
|---|---|---|
| Available for military service | 327,875 | 287,891 |
| Fit for military service | 275,842 | 239,862 |
| (All Greek Cypriot National Guard) | | |

*Military expenditure –* US$423m (2014)
*Conscription –* 18–50 years of age, Greek Cypriot males only; 24 months

## ECONOMY AND TRADE
The Greek Cypriot economy is dominated by the service sector, which accounted for 84.4 per cent of GDP in 2014; this was derived mainly from tourism and financial services. Tourism represents a major part of the total GDP, making the economy vulnerable to fluctuations. Shipping services are also important; about 20 per cent of the world's shipping is Cypriot-registered. Industry contributes 12.8 per cent of GDP and agriculture 2.8 per cent. The main products for export are citrus fruits, potatoes, pharmaceuticals, cement and garments. Imports are primarily consumer goods, fuel and lubricants, machinery and transport equipment. Over half of trade is with other EU countries.

Between 2009 and 2013, the economy contracted by a total of 8.2 per cent following a banking crisis triggered by excessive exposure to the damaged Greek economy. In 2013 Cyprus received a US$13bn (£7.6bn) economic bailout from the European Commission, the European Central Bank and the International Monetary Fund ('the Troika'). Conditions included the privatisation of state-owned enterprises and the downsizing and restructuring of the banking sector. The economy contracted again in 2014 and unemployment rose to 16 per cent, the highest in the EU. The economy is expected to contract again in 2015 before growing modestly in 2016. Tourism accounted for 20.6 per cent of GDP in 2013, with large numbers of Russian nationals visiting the island. Exploration for natural gas in Cypriot waters occurred in 2013 and is expected to continue in 2014 and 2015.

The Turkish Cypriot economy suffers from a small domestic market, international isolation and a bloated public sector. It is heavily dependent on financial support from the Turkish government. Services accounted for about 69.1 per cent of GDP in 2006, industry for 22.5 per cent and agriculture for 8.6 per cent. The main products for export are citrus fruits, dairy products, potatoes and textiles. The main imports are vehicles, fuel, cigarettes, food, minerals, chemicals and machinery.

*GNI –* US$21,878m; US$25,210 per capita (2013)
*Annual average growth of GDP – –*3.2 per cent (2014 est)
*Inflation rate – –*0.4 per cent (2013 est)
*Unemployment –* 14.7 per cent (2015 est)
*Total external debt –* US$95,280m (2013 est)
*Imports –* US$6,388m (2013)
*Exports –* US$2,075m (2013)

BALANCE OF PAYMENTS
*Trade –* US$4,313m deficit (2013)
*Current Account –* US$432m deficit (2014)

| Trade with UK | 2013 | 2014 |
|---|---|---|
| Imports from UK | £463,543,045 | £438,679,309 |
| Exports to UK | £183,429,689 | £132,020,027 |

## COMMUNICATIONS
*Airports and waterways –* 13; Larnaca and Paphos (Greek area); flight connections to Turkish area are via Turkey; principal ports are Limassol, Larnaca and Vasilikos (Greek area), and Famagusta and Kyrenia (Turkish area)
*Roadways –* The road network (8,564km in the Greek part of the island and 7,000km in the Turkish part) serves the main population centres
*Telecommunications –* 405,000 (Greek area) and 86,228 (Turkish area) fixed lines and 1.09 million (Greek area) and 147,522 (Turkish area) mobile subscriptions (2011); there were 433,900 internet users in 2009
*Internet code and IDD –* cy; 357 (from UK), 44 (to UK)
*Major broadcasters –* The state-run Cyprus Broadcasting Corporation competes with a number of privately owned television and radio stations; the Turkish north has its own public broadcaster, Bayrak Radio-TV
*Press –* Major daily newspapers include *Cyprus Mail* (English-language), *Politis* (Greek-language) and *Kibris Gazete* (Turkish-language)
*WPFI score –* 16,52 (24) (Greek area), 28,33 (76) (Turkish area)

# CZECH REPUBLIC

*Ceska Republika – Czech Republic*

Collapse of Austro-Hungarian Empire; creation of Czechoslovakia, an amalgamation of Bohemia, Moravia, Slovakia and Ruthenia

Liberated by Soviet and US forces

The Communist Party embarks on a reform programme (the Prague Spring) which is abandoned after Gustav Husak becomes leader

The Communist Party is defeated in first free elections

Joins NATO

Joins the EU

1526   1939   1948   1989   1992

1918   1945   1968-9   1990   1999   2004

Medieval kingdom of Bohemia comes under rule of the Habsburg dynasty

German forces invade Czech lands; Slovakia becomes a puppet state

Soviets take power in a coup

The Communist Party forced to concede its monopoly on power following mass protests

Leaders of the Czech and Slovak republics agree to dissolve the federation and form two sovereign states

*Area* – 78,867 sq. km
*Capital* – Prague (Praha); population, 1,310,000 (2015 est)
*Major cities* – Brno (Brünn), Ostrava, Plzen (Pilsen)
*Currency* – Koruna (Kc) of 100 haleru
*Population* – 10,644,842 rising at 0.16 per cent a year (2015 est); Czech (64.3 per cent), Moravian (5 per cent), Slovak (1.4 per cent) (2011)
*Religion* – Christian (Roman Catholic 10.4 per cent, Protestant 1.1 per cent) (est)
*Language* – Czech (official), Slovak
*Population density* – 136 per sq. km (2013)
*Urban population* – 73.4 per cent (2013 est)
*Median age (years)* – 40.9 (2014 est)
*National anthem* – 'Kde Domov Muj?' ['Where is My Homeland?']
*National day* – 28 October (Founding Day)
*Death penalty* – Abolished for all crimes (since 1990)
*CPI score* – 51 (53)

## CLIMATE AND TERRAIN
The landlocked republic is composed of Bohemia (the west and centre) and Moravia (the east). Bohemia contains the fertile plains of the river Elbe and the surrounding low mountains, while the hilly region of Moravia extends towards the basin of the river Danube. Roughly a third of the country is covered by forest. Elevation extremes range from 1,602m (Snezka) to 115m (river Elbe). The climate is continental, with warm, humid summers and cold, dry winters. The average temperature in Prague ranges from −1.4°C in January to 18.2°C in July and August.

## POLITICS
The 1992 constitution provided for the separation of the Czech Republic and Slovakia; federal laws remain in place unless superseded by Czech ones. The president is elected by popular vote for a five-year term, renewable once; prior to 2012 the president was elected by a joint session of both chambers of the legislature. The bicameral *Parlament* comprises a 200-member Chamber of Deputies, directly elected for a four-year term, and an 81-member senate directly elected for a six-year term, one-third being elected every two years. The council of ministers is appointed by the president on the recommendation of the prime minister.

Early legislative elections in October 2013 gave a combined majority to three centre-left parties – the Czech Social Democratic Party (CSSD), the Christian Democratic Union/Czech People's Party (KDU–CSL) and the Action of Dissatisfied Citizens (ANO) – which formed a coalition government under CSSD chairman Bohuslav Sobotka. The incumbent Civic Democratic Party (ODS) lost more than two-thirds of its seats. Partial senate elections in autumn 2012 saw the CSSD increase its majority from one seat to two. Milos Zeman was elected president in January 2013.

## HEAD OF STATE
*President,* Milos Zeman, *elected* 25 January 2013, *sworn in* 8 March 2013

SELECTED GOVERNMENT MEMBERS *as at April 2015*
*Prime Minister,* Bohuslav Sobotka
*First Deputy Prime Minister, Finance,* Andrej Babis
*Defence,* Martin Stropnicky
*Foreign Affairs,* Lubomir Zaoralek

EMBASSY OF THE CZECH REPUBLIC
26–30 Kensington Palace Gardens, London W8 4QY
T 020-7243 1115 E london@embassy.mzv.cz
W www.mzv.cz/london
*Ambassador Extraordinary and Plenipotentiary,* HE Michael Zantovsky, *apptd* 2009

BRITISH EMBASSY
Thunovska 14, 11800 Prague 1
T (+420) (2) 5740 2111 E ukinczechrepublic@fco.gov.uk
W www.gov.uk/government/world/czech-republic
*Ambassador Extraordinary and Plenipotentiary,* HE Jan Thompson, OBE, *apptd* 2013

## DEFENCE

| Aged 16–49, 2010 est | Males | Females |
| --- | --- | --- |
| Available for military service | 2,506,826 | 2,407,634 |
| Fit for military service | 2,072,267 | 1,988,839 |

*Military expenditure* – US$2,023m (2014)

## ECONOMY AND TRADE
Economic reforms and accession to the EU have produced a stable and successful market economy, as well as contributing to steady growth by expanding export markets and encouraging foreign investment. The global economic downturn caused the economy to contract in 2009, largely because of a reduced demand for the country's major exports. The economy ended two years of recession in 2014, growing by 2.4 per cent, thanks to the manufacturing sector, internal consumption, tourism and international investment.

Services account for 60 per cent of GDP, industry for 37.4 per cent and agriculture for 2.6 per cent. The principal agricultural products are cereal crops, sugar beet and potatoes; the timber industry is also important. The country has been industrialised since the 19th century, and motor vehicles, metals, machinery, glass and armaments are major products. Electricity is also exported. The principal trading partners are EU countries – especially Germany – and China and Russia.

*GNI* – US$199,407m; US$18,950 per capita (2013)
*Annual average growth of GDP* – 2.5 per cent (2014 est)
*Inflation rate* – 1.4 per cent (2013 est)
*Population below poverty line* – 8.6 per cent (2011 est)
*Unemployment* – 7 per cent (2015 est)
*Total external debt* – US$116,100m (2014 est)
*Imports* – US$144,320m (2013)
*Exports* – US$162,302m (2013)

BALANCE OF PAYMENTS
*Trade* – US$17,983m surplus (2013)
*Current Account* – US$1,266m surplus (2014 est)

| Trade with UK | 2013 | 2014 |
|---|---|---|
| Imports from UK | £1,880,722,377 | £2,021,561,826 |
| Exports to UK | £4,581,782,057 | £4,670,949,703 |

## COMMUNICATIONS

*Airports and waterways* – There are 41 airports, with the principal airport at Prague; the 664km of waterways include the Elbe, Vltava and Oder rivers

*Roadways and railways* – Extensive road (130,671km) and rail (9,469km) networks link the main population centres

*Telecommunications* – 2.1 million fixed lines and 12.97 million mobile subscriptions (2012); there were 6.681 million internet users in 2009

*Internet code and IDD* – cz; 420 (from UK), 44 (to UK)

*Major broadcasters* – The public broadcaster Ceska Televize (CT) runs two networks and a 24-hour news channel alongside two major private television stations; Czech public radio, Cesky Rozhlas (CRo), operates three national networks and local services

*Press* – Major daily newspapers include *Lidove Noviny, Mlada Fronta Dnes* and *Pravo*

*WPFI score* – 11,62 (13)

## EDUCATION AND HEALTH

Education is free and compulsory for all children from the age of six to 15.

*Gross enrolment ratio (percentage of relevant age group)* – primary 100 per cent; secondary 97 per cent; tertiary 64 per cent (2012 est)

*Health expenditure (per capita)* – US$1,367 (2013)

*Hospital beds (per 1,000 people)* – 6.8 (2011)

*Life expectancy (years)* – 78.31 (2013 est)

*Mortality rate* – 10.29 (2014 est)

*Birth rate* – 9.79 (2014 est)

*Infant mortality rate* – 2.63 (2014 est)

# DENMARK

*Kongeriget Danmark – Kingdom of Denmark*

*Area* – 43,094 sq. km (excluding the Faroe Islands and Greenland)

*Capital* – Copenhagen; population, 1,255,000 (2014)

*Major cities* – Aalborg, Aarhus, Esbjerg, Odense

*Currency* – Danish krone (DKr) of 100 ore

*Population* – 5,581,503 rising at 0.22 per cent a year (2015 est)

*Religion* – Christian (Lutheran 80 per cent, Roman Catholic 1 per cent), Muslim 4 per cent (est); the Evangelical Lutheran Church is the state church

*Language* – Danish (official), Faroese, Greenlandic, German; English is widely spoken as a second language

*Population density* – 132 per sq. km (2013)

*Urban population* – 87.2 per cent (2013)

*Median age (years)* – 41.6 (2014 est)

*National anthem* – 'Det er et Yndigt Land' ['There is a Lovely Land']

*National day* – 5 June (Constitution Day)

*Death penalty* – Abolished for all crimes (since 1978)

*CPI score* – 92 (1)

## CLIMATE AND TERRAIN

Denmark consists of most of the Jutland peninsula and 406 islands, mainly in the Baltic Sea or among the northern Frisian Islands in the North Sea. The largest islands are Sjaelland (Zealand), Fyn, Lolland, Faister and Bornholm. It is a low-lying country, indented by fjords on its east coast and with lagoons and sand dunes along the west coast; Lim Fjord nearly bisects the north of Jutland. Elevation extremes range from 171m (Mollehoj) to −7m (Lammefjord). The climate is temperate, with cold winters and warm summers. Average temperatures range from 1.1°C in January to 17.4°C in July.

## HISTORY AND POLITICS

The Danes were at the forefront of Viking expansionism from the eighth century. Denmark was unified in the tenth century and was the centre of a short-lived empire, also including Norway and England, created by Cnut (Canute) in the 11th century. The Union of Kalmar (1397) brought Norway and Sweden (including Finland) under Danish rule. Danish power waned during the 16th century, enabling Sweden to re-establish its independence in 1523, and Norway was ceded to Sweden under the Treaty of Kiel in 1814. Denmark was neutral during the First World War, but in the Second World War it was invaded and occupied by Germany until May 1945.

Denmark joined the European Community in 1973. In a 2000 referendum, it rejected adopting the euro.

In the 2011 legislative election, the Liberal Party remained the largest party in parliament, but a surge of support for the Red Bloc (a political alliance consisting of centre-left parties) gave them an overall majority with 97 seats. Helle Thorning-Schmidt, leader of the Social Democrats, formed a coalition with other member parties of the Red Bloc, and took office in October 2011. In January 2015, the resignation of the Socialist People's party caused the remaining members of the ruling coalition to form a minority government. In the June 2015 legislative elections, the centre-right Blue Bloc coalition, led by the Venstre party, gained a one seat majority.

The country is a constitutional monarchy, with a hereditary monarch as head of state. The head of government is the prime minister, who appoints the cabinet. The unicameral legislature, the *Folketing*, has 179 members, including two for the Faeroes and two for Greenland; members are elected for a four-year term by proportional representation.

### HEAD OF STATE

*HM The Queen of Denmark,* Queen Margrethe II, KG, *born* 16 April 1940, *acceded* 14 January 1972

*Heir,* HRH Crown Prince Frederik, *born* 26 May 1968

### SELECTED GOVERNMENT MEMBERS *as at September 2015*

*Prime Minister,* Lars Rasmussen

*Defence,* Carl Holst

*Finance,* Claus Frederiksen

*Foreign Affairs,* Kristian Jensen

### ROYAL DANISH EMBASSY

55 Sloane Street, London SW1X 9SR

T 020-7333 0200 E lonamb@um.dk W www.storbrittanien.um.dk

*Ambassador Extraordinary and Plenipotentiary,* HE Claus Grube, *apptd* 2013

## BRITISH EMBASSY

Kastelsvej 36–40, DK-2100 Copenhagen
T (+45) 3544 5200 E enquiry.copenhagen@fco.gov.uk
W www.gov.uk/government/world/denmark
*Ambassador Extraordinary and Plenipotentiary,* Vivien Life,
    apptd 2012

## DEFENCE

| Aged 16–49, 2010 est | Males | Females |
|---|---|---|
| Available for military service | 1,236,337 | 1,224,182 |
| Fit for military service | 1,014,560 | 1,003,921 |

*Military expenditure* – US$4,457m (2014)
*Conscription* – 18 years of age; 4–12 months

## ECONOMY AND TRADE

Denmark has a diversified and industrialised market economy with a high dependence on exports. It is a net exporter of food and energy (oil and natural gas). Slowing growth from 2007 and then the global downturn pushed the economy into recession in 2009; a modest recovery began in 2010 but the economy re-entered a technical recession at the beginning of 2011. The economy returned to growth in 2014 and is expected to grow by 1.6 per cent in 2015. The service sector contributes 77.5 per cent of GDP, industry 21.2 per cent and the highly efficient agricultural sector 1.3 per cent. Metals, pharmaceuticals, shipping and renewable energy are key industries.

The main trading partners are other EU countries, especially Germany and Sweden. Principal exports are machinery and instruments, meat and meat products, dairy products, fish, pharmaceuticals, furniture and windmills. The main imports are machinery and equipment, industrial raw materials and semi-manufactures, chemicals, grain and foodstuffs, and consumer goods.

*GNI* – US$324,263m; US$61,680 per capita (2013)
*Annual average growth of GDP* – 1.5 per cent (2014 est)
*Inflation rate* – 0.6 per cent (2014 est)
*Population below poverty line* – 13.4 per cent (2011)
*Unemployment* – 6.8 per cent (2015 est)
*Total external debt* – US$586,700m (2012)
*Imports* – US$98,374m (2013)
*Exports* – US$111,351m (2013)

BALANCE OF PAYMENTS
*Trade* – US$12,976m surplus (2013)
*Current Account* – US$18,097m surplus (2015 est)

| Trade with UK | 2013 | 2014 |
|---|---|---|
| Imports from UK | £2,922,042,816 | £2,787,299,840 |
| Exports to UK | £5,308,788,763 | £4,458,870,670 |

## COMMUNICATIONS

*Airports and waterways* – The principal airports are at Copenhagen, Aarhus, Aalborg and near Vejle; the main ports are Aarhus, Odense, Copenhagen, Aalborg and Esbjerg
*Roadways and railways* – There are 73,929km of roadways, including 1,143km of motorways, and 2,667km of railways, of which 640km are electrified
*Telecommunications* – 2.431 million fixed lines and 6.6 million mobile subscriptions (2012); there were 4.75 million internet users in 2009
*Internet code and IDD* – dk; 45 (from UK), 44 (to UK)
*Major broadcasters* – The public broadcaster is Danmarks Radio, which operates two television networks, and national and regional radio stations
*Press* – There are six major daily newspapers, including

*Morgenavisen Jyllands-Posten* (English-language pages), *Berlingske Tidende* and *Ekstra Bladet*
*WPFI score* – 8,24 (3)

## EDUCATION AND HEALTH

Education is free and compulsory for nine years.
*Gross enrolment ratio (percentage of relevant age group)* – primary 101 per cent; secondary 125 per cent; tertiary 80 per cent (2012)
*Health expenditure (per capita)* – US$6,270 (2013)
*Hospital beds (per 1,000 people)* – 3.5 (2010)
*Life expectancy (years)* – 79.09 (2014 est)
*Mortality rate* – 10.23 (2014 est)
*Birth rate* – 10.22 (2014 est)
*Infant mortality rate* – 4.1 (2014 est)

## THE FAROE ISLANDS

*Area* – 1,393 sq. km
*Capital* – Torshavn; population, 21,000 (2014 est)
*Population* – 49,947 at 0.49 per cent per year (2014 est)
*National day* – 29 July (Olaifest)
*Internet code and IDD* – fo; 298 (from UK), 44 (to UK)

The Faroe (Sheep) Islands are a group of 18 rugged islands (17 inhabited) and a few islets in the North Atlantic Ocean, between the Shetland Islands and Iceland. First settled in the ninth century, the islands were a Norwegian province and, with Norway, came under Danish rule in the 14th century. Since 1948 the Faeroes have been self-governing and are not part of the EU.

The sovereign is represented in the islands by a high commissioner, and the islands elect two representatives to the Danish legislature. The Faroese government *(Landsstyri)* is responsible for internal affairs. The parliament *(Loegting)* has 33 members, elected for a four-year term. In the 2011 election, the Union Party overtook the Republican Party to become the largest party in parliament; the incumbent prime minister Kaj Leo Johannesen continued to head a coalition government comprising the Union Party, the Social Democrats and the People's Party.
*Prime Minister,* Kaj Leo Johannesen

## ECONOMY AND TRADE

The economy has grown steadily in recent years, although it slowed during the global downturn. It remains highly dependent on fishing and fish processing; fish and fish products account for 95 per cent of exports. Offshore oil discoveries raise the possibility of future diversification and less dependence on Danish government subsidies.

BALANCE OF PAYMENTS
*Trade* – US$44m (2010)
*Current Account* – US$7m deficit (2003)

| Trade with UK | 2013 | 2014 |
|---|---|---|
| Imports from UK | £10,982,989 | £11,869,306 |
| Exports to UK | £206,976,990 | £191,120,750 |

BRITISH CONSULATE
P/F Damfar, PO Box 1154, Niels Finsengota 5, FR-110 Torshavn
T (+298) 35 00 77
*Honorary Consul,* Joannes Hansen

## GREENLAND (KALAALLIT NUNAAT)

*Area* – 2,166,086 sq. km
*Capital* – Nuuk (Godthab); population, 17,000 (2014)
*Population* – 57,728 rising at 0.02 per cent per year (2014 est)

*National day* – 21 June (longest day)
*Internet code and IDD* – gl; 299 (from UK), 44 (to UK)

Greenland, the world's largest island, lies between the Atlantic and Arctic oceans, to the east of Canada and to the west of Iceland. Most of Greenland is within the Arctic Circle, with permafrost covering about 80 per cent of the island, although this ice cap is beginning to melt (*see* North and South Poles). Elevation extremes range from 3,700m (Gunnbjorn) to 0m (Atlantic Ocean).

Greenland was first discovered by small groups of hunters and nomadic groups who migrated from Canada *c.*500 BC. In the late tenth century Icelanders established settlements along the south-eastern coast, but these colonies had died out by the 16th century. Danish colonisation began in the 18th century. Greenland was integrated into Denmark in 1953 and was granted internal autonomy in 1979; greater autonomy was granted in 2009. Greenland negotiated its withdrawal from the EU, without discontinuing relations with Denmark, and left in 1985. The USA maintains air bases on the island.

The sovereign is represented by a high commissioner, and Greenland elects two representatives to the Danish legislature. The Greenlandic government *(Landsstyri)* is elected by the parliament *(Landsting)*, which has 31 members, elected for a four-year term. In the 2013 election to the *Landsting*, the Siumut (Forward) party won over 40 per cent of the popular vote, making Aleqa Hammond the country's first female prime minister. Snap elections in December 2014, called after Hammond resigned following a corruption scandal and fears over the economy, were won by the governing centre-left Siumut party.
*Prime Minister,* Kim Kielsen

## ECONOMY AND TRADE
The economy is dependent on Danish subsidies (56 per cent of government revenue) and fishing; fish and fish products comprise 89 per cent of exports. Natural resources include zinc, iron ore, lead, coal, molybdenum, gold, platinum and uranium, some of which are mined. Mineral exploration and mining operations are being extended as the ice cap shrinks. This is also benefiting offshore oil exploration, and global warming is extending the growing season. Tourism is being encouraged.

| Trade with UK | 2013 | 2014 |
| --- | --- | --- |
| Imports from UK | £5,930,401 | £999,635 |
| Exports to UK | £147,699 | £606,307 |

# DJIBOUTI

*Jumhuriyat Jibuti/République de Djibouti* – Republic of Djibouti

*Area* – 23,200 sq. km
*Capital* – Djibouti; population, 522,000 (2014)
*Major cities* – Ali Sabin, Danan, Tadjoura
*Currency* – Djibouti franc (DJF) of 100 centimes
*Population* – 828,324 rising at 2.2 per cent a year (2015 est); Somali (Issa) 60 per cent, Afar 35 per cent (est)
*Religion* – Muslim 94 per cent, Christian 6 per cent
*Language* – French, Arabic (both official), Somali, Afar
*Population density* – 38 per sq. km (2013)
*Urban population* – 77.2 per cent (2013)
*Median age (years)* – 22.8 (2014 est)
*National anthem* – 'Jabuuti' ['Djibouti']
*National day* – 27 June (Independence Day)
*Death penalty* – Abolished for all crimes (since 1995)
*CPI score* – 34 (107)
*Life expectancy (years)* – 62.4 (2014 est)
*Mortality rate* – 7.84 (2014 est)
*Birth rate* – 24.08 (2014 est)
*Infant mortality rate* – 50.2 (2014 est)
*HIV/AIDS adult prevalence* – 0.2 per cent (2013 )

## CLIMATE AND TERRAIN
Djibouti is situated on the strait linking the Gulf of Aden with the Red Sea, close to busy shipping lanes. The coastal plain is separated from an inland plateau by the central mountains. Elevation extremes range from 2,028m (Moussa Ali) to −155m (Lake Assal). Although the climate is semi-arid with a hot season between April and October, occasional heavy rains can cause flash floods. The country is also prone to cyclones, drought and earthquakes. Djibouti experienced a fourth consecutive year of drought in 2014.

## POLITICS
Under the 1992 constitution, amended in 2010, the president is directly elected for a five-year term, renewable without limit. The president appoints the council of ministers. The unicameral National Assembly has 65 members, directly elected for a five-year term. The 2010 constitutional amendments provided for the establishment of a senate.

In the 2008 legislative elections, which were boycotted by the opposition, the Union for a Presidential Majority (UMP) retained all 65 seats in the legislature. The 2011 presidential election was boycotted by the opposition and President Guelleh won a third term in office. Though opposition parties took part in the February 2013 parliamentary elections, the ruling party took 49 of 65 seats; the Union of National Salvation issued a statement claiming the vote was rigged. New presidential elections are due to be held in 2017.

### HEAD OF STATE
*President,* Ismail Omar Guelleh, *elected* 9 April 1999, *re-elected* 2005, 2011

SELECTED GOVERNMENT MEMBERS *as at May 2015*
*Prime Minister,* Mohamed Kamil Abdoulkader
*Defence,* Hassan Darar Houffaneh
*Economy and Finance,* Hasan Ahmed Boulaleh
*Foreign Affairs,* Mahamoud Ali Youssouf
*Interior,* Hassan Omar

EMBASSY OF THE REPUBLIC OF DJIBOUTI
26 Rue Emile Ménier, 75116 Paris, France
T (+33) (1) 4727 4922 E webmaster@amb-djibouti.org
*Ambassador Extraordinary and Plenipotentiary,* HE Ayeid Mousseid Yahya, *apptd* 2015

BRITISH AMBASSADOR
HE Greg Dorey, *apptd* 2011, resident at Addis Ababa, Ethiopia

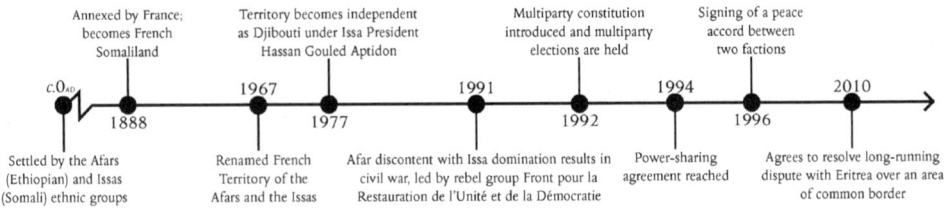

Annexed by France; becomes French Somaliland

Territory becomes independent as Djibouti under Issa President Hassan Gouled Aptidon

Multiparty constitution introduced and multiparty elections are held

Signing of a peace accord between two factions

c.0<sub>AD</sub>    1888    1967    1977    1991    1992    1994    1996    2010

Settled by the Afars (Ethiopian) and Issas (Somali) ethnic groups

Renamed French Territory of the Afars and the Issas

Afar discontent with Issa domination results in civil war, led by rebel group Front pour la Restauration de l'Unité et de la Démocratie

Power-sharing agreement reached

Agrees to resolve long-running dispute with Eritrea over an area of common border

## DEFENCE

| Aged 16–49, 2010 est | Males | Females |
|---|---|---|
| Available for military service | 170,386 | 221,411 |
| Fit for military service | 114,557 | 154,173 |

*Military expenditure* – US$40m (2008)

## ECONOMY AND TRADE
A barren country with few natural resources and little industry, Djibouti's chief asset is its location on major shipping lanes. It is a transit port for neighbouring landlocked countries (especially Ethiopia, 70 per cent of whose trade passes through Djibouti), an international trans-shipment and refuelling centre, and a military base for US and EU forces because of its strategic position. The country is dependent on foreign aid, has a very high level of unemployment and has to import nearly all its food. The service sector accounts for 80.5 per cent of GDP, industry for 16.6 per cent and agriculture for 2.9 per cent.

The main trading partners are Ethiopia (which takes 70 per cent of exports), Saudi Arabia, India and China. Principal exports are re-exports, hides and skins, and coffee (in transit). The main imports are food, beverages, transport equipment, chemicals and petroleum products.
*GNI* – US$1,120m; US$1,270 per capita (2009)
*Annual average growth of GDP* – 5.5 per cent (2014 est)
*Inflation rate* – 2.4 per cent (2013 est)
*Population below poverty line* – 18.8 per cent (2012 est)
*Unemployment* – 59 per cent (2007 est)
*Total external debt* – US$891.3m (2014 est)
*Imports* – US$560m (2013)
*Exports* – US$120m (2013)

BALANCE OF PAYMENTS
*Trade* – US$440m deficit (2013)
*Current Account* – US$175m deficit (2011)

| Trade with UK | 2013 | 2014 |
|---|---|---|
| Imports from UK | £6,748,776 | £13,194,267 |
| Exports to UK | £1,424,752 | £1,407,162 |

## COMMUNICATIONS
*Airports and waterways* – The main port and principal airport are located in Djibouti
*Roadways and railways* – 1,226km; the 100km Djibouti section of the Addis Ababa–Djibouti railway is controlled by both Djibouti and Ethiopia but is largely inoperable
*Telecommunications* – 18,000 fixed lines and 209,000 mobile telephones in use (2012); there were 25,900 internet users in 2009
*Internet code and IDD* – dj; 253 (from UK), 44 (to UK)
*Press* – The government owns the two major newspapers: La Nation (French-language) and Al-Qarn (Arabic-language)
*Major broadcasters* – Radiodiffusion-Télévision de Djibouti (RTD) is the national broadcaster and operates a radio station (Radio Djibouti) and television channel (Télé Djibouti 1).

Opposition parties operate media outlets from overseas, including La Voix de Djibouti radio
*WPFI score* – 71,04 (170)

# DOMINICA

*Commonwealth of Dominica*

*Area* – 751 sq. km
*Capital* – Roseau; population, 14,000 (2014 est)
*Currency* – East Caribbean dollar (EC$) of 100 cents
*Population* – 73,607 rising at 0.21 per cent a year (2015 est)
*Religion* – Christian (Roman Catholic 61 per cent, Pentecostal 6 per cent, Seventh-day Adventist 6 per cent, Baptist 4 per cent, Methodist 4 per cent) (est)
*Language* – English (official), Creole
*Population density* – 96 per sq. km (2013)
*Urban population* – 67.4 per cent (2013)
*Median age (years)* – 32.1 (2014 est)
*National anthem* – 'Isle of Beauty, Isle of Splendour'
*National day* – 3 November (Independence Day)
*Death penalty* – Retained (last used 1986)
*CPI score* – 58 (39)
*Life expectancy (years)* – 78.59 (2014 est)
*Mortality rate* – 7.94 (2014 est)
*Birth rate* – 15.53 (2014 est)
*Infant mortality rate* – 11.61 (2014 est)

## CLIMATE AND TERRAIN
Dominica, the most northerly of the Windward Islands, is 46km long and 25km wide, with a mountainous and forested centre. Its peaks include volcanic craters, one of which contains Boiling Lake, the world's second-largest thermally active lake. Elevation extremes range from 1,447m (Morne Diablotins) to 0m (Caribbean Sea). The climate is tropical, with an average temperature of 23.3°C. The island is located within the hurricane zone.

## HISTORY AND POLITICS
Dominica was discovered by Columbus in 1493, when it was a stronghold of the Caribs, the sole inhabitants of the island until the French founded settlements in the 18th century. It was ceded to the British in 1763 but passed back and forth

between France and Britain until 1805, after which British possession was unchallenged. From 1871 until the 1960s Dominica was administered by Britain as part of various federations of West Indian islands. Internal self-government from 1967 was followed on 3 November 1978 by independence as a republic.

The Dominica Labour Party (DLP) won the legislative election in 2014, the party's fourth general election victory in a row. Charles Savarin was elected president in 2013; the main opposition United Workers Party boycotted this election, claiming the process was unconstitutional.

Under the 1978 constitution, the president is elected by the legislature for a five-year term, renewable once. The unicameral House of Assembly has 30 members, 21 directly elected, and nine appointed senators; all members serve a five-year term.

## HEAD OF STATE
*President,* Charles Savarin, *elected* 2013

## SELECTED GOVERNMENT MEMBERS *as at May 2015*
*Prime Minister, Finance, Foreign Affairs, National Security,*
  Roosevelt Skerrit
*Defence,* Rayburn Blackmoore

## OFFICE OF THE HIGH COMMISSIONER FOR THE COMMONWEALTH OF DOMINICA
1 Collingham Gardens, London SW5 0HW
T 020-7370 5194 E info@dominicahighcommission.co.uk
W www.dominicahighcommission.co.uk
*High Commissioner,* vacant

## BRITISH HIGH COMMISSIONER
HE Victoria Dean, *apptd* 2013, resident at Bridgetown, Barbados

## ECONOMY AND TRADE
The economy, traditionally dependent on banana exports, struggled in the early 2000s as EU preferential access for the fruit was phased out; the industry also suffered serious hurricane damage in 2007. Economic restructuring from 2003 led to steady growth, with an emphasis on eco-agriculture and eco-tourism, until the global downturn caused the economy to contract in 2009, picking up only slightly in 2011 and 2012. Diversification into offshore financial services, medical education and light industry is also being encouraged, and exploitation of geothermal energy, fishing and forestry resources is planned.

Agriculture is the principal occupation, employing 40 per cent of the workforce but producing only 14.8 per cent of GDP. Services contribute 71.1 per cent of GDP and industry 14.1 per cent. The main trading partners are Japan, the USA, other Caribbean countries and China. Principal exports are bananas, soap, bay oil, vegetables and citrus fruits. The main imports are manufactured goods, machinery and equipment, food and chemicals.

*GNI –* US$462m; US$6,930 per capita (2013)
*Annual average growth of GDP –* 1.4 per cent (2015 est)
*Inflation rate –* 0 per cent (2013 est)
*Total external debt –* US$299m (2014)
*Imports –* US$203m (2013)
*Exports –* US$38m (2013)

## BALANCE OF PAYMENTS
*Trade –* US$165m deficit (2013)
*Current Account –* US$7m deficit (2015 est)

| Trade with UK | 2013 | 2014 |
| --- | --- | --- |
| Imports from UK | £5,570,890 | £4,940,200 |
| Exports to UK | £1,426,787 | £1,573,114 |

## COMMUNICATIONS
*Airports and waterways –* The principal airports are Melville Hall on the north-east tip of the island and Canefield, just outside Roseau; the main seaports are located at Portsmouth and Roseau
*Roadways –* 762km
*Telecommunications –* 14,600 fixed lines and 109,300 mobile subscriptions (2012); there were 28,000 internet users in 2009
*Internet code and IDD –* dm; 1 767 (from UK), 011 44 (to UK)
*Press –* There are no daily newspapers
*Major broadcasters –* There is no national television on the island, but cable television provider Marpim Telecom and Broadcasting covers parts of the island; DBS Radio is operated by the state broadcaster

# DOMINICAN REPUBLIC

*República Dominicana – Dominican Republic*

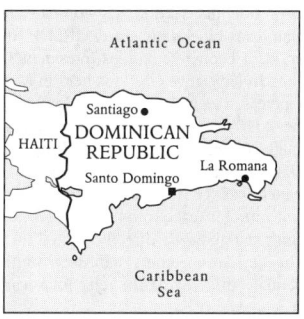

*Area –* 48,670 sq. km
*Capital –* Santo Domingo; population, 2,873,000 (2014)
*Major cities –* La Romana, San Pedro de Macorís, Santiago de los Caballeros, Los Alcarrizos
*Currency –* Dominican Republic peso (RD$) of 100 centavos
*Population –* 10,478,756 rising at 1.23 per cent a year (2015 est)
*Religion –* Christian (Roman Catholic 95 per cent), other 5 per cent
*Language –* Spanish (official)
*Population density –* 215 per sq. km (2013)
*Urban population –* 70.8 per cent (2013)
*Median age (years) –* 27.1 (2014 est)
*National anthem –* 'Himno Nacional' ['National Anthem']
*National day –* 27 February (Independence Day)
*Death penalty –* Abolished for all crimes (since 1966)
*CPI score –* 32 (115)
*Literacy rate –* 97.9 per cent (2015)
*Gross enrolment ratio (percentage of relevant age group) –* primary 103 per cent; secondary 76 per cent (2012)
*Health expenditure (per capita) –* US$315 (2013)
*Hospital beds (per 1,000 people) –* 1.7 (2011)
*Life expectancy (years) –* 77.8 (2014 est)
*Mortality rate –* 4.5 (2014 est)
*Birth rate –* 18.97 (2014 est)
*Infant mortality rate –* 19.63 (2014 est)

## CLIMATE AND TERRAIN
The republic forms the eastern two-thirds of the island of Hispaniola and is crossed from the north-west to the south-east by the Cordillera Central mountain range, which has a number of peaks over 3,000m. Elevation extremes range

from 3,175m (Pico Duarte) to −46m (Lake Enriquillo). The climate is maritime tropical, with an average temperature of 24.8°C.

## HISTORY AND POLITICS
The island was discovered by Columbus in 1492, and a Spanish colony was established in 1496. The eastern province of Santo Domingo remained under Spanish rule after the partition of Hispaniola in 1697, but was ceded to France in 1795. It was restored to Spain in 1809, but rebelled in 1821 and achieved independence briefly before being annexed by Haiti in 1822. Haitian rule ended in 1844 when independence was declared as the Dominican Republic, although the country was voluntarily under Spanish rule again from 1861 to 1865. A long dictatorship at the end of the 19th century was followed by revolution and bankruptcy, which led to occupation by US forces from 1916 until 1924. A military coup in 1930 established the dictatorship of Gen. Rafael Trujillo, whose corrupt rule continued until his assassination in 1961. After a period of political instability, a new constitution was adopted in 1966 and democracy was restored.

The 2012 presidential election was won by Danilo Medina of the Dominican Liberation Party (PLD); he replaced outgoing president Leonel Fernández (president 1996–2000 and 2004–12). In legislative elections held in May 2010 the ruling PLD increased its majority in both houses.

Under the 2010 constitution, the executive president is directly elected for a four-year term, which is not renewable. The bicameral National Congress comprises the Chamber of Deputies, which has 183 members, and the senate, with 32 members, one for each province and one for Santo Domingo. Both chambers are directly elected for a four-year term, but the current members will serve until 2016 so that presidential and legislative elections can be held simultaneously.

HEAD OF STATE
*President,* Danilo Medina, *elected* 2012, *sworn in* August 2012
*Vice-President,* Margarita Cedeno de Fernández

SELECTED GOVERNMENT MEMBERS *as at May 2015*
*Armed Forces,* Adm. Sigfrido Aramis Pared Perez
*Finance,* Simon Lizardo Mezquita
*Foreign Affairs,* Carlos Morales
*Interior,* Jose Ramon Fadul

EMBASSY OF THE DOMINICAN REPUBLIC
139 Inverness Terrace, London W2 6JF
T 020-7727 7091 E info@dominicanembassy.org.uk
W www.dominicanembassy.org.uk
*Ambassador Extraordinary and Plenipotentiary,* HE Federico Alberto Cuello Camilo, *apptd* 2011

BRITISH EMBASSY
Edificio Corominas Pepín, 7th–8th Floor, Ave 27 de Febrero No 233, Santo Domingo
T (+1) (829) 472 7111
W www.gov.uk/government/world/dominican-republic
*Ambassador Extraordinary and Plenipotentiary,* HE Christopher Campbell, *apptd* 2015

## DEFENCE

| Aged 16–49, 2010 est | Males | Females |
| --- | --- | --- |
| Available for military service | 2,580,083 | 2,464,698 |
| Fit for military service | 2,188,358 | 2,090,180 |

*Military expenditure* – US$399m (2014)

## ECONOMY AND TRADE
In recent years, tourism and the free trade zones have overtaken agriculture as the mainstay of the economy, and services now account for 61.6 per cent of GDP. Industry accounts for 32.1 per cent of GDP, agriculture for 6.3 per cent. The main crops are sugar, coffee, cotton, cocoa, tobacco, rice, vegetables and bananas, and the main industrial activities are tourism, sugar processing, mining and the production of textiles, cement and tobacco products. Remittances from expatriate workers represent nearly 10 per cent of GDP. The economy returned to growth in 2010–14 after the global recession and the country's budget deficit was halved from 2012–14. Despite strong growth, poverty rates remain high.

The main trading partner is the USA, which takes 38.9 per cent of exports and provides 44.7 per cent of imports. Principal exports are ferro-nickel, sugar, gold, silver, coffee, cocoa, tobacco, meats and consumer goods. The chief imports are food-stuffs, fuel, cotton and fabrics, chemicals and pharmaceuticals.
*GNI* – US$56,834m; US$5,770 per capita (2013)
*Annual average growth of GDP* – 5.3 per cent (2014 est)
*Inflation rate* – 3 per cent (2014 est)
*Population below poverty line* – 41.1 per cent (2013 est)
*Unemployment* – 15.4 per cent (2015 est)
*Total external debt* – US$19,720m (2014 est)
*Imports* – US$13,876m (2013)
*Exports* – US$4,622m (2013)

BALANCE OF PAYMENTS
*Trade* – US$9,254m deficit (2013)
*Current Account* – US$1,613m deficit (2015 est)

| Trade with UK | 2013 | 2014 |
| --- | --- | --- |
| Imports from UK | £74,138,343 | £78,999,784 |
| Exports to UK | £135,487,885 | £134,771,437 |

## COMMUNICATIONS
*Airports and waterways* – 16, the principal airport is at Santo Domingo; Santo Domingo, Rio Haina and Caucedo are the main seaports
*Roadways and railways* – There are 9,872km of surfaced roads, and 142km of railways
*Telecommunications* – 1.065 million fixed lines and 9.04 million mobile subscriptions (2012); there were 2.7 million internet users in 2009
*Internet code and IDD* – do; 1 809/829 (from UK), 011 44 (to UK)
*Major broadcasters* – The state-owned broadcaster is Corporacion Estatal de Radio y Television (CERTV)
*Press* – Five main daily newspapers are published in Spanish
*WPFI score* – 27,31 (63)

# ECUADOR

*República del Ecuador – Republic of Ecuador*

*Area* – 283,561 sq. km
*Capital* – Quito; population, 1,699,000 (2014 est)
*Major cities* – Cuenca, Guayaquil, Machala, Manta, Santo
   Domingo de los Colorados
*Currency* – US dollar (US$) of 100 cents
*Population* – 15,868,396 rising at 1.35 per cent a year
   (2015 est)
*Religion* – Christian (Roman Catholic 95 per cent), other
   5 per cent
*Language* – Spanish (official), Quechua, other Amerindian
   languages
*Population density* – 63 per sq. km (2013)
*Urban population* – 68.6 per cent (2013)
*Median age (years)* – 26.7 (2014 est)
*National anthem* – 'Salve, Oh Patria' ['We Salute You, Our
   Homeland']
*National day* – 10 August (Independence Day)
*Death penalty* – Abolished for all crimes (since 1906)
*CPI score* – 33 (110)

## CLIMATE AND TERRAIN

The Andes run north to south through the centre of Ecuador, dividing the coastal plain in the west from the low-lying rainforest in the east, and between two local Andean chains lie the central highlands. Elevation extremes range from 6,267m (Chimborazo) to 0m (Pacific Ocean). Other Andean peaks include Cotopaxi (5,896m) and Cayambe (5,790m) in the Eastern Cordillera. Ecuador is located in an earthquake zone and five of its volcanoes have erupted since 2000 – most recently Tungurahua in April 2014. The country has four different climatic zones and is one of the most biodiverse countries on earth; its territory includes the Galápagos Islands in the Pacific Ocean. The average temperature is 21.9°C.

## HISTORY AND POLITICS

The kingdom of the Caras, around Quito, was conquered by the Incas in the 15th century. After the Spanish defeated the Incas in Peru, Ecuador was conquered in 1534 and added to the Spanish viceroyalty of Peru. Independence from Spain was achieved in a revolutionary war that culminated in the battle of Mt Pichincha (1822). Ecuador then formed part of Gran Colombia with Colombia, Panama and Venezuela, but left this union to become a fully independent state in 1830. After independence, the country experienced periods of political instability interspersed with dictatorships and military rule. Democratic rule under civilian government was restored in 1979.

The exploitation of oil reserves funded economic and social transformation from the 1970s onwards but also caused rapid inflation and increased foreign debt. In recent years, these problems have worsened because of economic recession, leading to strikes and demonstrations. Civil unrest forced three presidents from office between 1997 and 2003.

Presidential and legislative elections were held in 2009 after a new constitution was approved by a national referendum in 2008, and in 2013 President Correa was elected for a third term – and his second four-year term – while his party, the left-wing PAIS Alliance, won 52 per cent of the legislative vote.

The 2008 constitution provides for an executive president who is directly elected for a four-year term, renewable once. The unicameral National Assembly has 137 members elected on a party-list proportional representation basis for a four-year term. The republic is divided into 24 provinces. In 2014, the National Assembly voted to abolish presidential term limits, potentially allowing President Correa to stand for a third presidential term in 2017.

## HEAD OF STATE

*President*, Rafael Correa, *took office* 15 January 2007,
   *re-elected* April 2009, February 2013
*Vice-President*, Jorge Espinel

SELECTED GOVERNMENT MEMBERS *as at May 2015*
*Finance*, Fausto Herrera Nicolalde
*Foreign Affairs*, Ricardo Patino
*National Defence*, Fernando Cueva

EMBASSY OF ECUADOR
Flat 3B, 3 Hans Crescent, London SW1X 0LS
T 020-7584 1367 E eecugranbretania@mmrree.gob.ec
W www.consuladoecuador.org.uk
*Ambassador Extraordinary and Plenipotentiary*, HE Juan
   Eduardo Falconi Puig, *apptd* 2013

BRITISH EMBASSY
PO Box 17-17-830, Citiplaza Building, Av. Naciones Unidas y
Republica de El Salvador, Piso 14, Quito
T (+593) (2) 2970 800 E quito.consular@fco.gov.uk
W www.gov.uk/government/world/ecuador
*Ambassador Extraordinary and Plenipotentiary*, HE Patrick
   Mullee, *apptd* 2012

## DEFENCE

| *Aged 16–49, 2010 est* | *Males* | *Females* |
| --- | --- | --- |
| Available for military service | 3,728,906 | 3,844,918 |
| Fit for military service | 2,834,213 | 3,269,535 |

*Military expenditure* – US$2,750m (2014)
*Conscription* – 18 years of age; 12 months (selective),
   currently suspended

## ECONOMY AND TRADE

Structural reforms in 2000, including the adoption of the US dollar in response to the severe economic crisis of 1999, paved the way for strong growth from 2002 to 2006. Growth has slowed since owing to the uncertainty created by windfall taxes imposed on foreign oil companies, a fall in oil production since 2007, the government defaulting on 30 per cent of public external debt in 2008, and the cancellation of a number of bilateral investment treaties in 2009. A decline in global oil prices is expected to restrict future growth, but the economy is still expected to grow by 4 per cent in 2015.

Oil is Ecuador's principal export, accounting for over half of export earnings and a third of government revenue in recent years. After oil, agriculture, fishing and forestry are the most important activities, providing products both for export and for the food- and wood-processing industries. The main exports are oil, bananas, cut flowers, fish, cacao, coffee, hemp and timber. The main imports are industrial materials, fuels and lubricants, and consumer goods. Principal trading partners are the USA and China. Faced with a widening trade deficit, Ecuador introduced a number of non-tariff trade barriers in December 2013.

*GNI* – US$82,734m; US$5,760 per capita (2013)
*Annual average growth of GDP* – 4 per cent (2014 est)
*Inflation rate* – 3.9 per cent (2014 est)
*Population below poverty line* – 25.6 per cent (2013 est)
*Unemployment* – 5.1 per cent (2015 est)
*Total external debt* – US$21,740m (2014)
*Imports* – US$27,146m (2013)
*Exports* – US$24,848m (2013)

BALANCE OF PAYMENTS
*Trade* – US$2,107m deficit (2013)
*Current Account* – US$3,387m deficit (2015 est)

| Trade with UK | 2013 | 2014 |
|---|---|---|
| Imports from UK | £248,074,961 | £110,935,002 |
| Exports to UK | £149,492,754 | £124,537,526 |

## COMMUNICATIONS

*Airports and waterways* – 104, with international flights operating to Quito and Guayaquil; the main ports are Guayaquil and Esmeraldas
*Roadways and railways* – There are 43,670km of roadways, 6,472km of which are surfaced, and 965km of railways
*Telecommunications* – 2.31 million fixed lines and 16.46 million mobile subscriptions (2012); there were 3.352 million internet users in 2009
*Internet code and IDD* – ec; 593 (from UK), 44 (to UK)
*Major broadcasters* – Six private television broadcasters dominate broadcasting, including TC Television and Ecuavisa
*Press* – Six newspapers are published daily, including *El Comercio, El Tiempo* and the Guayaquil-based daily *El Universo*
*WPFI* – 33,65 (108)

## EDUCATION AND HEALTH

Elementary education is free and compulsory until age 14.
*Literacy rate* – 98.8 per cent (2015 est)
*Gross enrolment ratio (percentage of relevant age group)* – primary 114 per cent; secondary 87 per cent (2012 est)
*Health expenditure (per capita)* – US$361 (2012)
*Hospital beds (per 1,000 people)* – 1.6 (2011)
*Life expectancy (years)* – 76.36 (2014 est)
*Mortality rate* – 5.04 (2014 est)
*Birth rate* – 18.87 (2014 est)
*Infant mortality rate* – 17.93 (2014 est)

## GALÁPAGOS ISLANDS

The Galápagos (Giant Tortoise) Islands, about 960km from the mainland, were annexed by Ecuador in 1832. The 12 large and several hundred smaller islands lie on the equator, and most form part of a national park where unique marine birds, iguanas and giant tortoises are conserved. This wildlife provided naturalist Charles Darwin (1809–82) with inspiration and research material for his theory of evolution by natural selection, expounded in *On the Origin of Species* (1859). The islands were declared a UNESCO World Heritage site in 1978.

# EGYPT

*Jumhuriyat Misr al-Arabiyah – Arab Republic of Egypt*

*Area* – 1,001,450 sq. km
*Capital* – Cairo; population, 18,419,000 (2014); stands on the Nile about 22km from the head of the delta
*Major cities* – Alexandria (founded 332 BC by Alexander the Great; the capital for over 1,000 years), Giza, Port Said, Shubra al-Khema, Suez
*Currency* – Egyptian pound (£E) of 100 piastres
*Population* – 88,487,396 rising at 1.79 per cent a year (2015 est); Egyptian (including Berber and Bedouin) 99.6 per cent (2006)
*Religion* – Muslim 90 per cent (almost all Sunni), Christian 10 per cent (mostly Coptic) (est)
*Language* – Arabic (official), English, French
*Population density* – 82 per sq. km (2013)
*Urban population* – 43.8 per cent (2013)
*Median age (years)* – 25.1 (2014 est)
*National anthem* – 'Biladi, Biladi, Biladi' ['My Homeland, My Homeland, My Homeland']
*National day* – 23 July (Revolution Day)
*Death penalty* – Retained
*CPI score* – 37 (94)

## CLIMATE AND TERRAIN

There are four broad regions: the Western Desert, which covers nearly two-thirds of the country to the west of the Nile valley; the Eastern Desert, which lies between the Nile and the mountains along the Red Sea coast; the fertile Nile valley and delta, where most of the population lives; and the Sinai peninsula, where a coastal plain on the Mediterranean rises to mountains in the south. The deserts are arid plateaux, with depressions in the Western Desert whose springs irrigate oases, while the Eastern Desert is dissected by wadis (dry watercourses). Elevation extremes range from 2,629m (Mt Catherine, Sinai) to −133m (Qattara depression). The country has a desert climate, with hot, dry summers and mild winters. Temperatures increase further south, and rainfall increases nearer the coast. Average daily temperatures range from 13°C in January to 30.4°C in August.

## POLITICS

The 1971 constitution was suspended after President Mubarak's resignation in 2011 and substantial changes to it were approved by referendum in March 2011. Following the ousting of President Mursi, a new constitution was approved in January 2014 which provides the army with greater political powers, established Sharia as the basis of the country's laws and provides for an executive president who is directly elected for a four-year term, which is renewable once.

Under the 2014 constitution the legislature is bicameral. The lower chamber, the House of Representatives, has 350 members directly elected for a five-year term and has the right to propose a referendum on the president's rule. The upper chamber, the Senate, has at least 150 members: three-quarters elected and a quarter appointed by the president.

The first legislative election since President Mubarak's departure from office was held in November 2011 and saw the Freedom and Justice Party (FJP, founded by the Muslim Brotherhood) win the most seats in the former unicameral People's Assembly but fail to win a majority. The People's Assembly was suspended in July 2013 and legislative elections under the new 2014 constitution were held in July 2014.

In the first presidential election in the country's history, FJP candidate Mohammed Mursi narrowly defeated the National Democratic Party candidate Ahmed Shafiq and was inaugurated on 30 June 2012. Following mass demonstrations, Mohammed Mursi was deposed by the army

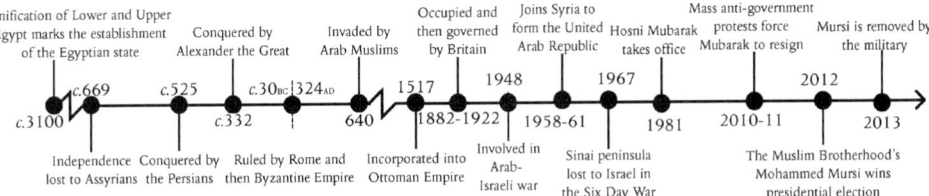

Unification of Lower and Upper Egypt marks the establishment of the Egyptian state — c.669 / c.3100

Conquered by Alexander the Great — c.525 / c.332

Invaded by Arab Muslims — c.30BC–324AD / 640

Occupied and then governed by Britain — 1517 / 1882–1922

Joins Syria to form the United Arab Republic — 1948 / 1958–61

Hosni Mubarak takes office — 1967 / 1981

Mass anti-government protests force Mubarak to resign — 2010–11

Mursi is removed by the military — 2012 / 2013

Independence lost to Assyrians

Conquered by the Persians

Ruled by Rome and then Byzantine Empire

Incorporated into Ottoman Empire

Involved in Arab–Israeli war

Sinai peninsula lost to Israel in the Six Day War

The Muslim Brotherhood's Mohammed Mursi wins presidential election

2010–11

in July 2013. In 2014, amid boycotts from opposition parties and claims that rivals had been intimidated, independent candidate and Commander-in-Chief of the Egyptian armed forces Abdel al-Sisi won the subsequent presidential election with 90 per cent of the vote.

## HEAD OF STATE
*President,* Abdel Fattah al-Sisi, *elected* 29 May 2014, *sworn in,* 8 June 2014
*Head of the Supreme Council of the Armed Forces, Defence,* Sedki Sobhi

SELECTED GOVERNMENT MEMBERS *as at May 2015*
*Prime Minister,* Ibrahim Mahlab
*Finance,* Hany Qadry
*Foreign Affairs,* Sameh Shukri
*Interior,* Magdy Abdel Ghafar

## EMBASSY OF THE ARAB REPUBLIC OF EGYPT
26 South Street, London W1K 1DW
**T** 020-7499 3304 **E** eg.emb_london@mfa.gov.eg
**W** www.egyptembassyuk.org
*Ambassador Extraordinary and Plenipotentiary,* HE Nasser Ahmed Ali, *apptd* 2014

## BRITISH EMBASSY
7 Ahmed Ragheb Street, Garden City, Cairo
**T** (+20) (2) 2791 6000 **E** consular.cairo@fco.gov.uk
**W** www.gov.uk/government/world/egypt
*Ambassador Extraordinary and Plenipotentiary,* HE John Casson, *apptd* 2014

## DEFENCE

| | Males | Females |
| --- | --- | --- |
| Aged 16–49, 2010 est | | |
| Available for military service | 21,012,199 | 20,145,021 |
| Fit for military service | 18,060,543 | 17,244,838 |

*Military expenditure* – US$4,961m (2014 est)
*Conscription* – 18–30 years of age, male only; 18–36 months

## ECONOMY AND TRADE
Economic liberalisation in recent years has attracted foreign investment and promoted exports, producing strong growth in GDP, but political uncertainty significantly reduced government revenues in 2012, and Egypt's attempts to obtain a multi-billion dollar loan from the IMF in 2012–13 failed. The country's budget deficit has concerned the IMF, though this is expected to fall to 8.7 per cent in 2014 from 13.3 per cent in 2013. In 2011 and 2012, the government drew down foreign exchange reserves by 50 per cent. Although the dams on the Nile have expanded the area of land under cultivation, other factors, such as population growth, put a greater strain on resources. The economy is predicted to grow by 4 per cent in 2015.

The services sector contributes 46.5 per cent to GDP and employs 47 per cent of the workforce. Tourism is the largest component of this sector (estimated to have contributed 7.5 per cent of GDP in 2014), along with Suez Canal revenues and expatriate remittances. Industry accounts for 38.9 per cent of GDP and 24 per cent of employment, but despite increasing industrialisation, agriculture still employs 29 per cent of the workforce, contributing 14.6 per cent of GDP. Egypt is a net importer of foodstuffs, especially grain, and a food security programme has been set up with the aim of achieving self-sufficiency.

The main cash crop is cotton, of which Egypt is one of the world's main producers. Other important crops are rice, maize, wheat, vegetables, fruit and livestock. Industry is centred on oil and gas extraction, processing hydrocarbons, cotton and other agricultural products, producing textiles, chemicals and pharmaceuticals. Oil is the backbone of the economy and helps, alongside considerable reserves of natural gas and the hydroelectric power produced by the Aswan and High dams, to make Egypt self-sufficient in energy.

The main trading partners are the USA, Italy, China and Germany. Principal exports are crude oil and petroleum products, cotton, textiles, metal products, chemicals and processed food. The main imports are machinery and equipment, foodstuffs, chemicals, wood products and fuels.
*GNI* – US$256,346m; US$3,140 per capita (2013)
*Annual average growth of GDP* – 2.2 per cent (2014 est)
*Inflation rate* – 10.2 per cent (2014 est)
*Population below poverty line* – 25.2 per cent (2011 est)
*Unemployment* – 12.6 per cent (2015 est)
*Total external debt* – US$55,860m (2014)
*Imports* – US$59,662m (2013)
*Exports* – US$28,493m (2013)

BALANCE OF PAYMENTS
*Trade* – US$31,169m deficit (2013)
*Current Account* – US$2,356m deficit (2014)

| Trade with UK | 2013 | 2014 |
| --- | --- | --- |
| Imports from UK | £943,486,208 | £1,051,824,760 |
| Exports to UK | £769,162,704 | £862,710,521 |

## COMMUNICATIONS
*Airports* – 72; the principal airports are at Cairo, Sharm el-Sheikh, Luxor, Alexandria and Hurghada
*Waterways* – Egypt has 3,500km of waterways, including the River Nile and Lake Nasser, the Alexandria–Cairo waterway, numerous small canals in the Nile delta and the Suez Canal (opened 1869; closed 1967–75); the main seaports are Alexandria, Damietta and Port Said on the Mediterranean Sea and Suez on the Red Sea
*Roadways and railways* – A road network of 126,742km and a rail network of 5,083km link the Nile valley and delta with the main development areas east and west of the river, but there are few routes in the interior
*Telecommunications* – 8.56 million fixed lines and 96.8 million mobile subscriptions (2012); there were 20.136 million internet users in 2009
*Internet code and IDD* – eg; 20 (from UK), 44 (to UK)
*Major broadcasters* – State-run national television channels and regional channels compete with the country's thriving

satellite television industry, which is watched throughout the Arab-speaking world

*Press* – A number of daily newspapers are published, including *Al-Ahram,* the oldest newspaper in the Arab world *WPFI score* – 50,17 (158)

## EDUCATION AND HEALTH

Education is free between the ages of six and 15.
*Literacy rate* – 91.1 per cent (2015 est)
*Gross enrolment ratio (percentage of relevant age group)* – primary 113 per cent; secondary 86 per cent; tertiary 30 per cent (2012 est)
*Health expenditure (per capita)* – US$151 (2011)
*Hospital beds (per 1,000 people)* – 0.5 (2012)
*Life expectancy (years)* – 73.45 (2014 est)
*Mortality rate* – 4.77 (2014 est)
*Birth rate* – 23.35 (2014 est)
*Infant mortality rate* – 22.41 (2014 est)

# EL SALVADOR

*República de El Salvador – Republic of El Salvador*

*Area* – 21,041 sq. km
*Capital* – San Salvador; population, 1,097,000 (2014)
*Major cities* – San Miguel, Santa Ana, Soyapango
*Currency* – US dollar (US$) of 100 cents
*Population* – 6,141,350 rising at 0.25 per cent a year (2015 est)
*Religion* – Christian (Roman Catholic 57 per cent, Protestant 21 per cent)
*Language* – Spanish (official), Nahua
*Population density* – 306 per sq. km (2013)
*Urban population* – 65.8 per cent (2013)
*Median age (years)* – 25.6 (2014 est)
*National anthem* – 'Himno Nacional de El Salvador' ['National Anthem of El Salvador']
*National day* – 15 September (Independence Day)
*Death penalty* – Retained for certain crimes (last used 1973)
*CPI score* – 39 (80)

## CLIMATE AND TERRAIN

El Salvador is mountainous, with narrow coastal plains and a central plateau. Many of its peaks are volcanoes; most are extinct, but Ilamatepec (or Santa Ana) erupted in 2005. There are also numerous volcanic lakes. Elevation extremes range from 2,730m (Cerro El Pital) to 0m (Pacific Ocean). The climate is tropical on the coast but more temperate at higher altitudes. The average annual temperature in San Salvador is 25.4°C. Earthquakes and volcanic activity are common, and the country is also susceptible to hurricanes and tropical storms.

## HISTORY AND POLITICS

El Salvador was part of the Aztec kingdom conquered in 1524 by Pedro de Alvarado, and formed part of the Spanish viceroyalty of Guatemala until 1821. It was part of a Central American federation of former Spanish provinces from 1823 until the federation's dissolution in 1838, becoming fully independent in 1840.

There was political unrest in the 1970s, and guerrilla activity by the left-wing Farabundo Martí National Liberation Front (FMLN), which intensified from 1977 amid reports of human rights abuses by government troops and right-wing death squads. Decades of military rule ended in 1979, but elections in 1982 were boycotted by left-wing parties and the right-wing Nationalist Republican Alliance (ARENA) took office. The civil war between the FMLN and the US-backed government lasted throughout the 1980s, until a UN-sponsored peace agreement was signed in 1992. The FMLN was recognised as a political party, and it won seats in the 1994 election.

In the 2015 legislative elections, the conservative Nationalist Republican Alliance (ARENA) became the largest single party, though the FMLN continued to govern as part of a coalition. The elections were marred by technical problems, long delays and allegations of fraud. In March 2014 the FMLN candidate and former guerrilla fighter Salvador Sanchez Ceren was elected president.

Under the 1983 constitution, the executive president is directly elected for a five-year term, which is not renewable. The unicameral legislative assembly has 84 members, who are directly elected for a three-year term. The president appoints the Council of State. The country is divided into 14 departments.

### HEAD OF STATE

*President,* Salvador Sanchez Ceren, *elected* 13 March 2014, *took office* 1 June 2014
*Vice-President,* Oscar Ortiz

SELECTED GOVERNMENT MEMBERS *as at May 2015*
*Defence,* David Payes
*Economy,* Tharsis Lopez
*Foreign Affairs,* Hugo Martinez

EMBASSY OF EL SALVADOR
8 Dorset Square, 1st & 2nd Floors, London NW1 6PU
T 020-7224 9800 E embajadalondres@rree.gob.sv
*Ambassador Extraordinary and Plenipotentiary,* HE Werner Matías Romero, *apptd* 2009

BRITISH EMBASSY
Edificio Torre Futura, 14th Floor, Colonia Escalon, San Salvador
T (+503) 2511 5757 E britishembassy.elsalvador@fco.gov.uk
W www.gov.uk/government/world/el-salvador
*Ambassador Extraordiniary and Plenipotentiary,* Bernhard Garside, *apptd* 2015

## DEFENCE

| Aged 16–49, 2010 est | Males | Females |
| --- | --- | --- |
| Available for military service | 1,449,214 | 1,611,248 |
| Fit for military service | 1,079,038 | 1,373,368 |

*Military expenditure* – US$263m (2014)
*Conscription* – 18 years of age; 12 months (selective)

## ECONOMY AND TRADE

The country is one of the most industrialised in Central America and has the region's third-largest economy despite being its smallest country and having few natural resources. Recovery after the civil war was set back by a series of natural disasters, but the economy has been transformed from a mainly agricultural to a service-based economy with a growing manufacturing sector. Government diversification efforts have promoted textile production, international port services and tourism. Even so, the value of expatriates' remittances accounted for 17 per of GDP in 2013. In September 2014, El Salvador was awarded US$277m by US government agency the Millennium Challenge Corporation with the aim of stimulating economic growth and reducing poverty. Though the country has struggled to attract foreign investment, increasing private demand is expected to help the economy grow by just over 2 per cent in 2015 and 2016.

Services, through tourism, commerce and financial services, contribute 64.9 per cent of GDP. Industry contributes 25.1 per cent of GDP, mostly through assembly for re-export, food processing, beverages, oil, chemicals, fertiliser, textiles, furniture and light metals. Agriculture contributes 10 per cent to GDP and employs 21 per cent of the workforce. The principal agricultural products are coffee, sugar, maize, rice, beans, oilseed, cotton, sorghum, beef and dairy products.

The main trading partners are the USA and other Central American states. Principal exports are offshore assembly products, coffee, sugar, textiles, garments, gold, ethanol, chemicals and electricity. The chief imports are raw materials, consumer goods, capital goods, fuels, foodstuffs, oil and electricity.

*GNI* – US$22,931m; US$3,720 per capita (2013)
*Annual average growth of GDP* – 1.7 per cent (2014 est)
*Inflation rate* – 0.9 per cent (2013 est)
*Population below poverty line* – 29.6 per cent (2013 est)
*Unemployment* – 6.5 per cent (2015 est)
*Total external debt* – US$15,460m (2014)
*Imports* – US$10,772m (2013)
*Exports* – US$5,491m (2013)

BALANCE OF PAYMENTS
*Trade* – US$5,281m deficit (2013)
*Current Account* – US$1,132m deficit (2015 est)

| Trade with UK | 2013 | 2014 |
|---|---|---|
| Imports from UK | £14,233,503 | £16,361,072 |
| Exports to UK | £13,714,884 | £12,605,456 |

## COMMUNICATIONS
*Airports and waterways* – Five; the principal ports are Cutuco and Acajutla, and ports in Honduras and Guatemala are also used
*Roadways and railways* – There are 3,247km of surfaced roads; the 283km rail network has not been in operation since 2005 due to lack of maintenance
*Telecommunications* – 1.06 million fixed lines and 8.65 million mobile subscriptions (2012); there were 746,000 internet users in 2009
*Internet code and IDD* – sv; 503 (from UK), 44 (to UK)
*Major broadcasters* – Broadcasting is dominated by private operators, including Teledos and Canal Cuatro; there are hundreds of radio broadcasters, including the state-run Radio Nacional de El Salvador
*Press* – There are four main daily newspapers: *La Prensa Gráfica, El Mundo, El Diario de Hoy* and *El Diario Co Latino*
*WPFI score* – 23,66 (45)

## EDUCATION AND HEALTH
Primary education is state-run, compulsory and free.
*Literacy rate* – 97.5 per cent (2011 est)

*Gross enrolment ratio (percentage of relevant age group)* – primary 113 per cent; secondary 69 per cent; tertiary 25 per cent (2012 est)
*Health expenditure (per capita)* – US$251 (2011)
*Hospital beds (per 1,000 people)* – 1.0 (2011)
*Life expectancy (years)* – 74.18 (2014 est)
*Mortality rate* – 5.67 (2014 est)
*Birth rate* – 16.79 (2014 est)
*Infant mortality rate* – 18.44 (2014 est)

# EQUATORIAL GUINEA

*República de Guinea Ecuatorial / République de Guinée Equatoriale – Republic of Equatorial Guinea*

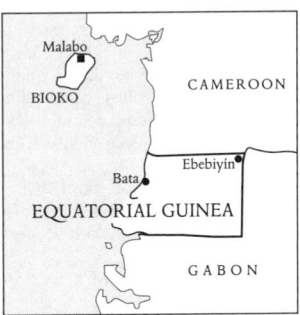

*Area* – 28,051 sq. km
*Capital* – Malabo, on Bioko; population, 145,000 (2014 est)
*Major towns* – Bata, the principal town and port of Río Muni; Ebebiyín
*Currency* – Central African CFA franc of 100 centimes
*Population* – 740,743 rising at 2.51 per cent a year (2015 est); predominantly Fang; indigenous Bubi now a minority on Bioko
*Religion* – Christian (Roman Catholic 87 per cent, other denominations 6 per cent), traditional indigenous religions 5 per cent (est); many Catholics also follow traditional beliefs
*Language* – Spanish, French (both official), Fang, Bubi
*Population density* – 27 per sq. km (2013)
*Urban population* – 39.8 per cent (2013)
*Median age (years)* – 19.4 (2014 est)
*National anthem* – 'Caminemos pisando las sendas de nuestra inmensa felicidad' ['Let Us Tread the Path of our Immense Happiness']
*National day* – 12 October (Independence Day)
*Death penalty* – Retained
*CPI score* – 20 (163)
*Literacy rate* – 98.3 per cent (2015 est)
*Life expectancy (years)* – 63.49 (2014 est)
*Mortality rate* – 8.39 (2014 est)
*Birth rate* – 33.83 (2014 est)
*Infant mortality rate* – 71.12 (2014 est)
*HIV / AIDS adult prevalence* – 6.2 per cent (2012 est)

## CLIMATE AND TERRAIN
The country consists of several islands off the Cameroon coast and a small area on the mainland, Río Muni, where 80 per cent of the population lives. The islands, of which Bioko is the largest, are of volcanic origin. The mainland rises from a narrow coastal plain to a mountainous interior plateau, and is covered in dense vegetation. Elevation extremes range from 3,008m (Pico Basile) to 0m (Atlantic Ocean). The climate is tropical, with a rainy season from July to January on Bioko, and from April to May and October to December on the mainland.

## HISTORY AND POLITICS

The island of Fernando Po (Bioko) was claimed by the Portuguese in 1494 and held until 1777, when it was ceded to Spain. The mainland territory of Río Muni came under Spanish rule in 1844, and the two territories became one colony, subsequently known as Spanish Guinea, in 1904. The colony became autonomous in 1963, and independent in 1968 under its present name.

The first president, Francisco Macías Nguema, established a one-party state in 1970. His brutal regime was overthrown in 1979 in a military coup led by his nephew, Col. Obiang Nguema. A military regime was established after the coup, and only presidential nominees were allowed to stand in the 1983 and 1988 elections. Constitutional amendments were introduced in 1991 to allow multiparty elections, but President Nguema and the Democratic Party of Equatorial Guinea (PDGE) have retained power since 1992; most elections have been boycotted by the opposition parties because of election irregularities and intimidation. The regime has been accused of human rights abuses and the suppression of political opposition, and in 2003 opposition leaders set up a 'government-in-exile' in Spain. There is also a separatist movement on Bioko.

In the 2013 legislative election, the PDGE retained its overwhelming majority in parliament. President Nguema won the 2009 presidential election with 95 per cent of the vote.

The 1991 constitution introduced a multiparty system. The president is directly elected for a seven-year term; constitutional amendments approved by referendum in November 2011 introduced a two-term limit. Constitutional amendments in 2012 created a bicameral system with a lower chamber, the House of Deputies, with 100 members, and an upper chamber, the Senate, containing 55 elected officials and 15 presidential appointments.

### HEAD OF STATE

*President,* Brig.-Gen. Teodoro Obiang Nguema Mbasogo, *took power* August 1979, *re-elected* 1989, 1996, 2002, 2009

### SELECTED GOVERNMENT MEMBERS *as at May 2015*

*Prime Minister,* Vicente Ehate Tomi
*Defence,* Teodoro Nguema Obiang Mangue
*Economy,* Eucario Bakale Angue
*Foreign Affairs,* Agapito Mba Mokuy

### EMBASSY OF THE REPUBLIC OF EQUATORIAL GUINEA

13 Park Place, St Jame's, London SW1A 1LP
T 020-7499 6867 E embarege-londres@embarege-londres.org
W www.embarege-londres.org
*Ambassador Extraordinary and Plenipotentiary,* HE Mari-Cruz Evuna Andeme, *apptd* 2012

### BRITISH HIGH COMMISSION

*High Commissioner,* HE Brian Olley, *apptd* 2013, resident at Yaounde, Cameroon

### DEFENCE

| Aged 16–49, 2010 est | Males | Females |
| --- | --- | --- |
| Available for military service | 151,147 | 150,345 |
| Fit for military service | 113,277 | 115,320 |

*Military expenditure –* US$167m (2014)
*Conscription –* 18 years of age; 24 months, although conscription is rarely enforced

## ECONOMY AND TRADE

Large oil and natural gas deposits discovered off Bioko in the 1990s have transformed the economy, which has grown dramatically since production began in 1996. The country has the reputation of being one of the most corrupt in the world; oil exploitation has not benefited much of the population as most businesses are owned by government officials or their families. The economy entered recession in 2013 and is expected to deliver negative growth in 2015. Major economic concerns include an undiversified economy and declining world oil prices.

Industry contributes 85.7 per cent of GDP, services 9.2 per cent and agriculture 5.1 per cent. The oil-driven growth in the GDP masks stagnation in other sectors; agriculture, once the mainstay of the economy, has declined to subsistence level owing to neglect and lack of investment. The main crops are coffee, cocoa, rice, fruit, nuts, livestock and timber. Industrial activities other than oil and natural gas production include fishing and timber processing.

The main trading partners are the USA, China and Japan. Principal exports are petroleum and timber. The main imports are oil industry and other industrial equipment.

*GNI –* US$11,051m; US$14,320 per capita (2013)
*Annual average growth of GDP –* –2.5 per cent (2014 est)
*Inflation rate –* 6 per cent (2013 est)
*Unemployment –* 10.7 per cent (2015 est)
*Total external debt –* US$1,385m (2014 est)
*Imports –* US$6,990m (2013)
*Exports –* US$13,981m (2013)

### BALANCE OF PAYMENTS

*Trade –* US$6,990m surplus (2013)
*Current Account –* US$2,764m deficit (2015 est)

| Trade with UK | 2013 | 2014 |
| --- | --- | --- |
| Imports from UK | £48,436,012 | £58,465,688 |
| Exports to UK | £1,094,072,743 | £1,187,448,248 |

### COMMUNICATIONS

*Airports –* The principal airport is based in Malabo
*Roadways –* 2,880km
*Telecommunications –* 14,900 fixed lines (2012) and 501,000 mobile subscriptions (2012); there were 14,400 internet users in 2009
*Internet code and IDD –* gq; 240 (from UK), 44 (to UK)
*Broadcasters –* Television and radio broadcasts are state-controlled
*Press – Ebano* is the government-run newspaper; privately owned newspapers are unable to publish regularly due to financial and political pressure
*WPFI score –* 66,23 (167)

## ERITREA

*Hagere Ertra – State of Eritrea*

*Area* – 117,600 sq. km
*Capital* – Asmara; population, 775,000 (2014)
*Major towns* – Assab, Keren, Massawa
*Currency* – Nakfa (Nfk) of 100 cents
*Population* – 6,527,689 rising at 2.25 per cent a year
(2015 est); Tigrinya (55 per cent), Tigre (30 per cent),
Saho (4 per cent), Kunama (2 per cent), Rashaida (2 per
cent), Bilen (2 per cent) (2010 est)
*Religion* – Muslim (Sunni) 50 per cent, Christian 40 per cent
(Eritrean Orthodox 24 per cent, Roman Catholic 10 per
cent), animist 2 per cent; only Christians of the Eritrean
Orthodox, Catholic and Lutheran churches, and Muslims
may meet freely
*Language* – Arabic, English, Tigrinya (all official), Tigre, Afar,
Kunama
*Population density* – 63 per sq. km (2013)
*Urban population* – 22.2 per cent (2013)
*Median age (years)* – 19.1 (2014 est)
*National anthem* – 'Ertra, Ertra, Ertra' ['Eritrea, Eritrea,
Eritrea']
*National day* – 24 May (Independence Day)
*Death penalty* – Retained (last used 1989)
*CPI score* – 18 (166)
*Literacy rate* – 93.2 per cent (2015 est)
*Gross enrolment ratio (percentage of relevant age group)* –
primary 42 per cent; secondary 30 per cent; tertiary
2 per cent (2012 est)
*Health expenditure (per capita)* – US$17 (2013)
*Hospital beds (per 1,000 people)* – 0.7 (2011)
*Life expectancy (years)* – 63.51 (2014 est)
*Mortality rate* – 7.65 (2014 est)
*Birth rate* – 30.69 (2014 est)
*Infant mortality rate* – 38.44 (2014 est)
*HIV / AIDS adult prevalence* – 1.3 per cent (2013 est)

## CLIMATE AND TERRAIN

The northern end of the Ethiopian Highlands extends into
central Eritrea, where the average altitude is over 2,000m.
The mountains fall in the west to a plateau, which then rises
to the hills on the Sudanese border. To the east of the
mountains, the land falls to the narrow coastal plain. The
coastal strip extending to the Djibouti border is low-lying,
while the border with Ethiopia runs along the edge of the
Danakil desert. Elevation extremes range from 3,018m
(Soira) to −75m (Danakil depression). Average temperatures
range from 23°C in January to 30.6°C in June.

## HISTORY AND POLITICS

Part of the Axum empire from the first century AD, the area
came under the control of the Ottoman Empire in the mid-
16th century. It was occupied by Italy in the late 19th
century and was the base for Italy's 1936 invasion of
Abyssinia (now Ethiopia). After the Italian defeat in North
Africa in 1941, Eritrea became a British protectorate until 15
September 1952, when a federation with Ethiopia
was established by the UN. In 1962, Ethiopia annexed
Eritrea outright.

The Eritrean Liberation Front (ELF) fought a guerrilla war
for independence from 1961, and the Eritrean People's
Liberation Front (EPLF) – a breakaway faction of the ELF –
emerged in the 1970s, becoming the dominant rebel group
in the 1980s. The EPLF joined with Ethiopian resistance
groups to fight the Mengistu regime, which was overthrown
in 1991. The EPLF secured the whole of Eritrea and formed
an autonomous provisional government. The new Ethiopian
government agreed to an Eritrean referendum on
independence, held in April 1993, which recorded a 99.89
per cent vote in favour. Independence was declared on 24
May 1993.

Following independence, a transitional government for
a four-year period was formed under Isaias Afewerki, and
the EPLF became the ruling political party, renaming itself
the People's Front for Democracy and Justice (PFDJ) in
1994. The post-independence regime has become
increasingly authoritarian, and since 2001 has dealt harshly
with anyone openly critical of the government. In 2015, the
UN reported that Eritreans are routinely subjected to a
number of abuses by the government, including torture,
sexual abuse and indefinite service in the country's military.

Few of the provisions outlined in the 1997 constitution
have been enacted and no presidential or legislative elections
have been held, so the transitional president, state council
(cabinet) and legislature remain in place. Under the
constitution, the president is elected for a five-year term by
the legislature, and the 150-member unicameral National
Assembly is directly elected for a four-year term. The
People's Front for Democracy and Justice (PFDJ) is the only
legal political party.

### HEAD OF STATE

*President, Chairman of the State Council and of the National
Assembly,* Isaias Afewerki, *elected by the National Assembly*
22 May 1993

SELECTED GOVERNMENT MEMBERS *as at May 2015*
*Defence,* Gen. Sebhat Ephrem
*Finance,* Berhane Habtemariam
*Foreign Affairs,* Osman Saleh

### EMBASSY OF THE STATE OF ERITREA

96 White Lion Street, London N1 9PF
T 020-7713 0096 E eriemba@eriembauk.com
*Ambassador Extraordinary and Plenipotentiary,* HE Estifanos
Habtemariam Ghebreyesus, *apptd* 2014

### BRITISH EMBASSY

PO Box 5584, 66–68 Mariam Ghimbi Street, Asmara
T (+291) (1) 120 145 E asmara.enquiries@fco.gov.uk
W www.gov.uk/government/world/eritrea
*Ambassador Extraordinary and Plenipotentiary,* HE David
Ward, *apptd* 2014

### FOREIGN RELATIONS

Since independence, Eritrea has been involved in disputes
with Yemen, Ethiopia and Djibouti over territory, while
Sudan has accused Eritrea of supporting rebels in eastern
Sudan. The dispute with Yemen was over the Hanish and
Mohabaka islands in the Red Sea; possession was divided
between Yemen and Eritrea by international arbitration.

There has been fighting with Ethiopia in disputes over
border territory, especially in the Tigray region, since 1998.
Fighting escalated in 1999–2000 into a war that left
thousands of people dead. An independent boundary
commission defined the international border between the
two countries in 2002, but both countries have failed to
abide by successive rulings.

Fighting broke out on the part of the border disputed with
Djibouti in 2008. Both countries agreed to seek a peaceful
settlement in 2010.

Following border disputes in early 2011, Ethiopia
announced that it would support Eritrean rebels fighting
President Afewerki.

In July 2011, a UN report accused Eritrea of planning to
attack an African Union Summit in Ethiopia; owing to
Eritrea's alleged support for Islamist insurgents in Somalia,
the UN further tightened sanctions in December 2011.
In March 2012 Ethiopia attacked three military camps in

Eritrea, claiming the country was supporting Ethiopian rebels who mounted attacks on western tourists.

Political repression has increasingly led to Eritreans seeking political asylum abroad. The number of Eritreans seeking asylum in the EU increased from 13,000 in 2013 to 37,000 in 2014; nearly a quarter of the number of refugees attempting to enter Europe via boat in 2014 were Eritrean.

## DEFENCE

| Aged 16–49, 2010 est | Males | Females |
| --- | --- | --- |
| Available for military service | 1,350,446 | 1,362,575 |
| Fit for military service | 896,096 | 953,757 |

*Military expenditure* – US$522 (2003 est)
*Conscription* – 18–40 years of age; 16 months

## ECONOMY AND TRADE
Over 30 years of conflict left the country's economy devastated, and the restrictive policies of the post-independent regime have hampered recovery. The command economy has concentrated business ownership in military and party hands. Agricultural output is restricted by lack of labour owing to the failure to demobilise the large army, the conflict with Ethiopia and the frequent droughts and ensuing famines. Nevertheless, agriculture and herding are the means of subsistence of around 80 per cent of the population. The industrial sector has contracted since trade with Ethiopia halted in 1998, and the principal ports have suffered from the loss of this transit trade. Development of the Zara mining project, a new gold mine in the centre of the country, began in 2013.

Mineral reserves include zinc, potash, gold, copper and possibly oil; these are not fully exploited at present, although mining production began in 2010. Industries include food processing, beverages, clothing and textiles, salt, cement and light manufacturing. The opening of a free trade zone at Massawa in 2008 may boost revenues, which are heavily dependent on remittances from expatriates.

The main trade partners are India, Italy, Saudi Arabia, China and Sudan. Principal exports are livestock, sorghum, textiles, food and light manufactures. The main imports are machinery, petroleum products, food and manufactured goods.
*GNI* – US$3,063m; US$490 per capita (2013)
*Annual average growth of GDP* – 2 per cent (2014 est)
*Inflation rate* – 13 per cent (2013 est)
*Population below poverty line* – 50 per cent (2004 est)
*Unemployment* – 9.0 per cent (2015 est)
*Total external debt* – US$1,049m (2014 est)

BALANCE OF PAYMENTS
*Trade* – US$418m deficit (2010)
*Current Account* – US$69m deficit (2015 est)

| Trade with UK | 2013 | 2014 |
| --- | --- | --- |
| Imports from UK | £7,133,569 | £3,174,404 |
| Exports to UK | £168,383 | £91,973 |

## COMMUNICATIONS
*Airports and waterways* – Four, with the main international airport at Asmara; the principal seaports are at Assab and Massawa
*Roadways and railways* – There are 4,101km of roadways, of which 874km are surfaced, and 306km of railways, which link Massawa to Sudan via Asmara
*Telecommunications* – There are 60,000 fixed lines and 305,300 mobile subscriptions (2012); there were 200,000 internet users in 2009

*Internet code and IDD* – er; 291 (from UK), 44 (to UK)
*Broadcasters* – Eritrea is the only country in Africa without any privately owned media; Eri TV, Voice of the Broad Masses of Eritrea and Radio Zara are state-run
*Press* – *Hadas Eritrea* and *Eritrea Profile* are the government-owned newspaper publications
*WPFI score* – 84,83 (180)

## ESTONIA

*Eesti Vabariik* – *Republic of Estonia*

*Area* – 45,228 sq. km
*Capital* – Tallinn; population, 392,000 (2014)
*Major towns* – Kohtla-Jarve, Narva, Parnu, Tartu
*Currency* – Euro (€) of 100 cents
*Population* – 1,265,420 falling at 0.55 per cent a year (2015 est); Estonian (68.7 per cent), Russian (24.8 per cent), Ukrainian (1.7 per cent), Belarusian (1 per cent), Finn (0.6 per cent) (2008)
*Religion* – Christian (Orthodox 16 per cent, Lutheran 10 per cent) (est)
*Language* – Estonian (official), Russian
*Population density* – 31 per sq. km (2013)
*Urban population* – 69.6 per cent (2013)
*Median age (years)* – 41.2 (2014 est)
*National anthem* – 'Mu Isamaa, Mu Onn Ja Room' ['My Fatherland, My Pride and Joy']
*National day* – 24 February (Independence Day)
*Death penalty* – Abolished for all crimes (since 1998)
*CPI score* – 69 (26)

## CLIMATE AND TERRAIN
The country is mostly a plain of lakes, marshes and forests, with a range of low hills in the south-east. Elevation extremes range from 318m (Suur Munamagi) to 0m (Baltic Sea). Part of the border with Russia runs through the large Lake Peipsi. The climate is maritime, with average temperatures ranging from −3.9°C in February to 17.7°C in July.

## HISTORY AND POLITICS
The area came under Swedish control between 1561 and 1629, and was ceded to the Russian Empire in 1721. An Estonian nationalist movement developed in the late 19th century and fought against occupying German forces during the First World War. Estonia declared its independence in February 1918 and defended it against Soviet forces until 1920, when independence was recognised by the USSR. However, the USSR annexed Estonia in 1940, and the country was subsequently occupied by German forces when they invaded the USSR in 1941. In 1944 the USSR expelled the Germans and reannexed the country, beginning a process of 'Sovietisation'.

There was a resurgence of nationalist sentiment in the 1980s, and in 1989 the Estonian Supreme Soviet declared the republic to be sovereign and its 1940 annexation by the USSR to be illegal. In 1990, the Communist Party's monopoly on power was abolished and, following multiparty elections in which pro-independence candidates won the majority of seats, a period of transition to independence was inaugurated, culminating in its declaration on 20 August 1991. The last Russian troops withdrew in 1994. Since independence, Estonia has pursued pro-Western policies. It joined NATO and the EU in 2004.

In 2011 Toomas Hendrik Ilves was re-elected president by an electoral assembly. In the 2015 legislative election, the Reform Party (ER), the main partner in the coalition government since 2005, remained the largest party and formed a coalition with the Social Democratic Party of Estonia (SDE) and Res Publica (IRL). Taavi Roivas remained prime minister.

Under the 1992 constitution, the president is elected for a five-year term by the legislature by a two-thirds majority or, if no candidate receives this majority after three rounds of voting, by an electoral assembly composed of the legislature members and 266 local government representatives. The unicameral legislature, the *Riigikogu,* has 101 members, directly elected for a four-year term. The prime minister is appointed by the president and nominates the government.

HEAD OF STATE
*President,* Toomas Hendrik Ilves, *elected by electoral assembly* 23 September 2006, *sworn in* 9 October 2006, *re-elected* 2011

SELECTED GOVERNMENT MEMBERS *as at May 2015*
*Prime Minister,* Taavi Roivas
*Defence,* Sven Mikser
*Finance,* Sven Sester
*Foreign Affairs,* Keit Pentus-Rosimannus
*Internal Affairs,* Hanno Pevkur

EMBASSY OF THE REPUBLIC OF ESTONIA
16 Hyde Park Gate, London SW7 5DG
T 020-7589 3428 E london@mfa.ee W www.estonia.gov.uk
*Ambassador Extraordinary and Plenipotentiary,* HE Lauri Bambus, *apptd* 2014

BRITISH EMBASSY
Wismari 6, Tallinn 10136
T (+372) 667 4700 E infotallinn@fco.gov.uk
W www.gov.uk/government/world/estonia
*Ambassador Extraordinary and Plenipotentiary,* HE Christopher Holtby OBE, *apptd* 2012

DEFENCE

| Aged 16–49, 2010 est | Males | Females |
| --- | --- | --- |
| Available for military service | 291,801 | 302,696 |
| Fit for military service | 210,854 | 251,185 |

*Military expenditure* – US$509m (2014)
*Conscription* – 18–27 years of age; 8–11 months, depending on education

ECONOMY AND TRADE
Economic reforms and restructuring since 1992 have resulted in a market economy, the growth of which was boosted by the country's accession to the EU in 2004. Estonia entered recession in 2008 after an investment and consumption slump, and a drop in demand for exports. Prudent financial management has enabled the economy to recover slowly, and it met the accession criteria for the eurozone, which Estonia joined in January 2011; it has since garnered one of the highest GDP growth rates in Europe. Weak growth in the eurozone and Russian economies is expected to restrict growth to 2 per cent in 2015.

Agriculture engages 4.2 per cent of the workforce and accounts for 3.6 per cent of GDP, the main products being cereals, vegetables, livestock, dairy products and fish. Industry accounts for 20.2 per cent of employment and 29.2 per cent of GDP, concentrating on engineering, electronics, wood and wood products, textiles, information technology and telecommunications; electronics and telecommunications are particularly strong. The services sector accounts for 75.6 per cent of employment and 67.2 per cent of GDP.

The main trading partners are other EU countries, particularly Finland, Sweden and Russia. Principal exports are machinery and electrical equipment, wood and wood products, metals, furniture, vehicles and parts, food products and textiles. The main imports are machinery and electrical equipment, fuels, foodstuffs, plastics and textiles. Estonia remains dependent on Russian natural gas supplies.
*GNI* – US$21,322m; US$17,690 per capita (2013)
*Annual average growth of GDP* – 1.2 per cent (2014 est)
*Inflation rate* – –0.1 per cent (2014 est)
*Population below poverty line* – 17.5 per cent (2011)
*Unemployment* – 9.2 per cent (2015 est)
*Total external debt* – US$22,790m (2014 est)
*Imports* – US$18,142m (2013)
*Exports* – US$16,291m (2013)

BALANCE OF PAYMENTS
*Trade* – US$3,146m deficit (2013)
*Current Account* – US$91m deficit (2015 est)

| Trade with UK | 2013 | 2014 |
| --- | --- | --- |
| Imports from UK | £320,734,691 | £268,627,725 |
| Exports to UK | £182,345,630 | £176,518,724 |

COMMUNICATIONS
*Airports and waterways* – 13, with the principal international airport in Tallinn; there are 335km of year-round navigable waterways, and the main seaports are at Tallinn, Parnu Reid and Haapsalu Jahtklubi
*Roadways and railways* – 10,427km, including 115km of motorways; 1,196km
*Telecommunications* – 448,200 fixed lines and 2.07 million mobile subscriptions (2012); there were 971,700 internet users in 2009
*Internet code and IDD* – ee; 372 (from UK), 44 (to UK)
*Major broadcasters* – Public broadcasters Eesti Televisioon and Eesti Radio compete with private-sector, usually Swedish- or Norwegian-owned broadcasters
*Press* – Major newspapers include *Postimees* (Estonian and Russian editions) and *Eesti Paevaleht*
*WPFI score* – 11,19 (10)

EDUCATION AND HEALTH
Primary and secondary level education is compulsory between the ages of seven and 15.
*Literacy rate* – 100 per cent (2015 est)
*Gross enrolment ratio (percentage of relevant age group)* – primary 98 per cent; secondary 107 per cent; tertiary 77 per cent (2012 est)
*Health expenditure (per capita)* – US$1,072 (2013)
*Hospital beds (per 1,000 people)* – 5.3 (2011)
*Life expectancy (years)* – 74.07 (2014 est)
*Mortality rate* – 13.69 (2014 est)
*Birth rate* – 10.29 (2014 est)
*Infant mortality rate* – 6.7 (2014 est)
*HIV/AIDS adult prevalence* – 1.3 per cent (2013 est)

# ETHIOPIA

*Ityop'iya Federalawi Demokrasiyawi Ripeblik – Federal Democratic Republic of Ethiopia*

*Area –* 1,104,300 sq. km
*Capital –* Addis Ababa; population, 3,168,000 (2014)
*Major cities –* Bahir Dar, Dese, Dire Dawa, Gonder, Mek'ele, Nazret
*Currency –* Birr (EB) of 100 cents
*Population –* 99,465,819 rising at 2.89 per cent a year (2015 est); Oromo (34.5 per cent), Amhara (26.9 per cent), Somali (6.2 per cent), Tigray (6.1 per cent), Sidama (4 per cent), Guragie (2.5 per cent), Welaita (2.3 per cent) (2007)
*Religion –* Christian 63 per cent (Ethiopian Orthodox 44 per cent, Protestant 19 per cent), Muslim 34 per cent (mostly Sunni) (est)
*Language –* Amharic, English, Arabic (all official), Oromo Tigrinya, Somali, Guaragigna, Sidamo
*Population density –* 94 per sq. km (2013)
*Urban population –* 17.5 per cent (2013)
*Median age (years) –* 17.6 (2014 est)
*National anthem –* 'Wodefit Gesgeshi Widd Innat Ityopp'ya' ['March Forward, Dear Mother Ethiopia']
*National day –* 28 May (defeat of Mengistu government, 1991)
*Death penalty –* Retained (last used 2007)
*CPI score –* 33 (110)

## CLIMATE AND TERRAIN

Ethiopia is dominated by a central plateau, rising to the mountains of the Ethiopian Highlands, which are divided by the Great Rift Valley. The western mountains are the source of the Blue Nile. The land drops to desert plains in the east (Ogaden) and north-east (Danakil desert). Elevation extremes range from 4,533m (Ras Dejen) to −125m (Danakil depression). There is a tropical monsoon climate, with variations according to altitude. The wet season is from April to September.

## POLITICS

The 1994 constitution provides for a federal government responsible for foreign affairs, defence and economic policy, and nine ethnically based states. The president is elected by both houses of the legislature for a six-year term, renewable once. The prime minister is appointed by the lower chamber of the legislature and appoints the government. The Federal Parliamentary Assembly is bicameral. The lower chamber, the House of People's Representatives, has 547 members, directly elected for a five-year term. The House of the Federation has 110 members, elected for a five-year term by the government councils of the nine states in the federation. These regional administrations have considerable autonomy and the right to secede.

In the 2015 legislative elections, the ruling Ehtiopian People's Revolutionary Demoratic Front won all 172 seats in the House of People's Representatives; observers and opposition groups claimed that the polls were not fair due to government restrictions on free speech. In 2012, Prime Minister Meles Zenawi died and was succeeded by Deputy Prime Minister Hailemariam Desalegn; Mulatu Teshome was elected president in 2013.

HEAD OF STATE
*President,* Mulatu Teshome, *elected* 7 October 2013

SELECTED GOVERNMENT MEMBERS *as at September 2015*
*Prime Minister,* Hailemariam Desalegn
*Deputy Prime Minister, Finance,* Debretsion Gebremichael
   *(Finance);* Aster Mamo; Demeke Mekonnen

EMBASSY OF THE FEDERAL DEMOCRATIC REPUBLIC OF ETHIOPIA
17 Princes Gate, London SW7 1PZ
T 020-7589 7212 E info@ethioembassy.org.uk
W www.ethioembassy.org.uk
*Ambassador Extraordinary and Plenipotentiary,* HE Berhanu Kebede, *apptd* 2006

BRITISH EMBASSY
Comoros Street, Addis Ababa 858
T (+251) (11) 61 70100 E britishembassy.addisababa@fco.gov.uk
W www.gov.uk/government/world/ethiopia
*Ambassador Extraordinary and Plenipotentiary,* HE Greg Dorey, *apptd* 2011

FOREIGN RELATIONS
Ethiopia intervened in Somalia in 2006 in support of the Somali transitional government. It formally withdrew its forces in January 2009, in accordance with a 2008 peace agreement between the Somali government and rebels. In January 2014, 4,000 Ethiopian troops reinforced African Union soldiers fighting the al-Qaeda-aligned al-Shabab group in northern Somalia.

For border disputes with Eritrea, *see* Eritrea.

## DEFENCE

| Aged 16–49, 2010 est | Males | Females |
| --- | --- | --- |
| Available for military service | 19,067,499 | 19,726,816 |
| Fit for military service | 11,868,084 | 12,889,260 |

*Military expenditure –* US$394m (2014)

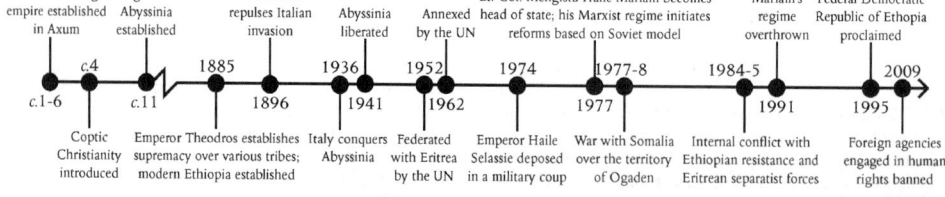

| Coastal trading empire established in Axum | Kingdom of Abyssinia established | Menelik II repulses Italian invasion | Abyssinia liberated | Annexed by the UN | Lt.-Col. Mengistu Haile Mariam becomes head of state; his Marxist regime initiates reforms based on Soviet model | Mariam's regime overthrown | Federal Democratic Republic of Ethopia proclaimed |
| --- | --- | --- | --- | --- | --- | --- | --- |
| c.4 | 1885 | 1936 | 1952 | 1974 | 1977-8 | 1984-5 | 2009 |
| c.1-6 | c.11 | 1896 | 1941 | 1962 | 1977 | 1991 | 1995 |
| Coptic Christianity introduced | Emperor Theodros establishes supremacy over various tribes; modern Ethiopia established | Italy conquers Abyssinia | Federated with Eritrea by the UN | Emperor Haile Selassie deposed in a military coup | War with Somalia over the territory of Ogaden | Internal conflict with Ethiopian resistance and Eritrean separatist forces | Foreign agencies engaged in human rights banned |

## ECONOMY AND TRADE

The economy is highly dependent on agriculture, and therefore reliant on the rains; recurring droughts led to famine conditions in 1984–5, 1992, 1997, 2000, 2002, 2009 and 2011. Although most foreign debt was cancelled in 2005, emergency IMF funding was needed to cushion the country from the effects of the global downturn. Ethiopia has experienced more than a decade of strong growth, with GDP growing by 93 per cent between 2007 and 2013, and the government has invested revenue in improving the country's infrastructure.

Agriculture and herding account for 47.7 per cent of GDP, and 85 per cent of the population is dependent upon the land for a living. The main crops are cereals, pulses, coffee, oilseed, cotton, sugar, potatoes, qat (or khat, a flowering plant chewed for its stimulant properties), cut flowers, livestock products and fish. Natural resources, including gold, platinum, copper, potash, oil and natural gas, are largely unexploited; most industrial activity involves the processing of agricultural products, gold mining and metalworking, and textiles. Work continues on the Grand Ethiopian Renaissance Dam on the Nile, which is intended to generate electricity for domestic consumption and export, and is due to be completed in 2017, despite claims from the Egyptian government the new dam could threaten Egypt's water supply.

The main trade partners are China, Saudi Arabia, the USA, Germany and Belgium. Principal exports are coffee, qat, gold, leather products, livestock and oilseeds. The main imports are food, livestock, petroleum and petroleum products, chemicals, machinery, vehicles, cereals and textiles.

*GNI* – US$41,511m; US$470 per capita (2013)
*Annual average growth of GDP* – 8.2 per cent (2014 est)
*Inflation rate* – 7.4 per cent (2014 est)
*Population below poverty line* – 39 per cent (2012 est)
*Unemployment* – 6.0 per cent (2015 est)
*Total external debt* – US$17,020m (2014 est)
*Imports* – US$12,641m (2012)
*Exports* – US$4,062m (2012)

BALANCE OF PAYMENTS
*Trade* – US$8,985m deficit (2012)
*Current Account* – US$3,781m deficit (2015 est)

| Trade with UK | 2013 | 2014 |
| --- | --- | --- |
| Imports from UK | £98,714,598 | £108,109,196 |
| Exports to UK | £69,968,579 | £44,283,506 |

## COMMUNICATIONS

*Airports and waterways* – 17; this landlocked country uses ports in Djibouti city and Berbera in Somalia
*Roadways and railways* – There are 6,064km of surfaced roads; the only railway line links Addis Ababa and Djibouti over 681km but is largely inoperable
*Telecommunications* – 797,500 fixed lines and 20.524 million mobile subscriptions (2012); there were 447,300 internet users in 2009
*Internet country code and IDD* – et; 251 (from UK), 44 (to UK)
*Major broadcasters* – The state-owned Ethiopian Television and Radio Ethiopia operate national and regional stations
*Press* – The number of privately owned newspapers has increased in recent years: *Addis Zemen* and *Ethiopian Herald* are the state-owned dailies, *The Daily Monitor* and *Addis Admass* are privately owned publications
*WPFI score* – 41,83 (142)

## EDUCATION AND HEALTH

Non-compulsory elementary and secondary education is provided by government schools in the major population centres; there are also mission schools.
*Literacy rate* – 69.5 per cent (2015 est)
*Gross enrolment ratio (percentage of relevant age group)* – primary 95 per cent; secondary 36 per cent; tertiary 8 per cent (2011 est)
*Health expenditure (per capita)* – US$25 (2013)
*Hospital beds (per 1,000 people)* – 6.3 (2011)
*Life expectancy (years)* – 60.75 (2014 est)
*Mortality rate* – 8.52 (2014 est)
*Birth rate* – 37.66 (2014 est)
*Infant mortality rate* – 55.77 (2014 est)
*HIV/AIDS adult prevalence* – 1.5 per cent (2013 )

# FIJI

*Matanitu ko Viti – Republic of Fiji*

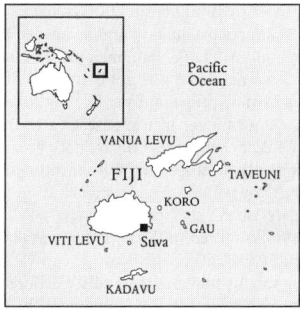

*Area* – 18,274 sq. km
*Capital* – Suva, on Viti Levu; population, 176,000 (2014)
*Major towns* – Lautoka, Nasinu, Nausori
*Currency* – Fijian dollar (F$) of 100 cents
*Population* – 909,389 rising at 0.67 per cent a year (2015 est); Fijian (57.3 per cent), Indian (37.6 per cent), Rotuman (1.2 per cent) (2007)
*Religion* – Christian 65 per cent (predominantly Methodist), Hindu 28 per cent, Muslim 6 per cent (predominantly Sunni) (est)
*Language* – English, Fijian (official), Hindustani
*Population density* – 48 per sq. km (2013)
*Urban population* – 53 per cent (2013)
*Median age (years)* – 27.9 (2014 est)
*National anthem* – 'Meda Dau Doka' ['God Bless Fiji']
*National day* – Second Monday of October (Independence Day)
*Death penalty* – Abolished for all crimes since 2015
*Life expectancy (years)* – 72.15 (2014 est)
*Mortality rate* – 6.0 (2014 est)
*Birth rate* – 19.86 (2014 est)
*Infant mortality rate* – 10.2 (2014 est)
*Gross enrolment ratio (percentage of relevant age group)* – primary 105 per cent; secondary 88 per cent (2012 est)

## CLIMATE AND TERRAIN

Fiji comprises a group of about 330 islands (around 110 are permanently inhabited) and over 500 islets in the South Pacific, about 1,770km north of New Zealand. The group extends 480km from east to west and 480km north to south. The international date line has been diverted to the east of the island group. The largest islands are Viti Levu and Vanua Levu. The terrain is mountainous and volcanic, with tropical rainforest and grassland, and most islands are surrounded by coral reefs. Elevation extremes range from 1,324m (Tomanivi, on Viti Levu) to 0m (Pacific Ocean). Fiji has a tropical maritime climate with high humidity and an average annual temperature of 24.3°C.

## HISTORY AND POLITICS

The islands were settled by Melanesian peoples. European contact began with the visit of the Dutch explorer Abel Tasman in 1643; later visitors included Captain Cook in 1774. The islands became a British colony in 1874, and sugar plantations, employing more than 60,000 indentured Indian labourers, were established. Fiji became independent as a constitutional monarchy on 10 October 1970, and became a republic after the 1987 coups.

The growing size and political strength of the ethnic Indian population caused political instability in the late 1980s. There were two coups in 1987 and one in 2000 as indigenous Fijians attempted to reassert their political dominance and entrench this in the constitution. A fourth coup occurred in 2006 over the government's proposed amnesty for those involved in the 2000 coup.

Since the 2006 coup a military regime headed by the coup leader, Commodore 'Frank' Bainimarama, has held power. Although President Iloilo was reinstated in 2007, when Bainimarama became prime minister, the regime has become increasingly authoritarian. In response to a court of appeal ruling in April 2009 stating that the military government was illegal, President Iloilo suspended the constitution, dismissed the judiciary, reappointed Bainimarama as interim prime minister and declared a state of emergency.

President Iloilo retired in 2009 and was replaced by the vice-president, Ratu Epeli Nailatikau.

Political instability and failure to hold elections caused Fiji to be suspended from the Commonwealth of Nations between 1987 and 1997, 2000 to 2001 and 2009 to 2014. The first legislative elections in eight years were held on 21 September 2014; the Fiji First Party emerged as the largest single party, winning 32 of the 50 seats in the legislature, in elections deemed credible by many international observers. Frank Bainimarama remained prime minister.

In September 2013, Fiji's fourth constitution was signed into law by President Nailatikau, the first to abolish race-based electoral rolls and seat quotas. It vests sole legislative authority in the single-chamber, 50-seat Parliament, which is due to convene following 2014 elections.

HEAD OF STATE
*President,* Ratu Epeli Nailatikau, *sworn in* 5 November 2009

SELECTED GOVERNMENT MEMBERS *as at May 2015*
*Prime Minister, Finance,* Commodore Voreqe ('Frank') Bainimarama
*Attorney-General, Finance,* Aiyaz Sayed-Khaiyum
*Defence,* Timoci Lesi Natuva
*Foreign Affairs,* Inoke Kubuabola

HIGH COMMISSION OF THE REPUBLIC OF FIJI
34 Hyde Park Gate, London SW7 5DN
T 020-7584 3661 E mail@fijihighcommission.org.uk
W www.fijihighcommission.org.uk
*High Commissioner,* HE Solo Mara, *apptd* 2011

BRITISH HIGH COMMISSION
47 Gladstone Road, Suva
T (+679) 322 9100 E publicdiplomacy@fco.gov.uk
W www.gov.uk/government/world/fiji
*High Commissioner,* HE Roderick Drummond, *apptd* 2013

## DEFENCE

| Aged 16–49, 2010 est | Males | Females |
|---|---|---|
| Available for military service | 233,240 | 222,587 |
| Fit for military service | 183,730 | 188,325 |

*Military expenditure* – US$52.2m (2012)

## ECONOMY AND TRADE

Fiji has abundant natural resources and one of the more developed economies in the region. However, the economy suffered after the 1987 coups because of the mass emigration of Indian Fijians, and is now contracting owing to structural problems, inefficiency and continuing political instability. Tourism, the mainstay of the economy, has declined since the 2006 coup and is expected to recover following the country's return to democracy. Low global sugar and gold prices present threats to long-term growth.

Agriculture, much of it at subsistence level, accounts for 12.7 per cent of GDP and employs 70 per cent of the workforce. The principal cash crop is sugar cane, but revenue has been affected by cuts in EU subsidies. The other main agricultural products are coconuts, cassava, rice, sweet potatoes, bananas, livestock and fish. The main industries are tourism, sugar processing, garment manufacturing, copra production, gold and silver mining, forestry and small cottage industries. The main trade partners are Australia, Singapore, New Zealand, the USA and the UK. Principal exports are sugar, garments, gold, timber, fish, molasses and coconut oil. The chief imports are manufactured goods, machinery and transport equipment, petroleum products, food and chemicals.

*GNI* – US$3,755m; US$4,370 per capita (2013)
*Annual average growth of GDP* – 3.8 per cent (2014 est)
*Inflation rate* – 0.5 per cent (2014)
*Unemployment* – 7.6 per cent (2015 est)
*Total external debt* – US$503.1m (2014 est)
*Imports* – US$2,822m (2013)
*Exports* – US$1,107m (2013)

BALANCE OF PAYMENTS
*Trade* – US$1,715m deficit (2013)
*Current Account* – US$355m deficit (2015 est)

| Trade with UK | 2013 | 2014 |
|---|---|---|
| Imports from UK | £7,959,645 | £9,755,302 |
| Exports to UK | £49,975,047 | £60,196,753 |

## COMMUNICATIONS

*Airports and waterways* – Four, including international airports at Suva and Nadi; the main seaports are Suva and Lautoka
*Roadways and railways* – There are 1,686km of surfaced roads, and 597km of railway track, principally used by the sugar industry
*Telecommunications* – 88,400 fixed lines and 858,800 mobile subscriptions (2012); there were 114,200 internet users in 2009
*Internet code and IDD* – fj; 679 (from UK), 44 (to UK)
*Major broadcasters* – There are two main television networks: national Fiji TV Ltd and the commercial Mai TV; Fiji Broadcasting Corporation is the state-owned radio broadcaster
*Press* – Daily newspapers include the *Fiji Times* (English language), *Sartaj* and *Shanti Dut* (Hindi)
*WPFI score* – 31,28 (93)

# FINLAND

*Suomen tasavalta / Republiken Finland – Republic of Finland*

*Area* – 338,145 sq. km
*Capital* – Helsinki (Helsingfors); population, 1,170,000 (2014)
*Major cities* – Espoo (Esbo), Oulu (Uleaborg), Tampere (Tammerfors), Turku (Aabo), Vantaa (Vanda)
*Currency* – Euro (€) of 100 cents
*Population* – 5,476,922 rising at 0.4 per cent a year (2015 est); Finnish (93.4 per cent), Swedish (5.6 per cent), Sami (0.1 per cent) (2006)
*Religion* – Christian (Lutheran 79 per cent, Orthodox 1 per cent), none 19 per cent
*Language* – Finnish, Swedish (both official)
*Population density* – 18 per sq. km (2013)
*Urban population* – 83.9 per cent (2013)
*Median age (years)* – 43.2 (2014 est)
*National anthem* – 'Maamme' / 'Vart Land' ['Our Land']
*National day* – 6 December (Independence Day)
*Death penalty* – Abolished for all crimes (since 1972)
*CPI score* – 89 (3)

## CLIMATE AND TERRAIN

Much of the centre of the country is a glaciated plateau of forests and lakes, with low hills along the eastern border with Russia and in the far north. Forests cover around 70 per cent of the country, including those of the coastal peatlands in the south-west. There are over 60,000 lakes, with an average depth of 7m. Elevation extremes range from 1,328m (Haltiatunturi, or Halti) to 0m (Baltic Sea). A quarter of the country lies north of the Arctic Circle; temperatures there can range from −9.4°C in February to 15.6°C in July. Average temperatures in Helsinki range from −6°C in February to 16°C in July.

Owing to isostatic uplift (the rise of land mass no longer depressed by the weight of glaciers), the surface area of Finland is growing by around 7 sq. km a year.

## HISTORY AND POLITICS

Finland was part of the Swedish Empire from the 12th century until it was ceded to Russia in 1809, when it became an autonomous grand duchy of the Russian Empire. After the Russian Revolution in 1917, Finland declared its independence. An attempted coup by Finnish Bolsheviks led to a short civil war that ended in their defeat in 1918, and in 1919 a republic was established. It resisted the 1939 invasion by the USSR but was defeated in 1940 and forced to cede territory; in the hope of recovering this territory it joined Germany's attack on the USSR in 1941. After agreeing an armistice with the USSR in 1944, Finland concluded a peace treaty in 1947 that conceded further territory to the USSR and obliged it to pay reparations. A Soviet-Finnish cooperation treaty in 1948 forced Finland

to demilitarise its Soviet border and to adopt a stance of neutrality; these terms lasted until the demise of the USSR in 1991.

Finland joined the EU in 1995 and the European Monetary Union in 1998.

In the 2015 legislative election, the Centre Party (KESK) emerged as the largest party, winning 49 of 200 parliamentary seats.

Under the 2000 constitution, the president is directly elected for a six-year term. There is a unicameral legislature, the *Eduskunta*, with 200 members directly elected for a four-year term. The prime minister is elected by the *Eduskunta* and appointed by the president.

HEAD OF STATE
*President*, Sauli Niinisto, *elected* 5 February 2012, *inaugurated* 1 March 2012

SELECTED GOVERNMENT MEMBERS *as at September 2015*
*Prime Minister*, Juha Sipila
*Deputy Prime Minister*, Timo Soini
*Defence*, Jussi Niinisto
*Finance*, Alexander Stubb
*Interior*, Petteri Orpo

EMBASSY OF FINLAND
38 Chesham Place, London SW1X 8HW
T 020-7838 6200 E sanomat.lon@formin.fi
W www.finemb.org.uk
*Ambassador Extraordinary and Plenipotentiary*, HE Pekka Huhtaniemi, *apptd* 2010

BRITISH EMBASSY
Itainen Puistotie 17, 00140 Helsinki
T (+358) (9) 2286 5100 E info.helsinki@fco.gov.uk
W www.gov.uk/government/world/finland
*Ambassador Extraordinary and Plenipotentiary*, HE Sarah Price, *apptd* 2014

## DEFENCE

| *Aged 16–49, 2010 est* | *Males* | *Females* |
| --- | --- | --- |
| Available for military service | 1,155,368 | 1,106,193 |
| Fit for military service | 955,151 | 912,983 |

*Military expenditure* – US$3,649m (2014)
*Conscription* – 18 years of age, male only; 6–12 months

## ECONOMY AND TRADE

The country has a highly industrialised market economy which has thrived as a result of its telecommunications and electronics industries, particularly the manufacture of mobile phones, as well as its traditional timber and metals industries. The economy entered recession in 2012, due to a lack of economic competitiveness, high wages and an ageing population. The economy is particularly vulnerable to fluctuations in trade with Russia, and has been harmed by the economic sanctions imposed on the country following the 2014 annexation of the Crimea. Modest growth of under 1 per cent is expected in 2015.

The main trade partners are Russia, Germany and Sweden. Principal exports are electrical and optical equipment, machinery, transport equipment, paper and pulp, chemicals, base metals and timber. The main imports are foodstuffs (especially grain), petroleum and petroleum products, chemicals, transport equipment, iron and steel, machinery, textile yarn and fabrics, and components for manufactured goods. Finland is a net importer of energy.

*GNI* – US$247,239m; US$48,820 per capita (2013)
*Annual average growth of GDP* – –0.2 per cent (2014 est)
*Inflation rate* – 1 per cent (2014 est)
*Unemployment* – 8.9 per cent (2015 est)
*Total external debt* – US$586,900m (2012)
*Imports* – US$77,579m (2013)
*Exports* – US$74,433m (2013)

BALANCE OF PAYMENTS
*Trade* – US$3,146m deficit (2013)
*Current Account* – US$623m deficit (2015 est)

| Trade with UK | 2013 | 2014 |
|---|---|---|
| Imports from UK | £1,507,011,142 | £1,598,007,678 |
| Exports to UK | £2,509,680,334 | £2,509,680,334 |

## COMMUNICATIONS
*Airports and waterways* – The principal airports are at Helsinki, Turku and Tampere; the main seaports are Helsinki, Kotka, Rauma and Turku
*Roadways and railways* – The 50,000km road network and 5,944km rail network are concentrated in the southern half of the country, where most of the population and industry are located
*Telecommunications* – 890,000 fixed lines and 9.32 million mobile telephone subscriptions (2012); there were 4.393 million internet users in 2009
*Internet code and IDD* – fi; 358 (from UK), 44 (to UK)
*Major broadcasters* – There are both commercial and state-owned broadcasters; the state broadcaster, Yleisradio Oy (YLE), is funded by licence fees and provides radio and television services in Swedish and Finnish, with radio in Sami (Lappish)
*Press* – Major publications include *Helsingin Sanomat* (Finnish), *Hufvudstadsbladet* (Swedish) and the English-language *Helsinki Times*
*WPFI score* – 7,52 (1)

## EDUCATION AND HEALTH
Basic education is free and compulsory for children from seven to 16 years.
*Gross enrolment ratio (percentage of relevant age group)* – primary 100 per cent; secondary 108 per cent; tertiary 94 per cent (2012 est)
*Health expenditure (per capita)* – US$4,449 (2013)
*Hospital beds (per 1,000 people)* – 5.5 (2011)
*Life expectancy (years)* – 79.69 (2014 est)
*Mortality rate* – 10.51 (2014 est)
*Birth rate* – 10.35 (2014 est)
*Infant mortality rate* – 3.36 (2014 est)

# FRANCE

*République française* – French Republic

*Area* – 551,500 sq. km (excluding overseas territories)
*Capital* – Paris; population, 10,764,000 (2014)
*Major cities* – Bordeaux, Lille, Lyon, Marseille, Montpellier, Nantes, Nice, Reims, Rennes, Strasbourg, Toulouse. The chief towns of Corsica are Ajaccio and Bastia
*Currency* – Euro (€) of 100 cents
*Population* – 66,553,766 (excluding overseas territories), rising at 0.43 per cent a year (2015 est)
*Religion* – Christian (Roman Catholic 83–88 per cent, Protestant 2 per cent), Muslim 5–10 per cent, Buddhist 1 per cent, Jewish 1 per cent (est)
*Language* – French (official)
*Population density* – 121 per sq. km (2013) (excluding overseas territories)
*Urban population* – 86.9 per cent (2013)
*Median age (years)* – 40.9 (2014 est)
*National anthem* – 'La Marseillaise' ['The Song of Marseille']
*National day* – 14 July (Fête de la Fédération/Fête Nationale)
*Death penalty* – Abolished for all crimes (since 1981)
*CPI score* – 69 (26)

## CLIMATE AND TERRAIN
The north and west consist of flat plains, particularly in the basins of the Somme, Seine, Loire and Garonne rivers, with some low hills. The centre of the south is occupied by the Massif Central plateau, which is divided by the valley of the Rhone and Soane rivers from the mountains – the French Alps, the Jura and the Vosges – on the eastern border. The Pyrenees range lies along the southern border with Spain. Elevation extremes range from 4,807m (Mt Blanc, Alps) to –2m (Rhône delta). The climate is generally temperate, though the south has a Mediterranean climate and the east a continental climate.

## POLITICS
Under the 1958 constitution, the head of state is a president directly elected for a five-year term, which is renewable once. The legislature, the *Parlement,* consists of the National Assembly and the senate. The National Assembly has 577 deputies, 555 for metropolitan France and 22 for the overseas departments and territories; members are directly elected for a five-year term. The senate has been enlarged gradually over the past decade; since the September 2011 elections there are 348 senators (328 for metropolitan France and the overseas departments, eight for overseas collectivities and territories, and 12 for French nationals abroad) elected by an electoral college to serve a six-year term, with half elected every three years.

The prime minister is nominated by the National Assembly and appointed by the president, as is the council of ministers. They are responsible to the legislature, but as the executive is constitutionally separate from the legislature, ministers may not sit in the legislature and must hand over their seats to a substitute.

The constitution was amended in 2003 to pave the way for the devolution to the 22 metropolitan regions and 96 metropolitan departments of powers over economic development, transport, tourism, culture and further education.

The 2012 presidential election was won in the second round by Socialist Party (PS) candidate François Hollande. In the 2012 legislative elections, the Socialist Party won an overall majority, defeating Nicolas Sarkozy's Union for a Popular Movement party by 86 seats. Following poor local election results for the PS, Manuel Valls replaced Jean-Marc Ayrault as prime minister on 1 April 2014 and instigated a major cabinet reshuffle.

| Remains province of Gaul until Frankish invasion | Civil war hinders attempt to establish European power | Republic declared; King Louis XVI executed | Second Republic declared after the congress of Vienna briefly restores monarchy | Third Republic declared | North occupied by Germany during the Second World War, with a pro-German government in the south | Joins European Monetary Union |
|---|---|---|---|---|---|---|

c.100 AD    843    1789    1804–14    1852    1914–18    1946–62    2005–8

c.500–600    1562–98    1792    1848    1870–1    1940–4    1999

| Conquered by the Romans | *Francia Occidentalis* becomes the basis of modern France | *Ancien régime* overthrown by French Revolution | Republic overthrown by Napoléon Bonaparte, who establishes the French Empire | Napoléon III declares second French Empire | Victorious in the First World War | Fourth Republic collapses in 1958; colonies granted independence | Population rejects EU constitution; country signs Lisbon Treaty |
|---|---|---|---|---|---|---|---|

## HEAD OF STATE
*President of the French Republic,* François Hollande, *elected* 6 May 2012

## SELECTED GOVERNMENT MEMBERS *as at May 2015*
*Prime Minister,* Manuel Valls
*Defence,* Jean-Yves Le Drian
*Finance,* Michel Sapin
*Foreign Affairs,* Laurent Fabius

## EMBASSY OF FRANCE
58 Knightsbridge, London SW1X 7JT
T 020-7073 1000 W www.ambafrance-uk.org
*Ambassador Extraordinary and Plenipotentiary,* HE Sylvie Bermann, *apptd* 2014

## BRITISH EMBASSY
35 rue du Faubourg St Honoré, 75383 Paris Cédex 08
T (+33) (1) 4451 3100 W www.gov.uk/government/world/france
*Ambassador Extraordinary and Plenipotentiary,* HE Sir Peter Ricketts, GCMG, GCVO, *apptd* 2012

## INSURGENCIES
Corsican separatists have pursued a campaign of bombings and shootings since the 1970s apart from a ceasefire in 2003–5 observed by the main separatist faction. The French government's proposals to combine the island's two departments and to give the Corsican regional parliament greater autonomy were narrowly rejected in a 2003 referendum.

## DEFENCE

| *Aged 16–49, 2010 est* | *Males* | *Females* |
|---|---|---|
| Available for military service | 14,563,662 | 14,238,434 |
| Fit for military service | 12,025,341 | 11,721,827 |

*Military expenditure* – US$62,289m (2014)

## ECONOMY AND TRADE
The economy is in transition from extensive government ownership and intervention to a more liberal and market-oriented form with many large, state-run companies becoming privatised; reform was initiated in response to poor economic growth and high unemployment. Implementation has been slow because of the constraints of eurozone membership, and strong resistance to the government's plans for privatisation and reform of labour, pensions and welfare. Since 2014, François Hollande's government has looked to liberalise the economy by extending working hours, introducing spending cuts and reducing tax for higher earners.

Over one-third of the land area of metropolitan France is utilised for agricultural production and a further quarter is covered by forests. Viniculture is extensive, although France has lost market share to other countries in recent years. Cognac, liqueurs and cider are also produced. Other important agricultural products include cereals, sugar beet, potatoes, beef, dairy products and fish. Agriculture employs 2.9 per cent of the workforce and contributes 1.7 per cent of GDP.

Oil is produced from fields in the Landes area, but France is a net importer of crude oil, for processing by its oil-refining industry. Natural gas is produced in the foothills of the Pyrenees.

Industry contributes 19.4 per cent of GDP, employing 24.3 per cent of the workforce. The sector is highly diversified and includes the production of machinery, iron, steel, aluminium, chemicals, vehicles, aircraft, electronic goods, textiles and processed food. The service sector contributes 78.9 per cent of GDP and employs 71.8 per cent of the workforce. Tourism is an important contributor to GDP: France is the most-visited country in the world.

The main trading partners are other EU countries, especially Germany. Principal exports are machinery, vehicles, aircraft, plastics, chemicals, pharmaceutical products, iron and steel, and beverages. The main imports are raw materials for industry (eg crude oil, chemicals, plastics), machinery, vehicles and aircraft.

*GNI* – US$2,657,720m; US$43,460 per capita (2013)
*Annual average growth of GDP* – 0.4 per cent (2014 est)
*Inflation rate* – 0.5 per cent (2014 est)
*Population below poverty line* – 7.9 per cent (2011)
*Unemployment* – 10.8 per cent (2015 est)
*Total external debt* – US$5,371,000m (2012)
*Imports* – US$671,019m (2013)
*Exports* – US$567,840m (2013)

## BALANCE OF PAYMENTS
*Trade* – US$102,919m deficit (2013)
*Current Account* – US$2,679m deficit (2015 est)

| Trade with UK | 2013 | 2014 |
|---|---|---|
| Imports from UK | £22,391,925,688 | £19,684,017,626 |
| Exports to UK | £24,979,429,650 | £24,991,613,287 |

## COMMUNICATIONS
*Airports* – 294; there are two international airports serving Paris, and many regional airports capable of accepting international flights
*Waterways* – The principal seaports are Marseille on the Mediterranean Sea, Bordeaux and Nantes on the Atlantic coast, and Le Havre, Calais and Dunkirk on the Channel coast; there are 8,501km of navigable inland waterways, 1,621km navigable by large vessels, and Paris, Rouen and Strasbourg are significant river ports. The French mercantile marine consisted in 2011 of 162 ships of 1,000 gross tonnage or over, 151 of which are registered overseas
*Roadways and railways* – There are 1,028,446km of roadways, including 11,416km of motorways, and 29,640km of railways
*Telecommunications* – 39.29 million fixed lines and 62.28 million mobile subscriptions (2012); there were 44.63 million internet users in 2009
*Internet code and IDD* – fr; 33 (from UK), 44 (to UK)
*Major broadcasters* – TV5 is an international French-language television channel co-financed by Belgium, Canada, France and Switzerland. The main domestic channel, TF1, was privatised in 1987. A global news channel, France 24, was launched in 2006 and broadcasts in French, English and Arabic

*Press* – France has over 100 daily newspapers, including *Le Monde*, *Le Figaro* and *Libération*
*WPFI score* – 21,15 (38)

## EDUCATION AND HEALTH

Education is compulsory and free between the ages of six and 16. There are three types of *lycée* – *général, technique* and *professionel* – and each leads to its own *baccalauréat* qualification. Specialist schools are numerous.
*Gross enrolment ratio (percentage of relevant age group)* – primary 107 per cent; secondary 110 per cent; tertiary 58 per cent (2012 est)
*Health expenditure (per capita)* – US$4,864 (2013)
*Hospital beds (per 1,000 people)* – 6.4 (2011)
*Life expectancy (years)* – 81.66 (2014 est)
*Mortality rate* – 9.06 (2014 est)
*Birth rate* – 12.49 (2014 est)
*Infant mortality rate* – 3.31 (2014 est)

## OVERSEAS DEPARTMENTS/REGIONS

French Guiana, Guadeloupe, Martinique and Réunion have had departmental status since 1946. They were given regional status with greater powers of self-government and elected assemblies in 1982, and were redesignated as Overseas Regions in 2003. Their regional and departmental status is identical to that of regions and departments of metropolitan France, and they can choose to replace these with a single structure by merging their regional and departmental assemblies. The French government is represented by a *prefect* in each. In referendums in 2010, French Guiana and Martinique rejected proposals for granting greater autonomy to their local governments.

### FRENCH GUIANA

*Area* – 83,534 sq. km
*Capital* – Cayenne; population, 57,229 (2011 est)
*Population* – 250,109 (2013 est)

Situated on the north-eastern coast of South America, French Guiana is flanked by Suriname to the west and by Brazil to the south and east. Under the administration of French Guiana are the Îles du Salut group of islands (St Joseph, Île Royal and Île du Diable). The European Space Agency rocket launch site is situated at Kourou and accounts for 25 per cent of GDP. Fishing, forestry and mining are the main activities, and the economy is dependent on government subsidies. The main exports are timber, shrimp and gold. Tourism is restricted by the lack of infrastructure, as much of the interior is only accessible by river.
*Prefect*, Éric Spitz, *apptd* 2013

### GUADELOUPE

*Area* – 1,705 sq. km
*Capital* – Basse-Terre; population, 11,730 (2011 est), on Guadeloupe
*Population* – 405,739 (2013)

The Guadeloupe archipelago consists of a number of islands in the Leeward Islands group in the West Indies, including Guadeloupe (or Basse-Terre), Grande-Terre, Marie-Galante, La Désirade and the Îles des Saintes. The main towns are Les Abymes, Pointe-à-Pitre (Grande-Terre) and Grand Bourg (Marie-Galante). The main industries are tourism, agriculture, sugar refining and rum distilling. Bananas, sugar, rum and vanilla are the main exports.
*Prefect*, Jacques Billant, *apptd* 2014

### MARTINIQUE

*Area* – 1,100 sq. km
*Capital* – Fort-de-France; population, 86,753 (2011 est)
*Population* – 386,486 (2013)

An island in the Windward Islands group in the West Indies, Martinique lies between Dominica in the north and St Lucia in the south. It is dominated by Mt Pelée (1,397m), an active volcano that last erupted in 1902. Tourism is a major industry. The main exports are bananas, rum and petroleum products.
*Prefect*, Fabrice Rigoulet-Rozel, *apptd* 2011

### MAYOTTE

*Area* – 374 sq. km
*Capital* – Mamoudzou; population, 58,197 (2012 est)
*Population* – 217,091 (2012 est)

Part of the Comoros archipelago, Mayotte remained a French dependency when the other three islands became independent as the Comoros Republic in 1975. It became a *collectivité territoriale* in 1976, and an Overseas Department/Region in 2011. The main products are vanilla, ylang-ylang (perfume essence), coffee, copra, lobster and shrimp. The economy is dependent on French subsidies.
*Prefect*, Seymour Morsy, *apptd* 2013

### RÉUNION

*Area* – 2,507 sq. km
*Capital* – St-Denis; population, 201,366 (2012 est)
*Population* – 840,974 (2013 est)

A French possession since 1638, Réunion lies in the Indian Ocean, about 650km east of Madagascar and 180km south-west of Mauritius. The main industries are tourism and sugar, and rum production.
*Prefect*, Dominique Sorain, *apptd* 2012

## TERRITORIAL COLLECTIVITIES

Overseas *collectivités* are administrative divisions with a degree of autonomy but without the status of a similar administrative division in metropolitan France; each has its own laws and an elected assembly and president. The French government is represented by a *prefect* or high commissioner in each. Constitutional changes in 2003 redesignated most of the former overseas territories as *collectivités*; New Caledonia is treated in this category because this is its *de facto* status at present, but its official designation depends upon the outcome of independence referendums to be held between 2014 and 2018.

### FRENCH POLYNESIA

*Area* – 4,167 sq. km
*Capital* – Papeete, on Tahiti; population, 133,000 (2014 est)
*Population* – 280,026 rising at 0.97 per cent a year (2014 est)

French Polynesia consists of over 118 volcanic or coral islands and atolls in the South Pacific. There are five archipelagos: the Society Islands (Windward Islands group includes Tahiti, Moorea, Makatea, Mehetia, Tetiaroa, Tubuai Manu; Leeward Islands group includes Huahine, Raiatea, Tahaa, Bora-Bora, Maupiti); the Tuamotu Islands (Rangiroa, Hao, Turéia etc); the Gambier Islands (Mangareva etc); the Tubuai Islands (Rimatara, Rurutu, Tubuai, Raivavae, Rapa etc); and the Marquesas Islands (Nuku-Hiva, Hiva-Oa, Fatu-Hiva, Tahuata, Ua Huka etc). Some of the atolls were

used by France for testing nuclear weapons between 1966 and 1996. The main industries are tourism, pearl-farming, deep-sea fishing, coconut products and vanilla production.
*High Commissioner,* Lionel Beffre, *apptd* 2013

## NEW CALEDONIA
*Area* – 18,575 sq. km
*Capital* – Nouméa; population, 181,000 (2014 est)
*Population* – 267,840 rising at 1.42 per cent a year (2014 est)

New Caledonia is a large island in the western Pacific, 1,120km off the eastern coast of Australia. Its dependencies are the Isle of Pines, the Loyalty Islands (Mahé, Lifou, Urea, etc), the Bélep Archipelago, the Chesterfield Islands, the Huon Islands and Walpole. New Caledonia was discovered in 1774 and annexed by France in 1853. Agitation for independence from the 1980s ended with the Nouméa accord in 1998, under which an increasing degree of autonomy will be transferred to the territory up to 2018, with a referendum on independence to be held between 2015 and 2018. The territory is divided into three provinces, each with a provincial assembly; these combine to form the territorial assembly.

A quarter of the world's nickel deposits are found in the territory, and nickel mining and smelting are the main industries, along with tourism and fishing. Ferronickel, nickel ore and fish are the main exports. About 20 per cent of food has to be imported.
*High Commissioner,* Vincent Bouvier, *apptd* 2014

## ST BARTHÉLEMY
*Area* – 21 sq. km
*Capital* – Gustavia
*Population* – 7,267 (2014 est)

The island lies in the Caribbean Sea about 240km north-west of Guadeloupe. It was settled by the French from 1648. France sold the island to Sweden in 1784 but bought it back again in 1878 and it was under the administration of Guadeloupe until 2007, when it became a *collectivité territoriale*. The economy is based on luxury tourism and duty-free commerce in luxury goods. Freshwater sources are limited, so all food and energy and most manufactured goods are imported.
*Prefect,* Philippe Chopin, *apptd* 2011

## ST MARTIN
*Area* – 54.4 sq. km
*Capital* – Marigot
*Population* – 31,530 (2014 est)

The territory occupies the northern part of the island of St Martin, 250km to the north-west of Guadeloupe; the southern part (Sint Maarten) is a territory of the Netherlands. The island was claimed for Spain by Columbus in 1493 but the Spanish relinquished it in 1648 to the Dutch and French, who divided the island between them. The French part was administered from Guadeloupe until it was made a *collectivité territoriale* in 2007. The economy is dependent on tourism, which employs 85 per cent of the workforce. Nearly all food, energy and manufactured goods are imported.
*Prefect,* Philippe Chopin, *apptd* 2011

## ST PIERRE AND MIQUELON
*Area* – 242 sq. km
*Capital* – St-Pierre; population, 5,000 (2014 est)
*Population* – 5,716 falling at 1.02 per cent a year (2014 est)

These two small groups of eight islands off the south coast of Newfoundland became a *collectivité territoriale* in 1985. The main industry of fishing and servicing fishing fleets has declined in step with the decline in cod stocks, and fish farming, crab fishing and agriculture are being developed. Tourism is of growing importance, but the economy is dependent on government subsidies.
*Prefect,* Jean-Christophe Bouvier, *apptd* 2014

## WALLIS AND FUTUNA ISLANDS
*Area* – 142 sq. km
*Capital* – Mata-Utu, on Uvea, the main island of the Wallis group; population, 1,000 (2014 est)
*Population* – 15,561 rising at 0.33 per cent a year (2014 est)

The two groups of islands (the Wallis Archipelago and the Îles de Horne) lie in the South Pacific, north-east of Fiji. They became a French protectorate from the 1840s and were administered from New Caledonia until 1961. The main products are copra, vegetables, bananas, livestock products, fish and timber.
*Administrator,* Michel Jeanjean, *apptd* 2010

## OVERSEAS TERRITORIES

### TERRITORY OF THE FRENCH SOUTHERN AND ANTARCTIC LANDS
Created in 1955 from former Réunion dependencies, the territory comprises the islands of Amsterdam (55 sq. km) and St Paul (7 sq. km), the Kerguelen Islands (7,215 sq. km) and Crozet Islands (352 sq. km) archipelagos, Adélie Land (about 500,000 sq. km) in the Antarctic continent and, since 2007, the islands of Bassas da India (80 sq. km), Europa (28 sq. km), les Glorieuses (5 sq. km), Juan de Nova (4.4 sq. km) and Tromelin (1 sq. km). The population consists only of staff of the meteorological and scientific research stations.
*Administrator,* Cécile Pozzo Di Borgo, *apptd* 2012

### THE FRENCH COMMUNITY OF STATES
The 1958 constitution envisaged the establishment of a French Community of States. A number of former French colonies in Africa have seceded from the community but for all practical purposes continue to enjoy the same close links with France as do those that remain formal members. Most former French African colonies are closely linked to France by financial, technical and economic agreements.

## GABON

*République Gabonaise – Gabonese Republic*

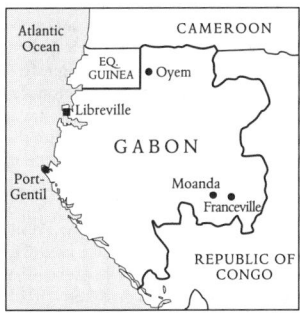

*Area* – 267,667 sq. km
*Capital* – Libreville; population, 695,000 (2014)

*Major towns* – Franceville (Masuku), Moanda, Oyem, Port-Gentil
*Currency* – Central African CFA franc of 100 centimes
*Population* – 1,705,336 rising at 1.93 per cent a year (2015 est); over 40 predominantly Bantu tribes, of which the Bapounou, Fang, Nzebi and Obamba are the largest tribal groupings
*Religion* – Christian 55–75 per cent, Muslim less than 1 per cent; many people combine elements of Christian and indigenous beliefs
*Language* – French (official), Fang, Myene, Nzebi, Bapounou, Bandjabi
*Population density* – 6 per sq. km (2013)
*Urban population* – 86.9 per cent (2013)
*Median age (years)* – 18.6 (2014 est)
*National anthem* – 'La Concorde' ['The Concord']
*National day* – 17 August (Independence Day)
*Death penalty* – Abolished for all crimes (since 2010)
*CPI score* – 37 (94)
*Literacy rate* – 89.1 per cent (2015 est)
*Health expenditure (per capita)* – US$441 (2013)
*Hospital beds (per 1,000 people)* – 6.3 (2010)
*Life expectancy (years)* – 52.06 (2014 est)
*Mortality rate* – 13.13 (2014 est)
*Birth rate* – 34.64 (2014 est)
*Infant mortality rate* – 47.03 (2014 est)
*HIV/AIDS adult prevalence* – 0.3 per cent (2013)

## CLIMATE AND TERRAIN

The country lies on the equator. It rises from a narrow coastal plain to a hilly interior; approximately 85 per cent of the land is rainforest, with savannah in the east and south, although by 2006 as much as half of the country's forest was being leased for timber. In 2002, 10 per cent of the country was designated as national park. Elevation extremes range from 1,575m (Mt Iboundji) to 0m (Atlantic Ocean). The climate is tropical, with an average temperature of 25.2°C. There are two wet seasons each year, from January to June and September to December.

## HISTORY AND POLITICS

The first Europeans to visit the region were the Portuguese in the 15th century; Dutch, French and English traders arrived soon after. Sovereignty was signed over to the French in 1839 by a local Mpongwe ruler. In 1849, slaves freed by the French formed a settlement which they called Libreville, now the capital. The country was occupied by the French in 1885 and became part of French Equatorial Africa in 1910. Gabon became autonomous within the French Community in 1958 and gained independence on 17 August 1960.

Omar Bongo succeeded to the presidency in 1967 after the death of the first president, and in 1968 he established a one-party state with the *Parti Démocratique Gabonais* (PDG) as the only party. By the late 1980s, the deteriorating economy was provoking unrest and demands for greater democracy, and in 1991 a multiparty system was reintroduced.

Under the multiparty system, the PDG has remained in power (amid allegations of electoral fraud) although it has included opposition party members in coalition governments since 1994. The PDG and its coalition partners retained the majority in the 2011 legislative election, which was boycotted by the main opposition party. President Bongo was re-elected for a sixth term of office in 2005; he died in June 2009, and was succeeded by his son, Ali-Ben Bongo, who was elected president in August 2009 amid allegations of vote-rigging. In January 2014 Daniel Ona Ondo replaced Raymond Ndong Sima as prime minister, with Sima having been in office since February 2012.

The 1991 constitution, amended in 1995, 1997 and 2003, provides for a president who is directly elected for a seven-year term; since 2003, there has been no limit on the number of terms a president may serve. The president appoints the prime minister, who then appoints the council of ministers. There is a bicameral *Parlement*, comprising the 120-member National Assembly (111 directly elected and nine appointed by the president, all for a five-year term) and the senate, which has 102 members elected for a six-year term by municipal and regional councillors.

HEAD OF STATE
*President*, Ali-Ben Bongo, *elected* 30 August 2009, *sworn in* 16 October 2009

SELECTED GOVERNMENT MEMBERS *as at May 2015*
*Prime Minister*, Daniel Ona Ondo
*Defence*, Ernest Mpouho Epigat
*Economy*, Regis Immongault Tatagani
*Foreign Affairs*, Emmanuel Issozet Ngondet
*Interior*, Guy-Bertrand Mapangou

EMBASSY OF THE GABONESE REPUBLIC
27 Elvaston Place, London SW7 5NL
T 020-7823 9986
*Ambassador Extraordinary and Plenipotentiary*, vacant

BRITISH HIGH COMMISSION
HE Brian Olley, *apptd* 2013, resident at Yaoundé, Cameroon

## DEFENCE

| Aged 16–49, 2010 est | Males | Females |
| --- | --- | --- |
| Available for military service | 350,640 | 351,718 |
| Fit for military service | 202,404 | 195,389 |

*Military expenditure* – US$254m (2013)

## ECONOMY AND TRADE

Gabon is one of the most prosperous countries in Africa, largely owing to its small population and abundance of oil and mineral resources. The economy is heavily dependent on oil (which contributes over 50 per cent of GDP) and other mineral resources, including manganese and uranium, and timber, but the government is investing in diversification to reduce vulnerability to fluctuating commodity prices and the gradual decline in oil production as reserves become exhausted. Despite the country's wealth, a large proportion of the population remains poor, and weak fiscal management has resulted in a high foreign debt which has had to be rescheduled several times. GDP growth is expected to accelerate to 7.2 per cent in 2015.

Industry contributes 61.7 per cent of GDP and employs 15 per cent of the workforce, mainly in oil and mineral extraction, oil refining, chemicals, ship repair, textiles, and processing agricultural and forestry products. Agriculture is largely at subsistence level, employing 60 per cent of the workforce but contributing only 3.7 per cent of GDP. It is restricted by the forest cover and lack of suitable land. The main products include cocoa, coffee, sugar, palm oil, rubber, cattle, timber and fish.

The main trading partners are France, Japan, the USA and China. Principal exports are crude oil (70 per cent), timber, manganese and uranium. The main imports are machinery and equipment, food, chemicals and construction materials.
*GNI* – US$16,428m; US$10,650 per capita (2013)
*Annual average growth of GDP* – 5.1 per cent (2014 est)
*Inflation rate* – 0.5 per cent (2013 est)

*Unemployment* – 17.6 per cent (2015 est)
*Total external debt* – US$3,741m (2014 est)
*Imports* – US$3,886m (2013)
*Exports* – US$9,514m (2013)

BALANCE OF PAYMENTS
*Trade* – US$5,628m surplus (2013)
*Current Account* – US$352m surplus (2015 est)

| *Trade with UK* | *2013* | *2014* |
| --- | --- | --- |
| Imports from UK | £59,624,588 | £51,002,536 |
| Exports to UK | £82,028,156 | £111,708,304 |

COMMUNICATIONS
*Airports and waterways* – 14, including international airports in Libreville and Port-Gentil; there are 1,600km of navigable waterways and the principal seaport is in Port-Gentil
*Roadways and railways* – 1,097km; 649km
*Telecommunications* – 17,000 fixed lines and 2.93 million mobile subscriptions (2012); there were 98,800 internet users in 2009
*Internet code and IDD* – ga; 241 (from UK), 44 (to UK)
*Broadcasters* – The state-controlled broadcaster, Radiodiffusion-Télévision Gabonaise, operates two television channels and two radio networks; Africa No. 1, a pan-African radio broadcaster, is based in Gabon
*Press* – The only two daily newspapers, *L'Union* and *Gabon Matin*, are operated by the government
*WPFI score* – 31.38 (95)

# THE GAMBIA

*Republic of The Gambia*

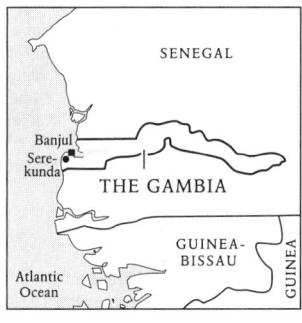

*Area* – 11,295 sq. km
*Capital* – Banjul; population, 489,000 (2014)
*Major towns* – Bakau, Brikama, Farafenni, Serekunda
*Currency* – Dalasi (D) of 100 butut
*Population* – 1,967,709 rising at 2.16 per cent a year (2015 est); Mandinka (42 per cent), Fulani (18 per cent), Wolof (16 per cent), Jola (10 per cent), Serahuli (Soninke) (9 per cent) (2003)
*Religion* – Sunni Muslim 90 per cent (majority Malikite Sufi), Christian 8 per cent (predominantly Roman Catholic), animist 2 per cent (est)
*Language* – English (official), Mandinka, Wolof, Fula
*Population density* – 183 per sq. km (2013)
*Urban population* – 58.4 per cent (2013)
*Median age (years)* – 20.2 (2014 est)
*National anthem* – 'For The Gambia, Our Homeland'
*National day* – 18 February (Independence Day)
*Death penalty* – Retained
*CPI score* – 29 (126)

CLIMATE AND TERRAIN
The Gambia consists of a narrow strip of land along the river Gambia, mostly comprising the basin and flood plain of the river, flanked by savannah and low hills. Elevation extremes range from 53m to 0m (Atlantic Ocean). The climate is tropical, with a wet season from June to November.

HISTORY AND POLITICS
The Gambia river basin was part of an area dominated from the 10th to 16th centuries by the Mali and Songhai kingdoms. The Portuguese reached the river Gambia in 1447 and established trading posts along the river. In 1816 a British garrison was stationed on an island at the river mouth; this became the capital of a small British colony, and a crown colony in 1843. The boundaries of the country were agreed by France and Britain in 1889; British territory would extend 10km from the upper river on either bank. The Gambia became independent on 18 February 1965 and a republic in 1970. The country withdrew from the Commonwealth in 2013, describing the organisation as 'neo-colonialist'.

The post-independence prime minister, Sir Dawda Jawara, was president from 1970 until 1994, when he was overthrown in a military coup. The coup leader, Lt. (later Col.) Yahya Jammeh, assumed the presidency and a civilian-military government was formed to govern in conjunction with the ruling military council. Civilian government was restored after elections in 1996 and 1997 following the approval of a new constitution. Jammeh was elected president and his Alliance for Patriotic Reorientation and Construction (APRC) won an overall majority of the legislative seats. Jammeh and the APRC have won all subsequent elections; the opposition and media are subject to harassment and detention without charge.

In the 2011 presidential election, Jammeh was re-elected with 71 per cent of the vote. The 2012 legislative election was won by the APRC, with 43 of the 48 elected seats. In December 2014, a military coup organised to depose President Jammeh while he was out of the country was defeated (*see* Events).

Under the 1997 constitution, the executive president is directly elected for a five-year term; there is no limit on re-election. The unicameral National Assembly has 53 members, of whom 48 are directly elected and five are appointed by the president, for a five-year term.

HEAD OF STATE
*President, Defence, Agriculture,* Col. Yahya Jammeh, *took power* July 1994, *elected* September 1996, *re-elected* 2001, 2006, 2012
*Vice-President, Women's Affairs,* Isatou Njie-Saidy

SELECTED GOVERNMENT MEMBERS *as at May 2015*
*Finance and Economic Affairs,* Abdou Kolley
*Foreign Affairs,* Neneh MacDouall-Gaye
*Interior,* Ousman Sonko
*Justice, Attorney-General,* Mama Fatima Singhateh

EMBASSY OF THE GAMBIA
92 Ledbury Road, London W11 2AH
T 020-7229 8066 E info@gambiaembassy.org.uk
W www.gambiaembassy.org.uk
*Ambassador Extraordinary and Plenipotentiary,* HE Elizabeth Ya Eli Harding, *apptd* 2013

BRITISH EMBASSY
PO Box 507, 48 Atlantic Road, Fajara, Banjul
T (+220) 449 5133 E ukinthegambia@fco.gov.uk
W www.gov.uk/government/world/gambia
*Ambassador Extraordinary and Plenipotentiary,* HE Colin Crorkin MBE, *apptd* 2014

## DEFENCE

| Aged 16–49, 2010 est | Males | Females |
|---|---|---|
| Available for military service | 423,306 | 438,641 |
| Fit for military service | 315,176 | 347,017 |

*Military expenditure* – US$14.1m (2014 )

## ECONOMY AND TRADE

The country has limited natural resources and agricultural land. Historically, the mainstay of the economy was re-export trade with neighbouring countries, but this has declined since the late 1990s, owing to the vagaries of government policies and trade and transport disputes with Senegal. There are high levels of public and foreign debt and the country is dependent on financial and technical aid from foreign donors. Remittances from Gambians working abroad and tourism are vital revenue sources. Increasing tourist numbers and a growing agricultural sector are expected to help the economy to grow by just under 7 per cent in 2015.

The services sector employs only 6 per cent of the workforce but contributes 59.5 per cent of GDP. About 75 per cent of the population is dependent on subsistence agriculture, which contributes 22.8 per cent of GDP. The chief product, peanuts, is also the main export and the basis of the main industrial activity, leaving the economy vulnerable to market fluctuations and the weather. Industry contributes 11.8 per cent to GDP, chiefly through processing peanuts, fish and hides, assembling agricultural machinery, metalworking, woodworking and the production of beverages and clothing.

The main trade partners are China, India, Brazil, EU countries and Senegal. Principal exports are peanut products, fish, cotton lint and palm kernels. The main imports are foodstuffs, manufactures, fuel, machinery and transport equipment.

*GNI* – US$874m; US$500 per capita (2013)
*Annual average growth of GDP* – 7.4 per cent (2013 est)
*Inflation rate* – 5.9 per cent (2014 est)
*Population below poverty line* – 48.4 per cent (2010 est)
*Unemployment* – 8.4 per cent (2015 est)
*Total external debt* – US$583.9m (2014 est)
*Imports* – US$351m (2013)
*Exports* – US$15m (2010)

BALANCE OF PAYMENTS
*Trade* – US$286m deficit (2010)
*Current Account* – US$92m deficit (2015 est)

| Trade with UK | 2013 | 2014 |
|---|---|---|
| Imports from UK | £29,481,129 | £20,208,767 |
| Exports to UK | £2,076,462 | £5,239,501 |

## COMMUNICATIONS

*Airports and waterways* – There is an international airport at Banjul; there are 390km of navigable waterways on the River Gambia
*Roadways* – 711km
*Telecommunications* – 64,200 fixed lines and 1.526 million mobile subscriptions (2012); there were 130,100 internet users in 2009
*Internet code and IDD* – gm; 220 (from UK), 44 (to UK)
*Major broadcasters* – Gambia Television (GRTS TV) and Radio Gambia are the state broadcasters; private television stations are banned while independent radio stations self-censor content
*Press* – Major publications include the *Daily Observer* and *The Standard; The Daily News* has been banned since 2012
*WPFI score* – 44,5 (151)

## EDUCATION AND HEALTH

Education is compulsory between the ages of seven and 12.
*Literacy rate* – 73.2 per cent (2015 est)
*Gross enrolment ratio (percentage of relevant age group)* – primary 85 per cent (2012 est); secondary 57 per cent (2010 est); tertiary 3 per cent (2011 est)
*Health expenditure (per capita)* – US$29 (2013)
*Hospital beds (per 1,000 people)* – 1.1 (2011)
*Life expectancy (years)* – 64.36 (2014 est)
*Mortality rate* – 7.26 (2014 est)
*Birth rate* – 31.75 (2014 est)
*Infant mortality rate* – 65.74 (2014 est)
*HIV/AIDS adult prevalence* – 1.3 per cent (2012 est)

# GEORGIA

*Sak'art'velo* – Georgia

*Area* – 69,700 sq. km
*Capital* – Tbilisi; population, 1,150,000 (2014)
*Major cities* – Batumi, Kutaisi, Poti, Rustavi, Zugdidi
*Currency* – Lari of 100 tetri
*Population* – 4,931,226 falling at 0.08 per cent a year (2015 est); Georgian (83.8 per cent), Azeri (6.5 per cent), Armenian (5.7 per cent), Russian (1.5 per cent) (2002)
*Religion* – Christian 89 per cent (Orthodox 84 per cent, Armenian–Gregorian 4 per cent, Catholic 1 per cent), Muslim 10 per cent (est)
*Language* – Georgian (official), Russian, Armenian, Azeri, Abkhaz (official in Abkhazia)
*Population density* – 78 per sq. km (2013)
*Urban population* – 53 per cent (2013)
*Median age (years)* – 37.7 (2014 est)
*National anthem* – 'Tavisupleba' ['Freedom']
*National day* – 26 May (Independence Day, 1918)
*Death penalty* – Abolished for all crimes (since 1997)
*CPI score* – 52 (50)
*Literacy rate* – 100 per cent (2015 est)
*Gross enrolment ratio (percentage of relevant age group)* – primary 103 per cent; secondary 101 per cent; tertiary 33 per cent (2013 est)
*Health expenditure (per capita)* – US$350 (2013)
*Hospital beds (per 1,000 people)* – 2.6 (2012)
*Life expectancy (years)* – 75.72 (2014 est)
*Mortality rate* – 10.77 (2014 est)
*Birth rate* – 12.93 (2014 est)
*Infant mortality rate* – 16.68 (2014 est)

## CLIMATE AND TERRAIN

Georgia lies in the western part of the Caucasus region, on the eastern shore of the Black Sea. It is mountainous, with the Great Caucasus mountain range along the northern border with Russia, and the Lesser Caucasus in the south. These are divided by the Kolkhida lowland in the west and the Mtkvari (Kura) river basin in the east, between which

| Converted to Christianity | | Invaded by Moguls | Ottoman and Persian empires compete for influence | | Russia invades; Georgia joins USSR as part of the Transcaucasian Soviet Socialist Republic | | Communist Party's monopoly on power abolished | Declares independence from USSR | Leaves COIS to join the EU-initiated Eastern Partnership |
| c.100 | | c.1000 | | 1801–4 | 1917 | | 1936 | | 1992–3 |
| | c.400 | | 1236 | 1500–1700 | | 1921–2 | | 1990 | 1991 | 2009 |
| Kingdom of Georgia comes under Roman influence | Independence established following domination by Persian, Arabs and Turks | | | Absorbed into Russian Empire | Independent nationalist government comes to power | | Country becomes separate republic | Authoritarian president Zviad Gamsakhurdia overthrown; an uprising forces the country to join Commonwealth of Independent States (COIS) |

runs the valley of the Mtkvari river. Elevation extremes range from 5,201m (Mt Shkhara) to 0m (Black Sea). The climate is almost tropical in summer, while cold winters affect both the mountains and valleys. Average temperatures range from −6.4°C in January to 18.6°C in August.

## POLITICS
The 1995 constitution provides for a federal republic with a unicameral legislature, to become bicameral 'following the creation of appropriate conditions'. It was amended in 2010 to transfer some of the president's powers to the legislature and prime minister. The president is directly elected for a five-year term, renewable once. The unicameral parliament has 150 members, 75 elected in single-member constituencies and 75 by proportional representation, who serve for a five-year term.

In November 2013, Irakli Garibashvili of the Georgian Dream party replaced Bidzina Ivanishvili as the country's prime minister, becoming the world's youngest elected leader at the time, aged 31. The October 2013 presidential election was won by ally Giorgi Margvelashvili, marking an end to a decade in power for outgoing president Mikheil Saakashvili.

## HEAD OF STATE
*President*, Giorgi Margvelashvili, *sworn in* 17 November 2014

## SELECTED GOVERNMENT MEMBERS *as at May 2015*
*Prime Minister*, Irakli Garibashvili
*Vice-Prime Ministers*, Giorgi Kvirikashvili *(Economy)*; Kakha Kaladze *(Energy)*
*Defence*, Mindia Janelidze
*Finance*, Nodar Khaduri

## EMBASSY OF GEORGIA
4 Russell Gardens, London W14 8EZ
T 020-7348 1941 E embassy@geoemb.plus.com
W www.uk.mfa.gov.ge
*Ambassador Extraordinary and Plenipotentiary*, HE Dr Revaz Gachechiladze, *apptd* 2014

## BRITISH EMBASSY
51 Krtsanisi Street, 0144 Tbilisi
T (+995) (32) 227 47 47 E british.embassy.tbilisi@fco.gov.uk
W www.gov.uk/government/world/georgia
*Ambassador Extraordinary and Plenipotentiary*, HE Alexandra Hall Hall, *apptd* 2013

## SECESSION
Fears that Georgian independence would deprive them of their own autonomy led to unilateral declarations of independence by the central region of South Ossetia (1991) and the north-western region of Abkhazia (1992) followed by a year of conflict in both separatist areas. In August 2008, clashes between Georgian troops and South Ossetian separatists escalated into a brief war between Georgia and Russia, in which Georgian forces were expelled from South Ossetia and Abkhazia. Russia has not fully complied with an EU-brokered ceasefire, maintaining a military presence in the areas and a 'buffer zone' around them; only Russia, Venezuela, Nicaragua and Nauru recognise their unilateral declarations of independence. Russia signed integration treaties with Abkhazia in 2014 and South Ossetia in 2015, paving the way for greater Russian involvement in the breakaway regions.

Relations between Georgia and Ajaria, a semi-autonomous region in the south-west and a key trade hub, deteriorated briefly in 2004 when Aslan Abashidze, Ajaria's leader since 1991, refused to recognise the authority of the newly elected President Saakashvili, and accused Georgia of planning to invade Ajaria. Public demonstrations against Abashidze forced him to resign. The Georgian parliament granted the Ajarian assembly powers over local affairs but the Georgian president retains the power to nominate the region's head of government and to dissolve its government and assembly.

## DEFENCE

| *Aged 16–49, 2010 est* | *Males* | *Females* |
| --- | --- | --- |
| Available for military service | 1,080,840 | 1,122,031 |
| Fit for military service | 893,003 | 931,683 |

*Military expenditure* – US$388m (2014 est)
*Conscription* – 18–34 years of age; 18 months

## ECONOMY AND TRADE
The economy grew rapidly from 2003, making good progress towards recovery following the near-collapse of the 1990s. Reform of the tax system nearly quadrupled government revenue, while added impetus in privatisation and anti-corruption programmes attracted foreign investment. However, the economy slowed in 2008 following the war with Russia and contracted in 2009 as the global economic downturn affected the regional economy and led to a decline in foreign investment and expatriates' remittances. The fuel crises in 2005–6 prompted the renovation of hydroelectric power plants and the repair of a pipeline from Azerbaijan; the country now meets the majority of its energy needs. In 2014, Georgia signed an association agreement with the EU which provided Georgian firms with greater access to European markets. Future economic growth is predicted to be depressed by the poorly performing Russian economy, which has reduced the value of remittances from expatriates.

Agriculture employs 55.6 per cent of the workforce and generates 9.1 per cent of GDP, with a concentration on grapes for winemaking, tea, citrus fruits and hazelnuts. Industry, which contributes 21.8 per cent of GDP, produces steel, aircraft, machine tools, electrical appliances, manganese, copper, chemicals, wood products and wine.

The main trading partners are Turkey, Azerbaijan and Armenia. Principal exports are scrap metal, wine, mineral water, mineral ores, vehicles, fruit and nuts. The main imports are fuels, vehicles, machinery and parts, food (especially grain) and pharmaceuticals.
*GNI* – US$15,641m; US$3,570 per capita (2013)
*Annual average growth of GDP* – 5 per cent (2014 est)

*Inflation rate* – 3.1 per cent (2014 est)
*Population below poverty line* – 14.8 per cent (2012)
*Unemployment* – 13.2 per cent (2015 est)
*Total external debt* – US$12,300m (2014 est)
*Imports* – US$7,885m (2013)
*Exports* – US$2,909m (2013)

BALANCE OF PAYMENTS
*Trade* – US$4,965m deficit (2013)
*Current Account* – US$1,579m deficit (2015 est)

| Trade with UK | 2013 | 2014 |
|---|---|---|
| Imports from UK | £47,278,641 | £57,786,731 |
| Exports to UK | £34,199,387 | £9,357,306 |

## COMMUNICATIONS
*Airports* – 18, including an international terminal in Tbilisi
*Roadways and railways* – 19,109km, including 69km of motorways; 1,612km
*Telecommunications* – 1.276 million fixed lines and 4.7 million mobile subscriptions (2012); there were 1.3 million internet users in 2009
*Internet code and IDD* – ge; 995 (from UK), 810 44 with no extra zeros (to UK)
*Major broadcasters* – Government-funded Georgian Public Broadcasting provides two television and two radio networks, alongside a host of private cable operators and major commercial stations
*Press* – Daily titles include *Sakartvelos Respublika*, *Rezonansi* and *24 Saati*
*WPFI score* – 27.7 (69)

## GERMANY

*Bundesrepublik Deutschland – Federal Republic of Germany*

*Area* – 357,022 sq. km
*Capital* – Berlin; population, 3,547,000 (2014)
*Major cities* – Bremen, Cologne, Dortmund, Dresden, Düsseldorf, Essen, Frankfurt, Hamburg, Hannover, Leipzig, Munich, Nuremberg, Stuttgart
*Currency* – Euro (€) of 100 cents

*Population* – 80,854,408 falling at 0.17 per cent a year (2015 est); German (91.5 per cent), Turkish (2.4 per cent) (est)
*Religion* – Protestant 34 per cent, Roman Catholic 34 per cent, Muslim 4 per cent, unaffiliated or other 29 per cent
*Language* – German (official)
*Population density* – 231 per sq. km (2013)
*Urban population* – 74.2 per cent (2013)
*Median age (years)* – 46.1 (2014 est)
*National anthem* – 'Das Deutschlandlied' ['The Song of Germany']
*National day* – 3 October (Unity Day)
*Death penalty* – Abolished for all crimes (since 1949 in FRG and 1987 in GDR)
*CPI score* – 79 (12)

## CLIMATE AND TERRAIN
The north of the country is low-lying, rising in the centre to uplands and Alpine foothills, then to the Bavarian Alps in the south. Elevation extremes range from 2,963m (Zugspitze, Bavaria) to −3.54m (Neuendorf bei Wilster). The Rhine, Weser and Elbe rivers flow from the south to the North Sea, the Oder and Neisse rivers flow north to the Baltic Sea, and the Danube flows east from its source in the south of the country to the Austrian border. Nearly a third of the land is covered by forest or woodland. The climate is temperate, with average temperatures ranging from 0.9°C in January to 18.2°C in July.

## POLITICS
The Basic Law was adopted in 1949 as the constitution of West Germany; at unification in 1990, Berlin and the five reformed *Länder* (states) of East Germany acceded to the Federal Republic. The president is elected for a five-year term by the *Bundesversammlung*, an electoral college comprising the members of the *Bundestag* (*see* below) and an equal number of representatives elected by the state legislatures. The bicameral legislature comprises a lower house, the Federal Assembly *(Bundestag)*, with 631 members elected by a mixed constituency and proportional representation system for a four-year term. The Federal Council *(Bundesrat)* has 69 members appointed by the governments of the *Länder* in proportion to their populations; their term of office is determined by their *Land's* constitution. The head of government is the chancellor, who is proposed by the president and elected by the *Bundestag*.

Angela Merkel, leader of the Christian Democratic Union of Germany and the Christian Social Union of Bavaria (CDU/CSU), became Germany's first female chancellor in 2005 at the head of a CDU/CSU and Social Democratic Party (SPD), governing without the latter following re-election in 2009. In 2013 the CDU again formed a 'grand coalition' with the SPD after the CDU fell five seats short of claiming a historic majority in the *Bundestag* with 41.5 per cent of the vote. Independent candidate Joachim Gauck won the 2012 presidential election, picking up 991 votes; he replaced Christian Wulf following the president's resignation amid allegations of corruption.

| German Confederation replaces Holy Roman Empire | Second German Empire formed; King of Prussia proclaimed emperor | World economic crisis precipitates the rise of the National Socialist movement led by Adolf Hitler | Germany invades Poland, beginning the Second World War | Communist GDR government collapses; Berlin declared capital of unified Germany | |
|---|---|---|---|---|---|
| 843 | 1866 | 1918 | 1933 | 1945 | 1999 |
| 1806 | 1871 | 1929 | 1939 | 1989-90 | |
| Treaty of Verdun establishes eastern part of Charlemagne's Frankish empire, the foundations of modern Germany | German Confederation dissolved, replaced by Prussian-dominated North German Federation | Abdication of Prussian emperor after defeat in First World War; Germany made a republic | Hitler becomes Chancellor | Germany surrenders to the Allied forces | Germany joins Eurozone |

HEAD OF STATE
*Federal President,* Joachim Gauck, *elected and sworn in*
23 March 2012

SELECTED GOVERNMENT MEMBERS *as at May 2015*
*Federal Chancellor,* Angela Merkel
*Defence,* Ursula von der Leyen
*Finance,* Wolfgang Schäuble
*Foreign Affairs,* Frank-Walter Steinmeier

EMBASSY OF THE FEDERAL REPUBLIC OF GERMANY
23 Belgrave Square, London SW1X 8PZ
T 020-7824 1300 W www.london.diplo.de
*Ambassador Extraordinary and Plenipotentiary,* HE Dr Peter
Ammon, *apptd* May 2014

BRITISH EMBASSY
Wilhelmstrasse 70/71, 10117 Berlin
T (+49) (30) 204 570 E ukingermany@fco.gov.uk
W www.gov.uk/government/world/germany
*Ambassador Extraordinary and Plenipotentiary,* HE Sir Simon
McDonald, KCMG, *apptd* 2010

FEDERAL STRUCTURE
Germany is a federal republic composed of 16 states *(Länder)*
(ten from the former Federal Republic of Germany (FRG),
five from the former German Democratic Republic (GDR),
and Berlin). Each *Land* has its own directly elected legislature
and government led by a minister-president (prime minister)
or equivalent. The 1949 Basic Law vests executive power
in the *Länder* governments except in those areas reserved for
the federal government.

| State *(Capital, where name differs)* | Population *(millions) (2011 est)* |
|---|---|
| Baden-Württemberg (Stuttgart) | 10.78 |
| Bavaria (Munich) | 12.50 |
| Berlin | 3.50 |
| Brandenburg (Potsdam) | 2.49 |
| Bremen | 0.60 |
| Hamburg | 1.79 |
| Hesse (Wiesbaden) | 6.00 |
| Lower Saxony (Hannover) | 7.90 |
| Mecklenburg-West Pomerania (Schwerin) | 1.60 |
| North Rhine-Westphalia (Düsseldorf) | 17.80 |
| Rhineland-Palitanate (Mainz) | 3.90 |
| Saarland (Saarbrücken) | 1.00 |
| Saxony (Dresden) | 4.10 |
| Saxony-Anhalt (Magdeburg) | 2.30 |
| Schleswig-Holstein (Kiel) | 2.80 |
| Thuringia (Erfurt) | 2.20 |

DEFENCE

| *Aged 16–49, 2010 est* | *Males* | *Females* |
|---|---|---|
| Available for military service | 18,529,299 | 17,888,543 |
| Fit for military service | 15,027,866 | 14,510,527 |

*Military expenditure* – US$46,455m (2014)

ECONOMY AND TRADE
Germany has the world's fifth largest economy and the
largest in Europe, but decades of strong economic
performance gave way in the 1990s to a severe recession,
largely an aftermath of reunification and of macroeconomic
stagnation. Although the economy as a whole began to grow
again in 2006, in the east it remains weak despite costly
modernisation and integration measures. However, the
revival was largely export-led and a decline in demand due to

the global economic downturn caused a recession in 2008–
9. The government's economic stimulus measures pushed the
budget deficit slightly beyond the eurozone's 3 per cent
threshold in 2010, although it remained at 1.7 per cent in
2011. The country achieved a budget surplus of 0.1 per cent
in 2012. While unemployment and government debt remains
low, the country suffers from a lack of internal investment.
The country is the world's third largest exporter and
Germany's reliance on exports means the economy has been
hampered by slowdowns in the eurozone, and Russian and
Chinese economies. Growth of under 2 per cent is expected
until 2019.

The country has a modern, diverse, highly industrialised
and technologically advanced market economy. The services
sector contributes 68.4 per cent of GDP, industry 30.8
per cent and agriculture 0.9 per cent. The industrial sector is
among the world's largest producers of iron, steel, coal,
cement, chemicals, machinery, vehicles, machine tools,
electronics, food and beverages, ships and textiles. Germany
depends on imports to meet its oil and natural gas needs, but
it remains a net exporter of electricity; in the wake of Japan's
Fukushima crisis in March 2011, the German government
revoked a decision to extend the life of the country's 17
nuclear power stations (which supply about 23 per cent of its
electricity). All stations are expected to close by 2022.

The main trading partners are the Netherlands, France,
the USA and China. Machinery, vehicles, chemicals, metals
and manufactures, foodstuffs and textiles are the principal
imports and exports.

*GNI* – US$3,509,989m; US$47,270 per capita (2013)
*Annual average growth of GDP* – 1.4 per cent (2014 est)
*Inflation rate* – 0.9 per cent (2013 est)
*Population below poverty line* – 15.5 per cent (2010 est)
*Unemployment* – 5.4 per cent (2015 est)
*Total external debt* – US$5,717,000m (2012 est)
*Imports* – US$1,192,751m (2013)
*Exports* – US$1,451,631m (2013)

BALANCE OF PAYMENTS
*Trade* – US$262,476m surplus (2013)
*Current Account* – US$286,778m surplus (2015 est)

| Trade with UK | 2013 | 2014 |
|---|---|---|
| Imports from UK | £30,672,802,617 | £31,573,030,419 |
| Exports to UK | £55,949,516,792 | £59,712,411,764 |

COMMUNICATIONS
*Airports* – 318; the busiest airport is at Frankfurt, other major
airports include Berlin, Munich and Bonn
*Waterways* – Around 20 per cent of domestic freight is
carried on 7,467km of inland waterways. The Rhine and the
Danube are linked by the Rhine–Maine–Danube (RMD)
canal, creating a through route from the North Sea to the
Black Sea. The Kiel canal links the North Sea and the Baltic
Sea. The main river ports are Duisburg, Frankfurt, Karlsruhe
and Mainz; the main seaports are Hamburg, Bremen,
Bremerhaven, Lübeck, Rostock and Wilhelmshaven
*Roadways and railways* – There is an extensive 645,000km
road network, including 12,800km of motorways; there are
41,981km of railways
*Telecommunications* – 50.7 million fixed lines and 107.7
million mobile subscriptions (2012); there were 65.13
million internet users in 2009
*Internet code and IDD* – de; 49 (from UK), 44 (to UK)
*Major broadcasters* – National and regional public television
competes with a large private sector, with about 90 per cent
of households having access to cable or satellite stations;
broadcasters include ARD (which operates Das Erste, the
main national public TV channel) and ZDF

*Press* – Major newspapers include *Frankfurter Allgemeine Zeitung, Süddeustche Zeitung* and *Die Welt*
*WPFI score* – 11,47 (12)

## EDUCATION AND HEALTH
Education is free and compulsory between the ages of six and 18.

The largest universities are in Munich, Berlin, Hamburg, Bonn, Frankfurt and Cologne. Germany's oldest university is Heidelberg, founded in 1386.

*Gross enrolment ratio (percentage of relevant age group)* – primary 100 per cent; secondary 101 per cent; tertiary 62 per cent (est 2012)
*Health expenditure (per capita)* – US$5,006 (2013)
*Hospital beds (per 1,000 people)* – 8.2 (2011)
*Life expectancy (years)* – 80.44 (2014 est)
*Mortality rate* – 11.29 (2014 est)
*Birth rate* – 8.42 (2014 est)
*Infant mortality rate* – 3.46 (2014 est)

# GHANA

*Republic of Ghana*

*Area* – 238,533 sq. km
*Capital* – Accra; population, 2,482,000 (2014)
*Major cities* – Kumasi, Sekondi-Takoradi, Tamale
*Currency* – Cedi (¢) of 100 pesewas
*Population* – 26,327,649 rising at 2.18 per cent a year (2015 est); Akan (47.5 per cent), Mole-Dagbon (16.6 per cent), Ewe (13.9 per cent), Ga-Dangme (7.4 per cent), Gurma (5.7 per cent), Guan (3.7 per cent), Grusi (2.5 per cent) (2010)
*Religion* – Christian 71 per cent, Muslim 18 per cent (predominantly Sunni), indigenous and other religions 11 per cent (est)
*Language* – English (official), Asante, Ewe, Fante, Boron, Dagomba, Dangme, Dagarte, Akyem, Ga, Akuapem
*Population density* – 114 per sq. km (2013)
*Urban population* – 53.2 per cent (2013)
*Median age (years)* – 20.8 (2014 est)
*National anthem* – 'God Bless Our Homeland Ghana'
*National day* – 6 March (Independence Day)
*Death penalty* – Retained (last used 1993)
*CPI score* – 48 (61)

## CLIMATE AND TERRAIN
Ghana consists mostly of plains dissected by the Volta river basin and the great central Lake Volta, rising to the Ashanti plateau in the west. There is dense rainforest in the south and west and forested hills in the north, with savannah in the east and far north. Elevation extremes range from 885m (Mt Afadjato) to 0m (Atlantic Ocean). The climate is tropical but with cooler temperatures on the south-east coast, and less rainfall in the south-east and north. Average temperatures range between 25.6°C in August and 29.94°C in March.

## HISTORY AND POLITICS
First reached by Europeans in the 15th century, after which it became a centre for gold and slave trading, the constituent parts of Ghana came under British administration at various times. The original Gold Coast colony was constituted in 1874 and Ashanti and the Northern Territories Protectorate in 1901. Trans-Volta-Togoland, part of the former German colony of Togo, was mandated to Britain by the League of Nations after the First World War and was integrated with the Gold Coast colony in 1956 following a plebiscite. The colony became independent as Ghana on 6 March 1957. It was proclaimed a republic in 1960.

Ghana became a one-party state in 1964 and from 1966 experienced long periods of military rule (1966–9, 1972–9, 1981–91) interspersed with short-lived civilian governments (1969–72, 1979–81). Flt. Lt. Jerry Rawlings, who had ousted the military regime in 1979 and deposed the civilian government in 1981, was elected president in 1992 when the country returned to multiparty politics after a referendum approved a new constitution.

Since the mid-1990s there have been intermittent clashes over land ownership between ethnic groups in the north; a state of emergency was in place there for two years after the last major outbreak of ethnic violence in 2002.

In the 2008 elections, John Atta Mills, the candidate of the National Democratic Congress (NDC), was elected president, and the NDC became the largest party in the legislature, winning half the seats. Vice-president John Dramani Mahama took over the presidency following the death of John Atta Mills in July 2012. In December 2012 Mahama was re-elected as president, and the NDC retained its majority in legislative elections. New presidential and legislative elections are scheduled for 2016.

Under the 1993 constitution, the executive president is directly elected for a four-year term, renewable once. The president appoints members of the council of ministers subject to approval by the legislature. The unicameral parliament has 230 members who are directly elected for a four-year term.

HEAD OF STATE
*President,* John Dramani Mahama, *apptd* 24 July 2012
*Vice-President,* Kwesis Amissah-Arthur

SELECTED GOVERNMENT MEMBERS *as at May 2015*
*Defence,* Benjamin Bewa-Nyog Kunbuor
*Finance,* Seth Terkper
*Foreign Affairs,* Hannah Tetteh
*Interior,* Mark Owen Woyongo

OFFICE OF THE HIGH COMMISSIONER FOR GHANA
13 Belgrave Square, London SW1X 8PN
T 020-7201 5900 W www.ghanahighcommissionuk.com
*High Commissioner,* HE Victor Emmanuel Smith, *apptd* 2014

BRITISH HIGH COMMISSION
PO Box 296, Osu Link, off Gamel Abdul Nasser Avenue, Accra
T (+233) (302) 213 250 E high.commission.accra@fco.gov.uk
W www.gov.uk/government/world/ghana
*High Commissioner,* HE Jon Benjamin, *apptd* 2014

## DEFENCE

| Aged 16–49, 2010 est | Males | Females |
| --- | --- | --- |
| Available for military service | 6,268,191 | 6,194,339 |
| Fit for military service | 4,136,406 | 4,220,761 |

*Military expenditure* – US$181m (2014 )

## ECONOMY AND TRADE

Ghana has abundant natural resources, but high foreign debt and budget, and trade deficits make it dependent on international financial and technical aid to fund its economic and social development programmes. It has benefited from tighter government management of the economy since 2001, and from debt relief in 2002 and 2006. Ghana was recategorised as a lower middle-income country in 2010. Between 2008 and 2014, the economy grew by an average of 6 per cent, with growth driven by the service sector and industry. In 2015, Ghana received a US$918m loan from the IMF to provide financial stability and aid job creation.

Agriculture, mostly at subsistence level, forms the basis of the economy, along with forestry and fishing. The sector employs 56 per cent of the workforce and generates 21.4 per cent of GDP. The main cash crops are cocoa, timber and tuna. Industry employs 15 per cent of the workforce and contributes 29.2 per cent of GDP, mainly from mining (gold, manganese, bauxite, diamonds), forestry, light manufacturing, aluminium smelting, food processing and shipbuilding. Services employ 29 per cent and account for 49.4 per cent of GDP. Hydroelectric power is generated at dams on Lake Volta and is transmitted to most of Ghana, and to Togo and Benin. Oil was discovered offshore in 2007 and production began in 2010. More oil projects are planned and the country is believed to have reserves totalling 700 million barrels.

The main export markets are EU countries, Ukraine and Malaysia. Principal exports are gold, oil, cocoa, timber, tuna, metals, minerals and diamonds. Imports are provided mainly by China, Nigeria, the USA, Singapore and the EU. The main imports are capital equipment, fuel and foodstuffs.

*GNI* – US$38,564m; US$1,770 per capita (2013)
*Annual average growth of GDP* – 4.5 per cent (2014 est)
*Inflation rate* – 15.5 per cent (2014 est)
*Population below poverty line* – 24.2 per cent (2012 est)
*Unemployment* – 5 per cent (2015 est)
*Total external debt* – US$16,020m (2014 est)
*Imports* – US$17,759m (2013)
*Exports* – US$13,691m (2013)

BALANCE OF PAYMENTS
*Trade* – US$4,067m deficit (2013)
*Current Account* – US$2,759m deficit (2015 est)

| Trade with UK | 2013 | 2014 |
|---|---|---|
| Imports from UK | £393,988,080 | £339,865,597 |
| Exports to UK | £289,329,024 | £261,554,096 |

## COMMUNICATIONS

*Airports and waterways* – Seven, including an international terminal in Accra; there are 1,293km of navigable waterways
*Roadways and railways* – 13,787km of surfaced roads; 947km
*Telecommunications* – 285,000 fixed lines and 25.62 million mobile subscriptions (2012); there were 1.29 million internet users in 2009
*Broadcasters* – Ghana has a diverse media environment, though journalists face occasional harassment from the government. Ghana Broadcasting Corporation (GBC) operates TV and radio stations, and competes with a number of private companies
*Press* – Major daily titles include *The Ghanaian Chronicle*, *Daily Guide* and *The Ghanaian Times*
*Internet code and IDD* – gh; 233 (from UK), 44 (to UK)
*WPFI score* – 15,5 (22)

## EDUCATION AND HEALTH

The government provides ten years of compulsory basic education for all children free of charge. Ghana has one of Africa's oldest universities, at Legon in Accra (established in 1948).

*Literacy rate* – 90.6 per cent (2015 est)
*Gross enrolment ratio (percentage of relevant age group)* – primary 109 per cent; secondary 61 per cent (2013 est); tertiary 12 per cent (2012 est)
*Health expenditure (per capita)* – US$100 (2013)
*Hospital beds (per 1,000 people)* – 0.9 (2011)
*Life expectancy (years)* – 65.75 (2014 est)
*Mortality rate* – 7.37 (2014 est)
*Birth rate* – 31.4 (2014 est)
*Infant mortality rate* – 38.52 (2014 est)
*HIV/AIDS adult prevalence* – 1.2 per cent (2013)

# GREECE

*Elliniki Dhimokratia – Hellenic Republic*

*Area* – 131,957 sq. km
*Capital* – Athens; population, 3,060,000 (2014)
*Major cities* – Iraklion (Heraklion) on Crete, Larisa, Patrai (Patras), Piraeus, Thessaloniki (Salonika)
*Currency* – Euro (€) of 100 cents
*Population* – 10,775,643 falling at 0.01 per cent a year (2015 est)
*Religion* – Christian (Greek Orthodox 98 per cent) (est)
*Language* – Greek (official)
*Population density* – 86 per sq. km (2013)
*Urban population* – 61.9 per cent (2013)
*Median age (years)* – 43.5 (2014 est)
*National anthem* – 'Ymnos eis tin Eleutherian' ['Hymn to Liberty']
*National day* – 25 March (Independence Day)
*Death penalty* – Abolished for all crimes (since 2004)
*CPI score* – 43 (69)

## CLIMATE AND TERRAIN

The main areas of Greece are: Macedonia, Thrace, Epirus, Thessaly, Continental Greece, the Peloponnese and Attica on the mainland and the island of Crete. The main island groups are the Sporades, the Dodecanese or Southern Sporades and the Cyclades in the Aegean Sea, and the Ionian islands, including Corfu, to the west of the mainland. Low-lying coastal areas rise to a hilly or mountainous interior on the mainland and the islands. The Pindos mountains form a spine down the centre of the mainland, continuing down the Peloponnese, which is divided from the mainland by the Gulf of Corinth, the largest of the gulfs and bays indenting the coast. Elevation extremes range from 2,917m (Mt Olympus) to 0m (Mediterranean Sea). The climate is temperate; the coastline and islands have a Mediterranean climate but weather is cooler at higher altitudes. The average temperature ranges from 6.4°C in January to 25°C in July.

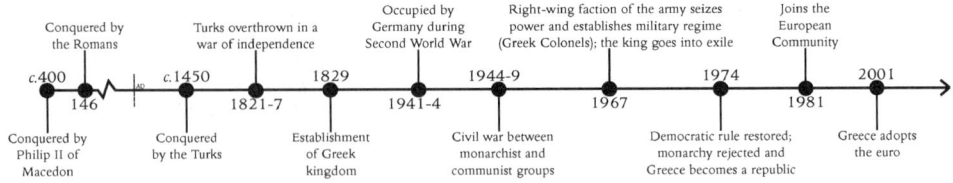

## POLITICS

Under the 1975 constitution, the head of state is the president, elected by the legislature for a five-year term, renewable once. The unicameral legislature, the *Vouli*, has 300 members directly elected for a four-year term.

The New Democracy party (ND) won the most seats in the 2012 legislative elections but was unable to form a coalition government; the party increased its number of seats in the subsequent election and ND leader Antonis Samaras was sworn into office on 20 June 2012. After three rounds of voting finishing in February 2015, Prokopis Pavlopoulos of the ND was elected president. In the early 2015 legislative elections, called after parliament failed to initially elect a president in 2014, Syriza became the largest party in the *Vouli*, gaining 149 seats, and formed a coalition with the far-right, anti-austerity Independent Greeks (ANEL). In July 2015, voters rejected the terms of a proposed EU bail out by 61.3 per cent to 38.7 per cent in a national referendum. On 20 September, the ruling coalition was re-elected following snap legislative elections.

HEAD OF STATE
*President of the Hellenic Republic,* Prokopis Pavlopoulos
    *elected* 18 February 2015, *sworn in* 13 March 2015

SELECTED GOVERNMENT MEMBERS *as at September 2015*
*Prime Minister,* Alexis Tsipras
*Finance,* George Chouliarakis
*Foreign Affairs,* Petros Molyviatis
*Interior,* Antonis Makrydimitris

EMBASSY OF GREECE
1A Holland Park, London W11 3TP
T 020-7229 3850 E gremb.lon@mfa.gr W www.mfa.gr/uk
*Ambassador Extraordinary and Plenipotentiary,* HE
    Konstantinos Bikas, *apptd* 2012

BRITISH EMBASSY
1 Ploutarchou Street, 106 75 Athens
T (+30) (210) 727 2600 E consular.athens@fco.gov.uk
W www.gov.uk/government/world/greece
*Ambassador Extraordinary and Plenipotentiary,* HE John
    Kittmer, *apptd* 2013

## DEFENCE

| Aged 16–49, 2010 est | Males | Females |
| --- | --- | --- |
| Available for military service | 2,485,389 | 2,469,854 |
| Fit for military service | 2,032,378 | 2,016,552 |

*Military expenditure* – US$5,318m (2014)
*Conscription* – 19–45 years of age, male only; 9–12 months

## ECONOMY AND TRADE

Greece experienced rapid economic growth in the final quarter of the 20th century, owing largely to increased tourism and its accession to the European Community. But in the 2000s, high government spending, low fiscal revenue and recession contributed to a growing budget deficit, which soared to over 15 per cent of GDP in 2009 and left the country particularly vulnerable in the global economic downturn. The New Democracy government's persistent failure to address the public finance crisis contributed to Greece's international debt rating being downgraded in late 2009. The following Panhellenic Socialist Movement (Pasok) government's austerity measures, and financial assistance from the IMF and other EU countries, saw the budget deficit reduced to 9 per cent of GDP in 2011, but unemployment rose by over 5 per cent causing many economists to doubt the effectiveness of the government's fiscal policies.

Against a backdrop of protests, in spring 2012 the government agreed new austerity measures and a 'debt swap' deal with private-sector lenders – all conditions of an EU bailout. Further austerity measures were agreed in April 2013 in order to pave the way for more bailout funds. A third bailout worth €86b (£60b) was negotiated with EU partners and passed by parliament on 14 August 2015. In 2014, the government balanced the 2013 budget (excluding debt repayments) and the economy recorded the first quarter of growth since 2008. The EU agreed to extend elements of Greece's bailout for four months in March 2015.

The service sector employs 72.4 per cent of the workforce and generates 80.6 per cent of GDP; much of this is derived from tourism, which accounts for about 18 per cent of GDP, and shipping. Greece is a net importer of energy, including oil for refining and re-export. Industrial activities, which contribute 15.9 per cent of GDP, include food and tobacco processing, textiles, chemicals, metal products, mining and petroleum production. Despite substantial industrialisation in the 20th century, agriculture still employs 12.9 per cent of the workforce, contributing 3.5 per cent of GDP. The most important agricultural products are cereals, vegetables, fruit, tobacco, beef and dairy products.

The main trading partners are Turkey, Russia and Italy and China. Principal exports are food and drink, manufactured goods, petroleum products, chemicals and textiles. The main imports are machinery, transport equipment, fuels and chemicals.

*GNI* – US$250,328m; US$22,690 per capita (2013)
*Annual average growth of GDP* – 0.6 per cent (2014 est)
*Inflation rate* – –1.3 per cent (2014 est)
*Population below poverty line* – 44.0 per cent (2013 est)
*Unemployment* – 27.9 per cent (2013 est)
*Total external debt* – US$568,700m (2013 est)
*Imports* – US$62,084m (2013)
*Exports* – US$36,269m (2013)

BALANCE OF PAYMENTS
*Trade* – US$25,815m deficit (2013)
*Current Account* – US$2,807m surplus (2015 est)

| Trade with UK | 2013 | 2014 |
| --- | --- | --- |
| Imports from UK | £916,600,704 | £982,283,227 |
| Exports to UK | £728,147,820 | £697,033,659 |

## COMMUNICATIONS

*Airports* – 68, the largest of which are at Athens, Thessaloniki, Iraklion (Crete) and Corfu town (Corfu)
*Waterways* – The main seaports are Piraeus, Thessaloniki and Patrai on the mainland, and Iraklion on Crete. An extensive

ferry system connects the islands to one another and to the mainland. The 6km Corinth canal across the Corinth isthmus shortens the sea journey by 325km

*Roadways and railways* – There are 41,357km of surfaced roads, including 1,091km of motorways; 2,548km of railways are state-owned (with the exception of the Athens–Piraeus Electric Railway). As of 2015, the Syriza government is reviewing a proposal to privatise the loss-making, state-controlled rail network operator TrainOSE

*Telecommunications* – 5.46 million fixed lines and 13.35 million mobile subscriptions (2012); there were 4.97 million internet users in 2009

*Internet code and IDD* – gr; 30 (from UK), 44 (to UK)

*Major broadcasters* – In 2013 state broadcaster ERT was closed as part of the country's ongoing austerity measures. A new public broadcaster, New Hellenic Radio, Internet and TV (NERIT), was established in 2014; private broadcasters include Mega TV and Athena 984 (radio)

*Press* – There are three major daily news publications: *Eleftherotypia, Ta Nea* and *Kathimerini*

*WPFI score* – 31,01 (91)

## EDUCATION AND HEALTH

Education is free and compulsory between the ages of six and 14, and is maintained by state grants.

*Literacy rate* – 99.4 per cent (2015 est)

*Gross enrolment ratio (percentage of relevant age group)* – primary 102 per cent; secondary 108 per cent (2011 est)

*Health expenditure (per capita)* – US$2,146 (2013)

*Hospital beds (per 1,000 people)* – 4.9 (2009)

*Life expectancy (years)* – 80.3 (2014 est)

*Mortality rate* – 11.0 (2014 est)

*Birth rate* – 8.8 (2014 est)

*Infant mortality rate* – 4.78 (2014 est)

# GRENADA

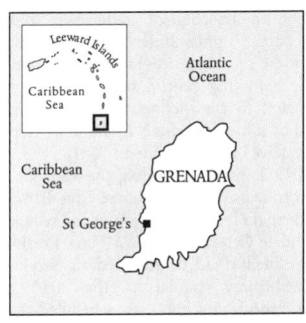

*Area* – 344 sq. km

*Capital* – St George's; population, 38,000 (2014)

*Currency* – East Caribbean dollar (EC$) of 100 cents

*Population* – 110,694 rising at 0.48 per cent a year (2015 est)

*Religion* – Christian (Roman Catholic 53 per cent, Anglican 14 per cent, other Protestant 33 per cent)

*Language* – English (official), Creole (small minority)

*Population density* – 311 per sq. km (2013)

*Urban population* – 39.8 per cent (2013)

*Median age (years)* – 29.9 (2014 est)

*National anthem* – 'Hail Grenada'

*National day* – 7 February (Independence Day)

*Death penalty* – Retained (last used 1978)

*Literacy rate* – 97.3 per cent (2008 est)

*Gross enrolment ratio (percentage of relevant age group)* – primary 103 per cent; secondary 108 per cent (2010 est)

*Life expectancy (years)* – 73.8 (2014 est)

*Mortality rate* – 8.04 (2013 est)

*Birth rate* – 16.3 (2014 est)

*Infant mortality rate* – 10.5 (2014 est)

## CLIMATE AND TERRAIN

The most southerly of the Windward Islands, Grenada comprises three islands: Grenada (the largest at 18km in length and 34km in width), Carriacou and Petite Martinique. Elevation extremes range from 840m (Mt St Catherine) to 0m (Caribbean Sea). The climate is subtropical, with the wettest weather from July to November. Grenada lies in a hurricane zone.

## HISTORY AND POLITICS

Discovered by Columbus in 1498 and named Concepción, Grenada was colonised from the mid-17th century by the French, who subdued the native Caribs; the island was ceded to Britain in 1763. It became a crown colony in 1877, a self-governing associated state in 1967 and an independent nation on 7 February 1974.

The government was overthrown in 1979 by the New Jewel Movement led by Maurice Bishop, and the People's Revolutionary Government (PRG) was set up, with Bishop as prime minister. In 1983, disagreements within the PRG led to the deposition and execution of Bishop, whose government was replaced by a revolutionary military council. These events prompted the intervention of Caribbean and US forces. After a period of interim government, democracy was restored and a general election held in 1984. Since the restoration of democracy, power has alternated between the New National Party (NNP) and the National Democratic Congress (NDC).

In 2013 the NNP won all 15 seats in parliamentary elections; Keith Mitchell returned as prime minister.

Under the 1974 constitution, reinstated in 1984, the head of state is Queen Elizabeth II, represented locally by a governor-general. The bicameral parliament consists of the House of Representatives, with 15 directly elected members, and a senate with 13 appointed members, ten of whom are appointed by the government and three by the opposition; both chambers serve a five-year term.

*Governor-General*, HE Cécile La Grenade, GCMG, OBE, apptd 2013

SELECTED GOVERNMENT MEMBERS *as at May 2015*
*Prime Minister, Finance, Energy*, Keith Mitchell
*Foreign Affairs*, Claris Modeste-Curwen

### HIGH COMMISSION FOR GRENADA
The Chapel, Archel Road, London W14 9QH
T 020-7385 4415 E office@grenada-highcommission.co.uk
W www.grenadahclon.co.uk
*High Commissioner*, HE Joslyn Raphael Whiteman, apptd 2013

### BRITISH HIGH COMMISSIONER
HE Victoria Dean, apptd 2013, resident at Bridgetown, Barbados

## ECONOMY AND TRADE

The economy has grown considerably in recent decades owing to diversification into tourism, offshore financial services and other service industries. Tourism and agriculture have recovered from severe hurricane damage in 2004 and 2005, but reconstruction has burdened the country with considerable debt, and the global downturn's effect on tourism and remittances caused the economy to contract in 2009 and stagnate in 2010–14.

Agriculture now employs only 11 per cent of the workforce and produces 5.9 per cent of GDP. Industry consists of processing agricultural products, textile manufacturing, light assembly operations and construction, and contributes 11 per cent of GDP. The service sector, including tourism and offshore financial services, accounts for 69 per cent of employment and 83.2 per cent of GDP.

The main trading partners are Trinidad and Tobago (44.3 per cent of imports), the USA and other Caribbean states. Principal exports are bananas, cocoa, nutmeg, fruit, vegetables, clothing and mace. Imports include food, manufactured goods, machinery, chemicals and fuels.

*GNI* – US$725m; US$7,490 per capita (2013)
*Annual average growth of GDP* – 1.1 per cent (2014 est)
*Inflation rate* – 0 per cent (2013 est)
*Total external debt* – US$679m (2013 est)
*Imports* – US$368m (2013)
*Exports* – US$33m (2013)

BALANCE OF PAYMENTS
*Trade* – US$336m deficit (2013)
*Current Account* – US$154m deficit (2015 est)

| Trade with UK | 2013 | 2014 |
| --- | --- | --- |
| Imports from UK | £5,687,830 | £6,098,547 |
| Exports to UK | £417,866 | £876,187 |

## COMMUNICATIONS

*Airports and waterways* – The main airport and port are based at St George's
*Roadways* – 687km of surfaced roads
*Telecommunications* – 28,500 fixed lines and 128,000 mobile subscriptions (2012); there were 25,000 internet users in 2009
*Internet code and IDD* – gd; 1 473 (from UK), 011 44 (to UK)
*Major broadcasters and press* – The Grenada Broadcasting Network is jointly owned by the government and the Caribbean Communications Network; there are no daily newspapers but several weeklies, including *Grenada Today* and *The Grenada Informer*

## GUATEMALA

*República de Guatemala* – Republic of Guatemala

*Area* – 108,889 sq. km
*Capital* – Guatemala City; population, 2,847,000 (2014)
*Major cities* – Mixco, Quezaltenango, Villa Nueva
*Currency* – Quetzal (Q) of 100 centavos
*Population* – 14,918,999 rising at 1.82 per cent a year (2015 est); mestizo and European (59.4 per cent), Mayan (40.3 per cent), indigenous non-Mayan (0.2 per cent) (2001)
*Religion* – Christian (Roman Catholic 65 per cent, Evangelical Protestant 43 per cent) (est)
*Language* – Spanish, 23 Amerindian languages (all official)
*Population density* – 144 per sq. km (2013)
*Urban population* – 50.7 per cent (2013)
*Median age (years)* – 21 (2014 est)
*National anthem* – 'Himno Nacional de Guatemala' ['National Anthem of Guatemala']
*National day* – 15 September (Independence Day)
*Death penalty* – Retained (last used 2000)
*CPI score* – 32 (115)

## CLIMATE AND TERRAIN

Narrow tropical plains on both the north (Caribbean) and south (Pacific) coasts rise to a mountainous interior in the centre and south. The mountains fall in the north to lowlands covered in tropical jungle. Elevation extremes range from 4,211m (Tajumulco volcano) to 0m (Pacific Ocean). There are 37 volcanoes, three active, in the central plateau. The climate is tropical but is cooler in the highlands. The wet season runs from May to September, when mudslides and hurricanes can occur. There are also frequent minor earth tremors and some earthquakes.

## HISTORY AND POLITICS

Mayan and Aztec civilisations flourished in the area until the Spanish conquest in 1523–4, after which the area became a Spanish colony. It gained independence in 1821, and formed part of a Central American federation of former Spanish provinces from 1823 to 1839. After independence, the country was ruled by a series of dictatorships and military regimes, interspersed with periods of democratic government. In 1960 a civil war between military governments, right-wing vigilantes and left-wing guerrillas began, lasting 36 years and during which over 200,000 people died or disappeared.

In 1996 the democratically elected civilian government concluded a peace agreement with the left-wing Guatemalan Revolutionary National Unity guerrillas that ended the civil war. In 1999, an independent commission found that 93 per cent of human rights abuses during the war had been instigated by the security forces, and in 2000 and 2004 the state formally admitted guilt in several human rights cases, paying damages to the victims. At present, only a small number of the military personnel found to be responsible for the atrocities have been prosecuted.

In the 2011 legislative election, the Patriotic Party (PP) won the most seats, but without an overall majority. The 2011 presidential election was won in the second round by the PP candidate Gen. Otto Perez Molina. President Molina and Vice-President Baldetti resigned in September 2015 following a bribery scandal. In the 2015 presidential elections, a runoff election was scheduled for October following an inconclusive round of voting in September.

Under the 1986 constitution, the executive president is directly elected for a four-year term, which is not renewable. He or she is responsible to the congress and appoints the cabinet. The unicameral Congress of the Republic has 158 members, who are directly elected for a four-year term.

HEAD OF STATE
*Interim President,* Alejandro Moldonado, *sworn in* 3 September 2015
*Vice-President,* vacant

SELECTED GOVERNMENT MEMBERS *as at September 2015*
*Defence,* William Mancilla
*Economy,* Ricardo Sagastume
*Foreign Relations,* Luis Castro

## EMBASSY OF GUATEMALA
13 Fawcett Street, London SW10 9HN
T 020-7351 3042 E inglaterra@minex.gob.gt
*Ambassador Extraordinary and Plenipotentiary,* HE Acisclo Valladares Molina, *apptd* 2010

## BRITISH EMBASSY
Edificio Torre Internacional, Nivel 11, 16 Calle 0–55, Zona 10, Guatemala City
T (+502) 2380 7300 E embassy@intelnett.com
W www.gov.uk/government/world/guatemala
*Ambassador Extraordinary and Plenipotentiary,* HE Sarah Dickson, *apptd* 2012

## DEFENCE

| Aged 16–49, 2010 est | Males | Females |
|---|---|---|
| Available for military service | 3,165,870 | 3,371,217 |
| Fit for military service | 2,590,843 | 2,926,544 |

*Military expenditure* – US$264m (2014)
*Conscription* – 18–50 years of age, male only; 12–24 months (selective)

## ECONOMY AND TRADE
IMF funding and foreign aid have underpinned the government's economic reforms and stabilisation programmes, but the trade deficit, poor infrastructure, security problems and high levels of corruption still deter foreign investment. The country suffers from a huge imbalance in wealth, and over half the population lives below the poverty line. Despite potential for tourism and increased regional integration and trade, economic growth is predicted to average 3.5 per cent between 2015 and 2019 due to low productivity.

Half of the population is dependent on agriculture, which contributes 13.3 per cent of GDP and accounts for a high proportion of exports. Industry accounts for 23.5 per cent of GDP, and the services sector, which includes tourism, for 63.2 per cent of GDP.

The main trading partners are the USA, El Salvador, Honduras and Mexico. The principal exports are coffee, sugar, petroleum, garments, bananas, other fruit, vegetables and cardamom. The chief imports are fuels, machinery and transport equipment, construction materials, grain, fertilisers and electricity.
*GNI* – US$48,862m; US$3,340 per capita (2013)
*Annual average growth of GDP* – 3.4 per cent (2014 est)
*Inflation rate* – 3.4 per cent (2014 est)
*Population below poverty line* – 53.7 per cent (2011 est)
*Unemployment* – 2.7 per cent (2015 est)
*Total external debt* – US$15,940m (2014 est)
*Imports* – US$14,368m (2013)
*Exports* – US$6,975m (2013)

BALANCE OF PAYMENTS
*Trade* – US$7,392m deficit (2013)
*Current Account* – US$1,026m deficit (2015 est)

| Trade with UK | 2013 | 2014 |
|---|---|---|
| Imports from UK | £31,229,824 | £35,346,495 |
| Exports to UK | £53,287,767 | £52,102,721 |

## COMMUNICATIONS
*Airports* – 16; the principal international airport is based in Guatemala City
*Waterways* – There are 990km of navigable waterways, of which only 260km are navigable all year round; the main seaports are at Quetzal on the Pacific Ocean and Santo Tomás de Castilla on the Gulf of Honduras

*Roadways and railways* – 6,797km of surfaced roads; 332km
*Telecommunications* – 1.744 million fixed lines and 20.787 million mobile subscriptions (2012); there were 2.279 million internet users in 2009
*Internet code and IDD* – gt; 502 (from UK), 44 (to UK)
*Major broadcasters* – Private broadcasters dominate the media; four national television stations, including Canal 3, share the same owner
*Press* – There are four main daily newspapers, including *Prensa Libre* and *el Periodico*
*WPFI score* – 37,92 (124)

## EDUCATION AND HEALTH
There are nine years of compulsory education.
*Literacy rate* – 95.4 per cent (2015 est)
*Gross enrolment ratio (percentage of relevant age group)* – primary 114 per cent; secondary 65 per cent (2011 est)
*Health expenditure (per capita)* – US$227 (2013)
*Hospital beds (per 1,000 people)* – 0.6 (2011)
*Life expectancy (years)* – 71.74 (2014 est)
*Mortality rate* – 4.82 (2014 est)
*Birth rate* – 25.46 (2014 est)
*Infant mortality rate* – 23.51 (2014 est)

# GUINEA

*République de Guinée – Republic of Guinea*

*Area* – 245,857 sq. km
*Capital* – Conakry; population, 1,886,000 (2014)
*Major cities* – Guéckédou, Kankan, Nzérékoré
*Currency* – Guinea franc (GNF) of 100 centimes
*Population* – 11,780,162 rising at 2.63 per cent a year (2015 est); Fulani (40 per cent), Malinke (30 per cent), Susu (20 per cent) (est)
*Religion* – Muslim 85 per cent (predominantly Sunni), Christian 8 per cent, traditional indigenous religions 7 per cent (est); some combine Islam or Christianity with indigenous beliefs
*Language* – French (official), Eastern Maninkakan, Guinea Kpelle, Northern Kissi, Pular, Susu, Toma
*Population density* – 48 per sq. km (2013)
*Urban population* – 36.4 per cent (2013)
*Median age (years)* – 18.7 (2014 est)
*National anthem* – 'Liberté' ['Freedom']
*National day* – 2 October (Independence Day)
*Death penalty* – Retained (last used 2001)
*CPI score* – 25 (145)
*Literacy rate* – 45.2 per cent (2015 est)
*Gross enrolment ratio (percentage of relevant age group)* – primary 91 per cent; secondary 38 per cent; tertiary 10 per cent (2012 est)
*Health expenditure (per capita)* – US$25 (2013)

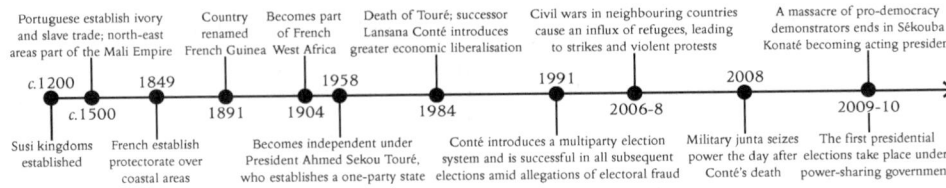

Portuguese establish ivory and slave trade; north-east areas part of the Mali Empire — *c.*1200

Country renamed French Guinea — 1849

Becomes part of French West Africa — 1958

Death of Touré; successor Lansana Conté introduces greater economic liberalisation — 1984

Civil wars in neighbouring countries cause an influx of refugees, leading to strikes and violent protests — 1991

A massacre of pro-democracy demonstrators ends in Sékouba Konaté becoming acting president — 2008

Susi kingdoms established — *c.*1500

French establish protectorate over coastal areas — 1891

Becomes independent under President Ahmed Sekou Touré, who establishes a one-party state — 1904

Conté introduces a multiparty election system and is successful in all subsequent elections amid allegations of electoral fraud — 2006-8

Military junta seizes power the day after Conté's death — 2009-10

The first presidential elections take place under power-sharing government

*Hospital beds (per 1,000 people)* – 0.3 (2011)
*Life expectancy (years)* – 59.6 (2014 est)
*Mortality rate* – 9.69 (2014 est)
*Birth rate* – 36.02 (2014 est)
*Infant mortality rate* – 55.24 (2014 est)
*HIV/AIDS adult prevalence* – 3.7 per cent (2013)

## CLIMATE AND TERRAIN

Guinea has a flat coastal plain that rises to the hilly Fouta Djallon plateau in the north-west, where the Gambia and Senegal rivers rise. East of the plateau is the central savannah, the source of the Niger river, with rainforest in the south-east. Elevation extremes range from 1,752m (Mt Nimba) to 0m (Atlantic Ocean). The climate is tropical, with a wet season from April to November; the average daily temperature is 26.1°C.

## POLITICS

Under the 2010 constitution, the executive president is directly elected for a five-year term, renewable once. The unicameral National Assembly has 114 members, who are directly elected for a five-year term. The president appoints the council of ministers.

The presidential election in 2010, the first democratic election since independence, was won by Alpha Condé; the second round of voting was delayed by allegations of fraud in the first round, and his victory sparked off several weeks of intercommunal violence. Delayed 2013 legislative elections resulted in Alpha Condé's ruling Rally of the Guinean People party (RPG) winning 53 seats and forming a coalition with smaller parties. The opposition Union of Democratic Forces in Guinea declared the result invalid and violent demonstrations occurred in the capital. In 2015, violent protests again broke out in Conakry following the announcement that overdue local elections would not take place until 2016. Opposition groups accused the government of planning to interfere with presidential elections due to take place in October 2015.

HEAD OF STATE
*President, Defence*, Alpha Condé, *elected* 7 November 2010, *sworn in* 21 December

SELECTED GOVERNMENT MEMBERS *as at May 2015*
*Prime Minister*, Mohamed Said Fofana
*Economy and Finance*, Mohamed Diaré
*Foreign Affairs*, François Fall
*Security*, Mahmoud Cissé

EMBASSY OF THE REPUBLIC OF GUINEA
258 Belsize Road, London NW6 4BT
T 020-7316 1861 E office@ambaguinee-london.co.uk
*Ambassador Extraordinary and Plenipotentiary*, Paul Goa Zoumanigui, *apptd* 2013

BRITISH EMBASSY
Villa 1, Residence 2000, Corniche Sud Conakry
T (+224) 6335 5329 E britembconakry@hotmail.com
W www.gov.uk/government/world/guinea
*Ambassador Extraordinary and Plenipotentiary*, HE Catherine Inglehearn, *apptd* 2015

## DEFENCE

| | Males | Females |
| --- | --- | --- |
| *Aged 16–49, 2010 est* | | |
| Available for military service | 2,359,203 | 2,329,784 |
| Fit for military service | 1,493,991 | 1,535,418 |

*Military expenditure* – US$255m (2014)
*Conscription* – 18–25 years of age; 18 months

## ECONOMY AND TRADE

Although Guinea is the second largest producer of bauxite in the world and despite an abundance of natural resources, decades of mismanagement and corruption have left the economy undeveloped. Foreign aid was suspended following the 2008 coup and resumed in 2012 following democratic elections in 2010. The economy is expected to experience negative growth in 2015 due to the economic effects of the 2014–15 Ebola outbreak. The epidemic is thought to have cost the economy US$540m (£348m), due to the disruption caused to trade and a reduction in investor confidence.

Mining is, however, attracting foreign investment and a new mining code introduced in September 2011 includes provisions to combat corruption. Agriculture, much of it at subsistence level, employs 76 per cent of the population and contributes 20.2 per cent of GDP. Industry accounts for 44.5 per cent of GDP, mostly through mining and the processing of minerals and agricultural produce.

The main trading partners are India, China and EU countries, especially Spain. Principal exports are bauxite, alumina, gold, diamonds, coffee, fish and other agricultural products. The main imports are petroleum products, metals, machinery, transport equipment, textiles, grain and other foodstuffs.

*GNI* – US$5,202m; US$460 per capita (2013)
*Annual average growth of GDP* – 2.5 per cent (2014 est)
*Inflation rate* – 11.9 per cent (2013 est)
*Population below poverty line* – 55.2 per cent (2012 est)
*Unemployment* – 3.1 per cent (2015 est)
*Total external debt* – US$843.5m (2014 est)
*Imports* – US$2,150m (2013)
*Exports* – US$1,300m (2013)

BALANCE OF PAYMENTS
*Trade* – US$850m deficit (2013)
*Current Account* – US$1,198m deficit (2015 est)

| *Trade with UK* | 2013 | 2014 |
| --- | --- | --- |
| Imports from UK | £160,671,703 | £36,707,376 |
| Exports to UK | £1,657,367 | £1,874,210 |

## COMMUNICATIONS

*Airports* – Four with surfaced runways; the principal airport is at Conakry
*Waterways* – The major seaports are Conakry and Kamsar; there are 1,300km of waterways
*Roadways and railways* – 4,342km of surfaced roadways, and 1,185km of railways
*Telecommunications* – 18,000 fixed lines and 4.781 million mobile telephone lines in use (2012); there were 95,000 internet users in 2009

*Internet code and IDD* – gn; 224 (from UK), 44 (to UK)
*Major broadcasters* – Radiodiffusion-Télévision Guinéenne is the principal, state-run broadcaster
*Press* – *Horoya* is the main government-owned daily
*WPFI score* – 32,56 (102)

# GUINEA-BISSAU

*Republica da Guine-Bissau* – *Republic of Guinea-Bissau*

*Area* – 36,125 sq. km
*Capital* – Bissau; population, 473,000 (2014)
*Currency* – West African CFA franc of 100 centimes
*Population* – 1,726,170 rising at 1.91 per cent a year (2015 est); Balanta (30 per cent), Fulani (20 per cent), Manjaca (14 per cent), Mandinga (13 per cent), Papel (7 per cent) (est)
*Religion* – Muslim 50 per cent, indigenous beliefs 40 per cent, Christian 10 per cent
*Language* – Portuguese (official), Creole
*Population density* – 61 per sq. km (2013)
*Urban population* – 45.3 per cent (2013)
*Median age (years)* – 19.8 (2014 est)
*National anthem* – 'Esta e a Nossa Patria Bem Amada' ['This is Our Beloved Country']
*National day* – 24 September (Independence Day)
*Death penalty* – Abolished for all crimes (since 1993)
*CPI score* – 19 (161)
*Literacy rate* – 77.3 per cent (2015 est)
*Gross enrolment ratio (percentage of relevant age group)* – primary 116 per cent (2011 est)
*Health expenditure (per capita)* – US$32 (2013)
*Hospital beds (per 1,000 people)* – 1.0 (2009)
*Life expectancy (years)* – 49.87 (2014 est)
*Mortality rate* – 14.54 (2014 est)
*Birth rate* – 33.83 (2014 est)
*Infant mortality rate* – 90.92 (2014 est)
*HIV/AIDS adult prevalence* – 3.9 per cent (2012 est)

## CLIMATE AND TERRAIN

Guinea-Bissau has a low coastal plain that rises to savannah in the east. The coast is heavily indented and covered with mangrove swamps. Elevation extremes range from 300m (in the north-east) to 0m (Atlantic Ocean). The climate is tropical, with a wet season from July to September.

## HISTORY AND POLITICS

A part of the ancient African empire of Mali, Guinea-Bissau was once the kingdom of Gabu, which became independent of the empire in 1546 and survived until 1867. In 1446, Portuguese traders discovered the coast and established slave trading there, subsequently administering Guinea-Bissau with the Cape Verde islands; it became a separate colony in 1879. After a guerrilla war led by the left-wing African Party

for the Independence of Guinea and Cape Verde (PAIGC), Guinea-Bissau declared independence unilaterally in 1973 and Portugal recognised this in 1974.

After independence Guinea-Bissau became a one-party socialist state under the PAIGC, led by Luis Cabral. He was deposed in 1980, in a military coup led by General Joao Vieira, and the country was under military rule until 1994. A multiparty system was introduced in 1991 after popular agitation, but the following 15 years saw a short civil war (1998–9) and two more military coups (1999, 2003); democratic government was restored in 2004–5.

The 2008 legislative election was won by the PAIGC, which formed a government in January 2009. The PAIGC candidate, Malam Bacai Sanha, was elected president in July 2009, but became seriously ill and died on 9 January 2012; he was temporarily replaced by Speaker of the National Assembly Raimundo Pereira. A military coup in April 2012 detained Pereira and the presidential front-runner, outgoing prime minister Carlos Gomes Jr; Guinea-Bissau has since been ruled by a Transitional National Council, headed by Manuel Serifo Nhamadjo, a former parliamentary speaker. The April 2014 legislative election was won by PAIGC, whose candidate, Jose Mario Vaz, was elected president in May 2014.

Under the 1999 constitution, the executive president is directly elected for a five-year term, which is renewable once. The president appoints the council of ministers. The unicameral National People's Assembly has 102 members, who are directly elected for a four-year term.

HEAD OF STATE
President, Jose Mario Vaz, *elected* 20 May 2014, *sworn in* 23 June 2014

SELECTED GOVERNMENT MEMBERS *as at May 2015*
*Prime Minister*, Domingos Simoes Pereira
*Economy*, Geraldo Martins
*Foreign Affairs*, Mario Lopes Da Rosa

EMBASSY OF THE REPUBLIC OF GUINEA-BISSAU
94 rue St Lazare, 75009 Paris, France
T (+33) (1) 4874 3639
*Ambassador Extraordinary and Plenipotentiary*, vacant

BRITISH CONSULATE
*Ambassador Extraordinary and Plenipotentiary*, HE Robert John Marshall, *apptd* 2011, resident at Dakar, Senegal

## DEFENCE

| Aged 16–49, 2010 est | Males | Females |
|---|---|---|
| Available for military service | 370,790 | 372,171 |
| Fit for military service | 205,460 | 212,277 |

*Military expenditure* – US$16.6m (2012)
*Conscription* – 18–25 years of age (selective)

## ECONOMY AND TRADE

The economy is in a poor state owing to decades of mismanagement and corruption, the devastating effects of the 1998–9 civil war and ongoing political instability. Successful elections in 2014 allowed the country to resume receiving international aid.

Although Guinea-Bissau has mineral resources, including oil, the high cost of exploiting these inhibits development and the economy is based almost exclusively on agriculture and fishing; drug trafficking is the most lucrative industry in the country. The agricultural sector employs 82 per cent of the population and contributes 45 per cent of GDP.

The small industrial sector generates 7.5 per cent of GDP, mainly through processing agricultural products and beer, and soft drink production.

The main trading partners are India (56.5 per cent of exports) and Nigeria. Principal exports include fish, cashew nuts, peanuts, palm kernels and timber. The main imports are foodstuffs, machinery and transport equipment, and fuels.
*GNI* – US$821m; US$590 per capita (2013)
*Annual average growth of GDP* – 2.6 per cent (2014 est)
*Inflation rate* – –1 per cent (2013 est)
*Unemployment* – 8.2 per cent (2015 est)
*Total external debt* – US$1,095,000m (2010 est)
*Imports* – US$240m (2013)
*Exports* – US$210m (2013)

BALANCE OF PAYMENTS
*Trade* – US$30m deficit (2013)
*Current Account* – US$111m deficit (2015 est)

| Trade with UK | 2013 | 2014 |
| --- | --- | --- |
| Imports from UK | £614,135 | £39,991,290 |
| Exports to UK | £11,930 | £24,411 |

## COMMUNICATIONS
*Airports* – Two; the principal airport is at Bissau
*Waterways* – The main rivers are navigable for part of their lengths, and shallow-draught craft can access much of the interior via creeks and inlets; Bissau is the main seaport
*Roadways* – There are 965km of surfaced roads
*Telecommunications* – 5,000 fixed lines and 1.1 million mobile subscriptions (2012); there were 37,100 internet users in 2009
*Internet code and IDD* – gw; 245 (from UK), 44 (to UK)
*Major broadcasters* – The state-run Radio Televisao de Guinea-Bissau is the main broadcaster
*Press* – Major newspapers include state-run weekly *No Pintcha* and the privately run *Gazeta de Noticias*
*WPFI score* – 28,7 (81)

# GUYANA

*Cooperative Republic of Guyana*

*Area* – 214,969 sq. km
*Capital* – Georgetown; population, 124,000 (2014 est)
*Major towns* – Linden, New Amsterdam
*Currency* – Guyana dollar (G$) of 100 cents
*Population* – 735,222 rising at 0.02 per cent a year (2015 est); Indo-Guyanese 43.5 per cent, Afro-Guyanese 30.2 per cent, mixed 16.7 per cent, Amerindian 9.1 per cent (2002)
*Religion* – Protestant 31 per cent, Hindu 28 per cent, Roman Catholic 8 per cent

*Language* – English (official), Amerindian dialects, Creole, Caribbean Hindustani (a dialect of Hindi), Urdu
*Population density* – 4 per sq. km (2013)
*Urban population* – 28.5 per cent (2013)
*Median age (years)* – 25 (2014 est)
*National anthem* – 'Dear Land of Guyana, of Rivers and Plains'
*National day* – 23 February (Republic Day)
*Death penalty* – Retained (last used 1993)
*CPI score* – 30 (124)
*Literacy rate* – 94.4 per cent (2015 est)
*Gross enrolment ratio (percentage of relevant age group)* – primary 75 per cent; secondary 101 per cent; tertiary 13 per cent (2012 est)
*Life expectancy (years)* – 67.81 (2014 est)
*Mortality rate* – 7.3 (2014 est)
*Birth rate* – 15.9 (2014 est)
*Infant mortality rate* – 33.56 (2014 est)
*HIV/AIDS adult prevalence* – 1.3 per cent (2012 est)

## CLIMATE AND TERRAIN
The land rises from a narrow coastal plain to forested highlands in the west and savannah on the southern border; about 90 per cent of the population lives on the coastal plain, which constitutes 5 per cent of the land area. Around 79 per cent of the country is covered by rainforest. Elevation extremes range from 2,835m (Mt Roraima) to 0m (Atlantic Ocean). The climate is tropical, with an average daily temperature of 26°C, and two wet seasons, from April to July and from November to January.

## HISTORY AND POLITICS
Carib and Arawak peoples inhabited the coastal region of Guyana when Dutch merchants founded the first European settlement in the late 16th century. Guyana became an important producer of sugar, grown on plantations worked first by African slaves and then, after the abolition of slavery in 1834, by indentured labourers, mostly from India. Several areas were ceded to Britain in 1815, and consolidated as British Guiana in 1831. The country became independent, as Guyana, on 26 May 1966, and became a republic in 1970.

Guyana's first political party, the People's Progressive Party (PPP), split along ethnic lines in the 1950s; the PPP continued as a predominantly Indian party under Cheddi Jagan, while those of African descent formed the People's National Congress (PNC), led by Forbes Burnham. Burnham dominated political life after independence, first as prime minister (1966–80) and then as executive president until his death in 1985. Under his autocratic rule, politics became characterised by suspect elections and a disregard for civil liberties and human rights. The PPP's electoral victory in 1992 ended the PNC's monopoly of power but persistent ethnic tensions continue to destabilise politics.

The 2011 legislative election was won by the PPP, securing its fifth consecutive term of office but without an overall majority; Donald Ramotar (PPP) became president, replacing Bharrat Jagdeo (also PPP). In the May 2015 legislative elections, the Partnership for National Unity and Alliance for Change coalition (APNU-AFC) emerged as the single largest party, and APNU's leader David Granger was sworn in as president.

Under the 1980 constitution, the executive president is nominated by the majority party in the legislature after each legislative election, and serves a five-year term, renewable once. The unicameral National Assembly has 65 members, of whom 53 are elected by proportional representation and 12 are regional representatives; they serve a five-year term.

HEAD OF STATE
*President,* David Granger, *sworn in* 16 May 2015

SELECTED GOVERNMENT MEMBERS *as at May 2015*
*Prime Minister,* Moses Nagamootoo
*Finance,* Ashni Kumar Singh
*Foreign Affairs,* Carolyn Rodrigues-Burkett
*Home Affairs,* Clement Rohee

HIGH COMMISSION FOR GUYANA
3 Palace Court, Bayswater Road, London W2 4LP
T 020-7229 7684 E info@guyanahclondon.co.uk
W www.guyanahclondon.co.uk
*High Commissioner,* HE Laleshwar Singh, *apptd* 1993

BRITISH HIGH COMMISSION
PO Box 10849, 44 Main Street, Georgetown
T (+1592) 226 5881 W www.gov.uk/government/world/guyana
*High Commissioner,* HE James Gregory Quinn, *apptd* 2015

## DEFENCE

| *Aged 16–49, 2010 est* | *Males* | *Females* |
|---|---|---|
| Available for military service | 189,840 | – |
| Fit for military service | 133,239 | 147,719 |

*Military expenditure* – US$31.2m (2013)

## ECONOMY AND TRADE

The economy grew from 2001 to 2008 owing to expansion in agriculture and mining, the cancellation of over one-third of Guyana's external debt, and increases in foreign direct investment and remittances from expatriate workers. Growth slowed in 2014 and is expected to remain depressed by declining global commodity prices. The exploitation of offshore oil deposits, which began in May 2015, could potentially add US$200m to the economy. In the longer term, poor infrastructure and skills shortages inhibit growth, especially attempts to develop tourism.

Agriculture accounts for 20.3 per cent of GDP and provides the raw materials for the major industries of sugar processing and rice milling. Non-agricultural activities include bauxite and gold mining, forestry, fishing and textile manufacturing; industry accounts for 39.2 per cent of GDP.

The main trading partners are the USA, Trinidad and Tobago, Canada and the UK. Principal exports include sugar, gold, bauxite, alumina, rice, shrimp, molasses, rum and timber. The main imports are manufactured goods, machinery, fuel and food.

*GNI* – US$2,849m; US$3,750 per capita (2013)
*Annual average growth of GDP* – 3.3 per cent (2014 est)
*Inflation rate* – 1.8 per cent (2013 est)
*Unemployment* – 10.8 per cent (2015 est)
*Total external debt* – US$1,846m (2011 est)
*Imports* – US$1,750m (2013)
*Exports* – US$1,380m (2013)

BALANCE OF PAYMENTS
*Trade* – US$370m deficit (2013)
*Current Account* – US$517m deficit (2015 est)

| *Trade with UK* | *2013* | *2014* |
|---|---|---|
| Imports from UK | £26,356,049 | £26,020,786 |
| Exports to UK | £70,055,879 | £61,999,690 |

## COMMUNICATIONS

*Airports and waterways* – 11; 330km of navigable waterways (principally the Berbice, Demerara and Essequibo rivers) form the main arteries of communication

*Roadways* – There are 590km of surfaced roads
*Telecommunications* – 154,200 fixed lines and 547,000 mobile subscriptions (2012); there were 189,600 internet users in 2009
*Internet code and IDD* – gy; 592 (from UK), 1 44 (to UK)
*Major broadcasters* – The state-owned National Communications Network operates national television and radio networks
*Press* – There are three major daily newspapers: the government-owned *Guyana Chronicle, Stabroek News* and *Kaieteur News*
*WPFI score* – 27,21 (62)

# HAITI

*République d'Haïti / Repiblik d'Ayiti* – Republic of Haiti

*Area* – 27,750 sq. km
*Capital* – Port-au-Prince; population, 2,376,000 (2014)
*Major cities* – Cap-Haïtien, Gonaïves, Pétionville
*Currency* – Gourde (G) of 100 centimes
*Population* – 10,110,019 rising at 1.17 per cent a year (2015 est)
*Religion* – Christian (Roman Catholic 80 per cent, Baptist 10 per cent, Pentecostal 4 per cent, Seventh-day Adventist 1 per cent); many Christians also practise Voodoo, recognised as an official religion in 2003
*Language* – French, Creole (both official)
*Population density* – 374 per sq. km (2013)
*Urban population* – 56.1 per cent (2013)
*Median age (years)* – 22.2 (2014 est)
*National anthem* – 'La Dessalinienne' ['The Song of Dessalines']
*National day* – 1 January (Independence Day)
*Death penalty* – Abolished for all crimes (since 1987)
*CPI score* – 19 (161)
*Literacy rate* – 82.1 per cent (2015 est)
*Health expenditure (per capita)* – US$77 (2013)
*Hospital beds (per 1,000 people)* – 1.3 (2007)
*Life expectancy (years)* – 63.18 (2014 est)
*Mortality rate* – 7.91 (2014 est)
*Birth rate* – 22.83 (2014 est)
*Infant mortality rate* – 49.43 (2014 est)
*HIV/AIDS adult prevalence* – 0.5 per cent (2013)

## CLIMATE AND TERRAIN

The country occupies the western third of the island of Hispaniola. The terrain is mountainous, with coastal plains and a large central plateau. Elevation extremes range from 2,680m (Chaîne de la Selle) to 0m (Caribbean Sea). The climate is tropical, and semi-arid where the eastern mountains block the trade winds, with two wet seasons (April–June, August–November) and a hurricane season from June to November.

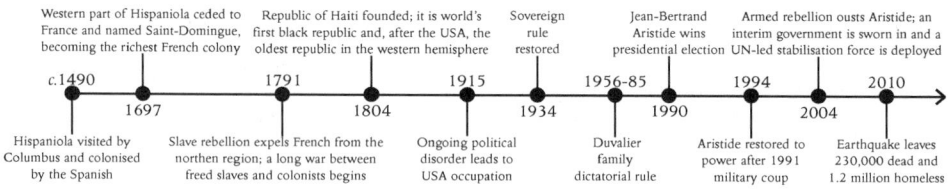

Western part of Hispaniola ceded to France and named Saint-Domingue, becoming the richest French colony — *c.1490*

Republic of Haiti founded; it is world's first black republic and, after the USA, the oldest republic in the western hemisphere — *1791*

Sovereign rule restored — *1915*

Jean-Bertrand Aristide wins presidential election — *1956-85*

Armed rebellion ousts Aristide; an interim government is sworn in and a UN-led stabilisation force is deployed — *1994* / *2010*

Hispaniola visited by Columbus and colonised by the Spanish — *1697*

Slave rebellion expels French from the northen region; a long war between freed slaves and colonists begins — *1804*

Ongoing political disorder leads to USA occupation — *1934*

Duvalier family dictatorial rule — *1990*

Aristide restored to power after 1991 military coup — *2004*

Earthquake leaves 230,000 dead and 1.2 million homeless

## POLITICS

Under the 1987 constitution, the president is directly elected for a five-year term that may not be renewed immediately. The bicameral National Assembly comprises a lower house, the Chamber of Deputies, with 99 members directly elected for a four-year term, and the senate, with 30 members directly elected for a six-year term; one-third of the senators are elected every two years. The president appoints the prime minister, who must be approved by the legislature.

The March 2011 presidential election was won in the second round of voting by Michel Martelly of the Repons Peyizan party. The Inite party won a majority in both the National Assembly and Chamber of Deputies in a legislative election dogged by allegations of irregularities. In 2014, following violent demonstrations in protest at the delays in holding new elections, which have been overdue since 2012, Prime Minister Laurent Lamothe resigned and was replaced by Evans Paul. New presidential elections are scheduled to take place on 25 October 2015.

### HEAD OF STATE
*President,* Michel Martelly, *elected* 20 March 2011, *sworn in* 14 May 2011

### SELECTED GOVERNMENT MEMBERS *as at May 2015*
*Prime Minister,* Evans Paul
*Economy and Finance,* Wilson Laleau
*Interior,* Ariel Henry

### EMBASSY OF THE REPUBLIC OF HAITI
14 Cavendish Place, London W1G 9DJ
T 020-7637 8985
*Ambassador Extraordinary and Plenipotentiary,* vacant

### BRITISH AMBASSADOR
HE Sharon Campbell, *apptd* 2015, resident at Santo Domingo, Dominican Republic

### ECONOMY AND TRADE
The country is the poorest in the western hemisphere, with most of the population living below the poverty line and over half in abject poverty. Its economy, damaged by years of political instability, violence and corruption as well as the natural disasters to which it is vulnerable, experienced moderate growth from 2005 and Haiti had its foreign debt written off in 2009 and 2010. But the 2010 earthquake reversed these gains, devastating the infrastructure and continuing the government's complete dependence on foreign aid. Disruption to the agricultural sector, caused by heavy rain and delays in the passing of the government's budget, suppressed growth in 2013 and 2014. Remittances from the estimated one in six Haitians who live abroad, principally in the USA, are the main source of foreign revenue, worth nearly 20 per cent of GDP. Two-fifths of the population depend on agriculture – predominantly small-scale subsistence farming – which contributes 24.7 per cent of GDP. Industrial activities include production of textiles and garments, sugar refining, flour milling and assembly of goods, especially vehicle parts, for re-export.

The main trading partners are the USA and Dominican Republic. Principal exports are garments (three-quarters of exports), manufactured goods, essential oils, cocoa, mangoes and coffee. The main imports are food, manufactured goods, machinery and transport equipment, fuels and raw materials.
*GNI* – US$7,911m; US$810 per capita (2013)
*Annual average growth of GDP* – 3.8 per cent (2014 est)
*Inflation rate* – 4.6 per cent (2014 est)
*Population below poverty line* – 58.5 per cent (2012 est)
*Unemployment* – 7.0 per cent (2015 est)
*Total external debt* – US$1,687m (2014 est)
*Imports* – US$3,400m (2013)
*Exports* – US$885m (2013)

BALANCE OF PAYMENTS
*Trade* – US$2,498m deficit (2013)
*Current Account* – US$275m deficit (2015 est)

| Trade with UK | 2013 | 2014 |
| --- | --- | --- |
| Imports from UK | £9,069,554 | £8,134,468 |
| Exports to UK | £3,302,530 | £3,676,296 |

### COMMUNICATIONS
*Airports and waterways* – Four; the international airports and main ports are at Port-au-Prince and Cap-Haitien
*Roadways* – Only 768km of the country's roads are surfaced
*Telecommunications* – 50,000 fixed lines (2010) and 6.095 million mobile subscriptions (2012); there were 1 million internet users in 2009
*Internet code and IDD* – ht; 509 (from UK), 44 (to UK)
*Major broadcasters* – The government-owned Television Nationale d'Haiti broadcasts in Creole, French and Spanish
*Press* – There are two daily newspapers, *Le Matin* and *Le Nouvelliste*
*WPFI score* – 25,08 (53)

## HONDURAS

*República de Honduras – Republic of Honduras*

*Area* – 112,090 sq. km
*Capital* – Tegucigalpa; population, 1,101,000 (2014)

*Major cities* – Choloma, El Progreso, La Ceiba, San Pedro Sula

*Currency* – Lempira of 100 centavos

*Population* – 8,746,673 rising at 1.68 per cent a year (2015 est); mainly mestizo, with Amerindian and black minorities

*Religion* – Christian (Roman Catholic 97 per cent, Protestant 3 per cent)

*Language* – Spanish (official), Amerindian dialects

*Population density* – 72 per sq. km (2013)

*Urban population* – 53.3 per cent (2013)

*Median age (years)* – 21.9 (2014 est)

*National anthem* – 'Himno Nacional de Honduras' ['National Anthem of Honduras']

*National day* – 15 September (Independence Day)

*Death penalty* – Abolished for all crimes (since 1956)

*CPI score* – 29 (126)

## CLIMATE AND TERRAIN

Honduras has a mountainous interior, falling to narrow coastal plains. Elevation extremes range from 2,870m (Cerro Las Minas) to 0m (Caribbean Sea). The climate is subtropical in the lowlands and temperate in the mountains. The average temperature is 24.4°C.

## HISTORY AND POLITICS

Honduras was home to part of the Mayan civilisation between the fourth and ninth centuries AD. Christopher Columbus first set foot on the American mainland at Trujillo in Honduras in 1502, but it was 1525 before Spanish colonisation began. In 1821, the country gained independence from Spain, and it was part of a Central American federation of former Spanish colonies from 1823 until it became fully independent in 1839. Thereafter the country underwent periods of political instability interspersed with military rule until 1982, when a civilian government took office. During the civil wars in Nicaragua and El Salvador, Honduras acted as a base for US forces and anti-Sandinista Contras, and there was a marked decline in its respect for human rights. The end of the civil wars led to a decline in the power of the army, which was brought under civilian control in 1999, but there are still very high levels of violent crime. In 2011 congress voted to allow troops to take on police responsibilities in an attempt to curb the high murder rate.

In November 2013, Juan Orlando Hernández of the National Party was declared the winner of the presidential election, winning 36 per cent of votes cast amid allegations of fraud.

Under the 1982 constitution, the executive president is directly elected for a four-year term, which is not renewable, and appoints the government. The unicameral National Congress has 128 members, directly elected for a four-year term.

HEAD OF STATE

*President*, Juan Orlando Hernández, *elected* 24 November 2013, *took office* 27 January 2014

*First Vice-President*, Ricardo Antonio Alvarez Arias

SELECTED GOVERNMENT MEMBERS *as at May 2015*

*Defence*, Samuel Reyes Rendon

*Finance*, Wilfredo Cerrato

*Foreign Relations*, Arturo Corrales

EMBASSY OF HONDURAS

4th Floor, 136 Baker Street, London W1U 6UD

**T** 020-7486 4880 **E** hondurasuk@lineone.net

*Ambassador Extraordinary and Plenipotentiary*, HE Ivan Romero-Martinez, *apptd* 2008

BRITISH AMBASSADOR

HE Sarah Dickson, *apptd* 2012, resident at Guatemala City, Guatemala

## DEFENCE

| *Aged 16–49, 2010 est* | *Males* | *Females* |
| --- | --- | --- |
| Available for military service | 2,045,914 | 1,991,418 |
| Fit for military service | 1,525,578 | 1,539,688 |

*Military expenditure* – US$254m (2014)

## ECONOMY AND TRADE

The country has a huge imbalance in wealth and high levels of corruption and violent crime, often connected with drug-trafficking. Remittances from expatriate workers are equivalent to one-fifth of GDP. Economic activity is heavily dependent on the USA; a drop in exports and remittances due to the global economic downturn contributed to the economy's contraction in 2009. Economic difficulties led to government workers and suppliers going without pay in the winter of 2012. In 2014, the IMF agreed to provide the government with loans totalling US$189m (£120.7m) in order to pay off increasing government debt.

Although still dependent on agriculture, fishing and forestry, whose products form the basis of industrial activity and are the main exports, the economy is gradually diversifying into offshore assembly for re-export and tourism. Agriculture employs 39.2 per cent of the workforce and contributes 14 per cent of GDP. Industry accounts for 27.4 per cent of GDP and 20.9 per cent of employment, and the services sector for 55.3 per cent of GDP and 39.8 per cent of employment.

The main trading partner is the USA, which takes 34.5 per cent of exports and provides 44.3 per cent of imports. Principal exports are garments, coffee, shrimp, wire harnessing, cigars, bananas, gold, palm oil, fruit, lobster and timber. The main imports are machinery and transport equipment, industrial raw materials, chemical products, fuels and foodstuffs.

*GNI* – US$17,129m; US$2,180 per capita (2013)

*Annual average growth of GDP* – 3 per cent (2014 est)

*Inflation rate* – 6.1 per cent (2014 est)

*Unemployment* – 4.1 per cent (2015 est)

*Population below poverty line* – 64.5 per cent (2013)

*Total external debt* – US$7,111m (2014 est)

*Imports* – US$9,169m (2013)

*Exports* – US$3,923m (2013)

BALANCE OF PAYMENTS

*Trade* – US$5,246m deficit (2013)

*Current Account* – US$1,304m deficit (2015 est)

| *Trade with UK* | *2013* | *2014* |
| --- | --- | --- |
| Imports from UK | £11,812,365 | £11,407,664 |
| Exports to UK | £63,810,030 | £69,568,012 |

## COMMUNICATIONS

*Airports* – 13; the principal airports are at Tegucigalpa, La Ceiba and San Pedro Sula

*Waterways* – Honduras has ports on its Caribbean (Puerto Castilla, Puerto Cortes, Tela) and Pacific (San Lorenzo) coasts, and 465km of navigable waterways (mostly by small boats)

*Roadways and railways* – There are 3,367km of surfaced roads, and 44km of railways

*Telecommunications* – 610,000 fixed lines and 7.37 million mobile subscriptions (2012); there were 731,700 internet users in 2009
*Internet code and IDD* – hn; 504 (from UK), 44 (to UK)
*Major broadcasters* – Televicentro operates several channels throughout the country; CBC Canal 6, Vica TV and Sotel Canal 11 are all private broadcasters; private radio stations include Radio America and Radio HRN
*Press* – There are four private daily newspapers, including *El Heraldo* and *La Prensa*
*WPFI score* – 39,27 (132)

## EDUCATION AND HEALTH

Primary and secondary education is free of charge and primary education is compulsory between the ages of six and 11.
*Literacy rate* – 97.2 per cent (2015 est)
*Gross enrolment ratio (percentage of relevant age group)* – primary 109 per cent; secondary 73 per cent; tertiary 20 per cent (2012 est)
*Health expenditure (per capita)* – US$193 (2011)
*Hospital beds (per 1,000 people)* – 0.7 (2012)
*Life expectancy (years)* – 70.91 (2014 est)
*Mortality rate* – 5.13 (2014 est)
*Birth rate* – 23.66 (2014 est)
*Infant mortality rate* – 18.72 (2014 est)

# HUNGARY

*Magyarorszag – Republic of Hungary*

*Area* – 93,028 sq. km
*Capital* – Budapest; population, 1,717,000 (2014)
*Major cities* – Debrecen, Gyor, Miskolc, Pecs, Szeged
*Currency* – Forint of 100 filler
*Population* – 9,897,541 falling at 0.22 per cent a year (2015 est); Hungarian (92.3 per cent), Roma (1.9 per cent) (2001). There are also smaller groups of ethnic Germans, Serbs, Romanians and Slovaks
*Religion* – Christian (Roman Catholic 37 per cent, Protestant 14 per cent), Jewish (less than 1 per cent) (est)
*Language* – Hungarian (official)
*Population density* – 109 per sq. km (2013)
*Urban population* – 70.4 per cent (2013)

*Median age (years)* – 41.1 (2014 est)
*National anthem* – 'Himnusz' ['Hymn']
*National day* – 20 August (St Stephen's Day)
*Death penalty* – Abolished for all crimes (since 1990)
*CPI score* – 54 (47)

## CLIMATE AND TERRAIN

Hungary lies mostly on the vast plain created by the Danube and Tisza rivers, with hills and mountains along the northern border. Elevation extremes range from 1,014m (Mt Kekes) to 78m (river Tisza). Lake Balaton lies in the west. Average temperatures range from −0.6°C in January to 21.1°C in July.

## POLITICS

The 1949 constitution was superseded in 2012 by a new constitution approved by the legislature in April 2011. Parliament has since acted to limit the powers of the constitutional court following clashes, notably on electoral law. The president is elected by the legislature for a five-year term, renewable once; under the new constitution, he or she nominates the prime minister who is then elected by parliament. The unicameral National Assembly has 199 members directly elected for a four-year term.

The 2010 legislative election was won by the opposition Fidesz and Christian Democratic People's Party bloc and it formed a government under Viktor Orban (prime minister 1998–2002), who was re-elected in 2014. After a by-election in February 2015, Fidesz lost its two-thirds 'super majority' which allowed the party to pass laws without the support of other parties. The 2010 presidential election was won outright at the first vote by Pal Schmitt of the Fidesz party, who subsequently resigned from office in April 2012 after admitting he had plagiarised much of his doctoral thesis; the Fidesz party elected Janos Ader as Schmitt's replacement.

### HEAD OF STATE

*President,* Janos Ader, *elected* 2 May 2012, *sworn in* 10 May 2012

### SELECTED GOVERNMENT MEMBERS *as at May 2015*
*Prime Minister,* Viktor Orban
*Deputy Prime Minister,* Zsolt Semjen
*Defence,* Csaba Hende
*Economy,* Mihaly Varga
*Foreign Affairs,* Peter Szijjarto

### EMBASSY OF THE REPUBLIC OF HUNGARY
35 Eaton Place, London SW1X 8BY
T 020-7201 3440 E mission.lon@mfa.gov.hu
W www.london.gov.hu
*Ambassador Extraordinary and Plenipotentiary,* HE Peter Szabadhegy, *apptd* 2014

### BRITISH EMBASSY
Harmincad Utca 6, 1051 Budapest
T (+36) (1) 266 2888 W www.gov.uk/government/world/hungary
*Ambassador Extraordinary and Plenipotentiary,* vacant

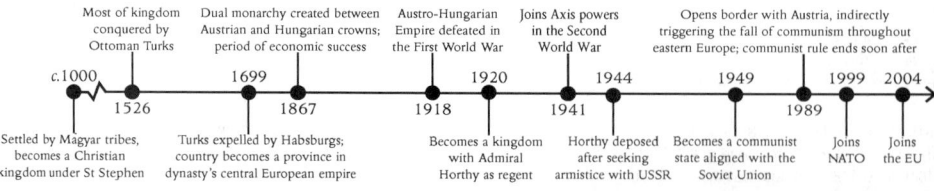

# DEFENCE

| Aged 16–49, 2010 est | Males | Females |
|---|---|---|
| Available for military service | 2,349,948 | 2,290,568 |
| Fit for military service | 1,902,639 | 1,897,378 |

*Military expenditure* – US$1,164m (2014 est)

## ECONOMY AND TRADE

Hungary made a successful transition to a market economy after 1989, attracting high levels of foreign direct investment, and over 80 per cent of GDP is now generated by the private sector. This strong economic growth started to slow in 2006–7, partly as a result of a government austerity programme intended to reduce the budget deficit and public debt. The global economic downturn left Hungary struggling to service both state and private debt in the face of rising interest rates and falling export demand, and the government had to obtain international assistance in 2008. By 2013 Hungary had cut its deficit to under 3 per cent of GDP, allowing the country to exit the EU's Excessive Deficit Procedure. Increases in tourism, household spending and car manufacturing are expected to allow the economy to achieve growth of over 2.5 per cent in 2015 and 2016, despite the poor performance of neighbouring eastern European economies.

Nearly half the land is under cultivation, but agriculture accounts for only 3.4 per cent of GDP; the main crops are cereals, sunflower seeds, vegetables, livestock and dairy products. Industry contributes 31.1 per cent of GDP; the main activities include mining, metallurgy, food processing, and the production of construction materials, textiles, chemicals (especially pharmaceuticals) and motor vehicles. The main trading partners are Germany, Austria, Russia and China. Machinery and manufactured goods account for 84.7 per cent of exports and 79.7 per cent of imports. The country is a net importer of fuels and electricity.

*GNI* – US$117,509m; US$13,260 per capita (2013)
*Annual average growth of GDP* – 2.8 per cent (2014 est)
*Inflation rate* – –0.2 per cent (2014 est)
*Unemployment* – 9.8 per cent (2015 est)
*Population below poverty line* – 14.3 per cent (2012)
*Total external debt* – US$164,800m (2014 est)
*Imports* – US$99,091m (2013)
*Exports* – US$108,426m (2013)

BALANCE OF PAYMENTS
*Trade* – US$9,335m surplus (2013)
*Current Account* – US$6,036m surplus (2015 est)

| Trade with UK | 2013 | 2014 |
|---|---|---|
| Imports from UK | £1,211,447,297 | £1,397,808,707 |
| Exports to UK | £2,596,619,794 | £2,408,449,252 |

## COMMUNICATIONS

*Airports and waterways* – 20, with the principal airport at Budapest; there are 1,622km of permanently navigable waterways, mainly on the river Danube, which has several major river ports and harbours including Budapest
*Roadways and railways* – There are 76,075km of surfaced roads, and 8,057km of railways (including a cross-border line to Austria jointly managed by the two countries)
*Telecommunications* – 2.96 million fixed lines and 11.58 million mobile subscriptions (2012); there were 6.176 million internet users in 2009
*Internet code and IDD* – hu; 36 (from UK), 44 (to UK)
*Major broadcasters* – Magyar Televizio operates two public channels alongside private channels TV2 and RTL Klub;

Duna TV operates satellite channels for Hungarian minorities living in neighbouring states
*Press* – There are four daily newspapers, including *Nepszabadsag, Magyar Hirlap* and *Magyar Nemzet*
*WPFI score* – 27.44 (65)

## EDUCATION AND HEALTH

Hungarians have ten years of compulsory education until age 16; a further two years at secondary level is optional.
*Literacy rate* – 98.8 per cent (2015 est)
*Gross enrolment ratio (percentage of relevant age group)* – primary 102 per cent; secondary 102 per cent; tertiary 60 per cent (2012 est)
*Health expenditure (per capita)* – US$1,056 (2013)
*Hospital beds (per 1,000 people)* – 7.2 (2011)
*Life expectancy (years)* – 75.46 (2014 est)
*Mortality rate* – 12.72 (2014 est)
*Birth rate* – 9.26 (2014 est)
*Infant mortality rate* – 5.09 (2014 est)

# ICELAND

*Lydveldid Island – Republic of Iceland*

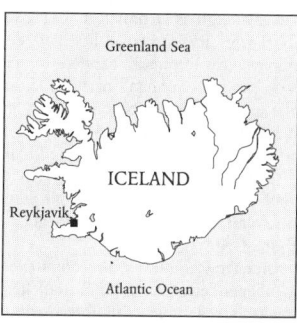

*Area* – 103,000 sq. km
*Capital* – Reykjavik; population, 184,000 (2014 est)
*Major towns* – Hafnarfjordur, Kopavogur
*Currency* – Icelandic kronur (Kr) of 100 aurar
*Population* – 331,918 rising at 1.21 per cent a year (2015 est)
*Religion* – Christian (Lutheran 76 per cent, Roman Catholic 3 per cent) (est)
*Language* – Icelandic (official), English, German
*Population density* – 3 per sq. km (2013)
*Urban population* – 93.9 per cent (2013)
*Median age (years)* – 36.4 (2014 est)
*National anthem* – 'Lofsongur' ['Hymn']
*National day* – 17 June (Independence Day)
*Death penalty* – Abolished for all crimes (since 1928)
*CPI score* – 79 (12)
*Military expenditure* – US$17.4m (2012)
*Gross enrolment ratio (percentage of relevant age group)* – primary 99 per cent; secondary 109 per cent; tertiary 81 per cent (2011 est)
*Life expectancy (years)* – 81.22 (2014 est)
*Mortality rate* – 7.13 (2014 est)
*Birth rate* – 13.09 (2014 est)
*Infant mortality rate* – 3.15 (2014 est)

## CLIMATE AND TERRAIN

Iceland is a volcanic island in the North Atlantic Ocean, to the east of Greenland and to the west of Norway, and its northernmost point reaches the Arctic Circle. Some parts of the coastline have narrow strips of low-lying land, others are sheer cliffs. An inland plateau of glaciers, lakes and lava fields covers most of the interior, with mountainous areas in the north and at the four glaciers in the centre and south. Elevation extremes range from 2,110m (Hvannadalshnukur, on the Oraefajokull volcano) to 0m (North Atlantic Ocean). There are geysers and hot springs owing to the numerous active volcanoes, which can create new islands, such as Surtsey in 1963; the volcano under the Eyjafjallajokull glacier has been active since March 2010. It is estimated that over the past 500 years, Iceland has emitted one-third of the Earth's total lava flow. The climate is influenced by the Gulf Stream; average temperatures range from −1.7°C in January to 9.3°C in July.

## HISTORY AND POLITICS

The first major settlement occurred from around AD 870 onwards, as turmoil in Scandinavia drove migrants to seek new homelands. Iceland hosted a flourishing Viking culture in the ninth and tenth centuries, becoming a fully Christian country in 1000. Iceland recognised Norwegian sovereignty in 1263 and, with Norway, came under Danish rule in 1397. When Norway was ceded to Sweden in 1814, Iceland remained Danish territory, achieving autonomy in domestic affairs in 1874. Although it became an independent state with the same sovereign as Denmark in 1918, Copenhagen continued to control its foreign policy and defence. The treaty of union with Denmark expired in 1943, while Denmark was under German occupation, and in a referendum Icelanders voted to become a fully independent republic, proclaimed on 17 June 1944.

The country's dependence on the fishing industry has led occasionally to fraught foreign relations. The introduction and extensions of an exclusive fishing limit around Iceland in 1958, 1972 and 1975 caused the so-called 'Cod War' disputes with the UK.

Post-independence politics was dominated by the conservative Independence Party (SSF) until January 2009, when the country's economic crisis forced the government first to call an early election, then to resign with immediate effect. Incumbent president Olafur Ragnar Grimsson was re-elected for a fifth term in June 2012. The Progressive and Independence parties won the April 2013 parliamentary elections with 19 seats each and formed a coalition government in May. In 2015, Iceland announced that it would withdraw its EU accession bid, having been a candidate country since 2010.

Under the 1944 constitution, the head of state is the president, who is directly elected for a four-year term, which is renewable. The unicameral legislature, the *Althing*, has 63 members, who are directly elected for a four-year term. Founded in AD 930, the *Althing* is the world's oldest functioning parliament.

### HEAD OF STATE

*President,* Olafur Ragnar Grimsson, *elected* 29 June 1996, re-elected 2000, 2004, 2008, 2012

SELECTED GOVERNMENT MEMBERS *as at May 2015*
*Prime Minister,* Sigmundur Gunnlaugsson
*Finance,* Bjarni Benediktsson
*Foreign Affairs,* Gunnar Bragi Sveinsson

EMBASSY OF ICELAND
2A Hans Street, London SW1X 0JE
T 020-7259 3999 E emb.london@mfa.is W www.iceland.is/uk
*Ambassador Extraordinary and Plenipotentiary,* HE Thordur Aegir Oskarsson, *apptd* 2014

BRITISH EMBASSY
Laufasvegur 31, 101 Reykjavík
T (+354) 550 5100 E info@britishembassy.is
W www.gov.uk/government/world/iceland
*Ambassador Extraordinary and Plenipotentiary and Consul-General,* HE Stuart Gill, *apptd* 2012

## ECONOMY AND TRADE

Iceland has a market economy with an extensive welfare system. While it remains heavily dependent on the fishing industry, which accounts for more than 6 per cent of GDP and 40 per cent of export earnings, there has been recent diversification into aluminium smelting, ferrosilicon production, software production, biotechnology and tourism, encouraged by the plentiful supply of geothermal power. A major area of diversification was into banking, but aggressive expansion in the 2000s led to over-exposure in foreign markets. In the 2008 global financial crisis, the three largest banks collapsed and the government required over US$10bn (£6.3bn) in loans to stabilise its currency and financial system. The economy contracted sharply, causing widespread unemployment and rapid inflation; GDP, however, rose steadily in 2011 and 2012 and the country has begun compensation payments to international claimants of failed Icelandic banks. In January 2013 Iceland awarded licences for oil and gas exploration and production in the waters off its north-east coast to Faroe Petroleum and Valiant Petroleum; Norway took a 25 per cent stake in both. EU accession negotiations started in 2010 but were suspended in 2013 amid concerns about loss of control of the fishing industry and the eurozone's ongoing financial troubles. The economy is forecast to grow by around 3 per cent in 2015 and 2016.

The main trading partners are the Netherlands, Norway and the USA. Principal exports are fish and fish products, aluminium, animal products, ferrosilicon and diatomite. The main imports are machinery, petroleum products, foodstuffs and textiles.

*GNI* – US$12,077m; US$46,400 per capita (2013)
*Annual average growth of GDP* – 2.9 per cent (2014 est)
*Inflation rate* – 2 per cent (2014 est)
*Unemployment* – 5.2 per cent (2015 est)
*Total external debt* – US$102,000m (2012 est)
*Imports* – US$4,787m (2013)
*Exports* – US$4,990m (2013)

BALANCE OF PAYMENTS
*Trade* – US$204m surplus (2013)
*Current Account* – US$108m surplus (2015 est)

| Trade with UK | 2013 | 2014 |
|---|---|---|
| Imports from UK | £193,550,899 | £191,543,179 |
| Exports to UK | £386,780,570 | £404,478,503 |

## COMMUNICATIONS

*Airports* – Seven, with the principal airports at Keflavik, near Reykjavik, in the south, and Akureyri in the north
*Roadways* – There are 4,782km of paved and oiled gravel roads
*Telecommunications* – 189,000 fixed lines and 346,000 mobile subscriptions (2012); there were 301,600 internet users in 2009
*Internet code and IDD* – is; 354 (from UK), 44 (to UK)
*Major broadcasters* – Icelandic National Broadcasting Service operates radio and television services across the country
*Press* – There are three major daily newspapers: *Frettabladid, Morgunbladid* and *DV*
*WPFI score* – 13,87 (21)

# INDIA

*Bharatiya Ganarajya – Republic of India*

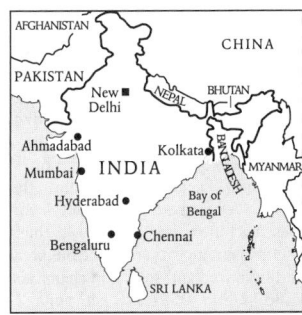

*Area* – 3,287,263 sq. km

*Capital* – New Delhi; population, 24,953,000 (2014)

*Major cities* – Ahmadabad, Bengaluru (Bangalore), Chennai (Madras), Hyderabad, Jaipur, Kanpur, Kolkata (Calcutta), Mumbai (Bombay), Pune, Surat

*Currency* – Indian rupee (Rs) of 100 paise

*Population* – 1,251,695,584 rising at 1.22 per cent a year (2015 est); Indo-Aryan (72 per cent), Dravidian (25 per cent) (2000 est)

*Religion* – Hindu 80 per cent, Muslim 13 per cent (Sunni 85 per cent, Shia 15 per cent), Christian 2 per cent, Sikh 2 per cent (est)

*Language* – Hindi (official national language), English, Assamese, Bengali, Bodo, Dogri, Gujarati, Kannada, Kashmiri, Konkani, Maithili, Malayalam, Manipuri, Marathi, Nepali, Oriya, Punjabi, Sanskrit, Santhali, Sindhi, Tamil, Telugu, Urdu (all official)

*Population density* – 421 per sq. km (2013)

*Urban population* – 32 per cent (2013)

*Median age (years)* – 27 (2014 est)

*National anthem* – 'Jana Gana Mana' ['Thou Art the Ruler of the Minds of all People']

*National day* – 26 January (Republic Day)

*Death penalty* – Retained

*CPI score* – 38 (85)

## CLIMATE AND TERRAIN

India has three well-defined regions: the mountain range of the Himalayas, the Indo-Gangetic plain and the southern peninsula. The Himalayas along the northern border reach 8,598m (Kangchenjunga), then drop to the northern plains formed by the basins of the Indus, Ganges and Brahmaputra rivers before rising to low hills running east to west that mark the division with the southern Deccan peninsula. The peninsula has narrow coastal plains rising to a central plateau, with the Western Ghats and Eastern Ghats ranges of hills lying along the west and east coasts respectively. The Thar Desert lies in the north-west. The climate varies from tropical in the south to temperate in the north. It is influenced by the south-west monsoon; the main rainy season is June to October. During the drier season from December to May, the weather is cooler until February and then becomes increasingly hot until the monsoon breaks. The average temperature in New Delhi ranges from 13.8°C in January to 34°C in June.

## POLITICS

Under the 1950 constitution, the president is elected for a five-year term by an electoral college consisting of members of both chambers of the legislature. The president appoints the prime minister, who is responsible to the legislature. The vice-president, who is elected by both chambers for a five-year term, is *ex-officio* chair of the upper chamber. The legislature, the *Sansad,* consists of two chambers. The upper chamber, the Council of States *(Rajya Sabha),* has up to 250 members, who serve a six-year term; up to 238 members are elected by the state legislative assemblies as individual terms expire, and the rest are nominated by the president. The House of the People *(Lok Sabha)* has 545 members; 543 are directly elected for a five-year term, and two representatives of the Anglo-Indian community are nominated by the president.

There are 28 states and seven union territories (including the national capital territory). Each state has its own executive, comprising a governor, who is appointed by the president for a five-year term, and a council of ministers. All states have a legislative assembly, and some also have a legislative council, elected directly for a maximum period of five years. The states have considerable autonomy, although the union government controls such matters as foreign policy, defence and external trade. The union territories are administered, except where otherwise provided by parliament, by a lieutenant-governor or an administrator appointed by the president.

The 2012 presidential election was won by Pranab Mukherjee. In the legislative elections held in May 2014 the Bharatiya Janata Party (BJP) won a landslide victory against the incumbent India National Congress (INC) and its coalition partners, establishing India's first majority government since 1984 with 282 seats in the *Lok Sabha.* The 2014 legislative election saw the largest turnout in history with 551 million votes cast.

HEAD OF STATE

*President,* Pranab Mukherjee, *elected* 19 July 2012, *took office* 25 July 2012

*Vice-President,* Hamid Ansari

SELECTED GOVERNMENT MEMBERS *as at May 2015*

*Prime Minister,* Narendra Modi

*Finance,* Arun Jaitley

*Home Affairs,* Raj Nath Singh

OFFICE OF THE HIGH COMMISSIONER FOR INDIA

India House, Aldwych, London WC2B 4NA

T 020-7836 8484 E info.london@hcilondon.in

W www.hcilondon.in

*High Commissioner,* HE Ranjan Mathai, *apptd* 2013

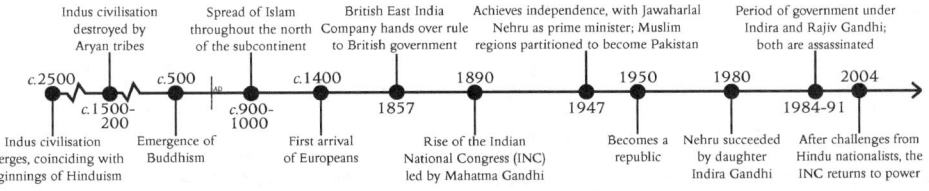

| Indus civilisation destroyed by Aryan tribes | Spread of Islam throughout the north of the subcontinent | British East India Company hands over rule to British government | Achieves independence, with Jawaharlal Nehru as prime minister; Muslim regions partitioned to become Pakistan | Period of government under Indira and Rajiv Gandhi; both are assassinated |

*c.*2500     *c.*500     *c.*1400     1890     1950     1980     2004

*c.*1500-200     *c.*900-1000     1857     1947     1984-91

| Indus civilisation emerges, coinciding with beginnings of Hinduism | Emergence of Buddhism | First arrival of Europeans | Rise of the Indian National Congress (INC) led by Mahatma Gandhi | Becomes a republic | Nehru succeeded by daughter Indira Gandhi | After challenges from Hindu nationalists, the INC returns to power |

BRITISH HIGH COMMISSION
Shantipath, Chanakyapuri, New Delhi 110021
T (+91) (11) 2419 2100 E web.newdelhi@fco.gov.uk
W www.gov.uk/government/world/india
*High Commissioner,* Sir James Bevan, KCMG, *apptd* 2011

## FOREIGN RELATIONS

Since partition, sovereignty over the predominantly Muslim state of Jammu and Kashmir has been disputed by India and Pakistan. A short war in 1947–8 resulted in the state being partitioned between the two countries; its status remains unresolved, despite further outbreaks of war in 1965 and 1971, low-level conflict for control of the Siachen glacier since 1985 and occasional increases in military exchanges, most recently in 1999–2002 and 2003. Tension was exacerbated by Pakistan's support of the Muslim insurgency in the Indian part of the state, which began in the late 1980s and has included terrorist attacks in Indian cities, and by both countries' acquisition of nuclear weapons. Moves towards a peaceful settlement began in 2003, when diplomatic missions were reopened and the resumption of transport links was initiated. Formal diplomatic talks began in 2004 and have achieved several accords intended to reduce tension between the two countries, although the status of Kashmir has yet to be addressed. Talks were temporarily suspended by the Indian government after the 2008 terrorist attacks on Mumbai, but resumed in 2010.

In the Sino-Indian war in 1962, India lost territory to China. In addition, China claims Arunachal Pradesh and does not recognise Indian sovereignty over Sikkim. Talks between India and China in 2003 resulted in India's formal recognition of the Tibetan Autonomous Region as a part of China and a cross-border trade agreement on Sikkim.

## DEFENCE

| Aged 16–49, 2010 est | Males | Females |
|---|---|---|
| Available for military service | 319,129,420 | 296,071,637 |
| Fit for military service | 249,531,562 | 240,039,958 |

*Military expenditure* – US$49,968m (2014)

## ECONOMY AND TRADE

The economy was closed for several decades after independence, with high import tariffs and limits on foreign investment intended to stimulate domestic growth. Since 1991, economic liberalisation and increased foreign investment have generated rapid expansion, with GDP growing by an average 7 per cent a year since 1997. Following a brief contraction in 2008–9 during the global economic downturn, growth exceeded 8 per cent in 2010, but slowed to a ten-year low in 2013 due to the economy performing poorly in a number of key areas. The economy grew by 7.4 per cent in 2014, despite an erratic monsoon season which damaged the agricultural sector. Decreasing inflation and rising demand for Indian exports is predicted to generate growth of around 8 per cent in 2015 and 2016.

India's large skilled workforce has enabled it to develop knowledge-based industries and become a global centre for manufacturing and services. Other areas of growth are pharmaceuticals, tourism and the provision of services to the burgeoning urban middle class. The service sector now accounts for 57.9 per cent of GDP and industry for 24.2 per cent, employing 31 per cent and 20 per cent of the workforce respectively.

Although about 1 per cent of the population has been lifted out of poverty each year since 1997, rural areas have benefited disproportionately little from the economic growth. Agriculture, forestry and fishing support 49 per cent of the population and contribute 17.9 per cent of GDP. The main food crops are rice, cereals (principally wheat) and pulses. The major cash crops include cotton, jute, tea and sugar cane. Agriculture and forestry are threatened by deforestation, soil erosion, over-grazing and desertification.

Despite recent advances, the economy faces a number of problems, chief among which is population growth. Economic constraints on continued growth include underinvestment in infrastructure, shortfalls in energy generation, excessive regulation and corruption.

The main trading partners are the USA, the UAE and China. Principal exports include petroleum products, precious stones, machinery, iron and steel, chemicals, vehicles and garments. Its main imports are crude oil, precious stones, machinery, fertiliser, iron and steel, and chemicals.

*GNI* – US$1,887,143m; US$1,570 per capita (2013)
*Annual average growth of GDP* – 5.6 per cent (2014 est)
*Inflation rate* – 6.4 per cent (2014 est)
*Population below poverty line* – 21.9 per cent (2012 est)
*Unemployment* – 3.8 per cent (2015 est)
*Total external debt* – US$425,300m (2014 est)
*Imports* – US$465,538m (2013)
*Exports* – US$314,684m (2013)

BALANCE OF PAYMENTS
*Trade* – US$151,395m deficit (2013)
*Current Account* – US$29,408m deficit (2015 est)

| Trade with UK | 2013 | 2014 |
|---|---|---|
| Imports from UK | £5,118,498,070 | £3,894,300,273 |
| Exports to UK | £6,186,087,737 | £6,566,708,818 |

## COMMUNICATIONS

*Airports* – There are 253 airports and airfields, principally at Delhi, Mumbai, Chennai and Kolkata
*Waterways* – The chief seaports are Mumbai, Kolkata, Haldia, Chennai, Cochin, Visakhapatnam, Mangalore and Tuticorin; there are 340 ships of over 1,000 tonnes in the merchant fleet. There are 485km of canals and the great rivers provide around 5,200km of navigable waterways
*Roadways and railways* – 79,116km of motorways and 155,716km of state highways; 64,600km
*Telecommunications* – 31.08 million fixed lines and 893.862 million mobile subscriptions (2012); there were 61.338 million internet users in 2009
*Internet code and IDD* – in; 91 (from UK), 44 (to UK)
*Major broadcasters* – The public-owned Doordarshan network operates several national, regional and local services, and All India Radio is the country's largest radio broadcaster
*Press* – Eight major daily newspapers make up a lively press sector; these include *The Times of India, The Hindu* and *India Today*
*WPFI score* – 40,49 (136)

## EDUCATION AND HEALTH

Education is free and became compulsory for children aged six to 14 years in April 2010.
*Literacy rate* – 90.2 per cent (2015 est)
*Gross enrolment ratio (percentage of relevant age group)* – primary 113 per cent; secondary 69 per cent (2011 est); tertiary 25 per cent (2012 est)
*Health expenditure (per capita)* – US$61 (2013)
*Hospital beds (per 1,000 people)* – 0.7 (2011)
*Life expectancy (years)* – 67.8 (2014 est)
*Mortality rate* – 7.35 (2014 est)
*Birth rate* – 19.89 (2014 est)
*Infant mortality rate* – 43.19 (2014 est)

# INDONESIA

*Republik Indonesia – Republic of Indonesia*

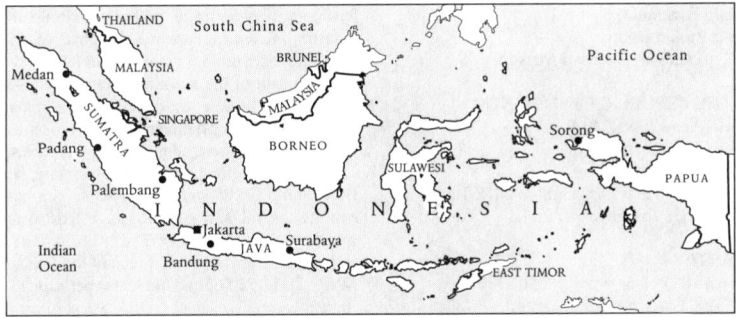

*Area* – 1,904,569 sq. km

*Capital* – Jakarta; population, 10,176,000 (2014 est)

*Major cities* – Bandung, Bekasi, Depok, Makasar, Medan, Palembang, Semarang, Surabaya, Tangerang

*Currency* – Rupiah (Rp) of 100 sen

*Population* – 255,993,674 rising at 0.92 per cent a year (2015 est); Javanese (40.6 per cent), Sundanese (15 per cent), Madurese (3.3 per cent), Minangkabau (2.7 per cent), Betawi (2.4 per cent), Bugis (2.4 per cent), Banten (2 per cent), Banjar (1.7 per cent) (2000)

*Religion* – Muslim 87 per cent (predominantly Sunni), Christian 7 per cent, Hindu 2 per cent (est)

*Language* – Bahasa Indonesia (official), English, Dutch, Javanese, over 580 languages and dialects

*Population density* – 138 per sq. km (2013)

*Urban population* – 52.2 per cent (2013)

*Median age (years)* – 29.2 (2014 est)

*National anthem* – 'Indonesia Raya' ['Great Indonesia']

*National day* – 17 August (Independence Day)

*Death penalty* – Retained

*CPI score* – 34 (107)

*Literacy rate* – 99 per cent (2015 est)

*Gross enrolment ratio (percentage of relevant age group)* – primary 109 per cent; secondary 81 per cent; tertiary 32 per cent (2012 est)

*Health expenditure (per capita)* – US$107 (2013)

*Hospital beds (per 1,000 people)* – 0.9 (2012)

*Life expectancy (years)* – 72.17 (2014 est)

*Mortality rate* – 6.34 (2014 est)

*Birth rate* – 17.04 (2014 est)

*Infant mortality rate* – 25.16 (2014 est)

## CLIMATE AND TERRAIN

Indonesia is an archipelago of over 17,500 islands, of which about 6,000 are inhabited. They include the islands of Sumatra, Java, Madura, Bali, Lombok, Sumbawa, Sumba, Flores, the Riouw-Lingga archipelago, Bangka and Billiton, part of the island of Borneo (Kalimantan), Sulawesi (formerly Celebes), the Maluku (formerly Moluccas) archipelago and others comprising the provinces of East and West Nusa Tenggara, and the western halves of the islands of New Guinea (Papua; formerly Irian Jaya) and Timor. Many of the islands have narrow coastal plains with hilly or mountainous interiors, and around half of the country is covered by tropical rainforest. Elevation extremes range from 4,884m (Puncak Jaya, in Papua) to 0m (Indian Ocean). The climate is tropical; the average temperature is 26.2°C and rainfall peaks in January and February, and is lowest in August.

The country is located near to an intersection of tectonic plates, making it susceptible to seismic activity such as earthquakes and volcanic eruptions; in January 2014 the eruption of Mt Kelud caused mass evacuations in East Java. Indonesia's weather patterns are being affected by climate change.

## HISTORY AND POLITICS

Hindu and Buddhist kingdoms existed in some parts of the Indonesian islands until the 14th century. Islam was introduced in the 13th century and spread over the next three centuries. Trading by the Portuguese began in the 16th century, but the Portuguese were displaced by the Dutch who, lured by the rich spice trade, came to dominate Indonesia by the early 20th century. Opposition to Dutch rule grew in the 1920s and the Japanese occupation of Indonesia during the Second World War strengthened nationalism, leading to a declaration of independence after liberation in 1945. This was not recognised by the Dutch, but after four years of guerrilla warfare they granted independence to the Netherlands Indies in 1949. Irian Jaya (now Papua) was annexed in 1963. Timor–Leste was invaded and annexed in 1975 but gained its independence in 2002.

Achmed Soekarno, the foremost proponent of self-rule since the 1920s, became president in 1949 but was deposed in 1966 in a military coup suppressed by General Suharto, who subsequently became president. Suharto remained in power until 1998 when, amid economic and social upheaval, he was succeeded by his deputy B. J. Habibie. Habibie was defeated in 1999 by Abdurrahman Wahid, in the first democratic elections for 44 years. President Wahid was impeached for alleged financial corruption and in 2001 the legislature appointed Megawati Soekarnoputri (daughter of Achmed Soekarno) to replace him.

The April 2014 legislative elections were won by the ruling Democratic Party and the July 2014 presidential election by their candidate, Joko Widodo. The results were subsequently challenged by his opponent Prabowo Subianto who alleged that widespread electoral fraud had taken place. In August, the Constitutional Court rejected the claims, allowing Widodo to form a cabinet in October 2014.

The 1959 constitution was amended in 2001 to provide for the establishment of the upper chamber of the legislature, and in 2002 to provide for the direct election of the president and the abolition of parliamentary seats reserved for the armed forces.

The executive president is directly elected for a five-year term, renewable once, and appoints the cabinet. The bicameral People's Consultative Assembly comprises the House of Representatives, which has 560 members directly elected for a five-year term, and the House of Representatives of the Regions, which has 132 members, four for each province, directly elected on a non-partisan basis for a five-year term.

HEAD OF STATE
*President elect,* Joko Widodo, *elected* 22 July 2014

SELECTED GOVERNMENT MEMBERS *as at May 2015*
*Defence,* Ryamizard Ryacudu
*Finance,* Bambang Brodjonegoro
*Foreign Affairs,* Retno Lestari Priansari Marsudi

EMBASSY OF THE REPUBLIC OF INDONESIA
38 Grosvenor Square, London W1K 2HW
T 020-7499 7661 E kbri@btconnect.com
W www.indonesianembassy.org.uk
*Ambassador Extraordinary and Plenipotentiary,* HE Teuku
Mohammad Hamzah Thayeb, *apptd* 2012

BRITISH EMBASSY
Jl Patra Kuningan Raya Blok L5-6, Jakarta 12950
T (+62) (21) 2356 5200 E jakarta.mcs@fco.gov.uk
W http://ukinindonesia.fco.gov.uk
*Ambassador Extraordinary and Plenipotentiary,* HE Moazzam
Malik, *apptd* 2014

INSURGENCIES
Separatist movements developed in several parts of Indonesia
after independence, including Maluku, which fought an
unsuccessful separatist war in the 1950s; Irian Jaya (now
Papua), which was granted greater autonomy in 2002,
although separatist agitation continues; Timor–Leste, from its
annexation in 1975 until independence in 2002; and Aceh
province in Sumatra, which was granted a degree of
autonomy in 2005.

Since the fall of Suharto in 1998, tensions between
different ethnic and religious groups have surfaced, and there
has been intercommunal violence in Kalimantan (1996–7,
1999, 2001), Sulawesi (1998–2000, 2001, 2005) and
Maluku (1999–2002, 2004).

At least two Muslim extremist groups are based in
Indonesia and claim links with al-Qaida. They have been
held responsible for bombings in Bali in 2002 and 2005,
and Jakarta in 2003, 2004 and 2009.

DEFENCE

| *Aged 16–49, 2010 est* | *Males* | *Females* |
| --- | --- | --- |
| Available for military service | 65,847,171 | 63,228,017 |
| Fit for military service | 54,264,299 | 53,274,361 |

*Military expenditure –* US$7,020m (2014)
*Conscription –* 18–45 years of age; 24 months (selective)

ECONOMY AND TRADE
The economy struggled from the late 1990s until recent
years, hit in succession by the Asian financial crisis, the
political turmoil following the fall of Suharto, a downturn in
tourism following the Bali bombings and a number of
natural disasters since 2004. President Yudhoyono's
government introduced significant economic reforms which
reduced debt, unemployment and inflation, and boosted
growth in 2004–8. Although growth slowed in 2008,
government stimulus measures countered the effect of the
global downturn in 2009 and by 2011 Indonesia's credit
rating was raised to investment grade due mainly to its low
rates of inflation and small current account surplus. The
economy slowed for a fourth consecutive year in 2014, but
it is predicted to accelerate in 2015 and 2016 due to
investment in infrastructure and the reform of expensive
government fuel subsidies. Indonesia will become a member
of the Asian Economic Community on 31 December 2015.

Natural resources include oil, tin, natural gas, nickel,
timber, bauxite, copper, coal, gold and silver. However, a lack
of investment in prospecting for new sources has led to a
decline in oil production and Indonesia has been a net
importer since 2004. The exploitation and processing of
mineral assets, production of textiles, clothing, cement,
fertilisers, plywood and rubber, and tourism are the main
industrial activities; industry accounts for 45.5 per cent of
GDP and services 45.5 per cent, employing 22.2 per cent and
47.9 per cent of the workforce respectively. Agriculture contributes only 14.2 per cent of GDP but employs 38.9 per cent
of the workforce. The main crops are rice, cassava, peanuts,
rubber, cocoa, coffee, palm oil, copra and livestock products.

The main trading partners are Singapore, Japan, China, the
USA, South Korea and other Pacific Rim nations. Principal
exports are oil and natural gas, electrical appliances, plywood, textiles and rubber. The main imports are machinery
and equipment, chemicals, fuel and foodstuffs.

*GNI –* US$852,561m; US$3,580 per capita (2013)
*Annual average growth of GDP –* 5.2 per cent (2014 est)
*Inflation rate –* 6.4 per cent (2014 est)
*Population below poverty line –* 11.3 per cent (2014)
*Unemployment –* 6 per cent (2015 est)
*Total external debt –* US$278,500m (2014 est)
*Imports –* US$186,351m (2013)
*Exports –* US$182,659m (2013)

BALANCE OF PAYMENTS
*Trade –* US$3,692m deficit (2013)
*Current Account –* US$27,058m decifit (2015 est)

| Trade with UK | 2013 | 2014 |
| --- | --- | --- |
| Imports from UK | £692,490,096 | £620,929,656 |
| Exports to UK | £1,202,629,426 | £1,089,989,728 |

COMMUNICATIONS
*Airports –* 186; each of the main islands has a major airport,
with most capable of accepting international flights
*Waterways –* There are nine major ports, usually the chief
towns of the major islands, and the merchant fleet contains
1,340 ships of over 1,000 tonnes
*Roadways and railways –* 283,102km; 5,042km
*Telecommunications –* 37.98 million fixed lines and 242
million mobile subscriptions (2012); there were 20 million
internet users in 2009
*Internet code and IDD –* id; 62 (from UK), 1 44/ 8 44 (to UK)
*Major broadcasters –* Radio and Televisi Republik Indonesia,
the country's principal broadcaster, operates six television
and two radio networks
*Press –* *The Jakarta Post* and *The Jakarta Globe* dominate a
competitive market that includes eight other dailies
*WPFI score –* 40,75 (138)

# IRAN

*Jomhuri-ye Eslami-ye Iran – Islamic Republic of Iran*

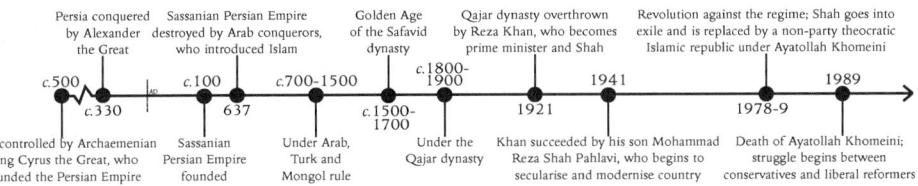

| | | | |
|---|---|---|---|
| Persia conquered by Alexander the Great | Sassanian Persian Empire destroyed by Arab conquerors, who introduced Islam | Golden Age of the Safavid dynasty | Qajar dynasty overthrown by Reza Khan, who becomes prime minister and Shah | Revolution against the regime; Shah goes into exile and is replaced by a non-party theocratic Islamic republic under Ayatollah Khomeini |

*c.*500 — *c.*100 — *c.*700–1500 — *c.*1800–1900 — 1941 — 1989

*c.*330 — 637 — *c.*1500–1700 — 1921 — 1978–9

| Area controlled by Archaemenian king Cyrus the Great, who founded the Persian Empire | Sassanian Persian Empire founded | Under Arab, Turk and Mongol rule | Under the Qajar dynasty | Khan succeeded by his son Mohammad Reza Shah Pahlavi, who begins to secularise and modernise country | Death of Ayatollah Khomeini; struggle begins between conservatives and liberal reformers |

*Area* – 1,648,195 sq. km

*Capital* – Tehran; population, 8,353,000 (2014)

*Major cities* – Ahvaz, Esfahan, Karaj, Mashhad, Qom, Shiraz, Tabriz

*Currency* – Iranian rial of 100 dinar

*Population* – 81,824,270 rising at 1.2 per cent a year (2015 est); Persian (61 per cent), Azeri (16 per cent), Kurdish (10 per cent), Lur (6 per cent), Arab (2 per cent), Baloch (2 per cent), Turkmen (2 per cent) (est)

*Religion* – Muslim (official) 99 per cent (Shia 90–95 per cent, Sunni 5–10 per cent) (est); small Zoroastrian, Jewish, Christian and Baha'i minorities

*Language* – Persian (official), Turkic, Kurdish, Luri, Balochi, Arabic, Turkish

*Population density* – 48 per sq. km (2013)

*Urban population* – 69.3 per cent (2013)

*Median age (years)* – 28.3 (2014 est)

*National anthem* – 'Sorud-e Melli-e Jomhouri-ye Eslami-ye Iran' ['National Anthem of the Islamic Republic of Iran']

*National day* – 1 April (Republic Day)

*Death penalty* – Retained

*CPI score* – 27 (136)

## CLIMATE AND TERRAIN

Apart from narrow coastal plains on the Gulf coasts and the shores of the Caspian Sea, the interior is a plateau consisting of barren desert in the centre and east. This is enclosed by high mountains in the west and north, with smaller ranges on the eastern border and the southern coast. Elevation extremes range from 5,671m (Kuh-e Damavand) to −28m (Caspian Sea). Earthquakes are frequent. The climate is arid or semi-arid in the interior, and subtropical on the Caspian shores. Average temperatures are 5.2°C in January and 29.8°C in July.

## POLITICS

Under the 1979 constitution, overall authority rests with the spiritual leader of the republic, who is appointed for life by the Assembly of Experts; this consists of 83 clerics who are directly elected and decide religious and spiritual matters. The executive president is directly elected for a four-year term, renewable once. Ministers are nominated by the president but must be approved by the legislature. The unicameral Consultative Council *(Majlis al-Shoura)* has 290 members who are directly elected for a four-year term on a non-party basis; five seats are reserved for religious minorities. Laws passed by the legislature must be approved by the Council of Guardians of the Constitution, six theologians appointed by the spiritual leader and six jurists nominated by the judiciary and approved by the legislature; it also has a supervisory role in elections. In 1997, Constitutional Surveillance Council, a five-member body, was established to supervise the proper application of constitutional laws.

Mahmoud Ahmadinejad won the presidential elections in 2005 and 2009. The results of the 2009 election were challenged by the other candidates, who alleged electoral fraud. Following massive protest rallies, the Council of Guardians confirmed Ahmadinejad's victory and ruled out an annulment; further popular protests were suppressed. After the protests in summer 2009, Ahmadinejad's government ruthlessly suppressed the opposition (the Green Movement) and purged liberals from official positions. Conservative candidates retained the majority of seats in the *Majlis* in the 2012 legislative election. In the 15 June 2013 presidential elections, moderate candidate Hassan Rouhani defeated the conservative mayor of Tehran Mohammed Baqer Qaliaf, gaining 50 per cent of the vote.

*Spiritual Leader of the Islamic Republic and C.-in-C. of Armed Forces,* Ayatollah Seyed Ali Khamenei, *appointed* June 1989

*President,* Hassan Rouhani, *elected* 15 June 2013

*First Vice-President,* Es'haq Jahangiri

SELECTED GOVERNMENT MEMBERS *as at May 2015*

*Defence,* Hossein Dehqan

*Economic Affairs and Finance,* Ali Tayebnia

*Foreign Affairs,* Mohammad Javad Zarif

EMBASSY OF THE ISLAMIC REPUBLIC OF IRAN
16 Prince's Gate, London SW7 1PT
T 020-7225 4208 W london.mfa.ir
*Ambassador Extraordinary and Plenipotentiary,* vacant

BRITISH EMBASSY
The Swedish Embassy and embassies of EU countries offer limited consular assistance to British citizens; Swedish Embassy, 27 Nastaran Street, Boostan Avenue, Tehran
T (+98) (21) 2371 2200
E ambassaden.teheran@foreign.ministry.se

## FOREIGN RELATIONS

Between 1980 and 1988, Iran was engaged in a bitter war with Iraq over the Shatt-al-Arab waterway. Iran remained neutral in the Gulf War (1991) and the Iraq War (2003), but it has been accused since of subverting reconstruction in Iraq by arming Shia insurgents.

Since the 1978 revolution, Iran's relations with the West, and especially the USA and the UK, have been strained. It has not cooperated with international efforts to achieve peace in the Middle East, and has long been suspected of sponsoring terrorism by Islamic fundamentalists, especially in Lebanon and Palestine, and now is believed to be supplying arms to the Taliban.

Since 2002 international relations have deteriorated further because of concerns over Iran's nuclear and ballistic missile programmes, especially its acquisition of the ability to enrich uranium. Iran insists that this is for power generation and is not a precursor to developing nuclear weapons, but refuses to halt the programme or cooperate with the International Atomic Energy Agency. The UN has passed six resolutions since 2006 calling on Iran to suspend uranium enrichment and reprocessing and to comply with its IAEA obligations and responsibilities; four of the resolutions imposed or extended sanctions on trade and travel. In an escalation of the nuclear row, the EU imposed an oil embargo on Iran in January 2012, after the country reportedly began to enrich uranium at its underground plant in Fordo. Following an attack on the British embassy in November

2011, economic sanctions were strengthened, and Britain closed its embassy in Tehran and expelled all Iranian diplomats from London.

## DEFENCE

| Aged 16–49, 2010 est | Males | Females |
|---|---|---|
| Available for military service | 23,619,215 | 22,628,341 |
| Fit for military service | 20,149,222 | 19,417,275 |

*Military expenditure –* US$12,719m (2012)\*
*Conscription –* 18 years of age, male only; 18 months

\* Figure does not include paramilitary spending

## ECONOMY AND TRADE

Iran was one of the best-performing economies in the Middle East owing to its vast reserves of oil and natural gas, but its performance has been deteriorating; the predominantly state-controlled economy is inefficient, with little diversification and only a limited, small-scale private sector. Unemployment and underemployment are serious problems, and there is a flourishing unofficial economy. Falling oil prices in 2008–10 and UN sanctions since 2008 have exacerbated Iran's economic problems. The election of the reformer Hassan Ruhani has coincided with a strengthened national currency and an increase in the value of the Tehran stock exchange. The economy left recession in 2014, primarily due to the demand for Iranian oil from the Far East. Inflation and the declining cost of oil is predicted to restrict growth to under 1 per cent in 2015.

Oil and gas extraction and processing dominate the economy, but other industries include petrochemicals, textiles, construction materials, food processing, metal fabrication and armaments. Agricultural production includes wheat, rice, other grains, sugar beet and sugar cane, fruit, nuts, cotton, dairy products, wool and caviar.

The main trading partners are China, the UAE, Turkey, South Korea and Japan. Principal exports are petroleum (80 per cent), chemical and petrochemical products, fruit and nuts, and carpets. The main imports are industrial raw materials and intermediate goods, capital goods, foodstuffs, consumer goods and technical services.

*GNI –* US$328,593m; US$5,780 per capita (2013)
*Annual average growth of GDP –* 1.5 per cent (2014 est)
*Inflation rate –* 17.2 per cent (2014 est)
*Population below poverty line –* 18.7 per cent (2007 est)
*Unemployment –* 13 per cent (2015 est)
*Total external debt –* US$10,170m (2014 est)
*Imports –* US$49,000m (2013)
*Exports –* US$82,000m (2013)

BALANCE OF PAYMENTS
*Trade –* US$33,000m surplus (2013)
*Current Account –* US$3,063m surplus (2015 est)

| Trade with UK | 2013 | 2014 |
|---|---|---|
| Imports from UK | £79,691,990 | £96,625,562 |
| Exports to UK | £31,911,854 | £40,369,851 |

## COMMUNICATIONS

*Airports and waterways –* 140, the principal airports are at Tehran and Shiraz; Iran's seaports include Asaluyeh, Bushehr and Abadan on the Persian Gulf, and Bandar Abbas on the Strait of Hormuz
*Roadways and railways –* There are 160,366km of roadways, including 1,948km of motorways, and 8,442km of railways
*Telecommunications –* 28.76 million fixed lines and 58.16 million mobile subscriptions (2012); there were 8.214 million internet users in 2009

*Internet code and IDD –* ir; 98 (from UK), 44 (to UK)
*Major broadcasters –* The state-run IRIB network operates national and international networks in an industry dominated by satellite channels
*Press –* Major daily newspapers include the English-language daily *Tehran Times,* the conservative *Kayhan* and reformist *Sharq*
*WPFI score –* 72,32 (173)

## EDUCATION AND HEALTH

Primary education, between age six and 14, is compulsory and free.
*Literacy rate –* 98.4 per cent (2015 est)
*Gross enrolment ratio (percentage of relevant age group) –* primary 106 per cent; secondary 86 per cent; tertiary 55 per cent (2012 est)
*Health expenditure (per capita) –* US$346 (2011)
*Hospital beds (per 1,000 people) –* 0.1 (2012)
*Life expectancy (years) –* 70.89 (2014 est)
*Mortality rate –* 5.94 (2014 est)
*Birth rate –* 18.23 (2014 est)
*Infant mortality rate –* 39.0 (2014 est)

# IRAQ

*Jumhuriyat al-Iraq / Komar-i Eraq – Republic of Iraq*

*Area –* 438,317 sq. km
*Capital –* Baghdad; population, 6,483,000 (2014)
*Major cities –* Arbil, Basra, Kirkuk, Mosul, Najaf, Sulaymaniyah
*Currency –* Iraqi dinar (NID) of 1,000 fils
*Population –* 37,056,169 rising at 2.93 per cent a year (2015 est); Arab (75–80 per cent), Kurdish (15–20 per cent) (est)
*Religion –* Muslim (official) 97 per cent (of which Shia 60–65 per cent, Sunni 32–37 per cent), Christian 0.8 per cent (predominantly Chaldean Catholic) (est)
*Language –* Arabic (official), Kurdish (official in Kurdish Autonomous Region), Turkoman, Assyrian, Armenian
*Population density –* 77 per sq. km (2013 est)
*Urban population –* 66.4 per cent (2013)
*Median age (years) –* 21.5 (2014 est)
*National anthem –* 'Mawtini' ['My Homeland']
*National day –* 14 July (Republic Day)
*Death penalty –* Retained
*CPI score –* 16 (170)

## CLIMATE AND TERRAIN

The north-west and south of Iraq consist of an almost barren desert plain. The area between the Euphrates and Tigris rivers, which run across the country from north-west to south-east, is fertile, irrigated and heavily cultivated. The rivers run through marshland to their outflow in the Persian

| Battle of Karbala | Ottomans, weakened by | Comes under | | Second Gulf War; | |
|---|---|---|---|---|---|
| States become part of the Assyrian Empire | Falls under Roman rule | marks split between Sunnis and Shias | First World War, cede control to British | control of Ba'ath Party | War with Iran | Saddam Hussein captured | Final US troops leave |

c.2350    c.550    637    1533    1921    1979    1991    2006

c.600    116–266    680    1916    1968    1980-8    2011

2003-4

| Summerians build city-states into an empire | Iraq falls under Persian rule | Persia conquered by Arab Muslims | Country comes under control of Ottoman Empire | Emir Faisal elected king | Saddam Hussein becomes president | First Gulf War | Execution of Saddam Hussein |

Gulf, on which Iraq has a 58km coastline. In the north-east the land rises to the Kurdistan mountains. Elevation extremes range from 3,611m to 0m (Persian Gulf). The climate is mostly desert, though colder and wetter in the mountains. Average temperatures from 8.9°C in January to 33.9°C in July and August.

## POLITICS

Under the 2005 constitution, the president is elected by the legislature for a four-year term, renewable once. The president nominates the prime minister, subject to the approval of the legislature. The unicameral Council of Representatives *(Majlis al-Nuwab)* has 325 members, of whom 82 must be women and 15 from minorities; members are directly elected for a four-year term.

In the March 2010 legislative elections, the Iraqi National Movement (al-Iraqiya) bloc led by former prime minister Iyad Allawi won the most seats. After several months of negotiations, the al-Iraqiya, SL and Kurdistan Alliance (KA) blocs agreed to form a coalition government under Nouri al-Maliki, and this was sworn in on 21 December. Jalal Talabani, the Kurdish president of the interim government in 2005 and re-elected to the office in 2006, was re-elected for a second term in November 2010. In the April 2014 legislative elections al-Maliki's coalition remained the largest political grouping and Fouad Massoum was elected president in July. However, the military victories of the Islamic State (IS) in the north of the country resulted in al-Maliki's resignation as prime minister on 14 August in favour of Haider al-Abadi. An inclusive unitary government was formed on 8 September.

### HEAD OF STATE

*President,* Fouad Massoum, *elected* 24 July 2014
*Vice-Presidents,* Iyad Allawi; Nouri al-Maliki; Osama al-Nujaifi

SELECTED GOVERNMENT MEMBERS *as at May 2015*
*Prime Minister,* Haider al-Abadi
*Finance,* Hoshyar al-Zebari
*Foreign Affairs,* Ibrahim al-Jaafari

EMBASSY OF THE REPUBLIC OF IRAQ
21 Queens Gate, London SW7 5JE
**T** 020-7590 7650 **E** lonemb@mofaml.gov.iq
**W** www.iraqembassy.org.uk
*Ambassador Extraordinary and Plenipotentiary,* HE Faik Ferik Abdileziz Nerweyi, *apptd* 2013

BRITISH EMBASSY
International Zone, Baghdad
**T** (+964) 790 192 6280 **E** baghdad.consularenquiries@fco.gov.uk
**W** www.gov.uk/government/world/iraq
*Ambassador Extraordinary and Plenipotentiary,* HE Frank Baker, OBE, *apptd* 2014

### INTERNAL UNREST

There are about 4 million Kurds in north-east Iraq, in areas adjoining the predominantly Kurdish areas in Iran and Turkey. Iraq's Kurdish nationalists have demanded an autonomous homeland, Kurdistan, since the 1960s, and turned to militant tactics in the 1970s. Their demands were opposed by Saddam Hussein's regime with great brutality. An uprising after the Gulf War (1991) was suppressed by Iraqi troops, prompting the creation of UN safe havens which enabled the Kurds to set up a semi-autonomous region in the north. An air exclusion zone was also established, but there was further conflict with Iraqi forces and between the two main Kurdish parties in the 1990s. During the war in 2003, Kurdish fighters fought alongside US troops in the north, taking control of the northern cities and establishing an administration in the area, which is now autonomous.

The Shias in southern Iraq also rebelled after the Gulf War and were brutally suppressed. The UN established an air exclusion zone over southern Iraq in 1992 to protect the population, but persecution continued until 2003.

After May 2003, there was insurgent activity throughout the country, particularly in the Baghdad area, the predominantly Sunni-populated towns in the centre and west of the country, and in and around Mosul. The level of violence dropped after 2007 because of the US military 'surge', a ceasefire by one of the main militias, the Mahdi Army, from August 2007, and a key Sunni militia, the Awakening movement, turning against al-Qaida. There was an upsurge of violence in 2008 as the government mounted offensives against militias in Basra, Mosul and parts of Baghdad, and another upsurge in 2009–10 in the run-up to the legislative election and in the months following its inconclusive result. The approximate number of deaths as at December 2010 was: Iraqi civilians 99,000–108,000; US troops 4,400; and other coalition troops 318. Sectarian violence has continued following the withdrawal of coalition troops; in 2012 Shia areas were targeted with numerous bomb and gun attacks. In 2013 a series of deadly bomb attacks marked the ten-year anniversary of the US-led invasion.

In January 2014, after seizing territory in the east of Syria, the IS captured the Iraqi cities of Fallujah and Ramadi. Mosul, Iraq's second largest city, Tikrit and the Kurdish city of Kirkuk were captured in June. Despite reports that the Iraqi army, supported by US air strikes and Iranian backed Shiite militias, regained territory from IS in 2015, Ramadi, a city less than 70 miles from Baghdad, was captured in May 2015. For further details, *see* Middle East, Events.

## DEFENCE

| Aged 16–49, 2010 est | Males | Females |
|---|---|---|
| Available for military service | 7,767,329 | 7,461,766 |
| Fit for military service | 6,591,185 | 6,421,717 |

*Military expenditure* – US$9,516m (2014)

## ECONOMY AND TRADE

The economy suffered three decades of state intervention, mismanagement, corruption, militarisation, war and international sanctions as well as the looting, insurgency and sabotage that followed the 2003 Allied invasion. With the improvement in the security situation, economic activity has increased, the institutions required to implement economic policy are being put in place and a debt reduction programme has been arranged. However, conflict and declining oil prices caused the economy to contract in 2014 and a further contraction is expected in 2015.

Oil is the main resource and export, providing more than 80 per cent of foreign exchange earnings. The conflict with IS has not significantly disrupted production. Other industries include chemicals, textiles, construction materials, food processing and metal fabrication.

The main trading partners are Turkey (25.3 per cent of imports), India (22.5 per cent of exports), China and Syria. Principal exports are crude oil (84 per cent), other crude materials, food and livestock. The main imports are food, medicine and manufactured goods.

*GNI* – US$213,115m; US$6,720 per capita (2013)
*Annual average growth of GDP* – –0.5 per cent (2014 est)
*Inflation rate* – 1.9 per cent (2013 est)
*Population below poverty line* – 18.9 per cent (2012 est)
*Unemployment* – 17.2 per cent (2015 est)
*Total external debt* – US$58,190m (2014 est)
*Imports* – 61,000m (2013)
*Exports* – 82,000m (2013)

BALANCE OF PAYMENTS
*Trade* – US$28,550m surplus (2013)
*Current Account* – US$16,636m deficit (2015 est)

| Trade with UK | 2013 | 2014 |
|---|---|---|
| Imports from UK | £407,091,596 | £376,513,415 |
| Exports to UK | £4,091,504 | £3,384,131 |

## COMMUNICATIONS

*Airports and waterways* – 72, the main international airport is at Baghdad; the 5,279km of waterways are primarily on the Tigris and Euphrates rivers
*Roadways and railways* – 59,623km; 2,370km
*Telecommunications* – 1.87 million fixed lines and 26.76 million mobile subscriptions (2012); there were 325,900 internet users in 2009
*Internet code and IDD* – iq; 964 (from UK), 44 (to UK)
*Major broadcasters* – State-run services include Al-Iraqiya (TV) and Republic of Iraq Radio; there are several private radio and television broadcasters
*Press* – There are more than 100 newspapers and periodicals, many with an ethnic or religious affiliation; publications include the state-run *Al-Sabah,* the private *Al-Mada* and the London-based *Al-Zaman*
*WPFI score* – 47,76 (156)

## EDUCATION AND HEALTH

Since 2003 the country's education system has been reviewed and over 2,500 schools have been refurbished. Primary education is compulsory.
*Literacy rate* – 81.5 per cent (2015 est)
*Health expenditure (per capita)* – US$305 (2013)
*Hospital beds (per 1,000 people)* – 1.3 (2012)
*Life expectancy (years)* – 71.42 (2014 est)
*Mortality rate* – 4.57 (2014 est)
*Birth rate* – 26.85 (2014 est)
*Infant mortality rate* – 37.53 (2014 est)

# IRELAND

*Eire – Ireland*

*Area* – 70,273 sq. km
*Capital* – Dublin *(Baile Atha Cliath);* population, 1,155,000 (2014)
*Major cities* – Cork (Corcaigh), Galway (Gaillimh), Limerick (Liumneach), Swords (Sord Cholm Cille), Waterford (Port Lairge)
*Currency* – Euro (€) of 100 cents
*Population* – 4,892,305 rising at 1.25 per cent a year (2015 est)
*Religion* – Christian (Roman Catholic 84 per cent, Anglican 3 per cent, Muslim 1 per cent (est)
*Language* – English, Irish (Gaelic) (both official)
*Population density* – 67 per sq. km (2013)
*Urban population* – 62.8 per cent (2015)
*Median age (years)* – 35.7 (2014 est)
*National anthem* – 'Amhran na bhFiann' ['The Soldier's Song']
*National day* – 17 March (St Patrick's Day)
*Death penalty* – Abolished for all crimes (since 1990)
*CPI score* – 74 (17)

## CLIMATE AND TERRAIN

The greatest length of the island of Ireland is 486km, from Torr Head in the north-east to Mizen Head in the south-west, and the greatest breadth is 280km, from Dundrum Bay in the east to Annagh Head in the west. Northern Ireland, in the north-east, is part of the UK. The republic has a central plain broken by hills and numerous lakes and bogs. It is surrounded by low mountains, including the Wicklow, Knockmealdown, Galty and Boggeragh mountains, and drained by the principal river, the Shannon (386km), which flows into the Atlantic Ocean. On the north coast of Achill Island (Co. Mayo) are the highest cliffs in the British Isles, 609m above sea level. Elevation extremes range from 1,041m (Carrauntoohil, Co. Kerry) to 0m (Irish Sea).

## POLITICS

Under the 1937 constitution, the president *(Uachtaran na Eireann)* is directly elected for a seven-year term, renewable once. The bicameral National Parliament *(Oireachtas)* consists of the House of Representatives *(Dail Eireann)* and the senate *(Seanad Eireann).* The *Dail* has 166 members, elected for a five-year term by proportional representation. The *Seanad* has 60 members, who serve a five-year term; of these, 11 are nominated by the prime minister *(Taoiseach)* and 49 are elected, six by the universities and 43 from panels of candidates representing various sectoral interests.

The *Taoiseach* is appointed by the president on the nomination of the *Dail,* while other members of the government are appointed by the president on the nomination of the *Taoiseach* with the previous approval of the *Dail.*

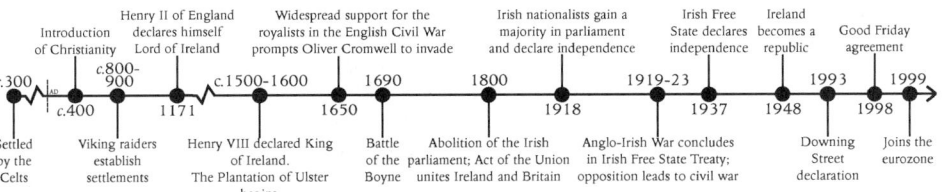

The timeline reads:

Introduction of Christianity — c.300 AD / c.400

Settled by the Celts

Henry II of England declares himself Lord of Ireland — c.800–900 / 1171

Viking raiders establish settlements

Widespread support for the royalists in the English Civil War prompts Oliver Cromwell to invade — c.1500–1600 / 1650

Henry VIII declared King of Ireland. The Plantation of Ulster begins.

Battle of the Boyne — 1690

Irish nationalists gain a majority in parliament and declare independence — 1800 / 1918

Abolition of the Irish parliament; Act of the Union unites Ireland and Britain

Irish Free State declares independence — 1919–23 / 1937

Anglo-Irish War concludes in Irish Free State Treaty; opposition leads to civil war

Ireland becomes a republic — 1948

Good Friday agreement — 1993 / 1998

Downing Street declaration

Joins the eurozone — 1999

The *Taoiseach* appoints a member of the government to be the deputy prime minister *(Tánaiste)*.

The 1997 presidential election was won by Mary McAleese, and she was confirmed in office unopposed in 2004. The coalition government of the Fianna Fail, Progressive Democrats and Green Party lost the early election called in February 2011 because of the country's economic crisis. The opposition Fine Gail (FG) won the most seats but without a majority, and formed a coalition government with the Labour Party; the FG leader, Enda Kenny, was elected prime minister. Labour Party candidate Michael D. Higgins won the 2011 presidential election. New legislative elections are due to take place by April 2016.

**HEAD OF STATE**
*President,* Michael D. Higgins, *elected* 27 October 2011, *confirmed in office* 11 November 2011

**SELECTED GOVERNMENT MEMBERS** *as at May 2015*
*Taoiseach (Prime Minister),* Enda Kenny
*Tanaiste (Deputy Prime Minister),* Joan Burton
*Defence,* Paul Kehoe
*Finance,* Michael Noonan

**EMBASSY OF IRELAND**
17 Grosvenor Place, London SW1X 7HR
T 020-7235 2171 E londonembassymail@dfa.ie
W www.embassyofireland.co.uk
*Ambassador Extraordinary and Plenipotentiary,* HE Daniel Mulhall, *apptd* 2013

**BRITISH EMBASSY**
29 Merrion Road, Ballsbridge, Dublin 4
T (+353) (1) 205 3700 W www.gov.uk/government/world/ireland
*Ambassador Extraordinary and Plenipotentiary,* HE Dominick Chilcott, CMG, *apptd* 2012

**DEFENCE**

| Aged 16–49, 2010 est | Males | Females |
| --- | --- | --- |
| Available for military service | 1,179,125 | 1,163,728 |
| Fit for military service | 977,631 | 965,900 |

*Military expenditure* – US$1,191m (2014)

**ECONOMY AND TRADE**
Since the 1980s Ireland's economy has been transformed from a mainly agricultural to a modern, export-led economy that experienced strong growth from the mid-1990s. But an over-inflated property sector and high levels of personal debt left the economy exposed in the 2008 global financial crisis, causing it to go into a deep recession. Despite passing austerity budgets in 2009 and 2010, in November 2010 the government agreed loan packages with the IMF and EU to avoid defaulting on its sovereign debt. After Enda Kenny took office in March 2011, austerity measures increased in order to reach Ireland's EU-IMF deficit targets; Ireland achieved growth of 1.4 per cent in 2011 and in 2012 the budget deficit was cut to 8.5 per cent of GDP. Towards the end of 2013, Ireland exited its EU-IMF bailout program after meeting deficit reduction targets and reducing banking debt. Ireland was the fastest growing economy in the eurozone in 2014 and is expected to grow by over 3 per cent in 2015.

Agriculture now accounts for 1.6 per cent of GDP and 5 per cent of employment; services contribute 71.4 per cent and industry 27 per cent of GDP, and the sectors account for 76 per cent and 19 per cent of employment respectively. Major industries include mining, pharmaceuticals, chemicals, computer hardware and software, food and drink production, and tourism. Although the Kinsale gas field off the south coast meets some of Ireland's gas needs, and hydroelectric power is generated from the Shannon barrage and other schemes, the country is a net importer of energy. The introduction of charges for tap water in 2014, a measure that was part of Ireland's bailout agreement with EU and IMF, was met with protests.

The main trading partners are the UK, other EU countries and the USA. Principal exports are machinery, computers, chemicals, pharmaceuticals, livestock and livestock products. The main imports are data processing equipment, other machinery, chemicals, petroleum and petroleum products, textiles and clothing.

*GNI* – US$172,106m; US$43,110 per capita (2013)
*Annual average growth of GDP* – 3.6 per cent (2014 est)
*Inflation rate* – 0.2 per cent (2014 est)
*Population below poverty line* – 5.5 per cent (2009 est)
*Unemployment* – 12.7 per cent (2015 est)
*Total external debt* – US$2,164,000m (2012)
*Imports* – US$65,997m (2013)
*Exports* – US$115,334m (2013)

**BALANCE OF PAYMENTS**
*Trade* – US$49,337m surplus (2013)
*Current Account* – US$10,719m surplus (2015 est)

| Trade with UK | 2013 | 2014 |
| --- | --- | --- |
| Imports from UK | £18,142,605,726 | £17,856,669,927 |
| Exports to UK | £15,330,869,484 | £11,710,620,969 |

**COMMUNICATIONS**
*Airports* – The principal airport is at Dublin, with others at Shannon, Waterford, Cork, Killarney, Galway and Knock
*Waterways* – There are 956km of waterways, although these are used only by leisure craft; the main ports are Cork, Dun Laoghaire, Galway, Limerick and Waterford
*Roadways and railways* – 96,036km, including 1,244km of motorways; 3,237km
*Telecommunications* – 2.007 million fixed lines and 4.906 million mobile subscriptions (2012); there were 3.04 million internet users in 2009
*Internet code and IDD* – ie; 353 (from UK), 44 or 048 for Northern Ireland (to UK)
*Major broadcasters* – The main radio and television broadcaster is the state-run Raidio Telefis Eireann (RTE), whose competitors include a handful of Irish commercial stations and British terrestrial and satellite services
*Press* – There are three national newspapers: the *Irish Times, Irish Independent* and *Irish Examiner*
*WPFI score* – 11,2 (11)

## EDUCATION AND HEALTH

Primary education is directed by the state and education is compulsory until age 16.

*Gross enrolment ratio (percentage of relevant age group)* – primary 104 per cent; secondary 119 per cent; tertiary 71 per cent (2012 est)

*Health expenditure (per capita)* – US$4,233 (2013)

*Hospital beds (per 1,000 people)* – 2.9 (2011)

*Life expectancy (years)* – 80.56 (2014 est)

*Mortality rate* – 6.45 (2014 est)

*Birth rate* – 15.18 (2014 est)

*Infant mortality rate* – 3.74 (2014 est)

## ISRAEL AND PALESTINIAN TERRITORIES

*Medinat Yisra'el/Dawlat Isra'il – State of Israel*

*Area* – 20,770 sq. km (includes Jerusalem and the Golan Heights)

*Capital* – The legislature and most government departments are in Jerusalem; population, 829,000 (2014). A resolution proclaiming Jerusalem as the capital of Israel was adopted by the *Knesset* in 1950. It is not, however, recognised as the capital by the UN because East Jerusalem is part of the Occupied Territories captured in 1967; the UN and international law consider Tel Aviv (2014 population, 3,559,000) to be the capital

*Major cities* – Haifa, Rishon Le'Zion

*Currency* – New Israeli Shekel (NIS) of 100 agora

*Population* – 8,049,314 rising at 1.56 per cent a year (2015 est); includes about 531,129 (est) settlers in the occupied areas. Since independence, Israel has had a policy of granting an immigration visa to every Jew who expresses a desire to settle in the country; between 1948 and 2009, over 3 million immigrants entered Israel from over 100 different countries

*Religion* – Jewish 75 per cent, Muslim 17 per cent (predominantly Sunni, Druze 2 per cent), Christian 2 per cent (predominantly Eastern Orthodox) (est)

*Language* – Hebrew, Arabic (both official), English

*Population density* – 372 per sq. km (2013)

*Urban population* – 92 per cent (2013)

*Median age (years)* – 29.9 (2014 est)

*National anthem* – 'Hatikvah' ['The Hope']

*National day* – Fifth day of Jewish month of Iyar (anniversary of Independence Day, 1948)

*Death penalty* – Retained for certain crimes (last used 1962)

*CPI score* – 60 (37)

## CLIMATE AND TERRAIN

Israel comprises the partly forested hill country of Galilee and parts of Judea and Samaria, the coastal plain from the Gaza Strip to north of Acre (including the plain of Esdraelon running from Haifa Bay to the south-east); the Negev, a triangular rocky desert in the south; and parts of the Jordan valley, including the Hula region, Lake Tiberias and the south-western part of the Dead Sea. Elevation extremes range from 1,208m (Har Meron) to −408m (Dead Sea), which is the Earth's deepest depression. The climate is temperate, with hotter, drier conditions in the south and east. Average temperatures range from 11.8°C in January to 27.8°C in August.

## POLITICS

Israel has no written constitution; most constitutional provision is set out in the basic law on government. The head of state is the president, elected by the legislature for a seven-year term, which is not renewable. The unicameral *Knesset* has 120 members elected by proportional representation for a four-year term. The prime minister is responsible to the *Knesset,* and appoints the cabinet, subject to the approval of the *Knesset.*

In the March 2015 parliamentary elections the Likud party won 30 seats and Prime Minister Benjamin Netanyahu formed a coalition government with the centre-right Kulanu (10 seats), the pro-settler Habayit Hayehudi (8 seats), the ultra-orthodox Shas (7 seats) and Yahadut Hatorah (6 seats) parties. The 2014 presidential election was won by Reuven Rivlin.

HEAD OF STATE

*President,* Reuven Rivlin, *elected* 10 June 2014, *sworn in* 27 July 2014

SELECTED GOVERNMENT MEMBERS *as at May 2015*

*Prime Minister,* Benjamin Netanyahu

*Defence,* Moshe Ya'alon

*Finance,* Moshe Kahlon

*Interior,* Silvan Shalom

EMBASSY OF ISRAEL

2 Palace Green, London W8 4QB

T 020-7957 9500 E info@london.mfa.gov.il

W http://london.mfa.gov.il

*Ambassador Extraordinary and Plenipotentiary,* HE Daniel Taub, *apptd* 2011

BRITISH EMBASSY

192 Hayarkon Street, Tel Aviv 6340502

T (+972) (3) 725 1222 E webmaster.telaviv@fco.gov.uk

W www.gov.uk/government/world/israel

*Ambassador Extraordinary and Plenipotentiary,* HE David Quarrey, *apptd* 2015

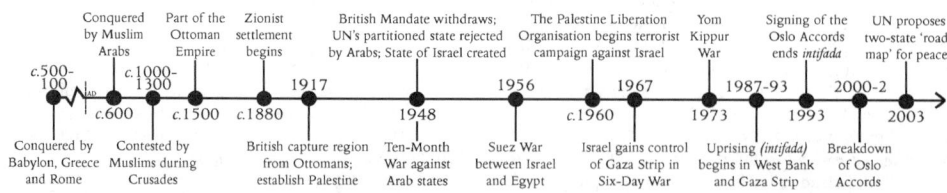

# DEFENCE

| Aged 16–49, 2010 est | Males | Females |
|---|---|---|
| Available for military service | 1,797,960 | 1,713,230 |
| Fit for military service | 1,517,510 | 1,446,132 |

*Military expenditure* – US$15,908m (2014)
*Conscription* – 18 years of age ( Jews and Druze only; Christians, Circassians and Muslims may volunteer); 21–48 months

## ECONOMY AND TRADE

Israel has a technically advanced market economy, having developed its agriculture and industry intensively since the 1970s despite limited natural resources. After a short recession in the early 2000s, structural reforms and tighter fiscal control were implemented, resulting in steady growth from 2003 to 2007, increased foreign investment and a rising demand for exports. Despite the high level of external debt, the economy proved resilient in the global downturn, although it contracted slightly in 2008–9. Its debt and deficits are covered by foreign aid and loans; the USA is the main source of economic and military aid and is Israel's main creditor, owed about half of its external debt. Israel's income inequality and poverty rates are among the highest of any developed nation. Israel is increasingly able to produce natural gas, with production adding to the country's GDP by 0.5 per cent in 2014. Economic growth of just over 4 per cent is expected between 2015 and 2019.

Israel has developed a strong technology sector, central to which are the aviation, electronics, biotechnology, communications and software industries. Other important industries include timber and paper, mineral and metal products, cement, chemicals, plastics, textiles, diamond cutting and tourism, which is reviving. The country is also an important producer of citrus fruits, vegetables, cotton, beef, poultry and dairy products. Service industries account for 71.9 per cent of GDP, industry for 25.7 per cent and agriculture for 2.4 per cent.

The main trading partners are the USA (28.8 per cent of exports), Hong Kong, EU states and China. Principal exports are high-technology machinery and equipment, software, cut diamonds, agricultural products, chemicals, textiles and clothing. The main imports are raw materials, military equipment, investment goods, rough diamonds, fuels, grain and consumer goods.

*GNI* – US$236,682m; US$33,930 per capita (2013)
*Annual average growth of GDP* – 2.5 per cent (2014 est)
*Inflation rate* – 0.5 per cent (2014 est)
*Population below poverty line* – 21 per cent (2012)
*Unemployment* – 6.9 per cent (2015 est)
*Total external debt* – US$99,750m (2014 est)
*Imports* – US$74,861m (2013)
*Exports* – US$66,607m (2013)

BALANCE OF PAYMENTS
*Trade* – US$8,260m deficit (2013)
*Current Account* – US$13,779m surplus (2015 est)

| Trade with UK | 2013 | 2014 |
|---|---|---|
| Imports from UK | £1,381,379,849 | £1,096,840,429 |
| Exports to UK | £1,871,167,906 | £1,182,095,950 |

## COMMUNICATIONS

*Airports and waterways* – 29, with the chief international airport Ben Gurion, between Tel Aviv and Jerusalem; the chief seaports are Haifa and Ashdod on the Mediterranean, and Eilat on the Red Sea
*Roadways and railways* – There are 18,566km of roadways, including 449km of motorway, and Israel State Railways operates a network of 975km
*Telecommunications* – 3.594 million fixed lines and 9.225 million mobile subscriptions (2012); there were 4.525 million internet users in 2009
*Internet code and IDD* – il; 972 (from UK), 44/012/013/014 (to UK)
*Major broadcasters* – The Israel Broadcasting Authority operates public television and radio services across the country; Galei Zahal Israel Defence Force (IDF) radio broadcasts to a mostly civilian audience
*Press* – Daily newspapers include *Yediot Aharonot, Ha'aretz* and *Jerusalem Post*
*WPFI score* – 32,09 (101)

## EDUCATION AND HEALTH

Education is compulsory between the ages of five and 16 and is free.
*Literacy rate* – 99.6 per cent (2011 est)
*Gross enrolment ratio (percentage of relevant age group)* – primary 105 per cent; secondary 102 per cent; tertiary 66 per cent (2011 est)
*Health expenditure (per capita)* – US$2,601 (2013)
*Hospital beds (per 1,000 people)* – 3.3 (2012)
*Life expectancy (years)* – 81.28 (2014 est)
*Mortality rate* – 5.54 (2014 est)
*Birth rate* – 18.44 (2014 est)
*Infant mortality rate* – 3.98 (2014 est)

# PALESTINIAN AUTONOMOUS AREAS

*Area* – The total area is 6,231 sq. km. The area which is fully autonomous is 412 sq. km, of which the Gaza Strip is 360 sq. km and the Jericho enclave 60 sq. km
*Capital* – Although Palestinians claim East Jerusalem as their capital, the administrative capital was established in 1994 in Gaza City; population, 479,400 (2005 est); since 2007 the president and transitional government have been located in Ramallah, on the West Bank; population, 69,479 (2009 est)
*Major towns* – Jabalia, Khan Yunis, Rafah in the Gaza Strip; Hebron, Jericho, Nablus and Ramallah on the West Bank
*Population* – 4,547,431 (2014 est) (Gaza Strip – 1,816,379; West Bank – 2,731,052)
*Religion* – Muslim 98 per cent (Sunni); small Jewish and Christian minorities (est)
*National anthem* – 'Fidai, Fidai' ['Freedom Fighter, Freedom Fighter']

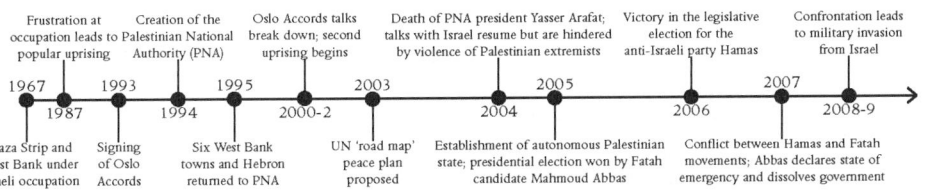

| Frustration at occupation leads to popular uprising | Creation of the Palestinian National Authority (PNA) | Oslo Accords talks break down; second uprising begins | Death of PNA president Yasser Arafat; talks with Israel resume but are hindered by violence of Palestinian extremists | Victory in the legislative election for the anti-Israeli party Hamas | Confrontation leads to military invasion from Israel |
|---|---|---|---|---|---|
| 1967 | 1993 | 1995 | 2003 | 2005 | 2007 |
| 1987 | 1994 | 2000-2 | 2004 | 2006 | 2008-9 |
| Gaza Strip and West Bank under Israeli occupation | Signing of Oslo Accords | Six West Bank towns and Hebron returned to PNA | UN 'road map' peace plan proposed | Establishment of autonomous Palestinian state; presidential election won by Fatah candidate Mahmoud Abbas | Conflict between Hamas and Fatah movements; Abbas declares state of emergency and dissolves government |

*Death penalty* – Retained
*Literacy rate* – 94.9 per cent (2010 est)

## POLITICS

The Interim Agreement of 1995 invested the Palestinian Authority with executive, legislative and judicial authority, but not sovereignty, in the autonomous areas.

The executive president is directly elected for a five-year term. The unicameral Palestinian Legislative Council *(Majlis al-Tashri'i)* has one seat reserved for the president and 132 seats for members elected from party lists for a five-year term. The president appoints the prime minister, who appoints the council of ministers, which must be approved by the legislature. In August 2013 Rami Hamdallah was appointed prime minister having served briefly in office in June 2013.

SELECTED GOVERNMENT MEMBERS *as at May 2015*
*President, Interior,* Mahmoud Abbas, *elected* 9 January 2005
*Prime Minister,* Rami Hamdallah
*Foreign Affairs,* Riyad Najib Abd-al-Rahman al-Maliki

PALESTINIAN GENERAL DELEGATION
5 Galena Road, London W6 0LT
T 020-8563 0008 W www.palestinianmissionuk.com
*General Delegate,* Prof. Manuel Hassassian

BRITISH CONSULATE-GENERAL
PO Box 19690, 15 Nashashibi Street, Sheikh Jarrah Quarter, East Jerusalem 97200
T (+972) (2) 541 4100 W www.gov.uk/government/world/the-occupied-palestinian-territories
*Consul-General,* Alastair McPhail, CMG OBE, *apptd* 2014

## ECONOMY AND TRADE

The *intifada,* and Israeli security restrictions in response to it, have damaged infrastructure and severely constrained economic activity in the Palestinian areas and external trade since 2000. Incomes had dropped and poverty risen sharply even before 2006, when the policies of the new Hamas government led to an embargo by international funding providers, and Israel stopped remitting customs dues collected on behalf of the Palestinian Authority. Emergency aid, provided through channels that bypass the Hamas government, was resumed in late 2006. The effects were most severe in Gaza, where the population is dependent on food aid. On the West Bank, some Israeli restrictions have been eased since 2007, and economic reforms made since 2008, underpinned by foreign aid donors, have stimulated economic development. The 2014 conflict in Gaza caused an estimated US$2.8bn (£1.8bn) worth of damage.

Most economic activity consists of small family businesses engaged in farming, quarrying and small-scale manufacturing of construction materials and textiles, metal goods, handicrafts and agricultural processing. The main exports are stone, fruit, olives, vegetables and flowers, and the main trading partners are Israel, Jordan and Egypt.

*Inflation rate* – 3.5 per cent (2012 est)
*Population below poverty line* – West Bank 18.3 per cent (2010 est); Gaza Strip 38 per cent (2010 est)
*Imports* – US$4,492m (2011)
*Exports* – US$759m (2011)

BALANCE OF PAYMENTS
*Trade* – US$3,733m deficit (2011)

| Trade with UK | 2013 | 2014 |
|---|---|---|
| Imports from UK | £3,605,004 | £1,012,813 |
| Exports to UK | £1,341,994 | £1,301,114 |

# ITALY

*Repubblica Italiana – Italian Republic*

*Area* – 301,340 sq. km
*Capital* – Rome; population, 3,697,000 (2014)
*Major cities* – Bari, Bologna, Florence, Genoa, Milan, Naples, Turin, Venice, Verona. The chief towns of Sicily and Sardinia are Palermo and Cagliari respectively
*Currency* – Euro (€) of 100 cents
*Population* – 61,855,120 rising at 0.27 per cent a year (2015 est)
*Religion* – Christian (Roman Catholic 80 per cent) (est); unaffiliated 20 per cent
*Language* – Italian (official), German, French, Slovene
*Population density* – 203 per sq. km (2013)
*Urban population* – 68.7 per cent (2013)
*Median age (years)* – 44.5 (2014 est)
*National anthem* – 'Il Canto degli Italiani' ['The Song of the Italians']
*National day* – 2 June (Republic Day)
*Death penalty* – Abolished for all crimes (since 1994)
*CPI score* – 43 (69)

## CLIMATE AND TERRAIN

Italy consists of a peninsula, the islands of Sicily, Sardinia, Elba and about 70 smaller islands. The smaller islands include Pantelleria, the Pelagian islands, the Aeolian islands, Capri, the Flegrean islands, the Pontine archipelago, the Tremiti islands and the Tuscan archipelago. Most of the islands are mountainous.

The peninsula is also largely mountainous, but between the spine of the Apennines and the eastern coastline are two large fertile plains: Emilia-Romagna in the north and Apulia in the south. Italy is divided from France and Switzerland by the Alps, and from Austria and Slovenia by both the Alps and the Dolomites. Three volcanoes, Vesuvius, Etna and Stromboli, are still active. Elevation extremes range from 4,748m (Mt Bianco di Courmayeur) to 0m (Mediterranean Sea). At the foot of the Alps lie the great lakes of Como, Maggiore and Garda. The chief rivers are the Po (651km) and the Adige, flowing through the northern plain to the Adriatic Sea, and the Arno (Florentine plain) and the Tiber (flowing through Rome to Ostia), which flow to the west coast. The climate is Mediterranean, with warm dry summers and mild winters.

## POLITICS

The 1948 constitution has been amended several times, notably in 2001 to provide for greater autonomy for the 20 regions in tax, education and environment matters. The president, who must be over 50 years of age, is elected for a seven-year term by an electoral college consisting of both chambers of the legislature and 58 regional representatives. The bicameral *Parlamento* comprises a 630-member

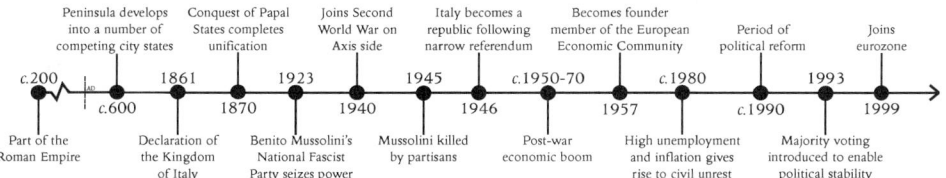

| Peninsula develops into a number of competing city states | Conquest of Papal States completes unification | Joins Second World War on Axis side | Italy becomes a republic following narrow referendum | Becomes founder member of the European Economic Community | Period of political reform | Joins eurozone |

c.200 — 1861 — 1923 — 1945 — c.1950-70 — c.1980 — 1993

c.600 — 1870 — 1940 — 1946 — 1957 — c.1990 — 1999

| Part of the Roman Empire | Declaration of the Kingdom of Italy | Benito Mussolini's National Fascist Party seizes power | Mussolini killed by partisans | Post-war economic boom | High unemployment and inflation gives rise to civil unrest | Majority voting introduced to enable political stability |

Chamber of Deputies and a senate with 315 members directly elected on a regional basis and a variable number of life senators, who are past presidents and senators appointed by incumbent presidents. Elected members of both chambers serve a five-year term. In 2015, parliament passed new legislation set to come into force in 2016 to ensure that the party that wins the most votes in a legislative election will be allocated a majority of seats. Any party that wins more than 40 per cent of the national vote will be awarded 340 seats. If no party reaches the threshold, there is a second-place run-off between the two parties with the most votes.

Having been elected the leader of the Democratic Party (PD) in December 2013, Matteo Renzi succeeded Enrico Letta as prime minister in February 2014, becoming the third prime minster in a row not to be directly elected by the Italian people. His PD-led coalition government was sworn in on 22 February. In January 2015, Sergio Mattarella was elected president by parliament following the resignation of Georgio Napolitano due to ill health.

HEAD OF STATE
*President*, Sergio Mattarella, *elected* 31 January 2015, *sworn in* 4 February 2015

SELECTED GOVERNMENT MEMBERS *as at May 2015*
*Prime Minister*, Matteo Renzi
*Defence*, Roberta Pinotti
*Foreign Affairs*, Paolo Gentiloni
*Interior*, Angelino Alfano

ITALIAN EMBASSY
14 Three Kings Yard, Davies Street, London W1K 4EH
T 020-7312 2200 E ambasciata.londra@esteri.it
W www.amblondra.esteri.it
*Ambassador Extraordinary and Plenipotentiary*, HE Pasquale Terracciano, *apptd* 2013

BRITISH EMBASSY
Via XX Settembre 80A, 00187 Rome
T (+39) (06) 4220 0001 W www.gov.uk/government/world/italy
*Ambassador Extraordinary and Plenipotentiary*, HE Christopher Prentice, CMG, *apptd* 2011

DEFENCE

| Aged 16–49, 2010 est | Males | Females |
| --- | --- | --- |
| Available for military service | 13,865,688 | 14,003,755 |
| Fit for military service | 11,247,446 | 11,348,695 |

*Military expenditure* – US$30,909m (2014)

ECONOMY AND TRADE
Economically, Italy is divided between a prosperous and industrially developed north and a largely agricultural and welfare-dependent south that has high unemployment levels. There is a large unofficial economy that is estimated to be worth 17 per cent of GDP, but measures to tackle this and wider structural reforms have made slow progress because of political opposition and sluggish economic performance. A large budget deficit and public debt of over 126 per cent of GDP in 2012 helped cause growth to reach −1.8 per cent in

2013. Unemployment reached 12.4 per cent, with youth unemployment increasing to 40 per cent. The economy is expected to grow in 2015 for the first time in four years.

Tourism is the largest industry. Other major industries include precision machinery, iron and steel, chemicals, food processing, textiles, motor vehicles, fashion clothing, footwear, ceramics and electrical goods. The services sector contributes 73.9 per cent of GDP, industry 23.9 per cent and agriculture 2.2 per cent. The main trading partners are other EU states, especially Germany and France. Principal exports are the products of the main industries, plus food, beverages, minerals and non-ferrous metals. The main imports are engineering and energy products, industrial raw materials and transport equipment.

*GNI* – US$2,001,518m; US$35,860 per capita (2013)
*Annual average growth of GDP* – −0.2 per cent (2014 est)
*Inflation rate* – 0.2 per cent (2014 est)
*Population below poverty line* – 29.9 per cent (2012 est)
*Unemployment* – 12.7 per cent (2015 est)
*Total external debt* – US$2,604,000m (2013 est)
*Imports* – US$477,292m (2013)
*Exports* – US$517,628m (2013)

BALANCE OF PAYMENTS
*Trade* – US$40,338m surplus (2013)
*Current Account* – US$48,409m surplus (2015 est)

| Trade with UK | 2013 | 2014 |
| --- | --- | --- |
| Imports from UK | £8,404,165,390 | £8,739,902,545 |
| Exports to UK | £15,330,869,484 | £16,673,779,082 |

COMMUNICATIONS
*Airports and waterways* – 98, including major airports at Rome, Milan, Naples and Venice, Palermo and Catania (Sicily), and Cagliari (Sardinia); the main seaports are Naples, Genoa, Livorno, Trieste, Venice, Palermo and Catania
*Roadways* – A 6,700km network of motorways *(autostrade)* covers the country but there are 487,700km of roads in total
*Railways* – There are 20,255km of railways; the main railway system is run by the state-owned *Ferrovia dello Stato*. In February 2015 it was agreed a new high-speed rail link between Lyon and Turin worth €26bn (£18bn) would be built by 2020, including a 57km tunnel through the Alps
*Telecommunications* – 21.656 million fixed lines and 97.225 million mobile subscriptions (2012); there were 29.24 million internet users in 2009
*Internet code and IDD* – it; 39 (from UK), 44 (to UK)
*Major broadcasters* – Rai is Italy's public radio and television broadcaster and competes with a number of private television broadcasters, the leading one being Mediaset, part of the media empire of former prime minister Silvio Berlusconi
*Press* – The press is highly regionalised; daily newspapers include *La Stampa* (Turin based), *La Repubblica* (Rome) and *Corriere della Sera* (Milan)
*WPFI score* – 27,94 (73)

EDUCATION AND HEALTH
Education is free and compulsory between the ages of six and 16.
*Literacy rate* – 99.9 per cent (2015 est)

*Gross enrolment ratio (percentage of relevant age group)* –
primary 100 per cent; secondary 101 per cent (2011 est);
tertiary 62 per cent (2012 est)
*Health expenditure (per capita)* – US$3,155 (2013)
*Hospital beds (per 1,000 people)* – 3.4 (2011)
*Life expectancy (years)* – 82.03 (2014 est)
*Mortality rate* – 10.1 (2014 est)
*Birth rate* – 8.84 (2014 est)
*Infant mortality rate* – 3.31 (2014 est)

# JAMAICA

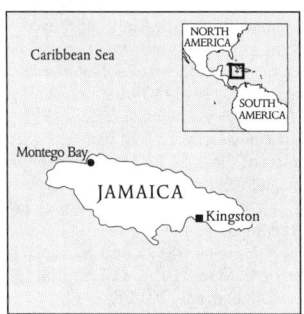

*Area* – 10,991 sq. km
*Capital* – Kingston; population, 587,000 (2014)
*Major towns* – Montego Bay, Portmore, Spanish Town
*Currency* – Jamaican dollar (J$) of 100 cents
*Population* – 2,950,210 rising at 0.68 per cent a year
(2015 est)
*Religion* – Christian (Protestant 64 per cent, Roman Catholic
2 per cent), Rastafarian 1 per cent (est)
*Language* – English (official), Jamaican patois
*Population density* – 251 per sq. km (2013)
*Urban population* – 52.2 per cent (2013)
*Median age (years)* – 24.9 (2014 est)
*National anthem* – 'Jamaica, Land We Love'
*National day* – 6 August (Independence Day)
*Death penalty* – Retained (last used 1988)
*CPI score* – 38 (85)

## CLIMATE AND TERRAIN
An island in the Caribbean Sea, south of Cuba and west
of Hispaniola, Jamaica is mostly mountainous and forested,
with a narrow coastal plain. Elevation extremes range from
2,256m (Blue Mountain Peak) to 0m (Caribbean Sea). The
climate is tropical, although more temperate inland. The
average temperature in Jamaica is 25.6°C.

## HISTORY AND POLITICS
Jamaica was visited by Columbus in 1494 and settled by
the Spanish from 1509. Captured by the British in 1655, it
became a crown colony in 1865. Jamaica became internally
self-governing in 1959 and independent in 1962.

Post-independence politics has been dominated by the
conservative Jamaican Labour Party (JLP) and social-
democratic People's National Party (PNP). Relations
between the two parties, often fraught, degenerated in the
1970s into violence that marred elections and political life
for some years. Despite the current political stability, there is
still widespread lawlessness, which now is often connected
to drug-trafficking.

In the 2011 legislative election, the PNP, narrowly
defeated by the JLP in the previous election, won a two-
thirds majority, picking up 42 of the 63 seats. The PNP
formed a government under Portia Simpson-Miller.

Under the 1962 constitution, the head of state is Queen
Elizabeth II, represented locally by a governor-general.
The bicameral parliament consists of the House of
Representatives, with 63 directly elected members, and the
senate of 21 appointed members, 13 nominated by the prime
minister and eight by the leader of the opposition; both
chambers serve five-year terms. The prime minister is the
leader of the majority party in the elected chamber.
*Governor-General*, HE Patrick Allen, GCMG, *apptd* 2009

SELECTED GOVERNMENT MEMBERS *as at May 2015*
*Prime Minister, Defence*, Portia Simpson-Miller
*Deputy Prime Minister, Finance*, Peter Phillips
*Foreign Affairs and Foreign Trade*, Arnold Nicholson
*National Security*, Peter Bunting

JAMAICAN HIGH COMMISSION
1–2 Prince Consort Road, London SW7 2BZ
T 020-7823 9911 E jamhigh@jhcuk.com W www.jhcuk.org
*High Commissioner*, HE Aloun Ndombet-Assamba, *apptd*
2012

BRITISH HIGH COMMISSION
PO Box 575, 28 Trafalgar Road, Kingston 10
T (+1) (876) 936 0700 E ppa.kingston@fco.gov.uk
W www.gov.uk/government/world/jamaica
*High Commissioner*, HE David Fitton, *apptd* 2013

## DEFENCE

| *Aged 16–49, 2010 est* | *Males* | *Females* |
| --- | --- | --- |
| Available for military service | 726,263 | 742,958 |
| Fit for military service | 590,673 | 596,414 |

*Military expenditure* – US$120m (2014)

## ECONOMY AND TRADE
The economy is weak owing to high interest rates, increased
foreign competition, high unemployment, growing internal
and external debt, and hurricane and storm damage in
2004, 2007 and 2008. Jamaica depends on foreign aid and
remittances from expatriates; remittances were worth nearly
20 per cent of GDP but declined to about 15 per cent after
the global downturn began. This hit the economy badly, and
IMF support was needed in 2010. Economic growth is
hindered by the high level of violent crime, corruption and a
debt-to-GDP ratio of 125 per cent. Tourism, accounting for
5 per cent of GDP, remains strong. Public debt is among the
highest in the developing world, while youth unemployment
and crime also threaten the economy. Economic growth of
just under 2 per cent is expected in 2015–16.

The economy is dominated by the service sector, which
makes up 72 per cent of GDP; industry accounts for 21.1
per cent, and agriculture for 6.9 per cent. Industries include
alumina and bauxite extraction, processing agricultural
produce and light manufacturing.

The main trading partners are the USA, Trinidad and
Tobago, Canada, Venezuela and the UK. Principal exports
are alumina, bauxite, sugar, bananas, rum, coffee, yams,
beverages, chemicals and clothing. The main imports are
food, consumer goods, industrial supplies, fuel, and parts and
accessories for capital goods.
*GNI* – US$14,321m; US$5,220 per capita (2013)
*Annual average growth of GDP* – 1.1 per cent (2014 est)
*Inflation rate* – 8.3 per cent (2014 est)
*Population below poverty line* – 17.6 per cent (2010 est)
*Unemployment* – 14.7 per cent (2015 est)
*Total external debt* – US$15,590m (2014 est)
*Imports* – US$6,200m (2013)
*Exports* – US$1,574m (2013)

## BALANCE OF PAYMENTS
Trade – US$4,626m deficit (2013)
Current Account – US$697m deficit (2015 est)

| Trade with UK | 2013 | 2014 |
|---|---|---|
| Imports from UK | £43,002,949 | £40,413,833 |
| Exports to UK | £57,750,311 | £51,106,669 |

## COMMUNICATIONS
Airports and waterways – The principal airports are at Kingston and Montego Bay; there are several harbours, Kingston being the main seaport
Roadways and railways – The island has 16,148km of roadways; the rail network is no longer in use
Telecommunications – 265,000 fixed lines and 2.665 million mobile telephone subscriptions (2012); there were 1.58 million internet users in 2009
Internet code and IDD – jm; 1 876 (from UK), 011 44 (to UK)
Major broadcasters – The state broadcaster was privatised in 1997 and now operates as Television Jamaica Ltd; Radio Jamaica Ltd (RJR) operates a number of stations
Press – There are three main daily newspapers: The Jamaica Gleaner, The Jamaica Star and the Jamaica Observer
WPFI score – 11,18 (9)

## EDUCATION AND HEALTH
In 2010 the Inter-American Development Bank provided US$45m in funding to enable the government to make improvements to the education system and expand compulsory schooling from age 16 to 18.
Literacy rate – 96.5 per cent (2015 est)
Gross enrolment ratio (percentage of relevant age group) – secondary 89 per cent (2011 est); tertiary 31 per cent (2012 est)
Health expenditure (per capita) – US$300 (2013)
Hospital beds (per 1,000 people) – 1.7 (2012)
Life expectancy (years) – 73.48 (2014 est)
Mortality rate – 6.67 (2014 est)
Birth rate – 18.41 (2014 est)
Infant mortality rate – 13.69 (2014 est)
HIV/AIDS adult prevalence – 1.7 per cent (2012 est)

# JAPAN

Nihon-koku/Nippon-koku – Japan

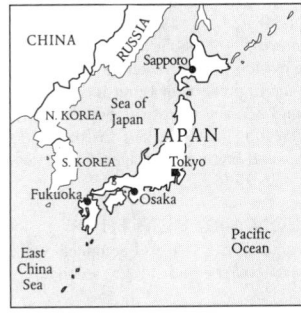

Area – 377,915 sq. km
Capital – Tokyo; population, 37,833,000 (2014)
Major cities – Fukuoka, Hiroshima, Kawasaki, Kobe, Kyoto (the ancient capital), Nagoya, Osaka, Saitama, Sapporo, Yokohama
Currency – Yen of 100 sen
Population – 126,919,659 falling at 0.16 per cent a year (2015 est)

Religion – Shinto 78.7 per cent, Buddhist 66.1 per cent, Christian 1.5 per cent (est); much of the population adheres to more than one religion, most commonly combining Shinto and Buddhist beliefs
Language – Japanese (official)
Population density – 349 per sq. km (2013)
Urban population – 92.5 per cent (2013)
Median age (years) – 46.1 (2014 est)
National anthem – 'Kimigayo' ['The Emperor's Reign']
National day – 23 December (Birthday of Emperor Akihito)
Death penalty – Retained
CPI score – 76 (15)

## CLIMATE AND TERRAIN
Japan consists of four large islands: Honshu (or Mainland), Shikoku, Kyushu and Hokkaido, and many smaller islands. Typically, the islands have coastal plains and wooded, mountainous interiors; 67 per cent of Japan's land area is forested. The mountains running across the mainland from the Sea of Japan to the Pacific Ocean include a number of volcanoes, mainly extinct or dormant. Elevation extremes range from 3,776m (Mt Fuji) to −4m (Hachiro-gata). The climate varies from temperate in the north to tropical in the south. Average temperatures range from 1°C in January to 23.7°C in August.

The islands are located at the intersection of three tectonic plates and are prone to seismic activity; 20 per cent of the world's major earthquakes occur in this area. A magnitude-9 earthquake and the ensuing tsunami devastated the north-east of Honshu in March 2011.

## POLITICS
The 1947 constitution established Japan as a constitutional monarchy with a hereditary emperor as head of state. The bicameral Diet comprises the House of Representatives (the lower house) and the House of Councillors. The House of Representatives has 480 members directly elected for a four-year term, including 180 by proportional representation. The House of Councillors has 242 members, including 96 elected by proportional representation, who serve six-year terms, with half elected every three years; unlike the lower house, it cannot be dissolved by the prime minister. The prime minister is formally elected by the House of Representatives and appoints the cabinet.

The Liberal Democrat Party (LDP) has dominated post-war politics, holding power continuously from 1955 to 1993, and then – usually as the main party in coalition governments – from 1994 to 2009. In 2010, it regained control of the upper house of the legislature from the Democratic Party of Japan (DPJ). In December 2012 the LDP returned to power, taking 294 seats in the parliamentary election while the DPJ won only 57; Shinzo Abe once again took the position of prime minister. Following snap legislative elections in December 2014, the LDP remained in power, in coalition with the Komeito (NKP), despite the DPJ increasing its seats to 73.

HEAD OF STATE
HIM The Emperor of Japan, Akihito, born 23 December 1933, succeeded 8 January 1989, enthroned 12 November 1990
Heir, HRH Crown Prince Naruhito Hironomiya, born 23 February 1960

SELECTED GOVERNMENT MEMBERS as at May 2015
Prime Minister, Shinzo Abe
Defence, Gen. Nakatani
Finance, Taro Aso
Foreign Affairs, Fumio Kishida

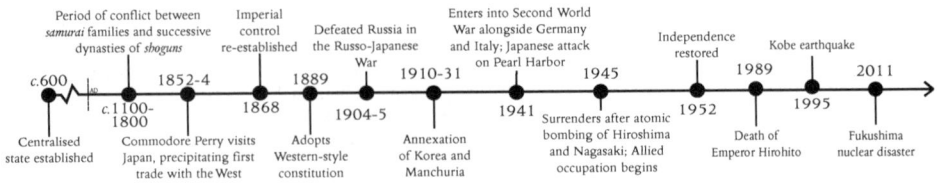

**EMBASSY OF JAPAN**
101–104 Piccadilly, London W1J 7JT
T 020-7465 6500 E info@ld.mofa.go.jp
W www.uk.emb-japan.go.jp
*Ambassador Extraordinary and Plenipotentiary,* HE Keiichi
  Hayashi, *apptd* 2011

**BRITISH EMBASSY**
No. 1 Ichiban-cho, Chiyoda-ku, Tokyo 102–8381
T (+81) (3) 5211 1100 E public-enquiries.tokyo@fco.gov.uk
W www.gov.uk/government/world/japan
*Ambassador Extraordinary and Plenipotentiary,* HE Tim
  Hitchens, *apptd* 2012

## DEFENCE

The constitution prohibits the maintenance of armed forces, although internal security forces were created in the 1950s and their mission was extended in 1954 to include the defence of Japan against aggression. In the 1990s, legislation was passed permitting limited participation by the armed forces in UN peacekeeping missions and allowing them to enter foreign conflicts in order to rescue Japanese nationals. A revision to the USA–Japan defence cooperation guidelines agreed in 1997 permits Japan to play a supporting role in US military operations in areas surrounding Japan; Japanese troops were also deployed in Iraq to assist with post-war reconstruction between 2003 and 2006.

| Aged 16–49, 2010 est | Males | Females |
| --- | --- | --- |
| Available for military service | 27,301,443 | 26,307,003 |
| Fit for military service | 22,390,431 | 21,540,322 |

*Military expenditure* – US$45,776m (2014)

## ECONOMY AND TRADE

Japan has the fourth-largest economy in the world after the USA, China and India. Its rapid post-war economic growth, based largely on car and consumer electronics manufacturing, experienced a marked contraction from 1990. Exacerbated by the 1997 Asian economic crisis, the recession lasted 14 years. Reforms introduced from 2001, particularly to the corporate and public sectors, improved economic growth from 2002 to 2007, but the economy went into recession again in 2008 owing to the global downturn. Government stimulus packages and an increase in global demand spurred the start of a recovery from late 2009. Following the 2011 earthquake and tsunami there was a drop in production; the economy has largely recovered in the following two years, but was less complete in the Tohoku region. Though the economy is benefiting from declining oil prices and a weak yen, a large public debt, which reached 240 per cent of GDP in 2014, and a series of tax rises, which began in 2014, and are scheduled to continue until 2017, are predicted to limit future growth.

High-technology industries remain the mainstay of the economy, producing vehicles, electronic equipment, machine tools, steel and other metals, ships, chemicals, textiles and processed food. Financial services is also a major sector, supplying a global market. Agriculture is constrained by the mountainous terrain but intensive cultivation produces high yields, and there is a large fishing industry. The service sector contributes 73.1 per cent of GDP, industry 25.7 per cent and agriculture 1.2 per cent.

The main trading partners are China, the USA, other Pacific Rim countries and the Gulf states. Principal exports include transport equipment, motor vehicles, semiconductors, electrical machinery and chemicals. The main imports are machinery and equipment, fuels, foodstuffs, chemicals, textiles and raw materials.

*GNI* – US$6,150,131m; US$46,330 per capita (2013)
*Annual average growth of GDP* – 1.3 per cent (2014 est)
*Inflation rate* – 2.7 per cent (2014 est)
*Population below poverty line* – 16.1 per cent (2013 est)
*Unemployment* – 4 per cent (2015 est)
*Total external debt* – US$3,017,000m (2012 est)
*Imports* – US$832,424m (2013)
*Exports* – US$714,613m (2013)

BALANCE OF PAYMENTS
*Trade* – US$81,568m deficit (2015 est)
*Current Account* – US$60,446m surplus (2012)

| Trade with UK | 2013 | 2014 |
| --- | --- | --- |
| Imports from UK | £4,499,893,258 | £4,329,744,154 |
| Exports to UK | £7,397,407,912 | £6,925,555,072 |

## COMMUNICATIONS

*Airports* – 142; the principal airports include Haneda (Tokyo), Narita, Kansai and Chubu
*Waterways* – Japan has a large merchant fleet, with 684 ships of over 1,000 tonnes in 2011; the main seaports are Tokyo, Osaka, Nagoya, Yokohama, Kobe and Kawasaki
*Roadways and railways* – There are 973,234km of roadways, including 7,803km of motorways, and 27,182km of railways
*Telecommunications* – 64.27 million fixed lines and 138.36 million mobile subscriptions (2012); there were 99.18 million internet users in 2009
*Internet code and IDD* – jp; 81 (from UK), 1 44/010 44/41 44/61 44 (to UK)
*Major broadcasters* – A public broadcaster, NHK, provides radio and television services; satellite and cable television is widespread and digital broadcasting is expanding
*Press* – Around 80 per cent of the population reads a daily newspaper, creating huge markets for publications such as *Asahi Shimbun* and English-language title *The Japan Times*
*WPFI score* – 26,95 (61)

## EDUCATION AND HEALTH

Elementary education is free and compulsory at elementary level (six-year course) and lower secondary (three-year course).
*Gross enrolment ratio (percentage of relevant age group)* – primary 102 per cent; secondary 102 per cent; tertiary 61 per cent (2012 est)
*Health expenditure (per capita)* – US$3,966 (2013)
*Hospital beds (per 1,000 people)* – 13.7 (2009)
*Life expectancy (years)* – 84.46 (2014 est)
*Mortality rate* – 9.38 (2014 est)
*Birth rate* – 8.07 (2014 est)
*Infant mortality rate* – 2.13 (2014 est)

# JORDAN

*Al-Mamlakah al-Urduniyah al-Hashimiyah – Hashemite Kingdom of Jordan*

*Area* – 89,342 sq. km
*Capital* – Amman; population, 1,148,000 (2014)
*Major cities* – Aqaba, Az Zarqa, Irbid
*Currency* – Jordanian dinar (JD) of 10 dirhams
*Population* – 8,117,564 rising at 0.83 per cent a year
(2015 est); Arab (98 per cent), Armenian (1 per cent),
Circassian (1 per cent) (est)
*Religion* – Muslim (Sunni) 97 per cent, Christian 2 per cent
(est)
*Language* – Arabic (official), English
*Population density* – 73 per sq. km (2013)
*Urban population* – 83.2 per cent (2013)
*Median age (years)* – 21.8 (2014 est)
*National anthem* – 'As-Salam al-Malaki al-Urdoni' ['Long
Live the King of Jordan']
*National day* – 25 May (Independence Day)
*Death penalty* – Retained
*CPI score* – 49 (55)

## CLIMATE AND TERRAIN

Most of the country is a desert plateau, with the valley of
the River Jordan and the Dead Sea in the west marking the
border with Israel. The Jordan Valley and its extension from
the Dead Sea to the Gulf of Aqaba are part of the Great
Rift Valley in Africa. The only hills lie in the south, along
the edge of the Great Rift Valley, although there is a hilly
outcrop in the centre of the desert. Elevation extremes range
from 1,854m (Jabal Umm ad Dami) to −408m (Dead Sea).
The climate is arid, but with a rainy season in the west from
November to April. Average daily temperatures range from
8.8°C in January to 28.3°C in August. Winters can be cold,
with frost and snow on the plateau.

## POLITICS

The 1952 constitution provides for a monarchy with a
hereditary king as head of state. The bicameral National
Assembly comprises a House of Deputies and a senate
or House of Notables. The House of Deputies has 120
members, directly elected for a four-year term; 12 seats are
now reserved for women. The senate has 55 members, who
are appointed by the king for a four-year term. The king
appoints the prime minister, who chooses the council of
ministers.

After the legislative election in November 2010, over
85 per cent of seats were won by pro-government candidates;
the announcement of this result led to rioting. Since January
2011, Jordan has experienced demonstrations similar to those
elsewhere in the Arab world, with protestors demanding
political reform, lower food prices and measures to tackle
unemployment. This led to the king dismissing the
government in February 2011 and to the appointment of four
prime ministers in 14 months. In October 2012 Abdullah
Ensour was appointed prime minister and reappointed to the
post in March 2013. Jordan took part in Saudi-led air strikes
against Houthi rebels in Yemen in March 2015.

### HEAD OF STATE

HM *The King of Jordan*, Abdullah II, *born* 30 January 1962,
*succeeded* 7 February 1999
*Crown Prince*, Hussein bin al-Abdullah, *born* 29 March 1982

SELECTED GOVERNMENT MEMBERS *as at May 2015*
*Prime Minister, Defence*, Abdullah Ensour
*Finance*, Umayya Toukan
*Foreign Affairs*, Nasser Judah
*Interior*, Hussein Majali

EMBASSY OF THE HASHEMITE KINGDOM OF
JORDAN
6 Upper Phillimore Gardens, London W8 7HA
T 020-7937 3685 E london@fm.gov.jo
W www.jordanembassy.org.uk
*Ambassador Extraordinary and Plenipotentiary*, HE Mazen
Kemel Homoud, *apptd* 2011

BRITISH EMBASSY
PO Box 87, Abdoun, Amman 11118
T (+962) (6) 590 9200 E amman.enquiries@fco.gov.uk
W www.gov.uk/government/world/jordan
*Ambassador Extraordinary and Plenipotentiary*, HE Edward
Oakden, CMG, *apptd* 2015

## DEFENCE

| *Aged 16–49, 2010 est* | *Males* | *Females* |
| --- | --- | --- |
| Available for military service | 1,674,260 | 1,611,315 |
| Fit for military service | 1,439,192 | 1,384,500 |

*Military expenditure* – US$1,268m (2014)

## ECONOMY AND TRADE

Jordan's economic development has been hindered by its lack
of natural resources, influxes of refugees from the West Bank
in 1967, Iraq since 2003, and Syria since 2013, and the
impact of conflict on its trade with Israel and Iraq. High
levels of poverty, unemployment and government debt are
long-term problems. Since 1999, King Abdullah has
implemented economic reforms, and these measures have
increased productivity and exports, begun to attract foreign
direct investment, and won agreement to debt rescheduling

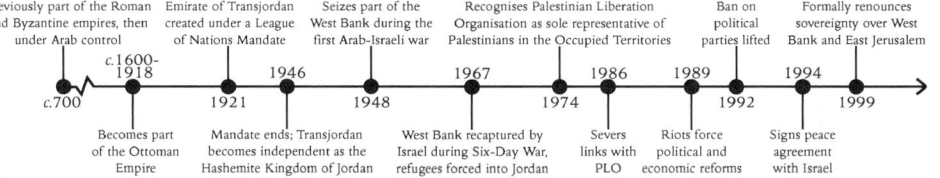

from international donors. Even so, the economy is still dependent on foreign aid, of which the USA is the largest provider, and in 2011 the government agreed two economic relief packages to improve the living conditions for the middle and poor classes. Decreasing oil prices and increasing private consumption is expected to produce growth of 3.5 per cent in 2015 and 3.9 per cent in 2016. The arrival of more than 1 million refugees from the conflict in Syria has put an additional strain on government finances.

Jordan has no oil reserves of its own and few water resources. Shale reserves and renewable energy sources are being explored by the government. The country also imports natural gas, but aims to become a net exporter of electricity via its national grid's links with those of Syria and Egypt. It is currently considering nuclear power generation to ensure an adequate future supply. Jordan has also begun joint ventures with Israel and Syria to guarantee water supplies.

The service sector, including tourism, accounts for 67.4 per cent of GDP. Industry generates 29.5 per cent, from activities that include garment manufacturing, fertilisers, potash and phosphate mining, pharmaceuticals, oil refining, cement, inorganic chemicals and light manufacturing. Agriculture, which accounts for 3.2 per cent of GDP, produces citrus and stone fruits, tomatoes, cucumbers, olives, sheep, poultry and dairy products.

The main trade partners are the USA, Iraq, India, China and Saudi Arabia. Principal exports are clothing, fertilisers, potash, phosphates, vegetables and pharmaceuticals. The main imports are crude oil, machinery, transport equipment, iron and cereals.

*GNI* – US$30,709m; US$4,950 per capita (2013)
*Annual average growth of GDP* – 3 per cent (2014 est)
*Inflation rate* – 2.8 per cent (2014 est)
*Unemployment* – 12.6 per cent (2015 est)
*Total external debt* – US$26,060m (2014 est)
*Imports* – US$21,701m (2013)
*Exports* – US$7,896m (2013)

BALANCE OF PAYMENTS
*Trade* – US$13,804m deficit (2013)
*Current Account* – US$2,907m deficit (2015 est)

| Trade with UK | 2013 | 2014 |
| --- | --- | --- |
| Imports from UK | £272,543,110 | £258,577,105 |
| Exports to UK | £26,889,601 | £82,123,321 |

## COMMUNICATIONS
*Airports* – 16; the largest airports are at Amman and Aqaba
*Waterways* – Amman is linked to Jordan's seaport at Aqaba, the Saudi Arabian port of Jeddah and the Syrian and Iraqi capitals by roads which are of considerable importance in the overland trade of the Middle East
*Roadways and railways* – 7,203km; 507km
*Telecommunications* – 435,000 fixed lines and 8.984 million mobile subscriptions (2012); there were 1.64 million internet users in 2009
*Internet code and IDD* – jo; 962 (from UK), 44 (to UK)
*Major broadcasters* – Jordan Radio and Television, the state-run broadcaster, operates three terrestrial television channels and a satellite channel as well as radio services in Arabic, English and French
*Press* – Major daily newspapers include *Ad Dustour, Al Ra'y* and *Al Ghadd*
*WPFI score* – 42,07 (143)

## EDUCATION AND HEALTH
*Literacy rate* – 99.2 per cent (2015 est)
*Gross enrolment ratio (percentage of relevant age group)* –

primary 98 per cent; secondary 88 per cent; tertiary 47 per cent (2012 est)
*Health expenditure (per capita)* – US$336 (2013)
*Hospital beds (per 1,000 people)* – 1.8 (2012)
*Life expectancy (years)* – 74.1 (2014 est)
*Mortality rate* – 3.8 (2014 est)
*Birth rate* – 25.23 (2014 est)
*Infant mortality rate* – 15.73 (2014 est)

# KAZAKHSTAN

*Qazaqstan Respublikasy – Republic of Kazakhstan*

*Area* – 2,724,900 sq. km
*Capital* – Astana (previously known as Akmola and Tselinograd); population, 741,000 (2014)
*Major cities* – Almaty (the former capital), Oskemen, Pavlodar, Qaraghandy, Semey, Shymkent, Taraz
*Currency* – Tenge of 100 tiyn
*Population* – 18,157,122 rising at 1.14 per cent a year (2015 est); Kazakh (63.1 per cent), Russian (23.7 per cent), Uzbek (2.8 per cent), Ukrainian (2.1 per cent), Uygur (1.4 per cent), Tatar (1.3 per cent), German (1.1 per cent) (2009). The Russian population is concentrated in the north of the country, where it forms a significant majority, and in Almaty
*Religion* – Muslim 70 per cent (predominantly Sunni), Christian 26 per cent (mostly Russian Orthodox) (est)
*Language* – Kazakh, Russian (both official)
*Population density* – 6 per sq. km (2013)
*Urban population* – 53.4 per cent (2013)
*Median age (years)* – 29.7 (2014 est)
*National anthem* – 'Menin Qazaqstanim' ['My Kazakhstan']
*National day* – 16 December (Independence Day)
*Death penalty* – Retained for certain crimes
*CPI score* – 29 (126)
*Literacy rate* – 99.8 per cent (2015 est)
*Gross enrolment ratio (percentage of relevant age group)* –
primary 106 per cent (2013 est); secondary 98 per cent; tertiary 45 per cent (2012 est)
*Health expenditure (per capita)* – US$589 (2013)
*Hospital beds (per 1,000 people)* – 7.2 (2012)
*Life expectancy (years)* – 70.24 (2014 est)
*Mortality rate* – 8.31 (2014 est)
*Birth rate* – 19.61 (2014 est)
*Infant mortality rate* – 21.61 (2014 est)

## CLIMATE AND TERRAIN
Kazakhstan stretches from the basin of the river Volga and the Caspian Sea in the west to the Altai and Tien Shan mountains in the east. The terrain consists of arid steppes and semi-deserts, flat in the west, hilly in the east and mountainous in the south-east. Elevation extremes range

from 6,995m (Khan Tangiri Shyngy) to −132m (Vpadina Kaundy). The country contains the northern part of the Aral Sea in the south-west, and Lake Balkhash and Lake Zaysan in the east. The Aral Sea has suffered significant pollution and desertification since the 1960s, creating the Aralkum desert. The climate is continental, and while arid in much of the country, it can be Siberian in the north. Average yearly temperatures in Astana range from −11.3°C in January to 23.1°C in July.

## HISTORY AND POLITICS

Kazakhstan was inhabited by nomadic tribes before being invaded by Genghis Khan and incorporated into his empire in 1218. After this empire disintegrated, feudal towns emerged based on large oases and the nomadic tribes formed federations led by khans. The towns affiliated in the late 15th century and established a Kazakh state which engaged in almost continuous warfare with the marauding khanates on its southern border. After turning to Russia for protection in the 1730s, the Kazakh khanates were formally incorporated into the Russian Empire in the early 19th century.

The 1917 Bolshevik revolution in Russia was followed by civil war in Kazakhstan, which became an autonomous republic within the USSR in 1920 and a full union republic in 1936. Kazakhstan suffered severely under Stalin's policies of agricultural collectivisation and 'sedentarisation', which forced nomadic tribes to become farmers; around 1.5 million people died of famine or disease. Later Soviet rule saw the country used as a test site for nuclear weapons.

Growing nationalism in the 1980s and a reformist leader led to economic and cultural reforms in 1989 and a declaration of sovereignty in 1990. Kazakhstan declared its independence in December 1991, and became a founding member of the Commonwealth of Independent States (CIS). It entered an economic, social and military union with Kyrgyzstan and Uzbekistan in 1994, and an economic and military pact with Russia in 1995, when it achieved nuclear-free status.

Nursultan Nazarbayev, the reformist communist leader of 1989, became head of state in 1990 and was re-elected in 1991, 1999, 2005 and 2011; the April 2011 election, in which he received 95 per cent of the vote, was criticised by international observers. A 2007 constitutional reform allows him to serve for an unlimited number of terms.

In 2006, three pro-government parties merged with Nazarbayev's Fatherland Republican Party (Otan), which subsequently changed its name to Nur-Otan. Nur-Otan won every seat in the lower legislative chamber in the 2007 legislative elections and retained 83 seats in the 2012 elections. In April 2014 Karim Massimov became prime minister for a second time, replacing Serik Akhmetov. President Nazarbayev was re-elected in the April 2015 presidential election and claimed to have won over 97 per cent of the popular vote, easily defeating his pro-government opponents. The elections were judged to be unsound by a number of human rights groups.

The president is directly elected; in 2007 the constitution was amended to reduce the presidential term from seven to five years, renewable once, although President Nazarbayev is exempt from this restriction. The bicameral parliament is composed of the assembly (Majlis) and the senate. The assembly has 107 members, 98 directly elected on a single constituency basis and nine seats reserved for ethnic groups; all serve a five-year term. The senate has 47 members, of whom 32 are indirectly elected and 15 are appointed for a six-year term, with half elected every three years. The president appoints the prime minister and other senior ministers.

### HEAD OF STATE

President, Nursultan Nazarbayev, elected 1 December 1991, confirmed in office by referendum 1995, re-elected 1999, 2005, 2011, 2015

SELECTED GOVERNMENT MEMBERS as at May 2015
Prime Minister, Karim Massimov
First Deputy Prime Minister, Bakytzhan Sagintayev
Defence, Imangali Tasmagambetov
Foreign Affairs, Erlan Idrissov
Internal Affairs, Kalmukhanbet Kasymov

### EMBASSY OF THE REPUBLIC OF KAZAKHSTAN

125 Pall Mall, London SW1Y 5EA
T 020-7925 1757 E london@mfa.kz W www.kazembassy.org.uk
Ambassador Extraordinary and Plenipotentiary, HE Erzhan Kazykhanov, apptd 2014

### BRITISH EMBASSY

62 Kosmonavtov Street, Astana
T (+7) (717) 255 6200 E ukinkz@fco.gov.uk
W www.gov.uk/government/world/kazakhstan
Ambassador Extraordinary and Plenipotentiary, HE Dr Carolyn Browne, apptd 2013

### DEFENCE

The CIS Mutual Defence Treaty of 1993, to which Kazakhstan is a signatory, retains a common air defence force, and Kazakh forces also take part in the CIS peacekeeping force on the Tajikistan–Afghanistan border. An agreement signed with Russia in 1995 provides for eventual reunification of the two states' armed forces. By 1996, all nuclear warheads had been returned to Russia, although Kazakhstan retained 48 SS-18 intercontinental ballistic missiles. Kazakhstan participates in the NATO partnership for peace programme.

| Aged 16–24, 2010 est | Males | Females |
| --- | --- | --- |
| Available for military service | 4,163,629 | 4,179,051 |
| Fit for military service | 2,909,999 | 3,528,169 |

Military expenditure – US$2,319m (2014)
Conscription – 18 years of age; 24 months

### ECONOMY AND TRADE

Economic reforms and privatisation in the 1990s enabled GDP to grow by at least 8 per cent a year from 2002 to 2007, although lower commodity prices and banking sector problems caused the economy to contract briefly in 2008–9. Growth has largely been achieved through exploitation of vast oil and natural gas reserves, particularly since the opening of export pipelines to Black Sea ports (in 2001) and China (2005), and Kazakhstan's use of the Azerbaijan–Turkey pipeline (from 2008); the country is also part of a four-country consortium developing another pipeline to China. As a result of the boom, the government has eliminated the budget deficit, but it is also trying to stimulate growth in other industries to reduce dependency on oil. The economy has been badly affected by weaknesses in the Russian economy and by falling commodity prices. A stimulus package worth around 7 per cent of GDP was introduced in December 2014.

Other mineral resources are considerable and there is a significant mining industry exploiting coal, iron ore, manganese, chrome, lead, zinc, copper, titanium, bauxite, silver, gold, phosphate and uranium deposits. A large and well-developed agricultural sector produces grain, wool, cotton and livestock as cash crops. The main industries are mineral extraction and processing and machine-building, especially agricultural machinery and electric motors. Services contribute 65.6 per cent of GDP, industry 29.5 per cent and agriculture 4.9 per cent, although agriculture employs 25.8 per cent of the workforce.

The main trading partners are China, Russia, Ukraine and EU states. Principal exports are oil and oil products, ferrous metals, chemicals, machinery, grain, wool, meat and coal. The main imports are machinery and equipment, metal products and foodstuffs. Kazakhstan became a founding member of the Eurasian Economic Union (EEU); a customs union with Russia and Belarus, in January 2015.

*GNI* – US$175,469m; US$11,550 per capita (2013)
*Annual average growth of GDP* – 4.6 per cent (2014 est)
*Inflation rate* – 6.7 per cent (2014 est)
*Population below poverty line* – 2.9 per cent (2013 est)
*Unemployment* – 5.7 per cent (2015 est)
*Total external debt* – US$163,200m (2014 est)
*Imports* – US$45,966m (2013)
*Exports* – US$81,912m (2013)

BALANCE OF PAYMENTS
*Trade* – US$35,945m surplus (2013)
*Current Account* – US$8,269m deficit (2015 est)

| Trade with UK | 2013 | 2014 |
|---|---|---|
| Imports from UK | £514,523,283 | £359,330,702 |
| Exports to UK | £458,253,307 | £370,099,465 |

## COMMUNICATIONS

*Airports* – 63; the largest airports are at Astana, Almaty and Atyrau
*Waterways* – There are important ports on the Caspian and Aral seas which permit international trade, while the Syr Darya and Irtysh rivers provide 4,000km of navigable waterways
*Roadways and railways* – 87,140km; 15,333km
*Telecommunications* – 4.34 million fixed lines and 28.731 million mobile subscriptions (2012); there were 5.299 million internet users in 2009
*Internet code and IDD* – kz; 7 (from UK), 810 44 (to UK)
*Major broadcasters* – There are 250 television and radio stations according to official statistics; the influential Khabar Agency, founded by the president's eldest daughter, Dariga Nazarbayeva, operates channels in both Russian and Kazakh
*Press* – Major newspapers include the government-backed Russian-language *Kazakhstanskaya Pravda* and the Kazakh-language *Egemen Kazakhstan*
*WPFI score* – 53,46 (160)

## KENYA

*Jamhuri ya Kenya – Republic of Kenya*

*Area* – 580,367 sq. km
*Capital* – Nairobi; population, 3,768,000 (2014)
*Major cities* – Eldoret, Kisumu, Mombasa, Nakuru
*Currency* – Kenyan shilling (Ksh) of 100 cents
*Population* – 45,925,301 rising at 1.93 per cent a year (2015 est); Kikuyu (22 per cent), Luhya (14 per cent), Luo (13 per cent), Kalenjin (12 per cent), Kamba (11 per cent), Kisii (6 per cent), Meru (6 per cent) (2009)
*Religion* – Christian 82 per cent (Protestant 47 per cent, Roman Catholic 23 per cent, other 12 per cent), Muslim 11 per cent
*Language* – English, Swahili (both official), indigenous languages
*Population density* – 78 per sq. km (2013)
*Urban population* – 24.8 per cent (2013)
*Median age (years)* – 19.1 (2014 est)
*National anthem* – 'Ee Mungu Nguvu Yetu' ['Oh God of All Creation']
*National day* – 12 December (Independence Day)
*Death penalty* – Retained (last used 1987)
*CPI score* – 25 (145)

## CLIMATE AND TERRAIN

The coastal plain and semi-desert plains in the east rise to mountainous highlands in the centre and west that are divided by the Great Rift Valley. Elevation extremes range from 5,199m (Mt Kenya) to 0m (Indian Ocean). The country includes part of Lake Victoria in the south-west and the Lake Turkana (Rudolph) in the north. Kenya is an equatorial country; the climate is tropical on the coast and arid in the interior, tempered by altitude. The average temperature is 25°C.

## HISTORY AND POLITICS

Fossils of early hominids found in the Lake Turkana region suggest that the area was inhabited some 2.6 million years ago. Arabs and Persians settled on the Kenyan coast from the eighth century AD. The Portuguese gained control of coastal areas in the 16th century but Arab overlordship was reasserted in the 18th century.

European exploration of the interior began in the 19th century and in 1895, Kenya became part of Britain's East African Protectorate, becoming a colony in 1920. Demands for internal self-government by white settlers were rejected in 1923, but from 1944 a nationalist group, the Kenya African Union (KAU), was founded to campaign for African rights. The Mau Mau rebellion of 1952–6, intended to drive white settlers from African tribal lands, resulted in a state of emergency that lasted until 1960, when preparations for majority African rule began. Kenya became independent in 1963, and a republic in 1964. President Jomo Kenyatta's death in 1978 brought Daniel arap Moi to power, and he remained president until 2002, when he was barred from standing for re-election.

Kenya was a one-party state ruled by the Kenya African National Union (KANU) between 1964 and 1991. A multiparty system was reintroduced after violent agitation and international pressure in the early 1990s but KANU maintained its grip on power until the 2002 elections, which were won by the National Rainbow Coalition (NARC). Despite the NARC's anti-corruption electoral platform, once in government it made little headway against endemic corruption, and government ministers were implicated in corruption scandals in 2005 and 2006. It is estimated that up to US$1,000m (£650m) of official funds were misappropriated in 2002–7.

After decades of stability, intercommunal violence and conflict over land and water rights have become more frequent since the 1990s, exacerbated by a rural food crisis since 2004 following persistent drought and crop failures.

The 2007 legislative elections were won by the Orange Democratic Movement (ODM), led by Raila Odinga. The announcement that President Kibaki had won the simultaneous presidential election triggered weeks of serious rioting; this developed into ethnic violence that left over 1,000 dead and 600,000 displaced. After international mediation, a power-sharing agreement was signed in February 2008; under this, Kibaki remained president and the post of prime minister was created for Raila Odinga, although this post was abolished in 2013.

In March 2013 Uhuru Kenyatta, the son of Kenya's first president, was elected president with 50.5 per cent of the vote; his Jubilee coalition became the largest bloc in both houses in the legislative elections. In October 2014 Uhuru Kenyatta is due to face International Criminal Court charges relating to 2007's post-election violence.

In recent years Kenya has suffered a number of terrorist attacks linked to Islamism, with the Somalian group al-Shabab attacking US, Israeli and Kenyan targets within the country. In September 2013, al-Shabab gunmen killed at least 62 people in the Westgate shopping mall and, in April 2015, 147 people in the Garissa University College attack.

The president is directly elected for a five-year term, renewable once. The bicameral parliament as defined in the 2010 constitution was first elected in 2013; members of both houses serve five-year terms. The lower chamber, the National Assembly, was increased to 350 members, of whom 290 are directly elected; 47 seats are reserved for women, directly elected from each county, 12 members are nominated pro rata by political parties to represent special interests including youth, persons with disabilities and workers, and the speaker is a member ex officio. The new upper chamber, the Senate, has 68 members: 47 are directly elected from each county, 16 seats are reserved for women, nominated pro rata by political parties, and four members are nominated to represent youth and persons with disabilities; the speaker is a member *ex officio*.

## HEAD OF STATE

*President, C-in-C of the Armed Forces,* Uhuru Kenyatta, *elected* 4 March 2013, *took office* 9 April 2013
*Vice-President,* William Ruto

SELECTED GOVERNMENT MEMBERS *as at May 2015*
*Defence,* Raychelle Omamo
*Foreign Affairs,* Amina Mohammed

## KENYA HIGH COMMISSION

45 Portland Place, London W1B 1AS
**T** 020-7636 2371 **E** info@kenyahighcom.org.uk
**W** www.kenyahighcom.org.uk
*High Commissioner,* HE Lazarus Ombai Amayo, *apptd* 2015

## BRITISH HIGH COMMISSION

PO Box 30465, Upper Hill Road, 00100 Nairobi
**T** (+254) (20) 284 4000 **E** nairobi.enquiries@fco.gov.uk
**W** www.gov.uk/government/world/kenya
*High Commissioner,* HE Dr Christian Turner, *apptd* 2012

## DEFENCE

| *Aged 16–49, 2010 est* | *Males* | *Females* |
| --- | --- | --- |
| Available for military service | 9,768,140 | 9,466,257 |
| Fit for military service | 6,361,268 | 6,106,870 |

*Military expenditure* – US$724m (2013)

## ECONOMY AND TRADE

Kenya acts as a regional trade and finance hub for its landlocked neighbours. However, its own economy is weak owing to endemic corruption, low commodity prices, low investor confidence and the frequent suspension of international aid because of successive governments' failure to tackle corruption. These problems are exacerbated by occasional severe droughts, and in 2008–9 the economy contracted owing to post-election violence and the global downturn, which reduced tourism, exports and expatriates' remittances. Peaceful elections in 2013, good climatic conditions for agriculture and the stability of the shilling are expected to promote economic growth in the short and medium term.

The country is overwhelmingly agricultural, with 75 per cent of the population engaged in agricultural and horticultural production; this sector contributes 29.3 per cent of GDP. The world's third largest producer of tea, Kenya also grows coffee, maize, wheat, sugar cane, fruit and vegetables. Natural resources include gold, limestone, soda ash, salt, rubies, garnets and hydroelectric power, which makes it self-sufficient in energy.

The industrial sector has grown over the past two decades, developing a manufacturing base in consumer goods (such as textiles) and agricultural products (such as dehydrated vegetables), as well as oil refining, commercial ship repair and the production of steel, aluminium, lead and cement. Tourism is an important source of income, though it is threatened by terrorism. Industry contributes 17.7 per cent to GDP and the service sector 53 per cent.

The main export markets are the UK, the Netherlands, Uganda, Tanzania, the USA and Pakistan, while imports come mainly from India, China, the UAE and South Africa. Principal exports are tea, horticultural products, coffee, petroleum products, fish and cement. The main imports are machinery and transport equipment, petroleum products, vehicles, iron and steel, resins and plastics.

*GNI* – US$40,526m; US$1,160 per capita (2013)
*Annual average growth of GDP* – 5.3 per cent (2014 est)
*Inflation rate* – 6.9 per cent (2014 est)
*Population below poverty line* – 43.4 per cent (2012 est)
*Unemployment* – 9.1 per cent (2015 est)
*Total external debt* – US$16,770m (2014 est)
*Imports* – US$16,358m (2013)
*Exports* – US$5,856m (2013)

## BALANCE OF PAYMENTS

*Trade* – US$10,503m deficit (2013)
*Current Account* – US$5,047m deficit (2015 est)

| *Trade with UK* | *2013* | *2014* |
| --- | --- | --- |
| Imports from UK | £438,959,978 | £398,032,518 |
| Exports to UK | £361,442,179 | £291,119,733 |

## COMMUNICATIONS

*Airports* – 16; the largest airports are at Nairobi, Mombasa and Eldoret
*Waterways* – The only significant inland waterway is the Kenyan portion of Lake Victoria; Kisumu is the main port
*Roadways and railways* – There are 11,189km of roadways; the Kenya Railways Corporation operates 2,066km of railways. In 2014, a Chinese company agreed to begin the construction of a new railway between Mombasa and Nairobi; the 610km line is due to be completed in 2018
*Telecommunications* – 251,600 fixed lines and 30.732 million mobile subscriptions (2012); there were 3.996 million internet users in 2009
*Internet code and IDD* – ke; 254 (from UK), 0 44 (to UK)

*Major broadcasters* – The state-run Kenya Broadcasting Corporation (KBC) competes with a range of commercial television and radio stations
*Press* – Daily newspapers include the English-language *Daily Nation* and *The Standard*, and *Taifa Leo* (Swahili)
*WPFI score* – 32,07 (100)

## EDUCATION AND HEALTH

The state provides eight years of free primary education.
*Literacy rate* – 85.9 per cent (2015 est)
*Health expenditure* – US$45 (2013)
*Hospital beds (per 1,000 people)* – 1.4 (2010)
*Life expectancy (years)* – 63.52 (2014 est)
*Mortality rate* – 7.0 (2014 est)
*Birth rate* – 28.27 (2014 est)
*Infant mortality rate* – 40.71 (2014 est)
*HIV/AIDS adult prevalence* – 0.7 per cent (2013)

# KIRIBATI

*Republic of Kiribati*

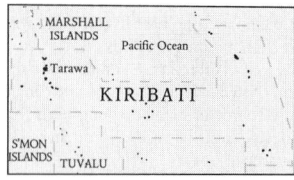

*Area* – 811 sq. km
*Capital* – Tarawa, on Bairiki; population, 46,000 (2014)
*Currency* – Australian dollar ($A) of 100 cents
*Population* – 105,711 rising at 1.15 per cent a year (2015 est); Micronesian (99.2 per cent), mixed (9.7 per cent) (2000)
*Religion* – Christian (Roman Catholic 56 per cent, Presbyterian 34 per cent, Mormon 5 per cent), Baha'i 3 per cent (est)
*Language* – English, Kiribati (Gilbertese) (both official)
*Population density* – 126 per sq. km (2013)
*Urban population* – 44.1 per cent (2013)
*Median age (years)* – 23.6 (2014 est)
*National anthem* – 'Teirake Kaini Kiribati' ['Stand up, Kiribati']
*National day* – 12 July (Independence Day)
*Death penalty* – Abolished for all crimes (since 1979)
*Gross enrolment ratio (percentage of relevant age group)* – primary 116 per cent; secondary 86 per cent (2011 est)
*Life expectancy (years)* – 65.47 (2014 est)
*Mortality rate* – 7.18 (2014 est)
*Birth rate* – 21.85 (2014 est)
*Infant mortality rate* – 35.37 (2014 est)

## CLIMATE AND TERRAIN

Kiribati (pronounced Kiri-bas) comprises 32 atolls and one island. About 20 are inhabited: Banaba island; the Kiribati (Gilbert) group (17); the Rawaki (Phoenix) Islands (8); and some of the Line Islands (11), including Kiritimati (Christmas Island). They are situated in the southern central Pacific Ocean, crossed by the Equator; the area was also crossed by the international date line until 1995, when the government unilaterally moved the date line eastwards so that the whole country shared the same day. Few of the atolls are more than 800m wide or more than 3m high, making the country particularly vulnerable to rising sea levels. The highest point is 81m (on Banaba) and the lowest is 0m (Pacific Ocean). The climate is tropical.

## HISTORY AND POLITICS

The islands were settled by Austronesian-speaking peoples in the first millennium BC, and Samoans, Fijians and Tongans migrated there in the 11th to 14th centuries. British settlers arrived in the islands in the early 19th century. In 1892, the Gilbert (Kiribati) and Ellice (Tuvalu) islands were proclaimed a British protectorate and in 1916 became a British colony which subsequently incorporated the Line Islands and Phoenix Islands. During the Second World War, Banaba and the Gilbert islands were occupied by the Japanese and were the scene of fierce fighting between Japanese and US troops. Some of the Line Islands were used for British nuclear weapons tests in the 1950s and 1960s. In 1975, the territories separated and the Gilbert, Phoenix and Line Islands became independent as the Republic of Kiribati in 1979.

Open-cast phosphate mining left Banaba unfit for human habitation and the population was evacuated in 1945, to be relocated to a northern island of Fiji. Overcrowding and lack of infrastructure have caused more general environmental degradation, especially in urban areas. However, the main problem is the rise in the sea level due to global warming; salination is already contaminating water supplies and agricultural land, causing villages to be relocated, and Kiribati is expected to be the first state to lose territory. The government is seeking permanent refugee status for its citizens in neighbouring countries.

Independent members gained the most number of seats in the 2011 legislative elections, picking up 17 of the 44 seats available; the Pillars of Truth group and United Coalition Party won 15 and 11 seats respectively. The incumbent president, Anote Tong, was re-elected for a third term in the 2012 presidential election.

Under the 1979 constitution, the executive president is directly elected for a four-year term, with a maximum of three terms; presidential candidates are selected by and from members of the legislature. The unicameral legislature, House of Assembly, has 46 members: 44 members directly elected for a four-year term, an appointed representative of the Banaban community in Fiji and the attorney-general. There are no formal political parties, but since the 1980s some associations of politicians formed for elections have proved durable enough to be given names.

### HEAD OF STATE

*President, Foreign Affairs,* Anote Tong, *elected* 4 July 2003, *sworn in* 6 July 2003, *re-elected* 2007, 2012
*Vice-President,* Teima Onorio

SELECTED GOVERNMENT MEMBERS *as at May 2015*
*Commerce, Industry and Co-Operatives,* Pinto Kaita
*Finance and Economic Development,* Tim Murdoch

KIRIBATI HONORARY CONSUL
The Great House, Llanddewi Rhydderich, Monmouthshire NP7 9UY
*Honorary Consul,* Michael Walsh

BRITISH HIGH COMMISSIONER
HE Roderick Drummond, *apptd* 2013, resident at Suva, Fiji

## ECONOMY AND TRADE

Since the phosphate deposits on Banaba ran out in 1979, the economy has been weak, dependent on coconuts, fish and tourism (over 20 per cent of GDP) as the main economic activities; development is hampered by remoteness, poor transport connections and the lack of funding, infrastructure and skills. Around 25 per cent of GDP comes from international aid (mainly from Australia), the sale of fishing licences, remittances from expatriates and monies from the trust fund established with phosphate mining revenues.

A financial sector is being developed. The main trading partners are Pacific Rim countries. The principal exports are copra (62 per cent), coconuts, seaweed and fish. The principal imports are foodstuffs, machinery and transport equipment, manufactured goods and fuel. Growth is expected to be slow in 2015 following the damage to infrastructure caused by Tropical Cyclone Pam (*see* Events).

GNI – US$258m; US$2,620 per capita (2013)
*Annual average growth of GDP* – 3 per cent (2014)
*Inflation rate* – 0.2 per cent (2007 est)
*Total external debt* – US$136m (2013 est)
*Imports* – US$112m (2013)
*Exports* – US$8m (2013)

BALANCE OF PAYMENTS
*Trade* – US$105m deficit (2013)
*Current Account* – US$41m deficit (2015 est)

| Trade with UK | 2013 | 2014 |
|---|---|---|
| Imports from UK | £132,736 | £31,641 |
| Exports to UK | £22,224 | £3,330 |

## COMMUNICATIONS
*Airports and waterways* – Four, with the main international airport on Tarawa, while another on Kiritimati operates regular services to Fiji and Hawaii; the main seaport is Betio, on Tarawa
*Roadways* – 670km
*Telecommunications* – 9,000 fixed lines and 16,000 mobile subscriptions (2012); there were 7,800 internet users in 2009
*Internet code and IDD* – ki; 686 (from UK), 44 (to UK)
*Media* – The government-run newspaper and radio stations offer a diverse range of views; *Te Uekera* is the principal weekly newspaper

# DEMOCRATIC PEOPLE'S REPUBLIC OF KOREA

*Choson-minjujuui-inmin-konghwaguk* – *Democratic People's Republic of Korea*

*Area* – 120,538 sq. km
*Capital* – Pyongyang; population, 2,856,000 (2014)
*Major cities* – Chongjin, Hamhung, Hungnam, Nampo

*Currency* – North Korean won of 100 chon
*Population* – 24,983,205 rising at 0.53 per cent a year (2015 est)
*Religion* – Religious activity is almost non-existent outside government-sponsored religious groups, although many believers are thought to worship in private. Historically, the main religions were Buddhism and Confucianism; Buddhism, Christianity and Chondo (a syncretic religion) are officially recognised.
*Language* – Korean (official)
*Population density* – 207 per sq. km (2013)
*Urban population* – 60.6 per cent (2013)
*Median age (years)* – 33.4 (2014 est)
*National anthem* – 'Aegukka' ['Patriotic Song']
*National day* – 9 September (Founding of the Democratic People's Republic of Korea, 1948)
*Death penalty* – Retained
*CPI score* – 8 (174)
*Literacy rate* – 100 per cent (2015 est)
*Health expenditure (per capita)* – $22 (2007)
*Life expectancy (years)* – 69.81 (2014 est)
*Mortality rate* – 9.18 (2014 est)
*Birth rate* – 14.51 (2014 est)
*Infant mortality rate* – 24.5 (2014 est)

## CLIMATE AND TERRAIN
The republic occupies the northern half of the Korean peninsula. The land rises from coastal plains in the west to mountains and hills that occupy 80 per cent of the land area. Elevation extremes range from 2,744m (Paektu-san) to 0m (Sea of Japan). The climate is temperate, though more extreme than in South Korea. Average temperatures range from −10.5°C in January to 21.3°C in July and August.

## HISTORY AND POLITICS
After the Korean war ended in 1953, Kim Il-sung continued the process of Soviet-style reform begun in 1946. He also developed *Juche* (self-reliance), an ideology demanding total economic independence. North Korea pursued an isolationist foreign policy for several decades, only signing a mutual assistance treaty with China in 1961 and improving relations with the USSR in 1985. It established diplomatic contacts with South Korea and Japan in 1990, raising hopes that it was abandoning its isolationism, but it remains a secretive, closed country under rigid state control.

Kim Il-sung died in 1994. His son Kim Jong-il became chairman of the National Defence Commission, designated as the highest post of the state, and general secretary of the Korean Workers' Party in 1997. The most recent elections to the Supreme People's Assembly took place in April 2009, and the assembly re-elected Kim Jong-il to his post. In September 2010 the Korean Workers' Party congress (the first for 44 years) renewed the top party leadership; Kim Jong-il's third son, Kim Jong-un, was appointed to senior political and military posts, before ascending to supreme leader following the death of Kim Jong-il in December 2012. In December 2013 Kim Jong-un's uncle Chang Song-thaek, a senior political figure within North Korea, was executed in a move seen by observers as an attempt to consolidate Kim's regime.

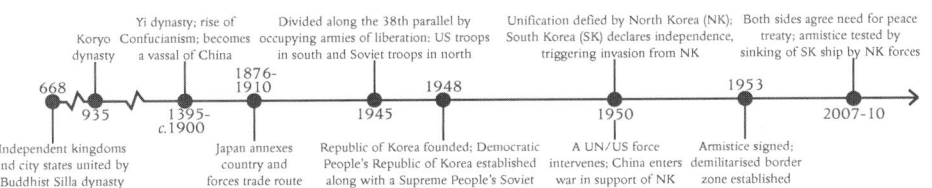

The communist Korean Workers' Party, founded in 1946 by Kim Il-sung, is the only permitted political party. However, political control and leadership is maintained by the cult of personality created by Kim Il-sung and continued by his successors Kim Jong-il and Kim Jong-un.

The 1972 constitution was amended in 1998 to designate leading state posts; it made Kim Il-sung the Eternal President and the chairmanship of the National Defence Commission (NDC), held by Kim Jong-il, the highest post in the state, while providing that the chairman of the Presidium of the Supreme People's Assembly would represent the state on formal occasions. A further amendment in 2009 named the NDC chairman as the 'supreme leader of the state'; it also removed all references to communism, and established the *songun* principle of military responsibility for all internal affairs.

There is a unicameral legislature, the Supreme People's Assembly, which has 687 members directly elected from a single list of candidates for a five-year term. The assembly elects a presidium and the premier, appointing the government on the recommendation of the premier. The Central People's Committee, which is also elected by the assembly, directs the administrative council (government), which implements the policy formulated by the committee.

HEAD OF STATE
*Eternal President,* Kim Il-sung (deceased)
*Eternal General Secretary,* Kim Jong-il (deceased)
*Supreme Leader,* Kim Jong-un
*President of the Presidium of the Supreme People's Assembly,* Kim Yong-nam

SELECTED GOVERNMENT MEMBERS *as at May 2015*
*Premier,* Pak Pong-ju
*Deputy Premiers,* Ri Chol-man; Rim Chol-ung; Ri Mu-yong; Ro Tu-chol; Kim Yong-jin
*Finance,* Choe Kwang-jin
*Foreign Affairs,* Ri Su-yong

EMBASSY OF THE DEMOCRATIC PEOPLE'S REPUBLIC OF KOREA
73 Gunnersbury Avenue, London W5 4LP
T 020-8992 4965 E prkinfo@yahoo.com
*Ambassador Extraordinary and Plenipotentiary,* HE Hak Bong Hyon, *apptd* 2012

BRITISH EMBASSY
Munsu Dong compound, Pyongyang
T (+850) (2) 381 7980 E pyongyang.enquiries@fco.gov.uk
W www.gov.uk/government/world/north-korea
*Ambassador Extraordinary and Plenipotentiary,* HE Michael Gifford, *apptd* 2012

INTERNATIONAL RELATIONS
The D. P. R. K's relations with other countries have been erratic over the past 20 years, largely owing to its nuclear ambitions and international reaction to these. It first agreed to freeze its nuclear development programme in return for fuel and development aid in 1994, only to restart the programme in 2002, claiming that other parties to the agreement had reneged on it. This pattern has been repeated several times, with the regime using the discontinuation of its nuclear and missile development programmes to bargain for aid from international agencies and regional powers. Six-nation talks to resolve the nuclear issues began in 2003 after North Korea withdrew from the Nuclear Non-proliferation Treaty, but North Korea has never fully complied with any of the agreements concluded at the talks. The consequent suspension of aid by other nations, and UN censure and sanctions after North Korea test-fired ballistic missiles and nuclear devices in 2006, 2009, 2012, 2013 and 2015 have been interpreted as acts of aggression by North Korea and met with a bellicose response from the regime.

## DEFENCE

| Aged 16–49, 2010 est | Males | Females |
| --- | --- | --- |
| Available for military service | 6,515,279 | 6,418,693 |
| Fit for military service | 4,836,567 | 5,230,137 |

*Conscription* – 18 years of age (presumed)

## ECONOMY AND TRADE

Although North Korea is rich in natural resources and had developed a heavy industry base in the first half of the 20th century, the economy is stagnant after decades of mismanagement, underinvestment, low export levels and the diversion of resources to military expenditure. Its long decline was compounded by the loss of Soviet support from 1991.

A series of natural disasters in the 1990s caused severe famine, obliging the government to request international aid. It is estimated that 3 million people have died since the 1990s as a result of the acute food shortages, which continue despite international food and fuel aid.

A redenomination of North Korea's currency in 2009 wiped out many people's savings, disrupted the nascent private sector, triggered rapid inflation and was met with unprecedented public protests that lasted some weeks. The country continues to develop special economic zones with China and South Korea. In 2015, the USA imposed further economic sanctions on a number of North Korean officials following the country's alleged hacking of the US division of Sony Pictures (*see* Events).

Industrial output is centred on mining, steel, chemicals and machine building, but antiquated machinery and fuel shortages have limited output to a fraction of pre-1990 levels. Agriculture is in an equally parlous state, as collective farming, lack of arable land and chronic shortages of fertilisers and agricultural machinery prevent the country from producing enough to feed its population. It has been dependent on massive amounts of food aid since the mid-1990s to avert a repeat of the 1995 famine, but chronic malnutrition is widespread. A relaxation of restrictions on private farming and markets in 2003 was partially rescinded in 2005 and a centralised rationing system was reinstated. South Korean assistance in developing infrastructure, industry, the Kaesong Industrial Zone and tourism has been limited by North Korea's restrictions, and was reduced or suspended when South Korea imposed sanctions on the North in 2010.

The main trading partners are China and South Korea. Principal exports are minerals, metallurgical products, armaments, textiles, and agricultural and fish products. The main imports are petroleum, coal, machinery and equipment, textiles and grain.

*Annual average growth of GDP* – 1 per cent (2013 est)

| Trade with UK | 2013 | 2014 |
| --- | --- | --- |
| Imports from UK | £557,274 | £279,379 |
| Exports to UK | £3,379,667 | £186,885 |

## COMMUNICATIONS

*Airports and waterways* – There are 39 airports, the largest of which is at Pyongyang. There are some 2,250km of waterways but these are navigable only by small craft; the main seaports are Chongjin, Nampo and Wonsan

*Roadways and railways* – There are 724km of paved roadways, and 5,242km of railways
*Telecommunications* – 1.18 million fixed lines and 1.7 million mobile subscriptions (2012)
*Internet code and IDD* – kp; 850 (from UK), 44 (to UK)
*Media* – There are no independent media outlets in North Korea; all television, radios and national newspapers are government organs
*WPFI score* – 83,25 (179)

# REPUBLIC OF KOREA

*Taehan-min'guk – Republic of Korea*

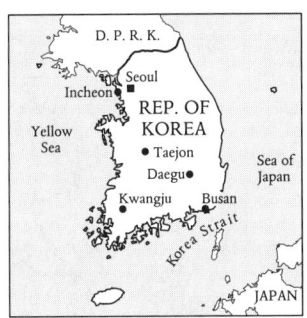

*Area* – 99,720 sq. km
*Capital* – Seoul; population, 9,775,000 (2014 est)
*Major cities* – Busan, Changwon, Daegu, Daejon, Gwangju, Incheon, Suwon, Urusan
*Currency* – South Korean won of 100 jeon
*Population* – 49,115,196 rising at 0.14 per cent a year (2015 est)
*Religion* – Buddhist 24 per cent (predominantly the Jogye order of the Seon (Zen) school), Christian (Protestant 24 per cent, Roman Catholic 8 per cent), none 43 per cent (est)
*Language* – Korean (official), English
*Population density* – 516 per sq. km (2013)
*Urban population* – 83.8 per cent (2013)
*Median age (years)* – 40.2 (2014 est)
*National anthem* – 'Aegukga' ['Patriotic Song']
*National day* – 15 August (Liberation Day)
*Death penalty* – Retained (last used 1997)
*CPI score* – 55 (43)

## CLIMATE AND TERRAIN
The country occupies the southern part of the mountainous Korean peninsula, with highlands and mountains accounting for around 70 per cent of the land area. Elevation extremes range from 1,950m (Halla-san) to 0m (Sea of Japan). The climate is temperate, although winters are very cold for the latitude. Average temperatures range from −2.5°C in January to 24.3°C in August. The rainy season lasts from June to September.

## HISTORY AND POLITICS
From 1948, South Korea experienced over 40 years of mostly authoritarian, often military, rule and great industrial development. Syngman Rhee, president from 1948, resigned in 1960 in the face of popular protests at corruption and electoral fraud. A military coup in 1961 brought General Park Chung-hee to power and he instigated a programme of industrial development; by the time of his assassination in 1979, Korea was a leading shipbuilding nation and producer of electronic goods.

Following riots against the interim government, General Chun Do-hwan assumed power in 1980 after martial law was declared. Pro-democracy agitation in the mid-1980s led to constitutional changes in 1987 and the first multiparty legislative elections in 1988, but despite the anti-corruption campaign of the new democratically elected president Roh Tae-woo, politics continued to be plagued by allegations of corruption and fraud, and was subject to military influence. The first civilian president and the first wholly civilian government since 1961 were appointed in 1993.

The 2007 presidential election was won by Lee Myung-bak, the Grand National Party (GNP) candidate. Lee Myung-bak's government reversed the 'sunshine policy' of greater political contact with the north in 2008; it imposed sanctions on North Korea in 2010, blaming the north for the sinking of one of its warships in March 2010. In the 2012 legislative election, the New Frontier Party, formerly known as the GNP, won a small overall majority in the National Assembly. In December 2012 Park Geun-hye was elected South Korea's first female president and assumed office in February 2013. Lee Wan-koo was appointed prime minister in January 2015, following the resignation of Chung Hong-won after 2014's *Sewol* ferry disaster, in which more than 300 people died. New presidential elections are due in 2017.

A new constitution was adopted when the Sixth Republic was inaugurated in 1988. Under this, the president is directly elected for a five-year term, which is not renewable. The president appoints the prime minister with the approval of the legislature, and members of the state council (cabinet) on the recommendation of the prime minister. The president is also empowered to take wide-ranging measures in an emergency, but must obtain the agreement of the legislature. The unicameral National Assembly has 300 members who are directly elected for a four-year term.

### HEAD OF STATE
*President*, Park Geun-hye, *elected* 19 December 2012, *sworn in* 25 February 2013

SELECTED GOVERNMENT MEMBERS *as at May 2015*
*Prime Minister*, Lee Wan-koo
*Deputy Prime Minister, Finance*, Choi Kyung-hwan
*Defence*, Gen. Han Min-koo
*Foreign Affairs*, Yun Byung-se

### EMBASSY OF THE REPUBLIC OF KOREA
60 Buckingham Gate, London SW1E 6AJ
T 020-7227 5500 E koreanembinuk@mofat.go.kr
W www.gbr.mofat.go.kr
*Ambassador Extraordinary and Plenipotentiary*, HE Sungnam Lim, *apptd* 2013

### BRITISH EMBASSY
Sejong-daero 19-gil 24, Jung-gu, Seoul 100–120
T (+82) (2) 3210 5500 E enquiry.seoul@fco.gov.uk
W www.gov.uk/government/world/south-korea
*Ambassador Extraordinary and Plenipotentiary*, HE Charles Hay, *apptd* 2015

### DEFENCE

| Aged 16–49, 2010 est | Males | Females |
| --- | --- | --- |
| Available for military service | 13,185,794 | 12,423,496 |
| Fit for military service | 10,864,566 | 10,168,709 |

*Military expenditure* – US$36,677m (2014)
*Conscription* – 20–30 years of age; 21–24 months (selective)

## ECONOMY AND TRADE

Industrialisation from the 1960s transformed South Korea from a predominantly agrarian country into one of the Asian 'miracle' economies by the 1980s. Initially based on shipbuilding and electrical goods, production shifted towards electronics and IT goods in the 1980s. By 1997 South Korea was the world's eleventh-largest economy, with an annual GDP growth rate of 8 per cent. However, the dominating conglomerates *(chaebols)* were experiencing difficulties which, exacerbated by the Asian financial crisis in 1997, caused a number to collapse in the late 1990s and the economy to contract sharply. Corporate and financial reforms were introduced and GDP growth resumed from the early 2000s. Slow growth in Europe, the US and China reduced South Korean growth in 2013 and 2014. Long-term challenges include an ageing population, reliance on a small number of large companies and a dependence on exports.

Services contribute 58.9 per cent to GDP, industry 38.7 per cent and agriculture 2.4 per cent. Major manufacturing industries include electronics, telecommunications, motor vehicles, chemicals, shipbuilding and steel. Tourism is of growing importance.

The main trading partners are China, Japan and the USA (the US–South Korea Trade Agreement was first signed in 2007 and ratified in 2011). Principal exports are semiconductors, telecommunications equipment, motor vehicles, computers, steel, ships and petrochemicals. The main imports are machinery, electronics and electronic equipment, oil, steel, transport equipment, organic chemicals and plastics.

*GNI* – US$1,135,889m; US$25,920 per capita (2013)
*Annual average growth of GDP* – 3.5 per cent (2014 est)
*Inflation rate* – 1.3 per cent (2014 est)
*Population below poverty line* – 14.6 per cent (2013 est)
*Unemployment* – 3.4 per cent (2015 est)
*Total external debt* – US$424,200m (2014 est)
*Imports* – US$515,561m (2013)
*Exports* – US$559,649m (2013)

BALANCE OF PAYMENTS
*Trade* – US$44,088m surplus (2013)
*Current Account* – US$102,147m surplus (2015 est)

| Trade with UK | 2013 | 2014 |
| --- | --- | --- |
| Imports from UK | £4,820,700,286 | £4,202,297,444 |
| Exports to UK | £3,264,866,180 | £3,959,165,605 |

## COMMUNICATIONS

*Airports and waterways* – 71, including international airports at Seoul (Kimpo), Kimhae (near Busan), Daegu, Cheju city and Incheon; Busan, Incheon and Pohang are the major ports, although development and operations at Incheon are hampered by tidal variations of 9–10m
*Roadways and railways* – There are 83,199km of roadways, of which 3,779km are motorways, and 3,381km of railway in commercial operation, of which 1,843km are electrified
*Telecommunications* – 30.1 million fixed lines and 53.625 million mobile telephone subscriptions (2012); there were 39.4 million internet users in 2009
*Internet code and IDD* – kr; 82 (from UK), 1 44/2 44 (to UK)
*Major broadcasters* – Korea has a number of public radio and television broadcasters, including Korea Broadcasting System (KBS) and Munhwa Broadcasting Corporation (MBC), as well as a diversified commercial sector
*Press* – Major newspapers include *Chosun Ilbo, Korea Daily* and English-language daily *Korea Herald*
*WPFI score* – 26,55 (60)

## EDUCATION AND HEALTH

Primary education is free and compulsory for nine years from the age of six.

*Gross enrolment ratio (percentage of relevant age group)* – primary 103 per cent; secondary 97 per cent; tertiary 98 per cent (2012 est)
*Health expenditure (per capita)* – US$1,880 (2013)
*Hospital beds (per 1,000 people)* – 10.3 (2009)
*Life expectancy (years)* – 79.8 (2014 est)
*Mortality rate* – 6.63 (2014 est)
*Birth rate* – 8.26 (2014 est)
*Infant mortality rate* – 3.93 (2014 est)

# KOSOVO

*Republika e Kosoves – Republic of Kosovo*

*Area* – 10,887 sq. km
*Capital* – Pristina; population, 205,133 (2012 est)
*Major towns* – Mitrovica, Pec, Prizren
*Currency* – Euro (€) of 100 cents; the Serbian dinar is also in circulation
*Population* – 1,870,981 (2015 est); Albanian (92 per cent), Serb, Bosniak, Turk, Ashkali, Egyptian, Roma and Gorani (8 per cent) (2008)
*Religion* – Muslim, Christian (Serbian Orthodox, Roman Catholic, Protestant)
*Language* – Albanian, Serbian (both official), Bosnian, Turkish, Romani
*Population density* – 168 per sq. km (2013)
*Median age (years)* – 27.8 (2014 est)
*National anthem* – 'Europe'
*National day* – 17 February (Independence Day)
*Death penalty* – Not since independence
*CPI score* – 33 (110)

## CLIMATE AND TERRAIN

Kosovo has a hilly central region which divides plains in the east and west. Mountains lie along the borders with Albania, Macedonia and Montenegro, and along much of the border with Serbia. Elevation extremes range from 2,656m (Gjeravica) to 297m (Drini i Bardhe river). The main rivers are the Drini i Bardhe in the west and the Iberi in the north. The climate is continental.

## POLITICS

Under the 2008 constitution, the president is elected by the legislature for a five-year term and can be re-elected once. The unicameral legislature, the Assembly of Kosovo, has 120 members, elected for a four-year term; 100 seats have directly elected members, ten seats are reserved for Serbs and ten for other minorities. The majority party or coalition nominates the prime minister, who is appointed by the president. Both the prime minister and the government must be approved by the legislature.

Serbia regains control after First Balkan War; becomes province of Serbia, then part of Yugoslavia — Stripped of its autonomy by Serbian government and Albanian majority; gradually excluded from public life — Insurgency by the Kosovan Liberation Army provokes Serbian military reprisals — NATO intervention; Serbia signs peace plan and withdraws forces — International Court of Justice rules declaration legal; it is accepted by UN but refused by Serbia

1389        1945        1991                1998            2008

1913        1989        c.1995              1999            2010

Battle of Kosovo; Serbian principalities become part of the Ottoman Empire — Becomes an autonomous republic within Serbia — Vote of independence declared illegal by Serbian government — Serbia begins systematic ethnic cleansing of country — Kosovan government declares independence; it goes unrecognised by the UN

In the June 2014 legislative elections, the ruling Democratic Party of Kosovo won the most seats and formed a governing coalition in December. Behgjet Pacolli was elected president unopposed in February 2011, but the constitutional court declared the election unconstitutional; Atifete Jahjaga was elected president in April 2011.

## HEAD OF STATE
*President,* Atifete Jahjaga, *elected* 7 April 2011

## SELECTED GOVERNMENT MEMBERS *as at May 2015*
*Prime Minister,* Isa Mustafa
*First Deputy Prime Minister, Foreign Affairs,* Hashim Thaci
*Finance,* Avdullah Hoti
*Interior,* Skender Hyseni

## EMBASSY OF THE REPUBLIC OF KOSOVO
8 John Street, London WC1N 2ES
T 020-3585 4167 E embassy.uk@rks-gov.net
W www.kosovoembassy.org.uk
*Ambassador Extraordinary and Plenipotentiary,* HE Lirim Greicevci, *apptd* 2012

## BRITISH EMBASSY
Ismail Qemali 6, Arberi, Dragodan, Pristina
T (+381) 3825 4700 E britishembassy.pristina@fco.gov.uk
W www.gov.uk/government/world/kosovo
*Ambassador Extraordinary and Plenipotentiary,* HE Ruairí O'Connell, *apptd* 2015

## ECONOMY AND TRADE
Under UN administration Kosovo began the transition to a market economy, and over half of state-owned businesses have been privatised. However, income levels are the lowest in Europe, and the economy is dependent on international and foreign aid and the remittances of expatriates, worth about 10 per cent and 14 per cent of GDP respectively. Agriculture is close to subsistence level and inefficient; industrial output has declined because of insufficient investment and an unemployment level of over 45 per cent encourages emigration. International agencies and foreign governments are working with the Kosovan government to stimulate economic growth, attract investment and reduce unemployment.

Kosovo joined the Central Europe Free Trade Area (CEFTA) in 2006, and its members are the main markets for exports of minerals and processed metal products, scrap metals, leather goods, machinery and appliances. Imports of foodstuffs, wood, fuels, chemicals, machinery and electrical equipment come mainly from EU and neighbouring countries. In 2011 Serbia and Bosnia resumed trade with Kosovo, while a free trade agreement was signed with Turkey in 2013. The country continues to negotiate trade liberalisation with the EU.

*GNI* – US$6,401m; US$3,940 per capita (2013)
*Annual average growth of GDP* – 2.7 (2014 est)
*Inflation rate* – 0.4 per cent (2014 est)
*Population below poverty line* – 29.7 per cent (2011 est)
*Unemployment* – 45.3 per cent (2011 est)
*Total external debt* – US$4,482m (2014 est)

## BALANCE OF PAYMENTS
*Current Account* – US$473m deficit (2015 est)

| Trade with UK | 2013 | 2014 |
| --- | --- | --- |
| Imports from UK | £3,639,089 | £3,782,414 |
| Exports to UK | £718,185 | £504,388 |

## COMMUNICATIONS
*Airports* – Three; the principal international terminal is at Pristina
*Roadways and railways* – 1,843km, including 38km of motorways; 430km
*Telecommunications* – 106,300 fixed lines (2006) and 562,000 mobile telephone subscriptions (2007)
*Internet code and IDD* – kv; 381 (from UK), 44 (to UK)
*Major broadcasters* – Kosovo Radio-Television is the country's public broadcaster
*Press* – Leading dailies include *Koha Ditore, Bota Sot* and *Kosova Sot*
*WPFI score* – 30,63 (87)

# KUWAIT

*Dawlat al-Kuwayt – State of Kuwait*

*Area* – 17,818 sq. km
*Capital* – Kuwait City (al-Kuwayt); population, 2,680,000 (2014)
*Major cities* – Al Ahmadi, As Salimiyah, Hawalli
*Currency* – Kuwaiti dinar (KD) of 1,000 fils
*Population* – 2,788,534 rising at 1.62 per cent a year (2015 est); Kuwaiti (45 per cent), other Arab (35 per cent), South Asian (9 per cent), Iranian (4 per cent) (est)
*Religion* – Muslim (official) (Sunni 77 per cent, the remainder predominantly Shia) (est); Christian, Hindu and Parsi minorities, mostly expatriates
*Language* – Arabic (official), English
*Population density* – 189 per sq. km (2013)
*Urban population* – 98.3 per cent (2013)
*Median age (years)* – 28.9 (2014 est)
*National anthem* – 'Al-Nasheed al-Watani' ['National Anthem']
*National day* – 25 February
*Death penalty* – Retained
*CPI score* – 44 (67)

## CLIMATE AND TERRAIN

Kuwait is an almost entirely flat desert plain, with elevation extremes ranging from 306m to 0m (Persian Gulf). Its territory includes the island of Bubiyan and others at the head of the Persian Gulf. The climate is arid, with little rainfall but high levels of humidity. Average temperatures range from 12.5°C in January to 37°C in July and August.

## HISTORY AND POLITICS

The area was under the nominal control of the Ottoman Empire from the late 16th century, but in 1756 an autonomous sheikhdom was founded that has been ruled by the al-Sabah family ever since. Kuwait entered into a treaty of friendship with Britain in 1899, in order to protect itself from Ottoman and Saudi domination, and it became a British protectorate in 1914. The borders with Saudi Arabia and Iraq were agreed between 1922 and 1933. Full independence was achieved in 1961, although Britain retained a military presence in the country until 1971.

An attempted Iraqi invasion shortly after independence in 1961 was discouraged by British troops in the Gulf. However, in August 1990 Iraq invaded and occupied Kuwait, proclaiming it a province of Iraq. In 1991, a short military campaign by a US-led alliance expelled the Iraqi forces, although there were further Iraqi incursions in 1993 before Iraq renounced its claim and recognised the new UN-demarcated border in 1994. Extensive damage was caused to the country's infrastructure and environment during the Iraqi occupation and reconstruction was a priority throughout the 1990s; in 2003, Kuwait was a base for forces involved in the Iraq War.

In recent years, there have been clashes between security forces and militant Islamists, some of whom are alleged to have links to al-Qaida.

Although Kuwait was the first Arab country in the Gulf to have an elected legislature, this was suspended from 1977–81, 1986–92, and in 1999, 2012 and 2013. The political system is subject to instability, with electoral boycotts by Islamist and liberal parties common; two elections were held in 12 months in 2008–9 owing to the legislature's efforts to subject the government to parliamentary scrutiny. Pro-reform demonstrations took place in spring 2011, forcing Sheikh Nasser al-Muhammad al-Ahmed al-Sabeh's government to resign from office; the cabinet was replaced by a new government headed by Sheikh Jaber Mubarak al-Hamad al-Sabah who retained power until the next election. The 2012 legislative election saw Islamists retain the largest bloc in the National Assembly, after which Sheikh Jaber was reappointed prime minister. In 2015, Kuwait participated in Saudi Arabian air strikes against Houthi rebels in Yemen.

The 1962 constitution was amended in 2005 to extend the franchise to women. The head of state is the emir, chosen from among the ruling family. He exercises executive power through the council of ministers; in 2003, the post of prime minister was separated from the role of heir to the throne for the first time. The unicameral National Assembly has 50 members directly elected for a four-year term. There are no political parties.

The country is divided into six governorates: Capital, Hawalli, al-Ahmadi, al-Jahrah, al-Farwaniya and Mubarak al-Kabeer.

## HEAD OF STATE

*HH The Emir of Kuwait,* Sheikh Sabah al-Ahmad al-Jaber al-Sabah, *born* 1929, *acceded* 29 January 2006
*Crown Prince,* HH Sheikh Nawaf al-Ahmad al-Jaber al-Sabah

SELECTED GOVERNMENT MEMBERS *as at May 2015*
*Prime Minister,* Sheikh Jaber al-Mubarak al-Hamad al-Sabah
*First Deputy Prime Minister, Foreign Affairs,* Sheikh Sabah al-Khaled al-Hamad al-Sabah
*Deputy Prime Minister, Defence,* Sheikh Khaled al-Jarrah al-Sabah
*Deputy Prime Minister, Interior,* Sheikh Mohammed al-Hamad al-Sabah

EMBASSY OF THE STATE OF KUWAIT
2 Albert Gate, London SW1X 7JU
T 020-7590 3400 E kuwait@dircon.co.uk
*Ambassador Extraordinary and Plenipotentiary,* HE Khaled al-Duwaisan, GCVO, *apptd* 1993

BRITISH EMBASSY
PO Box 2, Arabian Gulf Street, Safat 13001
T (+965) 2259 4320 E kuwait.generalenquiries@fco.gov.uk
W www.gov.uk/government/world/kuwait
*Ambassador Extraordinary and Plenipotentiary,* HE Matthew Lodge, *apptd* 2014

## DEFENCE

| Aged 16–49, 2010 est | Males | Females |
| --- | --- | --- |
| Available for military service | 1,002,480 | 616,958 |
| Fit for military service | 840,912 | 523,206 |

*Military expenditure* – US$5,644m (2013)
*Conscription* – Suspended

## ECONOMY AND TRADE

Oil was discovered in 1938 and the development of the oil industry after 1945 transformed the country from one of the poorest in the world to one of the richest. Petroleum accounts for 95 per cent of export revenues and 95 per cent of government income. Income from foreign reserves and investment is also high, cushioning the economy from the effects of dependency on oil. Economic reform is slow owing to the tensions between the government and legislature; a diversification fund worth US$130bn was established in 2010, though much of this money has yet to be spent. Kuwait has a rich sovereign wealth fund, worth around US$410bn (£260.4bn), but the economy remains vulnerable to long-term low oil prices and an undiversified economy.

The climate and terrain limit agriculture and, with the exception of fish, all food is imported; the primary sector contributes only 0.3 per cent of GDP. Services account for 50.2 per cent of GDP and industry for 49.4 per cent. Apart from the oil and petrochemical industries, activities include the production of cement and construction materials, shipbuilding and repair, water desalination and food processing.

The main export markets are South Korea, India, Japan, China and the USA, and the main sources of imports are the USA, China, Saudi Arabia and South Korea. Principal exports are oil and refined products, and fertilisers. The main imports are food, construction materials, vehicles and vehicle parts, and clothing.

*GNI* – US$132,166m (2010); US$45,130 per capita (2011)
*Annual average growth of GDP* – 1.4 per cent (2014 est)
*Inflation rate* – 2.5 per cent (2014 est)
*Unemployment* – 2.7 per cent (2015 est)
*Total external debt* – US$33,100m (2014 est)
*Imports* – US$29,644m (2013)
*Exports* – US$115,210m (2013)

**BALANCE OF PAYMENTS**
*Trade* – US$85,566m surplus (2013)
*Current Account* – US$21,114m surplus (2015 est)

| Trade with UK | 2013 | 2014 |
|---|---|---|
| Imports from UK | £531,108,877 | £542,951,786 |
| Exports to UK | £1,647,186,395 | £1,318,396,937 |

## COMMUNICATIONS
*Airports and waterways* – Four, with an international airport at Kuwait City; the main seaports are Ash Shu'aybah and Ash Shuwaykh
*Roadways* – There are 6,608km of roadways
*Telecommunications* – 510,000 fixed lines and 5.526 million mobile subscriptions; there were 1.1 million internet users in 2009
*Internet code and IDD* – kw; 965 (from UK), 44 (to UK)
*Major broadcasters* – Kuwaiti TV and Radio Kuwait are the public broadcasters and compete with commercial stations; satellite television is also widely watched
*Press* – Major dailies include *Al-Watan*, *Al-Qabas* and the *Kuwait Times*
*WPFI score* – 30,84 (90)

## EDUCATION AND HEALTH
Education is free and compulsory from six to 14 years.
*Literacy rate* – 99.5 per cent (2015 est)
*Health expenditure (per capita)* – US$1,507 (2013)
*Hospital beds (per 1,000 people)* – 2.2 (2012)
*Life expectancy (years)* – 77.64 (2014 est)
*Mortality rate* – 2.16 (2014 est)
*Birth rate* – 20.26 (2013 est)
*Infant mortality rate* – 7.51 (2014 est)

# KYRGYZSTAN

*Kyrgyz Respublikasy* – Kyrgyz Republic

*Area* – 199,951 sq. km
*Capital* – Bishkek; population, 850,000 (2015 est)
*Major city* – Osh
*Currency* – Som of 100 tyiyn
*Population* – 5,664,939 rising at 1.11 per cent a year (2015 est); Kyrgyz (64.7 per cent), Uzbek (13.6 per cent), Russian (12.5 per cent), Dungan (1 per cent), Ukrainian (1 per cent), Uygur (1 per cent) (est)
*Religion* – Muslim 75 per cent (predominantly Sunni), Christian (Russian Orthodox) 20 per cent, other 5 per cent
*Language* – Kyrgyz, Russian (both official), Uzbek, Dungan
*Population density* – 30 per sq. km (2013)
*Urban population* – 35.5 per cent (2013)
*Median age (years)* – 25.7 (2014 est)

*National anthem* – 'Kyrgyz Respublikasynyn Mamlekettik Gimni' ['National Anthem of the Kyrgyz Republic']
*National day* – 31 August (Independence Day)
*Death penalty* – Abolished for all crimes (since 2007)
*CPI score* – 27 (136)
*Literacy rate* – 99.7 per cent (2015 est)
*Gross enrolment ratio (percentage of relevant age group)* – primary 106 per cent (2012 est); secondary 88 per cent; tertiary 41 per cent (2011 est)
*Health expenditure (per capita)* – US$87 (2013)
*Hospital beds (per 1,000 people)* – 4.8 (2012)
*Life expectancy (years)* – 70.06 (2014 est)
*Mortality rate* – 6.74 (2014 est)
*Birth rate* – 23.33 (2014 est)
*Infant mortality rate* – 28.71 (2014 est)

## CLIMATE AND TERRAIN
Kyrgyzstan is a landlocked and mountainous country lying in the Tien Shan mountain range, with the Pamir mountains in the extreme south. Elevations range from 7,439m (Jengish Chokusu) to 132m (Kara-Darya), though most of the country lies at over 1,000m. The principal rivers are the Naryn and the Chu, and the vast Issyk-Kul lake lies in the north-east. The climate is continental but with temperatures and humidity moderated by the altitude; typical temperatures range from −12.6°C in January to 15.2°C in July. Rainfall is low for the altitude, owing to Kyrgyzstan's distance from the sea and the rain-shadow effect of the Himalayan and Pamir ranges.

## HISTORY AND POLITICS
After centuries of Turkic, Mongol and Chinese rule, the Kyrgyz became part of the Russian Empire in the 1860s and 1870s. After the October 1917 revolution in Russia, the area became part of the Turkestan autonomous republic within the USSR until 1924, when the Kirgiz Autonomous Region was formed. Soviet rule brought land reforms in the 1920s that resulted in the settlement of many of the nomadic Kyrgyz. Kyrgyzstan became an autonomous republic in 1926 and a constituent republic of the USSR in 1936.

Reform in the USSR in the 1980s provoked an upsurge in nationalism in Kyrgyzstan and agitation for independence. Following the attempted coup in Moscow in 1991, Kyrgyzstan became an independent republic and joined the Commonwealth of Independent States.

Since independence, there has been tension between the Kyrgyz and ethnic Uzbeks, concentrated around Osh, and between the Kyrgyz and Dungans (ethnic Chinese) near Bishkek. There have also been clashes between security forces and militant Islamists, active near the border with Tajikistan.

Askar Akayev, a pro-reform Communist, was president from 1990 until he was deposed in March 2005 in a popular uprising over alleged electoral fraud; the uprising was also fuelled by years of unrest over the dire economic situation, corruption, nepotism and crime. The opposition leader Kurmanbek Bakiyev was elected president in July 2005 and re-elected in 2009, but forced from office in April 2010 after attempts to suppress anti-government demonstrations left over 80 protesters dead.

An interim government was formed, but intercommunal violence between Kyrgyz and Uzbeks erupted in June 2010, spreading to Jalalabad; a referendum held in the same month approved a draft constitution granting greater powers to parliament at the expense of the president.

The 2010 legislative election was indecisive: the four main parties won roughly the same number of seats each. Two, the Social Democratic Party (SDPK) and Respublika, formed a coalition government with the Homeland party and took office in December. Former prime minister and SDPK leader Almazbek Atambayev won the 2011 presidential election, taking over from interim president Roza Otunbayeva. In March 2014, the government of Prime Minister Zhantoro Satybaldiyev resigned following allegations of corruption; reformist politician Joomart Otorbaev was elected to the premiership by a majority of the legislature.

Under the 2010 constitution, the president will be directly elected for a six-year term, which is not renewable. The unicameral Supreme Council has 120 members directly elected for a five-year term. The largest party in the legislature nominates the prime minister, and the president appoints the cabinet; the appointments are subject to the approval of the Supreme Council. New legislative elections are scheduled to take place in November 2015.

### HEAD OF STATE
*President,* Almazbek Atambayev, *sworn in* 1 December 2011

### SELECTED GOVERNMENT MEMBERS *as at May 2015*
*Prime Minister,* Joomart Otorbaev
*First Vice-Prime Minister,* Tayirbek Sarpashev
*Foreign Affairs,* Erlan Abdyldayev
*Internal Affairs,* Melis Turganbaev

### EMBASSY OF THE KYRGYZ REPUBLIC
Ascot House, 119 Crawford Street, London W1U 6BJ
T 020-7935 1462 E mail@kyrgyz-embassy.org.uk
W www.kyrgyz-embassy.org.uk
*Ambassador Extraordinary and Plenipotentiary,* vacant

### BRITISH EMBASSY
21 Erkindik Boulevard, Office 404, Bishkek, 720040, Kyrgyzstan
T (+996) 312 303 637 E ukinkyrgyzrepublic@fco.gov.uk
W www.gov.uk/government/world/kyrgyzstan
*Ambassador Extraordinary and Plenipotentiary,* HE Judith Margaret Farnworth, *apptd* 2011

### DEFENCE

| Aged 16–49, 2010 est | Males | Females |
| --- | --- | --- |
| Available for military service | 1,456,881 | 1,470,317 |
| Fit for military service | 1,119,224 | 1,257,263 |

*Military expenditure* – US$252m (2014)
*Conscription* – 18–27 years of age, male only; 12 months

### ECONOMY AND TRADE
Economic reforms in the early 1990s caused severe hardship, and although productivity and exports have grown since the late 1990s, poverty is widespread and unemployment high, particularly in the south. The economy, which is heavily dependent on gold exports, contracted in 2009 owing to the global downturn, and production and trade were reduced further by the political violence and disruption of 2010. Despite such damage to the infrastructure, the economy grew 1 per cent in 2013 increasing to 17.4 per cent in 2013. The government, with international support, is pursuing poverty-reduction and economic-growth programmes, but the greater foreign direct investment that these require may be deterred by political volatility, lack of transparency and the high level of organised crime. Kyrgyzstan became the fifth member of the Eurasian Economic Union (EEU) in May 2015 and membership is expected to help the economy to grow by 2 per cent in 2015.

The economy is predominantly agrarian, with agriculture accounting for 19.3 per cent of GDP and employing 48 per cent of the workforce. There are deposits of gold, uranium, mercury and natural gas. Apart from mining,

industry consists of hydroelectric power generation and light manufacturing, contributing 31.1 per cent of GDP; services contribute 49.6 per cent.

The main trading partners are China, Russia, the UAE, Kazakhstan and Uzbekistan. Principal exports are cotton, wool, meat, tobacco, gold, mercury, uranium, natural gas, hydroelectric power, machinery and shoes. The main imports are oil, gas, machinery and equipment, chemicals and foodstuffs.

*GNI* – US$6,085m; US$1,210 per capita (2013)
*Annual average growth of GDP* – 4.1 per cent (2014 est)
*Inflation rate* – 7.5 per cent (2014 est)
*Population below poverty line* – 38.0 per cent (2012 est)
*Unemployment* – 7.5 per cent (2015 est)
*Total external debt* – US$6,819m (2014 est)
*Imports* – US$6,070m (2013)
*Exports* – US$1,791m (2013)

### BALANCE OF PAYMENTS
*Trade* – US$4,279m deficit (2013)
*Current Account* – US$1,255m deficit (2015 est)

| Trade with UK | 2013 | 2014 |
| --- | --- | --- |
| Imports from UK | £3,026,539 | £501,915 |
| Exports to UK | £556,661 | £1,032,694 |

### COMMUNICATIONS
*Airports and waterways* – 18, with an international airport outside Bishkek; there are 600km of waterways
*Roadways and railways* – 34,000km; 470km
*Telecommunications* – 489,000 fixed lines and 6.8 million mobile subscriptions (2012); there were 2.195 million internet users in 2009
*Internet code and IDD* – kg; 996 (from UK), 44 (to UK)
*Major broadcasters* – Kyrgyz National TV and Radio Broadcasting Corporation runs various networks alongside a number of private broadcasters
*Press* – Major dailies include the government-owned *Slovo Kyrgyzstana Plus* and the private *Vecherniy Bishkek*
*WPFI score* – 30,69 (88)

## LAOS

*Sathalanalat Paxathipatai Paxaxon Lao – Lao People's Democratic Republic*

*Area* – 236,800 sq. km
*Capital* – Vientiane; population, 946,000 (2014)
*Major towns* – Luang Prabang, Pakse, Savannakhet
*Currency* – Kip (K) of 100 att
*Population* – 6,803,699 rising at 1.59 per cent a year (2014 est); there are (officially) 47 ethnic groups, including Lao (55 per cent), Khmou (11 per cent), Hmong (8 per cent) (2005)

*Religion* – Buddhist 67 per cent (predominantly Theravada), Christian 1.5 per cent; most of the remainder practise animist beliefs

*Language* – Lao (official), French, English, ethnic languages

*Population density* – 29 per sq. km (2013)

*Urban population* – 36.5 per cent (2013 est)

*Median age (years)* – 22 (2014 est)

*National anthem* – 'Pheng Xat Lao' ['Hymn of the Lao People']

*National day* – 2 December (Republic Day)

*Death penalty* – Retained (last used 1989)

*CPI score* – 25 (145)

*Literacy rate* – 90.2 per cent (2015 est)

*Gross enrolment ratio (percentage of age group)* – primary 121 per cent; secondary 50 per cent; tertiary 18 per cent (2013 est)

*Health expenditure (per capita)* – US$32 (2013)

*Hospital beds (per 1,000 people)* – 1.5 (2012)

*Life expectancy (years)* – 63.51 (2014 est)

*Mortality rate* – 7.74 (2014 est)

*Birth rate* – 24.76 (2014 est)

*Infant mortality rate* – 54.53 (2014 est)

## CLIMATE AND TERRAIN

Laos is mostly mountainous, the land rising from the Mekong river basin in the west to mountains in the north and east. Elevation extremes range from 2,817m (Phou Bia) to 70m (Mekong river). Much of the land is covered by rainforest. The climate is tropical, with a wet season from May to October, during which humidity levels are very high. Average temperatures in Vientiane range from 19.9°C in January to 26.3°C in June.

## HISTORY AND POLITICS

From the ninth to the 13th centuries, Laos was part of the Khmer Empire centred on Angkor in Cambodia. Small principalities developed from the 12th century and were united in the 14th century into the Lao kingdom of Lan Xang ('the land of a million elephants'), which dominated until 1713, when it split into the separate kingdoms of Luang Prabang, Vientiane and Champassac, which became tributaries of Siam (Thailand) in the late 18th century and then a protectorate of France from 1893.

Japanese occupation during the Second World War inspired a Lao nationalist movement, which proclaimed independence in 1945, but the French regained control of the country in 1946. Independence as a constitutional monarchy was granted in 1953, but much of the following 20 years was spent in civil war between the Communist Pathet Lao movement, backed first by China and then by North Vietnam, and royalists, who attracted US and Thai support from the early 1960s. A ceasefire in 1973 partitioned the country between the two sides, but in 1975 the Pathet Lao seized power in the rest of the country and proclaimed a republic, introducing a one-party state and initiating socialist policies. Greater economic liberalisation was introduced from the mid-1980s, and the first legislative elections since 1975 were held in 1989.

Ethnic Hmong minority groups have maintained a low-level insurgency against the communist regime since 1975. In 2000 and 2004, Laos suffered serious civil disturbances, including bombings and armed attacks on buses. These were variously attributed to Hmong insurgents and anti-government groups based abroad.

In the 2011 legislative election, Lao People's Revolutionary Party (LPRP) candidates won all but four of the seats, the remaining seats being taken by approved independent candidates. The legislature re-elected Choummaly Sayasone as president in June 2011 and approved a reshuffled council of ministers. In May 2014 a plane crash in northern Laos killed the defence minister and a deputy prime minister, along with other government officials.

Under the 1991 constitution, the head of state is a president elected by the legislature for a five-year term. The unicameral National Assembly has 132 members, who are party-approved candidates directly elected for a five-year term. The LPRP is the only legal political party, although it has given approval to non-partisan candidates for legislative seats. Party congresses are held every five years.

### HEAD OF STATE

*President,* Lt.-Gen. Choummaly Sayasone, *elected* 8 June 2006, *re-elected* 2011

*Vice-President,* Bounnhang Vorachit

### SELECTED GOVERNMENT MEMBERS *as at May 2015*

*Prime Minister,* Thongsing Thammavong

*Deputy Prime Ministers,* Bounpone Bouttanavong; Maj.-Gen. Asang Laoly; Somsavat Lengsavad; Thongloun Sisoulith

*(Foreign Affairs);* Phankham Viphavanh

### EMBASSY OF THE LAO PEOPLE'S DEMOCRATIC REPUBLIC

49 Porchester Terrace, London W2 3TS

T 020-7402 3770 E laosemblondon@gmail.com

*Ambassador Extraordinary and Plenipotentiary,* HE Sayakane Sisouvong, *apptd* 2014

### BRITISH EMBASSY

Rue J. Nehru, Phonexay, Saysettha District, Vientiane

T (+856) 030 770 0000 E britishembassy.vientiane@fco.gov.uk

W www.gov.uk/government/world/organisations/british-embassy-vientiane

*Ambassador Extraordinary and Plenipotentiary,* HE Hugh Evans, *apptd* 2015

### DEFENCE

| Aged 16–49, 2010 est | Males | Females |
| --- | --- | --- |
| Available for military service | 1,574,362 | 1,607,856 |
| Fit for military service | 1,111,629 | 1,190,035 |

*Military expenditure* – US$20.3m (2012 est)

*Conscription* – 18 years of age; 18 months

### ECONOMY AND TRADE

Economic liberalisation and a measure of private enterprise were introduced from 1986, producing growth averaging 6 per cent a year since 1988, except during the 1997 Asian financial crisis. Recent economic growth has been driven by foreign investment in dam and transport construction projects, hydroelectric power and mining. The country remains very poor, with only a rudimentary infrastructure, and is dependent on international aid and investment. Laos was admitted to the World Trade Organization in 2012. The economy grew by over 7 per cent in 2014, for the seventh year in a row. Future growth is expected to by supported by the recovery of the Thai economy following the 2014 coup. Laos was scheduled to form a common market with the other members of the Association of Southeast Asian Nations (ASEAN) in 2015.

Subsistence agriculture, principally rice, accounts for 23.7 per cent of GDP and about 73.1 per cent of employment. Deposits of copper, tin, gold and gypsum are exploited, as is the abundance of timber in the rainforests. Other activities include food processing, manufacture of garments and cement, and tourism. A hydroelectric dam on the Mekong river exports electricity to Thailand.

The main trading partners are Thailand (33 per cent of exports; 56 per cent of imports), Vietnam and China. Principal exports are timber products, coffee, electricity, tin, copper and gold. The main imports are machinery and equipment, vehicles, fuel and consumer goods.
*GNI* – US$9,838m; US$1,450 per capita (2013)
*Annual average growth of GDP* – 7.4 per cent (2014)
*Inflation rate* – 4.7 per cent (2014 est)
*Population below poverty line* – 22 per cent (2013 est)
*Unemployment* – 1.5 per cent (2015 est)
*Total external debt* – US$7,520 (2014 est)
*Imports* – US$2,900m (2013)
*Exports* – US$2,600m (2013)

BALANCE OF PAYMENTS
*Trade* – US$300m deficit (2013)
*Current Account* – US$257m deficit (2015 est)

| Trade with UK | 2013 | 2014 |
| --- | --- | --- |
| Imports from UK | £4,522,940 | £3,561,685 |
| Exports to UK | £43,869,089 | £29,009,193 |

## COMMUNICATIONS
*Airports and waterways* – Eight, with the largest airports at Vientiane and Luang Prabang; there are around 4,600km of navigable waterways, principally on the Mekong and its tributaries, although some are not passable in the dry season
*Roadways and railways* – There are 530km of paved roadways; the Friendship Bridge over the Mekong river connects with Thailand, and links up road routes from Singapore to China. A rail track across the bridge links the Thai and Laotian rail systems
*Telecommunications* – 112,000 fixed lines (2012) and 6.492 million mobile subscriptions (2011); there were 300,000 internet users in 2009
*Internet code and IDD* – la; 856 (from UK), 44 (to UK)
*Major broadcasters* – The state-run Lao National TV is the country's principal broadcaster
*Press* – There are three state-run news publications, including the *Vientiane Mai*
*WPFI score* – 71,25 (171)

# LATVIA

*Latvijas Republika – Republic of Latvia*

*Area* – 64,589 sq. km
*Capital* – Riga; population, 629,000 (2014)
*Major cities* – Daugavpils, Jelgava, Liepaja
*Currency* – Euro (€) of 100 cents
*Population* – 1,986,705 falling at 1.06 per cent a year (2015 est); Latvian (61.1 per cent), Russian

(26.2 per cent), Belarusian (3.5 per cent), Ukrainian (2.3 per cent), Polish (2.2 per cent), Lithuanian (1.3 per cent) (2013 est)
*Religion* – Christian (Lutheran 19.6 per cent, Orthodox 15.3 per cent, other 0.4 per cent), unspecified 63.7 per cent (2006)
*Language* – Latvian (official), Russian
*Population density* – 32 per sq. km (2013)
*Urban population* – 67.7 per cent (2013 est)
*Median age (years)* – 41.4 (2014 est)
*National anthem* – 'Dievs, Sveti Latviju' ['God Bless Latvia']
*National day* – 18 November (Independence Day)
*Death penalty* – Abolished for all crimes (since 2012)
*CPI score* – 55 (43)

## CLIMATE AND TERRAIN
Latvia is a flat, low-lying country on the eastern shore of the Baltic Sea, with low hills and many lakes in the south-east. Elevation extremes range from 312m (Gaizinkalns) to 0m (Baltic Sea). The climate is temperate, and average temperatures range from −3.2°C in February to 17.9°C in July.

## HISTORY AND POLITICS
Conquered and Christianised in the 13th century by the Teutonic Knights, Latvia was successively under Polish, Lithuanian and Swedish rule in the 16th and 17th centuries until it was incorporated into the Russian Empire in 1721. Under partial German occupation during the First World War, it declared its independence in 1918 and successfully defended this against the Bolsheviks in 1918–20. A dictatorship was established in 1934 following a period of political instability and economic depression. The USSR invaded and annexed Latvia in 1940, and regained control in 1944 after ousting the German forces that had invaded in 1941. Latvia suffered huge civilian losses during the Second World War, including the destruction of its large Jewish community. Many more Latvians died after the war in purges and deportations ordered by Stalin.

Agitation by nationalist groups grew from the mid-1980s. In May 1990 the legislature declared independence. The last Russian troops left in 1994 but a large Russian minority remains and there are intercommunal tensions. Latvia joined NATO and the EU in 2004.

In January 2014, Laimdota Straujuma was appointed prime minister following the resignation of Valdis Dombrovskis. In the October 2014 legislative election, the ruling coalition, led by the centre-right Unity party, retained its majority, despite the pro-Russian Harmony Centre remaining the largest single party. Raimonds Vejonis of the Green and Farmers' Union (ZZS) was elected president in June 2015 after winning the fifth round of voting.

The 1922 constitution was restored in 1993. The head of state is a president, who is elected by the legislature for a four-year term which may be renewed once. The president appoints the prime minister, who appoints the cabinet subject to approval by the legislature. The unicameral *Saeima* has 100 deputies who are directly elected for a four-year term. The next general election will take place in October 2014.

HEAD OF STATE
*President*, Raimonds Vejonis *(Defence), elected* 3 June 2015, *sworn in* 8 July 2015

SELECTED GOVERNMENT MEMBERS *as at May 2015*
*Prime Minister*, Laimdota Straujuma
*Finance*, Janis Reirs
*Foreign Affairs*, Edgars Rinkevics

## EMBASSY OF THE REPUBLIC OF LATVIA

45 Nottingham Place, London W1U 5LY
T 020-7312 0041 E embassy.uk@mfa.gov.lv
W www.mfa.gov.lv/london
*Ambassador Extraordinary and Plenipotentiary,* HE Andris
   Teikmanis, *apptd* 2013

## BRITISH EMBASSY

5 J. Alunana Iela, Riga LV1010
T (+371) 6777 4700 E britishembassy.riga@fco.gov.uk
W www.gov.uk/government/world/latvia
*Ambassador Extraordinary and Plenipotentiary,* HE Sarah
   Cowley, *apptd* 2013

## DEFENCE

| Aged 16–49, 2010 est | Males | Females |
| --- | --- | --- |
| Available for military service | 546,090 | 540,810 |
| Fit for military service | 401,691 | 447,638 |

*Military expenditure* – US$299m (2014)

## ECONOMY AND TRADE

The country made the transition from a planned to a market economy in the decade after independence, although a few large enterprises remain in state ownership. The economy grew rapidly from 2004 to 2007, but was severely affected by the global economic downturn because of its large current account deficit and private-sector debt. The economy contracted by 20 per cent in 2008–9 and was slow to return to growth. The IMF, the World Bank and the EU provided aid in 2008–9 to avoid devaluation of the lat in return for a 40 per cent cut in public spending. The IMF programme was successfully concluded in December 2011. The poor performance of the eurozone and Russian economies are predicted to weaken growth in 2015.

The economy has shifted towards service industries since independence. Services, especially transit services and banking, is the largest sector, contributing 70.4 per cent of GDP. Industry contributes 24.8 per cent of GDP and includes food processing and the manufacture of processed wood products, textiles, processed metals, pharmaceuticals, rail transport vehicles, synthetic fibres and electronics. The agricultural sector accounts for 4.8 per cent of GDP, employs 8.8 per cent of the workforce and specialises in rearing livestock, dairy farming and crops including grain, rapeseed, potatoes and other vegetables.

The main trading partners are other EU states and Russia, with exports contributing nearly a third of GDP. Principal exports are food products, timber and wood products, metals, machinery and equipment, and textiles. The main imports are machinery and equipment, consumer goods, chemicals, fuel and vehicles.

*GNI* – US$30,773m; US$15,280 per capita (2013)
*Annual average growth of GDP* – 2.7 per cent (2014)
*Inflation rate* – 0.7 per cent (2014 est)
*Unemployment* – 11.2 per cent (2015 est)
*Total external debt* – US$38,540m (2014 est)
*Imports* – US$16,781m (2013)
*Exports* – US$13,317m (2013)

BALANCE OF PAYMENTS
*Trade* – US$3,464m deficit (2013)
*Current Account* – US$626m deficit (2015 est)

| Trade with UK | 2013 | 2014 |
| --- | --- | --- |
| Imports from UK | £368,820,008 | £333,686,061 |
| Exports to UK | £513,712,768 | £401,360,202 |

## COMMUNICATIONS

*Airports and waterways* – There are 18 airports with the largest at Riga, Ventspils and Liepaja; there are major ports at Riga and Ventspils
*Roadways and railways* – 14,707km; 2,239km
*Telecommunications* – 501,000 fixed lines and 2.31 million mobile subscriptions (2012); there were 1.504 million internet users in 2009
*Internet code and IDD* – lv; 371 (from UK), 44 (to UK)
*Major broadcasters* – Latvian Television (LTV) and Latvian Radio are the state broadcasters
*Press* – Prominent daily newspapers include *Diena, Neatkariga Rita Avize* (both Latvian language) and *Telegraf* (mainly Russian)
*WPFI score* – 18,12 (28)

## EDUCATION AND HEALTH

Education is compulsory from the age of seven until 16 years, after which there is the option for a further three years of either secondary or vocational study.
*Literacy rate* – 100 per cent (2015 est)
*Gross enrolment ratio (percentage of relevant age group)* –
   primary 103 per cent; secondary 98 per cent; tertiary
   65 per cent (2012 est)
*Health expenditure (per capita)* – US$874 (2013)
*Hospital beds (per 1,000 people)* – 5.9 (2011)
*Life expectancy (years)* – 73.44 (2014 est)
*Mortality rate* – 13.6 (2014 est)
*Birth rate* – 9.79 (2014 est)
*Infant mortality rate* – 7.91 (2014 est)

# LEBANON

*Al-Jumhuriyah al-Lubnaniyah* – *Lebanese Republic*

*Area* – 10,400 sq. km
*Capital* – Beirut (Bayrut); population, 2,179,000 (2014)
*Major cities* – Sidon, Tripoli (Tarabulus)
*Currency* – Lebanese pound (L£) of 100 piastres
*Population* – 6,184,701 rising at 0.86 per cent a year
   (2015 est); Arab (95 per cent), Armenian (4 per cent) (est)
*Religion* – Muslim 54 per cent (27 per cent Shia, 27 per cent
   Sunni), Christian 40.5 per cent (includes 21 per cent
   Maronite Catholic, Druze 5.6 per cent, small numbers
   of Jews, Baha'is, Buddhists, Hindus and Mormons
*Language* – Arabic (official), French, English, Armenian
*Population density* – 437 per sq. km (2013)
*Urban population* – 87.5 per cent (2013 est)
*Median age (years)* – 29.3 (2014 est)
*National anthem* – 'Kulluna lil-watan' ['All of Us, For Our
   Country']
*National day* – 22 November (Independence Day)
*Death penalty* – Retained
*CPI score* – 27 (136)

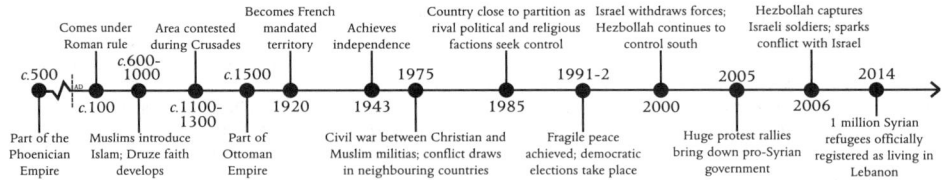

| | Comes under Roman rule | Area contested during Crusades | Becomes French mandated territory | Achieves independence | Country close to partition as rival political and religious factions seek control | Israel withdraws forces; Hezbollah continues to control south | Hezbollah captures Israeli soldiers; sparks conflict with Israel | |
|---|---|---|---|---|---|---|---|---|
| c.500 | c.600–1000 | c.1500 | | 1975 | 1991-2 | 2005 | 2014 | |
| c.100 | c.1100–1300 | 1920 | 1943 | 1985 | 2000 | 2006 | | |
| Part of the Phoenician Empire | Muslims introduce Islam; Druze faith develops | Part of Ottoman Empire | Civil war between Christian and Muslim militias; conflict draws in neighbouring countries | Fragile peace achieved; democratic elections take place | Huge protest rallies bring down pro-Syrian government | 1 million Syrian refugees officially registered as living in Lebanon | | |

## CLIMATE AND TERRAIN

A narrow plain along the Mediterranean Sea coast is backed by the Lebanon Mountains, along which the Anti-Lebanon range runs parallel, forming the border with Syria. Between the two ranges lies the fertile Bekaa valley, the northern extremity of Africa's Great Rift Valley. Elevations range from 3,088m (Qurnat as Sawda') to 0m (Mediterranean Sea). The climate is Mediterranean, although the mountains usually receive snow in winter. Average temperatures in Beirut are 7.4°C in January and 25.3°C in August.

## POLITICS

The constitution dates from 1926 but has been heavily amended, most significantly in 1943, when the National Covenant set out the division of power between the religious communities, and in 1990 to incorporate the provisions of the Ta'if accord. By convention, the presidency is held by a Maronite Christian, the prime minister is a Sunni Muslim and the speaker is a Shia Muslim.

The president is elected by the legislature for a six-year term, which is not renewable. The unicameral National Assembly has 128 members, directly elected for a four-year term; seats are divided equally between Christians and Muslims, whose quotas are subdivided by confession according to the distribution formalised in the 2008 election law. The prime minister is appointed by the president following consultation with the legislature.

In May 2008, a neutral candidate, General Michel Suleiman, the head of the armed forces, was elected president. After months of negotiation following the 2009 legislative election, the '14 March' leader Saad Hariri formed a national unity government which took office in November 2009. This government collapsed in January 2011 with the withdrawal of pro-Syria parties, and Najib Mikati was elected prime minister-designate later that month. In April 2013 Sunni politician Tamam Salam was nominated prime minister. In May 2014, Michel Suleiman's presidential term ended; political deadlock prevented a new appointment. New legislative elections, due to take place in 2014, have been delayed until June 2017 due to security concerns related to the conflict in Syria. Following the end of President Suleiman's term of office in May 2014, parliament has repeatedly failed to elect a new president, most recently in April 2015.

### HEAD OF STATE

*President,* Tamam Salam *(acting), apptd* 25 May 2014

### SELECTED GOVERNMENT MEMBERS *as at May 2015*
*Prime Minister,* Tamam Salam
*Deputy Prime Minister, Defence,* Samir Mokbel
*Finance,* Ali Hassan Khali

### EMBASSY OF LEBANON

21 Kensington Palace Gardens, London W8 4QN
T 020-7727 6696 W emb.leb@btinternet.com
*Ambassador Extraordinary and Plenipotentiary,* HE Inaam Osseiran, *apptd* 2008

### BRITISH EMBASSY

PO Box 11–471, Serail Hill, Beirut Central District, Beirut
T (+961) (1) 960 800 W www.gov.uk/government/world/lebanon
*Ambassador Extraordinary and Plenipotentiary,* HE Tom Fletcher, CMG, *apptd* 2011

### DEFENCE

| Aged 16–49, 2010 est | Males | Females |
|---|---|---|
| Available for military service | 1,081,016 | 1,115,349 |
| Fit for military service | 920,825 | 941,806 |

*Military expenditure* – US$2,121m (2014 est)

### ECONOMY AND TRADE

The civil war seriously damaged Lebanon's economy and infrastructure, as well as its role as an entrepôt and financial services centre for the region. Reconstruction was almost complete when the Israeli attacks in 2006 caused an estimated US$3.6bn (£2.1bn) of infrastructure damage. Recovery was hindered by internal instability, which also postponed the introduction of the economic reforms that were a condition of international funding for reconstruction. While GDP is expected to grow by around 2 per cent in 2015, the mass migration of refugees from Syria since 2011 has seriously increased income inequality and unemployment.

The service sector contributes 72.6 per cent of GDP, largely through banking and tourism, which are the two main economic activities. Industry accounts for 21.1 per cent, through food processing, wine production and the manufacture of jewellery, cement, textiles, mineral and chemical products, timber and furniture, oil refining and metal fabrication. Agriculture contributes 6.3 per cent of GDP, producing fruit, vegetables, tobacco and livestock.

The main export markets are the UAE, Saudi Arabia, Iraq and South Africa, while imports come mainly from China, Italy, France and the USA. Principal exports include jewellery, base metals, chemicals, consumer goods, fruit, vegetables, tobacco and construction materials. The main imports are petroleum products, cars, medicines, clothing, meat, livestock and consumer goods.

*GNI* – US$44,081m; US$9,870 per capita (2013)
*Annual average growth of GDP* – 2.3 per cent (2014)
*Inflation rate* – 1.5 per cent (2014 est)
*Unemployment* – 7.1 per cent (2015 est)
*Total external debt* – US$31,610m (2014 est)
*Imports* – US$21,236m (2013)
*Exports* – US$4,059m (2013)

### BALANCE OF PAYMENTS
*Trade* – US$17,176m deficit (2013)
*Current Account* – US$12,146m deficit (2015 est)

| Trade with UK | 2013 | 2014 |
|---|---|---|
| Imports from UK | £500,791,887 | £498,386,994 |
| Exports to UK | £36,279,279 | £43,594,637 |

## COMMUNICATIONS

*Airports and waterways* – There are five airports, including the international airport at Beirut; the principal seaports are Beirut and Tripoli

*Roadways and railways* – 170km of motorways; 401km

*Telecommunications* – 878,000 fixed lines and 4 million mobile subscriptions (2012); there were 1 million internet users in 2009

*Internet code and IDD* – lb; 961 (from UK), 44 (to UK)

*Major broadcasters* – Télé-Liban is the state-run broadcaster and competes with several commercial stations, including pro-Hezbollah al-Manar TV and the market-leading Lebanese Broadcasting Corporation and Future TV

*Press* – Leading dailies include *An-Nahar, Al-Safir* (both Arabic language) and *L'Orient-Le Jour* (French)

*WPFI score* – 31,81 (98)

## EDUCATION AND HEALTH

There are nine years of compulsory education.

*Literacy rate* – 99.1 per cent (2015 est)

*Gross enrolment ratio (percentage of relevant age group)* –
primary 113 per cent; secondary 75 per cent; tertiary 48 per cent (2013 est)

*Health expenditure (per capita)* – US$631 (2013)

*Hospital beds (per 1,000 people)* – 3.5 (2012)

*Life expectancy (years)* – 77.22 (2014 est)

*Mortality rate* – 4.95 (2014 est)

*Birth rate* – 14.8 (2014 est)

*Infant mortality rate* – 7.98 (2014 est)

# LESOTHO

*Kingdom of Lesotho*

*Area* – 30,355 sq. km

*Capital* – Maseru; population, 267,000 (2014)

*Major cities* – Leribe, Mafeteng, Quthing

*Currency* – Loti (M) of 100 lisente; the South African rand is also legal tender

*Population* – 1,947,701 rising at 0.32 per cent a year (2015 est); Sotho (99.7 per cent) (est)

*Religion* – Christian 80 per cent, indigenous beliefs 20 per cent

*Language* – English, Sesotho (both official), Zulu, Xhosa

*Population density* – 68 per sq. km (2013)

*Urban population* – 29 per cent (2013 est)

*Median age (years)* – 23.6 (2014 est)

*National anthem* – 'Lesotho Fatse la Bo Ntat'a Rona' ['Lesotho, Land of Our Fathers']

*National day* – 4 October (Independence Day)

*Death penalty* – Retained

*CPI score* – 49 (55)

*Military expenditure* – US$47.7m (2014)

## CLIMATE AND TERRAIN

Lesotho consists of a highland plateau with mountains in the east. The lower land in the west contains most of the arable land and 70 per cent of the population. Elevation extremes range from 3,482m (Thabana Ntlenyana) to 1,400m (the junction of the Orange and Makhaleng rivers). As 80 per cent of the country lies above 1,800m, the climate is temperate, with snow in the highlands in winter. Temperatures average 18.3°C in January and 7°C in June.

## HISTORY AND POLITICS

The area was organised into a single territory by Moshoeshoe the Great from the 1820s as the Sotho people came under pressure from both the expanding Zulu nation and the Boers. In 1868, after fighting two wars with the Boers, Moshoeshoe sought protection from the British government, and Basutoland became first a British territory (1868) and then a crown colony (1884).

The country gained independence in 1966 as the kingdom of Lesotho, under Moshoeshoe II and with Chief Lebua Jonathan as prime minister. Chief Jonathan was overthrown in a military coup in 1986; military rule ended with multiparty elections in 1993 and democratic rule was restored in 1994. The 1998 elections were also followed by severe disturbances, which were quelled by an intervention force from neighbouring countries. King Moshoeshoe II, deposed in 1990, was reinstated in 1995 but died in 1996; he was succeeded by King Letsie III, who had been king during his father's exile.

In the 2012 legislative election, the Democratic Congress (DC) party won the largest number of seats but did not gain a majority; Motsoahae Tom Thabane was appointed prime minister. In August 2014, an attempted military coup caused Thabane to briefly flee to South Africa. Following the coup attempt, early elections were held in February 2015 in an attempt to create a stable government. The DC, under Bethuel Pakalitha Mosisili, emerged again as the largest single party and was able to form a governing coalition.

Under the 1993 constitution, subsequently amended, the head of state is a hereditary monarch, with ceremonial duties but no executive or legislative powers. The bicameral parliament comprises the National Assembly, with 120 members elected for a five-year term, one-third by proportional representation, and the senate, whose 33 members comprise 22 principal chiefs and 11 members nominated by the king. The prime minister is the leader of the majority party in the legislature and appoints the council of ministers.

HEAD OF STATE

*HM The King of Lesotho*, King Letsie III, *acceded* 7 February 1996, *crowned* 31 October 1997

SELECTED GOVERNMENT MEMBERS *as at May 2015*

*Prime Minister,* Bethuel Pakalitha Mosisili

*Deputy Prime Minister,* Mothetjoa Metsing

*Finance,* 'Mamphono Khaketla

HIGH COMMISSION OF THE KINGDOM OF LESOTHO

7 Chesham Place, London SW1X 8HN

T 020-7235 5686 E hicom@lesotholondon.org.uk

W www.lesotholondon.org.uk

*High Commissioner,* HE Felleng Mamakeka Makeka, *apptd* 2013

BRITISH HIGH COMMISSION

*High Commissioner,* HE Judith Macgregor, CMG, LVO *apptd* 2013, resident at Pretoria (Tshwane), South Africa

## ECONOMY AND TRADE

The country is one of the poorest in the world, with 49 per cent of the population living below the poverty line. With few natural resources apart from water, the main sources of government revenue are customs dues from the South African customs union and, since 1998, the export of water and electricity to South Africa from the hydroelectric facilities created by the Lesotho Highlands Water Project. The economic situation worsened in the early 2000s with severe droughts and a decline in demand for mineworkers in South Africa.

This decline has been partially compensated for by the resumption of diamond mining in 2003, and the development of a small manufacturing base processing agricultural products, producing textiles and assembling garments, and of tourism, especially in the highlands. Lesotho's economy recovered well from the global economic crisis in 2008–9 with growth averaging nearly 5 per cent per year since 2010. The economy is heavily reliant on government consumption and diamond mining, which account for 37 per cent and 8.5 per cent of the economy's GDP respectively, and remittances supplied by migrants to South Africa. The economy is expected to grow by 4 per cent in 2015 and 2016; however, unemployment remains high, reaching 75 per cent in rural areas, and industry has been in decline since 2004.

Subsistence agriculture is the major employer and engages 86 per cent of the population, although productivity has declined in recent years because of drought, soil erosion and loss of labour due to HIV/AIDS.

Principal exports are clothing, footwear, road vehicles, wool and mohair, food and livestock. The main imports are food, construction materials, vehicles, machinery, medicines and petroleum products.

*GNI* – US$3,111m; US$1,500 per capita (2013)
*Annual average growth of GDP* – 4.3 per cent (2014)
*Inflation rate* – 6 per cent (2014 est)
*Unemployment* – 25 per cent (2008)
*Total external debt* – US$929.5m (2014 est)
*Imports* – US$2,284m (2013)
*Exports* – US$934m (2013)

BALANCE OF PAYMENTS
*Trade* – US$1,350m deficit (2013)
*Current Account* – US$114m deficit (2015 est)

| Trade with UK | 2013 | 2014 |
| --- | --- | --- |
| Imports from UK | £927,403 | £497,001 |
| Exports to UK | £76,024 | £97,432 |

## COMMUNICATIONS

*Airports* – There are three airports; the international airport is at Maseru
*Roadways* – There are 1,069km of surfaced roads
*Telecommunications* – 43,100 fixed lines and 1.312 million mobile subscriptions (2012); there were 76,800 internet users in 2009
*Internet code and IDD* – ls; 266 (from UK), 44 (to UK)
*Major broadcasters* – Radio is the most important medium, although only the state-run Radio Lesotho has national coverage; Lesotho Television, also state run, is the only television station, but South African broadcasts can be received
*Press* – A number of weekly newspapers are published in English and Sesotho
*WPFI score* – 28,36 (77)

## EDUCATION AND HEALTH

*Literacy rate* – 85.1 per cent (2015)
*Gross enrolment ratio (percentage of relevant age group)* –

primary 108 per cent (2013 est); secondary 53 per cent; tertiary 11 per cent (2012 est)
*Health expenditure (per capita)* – US$123 (2013)
*Hospital beds (per 1,000 people)* – 1.3 (2006)
*Life expectancy (years)* – 52.65 (2014 est)
*Mortality rate* – 14.91 (2014 est)
*Birth rate* – 25.92 (2014 est)
*Infant mortality rate* – 50.48 (2014 est)
*HIV/AIDS adult prevalence* – 22.85 per cent (2013 est)

# LIBERIA

*Republic of Liberia*

*Area* – 111,369 sq. km
*Capital* – Monrovia; population, 1,224,000 (2014)
*Currency* – Liberian dollar (L$) of 100 cents
*Population* – 4,195,666 rising at 2.47 per cent a year (2015 est); Kpelle (20.3 per cent), Bassa (13.4 per cent), Grebo (10 per cent), Gio (8 per cent), Mano (7.9 per cent), Kru (6 per cent), Loma (5.1 per cent), Kissi (4.8 per cent), Gola (4.4 per cent) (2008)
*Religion* – Christian 85.6 per cent, Muslim 12.2 per cent, traditional/other 0.8 per cent (2008)
*Language* – English (official), about 20 ethnic languages
*Population density* – 45 per sq. km (2013)
*Urban population* – 48.9 per cent (2013)
*Median age (years)* – 17.9 (2014 est)
*National anthem* – 'All Hail, Liberia, Hail!'
*National day* – 26 July (Independence Day)
*Death penalty* – Retained (last used 2000)
*CPI score* – 37 (94)
*Military expenditure* – US$15.6m (2014)
*Literacy rate* – 54.5 per cent (2015 est)
*Gross enrolment ratio (percentage of relevant age group)* – primary 96 per cent; secondary 38 per cent (2014 est); tertiary 12 per cent (2012 est)
*Health expenditure (per capita)* – US$44 (2013)
*Hospital beds (per 1,000 people)* – 0.8 (2010)
*Life expectancy (years)* – 58.21 (2014 est)
*Mortality rate* – 9.9 (2014 est)
*Birth rate* – 35.07 (2014 est)
*Infant mortality rate* – 69.19 (2014 est)
*HIV/AIDS adult prevalence* – 1.09 per cent (2013 est)

## CLIMATE AND TERRAIN

Liberia lies on the west African coast, just north of the equator. There are forested highlands and grassy plateaux in the interior and swampy plains on the coast, where several rivers enter the ocean. Elevation extremes range from 1,380m (Mt Wuteve) to 0m (Atlantic Ocean). The climate is tropical, with very high rainfall.

## HISTORY AND POLITICS

The land was purchased by the American Colonisation Society in 1821 and turned into a settlement for liberated black slaves from the USA, gaining recognition as an independent state in 1847.

In the first century of statehood, politics was dominated by the True Whig Party of the Americo-Liberian minority. Political stability ended in 1980 when a coup installed a military government under Samuel Doe. When civilian rule was restored in 1985, Doe became president, but his regime's arbitrary, corrupt rule combined with an economic collapse led to a revolt in 1989 by Charles Taylor's National Patriotic Forces of Liberia (NPFL) and the Armed Forces of Liberia (AFL). The country descended into a civil war that, apart from a respite in 1996–9, lasted until 2003. Around 250,000 people were killed and thousands were displaced. Following mediation by a number of African and European countries, all factions in the conflict signed a peace agreement in 2003 and a UN peacekeeping force was deployed. The disarming of militias was completed in 2005, and a truth and reconciliation commission was set up in 2006 and reported in 2009. In 2012 Taylor was found guilty of war crimes and sentenced to 50 years in jail to be served in a British prison.

After a period of transitional government, presidential and legislative elections were held in late 2005. In the legislative election, the Congress for Democratic Change (CDC) won the most seats but without an overall majority. The Unity Party leader Ellen Johnson Sirleaf was elected president in the second round of voting and took office in January 2006. Sirleaf regained the presidential nomination in the 2011 election, picking up 43.9 per cent of the overall vote. The Unity Party gained the most votes in the 2011 and 2014 legislative elections but lost control of the senate. New legislative and presidential elections are due in 2017.

Under the 1986 constitution, the head of state is an executive president who is directly elected for a six-year term, renewable once. There is a bicameral National Assembly, consisting of the House of Representatives, with 64 members directly elected for a six-year term, and a senate, with 30 members (two from each of the 15 counties) normally elected for a nine-year term, although half of the current senate will serve for only six years. The president appoints the cabinet, which must be approved by the legislature.

HEAD OF STATE
President, Ellen Johnson Sirleaf, elected 2005, re-elected 2011
Vice-President, Joseph N. Boakai

SELECTED GOVERNMENT MEMBERS, as at May 2015
Defence, Brownie Samukai
Finance, Amara Konneh
Foreign Affairs, Augustine Ngafuan

EMBASSY OF THE REPUBLIC OF LIBERIA
23 Fitzroy Square, London W1 6EW
T 020-7388 5489 E info@embassyofliberia.org.uk
W www.embassyofliberia.org.uk
Ambassador Extraordinary and Plenipotentiary, HE Rudolf
  von Ballmoos, apptd 2014

BRITISH AMBASSADOR
Leone Compound, 12th Street Beach-side, Sinkor, Monrovia
T (+231) (0)77530320 E monrovia.generalenquiries@fco.gov.uk
W www.gov.uk/government/world/libera
Ambassador Extraordinary and Plenipotentiary, HE David
  Belgrove, OBE, apptd 2014

## ECONOMY AND TRADE

The civil war devastated an economy already weakened by government mismanagement and corruption, and drove those with expertise and capital into exile. Since the war ended, foreign aid has been received to finance reconstruction, conditional on the adoption of anti-corruption measures, and economic activity has revived. Growth since 2006 has been driven by donor aid and exports, particularly of rubber and, since UN sanctions were lifted in 2006 and 2007 respectively, timber and diamonds. The country also benefited from substantial debt relief in 2010, and in 2011 the African Development Bank approved a grant of US$48m to support economic governance and competitiveness. Economic growth in 2015 and 2016 is expected to be restricted by the 2014 Ebola outbreak and a poor harvest. Inflation rose sharply in 2014 and the fiscal deficit is set to reach 12 per cent of GDP in 2015.

Agriculture was the main economic activity during the civil war but its contribution to GDP and its share of the labour market has declined as the industrial and service sectors have revived. Industry centres on the processing of rubber and palm oil, forestry and mining (diamonds and iron ore).

The main export markets are China, the USA and the EU countries, while imports come mainly from Singapore, South Korea, China and Japan. Principal exports are rubber, timber, iron, diamonds, cocoa and coffee. The main imports are fuels, chemicals, machinery, transport equipment, manufactured goods and foodstuffs.

GNI – US$1,743m; US$410 per capita (2013)
Annual average growth of GDP – 2.5 per cent (2014)
Inflation rate – 11.2 per cent (2014 est)
Total external debt – US$625.9m (2014 est)
Import – US$1,210m (2013)
Export – US$540m (2013)

BALANCE OF PAYMENTS
Trade – US$670m deficit (2013)
Current Account – US$826m deficit (2015 est)

| Trade with UK | 2013 | 2014 |
| --- | --- | --- |
| Imports from UK | £16,634,203 | £15,535,558 |
| Exports to UK | £3,018,623 | £2,527,520 |

## COMMUNICATIONS

Airports and waterways – There are two international airports, Robertsfield and Spriggs Payne, in Monrovia; the main seaports are Monrovia and Buchanan, and there is a merchant fleet of 2,771 ships of over 1,000 tonnes, including 2,581 foreign-owned ships registered in Liberia
Roadways and railways – There are 657km of surfaced roadways; owing to war damage, little of the 429km of railway track is operational, although reconstruction is underway
Telecommunications – 3,200 fixed lines (2011) and 2.394 million mobile subscriptions (2012); there were 20,000 internet users in 2009
Internet code and IDD – lr; 231 (from UK), 44 (to UK)
Major broadcasters – Media are largely privately owned, although the state-run Liberian Broadcasting System operates Radio Liberia; television broadcasters include Clar TV and Power TV
Press – There are two major daily newspapers, The Inquirer and The New Dawn, both privately owned
WPFI score – 30,78 (89)

# LIBYA

*Dawlat Libya – State of Libya*

*Area* – 1,759,540 sq. km
*Capital* – Tripoli (Tarabulus); population, 1,126,000 (2014)
*Major cities* – al-Hums, az-Zawiyah, Benghazi, Misratah,
Tarhunah, Zuwarah
*Currency* – Libyan dinar (LD) of 1,000 dirhams
*Population* – 6,411,776 rising at 2.23 per cent a year
(2015 est); Arab–Berber (97 per cent), with some Tuareg
in the south-west
*Religion* – Muslim 96.6 per cent (vast majority Sunni),
Christian 2.7 per cent, other 0.5 per cent
*Language* – Arabic (official), Berber dialects
*Population density* – 4 per sq. km (2013)
*Urban population* – 78.1 per cent (2013 est)
*Median age (years)* – 27.5 (2014 est)
*National anthem* – 'Libya, Libya, Libya'
*National day* – 23 October (Liberation Day)
*Death penalty* – Retained
*CPI score* – 18 (166)

## CLIMATE AND TERRAIN

Apart from hills on the north-west and north-east coasts
and in the far south, the country is made up of plains and
plateaux, with some depressions; 90 per cent is desert or
semi-desert. Elevation extremes range from 2,267m (Bikku
Bitti) to −47m (Sabkhat Ghuzayyil). The climate is
Mediterranean on the coast, and arid desert in the interior.
Average temperatures in Tripoli range from 12.9°C in
January to 30.4°C in July.

## POLITICS

Following the overthrow of the 'Leader of the Revolution',
Col. Muammar al-Gaddafi, the National Transitional Council
(NTC) set out plans for a 'political democratic regime to be
based upon the political multitude and multi-party system'.

In July 2012 the General National Congress was elected
and power was handed over from the transitional
government in August; Mohammed Magarief was elected
interim head of state. In October 2012, prime minister
elect Mustafa Abu Shagur failed in two attempts to gain
parliamentary approval for his government; the national

congress elected Ali Zidan prime minister in his place. In
May 2014 businessman Ahmed Maiteg was elected prime
minister but stood down one month later, when the Supreme
Court ruled his election unconstitutional.

Abdullah al-Thinni was appointed Libya's acting
prime minister in June 2014. In August, the House of
Representatives replaced the General National Congress as
the legislative body and its president, Akila Issa, became the
new head of state. Continuing political chaos saw the former
legislative body, the General National Congress, appoint
their own prime minister, Islamist Omar al-Hassi, on
25 August, resulting in two rival governments. Al-Thinni's
government resigned on 29 August in order to allow for
the formation of a national unity government; however,
al-Thinni was reappointed in September after Tripoli was
captured by rebel groups, forcing the government to relocate
to Tobruk. Talks between the two rival administrations, held
in Morocco in June 2015, failed to result in the formation of
a new national unity government.

HEAD OF STATE
*Chair of the House of Representatives,* Akila Issa

SELECTED GOVERNMENT MEMBERS *as at May 2015*
*Prime Minister,* Abdullah al-Thinni
*First Deputy Prime Minister,* Almahdi Hassan Muftah Allabad
*Second Deputy Prime Minister,* Abdulsalam al-Badri
*Third Deputy Prime Minister,* Abdulrahman al-Taher
*Economy,* Muneer Ali Assr

EMBASSY OF LIBYA
15 Knightsbridge, London SW1X 7LY
T 020-7201 8280 W www.libyanembassy.org
*Ambassador Extraordinary and Plenipotentiary,* HE Mahmud
Nacua, *apptd* 2012

BRITISH AMBASSADOR
*Ambassador Extraordinary and Plenipotentiary,* HE Peter
Millett, *apptd* 2015, resident at Tunis, Tunisia

## DEFENCE

| *Aged 16–49, 2010 est* | *Males* | *Females* |
| --- | --- | --- |
| Available for military service | 1,775,078 | 1,714,194 |
| Fit for military service | 1,511,144 | 1,458,934 |

*Military expenditure* – US$3,302m (2014 est)
*Conscription* – 16 to 49 years of age; 12–24 months (selective)

## ECONOMY AND TRADE

Normalisation of international relations stimulated economic
liberalisation and the start of a slow transition towards a
more market-orientated economy, as well as attracting more
foreign direct investment.

The state-controlled oil industry dominates the economy,
accounting for 95 per cent of export earnings and about
65 per cent of GDP and 80 per cent of government revenue;
as the population is small, this gives the country one of the
highest per capita GDPs in Africa, although the benefits are

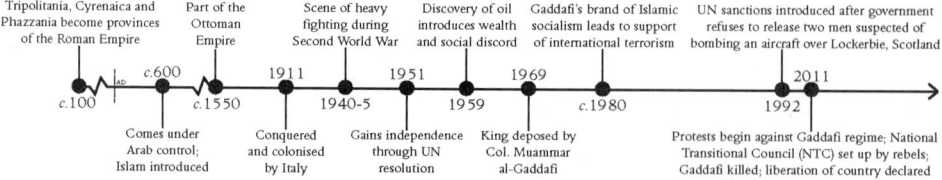

| Tripolitania, Cyrenaica and Phazzania become provinces of the Roman Empire | Part of the Ottoman Empire | Scene of heavy fighting during Second World War | Discovery of oil introduces wealth and social discord | Gaddafi's brand of Islamic socialism leads to support of international terrorism | UN sanctions introduced after government refuses to release two men suspected of bombing an aircraft over Lockerbie, Scotland |
| --- | --- | --- | --- | --- | --- |
| | *c.*600 | 1911 | 1951 | 1969 | 2011 |
| *c.*100 | *c.*1550 | 1940-5 | 1959 | *c.*1980 | 1992 |
| Comes under Arab control; Islam introduced | Conquered and colonised by Italy | Gains independence through UN resolution | King deposed by Col. Muammar al-Gaddafi | | Protests begin against Gaddafi regime; National Transitional Council (NTC) set up by rebels; Gaddafi killed; liberation of country declared |

not felt by much of the population. Production has become erratic since the start of the civil war in 2011, and many oil wells are now controlled by anti-government militias. The end of unilateral US sanctions in 2006 dramatically increased foreign investment in the energy and banking sectors. Attempts to diversify the economy have led to expansion of the service and construction sectors within the past five years, which together account for around 95 per cent of national revenue, to include the production of petrochemicals, iron, steel and aluminium in addition to food processing. Owing to the terrain and climate, agriculture is a small sector, contributing only 2 per cent of GDP with 80 per cent of food imported. Instability is predicted to restrict growth to 2 per cent in 2015.

The main trading partners are Italy, other EU countries, China and Turkey. Principal exports are crude oil, refined petroleum products, natural gas and chemicals. The main imports are machinery, semi-finished goods, food, transport equipment and consumer products.
*GNI* – US$61,985m; US$12,930 per capita (2009)
*Annual average growth of GDP* – –19.8 per cent (2014)
*Inflation rate* – 3.9 per cent (2014 est)
*Unemployment* – 9 per cent (2015 est)
*Total external debt* – US$3,904m (2014 est)
*Imports* – US$27,012m (2013)
*Exports* – US$43,989m (2013)

BALANCE OF PAYMENTS
*Trade* – US$18,064m deficit (2015)
*Current Account* – US$18,064m deficit (2015 est)

| Trade with UK | 2013 | 2014 |
| --- | --- | --- |
| Imports from UK | £269,209,815 | £165,634,321 |
| Exports to UK | £1,242,219,542 | £353,212,056 |

## COMMUNICATIONS
*Airports and waterways* – There are 68 airports; the principal airports are at Tripoli, Benghazi and Sebha, while the main seaports are Benghazi, Tripoli and Tubruq
*Roadways* – There are 57,214km of paved roads
*Telecommunications* – 814,000 million fixed lines and 9.59 million mobile subscriptions (2012); there were 353,900 internet users in 2009
*Internet code and IDD* – ly; 218 (from UK), 44 (to UK)
*Major broadcasters* – Launched in April 2011 following the uprising, Libyan Radio and TV (LRT) has been joined by more than 20, mainly privately owned, TV and radio stations
*Press* – Major dailies include *February* and *New Quryna* (Arabic language), and *The Tripoli Post* (English language)
*WPFI score* – 45,99 (154)

## EDUCATION AND HEALTH
There are six years of primary education and six of secondary, nine of which are compulsory.
*Literacy rate* – 100 per cent (2015 est)
*Health expenditure (per capita)* – US$433 (2013)
*Hospital beds (per 1,000 people)* – 3.7 (2012)
*Life expectancy (years)* – 76.04 (2014 est)
*Mortality rate* – 3.57 (2014 est)
*Birth rate* – 18.4 (2014 est)
*Infant mortality rate* – 11.87 (2014 est)

# LIECHTENSTEIN

*Fürstentum Liechtenstein – Principality of Liechtenstein*

*Area* – 160 sq. km
*Capital* – Vaduz; population, 5,000 (2014)
*Major town* – Schaan
*Currency* – Swiss franc of 100 rappen (or centimes)
*Population* – 37,624 rising at 0.84 per cent a year (2015 est)
*Religion* – Christian (Roman Catholic 75.9 per cent, Protestant Reformed 6.5 per cent, Lutheran 1.3 per cent), Muslim 5.4 per cent, other 9.8 per cent
*Language* – German (official); Alemannic is the main dialect
*Population density* – 231 per sq. km (2013)
*Median age (years)* – 42.4 (2014 est)
*National anthem* – 'Oben am Jungen Rhein' ['High Above the Young Rhine']
*National day* – 15 August (Feast of the Assumption)
*Death penalty* – Abolished for all crimes (since 1987)
*Gross enrolment ratio (percentage of relevant age group)* – primary 104 per cent; secondary 110 per cent; tertiary 42 per cent (2012 est)
*Life expectancy (years)* – 81.68 (2014 est)
*Mortality rate* – 7.02 (2014 est)
*Birth rate* – 10.53 (2014 est)
*Infant mortality rate* – 4.33 (2014 est)

## CLIMATE AND TERRAIN
Liechtenstein is a small, mountainous landlocked principality in the Alps. The land falls in the west, in the valley of the river Rhine, which forms the western border. Elevation extremes range from 2,599m (Grauspitz) to 430m (Ruggeller Riet). The climate is continental, with heavy snowfall in winter; average temperatures range from −0.8°C in January to 16.2°C in July and August.

## HISTORY AND POLITICS
Although there was a sovereign state within the present boundaries from the 14th century, the present state of Liechtenstein was formed from the lordships of Schellenberg and Vaduz in 1719. Part of the Holy Roman Empire, the principality became a member of the Confederation of the Rhine that succeeded the Empire in 1806, and then of the German Confederation from 1815 until 1866. It was the only German principality to remain outside the German Empire formed in 1871. The country abolished its armed forces and declared permanent neutrality in 1868. This was maintained in both World Wars.

Economic decline in the years following the First World War led Liechtenstein to adopt the Swiss currency in 1921 and to enter into a Swiss customs union in 1923. The country became extremely prosperous as an international finance centre after the Second World War. Since 2000 it has tightened its laws to prevent money laundering, and since

2008 it has started to meet international financial transparency standards.

Governments in the 20th and 21st centuries have been formed by the two main parties, the northern-based Progressive Citizens' Party (FBP) and the southern-based Fatherland Union (VU). Usually they have formed a coalition government, although the FBP formed a single-party government from 2001 to 2005. However, the government's power is limited by that of the monarchy, whose powers over the government and judiciary were increased by a 2003 referendum. Prince Hans Adam II remains head of state but in 2004 he handed over day-to-day responsibility for government to his son, Prince Alois.

The VU won an overall majority in the 2009 election. The coalition government formed with the FBP in 2005 continued, although the premiership passed from the FBP to the VU's Klaus Tschütscher. After the February 2013 legislative elections the FBP formed a coalition with the VU as the junior party.

Under the 1921 constitution, Liechtenstein is a constitutional monarchy, with the hereditary prince as head of state. The unicameral legislature, the *Landtag*, has 25 members directly elected for a four-year term. The cabinet is appointed by the prince on the advice of the *Landtag* and consists of the head of government and four ministers.

### HEAD OF STATE

*HSH The Prince of Liechtenstein,* Hans Adam II, *born* 14 February 1945, *succeeded* 13 November 1989
*Heir,* HSH Prince Alois, *born* 11 June 1968

SELECTED GOVERNMENT MEMBERS *as at May 2015*
*Head of Government, Finance,* Adrian Hasler
*Deputy Head of Government, Home Affairs, Justice, Economy,* Thomas Zwiefelhofer
*Foreign Affairs,* Aurelia Frick

BRITISH AMBASSADOR
HE David Moran, CMG, MVO, resident at Bern, Switzerland

### ECONOMY AND TRADE

Liechtenstein has a prosperous, highly industrialised and diversified economy. Its mainstay is the financial services sector, which, with other service industries such as tourism, employs over half of the workforce. A light industrial base produces electronics, metal manufactures, dental products, ceramics, pharmaceuticals, food products, precision and optical instruments, and employs 37 per cent of the workforce. Over half the workforce commutes daily from Austria, Switzerland and Germany.

Liechtenstein became a member of the European Free Trade Association in 1991, and of the European Economic Area in 1995. After completing 12 bilateral information-sharing agreements in 2009, Liechtenstein was removed from the OECD's 'grey list' of countries that have not implemented the organisation's model tax convention. In 2011 Liechtenstein joined the Schengen area. Most of its trade is with EU countries and Switzerland. The principal exports are its industrial products. The main imports are agricultural products, industrial raw materials, energy, machinery, metal goods, textiles, foodstuffs and vehicles.
*GNI* – US$4,816m; US$136,770 per capita (2009)
*Annual average growth of GDP* – 1.8 per cent (2012)
*Inflation rate* – −0.7 per cent (2012)
*Unemployment* – 2.5 per cent (2011)

| Trade with UK | 2013 | 2014 |
| --- | --- | --- |
| Imports from UK | £5,238,276 | £20,667,590 |
| Exports to UK | £4,227,166 | £8,138,768 |

### COMMUNICATIONS

*Transport* – Liechtenstein has no airports and only 380km of roads, 28km of waterways and 9km of rail track, which is part of the Austrian system connecting Austria and Switzerland
*Telecommunications* – 20,000 fixed lines and 38,000 mobile subscriptions (2012); there were 23,000 internet users in 2009
*Internet code and IDD* – li; 423 (from UK), 44 (to UK)
*Media* – The country has a very small media sector; its citizens rely on foreign broadcasters for most television and radio services. News publications include *Liechtensteiner Vaterland* and *Liechtensteiner Volksblatt*
*WPFI score* – 17.67 (27)

# LITHUANIA

*Lietuvos Respublika – Republic of Lithuania*

*Area* – 65,300 sq. km
*Capital* – Vilnius; population, 519,000 (2014)
*Major cities* – Kaunas, Klaipeda, Siauliai
*Currency* – Euro (€) of 100 cents
*Population* – 3,505,738 falling at 0.29 per cent a year (2014 est); Lithuanian (84.1 per cent), Polish (6.6 per cent), Russian (5.8 per cent), Belarusian (1.2 per cent) (2011 est)
*Religion* – Christian (Roman Catholic 77.2 per cent, Orthodox 4.1 per cent), none 6.1 per cent
*Language* – Lithuanian (official), Russian, Polish
*Population density* – 47 per sq. km (2013)
*Urban population* – 67.3 per cent (2013)
*Median age (years)* – 41.2 (2014 est)
*National anthem* – 'Tautiska Giesme' ['The National Song']
*National day* – 16 February (Independence Day)
*Death penalty* – Abolished for all crimes (since 1998)
*CPI score* – 58 (39)

### CLIMATE AND TERRAIN

Lithuania is a low-lying country with low hills in the west and south-east. It contains around 6,000 lakes and lagoons – over 2,800 of them sizeable – mostly lying in the east, although the Courland lagoon on the west coast is a major feature. Elevation extremes range from 294m (Aukstojas Hill) to 0m (Baltic Sea). The climate is mainly continental, and average temperatures range from −2.6°C in January to 18.1°C in July.

### HISTORY AND POLITICS

Lithuania became a nation in the 13th century. It remained pagan for far longer than the rest of Europe, only becoming fully Christian in the 15th century when the Samogitians and the Aukstaitiai, the two main ethnic groups in the region, were converted. In the 14th century, a grand duchy was formed that stretched from the Baltic to the Black Sea and eastwards almost as far as Moscow. It confederated with Poland in the 16th century, before coming under Russian rule in 1795. The country joined Poland in rebelling against Russian domination twice in the 19th century.

Occupied by Germany during the First World War, Lithuania declared its independence in 1918 and successfully defended its autonomy against the Bolsheviks in 1918–19. However, the province and city of Vilnius were occupied by the newly independent Poland from 1920 until 1939. The USSR invaded and annexed Lithuania in 1940, but the country revolted in 1941 and briefly established its own government before being invaded and occupied by the Germans in their 1941 offensive against the USSR. Around 210,000 Lithuanians, mainly Jews, were killed during the German occupation. Soviet troops ousted the Germans in 1944 and re-established Soviet control, against which Lithuanians carried on a guerrilla war until 1952.

Growing nationalist sentiment led to the formation of the pro-democracy *Sajudis* ('The Movement') in 1988 to campaign for greater autonomy. A unilateral declaration of independence in 1990 was blocked by the USSR but following the failed coup in Moscow in 1991, Lithuania declared its independence a second time, and this was internationally recognised. The last Russian troops left the country in 1993. Lithuania joined NATO and the EU in 2004.

In the 2012 legislative elections, the Social Democratic Party of Lithuania became the largest party but remained short of a majority. Its leader, Algirdas Butkevicius, became prime minister at the head of a four-party coalition government. Dalia Grybauskaite was re-elected in the 2014 presidential election.

Under the 1992 constitution, the head of state is a president, who is directly elected for a five-year term, renewable once. The unicameral *Seimas* has 141 members who are directly elected for a four-year term; 71 members are elected in first-past-the-post constituencies and 70 by proportional representation. The prime minister is appointed by the president with the approval of the *Seimas,* and ministers are appointed upon the recommendation of the prime minister.

HEAD OF STATE

*President,* Dalia Grybauskaite, *elected* 17 May 2009, *sworn in* 12 July 2009, *re-elected* 25 May 2014, *sworn in* 12 July 2014

SELECTED GOVERNMENT MEMBERS *as at May 2015*
*Prime Minister,* Algirdas Butkevicius
*Defence,* Juozas Olekas
*Foreign Affairs,* Linas Antanas Linkevicius
*Interior,* Saulius Skvernelis

EMBASSY OF THE REPUBLIC OF LITHUANIA
Lithuania House, 2 Bessborough Gardens, London SW1V 2JE
T 020-7592 2840 E amb.uk@urm.lt
W www.lithuanianembassy.co.uk/
*Ambassador Extraordinary and Plenipotentiary,* HE Asta Skaisgiryte Liauskiene, *apptd* 2012

BRITISH EMBASSY
2 Antakalnio, Vilnius LT-10308
T (+370) (5) 246 2900 E consular.vilnius@fco.gov.uk
W www.gov.uk/government/world/lithuania
*Ambassador Extraordinary and Plenipotentiary,* HE Claire Lawrence, *apptd* 2015

DEFENCE

| Aged 16–49, 2010 est | Males | Females |
| --- | --- | --- |
| Available for military service | 890,074 | 875,780 |
| Fit for military service | 669,111 | 724,803 |

*Military expenditure* – US$377m (2014)
*Conscription* – 18 years of age; 12 months

ECONOMY AND TRADE

Lithuania's transition to a market economy is nearly complete, with the private sector now accounting for about 80 per cent GDP. The transition initially caused a recession, but the economy recovered and grew steadily from 2004 to 2008 before being plunged into a deep recession, along with the other Baltic states, by the global economic downturn. Drastic government cuts in public spending and the halving of imports in 2009 restored the current account deficit, which had soared to 15 per cent of GDP in 2007–8, to a surplus. GDP grew 1.3 per cent in 2010 before jumping to 5.8 per cent in 2011, making the country one of the fastest growing economies in the EU. Despite high unemployment, successive governments dramatically increased the minimum wage in 2011 and 2013. The poor performance of the Russian and eurozone economies are predicted to restrict growth to just under 3 per cent in 2015. The country joined the eurozone on 1 January 2015.

The economy is diverse, and industries include metal-cutting machine tools, electric motors, domestic appliances, oil refining, shipbuilding, furniture making, textiles and amber extraction and jewellery making. Industry contributes 28.2 per cent to GDP, services 68.1 per cent and agriculture 3.7 per cent.

The main trading partners are Russia and other EU countries. Principal exports are mineral products, machinery and equipment, chemicals, textiles, foodstuffs and plastics. The main imports are mineral products, machinery, transport equipment, chemicals, textiles, clothing and metals.

*GNI* – US$44,060m; US$14,900 per capita (2013)
*Annual average growth of GDP* – 3 per cent (2014)
*Inflation rate* – 0.3 per cent (2014 est)
*Population below poverty line* – 20.6 per cent (2012 est)
*Unemployment* – 11 per cent (2015 est)
*Total external debt* – US$28,880m (2014 est)
*Imports* – US$35,211m (2013)
*Exports* – US$32,616m (2013)

BALANCE OF PAYMENTS
*Trade* – US$2,595m deficit (2013)
*Current Account* – US$91m surplus (2015 est)

| Trade with UK | 2013 | 2014 |
| --- | --- | --- |
| Imports from UK | £323,081,370 | £295,886,621 |
| Exports to UK | £889,016,060 | £958,107,323 |

COMMUNICATIONS

*Airports and waterways* – There are 22 airports, with the largest at Vilnius, Kaunas and Palanga; the main seaport is at Klaipeda
*Roadways and railways* – There are 72,297m of paved roadways, including 312km of motorways; a railway system of 1,767km links the major towns with Vilnius and Klaipeda
*Telecommunications* – 667,300 fixed lines and 5 million mobile subscriptions (2012); there were 1.96 million internet users in 2009
*Internet code and IDD* – lt; 370 (from UK), 44 (to UK)
*Major broadcasters* – Lithuania Radio and TV is the public broadcaster

*Press* – Major dailies include *Lietuvos Rytas, Respublika* and *Lietuvos Zinios*
*WPFI score* – 18,8 (31)

## EDUCATION AND HEALTH

Education is free and compulsory from seven to 16 years, with the system comprising primary school (four years), lower secondary school (six years) and upper secondary education (two years).

*Literacy rate* – 99.9 per cent (2015 est)
*Gross enrolment ratio (percentage of relevant age group)* –
  primary 99 per cent; secondary 106 per cent; tertiary
  74 per cent (2012 est)
*Health expenditure (per capita)* – US$966 (2013)
*Hospital beds (per 1,000 people)* – 7 (2011)
*Life expectancy (years)* – 75.98 (2014 est)
*Mortality rate* – 11.55 (2014 est)
*Birth rate* – 9.36 (2014 est)
*Infant mortality rate* – 6 (2014 est)

# LUXEMBOURG

*Groussherzogtom Lëtzebuerg/Grand-Duché de Luxembourg/*
*Großherzogtum Luxembourg – Grand Duchy of Luxembourg*

*Area* – 2,586 sq. km
*Capital* – Luxembourg; population, 107,000 (2014)
*Major towns* – Esch-sur-Alzette, Dudelange
*Currency* – Euro (€) of 100 cents
*Population* – 570,252 rising at 2.13 per cent a year
  (2015 est); Luxembourger (63.1 per cent), Portuguese
  (13.3 per cent), French (4.5 per cent), Italian (4.3 per
  cent), German (2.3 per cent), other EU 7.3 per cent (2000)
*Religion* – Roman Catholic 87 per cent, other 13 per cent
  (2000)
*Language* – Luxembourgish, French, German (all official)
*Population density* – 210 per sq. km (2013)
*Urban population* – 85.9 per cent (2013 est)
*Median age (years)* – 39.6 (2014 est)
*National anthem* – 'Ons Heemecht' ['Our Homeland']
*National day* – 23 June (official birthday of Grand Duchess
  Charlotte)
*Death penalty* – Abolished for all crimes (since 1979)
*CPI score* – 82 (9)
*Military expenditure* – US$297m (2014 est)
*Gross enrolment ratio (percentage of relevant age group)* –
  primary 97 per cent; secondary 100 per cent; tertiary
  20 per cent (2012 est)
*Health expenditure (per capita)* – US$7,980 (2013)
*Hospital beds (per 1,000 people)* – 5.4 (2010)
*Life expectancy (years)* – 80.01 (2014 est)
*Mortality rate* – 8.53 (2014 est)
*Birth rate* – 11.75 (2014 est)
*Infant mortality rate* – 4.28 (2014 est)

## CLIMATE AND TERRAIN

Luxembourg has the forested plateau of the Ardennes in the north, forming part of the Natural Germano-Luxembourg Park which extends east into Germany. The south of the country is mainly fertile farmland, and in the east is the wine-growing region of the Moselle valley. Elevation extremes range from 559m (Buurgplaatz) to 133m (Moselle river). The climate is modified continental, and average temperatures range from 2°C in January to 18.6°C in July.

## HISTORY AND POLITICS

The area was part of the Roman Empire and then became part of the Frankish Empire in the fifth century AD. It became autonomous within the Holy Roman Empire under Siegfried, Count of Ardennes, and was given the status of a duchy in 1354. Controlled by a succession of European powers after 1437 (when the House of Luxembourg died out), it was made a grand duchy under Dutch rule after the Napoleonic wars. Much of Luxembourg joined the Belgians in their revolt against the Netherlands in 1830; in 1838 the western, French-speaking region was assigned to Belgium, and the remainder became an independent grand duchy in 1839. The Treaty of London in 1867 confirmed its independence and neutrality. Occupation by Germany in both world wars prompted Luxembourg to give up its neutrality and it was a founding member of NATO in 1949.

Luxembourg entered into economic union with Belgium in 1921 and joined the Benelux economic union in 1948. It was a founder member of the EEC in 1958 and joined the eurozone in 1999.

Following a snap election in October 2013, the Democratic Party (DP) formed a small majority in the legislature. The elections were called after prime minister Jean-Claude Juncker of the Christian Social Party (CSV) stood down following revelations that his administration failed to prevent corruption within the security services.

Under the 1868 constitution, the head of state is a hereditary grand duke, whose role is now largely ceremonial. The unicameral legislature, the Chamber of Deputies, has 60 members directly elected for a five-year term. There is also a Council of State, which has 21 members nominated by the grand duke; this acts as the supreme administrative tribunal and has some legislative functions. The prime minister is appointed by the grand duke on the basis of the election results and appoints the cabinet.

HEAD OF STATE
HRH The Grand Duke of Luxembourg, Grand Duke Henri,
  born 16 April 1955; succeeded 7 October 2000
Heir, HRH Prince Guillaume, born 11 November 1981

SELECTED GOVERNMENT MEMBERS *as at May 2015*
*Prime Minister*, Xavier Bettel
*Deputy Prime Minister, Defence*, Etienne Schneider
*Finance*, Pierre Gramegna
*Interior*, Dan Kersch

EMBASSY OF LUXEMBOURG
27 Wilton Crescent, London SW1X 8SD
T 020-7235 6961 E londres.amb@mae.etat.lu
W http://londres.mae.lu
*Ambassador Extraordinary and Plenipotentiary*, HE Patrick
  Jean-Marie Engelberg, *apptd* 2013

BRITISH EMBASSY
5 Boulevard Joseph II, L-1840, Luxembourg
T (+352) 229 864 E britemb@internet.lu
W www.gov.uk/government/world/luxembourg
*Ambassador Extraordinary and Plenipotentiary*, HE Hon. Alice
  Walpole, *apptd* 2011

## ECONOMY AND TRADE

The economy is stable, with steady growth, low unemployment and low inflation providing an exceptionally high standard of living and the highest GDP per capita in the eurozone. The government offset the contraction in the economy in 2008–9 with economic stimulus measures, which led to a budget deficit in 2009 but growth resumed in 2010. Banking and financial services are the dominant sector, contributing 27 per cent of GDP. Steel production used to dominate the industrial sector, but this has diversified to include IT, telecommunications, freight transport, food processing, chemicals, metal products and engineering. Tourism accounts for 6.5 per cent of GDP. The small agricultural sector consists mainly of family-owned farms. Services account for 87.7 per cent of GDP, industry for 12 per cent and agriculture for 0.3 per cent. Around 60 per cent of the workforce commutes daily from France, Belgium and Germany. Banking sector reform in 2015 ended Luxembourg's culture of banking secrecy and new transparency laws are expected to have a negative effect on GDP, restricting growth to 2 per cent in 2015.

The main trading partners are other EU countries and China. Principal exports are the products of industrial activities. The main imports are minerals, metals, foodstuffs and quality consumer goods.

*GNI* – US$37,738m; US$69,900 per capita (2013)
*Annual average growth of GDP* – 2.7 per cent (2014)
*Inflation rate* – 0.8 per cent (2014 est)
*Unemployment* – 5.8 per cent (2015 est)
*Total external debt* – US$2,935,000m (2013 est)
*Imports* – US$23,912m (2013)
*Exports* – US$14,086m (2013)

BALANCE OF PAYMENTS
*Trade* – US$9,826m deficit (2013)
*Current Account* – US$2,582m surplus (2015 est)

| Trade with UK | 2013 | 2014 |
| --- | --- | --- |
| Imports from UK | £234,660,013 | £214,206,828 |
| Exports to UK | £362,340,966 | £444,024,235 |

## COMMUNICATIONS

*Transport* – Luxembourg has one airport with paved runways; there are 2,899km of road (including 152km of motorways), and 275km of railway. The Moselle river provides 37km of navigable waterway
*Telecommunications* – 266,700 fixed lines and 761,300 mobile subscriptions (2012); there are 424,500 internet users in 2009
*Internet code and IDD* – lu; 352 (from UK), 44 (to UK)
*Major broadcasters* – Luxembourg is the headquarters of the Société Européenne des Satellites (SES), which operates Europe's largest satellite operation; RTL Tele Letzebuerg is the country's principal and RTL Radio Letzebuerg are the public broadcasters
*Press* – Leading dailies include *Letzebuerger Journal, Luxemburger Wort* and *Tageblatt* (all German language)
*WPFI score* – 13,61 (19)

# MACEDONIA

*Republika Makedonija – Republic of Macedonia*

*Area* – 25,713 sq. km
*Capital* – Skopje; population, 501,000 (2014)
*Major cities* – Bitola, Kumanovo
*Currency* – Denar of 100 deni
*Population* – 2,096,015 rising at 0.20 per cent a year (2015 est); Macedonian (64.2 per cent), Albanian (25.2 per cent), Turkish (3.9 per cent), Roma (2.7 per cent), Serb (1.8 per cent) (2002 est)
*Religion* – Christian (Orthodox 64.8 per cent), Muslim 33.3 per cent (est)
*Language* – Macedonian, Albanian (both official), Turkish, Romani, Serbian (each official in different regions)
*Population density* – 84 per sq. km (2013)
*Urban population* – 59.5 per cent (2013)
*Median age (years)* – 36.8 (2014 est)
*National anthem* – 'Denes Nad Makedonija' ['Today Over Macedonia']
*National day* – 8 September (Independence Day)
*Death penalty* – Abolished for all crimes (since 1991)
*CPI score* – 45 (64)
*Literacy rate* – 97 per cent (2011 est)
*Gross enrolment ratio (percentage of relevant age group)* – primary 89 per cent; secondary 83 per cent; tertiary 38 per cent (2012 est)
*Health expenditure (per capita)* – US$312 (2013)
*Hospital beds (per 1,000 people)* – 4.5 (2011)
*Life expectancy (years)* – 75.8 (2014 est)
*Mortality rate* – 9.04 (2014 est)
*Birth rate* – 11.64 (2014 est)
*Infant mortality rate* – 7.9 (2014 est)

## CLIMATE AND TERRAIN

The landlocked country is a mountainous plateau divided by deep river valleys and basins, including the valleys of the Vardar river and its tributaries. Elevation extremes range from 2,764m (Golem Korab) to 50m (Vardar river). Lakes Ohrid and Prespa straddle the border with Albania, and Lake Doiran the border with Greece. The climate is continental, with average temperatures ranging from –0.7°C in January to 20.6°C in July and August.

## HISTORY AND POLITICS

The area of present-day Macedonia was part of the ancient Macedonian kingdom, which also included northern Greece and south-west Bulgaria, in the fourth century BC. Macedonia became a province of the Roman Empire in the second century BC, coming under the control of the Byzantine Empire from the fourth century AD. Slav peoples settled the area in the seventh century and mixed with the Greek, Illyrian, Thracian, Scythian and Turkish peoples.

From the ninth to the 14th centuries the area was under the rule successively of the Bulgars, Byzantium and the Serbs, and became part of the Ottoman Empire in the late 14th century. Following the Balkan wars of 1912 and 1913 the region was divided between Bulgaria, Serbia and Greece. After the First World War, the Serbian part was awarded to the newly created state that became Yugoslavia. During the Second World War, this area was occupied by Bulgaria from 1941 to 1944, and after liberation became a republic within the communist Federal Republic of Yugoslavia.

Nationalist sentiment grew throughout the 1980s, and in 1991 Macedonia declared its independence, which Yugoslavia recognised in 1992. International recognition was initially delayed by Greece's objections to the republic's name (Greece claims that its region of Macedonia is the only one entitled to the name), but the country joined the UN in 1993 as the Former Yugoslav Republic of Macedonia; Greece recognised it under this name and lifted its trade blockade in 1995, but in 2008 blocked the republic's membership of NATO.

Throughout the 1990s there was tension and sporadic violence with the large ethnic Albanian minority, aggrieved at their lack of civil rights. Instability in neighbouring Kosovo spilled over into Macedonia in 2001, sparking a two-month uprising by ethnic Albanian separatists. Peace talks facilitated by international bodies resulted in the Ohrid framework agreement, giving Albanians greater recognition within Macedonia and making Albanian an official language.

The 2009 presidential election was won in the second round by the VMRO-DPMNE candidate, Gjorge Ivanov. President Ivanov was re-elected in July 2014. In the legislative election in April 2014, the VMRO-DPMNE remained the largest bloc, forming a coalition government with the Democratic Union for Integration (BDI).

Macedonia experienced instability in 2015, following acquisitions made by the opposition Social Democrats that the government had illegally tapped the phones of 20,000 people, including politicians, journalists and judges. The accusations led to large protests both against and for the government, and the resignation of two ministers and a number of intelligence officers. Ethnic Albanian groups have also been targeted in anti-terrorism raids (*see* Events).

The 1991 constitution was amended in 2001 to incorporate provisions of the Ohrid agreement relating to ethnic Albanian rights, and several times since, most notably in 2004 to give ethnic Albanians greater local autonomy in areas where they predominate.

The head of state is a president, who is directly elected for a five-year term. The unicameral legislature, the *Sobranie*, has 123 members directly elected for a four-year term. The prime minister is appointed by the president. Government ministers are elected by the assembly but are not members of it.

## HEAD OF STATE

*President,* Gjorge Ivanov, *elected* 5 April 2009, *sworn in* 12 May 2009, *re-elected* 2 July 2014

SELECTED GOVERNMENT MEMBERS *as at June 2015*
*Prime Minister,* Nikola Gruevski
*Deputy Prime Ministers,* Vladimir Pesevski *(Economy);* Zoran Stavrevski *(Finance);* Fatmir Besimi; Musa Xhaferi
*Foreign Affairs,* Nikola Poposki
*Interior,* Mitko Chavkov

EMBASSY OF THE REPUBLIC OF MACEDONIA
Suites 2.1/2.2, Buckingham Court, 75–83 Buckingham Gate, London SW1E 6PE
**T** 020-7976 0535 **E** london@mfa.gov.mk
**W** www.missions.gov.mk/london
*Ambassador Extraordinary and Plenipotentiary,* HE Jovan Donev, *apptd* 2013

BRITISH EMBASSY
Todor Aleksandrov 165, Skopje 1000
**T** (+389) (2) 329 9299 **E** britishembassyskopje@fco.gov.uk
**W** www.gov.uk/government/world/macedonia
*Ambassador Extraordinary and Plenipotentiary,* HE Charles Garrett, *apptd* 2014

## DEFENCE

| *Aged 16–49, 2010 est* | *Males* | *Females* |
| --- | --- | --- |
| Available for military service | 532,196 | 511,964 |
| Fit for military service | 443,843 | 426,251 |

*Military expenditure* – US$133m (2014)

## ECONOMY AND TRADE

Macedonia was the least developed republic in the former Yugoslavia before 1991, and economic growth was initially hindered by the trade embargo by Greece (1993–5) and the 2001 ethnic Albanian uprising. Economic growth was steady from 2003 to 2008, although the economy contracted briefly in 2009 owing to the global downturn. Poverty and joblessness remains high (Macedonia's unemployment is among the highest in the world according to the IMF), although official figures may be overstated because of the size of the grey economy, estimated to be between 20 and 45 per cent of GDP. Small GDP growth was achieved in 2013, although the budget deficit increased by 4.2 per cent of GDP in the same year. Growth of 3 per cent is expected in 2015 and 2016, supported by infrastructure development and foreign investment.

Services produce 63.4 per cent of GDP, industry 26.2 per cent and agriculture 10.4 per cent. Food processing and winemaking are major industries, along with textiles, chemicals, iron, steel, cement, energy and pharmaceuticals. The main trading partners are Germany, Greece, Kosovo, Italy, and other Balkan and EU states. Principal exports are food, wine, tobacco, textiles, manufactured goods, iron and steel. The main imports are machinery and equipment, cars, chemicals, fuels and food.

*GNI* – US$10,257m; US$4,870 per capita (2013)
*Annual average growth of GDP* – 3.4 per cent (2014)
*Inflation rate* – –0.2 per cent (2014 est)
*Population below poverty line* – 30.4 per cent (2011)
*Unemployment* – 30 per cent (2013 est)
*Total external debt* – US$7,461m (2014 est)
*Imports* – US$6,600m (2013)
*Exports* – US$4,267m (2013)

BALANCE OF PAYMENTS
*Trade* – US$2,333m deficit (2013)
*Current Account* – US$203m deficit (2015 est)

| *Trade with UK* | 2013 | 2014 |
| --- | --- | --- |
| Imports from UK | £421,938,504 | £539,901,606 |
| Exports to UK | £46,727,859 | £40,837,030 |

## COMMUNICATIONS

*Airports* – The principal airports are at Skopje and Ohrid, and there are a further six airports around the country
*Roadways and railways* – There are 9,489km of paved roadways, including 259km of motorways; there are 699km of railways, of which 234km are electrified
*Telecommunications* – 407,900 fixed lines and 2.235 million mobile subscriptions (2012); there were 1.06 million internet users in 2009
*Internet code and IDD* – mk; 389 (from UK), 44 (to UK)
*Major broadcasters* – MTV and Macedonian Radio are the public broadcasters

*Media* – Leading dailies include *Nova Makedonija* (state subsidised), *Utrinski Vesnik* and *Dnevnik*
*WPFI score* – 36,26 (117)

# MADAGASCAR

*Repoblikan'i Madagasikara/République de Madagascar* – *Republic of Madagascar*

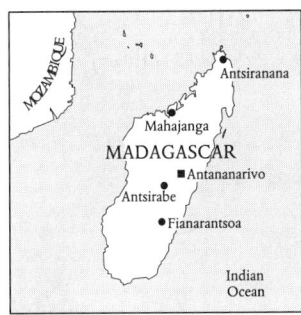

*Area* – 587,041 sq. km
*Capital* – Antananarivo; population, 2,487,000 (2014)
*Major cities* – Antsirabe, Fianarantsoa, Mahajanga, Toamasina
*Currency* – Ariary (MGA) of five iraimbilanja
*Population* – 23,812,681 rising at 2.58 per cent a year (2015 est); the people are of mixed Malayo-Indonesian, Arab and African origin. There are sizeable French, Chinese and Indian communities
*Religion* – Indigenous beliefs 52 per cent, Christian 41 per cent, Muslim 7 per cent
*Language* – Malagasy, French (both official), English
*Population density* – 39 per sq. km (2013)
*Urban population* – 33.8 per cent (2013 est)
*Median age (years)* – 19.2 (2014 est)
*National anthem* – 'Ry Tanindrazanay malala ô' ['Oh, Beloved Land of our Ancestors']
*National day* – 26 June (Independence Day)
*Death penalty* – Retained (no known use since 1958)
*CPI score* – 28 (133)

## CLIMATE AND TERRAIN

Madagascar, the fourth-largest island in the world, lies 386km off the south-east coast of Africa, from which it is separated by the Mozambique Channel. Coastal plains rise to a central plateau and mountains indented with river valleys. Elevation extremes range from 2,876m (Maromokotro) to 0m (Indian Ocean).

The climate is tropical on the coast, temperate in the interior and arid in the south; average temperatures range from 19.6°C in July to 24.9°C in December. Madagascar is subject to tropical cyclones, which cause flooding and wind damage, particularly on the coast.

## HISTORY AND POLITICS

The island was settled by peoples from South East Asia and East Africa from around the first century AD. Although first visited by Europeans *c.*1500, local kingdoms ruled until the early 19th century, when the Merina kingdom conquered the island. France made the island a protectorate in 1895 after the last indigenous resistance was defeated. During the Second World War, the British invaded in order to replace the pro-Vichy government with a Free French government. At the end of the war Madagascar was returned to France, which suppressed a nationalist uprising in 1947–8.

Nationalist agitation continued throughout the 1950s and resulted in independence in 1960.

The military took control in 1972 following civil disturbances, and in 1975 martial law was imposed after a coup. A Marxist one-party state was created with Lt.-Cdr. Didier Ratsiraka as president. Marxism was abandoned in 1980 and a new constitution introduced parliamentary democracy in 1992.

Didier Ratsiraka was defeated in the 1993 presidential elections but returned to office in 1997 after winning the 1996 election. He refused to accept his defeat in the 2001 presidential election and the six-month struggle between his supporters and those of Marc Ravalomanana, the successful candidate, brought the country close to civil war until, in July 2002, Ratsiraka went into exile and his supporters surrendered. President Ravalomanana was re-elected in 2006 and his I Love Madagascar party (TIM) retained its large majority in the 2007 legislative election.

A power struggle between President Ravalomanana and opposition leader Andry Rajoelina began in December 2008. Following an army mutiny and Ravalomanana's resignation, Rajoelina assumed power in March 2009 with the backing of the military and the high court, but the takeover provoked continued demonstrations and widespread international condemnation. The December 2013 presidential election was won by Hery Rajaonarimampianina, while Miaraka Amin'ny Prézidà Andry Rajoelina (MAPAR) emerged as the single largest party in the simultaneous legislative elections. In May 2015, parliament voted to impeach President Rajaonarimampianina amid claims that he had failed to enact promised political reforms; the supreme court annulled the decision on legal grounds in June.

Under the 2010 constitution, the president is directly elected and serves a five-year term, renewable once; the minimum age requirement for presidential candidates was lowered in 2010. The legislature is bicameral, comprising the National Assembly, which has 127 members directly elected for a four-year term, and the senate, which has 100 members, of whom two-thirds are appointed by the regional assemblies and one-third by the president; they serve a four-year term. The 258-member Congress of Transition and 65-member Higher Transition Council set up under 2009 agreements remain in office until elections give effect to the 2010 constitution.

HEAD OF STATE
*President,* Hery Rajaonarimampianina, *took office* 25 January 2014

SELECTED GOVERNMENT MEMBERS *as at June 2015*
*Prime Minister,* Jean Ravelonarivo
*Finance,* Francois Marie Rakotoarimanana
*Foreign Affairs,* Beatrice Attalah

EMBASSY OF THE REPUBLIC OF MADAGASCAR
Avenue de Tervuren 276,1150 Brussels, Belgium
T (+32) (0) 2770 1726 E info@madagascar-embassy.eu
W www.madagascar-embassy.eu
*Ambassador Extraordinary and Plenipotentiary,* HE Jeannot Rakotomalal, *apptd* 2007

BRITISH EMBASSY
Ninth Floor, Tour Zital, Ravoninahitriniarivo Street, Antananarivo 101
T (+261) (20) 223 3053 E BEAntananarivo@moov.mg
W www.gov.uk/government/world/madagascar
*Ambassador Extraordinary and Plenipotentiary,* HE Timothy Smart, *apptd* 2012

## DEFENCE

| Aged 16–49, 2010 est | Males | Females |
|---|---|---|
| Available for military service | 4,900,729 | 4,909,061 |
| Fit for military service | 3,390,071 | 3,682,180 |

*Military expenditure* – US$72.1m (2014)

## ECONOMY AND TRADE

Economic liberalisation and privatisation since the mid-1990s have resulted in slow but steady growth, although the political disturbances in 2002 and 2009–10, and cyclone devastation in 2000 and 2004, have been serious setbacks. President Ravalomanana's reforms and anti-corruption measures attracted increased international aid, and in 2004 half of the country's foreign debt was written off. International aid was suspended in 2010 following the 2009 coup; the country began to receive limited amounts of aid after a new government was appointed in 2014. Growth in the agricultural, tourism and mining sectors should allow the economy to expand by 5.4 per cent in 2015.

Agriculture, fishing and forestry are the mainstays of the economy, accounting for 28.1 per cent of GDP and employing 80 per cent of the workforce. The main cash crops include coffee, vanilla, fish, sugar cane, cocoa, cloves and pepper. The industrial sector contributes 17.4 per cent of GDP, through mining (chromite, graphite, sapphires), processing meat, fish and other agricultural products, manufacturing (textiles, paper, cement, chemicals), car assembly and oil refining. Tourism is of growing importance.

The main trading partners are France, China, the USA and India. Principal exports are agricultural products, textiles, chromite and petroleum products. The main imports are capital goods, petroleum, consumer goods and food.
*GNI* – US$10,179m; US$440 per capita (2013)
*Annual average growth of GDP* – 3 per cent (2014)
*Inflation rate* – 6.4 per cent (2014 est)
*Population below poverty line* – 75.3 per cent (2010 est)
*Unemployment* – 3.5 per cent (2015 est)
*Total external debt* – US$3,630m (2014 est)
*Imports* – US$3,198m (2013)
*Exports* – US$1,947m (2013)

BALANCE OF PAYMENTS
*Trade* – US$1,250m deficit (2013)
*Current Account* – US$343m deficit (2015)

| Trade with UK | 2013 | 2014 |
|---|---|---|
| Imports from UK | £12,157,525 | £8,417,402 |
| Exports to UK | £24,935,245 | £34,959,398 |

## COMMUNICATIONS

*Airports and waterways* – There are 26 airports, with the largest at Antananarivo and Mahajanga; there are 432km of navigable waterways
*Roadways and railways* – 5,613km; 854km
*Telecommunications* – 143,700 fixed lines and 8.56 million mobile subscriptions (2012); there were 319,900 internet users in 2009
*Internet code and IDD* – mg; 261 (from UK), 44 (to UK)
*Major broadcasters* – Television Malagasy (TVM) and Malagasy National Radio (RNM) are the state broadcasters and have a monopoly on national broadcasting; there are hundreds of private local radio and TV stations
*Press* – Daily titles include *Midi-Madagasikara, Madagascar-Tribune* and *La Gazette de la Grande Ile* (all French language)
*WPFI score* – 27,43 (64)

## EDUCATION AND HEALTH

Education is free and compulsory for nine years, but attendance is variable.
*Literacy rate* – 66.1 per cent (2015)
*Gross enrolment ratio (percentage of relevant age group)* – primary 145 per cent; secondary 38 per cent (2013 est); tertiary 4 per cent (2012 est)
*Health expenditure (per capita)* – US$20 (2013)
*Hospital beds (per 1,000 people)* – 0.2 (2010)
*Life expectancy (years)* – 65.2 (2014 est)
*Mortality rate* – 6.95 (2014 est)
*Birth rate* – 33.12 (2014 est)
*Infant mortality rate* – 44.88 (2014 est)

# MALAWI

*Dziko la Malawi – Republic of Malawi*

*Area* – 118,484 sq. km
*Capital* – Lilongwe; population, 867,000 (2014)
*Major cities* – Blantyre, the commercial and industrial centre; Mzuzu; Zomba, the former capital
*Currency* – Kwacha (K) of 100 tambala
*Population* – 17,964,697 rising at 3.32 per cent a year (2015 est); about nine ethnic groups, of which the largest are Chewa (32.6 per cent), Lomwe (17.6 per cent), Yao (13.5 per cent) and Angoni (Nguni) (11.5 per cent) (est)
*Religion* – Christian 82.6 per cent, Muslim 13 per cent, none 2.5 per cent, other 1.9 per cent (2008 est)
*Language* – English (official), Chichewa, Chinyanja, Chiyao, Chitumbuka
*Population density* – 174 per sq. km (2013)
*Urban population* – 16 per cent (2013 est)
*Median age (years)* – 16.3 (2014 est)
*National anthem* – 'Mulungu dalitsa Malawi' ['Oh God Bless Malawi']
*National day* – 6 July (Independence Day)
*Death penalty* – Retained (last used 1992)
*CPI score* – 33 (110)

## CLIMATE AND TERRAIN

The landlocked state lies along the western and southern shores of Lake Malawi (Nyasa). The northern and central regions are plateaux with rolling terrain, while the south is mainly hills and mountains. Elevation extremes range from 3,002m (Sapitwa) to 37m (junction of Shire river and Mozambique border). The climate is subtropical, with a wet season from November to April; average temperatures in Lilongwe range from 18.1°C in July to 25.2°C in November.

## HISTORY AND POLITICS

Until contact was made with European missionaries in the 19th century, Malawi was dominated by a succession of powerful tribes that included the Maravi, the Yao and the Nguni. The missionaries campaigned for official intervention to end the east-coast slave trade, which had begun in the early 19th century, and in 1891 Britain established the Nyasaland and District Protectorate over the area. Renamed the British Central Africa Protectorate in 1893, it became the British colony of Nyasaland in 1907. The country was joined with Northern and Southern Rhodesia (now Zambia and Zimbabwe) between 1953 and 1963. It became independent, as Malawi, in 1964, with Dr Hastings Banda as prime minister.

In 1966, the country became a one-party state ruled by the Malawi Congress Party (MCP) and Dr Banda became president, declaring himself president for life in 1971. In the early 1990s, increasing pro-democracy agitation and international pressure forced Banda to introduce multiparty democracy in 1994.

In the 2004 legislative election, the MCP became the largest party with 60 seats, but without an overall majority. The simultaneous presidential election was won by the United Democratic Front (UDF) candidate Bingu wa Mutharika, who appointed a coalition government made up of the UDF and smaller parties.

In 2005, President Bingu Mutharika resigned from the UDF over the hostility of the party and his predecessor, Bakili Muluzi, to his anti-corruption campaign and founded a new party, the Democratic Progressive Party (DPP). The 2009 legislative election was won by the DPP and President Mutharika was re-elected; Joyce Banda was appointed interim president following his death in April 2012. The DPP returned to power in the May 2014 legislative elections. Opposition parties claimed widespread electoral fraud had taken place, but the results were upheld by Malawi's electoral commission on 30 May. Peter Mutharika was elected president.

Under the 1995 constitution, the executive president is directly elected for a five-year term, renewable once. The unicameral National Assembly consists of 193 members, who are directly elected for a five-year term.

### HEAD OF STATE
*President,* Peter Mutharika *elected* 30 May 2014
*Vice-President,* Saulos Chilima

### SELECTED GOVERNMENT MEMBERS *as at June 2015*
*Finance,* Goodall Gondwe
*Foreign Affairs,* George Chaponda
*Home Affairs,* Atupele Muluzi

### HIGH COMMISSION OF THE REPUBLIC OF MALAWI
36 John Street, London WC1N 2AT
T 020-7421 6010 E malawihighcommission@btconnect.com
W www.malawihighcommission.co.uk
*High Commissioner,* Bernard Sande, *apptd* 2012

### BRITISH HIGH COMMISSION
Off Convention Drive, PO Box 30042, Lilongwe 3
T (+265) (1) 772 400 E bhclilongwe@fco.gov.uk
W www.gov.uk/government/world/malawi
*High Commissioner,* vacant

### DEFENCE

| | *Males* | *Females* |
|---|---|---|
| *Aged 16–49, 2010 est* | | |
| Available for military service | 3,514,809 | – |
| Fit for military service | 2,132,909 | 2,043,925 |

*Military expenditure* – US$51.9m (2014 est)

## ECONOMY AND TRADE
Malawi is one of the poorest countries in Africa. It has few natural resources and its agricultural land is under pressure because of population growth. It also experienced years of mismanagement under earlier governments, and corruption remains a problem despite the government's determination to eliminate it. These factors, high HIV/AIDS rates and the vulnerability of agricultural production to both drought and severe flooding, make the country heavily dependent on food and economic aid from international agencies and donor nations, although international aid was suspended in January 2014 after US$100m (£60m) was allegedly stolen from government funds. International aid has been suspended since 2013 following a major corruption scandal. Growth is anticipated to slow in 2014 after agriculture was damaged by the late arrival of rains and the damage done to infrastructure by consequent heavy flooding.

The economy is primarily agricultural, with 90 per cent of the workforce engaged in agriculture, which accounts for 30.1 per cent of GDP and 90 per cent of export revenue. Tobacco is the most important cash crop, providing 53 per cent of export earnings, along with tea, sugar, cotton, coffee and peanuts. The main industrial activities are agricultural processing, sawmill products, cement and consumer goods, now supplemented by mining uranium, of which exports began in 2009.

The main export markets are India, Germany, South Africa, Russia and Zimbabwe; imports come mainly from South Africa (31 per cent), Zambia, India and China. Apart from tobacco and other agricultural products, wood products and clothing are principal exports. The main imports are food, fuels, semi-manufactures, consumer goods and transport equipment.

*GNI* – US$4,418m; US$270 per capita (2013)
*Annual average growth of GDP* – 5.7 per cent (2014)
*Inflation rate* – 22.8 per cent (2014 est)
*Population below poverty line* – 50.7 per cent (2010 est)
*Unemployment* – 7.5 per cent (2015 est)
*Total external debt* – US$1,729m (2014 est)
*Imports* – US$2,831m (2013)
*Exports* – US$1,196m (2013)

BALANCE OF PAYMENTS
*Trade* – US$1,636m deficit (2013)
*Current Account* – US$168m deficit (2015 est)

| Trade with UK | 2013 | 2014 |
|---|---|---|
| Imports from UK | £15,329,055 | £13,887,679 |
| Exports to UK | £22,244,361 | £15,691,747 |

## COMMUNICATIONS
*Airports and waterways* – The main airports are at Blantyre and Lilongwe, with five smaller airports around the country; there are 700km of navigable waterways on Lake Malawi (Nyasa) and the Shire river
*Roadways and railways* – There are 6,951km of roadways, and 797km of railways, including a line linking the Zambian town of Chipata to the Indian Ocean coast at Nacala in Mozambique
*Telecommunications* – 227,300 fixed lines and 4.42 million mobile subscriptions (2012); there were 716,400 internet users in 2009
*Internet code and IDD* – mw; 265 (from UK), 44 (to UK)
*Major broadcasters* – Television Malawi (TVM) and Malawi Broadcasting Corporation (radio) are the state broadcasters
*Press* – *The Nation* and *The Daily Times* are the only daily national newspapers
*WPFI score* – 26,41 (59)

## EDUCATION AND HEALTH

The government is responsible for primary and secondary schools, technical education and primary teacher training.
*Literacy rate* – 75.1 per cent (2010 est)
*Gross enrolment ratio (percentage of relevant age group)* – primary 141 per cent; secondary 37 per cent (2013 est), tertiary 1 per cent (2011 est)
*Health expenditure (per capita)* – US$26 (2013)
*Hospital beds (per 1,000 people)* – 1.3 (2011)
*Life expectancy (years)* – 59.99 (2014 est)
*Mortality rate* – 8.74 (2014 est)
*Birth rate* – 41.8 (2014 est)
*Infant mortality rate* – 48.01 (2014 est)
*HIV/AIDS adult prevalence* – 10.25 per cent (2013 est)

# MALAYSIA

*Area* – 329,847 sq. km
*Capital* – Kuala Lumpur; population, 6,629,000 (2014); Putrajaya is the administrative capital
*Major cities* – Ampang Jaya, Ipoh, Johor Bahru, Klang, Kota Kinabalu, Kuantan, Kuching, Petaling Jaya, Shah Alam
*Currency* – Malaysian ringgit (RM) of 100 sen; also known as Malaysian dollar
*Population* – 30,513,848 rising at 1.44 per cent a year (2015 est); Malay (50.1 per cent), Chinese (22.6 per cent), indigenous (11.8 per cent), Indian (6.7 per cent) (2004 est)
*Religion* – Muslim 61.3 per cent, Buddhist 19.8 per cent, Christian 9.2 per cent, Hindu 6.3 per cent, Chinese traditional religions 1.3 per cent
*Language* – Bahasa Malaysia (Malay) (official), English, Cantonese, Mandarin, Tamil, Telugu, Malayalam, Punjabi, Thai, Iban, Kadazan
*Population density* – 90 per sq. km (2013)
*Urban population* – 74.2 per cent (2013 est)
*Median age (years)* – 27.7 (2014 est)
*National anthem* – 'Negaraku' ['My Country']
*National day* – 31 August (Independence Day)
*Death penalty* – Retained
*CPI score* – 52 (50)

## CLIMATE AND TERRAIN

Malaysia comprises the 11 states of peninsular Malaya plus the states of Sabah and Sarawak on the island of Borneo. The Malay peninsula, which extends from the isthmus of Kra to the Singapore Strait, is a plain with two highland areas in the north. The Malaysian part of Borneo is mostly high plateau, rising to mountains in western Sabah and eastern Sarawak, while Sarawak also has lower-lying land along the coast and in the Rajang valley; both states are densely forested. Elevation extremes range from 4,100m (Gunung Kinabalu,

Sabah) to 0m (Indian Ocean). The climate is tropical, experiencing the south-west monsoon from May to September and the north-east monsoon from November to March. The average temperature daily temperature is 25.9°C.

## POLITICS

The federal *Parlimen* has two houses, the House of Representatives and the Senate. The former is the lower house and has 222 members, directly elected for a five-year term. The senate has 70 members who serve a three-year term; the legislative assembly of each state elects two members, and 44 are nominated by the head of state.

The 1957 constitution provides for a federal government and a degree of autonomy for the state governments. Each of the 13 states has its own constitution, which must not be inconsistent with the federal constitution. The Malay rulers are either chosen or succeed to their position in accordance with the custom of their particular state; in other states of Malaysia, choice of the head of state is at the discretion of the *Yang di-Pertuan Agong* after consultation with the chief minister of the state. The ruler or governor acts on the advice of an executive council appointed on the advice of the chief minister and a single-chamber legislative assembly. The legislative assemblies are elected on the same basis as the lower chamber of the federal legislature.

The Barisan Nasional (BN) coalition remained in power after the 2013 legislative elections, despite the People's Alliance emerging as the largest single party in the House of Representatives. The BN retained its large majority in the Senate. The ethnic Chinese party the Malaysian Chinese Association (MCA) joined the coalition in June 2014.

The supreme head of state (Abdul Halim al-Marhum Badlishah) is elected by the nine hereditary rulers of the peninsular states from among their number and serves a five-year term.

HEAD OF STATE
*Supreme Head of State,* HM Abdul Halim Muadzam Shah ibni al-Marhum Badlishah, *sworn in* 13 December 2011
*Deputy Head of State,* HM Sultan Muhammad V

SELECTED GOVERNMENT MEMBERS *as at August 2015*
*Prime Minister, Finance,* Najib bin Tun Haji Abdul Razak
*Deputy Prime Minister,* Ahmad Zahid bin Hamidi
*Defence,* Hishammuddin bin Tun Hussein
*Foreign Affairs,* Anifah bin Haji Aman

MALAYSIAN HIGH COMMISSION
45 Belgrave Square, London SW1X 8QT
T 020-7235 8033 E mwlon@btconnect.com
W www.jimlondon.net
*High Commissioner,* HE Dato' Ahmad Rasidi Hazizi, apptd 2014

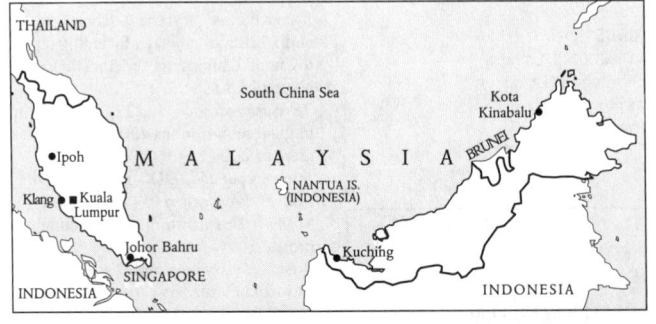

| c.800-1300 | c.1500 | 1867 | 1941-5 | 1946 | 1948 | 1957 | 1963 | 1965 | 1971 | 1981-2003 |

Portuguese, Dutch and British vie for control in the region

Occupied by Japan

Nine peninsular states federated as the Federation of Malaya

Forms Federation of Malaysia with Singapore, Sarawak and Sabah

UMNO becomes dominant partner in *Barisan Nasional* (National Front) government

Part of the Srivijaya Empire

Singapore, Penang and Malacca become crown colony

United Malays National Organisation (UMNO) founded to oppose postwar political settlement

Federation becomes independent

Singapore withdraws from federation

Mahathir bin Muhammad becomes prime minister and imposes authoritarian rule

## BRITISH HIGH COMMISSION

Level 27 Menara Binjai, 2 Jalan Binjai, Kuala Lumpur 50450
T (+60) (3) 2170 2200 E consular.kualalumpur@fco.gov.uk
W www.gov.uk/government/world/malaysia
*High Commissioner,* HE Victoria Treadell, CMG, MVO, *apptd* 2014

## DEFENCE

| Aged 16–49, 2010 est | Males | Females |
|---|---|---|
| Available for military service | 7,501,518 | 7,315,999 |
| Fit for military service | 6,247,306 | 6,175,274 |

*Military expenditure –* US$4,919m (2014)

## ECONOMY AND TRADE

The economy has grown vigorously since the 1970s, transforming the country into a diversified emerging economy. The government's goal is to achieve developed nation status by 2020. To this end, it has encouraged investment in high-technology industries, medical technology and pharmaceuticals, and growth as a regional financial hub, especially for Islamic finance. Growth in the tourism and manufacturing sectors is expected to shield the economy from the negative impact of falling oil prices in 2015. Malaysia was scheduled to form a common market with the other members of the Association of Southeast Asian Nations (ASEAN) in 2015.

The agricultural sector produces the raw materials for its highly developed industries. Industrial production includes rubber manufacturing, palm oil processing, electronics, tin mining and smelting, and logging and timber processing; in addition, oil is produced in Sabah and Sarawak, and refined in Sarawak. Tourism is a major industry. The services sector contributes 56 per cent of GDP, industry 34.7 per cent and agriculture 9.3 per cent.

The main trading partners are China, Singapore, Japan, the USA and other South East Asian countries. Principal exports are electronic equipment, petroleum and liquefied natural gas, timber and wood products, palm oil, rubber, textiles and chemicals. The main imports are electronics, machinery, petroleum products, plastics, vehicles, iron and steel products, and chemicals.

*GNI –* US$309,937m; US$10,430 per capita (2013)
*Annual average growth of GDP –* 5.9 per cent (2014)
*Inflation rate –* 3.1 per cent (2014 est)
*Unemployment –* 3.3 per cent (2015 est)
*Total external debt –* US$109,300m (2014 est)
*Imports –* US$205,898m (2013)
*Exports –* US$228,331m (2013)

## BALANCE OF PAYMENTS

*Trade –* US$22,434m surplus (2013)
*Current Account –* US$6,908m surplus (2015 est)

| Trade with UK | 2013 | 2014 |
|---|---|---|
| Imports from UK | £1,568,818,257 | £1,498,236,658 |
| Exports to UK | £1,684,623,665 | £1,743,263,073 |

## COMMUNICATIONS

*Airports –* There are 39 airports; the main international airports are at Kuala Lumpur, Kota Kinabalu, Kuching and Penang
*Waterways –* There are six main seaports in peninsular Malaysia, plus Kota Kinabalu (Sabah) and Kuching (Sarawak), and a merchant fleet of 315 ships of more than 1,000 tonnes; there are 7,200km of navigable waterways
*Roadways and railways –* 116,169km (including 1,821km of motorways); 1,849km
*Telecommunications –* 4.589 million fixed lines and 41.325 million mobile subscriptions (2012); there were 15.355 million internet users in 2009
*Internet country code and IDD –* my; 60 (from UK), 44 (to UK)
*Major broadcasters –* The state-run Radio Television Malaysia provides services in competition with commercial operators, which broadcast in Malay, Tamil, Chinese and English
*Press –* The four main national daily newspapers are in English: *The Star, The Sun, New Straits Times* and *The Malay Mail*
*WPFI score –* 43,29 (147)

## EDUCATION AND HEALTH

There are six years of compulsory education.
*Literacy rate –* 98.4 per cent (2015 est)
*Gross enrolment ratio (percentage of relevant age group) –* secondary 71 per cent; tertiary 37 per cent (2012 est)
*Health expenditure (per capita) –* US$423 (2013)
*Hospital beds (per 1,000 people) –* 1.9 (2012)
*Life expectancy (years) –* 74.52 (2014 est)
*Mortality rate –* 5 (2014 est)
*Birth rate –* 20.06 (2014 est)
*Infant mortality rate –* 13.69 (2014 est)

# MALDIVES

*Dhivehi Raajjeyge Jumhooriyyaa – Republic of Maldives*

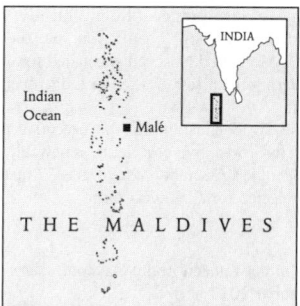

*Area –* 298 sq. km
*Capital –* Malé; population, 156,000 (2014)
*Currency –* Rufiyaa of 100 laarees
*Population –* 393,253 falling at 0.08 per cent a year (2015 est)

*Religion* – Sunni Muslim; public practice of other religions is illegal
*Language* – Dhivehi (official), English
*Population density* – 1,150 per sq. km (2013)
*Urban population* – 43.4 per cent (2013 est)
*Median age (years)* – 27.1 (2014 est)
*National anthem* – 'Gaumii Salaam' ['National Salute']
*National day* – 26 July (Independence Day)
*Death penalty* – Retained (no known use since 1952)
*Literacy rate* – 99.8 per cent (2015 est)
*Life expectancy (years)* – 75.15 (2014 est)
*Mortality rate* – 3.84 (2014 est)
*Birth rate* – 15.59 (2014 est)
*Infant mortality rate* – 24.59 (2014 est)

## CLIMATE AND TERRAIN
The republic is an archipelago of atolls in the Indian Ocean, 643km to the south-west of Sri Lanka. There are about 1,190 coral islands grouped into 26 clusters of atolls, about 200 of which are inhabited. The islands are all flat and low-lying; none is more than 2.4m above sea level, making them vulnerable to rising sea levels caused by climate change. The climate is tropical, affected by the dry north-east monsoon (January–March) and the wet south-west monsoon (May–November).

## HISTORY AND POLITICS
The Maldives were an independent sultanate from the mid-12th century. The sultan was overthrown by the Portuguese in 1558 but they were driven out in 1573 and the sultanate was re-established. In 1645, the islands became a dependency of Ceylon, which was under Dutch and then British rule. In 1887 they became an internally self-governing British protectorate. Independence was achieved in 1965, and in 1968 the Maldives became a republic under President Ibrahim Nasir.

The autocratic Nasir retired in 1978 and was succeeded by Maumoon Abdul Gayoom. His 30-year tenure, although equally autocratic, maintained political stability and economic development. However, unprecedented violence during anti-government demonstrations in 2003 and 2004 led to the legalising of political parties in 2005.

In the first multi-party legislative elections in 2009, the People's Party, led by Maumoon Abdul Gayoom, won control of the legislature through alliances with smaller parties. In the presidential elections of November 2013 Abdulla Gayoom of the Progressive Party of Maldives (PPM) and half brother of former dictator Maumoon Abdul Gayoom, defeated Mohamed Nasheed, the country's first democratically elected president from 2008–12. The March 2014 legislative elections were won by the PPM. In March 2015, Mohamed Nasheed was jailed for 13 years for illegally ordering the arrest of a senior judge during his time as president.

Under the 2008 constitution, the executive president is directly elected for a five-year term, renewable once. The unicameral People's Assembly *(Majlis)* has 77 members, who are directly elected for a five-year term.

### HEAD OF STATE
*President*, Abdulla Yameen Abdul Gayoom, *sworn in*
  17 November 2013
*Vice-President*, Mohamed Jameel Ahmed

SELECTED GOVERNMENT MEMBERS *as at June 2015*
*Defence*, Moosa Ali Jaleel
*Finance*, Abdula Jihad
*Foreign Affairs*, Dunya Maumoon

HIGH COMMISSION OF THE REPUBLIC OF MALDIVES
22 Nottingham Place, London W1U 5NJ
T 020-7224 2135 E info@maldiveshighcommission.org
W www.maldiveshighcommission.org
*High Commissioner (acting)*, Ahmed Shiaan

BRITISH HIGH COMMISSIONER
HE James Dauris, *apptd* 2014, resident at Colombo, Sri Lanka

## ECONOMY AND TRADE
Political stability and economic liberalisation have produced steady economic growth since the 1980s, except in 2005 owing to the devastation caused by the 2004 tsunami, and 2009, when tourist numbers and exports fell owing to the global economic downturn. Balance of payments difficulties forced the government to seek IMF standby funding in 2009; after the first two disbursements the IMF halted further funds due to the Maldives' growing budget deficit. The economy is heavily dependent on tourism and the economy is benefiting from increasing numbers of Chinese visitors in 2014, the government created a number of special economic zones to increase foreign investment and reduce dependancy on tourism. Agriculture and manufacturing are constrained by a shortage of cultivable land and domestic labour, so most food is imported. Industry is concentrated on clothing manufacture, fish processing, boat-building and handicrafts. Growth of over 6 per cent is predicted for 2016, though there is a widening fiscal deficit.

The main export markets are the UAE, Singapore and India. The only significant export is fish. Imports include petroleum products, ships, food and clothing, and are provided mainly by Thailand, France, Iran and Germany.
*GNI* – US$1,933m; US$5,600 per capita (2013)
*Annual average growth of GDP* – 4.5 per cent (2014)
*Inflation rate* – 4 per cent (2013 est)
*Population below poverty line* – 16 per cent (2008)
*Unemployment* – 12.2 per cent (2015 est)
*Total external debt* – US$793.6m (2013 est)
*Imports* – US$1,733m (2013)
*Exports* – US$167m (2013)

BALANCE OF PAYMENTS
*Trade* – US$1,567m deficit (2013)
*Current Account* – US$139m deficit (2015 est)

| Trade with UK | 2013 | 2014 |
| --- | --- | --- |
| Imports from UK | £8,291,086 | £11,444,990 |
| Exports to UK | £10,659,512 | £7,180,560 |

## COMMUNICATIONS
*Transport* – The country has seven airports, two of which handle international traffic; the main port is Malé and there are 88km of roads
*Telecommunications* – 23,140 fixed lines and 560,000 mobile subscriptions (2012); there were 86,400 internet users in 2009
*Internet code and IDD* – mv; 960 (from UK), to UK (44)
*Major broadcasters* – The state broadcaster Maldives National Broadcasting Corporation operates radio and TV stations; a small number of private broadcasters are permitted to operate
*Press* – Daily newspapers include *Miadhu News* and *Haveeru Daily*
*WPFI score* – 34,32 (112)

# MALI

*République de Mali – Republic of Mali*

*Area* – 1,240,192 sq. km
*Capital* – Bamako; population, 2,386,000 (2014)
*Major cities* – Kayes, Koutiala, Mopti, Ségou, Sikasso, Timbuktu
*Currency* – Franc CFA of 100 centimes
*Population* – 16,955,536 rising at 2.9 per cent a year (2015 est); Mandé (50 per cent), Peul (17 per cent), Voltaic (12 per cent), Tuareg and Moor (10 per cent), Songhai (6 per cent) (est); about 10 per cent are nomadic
*Religion* – Muslim 94.8 per cent, Christian 2.4 per cent, Animist 2 per cent
*Language* – French (official), Bambara, other African languages
*Population density* – 13 per sq. km (2013)
*Urban population* – 36.2 per cent (2013 est)
*Median age (years)* – 16 (2014 est)
*National anthem* – 'Le Mali' ['Mali']
*National day* – 22 September (Independence Day)
*Death penalty* – Retained (last used 1980)
*CPI score* – 32 (115)

## CLIMATE AND TERRAIN
The west African state is mainly savannah in the south and desert plains in the north, with some hills in the north-east; over 60 per cent is desert or semi-desert. The centre is drained by the Niger river and the south-west by the Senegal river. Elevation extremes range from 1,155m (Hombori Tondo) to 23m (Senegal river). The climate is subtropical in the south with a rainy season from June to November, and arid in the north. Average temperatures range from 21.4°C in January to 33.9°C in June.

## HISTORY AND POLITICS
Mali was successively part of the empire of the Malinke people from the 13th to 15th centuries, and of the Songhai Empire in the 15th to 16th centuries. With the fall of the Songhai Empire, it was divided between the Tuareg and the Fulani and Bambara kingdoms, and then the Tukolor and Samori kingdoms. It was conquered by the French in 1880–95 and became a French colony. In 1959, it formed the Federation of Mali with Senegal before becoming a separate independent state in 1960 under a one-party socialist regime.

In 1968, a military coup led by Lt. Moussa Traoré resulted in 23 years of oppressive military rule. Traoré was ousted as president in 1991 in a military coup led by Gen. Amadou Toumani Touré. Multiparty elections were held in 1992, returning the country to civilian government.

A degree of decentralisation was introduced in 1999, partly in response to rebellions in the north by the Tuareg

over land and cultural rights. Another rebellion in 2006 by Tuareg seeking greater autonomy for their region was settled within a few months, but a more militant faction carried on an insurrection from 2007 to 2009. In May 2014 Tuareg separatists occupied the northern towns Menaka, Agelhok, Anefis and Tessalit.

Amadou Toumani Touré, standing as an independent candidate, won the 2002 presidential elections, and was re-elected in 2007. In the 2007 legislative elections, the Alliance for Democracy in Mali (ADEMA), which had dominated government coalitions since 1992, won the largest number of seats and formed another coalition government. A military coup overthrew Touré's government in March 2012, claiming that the government had not supported the country's army against the advancing Tuareg-led rebellion. Cissé Mariam Kaidama Sidibé, the country's first female prime minister, was arrested shortly after the coup. In the subsequent 2013 presidential elections, former prime minister Ibrahim Boubacar Keita comfortably defeated rival candidate Soumaila Cissé. Following the resignation of prime ministers Oumar Tatam Ly in September 2013 and Moussa Mara in April 2015, Modibo Keita of the Alliance for Democracy in Mali party was appointed prime minister in January 2015.

Under the 1992 constitution, the president is directly elected for a five-year term, which is renewable once. The unicameral National Assembly has 160 members, 147 directly elected for a maximum of two terms and 13 to represent Malians abroad; all serve a five-year term. The president appoints the prime minister, who appoints the cabinet.

HEAD OF STATE
*President*, Ibrahim Boubacar Keita, *apptd* 4 September 2014

SELECTED GOVERNMENT MEMBERS *as at June 2015*
*Prime Minister*, Modibo Keita
*Economy and Finance*, Mamadou Igor Diarra
*Foreign Affairs*, Abdoulaye Diop

EMBASSY OF THE REPUBLIC OF MALI
Avenue Molière 487, 1050 Brussels, Belgium
T (+32) (2) 345 7432 E info@amba-mali.be W www.amba-mali.be
*Ambassador Extraordinary and Plenipotentiary*, vacant

BRITISH AMBASSADOR
Immeuble Semega, Route de Koulikoro, Hippodrome, BP 2069, Bamako
T (+223) 2021 3412 W www.gov.uk/government/world/mali
*Ambassador Extraordinary and Plenipotentiary*, HE Joanne Adamson, *apptd* 2014

## DEFENCE

| Aged 16–49, 2010 est | Males | Females |
| --- | --- | --- |
| Available for military service | 2,848,412 | 2,981,106 |
| Fit for military service | 1,825,779 | 1,968,563 |

*Military expenditure* – US$170m (2014)
*Conscription* – 18 years; 24 months (selective)

## ECONOMY AND TRADE
Mali is one of the world's poorest countries, with 660,000 children across the country at risk of malnutrition. Economic reform since the mid-1990s has produced steady growth, but Mali is heavily dependent on foreign aid and remittances from expatriates. The administration's purchase of a presidential jet for US$40m (£26.9m) and misappropriation

of defence budget funds led the IMF to temporarily suspend aid in 2014. Expected good harvests and the performance of the service sector are predicted to allow the economy to grow by over 5 per cent in 2015.

The economy is based primarily on subsistence farming and animal husbandry, which contribute 38 per cent of GDP and occupy 80 per cent of the population. Gold, phosphate and iron-ore mining, and cotton and food processing are the main activities in Mali's industrial sector, which accounts for 23.3 per cent of GDP. Export of hydro-electric power is expected to contribute to future earnings.

The main export markets are China and India; imports come mainly from France, Senegal and Côte d'Ivoire. Principal exports are cotton, gold and livestock. The main imports are fuel, machinery and equipment, construction materials, foodstuffs and textiles.

*GNI* – US$10,224m; US$670 per capita (2013)
*Annual average growth of GDP* – 5.9 per cent (2014)
*Inflation rate* – 1 per cent (2014 est)
*Population below poverty line* – 43.6 per cent (2010 est)
*Unemployment* – 8.3 per cent (2015 est)
*Total external debt* – US$3,737m (2014)
*Imports* – US$3,699m (2013)
*Exports* – US$2,601m (2013)

BALANCE OF PAYMENTS
*Trade* – US$1,098m deficit (2013)
*Current Account* – US$612m deficit (2015 est)

| Trade with UK | 2013 | 2014 |
| --- | --- | --- |
| Imports from UK | £10,122,395 | £14,831,732 |
| Exports to UK | £274,247 | £121,074 |

## COMMUNICATIONS
*Airports and waterways* – There are eight airports, with the largest at Bamako; the main port is Koulikoro on the Niger river
*Roadways and railways* – 5,522km; 593km
*Telecommunications* – 112,000 fixed lines and 14.613 million mobile subscriptions (2012); there were 249,800 internet users in 2009
*Internet code and IDD* – ml; 223 (from UK), 44 (to UK)
*Major broadcasters* – The public Office de la Radiodiffusion Télévision du Mali operates a number of radio and television channels in French and local vernacular languages
*Press* – There are five main daily newspapers, including *L'Essor*, the state-owned national daily
*WPFI score* – 36,33 (118)

## EDUCATION AND HEALTH
There are nine years of free, compulsory education beginning at age seven.
*Literacy rate* – 54.1 per cent (2015 est)
*Gross enrolment ratio (percentage of relevant age group)* – primary 84 per cent; secondary 45 per cent (2013 est); tertiary 7 per cent (2012 est)
*Health expenditure (per capita)* – US$53 (2013)
*Hospital beds (per 1,000 people)* – 0.1 (2010)
*Life expectancy (years)* – 54.95 (2014 est)
*Mortality rate* – 13.22 (2014 est)
*Birth rate* – 45.53 (2014 est)
*Infant mortality rate* – 104.34 (2014 est)
*HIV/AIDS adult prevalence* – 0.96 per cent (2013 est)

# MALTA

*Repubblika ta' Malta – Republic of Malta*

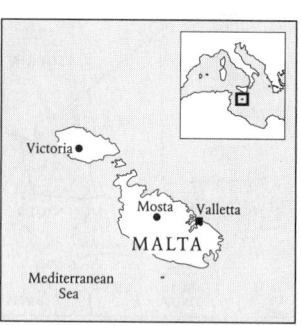

*Area* – 316 sq. km
*Capital* – Valletta; population, 197,000 (2014)
*Major towns* – Birkirkara, Mosta, Qormi, Saint Paul's Bay (San Pawl il-Bahar)
*Currency* – Euro (€) of 100 cents
*Population* – 412,655 rising at 0.33 per cent a year (2014 est)
*Religion* – Christian (Roman Catholic 90 per cent)
*Language* – Maltese, English (both official)
*Population density* – 1,323 per sq. km (2013)
*Urban population* – 95.2 per cent (2013 est)
*Median age (years)* – 40.9 (2014 est)
*National anthem* – 'L-Innu Malti' ['Hymn of Malta']
*National day* – 21 September (Independence Day)
*Death penalty* – Abolished for all crimes (since 2000)
*CPI score* – 55 (43)

## CLIMATE AND TERRAIN
Malta is an archipelago of six islands in the Mediterranean Sea; Malta, Gozo and Comino are the largest. The island of Malta has a coastal plain in the north-east, rising to low hills in the south-west. Elevation extremes range from 253m (Ta'Dmejrek) to 0m (Mediterranean Sea). Average temperatures range from 12.7°C in February to 27.2°C in August.

## HISTORY AND POLITICS
The islands were ruled successively by the Phoenicians, Greeks, Carthaginians, Romans, Arabs, Spanish and the Sovereign Military Order of Malta (known as the Knights of St John), which held them from 1530 until a French invasion in 1798. Liberated from French rule with British naval support in 1800, the island of Malta became a British colony in 1814, and was developed into a substantial naval base and dockyard. Malta was strategically important in both world wars, but particularly the second, when it was blockaded and subjected to aerial bombardment for five months. Its resistance led to the people of Malta being awarded the George Cross, the UK's highest award for civilian bravery, in 1942.

Malta gained its independence in 1964 and became a republic in 1974. In the 1970s it developed close links with communist and Arab states, but more pro-European and pro-US policies were adopted after the election of the Nationalist Party in 1987. Malta became a member of the EU in 2004, and adopted the euro in 2008. Since joining the EU, Malta has experienced a marked increase in illegal immigration from northern Africa.

In March 2013 the Labour Party returned to power after winning 39 seats in legislative elections. The party's leader

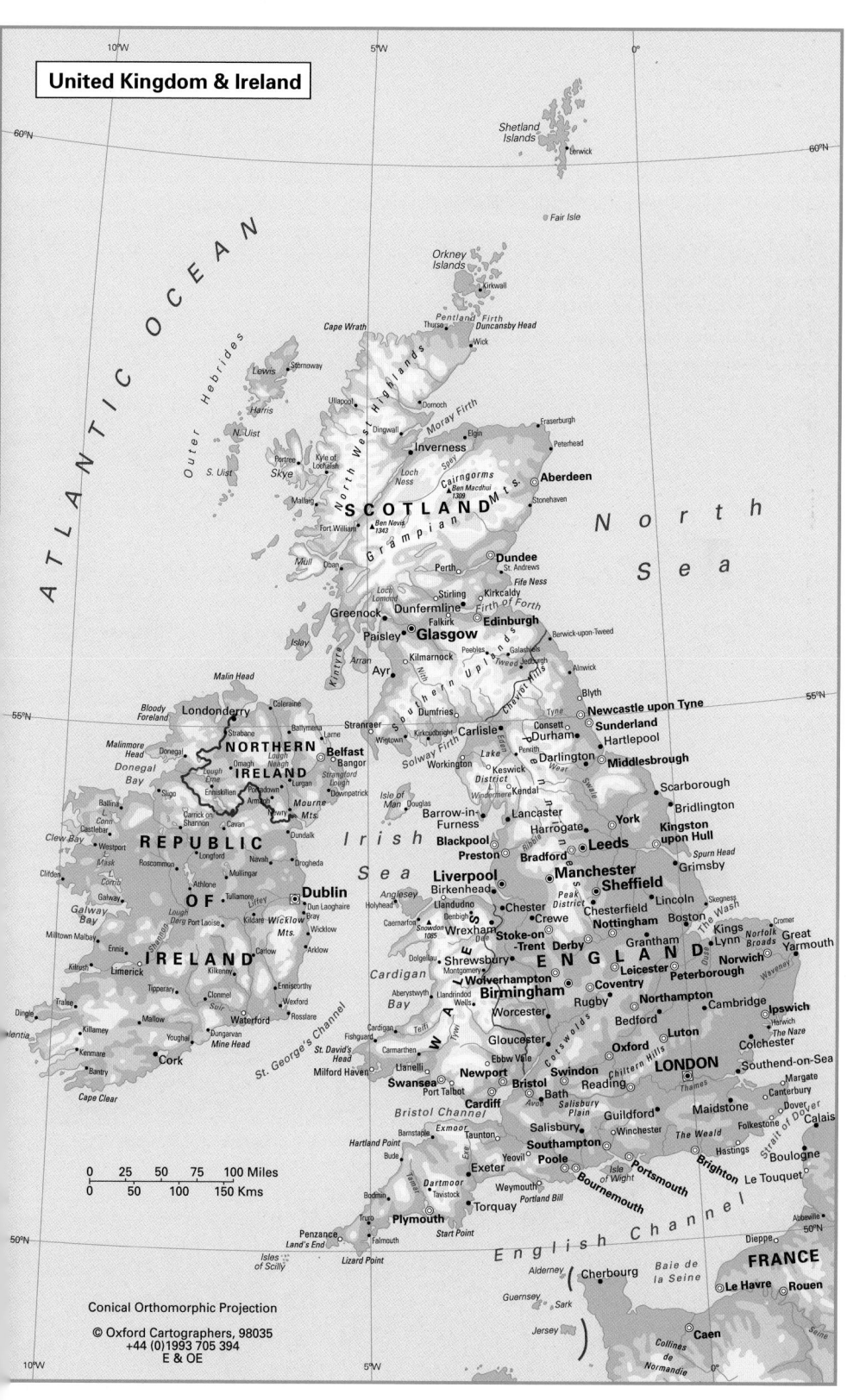

# United Kingdom & Ireland

Conical Orthomorphic Projection

© Oxford Cartographers, 98035
+44 (0)1993 705 394
E & OE

Europe

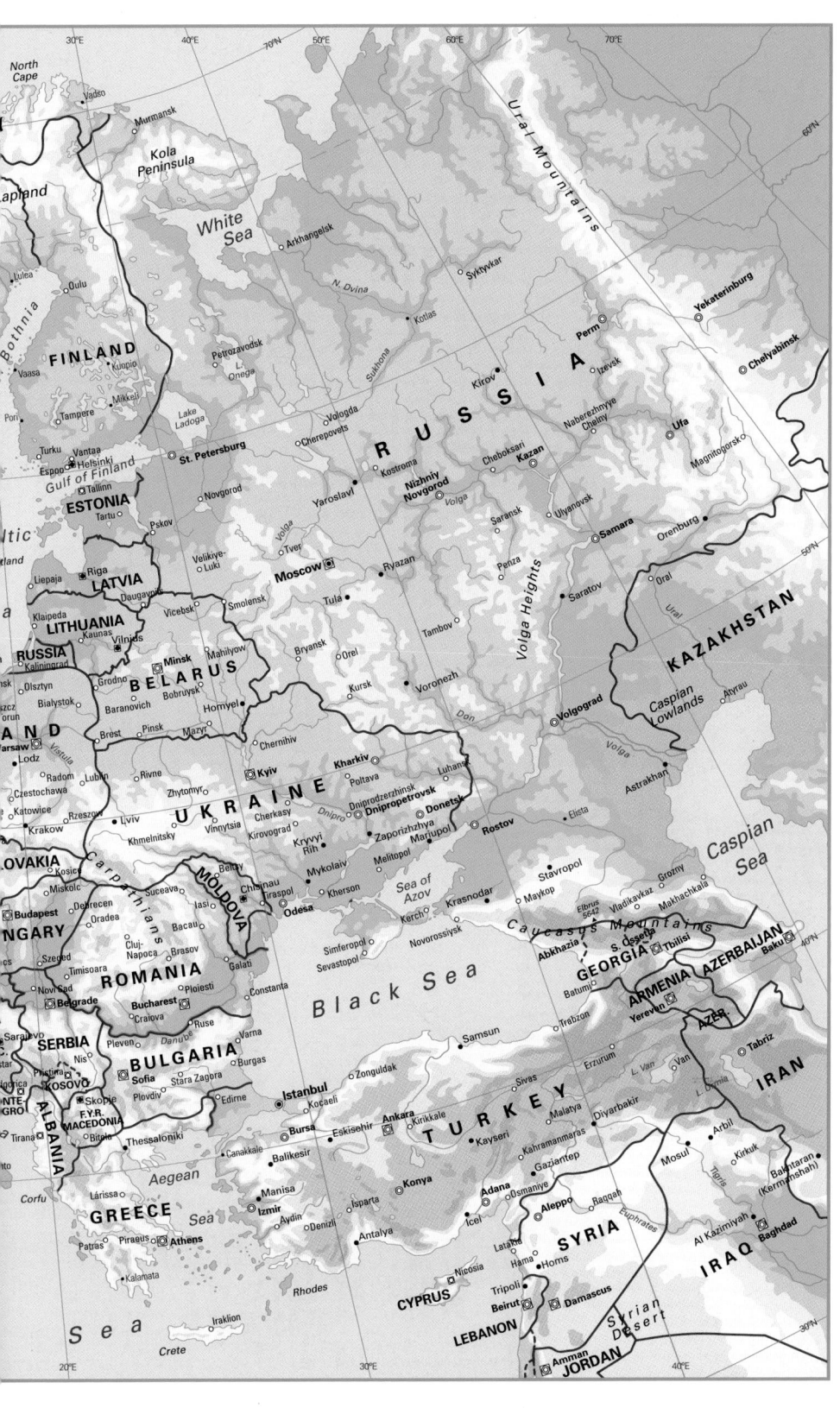

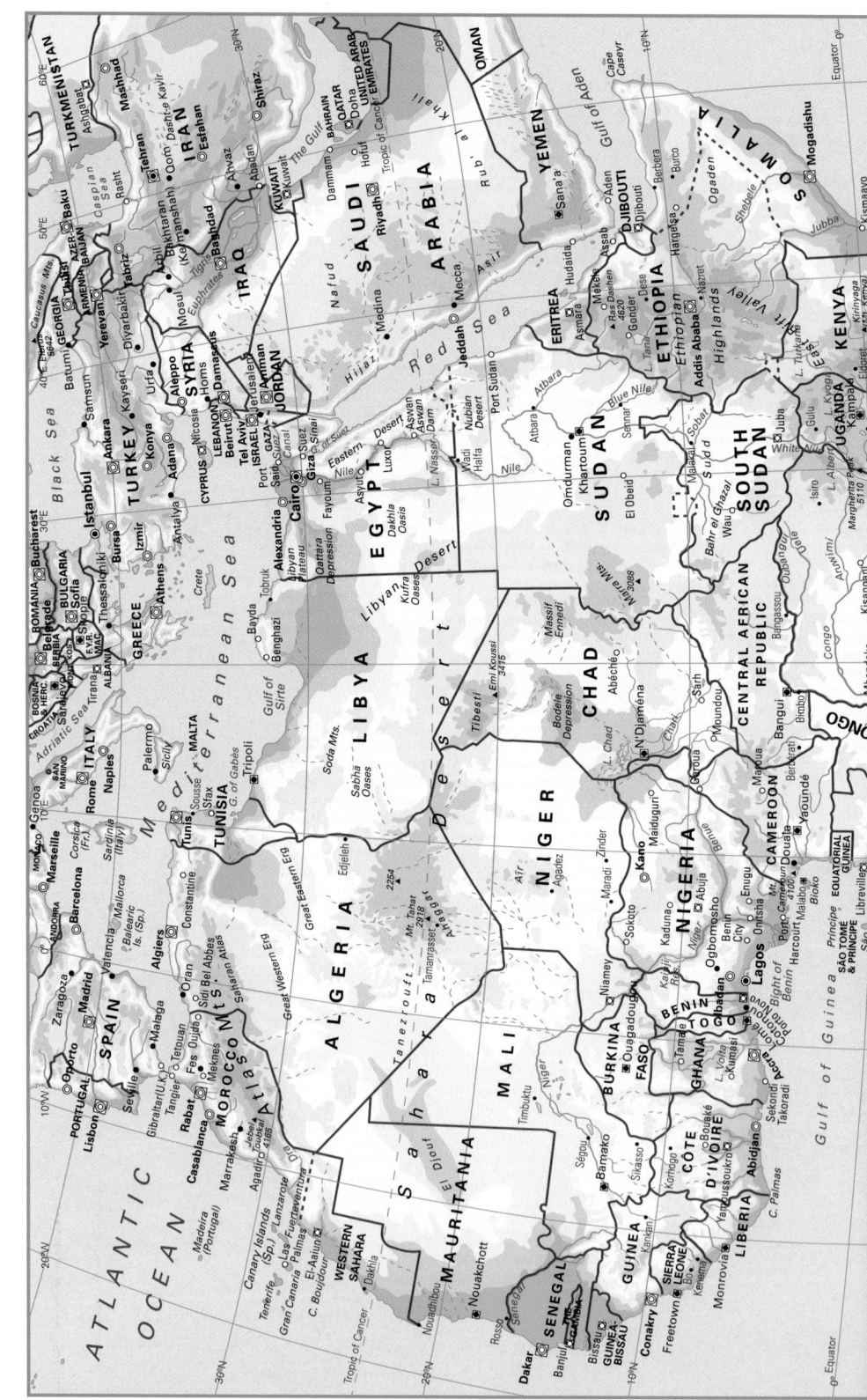

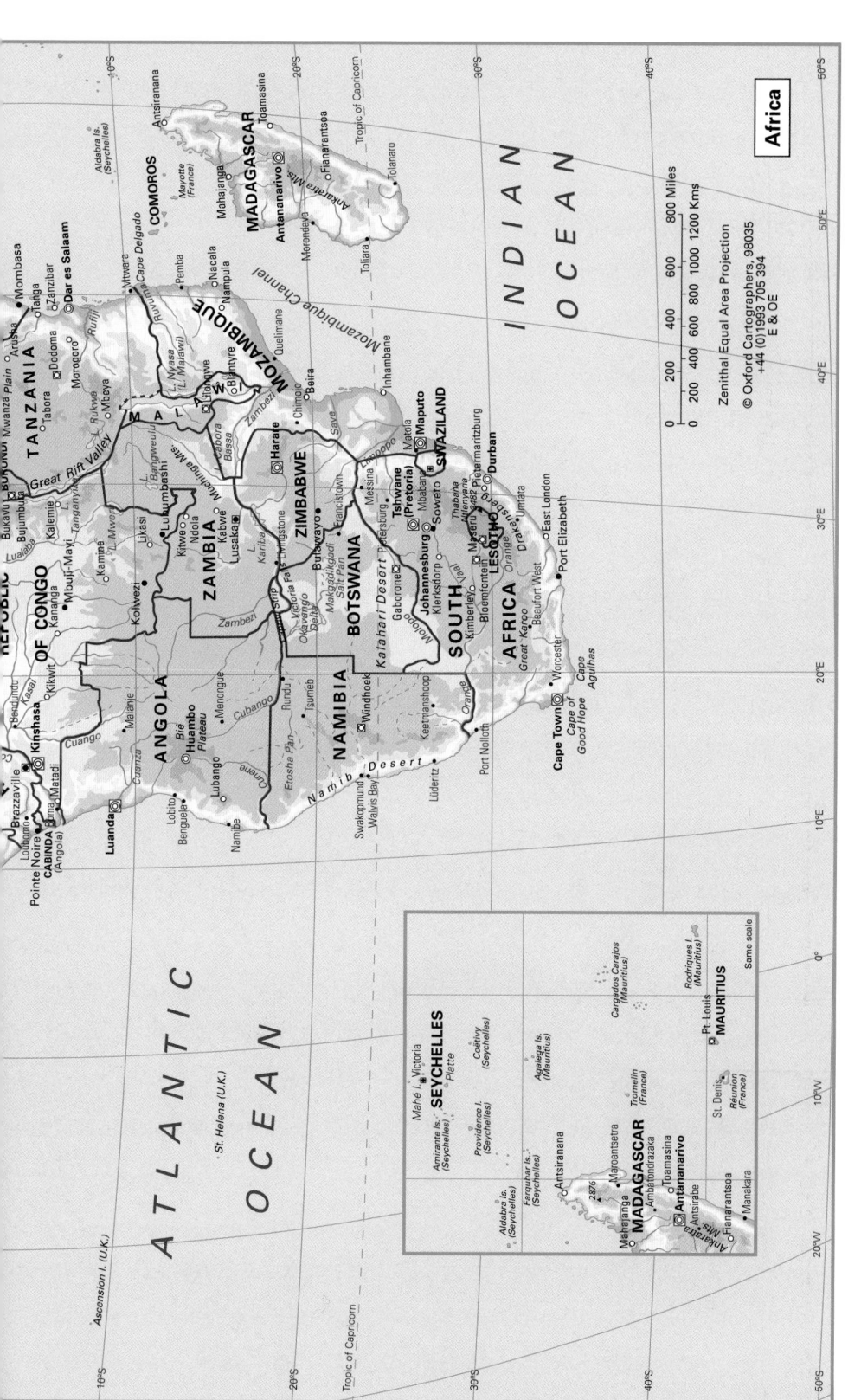

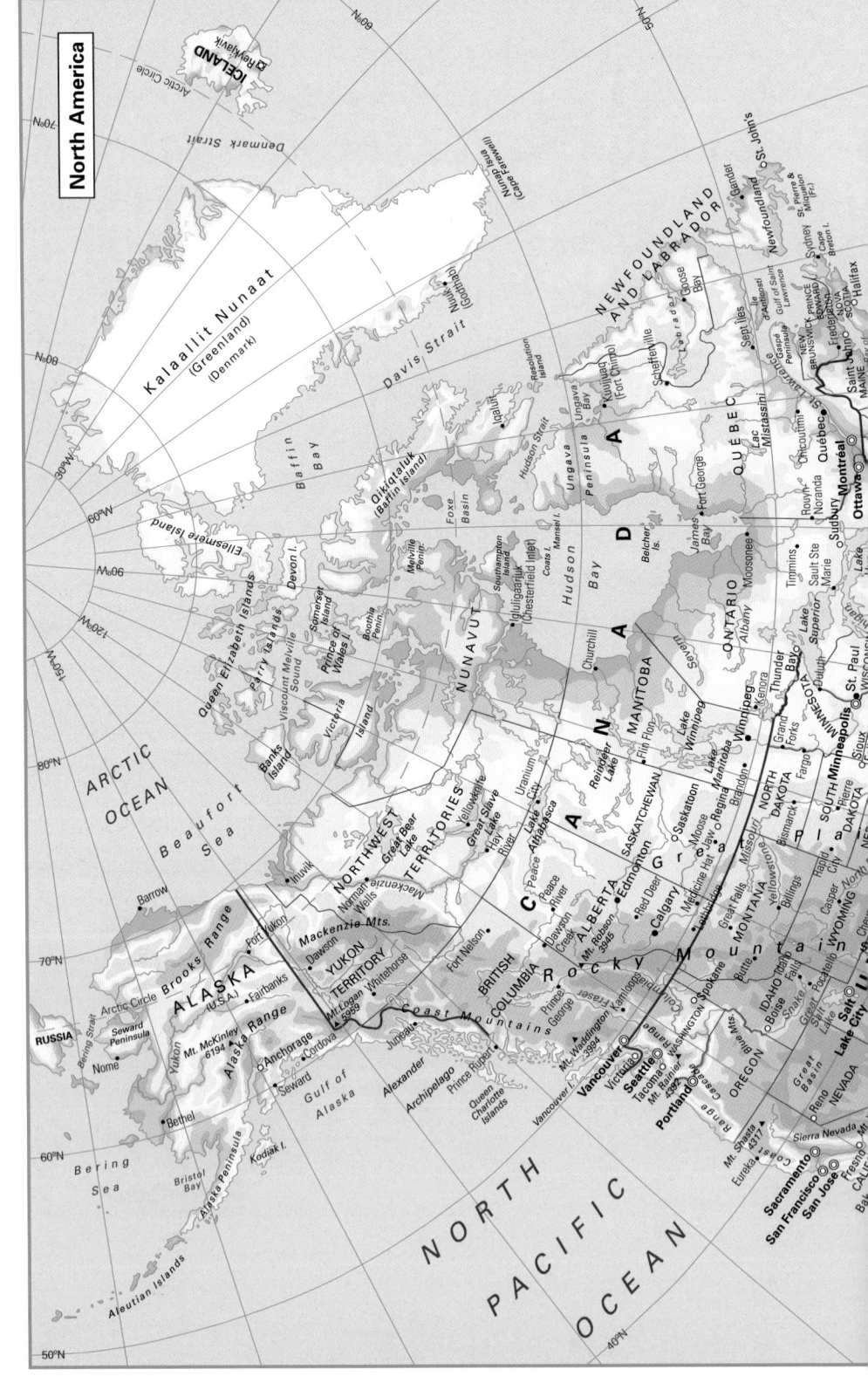

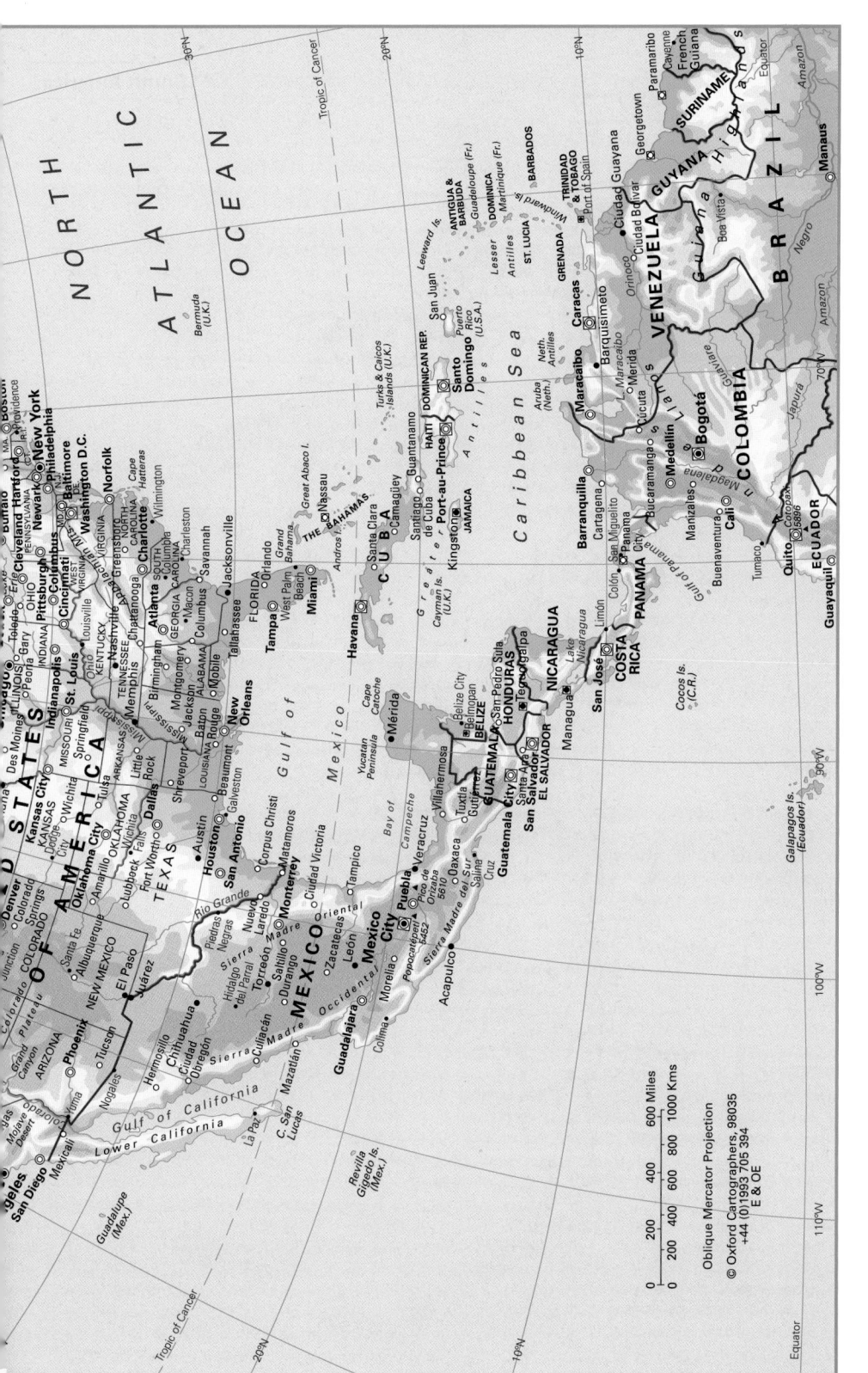

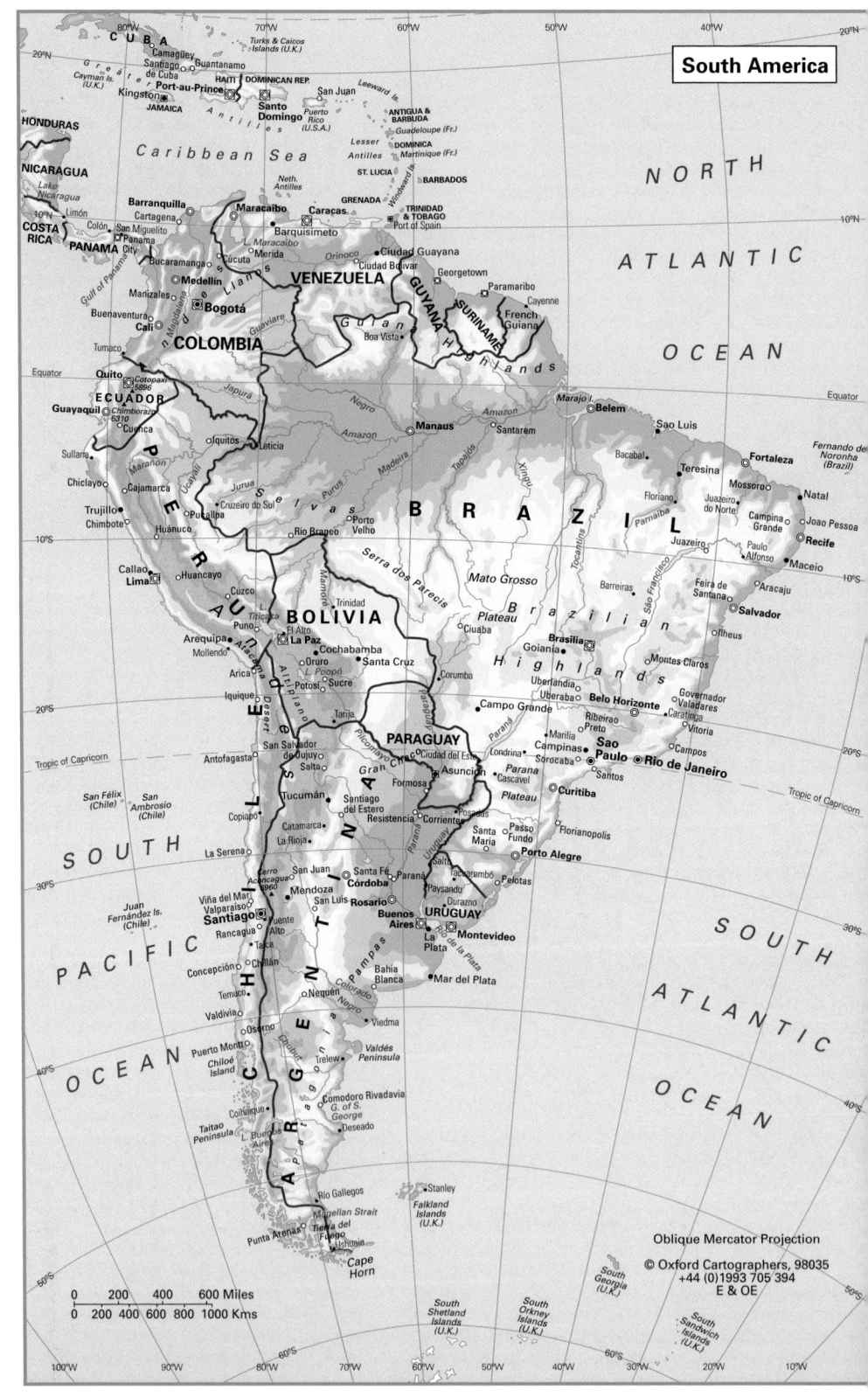

South America

CUBA
Camagüey
Santiago
de Cuba
Guantanamo
Turks & Caicos
Islands (U.K.)
Cayman Is.
(U.K.)
HAITI   DOMINICAN REP.
Port-au-Prince
Kingston
San Juan
Leeward Is.
HONDURAS
JAMAICA
Santo
Domingo
Puerto
Rico
(U.S.A.)
ANTIGUA &
BARBUDA
Antilles
Guadeloupe (Fr.)
Lesser
Antilles
DOMINICA
Martinique (Fr.)
NICARAGUA
Lake
Nicaragua
Caribbean Sea
Neth.
Antilles
ST. LUCIA
BARBADOS

NORTH

COSTA
RICA
Limón
Colón
San Miguelito
Panama
City
Barranquilla
Cartagena
PANAMA
Maracaibo
L. Maracaibo
Mérida
Caracas
Barquisimeto
GRENADA
TRINIDAD
& TOBAGO
Port of Spain

ATLANTIC

Gulf of Panama
Bucaramanga
Medellín
Manizales
Cúcuta
Orinoco
Ciudad Guayana
Ciudad Bolívar
Georgetown
Paramaribo
Cayenne

OCEAN

Buenaventura
Cali
Bogotá
VENEZUELA
Llanos
Guaviare
GUYANA
SURINAME
French
Guiana

Tumaco
COLOMBIA
Boa Vista
Guiana Highlands

Equator
Quito
Cotopaxi
5896
ECUADOR
Guayaquil
Chimborazo
6310
Cuenca
Iquitos
Leticia
Japurá
Negro
Manaus
Amazon
Marajó I.
Belem
Sao Luis

Equator

Sullana
Chiclayo
Cajamarca
Marañón
Amazon
Purus
Madeira
Santarem
Bacabal
Teresina
Mossoro
Fortaleza
Fernando de
Noronha
(Brazil)
Natal

Trujillo
Chimbote
Huánuco
Cruzeiro do Sul
Pucallpa
Jurua
Selvas
Porto
Velho
BRAZIL
Tapajos
Xingu
Floriano
Parnaiba
Juazeiro
do Norte
Campina
Grande
Joao Pessoa
Recife

Callao
Lima
Huancayo
PERU
Rio Branco
Mamore
Serra dos Parecis
Tocantins
Juazeiro
Sao Francisco
Paulo
Alfonso
Maceio

Cuzco
L. Titicaca
Puno
BOLIVIA
Trinidad
Mato Grosso
Barreiras
Feira de
Santana
Aracaju
Salvador

Arequipa
Mollendo
Atacama
El Alto
La Paz
Oruro
L. Poopó
Cochabamba
Santa Cruz
Brazilian
Plateau
Ciuaba
Goiania
Brasilia
Montes Claros
Ilheus

Arica
Iquique
Atacama Desert
Potosi
Sucre
Corumba
Uberlandia
Uberaba
Goiania
Highlands
Governador
Valadares
Caratinga
Vitoria

Antofagasta
Tarija
Pilcomayo
San Salvador
de Jujuy
PARAGUAY
Campo Grande
Belo Horizonte
Ribeirao
Preto
Campinas
Londrina
Sorocaba
Sao
Paulo
Rio de Janeiro

Tropic of Capricorn
San Félix
(Chile)
San
Ambrosio
(Chile)
Copiapó
Salta
Gran
Chaco
Ciudad del Este
Asuncion
Parana
Cascavel
Curitiba
Santos

Tropic of Capricorn

Catamarca
La Rioja
Tucumán
Santiago
del Estero
Resistencia
Formosa
Corrientes
Posadas
Parana
Plateau
Santa
Maria
Passo
Fundo
Florianopolis

Juan
Fernández Is.
(Chile)
La Serena
Cerro
Aconcagua
San Juan
Santa Fé
Parana
Uruguay
Salto
Tacuarembó
Porto Alegre
Pelotas

SOUTH
Viña del Mar
Valparaiso
Santiago
Rancagua
Mendoza
San Luis
Rosario
Córdoba
Paysandú
Durazno
URUGUAY
Buenos
Aires
Montevideo

PACIFIC
Puente
Alto
Talca
Chillán
Rancagua
PAMPAS
La
Plata
Rio de la Plata

Concepción
Temuco
Valdivia
Neuquen
Bahia
Blanca
Colorado
Negro
Mar del Plata

SOUTH

OCEAN
Osorno
Puerto Montto
Chiloé
Island
ARGENTINA
Viedma
Valdés
Peninsula
Trelew

ATLANTIC

Comodoro Rivadavia
G. of S.
George
Deseado

OCEAN

Taitao
Peninsula
Coihaique
L. Buenos
Aires
Rio Gallegos

Punta Arenas
Magellan Strait
Tierra del
Fuego
Stanley
Falkland
Islands
(U.K.)

Cape
Horn
South
Georgia
(U.K.)

Oblique Mercator Projection

© Oxford Cartographers, 98035
+44 (0)1993 705 394
E & OE

0   200   400   600 Miles
0   200 400 600 800 1000 Kms

South
Shetland
Islands
(U.K.)
South
Orkney
Islands
(U.K.)
South
Sandwich
Islands
(U.K.)

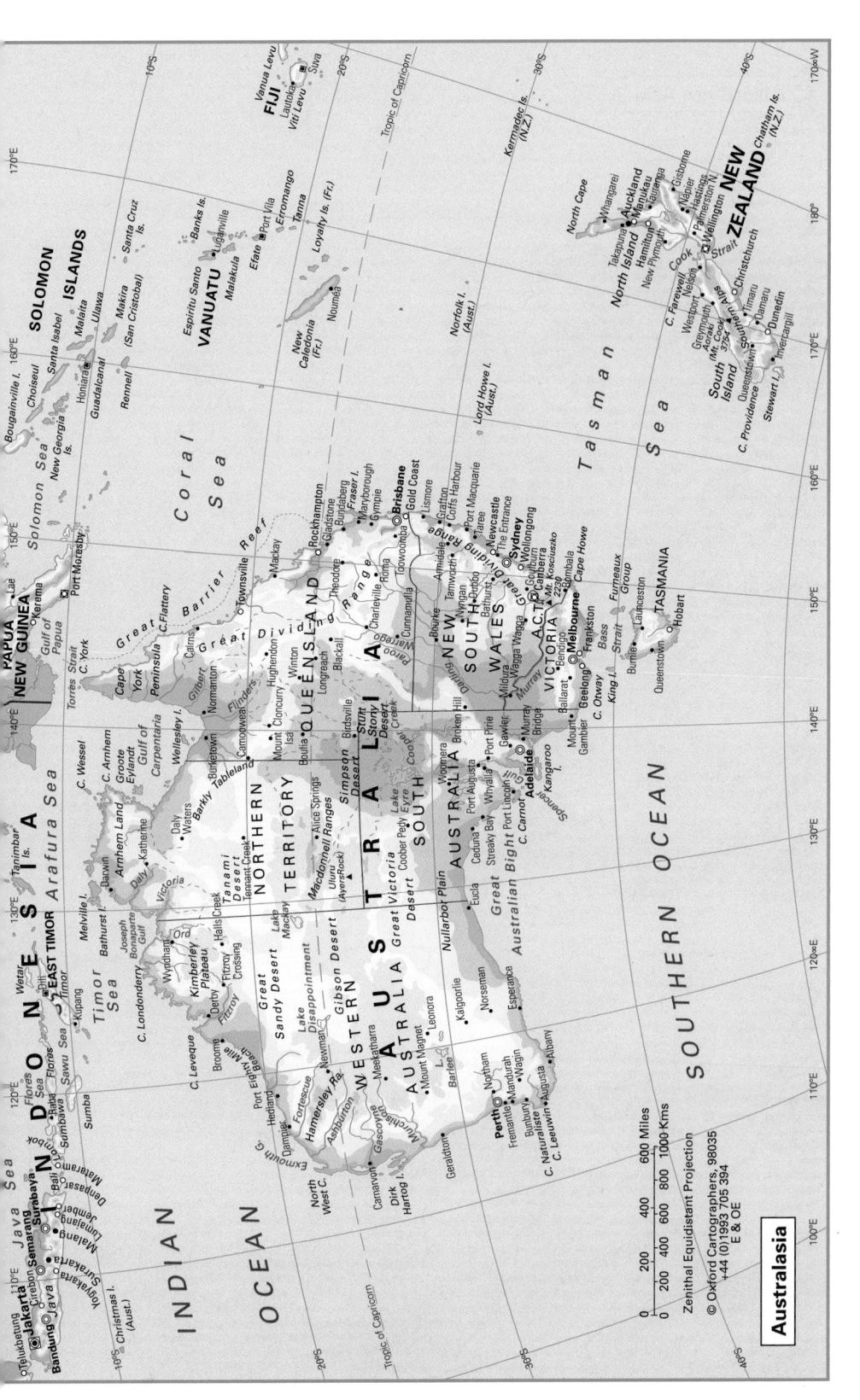

Australasia

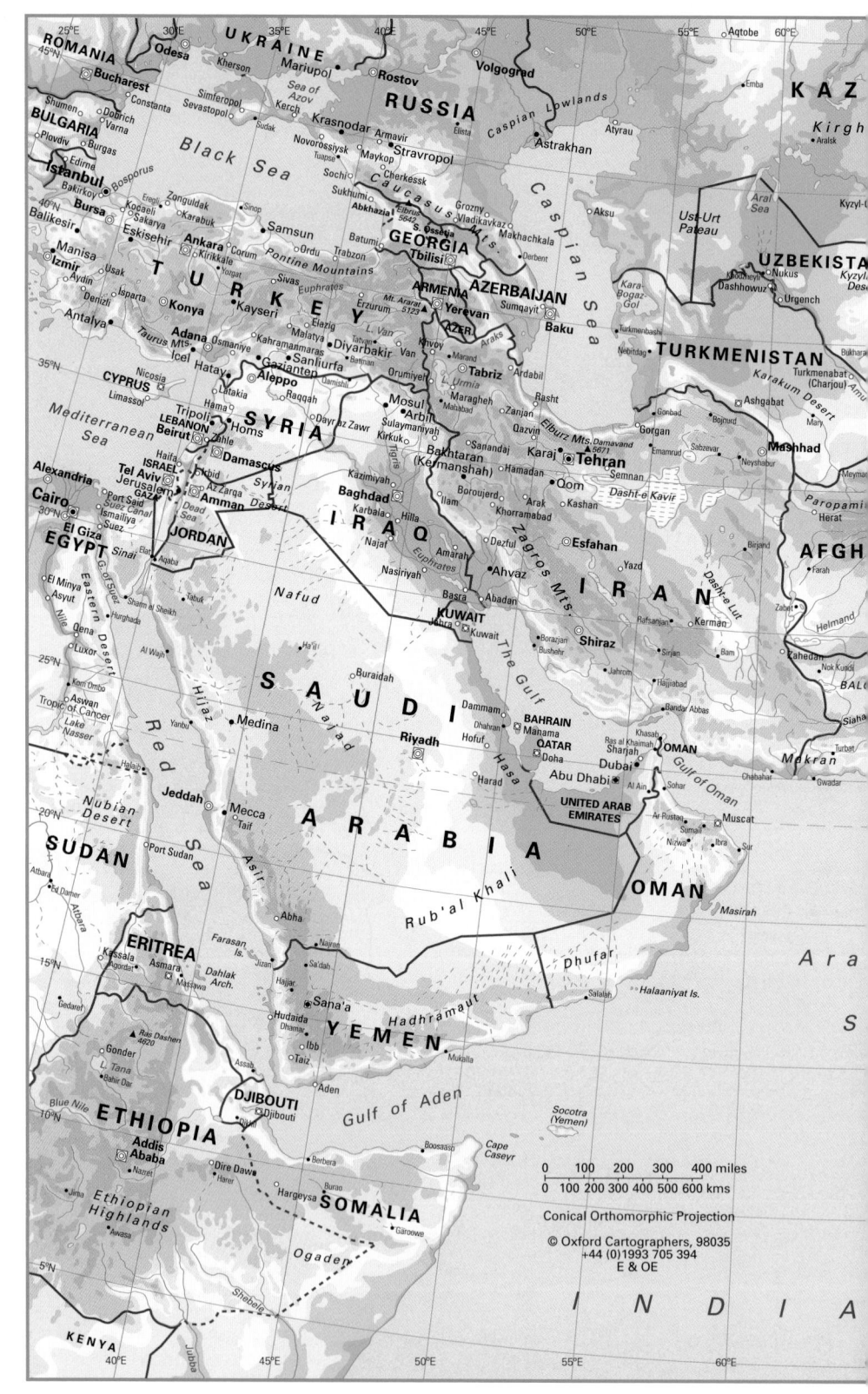

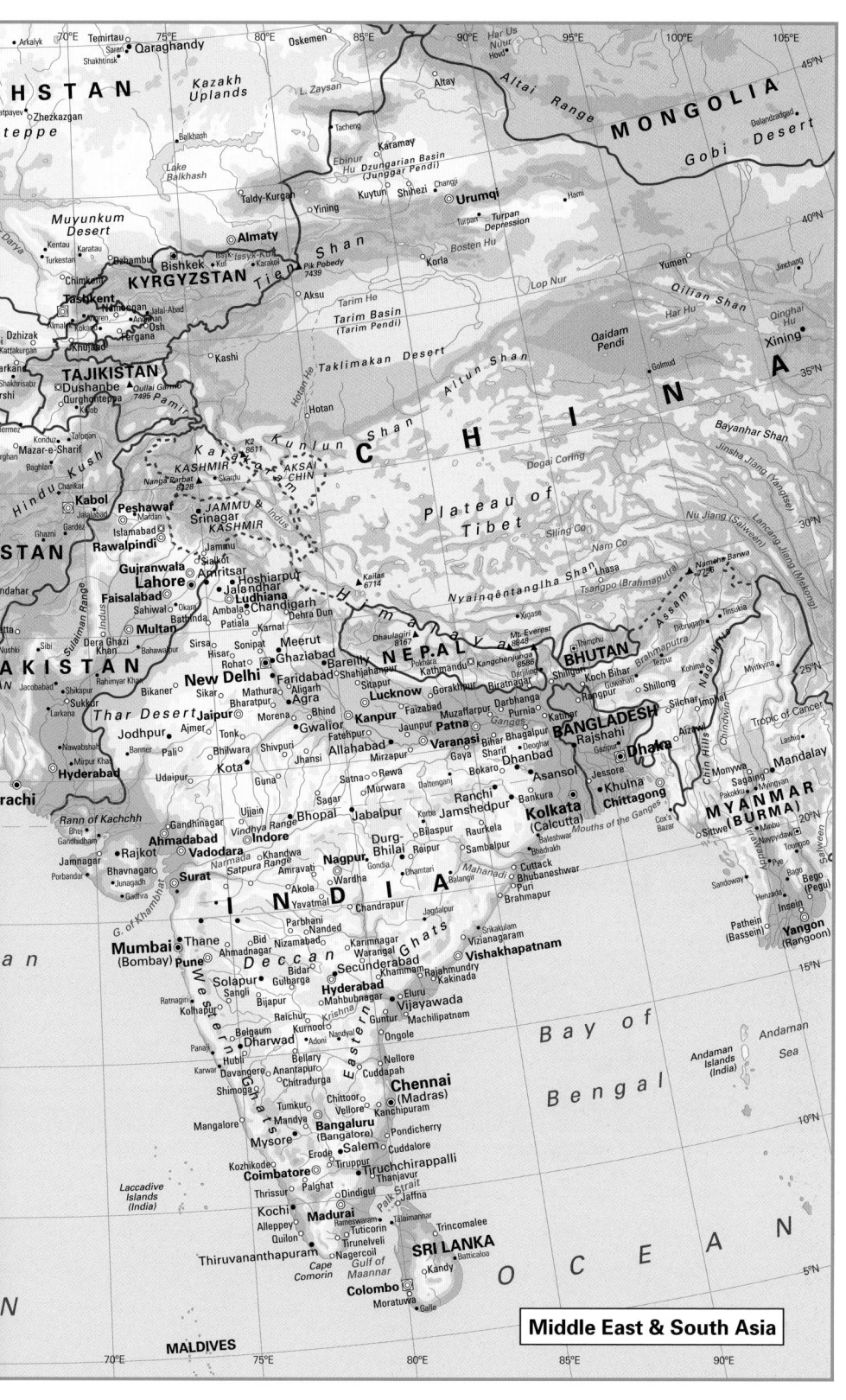

Middle East & South Asia

Pacific

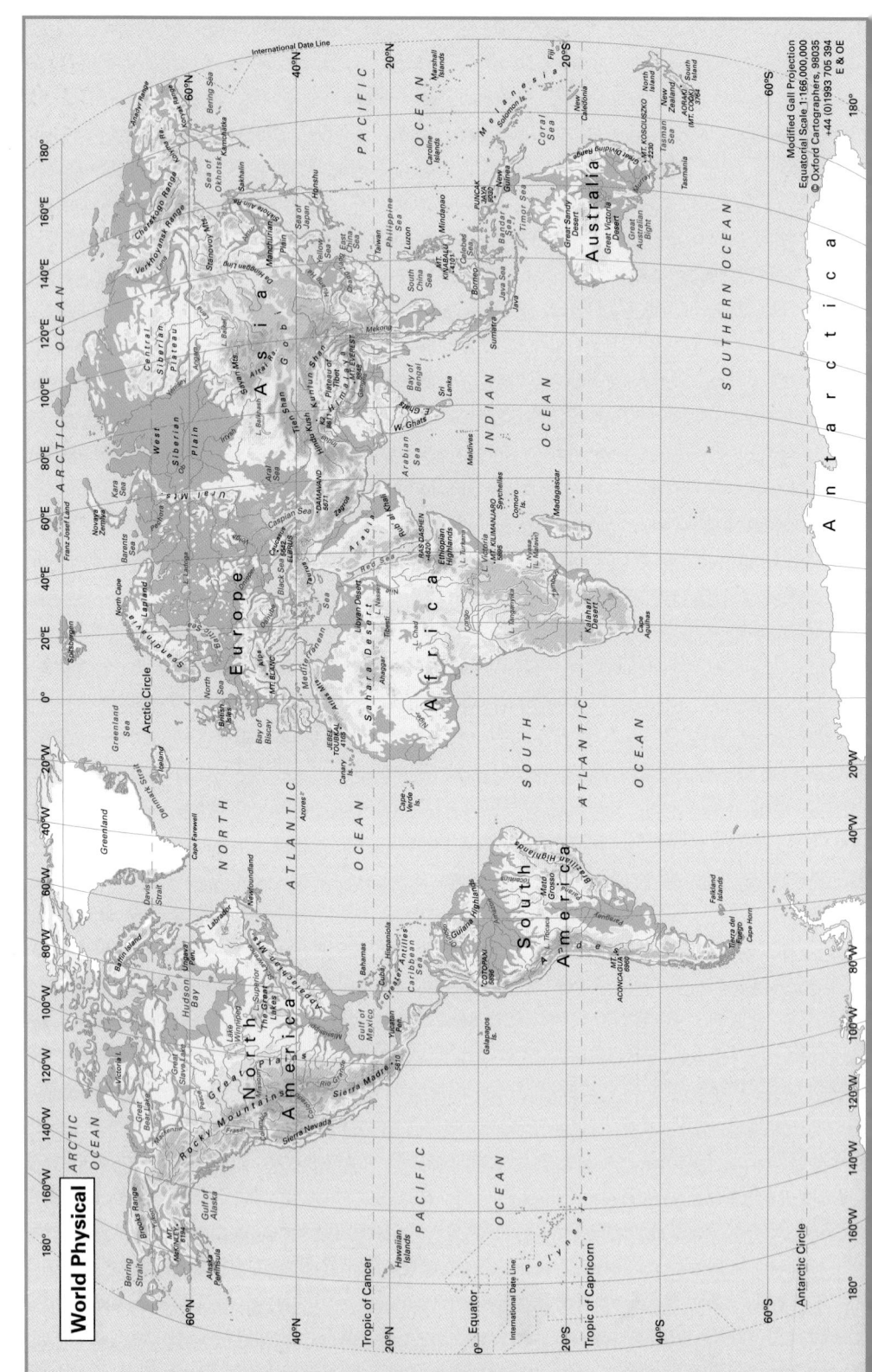

# World Physical

Modified Gall Projection
Equatorial Scale 1:166,000,000
© Oxford Cartographers, 98035
+44 (0)1993 705 394
E & OE

# World Political

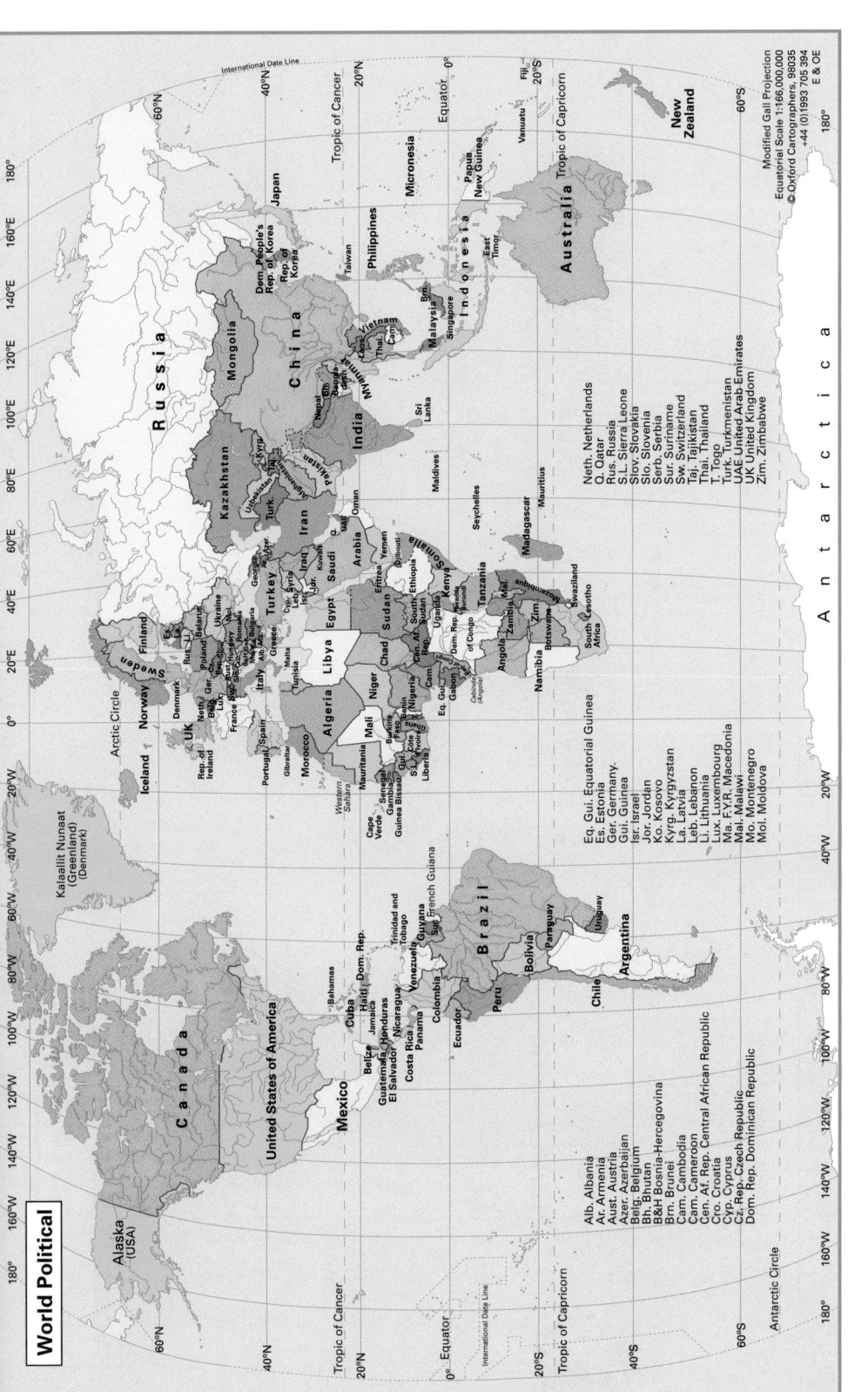

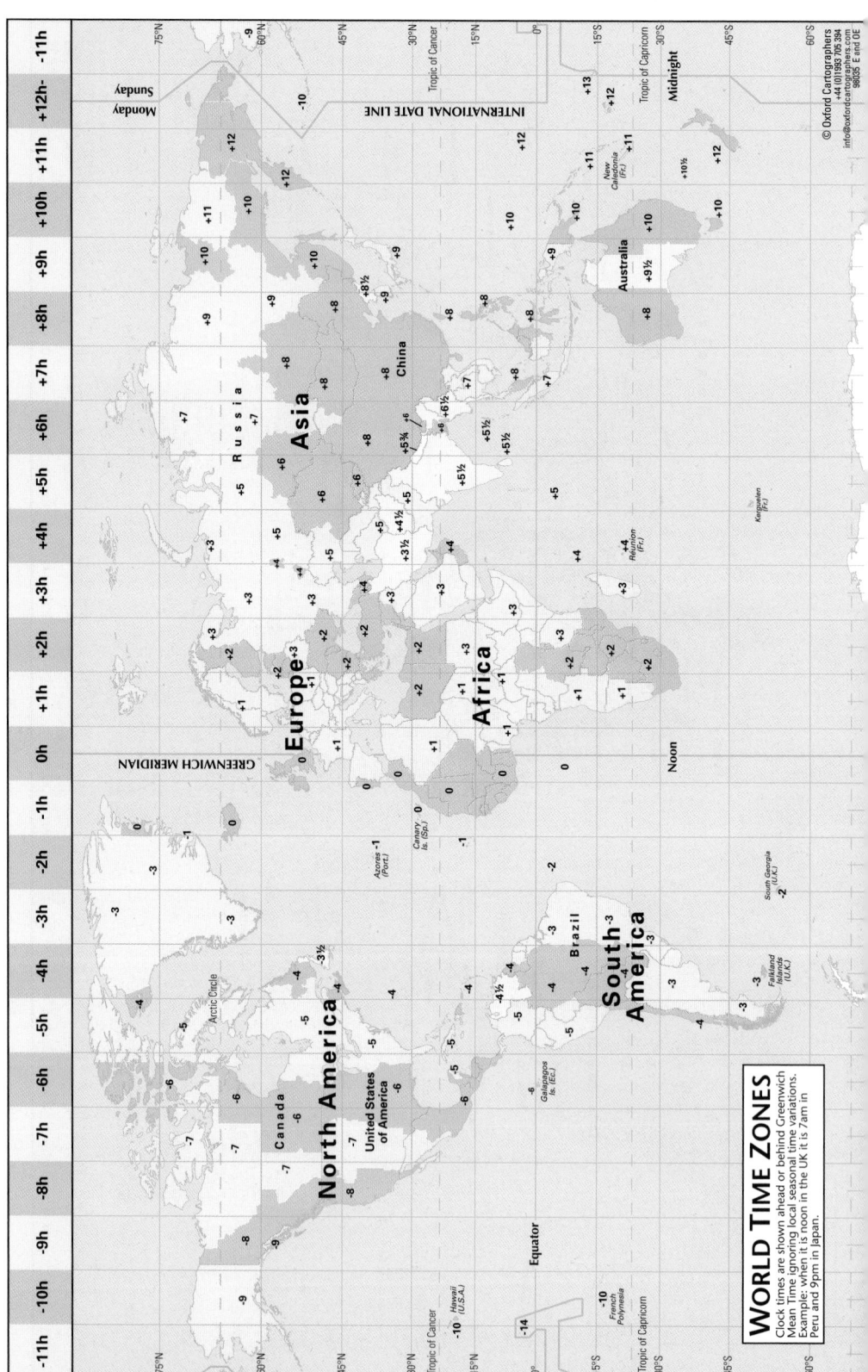

## WORLD TIME ZONES

Clock times are shown ahead or behind Greenwich Mean Time ignoring local seasonal time variations. Example: when it is noon in the UK it is 7am in Peru and 9pm in Japan.

© Oxford Cartographers
+44 (0)1993 705 394
info@oxfordcartographers.com
www.oxfordcartographers.com
9805 E and 0E

# FLAGS OF THE WORLD

The following four pages show the national flag of each country, as it is used for international purposes. In some cases this means that the state flag is shown. Where this is the case the country name is marked (†).

AFGHANISTAN

ALBANIA

ALGERIA

ANDORRA

ANGOLA

ANTIGUA AND BARBUDA

ARGENTINA

ARMENIA

AUSTRALIA

AUSTRIA

AZERBAIJAN

THE BAHAMAS

BAHRAIN

BANGLADESH

BARBADOS

BELARUS

BELGIUM

BELIZE

BENIN

BHUTAN

BOLIVIA†

BOSNIA AND HERCEGOVINA

BOTSWANA

BRAZIL

BRUNEI

BULGARIA

BURKINA FASO

BURUNDI

CAMBODIA

CAMEROON

CANADA

CAPE VERDE

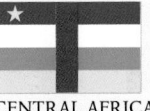
CENTRAL AFRICAN REPUBLIC

CHAD

CHILE

CHINA

COLOMBIA

THE COMOROS

DEM. REPUBLIC OF THE CONGO

REPUBLIC OF THE CONGO

COSTA RICA

CÔTE D'IVOIRE

CROATIA

CUBA

CYPRUS

CZECH REPUBLIC

DENMARK

DJIBOUTI

DOMINICA

DOMINICAN REPUBLIC

 EAST TIMOR

 ECUADOR

 EGYPT

 EL SALVADOR

 EQUATORIAL GUINEA

 ERITREA

 ESTONIA

 ETHIOPIA

 FIJI

 FINLAND

 FRANCE

 GABON

 THE GAMBIA

 GEORGIA

 GERMANY

 GHANA

 GREECE

 GRENADA

 GUATEMALA

 GUINEA

 GUINEA-BISSAU

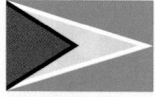 GUYANA

 HAITI†

 HONDURAS

 HUNGARY

 ICELAND

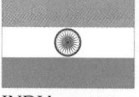 INDIA

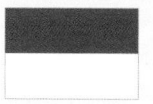 INDONESIA

 IRAN

 IRAQ

 IRELAND

 ISRAEL

 ITALY

 JAMAICA

 JAPAN

 JORDAN

 KAZAKHSTAN

 KENYA

 KIRIBATI

 DEM. PEOPLE'S REPUBLIC OF KOREA

 REPUBLIC OF KOREA

 KOSOVO

 KUWAIT

 KYRGYZSTAN

 LAOS

 LATVIA

 LEBANON

 LESOTHO

LIBERIA

LIBYA

 LIECHTENSTEIN

 LITHUANIA

 LUXEMBOURG

 MACEDONIA

 MADAGASCAR

 MALAWI

 MALAYSIA

 MALDIVES

 MALI

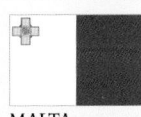 MALTA

 MARSHALL ISLANDS

 MAURITANIA

 MAURITIUS

 MEXICO

 FEDERATED STATES OF MICRONESIA

 MOLDOVA

 MONACO

 MONGOLIA

 MONTENEGRO

 MOROCCO

 MOZAMBIQUE

 MYANMAR

 NAMIBIA

 NAURU

 NEPAL

 THE NETHERLANDS

 NEW ZEALAND

 NICARAGUA

 NIGER

 NIGERIA

 NORWAY

 OMAN

 PAKISTAN

 PALAU

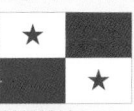 PANAMA

 PAPUA NEW GUINEA

 PARAGUAY

 PERU

 THE PHILIPPINES

 POLAND

 PORTUGAL

 QATAR

 ROMANIA

 RUSSIAN FEDERATION

 RWANDA

 ST CHRISTOPHER AND NEVIS

ST LUCIA

ST VINCENT AND THE GRENADINES

SAMOA

 SAN MARINO†

 SAO TOME AND PRINCIPE

 SAUDI ARABIA

 SENEGAL

 SERBIA†

 SEYCHELLES

 SIERRA LEONE

 SINGAPORE

 SLOVAKIA

 SLOVENIA

 SOLOMON ISLANDS

 SOMALIA

 SOUTH AFRICA

 SOUTH SUDAN

 SPAIN

SRI LANKA

 SUDAN

 SURINAME

 SWAZILAND

 SWEDEN

 SWITZERLAND

 SYRIA

 TAIWAN

 TAJIKISTAN

 TANZANIA

 THAILAND

 TOGO

 TONGA

 TRINIDAD AND TOBAGO

 TUNISIA

 TURKEY

 TURKMENISTAN

 TUVALU

 UGANDA

 UKRAINE

 UNITED ARAB EMIRATES

 UNITED KINGDOM

 UNITED STATES OF AMERICA

 URUGUAY

 UZBEKISTAN

 VANUATU

 VATICAN CITY STATE

 VENEZUELA

 VIETNAM

 YEMEN

 ZAMBIA

 ZIMBABWE

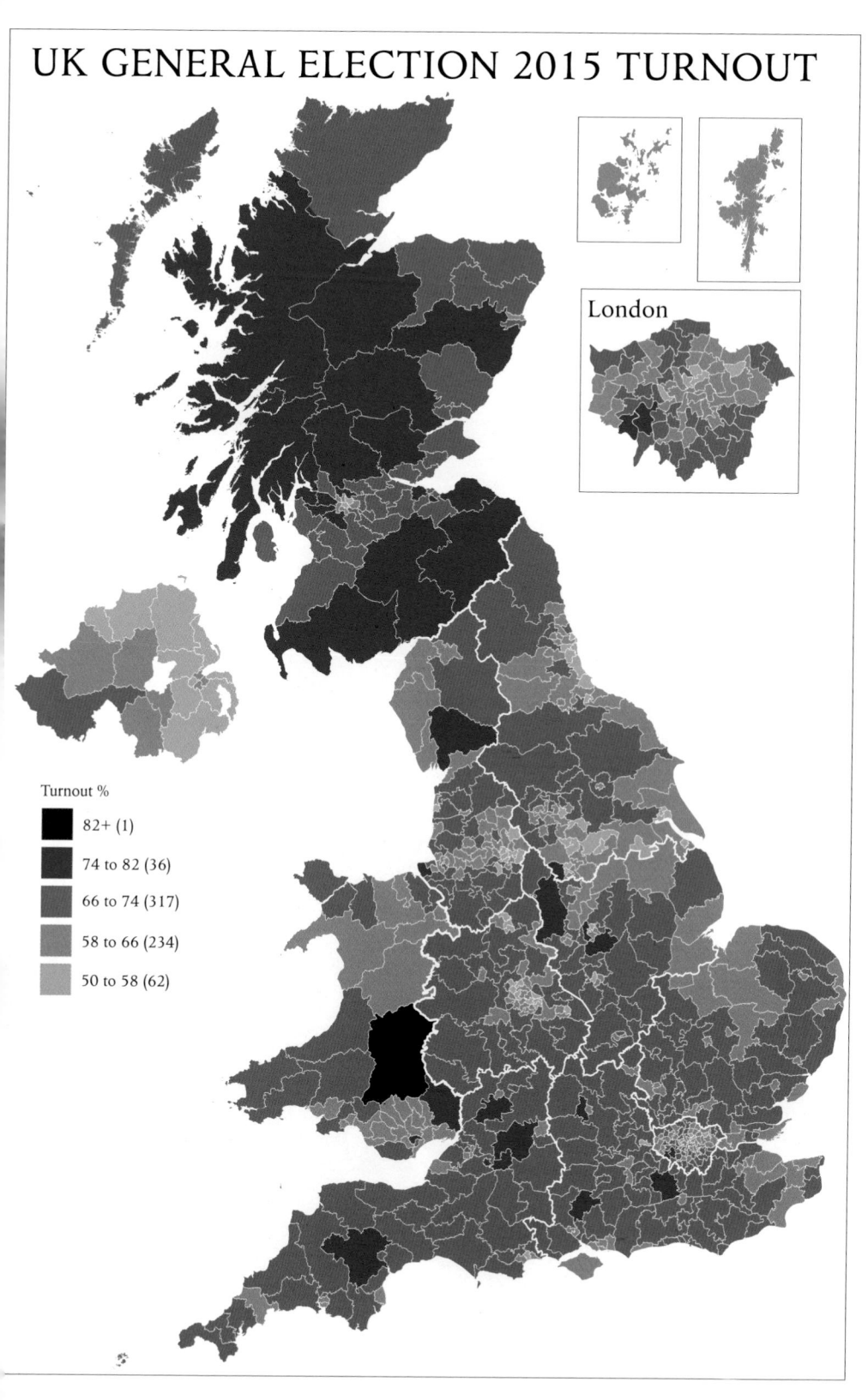

# UK GENERAL ELECTION 2015 TURNOUT

London

Turnout %

- 82+ (1)
- 74 to 82 (36)
- 66 to 74 (317)
- 58 to 66 (234)
- 50 to 58 (62)

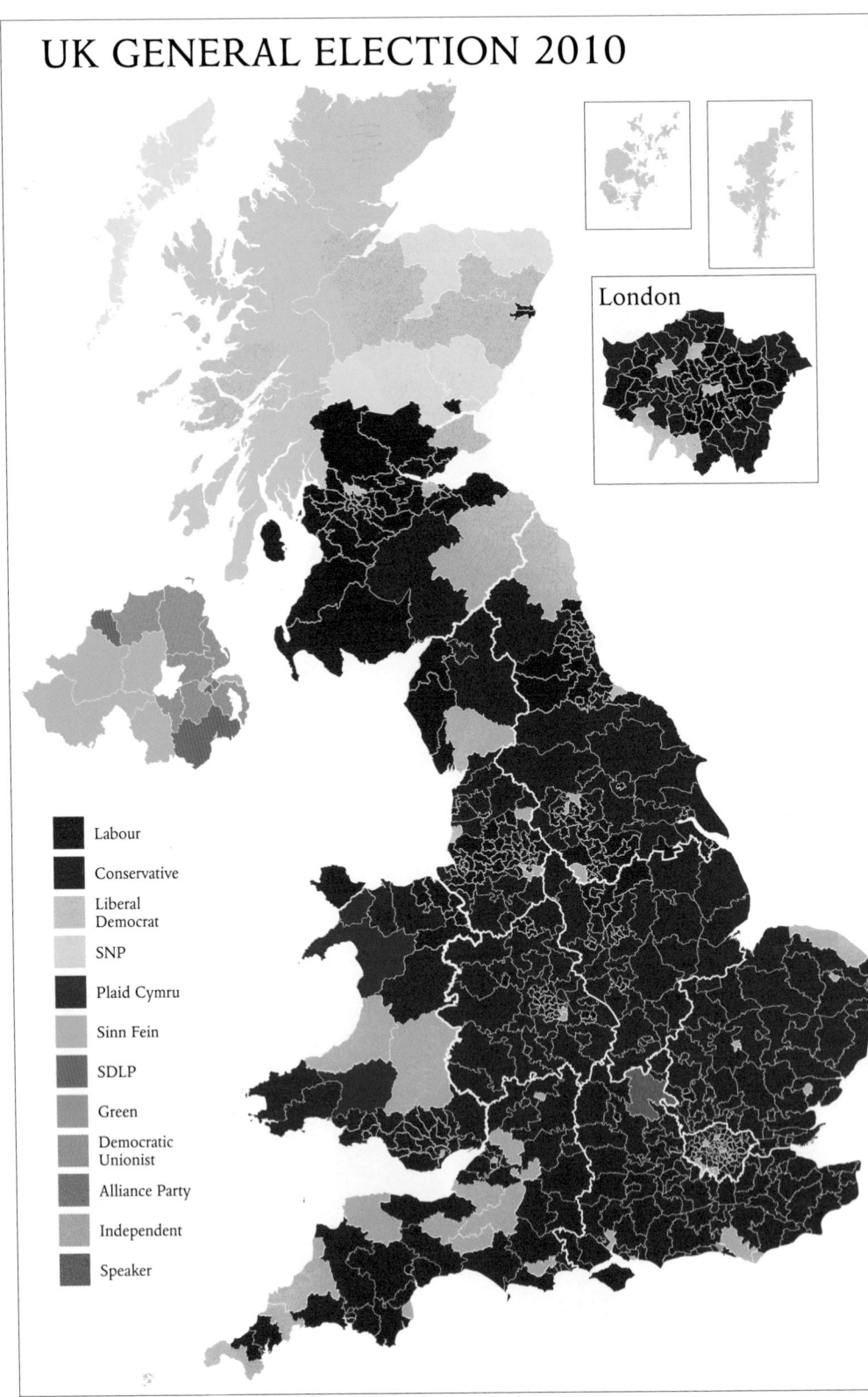

# UK GENERAL ELECTION 2010

London

Labour

Conservative

Liberal
Democrat

SNP

Plaid Cymru

Sinn Fein

SDLP

Green

Democratic
Unionist

Alliance Party

Independent

Speaker

# UK GENERAL ELECTION 2015

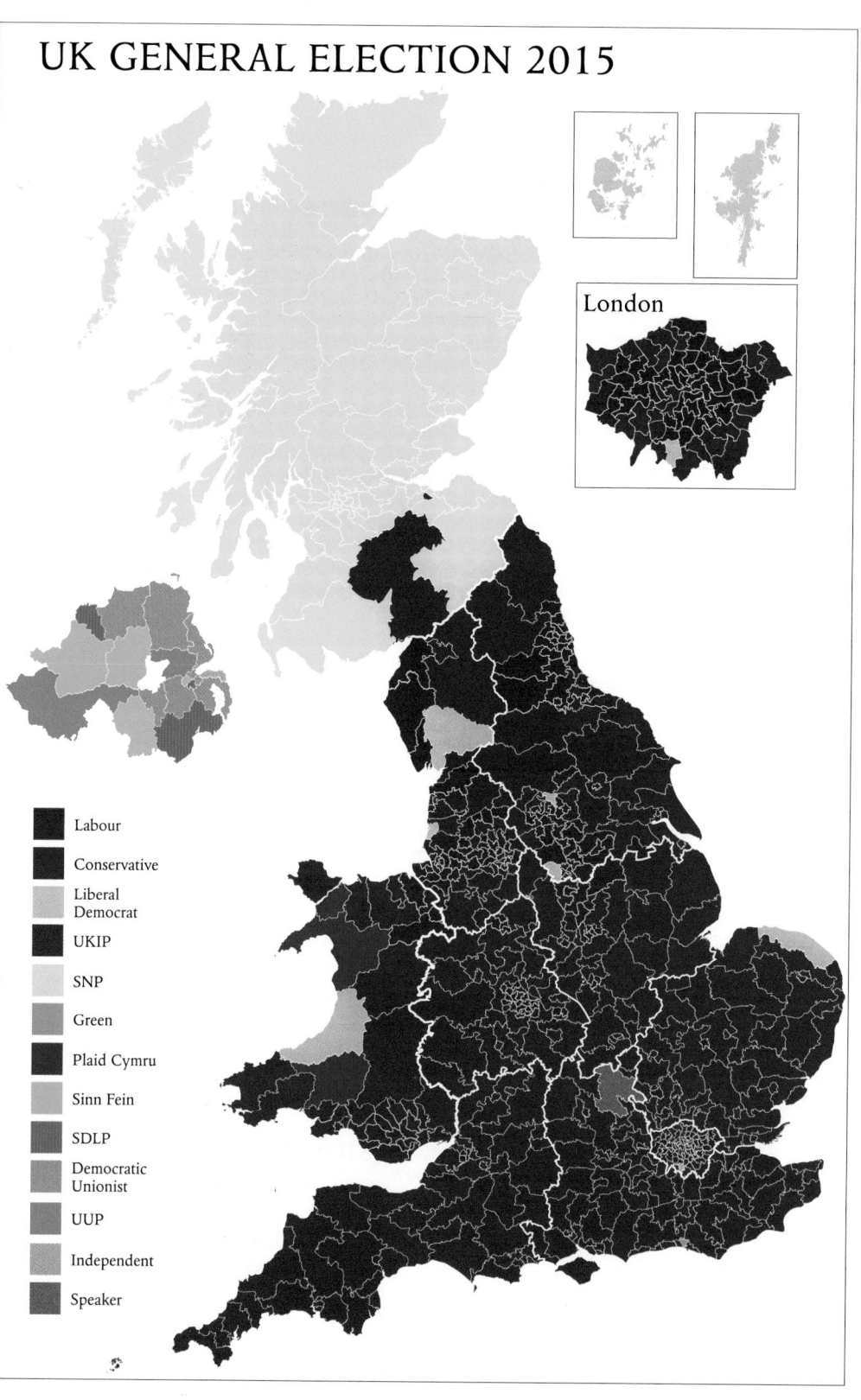

London

Labour
Conservative
Liberal
Democrat
UKIP
SNP
Green
Plaid Cymru
Sinn Fein
SDLP
Democratic
Unionist
UUP
Independent
Speaker

# UK GENERAL ELECTION 2015 STATISTICS

STATE OF THE PARTIES AFTER THE 2015 GENERAL ELECTION

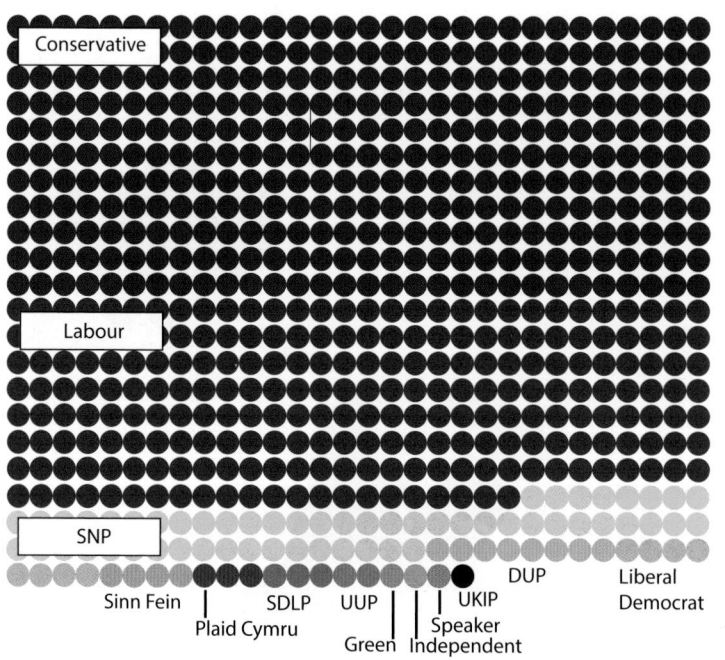

Conservative

Labour

SNP

Sinn Fein | Plaid Cymru | SDLP | UUP | Green Independent | Speaker | UKIP | DUP | Liberal Democrat

177 new MPs

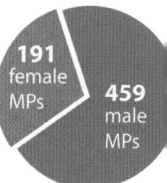

191 female MPs

459 male MPs

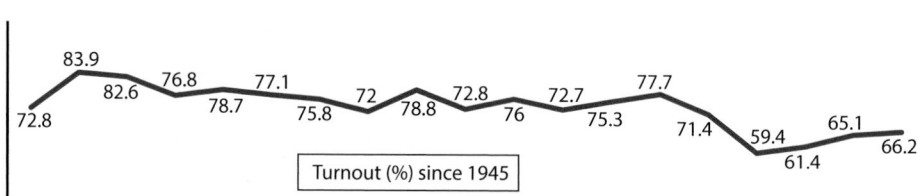

Turnout (%) since 1945

72.8  83.9  82.6  76.8  78.7  77.1  75.8  72  78.8  72.8  76  72.7  75.3  77.7  71.4  59.4  61.4  65.1  66.2

1945 1950 1951 1955 1959 1964 1966 1970 1974 1974 1979 1983 1987 1992 1997 2001 2005 2010 2015
                                        (Feb.)(Oct.)

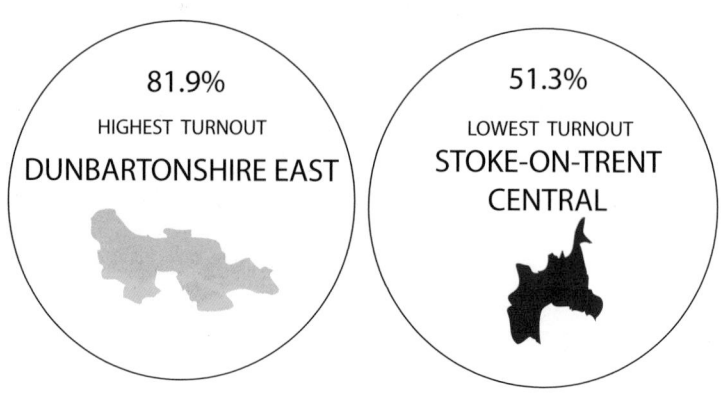

81.9%

HIGHEST TURNOUT

DUNBARTONSHIRE EAST

51.3%

LOWEST TURNOUT

STOKE-ON-TRENT CENTRAL

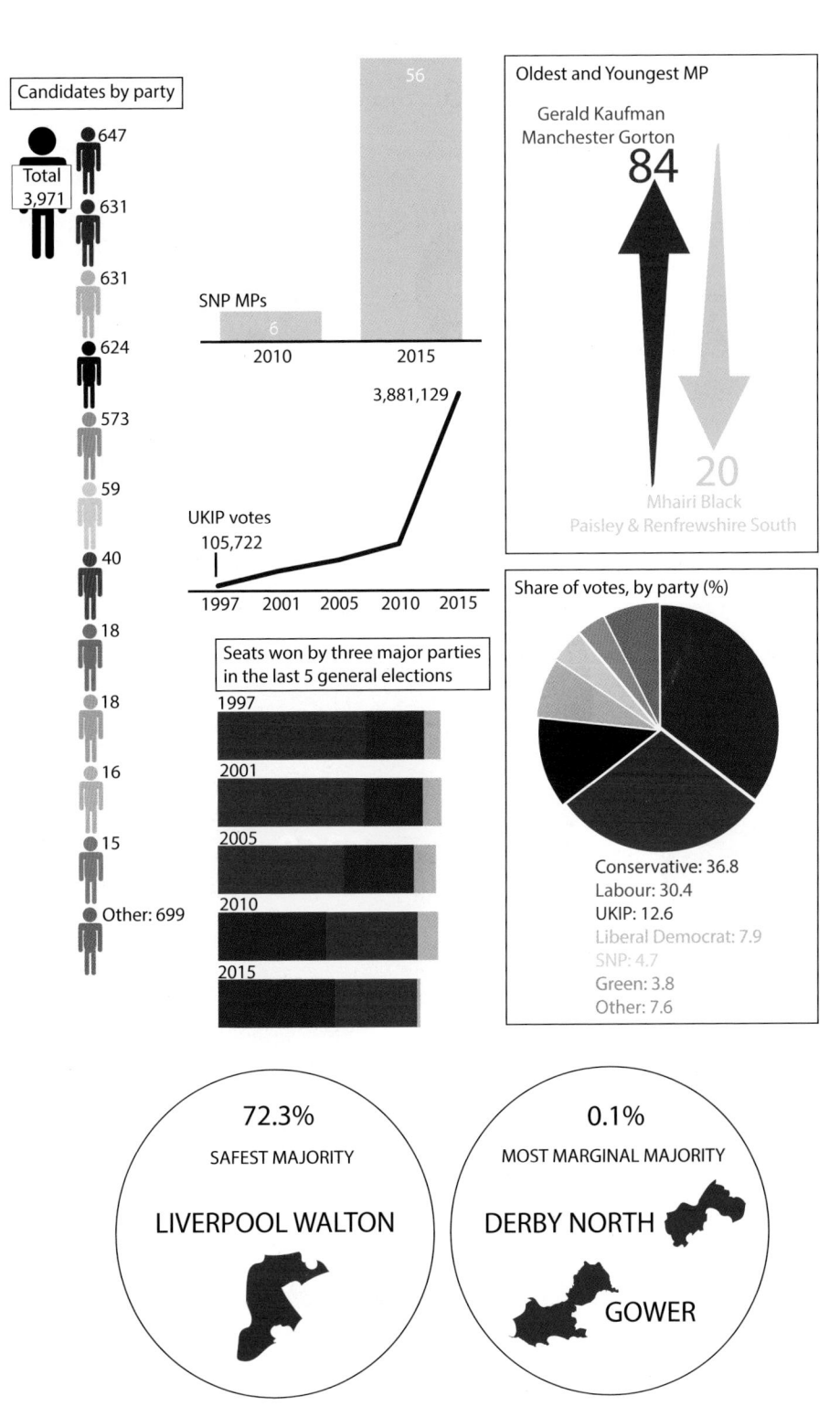

Candidates by party

Total 3,971

- 647
- 631
- 631
- 624
- 573
- 59
- 40
- 18
- 18
- 16
- 15
- Other: 699

SNP MPs

56

6

2010       2015

UKIP votes

3,881,129

105,722

1997   2001   2005   2010   2015

Seats won by three major parties in the last 5 general elections

1997
2001
2005
2010
2015

Oldest and Youngest MP

Gerald Kaufman
Manchester Gorton

84

20

Mhairi Black
Paisley & Renfrewshire South

Share of votes, by party (%)

Conservative: 36.8
Labour: 30.4
UKIP: 12.6
Liberal Democrat: 7.9
SNP: 4.7
Green: 3.8
Other: 7.6

72.3%

SAFEST MAJORITY

LIVERPOOL WALTON

0.1%

MOST MARGINAL MAJORITY

DERBY NORTH

GOWER

# GOVERNMENT DEPARTMENTAL BUDGETS 2015–16

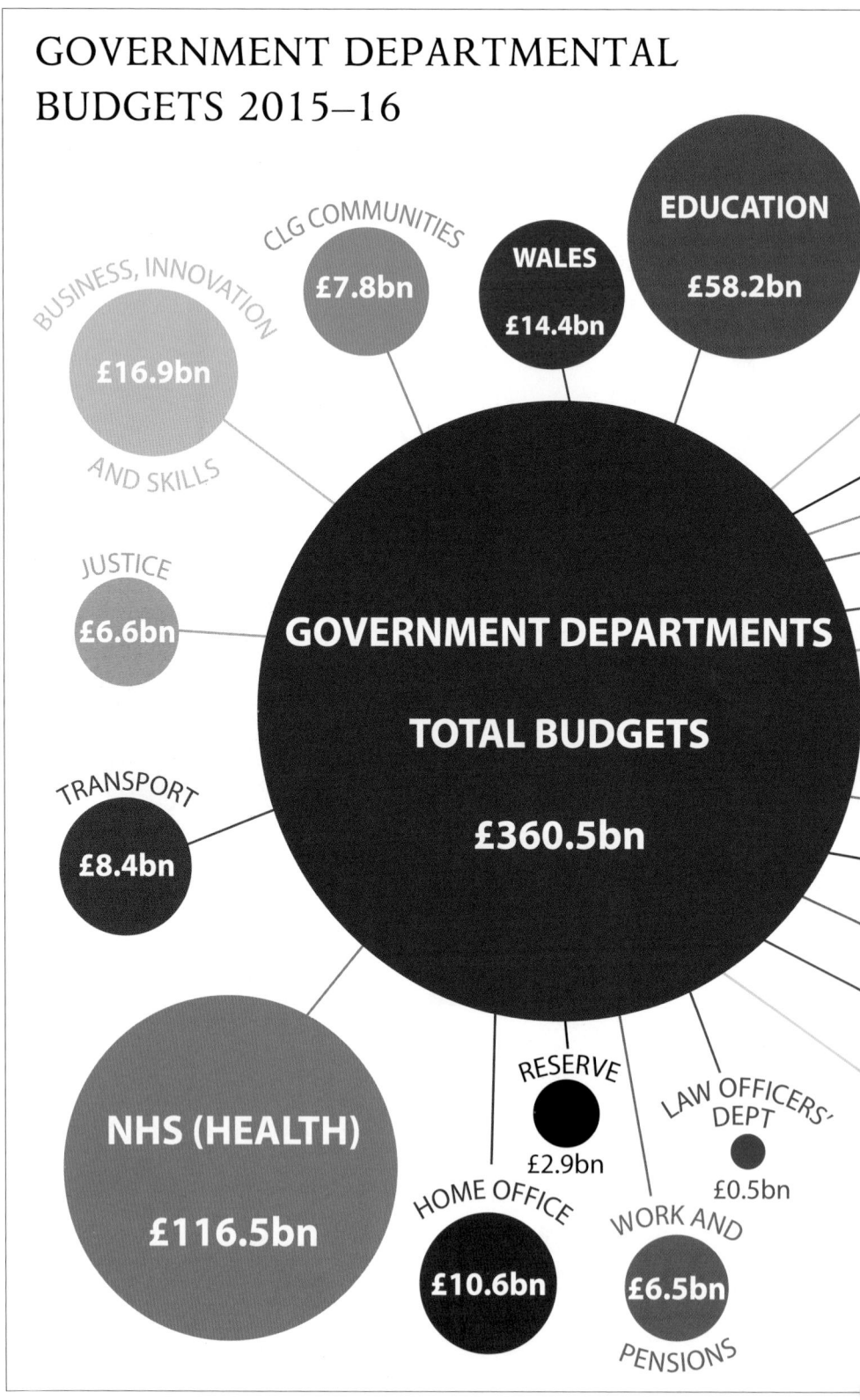

CLG COMMUNITIES
£7.8bn

WALES
£14.4bn

EDUCATION
£58.2bn

BUSINESS, INNOVATION AND SKILLS
£16.9bn

JUSTICE
£6.6bn

GOVERNMENT DEPARTMENTS

TOTAL BUDGETS

£360.5bn

TRANSPORT
£8.4bn

NHS (HEALTH)
£116.5bn

RESERVE
£2.9bn

HOME OFFICE
£10.6bn

LAW OFFICERS' DEPT
£0.5bn

WORK AND PENSIONS
£6.5bn

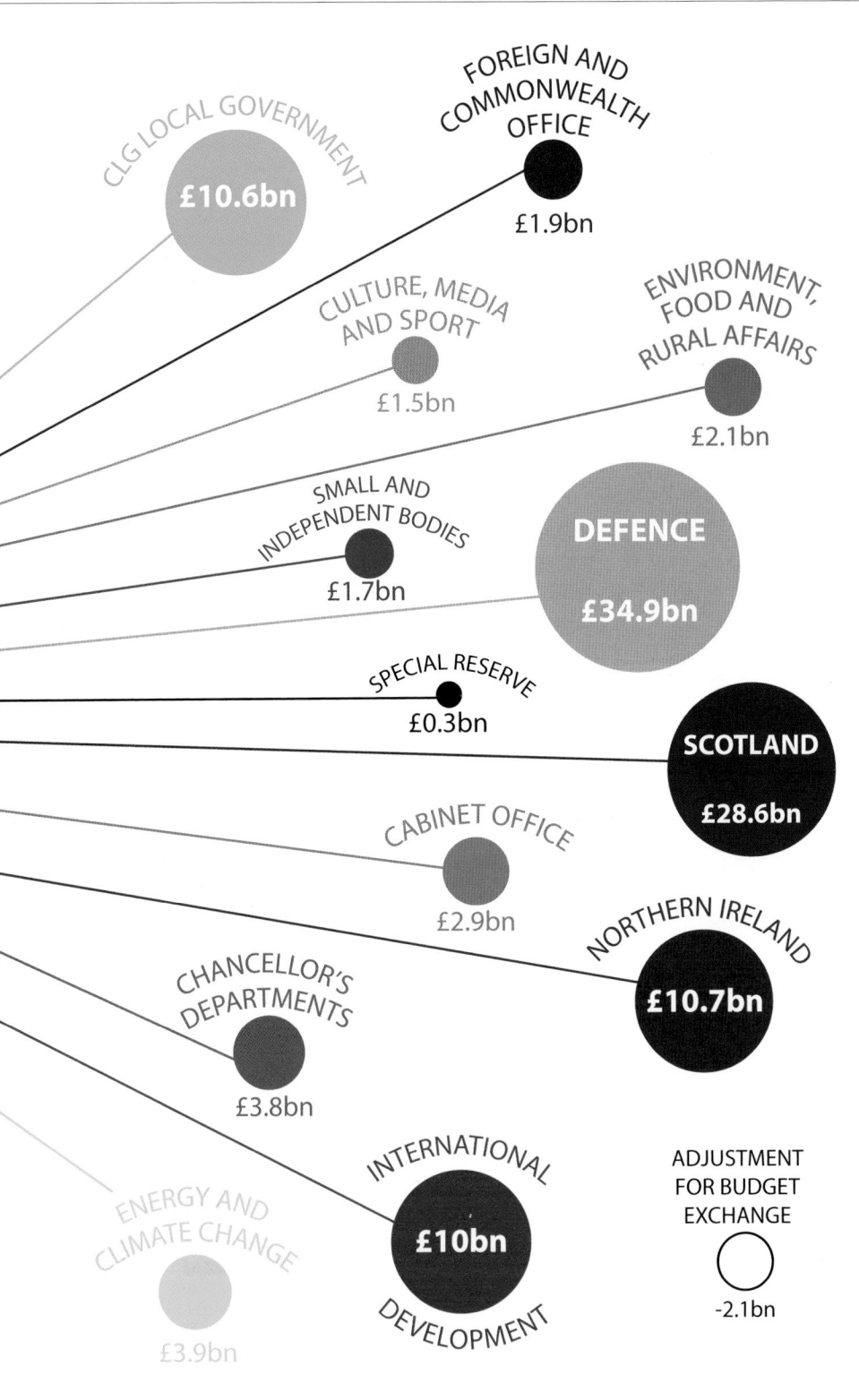

# WORLD PRESS FREEDOM INDEX, 2015

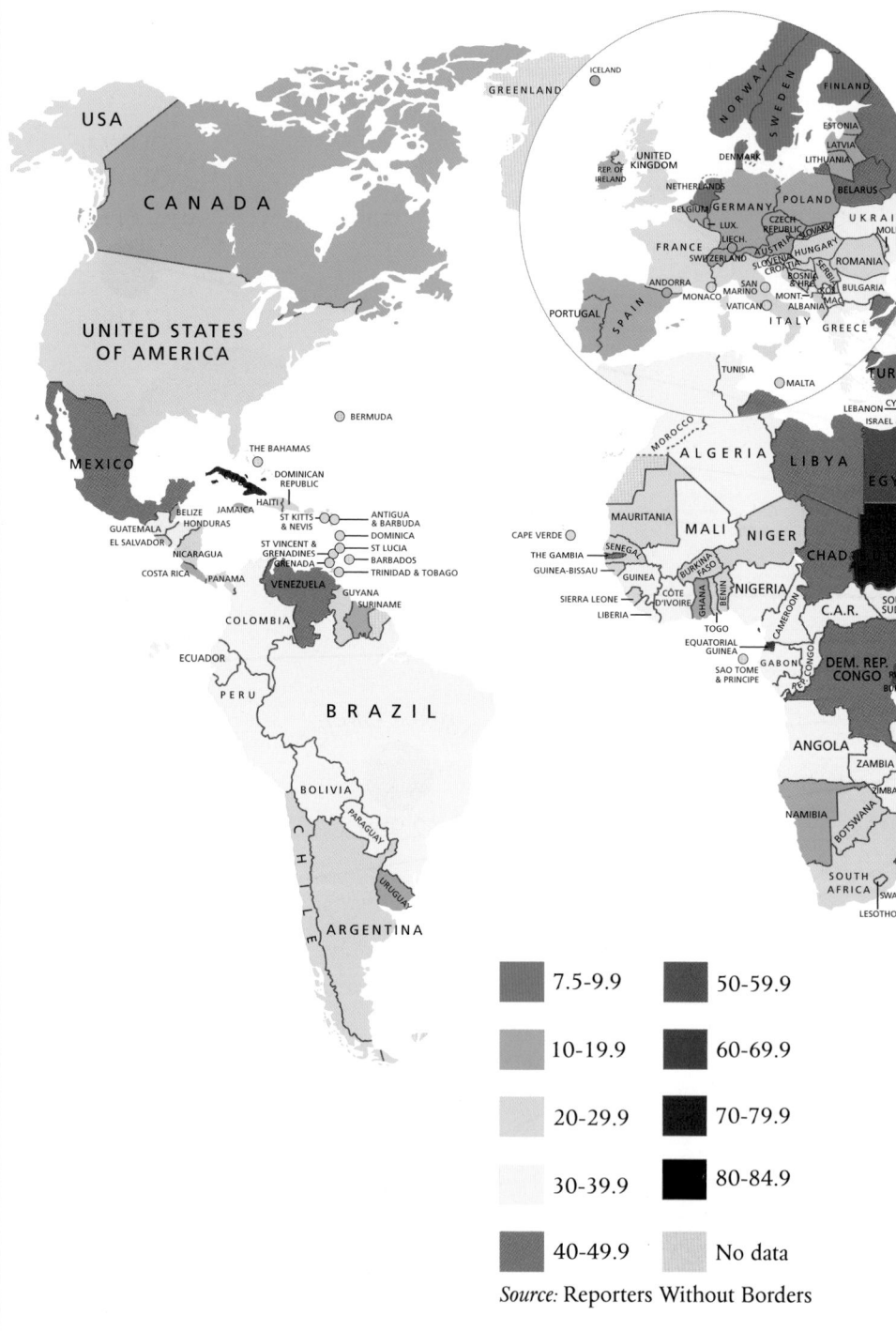

| | |
|---|---|
| 7.5-9.9 | 50-59.9 |
| 10-19.9 | 60-69.9 |
| 20-29.9 | 70-79.9 |
| 30-39.9 | 80-84.9 |
| 40-49.9 | No data |

*Source:* Reporters Without Borders

RUSSIAN FEDERATION

KAZAKHSTAN    MONGOLIA

KYRGYZ

UZBEKISTAN

TAJIK

AFGHANISTAN    D.R. KOREA

REP. KOREA

JAPAN

IRAQ    PAKISTAN    NEPAL

KUW    BANGLADESH    TAIWAN

SAUDI    BA    MYANMAR

ARABIA    QATAR    INDIA

UAE    OMAN    VIETNAM

ERE    YEMEN    THAILAND

DJIBOUTI    CAMBODIA

ETHIOPIA    THE PHILIPPINES    MARSHALL ISLANDS

KENYA    SRI LANKA    BRUNEI    PALAU    MICRONESIA

MALDIVES    MALAYSIA

SEYCHELLES    SINGAPORE    KIRIBATI

TANZANIA    NAURU

THE COMOROS    INDONESIA    PAPUA NEW GUINEA    SOLOMON ISLANDS    TUVALU

MALAWI    EAST TIMOR    SAMOA

MOZAMBIQUE    MADAGASCAR    VANUATU    FIJI

MAURITIUS    TONGA

AUSTRALIA

The World Press Freedom Index is a global indicator of media freedom; the index ranges from 0 to 100 indicating low or high levels of censorship respectively. Regional instability and political conflict typically affect the level of press freedom. However, the index is based on factors such as legislative and physical restrictions against journalists, rather than political systems.

NEW ZEALAND

In 2015 the country with the greatest press freedom was Finland, with a score of 7.52; the lowest was Eritrea with 84.86. The UK scored 20.

With the regional model a score between 1 and 100 is produced to indicate the level of press freedom, with 100 as the most restrictive:
1. Europe, 18.6
2. The Americas, 30.8
3. Africa, 35.9
4. Asia-Pacific, 42.6
5. Eastern Europe and Central Asia, 46.1
6. The Middle East and North Africa, 49.2

# WINNERS OF THE NOBEL PRIZE BY NATIONALITY

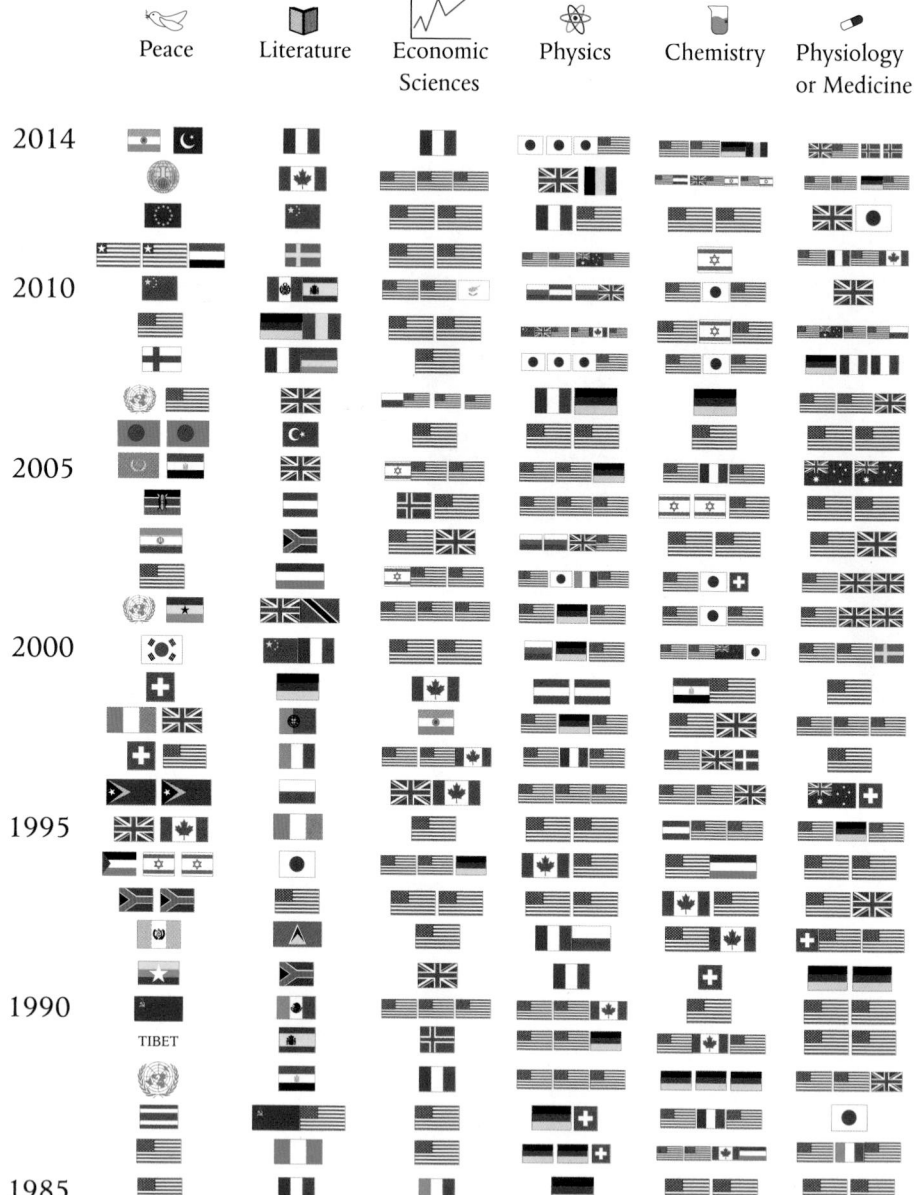

If more than one national flag is shown, this represents multiple laureates for the prize.
Flags that are connected represent a laureate's dual nationality.

Marie-Louise Coleiro Preca was confirmed as president in April 2014.

Under the 1974 constitution, the president is elected by the legislature for a five-year term, renewable once. The unicameral legislature, the House of Representatives, has 69 members directly elected for a five-year term; if a party wins the majority of votes in a general election without winning a majority of seats, new seats are created until that party holds a majority of one seat. The prime minister is appointed by the president and nominates the other ministers.

**HEAD OF STATE**
*President,* Marie-Louise Coleiro Preca, *elected* 1 April 2014, *took office* 4 April 2014

**SELECTED GOVERNMENT MEMBERS** *as at June 2015*
*Prime Minister,* Joseph Muscat
*Economy,* Christian Cardona
*Finance,* Edward Scicluna
*Foreign Affairs,* George Vella
*Home Affairs,* Carmelo Abela

**MALTA HIGH COMMISSION**
Malta House, 36–38 Piccadilly, London W1J 0LE
**T** 020-7292 4800 **E** maltahighcommission.london@gov.mt
**W** www.foreign.gov.mt/uk
*High Commissioner,* HE Norman Hamilton, *apptd* 2013

**BRITISH HIGH COMMISSION**
Whitehall Mansions, Ta' Xbiex Seafront, Ta' Xbiex XBX 1026
**T** (+356) 2323 0000 **E** bhcvalletta@fco.gov.uk
**W** www.gov.uk/government/world/malta
*High Commissioner,* HE Rob Luke, *apptd* 2012

**DEFENCE**

| *Aged 16–49, 2010 est* | *Males* | *Females* |
|---|---|---|
| Available for military service | 95,499 | 90,919 |
| Fit for military service | 79,645 | 75,684 |

*Military expenditure* – US$59.8m (2014)

**ECONOMY AND TRADE**
The mainstay of the economy for over a century was the dockyard, and shipbuilding and ship repairs remain significant industries, but since the 1980s Malta has developed into a tourist destination, financial services centre and freight trans-shipment point. Tourism is now the main source of income, followed by foreign trade and manufacturing, especially of electronics and pharmaceuticals. All were adversely affected by the global downturn in 2009, and new fiscal measures contributed further to a deterioration in public finances in 2011. An excessive deficit procedure against Malta was opened by the EU in 2013; the deficit is predicted to decrease significantly by 2016. The service sector accounts for 85.6 per cent of GDP, industry for 12.9 per cent and agriculture for 1.6 per cent.

The main trading partners are other EU states. Principal exports are electrical machinery, mechanical appliances, fish and shellfish, pharmaceuticals and printed material. The main imports are mineral fuels and oil, machinery, aircraft and other transport equipment, semi-manufactured goods, food, beverages and tobacco.
*GNI* – US$8,881m; US$20,980 per capita (2013)
*Annual average growth of GDP* – 2.2 per cent (2014)
*Inflation rate* – 1 per cent (2014 est)
*Population below poverty line* – 15.7 per cent (2013 est)
*Unemployment* – 6.6 per cent (2015 est)
*Total external debt* – US$51,080m (2013 est)

*Imports* – US$7,479m (2013)
*Exports* – US$5,182m (2013)

**BALANCE OF PAYMENTS**
*Trade* – US$2,297m deficit (2013)
*Current Account* – US$291m surplus (2015)

| *Trade with UK* | *2013* | *2014* |
|---|---|---|
| Imports from UK | £434,431,997 | £401,915,118 |
| Exports to UK | £109,138,448 | £124,276,402 |

**COMMUNICATIONS**
*Airports and waterways* – The international airport is at Luqa, south-west of Valletta; the main ports are Marsaxlokk (Malta's freeport) and Valletta, and there is a large merchant fleet of 1,650 ships of over 1,000 tonnes
*Roadways* – 2,704km
*Telecommunications* – 229,700 fixed lines and 539,500 mobile subscriptions (2012); there were 240,600 internet users in 2009
*Internet code and IDD* – mt; 356 (from UK), 44 (to UK)
*Major broadcasters* – Television Malta (TVM) and Radio Malta are the public broadcasters
*Press* – Daily national newspapers include *Times of Malta, Malta Independent* (both English language) and *L-Orizzont* (Maltese)
*WPFI score* – 24,16 (48)

**EDUCATION AND HEALTH**
Education is free at all levels and compulsory between the ages of five and 16.
*Literacy rate* – 99.0 per cent (2015 est)
*Gross enrolment ratio (percentage of relevant age group)* – primary 96 per cent; secondary 95 per cent; tertiary 41 per cent (2012 est)
*Life expectancy (years)* – 80.11 (2014 est)
*Mortality rate* – 8.96 (2014 est)
*Birth rate* – 10.24 (2014 est)
*Infant mortality rate* – 3.59 (2014 est)

# MARSHALL ISLANDS

*Republic of the Marshall Islands*

*Area* – 181 sq. km (plus 11,673 sq. km of lagoon waters)
*Capital* – Majuro; population, 31,000 (2014)
*Major towns* – Ebeye, Rita
*Currency* – US dollar (US$) of 100 cents
*Population* – 72,191 rising at 1.66 per cent a year (2015 est); mainly Micronesian. About 70 per cent of the population lives on Majuro and Kwajalein
*Religion* – Christian (Protestant 54.8 per cent, Assembly of God 25.8 per cent, Roman Catholic 8.4 per cent)
*Language* – Marshallese, English (both official)
*Population density* – 292 per sq. km (2013)
*Urban population* – 72.5 per cent (2013 est)
*Median age (years)* – 22.5 (2014 est)
*National anthem* – 'Forever Marshall Islands'
*National day* – 1 May (Constitution Day)
*Death penalty* – Abolished for all crimes (since 1986)
*Life expectancy (years)* – 72.58 (2014 est)
*Mortality rate* – 4.24 (2014 est)
*Birth rate* – 26.36 (2014 est)
*Infant mortality rate* – 21.39 (2014 est)

**CLIMATE AND TERRAIN**
The republic consists of two chains of 29 atolls, five islands and over 1,000 islets in the western Pacific Ocean. All of

the islands are low-lying (the highest point is 10m) and vulnerable to rising sea levels, which could submerge them by the mid-21st century. The climate is tropical, with a wet season from June to November.

## HISTORY AND POLITICS

The Marshall Islands were first claimed by Spain in 1592 but were left largely undisturbed. Subsequently they were seized by Germany and formally became a protectorate in 1886. Japan took control of the islands in 1914 on behalf of the Allied powers and administered them from 1920 until 1944, when they were captured by US forces. In 1947 the islands became part of the UN Trust Territory of the Pacific Islands, administered by the USA. Between 1946 and 1958, US nuclear weapons were tested on Bikini and Enewetak atolls. Enewetak has been partially decontaminated but Bikini is uninhabitable; the USA paid compensation to the test victims in the 1980s but the government is seeking further compensation to cover the medical care of radiation victims and rectify environmental damage.

The islands became internally self-governing in 1979, and US administration ended in 1986, when a compact of free association between the Republic of the Marshall Islands and the USA came into effect. Under this agreement, the USA recognised the republic as a sovereign and independent state but retained responsibility for external security and defence as well as giving financial help. UN trust territory status was terminated in 1990 and full independence was granted in December 1990. A renegotiated compact with the USA was signed in 2003. The USA retains control of the Kwajalein atoll, where it has a military base and missile tracking station.

There were no formal political parties in the 2011 legislative elections, with all 33 members of the chamber standing as independents. Christopher Loeak was elected president in the 2012 presidential election, beating the incumbent Jurelang Zedkaia by ten votes. New legislative elections were due in November 2015.

Under the 1979 constitution, the executive president is elected by the legislature from among its members to serve a four-year term. The unicameral legislature, the *Nitijela,* has 33 members, directly elected for a four-year term. There are no formal political parties, although groupings of like-minded independents have emerged in recent years. There is also a 12-member Council of Chiefs *(Iroij)* which has a consultative and advisory role.

HEAD OF STATE
*President,* Christopher Loeak, *elected* 4 January 2012, *sworn in* 12 January 2012

SELECTED GOVERNMENT MEMBERS *as at June 2015*
*Finance,* Jack Ading
*Foreign Affairs,* Tony A. de Brum
*Internal Affairs,* David Kabua

BRITISH AMBASSADOR
HE Asif Ahmad, *apptd* 2013, resident at Manila, the Philippines

## ECONOMY AND TRADE

The islands have few natural resources, apart from possible seabed mineral deposits, and the economy is dependent on aid from the USA, supplemented by ship registration fees and the sale of fishing licences. Most islanders live by subsistence farming and fishing, with coconuts, breadfruit and fish the main commercial crops. A small-scale industrial sector produces copra and handicrafts and processes tuna. Tourism

is being encouraged but has declined recently which, with a similar decline in fishing licence sales, has limited economic growth. The government is the largest employer. The main trading partners are Japan, the USA, New Zealand, Australia, China and Taiwan. Principal exports are copra and coconut products, handicrafts and fish. Main imports include food and fuel.

*GNI* – US$226m; US$4,310 per capita (2013)
*Annual average growth of GDP* – 3.2 per cent (2014 est)
*Inflation rate* – 12.9 per cent (2008 est)
*Unemployment* – 36 per cent (2006 est)
*Total external debt* – US$87m (2008 est)

| Trade with UK | 2013 | 2014 |
| --- | --- | --- |
| Imports from UK | £913,160 | £6,935,681 |
| Exports to UK | £2,636,317 | £402,414 |

## COMMUNICATIONS

*Airports and waterways* – There are four airports throughout the islands; Majuro is the main airport as well as the main port, with a merchant fleet of 1,593 ships of over 1,000 tonnes, 1,468 of which are foreign-owned
*Roadways* – There are 2,028km of surfaced roads
*Telecommunications* – 4,400 fixed lines and 3,800 mobile subscriptions (2010); there were 2,200 internet users in 2009
*Internet code and IDD* – mh; 692 (from UK), 011 44 (to UK)
*Media* – MBC TV is the state-run broadcaster; the English and Marshallese-language *Marshall Islands Journal* is published on a weekly basis

# MAURITANIA

*Al-Jumhuriyah al-Islamiyah al-Muritaniyah* – Islamic Republic of Mauritania

*Area* – 1,030,700 sq. km
*Capital* – Nouakchott; population, 945,000 (2014)
*Major towns* – Kaedi, Kiffa, Nouadhibou, Rosso, Zuwarat
*Currency* – Ouguiya (UM) of 5 khoums
*Population* – 3,596,702 rising at 2.23 per cent a year (2015 est)
*Religion* – Muslim 100 per cent (official, almost entirely Sunni) (est)
*Language* – Arabic (official), Pulaar, Soninke, Wolof, French
*Population density* – 4 per sq. km (2013)
*Urban population* – 42 per cent (2013 est)
*Median age (years)* – 19.9 (2014 est)
*National anthem* – 'National Anthem of Mauritania'
*National day* – 28 November (Independence Day)
*Death penalty* – Retained (last used 1987)
*CPI score* – 30 (124)
*Literacy rate* – 62.6 per cent (2015 est)

*Gross enrolment ratio (percentage of relevant age group)* – primary 97 per cent; secondary 30 per cent; tertiary 5 per cent (2013 est)
*Health expenditure (per capita)* – US$44 (2012)
*Hospital beds (per 1,000 people)* – 0.4 (2006)
*Life expectancy (years)* – 62.28 (2014 est)
*Mortality rate* – 8.35 (2014 est)
*Birth rate* – 31.83 (2014 est)
*Infant mortality rate* – 56.06 (2014 est)

## CLIMATE AND TERRAIN
About 60 per cent of the country is covered by the plains of the Sahara Desert, with some hills in the centre. The terrain is arid, apart from in the Senegal river valley on the southern border; most of the population lives there or on the coast at Nouakchott and Nouadhibou. Elevation extremes range from Kediet Ijill (915m) to −5m (Sebkhet Te-n-Dghamcha). There is a desert climate; the north of the country is virtually rainless, while the south receives some unreliable rainfall between June and October. Humidity can be high in the wet season, especially on the coast. Average temperatures range from 20.3°C in January to 33.9°C in June.

## HISTORY AND POLITICS
Eastern Mauritania was part of the Ghana Empire and then the Muslim Almoravid and Almohad empires from the 11th to the 13th century. The area became part of the French West Africa protectorate in 1903 and then a colony in 1920. The country became independent as the Islamic Republic of Mauritania on 28 November 1960.

Mauritania has experienced several military coups and periods of military rule since independence. The 1984 coup brought to power Col. Maaouya ould Sid Ahmed Taya, who restored civilian rule in 1992 with multi-party elections in which he was elected president. President Taya was deposed in a military coup in 2005 and after a period of transitional government, elections were held in late 2006 and early 2007.

The 2007 presidential election was won by Sidi ould Cheikh Abdallahi who was subsequently overthrown in a military coup after attempting to sack four military leaders. Democracy was restored with the 2009 presidential election, which was won by General Mohamed ould Abdelaziz, who had led the 2008 coup, but the 2011 legislative elections were postponed. In December 2013 Abdelaziz's Union for the Republic party won a majority in the first legislative elections since 2006, although the polls were widely boycotted by opposition parties. President Abdelaziz was elected for a further five-year term on 30 June 2014.

The 1991 constitution was amended in 2007 to reduce the term of the president, who is directly elected, to five years, renewable once. The bicameral legislature comprises the National Assembly (the lower house) and the senate. The National Assembly has 95 members who are directly elected for a five-year term. The senate has 56 members (including three representing Mauritanians abroad), who are indirectly elected for a six-year term; one-third is elected every two years.

HEAD OF STATE
*President,* Gen. Mohamed ould Abdelaziz, *elected* 18 July 2009, *sworn in* 5 August 2009, *re-elected* 30 June 2014

SELECTED GOVERNMENT MEMBERS *as at June 2015*
*Prime Minister,* Yahya ould Hademine
*Finance,* Mokhtar ould Diay
*Foreign Affairs,* Fatma Vall mint Soueinae
*Interior,* Mohamed ould Ahmed Salem

EMBASSY OF THE ISLAMIC REPUBLIC OF MAURITANIA
Carlyle House, 235 Vauxhall Bridge Road, London SW1V 1EJ
T 020-7233 6158 E info@mauritanianembassy.org.uk
W www.mauritanianembassy.org.uk
*Chargé d'Affaires,* Mohamed Yahya ould Sidi Haiba

BRITISH AMBASSADOR
HE Clive Alderton, *apptd* 2012, resident at Rabat, Morocco

## DEFENCE

| *Aged 16–49, 2010 est* | *Males* | *Females* |
| --- | --- | --- |
| Available for military service | 718,713 | 804,622 |
| Fit for military service | 480,042 | 581,473 |

*Military expenditure* – US$150m (2014)

## ECONOMY AND TRADE
Mauritania is one of the poorer countries in the region, with 40 per cent of the population living below the poverty line and unemployment at 30 per cent. Past economic mismanagement and droughts created a huge foreign debt, although the country has benefited from debt cancellation since 2000. The economy is expected to grow at around 5.5 per cent a year in 2015–16.

Natural resources include iron ore, copper, gold, gypsum, oil (offshore production at the Banda gas field was due to begin in 2015) and rich fishing waters, although the latter are threatened by over-exploitation. Agriculture and animal husbandry, mainly at subsistence level, are the mainstay of the economy, accounting for 17.1 per cent of GDP and engaging 50 per cent of the population. The main industries are fish processing, oil production and refining, and mining.

The main trading partners are China, EU countries and USA. Principal exports are iron ore, fish and fish products, gold, copper and oil. The main imports are machinery, petroleum products, capital goods, food and consumer goods.
*GNI* – US$4,116m; US$1,060 per capita (2013)
*Annual average growth of GDP* – 6.8 per cent (2014)
*Inflation rate* – 4.4 per cent (2014 est)
*Population below poverty line* – 40 per cent (2004 est)
*Unemployment* – 30.6 per cent (2015 est)
*Total external debt* – $3,996m (2014 est)
*Imports* – US$3,974m (2013)
*Exports* – US$2,680m (2013)

BALANCE OF PAYMENTS
*Trade* – US$1,294m deficit (2013)
*Current Account* – US$728m deficit (2015 est)

| *Trade with UK* | *2013* | *2014* |
| --- | --- | --- |
| Imports from UK | £55,898,171 | £13,584,487 |
| Exports to UK | £5,390,177 | £43,878,879 |

## COMMUNICATIONS
*Transport* – There are nine airports; the main seaports are Nouakchott and Nouadhibou; there are 3,158km of roadways and 728km of railways
*Telecommunications* – 65,100 fixed lines and 4.02; million mobile subscriptions (2012); there were 75,000 internet users in 2009
*Internet code and IDD* – mr; 222 (from UK), 44 (to UK)
*Major broadcasters* – Télévision de Mauritanie and Radio Mauritanie are the public broadcasters and offer programmes in Arabic and French; private broadcast media have been allowed to operate since 2011
*Press* – Major daily newspapers include the Arabic-language *Al-Sha'b* and the French-language *Horizons* (both state run)
*WPFI score* – 25,27 (55)

# MAURITIUS

*Republic of Mauritius*

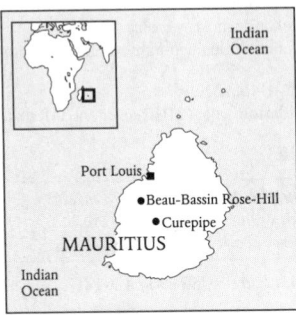

*Area* – 2,040 sq. km (includes Rodrigues and other islands)
*Capital* – Port Louis; population, 135,000 (2014)
*Major towns* – Beau-Bassin Rose-Hill, Curepipe, Quatre Bornes, Vacoas-Phoenix
*Currency* – Mauritius rupee of 100 cents
*Population* – 1,339,827 rising at 0.64 per cent a year (2015 est); Indo-Mauritian (68 per cent), Creole (27 per cent), Sino-Mauritian (3 per cent), Franco-Mauritian (2 per cent) (est)
*Religion* – Hindu 48.5 per cent, Christian (Roman Catholic 26.3 per cent), Muslim 17.3 per cent (2011 est)
*Language* – English (official), Creole, French, Bhojpuri
*Population density* – 639 per sq. km (2013)
*Urban population* – 41.8 per cent (2013 est)
*Median age (years)* – 33.9 (2014 est)
*National anthem* – 'Motherland'
*National day* – 12 March (Independence Day)
*Death penalty* – Abolished for all crimes (since 1995)
*CPI score* – 54 (47)

## CLIMATE AND TERRAIN

The republic is an island group in the Indian Ocean, approximately 885km east of Madagascar. The volcanic island of Mauritius rises from narrow coastal plains to a central plateau ringed by mountains. Elevation extremes range from 828m (Mt Piton) to 0m (Indian Ocean). The island of Rodrigues, formerly a dependency but now part of Mauritius, is about 563km east of Mauritius, with an area of 109 sq. km; the population is 37,922 (2011). The islands of Agalega and St Brandon are dependencies of Mauritius; their total population is about 350 (2011).

There is a tropical climate, modified by south-east trade winds, and little variation in temperature throughout the year. The cyclone season (December–April) brings rain but cyclones usually miss the islands.

## HISTORY AND POLITICS

The islands were first visited in the tenth century, but were settled only after 1638 by the Dutch, who introduced sugar cane cultivation; the colonists withdrew in 1710. A decade later they were replaced by the French, who established plantations that were worked by African slaves. In 1814 Mauritius was ceded to the British, who had occupied it in 1810. The British abolished slavery in 1834 and imported indentured Indian and Chinese labourers to work on the plantations. Independence was achieved on 12 March 1968 and the state became a republic in 1992.

The Militant Socialist Movement (MSM) under Sir Anerood Jugnauth held power from 1983 until 1995, and then returned to power in 2000 in coalition with the Mauritian Militant Movement (MMM). Jugnauth stood down

as party leader and prime minister in 2003; he was elected president later that year and again in 2008. The MSM-MMM coalition lost the 2005 election to the opposition Socialist Alliance, but the MSM returned to power in 2010 in the Alliance of the Future, led by the Mauritius Labour Party (MPT). President Jugnauth resigned from office in March 2012 and in July Rajkeswur Purryag was elected president. The December 2014 legislative elections were won by the Alliance Lepep, consisting of the MSM, Mauritian Social Democratic Party (PMSD) and the Mouvement Libérateur (ML). Sir Anerood Jugnauth of the MSM formed a new government and became prime minister for a third term.

The 1968 constitution was amended in 1992 to introduce a republican form of government, and in 2001 to give the island of Rodrigues a degree of autonomy.

The president is elected by the legislature for a five-year term, renewable once. The unicameral National Assembly has 62 elected members (including two representing Rodrigues) and eight appointed members, all of whom serve a five-year term; the electoral commission allocates the appointed seats on a 'best loser' basis to give more equitable representation to ethnic minorities. The prime minister is the leader of the majority party in the legislature.

Rodrigues has had an 18-member regional assembly, a chief commissioner and a chief executive since 2002.

HEAD OF STATE
*President*, Rajkeswur Purryag, *elected* 20 July 2014

SELECTED GOVERNMENT MEMBERS *as at June 2015*
*Prime Minister, Defence, Interior,* Sir Anerood Jugnauth
*Deputy Prime Minister,* Charles Xavier-Luc Duval
*Vice-Prime Ministers,* Ivan Collendavelloo, Showkutally Soodhun
*Foreign Affairs,* Marie Sinatambou

MAURITIUS HIGH COMMISSION
32–33 Elvaston Place, London SW7 5NW
T 020-7581 0294 E londonhc@govmu.org
W london.mauritius.gov.mu
*High Commissioner,* vacant

BRITISH HIGH COMMISSION
7th floor, Cascades Building, Edith Cavell Street, PO Box 1063, Port Louis
T (+230) 202 9400 E bhc@intnet.mu
W www.gov.uk/government/world/mauritius
*High Commissioner,* HE Jonathan Drew, MBE, *apptd* 2014

## DEFENCE

| *Aged 16–49, 2010 est* | *Males* | *Females* |
| --- | --- | --- |
| Available for military service | 343,628 | – |
| Fit for military service | 280,596 | 283,317 |

*Military expenditure* – US$32.9m (2014)

## ECONOMY AND TRADE

Since independence Mauritius has developed from an economy dependent on agriculture to one with prospering tourist, manufacturing (primarily of textiles and garments) and financial sectors. Although sugar remains an important commodity (sugar cane is grown on 90 per cent of cultivated land and produces 15 per cent of export earnings), both the sugar and textile industries are beginning to decline. Diversification into fish processing, information and communications technology, banking, hospitality and property development is being encouraged. The services sector accounts for 73.24 per cent of GDP, industry for 22.4 per cent and agriculture for 4.5 per cent.

The main trading partners are India, the UK and France. Principal exports are clothing, textiles, sugar, cut flowers, molasses and fish. The main imports are manufactured goods, capital equipment, food, fuels and chemicals.
*GNI* – US$12,046m; US$9,290 per capita (2013)
*Annual average growth of GDP* – 3.3 per cent (2014)
*Inflation rate* – 3.9 per cent (2014 est)
*Unemployment* – 8.1 per cent (2015 est)
*Total external debt* – US$5,700m (2014 est)
*Imports* – US$5,399m (2013)
*Exports* – US$2,872m (2013)

BALANCE OF PAYMENTS
*Trade* – US$2,527m deficit (2013)
*Current Account* – US$838m deficit (2015 est)

| Trade with UK | 2013 | 2014 |
| --- | --- | --- |
| Imports from UK | £62,683,581 | £59,301,513 |
| Exports to UK | £263,823,406 | £232,417,981 |

## COMMUNICATIONS
*Airports and waterways* – The international airport and the main port are at Port Louis
*Roadways* – 2,149km, including 75km of motorways
*Telecommunications* – 349,100 fixed lines and 1.485 million mobile subscriptions (2012); there were 290,000 internet users in 2009
*Internet code and IDD* – mu; 230 (from UK), 44 (to UK)
*Major broadcasters* – The state-owned Mauritius Broadcasting Corporation runs television and radio services funded through advertising and a licence fee
*Press* – Leading dailies include *L'Express, Le Mauricien* and *Le Matinal*
*WPFI score* – 27,69 (68)

## EDUCATION AND HEALTH
Twelve years of education are free and compulsory.
*Literacy rate* – 98.7 per cent (2015 est)
*Gross enrolment ratio (percentage of relevant age group)* – primary 108 per cent (2013 est); secondary 96 per cent (2012 est); tertiary 41 per cent (2013 est)
*Health expenditure (per capita)* – US$463 (2013)
*Hospital beds (per 1,000 people)* – 3.4 (2011)
*Life expectancy (years)* – 75.17 (2014 est)
*Mortality rate* – 6.85 (2014 est)
*Birth rate* – 13.46 (2014 est)
*Infant mortality rate* – 10.59 (2014 est)
*HIV/AIDS adult prevalence* – 1.1 per cent (2013 est)

# MEXICO

*Estados Unidos Mexicanos – United Mexican States*

*Area* – 1,964,375 sq. km
*Capital* – Mexico City; population, 20,843,000 (2014)
*Major cities* – Ciudad Juárez, Ecatepec, Guadalajara, León, Monterrey, Puebla, Tijuana
*Currency* – Peso of 100 centavos
*Population* – 121,736,809 rising at 1.18 per cent a year (2015 est)
*Religion* – Christian (Roman Catholic 82.7 per cent, Evangelical 8 per cent), none 4.7 per cent
*Language* – Spanish (official) indigenous languages including dialects of Mayan and Nahuatl
*Population density* – 63 per sq. km (2013)
*Urban population* – 78.7 per cent (2013 est)
*Median age (years)* – 27.3 (2014 est)
*National anthem* – 'Himno Nacional Mexicano' ['Mexican National Anthem']
*National day* – 16 September (Independence Day)
*Death penalty* – Abolished for all crimes (since 2005)
*CPI score* – 35 (103)

## CLIMATE AND TERRAIN
The Rio Grande river forms the eastern part of the border with the USA. South of this, coastal plains rise to a central plateau which lies between two spines of high mountains, the Western and the Eastern Sierra Madre, running from the north-west to south-east. The mountains include volcanoes such as Popocatepetl, and in the south are covered with dense jungle. The Yucatán peninsula in the south-east is low-lying, and marshy on the coast. The narrow Baja California peninsula, separated from the rest of the country by the Gulf of California, has a range of hills running along it. Elevation extremes range from 5,700m (Volcan Pico de Orizaba) to −10m (Laguna Salada). The north has a desert climate, while the south is tropical. The average temperature ranges from 16.1°C in January to 25.9°C in June and July.

## POLITICS
Under the 1917 constitution, the federal republic consists of 31 states and the federal capital. The head of state is an executive president, directly elected for a single six-year term. The bicameral legislature is the Congress of the Union: the lower house, the Chamber of Deputies, has 500 members, directly elected for a three-year term, and the senate has 128 members, directly elected for a six-year term. The president appoints the cabinet.

Each of the states has its own constitution and is administered by a governor, elected for a six-year term, and a state chamber of deputies, elected for a three-year term.

The Institutional Revolutionary Party's (PRI) political dominance ended at the 1997 election, when it lost its absolute majority in the lower house of the legislature, although it continued in government until 2000 and was again in power from 2003 until 2006. The presidential elections were won by Felipe Calderón of the Partido Accion Nacional (PAN) in 2006 and by Enrique Pena Nieto of the PRI in 2012. The PRI became the largest party in the Chamber of Deputies in the 2012 legislative election, picking up 93 more seats than nearest rival PAN. In the 2015 legislative elections, the PRI, along with its allies the Green Party and New Alliance Party, increased their majority in the Chamber of Deputies. The PRI remained the largest single party in the Senate.

HEAD OF STATE
*President,* Enrique Pena Nieto, *elected* 1 July 2012, *sworn in* 1 December 2012

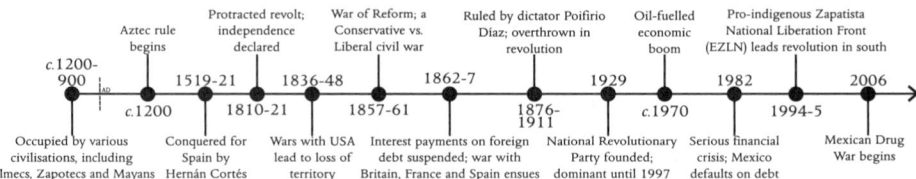

**Timeline:**

| | | | |
|---|---|---|---|
| Aztec rule begins | Protracted revolt; independence declared | War of Reform; a Conservative vs. Liberal civil war | Ruled by dictator Poifirio Díaz; overthrown in revolution |
| c.1200-900 | 1519-21 | 1836-48 | 1862-7 |

Oil-fuelled economic boom — Pro-indigenous Zapatista National Liberation Front (EZLN) leads revolution in south

1929    1982    2006

c.1200    1810-21    1857-61    1876-1911    c.1970    1994-5

Occupied by various civilisations, including Olmecs, Zapotecs and Mayans — Conquered for Spain by Hernán Cortés — Wars with USA lead to loss of territory — Interest payments on foreign debt suspended; war with Britain, France and Spain ensues — National Revolutionary Party founded; dominant until 1997 — Serious financial crisis; Mexico defaults on debt — Mexican Drug War begins

## SELECTED GOVERNMENT MEMBERS *as at June 2015*
*Defence,* Gen. Salvador Cienfuegos Zepeda
*Economy,* Ildefonso Guajardo
*Foreign Affairs,* José Antonio Meade
*Interior,* Miguel Angel Osorio Chong

## EMBASSY OF MEXICO
16 St George Street, London W1S 1FD
T 020-7499 8586 E mexuk@sre.gob.mx
W www.sre.gob.mx/reinounido
*Ambassador Extraordinary and Plenipotentiary,* HE Diego Gómez Pickering, *apptd* 2013

## BRITISH EMBASSY
Río Lerma 71, Col. Cuauhtémoc, 06500 Mexico City
T (+52) (55) 1670 3200 E ukinmexico@fco.gov.uk
W www.gov.uk/government/world/mexico
*Ambassador Extraordinary and Plenipotentiary,* HE Duncan Taylor CBE, *apptd* 2013

## DEFENCE

| Aged 16–49, 2010 est | Males | Females |
|---|---|---|
| Available for military service | 28,815,506 | 30,363,558 |
| Fit for military service | 23,239,866 | 25,642,549 |

*Military expenditure* – US$8,660m (2014)
*Conscription* – 18 years; 12 months

## ECONOMY AND TRADE
Mexico had a relatively closed economy until the mid-1980s, but increased trade and domestic liberalisation in the 1990s stimulated economic growth and development, particularly in the industrial sector. However, although it has free trade agreements with over 50 countries, covering 90 per cent of its trade, its economy is still closely tied to that of the USA and experienced a deep recession in 2009 as the global downturn affected its main export market. In November 2012 former president Felipe Calderón signed a comprehensive labour reform into law. The continued recovery of the US economy is set to help growth to average over 3.5 per cent during 2015–19.

Agriculture is diverse and productive; major crops include maize, wheat, soya beans, rice, beans, cotton, coffee, fruit, tomatoes, beef, poultry and dairy products. Agriculture accounts for 3.5 per cent of GDP and 13.4 per cent of employment. The main industries include production of food, beverages, tobacco, chemicals, iron and steel, textiles, clothing, motor vehicles, consumer durables, oil production, mining and tourism. Tourism is now the fourth-largest revenue earner. The services sector accounts for 60.1 per cent of GDP and industry for 36.4 per cent.

The main trading partner is the USA (78.8 per cent of exports; 49.1 per cent of imports). Canada is the other main export market, and China and Japan the other main source of imports. Principal exports include manufactured goods, oil and oil products, silver, fruit, vegetables, coffee and cotton.

The main imports include metalworking machines, steel mill products, agricultural machinery, electrical equipment, car parts for assembly, vehicle repair parts, aircraft and aircraft parts.
*GNI* – US$1,216,087m; US$9,940 per capita (2013)
*Annual average growth of GDP* – 2.4 per cent (2014)
*Inflation rate* – 3.8 per cent (2014 est)
*Population below poverty line* – 52.3 per cent (2012)
*Unemployment* – 4.8 per cent (2015 est)
*Total external debt* – US$438,400m (2014 est)
*Imports* – US$381,202m (2013)
*Exports* – US$380,107m (2013)

### BALANCE OF PAYMENTS
*Trade* – US$1,095m deficit (2013)
*Current Account* – US$26,595m deficit (2015 est)

| Trade with UK | 2013 | 2014 |
|---|---|---|
| Imports from UK | £1,109,626,951 | £1,048,883,274 |
| Exports to UK | £788,417,053 | £1,002,879,814 |

## COMMUNICATIONS
*Airports* – The main international airport is at Mexico City, with 242 others around the country
*Waterways* – Veracruz, Tampico and Coatzacoalcos are the chief seaports on the east coast, and Guaymas, Mazatlán, Lázaro Cárdenas and Salina Cruz on the Pacific; there are 2,900km of navigable rivers and coastal canals
*Roadways and railways* – There are 137,544km of paved roadways, including 7,176km of motorways – the Baluarte bridge, the highest cable-stayed bridge in the world, opened in 2012 and stretches 1,124m across the Durango-Mazatlán motorway in the north; there are 17,166km of railways
*Telecommunications* – 20.22 million fixed lines and 100.79 million mobile subscriptions (2012); there were 31.02 million internet users in 2009
*Internet code and IDD* – mx; 52 (from UK), 44 (to UK)
*Major broadcasters* – The Televisa group used to dominate broadcasting but now competes with other television channels and a huge number of independent radio stations
*Press* – Leading dailies include *Excelsior, La Jornada* and *Reforma*
*WPFI score* – 43,69 (148)

## EDUCATION AND HEALTH
Education is compulsory in Mexico for ten years from age six, although attainment varies among states.
*Literacy rate* – 99.0 per cent (2015 est)
*Gross enrolment ratio (percentage of relevant age group)* – primary 105 per cent; secondary 86 per cent; tertiary 29 per cent (2012 est)
*Health expenditure (per capita)* – US$664 (2013)
*Hospital beds (per 1,000 people)* – 1.5 (2011)
*Life expectancy (years)* – 75.43 (2014 est)
*Mortality rate* – 5.24 (2014 est)
*Birth rate* – 19.02 (2014 est)
*Infant mortality rate* – 12.58 (2014 est)

# FEDERATED STATES OF MICRONESIA

*Area* – 702 sq. km
*Capital* – Palikir, on Pohnpei; population, 7,000 (2014)
*Major towns* – Kolonia, Weno
*Currency* – US dollar (US$) of 100 cents
*Population* – 105,216 falling at 0.46 per cent a year (2015 est); Chuukese (49.3 per cent), Pohnpeian (29.8 per cent), Kosraen (6.3 per cent), Yapese (5.7 per cent), Yap outer islanders (5.1 per cent), Polynesian (1.6 per cent) (2000)
*Religion* – Christian (Roman Catholic 54.7 per cent, Protestant 41.1 per cent, Mormon 1.5 per cent)
*Language* – English (official), Chuukese, Kosraen, Pohnpeian, Yapese, Ulithian, Woleaian, Nukuoro, Kapingamarangi
*Population density* – 148 per sq. km (2013)
*Urban population* – 22.8 per cent (2013 est)
*Median age (years)* – 23.8 (2014 est)
*National anthem* – 'Patriots of Micronesia'
*National day* – 10 May (Constitution Day)
*Death penalty* – Abolished for all crimes (since 1986)
*Life expectancy (years)* – 72.35 (2014 est)
*Mortality rate* – 4.25 (2014 est)
*Birth rate* – 20.97 (2014 est)
*Infant mortality rate* – 21.93 (2014 est)

## CLIMATE AND TERRAIN

The republic consists of four major island groups totalling over 600 mountainous volcanic islands and low-lying atolls, extending over 2,900 sq. km of the western Pacific Ocean. Elevation extremes range from 791m (Dolohmwar) to 0m (Pacific Ocean). The climate is tropical, with only slight seasonal variations in temperatures; there is a stormy season between July and November. The islands are vulnerable to the effects of global warming, particularly an increase in the frequency and intensity of cyclones in the region.

## HISTORY AND POLITICS

Inhabited since around 4,000 BC by migrants from the Philippines and Indonesia, Micronesia experienced contact with Europeans from the 1520s, and the islands were colonised by Spain from the 16th century. German encroachment in the 1870s and 1880s was resisted until 1899, when Germany purchased the islands from Spain. The islands were occupied by Japan on behalf of the Allies during the First World War, and administered as a League of Nations mandated territory by Japan from 1920 until the Japanese defeat in the Second World War. In 1947 the islands became part of the UN Trust Territory of the Pacific, administered by the USA.

A constitution was adopted in 1979 and the islands became independent in 1986 under a compact of free association with the USA, by which the USA retains responsibility for defence and provides substantial financial aid; a renegotiated agreement came into force in 2004. The UN trusteeship was formally terminated in 1990.

Following simultaneous legislative and presidential elections in May 2015, Peter Christian was elected president. The 1979 constitution established a federal republic of four states: Chuuk, Kosrae, Pohnpei and Yap. The federal head of state is an executive president, who is elected by the federal legislature for a four-year term. The unicameral congress has 14 members, ten senators directly elected for a two-year term and four senators 'at large' (one from each state) elected for a four-year term; the president and vice-president must be selected from among the 'at large' senators. The federal cabinet is appointed by the president and approved by the congress. There are no formal political parties.

Each state has its own constitution, legislature and government.

### HEAD OF STATE
*President*, Peter Christian, *elected and sworn in* 11 May 2015
*Vice-President*, Yosiwo George

### SELECTED GOVERNMENT MEMBERS *as at June 2015*
*Attorney-General*, Maketo Robert
*Finance*, Finley S. Perman
*Foreign Affairs*, Lorin S. Robert

### BRITISH AMBASSADOR
HE Asif Ahmad, *apptd* 2013, resident at Manila, the Philippines

## ECONOMY AND TRADE

Micronesia has few natural resources apart from phosphate, which is not exploited, and is highly dependent on aid from the USA, which constitutes over a quarter of GDP. The main economic activities are subsistence farming and fishing, which account for 14 per cent of GDP, but both are threatened by climate change and over-fishing. The islands' remoteness and lack of facilities has constrained the development of tourism, the main industry; other industries include construction, fish processing, specialised aquaculture and handicrafts. Two-thirds of the workforce is employed by the government. The main trading partners are the USA and Japan. Principal exports are fish, garments, bananas and black pepper. The main imports are food, manufactured goods and machinery.

*GNI* – US$343m; US$3,280 per capita (2013)
*Annual average growth of GDP* – 0.6 per cent (2014)
*Inflation rate* – 3.4 per cent (2011)
*Total external debt* – US$93.6m (2013 est)

| Trade with UK | 2013 | 2014 |
| --- | --- | --- |
| Imports from UK | £32,263 | £16,693 |
| Exports to UK | £27,036 | £4,425 |

## COMMUNICATIONS

*Transport* – There are six airports, including major airports on the four main islands; the main seaports are Colonia (Yap), Kolonia (Pohnpei), Lele and Moen; there are 42km of paved roads
*Telecommunications* – 8,400 fixed lines and 27,600 mobile subscriptions; there were 17,000 internet users in 2010
*Internet code and IDD* – fm; 691 (from UK), 011 44 (to UK)
*Media* – The federal government produces a fortnightly information bulletin and state governments produce weekly news publications; the majority of television programming is imported

# MOLDOVA

*Republica Moldova – Republic of Moldova*

*Area –* 33,851 sq. km
*Capital –* Chisinau; population, 721,000 (2014)
*Major towns –* Balti, Tighina, Tiraspol
*Currency –* Moldovan leu (plural lei) of 100 bani
*Population –* 3,546,847 falling at 1.03 per cent a year
    (2015 est); Moldovan (75.8 per cent), Ukrainian (8.4 per
    cent), Russian (5.9 per cent), Gagauz (4.4 per cent),
    Romanian (2.2 per cent), Bulgarian (1.9 per cent) (2004)
*Religion –* Christian (Orthodox 97 per cent) (2013)
*Language –* Moldovan (official; linguistically identical to
    Romanian), Russian, Gagauz
*Population density –* 124 per sq. km (2013)
*Urban population –* 49.1 per cent (2013 est)
*Median age (years) –* 35.7 (2014 est)
*National anthem –* 'Limba Noastra' ['Our Language']
*National day –* 27 August (Independence Day)
*Death penalty –* Abolished for all crimes (since 1995)
*CPI score –* 35 (103)

## CLIMATE AND TERRAIN

The landlocked country consists of rolling steppe lying
mostly between the Prut and Dniester rivers. Elevation
extremes range from 430m (Dealul Balanesti) at the highest
point to 2m (river Dniester) at the lowest. The climate is
continental, and average temperatures range from −1.5°C in
January to 22.4°C in July.

## POLITICS

The 1997 constitution was amended in 2000 to increase the
powers of the legislature and the executive. The head of state
is a president who is elected by the legislature by a
three-fifths majority for a four-year term, renewable once.
The unicameral legislature, the *Parlamentul,* has 101
members, who are directly elected for a four-year term. The
prime minister and government are nominated by the
president.

The governments in the first decade after independence
were made up of moderate reformists, but there was a
resurgence in support for the Communist Party of Moldova
(PCM), which won the majority of seats in the 1998, 2001,
2005, 2009 (April and July) and 2010 legislative elections,

forming the government from 2005 to 2009. Pro-Western
parties formed coalition governments after legislative
elections in 2010 and 2014, despite the PCM emerging as
the single largest party in both elections. Following three
years in which parliament failed to elect a president, in March
2012 the stalemate was broken after independent candidate
Nicolae Timofti picked up 62 of 101 parliamentary votes
in an election boycotted by the PCM. In July 2015, Valeriu
Strelet was appointed prime minister after the previous
incumbent, Chiril Gaburici, was accused of faking academic
qualifications.

HEAD OF STATE
*President,* Nicolae Timofti, *took office* 23 March 2012

SELECTED GOVERNMENT MEMBERS *as at August 2015*
*Prime Minister,* Valeriu Strelet
*Deputy Prime Ministers,* Victor Osipov, Stephane Bride
    *(Economy);* Natalia Gherman *(Foreign Affairs)*
*Defence,* Anatol Salaru
*Finance,* Anatol Arapu

EMBASSY OF THE REPUBLIC OF MOLDOVA
5 Dolphin Square, Edensor Road, London W4 2ST
T 020-8995 6818 E embassy.london@mfa.md
W www.britania.mfa.gov.md
*Ambassador Extraordinary and Plenipotentiary,* HE Iulian
    Fruntasu, *apptd* 2011

BRITISH EMBASSY
18/1 Nicolae Iorga Str., Chisinau, MD-2012
T (+373) 222 225902 E enquiries.chisinau@fco.gov.uk
W www.gov.uk/government/world/moldova
*Ambassador Extraordinary and Plenipotentiary,* HE Philip
    Batson, *apptd* 2013

SECESSION
Moldovan nationalism in the late 1980s and possible
reunification with Romania alarmed the republic's Russian
and Ukrainian ethnic minorities in the Transdniestria region
(east of the Dniester) and the Gagauz (Turkish-speaking
Christians) in the south-west. Both areas declared
independence unilaterally in 1990, though this was not
recognised. The regions were granted a special status by the
1994 constitution, and the Gagauz have since exercised
a degree of autonomy over their political, economic and
cultural affairs.

In response to the Russian takeover of Crimea, in March
2014 President Timofti warned Russia against trying to
annex Transdniestria while also calling on the EU to fast-
track Moldova's entry into the organisation in order to deter
invasion.

## DEFENCE

| *Aged 16–49, 2010 est* | *Males* | *Females* |
| --- | --- | --- |
| Available for military service | 1,143,440 | 1,156,958 |
| Fit for military service | 875,224 | 969,903 |

*Military expenditure –* US$27.6m (2014)

| Becomes part of a larger Moldovan kingdom | Bessarabia granted to Russia | Area returned to USSR; becomes the Moldavian Soviet Socialist Republic | Recaptured by USSR | Joins Commonwealth of Independent States following collapse of USSR |
| --- | --- | --- | --- | --- |
| 106 | 1500-1800 | 1918 | 1990 | 1994 |
| 1350 | 1812 | 1940 | 1944 | 1991 |
| Part of the Roman province of Dacia (known as Bessarabia) | Territory contested by Ottoman and Russian empires | Becomes province of Romania following Russian Revolution | Area retaken by Romania 1941 | Parliament asserts its political and economic sovereignty | Referendum endorses independence |

## ECONOMY AND TRADE

Moldova is one of the poorest countries in Europe, despite moves towards a market economy since independence. With few natural resources and most industry lying in the breakaway Transdniestria region, the economy is dependent on agriculture and remittances from expatriate workers, remaining one of the poorest countries in Europe despite declining poverty levels. Following the global downturn, the economy recovered in 2011, posting growth of around 6 per cent, but remains susceptible to political uncertainty, increasing fuel prices and a weak investment market. EU integration has yielded generally positive results, though the economy is predicted to experience 0 per cent growth in 2015.

The agricultural sector accounts for 15.7 per cent of GDP. Principal crops include vegetables, fruit, wine, grain, sugar beet, sunflower seed, tobacco, beef and milk. Major industrial activities include food processing and production of sugar, vegetable oil, agricultural machinery, foundry equipment, domestic appliances, footwear and textiles. Industry accounts for 20 per cent of GDP and services for 64.3 per cent.

The main trading partners are Russia, Romania and Ukraine. Principal exports are foodstuffs, textiles and machinery. The main imports are mineral products and fuel, machinery and equipment, chemicals and textiles.

*GNI* – US$8,780m; US$2,470 per capita (2013)
*Annual average growth of GDP* – 1.8 per cent (2014)
*Inflation rate* – 4.7 per cent (2014 est)
*Population below poverty line* – 12.7 per cent (2013)
*Unemployment* – 5.4 per cent (2015 est)
*Total external debt* – US$6,778m (2014 est)
*Imports* – US$5,493m (2013)
*Exports* – US$2,399m (2013)

BALANCE OF PAYMENTS
*Trade* – US$3,094m deficit (2013)
*Current Account* – US$277m deficit (2015 est)

| Trade with UK | 2013 | 2014 |
| --- | --- | --- |
| Imports from UK | £44,760,375 | £39,579,307 |
| Exports to UK | £48,598,071 | £47,744,681 |

## COMMUNICATIONS

*Airports and waterways* – There are five airports, including the principal airport at Chisinau; there are 558km of navigable waterways on the Prut, Dniester and Danube rivers
*Roadways and railways* – 8,835m; 1,190km
*Telecommunications* – 1.206 million fixed lines and 4.08 million mobile subscriptions (2012); there were 1.333 million internet users in 2009
*Internet code and IDD* – md; 373 (from UK), 44 (to UK)
*Major broadcasters* – Public networks Moldova One (TV) and Radio Moldova broadcasts nationally alongside Russian and Romanian stations
*Press* – Major daily newspapers include *Timpul, Flux* (both in Moldovan) and *Kommersant Moldoviy* (Russian language)
*WPFI score* – 27,85 (72)

## EDUCATION AND HEALTH

*Literacy rate* – 100 per cent (2015 est)
*Gross enrolment ratio (percentage of relevant age group)* – primary 94 per cent; secondary 88 per cent; tertiary 41 per cent (2013 est)
*Health expenditure (per capita)* – US$263 (2013)
*Hospital beds (per 1,000 people)* – 6.2 (2012)
*Life expectancy (years)* – 70.12 (2014 est)
*Mortality rate* – 12.6 (2014 est)
*Birth rate* – 12.21 (2014 est)
*Infant mortality rate* – 12.93 (2014 est)

# MONACO

*Principauté de Monaco – Principality of Monaco*

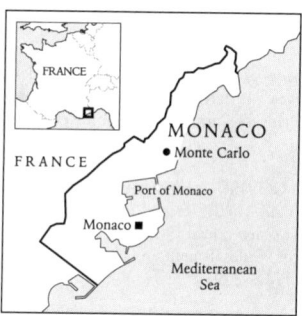

*Area* – 2 sq. km
*Capital* – Monaco
*Major town* – Monte Carlo
*Currency* – Euro (€) of 100 cents
*Population* – 30,535 growing at 0.12 per cent a year (2015 est); French (47 per cent), Monegasque (16 per cent), Italian (16 per cent) (est)
*Religion* – Christian (Roman Catholic 90 per cent)
*Language* – French (official), English, Italian, Monegasque
*Population density* – 18,916 per sq. km (2013)
*Urban population* – 100 per cent (2013)
*Median age (years)* – 51.1 (2014 est)
*National anthem* – 'Hymne Monegasque' ['Hymn of Monaco']
*National day* – 19 November (St Rainier's Day)
*Death penalty* – Abolished for all crimes (since 1962)
*Life expectancy (years)* – 89.57 (2014 est)
*Mortality rate* – 9.01 (2014 est)
*Birth rate* – 6.72 (2014 est)
*Infant mortality rate* – 1.81 (2014 est)

## CLIMATE AND TERRAIN

Monaco lies on 4km of steep, rugged coastline. It has been expanded by 0.3 sq. km with land reclaimed from the sea by infilling. Elevation extremes range from 140m (Mt Agel) to 0m (Mediterranean Sea). The climate is Mediterranean, with average temperatures ranging from 6.6°C in January to 22°C in August.

## HISTORY AND POLITICS

Monaco has been ruled by the Grimaldi family since the 13th century. Monarchical France recognised Monaco's independence in the 15th century, but Revolutionary France annexed it in 1793. Although the prince was restored to power in 1814, Monaco did not regain its independence until 1861. It was occupied by the Italians and subsequently by the Germans in the Second World War. The principality's foreign relations and security have been aligned to those of France since 1861 by various treaties; the terms were changed in 2005 to allow Monaco greater control over its foreign relations and internal administration.

The 1962 constitution was amended in 2002 to allow the throne to pass through the female line in the absence of male heirs. Legislative power is held jointly by the prince and a 24-member National Council, which is directly elected for a five-year term. Executive power is exercised by the prince and a six-member Council of Government, headed by a minister of state who is nominated by the prince and approved by the French government. The judicial code is based on that of France.

Michel Roger replaced Jean-Paul Proust as head of the Government in March 2010. In the 2013 legislative election, the Horizon Monaco Party won 20 seats, an overwhelming majority, in the legislature.

## HEAD OF STATE
*HSH The Prince of Monaco,* Prince Albert II (Alexandre Louis Pierre), *born* 14 March 1958, *succeeded* 6 April 2005
*Heir,* HSH Princess Caroline von Hannover, *born* 23 January 1957

## SELECTED GOVERNMENT MEMBERS *as at June 2015*
*Minister of State,* Michel Roger
*Finance and Economy,* Jean Castellini
*Foreign Affairs,* Gilles Tonelli
*Interior,* Paul Masseron

## EMBASSY OF THE PRINCIPALITY OF MONACO
7 Upper Grosvenor Street, London W1K 2LX
**T** 020-7318 1078 **E** embassy.uk@gouv.mc
**W** www.monaco-embassy-uk.gouv.mc
*Ambassador Extraordinary and Plenipotentiary,* Evelyne Genta, *apptd* 2010

## BRITISH HONORARY CONSULATE
Contact British Consulate Marseille, 24 Avenue du Prado, 13006 Marseille
**T** (+33) (0) 4 9115 7210

## ECONOMY AND TRADE
The economy has diversified away from its historic dependence on tourism and gambling, and over half its revenue now comes from financial services, retail, real estate, construction and light industry (chemicals, pharmaceuticals, cosmetics, medical devices, plastics, electronics).

As the state collects no taxes from individuals and little from businesses, it has become a tax haven for wealthy expatriates and foreign companies. The state retains monopolies in a number of sectors, including tobacco, the telephone network and the postal service. Since 1963 Monaco has been in a customs union with France, and through this it participates in the EU market. Over half its trade is with EU countries, particularly France and Italy.
*GNI* – US$6,075m; US$167,021 per capita (2011)
*Unemployment* – 0 per cent (2005 est)

## COMMUNICATIONS
*Transport* – The nearest international airport is the Côte d'Azur airport in Nice, France; the installation of a large floating jetty in 2002 doubled the port of Monaco's capacity to handle cruise ships; there are 77km of roads and a single railway station, Monaco-Monte Carlo
*Telecommunications* – 44,500 fixed lines and 33,200 mobile subscriptions (2012); there were 23,000 internet users in 2009
*Internet code and IDD* – mc; 377 (from UK), 44 (to UK)
*Media* – Monaco has one television station and the principality's news is covered by the French press

# MONGOLIA

*Mongol Uls – Mongolia*

*Area* – 1,564,116 sq. km
*Capital* – Ulaanbaatar; population, 1,334,000 (2014)
*Major towns* – Darhan, Erdenet
*Currency* – Tugrik of 100 mongo
*Population* – 2,992,908 rising at 1.31 per cent a year (2015 est); Khalkh (81.9 per cent), Kazak (3.8 per cent), Dorvod (2.7 per cent) and several others (2010 est)
*Religion* – Buddhist 53 per cent, none 38.6 per cent, Muslim 3 per cent, Shamanist 2.9 per cent, Christian 2.2 per cent (2010 est)
*Language* – Khalkha Mongol (official), Turkic, Russian
*Population density* – 2 per sq. km (2013)
*Urban population* – 70.4 per cent (2013 est)
*Median age (years)* – 27.1 (2014 est)
*National anthem* – 'Mongol ulsyn toriin duulal' ['National Anthem of Mongolia']
*National day* – 11 July (Revolution Day)
*Death penalty* – Abolished for all crimes (since 2012)
*CPI score* – 39 (80)
*Literacy rate* – 98.5 per cent (2015 est)
*Gross enrolment ratio (percentage of relevant age group)* – primary 109 per cent (2013 est); secondary 92 per cent (2010 est); tertiary 62 per cent (2013 est)
*Health expenditure (per capita)* – US$244 (2013)
*Hospital beds (per 1,000 people)* – 6.8 (2012)
*Life expectancy (years)* – 68.98 (2014 est)
*Mortality rate* – 6.38 (2014 est)
*Birth rate* – 20.88 (2014 est)
*Infant mortality rate* – 23.15 (2014 est)

## CLIMATE AND TERRAIN
The eastern part of Mongolia lies on a semi-desert plateau, with steppes rising to the Mongolian Altai and Hangai mountain ranges in the west. The Gobi desert covers the southern third of the country. Elevation extremes range from 4,374m (Nayramadlin Orgil) to 560m (Hoh Nuur). The country has long, cold winters, which quickly turn into short and warm summers. The wet season runs from June to September. Average temperatures range from −20.1°C in January to 18.5°C in July.

## POLITICS
The 1992 constitution was amended in 2000 to give the president the right to dissolve the legislature if it is unable to reach agreement on appointing a prime minister. The president is directly elected for a four-year term, which is renewable. The unicameral State Great Hural has 76 members who are directly elected for a four-year term. The prime minister is elected by the legislature and appoints the cabinet.

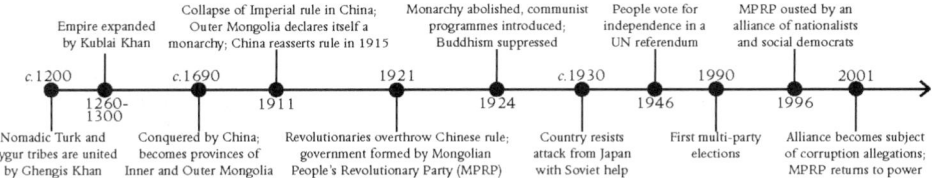

| | Collapse of Imperial rule in China; | Monarchy abolished, communist | People vote for | MPRP ousted by an |
|---|---|---|---|---|
| Empire expanded | Outer Mongolia declares itself a | programmes introduced; | independence in a | alliance of nationalists |
| by Kublai Khan | monarchy; China reasserts rule in 1915 | Buddhism suppressed | UN referendum | and social democrats |

c.1200    c.1690    1921    c.1930    1990    2001
1260-    1911    1924    1946    1996
1300

Nomadic Turk and | Conquered by China; | Revolutionaries overthrow Chinese rule; | Country resists | First multi-party | Alliance becomes subject
Uygur tribes are united | becomes provinces of | government formed by Mongolian | attack from Japan | elections | of corruption allegations;
by Ghengis Khan | Inner and Outer Mongolia | People's Revolutionary Party (MPRP) | with Soviet help | | MPRP returns to power

In the 2012 legislative election the Democratic Party (DP) became the largest single party and formed a coalition with the Mongolian People's Revolutionary Party (MPRP). The 2013 presidential election was won by the incumbent, Tsakhiagiin Elbegdorj (prime minister 1998, 2006–8). Prime Minister Norov Altankhuyag was dismissed by a vote in parliament on 5 November 2014 due to the country's poor economic performance; he was replaced by Chimed Saikhanbileg on 21 November.

## HEAD OF STATE
*President,* Tsakhiagiin Elbegdorj, *elected* 24 May 2009, re-elected 26 June 2013

SELECTED GOVERNMENT MEMBERS *as at June 2015*
*Prime Minister,* Chimed Saikhanbileg
*Deputy Prime Minister,* Ukhnaa Khurelsukh
*Defence,* Tserendash Tsolmon
*Justice,* Dambii Dorligjav

## EMBASSY OF MONGOLIA
7–8 Kensington Court, London W8 5DL
T 020-7937 0150 E office@embassyofmongolia.co.uk
W www.embassyofmongolia.co.uk
*Ambassador Extraordinary and Plenipotentiary,* HE Narkhuu Tulgu, *apptd* 2013

## BRITISH EMBASSY
Peace Avenue 30, Bayanzurkh District, Ulaanbaatar 13381
T (+976) (11) 458 133 E enquiries.mongolia@fco.gov.uk
W www.gov.uk/government/world/mongolia
*Ambassador Extraordinary and Plenipotentiary,* HE Catherine Arnold, *apptd* 2015

## DEFENCE

| Aged 16–49, 2010 est | Males | Females |
|---|---|---|
| Available for military service | 898,546 | 891,192 |
| Fit for military service | 726,199 | 756,628 |

*Military expenditure* – US$115m (2012 est)
*Conscription* – 18 to 25 years of age; 12 months

## ECONOMY AND TRADE
The economy suffered during the transition to a market economy but recovered before the global economic downturn in 2008. Declining commodity prices and export demand and soaring inflation caused difficulties that forced the government to seek an IMF loan in spring 2009. Mongolia has attracted foreign investment, particularly in mining, agricultural processing and infrastructure, but administrative corruption, dependency on imported energy supplies (mostly from Russia) and the vulnerability of the agrarian sector to climate extremes continue to hinder growth. GDP growth is anticipated to fall to 3 per cent in 2015 due to increasing inflation and falling demand for mining exports.

Deposits of copper, coal, molybdenum, fluorspar, tin, tungsten, uranium, gold and oil are being exploited; copper and gold sales are major drivers of recent economic growth (up 12.3 per cent in 2012 and 11.8 per cent in 2013). The agrarian sector, which makes up 16.3 per cent of GDP, engages 33 per cent of the workforce in agriculture and herding. The main products are grains, vegetables, forage crops, sheep, goats and other livestock. The main industries are construction, mining, processing animal products, and the production of oil, food and beverages, cashmere and natural yarns.

The main export market is China (90 per cent); the main import providers are China (37.8 per cent) and Russia (27.6 per cent). Principal exports are copper, clothing, livestock, animal products, cashmere, wool, hides, fluorspar, metals and coal. The main imports are machinery and equipment, fuels, cars, foodstuffs, industrial consumer goods, chemicals and construction materials.
*GNI* – US$10,706m; US$3,770 per capita (2013)
*Annual average growth of GDP* – 9.1 per cent (2014)
*Inflation rate* – 12.8 per cent (2014 est)
*Population below poverty line* – 27.4 per cent (2012)
*Unemployment* – 4.6 per cent (2015 est)
*Total external debt* – US$5,352m (2014 est)
*Imports* – US$6,355m (2013)
*Exports* – US$4,273m (2013)

## BALANCE OF PAYMENTS
*Trade* – US$2,082m deficit (2013)
*Current Account* – US$1,379m deficit (2015 est)

| Trade with UK | 2013 | 2014 |
|---|---|---|
| Imports from UK | £20,752,773 | £12,729,594 |
| Exports to UK | £7,274,020 | £6,342,985 |

## COMMUNICATIONS
*Airports and waterways* – The main airport is at Ulaanbaatar – there are 14 other airports around the country; the 580km of waterways are navigable in the summer months although Lake Hovsgol near the Russian border is the only waterway in commercial operation
*Roadways and railways* – 4,800km; 1,908km
*Telecommunications* – 176,700 fixed lines and 3.375 million mobile subscriptions (2012); there were 330,000 internet users in 2009
*Internet code and IDD* – mn; 976 (from UK), 1 44 (to UK)
*Major broadcasters* – Mongolian National Broadcaster (MNB) is the state-owned national television broadcaster: the publicly owned Mongolian Radio is the only radio station with national coverage
*Press* – Major national dailies include *Onoodor,* which has the biggest circulation, and *Unen* (Truth), the organ of the MPRP and the country's oldest newspaper
*WPFI score* – 25,25 (54)

# MONTENEGRO

*Crna Gora – Montenegro*

*Area* – 13,812 sq. km

*Capital* – Podgorica; population, 165,000 (2014)

*Major cities* – Cetinje (historic and cultural capital), Niksic, Pljevlja

*Currency* – Euro (€) of 100 cents

*Population* – 647,073 falling at 0.42 per cent a year (2015 est); Montenegrin (45 per cent), Serbian (28.7 per cent), Bosniak (8.7 per cent), Albanian (4.9 per cent) (2011)

*Religion* – Christian (Orthodox 72.1 per cent, Roman Catholic 3.4 per cent), Muslim 19.1 per cent

*Language* – Montenegrin (a version of Serbo-Croat) (official), Serbian, Bosnian, Albanian, Croatian

*Population density* – 46 per sq. km (2013)

*Urban population* – 63.7 per cent (2013 est)

*Median age (years)* – 39.2 (2014 est)

*National anthem* – 'Oj, Svijetla Majska Zoro' ['O, Bright Dawn of May']

*National day* – 13 July (Statehood Day)

*Death penalty* – Abolished for all crimes (since 2002)

*CPI score* – 42 (76)

*Literacy rate* – 99.2 per cent (2015 est)

*Mortality rate* – 9.3 (2014 est)

*Birth rate* – 10.59 (2014 est)

## CLIMATE AND TERRAIN

The terrain is mountainous in the north and centre of the country, intersected by deep canyons and river valleys, and falls to a narrow plain on the highly indented Adriatic coast. About 40 per cent of the country is forested. Elevation extremes range from 2,522m (Bobotov Kuk) to 0m (Adriatic Sea). The main rivers are the Piva (Drina), the Tara and the Lim. Lake Skadarsko straddles the border with Albania. The climate is Mediterranean on the coast, but more continental inland. Average temperatures in Podgorica range from 0.1°C in January to 20.2°C in July and August.

## HISTORY AND POLITICS

The area was part of the Roman province of Illyria, and then was settled by Slavs in the seventh century. In the late 12th century it was incorporated into the medieval kingdom of Serbia and so became part of the Ottoman Empire after Serbia's defeat by the Turks in 1389. When Serbia became independent in 1878, Montenegro followed and remained an independent monarchy until the end of the First World War. In 1918, Montenegro joined with Serbia and the former Austro-Hungarian provinces of Slovenia, Croatia and Bosnia-Hercegovina to form the Kingdom of Serbs, Croats and Slovenes, which was renamed Yugoslavia in 1929. Yugoslavia was occupied by Axis forces in 1941, and after liberation it reformed as a communist federal republic in 1945. When the

federation disintegrated in 1991, Serbia and Montenegro formed the Federal Republic of Yugoslavia, declared on 27 April 1992.

Montenegro's desire for independence led in 2002 to an EU-brokered agreement between the leaders of Serbia, Montenegro and the Federal Republic of Yugoslavia that restructured the republic into a union of two semi-independent states, named Serbia and Montenegro, with effect from March 2003. The agreement provided for the two republics to hold referendums on whether to retain or end the union after a minimum of three years. In a referendum held in Montenegro on 21 May 2006, 55.5 per cent voted in favour of independence, which was declared on 3 June and acknowledged by Serbia on 5 June. Montenegro joined the UN in June 2006, and formally applied for EU membership in 2008.

In the 2012 legislative election, the Coalition for a European Montenegro again won the most seats but failed to retain an overall majority. In December 2012 Milo Djukanovic became prime minister for the seventh time. In the 2013 presidential election, President Vujanovic was re-elected with 51.2 per cent of the vote.

Under the 2007 constitution, the president is directly elected for a five-year term, which is renewable once. The unicameral Assembly of the Republic of Montenegro has 81 members directly elected for a four-year term; five members are elected from the ethnic Albanian community. The prime minister appoints the cabinet, subject to the approval of the assembly.

### HEAD OF STATE

*President,* Filip Vujanovic, *elected* 11 May 2003, *re-elected* 6 April 2008, 7 April 2013

### SELECTED GOVERNMENT MEMBERS *as at June 2015*

*Prime Minister,* Milo Djukanovic

*Deputy Prime Ministers,* Rafet Husovic; Vujica Lazovic; Igor Luksic *(Foreign Affairs);* Dusko Markovic

*Defence,* Milica Pejanovic Djurisic

*Finance,* Radoje Zugic

### EMBASSY OF MONTENEGRO

47 De Vere Gardens, London W8 5AW

T 020-3302 7227 E unitedkingdom@mfa.gov.me

*Ambassador Extraordinary and Plenipotentiary,* HE Prof. Ljubisa Stankovic, *apptd* 2011

### BRITISH EMBASSY

Ulcinjska 8, Gorica C, 81000 Podgorica

T (+382) (20) 618 010 E podgorica@fco.gov.uk

W www.gov.uk/government/world/montenegro

*Ambassador Extraordinary and Plenipotentiary,* HE Ian Whitting, OBE, *apptd* 2013

### DEFENCE

| Aged 16–49, 2010 est | Males | Females |
| --- | --- | --- |
| Available for military service | – | – |
| Fit for military service | 149,159 | 131,823 |

*Military expenditure* – US$78.5m (2014)

### ECONOMY AND TRADE

Montenegro achieved fiscal autonomy from the Yugoslav federation in the 1990s. However, it faced the same problems as Serbia – slow growth, foreign debt, lack of foreign investment, high unemployment, corruption and organised crime – as well as having more limited health and education facilities, and a poor administrative capacity. Since independence, it has pursued international integration, prioritising in particular its bid for EU membership; negotiations for membership began in June 2012. It has privatised its aluminium industry and financial sector, and is attracting direct foreign investment in its growing tourism industry.

The development of the tourist industry is expected to help growth exceed 3 per cent during 2014–16.

The main agricultural products are tobacco, fruit and vegetables. Major industrial activities include production of steel, aluminium and consumer goods, processing of agricultural products and tourism. The main trading partners are EU and other Balkan countries.

*GNI* – US$4,504m; US$7,250 per capita (2013)
*Annual average growth of GDP* – 2.3 per cent (2014)
*Inflation rate* – 4 per cent (2012)
*Population below poverty line* – 11.3 per cent (2012 est)
*Unemployment* – 19.1 per cent (2015 est)
*Total external debt* – US$1,700m (2012 est)
*Imports* – US$2,354m (2013)
*Exports* – US$498m (2013)

BALANCE OF PAYMENTS
*Current Account* – US$873m deficit (2015 est)

| Trade with UK | 2013 | 2014 |
| --- | --- | --- |
| Imports from UK | £15,701,513 | £11,413,703 |
| Exports to UK | £3,364,783 | £3,329,309 |

COMMUNICATIONS
*Airports and waterways* – There are five airports, including international airports at Podgorica and Tivat; the major seaport is located at Bar
*Roadways and railways* – There are 5,365km of roadways and 250km of railway track linking the Adriatic port of Bar with Belgrade, via Podgorica
*Telecommunications* – 163,000 fixed lines and 1.13 million mobile subscriptions (2012); there were 280,000 internet users in 2009
*Internet code and IDD* – me; 382 (from UK), 44 (to UK)
*Major broadcasters* – The state-funded TV Montenegro and Radio Montenegro operate national stations
*Press* – Leading national papers include *Vijesti, Pobjeda, Republika* and *Dan*
*WPFI score* – 34,63 (114)

# MOROCCO

*Al-Mamlakah al-Maghribiyah – Kingdom of Morocco*

*Area* – 446,550 sq. km
*Capital* – Rabat; population, 1,932,000 (2014)
*Major cities* – Agadir, Casablanca, Fez, Marrakesh, Meknes, Tangier
*Currency* – Dirham (DH) of 100 centimes

*Population* – 33,322,699 rising at 1.02 per cent a year (2015 est); Arab–Berber (99 per cent) (est)
*Religion* – Muslim 99 per cent (predominantly Sunni)
*Language* – Arabic (official), French, Berber dialects
*Population density* – 74 per sq. km (2013)
*Urban population* – 57.8 per cent (2013 est)
*Median age (years)* – 28.1 (2014 est)
*National anthem* – 'Hymne Chérifien' ['Hymn of the Sharif']
*National day* – 30 July (Throne Day)
*Death penalty* – Retained (last used 1993)
*CPI score* – 39 (80)

## CLIMATE AND TERRAIN
Fertile coastal plains in the west rise to a mountainous centre, with ranges, including the Atlas range, running north-east to south-west. The Rif mountains lie along the northern, Mediterranean coast. Elevation extremes range from 4,165m (Jebel Toubkal) to −55m (Sebkha Tah). The climate is Mediterranean, becoming more extreme in the interior. Average temperatures range from 9.9°C in January to 26.8°C in July, although summer temperatures in the desert can reach over 40°C.

## HISTORY AND POLITICS
From the tenth century BC, the northern coast was settled by the Phoenicians. Morocco was part of the Roman Empire from the first century AD until it was invaded by first the Vandals and then the Visigoths in the fifth and sixth centuries. Arab conquest of the area began in the seventh century but Morocco was independent from about the ninth century, successfully resisting inclusion in the Ottoman Empire in the 16th century. The current Alawite dynasty was founded in the mid-17th century. Morocco remained isolated until the mid-19th century, when the country opened up to European trade. The subsequent growth in Spanish and French influence resulted in its partition into two protectorates from 1912. In the Second World War, Morocco was a base for the Allied offensives that drove German forces out of North Africa.

Nationalist campaigning for independence began in the 1940s. French and Spanish forces withdrew in 1956, leaving Morocco independent under Sultan Mohammed V, who adopted the title of king in 1957; the coastal towns of Ceuta and Melilla remain under Spanish control. King Hassan II, who ruled from 1961 to 1999, annexed the mineral-rich Western Sahara region in 1975.

Since the accession of King Mohammed VI in 1999, Morocco has been moving away from absolute monarchy, increasing civil liberties and addressing human rights issues. Pro-reform demonstrations in spring 2011 led to a referendum in July in which an overwhelming majority voted in favour of constitutional changes that would make the prime minister, rather than the king, the head of government.

In the 2011 legislative election the Justice and Development Party (PJD) became the largest party in the House of Representatives, but its leader Abdelilah Benkirane's government collapsed when one of three other parties withdrew from the coalition in April 2013; further resignations from the newly formed government followed in July.

The head of state is a hereditary constitutional monarch. The king appoints the prime minister, who appoints the members of the council of ministers. There is a bicameral legislature; the lower house, the House of Representatives *(Majlis al-Nuwab)* has 395 members who are directly elected for a five-year term. The House of Councillors *(Majlis al-Mustasharin)* has 270 members, elected by local councils, professional organisations and the 'salaried classes'; one-third of its members is elected every three years, to serve a nine-year term.

HEAD OF STATE
*HM The King of Morocco,* King Mohammed VI (Sidi Mohammed Ben Hassan), *born* 21 August 1963, *acceded* 23 July 1999, *crowned* 30 July 1999
*Heir,* HRH Crown Prince Moulay Hassan, *born* 2003

SELECTED GOVERNMENT MEMBERS *as at June 2015*
*Prime Minister,* Abdelilah Benkirane
*Economy and Finance,* Mohamed Boussaid
*Foreign Affairs,* Salaheddine Mezouar
*Interior,* Mohamed Hassad

EMBASSY OF THE KINGDOM OF MOROCCO
49 Queen's Gate Gardens, London SW7 5NE
T 020-7581 5001 E ambalondres@maec.gov.ma
W www.moroccanembassylondon.org.uk
*Ambassador Extraordinary and Plenipotentiary,* HH Princess Lalla Joumala Alaoui, *apptd* 2009

BRITISH EMBASSY
28 Avenue SAR Sidi Mohammed, Souissi 10105 (BP45), Rabat
T (+212) (0) 537 633 333 E rabat.consular@fco.gov.uk
W www.gov.uk/government/world/morocco
*Ambassador Extraordinary and Plenipotentiary,* Vacant

DEFENCE

| Aged 16–49, 2010 est | Males | Females |
|---|---|---|
| Available for military service | 8,252,682 | 8,691,419 |
| Fit for military service | 7,026,016 | 7,377,045 |

*Military expenditure* – US$4,050m (2014)
*Conscription* – 20 years of age; 18 months

## ECONOMY AND TRADE

Economic liberalisation since 1999 has attracted foreign direct investment, and the industrial and service sectors are being developed. Despite steady growth, Morocco remains a poor country, with unemployment at around 9 per cent, and in 2005 the king launched a poverty-alleviation programme. The remittances of expatriate workers are crucial to the domestic economy but these, along with tourism and export demand, declined in 2008–9 owing to the global downturn. Unemployment, poverty and illiteracy remain high in rural areas. The government has stabilised the country's finances by decreasing debt and reducing fuel subsidies. Falling oil prices and the performance of the secondary and tertiary sectors is expected to generate growth of over 4 per cent during 2015–19.

The large agrarian sector generates 14 per cent of GDP and engages 44.6 per cent of the workforce, producing cereals, citrus fruits, vegetables, wine, olives and livestock. It faces environmental problems such as desertification and soil erosion. Another major sector is the exploitation of mineral reserves, especially phosphate. Other industries include food processing, textiles, leather goods, construction and tourism. Industry accounts for 24.9 per cent of GDP and services for 61.1 per cent.

The main trading partners are EU countries, especially France and Spain. Principal exports are clothing, textiles, electrical components, inorganic chemicals, transistors, crude minerals, fertilisers, petroleum products, fruit and vegetables. The main imports are crude petroleum, fabrics, telecommunications equipment, wheat, gas and electricity.
*GNI* – US$101,551m; US$3,020 per capita (2013; includes Western Sahara)
*Annual average growth of GDP* – 3.5 per cent (2014)
*Inflation rate* – 1.1 per cent (2014 est)
*Population below poverty line* – 15 per cent (2007 est)

*Unemployment* – 9.4 per cent (2015 est)
*Total external debt* – US$35,540m (2014 est)
*Imports* – US$44,934m (2013)
*Exports* – US$21,847m (2013)

BALANCE OF PAYMENTS
*Trade* – US$21,999m deficit (2012)
*Current Account* – US$3,486m deficit (2015 est)

| Trade with UK | 2013 | 2014 |
|---|---|---|
| Imports from UK | £447,872,298 | £573,448,594 |
| Exports to UK | £505,809,249 | £602,131,395 |

## COMMUNICATIONS

*Airports and waterways* – The principal airports are at Rabat, Agadir, Casablanca and Marrakesh; the main ports are Tangier, Casablanca and Agadir, on the Atlantic coast
*Roadways and railways* – There are 41,116km of roadways, including 1,080km of motorways, and 2,067km of railways
*Telecommunications* – 3.28 million fixed lines and 39.02 million mobile subscriptions (2012); there were 13.213 million internet users in 2009
*Internet code and IDD* – ma; 212 (from UK), 44 (to UK)
*Major broadcasters* – The government owns Radio-Télévision Marocaine and has a stake in 2M, the other main television network
*Press* – There are a number of daily newspapers, including the semiofficial *Le Matin* (French language), *Al-Massae* and *Assabah* (both Arabic language)
*WPFI score* – 39,19 (130)

## EDUCATION AND HEALTH

Education is compulsory between the ages of six and 15.
*Literacy rate* – 83.2 per cent (2015 est)
*Gross enrolment ratio (percentage of relevant age group)* – primary 118 per cent (2014 est); secondary 69 per cent (2012 est); tertiary 16 per cent (2011 est)
*Health expenditure (per capita)* – US$189 (2013)
*Hospital beds (per 1,000 people)* – 0.9 (2012)
*Life expectancy (years)* – 76.51 (2014 est)
*Mortality rate* – 4.79 (2014 est)
*Birth rate* – 18.47 (2014 est)
*Infant mortality rate* – 24.52 (2014 est)

## WESTERN SAHARA

*Al-Jumhuriyya al-'Arabiyya as-Sahrawiyya ad-Dimuqratiyya – Sahrawi Arab Democratic Republic*
*Area* – 266,000 sq. km. Neighbours: Morocco (north), Algeria (north-east), Mauritania (east and south)
*Administrative centre* – El-Aaiun (Laayoune); population, 237,000 (2011 est)
*Population* – 538,811 rising at 2.96 per cent a year (2013 est)
*Religion* – Muslim (99 per cent) (est)
*Language* – Hassaniyya Arabic, Moroccan Arabic
*Flag* – Three horizontal stripes of black, white and green with a red crescent and a five-pointed star in the centre and a red triangle based on the hoist

Western Sahara came under Spanish rule in 1884, and became a province in 1934. Following Spain's withdrawal in 1976, Morocco and Mauritania annexed the territory and divided it between them. The Polisario Front declared Western Sahara's independence as the Sahrawi Arab Democratic Republic in 1976, and began a guerrilla war to win the territory, setting up a government in exile. In 1979, Mauritania withdrew from its part of the territory, which was annexed by Morocco.

A ceasefire was established in 1991 following both sides' agreement in 1988 to UN proposals for a peace settlement, which included holding a referendum on the future status of Western Sahara. But the precise terms of the referendum have proved a sticking point and an impasse was reached that has still not been overcome, despite further negotiations in 2001–4; Polisario agreed to a referendum offering the options of independence, semi-autonomy or integration for Western Sahara, but Morocco is only prepared to accept semi-autonomy or integration. Talks have taken place intermittently since 2007 but have made no progress.

# MOZAMBIQUE

*Republica de Mocambique – Republic of Mozambique*

*Area* – 799,380 sq. km
*Capital* – Maputo; population, 1,174,000 (2014)
*Major cities* – Beira, Chimoio, Matola, Nampula
*Currency* – New metical (MT) of 100 centavos
*Population* – 25,303,133 rising at 2.45 per cent a year
   (2015 est)
*Religion* – Christian (Roman Catholic 28.4 per cent, Zionist
   Christian 15.5 per cent, Protestant 12.2 per cent), none
   18.7 per cent, Muslim 17.9 per cent
*Language* – Portuguese (official), Emakhuwa, Xichangana,
   Elomwe, Cisena, Echuwabo
*Population density* – 33 per sq. km (2013)
*Urban population* – 31.7 per cent (2013)
*Median age (years)* – 16.9 (2014)
*National anthem* – 'Patria Amada' ['Beloved Fatherland']
*National day* – 25 June (Independence Day)
*Death penalty* – Abolished for all crimes (since 1990)
*CPI score* – 31 (119)
*Literacy rate* – 76.7 per cent (2015 est)
*Gross enrolment ratio (percentage of relevant age group)* –
   primary 105 per cent; secondary 26 per cent; tertiary
   5 per cent (2013 est)
*Health expenditure (per capita)* – US$40 (2013)
*Hospital beds (per 1,000 people)* – 0.7 (2011)
*Life expectancy (years)* – 52.6 (2014 est)
*Mortality rate* – 12.34 (2014 est)
*Birth rate* – 38.83 (2014 est)
*Infant mortality rate* – 72.42 (2014 est)
*HIV/AIDS adult prevalence* – 10.75 per cent (2013 est)

## CLIMATE AND TERRAIN

Coastal plains rise to plateaux in the centre and west, with mountains on the western borders. Elevation extremes range from 2,436m (Mt Binga) to 0m (Indian Ocean). A number of rivers run from the western highlands to the Indian Ocean coast, including the Zambezi, Limpopo, Save and Ruvuma. The climate is tropical, with average temperatures in Maputo ranging from 19.9°C in July to 26.6°C in November.

## HISTORY AND POLITICS

Between the first and fourth centuries Mozambique was settled by Bantu peoples. Trade with India and the Arabian peninsula grew and migrants from both these regions settled in the coastal areas. From the 16th century the Portuguese established settlements on the coast and along the Zambezi, trading in gold, ivory, spices and slaves, and in the late 19th century they succeeded in conquering the interior. The area was administered as part of Portuguese India from 1751, becoming a separate colony in the late 19th century and an overseas province of Portugal in 1951. Concessions to private companies that had operated as *de facto* rulers over much of the country were ended in 1930.

The *Frente de Libertacao de Mocambique* (Frelimo) was founded in 1962 to fight for independence, and a ten-year guerrilla war against Portuguese forces began in 1964. Independence was achieved in 1975, when a one-party socialist republic was set up. Opposition to this was led from 1977 by the *Resistencia Nacional de Mocambique* (Renamo) and a brutal civil war broke out that lasted until 1992. Mozambique joined the Commonwealth in 1995; although it had never been under British rule, it has close relationships and a shared experience with its neighbours, all former British colonies. Reconstruction of the economy and infrastructure progressed quickly after the civil war, although a series of natural catastrophes since 2000, high HIV/AIDS infection rates and remaining civil war landmines have slowed progress.

In 1990 Frelimo abandoned Marxist-Leninism and ended one-party rule, introducing a multiparty system. The first elections under the new constitution were held in 1994 and won by Frelimo. Frelimo retained power in the 1999, 2004 and 2009 elections, prompting allegations of vote-rigging by Renamo. The October 2014 presidential elections were won by Filipe Nyusi of the Frelimo party; Frelimo also won the simultaneous legislative election, retaining an overall majority despite losing seats.

Under the 2004 constitution, the executive president is directly elected for a five-year term, renewable once. The unicameral Assembly of the Republic has 250 members, who are directly elected for a five-year term. The president appoints the prime minister and the council of ministers.

HEAD OF STATE
*President,* Filipe Jacinto Nyusi, *elected* 24 October 2014,
   *sworn in* 15 January 2015

SELECTED GOVERNMENT MEMBERS *as at June 2015*
*Prime Minister,* Carlos Agostinho Do Rosario
*Finance,* Adriano Afonso Maleiane
*Foreign Affairs,* Oldemiro Julio Marques Baloi
*Interior,* Jaime Basilio Monteiro

HIGH COMMISSION FOR THE REPUBLIC OF
MOZAMBIQUE
21 Fitzroy Square, London W1T 6EL
T 020-7383 3800 E sectorconsular@mozambiquehc.co.uk
W www.mozambiquehighcommission.org.uk
*High Commissioner,* HE Carlos Dos Santos, *apptd* 2011

BRITISH HIGH COMMISSION
Avenida Vladmir Lenine, 310 Maputo City, Maputo, PO Box 55
T (+258) (21) 356 000 E maputo.consularenquiries@fco.gov.uk
W www.gov.uk/government/world/mozambique
*High Commissioner,* HE Joanna Kuenssberg, *apptd* 2014

## DEFENCE

| Aged 16–49, 2010 est | Males | Females |
| --- | --- | --- |
| Available for military service | 4,613,367 | – |
| Fit for military service | 2,677,473 | 2,941,073 |

*Military expenditure* – US$174m (2014)
*Conscription* – Men and women aged 18 to 35; 24 months (selective)

## ECONOMY AND TRADE

Political stability and economic liberalisation have attracted foreign direct investment and donor support, and achieved economic growth despite setbacks from devastating flooding (2000, 2001, 2007, 2008, 2010), droughts (2002, 2003, 2009, 2010) and an earthquake (2006). But the country remains dependent on foreign aid with over half of the population living below the poverty line. The huge foreign debt has been reduced to a more manageable size by debt cancellation and rescheduling, but there is a substantial ongoing trade imbalance. Mozambique grew at an average annual rate of 7 per cent between 2004 and 2014; growth is expected to rise to 7.5 per cent during 2015–19.

Agriculture and forestry are the mainstay of the economy, accounting for 28.9 per cent of GDP and engaging about 81 per cent of the workforce; shellfish, cashew nuts, cotton, sugar, citrus fruits and timber are important exports. There are considerable oil, gas, mineral and hydro-electric power resources, which are increasingly being exploited. Industries include aluminium, titanium, coal, zircon and natural gas extraction and smelting, food processing, production of beverages, chemicals, petroleum products and textiles. There are plans to expand titanium extraction and processing, and garment-manufacturing. Industry generates 24 per cent of GDP and services 47.1 per cent.

The main trading partners are South Africa, India and China. The country also benefits from trade with its landlocked neighbours. Principal exports are aluminium, agricultural products, timber and electricity. The main imports are machinery, vehicles, fuel, chemicals, metal products, foodstuffs and textiles.

*GNI* – US$15,751m; US$610 per capita (2013)
*Annual average growth of GDP* – 8.3 per cent (2014)
*Inflation rate* – 3 per cent (2014)
*Population below poverty line* – 52 per cent (2009 est)
*Unemployment* – 8.4 per cent (2015 est)
*Total external debt* – US$7,521m (2014 est)
*Imports* – US$8,600m (2013)
*Exports* – US$4,300m (2013)

BALANCE OF PAYMENTS
*Trade* – US$4,300m deficit (2013)
*Current Account* – US$696m deficit (2015 est)

| Trade with UK | 2013 | 2014 |
|---|---|---|
| Imports from UK | £45,250,709 | £41,281,566 |
| Exports to UK | £105,159,563 | £87,655,359 |

## COMMUNICATIONS

*Airports and waterways* – The principal airports are at Maputo and Beira, with 19 other airports around the country; the main seaports are Maputo, Beira and Nacala, which also handle trade for neighbouring countries
*Roadways and railways* – There are 6,303km of roadways and 4,787km of railways
*Telecommunications* – 88,100 fixed lines and 8.12 million mobile subscriptions (2012); there were 613,600 internet users in 2009
*Internet code and IDD* – mz; 258 (from UK), 44 (to UK)
*Major broadcasters* – Televisao de Mozambique (TVM) is the state-run television broadcaster; Radio Mozambique and Radio Cidade are the public radio broadcasters
*Press* – Leading national dailies include *Diario de Mocambique*, *O Pais* and *Noticias* (partly state owned)
*WPFI score* – 29,98 (85)

# MYANMAR

*Pyidaungzu Thammada Myanma Naingngandaw* – Republic of the Union of Myanmar

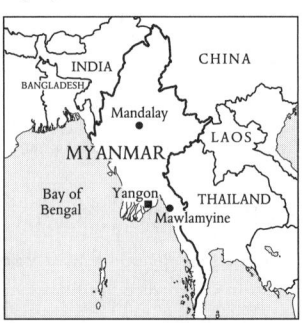

*Area* – 676,578 sq. km
*Capital* – Naypyitaw; population, 4,705,000 (2014)
*Major cities* – Bago, Mandalay, Mawlamyine (Moulmein), Pathein (Bassein), Yangon (Rangoon)
*Currency* – Kyat (K) of 100 pyas
*Population* – 56,320,206 rising at 1.01 per cent a year (2015 est); Burman (68 per cent), Shan (9 per cent), Karen (7 per cent), Rakhine (4 per cent), Chinese (3 per cent), Indian (2 per cent), Mon (2 per cent) (est)
*Religion* – Buddhist 89 per cent, Christian 4 per cent (Baptist 3 per cent, Roman Catholic 1 per cent), Muslim 4 per cent
*Language* – Burmese (official), numerous ethnic languages
*Population density* – 82 per sq. km (2013)
*Urban population* – 33.8 per cent (2013 est)
*Median age (years)* – 27.9 (2014 est)
*National anthem* – 'Kaba Ma Kyei' ['Till the End of the World, Myanmar']
*National day* – 4 January (Independence Day)
*Death penalty* – Retained (last used in the 1980s)
*CPI score* – 21 (156)

## CLIMATE AND TERRAIN

Central lowlands are ringed by mountains in the west, north (part of the foothills of the Himalayas) and east. The eastern range extends down the Kra isthmus that Myanmar shares with Thailand, forming a natural border. Elevation extremes range from 5,870m (Gamlang Razi) to 0m (Andaman Sea). The lowlands are drained by the Irrawaddy river and its chief tributary, the Chindwin, and the eastern mountains by the Salween. The Irrawaddy has a large delta on the Andaman coast. The climate is tropical, with a wet season from May to September. Average temperatures in Mandalay, representative of the interior lowlands, range from 18.4°C in January to 25.2°C in April and May, although temperatures in the interior can reach 44°C in May.

## POLITICS

Under the 2010 constitution, the head of state is a president elected by the legislature for a five-year term, renewable once. The president is also head of government and appoints ministers with the approval of the legislature. The bicameral People's Assembly comprises the 440-member House of Representatives, the lower chamber, and the 224-member House of Nationalities. In each chamber, 25 per cent of seats are reserved for the military and the rest are directly elected; both chambers serve a five-year term. Constitutional changes require approval by a 75 per cent majority.

In preparation for legislative elections in late 2010, several electoral laws were introduced in March 2010; these excluded many political activists, such as Aung San Suu Kyi,

| | | | | | | |
|---|---|---|---|---|---|---|
| Area invaded by Mongols, led by Kublai Khan | King Alaunghpaya reunites nation | Country annexed as part of British India following Anglo-Burmese war | Gains independence as Union of Burma | One-party socialist republic formally established | Aung San Suu Kyi's NLD wins a landslide victory in first multi-party elections for 30 years | |

c.1050    c.1400    1800–50    1937    1962    1988    2010

1287    1759    1885    1948    1972    1990

| | | | | | | |
|---|---|---|---|---|---|---|
| Unified by King Anawratha, who adopts Theravada Buddhism | Achieves unification; war with Thailand | Border disputes with British India spiral into series of wars | Becomes self-governing protectorate; occupied by Japanese in Second World War | Military coup; economy nationalised | State Law and Order Council takes control; state name changed to Myanmar | Aung San Suu Kyi released from house arrest |

from participation in the elections, set restrictive conditions for party registration, and tightly regulated campaigning and funding; the National League for Democracy (NLD) announced a boycott of the elections. Several members of the government resigned their military commissions to contest the elections as civilians, registering a new political party, the Union Solidarity and Development Party (USDP).

In November 2010, the USDP won 259 of the seats in the lower chamber and 129 of the seats in the upper chamber in elections that opposition groups claimed were fraudulent and were condemned internationally as a sham. The new legislature convened in January 2011, electing prime minister Thein Sein as president in February 2011. A new, nominally civilian government was sworn in on 30 March, and the dissolution of the State Peace and Development Council was announced. In April 2012, the NLD, led by Aung San Suu Kyi, contested 44 of the 46 seats in the lower house by-elections, winning 43 of them.

## HEAD OF STATE
*President, Chair of National Defence and Security Council,* Lt.-Gen. (retd) Thein Sein
*First Vice-President,* Adm. (retd) Nyan Tun
*Second Vice-President,* Mauk Kham

## SELECTED GOVERNMENT MEMBERS *as at June 2015*
*Defence,* Vice Senior Gen. Wai Lwin
*Foreign Affairs,* Gen. (retd) Wunna Maung Lwin
*Home Affairs,* Lt.-Gen. Ko Ko

## EMBASSY OF THE REPUBLIC OF THE UNION OF MYANMAR
19A Charles Street, London W1J 5DX
T 020-7499 4340
E ambassadoroffice@myanmarembassylondon.com
W www.myanmarembassylondon.com
*Ambassador Extraordinary and Plenipotentiary,* HE Kyaw Zwar Minn, *apptd* 2013

## BRITISH EMBASSY
80 Strand Road (Box 638), Rangoon
T (+95) (1) 370 865 E be.rangoon@fco.gov.uk
W www.gov.uk/government/world/burma
*Ambassador Extraordinary and Plenipotentiary,* HE Andrew Patrick, *apptd* 2013

## INSURGENCIES
Since independence in 1948 there have been various insurgencies, mostly by ethnic groups. These have included the Kachin, Kayin (Karen), Karenni, Wa, Shan, Mon, Arakan Chin and Kokang ethnic minorities. Since 1992, 18 ethnic groups have signed ceasefire agreements; the government is accused of breaking four of these since the November 2010 election. Some groups have achieved a degree of autonomy in their region; others have splintered, creating intra-ethnic tension. The country's ethnic minorities are believed to bear the brunt of the government's human rights abuses, with the Muslim Rohingya of western Burma considered one of the most oppressed peoples in the world; military offensives against insurgents have displaced over half a million people.

## DEFENCE

| Aged 16–49, 2010 est | Males | Females |
|---|---|---|
| Available for military service | 14,747,845 | 14,710,871 |
| Fit for military service | 10,451,515 | 11,181,537 |

*Military expenditure* – US$2,373m (2014)

## ECONOMY AND TRADE
Myanmar has fertile soil, occupies strategic trade routes between India, China and South East Asia, and has an abundance of natural resources such as natural gas (it is Asia's largest exporter), timber (it is the world's largest exporter of teak), precious gems (jade, pearls, rubies and sapphires) and oil, but the economy is characterised by mismanagement and corruption. The country became increasingly poverty-stricken under military rule and just under a third of children suffer from malnutrition. The economy suffers from unpredictable policies, market distortions and inadequate commercial, transport and energy infrastructure. The regime's repressiveness lost it development aid, and attracted economic and trade sanctions, though many US sanctions were lifted in 2012 following political reforms. There is a large grey economy and considerable unofficial cross-border trade. Growth of just under 8.5 per cent is expected in 2015 and 2016, due to structural reform and the positive performances of the neighbouring Indian and Thai economies. Myanmar is scheduled to form a common market with the other members of the Association of Southeast Asian Nations (ASEAN) in 2015.

Agriculture is the dominant economic activity, accounting for 38 per cent of GDP and engaging 70 per cent of the workforce; the most important export crops are rice, pulses, beans and fish. The main industries are forestry, mining and oil and gas extraction, and these have attracted some foreign investment; manufacturing and services are struggling, and the then growing tourist industry declined dramatically after the violent suppression of demonstrations in 2007. Industry contributes 20.3 per cent of GDP and services 41.7 per cent.

The main trading partners are Thailand (35 per cent of exports; 20.3 per cent of imports), China (24.5 per cent of exports; 40 per cent of imports), Singapore and India. Principal exports are natural gas, wood products, agricultural produce, clothing and gems. The main imports are fabric, petroleum products, fertiliser, plastics, machinery, transport equipment, construction materials, crude oil and food.

*Annual average growth of GDP* – 8.5 per cent (2014)
*Inflation rate* – 6.6 per cent (2014 est)
*Population below poverty line* – 32.7 per cent (2007 est)
*Unemployment* – 3.6 per cent (2015 est)
*Total external debt* – US$2,491m (2014 est)
*Imports* – US$9,109m (2011)
*Exports* – US$9,2380m (2011)

BALANCE OF PAYMENTS
*Trade* – US$221m surplus (2011)
*Current Account* – US$4,832m deficit (2015 est)

| Trade with UK | 2013 | 2014 |
|---|---|---|
| Imports from UK | £6,040,007 | £12,862,636 |
| Exports to UK | £36,876,749 | £44,900,710 |

## COMMUNICATIONS

*Airports and waterways* – The main airports are at Yangon and Mandalay; the 12,800km of navigable waterways include the Irrawaddy and Chindwin rivers, and the chief seaports are Yangon (Rangoon), Mawlamyine (Moulmein) and Akyab (Sittwe)

*Roadways and railways* – 34,377km of roadways and 5,031km of railways

*Telecommunications* – 556,000 fixed lines and 5.44 mobile subscriptions (2011); there were 110,000 internet users in 2009

*Internet code and IDD* – mm; 95 (from UK), 44 (to UK)

*Major broadcasters* – Democratic Voice of Burma, an opposition radio station broadcasting via short-wave from Norway, and foreign services such as the BBC and Voice of America, are key sources of information for the population; TV Myanmar is the state-run national broadcaster

*Press* – Leading dailies include the state-run *Kyehmon* and *Myanmar Alin;* legislation increasing journalistic freedom was passed in 2014

*WPFI score* – 42,08 (144)

## EDUCATION AND HEALTH

*Literacy rate* – 96.3 per cent (2015 est)

*Gross enrolment ratio (percentage of relevant age group)* – primary 114 per cent; secondary 50 per cent (2010 est); tertiary 13 per cent (2012 est)

*Health expenditure (per capita)* – US$14 (2013)

*Hospital beds (per 1,000 people)* – 0.6 (2006)

*Life expectancy (years)* – 65.6 (2013 est)

*Mortality rate* – 8.05 (2013 est)

*Birth rate* – 18.65 (2014 est)

*Infant mortality rate* – 44.91 (2014 est)

# NAMIBIA

*Republic of Namibia*

*Area* – 824,292 sq. km

*Capital* – Windhoek; population, 356,000 (2014)

*Major towns* – Oshakati, Rundu, Walvis Bay

*Currency* – Namibian dollar of 100 cents, at parity with South African rand

*Population* – 2,212,307 rising at 0.59 per cent a year (2015 est); Ovambo (50 per cent), Kavangos (9 per cent), Herero (7 per cent), Damara (7 per cent), Nama (5 per cent), Caprivian (4 per cent), San (Bushmen) (3 per cent), Baster (2 per cent) (est)

*Religion* – Christian 80–90 per cent (at least 50 per cent Lutheran), indigenous beliefs 10–20 per cent

*Language* – English (official), Afrikaans (lingua franca), Oshiwambo, Herero, Nama, other indigenous languages

*Population density* – 3 per sq. km (2013)

*Urban population* – 39.5 per cent (2013 est)

*Median age (years)* – 22.8 (2014 est)

*National anthem* – 'Namibia, Land of the Brave'

*National day* – 21 March (Independence Day)

*Death penalty* – Abolished for all crimes (since 1990)

*CPI score* – 49 (55)

*Literacy rate* – 89.9 per cent (2015 est)

*Gross enrolment ratio (percentage of relevant age group)* – primary 109 per cent (2012 est)

*Health expenditure (per capita)* – US$423 (2013)

*Hospital beds (per 1,000 people)* – 2.7 (2009)

*Life expectancy (years)* – 51.85 (2014 est)

*Mortality rate* – 13.6 (2014 est)

*Birth rate* – 20.28 (2014 est)

*Infant mortality rate* – 45.64 (2014 est)

*HIV/AIDS adult prevalence* – 14.3 per cent (2013 est)

## CLIMATE AND TERRAIN

The Namib desert runs along the Atlantic coast and is separated by a line of hills and high veldt from the Kalahari desert in the interior. Elevation extremes range from 2,606m (Konigstein) to 0m (Atlantic Ocean). Major rivers include the Orange, which forms the southern border with South Africa, and the Zambezi, which runs through the Caprivi Strip in the extreme north-east of the country. The climate is arid in the west and semi-arid in the centre and north-east; rainfall is sparse and droughts are frequent. The coast is cooler and frequently foggy. Average temperatures range from 14.9°C in July to 24.4°C in January.

## HISTORY AND POLITICS

Pre-colonial Namibia was inhabited by San and then by Bantu tribes. It was annexed by Germany in 1884 and named South West Africa. Indigenous uprisings against colonial settlement in the early 20th century were brutally suppressed, with some tribes suffering severe losses; the Herero and Nama were nearly wiped out. The territory was occupied by South Africa on behalf of the Allies in 1915 and after the First World War it became a League of Nations mandated territory, administered by South Africa.

The arrangement continued under the UN after the Second World War, but South Africa exceeded its mandate by effectively annexing the country, extending representation in the South African parliament to the white population in 1949, and applying apartheid in 1966. These actions were taken despite the UN's refusal to permit the country's incorporation into South Africa in 1946 and its termination of the mandate in 1966. In 1968, the UN changed the country's name to Namibia, and the South West Africa People's Organisation (SWAPO), which had campaigned for racial equality and independence since 1960, began a guerrilla war against South Africa.

South Africa's peace talks with Angola in 1988 led to agreement on independence for Namibia, and this was achieved on 21 March 1990; South Africa's Walvis Bay enclave was returned to Namibia in 1994.

The country has enjoyed stability since independence, apart from a brief period of secessionist violence in the Caprivi Strip in the late 1990s, and has been recognised by observers as having one of the freest media industries in Africa. Following agitation for an acceleration of land reform, the government programme moved from voluntary sales to expropriation of white-owned farms in 2005. The country's main problems arise from the demographic, economic and social impact of the high level of HIV/AIDS infection among the population.

SWAPO has been the dominant party since independence, holding the presidency and commanding a parliamentary majority without interruption. The November 2014 presidential election was won by Hage Geingob of SWAPO who collected 86.7 per cent of the vote; SWAPO retained its large majority in the simultaneous legislative election.

Under the 1990 constitution, the executive president is directly elected for a five-year term, renewable once. There is a bicameral parliament consisting of a National Assembly, with 72 members directly elected for a five-year term and up to six additional non-voting members appointed by the president, and a National Council, whose 26 members are elected by the regional councils from among their own members for a six-year term; the latter's main function is to review and consider legislation from the lower chamber. The president appoints the prime minister and the other ministers.

## HEAD OF STATE

*President,* Hage Geingob, *elected* 1 December 2014, *sworn in* 21 March 2015
*Vice-President,* Nickey Iyambo

SELECTED GOVERNMENT MEMBERS *as at June 2015*
*Prime Minister,* Saara Kuugongelwa-Amadhila
*Deputy Prime Minister,* Netumbo Nandi-Ndaitwah
*Defence,* Penda Ya Ndakolo
*Finance,* Calle Schlettwein

## HIGH COMMISSION FOR THE REPUBLIC OF NAMIBIA

6 Chandos Street, London W1G 9LU
T 020-7636 6244 E info@namibiahc.org.uk
W www.namibiahc.org.uk
*High Commissioner,* HE Steve Vemunavi Katjiuanjo, *apptd* 2013

## BRITISH HIGH COMMISSION

116 Robert Mugabe Avenue, PO Box 22202, Windhoek
T (+264) (61) 274 800 E general.windhoek@fco.gov.uk
W www.gov.uk/government/world/namibia
*High Commissioner,* HE Joanne Lomas, *apptd* 2015

## DEFENCE

| Aged 16–49, 2010 est | Males | Females |
| --- | --- | --- |
| Available for military service | 568,231 | – |
| Fit for military service | 351,431 | 311,513 |

*Military expenditure* – US$548m (2014)

## ECONOMY AND TRADE

Despite a high GDP per capita, Namibia has high levels of poverty and inequality. Its arid terrain limits agriculture, but the emphasis on environmental protection (enshrined in the constitution) is helping the development of tourism. The country has rich mineral deposits; extraction of these is the main industrial activity and minerals account for over 50 per cent of foreign exchange earnings. This leaves the economy vulnerable to global price fluctuations, and the government is encouraging foreign investment to help diversification. Other industries process the products of the farming and fisheries sectors. Agriculture operates mostly at subsistence level, accounting for 6.2 per cent of GDP.

The main trading partners are South Africa, the UK, Angola, Spain, Japan and China. Principal exports are diamonds, copper, gold, zinc, lead, uranium, cattle, processed fish and skins. The main imports are foodstuffs (particularly grain), petroleum products and fuel, machinery and equipment, and chemicals.
*GNI* – US$13,519m; US$5,870 per capita (2013)
*Annual average growth of GDP* – 4.3 per cent (2014)
*Inflation rate* – 5.6 per cent (2014 est)

*Population below poverty line* – 28.7 per cent (2010 est)
*Unemployment* – 19.1 per cent (2015 est)
*Total external debt* – US$5,480m (2014 est)
*Imports* – US$7,498m (2013)
*Exports* – US$3,480m (2013)

BALANCE OF PAYMENTS
*Trade* – US$4,018m deficit (2013)
*Current Account* – US$124m deficit (2015 est)

| Trade with UK | 2013 | 2014 |
| --- | --- | --- |
| Imports from UK | £55,174,571 | £47,662,613 |
| Exports to UK | £77,346,165 | £39,491,991 |

## COMMUNICATIONS

*Airports and waterways* – The main airports are at Windhoek and Odangwa, with 17 smaller airports around the country; the two main seaports are Walvis Bay and Luderitz
*Roadways and railways* – 6,387km; 2,626km
*Telecommunications* – 171,000 fixed lines and 2.435 million mobile subscriptions (2012); there were 127,500 internet users in 2009
*Internet code and IDD* – na; 264 (from UK), 44 (to UK)
*Major broadcasters* – The Namibian Broadcasting Corporation (NBC) is publicly owned and operates television and radio stations
*Press* – There are five national daily newspapers including *The Namibian* (English and Oshiwambo language), *Die Republikein* (Afrikaans) and the state-owned *New Era*
*WPFI score* – 12,5 (17)

# NAURU

*Republic of Nauru*

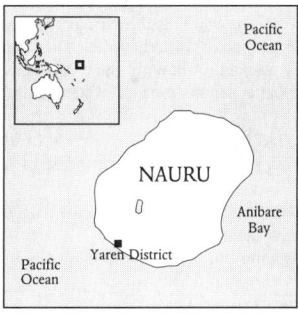

*Area* – 21 sq. km
*Capital* – Yaren District (unofficial)
*Currency* – Australian dollar (A$) of 100 cents
*Population* – 9,540 rising at 0.55 per cent a year (2015 est); Nauruan (58 per cent), other Pacific Islander (26 per cent), Chinese (8 per cent), European (8 per cent) (est)
*Religion* – Christian (Protestant 60.4 per cent, Roman Catholic 33 per cent)
*Language* – Nauruan (official), English
*Urban population* – 100 per cent (2013)
*Median age (years)* – 25.3 (2014 est)
*National anthem* – 'Nauru Bwiema' ('Song of Nauru')
*National day* – 31 January (Independence Day)
*Death penalty* – Retained (last used 1968)
*Life expectancy (years)* – 66.4 (2014 est)
*Mortality rate* – 5.9 (2014 est)
*Birth rate* – 25.61 (2014 est)
*Infant mortality rate* – 8.21 (2014 est)

## CLIMATE AND TERRAIN
Nauru is a low-lying island in the southern Pacific Ocean, 42km south of the equator and 4,000km north-east of Sydney, Australia. There is a fertile coastal plain but about 60 per cent of the land area consists of the central plateau, formed of phosphate, which has been extensively mined. The plateau rim is the highest point, at 61m; the lowest is 0m at sea level. The climate is tropical, with a rainy season from November to February.

## HISTORY AND POLITICS
Nauru was first settled by Polynesian and Melanesian groups. The first Europeans to visit the island were British whalers in 1798, and by 1888 Nauru was annexed by Germany. At the outbreak of the First World War, Nauru was occupied by Australia, which continued to administer the island under a League of Nations mandate from 1920. The island was occupied by the Japanese in 1942–3, but in 1947 UN trusteeship status superseded the mandate and Nauru continued to be administered by Australia until it became independent on 31 January 1968. A detention centre, established in partnership with Australia to house asylum seekers headed towards that country, has attracted controversy for its allegedly harsh conditions.

A financial crisis in 2003 caused some political instability, though a more stable period during Ludwig Scotty's second presidency (2004–7) saw the introduction of austerity measures and public sector reform. Scotty lost a vote of confidence in December 2007 and was replaced by Marcus Stephen. President Stephen resigned in 2011 amid allegations of corruption and was replaced first by Frederick Pitcherr and then former transport minister Sprent Dabwido; Baron Waqa won the 2013 presidential election. A third of the MPs elected in the 2013 legislative elections were new to parliament.

Under the 1968 constitution, the executive president is elected by the legislature from among its members for a three-year term. The unicameral parliament has 18 members, who are directly elected for a three-year term. The president appoints the cabinet. Although there are active political parties, most parliamentary candidates stand as independents.

### HEAD OF STATE
*President, Foreign Affairs,* Baron Waqa, *elected* 11 June 2013

### SELECTED GOVERNMENT MEMBERS *as at June 2015*
*Finance, Justice,* David Adeang
*Commerce, Industry and Environment,* Aaron Cook

### HONORARY CONSULATE
Romshed Courtyard, Underriver, Sevenoaks, Kent TN15 0SD
T 01732-746061 E nauru@weald.co.uk
*Honorary Consul,* Martin Weston

### BRITISH HIGH COMMISSIONER
HE Roderick Drummond, *apptd* 2013, resident at Suva, Fiji

## ECONOMY AND TRADE
Phosphate is the only resource and its extraction is the sole industry, but reserves will be exhausted in 30 years. Profits derived from the mining industry were invested in trust funds to provide for the post-mining future, but heavy spending from the funds has left the country virtually bankrupt, causing it to default on loans and have assets seized in 2004. The economy is dependent on international aid (principally from Australia) and revenue from the sale of fishing licences, but diversification efforts include offshore banking and small-scale tourism.

The main trading partners are Australia and New Zealand. The only export is phosphate. All food, fuel, manufactured goods, machinery and construction materials are imported.
*Unemployment* – 90 per cent (2004 est)
*Total external debt* – US$33.3m (2004 est)

| Trade with UK | 2013 | 2014 |
| --- | --- | --- |
| Imports from UK | £132,149 | £117,991 |
| Exports to UK | £121,502 | £92,316 |

## COMMUNICATION
*Transport* – The island has one international airport and 24km of roadways
*Telecommunications* – 1,900 fixed lines (2009) and 6,800 mobile phone subscriptions (2012)
*Internet code and IDD* – nr; 674 (from UK), 44 (to UK)
*Media* – The government-owned Nauru Television and Radio Nauru are the island's principal broadcasters; there are no daily newspapers

# NEPAL

*Sanghiya Loktantrik Ganatantra Nepal – Federal Democratic Republic of Nepal*

*Area* – 147,181 sq. km
*Capital* – Kathmandu; population, 1,142,000 (2014)
*Major cities* – Biratnagar, Lalitpur, Lumbini, Pokhara
*Currency* – Nepalese rupee (Rs) of 100 paisa
*Population* – 31,551,305 rising at 1.79 per cent a year (2015 est); Chhettri (16.6 per cent), Brahman-Hill (12.2 per cent), Magar (7.1 per cent), Tharu (6.6 per cent), Tamang (5.8 per cent), Newar (5 per cent), Kami (4.8 per cent), Yadav (4 per cent) (2001)
*Religion* – Hindu 81.3 per cent, Buddhist 9 per cent, Muslim 4.4 per cent, Kirant 3 per cent (practised by a large proportion of Nepal's Kirati population)
*Language* – Nepali (official), English, Maithali, Bhojpuri, Tharu, Tamang, Newar, Magar, Awadhi
*Population density* – 194 per sq. km (2013)
*Urban population* – 17.7 per cent (2013 est)
*Median age (years)* – 22.9 (2014 est)
*National anthem* – 'Sayaun Thunga Phool Ka' ['Hundreds of Flowers']
*National day* – 29 May (Republic Day)
*Death penalty* – Abolished for all crimes (since 1997)
*CPI score* – 29 (126)

## CLIMATE AND TERRAIN
The north of Nepal lies in the Himalayas, with the snowline at about 4,880m. The terrain descends from the mountains through a hilly central region with fertile valleys to the southern plains, the Terai, that lie in the valley of the Ganges.

Elevation extremes range from 8,850m (Mt Everest) to 70m (Kanchan Kalan). The climate varies from subtropical in the south to much cooler with severe winters in the north. Average temperatures range from 4.8°C in January to 19.1°C in June and July. The rainy season lasts from June to September.

## HISTORY AND POLITICS

Modern Nepal was formed from a number of small states that were conquered and unified in the 18th century by the Gurkha ruler Prithvi Naryan Shah. After war with the British in 1815–16, Nepal became a British-dependent buffer state; its independence was formally recognised in 1923.

Power was seized by Jung Bahdur in 1846. He assumed the title Rana and his family became hereditary chief ministers, reducing the monarchy to a purely ceremonial role and keeping the country isolated. In 1950–1, the Ranas were overthrown and the monarchy was restored to power. Apart from 1959–60, when a parliamentary system of government was in place, the kings ruled as absolute monarchs until 1990, when a new constitution was introduced that made the country a constitutional monarchy and multiparty parliamentary democracy.

However, factionalism led to frequent changes of government, causing political and social instability, which was exacerbated from 1996 by a Maoist insurgency led by the Nepal Communist Party. The insurgency began in the west and spread quickly. By 2006 the insurgents controlled 80 per cent of the country.

King Gyanendra's assumption of direct rule in 2005 led politicians to ally themselves with the Maoists to achieve the restoration of democracy, and in April 2006 the king reinstated the legislature after three months of violent pro-democracy protests. In November 2006 a peace accord was signed, an interim legislature was established in January 2007 and a multiparty government took office in April.

Elections to the constituent assembly took place in April 2008; the Communist Party of Nepal–Maoists (CPN-M) won the most seats and abolished the monarchy on 28 May 2008. The assembly elected Ram Baran Yadav of the Nepali Congress party as the country's first president in July. In legislative elections in November 2013, the Nepali Congress party became the largest party, winning 105 of the 240 seats allocated by the first past the post system and 91 of the 335 allocated by proportional representation. Congress leader Sushil Koirala was then elected prime minister by parliament.

The 2007 interim constitution is in force until a new constitution is drafted by the constituent assembly and is approved. The monarchy was abolished in May 2008 and the country declared a republic. The head of state is the president, who was elected by the constituent assembly. The legislature consists of 575 directly elected members and 26 appointed by the council of ministers. A new constitution was due to be drafted in 2015.

The prime minister is appointed by consensus among the political parties or elected by a two-thirds majority of the assembly. The council of ministers is responsible to the legislature.

### HEAD OF STATE

*President,* Ram Baran Yadav, *elected* 21 July 2008, *sworn in* 23 July 2008
*Vice-President,* Paramananda Jha

SELECTED GOVERNMENT MEMBERS *as at June 2015*
*Prime Minister, Defence,* Sushil Koirala
*Foreign Affairs,* Mahendra Bahadur Pande
*Finance,* Ram Sharan Mahat

### EMBASSY OF NEPAL

12A Kensington Palace Gardens, London W8 4QU
T 020-7229 1594 E eon@nepembassy.org.uk
W www.nepembassy.org.uk
*Ambassador Extraordinary and Plenipotentiary,* vacant

### BRITISH EMBASSY

PO Box 106, Lainchaur, Kathmandu
T (+977) (1) 441 0583 E bekathmandu@fco.gov.uk
W www.gov.uk/government/world/nepal
*Ambassador Extraordinary and Plenipotentiary,* HE John Rankin, *apptd* 2015

### DEFENCE

| Aged 16–49, 2010 est | Males | Females |
| --- | --- | --- |
| Available for military service | 6,941,152 | 7,618,397 |
| Fit for military service | 5,260,878 | 5,947,512 |

*Military expenditure* – US$305m (2014)

### ECONOMY AND TRADE

The country is one of the poorest in Asia, and the economy is dependent on foreign aid and trade with India. Tourism and hydroelectric power have potential for development, although this might compound growing environmental problems.

Agriculture is the main economic sector, generating 30.7 per cent of GDP and engaging about 75 per cent of the workforce; principal crops are pulses, rice, maize, wheat, sugar cane, jute, root crops, milk and meat. Industries other than tourism include carpets, textiles, cigarettes, cement and bricks, and the processing of rice, jute, sugar and oilseed. Industry accounts for 13.6 per cent of GDP and services for 55.7 per cent. The April 2015 earthquake (*see* Events) has severely damaged the economy. Costs of reconstruction are estimated to be around US$10bn (£6.5bn), around 50 per cent of Nepal's GDP.

The main export market is India (53.7 per cent); the main import providers are India (50.6 per cent) and South Korea. Principal exports are clothing, pulses, carpets, textiles, juice, pashmina and jute goods. The main imports are petroleum products, machinery, gold, electrical goods and medicine.
*GNI* – US$20,261m; US$730 per capita (2013)
*Annual average growth of GDP* – 5.5 per cent (2014)
*Inflation rate* – 8.4 per cent (2014 est)
*Population below poverty line* – 25.2 per cent (2011)
*Unemployment* – 2.7 per cent (2015 est)
*Total external debt* – US$3,549m (2014 est)
*Imports* – US$6,385m (2013)
*Exports* – US$920m (2013)

### BALANCE OF PAYMENTS

*Trade* – US$5,465m deficit (2013)
*Current Account* – US$88m surplus (2015 est)

| Trade with UK | 2013 | 2014 |
| --- | --- | --- |
| Imports from UK | £8,112,176 | £7,876,093 |
| Exports to UK | £16,205,634 | £14,505,099 |

### COMMUNICATIONS

*Airports* – The principal airport is at Kathmandu, and there are ten smaller airports around the country
*Roadways and railways* – 4,952km; 59km
*Telecommunications* – 834,000 fixed lines and 18.148 million mobile subscriptions (2013); there were 577,800 internet users in 2009
*Internet code and IDD* – np; 977 (from UK), 44 (to UK)

*Major broadcasters* – The state-run Nepal Television Corporation operates various channels across the country alongside numerous private operators
*Press* – Dailies include the semi-official *Gorkhapatra,* Nepal's oldest newspaper, and *The Rising Nepal,* plus the private *The Kathmandu Post*
*WPFI score* – 32,71 (105)

## EDUCATION AND HEALTH
*Literacy rate* – 86.9 per cent (2015 est)
*Gross enrolment ratio (percentage of relevant age group)* –
    primary 132.7 per cent; secondary 66.9 per cent
    (2014 est); tertiary 17.2 per cent (2013 est)
*Health expenditure (per capita)* – US$39 (2013)
*Hospital beds (per 1,000 people)* – 5 (2006)
*Life expectancy (years)* – 67.19 (2014 est)
*Mortality rate* – 6.62 (2014 est)
*Birth rate* – 21.07 (2014 est)
*Infant mortality rate* – 40.43 (2014 est)

# THE NETHERLANDS

*Koninkrijk der Nederlanden – Kingdom of the Netherlands*

*Area* – 41,543 sq. km
*Capital* – Amsterdam; population, 1,084,000 (2014)
*Seat of government* – The Hague (Den Haag or, in full,
    's-Gravenhage), population, 629,000 (2009 est)
*Major cities* – Almere, Eindhoven, Haarlem, Rotterdam,
    Tilburg, Utrecht
*Currency* – Euro (€) of 100 cents
*Population* – 16,947,904 rising at 0.41 per cent a year
    (2015 est); Dutch (80.7 per cent), Indonesian (2.4 per
    cent), Turkish (2.2 per cent), Moroccan (2 per cent),
    Surinamese (2 per cent) (2008 est)
*Religion* – Christian (Roman Catholic 28 per cent, Protestant
    18 per cent), Muslim 5 per cent
*Language* – Dutch (official), Frisian, Low Saxon, and
    Limburgish (official regional languages); English is widely
    spoken
*Population density* – 498 per sq. km (2013)
*Urban population* – 84 per cent (2013 est)
*Median age (years)* – 42.1 (2014 est)

*National anthem* – 'Het Wilhelmus' ['The William']
*National day* – 27 April (King's Day)
*Death penalty* – Abolished for all crimes (since 1982)
*CPI score* – 83 (8)

## CLIMATE AND TERRAIN
The Netherlands is a low-lying country; about a quarter is below sea level, making it susceptible to flooding despite the coastal defences and a network of dykes and canals. Its land area has been extended over the centuries by land reclamation (polders), found especially in the west around the huge freshwater lake of Yssel, created in the 1930s by damming the Zuider Zee. The country is crossed by three major European rivers, the Rhine, Maas (Meuse) and Scheldt, whose estuaries are in the south-west. Mount Scenery (862m), on the Caribbean island of Saba, is considered the highest point of the Kingdom of the Netherlands. Elevation extremes in the Netherlands itself range from 322m (Vaalserberg) to −7m (Zuidplaspolder). The climate is temperate, with average temperatures ranging from 3.5°C in January to 18°C in August.

## POLITICS
Under the 1983 constitution, the head of state is a hereditary constitutional monarch. The States-General *(Staten-Generaal)* consists of the First Chamber *(Eerste Kamer)* of 75 members, elected for a four-year term by the Provincial States; and the Second Chamber *(Tweede Kamer)* of 150 members, directly elected for a four-year term. The head of government is the prime minister, who is responsible to the legislature.

    Although it is a stable democracy, one party has rarely commanded a sufficient parliamentary majority to govern alone in the post-war period; governments have usually been coalitions of two or more parties. In the May 2015 election to the First Chamber, the VVD led by Mark Rutte retained its position as the largest party; since 2012 the VVD has been the largest party in the Second Chamber. In April 2013, Queen Beatrix abdicated in favour of Willem-Alexander, her eldest son.

HEAD OF STATE
*HM The King of the Netherlands,* King Willem-Alexander,
    *born* 27 April 1967; *succeeded* 30 April 2013
*Heiress,* HRH Princess Catharina-Amalia, *born* 7 December
    2003

SELECTED GOVERNMENT MEMBERS *as at June 2015*
*Prime Minister,* Mark Rutte
*Deputy Prime Minister,* Lodewijk Asscher
*Defence,* Jeanine Hennis-Plasschaert
*Foreign Affairs,* Bert Koenders

EMBASSY OF THE KINGDOM OF THE NETHERLANDS
38 Hyde Park Gate, London SW7 5DP
T 020-7590 3200 E lon@minbuza.nl
W www.dutchembassyuk.org
*Ambassador Extraordinary and Plenipotentiary,* HE Laetitia van
    den Assum, *apptd* 2012

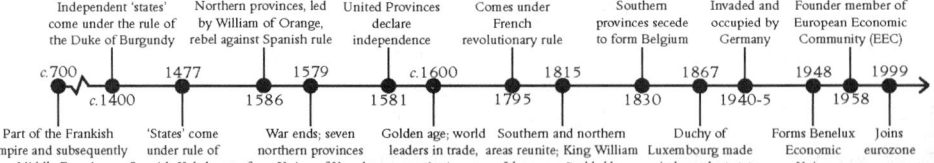

BRITISH EMBASSY
Lange Voorhout 10, The Hague, 2514 ED
T (+31) (70) 427 0427 E ukinnl@fco.gov.uk
W www.gov.uk/government/world/netherlands
*Ambassador Extraordinary and Plenipotentiary,* HE Sir
Geoffrey Adams, *apptd* 2013

## DEFENCE

| Aged 16–49, 2014 est | Males | Females |
|---|---|---|
| Available for military service | 3,911,098 | 3,817,031 |
| Fit for military service | 3,479,509 | 3,435,564 |

*Military expenditure* – US$10,086m (2014)

## ECONOMY AND TRADE

The Netherlands has a highly industrialised and diversified market economy, and is a major European transportation hub. The economy depends heavily on foreign trade and financial services, and contracted sharply in 2009 as exports fell by almost 25 per cent in the global economic downturn. The government nationalised two banks to stabilise the financial sector and introduced stimulus measures, creating a budget deficit; the implementation of new fiscal measures in early 2011, however, reduced the budget deficit, which remained at 3.8 per cent of GDP by the end of the year. The budget deficit decreased in 2013 and 2014, although unemployment rates remain high and growth in wages low. GDP growth of under 1 per cent is expected in 2015.

The highly mechanised agricultural sector employs only 2.3 per cent of the workforce but output supplies the food processing industries and the export as well as the domestic market. Flower bulbs and cut flowers are a major contributor to this sector, as is the fishing industry. The industrial sector contributes 22.3 per cent of GDP; major industries include food processing, and the manufacture of metal and engineering products, electrical machinery and equipment, chemicals, oil refining, construction and micro-electronics. The service industries represent 74.8 per cent of the economy. Other EU countries, China and Russia account for most overseas trade. Principal exports are machinery and equipment, chemicals, fuels and foodstuffs. The main imports are machinery and transport equipment, chemicals, fuels, foodstuffs and clothing.

*GNI* – US$858,027m; US$51,060 per capita (2013)
*Annual average growth of GDP* – 0.6 per cent (2014)
*Inflation rate* – 0.5 per cent (2014 est)
*Population below poverty line* – 9.1 per cent (2013)
*Unemployment* – 7.2 per cent (2015 est)
*Total external debt* – US$2,347,000m (2013 est)
*Imports* – US$507,478m (2013)
*Exports* – US$567,674m (2013)

BALANCE OF PAYMENTS
*Trade* – US$60,196m surplus (2013)
*Current Account* – US$78,090m surplus (2015 est)

| Trade with UK | 2013 | 2014 |
|---|---|---|
| Imports from UK | £23,875,601,316 | £22,621,338,613 |
| Exports to UK | £34,262,277,863 | £31,164,581,211 |

## COMMUNICATIONS

*Airports* – The principal airports are at Amsterdam, Rotterdam, Eindhoven and Maastricht, with a further 25 airports around the country
*Waterways* – The main seaport is Rotterdam, although there are a number of other ports on river estuaries or linked to the coast by the canals; 6,237km of inland waterways are navigable by ships of up to 50 tonnes. The large merchant fleet includes 744 ships of over 1,000 tonnes

*Roadways and railways* – There are 139,295km of roads, including 2,758km of motorways, and 3,013km of railways, of which 2,195km are electrified
*Telecommunications* – 7.086 million fixed lines and 19.643 million mobile subscriptions (2012); there were 14.872 million internet users in 2009
*Internet code and IDD* – nl; 31 (from UK), 44 (to UK)
*Major broadcasters* – A competitive broadcasting sector includes Nederlandse Omroep Stichting (NOS), which operates public radio and television stations
*Press* – Leading dailies include *Algemeen Dagblad, NRC Handelsblad* and *De Telegraaf*
*WPFI score* – 9,22 (4)

## EDUCATION AND HEALTH

Education is free and compulsory for 13 years.
*Gross enrolment ratio (percentage of relevant age group)* – primary 106 per cent; secondary 130 per cent; tertiary 77 per cent (2012 est)
*Health expenditure (per capita)* – US$6,145 (2013)
*Hospital beds (per 1,000 people)* – 4.7 (2009)
*Life expectancy (years)* – 81.12 (2014 est)
*Mortality rate* – 8.57 (2014 est)
*Birth rate* – 10.83 (2014 est)
*Infant mortality rate* – 3.66 (2014 est)

## OVERSEAS TERRITORIES

The Kingdom of the Netherlands consists of four autonomous elements: the Netherlands (European and Caribbean Netherlands), Aruba, Curacao and St Maarten; the latter two were part of the Netherlands Antilles until its dissolution on 10 October 2010. The other three islands of the Netherlands Antilles, the 'Caribbean Netherlands', comprising Bonaire, St Eustatius and Saba, are now autonomous special municipalities of the Netherlands.

### ARUBA

*Area* – 180 sq. km
*Capital* – Oranjestad; population, 29,000 (2014)
*Major town* – Sint Nicolaas
*Currency* – Aruban florin of 100 cents
*Population* – 110,663 rising at 1.36 per cent a year (2014 est)
*Language* – Dutch (official), Papiamento, Spanish, English
*National Day* – 18 March (Flag Day)

The Caribbean island was colonised by the Dutch in the 17th century. It was part of the Netherlands Antilles until 1986, when it became a separate, autonomous territory. The Dutch government is responsible for external affairs and represented by a resident governor. Internal government is in the hands of the prime minister and council of ministers, who are responsible to the 21-member unicameral legislature *(Staten)*, directly elected for a four-year term.

The principal economic activities are tourism and offshore financial services.
*Governor,* Fredis Refunjol, *apptd* 2004
*Prime Minister,* Mike Eman, *elected* 2009

### CURACAO

*Area* – 444 sq. km
*Capital* – Willemstad; population, 146,836 (2013 est)
*Currency* – Caribbean guilder of 100 cents
*Population* – 146,836 (2013 est)
*Language* – Dutch (official), Papiamento, English, Spanish

The island was colonised by the Dutch in the 17th century and was part of the Netherlands Antilles from 1954 until

10 October 2010, when it became a separate, autonomous territory. The Dutch government is responsible for external affairs and represented by a resident governor. Internal affairs are in the hands of a prime minister and council of ministers, who are responsible to the 21-member unicameral legislature *(Staten),* which serves a four-year term.

The principal economic activities are tourism, oil refining and offshore financial services.

*Governor,* Lucille George-Wout, *apptd* 2013
*Prime Minister,* Ivar Asjes, *elected* 2013

## ST MAARTEN

*Area* – 34 sq. km
*Capital* – Philipsburg
*Currency* – Caribbean guilder of 100 cents
*Population* – 31,530 (2014)
*Language* – Dutch, English (official), Spanish, Creole

The territory forms the southern part of the island of St Martin in the Caribbean; the north is French territory. Possession of the island was disputed between the Dutch and the Spanish until 1648, when the Spanish relinquished it to the Dutch and French, who divided it between them. The Dutch territory was part of the Netherlands Antilles from 1954 until 10 October 2010, when it became a separate, autonomous territory. The Dutch government is responsible for external affairs and represented by a governor. Internal affairs are in the hands of a prime minister and council of ministers, who are responsible to the 15-member unicameral legislature *(Staten),* which serves a four-year term.

The principal economic activities are tourism and sugar production.

*Governor,* Eugene Holiday, *apptd* 2010
*Prime Minister,* Marcel Gumbs, *apptd* 2014

# NEW ZEALAND

*Aotearoa – New Zealand*

*Area* – 267,710 sq. km (includes outlying islands)
*Capital* – Wellington; population, 380,000 (2014)
*Major cities* – Auckland, Christchurch, Dunedin, Hamilton, Manakau, North Shore, Tauranga, Waitakere
*Currency* – New Zealand dollar (NZ$) of 100 cents
*Population* – 4,438,393 rising at 0.82 per cent a year (2015 est); European (71.2 per cent), Maori (14.1 per cent), Asian (11.3 per cent), Pacific Islander (7.6 per cent) (2013)
*Religion* – Christian (Protestant 22.8 per cent, Roman Catholic 11.6 per cent, Anglican 10.8 per cent), Hindu 2.1 per cent
*Language* – English, Maori (both official)
*Population density* – 17 per sq. km (2013)
*Urban population* – 86.3 per cent (2013 est)

*Median age (years)* – 37.6 (2014 est)
*National anthem* – 'God Defend New Zealand'/'God Save the Queen'
*National day* – 6 February (Waitangi Day)
*Death penalty* – Abolished for all crimes (since 1989)
*CPI score* – 92 (2)

## CLIMATE AND TERRAIN

New Zealand consists of North Island, South Island and neighbouring coastal islands such as Stewart Island, and outlying islands that include the Chatham, Kermadec, Three Kings, Bounty, Antipodes, Snares, Auckland and Campbell groups in the South Pacific Ocean. The two larger islands, North Island and South Island, are separated by the relatively narrow Cook Strait. The island groups are much smaller and more widely dispersed.

Much of the North and South Islands is mountainous. The North Island mountains include several volcanoes, three of which are active. The principal range is the Southern Alps, extending the entire length of South Island to the west of the Canterbury Plains. There are geysers and hot springs in the Rotorua district and glaciers in the Southern Alps. Elevation extremes range from 3,754m (Aoraki/Mt Cook) to 0m (Pacific Ocean). The climate is temperate, though with marked regional variations; average temperatures range from 5.5°C in July to 15.5°C in February. The country is subject to seismic activity; a major earthquake devastated Christchurch in February 2011.

## HISTORY AND POLITICS

Settled by Polynesian tribes, the ancestors of the Maori, from about the tenth century, New Zealand was sighted by the Dutch navigator Abel Tasman in 1642 but he did not land. The British explorer James Cook surveyed the coastline in 1769, the year in which the islands were claimed by the British. The Maori accepted British sovereignty in 1840, under the Treaty of Waitangi, in return for land rights and the rights of British subjects. Large-scale European immigration and the 1860s gold rush led to encroachment by settlers and 'land wars' with the Maori in 1860 and 1872; Maori resistance was defeated but concessions such as parliamentary representation were won. A tribunal was set up in 1975 to consider grievances caused by breaches of the Waitangi Treaty, and in the 1990s the Maori were compensated for land lost to European settlers.

New Zealand was administered as part of Britain's New South Wales colony until 1841, when it became a separate colony. In 1907 it was granted dominion status; in 1931 the Statute of Westminster tacitly acknowledged its independence, which was formally confirmed in 1947.

New Zealand forces took part in the Boer War, both world wars, the Korean War and the Vietnam War. Since the UK's entry into the EEC in 1973, the focus of New Zealand's foreign and trade policies has shifted to Asia and the Pacific region.

Post-war politics has been dominated by the National Party and the Labour Party, either forming governments on their own or in coalition with smaller parties; coalitions have been the norm since a proportional representation voting system was introduced in 1993. The 2014 legislative elections were won by the New Zealand National Party, becoming the first party to secure a majority since the introduction of proportional representation in 1996.

There is no written constitution. The head of state is Queen Elizabeth II, represented by the governor-general, who is appointed on the advice of the New Zealand government. The unicameral House of Representatives currently has 122 members (usually 120), elected for a three-year term; there are 70 members from single-member constituencies, which include seven Maori constituencies, and 52 (usually 50) allocated from party lists; if a party wins a significantly larger proportion of constituency seats relative to their party list vote, this can result in an 'overhang' of extra seats. The prime minister and cabinet are appointed by the governor-general on the advice of the legislature.

GOVERNOR-GENERAL
Governor-General, HE Lt.-Gen. Sir Jerry Mateparae, *sworn in* August 2011

SELECTED GOVERNMENT MEMBERS *as at June 2015*
*Prime Minister,* John Key
*Deputy Prime Minister, Finance,* Bill English
*Defence,* Gerry Brownlee
*Internal Affairs,* Peter Dunne

NEW ZEALAND HIGH COMMISSION
New Zealand House, 80 Haymarket, London SW1Y 4TQ
T 020-7930 8422 E aboutnz@newzealandhc.org.uk
W www.nzembassy.com/uk
*High Commissioner,* HE Sir Lockwood Smith, *apptd* 2013

BRITISH HIGH COMMISSION
44 Hill Street, Thorndon, Wellington 6011
T (+64) (4) 924 2888 E consularmail.wellington@fco.gov.uk
W www.gov.uk/government/world/new-zealand
*High Commissioner,* HE Jonathan Sinclair, *apptd* 2014

DEFENCE
With Australia and the USA, New Zealand formed the ANZUS Pacific Security Treaty in 1951, but its non-nuclear military policy led to disagreements with the USA and France in 1985, and in 1986 the USA suspended its ANZUS obligations towards New Zealand.

| *Aged 16–49, 2010 est* | *Males* | *Females* |
| --- | --- | --- |
| Available for military service | 1,019,798 | 1,003,429 |
| Fit for military service | 843,526 | 828,779 |

*Military expenditure –* US$2,409m (2014)

ECONOMY AND TRADE
Since the 1980s industrial and service sectors have superseded the large, efficient agricultural sector. Growth has been driven by trade, particularly in agricultural products, but various factors had pushed the economy into recession in 2008 before the global downturn. The economy moved out of recession in 2009, and achieved 2–3 per cent growth during 2011–14; similar growth levels are expected in 2015.

The agricultural sector contributes 3.8 per cent of GDP and employs 7 per cent of the workforce. The main products are dairy products, meat, cereals, pulses, fruit, vegetables, wool and fish. The major industries are food processing, wood and paper products, textiles, machinery, transport equipment, financial services, mining, and tourism, which is overtaking agriculture as the main source of foreign exchange revenue. Non-metallic minerals such as coal, limestone and dolomite are heavily exploited, and gold and iron production is economically important. Natural gas deposits in offshore and onshore fields are used for electricity generation, though a significant amount of the country's energy is derived from sustainable sources such as hydro-electric power. Industry contributes 26.6 per cent of GDP and services 69.6 per cent.

The main trading partners are China, Australia, the USA and Japan. Principal exports are dairy products, meat, wood, wood products, fish and machinery. The main imports are machinery and equipment, vehicles and aircraft, petroleum, electronics, textiles and plastics.

*GNI –* US$247,040m; US$35,550 per capita (2012)
*Annual average growth of GDP –* 3.6 per cent (2014)
*Inflation rate –* 1.4 per cent (2014 est)
*Unemployment –* 5.9 per cent (2013 est)
*Total external debt –* US$87,160m (2014 est)
*Imports –* US$40,354m (2013)
*Exports –* US$41,074m (2013)

BALANCE OF PAYMENTS
*Trade –* US$435m deficit (2012)
*Current Account –* US$9,298m deficit (2015 est)

| *Trade with UK* | *2013** | *2014*** |
| --- | --- | --- |
| Imports from UK | £601,091,806 | £646,626,509 |
| Exports to UK | £845,900,198 | £889,462,550 |

* Includes Tokelau, Cook Islands and Niue
** Includes Cook Islands and Niue

COMMUNICATIONS
*Airports and waterways –* The principal airports are at Auckland, Wellington (North Island), Christchurch and Dunedin (South Island) and there are 35 smaller airports around the country; Tauranga, Christchurch, New Plymouth, Auckland and Napier are the main seaports
*Roadways and railways –* There are 62,759km of roadways, including 199km of motorways, and 4,128km of railways
*Telecommunications –* 1.88 million fixed lines and 4.82 million mobile subscriptions (2012); there were 3.4 million internet users in 2009
*Internet code and IDD –* nz; 64 (from UK), 44 (to UK)
*Major broadcasters –* The state-owned Television New Zealand and Radio New Zealand operate nationally; Niu FM is the national government-funded station for the Pacific island communities
*Press –* The Auckland-based *New Zealand Herald* has the largest circulation, alongside Wellington-based *Dominion Post* and Christchurch-based *The Press*
*WPFI score –* 10,06 (6)

EDUCATION AND HEALTH
Education is free of charge and compulsory between the ages of 5 and 16.
*Gross enrolment ratio (percentage of relevant age group)* – primary 99 per cent; secondary 120 per cent; tertiary 80 per cent (2012)
*Health expenditure (per capita) –* US$4,063 (2013)
*Hospital beds (per 1,000 people) –* 2.3 (2011)
*Life expectancy (years) –* 80.93 (2014 est)
*Mortality rate –* 7.3 (2014 est)
*Birth rate –* 13.4 (2014 est)
*Infant mortality rate –* 4.59 (2014 est)

TERRITORIES

TOKELAU
*Area –* 12 sq. km
*Population –* 1,337 (2014 est)

Tokelau consists of three atolls, Fakaofo, Nukunonu and Atafu, in the southern Pacific Ocean. Formerly part of Britain's Gilbert and Ellice Islands colony, Tokelau was transferred to New Zealand administration in 1926 and proclaimed part of New Zealand in 1949.

The territory is self-administering, but has rejected greater autonomy in two referendums (2006 and 2007). The Council for the Ongoing Government (cabinet) comprises three *Faipule* (village leaders) and three *Pulenuku* (village mayors), one from each atoll; the position of *Ulu-o-Tokelau* (leader) is rotated among the three *Faipule* members annually. The *General Fono,* which has 20 members elected for a three-year term, has legislative powers. Each atoll has a *Taupulega* (council of elders).

The economy is dependent on New Zealand budgetary aid, with some revenue derived from remittances and the sale of fishing rights, stamps, coins and the use of its internet suffix. The main activities are subsistence farming, copra production and handicrafts. In 2011 Tokelau changed its position within the international dateline in order to improve trade links with Australia and New Zealand.

*Administrator,* Jonathan Kings, *apptd* 2011

### THE ROSS DEPENDENCY

New Zealand has administrative responsibility for the Ross Dependency. This is defined as all the Antarctic islands and territories between 160° E. and 150° W. longitude which are situated south of the 60° S. parallel, including Edward VII Land and portions of Victoria Land (*see also* The North and South Poles).

### ASSOCIATED STATES
### COOK ISLANDS

*Area* – 236 sq. km
*Population* – 10,134 (2014 est)
*Capital* – Avarua, on Rarotonga

The Cook Islands consist of 15 volcanic islands and coral atolls in the southern Pacific Ocean. A former British protectorate, since 1965 the islands have been self-governing in free association with New Zealand.

Queen Elizabeth II has a representative on the islands, and the New Zealand government is represented by a high commissioner. There is a 24-member legislative assembly, and the House of Ariki, made up of 15 traditional leaders who advise on traditional matters. Executive power is exercised by a prime minister and a cabinet responsible to the legislature.

The main economic activities are tourism, agriculture (especially tropical fruits), fruit processing, fishing, garment manufacturing, handicrafts and pearl-farming; black pearls are the main export.

*HM Representative,* Sir Frederick Goodwin, KBE, *apptd* 2001
*Prime Minister,* Henry Puna *apptd* 2010

### NIUE

*Area* – 260 sq. km
*Population* – 1,190 (2014 est)
*Capital* – Alofi; population,1,000 (2014 est)

Although part of the Cook Islands group, Niue was administered separately after 1903. Since 1974 the island has been self-governing in free association with New Zealand.

A New Zealand high commissioner represents both the Queen and the New Zealand government. There is a 20-member legislative assembly; executive power is exercised by a prime minister and a three-member cabinet drawn from the assembly's members.

The principal economic activities are agriculture, fishing, tourism, handicrafts, food processing and the sale of postage stamps and the use of its internet suffix.

*New Zealand High Commissioner,* Ross Ardern, *apptd* 2014
*Premier,* Toke Talagi

# NICARAGUA

*República de Nicaragua – Republic of Nicaragua*

*Area* – 130,370 sq. km
*Capital* – Managua; population, 951,000 (2014)
*Major cities* – Chinandega, Estelí, León, Masaya, Tipitapa
*Currency* – Córdoba (C$) of 100 centavos
*Population* – 5,907,881 rising at 1 per cent a year (2015 est)
*Religion* – Christian (Roman Catholic 58.5 per cent, Protestant 23.2 per cent), none 15.7 per cent
*Language* – Spanish (official), English, Miskito
*Population density* – 51 per sq. km (2013)
*Urban population* – 58.1 per cent (2013 est)
*Median age (years)* – 24.2 (2014 est)
*National anthem* – 'Salve a ti, Nicaragua' ['Hail to Thee, Nicaragua']
*National day* – 15 September (Independence Day)
*Death penalty* – Abolished for all crimes (since 1979)
*CPI score* – 28 (133)

### CLIMATE AND TERRAIN

The narrow Pacific coastal plain is broken by active volcanoes and lakes Managua and Nicaragua. A mountainous central region separates it from the broad Atlantic coastal plain, which constitutes 60 per cent of the country and is covered by tropical rainforest. Elevation extremes range from 2,438m (Mogoton) to 0m (Pacific Ocean). The climate is generally tropical on the plains but cooler at altitude; the average temperature is 25.6°C. The country is subject to frequent earthquakes.

### HISTORY AND POLITICS

Nicaragua was originally populated by tribes related to the Aztec, Maya and other indigenous people. Fossilised footprints, the oldest in South America, indicate a human presence in Nicaragua dating back 6,000 years. Spanish colonisation began in 1523 but in the 17th and 18th centuries the British were the dominant presence on the Caribbean coast, with the Spanish controlling the Pacific plain. Independence from Spain was achieved in 1821 and the area was initially incorporated into Mexico. In 1823 it became part of a Central American federation of former Spanish provinces but seceded and became fully independent in 1838. British control of the Caribbean coast was ceded to Nicaragua in 1860.

In 1893, General José Santos Zelaya established a dictatorship that lasted until 1909, when he was overthrown by US troops. General Anastasio Somoza established a dictatorship in 1938 and ruled until his assassination in 1956, when he was succeeded as president by his sons Luis (1956–67) and Anastasio (1967–79). After 44 years in power, the family was overthrown in 1979 in a popular revolt led by the Frente Sandinista de Liberación Nacional (FSLN), popularly known as the Sandinistas.

The Sandinistas' socialist government redistributed land and promoted education and health services, but was opposed by US-backed right-wing guerrillas (the Contras). The civil war lasted from 1982 until 1990 (although there was a ceasefire from 1988), when the Sandinistas were unexpectedly defeated in elections by a coalition of opposition parties.

From 1990 to 2006, governments were liberal or liberal-dominated coalitions, keeping the FSLN from power even though it was often the largest party in the legislature. However, in the 2006 presidential and legislative elections, the FSLN candidate, Daniel Ortega (president 1984–90), was elected president and the FSLN became the largest party in the assembly. Ortega was re-elected in the 2011 presidential election, picking up over 62 per cent of the vote; his FSLN party won an outright majority in the country's legislative election, also in 2011.

In 2009 the Supreme Court lifted the ban on a president serving two consecutive terms and in January 2014 the National Assembly eliminated constitutional term limits for the presidency altogether, potentially allowing President Ortega to run for re-election in 2016. Opposition parties have labelled the changes undemocratic. The executive president is directly elected for a five-year term, which may be renewed only once. The unicameral National Assembly has 90 members directly elected for a five-year term; unsuccessful presidential and vice-presidential candidates may be awarded a seat if they receive more than the average percentage of the vote in each electoral district. The cabinet is appointed by the president.

### HEAD OF STATE

*President,* Daniel Ortega, *re-elected* 6 November 2011, *sworn in* 11 January 2012
*Vice-President,* Moises Omar Halleslevens

### SELECTED GOVERNMENT MEMBERS *as at June 2015*

*Defence,* Martha Elena Ruiz Sevilla
*Finance,* Ivan Acosta Montalvan
*Foreign Affairs,* Samuel Santos Lopez
*Interior,* Ana Isabel Morales Mazún

### EMBASSY OF NICARAGUA

Suite 31, Vicarage House, 58–60 Kensington Church Street, London W8 4DP
T 020-7938 2373
*Ambassador Extraordinary and Plenipotentiary,* HE Guisell Morales-Echaverry, *apptd* 2015

### BRITISH AMBASSADOR

*Ambassador Extraordinary and Plenipotentiary,* HE Christopher Campbell, resident at San José, Costa Rica

### DEFENCE

| Aged 16–49, 2010 est | Males | Females |
|---|---|---|
| Available for military service | 1,452,107 | 1,552,698 |
| Fit for military service | 1,227,757 | 1,335,653 |

*Military expenditure* – US$82.9m (2014)

### ECONOMY AND TRADE

Progress towards economic recovery and reconstruction after the civil war has been slow and the country remains the poorest in Central America. The economy contracted in 2009 as the global downturn reduced key commodity prices, export demand and remittances (worth almost 15 per cent of GDP). Although almost 80 per cent of debt was cancelled in 2004 and 2006, the government is dependent on foreign aid and 42.5 per cent of the population lives below the poverty line. The fiscal deficit is large and is predicted to grow as economic growth slows in 2015 and 2016.

Agriculture is the mainstay of the economy, accounting for 14.9 per cent of GDP and 31 per cent of employment. The main commercial crops are coffee, beef, shellfish, tobacco, sugar and peanuts. Industry includes food and timber processing, mining, the manufacture of chemicals, machinery, metal products, textiles, clothing and footwear, oil refining and tourism. Industry contributes 28.8 per cent of GDP and services 56.4 per cent.

The main trading partners are the USA and other central and south American countries. Principal exports are the main commercial crops and gold. The main imports are consumer goods, machinery and equipment, raw materials and petroleum products.

*GNI* – US$10,890m; US$1,790 per capita (2013)
*Annual average growth of GDP* – 4 per cent (2014)
*Inflation rate* – 6.1 per cent (2014 est)
*Population below poverty line* – 42.5 per cent (2009)
*Unemployment* – 6.5 per cent (2015 est)
*Total external debt* – US$10,250m (2014 est)
*Imports* – US$5,647m (2013)
*Exports* – US$2,408m (2013)

### BALANCE OF PAYMENTS

*Trade* – US$3,239m deficit (2013)
*Current Account* – US$832m deficit (2015 est)

| Trade with UK | 2013 | 2014 |
|---|---|---|
| Imports from UK | £6,092,469 | £5,125,259 |
| Exports to UK | £23,157,424 | £24,078,272 |

### COMMUNICATIONS

*Airports* – The main airport is at Managua, and there are a further 11 airports around the country
*Waterways* – The chief ports are Corinto (Pacific) and Bluefields and El Bluff (Caribbean); there are 2,220km of inland waterways, mostly on lakes Managua and Nicaragua
*Roadways* – There are 3,282km of roadways; the Inter-American Highway runs between Nicaragua's Honduran and Costa Rican borders, and the Inter-Oceanic Highway runs from Corinto on the Pacific coast via Managua to Rama, where there is a natural waterway to Bluefields on the Caribbean
*Telecommunications* – 320,000 fixed lines and 5.346 million mobile subscriptions (2012); there were 199,800 internet users in 2009
*Internet code and IDD* – ni; 505 (from UK), 44 (to UK)
*Major broadcasters* – There are several commercial television and radio broadcasters, including Nicavision Canal 12; Radio Nicaragua is publicly owned
*Press* – La Pensa and El Nuevo Diario are the country's two principal daily newspapers
*WPFI score* – 27,94 (74)

### EDUCATION AND HEALTH

*Literacy rate* – 91.6 per cent (2015 est)
*Gross enrolment ratio (percentage of relevant age group)* – primary 117 per cent; secondary 69 per cent (2010 est)
*Health expenditure (per capita)* – US$153 (2013)
*Hospital beds (per 1,000 people)* – 0.9 (2012)
*Life expectancy (years)* – 72.72 (2014 est)
*Mortality rate* – 5.07 (2014 est)
*Birth rate* – 18.41 (2014 est)
*Infant mortality rate* – 20.36 (2014 est)

# NIGER

*République du Niger – Republic of Niger*

*Area* – 1,267,000 sq. km
*Capital* – Niamey; population, 1,058,000 (2014)
*Major cities* – Agadez, Maradi, Zinder
*Currency* – Franc CFA of 100 centimes
*Population* – 18,045,729 rising at 3.25 per cent a year
    (2015 est); Hausa (55.4 per cent), Djerma (21 per cent),
    Tuareg (9.3 per cent), Fulani (8.5 per cent), Kanouri
    Manga (4.7 per cent) (2001)
*Religion* – Muslim 80 per cent, other (includes indigenous
    beliefs and Christian) 20 per cent
*Language* – French (official), Arabic, Hausa, Djerma
*Population density* – 14 per sq. km (2013)
*Urban population* – 18.3 per cent (2013 est)
*Median age (years)* – 15.1 (2014 est)
*National anthem* – 'La Nigérienne' ['The Nigerian']
*National day* – 18 December (Republic Day)
*Death penalty* – Retained (no known use since 1976)
*CPI score* – 35 (103)
*Literacy rate* – 26.6 per cent (2015 est)
*Gross enrolment ratio (percentage of relevant age group)* –
    primary 71 per cent; secondary 16 per cent; tertiary
    2 per cent (2012 est)
*Health expenditure (per capita)* – US$27 (2013)
*Hospital beds (per 1,000 people)* – 0.3 (2004–9)
*Life expectancy (years)* – 54.74 (2014 est)
*Mortality rate* – 12.73 (2014 est)
*Birth rate* – 46.12 (2014 est)
*Infant mortality rate* – 86.27 (2014 est)

## CLIMATE AND TERRAIN

Niger is mostly desert, with low hills in the north and
savannah in the south. Elevation extremes range from
2,022m (Mt Idoukal-n-Taghes/Bagzane) to 200m (Niger
River). The Niger valley in the south-west is the only
well-watered area. There is a desert climate, except in the
extreme south which is sub-tropical. Average temperatures
range from 19.3°C in January to 33.3°C in June.

## HISTORY AND POLITICS

The area was divided between several kingdoms formed by
different tribes (Tuareg, Songhai, Hausa, Fulani) from the
tenth to 19th centuries. French colonial expansion from
the 1880s brought the whole area under its control in 1898
and in 1904 it became part of French West Africa. The
country became autonomous in 1958 and achieved full
independence in 1960.

The first president introduced a one-party regime, which
continued under the military government installed after a
coup in 1974. Following popular agitation, civilian
government was reintroduced in 1989, other parties were
legalised in 1990, and multi-party elections held in 1993.

This political liberalisation was reversed following a military
coup in 1996 led by Brig. Ibrahim Barre Mainassara. He was
assassinated in 1999 by the military, who restored political
pluralism.

From 1990 there was a rebellion in the north by Tuareg
seeking greater social equality and political representation.
Peace agreements with rebel groups in 1995 and 1997
brought calm until 2007, when a new rebel group emerged,
seeking greater autonomy and access to mining revenue; this
group signed a ceasefire with the government in 2009.

After seeking to increase his powers in 2009, President
Mamadou Tandja (first elected in 1999) was deposed in
February 2010 by the military. A referendum on a new
constitution was held in October 2010, and presidential and
legislative elections were held in January 2011. The Nigerien
Party for Democracy and Socialism (PNDS-Tarayya) won the
most seats, but without a majority; in August 2013 a unity
government was declared under Prime Minister Brigi Rafini.
The PNDS-Tarayya leader Mahamadou Issoufou was elected
president in the second round of voting in March 2011.

The 2010 constitution reduced the president's powers and
restored the limit on presidential terms. The executive
president is directly elected for a five-year term, renewable
once. The unicameral National Assembly has 113 members
directly elected for a five-year term. The prime minister is
appointed by the president.

HEAD OF STATE
*President,* Mahamadou Issoufou, *elected* 12 March 2011,
    *took office* 7 April 2011

SELECTED GOVERNMENT MEMBERS *as at June 2015*
*Prime Minister,* Brigi Rafini
*Finance,* Gilles Bayet
*Foreign Affairs,* Aichatou Boulama
*Interior,* Massaoudou Hassoumi

HONORARY CONSULATE
MPC House, 15 Maple Mews, London NW6 5UZ
T 020-7328 8180 E consulate@nigerconsulateuk.org
W www.nigerconsulateuk.org
*Honorary Consul,* Muhammadu Dikko Ladan

BRITISH AMBASSADOR
HE Joanne Adamson, *apptd* 2014, resident at Bamako, Mali

## DEFENCE

| *Aged 16–49, 2010 est* | *Males* | *Females* |
| --- | --- | --- |
| Available for military service | 3,329,184 | 3,267,669 |
| Fit for military service | 2,194,570 | 2,219,416 |

*Military expenditure* – US$69.8m (2012)
*Conscription* – 18 years of age; 24 months (selective)

## ECONOMY AND TRADE

Niger is one of the poorest countries in the world, with
63 per cent of the population living below the poverty
line. Economic progress has been hampered by political
instability, recurrent droughts (most recently in 2009–10),
desertification, over-grazing and rapid population growth,
leaving the country dependent on foreign aid, which makes
up over half of government revenue. Its huge foreign debt
burden was much reduced by debt relief and cancellation in
2000 and 2005. While the country negotiated a US$121m
(£78m) extended credit facility agreement with the IMF
for 2012–15, Niger suffers from a lack of international
investment. Growth is predicted to reach 6 per cent in 2015
and 2016.

The mainstay of the economy is currently subsistence agriculture and herding, which accounts for 37.7 per cent of GDP and engages 90 per cent of the population; the main cash crops are cowpeas, cotton, vegetables, cereals and livestock. The most significant export is uranium, making the economy vulnerable to fluctuations in global prices; efforts are being made to diversify into exploitation of other mineral resources, including gold and oil. The other industries include processing agricultural products and manufacturing cement, bricks, soap, textiles and chemicals. Industry contributes 18.6 per cent of GDP and services 43.7 per cent.

The main trading partners are Nigeria (54.2 per cent of exports), South Korea and France. Principal exports are uranium ore, livestock, cowpeas and onions. The main imports are foodstuffs, machinery, vehicles and parts, petroleum and cereals.

*GNI* – US$7,118m; US$400 per capita (2013)
*Annual average growth of GDP* – 6.3 per cent (2014)
*Inflation rate* – –0.2 per cent (2014 est)
*Unemployment* – 4.9 per cent (2015 est)
*Total external debt* – US$2,851m (2014 est)
*Imports* – US$1,909m (2013)
*Exports* – US$1,613m (2013)

BALANCE OF PAYMENTS
*Trade* – US$295m deficit (2013)
*Current Account* – US$1,974m deficit (2015 est)

| Trade with UK | 2013 | 2014 |
| --- | --- | --- |
| Imports from UK | £6,603,887 | £6,735,074 |
| Exports to UK | £44,371 | £2,571,300 |

## COMMUNICATIONS

*Airports and waterways* – The principal airport is at Niamey and there are a further nine airports; the river Niger is navigable between September and March for 300km from Niamey to the Benin frontier
*Roadways* – There are 3,912km of roadways
*Telecommunications* – 100,500 fixed lines and 5.4 million mobile subscriptions (2012); there were 115,900 internet users in 2009
*Internet code and IDD* – ne; 227 (from UK), 44 (to UK)
*Major broadcasters* – The government-owned Télé-Sahel (TV) competes with a number of commercial stations; state-run La Voix du Sahel is the only radio station offering national coverage
*Press* – The state-run *Le Sahel* is the only national daily
*WPFI score* – 23,85 (47)

# NIGERIA

*Federal Republic of Nigeria*

*Area* – 923,768 sq. km
*Capital* – Abuja (since 1991); population, 2,301,000 (2014)
*Major cities* – Aba, Benin City, Ibadan, Ilorin, Kaduna, Kano, Lagos (the former capital), Port Harcourt, Warri, Zaria
*Currency* – Naira (N) of 100 kobo
*Population* – 181,562,056 rising at 2.45 per cent a year (2015 est); Hausa and Fulani (29 per cent), Yoruba (21 per cent), Igbo (18 per cent), Ijaw (10 per cent), Kanuri (4 per cent), Ibibio (3.5 per cent), Tiv (2.5 per cent) (est)
*Religion* – Muslim 50 per cent, Christian 40 per cent, indigenous beliefs 10 per cent
*Language* – English (official), Hausa, Yoruba, Igbo, Fula, over 500 other languages
*Population density* – 191 per sq. km (2013)
*Urban population* – 50.9 per cent (2013 est)
*Median age (years)* – 18.2 (2014 est)
*National anthem* – 'Arise O Compatriots, Nigeria's Call Obey'
*National day* – 1 October (Independence Day)
*Death penalty* – Retained
*CPI score* – 27 (136)

## CLIMATE AND TERRAIN

The north is arid savannah and semi-desert plains, which rise to central hills and plateaux. There are mountains along the south-eastern border, but the south is generally low-lying and covered in tropical rainforest, with mangrove swamps along the coast and hills in the south-east. Elevation extremes range from 2,419m (Chappal Waddi) to 0m (Atlantic Ocean). The river Niger flows across the country from the north-west to the south coast, where it forms a broad delta on the Gulf of Guinea. The climate is equatorial in the south, tropical in the centre and arid in the north. The north has one rainy season (June to September), while the south has two (March–July, September–October); average national temperatures range from 24.9°C in January to 30.4°C in April.

## POLITICS

The country is a federal democratic republic. Under the 1999 constitution, the executive president is directly elected for a four-year term, renewable once. The president appoints the federal executive council, which must be approved by the senate. The bicameral National Assembly comprises the 360-member House of Representatives and the 109-member senate, both elected for a four-year term.

The March 2015 presidential election was won by former military ruler Muhammadu Buhari of the All Progressives Congress (APC) – the first time an opposition candidate has unseated the incumbent at the ballot box. The APC also secured a majority in both houses during the simultaneous legislative elections. Despite some allegations of fraud, the elections were described as largely fair by the majority of observers.

HEAD OF STATE
*President,* Muhammadu Buhari, *elected* 31 March 2015, *sworn in* 5 May 2015
*Vice-President,* Yemi Osinbajo

SELECTED GOVERNMENT MEMBERS *as at June 2015*
*Finance,* Ngozi Okonjo-Iweala
*Foreign Affairs,* Aminu Wali
*Internal Affairs,* Patrick Abba Moro

HIGH COMMISSION FOR THE FEDERAL REPUBLIC OF NIGERIA
Nigeria House, 9 Northumberland Avenue, London WC2N 5BX
**T** 020-7839 1244 **E** information@nigeriahc.org.uk
**W** www.nigeriahc.org.uk
*High Commissioner,* HE Dr Dalhatu Sarki Tafida, *apptd* 2008

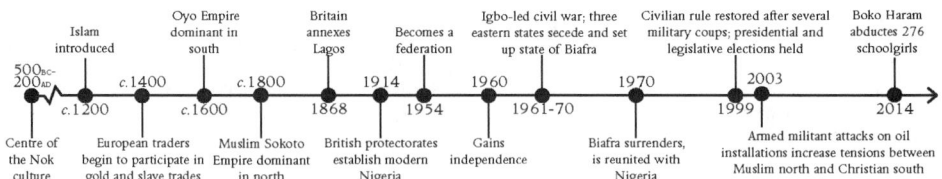

Islam introduced — 500BC-200AD

Centre of the Nok culture — *c.*1200

European traders begin to participate in gold and slave trades — *c.*1400

Oyo Empire dominant in south — *c.*1600

Muslim Sokoto Empire dominant in north — *c.*1800

British protectorates establish modern Nigeria — 1868

Britain annexes Lagos — 1914

Becomes a federation — 1954

Gains independence — 1960

Igbo-led civil war; three eastern states secede and set up state of Biafra — 1961-70

Biafra surrenders, is reunited with Nigeria — 1970

Civilian rule restored after several military coups; presidential and legislative elections held — 1999

Armed militant attacks on oil installations increase tensions between Muslim north and Christian south — 2003

Boko Haram abducts 276 schoolgirls — 2014

## BRITISH HIGH COMMISSION
19 Torrens Close, Mississippi, Maitama, Abuja
T (+234) (9) 462 2200 E ppainformation.abuja@fco.gov.uk
W www.gov.uk/government/world/nigeria
*High Commissioner,* HE Dr Andrew Pocock, CMG, apptd 2012

## FEDERAL STRUCTURE
The federal republic is divided into 36 states and the Federal Capital Territory: Abia, Adamawa, Akwa Ibom, Anambra, Bauchi, Bayelsa, Benue, Borno, Cross River, Delta, Ebonyi, Edo, Ekiti, Enugu, Gombe, Imo, Jigawa, Kaduna, Kano, Katsina, Kebbi, Kogi, Kwara, Lagos, Nassarawa, Niger, Ogun, Ondo, Osun, Oyo, Plateau, Rivers, Sokoto, Taraba, Yobe and Zamfara. Each state has an elected governor and legislature.

## DEFENCE

| Aged 16–49, 2010 est | Males | Females |
|---|---|---|
| Available for military service | 37,087,711 | 35,232,127 |
| Fit for military service | 20,839,976 | 19,867,683 |

*Military expenditure* – US$2,265m (2014)

## ECONOMY AND TRADE
In April 2014 a statistical 'revaluation' of the economy by the Nigerian government increased the size of the Nigerian economy by 89 per cent overnight, and Nigeria has now emerged as Africa's largest economy, with 2013 GDP estimated at US$502bn (£296bn). The country is the leading sub-Saharan oil producer, enjoying an oil boom in the 1970s and recently benefiting again from high oil prices. However, mismanagement and corruption mean the majority of the population has yet to derive much benefit. Past governments also failed to diversify the economy away from its dependence on oil, which accounts for 80 per cent of government revenue and 95 per cent of foreign exchange earnings. However, since 2008 economic reforms have been introduced to improve fiscal and monetary management, curb inflation and address regional agitation for wider distribution of oil revenues. Factors such as security and inadequate infrastructure remain obstacles to growth, but infrastructure improvements are a priority, especially in electricity supply and roads. The largely peaceful elections in 2015 are expected to boost the economy going forward, but declining oil prices are likely to depress economic growth to around 5 per cent in 2015.

The mainstay of the economy is agriculture, mostly at subsistence level, which generates 20.6 per cent of GDP and engages 70 per cent of the labour force. The main crops include cocoa, peanuts, cotton, palm oil, maize, rice, sorghum, millet and rubber. However, agricultural output has failed to keep pace with rapid population growth, changing Nigeria from a net food exporter to a food importer. Industrial activities include oil and natural gas production, mining (coal, tin, columbite), processing agricultural products, textiles, cement and other construction materials

and footwear. Industry contributes 25.6 per cent of GDP and services 53.8 per cent.

The main trading partners are China (20.8 per cent of imports), India, the USA, Brazil and the EU. Principal exports are oil and oil products, cocoa and rubber. The main imports are machinery, chemicals, transport equipment, manufactured goods, food and live animals.

*GNI* – US$469,729m; US$2,710 per capita (2013)
*Annual average growth of GDP* – 7 per cent (2014)
*Inflation rate* – 8.3 per cent (2014 est)
*Population below poverty line* – 70 per cent (2010 est)
*Unemployment* – 7.5 per cent (2015 est)
*Total external debt* – US$22,010m (2014 est)
*Imports* – US$44,598m (2013)
*Exports* – US$114,000m (2012)

### BALANCE OF PAYMENTS
*Trade* – US$63,000m surplus (2012)
*Current Account* – US$3,483m surplus (2015 est)

| Trade with UK | 2013 | 2014 |
|---|---|---|
| Imports from UK | £1,550,022,615 | £1,380,970,121 |
| Exports to UK | £3,199,207,278 | £2,491,384,158 |

## COMMUNICATIONS
*Airports and waterways* – There are 40 airports, including the principal airports at Lagos, Abuja, Kano and Port Harcourt; there are 8,600km of waterways, mostly on the Niger and Benue rivers; the main seaports are Lagos, Port Harcourt, Warri and Calabar
*Roadways and railways* – There are 28,980km of roadways; the Nigerian railway network, which is controlled by the Nigerian Railway Corporation, has 3,505km of track
*Telecommunications* – 418,200 fixed lines and 112.78 million mobile subscriptions (2012); there were 43.99 million internet users in 2009
*Internet code and IDD* – ng; 234 (from UK), 9 44 (to UK)
*Major broadcasters* – The Nigerian Television Authority (NTA) and Federal Radio Corporation of Nigeria (FRCN) are the public broadcasters
*Press* – *The Guardian* is one of the most influential news publications in the country; the government-backed *New Nigerian* prints separate editions in Lagos and Kaduna
*WPFI score* – 34,09 (111)

## EDUCATION AND HEALTH
*Literacy rate* – 72.8 per cent (2015 est)
*Gross enrolment ratio (percentage of relevant age group)* – primary 85 per cent; secondary 44 per cent (2010 est)
*Health expenditure (per capita)* – US$115 (2013)
*Hospital beds (per 1,000 people)* – 0.5 (2004–9)
*Life expectancy (years)* – 52.62 (2014 est)
*Mortality rate* – 13.16 (2014 est)
*Birth rate* – 38.03 (2014 est)
*Infant mortality rate* – 74.09 (2014 est)
*HIV/AIDS adult prevalence* – 3.17 per cent (2013 est)

# NORWAY

*Kongeriket Norge – Kingdom of Norway*

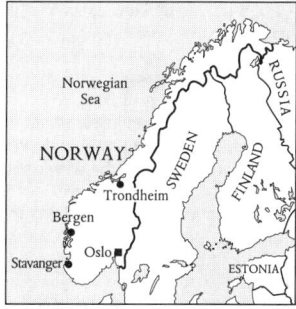

*Area* – 323,802 sq. km

*Capital* – Oslo; population, 970,000 (2014)

*Major cities* – Bergen, Stavanger, Trondheim

*Currency* – Krone of 100 ore

*Population* – 5,207,689 rising at 1.13 per cent per year (2015 est)

*Religion* – Christian (Lutheran 82.1 per cent, other 3.9 per cent), Muslim 2.3 per cent

*Language* – Bokmal and Nynorsk Norwegian (both official), Finnish, Sami (official in six municipalities)

*Population density* – 14 per sq. km (2013)

*Urban population* – 79.9 per cent (2013 est)

*Median age (years)* – 39.1 (2014 est)

*National anthem* – 'Ja, Vi Elsker Dette Landet' ['Yes, We Love This Country']

*National day* – 17 May (Constitution Day)

*Death penalty* – Abolished for all crimes (since 1979)

*CPI score* – 86 (5)

## CLIMATE AND TERRAIN

The terrain is mostly mountainous, with elevated, barren plateaux separated by deep, narrow valleys; the north is arctic tundra. The coastline is deeply indented with numerous fjords and fringed with thousands of rocky islands and islets; Geirangerfjord and Naeroyfjord are UNESCO World Heritage Sites. Elevation extremes range from 2,469m (Galdhopiggen) to 0m (Norwegian Sea).

Nearly half of the country lies north of the Arctic Circle, and at North Cape the sun does not appear to set between about 14 May and 29 July, causing the phenomenon known as the midnight sun; conversely, there is no apparent sunrise from about 18 November to 24 January. The climate is temperate on the coast but colder and wetter inland; average temperatures range from −6.6°C in January to 12.6°C in July, but winter temperatures in parts of the north can drop to −40°C.

## HISTORY AND POLITICS

Norway became a unified country under the rule of King Harald Fairhair in c.900 but dissolved after his death and was reunified by Olav II in c.1016–28. Canute brought Norway under Danish rule in 1028 but the throne reverted on his death to Magnus I. When the royal house died out in the 14th century, the Danish monarch was the nearest heir and in 1397 Norway, Denmark and Sweden were united under a single monarch in the Kalmar Union. Sweden seceded from the union in 1523, but Norway continued to be ruled by the Danish crown until 1814, when it was ceded to Sweden.

Although internal self-government was established in 1814, growing tension over constraints on the Norwegian government led to the union being dissolved, and Norway became independent in 1905. The first king of the newly independent country was a Danish prince, who took the throne as King Haakon VII.

The country was neutral in the First World War, but in the Second World War Norway was invaded and occupied by Germany from 1940 until 1945. Norway joined NATO in 1949 and was a founder member of the European Free Trade Association in 1960. Membership of the EU was rejected in referendums in 1972 and 1994.

After 1945, governments pursued policies of economic planning and an extensive welfare state. The Labour Party dominated politics from the 1930s to the early 1980s, governing either on its own or in coalition with smaller parties. It was returned to power in 2005. In September 2013 the Conservative Party formed a minority government with the right-wing Progress Party, despite the Labour Party remaining the largest single party in the legislature.

Norway is a constitutional monarchy with a hereditary monarch as head of state. Under the 1814 constitution, the unicameral *Storting* has 169 members who are directly elected for a four-year term; a 2007 constitutional amendment abolished a bicameral division within the *Storting*, which took effect from the 2009 election. The prime minister, who is responsible to parliament, appoints the cabinet.

HEAD OF STATE

*HM The King of Norway,* King Harald V, KG, GCVO, *born* 21 February 1937; *succeeded* 17 January 1991

*Heir,* HRH Crown Prince Haakon Magnus, *born* 20 July 1973

SELECTED GOVERNMENT MEMBERS *as at June 2015*

*Prime Minister,* Erna Solberg

*Defence,* Ine Marie Eriksen Soreide

*Finance,* Siv Jensen

*Foreign Affairs,* Borge Brende

ROYAL NORWEGIAN EMBASSY

25 Belgrave Square, London SW1X 8QD

T 020-7591 5500 E emb.london@mfa.no W www.norway.org.uk

*Ambassador Extraordinary and Plenipotentiary,* HE Mona Juul, *apptd* 2014

BRITISH EMBASSY

Thomas Heftyes Gate 8, 0244 Oslo

T (+47) 2313 2700 E britemb@online.no

W www.gov.uk/government/world/norway

*Ambassador Extraordinary and Plenipotentiary,* HE Sarah Gillett, CMG, CVO, *apptd* 2014

## DEFENCE

| *Aged 16–49, 2010 est* | *Males* | *Females* |
| --- | --- | --- |
| Available for military service | 1,079,043 | 1,051,210 |
| Fit for military service | 888,761 | 865,697 |

*Military expenditure* – US$6,773m (2014)

*Conscription* – men aged 19 to 35; 12 months

## ECONOMY AND TRADE

Norway's prosperity depends primarily upon oil and gas extraction, which accounts for nearly half of exports, and its fisheries. Oil production is declining, but oil and gas deposits in the Barents Sea and other areas are becoming more accessible as the Arctic ice cap retreats. Norway has planned for the time when reserves are exhausted by investing revenue from this sector in the world's largest sovereign wealth fund, valued at over US$830bn in January 2014. The state retains a majority share in key enterprises, including the oil industry. Lower oil prices in 2015 are expected to slow growth and potentially cause a contraction in the economy.

The nature of the terrain restricts agriculture, which generates 1.7 per cent of GDP. The main industries apart from oil and gas are fishing, forestry, food processing, shipbuilding, pulp and paper products, metals, chemicals, mining and textiles. Shipping freight services are also significant, with Norwegian companies controlling 4.5 per cent of the world's shipping fleet by tonnage. Industry contributes 41.8 per cent of GDP and services 56.5 per cent.

The main trading partners are the UK (24.5 per cent of exports), other EU countries, the USA and China. Principal exports are oil and petroleum products, machinery and equipment, metals, chemicals, ships and fish. The main imports are machinery and equipment, chemicals, metals and foodstuffs.

*GNI* – US$521,712m; US$102,610 per capita (2013)
*Annual average growth of GDP* – 1.8 per cent (2014)
*Inflation rate* – 2 per cent (2014 est)
*Unemployment* – 3.5 per cent (2015 est)
*Total external debt* – US$720,600m (2013)
*Imports* – US$89,988m (2013)
*Exports* – US$153,188m (2013)

BALANCE OF PAYMENTS
*Trade* – US$63,201m surplus (2013)
*Current Account* – US$31,949m surplus (2015 est)

| Trade with UK | 2013 | 2014 |
| --- | --- | --- |
| Imports from UK | £3,492,266,976 | £3,677,308,234 |
| Exports to UK | £16,804,317,358 | £14,990,782,938 |

## COMMUNICATIONS
*Airports and waterways* – There are 67 airports, including the principal airports at Oslo, Bergen, Stavanger and Trondheim; the main ports are Oslo, Bergen, Kristiansand, Tonsberg, Stavanger and Narvik, and there is a large merchant fleet, with 585 ships of over 1,000 tonnes registered in Norway and 974 registered abroad
*Roadways and railways* – 18,116km; 4,237km
*Telecommunications* – 1.465 million fixed lines and 5.732 million mobile subscriptions (2011); there were 4.431 million internet users in 2009
*Internet code and IDD* – no; 47 (from UK), 44 20 (to UK)
*Major broadcasters* – The public broadcaster NRK operates radio and television channels, in competition with a number of commercial rivals
*Press* – *VG* has the largest circulation among the country's daily news publications; other newspapers include *The Norway Post* and *Dagbladet*
*WPFI score* – 7,75 (2)

## EDUCATION AND HEALTH
Education from six to 16 is free and compulsory in the basic schools, and free from 16 to 19 years.
*Gross enrolment ratio (percentage of relevant age group)* – primary 99 per cent; secondary 111 per cent; tertiary 74 per cent (2012 est)
*Health expenditure (per capita)* – US$9,715 (2013)
*Hospital beds (per 1,000 people)* – 3.3 (2011)
*Life expectancy (years)* – 81.6 (2014 est)
*Mortality rate* – 8.19 (2014 est)
*Birth rate* – 12.09 (2014 est)
*Infant mortality rate* – 2.48 (2014 est)

## TERRITORIES

### SVALBARD
*Area* – 62,045 sq. km
*Population* – 1,872 (2014 est); Norwegian 55.4 per cent, Russian and Ukrainian 44.3 per cent

The Svalbard archipelago consists of Spitsbergen, North East Land, the Wiche Islands, Barents Island, Edge Island, Prince Charles Foreland, Hope Island and Bear Island. It lies north of the Arctic Circle, and glaciers and snow cover around 60 per cent of the area, although the west coast is ice-free for about half the year. Some 65 per cent of the Svalbard archipelago is protected to ensure biodiversity; there are seven national parks, six large nature reserves, 15 bird sanctuaries and one geotopic protected area. A global seed repository has been established on Spitsbergen. Norway's sovereignty was recognised by treaty in 1920 but the other signatories were granted equal rights to exploit mineral deposits, although this right is now only exercised by Russia. The territory is administered by a governor, who is responsible to the Ministry of Justice and Police. The main economic activities are coal mining, tourism, and research and education.

### JAN MAYEN ISLAND
*Area* – 377 sq. km
*Population* – The only residents are the staff of the radio and meteorological stations

The island is barren, volcanic and partially covered by glaciers, with no exploitable natural resources. It lies in the North Atlantic Ocean about 950km west of Norway and is home to the Beerenberg volcano, the northernmost active volcano on Earth. It was annexed by Norway in 1922 and integrated into the kingdom in 1930; since 1995 it has been administered by the governor of Nordland county.

### NORWEGIAN ANTARCTIC TERRITORY
The Norwegian Antarctic Territory consists of Queen Maud Land, Bouvet Island and Peter the First Island. Claimed in 1938, Queen Maud Land is a sector of the Antarctic continent which extends from 45° E. to 20° E. Peter the First Island was formally claimed in 1931 and is the only claimed area covered under the Antarctic Treaty that is not part of the main land mass. Bouvet Island was claimed in 1930 (*see also* The North and South Poles).

# OMAN

*Saltanat Uman – Sultanate of Oman*

*Area* – 309,500 sq. km
*Capital* – Muscat (Masqat); population, 812,000 (2014)

*Major cities* – Ibri, Salalah, Suhar, as-Suwayq
*Currency* – Omani Rial (OR) of 1,000 baisas
*Population* – 3,286,936 rising at 2.07 per cent a year
(2015 est)
*Religion* – Muslim 85.9 per cent (majority are Ibadhi, lesser
numbers of Sunni and Shia), Christian 6.5 per cent, Hindu
5.5 per cent
*Language* – Arabic (official), English, Baluchi, Urdu
*Population density* – 12 per sq. km (2013)
*Urban population* – 73.9 per cent (2013 est)
*Median age (years)* – 24.9 (2014 est)
*National anthem* – 'Nashid as-Salaam as-Sultani' ['The
Sultan's Anthem']
*National day* – 18 November (Birthday of Sultan Qaboos,
1940)
*Death penalty* – Retained
*CPI score* – 45 (64)

## CLIMATE AND TERRAIN

Oman lies at the south-eastern corner of the Arabian
peninsula and includes territory at the tip of the Musandam
peninsula, which is separated from the rest of the country by
the UAE. There are mountains in the north and the
south-west of the country, divided by high desert plateau;
over 80 per cent of the country is desert. The plateau
descends to a fertile plain on the Arabian Sea coast. Elevation
extremes range from 2,980m (Jabal Shams) to 0m (Arabian
Sea). The climate is arid, with high temperatures and
humidity throughout the year; temperatures are lower on
the coast, but the high humidity often makes coastal areas
the most inhospitable. Average temperatures range from
20.4°C in January to 30.4°C in June.

## HISTORY AND POLITICS

Oman began to build an empire in the Middle East from the
eighth century AD and remained largely unchallenged until
the arrival in 1506 of the Portuguese, who were ousted in
1650. An independent sultanate was established in 1749 by
the founder of the dynasty that still rules the country. By the
early 19th century, Omani rule extended to the east African
coast and parts of Persia and Balochistan (in modern
Pakistan). The kingdom came under British influence from
the late 19th century until 1951.

The country was divided from 1913, with religious
leaders in control of the interior and the sultan of the coastal
regions. The interior's attempts to assert its independence
led to clashes in the 1950s, but by 1959 the sultan had
established control over the whole country. An insurrection
in the south by left-wing rebels supported by South Yemen
began in 1965 and was defeated with British military
assistance in 1975. The discovery and subsequent
exploitation of oil in the mid-1960s led to the steady
economic transformation of Oman, and in 1970 the sultan
was overthrown in a bloodless coup by his son, Sultan
Qaboos bin Said al-Said, who initiated a modernisation
programme.

The country is still essentially an absolute monarchy,
although a degree of political liberalisation has occurred in
the past 20 years. In 1996 the sultan issued a Basic Statute
that is in effect a constitution; it established a succession
mechanism, codified the system of government and set up a
bicameral legislature. The first direct election to the
consultative council was held in 2000 and the first by
universal adult suffrage in 2003. In the 2011 election, all the
candidates contesting the 84 seats were independents.
Pro-reform demonstrations occurred prior to the October
2011 elections.

At present, legislation is proposed by the sultan and passed
by decree. The sultan is advised by the bicameral Council of

Oman, comprising the Consultative Council *(Majlis
al-Shura)*, which has 84 members directly elected for a
four-year term, and the Council of State *(Majlis al-Dawlah)*,
which has 59 members appointed by the sultan for a
four-year term. The Consultative Council has the right to
review legislation, question ministers and make policy
proposals. The Council of State is intended to facilitate
'constructive cooperation between the government and the
citizens'. There are no political parties.

### HEAD OF STATE

*HM The Sultan of Oman, Prime Minister,* Sultan Qaboos bin
Said al-Said, *succeeded following a coup,* 23 July 1970

### SELECTED GOVERNMENT MEMBERS *as at June 2015*
*Deputy Prime Minister,* Fahd bin Mamud al-Said
*Defence,* Badr bin Saud bin Hareb al-Busaidi
*Foreign Affairs,* Yusuf bin Alawi bin Abdullah
*Interior,* Sayyid Hamoud bin Faisal al-Busaidi

### EMBASSY OF THE SULTANATE OF OMAN
167 Queen's Gate, London SW7 5HE
T 020-7225 0001
*Ambassador Extraordinary and Plenipotentiary,* HE Abdul Aziz
al-Hinai, *apptd* 2009

### BRITISH EMBASSY
PO Box 185, Mina al-Fahal, 116 Muscat
T (+968) (24) 609 000 E muscat.enquiries@fco.gov.uk
W www.gov.uk/government/world/oman
*Ambassador Extraordinary and Plenipotentiary,* HE Jonathan
Wilks, *apptd* 2014

## DEFENCE

| *Aged 16–49, 2010 est* | *Males* | *Females* |
| --- | --- | --- |
| Available for military service | 985,957 | 737,812 |
| Fit for military service | 837,886 | 642,427 |

*Military expenditure* – US$9,623m (2014)

## ECONOMY AND TRADE

Although its production is more modest than other Gulf
states, oil and gas are the mainstay of Oman's economy. Oil
reserves are dwindling and development plans centre on
diversification, industrialisation and privatisation, with the
aim of reducing the oil sector's contribution to GDP to
9 per cent by 2020. Industrial development is focused on
natural gas production, metal manufacturing, petrochemicals
and trans-shipment ports, with plans also to develop tourism
and communication technology industries. Improved
training, especially in IT and business skills, is intended to
enable the local population to replace expatriate workers.
Growth of the non-oil sector is expected to produce growth
of just under 4 per cent in 2015–19.

Agriculture and fishing account for 1.3 per cent of GDP,
producing dates, limes, bananas, alfalfa and vegetables as well
as fish. The main industries apart from oil and natural gas
extraction are oil refining, liquefied natural gas production,
construction and production of cement, copper, steel,
chemicals and optic fibre. Industry accounts for 55.2 per cent
of GDP and services for 43.5 per cent.

The main trading partners are China, the UAE, Japan,
India and South Korea. Principal exports are petroleum,
re-exports, fish, metals and textiles. The main imports are
machinery, transport equipment, manufactured goods, food
and livestock.

GNI – US$54,687m; US$25,150 per capita (2012)
Annual average growth of GDP – 3.4 per cent (2014)
Inflation rate – 2.8 per cent (2014 est)
Unemployment – 8.1 per cent (2015 est)
Total external debt – US$11,300m (2014 est)
Imports – US$34,333m (2013)
Exports – US$56,429m (2013)

BALANCE OF PAYMENTS
Trade – US$22,096m surplus (2013)
Current Account – US$9,462m deficit (2015 est)

| Trade with UK | 2013 | 2014 |
| --- | --- | --- |
| Imports from UK | £555,431,881 | £551,269,885 |
| Exports to UK | £115,665,054 | £227,163,090 |

## COMMUNICATIONS
Airports and waterways – The main airports are at Muscat and Salalah; the main ports are Salalah and Port Qaboos at Mutrah, which has eight deep-water berths
Roadways – There are 29,685km of roadways, including 1,943km of motorways
Telecommunications – 305,000 fixed lines and 5.278 million mobile telephone subscriptions (2012); there were 1.465 million internet users in 2009
Internet code and IDD – om; 968 (from UK), 44 (to UK)
Media – Oman TV and Radio Oman are the state-run broadcasters; Al-Watan and the Oman Daily are the principal daily newspapers
WPFI score – 38,83 (127)

## EDUCATION AND HEALTH
Literacy rate – 99.2 per cent (2015 est)
Gross enrolment ratio (percentage of relevant age group) –
    primary 113 per cent (2013 est); secondary 94 per cent
    (2012 est); tertiary 28 per cent (2011 est)
Health expenditure (per capita) – US$678 (2013)
Hospital beds (per 1,000 people) – 1.7 (2012)
Life expectancy (years) – 74.97 (2014 est)
Mortality rate – 3.38 (2014 est)
Birth rate – 24.47 (2014 est)
Infant mortality rate – 14 (2014 est)

# PAKISTAN

Jamhuryat Islami Pakistan – Islamic Republic of Pakistan

Area – 796,095 sq. km
Capital – Islamabad; population, 1,297,000 (2014)
Major cities – Faisalabad, Gujranwala, Hyderabad, Karachi, Lahore, Multan, Peshawar, Quetta, Rawalpindi
Currency – Pakistan rupee of 100 paisa
Population – 199,085,847 rising at 1.46 per cent a year

(2015 est); Punjabi (44.7 per cent), Pashtun (15.4 per cent), Sindhi (14.1 per cent), Sariaki (8.4 per cent), Muhajirs (7.6 per cent), Balochi (3.6 per cent) (est)
Religion – Muslim 96.4 per cent (predominantly Sunni), other (includes Christian and Hindu) 3.6 per cent; Islam is the state religion
Language – English, Urdu (both official), Balochi, Brahui, Burushaski, Hindko, Punjabi, Pashto, Sindhi, Siraiki
Population density – 236 per sq. km (2013)
Urban population – 36.8 per cent (2013 est)
Median age (years) – 22.6 (2014 est)
National anthem – 'Qaumi Tarana' ['The Sacred Land']
National day – 23 March (Republic Day)
Death penalty – Retained
CPI score – 29 (126)

## CLIMATE AND TERRAIN
The arid Thar desert in the east gives way to the fertile Indus valley in the centre of the country. The terrain then rises to the Makran, Kirthar and Sulaiman mountain ranges in the west and the Karakoram and Himalayan ranges in the north. Elevation extremes range from 8,611m (K2) to 0m (Indian Ocean). The climate varies greatly across the country. For most areas, the rainy season runs from July to September and is accompanied by very high humidity. Average temperatures range from 8.8°C in January to 28.6°C in June. Pakistan is prone to earthquakes – the most recent major occurrences were in 2008 and 2013 – and flooding; following heavy monsoon rains in 2010 the entire length of the Indus valley was flooded, displacing millions of people.

## POLITICS
Pakistan is a federal republic. The 1973 constitution has been suspended and restored several times, amended in 1985, 2002 and 2003, and in 2010 was reinstated in its original form, returning some of the president's powers to the prime minister.

The president is elected by the legislature for a five-year term. The parliament (Majlis as-Shura) comprises a lower house, the National Assembly and the senate. The National Assembly has 342 members, of whom 60 are women and ten are elected by non-Muslim minorities; members serve a five-year term. The senate has 104 members, 92 elected by provincial assemblies, eight chosen by tribal agencies and four elected by the National Assembly; they serve a six-year term, with half elected every three years. The prime minister is nominated by and is responsible to the legislature.

There are four provinces: Balochistan, Khyber Pukhtoonkhwa (formerly North-West Frontier Province), Punjab and Sindh. Each has a provincial assembly and government. In addition, there are the Federally Administered Tribal Areas and the Islamabad Capital Territory.

The legislative elections originally scheduled for January 2008 were postponed to February after the assassination of Benazir Bhutto in December 2007. The two main opposition parties, Bhutto's Pakistan People's Party (PPP) and the Pakistan Muslim League–Nawaz Sharif (PML-N), won the most seats and formed a coalition government with two smaller parties; the PML-N withdrew from the coalition government in August 2008. The presidential election in July 2013 was won by Mamnoon Hussain, the first instance in Pakistan's history in which one elected civilian president was replaced by another. In the May 2013 legislative elections, the PML-N won the most seats but without a majority. However, 50 of the 70 reserved seats were assigned to PML supporters, giving the PML a majority in the chamber. Nawaz Sharif was elected prime minister in June 2013.

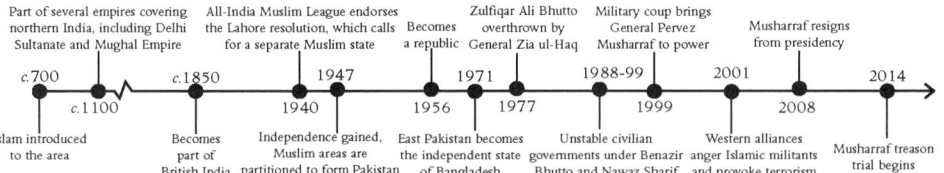

Part of several empires covering northern India, including Delhi Sultanate and Mughal Empire — *c.*700

*c.*1100 — Islam introduced to the area

All-India Muslim League endorses the Lahore resolution, which calls for a separate Muslim state — *c.*1850

1940 — Becomes part of British India

1947 — Becomes a republic

1956 — Independence gained, Muslim areas are partitioned to form Pakistan

Zulfiqar Ali Bhutto overthrown by General Zia ul-Haq — 1971

1977 — East Pakistan becomes the independent state of Bangladesh

Military coup brings General Pervez Musharraf to power — 1988-99

1999 — Unstable civilian governments under Benazir Bhutto and Nawaz Sharif

Musharraf resigns from presidency — 2001

2008 — Western alliances anger Islamic militants and provoke terrorism

2014 — Musharraf treason trial begins

## HEAD OF STATE
President, Mamnoon Hussain, *elected* 30 July 2013, *sworn in* 9 September 2013

SELECTED GOVERNMENT MEMBERS *as at June 2015*
Prime Minister, Defence, Nawaz Sharif
Finance, Muhammad Ishaq Dar
Education, Muhammad Baligh Ur Rehman

## HIGH COMMISSION FOR THE ISLAMIC REPUBLIC OF PAKISTAN
34–36 Lowndes Square, London SW1X 9JN
T 020-7664 924 E poldiv@phclondon.org W www.phclondon.org
High Commissioner (acting), HE Syed Ibne Abbas, *apptd* 2014

## BRITISH HIGH COMMISSION
Diplomatic Enclave, Ramna 5, PO Box 1122, Islamabad
T (+92) (51) 201 2000 E islamabad-general.enquiries@fco.gov.uk
W www.gov.uk/government/world/pakistan
High Commissioner, HE Philip Barton, *apptd* 2014

## INSURGENCIES
Balochistan, Punjab and Sindh provinces have all been affected since the 1980s by conflict between Shia and Sunni fundamentalists. Balochistan and, since the early 1990s, Sindh (especially Karachi) have experienced violence by armed militants seeking greater autonomy for each province.

Civil order has always been harder to maintain in Pukhtoonkhwa and the federally administered tribal areas than in the rest of the country. These areas became havens for the Taliban and al-Qaida fleeing Afghanistan after 2001, radicalising and destabilising increasingly wide areas. Government military and security forces are struggling to maintain control in over half of these areas. The government conceded the imposition of Shariah law in the Swat valley as part of a cease-fire agreement with the Taliban in early 2009, but when the Taliban attempted to extend its influence further into the country, the army began a counter-insurgency offensive to retake the area in April 2009, subsequently moving against the Taliban in other strongholds such as South Waziristan. These offensives led to an increase in militants' attacks in the major cities, while by 2010 the Taliban began to reassert its influence in some of the areas cleared by the army offensives in 2009. Islamist attacks continue to be carried out against civilian targets; in March 2014 peace talks with the Taliban resumed in Waziristan. The group continued to attack civilian targets in late 2014 and 2015.

## FOREIGN RELATIONS
Since partition, sovereignty over the predominantly Muslim state of Jammu and Kashmir has been disputed between Pakistan and India. A short war in 1947–8 resulted in the state being partitioned between the two countries; its status remains unresolved, despite further outbreaks of war in 1965 and 1971, low-level conflict for control of the Siachen glacier since 1985 and occasional increases in military exchanges, most recently in 1999–2002 and 2003. Tension was exacerbated by Pakistan's support of the Muslim insurgency in the Indian part of the state, which began in the 1980s, and by both countries' acquisition of nuclear weapons. Moves towards a peaceful settlement began in 2003, when diplomatic missions were reopened and the resumption of transport links was initiated. Formal diplomatic talks began in 2004 and have achieved several accords intended to reduce tension between the two countries. Talks were temporarily suspended by the Indian government after the Mumbai terrorist attacks in 2008, but resumed in 2010. In recent years the two countries have exchanged live fire across the Kashmiri border, including in 2014 and 2015.

## DEFENCE

| Aged 16–49, 2010 est | Males | Females |
| --- | --- | --- |
| Available for military service | 48,453,305 | 44,898,096 |
| Fit for military service | 37,945,440 | 37,381,549 |

*Military expenditure* – US$8,537m (2014)

## ECONOMY AND TRADE
Decades of political instability, inefficiency, corruption and high military expenditure have left Pakistan an under-developed country, averaging poor economic growth of 3.5 per cent between 2008 and 2015. In the 2000s economic reforms, international aid and greater foreign investment produced steady growth of 5–8 per cent a year until 2008, notably in the industrial and service sectors, and reduced poverty levels by 10 per cent between 2001 and 2007. However, slower growth in 2008 caused budget and fiscal deficits that forced Pakistan to seek IMF assistance. These problems have been exacerbated by the 2010 floods, which left millions homeless, destroyed crops and damaged infrastructure. A large proportion of the country's labour force works abroad, especially in the Middle East, providing valuable remittances but also causing use of child labour within Pakistan. The Sharif government has successfully implemented fiscal and energy reforms and growth of over 4 per cent is expected in 2015–16. Political instability remains a significant threat to further development.

Agriculture employs 45.1 per cent of the workforce, producing cotton, wheat, rice, sugar cane, vegetables, milk, meat and eggs, and contributes 25.1 per cent of GDP. Significant manufacturing industries include textiles and clothing, food processing, pharmaceuticals, construction materials, paper products, fertiliser and seafood. Industry accounts for 21.3 per cent of GDP and services for 53.6 per cent.

The main trading partners are China, the USA, the UAE, Saudi Arabia, Afghanistan and Kuwait. Principal exports are textiles (clothing, bed linen, cotton cloth and yarn), rice, leather goods, sports goods, chemicals, carpets and rugs. The main imports are petroleum, machinery, plastics, transport equipment, edible oils, paper, iron, steel and tea.
*GNI* – US$247,040m; US$1,360 per capita (2013)
*Annual average growth of GDP* – 4.1 per cent (2014)
*Inflation rate* – 8.6 per cent (2014 est)
*Population below poverty line* – 12.4 per cent (2011 est)

*Unemployment* – 5.4 per cent (2015 est)
*Total external debt* – US$62,330m (2014 est)
*Imports* – US$44,647m (2013)
*Exports* – US$25,121m (2013)

BALANCE OF PAYMENTS
*Trade* – US$19,526m deficit (2013)
*Current Account* – US$3,096m deficit (2014 est)

| Trade with UK | 2013 | 2014 |
|---|---|---|
| Imports from UK | £474,804,433 | £519,036,797 |
| Exports to UK | £916,338,926 | £1,078,500,827 |

## COMMUNICATIONS
*Airports and waterways* – The principal airports are at Karachi, Islamabad, Lahore, Peshawar and Sialkot, and 103 other airports; the main seaports are Karachi and Port Muhammad bin Qasim, and there is a deep-water port at Gwadar
*Roadways and railways* – 189,218km, including 708km of motorways; 7,791km
*Telecommunications* – 5.803 million fixed lines and 125 million mobile subscriptions (2012); there were 20.431 million internet users in 2009
*Internet code and IDD* – pk; 92 (from UK), 44 (to UK)
*Major broadcasters* – Radio Pakistan and Pakistan Television Corporation Ltd are the principal state broadcasters
*Press* – Leading dailies include *Daily Jang* (Urdu language), *Dawn* and *The Nation* (both English language)
*WPFI score* – 50,46 (159)

## EDUCATION AND HEALTH
Education is free to upper secondary level.
*Literacy rate* – 74.8 per cent (2015)
*Gross enrolment ratio (percentage of relevant age group)* – primary 92 per cent; secondary 38 per cent; tertiary 10 per cent (2013 est)
*Health expenditure (per capita)* – US$37 (2013)
*Hospital beds (per 1,000 people)* – 0.6 (2012)
*Life expectancy (years)* – 67.05 (2014 est)
*Mortality rate* – 6.58 (2014 est)
*Birth rate* – 23.19 (2014 est)
*Infant mortality rate* – 57.48 (2014 est)

# PALAU

*Beluu er a Belau – Republic of Palau*

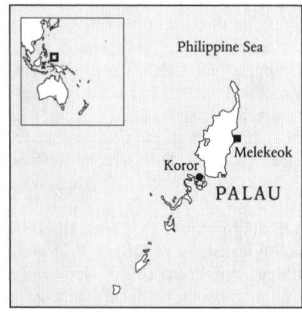

*Area* – 459 sq. km
*Capital* – Melekeok, on Babeldaob; population, 299 (2012)
*Major town* – Koror
*Currency* – US dollar (US$) of 100 cents
*Population* – 21,265 rising at 0.38 per cent a year (2015 est);

Palauan (72.5 per cent), Filipino (16.3 per cent), Chinese (1.6 per cent) (2005 est)
*Religion* – Christian (Roman Catholic 49.4 per cent, Protestant 30.9 per cent), Modekngei 8.7 per cent (indigenous to Palau; combines Animism and Christianity)
*Language* – Palauan (official in most islands), English (official in all islands), Tobi, Sonsoralese, Angaur (official in respective islands), Japanese (official in Angaur), Filipino, Chinese
*Population density* – 45 per sq. km (2013)
*Urban population* – 85.8 per cent (2013 est)
*Median age (years)* – 33 (2014 est)
*National anthem* – 'Belau rekid' ['Our Palau']
*National day* – 9 July (Constitution Day)
*Death penalty* – Abolished for all crimes (since 1994)
*Literacy rate* – 99.8 per cent (2015 est)
*Life expectancy (years)* – 72.6 (2014 est)
*Mortality rate* – 7.93 (2014 est)
*Birth rate* – 10.95 (2014 est)
*Infant mortality rate* – 11.46 (2014 est)

## CLIMATE AND TERRAIN
The republic consists of six island groups in the western Pacific Ocean; these comprise eight large islands and over 300 smaller islands or islets that are either volcanic and mountainous or coral and low-lying. Elevation extremes range from 242m (Mt Ngerchelchuus) to 0m (Pacific Ocean). The climate is tropical, with a wet season from May to November. The average temperature is 27.8°C.

## HISTORY AND POLITICS
Palau has been inhabited since the first millennium BC. In the 19th century, Spain and Germany vied for possession until 1889, when Spain sold the islands to Germany, which exploited the phosphate deposits and developed coconut plantations. Japan occupied the islands on behalf of the Allies in 1914 and administered them after the First World War under a League of Nations mandate. Japanese forces were ousted by US troops during the Second World War.

In 1947 the islands became part of the UN Trust Territory of the Pacific, administered by the USA. In 1982 a compact of free association was signed with the USA under which the USA retained responsibility for defence and foreign policy in return for providing economic aid; the compact was ratified in 1993 and entered into force when Palau became independent on 1 October 1994.

The latest presidential and legislative elections were held in 2012; Tommy Remengesau Jr was elected president.

Under the 1981 constitution, the executive president is directly elected for a four-year term, renewable once. The president appoints the cabinet. The bicameral National Congress comprises the House of Delegates, which has 16 members (one from each state), and the 13-member senate; members of both chambers stand for election as independents, and serve a four-year term. A council of indigenous chiefs, composed of the paramount chief from each of the 16 states, acts as an advisory body to the president on matters concerning traditional law and customs.

Each of the 16 constituent states has its own governor and legislature.

HEAD OF STATE
*President,* Tommy Remengesau Jr, *elected* 6 November 2012, *inaugurated* 17 January 2013
*Vice-President, Justice,* Antonio Bells

SELECTED GOVERNMENT MEMBERS *as at June 2015*
*Finance,* Elbuchel Sadang
*Minister of State,* Billy Kuartei

HONORARY CONSULATE OF THE REPUBLIC OF PALAU
Bankfoot Square, Bankfoot Street, Batley WF17 5LH
T 01924-470 786 W www.palauconsulate.org.uk

BRITISH AMBASSADOR
HE Asif Ahmad, *apptd* 2013, resident at Manila, the Philippines

## ECONOMY AND TRADE
The economy is reliant on economic aid from the USA and the government is keen to diversify. Tourism is now the main industry, catering for over 80,000 people a year, but the government is limiting development to protect the environment. The other main industries are handicrafts, construction and garment manufacturing. Subsistence agriculture and fishing remain important, engaging 20 per cent of the workforce and producing crops such as coconuts, copra, cassava and sweet potatoes as well as fish. Revenue is also derived from the sale of licences to foreign fishing fleets.

The main trading partners are the USA, Japan, Taiwan, Singapore and South Korea. Principal exports are shellfish, tuna, copra and clothing. The main imports are machinery and equipment, fuels, metals and foodstuffs.

*GNI* – US$229m; US$10,970 per capita (2013)
*Annual average growth of GDP* – 1.8 per cent (2014)
*Inflation rate* – 7.7 per cent (2013 est)
*Unemployment* – 4.2 per cent (2005 est)
*Total external debt* – US$67m (2014 est)

| Trade with UK | 2013 | 2014 |
|---|---|---|
| Imports from UK | £44,792 | £82,688 |
| Exports to UK | £11,270 | £1,215 |

## COMMUNICATIONS
*Airports and waterways* – There are three airports, on Koror, Peleliu and Angaur, which receive international flights from Guam, Japan, the Philippines and Taiwan; Koror is also the main seaport
*Roadways* – 36km
*Telecommunications* – 7,300 fixed lines and 17,150 mobile subscriptions (2012)
*Internet code and IDD* – pw; 680 (from UK), 011 44 (to UK)
*Media* – T8AA Eco Paradise (radio) is the public broadcaster; there are no TV stations based in Palau or daily newspapers

# PANAMA

*República de Panamá – Republic of Panama*

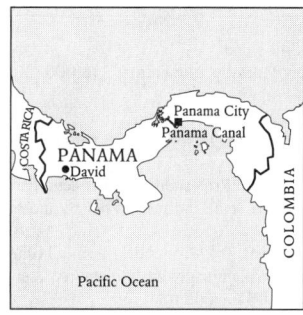

*Area* – 75,420 sq. km
*Capital* – Panama City; population, 1,638,000 (2014)
*Major cities* – Colón, David, San Miguelito
*Currency* – Balboa of 100 centésimos; at parity with the US dollar, which is used as paper currency. Both Panamanian and US coins are used

*Population* – 3,657,024 rising at 1.32 per cent a year (2015 est)
*Religion* – Christian (Roman Catholic 85 per cent, Protestant 15 per cent) (est)
*Language* – Spanish (official), English
*Population density* – 52 per sq. km (2013)
*Urban population* – 76.5 per cent (2013 est)
*Median age (years)* – 28.3 (2014 est)
*National anthem* – 'Himno Istmeño' ['Hymn of the Isthmus']
*National day* – 3 November (Independence Day)
*Death penalty* – Abolished for all crimes (since 1922)
*CPI score* – 37 (94)

## CLIMATE AND TERRAIN
Panama lies on the isthmus connecting North and South America. A mountain range runs along the centre, falling to coastal plains on both coasts. There is dense tropical rainforest in the east. Elevation extremes range from 3,475m (Volcan Baru) to 0m (Pacific Ocean). The climate is tropical, with a prolonged wet season from May to January. The average temperature is 23.8°C.

## HISTORY AND POLITICS
Panama was visited by Spanish explorers from 1502, and in 1519 became part of the Viceroyalty of New Andalucia, later New Grenada. When it gained its independence from Spain in 1821, Panama joined the confederacy of Gran Colombia (comprising Colombia, Venezuela, Ecuador, Peru and Bolivia). The confederacy split up in 1830 and Panama became part of Colombia until 1903, when it achieved its independence.

In the 1880s, the French attempted to construct a canal across Panama to link the Atlantic and Pacific oceans. In 1903 the USA bought the rights to build the canal, which was completed in 1914 and opened in 1919. The USA was also given control of the canal and land to either side of it, known as the Canal Zone, in perpetuity but, under a 1977 agreement, sovereignty over the Canal Zone was transferred to Panama on 31 December 1999.

Panama was under the military rule of General Omar Torrijos from 1968 until his death in 1981. In 1983, General Manuel Noriega seized power and instigated a period of military rule, supported by the USA until 1987. An internal coup to unseat Noriega was unsuccessful in 1988, but in 1989 US forces invaded and deposed him. Noriega surrendered in 1990 and in 1992 was tried and sentenced in the USA on drug-trafficking and money-laundering charges. He was extradited to Panama in 2011 to serve a further 20 years in prison.

The May 2014 presidential election was won by Juan Carlos Varela of the Panamenista party. In the simultaneous legislative election the four-party Alliance for Change coalition won the most seats.

Under the 1972 constitution, as amended in 1983, the executive president is directly elected for a five-year term, which is not renewable. The unicameral National Assembly has 71 members, who are directly elected for a five-year term. The president, who is responsible to the legislature, appoints the cabinet.

### HEAD OF STATE
*President,* Juan Carlos Varela, *elected* 4 May 2014, *sworn in* 1 July 2014
*Vice-President, Foreign Affairs,* Isabel St Malo de Alvarado

SELECTED GOVERNMENT MEMBERS *as at June 2015*
*Economy and Finance,* Dulcidio de la Guardia
*Interior,* Milton Henríquez

## EMBASSY OF PANAMA
40 Hertford Street, London W1J 7SH
T 020-7493 4646 E panama1@btconnect.com
W www.panamaconsul.co.uk
*Ambassador Extraordinary and Plenipotentiary,* HE Daniel
　Fabrega, *apptd* 2011

## BRITISH EMBASSY
Humboldt Tower, 4th Floor, Calle 53, Marbella, PO Box
0816-07946, Panama City
T (+507) 297 6550 W www.gov.uk/government/world/panama
*Ambassador Extraordinary and Plenipotentiary,* HE Daniel
　Fabrega, *apptd* 2014

## DEFENCE

| Aged 16–49, 2010 est | Males | Females |
|---|---|---|
| Available for military service | 890,006 | – |
| Fit for military service | 731,254 | 728,329 |

## ECONOMY AND TRADE
The economy is based on a large service sector and has
experienced steady growth in recent years, although this
slowed in 2009 because of the global economic downturn.
However, the distribution of wealth is uneven: over
one-quarter of the population lives below the poverty line,
although unemployment has reduced significantly from
12 per cent to 4.4 per cent of the labour force in 2012.
The economy has grown quickly since 2009, expanding by
7.5 per cent in 2013 and 7.3 per cent in 2014.

The service sector accounts for 83 per cent of GDP,
derived from the operation of the Panama Canal and the
Colón free trade zone, financial services, container ports, ship
registry and tourism. Enlargement of the canal to take more
and larger vessels is scheduled for completion in 2015.
Industry, which contributes 14.1 per cent of GDP, includes
construction, brewing, sugar refining and the manufacture of
cement and other construction materials. Agriculture, which
accounts for 2.9 per cent of GDP, is centred on bananas, rice,
maize, coffee, sugar cane, vegetables, livestock and shrimp.

The main trading partners are Ecuador, the USA, China,
Singapore, Japan and Brazil. Principal exports are gold,
bananas, shrimp, sugar, iron and steel waste, and fruit. The
main imports are fuel products, medicines, vehicles, iron and
steel rods, and mobile phones.
*GNI* – US$41,328m; US$10,700 per capita (2013)
*Annual average growth of GDP* – 6.6 per cent (2014)
*Inflation rate* – 2.9 per cent (2014 est)
*Population below poverty line* – 25.8 per cent (2013 est)
*Unemployment* – 4.3 per cent (2015 est)
*Total external debt* – US$15,470m (2014 est)
*Imports* – US$12,633m (2012)
*Exports* – US$785m (2011)

## BALANCE OF PAYMENTS
*Trade* – US$10,556m deficit (2012)
*Current Account* – US$4,941m deficit (2015 est)

| Trade with UK | 2013 | 2014 |
|---|---|---|
| Imports from UK | £184,917,422 | £180,697,164 |
| Exports to UK | £42,082,523 | £25,702,638 |

## COMMUNICATIONS
*Airports* – There are 57 airports; the principal airport is at
Panama City
*Waterways* – The Panama Canal connects the Pacific and
Atlantic oceans. Each year the canal handles about 5 per cent
of world trade and over 40 per cent of trade between Asia
and the east coast of the USA. The chief ports are Colón,
Cristóbal and Balboa, at either end of the canal. Because of
its role as a ship registry, there were 6,413 Panamanian- and
5,162 foreign-owned ships of over 1,000 tonnes registered
under its flag in 2011
*Roadways and railways* – 6,351km; 76km
*Telecommunications* – 640,000 fixed lines and 6.77 million
mobile subscriptions (2012); there were 959,800 internet
users in 2009
*Internet code and IDD* – pa; 507 (from UK), 44 (to UK)
*Major broadcasters* – The sector is dominated by private
firms, including Telemetro (TV) and RPC Radio
*Press* – *La Prensa, Panama News* and *El Siglo* are among the
leading daily newspapers
*WPFI score* – 28,98 (83)

## EDUCATION AND HEALTH
There are nine years of compulsory education.
*Literacy rate* – 98.1 per cent (2015 est)
*Gross enrolment ratio (percentage of relevant age group)* –
primary 99 per cent; secondary 73 per cent (2014 est);
tertiary 43 per cent (2012 est)
*Health expenditure (per capita)* – US$796 (2013)
*Hospital beds (per 1,000 people)* – 2.2 (2011)
*Life expectancy (years)* – 78.3 (2014 est)
*Mortality rate* – 4.77 (2014 est)
*Birth rate* – 18.61 (2014 est)
*Infant mortality rate* – 10.7 (2014 est)

# PAPUA NEW GUINEA

*Gau Hedinarai ai Papua-Matamata Guinea – Independent State
of Papua New Guinea*

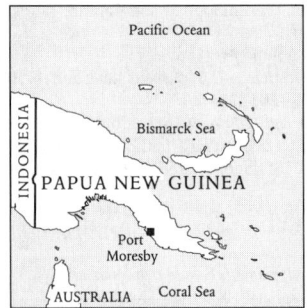

*Area* – 462,840 sq. km
*Capital* – Port Moresby; population, 338,000 (2014)
*Major town* – Arawa, Lae
*Currency* – Kina (K) of 100 toea
*Population* – 6,672,429 rising at 1.78 per cent a year
(2015 est)
*Religion* – Christian (Protestant 69.4 per cent, Roman
Catholic 27 per cent), indigenous beliefs and other
3.3 per cent
*Language* – English, Tok Pisin, Hiri Motu (all official), Motu;
836 indigenous languages are spoken, representing over
12 per cent of the world total
*Population density* – 16 per sq. km (2013)
*Urban population* – 12.6 per cent (2013 est)
*Median age (years)* – 22.4 (2014 est)
*National anthem* – 'O Arise, All You Sons'
*National day* – 16 September (Independence Day)
*Death penalty* – Retained (last used 1950)
*CPI score* – 25 (145)

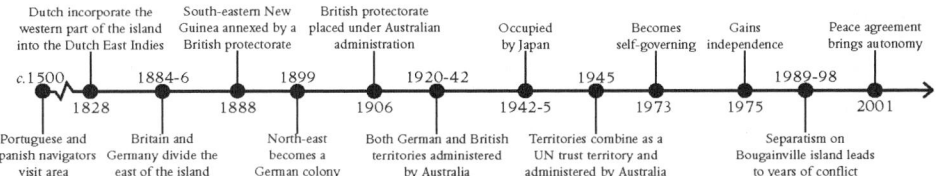

| Dutch incorporate the western part of the island into the Dutch East Indies | South-eastern New Guinea annexed by a British protectorate | British protectorate placed under Australian administration | | Occupied by Japan | Becomes self-governing | Gains independence | Peace agreement brings autonomy |

c.1500 — 1884–6 — 1899 — 1920–42 — 1945 — 1989–98

1828 — 1888 — 1906 — 1942–5 — 1973 — 1975 — 2001

| Portuguese and Spanish navigators visit area | Britain and Germany divide the east of the island | North-east becomes a German colony | Both German and British territories administered by Australia | Territories combine as a UN trust territory and administered by Australia | Separatism on Bougainville island leads to years of conflict |

## CLIMATE AND TERRAIN

Papua New Guinea lies in the south-western Pacific Ocean and consists of the eastern half of the island of New Guinea, the islands of Bougainville, New Britain and New Ireland, the Admiralty Islands, the D'Entrecasteaux Islands and the Louisiade archipelago. A range of densely forested mountains runs across the centre of the Papuan part of New Guinea, descending to coastal plains and swamps, and coral reefs. Elevation extremes range from 4,509m (Mt Wilhelm) to 0m (Pacific Ocean). There are a number of active volcanoes and the country is subject to frequent eruptions and earthquakes. Over 50 per cent of the country is forested, and 20 per cent is permanently or seasonally flooded. The climate is tropical and subject to the north-west monsoon (December–March) and south-east monsoon (May–October).

## POLITICS

The 1975 constitution was amended in 1998 to grant greater autonomy to Bougainville, and in March 2010 to expand the maximum number of cabinet ministers from 28 to 31. The head of state is Queen Elizabeth II, represented by a governor-general who is elected by the legislature for a six-year term. The unicameral National Parliament has 109 members, 20 from provincial electorates and the remainder from open electorates, who are directly elected for a five-year term. The prime minister is nominated by the legislature and appointed by the governor-general.

Factionalism and shifting alliances have caused political instability since independence, and a proportional representation element was introduced into the voting system in 2007 to try to increase the stability of governments. Following the 2007 legislative election, the National Alliance Party (NAP) leader, Sir Michael Somare, was elected prime minister for the fourth time, forming a new coalition government. Somare was convicted of financial irregularities in March 2011 and suspended for 14 days; former transport minister Peter O'Neill was elected as prime minister in August 2011. Legislative elections in 2012 saw the People's National Congress Party (PNC) gain the most seats but without a majority; following this, O'Neill announced that he would lead the government.

*Governor-General,* HE Sir Michael Ogio, GCMG, CBE *sworn in* 25 February 2012

SELECTED GOVERNMENT MEMBERS *as at June 2015*
*Prime Minister,* Peter O'Neill
*Deputy Prime Minister,* Leo Dion
*Foreign Affairs,* Rimbink Pato

## PAPUA NEW GUINEA HIGH COMMISSION

3rd Floor, 14 Waterloo Place, London SW1Y 4AR
T 020-7930 0922 E info@pnghighcomm.org.uk
W www.pnghighcomm.org.uk
*High Commissioner,* HE Winnie Kiap, *apptd* 2011

## BRITISH HIGH COMMISSION

Sec 411 Lot 1 & 2, Kiroki Street, Waigani, National Capital District, Port Moresby

T (+675) 325 1677 E uk.inpng@fco.gov.uk
W www.gov.uk/government/world/papua-new-guinea
*High Commissioner,* HE Simon Tonge, *apptd* 2014

## DEFENCE

| *Aged 16–49, 2010 est* | *Males* | *Females* |
| --- | --- | --- |
| Available for military service | 1,568,210 | 1,478,965 |
| Fit for military service | 1,130,951 | 1,137,753 |

*Military expenditure* – US$100m (2014)

## ECONOMY AND TRADE

Political instability, corruption, a weak economy and high unemployment and crime levels had brought the country to the brink of economic and social collapse in 2004. The economy has grown since, achieving 12 years of continuous growth as of 2014, owing to higher commodity prices and tight control of the national budget but the country does remain poor and underdeveloped. Foreign investment in oil and liquid natural gas extraction since 2004 has boosted economic growth; the export of liquefied natural gas to Asian economies began in March 2014.

About 85 per cent of the population practises subsistence farming, including some tribes in the interior so isolated that their economy is unmonetised. Mineral deposits, including copper, gold, silver, nickel, oil and natural gas, are abundant and constitute the main sources of revenue, although exploitation is forced to overcome difficult terrain and poor infrastructure. This has been addressed by the government, which passed legislation in 2011 for an offshore sovereign wealth fund to manage government surpluses from mineral, oil and natural gas projects. The main industries are mining, oil extraction and refining, forestry, processing of agricultural and forestry products, construction and tourism. Industry contributes 39 per cent of GDP and services 34.8 per cent.

The main trading partners are Australia, Singapore and Japan. Principal exports are oil, gold, copper ore, logs, palm oil, coffee, cocoa and shellfish. The main imports are machinery and transport equipment, manufactured goods, food, fuels and chemicals.

*GNI* – US$14,749m; US$2,010 per capita (2013)
*Annual average growth of GDP* – 5.8 per cent (2014)
*Inflation rate* – 5 per cent (2014 est)
*Population below poverty line* – 37 per cent (2002 est)
*Unemployment* – 2 per cent (2015 est)
*Total external debt* – US$30,870m (2014 est)
*Imports* – US$5,500m (2012)
*Exports* – US$5,951m (2013)

BALANCE OF PAYMENTS
*Trade* – US$628m surplus (2012)
*Current Account* – US$2,053m surplus (2015 est)

| Trade with UK | 2013 | 2014 |
| --- | --- | --- |
| Imports from UK | £48,935,941 | £15,635,590 |
| Exports to UK | £120,962,404 | £126,350,596 |

## COMMUNICATIONS

*Airports and waterways* – 21, the principal airports being at Port Moresby, Lae and Rabaul; there are 11,000km of navigable waterways

*Roadways* – 3,000km

*Telecommunications* – 139,000 fixed lines and 2.709 million mobile subscriptions (2012); there were 125,000 internet users in 2009

*Internet code and IDD* – pg; 675 (from UK), 44 (to UK)

*Major broadcasters* – The National Television Service and National Broadcasting Corporation (radio) are the public broadcasters

*Press* – There are two foreign-owned daily newspapers: *The National* (Australia) and *The Post-Courier* (Malaysia)

*WPFI score* – 25,87 (56)

## EDUCATION AND HEALTH

*Literacy rate* – 72.4 per cent (2015 est)

*Health expenditure (per capita)* – US$94 (2013)

*Life expectancy (years)* – 66.85 (2014 est)

*Mortality rate* – 6.53 (2014 est)

*Birth rate* – 24.89 (2014 est)

*Infant mortality rate* – 39.67 (2014 est)

*HIV/AIDS adult prevalence rate* – 0.65 per cent (2013 est)

# PARAGUAY

*República del Paraguay* – *Republic of Paraguay*

*Area* – 406,752 sq. km

*Capital* – Asunción; population, 2,307,000 (2014)

*Major cities* – Ciudad del Este, Lambaré, Limpio, San Lorenzo

*Currency* – Guaraní (Gs) of 100 céntimos

*Population* – 6,783,272 rising at 1.16 per cent a year (2015 est)

*Religion* – Christian (Roman Catholic 89.6 per cent, Protestant 6.2 per cent)

*Language* – Spanish, Guaraní (both official)

*Population density* – 17 per sq. km (2013)

*Urban population* – 63 per cent (2013)

*Median age (years)* – 26.8 (2014 est)

*National anthem* – 'Paraguayos, República o Muerte' ['Paraguayans, the Republic or Death']

*National day* – 15 May (Independence Day)

*Death penalty* – Abolished for all crimes (since 1992)

*CPI score* – 24 (150)

## CLIMATE AND TERRAIN

The country is divided by the river Paraguay into two distinct regions. The area east of the Paraguay is a fertile, grassy plateau where most of the population lives. The area to the west, the Gran Chaco, consists of a grassy and occasionally marshy plain that extends into neighbouring countries. Elevation extremes range from 842m (Cerro Pero) to 46m (the junction of the Paraguay and Paraná rivers). The climate varies from subtropical to temperate, with higher rainfall in the east and semi-arid conditions in the west. Average temperatures range from 18.2°C in July to 27.6°C in January.

## HISTORY AND POLITICS

Spanish colonisation of Paraguay began in the early 16th century and Asunción was founded in 1537. Paraguay became independent from Spain in 1811 under the dictator José Gaspar Rodriguez de Francia, who ruled until his death in 1840. His successors instigated a period of reform and modernisation which ended in 1865–70 with the catastrophic War of the Triple Alliance against Brazil, Uruguay and Argentina over access to the sea. The war resulted in the loss of over half the population as well as 150,000 sq. km of territory, and initiated a period of political instability that lasted until 1912. In the Chaco War of 1932–5, Paraguay gained territory in the west from Bolivia in a conflict that killed 100,000 people.

Political instability and conflict in the late 1940s ended with a coup in 1954 in which General Alfredo Stroessner seized power. His rule was autocratic and increasingly repressive, marked by corruption and human rights abuses. He was ousted in a coup in 1989 that paved the way for free multiparty elections to the presidency and legislature in 1993. These were won by the National Republican Association-Colorado Party (ANR-PC) and its presidential candidate, and the ANR-PC won all subsequent elections until 2008. Instability has prevailed since the 1990s, however, with the assassination of a vice-president, an attempted coup, widespread corruption and the growth of drug-trafficking, money-laundering and organised crime.

The 2008 presidential election was won by Fernando Lugo of the Patriotic Alliance for Change coalition (APC), the first president from outside the ANR-PC in 61 years; Lugo, however, was removed from office by impeachment of the senate in June 2012 for failing to manage fatal clashes over land evictions. He was replaced by vice-president Federico Franco. In the 2013 presidential and legislative elections, Horacio Cartes of the ANR-PC was elected president while the ANR-RC remained the largest party in both chambers.

Under the 1992 constitution, the executive president is directly elected for a five-year term, which is not renewable. The bicameral Congress consists of a 45-member senate and an 80-member Chamber of Deputies, both directly elected for a five-year term. The president, who is responsible to the legislature, appoints the council of ministers.

HEAD OF STATE

*President elect,* Horacio Cartes, *elected* 22 April 2013

*Vice-President elect,* Juan Afara Marques

SELECTED GOVERNMENT MEMBERS *as at June 2015*

*Defence,* Bernardino Soto Estigarribia

*Foreign Affairs,* Eladio Loizaga

*Interior,* Francisco de Vargas

EMBASSY OF THE REPUBLIC OF PARAGUAY

3rd Floor, 344 Kensington High Street, London W14 8NS

T 020-7610 4180 E embapar@btconnect.com

W www.paraguayembassy.co.uk

*Ambassador Extraordinary and Plenipotentiary,* HE Miguel Solano López, *apptd* 2009

**BRITISH EMBASSY**
Edificio Citicenter, Piso 5, Av. Mariscal López y Cruz del Chaco, Asunción
T (595) (21) 614 588 E BE-Asuncion.Enquiries@fco.gov.uk
W www.gov.uk/government/world/paraguay
*Ambassador Extraordinary and Plenipotentiary,* HE Dr Jeremy Hobbs, *apptd* 2013

## DEFENCE

| Aged 16–49, 2010 est | Males | Females |
| --- | --- | --- |
| Available for military service | 1,678,335 | 1,675,352 |
| Fit for military service | 1,409,859 | 1,433,037 |

*Military expenditure* – US$452m (2014)
*Conscription* – 18 years of age; 12–24 months (selective)

## ECONOMY AND TRADE

Paraguay's economy features a large informal sector and benefits from the proceeds of re-exporting to neighbouring countries. The economy started to slow in 2008, when drought reduced production of key exports, and went into recession in 2009, when the global downturn reduced export demand and commodity prices. Although growth resumed in 2010, in the longer term it is hampered by political instability, corruption, national and foreign debt, inadequate infrastructure and high crime levels. Strong export growth saw the economy expand in 2014, and growth is predicted to reach 4.5 per cent in 2015. About one third of the population lives below the poverty line, although this rate is higher in the cities because of migration from the countryside of families made landless by the commercialisation of agriculture and forest clearances.

The country has few mineral resources although exploration for oil and gas is underway. The economy is largely agricultural, much of it at subsistence level. Agricultural production, which accounts for 19.9 per cent of GDP and engages 26.5 per cent of the workforce, is centred on cotton, sugar cane, soya beans, maize, wheat, tobacco, cassava, fruit, vegetables and livestock products. The main industries are sugar refining, forestry, manufacturing (cement, textiles, beverages, wood products, steel) and hydro-electric power generation. Industry accounts for 17.6 per cent of GDP and services for 62.5 per cent.

The main trading partners are Brazil, China, Argentina, Russia and the USA. Principal exports are soya beans, feed, cotton, meat, edible oils, electricity, timber and leather. The main imports are road vehicles, consumer goods, tobacco and petroleum products.

*GNI* – US$27,275m; US$4,010 per capita (2013)
*Annual average growth of GDP* – 4 per cent (2014)
*Inflation rate* – 5.1 per cent (2014 est)
*Population below poverty line* – 23.8 per cent (2013 est)
*Unemployment* – 5.1 per cent (2015 est)
*Total external debt* – US$8,759m (2014 est)
*Imports* – US$12,142m (2013)
*Exports* – US$9,432m (2013)

BALANCE OF PAYMENTS
*Trade* – US$2,710m deficit (2013)
*Current Account* – US$531m deficit (2015 est)

| Trade with UK | 2013 | 2014 |
| --- | --- | --- |
| Imports from UK | £35,505,812 | £34,271,028 |
| Exports to UK | £6,655,439 | £4,969,150 |

## COMMUNICATIONS

*Airports and waterways* – 15, including the principal airport at Asunción; and around 3,100km of navigable waterways around the country

*Roadways and railways* – There are 4,860km of roadways and a small railway system of around 36km
*Telecommunications* – 376,000 fixed lines and 6.79 million mobile subscriptions (2012); there were 1.105 million internet users in 2009
*Internet code and IDD* – py; 595 (from UK), 44 (to UK)
*Major broadcasters* – The state-owned Radio Nacional del Paraguay and TV Publica operate alongside a wealth of private broadcasters
*Press* – Major daily newspapers include *ABC Color, La Nación* and *Ultima Hora*
*WPFI score* – 33,74 (109)

## EDUCATION AND HEALTH

Basic education is free and compulsory for nine years.
*Literacy rate* – 99 per cent (2015 est)
*Gross enrolment ratio (percentage of relevant age group)* – primary 95 per cent; secondary 70 per cent (2011 est); tertiary 35 per cent (2010 est)
*Health expenditure (per capita)* – US$395 (2013)
*Hospital beds (per 1,000 people)* – 1.3 (2011)
*Life expectancy (years)* – 76.8 (2014 est)
*Mortality rate* – 4.64 (2014 est)
*Birth rate* – 16.66 (2014 est)
*Infant mortality rate* – 20.75 (2014 est)

# PERU

*República del Perú – Republic of Peru*

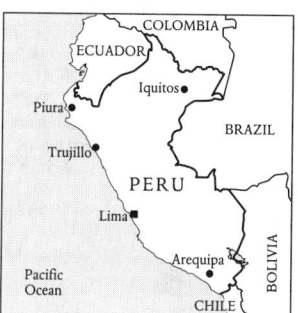

*Area* – 1,285,216 sq. km
*Capital* – Lima; population, 972,000 (2014)
*Major cities* – Arequipa, Chiclayo, Cuzco, Iquitos, Piura, Trujillo
*Currency* – Nuevo sol of 100 centimos
*Population* – 30,444,999 rising at 0.97 per cent a year (2015 est)
*Religion* – Christian (Roman Catholic 81.3 per cent, Protestant 12.5 per cent)
*Language* – Spanish, Quechua, Aymara (all official), other Amerindian languages
*Population density* – 24 per sq. km (2013)
*Urban population* – 77.9 per cent (2013)
*Median age (years)* – 27 (2014 est)
*National anthem* – 'Himno Nacional del Perú' ['National Anthem of Peru']
*National day* – 28 July (Independence Day)
*Death penalty* – Retained for certain crimes (last used 1979)
*CPI score* – 38 (85)

## CLIMATE AND TERRAIN

Peru has three main regions: the Costa, the coastal desert plain west of the Andes; the Sierra (mountain range) of the Andes, which runs parallel to the Pacific coast; and the

Montaña (or Selva), a vast area of jungle stretching from the eastern foothills of the Andes to the country's eastern and north-eastern borders. Elevation extremes range from 6,768m (Nevado Huascaran) to 0m (Pacific Ocean). The climate is arid in the west, temperate in the mountains and tropical in the east. Occasionally, due to the El Niño weather system, the northern districts experience a period of higher temperatures accompanied by torrential rain. The average temperature is 19.9°C.

## HISTORY AND POLITICS

The Inca Empire centred on Cuzco superseded earlier civilisations in Peru and flourished from the 13th to the 15th century, when the empire reached its zenith before falling to Spanish conquistadores led by Francisco Pizarro in 1532–3. The territory formed the Viceroyalty of Peru and its gold and silver mines made Peru the principal source of wealth in Spain's American empire. After 1810, Peru became the centre of Spanish colonial government as its other colonies rebelled. Although Peru declared its independence in 1821, this was achieved only with the final defeat of Spanish forces in 1824.

Peru entered into several border disputes with its neighbours in the 19th and 20th centuries, including the Pacific War (1879–83) in which it lost three southern coastal provinces to Chile. A border dispute with Ecuador was renewed in 1981, leading to a short, inconclusive war in 1995, but was resolved in 1998 following adjudication. A border dispute with Chile ended in 1999 with the implementation of accords first agreed in 1929.

Following independence, Peru alternated between periods of military dictatorship and democratic rule. Two left-wing insurgencies, by the Maoist *Sendero Luminoso* (Shining Path) and the *Movimento Revolucionario Tupac Amaru* (MRTA), began in the 1980s. The conflict caused about 69,000 deaths and saw human rights abuses by both the security forces and the guerrillas. By the late 1990s both insurgencies had been overcome, although a few Maoists remain active. The conflict has left a legacy of criminal violence, much of it related to drug production and trafficking.

Alberto Fujimori, elected president in 1990 on a platform of economic reform, subverted democratic institutions in Peru during his decade in power, suspending the legislature for three years, sacking judges and imposing order through an 'emergency national reconstruction government'. He fled to Japan in 2000 to escape corruption charges, but was extradited and convicted in 2007 of abuse of power and in 2009 of human rights abuses.

In the 2011 legislative election, the Peru Wins alliance gained the most seats but without a majority. The presidential election was won in June by the Peruvian Nationalist Party candidate Ollanta Humala. Prime Minister Rene Diaz and his government resigned in July 2014 after a corruption scandal and he was replaced by Ana Jara; the Jara government in turn resigned in March 2015 after losing a parliamentary vote of confidence following another corruption scandal. Pedro Cateriano Bellido was appointed prime minister on 3 April 2015, becoming the country's seventh prime minister in four years.

Under the 1993 constitution, the executive president is directly elected for a five-year term, renewable once. The unicameral legislature, the Congress of the Republic, has 130 members, directly elected for a five-year term. The president, who is responsible to the legislature, appoints the council of ministers.

### HEAD OF STATE

*President,* Ollanta Humala, *elected* 5 June 2011, *sworn in* 28 July 2011
*First Vice-President,* Marisol Espinoza

SELECTED GOVERNMENT MEMBERS *as at June 2015*
*President of Council of Ministers,* Pedro Cateriano Bellido
*Defence,* Jakke Valakivi Alvarez
*Economy and Finance,* Alonso Segura Vasi
*Foreign Affairs,* Ana Maria Sanchez Vargas de Rios

### EMBASSY OF PERU

52 Sloane Street, London SW1X 9SP
T 020-7235 1917 E postmaster@peruembassy-uk.com
W www.peruembassy-uk.com
*Ambassador Extraordinary and Plenipotentiary,* HE Julio Munoz-Deacon, *apptd* 2012

### BRITISH EMBASSY

Torre Parque Mar, Avenida José Larco 1301, Lima
T (+51) (1) 617 3000 E belima@fco.gov.uk
W www.gov.uk/government/world/peru
*Ambassador Extraordinary and Plenipotentiary,* HE Anwar Choudhury, *apptd* 2014

## DEFENCE

| *Aged 16–49, 2010 est* | *Males* | *Females* |
| --- | --- | --- |
| Available for military service | 7,385,588 | 7,727,623 |
| Fit for military service | 5,788,629 | 6,565,097 |

*Military expenditure* – US$2,797m (2014)

## ECONOMY AND TRADE

The Peruvian economy has been growing by an average of 5.6 per cent for the past five years, driven by exports of silver, copper, agricultural produce and fish. Tourism has also driven growth. Poverty remains widespread, but the benefits of economic growth are starting to be felt in the poorer regions and the poverty rate has declined by 23 per cent since 2002. The dependence on metal exports and imported foodstuffs makes the economy vulnerable to fluctuations in world prices. Growth is predicted to fall to just under 5 per cent during 2015–19 as global demand for Peruvian commodities falls.

Mineral resources, including copper, gold, silver, zinc, oil and natural gas, are abundant, and extracting and refining these is the mainstay of the economy. Other industries include steel and metal fabrication, fishing and fish processing, textiles and clothes manufacture and food processing. Agriculture is centred on asparagus, coffee, cocoa, cotton, sugar cane, rice, cereals, vegetables, fruit, coca, medicinal plants, meat and dairy products. Services contribute 56.2 per cent to GDP, industry 36.7 per cent and agriculture 7.1 per cent.

The main trading partners are the USA, China, Canada, Spain, Switzerland and other South American countries. Principal exports are copper, gold, zinc, tin, crude oil and petroleum products, natural gas, coffee, vegetables and fruit. The main imports are oil and petroleum products, chemicals, plastics, machinery, vehicles, telecommunications equipment, iron and steel, and food.

*GNI* – US$190,510m; US$6,270 per capita (2013)
*Annual average growth of GDP* – 3.6 per cent (2014)
*Inflation rate* – 3.3 per cent (2014 est)
*Population below poverty line* – 23.9 per cent (2013 est)
*Unemployment* – 4.1 per cent (2015 est)
*Total external debt* – US$56,470m (2014 est)
*Imports* – US$42,199m (2013)
*Exports* – US$41,484m (2013)

### BALANCE OF PAYMENTS

*Trade* – US$715m deficit (2013)
*Current Account* – US$8,706m deficit (2015 est)

| Trade with UK | 2013 | 2014 |
|---|---|---|
| Imports from UK | £167,717,958 | £170,640,153 |
| Exports to UK | £225,381,748 | £240,983,552 |

## COMMUNICATIONS

*Airports and waterways* – There are 59 airports, including the international airport at Lima; there are 8,808km of inland waterways, and the main seaports are Callao and Matarani
*Roadways and railways* – There are 18,698km of roadways, including sections of the east–west Andean Highway, linking the Pacific and Atlantic coasts, and the north–south Pan-American Highway running along the Pacific coast; the state-run railways have 1,907km of track
*Telecommunications* – 3.42 million fixed lines and 29.4 million mobile subscriptions (2012); there were 9.16 million internet users in 2009
*Internet code and IDD* – pe; 51 (from UK), 44 (to UK)
*Major broadcasters* – The state-owned TV Peru and Radio Nacional operate alongside a number of private broadcasters
*Press* – Major daily newspapers include *El Bocón, La República* and *Ojo*
*WPFI score* – 31,21 (92)

## EDUCATION AND HEALTH

Education is free and compulsory for 11 years.
*Literacy rate* – 98.9 per cent (2015 est)
*Gross enrolment ratio (percentage of relevant age group)* – primary 102 per cent; secondary 94 per cent (2013 est); tertiary 41 per cent (2010 est)
*Health expenditure (per capita)* – US$354 (2013)
*Hospital beds (per 1,000 people)* – 1.5 (2012)
*Life expectancy (years)* – 73.23 (2014 est)
*Mortality rate* – 5.99 (2014 est)
*Birth rate* – 18.57 (2014 est)
*Infant mortality rate* – 20.21 (2014 est)

# THE PHILIPPINES

*Republika ng Pilipinas – Republic of the Philippines*

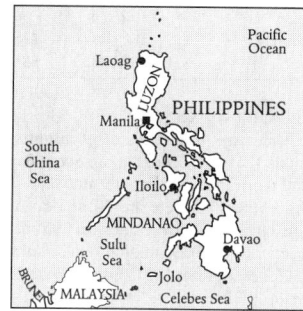

*Area* – 300,000 sq. km
*Capital* – Manila; population (Metro Manila, including Quezon City), 12,764,000 (2014)
*Major cities* – Bacolod, Cagayan de Oro, Cebu, Davao, General Santos (Dadiangas), Iloilo, Zamboanga
*Currency* – Philippine peso (P) of 100 centavos
*Population* – 100,998,376 rising at 1.61 per cent a year (2015 est); Tagalog (28.1 per cent), Cebuano (13.1 per cent), Ilocano (9 per cent), Bisaya (7.6 per cent), Hiligaynon Ilonggo (7.5 per cent), Bikol (6 per cent), Waray (3.4 per cent) (2000)
*Religion* – Christian (Roman Catholic 82.9 per cent, Evangelical 2.8 per cent), Muslim 5 per cent

*Language* – Filipino, English (both official), Tagalog, Cebuano, Ilocano, Hiligaynon, Bicol, Waray, Pampango, Pangasinan
*Population density* – 330 per sq. km (2013)
*Urban population* – 49.3 per cent (2013)
*Median age (years)* – 23.5 (2014 est)
*National anthem* – 'Lupang Hinirang' ['Chosen Land']
*National day* – 12 June (Independence Day)
*Death penalty* – Abolished for all crimes (since 2006)
*CPI score* – 38 (85)

## CLIMATE AND TERRAIN

The Philippines comprises over 7,100 islands in the western Pacific Ocean. The principal islands are Luzon, Mindanao, Mindoro, Samar, Negros, Palawan, Panay and Leyte; other groups include the Sulu islands, Babuyanes and Batanes, Calamian and Kalayaan islands. The islands mostly have mountainous interiors and narrow coastal plains. The mountain ranges are volcanic, and some volcanoes are still active. Elevation extremes range from 2,954m (Mt Apo) to 0m (Philippine Sea). The climate is tropical; the average temperature is 26.2°C, and relative humidity is high. The country is affected by the monsoons, which cause the rainy season between July and October. During this period the country is also susceptible to typhoons, which frequently cause widespread damage and loss of life.

## HISTORY AND POLITICS

The Philippine islands were settled first by Malays, then by Chinese, Indonesian and Arab traders. Islam was introduced in the 14th century and became the dominant religion in the south. The islands were discovered by Spain and then settled from 1565 by the Spanish, who introduced Roman Catholicism. Colonial rule lasted until 1898, when Spain ceded the colony to the USA following the Spanish-American War. The country became internally self-governing in 1935, was occupied by Japan from 1942 to 1944, and achieved independence from the USA in 1946.

Ferdinand Marcos was elected president in 1965, imposing martial law in 1972. His regime became increasingly repressive, corrupt and violent, and when he falsified election results in 1986 to prevent Corazon Aquino from taking office as president, a popular uprising forced him to flee the country. Aquino survived political unrest and ten attempted military coups to introduce a new constitution and entrench democratic politics.

Fidel Ramos, Aquino's successor in 1992, built on her work, raised the country's international profile and instigated peace talks with insurgents (*see* below). Joseph Estrada, elected president in 1998, was overthrown in 2001 in a popular uprising; his term was completed by Vice-President Gloria Arroyo. President Arroyo retained the presidency in the 2004 presidential election, but her popularity plummeted and her anti-corruption measures and economic reforms were undermined by corruption scandals and impeachment attempts.

The 2010 presidential election was won by Benigno ('Noynoy') Aquino III, son of former president Corazon Aquino. In the May 2013 legislative elections, the Liberal Party (LP) won the most seats in the house of representatives but without a majority.

Under the 1987 constitution, the executive president is directly elected for a six-year term, which is not renewable. There is a bicameral Congress. The lower house, the House of Representatives, has up to 250 directly elected members, plus 20 per cent are appointed from party and minority group lists; all serve a three-year term. The senate has 24 members directly elected for a six-year term, with half re-elected every three years.

The Autonomous Region of Muslim Mindanao comprises the provinces of Lanao del Sur and Maguindanao on Mindanao and the island provinces of Sulu, Tawi-Tawi and Basilan. It has a 24-member regional assembly and a governor.

## HEAD OF STATE

President, Benigno ('Noynoy') Aquino III, elected 10 May 2010, sworn in 30 June 2010
Vice-President, Jejomar Binay

## SELECTED GOVERNMENT MEMBERS as at June 2015

Defence, Voltaire Gazmin
Finance, Cesar Purisima
Foreign Affairs, Albert del Rosario
Trade and Industry, Gregory Domingo

## EMBASSY OF THE REPUBLIC OF THE PHILIPPINES

6–11 Suffolk Street, London SW1Y 4HG
T 020-7451 1780 E embassy@philemb.co.uk
W www.philembassy-uk.org
Ambassador Extraordinary and Plenipotentiary, HE Enrique Manalo, apptd 2011

## BRITISH EMBASSY

120 Upper McKinley Road, McKinley Hill, Taguig City 1634, Manila
T (+63) (2) 858 2200 E ukinthephilippines@fco.gov.uk
W www.gov.uk/government/world/philippines
Ambassador Extraordinary and Plenipotentiary, HE Asif Ahmad, apptd 2013

## INSURGENCIES

A communist insurgency by the New People's Army (NPA) began in the late 1960s. The NPA is based in Mindanao but has groups in rural areas throughout the country. Peace talks between the government and the NPA's political front, the National Democratic Front, stalled in 2004 but were resumed in early 2011.

There has been a Muslim (Moro) insurgency in the southern islands, particularly Mindanao, since the 1970s. The Moro National Liberation Front (MNLF) concluded a peace agreement with the government in 1996 that ended its insurgency and established the Autonomous Region of Muslim Mindanao (ARMM). The Moro Islamic Liberation Front (MILF) agreed a ceasefire with the government in 2003, but negotiations over a Muslim 'homeland' broke down in 2008; a resumption of violence in 2009 displaced over 300,000 people until another ceasefire was agreed and peace talks resumed in late 2009. Peace talks broke down in October 2011, however, after air strikes on MILF areas in Zamboanga left 35 people dead. In January 2014, the government agreed to create a new Muslim autonomous area called Bangsamoro in the south of the Philippines by 2016 in return for the disbanding of the MILF. Despite the agreement, MILF members are believed to been involved in an attack which killed more than 40 Filipino police officers in January 2015.

The radical Muslim separatist group Abu Sayyaf, based on Jolo and Basilan, is viewed as a terrorist organisation and the government refuses to negotiate with it. It pledged allegiance to Islamic State (IS) in October 2014.

## DEFENCE

| Aged 16–49, 2010 est | Males | Females |
| --- | --- | --- |
| Available for military service | 25,614,135 | 25,035,061 |
| Fit for military service | 20,142,940 | 21,427,792 |

Military expenditure – US$3,292m (2014 est)

## ECONOMY AND TRADE

The economy has survived the 2009 recession better than other Asian economies thanks to low dependence on exports, robust domestic consumption and remittances from four to five million overseas workers. Despite this, poverty has increased as economic expansion struggles to offset the high rate of population growth, and nearly a quarter of the population lives below the poverty line. The government announced a stimulus effort after growth slowed significantly in 2011. Growth averaged 6.6 per cent during 2012–14 and is expected to fall to 6.4 per cent in 2015–16. The Philippines was scheduled to form a common market with the other members of the Association of Southeast Asian Nations (ASEAN) in 2015.

Major industries include electronics assembly, manufacture of clothing, footwear, pharmaceuticals, chemicals and wood products, food processing, oil refining and fishing. The large agricultural sector employs 32 per cent of the workforce, producing sugar cane, coconuts, rice, maize, tropical fruits and livestock products. Agriculture accounts for 10.7 per cent of GDP, industry for 31.5 per cent and services for 57.8 per cent.

The main trading partners are Japan, the USA, China, South Korea and other Asian states. Principal exports are semiconductors and electronic products, clothing, copper products, petroleum products, coconut oil and fruit. The main imports are electronic products, fuels, machinery and transport equipment, iron and steel, fabrics, grains, chemicals and plastics.

GNI – US$229,463m; US$3,270 per capita (2013)
Annual average growth of GDP – 6.2 per cent (2014)
Inflation rate – 4.5 per cent (2014 est)
Population below poverty line – 25.2 per cent (2012 est)
Unemployment – 7.4 per cent (2015 est)
Total external debt – US$59,210m (2014 est)
Imports – US$65,048m (2013)
Exports – US$53,882m (2013)

## BALANCE OF PAYMENTS

Trade – US$11,166m deficit (2013)
Current Account – US$16,954m surplus (2015 est)

| Trade with UK | 2013 | 2014 |
| --- | --- | --- |
| Imports from UK | £374,262,443 | £365,106,153 |
| Exports to UK | £383,596,985 | £387,111,021 |

## COMMUNICATIONS

Airports and waterways – There are 89 airports; the main ports are Manila (Luzon), Cebu, Davao, Subic Bay, Batangas and Iloilo, and there are 3,219km of waterways
Roadways and railways – There are 54,481km of roadways and Philippine National Railway operates 995km of railways
Telecommunications – 3.939 million fixed lines and 103 million mobile subscriptions (2012); there were 8.28 million internet users in 2009
Internet code and IDD – ph; 63 (from UK), 44 (to UK)
Major broadcasters – The government-owned People's Television and Philippine Broadcasting Service (radio) compete with two major commercial broadcasters and over 600 radio stations
Press – Daily newspapers include the Daily Tribune, Malaya and Philippine Star
WPFI score – 41,19 (141)

## EDUCATION AND HEALTH

There are seven years of free and compulsory primary education, followed by three years of free but non-compulsory secondary education.
Literacy rate – 97.9 per cent (2015 est)

*Gross enrolment ratio (percentage of relevant age group)* – primary 106 per cent; secondary 85 per cent; tertiary 28.9 per cent (2011 est)
*Health expenditure (per capita)* – US$122 (2013)
*Hospital beds (per 1,000 people)* – 1 (2011)
*Life expectancy (years)* – 72.48 (2014 est)
*Mortality rate* – 4.92 (2014 est)
*Birth rate* – 24.24 (2014 est)
*Infant mortality rate* – 17.64 (2014 est)

# POLAND

*Rzeczpospolita Polska – Republic of Poland*

*Area* – 312,685 sq. km
*Capital* – Warsaw; population, 1,718,000 (2014)
*Major cities* – Bydgoszcz, Gdansk, Katowice, Krakow, Lodz, Lublin, Poznan, Szczecin, Wroclaw
*Currency* – Zloty of 100 groszy
*Population* – 38,562,189 falling at 0.09 per cent a year (2015 est)
*Religion* – Christian (Roman Catholic 87.2 per cent, Orthodox 1.3 per cent, Protestant 0.4 per cent)
*Language* – Polish (official)
*Population density* – 126 per sq. km (2013)
*Urban population* – 60.7 per cent (2013 est)
*Median age (years)* – 39.5 (2014 est)
*National anthem* – 'Mazurek Dabrowskiego' ['Dabrowski's Mazurka']
*National day* – 3 May (Constitution Day)
*Death penalty* – Abolished for all crimes (since 1997)
*CPI score* – 61 (35)

## CLIMATE AND TERRAIN
Poland lies mostly in a great plain crossed by the Oder, Neisse and Vistula rivers. The land rises to the Carpathian, Tatra and Sudeten mountains along the southern border. Elevation extremes range from 2,499m (Rysy) to −2m (Raczki Elblaskie). The climate is continental, and average temperatures range from −1.3°C in January to 18.5°C in July.

## POLITICS
Under the 1997 constitution, the head of state is the president, who is directly elected for a five-year term,

renewable once. The president nominates the prime minister and has the right to be consulted over the appointment of the foreign, defence and interior ministers. The National Assembly is bicameral; the lower house, the Diet *(Sejm)*, has 460 members elected by proportional representation for a four-year term. The senate has 100 members elected on a provincial basis for a four-year term.

In the 2011 legislative elections, Donald Tusk of the Civil Platform (PO) became the first Polish prime minister to be appointed for a second term since the fall of communism, continuing in coalition with the Polish People's Party (PSL). Prime Minister Tusk stood down in September 2014 to become President of the European Council and was succeeded by Ewa Kopacz. In the May 2015 presidential elections, Andrzej Duda of the conservative Law and Justice party (PiS) was elected after a second round of voting. New legislative elections were due in October 2015.

HEAD OF STATE
*President,* Andrzej Duda, *elected* 26 May 2015, *sworn in* 6 August 2015

SELECTED GOVERNMENT MEMBERS *as at June 2015*
*Prime Minister,* Ewa Kopacz
*Deputy Prime Minister, Economy,* Janusz Piechocinski
*Defence,* Tomasz Siemoniak
*Finance,* Mateusz Szczurek

EMBASSY OF THE REPUBLIC OF POLAND
47 Portland Place, London W1B 1JH
T 020-7291 3520 E london@msz.gov.pl
W www.london.polemb.net
*Ambassador Extraordinary and Plenipotentiary,* HE Witold Sobków, *apptd* 2012

BRITISH EMBASSY
ul. Kawalerii 12, 00-468 Warsaw
T (+48) (22) 311 0000 E info@britishembassy.pl
W www.gov.uk/government/world/poland
*Ambassador Extraordinary and Plenipotentiary,* HE Robin Barnett, CMG, *apptd* 2011

## DEFENCE

| Aged 16–49, 2010 est | Males | Females |
| --- | --- | --- |
| Available for military service | 9,531,855 | 9,298,593 |
| Fit for military service | 7,817,556 | 7,766,361 |

*Military expenditure* – US$10,499m (2014)

## ECONOMY AND TRADE
Poland's successful transition to a market economy in the 1990s came at the cost of high levels of public debt, unemployment and inflation, which were reduced by subsequent governments. The economy has grown steadily since 1992 and particularly since accession to the EU in 2004, avoiding recession in 2008–9. Further economic development is hindered by inefficiency, rigidity and low-level corruption, although the Tusk government is

| Foundation of Jagiellon dynasty brings greater power to the region | Semi-independent Congress Kingdom of Poland created, swiftly incorporated into the Russian Empire | Invaded by Germany and USSR | Eastern Poland ceded to USSR | Mass movement for civil rights emerges following popular discontent | Civil unrest forces multiparty elections and transition to market economy |
| --- | --- | --- | --- | --- | --- |
| c.800 | 1772-95 | 1918 | 1944-5 | 1947 | 1981 | 2004 |
| 1386 | 1814-5 | 1939 | 1945 | 1980 | 1989 |
| Emerges as independent kingdom | Territory partitioned by Russia, Prussia and Austria | Regains independence under the Treaty of Versailles | Liberated by Soviet forces | Soviet-influenced government declares a communist republic | Government declares martial law, forcing movement underground | Joins EU |

committed to further privatisation and restructuring public finances. Economic problems in the eurozone caused growth to slow in 2013 and 2014.

Poland has vast mineral resources, especially coal, and nearly half its area is fertile arable land. The large agricultural sector has been modernised but remains inefficient; it employs 12.9 per cent of the workforce but contributes only 3.7 per cent of GDP. The agricultural products are vegetables, fruit, wheat, meat, eggs and dairy products. The main industries are machine-building, iron and steel production, coal-mining, chemicals, shipbuilding, food processing, glass, beverages and textiles. Industry accounts for 32 per cent of GDP.

The main trading partners are other EU countries (especially Germany) and Russia. Principal exports include machinery and vehicles, manufactured and semi-manufactured goods, food and livestock. The main imports are machinery and vehicles, semi-manufactured goods, chemicals, minerals, fuels and lubricants.

*GNI* – US$510,000m; US$13,240 per capita (2013)
*Annual average growth of GDP* – 3.2 per cent (2014)
*Inflation rate* – 0.2 per cent (2014 est)
*Population below poverty line* – 17.1 per cent (2011 est)
*Unemployment* – 10.5 per cent (2015 est)
*Total external debt* – US$395,200m (2014 est)
*Imports* – US$205,174m (2013)
*Exports* – US$202,107m (2013)

BALANCE OF PAYMENTS
*Trade* – US$3,067m deficit (2013)
*Current Account* – US$8,861m deficit (2015 est)

| Trade with UK | 2013 | 2014 |
| --- | --- | --- |
| Imports from UK | £3,633,955,110 | £3,739,185,782 |
| Exports to UK | £7,840,741,375 | £7,658,272,207 |

## COMMUNICATIONS
*Airports and waterways* – The principal airports are at Warsaw, Krakow, Katowice and Wroclaw, and there are 83 smaller airports; the principal seaports are Gdansk, Gdynia, Swinoujscie and Szczecin, and there are 3,997km of navigable rivers and canals
*Roadways and railways* – 280,719km, including 2,418km of motorways; 19,428km
*Telecommunications* – 6.125 million fixed lines and 50.84 million mobile subscriptions (2012); there were 22.45 million internet users in 2009
*Internet code and IDD* – pl; 48 (from UK), 44 (to UK)
*Major broadcasters* – Telewizja Polska (TVP) and Polish Radio are the principal state broadcasters
*Press* – *Gazeta Wyborcza, Fakt* and *Rzeczpospolita* are the principal mass-circulation dailies
*WPFI score* – 12,71 (18)

## EDUCATION AND HEALTH
Elementary education (ages seven to 15) is free and compulsory. Secondary education is also free, but optional.
*Literacy rate* – 100 per cent (2015 est)
*Gross enrolment ratio (percentage of relevant age group)* – primary 101 per cent; secondary 98 per cent; tertiary 73 per cent (2012 est)
*Health expenditure (per capita)* – US$895 (2013)
*Hospital beds (per 1,000 people)* – 6.5 (2011)
*Life expectancy (years)* – 76.65 (2014 est)
*Mortality rate* – 10.37 (2014 est)
*Birth rate* – 9.77 (2014 est)
*Infant mortality rate* – 6.19 (2014 est)

# PORTUGAL

*República Portuguesa – Portuguese Republic*

*Area* – 92,090 sq. km
*Capital* – Lisbon; population, 2,869,000 (2014)
*Major cities* – Coimbra, Oporto
*Currency* – Euro (€) of 100 cents
*Population* – 10,825,309 rising at 0.09 per cent a year (2015 est)
*Religion* – Christian (Roman Catholic 81 per cent, other 3.3 per cent)
*Language* – Portuguese, Mirandese (both official)
*Population density* – 114 per sq. km (2013)
*Urban population* – 62.1 per cent (2013)
*Median age (years)* – 41.1 (2014 est)
*National anthem* – 'A Portuguesa' ['The Portuguese']
*National day* – 10 June (Portugal Day)
*Death penalty* – Abolished for all crimes (since 1976)
*CPI score* – 63 (31)

## CLIMATE AND TERRAIN
The terrain is mountainous north of the river Tagus, with rolling hills and plains in the south. Elevation extremes range from 2,351m (Ponta do Pico, Azores) to 0m (Atlantic Ocean). Forests of pine, cork oak and eucalyptus cover about 38 per cent of the country. The climate is temperate, with average temperatures ranging from 9.7°C in January to 22.5°C in August.

## HISTORY AND POLITICS
Part of the Roman Empire from the second century BC, the country was overrun by Vandals and Visigoths in the fifth century AD. The Visigoths were ousted by Muslims from north Africa in the eighth century, but Christian reconquest began in the tenth century and an independent Christian kingdom was established in the 12th century.

Portuguese navigators led the 15th-century European age of exploration and the country soon became a major commercial and colonial power, its empire expanding to include Brazil, parts of China and large areas of Africa. In 1807 Portugal was invaded by Napoleonic France and then became the base from which Allied forces liberated Portugal and Spain in the Peninsular War. The 19th century was politically turbulent, with power struggles between conservative and liberal politicians, and within different factions of the royal family. In 1910 an armed uprising in Lisbon drove King Manuel II into exile and a republic was declared.

A period of political instability ensued until the military intervened in 1926. The constitution of 1933 gave formal expression to the authoritarian *Estado Novo* (New State) introduced by Dr Antonio Salazar, prime minister from 1932 until 1968. Marcello Caetano succeeded Salazar in 1968 but the regime's failure to liberalise at home or to conclude wars in the African colonies resulted in the government's overthrow in a military coup in 1974. Great political turmoil followed in 1974–5, a period in which most of the country's colonies gained their independence. Elections in 1976 stabilised the situation and full civilian government was restored in 1982. Portugal joined the EEC in 1986 and adopted the euro in 2002.

The 2006 presidential election was won by the Social Democrat candidate Anibal Cavaco Silva (prime minister 1985–95), and he was re-elected in January 2011. The Socialist Party government, in power since 2005 but as a minority government since the 2009 election, resigned after its austerity programme was defeated in March 2011. In the legislative election in June, the Social Democratic Party (PSD) won the most seats but not an overall majority, and formed a coalition with the Democratic and Social Centre-People's Party and independents under the PSD leader Pedro Passos Coelho. New legislative elections are due to take place in late 2015.

Under the 1976 constitution, amended in 1982 and 1989, the head of state is a president who is directly elected for a five-year term, renewable once. The unicameral Assembly of the Republic has 230 members, directly elected by proportional representation for a four-year term. The prime minister, appointed by the president, is usually the leader of the largest party in the assembly.

HEAD OF STATE
*President of the Republic,* Anibal Cavaco Silva, *elected* 22 January 2006, *sworn in* 9 March 2006, *re-elected* 2011

SELECTED GOVERNMENT MEMBERS *as at June 2015*
*Prime Minister,* Pedro Passos Coelho
*Internal Administration,* Anabela Rodrigues
*Finance,* Maria Luis Albuquerque

EMBASSY OF PORTUGAL
11 Belgrave Square, London SW1X 8PP
T 020-7235 5331 E londres@mne.pt
W www.portuguese-embassy.co.uk
*Ambassador Extraordinary and Plenipotentiary,* HE Joao de Vallera, *apptd* 2011

BRITISH EMBASSY
Rua de Sao Bernardo 33, 1249-082 Lisbon
T (+351) (21) 392 4000 E portugal.consulate@fco.gov.uk
W www.gov.uk/government/world/portugal
*Ambassador Extraordinary and Plenipotentiary,* HE Kirsty Hayes, *apptd* 2014

DEFENCE

| Aged 16–49, 2010 est | Males | Females |
|---|---|---|
| Available for military service | 2,566,264 | 2,458,297 |
| Fit for military service | 2,103,080 | 2,018,004 |

*Military expenditure* – US$4,201m (2014)

ECONOMY AND TRADE
Portugal's economy was transformed after it joined the EU in 1986 into a diversified and increasingly service-based economy. The rapid growth of the 1990s slowed in 2001–8, and the global downturn pushed the economy into recession in 2009. Despite government austerity measures, a budget deficit treble the eurozone limit led to the country's credit rating being downgraded in 2010; in April 2011 the government obtained EU financial support. GDP fell in 2012 and 2013, as the government cut spending and increased tax to comply with the conditions of an EU-IMF financial rescue

package. Unemployment remains high at 15.3 per cent, with unemployment among the under-25s reaching 34.5 per cent. The government reduced the budget deficit from 10.1 per cent of GDP in 2009 to 4.8 per cent in 2014 and has agreed to lower the deficit to under 3 per cent in 2015 in order to comply with eurozone targets.

Around 12 per cent of the workforce is engaged in agriculture, contributing 2.6 per cent of GDP. The chief products are grain, fruit and vegetables, livestock, fish, dairy products, and timber and cork from the forests. The main industries are tourism, manufacturing (textiles, footwear, cork, pulp and paper, chemicals, motor vehicle components), metalworking, winemaking, oil refining, and shipbuilding and repair. Natural resources are being exploited to generate electricity from hydroelectric and solar sources to reduce dependence on imported fuel and energy. Industry accounts for 22.4 per cent of GDP and services for 75 per cent.

The main trading partners are other EU countries, particularly Spain, and Angola. Principal exports are agricultural products, food, wine, oil products, wood products, other industrial products, machinery and tools. The main imports include agricultural products, chemicals, vehicles, optical and precision instruments, and computer and IT components.

*GNI* – US$222,403m; US$21,260 per capita (2013)
*Annual average growth of GDP* – 1 per cent (2014)
*Inflation rate* – 0 per cent (2014 est)
*Population below poverty line* – 18.7 per cent (2012)
*Unemployment* – 15.3 per cent (2015 est)
*Total external debt* – US$508,300m (2013 est)
*Imports* – US$75,066m (2013)
*Exports* – US$62,841m (2013)

BALANCE OF PAYMENTS
*Trade* – US$12,225m deficit (2013)
*Current Account* – US$2,866m surplus (2015 est)

| Trade with UK | 2013 | 2014 |
|---|---|---|
| Imports from UK | £1,326,752,963 | £1,329,030,031 |
| Exports to UK | £1,934,827,268 | £2,223,233,681 |

COMMUNICATIONS
*Airports and waterways* – There are 43 airports, including international airports at Lisbon, Oporto, Faro, Santa Maria (Azores) and Funchal (Madeira); the main ports are Aveiro, Figueira da Foz, Leixoes, Lisbon, Setubal and Sines
*Roadways and railways* – 71,294km, including 2,613km of motorways; 3,319km
*Telecommunications* – 4.558 million fixed lines and 12.312 million mobile subscriptions (2012); there were 5.168 million internet users in 2009
*Internet code and IDD* – pt; 351 (from UK), 44 (to UK)
*Major broadcasters* – The monopoly of the public broadcaster RTP (TV) and RDP (radio) ended in 1992, and commercial stations now dominate the market
*Press* – Principal national newspapers include the daily titles *Diario de Noticias, Correio da Manha* and *Jornal de Noticias*
*WPFI score* – 17,11 (26)

EDUCATION AND HEALTH
Education is free and compulsory for nine years from the age of six. The university at Coimbra was founded in 1290.
*Literacy rate* – 99.6 per cent (2015 est)
*Gross enrolment ratio (percentage of relevant age group)* – primary 106 per cent; secondary 113 per cent; tertiary 69 per cent (2012 est)
*Health expenditure (per capita)* – US$2,037 (2013)
*Hospital beds (per 1,000 people)* – 3.4 (2011)
*Life expectancy (years)* – 79.01 (2014 est)

*Mortality rate* – 10.97 (2013 est)
*Birth rate* – 9.42 (2014 est)
*Infant mortality rate* – 4.48 (2014 est)

## AUTONOMOUS REGIONS

Madeira and the Azores are both autonomous regions, each with its own locally elected assembly and government.
MADEIRA is a group of islands in the Atlantic Ocean about 990km south-west of Lisbon, and consists of Madeira, Porto Santo and three uninhabited islands. Total area is 801 sq. km; population, 267,938 (2011 est). Funchal on Madeira, the largest island, is the capital.
THE AZORES is an archipelago of nine islands in the Atlantic Ocean 1,400–1,800km west of Lisbon, and consists of Flores, Corvo, Terceira, Sao Jorge, Pico, Faial, Graciosa, Sao Miguel and Santa Maria. Total area is 2,322 sq. km; population, 246,102 (2011 est). Ponta Delgada, on Sao Miguel, is the capital.

# QATAR

*Dawlat Qatar – State of Qatar*

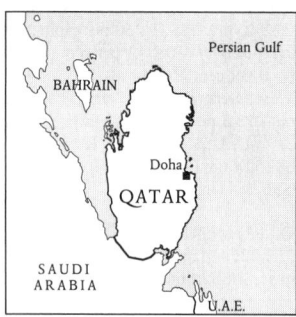

*Area* – 11,586 sq. km
*Capital* – Doha; population, 699,000 (2014)
*Major cities* – Ar Rayyan, al-Wakrah
*Currency* – Qatar riyal of 100 dirhams
*Population* – 2,194,817 rising at 3.07 per cent a year (2015 est); Arab (40 per cent), Indian (18 per cent), Pakistani (18 per cent), Iranian (10 per cent) (est)
*Religion* – Muslim 77.5 per cent (predominantly Sunni), Christian 8.5 per cent, other 14 per cent
*Language* – Arabic (official), English
*Population density* – 187 per sq. km (2013)
*Urban population* – 99.1 per cent (2013 est)
*Median age (years)* – 32.6 (2014 est)
*National anthem* – 'As-Salam al-Amiri' ['Peace to the Amir']
*National day* – 18 December
*Death penalty* – Retained
*CPI score* – 69 (26)
*Literacy rate* – 99.5 per cent (2015 est)
*Life expectancy (years)* – 78.38 (2014 est)
*Mortality rate* – 1.53 (2014 est)
*Birth rate* – 9.95 (2014 est)
*Infant mortality rate* – 6.42 (2014 est)

## CLIMATE AND TERRAIN

Qatar occupies a peninsula in the Persian Gulf and is mostly a low-lying desert plain, with sand dunes in the south. Elevation extremes range from 103m (Tuwayyir al-Hamir) to 0m (Persian Gulf). The country has a desert climate, with low rainfall and average temperatures ranging from 17.1°C in January to 36.6°C in July. Humidity along the coast often reaches 90 per cent in summer.

## HISTORY AND POLITICS

Towns on the Qatari coast developed into important trading centres from the 18th century. Persian rule of the area ended in the mid-18th century and after a period of conflict, the peninsula became a dependency of Bahrain in the 1850s. A revolt against Bahraini rule in the 1860s was suppressed, but Britain intervened in 1867, recognising the dependency as a separate entity. Nominally under the rule of the Ottoman Empire from 1871 until the outbreak of the First World War, Qatar became a British protectorate in 1916, when the al-Thani family was recognised as the ruling house. It became independent in 1971.

In 1972 Sheikh Ahmad was overthrown by the crown prince and prime minister, Sheikh Khalifa. Sheikh Khalifa was overthrown in 1995 by his son and heir, Sheikh Hamad, who has since introduced liberal reforms. Municipal elections, the first democratic polls since independence, were held in 1999. A referendum in 2003 approved a new constitution, which came into force in 2005. Elections to the partially elected consultative council established by the constitution have yet to take place. In June 2013 Sheikh Tamim bin Hamad al-Thani took over as emir after his father abdicated.

A new constitution came into force in 2005. The head of state is a hereditary absolute monarch, the amir. There is no legislature at present, although the 2005 constitution provides for a legislative council with 45 members, 30 directly elected and 15 appointed by the amir, and this will have legislative powers. At present there is an advisory council with 35 members appointed by the amir. There are no political parties. Women have been permitted to vote and stand for election since 1999.

HEAD OF STATE
*HH Emir of Qatar, Defence,* Sheikh Tamim bin Hamad al-Thani, *assumed power* 25 June 2013
*Crown Prince,* vacant

SELECTED GOVERNMENT MEMBERS *as at June 2015*
*Prime Minister, Interior,* HH Sheikh Abdullah bin Nasser bin Khalifa al-Thani
*Deputy Prime Minister,* Ahmed bin Abdullah bin Zaid al-Mahmoud
*Economy and Trade,* Ahmed bin Jassim bin Mohamed al-Thani
*Finance,* Ali Sherif al-Emadi

EMBASSY OF THE STATE OF QATAR
1 South Audley Street, London W1K 1NB
T 020-7493 2200 E amb@qatarembassy.org.uk
W www.qatarembassy.info
*Ambassador Extraordinary and Plenipotentiary,* HE Yousef Ali al-Khater, *apptd* 2014

BRITISH EMBASSY
West Bay, PO Box 3, Off Wahda Street near Rainbow Roundabout, Doha
T (+974) 4496 2000 E embassy.qatar@fco.gov.uk
W www.gov.uk/government/world/qatar
*Ambassador Extraordinary and Plenipotentiary,* Nicholas Hopton, *apptd* 2013

## DEFENCE

| *Aged 16–49, 2010 est* | *Males* | *Females* |
| --- | --- | --- |
| Available for military service | 389,487 | 165,572 |
| Fit for military service | 321,974 | 140,176 |

*Military expenditure* – US$1,877m (2010)
*Conscription* – Men aged 18 to 35; four months

## ECONOMY AND TRADE

The economy is based largely on the production of oil and gas, which account for more than 50 per cent of GDP, about 85 per cent of export earnings and 70 per cent of government revenues, and have made Qatar the world's highest per-capita income country. The state-owned Qatar General Petroleum Corporation controls the industry, and is responsible for oil production onshore and offshore. There has been substantial foreign investment in exploitation of Qatar's large gasfields, and the country is now the world's leading exporter of liquefied natural gas.

Other industries include oil refining, production of ammonia, fertilisers, petrochemicals, steel and cement, and ship repairing. Industry contributes 68 per cent of GDP and services 31.9 per cent.

The main export markets are Japan, South Korea and the USA; the chief sources of imports are EU states, the USA, UAE, Saudi Arabia, China and Japan. Principal exports are liquefied natural gas, petroleum products, fertilisers and steel. The main imports are machinery and transport equipment, food and chemicals.

*GNI* – US$189,004m; US$87,150 per capita (2013)
*Annual average growth of GDP* – 6.5 per cent (2014)
*Inflation rate* – 3.2 per cent (2014 est)
*Unemployment* – 0.6 per cent (2015 est)
*Total external debt* – US$158,000m (2014 est)
*Imports* – US$27,038m (2013)
*Exports* – US$136,855m (2013)

BALANCE OF PAYMENTS
*Trade* – US$109,817m surplus (2013)
*Current Account* – US$16,464m surplus (2015 est)

| Trade with UK | 2013 | 2014 |
| --- | --- | --- |
| Imports from UK | £1,467,285,083 | £1,674,374,760 |
| Exports to UK | £2,565,142,282 | £2,132,232,586 |

## COMMUNICATIONS

*Airports and waterways* – Doha is the principal airport and also the main seaport
*Roadways* – 9,830km
*Telecommunications* – 327,000 fixed lines and 2.6 million mobile subscriptions (2012); there were 563,800 internet users in 2009
*Internet code and IDD* – qa; 974 (from UK), 44 (to UK)
*Major broadcasters* – The country hosts the government-owned Al-Jazeera (TV) which broadcasts internationally in English and Arabic; Qatar TV and Qatar Broadcasting Service (QBS) are also public broadcasters
*Press* – *Al-Watan*, *Al-Rayah* and *Al-Sharq* are leading daily newspapers
*WPFI score* – 35,35 (115)

# ROMANIA

*Area* – 238,391 sq. km
*Capital* – Bucharest; population, 1,872,000 (2014)
*Major cities* – Brasov, Cluj-Napoca, Constanta, Craiova, Galati, Iasi, Timisoara
*Currency* – New leu (plural lei) of 100 bani
*Population* – 21,666,350 falling at 0.30 per cent a year (2015 est); Romanian (83.4 per cent), Hungarian (6.1 per cent), Roma (3.1 per cent) (2011); small minority of Sasi (Transylvanian Saxons)
*Religion* – Christian (Orthodox 81.9 per cent, Protestant 6.4 per cent, Roman Catholic 4.3 per cent)
*Language* – Romanian (official), Hungarian, Romani
*Population density* – 87 per sq. km (2013)
*Urban population* – 52.8 per cent (2013 est)
*Median age (years)* – 39.8 (2014 est)
*National anthem* – 'Desteapta-te, Romane' ['Wake Up, Romanian']
*National day* – 1 December (Unification Day)
*Death penalty* – Abolished for all crimes (since 1989)
*CPI score* – 43 (69)

## CLIMATE AND TERRAIN

The Carpathian mountain range runs south from the Ukrainian border into the centre of the country and then turns west (the Transylvanian Alps) and north. The mountains enclose the central Transylvanian plateau and divide it from the southern Wallachian plain, part of the basin of the river Danube, which runs along most of the southern border, and the eastern Moldavian plateau, through which the river Siret flows, and the Black Sea coast. The mountains are thickly forested. Elevation extremes range from 2,544m (Moldoveanu) to 0m (Black Sea). The climate is continental, with average temperatures ranging from −1.9°C in January to 20.9°C in July.

## POLITICS

The 1991 constitution was amended in 2003 to bring it into line with EU requirements. The president is directly elected for a five-year term, renewable once. The bicameral parliament comprises the Chamber of Deputies with 412 seats, of which 18 are reserved for ethnic minorities, and the senate with 176 seats. Both houses are directly elected for a four-year term by proportional representation. The prime minister is appointed by the president.

In the December 2012 legislative elections, the four-party Social Liberal Union won a significant majority in both chambers and the leader of the Social Democratic Party (PSD), Victor Ponta, was reappointed prime minister. The November 2014 presidential election was won by National Liberal Party (PNL) candidate Klaus Iohannis after a second round of voting.

HEAD OF STATE
*President of the Republic,* Klaus Iohannis, *elected* 16 November 2014, *sworn in* 21 December 2014

SELECTED GOVERNMENT MEMBERS *as at July 2015*
*Prime Minister,* Victor Ponta
*Vice-Prime Minister, Interior,* Gabriel Oprea
*Defence,* Mircea Dusa
*Finance,* Eugen Orlando Teodorovici

EMBASSY OF ROMANIA
Arundel House, 4 Palace Green, London W8 4QD
T 020-7937 9666 E londra@mae.ro W www.londra.mae.ro
*Ambassador Extraordinary and Plenipotentiary,* HE Dr Ion Jinga, *apptd* 2008

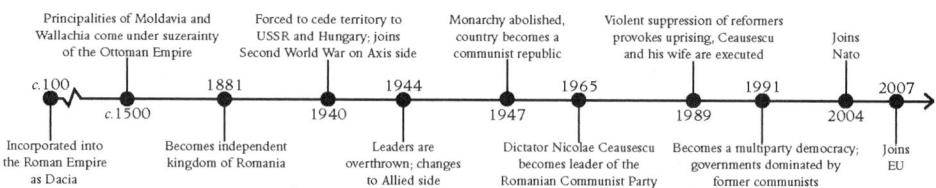

| | | | | |
|---|---|---|---|---|
| Principalities of Moldavia and Wallachia come under suzerainty of the Ottoman Empire | Forced to cede territory to USSR and Hungary; joins Second World War on Axis side | Monarchy abolished, country becomes a communist republic | Violent suppression of reformers provokes uprising, Ceausescu and his wife are executed | Joins Nato |
| c.100    1881    1944    1965    1991    2007 | | | | |
| c.1500    1940    1947    1989    2004 | | | | |
| Incorporated into the Roman Empire as Dacia | Becomes independent kingdom of Romania | Leaders are overthrown; changes to Allied side | Dictator Nicolae Ceausescu becomes leader of the Romanian Communist Party | Becomes a multiparty democracy; governments dominated by former communists    Joins EU |

## BRITISH EMBASSY
24 Strada Jules Michelet, 010463 Bucharest
T (+40) (21) 201 7200 E Press.Bucharest@fco.gov.uk
W www.gov.uk/government/world/romania
*Ambassador Extraordinary and Plenipotentiary,* HE Paul
 Brummell, *apptd* 2014

## DEFENCE
Under an agreement signed in 2005, the USA is allowed to
use military bases in Romania.

| Aged 16–49, 2010 est | Males | Females |
|---|---|---|
| Available for military service | 5,601,234 | 5,428,939 |
| Fit for military service | 4,550,409 | 4,507,880 |

*Military expenditure* – US$2,543m (2014)

## ECONOMY AND TRADE
Transition to a market economy made sluggish progress
until 2000, accelerating after 2004 in order to meet the
requirements for EU accession. Although the economy grew
steadily from 2000 to 2008, it was from a low base and
poverty remains high. The economy contracted sharply in
2009 owing to the global downturn, and the government
sought IMF and EU funding in spring 2009. Following
austerity measures the economy returned to positive growth
in 2011; economic growth increased from 0.6 per cent in
2012 to 3.5 per cent in 2013, driven by strong industrial
exports and a fecund agricultural harvest. Inflation fell to a
historic low of 1.6 per cent in December 2013. Deficit
reduction targets were met for a second consecutive year in
2014 and the economy is predicted to grow by just under
4 per cent between 2015 and 2019.
  Agriculture remains inefficient, employing 29 per cent of
the workforce but contributing only 12.4 per cent of GDP.
The principal crops are grains, sugar beet, sunflower seeds,
vegetables and livestock products. Vines and fruit are grown,
and extensive forests support an important timber industry.
There are reserves of natural gas and oil, but Romania is a net
importer of fossil fuels, although it exports electricity.
Mineral deposits, including coal, iron ore, bauxite, chromium
and uranium support a mining industry. Other industries
include manufacturing, electrical and light machinery and car
assembly, metallurgy, food processing and oil refining.
  The main trading partners are EU states (especially Italy
and Germany), Turkey and Russia. Principal exports include
machinery and equipment, textiles, footwear, metals and
metal products, minerals and fuels, chemicals and agricultural
products. The main imports are machines and equipment,
fuels, minerals, chemicals, textiles, base metals and
agricultural products.
*GNI* – US$180,846m; US$9,060 per capita (2013)
*Annual average growth of GDP* – 2.4 per cent (2014)
*Inflation rate* – 1.2 per cent (2014 est)
*Population below poverty line* – 22.2 per cent (2011 est)
*Unemployment* – 7.6 per cent (2015 est)
*Total external debt* – US$127,200m (2014 est)
*Imports* – US$73,452m (2013)
*Exports* – US$65,881m (2013)

## BALANCE OF PAYMENTS
*Trade* – US$7,571m deficit (2013)
*Current Account* – US$2,112m deficit (2015 est)

| Trade with UK | 2013 | 2014 |
|---|---|---|
| Imports from UK | £933,110,548 | £933,171,503 |
| Exports to UK | £1,444,157,159 | £1,511,208,421 |

## COMMUNICATIONS
*Airports and waterways* – The main airports are at Bucharest
and Timisoara; the main ports are Braila, Constanta, Galati
and Tulcea, with 1,599km of navigable waterways on the
river Danube and its tributaries and 132km of canals
*Roadways and railways* – 49,873km of surfaced roadways,
of which 337km are motorway; 10,777km of railways, over
one-third of which are electrified
*Telecommunications* – 4.68 million fixed lines and 22.7
million mobile subscriptions (2012); there were 7.79 million
internet users in 2009
*Internet code and IDD* – ro; 40 (from UK), 44 (to UK)
*Major broadcasters* – The state-owned Televiziunea (TVR)
and Radio Romania are the country's principal broadcasters
*Press* – There are several daily newspapers, including
*Adevarul, Libertatea* and *Evenimentul Zilei*
*WPFI score* – 24,9 (52)

## EDUCATION AND HEALTH
Primary and secondary education is free and compulsory for
ten years.
*Literacy rate* – 99.3 per cent (2015 est)
*Gross enrolment ratio (percentage of relevant age group)* –
 primary 94 per cent; secondary 95 per cent (2012 est);
 tertiary 52 per cent (2011 est)
*Health expenditure (per capita)* – US$504 (2013)
*Hospital beds (per 1,000 people)* – 6.1 (2011)
*Life expectancy (years)* – 74.69 (2014 est)
*Mortality rate* – 11.88 (2014 est)
*Birth rate* – 9.27 (2014 est)
*Infant mortality rate* – 10.16 (2014 est)

# RUSSIA

*Rossiyskaya Federatsiya – Russian Federation*

*Area* – 17,098,242 sq. km. Includes the Kaliningrad exclave,
 between Lithuania and Poland. Neighbours: Norway,
 Finland, Estonia, Latvia, Belarus, Ukraine (west), Georgia,
 Azerbaijan, Kazakhstan, China, Mongolia, North Korea
 (south)
*Capital* – Moscow; population, 12,063,000 (2014). Founded
 in around 1147, it became the centre of the rising
 Moscow principality and in the 15th century the capital of
 the whole of Russia (Muscovy). In 1703 Peter the Great
 transferred the capital to St Petersburg, but Moscow
 became the capital again in 1918
*Major cities* – Chelyabinsk, Kazan, Nizhniy Novgorod
 (Gorky 1932–90), Novosibirsk (Novonikolayevsk until
 1926), Omsk, Perm, Rostov, St Petersburg (Petrograd

1914–24; Leningrad 1924–91), Samara (Kuibyshev 1935–90), Ufa, Volgograd (Stalingrad 1925–61), Yekaterinburg (Sverdlovsk 1924–91)

*Currency* – Rouble of 100 kopeks
*Population* – 142,423,773 falling at 0.04 per cent a year (2015 est); Russian (77.7 per cent), Tatar (3.7 per cent), Ukrainian (1.4 per cent), Bashkir (1.1 per cent), Chuvash (1.1 per cent), and a further 150 nationalities (2010)
*Religion* – Russian Orthodox 74 per cent, Muslim 7 per cent; other groups include Buddhists, Hindus and Jews
*Language* – Russian (official); many minority languages
*Population density* – 9 per sq. km (2013)
*Urban population* – 74.2 per cent (2013 est)
*Median age (years)* – 38.9 (2014 est)
*National anthem* – 'Gosudarstvenny Gimn Rossiyskoy Federatsii' ['State Anthem of the Russian Federation']
*National day* – 12 June (Russia Day)
*Death penalty* – Retained (last used 1999)
*CPI score* – 27 (136)

## CLIMATE AND TERRAIN

Russia includes the easternmost areas of Europe and the whole of northern Asia. It lies mostly on plains which extend eastwards to the Ural mountains and then from the Urals to the Yenesei river. To the east of the Yenesei are plateaux, with lowlands in northern Siberia. Mountainous areas lie along the southern borders, in eastern Siberia and the Kamchatka peninsula. The terrain varies from the tundra of the Arctic region, through the taiga (the largest zone) of the north and centre, to the grassy plains (steppe) between the forests and the mountains. Elevation extremes range from 5,633m (Mt Elbrus, Caucasus) to −28m (Caspian Sea). Russia has the longest Arctic coastline in the world (over 27,000km); it also has Baltic, Black Sea and Pacific coastlines.

The most important rivers are the Volga, the Northern Dvina, the Neva, the Don and the Kuban in the European part, and in the Asiatic part the Ob, the Irtysh, the Yenisei, the Lena, the Amur and, further north, the Khatanga, Olenek, Yana, Indigirka and Kolyma. Lake Baikal in eastern Siberia is the deepest lake in the world. Part of the Caspian Sea lies within Russia.

The climate is mostly continental, but varies with latitude and terrain, from arctic conditions in the north to subtropical in the far east and on the Black Sea coast. Average national temperatures range from −25.2°C in January to 14.9°C in July. Rainfall is low to moderate in most of the country.

## POLITICS

The 1993 constitution introduced multiparty democracy and enshrines various human rights and civil liberties; amendments in 2008 extended the terms of office for the presidency and the State Duma from the 2012 elections. The head of state is a president, who is directly elected for a six-year term, renewable once consecutively. The bicameral Federal Assembly comprises the State Duma (lower house) of 450 members, all elected by proportional representation for a five-year term, and the Council of the Federation, which has 166 members (two from each member of the federation), appointed for terms of varying lengths. The president appoints the chairman of the council of ministers (prime minister), subject to the approval of the legislature, but is also entitled to chair sessions of the council.

In the 2011 legislative elections, the pro-Vladimir Putin United Russia party retained its overall majority in the *Duma* but with a reduced majority. Putin (elected president between 2000 and 2008) also retained the presidency in March 2012, picking up 63.6 per cent of the overall vote in a highly controversial presidential election. He was inaugurated as president in May 2012 and duly appointed former president Dmitry Medvedev to be chair of the Council of Ministers.

HEAD OF STATE
President, Vladimir Putin, *elected* 4 March 2012, *took office* 7 May 2012

SELECTED GOVERNMENT MEMBERS *as at June 2015*
*Chair of the Council of Ministers,* Dmitry Medvedev
*First Deputy Chair,* Igor Shuvalov
*Deputy Chairs,* Arkady Dvorkovich; Olga Golodets; Aleksandr Khloponin; Dmitry Kozak; Sergei Prikhodko; Dmitry Rogozin; Yury Trutnev

EMBASSY OF THE RUSSIAN FEDERATION
6–7 Kensington Palace Gardens, London W8 4QP
T 020-7229 6412 E info@rusemb.org.uk W www.rusemb.org.uk
*Ambassador Extraordinary and Plenipotentiary,* HE Alexander Yakovenko, *apptd* 2011

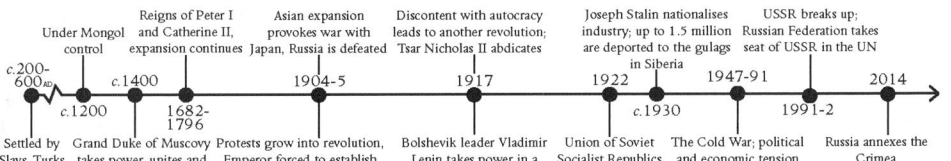

BRITISH EMBASSY
Smolenskaya Naberezhnaya 10, 121099 Moscow
T (+7) (495) 956 7200 E enquiriesukinrussia@fco.gov.uk
W www.gov.uk/government/world/russia
*Ambassador Extraordinary and Plenipotentiary*, HE Sir Tim
Barrow, KCMG, LVO, MBE, *apptd* 2011

INSURGENCIES
Chechnya occupies an area that is strategically important to
Russia because routes from central Russia to the Black Sea and
Caspian Sea, and oil and gas pipelines from neighbouring
countries, pass through it. The republic declared itself
independent in 1991 but its attempts to assert its
independence led to two wars with the federal government.
The first of these, in 1994–6, resulted in the signing of the
Khasavyurt accords. After the peace broke down and Russia
invaded Chechnya again in 1999, President Putin refused
negotiations and imposed direct rule from Moscow in 2000.
Rebels continued with terrorist attacks, although these have
decreased since 2007. Russia announced the end of
counter-terrorism operations in Chechnya in 2009, but has
had to reinstate these in some areas where rebels remain active.
The conflict in Chechnya has destabilised the whole of
the northern Caucasus, especially Ingushetia and Dagestan,
where violence has increased in recent years. The violence
has also affected other parts of Russia, where extremists
linked to Chechen separatists have carried out suicide
bombings and attacks such as the Moscow theatre siege in
2002, the Beslan school siege in 2004 and the bombing of
Moscow's metro system in 2010.

FEDERAL STRUCTURE
Following the break-up of the USSR in 1991, a new federal
treaty was signed in 1992 between the central government
and the autonomous republics of the Russian Federation.
Tatarstan and Bashkortostan signed the treaty in 1994 after
securing considerable legislative and economic autonomy.
The Russian Federation comprises 46 *oblasti* (regions),
nine *krai* (autonomous territories), 21 *respubliki* (autonomous
republics), four *okrugi* (autonomous areas), two cities with
federal status (Moscow and St Petersburg) and one
autonomous Jewish *oblast*, Yevrey. The *oblasti* are Amur,
Arkhangelsk, Astrakhan, Belgorod, Bryansk, Chelyabinsk,
Irkutsk, Ivanovo, Kaliningrad, Kaluga, Kemerovo, Kirov,
Kostroma, Kurgan, Kursk, Leningrad, Lipetsk, Magadan,
Moscow, Murmansk, Nizhny Novgorod, Novgorod,
Novosibirsk, Omsk, Orenburg, Orel, Penza, Pskov, Rostov,
Ryazan, Sakhalin, Samara, Saratov, Smolensk, Sverdlovsk,
Tambov, Tomsk, Tula, Tver, Tyumen, Ulyanovsk, Vladimir,
Volgograd, Vologda, Voronezh and Yaroslavl. The *krai* are
Altai, Kamchatka, Khabarovsk, Krasnodar, Krasnoyarsk,
Perm, Primorski, Stavropol and Zabaykalsk. The *respubliki*
are Adygeia, Altai, Bashkortostan, Buryatia, Chechnya,
Chuvashia, Dagestan, Ingushetia, Kabardino-Balkaria,
Kalmykiya, Karachayevo-Cherkessia, Karelia, Khakassia,
Komi, Mari-El, Mordovia, North Ossetia, Sakha, Tatarstan,
Tuva and Udmurtia. The *okrugi* are Chukotka,
Khanty-Mansi, Nenets and Yamalo-Nenets. On 11 April
2014, Russia recognised Crimea as a *respublika* and
Sevastopol as a federal city following the annexation of the
territory from the Ukraine.

DEFENCE
Since the demise of the USSR, Russia's armed forces have
been considerably reduced and major army reform is
ongoing.
The CIS Collective Security Treaty enables Russia to
station troops in Armenia, Belarus, Kazakhstan, Kyrgyzstan
and Tajikistan. The Black Sea fleet was divided between

Russian and Ukraine under an agreement signed in 1997.
In April 2010, the Strategic Arms Reduction Treaty (START)
was renewed by President Medvedev and US president
Obama; the bilateral treaty, originally drafted in 1991, is an
agreement between the two states to continue to significantly
reduce the number of operational strategic nuclear weapons.

| *Aged 16–49, 2013 est* | *Males* | *Females* |
| --- | --- | --- |
| Available for military service | 34,132,156 | 34,985,115 |
| Fit for military service | 23,597,728 | 23,017,006 |

*Military expenditure* – US$84,462m (2014 est)
*Conscription* – 18 to 27 years of age; 12 months

## ECONOMY AND TRADE
Under the Soviet regime, an essentially agrarian economy
in 1917 was transformed by the early 1960s into the
second-greatest industrial power in the world. However, by
the early 1970s the concentration of resources on the
military-industrial complex had caused stagnation in
the civilian economy. Economic reforms were introduced by
President Gorbachev, including the legalisation of small
private businesses, the reduction of state control over the
economy, and denationalisation and privatisation. Mass
privatisation of state industries began in 1992, and 80 per
cent of the economy had been privatised by 1996. The
largest and most economically significant industries, oil and
gas, were partially renationalised from 2004.
The transition to a market economy caused severe
economic crises in 1993 and 1998, but from 1999 to 2008
the economy sustained growth averaging 7 per cent a year.
Political and economic uncertainties, corruption, excessive
red tape and a lack of trust in institutions continue to inhibit
growth however. Other problems include the economy's
vulnerability to fluctuations in global prices of key
commodities and a dilapidated infrastructure. Some of these
factors exacerbated the impact on Russia of the global
financial crisis in autumn 2008, when a sharp fall in oil
prices coincided with turmoil in the banking system and
a 70 per cent drop in the stock market. Credit problems, an
severe drop in production and rising unemployment caused
a sharp contraction in the economy until late 2009, before
high oil prices boosted economic growth in 2011–12.
Russia joined the World Trade Organization in 2012,
providing greater access to foreign markets. Russia's
involvement in the Ukraine crisis caused a number of nations
to impose economic sanctions, including the US, the EU and
Japan. Sanctions have primarily targeted the energy, financial
and military sectors of the economy and have been credited
with dramatically reducing the value of the rouble since
2014. Growth is expected to fall to under 0 per cent in 2015
and forecasts through to 2030 have been revised down to an
estimate of 2.5 per cent per year.
Russia has some of the world's richest natural resources,
especially mineral deposits and timber. The recent growth in
the economy is founded on the exploitation and export of its
oil and natural gas reserves. Russia is now the world's leading
oil producer (surpassing Saudi Arabia in 2011) and exporter
of hydrocarbons, and the leading supplier to European
countries and China, a position that has led the country into
disputes with some of its neighbours; Ukraine, Georgia,
Lithuania, Czech Republic, Armenia, Azerbaijan, Poland and
Belarus have all had gas or oil supplies cut for short periods
during price negotiations.
Mining (coal, iron ore, aluminium and other non-ferrous
metals) and oil and natural gas extraction are concentrated in
the region south of Moscow, the Volga valley, the northern
Caucasus, the Urals, Siberia and the far east and north. Russia
is also keen to exploit the shrinking of the Arctic ice cap to
prospect for previously inaccessible deposits under the Arctic

Sea. The main industries are extracting and processing oil, gas and minerals, forestry, all forms of machine building (including transport, communications, agricultural, construction, and power generating and transmitting equipment), defence industries, shipbuilding, medical and scientific instruments, consumer durables, textiles and food processing.

The vast area and the great variety in climatic conditions are reflected in the structure of agriculture. In the far north, only reindeer breeding, hunting and fishing are possible; further south, forestry is combined with grain growing. In the southern half of the forest zone and in the adjacent forest-steppe zone, the acreage under grain crops is larger and agriculture more complex. The southern part of the Western Siberian plain is an important grain-growing and stock-breeding area. In the extreme south, cotton is cultivated. Vine, tobacco and other southern crops are grown on the Black Sea shore of the Caucasus.

The service sector is the largest, accounting for 59.7 per cent of GDP and employing 62.5 per cent of the workforce; industry contributes 36.3 per cent of GDP and employs 27.8 per cent; and agriculture accounts for 4 per cent of GDP and 9.7 per cent of employment.

Russia's main trading partners are China, EU countries (especially Germany) and Ukraine. Principal exports are oil and petroleum products, natural gas, metals, timber and wood products, chemicals, manufactured goods, military vehicles and defence equipment. The main imports are machinery, vehicles, pharmaceutical products, plastics, semi-finished metal products, meat, fruits and nuts, optical and medical equipment, iron and steel.

*GNI* – US$1,987,738m; US$13,850 per capita (2013)
*Annual average growth of GDP* – 0.5 per cent (2014)
*Inflation rate* – 9.1 per cent (2014 est)
*Population below poverty line* – 11 per cent (2013)
*Unemployment* – 5.8 per cent (2015 est)
*Total external debt* – US$683,600m (2014 est)
*Imports* – US$314,967m (2013)
*Exports* – US$527,266m (2013)

BALANCE OF PAYMENTS
*Trade* – US$212,299m surplus (2013)
*Current Account* – US$63,258m surplus (2015 est)

| Trade with UK | 2013 | 2014 |
| --- | --- | --- |
| Imports from UK | £5,181,577,615 | £4,033,589,272 |
| Exports to UK | £6,957,738,209 | £6,426,959,250 |

## COMMUNICATIONS

*Airports* – There are 594 airports; the principal international airports are at Moscow, St Petersburg and Novosibirsk
*Waterways* – Major ports include Kaliningrad on the Baltic Sea and Novorossiysk on the Black Sea. Two of the three northern ports, St Petersburg and Arkhangelsk, are icebound during winter; only Murmansk is accessible. There is a large merchant fleet of 1,143 ships of 1,000 tonnes and over, with a further 439 ships registered in other countries. There are 102,000km of waterways, supplemented by a 72,000km system of canals which provides a through route between the White Sea and Baltic Sea in the north and the Black Sea, Caspian Sea and the Sea of Azov in the south
*Roadways* – There are 927,721km of roadways, 39,143km of which are motorways
*Railways* – The railways are state run, with 87,157km of the network used for passenger transport plus 30,000km by industry
*Telecommunications* – 42.9 million fixed lines and 261.9 million mobile subscriptions (2011); there were 40.85 million internet users in 2009

*Internet code and IDD* – ru; 7 (from UK), 810 44 (to UK)
*Major broadcasters* – Broadcasting is dominated by the Russian State Television and Radio Broadcasting Company (VGTRK) and stations part-owned by the government or whose owners have close ties to it
*Press* – There are over 400 major newspapers printed every week, including *Komsomolskaya Pravda, Moskovsky Komsomolets* and *Izvestia*
*WPFI score* – 44,97 (152)

## EDUCATION AND HEALTH
There are 11 years of compulsory education: nine at basic school level and a further two at senior secondary level.
*Literacy rate* – 100 per cent (2010 est)
*Gross enrolment ratio (percentage of relevant age group)* – primary 101 per cent; secondary 95 per cent; tertiary 76 per cent (2012 est)
*Health expenditure (per capita)* – US$957 (2013)
*Hospital beds (per 1,000 people)* – 9.7 (2006)
*Life expectancy (years)* – 70.16 (2014 est)
*Mortality rate* – 13.83 (2014 est)
*Birth rate* – 11.87 (2014 est)
*Infant mortality rate* – 7.08 (2014 est)
*HIV/AIDS adult prevalence* – 1 per cent (2009 est)

# RWANDA

*Republika y'u Rwanda/République du Rwanda – Republic of Rwanda*

*Area* – 26,338 sq. km
*Capital* – Kigali; population, 1,223,000 (2014)
*Major towns* – Butare, Gisenyi, Gitarama, Ruhengeri
*Currency* – Rwanda franc of 100 centimes
*Population* – 12,661,733 rising at 2.56 per cent a year (2015 est); Hutu (84 per cent), Tutsi (15 per cent), Twa (1 per cent) (est)
*Religion* – Christian (Roman Catholic 49.5 per cent, Protestant 39.4 per cent, other 4.5 per cent)
*Language* – Kinyarwanda, French, English (all official), Swahili
*Population density* – 477 per sq. km (2013)
*Urban population* – 19.7 per cent (2013 est)
*Median age (years)* – 18.7 (2014 est)
*National anthem* – 'Rwanda Nziza' ['Rwanda, Our Beautiful Country']
*National day* – 1 July (Independence Day)
*Death penalty* – Abolished for all crimes (since 2007)
*CPI score* – 49 (55)
*Literacy rate* – 80.4 per cent (2015 est)
*Gross enrolment ratio (percentage of relevant age group)* – primary 134 per cent; secondary 33 per cent (2013 est); tertiary 7 per cent (2012 est)
*Health expenditure (per capita)* – US$71 (2013)
*Hospital beds (per 1,000 people)* – 1.6 (2007)

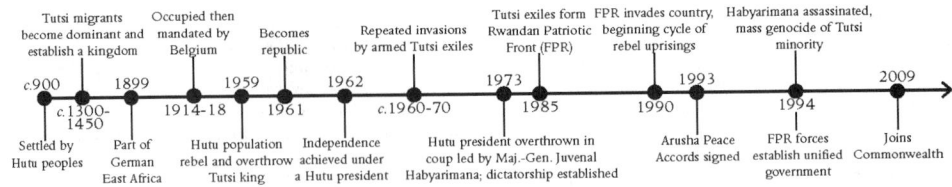

Tutsi migrants become dominant and establish a kingdom — *c.*900

Occupied then mandated by Belgium — 1899

Becomes republic — 1959

Repeated invasions by armed Tutsi exiles — 1962

Tutsi exiles form Rwandan Patriotic Front (FPR) — 1973

FPR invades country, beginning cycle of rebel uprisings — 1985

Habyarimana assassinated, mass genocide of Tutsi minority — 1993

2009

*c.*1300–1450

1914–18 — 1961

*c.*1960–70

1990

1994

Settled by Hutu peoples

Part of German East Africa

Hutu population rebel and overthrow Tutsi king

Independence achieved under a Hutu president

Hutu president overthrown in coup led by Maj.-Gen. Juvenal Habyarimana; dictatorship established

Arusha Peace Accords signed

FPR forces establish unified government

Joins Commonwealth

*Life expectancy (years)* – 59.26 (2014 est)
*Mortality rate* – 9.18 (2014 est)
*Birth rate* – 34.61 (2014 est)
*Infant mortality rate* – 59.59 (2014 est)
*HIV/AIDS adult prevalence* – 2.85 per cent (2013 est)

## CLIMATE AND TERRAIN
Landlocked Rwanda's terrain is mostly savannah uplands and mountains, including the volcanic Virunga range in the north-west. Elevation extremes range from 4,519m (Volcan Karisimbi) to 950m (Rusizi River). Rwanda's western border runs through Lake Kivu. The climate is temperate, with a wet season from October to May. The average temperature in Rwanda is 19.4°C.

## HISTORY AND POLITICS
The Rwandan Patriotic Front (FPR) won the 2003 legislative elections and retained an overall majority in the 2008 election, continuing in government in coalition with six other parties and a number of independent members. The FPR leader, Paul Kagame, was elected president in 2003, and re-elected in 2010, before gaining election to the senate in September 2011; he was succeeded in October by Pierre Damien Habumuremyi, who resigned as prime minister in July 2014.

Under the 2003 constitution, the president is directly elected for a seven-year term, renewable once. The bicameral parliament consists of the Chamber of Deputies (the lower house) and the senate. The Chamber of Deputies has 80 members, of whom 53 are directly elected, 24 are women members elected by the provinces, two represent youth organisations and one represents organisations of disabled people; all serve a five-year term. The senate has 26 members indirectly elected for an eight-year term. Political parties are barred from organising on an ethnic, regional or religious basis.

In 2006 the 12 provinces were replaced by five provinces: North, East, South, West and Kigali, with the aim of creating more ethnically diverse administrative areas.

HEAD OF STATE
*President,* Maj.-Gen. Paul Kagame, *appointed* 17 April 2000, *sworn in* 22 April 2000, *elected* 25 August 2003, *re-elected* 2010

SELECTED GOVERNMENT MEMBERS *as at June 2015*
*Prime Minister,* Anastase Murekezi
*Defence,* Gen. James Kabarebe
*Finance and Economic Planning,* Claver Gatete
*Foreign Affairs,* Louise Mushikiwabo

HIGH COMMISSION OF THE REPUBLIC OF RWANDA
120–122 Seymour Place, London W1H 1NR
T 020-7224 9832 E uk@rwandahc.org W www.rwandahc.org
*High Commissioner,* Williams Nkurunziza, *apptd* 2013

BRITISH HIGH COMMISSION
Parcelle No. 1131, Blvd de l'Umuganda, Kacyiru-Sud, BP 576 Kigali
T (+250) 252 556 000 E BHC.Kigali@fco.gov.uk
W www.gov.uk/government/world/rwanda
*High Commissioner,* HE William Gelling, OBE, *apptd* 2014

## DEFENCE

| Aged 16–49, 2010 est | Males | Females |
| --- | --- | --- |
| Available for military service | 2,625,917 | 2,608,110 |
| Fit for military service | 1,685,066 | 1,749,580 |

*Military expenditure* – US$85.9m (2014 est)

## ECONOMY AND TRADE
Rwanda is the most densely populated country in Africa, with few natural resources and minimal industry. Nearly half the population lives below the poverty line and economic growth, especially in food production, struggles to keep up with population growth. It is dependent on international aid but the demands of its high foreign debt have been reduced by debt relief. Regional instability, inadequate transport links with other countries and energy shortages hamper development, although electricity supply is expected to become more reliable when methane from Lake Kivu starts to be tapped.

Around 90 per cent of the population is engaged in agriculture, which is mainly at subsistence level and contributes 32.5 per cent of GDP. The main industries are mining, processing agricultural products, and small-scale manufacturing and tourism, which is now the main foreign exchange earner.

The main trading partners are China, Uganda and the Democratic Republic of the Congo. The main exports are coffee, tea, hides and tin ore. The principal imports are foodstuffs, machinery and equipment, steel, petroleum products and construction materials.

*GNI* – US$7,421m; US$630 per capita (2013)
*Annual average growth of GDP* – 6 per cent (2014)
*Inflation rate* – 2.4 per cent (2014 est)
*Population below poverty line* – 11 per cent (2013 est)
*Unemployment* – 0.6 per cent (2015 est)
*Total external debt* – US$1,901m (2014 est)
*Imports* – US$2,480m (2013)
*Exports* – US$689m (2013)

BALANCE OF PAYMENTS
*Trade* – US$1,529m deficit (2012)
*Current Account* – US$922m deficit (2015 est)

| Trade with UK | 2013 | 2014 |
| --- | --- | --- |
| Imports from UK | £9,776,267 | £6,736,575 |
| Exports to UK | £7,099,414 | £3,165,779 |

## COMMUNICATIONS
*Airports and waterways* – The principal airport is at Kigali; Lake Kivu is navigable by shallow boats, and provides access to the Democratic Republic of the Congo
*Roadways* – There are 1,207km of paved roads which links with those of neighbouring countries to provide access to Kenyan and Tanzanian ports
*Telecommunications* – 44,400 fixed lines and 5.69 million mobile subscriptions (2012); there were 450,000 internet users in 2009

*Internet code and IDD* – rw; 250 (from UK), 44 (to UK)
*Major broadcasters* – The state-owned Rwanda Broadcasting Agency operates Rwanda TV and Radio Rwanda, which broadcasts in English, French, Kinyarwanda and Swahili
*Press* – Leading newspapers include *The New Times* and *Rwanda Herald*
*WPFI score* – 56,57 (161)

# ST KITTS AND NEVIS

*Federation of St Christopher and Nevis (Federation of St Kitts and Nevis)*

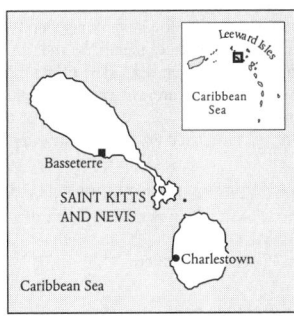

*Area* – 261 sq. km
*Capital* – Basseterre; population, 14,000 (2014)
*Major town* – Charlestown, the chief town of Nevis
*Currency* – East Caribbean dollar (EC$) of 100 cents
*Population* – 51,936 rising at 0.76 per cent a year (2015 est)
*Religion* – Christian (Anglican 50 per cent, Roman Catholic 25 per cent) (est)
*Language* – English (official)
*Population density* – 208 per sq. km (2013)
*Urban population* – 32.1 per cent (2013 est)
*Median age (years)* – 33.5 (2014 est)
*National anthem* – 'Oh Land of Beauty!'
*National day* – 19 September (Independence Day)
*Death penalty* – Retained (last used 2008)
*Life expectancy (years)* – 75.29 (2014 est)
*Mortality rate* – 7.08 (2014 est)
*Birth rate* – 13.64 (2014)
*Infant mortality rate* – 8.98 (2014 est)

## CLIMATE AND TERRAIN
The volcanic islands of St Kitts (St Christopher) (168 sq. km) and Nevis (93 sq. km) are part of the Leeward group in the eastern Caribbean Sea. The centre of St Kitts is forest-clad and mountainous, with the Great Salt Pond occupying the tip of its southern peninsula; elevation extremes range from 1,156m (Mt Liamuiga) to 0m (Caribbean Sea). Nevis, separated from the southern tip of St Kitts by a strait 3km wide, is dominated by Nevis Peak (985m). The climate is tropical, moderated by north-east trade winds, and a wet season occurs from May to September. The islands are in the hurricane belt.

## HISTORY AND POLITICS
The islands were inhabited by Carib, or Kalinago, people when discovered in 1493 by Christopher Columbus, who gave St Christopher its name. Colonisation by the British began in 1623–4, when St Kitts became the first British colony in the West Indies, and French settlement began shortly after. The island was held jointly from 1628 to 1713, although there were skirmishes between the British and French settlers in the 17th century; France dropped its claims

after 1783. Nevis was settled by the British from 1628. The two islands were part of the Leeward Islands colony from 1871 to 1956, and then of the West Indies Federation from 1958 to 1962. They achieved internal self-government in 1967 and became independent in September 1983.

The Labour Party, which has been in power since 1995, lost the 2015 National Assembly elections to the Team Unity coalition, which won seven of the 11 elected seats. Timothy Harris of the People's Labour Party was sworn in as prime minister on 22 February. In Nevis's 2013 assembly election the Concerned Citizens' Movement won three of the five elected seats.

Under the 1983 constitution, the head of state is Queen Elizabeth II, represented by a governor-general appointed on the advice of the prime minister. The unicameral National Assembly has 15 members: 11 directly elected for a five-year term, a speaker, and three appointed by the governor-general on the advice of the prime minister and the leader of the opposition. The prime minister, who is responsible to the legislature, and the cabinet are appointed by the governor-general.

Nevis is responsible for its own internal affairs. It has an eight-member Nevis Island assembly and is governed by the Nevis Island administration, headed by the premier.
*Governor-General,* HE Samuel Seaton, *apptd* 2015

SELECTED GOVERNMENT MEMBERS *as at June 2015*
*Prime Minister, Finance,* Timothy Harris
*Deputy Prime Minister,* Shawn Richards
*Foreign Affairs, National Security,* Mark Brantley

HIGH COMMISSION FOR ST KITTS AND NEVIS
10 Kensington Court, London W8 5DL
T 020-7937 9718 E info@sknhc.co.uk W www.stkittsnevisuk.com/
*High Commissioner,* HE Kevin Isaac, *apptd* 2011

BRITISH HIGH COMMISSIONER
HE Victoria Dean, *apptd* 2013, resident at Bridgetown, Barbados

## ECONOMY AND TRADE
The sugar industry was the mainstay of the economy for over 300 years but was closed down in 2005 after decades of operating at a loss. Tourism (the chief source of foreign exchange revenue), offshore financial services and manufacturing, especially distilling, food processing, clothing and electronics, are being developed. Services now account for 75.4 per cent of GDP, industry for 23 per cent and agriculture for 1.5 per cent. The economy of Nevis relies on farming, but a sea-island cotton industry is being developed for export. The economy is restricted by one of the world's highest public debt burdens (estimated at 81 per cent of GDP in 2014) and the country remains vulnerable to costly damage from natural disasters and shifts in tourism demand.

The main trading partners are the USA, the EU and Trinidad and Tobago. Principal exports are machinery, food, electronic equipment, beverages and tobacco. The main imports are machinery, manufactured goods, food and fuels.
*GNI* – US$752m; US$13,890 per capita (2013)
*Annual average growth of GDP* – 3.5 per cent (2014 est)
*Inflation rate* – 3 per cent (2014 est)
*Total external debt* – US$162.9m (2014 est)

BALANCE OF PAYMENTS
*Trade* – US$176m deficit (2012)
*Current Account* – US$99m deficit (2012)

| Trade with UK | 2013 | 2014 |
| --- | --- | --- |
| Imports from UK | £4,172,003 | £6,253,629 |
| Exports to UK | £137,498 | £140,495 |

## COMMUNICATIONS

*Airports* – There are two airports; the one on St Kitts can take most large jet aircraft

*Waterways* – Basseterre is a port of registry and has deep-water harbour facilities; there are regular ferries between Basseterre and Charlestown

*Roadways and railways* – The islands have 163km of surfaced roadways, and 50km of narrow-gauge railways on St Kitts

*Telecommunications* – 20,000 fixed lines and 84,000 mobile subscriptions (2012); there were 17,000 internet users in 2009

*Internet code and IDD* – kn; 1 869 (from UK), 011 44 (to UK)

*Media* – The government-owned broadcaster ZIZ operates national television and radio networks; *The Sun* is the sole daily newspaper

# ST LUCIA

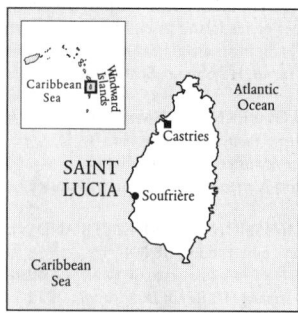

*Area* – 616 sq. km

*Capital* – Castries; population, 22,000 (2014)

*Currency* – East Caribbean dollar (EC$) of 100 cents

*Population* – 163,922 rising at 0.36 per cent a year (2015 est)

*Religion* – Christian (Roman Catholic 61.5 per cent, Seventh-day Adventists 10.4 per cent, Pentecostals 8.9 per cent, Baptists 2.2 per cent), Rastafarian 1.9 per cent (2010 est)

*Language* – English (official), French patois

*Population density* – 299 per sq. km (2013)

*Urban population* – 16.1 per cent (2013 est)

*Median age (years)* – 32.9 (2014 est)

*National anthem* – 'Sons and Daughters of Saint Lucia'

*National day* – 22 February (Independence Day)

*Death penalty* – Retained (last used 1996)

*Life expectancy (years)* – 77.41 (2014 est)

*Mortality rate* – 7.32 (2014 est)

*Birth rate* – 13.94 (2014 est)

*Infant mortality rate* – 11.75 (2014 est)

## CLIMATE AND TERRAIN

St Lucia is the second-largest island in the Windward group. The interior is mountainous and densely forested, with elevation extremes ranging from 950m (Mt Gimie) to 0m (Caribbean Sea). The area around the volcanic peaks of Gros Piton and Petit Piton is a UNESCO World Heritage Site. The climate is tropical, moderated by trade winds and with a wet season from July to November. The island is in the hurricane belt.

## HISTORY AND POLITICS

The original Arawak settlers were superseded by Caribs by AD 800. The island was sighted by Columbus in 1502

and European settlement began in the 1550s. Control was disputed between France and Britain from the mid-17th century until 1814, when the island was ceded to Britain. It achieved internal self-government in 1967 and became independent in 1979.

The St Lucia Labour Party (SLP) won the 2011 legislative election, defeating the incumbent United Workers' Party; SLP leader Kenny Anthony was sworn into office in November 2011.

Under the 1979 constitution, the head of state is Queen Elizabeth II, represented by a governor-general appointed on the advice of the prime minister. The bicameral parliament consists of the house of assembly and the senate. The senate has 11 members, six nominated by the government, three by the opposition and two by the governor-general. The House of Assembly has 17 elected members and an appointed speaker who serve a five-year term. The prime minister, who is responsible to the legislature, and the cabinet are appointed by the governor-general.

*Governor-General,* HE Dame Pearlette Louisy, *apptd* 1997

SELECTED GOVERNMENT MEMBERS *as at June 2015*
*Prime Minister, Finance, Economy,* Kenny Anthony
*Foreign Affairs,* Alva Baptiste
*Home Affairs,* Victor LaCorbiniere

HIGH COMMISSION FOR ST LUCIA
1 Collingham Gardens, London SW5 0HW
T 020-7370 7123 E enquiries@stluciahcuk.org
W www.stluciahcuk.org
*High Commissioner,* HE Ernest Hilaire, *apptd* 2012

BRITISH HIGH COMMISSIONER
HE Victoria Dean, *apptd* 2013, resident at Bridgetown, Barbados

## ECONOMY AND TRADE

The economy was dependent on bananas, but has diversified since preferential access to EU markets ended in 1999. Tourism and offshore financial services have been developed, and the manufacturing sector is the most diverse in the Caribbean, processing agricultural products, assembling electronic components and producing clothing, beverages and corrugated cardboard boxes. Services account for 82.5 per cent of GDP, industry for 14.5 per cent and agriculture for 3 per cent. Tourism is expected to contribute 45.4 per cent of GDP by 2015.

The main trading partners are the USA, Dominican Republic, and Trinidad and Tobago. Principal exports are bananas, clothing, cocoa, vegetables, fruit and coconut oil. The main imports are food, manufactured goods, machinery and transport equipment, chemicals and fuels.

*GNI* – US$1,287m; US$7,060 per capita (2013)

*Annual average growth of GDP* – –1.1 per cent (2014 est)

*Inflation rate* – 1 per cent (2014 est)

*Unemployment* – 20 per cent (2003 est)

*Total external debt* – US$498.2m (2014 est)

*Imports* – US$598m (2013)

*Exports* – US$171m (2013)

BALANCE OF PAYMENTS
*Trade* – US$527m deficit (2012)
*Current Account* – US$191m deficit (2012)

| Trade with UK | 2013 | 2014 |
| --- | --- | --- |
| Imports from UK | £14,272,546 | £12,835,316 |
| Exports to UK | £7,726,163 | £5,930,095 |

## COMMUNICATIONS

*Airports and waterways* – There are two airports in Castries and Vieux Fort; Castries also has a deep-water harbour
*Roadways* – 847km are surfaced
*Telecommunications* – 36,800 fixed lines and 227,000 mobile subscriptions (2012); there were 142,900 internet users in 2009
*Internet code and IDD* – lc; 1-758 (from UK), 011 44 (to UK)
*Media* – Television stations are privately owned and Radio Saint Lucia (RSL) is the state broadcaster; there are several newspapers but none daily

# ST VINCENT AND THE GRENADINES

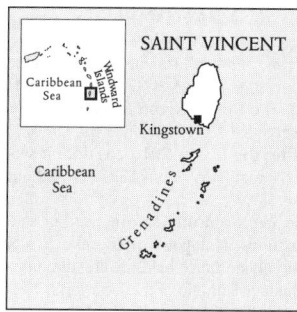

SAINT VINCENT

*Area* – 389 sq. km
*Capital* – Kingstown; population, 27,000 (2014)
*Currency* – East Caribbean dollar (EC$) of 100 cents
*Population* – 102,627 falling at 0.28 per cent a year (2015 est)
*Religion* – Christian (Anglican 47 per cent, Methodist 28 per cent and Roman Catholic 13 per cent), Hindu, Seventh-day Adventist
*Language* – English (official), French patois
*Population density* – 280 per sq. km (2013)
*Urban population* – 50.1 per cent (2013)
*Median age (years)* – 31.9 (2014)
*National anthem* – 'St Vincent! Land So Beautiful'
*National day* – 27 October (Independence Day)
*Death penalty* – Retained (last used 1995)
*CPI score* – 67 (29)
*Life expectancy (years)* – 74.86 (2014 est)
*Mortality rate* – 7.12 (2014 est)
*Birth rate* – 13.85 (2014 est)
*Infant mortality rate* – 13.07 (2014 est)

## CLIMATE AND TERRAIN

The state, which lies in the Windward group, consists of St Vincent and the 32 small islands and cays of the northern Grenadines, a chain stretching 64km across the eastern Caribbean Sea between St Vincent and Grenada. St Vincent itself is a mountainous and densely forested volcanic island. The Grenadines, of which the largest are Bequia, Canouan, Mayreau, Mustique and Union Island, are low-lying coral islands. Elevation extremes range from 1,234m (La Soufriére volcano, St Vincent) to 0m (Caribbean Sea). The climate is tropical, with a rainy season from May to November. The islands lie in the hurricane belt.

## HISTORY AND POLITICS

Settled successively by the Ciboney people, the Arawaks and the Caribs, St Vincent was sighted by Christopher Columbus in 1498. Although granted by Charles I to the Earl of

Carlisle in 1627, control was disputed between the British and the French until the islands were ceded to Britain in 1783. Internal self-government was granted in 1969, and independence as St Vincent and the Grenadines was achieved in 1979.

An early election in 2001 was won decisively by the opposition Unity Labour Party, which was returned for additional terms in 2005 and 2010. A referendum in 2009 rejected a draft constitution which proposed to replace the monarchy with a republic. Fresh legislative elections are due in December 2015.

Under the 1979 constitution, the head of state is Queen Elizabeth II, represented by a governor-general appointed on the advice of the prime minister. The unicameral House of Assembly has 21 members: 15 directly elected for a five-year term and six senators appointed by the governor-general (four on the advice of the government and two on the advice of the opposition). The prime minister, who is responsible to the legislature, and the cabinet are appointed by the governor-general.

*Governor-General,* Sir Frederick Ballantyne, GCMG, *apptd* 2002

SELECTED GOVERNMENT MEMBERS *as at June 2015*
*Prime Minister, Finance, National Security,* Ralph Gonsalves
*Deputy Prime Minister,* Girlyn Miguel

HIGH COMMISSION FOR ST VINCENT AND THE GRENADINES
10 Kensington Court, London W8 5DL
**T** 020-7565 2874 **E** info@svghighcom.co.uk
**W** www.svghighcom.co.uk
*High Commissioner,* HE Cenio E. Lewis, *apptd* 2001

BRITISH HIGH COMMISSIONER
HE Victoria Dean, *apptd* 2013, resident at Bridgetown, Barbados

## ECONOMY AND TRADE

Tourism (the development of which has been hampered by drug-related crime), manufacturing and offshore banking services have all expanded, although the economy contracted in 2009 owing to the global downturn. The economy is expected to improve in 2015 after a poor performance in 2014. Services now account for 70.6 per cent of GDP, industry for 20.9 per cent and agriculture for 8.5 per cent. Floods and mudslides caused by heavy rainfall in 2013 resulted in US$112m worth of damage.

The main export markets are Trinidad and Tobago and St Lucia. Imports come mostly from Singapore, Trinidad and Tobago, and the USA. Principal exports are bananas, vegetables, starch and tennis racquets. The main imports are foodstuffs, machinery and equipment, chemicals, fertilisers, minerals and fuel.
*GNI* – US$706m; US$6,460 per capita (2013)
*Annual average growth of GDP* – 1.7 per cent (2014 est)
*Inflation rate* – 5.4 per cent (2014 est)
*Total external debt* – US$248.7m (2014 est)
*Imports* – US$378m (2013)
*Exports* – US$48m (2013)

BALANCE OF PAYMENTS
*Trade* – US$314m deficit (2012)
*Current Account* – US$216m deficit (2012)

| Trade with UK | 2013 | 2014 |
| --- | --- | --- |
| Imports from UK | £14,048,947 | £11,679,434 |
| Exports to UK | £807,865 | £720,113 |

## COMMUNICATIONS

*Airports and waterways* – There are five airports; although none can accommodate international flights at present, an international airport is under construction and scheduled for completion in late 2014. The main harbour is at Kingstown

*Roadways* – 580km are surfaced

*Telecommunications* – 19,400 fixed lines and 135,500 mobile subscriptions (2012); there were 76,000 internet users in 2009

*Internet code and IDD* – vc; 1 784 (from UK), 011 44 (to UK)

*Media* – Television broadcasting is operated by the St Vincent and the Grenadines Broadcasting Corporation, and NBC Radio is partly government funded; there is one daily newspaper, *The Herald*

# SAMOA

*Malo Sa'oloto Tuto'atasi o Samoa* – *Independent State of Samoa*

*Area* – 2,831 sq. km

*Capital* – Apia, on Upolu; population, 37,000 (2014)

*Currency* – Tala (S$) of 100 sene

*Population* – 197,773 rising at 0.58 per cent a year (2015 est); Samoan (Polynesian) (92.6 per cent) (2001); the population also includes Euronesians, Chinese and Europeans

*Religion* – Christian (Congregational 31.8 per cent, Roman Catholic 19.4 per cent, Mormon 15.2 per cent, Methodist 13.7 per cent, Assemblies of God 8 per cent, Seventh-day Adventist 3.9 per cent) (2011 est)

*Language* – Samoan (official), English

*Population density* – 67 per sq. km (2013)

*Urban population* – 19.4 per cent (2013)

*Median age (years)* – 23.1 (2014 est)

*National anthem* – 'O le Fu'a o le Sa'olotoga o Samoa' ['The Banner of Freedom']

*National day* – 1 June (Independence Day celebration; independence was achieved on 1 January 1962)

*Death penalty* – Abolished for all crimes (since 2004)

*CPI score* – 52 (50)

*Literacy rate* – 99.6 per cent (2015 est)

*Life expectancy (years)* – 73.21 (2014 est)

*Mortality rate* – 5.32 (2014 est)

*Birth rate* – 21.29 (2014 est)

*Infant mortality rate* – 20.5 (2014 est)

## CLIMATE AND TERRAIN

Samoa consists of the islands of Savai'i, Upolu, Apolima, Manono, Fanuatapu, Namua, Nu'utele, Nu'ulua and Nu'usafe'e in the south Pacific Ocean. All the islands are volcanic in origin, with narrow coastal plains and mountainous, densely forested interiors. Elevation extremes range from 1,857m (Mauga Silisili, Savai'i) to 0m (Pacific Ocean). The climate is tropical, with a wet season from November to April; the average temperature is 27.6°C. The islands are vulnerable to cyclones and tsunamis.

## HISTORY AND POLITICS

Inhabited since *c.*1000 BC, Samoa was visited by European traders, explorers and missionaries from the 18th century. Germany, the UK and the USA disputed control of the islands until 1899, when the nine western islands (Western Samoa) became a German colony and the eastern islands American Samoa. Western Samoa was occupied by New Zealand on the outbreak of the First World War and became a mandated territory administered by New Zealand from 1920. Internal self-government was granted in 1959, and Western Samoa became independent on 1 June 1962. The state was treated as a member country of the Commonwealth until its formal admission in 1970. In 1997 the state dropped 'Western' from its name.

Former prime minister Tuiatua Tupua Tamasese Efi was elected head of state in June 2007 and re-elected unopposed in July 2012. The Human Rights Protection Party, which has been in power since 1981, remained the largest party in the legislature after the March 2011 election; it won 28 seats, the Tautua Samoa Party won 13 seats and independents won eight.

Under the 1962 constitution, the head of state is elected and has functions analogous to those of a constitutional monarch. Initially an office held for life, the monarch is now elected by the legislature for a five-year term. The unicameral legislative assembly *(Fono)* has 49 members elected for a five-year term; only members of the *Matai* (elected clan leaders) may stand for election. The prime minister is appointed by the monarch on the recommendation of the legislature and appoints the cabinet.

HEAD OF STATE

*Head of State,* Tuiatua Tupua Tamasese Efi, *elected* 16 June 2007, *re-elected* 20 July 2012

SELECTED GOVERNMENT MEMBERS *as at June 2015*

*Prime Minister, Finance, Foreign Affairs,* Tuilaepa Sailele Malielegaoi

*Deputy Prime Minister,* Fonotoe Nuafesili Pierre Lauofo

EMBASSY OF SAMOA

20 avenue de l'Oree, 1000 Brussels, Belgium

T (+32) (2) 660 8454 E samoanembassy@skynet.be

W www.samoaembassybelgium.com

*High Commissioner,* HE Dr Fatumanava Pa'olelei Luteru, *apptd* 2013

BRITISH HIGH COMMISSIONER

HE Victoria Treadell, CMG, MVO, *apptd* 2010, resident at Wellington, New Zealand

## ECONOMY AND TRADE

The economy is underdeveloped but has grown steadily in the past decade, diversifying away from its traditional dependence on fishing, agriculture, remittances from migrant workers and international aid. Economic strengths include a flexible labour market, stable external debt and low inflation. Agriculture and fishing generates 11.4 per cent of GDP, employing about two-thirds of the labour force and supplying about 90 per cent of exports. Manufacturing is branching out from small-scale processing of agricultural products into light manufacturing (particularly of motor vehicle components), and offshore financial services are being developed. Tourism has grown rapidly and accounts for about 25 per cent of GDP. Public finances were weakened by a tsunami in 2009 and a tropical cyclone in 2012, both of which caused severe damage. The economy is expected to grow by under 2.5 per cent in 2015 and income from tourism was expected to be boosted by the hosting of the Commonwealth Youth Games in 2015.

The main trading partners are American Samoa, New Zealand, Fiji, Australia and Singapore. Principal exports are fish, coconut oil and cream, copra, taro, vehicle parts, garments and beer. The main imports are machinery and equipment, industrial supplies and foodstuffs.

*GNI* – US$756m; US$3,970 per capita (2013)
*Annual average growth of GDP* – 2 per cent (2014 est)
*Inflation rate* – –1.2 per cent (2014 est)
*Total external debt* – US$368.3m (2011 est)
*Imports* – US$326m (2013)
*Exports* – US$24m (2013)

BALANCE OF PAYMENTS
*Trade* – US$274m deficit (2012)
*Current Account* – US$59m deficit (2015 est)

| Trade with UK | 2013 | 2014 |
| --- | --- | --- |
| Imports from UK | £176,423 | £81,603 |
| Exports to UK | £258,650 | £594,125 |

## COMMUNICATIONS

*Airports and waterways* – There is one international airport on Upolu; the southern island also contains the harbours of Apia and Mulifanua, and Salelologa, the harbour of Savai'i
*Roadways* – 332km are surfaced
*Telecommunications* – 35,300 fixed lines and 167,400 mobile subscriptions (2010); there were 9,000 internet users in 2009
*Internet code and IDD* – ws; 685 (from UK), 044 (to UK)
*Media* – The Samoa Broadcasting Corporation (TV) and National Radio 2AP are the state broadcasters; the *Samoa Observer* and *Samoa Times* are the only daily newspapers
*WPFI score* – 22,32 (40)

## SAN MARINO

*Repubblica di San Marino – Republic of San Marino*

*Area* – 61 sq. km
*Capital* – San Marino; population, 4,000 (2014 est)
*Currency* – Euro (€) of 100 cents
*Population* – 33,020 rising at 0.82 per cent a year (2015 est)
*Religion* – Christian (Roman Catholic 97 per cent) (est)
*Language* – Italian (official)
*Population density* – 524 per sq. km (2013)
*Urban population* – 94.2 per cent (2013)
*Median age (years)* – 43.6 (2014 est)
*National anthem* – 'Inno Nazionale della Repubblica' ['National Anthem of the Republic']

*Death penalty* – Abolished for all crimes (since 1865)
*National day* – 3 September (Republic Day)
*Life expectancy (years)* – 83.18 (2014 est)
*Mortality rate* – 8.31 (2014 est)
*Birth rate* – 8.7 (2014 est)
*Infant mortality rate* – 4.52 (2014 est)

## CLIMATE AND TERRAIN

A landlocked enclave in central Italy, the republic lies in the foothills of the Apennines, 20km from the Adriatic Sea. Elevation extremes range from 755m (Mt Titano) to 55m (Torrente Ausa). The climate is Mediterranean, with an average annual rainfall of 836mm.

## HISTORY AND POLITICS

The republic is said to have been founded in the fourth century by a Christian stonecutter seeking refuge from religious persecution. By the 12th century a self-governing commune was established, and a parliamentary constitution was adopted in 1600. The republic resisted papal claims and those of neighbouring dukedoms from the 15th to 18th centuries, and the papacy recognised its independence in 1631. In 1862 it signed a treaty with the newly united kingdom of Italy which recognised its integrity and sovereignty and accorded it the protection of Italy. San Marino became a member of the UN in 1992. A 2013 poll supported moves to join the EU, but the number of voters did not exceed the minimum 32 per cent of the electorate needed to enact the measure.

A coalition led by the Christian Democratic Party (PDCS) retained its majority in the November 2012 election.

The 1600 constitution has been amended several times. The joint heads of state are two captains-regent who are elected at six-monthly intervals (March and September) by the legislature, taking office the month after the election. Executive power is vested in the captains-regent and the Congress of State (cabinet), which is also elected by the legislature. The unicameral legislature, the Great and General Council, has 60 members, who are directly elected for a five-year term.

HEADS OF STATE
*Captains-Regent,* Andrea Belluzzi; Roberto Venturini

SELECTED GOVERNMENT MEMBERS *as at June 2015*
*Finance,* Giancarlo Capicchioni
*Foreign Affairs,* Pasquale Valentini
*Internal Affairs,* Giancarlo Venturini

EMBASSY OF THE REPUBLIC OF SAN MARINO
c/o Department of Foreign Affairs, Palazzo Begni – Contrado Ormerelli, 47890 San Marino
T 378 (0549) 88 2422 E dipartimentoaffariesteri@pa.sm
*Ambassador Extraordinary and Plenipotentiary,* HE Federica Bigi, *apptd* 2012

BRITISH AMBASSADOR
HE Christopher Prentice, CMG, *apptd* 2011, resident at Rome, Italy

## ECONOMY AND TRADE

Tourism and banking are the basis of the economy, and the service sector contributes 60.7 per cent of GDP. In 2009, investment outflows following Italy's tax amnesty, a money-laundering scandal at its largest bank and the global downturn contributed to a deep recession and growing budget deficit. The government is working to improve standards of financial transparency.

The principal agricultural products are grains, grapes, olives, cheeses and hides. The main industries, apart from tourism and banking, are quarrying, forestry, winemaking and the manufacture of clothing, electronics and ceramics. Sales of postage stamps and coins also generate significant revenue. San Marino is in a customs union with the EU.

*GNI* – US$1,572m; US$51,470 per capita (2008)
*Annual average growth of GDP* – 0 per cent (2014 est)
*Inflation rate* – 2.8 per cent (2012 est)
*Unemployment* – 7 per cent (2012 est)

| Trade with UK | 2013 | 2014 |
| --- | --- | --- |
| Imports from UK | £6,796,306 | £3,981,347 |
| Exports to UK | £2,796,436 | £6,879,356 |

## COMMUNICATIONS

*Roadways* – 292km
*Telecommunications* – 18,700 fixed lines and 36,000 mobile subscriptions (2011); there were 17,000 internet users in 2009
*Internet code and IDD* – sm; 378 (from UK), 44 (to UK)
*Media* – Broadcasting services are state-run; the two daily newspapers are *La Tribuna Sammarinese* and *San Marino Oggi*

# SAO TOME AND PRINCIPE

*Republica Democratica de Sao Tome e Principe* – Democratic Republic of Sao Tome and Principe

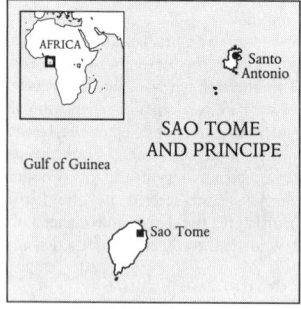

*Area* – 964 sq. km
*Capital* – Sao Tome; population, 71,000 (2014)
*Currency* – Dobra of 100 centimos
*Population* – 190,428 rising at 1.84 per cent a year (2015 est)
*Religion* – Christian (Roman Catholic 55.7 per cent, Adventist 4.1 per cent) (est)
*Language* – Portuguese (official), Creole dialects
*Population density* – 201 per sq. km (2013)
*Urban population* – 64.1 per cent (2013)
*Median age (years)* – 17.8 (2014 est)
*National anthem* – 'Independencia total' ['Total Independence']
*National day* – 12 July (Independence Day)
*Death penalty* – Abolished for all crimes (since 1990)
*CPI score* – 42 (76)
*Literacy rate* – 83.2 per cent (2015 est)
*Life expectancy (years)* – 64.22 (2014 est)
*Mortality rate* – 7.45 (2014 est)
*Birth rate* – 35.12 (2014 est)
*Infant mortality rate* – 49.16 (2014 est)

## CLIMATE AND TERRAIN

The republic consists of the islands of Sao Tome, Principe and several uninhabited islets off the west coast of Africa. The islands, which are volcanic in origin, are mountainous and thickly forested. Elevation extremes range from 2,024m

(Pico de Sao Tome) to 0m (Atlantic Ocean). The climate is tropical, with a wet season from October to May. The average temperature is 24.1°C.

## HISTORY AND POLITICS

The uninhabited islands were discovered by the Portuguese between 1469 and 1472, and settlement began in 1493. Agitation against Portuguese rule began in the late 1950s. The islands gained independence from Portugal in 1975 and became a one-party state under the rule of the Movement for the Liberation of Sao Tome and Principe (MLSTP). Close links with the communist bloc were scaled down in the 1980s as the economy deteriorated, and in 1990 the MLSTP abandoned Marxism and introduced political pluralism and economic liberalisation. The first multiparty elections were held in 1991.

In the 2010 legislative election, the opposition Independent Democratic Action (ADI) party became the largest party in the legislature and formed a ruling coalition. Manuel Pinto da Costa, the country's first post-independence president and former leader of the MLSTP, won the 2011 presidential election as an independent candidate. The ADI secured a majority in the legislature at the October 2014 elections and Patrice Trovoada was appointed prime minister in November, having previously served in the role during 2008–10.

Under the 1990 constitution, the president is directly elected for a five-year term, renewable once. The unicameral National Assembly has 55 members, directly elected for a four-year term. The prime minister is appointed by the president and nominates the cabinet.

Since 1995 Principe has been internally self-governing, with an eight-member regional council.

### HEAD OF STATE
*President,* Manuel Pinto da Costa, *elected* 7 August 2011, *sworn in* 3 September 2011

SELECTED GOVERNMENT MEMBERS *as at June 2015*
*Prime Minister,* Patrice Trovoada
*Defence,* Carlos Olímpio Stock
*Finance,* Américo D'Oliveira Ramos
*Foreign Affairs,* Manuel Salvador Dos Ramos

EMBASSY OF SAO TOME AND PRINCIPE
175 avenue de Tervuren, 1150 Brussels, Belgium
T (+32) (2) 734 8966 E ambassade@saotomeprincipe.be
*Ambassador Extraordinary and Plenipotentiary,* vacant

BRITISH AMBASSADOR
HE John Dennis, *apptd* 2014, resident at Luanda, Angola

## ECONOMY AND TRADE

The economy has benefited from cancellation of about 90 per cent of the country's external debt over the past decade. It is largely dependent on cocoa, but tourism is being encouraged in an attempt to diversify. A major economic shift will begin with the start of oil production from offshore reserves in the Gulf of Guinea. The fields are being developed jointly with Nigeria, and Sao Tome and Principe will receive 40 per cent of the revenue. Most of the population is engaged in subsistence farming and fishing.

The principal export markets are the Netherlands (30.5 per cent) and Belgium (20.4 per cent), and the main source of imports is Portugal (67.2 per cent). Principal exports are cocoa (80 per cent), copra, coffee and palm oil. The main imports are machinery and electrical equipment, foodstuffs and petroleum products.

*GNI* – US$284m; US$1,470 per capita (2013)
*Annual average growth of GDP* – 5 per cent (2014 est)

*Inflation rate* – 7 per cent (2014 est)
*Population below poverty line* – 66.2 per cent (2009 est)
*Total external debt* – US$416.4m (2014 est)
*Imports* – US$152,093m (2013)
*Exports* – US$6,938m (2013)

BALANCE OF PAYMENTS
*Trade* – US$48m deficit (2015 est)
*Current Account* – US$56m deficit (2012)

| Trade with UK | 2013 | 2014 |
|---|---|---|
| Imports from UK | £380,503 | £454,016 |
| Exports to UK | £1,135,977 | £13,798 |

## COMMUNICATIONS
*Airports and waterways* – There are two airports; the ports are Santo Antonio, on Principe, and Sao Tome
*Roadways* – 218km are surfaced but in poor condition
*Telecommunications* – 8,000 fixed lines and 122,000 mobile subscriptions (2012); there were 26,700 internet users in 2009
*Internet code and IDD* – st; 239 (from UK), 44 (to UK)
*Media* – Televisao Saotomense and Radio Nacional de Sao Tome e Principe are the state broadcasters; *Téla Nón Diario de Sao Tome e Principe* is the only daily newspaper

# SAUDI ARABIA

*Al-Mamlakah al-Arabiyah as-Suudiyah – Kingdom of Saudi Arabia*

*Area* – 2,149,690 sq. km
*Capital* – Riyadh; population, 6,195,000 (2014)
*Major cities* – At Taif, Dammam, Jeddah, Mecca, Medina, Tabuk
*Currency* – Saudi riyal (SR) of 100 halalas
*Population* – 27,752,316 rising at 1.46 per cent a year (2015 est); includes some 5,576,076 non-nationals (2013 est)
*Religion* – Muslim (Sunni 85–90 per cent, predominantly Wahhabi; Shia 10–15 per cent) (2012 est); public practice of other religions is forbidden
*Language* – Arabic (official)
*Population density* – 13 per sq. km (2013)
*Urban population* – 82.7 per cent (2013)
*Median age (years)* – 26.4 (2014)
*National anthem* – 'As-Salaam al-Malaki' ['The Royal Salute']
*National day* – 23 September (Unification Day)
*Death penalty* – Retained
*CPI score* – 49 (55)

## CLIMATE AND TERRAIN
Saudi Arabia comprises about 80 per cent of the Arabian peninsula. The Hejaz region (north-west) runs along the northern Red Sea coast to the Asir and contains the holy cities of Mecca and Medina. The mountainous Asir (southwest) and the coastal plain of the Tihama lie along the southern Red Sea coast from the Hejaz to the border with Yemen. The Nejd plateau extends over the centre, including the Nafud and Dahna deserts. The Hasa (east) is low-lying and largely desert. The Empty Quarter (south) is the world's largest sand desert. Elevation extremes range from 3,133m (Jabal Sawda) to 0m (Persian Gulf). There is a desert climate, with extremes of temperature in the interior; coastal areas are more temperate but extremely humid. Average temperatures range from 15.7°C in January to 32.9°C in August.

## HISTORY AND POLITICS
The Arabian peninsula was the birthplace of the Muslim faith in the seventh century and the base from which the religion and four Islamic Caliphates, the Rashidun, Umayyad, Abbasid and Fatimid, emerged. When the Fatimid empire declined in the 12th century, Arabia became isolated and internally divided. The rise of the al-Saud family began in the 18th century, when it united the Nejd in support of the Wahhabi religious movement. The modern state was the culmination of a 30-year campaign by Abd-al Aziz al-Saud (often known as Ibn Saud) to unite the four tribal regions of the Hejaz, Asir, Najd and Hasa; the Kingdom of Saudi Arabia was proclaimed on 23 September 1932.

The ruling family preserved stability for many years by suppressing dissent and resisting calls for greater democracy. Since 2003 demand for political reform has grown and become more militant. In 2005, the country's first nationwide elections were held for half the seats on municipal councils, with voting by universal male suffrage.

King Abdullah acceded to the throne after the death of his half-brother King Fahd in 2005. Following the death of King Abdullah in January 2015, his half-brother King Salman acceded to the throne. In April 2015, Mohammed bin Nayef, the former Saudi ambassador to the USA, was appointed crown prince.

There is no written constitution; constitutional practice is provided for by articles of government based on the Qur'an and the teachings and sayings of the Prophet Muhammad *(Sunnah)* and issued by royal decree.

Saudi Arabia is a hereditary monarchy. The king is head of government and appoints the council of ministers (established in 1953), whose term of office was fixed in 1993 at four years.

There is no legislature; the Consultative Council *(Majlis-al-Shura)* debates policy, proposes legislation in certain areas and makes recommendations to the king. The council's 150 members are appointed by the king and serve a four-year term. Its decisions are taken by majority vote. There are no political parties.

Each of the 13 provinces has a governor appointed by the king and a council of prominent local citizens to advise the governor on local government, budgetary and planning issues.

HEAD OF STATE
*The King of Saudi Arabia, Custodian of the Two Holy Mosques, Prime Minister*, King Salman bin Abdul Aziz al-Saud, *born* 31 December 1935, *succeeded* 23 January 2015
*HRH Crown Prince, Deputy Prime Minister, Defence*, Prince Mohammed bin Nayef bin Abdul Aziz al-Saud

SELECTED GOVERNMENT MEMBERS *as at June 2015*
*Economy*, Adel bin Mohammed bin Abdulqader Fakieh
*Finance*, Ibrahim bin Abdul Aziz al-Assaf
*Foreign Affairs*, Adel bin Ahmed al-Jubeir

**ROYAL EMBASSY OF SAUDI ARABIA**
30 Charles Street, London W1J 5DZ
T 020-7917 3000 E ukemb@mofa.gov.sa
W www.saudiembassy.org.uk
*Ambassador Extraordinary and Plenipotentiary,* HE HRH
Prince Mohamed bin Nawaf bin Abdul Aziz al-Saud,
*apptd* 2005

**BRITISH EMBASSY**
PO Box 94351, Diplomatic Quarter, Riyadh 11693
T (+966) (0) 11 4819 100 E consular.riyadh@fco.gov.uk
W www.gov.uk/government/world/saudi-arabia
*Ambassador Extraordinary and Plenipotentiary,* HE Simon
Collis, *apptd* 2015

## DEFENCE

| Aged 16–49, 2010 est | Males | Females |
| --- | --- | --- |
| Available for military service | 8,644,522 | 6,601,985 |
| Fit for military service | 7,365,624 | 5,677,819 |

*Military expenditure –* US$80,762m (2014)

## ECONOMY AND TRADE

The economy is based on oil extraction and processing, but since 1970 the government has used five-year development plans to encourage diversification, and the non-oil sector now accounts for 45 per cent of GDP. The 2010–14 development plan aims to increase natural gas production and to promote the growth of small- and medium-sized businesses, partly through further privatisation; it also partially opened the Saudi stock market to foreign investors. Growth is expected to fall to 2.5 per cent in 2015 and 1.8 per cent in 2016 as oil prices are expected to remain below US$100 a barrel, the price required for the country to balance its budget.

Oil extraction since the 1940s has brought great wealth. Saudi Arabia has the second-largest proven reserves of oil in the world (about 16 per cent of the world total) and the fifth-largest reserves of recoverable gas. The oil and gas industry contributes around 45 per cent of GDP and about 80 per cent of government revenue.

The main industries, apart from oil extraction and refining, include production of petrochemicals, ammonia, industrial gases, caustic soda, cement, fertiliser, plastics and metals, commercial ship and aircraft repair and construction. Industry accounts for 59.7 per cent of GDP and the service sector for 38.3 per cent. Agriculture contributes 2 per cent but is limited by the terrain, although productivity has been increased by extensive irrigation, desalination and the use of aquifers. The main products are grains, fruit, meat and dairy.

The main trading partners are China, the USA, Japan and South Korea. Oil and petroleum products constitute 90 per cent of exports. The principal imports are machinery and equipment, foodstuffs, chemicals, motor vehicles and textiles.
*GNI –* US$757,058m; US$26,260 per capita (2013)
*Annual average growth of GDP –* 3.6 per cent (2014 est)
*Inflation rate –* 2.9 per cent (2014 est)
*Unemployment –* 5.4 per cent (2015 est)
*Total external debt –* US$164,303m (2014 est)
*Imports –* US$163,902m (2013)
*Exports –* US$375,934m (2013)

**BALANCE OF PAYMENTS**
*Trade –* US$230,405m surplus (2012)
*Current Account –* US$6,547m deficit (2015 est)

| Trade with UK | 2013 | 2014 |
| --- | --- | --- |
| Imports from UK | £4,220,132,810 | £4,172,931,251 |
| Exports to UK | £2,618,632,244 | £2,050,338,991 |

## COMMUNICATIONS

*Airports –* There are 82 airports; the three international airports are at Riyadh, Jeddah (serving Mecca) and Dammam
*Waterways –* The main cargo ports are Jeddah on the Red Sea coast and Dammam on the Gulf coast; the main oil port (the world's largest) is Ras Tanura
*Roadways and railways –* The surfaced network totals 47,529km, including a 3,891km motorway system, and 1,378km of railways, operated by the state-run Saudi Railway Organisation
*Telecommunications –* 4.8 million fixed lines and 53 million mobile subscriptions (2012); there were 9.77 million internet users in 2009
*Internet code and IDD –* sa; 966 (from UK), 44 (to UK)
*Major broadcasters –* Saudi TV and Saudi Radio are the state-run broadcasters
*Press –* Leading daily newspapers include *Al-Riyadh*, *Al-Watan* and the English-language *Arab News*
*WPFI score –* 59,41 (164)

## EDUCATION AND HEALTH

With the exception of a few schools for expatriate children, all schools are segregated and supervised by the government.
*Literacy rate –* 99.3 per cent (2015 est)
*Gross enrolment ratio (percentage of relevant age group) –* primary 106 per cent; secondary 116 per cent; tertiary 58 per cent (2013 est)
*Health expenditure (per capita) –* US$808 (2013)
*Hospital beds (per 1,000 people) –* 2.1 (2012)
*Life expectancy (years) –* 74.82 (2014 est)
*Mortality rate –* 3.32 (2014 est)
*Birth rate –* 18.78 (2014 est)
*Infant mortality rate –* 14.58 (2014 est)

# SENEGAL

*République du Sénégal – Republic of Senegal*

*Area –* 196,722 sq. km
*Capital –* Dakar; population, 3,393,000 (2014)
*Major cities –* Kaolack, Mbour, Saint-Louis, Thiès, Touba, Ziguinchor
*Currency –* Franc CFA of 100 centimes
*Population –* 13,975,834 rising at 2.45 per cent a year (2015 est); Wolof (43.3 per cent), Pular (23.8 per cent), Serer (14.7 per cent), Jola (3.7 per cent), Mandinka (3 per cent), Soninke (1.1 per cent), European and Lebanese (1 per cent)
*Religion –* Muslim 94 per cent, Christian 5 per cent (est); most incorporate indigenous beliefs into their worship
*Language –* French (official), Fulani, Jola, Mandinka, Wolof
*Population density –* 73 per sq. km (2013)
*Urban population –* 43.1 per cent (2013 est)
*Median age (years) –* 18.4 (2014 est)

*National anthem* – 'Pincez Tous vos Koras, Frappez les Balafons' ['All Pluck Your Koras, Strike the Balafons']
*National day* – 4 April (Independence Day)
*Death penalty* – Abolished for all crimes (since 2004)
*CPI score* – 43 (69)

## CLIMATE AND TERRAIN

The terrain is generally low and rolling, with plains rising to hills in the south-east. There is desert in the north, savannah in the centre and tropical forest in the south. Elevation extremes range from 581m (near Nepen Diakha) to 0m (Atlantic Ocean). There are three rivers: the Senegal on the northern border, and the Gambia and the Casamance in the south. The climate is tropical, with a wet season from June to September; the average temperature is 28.4°C.

## HISTORY AND POLITICS

Senegal was part of the Mali Empire in the 14th to 15th centuries. The first European visitors were the Portuguese in 1445. The interior was colonised by the French in the mid-19th century and the territory became part of French West Africa in 1902. It became an autonomous state in 1958 and achieved independence as part of the Federation of Mali in June 1960, seceding to form the Republic of Senegal in August 1960. From 1966 to 1978, the country was a one-party state under the rule of the Senegalese Progressive Union (UPS), which changed its name to the Socialist Party (PS) in 1976.

In the early 1980s a separatist insurgency led by the Movement of Democratic Forces of Casamance (MFDC) began in the impoverished Casamance region south of the river Gambia. Splits and leadership changes among the separatists have prevented the implementation of peace agreements in 2001 and 2004, and clashes continue between government troops and rebels.

The Socialist Party's 40 years of political domination ended in 2000 with the election of Abdoulaye Wade, leader of the Senegalese Democratic Party (PDS), as president. President Wade lost the 2012 presidential election to the Alliance for the Republic–Yakaar leader Macky Sall, who picked up 65 per cent of the overall vote in the second round. In July 2014, Aminata Toure was dismissed as prime minister after her party performed poorly in local elections.

The 2001 constitution was amended in 2007 to re-establish the senate as the upper chamber of a bicameral legislature, but this was abolished in 2012 by the National Assembly. The National Assembly has 150 members, directly elected for a five-year term; 90 are elected by majority in single member constituencies and 60 are elected by proportional representation. The president is directly elected for a seven-year term, renewable once; the president appoints the prime minister, who nominates the other ministers.

### HEAD OF STATE

*President,* Macky Sall, *elected* 18 March 2012, *sworn in* 2 April 2012

### SELECTED GOVERNMENT MEMBERS *as at June 2015*

*Prime Minister,* Mohammed Dionne
*Finance and Economy,* Amadou Ba
*Foreign Affairs,* Mankeur Ndiaye
*Interior,* Abdoulaye Daouda Diallo

### EMBASSY OF THE REPUBLIC OF SENEGAL

39 Marloes Road, London W8 6LA
T 020-7938 4048
*Ambassador Extraordinary and Plenipotentiary,* HE Abdou Sourang, *apptd* 2007

### BRITISH EMBASSY

PO Box 6025, 20 rue du Docteur Guillet, Dakar
T (+221) 823 7392 E dakar.consularenquiries@fco.gov.uk
W www.gov.uk/government/world/senegal
*Ambassador Extraordinary and Plenipotentiary,* HE George Hodgson, *apptd* 2015

## DEFENCE

| Aged 16–49, 2010 est | Males | Females |
| --- | --- | --- |
| Available for military service | 2,699,196 | 3,018,565 |
| Fit for military service | 1,788,493 | 2,133,370 |

*Military expenditure* – US$240m (2014)
*Conscription duration* – 24 months (selective)

## ECONOMY AND TRADE

Despite steady growth since the mid-1990s and the cancellation of two-thirds of its foreign debt in recent years, Senegal remains poor. The country is heavily dependent on foreign aid and remittances from expatriate workers, but infrastructure projects and the development of the textiles, information technology, telecommunications services and tourism industries are government priorities. The government has announced a set of economic policies known as the Emerging Senegal Plan (ESP), which aims to turn Senegal into an emerging economy by 2035.

Agriculture and fishing are the mainstays of the economy, engaging 77.5 per cent of the workforce and contributing 15.6 per cent of GDP. The main industries are food and fish processing, mining (phosphate, iron, zircon, gold), oil refining, the production of fertiliser and construction materials, ship construction and tourism. Industry accounts for 23.8 per cent of GDP and services for 60.6 per cent.

The main trading partners are France, Mali, Nigeria, China and India. The principal exports are fish, groundnuts, petroleum products, phosphates and cotton. Principal imports are food, beverages, capital goods and fuels.

*GNI* – US$14,819m; US$1,050 per capita (2013)
*Annual average growth of GDP* – 4.5 per cent (2014 est)
*Inflation rate* – −0.7 per cent (2014 est)
*Population below the poverty line* – 46.7 per cent (2011 est)
*Unemployment* – 9.8 per cent (2015 est)
*Total external debt* – US$5,747m (2014 est)
*Imports* – US$6,067m (2013)
*Exports* – US$2,440m (2013)

### BALANCE OF PAYMENTS

*Trade* – US$3,501m deficit (2012)
*Current Account* – US$1,143m deficit (2015 est)

| Trade with UK | 2013 | 2014 |
| --- | --- | --- |
| Imports from UK | £319,993,639 | £299,877,163 |
| Exports to UK | £27,840,390 | £32,290,586 |

## COMMUNICATIONS

*Airports and waterways* – Dakar is the main port and the location of the principal airport (there are nine airports in total); seaport facilities are being modernised and there are 1,000km of navigable waterways, mainly on the Senegal, Saloum and Casamance rivers
*Roadways and railways* – 4,099km; 906km
*Telecommunications* – 338,200 fixed lines and 11.47 million mobile subscriptions (2012); there were 1.82 million internet users in 2009
*Internet code and IDD* – sn; 221 (from UK), 44 (to UK)
*Major broadcasters* – State-run Radiodiffusion Television Senegalaise operates the only free television channels and the main national and regional radio networks

*Press* – Leading daily newspapers include the French-language *Le Quotidien, L'Observateur* and *Sud Quotidien*
*WPFI score* – 27,77 (71)

## EDUCATION AND HEALTH
*Literacy rate* – 73.1 per cent (2015)
*Gross enrolment ratio (percentage of relevant age group)* –
   primary 84 per cent (2014 est); secondary 41 per cent
   (2011 est); tertiary 8 per cent (2010 est)
*Health expenditure (per capita)* – US$46 (2013)
*Hospital beds (per 1,000 people)* – 0.3 (2009)
*Life expectancy (years)* – 60.95 (2014 est)
*Mortality rate* – 8.65 (2014 est)
*Birth rate* – 35.09 (2014 est)
*Infant mortality rate* – 52.72 (2014 est)

# SERBIA

*Republika Srbija – Republic of Serbia*

*Area* – 77,474 sq. km
*Capital* – Belgrade; population, 1,181,000 (2014)
*Major cities* – Kragujevac, Nis, Novi Sad
*Currency* – Serbian dinar of 100 paras
*Population* – 7,176,794 falling at 0.46 per year (2015 est);
   Serb (83.3 per cent), Hungarian (3.5 per cent), Romany
   (2.1 per cent), Bosniak (2 per cent) (2011 est)
*Religion* – Christian (Serbian Orthodox 84.6 per cent,
   Roman Catholic 5 per cent, Protestant 1 per cent,
   Muslim 3.1 per cent (2011 est)
*Language* – Serbian (official), Hungarian, Romanian, Slovak,
   Ukrainian, Croatian (all official in different regions),
   Bosnian, Romani
*Population density* – 82 per sq. km (2013)
*Urban population* – 57.1 per cent (2013 est)
*Median age (years)* – 41.9 (2014 est)
*National anthem* – 'Boze Pravde' ['God of Justice']
*National day* – 15 February (Constitution Day)
*Death penalty* – Abolished for all crimes (since 2002)
*CPI score* – 41 (78)
*Literacy rate* – 98.5 per cent (2015 est)
*Gross enrolment ratio (percentage of relevant age group)* –
   primary 96 per cent; secondary 91 per cent; tertiary
   49.1 per cent (2011 est)

*Health expenditure (per capita)* – US$475 (2013)
*Hospital beds (per 1,000 people)* – 5.4 (2009)
*Life expectancy (years)* – 75.02 (2014 est)
*Mortality rate* – 13.71 (2014 est)
*Birth rate* – 9.13 (2014 est)
*Infant mortality rate* – 6.16 (2014 est)

## CLIMATE AND TERRAIN
The landlocked country is mountainous in the south, while
the north is dominated by the low-lying plains of the
Danube and its major tributaries, the Sava, the Tisa and the
Morava. Its highest point is 2,169m (Midzor) and its lowest
is 35m (the confluence of the Danube and Timok rivers).
The climate is continental; average temperatures range from
−0.5°C in January to 21.5°C in July and August.

## POLITICS
Under the 2006 constitution, the president is directly elected
for a five-year term, renewable once. The unicameral National
Assembly has 250 members, directly elected for a four-year
term. The prime minister is appointed by the president.
   Boris Tadic, leader of the Democratic Party (DS), was
elected president in 2004 and re-elected in 2008 but lost the
2012 presidential election to Tomislav Nikolic, leader of
the Serbian Progressive Party (SNS). The SNS-led coalition
won a majority in the 2014 legislative election, but required
support from a bloc led by the Socialist Party of Serbia (SPS)
to govern.

HEAD OF STATE
*President,* Tomislav Nikolic, *elected* 20 May 2012, *took office*
   31 May 2012

SELECTED GOVERNMENT MEMBERS *as at June 2015*
*Prime Minister, Interior,* Aleksandar Vucic
*First Deputy Prime Minister, Foreign Affairs,* Ivica Dacic
*Finance and Economy,* Dusan Vujovic

EMBASSY OF THE REPUBLIC OF SERBIA
28 Belgrave Square, London SW1X 8QB
T 020-7235 9049 E london@serbianembassy.org.uk
W www.serbianembassy.org.uk
*Ambassador Extraordinary and Plenipotentiary,* HE Ognjen
   Pribicevic, *apptd* 2014

BRITISH EMBASSY
Resavska 46, 11000 Belgrade
T (+381) (11) 306 0900 E belgrade.PPD@fco.gov.uk
W www.gov.uk/government/world/serbia
*Ambassador Extraordinary and Plenipotentiary,* HE Denis
   Keefe, *apptd* 2014

## DEFENCE

| | Males | Females |
| --- | --- | --- |
| *Aged 16–49, 2010 est* | | |
| Available for military service | – | – |
| Fit for military service | 1,395,426 | 1,356,415 |

*Military expenditure* – US$950m (2014)
*Conscription* – abolished in 2010

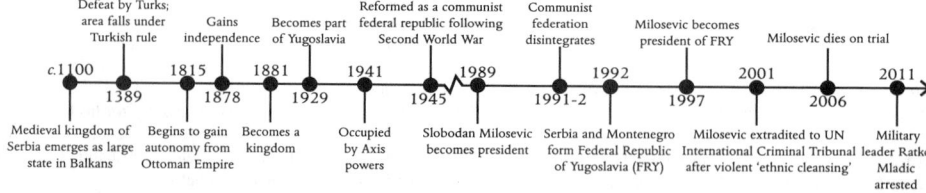

# ECONOMY AND TRADE

Economic mismanagement, UN sanctions in the 1990s along with damage to infrastructure and industry from NATO bombing in 1999 reduced the economy to about 50 per cent of its 1990 size by 1999. Since 2000, governments have pursued economic reforms and international reintegration, obtained international support for economic restructuring, rescheduled payments and received debt relief on much of its foreign debt. Progress has been intermittent, but most of the economy is now privatised.

Economic growth averaged 6 per cent until 2008 when it was severely affected by the global economic downturn. The government sought external fiscal support in 2008 and signed a standby agreement with the IMF in 2011–12 which was frozen after the country's 2012 budget deviated from the programme framework. Serbia gained EU candidate status in March 2012 and began accession negotiations in January 2014. After GDP contracted in 2014, the government accepted a €1.2bn (£85m) loan from the IMF in February 2015 after agreeing to implement a program of spending cuts. The economy is expected to contract in 2015.

Agriculture accounts for 8.2 per cent of GDP and employs 21.9 per cent of the workforce. The main agricultural products are wheat, maize, sugar beet, sunflowers, fruit, meat and milk. Industry includes food processing and production of base metals, furniture, machinery, chemicals, sugar, tyres, clothing and pharmaceuticals. Industry contributes 36.9 per cent of GDP and services 54.9 per cent.

The main trading partners are the EU, Russia and Bosnia and Hercegovina. Principal exports are iron and steel, rubber, clothing, wheat, fruit, vegetables and non-ferrous metals.

*GNI* – US$43,339m; US$6,050 per capita (2013)
*Annual average growth of GDP* – –0.5 per cent (2014 est)
*Inflation rate* – 2.3 per cent (2014 est)
*Population below poverty line* – 9.1 per cent (2013 est)
*Unemployment* – 27.7 per cent (2013 est)
*Total external debt* – US$28,630m (2014 est)
*Imports* – US$20,550m (2013)
*Exports* – US$14,610m (2013)

## BALANCE OF PAYMENTS
*Trade* – US$7,579m deficit (2012)
*Current Account* – US$1,926m deficit (2015 est)

| Trade with UK | 2013 | 2014 |
|---|---|---|
| Imports from UK | £136,587,458 | £120,967,481 |
| Exports to UK | £114,650,122 | £91,234,843 |

## COMMUNICATIONS

*Airports and waterways* – The main international airport is at Belgrade (there are ten airports in total); there are 587km of navigable waterways, and principal ports include Belgrade and Novi Sad on the Danube

*Roadways and railways* – 28,000km; 3,809km

*Telecommunications* – 2.977 million fixed lines and 9.14 million mobile subscriptions (2012); there were 4.11 million internet users in 2009

*Internet code and IDD* – rs; 381 (from UK), 44 (to UK)

*Major broadcasters* – Radio-Television Serbia (RTS) is the state-operated broadcaster

*Press* – National daily newspapers include *Blic*, *Danas* and *Politika*

*WPFI score* – 27,66 (67)

# SEYCHELLES

*République des Seychelles/Repiblik Sesel – Republic of Seychelles*

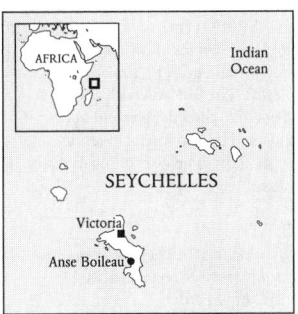

*Area* – 455 sq. km
*Capital* – Victoria, on Mahé; population, 26,000 (2014)
*Currency* – Seychelles rupee of 100 cents
*Population* – 92,430 rising at 0.83 per cent a year (2015 est)
*Religion* – Christian (Roman Catholic 76.2 per cent, Anglican 6.1 per cent), Hindu 2.4 per cent (2010 est)
*Language* – Seychellois Creole, English, French (all official)
*Population density* – 194 per sq. km (2013)
*Urban population* – 54.4 per cent (2013 est)
*Median age (years)* – 33.9 (2014 est)
*National anthem* – 'Koste Seselwa' ['Seychellois Unite']
*National day* – 18 June (Constitution Day)
*Death penalty* – Abolished for all crimes (since 1993)
*CPI score* – 55 (43)
*Literacy rate* – 99.1 per cent (2012 est)
*Gross enrolment ratio (percentage of relevant age group)* – primary 111 per cent; secondary 72 per cent; tertiary 3 per cent (2013 est)
*Life expectancy (years)* – 74.25 (2014 est)
*Mortality rate* – 6.90 (2014 est)
*Birth rate* – 14.54 (2014 est)
*Infant mortality rate* – 10.77 (2014 est)

## CLIMATE AND TERRAIN

Seychelles consists of 115 islands spread over 643,737 sq. km of the south-west Indian Ocean, north of Madagascar. There is a relatively compact granitic group of 32 islands, with high hills and mountains, of which Mahé is the largest and most populated (about 90 per cent of the population lives on Mahé), and an outlying coralline group, for the most part only slightly above sea-level. Elevation extremes range from 905m (Morne Seychellois) to 0m (Indian Ocean). The climate is tropical, with an average temperature of 27.3°C, and a wet season from November to March.

## HISTORY AND POLITICS

The uninhabited islands were proclaimed French territory in 1756, but settlement of the Mahé group began only in 1770. The group was a dependency of Mauritius, and was ceded to Britain with Mauritius in 1814. In 1903 these islands, together with the coralline group, were formed into a colony separate from Mauritius. On 29 June 1976, the islands became an independent republic.

Following a coup d'état in 1977, when France-Albert René became president, Seychelles became a one-party state ruled by the Seychelles People's Progressive Front (SPPF) in 1979. Opposition parties were permitted from 1991 and in 1993 President René reintroduced a multiparty constitution. Power has remained with the SPPF under the pluralist system, although opposition parties are beginning to achieve a greater share of the vote.

President René stepped down mid-term in 2004 and the rest of his term was served by the vice-president, James Michel, who was elected president in 2006 and re-elected in May 2011. In the 2011 legislative election, the People's Party (formerly SPPF) retained its overall majority.

Under the 1993 constitution, the executive president is directly elected for a five-year term, with a maximum of three consecutive terms. The unicameral National Assembly has up to 34 members: 25 directly elected by constituencies and up to nine allocated by proportional representation; members serve a five-year term. The council of ministers is appointed by the president.

HEAD OF STATE
*President, Defence,* James Michel, *assumed office* 14 April 2004, *elected* July 2006, *re-elected* 2011
*Vice-President,* Danny Faure

SELECTED GOVERNMENT MEMBERS *as at June 2015*
*Foreign Affairs,* Joel Morgan
*Internal Affairs,* Charles Bastienne

THE HIGH COMMISSION OF THE REPUBLIC OF SEYCHELLES
4th Floor, 132 Buckingham Palace Road, London SW1W 9SA
**T** 020-7730 2046 **E** seyhc.london@btconnect.com
*High Commissioner,* HE Marie-Pierre Lloyd, *apptd* 2012

BRITISH HIGH COMMISSION
PO Box 161, Oliaji Trade Centre, Victoria, Mahé
**T** (+248) 283 666 **E** bhcvictoria@fco.gov.uk
**W** www.gov.uk/government/world/seychelles
*High Commissioner,* HE Lindsay Skoll, *apptd* 2012

## DEFENCE

| Aged 16–49, 2010 est | Males | Females |
| --- | --- | --- |
| Available for military service | 26,257 | 23,996 |
| Fit for military service | 20,231 | 19,891 |

*Military expenditure* – US$15.1m (2013)

## ECONOMY AND TRADE
Seychelles prospered after independence owing to the development of tuna fishing and tourism, which employs about 30 per cent of the workforce and provides over 70 per cent of hard currency earnings. The economy struggled in 2008–9 owing to external debt, high deficits, food and oil price rises and the global recession, but recovered in 2010–11. By 2013 the IMF declared that Seychelles had a successful market-based economy with full employment and a fiscal surplus. Expansion in the tourism and financial service sectors is predicted to allow the economy to grow by just under 4 per cent during 2015–16.

Agriculture, small-scale manufacturing and offshore financial services are being developed to diversify the economy. Apart from fishing and tourism, the main industries involve processing fish, coconuts and vanilla, producing coir rope, furniture and beverages, boat-building and printing.

The main trading partners are EU countries, Saudi Arabia and Japan. The principal exports are canned tuna, frozen fish, cinnamon bark, copra and re-exports of petroleum products. The principal imports are machinery and equipment, foodstuffs, petroleum products and chemicals.
*GNI* – US$1,178m; US$13,210 per capita (2013)
*Annual average growth of GDP* – 3.7 per cent (2014 est)
*Inflation rate* – 2.3 per cent (2014 est)
*Unemployment* – 2 per cent (2006 est)
*Total external debt* – US$2,099m (2014 est)

*Imports* – US$930m (2013)
*Exports* – US$577m (2013)

BALANCE OF PAYMENTS
*Trade* – US$303m deficit (2012)
*Current Account* – US$266m deficit (2015 est)

| Trade with UK | 2013 | 2014 |
| --- | --- | --- |
| Imports from UK | £19,609,976 | £23,941,531 |
| Exports to UK | £74,458,419 | £65,608,596 |

## COMMUNICATIONS
*Airports and waterways* – The principal airport is at Mahé (there are seven airports in total); the main port is Victoria, and ferries run regularly between Mahé, Praslin and La Digue
*Roadways* – There are 490km of surfaced roads
*Telecommunications* – 28,900 fixed lines and 138,300 mobile subscriptions (2012); there were 32,000 internet users in 2008
*Media* – The state-run Seychelles Broadcasting Corporation operates various channels across the country; daily newspapers include *The Rising Sun* and the government-owned *Seychelles Nation*
*WPFI score* – 31,55 (96)

# SIERRA LEONE

*Republic of Sierra Leone*

*Area* – 71,740 sq. km
*Capital* – Freetown; population, 986,000 (2014)
*Major towns* – Bo, Kenema
*Currency* – Leone (Le) of 100 cents
*Population* – 5,879,098 rising at 2.35 per cent a year (2015 est); 20 ethnic groups, of which the largest are the Temne (35 per cent), Mende (31 per cent), Limba (8 per cent) and Kono (5 per cent) (2008)
*Religion* – Muslim 60 per cent, Christian 10 per cent, indigenous 30 per cent (est)
*Language* – English (official), Krio (Creole; lingua franca), Mende (in the south), Temne (in the north)
*Population density* – 84 per sq. km (2013)
*Urban population* – 40 per cent (2013 est)
*Median age (years)* – 19 (2014 est)
*National anthem* – 'High We Exalt Thee, Realm of the Free'
*National day* – 27 April (Independence Day)
*Death penalty* – Retained (last used 1998)
*CPI score* – 31 (119)

## CLIMATE AND TERRAIN
The land rises from mangrove swamps along the coast, to low-lying wooded country, and then to a mountainous plateau in the east. Elevation extremes range from 1,948m (Loma Mansa) to 0m (Atlantic Ocean). The climate is tropical, with a rainy season from May to November; rainfall

peaks in July and August, and is particularly heavy on the coast. The average temperature is 26.4°C.

## HISTORY AND POLITICS

In 1787 British philanthropists and abolitionists established a settlement for repatriated former slaves from Britain and its colonies on the Freetown peninsula. In 1808 the settlement was declared a crown colony and became the main base in west Africa for enforcing the 1807 Act outlawing the slave trade. In 1896 a protectorate was declared over the hinterland. The Freetown colony and the protectorate were united in 1951, and in 1961 Sierra Leone became independent.

The country became a republic in 1971 and a one-party state in 1978. Transition to a multiparty democracy began in 1991 but was aborted by a military coup in 1992. Civilian rule was restored with the 1996 elections. Another coup in May 1997 was short-lived, and the government was reinstated in March 1998 with the assistance of Economic Community of West African States (ECOWAS) troops.

The transition to multiparty and civilian rule was complicated by the civil war with the Revolutionary United Front (RUF), which began in 1991. Fighting continued until 2001, when a lasting ceasefire was agreed, and the war was declared over in 2002. An estimated 50,000 people were killed, 30,000 mutilated and a third of the population displaced between 1991 and 2002. A truth and reconciliation commission and a UN-supported war crimes tribunal were set up in 2002.

The 2012 presidential election was won by the incumbent, Ernest Bai Koroma, of the All People's Congress (APC). The APC won a majority of seats in the simultaneous legislative election, defeating the Sierra Leone People's Party.

Under the 1991 constitution, the executive president is directly elected for a five-year term, renewable once. The unicameral parliament has 124 members: 112 directly elected for a five-year term and 12 indirectly elected to represent the 12 provincial districts. The president, who is responsible to the legislature, appoints and chairs the cabinet.

HEAD OF STATE
*President,* Ernest Bai Koroma, *elected* 18 September 2007, re-elected 17 November 2012
*Vice-President,* Victor Foh

SELECTED GOVERNMENT MEMBERS *as at June 2015*
*Finance,* Kaifala Marah
*Foreign Affairs,* Samura Kamara
*Internal Affairs,* Joseph Dauda

SIERRA LEONE HIGH COMMISSION
41 Eagle Street, London WC1R 4TL
T 020-7404 0140 E info@slhc-uk.org.uk W www.slhc-uk.org.uk
*High Commissioner,* HE Edward Turay, *apptd* 2010

BRITISH HIGH COMMISSION
6 Spur Road, Freetown
T (+232) (0) 76 541 386 E freetown.general.enquiries@fco.gov.uk
W www.gov.uk/government/world/sierra-leone
*High Commissioner,* HE Peter West, *apptd* 2013

## DEFENCE

| Aged 16–49, 2010 est | Males | Females |
| --- | --- | --- |
| Available for military service | 1,183,093 | – |
| Fit for military service | 731,898 | 838,032 |

*Military expenditure* – US$39m (2014)

## ECONOMY AND TRADE

The country was devastated by a decade of civil war, and unemployment increased with the demobilisation of former combatants. Economic activity has grown since the end of the war but the country remains extremely poor, dependent on foreign aid and expatriates' remittances. It benefited from having around 90 per cent of its foreign debt written off in 2006.

There are significant mineral deposits and agricultural and fishery resources, although the lack of infrastructure hampers development. Diamonds account for about half of export earnings, but 42.5 per cent of GDP is generated by agriculture, much of which is at subsistence level. Industry consists mainly of mining (diamonds, rutile, bauxite), processing agricultural products, light manufacturing for the domestic market, oil refining and ship repair. Economic output was severely effected by the Ebola outbreak and the economy is expected to contract by 5 per cent in 2015.

The main export market is China (78.5 per cent), followed by Belgium; the chief import suppliers are China, India and South Africa. Principal exports are diamonds, rutile, cocoa, coffee and fish. The main imports are foodstuffs, machinery and equipment, fuels and lubricants, and chemicals.
*GNI* – US$4,050m; US$660 per capita (2013)
*Annual average growth of GDP* – 8 per cent (2014 est)
*Inflation rate* – 8.3 per cent (2014 est)
*Population below poverty line* – 52.9 per cent (2011)
*Unemployment* – 2.9 per cent (2015 est)
*Total external debt* – US$1,460m (2014 est)
*Imports* – US$1,780m (2013)
*Exports* – US$1,893m (2013)

BALANCE OF PAYMENTS
*Trade* – US$300m deficit (2010)
*Current Account* – US$582m deficit (2015 est)

| Trade with UK | 2013 | 2014 |
| --- | --- | --- |
| Imports from UK | £72,463,101 | £55,501,175 |
| Exports to UK | £13,595,671 | £7,333,867 |

## COMMUNICATIONS

*Airports and waterways* – There is an international airport at Freetown; Freetown, which has one of the world's largest natural harbours, is the main port and there are smaller ports at Pepel and Sherbro
*Roadways* – 904km are surfaced
*Telecommunications* – 18,000 fixed lines (2010) and 2.21 million mobile subscriptions (2012); there were 14,900 internet users in 2009
*Internet code and IDD* – sl; 232 (from UK), 44 (to UK)
*Media* – The Sierra Leone Broadcasting Corporation was formed in 2010 and is the country's principal TV and radio broadcaster; newspapers include *Awoko* and the *Standard Times*
*WPFI score* – 28,47 (79)

## EDUCATION AND HEALTH

The public University of Sierra Leone incorporates several campuses in Freetown, and Njala University was established in Bo in 2005; there are a number of other technical and teacher-training institutes throughout the country.
*Literacy rate* – 67.6 per cent (2015 est)
*Gross enrolment ratio (percentage of relevant age group)* – primary 134 per cent; secondary 45 per cent (2013 est)
*Health expenditure (per capita)* – US$96 (2013 est)
*Hospital beds (per 1,000 people)* – 0.4 (2006)
*Life expectancy (years)* – 57.39 (2014 est)
*Mortality rate* – 11.03 (2014 est)
*Birth rate* – 37.4 (2014 est)
*Infant mortality rate* – 73.29 (2014 est)
*HIV/AIDS adult prevalence* – 1.55 per cent (2013 est)

# SINGAPORE

*Xinjiapo    Gongheguo / Republik    Singapura / Cinkappur*
*Kutiyaracu* – Republic of Singapore

*Area* – 697 sq. km
*Capital* – Singapore; population, 5,517,000 (2014)
*Currency* – Singapore dollar (S$) of 100 cents
*Population* – 5,674,472 rising at 1.89 per cent a year
   (2015 est); Chinese (74.2 per cent), Malay (13.3 per cent),
   Indian (9.2 per cent) (2013 est)
*Religion* – Buddhist 33.9 per cent, Muslim 14.3 per cent,
   Taoist 11.3 per cent, Christian (Roman Catholic
   7.1 per cent, other Christian 11 per cent) (2010 est)
*Language* – Mandarin, English, Malay, Tamil (all official),
   Hokkien, Cantonese, Teochew
*Population density* – 7,713 per sq. km (2013)
*Urban population* – 100 per cent (2013 est)
*Median age (years)* – 33.8 (2014 est)
*National anthem* – 'Majulah Singapura' ['Onward, Singapore']
*National day* – 9 August (Independence Day)
*Death penalty* – Retained
*CPI score* – 84 (7)
*Literacy rate* – 99.8 per cent (2015)
*Health expenditure (per capita)* – US$2,507 (2013)
*Hospital beds (per 1,000 people)* – 2 (2011)
*Life expectancy (years)* – 84.38 (2014 est)
*Mortality rate* – 3.42 (2014 est)
*Birth rate* – 8.1 (2014 est)
*Infant mortality rate* – 2.53 (2014 est)

## CLIMATE AND TERRAIN

Singapore consists of the island of Singapore and 63 islets
situated off the southern extremity of the Malay peninsula,
from which it is separated by the Straits of Johor. The land
rises from the shore to a low, undulating central plateau.
Elevation extremes range from 166m (Bukit Timah) to 0m
(Singapore Strait). The state is just north of the Equator
and the climate is tropical, subject to monsoons in June to
September and December to March. The average temperature
is 27.6°C, and there is frequent rain and high humidity.

## HISTORY AND POLITICS

Singapore, a trading site since the 13th century, was
established as a British trading post by Sir Stamford Raffles in
1819 and was ceded to Britain in perpetuity in 1824. In 1826
it was incorporated with Penang and Malacca to form the
Straits Settlements and they became a crown colony in 1867.
Singapore became the commercial and financial hub of South
East Asia in the 19th century, and the principal British military
base in the Far East in the 1920s. In 1942, during the Second
World War, it fell to Japanese forces. Liberated in 1945, it
became a separate colony in 1946, and internal self-
government was introduced in 1959. It became part of the
Federation of Malaysia in 1963, before withdrawing to
become an independent sovereign state in 1965.

Although Singapore is a multiparty state, the People's
Action Party (PAP) has dominated politics since 1959;
opposition candidates were elected to parliament for the first
time in 1981.

Independent candidate Tony Tan was elected president in
August 2011, replacing PAP's Sellapan Rama Nathan. In the
2015 general election, PAP retained its large majority with
83 seats, but opposition parties won an unprecedented nine
seats. Lee Hsien Loong, the son of Lee Kuan Yew, continued
in office as prime minister, a post he has held since 2004.

The 1959 constitution was amended in 1965 to end the
affiliation with Malaysia and make Singapore a republic, and
in 1991 to make the presidency directly elected. The
president is directly elected for a six-year term, which is
renewable. The president appoints the prime minister and, on
his advice, the members of the cabinet. There is a unicameral
parliament with 87 directly elected members and up to nine
extra members from opposition parties (NCMPs) (currently
three), depending on their share of the vote; all members
serve a five-year term. Up to nine members can also be
nominated by the government for a two-year term (NMPs) to
bring the opposition numbers up to 18.

HEAD OF STATE
*President,* Tony Tan, *took office* 1 September 2011

SELECTED GOVERNMENT MEMBERS *as at*
*September 2015*
*Prime Minister,* Lee Hsien Loong
*Deputy Prime Minister,* Rear-Adm. Teo Chee Hean (*Home
   Affairs* ); Tharman Shanmugaratnam (*Finance*)
*Foreign Affairs,* Kasiviswanathan Shanmugam
*Finance,* Tharman Shanmugaratnam

HIGH COMMISSION FOR THE REPUBLIC OF
SINGAPORE
9 Wilton Crescent, London SW1X 8SP
**T** 020-7235 8315 **E** singhc_lon@sgmfa.gov.sg
**W** www.mfa.gov.sg/london
*High Commissioner,* HE Foo Chi Hsia, *apptd* 2014

BRITISH HIGH COMMISSION
100 Tanglin Road, Singapore 247919
**T** (+65) 6424 4200 **E** consular.singapore@fco.gov.uk
**W** www.gov.uk/government/world/organisations/british-high-
commission-singapore
*High Commissioner,* HE Scott Wightman, *apptd* 2015

## DEFENCE

| *Aged 16–49, 2010 est* | *Males* | *Females* |
| --- | --- | --- |
| Available for military service | 1,255,902 | – |
| Fit for military service | 1,018,839 | 1,087,134 |

*Military expenditure* – US$9,841m (2014)
*Conscription duration* – 24 months

## ECONOMY AND TRADE

Historically based on trade in raw materials from
surrounding countries and on trade in finished products, the
economy industrialised rapidly after independence and
diversified, becoming a regional financial and technology
centre and a tourist destination. Economic growth has rarely
flagged since 1965; although the global economic downturn
pushed the economy into recession in 2008, it recovered
strongly in 2010, before slowing to 1.9 per cent in 2012 and
4.1 per cent in 2013. Economic growth is expected to average
2.9 per cent in 2015 and 2016. Singapore was scheduled to
form a common market with the other members of the
Association of Southeast Asian Nations (ASEAN) in 2015.

Agriculture is limited and contributes little to GDP. Industries include manufacturing (especially consumer electronics, information technology products, biomedical sciences, pharmaceuticals and chemicals), engineering, oil refining, rubber processing, food processing and ship repair; industry contributes 25.3 per cent of GDP. The service sector (financial and business services, entrepôt trade, tourism) accounts for 74.7 per cent of GDP and employs 83.9 per cent of the workforce.

The main trading partners are Malaysia, China, Hong Kong, the USA and Indonesia. Principal exports are machinery and equipment (especially electronic), consumer goods, pharmaceuticals and other chemicals and mineral fuels. The main imports are machinery and equipment, mineral fuels, chemicals, food and consumer goods.

*GNI* – US$291,788m; US$54,040 per capita (2013)
*Annual average growth of GDP* – 3 per cent (2014 est)
*Inflation rate* – 1.5 per cent (2014 est)
*Unemployment* – 3.4 per cent (2015 est)
*Total external debt* – US$28,930m (2014 est)
*Imports* – US$373,016m (2013)
*Exports* – US$410,250m (2013)

BALANCE OF PAYMENTS
*Trade* – US$28,670m surplus (2012)
*Current Account* – US$61,172m surplus (2015 est)

| Trade with UK | 2013 | 2014 |
|---|---|---|
| Imports from UK | £4,261,564,528 | £3,793,023,554 |
| Exports to UK | £2,650,724,350 | £2,460,949,857 |

## COMMUNICATIONS

*Airports and waterways* – Singapore is one of the busiest seaports in the world, although there is a high risk of piracy in the South China Sea; it has a large merchant fleet of 1,599 ships of over 1,000 tonnes, with 344 registered in other countries, while 966 foreign-owned ships are registered in Singapore. There is one international airport, at Changi
*Roadways and railways* – There are 3,425km of roadways and an extensive light rail system on the island
*Telecommunications* – 1.99 million fixed lines and 8.06 million mobile subscriptions (2012); there were 3.24 million internet users in 2009
*Internet code and IDD* – sg; 65 (from UK), 1/2/8 44 (to UK)
*Major broadcasters* – TV and radio broadcasting is dominated by MediaCorp, owned by a state investment agency
*Press* – Singapore Press Holdings, which has close links to the ruling party, has a virtual monopoly on the newspaper industry and publishes 15 newspapers
*WPFI score* – 45,87 (153)

# SLOVAKIA

*Slovenska republika – Slovak Republic*

*Area* – 49,035 sq. km
*Capital* – Bratislava; population, 403,000 (2014)
*Major city* – Kosice
*Currency* – Euro (€) of 100 cents
*Population* – 5,445,027 rising at 0.02 per cent a year (2015 est); Slovak (80.7 per cent), Hungarian (8.5 per cent), Roma (2 per cent) (2011 est)
*Religion* – Christian (Roman Catholic 62 per cent, Protestant 8.2 per cent), none 13.4 (2011 est)
*Language* – Slovak (official), Hungarian, Roma, Ukrainian
*Population density* – 113 per sq. km (2013)
*Urban population* – 54.6 per cent (2013 est)
*Median age (years)* – 39.2 (2014 est)
*National anthem* – 'Nad Tatrou sa blýska' ['Lightning Over the Tatras']
*National day* – 1 September (Constitution Day)
*Death penalty* – Abolished for all crimes (since 1990)
*CPI score* – 50 (54)
*Literacy rate* – 99.45 per cent (2015)
*Gross enrolment ratio (percentage of relevant age group)* – primary 102 per cent; secondary 89 per cent; tertiary 54.2 per cent (2011 est)
*Health expenditure (per capita)* – US$1,454 (2013)
*Hospital beds (per 1,000 people)* – 6 (2011)
*Life expectancy (years)* – 76.69 (2014 est)
*Mortality rate* – 9.70 (2014 est)
*Birth rate* – 10.01 (2014 est)
*Infant mortality rate* – 5.35 (2014 est)

## CLIMATE AND TERRAIN

Slovakia is landlocked and mountainous, lying in the western Carpathian range which includes the Tatra and Beskid mountains to the north. The mountains fall to plains in the south-east and south-west; the latter is the plain of the river Danube and its tributary the Vah, which rises in the Tatras. Elevation extremes range from 2,655m (Gerlachovsky stit) to 94m (Bodrog river). The climate is temperate, with warm humid summers and cold dry winters. Average temperatures range from −2.4°C in January to 18.5°C in July.

## POLITICS

The 1993 constitution has been amended several times, most recently in 1999 to allow direct elections to the presidency. The president is directly elected for a five-year term, renewable once. The unicameral National Council has 150 members, who are directly elected for a four-year term by proportional representation. The prime minister, who is appointed by the president, nominates the cabinet.

The 2014 presidential election was won by Andrej Kiska. Direction-Social Democracy (Smer-SD) remained the largest party after the 2010 legislative election, but four centre-right parties held a majority of seats and formed a coalition government. Smer-SD won the 2012 legislative election, gaining an overall majority and forming a government under Robert Fico.

HEAD OF STATE
*President,* Andrej Kiska, *elected* 29 March 2014

SELECTED GOVERNMENT MEMBERS *as at June 2015*
*Prime Minister,* Robert Fico
*Defence,* Martin Glvac
*Foreign Affairs,* Miroslav Lajcak
*Interior,* Robert Kalinak

EMBASSY OF THE SLOVAK REPUBLIC
25 Kensington Palace Gardens, London W8 4QY
T 020-7313 6470 E emb.london@mzv.sk W www.mzv.sk/londyn
*Ambassador Extraordinary and Plenipotentiary,* Miroslav Wlachovsky, *apptd* 2011

Becomes part of
the Magyar
kingdom

Forms part of Czechoslovakia
after dissolution of
Austro-Hungarian Empire

Liberated by Soviet forces;
communist government takes
control

Czech and Slovak
republics gain
independence

Joins the
eurozone

*c.*800        *c.*1500        1938-9        1989        2004

*c.*900        1918        1945        1992-3        2009

Part of the kingdom
of Greater Moravia

Falls under Austrian
Habsburg rule

German annexation of
Czechoslovakia; Slovakia
becomes fascist state

Fall of communist
regime, Slovak
separatism gains ground

Joins NATO
and the EU

## BRITISH EMBASSY

Panska 16, Bratislava 811 01

T (+421) (2) 5998 2000 E bebra@internet.sk

W www.gov.uk/government/world/slovakia

*Ambassador Extraordinary and Plenipotentiary,* HE Andrew Gale, *apptd* 2014

## DEFENCE

| Aged 16–49, 2010 est | Males | Females |
|---|---|---|
| Available for military service | 1,405,310 | 1,369,897 |
| Fit for military service | 1,156,113 | 1,139,380 |

*Military expenditure* – US$988m (2014)

*Conscription* – suspended for peacetime in 2006

## ECONOMY AND TRADE

Slovakia has nearly completed the transition from a centrally planned to a free-market economy, following structural reforms and privatisation begun after 1998. As a result, foreign investment has risen, especially in the vehicle and electronics industries, and GDP grew steadily in 2000–8. The economy contracted in 2009 because of the global economic downturn, recovering in 2010. In 2012 a number of pro-growth economic reforms were scaled back to shore up government finances. The economy has been affected by the EU economic sanctions enacted against Russia which has seen Russian gas imports fall by 50 per cent since 2014. Economic growth of just under 3 per cent is expected in 2015.

Natural resources include brown coal and lignite, natural gas, oil, iron ore, copper and manganese. Major industries include production of metal and metal products, food and beverages, fuel and energy (electricity, gas, coke, oil and nuclear), chemicals and synthetic fibres, machinery, paper and printing, ceramics, transport vehicles, textiles and electrical and optical equipment. Industry accounts for 35.7 per cent of GDP, services 61.3 per cent and agriculture 2.9 per cent.

The main trading partners are other EU countries (especially Germany and the Czech Republic) and Russia. Principal exports are machinery and electrical equipment, vehicles, base metals, chemicals, minerals and plastics. The main imports are machinery and transport equipment, mineral products, vehicles, base metals, chemicals and plastics.

*GNI* – US$96,417m; US$17,810 per capita (2013)

*Annual average growth of GDP* – 2.4 per cent (2014 est)

*Inflation rate* – 0.3 per cent (2014 est)

*Population below the poverty line* – 20.5 per cent (2012 est)

*Unemployment* – 14.7 per cent (2015 est)

*Total external debt* – US$114,000m (2013 est)

*Imports* – US$83,637m (2013)

*Exports* – US$85,244m (2013)

## BALANCE OF PAYMENTS

*Trade* – US$805m surplus (2012)

*Current Account* – US$357m surplus (2015 est)

| Trade with UK | 2013 | 2014 |
|---|---|---|
| Imports from UK | £464,333,425 | £460,010,446 |
| Exports to UK | £1,808,298,067 | £1,916,672,491 |

## COMMUNICATIONS

*Airports and waterways* – The principal airport is at Bratislava and the main Danube ports are Bratislava and Komarno

*Roadways and railways* – 38,238km of surfaced roadways, including 417km of motorways; 3,622km of railways

*Telecommunications* – 975,000 fixed lines and 6.1 million mobile subscriptions (2012); there were 4.06 million internet users in 2009

*Internet code and IDD* – sk; 421 (from UK), 44 (to UK)

*Major broadcasters* – The public broadcasters Slovak TV and Slovak Radio operate national networks in competition with private companies

*Press* – The major daily newspapers, including *Pravda*, *Sme* and *Novy Cas*, are all privately owned

*WPFI score* – 11,66 (14)

# SLOVENIA

*Republika Slovenija – Republic of Slovenia*

*Area* – 20,273 sq. km

*Capital* – Ljubljana; population, 279,000 (2014)

*Major city* – Maribor

*Currency* – Euro (€) of 100 cents

*Population* – 1,983,412 falling at 0.26 per cent a year (2015 est); Slovene (83.1 per cent), Serb (2 per cent), Croat (1.8 per cent), Bosniak (1.1 per cent) (2002)

*Religion* – Christian (Roman Catholic 57.8 per cent, Orthodox 2.3 per cent), Muslim 2.4 per cent (2002)

*Language* – Slovene (official), Serbo-Croat; Hungarian and Italian are also official in designated municipalities

*Population density* – 102 per sq. km (2013)

*Urban population* – 49.8 per cent (2013)

*Median age (years)* – 43.5 (2014 est)

*National anthem* – 'Zdravljica' ['A Toast']

*National day* – 25 June (Statehood Day)

*Death penalty* – Abolished for all crimes (since 1989)

*CPI score* – 58 (39)

## CLIMATE AND TERRAIN

The Alps cover 42 per cent of the country, towards the north, and the south lies on the high Karst plateau. The only low-lying areas are the Pannonian plain in the east and north-east, and the short (47km) narrow coastal belt on the Adriatic Sea. Elevation extremes range from 2,864m

(Triglav) to 0m (Adriatic Sea). The climate is continental in most of the country but Mediterranean on the coast. Average temperatures range from 0.3°C in January to 19.7°C in July.

## POLITICS

Under the 1991 constitution, the president is directly elected for a five-year term. The unicameral National Assembly has 90 members directly elected for a four-year term. The National Council, which has 40 members indirectly elected for a five-year term, has an advisory role. The prime minister, who is nominated by the president and elected by the legislature, appoints the cabinet.

The November 2012 presidential election was won by Borut Pahor of the Social Democrats (SD), defeating the incumbent, Danilo Turk. The centre-left party of Miro Cerar (SMC) became the largest party after the 2014 legislative elections, and formed a governing coalition with the centre-left DeSUS and Social Democrat parties.

### HEAD OF STATE

*President,* Borut Pahor, *elected* 2 December 2012; *sworn in* 22 December 2012

SELECTED GOVERNMENT MEMBERS *as at June 2015*
*Prime Minister,* Miro Cerar
*Defence,* Andreja Katic
*Foreign Affairs,* Karl Erjavec

### EMBASSY OF THE REPUBLIC OF SLOVENIA

10 Little College Street, London SW1P 3SH
T 020-7222 5700 E vlo@gov.si W http://london.embassy.si
*Ambassador Extraordinary and Plenipotentiary,* HE Tadej Rupel, *apptd* 2014

### BRITISH EMBASSY

4th Floor, Trg Republike 3, 1000 Ljubljana
T (+386) (1) 200 3910 E info@british-embassy.si
W www.gov.uk/government/world/slovenia
*Ambassador Extraordinary and Plenipotentiary,* HE Sophie Honey, *apptd* 2013

### DEFENCE

| Aged 16–49, 2010 est | Males | Females |
| --- | --- | --- |
| Available for military service | 477,592 | 464,301 |
| Fit for military service | 392,075 | 380,077 |

*Military expenditure –* US$490m (2014)

### ECONOMY AND TRADE

Always the most prosperous republic of the former Yugoslavia, Slovenia's transition to a market economy was smoothed by good infrastructure and a well-educated workforce. Much of the economy remains in state ownership and taxes are high, deterring foreign investment and inhibiting its international competitiveness. The economy contracted sharply in 2009 owing to the global downturn and again experienced recession in 2012 and 2013. The European Commission has asked the country to reduce its budget deficit to 3 per cent by 2015 and the government is expected to pursue a privatisation programme. Growth of just over 2 per cent is expected in 2015.

Industry contributes 28.4 per cent of GDP, the service sector 69.5 per cent and agriculture 2.1 per cent. The main agricultural products are potatoes, hops, wheat, sugar beet, maize, grapes and livestock. Industries include mining and mineral processing (iron ore, aluminium, lead, zinc), electronics (including for military purposes), vehicles, electric power equipment, wood products, textiles, chemicals and machine tools.

The main trading partners are other EU countries (particularly Germany and Italy) and Austria. Principal exports are manufactured goods, machinery and transport equipment, chemicals and food. These items, along with fuels and lubricants, are also the main imports.

*GNI –* US$47,825m; US$23,210 per capita (2013)
*Annual average growth of GDP –* 1.4 per cent (2014 est)
*Inflation rate –* 0.5 per cent (2014 est)
*Population below the poverty line –* 13.5 per cent (2012 est)
*Unemployment –* 11.1 per cent (2015 est)
*Total external debt –* US$52,530m (2013 est)
*Imports –* US$29,380m (2013)
*Exports –* US$28,629m (2013)

BALANCE OF PAYMENTS
*Trade –* US$1,312m deficit (2012)
*Current Account –* US$3,033m surplus (2015 est)

| Trade with UK | 2013 | 2014 |
| --- | --- | --- |
| Imports from UK | £202,215,633 | £241,905,384 |
| Exports to UK | £319,630,490 | £313,049,932 |

### COMMUNICATIONS

*Airports and waterways –* The international airports are at Ljubljana, Maribor and Portoroz; Koper is the main port
*Roadways and railways –* 38,985km; 1,228km
*Telecommunications –* 825,000 fixed lines and 2.25 million mobile subscriptions (2012); there were 1.30 million internet users in 2009
*Internet code and IDD –* si; 386 (from UK), 44 (to UK)
*Media –* The public broadcaster RTV Slovenia operates TV and radio stations; daily newspapers include *Delo, Dnevnik* and *Slovenske Novice*
*WPFI score –* 20,55 (35)

### EDUCATION AND HEALTH

Education is free and compulsory between the ages of six and 15.

*Literacy rate –* 99.9 per cent (2015)
*Gross enrolment ratio (percentage of relevant age group) –* primary 99 per cent; secondary 98 per cent (2012 est); tertiary 84 per cent (2013 est)
*Health expenditure (per capita) –* US$2,085 (2013)
*Hospital beds (per 1,000 people) –* 4.6 (2011)
*Life expectancy (years) –* 77.83 (2014 est)
*Mortality rate –* 11.25 (2014 est)
*Birth rate –* 8.54 (2014 est)
*Infant mortality rate –* 4.04 (2014 est)

# SOLOMON ISLANDS

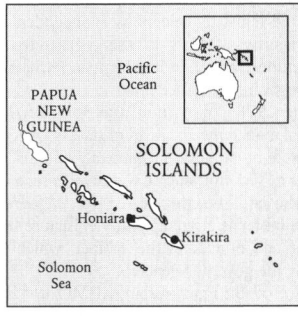

*Area –* 28,896 sq. km
*Capital –* Honiara, on Guadalcanal; population, 73,000 (2014)

*Currency* – Solomon Islands dollar (SI$) of 100 cents
*Population* – 622,469 rising at 2.02 per cent a year
(2015 est); Melanesian (95.3 per cent), Polynesian
(3.1 per cent), Micronesian (1.2 per cent) (2009 est)
*Religion* – Christian (Church of Melanesia 31.9 per cent,
Roman Catholic 19.6 per cent, Evangelical 17.1 per cent,
Seventh-day Adventist 11.7 per cent) (2009 est)
*Language* – English (official), Melanesian Pidgin (lingua
franca); around 120 indigenous languages exist
*Population density* – 20 per sq. km (2013)
*Urban population* – 21.4 per cent (2013)
*Median age (years)* – 21.6 (2014 est)
*National anthem* – 'God Save Our Solomon Islands'
*National day* – 7 July (Independence Day)
*Death penalty* – Abolished for all crimes (since 1966)
*Life expectancy (years)* – 74.89 (2014 est)
*Mortality rate* – 3.86 (2014 est)
*Birth rate* – 26.33 (2014 est)
*Infant mortality rate* – 16.17 (2014 est)

## CLIMATE AND TERRAIN

Forming a scattered archipelago of mountainous islands and
low-lying coral atolls in the south-west Pacific Ocean, the
Solomon Islands stretch about 1,448km in a south-easterly
direction from the Shortland Islands to the Santa Cruz islands.
The six biggest islands are Choiseul, New Georgia, Santa
Isabel, Guadalcanal, Malaita and Makira (San Cristobal). They
are characterised by thickly forested mountain ranges
intersected by deep, narrow valleys. Elevation extremes range
from 2,310m (Mt Popomanaseu) to 0m (Pacific Ocean). The
climate is tropical, with little variation in temperature, and a
wet season between November and April. The islands are
prone to seismic activity and tsunamis.

## HISTORY AND POLITICS

The islands were colonised by Austronesian people 30,000
years ago. Spanish explorers reached the islands in 1568 and
the area continued to be visited by Europeans intermittently
for about 300 years. Following the arrival of missionaries
and traders, Britain declared a protectorate in 1893 over
the southern islands; the northern islands were ceded to
Britain by Germany in 1899. After the Second World War,
campaigns began for self-government, which was achieved in
1976; independence followed in 1978.

Ethnic tension on Guadalcanal between the indigenous
Isatabus and migrants from the island of Malaita escalated
from 1998 into conflict between militant factions. Despite
a fragile peace following a ceasefire agreement signed in
October 2000, and elections in 2001, lawlessness and
corruption pervaded the country. An Australian-led regional
assistance mission restored public order and disarmed the
militias by late 2003.

In the 2014 legislative elections, independent candidates
won the majority of seats in the legislature and Prime
Minister Gordon Darcy Lilo lost his seat. Parliament elected
Manasseh Sogavare to replace him.

Under the 1978 constitution, the Solomon Islands is a
constitutional monarchy. The head of state is Queen Elizabeth
II, represented by a governor-general, who is chosen by
the legislature. The unicameral National Parliament has 50
members who are directly elected for a four-year term.
The prime minister is elected by the legislature from among
its members, and nominates the cabinet, which is formally
appointed by the governor-general.
*Governor-General,* Sir Frank Kabui, GCMG, *apptd* 2009

SELECTED GOVERNMENT MEMBERS *as at June 2015*
*Prime Minister,* Manasseh Sogavare
*Deputy Prime Minister, Home Affairs,* Douglas Ete

*Finance,* Snyder Rini
*Foreign Affairs,* Milner Tozaka

## HIGH COMMISSION FOR THE SOLOMON ISLANDS

17B Avenue Edouard Lacombe, 1040 Brussels, Belgium
T (+32) (2) 732 7085 E siembassy@compuserve.com
*High Commissioner,* vacant

## BRITISH HIGH COMMISSION

PO Box 676, Tanuli Ridge, Honiara
T (+677) 21705 E bhc@solomon.com.sb
W www.gov.uk/government/world/solomon-islands
*High Commissioner,* HE Dominic Meiklejohn, *apptd* 2012

## ECONOMY AND TRADE

The civil unrest of 1998–2003 left the country virtually
bankrupt but the restoration of law and order enabled the
economy to recover until its modest but steady growth was
curtailed by the global downturn and natural disasters in
2009 and 2010. The country's greater dependency since
2003 on foreign aid, principally from Australia, increased as
the downturn reduced government revenues.

Agriculture, much at subsistence level, is the largest
economic sector, accounting for 51.9 per cent of GDP and
engaging 75 per cent of the population. Abundant mineral
resources are largely undeveloped, although there are plans
to reopen a major gold mine. The main industries are fishing,
mining, forestry and processing agricultural products;
industry contributes 10 per cent of GDP.

The main trade partners are China, Australia and Singapore.
Principal exports are timber, fish, copra, palm oil and cocoa.
The main imports are food, machinery and equipment,
manufactured goods, fuels and chemicals.

*GNI* – US$897m; US$1,600 per capita (2013)
*Annual average growth of GDP* – 0.1 per cent (2014 est)
*Inflation rate* – 6.9 per cent (2014 est)
*Unemployment* – 3.9 per cent (2015 est)
*Total external debt* – US$228.1m (2012)
*Imports* – US$530m (2013)
*Exports* – US$440m (2013)

BALANCE OF PAYMENTS
*Trade* – US$30m deficit (2012)
*Current Account* – US$101m deficit (2015 est)

| Trade with UK | 2013 | 2014 |
| --- | --- | --- |
| Imports from UK | £4,516,327 | £1,517,116 |
| Exports to UK | £91,923 | £170,251 |

## COMMUNICATIONS

*Airports and waterways* – Air Niugini flies from Papua New
Guinea to Honiara; the main ports are Honiara and Viru
*Roadways* – 1,390km
*Telecommunications* – 8,060 fixed lines and 302,100 mobile
subscriptions (2012); there were 10,000 internet users in
2009
*Internet code and IDD* – sb; 677 (from UK), 44 (to UK)
*Media* – The Solomon Islands Broadcasting Corporation
(SIBC) operates public radio services and One Television
provides television programmes; the *Solomon Star* is the
single daily newspaper

# SOMALIA

*Jamhuuriyadda Federaalkaa Soomaaliya – Federal Republic of Somalia*

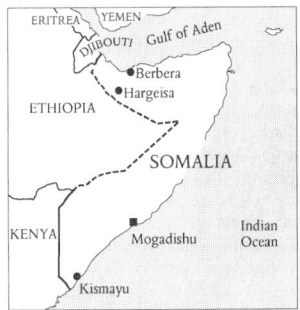

*Area* – 637,657 sq. km
*Capital* – Mogadishu; population, 2,014,000 (2014)
*Major cities* – Baidoa, Berbera, Burao, Hargeisa, Kismayu
*Currency* – Somali shilling of 100 cents; other currencies are also in circulation
*Population* – 10,616,380 (2014 est) rising at 1.83 per cent a year (2015 est)
*Religion* – Muslim (predominantly Sunni, including Sunni forms of Sufism)
*Language* – Somali (official), Arabic, Italian, English
*Population density* – 17 per sq. km (2013)
*Urban population* – 38.7 per cent (2013 est)
*Median age (years)* – 17.7 (2014 est)
*National anthem* – Qolobaa Calankeed ['Every Nation Has its Own Flag']
*National day* – 1 July (Foundation Day)
*Death penalty* – Retained
*CPI score* – 8 (174)
*Life expectancy (years)* – 51.58 (2014 est)
*Mortality rate* – 13.91 (2014 est)
*Birth rate* – 40.87 (2014 est)
*Infant mortality rate* – 100.14 (2014 est)

## CLIMATE AND TERRAIN
The country is mostly an arid and flat or undulating plateau, rising to hills in the north. Elevation extremes range from 2,416m (Shimbiris) to 0m (Indian Ocean). The climate is tropical, influenced by the north-east and south-west monsoons. Rainfall is greater in the south than the north, but is low and irregular throughout the country, leading to frequent droughts. The average temperature is 27.1°C.

## POLITICS
Hassan Sheikh Mohamud took office immediately following his presidential election victory in September 2012. Legislative elections could not be held in 2012 due to a lack of security; initial members of the parliament were chosen by 135 clan elders, themselves selected by the outgoing constituent assembly. Nominees were approved for 215 of the seats and were sworn into office on 21 August. A new

prime minister and cabinet were appointed by the president on 24 December 2014.

Under the 2012 provisional constitution the president is elected by the legislature for a four-year term. The president appoints the prime minister, who names the cabinet. The bicameral parliament has 225 directly elected members in the House of the People, who serve a four-year term; the Upper House has a maximum of 54 members, serving a four-year term and directly elected from the 18 regions of Somalia.

### HEAD OF STATE
*President,* Hassan Sheikh Mohamud, *elected* 10 September 2012 *sworn in* 16 September 2012

### SELECTED GOVERNMENT MEMBERS *as at June 2015*
*Prime Minister,* Omar Abdirashid Ali Sharmarke
*Deputy Prime Minister,* Mohamed Omar Arte
*Defence,* Abdulkadir Sheikh Ali Dini
*Finance,* Mohamed Ibrahim Adan
*Foreign Affairs,* Abdisalan Hadliye Omar

### SOMALI EMBASSY
Moran House, Suite 9, 449 High Road, Neasden, London NW10 2JJ
T 07852-280959 E somaliembassyuk@gmail.com
W http://www.uk.somaligov.net/
*Ambassador Extraordinary and Plenipotentiary,* HE Abdullahi Mohamed Ali Sanbaloshe, *apptd* 2013

### BRITISH AMBASSADOR
*Ambassador Extraordinary and Plenipotentiary,* HE Harriet Mathews, *apptd* 2015, resident at Nairobi, Kenya

## DEFENCE

| *Aged 16–49, 2010 est* | *Males* | *Females* |
| --- | --- | --- |
| Available for military service | 2,260,175 | 2,159,293 |
| Fit for military service | 1,331,894 | 1,357,051 |

## ECONOMY AND TRADE
The lack of central government before 2012 prevented broad-based economic development or assistance from international donors. Natural resources are not exploited and industry is virtually non-existent, but the lack of regulation led to a thriving and relatively sophisticated entrepreneurial economy, especially in livestock, remittance/money transfer services (in the absence of a banking sector) and telecommunications. Infrastructure has been developed by commercial concerns, with businesses building small airfields and using natural harbours for overseas trade, and the three main telecommunications companies jointly funding internet infrastructure.

Agriculture, primarily livestock-raising by nomads or semi-nomads, is the most important economic sector. It accounts for about 60.2 per cent of GDP and over half of export earnings, but is vulnerable to drought.

The main export markets are the UAE and Yemen; imports come mainly from Djibouti. Principal exports are livestock, bananas, hides, fish, charcoal and scrap metal. The main

imports are manufactured goods, petroleum products, foodstuffs, construction materials and qat.
*Annual average growth of GDP* – 2.6 per cent (2012 est)
*Total external debt* – US$3,055m (2012 est)
*Unemployment* – 8.5 per cent (2015 est)

BALANCE OF PAYMENTS

| Trade with UK | 2013 | 2014 |
| --- | --- | --- |
| Imports from UK | £10,742,217 | £8,352,393 |
| Exports to UK | £404,574 | £29,105 |

## COMMUNICATIONS

*Airports and waterways* – The international airports are at Mogadishu and Hargeisa; the main ports are Mogadishu, Kismayu and Merca in the south, and Berbera in the north. Piracy and armed robbery against ships in the Gulf of Aden and Indian Ocean are rife; despite a significant drop in 2012, the number of attacks still accounted for one quarter of the global total in 2012
*Roadways* – 2,608km are surfaced
*Telecommunications* – 100,000 fixed lines and 658,000 mobile subscriptions (2012); there were 106,000 internet users in 2009
*Internet code and IDD* – so; 252 (from UK), 44 (to UK)
*Broadcasters* – There is one state-operated TV station and two private broadcasters, with a number of radio stations operating on a regional basis
*Press* – There are various Mogadishu-based newspapers and an English-language weekly, *Somaliland Times,* but journalists are routinely threatened
*WPFI score* – 72,31 (172)

# SOUTH AFRICA

*Republic of South Africa*

*Area* – 1,219,090 sq. km
*Capital* – The seat of government is Pretoria (Tshwane): population, 1,991,000; the seat of the legislature is Cape Town: population, 3,624,000; and the seat of the judiciary is Bloemfontein: population, 496,000 (2014 est)
*Major cities* – Durban, Johannesburg, Port Elizabeth

*Currency* – Rand (R) of 100 cents
*Population* – 53,675,563 rising at 1.33 per cent a year (2015 est)
*Religion* – Christian 80 per cent (Zionist Christian 11.1 per cent, Charismatic 8.2 per cent, Roman Catholic 7.1 per cent, other 36 per cent), none 15.1 per cent
*Language* – Afrikaans, English, isiNdebele, isiXhosa, isiZulu, Sepedi, Sesotho, Setswana, siSwati, Tshivenda, Xitsonga (all official); the most widely spoken are isiZulu, isiXhosa and Afrikaans, but English is the lingua franca
*Population density* – 44 per sq. km (2013)
*Urban population* – 62.9 per cent (2013 est)
*Median age (years)* – 25.7 (2014 est)
*National anthems* – 'Nkosi Sikelel' iAfrika' ['God Bless Africa'], incorporating 'Die Stem van Suid Afrika' ['The Call of South Africa']
*National day* – 27 April (Freedom Day)
*Death penalty* – Abolished for all crimes (since 1997)
*CPI score* – 44 (67)

## CLIMATE AND TERRAIN

South Africa occupies the southernmost part of the African continent, with the exception of Lesotho and Swaziland. Its territory includes Prince Edward and Marion Islands, 1,920km to the south-east of Cape Town. The narrow coastal plain is separated by a mountainous escarpment, including the Drakensberg range, from a high inland plateau (the Great Karoo and the Highveld), an area of semi-arid scrubland in the west merging into grasslands or savannah in the centre and east. Elevation extremes range from 3,408m (Njesuthi) to 0m (Atlantic Ocean). The main rivers are the Orange and the Limpopo, and their tributaries. The country lies at the convergence of the Atlantic and Indian oceans, and the climate is influenced by the cold Benguela current along the west coast and the warm Agulhas current along the east, as well as by the altitude of the interior. These influences cause cooler, drier conditions in the west and almost subtropical warmth and rainfall in the east. Average temperatures range from 11.8°C in July to 23.4°C in January and February.

## POLITICS

Under the 1997 constitution, the executive president is elected by the National Assembly for a five-year term, renewable once. The president, who is responsible to the legislature, appoints the cabinet. The bicameral parliament consists of the National Assembly, the lower house and the National Council of Provinces. The National Assembly has 400 members directly elected by proportional representation for a five-year term. The National Council of Provinces has 90 members, ten for each province, selected by the provincial legislatures for a five-year term.

South Africa is divided into nine provinces: Eastern Cape, Free State, Gauteng, KwaZulu-Natal, Limpopo, Mpumalanga, Northern Cape, North-West and Western Cape. Each province has its own premier, legislature and constitution.

The African National Congress (ANC) has won all the legislative elections since 1994, but is increasingly racked by internal tensions and tainted by corruption allegations. In the May 2014 legislative elections, the ANC received 62.2

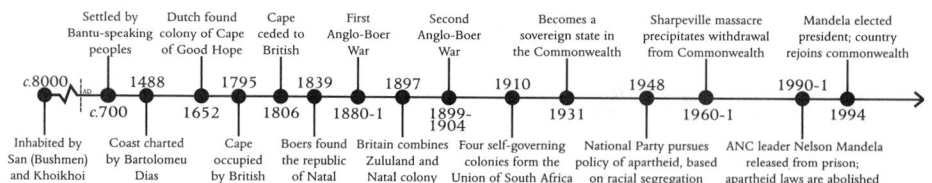

| Settled by Bantu-speaking peoples | Dutch found colony of Cape of Good Hope | Cape ceded to British | First Anglo-Boer War | Second Anglo-Boer War | Becomes a sovereign state in the Commonwealth | Sharpeville massacre precipitates withdrawal from Commonwealth | Mandela elected president; country rejoins commonwealth |
| --- | --- | --- | --- | --- | --- | --- | --- |
| *c.*8000 | 1488 | 1795 | 1839 | 1897 | 1910 | 1948 | 1990–1 |
| *c.*700 | 1652 | 1806 | 1880–1 | 1899–1904 | 1931 | 1960–1 | 1994 |
| Inhabited by San (Bushmen) and Khoikhoi | Coast charted by Bartolomeu Dias | Cape occupied by British | Boers found the republic of Natal | Britain combines Zululand and Natal colony | Four self-governing colonies form the Union of South Africa | National Party pursues policy of apartheid, based on racial segregation | ANC leader Nelson Mandela released from prison; apartheid laws are abolished |

per cent of the vote and its leader Jacob Zuma was elected president for the second time.

## HEAD OF STATE
*President,* Jacob Zuma, *elected* 6 May 2009, *sworn in* 9 May 2009, *re-elected* 21 May 2014, *sworn in* 24 May 2014
*Deputy President,* Cyril Ramaphosa

SELECTED GOVERNMENT MEMBERS *as at June 2015*
*Defence,* Nosiviwe Noluthando Mapisa-Nqakula
*Finance,* Nhlanhla Nene
*Home Affairs,* Malusi Knowledge Nkanyezi Gigaba

SOUTH AFRICAN HIGH COMMISSION
South Africa House, Trafalgar Square, London WC2N 5DP
T 020-7451 7299 W www.southafricahouseuk.com
*High Commissioner,* HE Obed Mlaba, *apptd* 2014

BRITISH HIGH COMMISSION
255 Hill Street, Arcadia 0028, Pretoria (Tshwane)
T (+27) (12) 421 7500
E pta.assistanceforbritishnationals@fco.gov.uk
W www.gov.uk/government/world/south-africa
*High Commissioner,* HE Judith Macgregor, CMG, LVO
*apptd* 2013

## DEFENCE
The South African National Defence Force (SANDF) was created in 1994 from the merger of the South African Defence Forces (SADF), the Umkhonto we Sizwe (MK) armed wing of the ANC, the Azanian People's Liberation Army (APLA) of the Pan Africanist Congress of Azania, and the defence forces of the four former 'independent' homelands.

| Aged 16–49, 2010 est | Males | Females |
|---|---|---|
| Available for military service | 13,439,781 | 12,473,641 |
| Fit for military service | 7,617,063 | 6,476,264 |

*Military expenditure* – US$3,895m (2014)

## ECONOMY AND TRADE
The economy varies between the sophisticated and well-developed, based on manufacturing, mining and financial services; the living eked out by the very poor, mostly through subsistence agriculture; and a large informal sector. Growth was strong until 2008, when the global economic downturn caused a contraction in the economy from which recovery is slowly being made, with 2 per cent growth achieved in 2014. State-owned enterprises are being used to create jobs and raise incomes. Industrial action and weakening demand from trading partners is expected to slow growth to 1.5 per cent in 2015–16.

Agriculture, forestry and fishing account for 2.4 per cent of GDP and employ 4 per cent of the workforce. Principal crops are maize, wheat, sugar cane, fruit and vegetables. Livestock farming, cotton and viticulture are also widespread.

The largest industry is mining; South Africa is the world's largest producer of gold, platinum and chromium, as well as producing diamonds, manganese, coal, copper, iron ore, tin, uranium and titanium. Other industries include car assembly, metalworking, food processing, ship repair and production of machinery, textiles, iron and steel, chemicals and fertiliser; manufacturing is concentrated most heavily around Johannesburg, Pretoria (Tshwane) and the major ports. Tourism is a significant industry, and South Africa is a major transit point for its landlocked neighbours. Industry contributes 28.5 per cent of GDP and services 69.1 per cent.

Fossil-fuel based electricity generation is being supplemented by nuclear power; one nuclear power station is in operation and others are planned. Water resources are inadequate to meet demand, so water is imported from the highlands of Lesotho.

The main trading partners are China, Germany, Saudi Arabia and the USA. Principal exports are gold, diamonds, platinum, other metals and minerals, and machinery and equipment. Principal imports are machinery and equipment, chemicals, petroleum products, scientific instruments and foodstuffs.

*GNI* – US$380,699m; US$7,190 per capita (2013)
*Annual average growth of GDP* – 1.4 per cent (2014 est)
*Inflation rate* – 6 per cent (2014 est)
*Unemployment* – 24.9 per cent (2013 est)
*Population below the poverty line* – 35.9 per cent (2012)
*Total external debt* – US$143,000m (2014 est)
*Imports* – US$101,2643m (2013)
*Exports* – US$83,531m (2013)

BALANCE OF PAYMENTS
*Trade* – US$14,047m deficit (2012)
*Current Account* – US$14,792m deficit (2015 est)

| Trade with UK | 2013 | 2014 |
|---|---|---|
| Imports from UK | £2,592,095,838 | £2,380,214,840 |
| Exports to UK | £3,311,178,404 | £4,631,019,548 |

## COMMUNICATIONS
*Airports and waterways* – 144 airports, with international airports at Johannesburg, Durban and Cape Town; Durban is the largest seaport, while other major ports are Cape Town, Port Elizabeth, East London, Saldanha, Mossel Bay and Richards Bay
*Roadways and railways* – There are 158,952km of surfaced roadways and 20,192km of railways, including the high-speed Gautrain which links Johannesburg's main international airport and Pretoria
*Telecommunications* – 4.03 million fixed lines and 68.4 million mobile subscriptions (2012); there were 4.42 million internet users in 2009
*Internet code and IDD* – za; 27 (from UK), 44 (to UK)
*Major broadcasters* – The South African Broadcasting Corporation (SABC) is the country's major, state-owned television and radio broadcaster
*Press* – *The Star* is Johannesburg's oldest daily newspaper, while the *Sunday Times* is the longest running weekly title; *Beeld* is a popular Afrikaans daily title
*WPFI score* – 22,06 (39)

## EDUCATION AND HEALTH
Education is compulsory between the ages of seven and 15.
*Literacy rate* – 99.0 per cent (2015 est)
*Gross enrolment ratio (percentage of relevant age group)* – primary 101 per cent; secondary 111 per cent (2013 est)
*Health expenditure (per capita)* – US$593 (2013)
*Hospital beds (per 1,000 people)* – 2.8 (2004–9)
*Life expectancy (years)* – 49.56 (2014 est)
*Mortality rate* – 17.49 (2014 est)
*Birth rate* – 18.94 (2014 est)
*Infant mortality rate* – 41.61 (2014 est)
*HIV/AIDS adult prevalence* – 19.05 per cent (2013 est)

# SOUTH SUDAN

*Republic of South Sudan*

*Area* – 644,329 sq. km
*Capital* – Juba; population, 307,000 (2014 est)
*Major cities* – Malakal, Wau
*Currency* – South Sudanese pound (SSDP) of 100 piastres
*Population* – 12,042,910 rising at 4.02 per cent a year (2015 est); Dinka (35.8 per cent), (Nuer 15.6 per cent) (2011 est)
*Religion* – Christian, animist (many animists also follow Christian practices)
*Language* – English (official), Arabic, indigenous languages
*Urban population* – 18.4 per cent (2013)
*Median age (years)* – 16.8 (2014 est)
*National anthem* – 'South Sudan Oyee!' ['Hooray!']
*National day* – 9 July (Independence Day)
*Death penalty* – Retained
*CPI score* – 15 (171)
*Literacy rate* – 27 per cent (2009)
*Infant mortality rate* – 68.16 (2014 est)

## CLIMATE AND TERRAIN

The White Nile, flowing north out of the uplands of central Africa, is the principal feature of the country, and formed part of the Sudd, a vast swamp of more than 100,000 sq. km. Divided by the river, the terrain rises from the plains on the northern border to wet southern highlands along the Kenya–Uganda divide to a maximum height of 3,187m (Mt Kinyeti). The climate is hot with seasonal rainfall and the average annual temperature is 27.7°C.

## HISTORY AND POLITICS

The history of the area is largely unrecorded until the early 19th century, as natural barriers prevented the invasions and occupations affecting northern Sudan. In the 19th century, Egypt attempted to extend its influence in the region but the south was only joined with the north with the arrival of the British in the late 19th century, becoming part of a joint Anglo-Egyptian condominium from 1899. Following the independence of Sudan in 1955, tensions between the dominant Arab, Muslim north and the black African, Christian and animist south led to civil war from 1955 to 1972, and again in 1983. A peace process began in 2000 and the parties to it – the government, the Sudan People's Liberation Army/Movement (SPLA/M) and the southern National Democratic Alliance – finalised a peace agreement in 2004. Under this, the southern parties joined a national unity government, a largely autonomous administration was set up in the south in October 2005 and a referendum on independence for the south was held after six years.

In the referendum in January 2011, the south voted overwhelmingly to separate from the north. In the run-up to independence on 9 July, disputes led to a deteriorating security situation in border areas, particularly over control of the oil-rich territory of Abyei.

In December 2013, fighting broke out between political factions after the finance minister was dismissed following corruption allegations in July. Thousands of people, including civilians, were killed and over a million people had been displaced by April 2014. President Kiir signed a peace treaty with rebel groups on 26 August 2015, officially ending the conflict. Legislative elections, originally due to take place in 2015, were delayed by the civil war and are now due to take place in 2017.

The transitional constitution came into force at independence and will remain in force until a permanent constitution is adopted. It provides for the current president of the government of South Sudan to become president of the independent republic, and for the National Legislative Assembly (comprising 170 members of the former South Sudan Legislative Assembly, plus 96 South Sudanese former members of the National Assembly to the Republic of Sudan; both these groups were directly elected in 2010) and the Council of States (comprising 20 former South Sudan members of the Council of States of the Republic of Sudan, plus 30 representatives appointed by the president). The president and the legislature will serve a four-year term.

HEAD OF STATE
*President*, Salva Kiir Mayardit, *sworn in under draft constitution* 9 July 2011
*Vice-President,* James Wani Igga

SELECTED GOVERNMENT MINISTERS *as at June 2015*
*Foreign Affairs,* Barnaba Marial Benjamin
*Internal Affairs (acting),* Augustino Jadalla

EMBASSY OF THE REPUBLIC OF SOUTH SUDAN
16 Upper Woburn Place, London WC1H 0BS
T 020-3741 8083 E info@embrss.org.uk W www.embrss.org.uk
*Ambassador Extraordinary and Plenipotentiary,* Sabit Abbe Alley, *apptd* 2013

BRITISH EMBASSY
EU Compound, Kololo Road, Thom Ping, Juba
T (+211) (0) 912 323 712 E ukin.southsudan@fco.gov.uk
W www.gov.uk/government/world/south-sudan
*Ambassador Extraordinary and Plenipotentiary,* HE Timothy Morris, *apptd* 2015

## ECONOMY AND TRADE

The troubled South Sudan economy, hindered by decades of civil war with the north, is based on subsistence agriculture which provides a living for the majority of the population. A lack of industry and infrastructure has forced the reliance on imports of goods and services from the north. The government derives 98 per cent of its budget from oil revenues. The country faces tough economical challenges and has received more than US$4bn in foreign aid since 2005, mainly from the UK, the Netherlands, the USA and Norway. Annual inflation rose to 79 per cent in May 2012 before falling dramatically to 1.7 per cent in 2013. A reduction in oil exports in 2013 led to reduced growth forecasts in 2014. The country consists of one of the richest agricultural areas in Africa with fertile soils and excellent water supplies. The economy is expected to contract sharply in 2015. Future economic development will hinge on the success of the current peace process and future international oil prices.

Subsistence crops include maize, rice millet, wheat, sugarcane, papayas, bananas and peanuts.

*GNI* – US$10,783m; US$950 per capita (2013 )
*Annual average growth of GDP* – –12.3 (2014 est)
*Population below the poverty line* – 51 per cent (2010 est)
*Imports* – US$4,160m (2010)
*Exports* – US$8,229m (2010)

## COMMUNICATIONS

*Airports* – There are three airports including an international terminal in Juba

*Roadways and railways* – There are 7,000km of mainly unpaved roadways in poor condition and 248km of railways

*Internet code and IDD* – ss; 211 (from UK), 44 (to UK)

*Media* – The country's fledgling media network faces political, social and logistical challenges; the government-run Southern Sudan TV and Radio is the country's sole network; *The Citizen* and *Juba Monitor* (both English language), and *Al-Masir* (Arabic) are the major daily newspapers

*WPFI score* – 38,04 (125)

# SPAIN

*Reino de España – Kingdom of Spain*

*Area* – 505,370 sq. km

*Capital* – Madrid; population, 6,133,000 (2014)

*Major cities* – Barcelona, Bilbao, Las Palmas (Gran Canaria), Málaga, Murcia, Palma (Majorca), Seville, Valencia, Zaragoza

*Currency* – Euro (€) of 100 cents

*Population* – 48,146,134 rising at 0.89 per cent a year (2015 est)

*Religion* – Christian (Roman Catholic 94 per cent) (est)

*Language* – Castilian (Spanish) (official), Catalan, Galician, Basque (all are official in certain regions)

*Population density* – 94 per sq. km (2013)

*Urban population* – 77.7 per cent (2013)

*Median age (years)* – 41.6 (2014 est)

*National anthem* – 'La Marcha Real' ['The Royal March']

*National day* – 12 October (marks Columbus's arrival in the Americas)

*Death penalty* – Abolished for all crimes (since 1995)

*CPI score* – 60 (37)

## CLIMATE AND TERRAIN

Spain occupies over 80 per cent of the Iberian peninsula, and includes two archipelagos and territories on or just off the Moroccan coast. The interior consists of an elevated plateau surrounded and traversed by mountain ranges: the Pyrenees on the border with France, the Cantabrian Mountains (north-west), the Sierra de Guadarrama, Sierra Morena, Montes de Toledo (centre) and the Sierra Nevada (south). Elevation extremes range from 3,718m (Pico de Teide, Tenerife, Canary Islands) to 0m (Mediterranean Sea). The principal rivers are the Duero, the Tajo (Tagus), the Guadiana, the Guadalquivir, the Ebro and the Miño. The climate is Mediterranean in the southern and eastern coastal areas, and temperate further inland and at altitude. Average temperatures range from 7°C in January to 23.1°C in July.

## POLITICS

The 1978 constitution has been amended at various times to devolve powers to the 19 autonomous regions. The head of state is a hereditary constitutional monarch. There is a bicameral legislature, the *Cortes Generales,* comprising a 350-member Congress of Deputies directly elected for a four-year term, and a senate with 264 members, 208 directly elected and 56 appointed by the assemblies of the autonomous regions, for a four-year term.

There are 19 autonomous regions: Andalucía, Aragón, Asturias, Balearic Islands, the Basque Country, Canary Islands, Cantabria, Castilla-La Mancha, Castilla y León, Catalonia, Ceuta, Extremadura, Galicia, La Rioja, Madrid, Melilla, Murcia, Navarre and Valencia. Each has its own elected legislature and government. In 2006 a referendum endorsed the *Cortes'* approval of greater autonomy for Catalonia.

In the 2011 early legislative elections the Popular Party won an overall majority in both houses. Mariano Rajoy, leader of the Popular Party (PP), was appointed prime minister in December 2011, replacing José Luis Rodríguez Zapatero. New legislative elections are due to take place in December in 2015.

### HEAD OF STATE

*HM The King of Spain,* King Felipe VI de Borbon y Grecia, *born* 30 January 1968, *acceded to the throne* 19 June 2014

*Heir,* HRH The Princess of the Asturias (Leonor de Borbon y Ortiz), *born* 31 October 2005

SELECTED GOVERNMENT MEMBERS *as at June 2015*

*Prime Minister,* Mariano Rajoy

*Vice-President,* Soraya Saenz de Santamaria

*Defence,* Pedro Morenes Eulate

*Foreign Affairs,* Jose Manuel Garcia-Margallo

*Interior,* Jorge Fernandez Diaz

### EMBASSY OF SPAIN

39 Chesham Place, London SW1X 8SB

T 020-7235 5555 E emb.londres@maec.es

W www.exteriores.gob.es/embajadas/londres

*Ambassador Extraordinary and Plenipotentiary,* HE Federico Trillo-Figueroa Martinez Conde, *apptd* 2012

### BRITISH EMBASSY

Torre Espacio, Paseo de la Castellana 259D, 28046 Madrid

T (+34) (91) 714 6300 E info.consulate@fco.gov.uk

W www.gov.uk/government/world/spain

*Ambassador Extraordinary and Plenipotentiary,* HE Simon Manley, CMG, *apptd* 2013

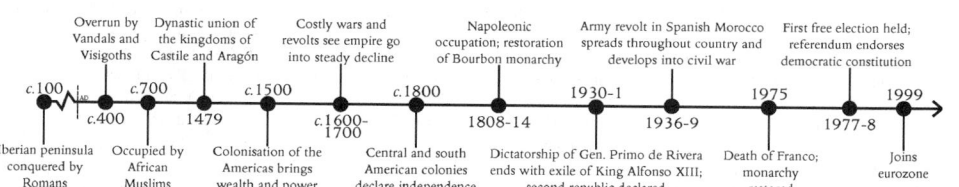

Overrun by Vandals and Visigoths — Dynastic union of the kingdoms of Castile and Aragón — Costly wars and revolts see empire go into steady decline — Napoleonic occupation; restoration of Bourbon monarchy — Army revolt in Spanish Morocco spreads throughout country and develops into civil war — First free election held; referendum endorses democratic constitution

c.100 — c.700 — c.1500 — c.1800 — 1930–1 — 1975 — 1999

c.400 — 1479 — c.1600–1700 — 1808–14 — 1936–9 — 1977–8

Iberian peninsula conquered by Romans — Occupied by African Muslims — Colonisation of the Americas brings wealth and power — Central and south American colonies declare independence — Dictatorship of Gen. Primo de Rivera ends with exile of King Alfonso XIII; second republic declared — Death of Franco; monarchy restored — Joins eurozone

## INSURGENCIES

The Basque separatist organisation ETA (*Euzkadi ta Azkatasuna* – Basque Nation and Liberty), formed in 1959, began a terrorist campaign of bombings, shootings and kidnappings in 1961 in an attempt to gain independence for the Basque country. ETA rejected regional autonomy for the Basque country in 1979 as insufficient and continued its campaign, but was greatly weakened in the early 1990s by increased cooperation between Spanish security forces and their European counterparts. ETA announced a permanent ceasefire in January 2011.

## DEFENCE

| Aged 16–49, 2010 est | Males | Females |
|---|---|---|
| Available for military service | 11,759,557 | 11,204,688 |
| Fit for military service | 9,603,939 | 9,116,928 |

*Military expenditure* – US$12,732m (2014)

## ECONOMY AND TRADE

Economic protectionism and isolation held back economic development until the mid-20th century, but the economy improved from the 1950s with industrialisation and the development of tourism. The mixed capitalist economy showed above-average growth, stimulated by liberalisation, privatisation and deregulation, from the mid-1990s until 2007. In 2008 it entered a severe recession because of the global economic downturn.

The downturn in construction and the property market left many banks struggling in 2010, and rising public-sector debt led to Spain's international credit rating being downgraded; the government introduced austerity measures in response but concern continues over the impact on the eurozone of Spain's sovereign debt.

Public debt continues to rise – from 60.1 per cent of GDP in 2010 to 93.4 per cent in 2013 – but rising labour productivity, decreasing labour costs and falling inflation have increased foreign investor interest. The government shored up struggling banks exposed to Spain's depressed domestic construction and real estate sectors by completing an EU-funded restructuring and recapitalisation programme in December 2013. Growth of nearly 3 per cent is expected in 2015 and 2016. Spain's unemployment, which reached 50 per cent in 2015, is among the highest in the EU.

The generally fertile country produces grains, vegetables, olives, sugar beets, citrus and other fruits, meat and dairy products. Viticulture is widespread. Spain also has one of Europe's largest fishing industries. The agricultural sector contributes 3.2 per cent of GDP and employs 2.9 per cent of the workforce. Abundant mineral resources include coal, iron ore, copper, zinc, lead, uranium and tungsten. Metal extraction and the manufacture of metal products, including steel, are major industries. A diverse industrial sector includes manufacturing (principally textiles, clothing, footwear, beverages, chemicals, cars, machine tools, clay products, pharmaceuticals and medical equipment), food processing, shipbuilding and tourism. Industry accounts for 25.4 per cent of GDP and the service sector for 71.4 per cent.

The main trading partners are other EU countries, especially France and Germany. Principal exports include machinery, vehicles, foodstuffs, pharmaceuticals, medicines and other consumer goods. The main imports are machinery and equipment, fuels, chemicals, semi-finished goods, foodstuffs, consumer goods, and measuring and medical control instruments.

*GNI* – US$1,395,916m; US$29,920 per capita (2013)
*Annual average growth of GDP* – 1.3 per cent (2014 est)
*Inflation rate* – −0.1 per cent (2014 est)
*Population below the poverty line* – 21.1 per cent (2012)
*Unemployment* – 26.3 per cent (2013 est)
*Total external debt* – US$2,278,000m (2012 est)
*Imports* – US$333,932m (2013)
*Exports* – US$310,996m (2013)

### BALANCE OF PAYMENTS

*Trade* – US$39,618m deficit (2012)
*Current Account* – US$3,348m surplus (2015 est)

| Trade with UK | 2013 | 2014 |
|---|---|---|
| Imports from UK | £8,476,818,760 | £8,803,488,623 |
| Exports to UK | £12,540,772,217 | £13,121,768,802 |

## COMMUNICATIONS

*Airports* – Of the 99 airports, the principal terminals are at Madrid, Barcelona, Alicante, Málaga, Valencia and Bilbao
*Waterways* – The main ports are Algeciras, Alicante, Barcelona, Bilbao, Cádiz, Santander and Valencia, and Las Palmas in the Canary Islands; there are also 1,000km of navigable inland waterways
*Roadways and railways* – 683,175km; 15,293km
*Telecommunications* – 19.22 million fixed lines and 50.66 million mobile subscriptions (2012); there were 28.12 million internet users in 2009
*Internet code and IDD* – es; 34 (from UK), 44 (to UK)
*Major broadcasters* – Public radio and television services are run by Radio Television Espanola (RTVE), which is funded by advertising and state subsidies
*Press* – Popular newspaper titles include *El Mundo, ABC, El País* and *El Periodico de Catalunya*
*WPFI score* – 19,95 (33)

## EDUCATION AND HEALTH

Education is free from age six to 18, and compulsory to the age of 16.

*Literacy rate* – 99.7 per cent (2015)
*Gross enrolment ratio (percentage of relevant age group)* – primary 103 per cent; secondary 131 per cent (2012 est); tertiary 86 per cent (2013 est)
*Health expenditure (per capita)* – US$2,581 (2013)
*Hospital beds (per 1,000 people)* – 3.1 (2011)
*Life expectancy (years)* – 81.47 (2014 est)
*Mortality rate* – 9.00 (2014 est)
*Birth rate* – 9.88 (2014 est)
*Infant mortality rate* – 3.33 (2014 est)

## ISLANDS AND ENCLAVES

THE BALEARIC ISLES form an archipelago off the east coast of Spain. There are four large islands (Majorca/Mallorca, Minorca, Ibiza and Formentera) and seven smaller ones (Aire, Aucanada, Botafoch, Cabrera, Dragonera, Pinto and El Rey). Area 4,992 sq. km; population 1,111,674 (2013 est). The archipelago forms a province of Spain. The capital is Palma, on Majorca.

THE CANARY ISLANDS are an archipelago in the Atlantic off the African coast, consisting of seven islands and six islets. Area 7,447 sq. km; population 2,118,679 (2013 est). The Canary Islands form two provinces of Spain: Las Palmas, comprising Gran Canaria, Lanzarote, Fuerteventura and six islets, with the seat of administration at Las Palmas, in Gran Canaria; and Santa Cruz de Tenerife, comprising Tenerife, La Palma, La Gomera and El Hierro, with the seat of administration at Santa Cruz, in Tenerife.

CEUTA is a fortified post on the Moroccan coast, opposite Gibraltar. Area 19 sq. km; population 84,180 (2013 est). Ceuta is an autonomous city of Spain.

ISLA DE FAISANES an uninhabited Franco-Spanish condominium, at the mouth of the Bidassoa in La Higuera bay.

MELILLA is a town on a rocky promontory of the Moroccan coast, connected with the mainland by a narrow isthmus. Area 13 sq. km; population 83,679 (2013 est). Melilla is an autonomous city of Spain.

## OVERSEAS TERRITORIES

The following territories, which are Spanish settlements on the Moroccan seaboard, come under direct Spanish administration. They are uninhabited other than by military personnel.
PENON DE ALHUCEMAS is a bay including six islands.
PENON DE LA GOMERA (or Peñón de Velez) is a fortified rocky islet.
THE CHAFFARINAS (or Zaffarines) is a group of three islands near the Algerian frontier.

## SRI LANKA

*Shri Lanka Prajatantrika Samajavadi Janarajaya/Ilankai Jananayaka Choshalichak Kutiyarachu – Democratic Socialist Republic of Sri Lanka*

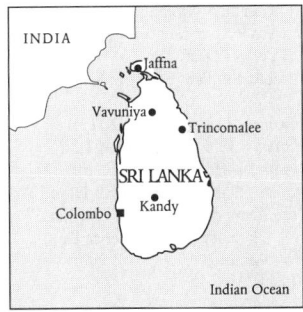

*Area* – 65,610 sq. km
*Capital* – Colombo; population, 704,000 (2014); the administrative capital is Jayewardenepura Kolte; population, 128,000 (2014 est)
*Major cities* – Dehiwala-Mount Lavinia, Jaffna, Kalmunai, Kandy, Moratuwa, Negombo, Trincomalee, Vavuniya
*Currency* – Sri Lankan rupee of 100 cents
*Population* – 22,053,488 rising at 0.84 per cent a year (2015 est); Sinhalese (74.9 per cent), Sri Lankan Tamil (11.2 per cent), Sri Lankan Moor (9.2 per cent), Indian Tamil (4.2 per cent) (2012 est)
*Religion* – Buddhist 70.2 per cent (predominantly Theravada), Hindu 12.6, Muslim 9.7 per cent, Christian 7.4 per cent (predominantly Roman Catholic) (2012 est)
*Language* – Sinhala (official), Tamil, English
*Population density* – 327 per sq. km (2013)
*Urban population* – 15.2 per cent (2013)
*Median age (years)* – 31.8 (2014 est)
*National anthem* – 'Sri Lanka Matha' ['Mother Sri Lanka']
*National day* – 4 February (Independence Day)
*Death penalty* – Retained (last used 1976)
*CPI score* – 38 (85)
*Literacy rate* – 98.8 per cent (2015 est)
*Gross enrolment ratio (percentage of relevant age group)* – primary 99 per cent (2011 est)
*Health expenditure (per capita)* – US$102 (2013)
*Hospital beds (per 1,000 people)* – 3.6 (2012)
*Life expectancy (years)* – 76.35 (2014 est)
*Mortality rate* – 6.06 (2014 est)
*Birth rate* – 16.24 (2014 est)
*Infant mortality rate* – 9.02 (2014 est)

## CLIMATE AND TERRAIN

Sri Lanka (formerly Ceylon) is an island in the Indian Ocean, separated from India by the narrow Palk Strait. The land is low-lying in the north and along the coasts, rising to a central massif with hills and mountains in the south and centre. Forests, jungle and scrub cover the greater part of the island. In areas over 600m above sea level, grasslands *(patanas* or *talawas)* are found. Elevation extremes range from 2,524m (Pidurutalagala) to 0m (Indian Ocean). The climate is tropical with little seasonal variation in conditions and humidity, which often reaches around 90 per cent. The island experiences the south-west monsoon from May to September and the north-east monsoon from October to January.

## HISTORY AND POLITICS

The Sinhalese colonised Sri Lanka in 500BC and were followed by Tamil Settlers in 200BC. The island was controlled by the Portuguese from 1505, the Dutch from 1658 and the British from 1802. Sri Lanka achieved independence as Ceylon in 1948.

The January 2015 presidential election was won by Maithripala Sirisena, the leader of a coalition of parties opposed to the ruling Sri Lanka Freedom Party (SLFP). After the legislative election in August 2015, the United National Front for Good Governance emerged as the single largest political grouping and formed a governing coalition with the SLFP.

The 1978 constitution was amended in 1983 to ban parties advocating separatism, in 1987 to create provincial councils, and in 2010 to remove the limit on presidential terms. The executive president is directly elected for a six-year term, which may be renewed. The unicameral parliament has 225 members directly elected by proportional representation for a six-year term. The president appoints the prime minister and cabinet.

Elected councils were set up in the nine provinces in 1987 in an attempt to defuse ethnic tensions. The Northern and Eastern provinces were merged into one from 1988 to 2006.

HEAD OF STATE
*President, Defence, Finance,* Maithripala Sirisena, *elected* 8 January 2015, *sworn in* 9 January 2015

SELECTED GOVERNMENT MEMBERS *as at September 2015*
*Prime Minister,* Ranil Wickremasinghe
*Home Affairs,* Vajira Abeywardena
*Foreign Affairs,* Mangala Samaraweera

HIGH COMMISSION OF THE DEMOCRATIC SOCIALIST REPUBLIC OF SRI LANKA
13 Hyde Park Gardens, London W2 2LU
T 020-7262 1841 E mail@slhc-london.co.uk
W www.srilankahighcommission.co.uk
*High Commissioner (acting),* HE Dr C. H. Talpahewa, *apptd* 2011

BRITISH HIGH COMMISSION
389 Bauddhaloka Mawatha, Colombo 7
T (+94) (11) 539 0639 E bhctrade@slt.lk
W www.gov.uk/government/world/sri-lanka
*High Commissioner,* HE James Dauris, *apptd* 2015

## DEFENCE

| Aged 16–49, 2010 est | Males | Females |
| --- | --- | --- |
| Available for military service | 5,342,147 | 5,466,409 |
| Fit for military service | 4,177,432 | 4,574,833 |

*Military expenditure* – US$1,843m (2014)

## ECONOMY AND TRADE

Despite the 26-year civil war and the 2004 Indian Ocean tsunami, which destroyed tourist resorts and the fishing industry, the economy saw sustained growth throughout the 2000s. The 2008–9 global downturn affected productivity only slightly, but high government debt and budget deficits obliged the government to seek an IMF loan, which in turn resulted in two years of strong growth. From 2010–11 Sri Lanka achieved 8 per cent growth, however, this dropped to 6 per cent in 2012. The once predominantly agricultural economy has become increasingly industrialised and diversified. Remittances from expatriate workers are also economically significant. Government debt of around 80 per cent of GDP is among the highest of developing nations, while a large trade deficit remains a concern. Increasing internal consumption and the success of the tourism industry, 6.2 per cent of GDP in 2015, is expected to allow the economy to grow by 7 per cent between 2015 and 2019.

Agriculture still accounts for 10.2 per cent of GDP and over 31.8 per cent of employment. The main crops are rice, sugar cane, grains, pulses, oilseed, spices, vegetables, fruit, tea, rubber, coconuts, livestock products and fish. Manufacturing is based on processing the main cash crops of rubber, tea, coconuts, tobacco and other commodities, and production of textiles, clothing, beverages and cement; other industries include oil refining and mining gemstones. Service industries such as telecommunications, banking and insurance, information technology services and tourism are also important. The service sector accounts for 56.7 per cent of GDP and industry for 33.1 per cent.

The main trading partners are India, the USA, China, Singapore and the UK. Principal exports are textiles and clothing, tea, rubber manufactures, spices, diamonds, emeralds, rubies, coconut products and fish. The main imports are oil, textile fabrics, machinery, transport equipment, building materials, mineral products and foodstuffs.

*GNI* – US$64,966m; US$3,170 per capita (2013)
*Annual average growth of GDP* – 7 per cent (2014 est)
*Inflation rate* – 3.8 per cent (2014 est)
*Population below poverty line* – 6.7 per cent (2013 est)
*Unemployment* – 4.5 per cent (2015 est)
*Total external debt* – US$27,110m (2014 est)
*Imports* – US$17,973m (2013)
*Exports* – US$9,397m (2013)

BALANCE OF PAYMENTS
*Trade* – US$9,606m deficit (2012)
*Current Account* – US$1,639m deficit (2015 est)

| Trade with UK | 2013 | 2014 |
| --- | --- | --- |
| Imports from UK | £166,534,377 | £165,153,076 |
| Exports to UK | £848,580,531 | £1,158,188,503 |

## COMMUNICATIONS

*Airports and waterways* – The principal airport is Bandaranaike International, to the north of the capital; Colombo is the main port although the first phase of a deep-water container port opened in 2010 at Hambantota
*Roadways and railways* – 16,977km; 1,449km
*Telecommunications* – 2.796 million fixed lines and 19.53 million subscriptions (2012); there were 1.78 million internet users in 2009
*Internet code and IDD* – lk; 94 (from UK), 44 (to UK)
*Media* – The state-owned Sri Lanka Rupavahini Corporation operates TV and radio stations; daily newspapers include *The Island* (English language), *Dinamina* (Sinhala) and *Virakesari* (Tamil)
*WPFI score* – 60,28 (165)

# SUDAN

*Jumhuriyat as-Sudan – Republic of the Sudan*

*Area* – 1,861,484 sq. km
*Capital* – Khartoum; population, 5,000,000 (2014)
*Major cities* – Kassala, Kusti, El Obeid, Nyala, Port Sudan
*Currency* – Sudanese pound (SDP) of 100 piastres
*Population* – 36,108,853 rising at 1.72 per cent a year (2015 est); Arab and Nubian peoples
*Religion* – Muslim 97 per cent (predominantly Sunni), Christian 3 per cent (est)
*Language* – Arabic, English (both official), Nubian, Ta Bedawie
*Population density* – 21 per sq. km (2013)
*Urban population* – 33.5 per cent (2013 est)
*Median age (years)* – 19.1 (2014 est)
*National anthem* – 'Nahnu Djund Allah Djund al-Watan' ['We Are the Army of God and of Our Land']
*National day* – 1 January (Independence Day)
*Death penalty* – Retained
*CPI score* – 11 (173)

## CLIMATE AND TERRAIN

Sudan is predominantly desert; the Libyan Desert in the west is separated from the rocky Nubian Desert in the east by the fertile valley of the Nile and its tributaries. There are mountains in the west and the south, and along the Red Sea coast. Elevation extremes range from 3,071m (Jabal Marrah) to 0m (Red Sea). The climate is arid on the desert plains, tropical in the south and cooler at altitude. There is a rainy season from April to October. Average temperatures range from 22.7°C in January to 31°C in May.

## POLITICS

Under the 2005 constitution, the executive president is directly elected for a five-year term, renewable once. The bicameral National Legislature comprises a National Assembly with 354 members, including 88 seats reserved for women, directly elected for a five-year term, and a Council of States of 32 members, two members from each state. The president appoints the cabinet.

President al-Bashir was re-elected following the April 2015 presidential election, with the president claiming to have won 95 per cent of the popular vote, while al-Bashir's National Congress party won the simultaneous legislative elections. Opposition groups alleged widescale vote-rigging had taken place.

HEAD OF STATE
*President, Prime Minister,* Field Marshal Omar al-Bashir, seized power 1989, elected 1996, re-elected 2000, sworn in under new constitution 9 July 2005, re-elected 2010, 2015
*First Vice-President,* Bakri Hassan Salih

Part of the Nubian empire | Islam introduced by Arab invaders | Egypt takes control of north | Declares independence | Second civil war breaks out | First multiparty elections for 24 years take place

c.1900   AD c.500   c.700   1889   1955-72   2005   2011
c.500   c.600   c.1800   1955   1983   2010

Part of the Egyptian empire | Country converts to Coptic Christianity | North conquered by Arab-African powers; the south remains independent | Country administered by Anglo-Egyptian condominium | First civil war between Muslim north and Christian and animist south | New constitution agreed; power-sharing government takes office | South Sudan becomes separate independent state

**SELECTED GOVERNMENT MEMBERS** *as at June 2015*
*Defence,* Mustafa Osman al-Obeid
*Finance,* Badr al-Din Mahmoud Abbas
*Foreign Affairs,* Ibrahim Ghandour
*Interior,* Ismat Abdul-Rahman Zain al-Abdin

## EMBASSY OF THE REPUBLIC OF THE SUDAN
3 Cleveland Row, London SW1A 1DD
T 020-7839 8080 E admin@sudanembassy.co.uk
W www.sudan-embassy.co.uk
*Ambassador Extraordinary and Plenipotentiary,* HE
  Mohammed Abdalla Ali Eltom, *apptd* 2014

## BRITISH EMBASSY
PO Box 801, Off Sharia Al Baladiya, Khartoum East
T (+249) (1)  8377 7105 E consular.khartoum@fco.gov.uk
W www.gov.uk/government/world/sudan
*Ambassador Extraordinary and Plenipotentiary,* HE Michael
  Aron, *apptd* 2015

## INSURGENCIES
In the western region of Darfur, tension between nomadic Arab livestock herders and black African farmers over land and grazing rights led to a rise in intercommunal violence in the 1990s. Between 2002 and 2009 black African rebels were ruthlessly suppressed by government forces, often operating through Arab militia ( *Janjaweed)* which carried out mass executions and forcible depopulation.

Two of the main rebel groups in Darfur signed peace agreements with the government, one in 2006 and the other in 2009. The International Criminal Court issued a warrant for the arrest of President al-Bashir for war crimes and crimes against humanity in 2009, and for genocide in 2010. In 2011, a related ethnic conflict broke out in the southern provinces of South Kordofan and the Blue Nile.

The conflicts have continued, with Darfur experiencing high levels of violence in December 2014, while fighting in South Kordofan and the Blue Nile intensified in 2015 as the government looked to make territorial gains before elections. As of 2015, 3 million people have been displaced by Sudan's conflicts, while approximately 7 million are thought to require international aid.

## DEFENCE

| Aged 16–49, 2010 est | Males | Females |
|---|---|---|
| Available for military service | 10,433,973 | 10,411,443 |
| Fit for military service | 6,475,530 | 6,840,885 |

*Military expenditure* – US$23,768m (2006 est)
*Conscription duration* – 12–24 months

## ECONOMY AND TRADE
Since 1997 Sudan has worked with the IMF to implement economic reforms which, despite the country's political instability and vulnerability to drought, have stabilised the economy. In 1999 Sudan began exporting oil, and increases in oil and agricultural production, light industry and exports have resulted in steady growth in GDP in recent years.

However, three quarters of its former oilfields are now controlled by South Sudan. The economy is expected to grow by 3.1 per cent in 2015 and 3.7 per cent in 2016.

Agriculture, much at subsistence level, provides employment for around 80 per cent of the workforce and contributes 26.8 per cent of GDP. Mechanised and traditional agriculture is practised in areas with sufficient rainfall and irrigation. The principal crops include cotton, groundnuts, sorghum, millet, wheat, sugar cane, tropical fruits and livestock. The country exports 75 to 80 per cent of the world's gum arabic. Industry consists of oil extraction and refining, cotton ginning, manufacture of textiles, cement, edible oils, sugar, soap, shoes, pharmaceuticals, armaments and vehicle assembly. Industry contributes 35.6 per cent of GDP and services 37.7 per cent.

The main trading partners are the UAE, China and India. Principal exports are oil and petroleum products, cotton, sesame, livestock, groundnuts, gum arabic and sugar. The main imports are foodstuffs, manufactured goods, refinery and transport equipment, medicines, chemicals, textiles and wheat.
*GNI* – US$58,767m; US$1,550 per capita (2013)
*Annual average growth of GDP* – 3 per cent (2014 est)
*Inflation rate* – 40.6 per cent (2014 est)
*Population below poverty line* – 15.5 per cent (2015 est)
*Unemployment* – 15.5 per cent (2015 est)
*Total external debt* – US$47,450m (2014 est)
*Imports* – US$9,918m (2013)
*Exports* – US$7,086m (2013)

BALANCE OF PAYMENTS
*Trade* – US$323m deficit (2015 est)
*Current Account* – US$290m deficit (2011)

| Trade with UK | 2013 | 2014 |
|---|---|---|
| Imports from UK | £99,702,261 | £71,240,441 |
| Exports to UK | £10,016,576 | £4,002,381 |

## COMMUNICATIONS
*Airports and waterways* – There are 16 airports, with the principal terminal at Khartoum; there are 4,068km of navigable waterways, including 1,723km on the White and Blue Nile rivers
*Roadways and railways* – 4,320km; 5,978km
*Telecommunications* – 425,000 fixed lines and 27.66 million mobile subscriptions (2012); there were 4.2 million internet users in 2008
*Internet and IDD* – sd; 249 (from UK), 44 (to UK)
*Media* – Sudan TV and Sudan Radio are the government-operated broadcasters; leading daily newspapers include *Al-Ra'y al-Amm, Al-Ayam* and *Al-Jareeda* (all Arabic-language)
*WPFI score* – 72,34 (174)

## EDUCATION AND HEALTH
Education is free of charge for most children, and compulsory for eight years; six years of primary education is followed by at least two years of secondary education.
*Literacy rate* – 89.6 per cent (2015 est)
*Gross enrolment ratio (percentage of relevant age group)* –
  primary 70 per cent; secondary 41 per cent (2012 est)
*Health expenditure (per capita)* – US$115 (2013)

*Hospital beds (per 1,000 people)* – 0.8 (2012)
*Life expectancy (years)* – 63.32 (2014 est)
*Mortality rate* – 7.87 (2014 est)
*Birth rate* – 30.01 (2014 est)
*Infant mortality rate* – 52.86 (2014 est)
*HIV/AIDS adult prevalence* – 0.24 per cent (2013 est)

# SURINAME

*Republiek Suriname – Republic of Suriname*

*Area* – 163,820 sq. km
*Capital* – Paramaribo; population, 234,000 (2014)
*Major towns* – Lelydorp, Nieuw Nickerie
*Currency* – Suriname dollar of 100 cents
*Population* – 579,633 rising at 1.08 per cent a year
(2015 est); Hindustani (37 per cent), Creole (31 per cent),
Javanese (15 per cent), Maroons (10 per cent), Amerindian
(2 per cent), Chinese (2 per cent) (est)
*Religion* – Hindu 27.4 per cent, Christian (Protestant,
predominantly Moravian, 25.2 per cent, Roman Catholic
22.8 per cent), Muslim 19.6 per cent, indigenous
5 per cent
*Language* – Dutch (official), English, Surinamese (Sranang
Tongo), Caribbean Hindustani (a dialect of Hindi),
Javanese
*Population density* – 3 per sq. km (2013)
*Urban population* – 70.5 per cent (2013 est)
*Median age (years)* – 28.6 (2014 est)
*National anthem* – 'God zij met ons Suriname' ['God Be With
Our Suriname']
*National day* – 25 November (Independence Day)
*Death penalty* – Abolished for all crimes (since 2015)
*CPI score* – 36 (100)
*Literacy rate* – 99.0 per cent (2015 est)
*Gross enrolment ratio (percentage of relevant age group)* –
primary 113 per cent; secondary 76 per cent (2013 est)
*Life expectancy (years)* – 71.69 (2014 est)
*Mortality rate* – 6.13 (2014 est)
*Birth rate* – 16.73 (2014 est)
*Infant mortality rate* – 27.07 (2014 est)
*HIV/AIDS adult prevalence* – 0.88 per cent (2013 est)

## CLIMATE AND TERRAIN

The narrow, swampy coastal plain is home to about 90 per
cent of the population. From the coastal belt, the land rises to
a hilly interior covered by tropical rainforest and savannah;
the rainforest contains a great diversity of flora and fauna.
Elevation extremes range from 1,230m (Juliana Top) to −2m
(coastal plain). The land is drained by several rivers, some of
which have been dammed to create large artificial lakes used
to generate hydro-electric power. The climate is tropical,
moderated by the north-east trade winds. There are two wet
seasons, from April to August and November to February.

## HISTORY AND POLITICS

Originally settled by Arawak and Carib peoples, the area
was visited by Spanish explorers in 1593. Early European
settlements failed, until a British colony was founded in
1651. The colony was ceded to the Dutch in 1667. Dutch
rule was interrupted by British occupation during the
French Revolutionary and Napoleonic wars, but was restored
in 1816. The colony, known as Dutch Guiana, became
autonomous in 1954, and achieved independence in 1975 as
Suriname.

The early years of independence were politically unstable,
with a period of military rule under Desi Bouterse following
a coup in 1980. Democratic, civilian rule was restored with
elections in 1987, but the military overthrew the government
in 1990 in a coup engineered by Bouterse. Democratic
elections in 1991 were won by the New Front for
Democracy and Development alliance, led by Ronald
Venetiaan, who became president. President Venetiaan
introduced an unpopular austerity programme, which
improved the economy but lost him the 1996 election.

Ronald Venetiaan was re-elected president in 2000 and
again in 2005. After the 2010 legislative election, the Mega
Combination bloc, dominated by Desi Bouterse's National
Democratic Party (NDP), held the most seats in the
legislature and formed a coalition government. Bouterse was
subsequently elected president by parliament. In the May
2015 legislative elections, the NDP emerged as the largest
single party, retaining a majority by one seat. In July,
President Bouterse was re-elected by the National Assembly.

Under the 1987 constitution, the executive president is
elected for a five-year term by a two-thirds majority in the
legislature or, if the required majority cannot be achieved, by
a specially convened United People's Assembly including
district and local council representatives. The vice-president
is elected in the same way. The unicameral National
Assembly has 51 members directly elected for a five-year
term. The council of ministers is appointed by the president
and chaired by the vice-president.

HEAD OF STATE
*President*, Desi Bouterse, *elected* 19 July 2010, *sworn in*
12 August 2010, *re-elected* 14 July, *sworn in* 12 August 2015
*Vice-President*, Robert Ameerali

SELECTED GOVERNMENT MEMBERS *as at June 2015*
*Defence*, Lamuré Latour
*Foreign Affairs*, Winston Lackin
*Internal Affairs*, Soewarto Moestadja

HONORARY CONSULATE OF THE REPUBLIC OF
SURINAME
89 Pier House, 31 Cheyne Walk, London SW3 5HG
T 07768-196 326 E ajethu@honoraryconsul.info
W www.honoraryconsul.info
*Honorary consul*, Amwedhkar Jethu

BRITISH AMBASSADOR
HE Andrew Ayre, *apptd* 2011, resident at Georgetown,
Guyana

## DEFENCE

| Aged 16–49, 2010 est | Males | Females |
| --- | --- | --- |
| Available for military service | 134,218 | 134,439 |
| Fit for military service | 109,445 | 112,538 |

## ECONOMY AND TRADE

Former president Venetiaan introduced policies that
contained rampant inflation and other economic problems,

and produced steady growth for a few years before the global downturn, which caused the economy to contract owing to reduced global prices for key commodities. The mainstays of the economy are mining, especially bauxite and gold, and oil and alumina production; these account for 85 per cent of exports and 25 per cent of government revenue, making the economy vulnerable to global price fluctuations. Bauxite reserves are declining, but oil production is increasing from existing offshore fields and onshore exploration has begun. Other industries include forestry, food processing and fishing. Industry accounts for 37.3 per cent of GDP and services for 54.1 per cent. Agriculture employs only 8 per cent of the population but produces 8.6 per cent of GDP.

The main trading partners are the USA, Belgium, the Netherlands and the UAE. Principal exports are alumina, gold, crude oil, timber, fish and shrimps, rice and bananas. The main imports are capital equipment, petroleum, food-stuffs, cotton and consumer goods.

*GNI* – US$5,053m; US$9,370 per capita (2013)
*Annual average growth of GDP* – 3.3 per cent (2014 est)
*Inflation rate* – 3.7 per cent (2014 est)
*Unemployment* – 12 per cent (2015 est)
*Total external debt* – US$1,037m (2014 est)
*Imports* – US$2,300m (2013)
*Exports* – US$2,550m (2013)

BALANCE OF PAYMENTS
*Trade* – US$769m surplus (2012)
*Current Account* – US$433m deficit (2015 est)

| Trade with UK | 2013 | 2014 |
|---|---|---|
| Imports from UK | £15,724,645 | £10,335,926 |
| Exports to UK | £655,563 | £262,605 |

## COMMUNICATIONS

*Airports and waterways* – The principal airport and seaport is at Paramaribo
*Roadways* – 4,304km
*Telecommunications* – 83,000 fixed lines and 977,000 mobile subscriptions (2012); there were 163,000 internet users in 2009
*Internet code and IDD* – sr; 597 (from UK), 44 (to UK)
*Media* – The government operates Radio SRS Suriname and two TV stations, Algemene Televisie Verzorging and Surinaamse Televisie Stichting; there are two privately owned daily newspapers, *De West* and *De Ware Tijd*
*WPFI score* – 18,2 (29)

# SWAZILAND

*Umbuso weSwatini – Kingdom of Swaziland*

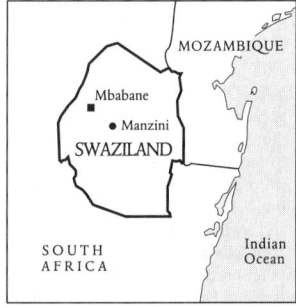

*Area* – 17,364 sq. km
*Capital* – Mbabane; population, 66,000 (2014). Lobamba is the legislative capital
*Major town* – Manzini
*Currency* – Lilangeni (E; plural *Emalangeni*) of 100 cents; the Lilangeni has a par value with the South African rand, which is also in circulation
*Population* – 1,435,613 rising at 1.11 per cent a year (2015 est)
*Religion* – Christian (Zionist 40 per cent, Roman Catholic 20 per cent), Muslim 10 per cent
*Language* – English, siSwati (both official)
*Population density* – 73 per sq. km (2013)
*Urban population* – 21.2 per cent (2013 est)
*Median age (years)* – 21 (2014 est)
*National anthem* – 'Nkulunkulu Mnikati wetibusiso temaSwati' ['Oh God, Bestower of Blessings on the Swazi']
*National day* – 6 September (Independence Day)
*Death penalty* – Retained (last used 1983)
*CPI score* – 43 (69)
*Literacy rate* – 94.8 per cent (2015 est)
*Gross enrolment ratio (percentage of relevant age group)* – primary 116 per cent; secondary 58 per cent (2011 est)
*Health expenditure (per capita)* – US$256 (2013)
*Hospital beds (per 1,000 people)* – 2.1 (2011)
*Life expectancy (years)* – 50.54 (2014 est)
*Mortality rate* – 13.75 (2014 est)
*Birth rate* – 25.18 (2014 est)
*Infant mortality rate* – 54.82 (2014 est)
*HIV/AIDS adult prevalence* – 27.36 per cent (2013 est)

## CLIMATE AND TERRAIN

The main regions of the landlocked country are: the densely forested and mountainous Highveld along the western border, with an average altitude of 1,219m; the Middleveld, a mixed farming area which averages about 609m in altitude, and the Lowveld, which was mainly scrubland until the introduction of sugar cane plantations, in the centre; and the Lubombo ridge, along the eastern edge of the country. Elevation extremes range from 1,862m (Emlembe) to 21m (Great Usutu river). Four rivers, the Komati, Usutu, Mbuluzi and Ngwavuma, flow from west to east.

The climate varies; the Highveld is humid and temperate, the Middleveld and Lubombo are subtropical, and the Lowveld is tropical and semi-arid. Average temperatures in Mbabane, in the Highveld, range from 15.8°C in July to 24°C in February.

## HISTORY AND POLITICS

The Swazi people are believed to have arrived in the area in the 16th century, and by the mid-17th century had developed a strong kingdom three times the size of the present country. This became a protectorate of the Boer republic of the Transvaal in 1884, and subsequently of Britain. The Kingdom of Swaziland became independent in 1968.

In 1973 King Sobhuza II suspended the constitution, banned political parties and assumed absolute power. The parliamentary system was replaced by traditional tribal communities *(tinkhundla)*. Sobhuza II died in 1982, and was succeeded by a son who was a minor. The regency between 1982 and 1986 led to power struggles within the royal family, but the real power passed to the Dlamini clan, which continues to dominate the government.

Swaziland has the highest levels of HIV/AIDS infection in the world, and as a consequence faces serious demo-graphic, economic and social problems.

The 2005 constitution retains the executive powers of the king; it appears to permit political parties while maintaining the ban on their members standing for election. The head of state is a hereditary king who is effectively an absolute monarch who rules by decree. There is a bicameral parliament comprising a 30-member senate and a 65-member House of Assembly; members of both serve a five-year term. Each of the country's 55 administrative districts *(tinkhundla)* directly elects one member to the House of Assembly and the king appoints ten members; there is also a provision for four female members to be regionally elected if the total percentage of women is less than 30 per cent. The members of the House of Assembly elect ten of their own number to the senate and a further 20 senators are appointed by the king.

HEAD OF STATE
*HM The King of Swaziland,* King Mswati III,
  crowned 25 April 1986

SELECTED GOVERNMENT MEMBERS *as at June 2015*
*Prime Minister,* Barnabas Sibusiso Dlamini
*Deputy Prime Minister,* Paul Dlamini
*Finance,* Martin Dlamini
*Foreign Affairs,* Mgwagwa Gamedze

KINGDOM OF SWAZILAND HIGH COMMISSION
20 Buckingham Gate, London SW1E 6LB
T 020-7630 6611 E enquiries@swaziland.org.uk
*High Commissioner,* HE Dumsile Sukati, *apptd* 2011

BRITISH HIGH COMMISSIONER
HE Judith Macgregor, CMG, LVO, *apptd* 2013, resident at
  Pretoria (Tshwane), South Africa

ECONOMY AND TRADE
The country is very poor, with 63 per cent of the population living below the poverty line. Customs dues from the South African Customs Union and remittances from expatriates working in South Africa are a vital supplement to the domestic economy; customs revenue dropped sharply in the global downturn and the government applied for international financial assistance. Overgrazing, soil depletion, drought and floods are potential future problems.

Subsistence agriculture occupies about 70 per cent of the population and contributes 7.2 per cent of GDP. Sugar cane, cotton, citrus fruits and pineapples are the main cash crops and the basis of industries producing sugar, canned fruit and soft drink concentrates. Coal mining has become less important since the 1980s with diversification into manufacturing such products as textiles, clothing, wood pulp and refrigerators. Industry contributes 47.4 per cent of GDP and services 45.4 per cent.

South Africa accounts for about 60 per cent of exports and over 90 per cent of imports. Principal exports are the products of agriculture and manufacturing. The main imports are vehicles, machinery, transport equipment, foodstuffs, petroleum products and chemicals.
*GNI* – US$3,738m; US$2,990 per capita (2013)
*Annual average growth of GDP* – 2.1 per cent (2014 est)
*Inflation rate* – 5.7 per cent (2014 est)
*Population below poverty line* – 63 per cent (2009)
*Unemployment* – 69 per cent (2006)
*Total external debt* – US$5,683m (2014 est)
*Imports* – US$1,946m (2012)
*Exports* – US$1,897m (2012)

BALANCE OF PAYMENTS
*Trade* – US$49m deficit (2012)
*Current Account* – US$14m surplus (2015 est)

| Trade with UK | 2013 | 2014 |
| --- | --- | --- |
| Imports from UK | £2,459,735 | £2,463,209 |
| Exports to UK | £5,897,800 | £12,605,625 |

COMMUNICATIONS
*Airports* – There is an international airport at Manzini, which is expected to be replaced by the new Mswati III International Airport
*Roadways and railways* – There are 1,078km of roads; 301km of railway connect with the Mozambique port of Maputo and the South African railway to Richards Bay and Durban
*Telecommunications* – 48,600 fixed lines and 805,000 mobile subscriptions (2012); there were 90,100 internet users in 2009
*Internet code and IDD* – sz; 268 (from UK), 44 (to UK)
*Media* – Swaziland Broadcasting and Information Service (radio) and Swazi TV are the state broadcasters; the only daily newspapers are *The Times of Swaziland* and *The Swazi Observer*
*WPFI score* – 47,28 (155)

# SWEDEN

*Konungariket Sverige – Kingdom of Sweden*

*Area* – 450,295 sq. km
*Capital* – Stockholm; population, 1,464,000 (2014)
*Major cities* – Gothenburg, Malmo, Uppsala
*Currency* – Swedish krona of 100 ore
*Population* – 9,801,616 rising at 0.8 per cent a year (2015 est)
*Religion* – Christian (Lutheran 87 per cent) (est)
*Language* – Swedish (official), Finnish, Sami
*Population density* – 24 per sq. km (2013)
*Urban population* – 85.5 per cent (2013 est)
*Median age (years)* – 41.2 (2014 est)
*National anthem* – 'Du Gamla, Du Fria' ['Thou Ancient, Thou Free']
*National day* – 6 June
*Death penalty* – Abolished for all crimes (since 1972)
*CPI score* – 87 (4)

CLIMATE AND TERRAIN
The terrain is mostly flat or rolling lowlands in the south and along the east coast, with mountains in the west. Elevation extremes range from 2,111m (Kebnekaise) to −2.4m (reclaimed bay of Lake Hammarsjon). There are many lakes, including Vanern, Vattern, Malaren and Hjalmaren in the south, and over 20,000 islands off the coast near Stockholm. The climate is temperate in the south and subarctic in the north; average temperatures range from −7°C in January and February to 14.5°C in July.

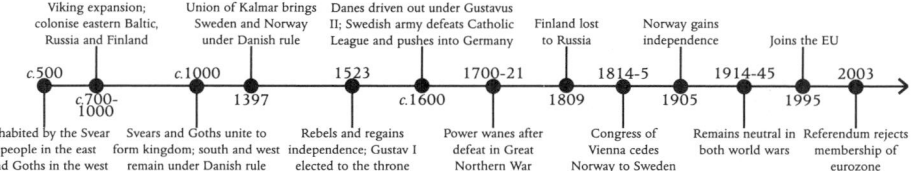

Viking expansion; colonise eastern Baltic, Russia and Finland — Union of Kalmar brings Sweden and Norway under Danish rule — Danes driven out under Gustavus II; Swedish army defeats Catholic League and pushes into Germany — Finland lost to Russia — Norway gains independence — Joins the EU

*c.*500    *c.*1000    1523    1700–21    1814–5    1914–45    2003
*c.*700–1000    1397    *c.*1600    1809    1905    1995

Inhabited by the Svear people in the east and Goths in the west — Svears and Goths unite to form kingdom; south and west remain under Danish rule — Rebels and regains independence; Gustav I elected to the throne — Power wanes after defeat in Great Northern War — Congress of Vienna cedes Norway to Sweden — Remains neutral in both world wars — Referendum rejects membership of eurozone

## POLITICS

Sweden is a hereditary constitutional monarchy. The 1975 constitution was amended in 1979 to vest the succession in the monarch's eldest child irrespective of sex. The unicameral legislature, the *Riksdag*, has 349 members directly elected by proportional representation for a four-year term. The prime minister appoints the council of ministers.

Legislative elections in September 2014 saw the Social Democrats remain the largest party in the *Riksdag* and form a minority government with support from the Green Party. The government's first budget was voted down in the legislature and Prime Minister Stefan Lofven announced plans to hold early elections in March 2015 to resolve the deadlock. However, in December 2014 an agreement was reached with the opposition centre-right Alliance coalition that would allow the government to continue to operate without holding early elections.

Sweden is divided into 21 counties *(lan)* and 290 municipalities *(kommun)*.

### HEAD OF STATE

*HM The King of Sweden,* King Carl XVI Gustaf, KG, *born* 30 April 1946, *succeeded* 15 September 1973
*Heir,* HRH Crown Princess Victoria Ingrid Alice Desiree, Duchess of Vastergotland, *born* 14 July 1977

### SELECTED GOVERNMENT MEMBERS *as at June 2015*
*Prime Minister,* Stefan Lofven
*Deputy Prime Minister,* Asa Romson
*Defence,* Peter Hultqvist
*Finance,* Magdalena Andersson

### EMBASSY OF SWEDEN
11 Montagu Place, London W1H 2AL
T 020-7917 6400 E ambassaden.london@gov.se
W www.swedenabroad.com/london
*Ambassador Extraordinary and Plenipotentiary,* HE Nicola Clase, *apptd* 2010

### BRITISH EMBASSY
PO Box 27819, Skarpogatan 6–8, 115 93 Stockholm
T (+46) (8) 671 3000 E info@britishembassy.se
W www.gov.uk/government/world/sweden
*Ambassador Extraordinary and Plenipotentiary,* HE David Cairns, *apptd* 2015

### DEFENCE
Sweden has a policy of non-alignment in peace and neutrality in war, and has declined to become a member of NATO.

| Aged 16–49, 2010 est | Males | Females |
| --- | --- | --- |
| Available for military service | 2,065,691 | 1,996,764 |
| Fit for military service | 1,709,055 | 1,650,432 |

*Military expenditure* – US$6,573m (2014)
*Conscription* – Abolished in practice as of 2009; retained for emergencies

## ECONOMY AND TRADE

Sweden developed from an agricultural to an industrial economy in the early 20th century. The prosperity that had funded the generous welfare state after 1946 ended in the early 1990s, when Sweden experienced a deep recession. It recovered to experience strong growth before briefly entering recession again in 2008–9 as a result of the global downturn. Despite improving results for the banking sector, growth slowed from 1 per cent in 2012–14, but should accelerate to 2.6 per cent in 2015 as the eurozone recovers and the weak value of the kronor boosts exports sales.

The main export-orientated industries are engineering and high-tech manufacturing, mining and forestry. Mineral resources include iron ore, copper, lead, zinc, sulphur, granite, marble, precious and heavy metals (the latter not exploited) and extensive deposits of low-grade uranium ore. The engineering sector provides 50 per cent of output and exports, particularly specialised machinery and systems such as electrical and electronic equipment and armaments, and motor vehicles and aircraft; other industries produce pharmaceuticals, plastics and chemicals.

Agriculture contributes 1.8 per cent of GDP, industry 33.4 per cent and services 64.8 per cent.

The main trading partners are other EU states, Norway and China. Principal exports include machinery, vehicles, paper products, pulp and wood, iron and steel products, and chemicals. The main imports are machinery, oil and petroleum products, chemicals, vehicles, iron and steel, foodstuffs and clothing.

*GNI* – US$592,410m; US$61,760 per capita (2013)
*Annual average growth of GDP* – 2.1 per cent (2014 est)
*Inflation rate* – –0.1 per cent (2014 est)
*Population below poverty line* – 14 per cent (2011 est)
*Unemployment* – 8.3 per cent (2015 est)
*Total external debt* – US$1,039,000m (2012)
*Imports* – US$159,665m (2013)
*Exports* – US$167,619m (2013)

### BALANCE OF PAYMENTS
*Trade* – US$8,896m surplus (2012)
*Current Account* – US$30,711m surplus (2015 est)

| Trade with UK | 2013 | 2014 |
| --- | --- | --- |
| Imports from UK | £5,576,121,106 | £5,449,853,573 |
| Exports to UK | £7,431,618,195 | £7,615,955,474 |

## COMMUNICATIONS
*Airports and waterways* – The principal airports are at Stockholm, Gothenburg, Lulea, Malmo and Umea; the main ports are Gothenburg, Helsingborg, Malmo and Stockholm
*Roadways and railways* – 135,444km; 11,633km
*Telecommunications* – 4.321 million fixed lines and 11.64 million mobile subscriptions (2012); there were 8.40 million internet users in 2009
*Internet code and IDD* – se; 46 (from UK), 44 (to UK)
*Major broadcasters* – The public broadcasters are Sveriges Television (SVT) and Sveriges Radio
*Press* – Major daily newspapers include *Aftonbladet, Dagens Nyheter* and *Goteborgs Posten*
*WPFI score* – 9,47 (5)

## EDUCATION AND HEALTH

The state education system provides nine years of free and compulsory schooling from the age of seven to 16 in the comprehensive elementary schools.

*Gross enrolment ratio (percentage of relevant age group)* – primary 102 per cent; secondary 98 per cent (2012 est); tertiary 65 per cent (2013 est)
*Health expenditure (per capita)* – US$5,680 (2013)
*Hospital beds (per 1,000 people)* – 2.7 (2011)
*Life expectancy (years)* – 81.89 (2014 est)
*Mortality rate* – 9.45 (2014 est)
*Birth rate* – 11.92 (2014 est)
*Infant mortality rate* – 2.6 (2014 est)

# SWITZERLAND

*Schweizerische Eidgenossenschaft/Confédération suisse/ Confederazione Svizzera/Confederaziun svizra – Swiss Confederation*

*Area* – 41,277 sq. km
*Capital* – Bern; population, 358,000 (2015)
*Major cities* – Basel, Geneva, Lausanne, Zurich
*Currency* – Swiss franc of 100 rappen (or centimes)
*Population* – 8,121,830 rising at 0.71 per cent a year (2015 est); German (65 per cent), French (18 per cent), Italian (10 per cent), Romansch (1 per cent) (est)
*Religion* – Christian (Roman Catholic 38.2 per cent, Protestant 26.9 per cent), Muslim 4.9 per cent, none 21.4 (2012 est)
*Language* – German, French, Italian, Romansch (all official), Albanian, English, Portuguese, Serbo-Croatian, Spanish
*Population density* – 205 per sq. km (2013)
*Urban population* – 73.8 per cent (2013)
*Median age (years)* – 42 (2014)
*National anthem* – 'Schweizerpsalm'/'Cantique suisse'/'Salmo svizzero'/'Psalm svizzer' ['Swiss Psalm']
*National day* – 1 August (Confederation Day)
*Death penalty* – Abolished for all crimes (since 1992)
*CPI score* – 86 (5)

## CLIMATE AND TERRAIN

Switzerland is the most mountainous country in Europe. The central plateau of hills, plains and over 1,500 lakes is enclosed by mountains. The Jura mountains lie in the northwest and the Alps, which cover two-thirds of the country, occupy the south and east. Elevation extremes range from 4,634m (Dufourspitze, Alps) to 195m (Lake Maggiore). Lakes Neuchâtel, Lucerne and Zurich lie wholly within the country, but Lake Maggiore is shared with Italy, Lake Geneva with France and Lake Constance with Germany and Austria. The Rhine, Rhône and Inn rivers all rise in the Alps. The climate is temperate, with conditions that vary with altitude.

Average temperatures range from −1.5°C in January to 15.2°C in July.

## HISTORY AND POLITICS

The area was conquered by the Romans in 58 BC and then overrun by Germanic tribes in the fourth century AD. It was a province of the medieval Holy Roman Empire from 1033. The Swiss confederation began in 1291 as a defensive alliance of three cantons to protect their autonomy, and expanded during the following centuries, becoming independent of the Habsburgs in the 14th century. Its independence was recognised by the Treaty of Westphalia in 1648. French revolutionary forces captured Switzerland in 1789 and named it the Helvetic Republic. Independence was restored in 1814, and the congress of Vienna (1815) joined Geneva, Neuchatel and Valais to the confederation and recognised the country's perpetual neutrality in international affairs.

Many policy decisions are submitted to national referendums. Although the federal government has pursued a policy of gradual integration with the EU and applied for membership in 1992, referendums have rejected membership of the European Economic Area (1992), approved bilateral trade agreements with the EU (2000) and rejected EU membership (2001).

Proportional representation, introduced in 1919, resulted in coalition governments throughout the 20th and into the 21st century. Apart from a 12-month period in 2007–8, since 1959 the federal government has been a coalition of four parties: the Swiss People's Party (SVP), the Social Democratic Party, the Christian Democratic People's Party and the Radical Democratic Party. The SVP, in coalition with the Democratic Centre Union, remained the largest party in the National Council in the 2011 legislative election. In December 2014 Simonetta Sommaruga of the Social Democratic Party of Switzerland was elected president and took office in January 2015.

Under the 1998 constitution, the head of state is a president elected annually (along with the vice-president) for a one-year term by the federal legislature from the members of the Federal Council; consecutive terms may not be served. The bicameral legislature, the Federal Assembly, has two chambers: the National Council has 200 members, directly elected for a four-year term; the Council of States has 46 members (two from each canton and one from each half-canton) directly elected within each canton for a four-year term.

Executive power is in the hands of a Federal Council of seven members, elected for a four-year term by the Federal Assembly after every legislative election. The Federal Council is chaired by the president. Not more than one person from the same canton may be elected a member of the Council; however, there is a tradition that Italian- and French-speaking areas should between them be represented on the council by at least two members.

SELECTED GOVERNMENT MEMBERS *as at June 2015*
*President of the Swiss Confederation*, Simonetta Sommaruga, *elected* 3 December 2014, *sworn in* 1 January 2015
*Vice-President*, Johann Schneider-Ammann
*Finance*, Eveline Widmer-Schlumpf
*Interior*, Alain Berset

EMBASSY OF SWITZERLAND
16–18 Montagu Place, London W1H 2BQ
T 020-7616 6000 E lon.swissembassy@eda.admin.ch
W www.eda.admin.ch/london
*Ambassador Extraordinary and Plenipotentiary*, HE Dominik Furgler, *apptd* 2013

## BRITISH EMBASSY

Thunstrasse 50, 3005 Bern
T (+41) (31) 359 7700 E info.berne@fco.gsi.gov.uk
W www.gov.uk/government/world/switzerland
*Ambassador Extraordinary and Plenipotentiary,* HE David
Moran, *apptd* 2014

## CONFEDERAL STRUCTURE

There are 23 cantons, three of which are subdivided, making
20 cantons and six half-cantons, or 26 in all. Each canton
and half-canton has its own government and a substantial
degree of autonomy. The main language in 19 of the cantons
is German; in six others it is French and one Italian.

## DEFENCE

| Aged 16–49, 2010 est | Males | Females |
| --- | --- | --- |
| Available for military service | 1,828,043 | 1,786,552 |
| Fit for military service | 1,493,509 | 1,459,450 |

*Military expenditure* – US$5,229m (2014)
*Conscription duration* – 18 weeks mandatory training, then
intermittent three-week refresher courses

## ECONOMY AND TRADE

Switzerland has a prosperous and stable market economy with
low unemployment and a highly skilled labour force. Its
prosperity is based on banking, financial services and export-
orientated industrial manufacturing. The economy went into
recession in 2009 owing to slower export demand and the
impact on the banking sector during the 2008 global financial
crisis. Growth remained slow between 2013 and 2015 due to
the poor performance of the eurozone and the strength of the
Swiss Franc, which helped make exports less competitive.
Although not an EU member, Switzerland has brought many
practices in line with the EU to maintain competitiveness, and
it is currently adopting OECD standards on tax administration
and transparency. The economy is expected to grow by
expansion of 1.7 per cent during 2016–19.

Agriculture is practised in the mountain valleys and the
central plateau, where grains, fruits and vegetables are grown.
Dairy farming and stock-raising are also important. The
industrial sector is noted for precision, electrical and
mechanical engineering, pharmaceuticals, chemicals,
telecommunications, food processing and packaging, and
graphics. Banking, insurance and tourism are the major
service industries. Agriculture contributes 0.8 per cent of
GDP, industry 26.7 per cent and services 72.5 per cent.

The main trading partners are EU countries (especially
Germany) and the USA. Principal exports are machinery,
chemicals, metals, watches and agricultural products. The
main imports are machinery, chemicals, vehicles, metals,
agricultural products and textiles.

*GNI* – US$733,437m; US$90,760 per capita (2013)
*Annual average growth of GDP* – 1.3 per cent (2014 est)
*Inflation rate* – –0.1 per cent (2014 est)
*Population below poverty line* – 7.6 per cent (2011 est)
*Unemployment* – 4.2 per cent (2015 est)
*Total external debt* – US$1,544,000m (2012)
*Imports* – US$191,705m (2013)
*Exports* – US$217,079m (2013)

BALANCE OF PAYMENTS
*Trade* – US$25,364m surplus (2012)
*Current Account* – US$39,711m surplus (2015)

| Trade with UK | 2013 | 2014 |
| --- | --- | --- |
| Imports from UK | £45,434,582,626 | £21,312,685,964 |
| Exports to UK | £8,081,040,878 | £8,927,457,335 |

## COMMUNICATIONS

*Airports and waterways* – The principal airports are at Zurich,
Basel, Bern and Geneva; the Rhine carries commercial
shipping on the 65km stretch from Basel-Rheinfelden and
Schaffhausen-Bodensee, and there are 12 navigable lakes
*Roadways and railways* – There are 71,464km of roadways,
including 1,415km of motorways, and 4,876km of railways
*Telecommunications* – 4.382 million fixed lines and 10.46
million mobile subscriptions (2012); there were 6.15 million
internet users in 2009
*Internet code and IDD* – ch; 41 (from UK), 44 (to UK)
*Major broadcasters* – The public-service Swiss Broadcasting
Corporation (SRG/SSR), which is funded mainly through
licence fees, dominates broadcasting
*Press* – Newspapers tend to be regional, reflecting linguistic
divisions: major titles include *Neue Zürcher Zeitung* (Zurich
based), *Le Temps* (Geneva) and *Corriere del Ticino* (Lugano)
*WPFI score* – 13,85 (20)

## EDUCATION AND HEALTH

Education is controlled by cantonal and communal
authorities and is free and compulsory from ages seven to 16.
*Gross enrolment ratio (percentage of relevant age group)* –
primary 103 per cent; secondary 96 per cent (2012 est);
tertiary 56 per cent (2013 est)
*Health expenditure (per capita)* – US$9,276 (2013)
*Hospital beds (per 1,000 people)* – 5.0 (2011)
*Life expectancy (years)* – 82.39 (2014 est)
*Mortality rate* – 8.10 (2014 est)
*Birth rate* – 10.48 (2014 est)
*Infant mortality rate* – 3.73 (2014 est)

# SYRIA

*Al-Jumhuriyah al-Arabiyah as-Suriyah* – *Syrian Arab Republic*

*Area* – 185,180 sq. km
*Capital* – Damascus; population, 2,574,000 (2014)
*Major cities* – Aleppo (Halab), Hama (Hamah), Homs (Hims),
Latakia (al-Ladhiqiyah)
*Currency* – Syrian pound (S£) of 100 piastres
*Population* – 17,064,854 falling at 0.16 per cent a year
(2015 est)
*Religion* – Muslim (Sunni 74 per cent, other 13 per cent,
including Alawite, Ismaili), Christian 10 per cent (est)
(of which Greek Orthodox is the largest denomination),
Druze 3 per cent
*Language* – Arabic (official), Kurdish, Armenian, Aramaic,
Circassian, French
*Population density* – 124 per sq. km (2013)
*Urban population* – 56.9 per cent (2013 est)
*Median age (years)* – 23.3 (2014 est)
*National anthem* – 'Homat al-Diyar' ['Guardians of the
Homeland']

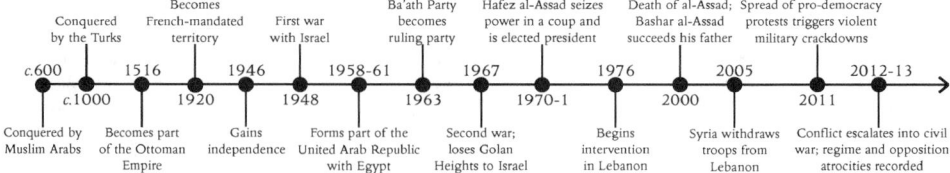

| | Becomes | | | Ba'ath Party | Hafez al-Assad seizes | | Death of al-Assad; | Spread of pro-democracy |
| Conquered | French-mandated | First war | | becomes | power in a coup and | | Bashar al-Assad | protests triggers violent |
| by the Turks | territory | with Israel | | ruling party | is elected president | | succeeds his father | military crackdowns |

| c.600 | 1516 | 1946 | 1958-61 | 1967 | 1976 | 2005 | 2012-13 |

| c.1000 | 1920 | 1948 | 1963 | 1970-1 | 2000 | 2011 |

| Conquered by | Becomes part | Gains | Forms part of the | Second war; | Begins | Syria withdraws | Conflict escalates into civil |
| Muslim Arabs | of the Ottoman | independence | United Arab Republic | loses Golan | intervention | troops from | war; regime and opposition |
| | Empire | | with Egypt | Heights to Israel | in Lebanon | Lebanon | atrocities recorded |

*National day* – 17 April (Independence Day)
*Death penalty* – Retained
*CPI score* – 20 (159)

## CLIMATE AND TERRAIN
There is a narrow coastal plain and ranges of mountains in the west, and the fertile basin of the river Euphrates in the north-east. The centre and south of the interior consist of semi-arid and desert plateaus. Elevation extremes range from 2,814m (Mt Hermon) to −200m (unnamed location near Lake Tiberias). There is a desert climate in much of the country, moderated by altitude in the mountains, and a Mediterranean climate on the coast. Average temperatures range from 6.4°C in January to 29.6°C in July.

## HISTORY AND POLITICS
In March 2011, protests against the ruling Assad regime broke out in a number of cities, including Damascus and Deraa. In May the army was used to restore order in a number of towns. Many soldiers and commanders unwilling to use force against civilians broke away from the government, forming the Free Syrian Army, which began fighting against the administration. Mounting civilian casualties escalated the conflict, leading to the involvement of a number of different anti-Assad groups, including the Kurdish People's Protection Units (YPG) operating in the north-east of the country, Islamist groups and Hezbollah fighters from neighbouring Lebanon.

Following a chemical attack on the town of Ghouta by the Syrian air force in August 2013, the Syrian government came under sustained international pressure to abandon its stockpile of chemical weapons. In April 2014, 92.5 per cent of the country's chemical weapons were confirmed to have been removed or destroyed by UN observers. The government continued to cede control of its territory in 2015, losing control of Idlib province to Islamists in March, the Jordanian and Iraqi borders to secular and Islamist groups in March and June, and control of the eastern areas of the country to Kurdish fighters in June.

In February 2012, a new constitution providing for multiparty elections was approved via a referendum. The majority of countries refused to recognise the outcome of the poll; exceptions included Russia and China.

HEAD OF STATE
*President,* Lt.-Gen. Bashar al-Assad, *elected* 27 June 2000, *confirmed by referendum* 10 July 2000, *re-elected* 2007, 2014
*Vice-President,* Najah al-Attar

SELECTED GOVERNMENT MEMBERS *as at June 2015*
*Prime Minister,* Wael Nader al-Halaqi
*Defence,* Gen. Fahad Jassim al-Freij
*Finance,* Ismail Ismail
*Foreign Affairs,* Walid al-Muallem

EMBASSY OF THE SYRIAN ARAB REPUBLIC
8 Belgrave Square, London SW1X 8PH
T 020-7245 9012 W www.syremb.com
Closed due to the conflict

## DEFENCE

| *Aged 16–49, 2010 est* | *Males* | *Females* |
| --- | --- | --- |
| Available for military service | 5,889,837 | 5,660,751 |
| Fit for military service | 5,055,510 | 4,884,151 |

*Military expenditure* – US$2,495m (2011)
*Conscription duration* – 18 months

## ECONOMY AND TRADE
The economy is state-controlled and predominantly state-owned, although unrest and international sanctions have slowed economic growth. Conflict-related problems include infrastructure damage, reduced domestic consumption, decreased production and sharply rising inflation. As of 2015, the continuing violence has displaced approximately 12.9 million Syrians. Around 12 million Syrians are thought to be in need of humanitarian aid, including 5.6 million children.

Oil and agriculture account for nearly half of GDP, but other activities, such as financial services, telecommunications, tourism and non-oil industry and trade, are becoming increasingly important. Gas is produced for domestic use, and phosphate is mined and processed; other non-oil industry includes the manufacture of textiles, processed food, beverages, tobacco and cement, and car assembly. Agriculture contributes 16.4 per cent of GDP, industry 22.7 per cent and services 60.9 per cent.

The main export markets are Iraq, Saudi Arabia, Kuwait and the UAE; imports come chiefly from Saudi Arabia, the UAE, Iran and Iraq. Principal exports are crude oil, minerals, petroleum products, fruit and vegetables, cotton fibre, textiles, clothing, meat, livestock and wheat. The main imports are machinery and transport equipment, electric power machinery, food and livestock, metals and metal products, chemicals, plastics, yarn and paper.
*GNI* – US$70,501m; US$2,610 per capita (2010)
*Annual average growth of GDP* – −2.3 per cent (2011 est)
*Inflation rate* – 34.8 per cent (2014 est)
*Population below poverty line* – 11.9 per cent (2006 est)
*Unemployment* – 8.5 per cent (2015 est)
*Total external debt* – US$11,640m (2014 est)
*Imports* – US$5,800m (2013)
*Exports* – US$3,000m (2013)

BALANCE OF PAYMENTS
*Trade* – US$5,700m deficit (2011)
*Current Account* – US$1,584m deficit (2009)

| *Trade with UK* | *2013* | *2014* |
| --- | --- | --- |
| Imports from UK | £16,863,847 | £11,647,986 |
| Exports to UK | £3,038,069 | £5,745,449 |

## COMMUNICATIONS
*Airports and waterways* – The principal airports are at Aleppo and Damascus; the main port is Latakia
*Roadways and railways* – 69,873km; 2,052km
*Telecommunications* – 4.425 million fixed lines and 12.93 million mobile subscriptions (2012); there were 4.47 million internet users in 2009

*Internet code and IDD* – sy; 963 (from UK), 44 (to UK)
*Major broadcasters* – Syrian Arab Republic Radio and Syrian TV are the public broadcasters; opposition groups operate TV and radio stations, including Al-Ghad (TV) and the Syrian Radio Network
*Press* – Only government-owned newspapers publish daily; leading titles include *Al-Baath, Al-Thawra* and *Tishrin*
*WPFI score* – 77,29 (177)

## EDUCATION AND HEALTH

Education is under state control. Elementary education is free at state schools and is compulsory from the age of seven.
*Literacy rate* – 96.4 per cent (2015 est)
*Gross enrolment ratio (percentage of relevant age group)* – primary 74 per cent; secondary 48 per cent (2013 est)
*Health expenditure (per capita)* – US$43 (2013)
*Hospital beds (per 1,000 people)* – 1.5 (2012)
*Life expectancy (years)* – 68.41 (2014 est)
*Mortality rate* – 6.51 (2014 est)
*Birth rate* – 22.76 (2014 est)
*Infant mortality rate* – 15.79 (2014 est)

# TAIWAN

*T'ai-wan* – *Taiwan (Republic of China)*

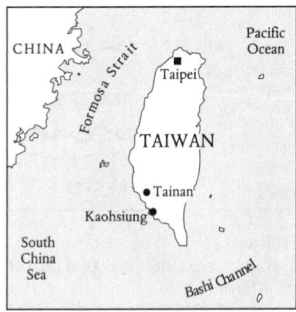

*Area* – 35,980 sq. km
*Capital* – Taipei; population, 2,667,000 (2014 est)
*Major cities* – Kaohsiung, Taichung, Tainan
*Currency* – New Taiwan dollar (NT$) of 100 cents
*Population* – 23,415,126 rising at 0.23 per cent a year (2015 est); Taiwanese 84 per cent, Mainland Chinese 14 per cent, indigenous 2 per cent (est)
*Religion* – Mixture of Buddhist and Taoist 93 per cent, Christian 4.5 per cent; many also practise Chinese folk beliefs
*Language* – Mandarin (official), Taiwanese (Min), Hakka dialects
*Population density* – 618 per sq. km (2001)
*Median age (years)* – 39.2 (2014 est)
*National anthem* – 'San Min Chu I' ['Three Principles of the People']
*National day* – 10 October (Republic Day)
*Death penalty* – Retained (last used 2011)
*CPI score* – 61 (35)
*Life expectancy (years)* – 79.84 (2014 est)
*Mortality rate* – 6.97 (2014 est)
*Birth rate* – 8.55 (2014 est)
*Infant mortality rate* – 4.49 (2014 est)

## CLIMATE AND TERRAIN

The island of Taiwan (formerly Formosa) lies 145km east of the Chinese mainland. Mountains run the length of the island, covering over half the terrain, with lowlands in the west. Elevation extremes range from 3,952m (Yu Shan) to 0m (South China Sea). Taiwan shares the tropical monsoon climate of southern China, with large seasonal variations in temperature, dry winters and wet summers. The typhoon season lasts from May to November, with particularly high humidity between July and September. Average temperatures in Taipei range from 16°C in January and February and 29°C in July and August.

Territories include the Penghu (Pescadores) islands (80.47 sq. km), some 56km west of Taiwan, as well as Kinmen (Quemoy) (109 sq. km) and Matsu (7 sq. km), which are only a few kilometres from mainland China.

## HISTORY AND POLITICS

Originally settled by Austronesian people 8,000 years ago, Chinese colonists arrived on the island from around the 12th century. The island was annexed by China in the 17th century, and ceded to Japan in 1895 at the end of the Sino-Japanese War. It was returned to China after Japan's defeat in the Second World War. The Kuomintang (KMT) government, led by Gen. Chiang Kai-shek, withdrew to Taiwan in 1949 after being defeated by the communists in mainland China. He was succeeded as president by his son, Gen. Chiang Ching-kuo, who ruled until his death in 1988. Martial law was lifted in 1987 after 38 years. In 1991 the Taiwanese government declared an end to the state of war with China, officially recognising the People's Republic of China for the first time, and ended emergency measures that had frozen political life in Taiwan since 1949.

Democratisation of the authoritarian one-party state began in the 1980s and led to the first multiparty elections in 1992. The 'Senior Parliamentarians' who had retained their seats since being elected on the mainland in 1948 were forcibly retired in 1991–2. From this point, power shifted away from the mainlanders to the native Taiwanese, and 50 years of KMT rule ended when the Democratic Progressive Party (DPP), which favours self-determination, won the presidency in 2000 and the 2001 legislative election.

The DPP retained the presidency and continued in government after the 2004 elections. However, in the 2008 elections the KMT returned to power, and the KMT candidate, Ma Ying-jeou, was elected president. The KMT retained its majority in the 2012 legislative election and Ma Ying-jeou was re-elected. The government resigned in November 2014 following poor local election results; former vice premier Mao Chi-kuo of the KMT was appointed prime minister.

Most nations acknowledge the position of the Chinese government that Taiwan is a province of the People's Republic of China, and as a result Taiwan has formal diplomatic relations with only 22 countries and no seat at the UN. China has sanctioned the use of force to prevent Taiwan declaring itself independent.

Contacts between Taiwan and China began in the 1980s and have led to a gradual relaxation of restrictions on direct economic, trade and transport links, and on travel and tourism. Since the KMT returned to power in 2008, Taiwan has sought greater economic cooperation and integration with China.

The 1947 constitution (which originally applied to the whole of China) has been amended a number of times since 1991. In 2004 an amendment provided for future proposed constitutional changes to be put to a referendum instead of the National Assembly (formerly the upper house of the legislature), which was disbanded under 2005 provisions that also reduced the number of legislative seats with effect from the 2008 election.

The president is directly elected for a four-year term, renewable once. The unicameral Legislative Yuan has 113 members: 73 directly elected, 34 elected proportionately by party and six elected by indigenous peoples in two constituencies; all serve a four-year term. The president appoints the premier and, on the premier's advice, the cabinet.

## HEAD OF STATE
*President*, Ma Ying-jeou, *elected* 22 March 2008, *re-elected* 14 January 2012
*Vice-President*, Wu Den-yih

## SELECTED GOVERNMENT MEMBERS *as at July 2015*
*Premier*, Mao Chi-kuo
*Defence*, Kao Kuang-chi
*Economy*, John Deng Chen-chung
*Foreign Affairs*, David Lin Yung-lo

## DEFENCE

| Aged 16–49, 2010 est | Males | Females |
| --- | --- | --- |
| Available for military service | 6,183,567 | 6,006,676 |
| Fit for military service | 5,074,173 | 4,951,088 |

*Military expenditure* – US$10,244m (2014)
*Conscription duration* – 24 months

## ECONOMY AND TRADE
Since the 1950s Taiwan has transformed itself from a mainly agricultural country into a highly developed industrial economy. This transition was driven by exports. There has been a gradual shift away from state domination of the economy, with a reduction in government influence on investment and foreign trade, and privatisation in the financial and industrial sectors. Taiwan's export markets suffered severely in the global economic downturn and the economy contracted sharply in 2008–9; despite achieving double-digit growth in 2010, growth slowed in 2011–14, averaging 3 per cent. The KMT's controversial policy of encouraging trade with China has lead to opposition, including large demonstrations in 2014.

Only a quarter of the land area is suitable for agriculture but the soil is very fertile, producing rice, corn, vegetables, fruit, tea, flowers, meat and dairy products. The industrial base includes electronics, communications and information technology products, oil refining, armaments, chemicals, textiles, iron and steel, machinery, cement, food processing, vehicles, consumer goods, pharmaceuticals and fishing. Agriculture contributes 1.7 per cent of GDP, industry 30.5 per cent and services 67.8 per cent.

The main trading partners are China (27.1 per cent of exports), Japan (17.6 per cent of imports), the USA and Hong Kong. Principal exports are electronic and computer equipment, flat panels, machinery, metals, textiles, plastics, chemicals and precision instruments. The main imports are electronic and electrical equipment, machinery, crude oil and precision instruments.
*Average annual growth of GDP* – 3.5 per cent (2014 est)
*Inflation rate* – 1.5 per cent (2014 est)
*Population below poverty line* – 1.5 per cent (2012 est)
*Unemployment* – 4.1 per cent (2015 est)
*Total external debt* – US$191,900m (2014 est)
*Imports* – US$251,500m (2010)
*Exports* – US$274,600m (2010)

## BALANCE OF PAYMENTS
*Trade* – US$23,100m surplus (2010)
*Current Account* – US$65,705m surplus (2015 est)

| Trade with UK | 2013 | 2014 |
| --- | --- | --- |
| Imports from UK | £1,192,943,273 | £1,095,920,618 |
| Exports to UK | £3,429,147,830 | £3,228,291,836 |

## COMMUNICATIONS
*Airports and waterways* – There are international airports at Taoyuan (near Taipei), Kaohsiung and Taichung; the main ports are Keelung, Kaohsiung and Taichung
*Roadways and railways* – 41,475km; 1,580km
*Telecommunications* – 15.998 million fixed lines and 29.46 million mobile subscriptions (2012); there were 16.15 million internet users in 2009
*Internet code and IDD* – tw; 886 (from UK), 2 44 (to UK)
*Broadcasters* – The government runs two non-profit public broadcasters, Public Television Service and CBS-Radio Taiwan International
*Press* – Major daily newspapers include *United Daily News*, *China Times* (both Chinese language) and *The China Post* (English)
*WPFI score* – 24,83 (51)

# TAJIKISTAN

*Jumhurii Tojikiston – Republic of Tajikistan*

*Area* – 143,100 sq. km
*Capital* – Dushanbe; population, 801,000 (2014)
*Major towns* – Khujand, Kulob
*Currency* – Somoni of 100 dirams
*Population* – 8,191,958 rising at 1.71 per cent a year (2015 est); Tajik (79.9 per cent), Uzbek (15.3 per cent), Russian (1.1 per cent), Kyrgyz (1.1 per cent) (2000)
*Religion* – Muslim (Sunni 85 per cent, Shia 5 per cent) (2003 est)
*Language* – Tajik (official), Russian
*Population density* – 59 per sq. km (2013)
*Urban population* – 26.6 per cent (2013 est)
*Median age (years)* – 23.5 (2014 est)
*National anthem* – 'Surudi Milli' ['National Anthem']
*National day* – 9 September (Independence Day)
*Death penalty* – Retained (last used 2004)
*CPI score* – 23 (152)
*Literacy rate* – 99.9 per cent (2015 est)
*Gross enrolment ratio (percentage of relevant age group)* – primary 102 per cent; secondary 87 per cent; tertiary 19.7 per cent (2011 est)
*Health expenditure (per capita)* – US$70 (2013)
*Hospital beds (per 1,000 people)* – 5.5 (2011)
*Life expectancy (years)* – 67.06 (2014 est)
*Mortality rate* – 6.28 (2014 est)
*Birth rate* – 24.99 (2014 est)
*Infant mortality rate* – 35.03 (2014 est)

## CLIMATE AND TERRAIN
Tajikistan is mountainous, with the Pamir highlands in the east and the high ridges of the Pamir-Altai ranges in the centre. More than half of the country lies above 3,000m.

Elevation extremes range from 7,495m (Qullai Ismoili Somoni) to 300m (Syr Darya river). The main rivers are the Syr Darya, flowing through the Fergana valley in the north, and the Amu Darya and its tributaries in the west and south. Most of the population lives on the fertile plains formed by these rivers. The climate is continental; average temperatures range from −8.6°C in January to 16.5°C in July.

## HISTORY AND POLITICS

The area that is now Tajikistan was first settled by Iranian peoples 3,000 years ago and was conquered by Alexander the Great in the fourth century BC, remaining under Greek and Greco-Persian rule for 200 years until the kingdom of Kushan was established throughout the Bactria region.

Tajikistan was invaded by Muslim Arabs in the eighth century AD, and Islam was the prevalent religion by the time of the Samanid Persian conquest in the ninth century. In 1868, the northern part was subsumed within the Russian Empire, while the south was annexed by the Bukhara khanate. At the time of the Russian revolution in 1917 the Central Asian territories attempted to establish their independence, but Bolshevik power was consolidated in the north by April 1918, and in the rest of Tajikistan by 1920. In 1924 the Tajikistan Autonomous Soviet Socialist Republic was formed as part of the Uzbek Republic, before Tajikistan was given the status of a full republic within the USSR in 1929.

Tajikistan declared its independence on 9 September 1991. In 1992, anti-government demonstrations escalated into a five-year civil war between government forces and Islamic and pro-democracy groups. A peace accord signed in 1997 was implemented by 2000. Political assassinations and bombings occurred after the end of the civil war, but the level of violence has dropped since 2002.

Former communists have dominated politics since 1991 and power is concentrated in the president's hands. Opposition parties are weak and face harassment; a number of opposition leaders have been arrested on criminal charges, moves that their supporters claim are politically motivated.

President Rakhmon has served as head of state since 1992, and was re-elected for a fourth term in 2013. The 2010 and 2015 legislative elections were won by the incumbent (former communist) People's Democratic Party of Tajikistan with an overwhelming majority, although international observers considered both polls flawed.

The 1994 constitution was amended in 1999 and 2003, following referendums, to introduce changes to the presidential term of office and the legislative structure. The executive president is directly elected for a single seven-year term, although the 2003 amendment permits the current incumbent to stand for two further terms. The bicameral parliament consists of the Assembly of Representatives (*Majlisi Namoyandogan*), which has 63 members directly elected for a five-year term, and the National Assembly (*Majlisi Milli*), which has 33 members, 25 elected by five regional assemblies and eight appointed by the president, to serve a five-year term. Administratively, Tajikistan is divided into two provinces and the Gorno-Badakhstan autonomous region.

### HEAD OF STATE

*President,* Emomali Rakhmon, *elected by Supreme Soviet* 19 November 1992, *elected* 6 November 1994, *re-elected* 1999, 2006, 2013

### SELECTED GOVERNMENT MEMBERS *as at July 2015*
*Prime Minister,* Kohir Rasulzoda
*First Deputy Prime Minister,* Davlatali Saidov

*Deputy Prime Ministers,* Murodali Alimardon; Azim Ibrohim; Marhabo Jabbarova
*Defence,* Mirzo Sherali

### EMBASSY OF THE REPUBLIC OF TAJIKISTAN
Grove House, 26–28 Hammersmith Grove, London W6 7BA
T 020-8834 1003 E info@tajembassy.org.uk
W www.tajembassy.org.uk
*Ambassador Extraordinary and Plenipotentiary,* HE Erkin Kasymov, *apptd* 2008

### BRITISH EMBASSY
65 Mirzo Tursunzoda Street, Dushanbe 734002
T (+992) 372 42221 E dushanbe.reception@fco.gov.uk
W www.gov.uk/government/world/tajikistan
*Ambassador Extraordinary and Plenipotentiary,* HE Hugh Philpott, *apptd* 2015

## DEFENCE

| Aged 16–49, 2010 est | Males | Females |
| --- | --- | --- |
| Available for military service | 2,012,790 | 2,020,618 |
| Fit for military service | 1,490,267 | 1,675,083 |

*Conscription duration –* 24 months

## ECONOMY AND TRADE

Since the civil war, there has been steady economic growth but the economy remains fragile owing to the inconsistent implementation of structural reforms, corruption, poor industrial and transport infrastructure, energy shortages and high foreign debt. The country has benefited from debt cancellation and is receiving substantial aid, primarily to develop industrial and transport infrastructure. The economy is dependent on remittances, with 90 per cent of the country's migrant workers residing in Russia. The economy is predicted to grow by an average of 4.4 per cent during 2015–16.

Agriculture accounts for 27.2 per cent of GDP but 46.5 per cent of employment. Cattle-raising and cotton-growing predominate; other crops are grain, fruit, grapes and vegetables. Abundant mineral deposits are not fully exploited. Industry consists of aluminium and hydro-electric power production, mining (zinc and lead) and production of cement and vegetable oil. Industry contributes 21.6 per cent of GDP and employs 10.7 per cent of the workforce. The services sector contributes the most to GDP at 51.2 per cent and employs 41.2 per cent of the workforce.

The main trading partners are China, Turkey and Russia. Principal exports are aluminium, electricity, cotton, fruit, vegetable oil and textiles. The main imports are petroleum products, aluminium oxide, machinery and equipment, and foodstuffs.

*GNI –* US$8,098m; US$990 per capita (2013)
*Annual average growth of GDP –* 6 per cent (2014 est)
*Inflation rate –* 6.3 per cent (2014 est)
*Population below poverty line –* 35.6 per cent (2013 est)
*Unemployment –* 10.5 per cent (2015 est)
*Total external debt –* US$3,821m (2014 est)

### BALANCE OF PAYMENTS
*Trade –* US$2,421m deficit (2012)
*Current Account –* US$604m deficit (2015 est)

| Trade with UK | 2013 | 2014 |
| --- | --- | --- |
| Imports from UK | £2,377,308 | £1,673,496 |
| Exports to UK | £993,417 | £498,940 |

## COMMUNICATIONS

*Airports and waterways* – The main airport is at Dushanbe and there are 16 others around the country; 200km of the river Vakhsh is navigable
*Roadways and railways* – 27,767km; 680km
*Telecommunications* – 393,000 fixed lines and 6.53 million mobile subscriptions (2012); there were 700,000 internet users in 2009
*Internet code and IDD* – tj; 992 (from UK), 810 44 (to UK)
*Media* – The state-run Tajik TV and Tajik Radio are the state broadcasters; major newspapers include the government-owned *Jumhuriyat* (Tajik language) and *Khalq Ovozi* (Uzbek)
*WPFI score* – 36,19 (116)

Most of the country lies on the central African plateau, from which rise mountains that run across the centre of the country from north-east to south-west. Peaks include Mt Kilimanjaro (5,895m), the highest point on the continent of Africa; the lowest point is 0m (Indian Ocean). Large areas of lakes Victoria, Tanganyika and Malawi (Nyasa) lie on the northern and western borders, and there are smaller lakes in the north-east and south-west. The Serengeti National Park covers an area of 9,656 sq. km in the north of the country. The climate is tropical, modified by altitude, with a rainy season from November to April except in coastal regions, which get most rain between March and May; rainfall is sporadic in the interior but more reliable and heavier on the coast.

# TANZANIA

*Jamhuri ya Muungano wa Tanzania* – *United Republic of Tanzania*

*Area* – 947,300 sq. km
*Capital* – Dodoma; population, 410,956 (2012)
*Major cities* – Arusha, Dar es Salaam, Mbeya, Mwanza, Zanzibar
*Currency* – Tanzanian shilling of 100 cents
*Population* – 51,045,882 rising at 2.79 per cent a year (2015 est); over 130 African ethnic groups on the mainland; Arab, African and mixed race on Zanzibar
*Religion* – mainland: Muslim 35 per cent, Christian 30 per cent, indigenous 35 per cent; Zanzibar: Muslim 99 per cent
*Language* – Swahili, English (both official), Arabic (especially on Zanzibar)
*Population density* – 56 per sq. km (2013)
*Urban population* – 27.6 per cent (2013 est)
*Median age (years)* – 17.4 (2014 est)
*National anthem* – 'Mungu ibariki Afrika' ['God Bless Africa']
*National day* – 26 April (Union Day)
*Death penalty* – Retained (last used 1994)
*CPI score* – 31 (119)

## CLIMATE AND TERRAIN

Tanzania comprises the former Tanganyika, on the mainland of east Africa, and the islands of Zanzibar, Pemba and Mafia.

## POLITICS

The 1977 constitution was amended in 1992 to introduce multiparty elections, and in 2000 to allow the president to nominate up to ten members of parliament. The executive president is directly elected for a five-year term, renewable once. The president is always from Tanganyika and the vice-president is always from Zanzibar. The unicameral National Assembly *(Bunge)* has 357 members: 239 directly elected, 102 seats reserved for women, ten appointed by the president (including five women), five chosen by Zanzibar's legislature, and the speaker. All serve a five-year term. The *Bunge* enacts laws that apply to the whole of Tanzania and laws that apply only to the mainland; laws that apply specifically to Zanzibar are enacted by the island's own legislature, the 81-member House of Representatives. Zanzibar also has its own directly elected president (who is a member of the Union government) and legislature.

In the 2010 national elections, Jakaya Kikwete was re-elected president, and the Revolutionary Party of Tanzania (CCM) retained its overwhelming majority in the legislature. The simultaneous presidential and legislative elections in Zanzibar were also won by the CCM, with CCM candidate Ali Mohamed Shein elected president. Fresh legislative and presidential elections are scheduled for October 2015.

HEAD OF STATE
*President of the United Republic,* Jakaya Kikwete,
　*elected* 14 December 2005, *took office* 21 December 2005,
　*re-elected* 2010
*Vice-President,* Mohammed Gharib Bilal
*President of Zanzibar,* Ali Mohamed Shein

SELECTED GOVERNMENT MEMBERS *as at June 2015*
*Prime Minister,* Mizengo Pinda
*Defence,* Hussein Mwinyi
*Finance,* Saada Mkuya Salum

HIGH COMMISSION OF THE UNITED REPUBLIC OF TANZANIA
3 Stratford Place, London W1C 1AS
T 020-7569 1470 E balozi@tanzania-online.gov.uk
W www.tanzania-online.gov.uk
*High Commissioner,* HE Peter Kallaghe, *apptd* 2010

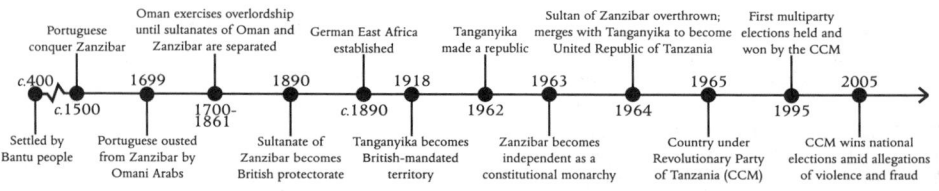

| Portuguese conquer Zanzibar | Oman exercises overlordship until sultanates of Oman and Zanzibar are separated | German East Africa established | Tanganyika made a republic | Sultan of Zanzibar overthrown; Zanzibar merges with Tanganyika to become United Republic of Tanzania | First multiparty elections held and won by the CCM |
| --- | --- | --- | --- | --- | --- |
| *c.*400 | 1699 | 1890 | 1918 | 1963 | 1965 | 2005 |
| *c.*1500 | 1700–1861 | *c.*1890 | 1962 | 1964 | 1995 |
| Settled by Bantu people | Portuguese ousted from Zanzibar by Omani Arabs | Sultanate of Zanzibar becomes British protectorate | Tanganyika becomes British-mandated territory | Zanzibar becomes independent as a constitutional monarchy | Country under Revolutionary Party of Tanzania (CCM) | CCM wins national elections amid allegations of violence and fraud |

BRITISH HIGH COMMISSION
PO Box 9200, Umoja House, Garden Avenue, Dar es Salaam
T (+255) (22) 229 0000 E bhc.dar@fco.gov.uk
W www.gov.uk/government/world/tanzania
*High Commissioner,* HE Dianna Patricia Melrose, *apptd* 2013

## DEFENCE

| Aged 16–49, 2010 est | Males | Females |
|---|---|---|
| Available for military service | 9,985,445 | – |
| Fit for military service | 5,860,339 | 5,882,279 |

*Military expenditure* – US$460m (2014 est)

## ECONOMY AND TRADE

State control has been dismantled gradually since the mid-1980s. Liberalisation and modernisation policies, supported by the World Bank, IMF and aid donors, have increased private-sector growth and investment. However, 36 per cent of the population still lives below the poverty line. In December 2014, international donors froze US$500m (£324.6m) worth of aid following a corruption scandal at the state-owned energy provider Tanesco.

Agriculture is the mainstay of the economy, accounting for 26.9 per cent of GDP, about 80 per cent of employment and 85 per cent of exports. It provides coffee, tea, cotton, pyrethrum, cashew nuts, grains, fruit and vegetables as well as the raw materials for industries producing sugar, beer, cigarettes and sisal twine. Zanzibar and Pemba produce cloves and clove oil, and coconuts and their derivatives. Increased output of minerals (chiefly diamonds, gold and iron) has driven recent economic growth, and salt, soda ash, cement, petroleum products, footwear, clothing, wood products and fertiliser are also produced. Tourism is a major source of revenue, especially for Zanzibar. Industry accounts for 25.2 per cent of GDP and services for 48 per cent.

The main trading partners are China, India, the UAE and Kenya. Principal exports are gold, coffee, cashew nuts, manufactures (especially clothing) and cotton. The main imports are consumer goods, machinery and transport equipment, industrial raw materials and crude oil.

*GNI* – US$30,218m; US$630 per capita (2013; mainland Tanzania only)
*Annual average growth of GDP* – 7.2 per cent (2014 est)
*Unemployment* – 3.4 per cent (2015 est)
*Inflation rate* – 6.2 per cent (2014 est)
*Total external debt* – US$15,350m (2014 est)
*Imports* – US$12,235m (2013)
*Exports* – US$5,043m (2013)

BALANCE OF PAYMENTS
*Trade* – US$6,191m deficit (2012)
*Current Account* – US$5,007m deficit (2015 est)

| Trade with UK | 2013 | 2014 |
|---|---|---|
| Imports from UK | £170,937,591 | £165,156,959 |
| Exports to UK | £41,791,304 | £28,620,326 |

## COMMUNICATIONS

*Airports* – The principal international airports are at Dar es Salaam, Kilimanjaro and Zanzibar
*Waterways* – The three great lakes (Tanganyika, Victoria and Nyasa) are the principal trade routes with neighbouring countries; the main seaports are Dar es Salaam, Tanga, Mtwara, Zanzibar, Mkoani and Wete (Pemba)
*Roadways and railways* – 86,472km; 3,689km
*Telecommunications* – 161,100 fixed lines (2011) and 27.22 million mobile subscriptions (2012); there were 678,000 internet users in 2009

*Internet code and IDD* – tz; 255 (from UK), 44 (to UK)
*Major broadcasters* – The state-run Tanzania Broadcasting Corporation operates TV and radio stations
*Press* – Newspapers include the government-owned *Daily News* (English language), and Swahili *Habari Leo* and *Uhuru*
*WPFI score* – 28,09 (75)

## EDUCATION AND HEALTH

Education is compulsory for seven years.
*Literacy rate* – 76.3 per cent (2015 est)
*Gross enrolment ratio (percentage of relevant age group)* – primary 90 per cent; secondary 33 per cent (2013 est)
*Health expenditure (per capita)* – US$49 (2013)
*Hospital beds (per 1,000 people)* – 0.7 (2010)
*Life expectancy (years)* – 61.24 (2014 est)
*Mortality rate* – 8.20 (2014 est)
*Birth rate* – 36.82 (2014 est)
*Infant mortality rate* – 43.74 (2014 est)
*HIV/AIDS adult prevalence* – 4.95 per cent (2013 est)

# THAILAND

*Ratcha Anachak Thai – Kingdom of Thailand*

*Area* – 513,120 sq. km
*Capital* – Bangkok (Krung Thep); population, 9,098,000 (2014)
*Major cities* – Chon Buri, Nonthaburi, Samut Prakan, Udon Thani
*Currency* – Baht of 100 satang
*Population* – 67,976,405 rising at 0.34 per cent a year (2015 est); Thai (95.9 per cent), Burmese (2 per cent) (2010 est)
*Religion* – Buddhist 93.6 per cent, Muslim 4.9 per cent, Christian 1.2 per cent (2010 est)
*Language* – Thai (official), English, Burmese
*Population density* – 131 per sq. km (2013)
*Urban population* – 34.8 per cent (2013 est)
*Median age (years)* – 36.2 (2014 est)
*National anthem* – 'Phleng Chat Thai' ['National Anthem of Thailand']
*National day* – 5 December (Birthday of the King)
*Death penalty* – Retained (last used 2009)
*CPI score* – 38 (85)

## CLIMATE AND TERRAIN

Thailand is divided geographically into four regions: the north is mountainous and forested; to the north-east is the semi-arid Korat plateau; the centre is a fertile plain lying in the Chao Phraya basin; and the south is the narrow, mountainous isthmus of Kra. Extremes of elevation range from 2,576m (Doi Inthanon) to 0m (Gulf of Thailand). The principal rivers are the Chao Phraya and its tributaries in the central plains and the Mekong on the north and eastern

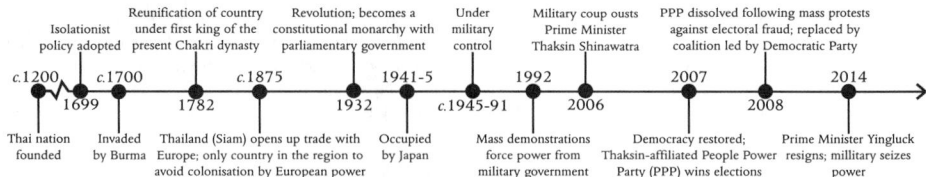

Timeline:

| | | | | | | |
|---|---|---|---|---|---|---|
| *c.*1200 | *c.*1700 | *c.*1875 | 1941-5 | 1992 | 2007 | 2014 |

Isolationist policy adopted — Reunification of country under first king of the present Chakri dynasty — Revolution; becomes a constitutional monarchy with parliamentary government — Under military control — Military coup ousts Prime Minister Thaksin Shinawatra — PPP dissolved following mass protests against electoral fraud; replaced by coalition led by Democratic Party

| 1699 | 1782 | 1932 | *c.*1945-91 | 2006 | 2008 |
|---|---|---|---|---|---|

Thai nation founded — Invaded by Burma — Thailand (Siam) opens up trade with Europe; only country in the region to avoid colonisation by European power — Occupied by Japan — Mass demonstrations force power from military government — Democracy restored; Thaksin-affiliated People Power Party (PPP) wins elections — Prime Minister Yingluck resigns; military seizes power

borders. The climate is tropical, with a monsoon season from June to October and high humidity.

## POLITICS

On 22 May 2014, the Royal Thai Armed Forces conducted a millitary coup after months of political tension between the ruling Pheu Thai Party and the opposition People's Democratic Reform Committee. Following the successful corruption proceedings filed against prime minister Yingluck and her subsequent removal from office on 7 May, martial law was declared by the military on 20 May before a new millitary government styled the National Council for Peace and Order was established. The military government announced the end of martial law in March 2015 and stated that a referendum on the creation of a new constitution would be held in 2016.

Thailand is a constitutional monarchy with a hereditary monarch as head of state. The 2007 constitution has been suspended by the millitary and the senate has been dissolved.

### HEAD OF STATE

*HM The King of Thailand,* King Bhumibol Adulyadej (Rama IX), *born* 5 December 1927, *succeeded* 9 June 1946
*Heir,* HRH Crown Prince Maha Vajiralongkorn, *born* 28 July 1952

### SELECTED GOVERNMENT MEMBERS *as at July 2015*

*Prime Minister,* Cdr-in-Chief Gen. Prayuth Chan-ocha
*Deputy Prime Ministers,* Pridiyathon Devakula; Wissanu Kruangam; Sommal Phasi *(Finance);* Thanasak Patimaprakorn *(Foreign Affairs);* Prawit Wongsuwan *(Defence);* Youngyuth Yutthamong

### ROYAL THAI EMBASSY

29–30 Queen's Gate, London SW7 5JB
T 020-789 2944 E csinfo@thaiembassyuk.org.uk
W www.thaiembassyuk.org.uk
*Ambassador Extraordinary and Plenipotentiary,* Kittiphong Na Ranong, *apptd* 2015

### BRITISH EMBASSY

14 Wireless Road, Bangkok 10330
T (+66) (0) 2 305 8333 E info.bangkok@fco.gov.uk
W www.gov.uk/government/world/thailand
*Ambassador Extraordinary and Plenipotentiary,* HE Mark Kent, *apptd* 2012

### INSURGENCY

The Muslim minority is concentrated in the isthmus of Kra. A separatist campaign in the region began in the 1970s but died down in the 1980s. Violence resumed in 2004 and has since claimed over 3,000 lives.

### FOREIGN RELATIONS

Sovereignty over border territory around the Hindu temple complex at Preah Vihear has been disputed with Cambodia for over a century. Although the temple complex was awarded to Cambodia in 1962, the status of adjacent territory remains unsettled. Tensions increased in 2008, when Cambodia had the temple listed as a UNESCO World Heritage Site, and there has been frequent sporadic fighting

in the area between the countries' troops. Despite talks between the Cambodian and Thai prime ministers in 2011, a resolution to the dispute has failed to materialise.

## DEFENCE

| *Aged 16–49, 2010 est* | *Males* | *Females* |
|---|---|---|
| Available for military service | 17,689,921 | 17,754,795 |
| Fit for military service | 13,308,372 | 14,182,567 |

*Military expenditure* – US$5,730m (2014)
*Conscription duration* – 24 months

## ECONOMY AND TRADE

Thailand was transformed from an agricultural to an export-orientated industrial economy in the last quarter of the 20th century, sustaining steady growth after its quick recovery from the 1997 economic crisis. The 2008 global economic downturn caused the export-dependent economy to contract sharply, and flooding in October and November 2011 reduced growth to only 0.1 per cent in 2011; growth increased to 5.5 per cent in 2012, however, as the industrial sector recovered and the private sector improved. The tourism sector contracted by around 6.5 per cent following the 2014 coup; this decrease is expected to depress growth to just over 4 per cent during 2015–19.

The agricultural sector generates 12.2 per cent of GDP and employs 32.2 per cent of the workforce. The main crops are rice, cassava, rubber, maize, sugar cane, coconuts and soya beans. In recent years fishing and livestock production have grown in importance. There are reserves of natural gas, lignite, tin, tungsten and lead.

The main industry is tourism, which has been the chief foreign exchange earner since the 1980s. Other industries include textiles and clothing, agricultural processing, beverages, tobacco, cement, mining and light manufacturing (jewellery, electrical appliances, computers and parts), furniture, plastics and cars, and vehicle parts. Industry contributes 43.3 per cent of GDP and services 44.5 per cent.

The main trading partners are Japan, China, the USA and the UAE. Principal exports are textiles and footwear, fish products, rice, rubber, jewellery, cars, computers and electrical appliances. The main imports are capital goods, intermediate goods and raw materials, consumer goods and fuels.
*GNI* – US$357,661m; US$5,340 per capita (2013)
*Annual average growth of GDP* – 1 per cent (2014 est)
*Inflation rate* – 2.1 per cent (2014 est)
*Population below poverty line* – 13.2 per cent (2011 est)
*Unemployment* – 0.9 per cent (2015 est)
*Total external debt* – US$140,700m (2014 est)
*Imports* – US$249,652m (2013)
*Exports* – US$224,863m (2013)

### BALANCE OF PAYMENTS

*Trade* – US$22,062m surplus (2012)
*Current Account* – US$17,085m surplus (2015 est)

| *Trade with UK* | 2013 | 2014 |
|---|---|---|
| Imports from UK | £2,362,742,894 | £1,458,876,840 |
| Exports to UK | £2,599,793,388 | £2,617,194,298 |

## COMMUNICATIONS

*Airports and waterways* – Bangkok is the main international airport and the main seaports are located in Bangkok and Sattahip; there are also 3,701km of navigable inland waterways (4,000km in total)
*Roadways and railways* – 180,053km (2006 total); 4,071km
*Telecommunications* – 6.391 million fixed lines and 84.08 million mobile subscriptions (2012); there were 17.48 million internet users in 2009
*Internet and IDD* – th; 66 (from UK), 1 44 (to UK)
*Major broadcasters* – The government and military both operate a number of TV and radio stations, including Thai TV3 and Radio Thailand
*Press* – Leading daily newspapers include the *Bangkok Post* and *The Nation* (both English language), and the *Daily News* (Thai)
*WPFI score* – 40,07 (134)

## EDUCATION AND HEALTH

Primary and lower secondary education is compulsory and free, and upper secondary education is free in government schools.
*Literacy rate* – 98.2 per cent (2015 est)
*Gross enrolment ratio (percentage of relevant age group)* – primary 93 per cent (2013 est); secondary 87 per cent (2012 est); tertiary 51 per cent (2013 est)
*Health expenditure (per capita)* – US$264 (2013)
*Life expectancy (years)* – 74.18 (2014 est)
*Mortality rate* – 7.72 (2014 est)
*Birth rate* – 11.26 (2014 est)
*Infant mortality rate* – 9.86 (2014 est)
*HIV/AIDS adult prevalence* – 1.09 per cent (2013 est)

# TIMOR–LESTE

*Republika Demokratika Timor Lorosa'e/Republica Democratica de Timor-Leste* – Democratic Republic of Timor-Leste

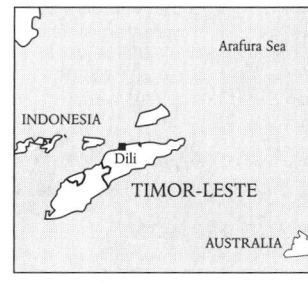

*Area* – 14,874 sq. km. Includes the enclave of Oecussi
*Capital* – Dili; population, 228,000 (2014)
*Major towns* – Baucau, Los Palos, Maliana, Pantemakassar (Oecussi), Same
*Currency* – US dollar (US$) of 100 cents
*Population* – 1,231,116 rising at 2.42 per cent a year (2012 est)

*Religion* – Christian (Roman Catholic 96.9 per cent, Protestant 2.2 per cent), Muslim 0.3 per cent (2005)
*Language* – Tetum, Portuguese (both official), Indonesian, English, around 16 indigenous languages
*Population density* – 79 per sq. km (2013)
*Urban population* – 29.1 per cent (2013 est)
*Median age (years)* – 18.5 (2014 est)
*National anthem* – 'Patria' ['Fatherland']
*National day* – 28 November (Independence Day)
*Death penalty* – Abolished for all crimes (since 1999)
*CPI score* – 28 (133)
*Literacy rate* – 82.4 per cent (2015 est)
*Gross enrolment ratio (percentage of relevant age group)* – primary 117 per cent; secondary 56 per cent; tertiary 16.7 per cent (2011 est)
*Health expenditure (per capita)* – US$59 (2013)
*Life expectancy (years)* – 67.39 (2014 est)
*Mortality rate* – 6.18 (2014 est)
*Birth rate* – 34.48 (2014 est)
*Infant mortality rate* – 38.79 (2014 est)

## CLIMATE AND TERRAIN

The republic comprises the eastern half of the island of Timor, plus the enclave of Oecussi, which lies on the northern coast, separated from the rest of the country by the Indonesian province of West Timor. The island, about 296km long and 72km wide, lies at the eastern end of the Malay archipelago and is the largest of the Lesser Sunda Islands. The interior is covered in forests and mountains. Elevation extremes range from 2,963m (Mt Tatamailau) to 0m (Timor Sea). The climate is tropical.

## POLITICS

The 2002 constitution established a parliamentary democracy. The president is directly elected for a five-year term, renewable once. The unicameral National Parliament has 65 members, directly elected for a five-year term. The council of ministers is nominated by the prime minister, who is appointed by the president.

The 2012 presidential election was won in the second round by Jose Maria Vasconcelos. In the 2012 legislative election, the National Congress for Timorese Reconstruction party (CNRT), emerged as the single largest party. The CNRT government resigned in February 2015 and was replaced by a coalition including the CNRT, Fretilin and Democratic parties.

HEAD OF STATE
*President,* Jose Maria Vasconcelos, *elected* 16 April 2012, *took office* 30 May 2012

SELECTED GOVERNMENT MEMBERS *as at July 2015*
*Prime Minister,* Rui Maria De Araujo
*Defence,* Cirilo Jose Cristovao
*Finance,* Santina Cardoso
*Foreign Affairs,* Hernani Coelho

| East Timor becomes Portuguese colony | The Revolutionary Front for an Independent East Timor (Fretilin) declares East Timor independent | Country votes for independence from Indonesia in a national plebiscite; Indonesian troops murder hundreds | Continuing instability causes UN to re-establish peacekeeping mission |
| --- | --- | --- | --- |
| c.1515 | 1974 | 1975-9 | 2002 | 2007 |
| 1702 | 1975 | 1999 | 2005-7 | |
| Discovered by Portuguese; partitioned between Portuguese and Dutch | Collapse of Portuguese rule | Indonesia invades, Fretilin engages in guerilla warfare; UN fails to recognise annexation | UN deploys peacekeeping troops and sets up a transitional administration | Becomes independent as the Democratic Republic of Timor-Leste | Violent protests against appointment of Xanana Gusmao |

EMBASSY OF THE DEMOCRATIC REPUBLIC OF
TIMOR-LESTE
4 Cavendish Square, London W1G 0PG
T 020-3440 9025
*Ambassador Extraordinary and Plenipotentiary,* HE Joaquim
Antonio Maria Lopes da Fonseca, *apptd* 2013

BRITISH EMBASSY
*Ambassador Extraordinary and Plenipotentiary,* HE Moazzam
Malik, *apptd* 2014, resident at Jakarta, Indonesia

## ECONOMY AND TRADE

An internationally funded programme in 2002–5 achieved
substantial reconstruction of the infrastructure destroyed
in the 1999 post-referendum violence, but the civil unrest
of 2006 caused further damage and disrupted economic
activity. Economic growth since independence is largely
owing to the exploitation of offshore oil and gas deposits,
which has boosted government revenue but has had little
impact on unemployment levels; there are no domestic
production facilities so oil and gas are piped to Australia for
processing. High levels of poverty and unemployment,
weak civil administration, a low skills base and inadequate
infrastructure all hinder development, although in late 2011
parliament passed an ambitious infrastructure-focused budget
which would allow the government to borrow for the first
time in ten years. Oil and gas revenues are declining, and the
economy is expected to contract in 2016 as a result.

Industry contributes 72.8 per cent of GDP, services 22.1
per cent, and agriculture 5.2 per cent, although it engages 64
per cent of the population. The main commercial crops are
coffee, timber, rice, maize, vegetables, tropical fruits and
vanilla. The main trading partners are Australia, Indonesia
and EU countries. Principal exports are coffee, oil, natural
gas, sandalwood and marble. The main imports are food,
fuels and machinery.
*GNI* – US$4,529m; US$3,940 per capita (2013)
*Annual average growth of GDP* – 6.6 per cent (2014 est)
*Inflation rate* – 0.5 per cent (2014 est)
*Population below poverty line* – 5 per cent (2015 est)
*Unemployment* – 5 per cent (2015 est)
*Imports* – 843,756m (2013)
*Exports* – 51,056 (2013)

BALANCE OF PAYMENTS
*Current Account* – US$443m surplus (2015 est)

| Trade with UK | 2013 | 2014 |
| --- | --- | --- |
| Imports from UK | £198,686 | £176,706 |
| Exports to UK | £52,857 | £84,122 |

## COMMUNICATIONS

*Airports and waterways* – The international airport and
seaport are at Dili
*Roadways* – There are 2,600 of paved roads, including one
major road linking the main townships on the northern coast
*Telecommunications* – 3,000 fixed lines and 621,000 mobile
subscriptions (2012); there were 2,100 internet users in
2009
*Internet code and IDD* – tl; 670 (from UK), 44 (to UK)
*Major broadcasters* – Televisao de Timor-Leste and Radio
Timor-Leste are the state-owned broadcasters
*Press* – Major daily newspapers include *Suara Timor Lorosae*
(Tetum language), *Diario Nacional* (Portuguese) and the
*Timor Post* (English)
*WPFI score* – 32,63 (103)

# TOGO

*République togolaise* – *Togolese Republic*

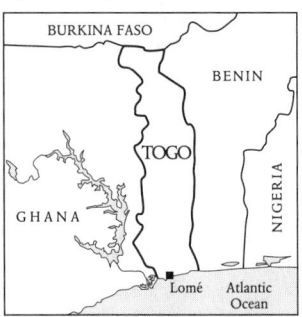

*Area* – 56,785 sq. km
*Capital* – Lomé; population, 930,000 (2014)
*Major cities* – Atakpamé, Kara, Sokodé
*Currency* – Franc CFA of 100 centimes
*Population* – 7,552,318 rising at 2.69 per cent a year
(2015 est); 37 tribes, largest of which are Ewe, Mina and
Kabre
*Religion* – Indigenous beliefs 51 per cent, Christian 29
per cent, Muslim 20 per cent
*Language* – French (official), Ewe, Mina (in the south), Kabye,
Dagomba (in the north)
*Population density* – 125 per sq. km (2013)
*Urban population* – 39 per cent (2013 est)
*Median age (years)* – 19.6 (2014 est)
*National anthem* – 'Salut à toi, pays de nos aïeux' ['Hail to
Thee, Land of Our Forefathers']
*National day* – 27 April (Independence Day)
*Death penalty* – Abolished for all crimes (since 2009)
*CPI score* – 29 (126)
*Literacy rate* – 85.1 per cent (2015 est)
*Gross enrolment ratio (percentage of relevant age group)* –
primary 140 per cent; secondary 46 per cent (2011 est)
*Health expenditure (per capita)* – US$54 (2013)
*Hospital beds (per 1,000 people)* – 0.7 (2011)
*Life expectancy (years)* – 64.06 (2014 est)
*Mortality rate* – 7.43 (2014 est)
*Birth rate* – 34.52 (2014 est)
*Infant mortality rate* – 46.73 (2014 est)
*HIV/AIDS adult prevalence* – 2.33 per cent (2013 est)

## CLIMATE AND TERRAIN

From hills in the centre of the country, the terrain declines
to savannah in the north and in the south to a plateau that
leads to a coastal plain with marshes and lagoons. Elevation
extremes range from 986m (Mt Agou) to 0m (Atlantic
Ocean). The climate in the south is tropical with two wet
seasons (March to July and September to November). In
the north it is semi-arid with one wet season (May to
September). The average temperature is 27.4°C.

## HISTORY AND POLITICS

Germany established a protectorate, Togoland, over the area
in 1884, and this was occupied on the outbreak of the First
World War by Britain and France. The country was divided
between Britain and France as a League of Nations mandate
after the war and the mandate was renewed by the UN in 1946.
In 1957, following a plebiscite, British Togoland integrated
with Ghana when it became independent. French Togoland
achieved independence as the Republic of Togo in 1960.

There was a military coup in 1963 led by Gnassingbé
Eyadéma, who installed a civilian president. In 1967

Eyadéma overthrew the government and became president himself, introducing a one-party state under his *Rassemblement du peuple togolais* (RPT). Violent demonstrations in 1990 forced the government to introduce a multiparty constitution in 1992. Eyadéma and the RPT were returned to power in the first multiparty elections in 1993 and in two subsequent elections.

After President Eyadéma's death in February 2005, military attempted to install his son, Faure Gnassingbé, who resigned as acting president following widespread condemnation of the move, only to be elected to the presidency in April 2005. Following reconciliation talks in 2006, the government and opposition leaders signed an accord providing for the participation of opposition parties, and a national unity government was appointed until a legislative election was held in 2007. The election was nevertheless won by the RPT; the 2013 election was won by President Gnassingbé's Union for the Republic (UNIR) party following the RPT's dissolution. President Gnassingbé won the April 2015 presidential election and was re-elected for a third term.

Under the 1992 constitution, the president is directly elected for a five-year term. The unicameral National Assembly has 81 members, who are directly elected for a five-year term. The prime minister is appointed by the president and appoints the cabinet in consultation with the president.

## HEAD OF STATE
*President, Defence,* Faure Gnassingbé, *elected* 24 April 2005, *sworn in* 4 May 2005, *re-elected* 2010, 2015

SELECTED GOVERNMENT MEMBERS *as at July 2015*
*Prime Minister,* Komi Selom Klassou
*Economy and Finance,* vacant
*Foreign Affairs,* vacant

## EMBASSY OF THE REPUBLIC OF TOGO
8 rue Alfred Roll, 75017 Paris, France
T (+33) (1) 4380 1213
*Ambassador Extraordinary and Plenipotentiary,* HE Calixte Batossie Madjoulba, *apptd* 2011

## BRITISH AMBASSADOR
HE Peter Jones, *apptd* 2011, resident at Accra, Ghana

## DEFENCE

| Aged 16–49, 2010 est | Males | Females |
|---|---|---|
| Available for military service | 1,577,572 | 1,589,715 |
| Fit for military service | 1,104,536 | 1,158,061 |

*Military expenditure* – US$59m (2011 est)
*Conscription duration* – 24 months (selective)

## ECONOMY AND TRADE
Progress on economic reform, intended to attract foreign investment and balance the budget, is slow, lacking impetus on privatisation and financial transparency. Resumption of aid to Togo, mostly suspended in the 1990s because of its human rights record, has increased since the 2007 election, and the country had 95 per cent of its external debt written off in 2010. Growth of 5.8 per cent is expected between 2015 and 2016.

The economy is predominantly based on agriculture, accounting for 27.6 per cent of GDP, engaging 65 per cent of the workforce and providing most of the country's exports as well as the raw materials for industry. Industrial activity centres on phosphate mining, agricultural processing and manufacture of cement, handicrafts, textiles and beverages. Industry accounts for 33.9 per cent of GDP and 5 per cent of employment. The service sector accounts for 38.5 per cent of GDP and employs 30 per cent of the workforce.

The main export markets are India, Lebanon, Burkina Faso and Benin; imports come mainly from China (40.4 per cent) and EU states. Principal exports are re-exports, cotton, phosphates, coffee and cocoa. The main imports are machinery and equipment, foodstuffs and petroleum products.

*GNI* – US$3,625m; US$530 per capita (2013)
*Annual average growth of GDP* – 5.6 per cent (2014 est)
*Inflation rate* – 1.1 per cent (2014 est)
*Unemployment* – 8.4 per cent (2015 est)
*Total external debt* – US$926.3m (2014 est)
*Imports* – US$2,108m (2013)
*Exports* – US$1,048m (2013)

BALANCE OF PAYMENTS
*Trade* – US$926m deficit (2014)
*Current Account* – US$225m deficit (2015 est)

| Trade with UK | 2013 | 2014 |
|---|---|---|
| Imports from UK | £90,972,300 | £181,603,038 |
| Exports to UK | £1,169,165 | £1,461,171 |

## COMMUNICATIONS
*Airports* – The principal airport is at Lomé
*Roadways and railways* – 2,447km; 568km
*Telecommunications* – 225,000 fixed lines in use and 3.52 million mobile subscriptions (2012); there were 356,300 internet users in 2009
*Internet code and IDD* – tg; 228 (from UK), 44 (to UK)
*Major broadcasters* – Public broadcasting is provided by Radio Togolaise, Television Togolaise and Telesports TV
*Press* – Major daily newspapers include *Togo-Presse, Liberté* and *Forum de la Semaine* (all French language)
*WPFI score* – 28,5 (80)

# TONGA

*Pule'anga Tonga – Kingdom of Tonga*

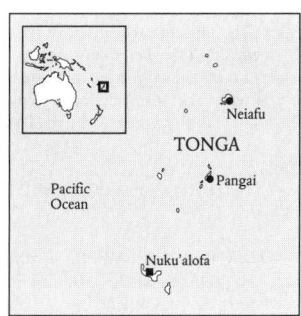

*Area* – 747 sq. km
*Capital* – Nuku'alofa, on Tongatapu; population, 25,000 (2014 est)
*Currency* – Pa'anga (T$) of 100 seniti
*Population* – 106,501 rising at 0.03 per cent a year (2015 est)
*Religion* – Christian (Free Wesleyan 36 per cent, Mormon 18 per cent, Roman Catholic 15 per cent, Free Church 12 per cent) (2006 est)
*Language* – English, Tongan (both official)

*Population density* – 146 per sq. km (2013)
*Urban population* – 23.6 per cent (2013 est)
*Median age (years)* – 22 (2014 est)
*National anthem* – 'Koe Fasi Oe Tu'i Oe Otu Tonga' ['Song of the King of the Tonga Islands']
*National day* – 4 November (Constitution Day)
*Death penalty* – Retained (last used 1982)
*Literacy rate* – 99.4 per cent (2015 est)
*Life expectancy (years)* – 75.82 (2014 est)
*Mortality rate* – 4.86 (2014 est)
*Birth rate* – 23.55 (2014 est)
*Infant mortality rate* – 12.36 (2014 est)

## CLIMATE AND TERRAIN
Tonga comprises over 170 islands in three groups, situated in the south Pacific Ocean some 724km east-south-east of Fiji. Most of the islands are of coral formation, but some are volcanic (Tofua, Kao and Niuafo'ou or 'Tin Can' Island). Elevation extremes range from 1,033m (on Kao Island) to 0m (Pacific Ocean). The climate is tropical, moderated by trade winds, with an average temperature of 25.4°C.

## HISTORY AND POLITICS
The islands were settled by Polynesians from *c*.1000 AD. They were visited by European explorers from the 17th century. The country was reunited in 1845 after a civil war, and a modern constitution adopted in 1875. Tonga became a British protectorate in 1900, and regained full independence on 4 June 1970.

A pro-democracy movement began in 1992 and gathered momentum throughout the 1990s, with the first political party being established in 1994. Following consultation on political and constitutional reform in 2005 and negotiations in 2007, a commission reported in 2009, recommending reducing the monarchy to a ceremonial role and introducing a popularly elected legislature. These constitutional changes took effect with the 2010 legislative election.

In the 2014 legislative election, the Democratic Party of the Friendly Islands (DPFI) won nine seats and independents the remaining eight. 'Akilisi Pohiva of the DPFI became prime minister, becoming the first commoner to hold the position.

The 1875 constitution was amended in 2003 to give greater powers to the king; the present king relinquished some of his executive powers in 2008 and most of the remainder in 2010, when new constitutional arrangements came into effect. The unicameral Legislative Assembly *(Fale Alea)* has 26 members: nine hereditary nobles elected by their peers, and 17 popularly elected representatives who serve a three-year term. The 14-member privy council acts as a cabinet. The prime minister is elected by the legislature.

HEAD OF STATE
*HM The King of Tonga*, King Tupou VI, *born* 12 July 1959, *acceded* 18 March 2012

SELECTED GOVERNMENT MEMBERS *as at July 2015*
*Prime Minister, Foreign Affairs,* Samiuela 'Akilisi Pohiva
*Deputy Prime Minister,* Siaosi Sovaleni
*Finance,* 'Aisake Valu Eke

TONGA HIGH COMMISSION
36 Molyneux Street, London W1H 5BQ
T 020-7724 5828
E office@tongahighcom.co.uk
*Acting High Commissioner,* HE Sione Sonata Tupou, *apptd* 2012

BRITISH HIGH COMMISSIONER
HE Roderick Drummond, *apptd* 2013, resident at Suva, Fiji

## ECONOMY AND TRADE
There are few natural resources and the country is dependent on foreign aid and remittances from Tongans working abroad. The government is encouraging the development of a private sector and committing increased funds towards education and health. Tourism is expected to increase from 2016 and this is expected to help the economy to grow by 2.6 per cent in 2016.

The main economic activities are agriculture, fishing and tourism, which is the second-largest source of foreign exchange revenue after remittances. The main crops are squashes, coconuts, bananas, vanilla beans, cocoa, coffee, ginger and black pepper. Fish is an important staple food. A small light industry sector processes agricultural produce.

The main export markets are South Korea, the USA and New Zealand; imports come chiefly from Fiji and New Zealand. Principal exports are squashes, fish, vanilla beans and root crops. The main imports are foodstuffs, machinery and transport equipment, fuels and chemicals.
*GNI* – US$472m; US$4,490 per capita (2013)
*Annual average growth of GDP* – 2.4 per cent (2014 est)
*Inflation rate* – 1.7 per cent (2014 est)
*Population below poverty line* – 24 per cent (2004)
*Unemployment* – 13 per cent (2004 est)
*Total external debt* – US$199.3m (2014 est)
*Imports* – US$210m (2013)
*Exports* – US$15m (2013)

BALANCE OF PAYMENTS
*Trade* – US$185m deficit (2012)
*Current Account* – US$32m deficit (2015 est)

| Trade with UK | 2013 | 2014 |
| --- | --- | --- |
| Imports from UK | £144,526 | £177,550 |
| Exports to UK | £24,685 | £219,605 |

## COMMUNICATIONS
*Airports and waterways* – There is one airport; the principal port is Nuku'alofa
*Roadways* – 680km, of which 184km are paved
*Telecommunications* – There are 30,000 main telephone lines in use (2012), 56,000 mobile subscriptions (2012); there were 8,400 internet users in 2009
*Internet code and IDD* – to; 676 (from UK), 44 (to UK)
*Media* – The government-run Tonga Broadcasting Commission operates TV and radio stations; there are no daily newspapers
*WPFI score* – 23,37 (44)

# TRINIDAD AND TOBAGO

*Republic of Trinidad and Tobago*

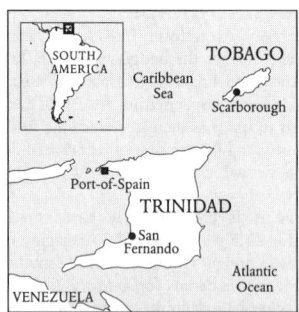

*Area* – 5,128 sq. km
*Capital* – Port of Spain, on Trinidad; population, 34,000 (2014)
*Major towns* – Chaguanas, San Fernando, Scarborough (Tobago)
*Currency* – Trinidad and Tobago dollar (T$) of 100 cents
*Population* – 1,222,363 falling at 0.13 per cent a year (2015 est)
*Religion* – Christian (Protestant 32.1 per cent, Roman Catholic 21.6 per cent, other 20.5 per cent), Hindu 18.2 per cent, Muslim 5 per cent, Jehovah's Witnesses 1.5 per cent (2011 est)
*Language* – English (official), Caribbean Hindustani (a dialect of Hindi), French, Spanish, Chinese
*Population density* – 261 per sq. km (2013)
*Urban population* – 14.2 per cent (2013 est)
*Median age (years)* – 34.4 (2014 est)
*National anthem* – 'Forged from the Love of Liberty'
*National day* – 31 August (Independence Day)
*Death penalty* – Retained (last used 1999)
*CPI score* – 38 (85)

## CLIMATE AND TERRAIN
Trinidad, the most southerly of the West Indian islands, lies 11km off the north coast of Venezuela. The island is mostly flat, with low mountains, the Northern Range, across almost its entire northern width and some low hills in the centre. Elevation extremes range from 940m (Mt Aripo) to 0m (Caribbean Sea). Pitch Lake, on the south-west coast, is the world's largest natural source of asphalt.

Tobago lies 30km north-east of Trinidad. The island has a range of hills, Main Ridge, running along its length; the highest point is 549m. Several islands, mainly, Chacachacare, Huevos, Monos and Gaspar Grande, lie west of Corozal Point, the north-west extremity of Trinidad.

The climate is tropical, with a wet season from June to December. Temperatures are constant all year round.

## HISTORY AND POLITICS
Trinidad is believed to be the oldest site of human habitation in the Caribbean archipelago, with excavated human remains dating back 7,200 years. The islands were home to a number of indigenous peoples, including the Nepuyo, Yaio and Caribs.

Trinidad and Tobago were discovered by Columbus in 1498. Trinidad was colonised in 1532 by Spain, capitulated to the British in 1797 and was ceded to Britain in 1802. Tobago was colonised by the Dutch from the 1630s but subsequently changed hands numerous times until it was ceded to Britain by France in 1814. The two islands were amalgamated into a single British colony in 1889. Internal self-government was granted in 1959 and independence was attained in 1962; the country became a republic in 1976.

The People's National Movement (PNM) has dominated post-independence politics, only out of office in 1986–91, 1995–2001, and since May 2010. The PNM won the 2009 election for the Tobago legislature, but lost the early general election in 2010 to the People's Partnership coalition, which took office under Kamla Persad-Bissessar, the country's first female prime minister. President Richards, first elected in 2003, was re-elected in 2008, and succeeded by independent candidate Anthony Carmona in February 2013. New legislative elections were scheduled for September 2015.

Under the 1976 constitution, the president is elected for a five-year term by an electoral college consisting of both houses of the legislature. The bicameral parliament comprises the House of Representatives and the senate. The former has 41 members directly elected for a five-year term. The senate

has 31 members, of whom 16 are appointed on the advice of the prime minister, six on the advice of the leader of the opposition and nine at the discretion of the president, to serve a five-year term.

Since 1980 Tobago has had internal self-government through its House of Assembly, which has 15 members, 12 directly elected and four appointed, who serve a four-year term.

HEAD OF STATE
*President,* Anthony Carmona, *elected* 15 February 2013, *took office* 18 March 2013

SELECTED GOVERNMENT MEMBERS *as at July 2015*
*Prime Minister,* Kamla Persad-Bissessar
*Attorney-General,* Garvin Nicholas
*Finance,* Larry Howai
*Foreign Affairs,* Winston Dookeran

HIGH COMMISSION OF THE REPUBLIC OF TRINIDAD AND TOBAGO
42 Belgrave Square, London SW1X 8NT
T 020-7245 9351 W www.tthighcommission.co.uk
*High Commissioner,* vacant

BRITISH HIGH COMMISSION
PO Box 778, 19 St Clair Avenue, St Clair, Port of Spain
T (+868) 350 0444
W www.gov.uk/government/world/trinidad-and-tobago
*High Commissioner,* HE Tim Stew, *apptd* 2015

## DEFENCE

| *All aged 16–49, 2010 est* | *Males* | *Females* |
| --- | --- | --- |
| Available for military service | 341,764 | 317,899 |
| Fit for military service | 269,824 | 261,735 |

## ECONOMY AND TRADE
The country is the most prosperous in the Caribbean, owing largely to its oil and natural gas reserves, but the government has encouraged diversification into petro-chemicals, aluminium, plastics, financial services and tourism to reduce its dependence on the energy sector. After years of steady growth, the economy contracted briefly in 2009 as export demand and oil prices fell. Crime and bureaucracy deter greater foreign investment.

The agricultural sector is small, accounting for 0.5 per cent of GDP; the main products are cocoa, rice, citrus fruits, coffee, vegetables and poultry. Apart from oil and gas extraction and processing, the main industries are tourism, food processing, production of chemicals, steel products, cement, beverages and cotton textiles.

The main trading partners are the USA (42.1 per cent of exports; 33.1 per cent of imports), Colombia, Argentina and Chile. Principal exports are oil and petroleum products, liquefied natural gas, chemicals, steel products, beverages, cereals and cereal products, sugar, cocoa, coffee, citrus fruits, vegetables and flowers. The main imports are fuels, lubricants, machinery, transport equipment, manufactured goods, food, chemicals and livestock.

*GNI* – US$21,133m; US$15,760 per capita (2013)
*Annual average growth of GDP* – 2.3 per cent (2014 est)
*Inflation rate* – 5.1 per cent (2014 est)
*Population below poverty line* – 17 per cent (2007 est)
*Unemployment* – 7.7 per cent (2015 est)
*Total external debt* – US$4,924m (2014 est)
*Imports* – US$8,799m (2013)
*Exports* – US$12,700m (2013)

BALANCE OF PAYMENTS
*Trade* – US$3,700m surplus (2012)
*Current Account* – US$1,508m surplus (2015 est)

| Trade with UK | 2013 | 2014 |
|---|---|---|
| Imports from UK | £128,434,980 | £118,012,967 |
| Exports to UK | £114,997,445 | £153,934,051 |

## COMMUNICATIONS
*Airports and waterways* – The international airport is at Port of Spain on Trinidad, and Tobago is served by Crown Point airport; the three main ports are Scarborough (Tobago), Port of Spain and Point Lisas
*Roadways* – 4,252km
*Telecommunications* – 287,000 fixed lines and 1.88 million mobile subscriptions (2012); there were 593,000 internet users in 2009
*Internet code and IDD* – tt; 1 868 (from UK), 011 44 (to UK)
*Media* – CTV and Talk City 91.1 (radio) are the state broadcasters; leading daily newspapers include *Newsday, Trinidad Guardian* and *Trinidad and Tobago Express*
*WPFI score* – 22,39 (41)

## EDUCATION AND HEALTH
Education is free at all state-owned and government-assisted denominational schools, and at certain faculties at the University of the West Indies.
*Literacy rate* – 99.6 per cent (2015 est)
*Gross enrolment ratio (percentage of relevant age group)* – primary 106 per cent (2010 est); secondary 90 per cent (2011 est)
*Health expenditure (per capita)* – US$965 (2013)
*Hospital beds (per 1,000 people)* – 2.7 (2012)
*Life expectancy (years)* – 72.29 (2014 est)
*Mortality rate* – 8.48 (2014 est)
*Birth rate* – 13.8 (2014 est)
*Infant mortality rate* – 24.82 (2014 est)
*HIV/AIDS adult prevalence* – 1.65 per cent (2013 est)

# TUNISIA

*Al-Jumhuriyah at-Tunisiyah – Tunisian Republic*

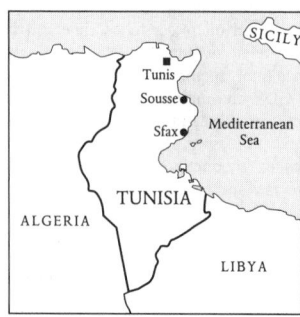

*Area* – 163,610 sq. km
*Capital* – Tunis; population, 1,978,000 (2014)
*Major cities* – Sfax, Sousse
*Currency* – Tunisian dinar of 1,000 millimes
*Population* – 11,037,225 rising at 0.89 per cent a year (2015 est)
*Religion* – Muslim 99.1 per cent (predominantly Sunni) (est); small minorities of Christians and Jews. Sunni Islam is the official religion
*Language* – Arabic (official), French, Berber

*Population density* – 70 per sq. km (2013)
*Urban population* – 66.7 per cent (2013 est)
*Median age (years)* – 31.4 (2014 est)
*National anthem* – 'Humat al-Hima' ['Defenders of the Homeland']
*National day* – 20 March (Independence Day)
*Death penalty* – Retained (last used 1991)
*CPI score* – 40 (79)

## CLIMATE AND TERRAIN
A central plain rises to mountains in the north, and in the semi-arid south merges into the Sahara desert. There are salt lakes in the west. Elevation extremes range from 1,544m (Jebel ech Chambi) to −17m (Shatt al Gharsah). The northern and coastal regions have a Mediterranean climate, while there is a desert climate in the south. Average temperatures range from 10.9°C in January to 30°C in August.

## HISTORY AND POLITICS
The area was ruled successively by the Phoenicians, Carthaginians, Romans, Byzantines and Arabs before becoming a largely autonomous part of the Ottoman Empire in the 16th century. In the 19th century French influence grew and it was formally declared a French protectorate in 1883. It was briefly occupied by Germany during the Second World War (1942–3), and became independent as a monarchy under the bey in 1956. In 1957 the bey was deposed and the country became a republic under one-party rule with Habib Bourguiba as president.

Multiparty legislative elections were held in 1981, but the ruling party, the Constitutional Democratic Rally (RCD), retained its grip on power until 2011. Although proclaimed president for life in 1975, President Bourguiba was deposed in 1987 on the grounds of senility by his prime minister Zine el-Abidine Ben Ali. Ben Ali was subsequently elected president in unopposed elections in 1989 and 1994, and in multiparty elections in 1999, 2004 and 2009.

Nationwide protests against Ben Ali's authoritarian regime and unemployment broke out in December 2010, forcing him to leave office and flee the country in January 2011. Moncef Marzouki was elected interim president by the new Constituent Assembly in December 2011; his nomination followed legislative elections in which the former opposition party al-Nahda won the most seats but not an overall majority. Attempts to implement some Islamic reforms by the moderate Islamist government resulted in protests by supporters of secularism and more violent demonstrations from Salafi Islamists.

In July 2013, the assassination of the Arab nationalist politician Mohamed Brahmi caused a general strike and calls for the government to resign. An interim government was created in December 2013, with new electoral laws approved in May 2014. In the October 2014 legislative elections, the secular Nidaa Tounes emerged as the single largest party, winning 85 seats. A coalition government was formed in February comprising Nidaa Tounes, Afek Tunis, the Islamist al-Nahda and the Free Patriotic Union.

The new constitution was implemented on 26 January 2014. The legislature, the Assembly of People's Representatives *(Majlis Nuwab al-Shab)*, is unicameral and directly elected for a five-year term. It has 217 seats, 18 of which are reserved for Tunisians abroad.

HEAD OF STATE
*President,* Beji Caid Essebsi, *elected* 22 December 2014, *sworn in* 31 December 2014

SELECTED GOVERNMENT MEMBERS *as at July 2015*
*Prime Minister,* Habib Essid
*Finance,* Slim Chaker
*Foreign Affairs,* Taieb Baccouche
*Interior,* Najem Gharsalli

## EMBASSY OF TUNISIA

29 Prince's Gate, London SW7 1QG
**T** 020-7584 8117 **E** london@tunisianembassy.co.uk
**W** http://www.at-londres.diplomatie.gov.tn/
*Ambassador Extraordinary and Plenipotentiary,* HE Nabil
Ammar, *apptd* 2012

## BRITISH EMBASSY

Rue du Lac Windermere, Les Berges du Lac, 1053 Tunis
**T** (+216) (71) 108 700 **E** britishembassytunis@fco.gov.uk
**W** www.gov.uk/government/world/tunisia
*Ambassador Extraordinary and Plenipotentiary,* HE Hamish
Cowell, *apptd* 2013

## DEFENCE

| *Aged 16–49, 2010 est* | *Males* | *Females* |
|---|---|---|
| Available for military service | 2,846,572 | 2,952,180 |
| Fit for military service | 2,397,716 | 2,484,097 |

*Military expenditure –* US$906m (2014)
*Conscription duration –* 12 months (selective)

## ECONOMY AND TRADE

The economy is diverse and an increasing proportion is
in private ownership, with further liberalisation planned.
Growth was steady from the late 1990s until 2008, although
the economy contracted in 2009 as export demand
dropped.

A focus on political problems in 2012 and 2013 led to a
neglect of the economy that resulted in several downgrades
of Tunisia's credit rating. Present economic problems include
budget and current account deficits, high unemployment,
and economic disparities between the more developed
coastal region and the impoverished interior. The economy
is likely to suffer further due to terrorist attacks on tourist
sites in March and June 2015 in which nearly 60 people
were killed.

Agriculture and fisheries account for 8.7 per cent of GDP;
the main products are olives, grain, tomatoes, citrus fruits,
sugar beets, dates, almonds, meat and dairy products. The
main industries are oil production, mining (principally
phosphates and iron ore), tourism, processing agricultural
products and manufacture of textiles, footwear and beverages.

The main trading partners are EU countries, especially
France and Italy. Principal exports are clothing, semi-finished
goods and textiles, agricultural products, mechanical goods,
phosphates and chemicals, hydrocarbons and electrical
equipment. The main imports are textiles, machinery and
equipment, hydrocarbons, chemicals and foodstuffs.

*GNI –* US$45,777m; US$4,200 per capita (2013)
*Annual average growth of GDP –* 2.8 per cent (2014 est)
*Inflation rate –* 5.7 per cent (2014 est)
*Population below poverty line –* 15.5 per cent (2010 est)
*Unemployment –* 16.6 per cent (2015 est)
*Total external debt –* US$29,560m (2014 est)
*Imports –* US$24,317m (2013)
*Exports –* US$17,061m (2013)

## BALANCE OF PAYMENTS

*Trade –* US$7,439m deficit (2012)
*Current Account –* US$2,917m deficit (2015 est)

| *Trade with UK* | *2013* | *2014* |
|---|---|---|
| Imports from UK | £160,165,273 | £160,487,196 |
| Exports to UK | £448,309,844 | £306,527,772 |

## COMMUNICATIONS

*Airports and waterways –* The principal airports are at Tunis,
Monastir and Djerba, and the main ports include Bizerte,
Sfax and Rades
*Roadways and railways –* 14,756km; 2,165km
*Telecommunications –* 1.105 million fixed lines and 12.84
million mobile subscriptions (2012); there were 3.50 million
internet users in 2009
*Internet code and IDD –* tn; 216 (from UK), 44 (to UK)
*Major broadcasters –* Al-Watania (TV) and Tunisian Radio are
the state broadcasters
*Press –* Major daily newspapers include *La Presse* (French
language), and *Esshafa* and *Assabah* (both Arabic)
*WPFI score –* 38,68 (126)

## EDUCATION AND HEALTH

There are 11 years of free and compulsory education.
*Literacy rate –* 98.1 per cent (2015 est)
*Gross enrolment ratio (percentage of relevant age group) –*
primary 110 per cent; secondary 91 per cent; tertiary
34 per cent (2013 est)
*Health expenditure (per capita) –* US$309 (2013)
*Hospital beds (per 1,000 people) –* 2.1 (2012)
*Life expectancy (years) –* 75.68 (2014 est)
*Mortality rate –* 5.94 (2014 est)
*Birth rate –* 16.9 (2014 est)
*Infant mortality rate –* 23.19 (2014 est)

# TURKEY

*Turkiye Cumhuriyeti – Republic of Turkey*

*Area –* 783,562 sq. km
*Capital –* Ankara (Angora), in Asia; population, 4,644,000
(2014)
*Major cities –* Adana, Antalya, Bursa, Gaziantep, Istanbul,
Izmir, Konya
*Currency –* Turkish lira (TL) of 100 kurus
*Population –* 79,414,269 rising at 1.26 per cent a year
(2015 est); Turkish (70–75 per cent), Kurdish (18
per cent) (2008 est)
*Religion –* Muslim (predominantly Sunni) 99.8 per cent (est)
*Language –* Turkish (official), Kurdish, Dimli, Azeri,
Kabardian
*Population density –* 97 per sq. km (2013)
*Urban population –* 73.4 per cent (2013 est)
*Median age (years) –* 29.6 (2014 est)
*National anthem –* 'Istiklal Marsi' ['The Independence
March']

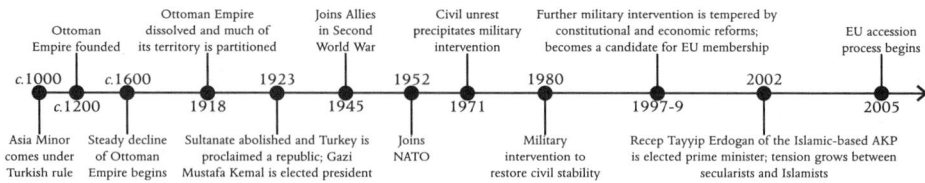

| Ottoman<br>Empire founded | Ottoman Empire<br>dissolved and much of<br>its territory is partitioned | Joins Allies<br>in Second<br>World War | Civil unrest<br>precipitates military<br>intervention | Further military intervention is tempered by<br>constitutional and economic reforms;<br>becomes a candidate for EU membership | EU accession<br>process begins |
| --- | --- | --- | --- | --- | --- |
| c.1000 | c.1600 | 1923 | 1952 | 1980 | 2002 |
| c.1200 | 1918 | 1945 | 1971 | 1997-9 | 2005 |
| Asia Minor<br>comes under<br>Turkish rule | Steady decline<br>of Ottoman<br>Empire begins | Sultanate abolished and Turkey is<br>proclaimed a republic; Gazi<br>Mustafa Kemal is elected president | Joins<br>NATO | Military<br>intervention to<br>restore civil stability | Recep Tayyip Erdogan of the Islamic-based AKP<br>is elected prime minister; tension grows between<br>secularists and Islamists |

*National day* – 29 October (Republic Day)
*Death penalty* – Abolished for all crimes (since 2004)
*CPI score* – 45 (64)

## CLIMATE AND TERRAIN
Turkey in Europe consists of the relatively low-lying area of Eastern Thrace, including the cities of Istanbul and Edirne, and is separated from Asia by the Bosporus at Istanbul and by the Sea of Marmara and the Dardanelles (a strait about 64km in length, with a width varying from 1.6km to 6.4km).

Turkey in Asia comprises the whole of Asia Minor or Anatolia. Western Anatolia consists of a high central plateau with narrow coastal plains fringed by mountains in the north and south. Eastern Anatolia is mountainous, the land falling to a plateau between the mountains and the Syrian border. Elevation extremes range from 5,166m (Mt Ararat) to 0m (Mediterranean Sea). The Euphrates and Tigris rivers rise in the eastern mountains, which also contain many lakes, including Lake Van. Anatolia is prone to earthquakes.

The climate is temperate, but more extreme in the interior. Average temperatures range from 0.2°C in January to 23.1°C in August.

## HISTORY AND POLITICS
The 1982 constitution has been amended several times, mostly recently in 2010; the 2010 amendments increase parliamentary control over the judiciary and the military. Since 2014, the president is directly elected for a four-year term, renewable once. The unicameral Turkish Grand National Assembly has 550 members who were directly elected for a four-year term. The prime minister is appointed by the president and appoints the cabinet.

Tension between secularists and Islamists has grown in recent years, particularly since the Islamic-based Justice and Development Party (AKP), led by Recep Tayyip Erdogan, came to power in 2002. Secularists' concerns about the AKP's agenda caused a four-month political crisis in 2007, preventing the election of a new president and leading outgoing President Sezer to refuse approval of constitutional amendments. The impasse was ended by early legislative elections in July 2007, in which the AKP won a greatly increased majority; it retained its overall majority in the legislative elections in June 2011.

In August 2014, incumbent prime minister Recep Tayyip Erdogan won the first direct election for a president. The June 2015 elections were won by the AKP, who secured 259 seats but lost their overall majority. The elections saw a Kurdish party, the People's Democratic Party, win 80 seats, becoming the first pro-Kurdish party to be elected to the legislature.

## HEAD OF STATE
*President,* Recep Tayyip Erdogan, *elected* 10 August 2014, *sworn in* 28 August 2014

SELECTED GOVERNMENT MEMBERS *as at July 2015*
*Prime Minister,* vacant
*Deputy Prime Ministers,* Yalcin Akdogan; Bulent Arinc; Ali Babacan; Numan Kurtulmus

*Finance,* Mehmet Simsek
*Foreign Affairs,* Mevlut Cavusoglu

### EMBASSY OF THE REPUBLIC OF TURKEY
43 Belgrave Square, London SW1X 8PA
**T** 020-7393 0202 **E** embassy.london@mfa.gov.tr
**W** www.london.emb.mfa.gov.tr
*Ambassador Extraordinary and Plenipotentiary,* HE Abdurrahman Bilgic, *apptd* 2014

### BRITISH EMBASSY
Sehit Ersan Caddesi 46/A, Cankaya, Ankara
**T** (+90) (312) 455 3344 **E** info.officer@fco.gov.uk
**W** www.gov.uk/government/world/turkey
*Ambassador Extraordinary and Plenipotentiary,* HE Richard Moore, *apptd* 2014

### INSURGENCIES
Turkey's 12 million Kurds are the majority population in the south-east of the country, and have sought greater political and cultural rights for many years. The Kurdistan Workers' Party (PKK) has fought a guerrilla war for an ethnic homeland in the south-east since 1984 and has been blamed for bombings in other parts of Turkey. Conflict on the Turkey–Iraq border has caused tension in relations with Iraq, especially in 2008 after Turkish military incursions into the autonomous Kurdish area in northern Iraq. The government started to seek a political solution to the violence in 2009, introducing measures to increase Kurdish language rights and reduce the military presence in the south-east.

Following a statement requesting a ceasefire by jailed PKK leader Abdullah Ocalan, Kurdish fighters withdrew from Turkey in 2013. In July 2015, the Turkish Air Force bombed PKK bases in Iraq following an apparent attack by the PKK near the Turkish town of Diyarbakir that killed two soldiers.

### DEFENCE

| Aged 16–49, 2010 est | Males | Females |
| --- | --- | --- |
| Available for military service | 21,079,077 | 20,558,696 |
| Fit for military service | 17,664,510 | 17,340,816 |

*Military expenditure* – US$22,618m (2014)
*Conscription duration* – 6–15 months

### ECONOMY AND TRADE
The economy combines modern industry and commerce with a traditional agriculture sector. The private sector is growing steadily following large-scale privatisations of basic industry, banking, transport and communications. Financial and fiscal reforms from 2002 achieved growth averaging over 5 per cent a year from 2005 to 2007, although large current account and trade deficits remain. Growth averaged 3.1 per cent between 2012 and 2015, and is expected to accelerate to 3.5 per cent in 2016.

The agricultural sector accounts for 8.2 per cent of GDP and employs 25.5 per cent of the workforce. The principal crops are tobacco, cotton, grain, olives, sugar beets, pulses, nuts, citrus and other fruits, and livestock products. A diverse industrial sector is dominated by textiles and clothing (which employ one-third of the industrial workforce), food processing, vehicle assembly, electronics, mining, iron and steel, oil, construction, timber and paper. Turkey is also a destination and a transit route for oil and gas from central Asian countries. Tourism is a major industry and source of foreign revenue. Industry contributes 26.9 per cent of GDP and services 64.9 per cent.

The main trading partners are EU countries (especially Germany), Russia, China and Iraq. Principal exports are clothing, foodstuffs, textiles, metal manufactures and transport equipment. The main imports are machinery, chemicals, semi-finished manufactures, fuels and transport equipment.
*GNI* – US$821,684m; US$10,970 per capita (2013)
*Annual average growth of GDP* – 3 per cent (2014 est)
*Inflation rate* – 8.9 per cent (2014 est)
*Population below poverty line* – 16.9 per cent (2010 est)
*Unemployment* – 9.7 per cent (2015 est)
*Total external debt* – US$407,100m (2014)
*Imports* – US$251,662m (2013)
*Exports* – US$151,798m (2013)

BALANCE OF PAYMENTS
*Trade* – US$84,083m deficit (2012)
*Current Account* – US$31,719m deficit (2015 est)

| Trade with UK | 2013 | 2014 |
| --- | --- | --- |
| Imports from UK | £4,343,502,632 | £3,723,253,786 |
| Exports to UK | £5,951,408,604 | £6,490,338,593 |

## COMMUNICATIONS
*Airports and waterways* – The principal airports are at Istanbul and Ankara, and the main ports are at Istanbul (Europe) and Izmir (Asia)
*Roadways and railways* – 352,268km; 12,008km
*Telecommunications* – 13.86 million fixed lines and 67.68 million mobile subscriptions (2012); there were 27.23 million internet users in 2009
*Internet code and IDD* – tr; 90 (from UK), 44 (to UK)
*Major broadcasters* – Turkish Radio Television (TRT) is the country's public broadcaster, and the country has over 300 private television channels and more than 1,000 private radio stations
*Press* – Major national daily newspapers include *Hurriyet, Milliyet* and *Cumhuriyet*
*WPFI score* – 44,16 (149)

## EDUCATION AND HEALTH
Education is free and compulsory from the ages of six to 14.
*Literacy rate* – 99.2 per cent (2015 est)
*Gross enrolment ratio (percentage of relevant age group)* – primary 100 per cent; secondary 86 per cent (2012 est); tertiary 79 per cent (2013 est)
*Health expenditure (per capita)* – US$608 (2013)
*Hospital beds (per 1,000 people)* – 2.5 (2011)
*Life expectancy (years)* – 73.29 (2014 est)
*Mortality rate* – 6.12 (2014 est)
*Birth rate* – 16.86 (2014 est)
*Infant mortality rate* – 21.43 (2014 est)

# TURKMENISTAN

*Area* – 488,100 sq. km
*Capital* – Ashgabat; population, 735,000 (2014)
*Major cities* – Dashoguz, Turkmenabat
*Currency* – Manat of 100 tennesi
*Population* – 5,231,422 rising at 1.14 per cent a year (2015 est); Turkmen (85 per cent), Uzbek (5 per cent), Russian (4 per cent) (2003)
*Religion* – Muslim 89 per cent (majority Sunni), Christian 9 per cent (mainly Eastern Orthodox) (est)
*Language* – Turkmen (official), Russian, Uzbek
*Population density* – 11 per sq. km (2013)
*Urban population* – 49.4 per cent (2013 est)
*Median age (years)* – 26.6 (2014 est)
*National anthem* – 'Garassyz, Bitarap Turkmenistanyn Dowlet Gimni' ['National Anthem of Independent, Neutral Turkmenistan']
*National day* – 27 October (Independence Day, 1991)
*Death penalty* – Abolished for all crimes (since 1999)
*CPI score* – 17 (169)
*Literacy rate* – 100 per cent (2011 est)
*Health expenditure (per capita)* – US$158 (2013)
*Hospital beds (per 1,000 people)* – 4.0 (2012)
*Life expectancy (years)* – 69.47 (2014 est)
*Mortality rate* – 6.16 (2014 est)
*Birth rate* – 19.46 (2014 est)
*Infant mortality rate* – 38.13 (2014 est)

## CLIMATE AND TERRAIN
Over 80 per cent of the country is taken up by the Kara Kum (Black Sands) desert. There are mountains in the south and along the Iranian border, and areas below sea level along the edges of the Caspian Sea. Elevation extremes range from 3,139m (Gora Ayribaba) to −81m (Vpadina Akchanaya, although Lake Sarygamysh sometimes has a lower elevation because of fluctuations in its water level). There is a subtropical desert climate. Average temperatures range from 1.8°C in January to 29.7°C in July.

## HISTORY AND POLITICS
Turkmenistan was conquered successively by the Persians, Greeks (under Alexander the Great), Parthians, Arabs and Mongols from the sixth century BC. From the early 19th century Turkmenistan was gradually incorporated into the Russian Empire. A Turkmen revolt against Russian rule in 1916 brought a period of autonomy until 1921, when Soviet control over Turkmenistan was established and it became an Autonomous Soviet Socialist Republic. Turkmenistan became a full republic of the USSR in 1925. It declared its independence from the USSR on 27 October 1991.

Saparmurat Niyazov became leader of the Turkmen Communist Party in 1985, and was elected president in

1990, becoming president for life in 2004. His autocratic regime, through harassment and authoritarianism, prevented the development of any effective political opposition or press freedom, rejecting political pluralism in favour of a cult of personality. After President Niyazov's death in 2006, Gurbanguly Berdimuhammedov was elected president, and was re-elected with an overwhelming majority in the 2012 presidential election. Parties supportive of the president won overwhelmingly in the 2013 legislative elections, whose outcome was criticised by human rights groups.

A new constitution was adopted in 2008 which encouraged multiparty politics and economic liberalisation, abolished the People's Council and increased the powers of the enlarged legislature. The executive president is directly elected for a five-year term. The unicameral parliament *(Majlis)* has 125 members directly elected for a five-year term.

The country is divided into five provinces (Ahal, Balkan, Dashhowuz, Lebap and Mary) and the city of Ashgabat.

## HEAD OF STATE
*President, Chair of the Council of Ministers,* Gurbanguly Berdimuhammedov, *elected* 14 February 2007, *re-elected* 2012

SELECTED GOVERNMENT MEMBERS *as at July 2015*
*Defence,* Begench Gundogdiyev
*Finance,* Annamuhammet Gocyyew
*Foreign Affairs,* Rashid Meredov

## EMBASSY OF TURKMENISTAN
131 Holland Park Avenue, London W11 4UT
T 020-7610 5239 E tkm-embassy-uk@btconnect.com
*Ambassador Extraordinary and Plenipotentiary,* HE Yazmurad N. Seryayev, *apptd* 2003

## BRITISH EMBASSY
Third Floor Office Building, Four Points Ak Altin Hotel, 744001 Ashgabat
T (+993) (12) 363 462 E beasb@online.tm
W www.gov.uk/government/world/turkmenistan
*Ambassador Extraordinary and Plenipotentiary,* Sanjay Wadvani, *apptd* 2013

## DEFENCE

| Aged 16–49, 2010 est | Males | Females |
| --- | --- | --- |
| Available for military service | 1,380,794 | 1,387,211 |
| Fit for military service | 1,066,649 | 1,185,538 |

*Conscription duration* – 12–24 months

## ECONOMY AND TRADE
Turkmenistan has large reserves of natural gas and some oil, but exports were restricted by a lack of export routes until 2009–10, when existing pipelines to Russia and Iran were supplemented by a new gas pipeline to China and a second pipeline to Iran; a trans-Caucasian route to European markets is also under exploration. Attempts to privatise the primarily state-run and inefficient economy have been made since 2012, but implementation has been slow. The slowdown in the Russian economy and falling oil prices caused the government to devalue the Manat by nearly 20 per cent in January 2015 in a bid to increase exports.

Agriculture is intensive around the irrigated oases, with half the irrigated land used to grow cotton. Agriculture accounts for 13.2 per cent of GDP and 48.2 per cent of employment; grain and livestock are the other main products. The principal industries are gas and oil production, petroleum products, textiles (including silk) and food processing. Industry contributes 49.3 per cent of GDP.

The main trading partners are China, Turkey, Russia, Ukraine, the UAE and the EU. Principal exports are gas, crude oil, petrochemicals, textiles and cotton fibre. The main imports are machinery and equipment, chemicals and foodstuffs.

*GNI* – US$36,050m; US$6,880 per capita (2013)
*Annual average growth of GDP* – 10.1 per cent (2014 est)
*Inflation rate* – 11 per cent (2014 est)
*Population below poverty line* – 0.2 per cent (2012 est)
*Unemployment* – 10.4 per cent (2015 est)
*Total external debt* – US$578.4m (2014 est)

BALANCE OF PAYMENTS
*Trade* – US$120m surplus (2003)
*Current Account* – US$4,945m deficit (2015 est)

| Trade with UK | 2013 | 2014 |
| --- | --- | --- |
| Imports from UK | £146,302,316 | £124,388,193 |
| Exports to UK | £279,693,839 | £213,772,918 |

## COMMUNICATIONS
*Airports and waterways* – The main airport is at Ashgabat; there are two important waterways, the Amu Darya river in the north-east and the Niyazov (formerly Kara Kum) canal, and the main port is Turkmenbashi, on the Caspian Sea
*Roadways and railways* – 47,577km; 2,980km
*Telecommunications* – 575,000 fixed lines and 3.95 million mobile subscriptions (2012); there were 80,400 internet users in 2009
*Internet code and IDD* – tm; 993 (from UK), 810 44 (to UK)
*Media* – The country's public broadcasters are Turkmen TV and Turkmen Radio; leading daily newspapers include *Neytralnyy Turkmenistan* (Russian language), and *Turkmenistan* and *Watan* (both Turkmen)
*WPFI score* – 80,83 (178)

# TUVALU

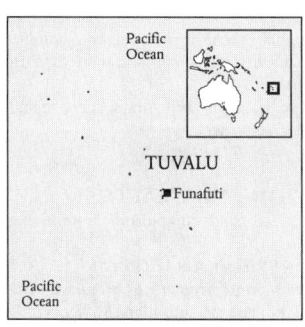

*Area* – 26 sq. km
*Capital* – Funafuti; population, 6,000 (2014 est)
*Currency* – The Australian dollar (A$) of 100 cents is legal tender; in addition there are Tuvalu dollar and cent coins in circulation
*Population* – 10,869 rising at 0.82 per cent a year (2015 est); Polynesian (96 per cent), Micronesian (4 per cent) (est)
*Religion* – Christian (Church of Tuvalu 97 per cent, Seventh-day Adventist 1.4 per cent, Baha'i 1 per cent (est)
*Language* – English, Tuvaluan (both official), Samoan, Kiribati (on Nui)
*Population density* – 329 per sq. km (2013)
*Urban population* – 51.4 per cent (2013 est)

*Median age (years)* – 24.9 (2014 est)
*National anthem* – 'Tuvalu mo te Atua' ['Tuvalu for the Almighty']
*National day* – 1 October (Independence Day)
*Death penalty* – Abolished for all crimes (since 1978)
*Life expectancy (years)* – 65.81 (2014 est)
*Mortality rate* – 8.90 (2014 est)
*Birth rate* – 23.74 (2014 est)
*Infant mortality rate* – 31.69 (2014 est)

## CLIMATE AND TERRAIN

Tuvalu comprises nine low-lying coral islands and atolls in the south-west Pacific Ocean. The highest elevation is 5m and the lowest is 0m (Pacific Ocean). The climate is tropical, with an average temperature of 28.4°C.

## HISTORY AND POLITICS

The islands were settled by Polynesians from Tonga 2,000 years ago. Europeans arrived in the 18th century and, as the Ellice Islands, Tuvalu came under the control of the British in 1877. They formed part of the Gilbert and Ellice Islands protectorate (later a colony) from 1892, but were granted separate status from the Gilbert Islands in 1975. The islands became independent as Tuvalu on 1 October 1978. The country is seriously affected by rising sea levels, which are threatening its economic viability.

There are no political parties; allegiances are influenced by personal and island loyalties. Politically stable as a democracy, there are frequent changes in government as support in parliament shifts, although incumbent Prime Minister Enele Sopoaga retained his seat in the March 2015 legislative elections.

Under the 1978 constitution, Tuvalu is a constitutional monarchy with Queen Elizabeth II as head of state, represented by a governor-general who is appointed on the advice of the prime minister. The unicameral legislature, the Parliament of Tuvalu, has 15 members who are directly elected for a four-year term. The prime minister is elected by the legislature from among its members, and appoints the cabinet, who must be members of parliament. Local government services are provided by elected island councils.

*Governor-General,* HE Sir Iakoba Italeli, GCMG, *apptd* 2013

SELECTED GOVERNMENT MEMBERS *as at July 2015*
*Prime Minister,* Enele Sopoaga
*Finance,* Maatia Toafa
*Foreign Affairs,* Taukelina Finikaso

HONORARY CONSULATE OF TUVALU
Tuvalu House, 230 Worple Road, London SW20 8RH
T 020-8879 0985 E tuvaluconsulate@netscape.net
*Honorary Consul,* Dr Iftikhar A. Ayaz

BRITISH HIGH COMMISSIONER
HE Roderick Drummond, *apptd* 2013, resident at Suva, Fiji

## ECONOMY AND TRADE

The main economic activities are subsistence agriculture and fishing, although agricultural productivity is threatened by the increasing salinity of the soil as the sea level rises; the only cash crop is coconuts. Tourism is limited by the state's remoteness. Most employment is in the public sector or abroad, often as merchant seamen; many families rely on remittances from expatriate workers. The government receives substantial annual income from a trust fund set up in 1987, and raises revenue through the sale of fishing licences, postage stamps and coins, and the leasing of its telephone code and internet suffix.

The main trading partners are Japan, the USA, New Zealand and Australia. The only exports are copra and fish. The main imports are food, livestock, fuels, machinery and manufactured goods.
*Annual average growth of GDP* – 2.2 per cent (2014 est)
*Inflation rate* – 3.8 per cent (2006 est)

BALANCE OF PAYMENTS
*Trade* – US$16m deficit (2007)

| Trade with UK | 2013 | 2014 |
|---|---|---|
| Imports from UK | – | – |
| Exports to UK | £49,542 | £161,254 |

## COMMUNICATIONS

*Airports and waterways* – Funafuti has an airfield, from which a regular service operates to Fiji and Kiribati, and it is also the main port
*Roadways* – 8km
*Telecommunications* – 1,450 fixed lines and 2,800 mobile subscriptions (2012); there were 4,200 internet users in 2008
*Internet code and IDD* – tv; 688 (from UK), 44 (to UK)
*Media* – The state-owned Tuvalu Media Corporation publishes a fortnightly newspaper and runs Radio Tuvalu, the main information source for islanders

# UGANDA

*Republic of Uganda*

*Area* – 241,038 sq. km
*Capital* – Kampala; population, 1,863,000 (2014)
*Major towns* – Entebbe, Gulu, Lira
*Currency* – Uganda shilling of 100 cents
*Population* – 37,101,745 rising at 3.24 per cent a year (2015 est); Baganda (16.9 per cent), Banyakole (9.5 per cent), Basoga (8.4 per cent), Bakiga (6.9 per cent), Iteso (6.4 per cent), Langi (6.1 per cent), Acholi (4.7 per cent), Bagisu (4.6 per cent), Lugbara (4.2 per cent), Bunyoro (2.7 per cent); other 29.6 per cent (2002)
*Religion* – Christian 83.9 per cent (Roman Catholic 41.9 per cent, Anglican 35.9 per cent, Pentecostal 4.6 per cent, Muslim 12.1 per cent (predominantly Sunni) (2002); indigenous beliefs are often blended into or observed alongside Christianity or Islam
*Language* – English (official), Luganda, Swahili, Arabic
*Population density* – 188 per sq. km (2013)
*Urban population* – 16.4 per cent (2013 est)
*Median age (years)* – 15.5 (2014 est)
*National anthem* – 'O Uganda, Land of Beauty!'
*National day* – 9 October (Independence Day)

*Death penalty* – Retained
*CPI score* – 26 (142)

## CLIMATE AND TERRAIN

Uganda lies on a high plateau with mountain ranges in the west, south-west and north-east. Elevation extremes range from 5,110m (Mt Stanley) to 621m (Lake Albert). Nearly 20 per cent of the country is covered by lakes, rivers and wetlands, and it contains about half of lakes Victoria, Edward and Albert (Mobuto), as well as lakes Kyoga, Kwania, George and Bisina (formerly Salisbury) and the course of the Nile from its outlet from Lake Victoria to the South Sudan border at Nimule. The climate is tropical, moderated by the altitude. There are two rainy seasons (March–May, October–December) in the south; the north is drier, semi-arid in places, with a single, longer rainy season.

## HISTORY AND POLITICS

Indigenous people had formed several kingdoms in the area by the 14th century. A British protectorate was established over the kingdom of Buganda in 1894 and gradually extended to other territory by 1914. Uganda became independent on 9 October 1962 as a federation of the kingdoms of Ankole, Buganda, Bunyoro, Busoga and Toro.

In 1963 Uganda was proclaimed a federal republic but in 1966 prime minister Milton Obote overthrew the president, ended the federal status and became executive president. In 1971 President Obote was deposed in an army coup led by Maj.-Gen. Idi Amin, who proclaimed himself head of state. His brutal dictatorship was overthrown in 1979 with military assistance from Tanzania.

Milton Obote was re-elected president in 1980 but political instability and human rights abuses continued. He was ousted by a military coup in 1985 amid a civil war with the rebel National Resistance Army (NRA) led by Yoweri Museveni. A military council was installed but the NRA captured Kampala in January 1986, securing control of the rest of the country in the following few months.

Museveni's 'Movement' system of government, under which political parties were allowed to exist but not to contest elections, was in place from 1986 until a 2005 referendum resulted in a return to multiparty politics. In multiparty elections held in February and March 2011, President Museveni was re-elected for a fourth term, and the National Resistance Movement retained its majority in parliament.

The Lord's Resistance Army (LRA), whose stated goals have proved inconsistent, began a low-level insurgency in northern Uganda in the late 1980s. Its activities have spread into north-eastern Congo (where most of the LRA is now located), southern Sudan, the Central African Republic and Kenya, despite offensives against LRA bases by Ugandan, Sudanese and Congolese forces since 2008. In Uganda, thousands have been massacred or mutilated, an estimated 20,000 children abducted to serve in its forces, and 1.7 million people displaced into camps.

Terrorist attacks by Islamic extremists have begun in recent years. Some were carried out by Somalian Islamists, as African Union peacekeepers (predominantly Ugandan) have prevented them establishing complete control of the Somalian capital, but other attacks were the work of the Allied Democratic Forces, based in the Democratic Republic of Congo, which seeks to create an Islamic state in Uganda. Prime Minister Mbabazi was sacked and replaced by Ruhakana Rugunda in September 2014. Legislative and presidential elections are scheduled for February 2016.

The 1995 constitution was amended in 2005 to allow multiparty elections. The president is directly elected for a five-year term; the two-term limit was abolished in 2005.

The unicameral parliament has 238 directly elected members and 137 (including 112 women) elected indirectly to represent particular groups; all serve a five-year term. The prime minister is appointed by the president, subject to the approval of parliament.

HEAD OF STATE
*President,* Yoweri Museveni, *sworn in* 29 January 1986, *elected* 9 May 1996, *re-elected* 2001, 2006, 2011
*Vice-President,* Edward Kiwanuka Sekandi

SELECTED GOVERNMENT MEMBERS *as at July 2015*
*Prime Minister,* Ruhakana Rugunda
*First Deputy Prime Minister,* Henry Muganwa Kajura
*Defence,* Crispus W. C. B. Kiyonga
*Finance,* Matia Kasaija

UGANDA HIGH COMMISSION
Uganda House, 58–59 Trafalgar Square, London WC2N 5DX
T 020-7839 5783 E info@ugandahighcommission.co.uk
W www.ugandahighcommission.co.uk
*High Commissioner,* HE Joyce Kikafunda, *apptd* 2013

BRITISH HIGH COMMISSION
PO Box 7070, 4 Windsor Loop, Kampala
T (+256) (31) 231 2000 E bhcinfo@starcom.co.ug
W www.gov.uk/government/world/uganda
*High Commissioner,* HE Alison Blackburne, *apptd* 2012

## DEFENCE

| *Aged 16–49, 2010 est* | *Males* | *Females* |
| --- | --- | --- |
| Available for military service | 7,249,271 | 7,025,439 |
| Fit for military service | 4,313,068 | 4,200,901 |

*Military expenditure* – US$322m (2014)

## ECONOMY AND TRADE

Economic reforms adopted since 1986 have produced steady economic growth, which was only slightly affected by the global downturn. However, there has been little industrialisation, so the economy is vulnerable to fluctuations in global commodity prices, especially that of coffee, its main export. Uganda's debt burden has been reduced by debt relief since 2000 but it is still dependent on foreign aid. High levels of government debt and the depreciation of the Uganda shilling depressed growth in 2014 and 2015.

Agriculture is the most important economic sector, contributing 21.9 per cent of GDP and engaging about 82 per cent of the workforce. The principal crops are coffee, tea, cotton, tobacco, cassava, potatoes, maize, millet, pulses, cut flowers and livestock products. Industrial activity centres on production of sugar, tobacco, cotton textiles, cement and steel, brewing and fishing. Tourism is growing, and oil has been discovered but is not yet being exploited.

The main export markets are neighbouring countries, the UAE and Rwanda; imports come chiefly from Kenya, the UAE, China and India. Principal exports are coffee, fish and fish products, tea, cotton, cut flowers, horticultural products and gold. Electricity is exported to Kenya, Tanzania and Rwanda. The main imports are capital equipment, vehicles, petroleum, medical supplies and cereals.

*GNI* – US$20,661m; US$550 per capita (2013)
*Annual average growth of GDP* – 5.9 per cent (2014 est)
*Inflation rate* – 4.3 per cent (2014 est)
*Population below poverty line* – 19.7 per cent (2013 est)
*Unemployment* – 3.5 per cent (2015 est)
*Total external debt* – US$4,095m (2014 est)
*Imports* – US$4,927m (2013)
*Exports* – US$2,847m (2013)

**BALANCE OF PAYMENTS**
*Trade* – US$2,369m deficit (2012)
*Current Account* – US$2,348m deficit (2015 est)

| Trade with UK | 2013 | 2014 |
|---|---|---|
| Imports from UK | £49,106,773 | £45,362,229 |
| Exports to UK | £16,710,183 | £12,598,090 |

## COMMUNICATIONS

*Airports and waterways* – There is an international airport at Entebbe; some of the lakes and parts of the river Nile provide navigable routes internally
*Roadways and railways* – 20,000km, including 3,624 of paved roadways; 1,244km
*Telecommunications* – 315,000 fixed lines and 16.36 million mobile subscriptions (2012); there were 3.2 million internet users in 2009
*Internet code and IDD* – ug; 256 (from UK), 0 44 (to UK)
*Media* – The Uganda Broadcasting Company is the main public-run broadcaster; major newspapers include the state-owned *New Vision,* as well as the privately owned *The Monitor* and *The Observer*
*WPFI score* – 31,65 (97)

## EDUCATION AND HEALTH

Education is a joint undertaking by the government, local authorities and voluntary agencies.
*Literacy rate* – 90.7 per cent (2015 est)
*Gross enrolment ratio (percentage of relevant age group)* – primary 107 per cent; secondary 27 per cent (2013 est); tertiary 4 per cent (2011 est)
*Health expenditure (per capita)* – US$59 (2013)
*Hospital beds (per 1,000 people)* – 0.5 (2010)
*Life expectancy (years)* – 54.46 (2014 est)
*Mortality rate* – 10.97 (2014 est)
*Birth rate* – 44.17 (2014 est)
*Infant mortality rate* – 60.82 (2014 est)
*HIV/AIDS adult prevalence* – 7.44 per cent (2013 est)

# UKRAINE

*Ukrayina* – Ukraine

*Area* – 603,550 sq. km
*Capital* – Kiev (Kyiv); population, 2,917,000 (2014)
*Major cities* – Dnipropetrovsk, Donetsk, Kharkiv, L'viv, Odesa, Zaporizhzhya
*Currency* – Hryvnia of 100 kopiykas
*Population* – 44,429,471 falling at 0.6 per cent a year (2015 est); Ukrainian (77.8 per cent), Russian (17.3 per cent); small Belarusian, Moldovan, Crimean Tatar, Bulgarian, Romanian, Polish, Hungarian and Greek minorities (2001 est)

*Religion* – Christian (Orthodox 70.6 per cent, Greek Catholic 5.7 per cent, Roman Catholic 1.3 per cent, Protestant 0.8 per cent), Muslim 0.7 per cent (est)
*Language* – Ukrainian (official), Russian
*Population density* – 79 per sq. km (2013)
*Urban population* – 69.3 per cent (2013 est)
*Median age (years)* – 40.6 (2014 est)
*National anthem* – 'Shche ne vmerla, Ukraina' ['Ukraine Has Not Yet Perished']
*National day* – 24 August (Independence Day)
*Death penalty* – Abolished for all crimes (since 1999)
*CPI score* – 26 (142)

## CLIMATE AND TERRAIN

Much of the country lies in a plain (steppe), with the Carpathian mountains in the west and mountains in the south of the Crimean peninsula. Elevation extremes range from 2,061m (Hora Hoverla) to 0m (Black Sea). The main rivers are the Dnieper, which runs through the centre of the country, the Dniester in the west, the Southern Buh and the Northern Donets (a tributary of the Don). The climate is continental, and Mediterranean in the southern Crimea. Average temperatures range from −2.9°C in January to 21.2°C in July.

## POLITICS

The 1996 constitution was amended in 2004 to transfer some powers from the president to the legislature *(Verkhovna Rada);* the constitutional court returned these powers to the president in late 2010 although in February 2014 the 2004 constitutional amendments were reinstated. The president is directly elected for a five-year term. The unicameral Supreme Council has 450 members, who are directly elected for a five-year term. The prime minister is appointed by the president, subject to the legislature's approval.

Following the decision of Viktor Yanukovych's government to abandon plans for an association agreement with the EU in November 2013, tens of thousands of pro-EU demonstrators protested in Kiev and other cities. The widespread and sometimes violent demonstrations, which left at least 77 protestors dead in Kiev, resulted in President Yanukovych leaving Ukraine and seeking asylum in Russia, causing opposition parties to form an interim government.

The speaker of the parliament, Oleksandr Turchynov, was appointed interim president on 22 February 2014. A national unity government was subsequently established, with Arseniy Yatsenyuk of the Fatherland party sworn in as prime minister on 26 February. In May 2014, Petro Poroshenko was elected president with 54.7 per cent of the popular vote. Arseniy Yatsenyuk was breifly replaced as prime minister by Volodymyr Groysman in May 2014 before being reinstated in July. Following early elections held in October 2014, the BPP remained the largest single party, winning 132 seats, and formed a coalition government in December.

In August 2015, parliament voted to provide greater autonomy to areas in the east of the country controlled by pro-Russian separatists. The decision caused the far-right Ukranian nationalist Radical Party to leave the ruling coalition in September.

HEAD OF STATE
*President,* Petro Poroshenko, *elected* 25 May 2014, *sworn in* 7 June 2014

SELECTED GOVERNMENT MEMBERS *as at September 2015*
*Prime Minister,* Arseniy Yatsenyuk
*Deputy Prime Ministers,* Vyacheslav Kirilenko; Yuriy Zubko

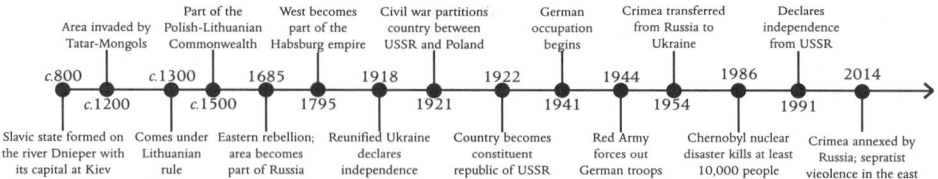

Finance, Natalie Jaresko
Foreign Affairs, Pavlo Klimkin

EMBASSY OF UKRAINE
60 Holland Park, London W11 3SJ
T 020-7727 6312 E emb_gb@mfa.gov.ua W www.ukremb.org.uk
Ambassador Extraordinary and Plenipotentiary, vacant

BRITISH EMBASSY
Desyatynna 9, Kiev 01025
T (+380) (44) 490 3660 E ukembinf@gmail.com
W www.gov.uk/government/world/ukraine
Ambassador Extraordinary and Plenipotentiary, HE Judith
  Gough, apptd 2015

FOREIGN RELATIONS
Following the disintegration of the USSR in 1991, relations between Ukraine and Russia were strained by disputes over the Black Sea fleet and the status of Crimea, a self-administered republic within Ukraine which had been part of Russia until 1954; these disputes often came to a head when Russia suspended gas supplies to Ukraine. However, in February 2014 armed pro-Russian groups seized government buildings in Crimea. The Crimea was formally annexed by the Russian government on the 18 March 2014 after a controversial independence vote in the Crimean parliament. Ukraine and a majority of UN member states do not accept the status of Crimea and Sevastopol as federal subjects of the Russian Federation.

From April, pro-Russian groups in the east of the Ukraine seized government buildings and two self-proclaimed pro-Russian states were established in the east of the country: the Donetsk People's Republic and the Luhansk People's Republic. Independence referendums were held on 11 May in both territories, with adminstrators claiming very large wins for supporters of independence. Both republics merged on 24 May to form The Federal State of Novorossiya. The breakaway states have not been recognised by Russia, Ukraine or the wider international community.

By June at least 270 people had been killed as these groups clashed with the Ukrainian military. While political tensions eased when the Russian government advised it would be pulling troops away from the Ukrainian border, violence between the Ukrainian army and separatist militias continued to occur. A Ukraine–European Union Association Agreement was formalised by the incoming government on 27 June 2014.

Tensions were reignited by the downing of Malaysian Airlines flight MH17 on Ukrainian soil on 17 July 2014, apparently by pro-Russian separatists. On 5 September, a ceasefire was agreed between the government and separatists, though fighting continued into 2015 and rebel forces captured the strategically important town of Debaltseve in February 2015.

DEFENCE

| Aged 16–49, 2010 est | Males | Females |
|---|---|---|
| Available for military service | 10,984,394 | 11,260,000 |
| Fit for military service | 6,893,551 | 8,792,504 |

Military expenditure – US$4,024m (2014)
Conscription duration – 12–18 months

ECONOMY AND TRADE
The first decade of independence was characterised by economic mismanagement and opposition to economic restructuring. When reform began in the late 1990s, it brought economic growth, with rises in output and exports and a reduction in inflation. However, slow progress has been a drag on the economy, leaving it vulnerable to external factors such as the global economic downturn; the economy contracted severely in 2009 and is now smaller than it was after independence in 1992. Economic growth slowed in 2012 amid allegations the Yanukovych regime mis-appropriated billions of dollars during its time in power.

After incurring debts worth US$1.9bn, with state-run Russian energy firm Gazprom, Russia ended its practice of supplying Ukraine with subsidised fossil fuels, greatly increasing domestic prices. In March 2015, the IMF approved a US$17.5bn (£11.28bn) loan to Ukraine in order to prevent the country from defaulting. The economy is expected to return to growth in 2016 despite the continuing conflict in the east.

The agricultural sector is large and productive, with over half the land under cultivation. The main crops are grain, sugar beet, sunflower seeds and vegetables; stock-raising and dairy farming are also important. Agriculture accounts for 12.1 per cent of GDP and 5.6 per cent of employment. There are large deposits of coal, iron ore and other minerals. The main industrial activities are mining and metal processing, manufacture of machinery and transport equipment and chemicals, electricity generation and food processing, especially sugar. Ukraine imports three-quarters of its oil and gas, principally from Russia; supplies have been suspended on occasion due to price disputes.

The main trading partners are Russia (25.6 per cent of exports; 32.4 per cent of imports), China, Germany and Turkey. Principal exports are ferrous and non-ferrous metals (especially steel), fuel and petroleum products, chemicals, machinery and transport equipment, and foodstuffs. The main imports are energy (primarily gas), machinery and equipment, and chemicals.

GNI – US$179,944m; US$3,960 per capita (2013)
Annual average growth of GDP – –6.5 per cent (2014 est)
Inflation rate – 11.3 per cent (2014 est)
Population below poverty line – 24.1 per cent (2010)
Unemployment – 8.3 per cent (2015 est)
Total external debt – US$153,600m (2014 est)
Imports – US$76,987m (2013)
Exports – US$63,321m (2013)

BALANCE OF PAYMENTS
Trade – US$15,848m deficit (2012)
Current Account – US$1,216m deficit (2015 est)

| Trade with UK | 2013 | 2014 |
|---|---|---|
| Imports from UK | £553,132,998 | £354,817,467 |
| Exports to UK | £379,483,944 | £395,703,673 |

## COMMUNICATIONS

*Airports and waterways* – The principal airports are at Kiev and Odesa; the main seaports are Mariupol on the Sea of Azov, and Kherson, Mykolayiv, Odesa and Sevastopol on the Black Sea

*Roadways and railways* – 169,095km; 21,619km

*Telecommunications* – 12.182 million fixed lines and 59.34 million mobile subscriptions (2012); there were 7.77 million internet users in 2009

*Internet code and IDD* – ua; 380 (from UK), 44 (to UK)

*Major broadcasters* – The National TV Company of Ukraine and the National Radio Company of Ukraine are the principal public broadcasters

*Press* – Major dailies include *Fakty i Kommentarii* (Ukrainian language), and *Silski Visti* and *Segodnya* (both Russian language)

*WPFI score* – 39,1 (129)

## EDUCATION AND HEALTH

*Literacy rate* – 99.8 per cent (2015)

*Gross enrolment ratio (percentage of relevant age group)* – primary 105 per cent; secondary 99 per cent; tertiary 79 per cent (2013 est)

*Health expenditure (per capita)* – US$313 (2013)

*Hospital beds (per 1,000 people)* – 9.0 (2012)

*Life expectancy (years)* – 69.14 (2014 est)

*Mortality rate* – 15.72 (2014 est)

*Birth rate* – 9.41 (2014 est)

*Infant mortality rate* – 8.1 (2014 est)

*HIV/AIDS adult prevalence* – 0.83 per cent (2013 est)

# UNITED ARAB EMIRATES

*Al-Imarat al-Arabiyah al-Muttahidah – United Arab Emirates*

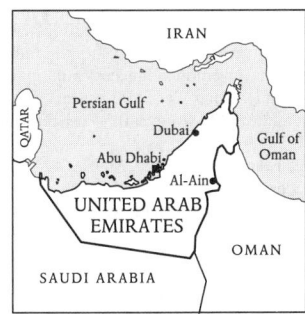

*Area* – 83,600 sq. km

*Capital* – Abu Dhabi; population, 1,114,000 (2014)

*Major cities* – Ajman, Al-Ain, Dubai, Sharjah

*Currency* – UAE dirham (Dh) of 100 fils

*Population* – 5,779,760 rising at 2.58 per cent a year (2015 est); Emirati (19 per cent), other Arab and Iranian (23 per cent), South Asian (50 per cent) (1982)

*Religion* – Muslim 76 per cent, Christian 9 per cent, other (primarily Hindu and Buddhist) 15 per cent (2005 est)

*Language* – Arabic (official), Persian, English, Hindi, Urdu

*Population density* – 112 per sq. km (2013)

*Urban population* – 84.9 per cent (2013 est)

*Median age (years)* – 30.3 (2014 est)

*National anthem* – 'Ishy Bilady' ['Long Live My Homeland']

*National day* – 2 December (Independence Day)

*Death penalty* – Retained

*CPI score* – 70 (25)

## CLIMATE AND TERRAIN

The United Arab Emirates (UAE) is situated in the south-east of the Arabian peninsula. Six of the emirates lie on the shore of the Gulf, between the Musandam peninsula in the east and the Qatar peninsula in the west, while the seventh, Fujairah, lies on the Gulf of Oman. A flat coastal plain merges into the desert of the interior, and there are mountains in the east. Elevation extremes range from 1,527m (Jabal Yibir) to 0m (Persian Gulf). There is a desert climate, although it is cooler in the mountains, with high humidity on the coast. Average temperatures range from 18.5°C in January to 34.4°C in July.

## HISTORY AND POLITICS

The United Arab Emirates (formerly the Trucial States) is composed of seven emirates. Six of these came together as an independent state on 2 December 1971 when they ended their individual special treaty relationships with the British government, and they were joined by Ras al-Khaimah on 10 February 1972.

Sheikh Zayed of Abu Dhabi was president from independence until his death in 2004. He was succeeded as Sultan of Abu Dhabi by his son, Sheikh Khalifa, who was also elected president of the UAE. The first national elections were held in 2006, when half the members of the Federal National Council (FNC) were elected by a small electoral college of 6,600 voters. The size of the electoral college increased significantly, to 129,274 voters (women comprised just under half of this total), in the most recent legislative election held in September 2011. President al-Nahyan was re-elected in the November 2014 presidential elections.

The 1971 provisional constitution, approved in 1996, was amended in 2008 to convert the FNC from a consultative into a legislative body and to extend its original two-year term to 2011. Overall authority lies with the Supreme Council, comprising the hereditary rulers of the seven emirates, each of whom also governs in his own territory. The president and vice-president are elected every five years by the Supreme Council from among its members. The president appoints the prime minister and the council of ministers. The unicameral FNC has 40 members, eight members each from Abu Dhabi and Dubai, six each from Sharjah and Ras al-Khaimah and four each for Ajman, Fujairah and Umm al-Qaiwain; half are elected by an electoral college and half are appointed by the rulers of each emirate.

HEAD OF STATE

*President,* HH Sheikh Khalifa bin Zayed al-Nahyan *(Abu Dhabi), elected* 3 November 2004, *re-elected* 2009, 2014

*Vice-President, Prime Minister, Defence,* HH Sheikh Mohammed bin Rashid al-Maktoum *(Dubai)*

SELECTED GOVERNMENT MEMBERS *as at July 2015*

*Deputy Prime Ministers,* Lt.-Gen. Sheikh Saif bin Zayed al-Nahyan *(Interior);* Sheikh Mansour bin Zayed al-Nahyan

*Finance,* HH Sheikh Hamdan bin Rashid al-Maktoum

*Foreign Affairs,* Sheikh Abdullah bin Zayed al-Nahyan

EMBASSY OF THE UNITED ARAB EMIRATES

30 Prince's Gate, London SW7 1PT

T 020-7581 1281 E informationuk@mofa.gov.ae

W www.uae-embassy.ae/uk

*Ambassador Extraordinary and Plenipotentiary,* HE Abdul Rahman Ghanem al-Mutaiwee, *apptd* 2009

BRITISH EMBASSY

PO Box 248, Khalid bin al-Waleed Street (Street 22), Abu Dhabi

T (+971) (2) 610 1100 E consular.UAE@fco.gov.uk

W www.gov.uk/government/world/united-arab-emirates

*Ambassador Extraordinary and Plenipotentiary,* HE Philip Parham, *apptd* 2014

FEDERAL STRUCTURE
The emirates are: Abu Dhabi, Ajman, Dubai, Fujairah, Ras al-Khaimah, Sharjah and Umm al-Qaiwain. Each emirate has its own government, judicial system and penal code. Abu Dhabi has an executive council chaired by the crown prince.

## DEFENCE

| Aged 16–49, 2010 est | Males | Females |
|---|---|---|
| Available for military service | 2,676,928 | 981,649 |
| Fit for military service | 2,229,366 | 842,759 |

*Military expenditure* – US$22,755m (2014)

## ECONOMY AND TRADE
Exploitation of the territories' oil reserves began in the 1960s and transformed the UAE from poor rural principalities into modern states with a high standard of living. Oil and gas production dominate the economy, although diversification means that output now accounts for 25 per cent of GDP and it is the most diversified of the Gulf states. The economy is also dependent on foreign workers, but the government aims to increase opportunities for its citizens through improved education and expansion of the private sector. The economy was badly hit by the global downturn, but its debt crisis has been alleviated by loans from federal and Abu Dhabi institutions. Government spending and the non-oil sector is expected to drive growth of 3.6 per cent during 2015–19.

Agriculture is limited by the terrain but the area under cultivation has been extended by irrigation and water desalination projects. The main products are dates, vegetables, watermelons, poultry, eggs and dairy products. Non-hydrocarbon industries include fishing, aluminium, cement, petrochemicals, fertilisers, commercial ship repair, construction materials, handicrafts, textiles, boat-building, financial services and tourism. Several free-trade zones are attracting foreign investment.

The main export markets are Japan, India and Iran; imports come chiefly from India, China, the USA and Germany. Principal exports are crude oil (45 per cent), natural gas, re-exports, dried fish and dates. The main imports are machinery and transport equipment, chemicals and food.
*GNI* – US$353,134m; US$38,360 per capita (2012)
*Annual average growth of GDP* – 4.3 per cent (2014 est)
*Inflation rate* – 2.2 per cent (2014 est)
*Population below poverty line* – 19.5 per cent (2003)
*Unemployment* – 3.6 per cent (2015 est)
*Total external debt* – US$173,300m (2014 est)
*Imports* – US$245,000m (2013)
*Exports* – US$365,000m (2013)

BALANCE OF PAYMENTS
*Trade* – US$80,000m surplus (2012)
*Current Account* – US$19,278m surplus (2015 est)

| Trade with UK | 2013 | 2014 |
|---|---|---|
| Imports from UK | £9,951,574,525 | £6,400,280,396 |
| Exports to UK | £2,542,817,845 | £2,598,547,122 |

## COMMUNICATIONS
*Airports and waterways* – There is an international airport in every emirate except Ajman, and significant ports in Jebel Ali, Khor Fakkan, Mina Khalid, Mina Rashid, Mina Saqr and Mina Zayed
*Roadways* – 4,080km
*Telecommunications* – 1.967 million fixed lines and 13.78 million mobile subscriptions (2012); there were 3.45 million internet users in 2009

*Internet code and IDD* – ae; 971 (from UK), 44 (to UK)
*Media* – Dubai Media Incorporated (TV) is the government-owned broadcaster; major newspapers include *Al-Bayan,* the *Khaleej Times* and *Gulf News*
*WPFI score* – 36,73 (120)

## EDUCATION AND HEALTH
Education is free in state schools and compulsory from ages six to 14.
*Literacy rate* – 99.4 per cent (2015 est)
*Health expenditure (per capita)* – US$1,569 (2013)
*Hospital beds (per 1,000 people)* – 1.1 (2012)
*Life expectancy (years)* – 77.09 (2014 est)
*Mortality rate* – 1.99 (2014 est)
*Birth rate* – 15.54 (2014 est)
*Infant mortality rate* – 10.92 (2014 est)

# UNITED KINGDOM

*United Kingdom of Great Britain and Northern Ireland*

*Area* – 243,610 sq. km
*Capital* – London; population, 10,189,000 (2014)
*Major cities* – Belfast, Birmingham, Cardiff, Edinburgh, Glasgow, Leeds, Liverpool, Manchester
*Currency* – Pound sterling (£) of 100 pence
*Population* – 64,088,222 rising at 0.54 per cent a year (2015 est)
*Religion* – Christian 59.5 per cent, Muslim 4.4 per cent, Hindu 1.3 per cent, none 25.7 per cent (2011 est); small Jewish, Sikh and Buddhist minorities
*Language* – English, Welsh, Scots, Scottish Gaelic, Irish
*Population density* – 265 per sq. km (2013)
*Urban population* – 79.9 per cent (2013 est)
*Median age (years)* – 40.4 (2014 est)
*National anthem* – 'God Save the Queen'
*Death penalty* – Abolished for all crimes (since 1998)
*CPI score* – 78 (14)

## CLIMATE AND TERRAIN
The terrain of Great Britain is higher in the north and west, with low mountains and rugged hills in Scotland, northern England and Wales; the land declines towards the south and east, with its lowest points in the south-east. Northern Ireland is more low-lying, with low mountains in the north and east. The heavily indented coastline varies in height between high cliffs and sea level. Elevation extremes range from 1,343m (Ben Nevis, Scotland) to −4m (the Fens, eastern England). Although Scotland contains numerous large lochs and northern England includes an area known as the Lake District, the largest freshwater lake is Lough Neagh in Northern Ireland. The main rivers are the Thames, the Severn and the Trent in England and Wales, and the Tay in Scotland.

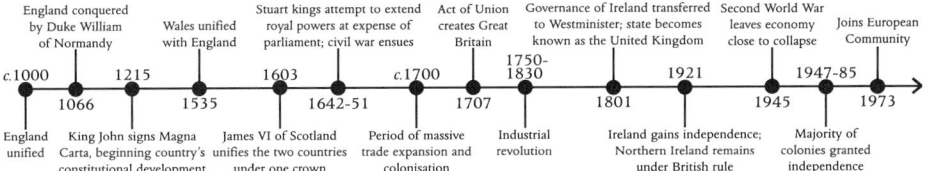

| England conquered by Duke William of Normandy | | Wales unified with England | Stuart kings attempt to extend royal powers at expense of parliament; civil war ensues | Act of Union creates Great Britain | Governance of Ireland transferred to Westminster; state becomes known as the United Kingdom | Second World War leaves economy close to collapse | Joins European Community |
|---|---|---|---|---|---|---|---|
| c.1000 | 1215 | | 1603 | c.1700 | 1750– 1830 | 1921 | 1947-85 |
| 1066 | | 1535 | 1642-51 | 1707 | 1801 | 1945 | 1973 |
| England unified | King John signs Magna Carta, beginning country's constitutional development | James VI of Scotland unifies the two countries under one crown | Period of massive trade expansion and colonisation | Industrial revolution | Ireland gains independence; Northern Ireland remains under British rule | Majority of colonies granted independence | |

The climate is temperate and extremes are rare, but the convergence of Atlantic, Arctic and European weather systems produces unusually changeable weather conditions. Average temperatures range from 4.4°C in January and December to 15.1°C in August.

## POLITICS

There is no written constitution. The head of state is a hereditary constitutional monarch. The bicameral parliament consists of the House of Commons, the lower house and the House of Lords. The House of Commons has 650 seats, directly elected for a five-year term. The House of Lords is appointed and numbers vary; in September 2014 it had 774 members, comprising 26 archbishops and bishops of the Church of England, 662 life peers and 86 hereditary peers. The prime minister is the leader of the majority party or coalition in the House of Commons.

Powers over certain internal matters were devolved in 1999 to Scotland, Wales and Northern Ireland, each of which has its own legislature and government; devolution was suspended in Northern Ireland several times between 2000 and 2007 owing to the breakdown of power-sharing arrangements.

The Labour government elected in 1945 pursued socialist economic and welfare policies, nationalising key industries, setting up the National Health Service and expanding the social security system. Economic decline continued until the 1980s, when it was reversed by the Conservative government led by Margaret Thatcher, the country's first woman prime minister. Her administration privatised nationalised industries, opened up welfare services to market forces and reduced the role of local government, polarising politics and public opinion. She also established a close relationship with the USA that was supportive of its foreign policy. This has been continued by her successors, most recently in the support for the US 'war on terror' and the deployment of British forces in Afghanistan since 2001, Iraq from 2003 to 2009, and in Libyan air space in 2011. In 2017 the UK is due to hold a referendum on whether to retain membership of the EU.

At the 2015 legislative election, the Conservative party won its first outright majority since 1996, winning 331 of 650 seats in the House of Commons. The Scottish Nationalist Party won 56 of the 59 seats contested in Scotland, easily surpassing the previous highest tally of 11 MPs it had elected at the 1974 general election.

### HEAD OF STATE

*HM The Queen of the United Kingdom of Great Britain and Northern Ireland*, Queen Elizabeth II, *born* 21 April 1926; *succeeded* 6 February 1952; *crowned* 2 June 1953
*Heir*, HRH The Prince of Wales (Prince Charles Philip Arthur George), *born* 14 November 1948

### SELECTED GOVERNMENT MEMBERS *as at July 2015*

*Prime Minister, First Lord of the Treasury, Civil Service,*
   David Cameron
*Chancellor of the Exchequer,* George Osborne
*Defence,* Michael Fallon
*Foreign and Commonwealth Affairs,* Philip Hammond

*Home Affairs,* Theresa May
*Justice, Lord Chancellor,* Michael Gove

### DEFENCE

| Aged 16–49, 2010 est | Males | Females |
|---|---|---|
| Available for military service | 14,856,917 | 14,307,316 |
| Fit for military service | 12,255,452 | 11,779,679 |

*Military expenditure* – US$60,482m (2014)

### ECONOMY AND TRADE

The UK has a highly developed and technologically advanced economy that is now dominated by services and trade. It was the first industrialised nation, developing an economy in the 19th century based on heavy industry, mass manufacturing and global trade. It became less predominant as industrialisation spread to other countries, and the demands of the Second World War caused a postwar industrial decline. In the 1980s, privatisation of state industries and constraints on public spending improved government finances, and primary industrial activities were increasingly replaced by service industries. After emerging from recession in the early 1990s, the economy experienced its longest-recorded period of expansion, outperforming the rest of the EU states, until 2008. The global economic downturn, tight credit and the end of the property boom caused the economy to go into recession from early 2008 until late 2009 and again at the start of 2012. The banking sector in particular was badly affected by the global financial crisis in 2008 and government intervention was necessary to stabilise the financial system, including nationalising or part-nationalising major banks. These measures left the government with a massive public-sector debt to service, and the new coalition government announced tight constraints on public spending from 2010. The budget deficit has fallen but remains high at nearly 7 per cent and public debt has continued to increase. The first Conservative budget since 1996 was passed in 2015 and included more welfare spending and spending cuts, a rise in the minimum wage and further boosts to improve productivity. Growth of 2.1 per cent is expected in 2015 and 2016.

The service sector, especially banking, insurance and business services, electronics, telecommunications and tourism, now contributes 78.8 per cent of GDP and employs 83.5 per cent of the workforce. Agriculture is intensive, highly mechanised and efficient, employing 1.3 per cent of the workforce, although contributing only 0.6 per cent of GDP. The UK has large but declining reserves of oil, gas and coal, and the country became a net importer of energy in 2005. Other industrial output is mostly of manufactured goods, including machine tools, electrical power equipment, automation and transport equipment, aircraft, ships, motor vehicles and parts, electronics and communications equipment, metals, chemicals, paper and paper products, food processing, textiles, clothing and other consumer goods.

The main trading partners are other EU countries, the USA and China. The principal exports are manufactured goods, fuels, chemicals, food, beverages and tobacco. The main imports are manufactured goods, machinery, fuels and foodstuffs.

*GNI* – US$2,671,727m; US$41,680 per capita (2013)
*Annual average growth of GDP* – 3.2 per cent (2014 est)
*Inflation rate* – 1.6 per cent (2014 est)
*Population below poverty line* – 16.2 per cent (2011 est)
*Unemployment* – 7.2 per cent (2015 est)
*Total external debt* – US$8,795,000m (2013)
*Imports* – US$645,516m (2013)
*Exports* – US$476,991m (2013)

BALANCE OF PAYMENTS
*Trade* – US$172,383m deficit (2012)
*Current Account* – US$135,579m deficit (2015 est)

## COMMUNICATIONS

*Airports* – There are 271 licensed civil airports, of which Heathrow (the world's fifth busiest international airport), Gatwick, Stansted and Manchester handle the highest volume of passengers

*Waterways* – Traditionally a seafaring nation, the UK has a large merchant navy, with 504 ships of over 1,000 tonnes registered in the UK and 308 ships registered overseas. The main ports are at Grimsby and Immingham, London, Milford Haven, Southampton, Tees and Hartlepool, Liverpool, Felixstowe, Forth, Dover and Belfast

*Roadways* – There are 394,428km of roadways, including 3,617km of motorways

*Railways* – The 16,454km of rail network is operated by 23 rail companies

*Telecommunications* – 33.01 million fixed lines and 82.11 million mobile subscriptions (2012); there were 51.44 million internet users in 2009

*Major broadcasters* – The British Broadcasting Corporation is a public service broadcaster and provides radio and television programmes, in competition with several commercial radio and television stations, including cable and satellite services

*Press* – The lively and occasionally controversial newspaper press publishes around ten newspapers daily, including *The Times*, *The Guardian* and *The Sun*

*WPFI score* – 20 (34)

## EDUCATION AND HEALTH

Full-time education is compulsory between the ages of five and 16 in Wales and Scotland and four and 16 in Northern Ireland. In England full-time education is compulsory between the ages of five until the end of the academic year of the pupil's 17th birthday.

*Gross enrolment ratio (percentage of relevant age group)* – primary 109 per cent; secondary 95 per cent (2012 est); tertiary 60 per cent (2013 est)
*Health expenditure (per capita)* – US$3,598 (2013)
*Hospital beds (per 1,000 people)* – 2.9 (2011)
*Life expectancy (years)* – 80.42 (2014 est)
*Mortality rate* – 9.34 (2014 est)
*Birth rate* – 12.22 (2014 est)
*Infant mortality rate* – 4.44 (2014 est)

## OVERSEAS TERRITORIES
*See* pages 932–940

# UNITED STATES OF AMERICA

*Area* – 9,826,675 sq. km
*Capital* – Washington, District of Columbia; population, 4,896,000 (2014)
*Major cities* – Boston, Chicago, Dallas, Houston, Los Angeles, New York, Philadelphia, Phoenix, San Antonio, San Diego, San Francisco, San Jose
*Currency* – US dollar (US$) of 100 cents
*Population* – 321,368,864 rising at 0.78 per cent a year (2015 est); white 79.9 per cent, black 12.8 per cent, Asian 4.4 per cent, Amerindian and Alaskan native 1 per cent, native Hawaiian and other Pacific islander 0.2 per cent; Hispanic 15.1 per cent (persons of Hispanic origin may be of any race or ethnic group) (2007 est)
*Religion* – Christian (Protestant 51.3 per cent, Roman Catholic 23.9 per cent, Mormon 1.7 per cent), Jewish 1.7 per cent, Buddhist 0.7 per cent, Muslim 0.6 per cent (est)
*Language* – English, Spanish, Hawaiian (official in Hawaii)
*Population density* – 35 per sq. km (2013)
*Urban population* – 82.9 per cent (2013 est)
*Median age (years)* – 37.6 (2014 est)
*National anthem* – 'The Star-Spangled Banner'
*National day* – 4 July (Independence Day)
*Death penalty* – Abolished in 18 states, District of Columbia and US insular territories
*CPI score* – 74 (17)

## CLIMATE AND TERRAIN

The coastline has a length of about 3,329km on the Atlantic Ocean, 12,268km on the Pacific, 1,705km on the Arctic and 2,624km on the Gulf of Mexico. The principal river is the Mississippi-Missouri-Red (5,970km long), traversing the whole country from Montana to its mouth in the Gulf of Mexico. The Rocky Mountains range runs the length of the western portion of the country. West of this, bordering the Pacific coast, the Cascade Mountains and Sierra Nevada form the outer edge of a high tableland, consisting partly of stony and sandy desert and partly of grazing land and forested mountains, and including the Great Salt Lake, which extends to the Rocky Mountains. A vast central plain lies between the Rockies and the hills and low mountains of the eastern states, where large forests still exist, remnants of the forests which formerly extended over the entire Atlantic slope. Elevation extremes range from 6,194m (Mt McKinley, Alaska) to −86m (Death Valley, California). The climate varies with latitude but is mostly temperate, with semi-arid conditions on the Great Plains and arid in the south-west. Average temperatures range from −4.8°C in January to 20°C in July.

Two states are detached: Alaska and Hawaii. Alaska occupies the north-western extremity of North America, separated from the rest of the USA by the Canadian province of British Columbia. The terrain is arctic tundra with mountain ranges, and the climate is arctic. The state of Hawaii is a chain of about 20 mountainous volcanic islands in the

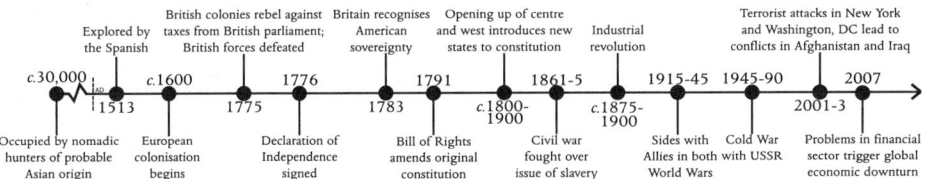

| | British colonies rebel against | Britain recognises | Opening up of centre | | Terrorist attacks in New York |
| Explored by | taxes from British parliament; | American | and west introduces new | Industrial | and Washington, DC lead to |
| the Spanish | British forces defeated | sovereignty | states to constitution | revolution | conflicts in Afghanistan and Iraq |

*c.*30,000    *c.*1600    1776    1791    1861-5    1915-45   1945-90    2007

1513    1775    1783    *c.*1800-1900    *c.*1875-1900    2001-3

| Occupied by nomadic | European | Declaration of | Bill of Rights | Civil war | Sides with Cold War | Problems in financial |
| hunters of probable | colonisation | Independence | amends original | fought over | Allies in both with USSR | sector trigger global |
| Asian origin | begins | signed | constitution | issue of slavery | World Wars | economic downturn |

north Pacific Ocean, of which the chief islands are Hawaii, Maui, Oahu, Kauai and Molokai. The climate is tropical.

The Pacific coast and Hawaii are prone to seismic activity. The Atlantic and Gulf of Mexico coasts frequently experience hurricanes.

## POLITICS

By the constitution of 17 September 1787 (which has been amended 15 times, most recently in 1992), the government of the USA is entrusted to three separate authorities: the federal executive (the president and cabinet), the legislature (Congress, which consists of a senate and a House of Representatives) and the judicature. The president is indirectly elected by an electoral college to serve a four-year term, and may serve a maximum of two consecutive terms. If a president dies in office, the vice-president serves the remainder of his term. The president appoints the cabinet officers and all the chief officials, subject to confirmation by the senate. He makes recommendations of a general nature to Congress, and when laws are passed, he may return them to Congress with a veto. But, if a measure so vetoed is again passed by both houses by a two-thirds majority in each house, it becomes law, notwithstanding the objection of the president.

Each of the 50 states has its own executive, legislature and judiciary. In theory, they are sovereign, but in practice their autonomy is increasingly circumscribed.

### PRESIDENTIAL ELECTIONS

Candidates for the presidency must be at least 35 years of age and a native citizen of the USA. The electoral college for each state is directly elected by universal adult suffrage in the November preceding the January in which the presidential term expires. The number of members of the electoral college is equal to the whole number of senators and representatives to which the state is entitled in the national congress. The electoral college for each state meets in its state in December and each member votes for a presidential candidate by ballot. The ballots are sent to Washington, DC, and opened on 6 January by the president of the senate in the presence of Congress. The candidate who has received a majority of the whole number of electoral votes cast is declared president for the ensuing term. If no one has a majority, then from the highest on the list (not exceeding three) the House of Representatives elects a president, the votes being taken by states, the representation from each state having one vote. A presidential term begins at noon on 20 January.

The 2008 presidential election was won by the Democrat candidate Barack Obama, the first African-American to hold the office; he was re-elected in November 2012. In the 2014 legislative elections, the Republican party retained its majority in the House of Representatives, winning 247 seats to the Democrats' 188; the Republicans also took control of the senate from the Democrats.

### HEAD OF STATE

*President,* Barack Obama, *elected* 2008, *sworn in* 20 January 2009, *re-elected* 6 November 2012, *sworn in* 20 January 2013

*Vice-President,* Joseph Biden

### SELECTED GOVERNMENT MEMBERS *as at July 2015*

*Defence,* Ashton Carter

*Interior,* Sally Jewel

*Secretary for Homeland Security,* Jeh Johnson

*Secretary of State,* John Kerry

*Treasury,* Jack Lew

### THE CONGRESS

Legislative power is vested in the bicameral Congress, comprising the senate and the House of Representatives. The senate has 100 members, two from each state, elected for a six-year term, with one-third elected every two years. The House of Representatives has 435 members directly elected in each state for a two-year term; a resident commissioner from Puerto Rico and a delegate each from American Samoa, the District of Columbia, Guam, the Northern Mariana Islands and the Virgin Islands serve as non-voting members of the house.

Members of the 114th Congress were elected on 6 November 2014 and sworn into office on 6 January 2015. As at July 2015, the 114th Congress is constituted as follows:

*Senate:* Republicans 54; Democrats 46

*House of Representatives:* Republicans 247; Democrats 188

*President of the Senate,* The Vice-President

*Senate majority leader,* Mitch McConnell *(R), Kentucky*

*Speaker of the House of Representatives,* John Boehner *(R), Ohio*

*House majority leader,* Kevin McCarthy *(R), California*

### THE JUDICATURE

The federal judiciary consists of three sets of federal courts: the Supreme Court at Washington, DC, consisting of a Chief Justice and eight Associate Justices; the US court of appeals, consisting of 179 circuit judges within 12 regional circuits and one federal circuit; and the 94 US district courts served by 678 district court judges.

### THE SUPREME COURT

US Supreme Court Building, Washington, DC 20543

*Chief Justice,* John Roberts, *apptd* 2005

### UNITED STATES EMBASSY

24 Grosvenor Square, London W1K 6AH

T 020-7499 9000 W http://london.usembassy.gov

*Ambassador Extraordinary and Plenipotentiary,* HE Matthew Barzun, *apptd* 2013

### BRITISH EMBASSY

3100 Massachusetts Avenue NW, Washington, DC 20008

T (+1) (202) 588 6500 E washi@fco.gov.uk

W www.gov.uk/government/world/usa

*Ambassador Extraordinary and Plenipotentiary,* Sir Peter Westmacott, KCMG, LVO, *apptd* 2012

### DEFENCE

Each military department is separately organised and functions under the direction, authority and control of the Secretary of Defence (except the Coast Guard, which is part of the Department of Homeland Security created in 2002).

## THE STATES OF THE UNION

The USA is a federal republic consisting of 50 states and the federal District of Columbia, and also of organised territories. Of the present 50 states, 13 are original states, seven were admitted without previous organisation as territories, and 30 were admitted after such organisation.

§ The 13 original states

(D) Democratic Party; (I) Independent; (R) Republican Party

| State (date and order of admission) | Area sq. km | Population* | Capital | Governor (end of term in office) |
|---|---|---|---|---|
| Alabama (AL) (1819, 22) | 135,767 | 4,833,722 | Montgomery | Robert Bentley (R), Jan. 2019 |
| Alaska (AK) (1959, 49) | 1,723,337 | 735,132 | Juneau | Bill Walker (I), Dec. 2018 |
| Arizona (AZ) (1912, 48) | 295,234 | 6,626,624 | Phoenix | Doug Ducey (R), Jan. 2019 |
| Arkansas (AR) (1836, 25) | 137,732 | 2,959,373 | Little Rock | Asa Hutchinson (R), Jan. 2019 |
| California (CA) (1850, 31) | 423,967 | 38,332,521 | Sacramento | Jerry Brown (D), Jan. 2019 |
| Colorado (CO) (1876, 38) | 269,601 | 5,268,367 | Denver | John Hickenlooper (D), Jan. 2019 |
| Connecticut (CT) § (1788, 5) | 14,357 | 3,596,080 | Hartford | Dan Malloy (D), Jan. 2019 |
| Delaware (DE) § (1787, 1) | 6,446 | 925,749 | Dover | Jack Markell (D), Jan. 2017 |
| Florida (FL) (1845, 27) | 170,312 | 19,552,860 | Tallahassee | Rick Scott (R), Jan. 2019 |
| Georgia (GA) § (1788, 4) | 153,910 | 9,992,167 | Atlanta | Nathan Deal (R), Jan. 2019 |
| Hawaii (HI) (1959, 50) | 28,313 | 1,404,054 | Honolulu | David Ige (D), Dec. 2018 |
| Idaho (ID) (1890, 43) | 216,443 | 1,612,136 | Boise | C. L. (Butch) Otter (R), Jan. 2019 |
| Illinois (IL) (1818, 21) | 149,995 | 12,882,135 | Springfield | Bruce Rauner (R), Jan. 2019 |
| Indiana (IN) (1816, 19) | 94,326 | 6,570,902 | Indianapolis | Mike Pence (R), Jan. 2017 |
| Iowa (IA) (1846, 29) | 145,746 | 3,090,416 | Des Moines | Terry Branstad (R), Jan. 2019 |
| Kansas (KS) (1861, 34) | 213,100 | 2,893,957 | Topeka | Sam Brownback (R), Jan. 2019 |
| Kentucky (KY) (1792, 15) | 104,656 | 4,395,295 | Frankfort | Steve Beshear (D), Dec. 2015 |
| Louisiana (LA) (1812, 18) | 135,659 | 4,625,470 | Baton Rouge | Bobby Jindal (R), Jan. 2016 |
| Maine (ME) (1820, 23) | 91,633 | 1,328,302 | Augusta | Paul LePage (R), Jan. 2019 |
| Maryland (MD) § (1788, 7) | 32,131 | 5,928,814 | Annapolis | Larry Hogan (R), Jan. 2019 |
| Massachusetts (MA) § (1788, 6) | 27,336 | 6,692,824 | Boston | Charlie Baker (R), Jan. 2019 |
| Michigan (MI) (1837, 26) | 250,487 | 9,895,622 | Lansing | Rick Snyder (R), Jan. 2019 |
| Minnesota (MN) (1858, 32) | 225,163 | 5,420,380 | St Paul | Mark Dayton (D), Jan. 2019 |
| Mississippi (MS) (1817, 20) | 125,438 | 2,991,207 | Jackson | Phil Bryant (R), Jan. 2016 |
| Missouri (MO) (1821, 24) | 180,540 | 6,044,171 | Jefferson City | Jeremiah ( Jay) Nixon (D), Jan. 2017 |
| Montana (MT) (1889, 41) | 380,831 | 1,015,165 | Helena | Steve Bullock (D), Jan. 2017 |
| Nebraska (NE) (1867, 37) | 200,330 | 1,868,516 | Lincoln | Pete Ricketts (R), Jan. 2019 |
| Nevada (NV) (1864, 36) | 286,380 | 2,790,136 | Carson City | Brian Sandoval (R), Jan. 2019 |
| New Hampshire (NH) § (1788, 9) | 24,214 | 1,323,459 | Concord | Maggie Hassan (D), Jan. 2019 |
| New Jersey (NJ) § (1787, 3) | 22,591 | 8,899,339 | Trenton | Chris Christie (R), Jan. 2018 |
| New Mexico (NM) (1912, 47) | 314,917 | 2,085,287 | Santa Fe | Susana Martinez (R), Jan. 2019 |
| New York (NY) § (1788, 11) | 141,297 | 19,651,127 | Albany | Andrew Cuomo (D), Jan. 2019 |
| North Carolina (NC) § (1789, 12) | 139,391 | 9,848,060 | Raleigh | Pat McCrory (R), Jan. 2017 |
| North Dakota (ND) (1889, 39) | 183,108 | 723,393 | Bismarck | Jack Dalrymple (R), Dec. 2016 |
| Ohio (OH) (1803, 17) | 116,098 | 11,570,808 | Columbus | John Kasich (R), Jan. 2019 |
| Oklahoma (OK) (1907, 46) | 181,037 | 3,850,568 | Oklahoma City | Mary Fallin (R), Jan. 2019 |
| Oregon (OR) (1859, 33) | 254,799 | 3,930,065 | Salem | Kate Brown (D), Jan. 2019 |
| Pennsylvania (PA) § (1787, 2) | 119,280 | 12,773,801 | Harrisburg | Tom Wolf (D), Jan. 2019 |
| Rhode Island (RI) § (1790, 13) | 4,001 | 1,051,511 | Providence | Gina Raimondo (D), Jan. 2019 |
| South Carolina (SC) § (1788, 8) | 82,933 | 4,774,839 | Columbia | Nikki R. Haley (R), Jan. 2019 |
| South Dakota (SD) (1889, 40) | 199,729 | 844,877 | Pierre | Dennis Daugaard (R), Jan. 2019 |
| Tennessee (TN) (1796, 16) | 109,153 | 6,495,978 | Nashville | Bill Haslam (R), Jan. 2019 |
| Texas (TX) (1845, 28) | 695,662 | 26,448,193 | Austin | Greg Abbott (R), Jan. 2019 |
| Utah (UT) (1896, 45) | 219,882 | 2,900,872 | Salt Lake City | Gary Herbert (R), Jan. 2017 |
| Vermont (VT) (1791, 14) | 24,906 | 626,630 | Montpelier | Peter Shumlin (D), Jan. 2017 |
| Virginia (VA) § (1788, 10) | 110,787 | 8,260,405 | Richmond | Terry McAuliffe (D), Jan. 2018 |
| Washington (WA) (1889, 42) | 184,661 | 6,971,406 | Olympia | Jay Inslee (D), Jan. 2017 |
| West Virginia (WV) (1863, 35) | 62,756 | 1,854,304 | Charleston | Earl Ray Tomblin (D), Jan. 2017 |
| Wisconsin (WI) (1848, 30) | 169,635 | 5,742,713 | Madison | Scott Walker (R), Jan. 2019 |
| Wyoming (WY) (1890, 44) | 253,335 | 582,658 | Cheyenne | Matthew Mead (R), Jan. 2019 |
| Dist. of Columbia (DC) (1791) | 177 | 646,449 | — | Muriel Bowser (D), Jan. 2019 *(Mayor)* |

### OUTLYING TERRITORIES AND POSSESSIONS

| | | | | |
|---|---|---|---|---|
| American Samoa | 199 | 54,343 | Pago Pago | Lolo Matalasi Moliga (I), Jan. 2017 |
| Guam | 544 | 161,785 | Hagatna | Eddie Calvo (R), Jan. 2019 |
| Northern Mariana Islands | 464 | 52,344 | Saipan | Eloy Inos (C), Jan. 2019 |
| Puerto Rico | 13,790 | 3,598,357 | San Juan | Alejandro Garcia Padilla (R), Jan. 2017 |
| US Virgin Islands | 1,910 | 103,574 | Charlotte Amalie | Kenneth Mapp (I), Jan. 2019 |

*States 2015 estimate; outlying territories 2015 estimate

The air force has primary responsibility for the Department of Defence space development programmes and projects.

| Aged 16–49, 2010 est | Males | Females |
|---|---|---|
| Available for military service | 73,270,043 | 71,941,969 |
| Fit for military service | 60,620,143 | 59,401,941 |

*Military expenditure* – US$609,914m (2014)

## ECONOMY AND TRADE

The USA is one of the world's leading industrial nations, with a sophisticated market economy that saw huge growth during the 20th century. Economic development was due in part to the mechanisation of the agrarian economy, expansion of the transport infrastructure and large amounts of relatively cheap migrant labour; more recently it has been driven by rapid advances in technology. In the late 20th century, the economy shifted emphasis from industry to services, and government involvement in the economy was steadily reduced.

The US sub-prime mortgage crisis in 2007 triggered a global economic downturn, and falling property prices and tight credit pushed the domestic economy into recession by mid-2008. Following the failure of several investment banks, Congress passed a US$700bn relief programme to stabilise the financial markets in October 2008, and in spring 2009 a US$787bn fiscal stimulus package and a record US$3.6 trillion budget for 2010 were approved. Despite these measures, the economy still experienced the collapse of key industries (such as vehicle manufacturing), and rising unemployment and inflation before growth restarted in late 2009 after the USA's longest and deepest recession since the 1930s, and grew by an average of 1.9 per cent during 2009–14. The economy is expected to grow by 2.5 per cent in 2015.

Agriculture is a major industry in the USA; principal crops are wheat, maize, other grains, fruit, vegetables, cotton, meat and dairy products. Agriculture, fishing and forestry contribute 1.6 per cent of GDP and employ 0.7 per cent of the workforce.

Mining and extraction are important to the economy. Large quantities of coal, iron ore, phosphate rock, copper, zinc and lead are mined. About one-third of the country's oil requirements are supplied by domestic production, principally from fields in the Gulf of Mexico. Natural gas is also produced. Despite its domestic oil and natural gas resources and its electricity generating capacity, the USA is a net importer of energy.

The industrial sector is highly diversified and technologically advanced. The main manufacturing industries produce steel, vehicles, aircraft and aerospace equipment, telecommunications equipment, chemicals, electronic equipment and consumer goods, and process food. Industry contributes 20.7 per cent of GDP and services account for 77.7 per cent of GDP.

The main trading partners are Canada, China, Mexico, Japan and Germany. Principal exports are capital goods (chiefly transistors, aircraft, vehicle parts, computers, telecommunications equipment), industrial supplies (eg organic chemicals), consumer goods (cars, medicines) and agricultural produce (soya beans, fruit, maize). The main imports are industrial goods (especially crude oil), consumer goods (cars, clothing, medicines, furniture, toys), capital goods (computers, telecommunications equipment, vehicle parts, office machines, electric power machinery) and agricultural products.

*GNI* – US$16,903,045m; US$53,470 per capita (2013)
*Annual average growth of GDP* – 2.4 per cent (2014 est)
*Inflation rate* – 2 per cent (2014 est)
*Population below poverty line* – 15.1 per cent (2010 est)

*Unemployment* – 6.8 per cent (2015 est)
*Total external debt* – US$15,680,000m (2012)
*Imports* – US$2,329,060m (2013)
*Exports* – US$1,579,050m (2012)

BALANCE OF PAYMENTS
*Trade* – US$789,830m deficit (2012)
*Current Account* – US$410,178m deficit (2015 est)

| Trade with UK | 2013 | 2014 |
|---|---|---|
| Imports from UK | £39,928,042,827 | £38,915,880,911 |
| Exports to UK | £32,060,071,905 | £32,829,183,284 |

## COMMUNICATIONS

*Airports* – There are 5,054 airports; nearly 200 are capable of handling international flights, the rest cater for the high domestic demand

*Waterways* – The main seaports are at Baton Rouge, Corpus Christi, Hampton Roads, Houston, Long Beach, Los Angeles, Miami, New Orleans, New York, Oaklands, Plaquemines, Port Canaveral, Port Everglades, Savannah, Seattle, Tampa and Texas City

*Roadways* – There are 4,304,715km of paved roadways, including 76,334km of motorways

*Railways* – There are 224,792km of railways

*Telecommunications* – 139 million fixed lines and 310 million mobile subscriptions (2012); there were 245 million internet users in 2009

*Internet code and IDD* – us; 1 (from UK), 011 44 (to UK)

*Major broadcasters* – The major television networks are ABC, CBS, NBC, CNN, Fox, MTV, HBO and the Public Broadcasting System, which serves around 350 local member stations and is partially funded by the government and private grants

*Press* – There are more than 1,500 daily newspapers, including *The Wall Street Journal, USA Today, The Washington Post* and *The New York Times*

*WPFI score* – 24,41 (49)

## EDUCATION AND HEALTH

All the states have compulsory school attendance laws. In general, children are obliged to attend school from seven to 16 years of age.

*Gross enrolment ratio (percentage of relevant age group)* – primary 98 per cent; secondary 94 per cent; tertiary 89 per cent (2012 est)
*Health expenditure (per capita)* – US$9,146 (2013)
*Hospital beds (per 1,000 people)* – 2.9 (2011)
*Life expectancy (years)* – 79.56 (2014 est)
*Mortality rate* – 8.15 (2014 est)
*Birth rate* – 13.42 (2014 est)
*Infant mortality rate* – 6.17 (2014 est)

## US TERRITORIES ETC

US insular areas are territories that are not part of one of the 50 US states or a federal district. The US Department of the Interior's Office of Insular Affairs has jurisdiction over American Samoa, Guam, the Northern Mariana Islands, the US Virgin Islands, part of Palmyra Atoll (4 sq. km) and Wake Atoll (6.4 sq. km), the latter shared with the US army's Space and Strategic Defence Command. The US Fish and Wildlife Service has jurisdiction over Baker Island (1.5 sq. km), Howland Island (2.5 sq. km), Jarvis Island (4.2 sq. km), Johnston Atoll (2.5 sq. km, shared with the Defence Threat Reduction Agency), Midway Atoll (5.2 sq. km), Navassa Island (7.8 sq. km), Kingman Reef and part of Palmyra Atoll. The Aleutian Islands (17,666 sq. km) form part of the Alaskan archipelago.

## AMERICAN SAMOA
*Territory of American Samoa*
*Area* – 199 sq. km
*Capital* – Pago Pago
*Population* – 54,343 falling at –0.35 per cent per year
(2015 est)
*National day* – 17 April (Flag Day)

American Samoa consists of the islands of Tutuila, Aunu'u, Ofu, Olosega, Ta'u, Rose Island and Swains Island. The islands were discovered by Europeans in the 18th century and the USA took possession in 1900. Those born in American Samoa are US non-citizen nationals, although some have acquired citizenship through service in the US armed forces or other naturalisation procedures. American Samoa is represented in Congress by a non-voting delegate, who is directly elected for a two-year term. Under the 1966 constitution, American Samoa has a measure of self-government, with certain powers reserved to the US Secretary of the Interior. The governor and deputy governor are directly elected for a four-year term. The bicameral legislative assembly comprises a 21-member House of Representatives (one appointed member and 20 members directly elected for a two-year term) and an 18-seat senate with members elected from among the traditional chiefs for a four-year term. Tuna fishing and canning are the principal economic activities.
*Governor,* Lolo Matalasi Moliga (I)

## GUAM
*Guåhan – Territory of Guam*
*Area* – 544 sq. km
*Capital* – Hagåtña (also known as Agana); population, 143,000 (2014 est)
*Population* – 161,785 rising at 0.44 per cent per year (2015 est); Chamorro (37.3 per cent), Filipino (26.3 per cent), white (7.1 per cent). The official languages are Chamorro (a language of the Malayo-Polynesian family with admixtures of Spanish) and English; most Chamorro residents are bilingual
*National day* – first Monday in March (Discovery Day)

Guam is the largest of the Mariana Islands, in the north Pacific Ocean. A Spanish colony for centuries, it was ceded to the USA in 1898 after the Spanish–American War. Guam was occupied by the Japanese in 1941 but was recaptured by US forces in 1944. Any person born in Guam is a US citizen. Guam is represented in Congress by a non-voting delegate, who is directly elected for a two-year term. Under the Organic Act of Guam 1950, Guam has statutory powers of self-government. The governor and lieutenant-governor are directly elected for a four-year term. The 15-member unicameral legislature is directly elected every two years. The main sources of revenue are tourism (particularly from Japan) and US military spending; the military installation is one of the most strategically important US bases in the Pacific.
*Governor,* Eddie Calvo (R)

| Trade with UK | 2013 | 2014 |
|---|---|---|
| Imports from UK | £1,849,855 | £3,252,376 |
| Exports to UK | £240,639 | £287,768 |

## NORTHERN MARIANA ISLANDS
*Commonwealth of the Northern Mariana Islands*
*Area* – 464 sq. km
*Seat of government* – Saipan
*Population* – 52,344 rising at 1.13 per cent per year (2015 est)
*National day* – 8 January (Commonwealth Day)

The USA administered the Northern Mariana Islands, a group of 14 islands in the north-west Pacific Ocean, as part of a UN trusteeship until the trusteeship agreement was terminated in 1986, when the islands became a common-wealth under US sovereignty. Those resident in 1976 or subsequently born in the islands are US citizens. The islands are represented in Congress by a non-voting representative, who is directly elected for a two-year term. Under the 1978 constitution, the islands are self-governing. The governor and lieutenant-governor are directly elected for a four-year term. The bicameral legislature comprises a 20-member House of Representatives and a nine-member senate; members are directly elected, representatives for two years and senators for four years. Tourism and manufacturing, especially of clothing, are the main industries.
*Governor,* Eloy Inos (C)

## PUERTO RICO
*Commonwealth of Puerto Rico*
*Area* – 13,790 sq. km
*Capital* – San Juan; population, 2,466,000m (2014). Other major towns are Bayamón, Carolina, Poncel
*Population* – 3,598,357 falling at –0.65 per cent per year (2015 est); most people are of Spanish descent. The official languages are Spanish and English
*National day* – 25 July (Constitution Day)

Puerto Rico (Rich Port) is an island of the Greater Antilles group in the Caribbean Sea and was discovered in 1493 by Columbus. It was a Spanish possession until 1898, when it was ceded to the USA after the Spanish–American War. Residents have been US citizens since 1917, and Puerto Rico is represented in Congress by a non-voting resident commissioner, who is directly elected for a four-year term. Under its 1952 constitution, Puerto Rico is a self-governing commonwealth. The governor is directly elected for a four-year term. The bicameral legislative assembly consists of a 31-member senate and a 53-member House of Representatives, whose members serve four-year terms. Tourism, pharmaceuticals, electronics, clothing and food processing are the main economic activities.
*Governor,* Alejandro Garcia Padilla (R)

## THE UNITED STATES VIRGIN ISLANDS
*Area* – 1,910 sq. km
*Capital* – Charlotte Amalie, on St Thomas; population, 52,000 (2014 est)
*Population* – 103,574 falling at –0.56 per cent per year (2015 est)
*National day* – 31 March (Transfer Day)

There are three main islands, St Thomas, St Croix and St John, and about 50 small islets or cays. These constituted the Danish part of the Virgin Islands from the 17th century until purchased by the USA in 1917. Those born in the US Virgin Islands are US nationals. The Virgin Islands are represented in Congress by a non-voting representative, who is directly elected for a two-year term. Under the provisions of the Revised Organic Act of 1954, the islands have powers of self-government. The governor and lieutenant-governor are directly elected for a four-year term. The unicameral senate has 15 members directly elected for a two-year term. Tourism, oil refining and manufacturing are the main industries.
*Governor,* Kenneth Mapp (I)

# URUGUAY

*República Oriental del Uruguay – Oriental Republic of Uruguay*

*Area –* 176,215 sq. km
*Capital –* Montevideo; population, 1,698,000 (2014)
*Major towns –* Ciudad de la Costa, Salto
*Currency –* Uruguayan peso of 100 centésimos
*Population –* 3,341,893 rising at 0.27 per cent a year
   (2015 est)
*Religion –* Christian 81 per cent (Roman Catholic
   45 per cent) (est)
*Language –* Spanish (official), Portunol or Brazilero
   (Portuguese-Spanish mix used along the northern
   border)
*Population density –* 19 per sq. km (2013)
*Urban population –* 92.7 per cent (2013 est)
*Median age (years) –* 34.3 (2014 est)
*National anthem –* 'Himno Nacional' ['National Anthem']
*National day –* 25 August (Independence Day)
*Death penalty –* Abolished for all crimes (since 1907)
*CPI score –* 73 (21)

## CLIMATE AND TERRAIN

The country consists mainly of undulating grassy plains,
with low hills. Elevation extremes range from 514m (Cerro
Catedral) to 0m (Atlantic Ocean). The principal river is the
Rio Negro (with its tributary, the Yi), flowing from north-
east to south-west into the Rio Uruguay; damming of the
Negro has created a reservoir that is the largest artificial lake
in South America. The climate is warm temperate, with
occasional cold and strong winds. Average temperatures
range from 11.5°C in July to 24.1°C in January.

## HISTORY AND POLITICS

The hostility of the indigenous Charrúa Amerindians when
the Rio de la Plata was first explored by the Spanish in 1516
discouraged colonisation until the 17th century. Although
initially settled by the Portuguese, the *Banda Oriental*, as the
territory lying on the eastern bank of the river Uruguay was
then called, was disputed between the Portuguese and the
Spanish until the late 18th century and then between Brazil
and Argentina after Spanish rule was overthrown. Uruguay's
independence was recognised in 1828 and a republic was
inaugurated in 1830. In the mid-19th century there was a
power struggle between the conservatives *(Blancos)* and
liberals *(Colorados)* which descended into civil war. From
1904 until the 1960s the country experienced political
stability and prosperity.

The period from 1962 to 1973 saw economic decline and
turmoil caused by the Marxist Tupamaros guerrillas. They
were crushed by a military dictatorship that held power
from 1973 until 1985, when a return to civilian rule was
agreed after violent anti-government protests at the regime's
repressive rule and the deteriorating economy.

The Colorado and National *(Blanco)* parties now both
occupy the centre ground, but their dominance of politics
has been eroded by left-wing parties such as New Space and
coalitions such as the Progressive Encounter-Broad Front
(EP-FA). The EP-FA won outright majorities in both
legislative chambers in the 2004 and the 2009 elections,
before losing its majority in the Chamber of Senators during
the 2014 elections. The November 2014 presidential
elections were won by Tabare Vazquez of the FA.

Under the 1997 constitution, the executive president is
directly elected for a five-year term, which is not renewable.
The president, who appoints the council of ministers, is
responsible to the legislature. The bicameral general assembly
consists of a Chamber of Representatives, with 99 members
directly elected for a five-year term, and the Chamber of
Senators, which has 31 members, 30 directly elected for a
five-year term and the vice-president as an *ex officio* member.

The republic is divided into 19 departments, each with an
elected governor and legislature.

HEAD OF STATE
*President,* Tabare Vazquez, *elected* 1 December 2014, *sworn in*
   1 March 2015
*Vice-President,* Raul Sendic

SELECTED GOVERNMENT MEMBERS *as at July 2015*
*Defence,* Eleuterio Fernandez Huidobro
*Economy and Finance,* Danilo Astori
*Foreign Affairs,* Rodolfo Nin Novoa
*Interior,* Eduardo Bonomi

EMBASSY OF URUGUAY
150 Brompton Road, London SW3 1HX
T 020-7584 2947 E cdlondres@mrree.gub.uy
*Ambassador Extraordinary and Plenipotentiary,* HE Fernando
   Lopez-Fabregat, *apptd* 2014

BRITISH EMBASSY
PO Box 16024, Calle Marco Bruto 1073, 11300 Montevideo
T (+598) (2) 622 3630 E ukinuruguay@adinet.com.uy
W www.gov.uk/government/world/uruguay
*Ambassador Extraordinary and Plenipotentiary,* HE Ben
   Lyster-Binns, *apptd* 2012

## DEFENCE

| *Aged 16–49, 2010 est* | *Males* | *Females* |
| --- | --- | --- |
| Available for military service | 771,159 | 780,932 |
| Fit for military service | 649,025 | 654,903 |

*Military expenditure –* US$915m (2014)

## ECONOMY AND TRADE

After years of steady growth, Uruguay suffered a severe
recession from 1998, largely owing to the economic
problems of Brazil and Argentina, its main export markets
and sources of tourists. The recession culminated in a
banking crisis in 2002; IMF loans, the rescheduling of
foreign debt repayments and the government's emergency
measures achieved a recovery and the economy grew
strongly from 2004 to 2008. The 2008 global downturn
slowed economic growth in 2009, but Uruguay avoided
recession, mainly through increased public expenditure.
Weak growth of 2.8 per cent is expected in 2015 and 2016
as the economy struggles with high levels of unemployment
and depressed growth in the Argentine and Brazilian
economies.

Ranching and livestock products (beef, mutton, wool) have been the mainstay of the economy since the mid-19th century, generating the prosperity that enabled Uruguay to develop an extensive welfare system in the early 20th century, although dependence on these products leaves the economy vulnerable to price fluctuations. Other crops include rice, grains, soya beans, citrus fruits, wine grapes, linseed and sunflower seed. Agricultural produce is the basis of the food processing and beverage industries. Other industries include fishing, forestry and the manufacture of electrical machinery, transport equipment, petroleum products, textiles and chemicals. Exploited minerals include clinker, dolomite, marble and granite. Tourism and offshore financial services also contribute substantially to revenue. Agriculture contributes 7.5 per cent of GDP, industry 20.4 per cent and services 72.1 per cent.

The main trading partners are China, Brazil, Argentina and the USA. Principal exports are meat, soya beans, cellulose, rice, wheat, timber, dairy products and wool. The main imports are crude and refined oil, vehicles and vehicle parts, mobile phones and insecticide.

*GNI* – US$51,717m; US$15,180 per capita (2013)
*Annual average growth of GDP* – 2.8 per cent (2014 est)
*Inflation rate* – 8.8 per cent (2014 est)
*Unemployment* – 7.1 per cent (2015 est)
*Total external debt* – US$17,540m (2014 est)
*Imports* – US$10,990m (2013)
*Exports* – US$8,844m (2013)

BALANCE OF PAYMENTS
*Trade* – US$2,041m deficit (2012)
*Current Account* – US$2,184m deficit (2015 est)

| Trade with UK | 2013 | 2014 |
| --- | --- | --- |
| Imports from UK | £157,756,337 | £110,919,034 |
| Exports to UK | £90,880,018 | £76,072,431 |

## COMMUNICATIONS
*Airports and waterways* – There are 11 airports, including an international airport near Montevideo; there are 1,600km of navigable waterways, mainly on the Uruguay and Negro rivers, and the main ports are located in Montevideo, Colonia, Fray Bentos and Paysandú
*Roadways and railways* – 7,743km; 1,641km
*Telecommunications* – 1.01 fixed lines in use and 5 million mobile subscriptions (2012); there were 1.41 million internet users in 2009
*Internet code and IDD* – uy; 598 (from UK), 44 (to UK)
*Major broadcasters* – State-run television and radio are operated by SODRE, the official broadcasting service
*Press* – Major daily newspapers include *El Pais, El Observador* and *El Telegrafo*
*WPFI score* – 15,94 (23)

## EDUCATION AND HEALTH
Primary and secondary education is compulsory and free, and technical and trade schools and evening courses for adult education are state-run.
*Literacy rate* – 99.0 per cent (2015 est)
*Gross enrolment ratio (percentage of relevant age group)* – primary 112 per cent; secondary 90 per cent; tertiary 63 per cent (2010 est)
*Health expenditure (per capita)* – US$1,431 (2013)
*Hospital beds (per 1,000 people)* – 2.5 (2012)
*Life expectancy (years)* – 76.81 (2014 est)
*Mortality rate* – 9.48 (2014 est)
*Birth rate* – 13.18 (2014 est)
*Infant mortality rate* – 8.97 (2014 est)

# UZBEKISTAN

*O'zbekiston Respublikasi – Republic of Uzbekistan*

*Area* – 447,400 sq. km
*Capital* – Tashkent; population, 2,241,000 (2014)
*Major cities* – Andijan, Bukhara, Karsi, Namangan, Nukus, Samarkand
*Currency* – Som of 100 tiyins
*Population* – 29,275,460 rising at 0.93 per cent a year (2015 est); Uzbek (80 per cent), Russian (5.5 per cent), Tajik (5 per cent), Kazakh (3 per cent), Karakalpak (2.5 per cent), Tatar (1.5 per cent) (1996 est)
*Religion* – Muslim 88 per cent (predominantly Sunni), Eastern Orthodox 9 per cent (est)
*Language* – Uzbek (official), Russian, Tajik
*Population density* – 71 per sq. km (2013)
*Urban population* – 36.3 per cent (2013 est)
*Median age (years)* – 27.1 (2014 est)
*National anthem* – 'O'zbekiston Respublikasining Davlat Madhiyasi' ['National Anthem of the Republic of Uzbekistan']
*National day* – 1 September (Independence Day, 1991)
*Death penalty* – Abolished for all crimes (since 2008)
*CPI score* – 18 (166)

## CLIMATE AND TERRAIN
Landlocked Uzbekistan has four regions: the Ustyurt plateau and Amu Darya delta in the west; the Kyzyl Kum desert east of the Aral Sea; the Tien Shan and Pamir mountains in the east and south-east; and the fertile Fergana valley in the east, crossed by the Syr Darya river. Elevation extremes range from 4,301m (Adelunga Toghi) to −12m (Sariqarnish Kuli). The country includes the southern part of the Aral Sea. There is a semi-arid desert climate, although it is colder in the mountains. Average temperatures range from −2.6°C in January to 27.3°C in July.

## HISTORY AND POLITICS
Settlements in the south developed as important transit points on the ancient 'Silk Road' in the first century BC. Bukhara and Samarkand became two of the most important cultural and academic centres in the Islamic world after the religion was introduced in the eighth century. In the 13th century the area became part of the Mongol Empire, with Samarkand as its capital during the reign of Amir Timur (Tamerlane). As the empire declined, independent principalities emerged. The three khanates in what is now Uzbekistan, Khiva, Kokand and Bukhara, were annexed by the Russian Empire in the second half of the 19th century. In 1917 a Bolshevik revolution broke out in Tashkent and by 1921 all of Uzbekistan had been absorbed into the USSR.

Uzbekistan declared its independence from the USSR on 1 September 1991 but post-independence political life has been dominated by the former communists. The main opposition parties, *Erk* (Freedom) and *Birlik* (Unity), were banned in 1992 and have since become inactive. The former communist leader Islam Karimov, who came to power in 1990, was elected president in 1991 and has retained the presidency since, in unopposed elections or through the extension of his term of office in referendums. He was re-elected in 2015 for a fourth term, despite the constitutional restriction to two terms.

All legislative elections since independence have been won by the People's Democratic Party (the former Communist Party) or its allies. After the latest legislative election in January 2015, the largest party in the legislative chamber was the pro-Karimov Liberal Democratic Party; opposition parties were barred from contesting the election.

The Islamic Movement of Uzbekistan (IMU), founded in 1996, has carried out armed attacks and bombings sporadically since 1999, but has little support. However, its activities have provided the government with an excuse to curtail human rights and suppress political opposition and protests.

The 1992 constitution was amended in 2002 to create a bicameral legislature and extend the president's term of office, and in 2011 to make the prime minister responsible to the legislature. The president is directly elected; his term of office was five years, renewable only once, but was extended to seven years. The legislature, the Supreme Assembly, became bicameral after the 2004–5 elections. The Legislative Chamber has 150 members, 135 directly elected and 15 members of the Ecological Movement of Uzbekistan. The senate has 101 members, 16 appointed by the president, 84 elected by regional deputies to represent the regions and the capital, and President Karimov. Members of both houses serve a five-year term. The president appoints the cabinet, which is chaired by the prime minister.

The country is divided into 12 provinces, the autonomous republic of Karakalpakstan, and the city of Tashkent.

## HEAD OF STATE

*President,* Islam Karimov, *elected* 29 December 1991, *elected by referendum for a five-year term* 1995, *re-elected* 2000, 2007, 2015

## SELECTED GOVERNMENT MEMBERS *as at July 2015*
*Prime Minister,* Shavkat Mirziyoev
*First Deputy Prime Minister, Finance,* Rustam Azimov
*Deputy Prime Ministers,* Elmira Basitkhanova; Gulomjon Ibragimov; Adham Ikromov; Ulugbek Rozukulov; Batir Zakirov

## EMBASSY OF THE REPUBLIC OF UZBEKISTAN
41 Holland Park, London W11 3RP
T 020-7229 7679 E info@uzbekembassy.org
W www.uzbekembassy.org
*Ambassador Extraordinary and Plenipotentiary,* HE Otabek Akbarov, *apptd* 2007

## BRITISH EMBASSY
Ul. Gulyamova 67, Tashkent 100000
T (+998) (71) 120 1500 E ukin.uzbekistan@fco.gov.uk
W www.gov.uk/government/world/uzbekistan
*Ambassador Extraordinary and Plenipotentiary,* HE Christopher Allan, OBE, *apptd* 2015

## DEFENCE

| | Males | Females |
|---|---|---|
| *Aged 16–49, 2010 est* | | |
| Available for military service | 7,887,292 | 7,886,459 |
| Fit for military service | 6,566,118 | 6,745,818 |

*Conscription duration* – 12 months

## ECONOMY AND TRADE
The economy remains centrally planned and control has increased in some areas, stifling economic activity. Economic growth and living standards are among the worst in the former Soviet republics, with over a quarter of the population living below the poverty line. The 2008 global downturn had little impact owing to the country's relative economic isolation. Economy growth is predicted to be slow post-2015 due to the poor performance of the Russian economy and low global prices for Central Asian commodities.

The economy is based on intensive agricultural production, particularly of cotton, made possible by extensive irrigation schemes. Vegetables, fruit, grain and livestock are also produced. The main industries are textile manufacture, food processing, machine building, metallurgy, mining (especially for gold), oil and natural gas production and chemicals. Oil and gas exports offer potential for greater economic growth and have attracted foreign interest, notably from Russia and China, but exploitation is hampered by a lack of modern oil pipelines and basic infrastructure. Agriculture contributes 18.5 per cent of GDP, industry 32 per cent and services 49.5 per cent.

The main trading partners are Russia, China, Kazakhstan and South Korea. Principal exports are oil and natural gas, cotton, gold, mineral fertilisers, metals, textiles, food products, machinery and motor vehicles. The main imports are machinery and equipment, foodstuffs, chemicals and metals.

*GNI* – US$56,855m; US$1,880 per capita (2013)
*Annual average growth of GDP* – 7 per cent (2014 est)
*Inflation rate* – 12.1 per cent (2014 est)
*Population below poverty line* – 17 per cent (2011 est)
*Unemployment* – 10.5 per cent (2015 est)
*Total external debt* – US$8,751m (2014 est)

BALANCE OF PAYMENTS
*Trade* – US$3,301m surplus (2011)
*Current Account* – US$169m surplus (2015 est)

| Trade with UK | 2013 | 2014 |
|---|---|---|
| Imports from UK | £42,170,101 | £25,195,471 |
| Exports to UK | £13,628,731 | £833,113 |

## COMMUNICATIONS
*Airports and waterways* – The principal airport is at Tashkent and there are 1,100km of waterways
*Roadways and railways* – 75,511km; 4,230km
*Telecommunications* – 1.963 million fixed lines and 20.27 million mobile subscriptions (2012); there were 4.69 million internet users in 2009
*Major broadcasters* – The National Television and Radio Company is the state-operated broadcaster; many private media outlets associated with President Karimov's daughter, Gulnara Karimova, have closed since 2013
*Press* – Leading dailies include *Khalq Sozi* (Uzbek language), and *Narodnoye Slovo* and *Pravda Vostoka* (both Russian language)
*WPFI score* – 61,14 (166)

## EDUCATION AND HEALTH
*Literacy rate* – 99.9 per cent (2015 est)
*Gross enrolment ratio (percentage of relevant age group)* –
    primary 93 per cent; secondary 105 per cent; tertiary 9 per cent (2011 est)
*Health expenditure (per capita)* – US$120 (2013)
*Hospital beds (per 1,000 people)* – 4.4 (2010)
*Life expectancy (years)* – 73.29 (2014 est)
*Mortality rate* – 5.29 (2014 est)

*Birth rate* – 17.02 (2014 est)
*Infant mortality rate* – 19.84 (2014 est)

# VANUATU

*Ripablik blong Vanuatu/République de Vanuatu – Republic of Vanuatu*

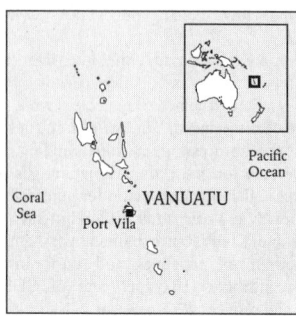

*Area* – 12,189 sq. km
*Capital* – Port Vila, on Efaté; population, 53,000 (2014 est)
*Major town* – Luganville, on Espiritu Santo
*Currency* – Vatu
*Population* – 272,264 rising at 1.95 per cent a year
    (2015 est); 98.5 per cent are Melanesian, the rest being
    mostly Micronesian, Polynesian and European (est)
*Religion* – Christian 82.4 per cent (Presbyterian 27.9 per
    cent, Anglican 15.1 per cent, Roman Catholic 12.4 per
    cent, Seventh-day Adventist 12.5 per cent) (2009 est)
*Language* – Bislama, English, French (all official); over
    100 local languages exist
*Population density* – 21 per sq. km (2013)
*Urban population* – 25.5 per cent (2013 est)
*Median age (years)* – 21.1 (2014 est)
*National anthem* – 'Yumi, Yumi, Yumi' ['We, We, We']
*National day* – 30 July (Independence Day)
*Death penalty* – Abolished for all crimes (since 1980)
*Literacy rate* – 95.7 per cent (2015 est)
*Life expectancy (years)* – 72.72 (2014 est)
*Mortality rate* – 4.14 (2014 est)
*Birth rate* – 25.69 (2014 est)
*Infant mortality rate* – 16.41 (2014 est)

## CLIMATE AND TERRAIN
Situated in the south Pacific Ocean, Vanuatu comprises 13 large and some 70 small islands, of either coral or volcanic origin, including the Banks Islands and Torres Islands in the north. The principal islands are Vanua Lava, Espiritu Santo, Maewo, Pentecost, Ambae, Malekula, Ambrym, Epi, Efaté, Erromango, Tanna and Aneityum. Most islands are mountainous and covered with dense rainforest. Elevation extremes range from 1,877m (Tabwemasana) to 0m (Pacific Ocean). The climate varies from tropical in the north of the archipelago to subtropical in the south, and all the islands experience cyclones.

## HISTORY AND POLITICS
Some of the islands of Vanuatu have been inhabited for over 4,000 years. Europeans first visited in the early 17th century, and Captain Cook named the islands the New Hebrides in 1774. In the 19th century, the British and the French established plantations, and from 1906 jointly administered the islands as the Condominium of the New Hebrides. This became independent as the Republic of Vanuatu in 1980.

In the 2012 legislative election the Vanuaaka Pati was the largest party in parliament. Vanuata has a history of producing unstable governments and three prime ministers have been deposed by parliamentary votes of no confidence since the 2012 elections: Sato Kilman in March 2013, Mona Kalosil in May 2014 and Joe Natuman in June 2015. Sato Kilman was re-elected prime minister by parliament in June. In the September 2014 presidential elections, independent candidate Baldwin Lonsdale was elected following eight rounds of voting.

Under the 1980 constitution, the head of state is a president who is elected for a five-year term by an electoral college consisting of the members of the legislature and the presidents of the six provincial governments. The unicameral parliament has 52 members, directly elected for a four-year term. The prime minister is elected by parliament from among its members, and appoints the council of ministers. The National Council of Chiefs advises on matters of custom.

### HEAD OF STATE
*President,* Baldwin Lonsdale, *elected* 22 September 2014

### SELECTED GOVERNMENT MEMBERS *as at July 2015*
*Prime Minister,* Sato Kilman
*Deputy Prime Minister,* Moana Carcasses
*Finance,* Willie Jimmy
*Internal Affairs,* Hosea Nevu

### EMBASSY OF VANUATU
Avenue de Tervueren 380, Chemin de Ronde 1150, Brussels
T (+32) (2) 771 7494 E info@vanuataembassy.be
*High Commissioner,* HE Roy Mickey Joy, *apptd* 2011

### BRITISH HIGH COMMISSIONER
HE Dominic Meiklejohn, *apptd* 2012, resident at Honiara, Solomon Islands

### ECONOMY AND TRADE
The economy is based on small-scale agriculture and fishing; 65 per cent of the population is employed on plantations or in subsistence agriculture. Subsistence crops include yams, taro, fruit and vegetables; the principal cash crops are coconuts, cocoa and coffee. Cattle are kept on the plantations. There is a small light industrial sector producing frozen food and fish and canned meat, and processing wood. Eco-tourism and offshore financial services are of growing importance. Australia and New Zealand supply revenue via aid and tourism.

The main export markets are Thailand (59.9 per cent) and Côte d'Ivoire; imports come chiefly from China, Singapore, the USA and Japan. Principal exports are copra, beef, cocoa, timber, kava and coffee. The main imports are machinery and equipment, foodstuffs and fuels.

*GNI* – US$790m; US$3,130 per capita (2013)
*Annual average growth of GDP* – 3.5 per cent (2014 est)
*Inflation rate* – 1.7 per cent (2014 est)
*Total external debt* – US$369.2m (2012 est)
*Imports* – US$311m (2013)
*Exports* – US$39m (2013)

BALANCE OF PAYMENTS
*Trade* – US$241m deficit (2012)
*Current Account* – US$107m deficit (2015 est)

| Trade with UK | 2013 | 2014 |
| --- | --- | --- |
| Imports from UK | £339,966 | £554,702 |
| Exports to UK | £459,377 | £8,038,885 |

## COMMUNICATIONS

*Airports and waterways* – The main international airport is at Port Vila and the main ports are located in Forari, Port Vila and Santo

*Roadways* – 1,070km, of which 256km are unpaved

*Telecommunications* – 5,800 main fixed lines and 137,000 mobile subscriptions (2012); there were 17,000 internet users in 2009

*Media* – Vanuatu Broadcasting and Television Corporation operates Television Blong Vanuatu

## VATICAN CITY STATE

*Status Civitatis Vaticanae or Sancta Sedes/stato Della Città del Vaticano or Santa Sede* – State of the Vatican City

ROME (ITALY)

Vatican Museums

St. Peter's Basilica

St. Peter's Square

ROME (ITALY)

*Area* – 0.44 sq. km (enclave only)

*Capital* – Vatican City

*Currency* – Euro (€) of 100 cents

*Population* – 842 (2014 est)

*Religion* – Christian (Roman Catholic)

*Language* – Latin (official), Italian, French

*National anthem* – 'Inno e Marcia Pontificale' ['Hymn and Pontifical March']

*National day* – 13 March (election of Pope Francis)

*Death penalty* – Abolished for all crimes (since 1969)

### HISTORY AND POLITICS

The Vatican City State is an independent sovereign state that consists of an enclave within the city of Rome and extraterritorial areas including offices and basilicas in Rome, the pope's summer residence and the location of Vatican Radio's transmitter. The Holy See, which comprises the pope and the departments that carry out the government of the Roman Catholic Church worldwide, has sovereign authority over the Vatican City State's territory, providing its government and diplomatic representation overseas.

The head of the Roman Catholic Church became a temporal ruler in the eighth century, holding territory in central Italy. The Papal States were annexed in 1860 by the newly unified kingdom of Italy, and Rome was captured by Italian troops in 1870–1, when the pope withdrew into the Vatican palace. In the Lateran treaties (1929), Italy recognised the pope's sovereignty over the city of the Vatican, and declared the state to be neutral and inviolable territory. The Vatican City State has special observer status at the United Nations.

The pope, the Sovereign Pontiff, is the head of state of the Vatican City, which is governed as an absolute monarchy. He is elected for life by a conclave consisting of those members of the Sacred College of Cardinals who are under the age of 80. Administration of the state is carried out by the Pontifical Commission and the Secretariat of State, which are appointed by the pope. All Vatican officials vacate their offices on the death of a pope. Pope Benedict XVI confirmed in office the president of the Pontifical Commission and the members of the Secretariat of State after his election. Pope Benedict XVI resigned in February 2013 and was succeeded by Pope Francis.

*Sovereign Pontiff,* His Holiness Pope Francis ( Jorge Mario Bergoglio), *born* 17 December 1936, *elected* 13 March 2013, *inaugurated* 19 March 2013

SECRETARIAT OF STATE *as at July 2015*

*Secretary of State,* Cardinal Pietro Parolin

*Substitute for General Affairs,* Archbishop Giovanni Becciu

*Secretary for Relations with States,* Archbishop Richard Gallagher

PONTIFICAL COMMISSION

*President,* Archbishop Giuseppe Bertello

APOSTOLIC NUNCIATURE

54 Parkside, London SW19 5NE

T 020-8944 7189

*Apostolic Nuncio,* HE Archbishop Antonio Mennini, *apptd* 2011

BRITISH EMBASSY TO THE HOLY SEE

Via XX Settembre 80/A, 00187 Rome

T (+39) (6) 4220 4000 E holysee@fco.gov.uk

W www.gov.uk/government/world/holy-see

*Ambassador Extraordinary and Plenipotentiary,* HE Nigel Baker, OBE, MVO, *apptd* 2011

### ECONOMY

The Vatican City budget is separate from that of the Holy See. The City's revenue is generated by museum admission charges and the sale of postage stamps, coins, medals, souvenirs and publications. The Holy See derives its income from investments, property, global banking and financial services and donations from Roman Catholics worldwide. Pope Francis began a process of reforming the Vatican Bank following a number of scandals. The annual collections known as Peter's Pence are used for charitable and overseas aid work and disaster relief.

## VENEZUELA

*República Bolivariana de Venezuela* – Bolivarian Republic of Venezuela

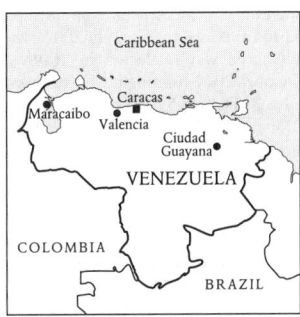

Caribbean Sea

Maracaibo

Caracas

Valencia

Ciudad Guayana

VENEZUELA

COLOMBIA

BRAZIL

*Area* – 912,050 sq. km

*Capital* – Caracas; population, 3,912,000 (2014)

*Major cities* – Barquisimeto, Ciudad Guayana, Maracaibo, Valencia

*Currency* – Bolívar fuerte (Bs. F) of 100 céntimos

*Population* – 29,275,460 rising at 1.39 per cent a year (2015 est)

*Religion* – Christian (Roman Catholic 96 per cent) (est)
*Language* – Spanish (official), several indigenous languages
*Population density* – 34 per sq. km (2013)
*Urban population* – 93.9 per cent (2013 est)
*Median age (years)* – 26.9 (2014 est)
*National anthem* – 'Gloria al Bravo Pueblo' ['Glory to the Brave People']
*National day* – 5 July (Independence Day)
*Death penalty* – Abolished for all crimes (since 1863)
*CPI score* – 19 (161)

## CLIMATE AND TERRAIN

The Andean mountains, of which the main range is the Sierra Nevada de Mérida, run across the north-west of the country, separating the northern coast from the central plains *(llanos)*. The Guiana Highlands occupy the south-east of the country. Elevation extremes range from 5,007m (Pico Bolivar) to 0m (Caribbean Sea). The Orinoco flows across the centre of the country to its delta on the Atlantic coast. Its upper waters are united with those of the Rio Negro (a Brazilian tributary of the Amazon) by a natural river or canal, known as the Brazo Casiquiare. The coastal lowlands contain many lagoons and lakes, including Lake Maracaibo (area 13,351 sq. km), the largest lake in South America. The climate varies from tropical to alpine, depending on altitude, and most areas experience a wet season from May to November. The average temperature is 25.8°C.

## HISTORY AND POLITICS

Columbus landed on the coast in 1498, and the first Spanish settlement was established at Cumaná in 1520. Venezuela became part of the Viceroyalty of New Granada in the early 18th century. There were several revolts against Spanish colonial rule, and a declaration of independence in 1811 was followed by several years of struggle until troops led by Simón Bolivar defeated the Spanish at the battle of Carabobo in 1821. Venezuela became part of Gran Colombia (with Colombia, Ecuador and Panama), and then an independent republic in 1830 under the first of a series of *caudillos* (military leaders). The first truly democratic elections were held in 1947 but the government was overthrown by the military within months. An enduring civilian democracy was established in 1958.

Oil revenues supported a buoyant economy in the 1970s but a price collapse in the mid-1980s led to economic difficulties and a number of attempted coups. After he came to power in 1998, President Hugo Chávez's economic and social reforms, and his authoritarian style polarised domestic opinion, provoking strikes and demonstrations, an attempted military coup in 2002 and a recall referendum in 2004, which he won.

President Chávez was re-elected in 2006. Despite re-election in October 2012, President Chávez was too ill to be re-inaugrated and died on 5 March 2013. Nicolas Maduro, also of the United Socialist Party of Venezuela (PSUV), was elected to succeed him in April 2013. In the 2010 legislative election, the PSUV and its allies won an overall majority, but lost its two-thirds majority (needed to change the constitution). President Maduro was granted the ability to rule by decree by parliament in March 2015 for nine months following the USA's announcement that Venezuela represented a threat to its national security. Legislative elections are due in December 2015.

Under the 1999 constitution, the executive president is directly elected for a six-year term; the limit on the number of successive terms was abolished in 2009. The unicameral National Assembly has 165 members, 162 directly elected and three representing indigenous people, who serve a five-year term. The president appoints the vice-president and the council of ministers.

The country is divided into 23 states, one capital district and one federal dependency composed of 11 island groups (72 individual islands). The states have considerable autonomy and each has its own legislature and elected governor.

HEAD OF STATE
*President*, Nicolas Maduro, *elected* 14 April 2013, *sworn in* 19 April 2013
*Executive Vice-President*, Jorge Arreaza

SELECTED GOVERNMENT MEMBERS *as at July 2015*
*Defence*, Vladimir Padrino
*Finance*, Rodolfo Marco Torres
*Interior and Justice*, Gustavo Gonzalez Lopez

EMBASSY OF THE BOLIVARIAN REPUBLIC OF VENEZUELA
1 Cromwell Road, London SW7 2HW
T 020-7584 4206 E embavenezuk@venezlon.co.uk
W www.venezlon.co.uk
*Ambassador Extraordinary and Plenipotentiary*, HE Rocio Maneiro, *apptd* 2014

BRITISH EMBASSY
Edificio Torre la Castellana, Piso 11, Avenida la Principal de la Castellana, Caracas 1601
T (+58) (212) 263 8411 E ukinvenezuela@fco.gov.uk
W www.gov.uk/government/world/venezuela
*Ambassador Extraordinary and Plenipotentiary*, HE John Saville, *apptd* 2014

## DEFENCE

| Aged 16–49, 2010 est | Males | Females |
| --- | --- | --- |
| Available for military service | 7,013,854 | 7,165,661 |
| Fit for military service | 5,614,743 | 6,074,834 |

*Military expenditure* – US$5,576m (2014)
*Conscription duration* – 30 months (selective)

## ECONOMY AND TRADE

Much of industry is state-owned, and since the Chávez regime came to power an increasing proportion of the private sector, some foreign-owned, has been nationalised, including oil, electricity, financial, steel, construction and agribusiness companies. Laws passed in December 2010 aimed to increase government control of the economy, which is struggling because of imbalances, high inflation and electricity shortages after a severe drought in 2009–10 left hydroelectric plants inoperable. High inflation, political instability and low global oil prices are expected to cause the economy to contract in 2015 and 2016.

Oil and gas are the mainstays of the economy, providing over 95 per cent of exports and over 45 per cent of government revenue, but heavy dependence on them makes the economy vulnerable to global price fluctuations.

Other major industries are mining (coal, iron ore, bauxite, gold), production of construction materials, textiles, steel and aluminium, food processing and vehicle assembly. Industry contributes 35.4 per cent of GDP and services 60.8 per cent. Agriculture comprises large-scale commercial farms and subsistence farming. Land distribution is uneven, and redistribution of land to the rural poor, breaking up larger estates, has begun. Agricultural products include maize, sorghum, sugar cane, rice, bananas, vegetables and coffee. There is an extensive beef and dairy farming industry. Agriculture provides 3.8 per cent of GDP and engages 7.3 per cent of the workforce.

The main trading partners are the USA (39.1 per cent of exports; 31.7 per cent of imports), Colombia, China and India.

Principal exports are oil, bauxite and aluminium, minerals, chemicals, agricultural products and basic manufactures. The main imports are agricultural products, raw materials, machinery, transport equipment and construction materials.

GNI – US$381,591m; US$12,550 per capita (2013)
Annual average growth of GDP – −3 per cent (2014 est)
Inflation rate – 69.8 per cent (2014 est)
Population below poverty line – 31.6 per cent (2011 est)
Unemployment – 8.6 per cent (2015 est)
Total external debt – US$69,660m (2014 est)
Imports – US$46,363m (2013)
Exports – US$86,700m (2013)

BALANCE OF PAYMENTS
Trade – US$37,340m surplus (2012)
Current Account – US$7,943m deficit (2015 est)

| Trade with UK | 2013 | 2014 |
| --- | --- | --- |
| Imports from UK | £290,068,639 | £200,586,726 |
| Exports to UK | £245,384,422 | £264,093,500 |

## COMMUNICATIONS
Airports and waterways – There are 127 airports, the principal terminals being at Caracas and Maracaibo; the main ports are Maracaibo, Puerto Cabello and Caracas-La Guaira
Roadways and railways – 32,308km; 806km
Telecommunications – 7.65 million fixed lines in use and 30.52 million mobile subscriptions (2012); there were 8.92 million internet users in 2009
Internet code and IDD – ve; 58 (from UK), 44 (to UK)
Major broadcasters – Venezolana de Television and Radio Nacional de Venezuela are the state broadcasters
Press – Major daily newspapers include El Mundo, El Nacional and Ultimas Noticias
WPFI score – 40,61 (137)

## EDUCATION AND HEALTH
There are nine years of compulsory education.
Literacy rate – 98.9 per cent (2015 est)
Gross enrolment ratio (percentage of relevant age group) – primary 102 per cent; secondary 93 per cent; tertiary 78 per cent (2013 est)
Health expenditure (per capita) – US$497 (2013)
Hospital beds (per 1,000 people) – 0.9 (2011)
Life expectancy (years) – 74.39 (2014 est)
Mortality rate – 5.27 (2014 est)
Birth rate – 19.42 (2014 est)
Infant mortality rate – 19.33 (2014 est)

# VIETNAM

Cong Hoa Xa Hoi Chu Nghia Viet Nam – Socialist Republic of Vietnam

Area – 331,210 sq. km
Capital – Hanoi; population, 3,470,000 (2014)
Major cities – Bien Hoa, Da Nang, Haiphong, Ho Chi Minh City (Saigon)
Currency – Dong of 10 ho or 100 xu
Population – 94,348,835 rising at 0.97 per cent a year (2015 est); Kinh (85.7 per cent), Tay (1.9 per cent), Thai (1.8 per cent), Muong (1.5 per cent), Khmer (1.5 per cent), Hmong (1.2 per cent), Nung (1.1 per cent) (2009)
Religion – Buddhist 9.3 per cent, Christian (Roman Catholic, 6.7 per cent, Protestant 0.5 per cent), Hoa Hao 1.5 per cent, Cao Dai 1.1 per cent, none 80.8 per cent (1999); Cao Dai is a syncretistic religion that combines elements of several faiths; Hoa Hao is a branch of Buddhism
Language – Vietnamese (official), English, French, Chinese, Khmer; Mon-Khmer and Malayo-Polynesian are spoken in mountain areas
Population density – 289 per sq. km (2013)
Urban population – 32.3 per cent (2013 est)
Median age (years) – 29.2 (2014 est)
National anthem – 'Tien Quan Ca' ['The Marching Song']
National day – 2 September (Independence Day)
Death penalty – Retained
CPI score – 31 (119)

## CLIMATE AND TERRAIN
The country is mostly mountainous, apart from the densely populated fertile plains around the deltas of the Hong (Red River) in the north and the Mekong in the south. Elevation extremes range from 3,144m (Fan Si Pan) to 0m (South China Sea). The climate is tropical and affected by the monsoon cycle. The wet season lasts from May to September, although the coast, being affected by typhoons and tropical storms, receives most rain between September and January.

## POLITICS
The 1992 constitution was amended in 2001 to allow small-scale capitalism greater freedom. The president is elected by the legislature to serve a five-year term. The unicameral National Assembly (Quoc-Hoi) has 500 members, who are directly elected for a five-year term. The head of government is the prime minister, who is responsible to the National Assembly, which appoints the council of ministers. However, effective power lies with the Communist Party of Vietnam. Its highest executive body is the Central Committee, elected by the national party congress held every five years. The politburo and the secretariat of the central committee, which exercise the real power, are elected at the party congress.

After the 2006 Communist Party Congress, the president and prime minister resigned to allow a younger leadership to be appointed; Nguyen Minh Triet was elected president to complete his predecessor's term of office, and he appointed Nguyen Tan Dung as prime minister. Both were re-elected to their posts in 2007, but the former lost the 2011 presidential race to Truong Tan Sang. In the May 2011 legislative election, the Communist Party and its allies held all the seats apart from four won by independent candidates.

HEAD OF STATE
President, Truong Tan Sang, elected 25 July 2011
Vice-President, Nguyen Thi Doan

SELECTED GOVERNMENT MEMBERS as at July 2015
Prime Minister, Nguyen Tan Dung
Deputy Prime Ministers, Hoang Trung Hai; Nguyen Xuan Phuc; Vu Duc Dam; Vu Van Ninh; Pham Binh Minh (Foreign Affairs)

*Finance,* Dinh Tien Dung
*Internal Affairs,* Nguyen Thai Binh

EMBASSY OF THE SOCIALIST REPUBLIC OF VIETNAM
12–14 Victoria Road, London W8 5RD
T 020-7937 1912 E vanphong@vietnamembassy.org.uk
W www.vietnamembassy.org.uk
*Ambassador Extraordinary and Plenipotentiary,* HE Van Thao Nguyen, *apptd* 2014

BRITISH EMBASSY
Central Building, 31 Hai Ba Trung, Hanoi
T (+84) (4) 3936 0500 E consularenquiries.vietnam@fco.gov.uk
W www.gov.uk/government/world/vietnam
*Ambassador Extraordinary and Plenipotentiary,* HE Giles Lever, *apptd* 2014

## DEFENCE

| Aged 16–49, 2010 est | Males | Females |
| --- | --- | --- |
| Available for military service | 25,649,738 | 24,995,692 |
| Fit for military service | 20,405,847 | 21,098,102 |

*Military expenditure* – US$4,251m (2014 est)
*Conscription duration* – 18–24 months

## ECONOMY AND TRADE

The economy struggled for a decade after 1975 owing to the devastation of war and the imposition of a centrally planned economy. Since economic liberalisation and international integration were adopted in 1986, the economy has grown substantially, albeit from a low base, and export-driven industries are being developed. The global downturn reduced economic growth in 2008–9, and in early 2012 the government introduced a three-fold economic reform programme, proposing a restructuring of the banking sector, public spending and state-owned enterprises. Vietnam was scheduled to form a common market with the other members of the Association of Southeast Asian Nations (ASEAN) in 2015.

Agriculture's contribution is gradually shrinking, but still accounts for 17.9 per cent of GDP and employs 48 per cent of the workforce. The main industries are food processing, clothing and footwear, machine building, coal mining, steel, cement, chemical fertiliser, glass, tyres and paper, and oil and gas production from large offshore reserves. Industry now contributes 38.1 per cent of GDP and services 44 per cent.

The main trading partners are China, Japan, South Korea and the USA. Principal exports are clothing, footwear, fish and seafood, crude oil, electronics, wood products, rice and machinery. The main imports are machinery and equipment, petroleum products, steel products, raw materials, electronics, plastics and vehicles.

*GNI* – US$156,447m; US$1,740 per capita (2013)
*Annual average growth of GDP* – 5.5 per cent (2014 est)
*Inflation rate* – 4.6 per cent (2014 est)
*Population below poverty line* – 11.3 per cent (2012 est)
*Unemployment* – 2.2 per cent (2015 est)
*Total external debt* – US$68,050m (2014 est)
*Imports* – US$131,260m (2013)
*Exports* – US$132,478m (2013)

BALANCE OF PAYMENTS
*Trade* – US$357m surplus (2012)
*Current Account* – US$9,816m surplus (2015 est)

| Trade with UK | 2013 | 2014 |
| --- | --- | --- |
| Imports from UK | £304,181,668 | £340,293,209 |
| Exports to UK | £2,895,918,023 | £2,474,409,713 |

## COMMUNICATIONS

*Airports and waterways* – The principal airports and ports are at Ho Chi Minh City, Hanoi and Da Nang
*Roadways and railways* – 148,338km; 2,632km
*Telecommunications* – 10.191 million fixed lines and 134.07 million mobile subscriptions (2012); there were 23.38 million internet users in 2009
*Internet code and IDD* – vn; 84 (from UK), 44 (to UK)
*Major broadcasters* – Vietnam Television (VTV) and Voice of Vietnam (radio) are the state-run broadcasters
*Press* – Leading newspapers include the Communist Party daily *Nhan Dahn, Vietnam Economic Times* and *Le Courrier du Vietnam*
*WPFI score* – 72,63 (175)

## EDUCATION AND HEALTH

*Literacy rate* – 98.1 per cent (2015 est)
*Gross enrolment ratio (percentage of relevant age group)* – primary 105 per cent (2013 est); secondary 77 per cent (2011 est); tertiary 25 per cent (2013 est)
*Health expenditure (per capita)* – US$111 (2013)
*Hospital beds (per 1,000 people)* – 2.0 (2010)
*Life expectancy (years)* – 72.91 (2014 est)
*Mortality rate* – 5.93 (2014 est)
*Birth rate* – 16.26 (2014 est)
*Infant mortality rate* – 18.99 (2014 est)

# YEMEN

*Al-Jumhuriyah al-Yamaniyah – Republic of Yemen*

*Area* – 527,968 sq. km
*Capital* – Sana'a; population, 2,833,000 (2014)
*Major cities* – Aden (the former capital of South Yemen), Hudaida (al-Hudaydah), Ibb, Mukulla, Taiz
*Currency* – Riyal of 100 fils
*Population* – 26,737,317 rising at 2.47 per cent a year (2015 est)
*Religion* – Muslim (Sunni 65 per cent, Shia 35 per cent) (2010 est)
*Language* – Arabic (official)
*Population density* – 46 per sq. km (2013)
*Urban population* – 33.5 per cent (2013 est)
*Median age (years)* – 18.6 (2014 est)
*National anthem* – 'Al-Jumhuriyah al-Muttahida' ['United Republic']
*National day* – 22 May (Unification Day)
*Death penalty* – Retained
*CPI score* – 19 (161)

## CLIMATE AND TERRAIN

A mountainous region in the west and south divides the desert plains of the interior from the narrow coastal plains. Elevation extremes range from 3,760m (Jabal an Nabi Shu'ayb) to 0m (Arabian Sea). There is a desert climate, which is particularly harsh in the east, but moderated in the western mountains by the monsoon. The coast experiences high humidity and the average temperature is 24.4°C.

The islands of Perim and Kamaran in the Red Sea, and Suqutra in the Gulf of Aden, are Yemeni territory. The border with Saudi Arabia, except for the north-west corner, is unclear and is being delineated following an agreement between the two countries.

## POLITICS

The president announced in March 2011 the drafting of a new constitution transferring powers from the presidency to the legislature. Under the 1991 constitution, the president is directly elected for a seven-year term, renewable once. The unicameral House of Representatives *(Majlis al-Nowab)* has 301 members directly elected for a six-year term. In addition, there is an advisory Shura council, whose 111 members are appointed by the president, who also appoints the prime minister.

In the 2003 legislative election, the ruling General People's Congress (GPC) won 238 seats and formed a coalition government with the Yemeni Alliance for Reform (YAR or al-Islah). Lt.-Gen. Ali Abdullah Saleh, president of North Yemen from 1978 and president of the united country since 1990, was forced to resign in December 2011 following sustained protests. He was replaced by former vice-president Abd-Rabbu Mansour Hadi after transitional presidential elections in 2012.

Following rising political tensions and violence in 2013 and 2014, in September 2014 Houthi rebels took control of the capital Sana'a after the Hadi administration failed to acquiesce to their demands for reform. The government resigned in January 2015 after the rebels rejected proposals for a new constitution. The Houthis announced that they had taken power in February and the deposed President Hadi fled to the southern city of Aden. In March, the group looked to annex territory in southern Yemen and were attacked by both Saudi Arabian airstrikes and by IS suicide bombers who targeted Shia mosques *(see* Events of the Year).

### HEAD OF STATE
*President,* Gen. Abd-Rabbu Mansour Hadi, *elected*
21 February 2012

### SELECTED GOVERNMENT MEMBERS *as at July 2015*
*Prime Minister,* vacant
*Defence,* Mahmoud Ahmed Salim al-Subaihi
*Foreign Affairs,* Riyadh Yassin

### EMBASSY OF THE REPUBLIC OF YEMEN
57 Cromwell Road, London SW7 2ED
**T** 020-7584 6607 **E** yemen.embassy@btconnect.com
*Ambassador Extraordinary and Plenipotentiary,* HE Abdulla Ali al-Radhi, *apptd* 2010

### BRITISH EMBASSY
PO Box 1287, 938 Thaher Himiyar Street, East Ring Road (opposite Mövenpick Hotel), Sana'a
**T** (+967) (1) 308 114 **E** britishembassysanaa@fco.gov.uk
**W** www.gov.uk/government/world/yemen
*Ambassador Extraordinary and Plenipotentiary,* HE Edmund Fitton Brown, *apptd* 2015

## DEFENCE

| Aged 16–49, 2010 est | Males | Females |
|---|---|---|
| Available for military service | 5,652,256 | 5,387,160 |
| Fit for military service | 4,056,944 | 4,116,895 |

*Military expenditure* – US$1,715m (2014)
*Conscription duration* – 24 months

## ECONOMY AND TRADE

Despite its oil industry, the mainstay of the economy, Yemen is one of the poorest countries in the Arab world. The government began an IMF restructuring programme in 2006 that aims to diversify the economy and attract foreign investment. Implementation has been hampered by popular protests, security problems internally and from piracy in nearby waters, corruption and rapid population growth. Falling oil prices nearly halved the government's revenue in 2009, although Yemen also benefited from its first exports of liquefied natural gas. Civil unrest in 2011 caused the economy to contract by 11 per cent. The economy has been devastated by the outbreak of conflict, particularly by the suspension by oil and gas exports.

Agriculture is largely of a subsistence nature, and, with herding and fishing, engages the majority of the population, contributing 9.2 per cent of GDP. Apart from oil and natural gas extraction and oil refining, industry consists of small-scale manufacturing of cotton textiles, leather goods, handi-crafts, aluminium products and cement, food processing and ship repair.

The main trading partners are China, India, the UAE and Thailand. Principal exports are crude oil, coffee, dried and salted fish, and liquefied natural gas. The main imports are food, livestock, machinery and equipment, and chemicals.
*GNI* – US$32,581m; US$1,330 per capita (2013)
*Annual average growth of GDP* – 1.9 per cent (2014 est)
*Inflation rate* – 11 per cent (2014 est)
*Population below poverty line* – 54 per cent (2003)
*Unemployment* – 16.6 per cent (2015 est)
*Total external debt* – US$8,002 m (2014 est)
*Imports* – US$12,500m (2013)
*Exports* – US$9,500m (2013)

### BALANCE OF PAYMENTS
*Trade* – US$3,475m deficit (2012)
*Current Account* – US$966m deficit (2015 est)

| Trade with UK | 2013 | 2014 |
|---|---|---|
| Imports from UK | £101,644,713 | £70,935,104 |
| Exports to UK | £57,975,042 | £2,657,679 |

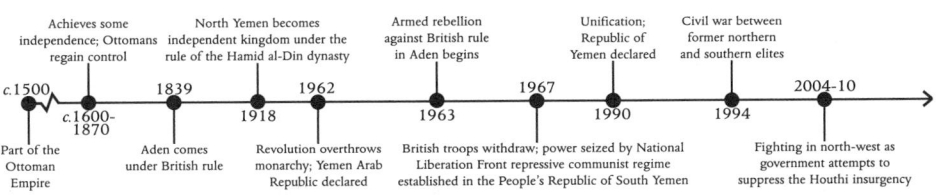

| | | | | |
|---|---|---|---|---|
| Achieves some independence; Ottomans regain control | North Yemen becomes independent kingdom under the rule of the Hamid al-Din dynasty | Armed rebellion against British rule in Aden begins | Unification; Republic of Yemen declared | Civil war between former northern and southern elites |

*c.*1500      1839      1962      1967      2004-10
*c.*1600-       1918      1963      1990      1994
1870

| Part of the Ottoman Empire | Aden comes under British rule | Revolution overthrows monarchy; Yemen Arab Republic declared | British troops withdraw; power seized by National Liberation Front repressive communist regime established in the People's Republic of South Yemen | Fighting in north-west as government attempts to suppress the Houthi insurgency |

## COMMUNICATIONS

*Airports and waterways* – Principal airports are at Sana'a and Aden and the main ports are at Aden, al-Hudaydah and al-Mukalla

*Roadways* – 71,300km, of which 6,200km are paved

*Telecommunications* – 1.1 million fixed lines and 13.9 million mobile subscriptions (2012); there were 2.35 million internet users in 2009

*Internet code and IDD* – ye; 967 (from UK), 44 (to UK)

*Media* – Republic of Yemen Television and Republic of Yemen Radio are the state-run broadcasters; leading daily newspapers include *Al-Thawra* (Arabic language), and the *Yemen Observer* and *Yemen Post* (both English language)

*WPFI score* – 66,36 (168)

## EDUCATION AND HEALTH

*Literacy rate* – 90.2 per cent (2015 est)

*Gross enrolment ratio (percentage of relevant age group)* – primary 101 per cent; secondary 49 per cent (2013 est)

*Health expenditure (per capita)* – US$74 (2013)

*Hospital beds (per 1,000 people)* – 0.7 (2012)

*Life expectancy (years)* – 64.83 (2014 est)

*Mortality rate* – 6.45 (2014 est)

*Birth rate* – 31.02 (2014 est)

*Infant mortality rate* – 50.41 (2014 est)

# ZAMBIA

*Republic of Zambia*

*Area* – 752,618 sq. km

*Capital* – Lusaka; population, 2,078,000 (2014)

*Major cities* – Kitwe, Ndola

*Currency* – Kwacha (K) of 100 ngwee

*Population* – 15,066,266 rising at 2.88 per cent a year (2015 est); over 70 ethnic groups, of which the Lozi, Bemba, Ngoni, Tonga, Luvale and Kaonde are the largest

*Religion* – Christian (Protestant 75.3 per cent, Roman Catholic 20.2 per cent) (2010 est)

*Language* – English (official), Bembe, Kaonde, Lozi, Lunda, Luvale, Nyanja, Tonga (national), over 70 other local languages

*Population density* – 20 per sq. km (2013)

*Urban population* – 40 per cent (2013 est)

*Median age (years)* – 16.7 (2014 est)

*National anthem* – 'Lumbanyeni Zambia' ['Stand and Sing of Zambia, Proud and Free']

*National day* – 24 October (Independence Day)

*Death penalty* – Retained (not used since 1997)

*CPI score* – 38 (85)

*Literacy rate* – 65.8 per cent (2015 est)

*Gross enrolment ratio (percentage of relevant age group)* – primary 115 per cent (2011 est)

*Health expenditure (per capita)* – US$93 (2013)

*Hospital beds (per 1,000 people)* – 2.0 (2010)

*Life expectancy (years)* – 51.83 (2014 est)

*Mortality rate* – 12.92 (2014 est)

*Birth rate* – 42.46 (2014 est)

*Infant mortality rate* – 66.62 (2014 est)

*HIV/AIDS adult prevalence* – 12.5 per cent (2013 est)

## CLIMATE AND TERRAIN

Landlocked Zambia lies on a forested plateau cut through by river valleys and with higher land in the north and north-east. Elevation extremes range from 2,301m (in the Mafinga Hills) to 329m (Zambezi river). The Zambezi and its tributaries are the main rivers. Lake Bangweulu and parts of Lakes Tanganyika, Mweru and Kariba lie within its boundaries. The climate is tropical, moderated by altitude, with a rainy season from October to April.

## HISTORY AND POLITICS

Most of the ethnic groups in Zambia migrated there between the 16th and the 18th centuries. Portuguese explorers arrived in the late 18th century and, with Arab traders, began slave-trading in the 19th century. The area came under British administration in 1889, was named Northern Rhodesia in 1911 and became a British protectorate in 1924. It was part of the Central African Federation with South Rhodesia (Zimbabwe) and Nyasaland (Malawi) from 1953 to 1963, when the federation was dissolved and Northern Rhodesia achieved internal self-government. It became an independent republic in 1964 under the name of Zambia.

Kenneth Kaunda of the United National Independence Party (UNIP) became president at independence and remained in power until 1991. Zambia was a one-party state ruled by the UNIP from 1972 until 1990, when pressure from opposition groups led to a new constitution, under which multiparty legislative and presidential elections were held in 1991.

The Patriotic Front (PF) won the 2011 legislative election, gaining enough seats for a small majority in the National Assembly. The PF's leader, Michael Sata, won the 2011 presidential election. After the death of President Sata in October 2014 following an illness, Edgar Lungu of the PF was elected in the January 2015 presidential elections, securing 48.3 per cent of the popular vote.

Under the 1991 constitution, the executive president is directly elected for a five-year term, renewable once. The unicameral National Assembly has 158 members: 150 directly elected, up to eight nominated by the president, and a speaker; all serve a five-year term. The president appoints the cabinet.

A new constitution is under debate, although it is unclear when it will be adopted.

HEAD OF STATE
*President, Defence,* Edgar Lungu, *elected* 24 January 2015, *sworn in* 25 January 2015
*Vice-President,* Inonge Wina

SELECTED GOVERNMENT MEMBERS *as at July 2015*
*Home Affairs,* Davies Mwila
*Finance,* Alexander Chikwanda
*Foreign Affairs,* Harry Kalaba

HIGH COMMISSION FOR THE REPUBLIC OF ZAMBIA
Zambia House, 2 Palace Gate, London W8 5NG
T 020-7589 6655 E info@zambiahc.org.uk
W www.zambiahc.org.uk
*High Commissioner,* HE Paul Lumbi, *apptd* 2013

## BRITISH HIGH COMMISSION

PO Box 5005, 5210 Independence Avenue, 15101 Ridgeway, Lusaka
T (+260) (21) 1423 2001251 133
E lusakageneralenquiries@fco.gov.uk
W www.gov.uk/government/world/zambia
*High Commissioner,* HE James Thornton, *apptd* 2012

## DEFENCE

| *Aged 16–49, 2010 est* | *Males* | *Females* |
| --- | --- | --- |
| Available for military service | 3,041,069 | 2,948,291 |
| Fit for military service | 1,745,656 | 1,688,670 |

*Military expenditure –* US$443m (2014)

## ECONOMY AND TRADE

The transition since the 1990s from a state-controlled to a free-market economy has improved productivity, especially in the now-privatised copper industry. The economy grew in 2010 due to high copper prices and a good maize crop harvest. It is also driven in particular by mining, hydro-electric power generation, construction and tourism. The economy is expected to grow by around 6.5 per cent in 2015 and 2016.

Copper is the main source of foreign earnings and increased demand in recent years for electronics has spurred investment and greater output, although weakening global copper prices caused a rapid depreciation of the kwacha in 2014. However, 85 per cent of the workforce remains engaged in agriculture, mostly at subsistence level, which accounts for 10.8 per cent of GDP. The main industries are copper and cobalt mining and processing, construction, food processing, beverages, chemicals, textiles, fertiliser and horticulture.

The main trading partners are China and South Africa. Principal exports are copper, cobalt, electricity, tobacco, cut flowers and cotton. The main imports are machinery, transport equipment, petroleum products, electricity, fertiliser, foodstuffs and clothing.

*GNI –* US$26,323m; US$1,810 per capita (2013)
*Annual average growth of GDP –* 6.5 per cent (2014 est)
*Inflation rate –* 7.8 per cent (2014 est)
*Unemployment –* 13.4 per cent (2015 est)
*Total external debt –* US$7,384m (2014 est)
*Imports –* US$10,165m (2013)
*Exports –* US$10,596m (2013)

### BALANCE OF PAYMENTS

*Trade –* US$550m surplus (2012)
*Current Account –* US$78m surplus (2015 est)

| Trade with UK | 2013 | 2014 |
| --- | --- | --- |
| Imports from UK | £88,176,187 | £64,712,402 |
| Exports to UK | £37,622,327 | £38,072,245 |

## COMMUNICATIONS

*Airports and waterways –* There are eight airports and 2,250km of navigable waterways on Lake Tanganyika and the Zambezi and Luapula rivers
*Roadways and railways –* 9,403km; 2,922km
*Telecommunications –* 82,500 fixed lines and 10.53 million mobile subscriptions (2012); there were 816,200 internet users in 2009
*Internet code and IDD –* zm; 260 (from UK), 44 (to UK)
*Media –* The state-run Zambia National Broadcasting Association operates TV and radio stations; major daily newspapers include the *Zambia Daily Mail, Times of Zambia* (both state-owned) and *The Post* (privately owned)
*WPFI score –* 34,35 (113)

# ZIMBABWE

*Republic of Zimbabwe*

*Area –* 390,757 sq. km
*Capital –* Harare; population, 1,495,000 (2014)
*Major cities –* Bulawayo, Chitungwiza, Gweru, Mutare
*Currency –* US dollars; other currencies, including the South African rand, are in use
*Population –* 14,229,541 rising at 2.21 per cent a year (2015 est); Shona (82 per cent), Ndebele (14 per cent) (est)
*Religion –* Christian (Apostolic 38 per cent, Pentecostal 21.1 per cent, Roman Catholic 8.4 per cent) (2011 est)
*Language –* English (official), Shona, Ndebele, numerous tribal dialects
*Population density –* 37 per sq. km (2013)
*Urban population –* 39.6 per cent (2013 est)
*Median age (years) –* 20.2 (2014 est)
*National anthem –* 'Simudzai Mureza wedu WeZimbabwe' ['Blessed be the Land of Zimbabwe']
*National day –* 18 April (Independence Day)
*Death penalty –* Retained
*CPI score –* 21 (156)

## CLIMATE AND TERRAIN

Zimbabwe lies mainly on a high plateau with a central high veld and mountains in the east. Elevation extremes range from 2,592m (Inyangani) to 162m (confluence of the Runde and Save rivers). The climate is tropical, moderated by altitude, with a wet season from November to March. Average temperatures range from 16.5°C in July to 25.4°C in November.

## POLITICS

Under the 2013 constitution, the term of the executive president was reduced from six years to five and is renewable once, however this does not apply retrospectively to the incumbent, Robert Mugabe. The bicameral parliament comprises the National Assembly and the senate. The former has 210 members directly elected for a five-year term plus 60 seats reserved for women. The senate has 80 members, who serve a five-year term: 62 elected (including six from each of the eight provinces) and 18 traditional chiefs.

The country is divided into eight provinces and two cities (Bulawayo and Harare) with provincial status. The provinces are: Manicaland, Mashonaland Central, Mashonaland East, Mashonaland West, Masvingo, Matabeleland North, Matabeleland South and Midlands.

An internationally brokered power-sharing arrangement was agreed between the Zimbabwe African National Union-Patriotic Front (ZANU-PF) and the Movement for Democratic Change (MDC) in September 2008 and January 2009, and the MDC's leader Morgan Tsvangirai was sworn in as prime minister at the head of a national unity government in February 2009. The 2013 presidential

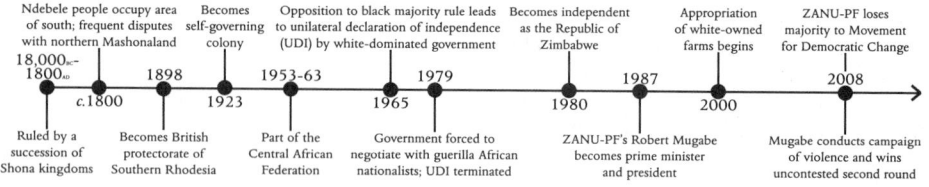

Ndebele people occupy area of south; frequent disputes with northern Mashonaland 18,000₀₀– 1800₀₀ · c.1800 · Becomes self-governing colony 1898 · 1923 · Opposition to black majority rule leads to unilateral declaration of independence (UDI) by white-dominated government 1953–63 · 1965 · Becomes independent as the Republic of Zimbabwe 1979 · 1980 · Appropriation of white-owned farms begins 1987 · 2000 · ZANU-PF loses majority to Movement for Democratic Change 2008

Ruled by a succession of Shona kingdoms · Becomes British protectorate of Southern Rhodesia · Part of the Central African Federation · Government forced to negotiate with guerilla African nationalists; UDI terminated · ZANU-PF's Robert Mugabe becomes prime minister and president · Mugabe conducts campaign of violence and wins uncontested second round

election was won by Robert Mugabe with 61.1 per cent of the vote; ZANU-PF won the legislative election. The office of prime minister was abolished under the 2013 constitution.

**HEAD OF STATE**
*President,* Robert Mugabe, *elected* 30 December 1987, *re-elected* 1990, 1996, 2002, 2008, 2013
*Vice-Presidents,* Emmerson Mnangagwa, Phelekezela Mphoko

SELECTED GOVERNMENT MEMBERS *as at July 2015*
*Defence,* Sydney Sekeramyi
*Finance,* Patrick Chinamasa
*Foreign Affairs,* Simbarashe Mumbengegwi

**EMBASSY OF THE REPUBLIC OF ZIMBABWE**
Zimbabwe House, 429 Strand, London WC2R 0JR
T 020-7836 7755 E zimlondon@zimfa.gov.zw
W www.zimlondon.gov.zw
*Ambassador Extraordinary and Plenipotentiary,* vacant

**BRITISH EMBASSY**
PO Box 4490, 3 Norfolk Road, Mount Pleasant, Harare
T (+263) (4) 8585 5200 E ukinfo.harare@fco.gov.uk
W www.gov.uk/government/world/zimbabwe
*Ambassador Extraordinary and Plenipotentiary,* HE Catriona Laing, CMG, *apptd* 2014

**DEFENCE**

| Aged 16–49, 2010 est | Males | Females |
| --- | --- | --- |
| Available for military service | 2,616,051 | 2,868,376 |
| Fit for military service | 1,528,166 | 1,646,041 |

*Military expenditure* – US$368m (2014)

**ECONOMY AND TRADE**
Poor governance, and in particular the seizure of almost all the white-owned commercial farms, caused a rapid contraction in the agriculture-based economy in the decade from the late 1990s; agricultural output and GDP halved, international aid was suspended because of the government's outstanding arrears on past loans, and the migration of professional and skilled labour and high levels of HIV/AIDS infection depleted the workforce. After the national unity government took office, the US dollar was adopted in 2009 and the Zimbabwe dollar phased out by late 2015, following years of rampant hyperinflation. Poverty and dependence on food aid is widespread.

Agriculture accounts for 20.1 per cent of GDP and engages two-thirds of the workforce. The most important crops are cotton and tobacco for export and maize for domestic consumption. Other crops include wheat, coffee, sugar cane, peanuts and livestock.

The mining sector is important to the economy as a foreign exchange earner. Almost all mineral production is exported. Gold is the most important product; others are coal, platinum, copper, nickel, tin, diamonds, iron ore and other metal and non-metal ores. Mining is now the largest industrial activity and supports a ferro-alloy industry and a

steel works. Manufacturing, traditionally highly dependent on the agricultural sector for raw materials, produces wood products, cement, chemicals, fertiliser, clothing, footwear, foodstuffs and beverages; output has dropped in some industries because of transport difficulties and power rationing. Industry generates 25.7 per cent of GDP and services 54.2 per cent.

The main trading partners are South Africa, China, the Democratic Republic of Congo and Botswana. Principal exports are platinum, cotton, tobacco, gold, ferro-alloys, textiles and clothing. The main imports are machinery and transport equipment, other manufactures, chemicals, fuels and food.

*GNI* – US$12,195m; US$860 per capita (2013)
*Annual average growth of GDP* – 3.1 per cent (2014 est)
*Inflation rate* – 6.5 per cent (2014 est)
*Population below poverty line* – 72.3 per cent (2011)
*Unemployment* – 5.6 per cent (2015 est)
*Total external debt* – US$9,361m (2014 est)
*Imports* – US$4,300m (2013)
*Exports* – US$3,552m (2013)

**BALANCE OF PAYMENTS**
*Trade* – US$600m deficit (2012)
*Current Account* – US$3,021m deficit (2015 est)

| Trade with UK | 2013 | 2014 |
| --- | --- | --- |
| Imports from UK | £27,134,044 | £25,184,497 |
| Exports to UK | £52,120,383 | £40,960,343 |

**COMMUNICATIONS**
*Airports* – The main airports are at Harare and Bulawayo, and there are 15 other airports
*Roadways and railways* – 18,481km; 3,427km
*Telecommunications* – 301,600 fixed lines and 12.61 million mobile subscriptions (2012); there were 1.42 million internet users in 2009
*Internet code and IDD* – zw; 263 (from UK), 44 (to UK)
*Major broadcasters* – The Zimbabwe Broadcasting Corporation operates the only official TV and radio stations; opposition groups operate a number of illegal radio stations, such as Voice of the People and Radio Dialogue from abroad
*Press* – The government publishes the only daily newspapers, *The Herald* and *The Chronicle*
*WPFI score* – 39,19 (131)

**EDUCATION AND HEALTH**
Education is compulsory at primary level, and the language of instruction is English.
*Literacy rate* – 91.7 per cent (2015 est)
*Gross enrolment ratio (percentage of relevant age group)* – primary 109 per cent; secondary 47 per cent (2012 est); tertiary 6 per cent (2013 est)
*Hospital beds (per 1,000 people)* – 1.7 (2011)
*Life expectancy (years)* – 55.68 (2014 est)
*Mortality rate* – 10.62 (2014 est)
*Birth rate* – 32.47 (2014 est)
*Infant mortality rate* – 26.55 (2014 est)
*HIV/AIDS adult prevalence* – 14.88 per cent (2013 est)

# THE NORTH AND SOUTH POLES

## THE ARCTIC

The Arctic is the region around the Earth's north pole; it includes the ice-covered Arctic Ocean, parts of Canada, the USA, Greenland, Iceland, Finland, Norway, Sweden and Russia. The area is commonly defined as lying north of the line of latitude known as the Arctic Circle (running at 66° 33' N.) or inside the 10°C July isotherm.

The climate is harsh, particularly during winter (October–March) when the Arctic receives little sunlight; the average monthly temperature in December, January and February is around −10 to −15°C. Continental areas, including Northern Canada and Alaska, can experience lows of −60°C in winter. In summer, the interior of Greenland remains subzero, while more southerly regions such as the Siberian tundra, can rise to 30°C. Coastal areas, including Iceland and Northern Scandinavia, have a milder, maritime climate with an average yearly temperature of 10°C. The Arctic is rarely as cold as the Antarctic since there is water, not land, underneath the Arctic ice. The water is warmer than the air above it, causing heat to rise and moderate the cold.

The polar bear is the region's apex predator. Other native species include varieties of caribou, lemming, wolf, hare and fox; around 200 bird species migrate to tundra areas in summer. Until recently, vegetation was limited to Arctic tundra, a biome consisting of around 1,700 species of low-lying shrubs, grasses, sedges, lichens and mosses. However, this tundra is slowly being replaced with flora typical of more southern locations, such as trees and evergreen shrubs. In 2013, a comprehensive study of these changes, the Arctic Biodiversity Assessment (W www.arcticbiodiversity.is), concluded that climate change and the effects of collective industrial development were degrading arctic biodiversity.

### ARCTIC SEA ROUTES
In 1906 Norwegian explorer Roald Amundsen first successfully navigated the Northwest passage, but the shallow waterways he encountered ensured that the route held little commercial potential until recently. Similarly, the Northern Sea route (formerly the Northeast passage) linking the Atlantic and Pacific oceans around Russia's Arctic coast, was first navigated by Finnish-Swedish explorer Adolf Erik Nordenskjold in 1878–9, but thereafter only icebreakers and Russian submarines regularly traversed it.

In summer 2007, the Northwest passage was declared open and ice-free for the first time since records began in late 1978; the first commercial ship travelled through it in September 2008. In August 2008 the Northwest passage and the Northern Sea route were open simultaneously for the first time, making the Arctic circumnavigable. Two German cargo vessels became the first to navigate the Northern Sea route in September 2009 and in August 2012 *The World* became the largest passenger ship to navigate the Northwest Passage, following Amundsen's route.

### CLIMATE CHANGE
The extent of ice in the Arctic has become a key measure of global climate change. The rate at which the ice melts grows exponentially: whereas the white ice reflects sunlight back into space, the darker seas absorb its heat, and the rising sea temperature melts the surrounding ice. The extent of sea ice reaches its greatest extent in March and retreats to its lowest point in September. The minimum ice extent in September 2014 was recorded as 5.02 million km²

(1.94 million miles²); 1.61 million km² (622,000 miles²) above the record minimum extent, which occurred in September 2012, and 1.68 million km² (650,000 miles²) below the 1979 to 2000 average minimum. Since 2010, estimates of sea ice thickness and volume have been obtained via the European Space Agency's CryoSat satellite. In October 2014 CryoSat measured approximately 7,500km³ (1,799 miles³) of sea ice at the end of the summer melt, only slightly reduced from 8,800km³ (2,111 miles³) in October 2013 and 12 per cent above the five-year average. However, it is estimated that in the early 1980s, October ice volume was around 20,000km³ (4,800 miles³).

### NATURAL RESOURCES
The Arctic's receding ice presents opportunities for national governments to lay claim to a wealth of hydrocarbon and mineral deposits. In 2008 the US Geological Survey estimated that 20 per cent of the world's undiscovered oil and gas reserves – as much as 90 billion barrels of oil, 44 billion barrels of natural gas liquids and 1,670 trillion cubic feet of natural gas – are located within the Arctic Circle. Under the 1982 UN Convention on the Law of the Sea, no state owns the pole or the ocean surrounding it: the five countries that border the Arctic Ocean – Canada, Denmark, Norway, Russia and the USA (a non-signatory) – are limited to an economic zone of 200 nautical miles from their coastline, unless able to prove that their continental shelf extends beyond that limit. Under the convention the countries have ten years from their date of ratification to assert a claim that their continental shelf extends into arctic territory. In August 2007, Russia planted a flag in the seabed below the pole, on the Lomonosov Ridge which spans much of the Arctic, and which Russia claims is an extension of the Eurasian continent and therefore part of its territory. However, Canadian geologists assert that Lomonosov is an extension of the North American continent, and therefore falls under their jurisdiction. In December 2014 Denmark followed Canada, Norway and Russia in submitting a claim under UNCLOS, arguing that the Lomonosov Ridge is an extension of Greenland's continental shelf.

## THE ANTARCTIC

The Antarctic is generally defined as the area lying within the Antarctic Convergence, the zone where cold northward-flowing Antarctic sea water sinks below warmer southward-flowing water. This zone fluctuates unevenly between latitudes of 48° S. and 61° S., typically extending further north in the Atlantic Ocean than in the Pacific. The Antarctic itself lies almost entirely within the Antarctic Circle; it has an area of around 14 million km², 98 per cent of which is permanently ice-covered. The average thickness of the grounded ice is 2,126m, but can reach 4,897m in places; it amounts to some 26.5 million km³, and represents around 90 per cent of the world's fresh water and 91 per cent of the world's glacier ice. Much of the sea freezes in winter, forming fast ice which breaks free of the coast in summer and drifts north as pack ice.

### CLIMATE AND TERRAIN
Antarctica is the highest, coldest and driest continent on Earth, with average coastal temperatures ranging from just above freezing in the summer (December–February) to −20°C in winter. Conditions on the interior plateau are more

severe, with katabatic (gravity-driven) winds and frequent cyclonic storms pushing average winter temperatures down to −65°C. The Vostok research station holds the record for the lowest surface temperature recorded on Earth at −89.2°C in 1983. Elevation extremes range from 4,897m (Vinson Massif) at the highest point to −2,540m (Bentley Subglacial Trench) at the lowest. The Transantarctic mountains bisect the continent north–south, dividing the west Antarctic ice-sheet – an ice-filled marine basin – from the significantly larger and more elevated east sheet. With average precipitation of just 140mm a year, Antarctica is considered a desert.

## CLIMATE CHANGE
While the recent decline in levels of ice in the Arctic has been clear and visible, concurrent changes in the Antarctic have been more complex. Despite reports of a recent thickening of the interior of the east ice-sheet due to increased snowfall, studies of data produced by the European Space Agency's Cryosat satellite indicate that the Antarctic ice-sheet as a whole has declined by more than 500km$^3$ (30 miles$^3$) a year since 2010, the majority of that loss having taken place in the west Antarctic. The continent appears to be gaining temporary sea ice in winter – which extended to a record 20.11 million km$^2$ (7.76 million miles$^2$) in September 2014 – probably due to increased meltwater from the land ice which re-freezes more easily than the ocean water below.

The British Antarctic Survey has found that the west coast of the Antarctic Peninsula has become one of the fastest-warming areas on the planet, with annual mean temperatures rising by around 3°C over the past 50 years. In 2009, a group of British geophysicists found that the retreat of the Pine Island Glacier in the Western Antarctic had quadrupled between 1995 and 2006. However, the temperatures recorded by the Amundsen-Scott station at the South Pole actually show a recent cooling, as do some studies of east Antarctica. It has been determined that these falling temperatures have been caused by the thinning of Antarctica's ozone layer that has in turn cooled the stratosphere above the continent. The historical use of chloro-fluorocarbons (CFCs) by humans has contributed to the destruction of Antarctica's ozone layer, as the clouds that form in the winter polar vortex – an area of very cold air above the continent – react with these CFCs to release chlorine which destroys ozone. Antarctic ozone levels are expected to recover by 2050 and this could result in warmer temperatures in the region.

## HISTORY AND DISCOVERY
The idea of Antarctica is much older than proof of the continent's existence. The notion of *Terra Australis*, a vast southern continent which counterbalanced the northern lands of Europe, Asia and North Africa, originated with Aristotle, and was depicted on a world map as early as 1531. The supposed land was gradually amended over the course of 16th-century exploration and further corrected after James Cook's circumnavigation of the globe in 1774. His journey from New Zealand to the Cape of Good Hope (via Tierra del Fuego), travelling at a high southern latitude (between 53° and 60°), confirmed that any land mass must be confined to the polar region.

The date of the first sighting of Antarctica is unclear. In 1820 three separate expeditions, from the UK, the USA and Russia, each claimed to have seen the continent within days of each other, and the argument has never been settled. The golden age of Antarctic exploration was prompted by the discovery of the magnetic North Pole in 1831, but it was not until the beginning of the 20th century that real progress was made. James Clark Ross was the first to identify the approximate location of the South Pole, but was unable to

reach it. British explorers Robert Scott in 1901–4 and Ernest Shackleton in 1907–9 got closer, but it was not until Norwegian adventurer Roald Amundsen pioneered a new route, through the Axel Heiberg Glacier, that the pole was reached in December 1911. Scott's second attempt was also successful, but he arrived a month later and perished with his team on the return journey.

## FLORA AND FAUNA
The only land animals to survive on the Antarctic continent are tiny invertebrates, including microscopic mites, lice, ticks, nematodes, rotifers and tardigrades. The largest land animal is the *Belgica antarctica*, a flightless midge just 2–6mm in size. The snow petrel, one of only three birds that breed exclusively in Antarctica, has been spotted at the South Pole. Large numbers of seals, penguins and other seabirds go ashore to breed in the summer; the emperor penguin is the only species that breeds ashore throughout the winter. Four species of albatross breed in South Georgia during the summer, but their numbers are in serious decline owing to the effects of longline fishing in the Southern Ocean region. Recent climate change has also affected the continent's wildlife, with the number of Adelie penguins falling significantly, as open-water species such as the chinstrap and gentoo penguins invade its Antarctic Peninsula habitat to take advantage of the warming temperatures.

By contrast, the Antarctic seas abound with life; recent expeditions identified over 700 previously unknown species. Krill, which congregates in large schools, is crucial to the ecosystem and provides a diet for migratory whales (including killer, humpback and blue whales), a number of species of seal, penguin, albatross and other, smaller birds. Each of these species is threatened by a substantial fall in recorded levels of krill since the 1970s, thought to be caused by warmer sea water and, paradoxically, the decimation of the blue whale through hunting in the first half of the 20th century: although whales eat krill, the iron in whale excrement is essential to the algae on which the krill feed. In 2010 a group of research bodies completed the Census of Antarctic Marine Life, an inventory of over 16,000 marine species compiled from 19 expeditions; scientists estimate that 39–58 per cent of the Antarctic's marine species are yet to be described.

With almost all of the Antarctic continent permanently covered in ice, only a small number of flowering plants, ferns and club mosses survive. Most of these are found on the sub-Antarctic islands, while only two species (a grass and a pearlwort) extend south of 60° S. Antarctic vegetation is dominated by lichens and mosses, with a few liverworts, algae and fungi surviving in the cracks and pore spaces of sandstone and granite rocks.

## ANTARCTIC LAW
The Antarctic Treaty was signed on 1 December 1959 when 12 states (Argentina, Australia, Belgium, Chile, France, Japan, New Zealand, Norway, South Africa, the Soviet Union, the UK and the USA) pledged to promote scientific and technical cooperation unhampered by politics. The signatories agreed to establish free use of the Antarctic continent for peaceful scientific purposes; freeze all territorial claims and disputes in the Antarctic; ban all military activities in the area; and prohibit nuclear explosions and the disposal of radioactive waste. The Antarctic Treaty was defined as covering areas south of latitude 60° S., excluding the high seas but including the ice shelves, and came into force in 1961. The treaty provides that any member of the UN can accede to it; it has since been signed by a further 39 states. In 1998 an extension to the treaty came into effect, placing a 50-year ban on mining, oil exploration and mineral extraction in Antarctica, and stipulating that all tourists, explorers and

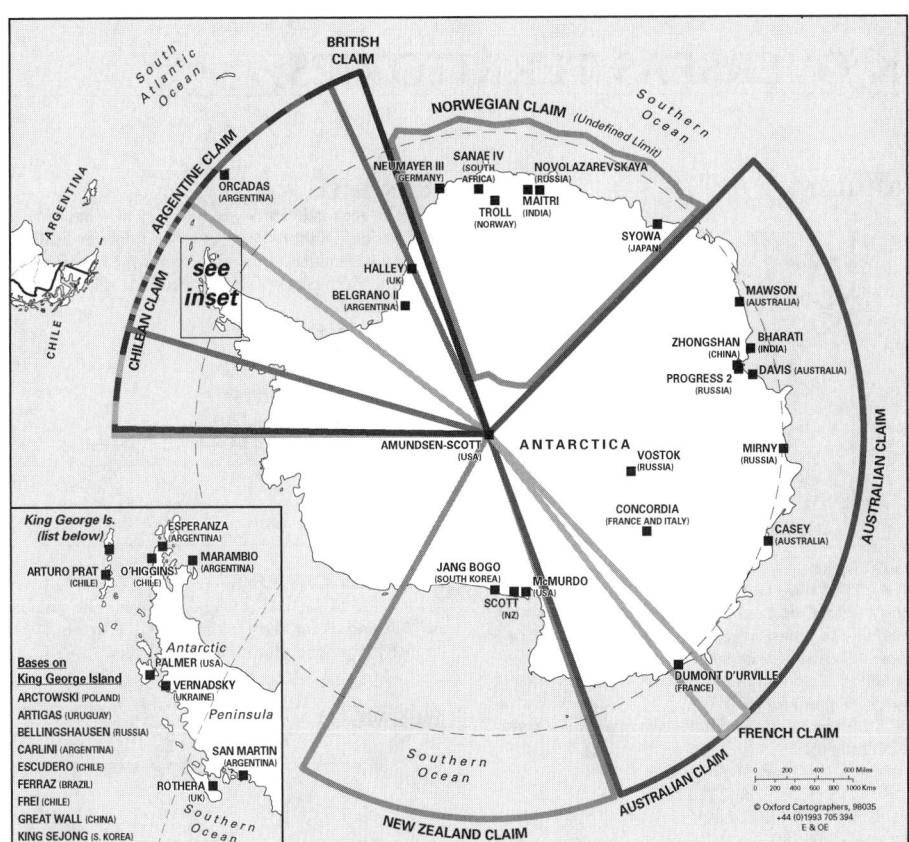

expeditions now require permission to enter the Antarctic from a relevant national authority. However, in recent years the region's coastal states have asserted often conflicting claims to oil- and gas-rich territory on the Antarctic seabed. Under the terms of the UN Convention on the Law of the Sea, each nation's sovereignty over its continental shelf extends up to 350 nautical miles beyond its territorial coasts; the UN Commission on the Limits of the Continental Shelf is examining evidence submitted in support of these claims.

## SCIENTIFIC RESEARCH

There are 20 nations with permanently manned research stations in Antarctica:

| Country | Number of research stations |
| --- | --- |
| Argentina | 6 |
| Russian Federation | 5 |
| Chile | 4 |
| Australia | 3 |
| USA | 3 |
| China | 2 |
| France | 2 |
| India | 2 |
| South Korea | 2 |
| UK | 2 |

Brazil, Germany, Italy (shared with France), Japan, New Zealand, Norway, Poland, South Africa, Ukraine and Uruguay each have a single station.

## POPULATION AND TOURISM

Antarctica has no indigenous inhabitants, although the continent maintains a population of tourists, scientists and research workers which peaks in the summer months at over 4,400.

Antarctic tourism is a growth industry. The first *Lonely Planet* guide to Antarctica was published in 1996, and ship-borne cruises typically depart from Argentina, Chile and the Falkland Islands. The continent has also become a popular venue for extreme sports enthusiasts: it is now possible to sky-dive, ski, ride a motorbike and fly a helicopter across the continent, and the Vinson Massif and other peaks have become desirable destinations for mountaineers. The huts built by Scott and Shackleton are also popular attractions. In 1991 the International Association of Antarctica Tour Operators (IAATO) was founded with the objective of providing a self-regulating code of conduct for all operators to follow, but membership is voluntary, and fears remain regarding tourism-related environmental damage. IAATO recorded 6,704 tourists in the 1992–3 summer season, rising to more than 46,000 in 2007–8 and dipping to 37,405 in 2013–14.

## THE BRITISH ANTARCTIC SURVEY

The British Antarctic Survey (BAS) is part of the Natural Environment Research Council and carries out the majority of Britain's scientific research in Antarctica. Over 400 staff are employed by BAS and the organisation supports five research stations, four of which are staffed throughout the winter months (two in South Georgia and two in Antarctica). *See* the BAS website (W www.antarctica.ac.uk) for further information.

# UK OVERSEAS TERRITORIES

## ANGUILLA

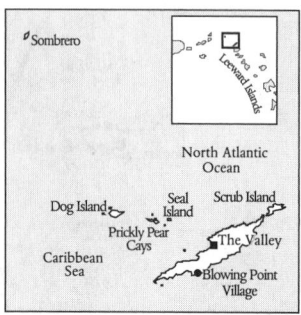

Sombrero
Leeward Islands
North Atlantic Ocean
Dog Island
Seal Island
Scrub Island
Prickly Pear Cays
The Valley
Caribbean Sea
Blowing Point Village

*Area* – 91 sq. km
*Capital* – The Valley; population, 1,000 (2014 est)
*Currency* – East Caribbean dollar (EC$) of 100 cents
*Population* – 16,086 rising at 2.06 per cent a year (2014 est)
*Religion* – Christian (Protestant 83.3 per cent, Roman Catholic 5.7 per cent) (est)
*Language* – English (official)
*Flag* – British blue ensign with the coat of arms and three dolphins in the fly
*National day* – 30 May (Anguilla Day)
*Life expectancy (years)* – 81.2 (2014 est)
*Mortality rate* – 4.54 (2014 est)
*Birth rate* – 12.68 (2014 est)
*Infant mortality rate* – 3.40 (2014 est)

### CLIMATE AND TERRAIN
Anguilla is a flat coralline island in the eastern Caribbean and one of the most northerly of the Leeward Islands. Elevation extremes range from 65m (Crocus Hill) to 0m (Caribbean Sea). The climate is tropical, modified by north-east trade winds, with temperatures ranging from 24.7°C in January to 27.4°C in August.

### HISTORY AND POLITICS
Anguilla has been a British colony since 1650. For much of its history it was linked administratively with St Kitts, but three months after the Associated State of Saint Christopher (St Kitts)-Nevis-Anguilla came into being in 1967, the Anguillans repudiated government from St Kitts. Final separation from St Kitts and Nevis was effected in December 1980 and Anguilla reverted to a British dependency.

The 1982 constitution (amended in 1990) provides for a governor, an executive council comprising four of the elected assembly members and two *ex-officio* members (the attorney-general and deputy governor), and a 12-member House of Assembly, consisting of a speaker, seven elected members, two nominated members and two *ex-officio* members (the attorney-general and deputy governor). The 2015 general election was won by the Anguilla United Front with six seats.

*Governor,* Christina Scott, *apptd* 2013
*Chief Minister,* Hon. Vicctor Banks

## ECONOMY
The main economic activity is tourism, which has stimulated construction. Offshore financial services, lobster fishing and expatriates' remittances are also important. Export earnings are mainly from sales of fish, lobsters, livestock, salt, concrete blocks and rum.
*Imports* – US$145m (2013)
*Exports* – US$4m (2013)

BALANCE OF PAYMENTS
*Trade* – US$141m deficit (2013)
*Current Account* – US$102.4m deficit (2011 est)

| Trade with UK | 2013 | 2014 |
| --- | --- | --- |
| Imports from UK | £1,602,879 | £5,124,105 |
| Exports to UK | £81,862 | £102,404 |

## COMMUNICATIONS
Some 82km of the road network are paved. The main ports are Blowing Point ferry terminal and Clayton J. Lloyd (formerly Wallblake) airport, near The Valley.

## BERMUDA

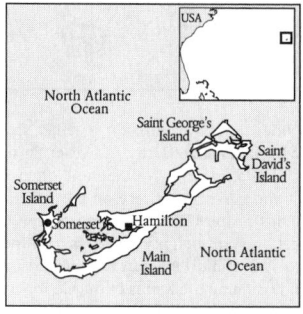

USA
North Atlantic Ocean
Saint George's Island
Saint David's Island
Somerset Island
Somerset
Hamilton
Main Island
North Atlantic Ocean

*Area* – 54 sq. km
*Capital* – Hamilton, on Main Island; population, 10,000 (2014 est)
*Currency* – Bermudian dollar (BD$) of 100 cents
*Population* – 69,839 rising at 0.52 per cent a year (2014 est)
*Religion* – Christian (Protestant 46.1 per cent, Roman Catholic 14.5 per cent) (est)
*Language* – English (official), Portuguese
*Population density* – 1,300 per sq. km (2013 est)
*Flag* – British red ensign with the coat of arms in the fly
*National day* – 24 May (Bermuda Day)
*Life expectancy (years)* – 81.04 (2014 est)
*Mortality rate* – 8.06 (2014 est)
*Birth rate* – 11.35 (2014 est)
*Infant mortality rate* – 2.48 (2014 est)
*GNI* – US$6,778m; US$104,610 per capita (2012)

### CLIMATE AND TERRAIN
Bermuda is a group of over 130 small islands, of which about 20 are inhabited, in the North Atlantic Ocean. All the islands are volcanic in origin, with hilly interiors, surrounded by coral reefs. Elevation extremes range from 76m (Town Hill)

to 0m (Atlantic Ocean). The climate is subtropical, regulated by the Gulf Stream, with average temperatures ranging from 16.7°C in February to 26.3°C in August.

## HISTORY AND POLITICS
Bermuda was discovered by the Spanish in 1503 but colonised by the British from the early 17th century, becoming a colony in 1684. Independence from the UK was rejected in a 1995 referendum.

Internal self-government was introduced in 1968. The governor is responsible for external affairs, defence, internal security and the police, although administrative matters for the police service have been delegated to the minister of labour, home affairs and public safety. The cabinet comprises the premier and six elected assembly members. The legislature consists of the senate of 11 appointed members and the House of Assembly with 36 members elected for a five-year term. At the 2012 election, opposition party One Bermuda Alliance won 19 of the 36 available seats, ousting the ruling Progressive Labour Party for the first time in 14 years. Michael Dunkley replaced Craig Cannonier as Alliance party leader and premier in May 2014.

*Governor,* HE George Fergusson, *apptd* 2012
*Premier,* Hon. Michael Dunkley

## ECONOMY
The economy is based on offshore financial services for international business (especially re-insurance), and tourism. Other activities include light manufacturing (re-exports of pharmaceuticals are the main export) and construction.

| Trade with UK | 2013 | 2014 |
| --- | --- | --- |
| Imports from UK | £69,067,907 | £47,074,879 |
| Exports to UK | £15,957,716 | £4,938,099 |

## COMMUNICATIONS
The main islands are connected by a series of bridges and causeways. There are 447km of roads, all of which are paved but only around half of which are public, and one airport, near Ferry Reach on St David's Island. The main ports are at Hamilton, Freeport and St George. The telephone system is extensive, and mobile telephone distribution is widespread.

# BRITISH ANTARCTIC TERRITORY

*See also* The North and South Poles

*Area* – 1,709,400 sq. km. This area is overlapped by territorial claims from Chile and Argentina. However, no claims are recognised internationally under the Antarctic Treaty of 1961
*Population* – There is no indigenous population. The British Antarctic Survey maintains two permanently staffed research stations, at Halley and Rothera; one part-time (summer-only) station at Signy (South Orkney Islands); and two summer-only logistics facilities, at Fossil Bluff (Alexander Island) and Sky Blu (Eastern Ellsworth Land). Several other countries maintain research stations in the territory
*Flag* – British white ensign, without the cross of St George, with the territory's coat of arms in the fly

## CLIMATE AND TERRAIN
The British Antarctic Territory (BAT) consists of the areas south of 60°S. latitude, between longitudes 20°W. and 80°W. The territory includes the South Orkney Islands, the South Shetland Islands, the mountainous Antarctic Peninsula and all adjacent islands, and the land mass extending to the South Pole. The highest point of the territory is 3,184m (Mt Jackson).

Only around 0.7 per cent of the territory remains ice-free, and the permanent ice-sheet that covers the remainder is, in places, nearly 5km thick. The climate is polar desert with very little precipitation, and the annual average temperature at the South Pole is −48°C.

## HISTORY AND POLITICS
Britain made its first territorial claim to part of the Antarctic in 1908. Since 1943, a permanent presence has been maintained, which became the British Antarctic Survey (BAS) in 1962. In the same year, the territory, originally a Dependency of the Falkland Islands, became a UK overseas territory in its own right, although it continued to be administered from the Falkland Islands until 1989 when the role of Commissioner of the British Antarctic Territory was created.

The BAT is administered by the Foreign and Commonwealth Office, and has a full suite of laws, legal and postal administrations. All activities are governed by the Antarctic Treaty of 1961, which has the objectives of keeping Antarctica demilitarised and promoting international scientific cooperation. The territory is self-financing from income-tax revenue and the sale of postage stamps and coins.

GOVERNMENT OF THE BRITISH ANTARCTIC TERRITORY
Polar Regions Department, Overseas Territories Directorate, Room 2/135, Old Admiralty Building, London SW1A 2AH
**T** 020-7008 1639 **E** polarregions@fco.gov.uk
*Commissioner (non-resident),* Dr Peter Hayes, *apptd* 2012
*Administrator,* Henry Burgess

# BRITISH INDIAN OCEAN TERRITORY

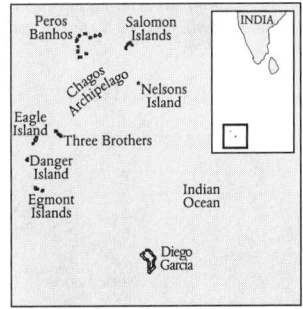

*Area* – 54,400 sq. km, of which 60 sq. km is land
*Currency* – US dollar (US$) of 100 cents
*Population* – No indigenous population now lives in the archipelago; around 4,000 military personnel and civilian contract employees (2004 est) are based at the joint UK–US naval support facility on Diego Garcia
*Flag* – Divided horizontally into blue and white wavy stripes, with the Union Flag in the canton and a crowned palm tree over all in the fly

## CLIMATE AND TERRAIN
The British Indian Ocean Territory (BIOT) comprises the Chagos Archipelago of 55 islands in six main groups,

situated on the Great Chagos Bank in the Indian Ocean. The largest and most southerly of the islands is Diego Garcia, a sand cay with an area of about 44 sq. km. The main island groups are Peros Banhos (29 islands with a total land area of 6.5 sq. km) and Salomon (11 islands with a total land area of 3.2 sq. km).

The flat and low terrain rarely rises more than 2m above sea-level, being only 15m at its highest point. The climate is hot and humid, although moderated by trade winds.

## HISTORY AND POLITICS

The Chagos Archipelago, originally colonised by the French, was one of the dependencies of Mauritius ceded to Britain in 1814 and was administered from Mauritius until 1965, when the BIOT was established. The islands of Farquhar, Desroches and Aldabra became part of the Seychelles when it became independent in 1976. Since the 1980s, successive Mauritian governments have claimed sovereignty over the remaining Chagos islands, arguing that they were annexed illegally.

Diego Garcia is used as a joint naval support facility by Britain and the USA. The islands' former inhabitants were forcibly relocated between 1967 and 1973 to allow for the construction of the naval base, most being resettled in Mauritius and the Seychelles. Since the 1990s they have taken legal action to obtain the right to return to and settle in the islands. In 2006, the Chagossians won a High Court case allowing them to return to the archipelago, but not to Diego Garcia. The House of Lords overturned this ruling on appeal in 2008; a case before the European Court of Human Rights was ruled inadmissable in December 2012 as the islanders had previously accepted financial compensation. The British government unilaterally, and controversially, declared the Chagos Archipelago a marine-protected area (MPA) in April 2010, a decision that was upheld by the High Court in 2013. In March 2015, a UN tribunal declared the creation of the MPA illegal and ordered the UK and Mauritius governments to renegotiate sovereignty of the area. In April, the UK government announced that it would defer any new judgements regarding the return of the Chagos islanders until after the 2015 general election.

*Commissioner (non-resident)*, Dr Peter Hayes, *apptd* 2012
*Administrator (non-resident)*, John McManus, *apptd* 2011

# BRITISH VIRGIN ISLANDS

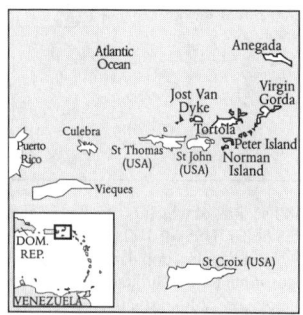

*Area* – 151 sq. km
*Capital* – Road Town, on Tortola; population, 13,000 (2011 est)
*Currency* – US dollar (US$) of 100 cents
*Population* – 32,680 rising at 2.36 per cent a year (2014 est)
*Religion* – Christian (Protestant 72.2 per cent, Roman Catholic 9.5 per cent) (est)

*Language* – English (official)
*Population density* – 156 per sq. km (2011)
*Flag* – British blue ensign with the coat of arms in the fly
*National day* – 1 July (Territory Day)
*Life expectancy (years)* – 78.29 (2014 est)
*Mortality rate* – 4.93 (2014 est)
*Birth rate* – 10.83 (2014 est)
*Infant mortality rate* – 13.45 (2014 est)

## CLIMATE AND TERRAIN

The easternmost part of the Virgin Islands archipelago in the Caribbean Sea, the British Virgin Islands comprise Tortola, Anegada, Virgin Gorda, Jost Van Dyke and about 40 islets and cays; 16 of the islands are inhabited. Apart from Anegada, which is flat, the British Virgin Islands are hilly with coral reefs offshore. The highest point of elevation is 521m (Mt Sage, on Tortola). The climate is subtropical, with little variation in average temperatures, which typically range between 23.4°C in January and February and 26.4°C in August and September. The hurricane season is from June to November.

## HISTORY AND POLITICS

Initially settled by Arawak Indians, the islands were named by Christopher Columbus in 1493 and colonised by the Dutch in the early 17th century. Annexed by the British in 1672, the islands were part of the Leeward Islands colony from 1872 to 1960. After a period of direct rule, a measure of self-government was introduced by the 1977 constitution and extended in 2000.

Under the 2007 constitution, the governor, appointed by the crown, retains responsibility for defence, security, external affairs and the civil service. The executive council comprises the premier, four other elected assembly members and the attorney-general. The House of Assembly consists of a speaker, one *ex-officio* member (the attorney-general) and 13 members elected for a four-year term.

The 2011 election was won by the National Democratic Party. Fresh elections are scheduled for November 2015.
*Governor*, HE John Duncan, OBE, *apptd* 2014
*Premier*, Hon. Orlando Smith, OBE

## ECONOMY

The main industries are tourism, which generates about 45 per cent of GDP, and offshore financial services. Other industries include construction and light manufacturing. The major exports are rum, fresh fish, fruit, livestock, gravel and sand. Chief imports are building materials, cars, foodstuffs and machinery.

| Trade with UK | 2013 | 2014 |
| --- | --- | --- |
| Imports from UK | £59,697,254 | £20,406,628 |
| Exports to UK | £47,438,592 | £19,793,893 |

## COMMUNICATIONS

The principal airport is on Beef Island, linked by bridge to Tortola, and there are also airfields on Anegada and Virgin Gorda. Road Harbour, at Road Town, is the main port, and ferry services connect the main islands. Much of the 200km of road is steep and narrow.

# CAYMAN ISLANDS

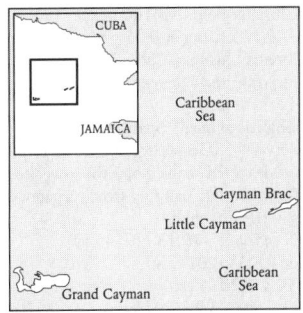

*Area* – 264 sq. km
*Capital* – George Town, on Grand Cayman; population, 31,000 (2014 est)
*Currency* – Caymanian dollar (CI$) of 100 cents
*Population* – 54,914 (2013 est) rising at 2.14 per cent a year (2014 est)
*Religion* – Christian (Protestant 67.8 per cent, Roman Catholic 14.1 per cent) (est)
*Language* – English (official), Spanish
*Population density* – 243.4 per sq. km (2013 est)
*Flag* – British blue ensign with the coat of arms in the fly
*National day* – First Monday in July (Constitution Day)
*Life expectancy (years)* – 81.02 (2014 est)
*Mortality rate* – 5.41 (2014 est)
*Birth rate* – 12.13 (2014 est)
*Infant mortality rate* – 6.21 (2014 est)
*Annual average growth of GDP* – 1.7 per cent (2014)

## CLIMATE AND TERRAIN

The Cayman Islands comprise Grand Cayman, Cayman Brac and Little Cayman. Situated around 240km south of Cuba, the low-lying islands are divided from Jamaica, 268km to the south-east, by the Cayman Trench, the deepest part of the Caribbean Sea. The average temperature is 27°C. Hurricane season is from July to November.

## HISTORY AND POLITICS

The territory derives its name from the Carib word *caymanas* (crocodile). The islands were ceded to Britain by Spain in 1670, and permanent settlement began in the 1730s. A dependency of Jamaica from 1863, the islands came under direct rule after 1962, and a measure of self-government was granted in 1972.

The 1972 constitution (revised in 1994 and 2009) provides for a governor, a legislative assembly and a cabinet. The governor is responsible for the police, civil service, internal security, defence, external affairs, and chairs the cabinet. The cabinet comprises two appointed official members (the deputy governor and attorney-general) and five of the assembly's elected members. The Legislative Assembly has 15 members elected for a four-year term and the two appointed official members of the cabinet, as well as a speaker.
*Governor,* HE Helen Kilpatrick, CB, *apptd* 2013
*Prime Minister,* Hon. Alden McLaughlin, MBE

CAYMAN ISLANDS GOVERNMENT OFFICE
6 Arlington Street, London SW1A 1RE
T 020-7491 7772 W www.gov.ky

## ECONOMY

The mainstays of the economy are offshore financial services (largely owing to the absence of direct taxation) and tourism. Government revenue is derived from fees and duties.

*Imports* – US$929m (2013)
*Exports* – US$30m (2013)

BALANCE OF PAYMENTS
*Trade* – US$899m deficit (2013)

| Trade with UK | 2013 | 2014 |
| --- | --- | --- |
| Imports from UK | £30,560,253 | £51,395,670 |
| Exports to UK | £103,567,552 | £87,810,033 |

## COMMUNICATIONS

The islands are served by airports at George Town and on Cayman Brac and by an airfield on Little Cayman. George Town is the main port. There are 785km of surfaced roads.

# FALKLAND ISLANDS

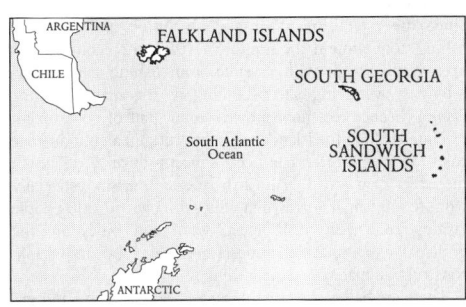

*Area* – 12,173 sq. km
*Capital* – Stanley, on East Falkland; population, 2,000 (2014 est)
*Currency* – Falkland Island pound (FK£) of 100 pence
*Population* – 2,840 (2012 est) static at 0 per cent a year (2009 est)
*Religion* – Christian 66 per cent, other 2 per cent (est)
*Language* – English
*Flag* – British blue ensign with coat of arms centred in the fly
*National day* – 14 June (Liberation Day)

## CLIMATE AND TERRAIN

The Falkland Islands consist of East Falkland (6,759 sq. km), West Falkland (5,413 sq. km) and around 700 small islands. Elevation extremes range from 705m (Mt Usbourne) to 0m (Atlantic Ocean). Average temperatures range from 1.3°C in July to 8°C in January, and annual rainfall is low (around 543.3mm per year).

## HISTORY AND POLITICS

The Falkland Islands have a long history of occupation by European countries, including France, Spain and the UK, which claimed sovereignty in 1765 and established its first settlement in 1766.

In 1820 the Falklands were claimed for the newly independent Argentina and a settlement was founded in 1826, but this was destroyed by the USA in 1831. In 1833 occupation was resumed by the British, and the islands were permanently colonised. Argentina continued to claim sovereignty over the islands (known to them as *las Islas Malvinas*), and invaded the islands on 2 April 1982. A British naval and military task force recaptured the islands on 14 June 1982. A small naval and military garrison remains in the islands. Argentina has reasserted its claims of sovereignty since 2007, and political tensions with the UK remain high. In a referendum in March 2013, the islanders voted overwhelmingly to remain a UK overseas territory; on a turnout of more than 90 per cent, 1,513 votes were cast in favour, with three against.

Under the 2009 constitution, the governor chairs an executive council consisting of three of the elected members of the legislative assembly and two *ex-officio* members, the chief executive and the financial secretary. The legislative assembly consists of eight members elected for a four-year term, the same two *ex-officio* members and a speaker. The last election was held in 2013. There are no political parties and all members sit as independents.

*Governor,* HE Colin Roberts, CVO, *apptd* 2014
*Chief Executive,* Keith Padgett, *apptd* 2012

**FALKLAND ISLANDS GOVERNMENT OFFICE**
Falkland House, 14 Broadway, London SW1H 0BH
**T** 020-7222 2542 **W** www.falklands.gov.fk

## ECONOMY

Since the establishment of a conservation and managed fishing zone around the islands in 1987, the economy has been transformed, with revenue from fishing and related activities overtaking sheep-farming as the main industry. Fishing licence fees now provide about half of government revenue, making the islands self-supporting in all but defence costs, although there has been concern since 2005 about the effect of overfishing on fish stocks. Tourism, especially wildlife tourism, has grown rapidly, with over 57,000 people visiting each year. Fish, meat, wool and hides are the principal exports. Chief imports are fuel, food and drink, construction materials and clothing.

There are believed to be substantial reserves of oil and gas offshore and the Falkland Islands government has licensed exploration for exploitable sites; a British exploration firm announced plans to commence oil production in 2018.

| Trade with UK | 2013 | 2014 |
| --- | --- | --- |
| Imports from UK | £52,063,585 | £71,054,767 |
| Exports to UK | £24,219,240 | £3,950,879 |

## COMMUNICATIONS

There is an international airport at Mt Pleasant, served by military flights to the UK and by commercial flights to Chile. The main port is Stanley Harbour and a regular shipping service operates to the UK. The road network is gradually expanding but only roads in and around Stanley are paved, and most longer internal journeys are by light aircraft. International telecommunications are possible through a satellite link, and the majority of households have internet access.

# GIBRALTAR

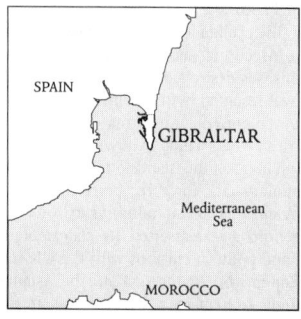

*Area* – 6.5 sq. km
*Capital* – Gibraltar
*Currency* – Gibraltar pound of 100 pence
*Population* – 29,185 rising at 0.25 per cent a year (2014 est)
*Religion* – Christian (Roman Catholic 78 per cent, other 10 per cent), Muslim 4 per cent, Jewish 2 per cent, Hindu 2 per cent (est)
*Language* – English (official), Spanish, Italian, Portuguese
*Population density* – 5,036 per sq. km (2013 est)
*Flag* – White with a red stripe along the lower edge; over all a red castle with a key hanging from its gateway
*National day* – 10 September
*Life expectancy (years)* – 79.13 (2014 est)
*Mortality rate* – 8.33 (2014 est)
*Birth rate* – 14.15 (2014 est)
*Infant mortality rate* – 6.29 (2014 est)

## CLIMATE AND TERRAIN

Gibraltar is a rocky promontory, 426m at its highest point, that juts southwards from the south-east coast of Spain, with which it is connected by a low isthmus. It is about 32km from the coast of Africa, across the Strait of Gibraltar.

## HISTORY AND POLITICS

Gibraltar was captured in 1704, during the War of the Spanish Succession, by a combined Dutch and English force, and was ceded to Britain in the Treaty of Utrecht (1713).

Spanish claims to the territory were a source of tension for many years, but after the overwhelming rejection of a joint sovereignty arrangement in a referendum in 2002, Spain moderated its attitude and the previously bilateral Anglo-Spanish talks about the territory became tripartite with the inclusion of Gibraltar from 2006.

Gibraltar is part of the EU (with the UK government responsible for enforcing EU directives affecting Gibraltar), but is not a full member and is exempt from the common policies on customs, commerce, agriculture, fisheries and VAT. Gibraltarians have voted in EU elections since 2004.

The 1969 constitution made provision for self-government in respect of certain domestic matters, but full internal autonomy came into effect with the 2006 constitution. This limited the governor's responsibilities to external affairs, defence, internal security and public service. The House of Assembly was restyled the Gibraltar Parliament, and may determine its own size; at present, it consists of an appointed speaker and 17 members elected for a four-year term. The government is formed by the chief minister (who is the leader of the majority party) and ministers from among the elected members of parliament.

The 2011 elections were won by the Gibraltar Social Democrats; the next general election is due to take place after October 2015.

*Governor,* HE Lt.-Gen. Sir James Benjamin Dutton, KCB, CBE, *apptd* 2013
*Chief Minister,* Hon. Fabian Picardo

**GOVERNMENT OF GIBRALTAR**
150 Strand, London WC2R 1JA
**T** 020-7836 0777 **W** www.gibraltar.gov.uk

## ECONOMY

The economy is dominated by tourism (especially retail for day visitors), offshore financial services and shipping, and these three sectors account for about 85 per cent of GDP. Diversification efforts have encouraged telecommunications in particular and Gibraltar has become a centre for internet businesses, especially online gambling. A shift from a predominantly public-sector to a private-sector economy has occurred in recent years, although government spending still

has a significant impact on the local economy. The chief sources of government revenue are port dues, the rent of the Crown Estate in the town VAT and duties on consumer items (although value added tax is not applied in the territory).
*Imports* – US$748m (2013)
*Exports* – US$279m (2013)

BALANCE OF PAYMENTS
*Trade* – US$469m deficit (2013)

| Trade with UK | 2013 | 2014 |
| --- | --- | --- |
| Imports from UK | £516,141,660 | £497,231,756 |
| Exports to UK | £6,207,655 | £283,327,649 |

## COMMUNICATIONS
Gibraltar has one international airport. The 29km road network is all surfaced; road links to Spain reopened in the 1980s. The port services the large shipping industry, cruise liners and a regular ferry service to Tangiers (Morocco).

# MONTSERRAT

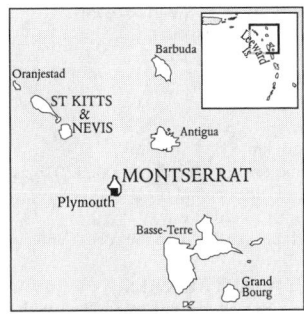

*Area* – 102 sq. km
*Capital* – Plymouth (abandoned 1997); the seat of government is now at Brades, in the north, population, 449 (2011 est); a new capital is under construction at nearby Little Bay
*Currency* – East Caribbean dollar (EC$) of 100 cents
*Population* – 5,215 rising at 0.48 per cent a year (2014 est)
*Religion* – Christian (Protestant 67 per cent, Roman Catholic 12 per cent)
*Language* – English (official)
*Population density* – 55 per sq. km (2005 est)
*Flag* – British blue ensign with the coat of arms in the fly
*National day* – Second Saturday in June (birthday of Queen Elizabeth II)
*Life expectancy (years)* – 73.9 (2014 est)
*Mortality rate* – 6.52 (2014 est)
*Birth rate* – 11.31 (2014 est)
*Infant mortality rate* – 13.66 (2014 est)

## CLIMATE AND TERRAIN
Montserrat is a mountainous volcanic island in the Leeward group in the Caribbean Sea. Its lowest point of elevation is 0m (Caribbean Sea); its highest point was 914m (Chances Peak), although a lava dome in a crater in the Soufrière Hills volcano is estimated to be over 930m. Volcanic activity since 1995 has left over half of the island devastated by lava flows and ash. The climate is tropical and the average temperature is 25.9°C.

## HISTORY AND POLITICS
Discovered by Columbus in 1493, Montserrat became a British colony in 1632. It was fought over by the French and

British throughout the 17th and 18th centuries, before being finally restored to Britain in 1783.

Continual volcanic activity by the Soufrière Hills volcano between 1995 and 2014 has left over half of the island uninhabitable, and prompted the migration of two-thirds of the population in the late 1990s. A 'special vulnerable area', to which access is restricted, covers two-thirds of the island and two maritime exclusion zones extend between 2km and 4km offshore.

The 1990 constitution was amended in 1999 after more than half of the constituencies were made uninhabitable by volcanic activity. Following modernisation talks, a new constitution came into force in September 2011, which established a new National Advisory Council to enhance democracy and governance. Under the new constitution, the cabinet is chaired by the governor and comprises the premier and three other elected members and two *ex-officio* members (the attorney-general and the financial secretary). The legislative assembly consists of nine members elected for a five-year term and two *ex-officio* members. In the 2014 general election the People's Democratic Movement won the most seats.
*Governor,* HE Adrian Davis, *apptd* 2011
*Prime Minister,* Hon. Reuben Meade

GOVERNMENT OF MONTSERRAT
180–186 Kings Cross Road, London WC1X 9DE T 020-7520 2622

## ECONOMY
Continuing volcanic activity has restricted economic activity to the northern third of the island and considerably impacted the agricultural sector. Activity includes mining and quarrying, construction (mostly public sector), financial and professional services, and tourism. In January 2013 the EU granted a £33.4m aid package to bolster recovery. Communications improved with the opening of Gerald's Airport in the north in 2005, allowing regular commercial air services to resume. There are port facilities at Little Bay, and a ferry service to and from Antigua was reintroduced in December 2009.
*Imports* – US$40m (2013)
*Exports* – US$2m (2013)

BALANCE OF PAYMENTS
*Trade* – US$38m deficit (2013)

| Trade with UK | 2013 | 2014 |
| --- | --- | --- |
| Imports from UK | £7,072,672 | £4,683,489 |
| Exports to UK | £103,258 | £47,107 |

# PITCAIRN ISLANDS

*Pitcairn, Henderson, Ducie and Oeno Islands*

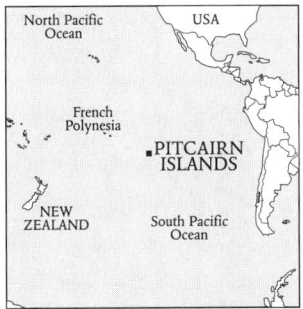

*Area* – 47 sq. km
*Capital* – Adamstown, on Pitcairn Island
*Currency* – New Zealand dollar (NZ$) of 100 cents
*Population* – 48 (2014 est)
*Religion* – Christian (Seventh-day Adventist)
*Language* – English, Pitkern (both official)
*Flag* – British blue ensign with the coat of arms in the fly
*National day* – 23 January (Bounty Day)

## CLIMATE AND TERRAIN

Pitcairn is the chief of a group of rugged islands situated in the South Pacific Ocean. The other main islands of the group are Henderson, lying 168km north-east of Pitcairn; Oeno, lying 120km north-west; and Ducie, lying 470km east. These are uninhabited. Henderson Island is a UNESCO World Heritage Site. The climate is tropical with an average temperature of 20.8°C.

## HISTORY AND POLITICS

Pitcairn was settled in 1790 by mutineers from the *Bounty* and their Tahitian companions. It became a British settlement under the British Settlements Act 1887.

Under the 2010 constitutional arrangements, the islands are administered by the governor (usually the British High Commissioner to New Zealand), in consultation with the island council, which manages internal affairs. The commissioner liaises between the governor and the council. The island council comprises ten members: the governor; two members appointed by the governor; one member appointed by the council itself; and six, including the mayor, who are elected. The mayor is elected every three years; elections for other council members are held every year in December.
*Governor (non-resident)*, HE Jonathan Sinclair, LVO *apptd* 2014 *(British High Commissioner to New Zealand)*
*Mayor*, Shawn Christian

## ECONOMY

The islanders live by subsistence fishing and horticulture, and the sale of honey and handicrafts, although tourism is being promoted. Apart from small fees charged for licences there are no taxes and government revenue is derived almost solely from the sale of postage stamps and .pn internet domain names, and income from investments. Since financial reserves became exhausted a few years ago the islands have received budgetary aid from the UK.

| Trade with UK | 2013 | 2014 |
| --- | --- | --- |
| Imports from UK | £351,598 | £10,103 |
| Exports to UK | £98,654 | £159,883 |

## COMMUNICATIONS

There is no airfield and the only means of access is by sea; cruise and container ships stop irregularly but a regular shipping supply route to French Polynesia was established in 2006. There are 6.4km of dirt roads on the islands. A telephone system and internet access have been introduced in recent years.

# ST HELENA, ASCENSION AND TRISTAN DA CUNHA

*Population* – 7,776 rising at 0.27 per cent (2014 est)
*Religion* – Christian (predominantly Protestant)
*Language* – English (official)
*National day* – Second Saturday in June (birthday of Queen Elizabeth II)
*Life expectancy (years)* – 79.21 (2014 est)
*Mortality rate* – 7.33 (2014 est)
*Birth rate* – 10.03 (2014 est)
*Infant mortality rate* – 14.71 (2014 est)

*ST HELENA*
*Area* – 122 sq. km
*Capital* – Jamestown; population, 1,000 (2014 est)
*Currency* – St Helena pound (£) of 100 pence
*Population* – 4,158 (2013 est)
*Flag* – British blue ensign with the coat of arms in the fly

## CLIMATE AND TERRAIN

St Helena is a rugged and volcanic island, with sheer cliffs rising to a central plateau. Mt Actaeon, at 818m, is the highest elevation. The climate is tropical but mild, tempered by trade winds, and the average temperature is 18.1°C.

## HISTORY AND POLITICS

St Helena is believed to have been discovered by the Portuguese navigator Joao da Nova in 1502. It was used as a port of call for vessels of all nations trading to the East until the late 19th century. From 1815 to 1821 the island was lent to the British government as a place of exile for Napoléon Bonaparte, who died there on 5 May 1821, and in 1834 it was annexed to the British crown. The Zulu chief Dinizulu was exiled to the island in 1890, and up to 6,000 Boer prisoners were held there between 1900 and 1903.

Under the 2009 constitution, government is administered by a governor, advised by an executive council comprising three *ex-officio* members (the chief secretary, financial secretary and attorney-general) and five elected members of the legislative council. The legislative council consists of 12 members elected for a four-year term, the three *ex-officio* members of the executive council and a speaker.
*Governor*, HE Mark Capes, *apptd* 2011

GOVERNMENT OF ST HELENA
16 Old Queen Street, London SW1H 9HP T 020-3170 8705

## ECONOMY AND TRADE

The island has few natural resources and its economy is dependent on an annual grant from the UK. The main economic activities are agriculture, the sale of fishing licences, fish processing and tourism. The only significant exports are coffee and frozen, canned and dried fish.

| Trade with UK | 2013 | 2014 |
|---|---|---|
| Imports from UK | £15,488,515 | £12,449,579 |
| Exports to UK | £74,446 | £319,309 |

## COMMUNICATIONS

Access is solely by sea to Jamestown port, provided by a regular supply ship. A long-promised international airport is scheduled for completion in 2016. Only 38km of the island's roads are paved. There are two local radio stations and two weekly newspapers.

## ASCENSION ISLAND

*Area* – 88 sq. km
*Capital* – Georgetown
*Currency* – St Helena pound (£) of 100 pence
*Population* – 880 (2011 est)

## CLIMATE AND TERRAIN

The island is a rocky volcanic peak that lies in the South Atlantic Ocean some 1,200km north-west of St Helena. The highest point (Green Mountain, 859m) is covered with lush vegetation. It is an important breeding place for the green turtle and a number of seabird species.

## HISTORY AND POLITICS

Ascension is said to have been discovered by Joao da Nova in 1501 and two years later it was visited on Ascension Day by Alphonse d'Albuquerque, who gave the island its present name. As HMS *Ascension* it remained under the supervision of the Board of Admiralty until 1922, when it was made a dependency of St Helena. The island was an important logistical centre in both world wars and during the Falklands conflict, and it has a continuing role as a military air base and in broadcasting, telecommunications and satellite tracking.

In 2002 new constitutional arrangements introduced a measure of self-government, and in 2009 Ascension ceased to be a dependency of St Helena. The governor, who is resident in St Helena, retains responsibility for defence, external affairs, internal security and public services. The governor, represented locally by the island administrator, chairs the island council, which consists of five elected members and two *ex-officio* members (the director of resources and the attorney-general).
*Administrator,* Marc Holland, *apptd* 2013

## ECONOMY

Before 2002 the island was administered and financed by commercial operators, including the BBC and Cable and Wireless, and the military. With the change in governance in 2002, a fiscal regime was introduced to finance public services through taxation. A private sector is developing following the sale of government-owned concerns to commercial operators and the establishment of a sports fishing industry.

## COMMUNICATIONS

Georgetown is the only port and there are regular scheduled shipping services, as well as regular air links to the UK and the USA by military aircraft and occasional charter flights. Ascension has 40km of roads. Telecommunication services are provided via satellite links. There is a local radio station and a weekly newspaper.

## TRISTAN DA CUNHA

*Area* – 98 sq. km
*Capital* – Edinburgh of the Seven Seas; population, 268 (2015 est)

*Currency* – Pound sterling (£) of 100 pence
*Population* – 263 (2014 est)
*Flag* – British blue ensign with the coat of arms in the fly

## CLIMATE AND TERRAIN

Tristan da Cunha is the chief of a group of islands in the South Atlantic Ocean which lie some 2,333km south-west of St Helena. All of the islands are volcanic and steep-sided with cliffs or narrow beaches. The island is home to the highest peak in the South Atlantic, Queens Mary's Peak, which rises to 2,060m above sea-level. Gough and Inaccessible Islands are UNESCO World Heritage Sites.

## HISTORY AND POLITICS

Tristan da Cunha was discovered in 1506 by the Portuguese navigator Tristao da Cunha. In 1816 the group was annexed to the British crown and a garrison was placed on Tristan da Cunha. When this force was withdrawn in 1817, four adults and two children remained at their own request and formed a settlement, which was joined in 1827 by five women from St Helena and afterwards by others from Cape Colony. Owing to its position on a major sea route the colony thrived, with an economy based on trade with passing ships, until the late 19th century, when the opening of the Suez Canal led to decline.

Tristan da Cunha and Inaccessible, Nightingale and Gough Islands were dependencies of St Helena from 1938 to 2009. They are administered by the governor of St Helena through a resident administrator, who is advised by an island council. This consists of eight members elected for a three-year term, of whom one must be a woman, and three appointed members.
*Administrator,* Alex Mitham, *apptd* 2013

## ECONOMY

The island is almost financially self-sufficient; UK government aid finances training scholarships and a resident medical officer at the hospital. The main activities are crayfish fishing, fish processing, agriculture and the sale of postage stamps and coins.

## COMMUNICATIONS

Communications with the outside world are by sea as there is no airport. Scheduled visits to the island are limited to about nine calls a year by fishing vessels from Cape Town and annual calls by a South African research vessel. Tristan da Cunha has 20km of roads, half of which are paved. There is a local radio station and a newspaper.

# SOUTH GEORGIA AND THE SOUTH SANDWICH ISLANDS

For map *see* Falkland Islands entry.

*Area* – 3,903 sq. km
*Capital* – King Edward Point (administrative centre), on South Georgia
*Currency* – Pound sterling (£) of 100 pence
*Population* – There is no indigenous population. The British Antarctic Survey maintains two permanently staffed research stations, at King Edward Point and on Bird Island, to the north-west of South Georgia; in addition, there are the government officers at King Edward Point and the curators of the museum at Grytviken, South Georgia
*Flag* – British blue ensign, with the coat of arms in the fly

## CLIMATE AND TERRAIN

Over half of South Georgia is permanently ice-covered, with many large glaciers. The main mountain range is the Allardyce, and elevation extremes range from 2,934m (Mt Paget) to 0m (Atlantic Ocean). The South Sandwich Islands are a chain of 11 uninhabited volcanic islands some 350km long.

## HISTORY AND POLITICS

South Georgia was used by whalers and sealers of many nationalities following its discovery by Captain Cook in 1775. Britain annexed South Georgia and the South Sandwich Islands in 1908 and since then they have been under continuous British occupation, apart from a brief period during the Falklands conflict in 1982; Argentina claims sovereignty over the territory. A small British army garrison was maintained on South Georgia until 2001, before being replaced by scientists from the British Antarctic Survey.

Under the present constitution, which came into effect in 1985, the commissioner is concurrently the governor of the Falkland Islands. A chief executive officer, also based in the Falkland Islands, is responsible for administration. Government officers are based in South Georgia.

*Commissioner (non-resident),* HE Colin Roberts, CVO, apptd 2014
*Senior Executive Officer (non-resident),* Martin Collins

## ECONOMY

A conservation and management fishing zone was established around the islands in 1993 and a licensing regime introduced for fishing vessels. Sale of fishing licences, passenger landing fees, harbour dues, and the sale of postage stamps and commemorative coins are the main sources of revenue. Tourism, especially wildlife tourism, is growing quickly, but prior permission to land on the islands must be sought.

# TURKS AND CAICOS ISLANDS

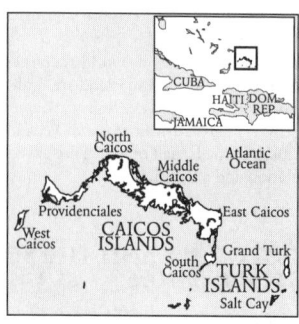

*Area* – 948 sq. km
*Capital* – Cockburn Town, on Grand Turk; population, 4,831 (2012 est)
*Currency* – US dollar (US$) of 100 cents
*Population* – 49,070 rising at 2.58 per cent a year (2014 est)
*Religion* – Christian (Protestant 72.8 per cent, Roman Catholic 11.4 per cent) (est)
*Language* – English (official)
*Population density* – 34.8 per sq. km (2013 est)
*Flag* – British blue ensign with the coat of arms in the fly
*National day* – 30 August (Constitution Day)
*Life expectancy (years)* – 79.55 (2014 est)
*Mortality rate* – 3.08 (2014 est)
*Birth rate* – 16.61 (2014 est)
*Infant mortality rate* – 10.97 (2014 est)

## CLIMATE AND TERRAIN

Around 40 islands and cays make up the the Turks and Caicos Islands, of which eight are permanently inhabited. The climate is marine tropical, moderated by trade winds; the average annual temperature is 26°C. Flamingo Hill on East Caicos is the highest elevation, at 48m.

## HISTORY AND POLITICS

The islands changed hands several times between the French, Spanish and British after their discovery in 1512 and before the arrival of the first settlers, a group of Bermudans, in the 1670s. They achieved separate colonial status under the administration of the Bahamas in 1848, and since 1973 the territory has had its own governor and internal self-government.

The constitution implemented in 2012 re-established home rule after the House of Assembly and 2006 constitution were suspended in 2009 following a corruption scandal. The constitution provides for a legislature consisting of 15 elected members, four members appointed by the governor and the island's attorney general. The UK remains responsible for defence, external affairs and international and offshore financial relations. The Progressive National Party (PNP) won elections held in November 2012, garnering eight seats to the People's Democratic Movement's seven, and elected government rule was reimplemented.

*Governor,* HE Peter Beckingham, apptd 2013

## ECONOMY

The main industries are offshore financial services, fishing and tourism, with over one million people visiting the island in 2013. The USA is the main source of tourists.

| Trade with UK | 2013 | 2014 |
| --- | --- | --- |
| Imports from UK | £1,789,452 | £2,082,430 |
| Exports to UK | £488,244 | £5,767 |

## COMMUNICATIONS

The principal airports are on the islands of Grand Turk and Providenciales and provide international air links; the main seaports are on Grand Turk and Providenciales. The islands have 24km of surfaced roads.

# THE YEAR 2014–15

The year under review covers the period from 1 August 2014 to 31 July 2015

# A CENTURY AGO IN *WHITAKER'S*

## EVENTS OF THE YEAR 1914–15

The following constitutes selected extracts from the Events of the Year chapter as recorded in the 1915 and 1916 editions of *Whitaker's Almanack,* published a century ago. The text has been reproduced in its original form, along with its idiosyncrasies of style and archaic spellings of names. The information in parentheses following the date is the name of the sub-section the extract was taken from.

### AUGUST 1914
3. **(United States)** On the outbreak of the European War, opinion in the U.S. was overwhelmingly in support of Great Britain and the Allies, except among German-Americans. 4. **(France)** The prime minister, detailing the negotiations leading to the war, referred gratefully to the British attitude. 11. **(Imperial Dominions)** In addition to the offer of 20,000 men and two submarines, accepted by the Home Government, the Canadian Government offered 1,000,000 bags of flour. The Government of Alberta offered 500,000 bushels of oats and a quick-firing battery. 12. **(Woman Suffrage)** Suffragist organisations suspended their work in order to devote their energies to relief measures. Subsequently militant suffragists in prison were unconditionally released.

### SEPTEMBER 1914
5. **(Imperial Politics)** Publication was made of the agreement between Great Britain, France, and Russia not to conclude peace separately. It was stated that Japan had joined in the agreement. 9. **(The King and Court)** The King sent messages to the Colonies and India expressing his gratification at the loyalty and devotion displayed.

### OCTOBER 1914
2. **(Imperial Dominions)** News was published of a riot on the arrival of the *Komagata Maru* with the returned Sikh immigrants, the later firing on the police owing to a decision to send them direct to the Punjab. 20. **(Russia)** The Tsar announced his decision to prohibit for ever in Russia the Government sale of alcohol.

### NOVEMBER 1914
11. **(Imperial Politics)** The new Session of Parliament was opened by the King. The Speech from the Throne was exceptionally brief, and emphasised the need for the concentration of national energy "on the prosecution to a victorious issue of the war on which we are engaged." 11. **(Crimes)** The German naval spy Lody, alias Inglis, sentenced by court-martial to be shot, executed at the Tower.

### DECEMBER 1914
8. **(United States)** President Wilson, in his annual Presidential Message to Congress, made an important statement with regard to national defences, and foreshadowed a scheme of optional military training for every citizen. Mr. Wilson emphasised America's prospective *rôle* of Peace-maker. 25. **(The King and Court)** Their majesties sent hearty good wishes for Christmas and the New Year to the officers and men of the Navy and Army both at home and abroad.

### JANUARY 1915
1. **(The King and Court)** The King sent a telegram to the French President expressing the hope that the New Year would witness a still greater drawing together of the bonds of warm friendship and alliance between Great Britain and France, to which M. Poincaré responded in similar terms of cordiality. 13. **(United States)** House of Representatives by 204 votes to 174 defeated the proposal to amend the Constitution so as to give the suffrage to women. 15. **(Sport)** Abandonment of the Oxford and Cambridge Boat Race officially announced. 25. **(Imperial Dominions)** Completion of the Canadian Northern Railway from Lake Superior to the Pacific coast.

### FEBRUARY 1915
4. **(Imperial Politics)** The Select Committee of the House of Commons to consider a scheme of pensions for disabled officers and men, and the widows and dependents of those killed in war, issued a Special Report recommending increased rates and pensions. 27. **(Other Countries)** Well-known Paris resort, the Moulin Rouge, totally destroyed by fire.

### MARCH 1915
1. **(Imperial Politics)** The Prime Minister, in an eloquent and fervent war speech, announced to the House of Commons the reply of Great Britain to the German "blockade," and stated that the British and French governments held themselves free to detain and take into port ships carrying goods of presumed enemy destination, ownership, or origin. Mr. Asquith asked the House to sanction votes of credit for £287,000,000. 22. **(Imperial Politics)** Sir Edward Grey, presiding at a lecture on the war, laid upon Germany, by her refusal to settle the dispute by a conference, the appalling responsibility for the war. One essential condition of peace must be the restoration of peace, and reparation to Belgium, and the admission of the claim of the Allies of the right to pursue a national existence in the enjoyment of their own liberty, as well as the liberty of other nationalities.

### APRIL 1915
6. **(The King and Court)** The King gave orders that no wine, spirits, or beer should be consumed in any of the Royal Households. 26. **(The King and Court)** Prince of Wales's Fund reached over £5,000,000.

### MAY 1915
10. **(United States)** Telegram sent to Washington by German Government placing the blame for the sinking of the *Lusitania* on the British Government, "which, through its plan of starving the civilian population, has forced Germany to adopt retaliatory measures." 22. **(Accidents and Disasters (General))** The worst disaster in the history of British railways took place at Quintin's Hill, a mile north of Gretna Green, on the Caledonian Line, a heavily laden troop train, going southward with 500 officers and men, running into a local passenger train, the Scotch express from Euston crashing into the wreckage of them both; 157 killed (among them many of the 7th Royal Scots, including 3 officers) and 200 injured. 31. **(Crimes)** The printer, publisher, and the writer of the letter in the Times entitled "The Need for Compulsion" charged at the Mansion House with publishing information that might be useful to the enemy; summons dismissed June 5.

### JUNE 1915
24. **(Labour)** Interview between the Executive Committee of the Miners' Federation and Mr. Lloyd George, who represented the urgent necessity of stopping all strikes and lock-outs, especially in trades connected with the production of war material. 29. **(Imperial Politics)** Mr. Walter Long introduced the National Registration Bill, providing for the registration of males and females between the ages of fifteen and sixty-five.

### JULY 1915
3. **(Labour)** The Government met miners' threat to strike on the 15th by issuing a proclamation under the Munitions Act, whereby it becomes an offence to strike, on penalty of £5 a day. Miners' Federation urged men to continue working, and leaders of South Wales miners strongly advised the men not to strike. 19. **(Sport)** Football association decided there shall be no International matches for the Challenge Cup. Amateur leagues and clubs to be allowed to arrange matches without cups, medals, or other awards, provided they do not interfere with those employed in war work.

# EVENTS OF THE YEAR 2014–15

## UK AFFAIRS

### AUGUST 2014

**4.** Across the UK and western Europe, commemorative events were held to mark the centenary of the outbreak of the First World War; Prince Charles, Prime Minister David Cameron, First Minister of Scotland Alex Salmond and Commonwealth heads of government attended a service at Glasgow Cathedral; the Queen attended a special service at Crathie Church while the Duchess of Cambridge, Prince Harry and the Archbishop of Canterbury laid lanterns at St Symphorien Military Cemetery in Mons, Belgium, the location of the first major engagement for British forces in the war. **5.** The foreign office minister Baroness Warsi resigned from the government, stating that its policy on the war in Gaza was 'morally indefensible'; Lady Warsi said that David Cameron's failure to condemn Israel's bombing of Gaza could lead to the radicalisation of British Muslims. RAF jets were scrambled to escort a Qatar Airways passenger plane to Manchester Airport after a passenger, who was arrested on landing, made a hoax bomb threat. **13.** A British Muslim rapper who left his home in Maida Vale, London, to join Islamic State (IS) and was pictured in Syria holding aloft a severed head; Abdel-Majed Abdel Bary, 23, posted the picture on Twitter. **19.** IS released a video online that showed the beheading of US journalist James Foley by a masked militant speaking with a British accent, thought to have been filmed on the outskirts of Raqqa, Syria; in the video entitled 'A Message to America', Foley – who went missing in Syria in 2012 – gave a message under duress to his family and blamed his death on the US bombing campaign of IS. **23.** MI5 and MI6 announced that they had identified the British jihadist accused of the beheading of the journalist James Foley; the masked militant was nicknamed 'Jihadi John' by hostages and the media, after John Lennon of the Beatles, due to the suspect being part of a British cell within IS. William Pooley, a British nurse living in Sierra Leone, tested positive for the deadly virus Ebola, with the number of cases in Africa at 2,615; it was the first reported case of a Briton contracting the virus, which resulted in death in 90 per cent of cases. **24.** The British nurse who had contracted Ebola was flown to the UK and began treatment in an isolation unit at the Royal Free Hospital in London. **28.** The Conservative MP Douglas Carswell defected to the UK Independence Party (UKIP) and quit as the MP for Clacton before announcing he would contest the subsequent by-election for the constituency; Mr Carswell stated he did not believe the prime minister was 'serious about the change we need', referring to the UK's future in Europe.

### SEPTEMBER 2014

**1.** A YouGov poll for Scottish independence put support for independence at 47 per cent against 53 per cent who wished to remain part of the UK, with 16 days until the historic referendum. **2.** IS released a video that showed the beheading of US journalist Steven Sotloff by what appeared to be the British jihadist nicknamed 'Jihadi John', who carried out the execution of James Foley; in a similar presentation to the previous video, the hostage read out a message to President Obama criticising US foreign policy against IS, before his execution and the subsequent threat by the militant to execute a British hostage (see 19 August). **3.** William Pooley, the British nurse being treated for Ebola contracted in Sierra Leone, was discharged from hospital after making a full recovery; the isolation unit underwent a complete

decontamination (see 24 August). **7.** In a YouGov poll for *The Sunday Times*, the 'yes' vote for Scottish independence took the lead for the first time with 51 per cent, which overturned a 22-point lead for the 'Better Together' campaign within a month. **8.** Kensington Palace announced that the Duchess of Cambridge was pregnant with her second child; William and Catherine's second child would become fourth in line to the throne, behind their first child Prince George. **11.** There was confusion in government regarding Britain's foreign policy when the foreign secretary, Philip Hammond, stated that air strikes in Syria had been excluded from consideration before the prime minister said that military action against IS in Syria had not been ruled out; the statement from Downing Street came after President Obama had pledged to destroy IS in Syria alongside a 'core coalition', including the UK. **14.** IS released a video that showed the beheading of British hostage David Haines, a 44-year-old aid worker captured in Syria in 2013; the video was entitled 'A Message to the Allies of America' and featured what appeared to be the same British militant from the previous IS videos, with Mr Haines stating under duress that the prime minister was 'entirely responsible for my execution', before his death, which was followed by a warning that a second British hostage would be next to die (see 2 September). **18.** In a new video released by IS, entitled 'Lend Me Your Ears', British journalist John Cantlie, delivered a message to camera against the UK and US governments and explained that the western media had misrepresented IS; unlike the previous videos released, the hostage was not executed. **19.** Scotland voted to remain in the UK following the referendum for Scottish independence, with the 'no' campaign winning 55 per cent, or 2,001,926 votes, compared with the 'yes' to independence result of 1,617,989, which represented the highest turnout for an election or referendum in the UK since the introduction of universal suffrage; David Cameron pledged to devolve more powers to the Scottish parliament while Alex Salmond, who led the campaign for independence, announced he would step down as Scottish first minister and resign as leader of the Scottish National Party. **26.** The UK parliament called for British air strikes against IS in Iraq after MPs and the leaderships of all three major political parties voted for military action by 524 votes to 43. **27.** Brooks Newmark, the Conservative MP for Braintree, resigned as the minister for civil society after a *Sunday Mirror* sting in which he shared sexually explicit images of himself with an undercover reporter posing as a young female activist on Twitter. At the UKIP conference, the Conservative MP for Rochester and Strood, Mark Reckless, announced that he had left the party and resigned as an MP in order to join UKIP, which triggered a by-election. **30.** RAF launched its first strikes on IS targets in support of Kurdish units in the north-west of Iraq; the successful strikes by two GR4 Tornados hit a 'heavy weapons position' and an armed pick-up truck.

### OCTOBER 2014

**3.** In similar scenes to previous videos, IS militants released another video that revealed the beheading of UK hostage Alan Henning, a taxi driver from Salford who was kidnapped in December 2013 while delivering aid to Syria (see 2 September). **7.** Four men, aged between 20 and 21, were arrested in London in anti-terrorism raids that were part of an investigation to prevent an IS plot to carry out attacks in the capital. **10.** The former Conservative MP Douglas Carswell became UKIP's first elected MP after he won the Clacton by-election with a majority of 12,404 votes over his former party (*see* 28 August). **21.** Three people died and five were injured as the remnants of Hurricane Gonzalo brought gusts of 108mph to the UK, having arrived from Bermuda. **24.** At a meeting of the European Council in Brussels, David Cameron insisted that the UK would not pay a £1.7bn bill demanded by the EU; the payment was requested after a Eurostat review, which analysed the economic performance of member states since 1995. **26.** The UK officially ended combat operations in Afghanistan when the last UK base, Camp Bastion, was handed over to Afghan security forces; the death toll of British troops stood at 453 in the conflict, which began in October 2001. **30.** The former Archbishop of York, Lord Hope of Thornes, resigned from his role as Honorary Assistant Bishop of Bradford; a report by Judge Sally Cahill QC had found that he had failed to act after he was informed of complaints against a cathedral dean, regarding allegations of sexual abuse. **31.** Fiona Woolf, the Lord Mayor of London, resigned as the head of an inquiry into historic child sex abuse after victims' groups said she was unsuitable for the role, citing her links with the ex-Home Secretary Lord Brittan, who was connected to the investigation; it followed Baroness Butler-Sloss's resignation in July 2014 as the first person appointed to lead the inquiry.

## NOVEMBER 2014

**6–7.** Police acting on intelligence from MI5 arrested four men in properties across west London and High Wycombe; the arrests prevented a suspected imminent Islamist attack on Remembrance Sunday. **11.** The final ceramic poppy was planted at the Tower of London on Remembrance Day to complete the installation of 888,246 hand-made poppies, each of which represented a British and colonial soldier who died during the First World War; 5 million people were believed to have visited *Blood Swept Lands and Seas of Red*. **20.** UKIP won the Rochester and Strood by-election in Kent, with the appointment of the Conservative defector Mark Reckless as their second MP, with 42.1 per cent of the votes. The shadow attorney general, Emily Thornberry, resigned from Labour's front bench after she sent a tweet during the Rochester and Strood by-election which showed a terraced house with three England flags and a white van outside, in a social media move branded by many as 'snobby'. **27.** A High Court judge ruled that the former chief whip Andrew Mitchell did call police officers 'f***ing plebs' during a row with PC Toby Rowland in 2012 when Mr Mitchell tried to leave Downing Street via the main gate on his bicycle; Mr Justice Mitting ordered Mr Mitchell to pay interim costs of £300,000. David Cameron said he hoped to get net migration into the UK below 100,000 before the general election in 2015 after figures showed that it rose to 260,000 in the year to June 2014, an increase of 78,000 on the previous year. **28.** Police were called to supermarkets across the UK during 'Black Friday', which saw crowd surges and fights as people sought bargains during the US-originated shopping day.

## DECEMBER 2014

**3.** In the Autumn Statement, the chancellor, George Osborne, announced that stamp duty would be cut for 98 per cent of homebuyers, with the previous system replaced by a graduated rate, similar to income tax; in an accompanying report, the Office for Budget Responsibility said the government plan was to reduce public spending from £5,650 per head in 2009–10 to £3,880 in 2019–20. **6.** A British-born US journalist was killed by al-Qaida militants in Yemen after a failed rescue operation by joint US and Yemeni special forces in the southern Shabwa region; Luke Somers was kidnapped in September 2013 and was

murdered by his captors, alongside another hostage, South African teacher Pierre Korkie, when the militants learned of the rescue attempt. **8.** UKIP suspended its general secretary, Roger Bird, after a prominent female member of the party, Natasha Bolter, claimed he had sexually harassed her, while she in turn resigned and ruled herself out of the running as the candidate for South Basildon; Mr Bird released a series of text messages which he claimed proved that he and Ms Bolter had had a consensual relationship, but she denied their relationship was of a sexual nature. **17.** The Reverend Libby Lane was named as the first female bishop for the Church of England (CofE) after the general synod had formally adopted legislation on 17 November allowing female bishops to be ordained; at the time of the announcement, 1,781 of the 7,798 full-time CofE priests were women. **22.** A council bin lorry careered into a busy shopping area after the driver lost consciousness in George Square, Glasgow, killing six people and injuring ten. **23.** The UKIP general secretary, Roger Bird, stood down by mutual consent despite being cleared of allegations that he had sexually harassed the parliamentary candidate Natasha Bolter. **29.** Ebola was diagnosed in Britain for the first time since the deadly virus's outbreak in West Africa, when a health worker returned from Sierra Leone; Pauline Cafferkey, who began to feel unwell during an internal flight to Glasgow, was placed in an isolation unit in London's Royal Free Hospital. **31.** In the Queen's New Year Honours list, 1,164 people were honoured for their services, including the actress Joan Collins who was made a Dame, OBEs for the actors James Corden and Sheridan Smith, an OBE for the athlete Steve Cram and a knighthood for the actor John Hurt.

## JANUARY 2015

**16.** The oldest Briton, believed to be the last person living in the UK born in the reign of Queen Victoria, died aged 114; Ethel Lang, born in Barnsley in 1900, lived through six monarchs and 22 prime ministers. **24.** The British nurse who was diagnosed with Ebola after volunteering in Sierra Leone was discharged from hospital after making a full recovery (*see* 29 December). **26.** The CofE consecrated its first female bishop in a ceremony at York Minster; in front of more than 1,000 people, the Rt. Revd Libby Lane was made Bishop of Stockport.

## FEBRUARY 2015

**7.** An early edition of Magna Carta was found in a Victorian scrapbook during a search of a council's archives in Sandwich, Kent, ahead of the 800th anniversary of the sealing of Magna Carta in 1215. **17.** Footage emerged which showed a group of Chelsea FC supporters on board a Paris Metro train who appeared to prevent a black man from boarding the carriage at Richelieu – Drouot station; the fans, in France for a match against Paris Saint-Germain, were heard to chant 'We're racist and that's the way we like it.' Three east London schoolgirls, aged between 15 and 16, flew to Turkey to cross the Syrian border to join IS; the pupils of Bethnal Green Academy were friends with a girl who had previously travelled to Syria in December 2014. **22.** Two former foreign secretaries, Jack Straw and Sir Malcolm Rifkind, were suspended from their parliamentary parties – but denied that they had broken any rules – after being secretly filmed offering their services for cash to a private Chinese firm, actually reporters from *The Daily Telegraph* and Channel 4's *Dispatches*; the MPs referred themselves to parliament's standards watchdog with Mr Straw stating he had fallen into a 'very skilful trap', while Ed Miliband called for a ban on MPs having second jobs. **25.** LCpl Joshua Leakey became the first living serviceman to be awarded the Victoria Cross – the highest British military honour – during the war in Afghanistan; LCpl Leakey, 27, of the Parachute Regiment, was awarded the medal for his valour during an assault on a

Taliban stronghold in Helmand province on 22 August 2013. **26.** The masked IS militant known as 'Jihadi John' was identified as Kuwaiti-born British man Mohammed Emwazi, in his mid-20s and from west London, who had been known to British security services.

## MARCH 2015

**2.** Former Royal Marine Konstandinos Erik Scurfield, 25, from Barnsley, became the first Briton to be killed while fighting against IS in Syria; Mr Scurfield, who was fighting alongside Kurdish forces, was said to have been 'horrified by the atrocities being carried out' by the militant group. **14.** Three British teenagers aged between 17 and 19 were stopped from travelling to Syria from Turkey after UK police alerted Turkish authorities; the trio were flown back to the UK and arrested on suspicion of preparing terrorist acts, before being released on bail. **17.** Three judges were sacked for viewing pornographic material using their official IT accounts; District Judge Timothy Bowles, Immigration Judge Warren Grant and Deputy District Judge and Recorder Peter Bullock were removed from office, while a fourth judge resigned before an official enquiry had been concluded. **18.** The chancellor, George Osborne, delivered his final Budget before the general election, in which he claimed Britain was 'walking tall' following five years of austerity; in a budget aimed at voters, Mr Osborne declared that if the Conservatives retained power in May, the first £1,000 of savings interest would be tax free, while new Help to Buy ISA accounts would allow first-time buyers to be topped up by the government by £50 for every £200 saved. **26.** The reburial service of King Richard III, whose skeleton was found under a Leicester car park in 2012, took place at Leicester Cathedral as the Archbishop of Canterbury presided over the service; more than 20,000 people viewed the king's coffin during the three days it was on display prior to the reburial service.

## APRIL 2015

**2.** The leaders of the seven major UK political parties clashed over the NHS, immigration and the deficit in the only televised debate to feature both David Cameron and Ed Miliband ahead of the general election in May; a YouGov poll suggested SNP leader Nicola Sturgeon won the debate with 28 per cent, followed by the UKIP leader Nigel Farage with 20 per cent. **23.** Lutfur Rahman was removed from his office as mayor of Tower Hamlets in east London after an election commissioner concluded that he had breached election rules and he was found guilty of electoral fraud; Mr Rahman, Britain's first elected Muslim mayor, was the first person since the 19th century to be found guilty of the Victorian misdeed of unlawful religious influence, having used religious intimidation to force voters to back him. **25.** Services around the world took place to remember the soldiers who fought at Gallipoli during the First World War, on the centenary of the Allied invasion during which 131,000 died; a dawn service was held at the landing in Turkey and Australian prime minister Tony Abbott described the 11,400 Australian and New Zealand Army Corps troops as 'founding heroes', while the Queen and Prince William were joined by senior government and military figures to lay wreaths at the Cenotaph in Whitehall. **29.** The final Ipsos MORI poll prior to the general election showed support for the SNP stood at 54 per cent, which suggested that the party could win all 59 Scottish seats. **30.** The three major political party leaders appeared on a BBC *Question Time* special just a week before the general election, where they faced separate inquisitions from the audience; an ICM poll suggested that 44 per cent believed David Cameron's appearance was the most successful, while 38 per cent considered Ed Miliband had made the most convincing case, although he encountered a hostile reception concerning the previous Labour government's economic record and attitude towards immigration.

## MAY 2015

**2.** Kensington Palace announced that the Duchess of Cambridge had given birth to a girl who was safely delivered at 08.34 at London's St Mary's Hospital; on 4 May the princess – fourth in line to the throne – was named Charlotte Elizabeth Diana. **7.** In the 2015 general election, David Cameron returned to Downing Street as prime minister after the Conservative party made gains in England and Wales to hold a slender majority, with 330 seats from 650 parliamentary constituencies, and in doing so became the first prime minister since 1900 to continue in office with a larger popular vote share after serving a full term; the result was considered a major shock as many polls suggested a hung parliament was the most likely outcome. Labour lost 26 seats to leave them with 232 MPs, the Liberal Democrats saw their 56 seats reduced to 8 and, despite claiming 12.7 per cent of the popular vote, UKIP's campaign ended with just one MP; the big winners were the SNP, who won 50 seats, almost wiping all other parties from the Scottish map and installing 56 SNP MPs in Parliament. **8.** Ed Miliband resigned as leader of the Labour party stating he was 'truly sorry' for the defeat, which also witnessed the shadow chancellor Ed Balls and the Labour leader in Scotland, Jim Murphy, fail to win their seats; Nick Clegg resigned as leader of the Liberal Democrat party citing that the results were 'immeasurably more crushing' than he had feared. Having failed to win the seat of Thanet South, Nigel Farage announced his resignation as UKIP leader but three days later stated that he would remain in the role after the party rejected his resignation. **9.** A second Briton, who had been trekking north of Kathmandu, was confirmed to have died following the 7.8-magnitude earthquake that struck Nepal on 25 April (*see* International Affairs, Asia, 25–26 April). **10.** The Queen joined around 1,000 veterans and their families to mark the 70th anniversary of VE Day in a service of thanksgiving at Westminster Abbey, while crowds gathered to watch a military parade pass through Westminster and a fly-past of Second World War aircraft; David Cameron and representatives of Allied nations and Commonwealth countries that fought alongside Britain also attended the service. **13.** After the UN estimated that 60,000 asylum seekers had attempted to cross the Mediterranean from North Africa in 2015, HMS *Bulwark*, a British warship, rescued more than 400 migrants from the Mediterranean after they were found 40 miles from the Libyan coast in inflatable boats. **27.** Former UK prime minister Tony Blair resigned as Middle East envoy representing the US, Russia, the UN and the EU. **28.** A year-long study by the Food Standards Agency that tested 4,000 samples of whole raw chickens purchased from UK stores found that 73 per cent tested positive for the food poisoning bug campylobacter.

## JUNE 2015

**2.** Four people aged between 18 and 27 were seriously injured in a crash between two carriages on the Smiler rollercoaster ride at Alton Towers theme park and were trapped for several hours, about 25ft above the ground, before being airlifted to trauma centres; one week after the accident, a 17-year-old passenger had her left leg amputated above the knee. **8.** HMS *Bulwark* arrived in Sicily carrying 1,200 migrants, which it had rescued the previous day from the Mediterranean; the migrants, from Syria, Pakistan and Africa, were packed into nine boats and were believed to have been sent on the dangerous journey illegally through people traffickers. **11.** The chancellor, George Osborne, revealed that the government planned to sell its 80 per cent stake in the Royal Bank of Scotland (RBS); in 2008 the government had provided RBS with a £45.5bn bailout package. **15.** The Queen and other senior members of the royal family, in addition to the Archbishop of Canterbury and the prime minister, attended a celebration event in Runnymede, Surrey, to mark the 800th anniversary of the sealing of the Magna Carta by King John of England. Three sisters from Bradford, along with their nine children aged between three and 15, were reported missing by their husbands and were believed to be in IS territory in Syria, where their brother was fighting with extremists. **25.** Figures released by the Office for National Statistics revealed that the UK population increased by almost half-a-million people to 64,596,800 in mid-2013 to mid-2014, which represented an 'above-average' increase; the median age of 40 was the highest ever estimated. **26.** In the Tunisian tourist resort of Sousse, a 28-year-old Tunisian student, linked with IS, pulled a Kalashnikov from a parasol and opened fire on holidaymakers on the beach, resulting in the deaths of 38 people, 30 of which were British (*see* International Affairs, Middle East).

JULY 2015
**5.** The Forth bridge in Scotland, which opened in 1890 and spans 1.5 miles, was awarded UNESCO World Heritage Site status. **7.** One decade on from the terrorist bombing of three Tube trains and a bus in London, a minute's silence was observed and services held to remember the 52 people who died and 700 injured in the atrocity. **8.** In the first Budget since the general election, the chancellor, George Osborne, announced a new National Living Wage to start at £7.20 an hour and rise to £9 an hour by 2020; the Budget froze working age benefits but increased the overall tax take to slow the pace of welfare cuts. **14.** A free vote on relaxing the fox hunting ban in England and Wales was postponed after the SNP MPs declared that they would vote against changing the law. **16.** The Independent Parliamentary Standards Authority (IPSA) announced that MPs' salaries would rise from £67,060 to £74,000. The health secretary, Jeremy Hunt, stated that the 'Monday to Friday culture' in parts of the NHS led to 6,000 deaths each year and that hospital doctors should work weekends. **17.** Tim Farron was announced as the new leader of the Liberal Democrats. Four people were killed in an explosion at a wood flour mill, which caused the collapse of the four-storey building in Bosley, Cheshire. **28.** The Labour peer Lord Sewel resigned from the House of Lords after he was filmed taking drugs with prostitutes in footage obtained by *The Sun on Sunday;* Lord Sewel apologised for the 'pain and embarrassment caused' by the footage. **31.** A private jet attempting to land at Blackbushe airport, Hampshire, crashed when it overshot the runway, resulting in the deaths of all four people on board; it transpired that the three deceased passengers were family members of the al-Qaida former leader Osama Bin Laden.

## ARTS AND MEDIA

AUGUST 2014
**14.** The Oxford English Dictionary's website, OxfordDictionaries.com, was updated with words including 'yolo' (you only live once), 'binge-watch' (to watch several episodes of a television series at one time) and 'amazeballs' (popularised by the television series *The Only Way is Essex*). **23.** Peter Capaldi made his feature-length debut as the 12th Doctor, when the eighth series of *Doctor Who* premiered on BBC One. **25.** In a BBC Radio 2 poll, listeners voted Led Zeppelin's 'Whole Lotta Love' the greatest guitar riff of all time. **26.** The British pop-star Kate Bush played her first live concert for 35 years when she appeared at London's Hammersmith Apollo; the three-hour set was the 56-year-old's first of a run of 22 shows that sold out in minutes. **31.** Rona Fairhead was selected to become the new chair of the BBC Trust, as the preferred candidate to replace Lord Patten who resigned in May; Mrs Fairhead became the first woman to chair the trust, overseeing the BBC.

SEPTEMBER 2014
**15.** An exhibition of cut-out art by the French artist Henri Matisse became the most successful exhibition in the history of the Tate Modern, with 562,622 visitors; *Henri Matisse: The Cut-Outs* was the first exhibition to be seen by over half-a-million people. **24.** A controversial exhibition that featured black actors in a recreation of a human zoo was cancelled following protests at its opening night; *Exhibit B,* curated by the Barbican at a venue below Waterloo station in London, had previously been shown in 12 cities but protestors deemed it offensive and racist.

OCTOBER 2014
**3.** The crew of the BBC driving programme *Top Gear,* including the presenter Jeremy Clarkson, were forced to flee Argentina while filming a special episode in the country after a crowd, who appeared angered by one of the car's number plates, pelted them with stones; the number plate, H982 FKL, seemed to refer to the Falklands conflict, but the BBC denied any intentional reference, blaming it on coincidence. **14.** The Man Booker Prize, worth £50,000, was won by the Australian author Richard Flanagan for his wartime novel *The Narrow Road to the Deep North*; the Duchess of Cornwall presented the prize for the novel set during the construction of the Thailand–Burma Death Railway in the Second World War. **29.** Edinburgh-based hip-hop trio Young Fathers won the 2014 Barclaycard Mercury Prize for the best album of the year with their debut album *Dead.*

NOVEMBER 2014
**23.** Band Aid 30's 'Do They Know It's Christmas?' – the fourth version of the track – went to number one in the charts in the UK and 62 other countries, while becoming the year's fastest-selling single; organised once more by Bob Geldof, the song, which featured artists such as One Direction, Ed Sheeran and Bono, was recorded with new lyrics to raise funds and awareness to combat the Ebola virus in West Africa. **31.** The Waterstones Book of the Year was named as *The Miniaturist* by debut novelist Jessie Burton; the novel, set in 17th-century Amsterdam, was the best-selling literary debut hardback of the decade.

DECEMBER 2014
**1.** The Turner Prize was won by Dublin-born film-artist Duncan Campbell for his 54-minute video *It for Others*; the work, which reflected on African art and included a dance sequence inspired by Karl Marx and comedic bottles of tomato ketchup, won the artist £25,000. **4.** For the first time since the British Museum acquired them in 1816, one of the Elgin Marbles was loaned out; a headless depiction of the river god Ilissos was lent to St Petersburg's State Hermitage Museum in Russia until January 2015. **21.** In a Classic FM poll, the German carol 'Silent Night' was voted the UK's favourite Christmas carol, ousting 'O Holy Night', which had held the top spot since 2003.

JANUARY 2015
**11.** At the Golden Globe Awards in California, British actor Eddie Redmayne won best actor in a drama for his role as Professor Stephen Hawking in *The Theory of Everything.* **19.** For the first time in 44 years, *The Sun* newspaper did not include a topless woman on Page Three; campaigners had criticised the feature for being sexist and outdated. **21.** The opening episode of the television adaption of Hilary Mantel's historical novel *Wolf Hall* was watched by 3.9 million viewers, becoming the most watched BBC Two drama in a decade. **22.** Days after apparently announcing an end to its Page Three feature, *The Sun* published a photo of a topless woman and mocked reports that said the feature would be dropped, with a trail on the front page reading 'We've had a

mammary lapse'. **27.** The Costa Book of the Year was awarded to Helen Macdonald for her memoir *H is for Hawk*, the author's account of training a goshawk following her father's death.

## FEBRUARY 2015

**1.** Two bronze sculptures that had formerly been credited to a Dutch sculptor were attributed to Michelangelo, becoming the only surviving bronzes by the Italian Master in the world; a group of scientists from Cambridge University identified Michelangelo's trademarks in the bronzes that depict naked, muscular men riding panthers. **3.** It was announced that a forgotten novel by Harper Lee would be published on 14 July 2015, 60 years after the Pulitzer prize-winning author had set it aside; the manuscript of *Go Set a Watchman*, which would be a sequel to *To Kill a Mockingbird*, was discovered in autumn 2014 (*see* 14 July). The 'highest ever' sales record was set in an impressionist and modern art sale at a total of £186m; five paintings by Monet sold in one hour for a collective £55.7m, while other artists including Matisse and Picasso were represented. **6.** An 1892 painting of two Tahitian girls by the French artist Paul Gauguin was sold for $300m (£197m), making it the most expensive work of art ever sold; *Nafea Faa Ipoipo?*, or *When Will You Marry?*, was reported to have been sold to a museum in Qatar. **8.** Eddie Redmayne won the best actor prize at the Bafta Awards for *The Theory of Everything*, with the film winning the award for outstanding British film. At the Grammy Awards in the USA, British soul singer Sam Smith won four awards including best record, best song and best new artist. **17.** Peter Oborne, the chief political commentator of *The Daily Telegraph* resigned from the newspaper over its coverage of HSBC and its tax-dodging scandal; Mr Oborne accused the paper of a 'form of fraud on its readers' and claimed the paper had not given attention to the HSBC scandal because of commercial interests. **22.** At the 87th Academy Awards in Hollywood, Eddie Redmayne won the best actor Oscar for *The Theory of Everything* while the dark comedy *Birdman* won four awards, including best film. **25.** At the Brit Awards, the 56-year-old pop icon Madonna fell off the stage at the start of her performance after a dancer attempted to remove a cape she was wearing; Ed Sheeran and Sam Smith shared two awards each while Paloma Faith was named best British female solo artist.

## MARCH 2015

**10.** The BBC suspended Jeremy Clarkson, the host of the flagship motoring show *Top Gear*, after a 'fracas' with a producer while on location on 4 March; the remaining *Top Gear* episodes were pulled from the BBC's schedule. **25.** The BBC confirmed that the *Top Gear* presenter Jeremy Clarkson was sacked for an 'unprovoked physical and verbal attack' on a producer, which left the victim in need of hospital treatment.

## APRIL 2015

**8.** The British Museum director Neil MacGregor announced that he would resign from the role at the end of the year having been in the position since 2002, during which time visitor attendance to the museum rose from 4.6 million a year to 6.7 million. **19.** The American actor and director Kevin Spacey stepped down as artistic director of the Old Vic after 11 years in charge. **29.** The Advertising Standards Authority (ASA) banned a controversial advertisement poster displayed throughout the London underground network, which featured a model in a bikini with the question 'Are You Beach Body Ready?'; about 360 complaints were made to the ASA, mostly suggesting that the poster, for Protein World weight-loss products, objectified women and promoted unhealthy body image.

## MAY 2015

**11.** Pablo Picasso's 1955 oil painting *Women of Algiers* became the most expensive painting sold at auction when it was bought for $160m (£102.6m) at Christie's in New York; in the same sale Alberto Giacometti's life-size *Man Pointing* set the record as the most expensive sculpture sold at auction when it sold for $141.3m (£90.6m). **18.** The BBC's Middle East correspondent Mark Lobel revealed that he and his news team were arrested in Qatar while reporting on migrant workers building stadiums for the 2022 FIFA World Cup, having been invited by the Qatari prime minister's office on an official tour; the crew were interrogated and jailed for two days before being released without charge, while the Qatari government accused the BBC of trespassing. **19.** A botanist and historian claimed a 400-year-old botany book contained the only known portrait of William Shakespeare made in his lifetime; Mark Griffiths claimed to identify Shakespeare aged 33 in an engraving while researching into the author of *The Herball or Generall Historie of Plantes*. **23.** In the Eurovision Song Contest held in Vienna, the UK entrant Electro Velvet finished 24th out of 27 participants with five points, while Sweden's Mans Zelmerlow won the competition with his song 'Heroes'.

## JUNE 2015

**3.** Ali Smith won the Baileys Women's Prize for Fiction for her 'tender, brilliant and witty' novel *How to Be Both*, a dual narrative concerning the lives of a teenage girl in the present day and a 15th-century Renaissance artist. **7.** For her performance as Queen Elizabeth II in *The Audience*, Dame Helen Mirren was named best actress at the Tony theatre awards in New York; the British play *The Curious Incident of the Dog in the Night-Time* won three awards: best play, best actor (Alex Sharp) and best directing (Marianne Elliot). **29.** A study by the industry ratings body the Broadcast Audience Research Council (BARB) revealed that the proportion of households with television ownership was at its lowest since 1972, at 93.7 per cent, due to the rise in laptops, smartphones and tablets; 1.72 million householders said they did not own a television. **30.** At the opening night of Rossini's *William Tell* at the Royal Opera House, the audience booed for over a minute after a rape scene, causing the orchestra to pause.

## JULY 2015

**14.** The long-lost novel by Pulitzer prize-winning author Harper Lee was released but was met with fury by some readers as the character Atticus Finch was recast as a racist; *Go Set a Watchman* had an initial US print run of 2 million and was released simultaneously in 70 countries. **22.** A critics poll conducted by the BBC named the 1941 film *Citizen Kane* as the greatest American film of all time.

# CRIMES AND LEGAL AFFAIRS

## AUGUST 2014

**11.** A 55-year-old university lecturer was brutally beaten at his home in Wimbledon, south-west London, when four masked men broke in and demanded money from the father of four. **16.** A man died after being found in a shipping container with 34 other people, including children, at Tilbury Docks; the survivors, alleged to be Afghan Sikhs, discovered when staff were alerted to the container by screaming and banging upon the freighter's arrival from Zeebrugge, Belgium. **25.** The mother of three-year-old Mikaeel Kular was jailed for 11 years after she admitted killing her son and hiding his body in a suitcase; the infant died after Rosdeep Adekoya, 34, beat him, before dumping the suitcase containing his body behind her sister's house in Kirkcaldy, Fife. **26.** The Office for National Statistics criticised the annual Crime Survey for England and Wales after almost four million crimes were left out of the official figures, which hid the rise in fraud; the inclusion of bank and credit card fraud would have allegedly increased the number of overall offences by 50 per cent from 7.3 million to 11 million crimes a year. An independent inquiry found that failings by social workers and police allowed 1,400 children in Rotherham to suffer years of abuse by gangs of men, almost all of whom were of Pakistani origin; Roger Stone, the leader of Rotherham council, resigned and offered apologies to girls as young as 11 who were regularly gang-raped, abducted and trafficked to other cities, while the gangs acted with virtual impunity between 1997 and 2003.

## SEPTEMBER 2014

**4.** An 82-year-old grandmother, Palmira Silva, was found beheaded in the garden of a house in Edmonton, London, in what was suspected to be a random attack; a 25-year-old man was arrested on suspicion of murder (*see* 23 June). **8.** An author claimed to have uncovered the identity of Jack the Ripper – the Victorian serial killer who murdered five women in the East End of London in 1888 – as 23-year-old Polish immigrant Aaron Kosminski; Russell Edwards, a self-confessed 'armchair detective', claimed to have solved the historic case after buying a blood-stained shawl of one of the victims in an auction and enlisting an expert in molecular biology, who discovered DNA of the suspect. **11.** A fire at Manchester Dogs' Home killed over 60 dogs, while around 150 dogs were rescued as more than 30 firefighters tackled the blaze; on 13 September, a 15-year-old boy was bailed after being arrested on suspicion of arson, while over £1.2m was raised to support the home. **15.** Two British tourists were found dead with severe blows to the head on the island of Koh Tao in Thailand; Thai police hunting for the murderers of David Miller, 24, and Hannah Witheridge, 23, offered a £13,000 reward for information, while a bloodstained garden hoe found nearby was believed to be the murder weapon. **16.** The South Yorkshire police and crime commissioner, Shaun Wright, resigned over the Rotherham child abuse scandal (*see* 26 August). **23.** Former Radio 1 DJ Dave Lee Travis was found guilty of indecently assaulting a young woman who was working on *The Mrs Merton Show* in 1995; three days later, Mr Travis, 69, was given a suspended sentence of three months. The National Crime Agency (NCA) revealed that its Operation Notarise inquiry had discovered more than 25,000 people in Britain suspected of viewing child abuse images online; the investigation had led to 660 arrests in July 2014 but the NCA stated that it would be unable to pursue all those identified.

## OCTOBER 2014

**1.** The Metropolitan Police confirmed that a body found in the River Brent in west London on 30 September was that of 14-year-old Alice Gross, who had gone missing on 28 August after leaving her home in Hanwell, west London. **4.** A 63-year-old woman who was accused of being an internet 'troll' after abusing the family of Madeleine McCann on Twitter was found dead in a Leicestershire hotel room; Brenda Leyland's body was discovered days after she was confronted by a Sky News reporter outside her home regarding her actions. **6.** A body found in Boston Manor Park, west London, was confirmed by police to be that of Arnis Zalkalns, a Latvian builder who was the prime suspect in the murder of the teenager Alice Gross; Mr Zalkalns was last seen at his home in Ealing six days after the disappearance of the 14-year-old, before his body was found a 20-minute walk from Miss Gross's body, with a post-mortem stating that his death was 'consistent with hanging'.

## NOVEMBER 2014

**1.** A 29-year-old British man, Rurik Jutting, was arrested for murdering two women after police discovered the victims in the former Merrill Lynch employee's apartment in the Wan Chai area of Hong Kong. **3.** A 16-year-old schoolboy, Will Cornick, was given a prison sentence of at least 20 years after he admitted stabbing his teacher, Ann Maguire, seven times at Corpus Christi Catholic College in Leeds. **6.** A man died after being stunned by a police Taser when he was found attacking a 22-year-old woman in an act of cannibalism at a hostel in Argoed, south Wales; Matthew Williams, 34, who had recently been released from prison for assault, murdered Cerys Yemm and had eaten an eye and part of her face before he was Tasered. **7.** Six Britons were arrested as part of an international operation in which the Silk Road 2.0 marketplace was shut down, with its founder held by the FBI in the USA; the website was closed alongside 400 others that were used to sell illegal items such as drugs and guns. **11.** Law student Erol Incedal, 26, was found guilty of possessing a bomb-making document following a terror trial at the Central Criminal Court; the trial, which was partially held in secret, saw claims that Mr Incedal was considering a Mumbai-style terror attack and had the address of a property owned by former prime minister Tony Blair. Harry Roberts, 78, who was jailed for life for murdering three police officers following an armed robbery in west London in 1966, was released from Littlehey Prison in Cambridgeshire; both the Met Police Federation chairman and the victims' relatives condemned the move. **17.** An antiques expert who appeared on a special edition of *Jim'll Fix It* alongside the notorious paedophile Jimmy Savile was revealed to be a child abuser active in the Paedophile Information Exchange, the BBC revealed; the feature, with expert Keith Harding, who died in June 2014, was set up by the production team, according to a man who was a boy when he was on the 1980 episode. **21.** Former *News of the World* editor Andy Coulson was released from Hollesley Bay Prison after serving almost five months for conspiracy to hack phones; Mr Coulson, who was found guilty during the phone-hacking trial of 2014, formerly worked as director of communications for the prime minister. **26.** Two brothers became the first British jihadists to be jailed for terrorism training in Syria after they admitted conspiracy to attend a camp in 2013; Mohommod Nawaz, 30, and Hamza Nawaz, 24, from Stratford, east London, were sentenced to four-and-a-half years and three years respectively after order officers stopped them when they returned to the UK in September carrying ammunition, phone pictures of a training camp and a training timetable.

## DECEMBER 2014

**8.** British businessman Shrien Dewani was cleared of murdering his wife, Anni Dewani, during their honeymoon in South Africa in November 2010, when she was shot dead in the back of their hijacked taxi; Judge Jeanette Traverso threw out the case after stating that the prosecution's evidence was 'far below the threshold' of what a reasonable court could convict on, while the victim's family said that the judicial system had failed them. **12.** A 46-year-old man, already serving three life sentences for attacks on two women, was jailed for life for the murder of Kent schoolgirl Claire Tiltman in 1993; Colin Ash-Smith stabbed his victim repeatedly in Greenhithe, 21 years before Judge Mr Justice Sweeney passed down the sentence. **16.** A British charity boss, identified as one of the UK's most prolific paedophiles, who preyed on vulnerable Kenyan street children, was convicted of eight charges of indecent and sexual assault in Gilgil; the prosecution of Simon Harris, 55, was the first to use legislation permitting British citizens to be tried for sex offences committed abroad against children if it was also an offence in that country.

## JANUARY 2015

**29.** A 44-year-old man appeared in Bristol Crown Court charged with the murder of Zac Evans, 19, in a machete attack outside a pub in Tuffley, Gloucester; Ewen Reynolds was additonally accused of injuring Mr Evans's friend in the incident, with a hearing scheduled for May 2015. **30.** Four Polish builders who brutally attacked a university lecturer in a raid at his home in Wimbledon, which left him 'unrecognisable', were jailed following a trial at Kingston Crown Court; two of the burglars were jailed for 19 years each while the others were given prison sentences of 13 years each (*see* 11 August).

FEBRUARY 2015
**6.** A British jihadist who faked his own death in order to return to the UK from Syria, where he had joined a militant group with links to IS, was given a 12-year custodial sentence; Imran Khawaja, 27, was arrested in Dover in June 2014 and admitted preparing for acts of terrorism, attending a camp, receiving training and possessing firearms. **27.** The former pop star Gary Glitter, real name Paul Gadd, was jailed for 16 years after being found guilty of sexually abusing three young girls between 1975 and 1980; the 70-year-old had been jailed in Vietnam in 2006 for molesting two girls aged 11 and 12. A 15-year-old boy was fatally stabbed on Caledonian Road in north London when three men attacked him while he was cycling with his friends; in the incident, which was captured on CCTV, the teenager managed to cycle away but collapsed, and paramedics pronounced him dead at the scene.

MARCH 2015
**17.** The Hillsborough police match commander, David Duckenfield, who was in charge of policing at Hillsborough stadium in 1989, admitted his failure to close a tunnel 'was the direct cause of the deaths of 96 people' during the Hillsborough disaster; Mr Duckenfield, 70, was giving evidence at the new Hillsborough inquests in Warrington when he accepted that he 'froze' during the afternoon of the FA Cup semi final, which led to the deaths of the Liverpool fans. **22.** Six people were arrested after they forced their way into a synagogue in north London in an incident police described as 'anti-Semitic'; one man was punched in the face as he tried to stop the inebriated intruders entering the Ahavas Torah synagogue, while one man made an anti-Semitic comment before security staff removed him. **29.** A retired British couple were found dead with bullet wounds at their home in Xalo, Alicante, Spain; Spanish police discovered former Olympic diver Peter Tarsey and his wife Jean, both 77, at their villa after an apparent burglary went wrong.

APRIL 2015
**7.** The police announced that the Hatton Garden Safe Deposit Company, an underground safe deposit facility in Hatton Garden, London's jewellery quarter, had been burgled with up to £200m including diamonds stolen; CCTV footage showed that the heist began on the Easter Bank Holiday weekend of 2 April when the burglars started to drill through the 50cm-thick vault walls with an industrial drill (*see* 19 May). **15.** The Crown Prosecution Service announced that the Labour peer Lord Janner would not face child sex abuse charges dating back to the 1970s and 1980s due to the severity of his dementia making him unfit to stand trial; the Labour party suspended the 86-year-old former MP for Leicester West who was accused of allegations relating to sex abuse charges against residents in Leicestershire children's homes.

MAY 2015
**5.** A former commander of the Provisional IRA was shot dead near Belfast city centre on his way to work at a local community centre; Gerard Davison, 47, who was shot a number of times, had been a senior member of the IRA until his expulsion in 2005. **7.** Ian Walters, a 51-year-old driving test examiner, was given a life term and ordered to serve a

minimum of 17 years after deliberately killing his wife in a car crash on the M1 in Leicestershire on 21 March 2014. **15.** According to files released by the National Archives following an application under the Freedom of Information Act, a former senior Conservative politician escaped prosecution for child abuse in the 1970s after he promised authorities he would not see the boy again; Victor Montagu, who died in 1995, was MP for South Dorset from 1941–62, and was let off with a caution by the director of public prosecutions in 1972 after indecently assaulting a boy for two years. **19.** Scotland Yard arrested nine suspects aged between 43 and 76, believed to be behind the Hatton Garden Safe Deposit raid; a number of high-value items were recovered when 200 police officers raided 12 addresses. **21.** The Trinity Mirror, which publishes the *Daily Mirror* and *Sunday Mirror,* was ordered by a high court judge to pay £1.2m in compensation to eight victims of phone-hacking, including the footballer Paul Gascoigne and the actress Sadie Frost. **22.** Anis Sardar, a 38-year-old cab driver from Wembley, became the first person to be convicted in a UK court for fighting in the Iraqi insurgency; Mr Sardar was sentenced to a minimum term of 38 years after a roadside bomb he built killed US Sergeant First Class Randy Johnson in Iraq in 2007.

JUNE 2015
**11.** A 14-year-old boy was arrested on suspicion of attempted murder after Vincent Uzomah, a 50-year-old supply teacher, was stabbed once in the stomach during a science lesson at Dixons Kings Academy, Bradford; on 10 August 2015 the boy, who bragged about the racially motivated attack on Facebook, was handed an 11-year extended sentence while Mr Uzomah said he had forgiven his attacker. **16.** The mile-wide island of Canna in the Small Isles, Scotland, reported its first crime for 50 years after items were stolen from the volunteer-run community shop. **18.** A 20-year-old man appeared in court charged with child destruction and grievous bodily harm with intent after he and an accomplice attacked his 32-week pregnant ex-girlfriend outside her home in Peckham; the 21-year-old lost her baby after she was kicked and stamped on by the two men who wore motorcycle helmets. **23.** Nicholas Salvador, who beheaded an 82-year-old widow in her garden in Edmonton, London, was cleared of murder on the grounds of insanity; the 25-year-old, who believed he was killing Adolf Hitler or a demon, was sent to Broadmoor high-security hospital indefinitely (*see* 4 September).

JULY 2015
**14.** Magdalena Luczak, who was jailed for a minimum of 30 years after being convicted of starving and beating her four-year-old son to death in 2012, was found dead in her cell at HMP Foston Hall. **19.** A 34-year-old man was charged with murder after a 79-year-old man was stabbed to death in a road-rage confrontation following a car crash in West Sussex; Don Lock had just been given the all-clear from cancer when he was killed on the A24 near Findon. **22.** Four Chelsea FC fans, including a director with the World Human Rights Forum, accused of refusing to allow a black man onto a Paris Metro carriage were banned from attending football matches for up to five years, while Chelsea FC imposed life bans from their matches (*see* UK Affairs, 17 February). **27.** The Metropolitan Police launched a criminal investigation after the former Deputy Lords Speaker Lord Sewel was filmed taking drugs with prostitutes (*see* UK Affairs, 28 July).

# ENVIRONMENT AND SCIENCE

AUGUST 2014
**6.** The *Rosetta* spacecraft became the first in history to go into orbit around a comet when it rendezvoused with the comet

67P/Churyumov-Gerasimenko, 405 million km from Earth and travelling at 55,000km/h; *Rosetta* would follow two triangular trajectories until it came within less than a mile from the comet, close enough to release a lander to float on to the surface. **11.** A study conducted at the Centre for Research in Epidemiology and Population Health at the Institut Gustave Roussy in France suggested that middle-aged women who walked for 30 minutes a day were 10 per cent less likely to develop breast cancer in later life than those who did no exercise. **12.** The world's first-known surviving newborn panda triplets were unveiled at Guangzhou's Chimelong safari park in China; the trio was born on 29 July, with Chinese zookeepers describing the cubs as a 'new wonder of the world'. **20.** Scientists at Harvard University, USA, discovered the reason why people struggle to fall asleep as they get older; published in the journal *Brain,* the study showed a depletion in the brain of neurons that act as a 'switch' to turn off conscious thoughts. **21.** The Met Office announced that the UK had enjoyed its warmest period from January to July on record; the eight-month period was the hottest and third wettest since records began in 1910, with one climate expert stating the data was proof of global warming affecting the UK. **25.** For the first time, a functioning organ was grown from scratch in a living animal when scientists grew working thymus glands within mice; published in the journal *Nature Cell Biology,* the procedure raised the prospects of a new treatment for transplant patients.

## SEPTEMBER 2014

**4.** Scientists unveiled the discovery of a dinosaur they named *Dreadnoughtus schrani,* which was 26m long and seven times as heavy as *Tyrannosaurus rex*; the 77 million-year-old skeleton, found in 2005 in Patagonia, Argentina, was not even fully grown, which meant it may be the largest-known land animal. **5.** In an experiment reported in the journal *PLOS One,* the word 'ciao' was read out from the electrical activity of one person's brain in the USA and transmitted to the brain of someone in France using powerful magnetic pulses; the experiment was believed to open up the future for telepathic-style communication. **22.** A study by climate scientists, published in the journal *Nature Geoscience,* revealed that the world had burned through two-thirds of its 'carbon budget' and the remaining third would be exhausted within 30 years at the present rate of emissions; the carbon budget refers to the maximum amount of greenhouse gas that scientists believe could be emitted cumulatively since the industrial revolution before the global average temperature rises more than 2°C and threatens the lives of millions of people. **30.** The World Wildlife Fund, together with the Zoological Society of London, revealed the number of wild animals on Earth – including lions in Mole National Park, Ghana, and forest elephants in west and central Africa – had halved in the past 40 years, while the human population had doubled; according to the *Living Planet Report,* which analysed 10,380 populations of 3,038 species, the average decline since 1970 was 52 per cent and freshwater species was 76 per cent.

## OCTOBER 2014

**6.** Prof. John O'Keefe, a British-American scientist, was awarded the Nobel Prize for Physiology or Medicine alongside two other scientists who discovered the brain's 'GPS system', or how the brain is able to navigate from one place to another; the discovery may help explain why patients who suffer from Alzheimer's disease are often unable to recognise their surroundings. **10.** Scientists at Harvard University, USA, hailed a major breakthrough in the cure for type 1 diabetes after they used stem cell technology to transform embryonic stem cells into functioning beta cells, which would eliminate the need for sufferers to inject insulin. **21.** As reported in the journal *Cell Transplantation,* a paralysed man was able to walk again following pioneering therapy led by a British research

team, which involved transplanting cells from his nasal cavity into his spinal cord; Darek Fidyka, from Poland, was left paralysed after being stabbed repeatedly in the back, but was able to walk with a frame and learned to drive following treatment. **22.** In Mongolia, the discovery of two almost complete dinosaur skeletons solved a mystery that had baffled palaeontologists for 50 years, as explained in the journal *Nature*; named *Deinocheirus mirificus,* meaning 'unusual, horrible hands', the dinosaur's previously discovered gigantic arms were matched with the skeleton to produce an 11m-long, 6-tonne beast with an elongated head, beak and humped sail on its back. **24.** Alan Eustace, a vice-president at Google, broke the world altitude record for a parachute jump after he jumped from a helium balloon over 40km (25 miles) above New Mexico, USA; Mr Eustace reached speeds of over 1,300km/h and exceeded the speed of sound, in turn breaking a record set in 2012 by Felix Baumgartner. **31.** Virgin Galactic's *SpaceShip Two* space tourism craft exploded and crashed during a manned test flight in California's Mojave Desert, which killed one of the two pilots.

## NOVEMBER 2014

**12.** The European probe *Philae* made the first historic landing on a comet when it landed on Comet 67P/Churyumov-Gerasimenko near the orbit of Jupiter, 250 million miles from Earth; the European Space Agency confirmed *Philae* had bounced twice off the comet's surface, back into space, but had finally settled and was 'talking' to them; the landing followed the *Rosetta* satellite's 4bn-mile, ten-year journey to understand materials in existence when the planets were formed 4.6bn years ago (*see* 6 August). **15.** The *Philae* lander sent a last stream of data to Earth before its battery lost power and it entered standby mode; the probe's battery was only receiving 1.5 hours of sunlight on its solar panels during the comet's 12-hour day, having landed pressed against a cliff in deep shadows (*see* 14 June).

## DECEMBER 2014

**2.** Published in the journal *Nature Communications,* analysis of DNA from the remains of King Richard III, which were found buried beneath a Leicester car park in 2012, showed that DNA passed down on the maternal side matched that of living relatives but genetic information passed down on the male side did not, which could cast doubt on the Tudor claim to the throne; analysis also showed that it was likely that Richard III had blond hair and blue eyes. A report by the Giraffe Conservation Foundation established that there were only 80,000 giraffes in Africa, which was a reduction of 40 per cent over the past 15 years. **4.** At 5.6m long and 2.9m tall, the world's most complete Stegosaurus, with 85 per cent of the skeleton intact, was unveiled at the Natural History Museum in London; 'Sophie' was the first complete dinosaur specimen to go on display at the museum in almost 100 years. **11.** Greenpeace apologised after undertaking a publicity stunt at the site of the ancient Nazca lines in Peru in order to increase pressure on UN negotiators meeting in Lima; Peruvian authorities said the environmental organisation had not received permission to enter the prohibited area and left footprints and a painted slogan among the geoglyphs.

## JANUARY 2015

**2.** A study published in the journal *Science* claimed two-thirds of cancer cases are the result of bad luck rather than poor lifestyle choices, such as smoking, or inherited factors; the study suggested that random mutations, which occur when cells are divided, is the biggest contributor to developing the disease. **5.** The Met Office confirmed that 2014 was the UK's warmest year since records began in 1910 and was additionally the warmest year in the Central England Temperature series, dating back to 1659; the UK's mean temperature was 9.9°C, which was 0.2°C higher than the

2006 record. **15.** The Mars robot *Beagle2,* which vanished on Christmas Day 2003 while attempting to land on the planet, was found intact on the surface of Mars; the UK-led probe was believed to have been destroyed in a high-velocity impact but it was discovered by NASA's *Mars Reconnaissance Orbiter.* **28.** After first being spotted on the River Otter in Devon in February 2014, a breeding family of beavers were permitted to remain living in the wild if they were found to be free of disease; Natural England's decision marked the first time an organisation had approved the re-introduction of a previously extinct mammal in England (*see* 23 March).

**FEBRUARY 2015**
**18.** Engineers in the UK discovered that limpets' teeth consisted of the strongest biological material ever tested; explained in the journal *Interface,* the teeth, consisting of an iron-based mineral called goethite and less than a millimetre long, were found to be stronger than spider silk and could help improve man-made composites used to build aircraft, cars and boats. **27.** Reported in the journal *Nature,* astronomers discovered a black hole 12 billion times as large as the Sun, which they hoped would provide an insight into galaxy formation in the early universe; the light from the black hole, known as SDSS J0100+2802, spent 12.8 billion years on its journey to reach Earth.

**MARCH 2015**
**13.** As reported in the journal *Nature,* scientists stated that they had genetically modified human embryos for the first time; the pioneering technology is illegal in much of the world but is permitted in Russia and parts of South America. **19.** Paleontologists revealed the discovery of a fossil of a crocodile-type predator which predated the dominance of the dinosaurs and walked on its hind legs across the continent known as Pangea; the *Carnufex carolinensis,* or 'Carolina Butcher', roamed North America 230 million years ago and grew to 3m (9ft) long. **20.** A solar eclipse was witnessed by millions of people across the UK and northern Europe with the period of greatest darkness occurring over a spot in the Norwegian Sea at 09.46 GMT; the next similar solar eclipse in the UK will not transpire until 2026. **23.** The only wild beavers in England were released back into the River Otter in Devon after being given a clean bill of health; tests revealed that the five beavers were free of bovine TB and a parasitic tapeworm. **27.** A Canadian physicist, Alexander Klotz, published his paper which calculated that it would take 38 minutes to drop through the centre of the Earth from one side to the other; the journey of approximately 7,900 miles would see the traveller reaching a top speed of 5 miles per second.

**APRIL 2015**
**9.** A report published in the journal *Nature* revealed that a study into more than 800 reefs in 64 locations around the world found that 83 per cent had lost over 50 per cent of their fish populations, most of the losses having occurred since the 1970s due to the rapid expansion of industrial fishing fleets and the increasing population of islands. **23.** Scientists researching a treatment for asthma, which kills three people per day in the UK, discovered a particular protein called the calcium-sensing receptor (CaSR) to be the cause of the condition; a study published in the journal *Science Translational Medicine* explained how drugs known as calcilytics can manipulate the CaSR and reverse the symptoms, which include airway narrowing, airway twitchiness and inflammation. **30.** Nasa's *Messenger* spacecraft ended its ten-year mission to Mercury when it smashed into a region of the planet's north pole, having spent four years orbiting it and completing 4,105 circuits; *Messenger* reached Mercury in 2011 having launched in August 2004 and sent back over 270,000 images, 10 terabytes of scientific

measurements and evidence for water ice hiding in the planet's shadowy polar craters.

**MAY 2015**
**10.** A study by the Canal & River Trust that analysed water vole sightings dating back to 1970, saw a 50 per cent reduction in water vole location sightings in the past 15 years compared with the 30 years before; the Trust attributed the decline to pollution from agriculture, destruction of the vole's soft bank habitats and predation by American mink. **12.** The Stroke Association reported that there had been a rise in the number of strokes among working-age men and women, with 6,221 hospital admissions for men aged 40–54 in England, an increase of 1,961 on 14 years earlier; experts stated that unhealthy lifestyles, a growing population and changes to hospital practice played a part, and insisted that strokes should not just be considered a disease of the elderly. **18.** Figures from the British Hedgehog Preservation Society showed that hedgehogs could be extinct within ten years if they continue to decline at their current rate; the data revealed that there were fewer than 1 million in Britain, having been as many as 30 million in the 1950s. **26.** Results published in the *Journal of Clinical Oncology* demonstrated that a genetically engineered version of a virus that normally causes cold sores could help fight skin cancer and lengthen patient survival by years; the treatment, known as T-VEC, was only effective for some melanoma patients and was not yet licensed.

**JUNE 2015**
**1.** At the American Society of Clinical Oncology, UK doctors presented the results of an international trial on 945 patients with advanced melanoma, which saw tumours shrink in 60 per cent of cases; the trial combined ipilimumab and nivolumab, which stopped the cancer advancing for nearly a year in 58 per cent of cases and was described by the chief clinician at Cancer Research UK as 'a whole new era for cancer treatments'. **10.** The robin was crowned Britain's national bird with 34 per cent of the vote after 200,000 people voted in a national poll. **14.** The European Space Agency (ESA) announced that its comet lander, *Philae,* had woken up and made contact with Earth, after Comet 67P had moved closer to the Sun to provide the probe with more energy; the ESA confirmed that contact was made for 85 seconds, seven months after the spacecraft had lost power. **29.** Councillors rejected an application by the energy firm Cuadrilla to start fracking at a site on the Fylde coast in Lancashire on the grounds of 'unacceptable noise impact' and the 'adverse urbanising effect on the landscape'; Cuadrilla, which wished to extract shale gas through the method known as fracking from the Little Plumpton site, said it was 'surprised and disappointed'. **30.** A leap second was added for the first time in three years, as the last minute of June had 61 seconds in it, with the time reading 23:59:60 UTC; leap seconds are added as basic means to keep the clock in sync with the Earth and its seasons.

**JULY 2015**
**1.** The UK saw the hottest July day on record as temperatures reached 36.7C (98F); the record, reached at Heathrow airport, surpassed the previous high from 2006. **14.** NASA's *New Horizons* spacecraft passed Pluto at 14km per second at a distance of 12,500km while the space agency released detailed images of the dwarf planet; the success of *New Horizons,* which launched in January 2006, marked the moment that a probe had visited all nine planets originally considered to be part of the Solar System. **23.** NASA's Kepler telescope identified a planet sharing many characteristics with Earth but with a 60 per cent larger radius; Kepler-452b, dubbed Earth 2.0, orbits at a similar distance from its star and is around 1,400 light years from Earth.

# SPORT

## AUGUST 2014

**2.** England's Nicola Adams became the first female Commonwealth Games boxing champion when she beat Northern Ireland's Michaela Walsh in the flyweight final in Glasgow; the victory was England's 50th gold medal at the games. **3.** The Commonwealth Games closed at Hampden Park, Scotland, as England finished first in the medal chart with 174 medals, 58 of which were gold; the hosts, Scotland, finished fourth with a record 19 golds from 53 medals. **10.** The Northern Irish world number one, Rory McIlroy, won the US PGA Championship at Valhalla, Kentucky; McIlroy became the first UK player to win back-to-back golf majors after fighting off three other players still in contention at the final hole, to win by one shot. **12.** At the European Championships in Zurich, 40-year-old Jo Pavey became the oldest woman ever to win gold in the competition after she finished first in the 10,000m. **17.** England won the Women's Rugby World Cup final in Paris after beating Canada 21–9 to end a run of three consecutive final defeats. On the final day of the European Championships in Zurich, Great Britain finished top of the medal table after Mo Farah added the 5,000m gold to his previous 10,000m victory; Greg Rutherford won gold in the long jump, while the men's 400m relay team and both sprint relay teams also won their finals to give Great Britain a record 12 gold medals. **21.** The former Cardiff City manager Malky Mackay was ruled out of contention for the managerial vacancy at Crystal Palace after text messages he sent were leaked, which contained racist, anti-Semitic, sexist and homophobic references; after Cardiff sent a dossier outlining their allegations to the Football Association, the League Managers' Association apologised, having described Mackay's texts as 'friendly text message banter'. **26.** Manchester United signed Argentinian winger Angel Di Maria from Real Madrid for a British club record transfer fee of £59.7m.

## SEPTEMBER 2014

**4.** The British number one tennis player Andy Murray was beaten in four sets by the world number one Novak Djokovic in the quarter-final of the US Open in New York. **7.** Serena Williams, the world number one, beat Caroline Wozniacki to win her sixth US Open and 18th Grand Slam, which moved the American to joint-fourth in the all-time list of major winners. **8.** The 14th seed, Marin Cilic, beat Japan's Kei Nishikori in straight sets in the final of the US Open to become the first Croat major champion since his coach Goran Ivanisevic at Wimbledon in 2001; the match marked the first final since the 2005 Australian Open that featured neither Djokovic, Murray, Roger Federer or Rafael Nadal. **10.** Prince Harry opened the Invictus Games for wounded servicemen and women at the Queen Elizabeth Olympic Park in London; the prince organised the event, which lasted four days and saw more than 400 competitors compete from 13 countries. **12.** In cricket, Yorkshire claimed their first County Championship title since 2001 when they beat Nottinghamshire at Trent Bridge. **24.** At the World Championships in Ponferrada, Spain, Sir Bradley Wiggins won his first cycling road world title with a victory by 26.23sec on a hilly 47.1km course in the time trial. **28.** Europe retained the Ryder Cup with a 16½–11½ victory against the United States in the 40th edition of the competition; the tournament, played at Gleneagles, marked the second occasion that Scotland hosted the Ryder Cup, in which the European captain Paul McGinley triumphed over the US captain Tom Watson.

## OCTOBER 2014

**5.** In the Formula 1 Japanese grand prix, the Marussia driver Jules Bianchi suffered a severe head injury following a horrific crash that left him unconscious; in a rain-affected race, the French driver lost control of his vehicle and crashed into a tractor that had been tending to a previous crash, which resulted in the race being red-flagged and declared over (*see* 18 July). **11.** In the Super League Grand Final at Old Trafford, Wigan's prop, Ben Flower, was sent off after just two minutes when he punched St Helen's Lance Hohaia and then punched him in the face again while the half-back was on the ground; on 14 October, the Rugby Football League gave Flower a six-month ban – the longest in Super League history – for his action in the match, which St Helens won 14–6.

## NOVEMBER 2014

**8.** In rugby union, England lost for a fourth consecutive time for the first time in eight years after New Zealand defeated them 21–24 at Twickenham, which marked the Kiwis' fifth victory in a row over England. **13.** A FIFA report into allegations of corruption in the bidding process of the 2018 and 2022 football World Cups – which cleared the winning nations Russia and Qatar, while accusing the English FA of flouting rules for its 2018 bid – was disputed by the US lawyer who had investigated the claims of corruption; Michael Garcia, who had conducted a two-year investigation into the bidding process, said the report contained 'numerous materially incomplete and erroneous representations' while he called for the full report to be published. Andy Murray was knocked out of the ATP World Tour Finals when he lost to Roger Federer 6–0 6–1 at the O2 Arena in London, which marked the Briton's worst defeat for seven years. **15.** Wayne Rooney won his 100th cap, becoming the ninth England player to do so, when he captained the team to a 3–1 victory over Slovenia at Wembley. **16.** Novak Djokovic, was awarded the ATP World Tour Final trophy and left to play an exhibition match against Andy Murray, after Roger Federer was forced to withdraw from the final with a back problem. **20.** Sheffield United retracted an offer to allow the convicted rapist Ched Evans to use their training facilities, following heavy criticism from fans, sponsors and personalities including the athlete Jessica Ennis-Hill; Mr Evans, a former Sheffield United player, was released in October 2014 having served half of a five-year prison sentence for rape in 2011. The Wigan Athletic chairman Dave Whelan was accused of anti-Semitism and condoning racism after he claimed in an interview with the *Guardian* that 'Jewish people chase money more than everybody else' and it was 'nothing' to call a Chinese person a 'chink'; Mr Whelan was attempting to defend the controversial managerial appointment of Malky Mackay when he made the misguided comments (*see* 21 August). **23.** Lewis Hamilton won his second drivers' World Championship after he finished first in the season-ending Formula 1 grand prix in Abu Dhabi; the Mercedes driver, 29, who was last crowned champion in 2008, became only the fourth British racer to win two titles. **27.** Australian Test batsman Phillip Hughes died, aged 25, after being hit on the top of the neck by a ball when at the wicket during a domestic match in Sydney on 25 November; Hughes collapsed after being struck and never regained consciousness following the accident.

## DECEMBER 2014

**7.** In snooker, Ronnie O'Sullivan beat Judd Trump 10–9 to win his fifth UK Championship title. **14.** The Formula 1 world champion Lewis Hamilton was named the BBC Sports Personality of the Year 2014; the driver earned 34 per cent of the vote, beating the golfer Rory McIlroy, who received 20 per cent of the vote. **17.** Michael Garcia, the FIFA independent ethics investigator, resigned in protest over the handling of his report into the 2018 and 2022 World Cup bidding; the UEFA president Michel Platini described the incident as a 'new failure for FIFA' while Michael Garcia cited a 'lack of leadership', a day after the organisation's appeal panel rejected his challenge of the summary of the report (*see* 13 November). **19.** Alastair Cook was removed as the England one-day captain and replaced by his fellow batsman Eoin Morgan.

## JANUARY 2015

**8.** Oldham Athletic withdrew an offer to sign Ched Evans following threats to the club's staff and their families while Mr Evans released a statement apologising for 'the effects of his actions' but maintained his innocence; the move was cancelled due to pressure from sponsors in addition to a member of staff at Oldham being threatened (*see* 20 November). **12.** The Real Madrid forward Cristiano Ronaldo won the Ballon d'Or award for world footballer of the year for the second year in a row; the Portugal captain, who scored 52 goals in 43 games in 2014, beat Barcelona's Lionel Messi and the Bayern Munich goalkeeper Manuel Neuer to the award. **18.** In Johannesburg, the South African batsman AB de Villiers recorded the fastest ever one-day international century, off 31 balls; the 30-year-old hit 8 fours and 10 sixes during an innings of 149 against West Indies to beat Corey Anderson's record of 36 balls. Shaun Murphy thrashed the Australian world number one Neil Robertson 10–2 in the Masters final at London's Alexandra Palace to become only the 10th player to complete snooker's triple crown. **24.** In one of the biggest FA Cup shocks in history, the League One side Bradford City recovered from two goals down to beat Chelsea 4–2 at Stamford Bridge in the fourth round. **29.** Andy Murray recovered from a set down to beat Tomas Berdych and reach his fourth Australian Open final. **30.** Serena Williams claimed her sixth Australian Open and 19th Grand Slam title after she beat Maria Sharapova for the 16th consecutive time. **31.** Novak Djokovic beat Andy Murray in the Australian Open final by three sets to one, which was the Serb's third win over Murray in the final and in turn brougtht him his eighth Grand Slam title; the defeat meant Murray had lost all four of his Australian Open finals.

## FEBRUARY 2015

**1.** In the Superbowl XLIX final the New England Patriots beat the Seattle Seahawks 28–24 to become the first team in Super Bowl history to trail by double digits in the second half and win. **6.** In the opening match of the Six Nations tournament, England recovered from being 10 points behind to defeat Wales at the Millennium Stadium in Cardiff. **8.** Côte d'Ivoire won the Africa Cup of Nations title for the first time since 1992 when their goalkeeper, Boubacar Barry, scored the winning penalty in a shootout against Ghana following a 0–0 draw in Equatorial Guinea. **10.** The broadcasters Sky and BT paid a record £5.136bn to show live Premier League games for three seasons from 2016–17. **14.** In their opening match of the ICC Cricket World Cup in Melbourne, England were defeated by Australia by 111 runs. **23.** FIFA recommended that the 2022 World Cup in Qatar should take place in November and December after deciding that a tournament in the summer would endanger the health of players and fans. **24.** The West Indies opener Chris Gayle hit the first double century in Cricket World Cup history in a match against Zimbabwe at Canberra, when he made 215.

## MARCH 2015

**1.** In the Six Nations, Ireland defeated England 19–9 in Dublin, which continued the hosts quest to complete the Grand Slam but ended England's hopes of the same pursuit. Jose Mourinho secured his first trophy since returning as the Chelsea manager after his team beat Tottenham 2–0 in the Capital Cup final at Wembley. **9.** England were knocked out of the ICC Cricket World Cup after losing to Bangladesh by 15 runs in Adelaide; the loss marked England's fourth defeat in five games and the third instance in which they had exited at the group stage in five tournaments. **10.** At the Cheltenham

Festival, the Irish trainer Willie Mullins made history by claiming four big race victories in one day, which included Faugheen winning the Champion Hurdle. **13.** The 7/1 chance Coneygree became the first novice to win the Cheltenham Gold Cup since 1974 when Nico de Boinville held off the challenges of Djakadam and Road to Riches in a thrilling finish. **21.** Having needed to win by 26 points to claim their first Six Nations title in four years, England fell one try short after beating France 55–35 at Twickenham; England's win in the 12-try contest was not enough to prevent Ireland – who had earlier beaten Scotland 40–10 – from clinching the title. **29.** Australia defeated New Zealand to win their fifth Cricket World Cup at the Melbourne Cricket Ground.

## APRIL 2015

**11.** Many Clouds won the 2015 Grand National by a length and three-quarters as jockey Leighton Aspell claimed his second consecutive victory in the historic race; Aspell became the first rider since Brian Fletcher on Red Rum in 1973 and 1974 to win consecutive Grand Nationals. Oxford beat Cambridge in the historic staging of the Women's Boat Race on the same day and course as the men, while Oxford also won the men's race. **12.** The 21-year-old American golfer Jordan Spieth equalled the lowest winning score in Masters history when he finished 18 under to win his first major at the prestigious Augusta course; England's Justin Rose finished joint-second as he ended 14 under while the world number one Rory McIlroy finished in fourth place on 12 under. **17.** In his 100th match, James Anderson overtook Ian Botham as England's highest Test wicket-taker with his 348th dismissal, against the West Indies in Antigua. **25.** The 40-year-old 20-time champion jockey AP McCoy ended his racing career at Sandown, having ridden more than 4,300 career winners.

## MAY 2015

**2.** Billed as the 'Fight of the Century', and the richest fight of all time, the American boxer Floyd Mayweather beat his Philippine rival Manny Pacquiao on points via a unanimous decision at the MGM Grand Garden Arena in Las Vegas, USA; Mayweather was awarded the WBO welterweight title and confirmed his status as the greatest pound-for-pound boxer of his generation. AFC Bournemouth won the Championship title by one point; Bournemouth sealed promotion to the top tier of English football for the first time, having been close to liquidation in 2008 and one game away from exiting the Football League in 2009. **3.** Chelsea FC won their fourth Premier League title with three games to spare after beating Crystal Palace 1–0. **4.** In snooker, Stuart Bingham defeated Shaun Murphy 18–15 at the Crucible to win his first World Championship, and at 38 years old, became the oldest world champion since Ray Reardon, who was 45 when he won in 1978. **15.** The England rugby union coach, Stuart Lancaster, said that Manu Tuilagi would not appear at the 2015 Rugby World Cup, after the Leicester Tigers centre was fined £6,205 for assaulting two female police officers; Mr Tuilagi was charged with two counts of assaulting a police officer, assault by beating and causing criminal damage, during an incident on 26 April. **16.** The Southampton winger Sadio Mane scored the fastest hat-trick in Premier League history when he hit three goals in two minutes and 56 seconds in a 6–1 win against Aston Villa. **24.** England all-rounder Ben Stokes hit the fastest Test century at Lord's after he hit 15 fours and three sixes in his 101 in the first Test against New Zealand. Having made his Premier League debut in 1998, in his final game for Liverpool, Steven Gerrard captained his side to a 3–1 defeat at Stoke, although he did score the consolation goal. **27.** Ahead of FIFA's presidential election, seven of its leading officials were arrested in Zurich at the behest of the US Department of Justice, which indicted 14 former and current FIFA officials and associates on charges of corruption following an FBI inquiry; Swiss prosecutors launched a second criminal case into the bids for the 2018 and 2022 World Cups. **30.** The England cricket captain Alistair Cook became England's leading Test run scorer after he overtook Graham Gooch's record of 8,900, which had stood since 1995; Cook, playing in his 114th Test, broke the record during the second day of the second Test against New Zealand at Headingley. Arsenal beat Aston Villa 4–0 at Wembley to retain the FA Cup, which they claimed for a record 12th time; Arsene Wenger won the trophy for a record-equalling sixth time, to stand alongside George Ramsay, who first won the competition in 1887. In rugby union, Saracens won their second Premiership title after beating Bath 28–16 at Twickenham.

## JUNE 2015

**2.** Sepp Blatter announced that he would resign as president of FIFA just days after his re-election after it emerged he was under investigation by US officials as part of their inquiry into corruption at FIFA; the 79-year-old stated that his 'mandate does not appear to be supported by everybody'. **3.** Rafael Nadal, known as the 'king of clay', was defeated for only the second time in 72 matches at the French Open after losing in straight-sets to Novak Djokovic in the quarter-finals. **6.** both clubs sought to win a treble after winning their domestic league and cup competitions, Barcelona beat Juventus 3–1 at Berlin's Olympic Stadium to win their third Champions League title in six years. At the French Open semi-finals, Novak Djokovic defeated Andy Murray in the fifth set following the British number one's fight-back from two sets down after a storm had halted play the previous day. At the 236th running of the Derby at Epsom, the Italian Frankie Dettori claimed his second victory in the race, on favourite *Golden Horn*. **7.** The Swiss eighth seed Stan Wawrinka shocked Novak Djokovic to win his first French Open final, by three sets to one. At the Lee Valley VeloPark, London, Sir Bradley Wiggins broke the cycling hour-record with a distance of 54.526km (33.88 miles). **21.** Andy Murray became the Queen's Club champion for a fourth time, beating Kevin Anderson 6–3, 6–4, after claiming victory over Victor Troicki in the rain-delayed semi-final earlier that day. **22.** The American golfer Jordan Spieth won the US Open at Chambers Bay to become the fourth-youngest player to win two majors, having won The Masters in April. **24.** In football's European Under-21 Championship, England were knocked out in the group stage after losing 3–1 to Italy, having previously beaten Sweden but lost to Portugal. **27.** For the third time in four years, a British cyclist won the Tour de France, as Chris Froome repeated his 2013 triumph and became the first Briton to win the prestigious event twice.

## JULY 2015

**4.** At the Women's World Cup in Canada, England beat Germany 1–0 to finish third, which marked the second best performance by an England football team at a World Cup since 1966. **10.** The seven-time Wimbledon champion Roger Federer beat Andy Murray in straight sets to reach his tenth Wimbledon final. **11.** Serena Williams won her sixth Wimbledon singles title and completed the 'Serena Slam' as the holder of all four major trophies after she defeated Spain's Garbiñe Muguruza; the straight-sets win marked the 33-year-old's 21st Grand Slam title. In Cardiff, England beat Australia to win the first Test of the 2015 Ashes series; the hosts won with a day to spare as they defeated the tourists with a 169-run victory. **12.** In a repeat of the 2014 final, Novak Djokovic beat Roger Federer to win the Wimbledon singles title; Djokovic, who was first seed, beat the second seed in four sets to claim his third Wimbledon and ninth Grand Slam title. **18.** Nine months after suffering severe head injuries in a crash at the 2014 Japanese Grand Prix, the French Formula 1 driver Jules Bianchi died, aged 25, having

been in a coma since the crash. **19.** Great Britain reached the Davis Cup semi-final for the first time in 34 years after Andy Murray beat France's Gilles Simon to give Britain a 3–1 lead in the best-of-five tie. Australia levelled the Ashes series with a 405-run victory over England at Lord's. **20.** At St Andrews, the American golfer Zach Johnson clinched his second major title following a three-man play-off in the 144th Open Championship. **25.** Dina Asher-Smith became the first British woman to run 100m in under 11 seconds when she set a new record of 10.99 secs at the Anniversary Games. **31.** England won the third Ashes Test to lead the series 2–1 after a convincing eight-wicket victory over Australia at Edgbaston.

# INTERNATIONAL AFFAIRS

## AFRICA

### AUGUST 2014

**1.** The Constitutional Court of Uganda annulled the 2014 Anti-Homosexuality Act after ruling it illegal. Sierra Leone and Liberia each declared a state of emergency following the deaths of 700 people across West Africa from Ebola. **5.** In the Democratic Republic of the Congo (DRC), opposition leader Jean-Bertrand Ewanga was arrested after demanding that President Joseph Kabila abide by constitutional presidential term limits. **11.** Anti-government protestors disrupted a court hearing during which South Africa's deputy president, Cyril Ramaphosa, was questioned about his role in the shooting of 34 striking miners in 2012. **21.** In Monrovia, Liberia, riots broke out after anti-Ebola measures caused 75,000 people to be barricaded into one of the city's poorest slums. Côte d'Ivoire closed its land borders with Liberia and Guinea due to the presence of Ebola in both countries. **22.** In Bambari, Central African Republic, the collapse of a gold mine run by Muslim Seleka militants killed 25 people. **26.** The DRC announced that Ebola had been detected in its Equateur province; it was later confirmed not to be the same strain of the disease present in West Africa. **27.** Three people were killed when anti-government rebels shot down a UN cargo helicopter near Bentiu, South Sudan. **29.** The first Ebola case in Senegal was confirmed in Dakar, making Senegal the fifth West African country to record a case of the disease. **30.** In Rwanda, four Tanzanian men were convicted of attempting to assassinate Kayumba Nyamwasa, a political rival of the Rwandan president Paul Kagame. The prime minister of Lesotho, Tom Thabane, fled to South Africa following a coup attempt.

### SEPTEMBER 2014

**2.** The Islamist group Boko Haram captured the town of Bama in northern Nigeria; 5,000 civilians were believed to have fled the attack. **6.** In Somalia, the Islamist group al-Shabab confirmed that its leader, Ahmed Abdi Godane, was killed by American airstrikes. **12.** In Lagos, 116 people were killed when a guest house built by one of the country's largest evangelical churches, the Synagogue Church of All Nations, collapsed. **18.** Amid growing hostility towards government attempts to prevent the spread of Ebola, a mob killed a group of eight aid workers and journalists near the village of Wome, Guinea. **19.** Kenyan officials arrested two Iranian nationals believed to have been plotting to carry out a terrorist attack in the country. **27.** In Mansoa, Guinea-Bissau, 22 people died when a vehicle carrying mourners to a funeral struck a landmine.

### OCTOBER 2014

**1.** In Guinea, the governor of Conakry, Soriba Sorel Camara, banned the public celebration of the Islamic festival Tabaski in order to prevent Ebola from being transmitted via large crowds. **10.** In Bangui, Central African Republic, 13 people, including a UN peacekeeper, died in clashes between

Christians and Muslims. **11.** In Cameroon, 27 people, including the wife of the country's vice-president, who had been captured by Boko Haram in July 2014, were freed; it was not disclosed if a ransom was paid. **13.** In Murufiti, Tanzania, 23 people were charged with murder after seven villagers were burned alive on suspicion of being witches. UNICEF denied claims by Kenya's Catholic Church that the tetanus vaccine had caused infertility. Former Madagascan president Marc Ravalomanana was arrested after returning to the country; a military coup had deposed him in 2009. **16.** Angola was elected to the UN Security Council for a two-year term, commencing on 1 January 2015. **21.** The World Health Organization declared Nigeria to be free of Ebola after no new cases were reported during a period of 42 days. **24.** The Rwandan government enacted a law to ban the BBC from the country, following the broadcast of a documentary questioning the Rwandan government's accounts of the country's genocide. **31.** In Gombe, Nigeria, three people were killed at a bus station when a Boko Haram bomb was detonated. In Beni, DRC, a mob killed and ate a man believed to have been a member of a Uganda-based Islamist group.

## NOVEMBER 2014

**1.** Malawian diplomat Thoko Banda declined to accept the role of ambassador to Zimbabwe due to his opposition to President Robert Mugabe's regime. In Potiskum, Nigeria, a suicide bomber killed 15 people during a Shia religious ceremony. **3.** In Kogi State, Nigeria, Islamist militants using explosives freed 144 prisoners, killing one person in the process. **6.** In Darfur, villagers reported that Sudanese soldiers had raped 200 women and girls; the military had accused locals of harbouring a soldier who had gone AWOL from a nearby barracks. **10.** In Potiskum, Nigeria, a suicide bomber killed 46 children in an attack on a school assembly. **12.** In Sierra Leone, 400 Ebola health workers went on strike after the government failed to pay a one-off 'hazard wage' of £63. **13.** Liberia ended the state of emergency introduced following the Ebola outbreak (*see* 1 August). **14.** In South Africa, four opposition MPs were injured during clashes with police after the country's president, Jacob Zuma, was cleared of embezzling $23m (£14m) of state funds. **17.** Nigerian officials sentenced 54 soldiers to death by firing squad after they refused to take part in the recapture of three Boko Haram towns in August. **18.** Takudzwa Goronga, 20-year-old nephew of Robert Mugabe, was found dead in a wardrobe in his room at Monash University in Melbourne, Australia. In Mombasa, rioting triggered by anti-terror raids on local mosques killed three people. **21.** In South Africa, decorated Paralympian Oscar Pistorius, 27, was convicted of the culpable homicide of his girlfriend Reeva Steenkamp on 14 February 2013 and sentenced to five years in prison. **23.** In Nigeria, near the border with Chad, Boko Haram militants killed 48 fisherman, murdering some by drowning. **24.** The eruption of Cape Verde's Pico do Fogo volcano closed three airports and necessitated the evacuation of hundreds of residents. In Morocco's Guelmim-Es Semara region, the flooding of the Tamsourt river killed 32 people.

## DECEMBER 2014

**2.** Boko Haram gunmen attacked the town of Damaturu, Nigeria, killing 39 people, before government forces intervened. Al-Shabab militants based in Somalia killed 36 people in Mandera County, Kenya. An Egyptian court sentenced 185 people to death for attacking a police station in Cairo in 2013. **5.** Prosecutors at the International Criminal Court withdrew charges against Kenyan president Uhuru Kenyatta relating to political violence that occurred in Kenya between 2007 and 2008. **8.** President Robert Mugabe was elected leader of the ZANU-PF party for the 35th year in a row. **12.** In the DRC, 129 people died and 232 were rescued after an overcrowded passenger ferry capsized while crossing

Lake Tanganyika. **18.** Boko Haram militants killed 35 people and kidnapped 172 women and children in Gumsuri, Nigeria. Cameroonian armed forces killed 116 Boko Haram fighters in the Amchide region in the north of the country. **25.** The AU military base at Mogadishu, Somalia, was attacked by eight Islamist fighters; three AU soldiers were killed. A series of attacks by Islamists across Nigeria, including the bombings of churches in Jos and Mandalla, killed 40 people. **29.** Following improved security in the country, the UN announced that it would begin delivering food aid to South Sudan via the Nile river for the first time. **30.** The Gambia's presidential guard defeated a millitary coup organised by Lieutenant-Colonel Lamin Sanneh; Lt-Col Sanneh was believed to have been killed during the failed uprising (*see* 6 November). **31.** In Somalia, US military drones carried out an attack that killed Tahliil Abdishakur, the leader of al-Shabab.

## JANUARY 2015

**5.** In Baga, Nigeria, Boko Haram captured a military base housing troops from Nigeria, Niger and Chad, which were sent to combat the group. **7.** In Somalia, al-Shabab executed four men it had accused of spying for the Central Intelligence Agency (CIA) and the Ethiopian government. Uganda confirmed that Dominic Ongwen, a commander in the Lord's Resistance Army rebel group, was captured by US forces in the Central African Republic. **13.** Zimbabwe's high court ruled that the practice of evicting farmers in Mazowe District in order to provide room for a game park should end. In Burkina Faso, MPs voted to cut their salaries in half following public anger at their $3,000 (£1,985) a month pay packet. **13–14.** Eastern areas of Malawi and Mozambique experienced widespread flooding after heavy rain, with 48 people killed and 23,000 forced to leave their homes. **18.** Mali announced that the country was free from Ebola after not recording a case for 42 days. **19.** In Niger, ten people died and 45 churches were set on fire during protests against the publication of cartoons of the Prophet Mohammed in the French satirical magazine *Charlie Hebdo* (*see* Europe, 13 January). **26.** In Nigeria, Boko Haram captured Maiduguri, the capital of Borno State; the army defeated a simultaneous attack on the city of Monguno. **27–29.** After two days of fighting, Chadian soldiers captured the town of Malumfatori in Nigeria from Boko Haram. **28.** The anti-government rebel group the South Sudan Democratic Army Cobra Faction announced that it would release 3,000 child soldiers pressganged into fighting for the militia. **30.** In South Africa, Eugene de Kock, the leader of an apartheid-era police unit that tortured and killed black activists, was parolled after serving 20 years of a 212-year prison sentence.

## FEBRUARY 2015

**5.** In Kahama district, Tanzania, flooding caused by a heavy storm killed 42 people and left 900 homeless near Lake Victoria. **12.** The Malawian government banned child marriages, raising the minimum marriage age to 18; around half of Malawian women marry before reaching adulthood. **20.** In Nigeria, a group of 158 women and children abducted by Boko Haram militants from Yobe state in July were released by the group; the Nigerian government did not disclose whether a ransom had been paid. In Mogadishu, Somalia, an al-Shabab car bomb detonated outside the Central Hotel, killing 20 people, including an MP and the city's deputy mayor. **22.** Following an inconclusive round of voting in January, the Union for the Development of the Comoros secured eight seats to win the country's legislative elections to the National Assembly. **23.** Liberia reopened its land borders and lifted curfews imposed after the 2014 Ebola outbreak following a reduction in the number of reported new infections in the country. **28.** In Lesotho's legislative elections, the ruling Democratic Congress secured 47 seats and formed a coalition government with six other parties.

MARCH 2015

**2.** Hifikepunye Pohamba, the outgoing Namibian president, was awarded the Mo Ibrahim Foundation prize for African leadership; the foundation cited President Pohamba's commitment to gender equality and the rule of law. **7.** Four suicide bombers attacked the city of Maiduguri, Nigeria, killing 54 people and wounding 143; the Nigerian government claimed Boko Haram carried out the attacks. **11.** In Côte d'Ivoire, former first lady Simone Gbagbo was sentenced to 20 years in prison for her role in promoting the post-election violence that killed 200 people in 2010. **12.** In Bardere, Somalia, a US drone strike killed al-Shabab leader Adan Garar; Garar was believed to have planned the attack on the 2013 Westgate shopping mall in Nairobi, Kenya, which killed 67 people. **27.** The Nigerian army recaptured the town of Gwoza in Borno state, which had served as a Boko Haram headquarters since it was seized by the group in 2014. **29.** In the Nigerian legislative elections, the All Progressives Congress (APC) party secured victory, winning 225 seats in the House of Representatives and 60 seats in the Senate; former military dictator Muhammadu Buhari of the APC won the simultaneous presidential election. **30.** The government of Guinea declared a 45-day 'health emergency' in five regions following reports that cases of the Ebola virus were on the increase in the country.

APRIL 2015

**3.** In Zimbabwe, former vice-president Joice Mujuru was expelled from the ruling Zimbabwe African National Union – Patriotic Front for allegedly planning a coup against President Robert Mugabe. In Nairobi, Kenya, nine al-Shabab gunmen attacked Garissa university and killed 147 students. **12–15.** In South Africa, six people were killed and businesses owned by Asian and African immigrants looted when anti-immigrant riots broke out in Durban and parts of Johannesburg. **16.** In the Sudan, Omar al-Bashir of the National Congress Party (NCP) was re-elected president, having served in office since 1996, in a vote widely considered to be unfair by international observers; the NCP remained the single largest party in the simultaneous legislative elections. **17.** In Kahama, Tanzania, an illegally operated gold mine collapsed, killing at least 19 people. **25.** In Togo, Faure Gnassingbé of the Union for the Republic party secured 58.7 of the popular vote to win the country's presidential election. **28.** In Benin, the ruling Cowry Forces for an Emerging Benin coalition won the 2015 legislative elections and remained the largest grouping in the National Assembly. **29.** Nigerian troops rescued 293 women and girls from Boko Haram camps in the Sambisa Forest in the north-east of the country; Boko Haram is thought to have kidnapped around 4,000 women across West Africa since 2014.

MAY 2015

**2.** The Nigerian army announced that it had rescued 234 women and girls from a Boko Haram stronghold in the Sambisa Forest. The government of the Republic of Congo banned women from wearing the Islamic niqab (full-face veil), claiming that the measure would help prevent religious extremism; Islamist rebels have been active in the east of the country since 1995. **5.** The government of Niger removed 4,000 Nigerian refugees who had been sheltering from Boko Haram fighters on an island in Lake Chad; the area was deemed unsafe following a number of Boko Haram ambushes. **8.** Burkina Faso and Niger agreed to exchange 18 towns in order to resolve a long-running border dispute; Burkina Faso received 14 towns and Niger four. **9.** The World Health Organization declared Liberia to be free of the Ebola virus after confirming that the country had not reported any new cases for 42 days. **10.** South Africa's main opposition party, the Democratic Alliance, elected its first black leader, Mmusi Maimane. **14.** The Allied Democratic Forces, a

Uganda-based Islamist group, killed 22 civilians during raids on villages in Beni, DRC. **20.** The government of Tanzania confirmed that 33 Burundians sheltering at the Nyarugusu refugee camp in Kigoma state were killed by an outbreak of cholera. **24.** In the Ethiopian legislative elections, the ruling Ethiopian People's Revolutionary Democratic Front coalition won every seat in the House of Peoples' Representatives. **29–30.** In Nigeria, Boko Haram fighters killed 13 people in an assault on the city of Maiduguri, before the Nigerian army repelled them; the following day, a Boko Haram suicide bomber killed 26 people during an attack on one of Maiduguri's largest mosques.

JUNE 2015

**1.** In Goma, Democratic Republic of the Congo, gunmen described as 'bandits' attacked the city's international airport; four government soldiers and three assailants were killed. **1–2.** In Maiduguri, Nigeria, a Boko Haram bomb detonated in a busy market, killing 50 people. **4.** In Accra, Ghana, around 150 people died after a fire broke out at a petrol station, causing a large explosion; the death toll was exacerbated by the fact that heavy rain and flooding had caused many homeless people to seek shelter in the petrol station. **13.** In Madagascar, the constitutional court threw out an attempt by parliament to impeach the country's leader, President Hery Rajaonarimampianina, in May, stating it had 'no legal foundation'. **18.** The government of Chad banned women from wearing the Islamic niqab (full-face veil), claiming that the measure would help prevent religious extremism. **21.** An al-Shabab suicide attack on Somalia's national intelligence agency in Mogadishu left three militants dead. **22.** In Maiduguri, Nigeria, 20 people died after a female Islamist suicide bomber attacked a fish market. **29.** Eleven people were killed in N'Djamena, Chad, after suspected Boko Haram fighters blew themselves up during a police raid.

JULY 2015

**1.** In Hwange National Park, Zimbabwe, Cecil, a 13-year-old male lion, was illegally shot and killed with a crossbow by American dentist Walter Palmer; the incident caused worldwide controversy, including protests outside Palmer's house in Minnesota, USA. **2.** In Mali, six UN peacekeepers from Burkina Faso were killed when Islamist rebels attacked their convoy near the town of Goundam. **5.** In Jos, Nigeria, 44 people were killed in simultaneous Boko Haram attacks on a restaurant and a mosque. **7.** In Zaria, Nigeria, a Boko Haram suicide bomber killed at least 25 civil servants during an attack on a government building. Al-Shabab gunmen killed 14 people, mostly quarry workers, in an attack on residential buildings in Mandera, Kenya. **8.** In Chad, Boko Haram militants killed 26 people during attacks on two villages near Lake Chad. **13.** In Burundi, the army killed 31 anti-government rebels and captured 170 during fighting in the north of the country. **21.** In the Burundi presidential elections, Pierre Nkurunziza of the National Council for Defense of Democracy – Forces for the Defense of Democracy (CNDD–FDD) was re-elected, securing 69.4 per cent of the popular vote. **25.** In Burundi, the ruling CNDD–FDD party won legislative elections, maintaining its majority in both the upper and lower houses. A suicide bomber killed at least 19 people in a crowded bar in Maroua, Cameroon. **27.** In Nara, Mali, 12 people died after Islamist gunmen attacked a military base; the Malian army repulsed the attack after several hours. **28.** In Addis Ababa, Ethiopia, President Barack Obama became the first US president to address the African Union; the president promised greater economic ties between the USA and Africa while urging African leaders to abide by their countries' constitutions. **29.** Wreckage thought to be from Malaysia Airlines Flight 370, which had gone missing on 8 March 2014, washed up on Réunion, a French overseas department in the Indian ocean; the French and Malaysian governments later confirmed the wreckage to be that of Flight 370.

## THE AMERICAS

### AUGUST 2014

**3.** Dr Kent Brantly, an American doctor who travelled to Sierra Leone to treat Ebola patients, became the first person to be treated for the disease in the USA. **9.** The Cuban government announced that US sanctions, imposed after the communist revolution, had cost Cuba $116.8bn (£76.2bn) over 55 years. **9–22.** In Ferguson, Missouri, USA, Michael Brown, a black 18-year-old, was shot and killed by Darren Wilson, a white police officer, in controversial circumstances; the shooting led to days of rioting and looting, as the city's black majority clashed with the town's mainly white police force and the state's National Guard. **12.** Eduardo Campos, the leader of the Brazilian Socialist Party and presidential candidate, was killed when his private jet crashed in the city of Santos. **15.** A ceremony was held in Panama to mark the 100th anniversary of the opening of the Panama Canal. **20.** In Guatemala, the chief of the country's defence staff and four other officers were killed in a helicopter crash near the border with Mexico. **24.** In the USA, 87 people were injured when the city of Napa was struck by a 6.0 magnitude earthquake, the largest earthquake to strike California in 25 years. **30.** In Bonanza, Nicaragua, emergency services rescued 22 miners who had become trapped underground by a landslide.

### SEPTEMBER 2014

**3.** In Missouri, USA, Governor Nixon ended the state of emergency declared in the city of Ferguson (see 9–22 August). **5.** The former president of El Salvador, Francisco Flores, was placed under house arrest; Flores was accused of embezzling $15m (£9m) between 1999 and 2004. **10.** President Obama announced that the USA would begin bombing IS targets in Syria and Iraq. The mayor of Toronto, Rob Ford, who admitted to drug and sexual harassment allegations in 2013, was diagnosed with cancer and announced he would not run for re-election. **11.** Venezuela closed its border with Colombia in order to combat petrol and food smuggling. In Valdivia, Chile, Congressman Rosauro Martinez was arrested over allegations that he ordered the killing of democracy campaigners during the Pinochet regime. **25.** Eric Holder resigned as the US Attorney General after serving for six years. **28.** Thomas Eric Duncan became the first person to be diagnosed with Ebola in the USA.

### OCTOBER 2014

**6.** The Supreme Court of the United States rejected appeals against the introduction of gay marriage in five states: Indiana, Oklahoma, Utah, Virginia and Wisconsin. **7.** The Canadian parliament voted to join US-led airstrikes against IS. In Guachaca, Colombia, lightning killed 11 members of an indigenous tribe at a religious ceremony. **10.** Vicente Carrillo, the leader of the Juarez Cartel, one of Mexico's largest organised crime gangs, was arrested in the northern city of Torren. **16.** Venezuela was elected to the UN Security Council for a two-year period of service, commencing on 1 January 2015. **20.** In Chile, Colonel Cristian Labbe, an aide to former dictator General Augusto Pinochet, was arrested on suspicion of involvement in the killing of 13 political prisoners during the 1970s. **21.** In Saint-Jean-sur-Richelieu, Quebec, Canada, Islamist Martin Couture-Rouleau injured two soldiers near a shopping centre with a car before police shot and killed him. In Mexico, 13 police forces were put under federal control due to fears that they had been infiltrated by drug cartels. **23.** In Canada, Michael Zehaf-Bibeau, an Islamist militant, shot and killed two men

guarding the Canadian parliament before being shot dead by the Sergeant-at-Arms of the Canadian House of Commons. **25.** In Queens, New York City, USA, Zale Thompson, a recent convert to Islam, attacked four policemen with an axe, injuring two before the two uninjured officers shot him dead. **30.** The Revolutionary Armed Forces of Colombia (FARC) admitted to harming civilians during the group's 50-year war with the Colombian government. In Wichita, Kansas, USA, four people died and five were injured when a light aircraft crashed into the Flight Safety International building at Mid-Continent airport.

### NOVEMBER 2014

**3.** In New York City, USA, the rebuilt World Trade Center opened 13 years after the September 11, 2001 terrorist attacks. **4.** In the US mid-term elections, the Republican party took control of the Senate for the first time since 2007; it retained control of the House of Representatives, winning 16 Democratic seats, its largest majority in the House since 1928. **6.** In Tahehyi, Paraguay, nine men were charged with murder after a woman was burned alive on suspicion of being a witch. **19.** In the USA, a state of emergency was declared in Missouri ahead of a decision to charge Darren Wilson with the murder of Michael Brown (see 9–22 August). In Brooklyn, New York City, USA, Ismaaiyl Brinsley shot and killed two off-duty police officers, Wenjian Liu and Rafael Ramos, before taking his own life. **21.** In the USA, Utah voted to reinstate executions via firing squad due to a shortage of lethal drugs previously used to execute criminals. **24.** Sony Pictures Entertainment was targeted by computer hackers who stole sensitive information, including details of executive salaries and private emails, and leaked copies of upcoming films online. **24–25.** In Ferguson, Missouri, a grand jury decided not to indict Darren Wilson for the death of Michael Brown; the decision sparked protests and disturbances in 170 US cities (see 9–22 August). **28.** In Cleveland, Ohio, USA, white police officers shot and killed a black 12-year-old boy believed to be holding a gun, which was subsequently shown to be a toy. **30.** After a second round of voting, Tabare Vazquez of the Broad Front Party won the Uruguayan presidential election.

### DECEMBER 2014

**2.** In Brazil, forensic scientists finished their investigation into whether former president Joao Goulart had been killed by poison in 1976; their findings indicated that Mr Goulart had died of natural causes. **4.** The US Department of Justice announced that it would launch a civil rights investigation into the death of Eric Garner, a black man who died after a white New York police officer placed him in a chokehold in July 2014. **8.** Uruguay agreed to re-settle six former Guantanamo Bay inmates who US authorities cleared of being al-Qaeda members. **9.** In the USA, the Senate Intelligence Committee reported that that the Central Intelligence Agency's Detention and Interrogation Program had involved the torture of a number of foreign prisoners between 2001 and 2006. **10.** In Brazil, the country's National Truth Commission reported that widespread torture, killings and kidnappings took place during the country's period of military dictatorship between 1964 and 1985. **17.** Following the release of Alan Gross, a US citizen imprisoned in Cuba since 2009 on espionage charges, President Obama and President Castro announced plans to normalise relations between the two countries. **23.** The US Food and Drug Administration recommended ending a 31-year-old policy that prevented sexually active gay and bisexual men from donating blood. **31.** In Hayden, Idaho, USA, a two-year-old boy accidently killed his mother with a gun he found in her handbag.

JANUARY 2015

**6.** Republican Congressman John Boehner won a third successive term as speaker of the House of Representatives, despite 25 members of his own party voting against him. Bob McDonnell, the former governor of Virginia, USA, was sentenced to two years in prison for accepting bribes worth $177,000 (£120,028). **7.** In Paraguay, Albino Jara, the leader of the rebel Armed Peasant Association, was killed during a firefight with soldiers near the town of Cuero Fresco. **16.** The USA relaxed the trade embargo with Cuba, legalising the sale of Cuban cigars. **20.** Alberto Nisman, an Argentine lawyer who had accused Cristina Fernández de Kirchner, the president of Argentina, of covering up Iran's alleged involvement in the bombing of a Jewish centre in 1994, was found dead in his home hours before he was due to give evidence in court. **27.** In the USA, Evgeny Buryakov, an employee of a Russian bank in New York City, was charged with spying for the Russian Foreign Intelligence Service (SVR); two Russian diplomats were also charged in absentia. **29.** Pedro Leonardo Mascheroni, an Argentine-born nuclear physicist, was sentenced to five years in prison in the USA for attempting to sell nuclear secrets to Venezuela.

FEBRUARY 2015

**5.** In New York City, USA, a federal court convicted Ross Ulbricht, the founder of the online black market Silk Road, of seven charges, including drug trafficking and money laundering (*see* 29 May). **6.** The government of Ecuador declared a state of emergency in the Galápagos Islands after the ship *The Floreana,* which carried 45,000l of fuel and other hazardous liquids, ran aground near the islands on 2 January. The Canadian supreme court ruled that assisted suicide should be legalised for patients suffering from debilitating and incurable illnesses. **8.** The Revolutionary Armed Forces of Colombia (FARC) invited the reigning Miss Universe, Colombian model Paulina Vega, to help the group conduct peace negotiations with the Colombian government; Miss Vega had previously stated that she wished to see the conflict between the two sides resolved. In Guatemala City, the eruption of the Fuego volcano closed the international airport and necessitated the evacuation of hundreds of people in the south of the country. **17.** In Port-au-Prince, Haiti, around 20 people were killed after a carnival float struck an overhead power line, electrocuting the performers and triggering a stampede. **25.** The government of Jamaica decriminalised the possession of small amounts of marijuana for personal use. Flooding displaced around 4,000 people from their homes in the town of Cobija, northern Bolivia, after the Acre river burst its banks following heavy rain. **26.** In Tyrone, Missouri, USA, 36-year-old Joseph Aldridge shot and killed seven people, including members of his own family, before taking his own life.

MARCH 2015

**1.** After legislative elections in El Salvador, the ruling Arena party remained the largest party in the Legislative Assembly, winning 32 seats. **3.** Chile's Villarrica volcano erupted in the south of the country, ejecting ash and lava thousands of feet into the air and necessitating the evacuation of around 3,000 people. **9.** President Obama signed an executive order declaring Venezuela a national security threat to the USA. In Washington D.C., USA, Israeli Prime Minister Benjamin Netanyahu addressed Congress, after being invited to do so by the Republican party, and condemned US attempts to sign a comprehensive nuclear agreement with Iran. **12.** Ted Cruz, US senator for Kentucky, announced that he would seek the Republican nomination for the US presidency in 2016. **14–15.** In Chile, large forest fires broke out near the ports of Valparaíso and Viña del Mar, necessitating the evacuation of 7,000 people and destroying 740 acres of forest. **15.** The Venezuelan parliament passed legislation allowing President Nicolas Maduro to rule by decree for nine months; Maduro had requested further powers following rising tensions between Venezuela and the US government. In Brazil, more than 1 million people across the country demonstrated against the government and called for the impeachment of President Dilma Rousseff, who had been accused of complicity in corruption at the state-owned oil firm Petrobras. **21.** In Havana, Cuba, 18 civil servants were sentenced to 15 years in prison for stealing and selling millions of dollars' worth of eggs on the black market. **23–25.** Flash floods and mudslides caused by heavy rain killed 17 people in the Atacama region of Chile, usually among the driest places in the world.

APRIL 2015

**1.** In the USA, the governor of California announced the introduction of mandatory water restrictions following the state's fourth consecutive year of drought. **7.** Rand Paul, US senator for Kentucky, announced that he would seek the Republican nomination for the US presidency in 2016. In Jalisco state, Mexico, 15 policemen were killed in an ambush by gunmen believed to be members of the New Generation Jalisco drug cartel. **10.** Twenty-one Haitian asylum seekers drowned after the boat they were travelling in sank in poor weather during their attempt to reach the neighbouring Turks and Caicos Islands. **12.** Hillary Clinton, the former US secretary of state, announced that she would seek to become the Democratic party candidate for the US presidency in 2016. **12–29.** In Baltimore, Maryland, USA, Freddie Gray, Jr., a 25-year-old African American, died on 19 January after receiving spinal injuries while being transported in police custody on 12 January; days of rioting followed, leading to 250 arrests and causing $9m (£5.8m) worth of damage. **13.** The US senator for Florida, Marco Rubio, announced that he would seek the Republican nomination for the US presidency in 2016. **15.** In Colombia, the supreme court convicted Sabas Pretelt and Diego Palacio, two former cabinet ministers, of corruption and ethical breaches; they were each sentenced to six years in prison. **23.** Former US army general and director of the Central Intelligence Agency David Petraeus pleaded guilty to sharing classified information with his biographer and lover; he was fined $100,000 (£64,678) and sentenced to two years' probation.

MAY 2015

**4.** Dr Ben Carson, a political commentator and former neurosurgeon, announced that he would seek to become the Republican party candidate for the US presidency in 2016. **7.** In Mexico City, police rescued around 100 Central American and Asian migrants who had been kidnapped by human traffickers; the migrants were captured by the gang while they were attempting to enter the USA. **8.** Roxana Baldetti, the vice-president of Guatemala, resigned following a corruption scandal involving the country's customs department; Ms. Baldetti was arrested on corruption charges relating to the case on 21 August. **11.** In Guyana, the People's National Congress Reform and A Partnership for National Unity (APNU–AFC) alliance won legislative elections, with 33 seats; in simultaneous presidential elections, David Granger of the APNU–AFC was elected after receiving 50.3 per cent of the popular vote. **19.** In Santa Barbara, California, USA, a pipeline owned by Plains All American Pipeline ruptured, spilling 2,500 barrels of oil into the Pacific ocean and onto nearby beaches, instigating a major clean-up operation. **23.** In Colombia, the FARC leftist rebel group suspended a unilateral ceasefire after 26 of its fighters were killed in government air and ground offensives. In Michoacán state, Mexico, 43 people died during a gun battle between armed drug gangs and security forces. **26.** In Ciudad Acuña, Mexico, at least 13 people were killed and 1,000 homes destroyed after a tornado struck the city. **28.** Spanish scientists investigating the death of the Chilean poet Pablo Neruda, who died in 1973, announced that they had found no evidence to suggest he had been poisoned; there were claims that Neruda was murdered under the orders of Chile's then-military dictator General Augusto Pinochet. **29.** The USA removed Cuba from its list of state sponsors of terrorism, continuing the process of rapprochement between the two countries (*see* 16 January). In New York, USA, Ross Ulbricht, the founder of the illegal black market website Silk Road, was sentenced to life in prison.

JUNE 2015

**5.** In New York state, two convicted murderers, Richard Matt, 49, and David Sweat, 35, escaped from the Clinton Correctional Facility; Matt was shot and killed by police in Malone, New York, on 26 June while Sweat was recaptured on 28 June. **7.** In Mexico, the ruling coalition led by the Institutional Revolutionary Party won legislative elections and majorities in both houses. **15.** Former governor of Florida Jeb Bush announced that he would seek to become the Republican party candidate for the US presidency in 2016. **16.** The billionaire entrepreneur and television personality Donald Trump announced that he would seek to become the Republican party candidate for the US presidency in 2016. **17.** In the USA, a gunman shot and killed nine African-Americans, including state senator Clementa C. Pinckney, during an attack on the Emanuel African Methodist Episcopal Church in Charleston, South Carolina. **24.** Peruvian authorities announced that they had discovered a mass grave containing the bodies of 17 farmers thought to have been killed by the Shining Path rebel group during the 1980s. **25.** Eighteen-year-old Maria Nelly Murillo and her one-year-old son, Yudier Moreno, were found alive five days after the plane they were travelling in crashed into the jungle in Choco province, Colombia. **26.** The US Supreme Court ruled that same-sex marriage would be legalised across the USA after judges voted 5-4 in favour of the decision; the ruling invalidated bans on same-sex marriage in 14 states. **30.** The governor of New Jersey Chris Christie announced that he would seek to become the Republican party candidate for the US presidency in 2016.

JULY 2015

**5–12.** Pope Francis conducted an eight-day tour of South America, visiting Ecuador, Paraguay and Argentina, and attracting millions of people to open-air masses. **6–11.** In Canada, wildfires broke out in Alberta, British Colombia and Saskatchewan; the blazes destroyed over 10,000 sq. miles of forest and necessitated the evacuation of around 10,000 residents. **10.** The Statehouse of South Carolina ceased to fly the battle flag of the Army of Northern Virginia, commonly referred to as the Confederate flag, on its property; the Confederate flag, historically associated with white supremacism by some, was linked to the 17 June church shooting in Charleston as the main suspect was seen to display the flag in various social media images. **12.** Joaquín 'El Chapo' Guzmán, leader of the Sinaloa drug cartel, escaped from the Altiplano maximum security prison near Mexico City; Guzmán had previously escaped from Jalisco prison in 2011. **18.** In Shelby, North Carolina, USA, Dylann Roof, a 21-year-old white supremacist, was arrested and later charged with carrying out the attack on the Emanuel African Methodist Episcopal Church in Charlestonthe (*see* 17 July). **23.** In Lafayette, Louisiana, John Russell Houser shot and killed two people before taking his own life during an attack on a cinema; it was reported that Houser had previously been committed for mental health reasons. **28.** The Peruvian army rescued 39 people, including 26 children, who had been kept as slaves by members of the Shining Path rebel group; some

of the rescued civilians had been held in captivity for up to 30 years. **31.** In Las Palomas, Colombia, a CN235 military transport plane crashed after reporting engine problems, killing 11 people.

## ASIA

AUGUST 2014

**4.** In Yunnan province, China, 367 people died and 12,000 houses were destroyed by an earthquake that measured 6.1 on the Richter scale. **6.** Major-General Harold Greene became the most senior US officer to die in combat since the Vietnam War when he was shot dead by an Afghan government soldier in Kabul; 15 other soldiers were injured during the attack. **14.** Pope Francis began a five-day visit to South Korea on his first trip to Asia as pontiff. **20.** The Sri Lankan government banned a team of UN inspectors, who were investigating the deaths of 40,000 civilians during the Sri Lankan civil war between 1983 and 2009, from entering the country. In Japan, landslides triggered by heavy rain killed 36 people near Hiroshima. **21.** In India, violent protests in Assam and Nagaland killed 20 people and forced thousands to flee their homes; the two states have been involved in a territorial dispute for 40 years. **25.** King Bhumibol Adulyadej of Thailand formally endorsed the military leader General Prayuth Chan-ocha as the country's new ruler following a bloodless military coup on 22 May 2014. **30.** Yun Tae Hyong, president of North Korea's Korean Daesong Bank, defected to Russia, fleeing with $3m (£1.9m) taken from President Kim Jong-un's personal bank account.

SEPTEMBER 2014

**2.** In Kaohsiung, Taiwan, an underground gas explosion killed 25 people and injured 300. In the Philippines, the justice panel of the lower house in congress voted against impeaching President Benigno Aquino III over corruption complaints and claims he had violated the constitution. **4.** In Ghazni, Afghanistan, a Taliban attack utilising truck bombs and rocket-propelled grenades killed 18 people and wounded 150. **5.** Heavy rains and flooding across Pakistan killed 231 people, with the majority of deaths occurring in Lahore. In India, 400 people died in the worst flooding for 50 years, with the highest death toll occuring in Indian Kashmir. **23.** The government of Laos enacted legislation to ban criticism of the ruling Communist Party on social media. **24.** Ilham Tohti, a prominent Uyghur academic, was sentenced to life in prison for 'inciting separatism' in Xinjiang province, China. **25.** Amid an ongoing dispute between the two countries over the sovereignty of the South Kuril Islands, Japan imposed sanctions on Russia following its annexation of Crimea and the visit of a Russian official to the Kuril Islands on 24 September. **26.** North Korean media reported that the country's leader, President Kim Jong-un, had been unable to attend a number of public events due to an illness that impaired his mobility. **30.** On Honshu island, Japan, the eruption of Mt Ontake killed 36 climbers.

OCTOBER 2014

**3.** The USA eased a 40-year ban on arms sales to Vietnam. In Hong Kong, Beijing loyalists attacked barricades erected by pro-democracy groups in Mong Kok. Around 30 people died during a stampede at a Dussehra Hindu festival in Patna, India. **5.** In West Kalimantan province, Indonesia, a collapse at an illegally operated gold mine killed 18 people. **8.** North and South Korean ships exchanged warning shots after a North Korean ship sailed over the countries' disputed maritime border. Typhoon Phanfone made landfall in Japan, killing ten people, including three US marines who were swept out to sea at Kadena Air Base. **8–12.** Cyclone Hudhud made landfall in India, first in the Andaman and Nicobar islands, before reaching the mainland four days later; the storm killed 46 people in Andhra Pradesh and caused £7.3bn worth of damage, making it the most destructive storm to hit the country since 2008. **9.** In Kashmir, shelling by the Indian and Pakistani armies killed five people and caused thousands to flee. **10.** Pakistani women's rights campaigner Malala Yousafzai, 17, and Indian Kailash Satyarthi, 60, a campaigner against child trafficking, were jointly awarded the Nobel prize for peace in Oslo. **16.** Malaysia was elected to the UN Security Council for a two-year period, commencing on 1 January 2015. **22.** Jeffrey Fowle, 56, was freed by the North Korean government after spending six months in prison; he was charged with deliberately leaving a Bible in a nightclub in Chongjin. **30.** In North Korea, 50 senior government officials were executed for a number of crimes, including watching South Korean TV soap operas. **31.** In India, Bangalore officially changed its name to Bengaluru, the name of the city in the local Kannada language.

NOVEMBER 2014

**2.** In Punjab province, Pakistan, near the Indian border, a suicide bombing by the Pakistani Taliban killed 45 people. **4.** In India, the high court overturned a 59-year-old law banning women from working as makeup artists on film sets. **9.** Two Americans, Kenneth Bae and Matthew Todd, were released by North Korea after being imprisoned for two years; the men had been accused of evangelising in the officially atheist country. **10.** In China, regulators connected the Shanghai and Hong Kong stock exchanges for the first time, allowing global investors greater access to the mainland economy. **11.** Lee Joon-seok, the former captain of the South Korean ferry *Sewol*, was sentenced to 36 years in prison for negligence following the sinking of the vessel in 2014, which killed 476; other senior officers received sentences of between 15 and 20 years. **13.** The Indian army sentenced seven soldiers to life imprisonment for the murder of three men in Indian-administered Kashmir in order to claim financial rewards. **19.** In India, a man who tested positive for Ebola after visting Liberia was placed in isolation in New Delhi's Indira Gandhi International airport. **21.** Chandigarh, India, the religious leader Satguru Maharaj Ji was arrested when police raided his group's compound in order to charge Maharaj with a 2006 murder; 450 of his followers were detained for attempting to prevent the arrest. **24.** In Kabul, Afghanistan, a suicide bomber killed 45 spectators and wounded more than 60 during an attack on a district youth tournament volleyball match.

DECEMBER 2014

**1.** In Chhattisgarh, India, Maoist insurgents killed 14 members of the Central Reserve Police Force during an ambush. **4.** North Korea ordered citizens who have the same name as the country's leader, Kim Jong-un, to change their names. China announced that it would end the practice of harvesting the organs of convicted criminals after their execution. **5–9.** Typhoon Hagupit made landfall in the Philippines, killing 25 people and destroying 1,000 homes. **11–15.** In Hong Kong, police began to successfully dismantle barricades at the largest protest sites within the city, ending the 2014 student protests (*see* 26 September). **16.** In Java, Indonesia, heavy rain caused mudslides that killed 51 people. In Peshawar, seven Pakistani Taliban gunmen attacked the Army Public School killing 145 people, including 132 children, in an event which became the deadliest terrorist attack to take place in Pakistan; Pakistani special forces killed all seven militants during the rescue operation that saved 960 people. **23.** In Bodoland, Assam, India, separatist Bodo rebels killed around 75 people, mainly from the Advasi ethnic group. In North Korea, the country's internet was taken

off-line for a period of nine hours, with a number of international hacking organisations claiming responsibility. **28.** Indonesia AirAsia Flight 8501 crashed into the Java Sea en route from Surabaya to Singapore, killing all 155 people on board; a combination of human and computer error was later found to have caused the crash.

JANUARY 2015

**1.** In Afghanistan, a rocket attack on a wedding party killed 20 people in Helmand province. In Shanghai, China, 36 people died during a crush caused by large crowds at a New Year's Eve celebration. The Eurasian Economic Union was founded, consisting of Armenia, Belarus, Kazakhstan, Russia and Ukraine. All 96 passengers and crew on board Adam Air Flight 574, which was travelling between Surabaya and Manado, Indonesia, were killed when the aircraft crashed into the Java Sea during poor weather. **5.** The former prime minister of Taiwan, Chen Shui-bian, was granted one month of medical parole from prison due to ill health; Mr Chen was sentenced to 20 years in prison for money laundering in 2009. In Helong, China, a deserter from the North Korean army killed four people after crossing the border into China to steal food and money. **21.** In Nepal, fighting broke out in parliament between opposing groups of MPs following the Maoist-led government's attempts to create ten new states divided along ethnic lines. **23.** The Thai parliament impeached the country's former prime minister, Yingluck Shinawatra, over corruption allegations involving the misappropriation of rice subsidies; she was banned from holding political office for five years. **28.** In North Waziristan, Pakistan, 53 Taliban were killed in air strikes carried out by the Pakistani air force. **30.** In Pakistan, a bomb planted in a Shia mosque in Singh province killed 20 worshippers. Kanagasabapathy Sripavan became the first Tamil since 1991 to be appointed chief justice of Sri Lanka.

FEBRUARY 2015

**4.** In Taipei, Taiwan, TransAsia Airways Flight 235 crashed shortly after takeoff from Songshan Airport, killing 43 people. **5.** In Hyderabad, India, police rescued at least 350 children who had been forced to work in leather and plastic factories for up to 12 hours a day. **11.** A Malaysian court sentenced Anwar Ibrahim, the leader of the opposition People's Justice party, to five years in prison for sodomy; Mr Ibrahim claimed the charges were untrue and politically motivated. **13.** In Shan state, Myanmar, 47 government soldiers were killed during fighting with ethnic Kokang rebels. **19.** Nineteen people were killed after Taliban militants armed with grenades attacked a Shia mosque in Peshwar, Pakistan. The Thai government banned foreigners from paying Thai women to act as surrogate mothers; the country had become a leading destination for fertility tourism. **25.** In Panjshir province, Afghanistan, more than 300 people were killed in avalanches triggered by heavy snowstorms. **26.** South Korea's constitutional court legalised adultery, overturning a 60-year ban that saw violators imprisoned for two years. **27.** In Dhaka, Bangledesh, Avijit Roy, an atheist American blogger, was stabbed to death by members of the Islamist group Ansarullah Bangla Team.

MARCH 2015

**1.** The ruling People's Democratic party of Tajikistan remained the largest party in the legislature, winning 65 per cent of the vote in parliamentary elections; a number of international monitors claimed that the government had influenced the results. **5.** In Seoul, South Korea, the US ambassador Mark Lippert was stabbed in the face and hand by a Korean nationalist protesting the presence of the US military in the Korean peninsula. In Mumbai, India, Bollywood film star Salman Khan was sentenced to five years in prison for killing a man during a hit and run incident in 2002; the Indian high court suspended the sentence on 7 March. **6.** In Taipei, Taiwan, Cheng Chieh was sentenced to death for killing four people and injuring 22 during a knife attack on the Taipei Metro on 21 May 2014. **11.** In the Andaman Sea, Indonesian and Malaysian authorities rescued around 2,000 Rohinja refugees fleeing Myanmar by boat after they were abandoned by people smugglers; around 8,000 Rohinja were thought to remain stranded at sea. **13.** In Karachi, Pakistan, gunmen from the Pakistani Taliban killed 43 Shia Muslims during an attack on a bus. The North Korean defence chief Hyon Yong-chol was executed by an anti-aircraft gun at the Kanggon Military Training Area north of Pyongyang; Mr Chol had been found guilty of treason. **15.** In Lahore, Pakistan, 15 people died when suicide bombers attacked two Roman Catholic churches; Jamaat-ul-Ahrar, a group associated with the Pakistani Taliban, claimed responsibility for the incident. **20.** In Uttar Pradesh, India, a train travelling between Dehradun and Varanasi derailed, killing 34 people. **27.** The Uzbekistan presidential elections were won by Islam Karimov of the Liberal Democratic Party; many international observers considered the elections to be unfair.

### APRIL 2015

**6.** In Bangladesh, 36 people were killed by tropical storms that hit the capital Dhaka and the north-west of the country. **7.** Twenty people were killed during a gun battle between police and timber smugglers in Andhra Pradesh, India. **11.** In Dhakar, Bangladesh, Muhammad Kamaruzzaman, a senior member of the Islamist Jamaat-e-Islami party, was executed for war crimes that he was alleged to have committed during Bangladesh's 1971 war of independence against Pakistan. **25–26.** In Nepal, an earthquake measuring 7.8 on the Richter scale with an epicentre south-east of the town of Lamjung killed at least 8,500 people and displaced over half a million; a major aftershock occurred on 26 April, with an epicentre near the Chinese border. **26.** Nursultan Nazarbayev won 97.8 per cent of the popular vote in the Kazakhstan presidential elections, securing a fifth consecutive term in office. **30.** An anti-terrorism court in Pakistan's Swat district sentenced ten people to life imprisonment after finding them guilty of the 2012 attack on Nobel Peace prize winner Malala Yousafzai, which left her and two other schoolgirls severely wounded.

### MAY 2015

**8.** In Gilgit-Baltistan, Pakistan, seven people, including the Philippine and Norwegian ambassadors to Pakistan, were killed in a helicopter crash. **9.** The North Korean government claimed that it had successfully test-fired a submarine-launched missile capable of carrying a nuclear warhead. **11.** The Malaysian government rescued and detained around 2,000 Bangladeshi and Rohingya refugees who had been abandoned at sea by people smugglers after Thailand, the preferred destination of the region's people smugglers, had made it more difficult for human traffickers to enter the country via boat. **13.** In Manila, the Philippines, the ignition of flammable chemicals caused a fire at a rubber slipper factory that killed 72 workers. **14.** In Karachi, Pakistan, eight members of the banned Islamist group Jundallah killed 46 Shia commuters on a bus; the Pakistani government claimed that Indian intelligence agencies were behind the attack. **20.** In South Korea, the first case of the Korean 2015 Middle East respiratory syndrome (MERS) was detected in a businessman travelling to South Korea from the Middle East. **26.** In Kabul, the Afghan military shot four Taliban militants when they attacked the Rabbani Guesthouse hotel with guns and rocket-propelled grenades.

### JUNE 2015

**1.** In Hubei province, China, 444 people died when the cruise ship *Eastern Star* capsized in poor weather in the Yangtze river. In Kashmir, the Indian army killed four Islamist militants who had attacked a military base near Tangdhar. **4.** In Manipur, India, 20 Indian soldiers were killed after separatist militants attacked the troops with rocket-propelled grenades. **5.** A magnitude 6.0 earthquake triggered landslides on Mount Kinabalu, Malaysia's highest mountain, killing 11 people and leaving 137 requiring rescue. **6.** Bangladesh and India signed an agreement to simplify their mutual international border by exchanging more than 150 enclaves of land; the existence of the enclaves had encouraged illegal migration, particularly of Bangladeshi workers into Indian Bengal. **9.** The start of the monsoon season in India ended a deadly heatwave that had killed 2,300 since the beginning of May and caused temperatures to rise to just under 50°C in states including Andhra Pradesh, Punjab and Uttar Pradesh; the higher than usual temperatures were caused by sparse pre-monsoon showers and the effects of the El Niño weather systems. **11.** In Tianjin, China, former security chief Zhou Yongkang was jailed for life after he was convicted of accepting bribes and abusing his power; Zhou became the most senior member of the Communist Party of China ever to be jailed. **20.** In Hunan province, China, hundreds of villagers attacked a police station and government buildings, leading to the arrests of 13 people, in response to a perceived mishandling of the death of a local woman; officials announced the cause of death to be pesticide poisoning, but relatives accused the woman's husband of involvement. **20–26.** In Sindh province, Pakistan, a severe heatwave killed around 800 people, including 780 in Karachi, when temperatures reached 45°C. **22.** In Kabul, six Taliban militants attacked the Afghan parliament, detonating a large suicide car bomb in the process and injuring 18 people; the security services killed all six assailants at the scene.

### JULY 2015

**2.** In the Philippines, the *Kim Nirvana* ferry travelling between the Camotes Islands and Ormoc port capsized, killing 36 people. **9–14.** In China, the approach of Typhoon Chan-hom, a category 4 storm, led to the evacuation of 1.1 million people across the country's south-eastern coast; no loss of life was reported, but the storm caused an estimated $410m (£264m) worth of damage. **16–31.** Tropical storms caused heavy flooding in the north of Myanmar, killing 21 people and displacing around 150,000. **27.** In Gurdaspur, India, ten people were killed when gunmen believed to be Islamist militants from the Indian-administered portion of Kashmir attacked a police station. **28.** South Korea announced the end of the 2015 MERS outbreak in the country; in total, 150 cases of the disease were reported, including 18 fatalities. Muhyiddin Yassin, the deputy prime minister of Malaysia, was dismissed by the country's prime minister following a high-profile scandal involving the misuse of a development fund by a number of senior politicians. **29.** The Afghan government announced that Mullah Mohammed Omar, the leader of the Taliban, who had not been seen in public since 2001, had been killed in 2013, ending years of speculation over his whereabouts.

## AUSTRALASIA AND THE PACIFIC

### AUGUST 2014

**12.** In Papua province, Indonesia, 21 people were arrested for allegedly participating in an independence movement which seeks to unite the province with Papua New Guinea. **29.** A volcanic eruption on East New Britain island, Papua New Guinea, ejected large amounts of ash and smoke, causing a number of airlines to reroute flights around the island.

SEPTEMBER 2014
**2.** Quincy Timberlake, a former presidential candidate in Kenya, was charged with murdering his three-year-old son in Adelaide, Australia; Timberlake claimed that his son died during a traditional exorcism. **14.** Prime minister Tony Abbott announced that Australia would send combat aircraft to the Middle East to combat the Islamic State (IS). **15.** The prime minister of New Zealand, John Key, denied that the New Zealand National Party had spied on the opposition Labour Party during the run-up to the country's general election (*see* 20 September). **17.** The Fiji First party, led by interim prime minister Frank Bainimarama, won the first legislative election in Fiji since 2006. **18.** In Sydney and Brisbane, 15 alleged Islamists were arrested on charges of planning the murder of an Australian citizen. **20.** In New Zealand, the Ruling National Party won the legislative elections, securing 60 of the 121 seats in the House of Representatives; John Key remained as prime minister. **23.** Islamist Abdul Numan Haider, 18, was shot dead outside a police station in Melbourne, Australia, after stabbing a police officer in the chest and face. **26.** The finance minister of Nauru announced that the country was bankrupt as a result of a $30m (£19.7m) dispute with the American hedge fund Firebird and could soon be unable to deliver essential services. **29.** Kiribati purchased 20sq. km of land in Fiji for A$9.3m (£4.73m) in order to improve the country's food security; agricultural land in Kiribati has been significantly eroded by rising sea levels. **31.** Australia lifted economic sanctions imposed on Fiji following the country's first democratic election in nine years (*see* 17 September).

OCTOBER 2014
**16.** New Zealand was elected to sit on the UN Security Council from 2015 for a two-year period, commencing on 1 January 2015. **20.** In French Polynesia, former president Gaston Flosse, who was sentenced to five years in prison for corruption in 2013, had his conviction quashed.

NOVEMBER 2014
**4.** In Guam, 56 per cent of the population voted in a referendum to allow people with certain medical conditions to use marijuana for treatment purposes. **15.** The ninth G20 summit took place in Brisbane, Australia. **17.** China and Australia signed a declaration of intent to form a major and wide-ranging free trade agreement, which will open up markets worth billions of dollars. In Nouméa, New Caledonia, thousands of demonstrators attended protests to support the territory's union with France. **21.** The government of Western Australia announced that it would stop providing basic services to 150 of the 270 remotest rural aboriginal communities. **25.** The parliament of Vanuatu was suspended after it was alleged that 16 opposition MPs had accepted bribes from opposition leader Moana Carcasses.

DECEMBER 2014
**1.** In Papua New Guinea, 30 men armed with guns and machetes looted Nadzab airport and held passengers hostage for two hours before escaping. **15–16.** In Martin Place, Sydney, Man Haron Monis, an Iranian refugee, took 18 people hostage in a cafe in order to demonstrate his support for IS; Monis and two hostages were killed when anti-terrorism police raided the building on 16 December after hearing gunshots.

JANUARY 2015
**13–27.** In Papua New Guinea, asylum seekers in an Australian-run detention centre embarked on a two-week hunger strike to protest their living conditions; the strike ended after guards confiscated personal property and moved 60 'ringleaders' to another facility. **19.** The Netherlands

and Brazil withdrew their ambassadors from Indonesia after both countries had one of their citizens executed for drug smuggling.

FEBRUARY 2015
**6.** Xanana Gusmão, the prime minister of East Timor, resigned ahead of a planned government reshuffle. **19–20.** Category 4 storm Cyclone Lam made landfall in Australia's Northern Territory, causing A$82.4m (£40m) worth of damage and displacing hundreds of residents. **20–26.** Cyclone Marcia, a category 5 cyclone, struck the Australian state of Queensland; the storm caused A$750m (£363.4m) worth of damage and left 60,000 homes without power. **23.** The Australian government stripped former entertainer and convicted sex offender Rolf Harris of his Order of Australia honour, originally awarded to him in 1989. **24.** New Zealand's Prime Minister John Key announced plans to send 143 non-combat troops to Iraq in order to help the Iraqi government fight IS militants.

MARCH 2015
**17.** In New South Wales, Australia, police charged the Roman Catholic Archbishop of Adelaide, Philip Wilson, with allegedly covering up child sex abuse committed by another priest, James Fletcher, during the 1970s. **19.** The Australian government announced that Norfolk Island, a territory which had exercised self-rule since 1979, would be governed directly from Canberra following a financial crisis on the island. **29–31.** Cyclone Maysak, a category 5 cyclone, made landfall in Micronesia, causing A$8.5m (£5.5m) worth of damage and displacing around 6,500 people.

APRIL 2015
**24.** Across Australia and New Zealand, record crowds, including 150,000 in Canberra, attended dawn ceremonies commemorating Australian and New Zealand Army Corps (ANZAC) day. **28.** In Nusakambangan, Indonesia, eight convicted drug smugglers from Australia, Brazil, Indonesia and Nigeria were executed by firing squad; Australia and Brazil withdrew their ambassadors from Indonesia in protest at the deaths.

MAY 2015
**1–3.** In Queensland, Australia, six people died in flooding after heavy rain caused the Albert and Logan rivers to burst their banks. **5.** Indonesia announced that it would ban migrant workers from working in 21 countries, mainly in the Middle East, following a number of high profile reports of abuse and exploitation dating back to 2011; around 1.8m Indonesian expats are believed to work in the Middle East. **27.** Tonga began an 11-day coronation ceremony for its new head of state King Tupou VI.

JUNE 2015
**8.** In New South Wales, James Sager, a 48-year-old man was arrested and charged with 17 offences after he destroyed a family home and four cars with a stolen bulldozer; Sager was believed to have a grudge against the owners of the property and to suffer from mental illness. John Momis, the president of the Autonomous Region of Bougainville, Papua New Guinea, was re-elected after winning 50 per cent of the popular vote. **10.** In Sumatra, Indonesia, the eruption of Mount Sinabung necessitated the evacuation of 10,000 people. **11.** Joe Natuman, the prime minister of Vanuatu, resigned following a vote of no confidence triggered by the defection of three MPs from the ruling Vanua'aku party. **30.** A C-130 Hercules military aircraft crashed into a residential neighbourhood in Medan, Indonesia, killing 142 people; a suspected engine failure is believed to have caused the incident.

## JULY 2015

**3.** In Adelaide, Phil Walsh, the coach of the Australian Football League team the Adelaide Crows, was stabbed to death in his home; Mr Walsh's 26-year-old son, Cy Walsh, was arrested and charged with the murder. **4.** Typhoon Nangka, a category 4 tropical storm, struck Guam and the Marshall Islands, causing severe flooding and power cuts in Majuro, the Marshall Islands' capital. **23.** It was announced that the Northern Territory would look to hold a referendum on becoming Australia's seventh state in 2018.

## EUROPE

### AUGUST 2014

**2.** The Greenpeace ship *Arctic Sunrise* was released by Russian authorities in Murmansk the ship had been held since September 2013 having been seized after its crew staged a protest near an offshore oil platform. **4.** The Ukrainian army recaptured the city of Yasynuvata from pro-Russian separatists. **6.** Russia banned imports of food from the EU and the USA following the imposition of sanctions by western governments in March 2014. **13.** Six French climbers, who had gone missing in bad weather, were found dead in the Graian Alps. **19.** Turkey demanded an end to German spying operations in the country; it had been reported in *Der Spiegel* that the BND, the German foreign intelligence service, had spied on its NATO partner for a number of years. **27.** Pro-Russian rebels captured the port of Novoazovsk in Ukraine.

### SEPTEMBER 2014

**1.** The Ukrainian army retreated from Luhansk International airport following an attack by pro-Russian separatists. In Bosnia, 13 former Serb police officers and soldiers were charged with murdering Croats and Muslims during the Yugoslavian civil war. **3.** France halted the delivery of two Mistral-class amphibious assault ships to Russia following the political unrest in the Ukraine. **5.** In Minsk, Belarus, the Ukrainian government and pro-Russian rebels agreed a temporary ceasefire. **8.** Pope Francis accepted the resignation of Cardinal Sean Brady, the head of the Catholic Church in Ireland; Cardinal Brady had faced criticism for his handling of Ireland's clerical sexual abuse scandal. **12.** The EU extended its programme of economic sanctions targeting Russian businesses; the industries affected included the financial, energy and defence sectors (*see* 6 August). **16.** The EU and Ukrainian government signed an association agreement, paving the way for Ukraine's future membership of the organisation. **17.** In Nyzhnya Krynka, Ukraine, ten civilians were killed by a rocket launched by pro-Russian rebels. **19.** France launched its first airstrikes against the Islamic State (IS) in Iraq. **21.** In Moscow, 26,000 people protested Russia's involvement in the war in Ukraine; similar protests occurred in cities around the world including Berlin, Boston and London. Pope Francis celebrated mass in Tirana during a visit to Albania, his first trip outside Italy and his first to a Muslim-majority country. **22.** In Moscow, around 20,000 people took part in further demonstrations against Russia's involvement in the war in Ukraine; similar protests took place in St Petersburg and other Russian cities. **29–30.** The Ukrainian government announced it had repelled an attack by pro-Russian rebels on Donbas airport.

### OCTOBER 2014

**1.** On the first day of the school year in Donbas, nine people were killed when Ukrainian army shells hit a school. **5.** In Grozny, Chechnya, five police officers died when a suicide bomber attacked a public festival. **9.** Estonia legalised gay marriage, becoming the first former Soviet country to do so. **12.** Romero Ramos, a nurse, became the first person outside of West Africa to contract Ebola after treating two missionaries in Madrid, Spain. **14.** The Turkish air force bombed militants belonging to the Kurdish Workers' Party in Hakkari province, close to the border with Iraq. **16.** Spain was elected to the UN Security Council for a twoyear term, commencing on 1 January 2015. **20.** Turkey announced that it would allow Kurdish fighters in Iraq to pass through its territory in order to combat IS in Syria. **29.** In Hungary, tens of thousands protested in Budapest following the government's decision to implement the world's first internet tax. In Italy, President Giorgio Napolitano became the first Italian head of state to give evidence at a criminal trial after attending a perjury trial involving the Sicilian Mafia.

### NOVEMBER 2014

**2–3.** Pro-Russian rebels held and elections in east Ukraine; rebel groups later claimed to have won the elections, though the results were not recognised by Western powers. **4.** Hans Neij, also known as TiAMO, one of the Swedish founders of the file sharing site Pirate Bay, was arrested on an international arrest warrant in Thailand on charges of aiding copyright infringement. **6–10.** In Germany, trade unions organised the longest rail strike in German history, with workers striking for four days following a pay dispute. **9.** Germany celebrated the 25th anniversary of the fall of the Berlin Wall. **10.** In Catalonia, Spain, a non-legally binding vote held by the autonomous region's government saw 80 per cent of participants vote for independence. **11.** The Romanian foreign minister, Titus Corlatean, resigned following a scandal that saw many Romanians living abroad unable to vote in the country's presidential election due to long delays at poleing stations. In Lithuania, a former air traffic controller was charged with passing defence secrets to the government of Belarus. **12.** Azerbaijan announced it had shot down an Armenian Mi-24 military helicopter that had flown into its airspace. he chief military commander of NATO, General Philip Breedlove, claimed Russian tanks had entered east Ukraine on 15 November. **17.** Miguel Macedo, Portugal's interior minister, resigned following allegations that he had provided visas in return for money. At a ceremony marking the 25th anniversary of the Velvet revolution in the Czech Republic, thousands of protestors heckled and threw eggs at President Milos Zeman, alleging that he is politically too close to Russia. **26.** The Spanish minister for health, Ana Mato, resigned after a judge accused her of receiving illegal payments. **30.** In a nationwide referendum, voters in Switzerland rejected a proposal to cut net immigration to no more than 0.2 per cent of the population.

### DECEMBER 2014

**1.** Donald Tusk became the first Polish president of the EU. Russia cancelled plans to route the South Stream gas pipeline through Bulgaria after the EU cited concerns around energy competition. **2.** In France, MPs voted to recognise Palestine as a state; the result was symbolic and would not bind the government. **4.** In Grozny, Chechnya, 20 people died during a gun battle between Islamist separatists and Russian security forces. **13.** The president of Hungary, Viktor Orban, called for the introduction of compulsory drug testing for politicians and journalists. In Greece, four gunmen from the millitant organisation Group of Popular Rebels fired 54 shots at the Israeli embassy in Athens in protest at Isreal's treatment of Palestinians. **15.** Denmark became the first country in the world to claim the North Pole as part of its territory. **18.** The EU removed Hamas from its official list of proscribed terrorist organisations. **19.** The USA imposed new sanctions on the Crimea peninsula following its annexation by Russia. **23.** The Ukrainian parliament voted to end the country's non-aligned status, paving the way for the country to join NATO in the future. **26.** The government of Ukraine and pro-Russian rebels exchanged 370 prisoners, the largest prisoner swap since hostilities between the two countries began in February 2014. **28.** The MS *Norman Atlantic,* an Italian owned, Greek operated ferry caught fire in the Adriatic Sea, killing 13 people. **30.** In Russia, anti-Putin activist Alexei Navalny was handed a three-and-a-half-year suspended sentence for corruption charges; 2,000 demonstrators protested the decision outside of the court. **31.** Five men held in a Guantanamo Bay detention centre for a decade were released and resettled in Kazakhstan.

## JANUARY 2015

**1.** Lithuania became the 19th country to adopt the euro. **2.** In Turkey, a member of the Marxist Revolutionary People's Liberation Party-Front (DHKP-C) was arrested after throwing a grenade at the offices of the Turkish president in Istanbul. **5.** Irish beef was approved for sale in the USA for the first time in 15 years; a ban had been implemented following the BSE outbreaks of the 1980s and 1990s. **6.** Protests against Muslim immigration into Europe occurred in a number of German cities, including Berlin, Cologne and Dresden; smaller counter-demonstrations were also held. In Turkey, a female suicide bomber belonging to the DHKP-C carried out an attack in Istanbul that killed a police officer. **7–8.** In Paris, two Islamist brothers, Cherif and Said Kouachi, shot and killed 13 people during an attack on the offices of French satirical newspaper *Charlie Hebdo,* which had previously published cartoons of the prophet Mohammed; in a related incident, Islamist Amedy Coulibaly shot and killed a jogger and police officer on 7 and 8 January respectively. **9.** The Kouachi brothers were shot and killed by French police after they had taken a man hostage in the town of Dammartin-en-Goële; Coulibay was also shot and killed by police after killing four out of the 15 people he had held captive in a Jewish supermarket. **10–11.** Large rallies took place throughout France to support the victims of the *Charlie Hebdo* attack (*see* August 7–9); in Paris, an estimated 3.7 million people attended the largest demonstration in French history. **13.** The first issue of *Charlie Hebdo* published since the attack on its offices carried a picture of the prophet Mohammed, causing worldwide controversy (*see* August 7–9). **16.** In Verviers, Belgium, police shot and killed two men alleged to have been members of an Islamist group which had been planning to attack police stations. **19.** In Grozny, capital of the Chechen Republic in Russia, 800,000 people – over half the region's population – demonstrated against the publication of cartoons depicting the prophet Mohammed in the French satirical newspaper *Charlie Hebdo.* **25.** In Greece, the far-left, anti-austerity Syriza party won the legislative elections, finishing two seats short of claming an overall majority. **26–28.** In Ukraine, pro-Russian rebels captured the strategically important Luhansk airport in Donetsk; two days later, the Ukrainian government claimed it had stopped the advance of soldiers from the regular Russian army near the town of Slavyanoserbsk.

## FEBRUARY 2015

**2.** Sergio Mattarella was elected president of Italy by the Italian parliament, becoming the first Sicilian to hold the position. **3.** In Paris, France, Islamist Moussa Coulibay stabbed three police officers outside a Jewish community centre before being arrested. **4.** Artillery shelling killed three people and damaged schools and a hospital in Donetsk, Ukraine; both the pro-Russian rebels and Ukrainian army denied responsibility. In The Hague, the Netherlands, the International Court of Justice ruled that the Serbian and Croatian militaries had not committed genocide during the violent breakup of the former Yugoslavia during the 1990s. Jean-Marie Le Pen, the former leader and honorary president of the far right National Front (NF) party in France, was suspended from the NF after allegedly making racist remarks.

**10.** Fifteen people were killed when pro-Russian rebels launched a missile, hitting a Ukrainian army base in Kramatorsk. **12.** In Minsk, Belarus, a cease-fire was negotiated between the Ukrainian government and pro-Russian rebels. **14–15.** In Copenhagen, Denmark, Omar Abdel Hamid El-Hussein, a 22-year-old Islamist with a criminal background, killed a Danish film director and a Jewish worshipper attending a synagogue; he was shot and killed by police a day later. **18.** Prokopis Pavlopoulos of the New Democracy party was elected president of Greece, having secured the votes of 79 per cent of MPs. **22.** After a by-election defeat, Hungary's governing party, Fidesz, lost its two-thirds parliamentary 'super majority', which had allowed the government to pass laws without support from other parties. **27.** In Moscow, Russia, an unidentified gunman shot and killed Boris Nemtsov, a member of parliament, opposition leader and the former deputy prime minister of Russia.

## MARCH 2015

**1.** In the Estonian parliamentary elections, the ruling Reform party remained the single largest party in the legislature, winning 30 seats. **3.** Slovenia became the 11th EU member state and the first post-communist state to legalise same-sex marriage and the adoption of children by same-sex couples. **4.** In Donetsk, Ukraine, a gas explosion in the pro-Russian rebel-controlled Zasyadko coal mine killed 33 people. **18.** Thousands of protestors attended anti-austerity demonstrations and marched on the European Central Bank in Frankfurt, Germany; around 200 protestors and 100 police officers were injured during clashes. In Paris, France, controversial French comedian Dieudonne M'bala M'bala was found guilty of condoning terrorism and given a two-month suspended prison sentence. **24.** Germanwings Flight 9525, en route from Barcelona to Düsseldorf, crashed 62 miles north-west of Nice in the Alps, killing all 150 passengers and crew on board; the flight's pilot, Andreas Lubitz, was suspected of planning the crash in order to commit suicide. **27.** In Rome, the Italian high court acquitted Amanda Knox and Raffaele Sollecito of murdering British student Meredith Kercher in November 2007. **31.** In Istanbul, Turkey, two gunmen from the banned Revolutionary People's Liberation Party–Front of Turkey attacked a courthouse and took a government prosecutor hostage; both gunmen and the hostage were killed when Special Forces stormed the building. **30.** Ukraine appointed Mikheil Saakashvili, the former president of Georgia and critic of Vladimir Putin, the governor of Odessa and after granting him Ukranian citizenship on 29 May.

## APRIL 2015

**1.** The Russian trawler *Dalniy Vostok* sank off the coast of the Kamchatka peninsula in the Sea of Okhotsk after colliding with ice; 57 of the ship's 132-member crew were killed. **2.** The French parliament banned fashion agencies from hiring underweight or dangerously thin models, in addition to making websites that promote anorexia illegal. **9.** In Milan, Italy, 57-year-old Claudio Giardiello, a defendant in a bankruptcy case, shot and killed three people during an attack on the Palace of Justice; he was arrested shortly after fleeing the scene. **12–16.** Across southern Siberia, wildfires lit by farmers and fuelled by dry weather and high winds spread out of control, killing 26 people, leaving around 6,000 homeless and destroying over 264,000 acres of land. **19.** In Finland, the Centre party won legislative elections, securing 49 seats and 21.1 per cent of the popular vote. **23.** In Veles, Macedonia, 14 African migrants died after being struck by a train after walking on train tracks while attempting to reach northern Europe. **24.** Armenia commemorated the 100th anniversary of the Armenian Genocide. In Cagliari, Italy, police arrested nine members of an al-Qaida-inspired terror cell which had allegedly plotted to attack a number of targets, including The Vatican. **24–25.** The Italian navy rescued 574 African migrants from unsafe boats off the Libyan coast and brought them to the Sicilian port of Augusta. **27.** The Polish government denied entry to the Night Wolves, a Russian nationalist motorcycle gang supported by Vladimir Putin; the group had planned to ride through former Eastern Bloc countries to Berlin in order to celebrate the end of the Second World War. **28.** Finland's navy announced it had dropped depth charges in waters near Helsinki upon detecting a suspected foreign submarine in the region.

MAY 2015

**1–3.** The Italian coastguard rescued 6,800 migrants attempting to cross the Mediterranean from Africa as people smugglers took advantage of good crossing conditions and calm seas. **4.** Jean-Marie Le Pen, the former leader of the far-right French National Front, was suspended from the party for allegedly making racist and anti-Semitic remarks. **15.** The prime minister of Luxembourg, Xavier Bettel, married Gauthier Destenay, a Belgian architect, becoming the first serving leader in the European Union to wed someone of the same sex. **22.** The Republic of Ireland legalised gay marriage via a referendum, becoming the first country in the world to legalise same-sex marriage through a popular vote; 62.07 per cent of the 1,201,607 votes cast were in favour of the proposal. **24.** In Poland, Andrzej Duda of the Law and Justice party was elected president after winning 51.6 per cent of the popular vote in a second round of voting. **29.** The Irish Naval Service patrol vessel *LÉ Eithne* rescued 300 African migrants who had become stranded in the Mediterranean Sea off the coast of Libya.

JUNE 2015

**5.** Greece advised that it would delay debt repayments of €300m (£216m) due on 10 June until the end of the month, becoming the first developed nation to delay a debt repayment to the IMF. **7.** German, Italian and Irish warships rescued more than 2,000 African migrants during a single operation off the coast of Libya. **13–14.** After heavy rainfall in Tbilisi, Georgia, the Vere river flooded, killing 20 people; the flood also struck Tbilisi Zoo, leaving half of its inhabitants – including big cats, wolves and a hippopotamus – either dead or on the loose. **15.** In a court in Lille, the former head of the IMF, Dominique Strauss-Kahn, was found not guilty of 'aggravated pimping', bringing an end to four years of accusations of sexual misconduct. **18–21.** In Belgium, the 200th anniversary of the Battle of Waterloo saw events including staged battle re-enactments and a concert for 200,000 visitors. **26.** In Saint-Quentin-Fallavier, France, the Islamist Yassine Salhi decapitated a man and injured two others during an attack on a chemicals factory; police arrested him later the same day.

JULY 2015

**1.** Greece became the first advanced economy to miss a payment to the IMF since the organisation's establishment in 1945. Gazprom, the Russian state gas producer, suspended shipments of gas to Ukraine following a payment dispute; natural gas accounts for around 40 per cent of Ukraine's energy consumption. **6.** In a referendum, 61 per cent of Greeks voted against accepting the IMF, European Central Bank and European Commission's proposed bailout; the Greek government had campaigned against the bailout, claiming it would impose further austerity measures on the already strained economy. **11.** Demonstrators pelted Aleksandar Vucic, the prime minister of Serbia, with stones when he attended a memorial for the victims of the Srebrenica massacre in Bosnia and Hercegovina; the Serbian army killed 8,000 Muslim Bosnians at Srebrenica in 1995.

**15.** In Lüneburg, Germany, Oskar Gröning, a former SS guard, was sentenced to four years in prison for his role in the killing of 300,000 Hungarian Jews at the Auschwitz concentration camp during the Second World War. **16.** The Greek parliament voted to accept a third bailout package worth $129bn (£91bn) from eurozone partners in exchange for implementing further austerity measures; the decision sparked serious rioting in Athens and other major Greek cities. **29–30.** In Calais, 3,500 migrants attempted to enter the UK via the Channel Tunnel, leading to the death of one Sudanese man; since June, the number of migrants trying to reach the UK from the controversial Sangatte refugee camp in Calais dramatically increased. **30.** In Sirnak province, south-eastern Turkey, three soldiers were killed after members of the Kurdistan Workers Party (PKK) ambushed a military convoy.

## MIDDLE EAST

AUGUST 2014

**1.** A planned 72-hour cease-fire between Israel and Hamas collapsed after Israel accused Hamas of kidnapping an Israeli soldier in Rafah; the two sides had been involved in a military conflict since July 2014. **3.** In Iraq, the Islamic State (IS) captured the Yazidi majority town of Sinjar, forcing 200,000 civilians to leave their homes. In Gaza, Israeli air strikes and shelling killed ten and wounded 30 at a UN-run school. In Tripoli, Libya, fighting between government forces and militants at the city's international airport killed at least 20 people. In Arsal, Lebanon, eight Lebanese soldiers were killed by Islamists near the Syrian border. **7.** Hamas announced it had executed 18 Palestinians suspected of spying for Israel. **10.** Around 40 people died when Sepahan Airlines Flight 5915 crashed shortly after take-off from Mehrabad International airport near Tehran. **14.** In Yemen, a plot to assassinate Ali Abdullah Saleh, the former Yemeni president, with explosives was uncovered by security forces. **15.** Greta Ramelli and Vanessa Marzullo, two Italian women kidnapped in Syria by Islamists in August, were freed. **16.** In Syria, IS executed 80 members of the minority Yazidi religion in the north of the country. **22.** In Diyala province, Iraq, 70 Sunni worshippers died when Shia militants attacked a mosque. **24.** Peter Curtis, a US journalist who had been held captive by a number of Islamist groups for two years, was released in Syria. **27.** A cease-fire between Israel and Hamas began, ending seven weeks of fighting.

SEPTEMBER 2014

**1–11.** The Syrian branch of al-Qaida captured 44 Fijian peacekeepers working for the UN; they were later released unharmed. Mohamed Ali Nasri, the deputy prime minister of Tunisia, survived an assassination attempt made by Islamist militants in the city of Kasserine. In Iraq, Shia militias and US air strikes drove IS out of the town of Amerli, near Baghdad. **4.** In Ghazni, Afghanistan, a Taliban attack utilising truck bombs and rocket-propelled grenades killed 18 people and wounded 150. **6.** In Raqqa, the Syrian air force bombed an IS-run bakery, killing 25 people. **7.** In Zintan, Libya, fighting between tribal groups and Islamists left 12 dead. **8.** Iran announced that Supreme Leader Ayatollah Ali Hosseini Khamenei had successfully undergone prostate surgery. **17.** Tunisian police killed two Islamists during clashes near the Algerian border. **19.** In Yemen, Shia Hothi rebels captured parts of the capital Sana'a, causing the resignation of the government. **21.** Mohammad Reza Rahimi, a former Iranian vice-president, was sentenced to five years in prison for his part in a £1.72bn embezzlement scheme in 2011. **24.** Approximately 250 sub-Saharan African migrants died when a boat bound for Europe capsized off the coast of Tripoli, Libya. **25.** Yemen released three Iranian Revolutionary Guard members who had been held on suspicion of aiding Shia insurgent groups within the country. **26.** Japan announced that nine Japanese nationals had travelled to Syria in order to join IS. **30.** A number of car bomb and mortar attacks on Shia districts in Baghdad killed 35 people.

## OCTOBER 2014

**1.** In Homs, Syria, two suicide bombers killed 39 people during an attack on a school. **3.** Israel reopened the Haram al-Sharif/Temple Mount, one of the holiest sites in Islam and Judaism, to Muslims; the site had been closed to Muslim visitors following the shooting of a right-wing Israeli activist on 29 October. **6.** In Libya, the Islamist group Ansar al-Sharia pledged its allegiance to IS and declared the city of Derna to be an Islamic emirate. **8.** Syria announced the existence of four chemical weapons facilities, which it had not previously revealed to UN weapons inspectors. **10.** In Sana'a, Yemen, a suicide bombing carried out by al-Qaida killed 50 worshippers participating in a Shia ceremony. IS captured the headquarters of Kurdish fighters defending the town of Kobane, Syria. **12.** Fighting between nationalist and Islamist militias in Zintan, Libya, killed 21 people. **13.** Khaled Bahah was appointed prime minister of Yemen after a deal was reached between the country's president and Hothi rebels (see 19 September). **23.** Thousands of people demonstrated in Ishahan, Iran, after eight women were injured in a series of acid attacks; Iranian police arrested four men suspected of involvement in the attacks. **25.** Israel introduced legislation to ban Palestinians from using buses in the West Bank due to security concerns. **29.** The Egyptian army began demolishing around 800 homes near the border with Gaza, in order to provide a buffer zone against weapons smugglers and militants.

## NOVEMBER 2014

**1.** In Iraq, IS murdered 85 members of the Albu Nimr tribe, which had been fighting the group alongside the Iraqi government. **3.** In Libya, fighting broke out in Benghazi after the army attempted to take the port from Islamist rebels. **5.** In Yemen, a US drone attack killed five senior members of al-Qaida. **18.** In west Jerusalem, four Israelis died after two Palestinian men attacked a mosque with guns and axes. Iraqi troops retook the Baiji oil refinery after driving out IS forces. **21.** In Egypt, the first doctor to be prosecuted for carrying out female genital mutilation, which led to the death of 13-year-old Suhair al-Bataa, was acquitted of manslaugher charges. **24.** Iran and the US agreed to extend talks over Tehran's nuclear programme for a further seven months. **28.** An Egyptian court sentenced 78 children aged between 13 and 17 to between two and five years in prison for protesting in favour of the Muslim Brotherhood. The UN declared a state of emergency in Gaza after two days of heavy rain caused widespread flooding and displaced 400,000 Palestinians. **29.** Hosni Mubarak, the former president of Egypt, was found not guilty of ordering the killing of hundreds of protestors during the Arab Spring.

## DECEMBER 2014

**1.** The Simon Wiesenthal Center, the Jewish human rights organisation, announced that wanted Nazi war criminal Alois Brunner had died in Syria in 2010. Islamist militants beheaded a policeman in Kef, Tunisia. **3.** Iran conducted its first air strikes against IS near the country's border with Iraq. **5.** In Baghdad and Kirkuk, a series of car bombs killed 33 people. **10.** In the United Arab Emirates, a court convicted 11 men of being al-Qaida members and for recruiting people to fight in Syria. **11.** Ziad Abu Ein, a minister in the Palestinian Authority, was killed during a confrontation with Israeli troops in Ramallah. **12.** In Israel, a Palestinian man threw acid into the faces of a family of five with four young

children; the attacker was shot and wounded by a passing civilian. **13.** In Iraq, IS captured the town of al-Wafa in Anbar province, killing 19 people. **14.** The Syrian army and allied Hezbollah fighters captured the town of Al Malah, killing 34 IS fighters. **16.** Peter Kassig, a US aid worker and convert to Islam, was beheaded by IS in Syria. **20.** In north-west Iraq, Kurdish and Yazidi fighters recaptured Mt Sinjar from IS (see 3 August). **25.** Israel approved the construction of 243 new settler homes in East Jerusalem. **26.** In al-Bab, Syria, attacks by the Syrian air force on IS-controlled areas killed 45 civilians. **28.** Bahrain officials arrested Sheikh Ali Salman, head of the country's largest Shia opposition group, on unspecified charges. **31.** In Ibb, Yemen, a suicide bomb killed 33 members of the Houthis, a Shia militant group.

## JANUARY 2015

**6.** In Anbar province, Iraq, 23 Iraqi soldiers were killed near a base where American troops were stationed during clashes between the Iraqi army and tribal fighters and IS. In Israel, Hussam Qawasmeh, a Palestinian, was convicted of the abduction and murder of three Israeli teenagers in Hebron, in September. **7.** In Sana'a, Yemen, a suicide bomber killed 30 people outside of a police training centre. In Mayadin, Syria, members of the religious police force established by IS were kidnapped by unknown gunmen. **19.** It was announced that Canadian soldiers had fired on IS militants in Syria, the first time Western troops had been involved in a ground battle during the conflict. **20.** In Syria, an Israeli drone strike killed Mohammad Ali Allahdadi, an Iranian general, as he visited a Hezbollah military base. **21.** IS demanded a ransom of $200m (£132m) after capturing two Japanese citizens near Dabiq, Syria. **22.** In Tel Aviv, Hamza Matrouk, a Palestinian man who had entered Israel illegally, stabbed 12 people on a bus before being arrested. The Yemeni government resigned in protest of the Hothi occupation of the capital Sana'a. **23.** The king of Saudi Arabia, Abdullah bin Abdulaziz Al Saud, 90, died; Crown Prince Salman bin Abdulaziz, 79, was proclaimed his successor. **25.** In Yemen, the Southern Movement, a nationalist organisation based in Aden, declared independence from the rest of the country following the Hothi military coup in Sana'a. **27.** Kurdish fighters drove the final IS fighters out of the town of Kobane; 1,600 people were estimated to have died during the four-month siege. **30.** In Egypt, Islamist militants allied to IS killed 26 policemen and soldiers in the Sinai Peninsula.

## FEBRUARY 2015

**1.** Peter Greste, an Australian Al-Jazeera journalist, was released from an Egyptian prison after spending 400 days behind bars; he was accused of supporting the banned Muslim Brotherhood. **3.** IS released photographs depicting the group's execution of the Royal Jordanian air force officer Muath al-Kasasbeh, originally captured by IS on 24 December 2014, in which the pilot could be seen being burned alive. **6.** In Yemen, Hothi rebels announced that they had overtaken the country's government and dissolved the national parliament in Sana'a. **8.** In Cairo, clashes between police and fans of the football team Zamalek SC killed 22 people; the government indefinitely suspend the Egyptian Premier League following the incident. Following the execution of one of their pilots, Royal Jordanian air force bombers attacked IS targets in Iraq for the first time; the attacks also targeted IS bases near the Syrian towns of Raqqa and Deir ez-Zor. **15.** IS released a video showing the execution of 21 Egyptian Coptic Christians who they had kidnapped near Sirte, Syria, in December 2014 and January 2015. **28.** In Baghdad, Iraq, a series of car bombs carried out by Sunni militants killed 19 people in predominantly Shia areas of the city.

MARCH 2015
**6.** In Idlib, Syria, 13 leaders of the al-Qaida affiliated Islamist group Nusra Front died in an apparent bomb blast while they attended a secret meeting; no group or nation claimed responsibility for the attack. **9.** In Tel Aviv, Israel, around 30,000 people took to the streets to protest against the government of Prime Minister Netanyahu days before the country's general election. **17.** In the Israeli general election, the centre-right Likud party, led by incumbent prime minister Benjamin Netanyahu, remained the largest party in the Knesset, winning 30 out of 120 seats. **18.** In Tunis, Tunisia, Islamist gunmen killed 23 people during an attack on the Bardo National Museum; the perpetrators, Tunisian citizens Yassine Labidi and Saber Khachnaoui, were killed at the scene by armed police officers. **20.** In Hasaka, Syria, two IS car bombs killed 20 Kurds celebrating Nowruz, the traditional start of the Iranian New Year. In Sana'a, Yemen, the al-Badr and al-Hashoosh Shi'ite mosques were simultaneously attacked by four suicide bombers, killing 142 people; IS claimed responsibility. **31.** The Saudia Arabian air force bombed the al-Mazrak refugee camp in Yemen in error, killing 40 civilians.

APRIL 2015
**2.** In Al Mukalla, Yemen, al-Qaida fighters freed 300 prisoners, including senior al-Qaida members, following an attack on the city's prison. In Sinai province, Egypt, 15 soldiers and two civilians were killed when IS-affiliated gunmen attacked military checkpoints near the town of Sheikh Zuweid. **12.** In Tripoli, Libya, IS gunmen attacked the South Korean embassy killing two guards, while an IS bomb damaged the Moroccan embassy building. **17.** Izzat Ibrahim al-Douri, the most senior member of Saddam Hussein's government to evade capture following the US-led invasion of Iraq in 2003, was killed by Iraqi troops near the city of Tikrit. **20.** In Sana'a, Yemen, Saudi Arabian air strikes detonated a Hothi rebel armoury, creating an explosion that killed 15 people. **26.** In Anbar province, Iraq, a series of bombings targeting government buildings, military checkpoints and Shi'a areas killed 22 people.

MAY 2015
**2.** In Anbar province, Iraq, IS suicide bombers killed 12 soldiers near a military checkpoint; simultaneous bomb attacks by IS in Baghdad killed a further 14 civilians. **6.** The Libyan government detained 600 African migrants from Somalia, Eritrea, Ghana and Mali who had been attempting to cross the Mediterranean and enter Italy. **9.** In Cairo, Hosni Mubarak, the former president of Egypt, was sentenced to three years in prison for embezzling $14m (£9.3m); Mubarak was originally convicted of the offence in May 2014, but the conviction was quashed on appeal in January 2015. **14.** In Benghazi, Libya, eight people were killed, including seven children, when a rocket hit a residential building; the Libyan army blamed Islamist militants for the attack. **16.** An Egyptian court banned organised associations of football fans after a number of violent incidents in 2014 and 2015; the government had also accused football fan organisations of having links to the banned Muslim Brotherhood. **19–21.** In Algeria, a military campaign in the mountainous Ferkioua region killed 25 members of the IS-affiliated Jund al-Khilafah rebel group. **20.** Israel ended a controversial three-month pilot programme of segregating Israeli and Palestinian bus commuters on safety grounds. In Syria, IS captured the town of Tadmur, causing over a thousand civilians to flee the area, and the adjacent ruins of Palmyra, a UNESCO World Heritage site (see 2–23 June). **30.** The Syrian airforce bombed civilian targets in Aleppo and the IS-controlled town of al-Bab, killing 72 people.

JUNE 2015
**1.** In Anbar province, Iraq, 45 police officers died when three suicide bombers attacked a military base. **2–23.** IS began destroying sections of the ancient city of Palmyra, including pre-Islamic Arabian statues and Roman-era shrines; the UNESCO Director-General Irina Bokova described the destruction as a 'war crime'. **7.** In Sana'a, Yemen, Saudi Arabian airstrikes on the country's military headquarters, controlled by Houthi rebels, killed 44 people and injured 100. **10.** The Tunisian navy rescued more than 350 migrants, who had attempted to sail from Libya to the Italian island of Lampedusa. **11.** The al-Nusra Front, an al-Qaida-affiliated Islamist group, executed at least 20 Druze villagers in Qalb Lawzah, Syria. **17.** Twenty people were killed in Sana'a, Yemen, after IS bombed a number of the city's Shia mosques. **18.** In Galilee, Israel, the Church of the Multiplication of the Loaves and Fish, purportedly the site of Jesus' feeding of the 5,000 miracle, was badly damaged in an arson attack; two Israeli settlers were arrested in relation to the crime. **21.** Kurdish troops captured the Syrian town of Ayn Issa and advanced to within 50km of IS's de facto capital of Raqqa. **26.** In Kuwait City, Kuwait, a suicide bomb attack on a Shia mosque killed 25 worshippers. In the tourist complex of Port El Kantaoui, Tunisia, Seifeddine Yacoubi, an Islamist, launched an attack on holidaymakers on the beach before entering the five-star Riu Imperial Marhaba Hotel; 38 tourists, including 30 British nationals, were killed, while a further 39 were injured, before police killed the assailant. **27.** Kurdish forces finally drove IS fighters out of the Syrian city of Kobani; the Islamists had launched a surprise assault on the town on 21 June. **30.** In Taiz, Yemen, an attack by al-Qaida supporters on a prison freed 1,200 inmates, including many suspected al-Qaida members.

JULY 2015
**1.** In North Sinai, simultaneous IS attacks on military checkpoints, including three suicide bombs, killed 60 Egyptian soldiers. **5.** Egypt launched air strikes and ground offensives in the north of the Sinai Peninsula, killing 63 IS-affiliated Islamists. In Yemen, air strikes launched by the Saudi Arabian air force struck a cattle market in Lahj province, killing 40 civilians. **12.** In Israel, Khader Adnan, the leader of the militant Islamist Jihad organisation Palestinian Islamic Jihad, was freed from prison after agreeing to end a 56-day hunger strike; Adnan had been held without charge following his arrest by Israeli forces during Operation Protective Edge in 2014. **14.** Iran agreed a nuclear non-proliferation treaty with the five permanent members of the UN security council plus Germany, ending six years of negotiations; the deal involved Iran storing less uranium and closing nuclear centrifuges, both of which can be used to build nuclear weapons, in return for Western countries lifting economic sanctions. **18.** In Khan Bani Saad, Iraq, 115 people celebrating the end of the Eid festival were killed after an IS suicide bomber attacked a marketplace. **22.** Israel introduced controversial 20-year jail sentences for people convicted of throwing stones at vehicles and roads; stone throwing has been a common Palestinian method of protesting against Israel since the 1980s. **23.** In Cairo, 21 people were killed when a cargo ship collided with a passenger boat hosting a wedding party on the river Nile. **28.** A court in Libya sentenced Saif al-Islam Gaddafi, son of former Libyan leader Colonel Muammar Gaddafi, after finding him guilty of committing war crimes during the 2011 Libyan civil war. **31.** In Jerusalem, Yishai Schlissel, a member of the conservative Haredi school of Judaism, attacked a gay pride march, stabbing and killing a 16-year-old girl and injuring six others; Schlissel had previously been imprisoned for attacking another gay pride march in 2005.

# OBITUARIES 2014–15

**Abse**, Dannie, CBE, poet, aged 91 – *b*. 22 September 1923, *d*. 28 September 2014

**Aghion**, Gaby, Egyptian-born founder of French fashion house Chloé, aged 93 – *b*. 3 March 1921, *d*. 27 September 2014

**Alba (18th)**, Duchess of, Spanish aristocrat, aged 88 – *b*. 28 March 1926, *d*. 20 November 2014

**Allenby (3rd)**, Viscount, aged 83 – *b*. 20 April 1931, *d*. 3 October 2014

**Anson**, Vice-Adm. Sir Edward, KCB, naval aviator: Flag Officer, Naval Air Command (1979–82); Chief of Staff to C-in-C Fleet (1982–4); Senior Naval Adviser, British Aerospace (1989–91), aged 85 – *b*. 11 May 1929, *d*. 22 September 2014

**Atkinson**, Frank, CBE, museum curator who created the Beamish 'living museum', which opened to visitors in 1972, aged 90 – *b*. 13 April 1924, *d*. 30 December 2014

**Baer**, Ralph, German-born American video game developer and inventor, aged 92 – *b*. 8 March 1922, *d*. 6 December 2014

**Barbour**, Very Revd Prof. Robin, KCVO, MC, Moderator of the General Assembly of Scotland (1979–80), Dean of the Chapel Royal in Scotland (1981–91), aged 93 – *b*. 11 May 1921, *d*. 18 October 2014

**Barnett**, Lord, PC, life peer; Labour MP for Heywood and Royton (1964–83) and Chief Secretary to the Treasury (1974–9), aged 91 – *b*. 14 October 1923, *d*. 1 November 2014

**Bellingham**, Lynda, OBE, actor, aged 66 – *b*. 31 May 1948, *d*. 19 October 2014

**Beltoise**, Jean-Pierre, French racing driver, aged 77 – *b*. 26 April 1937, *d*. 5 January 2015

**Bilk**, Acker, jazz clarinettist, aged 85 – *b*. 28 January 1929, *d*. 2 November 2014

**bin Abdulaziz**, King Abdullah, King of Saudi Arabia, aged 90 – *b*. 1 August 1924, *d*. 22 January 2015

**Black**, Cilla, OBE, pop singer and TV presenter, aged 72 – *b*. 27 May 1943, *d*.1 August 2015

**Black**, Tim, CBE, physician and co-founder of Marie Stopes International (1975), aged 77 – *b*. 7 January 1937, *d*. 11 December 2014

**Bonsall**, Sir Arthur, KCMG, CBE, director of GCHQ (1973–8), aged 97 – *b*. 25 June 1917, *d*. 26 November 2014

**Botín**, Emilio, Spanish banker; chair of Banco Santander Group (1986–2014), aged 79 – *b*. 1 October 1934, *d*. 9 September 2014

**Bradfield**, Sir John, CBE, senior bursar of Trinity College, Cambridge (1956–92), aged 89 – *b*. 20 May 1925, *d*. 13 October 2014

**Brittan of Spennithorne**, Lord, PC, QC, Conservative MP for Cleveland and Whitby (1974-83), Richmond (1983-8); Chief Secretary to the Treasury (1981–3); Home Secretary (1983–5); Vice-President of the European Commission (Mar–Sep 1999), aged 75 – *b*. 25 September 1939, *d*. 21 January 2015

**Bruce**, Jack, musician, aged 71 – *b*. 14 May 1943, *d*. 25 October 2014

**Bunce**, Michael, OBE, BBC TV editor, aged 79 – *b*. 24 April 1935, *d*. 31 December 2014

**Cabu**, French caricaturist, aged 76 – *b*. 13 January 1938, *d*. 7 January 2015

**Chapman**, Sir Sydney, Conservative MP for Birmingham Handsworth (1970–4) and Chipping Barnet (1979–95), instigator of the 'Plant a Tree in '73' campaign; Parliamentary Private Secretary to the Secretary of State for Transport (1979–81) and Social Services (1981–3); Lord Comissioner of HM Treasury (1990–2); Vice-Chamberlain of HM Household (1992–5), aged 78 – *b*. 17 October 1935, *d*. 9 October 2014

**Charbonnier**, Stéphane, editor and cartoonist for *Charlie Hebdo*, aged 47 – *b*. 21 August 1967, *d*. 7 January 2015

**Cheney**, Dorothy, American tennis player, aged 98 – *b*. 1 September 1916, *d*. 23 November 2014

**Chesworth**, John, dancer, choreographer and artistic director of the Rambert Dance Company (1974–80), aged 84 – *b*. 22 June 1930, *d*. 27 November 2014

**Churchill-Coleman**, George, OBE, QPM, head of the Metropolitan Police's anti-terrorist branch (1990–7), aged 76 – *b*. 17 November 1938, *d*. 10 January 2015

**Clarke**, Geoffrey, RA, sculptor and stained glass artist, aged 89 – *b*. 28 November 1924, *d*. 30 October 2014

**Clarke**, Warren, actor, aged 67 – *b*. 26 April 1947, *d*. 12 November 2014

**Clemens**, Brian, television screenwriter and producer; lead writer of the 1960s series *The Avengers,* aged 83 – *b*. 30 July 1931, *d*. 10 January 2015

**Close**, Brian, CBE, cricketer, aged 84 – *b*. 24 February 1931, *d*. 13 September 2015

**Collins**, Jackie, OBE, novelist, aged 77 – *b*. 4 October 1937, *d*. 19 September 2015

**Craven**, Wes, American film director, aged 76 – *b*. 2 August 1939, *d*. 30 August 2015

**d'Artois**, Sonya, MBE, Second World War SOE agent, aged 90 – *b*. 14 May 1924, *d*. 21 December 2014

**Davidge**, Christopher, Olympic oarsman, aged 85 – *b*. 5 November 1929, *d*. 22 December 2014

**de la Renta**, Oscar, fashion designer, aged 82 – *b*. 22 July 1932, *d*. 20 October 2014

**Devonshire**, Deborah, Dowager Duchess of, DCVO, youngest of the Mitford sisters and châtelaine of Chatsworth House, pivotal in its restoration, aged 94 – *b*. 31 March 1920, *d*. 24 September 2014

**Doar**, John, American lawyer who as Assistant Attorney-General of the US Federal Justice Department's Civil Rights Division (1965–7) secured convictions against seven members of the Ku Klux Klan who had been involved in lynching three civil rights activists in 1964, aged 92 – *b*. 3 December 1921, *d*. 11 November 2014

**Dobbin**, Jim, Labour MP for Heywood & Middleton (1997–2014), aged 73 – *b*. 7 May 1941, *d*. 7 September 2014

**Dorkenoo**, Efua, OBE, nurse, midwife and anti-FGM campaigner, aged 65 – *b*. 6 September 1949, *d*. 18 October 2014

**Ekberg**, Anita, Swedish actor, aged 83 – *b*. 29 September 1931, *d*. 11 January 2015

**Eveleigh**, Rt. Hon. Sir Edward, Lord Justice of Appeal (1977–85), aged 96 – *b*. 8 October 1917, *d*. 24 September 2014

**Fenner**, Dame Peggy (Edith), DBE, Conservative MP for Rochester & Chatham (1970–4 and 1979–83) and Medway (1983–97); aged 91 – *b*. 12 November 1922, *d*. 15 September 2014

**Fife (3rd)**, Duke of, aged 85 – *b*. 23 September 1929, *d*. 22 June 2015

**Forbes**, Elizabeth, music journalist and opera specialist who wrote the *Whitaker's* opera article for a considerable number of years, aged 90 – *b*. 3 August 1924, *d*. 22 October 2014

**Freeman**, John, MBE, PC, politician, journalist, diplomat and television executive, aged 99 – *b*. 19 February 1915, *d*. 20 December 2014

**Frutiger**, Adrian, Swiss typographer, aged 87 – *b*. 24 May 1928, *d*. 13 September 2015

**Glen Haig**, Dame Mary, DBE, Olympic fencer, president of the British Fencing Association (1974–86) and member of the International Olympic Committee (1982–93) aged 96 – *b*. 12 July 1918, *d*. 15 November 2014

**Grierson**, Sir Ronald, banker and industrialist, aged 93 – *b*. 6 August 1921, *d*. 23 October 2014

**Gunn**, Sheila, MBE, journalist and press adviser to former prime minister John Major (1995–7), aged 66 – *b.* 29 August 1948, *d.* 17 October 2014

**Halsey**, A. H., Professor of Social and Administrative Studies, University of Oxford (1978–90), aged 91 – *b.* 13 April 1923, *d.* 14 October 2014

**Harris**, Keith, entertainer and ventriloquist, aged 67 – *b.* 21 September 1947, *d.* 28 April 2015

**Henry**, Ron, footballer, aged 80 – *b.* 17 August 1934, *d.* 27 December 2014

**Herries of Terregles (14th)**, Lady, racehorse trainer, aged 76 – *b.* 12 June 1938, *d.* 25 November 2014

**Hodgson**, Sir Maurice, chairman of ICI (1978–82) and British Home Stores (1982–7), also chief executive of BHS (1982–5), aged 94 – *b.* 21 October 1919, *d.* 1 October 2014

**Hogwood**, Christopher, CBE, musician and scholar who founded the Academy of Ancient Music orchestra in 1973, aged 73 – *b.* 10 September 1941, *d.* 24 September 2014

**Hollom**, Sir Jasper, KBE, Deputy Governor of the Bank of England (1970–80), aged 96 – *b.* 16 December 1917, *d.* 29 August 2014

**Houston**, Maj.-Gen. David, CVO, CBE, Lord-Lieutenant for Sutherland (1991–2004), aged 85 – b. 24 February 1929, d. 10 November 2014

**Hughes**, Phillip, Australian cricketer, aged 25 – *b.*, 30 November 1988, *d.* 27 November 2014

**James of Holland Park**, Baroness (P. D. James), OBE, crime novelist, aged 94 – *b.* 3 August 1920, *d.* 22 November 2014

**Kay**, Bernard, actor, aged 86 – *b.* 23 February 1928, *d.* 25 December 2014

**Kennedy**, Charles, Liberal Democrat politician: MP for Ross, Skye and Lochaber (2005–15), Ross, Skye and Inverness West (1997–2005) and Ross, Cromarty and Skye (1983–97); Leader of the Liberal Democrats (1999–2006), aged 55 – *b.* 25 November 1959, *d.* 1 June 2015

**King**, B. B., American blues singer, songwriter and guitarist, aged 89 – *b.* 16 September 1925, *d.* 14 May 2015

**King**, Ben E., American R&B and soul singer, aged 76 – *b.* 28 September 1938, *d.* 30 April 2015

**Kirkbride**, Anne, actor, aged 60 – *b.* 21 June 1954, *d.* 19 January 2015

**Larson**, Glen A., American TV producer and writer, aged 77 – *b.* 3 January 1937, *d.* 14 November 2014

**Laws**, Dick, CBE, Director of the British Antarctic Survey (1973–87), aged 88 – *b.* 23 April 1926, *d.* 7 October 2014

**Lee**, Christopher, CBE, actor, aged 93 – *b.* 27 May 1922, *d.* 7 June 2015

**Lomax**, David, BBC reporter, aged 76 – *b.* 18 May 1938, *d.* 5 September 2014

**MacCormick**, Iain, Scottish National Party MP for Argyll (1974–9), aged 74 – *b.* 28 September 1939, *d.* 19 September 2014

**McFall**, Ray, owner of the Cavern Club, Liverpool (1959–66) who helped launch The Beatles, aged 88 – *b.* 14 November 1926, *d.* 8 January 2015

**MacKay**, Dave, footballer, aged 80 – *b.* 14 November 1934, *d.* 2 March 2015

**Macnee**, Patrick, actor, aged 93 – *b.* 6 February 1922, *d.* 25 June 2015

**Marlborough (11th)**, Duke of, aged 88 – *b.* 13 April 1926, *d.* 16 October 2014

**Meade**, Richard, OBE, equestrian rider and Olympic gold medallist, aged 76 – *b.* 4 December 1938, *d.* 8 January 2015

**Molitor**, Karl, Swiss downhill skier, aged 94 – *b.* 29 June 1920, *d.* 25 August 2014

**Nichols**, Mike, American film and theatre director, aged 83 – *b.* 6 November 1931, *d.* 19 November 2014

**Nimoy**, Leonard, actor, aged 83 – *b.* 26 March 1931, *d.* 27 February 2015

**Oilvero**, Magda, Spanish soprano, aged 104 – *b.* 25 March 1910, *d.* 8 September 2014

**Ollerenshaw**, Dame Kathleen, DBE, DPHIL, educationist and mathematician, aged 101 – *b.* 1 October 1912, *d.* 10 August 2014

**Partridge**, Pat, football referee, aged 81 – *b.* 30 June 1933, *d.* 31 October 2014

**Pasco**, Richard, actor, aged 88 – *b.* 18 July 1926, *d.* 12 November 2014

**Percival**, Lance, comic actor and entertainer, aged 81 – *b.* 26 July 1933, *d.* 6 January 2015

**Polak**, Prof. Dame Julia, DBE, endocrine pathologist, aged 75 – *b.* 29 June 1939, *d.* 11 August 2014

**Pratchett**, Sir Terry, OBE, fantasy writer, aged 66 – *b.* 28 April 1948, *d.* 12 March 2015

**Redfern**, David, photographer, aged 78 – *b.* 7 June 1936 *d.* 22 October 2014

**Reeve**, Sir Anthony, KCMG, KCVO, Ambassador to Jordan (1988–91) and High Commissioner to South Africa (1991–6), aged 76 – *b.* 20 October 1938, *d.* 6 November 2014

**Richardson**, Lt.-Gen. Sir Robert, KCB, CVO, CBE, GOC Berlin (1978–80); Vice Adj. Gen. and Director of Army Manning (1980–2); GOC NI (1982–5); Lieutenant of the Tower of London (1992–5), aged 85 – *b.* 2 March 1929, *d.* 21 November 2014

**Ryall**, David, actor, aged 79 – *b.* 5 January 1935, *d.* 25 December 2014

**Sacks**, Oliver, CBE, FRCP, neurologist, aged 82 – *b.* 9 July 1933, *d.* 30 August 2015

**Sample**, Joe, jazz musician, agted 75 – *b.* 1 February 1939, *d.* 12 September 2014

**Sata**, Michael, president of Zambia (2011–14), aged 77 – *b.* 6 July 1937, *d.* 28 October 2014

**Scott-Joynt**, Rt. Revd Michael, Bishop of Winchester (1995–2011), aged 71 – *b.* 15 March 1943, *d.* 27 September 2014

**Sewell**, Brian, art critic, aged 84 – *b.* 15 June 1931, *d.* 19 Sep 2015

**Shand Kydd**, William, businessman, jockey and racehorse owner, aged 77 – *b.* 12 May 1937, *d.* 27 December 2014

**Sharif**, Omar, Egyptian actor, aged 83 – *b.* 10 April 1032, *d.* 10 July 2015

**Shaw**, Colin, CBE, chief secretary of the BBC (1972–6), aged 85 – *b.* 2 November 1928, *d.* 18 September 2014

**Sheppard of Didgemere**, Lord, KCVO, industrialist and Conservative peer, aged 82 – *b.* 25 December 1932, *d.* 25 March 2015

**Staughton**, Sir Christopher, PC, Lord Justice of Appeal (1987–97), aged 81 – *b.* 24 May 1933, *d.* 15 October 2014

**Somerville**, Philip, milliner, aged 84 – *b.* 12 February 1930, *d.* 14 September 2014

**Sykes**, Rt. Revd Prof. Stephen, Bishop of Ely (1990–9), aged 75 – *b.* 1 August 1939, *d.* 24 September 2014

**Thorpe**, Jeremy, PC, Liberal MP for Devon North (1959–79) and leader of the Liberal Party (1967–76), aged 85 – *b.* 29 April 1929, *d.* 4 December 2014

**Timofeyeva**, Nina, Russian ballerina, aged 79 – *b.* 11 June 1935, *d.* 3 November 2014

**Townsend**, Lady Juliet, DCVO, Lady in Waiting to Princess Margaret (1965–71), High Sheriff of Northamptonshire (1991–2) and Lord-Lieutenant of Northamptonshire (1998–2014), aged 73 – *b.* 9 September 1941, *d.* 29 November 2014

**Tracey**, Sheila, BBC broadcaster and musician, aged 80 – *b.* 10 January 1934, *d.* 30 September 2014

**Tyler**, Dorothy, British high jumper who competed in four Olympic Games (1936, 1948, 1952 and 1956), aged 94 – *b.* 14 March 1920, *d.* 25 September 2014

**Vaux of Harrowden**, Lord, aged 74 – *b.* 1940, *d.* 16 December 2014

**Wellington (8th)**, Duke of, KG, LVO, OBE, MC, aged 99 – *b.* 2 July 1915, *d.* 31 December 2014

**Whitlam**, Gough, AC, QC, prime minister of Australia (1972–4), aged 98 – *b.* 11 July 1916, *d.* 21 October 2014

**Wynne**, David, OBE, sculptor, aged 88 – *b.* 25 May 1926, *d.* 4 September 2014

**Zapf**, Herman, German typeface designer and calligrapher, aged 96 – *b.* 8 November 1918, *d.* 4 June 2015

# ARCHAEOLOGY

Dr Nadia Durrani and Dr Neil Faulkner

## CANNIBAL CLUES AT GOUGH'S CAVE

New analysis of 14,700-year-old human remains from Gough's Cave in Somerset has confirmed that the site witnessed extensive cannibalism during the Magdalenian period (c.15,000–12,000 BC).

A recurring theme of Magdalenian sites in Europe is that human burials are rarely found, but fragmentary skeletal remains are often discovered mixed in with other occupational refuse. As these bones sometimes show traces of butchery, it has been suggested that during this period, communities may have disposed of their dead through ritual cannibalism, though the theory has remained controversial.

Fresh analysis of the Gough Cave remains is adding vital information to the debate. The evidence consists of some 205 fragments, representing at least six individuals, including a child aged around three years, two adolescents aged 12–14 and 14–16, and three adults. It has long been disputed whether the cut marks on their surfaces represent some kind of funerary defleshing, or whether the people were practising cannibalism, either for survival or ritual purposes. The new research, by the Natural History Museum, University College London and several Spanish universities, involved detailed examination of the bone fragments using focus variation microscope (which produced detailed 3D digital models of each cut mark) and scanning electron microscope technology.

The findings reveal much more extensive evidence of prehistoric processing of the remains, and across a wider range of body parts, than had been observed in any previous studies. Among the discoveries was clear evidence for defleshing, disarticulation, human chewing, crushing of spongy bone and the cracking of bones to extract marrow, according to lead researcher Dr Silvia Bello of the Natural History Museum. Of the post-cranial bones examined, some 58 per cent show cut marks, while 32 per cent indicate that the bones were being deliberately broken in order to extract highly nutritious marrow and grease within, and 53 per cent of the bones show evidence of chewing by human mouths.

Similar patterns of butchery marks are also seen on the bones of other large animals recovered from the site. However, the fact that the human skulls were then turned into cups or bowls makes it likely that their cannibalisation had a clear ritual element (as opposed to a purely nutritional purpose). This begs the question, still to be answered, whether ritual cannibalism was a regional ('Creswellian') phenomenon or a more widespread practice found throughout the Magdalenian world.

## NEW LIGHT ON THE MESOLITHIC

A wealth of prehistoric remains uncovered on the site of the Dunragit Bypass in Dumfries spanned 7,000 years and included what is probably the oldest house ever seen in south-west Scotland. Mesolithic (or Middle Stone Age, c.10,000–4000 BC) hunter-gatherers had constructed a circular post-built structure in about 6000 BC, as indicated by radiocarbon dates. The 'house' may have been used as a shelter while on hunting expeditions. Huge numbers of microliths – tiny (often sharp) flint tools – were knapped on the site, with some 13,500 tools and waste flakes found in an area of just 10m x 10m. Meanwhile, a perforated stone adze, used in woodworking, was also found during the excavations,

and may have been one of the tools used in the construction of the building. The site lies close to the sea – like many Mesolithic sites in Scotland – and it seems likely that the inhabitants exploited local fish and shellfish, as well as gathering and hunting in the hinterland.

Another new Mesolithic discovery has been Britain's earliest cremation burial. A team from Oxford Archaeology uncovered the remains while working at Langford in Essex. The archaeologists found some 118g of burnt human bone, together with large amounts of charcoal and three struck flints, within a 1m-wide pit, which its makers had then carefully backfilled. Three radiocarbon dates, obtained from two bone fragments and one charcoal sample, have confirmed that the burial dates from 5600 BC – much to the surprise of the researchers. Previously, only around 20 examples of Mesolithic human remains had been found in Britain, none of them cremated.

The discovery demonstrates that, despite the still largely nomadic lifestyles of the hunter-gatherer communities who lived in Britain at this time, they must have committed considerable skill and resources to the disposal of their dead: in order to cremate the bodies, they needed sufficient understanding and control of fire to achieve the necessary high temperatures, likely over 600°C.

Oxford Archaeology's Dr Louise Loe, who analysed the bone, identified the remains of at least one adult, although the total weight of bone is only about 7 per cent of what would be expected from a complete individual. Given the large amount of charcoal present, the deposit might represent the ritual burial of a portion of the burnt remains from the pyre, rather than the careful collection of all the cremated bone.

The burnt burial was discovered during archaeological work ahead of the construction of a new pipeline for Essex and Suffolk Water, which funded the excavations. A Bronze Age barrow, traces of an Early Roman farmstead, an Anglo-Saxon settlement and the remains of a medieval building were also identified during the project.

Still with the Mesolithic, traces of ancient wheat have been found in sediments submerged beneath the Solent. These 6,000-year-old grains suggest that Mesolithic Britain was not as cut off culturally from Europe as had previously been believed. This seems confirmed by another recent discovery: analysis of ancient DNA preserved in sediments that had once formed the surface of a now-sunken prehistoric landscape at Bouldnor Cliff has revealed the presence of einkorn, a variety of wheat known to have been cultivated in prehistoric southern England, but now seen to be present 2,000 years before farming took off in Britain.

These discoveries are highly significant. They imply strong cross-Channel links, with British hunter-gatherers maintaining extensive social and trading networks with Continental European farmers, probably taking advantage of the land bridges that, thanks to previously lower sea-levels, once connected Britain's south-east coast to the Continent. An additional implication may be that the transition to farming was a much more gradual, evolutionary process than previously assumed. As project co-leader Professor Vincent Gaffney of the University of Bradford points out, the einkorn find represents the start of a new chapter in British and European history, and demonstrates how the introduction of farming to Britain was a complex process.

Some of the new wealth of Mesolithic archaeology has turned up in surprising places. It had been assumed for example that the history of Chester began with the arrival of the Roman army in the early 70s AD. However, when the city's Roman amphitheatre (of which there were, in fact, two incarnations) was excavated between 2004 and 2006, evidence for much earlier human activity was recovered. Post-excavation analysis has now confirmed the surprising date. Beneath the seating of Chester's first amphitheatre (constructed as soon as the legionaries arrived, in the AD 70s), the team uncovered extensive pre-Roman remains.

The entire sequence was found to date back to around 5500 BC, when the area was occupied by nomadic Mesolithic hunter-gatherers. With the progression of time, the remains become increasingly complex – including evidence for Chester's earliest known house, a single Iron Age round-house, burnt down around 400–200 BC. Finally, from the Late Iron Age, just prior to the arrival of the Romans, the team uncovered extremely rare evidence of 'cord-rig earthworks', representing the remains of ridge-and-furrow ploughed fields.

## ROMANS AT SILCHESTER, COLCHESTER AND CHEDWORTH

The 18-year-long excavations of Insula IX at Silchester (*Calleva Atrebatum*) Roman town finally ended in August 2014. The 18 seasons, totalling 108 weeks, of the Silchester Town Life Project exposed some 3,000m² of the *insula* and provided a complete sample of the life of the settlement from the 1st century BC to the 5th century AD. The project revealed at least six main phases. These included the most complex 'town planning' ever seen in the archaeology of Late Iron Age Britain, arrangements which continued to influence the layout of the subsequent Roman town into the late 3rd century AD. Of particular importance was an imposing Iron Age structure 50m in length and 8m in width which had a large D-shaped enclosure on its northern side. Close to this, the team – over 250 volunteers in the final season, mainly from the University of Reading, some from other universities, some local volunteers – found a well containing water-logged plant remains that promise to shed light on environment and diet in the years immediately prior to the Roman conquest of AD 43. The excavation trench has now been backfilled and the land returned to pasture.

Grim evidence of the contested nature of that conquest has meanwhile emerged elsewhere. Two pieces of burnt and blackened bone – a fragment of human jaw-bone and a sliced-through fragment of tibia – have been excavated by the Colchester Archaeological Trust on a site close to Colchester High Street. Both bones were recovered from the remains of burnt buildings cleared away after the Boudican Revolt, and both appear to represent instances of violent death. Only one previous example of the possible remains of a victim of the revolt has been found in Colchester (*Camulodunum*) – during excavations about 95m north of the present site in 1965.

Equally suggestive of the trauma of the revolt was the discovery of a cache of jewellery, apparently squirrelled away by a wealthy Roman woman before her house was burnt down in AD 61. She may have perished in the revolt; she certainly never returned to recover the cache, which comprised rings, earrings, bracelets and armlets executed in gold and silver, along with the remains of a small jewellery box. From the same room as that in which the hoard was found came the remains of dates, figs, peas and grain, and also the remains of a collapsed shelf.

Meanwhile, the National-Trust owned property of Chedworth, in the heart of the Cotswolds, is one of England's best-preserved Roman villas. But despite having been excavated several times over the past 150 years, the villa was poorly understood, and indeed poorly presented to the public. In 2010, therefore, the National Trust launched a seven-year project to reinvestigate the site and to revamp it for the visitor.

The villa has three ranges – to the north, the west and the east – and for the first three years the focus was on the West Range. The excavation team uncovered a number of mosaics, a new, fully modern cover-building now stands over the entire length of the range, replacing the dark and dank Victorian cover-building, and so transforming the visitor experience.

From the summer of 2013, the research focus shifted to the North Range, believed to be even more spectacular than the West Range. Among the discoveries has been fragments of a once-major and spectacular mosaic that covered the floor of the North Range grand 'reception hall'. Analysis of marble found in the North Range revealed that it originated from imperial quarries on the Greek island of Euboea, so indicating that, certainly by the 4th century AD, Chedworth was a prestigious and wealthy establishment.

Work on the North Range is due to be completed by 2017, by which time – funding allowing – it is hoped that there will be enough research information to erect a new North Range cover-building.

## SECRETS OF THE STAFFORDSHIRE HOARD

The Staffordshire Hoard, famously discovered by a metal-detectorist in 2009, consists of over 3,500 items of Anglo-Saxon gold and silver metalwork, making it the largest of its type ever found in Britain. The analysis into this unparalleled hoard continues apace, and this year a pioneering research project undertaken at the British Museum has explored the metal-working techniques used by its makers. This project has revealed that the Early Medieval goldsmiths were using techniques far more sophisticated than previously appreciated.

It seems that the craftspeople had developed a complex chemical method of leeching out alloy from the surface of the gold objects, in order to give the impression that the items were of much purer gold than was in fact the case. (Gold objects are routinely made using alloys containing silver and copper; today's 18-carat gold, for example, is 75 per cent pure gold and 25 per cent other metals.) In some of the gold under analysis, the pieces were found to have a composition of 25–50 per cent silver at their core, but only 6–10 per cent silver on the surface. Such an intricate process of alloy extraction may have been a closely guarded secret among Anglo-Saxon goldsmiths, and certainly no description of how it was achieved survives from the period.

So were the goldsmiths manipulating their creations to cheat their patrons by passing off lower-quality material as pure gold? Not necessarily. The project revealed that in some cases the silver content was most likely reduced for artistic reasons, particularly on objects with decorated filigree, such as sword pommels. Here, their backing sheets have been enhanced, but the delicate patterns of the gold wires soldered onto them have not, so creating a striking contrast.

The sparkling findings were announced in October 2014 at Birmingham Museum and Art Gallery's launch of its new Staffordshire Hoard permanent gallery.

## VIKING DECAPITATIONS ANALYSED

One of the big discoveries of 2009 was a mass grave of decapitated men on Ridgeway Hill in Dorset (54 skeletons and 51 heads were found). As well as having been decapitated, the bodies had been tumbled into the grave without ceremony, making excavation a complex and time-consuming business. Though the victims had been stripped –

there was no evidence of clothing in the form of buckles or dress pins, for example – their arms had not been bound. The improvised grave was a disused Roman quarry-pit. Little more could be divined, however, during excavation.

The key discoveries only came later, in the laboratory, through scientific dating and detailed forensic analysis of the human remains. This analysis wrought significant results. All the bodies were of men, most of them aged 18–25 years old, though the youngest was early to mid-teens and the oldest in his 50s. Sample radiocarbon dates – from bones in the upper, middle and lower parts of the grave – gave consistent results of AD 970–1025, putting the event represented firmly in the context of a period of major wars between Anglo-Saxons and Vikings. Isotope analysis – which uses traces of minerals in bones and teeth to identify where someone lived – revealed the skeletons to belong to Scandinavians with a wide range of geographical origins and migratory histories. One man had filed his two front upper incisors, perhaps to mark his status as a warrior. The implication seemed to be that these were Viking prisoners of war who had been summarily executed by Anglo-Saxon enemies. But the interpretation is not straightforward.

That they were executed is beyond doubt, though it seems to have been done messily, with an average of four sword cuts per victim, centred on the neck, but in some cases striking the back of the head or the shoulder. Yet the victims appear not to have been bound, and if they were indeed warriors, why did they not resist? Some, moreover, seem to have been in poor health. One man, for example, had osteomyelitis and a leg so badly infected that the bone had grown to twice its normal thickness. There was also a marked absence of both healed trauma from earlier injuries and the multiple blows (other than the botched decapitations) usually associated with battlefield skeletal assemblages. So, while the best working hypothesis is that these skeletons represent Viking warriors, perhaps taken in a battle or a lynching and then executed, the interpretation remains open to question.

## MAGNA CARTA REUNITED AT 800
When 'bad' King John sealed (not signed) Magna Carta in June 1215, he was presented with at least 13 copies of the manuscript, to be dispatched across his kingdom. Of these originals, only four are known to have survived to the present day, held by Salisbury Cathedral, Lincoln Cathedral and two in the British Library.

This year, all four documents were united in a single place for the first time since their initial dispersal. As part of the celebrations marking the 800th anniversary of the charter's issue, the manuscripts were brought together at the British Library in order to allow leading experts to study them side by side as part of a major Arts and Humanities Research Council-funded research project looking at the context, production and reception of Magna Carta.

In addition to examining the handwriting of each of the scribes who created the documents, the researchers have been exploring the manuscripts' ownership history, and their similarities or differences to the hundreds of other King John charters examined during the course of the project. Findings include the discovery that one of the British Library manuscripts may have originally been sent to Canterbury Cathedral, after project member Professor David Carpenter of King's College London was able to demonstrate that the document's text matches that of a 1290s transcription of the charter then held by the cathedral.

## RICHARD III REINTERRED
Following the discovery of the remains of a body which proved to be that of King Richard III in a Leicester car park in September 2012, controversy raged as to where they should be reburied once osteological analyses had been completed. The last Yorkist king had been killed at the Battle of Bosworth in August 1485, and his naked corpse had then been publicly displayed in Leicester as proof that he was indeed dead. The body was then buried in the city's Greyfriars Church, and when this became the focus of recent archaeological investigations, there was speculation about the chances of the burial place being discovered. Circumstantial evidence – including marked curvature of the spine and multiple injuries to the head almost certainly received in combat – made it likely that the body recovered was indeed that of Richard III, but this became certain when DNA taken from the remains was shown to match that of a known surviving relative.

Despite the challenge from a small group – distant relatives of the deceased king who styled themselves as the 'Plantagenet Alliance' – arguing that the body should be reburied in York, a judicial review upheld the standard procedure in such cases that reburial of human remains should be local. Archaeologists considered this to be the right decision, since the group in question could not reasonably claim to 'speak for' a 500-year-old individual with, potentially, millions of collateral descendants. The remains were carried in procession to Leicester Cathedral on 22 March 2015, and reburied on 26 March at a religious ceremony led by the Archbishop of Canterbury and the Bishop of Leicester. The British Royal Family was represented, and the family of Richard III by the actor Benedict Cumberbatch, a distant relative, who read a poem by poet laureate Carol Ann Duffy. Thousands had lined the streets, many holding white roses (symbols of the House of York), during the funeral procession, and thousands more viewed the coffin as it lay in state for three days in the cathedral.

On the site of the original excavation, meantime, a new £4m King Richard III Visitor Centre had just opened. Occupying the old Leicester Grammar School, the centre is just 100m from Leicester Cathedral, where the King's remains now lie. A comprehensive exhibition, 'Dynasty, Death and Discovery', offers a detailed insight into the life and times of the last Yorkist king, with a special focus on his death. The site of his medieval burial has been incorporated into the centre, so that visitors look down into the grave through a glass floor, while a replica CT scanner houses a life-size model of the King's skeleton, allowing a close-up view of his deformed spine and fatal injuries. Expectations are for 80,000 visitors a year, making the former king one hard-working royal from the perspective of the city of Leicester.

Rarely has any archaeological discovery had such a sensational impact, and the huge popular interest has revived the old argument about Richard III's reputation. One broadsheet newspaper columnist denounced the reburial for its misplaced and anachronistic deference towards royalty, repeating the common (and Shakespearean) view that Richard was some sort of 'monster' and a 'child-murdering tyrant'. In fact, the measures taken by the King to secure the Yorkist monarchy were typical of the Wars of the Roses, a period of ferocious struggle inside a deeply fractured aristocracy; the succession of minors was, in the circumstances, almost inconceivable, and Richard enjoyed the broad backing of the dominant Yorkist faction for what was, in effect, an attempt to discourage a renewal of civil war. Nonetheless, the passionate response of so many thousands to the discovery, study and reburial of the body of a deceased king may not always have been entirely rational and measured.

## RADIOCARBON REVOLUTIONISED
Scientists at the University of Liverpool have been hard at work developing a fast, portable new radiocarbon-dating technology that is set to revolutionise field archaeology.

Radiocarbon dating is used to establish the age of organic materials by measuring the quantity of remaining carbon 14 (the radioactive carbon isotope that decays at a fairly constant rate after the organism dies). Since its development in the 1940s, this method has been an invaluable tool to archaeologists – but the current cost and the time needed for materials to be sent away and analysed in specialist laboratories means that projects tend to take as few samples as possible.

Now, funded by a £96,000 grant from Arts Council England, a team led by Professor Steve Taylor has been working with Norton Priory Museum and Gardens to create a prototype portable quadruple mass spectrometer (QMS). This will allow analysis to take place on site, meaning that archaeologists can obtain results more quickly and then use this information to make decisions about the excavation while it is still in progress.

The prototype has so far been used to test medieval and post-medieval animal bone samples from Norton Priory, the most excavated monastic site in Europe. While fine-tuning of the technology was ongoing throughout 2015, the researchers report that their results show 'encouraging levels of agreement' with conventional methods, and that they hope to reduce the amount of time it takes to obtain data from bone samples from multiple weeks to two days.

The first portable QMS unit is expected to be made commercially available to archaeologists in 2016, and will be based at Norton Priory Museum and Gardens.

## ENGLISH HERITAGE SPLITS

English Heritage, the government heritage agency formed in 1983, has split into two distinct bodies. Its statutory duties are now carried out by Historic England, which is headed by a former director of Somerset House, Duncan Wilson. The main remit of Historic England is to protect the historical environment of England by preserving and listing historic buildings and ancient monuments, and advising central and local government. Meanwhile, the name 'English Heritage' has been retained for a new charity that manages the national collection of over 400 historic sites, as well as the London blue-plaques scheme. It is headed by Kate Mavor, previously chief executive of the National Trust for Scotland.

The two organisations came into being on 1 April 2015 when Simon Thurley, the chief executive of (the former) English Heritage for 13 years, stepped down to take up a senior research fellowship at the Institute of Historical Research.

## THE HISTORICAL TV SENSATION OF 2015

And finally, with Channel 4's *Time Team* (1994–2014) having finally ceased production, viewers got their historical fix not from a documentary but from the much-acclaimed drama *Wolf Hall*. Shown on BBC Two over six parts, it was based on the novel of the same name by Hilary Mantel. Set in the period from 1500 to 1535, *Wolf Hall* is a fictionalised biography documenting the rapid rise to power of the Protestant commoner Thomas Cromwell, who became the chief minister of Henry VIII, against the background of the fall of both Cardinal Wolsey and Sir Thomas More.

There were the usual quibbles, including the use of Montacute House in Somerset as one of the principal locations, even though it was not built until 50 years after Thomas Cromwell's death, and the hanging of time-faded tapestries on the walls of the set instead of the vibrantly colourful works that they would have been before sunlight and age muted the tones. These complaints miss the point. TV drama is precisely that, and the real question is the degree to which the writers, actors and producers involved succeeded in reconstructing the essential character of the period, events and personalities depicted. The general consensus is that those behind *Wolf Hall* did so with spectacular success, setting a new benchmark for historical drama and reconstruction. Costing over £7m to make, it reached audiences of almost 6 million.

# ARCHITECTURE

*John Hitchman*

THE LEADENHALL BUILDING, LEADENHALL
STREET, LONDON
*Architect:* Rogers Stirk Harbour + Partners

London's skyline has changed enormously in recent years and the rash of tower building started during the gradual recovery from the economic crash of 2008/9 shows no sign of abating. In the central district, a companion piece to the recently completed Shard at London Bridge is now the second-tallest structure in London at 225m, squeezed onto a sensitive and tight site opposite the ground-breaking Lloyd's building (1986) on Leadenhall Street. In the manner of the Shard and several other high-profile towers in the City, it has instantly acquired its own nickname, in this case the 'Cheesegrater', on account of the distinctive inclination of its south-facing elevation and the resulting tapering glazed office element.

The reasoning behind the distinctive massing can be traced to one significant constraint in the form of the St Paul's Cathedral viewing corridors: one particular concern for the architects centred around the potential intrusion on views of the St Paul's dome, when seen from the west, of a standard rectangular tower. In order to counter any objection on this account, the façade leans back, withdrawing from the potential for conflict and by so doing almost disappearing from the passing pedestrian's awareness in a way that would certainly not have been the case had the building risen vertically from the site boundary.

The triangular wedge of air space that is thus given back to the street is coupled with a release of the majority of the

*Fig. 1.* The Leadenhall Building (section), Rogers Stirk Harbour + Partners

ground plane beneath the tower to the public realm in the form of a part-paved, part-soft landscaped 'Galleria' opening out into the adjoining St Helen's Square at the junction with St Mary Axe. The enormous undercroft created by withdrawing the lowest office floor up to level 6 enables the essential structural elements of the main office volume to become clearly expressed at the base, the vertical columns and diagonal bracing members emerging from the glazed cladding above to form a bold, open framework defining the site boundaries.

The structural beams supporting the overhead office floor and a restaurant floor that partly emerges beneath it at level 5 are clearly expressed on the soffit, while banks of escalators emerge from the glazed elevations at the rear, spilling down onto the paved approach. The general demeanour of the space is stark and distinctly no-nonsense; the hard grey surfaces of the steel structure and stone paving are only partially offset by the few trees and grassed areas to one side, with the glazed origins of the escalators somewhat mysterious. It is as though a huge spaceship has landed and lowered two enormous moving pathways for aliens to descend from the hidden interior.

Each of the two banks of three escalators rises either side of a central walkway that passes through the building to emerge on the far side in a small paved piazza, which borders the narrow service road to the rear, Undershaft. The left-hand bank of escalators rises to level 3 and leads into the main upper reception area and lift lobby for general tenants; the right-hand bank is shorter and provides access to the designated Aon reception area at level 2 (the insurance firm pre-let 50 per cent of the office floor area).

The layout of the office floors is based on the concept of served and servant spaces, where large rectangular open floor plates, offering maximum flexibility, are provided for the offices, supported by separate core elements accommodating passenger and goods lifts, toilets, plant and services risers. The strategic sloping of the street façade gives rise to an incrementally diminishing series of floor plates as the perimeter draws closer to the principal firefighting and escape cores, one located in each of the rear corners of the office element.

The cores help to stiffen the glazed A-shaped office tower structure and work in conjunction with an externally expressed braced ladder frame rising through the entire height of the structure, with each floor level articulated by an individual triangulated sub-frame set within the vertical risers of the ladder. The floors of the office element are supported off a primary structural mega-frame, the diagonal bracing members of which are clearly visible through the glazed envelope, with major horizontal interventions occurring every seven storeys; this emphasises the proportions of the frame and the angle of the sloping façade neatly coinciding with the junctions of the diagonal bracing members every 14 floors.

Rising up the north side of the office floors, and connected via a narrow bridge link, glazed at each end, is the secondary support core of elevators and toilet pods. This is not a consistently maintained volume, however, as the individual banks of elevators, arranged in groups of four and allocated to different sections of the building, terminate at the appropriate floor levels, rising to full height only on the east elevation. Expressed on the ends as another version of the 'ladder', the secondary core structure comprises a series of complex cross-braced steel 'tables', each a storey high and painted bright yellow, either side of which rise the glazed wall climber lifts and the male and female toilet pods. These were prefabricated off-site and craned into position as finished units. Slotted into the lobby area between the lifts in alternating locations to avoid the lift landing doors in each particular section, male and female pods are coloured blue and red. As all is visible through the glazing, colour is an important feature of this secondary element; the red, blue, yellow and other colours applied to the 'everything on view' lift machinery is a now-familiar characteristic of much 'hi-tech' design.

High standards of environmental performance have been a top priority and the building achieves a BREEAM 'Excellent' rating, the thermal performance aided by the use of a triple-glazed envelope of single outer and double-glazed inner leaves. The asymmetry generated by the wedge shape of the office component required significant structural engineering input to deal with the resulting imbalance of loading conditions both within the frame and through to the basement and foundations. Particular subtleties were required to handle the expansion and contraction developed by the reaction of the south-facing slope to solar gain, while a technique of 'active alignment' used by contractor Laing O'Rourke and engineer Arup ensured that as construction progressed upwards, the southern triangular mega-frame subsided vertically against the core structure rather than leaning over as a result of differential loading across the floor plan from south to north.

Design work started before the financial crash and subsequent recession, and the work was put on hold during 2007–10 until conditions improved from a commercial standpoint; the confidence to proceed with a start on site in July 2011 was bolstered by the 50 per cent pre-let to Aon. Providing nearly 85,000m² of office space over more than 40 floors, the building rises to a height of 225m and was completed in July 2015 at a cost of approximately £500m. The 'Cheesegrater' thus takes its place as one of the more significant new buildings to emerge in the City office cluster in recent years; one that demonstrates the highest pedigree in design quality with a clarity of spatial and functional organisation allied to a robust expression of structure and a welcome degree of concern for its relationships with the immediate street environment, as well as with the wider city context.

## WHITWORTH ART GALLERY EXTENSION, MANCHESTER
*Architect:* MUMA (McInnes Usher McKnight Architects)

Manchester's Whitworth Art Gallery houses one of the more important regional collections of fine art, textiles and wallpaper. In recent years it has considerably increased its national profile and visitor numbers thanks to an enterprising programme of exhibitions and educational initiatives. A footfall of 86,000 in 2006 had by 2008 jumped to 139,000 and, with an ever-growing collection to be housed on site, it was felt that there was a pressing need to expand. A competition was therefore launched in 2009 to seek a design proposal for refurbishment and extension that would enable the gallery to reach a wider audience, rationalise and make better use of the existing gallery spaces and develop a more engaged relationship with the surrounding green spaces of Whitworth Park, which it borders on the south and west sides.

The Whitworth started life as Grove House in the late 1880s and was soon converted to gallery use. A number of early additions were made by James Beaumont and the 1908 remodelling of the Oxford Road frontage followed, creating the current grandly scaled and detailed Victorian elevation

whose dark red brickwork and terracotta have been restored to their former glory and now overlook a new sculpture terrace. Substantial modifications were made to the interiors in the 1960s by the architect John Bickerdike, including the insertion of false ceilings in two of the vaulted galleries at the rear and a reordering of the central gallery spaces to accord with contemporary preferences for layout and circulation. An interior sculpture court was created at first floor level in 1995 by Ahrends, Burton and Koralek, which introduced increased daylight while preserving the essential symmetry of the plan established by the main entrance frontage.

The brief issued with the competition suggested the possible use of a site to the south-west of the gallery; rather than follow this suggestion, the winning design by architect MUMA continues and reinforces the underlying axial symmetry of the plan with a U-shaped extension that provides two new projecting wings of accommodation linked by a new two-level glazed promenade. The new structure is planted onto the rear of the western wall of the gallery and embraces a substantial landscaped court, to be developed as the 'Art Garden', open to the park beyond. The garden provides the opportunity for a second entrance to the galleries from the park at the rear. This strategy has enabled a range of mature trees along the south side that would otherwise have been at risk to be preserved, and retains the longer-term potential for a more complete reassertion of the central axis for primary circulation in the future. This is currently compromised by the 1960s modifications to the Gulbenkian and Pilkington galleries situated at the heart of the building that conservation officers were keen to retain untouched.

As part of the latest transformation, the suspended ceilings previously introduced to the exhibition galleries at the rear have been removed to reveal once again the handsome vaulted ceilings with roof-lights that allow daylight to flood in from above. The lecture theatre that occupied one of the three major spaces at the rear has been relocated into the restored Grand Hall, a finely proportioned room occupying most of the first floor of the Victorian frontage, formerly used unproductively for storage. With the three large rooms restored and returned to exhibition use, a wide opening has been punched through the rear wall of the central space in order to provide open access to the new promenade extension. The park gradually slopes away from the main road frontage so that the main ground-floor level established at the entrance foyer is consequently a storey height above the park level at the rear. Visitors proceeding through this new opening therefore find themselves at first-floor level and confronted with a view out over the Art Garden and onto the park and mature trees beyond.

The full-height glazing to the promenade draws the landscape setting into the heart of the building, providing a green backdrop to act as a counterfoil to the precision of the interiors, and an opportunity to relax the concentration implicit in the viewing of works of art. The glazing is shielded from the western sun by a high-level projecting brise-soleil, a delicate veil of alternating 5mm-thick straight and L-shaped fins of stainless steel. The Promenade provides a generously wide link, at ground and first-floor levels, between the two new projecting wings that enclose the garden area, each of which differs from the other in architectural appearance, both in terms of massing and in their degree of openness / enclosure.

The south wing is the smaller and lower of the two, extending the language of full-height glazing around a first-floor cafe and with highly reflective polished stainless steel triangular mullions reducing the feeling of enclosure to give visitors the experience of being in a sleek glass box suspended within the parkland setting. At the lower level, along the promenade and around the kitchen, toilet facilities and a learning studio that occupy the space below the cafe, red brick is predominant, with chunky triangular brick piers framing double-glazed windows looking out over the garden. Full-length internal and external bench seats, oak-veneered internally and stone-clad externally, fill the openings between the columns, modulating the transition to the flamed-finish stone floor of the internal promenade and a natural sandstone perimeter paving strip externally around the garden.

A degree of excavation at the rear has enabled the creation of a new storage area below the main galleries where the collection can be viewed by members of the public. The Collection Centre is accessed from the lower-level promenade and made visible through a series of arched openings in the brick wall that previously formed the back wall of the gallery.

At the north end of the new two-storey promenade, a grand staircase has been inserted linking the entry level, with its new access from the garden, to the upper-level galleries and the new Landscape Gallery that occupies the first floor of the north wing. This is a much more substantial and enclosed volume, presenting a blank wall to the side street capped by a large overhanging roof light-box that admits cool north light into the gallery interior. The expanse of red brick introduced to the north elevation has been enlivened by a mix of decorative bricklaying techniques and white faience inserts that are intended to reference some of the weaving and stitching techniques employed in the gallery's textile collection. A large deep-set window bay set into the west-facing end wall of the Landscape Gallery provides a full-height vision of the surrounding park and trees, while the study centre that occupies the same plan area at the ground floor is opened up to the Art Garden through a long horizontal slot-window along the south side.

With annual visitor numbers having accelerated again to some 190,000 by 2013, this imaginative extension has ensured that the Whitworth can now accommodate its increased level of patronage in comfort and style and will no doubt gain hugely from a transformed relationship with its mature landscape setting.

## THEATRE ROYAL EXTENSION, HOPE STREET, GLASGOW
*Architect:* Page/Park Architects

Glasgow's Theatre Royal, home of Scottish Opera since 1974, dates from 1867 and is the longest-running theatre in Glasgow, boasting a fine traditionally designed Victorian auditorium. This opulent interior was the subject of a major restoration and refurbishment project in 1997, aimed at rejuvenating the French Renaissance-style gilded decorative plasterwork, but outside the splendid auditorium, however, like many similar Victorian theatres, it continued to suffer from cramped and poorly laid out front-of-house public areas, sub-standard access arrangements and poor ventilation.

The opportunity for a radical overhaul arose as a result of adjoining commercial developments that released a small gap site adjacent to the theatre on Cowcaddens Road. Accordingly the theatre management developed a brief for a new vision for the theatre, whose ambition was to create a series of spacious, attractive new foyers capable of dealing with the pressures of a 1,500-strong audience, as well as to provide opportunities for education, community projects and interaction. The design solution proposed by the architects was to demolish part of the existing building, housing a cafe and offices, which was set to one side of the main entrance on Hope Street, and redevelop on the combined plots so as to

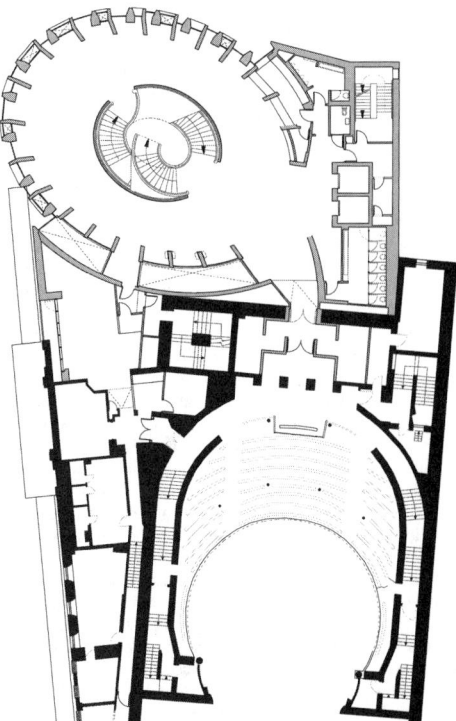

*Fig. 2.* Glasgow Theatre Royal Extension (upper level plan), Page/Park Architects

make full use of the potential offered by the strategic corner site that would be generated.

The new extension takes the form of a glazed and pillared elliptical drum, set between two flanking structures with its long axis aligned with the intersecting angle of the street corner. The deep-set narrow window slots are framed between metal-clad projecting reveals that link alternately at top and bottom in a lively dance around the perimeter, terminated at each end by the solid walls of the flanking structures that link to the theatre's main entrance on the Hope Street frontage and nudge up to the modern office block on the Cowcaddens Road side. The main floor levels of the drum are cantilevered out over the pavement in order to shelter the ground-floor approaches, while its topmost level is set well back to create an open roof terrace, which is accessible to the public.

The structural demands of the cantilever required the provision of deep fin-like columns to deal with the transfer of loads, but these have been put to good use as the deep reveals of the perimeter bay windows. The full-height glazed slots provide fine views out over the surrounding townscape that includes a splendidly detailed architectural statement on the opposite corner – Honeyman, Keppie and Mackintosh's fine 1903 tenement building in red sandstone, built for the Civic Improvement Trust. Externally the structural framework of the drum is covered in gold-coloured copper cladding and the building thus glistens and glints with reflected light in a decidedly theatrical, attention-grabbing manner.

The solid wings either side of this shiny centrepiece are clad in smooth white polished concrete panels, the block forms stepping up and down as a way of easing the transition in height between the drum and the adjoining buildings; the tall office building sits to one side and the modelled classical frontage of the theatre entrance to the other. On the Hope Street frontage, the flanking wing accommodates a couple of offices and at the ground floor provides circulation links between the entrance foyer and the new wing. On the Cowcaddens Road side, a stair and lift core with a bar, catering and toilet facilities is tucked in along the flank wall and linked to the upper foyer levels and the rear of the auditorium.

The main glory of the interior is an eye-catchingly sinuous spiral staircase that winds up through a central elliptical void, the flights doubling-up between first and second-floor levels in a visually arresting intertwining of forms. The stair is finished with a dark red carpet and a similar dark-hued leather finish has been applied to the internal sides of the solid balustrades, the inner section of the side wall capping pieces and even wrapped around the tubular handrail. The stair is clad on the outside with birch ply panels carefully cut and moulded to follow the curves of the stair, while the soffit has a Bute fabric finish on an acoustic foam backing, again in bright red. Interestingly, the birch ply panels were manufactured by Scottish Opera's own in-house scenery workshop, with the accuracy and tight tolerances achieved standing as a tribute to the skill of joiners more used to constructing scenic flights of imagination.

The column-free foyer levels provide a generous promenade around the central staircase and are finished with polished limestone tiles. A cantilevered clear glass balustrade around the stairwell allows a full appreciation of the internal spaces with views up and down. Access into the rear of the auditorium is provided at ground, first, second and fourth-floor levels, while at the intermediate third level, tucked in behind the steep rake of the upper tier, a separate dedicated suite has been provided for community support work and related educational activities. At the top level, the drum has been brought back from the perimeter to enclose just the central stair void and, with the foyer occupying a little less than half of the overall floor plate, a generous roof terrace has been created – a wonderful spot to enjoy an interval drink if the weather is clement.

Completed in December 2014, the new extension is already proving a popular addition to the theatre's front-of-house facilities, its exuberant form and finishes and the opportunities provided to mingle with the crowds, to see and be seen, all contributing to a vibrant theatre experience. Its dynamic contribution to the surrounding townscape, where it provides a bold counterfoil to the domed sandstone corner turret of the historic tenement opposite, is an obvious bonus for the city of Glasgow.

## ST JOHN BOSCO ARTS COLLEGE, CROXTETH, LIVERPOOL
*Architect:* BDP

With continually increasing demands for the provision of more school places set against a backdrop of stringent cost-cutting and budgetary constraints, and a perceptible lack of understanding among the political classes as to the value of good design, school building has become one of the most highly politicised areas of architectural practice in recent years. The frequent overhaul of government funding initiatives has been central to the debate about how to properly evaluate the benefits of high-quality design in terms of the impact upon educational outcomes, with quality all too often losing out to quantity as a basis for decision making. For the St John Bosco School, for example, the precipitate axing of the 'Building Schools for the Future' programme forced a complete redesign of the project.

New school buildings are, of necessity, in response to many varied influences and contexts, taking on many

different forms, so no one example can be held to adequately represent current trends. One of the more radical approaches can be seen in the design for this new Arts College building, recently completed for Liverpool City Council on the site of its soon-to-be-demolished predecessor in the suburb of Croxteth, a 1,100-place Catholic girls' secondary school that opened its doors to students at the start of the new academic year in September 2014.

One of the key aspects of the new building is its flexibility. This extends not merely to the potential to re-jig the circulation layout or to combine or divide teaching spaces but encompasses the potential to completely reconfigure the interior, perhaps even for an entirely different use, if future circumstances made it desirable. This has been done by separating the internal structures of walls, floors, ceilings, stairs and the like from the enclosing envelope, an enormous single-span box in many ways indistinguishable from a factory shed. A completely column-free interior space has been created through the use of steel portal frames spanning 55m on a 7.65m grid spacing to generate an interior volume 55m wide by 99m long and three storeys high. The frames utilise flat-bottomed steel trusses varying in height from 1.7m at the eaves to 4m at the ridge. Strip roof-lights are built into the metal deck-supported roof finish and surfaces are white, to exploit the daylight flowing into the heart of the building.

Within this large, simple volume the architects have created a stimulating multi-functional arrangement of learning, research and social environments catering for a broad range of academic programmes and providing visual stimulus through the use of bold graphics, selected bright colours and opportunities for social interaction, allied to a series of open circulation routes that offer views across the internal spaces.

The majority of the teaching areas are arranged in an independent U-shaped two-storey structure occupying three sides of the rectangular interior. There is a mix of traditional cellular and less formal teaching spaces, typically arranged in clusters of three or six classrooms set out around a central open-plan breakout space. Different clusters are allocated to general teaching, to science, to art and textiles and ICT, and to the sixth form, while a further group of rooms at ground level, accessed separately from the main entrance lobby, provides conference and teacher training facilities.

In the remaining central space, overlooked by balcony circulation routes at first and second-floor levels, a free-standing stepped, angled and faceted structure, in bright green, provides a sculptural focus for the school's activities and divides the ground floor into different zones. Called 'the Hill', its stepped flanks provide a readymade auditorium and a place for school assemblies, while the adjacent open seating area at first-floor level, which extends into bridge links to the surrounding teaching areas, encloses a ground-floor community space, headteacher's and administrative rooms, toilets and a special educational needs facility. Tucked in behind the Hill, in a triangle of space open to the roof, a learning resource centre continues the colourful theme with white circular tables and bright fuchsia-pink chairs and cabinets.

The final surprise element in the mix is a faceted stand-alone box-like volume set into a gap in the range of teaching spaces along the north side of the building. This bright yellow object is the 'Salesian pod', its title derived from the Salesian nuns, members of the order founded by St John Bosco, who was canonised in 1934 with a citation as 'Father and Teacher of Youth'. The pod is a highly visible expression of the school's faith basis and provides rooms at ground and first floor for quieter supporting activities.

Externally the frame is clad at the upper levels with factory-insulated panels that introduce both colour and pattern to break down the monolithic visual appearance of the building's mass. Brickwork walls surround the teaching and support spaces at ground level to provide an air of greater permanence and the necessary robustness, but where the main central space occurs this turns to glazing, first a single-storey glazed wall featuring the school name in storey-high super-graphics and then around the main entrance opening up to near full height, allowing light into the interior and providing glimpses of the colourful sculpted interior to the outside world.

From a purely bean-counting perspective, the major achievement of the architects has been to create not only 15 per cent more space than called for by the previous funding regime but at a much reduced construction cost of £16.5m, substantially under the target square metre cost set by the Education Funding Agency. Arguably of greater long-term significance, however, from the educational standpoint, the students of the St John Bosco College have been given a creative, stimulating and distinctive environment in which to learn and develop their potential, an asset that might well be regarded as priceless.

THE DERBY ARENA, DERBY
*Architect:* FaulknerBrowns Architects

The medal-winning achievements of the GB cycling team during the 2012 Olympics did much to bring the distinctive features of that hitherto rather specialised and esoteric sporting venue – the velodrome – to wider public attention. The very special architectural attributes of the Olympic Velodrome owed much to the fact that it was focused solely on providing optimum conditions for the track cyclists and could rely on capacity audiences for its high-profile events. While cycling as a spectator sport has continued its upward trajectory in terms of general popularity, it nevertheless remains an activity that commands a limited paying clientele for competitions. The question inevitably arises – how can such a single sport-specific environment be adapted so that the economics involved are not prohibitive in relation to predicted revenue?

The new Derby Arena, recently completed on a site close to the Derby County football stadium and fronting onto a nature reserve bounded by the River Derwent, is a bold attempt to massage the unforgiving elements of a velodrome into a multi-purpose arena format capable of hosting a wide range of sporting activities as well as non-sports based social, cultural and entertainment events. The key to the problem has been how to manage the large infield area circumscribed by the tightly banked loop of the cycle track, as well as countering the sterilising effect of the vertical height occupied by the track, particularly around the raking corners at each end. At the Olympic Velodrome the infield was placed at the same level as the inside of the track, with access from below via ramps. The solution adopted at Derby has been to lower the entire infield area, with the exception of a semi-circular section at one end, by a whole storey.

This enables sports competitors, visitors and audiences alike to walk into the central multi-purpose area on the level from the main entrance, while the remaining semi-circular portion of the oval that occupies the upper level is considered adequate for the maintenance and preparation activities of the cyclists and can be accessed via a ramp from the main floor level. The resulting flat-floored sports hall and events arena can cater for a range of indoor sports as well as provide seating for up to 3,500 people for pop concerts and the like, with the cyclists' 'D' providing a handy 'stage' for performers if required.

The main entrance is positioned axially, centred on the 'straight' of the track, and is linked with a small cafe. Cycling and events changing areas are positioned around the curved perimeter at the 'stage' end, with cycle storage provided immediately under the raised 'D', while changing rooms for other sports are located at the opposite end. Storage facilities and plant rooms occupy the ground-floor areas in the opposite half of the floor plan on the other side of the sports hall. Here, because the steep banking of the cycle track always makes it difficult to arrange seating evenly around the circumference, a bank of fixed seating has been positioned along one side of the central straight section of track, the tiered seating rising up over a first-floor concourse, raising the potential audience capacity to 5,000.

A narrow ramped concourse wraps around the curved ends, providing a circulation route from one side to the other and leading to a sizeable fitness gym that takes most of the available wedge of space over the entrance and has a shallow balcony overlooking the track. On the level above, a suite of meeting and multi-function rooms together with a bike 'spinning' studio and toilets are slotted in behind two supplementary rows of seating for spectators. The planning is simple, clear and efficient, though obviously deriving its format entirely from the geometry and dimensions of the 250m cycle track and its flat inboard safety zone.

The massive steel trussed roof spanning the entire internal volume speaks of simple value-engineered structural design and lacks the sophistication of its Olympic precursor, but in a cost-conscious environment it does its job without undue fuss. The exterior elevations are wrapped tightly around the lozenge-shaped plan and feature long horizontal strips of aluminium cladding in white, brown and shades of yellow ochre, alternating in a random fashion. They appear clearly intended to act as a visual metaphor for the polished timber planking of the cycle track inside. The continuously curving surface of the cladding forms a closed casket, propped up around the ground level entrance screen by V-shaped pairs of raking columns spaced around the perimeter.

At points around the circumference, the horizontal strips are prised apart to allow glazed inserts to provide daylight to the interiors; at other locations, narrow slots are cut into the surface to act as louvres. The striated colouring of the smooth metallic skin gives the building an unusual appearance and it is certainly striking, viewed either at close quarters or as a backdrop to the natural landscape to the rear. The 15,000m² arena has been realised at a very economical build cost of £24m and, having opened on 20 March 2015, is already hosting a wide range of sporting, entertainment and cultural events. The Arena will no doubt prove its value as a new multi-purpose venue for the Derby area and its innovative layout may well furnish some useful design ideas to influence other similar projects in the future.

## AWARDS

THE RIBA STIRLING PRIZE 2014
Everyman Theatre, Liverpool; Haworth Tompkins

*The Stirling Shortlist*
Library of Birmingham; Mecanoo
London Aquatics Centre; Zaha Hadid Architects
London Bridge Tower (The Shard); Renzo Piano Building Workshop
LSE Saw Swee Hock Student Centre, London; O'Donnell + Tuomey
Manchester School of Art; Feilden Clegg Bradley Studios

RIBA SPECIAL AWARDS 2014
*The Manser Medal* – Stormy Castle (private house), Gower Peninsula, Wales; Loyn & Co.
*The Stephen Lawrence Prize* – House No. 7, Isle of Tiree, Hebrides; Denizen Works

BRITISH CONSTRUCTION INDUSTRY AWARDS 2014

*Prime Minister's Better Public Building Award* – Medmerry Managed Realignment, Chichester, West Sussex (coastal protection/management scheme); Principal Designer – Jacobs

*Major Project Award (over £50m)* – London Aquatics Centre; Zaha Hadid Architects

*Building Award (£10m-£50m)* – Bonhams (auction rooms), New Bond Street, London; Lifschutz Davidson Sandilands

*Small Building Award (up to £10m)* – Ortus (event and learning centre), Camberwell, London; Duggan Morris Architects

*Sustainability Award* – The Bridge Scottish Water Stepps, Glasgow (National Operations Centre); Reiach and Hall Architects

RIAS AWARDS 2014

*RIAS Andrew Doolan Best Building in Scotland Award* – Advocate's Close (mixed-use development), Old Town, Edinburgh; Morgan McDonnell Architecture

RIBA SPECIAL AWARDS 2015

*Royal Gold Medal* – Sheila O'Donnell and John Tuomey

CIVIC TRUST AWARDS 2015

*Special Award for Sustainability* – Chester Balmore, Camden, London (residential and mixed-use); Rick Mather Architects

*Michael Middleton Award (Conservation)* – Somerset House West Wing and Ground Floor East Wing, London; Forme UK LLP (Interior Design)

*Special Award for Community Engagement* – Black Cultural Archives, Brixton, London; Pringle Richards Sharratt

*Special Award for Scotland* – Maggie's Cancer Caring Centre, Airdrie, Lanarkshire; Reiach and Hall Architects

*National Panel Special Award* – Abode at Great Kneighton, Cambridge (residential); Proctor and Matthews Architects

*Selwyn Goldsmith Award (Universal Design)* – Library of Birmingham; Mecanoo

*Special Award for Brick* – Saw Swee Hock Student Centre, Westminster, London; O'Donnell + Tuomey

# ART

Eddy Frankel

## ALL HAIL THE SALES

Another year, another set of auction records blown to smithereens. Just when you think that the market has peaked, that no one could possibly eclipse how much some billionaire has just paid for a painting, in swoops another headline sale, leaving everything else in its dust. It's jaw-dropping how recession-proof the art market is, really. Whatever is happening out in the real world, it appears that the auction houses can always rustle up another masterpiece to sell for more money than most of us could ever dream of seeing. And this year was no different, with both the big players – Christie's and Sotheby's – racking up record-breaking sales.

The biggest price tag came courtesy of Pablo Picasso, whose 1955 painting *Les Femmes d'Alger (Version 0)* sold for a quite astonishing $179m (£115m) at Christie's in New York. It eclipsed last year's $142m (£91m) sale of a Francis Bacon triptych, again at Christie's, and became the most expensive painting ever sold at auction. Depending on who you ask, the Picasso painting is either a masterpiece worth whatever anyone is willing to pay for it, or – slightly more reasonably – a bit of a jumbled, mid-period mess that would struggle to earn a space on many a modern art museum wall.

So dead artists are safe bets, but really old living ones aren't too dangerous either – hence octogenarian German painter Gerhard Richter making headlines yet again this year. His 1986 *Abstraktes Bild* painting – a vast canvas of multicoloured layered streaks – sold for £30.4m at Sotheby's in London in February, more than £10m above its higher estimate and the most ever paid for a painting by a living artist. The winning bidder was jumping up in increments of £2m, drawing gasps of amazement from people in the room. But while £30.4m is not quite the $58m paid for Jeff Koons' balloon dog sculpture last year, Sotheby's will not be complaining about adding another record sale. The same cannot be said for the artist, however. After *Abstraktes Bild* was sold, Richter was quoted in the German newspaper *Die Zeit* as saying: 'The records keep being broken and every time my initial reaction is one of horror.' He went on to describe it as both 'shocking' and 'foolish', a sentiment that probably resonates with most outside observers.

Another shock is how relatively little it appears that art by women is worth. A 1932 painting by American artist Georgia O'Keeffe, *Jimson Weed/White Flower No 1*, sold for $44m (£28m) at Sotheby's in New York in November 2014. While it is the most ever paid for a work by a female artist (almost quadrupling the previous record, $11.9m (£7.7m) for a Joan Mitchell painting), questions should probably be asked about why gender still has such a massive impact on the value of art in this day and age.

There were record sales, with Sotheby's reaching its highest total ever achieved in contemporary art in early July, and record revenue for the auction houses too. Christie's and Sotheby's both announced that 2014 had been their best year in terms of revenue. Sales rose at Christie's by 12 per cent to £5.1bn, while Sotheby's ran away with the lead, making £6bn, an 18 per cent increase on the previous year. It would appear that this upturn in fortunes is all thanks to new customers. Both auction houses have been expanding their operations, from New Delhi to mainland China, and local markets appear keen to invest. So keen, in fact, that Sotheby's reckons that a third of its clients last year were new.

Good news? Maybe not. Despite record revenues, the chief executives of both major auction houses resigned within two weeks of each other. William Ruprecht left Sotheby's in November to be replaced by Tad Smith, who was tasked with slashing costs, and Steven Murphy was replaced by Patricia Barbizet at Christie's. Bonhams, meanwhile, announced that it was closing one of its regional sales rooms. Cost-cutting? Resignations? Closures? What could be going wrong? Perhaps unsurprisingly, the answer appears to be greed. In a desperate, vicious fight for market share, the auction houses have been playing a dangerous game of brinkmanship; offering sellers ever higher guarantees, dropping their fees and outbidding each other for the right to sell headline works. *Fortune* magazine even thinks that Christie's lost money on the famous Jeff Koons balloon dog last year. A loss, on the most expensive work of art by a living artist! Combined with the fact that many major lots have not been selling at recent auctions, it makes for uneasy viewing. While revenues are up, profits seem to be going down across the board. It may be hard to feel any sympathy for them, but it's interesting that as the market booms, the margins get tighter and the middlemen of the auction world are feeling the squeeze.

Middle men may be the problem – as impressive as some of this year's record sales have been, the real money was in private sales. None were more remarkable than when Paul Gauguin's 1892 *When Will You Marry?* was sold privately to an anonymous bidder – believed to be a Qatari royal – for no less than $300m (£193m).

## CUTS AT THE MUSEUMS

Many on the non-commercial side of the art world were desperately hoping for an end to half a decade of cuts to funding, but when the general election rolled around on May 7, most were left disappointed. The Conservatives were voted back in on a programme that would almost certainly leave the arts floundering. Even before the election, arts minister Ed Vaizey ominously warned that 'no party can promise to maintain arts funding', encouraging institutions to find more 'imaginative' ways to make money. *The Guardian* art critic Jonathan Jones opined that five more years of Tory government would 'reduce the arts to a national joke'.

Not that the situation would have necessarily been much better under Labour; Ed Miliband certainly did not promise to increase the current arts budget, but rather to maintain it as it is. But it's too early to tell if things will be as bad as all that, though it is impossible to ignore the fact that funding to Arts Council England has been in steady decline since 2010. What this will mean is a stronger engagement with philanthropists, a reliance on generous benefactors rather than government funding. As it stands, most just seem to be getting on with the job of looking around for funding.

The outgoing director of the Museums Association, David Anderson, gave a damning verdict on the state of the arts in the UK. 'Austerity is killing local museums,' he said in a pre-election debate, pointing out that 70 per cent of funding goes to London museums. 'The cultural funding model we have is failing.'

One manifestation of the danger to the arts in the UK came in the shape of regular protests by staff at the National Gallery in London. The museum has been pushed to privatise various services and to freeze (the already very low) wages for staff, leading to demonstrations in Trafalgar Square and widespread walkouts; the National Gallery has been plunged into chaos by cuts and privatisation.

Another manifestation is the sudden exodus of seemingly every major museum director in London. During the year under review it was announced that Penelope Curtis was leaving Tate Britain and that Neil MacGregor (British Museum), Sandy Nairne (National Portrait Gallery) and Sir Nicholas Penny (National Gallery) were departing their posts; Chris Dercon will be leaving Tate Modern in two years for a role at the Volksbuhne Theatre in Berlin. This group of museum directors is jumping ship at a pivotal time, with many believing that they would rather not have to deal with potential cuts in funding.

The real danger though – as it has been over the past few years – is the prospect of losing so many valuable works of art currently residing in British museums to overseas investors. A beautiful Paul Cézanne landscape which has been on view at the Fitzwilliam Museum in Cambridge for over 30 years has had a temporary export ban put on it by the government in the hope that £13.5m can be raised to save it. A ban has also been placed on a painting by Jan Brueghel the Elder of the Garden of Eden, which is hanging in Alnwick Castle for the time being. The Ashmolean Museum in Oxford is trying to do something similar to save a J. M. W. Turner painting of the city, though it is not overseas investors who are trying to get their hands on that. The painting was on loan, and has been sold in order to cover death duties. There is positive news though, as millionaire Hamish Parker donated over £1m to the British Museum to enable it to buy a set of prints by Pablo Picasso.

There was more good news as figures released by the Association of Leading Visitor Attractions showed that there had been a 7 per cent increase in visitors on the previous year. The British Museum tops the list, as ever, followed closely by the National Gallery, the Southbank Centre and Tate Modern. Another reason to celebrate came in the form of the re-opening of the Wallace Collection in September. After two years out of the spotlight, and a £5m refurbishment, Frans Hals' *Laughing Cavalier* and Diego Velázquez's *The Lady with a Fan* were finally back on display for everyone to see.

Away from London, for once, the Whitworth Art Gallery in Manchester was named by the Art Fund as the UK's Museum of the Year. Its recent renovation has helped make the 126-year-old building one of the finest art destinations in the country. It's just one of the attractions making Manchester the place to be this year. There was also the opening of Home, a £25m arts complex that is the biggest outside of London. It is symbolic of the much-needed de-centralisation of the arts in the UK, something which Arts Council England clearly recognises, as it announced in May that there would be a 'significant shift' in investment outside of London. How that manifests itself remains to be seen, but at least it's a start.

Anger reared its head back in London as climate change activists continued their series of protests against BP's sponsorship of the Tate museums. Campaigner Mel Evans released a book in April 2015, elaborating on the allegedly dirty relationship between the arts and oil companies, and then in June, a group of activists occupied the Tate Modern Turbine Hall. The Liberate Tate group staged a 25-hour protest, covering the floor with countless words of warning about climate change. The Tate tried to treat it as an art performance rather than a protest, but it was still rather embarrassing.

In a victory for common sense, and one of the best pieces of news in the world of museums this year: the National Gallery has banned selfie sticks. No more trying to think deep thoughts about beautiful paintings while tourists bash you in the head as they take pictures of themselves instead of the art. Hurrah indeed.

## SHOOTING GALLERIES

The year under review was a stable one in the commercial art world compared with the years of turbulence that have preceded it. Throughout the recession, galleries have expanded and shrunk at a phenomenal rate. Only last year, we saw gallerists opening up spaces in Mayfair, closing spaces in east London, expanding into China, closing in China . . . It was exhausting. It is probably a sign of the stability of the financial markets that the waters were relatively calm in the UK this year.

Marian Goodman became the latest American gallerist to open a flagship London space, with her enormous and incredibly glitzy Golden Square gallery. She brought with her stars like John Baldessari and – yes, him again – Gerhard Richter. She follows in the footsteps of David Zwirner, Pace Gallery, Michael Werner and the ever-present Larry Gagosian, who has started work on his third London gallery, due to open in October 2015.

But are all these new American galleries in London doing well? Not necessarily, with David Zwirner recently complaining that London does not have the same 'density of collectors' as New York. That means a lot of galleries are vying for a slice of a much smaller pie than they are used to. It's a competitive city for gallerists. The result is galleries like Zwirner's going into the secondary market, which is an increasingly lucrative area for targeting the mega-rich, who tend to steer away from new artists, towards safer sure-fire investments like impressionist or modern works. Things cannot be going too badly though, because although there have been few major openings in the London gallery world, there have also been no closures, unless you count White Cube shutting its Sao Paulo operation after its three-year lease ran out.

London's Lisson Gallery bucked the trend slightly, opening its New York space earlier in the year, hoping to get a taste of the USA's big bucks. Work was also finally started on Damien Hirst's much-talked-about Newport Street Gallery in London, which will stage group and solo shows of art from the YBA's own collection. It is due to be completed in October 2015.

One sign of last year's gallery turbulence has remained, though: artists continued to switch allegiances between galleries. British artist Cecily Brown has left Gagosian for White Cube, American artist Sterling Ruby has left Hauser & Wirth to join with several galleries and another American, Mark Bradford, has left White Cube. They are only the tip of an art transfer market that suddenly seems extremely active. It may all resemble soap opera shenanigans, but it shows the opportunistic, shifting landscape of the contemporary gallery scene. Perhaps the days when an artist would get scooped up by a gallerist and be nurtured into success over many decades are numbered.

## CRIME AND A BIT OF PUNISHMENT

Wherever there is money, there is crime, and there is an awful lot of money in the art world. Most dramatic of all the heists this year was the audacious crook who walked into the Beaux Arts gallery in Mayfair in June, wrapped a £40,000 Elisabeth Frink statue in some newspaper and then walked right back out.

There was some vandalism too, though it is difficult to know if vandalising some vandalism really counts. The subject of that cryptic sentence is, of course, the notorious and mischievous street artist Banksy. Within 24 hours of daubing a mural called *Girl with the Pierced Eardrum* on a wall near Bristol's Hanover Square back in October 2014, someone had chucked a load of black paint on it. A work of his in Germany was then defaced in March, while an image by the reclusive graffiti artist of a pouting girl in north London was covered over to make it look like she was wearing a burka.

Elsewhere, art investor Jonathan Weal was forced to admit that he had been concealing a lost masterpiece by J. M. W. Turner during bankruptcy proceedings. He assumed that hiding in plain sight was the best plan of action, but perhaps the sight was too plain when he appeared on TV expressing joy that his Turner painting had been authenticated. Unfortunately, the receiver who had dealt with his recent bankruptcy claim was watching television and caught him in the act. The painting has been taken in trust.

Meanwhile, art dealer David Carter admitted selling fakes both online and from his Hayle Gallery in Cornwall and a top Mayfair art dealer was sued by his own clients for not coughing up cash from sales. Timothy Sammons stood accused of not paying clients for sales of works by the likes of Canaletto, Chagall and Picasso.

And finally, though not a crime on a judicial level, Londoners were up in arms when it was announced that Eduardo Paolozzi's mosaic murals in Tottenham Court Road tube station were being pulled down due to refurbishment. Months went by before Transport for London eventually came out and put everyone's minds at ease, announcing that the vast majority of the mosaics had been saved and would be given a new home. Phew.

## ALL'S FAIR IN ART AND WAR

There was a particularly appropriate neologism doing the rounds this year: 'fairtigue'. It describes the exhaustion that you experience due to the seemingly endless array of art fairs that clog up the London calendar in autumn. Between the two Frieze fairs, Art15, the Affordable Art Fair, London Art Fair, Start Art Fair, 1:54 and countless other satellite fairs, London is very much in danger of fair burnout.

Frieze tried to shake things up this year by adding a performance element to its usual main fair. The idea was to 'create moments of interruption or immersion within the fair's environment' through performance pieces by various artists. It ended up adding a wonderfully surreal, unsellable edge to the fair's otherwise rampant commercialism. Frieze also announced that its founding directors, Matthew Slotover and Amanda Sharp, would be replaced by Victoria Siddall. Stephanie Dieckvoss, esteemed director of Art14, passed on the reins to Kate Bryan for Art15.

Elsewhere in the commercial fair world, the 1:54 Contemporary African Art Fair had such a successful first spell in London that it expanded into New York in May. London additionally hosted yet another new fair, Photo London, which opened for a limited time in May. Fairtigue indeed.

In terms of art festivals, the UK had a respectable showing too. Notably, Sarah Lucas represented Great Britain at the glamorous Venice Biennale with a well-received show of fleshy sculptures and art works. Back in Blighty, the Folkestone Triennial was back and made headlines when artist Michael Sailstorfer buried 30 pieces of 24-carat gold bullion in the sand of the Outer Harbour Beach. Visitors (many with metal detectors) were scouring the sand for weeks!

## THE LIVES OF ARTISTS

The general election had an impact on everyone. Not least artist (yes, singular) Bob and Roberta Smith, who stood against Michael Gove in Surrey Heath. He was standing to help protect arts funding and education; it did not go particularly well. Another artist trying to give back to society was old favourite Banksy, albeit in typically elusive style. An image he stencilled on the door of a Bristol youth centre was crowbarred off by youth centre workers and sold to save the centre from closure. Banksy wrote that 'as far as I'm concerned, you can keep it'. Elsewhere, another of his works – a satirical image depicting pigeons with anti-immigration views – was removed due to complaints of racism from local residents in Clacton-on-Sea. His art may not be the best, but he certainly gets people talking.

That's a skill shared by another British artist, Sir Anish Kapoor, who this year installed his large-scale sculptures in the Palace of Versailles in Paris. For some unfathomable reason, the French took exception to one sculpture which apparently depicted Marie Antoinette's vagina. It was vandalised, and those who were not amused were very upset. Speaking of controversy, Tracey Emin's famous *My Bed* finally reappeared after 15 years in some warehouse to be displayed at Tate Britain. A welcome return for some; a tiresome sight for others.

But perhaps most controversial of all was playwright/artist Brett Bailey's short-lived attempt to stage *Exhibit B* at the Barbican Centre in September. It involved shackled black actors in cages displayed for viewers' (dis)pleasure. It was intended as a critique of European slavery, referencing 19th-century human zoos. The installation got five-star reviews in Edinburgh, but the satire was lost on many, and protests forced its early closure in September 2014.

Elsewhere, Scottish artist Duncan Campbell won the Turner prize for his compelling, critical film pieces; Israeli painter Matan Ben Cnaan won the BP portrait award for his photo-realist depiction of a daughter and son posing with a mean-looking hound; and Mikhael Subotzky and Patrick Waterhouse won the Deutsche Börse photography prize at the Photographers' Gallery for their depiction of the changing fortunes of a South African tower block.

The most talked about artist of the year, however, must be Paul Cummins, whose installation of poppies at the Tower of London to commemorate the centenary of the First World War was nothing short of a public art blockbuster. The local council even implored visitors to stay away from *Blood Swept Lands and Seas of Red*, which filled the grounds of the tower with almost 900,000 ceramic poppies, but to no avail. People flocked there, even started petitions to stop the artwork from being removed at the end of its stint. That an installation can connect so directly to the public is a powerful statement of the importance of art in British life. Long may it continue.

# BUSINESS AND FINANCE

*Lisa Carden*

## AN APPLE A DAY. . .

The past 12 months have seen some of the biggest names in both world and UK business in the headlines – and the publicity will have been more welcome for some than others.

In January 2015, Apple posted the biggest quarterly profit in history (£11.8bn), thanks to the enormous demand for its iPhone products; to date, a staggering 75 million have been sold and as at December 2014, the company held £93bn in cash reserves. Apple's deal with China Mobile earlier that year, which allowed the US tech giant to sell its products with the world's largest carrier, has no doubt played a vital role in that phenomenal success. What's next? 'Wearable technology' is likely to be a major focal point for Apple and its competitors; one such example, the Apple Watch, was launched to much fanfare in April 2015, and functions as a normal timepiece as well as having a host of additional functions.

China also proved to be fruitful territory for Jaguar Land Rover (JLR), which celebrated five successive years of growth in early 2015. Over 122,000 vehicles – more than a quarter of its total sales in 2014 – went to China, a rise of nigh on 30 per cent and testament to the region's consistent demand for high-end Western brands. JLR's success also translated into good news for the West Midlands, as the company announced plans to create over 1,000 new jobs in the area. Its Energy Manufacturing Centre, in which £500m has been invested, opened in Wolverhampton in late October 2014. There was even more good news for British engineering in April 2015, when Rolls-Royce announced that it had secured the largest order in its history: it would be paid £6.1bn for building the 200 engines required by the Emirates airline for 50 of its A380 aircraft. It was an impressive year all round for Rolls-Royce as, just a few weeks earlier, the company sealed a contract worth £670m with Air China for engines destined for 15 Boeing Dreamliners.

## ALL CHANGE

The picture was significantly less rosy for two of the best-known names on the UK's high streets, namely HSBC and Tesco.

Tesco, for many years the juggernaut of the UK's supermarket sector, had an extremely uncomfortable spell in the spotlight in autumn 2014, when it became clear – following the intervention of a whistleblower – that the company had misreported its profits by £250m. In the space of one business day, 22 September, £2bn was wiped off the company's stock market value, and shares fell by 11.5 per cent. Dave Lewis, appointed CEO just a few weeks previously, announced an investigation and referred the situation to the Financial Conduct Authority (FCA); at the time of writing, the Serious Fraud Office's investigation is ongoing.

This turn of events was the tin lid on a grim few years for Tesco. Its market share has been gradually eroded over recent times with the march of their continental cost-cutting rivals, Aldi and Lidl, and since the departure of Sir Terry Leahy in 2011, it was generally thought that the business had lost its way. This view was given added credence on 22 April 2015 when the business posted its largest-ever loss, to the tune of £6.4bn. A few weeks earlier in January, Tesco had signalled

all was not well when it announced plans to close 43 stores, and abandoned plans to build another 49. While some communities have actively fought off developments by large supermarket chains, others have welcomed them, deciding that they had a role to play in revitalising moribund town centres. In the light of Tesco's decision, however, these locations have yet another empty shop to fill, or a now purpose-less location to redevelop.

All of the main UK supermarkets have embarked on a series of price cuts in order to attract and retain an increasingly discount-hungry customer base, but suppliers have been put under extreme pressure in the process. (Indeed as the Tesco profit disaster was emerging last year, the anti-poverty organisation War on Want went public with its concerns about the implications of a price war.) Dairy farmers in particular have been very hard hit as supermarkets sought to cut customers' weekly shopping bills: in January 2015, the National Farmers' Union (NFU) claimed that milk was now cheaper than bottled water (four pints of milk now typically retail for just 89p). It will come as no surprise that the number of dairy farmers is at its lowest ever: there are under 10,000 left in the UK, according to the NFU and, if the patterns of the last decade are repeated, just 5,000 will remain by 2025.

HSBC also found itself under an intense spotlight when it became apparent that its Swiss arm had been helping wealthy customers to avoid paying tax in more than 200 countries, including the UK. A whistleblower began to collect data on this issue in 2007 and by 2010 the French government was able to inform its neighbours about the widespread tax avoidance ongoing in Geneva. Although money has been retrieved in some cases – in France, for example, more than £185m in taxes and fines were recouped from 3,000 clients, while the UK's HMRC recovered over £135m from more than 1,000 HSBC customers – prosecutions have been remarkably thin on the ground, with just one made in the UK to date. Matters came to a head in June 2015 when the bank paid 40m Swiss francs in what was termed 'compensation' to the Geneva authorities for its actions. Later that month, HSBC announced that it would be shedding 8,000 UK jobs and also rebranding its local branches as part of an extensive restructure. The bank may even move its HQ from the UK, but nothing had been confirmed at the time of writing. Unions took an expectedly dim view of the developments.

## WORRYING TIMES FOR WONGA *ET AL*

The much maligned 'pay-day' lenders have also been through the mill over the past 12 months, but sympathy has been conspicuously absent. The standard business model for such companies is to offer cash-poor customers short-term loans at eye-wateringly high interest rates. If customers did not pay back the loan on time, the penalty fees levied made what could have been an initially small loan sum spiral upwards very quickly indeed. While public concern about these companies had been growing for some time, in November 2014 the FCA instituted a cap on loans, stipulating that interest and fees could not exceed 0.8 per cent per day and that the total cost of the loan be fixed at 100 per cent of the original sum. Critics of the move said that it did not go far enough – Wonga, for example, perhaps the best known of these firms, did indeed drop its interest rate in December 2014, but from over 5,800 per cent to just over 1,500 per cent – and the FCA had to step in again when it became apparent that several of these loan brokers were raiding their customers' bank accounts in order to recoup fees and then sharing those bank details with other companies. An FCA report in March 2015 showed that there was still much work to do in terms of regulating this sector: reports of threatening communications with customers, unfair practices and unclear terms and conditions were still extremely common. Many companies ceased trading, and even the market-leading Wonga has wobbled: in October 2014, it announced that it was writing off over £200m worth of loans that had been made to customers who should never have received them in the first place under newly tightened rules ('affordability checks'). Six months later it reported a pre-tax loss of £37m for 2014 and warned the markets that 2015 was likely to be similarly bleak.

Household debt in general continues to be a significant issue for the lowest earners in the UK. Many clients of pay-day lenders are under extreme financial pressure and there has been concern in some quarters that tighter controls on these lenders may drive the desperate to use loan sharks. Credit unions have been suggested as one way forward: these community-owned organisations typically provide savings and loans (although some also offer current accounts and mortgages) and it is estimated that there are currently 500 operating across the UK.

ANY LIFE IN THE LIVING WAGE?
The UK has had a minimum wage – a legally mandated hourly earnings 'floor' for the lowest paid since 1999. The concept of the 'living' wage, described by *The Economist* magazine in November 2014 as 'the minimum necessary to meet housing, food and other basic needs', has been much discussed in recent times, however, as a way of further boosting pay for those struggling to make ends meet. Take-up was mixed: while some public- and private-sector organisations – including such varied names as Nestlé, Save the Children, KPMG and even Chelsea Football Club – had adopted it, it was gaining little traction in sectors such as retail, where pay is typically low and employees often need to rely on tax credits to boost their income.

The situation changed dramatically in early July 2015, however, when George Osborne, in his first Budget since the General Election, announced that a new national living wage would become the new norm as of April 2016 for all workers over 25-years-old. Rates will begin at £7.25 per hour, and are expected to rise to £9 by 2020. But will such a change really make a difference? Critics have argued not, maintaining that the new standard does not go far enough. One employer arguably going the extra mile is IKEA, which announced on 20 July its intention to pay 4,500 staff a living wage of £9.15 per hour in London and £ 7.85 elsewhere, also as of April 2016.

FOOD, GLORIOUS FOOD: BRITAIN'S STELLAR EXPORT
While for many years British cuisine has been the butt of jokes, the UK's interest in food and drink has never been higher. Millions of cookbooks are snapped up by eager readers every year and the current vogue for 'clean' eating saw one book, *Deliciously Ella* by the food blogger Ella Woodward, reprinted an astonishing six times before its official publication date in order to meet demand. Over 30,000 copies were sold in one week alone in late January 2015.

Baking, once viewed as the domain of fairycake-wielding toddlers or patient grandparents, has also soared in popularity in recent years thanks to a raft of TV programmes

and celebrity exponents. But beyond the bunting and nostalgia, the food market is serious business, and the organic sector in particular has played a part in its burgeoning importance. First gaining traction in the 1990s, the demand for organic products has broadly managed to avoid the overall slumps in food pricing and spending over the past year. In fact, a Soil Association report published in February 2015 showed that sales of organic items actually rose in 2014 by 4 per cent, and that the organic market was worth over £1.8bn. That said, organic items represent just a tiny proportion of the wider food market, which the Food and Drink Federation estimates to be £92bn. And Fairtrade products, which guarantee income for producers in developing countries, had their first fall in sales for 20 years, as cash-strapped shoppers tightened their belts.

Food and farming remains the biggest manufacturing sector in the UK and, according to government statistics, employs one in eight people. New products have been helping to boost local economies across the country: for example, the government announced that sales of English and Welsh sparkling wine were on track to reach just shy of £100m during 2015, and exports were growing to traditional competitors such as France and Australia. North of the border, whisky continues to reign supreme, with research published by the Scotch Whisky Association reporting that the industry contributed more than £5bn to the UK economy, supporting 40,000 jobs in the process (11,000 of which directly). In fact, food and drinks exports account for £18.9bn, according to official figures. In order to maintain that momentum, in February 2015 the Department for Environment, Food and Rural Affairs announced the launch of its Food Stars programme, in which 50 businesses from across the UK would receive expert backing to help develop their product range and international reach.

When it comes to high street name recognition, however, most of us will have encountered a Thorntons store when in need of a chocolate fix. The confectionery company has been in operation for more than a century and for many years was a popular choice for those looking for boxed chocolate gifts. Tastes have changed, however, and while Britain's appetite for sweet things remains undiminished, serious chocolate lovers have begun to hanker for higher-end offerings, including the increasingly popular 'bean to bar' products first created in small chocolateries (and now adopted by chocolate producers of all sizes). Thorntons has struggled in the face of changing consumer preferences and difficult trading conditions, most notably a period of rapid expansion in the mid-2000s, and in June 2015 the company was sold to the Italian confectionary giant Ferrero – the world's fourth-biggest chocolate brand according to Euromonitor research – for over £100m. While UK store numbers are likely to be reviewed, Ferrero said that the Thorntons factory in Derbyshire would remain open and its brand maintained.

TROUBLED WATERS FOR THE OIL INDUSTRY
The precipitous fall in the price of oil over the period under review allowed the UK's drivers to fill up more cheaply than at any point in recent years, but it was not all good news. In fact, the slump was just another worry for the UK's offshore oil and gas companies, which lost over £5bn in 2014 according to the industry body, Oil and Gas UK, even though production levels remained high at more than 1 million barrels equivalent per day. Just as oil prices were plummeting – they reached a record low of under $50 (£32) per barrel in January 2015 – production costs soared to £18.50 per barrel, not including tax, investment and decommissioning costs. The upshot? The North Sea oil reserves as yet untapped would remain in the ground. While

cost management would help the situation considerably, significant investment will be needed to take the industry forward as everyday life becomes ever more energy-intensive.

Wind turbines have been one source of alternative energy for the UK but have encountered local opposition from those who view them as blots on the landscape. Proponents of this view were no doubt heartened by the new Conservative government's decision to end onshore windfarm subsidies in 2016, a year earlier than had been previously planned under the former Coalition agreement with the Liberal Democrats. The news, announced in June 2015, was not welcomed everywhere; the devolved government in Scotland, which was likely to host the vast majority of potential windfarms, said that it had not been consulted on the move, while the European Commission reminded Whitehall that the UK would miss its 2020 renewable energy targets.

'Fracking' or hydraulic fracturing, a drilling technique used to extract natural gas from shale, has been another contentious energy issue over the past 12 months. Although widespread in the USA – where its use is likely to mean that the country will become a net exporter of natural gas by 2020 – and championed by the Conservative government, fracking has attracted a good deal of opposition in the UK due to safety and environmental concerns. In June 2015, county councillors in Lancashire rejected a bid by Cuadrilla, an oil and gas exploration company, to begin operations in the Fylde area. In fact, there is some dispute as to whether gas from shale is the silver bullet that its supporters have suggested: in a November 2014 report, in fact, the UK Energy Research Centre stated that while natural gas could be a 'bridging' fuel to be used in attempts to transition to a low-carbon economy, ultimately increased investment in other energy sources was urgently needed alongside increased gas storage.

Energy issues were a headache on the domestic front as well. Bills have been climbing inexorably for years – even when wholesale gas prices have fallen – but in February 2015 it became clear that many customers on a dual-fuel standard tariff had been overcharged for their gas and electricity supplies by the 'Big Six' energy firms (namely Centrica, E.ON, EDF Energy, npower, SSE and Scottish Power). A report by the Competition and Markets Authority found that while some customers were willing or able to actively shop around for the best prices, those who preferred to stick with a longstanding provider or who lacked the knowledge or resources to switch were up to £234 per year worse off. It has been a turbulent time for the Big Six: criticised by the energy regulator Ofgem in February 2015, their profits have taken a tumble this year – but remain substantial. Centrica, for example, which owns British Gas, reported a 35 per cent reduction in profits for 2014, but they were still £1.75bn; npower's operating profits for the same year also fell, this time by over 20 per cent on 2013, but still totalled £162.5m.

## CHEERS FOR CHARLOTTE

As was the case when Prince George was born in 2013, the arrival of Princess Charlotte in May 2015 was good news not only for the Royal Family. Retailers raked in over £200m on George-related items, yet merchandise inspired by his little sister could well dwarf that over the years ahead: the Centre for Retail Research estimated that £25m would be spent on souvenirs in the weeks directly following her arrival, and companies ranging from Denby to Marks & Spencer had a range of commemorative products ready to roll. In the case of the princess, however, it is probably fashion retailers and designers who will be hoping for a sales uplift once she is spotted in any of their wares. If the 'George Effect' is anything to go by – clothes he is seen wearing tend to sell out online within minutes – they may well be richly rewarded.

## EMERGENCY GREXIT

While world growth remains modest – it is forecast by the International Monetary Fund (IMF) to be 3.5 per cent in 2015, and 3.8 per cent in 2016 – the picture is very mixed across and even within regions. UK growth is forecast to be 2.7 per cent in 2015, for example, but 1.5 per cent in the Eurozone. The big unknown, however, is what will happen to the monetary union if Greece should leave.

The Greek economy has been on the brink of disaster since 2010 and it has been bailed out by its Eurozone neighbours and the IMF numerous times: it is estimated that it owes more than €300bn to a mix of international partners and private investors. In June 2015, however, the wheels finally came off when the European Central Bank ended emergency funding and Greece failed to make a repayment of €1.6bn to the IMF, becoming the first developed country to do so.

Banks in the country shut for a week over late June/early July in the run-up to a referendum called by the left-wing, anti-austerity government so that the country could vote on a bail-out plan offered by international creditors. When the Greek people voted on 5 July, their response was clear: 60 per cent of those who participated in the poll rejected the rescue package on offer. A subsequent – and some might argue equally punishing – pay-back arrangement was subsequently arranged with Eurozone leaders, and for the moment it would see that Greece's departure from the Eurozone ('Grexit') has been staved off yet again (at least temporarily).

But what would a 'Grexit' mean for the UK? British financial institutions are reasonably well insulated from any knock-on effects of such an event, but there are serious concerns about the potentially toxic impact it might have on economic confidence generally, and on countries such as Italy and Spain in particular. A worst-case scenario could be another crippling financial crisis – and the ripple effects would spread far and wide. For the moment, all eyes are on Athens.

# CONSERVATION

## NATURAL ENVIRONMENT

*Peter Marren*

### THE GREAT RED HOPE

The native red squirrel is one of our most endangered wild mammals. It faces competition for food from the introduced American grey squirrel, which also carries the squirrel pox virus, fatal to red squirrels. Where the two are in competition, the larger grey squirrel invariably wins. As a result, in England and Wales the red has been pushed to the margins and survives in small, isolated pockets of woodland, although it is still widespread in northern Scotland, especially in pine forests. In Ireland it has been much the same story. Though still widespread there too, the red has often been ousted by the grey, the latter being descended from a single introduction in 1911. Until recently this trend was increasing and the future of the Irish red squirrel seemed to be in doubt.

The first sign of a perhaps growing resistance to squirrel pox has been discovered within the small colony of red squirrels at Formby in Merseyside. This colony was devastated by an outbreak of the pox in 2008 which killed four out of every five squirrels. Although the colony has since partially recovered, further outbreaks are inevitable. Fortunately, scientists at Liverpool University have identified individual squirrels that have contracted the virus but survived. This does not necessarily mean that the animal is developing immunity but it could be a sign that the population is becoming more resistant, in the same way that rabbits developed some resistance to the myxomatosis virus (showing symptoms of the disease but surviving it). To safeguard the population further, conservationists hope to create a buffer around Formby by a concerted attempt to kill all grey squirrels in the surrounding area.

There is hope in the Irish Midlands too, where the grey squirrel has unexpectedly gone into decline while the red is commoner now than at any time during the past 30 years. The most likely reason is predation by pine martens. Research suggests that the presence of martens is critical in deciding whether the red or the grey squirrel wins out. Martens are on the increase again after a long period of persecution, and it is hoped that their spread will come to the rescue of the beleaguered native squirrel.

### NATIVE BAT DISCOVERY

A new discovery brings the number of bat species breeding in the UK to 17 – representing a full third of our native mammal fauna. An unusual bat later identified as Geoffroy's bat, a European species, was discovered in well-wooded countryside near Bath in 2014 while another individual was noted on the Sussex Downs. Geoffroy's bat is now known to be migratory and its appearance in suitable habitat in southern England strongly suggests that it is an overlooked native species. It is a middle-sized bat with reddish-brown fur, similar to the native Natterer's bat from which it is most easily distinguished by a characteristic notch in its ears. In Europe it is a woodland bat which sometimes visits cattle sheds and stables to 'glean' insects from the walls.

This is the third new bat to be discovered in the past 20 years. In the 1990s a new species of pipistrelle, the soprano pipistrelle, was detected after its distinctly high-pitched calls were heard on bat detectors. It is now known to be widespread in Britain. Another species, Alcathoe's bat, which was new to science when discovered in Greece in 2001, was first found in Britain in 2010 but is thought to have been with us, undetected, all along. It too is a critical species, closely related to the whiskered bat. A fourth species, Nathusius' pipistrelle, which is slightly larger than the common pipistrelle and with longer fur, was once thought to be a rare migrant but is now known to breed in the UK and sometimes stay with us all year round.

All British bats are protected by law but they still face many problems, including eviction from roof spaces and lofts, and the difficulty of finding enough flying insects in today's intensively managed countryside.

### RESTORING OUR LONG-LOST LYNX

The lynx is Britain's lost big (well, middle-sized) cat. Fossil evidence indicates that the animal was once widespread but that it died out about 1,000 years ago, not from loss of habitat but (presumably) from hunting and persecution. The Lynx UK Trust has now been formed to spearhead attempts to bring it back. The trust argues that restoring the lynx would benefit our natural ecology by helping to control the spiralling numbers of deer in our woods – and so reduce traffic collisions and help woodland regeneration. Judging by a survey carried out by the trust in 2015, the introduction would have public support: 90 per cent of the respondents gave the project the thumbs-up. The economic benefits, say the trust, might be as much as £20m a year.

The trust has identified four areas, all on private land, which are suitable – in Northumberland, Aberdeenshire, Cumbria and Thetford Forest in Norfolk. It proposes to apply formally for a licence later in 2015 to release six cats at each site for a trial period. If the licence were to be approved, the trial could begin within months.

The government's conservation agencies are cautious about the plan. Natural England warns that the proposal needs 'serious consideration in terms of its impacts' while Scottish Natural Heritage notes that any application to release lynx would need to be supported by 'a significant amount of evidence'. The National Sheep Association vowed to fight the proposal tooth and nail, as, doubtless, will other farming interests. 'Sheep farming is fairly marginal for a lot of people', it reminds us. 'They need encouragement, not added burdens and risks.' In Europe, lynx are not significant predators of sheep; in Germany for example, losses amount to one or two sheep lost per cat, per year. Whether or not the government looks kindly on the trust's application, in the longer term the prospects of a reintroduction of the lynx looks favourable – much more so than dreams of reintroducing wolves or bears.

Meanwhile, Devon's wild beavers have won a reprieve after DEFRA (the Department for Environment, Food and Rural Affairs) changed its mind over their capture and removal. The animals, which are either escapees or were illegally introduced into the wild, live in the catchment of the river Otter. Having been examined and found free of disease, they have been allowed to stay, at least for the next five years. On the river Tay, too, beavers are thriving and have increased to about 200 individuals. At the formal introduction site in Knapdale, Argyll, on the other hand, the animals are doing less well. Of the 16 adults released there, half have gone missing and, of 14 kits born in the wild, only one or two have survived. Nevertheless, the population is considered to be 'stable'. One way or another, the beaver looks set to stay, although not in a way foreseen by planners.

## GROUSE AND HEN HARRIERS

The hen harrier is Britain's most persecuted bird of prey. According to the Royal Society for the Protection of Birds (RSPB), England could support around 300 pairs but only a handful have managed to nest successfully in recent years. In 2015, five of the few nesting males in northern England disappeared (the males bring food to the nest while the female guards the eggs and brood). It is not thought probable that the birds deserted their nests and it is much more likely that they were shot, trapped or poisoned by gamekeepers and their bodies disposed of. This killing is, of course, illegal; the birds are fully protected by law.

The reason why the hen harrier has been targeted so ruthlessly is that it will raid the nests of red grouse and carry away chicks. Although their more usual prey is meadow pipits and voles, a pair of hen harriers can wreck the chances of a successful grouse shoot. One possible compromise is diversionary feeding, in which carrion is put out on a feeding post to divert the harriers away from the grouse nests. This seems to work best when harrier numbers are low but it has not always resulted in increased game bags of grouse. In Orkney, where the birds are not persecuted, harrier numbers have nonetheless fallen due to agricultural improvement, over-stocking of sheep and the consequent fall in numbers of voles and pipits.

Another possible compromise, which is supported by the Game and Wildlife Conservation Trust and the Hawk and Owl Trust, is 'brood management', in which harrier chicks are removed from the nest to be raised in an aviary for later release. Others are sceptical of such methods, given the lack of trust between grouse moor owners and conservationists, and given the very low numbers of hen harriers in England. The RSPB's current position is that, before brood management can happen, hen harrier numbers must first increase to a more acceptable level. It calls for 'a robust licensing system to govern grouse moor management to deliver environmental outcomes'.

The RSPB's former head of conservation, Mark Avery, has raised the stakes by organising a Hen Harrier Day just before the start of the grouse shooting season. An e-petition for a complete ban on driven grouse shooting in England collected over 22,000 signatures and won a defensive reply from DEFRA. In his new book, *Inglorious* – named in reference to the 'Glorious Twelfth' (12 August being the traditional start of the shooting season) – Avery argues that the claims of grouse moor owners to be wise custodians of the land are spurious. Many moors are over-burned and over-drained to their detriment as habitats and as stores of carbon – much of which is lost in smoke every winter. The battle lines are drawn.

## THE ADVANCE OF ASH DIEBACK

Ash trees are being afflicted by a disease caused by a fungus, *Hymenoscyphus fraxineus,* spread by tiny windblown spores from infected leaves. The disease causes leaf loss, bark lesions and the eventual death of the tree. Once a tree is infected, there is no known remedy. Dieback was brought to Britain on diseased ash saplings imported from tree nurseries in the Netherlands. It has spread partly through the movement of infected saplings and partly by natural processes. Ash trees in woods as well as nursery and planted trees are dying as a result.

Although the disease is advancing more slowly than was initially feared, it is now established throughout Britain in at least 1,000 sites, and little or nothing can be done to prevent its spread. The worst-hit areas are south-east England and East Anglia; current forecasts predict that most ash trees in Sussex and Kent will be lost by 2018, as well as half those in Norfolk, Suffolk and Essex. The impact on the landscape will be almost unimaginable and certainly worse than Dutch elm disease in the 1970s. The disease kills saplings and young trees very quickly; older trees may resist for a time though, in Denmark, only 1 per cent survived.

The best hope lies in the possibility that some strains of native ash are resistant to the disease. The newly formed Living Ash Project is attempting to identify such strains and to propagate them for replacement planting. But most woodland ash trees are wild, naturally regenerated trees – ash reproduces prolifically from seed – and were not planted by human agency. Our wonderful variety of wild ash trees, some of which are hundreds of years old, are irreplaceable.

Ash dieback is not the only problem faced by trees. In the London area, trees have been defoliated by caterpillars of the oak processionary moth, a European species which has crossed the Channel, possibly aided by the warming climate. The moth is a health risk since the caterpillars are covered in hairs that can cause skin rashes. They live in silken nests in the trees, which protect them from chemical sprays. One wood near Pangbourne was sprayed from the air by helicopter with 'Bt', a toxin produced by bacteria. Unfortunately such methods kill harmless insects too, which in this case included purple emperor and white admiral butterflies.

## RESTORATION BY BILLIONAIRE

For at least a century, the central ecological problem of the Scottish Highlands has been the unsustainably large numbers of grazing animals, notably domestic sheep and wild red deer. Numbers of the latter are routinely kept high to facilitate stalking – the means by which many Highland estates draw their income. The result has been dying woodlands that fail to regenerate except behind a deer-proof fence and the virtual loss of an entire habitat (subalpine scrub).

That may be changing because of a new kind of landowner: foreign billionaires who buy the land as an investment but bring with them new ideas based on the premise of a more sustainable approach to the land. A key player in this regard is the clothing magnate Anders Holch Povlsen who, in 2006, bought the 43,000-acre Glenfeshie estate in the Cairngorms and has now bought the Ben Loyal and Kinloch estates in Sutherland comprising another 40,000 acres of overgrazed moorland and mountain. He also owns the 30,000-acre Braeroy estate near Fort William.

Under the stewardship of his factor Thomas MacDonell, and with the advice of Scottish Natural Heritage, Glenfeshie – the home of Sir Edwin Landseer's *The Monarch of the Glen* – has been transformed. With deer numbers now under control, the pine and birch woods and natural scrublands of willow and juniper have regained vitality and are once again in good ecological health, with a resulting increase in birds such as black grouse. The estate is well on the way to achieving its target of doubling the amount of woodland over the next five years, mainly by natural regeneration.

Povlsen hopes to bring the same kind of ecological restoration to the far north of Scotland. This area, too, has long been denuded of woodland cover apart from plantations of alien spruce. At present there is little or no regeneration in the natural woodland of birch and rowan – the most northerly woods in Britain – despite the rain of seeds and berries from the ageing trees. With a reduction in deer numbers, the bare slopes of Ben Loyal could once again be clothed in trees, the spawning and feeding grounds for fish could be improved and the peat bogs restored to their original, actively growing condition.

At the 23,000-acre Alladale estate in Sutherland, an alternative form of restoration is being attempted by its owner, Paul Lister, heir to the MFI furniture company, who bought the estate in 2003. Inspired by South Africa's game reserves, his long-term goal is to create a wilderness reserve large enough to support many of our lost mammals, perhaps even bears and wolves. He has introduced elk (or moose) and wild boar on a trial basis and planted 800,000 native trees on the hitherto bare hillsides. Red deer numbers are controlled by shooting but Lister would far rather that bear, wolf and lynx did the job for him. As for other lost animals, Highland cattle stand in for the extinct aurochs and rugged Highland ponies for the lost wild horse, the tarpan. Unfortunately the project depends on enclosures and fences; plans to extend a 50-mile fence around the whole estate would fall foul of walkers' traditional – and now statutory – freedom to roam in the Highlands.

## NEW BRITISH BUTTERFLIES?
The summers of 2013 and 2014 brought a record number of continental swallowtail butterflies to Britain. As a native species, the swallowtail is confined to the Norfolk Broads but the slightly paler continental form is an occasional migrant to the south coast and may once have bred in the London area. It may now be in the process of establishing itself more firmly. Unlike the native form, which is confined to wild marshland, the continental swallowtail will lay on fennel and even carrots in gardens and allotments. Its boldly striped caterpillar was found in gardens in Eastbourne and elsewhere and in some of them survived the winter as chrysalids to emerge into butterflies the following spring. Whether this is the start of a successful invasion or the result of an unusually warm summer remains to be seen.

A much less predictable visitor appeared in small numbers, mainly in eastern England, in 2014: the scarce or yellow-legged tortoiseshell, a species hitherto recorded only once in Britain. Around 20 were spotted in places as far apart as Kent and Yorkshire, with the majority of sightings in Norfolk. One butterfly was found indoors in a cupboard, apparently attempting to hibernate, and several were seen flying in spring 2015 having overwintered safely. This species has increased in western Europe recently and it is thought that our visitors arrived on a favouring wind from the Netherlands. Whether or not it manages to produce another generation in Britain and thus become an at least temporary resident, the scarce tortoiseshell is the first new species of British butterfly arriving here by its own means for more than 60 years.

New butterflies are rare but new moths are becoming commonplace. Since 2000, 27 new species have colonised Britain while a further 89 species established breeding colonies during the last century, some of them from migration, others from accidental imports with foodstuffs or the horticultural trade. On the other hand, at least four native species of larger moth have died out in the recent past and many more face an uncertain future.

## OPPOSITION TO NEW EU WILDLIFE LAWS
The European Commission (EC) is set to review its Nature Directives, set up between 1979 and 1992, after a 12-week public consultation beginning in May 2015. These directives are twofold: the Habitats Directive, which protects habitats and a range of species of plants and animals; and the Birds Directive, which protects most of Europe's wild birds. The EC also established a Europe-wide network of protected sites known as Natura 2000. There are 800 of these in the UK, including such well-known places as the New Forest, the Severn Estuary, Snowdonia and the North Antrim coast, which includes the Giant's Causeway. The review will assess their cost-effectiveness, the extent to which they are a burden to businesses and whether such goals could not be better met at national level.

Not unnaturally, conservationists fear that the unstated goal is to weaken the laws protecting wildlife to make them more 'business-friendly'. Most conservation bodies are broadly satisfied with the directives, believing they provide social benefits as well as safeguarding rare habitats and wildlife. They believe the potential changes represent the single biggest threat to biodiversity and species in a generation. According to Kate Jennings, head of the RSPB's policy unit, before the directives, protected sites were being lost at a rate of 15 per cent a year; afterwards, the rate had fallen to just 1 per cent. Moreover, action plans drawn up under the Birds Directive have saved many European species from the brink of extinction, among them the griffon vulture, Bonelli's eagle, Dalmatian pelican and (not-so-common) common crane.

Orders for a thorough overhaul of the Nature Directives have come from the top: the new EC president Jean-Claude Juncker, who has been given strong support from Dutch farming lobbies. The new UK government has also lent him its support despite a recent review by DEFRA which found that the directives were largely working well. Even the European Union's own environment department is unenthusiastic about changing the rules, asserting that it 'would rather modernise than bury' them. Also, businesses may not necessarily welcome a change. According to Jennings, the majority of developers value regulatory certainty over confusingly moving goalposts.

The political context of this review is a wider agenda of deregulation. If the directives are weakened or delegated to national governments, then other European environmental directives may follow, such as that governing the level of emissions or the water framework directive.

Another straw in the wind may be the government's new, more 'business-friendly' line on fracking. Before the 2015 election, the government was minded to disallow fracking on protected sites such as Sites of Special Scientific Interest, Areas of Outstanding National Beauty and National Parks. By July, however, it seemed to have forgotten that promise and instead announced that fracking will be allowed below protected sites so long as the drilling rigs are stationed just outside their boundaries.

## IS THE NEW 'NATURE WRITING' NATURAL HISTORY?
A new genre of literature is appearing on the bookshelves: nature writing. Propelled by the success of *H is for Hawk* by Helen Macdonald and *The Old Ways* and *The Wild Places* by Robert Macfarlane, the new writing focuses not on traditional natural history so much as the author's experience of the natural world – and by extension the relationship between it and the human world. A host of new books have appeared in this style, such as Tim Dee's *Four Fields,* Rob Cowen's *Common Ground* and Patrick Barkham's *Coastlines*. In each, nature is not so much the object – a matter of facts and figures – but the subject, based on a sensitive inter-connection between humans and the wild.

This sudden flowering of nature writing and the unprecedented sales of Macfarlane's books in particular suggest a feeling of lost connection among readers, and perhaps a longing to rediscover the simple pleasures of walking, observing and keeping wild animals as pets. Such writing has a long pedigree, reaching its Victorian apogee with the works of Richard Jefferies and, nearer our own time, J. A. Baker, author of *The Peregrine,* and the nature writer Richard Mabey. The new style is confessional, unashamedly emotional and, at its best, draws the reader in by lyrical description which borders on poetry.

The new writing has underlined the distinction between writing subjectively about the human experience and objectively about wild animals, plants and their habitats. In terms of sales, the latter has been left high and dry. The former is closer to English literature than to science – although Mabey in particular was scrupulous in being true to nature and the facts of biology. The new writing does not even require the writer to have a deep knowledge of the subject. Some of it could equally be described as imaginative travel writing, lifestyle journalism or even a form of philosophy. The traditional, self-effacing naturalist is left looking old-fashioned and out of time.

Taken as a whole, 'nature writing' must say something about our relationship with what is left of the natural world. Whether or not it remains in fashion, it does at least rescue the subject from television and its dumbed-down, soundbite-based outlook.

### ATLASES GALORE

One of the activities that British naturalists most enjoy is putting dots on maps. All but the most obscure groups of terrestrial wildlife have been mapped at various scales, from birds and mammals, to butterflies, grasshoppers and even woodlice. In each case the crowning moment is the production of a printed atlas, usually recording species over the whole of the UK on a scale of 10km squares. In the case of birds and butterflies, the whole exercise is repeated at intervals of ten years or so. Traditionally, atlases cover Ireland as well as Britain.

During the past year, three remarkable atlases have been published. *The Atlas of Dragonflies in Britain and Ireland* places dragonflies on the same scale of popularity as butterflies. It devotes 400 pages to our small fauna of 56 species, including details of dragonfly lifestyles and habitats, the effect of a changing climate and attempts to conserve them. Volunteers contributed over a million records over a five-year period.

It took two fat volumes to cover the *Atlas of British and Irish Bryophytes*. Here, a relatively small band of specialists, has mapped these mostly small and elusive plants in the same detail as flowering plants and established a benchmark that would be hard to match anywhere in the world. Not to be outdone, the Botanical Society of Britain and Ireland has produced *Hybrid Flora of the British Isles,* mapping every known hybrid species known to exist outside gardens, and described as the final frontier in British field botany. That hybrids, too, can be mapped at the same level of detail as other plants indicates that there is no shortage of expert botanists in 21st-century Britain.

## BUILT HERITAGE

*Matthew Saunders*

### ENGLISH HERITAGE AND HISTORIC ENGLAND

On 1 April 2015, the long-expected split of English Heritage, first set up under the aegis of Michael Heseltine in 1983, took place. A body called the English Heritage Trust was granted a licence by the Historic Buildings and Monuments Commission and subsequently took into care the 420 abbeys, castles and other sites either owned by, or in the guardianship of, the state. The Chairman is Vice-Admiral Sir Tim Laurence (husband of HRH the Princess Royal) and the new Chief Executive, Kate Mavor, was latterly Chief Executive at the National Trust for Scotland. The new English Heritage Trust received a one-off grant of £88m from the Treasury – £52m to address the 'most severe conservation defects' among the 420 locations, £28m to improve interpretation and presentation, and £8.8m to

ease the transition. The business plan presupposes additional earned income of £58m in the eight years from 2015, alongside another £62m raised in philanthropic donations and an 86 per cent increase in membership from the present 700,000 to 1.3 million. The expectation of the Treasury is that the English Heritage Trust will have been weaned off public subsidy altogether by 2022–3. There was an early boost in that respect with the sale of Apethorpe Hall in Northamptonshire to the French businessman Baron von Pfetten. The Hall, one of the most important of all the nation's Buildings at Risk, had been compulsorily purchased on behalf of English Heritage in 2004 after years of dereliction; £3.5m was spent on buying it and a further £8m on repairs. While only £2.5m has been repaid through the change of hands, Baron von Pfetten has committed to completing the repairs and opening the house to the public for 50 days each year, starting in July 2015.

The other half of the 'old' English Heritage has become Historic England, which performs all the advocacy, research, designation (ie listing and scheduling) and grant-giving roles, although on the latter the annual budget is a mere £11m. It shares its Chairman, Sir Laurie Magnus, with the Historic Buildings and Monuments Commission, which retains overarching control over both bodies. The Chief Executive is Duncan Wilson, an archaeologist and accountant who has been in successive charge of three major historic buildings: Somerset House, the World Heritage site at Greenwich and Alexandra Palace in North London. Historic England has also hit the ground running with the introduction of 'heritage action zones', where it will 'work with local people to unlock the potential of the historic environment in areas of economic need'; the partial reintroduction of the Blue Plaque scheme; and the issue of formal guidance, both general and specific, for the conversion of farm buildings. And in Wales, there is another new face – Kate Clark, the new Chief Executive of Cadw, the Historic Environment arm of the Welsh Assembly. She arrived just in time to assist in the introduction of the Historic Environment (Wales) Bill in the Assembly, which showed England the way forward when it came to making the Register of Park and Gardens statutory, lending statutory underpinning to an expert panel and making it easier to stop unauthorised works at a scheduled site.

### LOTTERY WINNINGS

The body which continued to flourish more than any other, buoyed by £400m per year from the National Lottery, has been the Heritage Lottery Fund (HLF). The new Chairman, appointed in March 2015, is Sir Peter Luff, previously MP for Mid Worcestershire. It has been able to offer (first round) grants both modest and spectacular, the latter including St Wilfrid's Harrogate, one of Temple Moore's great masterpieces (£1.6m); the projected International Bomber Command Centre in Lincolnshire (£3.1m); a new exhibition for the Roman Baths at Bath (£3.5m); Cleveland Pools, Bath (£4.1m), the oldest swimming pool in Britain (1815); the National Botanic Gardens of Wales (£3.7m); Canterbury Cathedral (£11.9m); Gloucester Cathedral (£4.5m); a new Museum for Blackpool (£13.7m); Plymouth History Centre (£12.9m), to be housed in the existing museum and an adjacent church; Nottingham Castle (£13m), to include strengthening of the remarkable caves underneath; Hay Castle at Hay-on-Wye (£4.9m), to put back the roof missing since 1939; the Guildhall, Stratford–upon–Avon (£1.4m), to open up a building presently closed to the public; the Warwick Bridge Corn Mill, Cumbria (£1.4m), to rescue a Building at Risk; the Garden Museum, Lambeth (£3.5m), which includes the establishment of the first Archive of Garden Design; the Crescent in Buxton, Derbyshire, where a further grant has brought the HLF contribution to the rescue of this outstanding design by Carr of York to £23.9m; the Sculpture Heritage Project (£2.8m), to set up an online photographic catalogue of all publicly owned sculpture in the UK; the Charterhouse, Coventry (£4.7m), on the site of the city's Carthusian monastery; and the Painted Hall, Greenwich, completed by Sir James Thornhill between 1708 and 1727 (£2.8m).

HLF-funded schemes that re-opened or opened afresh in 2015 included the Whitworth Art Gallery, Manchester; the Huguenot Heritage Centre at Rochester; Tamworth Castle; Lincoln Castle; Keswick Museum; the Town Hall, Merthyr Tydfil (as a new arts centre); the former palace of the Prince Bishops at Auckland Castle, County Durham; Sewerby Hall, Bridlington; the National Black Heritage Centre in Brixton; All Souls Church, Bolton, owned by the Churches Conservation Trust and now a centre for community facilities; Shrewsbury Museum; Bletchley Park in Buckinghamshire, the famous code-breaking centre; and Colchester Castle.

HLF and the Art Fund were the key players in the decision, announced in 2015, that has saved the Wedgwood Collection of some 80,000 ceramics and the associated archive, which had been caught up in a dispute over the pension fund of the bankrupt company. The Collection will now pass into the care of the V&A. HLF will also no doubt play a critical role in the developing scheme to save one of the greatest of all the 18th-century houses, the stupendous Wentworth Woodhouse in Yorkshire, where years of uncertainty look as if they might finally be coming to an end.

## CHURCH DONATIONS ON THE UP

Amid tightening austerity elsewhere, the government has found useful sums for historic places of worship. Following the announcement in the 2014 Budget of a direct grant of £20m for the 'repair and enhancement of cathedrals', some £55m in total was found in 2014 and 2015 for a Church Roofs Repair Fund for parish churches. Some of that money came from the fines imposed on the banks after the LIBOR scandal. Among churches that have fallen out of use, the Grade I listed Merston in Sussex passed to the Churches Conservation Trust while in Wales, Castlemartin in Pembrokeshire has gone to the Friends of Friendless Churches. A Norfolk Diocesan Trust has been established, which it is hoped will take into care some 20 mostly medieval churches in that county where the congregations are struggling – there are similar moves in Lincolnshire,

Devon and Cumbria. The long-derelict Grade II* listed All Saints at Hawkhurst in Kent, designed by Sir Gilbert Scott, is to be converted into flats. The Church in Wales has declared itself convinced that the yew tree in the churchyard at St Cynog's in Defynnog, Powys, is, at 5,000 years, the oldest in the country.

## DOORS NOW OPEN

Among the new attractions which opened during the year under review are Miranda House at 58 Grafton Way in London's West End, home of the Venezuelan independence hero Francisco de Miranda, reopened after having been closed for years, and the New Museum of the Mind at Bethlem Royal Hospital at Beckenham. There has been a tentative start to creating a visitor centre at the appallingly vandalised Gwrych Castle near Abergele in Conwy. The palace of the Bishop of Carlisle, Rose Castle in Cumbria, now seems safe in the hands of the Rose Castle Foundation. The Museum of London has announced that it is to explore the feasibility of a move into the former Smithfield Market, reprieved from demolition over the course of the year after a public inquiry. The English-based Landmark Trust has taken on its first Belgian property, the former farmhouse at Hougoumont that was repeatedly fought over during the Battle of Waterloo in 1815. But there is bad news too – a fire in the estate offices at Castle Ashby in Northamptonshire has destroyed many important archives while in Kent, the local authority seems determined to shut the present museum in Orpington Priory.

During the year under review, the London Society has been re-launched, there is a new society dedicated to the great theatre designer Frank Matcham, and the Garden History Society and the Association of Gardens Trusts have merged. A Building Limes Forum has been established with a base in Edinburgh. Scholarship has advanced with significant new biographies of G. F. Bodley (by Michael Hall), E. S. Prior (David Valinsky) and W. A. and W. E. Nesfield (Shirley Rose Evans). There have been major overviews of stained glass in Wales (Martin Crampin) and that from the Arts and Crafts school (Peter Cormack) and important local studies of the country houses of Dorset (Michael Hill), Newstead Abbey in Nottinghamshire (Thoroton Society) and the Welsh slate industry (David Gwyn). There were also revised and greatly expanded editions in the Pevsner 'Buildings of Britain' series on Cambridgeshire, Somerset (two volumes), Cornwall, Bedfordshire (and Peterborough), Powys, Lothian and Suffolk (two volumes).

# DANCE

*Hanna Weibye*

Despite positive outcomes for dance in the 2014 Arts Council England funding round, the Conservative victory in the 2015 general election left dance, like many other publicly funded art forms, nervous about the prospect of further budget cuts. Unlike his recent predecessors, new culture secretary John Whittingdale has a track record of interest in the brief; he spent a decade as chair of the select committee on culture, media and sport, and sits on the all-party parliamentary dance committee. As chair of the select committee, he oversaw a report published in November 2014 which recommended that Arts Council England should do even more to rectify the current arts funding imbalance that significantly favours London, and which encouraged the Department for Culture, Media and Sport to work with local authorities to encourage local arts funding initiatives. For dance companies, this suggests that strong efforts in outreach/education and regional touring will continue to be conditions of government funding.

In March 2015, it was announced that Dance UK and three other industry umbrella organisations would receive an ACE grant of £650,000 a year for three years to work as a consortium to support a more coherent national approach to the delivery of dance services.

In April the BBC launched Young Dancer, a televised contest along the lines of the BBC's well-established annual Young Musician competition. The winner was the youngest contestant, 17-year-old Connor Scott from Northumberland, a raw talent in the contemporary category who was not even in professional dance training at the time. The support and encouragement given to the young dancers by the judges was heartening – the exaggerated harshness popular on TV talent shows would have been inappropriate here. But with the overall standard of talent not high and students of the country's elite ballet schools notably absent, it was generally felt that the contest would need some refining before it equals Young Musician in status.

The British choreographer Christopher Wheeldon directed and choreographed a new stage musical, *An American in Paris* (based on the 1950 film), which opened at the Théâtre du Chatelet in Paris in December 2014 before transferring to Broadway in March. It garnered multiple awards, including a Tony award for best choreography. Royal Ballet principal Leanne Cope created the principal female role, Lise, receiving a year's leave from the company to do so.

Maya Plisetskaya, one of the great Bolshoi ballerinas of the 20th century, died in May 2015, aged 89. The fiery Plisetskaya was renowned for her interpretation of Odette/Odile in *Swan Lake*, although her relationship with the work was famously soured by years of being required to perform it for visiting dignitaries. Her more personal legacy to the ballet world was the *Carmen Suite* she commissioned from the Cuban choreographer Alberto Alonso in 1966, with music from her composer husband Rodion Shchedrin – one of the most successful episodes in her campaign to transcend the narrow limits of the Bolshoi's ballet programming under Yury Grigorovich.

Dance critic Mary Clarke died in March at the age of 91. Clarke was involved with the magazine *Dancing Times* for nearly 60 years, 45 of those as its editor; she also served as *The Guardian* dance critic for 17 years, and authored many books on ballet and dance.

Frank Doran stepped down as MP for Aberdeen North at the 2015 general election. A key force behind the all-party parliamentary dance group, Doran had been a tireless parliamentary advocate for dance, in particular helping to secure a £5.5 million investment in Youth Dance England in 2007. His support was honoured with the Jane Attenborough Dance UK Industry Award at the 2014 Critics Circle National Dance Awards, the first time the award had gone to a politician.

Sylvie Guillem, sometime star of Paris Opéra and principal of the Royal Ballet and latterly a major performer and commissioner of contemporary dance, announced in October 2014 that she would be retiring from the stage in 2015, aged 50. The final London performances of two of her most hauntingly beautiful shows, *PUSH* with Russell Maliphant and *Sacred Monsters* with Akram Khan, were seen in 2014. For her farewell, Guillem, never one to rest on her laurels, created a new show, *Life in Progress*, in partnership with Sadler's Wells, featuring commissions from Khan and Maliphant alongside William Forsythe's *Duo* (1996) and Mats Ek's *Bye* (2011). Khan's *technê* used Guillem's lanky body in skittish, insectoid movements that made the piece difficult to warm to. After a gentle start, Maliphant's joyful *Here and After*, which referenced steps from Guillem and Maliphant's earlier collaborations, set Guillem and Emanuela Montanari running round a stage which kept changing shape thanks to the visionary lighting of Michael Hulls. Immense demand for tickets led to the show playing extra dates at the Coliseum in July 2015, and visiting the Edinburgh International Festival in August and Birmingham in September, as well as touring internationally. Guillem's final performance will be given in December 2015 in Japan, a country with which she has long had a special relationship.

## THE ROYAL BALLET

The company mounted 11 different productions this season: six story ballets, one all-Ashton bill, three mixed bills of 20th century and contemporary ballets, and Wayne McGregor's new full-length production, *Woolf Works*. The season opened with the ever-popular *Manon*, and December saw a return of Christopher Wheeldon's 2011 *Alice's Adventures in Wonderland*. Founder choreographer Sir Frederick Ashton was well-represented with *Onegin* and *La fille mal gardée*, in which the company's Russian principals made role debuts: Natalia Osipova was an impressively passionate Tatiana in *Onegin*, while Vadim Muntagirov's sparkling Colas in *Fille* capped a year of new roles for the young principal that included Des Grieux *(Manon)* and Lensky *(Onegin)*. Carlos Acosta's production of *Don Quixote*, premiered in 2013, proved its mettle by getting a swift revival, while a final farewell was said to Anthony Dowell's 1987 production of *Swan Lake*.

The November mixed bill of Ashton works included a truly marvellous performance of his 1946 *Symphonic Variations*, anchored by the serene grace of Vadim Muntagirov. *Song of the Earth*, a one-act ballet set to Mahler's *Lied von der Erde* by the Royal Ballet's other great director-choreographer, Kenneth MacMillan, was performed in two different mixed programmes, alongside works by George Balanchine and Jerome Robbins.

Only three new works were performed on the Royal Opera House main stage. Artist-in-residence Liam Scarlett contributed a one-act narrative ballet, *The Age of Anxiety,* with a Bernstein score based on the W H Auden poem of the same name and exploring the intense but uneasy interactions of four characters in a 1940s New York bar over the course of one evening. Hofesh Shechter's *Untouchable* was a rare collaboration between the Royal Ballet and a choreographer who has neither a company connection nor a grounding in classical ballet. Shechter used the corps de ballet rather than principals for a piece which relied for effect on its suggestion of an aggressive group dynamic.

The most ambitious and talked-about event of the year was the May premiere of McGregor's *Woolf Works*, a triptych of one-act ballets each based on a different novel by Virginia Woolf, and linked only by the figure of Woolf herself. One of the dancers playing Woolf was retired ballerina Alessandra Ferri, whose appearance at the age of 52 was considered a great coup for McGregor. McGregor demonstrated a newly lyrical, narrative quality to his choreography in the first act, 'I Now, I Then' (based on *Mrs Dalloway*), which was beautifully led by Ferri as Mrs Dalloway/Woolf and Edward Watson as Septimus, the tortured war veteran. The second act, 'Becomings', based on *Orlando*, was a total contrast, featuring steampunk black and gold costumes and intricate designs with lasers (by Lucy Carter). The choreography was in the trademark hyperkinetic McGregor style and utilised the remarkable physiques of Natalia Osipova, Steven McRae and Sarah Lamb. The final act, 'Tuesday', based on *The Waves*, returned to the more lyrical style of the first act, affectingly portraying Woolf's mental state in the weeks before her suicide in the summer of 1941. Public and critical reaction was divided. The majority hailed the work as a triumph and McGregor as a genius, and unsold tickets were quickly snapped up after the first performance garnered several five-star reviews. But a significant minority of critics felt *Woolf Works* was stylistically and psychologically flawed, an inappropriate reaction both to Woolf's sharp prose and to her struggle with mental illness.

The Linbury Studio Theatre saw new works by Royal Ballet dancer Ludovic Ondiviela (*Cassandra*, 2014) and Shobana Jeyasingh, whose *Bayadère – The Ninth Life* interrogated the orientalism of the 19th-century ballet *La Bayadère*.

## ENGLISH NATIONAL BALLET

At an October 2014 press conference, company director Tamara Rojo and Alastair Spalding, chief executive of Sadler's Wells, announced that English National Ballet (ENB) would be Associate Ballet Company at the Wells and perform two seasons a year there, the first ballet company to have such a relationship with the contemporary dance powerhouse. In a further bold move, Akram Khan has been commissioned to create a new *Giselle* for the company, to be premiered in autumn 2016.

Another significant announcement, in May 2015, concerned plans for a new joint home for the company and the English National Ballet School in east London, which will be a distinct improvement over the company's current, cramped Kensington premises. The move to the new location, near Canning Town, is planned for autumn 2018.

Perhaps to conserve money for all these future projects, and a large international tour in summer 2015, the 2014–15 season at ENB featured only three full-scale adult productions, plus a new children's ballet, *My First Swan Lake*. *Coppélia* and *Swan Lake* toured the regions in the autumn, when fans in Milton Keynes were upset by Alina Cojocaru's last-minute withdrawal from a performance in order to dance in a Bolshoi Theatre performance of John Neumeier's *La Dame aux camélias*. It may not have comforted those fans deprived of their chance to see the top ballerina, but the whole company was on fine form in *Swan Lake*, and for its London run in January Rojo secured attractive international

guest principals: Royal Danish Ballet's Alban Lendorf partnered Rojo and Ivan Vasiliev partnered Cojocaru.

The Modern Masters programme performed at Sadler's Wells in March 2015 was the first in the ENB's new partnership with the theatre, and had been cannily designed to impress both critics and punters. Jiří Kylián's 1991 *Petite Mort* is one of the Czech choreographer's best-known and -loved pieces, while it was a coup for ENB to give the UK premiere of *Spring and Fall*, a frothy pastoral piece by John Neumeier, artistic director of Hamburg Ballet. Cojocaru, one of Neumeier's favourite ballerinas, danced the principal female role opposite Alejandro Virelles, who joined the company from Boston Ballet for the 2014–15 season. The bill was rounded off with a high-octane performance of William Forsythe's *In the Middle, Somewhat Elevated* (1983). The company's strong showing in this demanding piece was further evidence that ENB under Rojo's leadership is reaching new heights of technical excellence.

## IN THE REGIONS

Birmingham Royal Ballet continued to perform an impressively wide repertoire. Alongside *Beauty and the Beast*, *The Nutcracker*, *Coppélia* and *Sylvia*, the company mounted a number of mixed programmes, which included a well-received Balanchine *Serenade* alongside works by David Bintley and Kenneth MacMillan. One of the season's two premieres was a re-creation by Dame Gillian Lynne of Robert Helpmann's groundbreaking 1944 *Miracle in the Gorbals*, one of the first British ballets on a contemporary vernacular subject. Lynne, who danced in the original but couldn't remember any of the steps, used the same set, score and scenario to create an effective piece of dance-drama that nonetheless, in the post-MacMillan era, did not quite have the impact Helpmann's expressionist style had had on contemporaries. The other new ballet was director David Bintley's one-act *The King Dances*, about Louis XIV and his relationship with dance.

Scottish Ballet's big production this season was an ambitious Christmas revival of *The Nutcracker*, a popular 1970s production by the company's late director Peter Darrell which had been retired from the repertory in 1997. Veteran dance theatre designer Lez Brotherston supplied lavish new designs that stayed true to the best features of the original, including the bauble-hung backdrop in the Kingdom of the Sweets, and the childlike charm of Darrell's classic story treatment made up for the occasional dullness in choreography. The company wrung continued value out of other narrative ballets in its repertory, touring its 2008 Krzysztof Pastor *Romeo and Juliet* to China and Japan in early 2015, and reviving its highly popular *Streetcar Named Desire* in Scotland, London and on tour in the USA. A new David Dawson version of *Swan Lake* was announced for 2016, the first time the company will have performed the classic since 1995. The only new commission performed in the 2014–15 season was Helen Pickett's *The Crucible*, based on the Arthur Miller play; it was accompanied by the UK premiere of Christopher Bruce's setting of Dylan Thomas's *Ten Poems*, in a double bill which was praised more for its ambition than its execution.

Northern Ballet were dizzyingly busy: ballets mounted included the UK premiere of Jean-Christophe Maillot's *Romeo and Juliet*; *Dracula*, *Cinderella*, *Wuthering Heights* and *The Great Gatsby*, all by David Nixon; and *Madam Butterfly*, a joint effort between Nixon, Northern Ballet and Christopher Hampson's company Perpetuum Mobile. Several short pieces were created for a 45th anniversary gala in March, one of which, *A Northern Trilogy* by Jonathan Watkins, was also performed in the company's London appearance. Watkins is creating a full-length *1984* for the company which will premiere in September 2015.

CONTEMPORARY DANCE

The contemporary dance scene continues to be dominated by London and the south-east, thanks in no small part to the might of Sadler's Wells as both venue and production house. In October 2014, the second Wells's Composer evening featured the orchestral music of Thomas Adès, played by the Britten Sinfonia and conducted by Adès himself. Wayne McGregor restaged his *Outlier* (2011), originally made for New York City Ballet, on dancers from his own company, Random Dance, accompanied by Thomas Gould in a splendid rendition of Adès's violin concerto 'Concentric Paths'. In both *Life Story*, choreographed by Karole Armitage in 1999, and *The Grit in the Oyster,* a new commission from British choreographer Alexander Whitley, Adès's music stole the show from the dance, and it was left to *Polaris*, a new commission from Crystal Pite, to demonstrate that dance was capable of matching Adès's music for complexity and drama. With 60 dancers moving together like one great tentacular beast, Pite's cinematically intense choreography was one of the hits of the season and contributed to her Olivier award for outstanding achievement in dance. The award also honoured Pite's *The Tempest Replica* (performed in April 2014) and her haunting, clever duet *A Picture of You Falling* (2008), which received its UK premiere on the Sadler's Wells Associates bill in February and was widely considered the highlight of that show.

The February Associates bill also featured an underwhelming Charlie Chaplin piece, *Smile*, by Kate Prince and Tommy Franzén, and a new Hofesh Shechter piece, *the barbarians in love,* the first of a planned trilogy. The latter eschewed the rock concert antics of some of his earlier pieces and instead explored themes of aging, adultery and creative impotence through a recorded conversation between Shechter and a disembodied female narrator.

With money from 14–18 NOW, the government's World War I Centenary art fund, BalletBoyz and Sadler's Wells commissioned *Young Men,* a full-length work choreographed by Iván Pérez with original music by Keaton Henson, which premiered at the Wells in January. It contained some good material and fine dancing, but was generally felt to be longer than the material could support. War was big this season, with several significant commissions; most of the major companies devoted at least one programme to the theme, but the war piece which garnered the most positive reaction was Rosie Kay's *5 Soldiers,* a revival of a 2010 piece by a small independent dance company which drew on Kay's work with injured soldiers in rehabilitation facilities.

Rambert balanced heritage programming and new commissions in a series of mixed programmes performed in London and on tour. Four new works were premiered in 2014–15: Mark Baldwin's *The Strange Charm of Mother Nature,* an engaging abstract piece evoking the whirling movement of subatomic particles; Shobana Jeyasingh's *Terra Incognita,* whose elegant design by Jean-Marc Puissant in some measure made up for Gabriel Prokofiev's ear-assaulting score; *Frames* by Alexander Whitley, which was also hampered by a difficult score and awkward metal props; and Mark Baldwin's *Dark Arteries,* a piece evoking the past and present of Welsh mining communities, and featuring an impressive original score by Gavin Higgins that was performed live on stage by the Tredegar Town Band.

Matthew Bourne's company, New Adventures, was very active, performing a Christmas run of *Edward Scissorhands* at Sadler's Wells, completing its extended *Lord of the Flies* tour, and reviving *The Car Man* (2000) on tour and in London.

Akram Khan Company had a busy year. Popular shows *DESH, Sacred Monsters* and *Gnosis* were revived in 2014, and Khan premiered a new show, *TOROBAKA,* with flamenco live wire Israel Galván, in which the two dancers traded rhythms from their respective dance traditions.

In addition to its usual schedule of touring and performances at The Place in London, Richard Alston Dance Company celebrated its 20th anniversary with a run at Sadler's Wells which included a new piece, *Nomadic,* in which 80-year-old Alston collaborated with young hip-hop choreographer Ajani Johnson-Goffe.

VISITORS

After the Mariinsky season at Covent Garden in summer 2014, Russian companies were notable by their absence in 2014–15. Russian dancers, however, did come; in August 2014, Natalia Osipova (formerly of the Bolshoi and Mikhailovsky, now of the Royal Ballet) mounted a show at the London Coliseum with former fiancé Ivan Vasiliev called *Solo For Two.* Despite the pair's acknowledged greatness as ballet dancers, their efforts at contemporary dance in reworked pieces by Sidi Larbi Charkaoui and Ohad Naharin did not impress particularly, although the final piece, Arthur Pita's *Facada,* provided deliciously black entertainment by casting Osipova as a jilted bride with murderous intentions towards her former fiancé.

The great Mariinsky and American Ballet Theatre ballerina Diana Vishneva brought a solo show, *Beauty in Motion,* to the London Coliseum, but its two character-driven pieces, by Jean-Christophe Maillot and Carolyn Carlson, were affected, convoluted and poorly scored, and did not display Vishneva's considerable talent to best effect.

Another visiting ballerina was Wendy Whelan, who retired from New York City Ballet last year and is now exploring the world of contemporary dance. Not all of the pieces on the bill of five specially commissioned new works that she performed at the Linbury Studio Theatre with Royal Ballet principal Edward Watson were hits, but the collaboration was praised for its vision.

Several European companies brought major productions to London. Mats Ek's 2013 version for Royal Swedish Ballet of one of the most beloved story ballets took a very different tack to its predecessors, changing the title to *Juliet and Romeo* and using the lesser-known Tchaikovsky score in preference to the iconic Prokofiev. The Swedes brought it to Sadler's Wells in September, as part of the Northern Light season of Scandinavian choreography, where it impressed and mystified audiences in equal measure and won an Olivier award for best new dance production.

Dutch National Ballet gave the UK premiere of Christopher Wheeldon's 2012 production of *Cinderella* at the London Coliseum in July. Though it featured some lovely design concepts by puppeteer Basil Twist, it was marred by a complicated story treatment, and Wheeldon's undoubted talent for pretty and diverting choreography was too little in evidence.

Tanztheater Wuppertal, always welcome visitors, gave the UK premieres of three pieces by its late director Pina Bausch: the dreamy *Sweet Mambo* (2009) at the Edinburgh International Festival 2014; and two sprawling pieces from Bausch's spiky middle period at Sadler's Wells in April: *Ahnen* (1987) and *Auf dem Gebirge hat man ein Geschrei gehört* (1984).

# NEW PRODUCTIONS

ROYAL BALLET

Founded 1931 as the Vic-Wells Ballet

Royal Opera House, Covent Garden, London WC2E 9DD

*The Age of Anxiety* (Liam Scarlett), 7 November 2014. A one-act work. *Music,* Leonard Bernstein; *design,* John Macfarlane; *lighting design,* Jennifer Tipton. Cast led by Bennet Gartside, Steven McRae, Laura Morera and Tristan Dyer

*Untouchable* (Hofesh Shechter), 27 March 2015. A one-act work. *Music,* Hofesh Shechter and Nell Catchpole; *design,* Holly Waddington; *lighting design,* Lee Curran

*Woolf Works* (Wayne McGregor), 11 May 2015. A full-length work in three parts. *Music,* Max Richter; *design,* Cigüe, We Not I, Wayne McGregor, Moritz Junge; *lighting design,* Lucy Carter. Cast led by Alessandra Ferri, Sarah Lamb, Natalia Osipova, Edward Watson and Federico Bonelli

### BIRMINGHAM ROYAL BALLET
Founded 1946 as the Sadler's Wells Opera Ballet
Birmingham Hippodrome, Thorp Street, Birmingham B5 4AU

*Miracle in the Gorbals* (Gillian Lynne, after Robert Helpmann), 8 October 2014. A one-act work. *Music,* Arthur Bliss; *design,* Adam Wiltshire after Edward Burra; *lighting design,* Peter Teigen. Cast led by Ian Mackay, Elisha Willis and Cesar Morales

*The King Dances* (David Bintley), 17 June 2015. A one-act work. *Music,* Stephen Montague; *design,* Katrina Lindsay; *lighting design,* Peter Mumford. Cast led by William Bracewell

### ENGLISH NATIONAL BALLET
Founded 1950 as Festival Ballet
Markova House, 39 Jay Mews, London SW7 2ES

*My First Swan Lake* (George Williamson, after Petipa/Ivanov), 2 April 2015, Peacock Theatre, London. A full-length work for children. *Music,* Tchaikovsky

### NORTHERN BALLET
Founded 1969 as Northern Ballet Theatre
2 St Cecilia Street, Quarry Hill, Leeds LS2 7PA

*A Northern Trilogy* (Jonathan Watkins), 14 March 2015. A one-act work. *Soundtrack,* Stanley Holloway; *design,* Julie Anderson; *lighting design,* Alastair West

### SCOTTISH BALLET
Founded 1956 as the Western Theatre Ballet, Bristol; moved to Glasgow as Scottish Theatre Ballet 1969
Tramway, 25 Albert Drive, Glasgow G41 2PE

*The Nutcracker* (Peter Darrell), 13 December 2014. A full-length work. *Music,* Tchaikovsky; *design,* Lez Brotherston; *lighting design,* Peter Thomson. Cast led by Erik Cavallari and Sophie Martin

*The Crucible* (Helen Pickett), 25 September 2014. A one-act work. *Music,* Bernard Herrman and others; *design,* Charles Heightchew Jr; *lighting design,* George Thomson

### RAMBERT
Founded 1926 as the Marie Rambert Dancers
944 Chiswick High Road, London W4 1SH

*The Strange Charm of Mother Nature* (Mark Baldwin), 24 September 2014. A one-act work. *Music,* Cheryl Frances-Hoad, Igor Stravinsky, J S Bach; *design,* Mark Baldwin, Katie Paterson, Stevie Stewart; *lighting design,* Mark Henderson

*Terra Incognita* (Shobana Jeyasingh), 18 November 2014. A one-act work. *Music,* Gabriel Prokofiev; *design,* Jean-Marc Puissant; *lighting design,* Lucy Carter

*Frames* (Alexander Whitley), 5 March 2015. A one-act work. *Music,* Daniel Bjarnasson; *design,* Revital Cohen, Tuur Van Balen; *lighting design,* Lee Curran

*Dark Arteries* (Mark Baldwin), 12 May 2015. A one-act work. *Music,* Gavin Higgins; *design,* Michael Howells; *lighting design,* Michael Mannion

### SADLER'S WELLS – LONDON'S DANCE HOUSE
Rosebery Avenue, London EC1R 4TN

*The Grit in the Oyster* (Alexander Whitley), 30 October 2014. A one-act work. *Music,* Thomas Adès; *design,* Jean-Marc Puissant; *lighting design,* Lee Curran

*Polaris* (Crystal Pite), 30 October 2014. A one-act work. *Music,* Thomas Adès; *design,* Jay Gower Taylor; *lighting design,* Tom Visser

*Young Men* (Iván Pérez), 14 January 2014. A full-length work. *Music,* Keaton Henson; *design,* Carlijn Petermeijer; *lighting design,* Jackie Shemesh

*Smile* (Kate Prince and Tommy Franzén), 5 February 2015. A one-act work. *Music,* D J Walde; *design,* Ben Stones; *lighting design,* Adam Carrée. Lead performer, Tommy Franzén

*the barbarians in love* (Hofesh Shechter), 5 Feburary 2015. A one-act work. *Music,* Hofesh Shechter; *design,* Merle Hensel; *lighting design,* Lee Curran

*technê* (Akram Khan), 27 May 2015. UK premiere of a one-act work. *Music,* Alies Sluiter with Prathap Ramachandra and Grace Savage; *design,* Kimie Kakano; *lighting design,* Adam Carrée and Lucy Carter. Lead performer, Sylvie Guillem

*Here and After* (Russell Maliphant), 27 May 2015. UK premiere of a one-act work. *Music,* Andy Cowton; *design,* Stevie Stewart; *lighting design,* Michael Hulls. Lead performers, Sylvie Guillem and Emanuela Montanari

## AWARDS

### CRITICS CIRCLE NATIONAL DANCE AWARDS 2014
*Best Classical Choreography* – Christopher Wheeldon for *The Winter's Tale* (Royal Ballet)
*Best Modern Choreography* – Akram Khan for *Dust* (English National Ballet)
*Outstanding Female Performance* (Classical) – Natalia Osipova (*Giselle*), *Giselle* (Royal Ballet)
*Outstanding Male Performance* (Classical) – Xander Parish (*Apollo*), *Apollo* (Mariinsky Ballet)
*Outstanding Male Performance* (Modern) – Jonathan Goddard (*Dracula*), *Dracula* (Mark Bruce Company)
*Outstanding Female Performance* (Modern) – Wendy Houstoun, *Pact with Pointlessness*
*Grishko Award for Emerging Artist* – Francesca Hayward
*Best Independent Company* – Mark Bruce Company
*Jane Attenborough Dance UK Industry Award* – Frank Doran, MP
*Stef Stefanou Award for Outstanding Company* – English National Ballet
*Grishko Award for Best Female Dancer* – Natalia Osipova
*Dancing Times Award for Best Male Dancer* – Jonathan Goddard
*De Valois Award for Outstanding Achievement* – Carlos Acosta

### BBC YOUNG DANCER 2015
Connor Scott

# FILM

*Omer Ali*

## WHIPPED INTO SHAPE

Two bestselling novels of the last five years became two of the most high-profile films of the period under review: *Gone Girl* and *Fifty Shades of Grey*. British author E. L. James' BDSM primer was first published in 2011 and had dragged its feet in hitting our screens until it was placed under the stewardship of artist-director Sam Taylor-Johnson.

Dakota Johnson plays Anastasia Steele, the college graduate who takes her friend's place at a job interview and finds herself drawn into the sex games of boss Christian Grey (Jamie Dornan). Released in time for Valentine's Day 2015, the film's visuals stray into soft-core territory, but Taylor-Johnson is not unaware of much of the book's ridiculousness.

Sexual politics are to the fore of American author Gillian Flynn's 2012 thriller *Gone Girl*, filmed by David Fincher. Ben Affleck and Rosamund Pike star as warring couple Nick and Amy Dunne, who retreat to the former's hometown when they both lose their jobs. He opens a bar with his twin sister Margo and appears to enter a funk, from which he's brutally shaken when Amy goes missing – all the clues suggest she has been murdered by Nick.

Fincher is a master at taking on adapted material, but here he leaves the script to speak for itself; Flynn adapted her own book and she's shaved some infelicities from the plot, but much of its richer territory has also been lost: Nick's ageing father is seemingly cast aside, while the backdrop of job losses and foreclosures only shows through the muted suburban setting.

## AMERICAN SNIPING

While *Gone Girl* and *Fifty Shades* were based on works of fiction, non-fiction routinely provides the sort of heavyweight material that wins awards. The transition from page to screen is not without risk, however, notably when dealing with recent history.

Clint Eastwood's *American Sniper* stars Bradley Cooper as US Navy Seal Chris Kyle, who was credited with 160 confirmed kills during four tours of Iraq. The film draws on a deep well of patriotism and made nearly $250m (£160m) in its first three weeks in US cinemas – making it the country's highest-grossing war movie, outstripping *Saving Private Ryan* (1998). However, *American Sniper* attracted much criticism for drawing a direct line between the events of 9/11 and the war in Iraq; based on Kyle's autobiography, the film undoubtedly sugarcoats its subject's character, while painting his victims in stark black and white (routinely the former), even inventing a nemesis to drive the narrative forward. History may be written by the victors, but it can always be rewritten by Hollywood, it seems.

## BRITISH LEADS

Despite emerging as a dark horse prior to awards season, *American Sniper* failed to outgun the likes of *The Theory of Everything,* James Marsh's polite portrayal of physicist Stephen Hawking's adult life. Based on ex-wife Jane Wilde Hawking's emotional account of the couple's relationship, this comic-book retread of the facts was praised for star Eddie Redmayne's physical transformation during the film, though it is no less impressive for Felicity Jones' performance as Jane.

Redmayne's main British challenger at award time was Benedict Cumberbatch for his touching portrayal of mathematician Alan Turing in *The Imitation Game,* directed by Norwegian Morten Tyldum. Liberties were taken with biographer Andrew Hodges' source material, but the outcome was no less affecting for that, although Keira Knightley had little to work with as a sympathetic fellow codebreaker.

Fellow Brit David Oyelowo should have been recognised alongside them after his outstanding take on US civil rights leader Martin Luther King Jr for director Ava DuVernay's *Selma*. Focusing on events in 1965, when the Alabama town became the focal point in the battle to secure the vote for black Americans, scriptwriter Paul Webb walks a remarkable tightrope in replicating King's tone considering the filmmakers were unable to quote his original words for copyright reasons.

Oyelowo is joined on-screen by compatriots Tom Wilkinson – as President Lyndon B. Johnson – and Tim Roth (Alabama governor George Wallace), as well as TV star Oprah Winfrey as Annie Lee Cooper, whose contribution seems to fade as the film does. To its credit, *Selma* neither tries to obscure the truth nor manipulate reality in order to offer simple answers.

Timothy Spall was also largely ignored in the UK and US for his unforgettable turn as J. M. W. Turner (Spall was hailed as best actor at Cannes 2014). For this portrait of *Mr. Turner,* director Mike Leigh concentrates on the painter's later life, recreating incidents at the Royal Academy or Margate, alongside settings from Turner's best-known paintings.

## MORE AND MOORE

Another of the year's stand-out stars was Oscar Isaac, who appeared alongside Alicia Vikander in writer Alex Garland's directorial debut *Ex Machina,* and with Oyelowo in writer-director J. C. Chandor's measured *A Most Violent Year.* In the former, Isaac is a tech boss who develops a remarkably human robot, while in the latter he is a domestic oil distributor trying to establish his company in a corrupt (and violent) 1981 New York. Having caught the eye of Oyelowo's ambitious assistant district attorney, Isaac's character decides he must succeed without the help of his wife Jessica Chastain's apparently criminal family.

Another trio of top performances front *Foxcatcher,* director Bennett Miller's bleak depiction of US wrestling's biggest scandal. Steve Carell stars as millionaire John du Pont, who invites Olympic wrestler Mark Schultz (Channing Tatum) to train US athletes at his Foxcatcher Farm; as events turn increasingly dark, Mark is joined by his older brother Dave, another gold-medal winner.

Actor Mark Ruffalo is deliciously watchful in the latter role, while Miller also draws a quietly menacing performance from comic actor Carell, though again not one without controversy. While the movie is based upon Mark Schultz's autobiographical account, Schultz bridled at Miller's introduction of a homosexual element to du Pont's behaviour, as did some gay critics. Director and stars were nominated for a number of major awards; Miller won best director at Cannes 2014.

Meanwhile, Julianne Moore was a shoo-in for best actress at many of 2015's biggest award ceremonies for her lead in *Still Alice.* Based on neuroscientist Lisa Genova's self-published 2007 novel, Moore stars as the eponymous

Harvard professor who discovers she has early-onset Alzheimer's. Kristen Stewart and Alec Baldwin appear as members of Alice's family, but the focus is on Moore: she won more than 20 awards for her performance.

## WOMEN ON THE VERGE

Female leads dominated many of the year's stand-out art-house films, notably French director Olivier Assayas' *Clouds of Sils Maria,* in which middle-aged actress Maria Enders (played by Juliette Binoche) revisits the stage role that made her famous as a young woman. Chloë Grace Moretz plays the star who now takes on that role, but the revelation here is Kristen Stewart as Enders' PA. In the give-and-take between her character and Enders, she and Binoche push each other to career-best performances.

Then there was *Girlhood,* Céline Sciamma's electric portrayal of growing up in the tower blocks of the Paris banlieues, where young women have to find their own place in the shadow of men and society. Karidja Touré, Assa Sylla, Lindsay Karamoh and Mariétou Touré as the four leads manage to be fierce, vulnerable and likeable – no small achievement.

Like *Gone Girl,* redundancy is at the centre of Belgian brothers Jean-Pierre and Luc Dardenne's harrowing *Two Days, One Night,* about a young woman, Sandra, who is given one weekend to try and get her workmates to vote to reinstate her job. Marion Cotillard excels as Sandra, who is struggling with depression, as she drives around the countryside dropping in on colleagues, supported by her husband (Fabrizio Rongione); against a backdrop of universal recession, many of them cannot afford to give up the bonuses that they received in the restructuring.

*Ida* is another small-scale road movie confronting big ideas. Set in Poland in 1962, young nun Ida (played by novice actor Agata Trzebuchowska) is about to take her vows when she is sent out to meet her formidable Jewish aunt (Agata Kulesza). Each shot of director Pawel Pawlikowski's black-and-white film is artfully framed, bolstered by brave performances from the two female leads, thrown together by shared history and politics.

## INTERNATIONAL INTRIGUE

*Ida* was duly rewarded at the Oscars and the BAFTAs, disappointing fans of Russian drama *Leviathan.* Despite part-funding from the Russian government, director Andrey Zvyagintsev's film unflinchingly presents a world of record-breaking alcoholism, abuse and (state and religious) corruption as his protagonists try to save their family home from development.

While the film's critical acclaim was seen as a snub to Russia's President Putin, it was nothing compared to the firestorm provoked by *The Interview.* Seth Rogen and Evan Goldberg's typically silly movie stars Rogen and James Franco as journalists sent to kill North Korean leader Kim Jong-un.

In the summer of 2014, North Korea threatened action against the USA if the film was released; in November, one month ahead of the film's US release, the servers of production company Sony Pictures were hacked, and other films and embarrassing emails were leaked; in December, cinemas showing the movie were warned that they faced attack. The FBI identified North Korea as the culprit, although some experts were less convinced; the film received a limited cinema outing alongside online rentals, becoming Sony's most-successful digital release.

No doubt the fallout will make for the basis of a film itself one day, but there can be few more gripping real-life dramas than that played out in director-producer Laura Poitras' account of whistleblower Edward Snowden's dramatic allegations of illegal intelligence-gathering practices by the US National Security Agency and Britain's GCHQ. *Citizenfour* focuses on a week in mid-2013 when the intelligence analyst met her and *Guardian* journalists Glenn Greenwald and Ewen MacAskill in a hotel room in Hong Kong. The atmosphere is understandably paranoid and Snowden's revelations provoked fierce political debate in the USA; the film scooped the 2015 Oscar for best documentary.

Documentaries don't always catch the public's imagination, but director Asif Kapadia has proven himself a sure draw since his 2010 film about Formula One star Ayrton Senna. Now the British film-maker turned his lens on musician Amy Winehouse, who died in 2011 aged 27. His moving study assembled from archive footage earned five-star reviews and recorded the biggest-ever opening weekend for a British documentary in the UK, making the top ten of the all-time chart for non-concert film documentaries.

## HOME PLEASURES

The highest-grossing British film in the domestic market in 2014 was teen comedy *The Inbetweeners 2.* Based on the E4 sitcom, the movie broke the record set by its predecessor for the highest-grossing opening day for a comedy in the UK. It was a record that lively Brit comedy *Pride,* about LGBT support for the miners in 1984, could not hope to match, though the film had much support come awards time.

French-born director Yann Demange went back a decade further for his gripping Northern Ireland drama *'71.* Jack O'Connell is a young British soldier who becomes separated from his squad at the height of the Troubles; as he tries to survive in a maze of Belfast streets, pubs and estates, Demange and writer Gregory Burke reveal the complex web of recent conflict.

On the lighter side, animated animals provided a great deal of home-grown fun. With Hamish McColl, director Paul King adapted Michael Bond's Paddington books; Ben Whishaw voices the immigrant bear, while Hugh Bonneville and Sally Hawkins are the human parents who take him in. Shaun the Sheep then visited the city, for Aardman Animations' latest stop-motion big-screen outing.

## STELLAR EFFECTS

Christmas 2014 was dominated by the third and final instalment of director Peter Jackson's J. R. R. Tolkien adaptation, *The Hobbit: The Battle of the Five Armies,* outstripping Ridley Scott's overblown biblical epic *Exodus: Gods and Kings,* starring Christian Bale. Despite unspectacular notices, the three Hobbit films grossed $2.9bn (£1.9bn) worldwide, on a par with the Lord of the Rings trilogy's (unadjusted) total box office revenue a decade previously.

Spectacular effects were to the fore in *Interstellar,* director Christopher Nolan's apocalyptic vision. When the future of humanity is threatened due to crop blight, the only answer is a mission into space to identify another habitable planet. Matthew McConaughey is outstanding as a former pilot who undertakes the journey alongside Anne Hathaway's biologist. Nolan's now-trademark mix of paranormal events, time shifts and inter-dimensional wizardry may have dented some of the film's entertainment value, but it remains a stunning achievement nonetheless, ranking alongside the previous year's *Gravity.*

## THE BEAT GOES ON

The effects-laden trailer for *Birdman* may have led cinemagoers to expect an offbeat superhero flick. In the event, director Alejandro González Iñárritu's take on theatre-land egos and the fickleness of Hollywood saved its CGI for a brief, stand-out moment, relying instead on the fireworks generated by an all-star cast.

Michael Keaton plays the one-time star of the Birdman superhero movies, Riggan Thomson, who hopes to shed his alter ego and regain some credibility by staging his own adaptation of Raymond Carver's short story 'What We Talk About When We Talk About Love' on Broadway. When one of the production's stars is knocked out by a falling stage light – an accident Thomson believes he caused himself – method actor Mike Shiner (Edward Norton) steps into the breach. Shiner pushes the production and Thomson to the brink with his unpredictable behaviour, insisting on drinking real alcohol on stage and seeking similar authenticity in a love scene.

Keaton and Norton produce some of their best performances of recent times, ably supported by Naomi Watts and Andrea Riseborough as their co-stars, Emma Stone as Thomson's daughter and Lindsay Duncan as a bitter theatre critic. But the film is dominated by Emmanuel Lubezki's camerawork, which creates the effect that most of the film was filmed in one shot, bolstered by a skittering drum score that keeps you on the edge of your seat.

Drumming dominates *Whiplash,* Damien Chazelle's second feature based on the writer-director's experience of being in a highly competitive high-school band. Chazelle's concept debuted as a short film at the 2013 Sundance Film Festival, starring J. K. Simmons as a bullying bandleader. It attracted financing for a full-length feature, again starring Simmons, this time with Miles Teller as his determined drummer protégé. A world away from Clint Eastwood's *Bird* (1988), *Whiplash* depicts jazz training with boot-camp intensity: bloodied hands soak in ice buckets and Teller's character insists he can play after being involved in a vicious car accident.

## BLOCKBUSTER HOLIDAY THRILLS

Summer 2015 revisited some old favourites for its biggest thrills. Robert Downey Jr (Iron Man), Scarlett Johansson (Black Widow), Chris Hemsworth (Thor), Mark Ruffalo (Hulk) and Chris Evans (Captain America) were among those who reassembled under director Joss Whedon for the snappy *Avengers: Age of Ultron,* in which the Marvel Comics characters battle Ultron, a mechanical artifical intelligence that is bent on destroying human life.

Former cop Max Rockatansky wheeled back onto our screens for the riotous *Mad Max: Fury Road.* Australian writer-director George Miller returns to the apocalyptic wasteland he first created in 1979 and Tom Hardy ably dons Mel Gibson's boots for the surprising fourth in the series, helping Charlize Theron's formidable war rig driver Imperator Furiosa escape from Immortan Joe's citadel with a cab-load of the latter's wives. Nicholas Hoult and model Rosie Huntington-Whiteley also appear among the noisy, freewheeling mayhem.

Two other venerable franchises returned for fifth instalments. July 2015 saw Arnold Schwarzenegger step into a machine-tooled *Terminator: Genisys,* followed by Tom Cruise's breezy return for *Mission: Impossible – Rogue Nation,* directed by Christopher McQuarrie, who wrote the screenplay for *The Usual Suspects,* with J. J. Abrams on board as co-producer.

But they were surpassed by *Jurassic World,* set 22 years after the events of *Jurassic Park* (1993), which was based on the novel by Michael Crichton. The prehistoric theme park has been reborn bigger and better, much like its dinosaur subjects. It's not long before their newest genetically modified draw, *Indominus rex,* breaks free, unleashing two hours of valuable mayhem: the film had the biggest worldwide opening weekend of all time, grossing $500m (£320m), racing to $1bn (£640m) in record time and into the top five all-time highest earners.

# AWARDS

## 71ST VENICE INTERNATIONAL FILM FESTIVAL
Golden Lion – *A Pigeon Sat on a Branch Reflecting on Existence* (Roy Andersson)
Grand Jury Prize – *The Look of Silence* (Joshua Oppenheimer)

## BRITISH ACADEMY FILM AWARDS 2015
Best Film – *Boyhood* (Richard Linklater)
Director – Richard Linklater *(Boyhood)*
Outstanding British Film – *The Theory of Everything* (James Marsh)
Outstanding Debut by a British Writer, Director or Producer – Stephen Beresford and David Livingstone *(Pride)*
Documentary – *Citizenfour* (Laura Poitras)
Original Screenplay – *The Grand Budapest Hotel* (Wes Anderson)
Adapted Screenplay – *The Theory of Everything* (Anthony McCarten)
Film Not in the English Language – *Ida* (Pawel Pawlikowski)
Animated Film – *The Lego Movie* (Phil Lord and Christopher Miller)
Leading Actor – Eddie Redmayne *(The Theory of Everything)*
Leading Actress – Julianne Moore *(Still Alice)*
Supporting Actor – J. K. Simmons *(Whiplash)*
Supporting Actress – Patricia Arquette *(Boyhood)*
Fellowship – Mike Leigh
Outstanding British Contribution to Cinema – BBC Films

## 65TH BERLIN INTERNATIONAL FILM FESTIVAL
Golden Bear – *Taxi* (Jafar Panahi)
Grand Jury Prize – *El Club* (Pablo Larraín)
Silver Bear for Best Director – *Aferim!* (Radu Jude)

## 87TH ACADEMY AWARDS
Best Picture – *Birdman* (Alejandro González Iñárittu)
Directing – Alejandro González Iñárittu *(Birdman)*
Actor in a Leading Role – Eddie Redmayne *(The Theory of Everything)*
Actress in a Leading Role – Julianne Moore *(Still Alice)*
Actor in a Supporting Role – J. K. Simmons *(Whiplash)*
Actress in a Supporting Role – Patricia Arquette *(Boyhood)*
Animated Feature Film – *Big Hero 6* (Don Hall and Chris Williams)
Writing (Original Screenplay) – *Birdman* (Alejandro González Iñárittu)
Writing (Adapted Screenplay) – *The Imitation Game* (Graham Moore)
Foreign Language Film – *Ida* (Pawel Pawlikowski)
Documentary Feature – *Citizenfour* (Laura Poitras)

## CANNES FILM FESTIVAL 2015
Palme d'Or – *Dheepan* (Jacques Audiard)
Grand Prix – *Son of Saul* (Laszlo Nemes)
Jury Prize – *The Lobster* (Yorgos Lanthimos)
Best Director – Hou Hsiao-Hsien *(The Assassin)*
Best Actor – Vincent Lindon *(La Loi du Marché)*
Best Actress – Emmanuelle Bercot *(Mon Roi)* and Rooney Mara *(Carol)*
Best Screenplay – *Chronic* (Michel Franco)
Caméra d'Or – *La Tierra y la Sombra* (César Augusto Acevedo)
Un Certain Regard – *Rams* (Grimur Hakonarson)

# LITERATURE

Nick Rennison

## FICTION

The highlight of the year was provided by a novel written nearly 60 years ago by a woman now approaching her 90th birthday. Excitement over the publication in July 2015 of Harper Lee's *Go Set a Watchman* (Heinemann), the prequel to her classic work of American fiction, *To Kill a Mockingbird*, was intense. Bookshops opened at midnight to sell it; readers rushed to buy it. There had been controversy over the circumstances in which the manuscript was discovered and some people had voiced reservations about the 89-year-old Lee's ability to give considered consent to its publication, but its appearance in print was undoubtedly a major literary event.

In Britain, several much-admired writers produced new novels. Kazuo Ishiguro turned to historical fantasy in *The Buried Giant* (Faber), his first novel in a decade. Nick Hornby celebrated 1960s popular entertainment in *Funny Girl* (Viking). Ian McEwan's *The Children Act* (Cape) was about a high court judge facing crises in both her professional and her private life. Kate Atkinson's *A God in Ruins* (Doubleday) was a companion work to her previous novel, *Life After Life*. In *The Dust That Falls from Dreams* (Harvill Secker), Louis de Bernières explored the impact of the First World War on four sisters and the men they know and love.

Other notable novels included Sarah Hall's *The Wolf Border* (Faber), about an attempt to reintroduce wolves into the Lake District; Caryl Phillips' *The Lost Child* (Oneworld) in which a contemporary story counterpointed the author's re-working of material from *Wuthering Heights;* and Irvine Welsh's *A Decent Ride* (Cape), a darkly funny tale of alcoholic, sexual and pharmaceutical excess set in an Edinburgh that the tourists don't see. Amitav Ghosh brought his 'Ibis' trilogy, set in 19th-century India and China, to a successful conclusion with *Flood of Fire* (John Murray). Michel Faber made skilful use of themes and ideas from science fiction in *The Book of Strange New Things* (Canongate), a story set in the future about a Christian missionary who is sent to work with an alien culture. David Mitchell's *The Bone Clocks* (Sceptre) also possessed elements of science fiction but, like much of Mitchell's fiction, ultimately defied categorisation. One of the most ambitious debut novels of the year was *Death and Mr Pickwick* (Cape), in which Stephen Jarvis took the story of the genesis of *The Pickwick Papers* and turned it into a sprawling study of genius and plagiarism.

Across the other side of the Atlantic, three acclaimed women writers attracted attention with new work. In *Lila* (Virago), Marilynne Robinson revisited the characters from her earlier novels *Home* and *Gilead,* telling the story of an elderly preacher's much younger wife in the poetic prose for which she is renowned. Anne Tyler published her 20th novel in a 50-year career: *A Spool of Blue Thread* (Chatto) was another of her deceptively simple but highly revealing chronicles of domestic life. Two volumes of Jane Smiley's planned 'Last Hundred Years' trilogy both appeared in the period under review. *Some Luck* (Mantle) and *Early Warning* (Mantle) shone the spotlight on several generations of an Iowa family. Anthony Doerr's *All the Light We Cannot See* (Fourth Estate), a powerful story set in occupied France, was the winner of the 2015 Pulitzer prize for fiction.

The 2014 Nobel prize in literature was won by the French novelist Patrick Modiano. Following his success, the British publisher Bloomsbury began to bring out paperback editions of his novels, including *The Night Watch* and *Ring Roads.* Two new novels by Nobel laureates were published in 2015: Mario Vargas Llosa's *The Discreet Hero* (Faber) told the intertwining stories of two middle-aged men in the author's native Peru; Toni Morrison's *God Help the Child* (Chatto) follows its central character as she is forced to question her identity as a black woman.

Milan Kundera has often been suggested as a possible candidate for the Nobel award. *The Festival of Insignificance* (Faber) was the Czech writer's first novel to be published in English translation in a dozen years. Karl Ove Knausgaard's *Dancing in the Dark* (Harvill Secker) was the fourth volume of his much-acclaimed, ongoing autobiographical novel. *The Green Road* (Cape) by Anne Enright, Irish winner of the 2007 Man Booker prize, was the story of a scattered family coming together again when its matriarch decides to sell the house on the Atlantic coast where her children grew up. *Amnesia* (Faber) by Peter Carey set radicals and internet hackers against the political establishment.

In shorter fiction, the publication of Hilary Mantel's collection of stories, *The Assassination of Margaret Thatcher* (Fourth Estate) briefly reawakened the controversy that had attended the earlier newspaper publication of the title story. American author Edith Pearlman confirmed her status as one of the greatest living practitioners of the short story with the publication of *Honeydew* (John Murray). The Sunday Times EFG short story award, the richest prize in the world for a single short story, now in its sixth year, was won for the first time by a woman: Chinese-American writer Yiyun Li took it for her story 'A Sheltered Woman'.

And, finally, the bestselling work of fiction, by far, in the months preceding the return of Scout and Atticus Finch was E. L. James's *Grey* (Arrow). While this is a book that critics feel free to mock, readers buy in the hundreds of thousands. Some think that telling her story once (in *Fifty Shades of Grey* and its sequels) was more than enough but James revisited events from the perspective of the male character Christian Grey and found the same level of astonishing commercial success that she had before.

In crime fiction, the past seems to have become almost as popular a setting for tales of murder as the present. C. J. Sansom's *Lamentation* (Mantle) was the sixth to feature Tudor investigator Matthew Shardlake; M. J. Carter's *The Infidel Stain* (Fig Tree) was the second novel about her mismatched Victorian investigators Blake and Avery; and Philip Kerr's *The Lady from Zagreb* (Quercus) was the latest in his series about his Nazi-era detective Bernie Gunther. Many of the best crime writers, of course, concentrate on a series character and the period under review saw new cases for Mark Billingham's London police officer Tom Thorne in *Time of Death* (Little, Brown), for Peter James's Brighton-based Detective Superintendent Roy Grace in *You Are Dead* (Macmillan) and for Temperance Brennan, the forensic anthropologist created by the American novelist Kathy Reichs, in *Speaking in Bones* (Heinemann). Two well-known Italian police officers also made their latest appearances in 2015: Donna Leon's *Falling in Love* (Heinemann) was her 24th Commissario Brunetti novel and Andrea Camilleri's *Game of Mirrors* (Mantle) was another adventure for the Sicilian Inspector Montalbano.

*The House of Wolfe* (No Exit) by James Carlos Blake was the third in a sequence of novels set on the border of the USA and Mexico, the second of which (*The Rules of Wolfe*) was shortlisted for the 2015 CWA Goldsboro Gold Dagger for the year's best crime novel. Others on the shortlist for that prestigious prize included Attica Locke's *Pleasantville* (Serpent's Tail) and *The Shut Eye* (Bantam), by previous winner Belinda Bauer.

The year's bestselling crime novel was *The Girl on the Train* (Doubleday) by Paula Hawkins, soon to be made into a film. S. J. Watson's *Second Life* (Doubleday) was a psychological thriller by the author of the bestselling *Before I Go to Sleep;* Kate Hamer's *The Girl in the Red Coat* (Faber) was a much-admired debut novel; and Val McDermid's *The Skeleton Road* (Little, Brown) followed her new character, Detective Chief Inspector Karen Pirie, on an investigation which led her from an Edinburgh garret to a village in Croatia haunted by past violence. Sophie Hannah's *The Monogram Murders* (HarperCollins), the first new Hercule Poirot novel to receive the approval of Agatha Christie's literary estate, met with a mixed response from readers. Some welcomed the return of a much-loved character with delight; others questioned Hannah's interpretation of the Belgian sleuth.

In science fiction, the 2015 Arthur C. Clarke award was presented to the Canadian writer Emily St John Mandel for her hauntingly original novel *Station Eleven* (Picador), set before and after a lethal flu pandemic which kills 99 per cent of humanity. Other notable works of science fiction included William Gibson's *The Peripheral* (Penguin); Paolo Bacigalupi's *The Water Knife* (Orbit), set in a future where water is more precious than gold; *Seveneves* (The Borough Press) by Neal Stephenson; *The Long Utopia* (Doubleday) by Stephen Baxter and the late Terry Pratchett; and *Ancillary Sword* (Orbit), the second volume of Ann Leckie's sophisticated space opera, which won the British Science Fiction Association award for 2014. *The Annihilation Score* (Orbit) by Charles Stross was another volume of the 'Laundry Files' – records of the work of a secretive government agency fighting occult powers. Realism and surrealism rubbed shoulders in China Miéville's collection of shorter works, *Three Moments of an Explosion* (Macmillan), and Neil Gaiman's *Trigger Warning* (Headline), included both a tale in which the author revisited the world of his novel *American Gods* and a Doctor Who story. The latest Doctor Who book was written by A. L. Kennedy, winner of the Costa book of the year award in 2007. *Doctor Who: The Drosten's Curse* (BBC) was a witty tale which went a long way towards satisfying both hardened Whovians and admirers of Kennedy's stylish prose.

In fantasy fiction, Anthony Ryan's 'Raven's Shadow' trilogy came to a conclusion with *Queen of Fire* (Orbit); Joe Abercrombie's 'Shattered Sea' books reached a third volume with *Half a War* (Harper Voyager); and *The Liar's Key* (Harper Voyager) was the second book in Mark Lawrence's 'Red Queen's War' sequence. *Foxglove Summer* (Gollancz) was the latest in Ben Aaronovitch's series of novels set in an alternative London. Two masters of horror fiction, one English and one American, published new titles in 2015. Clive Barker's *The Scarlet Gospels* (Macmillan) was his first novel in four years; Stephen King's *Finders Keepers* (Hodder) was about a reader whose obsession with a reclusive cult writer goes a little too far.

NON-FICTION

The success of Helen Macdonald's *H is for Hawk* (Cape), which won both the 2014 Costa book of the year award and the 2014 Samuel Johnson prize for non-fiction, provided an indication of the increasing popularity of books on natural history. There has been a marked renaissance in such writing

recently. Michael McCarthy's *The Moth Snowstorm* (John Murray) was a lyrical exploration of the joy that human beings can experience in the natural world; Rob Cowen investigated the wildlife and history of just one square mile of land in *Common Ground* (Hutchinson); and Matthew Oates' *In Pursuit of Butterflies* (Bloomsbury) combined erudition and enthusiasm in an account of a 50-year obsession. Robert Macfarlane's *Landmarks* (Hamish Hamilton) was a fascinating study of the ways in which our sense of landscape is shaped by the words that we use to describe it.

Neurologist Oliver Sacks' memoir *On the Move* (Picador) provided an exhilarating reconstruction of his younger, biker self. Other successful autobiographical works included *Please, Mister Postman* (Bantam), the second volume of Labour politician Alan Johnson's recollections of life in the 1960s and 1970s; actor Alan Cumming's family memoir *Not My Father's Son* (Canongate); and ex-footballer Roy Keane's *The Second Half* (Weidenfeld), written in collaboration with the novelist Roddy Doyle.

2015 marked the 150th anniversary of the publication of *Alice's Adventures in Wonderland* and several books reflected this. Robert Douglas-Fairhurst's *The Story of Alice* (Harvill Secker) explored the cultural context within which Carroll's classic was created and Edward Wakeling's *Lewis Carroll: The Man and his Circle* (I. B. Tauris) was a new biography of the writer. Other notable biographies included Peter Ackroyd's *Alfred Hitchcock* (Chatto), a new interpretation of the great director, Richard Davenport-Hines' *Universal Man: The Seven Lives of John Maynard Keynes* (Collins); *Romantic Outlaws* (Hutchinson) by Charlotte Gordon, which examined the lives of Mary Wollstonecraft and her daughter Mary Shelley; and Jean Moorcroft Wilson's *Edward Thomas: From Adlestrop to Arras* (Bloomsbury), a new life of the First World War poet. Ruth Scurr's *John Aubrey: My Own Life* (Chatto) and Hugh Aldersey-Williams' *The Adventures of Sir Thomas Browne in the 21st Century* (Granta) were imaginative introductions to the lives and works of two eccentric 17th-century masters of English prose.

As the title indicated, no history book published in the year could have been more wildly ambitious than Yuval Noah Harari's *Sapiens: A Brief History of Humankind* (Vintage), an attempt to encompass the history of our species from prehistory to the present day that won its Israeli author a worldwide audience. New works by well-known historians included Noel Malcolm's *Agents of Empire* (Allen Lane), a panoramic portrait of the relationships between the west and the Ottoman Empire in the 16th century; Antony Beevor's *Ardennes 1944: Hitler's Last Gamble* (Viking), about the Battle of the Bulge; John Julius Norwich's *Sicily: A Short History from the Ancient Greeks to Cosa Nostra* (John Murray); David Starkey's *Magna Carta* (Hodder), published to mark the 800th anniversary of the signing of the Great Charter at Runnymede; and Helen Castor's *Joan of Arc* (Faber).

POETRY

In June 2015, Simon Armitage took up his new role as Oxford Professor of Poetry with a promise to 'address the obstacles and opportunities brought about by changes in education, changes in reading habits, the internet . . . and the (alleged) long, lingering decline of the book'. It was a laudably ambitious statement of intent and those devoted to poetry as an art form will wish him well. The year under review saw plenty of interesting and original work, and it is only possible to highlight a very small percentage of it. The intriguingly titled *Bedouin of the London Evening* (Bloodaxe) was the collected poems of Rosemary Tonks, whose writing had won critical acclaim in the 1960s before she disappeared from public view for more than 40 years. Her death in 2014 and this volume heralded a renewal of interest in her work.

Clive James's *Sentenced to Life* (Picador) was a valedictory collection of verses, nearly all of them concerned with mortality. Seriously ill and facing death, James produced poetry of poignancy, dark humour and technical virtuosity. Sophie Hannah's *Marrying the Ugly Millionaire* (Carcanet) was a volume of new poems and others selected from previous collections and Simon Armitage himself published a new selection of his poems in *Paper Aeroplane* (Faber). Other collections included *Faithful and Virtuous Night* (Carcanet) by the veteran New York poet Louise Gluck; Christopher Reid's *The Curiosities* (Faber), 71 poems which all had titles beginning with the letter 'C'; *Kim Kardashian's Marriage* (Faber), a second volume by Sam Riviere, winner of the 2012 Forward prize for best first collection; and Sarah Howe's *Loop of Jade* (Chatto), which introduced a compelling new voice. *Breezeway* (Carcanet) was a further volume of teasing, sophisticated verse by the American poet John Ashbery; Paul Muldoon's *One Thousand Things Worth Knowing* (Faber) was the latest work by the admired Irish poet; and Sean O'Brien gathered together a rich variety of his recent poems in *The Beautiful Librarians* (Picador). The 2014 Forward prize for poetry for best collection was awarded to Kei Miller for his volume *The Cartographer Tries to Map a Way to Zion* (Carcanet), in a ceremony which also honoured one of its judges, the Welsh poet Dannie Abse, who died that year. Britain's other major poetry award, the T. S. Eliot prize, went in January 2015 to David Harsent for his haunting and powerful *Fire Songs* (Faber).

## CHILDREN'S

Bucking the current trend in other areas of publishing, the sales of children's books in 2014 increased by 11 per cent. In many ways, we are living through a 'golden age' of children's literature. Certainly, the diversity of titles available is such that it is impossible to do more than highlight a tiny handful of the novels for all ages of children which were published during the 12 months under review. *Five Children on the Western Front* (Faber) by Kate Saunders took the characters from the classic Edith Nesbit novel of the Edwardian era and imagined what might have happened to them in the Great War that destroyed the world in which they grew up. *A Song for Ella Grey* (Hodder) by David Almond was a re-telling of the myth of Orpheus set in contemporary Tyneside. St Trinian's met Agatha Christie in *Arsenic for Tea* (Corgi Childrens), Robin Stevens' second mystery in her ongoing 'Murder Most Unladylike' series about two schoolgirl detectives. *Opal Plumstead* (Doubleday Children's), the tale of a young girl in Edwardian England, was the 100th book by Jacqueline Wilson, one of the most popular of all contemporary children's writers. Other titles which were greeted with enthusiasm by readers and critics alike included *My Name's Not Friday* (David Fickling) by Jon Walter, a story set during the American Civil War; Frances Hardinge's atmospheric and dark fantasy *The Lie Tree* (Macmillan Children's); Michael Morpurgo's *Listen to the Moon* (HarperCollins Children's); *An Island of Our Own* (Scholastic) by Sally Nicholls, the story of three siblings on a treasure hunt for an inheritance from an eccentric great-aunt; and Marcus Sedgwick's ingenious and multi-stranded novel *The Ghosts of Heaven* (Orion Children's). In June 2015, Malorie Blackman relinquished the role of Children's Laureate, which she had performed so well for two years, and the title passed to the author and illustrator Chris Riddell.

## NEWS

There are now fewer bookshops in Britain than ever before. The number of independent bookshops in the country continued to decline and, by the beginning of 2015, it had dropped below 1,000. However, there were welcome signs that those that survive can thrive. During Independent Bookshop Week in June 2015, the predominant feeling was one of optimism and the programme of events, author signings, literary lunches and reading group sessions was a celebration of the benefits that an independent bookshop can bring to its local community.

News from the chain booksellers was mixed. Although sales dipped in 2014 for Waterstones, the country's largest bookseller, losses, which had been substantial in previous years, were reduced. The company remained bullish and had plans to open new stores. The academic chain Blackwell's returned to the black after nearly a decade in the red and announced plans early in 2015 to turn the company, like John Lewis, into a staff-owned business. Foyles, which welcomed a new chief executive in April 2015, announced a sales increase in 2014 of 2.2 per cent but the company had nonetheless slipped into the red during the financial year, largely due to the costs associated with the removal of its flagship London shop from one site to another in Charing Cross Road.

Amazon maintained its dominance in the book trade worldwide. There were continuing concerns about its tax arrangements in the UK and an EU commission announced that it was to examine the company's market position in ebooks where, it was suggested, Amazon unfairly restricted competition. To some people, including prominent writers, the online company remained a bugbear. In a blogpost, the science fiction novelist Ursula Le Guin stated unequivocally that 'every book purchase made from Amazon is a vote for a culture without content and without contentment'. To the majority of book buyers, the company remained a much-used, if not much-loved, resource.

It was Amazon, of course, which led the way in ebook sales, which now account for 30 per cent of total book sales, rising to 50 per cent of adult fiction. Since book sales in the UK were up by 4 per cent to £2.2bn in 2014, this is a sizeable turnover but there were definite signs that love of the printed book was reasserting itself. At the beginning of 2015, Douglas McCabe of Enders Analysis, the UK-based media research firm, was quoted as saying, 'The rapid growth of ebook sales has quite dramatically slowed and there is some evidence it has gone into reverse.'

Prophets of doom have been raising their voices in the book trade since, it sometimes seems, the days of Dickens; but it is not too difficult to detect silver linings around the clouds they delight in depicting. Publishing may be an increasingly competitive business but there is still room for small independent firms to make a mark. The longlist of the 2015 Bailey's women's prize for fiction, for example, included not one but two titles published by the tiny Legend Press. Other small publishers with interesting lists – such as Periscope Books, And Other Stories, Snowbooks, Bitter Lemon, Dedalus Books and Bluemoose Books – have succeeded in carving out niches for themselves in the literary world. This can only be good news for the overall health of the British book trade.

In the course of the year under review there were several literary discoveries to celebrate. In Spain in March 2015, historians working at the Convento de las Monjas Trinitarias Descalzas in Madrid announced that they had identified some remains in its crypt as those of Miguel de Cervantes, author of *Don Quixote* and one of the giants of world literature. It was known that Cervantes had been buried in the crypt when he died in 1616 but the exact location had been lost. A suitable final resting place can now be found for Spain's greatest writer. A rather different kind of find was made in the autumn of 2014 in the small French town of St Omer. A scholar named Rémy Cordonnier was rooting through the archives in the town's library when he came across a volume catalogued simply as a book of Shakespeare's plays. It turned out to be the rare and valuable First Folio edition, dating from 1623, and a welcome addition to the 230 copies of the work already known to exist. More recently, in July 2015, an antiquarian book dealer announced that the bound volumes of the Victorian magazine *All the Year Round* he had purchased the previous year had proved to contain a series of annotations in the hand of its long-time editor, Charles Dickens. Contributions to the magazine were all anonymous but Dickens, in what must have been his own set, had carefully noted who had written what. This meant that works, hitherto unidentified, could now be attributed to a large number of 19th-century writers, including such well-known names as Wilkie Collins, Lewis Carroll and Elizabeth Gaskell. One scholar went so far as to call the discovery the 'Rosetta Stone of Victorian literature'.

FAREWELLS
Not one but two queens of crime fiction were lost to us during the period under review. P. D. James, creator of the poet and policeman Adam Dalgliesh, died in November 2014 at the age of 94. Ruth Rendell, her younger contemporary, who also wrote under the name of Barbara Vine, followed her into literary history in May 2015. Books by both of them will continue to be enjoyed for many years to come. Another much-loved novelist, who wrote in a different genre, died in March 2015. Terry Pratchett, who had been diagnosed with early-onset Alzheimer's disease in 2007, had continued to produce his Discworld novels and other science fiction until shortly before his death. The world also lost a writer of international significance in Günter Grass, the Nobel prize-winning German author of *The Tin Drum* and *The Flounder*.

Others who died in these 12 months included Colleen McCullough, the Australian author of *The Thorn Birds* and the 'Masters of Rome' series; the South African novelist André Brink, author of *A Dry White Season* and *Rumours of Rain*, the American novelists Kent Haruf (*Plainsong*), Robert Stone (*Dog Soldiers*) and James Salter (*A Sport and a Pastime*); the Turkish novelist Yaşar Kemal (*Memed, My Hawk*); the American poet and musician Rod McKuen; the Scottish poet and translator Alastair Reid and the Welsh poet Dannie Abse; the poet and critic Jon Stallworthy; the children's authors Gene Kemp and Pauline Fisk; the literary editor Karl Miller and the literary critic John Bayley, author of memoirs of his wife, Iris Murdoch; the Swedish poet and winner of the 2011 Nobel prize in literature Tomas Tranströmer; the historian and biographer of Winston Churchill, Martin Gilbert; the centenarian literary critic M. H. Abrams, editor of the *The Norton Anthology of English Literature;* Martyn Goff and Ion Trewin, two men who were key figures in the success

of the Booker prize; the expert on children's literature Mary Cadogan; Candida Lycett Green, who wrote many books on the English countryside and edited a multi-volume edition of the letters of her father, John Betjeman; the fantasy novelist Graham Joyce; and the science fiction and fantasy writer Tanith Lee.

## AWARDS

MAN BOOKER PRIZE 2014
Richard Flanagan – *The Narrow Road to the Deep North*

SHORTLIST
Joshua Ferris – *To Rise Again at a Decent Hour*
Karen Joy Fowler – *We Are All Completely Beside Ourselves*
Howard Jacobson – *J*
Neel Mukherjee – *The Lives of Others*
Ali Smith – *How to Be Both*

COSTA BOOK AWARDS 2014
*Book of the Year Award*, Helen Macdonald – *H is for Hawk*
*Novel Award*, Ali Smith – *How to Be Both*
*First Novel Award*, Emma Healey – *Elizabeth is Missing*
*Children's Book Award*, Kate Saunders – *Five Children on the Western Front*
*Poetry Award*, Jonathan Edwards – *My Family and Other Superheroes*
*Biography Award*, Helen Macdonald – *H is for Hawk*

BAILEYS WOMEN'S PRIZE FOR FICTION 2015
Ali Smith – *How to Be Both*

SHORTLIST
Rachel Cusk – *Outline*
Laline Paull – *The Beest*
Kamila Shamsie – *A God in Every Stone*
Anne Tyler – *A Spool of Blue Thread*
Sarah Waters – *The Paying Guests*

CILIP CARNEGIE MEDAL IN CHILDREN'S LITERATURE 2015
Tanya Landman – *Buffalo Soldier*

SHORTLIST
Brian Conaghan – *When Mr Dog Bites*
Sarah Crossan – *Apple and Rain*
Sally Gardner – *Tinder*
Frances Hardinge – *Cuckoo Song*
Elizabeth Laird – *The Fastest Boy in the World*
Geraldine McCaughrean – *The Middle of Nowhere*
Patrick Ness – *More Than This*

# MEDIA

*Steve Clarke*

## TELEVISION

All media commentators know that the way we watch television is changing. The amount of traditional TV watching – so-called live, linear consumption – is being diluted by internet-driven platforms. Many people use catch-up services such as the BBC iPlayer and on-demand brands like YouTube and Netflix, now in more than one in ten UK homes. Young people were continuing to watch less TV on television sets than in the days before smartphones and tablet computers. Apparently the behaviour of older viewers was also undergoing change.

During the year under review, research firm Enders Analysis estimated that the amount of time British children spent watching conventional TV fell by 22 per cent between 2010 and 2014. This 'generation gap' appeared to be getting wider, according to media regulator Ofcom, which noted: 'While younger audiences have always watched less television than older audiences, our audience research suggests that the connected generation are watching increasingly less television, and that they may be taking these habits with them as they age.' Among 16–34-year-olds, live viewing fell 15 per cent between 2010 and 2014; for 35–54-year-olds, the figure was 10 per cent. 'The habits of the parents are changing too,' said Enders Analysis' Toby Syfret. Only for the over 55s did conventional TV set viewing remain steady, with a fall of just 1 per cent. Even so, as much as 88 per cent per cent of viewing in 2014–15 consisted of live broadcast TV.

### BAKE OFF COOKS UP A HUGE AUDIENCE

*The Great British Bake Off* was one of the year's most popular programmes in what was a strong 2014–15 for BBC One. The October final was watched by an average of 12.3 million viewers as outsider Nancy Birtwhistle out-baked hot favourite Richard Burr. The show had come a long way since it started on BBC Two in 2010 with a lowly 2 million viewers. 'Whoever would have thought a show about baking would be the highest-rating show of the year outside of the World Cup?' wondered BBC One controller Charlotte Moore.

While the power of TV soap operas to generate huge audiences was declining, season 12 of *Strictly Come Dancing* once again beat ITV's *The X Factor*. Ratings, however, were down on the previous year for the dance competition – an average audience of 10 million for the December final against 11.5 million a year earlier. *EastEnders'* 30th anniversary in February was watched by 3 million more viewers than usual, with 10.8 million tuning in for the special live episodes.

### WOLF HALL DEFIES THE CYNICS

BBC Two's extravagantly promoted *Wolf Hall* launched on 21 January 2015 and attracted 4 million viewers. It instantly became the channel's most popular drama for a decade and critics praised the six-part serial, which was adapted by screenwriter Peter Straughan from Dame Hilary Mantel's Booker-prize winning novels *Wolf Hall* and *Bring Up the Bodies*. Even cynics were won over by *Wolf Hall* and its all-star British cast. In America, *The New Yorker's* critic, Emily Nussbaum, expected the worst – another run-of-the-mill British costume piece. 'Instead, the show's deliberately paced

six hours turn out to be riveting, precisely because they are committed, without apology or, often, much explanation, to the esotericism of their subject matter,' she wrote. Mark Rylance was outstanding as the scheming Tudor courtier, Thomas Cromwell. The performances of Damian Lewis as Henry VIII and Claire Foy as his second wife, Anne Boleyn, were also praised. *Wolf Hall* was directed by Peter Kosminsky, whose usual forte was contemporary drama-documentary.

On BBC One, one of the year's most successful dramas was *Poldark*, a revival of the swashbuckling historical stories written by Winston Graham. Making much of gorgeous English landscapes, *Poldark* was set in 18th-century Cornwall; an original series of the television adaptation was first broadcast by the BBC in the mid-1970s. Critics were surprised by how skilfully the new adaption was executed. The eponymous hero was played with brooding, chest-bearing machismo by Aidan Turner. He quickly became a pin-up for female fans. Ross Poldark's stoical, low-born wife, the auburn-haired Demelza, performed by Eleanor Tomlinson, was a perfect foil for what *The Guardian's* Sam Wollaston reckoned was a 'pacier and racier' version than the original. A second season was quickly commissioned.

Many reviewers considered BBC One's *The Missing* to be the most absorbing whodunnit of 2014–15. It starred James Nesbitt as a devoted family man whose son goes missing in France; the eight-part thriller was widely regarded as hauntingly brilliant. Critics also praised screenwriter Paul Abbott's latest show, Channel 4's *No Offence*, set in a Manchester police station and starring Joanna Scanlan as the unorthodox DI Vivienne Deering.

The BBC Two drama *Marvellous*, based on the real-life story of Neil Baldwin, who was employed as the kit man for Stoke City FC, provided a showcase for another master-class in acting – Toby Jones, who played Baldwin, was outstanding. This unusual and empathetic film written by Peter Bowker deservedly won several awards. ITV, meanwhile, gave Sheridan Smith the opportunity to shine in a three-part biopic based on the early singing career of the late Liverpool showbiz legend. *Cilla*, written by Jeff Pope, 'was one of those extraordinary performances, like Julie Walters as Mo Mowlam, when an actress does more than play a real character; she becomes her, to the extent that it's hard for the viewer not to forget they're not actually watching a young Cilla Black,' opined *The Guardian*. It was the most popular new drama on any channel during 2014.

During the period under review, ITV struggled to compete with BBC One. The eagerly awaited second season of crime drama *Broadchurch* failed to live up to expectations. Arguably ITV's classiest drama was *The Lost Honour of Christopher Jefferies*, written by Peter Morgan and directed by Roger Michell. Jason Watkins' performance as the former Bristol schoolteacher who was wrongly accused of murdering one of his young female tenants was widely praised. The film showed how Jefferies fought back against Fleet Street to restore his reputation after the press sought to destroy his character.

HBO's cult fantasy series *Game of Thrones* finally went seriously mainstream in the UK. Season five's opening episode achieved record ratings for Sky Atlantic: more than 1.5 million saw the show, reportedly 43 times the usual Sky Atlantic peak-time audience. A Channel 4 series, *Humans,* in which robots lived side-by-side with ordinary families, gave the network its biggest audience for a drama in two decades (some 4 million viewers).

## CLARKSON DRIVEN AWAY FROM *TOP GEAR*
In March 2015, the BBC was caught up in a real-life drama of its own when *Top Gear* presenter Jeremy Clarkson was suspended for punching one of the motor show's producers at a Yorkshire hotel. According to eyewitnesses, Clarkson verbally abused producer Oisin Tymon for 40 minutes because there was no hot food available, before striking him in the face. Despite an online petition calling for his reinstatement signed by more than a million people, the BBC said that his contract would not be renewed. In June, former *The Big Breakfast* presenter Chris Evans was announced as Clarkson's replacement in a revamped *Top Gear* likely to feature a female co-presenter. Clarkson and his erstwhile colleagues, fellow presenters Richard Hammond and James May alongside executive producer Andy Wilman, were expected to sign a deal with either ITV or Netflix for a new motoring show.

Front-of-screen talent is often crucial to a show's success. The return of Simon Cowell to *The X Factor* jury in the autumn, however, failed to provide a sustained improvement in the ITV show's ratings. The final in December 2014 slumped to its lowest audience for a decade: an average of 9.1 million viewers, a 35 per cent per cent share of the audience, watched Ben Haenow win the show. The final of *Britain's Got Talent* proved more satisfying for ITV: on 1 June, the programme drew an average of 11.7 million viewers, at the time the only show on British television to top 11 million viewers in 2015.

## ELECTION – NO RE-RUN OF 2010-STYLE DEBATES
For audiences addicted to news and current affairs, the spring general election campaign failed to live up to the excitement generated by the televised live leaders' debates in 2010. Prime Minister David Cameron and his advisers were determined to avoid a repeat of the previous election's TV coverage. They believed that the strong showing of Liberal Democrat leader Nick Clegg in the 2010 debates had contributed to the Conservatives' failure to win an outright victory.

Cameron declined broadcasters' invitations to participate in a live TV head-to-head encounter with Clegg and Labour's Ed Miliband. Following lengthy negotiations with the TV networks, the prime minister was interviewed live by Jeremy Paxman in a programme shown simultaneously by Channel 4 and Sky News. Miliband was grilled separately by the ex-*Newsnight* interrogator on the same show. Both politicians faced questions from a studio audience chaired by Sky News' Kay Burley. Commentators agreed that Paxman's tough style of interviewing was one of the few moments during the lengthy election campaign when Cameron was caught off-guard on camera. Challenged on the growth of food banks during the five years of his coalition government and so-called zero-hours employment contracts, the prime minister was unable to give convincing answers.

Critics welcomed the veteran TV interviewer back. 'Journalistic rottweiler Jeremy Paxman returned to our screens after a nine-month hiatus since leaving *Newsnight* determined to prove he is still top dog when it comes to taking politicians to task,' reported the *Daily Mail*. On ITV, a two-hour live leaders' debate, chaired by Julie Etchingham, was the only programme of the campaign featuring all the main party leaders speaking together in the same studio. The verdict was that the Scottish National Party leader Nicola Sturgeon was the clear winner. Sturgeon and the two other female leaders, the Green Party's Natalie Bennett and Plaid

Cymru's Leanne Wood, seemed more in touch with public concerns than the men.

Another TV highlight of what most pundits thought was a highly stage-managed campaign was a special edition of BBC One's *Question Time*. Commentators agreed that the studio audience in Leeds were far better at putting Cameron, Miliband and Clegg on the spot than most TV professionals. And for once the political parties' spin doctors were not manipulating the agenda. Few politicians will ever forget 10pm on 7 May when the broadcasters' exit poll was announced. This predicted a small Conservative majority (in defiance of weeks of opinion polls forecasting political stalemate and a hung parliament). The moment was unquestionably the single most dramatic act of the 2015 general election.

## NEW LICENCE FEE DEAL FORCED ON BBC
Within days of the election, many opinion formers were convinced that the new Conservative government spelled trouble for the BBC. This view was strengthened by the appointment of the right-leaning John Whittingdale as the new Secretary of State for Culture, Media and Sport. In the past he had famously described the BBC licence fee as 'worse than the poll tax'. With right-of-centre newspapers like the *Daily Mail*, *The Sun* and *The Times* all campaigning to reduce the size of the BBC, press owners like Rupert Murdoch hoped that the Conservatives would seize the review of the BBC's Royal Charter as an opportunity to shrink the Corporation.

In July it emerged that in a rushed, behind-closed-doors series of talks – there was no public consultation – the BBC was forced to agree a new five-year licence fee deal. Tony Hall, the BBC director-general, speaking on Radio 4's *Today* show, claimed a victory for licence fee payers. Others, including former director-general John Birt, criticised the arrangement and the process leading up to it. Lord Patten, the former BBC Trust chairman, described the deal as 'quick and dirty'.

At the heart of the new agreement is the obligation for the BBC to finance free licence fees for over-75s. Previously, this expense came from Treasury coffers. The annual cost was reckoned to be at least £650m. In return, increases to the licence fee – frozen since 2010 – would be linked to inflation. Additionally, the BBC no longer had to pay for rolling out broadband in UK rural areas and a loophole allowing people to watch BBC catch-up services without having to pay the licence fee was closed.

A BBC green paper was published later in July. Whittingdale told parliament that the scale and scope of the BBC had grown exponentially in the last decade and asked 'whether this particular range of services best serves licence fee payers'. The BBC criticised the green paper and said it could 'herald a much diminished, less popular BBC', which 'would be bad for Britain'. Lord Fowler, the Conservative peer, said that the BBC faced 'an unprecedented threat' from the government. A number of celebrities rallied to the BBC's defence, including Sir David Attenborough and the newly knighted Sir Lenny Henry.

# RADIO

BBC Radio, dominant for so long, faced fresh threats during 2014–15. The aforementioned green paper said that Radio 1 and Radio 2 were 'arguably less distinctive' than BBC Radio 6 Music. The document claimed that there was a 'sizeable crossover in audiences' between Radio 1 and Radio 2. The head of BBC Radio, Helen Boaden, denied this. In a blog she said that less than 10 per cent of the tracks played on Radio 1 could be heard on its closest commercial equivalent,

Capital. Similarly, around 60 per cent of songs played on Radio 2 were not heard on any comparable commercial station.

For Radio 1, there were other problems too. In June, Radio 1 controller Ben Cooper admitted that the station had a 'real challenge on its hands' due to online competition from music-streaming services like Spotify and the newly launched Apple Music. RAJAR figures published in February showed the scale of his difficulty. Radio 1's audience was at a 12-year low. Breakfast DJ Nick Grimshaw had mislaid some 1.24 million listeners, or 18 per cent of the audience inherited from Chris Moyles in 2012. His weekly audience was down from 6.7 million listeners to 5.5 million in the first three months of 2015. Part of the problem was that Grimshaw was not attracting enough listeners under-30, Radio 1's target audience.

## FEAR GRIPS RADIO 1

Cooper had previously predicted that 'traditional radio for young people is dead in about a generation'. Clearly Radio 1 was trying hard to adapt to the online world. In November the station launched its own video site, accessed via the BBC iPlayer. The Radio 1 controller explained: 'What you'll find on iPlayer will focus on Radio 1 live events, our family of brilliant presenters and, of course, the lives of our young audience. Underpinning much of this is our dedication to discovering the best new music.'

Speaking in March, however, Cooper suggested that there was still a huge amount of work to do. 'The BBC needs to stop thinking about TV channels and radio stations and think about content for certain demographics. If we don't adapt, we will die,' he said. 'As a person running a traditional radio station, you should be afraid, you should be very afraid.'

Change was the order of the day at the other end of the radio market, too. Following a six-month search, in September 2014 the appointment of Alan Davey as new controller of Radio 3 was announced. He promised that the station would not be 'dumbing down' and pledged to play 'serious, interesting, life-changing and complex music'. Some commentators, however, thought it was too late. Interviewed by the *Financial Times* shortly after the announcement that Davey had got the job, Sarah Spilsbury of lobby group Friends of Radio 3 said that the station had become 'more like local radio', with listeners phoning to request particular songs. 'People are moving over to buying internet radios [and saying] there are classical stations all over Europe that I'd rather listen to,' she claimed.

## RADIO 2 – MORE FEMALE PRESENTERS NEEDED

Britain's most popular station, Radio 2, was criticised for the lack of female presenters in its daytime weekday line-up. Responding on Radio 4's *Feedback* in November, station controller Bob Shennan said: 'What you have got to understand about these daytime programmes is they are massively popular. Chris Evans has an audience nearly the size of Radio 1, Ken Bruce has an audience over 8 million, Jeremy Vine's show is the biggest current affairs show on BBC radio, Simon Mayo has the biggest-ever drivetime audience.' Shennan added that many new female presenters had been hired by Radio 2, including Vanessa Feltz, Jo Whiley, Sara Cox and Anneka Rice. Radio 2's most popular presenter, Chris Evans, insisted that he had no intention of giving up his breakfast show when his new role fronting *Top Gear* began.

In the period under review, Radio 4's listening figures were broadly static. There was praise for Dr Atul Gawande's *Reith Lectures* examining the future of medicine, Neil MacGregor's take on 600 years of German history and a

marathon ten-hour broadcast of Tolstoy's *War and Peace* on New Year's Day.

In the summer it was announced that Jim Naughtie was quitting as one of the *Today* presenters. His instantly recognisable Caledonian tones had been part of the early morning news and current affairs show for 21 years. Writing in *The Guardian*, John Plunkett mourned his departure. 'His critics might have it that his famously verbose line of questioning – one inquiry to Condoleezza Rice hit 183 words before reaching the final question mark – might put you to sleep,' suggested Plunkett, but his exit would make *Today* a duller programme. Naughtie's replacement was the BBC's political editor, Nick Robinson, keen to do the job despite undergoing treatment for lung cancer.

## PROTECT THE LICENCE FEE

As speculation intensified over the future of the licence fee following the unexpected election of a majority Conservative government, *The Daily Telegraph*'s radio critic, Gillian Reynolds, reminded readers what was at stake for radio fans. 'Should the BBC be funded by subscription rather than the licence fee? Yes, if you want to murder BBC radio. Goodbye to *In Our Time,* farewell *Friday Night Is Music Night* and the Proms, adieu to the best film programme anywhere, *Kermode and Mayo's Film Review* on 5 Live. Make your own list.'

In the commercial sector, digital stations were growing their audiences. With almost 40 per cent of radio listening now via digital, there were record listening figures for digital-only commercial stations including Absolute 80s and Planet Rock, according to RAJAR figures. Absolute 80s achieved an average of 1.45 million listeners a week and 1.25 million tuned in to Planet Rock in the first three months of 2015.

In London during 2014–15, digital listening had overtaken analogue, with a 46.8 per cent share ahead of FM and AM's 46.2 per cent. Outside the capital, analogue remained dominant, with 54.3 per cent of all listening, down from 57.8 per cent in 2014. Switchover to all-digital broadcasts was still some way off and not expected until 2020 at the earliest. Nevertheless Ford Ennals, the CEO of Digital Radio UK, was upbeat: 'The surge of digital listening to almost 40 per cent share is a landmark moment for digital radio, and shows the achievability of the 50 per cent listening criterion set by government for a radio switchover.'

## DIGITAL'S SECOND WAVE

In March 2015, Ofcom announced that the long-awaited second national commercial digital radio platform would be Sound Digital, which had beat rival consortium Listen2Digital. The move paved the way for a new wave of digital radio stations, expected on air in spring 2016. Virgin Radio, rebranded as Absolute Radio in 2008, would return. Three spin-off talkSPORT stations – talkRADIO, talkSPORT 2 and talkBUSINESS, backed by Bloomberg – were planned. In all, Sound Digital would launch 14 radio stations, some of which were already broadcasting on the existing DAB (Digital Audio Broadcasting) platform.

# THE PRESS

The year's biggest domestic story for the press was the general election. While newspaper circulations continued to fall, their influence in informing and influencing their readers' voting decisions was an area of much debate. With the exception of the *Daily Mirror* and *The Guardian,* much of the British daily press came out firmly in support of David Cameron's Conservative Party. The *Daily Express* supported UKIP; owner Richard Desmond made a donation of £1m to Nigel Farage's party. This infuriated the National

Union of Journalists, which pointed out that those working at the *Daily Express* had not received a pay rise since 2008. *The Daily Telegraph,* always stout allies of the Tories during an election campaign, took the unusual step of emailing readers and urging them to vote Conservative.

## PRESS ATTACKS 'RED ED' IN ELECTION
Whether newspapers' leader columns and their overall coverage of politics makes any real difference to the outcome of an election is questionable. Some commentators, however, thought the vilification of Labour leader Ed Miliband in *The Sun* and *Daily Mail* was even more pronounced than their attempt to destroy the credibility of Neil Kinnock in the 1992 election. It was not only Miliband that much of Fleet Street had it in for. London School of Economics media blogger Professor Charlie Beckett observed: 'The right-wing newspapers who were panicked by an apparently close race redoubled their efforts to drive home the horrors of Ed, Nicola and Nigel.'

Influential or otherwise at affecting public opinion, as Peter Preston pointed out in *The Observer,* the fall in newspaper circulations since the last general election was dramatic. In March 2010, national dailies sold 10.9 million copies. In March 2015, they averaged 7.6 million. Sales of *The Sun* were down from 3 million to 1.9 million, the *Daily Mail* from 2.1 million to 1.6 million, *The Daily Telegraph* from 678,000 to 480,000. Circulation at *The Guardian* fell from 283,000 to 175,000, *The Independent* from 184,000 to 59,000 and *The Times* from 502,000 to 391,000. 'The job of the professional journalist is as dead as the elevator operator,' opined American TV producer Michael Rosenblum, speaking at a conference on mobile journalism in the spring.

## WE'RE ALL JOURNALISTS NOW
Rosenblum's argument that anyone with a mobile phone could be a reporter sounded convincing but, despite declining sales, not all forecasters were pessimistic regarding the outlook for newspapers. The experienced media analyst Lorna Tilbian, writing in the spring, suggested that newspapers 'will not only survive, but prosper'. In an article for the News Media Association website, she observed: 'There is real cause for optimism at several national newspapers which have hit an inflection point whereby the decline in physical advertising is being more than offset by growth in digital advertising. Regional newspaper publishers too are showing clear signs of stabilisation as overall rates of revenue decline have decelerated and revenues from digital activities have risen rapidly.'

## ALL CHANGE AT THE GUARDIAN
In 2014–15, *The Guardian's* long-standing editor, Alan Rusbridger, stood down following 20 years at the helm. Reflecting on the changes that his leadership had witnessed, he said: 'Two-thirds of our readership is now outside of the UK: we publish continuously. Virtually all our readers can themselves now be publishers and can connect with one another, and anyone else, as well as us. They contribute to *The Guardian* in ways that were unimaginable even 15 years ago.' Rusbridger's successor was a veteran at the paper, Katharine Viner.

The Guardian's broadsheet competitor, *The Daily Telegraph,* was the subject of headlines itself when in February Peter Oborne, the paper's chief political commentator, resigned. He claimed that the interests of advertisers were taking precedence over editorial values. Oborne cited the lack of coverage of problems at HSBC bank. Commentator Roy Greenslade suggested that the owners of the *Telegraph,* the Barclay family, were at fault: 'Newspaper proprietorship gives unaccountable rights to

owners. For once, the Barclays are being held to account. Oborne, the maverick, has shone a light on a dark reality.'

Largely on the basis of his columns in *The Guardian* and *London Evening Standard,* Greenslade is regarded as one of Britain's most incisive media pundits. In March, four *Sun* journalists were acquitted on a charge of paying public officials for information. Writing in *The Guardian,* Greenslade remarked: 'We will look back on this in a decade and wonder that it ever happened. Phone hacking was one thing – a crime. Paying for stories is another – not, in my view and that of the Old Bailey jurors, a crime.'

## TRINITY MIRROR FINED FOR PHONE HACKING
Hacking, however, had not gone away. In the year under review it emerged that illegally listening to celebrities' voice messages on their mobiles was endemic at the *Daily Mirror* and *Sunday Mirror* and at *The Sunday People* from 1999 until 2009. The papers' publisher, Trinity Mirror, was ordered to pay compensation to numerous victims. The scale of the payments, ordered by Mr Justice Mann, was regarded as high compared with the amounts paid to those whose phones were hacked by papers owned by Rupert Murdoch. Eight victims, including Sadie Frost, Paul Gascoigne and Shane Richie, received a total of £1.2m.

## JE SUIS CHARLIE
By far the most tragic and shocking of events affecting press during the year under review was the terrorist attack by Islamic extremists on the Paris offices of the French satirical magazine *Charlie Hebdo.* A total of 12 people were killed. Among the dead were the cartoonist Charb (Stéphane Charbonnier), who was also editor-in-chief, and four other cartoonists working for the magazine. France's President Hollande described the massacre as 'an act of indescribable barbarity'. The impact of the killings on journalists around the world is hard to overstate. An estimated two million people gathered in Paris for a rally of national unity attended by more than 40 world leaders, including David Cameron. The next issue of *Charlie Hebdo* was published in six languages and sold 7.75 million copies; the typical print run was 60,000.

# THE INTERNET

It became clear in the year under review that the smartphone had become totally ubiquitous. Accountancy firm Deloitte said that by May, 76 per cent of UK adults used a smartphone. Meanwhile British adults were spending more than 20 hours online per week, according to Ofcom's annual survey of media usage. This was twice as much as ten years earlier.

2014 saw the biggest increase in time spent online in a decade, said the regulator. Inevitably young people aged 16–24 were the internet's biggest users; Ofcom said that they spent an average of 27 hours and 36 minutes a week online. 'Instant messaging has become a popular way of keeping in touch, driven by services including WhatsApp, Facebook Messenger and BBM,' observed the media watchdog.

## SOCIAL MEDIA'S UPWARD CURVE
The use of social media continued to surge. Ofcom said that 72 per cent of internet users aged 16 or over possessed a social media profile. Some 81 per cent of these users log into social media websites or apps – including Facebook, Twitter, LinkedIn, Instagram or Tumblr – at least once a day, up from 30 per cent in 2007. Social media had seen the biggest growth among 35–44-year-olds; 80 per cent of internet users in this age group were on social media, Ofcom recorded. It was not, however, all plain sailing for the technology giants in 2014–15.

In September the long-heralded Apple Watch was finally unveiled. Commentators, however, were sceptical that the device, retailing at a starting price of £230, would have the same impact as the iPhone or the iPad. 'Apart from some of the fitness monitoring capabilities, it is difficult to think of many things that are done better on a watch face than on a smartphone screen,' noted the BBC's technology correspondent, Rory Cellan-Jones. He added: 'I am convinced that Apple will be the giant of the smartwatch sector within a couple of months. What I'm less clear about is whether clever watches are anything more than a niche product for gadget fans and fitness addicts – unlike smartphones which are becoming essential for everyone.'

## TAYLOR SWIFT CHEWS UP APPLE
The June launch of Apple's new streaming service, Apple Music, a direct rival to Spotify, represented a major upheaval for Apple's digital music business. Until now Apple had focused on selling music downloads via the company's iTunes Store. iTunes remained open but Apple's plan was to encourage music fans to pay a monthly subscription to access its entire catalogue of music, rather than buy songs individually. The move also suggested that the boundaries between the internet and radio were becoming still more porous. Apple Music featured 'radio' station, Beats 1, offering 24-hour live music – albeit over the internet rather than the airwaves – from studios in Los Angeles, New York and London. DJs Zane Lowe – poached from BBC Radio 1 earlier in the year – Julie Adenuga and Ebro Darden were featured alongside guest DJs such as fellow Apple employee Dr Dre, along with Elton John, Disclosure, St Vincent, Pharrell Williams and Drake.

Some members of the music community were unimpressed by Apple's plan to avoid paying royalties to labels and music publishers during a three-month free trial for Apple Music. In a high-profile controversy, the multi-million selling singer Taylor Swift threatened to hold back her latest album, 1989, from Apple in protest at the technology giant's 'shocking and disappointing' decision not to pay for songs streamed during the trial. To the surprise of many commentators, Apple backed down. In three tweets Eddy Cue, senior vice president for internet software and services, wrote: 'Apple will always make sure that artists are paid. Apple Music will pay artists for streaming, even during [a] customer's free trial period. We hear you taylorswift13 and indie artists. Love, Apple.'

## UBER DRIVES WEB TRAFFIC
Another technology company to infuriate people during the year under review was Uber. Strictly speaking, Uber was not an internet company at all. The fast-expanding San Francisco-based firm created an app enabling people to arrange taxis on their mobiles and pay less for the service than through established companies. Traditional cab drivers claimed that Uber was driving them out of business, while technology experts said that Uber occupied a strange place in the tech industry. Journalist Bobbie Johnson commented: 'Among a legion of highly detested companies, in a highly detested business, it is the thing people hate the most. And the reactions against it are powerful, instinctive and often hard to articulate.' In London, mayor Boris Johnson was verbally abused by black cab drivers who wanted him to revoke Uber's licence. But the mayor claimed he was powerless to halt the operator's onward march. 'It would make no difference whatever. They'd go to a magistrate and be back on the roads tomorrow,' he said. 'Everywhere I go I see yellow lights on. I can see the business is dying and that grieves me. But it is very difficult to fight a huge change in consumer preference.'

## SOCIAL MEDIA FAILS TO 'WIN' ELECTION
Despite the apparent popularity of youth-friendly news websites like Vice and Buzzfeed, May's general election failed to live up to the hype as 'Britain's first social media election'. While there was little doubt that social media-led campaigns had helped the Scottish Nationalists in September's independence referendum, the general election was a very different story. Newspaper and TV dominated the news agenda – with one notable exception, the Labour leader Ed Miliband's interview with comedian and equality campaigner Russell Brand. The move attracted extensive traffic to Brand's YouTube channel, The Trews, reckoned to have 1.1. million subscribers.

## GIRL ONLINE GOES MAINSTREAM
Brand had started his career on TV and radio but in 2014–15 more YouTube stars were entering the mainstream. One of the most well-known was fashion vlogger Zoe 'Zoella' Sugg, who was reportedly earning £20,000 a month from YouTube advertising. Such was her popularity with adolescent girls that her debut novel, Girl Online, sold 78,000 copies in its first week of publication.

Sugg's successes disguised the fact that even some of the most successful online giants were struggling with their business models. In April, Twitter's shares fell nearly 20 per cent in an hour after its first quarter results were leaked by an unknown financial analytics company. The firm used the microblogging site to announce that Twitter's losses were 23 per cent greater than in the same period last year. It was Twitter's weakest quarterly revenue growth since it made its stock market debut in November 2013.

# CLASSICAL MUSIC AND OPERA

*Leonora Dawson-Bowling*

## ANNIVERSARIES

The start of the 2014–15 season witnessed the continued celebration of the 300th anniversary of C. P. E. Bach's birth; the 250th anniversary of Rameau's death (Les Arts Florissants performed two fully choreographed and staged court ballets by Rameau – *Daphnis et Églé* and *La Naissance d'Osiris*); the 150th anniversary of Richard Strauss' birth (his *Four Last Songs* among other works were ubiquitous, featuring in the BBC Proms as well as the BBC National Orchestra of Wales and Bournemouth Symphony Orchestra's 2014–15 season); and the 100th anniversary of Sir Andrzej Panufnik (most notably Kings Place's Panufnik centenary celebration, which examined the resonances between his music and that of his daughter, Roxanna Panufnik).

The centenary of the start of the First World War also continued to be marked. In particular, the Bournemouth Symphony Orchestra and Chorus performed Elgar's *For the Fallen* and Finzi's *Intimations of Immortality,* as well as pieces by George Butterworth and Cecil Coles (who both died in the trenches), while the London Symphony Orchestra (LSO) commemorated the anniversary with a new work, *Equal Voices,* by Sally Beamish, setting poetry by Andrew Motion. The City of Birmingham Symphony Orchestra, in the lead-up to its centenary in 2020, continued its programme exploring the decade a century earlier, year by year. It therefore also focused on the Great War, presenting poignant works that Elgar wrote during the period, the stunning *Three Pieces* by Alban Berg, and the overwhelmingly beautiful music that Manuel de Falla created amidst the turmoil.

The 150th anniversaries of two big Scandinavian composers, Carl Nielsen and Jean Sibelius, were celebrated in 2015. Nielsen's symphonies were performed in full by the BBC Symphony Orchestra and by the BBC Philharmonic (later to be recorded by Chandos). The Philharmonia meanwhile embarked on a two-year Nielsen symphony cycle. The Royal Scottish National Orchestra also performed his *Symphony No. 4* ('The Inextinguishable') as well as his *Violin Concerto* with James Ehnes while his *Clarinet Concerto* was performed both by Sabine Meyer and the Royal Philharmonic Orchestra and by Julian Bliss and the Royal Northern Sinfonia. The Philharmonia also presented the 'Ashkenazy Sibelius series' exploring a range of Sibelius' works including lesser-known, smaller vignettes while Sir Simon Rattle and the Berlin Philharmonic performed complete cycle of Sibelius symphonies and his *Concerto for Violin and Orchestra* (with Leonidas Kavakos) during a week-long residency at the Barbican and Southbank Centre. The 2014–15 season also celebrated two composer birthdays with explorations of their musical output. Sir Harrison Birtwistle's 80th was especially honoured in a three-day festival by the London Sinfonietta, which had commissioned 20 of his works over the years, and Pierre Boulez's 90th birthday acknowledgements included the BBC Symphony Orchestra's 'Total Immersion: Pierre Boulez at 90' (a day of concerts, talk and film), a BBC Scottish Symphony Orchestra birthday concert and a three-day retrospective at the Aldeburgh Festival.

The 2014–15 season also saw a 90th anniversary celebrated by the BBC Singers, while the Royal Liverpool Philharmonic Orchestra celebrated its 175th.

## OTHER HIGHLIGHTS

Nationalities were a strong theme in the 2014–15 season. In the 'UK-Russia year of culture', Russian music was to be found in abundance. The LSO and its Russian principal conductor Valery Gergiev used the theme 'Heartland of Russia' to explore works of varying prominence by Tishchenko, Prokofiev, Shostakovich, Tchaikovsky, Balakirev, Rachmaninov and Glazunov. The Philharmonia under the direction of Jakub Hrůša featured music by Tchaikovsky and the 'Mighty Five' group of composers: Mussorgsky, Balakirev, Borodin, Cui and Rimsky-Korsakov. The Philharmonia and pianist Daniil Trifonov also embarked on a two-year project performing all of Rachmaninov's major piano and orchestra works and the London Philharmonic Orchestra (LPO) staged a year-long 'Inside Out' festival exploring his major orchestral masterpieces alongside less familiar works such as a selection of song arrangements, the *Spring Cantata* and a semi-staged production of *The Miserly Knight.* The Hallé performed all six of Shostakovich's concertos while the BBC Scottish Symphony Orchestra presented three of his landmark symphonies *(Symphonies Nos. 5, 10 and 15).* Shostakovich's fifth symphony was also a highlight of the Bournemouth Symphony Orchestra's season alongside the last of their Prokofiev symphony cycle.

Austrian themes were also explored by the Britten Sinfonia, which presented passionate 'Songs of Vienna' and themes of loss and longing through the music of Richard Strauss, Schoenberg, Berg and Mahler, while Kings Place's 'Vienna Revisited' weekend similarly focused on Schoenberg and his Viennese contemporaries. At Wigmore Hall, the Florian Boesch Residency also explored works by composers raised in the old Austro-Hungarian Empire (Mahler and Schoenberg among others) while the Hall's associate artists, the Takács Quartet, went back further, performing masterworks from the Viennese Classical tradition (including Beethoven, Schubert and Mozart).

Mozart, Schubert and Mahler also formed individual composer focuses for a number of orchestras and venues. Wigmore Hall commenced a two-year 'Mozart Odyssey', training the spotlight on the composer's chamber music and also presented performances of Schubert's *Winterreise* (Simon Keenlyside and Emanuel Ax), two late Schubert piano sonatas (András Schiff) and the ongoing Bostridge-Drake Schubert *Lieder* series. At the Southbank, the 'Barenboim Project 2015' featured a cycle of Schubert piano sonatas. And the BBC National Orchestra of Wales continued its Mahler symphony series while the BBC Philharmonic performed his works as complementary counterparts within its Nielsen symphony cycle.

Wigmore Hall also travelled through Czech musical soundscapes with the Pavel Haas Quartet's 'Bohemia' series while Kings Place especially focused on the music of Dvořák in its short 'Dvořák Explored' series. In addition, Kings Place's 'Swept Away' series looked at the 1920–30s Berlin music scene where jazz, popular music and serialism met, and many of the works were then banned or burnt by the Third Reich and the composers exiled. The Philharmonia meanwhile turned to another European capital in its 'City of Light: Paris 1900–1950' series, using music from Debussy to Messiaen to explore the cultural and socio-political context that drew the leading artists to Paris from across Europe, from La Belle Époque and Les Années Folles to the aftermath of the Second World War.

The notion of emigrating composers was also explored by the City of London Sinfonia 'Émigré' series, and the

Orchestra of the Age of Enlightenment's 'Flying the Flag' series delved into national styles, lost nations and turning points in their musical and political histories. The Southbank Festival 'Changing Britain 1945–2015' also explored society, culture and politics, setting music from the last 70 years in context (with works by Britten, Walton, Richard Rodney Bennett, Judith Weir, Michael Nyman and Jonathan Dove) while the BBC Philharmonic focused more broadly on 'British Masters' (with works by David and Colin Matthews, Elgar, Vaughan Williams, Walton and Delius).

The Royal Scottish National Orchestra chose to look across the Atlantic to 20th-century American composers (John Adams, Bernstein, Barber and Gershwin) while Sarah Connolly also performed Copland's *Eight Poems of Emily Dickinson* in an American-themed concert with the Britten Sinfonia.

Elsewhere, in early music, love and intrigue, war and betrayal were explored during the Barbican's season through works by Monteverdi (Academy of Ancient Music and Les Arts Florissants) and Gesualdo (i Fagiolini). The Barbican's 'Baroque exploration' further included Rameau staged ballets, Handel operas and a rare performance of Vivaldi's *L'Oracolo in Messenia*. In addition, Wigmore Hall initiated its two-year series 'Henry Purcell: A Retrospective' while the Cardinall's Musick presented a Fayrfax celebration across the season.

Also looking back to the Renaissance, the BBC Philharmonic and the City of London Sinfonia both celebrated the 450th anniversary of Shakespeare's birth with series that included music for film and theatre (by Mendelssohn, Finzi, Walton, Korngold, Shostakovich and Owain Park) inspired by the Bard's work.

Beethoven featured strongly in the 2014–15 season. At Sage Gateshead, Saleem Ashkar performed 32 of Beethoven's piano sonatas while Renaud Capuçon and Frank Braley performed Beethoven's complete violin sonatas at the Southbank's Queen Elizabeth Hall. At Wigmore Hall, Maria João Pires, Augustin Dumay and Antonio Meneses worked through a selection of Beethoven's piano trios and the Elias String Quartet continued with its 'Beethoven Project'. Kings Place contrastingly presented 'Beethoven Plus', a series where ten contemporary composers (including Jonathan Dove, Judith Bingham and Kurt Schwertsik) wrote five-minute pieces inspired by and to accompany Beethoven's ten violin sonatas. Steven Osborne and the BBC Scottish Symphony Orchestra completed their Beethoven piano concerto cycle, the orchestra also celebrating chief conductor Donald Runnicles' 60th birthday with a performance of the mighty *Symphony No. 9*. Both the City of Birmingham Symphony Orchestra and the Royal Northern Sinfonia undertook a full Beethoven symphony cycle.

The work of James MacMillan was also prevalent throughout the season. The City of Birmingham Symphony Orchestra and Chorus gave the UK premiere of MacMillan's *St Luke Passion* followed by a London premiere of the same by the Britten Sinfonia and Britten Sinfonia Voices. The Royal Liverpool Philharmonic also premiered his *Little Mass,* the Philharmonia presented the UK premiere of his *Percussion Concerto* and the BBC Scottish Symphony Orchestra performed a MacMillan piano concerto cycle alongside other recent and contemporary works by Foulds, Stenhammar, John Adams and Magnus Lindberg.

The 2014–15 season also warmly acknowledged the recent passing of two influential composers: the BBC Scottish Symphony Orchestra presented a two-day celebration of the late Elliott Carter and Sir John Tavener was feted in the BBC Symphony Orchestra's 'Total Immersion: John Tavener Remembered' events; the Britten Sinfonia explored several of his pieces, including the world premiere of his last major concert work, *Flood of Beauty,* and *Kaleidoscopes,* Tavener's theatrical oboe concerto written for the orchestra in 2006.

Kings Place's yearly 'Unwrapped' series also opted for a more contemporary focus in 2015, turning its attentions to minimalism, while the Southbank hosted 'Metal Wood Skin: The Colin Currie Percussion Festival' to celebrate its artist-in-residence and the many new works written for percussion as a solo voice.

## FESTIVALS

The 120th BBC Proms during summer 2014 presented a number of epic works, including semi-staged performances of *Der Rosenkavalier, Salome* and *Elektra,* (in Strauss' anniversary year), Elgar's *The Kingdom,* seven Mahler symphonies, Britten's *War Requiem* and Beethoven's *Missa Solemnis,* performed by the usual impressive array of homegrown and international talent. There were also 80th birthday Proms for composers Sir Harrison Birtwistle and Sir Peter Maxwell Davies as well as a pop-operatic tragedy *A Man from the Future,* a tribute to Alan Turing (mathematician and wartime code-breaker who committed suicide after being prosecuted for his homosexuality), written by the Pet Shop Boys and performed by them and the BBC Concert Orchestra and Singers. Other firsts included the first CBeebies Prom, BBC Sport Prom, and the first collaboration with the National Theatre in the shape of a *War Horse* Prom (featuring the Military Wives Choir).

Throughout the 68th Edinburgh International Festival (August–September 2014) ran the theme of the relationship between conflict and cultural transcendence, with works including Britten's pacifist opera *Owen Wingrave* and his *War Requiem,* Shostakovich's *Leningrad Symphony,* Tchaikovsky's *1812 Overture,* Bernstein's *Kaddish Symphony* (written in memory of President John F. Kennedy) and a Kronos Quartet multimedia collaboration with composer Aleksandra Vrebalov and filmmaker Bill Morrison, *Beyond Zero: 1914–1918,* exploring art created before, during and after the Great War. The festival also acknowledged the Commonwealth Games in Glasgow with performers from Australia, New Zealand, South Africa and Canada, and a gala event celebrating 20 years of democracy in South Africa.

In November, the 37th Huddersfield Contemporary Music Festival offered 37 world premieres, including works by Scottish composer-in-residence James Dillon, and 79 UK premieres, and added two new venues to its list. The opening concert presented works by Christian Wolff, American experimentalist and disciple of John Cage in honour of Wolff's 80th birthday. The 70th birthday of saxophonist and improviser Evan Parker was also celebrated in his per-formance of three projects, including new commission *Twelve for Twelve Musicians* composed by Parker himself. There was also a strong music theatre strand to the festival with a new production of Salvatore Sciarrino's *Lohengrin,* a new chamber opera *Buenos Aires* by Simon Steen-Andersen and Christopher Fox's *Widerstehen,* an opera in memory of Fox's resistance-fighter aunt who was executed by the Nazis. Other highlights included the Aurora Orchestra's performance of experi-mentalist Michael Gordon's hypnotic *Timber,* a concert-length piece written for six amplified simantras (traditional Greek wooden instruments), and a new take by ensemble Apartment House on the 1975 Brian Eno album *Another Green World* (which had innovatively focused more on instrumental parts than contemporaneous albums) performed alongside *Ornamentik* by Tom Phillips, Eno's former teacher.

In the summer of 2015, the Garsington Opera featured Mozart's *Così fan Tutte* alongside two 20th-century seminal operas – Britten's *Death in Venice* and a new production of Strauss' bourgeois comedy *Intermezzo.* The Britten was notably conducted by Steuart Bedford, who had conducted the world premiere in 1973. The festival also joined forces with the Royal Shakespeare Company for the first time to present *A Midsummer Night's Dream* (abridged) enriched by Mendelssohn's incidental music. The concurrent Grange Park

Opera festival presented performances of Jerry Bock and Sheldon Harnick's *Fiddler on the Roof*, Tchaikovsky's *Eugene Onegin*, Puccini's *La Bohème* and Saint-Saëns' *Samson et Dalila*. At the same time, the Cotswolds-based Longborough Festival Opera followed the previous year's 'Ring Cycle' with a staging of Wagner's *Tristan und Isolde*. The other operas performed were Donizetti's *Don Pasquale*, Verdi's *Rigoletto* and Handel's *Xerxes*.

The 68th Aldeburgh Festival in June opened with a Birtwistle operatic mythological double bill of *The Corridor* preceded by the world premiere of *The Cure*. Meanwhile, the Multi-Story orchestra, working with local school choirs and reaching out to a broader, less traditional audience, presented a concert in an Ipswich car park. The middle weekend focused particularly on Bach with the Monteverdi Choir presenting three Bach concerts, while modernist Pierre Boulez's 90th birthday was celebrated in a three-day retrospective of his work. As one of the artists-in-residence, composer George Benjamin's other talents as conductor, pianist and advocate of next-generation composers were also plain to see throughout the festival. The festival also included founder Britten's only full-length ballet, *The Prince of Pagodas*.

The 71st Cheltenham Music Festival (June–July) introduced 22 world premieres including works by Charlotte Bray, Jonathan Dove and Matthew Martin. Themes of the festival included 'Revisiting 1945' (with works by Strauss, Messiaen, Howells and Tippett), 'Paris – City of Love and Lights' (with music by Poulenc, Satie and Messiaen, and Claire Martin's 'April in Paris', a Parisian cabaret concert) and a film strand with a Britten Sinfonia-accompanied screening of *Psycho* and the Orlando Consort's new soundtrack to Dreyer's 1928 silent film *La Passion de Jeanne d'Arc*.

Joan of Arc also featured in the July Buxton Festival, Verdi's *Giovanna d'Arco* being one of the festival operas along with Donizetti's *Lucia di Lammermoor*, Purcell's *Dido and Aeneas* and a concert performance of Charpentier's *Louise*. The festival was also host to over 100 concerts and recitals from performers including pianist Stephen Hough and the English Chamber Orchestra.

## OBITUARIES

In September 2014, conductor, musicologist, keyboardist and Radio 3 broadcaster Christopher Hogwood died of a brain tumour at the age of 73. A leading light in promoting 'historically informed performances' to the mainstream, in 1973 he founded the Academy of Ancient Music, which made many of the first recordings on period instruments. Whether in his performances, editions or academia, he liked to consider not only the composer's intentions but also the circumstances of a work's first performances and the processes of its composition, revision and adaptation. But he did not feel shackled exclusively to early music and was latterly also regarded as a Martinů specialist.

In February 2015, composer-pianist John McCabe died aged 75 after a long illness from brain cancer. After being badly burnt as a child, McCabe was home schooled and spent much time listening to music, learning the piano and experimenting with composition. After studies in Manchester and Munich, he became a pianist and composer of great renown. His recording legacy includes Haydn's piano sonatas and Nielsen's complete piano works, and composers such as John Casken, Sir Richard Rodney Bennett and George Benjamin all wrote solos and concertos for him. As a composer, he explored elements of serialism, drew on rock and jazz idioms, and latterly moved somewhat in the direction of minimalism. His compositions, which ranged from solo works to ballets and a children's opera, found inspiration in particular from British and foreign countryside as well as architecture, poetry and works of art. He was also an effective crusader for British music and performers.

The following June, composer James Horner died in a plane crash, aged 61. The American composer of scores for more than 100 Hollywood films, including *Aliens*, *Braveheart*, *Apollo 13* and *Titanic*, originally wanted to be a 'straight' classical composer but discovered that composing for film was freeing and unfettered by musical labels. He did, however, retain his interest in classical composition and had just had his double concerto for violin and cello premiered by Mari and Håkon Samuelsen and the Liverpool Philharmonic Orchestra in November 2014.

David Trendell, organist, early music specialist, director of music at King's College London and great inspiration to future generations of choral singers, died unexpectedly of a brain haemorrhage aged 50; Peter Cropper, founder and vibrant, fearless leader of the Lindsay Quartet for almost four decades, died aged 69; Patrick Gowers, composer who drew on aspects of jazz harmony and 20th-century French music, and mainly known for his film scores, died aged 78; Frans Brüggen, Dutch recorder player, flautist, musicologist, conductor and pioneer of the early music revival, died aged 79; Peter Sculthorpe, Australian composer who created a distinct identity for antipodean composition and pioneered the use of aboriginal music in the concert hall, died aged 85; James Erb, American composer, arranger, musicologist and conductor, particularly known for his arrangement of *Shenandoah*, died aged 88; Gunther Schuller, American composer of synthesised classical and jazz or 'Third Stream' music, orchestral conductor, French horn player and academic, died aged 89; Denys Darlow, composer, organist, festival founder/organiser and leading figure in the early music revival, died aged 93; Manitas de Plata, legendary French flamenco guitarist, died also aged 93; Knut Nystedt, Norwegian composer and conductor best known for his choral and church compositions, died aged 99; Roy Douglas, composer and arranger best known for his close working relationships supporting Walton and Vaughan Williams, died aged 107.

## NEW APPOINTMENTS AND HONOURS

Following the departure of Thomas Zehetmair, in September 2014, Lars Vogt took up the position of music director designate with the Royal Northern Sinfonia ahead of his full music directorship in the 2015–16 season. At the same time, Alexander Martin took up the role of Welsh National Opera chorus master while Dutch conductor Frank Zielhorst was appointed Leverhulme young conductor-in-association with Bournemouth Symphony Orchestra for the 2014–15 season. In January 2015, Alexander Shelley took up the baton as associate conductor of the Royal Philharmonic and the following April, Sir Andrew Davis was appointed conductor emeritus by the Royal Liverpool Philharmonic, following in the footsteps of the likes of Sir Charles Mackerras and Vernon Handley. In June of the same year, Stuart Stratford became the new music director for Scottish Opera.

In December 2014, the Southbank Centre announced the BBC Concert Orchestra as its new associate orchestra, with the orchestra opening the Southbank 'Changing Britain 1945–2015' festival the following month.

At the start of the 2014–15 season, Finnish composer Magnus Lindberg took up his three-year position as composer-in-residence for the LPO and Swedish composer B. Tommy Andersson was appointed the new composer-in-association for the BBC National Orchestra of Wales for the 2014–15 season. In November 2014, Brett Dean was appointed the new artist-in-association with the BBC Symphony Orchestra until the end of the 2016–17 season; the role involves him in the orchestra as composer, conductor and soloist on viola. And in January 2015, master of the Queen's music Judith Weir was appointed new associate composer of the BBC Singers for a three-year tenure.

In the Queen's New Year's and Birthday Honours, conductor Sir Neville Marriner was made one of only 65 Companions of Honour and composers James MacMillan and Karl Jenkins both received knighthoods. CBEs were presented to composer Mark-Anthony Turnage, Simon Halsey (City of Birmingham Symphony chorus director), opera directors Richard Jones and Jonathan Kent, Jude Kelly (artistic director of the Southbank Centre), David Whelton (managing director of the Philharmonia), Alan Davey (Radio 3 controller) and Roger Wright (chief executive of Aldeburgh Music and former Radio 3 controller and BBC Proms director). OBEs were awarded to Jeffrey Skidmore (conductor and artistic director of Ex Cathedra), John Lubbock (founder and artistic director of the Orchestra of St John's and charity 'Music for Autism') and violinist Rodney Friend (founder of the Solomon Trio and youngest-ever leader of the LPO). MBEs were given to Frances Hickox (co-founder of the St Endellion festival), Peter Holman (co-founder of the Parley of Instruments), Alan Fearon (founder and chorus master of the Chorus of the Royal Northern Sinfonia), Michael Bochmann (violin and chamber music professor – Trinity Laban Conservatoire) and clarinettist-conductor Michael Collins.

COMPETITIONS

In March 2015, the Wigmore Hall International String Quartet Competition was won by the Van Kuijk Quartet from France, along with the Haydn performance prize, and the second prize was jointly awarded to the Verona Quartet (USA) and Piatti Quartet (UK), the latter also winning the Mark-Anthony Turnage performance prize. Third prize went to the Aizuri Quartet (USA).

In April 2015, 24-year-old soprano Gemma Lois Summerfield won first prize at the Kathleen Ferrier Awards as well as the song prize for her performance of a Sibelius song. Second prize was awarded to soprano Soraya Mafi while the latter's pianist, Ian Tindale was awarded the accompanist's prize.

The same month, at the Handel Singing Competition, Spanish baritone Josep-Ramon Olivé won both first prize and the audience prize and Russian mezzo-soprano Maria Ostroukhova was awarded second prize. In June, soprano Nadine Koutcher from Belarus carried off first prize at the BBC Cardiff Singer of the World Competition, with South Korean bass Jongmin Park winning the song prize and Mongolian baritone Amartuvshin Enkhbat winning the audience prize.

In July, at the 28th St Albans International Organ Competition, Johannes Zeinler from Austria won first prize in the interpretation competition while second prize was awarded to Davide Mariano (Italy) along with the Peter Hurford Bach prize. Zita Nauratyill (Hungary) won the Paul Patterson prize for the best performance of the commissioned work as well as the audience prize, and Thomas Gaynor (New Zealand) won the Douglas May award for best performance of a competition work in the quarter-/semi-final round. David Cassan (France) won the improvisation competition.

## OPERA PRODUCTIONS

The list below summarises each opera company's activities and the date in parentheses indicates the year that the current production entered their repertory.

ROYAL OPERA
Founded 1946
W www.roh.org.uk

REPERTORY: *La Bohème* (1974), *La Traviata* (1994), *Rigoletto* (2001), *Madama Butterfly* (2003), *Die Zauberflöte* (2003), *Il Barbiere di Siviglia* (2005), *Il Turco in Italia* (2005), *L'Elisir d'Amore* (2007), *Der fliegende Holländer*

(2009), *Tristan und Isolde* (2009), *Anna Nicole* (2011), *Falstaff* (2012), *La Don Giovanni* (2014)
NEW PRODUCTIONS: *I due Foscari* (Verdi), 14 October 2014. Conductor, Antonio Pappano/Renato Balsadonna; director, Thaddeus Strassberger. Plácido Domingo (Francesco Foscari), Francesco Meli (Jacopo Foscari), Maria Agresta (Lucrezia Contarini), Maurizio Muraro (Jacopo Loredano), Samuel Sakker (Barbarigo), Rachel Kelly (Pisana)
*Idomeneo* (Mozart), 3 November 2014. Conductor, Marc Minkowski; director, Martin Kušej. Matthew Polenzani (Idomeneo), Franco Fagioli (Idamente), Sophie Bevan (Ilia), Malin Byström (Elettra), Stanislas de Barbeyrac (Arbace), Krystian Adam (High Priest of Neptune), Graeme Broadbent (Voice of Neptune)
*Un Ballo in Maschera* (Verdi), 18 December 2014. Conductor, Daniel Oren; director, Katharina Thoma. Joseph Calleja (Riccardo), Liudmyla Monastyrska (Amelia), Dmitri Hvorostovsky (Renato), Marianne Cornetti (Ulrica), Rosemary Joshua (Oscar), Anatoli Sivko (Sam), James Platt/Jihoon Kim (Tom), Samuel Johnson (Silvano), Samuel Sakker (Minister of Justice)
*Andrea Chénier* (Giordano), 20 January 2015. Conductor, Antonio Pappano; director, David McVicar. Jonas Kaufmann (Andrea Chénier), Željko Lučić (Carlo Gérard), Eva-Maria Westbroek (Maddalena de Coigny), Denyce Graves (Bersi), Elena Zilio (Madelon), Rosalind Plowright (Countessa de Coigny), Roland Wood (Roucher), Peter Coleman-Wright (Pietro Fléville), Adrian Clarke (Mathieu), Carlo Bosi (L'Incredibile)
*Rise and Fall of the City of Mahagonny* (Weill), 10 March 2015. Conductor, Mark Wigglesworth; director, John Fulljames. Anne Sofie von Otter (Leokadja Begbick), Peter Hoare (Fatty), Willard White (Trinity Moses), Christine Rice (Jenny Smith), Kurt Streit (Jimmy McIntyre), Jeffrey Lloyd-Roberts (Jack O'Brien), Darren Jeffrey (Bank Account Billy), Neal Davies (Alaska Wolf Joe), Hubert Francis (Toby Higgins)
*Król Roger* (Szymanowski), 1 May 2015. Conductor, Antonio Pappano; director, Kasper Holten. Mariusz Kwiecień (Król Roger II), Saimir Pirgu (Shepherd), Georgia Jarman (Roxana), Kim Begley (Edrisi), Alan Ewing (Archbishop), Agnes Zwierko (Deaconess)
*Guillaume Tell* (Rossini), 29 June 2015. Conductor, Antonio Pappano; director, Damiano Michieletto. Gerald Finley (Guillaume Tell), John Osborn (Arnold Melcthal), Malin Byström (Mathilde), Alexander Vinogradov (Walter Furst), Sofia Fomina (Jemmy), Nicolas Courjal (Gesler), Eric Halfvarson (Melcthal), Michael Colvin (Rodolphe), Mikeldi Atxalandabaso (Ruodi), Enkelejda Shkosa (Hedwige)

ENGLISH NATIONAL OPERA
Founded 1931
W www.eno.org

REPERTORY: *Xerxes* (1985), *La Bohème* (2009), *The Marriage of Figaro* (2011), *La Traviata* (2013)
NEW PRODUCTIONS: *Otello* (Verdi), 13 September 2014. Conductor, Edward Gardner; director, David Alden. Stuart Skelton (Otello), Leah Crocetto (Desdemona), Jonathan Summers (Iago), Allan Clayton (Cassio), Peter Van Hulle (Roderigo), Barnaby Rea (Lodovico), Charles Johnston (Montano), Pamela Helen Stephen (Emilia)
*The Girl of the Golden West* (Puccini), 2 October 2014. Conductor, Keri-Lynn Wilson; director, Richard Jones. Susan Bullock (Minnie), Craig Colclough (Jack Rance), Peter Auty (Dick Johnson), Graham Clark/Richard Roberts (Nick), Leigh Melrose (Sonora), Nicholas Crawley (Larkens), Adrian Dwyer (Trin), Jonathan McGovern (Sid), Charles Rice (Handsome), Richard Roberts/Philip Sheffield (Harry), Sam Furness (Joe), Alexander Robin Baker (Happy), Nicholas Masters (Ashby), George Humphreys (Jake Wallace), Clare Presland (Wowkle)

*The Gospel According to the Other Mary* (Adams), 21 November 2014. Conductor, Joana Carneiro; director, Peter Sellars. Patricia Bardon (Mary Magdalene), Meredith Arwady (Martha), Russell Thomas (Lazarus), Daniel Bubeck, Brian Cummings, Nathan Medley (Counter-tenors)

*The Mastersingers of Nuremberg* (Wagner), 7 February 2015. Conductor, Edward Gardner; director, Richard Jones. Iain Paterson (Hans Sachs), Rachel Nicholls (Eva), Andrew Shore (Beckmesser), James Creswell (Pogner), Gwyn Hughes Jones (Walther von Stolzing), Nicky Spence (David), David Stout (Kothner), Madeleine Shaw (Magdalene), Nicholas Crawley (Night Watchman)

*Indian Queen* (Purcell), 26 February 2015. Conductor, Laurence Cummings; director, Peter Sellars. Julia Bullock (Teculihuatzin/Doña Luisa), Lucy Crowe (Doña Isabel), Vince Yi (Hunahpú), Anthony Roth Costanzo (Ixbalanqué), Noah Stewart (Don Pedro de Alvarado), Thomas Walker (Don Pedrarias Dávila), Luthando Qave (Sacerdote Maya), Maritxell Carrero (Leonor)

*Between Worlds* (Tansy Davies), 11 April 2015. Conductor, Gerry Cornelius; director, Deborah Warner. Andrew Watts (Shaman), Eric Greene (Janitor), Rhian Lois (Younger Woman), Clare Presland (Realtor), William Morgan (Younger Man), Philip Rhodes (Older Man), Susan Bickley (Mother)

*The Pirates of Penzance* (Gilbert and Sullivan), 9 May 2015. Conductor, David Parry/Timothy Henty; director, Mike Leigh. Andrew Shore (Major-General Stanley), Joshua Bloom (Pirate King), Robert Murray (Frederic), Jonathan Lemalu (Sergeant of Police), Claudia Boyle (Mabel), Rebecca de Pont Davies (Ruth), Alexander Robin Baker (Samuel), Soraya Mafi (Edith), Anghorad Lyddon (Kate)

*Queen of Spades* (Tchaikovsky), 6 June 2015. Conductor, Edward Gardner; director, David Alden. Peter Hoare (Hermann), Giselle Allen (Lisa), Dame Felicity Palmer (Countess), Nicholas Pallesen (Prince Yeletsky), Gregory Dahl (Count Tomsky), Catherine Young (Pauline), Colin Judson (Tchenkalinsky), Wyn Pencarreg (Sourin), Valerie Reid (Governess), Katie Bird (Mascha), Peter Van Hulle (Tchaplitsky), Charles Johnston (Narumov)

## OPERA NORTH
Founded 1978
W www.operanorth.co.uk

REPERTORY: *La Vida Breve* (2004), *The Bartered Bride* (2012), *Carousel* (2012)
NEW PRODUCTIONS: *La Traviata* (Verdi), 20 September 2014. Conductors, Oliver von Dohnányi/Justin Doyle; director, Alessandro Talevi. Anna Jeruc-Kopec (Violetta Valéry), Victoria Sharp (Flora Bervoix), Louise Collett (Annina), Ji-Min Park (Alfredo Germont), Stephen Gadd (Giorgio Germont), Daniel Norman (Gastone), Peter Savidge (Baron Douphol), Nicholas Butterfield (Marquis d'Obigny), Dean Robinson (Doctor Grenvil)

*The Coronation of Poppea* (Monteverdi), 4 October 2014. Conductor, Laurence Cummings; director, Tim Albery. Sandra Piques Eddy (Poppea), James Laing (Nerone), Catherine Hopper (Ottavia), James Creswell (Seneca), Christopher Ainslie (Ottone), Katherine Manley (Drusilla), Fiona Kimm (Arnalta), Ciara Hendrick (Fortuna/Valletto), Claire Pascoe (Virtù), Emilie Renard (Amore), Daniel Norman (Liberto), Nicholas Sharratt (Lucano), Owen Willetts (Famigliari), Warren Gillespie (Famigliari), Dominic Barberi (Famigliari)

*The Marriage of Figaro* (Mozart), 24 January 2015. Conductors, Alexander Shelley/Anthony Kraus; director, Jo Davies. Richard Burkhard (Figaro), Silvia Moi (Susanna), Quirijn de Lang (Count Almaviva), Ana Maria Labin (Countess Almaviva), Helen Sherman (Cherubino), Henry Waddington/Dean Robinson (Doctor Bartolo), Joseph Shovelton (Don Basilio), Gaynor Keeble (Marcellina), Jeremy

Peaker (Antonio), Ellie Laugharne (Barbarina), Nicholas Watts (Don Curzio)

*Gianni Schicchi* (Puccini), 18 February 2015. Conductors, Jac van Steen/Martin Pickard; director, Christopher Alden. Christopher Purves (Gianni Schicchi), Jennifer France (Lauretta), Jesús Álvarez (Rinuccio), Victoria Sharp (Nella), Claire Pascoe (La Ciesca), Elizabeth Sikora (Zita), Daniel Norman (Gherardo), Peter Savidge (Marco), Jeremy Peaker (Ser Amantio di Nicolao), Dean Robinson (Betto di Signa), Brian Bannatyne-Scott (Simon), Tim Claydon (Dante/Buoso Donati)

*Swanhunter* (Dove and Middleton), 2 April 2015. Conductors, Justin Doyle/Ian Ryan; director, Hannah Mulder. Adrian Dwyer (Lemminkäinen), Ann Taylor (Mother), Suzanne Shakespeare (Swan/Chorus), Rebecca Afonwy-Jones (Louhi/Chorus), Christopher Diffey (Dog/Soppy Hat/Death's Son), Matthew Hargreaves (Dog/Death/Smith/Chorus)

CONCERT PERFORMANCES: *The Flying Dutchman* (Wagner), 27 June 2015. Conductor, Richard Farnes; director, Peter Mumford. Béla Perencz (The Dutchman), Alwyn Mellor (Senta), Mats Almgren (Daland), Mati Turi (Erik), Ceri Williams (Mary), Mark Le Brocq (Steersman)

## SCOTTISH OPERA
Founded 1962
W www.scottishopera.org.uk

REPERTORY: *Madama Butterfly* (2000), *Il Trovatore* (2001), *Macbeth* (2005)
NEW PRODUCTIONS: *La Cenerentola* (Rossini), 15 October 2014. Conductors, William Lacey/Oliver Rundell; director, Sandrine Anglade. Victoria Yarovaya (Angelina), Nico Darmanin (Don Ramiro), Richard Burkhard (Dandini), Graeme Danby (Don Magnifico), John Molloy (Alidoro), Rebecca Bottone (Clorinda), Máire Flavin (Tisbe)

*Inés de Castro* (MacMillan), 22 January 2015. Conductors, James MacMillan/Derek Clark; director, Olivia Fuchs. Stephanie Corley (Inés de Castro), Peter Wedd (Pedro), Susannah Glanville (Blanca), Paul Carey Jones (Pacheco), Brindley Sherratt (The King), Kathleen Wilkinson (Nurse/Old Woman), Gary Griffiths (Executioner)

*Orfeo ed Euridice* (Gluck), 19 February 2015. Conductor, Kenneth Montgomery; director, Ashley Page. Caitlin Hulcup (Orfeo), Lucy Hall (Euridice), Ana Quintans (Amor)

*Jenůfa* (Janáček), 7 April 2015. Conductor, Stuart Stratford; director, Annilese Miskimmon. Lee Bisset (Jenůfa), Kathryn Harries (Kostelnička Buryjovka), Peter Wedd (Laca Klemeň), Sam Furness (Števa Buryja), Anne-Marie Owens (Grandmother Buryjovka), William Robert Allenby (Stárek), Jonathan May (Mayor), Sarah Pring (Mayor's Wife), Rosalind Coad (Karolka), Louise Kemeny (Jano)

## WELSH NATIONAL OPERA
Founded 1946
W www.wno.org.uk

REPERTORY: *Carmen* (1997), *Hansel and Gretel* (1998), *The Magic Flute* (2005)
NEW PRODUCTIONS: *William Tell* (Rossini), 12 September 2014. Conductors, Carlo Rizzi/Andrew Greenwood; director, David Pountney. David Kempster (William Tell), Barry Banks (Arnold), Gisela Stille (Mathilde), Clive Bayley (Gesler), Fflur Wyn (Jemmy), Leah-Marian Jones (Hedwige), Richard Wiegold (Melchthal/Walter), Luciano Botelho (Ruodi), Nicky Spence (Rodolphe), Aidan Smith (Leuthold)

*Moses in Egypt* (Rossini), 3 October 2014. Conductors, Carlo Rizzi/Simon Phillippo; director, David Pountney. Miklós Sebestyén (Mosè), David Alegret (Osiride), Christine Rice/Linda Richardson (Amaltea), Barry Banks (Aronne),

Andrew Foster-Williams (Faraone), Leah-Marian Jones (Amenofi), Claire Booth (Elcia), Nicky Spence (Mambre) *Peter Pan* (Richard Ayres), 16 May 2015. Conductor, Erik Nielsen; director, Keith Warner. Iestyn Morris (Peter Pan), Marie Arnet (Wendy), Ashley Holland (Mr Darling/Captain Hook), Hilary Summers (Mrs Darling/Tiger Lily), Nicholas Sharratt (John), Rebecca Bottone (Michael), Mark Le Brocq (Smee), Aidan Smith (Nana)
*Pelléas and Mélisande* (Debussy), 29 May 2015. Conductor, Lothar Koenigs; director, David Pountney. Jacques Imbrailo (Pelléas), Jurgita Adomonyté (Mélisande), Christopher Purves (Golaud), Leah-Marian Jones (Genevieve), Scott Wilde (Arkel), Rebecca Bottone (Yniold)

### GLYNDEBOURNE
Founded 1934
W www.glyndebourne.com

REPERTORY: *Carmen* (2002), *L'Heure Espagnole/L'Enfant et les Sortilèges* (2012), *The Rape of Lucretia* (2013)
NEW PRODUCTIONS: *Poliuto* (Donizetti), 21 May 2015. Conductor, Enrique Mazzola; director, Mariame Clément. Michael Fabiano (Poliuto), Ana María Martínez (Paolina), Igor Golovatenko (Severo), Matthew Rose (Callistene), Timothy Robinson (Felice), Emanuele d'Aguanno (Nearco)
*Die Entführung aus dem Serail* (Mozart), 13 June 2015. Conductor, Robin Ticciati; director, David McVicar. Sally Matthews (Konstanze), Edgaras Montvidas (Belmonte), Tobias Kehrer (Osmin), Mari Eriksmoen (Blonde), Brenden Gunnell (Pedrillo)
*Saul* (Handel), 23 July 2015. Conductor, Ivor Bolton; director, Barrie Kosky. Christopher Purves/Henry Waddington (Saul), Iestyn Davies (David), Lucy Crowe (Merab), Sophie Bevan (Michal), Paul Appleby (Jonathan), Benjamin Hulett (High Priest), John Graham-Hall (Witch of Endor)
GLYNDEBOURNE TOUR: *The Turn of the Screw* (2006), *La Finta Giardiniera* (2014), *La Traviata* (2014)

## AWARDS

### GRAMOPHONE AWARDS 2014
SPECIAL AWARDS
Artist of the Year – Leonidas Kavakos (violin)
Label of the Year – Delphian Records
Lifetime Achievement – Sir James Galway (flute)
Outstanding Achievement – Sir Neville Marriner (conductor)
Young Artist of the Year – Nightingale String Quartet
RECORDING AWARDS
Baroque Instrumental – CPE Bach *Württemberg Sonatas:* Mahan Esfahani (harpsichord)
Baroque Vocal – C. P. E. Bach *Magnificat; Heilig ist Gott; Symphony in D major:* Elizabeth Watts, Wiebke Lehmkuhl, Lothar Odinius, Markus Eiche, RIAS Kammerchor, Akademie für Alte Musik Berlin/Hans-Christoph Rademann
Chamber – Schubert *String Quintet in C Major, String Quartet No. 14 'Death and the Maiden':* Pavel Haas Quartet with Danjulo Ishizaka (cello)
Choral – Mozart *Requiem; Misericordias Domini:* Joanne Lunn, Rowan Hellier, Thomas Hobbs, Matthew Brook, Dunedin Consort/John Butt
Concerto – Prokofiev *Complete Piano Concertos:* Jean-Efflam Bavouzet (piano), BBC Philharmonic Orchestra/Gianandrea Noseda
Contemporary – Benjamin *Written on Skin:* Christopher Purves, Barbara Hannigan , Bejun Mehta, Orchestra of the Royal Opera House, Covent Garden/George Benjamin; Katie Mitchell (stage director); Margaret Williams (video director)

Early – Marenzio *Primo Libro di Madrigali:* La Compagnia del Madrigale
Instrumental – Volodos *Plays Mompou* (various works): Arcadi Volodos (piano)
Opera – Ravel *L'Heure Espagnole; L'Enfant et les Sortilèges:* Stéphanie d'Oustrac, Alek Shrader, François Piolino, Elliot Madore, Paul Gay, Khatouna Gadelia, Elodie Méchain, Glyndebourne Chorus; LPO/Kazushi Ono; Laurent Pelly (stage director); François Roussillon (video director)
Orchestral (Recording of the Year) – Brahms *The Symphonies* (and other works): Leipzig Gewandhaus Orchestra/Riccardo Chailly
Recital – *Arise my Muse:* Iestyn Davies (countertenor), Richard Egarr (harpsichord); Wigmore Hall Live
Solo Vocal – Schubert *Winterreise:* Jonas Kaufmann (tenor), Helmut Deutsch (piano)

### BBC MUSIC MAGAZINE AWARDS 2015
Concerto and Recording of the Year – Beethoven *Piano Concertos Nos. 2 & 4:* Leif Ove Andsnes (piano), Mahler Chamber Orchestra
Orchestral – Bruckner *Symphony No. 9:* Lucerne Festival Orchestra/Claudio Abbado
Opera – Wagner *Die Meistersinger von Nürnberg:* Gerald Finley, Marco Jentzsch. Glyndebourne Chorus, LPO/Vladimir Jurowski
Vocal – *Stella di Napoli* (arias by Puccini, Bellini, Donizetti, Mercadante, etc): Joyce DiDonato (mezzo-soprano), Orchestre et Choeur de L'Opéra de Lyon/Riccardo Minasi
Choral – Elgar *The Dream of Gerontius; Sea Pictures:* Sarah Connolly (mezzo-soprano), Stuart Skelton (tenor), David Soar (bass), BBC Symphony Orchestra and Chorus/Sir Andrew Davis
Chamber – Beethoven *Piano Trios Op. 70 No. 2 & Op. 97 'Archduke':* Alexander Melnikov (piano), Isabelle Faust (violin), Jean-Guihen Queyras (cello)
Instrumental – *Dances* (works by J. S. Bach, Chopin, Scriabin, Granados, Albéniz, Gould and Schulz-Evler): Benjamin Grosvenor (piano)
JURY AWARDS
Newcomer – C. P. E. Bach *Württemberg Sonatas:* Mahan Esfahani (harpsichord)
Premiere Recording – Unsuk Chin *3 Concertos (Piano Concerto; Cello Concerto; Šu for Sheng and Orchestra):* Alban Gerhardt (cello), Wu Wei (sheng), Sunwook Kim (piano), Seoul Philharmonic Orchestra/Myung-Whun Chung
DVD – *Becoming Traviata:* Philippe Béziat (film director), Natalie Dessay (soprano), Jean-François Sivadier (opera director), Louis Langrée (conductor)

### ROYAL PHILHARMONIC SOCIETY AWARDS 2015
Audiences and Engagement – Philharmonia iOrchestra (SW England)
Chamber Music and Song – Oxford Lieder Festival
Chamber-Scale Composition – Graham Fitkin *Distil*
Concert Series and Festivals – Birtwistle at 80 (Barbican)
Conductor – Andris Nelsons
Creative Communication – Royal Opera *The Opera Machine*
Ensemble – London Contemporary Orchestra
Instrumentalist – Colin Currie
Large-Scale Composition – Hans Abrahamsen *Let Me Tell You.*
Learning and Participation – Britten's *War Requiem* (Southbank Centre)
Opera and Music Theatre – English National Opera
Singer – Christian Gerhaher
Young Artists – Mary Bevan

# POP MUSIC

*Piers Martin*

## SMITH AND SHEERAN SHINE

Last year, for the first time, not one album by a British artist managed to sell a million copies in the UK, a figure that appeared to tally with the declining fortunes of the music industry. During the year under review, however, both Ed Sheeran and Sam Smith achieved this, and also enjoyed considerable success in the US. Released in June 2014, Sheeran's second album *x* – known as *Multiply* – comfortably became the year's biggest record, spending 12 weeks at number one in the UK and selling 1.7 million copies in the six months to Christmas. By February 2015, the flame-haired 24-year-old from Framlingham in Suffolk had sold 5.8 million copies of *x* worldwide and topped the Billboard 200 chart in the US as well as those in Canada and Australia. That same month Sheeran won Brit awards for British Album and Male Solo Artist, while the streaming service Spotify announced *x* as the most streamed album of 2014, having been played some 430 million times. On *x*, Sheeran enlisted US heavyweights such as Pharrell Williams and Rick Rubin to give his homespun confessional pop a meatier flavour and a contemporary hip-hop edge, which served to broaden his appeal while accentuating his easy-going manner and boyish charm. The campaign for *x* culminated in Sheeran playing three sold-out shows at London's Wembley Stadium in July 2015, where he performed for 80,000 fans each night.

As the winner of BBC Music's Sound of 2014 competition and the recipient of the critics' choice award at the 2014 Brits, Sam Smith's path to glory was laid out before him, but few could have predicted just how popular his debut album *In the Lonely Hour* would become. The 23-year-old Londoner's melancholy take on soul and R&B, best realised in the radio-friendly gospel of his number one single 'Stay With Me', translated into 2014's second best-selling album in the UK (1.2 million copies), and third best-selling in the US; Smith was the only artist to sell over a million albums in both countries in 2014. By June 2015, sales of *In the Lonely Hour* had reached 1.8 million in the UK and 2 million in the US, and Smith's success had been acknowledged at the Brit awards, where he scooped awards for British Breakthrough Act and British Global Success, and at the 57th Grammy awards, where Smith won a remarkable four trophies, including gongs for Album of the Year and Best Pop Vocal Album. The ubiquity of 'Stay With Me' attracted the attention of representatives of the US musician Tom Petty, who noticed similarities between that song and Petty's 1989 hit 'I Won't Back Down'. In January 2015, both parties admitted that the similarities were purely a coincidence, but not before Petty was awarded a 12.5 per cent share of the royalties for 'Stay With Me'.

Figures released by the British Phonographic Industry (BPI) revealed that Smith and Sheeran's popularity in the UK helped UK artists to claim 12.2 per cent of overall music consumption in 2014, up from 10.4 per cent in 2013.

## STREAMING: THE SAVIOUR?

This was the year that the music industry decided to throw its weight – cautiously at first – behind streaming, in the face of dwindling returns from traditional revenue sources. Total UK industry income for 2014 fell 4.1 per cent to below £700m for the first time, to £699.6m, according to BPI figures; sales of physical albums, chiefly on CD, fell by 7.2 per cent, although physical formats still account for two-thirds of all albums sold. Perhaps more surprising, sales of digital downloads of albums and single tracks fell 11.8 per cent and 12.5 per cent respectively, the first time that a decrease has been recorded since online sales began in 2004, leading to a 12.2 per cent fall for digital in the total market share. The shift towards streaming by consumers now seems irreversible and the industry, lacking an alternative financial plan, must do what it can to maximise revenue from the raft of streaming services that have emerged in recent years. In the UK, for example, income from subscription and ad-supported streaming on platforms such as Spotify, Deezer and Rdio rose by 50 per cent in 2014, the BPI noted, while the number of streams in 2014 totalled 14.8 billion, an increase of 97.6 per cent on 2013's figure of 7.5 billion.

As one example of consumers' rapidly changing listening habits, records were set in December when 'Uptown Funk' by producer Mark Ronson was streamed 2 million times in its first week of release. The brassy disco hit, sung by Bruno Mars, went on to spend seven weeks at number one in the UK, where Ronson won the Brit award for British Single, and 14 consecutive weeks at the top of the chart in the US, where the track was streamed a record 4.8 million times in one week. Later, 'Uptown Funk' became the most streamed song of the first half of 2015 in the UK, with over 45 million plays. The track proved to be greater than the album it trailed, *Uptown Special,* which fared respectably and featured lyrics by US author Michael Chabon and a guest turn by Stevie Wonder. In March, meanwhile, US rapper Kendrick Lamar's second album, *To Pimp a Butterfly,* was streamed a record 9.6 million times on its day of release, data provided by Spotify revealed.

With streaming forecast to grow exponentially – the BPI predicts 25 billion streams in 2015, doubling to 50 billion when streaming tracks via YouTube are included – this year saw a number of high-profile streaming services enter what is becoming an increasingly competitive market at risk of saturation. In addition to the market leader Spotify, which claims to have more than 60 million users, including 20 million paying subscribers, new arrivals included Tidal (launched in March), Apple Music (June) and Amazon's Prime Music (July). Partly owned by rapper and mogul Jay Z, Tidal's launch was attended by a panoply of pop and rock stars such as Madonna, Daft Punk, Kanye West, Calvin Harris and Jack White, who each own a percentage of the service, which promises exclusive content for subscribers and greater transparency in its royalty payments to artists. But with anticipation growing over the arrival of Apple Music, Tidal appeared to be on the back foot from the start, and by July its interim CEO had left and Madonna found herself fielding questions in interviews about the health of the enterprise.

## ANOTHER BITE FOR APPLE

Streaming is uncharted territory for the music industry, which, rather than setting its own agenda, has been forced to react to the decisions of the software companies that own the streaming sites and develop the technology. What's more, the crucial issue of how much to pay artists and rights holders for streaming their songs has yet to be fully resolved. When Apple Music launched on June 30 with an announcement, it came under fire for its policy of not paying artists during the service's three-month free trial, instead only offering royalties once users begin paying the £9.99 monthly charge. Taylor Swift, arguably the world's biggest pop star, publicly threatened to withdraw her hit album *1989* from Apple

Music in protest at this policy, which she denounced as 'shocking' because it asked artists to 'work for nothing'. The next day, Apple announced that it would in fact now pay artists during the free trial period. Swift then allowed her album to be included on the service. Some wondered if the exchange had been a promotional stunt, not least because Swift's catalogue is still unavailable on Spotify, Apple Music's main rival, after the singer removed it in November. That month, *1989,* Swift's fifth, more pop-focused album, sold 1.2 million copies in its first week in the US, the first album to do this since 2002 and her fourth US number one album in a row.

Apple Music already has a distinct advantage over other streaming sites because most users are familiar with Apple's operating system and its iTunes service, and many use its iPhone handset, so using Apple Music would, the company hoped, be second nature. In addition to the streaming platform, Apple Music launched a global internet radio station called Beats 1, helmed by former BBC Radio 1 DJ Zane Lowe, and made much of its promise of exclusive content and curated playlists. In July, online retail giant Amazon rolled out its Prime Music streaming service in the UK, making it available to Amazon Prime customers who pay the annual £79 subscription. At the time of the launch, Amazon had yet to secure the rights to include artists signed to the Universal Music Group, such as Eminem, Kanye West and Abba. Rumours abound that Facebook is also planning to enter the music streaming market.

Streaming is not to everyone's taste, however. In June, Neil Young pulled his music from all platforms due to his dismay at the poor sound quality of the audio files used by streaming sites. 'I don't feel right allowing this to be sold to my fans. It's bad for my music,' the 69-year-old Canadian rocker wrote in a post on Facebook. Young has long campaigned for better audio quality and in October 2014 he launched his own digital music device, the PonoPlayer, a portable unit shaped like a Toblerone that could store hundreds of high-quality lossless-audio files. Six months later, it has yet to really catch on.

In April 2015, Geoff Barrow of the Bristol band Portishead raised eyebrows when he claimed he had received, after tax, just £1,700 when his music had been streamed 34,000,000 times. 'I've got nothing against streaming a record, but I've got a lot against people giving my work away for free,' he said, questioning the integrity of his record label, Universal. In September, Radiohead frontman Thom Yorke sidestepped the system altogether when he released his second solo album, *Tomorrow's Modern Boxes,* as an experiment via the BitTorrent file-sharing site. Users could either pay $6 for the full album or download a free bundle containing a single track, 'A Brain in a Bottle', and its accompanying video. By the end of 2014, BitTorrent claimed that the bundle had been downloaded 4.4 million times, though did not specify how many users had paid for the album.

## LIVE SPECTACLES
In August, the reclusive British singer Kate Bush performed a series of 22 sold-out concerts at London's Hammersmith Apollo. Titled 'Before the Dawn', these were her first live shows since 1979's 'Tour of Life', when she was 20 years old, and largely drew on material from her *Hounds of Love* and *Aerial* albums to create a highly conceptual event. The ambitious multimedia show used puppetry, video, 3D animation, dancers and a world-class rock ensemble to bring Bush's singular vision to life, notably during 'The Ninth Wave' song cycle, taken from 1985's *Hounds of Love,* in which a shipwrecked Bush plunges into an icy sea before being rescued by strange subaquatic creatures. 'Before the

Dawn' received rapturous reviews, which helped propel her back catalogue into the charts. The surge in interest resulted in Bush becoming the first female artist in history to have eight of her albums in the Top 40 at the same time; only Elvis Presley and The Beatles have bettered this. With the concert series completed in September, Bush withdrew from public life once more.

Throughout the year the American rapper Kanye West continued to cut a compellingly contentious figure whose every action and proclamation, however trivial or self-serving, was reported and analysed by an infatuated media. In January, West surprised many when he teamed up with Paul McCartney for two singles, the sentimental ballads 'Only One' and 'FourFiveSeconds', which features Rihanna, and led to some younger West fans taking to Twitter to ask, 'Who is this Paul McCartney?' When West was announced as the Saturday-night headliner at June's Glastonbury Festival, some 135,000 outraged festival-goers signed a petition calling for the rapper to be removed from the prestigious slot. At the festival, West's hugely anticipated set, performed solo beneath a lowered bank of white lights and, later, above the stage from the platform of a cherry-picker, divided opinion from critics and fans, many of whom deemed the show self-indulgent and under-rehearsed, and criticised West for failing to engage with the crowd. Towards the end of the set West declared, 'You are now watching the greatest living rock star on the planet.' A moment of light relief occurred when the comedian Simon Brodkin, in his Lee Nelson guise, ran onstage and appeared to spar with West, only to be escorted off by security.

The festival also saw Florence + the Machine pushed up the bill to headline the Pyramid Stage on the Friday, following the cancellation of US rockers Foo Fighters after frontman Dave Grohl broke his leg onstage at a concert in Gothenburg two weeks earlier. This capped a triumphant June for Florence Welch, whose stirring third album *How Big, How Blue, How Beautiful* topped charts in the UK and US upon its release.

## VINYL RESURGENCE
The continuing resurgence in sales of vinyl records was recognised by the Official Chart Company in April with the announcement of the first-ever weekly Official Vinyl Chart for albums and singles. Sales of the format reached a 20-year high in 2014, with 1.3 million LPs sold, an increase of 69 per cent year-on-year, though this accounts for just 1.5 per cent of total album sales, suggesting that the format is still very much a niche concern. Nevertheless, in November, Pink Floyd's 15th and final album *The Endless River* sold 6,000 vinyl copies in its first week of release, making it the fastest-selling LP since 1997. Other big vinyl sellers this year included new albums by Noel Gallagher's High Flying Birds *(Chasing Yesterday),* Jamie xx *(In Colour)* and the self-titled debut by Brighton duo Royal Blood. With an infectious style similar to the garage-rock of The White Stripes, Royal Blood's rapid ascent this year helped their album to become the fastest-selling rock debut in three years when it sold 66,000 copies in its first week in August. In general, though, the vinyl chart continues to log the enduring popularity of albums by Pink Floyd, Nirvana, Oasis and Led Zeppelin, whose catalogues are regularly plundered for reissue in a bid to attract this new generation of vinyl consumers.

## CULT FIGURES OLD AND NEW
In August 2014, a lime-green blimp bearing the logo of the cult electronic producer Aphex Twin was spotted floating over Hackney in east London, signalling the arrival of the Cornishman's first new album in 13 years. Released in September, *Syro* found Richard James in good humour and

exploring familiar themes, though some argued that the 43-year-old had nothing new to say. The album entered the UK top ten and in February won a Grammy for Best Dance/Electronic Album. Appearing to enjoy his return to the spotlight, James began to upload scores of unreleased tracks from his fabled archive, spanning three decades, to the SoundCloud online platform, direct to his hundreds of thousands of fans.

The Icelandic singer Björk hit the headlines in January when her ninth album *Vulnicura* was leaked two months before its official release date, prompting her to make it available online immediately. An intensely personal collection of songs detailing the break-up of her relationship with the American artist Matthew Barney, the orchestral electronics and raw emotion of Vulnicura – a construct of 'vulnerable' and 'cure', perhaps – challenged listeners to empathise with the singer. Less impressive, it seems, was the career-spanning exhibition 'Björk' at New York's Museum of Modern Art (MoMA), a populist look at the singer's life which opened in March and aimed to emulate the success of the wildly popular 'David Bowie Is' retrospective. *The Guardian* called it 'a strangely unambitious hotchpotch', while ARTnews felt that the show 'turns MoMA into Planet Hollywood'.

Easing with some elegance into Björk's slipstream, the singer and dancer FKA twigs released her debut *LP1* in August to considerable acclaim. On record, Tahliah Barnett, 27, originally from Gloucestershire, conjured intoxicating electronic erotica that, when performed live and combined with her sensual modern-dance routines, helped to fashion her FKA twigs persona into an alluring proposition. Barnett found herself attracting unwanted press attention following her engagement to the *Twilight* actor Robert Pattinson.

In July, meanwhile, the veteran Nottingham post-punk duo Sleaford Mods sealed a remarkable 12 months with the release of their eighth album *Key Markets*. Its predecessor, *Divide and Exit,* came out in May 2014 and in the period between, Sleaford Mods' witty and aggressive songs about small-town life, delivered in Jason Williamson's East Midlands sneer, seemed to capture the mood of a certain tranche of the record-buying public. Having plugged away on their own terms for years, Williamson and Andrew Fearn, both in their mid-40s, were able to give up their office-bound day jobs and focus on becoming professional musicians. Williamson could also be found ranting feverishly on new albums by 90s dance heavyweights The Prodigy and Leftfield.

## AWARDS

### BRIT AWARDS 2015
British Male Solo Artist – Ed Sheeran
British Female Solo Artist – Paloma Faith
British Group – Royal Blood
British Single – Mark Ronson featuring Bruno Mars, 'Uptown Funk'
British Album – Ed Sheeran, *x*
Critics' Choice – James Bay
International Male Solo Artist – Pharrell Williams

International Female Solo Artist – Taylor Swift
British Breakthrough Act – Sam Smith
International Group – Foo Fighters
British Global Success – Sam Smith
British Producer – Paul Epworth

### MERCURY MUSIC PRIZE 2014
Young Fathers, *Dead*

### NME AWARDS 2015
British Band – Kasabian
Album – Kasabian, *48:13*
Track – Jamie T, 'Zombie'
Solo Artist – Jake Bugg
Live Band – Royal Blood
New Band – Royal Blood
International Band – Foo Fighters
Festival – Glastonbury
Worst Band – 5 Seconds of Summer
Villain of the Year – Nigel Farage

### EUROVISION SONG CONTEST WINNER 2015
Måns Zelmerlöw, 'Heroes' (Sweden)

### MUSIC OF BLACK ORIGIN (MOBO) AWARDS 2014
Best Female – Jessie J
Best Male– Sam Smith
Best Song – Sam Smith, 'Stay With Me'
Best Album – Sam Smith, *In the Lonely Hour*
Best Newcomer – Ella Eyre
Best International – Beyoncé
Best Gospel – Living Faith Connections Choir
Best Jazz – Zara McFarlane
Best Reggae – Stylo G
Best African Act – Fuse ODG
Best R&B/Soul – Sam Smith
Best Hip-Hop – Krept and Konan
Best Grime – Stormzy

### IVOR NOVELLO AWARDS 2015
PRS for Music Most Performed Work – Clean Bandit, 'Rather Be'
Best Television Soundtrack – Natalie Holt and Martin Phipps, *The Honourable Woman*
Best Contemporary Song – Clean Bandit, 'Rather Be'
Best Original Film Score – David Holmes, *'71*
The Ivors Inspiration Award – James Dean Bradfield, Sean Moore and Nicky Wire (Manic Street Preachers)
Album Award – Bombay Bicycle Club, *So Long, See You Tomorrow*
PRS for Music Outstanding Contribution to British Music – Boy George
Best Song Musically and Lyrically – Hozier, 'Take Me to Church'
Songwriter of the Year – Ed Sheeran
Outstanding Song Collection – Albert Hammond
Lifetime Achievement – Geezer Butler, Tony Iommi, Ozzy Osbourne and Bill Ward (Black Sabbath)
PRS for Music Special International Award – Paul Williams

# PARLIAMENT

*Patrick Robathan*

The final session of the 2010 parliament saw the coalition government defeated on a further ten occasions in the House of Lords, mainly on the criminal justice and courts bill. By agreeing to so many urgent questions, the total that the Speaker, John Bercow, granted over the whole parliament rose to an unprecedented 159, meaning a relevant minister had to come to the Commons to answer for the government, with no prior notice. The coalition remained united until the end of the session – although the presentation of what many saw as an alternative budget by the Liberal Democrat chief secretary to the Treasury put this under some strain – and most of their legislative programme was approved. The session ended with the defeat of what many MPs saw as an attempt by the government to prevent the re-election of the incumbent Speaker following the general election.

When MPs returned to Westminster on 13 October, 2014 health secretary Jeremy Hunt updated MPs on the government's response to the ebola epidemic in west Africa. Scotland secretary Alistair Carmichael made a statement about the position of Scotland within the UK, following the referendum on Scottish independence, publishing a factual summary of the proposals for further devolution from each of the three pro-UK parties and promising to 'reach an agreement that will provide the enhanced powers to the people of Scotland and accountability for the Scottish parliament while retaining the strength and benefits of being part of the United Kingdom.' Labour MP Grahame Morris introduced a debate calling for the recognition of the state of Palestine alongside the state of Israel, which, although not binding on the government, was passed by 274 votes to 12. On 16 October, the minister for business and enterprise, Matthew Hancock, responded to an urgent question on the proposal for Tata Steel to sell its long products division. Foreign secretary Philip Hammond made a statement on Iraq and Syria following the killing of Alan Henning, David Haines and two American hostages.

On 22 October the home secretary, Theresa May, responded to an urgent question from her Labour shadow Yvette Cooper about the removal of foreign offenders. On 23 October Jeremy Hunt replied to an urgent question from his Labour shadow, Andy Burnham, on the Five Year Forward View for the NHS.

On 27 October, the day after British forces concluded their combat mission in Afghanistan, prime minister David Cameron reported back on the European Council. The Labour work and pensions spokesperson, Kate Green, moved a motion calling for welfare reform minister Lord Freud to be dismissed following his reported remark that the work of disabled people was not worth the minimum wage; it was defeated by 302 votes to 243. On 30 October, immigration minister James Brokenshire responded to an urgent question about why the government had decided not to support search and rescue operations for refugees and migrants in the Mediterranean.

On 3 November, Theresa May made a statement on the independent inquiry into child abuse, following the resignation of the panel's chair, Fiona Woolf. On 4 November, communities and local government secretary Eric Pickles made a statement about the London borough of Tower Hamlets and his decision to put in place a team of three commissioners to oversee certain functions of the

council until 31 March 2017. On 5 November, Matthew Hancock replied to an urgent question about the government's response to the 2,600 job cuts announced by Rolls-Royce (Aerospace Group). On 6 November, energy and climate change secretary Edward Davey delivered the government's annual energy statement.

On 10 November, the chancellor, George Osborne, responded to an urgent question clarifying his agreement on the European Union budget surcharge. On 11 November Theresa May replied to an urgent question on the Wanless review into how the Home Office had acted on information it received in the 1980s about child abuse. Justice secretary Chris Grayling made a statement on possible recording of telephone calls between prisoners and their constituency MPs.

On 17 November, defence minister Julian Brazier replied to an urgent question on army reserve recruitment. David Cameron reported on the G20 summit in Brisbane and the murder of American aid worker Peter Kassig. Environment secretary Elizabeth Truss made a statement on a confirmed case of avian flu at a duck-breeding farm in east Yorkshire: 'the risk to public health is very low'.

On 25 November the prime minister made a statement on the publication of the intelligence and security committee report into the murder of Fusilier Lee Rigby. Philip Hammond made a statement on the negotiations between the E3+3 and Iran regarding the future of Iran's nuclear programme. Work and pensions secretary Iain Duncan Smith made a statement about the roll-out of the next part of universal credit. On 27 November, Alistair Carmichael made a statement on further devolution in Scotland and the publication of the heads of agreement resulting from Lord Smith's five-party talks, which would lead to draft legislation in January. Defence secretary Michael Fallon made the quarterly statement on Afghanistan: 'the campaign was long, but it was worthwhile, and we believe that we have given Afghanistan the best chance of a safer future'.

On 1 December, Patrick McLoughlin made a statement about plans to invest £15bn in England's strategic road network. Jeremy Hunt made a statement on the implementation of the NHS Five Year Forward View: 'a long-term plan for the economy; a long-term plan for the NHS'. On 2 December the Speaker granted an emergency debate to the Conservative chair of the foreign affairs committee on the ban by China on that committee visiting Hong Kong.

## AUTUMN STATEMENT

Chancellor George Osborne delivered the final Autumn Statement of the 2010 parliament on 3 December. The main points were:

- the UK's is the fastest growing G7 economy
- 3 per cent growth forecast for 2014 and 2.4 per cent growth for 2015
- unemployment forecast to fall to 5.4 per cent in 2015
- inflation predicted to be 1.5 per cent in 2014, falling to 1.2 per cent in 2015
- reform of stamp duty on residential property
- borrowing forecast to fall from £97.5bn in 2013–14 to £91.3bn in 2014–15
- deficit projected to fall to £75.9bn in 2015–6
- fuel duty to be frozen
- personal tax allowance to increase to £10,600 in April 2015
- higher rate income tax threshold to rise to £42,385 in 2015

- new £90,000 charge for non-domiciled residents who have lived in the UK for 17 of the past 20 years
- £2bn extra for the NHS every year until 2020
- corporation tax to be devolved to Northern Ireland if the Stormont executive can manage the 'financial implications'
- income tax to be devolved in full to the Scottish parliament

The chancellor said: 'Four-and-a-half years ago, our economy was in crisis. People questioned whether Britain could remain among the front-rank economic nations of the world, but we set a course to restore stability, to get on top of our debts and to show that Britain was not going to be counted out. Now Britain is on course for surplus, on course for lower taxes, on course for more jobs, on course for higher growth and on course for a truly national recovery – a long-term economic plan on course to prosperity.' Shadow chancellor Ed Balls countered: 'We need a recovery for the many, not just a few. We need to balance the books fairly. We need a long-term plan to save our NHS. That is the autumn statement that we needed. It will take a Labour government to deliver it.'

On 4 December, pensions minister Steve Webb announced the annual pensions and benefits uprating for 2015–16, with the basic state pension increasing by 2.5 per cent.

On 8 December, Foreign Office minister Tobias Ellwood replied to an urgent question from the Labour chair of the home affairs committee, Keith Vaz, on the death of Luke Somers and the safety of British citizens in Yemen. On 10 December James Brokenshire responded to an urgent question about the resettlement of vulnerable Syria refugees. Education secretary Nicky Morgan made a statement on the next phase of the government's plan for education, preparing young people for the world of work.

On 15 December Michael Fallon replied to an urgent question from his Labour shadow Vernon Coaker on the role of UK armed forces in Iraq. Northern Ireland secretary Theresa Villiers responded to an urgent question from her Labour shadow Ivan Lewis on the talks process in Northern Ireland following the prime minister's visit: 'ultimately, whether an overall agreement is reached will be down to Northern Ireland's political leaders. They have the chance to show that, once again, they can move Northern Ireland forward towards a better future in which politics works, the economy grows and society is stronger and more united. That is the prize on offer.' On 16 December the Leader of the Commons, William Hague, made a statement on the implications of devolution for England: 'whichever option is ultimately decided upon must be clear, decisive and effective in producing fairness for the whole United Kingdom'. For Labour, Sadiq Khan said: 'we must consider the unintended consequences of our actions and think through the way changes are interrelated and interdependent. There should be no more backroom stitch-ups.' On 17 December Michael Fallon made a statement on the report into the al-Sweady inquiry into allegations that British forces tortured and executed up to 20 Iraqi men and mistreated nine others in 2004: 'it is now beyond doubt that those allegations were without foundation'. On 18 December Jeremy Hunt replied to an urgent question on plans to help accident and emergency (A&E) departments and ambulance services cope with winter pressures. Matthew Hancock responded to an urgent question on the publication of the government's anti-corruption plan. Local government minister Kris Hopkins made a statement on funding for local authorities in England in 2015: 'we have kept the overall reduction to 1.8 per cent – lower than last year, and one of the lowest levels of reduction under this government.'

On 5 January 2015, Patrick McLoughlin replied to an urgent question on the major disruptions to Britain's rail network over the Christmas period, which he described as 'totally unacceptable'. Jeremy Hunt made a statement about the UK's Ebola preparedness and the care being given to Pauline Cafferkey, an NHS nurse being treated for Ebola at the Royal Free Hospital in London. On 7 January Jeremy Hunt replied to an urgent question on the major incidents declared at a number of hospitals and on A&E performance in England. Theresa Villiers made a statement on the political talks in Northern Ireland culminating in the Stormont House agreement on 23 December: 'this agreement gives the five parties in the devolved executive the chance to refocus and work together with renewed confidence for a more prosperous, more stable, more united and more secure future'.

On 12 January Foreign Office minister Hugo Swire replied to an urgent question on the situation in Nigeria. On 13 January Edward Davey responded to an urgent question on the Nuclear Decommissioning Authority announcement of a change to its commercial model at Sellafield. On 14 January Theresa May made a statement about the terrorist attacks in Paris, and the threat from terrorism in the UK.

On 21 January Tobias Ellwood replied to an urgent question on clashes between the Houthis and Yemeni security forces in Yemen. On 22 January Theresa May responded to an urgent question on the child abuse inquiry; the second nominee to chair the inquiry had, like the first, resigned after it became apparent that they did not command the full confidence of victims. Scottish Office minister David Mundell made a statement about the further devolution process in Scotland and the publication of draft clauses to implement the Smith commission agreement.

On 27 January Theresa Villiers replied to an urgent question from Democratic Unionist MP Ian Paisley about recent developments relating to the 'on-the-run' letters: 'there is no amnesty, immunity or exemption from prosecution . . . if the evidence is sufficient to warrant prosecution, they will be prosecuted.' On 28 January Jeremy Hunt replied to an urgent question about guidance issued by NHS England on declaring a major incident: 'the Opposition have tried to spin as part of their policy to "weaponise the NHS" – this government will support NHS workers, not try to turn their efforts into a political football'. On 29 January Nicky Morgan updated the Commons on progress in implementing the recommendations contained in Peter Clarke's report on Birmingham schools. The minister for universities, science and cities, Greg Clark, made a statement about growth deals, 'which will fuel the resurgence of our local economies'. MPs passed without division a motion moved by David Davis (C.) that 'this House regrets that the Iraq inquiry has decided to defer publication of its report until after 7 May 2015'.

On 2 February the care services minister Norman Lamb answered an urgent question on the availability of child and adolescent mental health in-patient beds. On 4 February Theresa May announced the appointment of Justice Lowell Goddard, a judge of the High Court of New Zealand, as the chairman of the independent inquiry into child sexual abuse. She had also decided to set up a new statutory inquiry under the 2005 Act with a new panel. Eric Pickles made a statement on Louise Casey's inspection of Rotherham council, which had revealed the council's failure to accept, understand or combat the crimes of child sexual exploitation, proposing an intervention package to restore good local governance.

On 9 February the financial secretary to the Treasury, David Gauke, answered an urgent question on tax avoidance and evasion by HSBC. On 10 February Philip Hammond made a statement on the situation in Ukraine: 'civilised nations do not behave in the way Russia under Putin has behaved towards Ukraine'. On 11 February Jeremy Hunt made a statement on the government's response to Sir Robert Francis' report on NHS whistleblowing and on progress in implementing previous recommendations from the public inquiry into the failures of care at Mid Staffordshire NHS Foundation Trust: 'today is about tackling that culture challenge head on so that we build an NHS that supports staff to deliver the highest standards of safe and compassionate care and that avoids the mistakes that have led to both unacceptable waste and unspeakable tragedy.'

On 23 February George Osborne replied to an urgent question on the HSBC tax avoidance scandal: 'unlike the previous government, this government are taking action now and will do so again at the Budget'. David Cameron reported back on the European Council meeting. On 25 February Michael Fallon responded to an urgent question on the deployment of UK personnel to train Ukrainian forces: 'where we can help a friend with non-lethal equipment, we should do so'. On 26 February Jeremy Hunt updated the Commons on the NHS investigations into Jimmy Savile, publishing a further 16 investigations into his activities, including the main report from Stoke Mandeville hospital: 'we must show by our deeds as well as our words that we have learned the necessary lessons'.

On 2 March Theresa May responded to an urgent question on the government's counter-terrorism policy and the implications for individuals travelling to the Iraq/Syria conflict zones: 'tackling the extremist threat needs everyone to play their part. It requires educational institutions, social media companies, communities, religious leaders and families to help to protect people vulnerable to radicalisation and to confront this poisonous ideology.' On 3 March Nicky Morgan answered an urgent question on the serious case review into child sexual exploitation in Oxfordshire. Jeremy Hunt made a statement on the investigation into the care of mothers and babies at the University Hospitals of Morecambe Bay NHS Foundation Trust: 'despite many challenges, NHS staff have made excellent progress recently in improving the quality of care, with the highest ever ratings from the public for safety and compassionate care. The tragedy must strengthen our resolve to deliver real and lasting culture change so that these mistakes are never repeated.' Local government minister Brandon Lewis updated the Commons on the government's ambition to create a new garden city at Ebbsfleet.

On 9 March the Speaker made a statement on the serious breach of security over the weekend in the Palace of Westminster. On 10 March Eric Pickles made a statement on the troubled families programme. The minister for the Cabinet Office, Francis Maude, made a statement on trade unions in the civil service, eight departments having notified trade unions that they intend to end the practice of deducting union subscriptions from salaries. On 12 March the international development secretary Justine Greening updated the Commons on the Ebola outbreak in west Africa.

THE BUDGET AND FINANCE BILL 2015
Chancellor George Osborne delivered his sixth budget on 18 March. The main points included:
- the UK economy grew 2.6 per cent in 2014, faster than any other advanced economy but lower than the 3 per cent predicted in December 2014; 2.5 per cent growth forecast in 2015
- inflation projected to fall to 0.2 per cent in 2015
- borrowing forecast to fall from £97.5bn in 2013–14 to £90.2bn in 2014–15
- debt as a share of GDP to fall from 80.4 per cent in 2014 to 80.2 per cent in 2015–16
- the public spending squeeze to end in 2019–20, a year earlier than planned
- duty on beer cut by 1p a pint and on cider by 2p; 2 per cent cut in duty on spirits; duty on wine frozen

- no changes to gambling taxes
- tobacco duties set to rise by 2 per cent above inflation
- a new 'horse racing betting right' to replace the horse race betting levy
- petrol duty to be frozen; September's planned increase cancelled
- annual tax returns on paper to be replaced by digital accounts
- a new 'help to buy' ISA for first-time buyers to allow the government to add £50 to every £200 saved for a house deposit
- a review of business rates
- mental health services to get £1.25bn in extra funding
- Greater Manchester councils to be allowed to keep 100 per cent of growth in business rates
- a new intercity rail franchise for south-west England

Mr Osborne said: 'I present the Budget of an economy that is stronger in every way than the one we inherited – the Budget of an economy taking another big step from austerity to prosperity. We cut the deficit, and confidence is returning. We limited spending, made work pay and backed business, and growth is returning. We gave people control over their savings and helped people own their own homes, and optimism is returning. We have provided clear and decisive economic leadership, and from the depths Britain is returning ... This is the Budget for Britain, the come-back country.' The leader of the Opposition, Ed Miliband, responded, 'never has the gap between the chancellor's rhetoric and the reality of people's lives been greater ... This is a Budget that people will not believe from a government who are not on their side.' After three days of debate the Budget was approved by 334 votes to 250. All stages of a much reduced finance bill were taken in the Commons on 25 March, with the third reading being passed by 307 votes to 226.

On 19 March the chief secretary to the Treasury, Danny Alexander, made a statement on fiscal responsibility and fairness, widely derided as the alternative Liberal Democrat budget statement: 'combining fiscal responsibility with fairness – that is the approach that we as Liberal Democrats have brought to the coalition government ... That is the approach that will deliver a stronger economy and a fairer society.' His Labour shadow Chris Leslie thought, 'what a farce! Why has he been allowed to use the government dispatch box for his party political pleading?'

On 23 March the Speaker announced that the present acting Clerk of the House, David Natzler, should be recommended for appointment as Clerk of the House. David Cameron reported on the outcome of the European Council meeting. Francis Maude made a statement on government savings from efficiency and reform: 'we have shown that we can get more and better for less'. On 24 March, environment minister George Eustice replied to an urgent question on the delivery of the digital-only system for processing the basic payment scheme via the Rural Payments Agency. Francis Maude made a statement on the government's national cyber-security programme: 'we want Britain to benefit from the best digital economy in the world – effective cyber-security is central to that success.' On 26 March, the final day of the 2010 parliament, police minister Mike Penning replied to an urgent question about Lord Justice Pitchford's public inquiry into undercover policing; the inquiry would review and publish the terms of reference for the inquiry by the end of July. Public health minister Jane Ellison responded to an urgent question on the publication of the Penrose inquiry. The final act of the parliament was to debate a motion moved by William Hague to allow for a secret ballot to elect the Speaker in the new parliament, as recommended by the procedure committee; this was defeated by 228 votes to 202. In the Lords, the finance bill was approved and all outstanding bills received royal assent. Parliament was then prorogued for the general election on 7 May 2015, which produced a result that few people foresaw: a majority of 12 for the Conservative party.

## STATE OPENING OF PARLIAMENT AND THE QUEEN'S SPEECH

The Queen's Speech on 27 May, the first Conservative Queen's Speech in nearly two decades, contained details of 26 bills. David Cameron called it a programme 'for working people, from a one-nation government that will bring our country together. We have a clear mandate from the British people, a long-term economic plan that is working, a detailed and compelling manifesto, and we will not waste a single moment in getting on with the task.' The acting Labour leader Harriet Harman felt, 'we fear that the reality of this Queen's Speech will be very different from the rhetoric. At a time when our economy, our constitution and our public services are fragile, we fear that this Tory government will make things worse.' For the Scottish National Party – now officially the third party in the Commons – Angus Robertson thought 'the problem with the Queen's Speech is that there is no recognition in it of the fact that Scotland completely rejected the Tory agenda . . . At a time when people are suffering from the impact of austerity, the Tories are focused on the wrong issues.' After six days of debate a SNP motion of regret was defeated by 318 votes to 60 and the Queen's Speech was approved by 326 votes to 279.

On 28 May the Speaker ruled in response to a point of order from Alex Salmond (SNP) about whether the changes to standing orders the government proposed to bring forward on English votes for English laws (EVEL) would breach the principle that all members of the Commons were equal before the chair: 'I would not accept the motion if it breached the rules of the House, but it is not for the chair to judge the merits of a proposal. It is for the House to decide whether to agree to the government's proposal.' The new culture secretary, John Whittingdale, responded to an urgent question on indictments against FIFA officials: 'this is merely the latest sorry episode to suggest that FIFA is a deeply flawed and corrupt organisation'. On 1 June John Whittingdale returned to the subject following the election of Sepp Blatter as president of FIFA: 'for the good of the game, we must work together to bring about change . . . it is time for Sepp Blatter to go'. On 3 June the Commons paid tribute to the former Liberal Democrat leader Charles Kennedy. On 4 June, health minister Ben Gummer replied to an urgent question on the NHS Success Regime.

On 8 June James Brokenshire replied to an urgent question on the discovery and detention of 68 migrants by the Border Force at Harwich international port, stressing that 'the government are clear that the EU's approach to migratory flows must include the proper management of the external border, the prompt return of those not in genuine need of protection and action to tackle the efforts of the smugglers and traffickers who profit from human misery'. This was followed by the second reading of the Scotland bill, which David Mundell felt represented 'the fulfilment of a promise to the people of Scotland that a no vote in the referendum was not a vote for no change and it delivers on the all-party Smith commission agreement'. Angus Robertson was sceptical: 'in the weeks ahead, the House of Commons will debate amendments that can strengthen the bill. I hope that the government will deliver on their vow, accept the verdict of the electorate and ensure that the bill does deliver what the Scottish people require.' The bill was in committee of the whole house on 15, 29 and 30 June and 6 July. Although some 500 amendments were tabled, none were passed;

Tommy Sheppard (SNP) expressing frustration that Mr Mundell appeared to be resisting any amendment which was contrary to his point of view. On 9 June the European Union referendum bill had its second reading. Foreign secretary Philip Hammond suggested that 'this bill delivers the simple in/out referendum that we promised'. It was passed by 544 votes to 53 (all SNP). The bill was in committee of the whole house on 16 and 18 June. On 10 June David Cameron reported on the G7 meeting in Germany. On 11 June home secretary Theresa May made a statement on the publication of the Anderson Report and parliamentary consideration of investigatory powers, reiterating that the government intended to bring forward legislation. The economic secretary to the Treasury, Harriett Baldwin, made a statement on plans to sell the government's stake in Royal Bank of Scotland and on the sale of half of the government's remaining stake in Royal Mail, stressing that the government would dispose of all their shares in Royal Mail during this parliament.

On 22 June, energy and climate change secretary Amber Rudd made a statement on ending new subsidies for onshore wind: 'an important part of our current and future low-carbon energy mix, but we are reaching the limits of what is affordable and what the public are prepared to accept'. On 24 June Theresa May replied to an urgent question on the management of the border in Calais, where striking French workers had caused significant disruption: 'the most important step to resolving the situation in the Mediterranean is breaking the link between migrants making this dangerous journey and achieving settlement in Europe'. On 25 June transport secretary Patrick McLoughlin made a statement on Network Rail and the chairman stepping down to be replaced by the current transport commissioner in London, Sir Peter Hendy; electrification of Midland Main Line and the trans-Pennine route between Leeds and Manchester would be paused; commuter rail fares would continue to be capped in real terms for the whole of this parliament.

On 29 June David Cameron made a statement on the killing of British nationals in Tunisia, announcing a national one-minute silence the following Friday and pledging that 'we must step up our own efforts to support our agencies in tracking vital online communications, and we will bring forward a draft bill to achieve this'. On the outcome of the European Council, he said: 'we will put the Common Market back at the heart of our membership, get off the treadmill to ever-closer union, address the issue of migration to Britain from the rest of the EU and protect Britain's place in the single market for the long term'. George Osborne made a statement on developments in the financial crisis in Greece and how they might affect British citizens. On 1 July Patrick McLoughlin made a statement on the publication of the final Davies commission report on runway capacity in south-east England, which had concluded that 'Heathrow offers a stronger solution to the UK's aviation capacity and connectivity needs than a second runway at Gatwick', and said he would come back to parliament in autumn 2015 to provide a clear direction on the government's plans. Work and pensions secretary Iain Duncan Smith announced that he would bring forward legislation to remove the existing measures and targets in the Child Poverty Act 2010 but introduce a statutory duty to report on measures of worklessness and educational attainment: 'we need to move from a low wage, high tax, high welfare society to a higher wage, lower tax, lower welfare society'. On 2 July the leader of the Commons, Chris Grayling, made a statement setting out proposals on EVEL – 'we are committed to delivering a balanced and fair constitutional settlement for all the people of the United Kingdom' – and promising to lay draft orders 'in the next few days' for full debate and decision shortly before the summer recess. His Labour shadow Angela Eagle felt: 'It is hard not to conclude that the proposals are not an attempt to address the West Lothian question, but rather a cynical attempt by a government with an overall majority of just 12 to use procedural trickery to manufacture themselves a very much larger one.' The SNP chief whip Pete Wishart called it 'a lot of constitutional bilge and unworkable garbage!'

On 6 July John Whittingdale answered an urgent question on government proposals on concessionary television licences: 'the BBC will take on the cost of providing free television licences for those households with over-75s, phased in from 2018–19, with the BBC taking on the full costs from 2020–21'. George Osborne updated the Commons on the situation in Greece following the referendum there rejecting the creditors' terms: 'the situation risks going from bad to worse, and Britain will be affected the longer the Greek crisis lasts and the worse it gets'. On 7 July the Speaker granted Alistair Carmichael (Liberal Democrat) an emergency debate on EVEL.

## THE SECOND 2015 BUDGET

On 8 July George Osborne presented the first Conservative Budget for 18 years. The key points were:
- a new national living wage of over £9 an hour by 2020
- the government to run a surplus in 2019–20
- the personal tax allowance to increase to £11,000 in April 2016 and the higher rate threshold to £43,000 in 2016–17
- defence spending to be protected
- the family home to be taken out of inheritance tax
- corporation Tax to be cut to 19 per cent in 2017 and 18 per cent in 2020
- insurance premium tax to increase to 9.5 per cent
- permanent non-domiciled status to be ended
- £30m of funding for transport for northern England
- 30 hours of free childcare for three- and four-year-olds
- student maintenance grants to be replaced with loans
- public sector pay to increase by 1 per cent

The chancellor said: 'A Budget that puts security first: the economic security of a country that lives within its means; the financial security of lower taxes and a new national living wage; the national security of a Britain that defends itself and its values. One purpose, one policy, one nation.' Harriet Harman felt 'it does not put working people first; it ducks the big decisions on infrastructure and fails to give businesses the productivity boost they need. He says that he stands up for working people; what he does is make them worse off.' For the SNP, Stewart Hosie said 'it was less of a plan to boost productivity and more a sermon from the high priest of an austerity cult . . . This was not the Budget the country needed and it was not the Budget that those who have suffered most over the past five years should have had to endure.' After five days of debate the Budget was approved by 320 votes to 290. The finance bill was introduced on 14 July and received its second reading on 21 July by 301 votes to 75.

On 13 July the government was defeated in the House of Lords when a motion for a delay to the enactment of the 'waiting days' amendment to universal credit regulations was passed by 11 votes, and they suffered three defeats on amendments to the cities and local government devolution bill. On 14 July Theresa May updated the Commons on action to tackle illegal immigration: 'we are continuing our close collaboration with the French authorities to bolster the security of the ports in northern France; working closely with them to mitigate the consequences of irresponsible French strikers; providing the assistance our hard-working hauliers and the travelling public deserve; and leading the international efforts to tackle this problem in the longer term'. Chris Grayling announced that the government had decided not to press ahead with a motion on relaxing the rules on hunting with dogs, which Pete Wishart described as 'an utter and absolute shambles'. In the Lords the government proposal in the psychoactive substances bill to make supplying new psychoactive substances in prisons an aggravating offence was defeated by 38 votes. On 15 July Philip Hammond made a statement on the outcome of the nuclear negotiations with Iran: 'we now have a common responsibility to ensure that the wider potential benefits of this deal for the region and for the international community as a whole are delivered.' Theresa May made a statement on her decision not to authorise water cannon for use by the police in England and Wales. The Commons began the first of two days of debate on EVEL (the second was scheduled for September, when the substantive motions would be put and debated). In the Lords the government were defeated when an amendment to the cities and local government devolution bill to insert a clause lowering the age for voting in local government elections from 18 to 16 was passed by 67 votes. On 16 July Jeremy Hunt made a statement on measures to improve the safety culture in the NHS, strengthening its transition to a modern, patient-centric healthcare system and the publication of Lord Rose's report 'Better leadership for tomorrow'. John Whittingdale published his consultation paper on the BBC charter review.

On 20 July Ben Gummer replied to an urgent question on the support available to recipients of contaminated blood. The welfare reform and work bill passed its second reading by 308 votes to 124, but some 48 Labour MPs defied their leadership to vote against. In the Lords an amendment to the charities (protection and social investment) bill to insert a clause ensuring that charities are able to dispose of their assets in a way consistent with their charitable purposes was passed by 83 votes, against the wishes of the government. On 21 July, employment minister Priti Patel answered an urgent question on Department for Work and Pensions data on the number of people in receipt of benefit who have died since November 2011: 'the government intend to publish mortality statistics, but before doing so the statistics need to meet the high standards expected of official statistics. Once we have completed that important work, we will publish them.' The Commons then rose for the summer recess. The government suffered their ninth and tenth defeats in the Lords in the first eight weeks of the new parliament when an amendment to the cities and local government devolution bill to prevent the transfer of regulatory functions for the health service to devolved bodies was passed against their wishes by 65 votes, and a proposal to appoint a joint committee to produce a report on the constitutional implications of the government's revised proposals on EVEL by 30 March 2016 was passed by 181 votes. The House of Lords rose for the summer recess on 22 July.

On 7 September David Cameron updated MPs on the situation in the Middle East, confirming that he had authorised an RAF drone strike in Syria which had killed two British IS fighters, and on the refugee crisis in Europe, pledging that the UK would take 20,000 refugees from the camps in the Middle East over the next five years. He also experienced the first defeat for his government in the Commons when 37 Conservative MPs voted against government plans to amend the European Union referendum bill to change the rules limiting government activity during the campaign period, leading to a defeat by 312 votes to 285. On 8 September Theresa Villliers told MPs that despite a request from the DUP, the government did not think the time was right to suspend Northern Ireland's devolved institutions, but that if circumstances changed, the government would review its options. On 11 September Labour MP Rob Marris' private members bill on assisted dying was defeated on a free vote at second reading by 330 votes to 118.

# PUBLIC ACTS OF PARLIAMENT

Public acts included in this list are those which received the royal assent after 20 July 2014. The date stated after each act is the date on which it came into operation. For further information *see* W www.legislation.gov.uk

*Childcare Payments Act 2014 ch. 28* (17 December 2014) makes provision for and in connection with the making of payments to persons towards the costs of childcare; and to restrict the availability of an exemption from income tax in respect of the provision for an employee of childcare, or vouchers for obtaining childcare, under a scheme operated by or on behalf of the employer.

*Taxation of Pensions Act 2014 ch. 30* (17 December 2014) makes provision in connection with the taxation of pensions.

*Stamp Duty Land Tax Act 2015 ch. 1* (12 February 2015) makes provision about stamp duty land tax on residential property transactions and for connected purposes.

*Criminal Justice and Courts Act 2015 ch. 2* (12 February 2015) makes provision about how offenders are dealt with before and after conviction; to create offences invoicing ill-treatment or wilful neglect by a person providing health care or social care; to create an offence of the corrupt or other improper exercise of police powers and privileges; to make provision about offences committed by disqualified drivers; to create an offence of disclosing private sexual photographs or films with intent to cause distress; to amend the offence of meeting a child following sexual grooming; to amend the offence of possession of extreme pornographic images; to make provision about the proceedings and powers of courts and tribunals; to make provision about judicial review; and for connected purposes.

*Social Action, Responsibility and Heroism Act 2015 ch. 3* (12 February 2015) makes provision as to matters to which a court must have regard in determining a claim in negligence or breach of statutory duty.

*Insurance Act 2015 ch. 4* (12 February 2015) makes new provision about insurance contracts; to amend the Third Parties (Rights Against Insurers) Act 2010 in relation to the insured persons to whom that Act applies; and for connected purposes.

*National Insurance Contributions Act 2015 ch. 5* (12 February 2015) makes provision in relation to national insurance contributions; and for connected purposes.

*Counter-Terrorism and Security Act 2015 ch. 6* (12 February 2015) makes provision in relation to terrorism; to make provision about retention of communications data, about information, authority to carry and security in relation to air, sea and rail transport and about reviews by the Special Immigration Appeals Commission against refusals to issue certificates of naturalisation; and for connected purposes.

*Infrastructure Act 2015 ch. 7* (12 February 2015) makes provision for strategic highways companies and the funding of transport services by land; to make provision for the control of invasive non-native species; to make provision about nationally significant infrastructure projects; to make provision about town and country planning; to make provision about the Homes and Communities Agency and Mayoral development corporations; to make provision about the Greater London Authority so far as it exercises functions for the purposes of housing and regeneration; to make provision about HM Land Registry and local land charges; to make provision to enable building regulations to provide for off-site carbon abatement measures; to make provision for giving members of communities the right to buy stakes in local renewable electricity generation facilities; to make provision about maximising economic recovery of petroleum in the United Kingdom; to provide for a levy to be charged on holders of certain energy licences; to enable HM Revenue and Customs to exercise functions in connection with the Extractive Industries Transparency Initiative; to make provision about onshore petroleum and geothermal energy; to make provision about renewable heat incentives; to make provision about the reimbursement of persons who have paid for electricity connections; to make provision to enable the Public Works Loan Commissioners to be abolished; and for connected purposes.

*Pension Schemes Act 2015 ch. 8* (3 March 2015) makes provision about pension schemes, including provision designed to encourage arrangements that offer people different levels of certainty in retirement or that invoice different ways of sharing or pooling risk and provision designed to give people greater flexibility in accessing benefits and to help them make informed decisions about what to do with benefits.

*Serious Crime Act 2015 ch. 9* (3 March 2015) amends the Proceeds of Crime Act 2002, the Computer Misuse Act 1990, Part 4 of the Policing and Crime Act 2009, section 1 of the Children and Young Persons Act 1933, the Sexual Offences Act 2003, the Street Offences Act 1959, the Female Genital Mutilation Act 2003, the Prohibition of Female Genital Mutilation (Scotland) Act 2005, the Prison Act 1952 and the Terrorism Act 2006; to make provision about involvement in organised crime groups and about serious crime prevention orders; to make provision for the seizure and forfeiture of drug-cutting agents; to make it an offence to possess an item that contains advice or guidance about committing sexual offences against children; to create an offence in relation to controlling or coercive behaviour in intimate or family relationships; to make provision for the prevention or restriction of the use of communication devices by persons detained in custodial institutions; to make provision approving for the purposes of section 8 of the European Union Act 2011 certain draft decisions under Article 352 of the Treaty on the Functioning of the European Union relating to serious crime; to make provision about codes of practice that relate to the exercise and performance, in connection with the prevention or detection of serious crime, of powers and duties in relation to communications; and for connected purposes.

*Supply and Appropriation (Anticipation and Adjustments) Act 2015 ch. 10* (26 March 2015) authorises the use of resources for the years ending with 31 March 2014, 31 March 2015 and 31 March 2016; to authorise the issue of sums out of the Consolidated Fund for the years ending with 31 March 2015 and 31 March 2016; and to appropriate the supply authorised by this Act for the years ending with 31 March 2014 and 31 March 2015.

*Finance Act 2015 ch. 11* (26 March 2015) grants certain duties, alters other duties, and amends the law relating to the National Debt and the Public Revenue, and to make further provision in connection with finance.

*International Development (Official Development Assistance Target) Act 2015 ch. 12* (26 March 2015) makes provision about the meeting by the UK of the target for official development assistance (ODA) to constitute 0.7 per cent of gross national income; to make provision for independent verification that ODA is spent efficiently and effectively; and for connected purposes.

*Mutuals' Deferred Shares Act 2015 ch. 13* (26 March 2015) enables the law relating to societies registered and incorporated under the Friendly Societies Act 1992 and certain mutual insurers to be amended to permit or facilitate the issue of deferred shares; and to restrict the voting rights of members who hold such shares.

*House of Lords (Expulsion and Suspension) Act 2015 ch. 14* (26 March 2015) makes provision empowering the House of Lords to expel or suspend members.

*Consumer Rights Act 2015 ch. 15* (26 March 2015) amends the law relating to the rights of consumers and protection of their interests; to make provision about investigatory powers for enforcing the regulation of traders; to make provision about private actions in competition law and the Competition Appeal Tribunal; and for connected purposes.

*Specialist Printing Equipment and Materials (Offences) Act 2015 ch. 16* (26 March 2015) makes provision for an offence in respect of supplies of specialist printing equipment and related materials; and for connected purposes.

*Self-build and Custom Housebuilding Act 2015 ch. 17* (26 March 2015) places a duty on certain public authorities to keep a register of individuals and associations of individuals who wish to acquire serviced plots of land to bring forward self-build and custom housebuilding projects and to place a duty on certain public authorities to have regard to those registers in carrying out planning and other functions.

*Lords Spiritual (Women) Act 2015 ch. 18* (26 March 2015) makes time-limited provision for vacancies among the Lords Spiritual to be filled by bishops who are women.

*Armed Forces (Service Complaints and Financial Assistance) Act 2015 ch. 19* (26 March 2015) makes provision about service complaints; about financial assistance for the armed forces community; and for connected purposes.

*Deregulation Act 2015 ch. 20* (26 March 2015) makes provision for the reduction of burdens resulting from legislation for businesses or other organisations for individuals; to make provision for the repeal of legislation which no longer has practical use; to make provision about the exercise of regulatory functions; and for connected purposes.

*Corporation Tax (Northern Ireland) Act 2015 ch. 21* (26 March 2015) makes provision for and in connection with the creation of a Northern Ireland rate of corporation tax.

*Local Government (Review of Decisions) Act 2015 ch. 22* (26 March 2015) makes provision about the procedure for conducting investigations under Part 3 of the Local Government Act 1974; and to make provision for cases where an authority to which that Part applies takes a decision that affects the holding of an event for a reason relating to health or safety.

*Control of Horses Act 2015 ch. 23* (26 March 2015) makes provision for the taking of action in relation to horses which are on land in England without lawful authority; and for connected purposes.

*House of Commons Commission Act 2015 ch. 24* (26 March 2015) amends the House of Commons (Administration) Act 1978 so as to make provision about the membership of the House of Commons Commission, so as to confer a new strategic function on the Commission, and so as to make provision about the exercise of functions on behalf of the Commission or its members.

*Recall of MPs Act 2015 ch. 25* (26 March 2015) makes provision about the recall of members of the House of Commons; and for connected purposes.

*Small Business, Enterprise and Employment Act 2015 ch. 26* (26 March 2015) makes provision about improved access to finance for businesses and individuals; to make provision about regulatory provisions relating to business and certain voluntary and community bodies; to make provision about the exercise of procurement functions by certain public authorities; to make provision for the creation of a Pubs Code and Adjudicator for the regulation of dealings by pub-owning businesses with their tied pub tenants; to make provision about the regulation of the provision of childcare; to make provision about information relating to the evaluation of education; to make provision about the regulation of companies; to make provision about company filing requirements; to make provision about the disqualification from appointments relating to companies; to make provision about insolvency; to make provision about the law relating to employment; and for connected purposes.

*Local Government (Religious etc. Observances) Act 2015 ch. 27* (26 March 2015) makes provision about the inclusion at local authority meetings of observances that are, and about powers of local authorities in relation to events that to any extent are, religious or related to a religious or philosophical belief.

*Health and Social Care (Safety and Quality) Act 2015 ch. 28* (26 March 2015) makes provision about the safety of health and social care services in England; to make provision about the integration of information relating to users of health and social care services in England; to make provision about the sharing of information relating to an individual for the purposes of providing that individual with health or social care services in England; to make provision about the objectives of the regulatory bodies for health and social care professions and the Professional Standards Authority for Health and Social Care; to make provision about the disposal of cases concerning a person's fitness to practise a health or social care profession; and for connected purposes.

*Health Service Commissioner for England (Complaint Handling) Act 2015 ch. 29* (26 March 2015) makes provision about the handling of complaints by the Health Service Commissioner for England; to require the Commissioner to notify the complainant of the reason for the delay if the investigation of the complaint is not concluded within a 12 month period to require the Commissioner to lay before Parliament an annual report giving details of how long investigations of complaints have taken to be concluded and progress towards meeting a target of concluding investigations within a 12 month period; and for connected purposes.

*Modern Slavery Act 2015 ch. 30* (26 March 2015) makes provision about slavery, servitude and forced or compulsory labour and about human trafficking, including provision for the protection of victims; to make provision for an Independent Anti-slavery Commissioner; and for connected purposes.

*Supply and Appropriation (Main Estimates) Act 2015 ch. 31* (21 July 2015) authorises the use of resources for the year ending with 31 March 2016; to authorise both the issue of sums out of the Consolidated Fund and the application of income for that year; and to appropriate the supply authorised for that year by this Act and by the Supply and Appropriation (Anticipation and Adjustments) Act 2015.

*European Union (Finance) Act 2015 ch. 32* (21 July 2015) approves for the purposes of section 7(1) of the European Union Act 2011 the decision of the Council of 26 May 2014 on the system of own resources of the European Union; and to amend the definition of 'the Treaties' in section 1(2) of the European Communities Act 1972 so as to include that decision.

# SCIENCE AND DISCOVERY

*Storm Dunlop*

## DEFEATED BY DUST
In March 2014, there was worldwide interest when an international team led by the Harvard-Smithsonian Center for Astrophysics announced that, using the BICEP2 instrumentation at the South Pole, they had detected definite evidence of cosmic inflation, the exponential expansion of the universe immediately after the Big Bang, 13.82 billion years ago. Such a discovery would imply confirmation of the existence of gravitational waves, and suggest the existence of a particle called the graviton. However, there was widespread doubt about the discovery, because the effect was far greater than predicted and did not agree with the results from other sensitive experiments, which had not detected any such effects.

In January 2015, the original BICEP2 team and scientists working on data from the European Space Agency's (ESA) Planck spaceprobe confirmed that the original attribution of the observed signal (known technically as B-mode polarisation) to gravitational waves was incorrect. This was shown by the highly sensitive and detailed mapping by Planck of the polarisation arising from dust in our own Milky Way galaxy. New data from the Keck Array (also located at the South Pole) was available to the combined team.

The new study did, however, detect another source of B-mode polarisation, dating back to the early universe. This signal, first detected in 2013 and on much smaller scales, is attributed to gravitational lensing by the massive structures that populated the early universe and deflect photons from the cosmic microwave background during their passage towards us. The combined results from the three experiments put this effect on a very firm basis. Evidence for gravitational waves produced by the assumed inflationary phase immediately after the Big Bang remains to be established, although the new results set a clear upper limit for the size of any such signal.

## HOW LOW CAN YOU GO?
On 10 April 2015, a team at Stanford University, California, announced in *Physical Review Letters* that they had achieved the lowest temperature ever obtained. The temperature, $5 \times 10^{-11}$K (0.00000000005 K), in a gas of some 100,000 rubidium atoms, is just fractionally above absolute zero, 0 K (-273.15°C), at which all molecular motion ceases. It was achieved by using a laser to decelerate individual rubidium atoms by an amount proportional to their initial velocity.

## LHC RESTARTS
On 5 April 2015, the Large Hadron Collider (LHC) at CERN restarted after a break of more than two years for upgrades and repairs, with protons circulating in both directions around the 27-km ring. Actual collisions at the greatly increased (essentially doubled) energy of 13 TeV ($13 \times 10^{12}$ electron volts) between the two contra-circulating beams began on 3 June 2015. It is anticipated that the higher energies will reveal a new domain of sub-atomic physics beyond the current Standard Model. Expectations are that the collisions may reveal new forms of particle, including the theoretical 'partner' particles to those governed by the Standard Model, and which are predicted by supersymmetry.

On 14 July 2015, scientists at the LHC announced findings (which will be communicated to *Physical Review Letters*) that the LHCb experiment had confirmed the existence of a new particle, the pentaquark, consisting of five quarks. Although originally predicted by Murray Gell-Mann and George Zweig in 1964, the pentaquark has been the subject of numerous searches since then and several claims that it had been detected, all of which were subsequently discounted by further experiments. The scientists are confident that their results may only be explained by the existence of the pentaquark. It remains to be established whether the new discovery consists of a single particle, containing five individual quarks, or a weakly bonded pair formed of a meson (one quark and one antiquark) and a baryon (three quarks).

## ROSETTA AND THE 'RUBBER DUCK'
On 6 August 2014, the ESA's Rosetta spacecraft made a rendezvous with periodic comet 67P/Churyumov-Gerasimenko – generally known as '67P' – after a ten-year journey. The comet, which unexpectedly had a 'rubber-duck'-like shape, consisting of a 'head' and a 'body', currently has an orbital period of 6.45 years. Rosetta went into orbit around the comet on 10 September. On 12 November, Rosetta released the Philae probe, which then touched down on the surface, becoming the first spaceprobe to land on a comet. Unfortunately, the mechanisms (a gas thruster, harpoons and ice screws) intended to secure the probe in place malfunctioned, and Philae 'bounced' twice across the surface, ending on its side, wedged in a location where the solar panels were partially shielded from sunlight. However, before its batteries ran down on 15 November 2014, the probe was able to carry out almost all of its suite of observations and broadcast data to the orbiter. On 30 July 2015, in a special issue of *Science*, in a surprising development, it was announced that Philae had discovered a rich array of carbon compounds. One, hydroxyethanal, may initiate the prebiotic formation of sugars, and methanenitrile is a key molecule in the prebiotic synthesis of amino acids and nucleobases. The chemicals have even been described as 'a frozen primordial soup'. The presence of these compounds suggests that comets may have been the source of materials essential to the development of life on Earth.

Other preliminary results were released on 22 January 2015, together with some remarkable photographs. The size of the 'body' is about $4.1 \times 3.3 \times 1.8$km and the 'head' is about $2.6 \times 2.3 \times 1.8$km. The whole comet rotates once in slightly more than 12.4 hours. Measurements of its gravity give a mass of 10 billion tonnes, with a density of about 470kg per cubic metre. This is so low (less than half that of water) that 67P must be highly porous, with some 70–80 per cent empty space and possibly large voids below the surface, which is exceptionally dark, with an albedo (reflectivity) of just 6 per cent. The images required special processing to bring out the details. One significant early finding concerns the deuterium/hydrogen (D/H) ratio of the comet's water. This is higher than the ratio in Earth's water, casting doubt on the hypothesis that water on Earth originates from the impact of water-bearing comets early in the planet's history.

## DWARF PLANETS UNDER INVESTIGATION
For the first time two of the Solar System's dwarf planets are being investigated, both by NASA spaceprobes. On 6 March 2015, the Dawn spaceprobe began to orbit the dwarf planet Ceres, after being launched on 27 September 2007 and spending about a year in 2011–2012 very successfully mapping the asteroid Vesta. The largest of the bodies in the Main Belt between Mars and Jupiter, Ceres is essentially spherical and 950km in diameter. It is very different from the asteroid Vesta, and is suspected to have a rocky core,

surrounded by an icy mantle, and possibly a layer of liquid water. The mission is expected to last about 18 months, with the probe eventually orbiting at an altitude of 325km.

On 14 July 2015, the New Horizons spaceprobe made a fly-by of dwarf planet Pluto and its five satellites. Images from the Hubble Space Telescope revealed the satellites Nix and Hydra in 2005, Kerberos in 2011 and Styx in 2012. The last two have since been confirmed by the New Horizons spaceprobe. All (and the much larger satellite, Charon) are light in colour, possibly icy, except Kerberos, which is extremely dark. Nix and Hydra tumble erratically in their orbit; Styx and Kerberos are suspected to do the same. Saturn's moon Hyperion is the only other satellite known to exhibit such behaviour, thought to arise because the satellites are non-spherical and suffer differential tidal forces.

Although New Horizons sped past Pluto on 14 July 2015, and recorded details of the surface features of both Pluto and Charon, the low power available and the great distance means that it will take 16 months for all the data gathered to be transmitted to Earth, so it will be many years before the information is fully analysed. One result, prior to the fly-by, was that Pluto was found to be slightly larger than previously thought, with a diameter of 2,370km instead of 2,320km. This finding means that rather than the object known as Eris, Pluto is reinstated as the largest object in the Kuiper Belt of distant, icy objects (the Trans-Neptunian Objects, or TNOs). Charon's diameter is unchanged at 1,208km, while that of Nix is about 35km and Hydra, 45km. Ionised nitrogen was found to be streaming from the planet while the probe was still five days away from closest encounter.

Very early results of the fly-by showed that Pluto has areas of terrain with no impact craters, including smooth, polygonal areas bounded by troughs, somewhat resembling a large version of the patterned ground found in Earth's polar regions. The general lack of craters suggests that the terrain has been resurfaced by relatively recent geological activity, possibly within the last 100 million years. There are mountains some 3,300m high and these must consist of water-ice, because solid methane and nitrogen, expected on the surface, have insufficient strength to sustain such high elevations. (Both methane and nitrogen ice have been detected at Pluto's pole.) Charon has more craters but also a system of cliffs and troughs running for some 1,000km across the surface and a canyon that may be 6–9km deep. The discovery of active processes on such small, cold bodies is of major significance, because they are unaffected by tidal forces exerted by a nearby giant planet – as is believed to account for activity observed on certain satellites of Jupiter and Saturn. One possible heat source may be an internal ocean that is gradually freezing, releasing heat in the process.

## MESSENGER AND MERCURY

NASA's highly successful Messenger mission came to an end on 30 April 2015, when the probe, its fuel exhausted, crashed into the north polar region of the planet. Its impact velocity was about 14,000kph and it is believed to have created a crater some 50–60m across. The crater is invisible from Earth, but should be detected when the joint European/Japanese BepiColombo mission (to be launched in 2017) arrives on 1 January 2024.

## HINTS AT THE PAST FROM EARTH'S INNERMOST CORE

For many years, the conventional picture of Earth's interior held that it consisted of the rigid crust (or lithosphere); the mantle, rigid in its outer layer, but viscous at greater depths; a liquid outer core; and a solid inner core. In February 2015, researchers from the USA and China announced in *Nature*

*Geoscience* that they had discovered evidence that the solid inner core (which is about the size of the Moon) is itself divided into two parts. Seismic data suggests that the crystals in the two regions are aligned in different directions, at right-angles to one another. The crystals of the 'inner inner core' have an east–west orientation, unlike those of the 'outer inner core' which are oriented north–south. This distinct difference, together with other evidence, suggests that a major alteration in Earth's magnetic axis occurred early in the planet's history and that initially, some half a billion years ago, the orientation was equatorial, before switching to the current polar direction.

## THE ORIGIN OF PLATE TECTONICS

Earth is unique among the planets in exhibiting highly active plate tectonics, but the origin of the process has been controversial for decades. In a paper published in *Nature* on 17 September 2014, a team from the University of Sydney proposed a mechanism to account for the initiation of plate tectonics. The geological record suggests that when the Earth's crust first formed, it was immobile. At present, tectonic plates form at oceanic ridges where the material is hot and buoyant. As the plates move away from the ridges they cool, become denser and eventually sink back into the mantle. But on the early Earth the interior was far hotter, there was far more volcanic activity, and the plates did not become cool and dense enough to sink.

The new suggestion is that thick, buoyant continents formed in the centres of the immobile plates. These early continents spread horizontally because they were buoyant, and created major stresses on neighbouring plates. Eventually they spread to such an extent that adjacent plates were forced down around their edges. As Earth's interior cooled, the crust and plate mantle became denser, until eventually a self-sustaining process was established.

## 'STOP/GO' IN TECTONIC PLATES

Another mystery concerning tectonic plates is that although their motions are normally slow and take place over tens or even hundreds of millions of years, they may occasionally show abrupt motion over 'just' a million years. In a paper published on 19 January 2015 in the *Proceedings of the National Academy of Sciences,* researchers from Yale University, the University of California, Los Angeles and the Université de Lyon in France propose that these sudden motions are the result of two processes: dense crustal plugs and weakening of mineral grains. It is generally believed that tectonic plates are 'pulled' by the subduction of the underlying slabs in which the material cools and becomes denser, and thus sink down into the mantle. This process would normally proceed smoothly, but occasionally the subducting slabs become detached from their plates and exhibit sudden movement. It is proposed that thick crust is swept into the subduction zone, creating a plug that causes the underlying slab to break. The process is accentuated when mineral grains in the slab begin to shrink, causing it to weaken dramatically. When rupture occurs the plates shift abruptly horizontally. With the release of tension, the continental rocks may suddenly rise vertically.

## THE WAXING AND WANING OF SEAFLOOR VOLCANIC ACTIVITY

Seafloor volcanic activity along the mid-ocean ridges has been generally assumed to be generating lava at a steady rate. But a study published by workers from Columbia University in February 2015 in the journal *Geophysical Research Letters* suggests that undersea volcanoes erupt in regular cycles, which range from two weeks to 100,000 years in length. These surges in activity appear to be related to both short- and long-term changes in the Earth's orbit and sea-level changes. These pulses of activity occur almost exclusively in the first six months of the year. In addition, the long-term alterations in activity possibly assist in triggering climate change. Although it had always been assumed that the large quantities of carbon dioxide emitted by volcanoes on land might influence climate, the contribution of seafloor volcanoes had never been established.

The team monitored present-day activity using highly sensitive seismographs, and also examined long-term volcanic activity reaching back 700,000 years. The long-term data appears to show a periodicity of about 100,000 years. This has long been known as the dominant period of the astronomical Milankovitch cycles, related to changes in the ellipticity of the Earth's orbit and axial tilt and the tidal forces exerted on the Earth as it rotates. Ice begins to accumulate as the orbital eccentricity increases, giving rise to an ice age, but when the eccentricity is greatest, there is a sudden warming pulse. When the ice caps are at their maximum extent, volcanic activity on land is suppressed. Conversely, when water is locked into ice caps, sea levels are lowered. It is thought that the lessened force on the seafloor causes undersea volcanic activity to increase, releasing a major pulse of $CO_2$, which suddenly traps heat in the atmosphere, causing melting of the ice, which in turn then releases pressure on land volcanoes. Earth's climate enters a sudden warm phase. The examination of the long-term volcanic activity appears to confirm this scenario. At present, the Earth's orbital eccentricity is close to its minimum, so seafloor volcanism is quiescent.

But seafloor volcanism also responds to much shorter tidal effects. The study shows that volcanism exhibits fortnightly changes in activity. This is directly related to the combined tidal effects of the Sun and Moon. When sea levels are lowest, there is increased volcanic activity. In addition, all known modern eruptions occur in the period from January to June. In January, Earth is at its closest point to the Sun, so tidal forces are at a maximum, just as they are when Earth's orbit is most eccentric in the far longer 100,000-year cycle.

## THE 'HIATUS' THAT WASN'T
Climate-change and global-warming sceptics have seized upon an apparent plateau in the record of global temperatures in recent years to bolster their argument that such effects are not taking place. In 2013, the Intergovernmental Panel on Climate Change (IPCC) estimated that the surface warming rate from 1998 to 2012 was around one-third to one-half of the average rate from 1951 to 2012. On 11 September 2014, an article by the European Commission's Joint Research Centre showed that the apparent hiatus consisted of a combination of a natural cooling phase, known as multidecadal variability, and a decrease in the secular warming trend. That study did not identify the reason for the latter effect. On 4 June 2015, however, researchers from the National Oceanic and Atmospheric Administration's National Centers for Environmental Information in Asheville, North Carolina published results suggesting that the apparent decrease in the secular trend was not real, but was instead an artefact of incomplete and biased data. The investigators found gaps and bias in both land and sea temperatures, the largest bias affecting sea surface temperatures. When corrected data was substituted for the data used by the IPCC, there was no decrease in the secular warming, which instead exhibited a consistent overall rise.

## GETTING INTO HOT WATER
In the debate about global warming, the effect on the oceans is often ignored, apart from the fact that corals are likely to be adversely affected by higher temperatures. In a report published on 3 July 2015, researchers from the Alfred Wegener Institute, Helmholtz Centre for Polar and Marine Research found that even if it is possible to limit the rise in air temperature to 2°C by 2100, the situation regarding several marine ecosystems would be critical.

Temperatures have risen dramatically in the uppermost layer of the oceans, even to a depth of 700m. From the 1970s, the oceans have absorbed about 93 per cent of the additional heating produced by $CO_2$ emissions, and in the last decade some oceanic species have migrated as much as 400km closer to the poles. Even if, by the year 2100, it is possible to limit the air temperature rise to 2°C, with the increased acidification of oceanic waters through the absorption of $CO_2$, the situation will become critical for warm-water corals and bivalves at tropical and temperate latitudes, which will be unable to form their calcium carbonate skeletons. If the temperature rise exceeds 2°C, most other ecosystems and marine lifeforms will be very adversely affected, many beyond hope of recovery.

## DID VOLCANISM HAVE THE MOST IMPACT?
On 20 December 2014, a team of scientists from Princeton University published in *Science* a definitive geological timescale for the eruption of the Deccan Trap lavas in India. The study confirms that there was a series of massive eruptions 66 million years ago. The effects of this enormous eruption event challenge the widely held theory that the extinction of the non-avian dinosaurs was caused solely by the Chicxulub impact event occurring at the Cretaceous-Palaeogene (K-Pg) boundary.

The main phase of the eruption of the Deccan Traps began approximately 250,000 years before the extinction event, following a weaker earlier phase that lasted about 1 million years. The principal phase lasted some 750,000 years, during which time the volcanoes erupted about 1.1 million $km^3$ of lava. This was about 80–90 per cent of the overall volume of the Deccan Traps. Such an eruptive event would have introduced enormous quantities of gasses into the atmosphere and produced major alterations in Earth's overall climate.

The new research used sophisticated methods of uranium-lead dating to obtain more precise dates than had previously been available. The samples were taken from zircon crystals, which are known to contain a lot of uranium but no lead when they crystallise.

Four of the five known major extinction events in geological history coincide with major eruptive episodes. The K-Pg extinction is the only one known to occur at about the same time as an asteroidal impact.

### *BRONTOSAURUS* IS BACK!
In April 2015, it was announced in the journal *PeerJ* that the 'iconic' name *Brontosaurus,* commonly employed by the public for a whole family of dinosaurs, and which had actually been rejected by palaeontologists about a century ago, had been resurrected. During the 'Bone Wars' of the late 1800s, the team headed by Othniel Charles Marsh discovered two sauropod skeletons, which he considered to be distinct and so named *Apatosaurus ajax* and *Brontosaurus excelsus*. In 1903, after additional specimens had been found, it was thought that the two skeletons were different species within the same scientific genus. As the name *Apatosaurus* had been used first, it took precedence. *Brontosaurus excelsus* thus became *Apatosaurus excelsus:* a distinct species within the *Apatosaurus* genus. But the name *Brontosaurus* remained in common use, probably partly because of its evocative meaning of 'thunder lizard'.

Now an international team of researchers led by Emanuel Tschopp of the New University of Lisbon in Portugal have used statistical techniques to evaluate the differences between the various species and genera of large diplodocid dinosaurs, including the many specimens that have been discovered in recent years. They found conclusive evidence that specimens of *Brontosaurus* formed a completely distinct genus of dinosaur, so that now there are two distinct genera: *Apatosaurus* and *Brontosaurus*.

## MORE NEW HOMININS
In late May 2015, it was announced in *Nature* that a previously unknown species of hominin had been discovered in the Afar region of Ethiopia by an international team led by Dr Yohannes Haile-Selassie of the Cleveland Museum of Natural History in the USA. The jaw bones and teeth have an age of between 3.3 and 3.5 million years. This implies that the species, named *Australopithecus deyiremeda,* existed at the same time as three other, previously known, early hominin species. The most famous of these is *Australopithecus afarensis* ('Lucy'), dated to 2.9–3.8 million years ago, once thought to be a direct human ancestor. In addition there were *Kenyanthropus platyops* found in Kenya in 2001 and *Australopithecus bahrelghazali* discovered in Chad, although there is considerable controversy whether the last does indeed constitute a new species. There is still, in fact, a major debate about whether these fossils represent truly separate species, or belong to a single species with a range of features, just as present-day *Homo sapiens* displays a wide range of regional differences.

Earlier, 4 March 2015 saw the announcement of the discovery in Ethiopia of what is thought to be the earliest fossil of the genus *Homo,* with an age of some 2.8 million years, predating the earliest previous human find by about 400,000 years.

## THE EARLIEST TOOL-MAKERS
On 20 May 2015, an international team of researchers announced in *Nature* that they had discovered the earliest known stone tools. The finds, in the Turkana region of Kenya, have been dated to no less than 3.3 million years ago. This predates the oldest tools previously known by about 700,000 years and suggests that certain proto-humans possessed the necessary cognitive and motor abilities to fashion such tools and that the techniques were not exclusively confined to any of the various *Homo* species, the earliest of which did not appear until about half a million years later.

The actual species that created the tools is currently unknown, but a possible answer may lie in the hominin species known as *Kenyanthropus platytops,* also dated to 3.3 million years ago, and originally discovered in 1999 about 1km from the tool site. Further fragmentary *K. platyops* fossils have been found just a few hundred metres away. Because it is now suspected that there were several hominin species in the same general area, there is also the possibility that the toolmaker was *Australopithecus afarensis,* or even an unknown early species of *Homo.*

There is limited evidence of even earlier tool use from the discovery in 2009 at Dikika in Ethiopia of animal bones bearing slashes and cut marks, suggesting that tools were used to remove flesh from the bones or to crush them to obtain access to the nutrient-rich marrow. These bones have been dated to 3.39 million years ago, but no actual tools have been found at the site so it is unknown if the tools were actually manufactured or simply sharp-edged rocks.

## WAS 'OUT OF AFRICA' EARLIER?
For many years it has been accepted that *Homo sapiens* evolved in Africa some 200,000 years ago, but did not leave the continent until about 60,000 years ago. It is considered that the more primitive *Homo erectus* left Africa much earlier and reached as far as Indonesia. (It is believed that *Homo erectus* gave rise to both the Neanderthals and the Denisovans.) However, there are increasing signs from new

fossil discoveries that the date at which our human species left Africa was very much earlier than previously thought.

In July 2014, researchers from the University of Hawaii and Guangxi Museum of Nationalities in Nanning, China reported the discovery of two teeth from the Luna cave in China's Guangxi Zhuang region. Based on their proportions, the researchers propose that these were from *Homo sapiens* and, from calcite deposits, can be dated to between 75,000 and 125,000 years ago. Another suggestive fossil from China is a jawbone found at Zhirendong, a cave in Guizhou province, with an age of 100,000 years, described by Erik Trinkaus of Washington University in St Louis, Missouri. Trinkhaus has doubts about the teeth from the Luna cave but maintains that the Zhirendong fossil came from *Homo sapiens.*

Fossils that are undoubtedly anatomically modern human have been found at Tam Pa Ling in the Annamite Mountains of Laos and were described on 8 April 2015 in *PLOS One* by researchers from the University of Illinois at Urbana-Champaign and the National Museum of Natural History in Paris. The modern human skull was originally found in 2009 and the nearby jawbone, which exhibits both modern and archaic features, in 2010. The age of both fossils lies between 46,000 and 63,000 years. Although it has been suggested that the mixture of features in the fossils indicates that *Homo sapiens* interbred with more primitive hominins already present in the area, it is probably more likely that the apparent differences reflect variations within a single species.

The great diversity of hominin species in the Far East is demonstrated by a much older fossil jawbone recovered by fishermen some 25km offshore from Taiwan. This fossil, known as the Penghu jawbone, is very robust and appears to have an age of about 200,000 years, or just possibly as much as 450,000 years. It may be a late example of a fossil from the species known as *Homo erectus,* which is believed to have been present in eastern Asia as late as 400,000 years ago.

## WHERE DO YOU GET YOUR ENERGY FROM?
In a landmark decision, on 5 February 2015, MPs approved the use of a modified form of in-vitro fertilisation to combat mitochondrial diseases. The treatment creates an embryo from the DNA of the two parents, together with the healthy mitochondria from a third woman. The decision was ratified by the House of Lords on 24 February 2015. Mitochondria, which have their own small, separate set of DNA, completely different from the DNA that determines a person's genetic structure, are passed to a child from the mother alone. They are an essential part of the energy-conversion process occurring in every cell. Diseases caused by faulty mitochondria are particularly debilitating and often result in early death. The technique has been developed at Newcastle University, and the UK became the first country to sanction use of this method. Because the technique introduces permanent changes into the germ line – any improvement being passed on by female patients to their children – certain religious and other groups have voiced various ethical reservations.

On 16 July 2015, a team of scientists from Oregon Health and Science University announced in *Nature* that they had developed two laboratory techniques for harvesting cells with healthy mitochondria from affected patients. Both methods produced healthy stem cells which should, in theory, have the capacity to develop into any type of cell found in the body. If such stem cells could be turned into the desired cell type, they could then be transplanted into the patient to repair defective tissue. Such a technique would offer hope of a cure to existing sufferers from mitochondrial disease. The healthy mitochondria produced by such a technique, however, would not be passed to subsequent generations. Any treatments based on such techniques, however, are unlikely to be developed in the near future.

## THE KEY TO THE COMMON COLD?

On 4 February 2015, a group of researchers from the University of Leeds and the University of York announced in *Proceedings of the National Academy of Sciences* the discovery of the genetic code that determines the method of infection of a significant class of viruses, including the common cold and polio. They were able to determine the function of this code, part of the sequence of ribonucleic acid (RNA) that constitutes the genome of this group of viruses. The researchers were not only able to decipher the effect of the code but also prove that altering the code would disrupt the assembly of virus particles, preventing them from functioning and thus causing disease. The code for virus assembly was 'hidden' within the strand of letters forming the virus genome that creates virus proteins and which has been understood for decades.

The class of viruses concerned are single-strand RNA viruses, which, although the simplest form of virus, remain some of the most potent infectious agents. Quite apart from rhinoviruses, which cause the common cold and also cause more infections per year than any other virus, the group of single-stranded RNA viruses also includes highly debilitating diseases such as polio and chikungunya. The latter disease was once confined to the tropics, being spread primarily by the *Aedes aegypti* mosquito, but in about 2005 mutated into a form that could be transmitted by *Aedes albopictus,* the Asian tiger mosquito. This is able to survive in temperate regions. The Asian strain of chikungunya has spread to the Caribbean and Florida, and is poised to invade the south-eastern USA. The West African strain, a variant, has been detected in Italy and southern France. This one disease poses a major global health problem, so any result that may help in devising means to combat the virus is of major significance.

The methods used to determine the RNA sequence are of great importance in themselves and will be applicable to the study of other major human and animal diseases. The discovery took the form of three steps: first, the determination at a single-molecule level of how the core of the RNA virus packs itself into the outer viral shell; second, the creation of mathematical algorithms able to determine the code that governs the processes at work, and the creation of computer models of the coding system; third, actually 'cracking' the code by using single-molecule fluorescence spectroscopy to observe the codes being used in a single-strand RNA virus. These methods of single-molecule detection and computer modelling offer great potential for future investigations of similar viruses.

## LESSONS FROM EBOLA

The Ebola epidemic, which began in December 2013 and caused more than 11,000 deaths, mainly in the West-African states of Liberia, Guinea and Sierra Leone, produced worldwide alarm and extreme measures to prevent it becoming a global pandemic. It was the stimulus for unprecedented scientific research, into treatment and potential vaccines. Previously, research had been concentrated on vaccines against the Mayinga strain of virus from the outbreak in Zaire in 1976. In March 2015, *The Lancet* carried the report that a team of researchers in China, led by Professor Fengcai Zhu, had successfully tested a vaccine against the strain of virus responsible for the latest outbreak (known as the West African Makona strain of Ebola Zaire virus), and which produced a satisfactory immune response in trial participants. The vaccine was developed by the Beijing Institute of Biotechnology, and Tianjin CanSino Biotechnology in Tianjin, China.

In April 2015, *Nature* reported that an interdisciplinary team from the University of Texas Medical Branch at Galveston and Profectus BioSciences, Inc. had developed a quick-acting vaccine, effective with a single dose against the West-African Makona strain.

In June 2015, researchers from Harvard Medical School, Partners in Health and Boston Children's Hospital announced in *The Lancet* that they had developed a rapid diagnostic test, capable of being used in the field, and able to produce a diagnosis within minutes. Previously, laboratory tests were required and results might not be available for days.

On 31 July 2015, it was announced in *The Lancet* that a vaccine, initially developed by the Public Health Agency in Canada and then by the pharmaceutical company Merck, proved to be 100 per cent effective against Ebola in the field trials in Guinea, when contacts of an infected person were vaccinated immediately.

Although none of these developments came in time to be employed in the West-African outbreak, they illustrate how modern techniques offer the potential for the rapid development of vaccines and other tools that are effective, not just against known strains of a virus, but also against the latest forms of most immediate concern.

The World Health Organization (WHO) announced the West-African outbreak only in March 2014, and has been subject to considerable criticism for the delay and for what was widely perceived as an inadequate response. The WHO commissioned an independent report, published in early July 2015, confirming the failure and suggesting remedies, some of which have already been implemented, to try to ensure that swifter warning and action is taken in future. The report recommended the formtation of a Centre for Emergency Preparedness and Response. Individual countries (including the USA and UK) have announced increased research into the prevention and treatment of such potentially devastating epidemics that could evolve into worldwide pandemics.

## TWO DOWN, ONE TO GO

On 15 November 2014, the US Centers for Disease Control and Prevention announced a major success in the battle to eliminate polio globally. Thanks to extensive vaccination campaigns, the second of the three types of polio virus appears to have been eliminated. Type 3 polio virus has not been detected 'in the wild' for more than two years. (Type 2 polio virus was eradicated in 2013.) The remaining form, Type 1, a severe form, is found in just three countries, Afghanistan, Nigeria and Pakistan. Although there are signs that it may have been conquered in Nigeria, the principal threat from the virus remains the sources in Pakistan, because of the violent campaign by the Pakistani Taliban against vaccination. Despite recent success in the major source areas, Type 1 has now spread to all parts of Pakistan, which increases the threat that it will be reintroduced to other countries.

In August 2014, a report in *Science* announced that trials in India had demonstrated that the most effective method of eradication was the administration of both the oral form and the injection of the vaccine containing the inactivated virus.

## A CANCER BLOOD TEST?

On 26 July 2014, scientists at the University of Bradford announced the development of a simplified blood test which may be capable of detecting a whole range of cancers, possibly even a universal test. They found that patients with cancer have DNA that is more easily damaged by ultraviolet light.

The technique involves exposing white blood cells, which are involved in combating all diseases including cancers, to ultraviolet light. Although the trial involved only three forms of cancer, it was shown that in the presence of cancer, the DNA in the white blood cells was more readily damaged. The technique offers promise of a rapid and relatively easy form of cancer detection, but requires many more trials before it can be shown to be fully effective.

# SPORTS RESULTS

## ALPINE SKIING

### WORLD CUP 2014–15

MEN
*Downhill:* Kjetel Jansrud (Norway), 605pts
*Slalom:* Marcel Hirscher (Austria), 614pts
*Giant Slalom:* Marcel Hirscher (Austria), 690pts
*Super G:* Kjetel Jansrud (Norway), 556pts
*Combined:* Carlo Janka (Switzerland), 140pts
*Overall:* Marcel Hirscher (Austria), 1,448pts

WOMEN
*Downhill:* Lindsey Vonn (USA), 502pts
*Slalom:* Mikaela Shiffrin (USA), 679pts
*Giant Slalom:* Anna Fenninger (Austria), 542pts
*Super G:* Lindsey Vonn (USA), 540pts
*Combined:* Anna Fenninger (Austria), 100pts
*Overall:* Anna Fenninger (Austria), 1,553pts

## AMERICAN FOOTBALL

*AFC Championship 2014-15:* New England Patriots beat
  Indianapolis Colts 45–7
*NFC Championship 2014-15:* Seattle Seahawks beat Green
  Bay Packers 28–22 (OT)
*XLIX Superbowl:* New England Patriots beat Seattle
  Seahawks 28–24

## ANGLING

### NATIONAL CHAMPIONSHIPS 2015
*Individual:* David Cooper
*Individual (ladies):* Lisa Ford

TEAMS
*Division 1:* Daiwa Dorking
*Division 2:* Derbyshire Angling Federation

## ASSOCIATION FOOTBALL

### LEAGUE COMPETITIONS 2014–15

ENGLAND AND WALES
*Premier League*
1. Chelsea, 87pts
2. Manchester City, 79pts
3. Arsenal, 75pts
4. Manchester United, 70pts
*Relegated:* Hull City, Burnley, Queens Park Rangers

*Championship*
1. AFC Bournemouth, 90pts
2. Watford, 89pts
*Play-off winner and third promotion place:* Norwich City
*Relegated:* Millwall, Wigan Athletic, Blackpool

*League One*
1. Bristol City, 99pts
2. Milton Keynes Dons, 91pts
*Play-off winner and third promotion place:* Preston North End
*Relegated:* Notts County, Crawley Town, Leyton Orient,
  Yeovil Town

*League Two*
1. Burton Albion, 94pts
2. Shrewsbury Town, 89pts
3. Bury, 85pts
*Play-off winner and fourth promotion place:* Southend United
*Relegated:* Cheltenham Town, Tranmere Rovers

*National League*
1. Barnet, 92pts
*Play-off winner and second promotion place:* Bristol Rovers
*Relegated:* Alfreton Town, Dartford, Telford United,
  Nuneaton Town*
*Relegated teams go down to National League North or South
dependent on location

*Welsh Premier League*
1. The New Saints, 77pts
2. Bala Town, 59pts
3. Airbus UK Broughton, 58pts

SCOTLAND
*Scottish Premiership*
1. Celtic, 92pts
2. Aberdeen, 75pts
*Relegated:* St Mirren

*Scottish League One*
1. Greenock Moton, 69pts
*Relegated:* Stirling Albion

*Scottish Championship*
1. Heart of Midlothian, 91pts
*Relegated:* Cowdenbeath

*Scottish League Two*
1. Albion Rovers, 71pts
*Also promoted:* Stenhousemuir
*Bottom:* Montrose

NORTHERN IRELAND
*NFIL Premiership*
1. Crusaders, 82pts
2. Linfield, 72pts
3. Glenavon, 66pts

REPUBLIC OF IRELAND
*2014–15 League of Ireland:* 1. Dundalk, 74pts; 2. Cork City,
  72pts; 3. St Patrick's Athletic, 65pts

FRANCE
*Ligue 1:* 1. Paris Saint-Germain, 83pts; 2. Lyon, 75pts;
  3. Monaco, 71pts

GERMANY
*Bundesliga:* 1. Bayern Munich, 79pts; 2. VfL Wolfsburg, 69pts;
  3. Borussia Monchengladbach, 66pts

ITALY
*Serie A:* 1. Juventus, 87pts; 2. Roma, 70pts; 3. Lazio, 69pts

NETHERLANDS
*Eredivisie:* 1. PSV Eindhoven, 88pts; 2. Ajax, 71pts;
  3. AZ Alkmaar, 62pts

SPAIN
*La Liga:* 1. Barcelona, 94pts; 2. Real Madrid, 92pts;
  3. Atletico Madrid, 78pts

### CUP COMPETITIONS 2014–15
ENGLAND
*FA Cup final 2015:* Arsenal beat Aston Villa 4–0
*League Cup final 2015:* Chelsea beat Tottenham Hotspur 2–0
*Football League Trophy final 2015:* Bristol City beat Walsall
  2–0

*FA Vase final 2015:* North Shields beat Glossop North End 2–1
*FA Trophy final 2015:* North Ferriby United beat Wrexham 5–4 on penalties (3–3 aet)
*Community Shield 2015:* Arsenal beat Chelsea 1–0

## WOMEN
*FA Cup final 2015:* Chelsea beat Notts County 1–0
*Women's Super League 2014:* 1. Liverpool, 26pts (GD +9); 2. Chelsea, 26pts (GD +7); 3. Birmingham City, 25pts
*Premier League Cup final 2015:* Charlton Athletic beat Sheffield FC 4–2 on penalties (0–0 aet)

## WALES
*FAW Welsh Cup final 2015:* The New Saints beat Newtown 2–0
*Welsh League Cup final 2015:* The New Saints beat Bala Town 3–0

## SCOTLAND
*Scottish Cup final 2015:* Inverness Caledonian Thistle beat Falkirk 2–1
*League Cup final 2015:* Celtic beat Dundee United 2–0

## NORTHERN IRELAND
*Irish Cup final 2015:* Glentoran beat Portadown 1–0

## EUROPE
*Champions League final 2015:* Barcelona beat Juventus 3–1
*Europa League final 2015:* Sevilla beat Dnipro Dnipropetrovs 3–2

## FIFA BALLON D'OR*
2014 – Cristiano Ronaldo (Portugal)
2013 – Cristiano Ronaldo (Portugal)
2012 – Lionel Messi (Argentina)
2011 – Lionel Messi (Argentina)
2010 – Lionel Messi (Argentina)
2009 – Lionel Messi (Argentina)
2008 – Cristiano Ronaldo (Portugal)
2007 – Kaká (Brazil)
2006 – Fabio Cannavaro (Italy)
2005 – Ronaldinho (Brazil)

* Pre-2010, known as the FIFA World Player of the Year award

## 2015 WOMEN'S FIFA WORLD CUP FINALS
Canada, 6 June–5 July

### GROUP A

| | P | W | D | L | F | A | GD | PTS |
| --- | --- | --- | --- | --- | --- | --- | --- | --- |
| Canada | 3 | 1 | 2 | 0 | 2 | 1 | 1 | 5 |
| China | 3 | 1 | 1 | 1 | 3 | 3 | 0 | 4 |
| Netherlands | 3 | 1 | 1 | 1 | 2 | 2 | 0 | 4 |
| New Zealand | 3 | 0 | 2 | 1 | 2 | 3 | −1 | 2 |

Canada beat China 1–0
Netherlands beat New Zealand 1–0
China beat Netherlands 1–0
Canada drew with New Zealand 0–0
Netherlands drew with Canada 1–1
China drew with New Zealand 2–2

### GROUP B

| | P | W | D | L | F | A | GD | PTS |
| --- | --- | --- | --- | --- | --- | --- | --- | --- |
| Germany | 3 | 2 | 1 | 0 | 15 | 1 | 14 | 7 |
| Norway | 3 | 2 | 1 | 0 | 8 | 2 | 6 | 7 |
| Thailand | 3 | 1 | 0 | 2 | 3 | 10 | −7 | 3 |
| Ivory Coast | 3 | 0 | 0 | 3 | 3 | 16 | −13 | 0 |

Norway beat Thailand 4–0
Germany beat Ivory Coast 10–0
Germany drew with Norway 1–1
Thailand beat Ivory Coast 3–2
Germany beat Thailand 4–0
Norway beat Ivory Coast 3–1

### GROUP C

| | P | W | D | L | F | A | GD | PTS |
| --- | --- | --- | --- | --- | --- | --- | --- | --- |
| Japan | 3 | 3 | 0 | 0 | 4 | 1 | 3 | 9 |
| Cameroon | 3 | 2 | 0 | 1 | 9 | 3 | 6 | 6 |
| Switzerland | 3 | 1 | 0 | 2 | 11 | 4 | 7 | 3 |
| Ecuador | 3 | 0 | 0 | 3 | 1 | 17 | −16 | 0 |

Cameroon beat Ecuador 6–0
Japan beat Switzerland 1–0
Switzerland beat Ecuador 10–1
Japan beat Cameroon 2–1
Japan beat Ecuador 1–0
Cameroon beat Switzerland 2–1

### GROUP D

| | P | W | D | L | F | A | GD | PTS |
| --- | --- | --- | --- | --- | --- | --- | --- | --- |
| USA | 3 | 2 | 1 | 0 | 4 | 1 | 3 | 7 |
| Australia | 3 | 1 | 1 | 1 | 4 | 4 | 0 | 4 |
| Sweden | 3 | 0 | 3 | 0 | 4 | 4 | 0 | 3 |
| Nigeria | 3 | 0 | 1 | 2 | 3 | 6 | −3 | 1 |

Sweden drew with Nigeria 3–3
USA beat Australia 3–1
Australia beat Nigeria 2–0
USA drew with Sweden 0–0
USA beat Nigeria 1–0
Australia drew with Sweden 1–1

### GROUP E

| | P | W | D | L | F | A | GD | PTS |
| --- | --- | --- | --- | --- | --- | --- | --- | --- |
| Brazil | 3 | 3 | 0 | 0 | 4 | 0 | 4 | 9 |
| Rep. of Korea | 3 | 1 | 1 | 1 | 4 | 5 | −1 | 4 |
| Costa Rica | 3 | 0 | 2 | 1 | 3 | 4 | −1 | 2 |
| Spain | 3 | 0 | 1 | 2 | 2 | 4 | −2 | 1 |

Spain drew with Costa Rica 1–1
Brazil beat Rep. of Korea 2–0
Brazil beat Spain 1–0
Rep. of Korea drew with Costa Rica 2–2
Brazil beat Costa Rica 1–0
Rep. of Korea beat Spain 2–1

### GROUP F

| | P | W | D | L | F | A | GD | PTS |
| --- | --- | --- | --- | --- | --- | --- | --- | --- |
| France | 3 | 2 | 0 | 1 | 6 | 2 | 4 | 6 |
| England | 3 | 2 | 0 | 1 | 4 | 3 | 1 | 6 |
| Colombia | 3 | 1 | 1 | 1 | 4 | 3 | 1 | 4 |
| Mexico | 3 | 0 | 1 | 2 | 2 | 8 | −6 | 1 |

France beat England 1–0
Colombia drew with Mexico 1–1
Colombia beat France 2–0
England beat Mexico 2–1
France beat Mexico 5–0
England beat Colombia 2–1

### RANKING OF THIRD-PLACE TEAMS

| | P | W | D | L | F | A | GD | PTS |
| --- | --- | --- | --- | --- | --- | --- | --- | --- |
| Colombia (F) | 3 | 1 | 1 | 1 | 4 | 3 | 1 | 4 |
| Netherlands (A) | 3 | 1 | 1 | 1 | 2 | 2 | 0 | 4 |
| Switzerland (C) | 3 | 1 | 0 | 2 | 11 | 4 | 7 | 3 |
| Sweden (D) | 3 | 0 | 3 | 0 | 4 | 4 | 0 | 3 |
| Thailand (B) | 3 | 1 | 0 | 2 | 3 | 10 | −7 | 3 |
| Costa Rica (E) | 3 | 0 | 2 | 1 | 3 | 4 | −1 | 2 |

LAST 16
Germany beat Sweden 4–1
China beat Cameroon 1–0
Australia beat Brazil 1–0
France beat Rep. of Korea 3–0
Canada beat Switzerland 1–0
England beat Norway 2–1
USA beat Colombia 2–0
Japan beat Netherlands 2–1

QUARTER-FINALS
Germany beat France 5–4 on penalties (1–1 aet)
USA beat China 1–0
Japan beat Australia 1–0
England beat Canada 2–1

SEMI-FINALS
USA beat Germany 2–0
Japan beat England 2–1

3RD PLACE PLAY-OFF
England beat Germany 1–0 (aet)

FINAL
USA beat Japan 5–2

# ATHLETICS

EUROPEAN CROSS COUNTRY CHAMPIONSHIPS
Samokov, Bulgaria, 14 December 2014

SENIOR MEN (10,010m)
*Individual:* Polat Kemboi Arikan (Turkey), 32min 19sec
*Team:* Turkey, 33pts

U23 MEN (7,782m)
*Individual:* Ilgizar Safiulin (Russia), 25min 31sec
*Team:* Russia, 16pts

U20 MEN (6,085m)
*Individual:* Yemaneberhan Crippa (Italy), 20min 07sec
*Team:* Italy, 18pts

SENIOR WOMEN (7,782m)
*Individual:* Gemma Steel (Great Britain), 28min 27sec
*Team:* Great Britain, 21pts

U23 WOMEN (6,085m)
*Individual:* Rhona Auckland (Great Britain), 22min 23sec
*Team:* Russia

U20 WOMEN (3,857m)
*Individual:* Emine Hatun Tuna (Turkey), 14min 13sec
*Team:* Great Britain, 18pts

ENGLISH NATIONAL CROSS COUNTRY
CHAMPIONSHIPS
Parliament Hill, London, 21 February 2015

SENIOR MEN
*Individual:* Charlie Hulson (Sale Harriers Manchester),
    39min 12sec
*Team:* Notts, 213pts

JUNIOR MEN
*Individual:* Jonathan Davies (Reading), 33min 26sec
*Team:* Tonbridge, 53pts

SENIOR WOMEN
*Individual:* Lillian Partridge (Aldershot Farnham & Dist),
    30min 07sec
*Team:* Aldershot Farnham & Dist, 38pts

JUNIOR WOMEN
*Individual:* Rebecca Murray (Bedford & County),
    22min 48sec
*Team:* Aldershot Farnham & Dist, 34pts

EUROPEAN ATHLETICS INDOOR CHAMPIONSHIPS
Prague, Czech Republic, 5–8 March 2015

MEN
*60m:* Richard Kilty (Great Britain), 6.51sec
*400m:* Pavel Maslák (Czech Rep.), 45.33sec
*800m:* Marcin Lewandowski (Poland), 1min 46.67sec
*1500m:* Jakub Holusa (Czech Rep.), 3min 37.68sec
*3000m:* Ali Kaya (Turkey), 7min 38.42sec
*60m Hurdles:* Pascal Martinot-Lagarde (France), 7.49sec
*4 × 400m:* Belgium, 3min 02.87sec
*High Jump:* Daniil Tsyplakov (Russia), 2.31m
*Pole Vault:* Renaud Lavillenie (France), 6.04m
*Long Jump:* Michel Tornéus (Sweden), 8.30m
*Triple Jump:* Nelson Évora (Portugal), 17.21m
*Shot:* David Storl (Germany), 21.23m
*Heptathlon:* Ilya Shkurenyov (Russia), 6,353pts

WOMEN
*60m:* Dafne Schippers (Netherlands), 7.05sec
*400m:* Nataliya Pyhyda (Ukraine), 51.96sec
*800m:* Selina Büchel (Switzerland), 2min 01.95sec
*1500m:* Sifan Hassan (Netherlands), 4min 09.04sec
*3000m:* Yelena Korobkina (Russia), 8min 47.62sec
*60m Hurdles:* Alina Talay (Belarus), 7.85sec
*4 × France, 3min 31.61sec
*High Jump:* Mariya Kuchina (Russia), 1.97m
*Pole Vault:* Anzhelika Sidorova (Russia), 4.80m
*Long Jump:* Ivana Španović (Serbia), 6.98m
*Triple Jump:* Yekaterina Koneva (Russia), 14.69m
*Shot:* Anita Márton (Hungary), 19.23m
*Pentathlon:* Katarina Johnson-Thompson (Great Britain),
    5,000pts

IAAF WORLD CROSS COUNTRY CHAMPIONSHIPS
Guiyang, China, 28 March 2015

SENIOR
*Men (12km):* Geoffrey Kipsang (Kenya), 34min 52sec
*Team:* Ethiopia and Kenya, 20pts
*Women (8km):* Agnes Jebet Tirop (Kenya), 26min 01sec
*Team:* Ethiopia, 17pts

JUNIOR
*Men:* Yasin Haji (Ethiopia), 23min 42sec
*Team:* Kenya, 19pts
*Women:* Letesenbet Gidey (Ethiopia), 19min 48sec
*Team:* Ethiopia, 11pts

LONDON MARATHON
London, 26 April 2015

*Men:* Eliud Kipchoge (Kenya), 2hr 04min 42sec
*Women:* Tigist Tufa (Ethiopia), 2hr 23min 22sec

BRITISH CHAMPIONSHIPS
Alexander Stadium, Birmingham, 3–5 July 2015

MEN
*100m:* Chijindu Ujah (Enfield), 10.10sec
*200m:* Zharnel Hughes (Shaftesbury), 20.42sec
*400m:* Rabah Yousif (Newham), 45.01sec
*800m:* Kyle Langford (Shaftesbury), 1min 49.70sec
*1500m:* Charlie Grice (Brighton), 3min 50.66sec
*5000m:* Thomas Farrell (Border), 13min 42.20sec
*3000m Steeplechase:* Rob Mullett (Lewes), 8min 38.95sec

*110m Hurdles:* Lawrence Clarke (WSE Houns), 13.55sec
*400m Hurdles:* Niall Flannery (Newham), 50.16sec
*5000m Walk:* Tom Bosworth (Tonbridge), 19min 00.73sec
*High Jump:* Robbie Grabarz (Newham), 2.28m
*Pole Vault:* Steven Lewis (Newham), 5.35m
*Long Jump:* Greg Rutherford (Milton Keynes), 8.11m
*Triple Jump:* Julian Reid (Birchfield), 16.95m
*Shot:* Scott Lincoln (York), 18.54m
*Discus:* Brett Morse (Cardiff), 58.83m
*Hammer:* Nick Miller (Border), 75.88m
*Javelin:* Bonne Buwembo (Enfield), 70.34m

WOMEN
*100m:* Diana Asher-Smith (Blackheath), 11.08sec
*200m:* Margaret Adeoye (Enfield), 23.51sec
*400m:* Anyika Onuora (Liverpool), 51.87sec
*800m:* Lynsey Sharp (Edinburgh), 2min 02.40sec
*1500m:* Laura Muir (Dundee), 4min 10.37sec
*5000m:* Stephanie Twell (Aldershot Farnham and Dist),
    15min 38.01sec
*3000m Steeplechase:* Lennie Waite (Aldershot Farnham and
    Dist.), 10min 15.04sec
*100m Hurdles:* Tiffany Porter (Woodford), 12.83sec
*400m Hurdles:* Eilidh Child (Pitreavie), 55.57sec
*5000m Walk:* Johanna Atkinson (Middlesbrough),
    22min 03.55sec
*High Jump:* Isobel Pooley (Aldershot Farnham and Dist.),
    1.97m
*Pole Vault:* Holly Bradshaw (Blackburn), 4.50m
*Long Jump:* Shara Proctor (Birchfield), 6.86m
*Triple Jump:* Sineade Gutzmore (Birchfield), 13.35m
*Shot:* Rachel Wallader (WSE Houns), 17.42m
*Discus:* Jade Lally (Shaftesbury), 57.37m
*Hammer:* Sophie Hitchon (Blackburn), 71.10m
*Javelin:* Izzy Jeffs (North Devon), 53.50m

15TH IAAF WORLD CHAMPIONSHIPS IN
ATHLETICS
Beijing, China, 22–30 August 2015

MEN
*100m:* Usain Bolt (Jamaica), 9.79sec
*200m:* Usain Bolt (Jamaica), 19.55sec
*400m:* Wayde van Niekerk (South Africa), 43.48sec
*800m:* David Rudisha (Kenya), 1min 45.84sec
*1500m:* Asbel Kiprop (Kenya), 3min 34.40sec
*5000m:* Mohamed Farah (Great Britain), 13min 50.38sec
*10,000m:* Mohamed Farah (Great Britain), 27min 01.13sec
*3000m Steeplechase:* Ezekiel Kemboi (Kenya), 8min 11.28sec
*110m Hurdles:* Sergey Shubenkov (Russia), 12.98sec
*400m Hurdles:* Nicholas Bett (Kenya), 47.79sec
*4 × 100m:* Jamaica, 37.36sec
*4 × 400m:* USA, 2min 57.82sec
*20km Walk:* Miguel Angel Lopez (Spain), 1hr 19min 14sec
*50km Walk:* Matej Tóth (Slovakia), 3hr 40min 32sec
*Marathon:* Ghirmay Ghebreslassie (Eritrea), 2hr 12min 28sec
*High Jump:* Derek Drouin (Canada), 2.34m
*Pole Vault:* Shawnacy Barber (Canada), 5.90m
*Long Jump:* Greg Rutherford (Great Britain), 8.41m
*Triple Jump:* Christian Taylor (USA), 18.21m
*Shot:* Joe Kovacs (USA), 21.93m
*Discus:* Piotr Malachowski (Poland), 67.40m
*Hammer:* Pawel Fajdek (Poland), 80.88m
*Javelin:* Julius Yego (Kenya), 92.72m
*Decathlon:* Ashton Eaton (USA), 9,045pts
*800m Masters:* David Heath (Great Britain), 2min 00.92sec

WOMEN
*100m:* Shelly-Ann Fraser-Pryce (Jamaica), 10.76sec
*200m:* Dafne Schippers (Netherlands), 21.63sec

*400m:* Allyson Felix (USA), 49.26sec
*800m:* Maryna Arzamasova (Belarus), 1min 58.03sec
*1500m:* Genzebe Dibaba (Ethiopia), 4min 08.09sec
*5000m:* Almaz Ayana (Ethiopia), 14min 26.83sec
*10,000m:* Vivian Cheruiyot (Kenya), 31min 41.31sec
*3000m Steeplechase:* Hyvin Kiyeng Jepkemoi (Kenya),
    9min 19.11sec
*100m Hurdles:* Danielle Williams (Jamaica), 12.57sec
*400m Hurdles:* Zuzana Hejnová (Czech Rep.), 53.50sec
*4 × 100m:* Jamaica, 41.07sec
*4 × 400m:* Jamaica, 3min 19.13sec
*20km Walk:* Hong Liu (China), 1hr 27min 45sec
*Marathon:* Mare Dibaba (Ethiopia), 2hr 27min 35sec
*High Jump:* Maria Kuchina (Russia), 2.01m
*Pole Vault:* Yarisley Silva (Cuba), 4.90m
*Long Jump:* Tianna Bartoletta (USA), 7.14m
*Triple Jump:* Caterine Ibargüen (Columbia), 14.90m
*Shot:* Christina Schwanitz (Germany), 20.37m
*Discus:* Denia Caballero (Cuba), 69.28m
*Hammer:* Anita Wlodarczyk (Poland), 80.85m
*Javelin:* Kathrina Molitor (Germany), 67.69sec
*Heptathlon:* Jessica Ennis-Hill (Great Britain), 6,669pts
*400m Masters:* Sarah Louise Read Cayton (Great Britain),
    1min 00.05sec

## BADMINTON

WORLD CHAMPIONSHIPS 2015
Jakarta, Indonesia 10–16 August

*Men's Singles:* Chen Long (China) beat Lee Chong Wei
    (Malaysia) 2–0
*Women's Singles:* Carolina Marin (Spain) beat Saina Nehwal
    (India) 2–0
*Men's Doubles:* Mohammad Ahsan and Hendra Setiawan
    (Indonesia) beat Liu Xiaolong and Qiu Zihan (China)
    2–0
*Women's Doubles:* Tian Qing and Zhao Yunlei (China) beat
    Christinna Pedersen and Kamilla Rytter Juhl (Denmark)
    2–1
*Mixed Doubles:* Zhang Nan and Zhao Yunlei (China) beat
    Liu Cheng and Bao Yixin (China) 2–0

ALL-ENGLAND CHAMPIONSHIPS 2015
Birmingham, March

*Men's Singles:* Chen Long (China) beat Jan Jorgensen
    (Denmark) 2–1
*Women's Singles:* Carolina Marin (Spain) beat Saina Nehwal
    (India) 2–1
*Men's Doubles:* Mathias Boe and Carsten Mogensen
    (Denmark) beat Fu Haifeng and Zhang Nan (China) 2–0
*Women's Doubles:* Bao Yixin and Tang Yuanting (China) beat
    Wang Xiaoli and Yu Yang (China) 2–0
*Mixed Doubles:* Zhang Nan and Zhao Yunlei (China) beat
    Tontowi Ahmad and Lilyana Natsir (Indonesia) 2–0

ENGLISH NATIONAL CHAMPIONSHIPS 2015
Milton Keynes, February

*Men's Singles:* Sam Parsons beat Andrew Smith 2–0
*Women's Singles:* Nicola Cerfontyne beat Fontaine Chapman
    2–0
*Men's Doubles:* Marcus Ellis and Chris Langridge beat
    Matthew Nottingham and Harley Towler 2–1
*Women's Doubles:* Heather Olver and Lauren Smith beat
    Jennifer Moore and Victoria Williams 2–0
*Mixed Doubles:* Chris Adcock and Gabrielle Adcock beat
    Gary Fox and Lauren Smith 2–0

SCOTTISH NATIONAL CHAMPIONSHIPS 2015
Perth, February

*Men's Singles:* Keiran Merrilees beat Matthew Carder 2–1
*Women's Singles:* Kirsty Gilmour beat Holly Newall 2–0
*Men's Doubles:* Martin Cambell and Patrick MacHugh beat
 Robert Blair and Gordon Thomson 2–0
*Women's Doubles:* Imogen Bankier and Kirsty Gilmour beat
 Rebekka Findlay and Caitlin Pringle 2–0
*Mixed Doubles:* Robert Blair and Imogen Bankier beat
 Adam Hall and Julie MacPherson 2–0

WELSH NATIONAL CHAMPIONSHIPS 2015
Cardiff, February

*Men's Singles:* Daniel Font beat Tsung Fong Mo 2–0
*Women's Singles:* Carissa Turner beat Aimee Moran 2–0
*Men's Doubles:* Daniel Font and Joe Morgan beat Oliver
 Gwilt and Nic Strange 2–0
*Women's Doubles:* Sarah Thomas and Carissa Turner beat
 Amiee Moran and Ellen Mahenthiralingam 2–0
*Mixed Doubles:* Oliver Gwilt and Emillie Gwilt beat Joe
 Morgan and Sarah Thomas 2–0

## BASEBALL

*American League Championship Series 2014:* Kansas City
 Royals beat Baltimore Orioles 4–0
*National League Championship Series 2014:* San Francisco
 Giants beat St Louis Cardinals 4–1
*World Series 2014:* San Francisco Giants beat Kansas City
 Royals 4–3

## BASKETBALL

BRITISH

MEN
*BBL Play-off final 2015:* Newcastle Eagles beat London
 Lions 96–84
*BBL Trophy final 2015:* Newcastle Eagles beat Leicester
 Riders 96–90
*BBL Cup final 2015:* Newcastle Eagles beat Glasgow Rocks
 84–71
*BBL Champions 2014–15:* Newcastle Eagles

WOMEN
*WBBL Champions 2014–15:* Westfield Heath Sheffield
 Hatters
*WBBL Play-off final 2014–15:* Westfield Heath Sheffield
 Hatters beat Nottingham Wildcats 84–69
*WBBL Trophy 2015:* Westfield Heath Sheffield Hatters beat
 Nottingham Wildcats 76–62

USA – NATIONAL BASKETBALL LEAGUE (NBA)
*Eastern Conference final 2015:* Cleveland Cavaliers beat
 Atlanta Hawks 4–0
*Western Conference final 2015:* Golden State Warriors beat
 Houston Rockets 4–1
*NBA final 2014:* Golden State Warriors beat Cleveland
 Cavaliers 4–2

## BOWLS — INDOOR

WORLD CHAMPIONSHIPS 2015
Great Yarmouth, Norfolk, January

*Men's Singles:* Alex Marshall (Scotland) beat Andy Thomson
 (England) 2–0

*Women's Singles:* Laura Thomas (Wales) beat Katherine
 Rednall (England) 2–0
*Men's Pairs:* Robert Paxton and Simon Skelton (England)
 beat Paul Foster and Alex Marshall (Scotland) 3 –1
*Mixed Pairs:* Robert Paxton and Marion Purcell
 (England/Wales) beat Paul Foster and Laura Thomas
 (Scotland/Wales) 2–1

BRITISH ISLES INDOOR BOWLS CHAMPIONSHIPS
2015
Stanley, March

*Singles:* J. Walker (England) beat D. Doubler (Wales) 21–19
*Pairs:* Scotland beat Wales 23–19
*Triples:* Wales beat England 18–15
*Fours:* Ireland beat England 17–12

ENGLISH NATIONAL CHAMPIONSHIPS 2015
Melton & District IBC, Melton Mowbray , March–April

*Singles:* G. Harlow beat D. Hubbard 21–18
*Pairs:* Desborough beat Riverain 17–15
*Triples:* Cyphers beat Wellingborough 22–15
*Fours:* St Neots beat Bournemouth 21–20
*Liberty Trophy (Inter-County Championship) final:*
 Northamptonshire beat Lincolnshire 110–107
*Champion of Champions (Warner Lakeside, January–February):*
 P. Hartley beat S. Mitchinson 21–12

SCOTTISH NATIONAL CHAMPIONSHIPS 2015
Prestwick, March

*Singles:* East Lothian beat Elgin 21–20
*Pairs:* Arbroath beat Prestwick 22–18
*Triples:* Elgin beat Cumbernauld 20–19
*Fours:* West Lothian beat East Lothian 20–19

## BOWLS — OUTDOOR

BRITISH ISLES CHAMPIONSHIPS 2014
Royal Leamington Spa, June

*Singles:* Wales beat Jersey 21–18
*Pairs:* England beat Scotland 21–14
*Triples:* Ireland beat Scotland 21–14

ENGLISH NATIONAL CHAMPIONSHIPS 2015
Royal Leamington Spa, August

*Singles:* Cumbria beat Yorkshire 21–19
*Pairs:* Somerset beat Buckinghamshire 20–16
*Triples:* Huntingdonshire beat Leicestershire 16–10
*Fours:* Worcestershire beat Devon 19–15
*Middleton Cup:* Devon beat Cumbria 125–113

SCOTTISH NATIONAL CHAMPIONSHIPS 2015
Ayr, August

*Singles:* I. McLean beat S. McCubbin 21–15
*Pairs:* West End Stranraer beat Mauchline 15–13
*Triples:* Inverkeithing beat Crooks Moss 12–8
*Fours:* West Kilbride beat Bainfield 16–10

WELSH NATIONAL CHAMPIONSHIPS 2015
Llandrindod Wells, August

*Singles:* J. Tomlinson beat R. Weale 21–16
*Pairs:* Penylan beat Llanbradach 26–14
*Triples:* Presteigne beat Gilfach Bargoed 17–12
*Fours:* RTB Ebbw Vale beat Merthyr West End 23–15

# BOXING

WORLD CHAMPIONS
as at 19 August 2015

WORLD BOXING COUNCIL (WBC)
*Heavy:* Deontay Wilder (USA)
*Cruiser:* Grigory Drozd (Russia)
*Light-heavy:* Adonis Stevenson (Canada)
*Supermiddle:* Badou Jack (Sweden)
*Middle:* Miguel Cotto (Puerto Rico)
*Interim Middle:* Gennady Golovkin (Kazakhstan)
*Superwelter:* Floyd Mayweather Jr (USA)
*Welter:* Floyd Mayweather Jr (USA)
*Superlight:* vacant
*Light:* Jorge Linares (Venezuela)
*Superfeather:* Takashi Miura (Japan)
*Feather:* Gary Russell Jr (USA)
*Superbantam:* Leo Santa Cruz (Mexico)
*Bantam:* Shinsuke Yamanaka (Japan)
*Superfly:* Carlos Cuadras (Mexico)
*Fly:* Roman Gonzalez (Nicaragua)
*Lightfly:* Pedro Guevara (Mexico)
*Miniflyweight:* Wanheng Menayothin (Thailand)

WORLD BOXING ASSOCIATION (WBA)
*Heavy:* Wladimir Klitschko (Ukraine)
*Cruiser:* Dennis Lebedev (Russia)
*Light-heavy:* Sergey Kovalev (Russia)
*Supermiddle:* Andre Ward (USA)
*Middle:* Gennady Golovkin (Kazakhstan)
*Superwelter:* Floyd Mayweather Jr (USA)
*Welter:* Floyd Mayweather Jr (USA)
*Superlight:* Danny Garcia (USA)
*Light:* Darleys Perez (Colombia)
*Superfeather:* Takashi Uchiyama (Japan)
*Feather:* Jesus Andres Cuellar (Argentina)
*Superbantam:* Guillermo Rigondeaux (Cuba)
*Bantam:* Juan Carlos Payano (Dominican Republic)
*Superfly:* Kohei Kono (Japan)
*Fly:* Juan Francisco Estrada (Mexico)
*Lightfly:* Ryoichi Taguchi (Japan)
*Minimum:* Hekkie Budler (South Africa)

WORLD BOXING ORGANISATION (WBO)
*Heavy:* Wladimir Klitschko (Ukraine)
*Junior-heavy:* Marco Huck (Germany)
*Light-heavy:* Sergey Kovalev (Russia)
*Supermiddle:* Arthur Abraham (Armenia)
*Middle:* Andy Lee (Rep. of Ireland)
*Junior-middle:* vacant
*Welter:* Timothy Bradley (USA)
*Junior-welter:* Terence Crawford (USA)
*Light:* Terry Flanagan (Great Britain)
*Junior-light:* Roman Martinez (Puerto Rico)
*Feather:* Vasyl Lomachenko (Ukraine)
*Junior-feather:* Guillermo Rigondeaux (Cuba)
*Bantam:* Pungluang Sor Singyu (Thailand)
*Junior-bantam:* Naoya Inoue (Japan)
*Fly:* Juan Francisco Estrada (Mexico)
*Junior-fly:* Donnie Nietes (Philippines)
*Mini-fly:* Kosei Tanaka (Japan)

INTERNATIONAL BOXING FEDERATION (IBF)
*Heavy:* Wladimir Klitschko (Ukraine)
*Cruiser:* Yoan Pablo Hernandez (Germany)
*Light-heavy:* Sergey Kovalev (Russia)
*Supermiddle:* James De Gale (Great Britain)

*Middle:* David Lemieux (Canada)
*Junior-middle:* Cornelius Bundrage (USA)
*Welter:* Kell Brook (Great Britain)
*Junior-welter:* Cesar Cuenca (Argentina)
*Light:* vacant
*Junior—lightweight:* Jose Pedraza (USA)
*Feather:* Lee Selby (Great Britain)
*Junior-feather:* Carl Frampton (Great Britain)
*Bantam:* Randy Caballero (USA)
*Fly:* Amnat Ruenroeng (Thailand)
*Junior-fly:* Javier Mendoza (Mexico)
*Mini-fly:* Katsunari Takayama (Japan)

BRITISH CHAMPIONS
*Heavy:* Tyson Fury
*Cruiser:* Ola Afolabi
*Light-heavy:* Nathan Cleverly
*Super-middle:* James De Gale
*Middle:* Martin Murray
*Light-middle:* Brian Rose
*Welter:* Kell Brook
*Light-welter:* Willie Limond
*Light:* Ricky Burns
*Super-feather:* Stephen Smith
*Feather:* Lee Selby
*Super-bantam:* Carl Frampton
*Bantam:* Jamie McDonnell
*Super-fly:* Paul Butler
*Fly:* Kevin Satchell

# CHESS

*FIDE World Champion 2014:* Magnus Carlsen (Norway)
*British Champion 2015:* Jonathan Hawkins
*British Women's Champion 2015:* Akshaya Kalaiyalahan

# CRICKET

TEST SERIES

WEST INDIES V ENGLAND
*Antigua* (13–18 April): England drew with West Indies.
    West Indies 295 and 350–7; England 399 and 333–7
*St Georges* (21–26 April): England beat West Indies by
    9 wickets. England 464 and 144–1; West Indies 299
    and 307
*Bridgetown* (1–4 May): West Indies beat England by 5 wickets.
    West Indies 189 and 194–5; England 257 and 123

ENGLAND V NEW ZEALAND
*Lord's* (21–25 May): England beat New Zealand by 124
    runs. England 389 and 478; New Zealand 523 and 220
*Headingley* (29 May–2 June): New Zealand beat England
    by 199 runs. England 350 and 255; New Zealand 350
    and 454–8 dec.

ENGLAND V AUSTRALIA (THE ASHES)
*Cardiff* (8–11 July): England beat Australia by 169 runs.
    England 430 and 289; Australia 308 and 242
*Lord's* (16–19 July): Australia beat England by 405 runs.
    England 312 and 103; Australia 556–8 dec. and 242–2
*Edgbaston* (29–31 July): England beat Australia by 8 wickets.
    England 281 and 124–2; Australia 136 and 265
*Old Trafford* (6–8 August): England beat Australia by an
    innings and 78 runs. England 391–9 dec.; Australia 60
    and 253
*Kia Oval* (20–23 August): Australia beat England by an
    innings and 46 runs. Australia 481; England 149 and 286

ONE-DAY INTERNATIONALS

SRI LANKA V ENGLAND

*Colombo* (26 November): Sri Lanka beat England by 25 runs. Sri Lanka 317–6; England 292

*Colombo* (29 November): Sri Lanka beat England by 8 wickets. Sri Lanka 186–2; England 185

*Hambantota* (3 December): England beat Sri Lanka by 5 wickets (D/L). England 236–5; Sri Lanka 242–8

*Colombo* (7 December): Sri Lanka beat England by 6 wickets. Sri Lanka 267–4; England 265

*Pallekele* (10 December): England beat Sri Lanka by 5 wickets. England 240–5; Sri Lanka 239

*Pallekele* (13 December): Sri Lanka beat England by 90 runs. Sri Lanka 292–7; England 202

*Colombo* (16 December): Sri Lanka beat England by 87 runs. Sri Lanka 302–6; England 215

ENGLAND V AUSTRALIA AND INDIA TRIANGULAR SERIES

*Sydney* (16 January): Australia beat England by 3 wickets. Australia 235–7; England 234

*Brisbane* (20 January): England beat India by 9 wickets. England 156–1; India 153

*Hobart* (23 January): Australia beat England by 3 wickets. Australia 304–7; England 303–8

*Perth* (30 January): England beat India by 3 wickets. England 201–7; India 200

*Perth* (1 February): Australia beat England by 112 runs. Australia 278–8; England 16

REP. OF IRELAND V ENGLAND

*Dublin* (8 May): Match abandoned

ENGLAND V NEW ZEALAND

*Edgbaston* (9 June): England beat New Zealand by 210 runs. England 408–9; New Zealand 198

*Kia Oval* (12 June): New Zealand beat England by 13 runs (D/L). New Zealand 398–5; England 365–9

*The Rose Bowl* (14 June): New Zealand beat England by 3 wickets. New Zealand 306–7; England 302

*Trent Bridge* (17 June): England beat New Zealand by 7 wickets. England 350–3; New Zealand 349–7

*Chester-le-Street* (20 June): England beat New Zealand by 3 wickets (D/L). England 192–7; New Zealand 283–9

ENGLAND V AUSTRALIA

*The Rose Bowl* (3 September): Australia beat England by 59 runs. Austalia 305–6; England 246

*Lord's* (5 September): Australia beat England by 64 runs. Austalia 309–7; England 245

*Old Trafford* (8 September): England beat Australia by 93 runs. England 300–8; Australia 207

*Headingley* (11 September): England beat Australia by 3 wickets. England 304–7; Australia 299–7

*Old Trafford* (13 September): Australia beat England by 8 wickets. Austalia 140–2; England 138

TWENTY20 INTERNATIONALS

ENGLAND V NEW ZEALAND

*Old Trafford* (23 June): England beat New Zealand by 56 runs. England 191–7; New Zealand 135

ENGLAND V AUSTRALIA

*Cardiff* (31 August): England beat Australia by 5 runs. England 182–5; Austaralia 177–8

ICC WORLD CUP

Australia and New Zealand, February–March 2015

*Pool A*

| | Matches | Won | Lost | N/R | Pts | Net RR |
|---|---|---|---|---|---|---|
| New Zealand | 6 | 6 | 0 | 0 | 12 | +2.564 |
| Australia | 6 | 4 | 1 | 1 | 9 | +2.257 |
| Sri Lanka | 6 | 4 | 2 | 0 | 8 | +0.371 |
| Bangladesh | 6 | 3 | 2 | 1 | 7 | +0.136 |
| England | 6 | 2 | 4 | 0 | 4 | —0.753 |
| Afghanistan | 6 | 1 | 5 | 0 | 2 | —1.853 |
| Scotland | 6 | 0 | 6 | 0 | 0 | —2.218 |

*Pool B*

| | Matches | Won | Lost | N/R | Pts | Net RR |
|---|---|---|---|---|---|---|
| India | 6 | 6 | 0 | 0 | 12 | +1.827 |
| South Africa | 6 | 4 | 2 | 0 | 8 | +1.707 |
| Pakistan | 6 | 4 | 2 | 0 | 8 | –0.085 |
| West Indies | 6 | 3 | 3 | 0 | 6 | –0.053 |
| Rep. of Ireland | 6 | 3 | 3 | 0 | 6 | –0.933 |
| Zimbabwe | 6 | 1 | 5 | 0 | 2 | —0.527 |
| United Arab Emirates | 6 | 0 | 6 | 0 | 0 | —2.032 |

QUARTER-FINALS

*Sydney* (18 March): South Africa beat Sri Lanka by 9 wickets. South Africa 134–1; Sri Lanka 133

*Melbourne* (19 March): India beat Bangladesh by 109 runs. India 302–6; Bangladesh 193

*Adelaide* (20 March): Australia beat Pakistan by 6 wickets. Australia 216–4; Pakistan 213

*Wellington* (21 March): New Zealand beat West Indies by 143 runs. New Zealand 393–6; West Indies 250

SEMI-FINALS

*Auckland* (24 March): New Zealand beat South Africa by 4 runs (D/L). New Zealand 299–6; South Africa 281–5

*Sydney* (26 March): Australia beat India by 95 runs. Australia 328–7; India 233

FINAL

*Melbourne* (29 March): Australia beat New Zealand by 7 wickets. Australia 186–3; New Zealand 183

ENGLAND AND WALES DOMESTIC COMPETITIONS

*LV County Championship 2014, Division 1:* Yorkshire, 246pts; *Relegated* Lancashire, 143pts; Northamptonshire, 67pts – *Division 2:* Worcestershire, 235pts; *Promoted* Hampshire, 207pts

*Royal London One-Day Cup final 2015:* Gloucestershire beat Surrey by 6 runs. Gloucester 220; Surrey 214

*Natwest T20 Blast:* Lancashire Lightning beat Northants Steelbacks by 13 runs. Lancashire Lightning 166–7; Northants Steelbacks 153–6

OTHER INTERNATIONAL DOMESTIC CHAMPIONSHIPS

*Australia: Sheffield Shield final 2014–15:* Western Australia drew with Victoria. Western Australia 421; Victoria 381. *Matador BBQ's One-Day Cup final 2014–15:* Western Australia beat New South Wales by 64 runs. Western Australia 255–6; New South Wales 191. *Twenty20 Big Bash League final 2014–15:* Perth Scorchers beat Sydney Sixers by 4 wickets. Perth Scorchers 148–6; Sydney Sixers 147–5

*Bangladesh: BCL 2014–15 final:* Rangpur beat Dhaka Metropolis by 102 runs. Rangpur 491 and 306; Dhaka Metropolis 437 and 258.

*India: Irani Cup final 2014–15:* Karnataka beat Rest of India by 246 runs. Karnataka 244 and 422; Rest of India 264 and 156. *Deodhar Trophy 2014–15:* East Zone beat West Zone by 24 runs. East Zone 269–8; West Zone 245.

*Duleep Trophy final 2014–15:* Central Zone beat South Zone by 9 runs. Central Zone 276 and 403; South Zone 379 and 291. *Ranji Trophy Elite final 2014–15:* Karnataka beat Tamil Nadu by an innings and 217 runs. Karnataka 762; Tamil 134 and 411. *Syed Mushtaq Ali Trophy 2014–15:* Gujurat beat Punjab by two wickets. Gujurat 123–8; Punjab 117–9. *Vijay Hazare Trophy final 2014–15:* Karnataka beat Punjab by 156 runs. Karnataka 359–7; Punjab 203. *Indian Premier League Twenty20 final 2015:* Mumbai Indians beat Chennai Super Kings by 41 runs. Mumbai Indians 202–5; Chennai Super Kings 161–8

*New Zealand: Plunket Shield 2014–15:* Canterbury 122pts. *Ford Trophy final 2014–15:* Central Districts beat Auckland by 78 runs. Central Districts 271–7; Auckland 193. *Georgie Pie Super Smash final 2014–15:* Wellington beat Auckland by 6 runs. Wellington 186–6; Auckland 180–9

*Pakistan: Quaid-e-Azam Trophy final 2014–15:* Sui Northern Gas Pipelines drew with National Bank of Pakistan. Northern Gas 543 and 28–0; National Bank of Pakistan 242 and 508; Sui Northern win based on first innings lead. *Haier Super8 T20Cup final 2014–15:* Sialkot Stallions beat Lahore Lions by 74 runs. Silalkot 197–9; Lahore Lions 123–8. *President's Trophy final 2014–15:* State Bank of Pakistan beat National Bank of Pakistan by 2 wickets. State Bank 283–8; National Bank 279–6

*South Africa: Sunfoil Series 2014–15:* Lions, 151.64pts. *Momentum One-day Cup final 2014–15:* Titans beat Cape Cobras. Titans 288–5; Cobras 285–8. *Ram Slam T20 Challenge final 2014–15:* Cape Cobras beat Knights by 33 runs. Cape Cobras 158–4; Knights 125–9

*Sri Lanka: Premier Limited Overs Tournament 2014–15:* Colts CC beat Sinhalese Sports Club by 56 runs. Colts 251–9; Sinhalese 195

*West Indies: NagicoSuper50 final 2014–15:* Trinidad and Tobago beat Guyana by 135 runs. Trinidad and Tobago 200–8; Guyana 65. *Regional 4-Day Tournament 2014–15:* Guyana, 148 pts. *Caribbean Premier League T20 final 2014–15:* Trinidad and Tobago Red Steel beat Barbados Tridents by 20 runs. Trinidad 178–5; Barbados 158–4

*Zimbabwe: Pro50 Championship final 2014–15:* Mashonaland Eagles beat Matabeleland Tuskers by 4 wickets. Eagles 268–6; Tuskers 266–7

## CURLING

**MEN'S WORLD CHAMPIONSHIP 2015**
Halifax, Canada, March–April

*Final:* Sweden beat Norway 9–5

**WOMEN'S WORLD CHAMPIONSHIP 2015**
Sapporo, Japan, March

*Final:* Switzerland beat Canada 5–3

## CYCLING

*Vuelta a España 2015:* Fabio Aru (Italy)
*Giro d'Italia 2015:* Alberto Contador (Spain)
*Tour de France 2015:* Chris Froome (Great Britain)

**BRITISH NATIONAL ROAD RACE CHAMPIONSHIPS 2015**
Lincolnshire, June

**MEN**
*Road Race:* Peter Kennaugh

**WOMEN**
*Road Race:* Lizzie Armitstead

**UCI TRACK CYCLING WORLD CHAMPIONSHIPS 2015**
Saint-Quentin-en-Yvelines, France, March

**MEN**
*Points Race:* Artur Ershov (Russia)
*Sprint:* Grégory Baugé (France)
*1km Time Trial:* François Pervis (France)
*Individual Pursuit:* Stefan Küng (Switzerland)
*Scratch Race:* Lucas Liss (Germany)
*Keirin:* François Pervis (France)
*Team Pursuit:* New Zealand
*Madison:* Bryan Coquard and Morgan Kneisky (France)
*Team Sprint:* France
*Omnium:* Fernando Gaviria (Colombia)

**WOMEN**
*Points Race:* Stephanie Pohl (Germany)
*Sprint:* Kristina Vogel (Germany)
*500m Time Trial:* Anastasiia Voinova (Russia)
*Individual Pursuit:* Rebecca Wiasak (Australia)
*Scratch Race:* Kirsten Wild (Netherlands)
*Keirin:* Anna Meares (Australia)
*Team Pursuit:* Australia
*Team Sprint:* China
*Omnium:* Annette Edmondson (Australia)

## DARTS

*BDO World Championship 2015:* Scott Mitchell (England) beat Martin Adams (England) 7–6
*PDC World Championship 2015:* Gary Anderson (Scotland) beat Phil Taylor (England) 7–6

## EQUESTRIANISM

*Burghley Horse Trials 2014:* Andrew Nicholson (New Zealand) on Avebury
*Badminton Horse Trials 2015:* William Fox-Pitt (Great Britain) on Chilli Morning
*British Open Horse Trials 2015: (Gatcombe Park):* Christopher Burton (Australia) on TS Jamaimo

## ETON FIVES

*Amateur Championship (Kinnaird Cup) final 2015:* T. Dunbar and S. Cooley beat J. Toop and M. Wiseman 3–1
*Alan Barber Cup final 2015:* Old Olavians beat Old Salopians 2–1
*Marsh Insurance Schools' Championship 2015:* Boys: Eton beat Shrewsbury 3–0; Girls: Highgate 1s beat Highgate 2s 3–0
*Preparatory Schools' Tournament 2015:* Summer Fields beat Highgate 2–0
*National Ladies' Championships 2015 final:* K. Hird and C. Cooley beat D. Redmond and L. Redmond 3–0

## FENCING

**BRITISH CHAMPIONSHIPS 2015**
Sheffield, April

**MEN**
*Individual Foil:* Richard Kruse
*Individual Epée:* Tom Edwards
*Individual Sabre:* James Honeybone

WOMEN
*Individual Foil:* Ayesha Fihosy
*Individual Epée:* Hannah Lawrence
*Individual Sabre:* Joanna Hutchinson

EUROPEAN CHAMPIONSHIPS 2015
Montreux, Switzerland, June

MEN
*Individual Foil:* Andrea Cassarà (Italy)
*Individual Epée:* Gauthier Grumier (France)
*Individual Sabre:* Aron Szilagyi (Hungary)
*Team Foil:* France
*Team Epée:* France
*Team Sabre:* Germany

WOMEN
*Individual Foil:* Elisa Di Francisca (Italy)
*Individual Epée:* Violetta Kolobova (Russia)
*Individual Sabre:* Sofiya Velikaya (Russia)
*Team Foil:* Italy
*Team Epée:* Romania
*Team Sabre:* Russia

WORLD CHAMPIONSHIPS 2015
Moscow, Russia, 13–19 July

MEN
*Individual Foil:* Yuki Ota (Japan)
*Individual Epée:* Géza Imre (Hungary)
*Individual Sabre:* Aleksey Yakimenko (Russia)
*Team Foil:* Italy
*Team Epée:* Ukraine
*Team Sabre:* Italy

WOMEN
*Individual Foil:* Inna Deriglazova (Russia)
*Individual Epée:* Rossella Fiamingo (Italy)
*Individual Sabre:* Sofiya Velikaya (Russia)
*Team Foil:* Italy
*Team Epée:* China
*Team Sabre:* Russia

## FIGURE SKATING

BRITISH CHAMPIONSHIPS 2014/15
Sheffield, November 2014

*Men:* Phillip Harris
*Women:* Karly Robertson
*Pairs:* Caitlin Yankowskas and Hamish Gaman
*Ice Dance:* Olivia Smart and Joseph Buckland

EUROPEAN CHAMPIONSHIPS 2015
Stockholm, Sweden, January–February

*Men:* Javier Fernández (Spain)
*Women:* Elizaveta Tuktamysheva (Russia)
*Pairs:* Yuko Kavaguti and Alexander Smirnov (Russia)
*Ice Dance:* Gabriella Papadakis and Guillaume Cizeron
(France)

WORLD CHAMPIONSHIPS 2015
Shanghai, China, March

*Men:* Javier Fernández (Spain)
*Women:* Elizaveta Tuktamysheva (Russia)
*Pairs:* Meagan Duhamel and Eric Radford (Canada)
*Ice Dance:* Gabriella Papadakis and Guillaume Cizeron
(France)

## GOLF (MEN)

THE MAJOR CHAMPIONSHIPS 2015
*US Masters* (Augusta, 9–12 April): Jordan Spieth (USA), 270
*US Open* (Merion, 18–21 June): Jordan Spieth (USA), 275
*The Open* (Muirfield, 16–20 July): Zach Johnson (USA),
273
*US PGA Championship* (Oak Hill Country Club, 13–16
August): Jason Day (Australia), 268

WORLD RANKINGS
*as at 21 September 2015*

1. Jason Day (Australia); 2. Rory McIlroy (Northern Ireland);
3. Jordan Spieth (USA); 4. Bubba Watson (USA);
5. Rickie Fowler (USA)

PGA EUROPEAN TOUR 2014
*ISPS Handa Wales Open* (Newport, Wales): Joost Luiten
(Netherlands), 270
*Alfred Dunhill Championship* (St Andrews, Scotland): Oliver
Wilson (England), 271
*Portugal Masters* (Villamoura): Alexander Lévy (France),
124*
*Volvo World Match Play Championship* (London GC,
England): Mikko Ilonen (Finland), 3 & 1
*Hong Kong Open* (Hong Kong GC): Scott Hend (Australia),
267
*Perth International* (Lake Karrinyup Country Club, Australia):
Thorbjrn Olesen (Denmark), 271
*BMW Masters* (Lake Malaren GC, Shanghai): Marcel Siem
(Germany), 272
*WGC-HSBC Champions* (Sheshan GC, Shanghai): Bubba
Watson (USA), 277
*Turkish Airlines Open* (Montgomerie Maxx Royal, Belek,
Turkey): Brooks Koepka (USA), 271
*DP World Tour Championship* (Jumeirah Golf Estates, Earth
Course, Dubai): Henrik Stenson (Sweden), 272
*Nedbank Golf Challenge* (Sun City, South Africa): Danny
Willett (England), 270
*Alfred Dunhill Championship* (Leopard Creek GC, South
Africa): Branden Grace (South Africa), 268

* Course shortened to 36 holes due to poor weather

TEAM CHAMPIONSHIPS
*2014 Ryder Cup:* (Gleneagles) Europe beat USA 16½–11½

PGA EUROPEAN TOUR 2015
*South African Open* (Glendower GC, South Africa): Andy
Sullivan (England),
277
*Abu Dhabi HSBC Golf Championship* (Abu Dhabi GC): Gary
Stal (France), 269
*Commercial Bank Qatar Masters* (Doha GC): Branden Grace
(South Africa), 269
*Omega Dubai Desert Classic* (Emirates): Rory McIlroy
(Northern Ireland), 266
*Maybank Malaysian Open* (Kuala Lumpur): Anirban Lahiri
(India), 272
*True Thailand Classic* (Black Mountain GC, Thailand):
Andrew Dodt (Australia), 272
*Hero India Open* (Dehli GC, India): Anirban Lahiri (India),
277
*Joburg Open* (Royal Johannesburg and Kensington): Andy
Sullivan (England), 270
*WGC-Cadillac Championship* (Trump National Doral GC,
USA): Dustin Johnson (USA), 279
*Africa Open* (East London): Trevor Fisher Jr (South Africa),
264

*Tshwane Open* (Pretoria GC, South Africa): George Coetzee (South Africa), 266

*Trophée Hassan II* (Agadir, Morocco): Richie Ramsay (Scotland), 278

*Shenzhen International* (Genzon GC, China): Kiradech Aphibarnrat (Thailand), 276

*Volvo China Open* (Tomson Shanghai Pudong GC, China): Wu Ashun (China), 279

*WGC – Cadillac Match Play Championship* (TPC Holding Park, USA): Rory McIlroy (Northern Ireland), 4 & 2

*AfrAsia Bank Mauritius Open* (Heritage Golf Club, Mauritius): George Coetzee (South Africa), 271

*Open de España* (Real Club de Golf El Prat, Barcelona): James Morrison (England), 278

*BMW PGA Championship* (Wentworth, England): An Byeong-hun (Rep. of Korea), 267

*Irish Open* (Royal County Down): Sren Kjeldsen (Denmark), 282

*Nordea Masters* (PGA Sweden National GC, Sweden): Alexander Norén (Sweden), 276

*Lyoness Open* (Diamond CC, Austria):Chris Wood (England), 273

*BMW International Open* (Golfclub München Eichenried, Germany): Pablo Larrazábal (Spain), 271

*Alstom Open de France* (Le Golf National): Bernd Wiesberger (Austria), 279

*Aberdeen Asset Management Scottish Open* (Royal Aberdeen GC): Rickie Fowler (USA), 268

*Omega European Masters* (Crans-sur-Sierre, Switzerland): Danny Willett (England), 263

*Saltire Energy Paul Lawrie Matchplay* (Murcar Links GC, Scotland), Kiradech Aphibarnrat (Thailand), 1 up

*Madeira Islands Open* (Clube de Golf do Santo da Serra, Portugal): Roope Kakko (Finland)

*WGC-Bridgestone Invitational* (Firestone Country Club, USA): Shane Lowry (Rep. of Ireland), 269

*Made in Denmark* (Himmerland): David Horsey (England), 271

*D+ D Real Czech Masters* (Prague): Thomas Pieters (Belgium), 268

*M2M Russian Open* (Moscow): Lee Slattery (England), 269

*KLM Open* (Netherlands): Thomas Pieters (Belgium), 261

*Italian Open* (Turin): Rikard Karlberg (Sweden), 269

AMATEUR CHAMPIONSHIPS 2015

*British Amateur Championship* (Carnoustie GC): Romain Langasque (France)

*English Amateur Championship* (Alwoodley GC): Joe Dean

*Brabazon Trophy (English Open Strokeplay)* (Notts Golf Club, Hollinwell): Cormac Sharvin (Rep. of Ireland), 281

*Scottish Amateur Championship* (Muirfield): Robert MacIntyre

*Scottish Open Amateur Stroke Play Championship* (Moray GC): Marco Penge (England), 278

*Welsh Amateur Championship* (Prestatyn GC): Theo Baker (stroke-play) and David Boote (match-play)

*Welsh Open Stroke Play* (Ashburnham): Jimmy Mullen (England), 273

*Irish Amateur Open Championship* (Royal Dublin): Gavin Moynihan (Rep. of Ireland), 284

*Irish Amateur Close Championship* (Tramore): Tiarnan McLarnon

*Lytham Trophy* (Royal Lytham Golf Club): Marcus Kinhult (Sweden), 280

*Berkshire Trophy* (The Berkshire): Billy McKenzie (England), 278

# GOLF (WOMEN)

THE MAJOR CHAMPIONSHIPS 2015

*ANA Inspiration* (Rancho Mirage, USA, 2–5 April): Brittany Lincicome (USA), 279

*KPMG WPGA Championship* (Westchester GC, USA, 11–14 June): Inbee Park (Rep. of Korea), 273

*US Women's Open* (Lancaster Country Club, USA, 9–12 July): Chun In-gee (Rep. of Korea), 272

*Ricoh British Open* (The Trump Turnberry Resort, Scotland): Inbee Park (Rep. of Korea), 276

*Evian Championship* (Evian-les-Bains, France): Lydia Ko (New Zealand), 268

EUROPEAN LPGA TOUR 2014

*Open De España Femenino* (Tenerife): Connie Chen (South Africa), 276

*Lacoste Ladies Open De France* (Chantaco): Azahara Munoz (Spain), 269

*South Africa Womens' Open* (San Lameer Country Club, South Africa), Lee-Ann Pace (South Africa), 211

*Sanya Ladies Open* (Yalong Bay, China): Xi Yu Lin (China), 202

*Xiamen Open* (Xiamen Golf and Country Club, China): Ssu-Chia Cheng (Chinese Tapei), 206

*Hero Women's Indian Open* (Delhi GC): Gwladys Nocera (France), 208

Buick Championship Pro-AM (Shanghai Qizhong Garden Golf, China): S. Feng (China) and L. Zhang (China), 130

*Omega Dubai Ladies Masters* (Emirates GC): Shanshan Feng (China), 269

EUROPEAN LPGA TOUR ORDER OF MERIT 2014

1. Charley Hull (England); 2. Gwladys Nocera (France); 3. Lee-Anne Pace (South Africa); 4. Nikki Campbell (Australia); 5. Carlota Ciganda (Spain)

EUROPEAN LPGA TOUR 2015

*ISPS HANDA New Zealand Women's Open* (Clearwater): Mi Hyang Lee (South Korea), 207

*Volvik RACV Ladies' Masters* (Royal Pines, Australia): Su-Hyun Oh (Australia), 285

*ISPS HANDA Women's Australian Open* (Victoria GC): Lydia Ko (New Zealand), 283

*ISPS HANDA New Zealand Women's Open* (Clearwater): Lydia Ko (New Zealand), 202

*World Ladies' Championship* (Mission Hills, China): So Yeon Ryu (Rep. of Korea), 279

*Lalla Meryem Cup* (Golf de l'Ocean, Morocco): Gwladys Nocera (France), 271

*Buick Invitational* (Shanghai Qizhong Garden GC, China): Shanshan Feng (China), 271

*Turkish Airlines Ladies Open* (CaryaGC, Belek): Melissa Reid (England), 281

*Deloitte Ladies Open* (The International, Netherlands): Christel Boeljon (Netherlands), 209

*ISPS HANDA Ladies European Masters* (Buckinghamshire GC, England): Beth Allen (USA), 276

*Aberdeen Asset Management Ladies Scotland Open* (Dundonald Links Troon, Scotland): Rebecca Artis (Australia), 210

*Tipssport Golf Masters* (Golf Park Plzen, Czech Republic): Hannah Burke (England), 200

*Helsingborg Open* (Sweden): Nicole Broch Larsen (Denmark), 280

*Solheim Cup* (Baden-Wurttenburg, Germany): USA beat Europe 14½–13½

TEAM CHAMPIONSHIPS 2014

*Curtis Cup* (St Louis Country Club, USA): USA beat Great Britain and Ireland 13 to 7

AMATEUR CHAMPIONSHIPS 2015

*British Open Championship* (Royal St George's GC): Celine Boutier (France)

*Ladies' British Open Stroke Play Championship* (Prestwick): Aditi Ashok (India), 285

*English Close Championship* (Hunstanton): Bronte Law, 275

*English Open Stroke Play Championship* ( St Anne's Old Links): Samantha Giles (England), 289

*Helen Holm (Scottish Open Stroke Play Championship)* (Troon): Olivia Mahaffey (Rep. of Ireland), 220

*Scottish Ladies Close Championship* (Monifieth): Gillian Paton (Scotland), 145

*Welsh Open Stroke Play Championship* (Southerndown): Olivia Mahaffey (Rep.of Ireland), 221

*Welsh Close Match Play Championship* (Vale of Llangollen): Katherine O'Connor

*Irish Open Strokeplay Championship* (Dun Loaghaire): Chloe Ryan (Rep. of Ireland), 221

*Irish Close Championship* (Rosapenna GC): Sarah Helly

## GREYHOUND RACING

2014
*Grand National* (Sittingbourne): Cornamaddy Jumbo
*Williamhill.com St Leger* (Wimbledon): Roxholme Dream

2015
*The Coral Regency* (Hove): Touch Tackle
*Ladbrokes Golden Jacket* (Crayford): Wiki Waki Woo
*The Williamhill.com Derby* (Wimbledon): Rio Quattro

## GYMNASTICS

EUROPEAN ARTISTIC CHAMPIONSHIPS 2015
Montpellier, France, April

MEN
*All-Around:* Oleg Verniaiev (Ukraine)
*Floor:* Kristian Thomas (Great Britain)
*Pommel Horse:* Louis Smith (Great Britain)
*Rings:* Eleftherios Petrounias (Greece)
*Vault:* Nikita Nagornyy (Russia)
*Parallel Bars:* Oleg Verniaiev (Ukraine)
*Horizontal Bar:* Marijo Moznik (Croatia)

WOMEN
*All-Around:* Maria Kharenkova (Russia)
*Floor:* Giulia Steingruber (Switzerland)
*Beam:* Maria Kharenkova (Russia)
*Vault:* Giulia Steingruber (Switzerland)
*Uneven Bars:* Daria Spiridonova (Russia)

BRITISH CHAMPIONSHIPS 2015
Liverpool, March

MEN
*All-Around:* Daniel Purvis
*Floor:* Daniel Purvis
*Pommel Horse:* Louis Smith
*Rings:* Daniel Purvis
*Vault:* Kristian Thomas
*Parallel Bars:* Ashley Watson
*High Bar:* Kristian Thomas

WOMEN
*All-Around:* Amy Tinkler
*Floor:* Claudia Fragapane
*Beam:* Angel Romaeo
*Vault:* Claudia Fragapane
*Uneven Bars:* Rebecca Downie

## HOCKEY

MEN
*England Hockey League 2014–15: Premier Division:* East Grinstead Men's 1s, 44pts; *Conference East:* Holcombe Men's 1s, 52pts; *Conference North:* Bowdon Men's 1s, 50pts; *Conference West:* Team Bath Buccaneers Men's 1s, 47pts

*England Hockey League Championship final 2015:* Wimbledon Men's 1s beat East Grinstead Men's 1s 8–5

*England Hockey League Cup final 2013–14:* Reading beat Surbiton 5–1

*County Championship 2013–14: A Division:* Yorkshire beat Durham 8–2; *B Division:* Northumberland beat Kent 5–4; *C Division:* Surrey beat Nottinghamshire 6–4

WOMEN
*England Hockey League 2014–15: Premier Division:* Surbiton Ladies' 1s 48pts; *Conference East:* East Grinstead Ladies' 1's, 45pts; *Conference North:* Wakefield Ladies' 1s, 47pts; *Conference West:* Slough Ladies' 1s, 45pts

*England Hockey League Championship final 2014–15:* Surbiton Ladies' 1s beat Canterbury Ladies' 1s 2–1

*England Hockey League Cup final 2013–14:* Surbiton Ladies' 1s beat Clifton 2–1

## HORSE RACING

### NATIONAL HUNT
HENNESSY GOLD CUP
(1957) Newbury, 3 miles and about 2½ f

2010 Diamond Harry (7y), D. Jacob
2011 Carruthers (8y), M. Batchelor
2012 Bobs Worth (7y), B. Geraghty
2013 Triolo D'Alene (6y), B. Geraghty
2014 Many Clouds (7y), L. Aspell

TINGLE CREEK CHASE
(1957) Sandown, 2 miles

2010 Master Minded (7y), N. Fehily
2011 Sizing Europe (9y), A. E. Lynch
2012 Sprinter Sacre (6y), B. Geraghty
2013 Sire de Grugy (7y), J. Moore
2014 Dodging Bullets (6y), S. Twiston-Davies

KING GEORGE VI CHASE
(1937) Kempton, about 3 miles

2010 Long Run (6y), S. Waley-Cohen*
2011 Kauto Star (11y), R. Walsh
2012 Long Run (7y), S. Waley-Cohen
2013 Silviniaco Conti (7y), N. Fehily
2014 Silviniaco Conti (8y), N. Fehily
* Race took place on 15 January 2011, after original meeting was postponed due to snow and frost

CHAMPION HURDLE
(1927) Cheltenham, 2 miles and about ½ f

2011 Hurricane Fly (7y), R. Walsh
2012 Rock On Ruby (7y), N. Fehily
2013 Hurricane Fly (9y), R. Walsh
2014 Jezki (6y), B. Geraghty
2015 Faugheen (7y), R. Walsh

QUEEN MOTHER CHAMPION CHASE
(1959) Cheltenham, about 2 miles

2011 Sizing Europe (9y), A. E. Lynch
2012 Finian's Rainbow (9y), B. Geraghty
2013 Sprinter Sacre (7y), B. Geraghty
2014 Sire de Grugy (8y), J. Moore
2015 Dodging Bullets (7y), S. Twiston-Davies

CHELTENHAM GOLD CUP
(1924) 3 miles and about 2½ f

2011 Long Run (6y), S. Waley-Cohen
2012 Synchronised (9y), A. P. McCoy
2013 Bobs Worth (8y), B. Geraghty
2014 Lord Windermere (8y), D. Russell
2015 Coneygree (8y), N. de Boinville

GRAND NATIONAL
(1837) Liverpool, 4 miles and about 4 f

2011 Ballabriggs (10y), J. Maguire
2012 Neptune Collonges (11y), D. Jacob
2013 Auroras Encore (11y), R. Mania
2014 Pineau de Re (11y), L. Aspell
2015 Many Clouds (8y), L. Aspell

BET365 GOLD CUP
(1957) Sandown, 3 miles and about 5 f

2011 Poker De Sivola (8y), T. Murphy
2012 Tidal Bay (11y), D. Jacob

2013 Quentin Collonges (9y), A. Tinkler
2014 Hadrians Approach (7y), B. Geraghty
2015 Just A Par (8y), S. Bowen

STATISTICS
WINNING NATIONAL HUNT TRAINERS 2014–15

| | |
|---|---|
| P. F. Nicholls | £3,128,873 |
| N. J. Henderson | 1,793,517 |
| P. J. Hobbs | 1,435,431 |
| W. P. Mullins | 1,309,857 |
| D. E. Pipe | 1,176,751 |
| A. King | 1,045,054 |
| O. Sherwood | 1,023,874 |
| J. J. O'Neill | 876,894 |
| N. A. Twiston-Davies | 821,665 |
| V. Williams | 791,622 |

WINNING NATIONAL HUNT JOCKEYS 2014–15

| | 1st | 2nd | 3rd | Unpl. | Total mts |
|---|---|---|---|---|---|
| A. P. McCoy | 231 | 149 | 110 | 337 | 827 |
| R. Johnson | 153 | 164 | 120 | 422 | 859 |
| T. Scudamore | 150 | 100 | 83 | 352 | 685 |
| S. Twiston-Davies | 145 | 118 | 99 | 396 | 758 |
| B. Hughes | 106 | 94 | 82 | 372 | 654 |
| N. Fehily | 85 | 63 | 82 | 247 | 477 |
| A. Coleman | 82 | 78 | 81 | 412 | 653 |
| G. Sheehan | 73 | 47 | 42 | 239 | 401 |
| P. Moloney | 72 | 64 | 70 | 326 | 532 |
| P. Brennan | 67 | 64 | 50 | 261 | 442 |

The above statistics have been provided by *Timeform*, publishers of the *Racehorses* and *Chasers and Hurdlers* annuals

## THE FLAT

THE CLASSICS
ONE THOUSAND GUINEAS
(1814) Rowley Mile, Newmarket, for three-year-old fillies

| Year | Winner | Betting | Owner | Jockey | Trainer | Runners |
|---|---|---|---|---|---|---|
| 2010 | Special Duty | 9–2 | K. Abdulla | S. Pasquier | Mrs C. Head-Maarek | 17 |
| 2011 | Blue Bunting | 16–1 | Godolphin | F. Dettori | M. Al Zarooni | 18 |
| 2012 | Homecoming Queen | 25–1 | J. Magnier, M. Tabor and D. Smith | R. Moore | A. O'Brien | 17 |
| 2013 | Sky Lantern | 9–1 | B. Keswick | R. Hughes | R. Hannon | 15 |
| 2014 | Miss France | 7–1 | Ballymore Thoroughbred | M. Guyon | A. Fabre | 17 |
| 2015 | Legatissimo | 13–2 | J. Magnier, M. Tabor and D. Smith | R. Moore | D. Wachman | 13 |

TWO THOUSAND GUINEAS
(1809) Rowley Mile, Newmarket, for three-year-olds

| Year | Winner | Betting | Owner | Jockey | Trainer | Runners |
|---|---|---|---|---|---|---|
| 2010 | Makfi | 33–1 | M. Offenstadt | C-P. Lemaire | M. Delzangles | 19 |
| 2011 | Frankel | 1–2 | K. Abdulla | T. Queally | Sir H. Cecil | 13 |
| 2012 | Camelot | 15–8 | D. Smith | J. P. O'Brien | A. O'Brien | 18 |
| 2013 | Dawn Approach | 11–8 | Godolphin | K. Manning | J. S. Bolger | 13 |
| 2014 | Night of Thunder | 40–1 | S. Manana | K. Fallon | R. Hannon Jr | 14 |
| 2015 | Gleneagles | 4–1 | D. Smith, J. Magnier and M. Tabor | R. Moore | A. O'Brien | 18 |

THE DERBY
(1780) Epsom, 1 mile and about 4 f, for three-year-olds

The first winner was Sir Charles Bunbury's Diomed in 1780. The owners with the record number of winners are Lord Egremont, who won in 1782, 1804, 1805, 1807, 1826 (also won five Oaks); and Aga Khan III, who won in 1930, 1935, 1936, 1948, 1952. Other winning owners are: Duke of Grafton (1802, 1809, 1810, 1815); Mr J. Bowes (1835, 1843, 1852, 1853); Sir J. Hawley (1851, 1858, 1859, 1868); the 1st Duke of Westminster (1880, 1882, 1886, 1899); and Sir Victor Sassoon (1953, 1957, 1958, 1960).

The Derby was run at Newmarket in 1915–18 and 1940–5.

| Year | Winner | Betting | Owner | Jockey | Trainer | Runners |
|------|--------|---------|-------|--------|---------|---------|
| 2010 | Workforce | 6–1 | K. Abdulla | R. Moore | M. Stoute | 12 |
| 2011 | Pour Moi | 4–1 | Mrs J. Magnier, M. Tabor and D. Smith | M. Barzalona | A. Fabre | 13 |
| 2012 | Camelot | 8–13 | D. Smith | J. P. O'Brien | A. P. O'Brien | 9 |
| 2013 | Ruler Of The World | 7–1 | Mrs J. Magnier, M. Tabor and D. Smith | R. Moore | A. P. O'Brien | 12 |
| 2014 | Australia | 11–8 | D. Smith, S. Magnier, M. Tabor and T. Ah Khing | J. O'Brien | A. P. O'Brien | 16 |
| 2015 | Golden Horn | 13–2 | Anthony Oppenheimer | F. Dettori | J. Gosden | 12 |

## THE OAKS
(1779) Epsom, 1 mile and about 4 f, for three-year-old fillies

| Year | Winner | Betting | Owner | Jockey | Trainer | Runners |
|------|--------|---------|-------|--------|---------|---------|
| 2010 | Snow Fairy | 9–1 | Anamoine Ltd. | R. Moore | E. A. L. Dunlop | 15 |
| 2011 | Dancing Rain | 20–1 | M. J. and L. A. Taylor | J. Murtagh | W. Haggas | 13 |
| 2012 | Was | 20–1 | D. Smith, Mrs J. Magnier and M. Tabor | S. Heffernan | A. O'Brien | 12 |
| 2013 | Talent | 20–1 | J. L. Rowsell and M. H. Dixon | R. Hughes | R. Beckett | 11 |
| 2014 | Taghrooda | 5–1 | H. Al Maktoum | P. Hanagan | J. Gosden | 17 |
| 2015 | Qualify | 50–1 | C. Regalado-Gonzalez | C. O'Donoghue | A. O'Brien | 11 |

## ST LEGER
(1776) Doncaster, 1 mile and about 6 f, for three-year-olds

| Year | Winner | Betting | Owner | Jockey | Trainer | Runners |
|------|--------|---------|-------|--------|---------|---------|
| 2009 | Mastery | 14–1 | Godolphin | T. Durcan | S. Bin Suroor | 8 |
| 2010 | Arctic Cosmos | 12–1 | Ms R. Hood and R. Geffen | W. Buick | J. Gosden | 10 |
| 2011 | Masked Marvel | 15–2 | B. E. Neilsen | W. Buick | J. Gosden | 9 |
| 2012 | Encke | 25–1 | Godolphin | M. Barzalona | M. Al Zarooni | 9 |
| 2013 | Leading Light | 7–2 | D. Smith, S. Magnier and M. Tabor | J. O'Brien | A. P. O'Brien | 11 |
| 2014 | Kingston Hill | 9–4 | P. Smith | A. Atzeni | R. Varian | 12 |

## RESULTS

### CAMBRIDGESHIRE HANDICAP
(1839) Newmarket, 1 mile and 1 f

2010 Credit Swap (5y), J. Crowley
2011 Prince of Johanne (5y), J. Fahy
2012 Bronze Angel (3y), W. Buick
2013 Educate (4y), J. Murtagh
2014 Bronze Angel (5y), L. Steward

### PRIX DE L'ARC DE TRIOMPHE
(1920) Longchamp, Paris, 1½ miles

2010 Workforce (3y), R. Moore
2011 Danedream (3y), A. Starke
2012 Solemia (4y), O. Peslier
2013 Educate (4y), J. Murtagh
2014 Bronze Angel (5y), L. Steward

### CESAREWITCH
(1839) Newmarket, 2 miles and about 2 f

2010 Aaim To Prosper (6y), L-P. Beuzelin
2011 Never Can Tell (4y), L. Dettori
2012 Aaim To Prosper (8y), K. Fallon
2013 Scatter Dice (4y), S. de Sousa
2014 Big Easy (7y), T. Queally

### CHAMPION STAKES
(1877) Newmarket, 1 mile and 2 f

2010 Twice Over (5y), T. Queally

2011 Cirrus des Aigles (5y), C. Soumillon
2012 Frankel (4y), T. Queally
2013 Farhh (5y), S. de Sousa
2014 Noble Mission (5y), J. Doyle

### DUBAI WORLD CUP
(1996) Dubai, 1 mile and 2 f

2011 Victoire Pisa (4y), M. Dimuro
2012 Monterosso (5y), M. Barzalona
2013 Animal Kingdom (5y), J. Rosario
2014 African Story (7y), S. de Sousa
2015 Prince Bishop (8y), W. Buick

### LINCOLN HANDICAP
(1965) Doncaster, 1 mile

2011 Sweet Lightning (6y), J. Murtagh
2012 Brae Hill (6y), T. Hamilton
2013 Levitate (5y). D. Egan
2014 Ocean Tempest (5y), A. Kirby
2015 Gabrial (6y), T. Hamilton

### JOCKEY CLUB STAKES
(1894) Newmarket, 1½ miles

2011 Dandino (5y), P. Mulrennan
2012 Al Kazeem (4y), J. Doyle
2013 Universal (4y), J. Fanning
2014 Gospel Club (5y), R. Moore
2015 Second Step (4y), A. Atzeni

PRIX DU JOCKEY CLUB
(1836) Chantilly, 1 mile and about 2½ f, for three-year-olds

2010 Lope de Vega, M. Guyon
2011 Reliable Man, G. Mosse
2012 Saonois, A. Hamelin
2013 Intello, O. Peslier
2014 The Grey Gatsby (3y), R. Moore

ASCOT GOLD CUP
(1807) Ascot, 2 miles and about 4 f

2011 Fame and Glory (5y), J. Spencer
2012 Colour Vision (4y), L. Dettori
2013 Estimate (4y), R. Moore
2014 Leading Light (4y), J. O'Brien
2015 New Bay (3y), V. Cheminaud

IRISH DERBY
(1866) Curragh, 1½ miles, for three-year-olds

2011 Treasure Beach, C. O'Donoghue
2012 Camelot, J. P. O'Brien
2013 Trading Leather, K. Manning
2014 Australia, J. O'Brien
2015 Jack Hobbs, W. Buick

ECLIPSE STAKES
(1886) Sandown, 1 mile and about 2 f

2011 So You Think (5y), S. Heffernan
2012 Nathaniel (4y), W. Buick
2013 Al Kazeem (5y), J. Doyle
2014 Mukhadram (5y), P. Hanagan
2015 Golden Horn (3y), F. Dettori

KING GEORGE VI AND QUEEN ELIZABETH
DIAMOND STAKES
(1952) Ascot, 1 mile and about 4 f

2011 Nathaniel (3y), W. Buick
2012 Danedream (4y), A. Starke
2013 Novellist (4y), J. Murtagh
2014 Taghrooda (3y), P. Hanagan
2015 Postponed (4y), A. Atzeni

GOODWOOD CUP
(1812) Goodwood, about 2 miles

2011 Opinion Poll (5y), L. Dettori
2012 Saddler's Rock (4y), J. Murtagh
2013 Brown Panther (5y), R. Kingscote
2014 Cavalryman (8y), K. Fallon
2015 Big Orange (4y), J. Spencer

STATISTICS
WINNING FLAT OWNERS 2014

| | |
|---|---|
| Hamdan Al Maktoum | £3,382,405 |
| Godolphin | 3,077,833 |
| Mr K. Abdullalah | 2,172,671 |
| Sheikh Hamdan bin Mohammed Al Maktoum | 1,700,857 |
| D. Smith/Mrs J. Magnier/M. Tabor/T. Ah Khing | 1,284,698 |
| Al Shaqab Racing | 1,079,274 |
| Cheveley Park Stud | 997,705 |
| Mrs S. Power | 996,860 |
| Mr Saeed Manana | 879,790 |
| Dr Marwan Koukash | 790,518 |

WINNING FLAT TRAINERS 2014

| | |
|---|---|
| R. Hannon | £4,311,729 |
| J. Gosden | 3,927,739 |
| M. Johnston | 2,797,375 |
| A. O'Brien | 2,749,223 |
| R. A. Fahey | 2,597,374 |
| R. Varian | 2,146,645 |
| Sir Michael Stoute | 2,115,984 |
| W. Haggas | 2,066,155 |
| A. Balding | 1,834,784 |
| D. O'Meara | 1,682,346 |

WINNING FLAT SIRES 2014

| | Races won | Stakes |
|---|---|---|
| Galileo by Sadler's Wells | 78 | £4,343,147 |
| Invincible Spirit by Green Desert | 139 | 2,621,915 |
| Dubawi by Dubai Millennium | 106 | 2,314,586 |
| Shamardal by Giant's Causeway | 114 | 2,123,639 |
| Oasis Dream by Great Desert | 114 | 1,660,638 |
| Dutch Art by Medicean | 74 | 1,431,215 |
| Sea The Stars by Cape Cross | 37 | 1,325,480 |
| Dansili by Danehill | 74 | 1,274,287 |
| Mastercraftsman by Dane Hill Dancer | 40 | 1,272,918 |
| Dark Angel by Acclamation | 81 | 1,228,203 |

WINNING FLAT JOCKEYS 2014

| | 1st | 2nd | 3rd | Unpl. | Total mts |
|---|---|---|---|---|---|
| A. Kirby | 192 | 165 | 145 | 696 | 1,198 |
| L. Morris | 189 | 212 | 190 | 933 | 1,524 |
| J. Fanning | 168 | 156 | 146 | 707 | 1,177 |
| R. Hughes | 166 | 153 | 107 | 515 | 941 |
| R. Moore | 162 | 120 | 84 | 408 | 774 |
| G. Baker | 162 | 102 | 110 | 453 | 827 |
| G. Lee | 159 | 133 | 108 | 671 | 1,071 |
| W. Buick | 125 | 97 | 94 | 376 | 692 |
| A. Atzeni | 125 | 95 | 100 | 384 | 704 |
| JJ. Doyle | 121 | 131 | 70 | 361 | 683 |

The above statistics have been provided by *Timeform*, publishers of the *Racehorses* and *Chasers and Hurdlers* annuals

## ICE HOCKEY

MEN'S WORLD CHAMPIONSHIP 2015
Prague, Czech Republic, May
*Final:* Canada beat Russia 6–1

WOMEN'S WORLD CHAMPIONSHIP 2015
Malmo, Sweden, April–May
*Final:* United States beat Canada 7–5

DOMESTIC COMPETITIONS
*Elite League Champions 2014–15:* Sheffield Steelers
*Play-off Champions 2015:* Coventry Blaze
*Challenge Cup final 2014–15:* Cardiff Devils beat Sheffield
   Steelers 2–1

NATIONAL HOCKEY LEAGUE
*Stanley Cup final 2014–15:* Chicago Blackhawks beat Tampa
   Bay 2–0

## JUDO

EUROPEAN CHAMPIONSHIPS 2015
Baku, Azerbaijan, June (part of inaugural 2015 European
Games)

MEN
*Heavyweight* (over 100kg): Adam Okruashvili (Georgia)
*Light-heavyweight* (100kg): Henk Grol (Netherlands)
*Middleweight* (90kg): Kirill Denisov (Russia)

*Welterweight* (81kg): Avtandil Tchrikishvili (Georgia)
*Lightweight* (73kg): Sagi Muki (Israel)
*Junior Lightweight* (66kg): Kamal Khan-Magomedov (Russia)
*Bantamweight* (60kg): Beslan Mudranov (Russia)

WOMEN
*Heavyweight* (over 78kg): Émilie Andéol (France)
*Light-heavyweight* (78kg): Marhinde Verkerk (Netherlands)
*Middleweight* (70kg): Kim Polling (Netherlands)
*Welterweight* (63kg): Martyna Trajdos (Germany)
*Lightweight* (57kg): Telma Monteiro (Portugal)
*Junior Lightweight* (52kg): Andreea Chitu (Romania)
*Bantamweight* (48kg): Charline van Snick (Belgium)

BRITISH OPEN CHAMPIONSHIPS 2014
Sheffield, December

MEN
*Heavyweight* (over 100kg): Theodore Spalding-McIntosh
*Light-heavyweight* (100kg): Benjamin Fletcher
*Middleweight* (90kg): Gary Hall
*Welter* (81kg): Owen Livesey
*Lightweight* (73kg): Jan Gosiewski
*Junior Lightweight* (66kg): Colin Oates
*Bantamweight* (60kg): Ashley McKenzie

WOMEN
*Heavyweight* (over 78kg): Sarah Adlington
*Light-heavyweight* (78kg): Natalie Powell
*Middleweight* (70kg): Sally Conway
*Welter* (63kg): Alice Schlesinger
*Lightweight* (57kg): Nekoda Davis
*Junior Lightweight* (52kg): Chelsie Giles
*Bantamweight* (48kg): Kelly Staddon

# MOTORCYCLING

MOTOGP 2014
*Qatar* (Doha): Marc Marquez (Spain), Honda
*USA* (Austin): Marc Marquez (Spain), Honda
*Spain* (Jerez): Marc Marquez (Spain), Honda
*France* (Le Mans): Marc Marquez (Spain), Honda
*Italy* (Mugello): Marc Marquez (Spain), Honda
*Catalonia* (Barcelona): Marc Marquez (Spain), Honda
*Netherlands* (Assen): Marc Marquez (Spain), Honda
*Germany* (Sachsenring): Marc Marquez (Spain), Honda
*USA* (Indianapolis): Marc Marquez (Spain), Honda
*Czech Republic* (Brno): Dani Pedrosa (Spain), Honda
*Britain* (Silverstone): Marc Marquez (Spain), Honda
*San Marino* (Misano): Valentino Rossi (Italy), Yamaha
*Spain* (Aragon): Jorge Lorenzo (Spain), Yamaha
*Japan* (Motegi):Jorge Lorenzo (Spain), Yamaha
*Australia* (Phillip Island): Valentino Rossi (Italy), Yamaha
*Malaysia* (Sepang):Marc Marquez (Spain), Honda
*Spain* (Valencia): Marc Marquez (Spain), Honda
*Riders' Championship 2014*: 1. Marc Marquez (Spain),
   Honda, 362pts; 2. Valentino Rossi (Italy), Yamaha,
   295pts; 3. Jorge Lorenzo (Spain),Yamaha, 263pts

MOTOGP 2015
*Qatar* (Doha): Valentino Rossi (Italy), Yamaha
*USA* (Austin): Marc Marquez (Spain), Honda
*Argentina* (Buenos Aires): Valentino Rossi (Italy), Yamaha
*Spain* (Jerez): Jorge Lorenzo (Spain), Yamaha
*France* (Le Mans): Jorge Lorenzo (Spain), Yamaha
*Italy* (Mugello): Jorge Lorenzo (Spain), Yamaha
*Catalonia* (Barcelona): Jorge Lorenzo (Spain), Yamaha
*Netherlands* (Assen): Valentino Rossi (Italy), Yamaha
*Germany* (Sachsenring): Marc Marquez (Spain), Honda
*USA* (Indianapolis): Marc Marquez (Spain), Honda

*Czech Republic* (Brno): Jorge Lorenzo (Spain), Yamaha
*Britain* (Silverstone): Valentino Rossi (Italy), Yamaha
*San Marino* (Misano): Marc Marquez (Spain), Honda

MOTO2 2014
*Qatar* (Doha): Esteve Rabat (Spain), Kalex
*USA* (Austin): Maverick Viñales (Spain), Kalex
*Argentina* (Santiago del Estero): Esteve Rabat (Spain), Kalex
*Spain* (Jerez): Mika Kallio (Finland), Kalex
*France* (Le Mans): Mika Kallio (Finland), Kalex
*Italy* (Mugello): Esteve Rabat (Spain), Kalex
*Catalonia* (Barcelona): Esteve Rabat (Spain), Kalex
*Netherlands* (Assen): Anthony West (Australia), Speed Up
*Germany* (Sachsenring): Dominique Aegerter (Switzerland),
   Suter
*USA* (Indianapolis): Mika Kallio (Finland), Kalex
*Czech Republic* (Brno): Esteve Rabat (Spain), Kalex
*Britain* (Silverstone): Esteve Rabat (Spain), Kalex
*San Marino* (Misano): Esteve Rabat (Spain), Kalex
*Spain* (Aragon): Maverick Viñales (Spain), Kalex
*Japan* (Motegi): Thomas Luthi (Switzerland), Suter
*Australia* (Phillip Island): Maverick Viñales (Spain), Kalex
*Malaysia* (Sepang): Maverick Viñales (Spain), Kalex
*Spain* (Valencia): Thomas Luthi (Switzerland), Suter
*Riders' Championship 2014*: 1. Esteve Rabat (Spain),
   Kalex, 346pts; 2. Mika Kallio (Finland), Kalex, 289pts;
   3. Maverick Viñales (Spain), Kalex, 274pts

MOTO2 2015
*Qatar* (Doha): Jonas Folger (Germany), Kalex
*USA* (Austin): Sam Lowes (Great Britain), Speed Up
*Argentina* (Buenos Aires): Johann Zarco (France), Kalex
*Spain* (Jerez): Jonas Folger (Germany), Kalex
*France* (Le Mans): Thomas Luthi (Switzerland), Kalex
*Italy* (Mugello): Esteve Rabat (Spain), Kalex
*Catalonia* (Barcelona): Johann Zarco (France), Kalex
*Netherlands* (Assen): Johann Zarco (France), Kalex
*Germany* (Sachsenring): Xavier Siméon (Belgium), Kalex
*USA* (Indianapolis): Alex Rins (Spain), Kalex
*Czech Republic* (Brno): Johann Zarco (France), Kalex
*Britain* (Silverstone): Johann Zarco (France), Kalex
*San Marino* (Misano): Johann Zarco (France), Kalex

MOTO3 GRAND PRIX 2014
*Qatar* (Doha): Jack Miller (Australia), KTM
*USA* (Austin): Jack Miller (Australia), KTM
*Argentina* (Santiago del Estero): Romano Fenati (Italy),
   KTM
*Spain* (Jerez): Romano Fenati (Italy), KTM
*France* (Le Mans): Jack Miller (Australia), KTM
*Italy* (Mugello): Romano Fenati (Italy), KTM
*Catalonia* (Barcelona): Álex Márquez (Spain), Honda
*Netherlands* (Assen): Álex Márquez (Spain), Honda
*Germany* (Sachsenring): Jack Miller (Australia), KTM
*USA* (Indianapolis): Efren Vazquez (Spain), Honda
*Czech Republic* (Brno): Alexis Masbou (France), Honda
*Britain* (Silverstone): Alexis Rins (Spain), Honda
*San Marino* (Misano): Alexis Rins (Spain), Honda
*Spain* (Aragon): Romano Fenati (Italy), KTM
*Japan* (Motegi): Álex Márquez (Spain), Honda
*Australia* (Phillip Island): Jack Miller (Australia), KTM
*Malaysia* (Sepang): Efrén Vázquez (Spain), Honda
*Spain* (Valencia): Jack Miller (Australia), KTM
*Riders' Championship 2014*: 1. Álex Márquez (Spain),
   Honda, 278pts; 2. Jack Miller (Australia), KTM, 276pts;
   3. Alexis Rins (Spain), Honda, 237pts

MOTO3 2015
*Qatar* (Doha): Alexis Masbou (France), Honda
*USA* (Austin): Danny Kent (Great Britain), Honda

*Argentina* (Buenos Aires): Danny Kent (Great Britain), Honda
*Spain* (Jerez): Danny Kent (Great Britain), Honda
*France* (Le Mans): Romano Fenati (Italy), KTM
*Italy* (Mugello):Miguel Oliveira (Portugal), KTM
*Catalonia* (Barcelona): Danny Kent (Great Britain), Honda
*Netherlands* (Assen): Miguel Oliveira (Portugal), KTM
*Germany* (Sachsenring): Danny Kent (Great Britain), Honda
*USA* (Indianapolis): Livio Loi (Belgium), Honda
*Czech Republic* (Brno): Niccolò Antonelli (Italy), Honda
*Britain* (Silverstone): Danny Kent (Great Britain), Honda
*San Marino* (Misano): Enea Bastianini (Italy), Honda

ISLE OF MAN TOURIST TROPHY 2015
*Senior:* John McGuinness (England), Honda
*Supersport:* Race 1 – Ian Hutchinson (England), Yamaha;
  Race 2 – Ian Hutchinson (England), Yamaha

WORLD SUPERBIKES 2014
*Australia* (Phillip Island): Race 1 – Eugene Laverty (Ireland),
  Voltcom Crescent Suzuki; Race 2 – Sylvain Guintoli
  (France), Aprilia
*Spain* (Aragon): Race 1 – Tom Sykes (Great Britain),
  Kawasaki; Race 2 – Tom Sykes (Great Britain), Kawasaki
*Netherlands* (Assen): Race 1 – Sylvain Guintoli (France),
  Aprillia; Race 2 – Jonathan Rea (Great Britain), Pata
  Honda World Superbike
*Italy* (Imola): Race 1 – Jonathan Rea (Great Britain), Pata
  Honda World Superbike; Race 2 – Jonathan Rea (Great
  Britain), Pata Honda World Superbike
*Great Britain* (Donington): Race 1 – Tom Sykes (Great
  Britain), Kawasaki; Race 2 – Tom Sykes (Great Britain),
  Kawasaki
*Malaysia* (Sepang): Race 1 – Marco Melandri (Italy),
  Aprilia; Race 2 – Marco Melandri (Italy), Aprilia
*Italy* (Rimini): Race 1 – Tom Sykes (Great Britain), Kawasaki;
  Race 2 – Tom Sykes (Great Britain), Kawasaki
*Portugal* (Algarve): Race 1 – Tom Sykes (Great Britain),
  Kawasaki; Race 2 – Jonathan Rea (Great Britain), Pata
  Honda World Superbike
*USA* (Monterey): Race 1 – Marco Melandri (Italy), Aprilia;
  Race 2 – Tom Sykes (Great Britain), Kawasaki
*Spain* (Jerez): Race 1 – Marco Melandri (Italy), Aprilia;
  Race 2 – Marco Melandri (Italy), Aprilia
*France* (Magny-Cours): Race 1 – Sylvain Guintoli (France),
  Aprilia; Race 2 – Marco Melandri (Italy), Aprilia
*Qatar* (Doha): Race 1 – Sylvain Guintoli (France), Aprilia;
  Race 2 – Sylvain Guintoli (France), Aprilia
*Rider's World Championship 2014:* 1. Sylvain Guintoli
  (France), Aprilia, 416pts; 2. Tom Sykes (Great Britain),
  Kawasaki, 410pts; 3. Jonathan Rea (Great Britain), Pata
  Honda World Superbike, 334pts

WORLD SUPERBIKES 2015
*Australia* (Phillip Island): Race 1 – Jonathan Rea (Great
  Britain) Kawasaki; Race 2 – Leon Haslam (Great Britain),
  Aprilia
*Thailand* (Buriram): Race 1 – Jonathan Rea (Great Britain)
  Kawasaki; Race 2 – Jonathan Rea (Great Britain),
  Kawasaki
*Spain* (Aragon): Race 1 – Jonathan Rea (Great Britain)
  Kawasaki; Race 2 – Chaz Davies (Great Britain), Aruba.it
  Racing–Ducati SBK
*Netherlands* (Assen): Race 1 – Jonathan Rea (Great Britain)
  Kawasaki; Race 2 – Jonathan Rea (Great Britain),
  Kawasaki
*Italy* (Imola): Race 1 – Jonathan Rea (Great Britain), Kawasaki;
  Race 2 – Jonathan Rea (Great Britain), Kawasaki
*Great Britain* (Donington): Race 1 – Tom Sykes (Great
  Britain), Kawasaki; Race 2 – Tom Sykes (Great Britain),
  Kawasaki

*Portugal* (Algarve): Race 1 – Jonathan Rea (Great Britain),
  Kawasaki; Race 2 – Jonathan Rea (Great Britain), Kawasaki
*Italy* (Rimini): Race 1 – Tom Sykes (Great Britain), Kawasaki;
  Race 2 – Jonathan Rea (Great Britain), Kawasaki
*USA* (Monterey): Race 1 – Chaz Davies (Great Britain),
  Aruba.it Racing–Ducati SB; Race 2 – Chaz Davies (Great
  Britain), Aruba.it Racing–Ducati SBK
*Malaysia* (Sepang): Race 1 – Jonathan Rea (Great Britain),
  Kawasaki; Race 2 – Chaz Davies (Great Britain), Aruba.it
  Racing–Ducati SBK
*Spain* (Jerez): Race 1 – Tom Sykes (Great Britain), Kawasaki;
  Race 2 – Chaz Davies (Great Britain), Aruba.it Racing-
  Ducati SBK

## MOTOR RACING

FORMULA 1 GRAND PRIX 2014
*Australia* (Melbourne): Nico Rosberg (Germany), Mercedes
*Malaysia* (Sepang): Lewis Hamilton (Great Britain),
  Mercedes
*Bahrain* (Sakhir): Lewis Hamilton (Great Britain), Mercedes
*China* (Shanghai): Lewis Hamilton (Great Britain), Mercedes
*Spain* (Barcelona): Lewis Hamilton (Great Britain), Mercedes
*Monaco* (Monte Carlo): Nico Rosberg (Germany), Mercedes
*Canada* (Montreal): Daniel Ricciardo (Australia), RBR-
  Renault
*Austria* (Spielberg): Nico Rosberg (Germany), Mercedes
*Great Britain* (Silverstone): Lewis Hamilton (Great Britain),
  Mercedes
*Germany* (Nürburgring): Nico Rosberg (Germany),
  Mercedes
*Hungary* (Hungaroring): Daniel Ricciardo (Australia),
  RBR-Renault
*Belgium* (Spa): Daniel Ricciardo (Australia), RBR-Renault
*Italy* (Monza): Lewis Hamilton (Great Britain), Mercedes
*Singapore* (Morina Bay):Lewis Hamilton (Great Britain),
  Mercedes
*Japan* (Suzuka): Lewis Hamilton (Great Britain), Mercedes
*Russia* (Sochi): Lewis Hamilton (Great Britain), Mercedes
*USA* (Austin): Lewis Hamilton (Great Britain), Mercedes
*Brazil* (Sao Paulo): Nico Rosberg (Germany), Mercedes
*Abu Dhabi* (Yas Marina): Lewis Hamilton (Great Britain),
  Mercedes
*Drivers' World Championship 2014:* 1. Lewis Hamilton
  (Great Britain), Mercedes, 384pts; 2. Nico Rosberg
  (Germany), Mercedes, 317pts; 3. Daniel Riccardo
  (Australia), RBR-Renault, 238pts
*Constructors' World Championship 2014:* 1. Mercedes,
  701pts; 2. RBR-Renault, 405pts; 3. Williams-Mercedes,
  320pts

FORMULA 1 GRAND PRIX 2015
*Australia* (Melbourne): Lewis Hamilton (Great Britain),
  Mercedes
*Malaysia* (Sepang): Sebastian Vettel (Germany), Ferrari
*China* (Shanghai): Lewis Hamilton (Great Britain),
  Mercedes
*Bahrain* (Sakhir): Lewis Hamilton (Great Britain), Mercedes
*Spain* (Barcelona): Nico Rosberg (Germany), Mercedes
*Monaco* (Monte Carlo): Nico Rosberg (Germany), Mercedes
*Canada* (Montreal): Lewis Hamilton (Great Britain),
  Mercedes
*Austria* (Spielberg): Nico Rosberg (Germany), Mercedes
*Great Britain* (Silverstone): Lewis Hamilton (Great Britain),
  Mercedes
*Hungary* (Hungaroring): Sebastian Vettel (Germany), Ferrari
*Belgium* (Spa): Lewis Hamilton (Great Britain), Mercedes
*Italy* (Monza): Lewis Hamilton (Great Britain), Mercedes
*Singapore* (Marina Bay): Sebastian Vettel (Germany), Ferrari

INDIANAPOLIS 500 2015
Indianapolis, USA, 24 May
Juan Pablo Montoya (Colombia), Team Penske

LE MANS 24-HOUR RACE 2015
Le Mans, France, 10–14 June
Earl Bamber (New Zealand), Nick Tandy (Great Britain) and
    Nico Hülkenberg (Germany), Porsche Team

## MOTOR RALLYING

WORLD RALLY CHAMPIONSHIP 2014
*Monte Carlo:* Sébastien Ogier (France), Volkswagen
*Sweden:* Jari-Matti Latvala (Finland), Volkswagen
*Mexico:* Sébastien Ogier (France), Volkswagen
*Portugal:* Sébastien Ogier (France), Volkswagen
*Argentina:* Jari-Matti Latvala (Finland), Volkswagen
*Italy:* Sébastien Ogier (France), Volkswagen
*Poland:* Sébastien Ogier (France), Volkswagen
*Finland:* Jari-Matti Latvala (Finland), Volkswagen
*Germany:* Thierry Neuville (Belgium), Hyundai
*Australia:* Sébastien Ogier (France), Volkswagen
*Spain:* Sébastien Ogier (France), Volkswagen
*Great Britain:* Sébastien Ogier (France), Volkswagen
*Drivers' World Championship 2014:* 1. Sébastien Ogier
    (France), Volkswagen, 267pts; 2. Jari-Matti Latvala
    (Finland), Volkswagen, 218pts; 3. Andreas Mikkelsen
    (Norway), Volkswagen, 150pts
*Manufacturers' World Championship 2014:* 1. Volkswagen,
    447pts; 2. Citroën, 210pts; 3. M-Sport , 208pts

WORLD RALLY CHAMPIONSHIP 2015
*Monte Carlo:* Sébastien Ogier (France), Volkswagen
*Sweden:* Sébastien Ogier (France), Volkswagen
*Mexico:* Sébastien Ogier (France), Volkswagen
*Argentina:* Kris Meeke (Great Britain), Citroën
*Portugal:* Jari-Matti Latvala (Finland), Volkswagen
*Italy:* Sébastien Ogier (France), Volkswagen
*Poland:* Sébastien Ogier (France), Volkswagen
*Finland:* Jari-Matti Latvala (Finland), Volkswagen
*Germany:* Sébastien Ogier (France), Volkswagen
*Australia:* Sébastien Ogier (France), Volkswagen

DAKAR RALLY RAID 2015
Argentina, Chile, 4–17 January

*Motorcycle:* Marc Coma (Spain), KTM
*Quad:* Rafa   Sonik (Poland), Yamaha
*Car:* Nasser Al-Attiyah (Qatar), Mini
*Truck:* Ayrat Mardeev (Russia), Kamaz

## NETBALL

*Superleague Grand Final 2015:* Surrey Storm beat
    Hertfordshire Mavericks 56–36

NETBALL WORLD CUP 2015
Sydney, Australia 7–18 August 2015
*Semi-Final I:* New Zealand beat England 50–39
*Semi-Final II:* Australia beat Jamaica 67–56
*Bronze Medal Match:* England beat Jamaica 64–44
*Gold Medal Match:* Australia beat New Zealand 58–55

## NORDIC EVENTS

BIATHLON WORLD CUP 2014–15

MEN
*Overall:* Martin Fourcade (France), 1,402pts

WOMEN
*Overall:* Darya Domracheva (Belarus), 1,092pts

BIATHLON WORLD CHAMPIONSHIPS 2015
Kontiolahti, Finland, March

MEN
*20km Individual:* Martin Fourcade (France)
*10km Sprint:* Johannes Thingnes Bo (Norway)
*12.5km Pursuit:* Eric Lesser (Germany)
*15km Mass Start:* Jakov Fak (Slovenia)
*4 × 7.5km Relay (Team):* Germany

WOMEN
*15km Individual:* Ekaterina Yurlova (Russia)
*7.5km Sprint:* Marie Dorin Habert (France)
*10km Pursuit:* Marie Dorin Habert (France)
*12.5km Mass Start:* Valj Semerenko (Ukraine)
*4 × 6km Relay (Team):* Germany

NORDIC WORLD CUP 2014–15
*World Cup:* Eric Frenzel (Germany), 945pts
*Nation Cup:* Germany, 4,458pts

## POLO

*Prince of Wales Trophy 2015:* La Indiana beat El Remanso
    14–13
*Queen's Cup final 2015:* King Power Foxes beat Dubai 11–10
*Warwickshire Cup 2015:* Apes Hill Club beat HB Polo 8–6
*Gold Cup (British Open) final 2015:* King Power Foxes beat
    UAE 14–8

## RACKETS

*Noel Bruce Cup 2014:* Charlie Danby and Alex Titchener-
    Barrett (Harrow I) beat James Coyne and James Fuller
    (Wellington I) 4–2
*Amateur Singles Championship final 2014:* Alex Titchener-
    Barrett beat Tom Billings 3–0
*The Foster Cup final 2014 (public schools' singles championship):*
    C. Braham (Eton) beat T. Morales (Eton) 4–0
*British Professional Singles Championship final 2015:*
    Will Hopton beat Ben Snell 3–0
*British Open Singles Championship final 2015:* Jamie Stout beat
    Will Hopton 4–0
*British Open Doubles Championship final 2015:* J. Stout and
    J. J. S. Larken beat B. Snell and N. C. W. James 4–0
*Amateur Doubles Championship 2015:* Richard Owen and
    Alex Duncliffe-Vines beat Tim Cockcroft and Alex
    Titchener-Barrett 3–2

## REAL TENNIS

MEN
*British Open Singles final 2014:* Camden Riviere (USA) beat
    Steve Virgona (Australia) 3–2
*British Open Doubles final 2014:* Tim Chisholm (USA) and
    Camden Riviere (USA) beat Rob Fahey (Australia) and
    Bryn Sayers (Great Britain) 3–1
*Henry Leaf Cup final 2015 (public schools' old boys' doubles
    championship):* John Prenn and Charles Danby beat
    Harry Eddis and Horatio Cary 2–1
*World Championship 2015:* Tim Chisholm and Camden
    Riviere beat Rob Fahey and Steve Virgona 5–0

WOMEN
*British Open Singles Championship final 2015:* Claire Fahey
    (Great Britain) beat Sarah Vigrass (Great Britain) 2–0

*British Open Doubles Championship final 2015:* Claire Fahey (Great Britain) and Sarah Vigrass (Great Britain) beat Frederika Adam (USA) and Irina Dulbish (Russia) 2–0

# ROWING

## HENLEY ROYAL REGATTA 2015
*Grand Challenge Cup:* Leander Club and Molesey Boat Club beat Ruder Club Hansa von 1898 e.V. Dortmund (Germany) by 2¾ lengths

*Stewards' Challenge Cup:* Leander Club and University of London beat Nautical Club of Ioannina and Nautical Club of Kastoria (Greece) by 2 lengths

*Queen Mother Challenge Cup:* Leander Club and Agecroft Rowing Club beat Rostocker Ruder-Club and Potsdamer Ruder-Gesellschaft e.V. (Germany) by 5 lengths

*Silver Goblets and Nickalls' Challenge Cup:* J.C. Foad & M.K. Langridge (Molesey Boat Club and Leander Club) beat O.R.G. Cook & S.G. Innes (University of London and Leander Club) by 5 lengths

*Double Sculls Challenge Cup:* J.E. Collins & J.F.L. Walton (Leander Club) beat J.M. Thompson & J.E. Smith (South Africa) by 2? lengths

*Diamond Challenge Sculls:* A.M.O Drysdale (New Zealand) beat G. Csepregi (Hungary) by 5 lengths

*Remenham Challenge Cup:* Western Rowing Club (Canada) beat Leander Club and Imperial College London by 2¾ lengths

*Princess Grace Challenge Cup:* Imperial College London and Tees Rowing Club beat Molesey Boat Club easily

*Princess Royal Challenge Cup:* M. Knapkova (Czech Republic) beat L.I. Scheenaard (Netherlands) by 2¾ lengths

*Ladies' Challenge Plate:* Yale University (USA) beat University of Washington (USA) by 2¼ lengths

*Visitors' Challenge Cup:* University of California, Berkeley (USA) beat Sydney Rowing Club (Australia) by 1¾ lengths

*Prince of Wales Challenge Cup:* Leander Club beat Leander Club and Oxford Brookes University by 1½ lengths

*Thames Challenge Cup:* Thames Rowing Club 'A' beat Rudern, Tennis und Hockey Club Bayer Leverkusen (Germany) by 3 lengths

*Wyfold Challenge Cup:* Molesey Boat Club beat The Tideway Scullers' School by 2 lengths

*Britannia Challenge Cup:* Sydney Rowing Club (Australia) beat Thames Rowing Club by 4 lengths

*Temple Challenge Cup:* Amsterdamsche Studenten Roeivereeniging Nereus (Netherlands) beat Université de Lyon (France) by 4¾ lengths

*Prince Albert Challenge Cup:* University of Washington (USA) beat Yale University (USA) by 1 length

*Princess Elizabeth Challenge Cup:* St Paul's School beat Westminster School by 1⅔ lengths

*Fawley Challenge Cup:* Sir William Borlase's Grammar School beat Nottingham Rowing Club by 1¼ lengths

## THE 161ST UNIVERSITY BOAT RACE
Putney–Mortlake, 4 miles, 1 f, 180 yd, 11 April 2015

### MEN
Oxford beat Cambridge by 6 lengths; 17min 35sec
Cambridge have won 81 times, Oxford 79 and there has been one dead heat. The record time is 16min 19sec, rowed by Cambridge in 1998.

### WOMEN
Oxford beat Cambridge by 6½ lengths; 19min 45sec
Cambridge have won 41 times, Oxford 29

## BRITISH ROWING SENIOR CHAMPIONSHIPS 2014
Nottingham, October
*Open Double Sculls:* Leander Club

*Women's Double Sculls:* Imperial College London
*Open Coxless Fours:* Molesey Boat Club
*Women's Coxless Fours:* Army Rowing Club, London Rowing Club, Imperial College London and Minerva Bath Rowing Club

*Open Quadruple Sculls:* Sir William Borlase's Grammar School, Agecroft Rowing Club and Reading University

*Women's Quadruple Sculls:* London Rowing Club, Imperial College London, Minerva Bath Rowing Club and Army Rowing Club

*Open Eights:* Leander Club
*Women's Eights:* Leander Club
*Open Legs, Trunk and Arms Single Sculls:* Event not held in 2014 due to poor weather

*Open Trunks and Arms Single Sculls:* Event not held in 2014 due to poor weather

*Women's Trunk and Arms Single Sculls:* Event not held in 2014 due to poor weather

*Open Arms and Shoulders Single Sculls:* Event not held in 2014 due to poor weather

*Women's Arms and Shoulders Single Sculls:* Event not held in 2014 due to poor weather

## OTHER ROWING EVENTS
*Wingfield Sculls 2014: Men,* T.P. Richards (Imperial College); *Women,* M. Wilson (Imperial College)

*Oxford Summer Eights 2015: Men,* Oriel; *Women,* Wadham
*Torpid Races 2015: Men,* Pembroke; *Women,* Wadham
*Head of the River 2015: Men,* Leander; *Women,* Army BC/Imperial College BC/London RC/Marlow RC/Minerva-Bath RC/Oxford Brookes University BC/Southampton Coalporters ARC

# RUGBY FIVES

*National Open Singles Championship final 2014:* W. Ellison beat D. Grant 2–1

*National Ladies' Singles Championship final 2014:* C. Knowles beat T. Mills 2–0

*National Ladies' Doubles Championship final 2014:* K. Briedenhann and T. Mills beat M. Raynor and A. Steel 2–0

*National Open Doubles Championship final 2015:* D. Tristao and W. Ellison beat T. Dean and E. Kay 2–0

*National Club Championship final 2015:* Wessex Club beat Old Paulines 115–84

*National Schools' Singles Championship final 2015:* T. Watkinson (Winchester) beat S. Whitehorn (Derby Moor) 2–1

*National Schools' Doubles Championship final 2015:* Derby Moor I beat Edinburgh Academy I 2–0

*Varsity Match 2015:* Cambridge Sparrows beat Oxford Beavers 151–86

# RUGBY LEAGUE

*Super League Grand Final 2014:* St Helens beat Wigan Warriors 14–6

*Ladbrokes Challenge Cup final 2015:* Leeds Rhinos beat Hull KR 50–0

*World Club Series 2015:* South Sydney Rabbitohs beat St Helens 39–0

## AMATEUR COMPETITIONS 2014
*National Conference League Premier Division Grand Final:* West Hull beat Wath Brow Hornets 20–8

*Division One Champions:* West Hull
*Division Two Champions:* Kells
*BARLA National Cup final:* Egremont beat Sharlston Rovers 34–16

*Varsity Match 2015:* Oxford beat Cambridge 42–0

# RUGBY UNION

## SIX NATIONS' CHAMPIONSHIP 2015

| 6 February | Cardiff | England beat Wales 21–16 |
| | Rome | Ireland beat Italy 26–3 |
| 7 February | Saint-Denis | France beat beat Scotland 15–8 |
| 14 February | Twickenham | England beat Italy 47–17 |
| | Dublin | Ireland beat France 18–11 |
| 15 February | Edinburgh | Wales beat Scotland 26–23 |
| 28 February | Edinburgh | Italy beat Scotland 22–19 |
| 1 March | Saint-Denis | Wales beat France 20–13 |
| | Dublin | Ireland beat England 19–9 |
| 14 March | Cardiff | Wales beat Ireland 23–16 |
| | Twickenham | England beat Scotland 25–13 |
| 15 March | Rome | France beat Italy 29–0 |
| 21 March | Rome | Wales beat Italy 61–20 |
| | Edinburgh | Ireland beat Scotland 40–10 |
| | Twickenham | England beat France 55–35 |

*Final standings:* 1. Ireland, 8pts; 2. England, 8pts; 3. Wales, 8pts; 4. France, 4pts; 5. Italy, 2pts; 6. Scotland, 0pts

## EUROPEAN COMPETITIONS 2014–15
*European Rugby Champions Cup final:* Toulon beat Clermont 24–18
*European Rugby Challenge Cup final:* Gloucester beat Edinburgh 19–13

## DOMESTIC COMPETITIONS 2014–15

### ENGLAND
*Aviva Premiership:* Northampton Saints, 76pts
*Aviva Premiership final:* Saracens beat Bath 28–16
*RFU Championship:* Bristol, 103pts
*RFU Championship final:* Worcester Warriors beat Bristol Rugby 29–28 (at Bristol); Worcester Warriors drew with Bristol Rugby 21–20 (at Worcester). Worcester Warriors won 59–58 on agg.
*National League: Division 1,* Ealing Trailfinders, 1336pts; *Promotion from Division 2 (North):* Hull Ionians; *Promotion from Division 2 (South):* Henley Hawks
*British and Irish Cup final:* Worcester Warriors beat Doncaster Knights 35–5
*County Championship final (Bill Beaumont Cup):* Cornwall beat Lancashire 18–13
*County Shield final:* Leicestershire beat Cumbria 34–17
*133rd Varsity Match:* Oxford beat Cambridge 43–6

### ANGLO-WELSH
*LV Cup final:* Saracens beat Exeter Chiefs 23–20

### CELTIC
*Guiness Pro12:* Glasgow Warriors, 75pts
*Guiness Pro12 final:* Glasgow Warriors beat Munster 23–13

### SCOTLAND
*Premiership champions:* Heriots; *National League champions:* Selkirk RFC
*BT Cup final:* Boroughmuir beat Harwich 55–17

### WALES
*Premiership:* Pontypridd, 94pts; *National League:* League 1 (East), Penallta, 99pts; (West), Newcastle Emlyn, 82pts; (North) Pwllheli RFC, 92pts
*WRU Challenge Cup final:* Bridgend beat Pontypridd 19–15

### IRELAND
All Ireland League: Division 1A, Lansdowne, 65pts; Division 1B, Galwegians, 67pts; Division 2A, Old Wesley, 61pts; Division 2B, Highfield, 67pts

# SHOOTING

## 146TH NATIONAL RIFLE ASSOCIATION IMPERIAL MEETING
Bisley, 16–18 July 2015

*Queen's Prize:* D. P. Calvert, 294.29 v-bulls
*Grand Aggregate:* G. C. D Barnett, 700.102 v-bulls
*Prince of Wales Prize:* J. D. Warburton, 75.14 v-bulls
*St George's Vase:* D. P. Calvert , 149.21 v-bulls
*All Comers' Aggregate:* J. D. Warburton, 372.55 v-bulls
*Kolapore Cup:* Great Britain, 1172.131 v-bulls
*Chancellor's Trophy:* Cambridge University, 1148.102 v-bulls
*National Trophy:* England, 2061.247 v-bulls
*Musketeers Cup:* Newcastle University, 568.54 v-bulls
*County Championship Long Range:* Surrey, 588.79 v-bulls
*Mackinnon Challenge Cup:* England, 1142.100 v-bulls
*The Albert:* A. R. McLeod, 220.30 v-bulls
*Hopton Challenge Cup:* J. M. B Baillie-Hamilton, 981.99 v-bulls

# SNOOKER

## 2014–15
*Shanghai Masters:* Stuart Bingham (England) beat Mark Allen (Northern Ireland) 10–3
*UK Championship* (York): Ronnie O'Sullivan (England) beat Judd Trump (England) 10–9
*Masters* (Alexandra Palace): Shaun Murphy (England) beat Neil Robertson (Australia) 10–2
*Welsh Open* (Newport): John Higgins (Scotland) beat Ben Woollaston (England) 9–3
*German Masters* (Berlin): Mark Selby (England) beat Shaun Murphy (England) 9–7
*China Open* (Beijing): Mark Selby (England) beat Gary Wilson (England) 10–2
*World Championship* (Sheffield): Shaun Murphy (England) beat Stuart Bingham (England) 18–15
*Australian Open* (Bendigo): Judd Trump (England) beat Neil Robertson (Australia) 9–5
*Players Tour Championship* (Bangkok, Thailand): Joe Perry (England) beat Mark Williams (Wales) 4–3
*Wuxi Classic* (China): Neil Robertson (Australia) beat Joe Perry (England) 10–9
*International Championship* (Chengdu, China): Ricky Walden (England) beat Mark Allen (Northern Ireland) 10–7

# SPEED SKATING

## WORLD ALL-ROUND CHAMPIONSHIPS 2015
Calgary, Canada, 7–8 March

### MEN
*Gold:* Sven Kramer (Netherlands); *Silver:* Denis Yuskov (Russia); *Bronze:* Sverre Lunde Pedersen (Norway)
*500m:* Denny Morrison (Canada), 34.98sec
*1500m:* Denis Yuskov (Russia), 1min 42.92sec
*5000m:* Sven Kramer (Netherlands), 6min 07.49sec
*10,000m:* Sven Kramer (Netherlands), 12min 56.70sec

### WOMEN
*Gold:* Martina Sáblíková (Czech Rep.); *Silver:* Ireen Wüst (Netherlands); *Bronze:* Ida Njåtun (Norway)
*500m:* Helen Richardson (USA), 37.11sec
*1500m:* Ida Njåtun (Norway), 1min 52.71sec
*3000m:* Martina Sáblíková (Czech Rep.), 3min 55.10sec
*5000m:* Martina Sáblíková (Czech Rep.), 6min 51.21sec

EUROPEAN ALL-ROUND CHAMPIONSHIPS 2015
Chelyabinsk, Russia, 10–11 January

MEN
Gold: Sven Kramer (Netherlands); Silver: Koen Verweij
  (Netherlands); Bronze: Denis Yuskov (Russia)
500m: Koen Verweij (Netherlands), 36.20sec
1500m: Denis Yuskov (Russia), 1min 46.22sec
5000m: Sven Kramer (Netherlands), 6min 17.32sec
10,000m: Sven Kramer (Netherlands), 13min 07.27sec

WOMEN
Gold: Ireen Wüst (Netherlands); Silver: Martina Sáblíková
  (Czech Republic); Bronze: Linda de Vries (Netherlands)
500m: Ireen Wüst (Netherlands), 39.24sec
1500m: Ireen Wüst (Netherlands), 1min 56.05sec
3000m: Martina Sáblíková (Czech Rep.), 4min 05.23sec
5000m: Martina Sáblíková (Czech Rep.), 7min 00.70sec

WORLD SHORT TRACK CHAMPIONSHIPS 2015
Moscow, Russia, 13–15 March

MEN
500m: Dajing Wu (China), 41.032sec
1000m: Park Se-yeong (Rep. of Korea), 1min 25.155sec
1500m: Semion Elistratov (Russia), 2min 18.096sec
3000m: Sjinkie Knegt (Netherlands), 5min 05.321sec
5000m relay: China, 6min 55.228sec
Overall: Sjinkie Knegt (Netherlands), 63pts

WOMEN
500m: Fan Kexin (China), 43.886sec
1000m: Choi Min-jeong (Rep. of Korea), 1min 32.730sec
1500m: Arianna Fontana (Italy), 2min 31.392sec
3000m: Choi Min-jeong (Rep. of Korea), 5min 40.480sec
3000m relay: Rep. of Korea, 4min 18.550sec
Overall: Choi Min-jeong (Rep. of Korea), 89pts

EUROPEAN SHORT TRACK CHAMPIONSHIPS 2015
Dordrecht, Netherlands, 23–25 January

MEN
500m: Victor An (Russia), 41.780sec
1,000m: Sjinkie Knegt (Netherlands), 1min 27.775sec
1,500m: Sjinkie Knegt (Netherlands), 2min 20.320sec
3,000m: Vladislav Bykanov (Israel), 4min 54.151sec
5,000m relay: Russia, 7min 04.153sec
Overall: Sjinkie Knegt (Netherlands), 97pts

WOMEN
500m: Elise Christie (Great Britain), 43.295sec
1,000m: Sofia Prosvirnova (Russia), 1min 35.039sec
1,500m: Elise Christie (Great Britain), 2min 42.939sec
3,000m: Patrycja Maliszewsk (Poland), 5min 23.622sec
3,000m relay: Russia, 4min 18.084sec
Overall: Elise Christie (Great Britain), 89pts

SQUASH

MEN
World Championship 2014: Ramy Ashour (Egypt) beat
  Mohamed El Shorbagy (Egypt) 3–2
European Individual Closed Championship 2015: Gregory
  Gaultier (France) beat Borja Golán (Spain) 3–1
European Team Championship 2015: France beat England 2–1
British National Championship 2015: Nick Matthew
  (England) beat Daryl Selby (England) 3–0
British Grand Prix 2015: Mohamed El Shorbagy (Egypt)
  beat Nick Matthew (England) 3–1

WOMEN
World Championship 2014: Nicol David (Malaysia) beat
  Raneem El Weleily (Egypt) 3–2

World Team Championship 2015: England beat Malaysia 2–1
European Individual Closed Championship 2015: Camille
  Serme (France) beat Line Hansen (Denmark) 3–0
European Team Championship 2015: England beat France 2–1
British National Championship 2015: Sarah Jane Perry
  (England) beat Laura Massaro (England) 3–2

SWIMMING

WORLD AQUATICS CHAMPIONSHIPS 2015
Kazan, Russia 24 July–9 August

MEN
50m freestyle: Florent Manaudou (France), 21.19sec
100m freestyle: Ning Zetao (China), 47.84sec
200m freestyle: James Guy (Great Britain), 1min 45.14sec
400m freestyle: Sun Yang (China), 3min 42.58sec
800m freestyle:Sun Yang (China), 7min 39.96sec
1,500m freestyle: Gregorio Paltrinieri (Italy), 14min 39.67sec
50m backstroke: Camille Lacourt (France), 24.23sec
100m backstroke: Mitch Larkin (Australia), 52.40sec
200m backstroke: Mitch Larkin (Australia), 1min 53.58sec
50m breaststroke: Adam Peaty (Great Britain), 26.51sec
100m breaststroke: Adam Peaty (Great Britain), 58.52sec
200m breaststroke: Marco Koch (Germany), 2min 07.76sec
50m butterfly: Florent Manaudou (France), 22.97sec
100m butterfly: Chad le Clos (South Africa), 50.56sec
200m butterfly: László Cseh (Hungary), 1min 53.48sec
200m medley: Ryan Lochte (USA), 1min 55.81sec
400m medley: Daiya Seto (Japan), 4min 08.50sec
4 × 100m freestyle relay: France, 3min 10.74sec
4 × 200m freestyle relay: Great Britain, 7min 04.33sec
4 × 100m medley relay: USA, 3min 29.93sec

WOMEN
50m freestyle: Bronte Campbell (Australia), 24.12sec
100m freestyle: Bronte Campbell (Australia), 52.52sec
200m freestyle: Katie Ledecky (USA), 1min 55.16sec
400m freestyle: Katie Ledecky (USA), 3min 59.13sec
800m freestyle: Katie Ledecky (USA), 8min 07.39sec
1,500m freestyle: Katie Ledecky (USA), 15min 25.48sec
50m backstroke: Fu Yuanhui (China), 27.11sec
100m backstroke: Emily Seebohm (Australia), 58.26sec
200m backstroke: Emily Seebohm (Australia), 2min 05.81sec
50m breaststroke: Jennie Johansson (Sweden), 30.05sec
100m breaststroke: Yuliya Yefimova (Russia), 1min 05.66sec
200m breaststroke: Kanako Watanabe (Japan), 2min 21.15sec
50m butterfly: Sarah Sjöström (Sweden), 24.96sec
100m butterfly: Sarah Sjöström (Sweden), 56.64sec
200m butterfly: Natsumi Hoshi (Japan), 2min 05.56sec
200m medley: Katinka Hosszú (Hungary), 2min 06.12sec
400m medley: Katinka Hosszú (Hungary), 4min 30.39
4 × 100m freestyle relay: Australia, 3min 31.48sec
4 × 200m freestyle relay: USA, 7min 45.37sec
4 × 100m medley relay: China, 3min 54.41sec

MIXED
4 × 100m mixed freestyle relay: USA, 3min 23.05sec
4 × 100m mixed medley relay: Great Britain, 3min 41.71sec

BRITISH CHAMPIONSHIPS 2015
London Aquatics Centre, 14–18 April

MEN
50m freestyle: Benjamin Proud (Plymouth), 21.99sec
100m freestyle: Calum Jarvis (Bath), 48.79sec
200m freestyle: James Guy (Millfield), 1min 46.32sec
400m freestyle: James Guy (Millfield), 3min 44.16sec
1,500m freestyle: Stephen Milne (Perth City), 14min 58.25sec

*100m backstroke:* Chris Walker-Hebborn (Ellesmere College), 53.88sec
*200m backstroke:* Craig McNally (Warrender), 1min 57.58sec
*100m breaststroke:* Adam Peaty (Derby), 57.92sec
*200m breaststroke:* Adam Peaty (Derby), 2min 08.34sec
*100m butterfly:* Thomas Laxton (Loughborough University), 52.40sec
*200m butterfly:* Cameron Brodie (University of Stirling), 1min 57.71sec
*200m medley:* Roberto Pavoni (Loughborough University), 1min 57.79sec
*400m medley:* Daniel Wallace (Warrender), 4min 12.78sec

WOMEN
*50m freestyle:* Francesca Halsall (Loughborough University), 24.37sec
*100m freestyle:* Siobhan-Marie O'Connor (Bath University), 53.83sec
*200m freestyle:* Jazmin Carlin (Bath University), 1min 56.88sec
*400m freestyle:* Jazmin Carlin (Swansea University), 4min 03.51sec
*800m freestyle:* Jazmin Carlin (Swansea University), 8min 21.58sec
*100m backstroke:* Elizabeth Simmonds (Bath University), 1min 00.03sec
*200m backstroke:* Elizabeth Simmonds (Bath University), 2min 08.38sec
*100m breaststroke:* Sophie Taylor (London Aquatic), 1min 07.39sec
*200m breaststroke:* Molly Renshaw (Loughboorough University), 2min 25.75sec
*100m butterfly:* Rachael Kelly (Loughborough University), 57.72sec
*200m butterfly:* Hannah Miley (Garioch), 2min 08.63sec
*200m medley:* Siobhan-Marie O'Connor (Bath University), 2min 09.51sec
*400m medley:* Hannah Miley (Gairoch), 4min 32.16sec

## TABLE TENNIS

WORLD CHAMPIONSHIPS 2014: TEAM
Tokyo, Japan, 28 April–5 May

*Men's team:* China beat Germany 3–1
*Women's team:* China beat Japan 3–0

WORLD CHAMPIONSHIPS 2014: INDIVIDUAL
Suzhou, China, 26 April–3 May

*Men's singles:* Ma Long (China) beat Fang Bo (China) 5–1
*Women's singles:* Ding Ning (China) beat Lui Shiwen (China) 4–3
*Men's doubles:* Xu Xin (China) and Zhang Jike (China) beat Fan Zhendong (China) and Zhou You (China) 5–1
*Women's doubles:* Liu Shiwen (China) and Zhu Yuling (China) beat Ding Ning (China) and Li Xiaoxia (China) 4–3
*Mixed doubles:* Xu Xin (China) and Yang Ha-eun (Rep. of Korea) beat Maharu Yoshimura (Japan) and Kasumi Ishikawa (Japan) 4–0

ENGLISH NATIONAL CHAMPIONSHIPS 2014–15
*Men's singles:* L.Pitchford beat P. Drinkhall 4–3
*Women's singles:* K.Sibley beat T.Ho 4–2
*Men's doubles:* L. Pitchford and P. Drinkhall beat D. Reed and S.Walker 3–2
*Women's doubles:* T. Ho and M. Tsaptsinos beat K Fevre and E. Vickers 3–1
*Mixed doubles:* S. Walker and T. Ho beat D. Reed and K. Sibley 3–1

## TENNIS

AUSTRALIAN OPEN CHAMPIONSHIPS 2015
Melbourne, 19 January–1 February

*Men's Singles:* Novak Djokovic (Serbia) beat Andy Murray (Great Britain) 7–6, 6–7, 6–3, 6–0
*Women's Singles:* Serena Williams (USA) beat Maria Sharapova (Russia) 6–3, 7–6
*Men's Doubles:* Simone Bolelli (Italy) and Fabio Fognini (Italy) beat Pierre-Hugues Herbert (France) and Nicolas Mahut (France) 6–4, 6–4
*Women's Doubles:* Bethanie Mattek-Sands (USA) and Lucie Šafářová (Czech Rep.) beat Chan Yung-jan (Chinese Taipei) and Zheng Jie (China) 6–4, 7–6
*Mixed Doubles:* Martina Hingis (Switzerland) and Leander Paes (India) beat Kristina Mladenovic (France) and Daniel Nestor (Canada) 6–4, 6–3

FRENCH OPEN CHAMPIONSHIPS 2015
Paris, 24 May–7 June

*Men's Singles:* Stan Wawrinka (Switzerland) beat Novak Djokovic (Serbia) 4–6, 6–4, 6–3, 6–4
*Women's Singles:* Serena Williams (USA) beat Lucie Šafářová (Czech Rep.) 6–3, 6–7, 6–2
*Men's Doubles:* Ivan Dodig (Croatia) and Marcelo Melo (Brazil) beat Mike Bryan (USA) and Bob Bryan (USA) 6–7, 7–6, 7–5
*Women's Doubles:* Bethanie Mattek-Sands (USA) and Lucie Šafářová (Czech Rep.) beat Casey Dellacqua (Australia) and Yaroslava Shvedova (Kazakhstan) 3–6, 6–4, 6–2
*Mixed Doubles:* Bethanie Mattek-Sands (USA) and Mike Bryan (USA) beat Lucie Hradecká (Czech Rep.) and Marcin Matkowski (Poland) 7–6, 6–1

ALL-ENGLAND CHAMPIONSHIPS 2015
Wimbledon, 29 June–12 July

*Men's Singles:* Novak Djokovic (Serbia) beat Roger Federer (Switzerland) 7–6, 6–7, 6–4, 6–3
*Ladies' Singles:* Serena Williams (USA) beat Garbiñe Muguruza (Spain) 6–4, 6–4
*Men's Doubles:* Jean-Julien Rojer (Netherlands) and Horia Tecău (Romania) beat Jamie Murray (Great Britain) and John Peers (Australia) 7–5, 6–4, 6–4
*Ladies' Doubles:* Martina Hingis (Switzerland) and Sania Mirza (India) beat Ekaterina Makarova (Russia) and Elena Vesnina (Russia) 5–7, 7–6, 7–5
*Mixed Doubles:* Martina Hingis (Switzerland) and Leander Paes (India) beat Alexander Peya (Austria) and Tímea Babos (Hungary) 6–1, 6–1

US OPEN CHAMPIONSHIPS 2015
New York, 31 August–13 September

*Men's Singles:* Novak Djokovic (Serbia) beat Roger Federer (Switzerland) 6–4, 5–7, 6–4, 6–4
*Women's Singles:* Flavia Pennetta (Italy) beat Roberta Vinci (Italy) 7–6, 6–2
*Men's Doubles:* Pierre-Hugues (France) and Nicolas Mahut (France) beat Jamie Murray (Great Britain) and John Peers (Australia) 6–4, 6–4
*Women's Doubles:* Martina Hingis (Switzerland) and Sania Mirza (India) beat Casey Dellacqua (Australia) and Yaroslava Shvedova (Kazakhstan) 6–3, 6–3
*Mixed Doubles:* Martina Hingis (Switzerland) and Leander Paes (India) beat Bethanie Mattek-Sands (USA) and Sam Querrey (USA) 6–4, 3–6, 10–7

TEAM CHAMPIONSHIPS
*Davis Cup final 2014:* Switzerland beat France 3–1
*Fed Cup final 2014:* Czech Rep. beat Germany 3–1

# SPORTS RECORDS

## ATHLETICS WORLD RECORDS
*As at 1 September 2015*

All the world records given below have been accepted by the International Amateur Athletic Federation. Fully automatic timing to 1/100th second is mandatory up to and including 400 metres. For distances up to and including 10,000 metres, records will be accepted to 1/100th second if timed automatically, and to 1/10th if hand timing is used.

### MEN

| TRACK EVENTS | hr | min | sec |
|---|---|---|---|
| *100m* | | | 9.58 |
| Usain Bolt (Jamaica), 2009 | | | |
| *200m* | | | 19.19 |
| Usain Bolt (Jamaica), 2009 | | | |
| *400m* | | | 43.18 |
| Michael Johnson (USA), 1999 | | | |
| *800m* | | 1 | 40.91 |
| David Rudisha (Kenya), 2012 | | | |
| *1000m* | | 2 | 11.96 |
| Noah Ngeny (Kenya), 1999 | | | |
| *1500m* | | 3 | 26.00 |
| Hicham El Guerrouj (Morocco), 1998 | | | |
| *1 mile* | | 3 | 43.13 |
| Hicham El Guerrouj (Morocco), 1999 | | | |
| *2000m* | | 4 | 44.79 |
| Hicham El Guerrouj (Morocco), 1999 | | | |
| *3000m* | | 7 | 20.67 |
| Daniel Komen (Kenya), 1996 | | | |
| *5000m* | | 12 | 37.35 |
| Kenenisa Bekele (Ethiopia), 2004 | | | |
| *10,000m* | | 26 | 17.53 |
| Kenenisa Bekele (Ethiopia), 2005 | | | |
| *20,000m* | | 56 | 26.0 |
| Haile Gebrselassie (Ethiopia), 2007 | | | |
| *21,285m* | 1 | 00 | 00.0 |
| Haile Gebrselassie (Ethiopia), 2007 | | | |
| *25,000m* | 1 | 12 | 25.4 |
| Moses Mosop (Kenya), 2011 | | | |
| *30,000m* | 1 | 26 | 47.4 |
| Moses Mosop (Kenya), 2011 | | | |
| *Marathon* | 2 | 02 | 57 |
| Dennis Kipruto Kimetto (Kenya), 2014 | | | |
| *110m Hurdles (1.07m)* | | | 12.80 |
| Aries Merritt (USA), 2012 | | | |
| *400m Hurdles (0.97m)* | | | 46.78 |
| Kevin Young (USA), 1992 | | | |
| *3000m Steeplechase* | | 7 | 53.63 |
| Saif Saeed Shaheen (Qatar), 2004 | | | |

| RELAYS | | min | sec |
|---|---|---|---|
| *4 × 100m* | | | 36.84 |
| Jamaica, 2012 | | | |
| *4 × 200m* | | 1 | 18.63 |
| Jamaica, 2014 | | | |
| *4 × 400m* | | 2 | 54.29 |
| USA, 1993 | | | |
| *4 × 800m* | | 7 | 02.43 |
| Kenya, 2006 | | | |
| *4 × 1,500m* | | 14 | 22.22 |
| Kenya, 2014 | | | |

| FIELD EVENTS | m | ft | in |
|---|---|---|---|
| *High Jump* | 2.45 | 8 | 0½ |
| Javier Sotomayor (Cuba), 1993 | | | |
| *Pole Vault* | 6.16 | 20 | 2½ |
| Renaud Lavillenie (France), 2014 | | | |
| *Long Jump* | 8.95 | 29 | 4½ |
| Mike Powell (USA), 1991 | | | |
| *Triple Jump* | 18.29 | 60 | 0¼ |
| Jonathan Edwards (Great Britain), 1995 | | | |
| *Shot* | 23.12 | 75 | 10¼ |
| Randy Barnes (USA), 1990 | | | |
| *Discus* | 74.08 | 243 | 0 |
| Jürgen Schult (GDR), 1986 | | | |
| *Hammer* | 86.74 | 284 | 7 |
| Yuriy Sedykh (USSR), 1986 | | | |
| *Javelin* | 98.48 | 323 | 1 |
| Jan Zelezny (Czech Rep.), 1996 | | | |
| *Decathlon*† | | | 9,045pts |
| Yohann Diniz (France), 2011 | | | |
| Ashton Eaton (USA), 2015 | | | |

† Ten events comprising 100m, long jump, shot, high jump, 400m, 110m hurdles, discus, pole vault, javelin, 1500m

### WOMEN

| TRACK EVENTS | hr | min | sec |
|---|---|---|---|
| *100m* | | | 10.49 |
| Florence Griffith-Joyner (USA), 1988 | | | |
| *200m* | | | 21.34 |
| Florence Griffith-Joyner (USA), 1988 | | | |
| *400m* | | | 47.60 |
| Marita Koch (GDR), 1985 | | | |
| *800m* | | 1 | 53.28 |
| Jarmila Kratochvilova (Czechoslovakia), 1983 | | | |
| *1000m* | | 2 | 28.98 |
| Svetlana Masterkova (Russia), 1996 | | | |
| *1500m* | | 3 | 50.07 |
| Genzebe Dibaba (Ethiopia), 2015 | | | |
| *1 mile* | | 4 | 12.56 |
| Svetlana Masterkova (Russia), 1996 | | | |
| *2000m* | | 5 | 25.36 |
| Sonia O'Sullivan (Ireland), 1994 | | | |
| *3000m* | | 8 | 06.11 |
| Wang Junxia (China), 1993 | | | |
| *5000m* | | 14 | 11.15 |
| Tirunesh Dibaba (Ethiopia), 2008 | | | |
| *10,000m* | | 29 | 31.78 |
| Wang Junxia (China), 1993 | | | |
| *20,000m* | 1 | 5 | 26.6 |
| Tegla Loroupe (Kenya), 2000 | | | |
| *18,517* | 1 | 00 | 00.0 |
| Dire Tune (Ethiopia), 2008 | | | |
| *25,000m* | 1 | 27 | 05.9 |
| Tegla Loroupe (Kenya), 2002 | | | |
| *30,000m* | 1 | 45 | 50.0 |
| Tegla Loroupe (Kenya), 2003 | | | |
| *Marathon* | 2 | 15 | 25 |
| Paula Radcliffe (Great Britain), 2003 | | | |
| *100m Hurdles (0.84m)* | | | 12.21 |
| Yordanka Donkova (Bulgaria), 1988 | | | |
| *400m Hurdles (0.76m)* | | | 52.34 |
| Yuliya Pechonkina (Russia), 2003 | | | |

| *3000m Steeplechase* | 8 | 58.81 |
|---|---|---|
| Gulnara Galkina (Russia), 2008 | | |

| RELAYS | min | sec |
|---|---|---|
| *4 × 100m* | | 40.82 |
| USA, 2012 | | |
| *4 × 200m* | 1 | 27.46 |
| USA, 2000 | | |
| *4 × 400m* | 3 | 15.17 |
| USSR, 1988 | | |
| *4 × 800m* | 7 | 50.17 |
| USSR, 1984 | | |
| *4 × 1500m* | 16 | 33.58 |
| Kenya, 2014 | | |

| FIELD EVENTS | m | ft | in |
|---|---|---|---|
| *High Jump* | 2.09 | 6 | 10¼ |
| Stefka Kostadinova (Bulgaria), 1987 | | | |
| *Pole Vault* | 5.06 | 16 | 7 ¼ |
| Yelena Isinbayeva (Russia), 2009 | | | |
| *Long Jump* | 7.52 | 24 | 8¼ |
| Galina Chistyakova (USSR), 1988 | | | |
| *Triple Jump* | 15.50 | 50 | 10¼ |
| Inessa Kravets (Ukraine), 1995 | | | |
| *Shot* | 22.63 | 74 | 3 |
| Natalya Lisovskaya (USSR), 1987 | | | |
| *Discus* | 76.80 | 252 | 0 |
| Gabriele Reinsch (GDR), 1988 | | | |
| *Hammer* | 81.08 | 266 | 0 |
| Anita Wlodarczyk (Poland), 2015 | | | |
| *Javelin* | 72.28 | 237 | 2 |
| Barbora Spotakova (Czech Rep.), 2008 | | | |
| *Heptathlon*† | | | 7,291pts |
| Jackie Joyner-Kersee (USA), 1988 | | | |

† Seven events comprising 100m hurdles, shot, high jump, 200m, long jump, javelin, 800m

## ATHLETICS NATIONAL (UK) RECORDS
*As at 1 September 2015*

Records set anywhere by athletes eligible to represent Great Britain and Northern Ireland.

### MEN

| TRACK EVENTS | hr | min | sec |
|---|---|---|---|
| *100m* | | | 9.87 |
| Linford Christie, 1993 | | | |
| *200m* | | | 19.87 |
| John Regis, 1994 | | | |
| *400m* | | | 44.36 |
| Iwan Thomas, 1997 | | | |
| *800m* | | 1 | 41.73 |
| Sebastian Coe, 1981 | | | |
| *1000m* | | 2 | 12.18 |
| Sebastian Coe, 1981 | | | |
| *1500m* | | 3 | 28.81 |
| Mohamed Farah, 2013 | | | |
| *1 mile* | | 3 | 46.32 |
| Steve Cram, 1985 | | | |
| *2000m* | | 4 | 51.39 |
| Steve Cram, 1985 | | | |
| *3000m* | | 7 | 32.79 |
| David Moorcroft, 1982 | | | |
| *5000m* | | 12 | 53.11 |
| Mohamed Farah, 2011 | | | |
| *10,000m* | | 26 | 46.57 |
| Mohamed Farah, 2011 | | | |
| *20,000m* | | 57 | 28.7 |
| Carl Thackery, 1990 | | | |
| *20,855m* | 1 | 00 | 00.0 |
| Carl Thackery, 1993 | | | |
| *25,000m* | 1 | 15 | 22.6 |
| Ron Hill, 1965 | | | |
| *30,000m* | 1 | 31 | 30.4 |
| Jim Alder, 1970 | | | |
| *Marathon* | 2 | 07 | 13 |
| Steve Jones, 1985 | | | |
| *3000m Steeplechase* | | 8 | 07.96 |
| Mark Rowland, 1988 | | | |
| *110m Hurdles* | | | 12.91 |
| Colin Jackson, 1993 | | | |
| *400m Hurdles* | | | 47.82 |
| Kriss Akabusi, 1992 | | | |

| RELAYS | min | sec |
|---|---|---|
| *4 × 100m* | | 37.73 |
| GB team, 1999 | | |
| *4 × 200m* | 1 | 21.29 |
| GB team, 1989 | | |
| *4 × 400m* | 2 | 56.60 |
| GB team, 1996 | | |
| *4 × 800m* | 7 | 03.89 |
| GB team, 1982 | | |

| FIELD EVENTS | m | ft | in |
|---|---|---|---|
| *High Jump* | 2.37 | 7 | 9¼ |
| Steve Smith, 1993 | | | |
| Robbie Grabarz, 2012 | | | |
| *Pole Vault* | 5.82 | 19 | 1 |
| Steven Lewis, 2012 | | | |
| *Long Jump* | 8.51 | 27 | 11 |
| Greg Rutherford, 2014 | | | |
| *Triple Jump* | 18.29 | 60 | 0¼ |
| Jonathan Edwards, 1995 | | | |
| *Shot* | 21.92 | 71 | 11 |
| Carl Myerscough, 2003 | | | |
| *Discus* | 68.24 | 223 | 10 |
| Lawrence Okoye, 2012 | | | |
| *Hammer* | 77.55 | 254 | 5 |
| Nick Miller, 2015 | | | |
| *Javelin* | 91.46 | 300 | 1 |
| Steve Backley, 1992 | | | |
| *Decathlon* | | | 8,847pts |
| Daley Thompson, 1984 | | | |

| WALKING (TRACK) | hr | min | sec |
|---|---|---|---|
| *20,000m* | 1 | 23 | 26.5 |
| Ian McCombie, 1990 | | | |
| *30,000m* | 2 | 19 | 18 |
| Christopher Maddocks, 1984 | | | |
| *50,000m* | 4 | 05 | 44.6 |
| Paul Blagg, 1990 | | | |
| *26,037m* | 2 | 00 | 00.0 |
| Ron Wallwork, 1971 | | | |

### WOMEN

| TRACK EVENTS | min | sec |
|---|---|---|
| *100m* | | 10.99 |
| Dina Asher-Smith, 2015 | | |
| *200m* | | 22.07 |
| Dina Asher-Smith, 2015 | | |
| *400m* | | 49.41 |
| Christine Ohuruogu, 2013 | | |
| *800m* | 1 | 56.21 |
| Kelly Holmes, 1995 | | |
| *1500m* | 3 | 57.90 |
| Kelly Holmes, 2004 | | |
| *1 mile* | 4 | 17.57 |
| Zola Budd, 1985 | | |

| | min | sec |
|---|---|---|
| *3000m* | 8 | 22.20 |
| Paula Radcliffe, 2002 | | |
| *5000m* | 14 | 29.11 |
| Paula Radcliffe, 2004 | | |
| *10,000m* | 30 | 01.09 |
| Paula Radcliffe, 2002 | | |
| *Marathon* 2 | 15 | 25 |
| Paula Radcliffe, 2003 | | |
| *100m Hurdles* | | 12.51 |
| Tiffany Porter, 2014 | | |
| *400m Hurdles* | | 52.74 |
| Sally Gunnell, 1993 | | |
| *3000m Steeplechase* | 9 | 24.24 |
| Barbara Parker, 2012 | | |

| RELAYS | min | sec |
|---|---|---|
| *4 × 100m* | | 42.10 |
| GB team, 2015 | | |
| *4 × 200m* | 1 | 29.61 |
| GB team, 2014 | | |
| *4 × 400m* | 3 | 20.04 |
| GB team, 2007 | | |
| *4 × 800m* | 8 | 13.46 |
| GB team, 2013 | | |

| FIELD EVENTS | m | ft | in |
|---|---|---|---|
| *High Jump* | 1.97 | 6 | 5 |
| Isobel Pooley, 2015 | | | |
| *Pole Vault* | 4.71 | 15 | 6 |
| Holly Bleasdale, 2012 | | | |
| *Long Jump* | 7.07 | 23 | 2 |
| Shara Proctor, 2015 | | | |
| *Triple Jump* | 15.15 | 49 | 8½ |
| Ashia Hansen, 1997 | | | |
| *Shot* | 19.36 | 63 | 6¼ |
| Judy Oakes, 1988 | | | |
| *Discus* | 67.48 | 221 | 5 |
| Margaret Ritchie, 1981 | | | |
| *Hammer* | 73.86 | 242 | 3 |
| Sophie Hitchon, 2015 | | | |
| *Javelin* | 66.17 | 217 | 1 |
| Goldie Sayers, 2012 | | | |
| *Heptathlon* | | | 6,955pts |
| Jessica Ennis-Hill, 2012 | | | |

## SWIMMING WORLD RECORDS
*50m-pool. As at 27 July 2015*

| MEN | min | sec |
|---|---|---|
| *50m Freestyle* | | 20.91 |
| Cesar Cielo Filho (Brazil), 2009 | | |
| *100m Freestyle* | | 46.91 |
| Cesar Cielo Filho (Brazil), 2009 | | |
| *200m Freestyle* | 1 | 42.00 |
| Paul Biedermann (Germany), 2009 | | |
| *400m Freestyle* | 3 | 40.07 |
| Paul Biedermann (Germany), 2009 | | |
| *800m Freestyle* | 7 | 32.12 |
| Zhang Lin (China), 2009 | | |
| *1,500m Freestyle* | 14 | 31.02 |
| Sun Yang (China), 2012 | | |
| *50m Breaststroke* | | 26.67 |
| Cameron Van Der Burgh (South Africa), 2009 | | |
| *100m Breaststroke* | | 57.92 |
| Adam Peaty (Great Britain), 2015 | | |

| | min | sec |
|---|---|---|
| *200m Breaststroke* | 2 | 07.01 |
| Akihiro Yamaguchi (Japan), 2012 | | |
| *50m Butterfly* | | 22.43 |
| Rafael Munoz (Spain), 2009 | | |
| *100m Butterfly* | | 49.82 |
| Michael Phelps (USA), 2009 | | |
| *200m Butterfly* | 1 | 51.51 |
| Michael Phelps (USA), 2009 | | |
| *50m Backstroke* | | 24.04 |
| Liam Tancock (Great Britain), 2009 | | |
| *100m Backstroke* | | 51.94 |
| Aaron Peirsol (USA), 2009 | | |
| *200m Backstroke* | 1 | 51.92 |
| Aaron Peirsol (USA), 2009 | | |
| *200m Medley* | 1 | 54.00 |
| Ryan Lochte (USA), 2011 | | |
| *400m Medley* | 4 | 03.84 |
| Michael Phelps (USA), 2008 | | |
| *4 × 100m Freestyle relay* | 3 | 08.24 |
| USA, 2008 | | |
| *4 × 200m Freestyle relay* | 6 | 58.55 |
| USA, 2009 | | |
| *4 × 100m Medley relay* | 3 | 27.28 |
| USA, 2009 | | |

| WOMEN | min | sec |
|---|---|---|
| *50m Feestyle* | | 23.73 |
| Britta Steffen (Germany), 2009 | | |
| *100m Freestyle* | | 52.07 |
| Britta Steffen (Germany), 2009 | | |
| *200m Freestyle* | 1 | 52.98 |
| Federica Pellegrini (Italy), 2009 | | |
| *400m Freestyle* | 3 | 58.37 |
| Katie Ledecky (USA), 2014 | | |
| *800m Freestyle* | 8 | 11.00 |
| Katie Ledecky (USA), 2014 | | |
| *1,500m Freestyle* | 15 | 28.36 |
| Katie Ledecky (USA), 2014 | | |
| *50m Breaststroke* | | 29.48 |
| Ruta Meilutyte (Lithuania), 2013 | | |
| *100m Breaststroke* | 1 | 04.35 |
| Ruta Meilutyte (Lithuania), 2013 | | |
| *200m Breaststroke* | 2 | 19.11 |
| Rikke Moeller-Pedersen (Denmark), 2013 | | |
| *50m Butterfly* | | 24.43 |
| Sarah Sjostrom (Sweden), 2014 | | |
| *100m Butterfly* | | 55.98 |
| Dana Vollmer (USA), 2012 | | |
| *200m Butterfly* | 2 | 01.81 |
| Liu Zigi (China), 2009 | | |
| *50m Backstroke* | | 27.06 |
| Zhao Jing (China), 2009 | | |
| *100m Backstroke* | | 58.12 |
| Gemma Spofforth (Great Britain), 2009 | | |
| *200m Backstroke* | 2 | 04.06 |
| Missy Franklin (USA), 2012 | | |
| *200m Medley* | 2 | 06.15 |
| Ariana Kukors (USA), 2009 | | |
| *400m Medley* | 4 | 28.43 |
| Ye Shiwen (China), 2012 | | |
| *4 × 100m Freestyle relay* | 3 | 30.98 |
| Australia, 2014 | | |
| *4 × 200m Freestyle relay* | 7 | 42.08 |
| China, 2009 | | |
| *4 × 100m Medley relay* | 3 | 52.05 |
| USA, 2012 | | |

# THEATRE

*Matt Trueman*

## WEST END TOLLS

This was the year that the West End broke the £200 barrier. In July 2015, *The Stage's* annual ticket survey found that a premium seat for *The Book of Mormon* at the Prince of Wales Theatre was £202.25, marking a £50 price hike in a single year. It means that the most expensive seats in London have more than doubled in price in only three years (*Billy Elliot's* top tier was £97.50 in 2012).

Soaring prices can be taken as a mark of the West End's resilience – and, once again, the Society of London Theatre announced record attendance and box office figures for the 2014 calendar year – but it is also a sign of a shifting business model, one with greater disparity between premium and cheap seats, as well as increased flexibility through airline-style pricing and cut-price deals. Producers claim their hands are tied: rents are rising and talent fees are higher than ever.

It is ironic, then, that so many star-led shows should falter onstage. Lindsay Lohan had critics sharpening their claws ahead of her stage debut in David Mamet's *Speed-the-Plow* but she was the surprise – or at least, not the let-down – in Lindsay Posner's limp, rudderless revival of the Hollywood satire. 'A minor revelation,' *The Guardian* beamed. 'Can act a bit,' ventured *The Times*.

More Mamet came via *American Buffalo* – a big, starry, sell-out hit at Wyndham's Theatre. John Goodman played Don, the amiable Chicagoan junk shop owner taken in by schemester, Teach, played by a purple-suited, handlebar-moustachioed Damian Lewis. Tom Sturridge completed the trio as a young junkie, Bob, but the three seemed at odds with each other, acting in different registers, almost different eras, on Paul Wills' crowded resale-shop set.

Meanwhile, Bradley Cooper, once voted the world's sexiest man, turned himself into Joseph Merrick, the Elephant Man, without prosthetics, in a captivating feat of physical acting – hand bent backward, shoulders sloped, jaw sliding to the side – albeit in a hoary old 1977 play that did not need reviving. That pattern repeated. Why did Richard Bean's slight two-hander *The Mentalists* become a comic vehicle for Stephen Merchant? What possessed David Suchet to drag up as Lady Bracknell? And who thought Mary Chase's sweet but inert Pulitzer winner *Harvey* was worth restaging, let alone with James Dreyfus and Maureen Lipman in the leads? There's hope for big stars yet. Nicole Kidman, Sir Kenneth Branagh and Dame Judi Dench are due before the year's end.

However, the commercial sector looked largely resurgent, full of hit musicals and quality drama. True, the biggest houses, the Dominion and the Palladium, have struggled to replace their long-runners, but a wave of new productions came in. *Cats* returned with its very own Pussycat Doll, Nicole Scherzinger, in tow. Broadway imports *Memphis*, a celebration of early rock 'n' roll, and the Carole King jukebox musical *Beautiful*, both fared well, with Beverley Knight and Katie Brayben cementing their stardom in big leading roles, but it was an all-British affair, the Kinks-inspired *Sunny Afternoon*, that led the Olivier awards after transferring into the West End from the Hampstead Theatre. Rightly so; led by John Dagleish and George Maguire, it was swaggering, riotous entertainment.

So was *Made in Dagenham*, a musical sprung from the factory floor (via a hit Brit flick) that motored along thanks to Richard Thomas' tunes and Richard Bean's wit. Gemma Arterton made the role of Rita O'Grady her own as she led her colleagues on strike and all the way to parliament in this populist, political piece. The show closed six months later, without the Olivier nomination it deserved.

*Bend It Like Beckham* may yet go the same way, but Gurinder Chadha's staging of her own hit film won a slew of five-star reviews. Despite the occasional naff bit of soccer stagecraft, it proved a joyous celebration of multiculturalism and feminism, smack bang in the middle of the mainstream. It was everything Stratford East's staging of the *The Infidel* wanted to be, but David Baddiel's story tripped into schmaltz and stereotype in the move from the screen, losing all its hangdog humour. *Adrian Mole,* at the Leicester Curve, also stuttered; it never found a way to replicate the diary form that made Sue Townsend's books such a hoot. *Women on the Verge of a Nervous Breakdown,* a onetime Broadway flop, flopped again at the Playhouse.

Small-scale musicals led the way. Imelda Staunton was outstanding in *Gypsy* as a feisty, frayed gumball of a Mama Rose. There was Josie Rourke's gorgeous revival of Cy Coleman's sleuth-spoof *City of Angels*, with a lush Robert Jones design that slid from grayscale to technicolour as it swerved between fiction and reality. *Here Lies Love,* at the National, saw David Byrne and Fatboy Slim disco-tize the life and times of Imelda Marcos. Jamie Lloyd's *Assassins,* given a Marvel Comics Suicide Squad twist, was extraordinary; a site-specific *Sweeney Todd,* staged in a tiny south London pie shop, transferred into town on Stephen Sondheim's own recommendation. Cameron Mackintosh constructed a pie shop of his own on Shaftesbury Avenue. It explains the producer's desire to transform the Ambassadors Theatre into a flexible 400-seat studio space, capable of holding smaller-scale transfers; he plans to rename it the Sondheim Theatre.

It's true that transfers rule the roost, these days. *A View from the Bridge* and *King Charles III* both came in and earned moves to Broadway in the process. They follow a brilliant year for British talent in New York: *The Curious Incident of the Dog in the Night-Time, Wolf Hall, The Audience* and *Skylight* pulled in nine Tony awards between them.

Back at home, the Royal Shakespeare Company (RSC) transferred Tom Morton-Smith's bio-epic *Oppenheimer* into town, with John Heffernan's gaunt, haunted physicist at its centre, then followed it with an old-hat *Death of a Salesman,* with Antony Sher's Willy Loman smartly read but over-stewed. Very RSC, as it were. 1927's smartphone satire *Golem,* staged using the company's characteristic live-animation style, moved into the Trafalgar Studios, where James McAvoy had previously drawn huge crowds to an obscure Peter Barnes play, *The Ruling Class.* Not without good reason: at one point, the Scot rode a unicycle in his underpants.

## BY WHOM, FOR WHOM?

McAvoy was one of those to wade into a debate about the make-up of British theatre. In February, he argued that working-class actors were being frozen out of the industry; in May, a survey revealed that only one in ten British actors came from a working-class background.

Posh public-schoolboys – Eddie Redmayne, Benedict Cumberbatch, Tom Hiddleston and co. – were making the headlines, but their working class counterparts were struggling to cut through. That, in turn, impacts upon the work being staged – and so the wheel turns. 'Where are the Albert Finneys and the Glenda Jacksons?' asked shadow culture secretary Chris Bryant.

Representation was the big question of the year under review. Who gets to make theatre? Who gets to stand onstage? Whose stories get told and who decides? Plenty of navel-gazing, perhaps, but about time too as theatre's track record on diversity came under scrutiny. ACT For Change was set up in January 2014 by the actor Danny Lee Wynter, in response to a BBC trailer without a single non-white actor featured. It had theatre in its sights as well and, in June 2015, hosted a conference in the Olivier Theatre aimed at asking questions of diversity in theatre – not just in terms of race, but in terms of disability, class and gender too.

Meanwhile, Lucy Kerbel's organisation, TONIC Theatre, was pushing the question of gender. Its research found that women account for 37 per cent of artistic directors, a figure that drops to 24 per cent at theatres in receipt of more than £500,000 from the Arts Council. Female playwrights are grossly underrepresented, with less than a third of produced plays written by a woman, and only 12.5 per cent of adaptations. TONIC commissioned a series of plays with all-female casts for young people, seeking to increase opportunities for girls in school plays.

It is important to ask who is making theatre, but also who is watching. The Warwick Commission report, released in February, found that a third of theatregoers come from the wealthiest, best educated and least ethnically diverse section of the population. This fact, arguably, underpinned Rufus Norris' first season at the National Theatre (NT). He sought to open the theatre up, to insist that it was a medium for all, and his programming reflected that.

Sir Nicholas Hytner's reign came to an end in April. After a decade of massive expansion, commercial success, NT Live and a £70m refurbishment, Hytner's programming maintained an air of middle-class intellectualism. His last season gave us George Bernard Shaw's verbose four-hour treatise *Man and Superman* and a new Tom Stoppard play, his first in nine years, that tied the mystery of mind–body dualism to a banking system built on big data. *The Hard Problem* – a nod, perhaps, to writer's block – was, however, disappointing. Hytner's tenure ended with a raucous food-fight (the culmination of Sam Holcroft's deconstructed family farce, *Rules for Living*).

Norris began with *Everyman,* a medieval morality play with Oscar nominee Chiwetel Ejiofor in the title role. In Carol Ann Duffy's version, he was a blue-suited city slicker suddenly facing his reckoning and Norris' own production was as good-looking as it was plain-speaking. Intellectualism – with a similar message – came courtesy of Caryl Churchill's *Light Shining in Buckinghamshire,* staged by Lyndsey Turner on a vast Es Devlin-designed table. It became a push for a new politics; not parliamentary representation but a new, people-led democracy. Elsewhere, *The Red Lion* – Patrick Marber's first play in a decade – looked at the national game at grass roots level; Stephen Adly Guirgis' *The Motherfucker with the Hat,* a Broadway import, questioned privilege, race and addiction; and Alexander Zeldin's *Beyond Caring,* in the Shed, picked at zero-hour contracts. The National looked increasingly like a theatre for the nation.

## REINVENTING THE WHEEL OF TRAGEDY

The year has been strangely short on Shakespeare, though Benedict Cumberbatch is a hotly anticipated Hamlet, due in August. With nothing at the National and both the RSC and the Globe focusing elsewhere, it's been a welcome break from the Bard.

There were three stagings of The Merchant of Venice, though. Rupert Goold's Vegas-set production revived by the Almeida, with Susannah Fielding's doll-like Portia, prize in a reality TV show, winning the Ian Charleson award. Jonathan Pryce gave us a complex Shylock at the Globe, a tyrant at home and a victim in public, while at the RSC the role was taken by a Palestinian actor, Makram J. Khoury, with Patsy Ferran – still only a year out of RADA and already tipped for greatness – as Portia.

It was a year for women protagonists: the Donmar gave us an all-female *Henry IV;* Maxine Peake played an androgynous Hamlet in Manchester; Michelle Terry was a flirtatious Rosalind at the Globe; and Mariah Gale was a dignified, quakerish Isabella in *Measure for Measure.* Hers was an astonishing performance, taking the part unarmed: drab costume, no character tics or audience interaction – none of the things groundlings go in for. By the end, she had us rapt; charisma born of conviction alone. Lucian Msamati became the RSC's first black Iago, with Hugh Quarshie dismantling the notion of Othello as the 'noble Moor'.

Mostly, though, the RSC's focus was on Shakespeare's contemporaries, as was the Globe's, at least indoors in the Sam Wanamaker Playhouse. It meant a smorgasbord of John Ford: the first production of *Love's Sacrifice* since the 1630s, an Othello-like story of induced jealousy; *The Broken Heart,* a convoluted revenge tragedy in which a queen dies of an actual broken heart; and, his most famous, *'Tis Pity She's a Whore.* In Stratford, *The Jew of Malta* was a counterpoint to *Merchant,* with Jasper Britton a multifaceted Barabas. Trevor Nunn returned to the RSC for the first time with Ben Jonson's *Volpone.*

You could see this as a year of revisions; directors trying to shift our expectations in terms of the sorts of classics that we stage and the ways in which we stage them. The Barbican ran an Ibsen season and a Beckett season, collecting international approaches to these two literary behemoths. Thomas Ostermeier opened *An Enemy of the People* up into an actual public debate, while Australian wunderkind Simon Stone contemporised *The Wild Duck* and caged it in Perspex. Irina Brook's Iggy Pop-inspired *Peer Gynt* was less successful. Its Becketts included a dead duck *Waiting for Godot* from Sydney, with Hugo Weaving and Richard Roxburgh hampered by the Beckett estate's strictures, and a cartoonish *Krapp's Last Tape* from Robert Wilson. Pan Pan Theatre played *All That Fall* to an audience in rocking chairs. Olwen Fouéré tackled his prose in *Lessness.*

It was the ancient Greeks that got the biggest reworking, though. Not courtesy of Dame Kristin Scott Thomas, whose Old Vic *Electra* looked and felt like every Greek tragedy of the last 20 years: ashen-faced in an ashen world, frequently tipping into histrionics. Helen McCrory's *Medea* at the National felt fresher; this warrior mother, identifiable as an immigrant, paced the stage with frenzied purpose. Carrie Cracknell's production – scored by Alison Goldfrapp, with a juddering, shuddering zombie chorus – had a similar feel.

Pared-back clarity was what tended to work, in keeping with an age of austerity. Ivo van Hove whittled *Antigone* down into a kind of ritual: an enacted event on a bare stage, using microphones as masks and asking us, his audience, to really listen. His Antigone – a wispy Juliette Binoche – and his Kreon (Patrick O'Kane) were incorrigible in their opposition. Out of their stubborn constancy comes only tragedy.

Robert Icke's thrilling *Oresteia* – the start of a Greek season at the Almeida with *Bakkhai* and *Medea* to follow – put Aeschylus' vast trilogy through a press. Icke drew out its patterns: the spin cycles of revenge. It centred on a family dining table, at which the number of empty seats increased. Angus Wright's upright statesman Agamemnon cradled his daughter through a lethal injection. Clytemnestra battered him to death in the bath. Her son dispatched his mother and her lover, spurred on by his sister. The final act, a rug pull, places everything in court.

Writers too found themselves subject to revision. Terence Rattigan's debut play *First Episode,* written when he was an Oxford undergraduate, had its first revival since 1934. A portrait of student life and student drama, with an undercurrent of homosexuality, it is not without merit, despite Rattigan himself disowning it. There was juvenilia from Joe Orton too, with his 1959 piece *Fred and Madge,* which sits in a strain of British absurdism but lacks the manic glee of his best work.

A 'lost' Arthur Miller too, in his centenary year: *The Hook,* a film script abandoned over studio censorship in 1949, was collected from archived drafts and adapted for the stage by Ron Hutchinson. A tale of union corruption in the New York docks, Miller's script would spawn *On the Waterfront* and his own *A View from the Bridge,* though without either's precision and scope.

## ELECTION SPECIAL

In an election year, after five years of coalition government, it will come as no surprise that new work was dominated by politics. On election night itself, More4 hosted a live-broadcast of James Graham's *The Vote* from the Donmar Warehouse – a farce set, rather brilliantly, in a polling station with a host of famous faces playing the voters: Dame Judi Dench, Bill Paterson, Rosalie Craig and a three-second cameo from Jude Law, among others.

At the Royal Court, Vicky Featherstone announced a season loosely linked by the idea of revolution. Rory Mullarkey imagined the squeezed middle popping in *The Wolf from the Door,* a surreal satire in which Women's Institute members and rural pastors marched on Westminster. Molly Davies' *God Bless the Child* imagined a primary school rebellion. The kids themselves got Enda Walsh's stilted revision of Roald Dahl's *The Twits,* turned into an attack on entrenched privilege.

Meanwhile, Tim Price dramatised the Anonymous hacking collective, putting the internet onstage. Previously, *The Nether* took another tack: Jennifer Haley's play imagined a black hole of the internet where consenting adults could play out paedophilic fantasies. A smash West End transfer followed.

At the Almeida, Alecky Blythe's piece about the London riots, *Little Revolution,* turned its gaze on its own process, as the verbatim theatremaker fretted about the framing of the riots as 'mindless violence' – including her own portrayal of it. Steve Waters' *Temple* also looked at protest, zooming in on Occupy London and, particularly, the dilemma of the dean of St Paul's, who closed the cathedral and, ultimately, sided with the City of London Corporation. It was a sharp illustration of the creep of consumer-capitalism: the religion of our times.

Property prices came under scrutiny in *Radiant Vermin,* a warped Philip Ridley fairytale in which a young couple discover that killing the homeless improves their home and before long, they're eyeing a new kitchen, TV room and en-suite. As the speed of capitalism increases, the two actors take on more characters than they can handle. Mike Bartlett's *Game* looked at a similar hand-out: a young, unemployed couple gets a house in exchange for acting as live targets in a paintball-style shooting range. It skewered everything from rising inequality to benefit cheats, from austerity to virtual reality via provision for veterans – albeit without turning it into a satisfying drama. His miniature *Bull,* a companion piece to his 2009 play *Cock,* turned workplace politics into a bullfight, imagining two colleagues wearing one another down.

New work has become the most prominent part of Britain's theatre culture. One survey released this year found that, in 2013, new work had overtaken revivals for the first time since records began, accounting for 59 per cent of shows. With that has come a formal boldness and plays – as evidenced above – tend to find their own particular form and shape.

Tim Crouch's *Adler & Gibb* was art about art about art: a play about a biopic film about a conceptual artist whose work, like Marcel Duchamp's, challenged the very definitions of art. It progressed from a bare stage and actors' bodies through embodied and enacted naturalism and on into the hyper-realism and dislocated language of film – exploring the semiotics of storytelling and art's tendency to eat its own tail in its incessant, commercial quest for novelty.

*Carmen Disruption* also used art to talk about the world. Simon Stephens' play – a set of interwoven monologues – turned Bizet's *Carmen* into contemporary lives: Carmen as rent-boy; Escamillo as unrepentant, zombie banker; Don José as a cabbie, teetering into crime to get by; and an opera singer, travelling the world to play Carmen, staying in identikit hotels in identikit cities, living a life on repeat. It shows an individualistic world, run by machines and forcing its young and its vulnerable to sell themselves to survive, while the rich live in a global playground.

There's no pretending one doesn't know the other side of the coin – that was the message behind *Pomona,* Alistair McDowall's break-out hit at the Orange Tree. A strange play that let gaming culture segue into real life until fiction and reality were indistinguishable, it followed two teenagers playing out a sci-fi fantasy while, in the middle of an industrial wasteland in Manchester, there exists a terrible sci-fi reality: a brothel that trades in body parts.

One of the year's most controversial plays was *An Audience with Jimmy Savile.* Though Jonathan Maitland's play was dramatically flat-footed, its power was in Alistair McGowan's impersonation, so uncanny a presence that the audience gasped on his first entrance. What McGowan made you realize is that Savile was a confounding combination of oddities: the tinfoil tracksuits, the cigar, the open sexuality, jovial and matey one second, threatening and litigious the next.

## BUILDINGS AND BYE-BYES

In March, Battersea Arts Centre (BAC) suffered an enormous fire that destroyed its Grand Hall, a major renovation of which was nearing completion. The space, the biggest in the building, had hosted much of the organisation's profitable work, but the front of the building was able to re-open for performances the following day – a symbol of the BAC's spirit. A crowd-funding campaign raised more than £75,000 before chancellor George Osborne pledged £1m to the building's restoration.

Another major loss for the UK's experimental theatre scene was the Arches in Glasgow. The nightclub that ran alongside the arts venue, making it viable, lost its late licence following police complaints about disorder and drug use. Within a month, the venue had gone into administration, to the dismay of artists in Scotland and beyond. More positive was the announcement of a £78m flexible performance space in Manchester. The Factory will replace the old Granada Studios and become a focal point of the Manchester International Festival. This year saw the opening of HOME, an arts centre with a focus on Eurocentric theatre that brings together the Cornerhouse Cinema and the Library Theatre.

Kevin Spacey, artistic director at the Old Vic for the past 11 years, stepped down in May, handing over to Matthew Warchus, but not before picking up a special Olivier award and, in one of the strangest acceptance speeches of all time, duetting with Beverley Knight on Simon and Garfunkel's 'Bridge Over Troubled Water'. Could a musical be on the cards?

# AWARDS

## 2015 LAURENCE OLIVIER AWARDS

Best Actor – Mark Strong for *A View from the Bridge* at the Young Vic and Wyndham's Theatre

Best Actress – Penelope Wilton for *Taken at Midnight* at the Theatre Royal Haymarket

Best Actor in a Supporting Role – Nathaniel Parker for *Wolf Hall/Bring Up the Bodies* at the Aldwych Theatre

Best Actress in a Supporting Role – Dame Angela Lansbury for *Blithe Spirit* at the Gielgud Theatre

Best New Play – *King Charles III* by Mike Bartlett at the Almeida and Wyndham's Theatre

Best Revival – *A View from the Bridge* at the Young Vic and Wyndham's Theatre

Best Actor in a Musical – John Dagleish for *Sunny Afternoon* at the Hampstead Theatre and the Harold Pinter Theatre

Best Actress in a Musical – Katie Brayben for *Beautiful* at the Aldwych Theatre

Best Actor in a Supporting Role in a Musical – George Maguire for *Sunny Afternoon* at the Hampstead Theatre and the Harold Pinter Theatre

Best Actress in a Supporting Role in a Musical – Lorna Want for *Beautiful* at the Aldwych Theatre

Best New Musical – *Sunny Afternoon* at the Hampstead Theatre and the Harold Pinter Theatre

Best Musical Revival – *City of Angels* at the Donmar Warehouse

Best New Comedy – *The Play That Goes Wrong* at the Duchess Theatre

Best New Dance Production – *32 Rue Vandenbranden* by Peeping Tom at the Barbican

Outstanding Achievement in Dance – Crystal Pite for her choreography in *The Associates* at Sadler's Wells

Best New Opera Production – *The Mastersingers of Nuremberg* at the London Coliseum

Outstanding Achievement in Opera – Richard Jones for directing *Rodelinda, The Girl of the Golden West* and *The Mastersingers of Nuremberg* for English National Opera at the London Coliseum

Outstanding Achievement in an Affiliate Theatre – *Bull* at the Young Vic

Outstanding Achievement in Music – Ray Davies for *Sunny Afternoon* at the Hampstead Theatre and the Harold Pinter Theatre

Best Entertainment and Family – *La Soiree* at La Soiree Spiegeltent

Best Director – Ivo van Hove for *A View from the Bridge* at the Young Vic and Wyndham's Theatre

Best Theatre Choreographer – Sergio Trujillo for *Memphis: The Musical* at the Shaftesbury Theatre

Best Set Design – Es Devlin for *The Nether* at the Duke of York's Theatre

Best Lighting Design – Howard Harrison for *City of Angels* at the Donmar Warehouse

Best Sound Design – Gareth Owen for *Memphis: The Musical* at the Shaftesbury Theatre

Best Costume Design – Christopher Oram for *Wolf Hall/Bring Up the Bodies* at the Aldwych Theatre

This Morning Audience Award – *Wicked* at the Apollo Victoria

Special Award – Sylvie Guillem

Special Award – Kevin Spacey

## CRITICS' CIRCLE AWARDS 2014

Best Actor – Mark Strong for *A View from the Bridge* at the Young Vic

Best Actress – Helen McCrory for *Medea* at the National Theatre

The John and Wendy Trewin Award for Best Shakespearean Performance – Antony Sher for *Henry IV Parts I & II* at the Royal Shakespeare Theatre and the Barbican

The Jack Tinker Award for Most Promising Newcomer – Patsy Ferran for *Blithe Spirit* at the Apollo Theatre and *Treasure Island* at the National Theatre

Best New Play – *King Charles III* by Mike Bartlett at the Almeida and Wyndham's Theatre

The Peter Hepple Award for Best Musical – *Gypsy* at the Chichester Festival Theatre and the Savoy Theatre

Best Director – Ivo van Hove for *A View from the Bridge* at the Young Vic

Best Designer – Es Devlin for *The Nether* at the Royal Court and Paul Barritt for *Golem* at the Young Vic

Most Promising Playwright – Barney Norris for *Visitors* at the Arcola Theatre and the Bush Theatre

## EVENING STANDARD THEATRE AWARDS 2014

Best Actor – Tom Hiddleston for *Coriolanus* at the Donmar Warehouse

The Natasha Richardson Award for Best Actress – Gillian Anderson for *A Streetcar Named Desire* at the Young Vic

Best Play – *The James Plays* by Rona Munro at the National Theatre

The Ned Sherrin Award for Best Musical – *The Scottsboro Boys* at the Young Vic

The Milton Shulman Award for Best Director – Jeremy Herrin for *Wolf Hall/Bring Up the Bodies* at the Aldwych Theatre

Best Design – Es Devlin for *American Psycho* at the Almeida Theatre

Revival of the Year – *Skylight* at Wyndham's Theatre

The Charles Wintour Award for Most Promising Playwright – Beth Steel for *Wonderland* at the Hampstead Theatre

Emerging Talent Award – Laura Jane Matthewson for *Dogfight* at the Southwark Playhouse

Beyond Theatre Award – *Here Lies Love* at the National Theatre

Editor's Award – Kate Bush for *Before the Dawn*

The Lebedev Special Award – Tom Stoppard

# WEATHER

In the UK during the period July 2014–June 2015 sunshine was abundant; the 12-month period was the 2nd sunniest on record with 1,555 hours sunshine hours and the sunniest since 1955/6. Winter was the sunniest on record with 194 hours, outdoing the previous high of 189 hours set in 2001. High sunshine amounts extended well into spring, with a record breaking 212 hours recorded in April. Sunshine for April was also record breaking across England and Northern Ireland.

The UK's mean summer temperature was above average at 14.8°C, although summer 2013 was significantly warmer at 15.2°C. A very warm autumn followed, with a mean temperature of 10.9°C making it the third warmest and highest since 2011. Winter and spring were close to average.

Rainfall total over the year 2014–15 was 1,180mm, 5 per cent above normal; the previous 12-months had been much wetter with 1,311mm recorded. August and October were the 8th and 16th wettest on record respectively but between these September was the driest on record with only 22.8mm recorded.

## NEWSWORTHY EVENTS

Heavy showers over July 7/8 caused flooding across England and Wales. Rising temperatures peaked on 18th. This 'heatwave' (18–20 July) brought thunderstorms, localised flooding and reports of lightning damage; Norwich Airport recorded 45.8mm of rain in only one hour. Thunderstorms returned on the 28th with flash flooding across parts of south-east England.

Despite a high of 27.2°C in London on August 7, the first half of the month was unsettled. Ex-Hurricane Bertha passed over the country on the 10th giving a spell of unseasonably strong winds and heavy rain, again causing localised flooding across the country. Later in the month, cool conditions brought several cold nights.

High pressure gave mostly settled conditions during September. Despite this, thunderstorms in southern England during the 19th–20th caused flooding on a few roads and at Lacock (Wiltshire) 115.4mm of rain fell over 24 hours.

October was unsettled and very windy at times; rainfall accumulations were sufficient to give localised flooding in southern England and the Midlands over the 12th/13th. Ex-Hurricane Gonzalo brought heavy rainfall and strong winds across the country during the 20th/21st. Over a three-day period beginning on the 25th, exceptionally high rainfall totals across western Scotland gave accumulations of up to 200mm in places.

Heavy rain and strong winds affected the UK during the first half of November. The remainder of the month was more settled and very mild.

On December 10 an active low pressure system with 70mph gusts brought widespread transport disruption and 30,000 homes on the Western Isles went without power. Southern and central Scotland were affected by snow on the 12th and snow fell across the Midlands, Nottinghamshire, Derbyshire and the Pennines on Boxing Day.

The New Year began with extremely active depressions bringing very strong winds across Scotland and Northern Ireland. Gusts over 100mph occurred January 8–15 across northern Scotland and the Western Isles bringing disruption to both transport and power supplies. Later in the month snowfall affected Northern England and Scotland causing disruption at Manchester Airport on the 29th.

Snow and ice caused some disruption across the country in early February. Northern areas were affected by snow and strong winds later in the month.

Early March became very wet and windy across Scotland and Northern Ireland. Cluanie Inn (the Highlands) recorded 102.8mm of rainfall over a 24-hour period ending on the 6th and South Uist (the Highlands) recorded a wind gust of 89mph on the 9th. After a spell of settled weather, gales returned at the end of the month to these regions with parts of England and Wales also affected.

High pressure dominated much of April giving poor air quality across south-east England on 9th/10th due to a combination of local traffic fumes, pollution from Europe and Saharan dust. Cold air 'flooded' the UK on the 25th giving rise to snow fall over the Grampians and the east Highlands and overnight frosts elsewhere.

Heavy rain and strong winds affected the UK during the first ten days of May. Localised flooding affected parts of Northern Ireland and snow fell on the Scottish Highlands on May 2. After a quiescent spell of weather south-east England was affected by strong winds and rain at the end of the month.

June began unsettled with strong winds and heavy rain across a large part of the country. Localised flooding caused difficulties on some roads in Wales and winds gusting up to 60mph were reported at coastal locations. The remainder of the month was made up of thundery periods interspersed with warm and settled spells of weather. In England health warnings for heat were issued on the last day of the month. A high of 32.5°C was recorded at Heathrow (Greater London) on June 30. A minimum of −1.9°C was recorded at Katesbridge (County Down) on the 9th and Resallach (Sutherland) on the 14th.

## THE YEAR 2014

The 12-month period January–December 2014 was the UK's warmest year on record with a mean temperature of 9.9°C, which is 1.1°C above the long-term average and replaces the previous high of 9.7°C set in 2006. A total of eight of the UK's top-ten warmest years have all occurred since 2002. It was also the warmest year on record (10.93°C), based on the mean Central England Temperature, beating the previous highest set in 2006 (10.87°C). This data set began in 1659 and is the world's longest running instrumental temperature series.

## WEATHER STATISTICS 2014

| | Mean Temp. °C | Diff. from normal °C* | Rainfall mm | Percentage of normal* | Sunshine hours | Percentage of normal* |
|---|---|---|---|---|---|---|
| England | 10.8 | +1.1 | 985 | 117 | 1,596 | 106 |
| Wales | 10.1 | +1.0 | 1,553 | 110 | 1,507 | 109 |
| Scotland | 8.4 | +1.0 | 1,757 | 116 | 1,151 | 98 |
| Northern Ireland | 9.6 | +0.7 | 1,297 | 114 | 1,268 | 103 |
| United Kingdom | 9.9 | +1.0 | 1,300 | 116 | 1,427 | 104 |

* The standard reference period ('normal') for 2011–20 is the average for the 30-year period 1981–2010.

Despite this, no individual month broke a record for temperature in England, Wales, Scotland or Northern Ireland. Although, bar August, each month consistently surpassed its average mean monthly temperature, and significantly so during the first four months of the year. Mean temperatures in Northern Ireland were much closer to normal, unlike England, Wales and Scotland where 2014 set a new record for each.

Rainfall totalled 1,300mm, 16 per cent above the 1981–2010 normal and was the UK's fourth wettest on record and the wettest since 2012. September set a new record for dryness with a total of just 23mm – the normal is 94mm.

Sunshine, averaged over the UK, totalled 1,427 hours, 4 per cent above normal, and was the sunniest since 2010. Most months were close to their average, with the exception of March (124 per cent), July (129 per cent), December (142 per cent) and May (80 per cent). December was the sunniest since 2001 and the 2nd sunniest on record. May was the dullest since 1991.

## UK TEMPERATURE

The summer of 2014 was joint 15th warmest with a mean temperature of 14.8°C – the normal is 14.4°C – and the warmest since 2013 (15.2°C). The highest temperature of the year was 32.3°C at Gravesend (Kent) on July 18. The lowest summer night-time air minimum occurred at Braemar (Aberdeenshire) with −2.1°C on August 25.

Autumn was the 3rd warmest in the UK with a mean temperature of 10.9°C and the warmest since 2011 (11.3°C) – the normal is 9.5°C. It was also the 3rd warmest autumn across Scotland (9.3°C), England (11.8°C) and Wales (11.1°C). In Northern Ireland the mean temperature was 10.3°C. The highest air temperature for the season was 26.3°C recorded at Wiggonholt (West Sussex) on September 18. The lowest was −4.6°C recorded at Cromdale (Moray) on November 26.

Winter was close to average with a mean temperature of 3.9°C, the normal is 3.8°C; the previous winter was much warmer (5.2°C). The highest temperature, over the season, was 16.5°C at Exeter Airport (Devon) on January 9 and the lowest, −13.7°C, at Loch Glascarnoch (the Highlands), on January 19.

Spring was also close to average with a mean temperature of 7.7°C, the normal is 7.8°C, and was the coolest since 2010 (7.6°C). The highest temperature was 25.6°C recorded at Faversham (Kent) on April 15; the lowest for the season, in April, was −8.0°C on the 27th at Katesbridge (County Down).

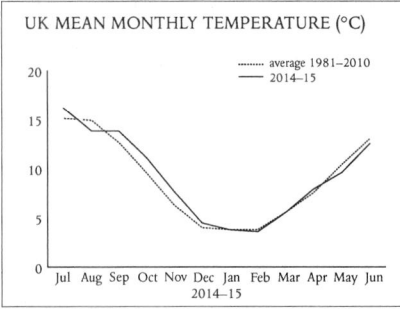

UK MEAN MONTHLY TEMPERATURE (°C)

## UK RAINFALL

Summer rainfall averaged 258.3mm across the UK and was the wettest since 2012 (379.2mm) – the normal is 233.7mm. The highest 24-hour total (each 24-hour period commences at 9am GMT on the day indicated) at a single location was 135.6mm at Torridon (Wester Ross) on August 11.

Autumn averaged 304.9mm and was the driest since 2007 (233.8mm); the normal is 336.5mm. September's record breaking dryness made the overall figure for autumn drier than average despite a very wet October. The highest 24-hour total was 141.3mm recorded at Gruline (Isle of Mull) on November 6.

Total winter rainfall amounted to 365.1mm; the normal is 326.7mm, and was in stark contrast to the previous winter which totalled 544.9mm. It was particularly wet across western and northern Scotland; some West Highland locations received a total of 1,400mm over the season. Amounts in eastern and southern areas of the UK were nearer to average. Honister Pass (Cumbria) recorded 145.2mm over a 24-hour period on December 22.

Despite a dry April, spring rainfall was above average at 251.4mm and the wettest since 2006 (291.2mm) – the normal is 231.3mm. It was Scotland's 2nd wettest spring on record with 401.3mm and wettest since 1986 (409.5mm). Over a 24-hour period Alltdearg House on the Isle of Skye recorded a total of 122.2mm on March 6.

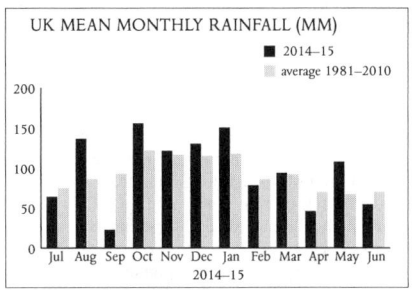

UK MEAN MONTHLY RAINFALL (MM)

## UK SUNSHINE

Total summer sunshine was well above average amounting to 572.5 hours, the normal is 505.6 hours. However, the previous summer was sunnier with 577.7 hours.

Overall, the autumn across the UK was dull with a total of 258.1 hours – the normal is 273.9 hours – and the dullest since 2001 (252.1 hours). However, seen in isolation, sunshine totals for Northern Ireland and Wales were slightly better than average.

Winter was the sunniest on record with 194.1 hours; the normal is 155.8 hours.

Spring was the 6th sunniest with 512.2 hours – the normal is 435.7 hours – and was the sunniest since 2011 (516.1 hours). April's sunshine of 212.2 hours broke the previous record set in 1942 of 204.6 hours. New records for April sunshine were also set in England and particularly Northern Ireland, where its total of 209.6 hours toppled the previous highest of 206.3 hours set in 1962.

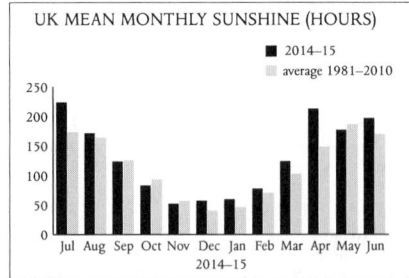

UK MEAN MONTHLY SUNSHINE (HOURS)

# UK WEATHER STATIONS

Given below are temperature, rainfall and sunshine at selected climatological stations for July 2014 to June 2015.

*Ht*   height of station above mean sea-level   *Rain*   total monthly rainfall
*Temp.*   mean monthly air temperature   *Sun*   total monthly sunshine duration

|  | Ht | July 2014 Temp. | Rain | Sun | August 2014 Temp. | Rain | Sun | September 2014 Temp. | Rain | Sun | October 2014 Temp. | Rain | Sun |
|---|---|---|---|---|---|---|---|---|---|---|---|---|---|
|  | m | °C | mm | hrs | °C | mm | hrs | °C | mm | hrs | °C | mm | hrs |
| Stornoway | 15 | 15.2 | 66 | 194 | 13.1 | 141 | 144 | 12.9 | 48 | 101 | 9.8 | 198 | 77 |
| Nairn | 23 | 15.9 | 35 | 205 | 13.7 | 175 | 139 | 14 | 22 | 98 | 10.7 | 109 | 72 |
| Leuchars | 10 | 16 | 43 | 208 | 13.9 | 113 | 158 | 13.9 | 17 | 101 | 10.9 | 123 | 80 |
| Paisley | 32 | 16.7 | 49 | 240 | 14.4 | 94 | 187 | 14.5 | 15 | 136 | 10.7 | 162 | 77 |
| Armagh | 62 | 16.5 | 56 | 155 | 14.1 | 119 | 161 | 13.8 | 3 | 102 | 10.7 | 103 | 91 |
| Bradford | 34 | 17.4 | 38 | 215 | 14.5 | 126 | 171 | 14.2 | 18 | 113 | 11.7 | 98 | 72 |
| Valley | 10 | 17 | 48 | 251 | 15.2 | 109 | 184 | 15.5 | 8 | 174 | 13.1 | 159 | 88 |
| Shawbury | 72 | 17.3 | 33 | 248 | 14.6 | 89 | 159 | 14.3 | 17 | 124 | 11.8 | 69 | 72 |
| Ross-on-Wye | 67 | 18.3 | 30 | 254 | 15.6 | 110 | 178 | 15.8 | 20 | 126 | 12.9 | 93 | 76 |
| Lowestoft | 18 | 18.4 | 59 | 210 | 16.5 | 95 | 247 | 16 | 19 | 134 | 14.1 | 64 | 133 |
| Heathrow | 25 | 20.4 | 50 | 246 | 17.2 | 98 | 184 | 17.2 | 11 | 135 | 14.3 | 76 | 104 |
| Hurn | 10 | 18.5 | 24 | 275 | 15.9 | 90 | 198 | 15.6 | 20 | 132 | 13.3 | 138 | 81 |
| Camborne | 87 | 17.3 | 29 | 205 | 15.6 | 93 | 200 | 16 | 8 | 178 | 13.9 | 123 | 78 |
| Eastbourne | 7 | 18.8 | 63 | 236 | 17.1 | 100 | 237 | 16.9 | 10 | 185 | 14.4 | 155 | 120 |
| Aberporth | 133 | 16.4 | 20 | 206 | 14.9 | 107 | 169 | 15.1 | 13 | 174 | 12.4 | 111 | 77 |
| Waddington | 68 | 18.5 | 19 | 219 | 15.8 | 62 | 172 | 15.1 | 10 | 99 | 12.4 | 89 | 79 |

|  | Ht | November 2014 Temp. | Rain | Sun | December 2014 Temp. | Rain | Sun | January 2015 Temp. | Rain | Sun | February 2015 Temp. | Rain | Sun |
|---|---|---|---|---|---|---|---|---|---|---|---|---|---|
|  | m | °C | mm | hrs | °C | mm | hrs | °C | mm | hrs | °C | mm | hrs |
| Stornoway | 15 | 8.4 | 90 | 53 | 4.9 | 168 | 20 | 4.4 | 199 | 30 | 5 | 115 | 45 |
| Nairn | 23 | 7.4 | 44 | 51 | 4.1 | 115 | 54 | 3.4 | 78 | 63 | 4.2 | 23 | 88 |
| Leuchars | 10 | 7.5 | 100 | 43 | 3.6 | 44 | 69 | 3.4 | 72 | 70 | 4.2 | 26 | 117 |
| Paisley | 32 | 7.8 | 79 | 58 | 4.6 | 176 | 46 | 3.8 | 211 | 57 | 4.4 | 105 | 78 |
| Armagh | 62 | 7.1 | 149 | 59 | 4.5 | 99 | 53 | 3.7 | 94 | 62 | 4.1 | 53 | 63 |
| Bradford | 34 | 8 | 96 | 41 | 4.9 | 115 | 54 | 4 | 109 | 59 | 4.1 | 34 | 70 |
| Valley | 10 | 9.6 | 59 | 88 | 7.5 | 68 | 44 | 6.1 | 77 | 60 | 5.3 | 37 | 86 |
| Shawbury | 72 | 8 | 77 | 60 | 4.9 | 73 | 72 | 4.3 | 60 | 73 | 4 | 25 | 56 |
| Ross-on-Wye | 67 | 8.6 | 113 | 53 | 5.6 | 35 | 71 | 5.3 | 73 | 91 | 4.5 | 33 | 86 |
| Lowestoft | 18 | 9.8 | 127 | 51 | 5.8 | 58 | 75 | 4.6 | 45 | 72 | 4.7 | 44 | 97 |
| Heathrow | 25 | 9.7 | 128 | 51 | 6.1 | 38 | 72 | 5.2 | 63 | 62 | 4.9 | 39 | 62 |
| Hurn | 10 | 9.3 | 164 | 59 | 5.5 | 46 | 74 | 5.5 | 102 | 78 | 4 | 53 | 71 |
| Camborne | 87 | 10.1 | 153 | 78 | 8 | 64 | 54 | 7.5 | 147 | 51 | 5.9 | 82 | 91 |
| Eastbourne | 7 | 11 | 157 | 56 | 6.7 | 58 | 73 | 6.1 | 153 | 59 | 5.2 | 76 | 97 |
| Aberporth | 133 | 8.8 | 123 | 81 | 6.9 | 83 | 46 | 5.7 | 94 | 45 | 4.7 | 59 | 70 |
| Waddington | 68 | 8.2 | 66 | 53 | 5.1 | 50 | 81 | 4.3 | 21 | 84 | 4 | 24 | 92 |

|  | Ht | March 2015 Temp. | Rain | Sun | April 2015 Temp. | Rain | Sun | May 2015 Temp. | Rain | Sun | June 2015 Temp. | Rain | Sun |
|---|---|---|---|---|---|---|---|---|---|---|---|---|---|
|  | m | °C | mm | hrs | °C | mm | hrs | °C | mm | hrs | °C | mm | hrs |
| Stornoway | 15 | 5.4 | 167 | 111 | 6.9 | 65 | 184 | 8.2 | 121 | 169 | 10.6 | 99 | 94 |
| Nairn | 23 | 5.9 | 38 | 159 | 8 | 37 | 202 | 8.7 | 52 | 188 | 11.9 | 56 | 143 |
| Leuchars | 10 | 5.9 | 37 | 132 | 8 | 25 | 234 | 9.5 | 78 | 176 | 12.8 | 36 | 151 |
| Paisley | 32 | 6.1 | 153 | 105 | 8.2 | 48 | 236 | 9.7 | 135 | 198 | 13 | 62 | 164 |
| Armagh | 62 | 6.2 | 59 | 138 | 8.3 | 62 | 204 | 10 | 116 | 140 | 13.3 | 29 | 183 |
| Bradford | 34 | 5.9 | 80 | 105 | 8.8 | 31 | 207 | 10.3 | 101 | 171 | 13.5 | 31 | 202 |
| Valley | 10 | 6.7 | 59 | 147 | 8.9 | 36 | 233 | 10.5 | 111 | 185 | 13.4 | 28 | 239 |
| Shawbury | 72 | 6.1 | 49 | 110 | 8.7 | 13 | 223 | 10.6 | 66 | 127 | 14 | 40 | 237 |
| Ross-on-Wye | 67 | 7.2 | 48 | 112 | 10.3 | 14 | 228 | 11.8 | 71 | 184 | 15.2 | 19 | 239 |
| Lowestoft | 18 | 6.9 | 24 | 157 | 8.5 | 21 | 242 | 11.6 | 58 | 221 | 14.6 | 23 | 247 |
| Heathrow | 25 | 7.9 | 24 | 141 | 11.2 | 16 | 212 | 13.2 | 42 | 189 | 16.8 | 12 | 197 |
| Hurn | 10 | 6.8 | 25 | 116 | 9.8 | 20 | 158 | 11.9 | 69 | 160 | 15.1 | 30 | 231 |
| Camborne | 87 | 7.6 | 45 | 147 | 10 | 15 | 212 | 11.2 | 64 | 162 | 13.8 | 38 | 229 |
| Eastbourne | 7 | 7.4 | 21 | 165 | 9.7 | 11 | 259 | 12 | 67 | 217 | 15 | 20 | 288 |
| Aberporth | 133 | 6.3 | 54 | 138 | 9.1 | 26 | 222 | 10.3 | 83 | 164 | 13.5 | 39 | 227 |
| Waddington | 68 | 6.4 | 24 | 137 | 9.4 | 14 | 216 | 11.1 | 63 | 169 | 14.4 | 35 | 209 |

# METEOROLOGICAL OBSERVATIONS IN LONDON *(Hampstead Weather Station)*

Minimum temperature is the lowest air temperature recorded over a 24-hour period ending at 9am on the day indicated; maximum temperature is the highest air temperature recorded over a 24-hour period beginning at 9am on the day indicated. Daily rainfall totals are for 24-hour periods commencing at 9am on the day indicated and include any solid precipitation, such as snow and hail, which is melted and measured in the same way as rainfall. A reading which is not available is indicated by '–'. If this occurs during the month the next reading will be for the accumulation over the relevant period. All times are GMT.

*July 2014*

| Day | Minimum Temperature (°C) | Maximum Temperature (°C) | Daily Total Rainfall (mm) |
|---|---|---|---|
| 1 | 11.0 | 21.5 | 0.0 |
| 2 | 10.3 | 23.7 | 0.0 |
| 3 | 12.9 | 25.2 | 0.0 |
| 4 | 13.6 | 25.7 | 5.2 |
| 5 | 15.5 | 21.1 | 0.0 |
| 6 | 13.3 | 21.4 | 0.6 |
| 7 | 9.8 | 21.1 | 0.6 |
| 8 | 10.6 | 19.9 | 3.8 |
| 9 | 11.3 | 22.1 | 0.0 |
| 10 | 13.8 | 17.4 | 6.0 |
| 11 | 11.4 | 19.0 | 0.2 |
| 12 | 13.1 | 26.9 | 18.4 |
| 13 | 16.2 | 24.0 | 0.0 |
| 14 | 10.7 | 23.7 | 0.0 |
| 15 | 16.6 | 24.9 | 0.0 |
| 16 | 13.2 | 25.9 | 0.0 |
| 17 | 15.9 | 27.2 | 10.8 |
| 18 | 16.8 | 30.5 | 3.8 |
| 19 | 18.9 | 27.5 | 0.0 |
| 20 | 17.1 | 24.8 | 0.0 |
| 21 | 15.0 | 25.1 | 0.0 |
| 22 | 13.8 | 26.0 | 0.0 |
| 23 | 14.4 | 27.9 | 0.0 |
| 24 | 14.7 | 28.4 | 0.0 |
| 25 | 15.3 | 26.8 | 2.6 |
| 26 | 15.5 | 28.6 | 0.0 |
| 27 | 17.6 | 25.1 | 0.0 |
| 28 | 14.7 | 23.4 | 0.0 |
| 29 | 14.5 | 26.1 | 0.0 |
| 30 | 12.7 | 24.8 | 0.0 |
| 31 | 13.8 | 24.9 | 0.0 |

*August 2014*

| Day | Minimum Temperature (°C) | Maximum Temperature (°C) | Daily Total Rainfall (mm) |
|---|---|---|---|
| 1 | 15.0 | 23.9 | 0.0 |
| 2 | 15.7 | 23.1 | 0.0 |
| 3 | 11.7 | 23.4 | 0.0 |
| 4 | 13.0 | 23.7 | 0.0 |
| 5 | 12.3 | 23.5 | 8.6 |
| 6 | 15.7 | 24.8 | 0.0 |
| 7 | 13.8 | 25.3 | 0.0 |
| 8 | 15.8 | 23.3 | 8.0 |
| 9 | 12.5 | 22.6 | 4.4 |
| 10 | 14.2 | 21.0 | 18.2 |
| 11 | 11.7 | 20.5 | 14.4 |
| 12 | 11.3 | 19.1 | 2.0 |
| 13 | 10.5 | 21.5 | 0.0 |
| 14 | 11.8 | 20.4 | 1.2 |
| 15 | 11.5 | 20.5 | 0.0 |
| 16 | 10.6 | 19.5 | 0.0 |
| 17 | 13.0 | 19.9 | 0.4 |
| 18 | 10.1 | 19.9 | 0.6 |
| 19 | 9.3 | 17.9 | 0.0 |
| 20 | 7.8 | 18.6 | 0.0 |
| 21 | 7.0 | 17.5 | 0.0 |
| 22 | 11.1 | 20.2 | 0.0 |
| 23 | 8.4 | 18.4 | 0.0 |
| 24 | 6.8 | 17.6 | 3.0 |
| 25 | 12.5 | 16.3 | 36.6 |
| 26 | 13.0 | 17.3 | 8.6 |
| 27 | 9.9 | 19.5 | 1.8 |
| 28 | 15.7 | 21.6 | 0.0 |
| 29 | 12.8 | 19.6 | 1.0 |
| 30 | 13.5 | 19.0 | 0.0 |
| 31 | 11.7 | 21.9 | 0.0 |

*September 2014*

| Day | Minimum Temperature (°C) | Maximum Temperature (°C) | Daily Total Rainfall (mm) |
|---|---|---|---|
| 1 | 11.2 | 17.8 | 5.2 |
| 2 | 11.9 | 21.6 | 0.0 |
| 3 | 14.1 | 22.3 | 0.0 |
| 4 | 12.7 | 19.7 | 0.0 |
| 5 | 14.0 | 19.9 | 0.0 |
| 6 | 15.5 | 21.0 | 0.0 |
| 7 | 13.1 | 21.2 | 0.0 |
| 8 | 10.4 | 21.8 | 0.0 |
| 9 | 10.7 | 21.7 | 0.0 |
| 10 | 10.8 | 19.9 | 0.0 |
| 11 | 10.0 | 17.4 | 0.0 |
| 12 | 12.2 | 22.1 | 0.0 |
| 13 | 11.6 | 20.7 | 0.0 |
| 14 | 11.6 | 20.1 | 0.0 |
| 15 | 12.1 | 22.1 | 0.0 |
| 16 | 13.1 | 23.2 | 0.0 |
| 17 | 14.8 | 19.8 | 0.0 |
| 18 | 14.1 | 24.8 | 10.2 |
| 19 | 14.9 | 22.9 | 15.8 |
| 20 | 15.3 | 17.8 | 0.4 |
| 21 | 10.7 | 17.4 | 0.0 |
| 22 | 7.1 | 18.5 | 0.0 |
| 23 | 7.6 | 18.2 | 2.2 |
| 24 | 11.1 | 18.5 | 0.4 |
| 25 | 6.2 | 17.7 | 0.0 |
| 26 | 10.4 | 20.8 | 0.0 |
| 27 | 12.5 | 20.5 | 0.0 |
| 28 | 14.3 | 23.0 | 0.0 |
| 29 | 13.2 | 17.8 | 1.6 |
| 30 | 13.4 | 21.5 | 0.2 |

*October 2014*

| Day | Minimum Temperature (°C) | Maximum Temperature (°C) | Daily Total Rainfall (mm) |
|---|---|---|---|
| 1 | 14.0 | 19.6 | 0.0 |
| 2 | 13.0 | 20.6 | 0.0 |
| 3 | 12.5 | 21.1 | 0.0 |
| 4 | 14.3 | 17.0 | 6.8 |
| 5 | 3.8 | 15.3 | 0.0 |
| 6 | 9.1 | 12.0 | 9.6 |
| 7 | 8.1 | 14.5 | 2.0 |
| 8 | 8.1 | 16.9 | 1.4 |
| 9 | 10.6 | 16.8 | 2.0 |
| 10 | 8.4 | 17.2 | 3.8 |
| 11 | 10.5 | 16.8 | 0.2 |
| 12 | 7.3 | 13.9 | 30.8 |
| 13 | 9.8 | 14.0 | 35.4 |
| 14 | 11.5 | 13.3 | 0.0 |
| 15 | 10.8 | 14.2 | 9.6 |
| 16 | 11.2 | 16.8 | 1.2 |
| 17 | 12.5 | 18.7 | 0.2 |
| 18 | 14.6 | 18.8 | 3.0 |
| 19 | 14.6 | 18.7 | 0.0 |
| 20 | 11.6 | 16.1 | 2.2 |
| 21 | 10.7 | 13.3 | 0.8 |
| 22 | 5.5 | 13.2 | 0.0 |
| 23 | 8.3 | 15.9 | 2.4 |
| 24 | 12.3 | 15.7 | 0.4 |
| 25 | 6.6 | 15.1 | 0.0 |
| 26 | 9.9 | 14.4 | 0.0 |
| 27 | 11.7 | 18.2 | 0.2 |
| 28 | 11.9 | 18.0 | 0.2 |
| 29 | 11.0 | 14.6 | 2.4 |
| 30 | 11.3 | 17.1 | 0.0 |
| 31 | 13.4 | 22.3 | 0.0 |

*November 2014*

| Day | Minimum Temperature (°C) | Maximum Temperature (°C) | Daily Total Rainfall (mm) |
|---|---|---|---|
| 1 | 14.9 | 17.5 | 0.2 |
| 2 | 11.8 | 14.3 | 8.8 |
| 3 | 8.9 | 9.1 | 4.4 |
| 4 | 4.3 | 12.5 | 8.2 |
| 5 | 4.3 | 10.6 | 0.2 |
| 6 | 1.3 | 12.1 | 5.0 |
| 7 | 5.6 | 12.1 | 0.0 |
| 8 | 6.9 | 13.1 | 14.2 |
| 9 | 7.1 | 12.5 | 0.0 |
| 10 | 7.0 | 12.8 | 0.2 |
| 11 | 8.5 | 13.1 | 3.6 |
| 12 | 10.1 | 12.7 | 0.6 |
| 13 | 9.2 | 12.5 | 10.0 |
| 14 | 10.2 | 14.0 | 6.8 |
| 15 | 6.8 | 12.2 | 0.2 |
| 16 | 7.8 | 10.1 | 9.6 |
| 17 | 6.6 | 9.1 | 1.4 |
| 18 | 6.3 | 12.8 | 0.8 |
| 19 | 7.1 | 11.4 | 0.2 |
| 20 | 5.8 | 10.8 | 0.2 |
| 21 | 5.1 | 12.1 | 1.8 |
| 22 | 6.8 | 13.5 | 18.0 |
| 23 | 7.9 | 7.9 | 19.8 |
| 24 | 1.4 | 8.8 | 0.2 |
| 25 | 2.2 | 7.9 | 6.8 |
| 26 | 4.3 | 9.9 | 5.0 |
| 27 | 7.4 | 11.2 | 0.0 |
| 28 | 7.7 | 11.7 | 0.2 |
| 29 | 9.1 | 12.6 | 0.2 |
| 30 | 6.2 | 12.0 | 0.0 |

*December 2014*

| Day | Minimum Temperature (°C) | Maximum Temperature (°C) | Daily Total Rainfall (mm) |
|---|---|---|---|
| 1 | 6.0 | 6.3 | 0.6 |
| 2 | 4.9 | 6.8 | 0.4 |
| 3 | 2.8 | 7.8 | 0.2 |
| 4 | 2.7 | 3.1 | 1.8 |
| 5 | 2.5 | 5.1 | 0.4 |
| 6 | −1.1 | 7.9 | 0.4 |
| 7 | −0.3 | 9.6 | 0.6 |
| 8 | 1.6 | 6.5 | 0.0 |
| 9 | −0.7 | 11.0 | 3.0 |
| 10 | 0.0 | 8.4 | 0.0 |
| 11 | 4.5 | 9.3 | 14.0 |
| 12 | 4.3 | 7.5 | 0.2 |
| 13 | −0.1 | 7.0 | 0.0 |
| 14 | −0.3 | 9.1 | 1.2 |
| 15 | 2.5 | 7.8 | 0.2 |
| 16 | 1.1 | 9.6 | 10.8 |
| 17 | 1.4 | 12.1 | 0.0 |
| 18 | 9.6 | 12.7 | 3.0 |
| 19 | 8.0 | 9.2 | 0.0 |
| 20 | 3.8 | 9.4 | 0.4 |
| 21 | 3.6 | 12.5 | 0.0 |
| 22 | 6.8 | 12.3 | 0.0 |
| 23 | 10.1 | 12.0 | 1.2 |
| 24 | 8.7 | 8.7 | 0.0 |
| 25 | 1.8 | 8.1 | 0.0 |
| 26 | 0.0 | 7.9 | 15.0 |
| 27 | 0.4 | 3.1 | 0.2 |
| 28 | 0.5 | 5.0 | 0.0 |
| 29 | −2.4 | 5.9 | 0.2 |
| 30 | −2.3 | 5.3 | 0.2 |
| 31 | −1.5 | 7.2 | 0.4 |

*January 2015*

| Day | Minimum Temperature (°C) | Maximum Temperature (°C) | Daily Total Rainfall (mm) |
|---|---|---|---|
| 1 | 1.4 | 11.8 | 2.0 |
| 2 | 7.1 | 8.7 | 13.6 |
| 3 | 3.6 | 4.8 | 4.8 |
| 4 | −0.9 | 5.9 | 0.2 |
| 5 | 0.2 | 8.7 | 0.0 |
| 6 | 5.9 | 9.1 | 1.6 |
| 7 | 1.3 | 10.2 | 7.0 |
| 8 | 4.7 | 10.8 | 10.6 |
| 9 | 5.6 | 14.3 | 0.4 |
| 10 | 10.0 | 13.0 | 0.6 |
| 11 | 1.9 | 8.8 | 0.6 |
| 12 | 2.9 | 11.1 | 15.4 |
| 13 | 6.3 | 9.0 | 1.4 |
| 14 | 1.5 | 9.6 | 9.2 |
| 15 | 1.9 | 8.4 | 0.0 |
| 16 | 3.8 | 6.8 | 0.4 |
| 17 | −1.9 | 6.9 | 1.4 |
| 18 | 0.8 | 3.5 | 0.0 |
| 19 | −1.2 | 5.2 | 0.2 |
| 20 | −2.3 | 4.4 | 0.0 |
| 21 | −1.6 | 2.5 | 0.0 |
| 22 | −0.4 | 4.2 | 0.0 |
| 23 | −2.8 | 7.5 | 5.4 |
| 24 | −1.9 | 6.9 | 0.2 |
| 25 | −0.6 | 8.4 | 0.0 |
| 26 | 0.5 | 9.4 | 0.2 |
| 27 | 1.9 | 9.3 | 0.0 |
| 28 | 3.6 | 9.2 | 4.8 |
| 29 | 0.7 | 5.8 | 2.6 |
| 30 | 0.3 | 5.7 | 0.2 |
| 31 | −0.7 | 3.9 | 3.4 |

*February 2015*

| Day | Minimum Temperature (°C) | Maximum Temperature (°C) | Daily Total Rainfall (mm) |
|---|---|---|---|
| 1 | 0.3 | 4.7 | 0.0 |
| 2 | −3.6 | 2.6 | 1.1 |
| 3 | −2.2 | 3.0 | 0.7 |
| 4 | −0.6 | 3.8 | 1.2 |
| 5 | 0.1 | 4.1 | 0.2 |
| 6 | −1.0 | 4.6 | 0.2 |
| 7 | −0.6 | 4.4 | 0.0 |
| 8 | 1.8 | 8.6 | 0.0 |
| 9 | 1.0 | 9.6 | 0.0 |
| 10 | 3.7 | 5.8 | 0.0 |
| 11 | 3.8 | 4.3 | 0.0 |
| 12 | 2.4 | 6.5 | 0.2 |
| 13 | 1.8 | 8.4 | 7.6 |
| 14 | 3.7 | 7.6 | 0.0 |
| 15 | 4.7 | 9.5 | 0.2 |
| 16 | 1.1 | 7.9 | 5.8 |
| 17 | 1.2 | 8.9 | 0.0 |
| 18 | 0.7 | 10.1 | 0.0 |
| 19 | 3.1 | 7.5 | 9.2 |
| 20 | 4.0 | 6.2 | 2.0 |
| 21 | 0.7 | 6.7 | 0.2 |
| 22 | −1.8 | 8.4 | 7.0 |
| 23 | 0.8 | 8.3 | 0.8 |
| 24 | 2.7 | 9.6 | 2.4 |
| 25 | 3.7 | 11.5 | 0.4 |
| 26 | 6.1 | 10.3 | 6.6 |
| 27 | −0.6 | 9.1 | 0.2 |
| 28 | 2.4 | 9.9 | 4.2 |

*March 2015*

| Day | Minimum Temperature (°C) | Maximum Temperature (°C) | Daily Total Rainfall (mm) |
|---|---|---|---|
| 1 | 6.0 | 10.9 | 3.6 |
| 2 | 1.6 | 8.4 | 0.0 |
| 3 | 2.3 | 8.8 | 0.0 |
| 4 | 0.7 | 10.7 | 0.0 |
| 5 | 0.2 | 11.2 | 0.0 |
| 6 | 3.5 | 12.3 | 0.0 |
| 7 | 5.8 | 16.1 | 0.0 |
| 8 | 5.9 | 11.6 | 0.0 |
| 9 | 2.5 | 9.2 | 0.0 |
| 10 | 3.4 | 12.2 | 0.0 |
| 11 | 2.9 | 13.0 | 0.0 |
| 12 | 5.1 | 14.2 | 0.0 |
| 13 | 5.8 | 10.8 | 0.0 |
| 14 | 1.3 | 8.2 | 0.0 |
| 15 | 3.7 | 6.0 | 2.6 |
| 16 | 3.7 | 7.9 | 0.8 |
| 17 | 4.2 | 11.6 | 0.0 |
| 18 | 2.4 | 10.0 | 0.0 |
| 19 | 4.0 | 6.9 | 0.0 |
| 20 | 3.7 | 12.3 | 0.0 |
| 21 | 3.7 | 7.1 | 0.0 |
| 22 | 2.4 | 8.8 | 0.0 |
| 23 | 0.6 | 11.0 | 0.4 |
| 24 | 3.8 | 9.4 | 1.0 |
| 25 | 0.1 | 9.9 | 6.4 |
| 26 | 3.2 | 11.7 | 1.0 |
| 27 | 1.9 | 12.5 | 0.0 |
| 28 | 6.1 | 13.2 | 2.2 |
| 29 | 8.0 | 13.0 | 4.0 |
| 30 | 4.4 | 11.6 | 1.4 |
| 31 | 7.3 | 12.6 | 0.2 |

*April 2015*

| Day | Minimum Temperature (°C) | Maximum Temperature (°C) | Daily Total Rainfall (mm) |
|---|---|---|---|
| 1 | 2.9 | 10.1 | 4.6 |
| 2 | 4.8 | 11.5 | 3.4 |
| 3 | 5.6 | 11.4 | 3.2 |
| 4 | 6.7 | 8.9 | 0.0 |
| 5 | 4.8 | 12.8 | 0.0 |
| 6 | 2.9 | 16.1 | 0.0 |
| 7 | 3.0 | 17.9 | 0.0 |
| 8 | 6.4 | 16.8 | 0.0 |
| 9 | 5.2 | 16.9 | 0.0 |
| 10 | 6.1 | 20.8 | 0.0 |
| 11 | 9.2 | 13.5 | 0.6 |
| 12 | 4.3 | 17.4 | 0.0 |
| 13 | 5.6 | 15.9 | 0.0 |
| 14 | 5.8 | 21.8 | 0.0 |
| 15 | 9.3 | 23.9 | 0.0 |
| 16 | 7.0 | 16.0 | 0.0 |
| 17 | 6.5 | 14.4 | 0.0 |
| 18 | 3.3 | 13.8 | 0.0 |
| 19 | 3.5 | 11.3 | 0.0 |
| 20 | 3.5 | 17.7 | 0.0 |
| 21 | 3.7 | 17.8 | 0.0 |
| 22 | 4.1 | 15.1 | 0.0 |
| 23 | 6.4 | 15.9 | 0.0 |
| 24 | 5.9 | 17.1 | 2.5 |
| 25 | 10.2 | 17.9 | 5.5 |
| 26 | 5.6 | 9.9 | 0.0 |
| 27 | 2.6 | 11.8 | 0.0 |
| 28 | 2.3 | 13.0 | 0.2 |
| 29 | 5.9 | 12.8 | 3.8 |
| 30 | 3.4 | 15.1 | – |

*May 2015*

| Day | Minimum Temperature (°C) | Maximum Temperature (°C) | Daily Total Rainfall (mm) |
|---|---|---|---|
| 1 | 3.9 | 12.9 | – |
| 2 | 4.2 | 13.6 | – |
| 3 | 7.8 | 18.9 | – |
| 4 | 10.5 | 17.9 | – |
| 5 | 11.0 | 14.8 | – |
| 6 | 6.7 | 13.5 | – |
| 7 | 8.1 | 17.1 | – |
| 8 | 7.3 | 16.2 | – |
| 9 | 10.4 | 17.2 | – |
| 10 | 8.0 | 18.1 | – |
| 11 | 12.3 | 20.8 | – |
| 12 | 9.7 | 16.7 | – |
| 13 | 5.3 | 19.1 | – |
| 14 | 6.9 | 10.8 | – |
| 15 | 6.3 | 15.2 | – |
| 16 | 9.9 | 18.1 | – |
| 17 | 5.6 | 16.5 | – |
| 18 | 8.1 | 14.5 | – |
| 19 | 6.1 | 13.7 | 3.6 |
| 20 | 3.5 | 15.1 | 0.0 |
| 21 | 4.7 | 19.0 | 0.0 |
| 22 | 7.1 | 18.9 | 0.0 |
| 23 | 11.7 | 16.6 | 0.6 |
| 24 | 10.9 | 18.9 | 0.0 |
| 25 | 7.6 | 15.7 | 0.0 |
| 26 | 8.3 | 19.5 | 0.0 |
| 27 | 5.9 | 19.3 | 0.0 |
| 28 | 10.5 | 16.5 | 0.0 |
| 29 | 8.4 | 14.1 | – |
| 30 | 5.6 | 16.8 | – |
| 31 | 9.8 | 14.9 | – |

*June 2015*

| Day | Minimum Temperature (°C) | Maximum Temperature (°C) | Daily Total Rainfall (mm) |
|---|---|---|---|
| 1 | 6.4 | 15.0 | – |
| 2 | 10.2 | 18.1 | – |
| 3 | 10.2 | 18.2 | – |
| 4 | 8.4 | 22.4 | 0.4 |
| 5 | 12.4 | 23.1 | 0.0 |
| 6 | 7.8 | 18.6 | 0.0 |
| 7 | 6.9 | 19.5 | 0.0 |
| 8 | 7.8 | 18.1 | 0.0 |
| 9 | 5.8 | 14.3 | 0.0 |
| 10 | 8.2 | 18.2 | 0.0 |
| 11 | 8.1 | 22.8 | 0.0 |
| 12 | 11.1 | 25.6 | 0.2 |
| 13 | 13.8 | 17.8 | 0.0 |
| 14 | 12.0 | 17.5 | 0.2 |
| 15 | 9.9 | 19.2 | 0.0 |
| 16 | 9.0 | 22.3 | 0.0 |
| 17 | 11.1 | 24.1 | 0.2 |
| 18 | 12.8 | 20.4 | 0.0 |
| 19 | 9.8 | 20.4 | 0.0 |
| 20 | 11.0 | 18.5 | 2.2 |
| 21 | 13.3 | 19.5 | 2.6 |
| 22 | 9.6 | 17.2 | 0.6 |
| 23 | 9.8 | 19.8 | 0.0 |
| 24 | 11.2 | 23.0 | 0.0 |
| 25 | 10.9 | 24.0 | 0.0 |
| 26 | 13.2 | 26.3 | 0.0 |
| 27 | 11.6 | 24.1 | 0.0 |
| 28 | 15.0 | 20.1 | 1.2 |
| 29 | 11.7 | 25.1 | 0.0 |
| 30 | 13.1 | 29.5 | 0.0 |

# TIME AND SPACE

ASTRONOMY

TIME MEASUREMENT AND CALENDARS

TIDES AND TIDAL PREDICTIONS

# ASTRONOMY

The following pages give astronomical data for each month of the year 2016. There are four pages of data for each month. All data are given for 0h Greenwich Mean Time (GMT), ie at the midnight at the beginning of the day named. This applies also to data for the months when British Summer Time is in operation (for dates, *see* below).

The astronomical data are given in a form suitable for observation with the naked eye or with a small telescope. These data do not attempt to replace the *Astronomical Almanac* for professional astronomers.

A fuller explanation of how to use the astronomical data is given on pages 1115–1117.

## CALENDAR FOR EACH MONTH

The calendar for each month comprises dates of general interest plus the dates of birth or death of well-known people. The theme for this edition is 'politics and elections' to tie-in with the 2015 General Election. For key religious, civil and legal dates *see* page 7. For details of flag-flying days *see* page 19. For royal birthdays *see* pages 19 and 20–1. For public holidays *see also* pages 8 and 9.

Fuller explanations of the various calendars can be found under Time Measurement and Calendars.

The zodiacal signs through which the Sun is passing during each month are illustrated. The date of transition from one sign to the next, to the nearest hour, is given under Astronomical Phenomena.

## JULIAN DATE

The Julian date on 2016 January 0.0 is 2457387.5. To find the Julian date for any other date in 2016 (at 0h GMT), add the day-of-the-year number on the extreme right of the calendar for each month to the Julian date for January 0.0.

## BRITISH SUMMER TIME

British Summer Time is the legal time for general purposes during the period in which it is in operation (*see also* page 1120). During this period, clocks are kept one hour ahead of Greenwich Mean Time. The hour of changeover is 01h Greenwich Mean Time. The duration of Summer Time in 2016 is from March 27 01h GMT to October 30 01h GMT.

## SEASONS

The seasons are defined astronomically as follows:

*Spring* from the vernal equinox to the summer solstice
*Summer* from the summer solstice to the autumnal equinox
*Autumn* from the autumnal equinox to the winter solstice
*Winter* from the winter solstice to the vernal equinox

The time when seasons start in 2016 are:

*Northern Hemisphere*

| | |
|---|---|
| *Vernal Equinox* | March 20d 04h 30m GMT |
| *Summer Solstice* | June 20d 22h 34m GMT |
| *Autumnal Equinox* | September 22d 14h 21m GMT |
| *Winter Solstice* | December 21d 10h 44m GMT |

*Southern Hemisphere*

| | |
|---|---|
| *Autumnal Equinox* | March 20d 04h 30m GMT |
| *Winter Solstice* | June 20d 22h 34m GMT |
| *Vernal Equinox* | September 22d 14h 21m GMT |
| *Summer Solstice* | December 21d 10h 44m GMT |

The longest day of the year, measured from sunrise to sunset, is at the summer solstice. The longest day in the UK will fall on 20 June in 2016.

The shortest day of the year is at the winter solstice. The shortest day in the UK will fall on 21 December in 2016.

The equinox is the point at which day and night are of equal length all over the world.

In popular parlance, the seasons in the northern hemisphere comprise the following months:

| | |
|---|---|
| *Spring* | March, April, May |
| *Summer* | June, July, August |
| *Autumn* | September, October, November |
| *Winter* | December, January, February |

The March equinox can fall as early as 19 March but this has not happened since 1796 and it will not happen again until 2044. This equinox in 2007 was on 21 March, however in 2008 it occurred on 20 March and will not revert to 21 March again until 2102.

In 2008 the June solstice occurred on 20 June, the first time since 1897. The June solstice in 1975 was on 22 June, but it will not occur on this date again until 2203.

# JANUARY 2016

FIRST MONTH, 31 DAYS. *Janus*, god of the portal, facing two ways, past and future

| | | | |
|---|---|---|---|
| 1 | *Friday* | Great Britain and Ireland unite as the United Kingdom of Great Britain and Ireland 1801 | day 1 |
| 2 | *Saturday* | José Antonio Remón Cantera, the president of Panama, is killed at a race track 1955 | 2 |
| 3 | *Sunday* | Joseph Jenkins Roberts is sworn in as the first president of Liberia 1848 | 3 |
| | | | |
| 4 | *Monday* | The Fabian Society, Britain's oldest political think tank, is founded 1884 | week 1 day 4 |
| 5 | *Tuesday* | The German Worker's Party, predecessor of the Nazi party, is founded in Munich 1919 | 5 |
| 6 | *Wednesday* | Theodore Roosevelt, the 26th US president and the first to win a Nobel Peace Prize *d.* 1919 | 6 |
| 7 | *Thursday* | Robert Devereux, 2nd Earl of Essex, leads a failed rebellion against Queen Elizabeth I 1601 | 7 |
| 8 | *Friday* | François Mitterrand, France's 21st and longest-serving president *d.* 1996 | 8 |
| 9 | *Saturday* | Anthoney Eden resigns as prime minister following the Suez Crisis 1957 | 9 |
| 10 | *Sunday* | Thomas Paine anonymously publishes *Common Sense* in support of American independence 1776 | 10 |
| | | | |
| 11 | *Monday* | Arthur Scargill, trade unionist, president National Union of Mineworkers (1982–2002) *b.* 1938 | week 2 day 11 |
| 12 | *Tuesday* | Edmund Burke, Irish philosopher and Whig politician who opposed the French Revolution *b.* 1729 | 12 |
| 13 | *Wednesday* | The Independent Labour party is founded in Bradford by James Keir Hardie 1893 | 13 |
| 14 | *Thursday* | Marshal Josip Broz Tito was elected as the first president of Yugoslavia 1953 | 14 |
| 15 | *Friday* | Rosa Luxemburg, revolutionary Marxist of Polish-Jewish descent, is assassinated in Berlin 1919 | 15 |
| 16 | *Saturday* | Ivan the Terrible is crowned Tsar of All the Russias 1547 | 16 |
| 17 | *Sunday* | Benjamin Franklin, Founding Father of the USA, who invented bifocals *b.* 1706 | 17 |
| | | | |
| 18 | *Monday* | Sir Edmund Barton, the first prime minister of Australia *b.* 1849 | week 3 day 18 |
| 19 | *Tuesday* | The US senate votes against participation in the League of Nations 1920 | 19 |
| 20 | *Wednesday* | Christian II is deposed from the thrones of Denmark and Norway 1523 | 20 |
| 21 | *Thursday* | On his first day in office, US president Jimmy Carter pardons Vietnam War draft evaders 1977 | 21 |
| 22 | *Friday* | Ramsay MacDonald becomes the first Labour prime minister of the UK 1924 | 22 |
| 23 | *Saturday* | William Pitt the Younger, the youngest British prime minister aged 24 *d.* 1806 | 23 |
| 24 | *Sunday* | Frederick II (Frederick the Great), who introduced the potato to the Kingdom of Prussia *b.* 1712 | 24 |
| | | | |
| 25 | *Monday* | The League of Nations is established at the Paris Peace Conference 1919 | week 4 day 25 |
| 26 | *Tuesday* | India officially becomes an independent republic and its first president is sworn in 1950 | 26 |
| 27 | *Wednesday* | The body of Vladimir Lenin is placed in a mausoleum in Red Square 1924 | 27 |
| 28 | *Thursday* | Sir Thomas Warner establishes Saint Kitts as the first British colony in the Caribbean 1624 | 28 |
| 29 | *Friday* | George III, whose life was longer than any monarch who preceded him *d.* 1820 | 29 |
| 30 | *Saturday* | Charles I is executed for treason outside the Banqueting House, Whitehall, London 1649 | 30 |
| 31 | *Sunday* | Guy Fawkes leaps to his death from the gallows before he could be hung for treason 1606 | 31 |

## ASTRONOMICAL PHENOMENA

*d  h*

2 23 Earth at perihelion
3 19 Mars 1° South of the Moon
6 24 Venus 3° South of the Moon
7 05 Saturn 3° South of the Moon
9 04 Saturn 0.1° South of Venus
10 18 Mercury 2° South of the Moon
16 06 Uranus 1° North of the Moon
28 01 Jupiter 1° North of the Moon

## MINIMA OF ALGOL

| d | h | d | h | d | h |
|---|---|---|---|---|---|
| 1 | 11.9 | 12 | 23.2 | 24 | 10.5 |
| 4 | 08.8 | 15 | 20.0 | 27 | 07.3 |
| 7 | 05.6 | 18 | 16.9 | 30 | 04.2 |
| 10 | 02.4 | 21 | 13.7 | | |

## CONSTELLATIONS

The following constellations are near the meridian at

| | d | h | | d | h |
|---|---|---|---|---|---|
| December | 1 | 24 | January | 16 | 21 |
| December | 16 | 23 | February | 1 | 20 |
| January | 1 | 22 | February | 15 | 19 |

Draco (below the Pole), Ursa Minor (below the Pole), Camelopardalis, Perseus, Auriga, Taurus, Orion, Eridanus and Lepus

## THE MOON

| Phases, Apsides and Node | d | h | m |
|---|---|---|---|
| ◐ Last Quarter | 2 | 05 | 30 |
| ● New Moon | 10 | 01 | 31 |
| ◑ First Quarter | 16 | 23 | 26 |
| ○ Full Moon | 24 | 01 | 46 |
| | | | |
| Apogee (404,277km) | 2 | 11 | 53 |
| Perigee (369,619km) | 15 | 02 | 14 |
| Apogee (404,553km) | 30 | 09 | 10 |

Mean longitude of ascending node on 1st, 176°

# THE SUN

Diam. 32.5″

| Day | Right Ascension h | m | s | Dec. ° | Equation of time m | s | Rise 52° h | m | Rise 56° h | m | Transit h | m | Set 52° h | m | Set 56° h | m | Sidereal time h | m | s | Transit of first point of Aries h | m | s |
|---|---|---|---|---|---|---|---|---|---|---|---|---|---|---|---|---|---|---|---|---|---|---|
| 1 | 18 | 43 | 28 | 23.1 | −3 | 06 | 8 | 08 | 8 | 30 | 12 | 03 | 15 | 59 | 15 | 36 | 6 | 40 | 22 | 17 | 19 | 38 |
| 2 | 18 | 47 | 53 | 23.0 | −3 | 34 | 8 | 08 | 8 | 30 | 12 | 04 | 16 | 00 | 15 | 38 | 6 | 44 | 18 | 17 | 15 | 42 |
| 3 | 18 | 52 | 17 | 22.9 | −4 | 02 | 8 | 07 | 8 | 30 | 12 | 04 | 16 | 01 | 15 | 39 | 6 | 48 | 15 | 17 | 11 | 45 |
| 4 | 18 | 56 | 42 | 22.8 | −4 | 30 | 8 | 07 | 8 | 30 | 12 | 05 | 16 | 02 | 15 | 40 | 6 | 52 | 12 | 17 | 07 | 48 |
| 5 | 19 | 01 | 05 | 22.7 | −4 | 57 | 8 | 07 | 8 | 29 | 12 | 05 | 16 | 04 | 15 | 41 | 6 | 56 | 08 | 17 | 03 | 52 |
| 6 | 19 | 05 | 29 | 22.6 | −5 | 24 | 8 | 07 | 8 | 29 | 12 | 06 | 16 | 05 | 15 | 43 | 7 | 00 | 05 | 16 | 59 | 55 |
| 7 | 19 | 09 | 52 | 22.5 | −5 | 51 | 8 | 06 | 8 | 28 | 12 | 06 | 16 | 06 | 15 | 44 | 7 | 04 | 01 | 16 | 55 | 59 |
| 8 | 19 | 14 | 15 | 22.3 | −6 | 17 | 8 | 06 | 8 | 28 | 12 | 07 | 16 | 07 | 15 | 46 | 7 | 07 | 58 | 16 | 52 | 02 |
| 9 | 19 | 18 | 37 | 22.2 | −6 | 43 | 8 | 05 | 8 | 27 | 12 | 07 | 16 | 09 | 15 | 47 | 7 | 11 | 54 | 16 | 48 | 06 |
| 10 | 19 | 22 | 59 | 22.1 | −7 | 08 | 8 | 05 | 8 | 26 | 12 | 07 | 16 | 10 | 15 | 49 | 7 | 15 | 51 | 16 | 44 | 09 |
| 11 | 19 | 27 | 20 | 21.9 | −7 | 32 | 8 | 04 | 8 | 25 | 12 | 08 | 16 | 12 | 15 | 51 | 7 | 19 | 47 | 16 | 40 | 13 |
| 12 | 19 | 31 | 40 | 21.8 | −7 | 56 | 8 | 04 | 8 | 24 | 12 | 08 | 16 | 13 | 15 | 52 | 7 | 23 | 44 | 16 | 36 | 16 |
| 13 | 19 | 36 | 00 | 21.6 | −8 | 20 | 8 | 03 | 8 | 23 | 12 | 09 | 16 | 14 | 15 | 54 | 7 | 27 | 41 | 16 | 32 | 19 |
| 14 | 19 | 40 | 19 | 21.4 | −8 | 42 | 8 | 02 | 8 | 23 | 12 | 09 | 16 | 16 | 15 | 56 | 7 | 31 | 37 | 16 | 28 | 23 |
| 15 | 19 | 44 | 38 | 21.3 | −9 | 05 | 8 | 01 | 8 | 21 | 12 | 09 | 16 | 18 | 15 | 58 | 7 | 35 | 34 | 16 | 24 | 26 |
| 16 | 19 | 48 | 56 | 21.1 | −9 | 26 | 8 | 01 | 8 | 20 | 12 | 10 | 16 | 19 | 15 | 59 | 7 | 39 | 30 | 16 | 20 | 30 |
| 17 | 19 | 53 | 13 | 20.9 | −9 | 47 | 8 | 00 | 8 | 19 | 12 | 10 | 16 | 21 | 16 | 01 | 7 | 43 | 27 | 16 | 16 | 33 |
| 18 | 19 | 57 | 30 | 20.7 | −10 | 07 | 7 | 59 | 8 | 18 | 12 | 10 | 16 | 22 | 16 | 03 | 7 | 47 | 23 | 16 | 12 | 37 |
| 19 | 20 | 01 | 46 | 20.5 | −10 | 26 | 7 | 58 | 8 | 17 | 12 | 11 | 16 | 24 | 16 | 05 | 7 | 51 | 20 | 16 | 08 | 40 |
| 20 | 20 | 06 | 01 | 20.3 | −10 | 44 | 7 | 57 | 8 | 15 | 12 | 11 | 16 | 26 | 16 | 07 | 7 | 55 | 16 | 16 | 04 | 44 |
| 21 | 20 | 10 | 15 | 20.1 | −11 | 02 | 7 | 56 | 8 | 14 | 12 | 11 | 16 | 27 | 16 | 09 | 7 | 59 | 13 | 16 | 00 | 47 |
| 22 | 20 | 14 | 29 | 19.8 | −11 | 19 | 7 | 54 | 8 | 13 | 12 | 11 | 16 | 29 | 16 | 11 | 8 | 03 | 10 | 15 | 56 | 50 |
| 23 | 20 | 18 | 42 | 19.6 | −11 | 36 | 7 | 53 | 8 | 11 | 12 | 12 | 16 | 31 | 16 | 13 | 8 | 07 | 06 | 15 | 52 | 54 |
| 24 | 20 | 22 | 54 | 19.4 | −11 | 51 | 7 | 52 | 8 | 10 | 12 | 12 | 16 | 32 | 16 | 15 | 8 | 11 | 03 | 15 | 48 | 57 |
| 25 | 20 | 27 | 05 | 19.2 | −12 | 06 | 7 | 51 | 8 | 08 | 12 | 12 | 16 | 34 | 16 | 17 | 8 | 14 | 59 | 15 | 45 | 01 |
| 26 | 20 | 31 | 15 | 18.9 | −12 | 20 | 7 | 49 | 8 | 06 | 12 | 12 | 16 | 36 | 16 | 19 | 8 | 18 | 56 | 15 | 41 | 04 |
| 27 | 20 | 35 | 25 | 18.7 | −12 | 33 | 7 | 48 | 8 | 05 | 12 | 13 | 16 | 38 | 16 | 21 | 8 | 22 | 52 | 15 | 37 | 08 |
| 28 | 20 | 39 | 34 | 18.4 | −12 | 45 | 7 | 47 | 8 | 03 | 12 | 13 | 16 | 40 | 16 | 23 | 8 | 26 | 49 | 15 | 33 | 11 |
| 29 | 20 | 43 | 42 | 18.1 | −12 | 57 | 7 | 45 | 8 | 01 | 12 | 13 | 16 | 41 | 16 | 25 | 8 | 30 | 45 | 15 | 29 | 15 |
| 30 | 20 | 47 | 49 | 17.9 | −13 | 07 | 7 | 44 | 8 | 00 | 12 | 13 | 16 | 43 | 16 | 28 | 8 | 34 | 42 | 15 | 25 | 18 |
| 31 | 20 | 51 | 56 | 17.6 | −13 | 17 | 7 | 42 | 7 | 58 | 12 | 13 | 16 | 45 | 16 | 30 | 8 | 38 | 39 | 15 | 21 | 21 |

## DURATION OF TWILIGHT (in minutes)

| Latitude | 52° | 56° | 52° | 56° | 52° | 56° | 52° | 56° |
|---|---|---|---|---|---|---|---|---|
| | 1 January | | 11 January | | 21 January | | 31 January | |
| Civil | 41 | 47 | 40 | 45 | 38 | 43 | 37 | 41 |
| Nautical | 84 | 96 | 82 | 93 | 80 | 90 | 78 | 87 |
| Astronomical | 125 | 141 | 123 | 138 | 120 | 134 | 117 | 130 |

## THE NIGHT SKY

*Mercury* is an evening object low in the south-west for the first week of January. It moves into the morning sky after inferior conjunction on the 14th and may be spotted in the last week of the month. Mercury's emergence now allows us take in all five classical planets in one sweep before sunrise until about mid-February. Such an opportunity last occurred in December 2004 when the five were in the right order of their increasing distance from the Sun.

*Venus* starts the year in Scorpius but quickly crosses into Ophiuchus before ending the month in Sagittarius. It rises about three hours before the Sun at the beginning of January but only about 90 minutes beforehand on the 31st. The Moon, Venus, and Saturn form an impressive trio on the 7th with the two planets only a Moon's width apart on the 9th.

*Mars* rises during the early hours and crosses from Virgo into Libra on the 17th. The planet's deep orange tint now becomes quite pronounced as it brightens from magnitude +1.3 to +0.8. The Moon is near Mars on the 3rd.

*Jupiter*, magnitude −2.2, rises during the late evening and can be found in Leo. It is stationary on the 8th and then begins to retrograde. The Moon is near Jupiter on the morning of January 1st but much closer on the 28th.

*Saturn*, magnitude +0.5, is in Ophiuchus and rises more than two hours before the Sun.

# THE MOON

| Day | R.A. h m | Dec. ° | Hor. Par. ' | Diam. ' | Sun's Co-Long. ° | PA of Br. Limb ° | Ph. % | Age d | Rise 52° h m | Rise 56° h m | Transit h m | Set 52° h m | Set 56° h m |
|---|---|---|---|---|---|---|---|---|---|---|---|---|---|
| 1 | 11 48 | +1.5 | 54.4 | 29.7 | 164 | 113 | 62 | 20.7 | — | — | 5 17 | 11 26 | 11 25 |
| 2 | 12 33 | −2.3 | 54.3 | 29.6 | 177 | 113 | 52 | 21.7 | 0 01 | 0 03 | 5 59 | 11 48 | 11 45 |
| 3 | 13 18 | −5.9 | 54.3 | 29.6 | 189 | 112 | 43 | 22.7 | 1 03 | 1 09 | 6 42 | 12 11 | 12 05 |
| 4 | 14 04 | −9.3 | 54.4 | 29.7 | 201 | 111 | 34 | 23.7 | 2 06 | 2 15 | 7 25 | 12 37 | 12 27 |
| 5 | 14 52 | −12.4 | 54.8 | 29.8 | 213 | 109 | 25 | 24.7 | 3 09 | 3 21 | 8 11 | 13 06 | 12 53 |
| 6 | 15 41 | −15.0 | 55.2 | 30.1 | 225 | 107 | 17 | 25.7 | 4 12 | 4 27 | 8 58 | 13 39 | 13 24 |
| 7 | 16 32 | −17.0 | 55.8 | 30.4 | 237 | 105 | 10 | 26.7 | 5 13 | 5 30 | 9 48 | 14 20 | 14 03 |
| 8 | 17 25 | −18.1 | 56.5 | 30.8 | 250 | 104 | 5 | 27.7 | 6 11 | 6 30 | 10 40 | 15 08 | 14 50 |
| 9 | 18 21 | −18.4 | 57.1 | 31.1 | 262 | 108 | 1 | 28.7 | 7 04 | 7 23 | 11 34 | 16 05 | 15 47 |
| 10 | 19 17 | −17.6 | 57.8 | 31.5 | 274 | 162 | 0 | 0.1 | 7 52 | 8 08 | 12 28 | 17 10 | 16 54 |
| 11 | 20 14 | −15.8 | 58.3 | 31.8 | 286 | 239 | 1 | 1.1 | 8 33 | 8 47 | 13 23 | 18 20 | 18 08 |
| 12 | 21 10 | −13.1 | 58.8 | 32.0 | 298 | 246 | 5 | 2.1 | 9 08 | 9 19 | 14 17 | 19 35 | 19 25 |
| 13 | 22 06 | −9.5 | 59.1 | 32.2 | 311 | 247 | 10 | 3.1 | 9 40 | 9 47 | 15 10 | 20 51 | 20 46 |
| 14 | 23 00 | −5.5 | 59.3 | 32.3 | 323 | 247 | 18 | 4.1 | 10 09 | 10 12 | 16 02 | 22 08 | 22 07 |
| 15 | 23 55 | −1.1 | 59.3 | 32.3 | 335 | 247 | 28 | 5.1 | 10 36 | 10 36 | 16 54 | 23 25 | 23 28 |
| 16 | 0 49 | +3.4 | 59.3 | 32.3 | 347 | 247 | 39 | 6.1 | 11 04 | 11 00 | 17 46 | — | — |
| 17 | 1 43 | +7.6 | 59.2 | 32.2 | 359 | 249 | 50 | 7.1 | 11 34 | 11 25 | 18 39 | 0 41 | 0 48 |
| 18 | 2 38 | +11.4 | 59.0 | 32.1 | 11 | 251 | 62 | 8.1 | 12 07 | 11 55 | 19 32 | 1 56 | 2 07 |
| 19 | 3 34 | +14.6 | 58.7 | 32.0 | 24 | 254 | 72 | 9.1 | 12 44 | 12 29 | 20 27 | 3 09 | 3 24 |
| 20 | 4 30 | +16.8 | 58.4 | 31.8 | 36 | 257 | 82 | 10.1 | 13 28 | 13 11 | 21 23 | 4 19 | 4 35 |
| 21 | 5 28 | +18.1 | 58.0 | 31.6 | 48 | 260 | 89 | 11.1 | 14 19 | 14 02 | 22 18 | 5 21 | 5 39 |
| 22 | 6 25 | +18.3 | 57.6 | 31.4 | 60 | 262 | 95 | 12.1 | 15 17 | 15 00 | 23 12 | 6 16 | 6 34 |
| 23 | 7 21 | +17.5 | 57.1 | 31.1 | 72 | 259 | 99 | 13.1 | 16 19 | 16 04 | — | 7 02 | 7 19 |
| 24 | 8 15 | +15.8 | 56.6 | 30.8 | 84 | 206 | 100 | 14.1 | 17 25 | 17 12 | 0 05 | 7 41 | 7 54 |
| 25 | 9 08 | +13.2 | 56.0 | 30.5 | 96 | 123 | 99 | 15.1 | 18 31 | 18 21 | 0 54 | 8 14 | 8 25 |
| 26 | 9 58 | +10.1 | 55.5 | 30.3 | 108 | 115 | 96 | 16.1 | 19 37 | 19 31 | 1 42 | 8 42 | 8 49 |
| 27 | 10 46 | +6.7 | 55.0 | 30.0 | 121 | 114 | 92 | 17.1 | 20 42 | 20 39 | 2 28 | 9 07 | 9 11 |
| 28 | 11 33 | +3.0 | 54.6 | 29.8 | 133 | 113 | 85 | 18.1 | 21 46 | 21 46 | 3 11 | 9 30 | 9 31 |
| 29 | 12 18 | −0.8 | 54.4 | 29.6 | 145 | 113 | 78 | 19.1 | 22 49 | 22 52 | 3 54 | 9 52 | 9 50 |
| 30 | 13 03 | −4.5 | 54.2 | 29.5 | 157 | 112 | 70 | 20.1 | 23 51 | 23 58 | 4 37 | 10 15 | 10 10 |
| 31 | 13 49 | −8.0 | 54.2 | 29.6 | 169 | 110 | 61 | 21.1 | — | — | 5 19 | 10 39 | 10 31 |

# MERCURY

| Day | R.A. h m | Dec ° | Mag. | Diam. " | Phase % | Rise h m | Transit h m | Set h m |
|---|---|---|---|---|---|---|---|---|
| 1 | 20 05.5 | −21.1 | −0.3 | 7 | 49 | 9 26 | 13 22 | 17 19 |
| 3 | 20 10.0 | −20.4 | −0.1 | 8 | 40 | 9 17 | 13 18 | 17 19 |
| 5 | 20 11.8 | −19.7 | +0.3 | 8 | 30 | 9 06 | 13 11 | 17 16 |
| 7 | 20 10.5 | −19.2 | +0.9 | 9 | 21 | 8 52 | 13 01 | 17 09 |
| 9 | 20 06.0 | −18.7 | +1.7 | 9 | 12 | 8 37 | 12 47 | 16 58 |
| 11 | 19 58.4 | −18.5 | +2.8 | 10 | 6 | 8 19 | 12 31 | 16 43 |
| 13 | 19 48.5 | −18.4 | +4.1 | 10 | 2 | 8 01 | 12 13 | 16 25 |
| 15 | 19 37.4 | −18.4 | +4.6 | 10 | 1 | 7 42 | 11 54 | 16 06 |
| 17 | 19 26.5 | −18.5 | +3.6 | 10 | 3 | 7 24 | 11 36 | 15 46 |
| 19 | 19 16.9 | −18.8 | +2.5 | 10 | 8 | 7 09 | 11 19 | 15 28 |
| 21 | 19 09.6 | −19.0 | +1.7 | 10 | 14 | 6 56 | 11 05 | 15 12 |
| 23 | 19 04.8 | −19.3 | +1.1 | 9 | 21 | 6 46 | 10 53 | 14 59 |
| 25 | 19 02.7 | −19.7 | +0.7 | 9 | 28 | 6 39 | 10 43 | 14 48 |
| 27 | 19 02.9 | −20.0 | +0.4 | 8 | 34 | 6 34 | 10 36 | 14 39 |
| 29 | 19 05.2 | −20.3 | +0.3 | 8 | 41 | 6 30 | 10 31 | 14 32 |
| 31 | 19 09.4 | −20.5 | +0.1 | 8 | 46 | 6 29 | 10 28 | 14 27 |

Rising and setting times are for latitude 54°

# VENUS

| Day | R.A. h m | Dec ° | Mag. | Diam. " | Phase % | Rise h m | Transit h m | Set h m |
|---|---|---|---|---|---|---|---|---|
| 1 | 16 00.6 | −18.6 | −5.4 | 15 | 77 | 6 00 | 9 20 | 13 33 |
| 6 | 16 25.8 | −19.8 | −5.3 | 15 | 79 | 5 20 | 9 25 | 13 30 |
| 11 | 16 51.5 | −20.8 | −5.2 | 15 | 80 | 5 33 | 9 31 | 13 29 |
| 16 | 17 17.6 | −21.6 | −5.1 | 14 | 81 | 5 45 | 9 37 | 13 30 |
| 21 | 17 43.9 | −22.2 | −5.0 | 14 | 83 | 5 55 | 9 44 | 13 33 |
| 26 | 18 10.5 | −22.4 | −4.9 | 14 | 84 | 6 04 | 9 51 | 13 38 |
| 31 | 18 37.1 | −22.4 | −4.9 | 13 | 85 | 6 11 | 9 58 | 13 45 |

# MARS

| Day | R.A. h m | Dec ° | Mag. | Diam. " | Phase % | Rise h m | Transit h m | Set h m |
|---|---|---|---|---|---|---|---|---|
| 1 | 13 47.5 | −9.5 | +1.3 | 6 | 91 | 1 56 | 7 06 | 12 16 |
| 6 | 13 58.0 | −10.4 | +1.2 | 6 | 91 | 1 53 | 6 57 | 12 01 |
| 11 | 14 08.4 | −11.4 | +1.1 | 6 | 91 | 1 49 | 6 48 | 11 47 |
| 16 | 14 18.7 | −12.3 | +1.1 | 6 | 91 | 1 45 | 6 39 | 11 32 |
| 21 | 14 29.3 | −13.1 | +1.0 | 6 | 90 | 1 40 | 6 29 | 11 17 |
| 26 | 14 39.0 | −13.9 | +0.9 | 7 | 90 | 1 36 | 6 19 | 11 03 |
| 31 | 14 48.9 | −14.7 | +0.8 | 7 | 90 | 1 31 | 6 10 | 10 48 |

# SUNRISE AND SUNSET

| | London 0° 05' / 51° 30' | | Bristol 2° 35' / 51° 28' | | Birmingham 1° 55' / 52° 28' | | Manchester 2° 15' / 53° 28' | | Newcastle 1° 37' / 54° 59' | | Glasgow 4° 14' / 55° 52' | | Belfast 5° 56' / 54° 35' | |
|---|---|---|---|---|---|---|---|---|---|---|---|---|---|---|
| d | h m | h m | h m | h m | h m | h m | h m | h m | h m | h m | h m | h m | h m | h m |
| 1 | 8 06 | 16 02 | 8 16 | 16 12 | 8 18 | 16 04 | 8 25 | 16 00 | 8 31 | 15 49 | 8 47 | 15 53 | 8 46 | 16 08 |
| 2 | 8 06 | 16 03 | 8 16 | 16 13 | 8 18 | 16 05 | 8 25 | 16 01 | 8 31 | 15 50 | 8 47 | 15 55 | 8 46 | 16 09 |
| 3 | 8 06 | 16 04 | 8 16 | 16 14 | 8 18 | 16 06 | 8 25 | 16 02 | 8 31 | 15 51 | 8 47 | 15 56 | 8 46 | 16 11 |
| 4 | 8 06 | 16 05 | 8 15 | 16 15 | 8 18 | 16 07 | 8 24 | 16 03 | 8 30 | 15 52 | 8 46 | 15 57 | 8 45 | 16 12 |
| 5 | 8 05 | 16 06 | 8 15 | 16 16 | 8 17 | 16 09 | 8 24 | 16 05 | 8 30 | 15 54 | 8 46 | 15 59 | 8 45 | 16 13 |
| 6 | 8 05 | 16 07 | 8 15 | 16 17 | 8 17 | 16 10 | 8 24 | 16 06 | 8 30 | 15 55 | 8 45 | 16 00 | 8 45 | 16 14 |
| 7 | 8 05 | 16 08 | 8 14 | 16 19 | 8 17 | 16 11 | 8 23 | 16 07 | 8 29 | 15 56 | 8 45 | 16 01 | 8 44 | 16 16 |
| 8 | 8 04 | 16 10 | 8 14 | 16 20 | 8 16 | 16 12 | 8 23 | 16 09 | 8 28 | 15 58 | 8 44 | 16 03 | 8 43 | 16 17 |
| 9 | 8 04 | 16 11 | 8 13 | 16 21 | 8 16 | 16 14 | 8 22 | 16 10 | 8 28 | 15 59 | 8 44 | 16 05 | 8 43 | 16 19 |
| 10 | 8 03 | 16 12 | 8 13 | 16 23 | 8 15 | 16 15 | 8 21 | 16 12 | 8 27 | 16 01 | 8 43 | 16 06 | 8 42 | 16 20 |
| 11 | 8 03 | 16 14 | 8 12 | 16 24 | 8 14 | 16 17 | 8 21 | 16 13 | 8 26 | 16 02 | 8 42 | 16 08 | 8 41 | 16 22 |
| 12 | 8 02 | 16 15 | 8 12 | 16 26 | 8 14 | 16 18 | 8 20 | 16 15 | 8 25 | 16 04 | 8 41 | 16 09 | 8 41 | 16 24 |
| 13 | 8 01 | 16 17 | 8 11 | 16 27 | 8 13 | 16 20 | 8 19 | 16 16 | 8 25 | 16 06 | 8 40 | 16 11 | 8 40 | 16 25 |
| 14 | 8 00 | 16 18 | 8 10 | 16 28 | 8 12 | 16 21 | 8 18 | 16 18 | 8 24 | 16 07 | 8 39 | 16 13 | 8 39 | 16 27 |
| 15 | 8 00 | 16 20 | 8 10 | 16 30 | 8 11 | 16 23 | 8 17 | 16 19 | 8 23 | 16 09 | 8 38 | 16 15 | 8 38 | 16 29 |
| 16 | 7 59 | 16 21 | 8 09 | 16 32 | 8 10 | 16 24 | 8 16 | 16 21 | 8 22 | 16 11 | 8 37 | 16 17 | 8 37 | 16 30 |
| 17 | 7 58 | 16 23 | 8 08 | 16 33 | 8 10 | 16 26 | 8 15 | 16 23 | 8 20 | 16 13 | 8 36 | 16 19 | 8 36 | 16 32 |
| 18 | 7 57 | 16 25 | 8 07 | 16 35 | 8 09 | 16 28 | 8 14 | 16 25 | 8 19 | 16 15 | 8 34 | 16 20 | 8 35 | 16 34 |
| 19 | 7 56 | 16 26 | 8 06 | 16 36 | 8 07 | 16 29 | 8 13 | 16 26 | 8 18 | 16 16 | 8 33 | 16 22 | 8 33 | 16 36 |
| 20 | 7 55 | 16 28 | 8 05 | 16 38 | 8 06 | 16 31 | 8 12 | 16 28 | 8 17 | 16 18 | 8 32 | 16 24 | 8 32 | 16 38 |
| 21 | 7 54 | 16 30 | 8 04 | 16 40 | 8 05 | 16 33 | 8 11 | 16 30 | 8 16 | 16 20 | 8 30 | 16 26 | 8 31 | 16 40 |
| 22 | 7 53 | 16 31 | 8 03 | 16 41 | 8 04 | 16 35 | 8 10 | 16 32 | 8 14 | 16 22 | 8 29 | 16 28 | 8 30 | 16 41 |
| 23 | 7 52 | 16 33 | 8 02 | 16 43 | 8 03 | 16 36 | 8 08 | 16 34 | 8 13 | 16 24 | 8 28 | 16 30 | 8 28 | 16 43 |
| 24 | 7 51 | 16 35 | 8 00 | 16 45 | 8 02 | 16 38 | 8 07 | 16 35 | 8 11 | 16 26 | 8 26 | 16 32 | 8 27 | 16 45 |
| 25 | 7 49 | 16 36 | 7 59 | 16 47 | 8 00 | 16 40 | 8 06 | 16 37 | 8 10 | 16 28 | 8 24 | 16 34 | 8 25 | 16 47 |
| 26 | 7 48 | 16 38 | 7 58 | 16 48 | 7 59 | 16 42 | 8 04 | 16 39 | 8 08 | 16 30 | 8 23 | 16 37 | 8 24 | 16 49 |
| 27 | 7 47 | 16 40 | 7 57 | 16 50 | 7 58 | 16 44 | 8 03 | 16 41 | 8 07 | 16 32 | 8 21 | 16 39 | 8 22 | 16 51 |
| 28 | 7 45 | 16 42 | 7 55 | 16 52 | 7 56 | 16 45 | 8 01 | 16 43 | 8 05 | 16 34 | 8 19 | 16 41 | 8 21 | 16 53 |
| 29 | 7 44 | 16 43 | 7 54 | 16 54 | 7 55 | 16 47 | 8 00 | 16 45 | 8 03 | 16 36 | 8 18 | 16 43 | 8 19 | 16 55 |
| 30 | 7 43 | 16 45 | 7 52 | 16 55 | 7 53 | 16 49 | 7 58 | 16 47 | 8 02 | 16 38 | 8 16 | 16 45 | 8 17 | 16 57 |
| 31 | 7 41 | 16 47 | 7 51 | 16 57 | 7 52 | 16 51 | 7 57 | 16 49 | 8 00 | 16 40 | 8 14 | 16 47 | 8 16 | 16 59 |

# JUPITER

| Day | R.A. h m | Dec ° | Mag. | Diam. " | Rise h m | Transit h m | Set h m |
|---|---|---|---|---|---|---|---|
| 1 | 11 36.0 | +3.9 | -2.2 | 39 | 22 27 | 4 55 | 11 19 |
| 11 | 11 36.3 | +4.0 | -2.2 | 40 | 21 48 | 4 16 | 10 41 |
| 21 | 11 35.5 | +4.1 | -2.3 | 41 | 21 07 | 3 36 | 10 01 |
| 31 | 11 33.5 | +4.4 | -2.4 | 42 | 20 24 | 2 54 | 9 21 |

Equatorial Diam. 41″, Polar Diam. 38″

# SATURN

| Day | R.A. h m | Dec ° | Mag. | Diam. " | Rise h m | Transit h m | Set h m |
|---|---|---|---|---|---|---|---|
| 1 | 16 38.4 | -20.5 | +0.5 | 15 | 5 56 | 9 56 | 13 57 |
| 11 | 16 42.8 | -20.6 | +0.5 | 15 | 5 22 | 9 22 | 13 21 |
| 21 | 16 47.0 | -20.7 | +0.6 | 16 | 4 47 | 8 46 | 12 45 |
| 31 | 16 50.7 | -20.8 | +0.6 | 16 | 4 13 | 8 11 | 12 09 |

Equatorial Diam. 15″, Polar Diam. 14″
Rings – major axis 35″ minor axis 15″, Tilt 26°

# URANUS

| Day | R.A. h m | Dec ° | Mag. | Diam. " | Rise h m | Transit h m | Set h m |
|---|---|---|---|---|---|---|---|
| 1 | 1 01.2 | +5.8 | +6.1 | 4 | 11 43 | 18 18 | 0 57 |
| 11 | 1 01.6 | +5.9 | +6.1 | 4 | 11 03 | 17 39 | 0 18 |
| 21 | 1 02.2 | +6.0 | +6.2 | 3 | 10 24 | 17 00 | 23 36 |
| 31 | 1 03.2 | +6.1 | +6.2 | 3 | 9 45 | 16 22 | 22 58 |

# NEPTUNE

| Day | R.A. h m | Dec ° | Mag. | Diam. " | Rise h m | Transit h m | Set h m |
|---|---|---|---|---|---|---|---|
| 1 | 22 37.3 | -9.6 | +7.9 | 2 | 10 45 | 15 54 | 21 04 |
| 11 | 22 38.3 | -9.5 | +7.9 | 2 | 10 06 | 15 16 | 20 26 |
| 21 | 22 39.4 | -9.3 | +8.0 | 2 | 9 27 | 14 38 | 19 49 |
| 31 | 22 40.6 | -9.2 | +8.0 | 2 | 8 48 | 14 00 | 19 11 |

# FEBRUARY 2016

SECOND MONTH, 28 or 29 DAYS. *Februa*, Roman festival of Purification

| | | | |
|---|---|---|---|
| 1 | *Monday* | Boris Yeltsin, who in 1991 became the first democratically elected Russian president *b.* 1931 | week 5 day 32 |
| 2 | *Tuesday* | Mehmed VI, the 36th and last Sultan of the Ottoman Empire *b.* 1861 | 33 |
| 3 | *Wednesday* | Prime Minister Harold Macmillan delivers his 'winds of change' speech in Cape Town 1960 | 34 |
| 4 | *Thursday* | George Washington is elected as the first president of the USA 1789 | 35 |
| 5 | *Friday* | Leopold II of Belgium establishes himself as Sovereign of the Congo Free State 1885 | 36 |
| 6 | *Saturday* | Tony Blair becomes Labour's longest-serving prime minister after 2,838 days in office 2005 | 37 |
| 7 | *Sunday* | The European Union is established with the signing of the Maastricht Treaty 1992 | 38 |
| 8 | *Monday* | Mary, Queen of Scots is executed for treason for her part in the Babington Plot 1587 | week 6 day 39 |
| 9 | *Tuesday* | Jefferson Davis is elected president of the Confederate States of America 1861 | 40 |
| 10 | *Wednesday* | North Korea publicly announces that it has developed nuclear weapons 2005 | 41 |
| 11 | *Thursday* | Traditional date of the foundation of Japan by Jimmu, on his accession as emperor in 660 BC | 42 |
| 12 | *Friday* | Abraham Lincoln, 16th US president who led the country through its civil war *b.* 1809 | 43 |
| 13 | *Saturday* | Australian prime minister Kevin Rudd apologises to the country's 'Stolen Generations' 2008 | 44 |
| 14 | *Sunday* | Rafik Hariri, former prime minister of Lebanon, is assassinated 2005 | 45 |
| 15 | *Monday* | Canada inaugurates a new national flag with a red maple leaf design 1965 | week 7 day 46 |
| 16 | *Tuesday* | Fidel Castro is sworn in as prime minister of Cuba after leading the Cuban Revolution 1959 | 47 |
| 17 | *Wednesday* | The Blaine Act ends 13 years of prohibition in the USA 1933 | 48 |
| 18 | *Thursday* | Victor Emmanuel II becomes the first king of a united Italy since the 6th century 1861 | 49 |
| 19 | *Friday* | The institution of serfdom is abolished in Russia by Tsar Alexander II 1861 | 50 |
| 20 | *Saturday* | Gordon Brown, prime minister and leader of the Labour Party (2007–10) *b.* 1951 | 51 |
| 21 | *Sunday* | John Rawls, American political philosopher and author of *A Theory of Justice b.* 1971 | 52 |
| 22 | *Monday* | A union between Syria and Egypt creates the United Arab Republic 1958 | week 8 day 53 |
| 23 | *Tuesday* | The 1950 General Election takes place with a record 83.9 per cent turnout and victory for Labour | 54 |
| 24 | *Wednesday* | Mexico declares independence from Spain during the Mexican War of Independence 1821 | 55 |
| 25 | *Thursday* | Nikita Khrushchev, leader of the Soviet Union, denounces Stalin and the cult of personality 1956 | 56 |
| 26 | *Friday* | Golda Meir is elected as the Alignment party leader ahead of becoming prime minister of Israel 1969 | 57 |
| 27 | *Saturday* | Benjamin Disraeli becomes prime minister of the UK for the first time 1868 | 58 |
| 28 | *Sunday* | Olof Palme, prime minister of Sweden (1969–76), is assassinated 1986 | 59 |
| 29 | *Monday* | Morarji Desai, fifth prime minister of India and independence activist *b.* 1896 | week 9 day 60 |

## ASTRONOMICAL PHENOMENA

d  h
1  09  Mars 3° South of the Moon
3  19  Saturn 3° South of the Moon
6  08  Venus 4° South of the Moon
6  17  Mercury 4° South of the Moon
7  01  Mercury Greatest elongation West
12  14  Uranus 2° North of the Moon
24  04  Jupiter 2° North of the Moon
29  18  Mars 4° South of the Moon

## MINIMA OF ALGOL

| d | h | d | h | d | h |
|---|---|---|---|---|---|
| 2 | 01.0 | 13 | 12.3 | 24 | 23.6 |
| 4 | 21.8 | 16 | 09.1 | 27 | 20.4 |
| 7 | 18.6 | 19 | 05.9 | | |
| 10 | 15.4 | 22 | 02.7 | | |

## CONSTELLATIONS

The following constellations are near the meridian at

| | d | h | | d | h |
|---|---|---|---|---|---|
| January | 1 | 24 | February | 15 | 21 |
| January | 16 | 23 | March | 1 | 20 |
| February | 1 | 22 | March | 16 | 19 |

Draco (below the Pole), Camelopardalis, Auriga, Taurus, Gemini, Orion, Canis Minor, Monoceros, Lepus, Canis Major and Puppis

## THE MOON

| Phases, Apsides and Node | | d | h | m |
|---|---|---|---|---|
| ◗ | Last Quarter | 1 | 03 | 28 |
| ● | New Moon | 8 | 14 | 39 |
| ◖ | First Quarter | 15 | 07 | 46 |
| ○ | Full Moon | 22 | 18 | 20 |

| | | | |
|---|---|---|---|
| Perigee (364,360km) | 11 | 02 | 41 |
| Apogee (405,383km) | 27 | 03 | 28 |

Mean longitude of ascending node on 1st, 174°

# THE SUN

Diam. 32.4″

| Day | Right Ascension | | | Dec. − | Equation of time | Rise 52° | | Rise 56° | | Transit | | Set 52° | | Set 56° | | Sidereal time | | | Transit of first point of Aries | | |
|---|---|---|---|---|---|---|---|---|---|---|---|---|---|---|---|---|---|---|---|---|---|
| | h | m | s | ° | m s | h | m | h | m | h | m | h | m | h | m | h | m | s | h | m | s |
| 1 | 20 | 56 | 01 | 17.3 | −13 26 | 7 | 41 | 7 | 56 | 12 | 14 | 16 | 47 | 16 | 32 | 8 | 42 | 35 | 15 | 17 | 25 |
| 2 | 21 | 00 | 06 | 17.0 | −13 35 | 7 | 39 | 7 | 54 | 12 | 14 | 16 | 49 | 16 | 34 | 8 | 46 | 32 | 15 | 13 | 28 |
| 3 | 21 | 04 | 10 | 16.7 | −13 42 | 7 | 38 | 7 | 52 | 12 | 14 | 16 | 51 | 16 | 36 | 8 | 50 | 28 | 15 | 09 | 32 |
| 4 | 21 | 08 | 14 | 16.5 | −13 49 | 7 | 36 | 7 | 50 | 12 | 14 | 16 | 52 | 16 | 38 | 8 | 54 | 25 | 15 | 05 | 35 |
| 5 | 21 | 12 | 16 | 16.2 | −13 55 | 7 | 34 | 7 | 48 | 12 | 14 | 16 | 54 | 16 | 41 | 8 | 58 | 21 | 15 | 01 | 39 |
| 6 | 21 | 16 | 18 | 15.9 | −14 00 | 7 | 33 | 7 | 46 | 12 | 14 | 16 | 56 | 16 | 43 | 9 | 02 | 18 | 14 | 57 | 42 |
| 7 | 21 | 20 | 19 | 15.5 | −14 04 | 7 | 31 | 7 | 44 | 12 | 14 | 16 | 58 | 16 | 45 | 9 | 06 | 14 | 14 | 53 | 46 |
| 8 | 21 | 24 | 19 | 15.2 | −14 08 | 7 | 29 | 7 | 42 | 12 | 14 | 17 | 00 | 16 | 47 | 9 | 10 | 11 | 14 | 49 | 49 |
| 9 | 21 | 28 | 18 | 14.9 | −14 11 | 7 | 27 | 7 | 40 | 12 | 14 | 17 | 02 | 16 | 49 | 9 | 14 | 08 | 14 | 45 | 52 |
| 10 | 21 | 32 | 17 | 14.6 | −14 13 | 7 | 26 | 7 | 38 | 12 | 14 | 17 | 04 | 16 | 52 | 9 | 18 | 04 | 14 | 41 | 56 |
| 11 | 21 | 36 | 15 | 14.3 | −14 14 | 7 | 24 | 7 | 36 | 12 | 14 | 17 | 05 | 16 | 54 | 9 | 22 | 01 | 14 | 37 | 59 |
| 12 | 21 | 40 | 12 | 13.9 | −14 14 | 7 | 22 | 7 | 33 | 12 | 14 | 17 | 07 | 16 | 56 | 9 | 25 | 57 | 14 | 34 | 03 |
| 13 | 21 | 44 | 08 | 13.6 | −14 14 | 7 | 20 | 7 | 31 | 12 | 14 | 17 | 09 | 16 | 58 | 9 | 29 | 54 | 14 | 30 | 06 |
| 14 | 21 | 48 | 03 | 13.3 | −14 13 | 7 | 18 | 7 | 29 | 12 | 14 | 17 | 11 | 17 | 00 | 9 | 33 | 50 | 14 | 26 | 10 |
| 15 | 21 | 51 | 58 | 12.9 | −14 11 | 7 | 16 | 7 | 27 | 12 | 14 | 17 | 13 | 17 | 03 | 9 | 37 | 47 | 14 | 22 | 13 |
| 16 | 21 | 55 | 52 | 12.6 | −14 08 | 7 | 14 | 7 | 24 | 12 | 14 | 17 | 15 | 17 | 05 | 9 | 41 | 43 | 14 | 18 | 17 |
| 17 | 21 | 59 | 45 | 12.3 | −14 05 | 7 | 12 | 7 | 22 | 12 | 14 | 17 | 17 | 17 | 07 | 9 | 45 | 40 | 14 | 14 | 20 |
| 18 | 22 | 03 | 37 | 11.9 | −14 01 | 7 | 10 | 7 | 20 | 12 | 14 | 17 | 18 | 17 | 09 | 9 | 49 | 37 | 14 | 10 | 23 |
| 19 | 22 | 07 | 29 | 11.6 | −13 56 | 7 | 08 | 7 | 17 | 12 | 14 | 17 | 20 | 17 | 11 | 9 | 53 | 33 | 14 | 06 | 27 |
| 20 | 22 | 11 | 20 | 11.2 | −13 50 | 7 | 06 | 7 | 15 | 12 | 14 | 17 | 22 | 17 | 13 | 9 | 57 | 30 | 14 | 02 | 30 |
| 21 | 22 | 15 | 10 | 10.8 | −13 44 | 7 | 04 | 7 | 13 | 12 | 14 | 17 | 24 | 17 | 16 | 10 | 01 | 26 | 13 | 58 | 34 |
| 22 | 22 | 19 | 00 | 10.5 | −13 37 | 7 | 02 | 7 | 10 | 12 | 14 | 17 | 26 | 17 | 18 | 10 | 05 | 23 | 13 | 54 | 37 |
| 23 | 22 | 22 | 49 | 10.1 | −13 30 | 7 | 00 | 7 | 08 | 12 | 13 | 17 | 28 | 17 | 20 | 10 | 09 | 19 | 13 | 50 | 41 |
| 24 | 22 | 26 | 37 | 9.7 | −13 22 | 6 | 58 | 7 | 05 | 12 | 13 | 17 | 30 | 17 | 22 | 10 | 13 | 16 | 13 | 46 | 44 |
| 25 | 22 | 30 | 25 | 9.4 | −13 13 | 6 | 56 | 7 | 03 | 12 | 13 | 17 | 31 | 17 | 24 | 10 | 17 | 12 | 13 | 42 | 48 |
| 26 | 22 | 34 | 13 | 9.0 | −13 04 | 6 | 54 | 7 | 01 | 12 | 13 | 17 | 33 | 17 | 26 | 10 | 21 | 09 | 13 | 38 | 51 |
| 27 | 22 | 37 | 59 | 8.6 | −12 54 | 6 | 52 | 6 | 58 | 12 | 13 | 17 | 35 | 17 | 29 | 10 | 25 | 05 | 13 | 34 | 55 |
| 28 | 22 | 41 | 45 | 8.3 | −12 43 | 6 | 49 | 6 | 56 | 12 | 13 | 17 | 37 | 17 | 31 | 10 | 29 | 02 | 13 | 30 | 58 |
| 29 | 22 | 45 | 31 | 7.9 | −12 32 | 6 | 47 | 6 | 53 | 12 | 12 | 17 | 39 | 17 | 33 | 10 | 32 | 59 | 13 | 27 | 01 |

## DURATION OF TWILIGHT (in minutes)

| Latitude | 52° | 56° | 52° | 56° | 52° | 56° | 52° | 56° |
|---|---|---|---|---|---|---|---|---|
| | 1 February | | 11 February | | 21 February | | 31 February | |
| Civil | 37 | 41 | 35 | 39 | 34 | 38 | 34 | 37 |
| Nautical | 77 | 86 | 75 | 83 | 74 | 81 | 73 | 80 |
| Astronomical | 117 | 130 | 114 | 126 | 113 | 124 | 112 | 124 |

## THE NIGHT SKY

*Mercury* is a morning object and reaches greatest elongation west (26°) on the 7th. However, it is quite low and will be lost to view after the first ten days or so of February. A slender Moon joins Mercury and Venus on the 6th.

*Venus* remains a striking herald of the approaching sunrise but is now getting rather low. A clear south-eastern horizon is a prerequisite to seeing Venus easily by the end of February, when its altitude is only 2° at the beginning of civil twilight. Venus crosses from Sagittarius into Capricornus on the 17th.

*Mars* rises not long after the witching hour at the end of February and will have brightened to magnitude +0.3 by then.

The Red Planet is at western quadrature on the 7th when telescope users will note its gibbous phase. The Last Quarter Moon is nearby on February 1st.

*Jupiter* rises during the early evening and climbs above the eastern horizon not long after sunset by the end of the month. The Moon is near Jupiter on the 23rd, making for a dramatic sight. Jupiter brightens a little this month from magnitude −2.4 to −2.5.

*Saturn* rises 3.5 hours before the Sun at the beginning of February and an hour earlier by the end of the month. The waning Moon is near Saturn on the 3rd and 4th.

## THE MOON

| Day | R.A. h m | Dec ° | Hor. Par. ' | Diam. ' | Sun's Co-Long. ° | PA of Br. Limb ° | Ph. % | Age d | Rise 52° h m | Rise 56° h m | Transit h m | Set 52° h m | Set 56° h m |
|---|---|---|---|---|---|---|---|---|---|---|---|---|---|
| 1 | 14 35 | −11.2 | 54.4 | 29.7 | 181 | 108 | 51 | 22.1 | 0 53 | 1 04 | 6 03 | 11 06 | 10 55 |
| 2 | 15 23 | −13.9 | 54.8 | 29.9 | 194 | 105 | 42 | 23.1 | 1 55 | 2 09 | 6 49 | 11 37 | 11 23 |
| 3 | 16 13 | −16.1 | 55.3 | 30.1 | 206 | 102 | 33 | 24.1 | 2 56 | 3 12 | 7 37 | 12 14 | 11 58 |
| 4 | 17 04 | −17.6 | 56.0 | 30.5 | 218 | 99 | 24 | 25.1 | 3 55 | 4 13 | 8 27 | 12 58 | 12 39 |
| 5 | 17 58 | −18.3 | 56.8 | 30.9 | 230 | 95 | 15 | 26.1 | 4 51 | 5 09 | 9 20 | 13 49 | 13 31 |
| 6 | 18 54 | −18.0 | 57.6 | 31.4 | 242 | 92 | 8 | 27.1 | 5 42 | 5 58 | 10 14 | 14 50 | 14 33 |
| 7 | 19 51 | −16.6 | 58.4 | 31.8 | 254 | 90 | 3 | 28.1 | 6 26 | 6 41 | 11 09 | 15 59 | 15 44 |
| 8 | 20 48 | −14.3 | 59.1 | 32.2 | 267 | 97 | 1 | 29.1 | 7 05 | 7 17 | 12 05 | 17 13 | 17 02 |
| 9 | 21 45 | −11.0 | 59.7 | 32.5 | 279 | 226 | 0 | 0.6 | 7 39 | 7 48 | 13 00 | 18 30 | 18 23 |
| 10 | 22 42 | −7.0 | 60.0 | 32.7 | 291 | 245 | 3 | 1.6 | 8 10 | 8 15 | 13 54 | 19 50 | 19 47 |
| 11 | 23 38 | −2.6 | 60.2 | 32.8 | 303 | 247 | 8 | 2.6 | 8 39 | 8 40 | 14 48 | 21 09 | 21 11 |
| 12 | 0 34 | +2.0 | 60.1 | 32.8 | 315 | 248 | 15 | 3.6 | 9 08 | 9 05 | 15 41 | 22 28 | 22 34 |
| 13 | 1 29 | +6.4 | 59.8 | 32.6 | 328 | 250 | 25 | 4.6 | 9 38 | 9 31 | 16 35 | 23 45 | 23 54 |
| 14 | 2 25 | +10.4 | 59.4 | 32.4 | 340 | 252 | 35 | 5.6 | 10 10 | 10 00 | 17 29 | — | — |
| 15 | 3 21 | +13.8 | 58.9 | 32.1 | 352 | 256 | 46 | 6.6 | 10 46 | 10 32 | 18 24 | 0 59 | 1 13 |
| 16 | 4 18 | +16.3 | 58.4 | 31.8 | 4 | 259 | 58 | 7.6 | 11 28 | 11 12 | 19 19 | 2 10 | 2 26 |
| 17 | 5 14 | +17.8 | 57.9 | 31.5 | 16 | 263 | 68 | 8.6 | 12 16 | 11 59 | 20 13 | 3 14 | 3 32 |
| 18 | 6 11 | +18.3 | 57.3 | 31.2 | 28 | 268 | 78 | 9.6 | 13 10 | 12 52 | 21 07 | 4 10 | 4 29 |
| 19 | 7 06 | +17.7 | 56.8 | 31.0 | 41 | 272 | 86 | 10.6 | 14 10 | 13 53 | 21 58 | 4 58 | 5 16 |
| 20 | 8 00 | +16.3 | 56.3 | 30.7 | 53 | 275 | 92 | 11.6 | 15 13 | 14 59 | 22 48 | 5 40 | 5 54 |
| 21 | 8 52 | +14.0 | 55.9 | 30.4 | 65 | 277 | 97 | 12.6 | 16 18 | 16 07 | 23 36 | 6 14 | 6 26 |
| 22 | 9 42 | +11.2 | 55.4 | 30.2 | 77 | 274 | 99 | 13.6 | 17 23 | 17 16 | — | 6 44 | 6 52 |
| 23 | 10 31 | +7.8 | 55.0 | 30.0 | 89 | 139 | 100 | 14.6 | 18 28 | 18 24 | 0 22 | 7 10 | 7 15 |
| 24 | 11 18 | +4.2 | 54.7 | 29.8 | 101 | 114 | 99 | 15.6 | 19 33 | 19 32 | 1 06 | 7 34 | 7 36 |
| 25 | 12 04 | +0.5 | 54.4 | 29.6 | 113 | 112 | 95 | 16.6 | 20 36 | 20 38 | 1 50 | 7 56 | 7 56 |
| 26 | 12 49 | −3.2 | 54.2 | 29.5 | 126 | 110 | 91 | 17.6 | 21 39 | 21 44 | 2 32 | 8 19 | 8 15 |
| 27 | 13 34 | −6.8 | 54.1 | 29.5 | 138 | 109 | 84 | 18.6 | 22 41 | 22 50 | 3 15 | 8 43 | 8 36 |
| 28 | 14 20 | −10.1 | 54.1 | 29.5 | 150 | 107 | 77 | 19.6 | 23 43 | 23 54 | 3 58 | 9 08 | 8 59 |
| 29 | 15 07 | −13.0 | 54.3 | 29.6 | 162 | 104 | 69 | 20.6 | — | — | 4 43 | 9 37 | 9 24 |

## MERCURY

| Day | R.A. h m | Dec ° | Mag. | Diam. " | Phase % | Rise h m | Transit h m | Set h m |
|---|---|---|---|---|---|---|---|---|
| 1 | 19 12.0 | −20.6 | +0.1 | 8 | 49 | 6 28 | 10 27 | 14 26 |
| 3 | 19 18.3 | −20.8 | 0.0 | 7 | 53 | 6 28 | 10 26 | 14 23 |
| 5 | 19 25.7 | −20.9 | 0.0 | 7 | 58 | 6 28 | 10 26 | 14 22 |
| 7 | 19 34.0 | −21.0 | 0.0 | 7 | 62 | 6 29 | 10 26 | 14 23 |
| 9 | 19 43.1 | −20.9 | 0.0 | 7 | 65 | 6 31 | 10 28 | 14 25 |
| 11 | 19 52.9 | −20.9 | −0.1 | 6 | 68 | 6 32 | 10 30 | 14 28 |
| 13 | 20 03.1 | −20.7 | −0.1 | 6 | 71 | 6 33 | 10 32 | 14 32 |
| 15 | 20 13.8 | −20.4 | −0.1 | 6 | 73 | 6 34 | 10 35 | 14 37 |
| 17 | 20 24.9 | −20.1 | −0.1 | 6 | 75 | 6 35 | 10 39 | 14 42 |
| 19 | 20 36.3 | −19.7 | −0.1 | 6 | 78 | 6 35 | 10 42 | 14 49 |
| 21 | 20 47.9 | −19.2 | −0.1 | 6 | 79 | 6 36 | 10 46 | 14 57 |
| 23 | 20 59.8 | −18.6 | −0.2 | 6 | 81 | 6 35 | 10 50 | 15 05 |
| 25 | 21 11.8 | −17.9 | −0.2 | 5 | 83 | 6 35 | 10 54 | 15 14 |
| 27 | 21 24.0 | −17.1 | −0.2 | 5 | 85 | 6 34 | 10 59 | 15 23 |
| 29 | 21 36.4 | −16.3 | −0.3 | 5 | 86 | 6 33 | 11 03 | 15 33 |

Rising and setting times are for latitude 54°

## VENUS

| Day | R.A. h m | Dec ° | Mag. | Diam. " | Phase % | Rise h m | Transit h m | Set h m |
|---|---|---|---|---|---|---|---|---|
| 1 | 18 42.5 | −22.4 | −4.8 | 13 | 85 | 6 12 | 9 59 | 13 46 |
| 6 | 19 09.1 | −22.0 | −4.8 | 13 | 86 | 6 16 | 10 06 | 13 56 |
| 11 | 19 35.6 | −21.4 | −4.7 | 13 | 87 | 6 19 | 10 13 | 14 07 |
| 16 | 20 01.8 | −20.5 | −4.6 | 13 | 88 | 6 19 | 10 19 | 14 20 |
| 21 | 20 27.6 | −19.4 | −4.6 | 12 | 89 | 6 17 | 10 26 | 14 35 |
| 26 | 20 53.1 | −18.0 | −4.5 | 12 | 90 | 6 13 | 10 31 | 14 50 |

## MARS

| Day | R.A. h m | Dec ° | Mag. | Diam. " | Phase % | Rise h m | Transit h m | Set h m |
|---|---|---|---|---|---|---|---|---|
| 1 | 14 50.9 | −14.9 | +0.8 | 7 | 90 | 1 30 | 6 08 | 10 46 |
| 6 | 15 00.6 | −15.6 | +0.7 | 7 | 90 | 1 24 | 5 58 | 10 31 |
| 11 | 15 10.1 | −16.2 | +0.7 | 7 | 90 | 1 18 | 5 48 | 10 17 |
| 16 | 15 19.3 | −16.9 | +0.6 | 8 | 90 | 1 12 | 5 37 | 10 02 |
| 21 | 15 28.3 | −17.5 | +0.5 | 8 | 90 | 1 05 | 5 26 | 9 48 |
| 26 | 15 36.9 | −18.0 | +0.4 | 8 | 90 | 0 57 | 5 15 | 9 33 |

# SUNRISE AND SUNSET

| d | London 0° 05' 51° 30' | | Bristol 2° 35' 51° 28' | | Birmingham 1° 55' 52° 28' | | Manchester 2° 15' 53° 28' | | Newcastle 1° 37' 54° 59' | | Glasgow 4° 14' 55° 52' | | Belfast 5° 56' 54° 35' | |
|---|---|---|---|---|---|---|---|---|---|---|---|---|---|---|
|  | h m | h m | h m | h m | h m | h m | h m | h m | h m | h m | h m | h m | h m | h m |
| 1 | 7 40 | 16 49 | 7 49 | 16 59 | 7 50 | 16 53 | 7 55 | 16 51 | 7 58 | 16 42 | 8 12 | 16 49 | 8 14 | 17 01 |
| 2 | 7 38 | 16 51 | 7 48 | 17 01 | 7 49 | 16 55 | 7 53 | 16 53 | 7 56 | 16 45 | 8 10 | 16 51 | 8 12 | 17 03 |
| 3 | 7 36 | 16 52 | 7 46 | 17 03 | 7 47 | 16 57 | 7 52 | 16 55 | 7 55 | 16 47 | 8 08 | 16 54 | 8 10 | 17 05 |
| 4 | 7 35 | 16 54 | 7 45 | 17 04 | 7 45 | 16 59 | 7 50 | 16 57 | 7 53 | 16 49 | 8 07 | 16 56 | 8 08 | 17 07 |
| 5 | 7 33 | 16 56 | 7 43 | 17 06 | 7 44 | 17 00 | 7 48 | 16 59 | 7 51 | 16 51 | 8 05 | 16 58 | 8 07 | 17 09 |
| 6 | 7 32 | 16 58 | 7 41 | 17 08 | 7 42 | 17 02 | 7 46 | 17 01 | 7 49 | 16 53 | 8 03 | 17 00 | 8 05 | 17 12 |
| 7 | 7 30 | 17 00 | 7 40 | 17 10 | 7 40 | 17 04 | 7 44 | 17 02 | 7 47 | 16 55 | 8 00 | 17 02 | 8 03 | 17 14 |
| 8 | 7 28 | 17 02 | 7 38 | 17 12 | 7 38 | 17 06 | 7 43 | 17 04 | 7 45 | 16 57 | 7 58 | 17 05 | 8 01 | 17 16 |
| 9 | 7 26 | 17 03 | 7 36 | 17 13 | 7 36 | 17 08 | 7 41 | 17 06 | 7 43 | 16 59 | 7 56 | 17 07 | 7 59 | 17 18 |
| 10 | 7 25 | 17 05 | 7 35 | 17 15 | 7 35 | 17 10 | 7 39 | 17 08 | 7 41 | 17 01 | 7 54 | 17 09 | 7 57 | 17 20 |
| 11 | 7 23 | 17 07 | 7 33 | 17 17 | 7 33 | 17 12 | 7 37 | 17 10 | 7 39 | 17 03 | 7 52 | 17 11 | 7 55 | 17 22 |
| 12 | 7 21 | 17 09 | 7 31 | 17 19 | 7 31 | 17 14 | 7 35 | 17 12 | 7 37 | 17 06 | 7 50 | 17 13 | 7 53 | 17 24 |
| 13 | 7 19 | 17 11 | 7 29 | 17 21 | 7 29 | 17 16 | 7 33 | 17 14 | 7 35 | 17 08 | 7 48 | 17 15 | 7 51 | 17 26 |
| 14 | 7 17 | 17 13 | 7 27 | 17 23 | 7 27 | 17 18 | 7 31 | 17 16 | 7 32 | 17 10 | 7 45 | 17 18 | 7 49 | 17 28 |
| 15 | 7 15 | 17 14 | 7 25 | 17 24 | 7 25 | 17 19 | 7 29 | 17 18 | 7 30 | 17 12 | 7 43 | 17 20 | 7 46 | 17 30 |
| 16 | 7 13 | 17 16 | 7 23 | 17 26 | 7 23 | 17 21 | 7 27 | 17 20 | 7 28 | 17 14 | 7 41 | 17 22 | 7 44 | 17 32 |
| 17 | 7 11 | 17 18 | 7 21 | 17 28 | 7 21 | 17 23 | 7 25 | 17 22 | 7 26 | 17 16 | 7 39 | 17 24 | 7 42 | 17 34 |
| 18 | 7 10 | 17 20 | 7 19 | 17 30 | 7 19 | 17 25 | 7 23 | 17 24 | 7 24 | 17 18 | 7 36 | 17 26 | 7 40 | 17 36 |
| 19 | 7 08 | 17 22 | 7 17 | 17 32 | 7 17 | 17 27 | 7 20 | 17 26 | 7 21 | 17 20 | 7 34 | 17 29 | 7 38 | 17 38 |
| 20 | 7 06 | 17 23 | 7 15 | 17 34 | 7 15 | 17 29 | 7 18 | 17 28 | 7 19 | 17 22 | 7 32 | 17 31 | 7 35 | 17 41 |
| 21 | 7 04 | 17 25 | 7 13 | 17 35 | 7 13 | 17 31 | 7 16 | 17 30 | 7 17 | 17 24 | 7 29 | 17 33 | 7 33 | 17 43 |
| 22 | 7 02 | 17 27 | 7 11 | 17 37 | 7 11 | 17 33 | 7 14 | 17 32 | 7 14 | 17 26 | 7 27 | 17 35 | 7 31 | 17 45 |
| 23 | 6 59 | 17 29 | 7 09 | 17 39 | 7 08 | 17 35 | 7 12 | 17 34 | 7 12 | 17 29 | 7 24 | 17 37 | 7 29 | 17 47 |
| 24 | 6 57 | 17 31 | 7 07 | 17 41 | 7 06 | 17 36 | 7 09 | 17 36 | 7 10 | 17 31 | 7 22 | 17 39 | 7 26 | 17 49 |
| 25 | 6 55 | 17 32 | 7 05 | 17 43 | 7 04 | 17 38 | 7 07 | 17 38 | 7 07 | 17 33 | 7 20 | 17 42 | 7 24 | 17 51 |
| 26 | 6 53 | 17 34 | 7 03 | 17 44 | 7 02 | 17 40 | 7 05 | 17 40 | 7 05 | 17 35 | 7 17 | 17 44 | 7 22 | 17 53 |
| 27 | 6 51 | 17 36 | 7 01 | 17 46 | 7 00 | 17 42 | 7 03 | 17 42 | 7 03 | 17 37 | 7 15 | 17 46 | 7 19 | 17 55 |
| 28 | 6 49 | 17 38 | 6 59 | 17 48 | 6 58 | 17 44 | 7 00 | 17 44 | 7 00 | 17 39 | 7 12 | 17 48 | 7 17 | 17 57 |
| 29 | 6 47 | 17 40 | 6 57 | 17 50 | 6 55 | 17 46 | 6 58 | 17 46 | 6 58 | 17 41 | 7 10 | 17 50 | 7 15 | 17 59 |

## JUPITER

| Day | R.A. h m | Dec ° | Mag. | Diam. " | Rise h m | Transit h m | Set h m |
|---|---|---|---|---|---|---|---|
| 1 | 11 33.2 | +4.4 | -2.4 | 43 | 20 20 | 2 50 | 9 17 |
| 11 | 11 30.1 | +4.8 | -2.4 | 43 | 19 35 | 2 08 | 8 37 |
| 21 | 11 26.1 | +5.2 | -2.5 | 44 | 18 49 | 1 24 | 7 56 |

Equatorial Diam. 44″, Polar Diam. 41″

## SATURN

| Day | R.A. h m | Dec ° | Mag. | Diam. " | Rise h m | Transit h m | Set h m |
|---|---|---|---|---|---|---|---|
| 1 | 16 51.0 | -20.8 | +0.6 | 16 | 4 09 | 8 07 | 12 05 |
| 11 | 16 54.2 | -20.9 | +0.5 | 16 | 3 33 | 7 31 | 11 29 |
| 21 | 16 56.8 | -20.9 | +0.5 | 16 | 2 57 | 6 54 | 10 52 |

Equatorial Diam. 16″, Polar Diam. 15″
Rings – major axis 36″ minor axis 16″, Tilt 26°

## URANUS

| Day | R.A. h m | Dec ° | Mag. | Diam. " | Rise h m | Transit h m | Set h m |
|---|---|---|---|---|---|---|---|
| 1 | 1 03.3 | +6.1 | +6.2 | 3 | 9 42 | 16 18 | 22 55 |
| 11 | 1 04.6 | +6.2 | +6.2 | 3 | 9 03 | 15 40 | 22 17 |
| 21 | 2 06.1 | +6.4 | +6.2 | 3 | 8 24 | 15 02 | 21 40 |

## NEPTUNE

| Day | R.A. h m | Dec ° | Mag. | Diam. " | Rise h m | Transit h m | Set h m |
|---|---|---|---|---|---|---|---|
| 1 | 22 40.8 | -9.2 | +8.0 | 2 | 8 44 | 13 56 | 19 07 |
| 11 | 22 42.1 | -9.1 | +8.0 | 2 | 8 06 | 13 18 | 18 30 |
| 21 | 22 43.5 | -8.9 | +8.0 | 2 | 7 27 | 12 40 | 17 53 |

# MARCH 2016

THIRD MONTH, 31 DAYS. *Mars*, Roman god of battle

| | | | |
|---|---|---|---|
| 1 | *Tuesday* | The Syrian regional Ba'ath party takes power in Syria following a coup d'état 1966 | day 61 |
| 2 | *Wednesday* | Ho Chi Minh is elected as the first president of Vietnam 1945 | 62 |
| 3 | *Thursday* | The Statute of Rhuddlan introduces the English common law system to Wales 1234 | 63 |
| 4 | *Friday* | In Frankfurt, Frederick Barbarossa (Frederick I) is elected King of Germany 1152 | 64 |
| 5 | *Saturday* | Winston Churchill gives his 'Iron Curtain' speech, condemning the Soviet Union's policy 1946 | 65 |
| 6 | *Sunday* | Ghana became the first black African country to gain independence from Britain 1957 | 66 |
| 7 | *Monday* | In a referendum 98 per cent of Moldovans voted to remain an independent nation 1994 | week 10 day 67 |
| 8 | *Tuesday* | William Taft, the 27th president, and later, tenth chief justice of the USA *d.* 1930 | 68 |
| 9 | *Wednesday* | Northern Ireland votes to remain part of the UK in the sovereignty referendum 1973 | 69 |
| 10 | *Thursday* | The 1959 11-day Tibetan uprising against Chinese occupation, begins | 70 |
| 11 | *Friday* | Sho Tai, the last king of the Ryukyu Kingdom, abdicates the throne 1879 | 71 |
| 12 | *Saturday* | The *Anschluss* begins when Nazi troops march into Austria 1938 | 72 |
| 13 | *Sunday* | Charles Grey, prime minister, whose government abolished slavery in the British Empire *b.* 1764 | 73 |
| 14 | *Monday* | Gerry Adams, president of Sinn Fein, is injured in an assassination attempt 1984 | week 11 day 74 |
| 15 | *Tuesday* | Julius Caesar, dictator of the Roman Republic, is assassinated on the Ides of March 44 BC | 75 |
| 16 | *Wednesday* | Harold Wilson resigns as prime minister and leader of the Labour Party 1976 | 76 |
| 17 | *Thursday* | Parliament abolishes the monarchy in England after the execution of Charles I 1649 | 77 |
| 18 | *Friday* | The Paris Commune is established after the end of Franco–Prussian War 1871 | 78 |
| 19 | *Saturday* | Egon Krenz, the last Communist leader of East Germany *b.* 1937 | 79 |
| 20 | *Sunday* | Namibia becomes independent of South Africa after 75 years of occupation 1990 | 80 |
| 21 | *Monday* | Otto von Bismarck is appointed as the first chancellor of the German Empire 1871 | week 12 day 81 |
| 22 | *Tuesday* | The Arab League is founded in Cairo with six members 1945 | 82 |
| 23 | *Wednesday* | The Labour government of James Callaghan survives a vote of no confidence 1977 | 83 |
| 24 | *Thursday* | Death of Harun al-Rashid, caliph of the Abbasid empire AD 809 | 84 |
| 25 | *Friday* | The Slave Trade Act, abolishing the slave trade in the British Empire, receives royal assent 1807 | 85 |
| 26 | *Saturday* | The Social Democrat Party (SDP), which later merged with the Liberal Party, is founded 1981 | 86 |
| 27 | *Sunday* | Jiang Zemin is appointed as the fifth president of the People's Republic of China 1993 | 87 |
| 28 | *Monday* | James Callaghan's Labour government loses a parliamentary vote of no confidence 1979 | week 13 day 88 |
| 29 | *Tuesday* | The 14th Earl of Derby, prime minister and longest-serving Conservative Party leader *b.* 1799 | 89 |
| 30 | *Wednesday* | Airey Neave, the shadow Northern Ireland secretary, is killed by a car bomb 1979 | 90 |
| 31 | *Thursday* | A snap general election in 1966 returns Harold Wilson's Labour government with a majority of 96 | 91 |

## ASTRONOMICAL PHENOMENA

   *d  h*
  2  07  Saturn 4° South of the Moon
  7  11  Venus 4° South of the Moon
  8  05  Mercury 4° South of the Moon
  8  11  Jupiter at opposition
  9  02  Total eclipse of the Sun
11  01  Uranus 2° North of the Moon
20  04  Equinox
22  04  Jupiter 2° North of the Moon
23  12  Penumbral eclipse of the Moon
28  19  Mars 4° South of the Moon
29  15  Saturn 4° South of the Moon

## MINIMA OF ALGOL

| *d* | *h* | *d* | *h* | *d* | *h* |
|---|---|---|---|---|---|
| 1 | 17.2 | 13 | 04.5 | 24 | 15.8 |
| 4 | 14.0 | 16 | 01.3 | 27 | 12.6 |
| 7 | 10.8 | 18 | 22.1 | 30 | 09.4 |
| 10 | 07.7 | 21 | 19.0 | | |

## CONSTELLATIONS

The following constellations are near the meridian at

| | *d* | *h* | | *d* | *h* |
|---|---|---|---|---|---|
| February | 1 | 24 | March | 16 | 21 |
| February | 15 | 23 | April | 1 | 20 |
| March | 1 | 22 | April | 15 | 19 |

Cepheus (below the Pole), Camelopardalis, Lynx, Gemini, Cancer, Leo, Canis Minor, Hydra, Monoceros, Canis Major and Puppis

## THE MOON

| *Phases, Apsides and Node* | | *d* | *h* | *m* |
|---|---|---|---|---|
| ◑ | Last Quarter | 1 | 23 | 11 |
| ● | New Moon | 9 | 01 | 54 |
| ◐ | First Quarter | 15 | 17 | 03 |
| ○ | Full Moon | 23 | 12 | 01 |
| ◑ | Last Quarter | 31 | 15 | 17 |

| | | | |
|---|---|---|---|
| Perigee (359,510km) | 10 | 07 | 04 |
| Apogee (406,125km) | 25 | 14 | 17 |

Mean longitude of ascending node on 1st, 172°

# THE SUN

Diam. 32.2″

| Day | Right Ascension | | | Dec. | Equation of time | | Rise 52° | | Rise 56° | | Transit | | Set 52° | | Set 56° | | Sidereal time | | | Transit of first point of Aries | | |
|---|---|---|---|---|---|---|---|---|---|---|---|---|---|---|---|---|---|---|---|---|---|---|
| | h | m | s | ° | m | s | h | m | h | m | h | m | h | m | h | m | h | m | s | h | m | s |
| 1 | 22 | 49 | 16 | −7.5 | −12 | 21 | 6 | 45 | 6 | 51 | 12 | 12 | 17 | 40 | 17 | 35 | 10 | 36 | 55 | 13 | 23 | 05 |
| 2 | 22 | 53 | 01 | −7.1 | −12 | 09 | 6 | 43 | 6 | 48 | 12 | 12 | 17 | 42 | 17 | 37 | 10 | 40 | 52 | 13 | 19 | 08 |
| 3 | 22 | 56 | 45 | −6.7 | −11 | 57 | 6 | 41 | 6 | 45 | 12 | 12 | 17 | 44 | 17 | 39 | 10 | 44 | 48 | 13 | 15 | 12 |
| 4 | 23 | 00 | 28 | −6.4 | −11 | 44 | 6 | 38 | 6 | 43 | 12 | 12 | 17 | 46 | 17 | 41 | 10 | 48 | 45 | 13 | 11 | 15 |
| 5 | 23 | 04 | 12 | −6.0 | −11 | 30 | 6 | 36 | 6 | 40 | 12 | 11 | 17 | 48 | 17 | 43 | 10 | 52 | 41 | 13 | 07 | 19 |
| 6 | 23 | 07 | 55 | −5.6 | −11 | 17 | 6 | 34 | 6 | 38 | 12 | 11 | 17 | 49 | 17 | 46 | 10 | 56 | 38 | 13 | 03 | 22 |
| 7 | 23 | 11 | 37 | −5.2 | −11 | 03 | 6 | 32 | 6 | 35 | 12 | 11 | 17 | 51 | 17 | 48 | 11 | 00 | 34 | 12 | 59 | 26 |
| 8 | 23 | 15 | 19 | −4.8 | −10 | 48 | 6 | 29 | 6 | 33 | 12 | 11 | 17 | 53 | 17 | 50 | 11 | 04 | 31 | 12 | 55 | 29 |
| 9 | 23 | 19 | 01 | −4.4 | −10 | 33 | 6 | 27 | 6 | 30 | 12 | 10 | 17 | 55 | 17 | 52 | 11 | 08 | 28 | 12 | 51 | 32 |
| 10 | 23 | 22 | 42 | −4.0 | −10 | 18 | 6 | 25 | 6 | 28 | 12 | 10 | 17 | 56 | 17 | 54 | 11 | 12 | 24 | 12 | 47 | 36 |
| 11 | 23 | 26 | 23 | −3.6 | −10 | 03 | 6 | 23 | 6 | 25 | 12 | 10 | 17 | 58 | 17 | 56 | 11 | 16 | 21 | 12 | 43 | 39 |
| 12 | 23 | 30 | 04 | −3.2 | −9 | 47 | 6 | 20 | 6 | 22 | 12 | 10 | 18 | 00 | 17 | 58 | 11 | 20 | 17 | 12 | 39 | 43 |
| 13 | 23 | 33 | 44 | −2.8 | −9 | 31 | 6 | 18 | 6 | 20 | 12 | 09 | 18 | 02 | 18 | 00 | 11 | 24 | 14 | 12 | 35 | 46 |
| 14 | 23 | 37 | 24 | −2.4 | −9 | 14 | 6 | 16 | 6 | 17 | 12 | 09 | 18 | 03 | 18 | 02 | 11 | 28 | 10 | 12 | 31 | 50 |
| 15 | 23 | 41 | 04 | −2.0 | −8 | 57 | 6 | 13 | 6 | 14 | 12 | 09 | 18 | 05 | 18 | 04 | 11 | 32 | 07 | 12 | 27 | 53 |
| 16 | 23 | 44 | 44 | −1.7 | −8 | 40 | 6 | 11 | 6 | 12 | 12 | 09 | 18 | 07 | 18 | 06 | 11 | 36 | 03 | 12 | 23 | 57 |
| 17 | 23 | 48 | 23 | −1.3 | −8 | 23 | 6 | 09 | 6 | 09 | 12 | 08 | 18 | 09 | 18 | 08 | 11 | 40 | 00 | 12 | 20 | 00 |
| 18 | 23 | 52 | 02 | −0.9 | −8 | 06 | 6 | 07 | 6 | 07 | 12 | 08 | 18 | 10 | 18 | 10 | 11 | 43 | 57 | 12 | 16 | 03 |
| 19 | 23 | 55 | 41 | −0.5 | −7 | 48 | 6 | 04 | 6 | 04 | 12 | 08 | 18 | 12 | 18 | 13 | 11 | 47 | 53 | 12 | 12 | 07 |
| 20 | 23 | 59 | 20 | −0.1 | −7 | 31 | 6 | 02 | 6 | 01 | 12 | 07 | 18 | 14 | 18 | 15 | 11 | 51 | 50 | 12 | 08 | 10 |
| 21 | 0 | 02 | 59 | +0.3 | −7 | 13 | 6 | 00 | 5 | 59 | 12 | 07 | 18 | 16 | 18 | 17 | 11 | 55 | 46 | 12 | 04 | 14 |
| 22 | 0 | 06 | 37 | +0.7 | −6 | 55 | 5 | 57 | 5 | 56 | 12 | 07 | 18 | 17 | 18 | 19 | 11 | 59 | 43 | 12 | 00 | 17 |
| 23 | 0 | 10 | 16 | +1.1 | −6 | 37 | 5 | 55 | 5 | 53 | 12 | 06 | 18 | 19 | 18 | 21 | 12 | 03 | 39 | 11 | 56 | 21 |
| 24 | 0 | 13 | 54 | +1.5 | −6 | 19 | 5 | 53 | 5 | 51 | 12 | 06 | 18 | 21 | 18 | 23 | 12 | 07 | 36 | 11 | 52 | 24 |
| 25 | 0 | 17 | 33 | +1.9 | −6 | 00 | 5 | 50 | 5 | 48 | 12 | 06 | 18 | 22 | 18 | 25 | 12 | 11 | 32 | 11 | 48 | 28 |
| 26 | 0 | 21 | 11 | +2.3 | −5 | 42 | 5 | 48 | 5 | 45 | 12 | 06 | 18 | 24 | 18 | 27 | 12 | 15 | 29 | 11 | 44 | 31 |
| 27 | 0 | 24 | 49 | +2.7 | −5 | 24 | 5 | 46 | 5 | 43 | 12 | 05 | 18 | 26 | 18 | 29 | 12 | 19 | 26 | 11 | 40 | 34 |
| 28 | 0 | 28 | 28 | +3.1 | −5 | 06 | 5 | 43 | 5 | 40 | 12 | 05 | 18 | 28 | 18 | 31 | 12 | 23 | 22 | 11 | 36 | 38 |
| 29 | 0 | 32 | 06 | +3.5 | −4 | 48 | 5 | 41 | 5 | 38 | 12 | 05 | 18 | 29 | 18 | 33 | 12 | 27 | 19 | 11 | 32 | 41 |
| 30 | 0 | 35 | 45 | +3.9 | −4 | 30 | 5 | 39 | 5 | 35 | 12 | 04 | 18 | 31 | 18 | 35 | 12 | 31 | 15 | 11 | 28 | 45 |
| 31 | 0 | 39 | 23 | +4.2 | −4 | 12 | 5 | 36 | 5 | 32 | 12 | 04 | 18 | 33 | 18 | 37 | 12 | 35 | 12 | 11 | 24 | 48 |

## DURATION OF TWILIGHT (in minutes)

| Latitude | 52° | 56° | 52° | 56° | 52° | 56° | 52° | 56° |
|---|---|---|---|---|---|---|---|---|
| | 1 March | | 11 March | | 21 March | | 31 March | |
| Civil | 34 | 37 | 34 | 37 | 34 | 37 | 34 | 38 |
| Nautical | 73 | 80 | 73 | 80 | 74 | 81 | 75 | 84 |
| Astronomical | 112 | 124 | 113 | 125 | 115 | 128 | 120 | 135 |

## THE NIGHT SKY

*Mercury* is not visible this month.

*Venus* is now a very difficult object and can be considered lost to view for the casual observer. It remains poorly placed to be seen easily until mid-August when it returns to the evening sky.

*Mars* crosses from Libra into Scorpius on March 13th and rises not long after midnight. It surges in brightness during February to magnitude −0.5. The Moon is close by on the 1st but a little more distant when in the area again on the 29th.

*Jupiter,* magnitude −2.5, reaches opposition on March 8th in eastern Leo and is visible all night. The Moon is just one day from full when near Jupiter on March 22nd.

*Saturn* is a morning object in Ophiuchus where it reaches its first stationary point on the 25th and then begins to retrograde. Saturn is 3° from the Moon on the 2nd and forms a wide group with it and Mars on the 29th.

*A total solar eclipse* on March 9th passes over Sumatra, Borneo, Sulawesi, and a narrow span of the Pacific Ocean. Australia, eastern Asia, and Pacific regions, including Hawaii, will experience a partial eclipse.

*A penumbral lunar eclipse* on March 23rd is visible from the Americas, Asia, and Australia. The Moon clips the northern edge of the Earth's penumbral shadow so some subtle shading of the Moon's southern hemisphere may be noticed.

# THE MOON

| Day | R.A. h m | Dec. ° | Hor. Par. ' | Diam. ' | Sun's Co-Long. ° | PA of Br. Limb ° | Ph. % | Age d | Rise 52° h m | Rise 56° h m | Transit h m | Set 52° h m | Set 56° h m |
|---|---|---|---|---|---|---|---|---|---|---|---|---|---|
| 1 | 15 56 | −15.3 | 54.7 | 29.8 | 174 | 101 | 60 | 21.6 | 0 43 | 0 57 | 5 29 | 10 11 | 9 56 |
| 2 | 16 46 | −17.1 | 55.2 | 30.1 | 186 | 97 | 50 | 22.6 | 1 42 | 1 58 | 6 17 | 10 50 | 10 33 |
| 3 | 17 38 | −18.0 | 55.9 | 30.5 | 199 | 93 | 40 | 23.6 | 2 38 | 2 55 | 7 08 | 11 36 | 11 19 |
| 4 | 18 31 | −18.1 | 56.7 | 30.9 | 211 | 89 | 30 | 24.6 | 3 30 | 3 47 | 8 00 | 12 31 | 12 14 |
| 5 | 19 27 | −17.3 | 57.6 | 31.4 | 223 | 85 | 21 | 25.6 | 4 16 | 4 32 | 8 53 | 13 35 | 13 19 |
| 6 | 20 23 | −15.4 | 58.6 | 31.9 | 235 | 81 | 13 | 26.6 | 4 57 | 5 11 | 9 48 | 14 46 | 14 33 |
| 7 | 21 20 | −12.5 | 59.5 | 32.4 | 247 | 78 | 6 | 27.6 | 5 34 | 5 44 | 10 43 | 16 02 | 15 53 |
| 8 | 22 17 | −8.8 | 60.2 | 32.8 | 260 | 75 | 2 | 28.6 | 6 07 | 6 13 | 11 38 | 17 21 | 17 16 |
| 9 | 23 14 | −4.5 | 60.7 | 33.1 | 272 | 86 | 0 | 0.1 | 6 37 | 6 40 | 12 34 | 18 43 | 18 42 |
| 10 | 0 12 | +0.1 | 61.0 | 33.2 | 284 | 251 | 1 | 1.1 | 7 07 | 7 06 | 13 29 | 20 05 | 20 08 |
| 11 | 1 09 | +4.8 | 60.9 | 33.2 | 296 | 252 | 5 | 2.1 | 7 37 | 7 32 | 14 25 | 21 26 | 21 34 |
| 12 | 2 07 | +9.1 | 60.6 | 33.0 | 308 | 254 | 12 | 3.1 | 8 10 | 8 01 | 15 21 | 22 45 | 22 56 |
| 13 | 3 05 | +12.8 | 60.0 | 32.7 | 321 | 257 | 21 | 4.1 | 8 45 | 8 33 | 16 17 | 23 58 | — |
| 14 | 4 03 | +15.6 | 59.3 | 32.3 | 333 | 261 | 31 | 5.1 | 9 26 | 9 11 | 17 13 | — | 0 14 |
| 15 | 5 01 | +17.4 | 58.6 | 31.9 | 345 | 265 | 42 | 6.1 | 10 13 | 9 56 | 18 09 | 1 06 | 1 24 |
| 16 | 5 58 | +18.2 | 57.8 | 31.5 | 357 | 269 | 53 | 7.1 | 11 06 | 10 48 | 19 03 | 2 06 | 2 25 |
| 17 | 6 54 | +17.9 | 57.0 | 31.1 | 9 | 274 | 64 | 8.1 | 12 04 | 11 47 | 19 55 | 2 57 | 3 15 |
| 18 | 7 48 | +16.7 | 56.4 | 30.7 | 21 | 278 | 73 | 9.1 | 13 06 | 12 51 | 20 45 | 3 40 | 3 55 |
| 19 | 8 40 | +14.6 | 55.8 | 30.4 | 34 | 282 | 82 | 10.1 | 14 10 | 13 58 | 21 33 | 4 16 | 4 29 |
| 20 | 9 30 | +11.9 | 55.3 | 30.1 | 46 | 285 | 89 | 11.1 | 15 14 | 15 05 | 22 19 | 4 47 | 4 56 |
| 21 | 10 18 | +8.7 | 54.9 | 29.9 | 58 | 288 | 94 | 12.1 | 16 19 | 16 13 | 23 04 | 5 14 | 5 20 |
| 22 | 11 05 | +5.2 | 54.6 | 29.7 | 70 | 291 | 98 | 13.1 | 17 23 | 17 20 | 23 47 | 5 38 | 5 41 |
| 23 | 11 51 | +1.5 | 54.3 | 29.6 | 82 | 299 | 100 | 14.1 | 18 26 | 18 27 | — | 6 01 | 6 01 |
| 24 | 12 36 | −2.2 | 54.1 | 29.5 | 94 | 97 | 100 | 15.1 | 19 29 | 19 34 | 0 30 | 6 23 | 6 21 |
| 25 | 13 22 | −5.8 | 54.0 | 29.4 | 107 | 103 | 98 | 16.1 | 20 32 | 20 39 | 1 12 | 6 47 | 6 41 |
| 26 | 14 07 | −9.2 | 54.0 | 29.4 | 119 | 103 | 95 | 17.1 | 21 34 | 21 44 | 1 55 | 7 11 | 7 03 |
| 27 | 14 54 | −12.2 | 54.1 | 29.5 | 131 | 101 | 89 | 18.1 | 22 34 | 22 48 | 2 39 | 7 39 | 7 27 |
| 28 | 15 42 | −14.8 | 54.3 | 29.6 | 143 | 99 | 83 | 19.1 | 23 34 | 23 49 | 3 25 | 8 10 | 7 56 |
| 29 | 16 31 | −16.7 | 54.7 | 29.8 | 155 | 96 | 75 | 20.1 | — | — | 4 12 | 8 47 | 8 30 |
| 30 | 17 22 | −17.9 | 55.2 | 30.1 | 167 | 92 | 66 | 21.1 | 0 30 | 0 47 | 5 00 | 9 29 | 9 12 |
| 31 | 18 14 | −18.2 | 55.8 | 30.4 | 180 | 88 | 57 | 22.1 | 1 22 | 1 40 | 5 50 | 10 20 | 10 03 |

## MERCURY

| Day | R.A. h m | Dec ° | Mag. | Diam. '' | Phase % | Rise h m | Transit h m | Set h m |
|---|---|---|---|---|---|---|---|---|
| 1 | 21 42.6 | −15.8 | −0.3 | 5 | 87 | 6 33 | 11 05 | 15 39 |
| 3 | 21 55.2 | −14.9 | −0.4 | 5 | 88 | 6 31 | 11 10 | 15 50 |
| 5 | 22 07.8 | −13.8 | −0.5 | 5 | 90 | 6 29 | 11 15 | 16 01 |
| 7 | 22 20.7 | −12.7 | −0.5 | 5 | 91 | 6 27 | 11 20 | 16 13 |
| 9 | 22 33.6 | −11.4 | −0.6 | 5 | 93 | 6 25 | 11 25 | 16 26 |
| 11 | 22 46.7 | −10.1 | −0.8 | 5 | 94 | 6 22 | 11 30 | 16 39 |
| 13 | 22 59.9 | −8.7 | −0.9 | 5 | 95 | 6 20 | 11 36 | 16 53 |
| 15 | 23 13.3 | −7.2 | −1.0 | 5 | 97 | 6 17 | 11 41 | 17 07 |
| 17 | 23 26.8 | −5.7 | −1.2 | 5 | 98 | 6 14 | 11 47 | 17 21 |
| 19 | 23 40.6 | −4.1 | −1.4 | 5 | 99 | 6 10 | 11 53 | 17 37 |
| 21 | 23 54.5 | −2.4 | −1.6 | 5 | 99 | 6 07 | 11 59 | 17 52 |
| 23 | 0 08.6 | −0.6 | −1.8 | 5 | 100 | 6 04 | 12 05 | 18 08 |
| 25 | 0 22.8 | +1.2 | −1.9 | 5 | 100 | 6 00 | 12 12 | 18 25 |
| 27 | 0 37.3 | +3.1 | −1.8 | 5 | 99 | 5 56 | 12 18 | 18 42 |
| 29 | 0 51.9 | +5.0 | −1.7 | 5 | 98 | 5 52 | 12 25 | 18 59 |
| 31 | 1 06.5 | +6.9 | −1.6 | 5 | 96 | 5 48 | 12 32 | 19 17 |

Rising and setting times are for latitude 54°

## VENUS

| Day | R.A. h m | Dec ° | Mag. | Diam. '' | Phase % | Rise h m | Transit h m | Set h m |
|---|---|---|---|---|---|---|---|---|
| 1 | 21 13.2 | −16.8 | −4.5 | 12 | 91 | 6 09 | 10 36 | 15 02 |
| 6 | 21 37.9 | −15.0 | −4.4 | 12 | 92 | 6 03 | 10 41 | 15 19 |
| 11 | 22 02.2 | −13.1 | −4.3 | 12 | 93 | 5 56 | 10 45 | 15 35 |
| 16 | 22 26.0 | −11.1 | −4.3 | 12 | 93 | 5 48 | 10 49 | 15 51 |
| 21 | 22 49.5 | −8.9 | −4.3 | 11 | 94 | 5 39 | 10 53 | 16 08 |
| 26 | 23 12.7 | −6.6 | −4.2 | 11 | 95 | 5 29 | 10 57 | 16 24 |
| 31 | 23 35.6 | −4.2 | −4.2 | 11 | 95 | 5 19 | 11 00 | 16 41 |

## MARS

| Day | R.A. h m | Dec ° | Mag. | Diam. '' | Phase % | Rise h m | Transit h m | Set h m |
|---|---|---|---|---|---|---|---|---|
| 1 | 15 43.5 | −18.4 | +0.3 | 9 | 90 | 0 51 | 5 06 | 9 21 |
| 6 | 15 51.3 | −18.8 | +0.2 | 9 | 90 | 0 42 | 4 54 | 9 06 |
| 11 | 15 58.6 | −19.3 | 0.0 | 10 | 91 | 0 33 | 4 42 | 8 51 |
| 16 | 16 05.3 | −19.6 | −0.1 | 10 | 91 | 0 22 | 4 29 | 8 36 |
| 21 | 16 11.4 | −20.0 | −0.2 | 11 | 91 | 0 11 | 4 15 | 8 20 |
| 26 | 16 16.6 | −20.3 | −0.4 | 11 | 92 | 23 59 | 4 01 | 8 03 |
| 31 | 16 21.0 | −20.6 | −0.5 | 12 | 93 | 23 46 | 3 46 | 7 46 |

# SUNRISE AND SUNSET

| | London | | | | Bristol | | | | Birmingham | | | | Manchester | | | | Newcastle | | | | Glasgow | | | | Belfast | | | |
|---|---|---|---|---|---|---|---|---|---|---|---|---|---|---|---|---|---|---|---|---|---|---|---|---|---|---|---|---|
| | 0° 05′ | | 51° 30′ | | 2° 35′ | | 51° 28′ | | 1° 55′ | | 52° 28′ | | 2° 15′ | | 53° 28′ | | 1° 37′ | | 54° 59′ | | 4° 14′ | | 55° 52′ | | 5° 56′ | | 54° 35′ | |
| d | h | m | h | m | h | m | h | m | h | m | h | m | h | m | h | m | h | m | h | m | h | m | h | m | h | m | h | m |
| 1 | 6 | 45 | 17 | 41 | 6 | 55 | 17 | 51 | 6 | 53 | 17 | 47 | 6 | 56 | 17 | 48 | 6 | 55 | 17 | 43 | 7 | 07 | 17 | 52 | 7 | 12 | 18 | 01 |
| 2 | 6 | 43 | 17 | 43 | 6 | 53 | 17 | 53 | 6 | 51 | 17 | 49 | 6 | 54 | 17 | 49 | 6 | 53 | 17 | 45 | 7 | 05 | 17 | 54 | 7 | 10 | 18 | 03 |
| 3 | 6 | 40 | 17 | 45 | 6 | 50 | 17 | 55 | 6 | 49 | 17 | 51 | 6 | 51 | 17 | 51 | 6 | 51 | 17 | 47 | 7 | 02 | 17 | 56 | 7 | 07 | 18 | 05 |
| 4 | 6 | 38 | 17 | 47 | 6 | 48 | 17 | 57 | 6 | 47 | 17 | 53 | 6 | 49 | 17 | 53 | 6 | 48 | 17 | 49 | 7 | 00 | 17 | 58 | 7 | 05 | 18 | 07 |
| 5 | 6 | 36 | 17 | 48 | 6 | 46 | 17 | 58 | 6 | 44 | 17 | 55 | 6 | 47 | 17 | 55 | 6 | 46 | 17 | 51 | 6 | 57 | 18 | 01 | 7 | 02 | 18 | 09 |
| 6 | 6 | 34 | 17 | 50 | 6 | 44 | 18 | 00 | 6 | 42 | 17 | 57 | 6 | 44 | 17 | 57 | 6 | 43 | 17 | 53 | 6 | 55 | 18 | 03 | 7 | 00 | 18 | 11 |
| 7 | 6 | 32 | 17 | 52 | 6 | 42 | 18 | 02 | 6 | 40 | 17 | 58 | 6 | 42 | 17 | 59 | 6 | 41 | 17 | 55 | 6 | 52 | 18 | 05 | 6 | 58 | 18 | 13 |
| 8 | 6 | 29 | 17 | 54 | 6 | 39 | 18 | 04 | 6 | 37 | 18 | 00 | 6 | 40 | 18 | 01 | 6 | 38 | 17 | 57 | 6 | 49 | 18 | 07 | 6 | 55 | 18 | 15 |
| 9 | 6 | 27 | 17 | 55 | 6 | 37 | 18 | 05 | 6 | 35 | 18 | 02 | 6 | 37 | 18 | 03 | 6 | 36 | 17 | 59 | 6 | 47 | 18 | 09 | 6 | 53 | 18 | 17 |
| 10 | 6 | 25 | 17 | 57 | 6 | 35 | 18 | 07 | 6 | 33 | 18 | 04 | 6 | 35 | 18 | 05 | 6 | 33 | 18 | 01 | 6 | 44 | 18 | 11 | 6 | 50 | 18 | 19 |
| 11 | 6 | 23 | 17 | 59 | 6 | 33 | 18 | 09 | 6 | 31 | 18 | 06 | 6 | 32 | 18 | 06 | 6 | 31 | 18 | 03 | 6 | 42 | 18 | 13 | 6 | 48 | 18 | 21 |
| 12 | 6 | 20 | 18 | 00 | 6 | 30 | 18 | 10 | 6 | 28 | 18 | 07 | 6 | 30 | 18 | 08 | 6 | 28 | 18 | 05 | 6 | 39 | 18 | 15 | 6 | 45 | 18 | 23 |
| 13 | 6 | 18 | 18 | 02 | 6 | 28 | 18 | 12 | 6 | 26 | 18 | 09 | 6 | 28 | 18 | 10 | 6 | 26 | 18 | 07 | 6 | 37 | 18 | 17 | 6 | 43 | 18 | 24 |
| 14 | 6 | 16 | 18 | 04 | 6 | 26 | 18 | 14 | 6 | 24 | 18 | 11 | 6 | 25 | 18 | 12 | 6 | 23 | 18 | 09 | 6 | 34 | 18 | 19 | 6 | 40 | 18 | 26 |
| 15 | 6 | 14 | 18 | 06 | 6 | 24 | 18 | 16 | 6 | 21 | 18 | 13 | 6 | 23 | 18 | 14 | 6 | 21 | 18 | 11 | 6 | 31 | 18 | 21 | 6 | 38 | 18 | 28 |
| 16 | 6 | 11 | 18 | 07 | 6 | 21 | 18 | 17 | 6 | 19 | 18 | 15 | 6 | 20 | 18 | 16 | 6 | 18 | 18 | 13 | 6 | 29 | 18 | 23 | 6 | 35 | 18 | 30 |
| 17 | 6 | 09 | 18 | 09 | 6 | 19 | 18 | 19 | 6 | 17 | 18 | 16 | 6 | 18 | 18 | 18 | 6 | 16 | 18 | 15 | 6 | 26 | 18 | 25 | 6 | 33 | 18 | 32 |
| 18 | 6 | 07 | 18 | 11 | 6 | 17 | 18 | 21 | 6 | 14 | 18 | 18 | 6 | 16 | 18 | 19 | 6 | 13 | 18 | 17 | 6 | 23 | 18 | 27 | 6 | 30 | 18 | 34 |
| 19 | 6 | 05 | 18 | 12 | 6 | 15 | 18 | 22 | 6 | 12 | 18 | 20 | 6 | 13 | 18 | 21 | 6 | 10 | 18 | 19 | 6 | 21 | 18 | 29 | 6 | 28 | 18 | 36 |
| 20 | 6 | 02 | 18 | 14 | 6 | 12 | 18 | 24 | 6 | 09 | 18 | 22 | 6 | 11 | 18 | 23 | 6 | 08 | 18 | 21 | 6 | 18 | 18 | 32 | 6 | 25 | 18 | 38 |
| 21 | 6 | 00 | 18 | 16 | 6 | 10 | 18 | 26 | 6 | 07 | 18 | 23 | 6 | 08 | 18 | 25 | 6 | 05 | 18 | 23 | 6 | 16 | 18 | 34 | 6 | 23 | 18 | 40 |
| 22 | 5 | 58 | 18 | 17 | 6 | 08 | 18 | 27 | 6 | 05 | 18 | 25 | 6 | 06 | 18 | 27 | 6 | 03 | 18 | 25 | 6 | 13 | 18 | 36 | 6 | 20 | 18 | 42 |
| 23 | 5 | 55 | 18 | 19 | 6 | 05 | 18 | 29 | 6 | 02 | 18 | 27 | 6 | 03 | 18 | 29 | 6 | 00 | 18 | 27 | 6 | 10 | 18 | 38 | 6 | 18 | 18 | 44 |
| 24 | 5 | 53 | 18 | 21 | 6 | 03 | 18 | 31 | 6 | 00 | 18 | 29 | 6 | 01 | 18 | 30 | 5 | 58 | 18 | 29 | 6 | 08 | 18 | 40 | 6 | 15 | 18 | 46 |
| 25 | 5 | 51 | 18 | 22 | 6 | 01 | 18 | 33 | 5 | 58 | 18 | 30 | 5 | 59 | 18 | 32 | 5 | 55 | 18 | 31 | 6 | 05 | 18 | 42 | 6 | 13 | 18 | 48 |
| 26 | 5 | 49 | 18 | 24 | 5 | 59 | 18 | 34 | 5 | 55 | 18 | 32 | 5 | 56 | 18 | 34 | 5 | 53 | 18 | 33 | 6 | 02 | 18 | 44 | 6 | 10 | 18 | 50 |
| 27 | 5 | 46 | 18 | 26 | 5 | 56 | 18 | 36 | 5 | 53 | 18 | 34 | 5 | 54 | 18 | 36 | 5 | 50 | 18 | 35 | 6 | 00 | 18 | 46 | 6 | 08 | 18 | 52 |
| 28 | 5 | 44 | 18 | 28 | 5 | 54 | 18 | 38 | 5 | 51 | 18 | 36 | 5 | 51 | 18 | 38 | 5 | 48 | 18 | 36 | 5 | 57 | 18 | 48 | 6 | 05 | 18 | 53 |
| 29 | 5 | 42 | 18 | 29 | 5 | 52 | 18 | 39 | 5 | 48 | 18 | 37 | 5 | 49 | 18 | 40 | 5 | 45 | 18 | 38 | 5 | 55 | 18 | 50 | 6 | 03 | 18 | 55 |
| 30 | 5 | 40 | 18 | 31 | 5 | 50 | 18 | 41 | 5 | 46 | 18 | 39 | 5 | 46 | 18 | 41 | 5 | 42 | 18 | 40 | 5 | 52 | 18 | 52 | 6 | 00 | 18 | 57 |
| 31 | 5 | 37 | 18 | 33 | 5 | 47 | 18 | 43 | 5 | 44 | 18 | 41 | 5 | 44 | 18 | 43 | 5 | 40 | 18 | 42 | 5 | 49 | 18 | 54 | 5 | 58 | 18 | 59 |

## JUPITER

| Day | R.A. | | Dec | Mag. | Diam. | Rise | | Transit | | Set | |
|---|---|---|---|---|---|---|---|---|---|---|---|
| | h | m | ° | | ″ | h | m | h | m | h | m |
| 1 | 11 | 22.0 | +5.7 | −2.5 | 44 | 18 | 07 | 0 | 45 | 7 | 19 |
| 11 | 11 | 17.2 | +6.2 | −2.5 | 44 | 17 | 20 | 0 | 01 | 6 | 38 |
| 21 | 11 | 12.5 | +6.7 | −2.5 | 44 | 16 | 33 | 23 | 13 | 5 | 57 |
| 31 | 11 | 08.2 | +7.1 | −2.4 | 44 | 15 | 47 | 22 | 30 | 5 | 16 |

Equatorial Diam. 44″, Polar Diam. 41″

## SATURN

| Day | R.A. | | Dec | Mag. | Diam. | Rise | | Transit | | Set | |
|---|---|---|---|---|---|---|---|---|---|---|---|
| | h | m | ° | | ″ | h | m | h | m | h | m |
| 1 | 16 | 58.6 | −21.0 | +0.5 | 17 | 2 | 24 | 6 | 21 | 10 | 18 |
| 11 | 17 | 00.0 | −21.0 | +0.5 | 17 | 1 | 46 | 5 | 43 | 9 | 40 |
| 21 | 17 | 00.7 | −21.0 | +0.4 | 17 | 1 | 07 | 5 | 04 | 9 | 01 |
| 31 | 17 | 00.6 | −21.0 | +0.4 | 17 | 0 | 28 | 4 | 25 | 8 | 22 |

Equatorial Diam. 17″, Polar Diam. 15″
Rings – major axis 38″ minor axis 17″, Tilt 26°

## URANUS

| Day | R.A. | | Dec | Mag. | Diam. | Rise | | Transit | | Set | |
|---|---|---|---|---|---|---|---|---|---|---|---|
| | h | m | ° | | ″ | h | m | h | m | h | m |
| 1 | 1 | 07.6 | +6.5 | +6.2 | 3 | 7 | 49 | 14 | 28 | 21 | 07 |
| 11 | 1 | 09.4 | +6.7 | +6.2 | 3 | 7 | 11 | 13 | 51 | 20 | 31 |
| 21 | 1 | 11.4 | +6.9 | +6.2 | 3 | 6 | 32 | 13 | 14 | 19 | 55 |
| 31 | 1 | 13.5 | +7.1 | +6.2 | 3 | 5 | 54 | 12 | 36 | 19 | 19 |

## NEPTUNE

| Day | R.A. | | Dec | Mag. | Diam. | Rise | | Transit | | Set | |
|---|---|---|---|---|---|---|---|---|---|---|---|
| | h | m | ° | | ″ | h | m | h | m | h | m |
| 1 | 22 | 44.8 | −8.8 | +8.0 | 2 | 6 | 52 | 12 | 06 | 17 | 20 |
| 11 | 22 | 46.2 | −8.7 | +8.0 | 2 | 6 | 13 | 11 | 28 | 16 | 43 |
| 21 | 22 | 47.6 | −8.5 | +8.0 | 2 | 5 | 35 | 10 | 50 | 16 | 05 |
| 31 | 22 | 48.9 | −8.4 | +8.0 | 2 | 4 | 56 | 10 | 12 | 15 | 28 |

# APRIL 2016

FOURTH MONTH, 30 DAYS. *Aperire*, to open; Earth opens to receive seed.

| | | | |
|---|---|---|---|
| **1** | *Friday* | Slobodan Milosevic, former president of Yugoslavia, is arrested for war crimes 2001 | day 92 |
| **2** | *Saturday* | Georges Pompidou, prime minister and later president of France *d.* 1974 | 93 |
| **3** | *Sunday* | Edward II (the Confessor), is crowned at Winchester Cathedral 1043 | 94 |

| | | | |
|---|---|---|---|
| **4** | *Monday* | Martin Luther King, Jr, American civil rights activist, is assassinated in Memphis 1968 | week 14 day 95 |
| **5** | *Tuesday* | Winston Churchill resigns as prime minister citing poor health 1955 | 96 |
| **6** | *Wednesday* | The presidents of Burundi and Rwanda die when their plane is shot down 1994 | 97 |
| **7** | *Thursday* | John Stonehouse, MP, resigns the Labour whip, leaving the government in a minority 1976 | 98 |
| **8** | *Friday* | Jomo Kenyatta is sentenced to hard labour after the Mau Mau rebellion in Kenya 1953 | 99 |
| **9** | *Saturday* | The Conservatives win the 1992 general election despite Labour being ahead in the polls | 100 |
| **10** | *Sunday* | Bobby Sands was elected as the MP for Fermanagh and South Tyrone 1981 | 101 |

| | | | |
|---|---|---|---|
| **11** | *Monday* | William III and Mary II are crowned joint sovereigns of Britain at Westminster Abbey 1689 | week 15 day 102 |
| **12** | *Tuesday* | Seneca the Younger, Roman stoic philosopher and statesman, commits suicide AD 65 | 103 |
| **13** | *Wednesday* | The Roman Catholic Relief Act, allowing catholics to sit in parliament, receives royal assent 1829 | 104 |
| **14** | *Thursday* | US president Abraham Lincoln, is fatally shot at Ford's Theatre, Washington 1865 | 105 |
| **15** | *Friday* | Pol Pot, Cambodian communist dictator who led the Khmer Rouge *d.* 1998 | 106 |
| **16** | *Saturday* | Conservative MP Harvey Proctor is accused of committing four acts of gross indecency 1987 | 107 |
| **17** | *Sunday* | Bernadette Devlin, aged 21, becomes Britain's youngest ever female MP 1969 | 108 |

| | | | |
|---|---|---|---|
| **18** | *Monday* | Michael D. Higgins, president of Ireland who made the first state visit to the UK *b.* 1941 | week 16 day 109 |
| **19** | *Tuesday* | William Wilberforce's first bill to abolish the slave trade is defeated by 163 votes to 88 1791 | 110 |
| **20** | *Wednesday* | Conservative minister Enoch Powell delivers his controversial 'Rivers of Blood' speech 1968 | 111 |
| **21** | *Thursday* | The Haitian Revolution against slavery, which establishes the Republic of Haiti, begins 1791 | 112 |
| **22** | *Friday* | François 'Papa Doc' Duvalier, president of Haiti, dies after 14 years in office 1971 | 113 |
| **23** | *Saturday* | Charles II, son of the executed Charles I, is crowned at Westminster Abbey 1661 | 114 |
| **24** | *Sunday* | Philippe Pétain, Chief of State of Vichy France (1940–4) who was convicted of treason *b.* 1856 | 115 |

| | | | |
|---|---|---|---|
| **25** | *Monday* | Oliver Cromwell, MP, military leader and Lord Protector of the Commonwealth *b.* 1599 | week 17 day 116 |
| **26** | *Tuesday* | Paul von Hindenburg becomes the first directly elected president of the Weimar Republic 1925 | 117 |
| **27** | *Wednesday* | Betty Boothroyd becomes the first female Speaker of the House of Commons 1992 | 118 |
| **28** | *Thursday* | António Salazar, prime minister of Portugal (1932–68) *b.* 1889 | 119 |
| **29** | *Friday* | The Easter Rising in Dublin by Irish Republicans against British rule, is suppressed 1916 | 120 |
| **30** | *Saturday* | Adolf Hitler and his wife Eva Braun commit suicide in the Führerbunker, Berlin 1945 | 121 |

## ASTRONOMICAL PHENOMENA

*d  h*

7 14 Uranus 2° North of the Moon
8 08 Moon occults Venus (Sun nearby, so view with great care)
18 14 Mercury Greatest elongation East
18 05 Jupiter 2° North of the Moon
25 04 Mars 5° South of the Moon
25 19 Saturn 3° South of the Moon

## MINIMA OF ALGOL

| d | h | d | h | d | h |
|---|---|---|---|---|---|
| 2 | 06.2 | 13 | 17.5 | 25 | 04.8 |
| 5 | 03.1 | 16 | 14.3 | 28 | 01.6 |
| 7 | 23.9 | 19 | 11.2 | 30 | 22.4 |
| 10 | 20.7 | 22 | 08.0 | | |

## CONSTELLATIONS

The following constellations are near the meridian at

| | d | h | | d | h |
|---|---|---|---|---|---|
| March | 1 | 24 | April | 15 | 21 |
| March | 16 | 23 | May | 1 | 20 |
| April | 1 | 22 | May | 16 | 19 |

Cepheus (below the Pole), Cassiopeia (below the Pole), Ursa Major, Leo Minor, Leo., Sextans, Hydra and Crater

## THE MOON

| Phases, Apsides and Node | d | h | m |
|---|---|---|---|
| ● New Moon | 7 | 11 | 24 |
| ◑ First Quarter | 14 | 03 | 59 |
| ○ Full Moon | 22 | 05 | 24 |
| ◐ Last Quarter | 30 | 03 | 29 |

| | | | |
|---|---|---|---|
| Perigee (357,163km) | 7 | 17 | 36 |
| Apogee (406,351km) | 21 | 16 | 05 |

Mean longitude of ascending node on 1st, 171°

# THE SUN

Diam. 31.9″

| Day | Right Ascension | | | Dec. + | Equation of time | | Rise 52° | | Rise 56° | | Transit | | Set 52° | | Set 56° | | Sidereal time | | | Transit of first point of Aries | | |
|---|---|---|---|---|---|---|---|---|---|---|---|---|---|---|---|---|---|---|---|---|---|---|
| | h | m | s | ° | m | s | h | m | h | m | h | m | h | m | h | m | h | m | s | h | m | s |
| 1 | 0 | 42 | 53 | 4.6 | −3 | 54 | 5 | 36 | 5 | 32 | 12 | 04 | 18 | 33 | 18 | 37 | 11 | 38 | 59 | 11 | 20 | 52 |
| 2 | 0 | 46 | 32 | 5.0 | −3 | 37 | 5 | 34 | 5 | 30 | 12 | 04 | 18 | 34 | 18 | 39 | 11 | 42 | 55 | 11 | 16 | 55 |
| 3 | 0 | 50 | 11 | 5.4 | −3 | 19 | 5 | 32 | 5 | 27 | 12 | 03 | 18 | 36 | 18 | 41 | 11 | 46 | 52 | 11 | 12 | 59 |
| 4 | 0 | 53 | 50 | 5.8 | −3 | 02 | 5 | 30 | 5 | 24 | 12 | 03 | 18 | 38 | 18 | 43 | 11 | 50 | 48 | 11 | 09 | 02 |
| 5 | 0 | 57 | 29 | 6.1 | −2 | 44 | 5 | 27 | 5 | 22 | 12 | 03 | 18 | 40 | 18 | 45 | 11 | 54 | 45 | 11 | 05 | 05 |
| 6 | 1 | 01 | 09 | 6.5 | −2 | 27 | 5 | 25 | 5 | 19 | 12 | 03 | 18 | 41 | 18 | 47 | 11 | 58 | 41 | 11 | 01 | 09 |
| 7 | 1 | 04 | 48 | 6.9 | −2 | 11 | 5 | 23 | 5 | 17 | 12 | 02 | 18 | 43 | 18 | 49 | 12 | 02 | 38 | 10 | 57 | 12 |
| 8 | 1 | 08 | 28 | 7.3 | −1 | 54 | 5 | 20 | 5 | 14 | 12 | 02 | 18 | 45 | 18 | 51 | 12 | 06 | 34 | 10 | 53 | 16 |
| 9 | 1 | 12 | 08 | 7.6 | −1 | 38 | 5 | 18 | 5 | 11 | 12 | 02 | 18 | 46 | 18 | 53 | 12 | 10 | 31 | 10 | 49 | 19 |
| 10 | 1 | 15 | 49 | 8.0 | −1 | 22 | 5 | 16 | 5 | 09 | 12 | 01 | 18 | 48 | 18 | 55 | 12 | 14 | 28 | 10 | 45 | 23 |
| 11 | 1 | 19 | 30 | 8.4 | −1 | 06 | 5 | 14 | 5 | 06 | 12 | 01 | 18 | 50 | 18 | 57 | 12 | 18 | 24 | 10 | 41 | 26 |
| 12 | 1 | 23 | 11 | 8.7 | −0 | 50 | 5 | 11 | 5 | 04 | 12 | 01 | 18 | 52 | 18 | 59 | 12 | 22 | 21 | 10 | 37 | 30 |
| 13 | 1 | 26 | 52 | 9.1 | −0 | 35 | 5 | 09 | 5 | 01 | 12 | 01 | 18 | 53 | 19 | 01 | 12 | 26 | 17 | 10 | 33 | 33 |
| 14 | 1 | 30 | 33 | 9.5 | −0 | 20 | 5 | 07 | 4 | 59 | 12 | 00 | 18 | 55 | 19 | 04 | 12 | 30 | 14 | 10 | 29 | 36 |
| 15 | 1 | 34 | 15 | 9.8 | −0 | 05 | 5 | 05 | 4 | 56 | 12 | 00 | 18 | 57 | 19 | 06 | 12 | 34 | 10 | 10 | 25 | 40 |
| 16 | 1 | 37 | 57 | 10.2 | +0 | 09 | 5 | 03 | 4 | 54 | 12 | 00 | 18 | 58 | 19 | 08 | 12 | 38 | 07 | 10 | 21 | 43 |
| 17 | 1 | 41 | 40 | 10.5 | +0 | 23 | 5 | 00 | 4 | 51 | 12 | 00 | 19 | 00 | 19 | 10 | 12 | 42 | 03 | 10 | 17 | 47 |
| 18 | 1 | 45 | 23 | 10.9 | +0 | 37 | 4 | 58 | 4 | 49 | 11 | 59 | 19 | 02 | 19 | 12 | 12 | 46 | 00 | 10 | 13 | 50 |
| 19 | 1 | 49 | 06 | 11.2 | +0 | 50 | 4 | 56 | 4 | 46 | 11 | 59 | 19 | 04 | 19 | 14 | 12 | 49 | 57 | 10 | 09 | 54 |
| 20 | 1 | 52 | 50 | 11.6 | +1 | 03 | 4 | 54 | 4 | 44 | 11 | 59 | 19 | 05 | 19 | 16 | 12 | 53 | 53 | 10 | 05 | 57 |
| 21 | 1 | 56 | 34 | 11.9 | +1 | 15 | 4 | 52 | 4 | 41 | 11 | 59 | 19 | 07 | 19 | 18 | 12 | 57 | 50 | 10 | 02 | 01 |
| 22 | 2 | 00 | 19 | 12.3 | +1 | 27 | 4 | 50 | 4 | 39 | 11 | 59 | 19 | 09 | 19 | 20 | 13 | 01 | 46 | 9 | 58 | 04 |
| 23 | 2 | 04 | 04 | 12.6 | +1 | 39 | 4 | 48 | 4 | 36 | 11 | 58 | 19 | 10 | 19 | 22 | 13 | 05 | 43 | 9 | 54 | 07 |
| 24 | 2 | 07 | 49 | 12.9 | +1 | 50 | 4 | 46 | 4 | 34 | 11 | 58 | 19 | 12 | 19 | 24 | 13 | 09 | 39 | 9 | 50 | 11 |
| 25 | 2 | 11 | 35 | 13.2 | +2 | 00 | 4 | 44 | 4 | 32 | 11 | 58 | 19 | 14 | 19 | 26 | 13 | 13 | 36 | 9 | 46 | 14 |
| 26 | 2 | 15 | 22 | 13.6 | +2 | 10 | 4 | 41 | 4 | 29 | 11 | 58 | 19 | 15 | 19 | 28 | 13 | 17 | 32 | 9 | 42 | 18 |
| 27 | 2 | 19 | 09 | 13.9 | +2 | 20 | 4 | 39 | 4 | 27 | 11 | 58 | 19 | 17 | 19 | 30 | 13 | 21 | 29 | 9 | 38 | 21 |
| 28 | 2 | 22 | 56 | 14.2 | +2 | 29 | 4 | 37 | 4 | 24 | 11 | 58 | 19 | 19 | 19 | 32 | 13 | 25 | 26 | 9 | 34 | 25 |
| 29 | 2 | 26 | 44 | 14.5 | +2 | 38 | 4 | 35 | 4 | 22 | 11 | 57 | 19 | 20 | 19 | 34 | 13 | 29 | 22 | 9 | 30 | 28 |
| 30 | 2 | 30 | 33 | 14.8 | +2 | 45 | 4 | 34 | 4 | 20 | 11 | 57 | 19 | 22 | 19 | 36 | 13 | 33 | 19 | 9 | 26 | 32 |

## DURATION OF TWILIGHT (in minutes)

| Latitude | 52° | 56° | 52° | 56° | 52° | 56° | 52° | 56° |
|---|---|---|---|---|---|---|---|---|
| | 1 April | | 11 April | | 21 April | | 31 April | |
| Civil | 34 | 38 | 35 | 39 | 37 | 42 | 39 | 44 |
| Nautical | 76 | 84 | 79 | 89 | 83 | 96 | 89 | 106 |
| Astronomical | 120 | 136 | 127 | 147 | 137 | 165 | 152 | 204 |

## THE NIGHT SKY

*Mercury* leaps out of the evening twilight and reaches greatest elongation east (19.9°) on the 18th. The planet is visible right throughout April in the western sky after sunset but is brightest at the beginning of this apparition. The 32.5-hour-old Moon lies 6° to the left of Mercury on the 8th.

A chance sighting of *Venus* in the dawn sky can be discounted this month as the planet is now rising less than 20 minutes before the Sun.

*Mars* brightens from magnitude −0.5 to −1.4 and appears above the south-eastern horizon during the late evening by the end of April. It moves into Ophiuchus on the 3rd where it is stationary on the 17th and then starts to retrograde, before returning to Scorpius on the 30th. The bright ember is unmistakable 4° below the Moon when both rise on the evening of April 25th.

*Jupiter* is high in the south-east after nightfall and currently shines at magnitude −2.4 under the body of Leo.

*Saturn* is rising only half an hour after Mars all month and lies in the southern part of Ophiuchus. The northern aspect of the rings is currently tipped more than 26° earthward. Saturn is 4° to the lower right of the Moon on April 26th.

# THE MOON

| Day | R.A. | | Dec. | Hor. Par. | Diam. | Sun's Co-Long. | PA of Br. Limb | Ph. | Age | Rise | | | | Transit | | Set | | | |
|---|---|---|---|---|---|---|---|---|---|---|---|---|---|---|---|---|---|---|---|
| | | | | | | | | | | 52° | | 56° | | | | 52° | | 56° | |
| | h | m | ° | ' | ' | ° | ° | % | d | h | m | h | m | h | m | h | m | h | m |
| 1 | 19 | 05 | −17.8 | 56.5 | 30.8 | 191 | 84 | 47 | 23.0 | 1 | 22 | 1 | 40 | 5 | 50 | 10 | 20 | 10 | 03 |
| 2 | 19 | 59 | −16.3 | 57.4 | 31.3 | 204 | 80 | 37 | 24.0 | 2 | 09 | 2 | 26 | 6 | 42 | 11 | 18 | 11 | 02 |
| 3 | 20 | 54 | −14.0 | 58.4 | 31.8 | 216 | 76 | 26 | 25.0 | 2 | 51 | 3 | 06 | 7 | 34 | 12 | 23 | 12 | 09 |
| 4 | 21 | 50 | −10.7 | 59.3 | 32.3 | 228 | 72 | 17 | 26.0 | 3 | 29 | 3 | 40 | 8 | 28 | 13 | 35 | 13 | 24 |
| 5 | 22 | 46 | −6.7 | 60.2 | 32.8 | 240 | 69 | 9 | 27.0 | 4 | 02 | 4 | 10 | 9 | 21 | 14 | 51 | 14 | 44 |
| 6 | 23 | 43 | −2.2 | 60.9 | 33.2 | 252 | 66 | 3 | 28.0 | 4 | 33 | 4 | 38 | 10 | 16 | 16 | 11 | 16 | 08 |
| 7 | 0 | 40 | +2.5 | 61.3 | 33.4 | 265 | 54 | 0 | 29.0 | 5 | 03 | 5 | 04 | 11 | 11 | 17 | 33 | 17 | 34 |
| 8 | 1 | 39 | +7.1 | 61.4 | 33.5 | 277 | 272 | 0 | 0.5 | 5 | 33 | 5 | 30 | 12 | 07 | 18 | 56 | 19 | 01 |
| 9 | 2 | 38 | +11.3 | 61.1 | 33.3 | 289 | 262 | 3 | 1.5 | 6 | 05 | 5 | 57 | 13 | 04 | 20 | 18 | 20 | 28 |
| 10 | 3 | 38 | +14.6 | 60.6 | 33.0 | 301 | 263 | 9 | 2.5 | 6 | 39 | 6 | 28 | 14 | 03 | 21 | 38 | 21 | 51 |
| 11 | 4 | 38 | +16.9 | 59.8 | 32.6 | 313 | 266 | 17 | 3.5 | 7 | 19 | 7 | 05 | 15 | 01 | 22 | 51 | 23 | 08 |
| 12 | 5 | 38 | +18.1 | 59.0 | 32.1 | 326 | 271 | 27 | 4.5 | 8 | 05 | 7 | 48 | 15 | 59 | 23 | 57 | — | |
| 13 | 6 | 36 | +18.2 | 58.0 | 31.6 | 338 | 275 | 37 | 5.5 | 8 | 58 | 8 | 39 | 16 | 56 | — | | 0 | 15 |
| 14 | 7 | 32 | +17.2 | 57.1 | 31.1 | 350 | 279 | 48 | 6.5 | 9 | 56 | 9 | 38 | 17 | 50 | 0 | 53 | 1 | 11 |
| 15 | 8 | 25 | +15.4 | 56.3 | 30.7 | 2 | 283 | 58 | 7.5 | 10 | 58 | 10 | 41 | 18 | 42 | 1 | 40 | 1 | 56 |
| 16 | 9 | 16 | +12.8 | 55.6 | 30.3 | 15 | 286 | 68 | 8.5 | 12 | 02 | 11 | 48 | 19 | 31 | 2 | 19 | 2 | 33 |
| 17 | 10 | 05 | +9.7 | 55.1 | 30.0 | 27 | 289 | 77 | 9.5 | 13 | 06 | 12 | 57 | 20 | 18 | 2 | 51 | 3 | 01 |
| 18 | 10 | 52 | +6.3 | 54.6 | 29.8 | 39 | 292 | 84 | 10.5 | 14 | 11 | 14 | 04 | 21 | 02 | 3 | 19 | 3 | 26 |
| 19 | 11 | 38 | +2.6 | 54.3 | 29.6 | 51 | 294 | 91 | 11.5 | 15 | 15 | 15 | 11 | 21 | 46 | 3 | 43 | 3 | 48 |
| 20 | 12 | 23 | −1.1 | 54.1 | 29.5 | 63 | 296 | 95 | 12.5 | 16 | 18 | 16 | 18 | 22 | 28 | 4 | 06 | 4 | 08 |
| 21 | 13 | 08 | −4.8 | 54.0 | 29.4 | 75 | 302 | 99 | 13.5 | 17 | 21 | 17 | 24 | 23 | 11 | 4 | 29 | 4 | 27 |
| 22 | 13 | 54 | −8.3 | 54.0 | 29.4 | 88 | 338 | 100 | 14.5 | 18 | 24 | 18 | 30 | 23 | 53 | 4 | 51 | 4 | 46 |
| 23 | 14 | 40 | −11.4 | 54.0 | 29.4 | 100 | 82 | 100 | 15.5 | 19 | 26 | 19 | 36 | — | | 5 | 15 | 5 | 08 |
| 24 | 15 | 28 | −14.1 | 54.2 | 29.5 | 112 | 91 | 97 | 16.5 | 20 | 28 | 20 | 40 | 0 | 37 | 5 | 41 | 5 | 31 |
| 25 | 16 | 16 | −16.3 | 54.4 | 29.7 | 124 | 92 | 93 | 17.5 | 21 | 28 | 21 | 43 | 1 | 22 | 6 | 12 | 5 | 58 |
| 26 | 17 | 07 | −17.7 | 54.8 | 29.9 | 136 | 89 | 88 | 18.5 | 22 | 25 | 22 | 42 | 2 | 09 | 6 | 46 | 6 | 30 |
| 27 | 17 | 58 | −18.4 | 55.2 | 30.1 | 148 | 86 | 81 | 19.5 | 23 | 18 | 23 | 37 | 2 | 57 | 7 | 26 | 7 | 09 |
| 28 | 18 | 50 | −18.1 | 55.8 | 30.4 | 161 | 83 | 72 | 20.5 | — | | — | | 3 | 46 | 8 | 14 | 7 | 56 |
| 29 | 19 | 43 | −17.0 | 56.5 | 30.8 | 173 | 79 | 63 | 21.5 | 0 | 06 | 0 | 25 | 4 | 36 | 9 | 08 | 8 | 51 |
| 30 | 20 | 37 | −15.0 | 57.2 | 31.2 | 185 | 75 | 52 | 22.5 | 0 | 50 | 1 | 05 | 5 | 27 | 10 | 10 | 9 | 54 |

# MERCURY

| Day | R.A. | | Dec | Mag. | Diam. | Phase | Rise | | Transit | | Set | |
|---|---|---|---|---|---|---|---|---|---|---|---|---|
| | h | m | ° | | " | % | h | m | h | m | h | m |
| 1 | 1 | 13.5 | +7.8 | −1.5 | 5 | 94 | 5 | 46 | 12 | 35 | 19 | 25 |
| 3 | 1 | 28.1 | +9.6 | −1.4 | 5 | 90 | 5 | 42 | 12 | 41 | 19 | 42 |
| 5 | 1 | 42.4 | +11.4 | −1.3 | 6 | 86 | 5 | 38 | 12 | 48 | 19 | 59 |
| 7 | 1 | 56.3 | +13.1 | −1.1 | 6 | 80 | 5 | 34 | 12 | 53 | 20 | 15 |
| 9 | 2 | 09.7 | +14.7 | −0.9 | 6 | 73 | 5 | 29 | 12 | 59 | 20 | 30 |
| 11 | 2 | 22.3 | +16.1 | −0.8 | 6 | 66 | 5 | 25 | 13 | 03 | 20 | 43 |
| 13 | 2 | 34.0 | +17.4 | −0.5 | 7 | 59 | 5 | 20 | 13 | 06 | 20 | 54 |
| 15 | 2 | 44.7 | +18.5 | −0.3 | 7 | 51 | 5 | 15 | 13 | 09 | 21 | 03 |
| 17 | 2 | 54.1 | +19.4 | 0.0 | 7 | 44 | 5 | 11 | 13 | 10 | 21 | 09 |
| 19 | 3 | 02.3 | +20.1 | +0.3 | 8 | 38 | 5 | 06 | 13 | 09 | 21 | 13 |
| 21 | 3 | 09.1 | +20.6 | +0.6 | 8 | 31 | 5 | 01 | 13 | 08 | 21 | 15 |
| 23 | 3 | 14.4 | +21.0 | +0.9 | 9 | 25 | 4 | 55 | 13 | 05 | 21 | 13 |
| 25 | 3 | 18.2 | +21.2 | +1.3 | 9 | 20 | 4 | 50 | 13 | 00 | 21 | 09 |
| 27 | 3 | 20.5 | +21.1 | +1.8 | 10 | 15 | 4 | 45 | 12 | 54 | 21 | 01 |
| 29 | 3 | 21.4 | +20.9 | +2.3 | 10 | 11 | 4 | 39 | 12 | 46 | 20 | 51 |

Rising and setting times are for latitude 54°

# VENUS

| Day | R.A. | | Dec | Mag. | Diam. | Phase | Rise | | Transit | | Set | |
|---|---|---|---|---|---|---|---|---|---|---|---|---|
| | h | m | ° | | " | % | h | m | h | m | h | m |
| 1 | 23 | 40.0 | −3.8 | −4.2 | 11 | 96 | 5 | 17 | 11 | 00 | 16 | 44 |
| 6 | 0 | 02.7 | −1.3 | −4.1 | 11 | 96 | 5 | 07 | 11 | 03 | 17 | 00 |
| 11 | 0 | 25.4 | +1.1 | −4.1 | 11 | 97 | 4 | 56 | 11 | 06 | 17 | 17 |
| 16 | 0 | 48.1 | +3.6 | −4.1 | 11 | 97 | 4 | 46 | 11 | 09 | 17 | 33 |
| 21 | 1 | 10.8 | +6.0 | −4.0 | 11 | 98 | 4 | 35 | 11 | 12 | 17 | 50 |
| 26 | 1 | 33.8 | +8.3 | −4.0 | 11 | 98 | 4 | 25 | 11 | 15 | 18 | 07 |

# MARS

| Day | R.A. | | Dec | Mag. | Diam. | Phase | Rise | | Transit | | Set | |
|---|---|---|---|---|---|---|---|---|---|---|---|---|
| | h | m | ° | | " | % | h | m | h | m | h | m |
| 1 | 16 | 21.8 | −20.6 | −0.5 | 12 | 93 | 23 | 43 | 3 | 43 | 7 | 42 |
| 6 | 16 | 25.0 | −20.9 | −0.7 | 12 | 93 | 23 | 29 | 3 | 26 | 7 | 24 |
| 11 | 16 | 27.1 | −21.1 | −0.8 | 13 | 94 | 23 | 13 | 3 | 09 | 7 | 05 |
| 16 | 16 | 28.0 | −21.3 | −1.0 | 14 | 95 | 22 | 56 | 2 | 50 | 6 | 45 |
| 21 | 16 | 27.7 | −21.4 | −1.2 | 15 | 96 | 22 | 38 | 2 | 30 | 6 | 24 |
| 26 | 16 | 26.0 | −21.6 | −1.3 | 15 | 97 | 22 | 18 | 2 | 09 | 6 | 02 |

# SUNRISE AND SUNSET

| | London | | | | Bristol | | | | Birmingham | | | | Manchester | | | | Newcastle | | | | Glasgow | | | | Belfast | | | |
|---|---|---|---|---|---|---|---|---|---|---|---|---|---|---|---|---|---|---|---|---|---|---|---|---|---|---|---|---|
| | 0° 05′ | | 51° 30′ | | 2° 35′ | | 51° 28′ | | 1° 55′ | | 52° 28′ | | 2° 15′ | | 53° 28′ | | 1° 37′ | | 54° 59′ | | 4° 14′ | | 55° 52′ | | 5° 56′ | | 54° 35′ | |
| d | h | m | h | m | h | m | h | m | h | m | h | m | h | m | h | m | h | m | h | m | h | m | h | m | h | m | h | m |
| 1 | 5 | 35 | 18 | 34 | 5 | 45 | 18 | 44 | 5 | 41 | 18 | 43 | 5 | 42 | 18 | 45 | 5 | 37 | 18 | 44 | 5 | 47 | 18 | 56 | 5 | 55 | 19 | 01 |
| 2 | 5 | 33 | 18 | 36 | 5 | 43 | 18 | 46 | 5 | 39 | 18 | 44 | 5 | 39 | 18 | 47 | 5 | 35 | 18 | 46 | 5 | 44 | 18 | 58 | 5 | 53 | 19 | 03 |
| 3 | 5 | 30 | 18 | 38 | 5 | 40 | 18 | 48 | 5 | 37 | 18 | 46 | 5 | 37 | 18 | 49 | 5 | 32 | 18 | 48 | 5 | 42 | 19 | 00 | 5 | 50 | 19 | 05 |
| 4 | 5 | 28 | 18 | 39 | 5 | 38 | 18 | 49 | 5 | 34 | 18 | 48 | 5 | 34 | 18 | 51 | 5 | 30 | 18 | 50 | 5 | 39 | 19 | 02 | 5 | 48 | 19 | 07 |
| 5 | 5 | 26 | 18 | 41 | 5 | 36 | 18 | 51 | 5 | 32 | 18 | 50 | 5 | 32 | 18 | 52 | 5 | 27 | 18 | 52 | 5 | 36 | 19 | 04 | 5 | 45 | 19 | 09 |
| 6 | 5 | 24 | 18 | 43 | 5 | 34 | 18 | 53 | 5 | 30 | 18 | 51 | 5 | 30 | 18 | 54 | 5 | 25 | 18 | 54 | 5 | 34 | 19 | 06 | 5 | 43 | 19 | 11 |
| 7 | 5 | 21 | 18 | 44 | 5 | 32 | 18 | 54 | 5 | 27 | 18 | 53 | 5 | 27 | 18 | 56 | 5 | 22 | 18 | 56 | 5 | 31 | 19 | 08 | 5 | 40 | 19 | 13 |
| 8 | 5 | 19 | 18 | 46 | 5 | 29 | 18 | 56 | 5 | 25 | 18 | 55 | 5 | 25 | 18 | 58 | 5 | 20 | 18 | 58 | 5 | 29 | 19 | 10 | 5 | 38 | 19 | 14 |
| 9 | 5 | 17 | 18 | 48 | 5 | 27 | 18 | 58 | 5 | 23 | 18 | 57 | 5 | 23 | 19 | 00 | 5 | 17 | 19 | 00 | 5 | 26 | 19 | 12 | 5 | 35 | 19 | 16 |
| 10 | 5 | 15 | 18 | 49 | 5 | 25 | 18 | 59 | 5 | 21 | 18 | 58 | 5 | 20 | 19 | 01 | 5 | 15 | 19 | 02 | 5 | 24 | 19 | 14 | 5 | 33 | 19 | 18 |
| 11 | 5 | 13 | 18 | 51 | 5 | 23 | 19 | 01 | 5 | 18 | 19 | 00 | 5 | 18 | 19 | 03 | 5 | 12 | 19 | 04 | 5 | 21 | 19 | 16 | 5 | 30 | 19 | 20 |
| 12 | 5 | 10 | 18 | 53 | 5 | 21 | 19 | 03 | 5 | 16 | 19 | 02 | 5 | 15 | 19 | 05 | 5 | 10 | 19 | 06 | 5 | 18 | 19 | 18 | 5 | 28 | 19 | 22 |
| 13 | 5 | 08 | 18 | 54 | 5 | 18 | 19 | 04 | 5 | 14 | 19 | 04 | 5 | 13 | 19 | 07 | 5 | 07 | 19 | 08 | 5 | 16 | 19 | 20 | 5 | 26 | 19 | 24 |
| 14 | 5 | 06 | 18 | 56 | 5 | 16 | 19 | 06 | 5 | 12 | 19 | 05 | 5 | 11 | 19 | 09 | 5 | 05 | 19 | 10 | 5 | 13 | 19 | 22 | 5 | 23 | 19 | 26 |
| 15 | 5 | 04 | 18 | 58 | 5 | 14 | 19 | 08 | 5 | 09 | 19 | 07 | 5 | 09 | 19 | 11 | 5 | 03 | 19 | 11 | 5 | 11 | 19 | 24 | 5 | 21 | 19 | 28 |
| 16 | 5 | 02 | 18 | 59 | 5 | 12 | 19 | 09 | 5 | 07 | 19 | 09 | 5 | 06 | 19 | 12 | 5 | 00 | 19 | 13 | 5 | 08 | 19 | 26 | 5 | 18 | 19 | 30 |
| 17 | 5 | 00 | 19 | 01 | 5 | 10 | 19 | 11 | 5 | 05 | 19 | 10 | 5 | 04 | 19 | 14 | 4 | 58 | 19 | 15 | 5 | 06 | 19 | 28 | 5 | 16 | 19 | 32 |
| 18 | 4 | 58 | 19 | 03 | 5 | 08 | 19 | 13 | 5 | 03 | 19 | 12 | 5 | 02 | 19 | 16 | 4 | 55 | 19 | 17 | 5 | 03 | 19 | 30 | 5 | 14 | 19 | 34 |
| 19 | 4 | 56 | 19 | 04 | 5 | 06 | 19 | 14 | 5 | 01 | 19 | 14 | 4 | 59 | 19 | 18 | 4 | 53 | 19 | 19 | 5 | 01 | 19 | 32 | 5 | 11 | 19 | 36 |
| 20 | 4 | 53 | 19 | 06 | 5 | 03 | 19 | 16 | 4 | 58 | 19 | 16 | 4 | 57 | 19 | 20 | 4 | 51 | 19 | 21 | 4 | 59 | 19 | 34 | 5 | 09 | 19 | 37 |
| 21 | 4 | 51 | 19 | 08 | 5 | 01 | 19 | 18 | 4 | 56 | 19 | 17 | 4 | 55 | 19 | 21 | 4 | 48 | 19 | 23 | 4 | 56 | 19 | 36 | 5 | 07 | 19 | 39 |
| 22 | 4 | 49 | 19 | 09 | 4 | 59 | 19 | 19 | 4 | 54 | 19 | 19 | 4 | 53 | 19 | 23 | 4 | 46 | 19 | 25 | 4 | 54 | 19 | 38 | 5 | 04 | 19 | 41 |
| 23 | 4 | 47 | 19 | 11 | 4 | 57 | 19 | 21 | 4 | 52 | 19 | 21 | 4 | 51 | 19 | 25 | 4 | 44 | 19 | 27 | 4 | 51 | 19 | 40 | 5 | 02 | 19 | 43 |
| 24 | 4 | 45 | 19 | 13 | 4 | 55 | 19 | 23 | 4 | 50 | 19 | 23 | 4 | 48 | 19 | 27 | 4 | 41 | 19 | 29 | 4 | 49 | 19 | 42 | 5 | 00 | 19 | 45 |
| 25 | 4 | 43 | 19 | 14 | 4 | 53 | 19 | 24 | 4 | 48 | 19 | 24 | 4 | 46 | 19 | 29 | 4 | 39 | 19 | 31 | 4 | 47 | 19 | 44 | 4 | 58 | 19 | 47 |
| 26 | 4 | 41 | 19 | 16 | 4 | 51 | 19 | 26 | 4 | 46 | 19 | 26 | 4 | 44 | 19 | 31 | 4 | 37 | 19 | 33 | 4 | 44 | 19 | 46 | 4 | 55 | 19 | 49 |
| 27 | 4 | 39 | 19 | 18 | 4 | 49 | 19 | 28 | 4 | 44 | 19 | 28 | 4 | 42 | 19 | 32 | 4 | 35 | 19 | 35 | 4 | 42 | 19 | 48 | 4 | 53 | 19 | 51 |
| 28 | 4 | 37 | 19 | 19 | 4 | 47 | 19 | 29 | 4 | 42 | 19 | 30 | 4 | 40 | 19 | 34 | 4 | 32 | 19 | 37 | 4 | 40 | 19 | 50 | 4 | 51 | 19 | 53 |
| 29 | 4 | 35 | 19 | 21 | 4 | 46 | 19 | 31 | 4 | 40 | 19 | 31 | 4 | 38 | 19 | 36 | 4 | 30 | 19 | 39 | 4 | 37 | 19 | 53 | 4 | 49 | 19 | 55 |
| 30 | 4 | 34 | 19 | 23 | 4 | 44 | 19 | 32 | 4 | 38 | 19 | 33 | 4 | 36 | 19 | 38 | 4 | 28 | 19 | 41 | 4 | 35 | 19 | 55 | 4 | 47 | 19 | 56 |

## JUPITER

| Day | R.A. | | Dec | Mag. | Diam. | Rise | | Transit | | Set | |
|---|---|---|---|---|---|---|---|---|---|---|---|
| | h | m | ° | | ″ | h | m | h | m | h | m |
| 1 | 11 | 07.8 | +7.2 | −2.4 | 44 | 15 | 43 | 22 | 25 | 5 | 12 |
| 11 | 11 | 04.2 | +7.5 | −2.4 | 43 | 14 | 58 | 21 | 42 | 4 | 31 |
| 21 | 11 | 01.6 | +7.8 | −2.3 | 42 | 14 | 14 | 21 | 00 | 3 | 50 |

Equatorial Diam. 42″, Polar Diam. 40″

## SATURN

| Day | R.A. | | Dec | Mag. | Diam. | Rise | | Transit | | Set | |
|---|---|---|---|---|---|---|---|---|---|---|---|
| | h | m | ° | | ″ | h | m | h | m | h | m |
| 1 | 17 | 00.6 | −21.0 | +0.4 | 17 | 0 | 24 | 4 | 21 | 8 | 18 |
| 11 | 16 | 59.8 | −20.9 | +0.3 | 18 | 23 | 40 | 3 | 41 | 7 | 38 |
| 21 | 16 | 58.3 | −20.9 | +0.3 | 18 | 22 | 58 | 3 | 00 | 6 | 58 |

Equatorial Diam. 18″, Polar Diam. 16″
Rings – major axis 40″ minor axis 18″, Tilt 26°

## URANUS

| Day | R.A. | | Dec | Mag. | Diam. | Rise | | Transit | | Set | |
|---|---|---|---|---|---|---|---|---|---|---|---|
| | h | m | ° | | ″ | h | m | h | m | h | m |
| 1 | 1 | 13.7 | +7.2 | +6.2 | 3 | 5 | 50 | 12 | 33 | 19 | 15 |
| 11 | 1 | 15.9 | +7.4 | +6.2 | 3 | 5 | 11 | 11 | 55 | 18 | 39 |
| 21 | 1 | 18.0 | +7.6 | +6.2 | 3 | 4 | 33 | 11 | 18 | 18 | 03 |

## NEPTUNE

| Day | R.A. | | Dec | Mag. | Diam. | Rise | | Transit | | Set | |
|---|---|---|---|---|---|---|---|---|---|---|---|
| | h | m | ° | | ″ | h | m | h | m | h | m |
| 1 | 22 | 49.0 | −8.4 | +8.0 | 2 | 4 | 52 | 10 | 08 | 15 | 24 |
| 11 | 22 | 50.2 | −8.3 | +7.9 | 2 | 4 | 13 | 9 | 30 | 14 | 47 |
| 21 | 22 | 51.3 | −8.2 | +7.9 | 2 | 3 | 34 | 8 | 52 | 14 | 09 |

# MAY 2016 ♊

FIFTH MONTH, 31 DAYS. *Maia*, goddess of growth and increase

| 1 | *Sunday* | The kingdoms of England and Scotland unite, forming the Kingdom of Great Britain 1707 | day 122 |

| 2 | *Monday* | In the 1997 general election, the Conservative party suffers its worst defeat since 1906 | week 18 day 123 |
| 3 | *Tuesday* | Joseph McCarthy, US Senator who raised fears of Communist subversion in the Cold War *d.* 1957 | 124 |
| 4 | *Wednesday* | Ken Livingstone, an Independent candidate, is appointed as London's first elected mayor 2000 | 125 |
| 5 | *Thursday* | Napoleon Bonaparte dies having spent six years of his life in exile on the island of St Helena 1821 | 126 |
| 6 | *Friday* | Maximilien Robespierre, French revolutionary prominent during the Reign of Terror *b.* 1758 | 127 |
| 7 | *Saturday* | The Equal Franchise Act ensures women over the age of 21 receive the vote 1928 | 128 |
| 8 | *Sunday* | The publication of the Peoples Charter begins the Chartist movement 1838 | 129 |

| 9 | *Monday* | German philosopher Karl Marx is exiled from Prussia 1849 | week 19 day 130 |
| 10 | *Tuesday* | Winston Churchill becomes prime minister after the resignation of Neville Chamberlain 1940 | 131 |
| 11 | *Wednesday* | Spencer Perceval becomes the first and only British prime minister to be assassinated 1812 | 132 |
| 12 | *Thursday* | Leader of the Labour Party John Smith suffers a fatal heart attack and dies in office 1994 | 133 |
| 13 | *Friday* | The 2nd Marquess of Rockingham, Whig politician who twice served as prime minister *b.* 1730 | 134 |
| 14 | *Saturday* | The Soviet Union establishes the Warsaw Pact with its Eastern Bloc allies 1955 | 135 |
| 15 | *Sunday* | Édith Cresson becomes the first woman to be appointed Prime Minister of France 1991 | 136 |

| 16 | *Monday* | Deputy Prime Minister John Prescott punches an egg-throwing protestor in Rhyl, Wales 2001 | week 20 day 137 |
| 17 | *Tuesday* | Vidkun Quisling founds *Nasjonal Samling* [National Unity], the Norwegian fascist party 1933 | 138 |
| 18 | *Wednesday* | Napoleon Bonaparte is declared Napoleon I, Emperor of the French 1804 | 139 |
| 19 | *Thursday* | Pol Pot, Cambodian communist dictator who led the Khmer Rouge *b.* 1925 | 140 |
| 20 | *Friday* | Moshe Dayan, Israeli military leader who was defence minister during the Six-Day War *b.* 1915 | 141 |
| 21 | *Saturday* | President Suharto of Indonesia resigns after 31 years in office 1998 | 142 |
| 22 | *Sunday* | US President Lyndon Johnson formally presents his 'Great Society' reform package 1964 | 143 |

| 23 | *Monday* | Northern Ireland and the Republic of Ireland vote in favour of the Good Friday Agreement 1998 | week 21 day 144 |
| 24 | *Tuesday* | Harold Wilson, Labour Party leader and prime minister who won four general elections *d.* 1995 | 145 |
| 25 | *Wednesday* | Britain's last all-Liberal government forms a wartime coalition with the Conservatives 1915 | 146 |
| 26 | *Thursday* | John Stuart, 3rd Earl of Bute becomes the first Scottish and first Tory prime minister 1762 | 147 |
| 27 | *Friday* | Jawaharlal Nehru, first prime minister of an independent India *d.* 1964 | 148 |
| 28 | *Saturday* | Lord John Russell, British prime minister who proposed the 1832 Reform Act *d.* 1878 | 149 |
| 29 | *Sunday* | The Fall of Constantinople, bringing an end to the Byzantine Empire 1453 | 150 |

| 30 | *Monday* | Women over the age of 21 vote for the first time in a general election 1929 | week 22 day 151 |
| 31 | *Tuesday* | Four separate British colonies form the Union of South Africa 1910 | 152 |

ASTRONOMICAL PHENOMENA

| d | h | |
|---|---|---|
| 5 | 03 | Uranus 2° North of the Moon |
| 6 | 04 | Venus 3° North of the Moon |
| 9 | 15 | Transit of Mercury *see* page 1114 |
| 13 | 21 | Venus 0.4° North of Mercury |
| 15 | 10 | Jupiter 2° North of the Moon |
| 22 | 22 | Saturn 3° South of the Moon |
| 22 | 11 | Mars at opposition |

MINIMA OF ALGOL

| d | h | d | h | d | h |
|---|---|---|---|---|---|
| 3 | 19.3 | 15 | 06.5 | 26 | 17.8 |
| 6 | 16.1 | 18 | 03.3 | 29 | 14.6 |
| 9 | 12.9 | 21 | 00.2 | | |
| 12 | 09.7 | 23 | 21.0 | | |

CONSTELLATIONS

The following constellations are near the meridian at

| | d | h | | d | h |
|---|---|---|---|---|---|
| April | 1 | 24 | May | 16 | 21 |
| April | 15 | 23 | June | 1 | 20 |
| May | 1 | 22 | June | 15 | 19 |

Cepheus (below the Pole), Cassiopeia (below the Pole), Ursa Minor, Ursa Major, Canes Venatici, Coma Berenices, Bootes, Leo, Virgo, Crater, Corvus and Hydra

THE MOON

| *Phases, Apsides and Node* | | d | h | m |
|---|---|---|---|---|
| ● | New Moon | 6 | 19 | 30 |
| ◐ | First Quarter | 13 | 17 | 02 |
| ○ | Full Moon | 21 | 21 | 14 |
| ◑ | Last Quarter | 29 | 12 | 12 |

| Perigee (357,827km) | 6 | 04 | 13 |
| Apogee (405,933km) | 18 | 22 | 06 |

Mean longitude of ascending node on 1st, 169°

# THE SUN

Diam. 31.7″

| Day | Right Ascension h | m | s | Dec. + ° | Equation of time m | s | Rise 52° h | m | Rise 56° h | m | Transit h | m | Set 52° h | m | Set 56° h | m | Sidereal time h | m | s | Transit of first point of Aries h | m | s |
|---|---|---|---|---|---|---|---|---|---|---|---|---|---|---|---|---|---|---|---|---|---|---|
| 1 | 2 | 34 | 22 | 15.1 | +2 | 53 | 4 | 32 | 4 | 18 | 11 | 57 | 19 | 24 | 19 | 38 | 13 | 37 | 15 | 9 | 22 | 35 |
| 2 | 2 | 38 | 12 | 15.4 | +3 | 00 | 4 | 30 | 4 | 15 | 11 | 57 | 19 | 25 | 19 | 40 | 13 | 41 | 12 | 9 | 18 | 38 |
| 3 | 2 | 42 | 02 | 15.7 | +3 | 06 | 4 | 28 | 4 | 13 | 11 | 57 | 19 | 27 | 19 | 42 | 13 | 45 | 08 | 9 | 14 | 42 |
| 4 | 2 | 45 | 53 | 16.0 | +3 | 12 | 4 | 26 | 4 | 11 | 11 | 57 | 19 | 29 | 19 | 44 | 13 | 49 | 05 | 9 | 10 | 45 |
| 5 | 2 | 49 | 44 | 16.3 | +3 | 17 | 4 | 24 | 4 | 09 | 11 | 57 | 19 | 30 | 19 | 46 | 13 | 53 | 01 | 9 | 06 | 49 |
| 6 | 2 | 53 | 36 | 16.6 | +3 | 22 | 4 | 22 | 4 | 07 | 11 | 57 | 19 | 32 | 19 | 48 | 13 | 56 | 58 | 9 | 02 | 52 |
| 7 | 2 | 57 | 29 | 16.9 | +3 | 26 | 4 | 20 | 4 | 04 | 11 | 57 | 19 | 34 | 19 | 50 | 14 | 00 | 55 | 8 | 58 | 56 |
| 8 | 3 | 01 | 22 | 17.1 | +3 | 29 | 4 | 19 | 4 | 02 | 11 | 57 | 19 | 35 | 19 | 52 | 14 | 04 | 51 | 8 | 54 | 59 |
| 9 | 3 | 05 | 15 | 17.4 | +3 | 32 | 4 | 17 | 4 | 00 | 11 | 56 | 19 | 37 | 19 | 54 | 14 | 08 | 48 | 8 | 51 | 03 |
| 10 | 3 | 09 | 10 | 17.7 | +3 | 34 | 4 | 15 | 3 | 58 | 11 | 56 | 19 | 39 | 19 | 56 | 14 | 12 | 44 | 8 | 47 | 06 |
| 11 | 3 | 13 | 04 | 17.9 | +3 | 36 | 4 | 14 | 3 | 56 | 11 | 56 | 19 | 40 | 19 | 58 | 14 | 16 | 41 | 8 | 43 | 09 |
| 12 | 3 | 17 | 00 | 18.2 | +3 | 37 | 4 | 12 | 3 | 54 | 11 | 56 | 19 | 42 | 20 | 00 | 14 | 20 | 37 | 8 | 39 | 13 |
| 13 | 3 | 20 | 56 | 18.4 | +3 | 38 | 4 | 10 | 3 | 52 | 11 | 56 | 19 | 43 | 20 | 02 | 14 | 24 | 34 | 8 | 35 | 16 |
| 14 | 3 | 24 | 52 | 18.7 | +3 | 38 | 4 | 09 | 3 | 50 | 11 | 56 | 19 | 45 | 20 | 03 | 14 | 28 | 30 | 8 | 31 | 20 |
| 15 | 3 | 28 | 49 | 18.9 | +3 | 38 | 4 | 07 | 3 | 49 | 11 | 56 | 19 | 46 | 20 | 05 | 14 | 32 | 27 | 8 | 27 | 23 |
| 16 | 3 | 32 | 46 | 19.1 | +3 | 37 | 4 | 06 | 3 | 47 | 11 | 56 | 19 | 48 | 20 | 07 | 14 | 36 | 24 | 8 | 23 | 27 |
| 17 | 3 | 36 | 45 | 19.4 | +3 | 35 | 4 | 04 | 3 | 45 | 11 | 56 | 19 | 49 | 20 | 09 | 14 | 40 | 20 | 8 | 19 | 30 |
| 18 | 3 | 40 | 43 | 19.6 | +3 | 33 | 4 | 03 | 3 | 43 | 11 | 56 | 19 | 51 | 20 | 11 | 14 | 44 | 17 | 8 | 15 | 34 |
| 19 | 3 | 44 | 42 | 19.8 | +3 | 31 | 4 | 01 | 3 | 42 | 11 | 56 | 19 | 52 | 20 | 13 | 14 | 48 | 13 | 8 | 11 | 37 |
| 20 | 3 | 48 | 42 | 20.0 | +3 | 27 | 4 | 00 | 3 | 40 | 11 | 57 | 19 | 54 | 20 | 14 | 14 | 52 | 10 | 8 | 07 | 40 |
| 21 | 3 | 52 | 42 | 20.2 | +3 | 24 | 3 | 59 | 3 | 38 | 11 | 57 | 19 | 55 | 20 | 16 | 14 | 56 | 06 | 8 | 03 | 44 |
| 22 | 3 | 56 | 43 | 20.4 | +3 | 20 | 3 | 57 | 3 | 37 | 11 | 57 | 19 | 57 | 20 | 18 | 15 | 00 | 03 | 7 | 59 | 47 |
| 23 | 4 | 00 | 44 | 20.6 | +3 | 15 | 3 | 56 | 3 | 35 | 11 | 57 | 19 | 58 | 20 | 19 | 15 | 03 | 59 | 7 | 55 | 51 |
| 24 | 4 | 04 | 46 | 20.8 | +3 | 10 | 3 | 55 | 3 | 34 | 11 | 57 | 19 | 59 | 20 | 21 | 15 | 07 | 56 | 7 | 51 | 54 |
| 25 | 4 | 08 | 48 | 21.0 | +3 | 04 | 3 | 54 | 3 | 32 | 11 | 57 | 20 | 01 | 20 | 23 | 15 | 11 | 53 | 7 | 47 | 58 |
| 26 | 4 | 12 | 51 | 21.2 | +2 | 58 | 3 | 53 | 3 | 31 | 11 | 57 | 20 | 02 | 20 | 24 | 15 | 15 | 49 | 7 | 44 | 01 |
| 27 | 4 | 16 | 54 | 21.3 | +2 | 51 | 3 | 52 | 3 | 29 | 11 | 57 | 20 | 03 | 20 | 26 | 15 | 19 | 46 | 7 | 40 | 05 |
| 28 | 4 | 20 | 58 | 21.5 | +2 | 44 | 3 | 51 | 3 | 28 | 11 | 57 | 20 | 05 | 20 | 27 | 15 | 23 | 42 | 7 | 36 | 08 |
| 29 | 4 | 25 | 02 | 21.6 | +2 | 36 | 3 | 50 | 3 | 27 | 11 | 57 | 20 | 06 | 20 | 29 | 15 | 27 | 39 | 7 | 32 | 11 |
| 30 | 4 | 29 | 07 | 21.8 | +2 | 28 | 3 | 49 | 3 | 26 | 11 | 57 | 20 | 07 | 20 | 30 | 15 | 31 | 35 | 7 | 28 | 15 |
| 31 | 4 | 33 | 12 | 21.9 | +2 | 19 | 3 | 48 | 3 | 25 | 11 | 58 | 20 | 08 | 20 | 31 | 15 | 35 | 32 | 7 | 24 | 18 |

## DURATION OF TWILIGHT (in minutes)

| Latitude | 52° | 56° | 52° | 56° | 52° | 56° | 52° | 56° |
|---|---|---|---|---|---|---|---|---|
| | 1 May | | 11 May | | 21 May | | 31 May | |
| Civil | 39 | 44 | 41 | 48 | 44 | 53 | 46 | 57 |
| Nautical | 89 | 106 | 97 | 120 | 106 | 141 | 115 | 187 |
| Astronomical | 152 | 204 | 176 | TAN | TAN | TAN | TAN | TAN |

## THE NIGHT SKY

*Mercury* passes through inferior conjunction on May 9th when it will be seen to transit the Sun. The entire event is visible from Western Europe, Africa, South America and the eastern states of North America. Bordering these regions will see some of the transit, but not Australasia. *See* page 1114 for more details and timings. Mercury will not be visible for the rest of May.

*Venus* is not visible this month as it is rising at roughly the same time as the Sun.

*Mars* reaches opposition in Scorpius on May 22nd where it burns at magnitude −2.1 and shows an 18 arc-second disk in a telescope. The Full Moon is 5° from Mars on the 21st. Mars crosses into Libra on May 28th.

*Jupiter* is high in the southern sky in Leo as dusk falls and remains visible for the first half of the night. The giant planet is stationary on the 10th after which its direct motion resumes. The Moon is just past First Quarter when near Jupiter on May 14th and 15th.

*Saturn* in Ophiuchus, rises less than 30 minutes after Mars. The planet will brighten a little from magnitude +0.2 to 0.0 during the month. The Moon is just a day past full when near Saturn on May 22nd.

## THE MOON

| Day | R.A. h m | Dec. ° | Hor. Par. ' | Diam. ' | Sun's Co-Long. ° | PA of Br. Limb ° | Ph. % | Age d | Rise 52° h m | Rise 56° h m | Transit h m | Set 52° h m | Set 56° h m |
|---|---|---|---|---|---|---|---|---|---|---|---|---|---|
| 1 | 21 31 | −12.1 | 58.1 | 31.7 | 197 | 72 | 41 | 23.5 | 1 28 | 1 41 | 6 19 | 11 17 | 11 04 |
| 2 | 22 25 | −8.4 | 59.0 | 32.1 | 209 | 69 | 31 | 24.5 | 2 01 | 2 11 | 7 11 | 12 28 | 12 19 |
| 3 | 23 20 | −4.2 | 59.8 | 32.6 | 222 | 67 | 21 | 25.5 | 2 32 | 2 39 | 8 03 | 13 44 | 13 39 |
| 4 | 0 15 | +0.4 | 60.5 | 33.0 | 234 | 65 | 12 | 26.5 | 3 01 | 3 04 | 8 56 | 15 03 | 15 02 |
| 5 | 1 12 | +5.0 | 61.0 | 33.3 | 246 | 63 | 5 | 27.5 | 3 29 | 3 28 | 9 50 | 16 24 | 16 27 |
| 6 | 2 11 | +9.4 | 61.3 | 33.4 | 258 | 55 | 1 | 28.5 | 3 59 | 3 54 | 10 45 | 17 46 | 17 53 |
| 7 | 3 11 | +13.3 | 61.2 | 33.3 | 271 | 319 | 0 | 29.5 | 4 32 | 4 23 | 11 43 | 19 08 | 19 20 |
| 8 | 4 12 | +16.1 | 60.8 | 33.1 | 283 | 276 | 2 | 1.0 | 5 09 | 4 56 | 12 42 | 20 27 | 20 42 |
| 9 | 5 13 | +17.9 | 60.1 | 32.8 | 295 | 274 | 7 | 2.0 | 5 52 | 5 36 | 13 42 | 21 39 | 21 56 |
| 10 | 6 14 | +18.4 | 59.2 | 32.3 | 307 | 277 | 14 | 3.0 | 6 43 | 6 25 | 14 42 | 22 42 | 23 00 |
| 11 | 7 13 | +17.8 | 58.3 | 31.8 | 320 | 280 | 23 | 4.0 | 7 40 | 7 22 | 15 39 | 23 35 | 23 52 |
| 12 | 8 09 | +16.2 | 57.3 | 31.3 | 332 | 284 | 32 | 5.0 | 8 43 | 8 26 | 16 34 | — | — |
| 13 | 9 02 | +13.8 | 56.5 | 30.8 | 344 | 287 | 42 | 6.0 | 9 48 | 9 34 | 17 26 | 0 18 | 0 33 |
| 14 | 9 52 | +10.8 | 55.7 | 30.4 | 356 | 290 | 53 | 7.0 | 10 55 | 10 43 | 18 15 | 0 53 | 1 05 |
| 15 | 10 40 | +7.4 | 55.1 | 30.0 | 8 | 292 | 62 | 8.0 | 12 01 | 11 53 | 19 00 | 1 23 | 1 32 |
| 16 | 11 26 | +3.7 | 54.6 | 29.7 | 21 | 293 | 71 | 9.0 | 13 05 | 13 01 | 19 44 | 1 49 | 1 55 |
| 17 | 12 12 | +0.0 | 54.3 | 29.6 | 33 | 294 | 80 | 10.0 | 14 09 | 14 08 | 20 27 | 2 12 | 2 15 |
| 18 | 12 57 | −3.7 | 54.1 | 29.5 | 45 | 295 | 87 | 11.0 | 15 12 | 15 14 | 21 09 | 2 35 | 2 34 |
| 19 | 13 42 | −7.3 | 54.0 | 29.4 | 57 | 296 | 92 | 12.0 | 16 15 | 16 21 | 21 52 | 2 57 | 2 53 |
| 20 | 14 28 | −10.6 | 54.1 | 29.5 | 69 | 298 | 97 | 13.0 | 17 18 | 17 27 | 22 35 | 3 20 | 3 13 |
| 21 | 15 15 | −13.5 | 54.2 | 29.6 | 82 | 308 | 99 | 14.0 | 18 20 | 18 32 | 23 20 | 3 45 | 3 35 |
| 22 | 16 04 | −15.9 | 54.5 | 29.7 | 94 | 21 | 100 | 15.0 | 19 21 | 19 36 | — | 4 14 | 4 01 |
| 23 | 16 54 | −17.5 | 54.8 | 29.9 | 106 | 74 | 99 | 16.0 | 20 20 | 20 37 | 0 06 | 4 46 | 4 31 |
| 24 | 17 46 | −18.4 | 55.2 | 30.1 | 118 | 80 | 96 | 17.0 | 21 16 | 21 34 | 0 54 | 5 25 | 5 08 |
| 25 | 18 38 | −18.4 | 55.6 | 30.3 | 130 | 80 | 91 | 18.0 | 22 06 | 22 25 | 1 43 | 6 10 | 5 52 |
| 26 | 19 31 | −17.5 | 56.1 | 30.6 | 143 | 77 | 85 | 19.0 | 22 51 | 23 08 | 2 34 | 7 03 | 6 44 |
| 27 | 20 24 | −15.7 | 56.7 | 30.9 | 155 | 74 | 76 | 20.0 | 23 31 | 23 45 | 3 24 | 8 02 | 7 45 |
| 28 | 21 17 | −13.1 | 57.3 | 31.2 | 167 | 72 | 67 | 21.0 | — | — | 4 15 | 9 06 | 8 53 |
| 29 | 22 10 | −9.7 | 58.0 | 31.6 | 179 | 69 | 56 | 22.0 | 0 05 | 0 16 | 5 06 | 10 15 | 10 05 |
| 30 | 23 03 | −5.7 | 58.7 | 32.0 | 191 | 67 | 45 | 23.0 | 0 36 | 0 44 | 5 57 | 11 28 | 11 21 |
| 31 | 23 57 | −1.4 | 59.4 | 32.4 | 204 | 66 | 34 | 24.0 | 1 04 | 1 08 | 6 48 | 12 43 | 12 40 |

## MERCURY

| Day | R.A. h m | Dec ° | Mag. | Diam. " | Phase % | Rise h m | Transit h m | Set h m |
|---|---|---|---|---|---|---|---|---|
| 1 | 3 20.8 | +20.6 | +2.9 | 11 | 7 | 4 33 | 12 37 | 20 39 |
| 3 | 3 19.0 | +20.0 | +3.5 | 11 | 4 | 4 27 | 12 27 | 20 24 |
| 5 | 3 16.2 | +19.4 | +4.2 | 12 | 2 | 4 21 | 12 16 | 20 07 |
| 7 | 3 12.6 | +18.6 | +5.0 | 12 | 1 | 4 15 | 12 05 | 19 50 |
| 9 | 3 08.5 | +17.7 | +5.9 | 12 | 0 | 4 09 | 11 53 | 19 32 |
| 11 | 3 04.3 | +16.8 | +5.6 | 12 | 0 | 4 03 | 11 41 | 19 14 |
| 13 | 3 00.2 | +16.0 | +4.8 | 12 | 1 | 3 57 | 11 29 | 18 57 |
| 15 | 2 56.6 | +15.1 | +4.1 | 12 | 3 | 3 51 | 11 18 | 18 41 |
| 17 | 2 53.7 | +14.4 | +3.5 | 12 | 5 | 3 45 | 11 07 | 18 27 |
| 19 | 2 51.6 | +13.8 | +3.0 | 12 | 7 | 3 39 | 10 58 | 18 14 |
| 21 | 2 50.6 | +13.3 | +2.5 | 11 | 10 | 3 33 | 10 49 | 18 03 |
| 23 | 2 50.6 | +13.0 | +2.1 | 11 | 13 | 3 27 | 10 42 | 17 55 |
| 25 | 2 51.7 | +12.8 | +1.8 | 10 | 17 | 3 22 | 10 36 | 17 48 |
| 27 | 2 53.9 | +12.8 | +1.5 | 10 | 20 | 3 16 | 10 30 | 17 44 |
| 29 | 2 57.2 | +12.9 | +1.3 | 10 | 24 | 3 11 | 10 26 | 17 41 |
| 31 | 3 01.5 | +13.2 | +1.1 | 9 | 27 | 3 05 | 10 23 | 17 40 |

Rising and setting times are for latitude 54°

## VENUS

| Day | R.A. h m | Dec ° | Mag. | Diam. " | Phase % | Rise h m | Transit h m | Set h m |
|---|---|---|---|---|---|---|---|---|
| 1 | 1 57.0 | +10.6 | −4.0 | 11 | 99 | 4 15 | 11 19 | 18 24 |
| 6 | 2 20.5 | +12.8 | −4.0 | 11 | 99 | 4 06 | 11 23 | 18 41 |
| 11 | 2 44.4 | +14.9 | −3.9 | 10 | 99 | 3 57 | 11 27 | 18 58 |
| 16 | 3 08.7 | +16.8 | −3.9 | 10 | 99 | 3 49 | 11 32 | 19 15 |
| 21 | 3 33.5 | +18.5 | −3.9 | 10 | 100 | 3 43 | 11 37 | 19 32 |
| 26 | 3 58.7 | +20.0 | −3.9 | 10 | 100 | 3 37 | 11 42 | 19 48 |
| 31 | 4 24.4 | +21.3 | −3.9 | 10 | 100 | 3 34 | 11 48 | 20 03 |

## MARS

| Day | R.A. h m | Dec ° | Mag. | Diam. " | Phase % | Rise h m | Transit h m | Set h m |
|---|---|---|---|---|---|---|---|---|
| 1 | 16 22.9 | −21.7 | −1.5 | 16 | 98 | 21 56 | 1 46 | 5 38 |
| 6 | 16 18.5 | −21.7 | −1.6 | 17 | 99 | 21 33 | 1 22 | 5 14 |
| 11 | 16 12.9 | −21.7 | −1.8 | 17 | 99 | 21 08 | 0 56 | 4 48 |
| 16 | 16 06.3 | −21.7 | −1.9 | 18 | 100 | 20 42 | 0 30 | 4 22 |
| 21 | 15 59.0 | −21.6 | −2.0 | 18 | 100 | 20 14 | 0 03 | 3 56 |
| 26 | 15 51.5 | −21.5 | −2.0 | 19 | 100 | 19 46 | 23 38 | 3 29 |
| 31 | 15 44.0 | −21.4 | −2.0 | 19 | 100 | 19 18 | 23 11 | 3 03 |

# SUNRISE AND SUNSET

| | London | | | | Bristol | | | | Birmingham | | | | Manchester | | | | Newcastle | | | | Glasgow | | | | Belfast | | | |
|---|---|---|---|---|---|---|---|---|---|---|---|---|---|---|---|---|---|---|---|---|---|---|---|---|---|---|---|---|
| | 0° 05′ | | 51° 30′ | | 2° 35′ | | 51° 28′ | | 1° 55′ | | 52° 28′ | | 2° 15′ | | 53° 28′ | | 1° 37′ | | 54° 59′ | | 4° 14′ | | 55° 52′ | | 5° 56′ | | 54° 35′ | |
| d | h | m | h | m | h | m | h | m | h | m | h | m | h | m | h | m | h | m | h | m | h | m | h | m | h | m | h | m |
| 1 | 4 | 32 | 19 | 24 | 4 | 42 | 19 | 34 | 4 | 36 | 19 | 35 | 4 | 34 | 19 | 39 | 4 | 26 | 19 | 43 | 4 | 33 | 19 | 57 | 4 | 45 | 19 | 58 |
| 2 | 4 | 30 | 19 | 26 | 4 | 40 | 19 | 36 | 4 | 34 | 19 | 36 | 4 | 32 | 19 | 41 | 4 | 24 | 19 | 44 | 4 | 31 | 19 | 59 | 4 | 42 | 20 | 00 |
| 3 | 4 | 28 | 19 | 27 | 4 | 38 | 19 | 37 | 4 | 32 | 19 | 38 | 4 | 30 | 19 | 43 | 4 | 22 | 19 | 46 | 4 | 28 | 20 | 01 | 4 | 40 | 20 | 02 |
| 4 | 4 | 26 | 19 | 29 | 4 | 36 | 19 | 39 | 4 | 30 | 19 | 40 | 4 | 28 | 19 | 45 | 4 | 19 | 19 | 48 | 4 | 26 | 20 | 02 | 4 | 38 | 20 | 04 |
| 5 | 4 | 24 | 19 | 31 | 4 | 34 | 19 | 41 | 4 | 28 | 19 | 42 | 4 | 26 | 19 | 47 | 4 | 17 | 19 | 50 | 4 | 24 | 20 | 04 | 4 | 36 | 20 | 06 |
| 6 | 4 | 23 | 19 | 32 | 4 | 33 | 19 | 42 | 4 | 26 | 19 | 43 | 4 | 24 | 19 | 48 | 4 | 15 | 19 | 52 | 4 | 22 | 20 | 06 | 4 | 34 | 20 | 08 |
| 7 | 4 | 21 | 19 | 34 | 4 | 31 | 19 | 44 | 4 | 25 | 19 | 45 | 4 | 22 | 19 | 50 | 4 | 13 | 19 | 54 | 4 | 20 | 20 | 08 | 4 | 32 | 20 | 09 |
| 8 | 4 | 19 | 19 | 35 | 4 | 29 | 19 | 45 | 4 | 23 | 19 | 46 | 4 | 20 | 19 | 52 | 4 | 11 | 19 | 56 | 4 | 18 | 20 | 10 | 4 | 30 | 20 | 11 |
| 9 | 4 | 17 | 19 | 37 | 4 | 28 | 19 | 47 | 4 | 21 | 19 | 48 | 4 | 18 | 19 | 54 | 4 | 09 | 19 | 58 | 4 | 16 | 20 | 12 | 4 | 28 | 20 | 13 |
| 10 | 4 | 16 | 19 | 39 | 4 | 26 | 19 | 49 | 4 | 19 | 19 | 50 | 4 | 17 | 19 | 55 | 4 | 07 | 19 | 59 | 4 | 14 | 20 | 14 | 4 | 27 | 20 | 15 |
| 11 | 4 | 14 | 19 | 40 | 4 | 24 | 19 | 50 | 4 | 18 | 19 | 51 | 4 | 15 | 19 | 57 | 4 | 06 | 20 | 01 | 4 | 12 | 20 | 16 | 4 | 25 | 20 | 17 |
| 12 | 4 | 13 | 19 | 42 | 4 | 23 | 19 | 52 | 4 | 16 | 19 | 53 | 4 | 13 | 19 | 59 | 4 | 04 | 20 | 03 | 4 | 10 | 20 | 18 | 4 | 23 | 20 | 19 |
| 13 | 4 | 11 | 19 | 43 | 4 | 21 | 19 | 53 | 4 | 14 | 19 | 55 | 4 | 11 | 20 | 00 | 4 | 02 | 20 | 05 | 4 | 08 | 20 | 20 | 4 | 21 | 20 | 20 |
| 14 | 4 | 10 | 19 | 45 | 4 | 20 | 19 | 55 | 4 | 13 | 19 | 56 | 4 | 10 | 20 | 02 | 4 | 00 | 20 | 07 | 4 | 06 | 20 | 22 | 4 | 19 | 20 | 22 |
| 15 | 4 | 08 | 19 | 46 | 4 | 18 | 19 | 56 | 4 | 11 | 19 | 58 | 4 | 08 | 20 | 04 | 3 | 58 | 20 | 08 | 4 | 04 | 20 | 24 | 4 | 18 | 20 | 24 |
| 16 | 4 | 07 | 19 | 48 | 4 | 17 | 19 | 58 | 4 | 10 | 19 | 59 | 4 | 07 | 20 | 05 | 3 | 57 | 20 | 10 | 4 | 02 | 20 | 25 | 4 | 16 | 20 | 25 |
| 17 | 4 | 05 | 19 | 49 | 4 | 15 | 19 | 59 | 4 | 08 | 20 | 01 | 4 | 05 | 20 | 07 | 3 | 55 | 20 | 12 | 4 | 01 | 20 | 27 | 4 | 14 | 20 | 27 |
| 18 | 4 | 04 | 19 | 51 | 4 | 14 | 20 | 01 | 4 | 07 | 20 | 02 | 4 | 04 | 20 | 08 | 3 | 53 | 20 | 14 | 3 | 59 | 20 | 29 | 4 | 13 | 20 | 29 |
| 19 | 4 | 02 | 19 | 52 | 4 | 13 | 20 | 02 | 4 | 05 | 20 | 04 | 4 | 02 | 20 | 10 | 3 | 52 | 20 | 15 | 3 | 57 | 20 | 31 | 4 | 11 | 20 | 30 |
| 20 | 4 | 01 | 19 | 54 | 4 | 11 | 20 | 03 | 4 | 04 | 20 | 05 | 4 | 01 | 20 | 12 | 3 | 50 | 20 | 17 | 3 | 56 | 20 | 33 | 4 | 10 | 20 | 32 |
| 21 | 4 | 00 | 19 | 55 | 4 | 10 | 20 | 05 | 4 | 03 | 20 | 07 | 3 | 59 | 20 | 13 | 3 | 49 | 20 | 19 | 3 | 54 | 20 | 34 | 4 | 08 | 20 | 34 |
| 22 | 3 | 59 | 19 | 56 | 4 | 09 | 20 | 06 | 4 | 01 | 20 | 08 | 3 | 58 | 20 | 15 | 3 | 47 | 20 | 20 | 3 | 52 | 20 | 36 | 4 | 07 | 20 | 35 |
| 23 | 3 | 57 | 19 | 58 | 4 | 08 | 20 | 07 | 4 | 00 | 20 | 10 | 3 | 56 | 20 | 16 | 3 | 46 | 20 | 22 | 3 | 51 | 20 | 38 | 4 | 05 | 20 | 37 |
| 24 | 3 | 56 | 19 | 59 | 4 | 06 | 20 | 09 | 3 | 59 | 20 | 11 | 3 | 55 | 20 | 17 | 3 | 44 | 20 | 23 | 3 | 49 | 20 | 39 | 4 | 04 | 20 | 38 |
| 25 | 3 | 55 | 20 | 00 | 4 | 05 | 20 | 10 | 3 | 58 | 20 | 12 | 3 | 54 | 20 | 19 | 3 | 43 | 20 | 25 | 3 | 48 | 20 | 41 | 4 | 03 | 20 | 40 |
| 26 | 3 | 54 | 20 | 01 | 4 | 04 | 20 | 11 | 3 | 57 | 20 | 14 | 3 | 53 | 20 | 20 | 3 | 42 | 20 | 26 | 3 | 47 | 20 | 42 | 4 | 01 | 20 | 41 |
| 27 | 3 | 53 | 20 | 03 | 4 | 03 | 20 | 13 | 3 | 56 | 20 | 15 | 3 | 52 | 20 | 22 | 3 | 40 | 20 | 28 | 3 | 45 | 20 | 44 | 4 | 00 | 20 | 43 |
| 28 | 3 | 52 | 20 | 04 | 4 | 02 | 20 | 14 | 3 | 55 | 20 | 16 | 3 | 51 | 20 | 23 | 3 | 39 | 20 | 29 | 3 | 44 | 20 | 45 | 3 | 59 | 20 | 44 |
| 29 | 3 | 51 | 20 | 05 | 4 | 01 | 20 | 15 | 3 | 54 | 20 | 17 | 3 | 49 | 20 | 24 | 3 | 38 | 20 | 31 | 3 | 43 | 20 | 47 | 3 | 58 | 20 | 45 |
| 30 | 3 | 50 | 20 | 06 | 4 | 00 | 20 | 16 | 3 | 53 | 20 | 19 | 3 | 48 | 20 | 25 | 3 | 37 | 20 | 32 | 3 | 42 | 20 | 48 | 3 | 57 | 20 | 47 |
| 31 | 3 | 49 | 20 | 07 | 4 | 00 | 20 | 17 | 3 | 52 | 20 | 20 | 3 | 48 | 20 | 27 | 3 | 36 | 20 | 33 | 3 | 41 | 20 | 50 | 3 | 56 | 20 | 48 |

## JUPITER

| Day | R.A. | | Dec | Mag. | Diam. | Rise | | Transit | | Set | |
|---|---|---|---|---|---|---|---|---|---|---|---|
| | h | m | ° | | ″ | h | m | h | m | h | m |
| 1 | 11 | 00.0 | +7.9 | −2.3 | 41 | 13 | 33 | 20 | 20 | 3 | 10 |
| 11 | 10 | 59.5 | +7.9 | −2.2 | 40 | 12 | 53 | 19 | 40 | 2 | 30 |
| 21 | 11 | 00.2 | +7.8 | −2.1 | 39 | 12 | 15 | 19 | 01 | 1 | 51 |
| 31 | 11 | 02.0 | +7.6 | −2.1 | 37 | 11 | 38 | 18 | 23 | 1 | 12 |

Equatorial Diam. 39″, Polar Diam. 37″

## SATURN

| Day | R.A. | | Dec | Mag. | Diam. | Rise | | Transit | | Set | |
|---|---|---|---|---|---|---|---|---|---|---|---|
| | h | m | ° | | ″ | h | m | h | m | h | m |
| 1 | 16 | 56.3 | −20.8 | +0.2 | 18 | 22 | 17 | 2 | 19 | 6 | 17 |
| 11 | 16 | 53.8 | −20.7 | +0.1 | 18 | 21 | 34 | 1 | 37 | 5 | 35 |
| 21 | 16 | 50.9 | −20.7 | +0.1 | 18 | 20 | 51 | 0 | 54 | 4 | 54 |
| 31 | 16 | 47.8 | −20.6 | 0.0 | 18 | 20 | 08 | 0 | 12 | 4 | 12 |

Equatorial Diam. 18″, Polar Diam. 17″
Rings – major axis 41″ minor axis 18″, Tilt 26°

## URANUS

| Day | R.A. | | Dec | Mag. | Diam. | Rise | | Transit | | Set | |
|---|---|---|---|---|---|---|---|---|---|---|---|
| | h | m | ° | | ″ | h | m | h | m | h | m |
| 1 | 1 | 20.1 | +7.8 | +6.2 | 3 | 3 | 55 | 10 | 41 | 17 | 27 |
| 11 | 1 | 22.1 | +8.0 | +6.2 | 3 | 3 | 16 | 10 | 04 | 16 | 51 |
| 21 | 1 | 23.9 | +8.2 | +6.2 | 3 | 2 | 38 | 9 | 26 | 16 | 15 |
| 31 | 1 | 25.7 | +8.4 | +6.2 | 3 | 1 | 59 | 8 | 49 | 15 | 38 |

## NEPTUNE

| Day | R.A. | | Dec | Mag. | Diam. | Rise | | Transit | | Set | |
|---|---|---|---|---|---|---|---|---|---|---|---|
| | h | m | ° | | ″ | h | m | h | m | h | m |
| 1 | 22 | 52.2 | −8.1 | +7.9 | 2 | 2 | 55 | 8 | 13 | 13 | 32 |
| 11 | 22 | 53.0 | −8.0 | +7.9 | 2 | 2 | 16 | 7 | 35 | 12 | 53 |
| 21 | 22 | 53.6 | −8.0 | +7.9 | 2 | 1 | 37 | 6 | 56 | 12 | 15 |
| 31 | 22 | 54.0 | −7.9 | +7.9 | 2 | 0 | 58 | 6 | 17 | 11 | 36 |

# JUNE 2016

SIXTH MONTH, 30 DAYS. *Junius*, Roman *gens* (family)

| | | | |
|---|---|---|---|
| 1 | Wednesday | End of the 'Cod War' between Britain and Iceland over fishing rights in the Atlantic 1976 | day 153 |
| 2 | Thursday | As a display of resistance to German nationalism the first Prague Slavic Congress begins 1848 | 154 |
| 3 | Friday | Ayatollah Khomeini, first leader of Iran after the 1979 revolution which ousted the Shah *d.* 1989 | 155 |
| 4 | Saturday | Suffragette Emily Davidson steps in front of King George V's horse and is killed 1913 | 156 |
| 5 | Sunday | Ronald Reagan, 40th US president who was an actor before moving into politics *d.* 2004 | 157 |
| 6 | Monday | The UK votes to stay in the European Economic Community in the 1975 referendum | week 23 day 158 |
| 7 | Tuesday | The Norwegian parliament dissolves the union between Norway and Sweden 1905 | 159 |
| 8 | Wednesday | Conservative MP Jonathan Aitken is sentenced to 18 months in prison for perjury 1999 | 160 |
| 9 | Thursday | Roman Emperor Nero commits suicide, ending the Julio-Claudian dynasty AD 68 | 161 |
| 10 | Friday | Alexander the Great, creator of one of the largest empires in the ancient world *d.* 323 BC | 162 |
| 11 | Saturday | Margaret Thatcher wins her third consecutive term as prime minister 1987 | 163 |
| 12 | Sunday | Nelson Mandela is sentenced to life imprisonment 1964 | 164 |
| 13 | Monday | Charles the Fat, great-grandson of Charlemagne and the last Carolingian Emperor *b.* AD 839 | week 24 day 165 |
| 14 | Tuesday | Che Guevara, Argentine Marxist revolutionary, key figure in the Cuban Revolution *b.* 1928 | 166 |
| 15 | Wednesday | The Magna Carta is signed by King John (Lackland) at Runnymede 1215 | 167 |
| 16 | Thursday | Enoch Powell, Conservative MP known for his 'Rivers of Blood' speech *b.* 1912 | 168 |
| 17 | Friday | An IRA bomb explodes at the Houses of Parliament, injuring 11 people 1974 | 169 |
| 18 | Saturday | The 1970 general election allows people to vote from the age of 18 for the first time | 170 |
| 19 | Sunday | King James I of England and VI of Scotland, who united the two crowns in one person *b.* 1566 | 171 |
| 20 | Monday | The 1st Duke of Monmouth leads the Monmouth Rebellion against James II 1685 | week 25 day 172 |
| 21 | Tuesday | Niccolò Machiavelli, author of *The Prince,* from who the word 'Machiavellanism' originates *d.* 1527 | 173 |
| 22 | Wednesday | Former Liberal Party leader Jeremy Thorpe is cleared of attempted murder 1979 | 174 |
| 23 | Thursday | Two British spies, Guy Burgess and Donald Maclean, defect to the USSR 1951 | 175 |
| 24 | Friday | Grover Cleveland, the only US president to serve two non-consecutive terms *d.* 1908 | 176 |
| 25 | Saturday | The House of Lords, persuaded by the Duke of Wellington, abolishes the Corn Laws 1846 | 177 |
| 26 | Sunday | John F. Kennedy delivers his 'Ich bin ein Berliner' speech to West German citizens 1963 | 178 |
| 27 | Monday | The UN court of justice rules that US support of the Contras in Nicaragua is unlawful 1986 | week 26 day 179 |
| 28 | Tuesday | Archduke Franz Ferdinand of Austria is assassinated by Gavrilo Princip in Sarajevo 1914 | 180 |
| 29 | Wednesday | Isabel Peron, third wife of Juan Peron, is sworn in as interim president of Argentina 1964 | 181 |
| 30 | Thursday | Montezuma II, the last emperor of the Aztecs *d.* 1520 | 182 |

## ASTRONOMICAL PHENOMENA

| d | h | |
|---|---|---|
| 1 | 14 | Uranus 2° North of the Moon |
| 3 | 10 | Mercury 1° North of the Moon |
| 3 | 07 | Saturn at opposition |
| 5 | 09 | Mercury Greatest elongation West |
| 5 | 01 | Venus 5° North of the Moon |
| 11 | 20 | Jupiter 1° North of the Moon |
| 19 | 00 | Saturn 3° South of the Moon |
| 20 | 23 | Solstice |
| 28 | 23 | Uranus 3° North of the Moon |

## MINIMA OF ALGOL

| d | h | d | h | d | h |
|---|---|---|---|---|---|
| 1 | 11.4 | 12 | 22.7 | 24 | 09.9 |
| 4 | 08.2 | 15 | 19.5 | 27 | 06.8 |
| 7 | 05.1 | 18 | 16.3 | 30 | 03.6 |
| 10 | 01.9 | 21 | 13.1 | | |

## CONSTELLATIONS

The following constellations are near the meridian at

| | d | h | | d | h |
|---|---|---|---|---|---|
| May | 1 | 24 | June | 15 | 21 |
| May | 16 | 23 | July | 1 | 20 |
| June | 1 | 22 | July | 16 | 19 |

Cassiopeia (below the Pole), Ursa Minor, Draco, Ursa Major, Canes Venatici, Bootes, Corona, Serpens, Virgo and Libra

## THE MOON

| Phases, Apsides and Node | | d | h | m |
|---|---|---|---|---|
| ● | New Moon | 5 | 03 | 00 |
| ◑ | First Quarter | 12 | 08 | 10 |
| ○ | Full Moon | 20 | 11 | 02 |
| ◐ | Last Quarter | 27 | 18 | 19 |
| | Perigee (361,140km) | 3 | 10 | 55 |
| | Apogee (405,024km) | 15 | 12 | 01 |

Mean longitude of ascending node on 1st, 168°

# THE SUN

Diam. 31.5″

| Day | Right Ascension h | m | s | Dec. + ° | Equation of time m | s | Rise 52° h | m | Rise 56° h | m | Transit h | m | Set 52° h | m | Set 56° h | m | Sidereal time h | m | s | Transit of first point of Aries h | m | s |
|---|---|---|---|---|---|---|---|---|---|---|---|---|---|---|---|---|---|---|---|---|---|---|
| 1 | 4 | 37 | 18 | 22.1 | +2 | 10 | 3 | 47 | 3 | 24 | 11 | 58 | 20 | 09 | 20 | 33 | 15 | 39 | 28 | 7 | 20 | 22 |
| 2 | 4 | 41 | 24 | 22.2 | +2 | 01 | 3 | 46 | 3 | 23 | 11 | 58 | 20 | 10 | 20 | 34 | 15 | 43 | 25 | 7 | 16 | 25 |
| 3 | 4 | 45 | 30 | 22.3 | +1 | 51 | 3 | 45 | 3 | 22 | 11 | 58 | 20 | 11 | 20 | 35 | 15 | 47 | 22 | 7 | 12 | 29 |
| 4 | 4 | 49 | 37 | 22.5 | +1 | 41 | 3 | 45 | 3 | 21 | 11 | 58 | 20 | 12 | 20 | 36 | 15 | 51 | 18 | 7 | 08 | 32 |
| 5 | 4 | 53 | 44 | 22.6 | +1 | 30 | 3 | 44 | 3 | 20 | 11 | 58 | 20 | 13 | 20 | 38 | 15 | 55 | 15 | 7 | 04 | 36 |
| 6 | 4 | 57 | 52 | 22.7 | +1 | 19 | 3 | 43 | 3 | 19 | 11 | 59 | 20 | 14 | 20 | 39 | 15 | 59 | 11 | 7 | 00 | 39 |
| 7 | 5 | 01 | 59 | 22.8 | +1 | 08 | 3 | 43 | 3 | 18 | 11 | 59 | 20 | 15 | 20 | 40 | 16 | 03 | 08 | 6 | 56 | 42 |
| 8 | 5 | 06 | 07 | 22.9 | +0 | 57 | 3 | 42 | 3 | 18 | 11 | 59 | 20 | 16 | 20 | 41 | 16 | 07 | 04 | 6 | 52 | 46 |
| 9 | 5 | 10 | 16 | 22.9 | +0 | 45 | 3 | 42 | 3 | 17 | 11 | 59 | 20 | 17 | 20 | 42 | 16 | 11 | 01 | 6 | 48 | 49 |
| 10 | 5 | 14 | 24 | 23.0 | +0 | 33 | 3 | 42 | 3 | 16 | 11 | 59 | 20 | 18 | 20 | 43 | 16 | 14 | 57 | 6 | 44 | 53 |
| 11 | 5 | 18 | 33 | 23.1 | +0 | 21 | 3 | 41 | 3 | 16 | 12 | 00 | 20 | 18 | 20 | 44 | 16 | 18 | 54 | 6 | 40 | 56 |
| 12 | 5 | 22 | 42 | 23.2 | +0 | 09 | 3 | 41 | 3 | 16 | 12 | 00 | 20 | 19 | 20 | 44 | 16 | 22 | 51 | 6 | 37 | 00 |
| 13 | 5 | 26 | 51 | 23.2 | −0 | 04 | 3 | 41 | 3 | 15 | 12 | 00 | 20 | 20 | 20 | 45 | 16 | 26 | 47 | 6 | 33 | 03 |
| 14 | 5 | 31 | 00 | 23.3 | −0 | 17 | 3 | 40 | 3 | 15 | 12 | 00 | 20 | 20 | 20 | 46 | 16 | 30 | 44 | 6 | 29 | 07 |
| 15 | 5 | 35 | 09 | 23.3 | −0 | 29 | 3 | 40 | 3 | 15 | 12 | 00 | 20 | 21 | 20 | 46 | 16 | 34 | 40 | 6 | 25 | 10 |
| 16 | 5 | 39 | 19 | 23.4 | −0 | 42 | 3 | 40 | 3 | 14 | 12 | 01 | 20 | 21 | 20 | 47 | 16 | 38 | 37 | 6 | 21 | 13 |
| 17 | 5 | 43 | 28 | 23.4 | −0 | 55 | 3 | 40 | 3 | 14 | 12 | 01 | 20 | 22 | 20 | 47 | 16 | 42 | 33 | 6 | 17 | 17 |
| 18 | 5 | 47 | 37 | 23.4 | −1 | 08 | 3 | 40 | 3 | 14 | 12 | 01 | 20 | 22 | 20 | 48 | 16 | 46 | 30 | 6 | 13 | 20 |
| 19 | 5 | 51 | 47 | 23.4 | −1 | 21 | 3 | 40 | 3 | 14 | 12 | 01 | 20 | 22 | 20 | 48 | 16 | 50 | 26 | 6 | 09 | 24 |
| 20 | 5 | 55 | 57 | 23.4 | −1 | 34 | 3 | 40 | 3 | 14 | 12 | 01 | 20 | 23 | 20 | 49 | 16 | 54 | 23 | 6 | 05 | 27 |
| 21 | 6 | 00 | 06 | 23.4 | −1 | 47 | 3 | 40 | 3 | 15 | 12 | 02 | 20 | 23 | 20 | 49 | 16 | 58 | 20 | 6 | 01 | 31 |
| 22 | 6 | 04 | 16 | 23.4 | −2 | 00 | 3 | 41 | 3 | 15 | 12 | 02 | 20 | 23 | 20 | 49 | 17 | 02 | 16 | 5 | 57 | 34 |
| 23 | 6 | 08 | 25 | 23.4 | −2 | 13 | 3 | 41 | 3 | 15 | 12 | 02 | 20 | 23 | 20 | 49 | 17 | 06 | 13 | 5 | 53 | 38 |
| 24 | 6 | 12 | 34 | 23.4 | −2 | 25 | 3 | 41 | 3 | 15 | 12 | 02 | 20 | 23 | 20 | 49 | 17 | 10 | 09 | 5 | 49 | 41 |
| 25 | 6 | 16 | 44 | 23.4 | −2 | 38 | 3 | 42 | 3 | 16 | 12 | 03 | 20 | 23 | 20 | 49 | 17 | 14 | 06 | 5 | 45 | 44 |
| 26 | 6 | 20 | 53 | 23.4 | −2 | 51 | 3 | 42 | 3 | 16 | 12 | 03 | 20 | 23 | 20 | 49 | 17 | 18 | 02 | 5 | 41 | 48 |
| 27 | 6 | 25 | 02 | 23.3 | −3 | 03 | 3 | 42 | 3 | 17 | 12 | 03 | 20 | 23 | 20 | 49 | 17 | 21 | 59 | 5 | 37 | 51 |
| 28 | 6 | 29 | 11 | 23.3 | −3 | 16 | 3 | 43 | 3 | 17 | 12 | 03 | 20 | 23 | 20 | 49 | 17 | 25 | 55 | 5 | 33 | 55 |
| 29 | 6 | 33 | 19 | 23.2 | −3 | 28 | 3 | 43 | 3 | 18 | 12 | 03 | 20 | 23 | 20 | 49 | 17 | 29 | 52 | 5 | 29 | 58 |
| 30 | 6 | 37 | 28 | 23.2 | −3 | 40 | 3 | 44 | 3 | 19 | 12 | 04 | 20 | 23 | 20 | 48 | 17 | 33 | 49 | 5 | 26 | 02 |

## DURATION OF TWILIGHT (in minutes)

| Latitude | 52° | 56° | 52° | 56° | 52° | 56° | 52° | 56° |
|---|---|---|---|---|---|---|---|---|
| | 1 June | | 11 June | | 21 June | | 31 June | |
| Civil | 46 | 58 | 48 | 61 | 49 | 63 | 48 | 61 |
| Nautical | 116 | TAN | 124 | TAN | 127 | TAN | 124 | TAN |
| Astronomical | TAN | TAN | TAN | TAN | TAN | TAN | TAN | TAN |

## THE NIGHT SKY

*Mercury* is a morning sky object but is not well placed for observation this month. It reaches greatest elongation west (24°) on June 5th.

*Venus* is at superior conjunction on June 6th and then moves into the evening sky. However, it is still that bit too close to the solar glare to be seen at any stage this month.

*Mars* is low in the south-east in Libra these evenings. The planet is stationary on the 30th after which its direct motion resumes. Mars very slowly fades from magnitude −2.0 to −1.4 during June but still far outshines the stars in this region of sky.

*Jupiter* is in the south-west after sunset and now starts its slow slide towards the Sun over the next few months. It sets before midnight by the end of June and also fades a little to magnitude −1.9 in this time. The Moon is close to Jupiter on the 11th.

*Saturn* reaches opposition on June 3rd in Ophiuchus when at magnitude 0.0. Telescope users will see the planet's disk just over 18 arc-seconds in diameter and the rings tipped more than 26° earthward. Saturn can be found just below the Full Moon during the brief hours of darkness on June 18th.

# THE MOON

| Day | R.A. | | Dec. | Hor. Par. | Diam. | Sun's Co-Long. | PA of Br. Limb | Ph. | Age | Rise 52° | | Rise 56° | | Transit | | Set 52° | | Set 56° | |
|---|---|---|---|---|---|---|---|---|---|---|---|---|---|---|---|---|---|---|---|
| | h | m | ° | ′ | ′ | ° | ° | % | d | h | m | h | m | h | m | h | m | h | m |
| 1 | 0 | 51 | +3.2 | 60.0 | 32.7 | 216 | 66 | 23 | 25.0 | 1 | 31 | 1 | 32 | 7 | 39 | 14 | 00 | 14 | 02 |
| 2 | 1 | 47 | +7.6 | 60.4 | 32.9 | 228 | 66 | 14 | 26.0 | 1 | 59 | 1 | 56 | 8 | 32 | 15 | 20 | 15 | 25 |
| 3 | 2 | 45 | +11.7 | 60.7 | 33.1 | 240 | 66 | 7 | 27.0 | 2 | 29 | 2 | 22 | 9 | 27 | 16 | 40 | 16 | 49 |
| 4 | 3 | 45 | +15.0 | 60.7 | 33.1 | 253 | 62 | 2 | 28.0 | 3 | 02 | 2 | 51 | 10 | 24 | 17 | 59 | 18 | 13 |
| 5 | 4 | 46 | +17.3 | 60.4 | 32.9 | 265 | 18 | 0 | 29.0 | 3 | 41 | 3 | 26 | 11 | 23 | 19 | 15 | 19 | 32 |
| 6 | 5 | 48 | +18.5 | 59.9 | 32.6 | 277 | 292 | 1 | 0.5 | 4 | 27 | 4 | 10 | 12 | 23 | 20 | 24 | 20 | 42 |
| 7 | 6 | 49 | +18.4 | 59.2 | 32.2 | 289 | 285 | 5 | 1.5 | 5 | 21 | 5 | 04 | 13 | 23 | 21 | 24 | 21 | 42 |
| 8 | 7 | 47 | +17.2 | 58.3 | 31.8 | 302 | 285 | 11 | 2.5 | 6 | 23 | 6 | 05 | 14 | 21 | 22 | 12 | 22 | 29 |
| 9 | 8 | 43 | +15.0 | 57.4 | 31.3 | 314 | 288 | 18 | 3.5 | 7 | 29 | 7 | 13 | 15 | 15 | 22 | 52 | 23 | 06 |
| 10 | 9 | 35 | +12.1 | 56.6 | 30.8 | 326 | 290 | 27 | 4.5 | 8 | 37 | 8 | 24 | 16 | 07 | 23 | 25 | 23 | 36 |
| 11 | 10 | 25 | +8.8 | 55.8 | 30.4 | 338 | 292 | 37 | 5.5 | 9 | 45 | 9 | 35 | 16 | 55 | 23 | 53 | 0 | 00 |
| 12 | 11 | 13 | +5.1 | 55.1 | 30.0 | 351 | 293 | 46 | 6.5 | 10 | 52 | 10 | 46 | 17 | 40 | — | | — | |
| 13 | 11 | 59 | +1.3 | 54.6 | 29.8 | 3 | 294 | 56 | 7.5 | 11 | 57 | 11 | 54 | 18 | 24 | 0 | 18 | 0 | 22 |
| 14 | 12 | 44 | −2.5 | 54.3 | 29.6 | 15 | 294 | 65 | 8.5 | 13 | 01 | 13 | 02 | 19 | 07 | 0 | 40 | 0 | 41 |
| 15 | 13 | 29 | −6.2 | 54.2 | 29.5 | 27 | 293 | 74 | 9.5 | 14 | 04 | 14 | 08 | 19 | 49 | 1 | 03 | 1 | 00 |
| 16 | 14 | 15 | −9.6 | 54.2 | 29.5 | 39 | 292 | 82 | 10.5 | 15 | 07 | 15 | 14 | 20 | 32 | 1 | 25 | 1 | 20 |
| 17 | 15 | 02 | −12.6 | 54.3 | 29.6 | 52 | 292 | 89 | 11.5 | 16 | 09 | 16 | 20 | 21 | 16 | 1 | 49 | 1 | 41 |
| 18 | 15 | 50 | −15.2 | 54.5 | 29.7 | 64 | 291 | 94 | 12.5 | 17 | 11 | 17 | 25 | 22 | 02 | 2 | 16 | 2 | 05 |
| 19 | 16 | 40 | −17.1 | 54.9 | 29.9 | 76 | 294 | 98 | 13.5 | 18 | 12 | 18 | 28 | 22 | 49 | 2 | 47 | 2 | 32 |
| 20 | 17 | 32 | −18.3 | 55.3 | 30.1 | 88 | 313 | 100 | 14.5 | 19 | 09 | 19 | 28 | 23 | 39 | 3 | 23 | 3 | 07 |
| 21 | 18 | 24 | −18.6 | 55.7 | 30.4 | 100 | 49 | 100 | 15.5 | 20 | 02 | 20 | 22 | — | | 4 | 06 | 3 | 48 |
| 22 | 19 | 18 | −18.0 | 56.2 | 30.6 | 113 | 69 | 98 | 16.5 | 20 | 50 | 21 | 08 | 0 | 29 | 4 | 57 | 4 | 37 |
| 23 | 20 | 12 | −16.4 | 56.7 | 30.9 | 125 | 71 | 94 | 17.5 | 21 | 33 | 21 | 48 | 1 | 21 | 5 | 54 | 5 | 36 |
| 24 | 21 | 06 | −14.0 | 57.2 | 31.2 | 137 | 70 | 87 | 18.5 | 22 | 09 | 22 | 22 | 2 | 12 | 6 | 58 | 6 | 42 |
| 25 | 21 | 59 | −10.7 | 57.7 | 31.5 | 149 | 69 | 79 | 19.5 | 22 | 41 | 22 | 50 | 3 | 04 | 8 | 06 | 7 | 54 |
| 26 | 22 | 51 | −6.9 | 58.2 | 31.7 | 161 | 68 | 70 | 20.5 | 23 | 10 | 23 | 15 | 3 | 55 | 9 | 18 | 9 | 10 |
| 27 | 23 | 44 | −2.7 | 58.7 | 32.0 | 174 | 67 | 59 | 21.5 | 23 | 37 | 23 | 39 | 4 | 45 | 10 | 31 | 10 | 27 |
| 28 | 0 | 37 | +1.8 | 59.1 | 32.2 | 186 | 67 | 48 | 22.5 | — | | — | | 5 | 36 | 11 | 46 | 11 | 46 |
| 29 | 1 | 31 | +6.2 | 59.5 | 32.4 | 198 | 68 | 36 | 23.5 | 0 | 03 | 0 | 02 | 6 | 27 | 13 | 03 | 13 | 07 |
| 30 | 2 | 27 | +10.3 | 59.8 | 32.6 | 210 | 69 | 26 | 24.5 | 0 | 31 | 0 | 26 | 7 | 19 | 14 | 21 | 14 | 29 |

## MERCURY

| Day | R.A. | | Dec | Mag. | Diam. | Phase | Rise | | Transit | | Set | |
|---|---|---|---|---|---|---|---|---|---|---|---|---|
| | h | m | ° | | ″ | % | h | m | h | m | h | m |
| 1 | 3 | 04.0 | +13.4 | +1.0 | 9 | 29 | 3 | 03 | 10 | 22 | 17 | 40 |
| 3 | 3 | 09.8 | +13.9 | +0.8 | 9 | 33 | 2 | 58 | 10 | 20 | 17 | 42 |
| 5 | 3 | 16.5 | +14.4 | +0.6 | 8 | 37 | 2 | 53 | 10 | 19 | 17 | 45 |
| 7 | 3 | 24.2 | +15.1 | +0.4 | 8 | 41 | 2 | 49 | 10 | 19 | 17 | 50 |
| 9 | 3 | 32.8 | +15.8 | +0.3 | 8 | 45 | 2 | 45 | 10 | 20 | 17 | 56 |
| 11 | 3 | 42.3 | +16.6 | +0.1 | 7 | 49 | 2 | 42 | 10 | 22 | 18 | 04 |
| 13 | 3 | 52.7 | +17.4 | 0.0 | 7 | 53 | 2 | 39 | 10 | 25 | 18 | 12 |
| 15 | 4 | 04.0 | +18.3 | −0.2 | 7 | 58 | 2 | 36 | 10 | 29 | 18 | 22 |
| 17 | 4 | 16.3 | +19.2 | −0.3 | 6 | 63 | 2 | 34 | 10 | 33 | 18 | 33 |
| 19 | 4 | 29.5 | +20.1 | −0.5 | 6 | 68 | 2 | 34 | 10 | 39 | 18 | 46 |
| 21 | 4 | 43.7 | +20.9 | −0.7 | 6 | 73 | 2 | 34 | 10 | 45 | 18 | 59 |
| 23 | 4 | 58.9 | +21.7 | −0.8 | 6 | 78 | 2 | 35 | 10 | 53 | 19 | 12 |
| 25 | 5 | 15.0 | +22.4 | −1.0 | 6 | 83 | 2 | 38 | 11 | 01 | 19 | 26 |
| 27 | 5 | 32.0 | +23.1 | −1.2 | 5 | 87 | 2 | 42 | 11 | 11 | 19 | 41 |
| 29 | 5 | 49.7 | +23.6 | −1.4 | 5 | 92 | 2 | 48 | 11 | 21 | 19 | 55 |

Rising and setting times are for latitude 54°

## VENUS

| Day | R.A. | | Dec | Mag. | Diam. | Phase | Rise | | Transit | | Set | |
|---|---|---|---|---|---|---|---|---|---|---|---|---|
| | h | m | ° | | ″ | % | h | m | h | m | h | m |
| 1 | 4 | 29.6 | +21.6 | −3.9 | 10 | 100 | 3 | 33 | 11 | 50 | 20 | 06 |
| 6 | 4 | 55.8 | +22.6 | −3.9 | 10 | 100 | 3 | 32 | 11 | 56 | 20 | 20 |
| 11 | 5 | 22.3 | +23.3 | −3.9 | 10 | 100 | 3 | 33 | 12 | 03 | 20 | 33 |
| 16 | 5 | 49.0 | +23.8 | −3.9 | 10 | 100 | 3 | 37 | 12 | 10 | 20 | 43 |
| 21 | 6 | 15.9 | +23.9 | −3.9 | 10 | 100 | 3 | 43 | 12 | 17 | 20 | 52 |
| 26 | 6 | 42.8 | +23.8 | −3.9 | 10 | 100 | 3 | 51 | 12 | 24 | 20 | 57 |

## MARS

| Day | R.A. | | Dec | Mag. | Diam. | Phase | Rise | | Transit | | Set | |
|---|---|---|---|---|---|---|---|---|---|---|---|---|
| | h | m | ° | | ″ | % | h | m | h | m | h | m |
| 1 | 15 | 42.5 | −21.4 | −2.0 | 19 | 99 | 19 | 12 | 23 | 06 | 2 | 58 |
| 6 | 15 | 35.6 | −21.2 | −1.9 | 18 | 99 | 18 | 45 | 22 | 39 | 2 | 32 |
| 11 | 15 | 29.6 | −21.1 | −1.8 | 18 | 98 | 18 | 18 | 22 | 13 | 2 | 08 |
| 16 | 15 | 24.9 | −21.0 | −1.7 | 18 | 97 | 17 | 52 | 21 | 48 | 1 | 44 |
| 21 | 15 | 21.4 | −20.9 | −1.6 | 17 | 96 | 17 | 28 | 21 | 25 | 1 | 21 |
| 26 | 15 | 19.4 | −20.9 | −1.5 | 17 | 94 | 17 | 06 | 21 | 03 | 0 | 59 |

# SUNRISE AND SUNSET

| | London 0° 05' | 51° 30' | Bristol 2° 35' | 51° 28' | Birmingham 1° 55' | 52° 28' | Manchester 2° 15' | 53° 28' | Newcastle 1° 37' | 54° 59' | Glasgow 4° 14' | 55° 52' | Belfast 5° 56' | 54° 35' |
|---|---|---|---|---|---|---|---|---|---|---|---|---|---|---|
| d | h m | h m | h m | h m | h m | h m | h m | h m | h m | h m | h m | h m | h m | h m |
| 1 | 3 49 | 20 08 | 3 59 | 20 18 | 3 51 | 20 21 | 3 47 | 20 28 | 3 35 | 20 35 | 3 40 | 20 51 | 3 55 | 20 49 |
| 2 | 3 48 | 20 09 | 3 58 | 20 19 | 3 50 | 20 22 | 3 46 | 20 29 | 3 34 | 20 36 | 3 39 | 20 52 | 3 54 | 20 51 |
| 3 | 3 47 | 20 10 | 3 57 | 20 20 | 3 49 | 20 23 | 3 45 | 20 30 | 3 33 | 20 37 | 3 38 | 20 53 | 3 53 | 20 52 |
| 4 | 3 47 | 20 11 | 3 57 | 20 21 | 3 49 | 20 24 | 3 44 | 20 31 | 3 32 | 20 38 | 3 37 | 20 55 | 3 52 | 20 53 |
| 5 | 3 46 | 20 12 | 3 56 | 20 22 | 3 48 | 20 25 | 3 44 | 20 32 | 3 31 | 20 39 | 3 36 | 20 56 | 3 51 | 20 54 |
| 6 | 3 45 | 20 13 | 3 56 | 20 23 | 3 47 | 20 26 | 3 43 | 20 33 | 3 31 | 20 40 | 3 35 | 20 57 | 3 51 | 20 55 |
| 7 | 3 45 | 20 14 | 3 55 | 20 24 | 3 47 | 20 27 | 3 42 | 20 34 | 3 30 | 20 41 | 3 34 | 20 58 | 3 50 | 20 56 |
| 8 | 3 44 | 20 15 | 3 55 | 20 25 | 3 46 | 20 28 | 3 42 | 20 35 | 3 30 | 20 42 | 3 34 | 20 59 | 3 49 | 20 57 |
| 9 | 3 44 | 20 16 | 3 54 | 20 26 | 3 46 | 20 28 | 3 41 | 20 36 | 3 29 | 20 43 | 3 33 | 21 00 | 3 49 | 20 58 |
| 10 | 3 44 | 20 16 | 3 54 | 20 26 | 3 46 | 20 29 | 3 41 | 20 37 | 3 28 | 20 44 | 3 33 | 21 01 | 3 48 | 20 59 |
| 11 | 3 43 | 20 17 | 3 54 | 20 27 | 3 45 | 20 30 | 3 41 | 20 37 | 3 28 | 20 45 | 3 32 | 21 02 | 3 48 | 20 59 |
| 12 | 3 43 | 20 18 | 3 53 | 20 28 | 3 45 | 20 31 | 3 40 | 20 38 | 3 28 | 20 45 | 3 32 | 21 02 | 3 48 | 21 00 |
| 13 | 3 43 | 20 18 | 3 53 | 20 28 | 3 45 | 20 31 | 3 40 | 20 39 | 3 27 | 20 46 | 3 32 | 21 03 | 3 47 | 21 01 |
| 14 | 3 43 | 20 19 | 3 53 | 20 29 | 3 45 | 20 32 | 3 40 | 20 39 | 3 27 | 20 47 | 3 31 | 21 04 | 3 47 | 21 01 |
| 15 | 3 43 | 20 19 | 3 53 | 20 29 | 3 44 | 20 32 | 3 40 | 20 40 | 3 27 | 20 47 | 3 31 | 21 04 | 3 47 | 21 02 |
| 16 | 3 43 | 20 20 | 3 53 | 20 30 | 3 44 | 20 33 | 3 40 | 20 40 | 3 27 | 20 48 | 3 31 | 21 05 | 3 47 | 21 02 |
| 17 | 3 43 | 20 20 | 3 53 | 20 30 | 3 44 | 20 33 | 3 40 | 20 41 | 3 27 | 20 48 | 3 31 | 21 05 | 3 47 | 21 03 |
| 18 | 3 43 | 20 21 | 3 53 | 20 30 | 3 44 | 20 33 | 3 40 | 20 41 | 3 27 | 20 49 | 3 31 | 21 06 | 3 47 | 21 03 |
| 19 | 3 43 | 20 21 | 3 53 | 20 31 | 3 44 | 20 34 | 3 40 | 20 41 | 3 27 | 20 49 | 3 31 | 21 06 | 3 47 | 21 03 |
| 20 | 3 43 | 20 21 | 3 53 | 20 31 | 3 45 | 20 34 | 3 40 | 20 42 | 3 27 | 20 49 | 3 31 | 21 06 | 3 47 | 21 04 |
| 21 | 3 43 | 20 21 | 3 53 | 20 31 | 3 45 | 20 34 | 3 40 | 20 42 | 3 27 | 20 49 | 3 31 | 21 06 | 3 47 | 21 04 |
| 22 | 3 43 | 20 21 | 3 54 | 20 31 | 3 45 | 20 34 | 3 40 | 20 42 | 3 28 | 20 50 | 3 32 | 21 06 | 3 48 | 21 04 |
| 23 | 3 44 | 20 22 | 3 54 | 20 31 | 3 45 | 20 34 | 3 41 | 20 42 | 3 28 | 20 50 | 3 32 | 21 07 | 3 48 | 21 04 |
| 24 | 3 44 | 20 22 | 3 54 | 20 31 | 3 46 | 20 34 | 3 41 | 20 42 | 3 28 | 20 50 | 3 32 | 21 07 | 3 49 | 21 04 |
| 25 | 3 44 | 20 22 | 3 55 | 20 31 | 3 46 | 20 34 | 3 41 | 20 42 | 3 29 | 20 50 | 3 33 | 21 06 | 3 49 | 21 04 |
| 26 | 3 45 | 20 22 | 3 55 | 20 31 | 3 47 | 20 34 | 3 42 | 20 42 | 3 29 | 20 49 | 3 33 | 21 06 | 3 49 | 21 04 |
| 27 | 3 45 | 20 21 | 3 56 | 20 31 | 3 47 | 20 34 | 3 42 | 20 42 | 3 30 | 20 49 | 3 34 | 21 06 | 3 50 | 21 04 |
| 28 | 3 46 | 20 21 | 3 56 | 20 31 | 3 48 | 20 34 | 3 43 | 20 41 | 3 30 | 20 49 | 3 34 | 21 06 | 3 50 | 21 03 |
| 29 | 3 46 | 20 21 | 3 57 | 20 31 | 3 48 | 20 34 | 3 44 | 20 41 | 3 31 | 20 49 | 3 35 | 21 05 | 3 51 | 21 03 |
| 30 | 3 47 | 20 21 | 3 57 | 20 31 | 3 49 | 20 34 | 3 44 | 20 41 | 3 32 | 20 48 | 3 36 | 21 05 | 3 52 | 21 03 |

## JUPITER

| Day | R.A. h m | Dec ° | Mag. | Diam. " | Rise h m | Transit h m | Set h m |
|---|---|---|---|---|---|---|---|
| 1 | 11 02.2 | +7.6 | −2.1 | 37 | 11 35 | 18 20 | 1 09 |
| 11 | 11 05.1 | +7.2 | −2.0 | 36 | 11 00 | 17 43 | 0 30 |
| 21 | 11 08.9 | +6.8 | −1.9 | 35 | 10 27 | 17 08 | 23 48 |

Equatorial Diam. 36", Polar Diam. 33"

## SATURN

| Day | R.A. h m | Dec ° | Mag. | Diam. " | Rise h m | Transit h m | Set h m |
|---|---|---|---|---|---|---|---|
| 1 | 16 47.5 | −20.6 | 0.0 | 18 | 20 04 | 0 08 | 4 08 |
| 11 | 16 44.3 | −20.5 | 0.0 | 18 | 19 21 | 23 22 | 3 26 |
| 21 | 16 41.3 | −20.4 | +0.1 | 18 | 18 38 | 22 39 | 2 44 |

Equatorial Diam. 18", Polar Diam. 17"
Rings – major axis 42" minor axis 18", Tilt 26°

## URANUS

| Day | R.A. h m | Dec ° | Mag. | Diam. " | Rise h m | Transit h m | Set h m |
|---|---|---|---|---|---|---|---|
| 1 | 1 25.8 | +8.4 | +6.2 | 3 | 1 55 | 8 45 | 15 34 |
| 11 | 1 27.3 | +8.5 | +6.2 | 3 | 1 16 | 8 07 | 14 57 |
| 21 | 1 28.6 | +8.6 | +6.2 | 3 | 0 38 | 7 29 | 14 20 |

## NEPTUNE

| Day | R.A. h m | Dec ° | Mag. | Diam. " | Rise h m | Transit h m | Set h m |
|---|---|---|---|---|---|---|---|
| 1 | 22 54.0 | −7.9 | +7.9 | 2 | 0 54 | 6 13 | 11 32 |
| 11 | 22 54.2 | −7.9 | +7.9 | 2 | 0 15 | 5 34 | 10 53 |
| 21 | 22 54.1 | −7.9 | +7.9 | 2 | 23 32 | 4 55 | 10 14 |

# JULY 2016

SEVENTH MONTH, 31 DAYS. *Julius* Caesar, formerly *Quintilis*, fifth month of Roman pre-Julian calendar

| 1 | Friday | Hong Kong is returned to China, ending 156 years of British colonial governance 1997 | day 183 |
|---|--------|-----|-----|
| 2 | Saturday | President Johnson signs the Civil Rights Act in a televised ceremony at the White House 1964 | 184 |
| 3 | Sunday | Louis XI (the Prudent) who was King of France (1461–83) *b.* 1423 | 185 |

| 4 | Monday | William Petty becomes the first Irish-born prime minister of the UK 1782 | week 27 day 186 |
|---|--------|-----|-----|
| 5 | Tuesday | Clement Attlee's Labour Party wins the general election two months after VE Day 1945 | 187 |
| 6 | Wednesday | George W. Bush, 43rd US president, who launched the War on Terror *b.* 1946 | 188 |
| 7 | Thursday | Israel begins Operation Protective Edge in the Hamas-controlled Gaza Strip 2014 | 189 |
| 8 | Friday | Kim Jong-il becomes the first 'Supreme Leader' of North Korea 1994 | 190 |
| 9 | Saturday | South Sudan becomes independent of Sudan following a referendum 2011 | 191 |
| 10 | Sunday | The Bahamas gains independence after 325 years of British rule 1973 | 192 |

| 11 | Monday | Robert the Bruce, King of Scots who fought for Scotland's independence *b.* 1274 | week 28 day 193 |
|---|--------|-----|-----|
| 12 | Tuesday | Ranjit Singh founds the Sikh Empire, based in the Punjab region 1799 | 194 |
| 13 | Wednesday | The Congress of Berlin, to determine the territories of the Balkan peninsula states, ends 1878 | 195 |
| 14 | Thursday | Gerald Ford, appointed vice-president and later US president (38th) without election *b.* 1913 | 196 |
| 15 | Friday | Emmeline Pankhurst, suffragette who helped women win the right to vote *b.* 1858 | 197 |
| 16 | Saturday | Richard of Bordeaux is crowned Richard II of England 1377 | 198 |
| 17 | Sunday | The Russian Imperial family of Tsar Nicholas II are executed 1918 | 199 |

| 18 | Monday | The Ballot Act 1872, requiring that elections are held by secret ballot, receives royal assent | week 29 day 200 |
|---|--------|-----|-----|
| 19 | Tuesday | Syngman Rhee, first president of South Korea, in office during the Korean War *d.* 1965 | 201 |
| 20 | Wednesday | Otto John, the head of West Germany's intelligence service, defects to East Germany 1954 | 202 |
| 21 | Thursday | Sirimavo Bandaranaike becomes the first female head of government, in Ceylon 1960 | 203 |
| 22 | Friday | A military coup in Gambia deposes president Dawda Jawara, who is exiled 1994 | 204 |
| 23 | Saturday | The government of Abkhazia declares its independence from Georgia 1992 | 205 |
| 24 | Sunday | French president Charles de Gaulle declares 'Long live free Quebec!' on a visit to Canada 1967 | 206 |

| 25 | Monday | Arthur Balfour, prime minister who succeeded his uncle, Lord Salisbury *b.* 1848 | week 30 day 207 |
|---|--------|-----|-----|
| 26 | Tuesday | The Labour Party wins the 1945 general election, less than two months after VE Day | 208 |
| 27 | Wednesday | The first article of impeachment charging President Nixon with obstruction of justice is approved 1974 | 209 |
| 28 | Thursday | Gen. José de San Martín proclaims Peru independent from Spain after occupying Lima 1821 | 210 |
| 29 | Friday | A constitutional referendum in Greece votes in favour of abolishing the monarchy 1973 | 211 |
| 30 | Saturday | William Penn, Quaker and founder of the Province of Pennsylvania *d.* 1718 | 212 |
| 31 | Sunday | The IRA declares a complete ceasefire after 25 years of armed operations 1994 | 213 |

## ASTRONOMICAL PHENOMENA

| d | h | |
|---|---|---|
| 4 | 16 | Earth at aphelion |
| 9 | 10 | Jupiter 1° North of the Moon |
| 16 | 18 | Venus 0.5° South of Mercury |
| 16 | 05 | Saturn 3° South of the Moon |
| 26 | 04 | Uranus 3° North of the Moon |

## MINIMA OF ALGOL

| d | h | d | h | d | h |
|---|---|---|---|---|---|
| 3 | 00.4 | 14 | 11.6 | 25 | 22.9 |
| 5 | 21.2 | 17 | 08.4 | 28 | 19.7 |
| 8 | 18.0 | 20 | 05.2 | 31 | 16.5 |
| 11 | 14.8 | 23 | 02.1 | | |

## CONSTELLATIONS

The following constellations are near their meridian at

| | d | h | | d | h |
|---|---|---|---|---|---|
| June | 1 | 24 | July | 16 | 21 |
| June | 15 | 23 | August | 1 | 20 |
| July | 1 | 22 | August | 16 | 19 |

Ursa Minor, Draco, Corona, Hercules, Lyra, Serpens, Ophiuchus, Libra, Scorpius and Sagittarius

## THE MOON

| Phases, Apsides and Node | d | h | m |
|---|---|---|---|
| ● New Moon | 4 | 11 | 01 |
| ◐ First Quarter | 12 | 00 | 52 |
| ○ Full Moon | 19 | 22 | 57 |
| ◑ Last Quarter | 26 | 23 | 00 |
| | | | |
| Perigee (365,983km) | 1 | 06 | 40 |
| Apogee (404,269km) | 13 | 05 | 24 |
| Perigee (369,662km) | 27 | 11 | 37 |

Mean longitude of ascending node on 1st, 166°

# THE SUN

Diam. 31.5″

| Day | Right Ascension | | | Dec. + | Equation of time | | Rise 52° | | Rise 56° | | Transit | | Set 52° | | Set 56° | | Sidereal time | | | Transit of first point of Aries | | |
|---|---|---|---|---|---|---|---|---|---|---|---|---|---|---|---|---|---|---|---|---|---|---|
| | h | m | s | ° | m | s | h | m | h | m | h | m | h | m | h | m | h | m | s | h | m | s |
| 1 | 6 | 41 | 36 | 23.1 | −3 | 51 | 3 | 45 | 3 | 19 | 12 | 04 | 20 | 23 | 20 | 48 | 17 | 37 | 45 | 5 | 22 | 05 |
| 2 | 6 | 45 | 44 | 23.0 | −4 | 03 | 3 | 45 | 3 | 20 | 12 | 04 | 20 | 22 | 20 | 47 | 17 | 41 | 42 | 5 | 18 | 09 |
| 3 | 6 | 49 | 52 | 22.9 | −4 | 14 | 3 | 46 | 3 | 21 | 12 | 04 | 20 | 22 | 20 | 47 | 17 | 45 | 38 | 5 | 14 | 12 |
| 4 | 6 | 54 | 00 | 22.9 | −4 | 25 | 3 | 47 | 3 | 22 | 12 | 04 | 20 | 21 | 20 | 46 | 17 | 49 | 35 | 5 | 10 | 15 |
| 5 | 6 | 58 | 07 | 22.8 | −4 | 36 | 3 | 48 | 3 | 23 | 12 | 05 | 20 | 21 | 20 | 46 | 17 | 53 | 31 | 5 | 06 | 19 |
| 6 | 7 | 02 | 14 | 22.7 | −4 | 46 | 3 | 48 | 3 | 24 | 12 | 05 | 20 | 20 | 20 | 45 | 17 | 57 | 28 | 5 | 02 | 22 |
| 7 | 7 | 06 | 20 | 22.6 | −4 | 56 | 3 | 49 | 3 | 25 | 12 | 05 | 20 | 20 | 20 | 44 | 18 | 01 | 24 | 4 | 58 | 26 |
| 8 | 7 | 10 | 26 | 22.5 | −5 | 05 | 3 | 50 | 3 | 26 | 12 | 05 | 20 | 19 | 20 | 43 | 18 | 05 | 21 | 4 | 54 | 29 |
| 9 | 7 | 14 | 32 | 22.3 | −5 | 14 | 3 | 51 | 3 | 27 | 12 | 05 | 20 | 19 | 20 | 43 | 18 | 09 | 18 | 4 | 50 | 33 |
| 10 | 7 | 18 | 37 | 22.2 | −5 | 23 | 3 | 52 | 3 | 28 | 12 | 05 | 20 | 18 | 20 | 42 | 18 | 13 | 14 | 4 | 46 | 36 |
| 11 | 7 | 22 | 42 | 22.1 | −5 | 31 | 3 | 53 | 3 | 29 | 12 | 05 | 20 | 17 | 20 | 41 | 18 | 17 | 11 | 4 | 42 | 40 |
| 12 | 7 | 26 | 46 | 21.9 | −5 | 39 | 3 | 54 | 3 | 31 | 12 | 06 | 20 | 16 | 20 | 40 | 18 | 21 | 07 | 4 | 38 | 43 |
| 13 | 7 | 30 | 50 | 21.8 | −5 | 46 | 3 | 55 | 3 | 32 | 12 | 06 | 20 | 15 | 20 | 39 | 18 | 25 | 04 | 4 | 34 | 46 |
| 14 | 7 | 34 | 53 | 21.6 | −5 | 53 | 3 | 56 | 3 | 33 | 12 | 06 | 20 | 14 | 20 | 37 | 18 | 29 | 00 | 4 | 30 | 50 |
| 15 | 7 | 38 | 56 | 21.5 | −5 | 59 | 3 | 58 | 3 | 35 | 12 | 06 | 20 | 14 | 20 | 36 | 18 | 32 | 57 | 4 | 26 | 53 |
| 16 | 7 | 42 | 58 | 21.3 | −6 | 05 | 3 | 59 | 3 | 36 | 12 | 06 | 20 | 13 | 20 | 35 | 18 | 36 | 53 | 4 | 22 | 57 |
| 17 | 7 | 47 | 00 | 21.2 | −6 | 10 | 4 | 00 | 3 | 38 | 12 | 06 | 20 | 11 | 20 | 34 | 18 | 40 | 50 | 4 | 19 | 00 |
| 18 | 7 | 51 | 01 | 21.0 | −6 | 15 | 4 | 01 | 3 | 39 | 12 | 06 | 20 | 10 | 20 | 32 | 18 | 44 | 47 | 4 | 15 | 04 |
| 19 | 7 | 55 | 02 | 20.8 | −6 | 19 | 4 | 03 | 3 | 41 | 12 | 06 | 20 | 09 | 20 | 31 | 18 | 48 | 43 | 4 | 11 | 07 |
| 20 | 7 | 59 | 02 | 20.6 | −6 | 22 | 4 | 04 | 3 | 42 | 12 | 06 | 20 | 08 | 20 | 29 | 18 | 52 | 40 | 4 | 07 | 11 |
| 21 | 8 | 03 | 01 | 20.4 | −6 | 25 | 4 | 05 | 3 | 44 | 12 | 06 | 20 | 07 | 20 | 28 | 18 | 56 | 36 | 4 | 03 | 14 |
| 22 | 8 | 07 | 00 | 20.2 | −6 | 28 | 4 | 06 | 3 | 45 | 12 | 06 | 20 | 06 | 20 | 26 | 19 | 00 | 33 | 3 | 59 | 17 |
| 23 | 8 | 10 | 59 | 20.0 | −6 | 30 | 4 | 08 | 3 | 47 | 12 | 06 | 20 | 04 | 20 | 25 | 19 | 04 | 29 | 3 | 55 | 21 |
| 24 | 8 | 14 | 57 | 19.8 | −6 | 31 | 4 | 09 | 3 | 49 | 12 | 07 | 20 | 03 | 20 | 23 | 19 | 08 | 26 | 3 | 51 | 24 |
| 25 | 8 | 18 | 54 | 19.6 | −6 | 32 | 4 | 11 | 3 | 50 | 12 | 07 | 20 | 02 | 20 | 21 | 19 | 12 | 22 | 3 | 47 | 28 |
| 26 | 8 | 22 | 51 | 19.4 | −6 | 32 | 4 | 12 | 3 | 52 | 12 | 07 | 20 | 00 | 20 | 20 | 19 | 16 | 19 | 3 | 43 | 31 |
| 27 | 8 | 26 | 47 | 19.2 | −6 | 32 | 4 | 13 | 3 | 54 | 12 | 07 | 19 | 59 | 20 | 18 | 19 | 20 | 16 | 3 | 39 | 35 |
| 28 | 8 | 30 | 42 | 18.9 | −6 | 30 | 4 | 15 | 3 | 56 | 12 | 07 | 19 | 57 | 20 | 16 | 19 | 24 | 12 | 3 | 35 | 38 |
| 29 | 8 | 34 | 37 | 18.7 | −6 | 29 | 4 | 16 | 3 | 58 | 12 | 06 | 19 | 56 | 20 | 14 | 19 | 28 | 09 | 3 | 31 | 42 |
| 30 | 8 | 38 | 32 | 18.5 | −6 | 27 | 4 | 18 | 3 | 59 | 12 | 06 | 19 | 54 | 20 | 12 | 19 | 32 | 05 | 3 | 27 | 45 |
| 31 | 8 | 42 | 25 | 18.2 | −6 | 24 | 4 | 19 | 4 | 01 | 12 | 06 | 19 | 52 | 20 | 10 | 19 | 36 | 02 | 3 | 23 | 48 |

## DURATION OF TWILIGHT (in minutes)

| Latitude | 52° | 56° | 52° | 56° | 52° | 56° | 52° | 56° |
|---|---|---|---|---|---|---|---|---|
| | 1 July | | 11 July | | 21 July | | 31 July | |
| Civil | 48 | 61 | 47 | 58 | 44 | 53 | 42 | 49 |
| Nautical | 124 | TAN | 117 | TAN | 107 | 146 | 98 | 123 |
| Astronomical | TAN | TAN | TAN | TAN | TAN | TAN | 182 | TAN |

## THE NIGHT SKY

*Mercury* is at superior conjunction on the 7th and then moves into the evening sky. It will be too deep in the twilight to be seen this month though.

*Venus* might be spotted barely above the north-west horizon just before the end of civil twilight the last few days of July. The observation calls for an exceptional horizon though and may first require sweeping with binoculars to tease out the planet's elusive spark.

*Mars* sets before midnight at the end of July but is still quite prominent among the stars of Libra. The planet's slow fade from magnitude −1.4 to −0.8 during the month is due to Earth's faster motion round the Sun as we leave Mars behind in its orbit. The Moon lies 7° above Mars on the evening of the 14th.

*Jupiter,* magnitude −1.7, sinks lower towards the west these evenings and will set only 90 minutes after the Sun by the end of July. The planet is 5° to the Moon's right after sunset on the 9th.

*Saturn,* magnitude +0.2, is in the southern sky in Ophiuchus after dark. It sets during the early hours at the beginning of July but just after midnight by the end of the month. The Moon is just under 5° from Saturn on July 15th.

# THE MOON

| Day | R.A. | | Dec. | Hor. Par. | Diam. | Sun's Co-Long. | PA of Br. Limb | Ph. | Age | Rise | | | | Transit | | Set | | | |
|---|---|---|---|---|---|---|---|---|---|---|---|---|---|---|---|---|---|---|---|
| | | | | | | | | | | 52° | | 56° | | | | 52° | | 56° | |
| | h | m | ° | ′ | ′ | ° | ° | % | d | h | m | h | m | h | m | h | m | h | m |
| 1 | 3 | 24 | +13.8 | 59.9 | 32.6 | 222 | 71 | 16 | 25.5 | 1 | 02 | 0 | 53 | 8 | 14 | 15 | 38 | 15 | 50 |
| 2 | 4 | 23 | +16.5 | 59.9 | 32.6 | 235 | 73 | 8 | 26.5 | 1 | 37 | 1 | 24 | 9 | 10 | 16 | 53 | 17 | 09 |
| 3 | 5 | 24 | +18.1 | 59.6 | 32.5 | 247 | 73 | 3 | 27.5 | 2 | 18 | 2 | 03 | 10 | 08 | 18 | 04 | 18 | 23 |
| 4 | 6 | 24 | +18.6 | 59.2 | 32.3 | 259 | 57 | 0 | 28.5 | 3 | 07 | 2 | 49 | 11 | 07 | 19 | 08 | 19 | 27 |
| 5 | 7 | 24 | +17.9 | 58.7 | 32.0 | 271 | 310 | 0 | 29.5 | 4 | 05 | 3 | 46 | 12 | 05 | 20 | 02 | 20 | 20 |
| 6 | 8 | 21 | +16.1 | 58.0 | 31.6 | 284 | 293 | 3 | 0.9 | 5 | 08 | 4 | 51 | 13 | 02 | 20 | 47 | 21 | 02 |
| 7 | 9 | 15 | +13.5 | 57.2 | 31.2 | 296 | 291 | 8 | 1.9 | 6 | 16 | 6 | 02 | 13 | 55 | 21 | 24 | 21 | 36 |
| 8 | 10 | 07 | +10.2 | 56.4 | 30.8 | 308 | 292 | 14 | 2.9 | 7 | 25 | 7 | 14 | 14 | 46 | 21 | 54 | 22 | 03 |
| 9 | 10 | 56 | +6.6 | 55.7 | 30.4 | 320 | 293 | 22 | 3.9 | 8 | 34 | 8 | 26 | 15 | 33 | 22 | 21 | 22 | 27 |
| 10 | 11 | 44 | +2.8 | 55.1 | 30.0 | 333 | 293 | 31 | 4.9 | 9 | 41 | 9 | 37 | 16 | 19 | 22 | 45 | 22 | 47 |
| 11 | 12 | 30 | −1.0 | 54.7 | 29.8 | 345 | 293 | 40 | 5.9 | 10 | 47 | 10 | 46 | 17 | 02 | 23 | 07 | 23 | 07 |
| 12 | 13 | 15 | −4.8 | 54.4 | 29.6 | 357 | 292 | 49 | 6.9 | 11 | 51 | 11 | 53 | 17 | 45 | 23 | 30 | 23 | 26 |
| 13 | 14 | 01 | −8.3 | 54.2 | 29.6 | 9 | 291 | 59 | 7.9 | 12 | 54 | 13 | 00 | 18 | 28 | 23 | 53 | 23 | 46 |
| 14 | 14 | 47 | −11.5 | 54.3 | 29.6 | 22 | 289 | 68 | 8.9 | 13 | 56 | 14 | 06 | 19 | 11 | — | | — | |
| 15 | 15 | 35 | −14.3 | 54.5 | 29.7 | 34 | 287 | 77 | 9.9 | 14 | 58 | 15 | 11 | 19 | 56 | 0 | 19 | 0 | 09 |
| 16 | 16 | 24 | −16.5 | 54.8 | 29.9 | 46 | 284 | 84 | 10.9 | 15 | 59 | 16 | 15 | 20 | 43 | 0 | 48 | 0 | 34 |
| 17 | 17 | 15 | −17.9 | 55.3 | 30.1 | 58 | 282 | 91 | 11.9 | 16 | 58 | 17 | 16 | 21 | 31 | 1 | 21 | 1 | 06 |
| 18 | 18 | 08 | −18.6 | 55.8 | 30.4 | 70 | 280 | 96 | 12.9 | 17 | 54 | 18 | 13 | 22 | 22 | 2 | 02 | 1 | 43 |
| 19 | 19 | 01 | −18.3 | 56.4 | 30.7 | 83 | 284 | 99 | 13.9 | 18 | 45 | 19 | 03 | 23 | 13 | 2 | 48 | 2 | 29 |
| 20 | 19 | 56 | −17.0 | 57.0 | 31.1 | 95 | 349 | 100 | 14.9 | 19 | 30 | 19 | 47 | — | | 3 | 43 | 3 | 25 |
| 21 | 20 | 51 | −14.8 | 57.5 | 31.4 | 107 | 62 | 99 | 15.9 | 20 | 09 | 20 | 24 | 0 | 06 | 4 | 45 | 4 | 29 |
| 22 | 21 | 45 | −11.8 | 58.0 | 31.6 | 119 | 67 | 95 | 16.9 | 20 | 44 | 20 | 54 | 0 | 58 | 5 | 54 | 5 | 40 |
| 23 | 22 | 39 | −8.1 | 58.5 | 31.9 | 131 | 67 | 90 | 17.9 | 21 | 14 | 21 | 21 | 1 | 50 | 7 | 06 | 6 | 56 |
| 24 | 23 | 32 | −3.9 | 58.8 | 32.0 | 144 | 67 | 82 | 18.9 | 21 | 42 | 21 | 46 | 2 | 42 | 8 | 20 | 8 | 14 |
| 25 | 0 | 26 | +0.6 | 59.1 | 32.2 | 156 | 68 | 72 | 19.9 | 22 | 09 | 22 | 09 | 3 | 33 | 9 | 36 | 9 | 34 |
| 26 | 1 | 19 | +5.0 | 59.2 | 32.3 | 168 | 69 | 61 | 20.9 | 22 | 37 | 22 | 32 | 4 | 24 | 10 | 52 | 10 | 54 |
| 27 | 2 | 14 | +9.2 | 59.3 | 32.3 | 180 | 71 | 50 | 21.9 | 23 | 06 | 22 | 58 | 5 | 16 | 12 | 09 | 12 | 15 |
| 28 | 3 | 10 | +12.8 | 59.3 | 32.3 | 192 | 73 | 39 | 22.9 | 23 | 38 | 23 | 27 | 6 | 09 | 13 | 25 | 13 | 36 |
| 29 | 4 | 07 | +15.7 | 59.2 | 32.3 | 205 | 77 | 28 | 23.9 | — | | — | | 7 | 03 | 14 | 40 | 14 | 53 |
| 30 | 5 | 06 | +17.7 | 59.0 | 32.2 | 217 | 80 | 18 | 24.9 | 0 | 16 | 0 | 02 | 7 | 59 | 15 | 51 | 16 | 07 |
| 31 | 6 | 05 | +18.5 | 58.7 | 32.0 | 229 | 84 | 10 | 25.9 | 1 | 01 | 0 | 43 | 8 | 56 | 16 | 56 | 17 | 14 |

# MERCURY

| Day | R.A. | | Dec | Mag. | Diam. | Phase | Rise | | Transit | | Set | |
|---|---|---|---|---|---|---|---|---|---|---|---|---|
| | h | m | ° | | ″ | % | h | m | h | m | h | m |
| 1 | 6 | 08.1 | +23.9 | −1.6 | 5 | 95 | 2 | 56 | 11 | 31 | 20 | 08 |
| 3 | 6 | 27.0 | +24.1 | −1.8 | 5 | 98 | 3 | 05 | 11 | 43 | 20 | 20 |
| 5 | 6 | 46.0 | +24.1 | −2.0 | 5 | 99 | 3 | 16 | 11 | 54 | 20 | 31 |
| 7 | 7 | 05.0 | +24.0 | −2.2 | 5 | 100 | 3 | 29 | 12 | 05 | 20 | 40 |
| 9 | 7 | 23.8 | +23.6 | −2.0 | 5 | 99 | 3 | 43 | 12 | 16 | 20 | 48 |
| 11 | 7 | 42.2 | +23.1 | −1.7 | 5 | 98 | 3 | 58 | 12 | 26 | 20 | 53 |
| 13 | 8 | 00.1 | +22.4 | −1.5 | 5 | 96 | 4 | 13 | 12 | 36 | 20 | 57 |
| 15 | 8 | 17.3 | +21.6 | −1.2 | 5 | 94 | 4 | 29 | 12 | 45 | 21 | 00 |
| 17 | 8 | 33.8 | +20.6 | −1.0 | 5 | 92 | 4 | 45 | 12 | 54 | 21 | 01 |
| 19 | 8 | 49.6 | +19.6 | −0.9 | 5 | 89 | 5 | 00 | 13 | 01 | 21 | 01 |
| 21 | 9 | 04.7 | +18.5 | −0.7 | 5 | 87 | 5 | 15 | 13 | 08 | 21 | 00 |
| 23 | 9 | 19.0 | +17.3 | −0.6 | 5 | 84 | 5 | 29 | 13 | 15 | 20 | 58 |
| 25 | 9 | 32.6 | +16.0 | −0.5 | 6 | 81 | 5 | 43 | 13 | 20 | 20 | 55 |
| 27 | 9 | 45.6 | +14.8 | −0.3 | 6 | 79 | 5 | 57 | 13 | 25 | 20 | 52 |
| 29 | 9 | 58.0 | +13.5 | −0.2 | 6 | 76 | 6 | 09 | 13 | 29 | 20 | 48 |
| 31 | 10 | 09.7 | +12.1 | −0.2 | 6 | 73 | 6 | 21 | 13 | 33 | 20 | 43 |

Rising and setting times are for latitude 54°

# VENUS

| Day | R.A. | | Dec | Mag. | Diam. | Phase | Rise | | Transit | | Set | |
|---|---|---|---|---|---|---|---|---|---|---|---|---|
| | h | m | ° | | ″ | % | h | m | h | m | h | m |
| 1 | 7 | 09.5 | +23.4 | −4.0 | 10 | 99 | 4 | 01 | 12 | 31 | 21 | 01 |
| 6 | 7 | 36.1 | +22.7 | −4.0 | 10 | 99 | 4 | 14 | 12 | 38 | 21 | 02 |
| 11 | 8 | 02.3 | +21.7 | −4.0 | 11 | 99 | 4 | 28 | 12 | 44 | 21 | 00 |
| 16 | 8 | 28.0 | +20.4 | −4.0 | 11 | 98 | 4 | 43 | 12 | 50 | 20 | 57 |
| 21 | 8 | 53.4 | +18.9 | −4.0 | 11 | 98 | 5 | 00 | 12 | 56 | 20 | 52 |
| 26 | 9 | 18.2 | +17.2 | −4.1 | 11 | 97 | 5 | 16 | 13 | 01 | 20 | 45 |
| 31 | 9 | 42.5 | +15.3 | −4.1 | 11 | 97 | 5 | 34 | 13 | 06 | 20 | 37 |

# MARS

| Day | R.A. | | Dec | Mag. | Diam. | Phase | Rise | | Transit | | Set | |
|---|---|---|---|---|---|---|---|---|---|---|---|---|
| | h | m | ° | | ″ | % | h | m | h | m | h | m |
| 1 | 15 | 18.9 | −21.0 | −1.4 | 16 | 93 | 16 | 46 | 20 | 42 | 0 | 38 |
| 6 | 15 | 19.8 | −21.2 | −1.3 | 16 | 92 | 16 | 28 | 20 | 23 | 0 | 19 |
| 11 | 15 | 22.1 | −21.4 | −1.2 | 15 | 91 | 16 | 12 | 20 | 05 | 0 | 00 |
| 16 | 15 | 25.7 | −21.6 | −1.1 | 15 | 90 | 15 | 57 | 19 | 49 | 23 | 42 |
| 21 | 15 | 30.5 | −21.9 | −1.0 | 14 | 89 | 15 | 44 | 19 | 34 | 23 | 22 |
| 26 | 15 | 36.4 | −22.3 | −0.9 | 14 | 88 | 15 | 33 | 19 | 20 | 23 | 06 |
| 31 | 15 | 43.4 | −22.7 | −0.8 | 13 | 88 | 15 | 23 | 19 | 07 | 22 | 50 |

# SUNRISE AND SUNSET

| | London | | Bristol | | Birmingham | | Manchester | | Newcastle | | Glasgow | | Belfast | |
|---|---|---|---|---|---|---|---|---|---|---|---|---|---|---|
| | 0° 05′ | 51° 30′ | 2° 35′ | 51° 28′ | 1° 55′ | 52° 28′ | 2° 15′ | 53° 28′ | 1° 37′ | 54° 59′ | 4° 14′ | 55° 52′ | 5° 56′ | 54° 35′ |
| d | h m | h m | h m | h m | h m | h m | h m | h m | h m | h m | h m | h m | h m | h m |
| 1 | 3 48 | 20 20 | 3 58 | 20 30 | 3 50 | 20 33 | 3 45 | 20 40 | 3 33 | 20 48 | 3 37 | 21 05 | 3 53 | 21 02 |
| 2 | 3 48 | 20 20 | 3 59 | 20 30 | 3 50 | 20 33 | 3 46 | 20 40 | 3 33 | 20 47 | 3 38 | 21 04 | 3 53 | 21 02 |
| 3 | 3 49 | 20 20 | 3 59 | 20 29 | 3 51 | 20 32 | 3 47 | 20 40 | 3 34 | 20 47 | 3 38 | 21 03 | 3 54 | 21 01 |
| 4 | 3 50 | 20 19 | 4 00 | 20 29 | 3 52 | 20 32 | 3 47 | 20 39 | 3 35 | 20 46 | 3 39 | 21 03 | 3 55 | 21 01 |
| 5 | 3 51 | 20 19 | 4 01 | 20 28 | 3 53 | 20 31 | 3 48 | 20 38 | 3 36 | 20 45 | 3 40 | 21 02 | 3 56 | 21 00 |
| 6 | 3 52 | 20 18 | 4 02 | 20 28 | 3 54 | 20 31 | 3 49 | 20 38 | 3 37 | 20 45 | 3 42 | 21 01 | 3 57 | 20 59 |
| 7 | 3 53 | 20 17 | 4 03 | 20 27 | 3 55 | 20 30 | 3 50 | 20 37 | 3 38 | 20 44 | 3 43 | 21 00 | 3 58 | 20 59 |
| 8 | 3 54 | 20 17 | 4 04 | 20 27 | 3 56 | 20 29 | 3 51 | 20 36 | 3 39 | 20 43 | 3 44 | 21 00 | 3 59 | 20 58 |
| 9 | 3 55 | 20 16 | 4 05 | 20 26 | 3 57 | 20 28 | 3 52 | 20 35 | 3 41 | 20 42 | 3 45 | 20 59 | 4 00 | 20 57 |
| 10 | 3 56 | 20 15 | 4 06 | 20 25 | 3 58 | 20 28 | 3 54 | 20 35 | 3 42 | 20 41 | 3 46 | 20 58 | 4 02 | 20 56 |
| 11 | 3 57 | 20 14 | 4 07 | 20 24 | 3 59 | 20 27 | 3 55 | 20 34 | 3 43 | 20 40 | 3 48 | 20 56 | 4 03 | 20 55 |
| 12 | 3 58 | 20 14 | 4 08 | 20 23 | 4 00 | 20 26 | 3 56 | 20 33 | 3 44 | 20 39 | 3 49 | 20 55 | 4 04 | 20 54 |
| 13 | 3 59 | 20 13 | 4 09 | 20 23 | 4 01 | 20 25 | 3 57 | 20 32 | 3 46 | 20 38 | 3 50 | 20 54 | 4 05 | 20 53 |
| 14 | 4 00 | 20 12 | 4 10 | 20 22 | 4 02 | 20 24 | 3 58 | 20 31 | 3 47 | 20 37 | 3 52 | 20 53 | 4 07 | 20 52 |
| 15 | 4 01 | 20 11 | 4 11 | 20 21 | 4 04 | 20 23 | 4 00 | 20 29 | 3 48 | 20 36 | 3 53 | 20 52 | 4 08 | 20 51 |
| 16 | 4 02 | 20 10 | 4 13 | 20 20 | 4 05 | 20 22 | 4 01 | 20 28 | 3 50 | 20 34 | 3 55 | 20 50 | 4 09 | 20 49 |
| 17 | 4 04 | 20 09 | 4 14 | 20 18 | 4 06 | 20 21 | 4 02 | 20 27 | 3 51 | 20 33 | 3 56 | 20 49 | 4 11 | 20 48 |
| 18 | 4 05 | 20 07 | 4 15 | 20 17 | 4 08 | 20 19 | 4 04 | 20 26 | 3 53 | 20 32 | 3 58 | 20 47 | 4 12 | 20 47 |
| 19 | 4 06 | 20 06 | 4 16 | 20 16 | 4 09 | 20 18 | 4 05 | 20 25 | 3 54 | 20 30 | 3 59 | 20 46 | 4 14 | 20 45 |
| 20 | 4 08 | 20 05 | 4 18 | 20 15 | 4 10 | 20 17 | 4 07 | 20 23 | 3 56 | 20 29 | 4 01 | 20 44 | 4 15 | 20 44 |
| 21 | 4 09 | 20 04 | 4 19 | 20 14 | 4 12 | 20 16 | 4 08 | 20 22 | 3 57 | 20 27 | 4 03 | 20 43 | 4 17 | 20 42 |
| 22 | 4 10 | 20 03 | 4 20 | 20 12 | 4 13 | 20 14 | 4 10 | 20 20 | 3 59 | 20 26 | 4 04 | 20 41 | 4 18 | 20 41 |
| 23 | 4 12 | 20 01 | 4 22 | 20 11 | 4 15 | 20 13 | 4 11 | 20 19 | 4 01 | 20 24 | 4 06 | 20 40 | 4 20 | 20 39 |
| 24 | 4 13 | 20 00 | 4 23 | 20 10 | 4 16 | 20 11 | 4 13 | 20 17 | 4 02 | 20 23 | 4 08 | 20 38 | 4 22 | 20 38 |
| 25 | 4 14 | 19 58 | 4 25 | 20 08 | 4 17 | 20 10 | 4 14 | 20 16 | 4 04 | 20 21 | 4 10 | 20 36 | 4 23 | 20 36 |
| 26 | 4 16 | 19 57 | 4 26 | 20 07 | 4 19 | 20 08 | 4 16 | 20 14 | 4 06 | 20 19 | 4 11 | 20 34 | 4 25 | 20 34 |
| 27 | 4 17 | 19 55 | 4 27 | 20 05 | 4 20 | 20 07 | 4 17 | 20 13 | 4 07 | 20 17 | 4 13 | 20 33 | 4 27 | 20 33 |
| 28 | 4 19 | 19 54 | 4 29 | 20 04 | 4 22 | 20 05 | 4 19 | 20 11 | 4 09 | 20 16 | 4 15 | 20 31 | 4 28 | 20 31 |
| 29 | 4 20 | 19 52 | 4 30 | 20 02 | 4 23 | 20 04 | 4 20 | 20 09 | 4 11 | 20 14 | 4 17 | 20 29 | 4 30 | 20 29 |
| 30 | 4 22 | 19 51 | 4 32 | 20 01 | 4 25 | 20 02 | 4 22 | 20 08 | 4 12 | 20 12 | 4 19 | 20 27 | 4 32 | 20 27 |
| 31 | 4 23 | 19 49 | 4 33 | 19 59 | 4 27 | 20 00 | 4 24 | 20 06 | 4 14 | 20 10 | 4 20 | 20 25 | 4 33 | 20 26 |

## JUPITER

| Day | R.A. | | Dec | Mag. | Diam. | Rise | | Transit | | Set | |
|---|---|---|---|---|---|---|---|---|---|---|---|
| | h | m | ° | | ″ | h | m | h | m | h | m |
| 1 | 11 | 13.4 | +6.3 | −1.9 | 34 | 9 | 55 | 16 | 33 | 23 | 11 |
| 11 | 11 | 18.8 | +5.7 | −1.8 | 33 | 9 | 24 | 15 | 59 | 22 | 33 |
| 21 | 11 | 24.7 | +5.1 | −1.8 | 33 | 8 | 55 | 15 | 26 | 21 | 56 |
| 31 | 11 | 31.1 | +4.4 | −1.7 | 32 | 8 | 26 | 14 | 53 | 21 | 19 |

Equatorial Diam. 33″, Polar Diam. 31″

## SATURN

| Day | R.A. | | Dec | Mag. | Diam. | Rise | | Transit | | Set | |
|---|---|---|---|---|---|---|---|---|---|---|---|
| | h | m | ° | | ″ | h | m | h | m | h | m |
| 1 | 16 | 38.6 | −20.4 | +0.2 | 18 | 17 | 56 | 21 | 57 | 2 | 03 |
| 11 | 16 | 36.3 | −20.3 | +0.2 | 18 | 17 | 14 | 21 | 16 | 1 | 21 |
| 21 | 16 | 34.4 | −20.3 | +0.3 | 18 | 16 | 32 | 20 | 34 | 0 | 40 |
| 31 | 16 | 33.2 | −20.3 | +0.3 | 18 | 15 | 52 | 19 | 54 | 0 | 00 |

Equatorial Diam. 18″, Polar Diam.16″
Rings – major axis 41″ minor axis 18″, Tilt 26°

## URANUS

| Day | R.A. | | Dec | Mag. | Diam. | Rise | | Transit | | Set | |
|---|---|---|---|---|---|---|---|---|---|---|---|
| | h | m | ° | | ″ | h | m | h | m | h | m |
| 1 | 1 | 29.6 | +8.7 | +6.2 | 3 | 23 | 59 | 6 | 51 | 13 | 42 |
| 11 | 1 | 30.3 | +8.8 | +6.1 | 4 | 23 | 20 | 6 | 12 | 13 | 04 |
| 21 | 1 | 30.7 | +8.8 | +6.1 | 4 | 22 | 41 | 5 | 33 | 12 | 25 |
| 31 | 1 | 30.8 | +8.8 | +6.1 | 4 | 22 | 02 | 4 | 54 | 11 | 46 |

## NEPTUNE

| Day | R.A. | | Dec | Mag. | Diam. | Rise | | Transit | | Set | |
|---|---|---|---|---|---|---|---|---|---|---|---|
| | h | m | ° | | ″ | h | m | h | m | h | m |
| 1 | 22 | 53.9 | −8.0 | +7.9 | 2 | 22 | 53 | 4 | 15 | 9 | 34 |
| 11 | 22 | 53.5 | −8.0 | +7.8 | 2 | 22 | 13 | 3 | 36 | 8 | 54 |
| 21 | 22 | 52.9 | −8.1 | +7.8 | 2 | 21 | 34 | 2 | 56 | 8 | 14 |
| 31 | 22 | 52.1 | −8.1 | +7.8 | 2 | 20 | 54 | 2 | 16 | 7 | 33 |

# AUGUST 2016

EIGHTH MONTH, 31 DAYS. *Augustus*, formerly *Sextilis*, sixth month of Roman pre-Julian calendar

| 1 | Monday | Hutton Inquiry into the death of former UN weapons inspector Dr David Kelly begins 2003 | week 31 day 214 |
| 2 | Tuesday | William II (Rufus) dies after being shot by an arrow while hunting 1100 | 215 |
| 3 | Wednesday | Stanley Baldwin, Conservative prime minister three times between the World Wars *b.* 1867 | 216 |
| 4 | Thursday | Idi Amin orders the expulsion of Uganda's 60,000 Asian population 1972 | 217 |
| 5 | Friday | Plaid Genedlaethol Cymru (National Party of Wales), now Plaid Cymru, is formed 1925 | 218 |
| 6 | Saturday | Jamaica becomes independent of the UK 1962 | 219 |
| 7 | Sunday | An Act is passed to make it illegal to employ anyone aged under 21 to sweep chimneys 1840 | 220 |

| 8 | Monday | George Canning, foreign secretary who had a duel with Lord Castlereagh *d.* 1827 | week 32 day 221 |
| 9 | Tuesday | Richard Nixon becomes the first US president to resign, after the Watergate scandal 1974 | 222 |
| 10 | Wednesday | Herbert Hoover, US president who presided over the Wall Street Crash *b.* 1874 | 223 |
| 11 | Thursday | MPs in the House of Commons vote for receiving an annual salary, initially set at £400 1911 | 224 |
| 12 | Friday | The East German army begins to close the border with West Berlin 1961 | 225 |
| 13 | Saturday | Fidel Castro, Cuban politician and revolutionary, President of Cuba (1976–2008) *b.* 1927 | 226 |
| 14 | Sunday | Guangxu Emperor of China (1875–1908) and 11th emperor of the Qing dynasty *b.* 1871 | 227 |

| 15 | Monday | Napoleon Bonaparte, Emperor of the French, who led the Napoleonic Wars *b.* 1769 | week 33 day 228 |
| 16 | Tuesday | The Peterloo Massacre takes place in Manchester, when cavalry charge a crowd 1819 | 229 |
| 17 | Wednesday | US president Bill Clinton admits he had an 'improper' relationship with Monica Lewinsky 1998 | 230 |
| 18 | Thursday | Genghis Khan, founder of the Mongol Empire, the largest contiguous empire in history *d.* 1227 | 231 |
| 19 | Friday | Bill Clinton, 42nd US president and aged 46 the third-youngest to take office *b.* 1946 | 232 |
| 20 | Saturday | Slobodan Milosevic, Yugoslavian president (1997–2000) who died while on trial for war crimes *b.* 1941 | 233 |
| 21 | Sunday | A coup d'état by Gustav III ends the Age of Liberty and parliamentary rule in Sweden 1772 | 234 |

| 22 | Monday | Ida Siekmann becomes the first person to die while attempting to cross the Berlin wall 1961 | week 34 day 235 |
| 23 | Tuesday | The Baltic Way, a 2 million-strong human chain demonstration against Soviet occupation occurs 1989 | 236 |
| 24 | Wednesday | Brazilian president Getulio Vargas commits suicide hours after resigning 1954 | 237 |
| 25 | Thursday | George Rockwell, founder of the American Nazi Party, is shot dead in Virginia 1967 | 238 |
| 26 | Friday | Sir Robert Walpole, the first and longest-serving prime minister of Great Britain *b.* 1676 | 239 |
| 27 | Saturday | The Treaty of Montevideo is signed in which Brazil and Argentina recognise the independence of Uruguay 1828 | 240 |
| 28 | Sunday | Martin Luther King, Jr. delivers his 'I Have a Dream' speech, calling for an end to racism 1963 | 241 |

| 29 | Monday | The New Jersey legislature establishes the first Native American reservation 1758 | week 35 day 242 |
| 30 | Tuesday | East Timor votes for independence from Indonesia in a referendum 1999 | 243 |
| 31 | Wednesday | The Federation of Malaya becomes an independent sovereign country within the Commonwealth 1957 | 244 |

## ASTRONOMICAL PHENOMENA

*d  h*
4 06  Venus 3° North of the Moon
4 22  Mercury 0.6° North of the Moon
6 04  Jupiter 0.2° North of the Moon
12  –  Perseid meteor peak
12 12  Saturn 4° South of the Moon
16 21  Mercury Greatest elongation East
20 12  Pallas at opposition
22 10  Uranus 3° North of the Moon
25 18  Saturn 4° North of Mars
27 05  Venus 5° North of Mercury
27 22  Jupiter 0.1° South of Venus

## MINIMA OF ALGOL

| d | h | d | h | d | h |
|---|---|---|---|---|---|
| 3 | 13.3 | 15 | 00.5 | 26 | 11.8 |
| 6 | 10.1 | 17 | 21.4 | 29 | 08.6 |
| 9 | 06.9 | 20 | 18.2 | | |
| 12 | 03.7 | 23 | 15.0 | | |

## CONSTELLATIONS

The following constellations are near their meridian at

| | d | h | | d | h |
|---|---|---|---|---|---|
| July | 1 | 24 | August | 16 | 21 |
| July | 16 | 23 | September | 1 | 20 |
| August | 1 | 22 | September | 15 | 19 |

Draco, Hercules, Lyra, Cygnus, Sagitta, Ophiuchus, Serpens, Aquila and Sagittarius

## THE MOON

| Phases, Apsides and Node | d | h | m |
|---|---|---|---|
| ● New Moon | 2 | 20 | 45 |
| ◑ First Quarter | 10 | 18 | 21 |
| ○ Full Moon | 18 | 09 | 27 |
| ◐ Last Quarter | 25 | 03 | 41 |

| Apogee (404,262km) | 10 | 00 | 05 |
| Perigee (367,050km) | 22 | 01 | 19 |

Mean longitude of ascending node on 1st, 164°

# THE SUN

Diam. 31.6″

| Day | Right Ascension | | | Dec. + | Equation of time | | Rise 52° | | 56° | | Transit | | Set 52° | | 56° | | Sidereal time | | | Transit of first point of Aries | | |
|---|---|---|---|---|---|---|---|---|---|---|---|---|---|---|---|---|---|---|---|---|---|---|
| | h | m | s | ° | m | s | h | m | h | m | h | m | h | m | h | m | h | m | s | h | m | s |
| 1 | 8 | 46 | 19 | 18.0 | −6 | 21 | 4 | 21 | 4 | 03 | 12 | 06 | 19 | 51 | 20 | 09 | 19 | 39 | 58 | 3 | 19 | 52 |
| 2 | 8 | 50 | 11 | 17.7 | −6 | 17 | 4 | 22 | 4 | 05 | 12 | 06 | 19 | 49 | 20 | 07 | 19 | 43 | 55 | 3 | 15 | 55 |
| 3 | 8 | 54 | 03 | 17.5 | −6 | 12 | 4 | 24 | 4 | 07 | 12 | 06 | 19 | 47 | 20 | 05 | 19 | 47 | 51 | 3 | 11 | 59 |
| 4 | 8 | 57 | 55 | 17.2 | −6 | 07 | 4 | 26 | 4 | 09 | 12 | 06 | 19 | 46 | 20 | 03 | 19 | 51 | 48 | 3 | 08 | 02 |
| 5 | 9 | 01 | 45 | 16.9 | −6 | 01 | 4 | 27 | 4 | 10 | 12 | 06 | 19 | 44 | 20 | 00 | 19 | 55 | 45 | 3 | 04 | 06 |
| 6 | 9 | 05 | 36 | 16.6 | −5 | 55 | 4 | 29 | 4 | 12 | 12 | 06 | 19 | 42 | 19 | 58 | 19 | 59 | 41 | 3 | 00 | 09 |
| 7 | 9 | 09 | 25 | 16.4 | −5 | 48 | 4 | 30 | 4 | 14 | 12 | 06 | 19 | 40 | 19 | 56 | 20 | 03 | 38 | 2 | 56 | 13 |
| 8 | 9 | 13 | 14 | 16.1 | −5 | 40 | 4 | 32 | 4 | 16 | 12 | 06 | 19 | 39 | 19 | 54 | 20 | 07 | 34 | 2 | 52 | 16 |
| 9 | 9 | 17 | 02 | 15.8 | −5 | 32 | 4 | 33 | 4 | 18 | 12 | 06 | 19 | 37 | 19 | 52 | 20 | 11 | 31 | 2 | 48 | 19 |
| 10 | 9 | 20 | 50 | 15.5 | −5 | 23 | 4 | 35 | 4 | 20 | 12 | 05 | 19 | 35 | 19 | 50 | 20 | 15 | 27 | 2 | 44 | 23 |
| 11 | 9 | 24 | 37 | 15.2 | −5 | 14 | 4 | 37 | 4 | 22 | 12 | 05 | 19 | 33 | 19 | 47 | 20 | 19 | 24 | 2 | 40 | 26 |
| 12 | 9 | 28 | 24 | 14.9 | −5 | 04 | 4 | 38 | 4 | 24 | 12 | 05 | 19 | 31 | 19 | 45 | 20 | 23 | 20 | 2 | 36 | 30 |
| 13 | 9 | 32 | 10 | 14.6 | −4 | 53 | 4 | 40 | 4 | 26 | 12 | 05 | 19 | 29 | 19 | 43 | 20 | 27 | 17 | 2 | 32 | 33 |
| 14 | 9 | 35 | 55 | 14.3 | −4 | 42 | 4 | 41 | 4 | 28 | 12 | 05 | 19 | 27 | 19 | 41 | 20 | 31 | 14 | 2 | 28 | 37 |
| 15 | 9 | 39 | 40 | 14.0 | −4 | 31 | 4 | 43 | 4 | 30 | 12 | 05 | 19 | 25 | 19 | 38 | 20 | 35 | 10 | 2 | 24 | 40 |
| 16 | 9 | 43 | 25 | 13.7 | −4 | 18 | 4 | 45 | 4 | 32 | 12 | 04 | 19 | 23 | 19 | 36 | 20 | 39 | 07 | 2 | 20 | 44 |
| 17 | 9 | 47 | 09 | 13.4 | −4 | 06 | 4 | 46 | 4 | 34 | 12 | 04 | 19 | 21 | 19 | 33 | 20 | 43 | 03 | 2 | 16 | 47 |
| 18 | 9 | 50 | 52 | 13.0 | −3 | 52 | 4 | 48 | 4 | 36 | 12 | 04 | 19 | 19 | 19 | 31 | 20 | 47 | 00 | 2 | 12 | 50 |
| 19 | 9 | 54 | 35 | 12.7 | −3 | 39 | 4 | 49 | 4 | 38 | 12 | 04 | 19 | 17 | 19 | 29 | 20 | 50 | 56 | 2 | 08 | 54 |
| 20 | 9 | 58 | 17 | 12.4 | −3 | 24 | 4 | 51 | 4 | 39 | 12 | 04 | 19 | 15 | 19 | 26 | 20 | 54 | 53 | 2 | 04 | 57 |
| 21 | 10 | 01 | 59 | 12.1 | −3 | 10 | 4 | 53 | 4 | 41 | 12 | 03 | 19 | 13 | 19 | 24 | 20 | 58 | 49 | 2 | 01 | 01 |
| 22 | 10 | 05 | 40 | 11.7 | −2 | 55 | 4 | 54 | 4 | 43 | 12 | 03 | 19 | 11 | 19 | 21 | 21 | 02 | 46 | 1 | 57 | 04 |
| 23 | 10 | 09 | 21 | 11.4 | −2 | 39 | 4 | 56 | 4 | 45 | 12 | 03 | 19 | 08 | 19 | 19 | 21 | 06 | 42 | 1 | 53 | 08 |
| 24 | 10 | 13 | 02 | 11.0 | −2 | 23 | 4 | 58 | 4 | 47 | 12 | 03 | 19 | 06 | 19 | 16 | 21 | 10 | 39 | 1 | 49 | 11 |
| 25 | 10 | 16 | 42 | 10.7 | −2 | 07 | 4 | 59 | 4 | 49 | 12 | 02 | 19 | 04 | 19 | 14 | 21 | 14 | 36 | 1 | 45 | 15 |
| 26 | 10 | 20 | 22 | 10.3 | −1 | 50 | 5 | 01 | 4 | 51 | 12 | 02 | 19 | 02 | 19 | 11 | 21 | 18 | 32 | 1 | 41 | 18 |
| 27 | 10 | 24 | 01 | 10.0 | −1 | 33 | 5 | 03 | 4 | 53 | 12 | 02 | 19 | 00 | 19 | 09 | 21 | 22 | 29 | 1 | 37 | 21 |
| 28 | 10 | 27 | 40 | 9.6 | −1 | 15 | 5 | 04 | 4 | 55 | 12 | 01 | 18 | 58 | 19 | 06 | 21 | 26 | 25 | 1 | 33 | 25 |
| 29 | 10 | 31 | 19 | 9.3 | −0 | 57 | 5 | 06 | 4 | 57 | 12 | 01 | 18 | 55 | 19 | 04 | 21 | 30 | 22 | 1 | 29 | 28 |
| 30 | 10 | 34 | 57 | 8.9 | −0 | 39 | 5 | 07 | 4 | 59 | 12 | 01 | 18 | 53 | 19 | 01 | 21 | 34 | 18 | 1 | 25 | 32 |
| 31 | 10 | 38 | 35 | 8.6 | −0 | 21 | 5 | 09 | 5 | 01 | 12 | 00 | 18 | 51 | 18 | 59 | 21 | 38 | 15 | 1 | 21 | 35 |

## DURATION OF TWILIGHT (in minutes)

| Latitude | 52° | 56° | 52° | 56° | 52° | 56° | 52° | 56° |
|---|---|---|---|---|---|---|---|---|
| | 1 August | | 11 August | | 21 August | | 31 August | |
| Civil | 41 | 49 | 39 | 45 | 37 | 42 | 35 | 40 |
| Nautical | 97 | 121 | 90 | 107 | 84 | 97 | 79 | 90 |
| Astronomical | 179 | TAN | 154 | 210 | 139 | 168 | 128 | 148 |

## THE NIGHT SKY

*Mercury* is in the evening sky and reaches greatest elongation east (27°) on the 16th but is still hopelessly low after sunset to be seen from the UK.

*Venus* should put in an appearance in the evening sky from mid-August but it will be a very difficult sighting as Venus lies almost on the horizon at the end of civil twilight. This is disappointing as Venus is less than 5 arc-minutes from Jupiter on the 27th.

*Mars* moves from Libra into Scorpius on August 2nd, through Ophiuchus between the 21st and 27th, and then back to Scorpius. The Red Planet, magnitude −1.7, passes within 2° of Antares, magnitude +1.1, on August 24th. Mars sets around three hours after the Sun during the month.

*Jupiter,* magnitude −1.7, sets 1.5 hours after the Sun at the beginning of August but only 30 minutes after by the 31st. The three-day old Moon is nearby on the 5th. Jupiter moves from Leo into Virgo on August 9th.

*Saturn,* magnitude +0.4, is stationary in Ophiuchus on August 13th after which its direct motion resumes. The planet sets late-evening by the end of August. The Moon lies 4.5° to the upper left of Saturn on the 12th and Mars passes about 4.5° from Saturn on the 25th.

The *Perseid meteor* shower peaks on August 11th/12th this year. Moonset is before local midnight so the second half of the night will offer a good dark sky period to catch this annual display.

# THE MOON

| Day | R.A. | | Dec. | Hor. Par. | Diam. | Sun's Co-Long. | PA of Br. Limb | Ph. | Age | Rise 52° | | Rise 56° | | Transit | | Set 52° | | Set 56° | |
|---|---|---|---|---|---|---|---|---|---|---|---|---|---|---|---|---|---|---|---|
| | h | m | ° | ' | ' | ° | ° | % | d | h | m | h | m | h | m | h | m | h | m |
| 1 | 07 | 03 | +18.2 | 58.4 | 31.8 | 241 | 86 | 4 | 26.9 | 1 | 53 | 1 | 34 | 9 | 53 | 17 | 52 | 18 | 11 |
| 2 | 08 | 00 | +16.9 | 57.9 | 31.5 | 254 | 84 | 1 | 27.9 | 2 | 53 | 2 | 34 | 10 | 50 | 18 | 41 | 18 | 57 |
| 3 | 08 | 56 | +14.6 | 57.3 | 31.2 | 266 | 353 | 0 | 28.9 | 3 | 58 | 3 | 42 | 11 | 44 | 19 | 21 | 19 | 35 |
| 4 | 09 | 48 | +11.6 | 56.7 | 30.9 | 278 | 296 | 1 | 0.4 | 5 | 06 | 4 | 54 | 12 | 36 | 19 | 54 | 20 | 04 |
| 5 | 10 | 39 | +8.1 | 56.1 | 30.6 | 290 | 293 | 5 | 1.4 | 6 | 15 | 6 | 06 | 13 | 25 | 20 | 23 | 20 | 30 |
| 6 | 11 | 27 | +4.3 | 55.5 | 30.2 | 303 | 292 | 10 | 2.4 | 7 | 24 | 7 | 18 | 14 | 12 | 20 | 48 | 20 | 51 |
| 7 | 12 | 14 | +0.4 | 55.0 | 30.0 | 315 | 292 | 17 | 3.4 | 8 | 30 | 8 | 28 | 14 | 56 | 21 | 11 | 21 | 12 |
| 8 | 13 | 00 | −3.4 | 54.6 | 29.7 | 327 | 291 | 25 | 4.4 | 9 | 36 | 9 | 37 | 15 | 40 | 21 | 34 | 21 | 31 |
| 9 | 13 | 46 | −7.0 | 54.3 | 29.6 | 339 | 290 | 33 | 5.4 | 10 | 40 | 10 | 44 | 16 | 23 | 21 | 57 | 21 | 51 |
| 10 | 14 | 32 | −10.4 | 54.2 | 29.6 | 352 | 288 | 43 | 6.4 | 11 | 43 | 11 | 50 | 17 | 06 | 22 | 21 | 22 | 13 |
| 11 | 15 | 19 | −13.3 | 54.3 | 29.6 | 4 | 285 | 52 | 7.4 | 12 | 45 | 12 | 56 | 17 | 50 | 22 | 49 | 22 | 37 |
| 12 | 16 | 07 | −15.6 | 54.6 | 29.7 | 16 | 282 | 61 | 8.4 | 13 | 46 | 13 | 59 | 18 | 36 | 23 | 20 | 23 | 06 |
| 13 | 16 | 57 | −17.4 | 55.0 | 30.0 | 28 | 279 | 71 | 9.4 | 14 | 46 | 15 | 01 | 19 | 23 | 23 | 57 | 23 | 39 |
| 14 | 17 | 49 | −18.3 | 55.5 | 30.3 | 40 | 275 | 79 | 10.4 | 15 | 42 | 16 | 00 | 20 | 12 | — | | — | |
| 15 | 18 | 42 | −18.4 | 56.2 | 30.6 | 53 | 271 | 87 | 11.4 | 16 | 35 | 16 | 53 | 21 | 03 | 0 | 39 | 0 | 21 |
| 16 | 19 | 36 | −17.5 | 56.9 | 31.0 | 65 | 267 | 93 | 12.4 | 17 | 23 | 17 | 40 | 21 | 55 | 1 | 30 | 1 | 13 |
| 17 | 20 | 31 | −15.7 | 57.7 | 31.4 | 77 | 265 | 97 | 13.4 | 18 | 05 | 18 | 20 | 22 | 48 | 2 | 29 | 2 | 13 |
| 18 | 21 | 26 | −12.9 | 58.3 | 31.8 | 89 | 272 | 100 | 14.4 | 18 | 42 | 18 | 54 | 23 | 41 | 3 | 36 | 3 | 21 |
| 19 | 22 | 21 | −9.4 | 58.9 | 32.1 | 101 | 62 | 100 | 15.4 | 19 | 15 | 19 | 24 | — | | 4 | 47 | 4 | 36 |
| 20 | 23 | 16 | −5.2 | 59.4 | 32.4 | 114 | 68 | 97 | 16.4 | 19 | 45 | 19 | 49 | 0 | 34 | 6 | 03 | 5 | 56 |
| 21 | 0 | 11 | −0.7 | 59.6 | 32.5 | 126 | 69 | 92 | 17.4 | 20 | 13 | 20 | 14 | 1 | 26 | 7 | 20 | 7 | 17 |
| 22 | 1 | 06 | +3.8 | 59.7 | 32.6 | 138 | 70 | 84 | 18.4 | 20 | 41 | 20 | 38 | 2 | 19 | 8 | 38 | 8 | 39 |
| 23 | 2 | 01 | +8.1 | 59.7 | 32.5 | 150 | 72 | 74 | 19.4 | 21 | 10 | 21 | 03 | 3 | 12 | 9 | 56 | 10 | 01 |
| 24 | 2 | 57 | +11.9 | 59.5 | 32.4 | 162 | 75 | 64 | 20.4 | 21 | 41 | 21 | 31 | 4 | 05 | 11 | 14 | 11 | 23 |
| 25 | 3 | 54 | +15.0 | 59.2 | 32.3 | 174 | 78 | 52 | 21.4 | 22 | 17 | 22 | 04 | 5 | 00 | 12 | 30 | 12 | 43 |
| 26 | 4 | 52 | +17.2 | 58.8 | 32.1 | 187 | 82 | 41 | 22.4 | 23 | 00 | 22 | 43 | 5 | 55 | 13 | 42 | 13 | 57 |
| 27 | 5 | 50 | +18.3 | 58.4 | 31.8 | 199 | 87 | 30 | 23.4 | 23 | 48 | 23 | 30 | 6 | 51 | 14 | 48 | 15 | 06 |
| 28 | 6 | 48 | +18.3 | 58.0 | 31.6 | 211 | 91 | 21 | 24.4 | — | | — | | 7 | 47 | 15 | 47 | 16 | 05 |
| 29 | 7 | 44 | +17.3 | 57.5 | 31.3 | 223 | 96 | 13 | 25.4 | 0 | 44 | 0 | 26 | 8 | 43 | 16 | 37 | 16 | 54 |
| 30 | 8 | 39 | +15.3 | 57.0 | 31.1 | 236 | 99 | 6 | 26.4 | 1 | 46 | 1 | 30 | 9 | 37 | 17 | 19 | 17 | 34 |
| 31 | 9 | 32 | +12.6 | 56.5 | 30.8 | 248 | 102 | 2 | 27.4 | 2 | 53 | 2 | 38 | 10 | 28 | 17 | 54 | 18 | 05 |

## MERCURY

| Day | R.A. | | Dec | Mag. | Diam. | Phase | Rise | | Transit | | Set | |
|---|---|---|---|---|---|---|---|---|---|---|---|---|
| | h | m | ° | | " | % | h | m | h | m | h | m |
| 1 | 10 | 15.4 | +11.5 | −0.1 | 6 | 72 | 6 | 27 | 13 | 35 | 20 | 41 |
| 3 | 10 | 26.2 | +10.2 | 0.0 | 6 | 70 | 6 | 37 | 13 | 37 | 20 | 36 |
| 5 | 10 | 36.5 | +8.8 | 0.0 | 6 | 67 | 6 | 47 | 13 | 39 | 20 | 30 |
| 7 | 10 | 46.2 | +7.5 | +0.1 | 6 | 65 | 6 | 57 | 13 | 41 | 20 | 25 |
| 9 | 10 | 55.4 | +6.3 | +0.1 | 7 | 62 | 7 | 05 | 13 | 42 | 20 | 18 |
| 11 | 11 | 04.0 | +5.0 | +0.2 | 7 | 59 | 7 | 12 | 13 | 43 | 20 | 12 |
| 13 | 11 | 12.0 | +3.8 | +0.2 | 7 | 57 | 7 | 19 | 13 | 43 | 20 | 05 |
| 15 | 11 | 19.4 | +2.6 | +0.3 | 7 | 54 | 7 | 25 | 13 | 42 | 19 | 58 |
| 17 | 11 | 26.2 | +1.5 | +0.3 | 7 | 51 | 7 | 30 | 13 | 40 | 19 | 51 |
| 19 | 11 | 32.2 | +0.5 | +0.4 | 8 | 48 | 7 | 33 | 13 | 38 | 19 | 43 |
| 21 | 11 | 37.5 | −0.4 | +0.5 | 8 | 44 | 7 | 35 | 13 | 35 | 19 | 35 |
| 23 | 11 | 41.9 | −1.3 | +0.6 | 8 | 41 | 7 | 36 | 13 | 32 | 19 | 27 |
| 25 | 11 | 45.4 | −2.0 | +0.7 | 9 | 37 | 7 | 36 | 13 | 27 | 19 | 18 |
| 27 | 11 | 47.9 | −2.6 | +0.8 | 9 | 33 | 7 | 33 | 13 | 21 | 19 | 09 |
| 29 | 11 | 49.2 | −3.1 | +1.0 | 9 | 28 | 7 | 28 | 13 | 14 | 19 | 00 |
| 31 | 11 | 49.2 | −3.3 | +1.2 | 9 | 24 | 7 | 21 | 13 | 06 | 18 | 51 |

Rising and setting times are for latitude 54°

## VENUS

| Day | R.A. | | Dec | Mag. | Diam. | Phase | Rise | | Transit | | Set | |
|---|---|---|---|---|---|---|---|---|---|---|---|---|
| | h | m | ° | | " | % | h | m | h | m | h | m |
| 1 | 9 | 47.3 | +14.9 | −4.1 | 11 | 96 | 5 | 37 | 13 | 07 | 20 | 35 |
| 6 | 10 | 11.1 | +12.8 | −4.2 | 11 | 96 | 5 | 54 | 13 | 11 | 20 | 26 |
| 11 | 10 | 34.5 | +10.6 | −4.2 | 11 | 95 | 6 | 12 | 13 | 14 | 20 | 16 |
| 16 | 10 | 57.4 | +8.2 | −4.2 | 11 | 94 | 6 | 29 | 13 | 17 | 20 | 05 |
| 21 | 11 | 20.1 | +5.7 | −4.3 | 11 | 94 | 6 | 46 | 13 | 20 | 19 | 54 |
| 26 | 11 | 42.5 | +3.2 | −4.3 | 12 | 93 | 7 | 02 | 13 | 23 | 19 | 43 |
| 31 | 12 | 04.8 | +0.7 | −4.4 | 12 | 92 | 7 | 19 | 13 | 26 | 19 | 31 |

## MARS

| Day | R.A. | | Dec | Mag. | Diam. | Phase | Rise | | Transit | | Set | |
|---|---|---|---|---|---|---|---|---|---|---|---|---|
| | h | m | ° | | " | % | h | m | h | m | h | m |
| 1 | 15 | 44.9 | +22.8 | −0.8 | 13 | 87 | 15 | 21 | 19 | 04 | 22 | 47 |
| 6 | 15 | 53.0 | −23.2 | −0.7 | 13 | 87 | 15 | 12 | 18 | 53 | 22 | 33 |
| 11 | 16 | 02.0 | −23.6 | −0.6 | 12 | 86 | 15 | 05 | 18 | 42 | 22 | 19 |
| 16 | 16 | 11.8 | −24.0 | −0.5 | 12 | 86 | 14 | 58 | 18 | 32 | 22 | 06 |
| 21 | 16 | 22.3 | −24.4 | −0.4 | 11 | 85 | 14 | 52 | 18 | 23 | 21 | 53 |
| 26 | 16 | 33.5 | −24.8 | −0.4 | 11 | 85 | 14 | 46 | 18 | 14 | 21 | 42 |
| 31 | 16 | 45.3 | −25.1 | −0.3 | 11 | 85 | 14 | 41 | 18 | 06 | 21 | 31 |

# SUNRISE AND SUNSET

| | London | | | | Bristol | | | | Birmingham | | | | Manchester | | | | Newcastle | | | | Glasgow | | | | Belfast | | | |
|---|---|---|---|---|---|---|---|---|---|---|---|---|---|---|---|---|---|---|---|---|---|---|---|---|---|---|---|---|
| | 0° 05′ | | 51° 30′ | | 2° 35′ | | 51° 28′ | | 1° 55′ | | 52° 28′ | | 2° 15′ | | 53° 28′ | | 1° 37′ | | 54° 59′ | | 4° 14′ | | 55° 52′ | | 5° 56′ | | 54° 35′ | |
| d | h m | | h m | | h m | | h m | | h m | | h m | | h m | | h m | | h m | | h m | | h m | | h m | | h m | | h m | |
| 1 | 4 25 | | 19 48 | | 4 35 | | 19 58 | | 4 28 | | 19 59 | | 4 25 | | 20 04 | | 4 16 | | 20 08 | | 4 22 | | 20 23 | | 4 35 | | 20 24 | |
| 2 | 4 26 | | 19 46 | | 4 36 | | 19 56 | | 4 30 | | 19 57 | | 4 27 | | 20 02 | | 4 18 | | 20 06 | | 4 24 | | 20 21 | | 4 37 | | 20 22 | |
| 3 | 4 28 | | 19 44 | | 4 38 | | 19 54 | | 4 31 | | 19 55 | | 4 29 | | 20 00 | | 4 20 | | 20 04 | | 4 26 | | 20 19 | | 4 39 | | 20 20 | |
| 4 | 4 29 | | 19 43 | | 4 39 | | 19 52 | | 4 33 | | 19 53 | | 4 30 | | 19 59 | | 4 21 | | 20 02 | | 4 28 | | 20 17 | | 4 40 | | 20 18 | |
| 5 | 4 31 | | 19 41 | | 4 41 | | 19 51 | | 4 35 | | 19 52 | | 4 32 | | 19 57 | | 4 23 | | 20 00 | | 4 30 | | 20 15 | | 4 42 | | 20 16 | |
| 6 | 4 32 | | 19 39 | | 4 42 | | 19 49 | | 4 36 | | 19 50 | | 4 34 | | 19 55 | | 4 25 | | 19 58 | | 4 32 | | 20 13 | | 4 44 | | 20 14 | |
| 7 | 4 34 | | 19 37 | | 4 44 | | 19 47 | | 4 38 | | 19 48 | | 4 35 | | 19 53 | | 4 27 | | 19 56 | | 4 34 | | 20 10 | | 4 46 | | 20 12 | |
| 8 | 4 35 | | 19 35 | | 4 46 | | 19 45 | | 4 39 | | 19 46 | | 4 37 | | 19 51 | | 4 29 | | 19 54 | | 4 36 | | 20 08 | | 4 48 | | 20 10 | |
| 9 | 4 37 | | 19 34 | | 4 47 | | 19 43 | | 4 41 | | 19 44 | | 4 39 | | 19 49 | | 4 31 | | 19 52 | | 4 37 | | 20 06 | | 4 49 | | 20 08 | |
| 10 | 4 39 | | 19 32 | | 4 49 | | 19 42 | | 4 43 | | 19 42 | | 4 41 | | 19 47 | | 4 32 | | 19 50 | | 4 39 | | 20 04 | | 4 51 | | 20 06 | |
| 11 | 4 40 | | 19 30 | | 4 50 | | 19 40 | | 4 44 | | 19 40 | | 4 42 | | 19 45 | | 4 34 | | 19 48 | | 4 41 | | 20 01 | | 4 53 | | 20 03 | |
| 12 | 4 42 | | 19 28 | | 4 52 | | 19 38 | | 4 46 | | 19 38 | | 4 44 | | 19 43 | | 4 36 | | 19 45 | | 4 43 | | 19 59 | | 4 55 | | 20 01 | |
| 13 | 4 43 | | 19 26 | | 4 53 | | 19 36 | | 4 48 | | 19 36 | | 4 46 | | 19 41 | | 4 38 | | 19 43 | | 4 45 | | 19 57 | | 4 57 | | 19 59 | |
| 14 | 4 45 | | 19 24 | | 4 55 | | 19 34 | | 4 49 | | 19 34 | | 4 47 | | 19 39 | | 4 40 | | 19 41 | | 4 47 | | 19 55 | | 4 58 | | 19 57 | |
| 15 | 4 46 | | 19 22 | | 4 57 | | 19 32 | | 4 51 | | 19 32 | | 4 49 | | 19 36 | | 4 42 | | 19 39 | | 4 49 | | 19 52 | | 5 00 | | 19 55 | |
| 16 | 4 48 | | 19 20 | | 4 58 | | 19 30 | | 4 53 | | 19 30 | | 4 51 | | 19 34 | | 4 44 | | 19 36 | | 4 51 | | 19 50 | | 5 02 | | 19 52 | |
| 17 | 4 50 | | 19 18 | | 5 00 | | 19 28 | | 4 54 | | 19 28 | | 4 53 | | 19 32 | | 4 45 | | 19 34 | | 4 53 | | 19 48 | | 5 04 | | 19 50 | |
| 18 | 4 51 | | 19 16 | | 5 01 | | 19 26 | | 4 56 | | 19 26 | | 4 54 | | 19 30 | | 4 47 | | 19 32 | | 4 55 | | 19 45 | | 5 06 | | 19 48 | |
| 19 | 4 53 | | 19 14 | | 5 03 | | 19 24 | | 4 58 | | 19 24 | | 4 56 | | 19 28 | | 4 49 | | 19 30 | | 4 57 | | 19 43 | | 5 08 | | 19 46 | |
| 20 | 4 54 | | 19 12 | | 5 04 | | 19 22 | | 4 59 | | 19 21 | | 4 58 | | 19 25 | | 4 51 | | 19 27 | | 4 59 | | 19 40 | | 5 09 | | 19 43 | |
| 21 | 4 56 | | 19 10 | | 5 06 | | 19 20 | | 5 01 | | 19 19 | | 5 00 | | 19 23 | | 4 53 | | 19 25 | | 5 01 | | 19 38 | | 5 11 | | 19 41 | |
| 22 | 4 58 | | 19 08 | | 5 08 | | 19 17 | | 5 03 | | 19 17 | | 5 01 | | 19 21 | | 4 55 | | 19 22 | | 5 03 | | 19 35 | | 5 13 | | 19 39 | |
| 23 | 4 59 | | 19 05 | | 5 09 | | 19 15 | | 5 04 | | 19 15 | | 5 03 | | 19 19 | | 4 57 | | 19 20 | | 5 05 | | 19 33 | | 5 15 | | 19 36 | |
| 24 | 5 01 | | 19 03 | | 5 11 | | 19 13 | | 5 06 | | 19 13 | | 5 05 | | 19 16 | | 4 58 | | 19 18 | | 5 07 | | 19 30 | | 5 17 | | 19 34 | |
| 25 | 5 02 | | 19 01 | | 5 12 | | 19 11 | | 5 08 | | 19 11 | | 5 07 | | 19 14 | | 5 00 | | 19 15 | | 5 09 | | 19 28 | | 5 19 | | 19 31 | |
| 26 | 5 04 | | 18 59 | | 5 14 | | 19 09 | | 5 09 | | 19 08 | | 5 08 | | 19 12 | | 5 02 | | 19 13 | | 5 10 | | 19 25 | | 5 20 | | 19 29 | |
| 27 | 5 05 | | 18 57 | | 5 16 | | 19 07 | | 5 11 | | 19 06 | | 5 10 | | 19 09 | | 5 04 | | 19 10 | | 5 12 | | 19 23 | | 5 22 | | 19 27 | |
| 28 | 5 07 | | 18 55 | | 5 17 | | 19 05 | | 5 13 | | 19 04 | | 5 12 | | 19 07 | | 5 06 | | 19 08 | | 5 14 | | 19 20 | | 5 24 | | 19 24 | |
| 29 | 5 09 | | 18 52 | | 5 19 | | 19 02 | | 5 14 | | 19 02 | | 5 14 | | 19 05 | | 5 08 | | 19 05 | | 5 16 | | 19 18 | | 5 26 | | 19 22 | |
| 30 | 5 10 | | 18 50 | | 5 20 | | 19 00 | | 5 16 | | 18 59 | | 5 15 | | 19 02 | | 5 10 | | 19 03 | | 5 18 | | 19 15 | | 5 28 | | 19 19 | |
| 31 | 5 12 | | 18 48 | | 5 22 | | 18 58 | | 5 18 | | 18 57 | | 5 17 | | 19 00 | | 5 12 | | 19 00 | | 5 20 | | 19 13 | | 5 30 | | 19 17 | |

## JUPITER

| Day | R.A. | | Dec | Mag. | Diam. | Rise | | Transit | | Set | |
|---|---|---|---|---|---|---|---|---|---|---|---|
| | h | m | ° | | ″ | h | m | h | m | h | m |
| 1 | 11 | 31.8 | +4.3 | −1.7 | 32 | 8 | 23 | 14 | 49 | 21 | 16 |
| 11 | 11 | 38.7 | +3.5 | −1.7 | 32 | 7 | 55 | 14 | 17 | 20 | 39 |
| 21 | 11 | 46.0 | +2.7 | −1.7 | 31 | 7 | 27 | 13 | 45 | 20 | 03 |
| 31 | 11 | 53.5 | +1.9 | −1.7 | 31 | 7 | 00 | 13 | 13 | 19 | 26 |

Equatorial Diam. 31″, Polar Diam. 29″

## SATURN

| Day | R.A. | | Dec | Mag. | Diam. | Rise | | Transit | | Set | |
|---|---|---|---|---|---|---|---|---|---|---|---|
| | h | m | ° | | ″ | h | m | h | m | h | m |
| 1 | 16 | 33.1 | −20.3 | +0.4 | 18 | 15 | 48 | 19 | 50 | 23 | 56 |
| 11 | 16 | 32.6 | −20.3 | +0.4 | 17 | 15 | 08 | 19 | 10 | 23 | 12 |
| 21 | 16 | 32.7 | −20.3 | +0.5 | 17 | 14 | 29 | 18 | 31 | 22 | 33 |
| 31 | 16 | 33.5 | −20.4 | +0.5 | 17 | 13 | 51 | 17 | 52 | 21 | 54 |

Equatorial Diam. 17″, Polar Diam. 16″
Rings – major axis 39″ minor axis 17″, Tilt 26°

## URANUS

| Day | R.A. | | Dec | Mag. | Diam. | Rise | | Transit | | Set | |
|---|---|---|---|---|---|---|---|---|---|---|---|
| | h | m | ° | | ″ | h | m | h | m | h | m |
| 1 | 1 | 30.8 | +8.8 | +6.1 | 4 | 21 | 58 | 4 | 50 | 11 | 42 |
| 11 | 1 | 30.6 | +8.8 | +6.1 | 4 | 21 | 18 | 4 | 10 | 11 | 03 |
| 21 | 1 | 30.1 | +8.8 | +6.1 | 4 | 20 | 39 | 3 | 31 | 10 | 22 |
| 31 | 1 | 29.3 | +8.7 | +6.1 | 4 | 19 | 59 | 2 | 50 | 9 | 42 |

## NEPTUNE

| Day | R.A. | | Dec | Mag. | Diam. | Rise | | Transit | | Set | |
|---|---|---|---|---|---|---|---|---|---|---|---|
| | h | m | ° | | ″ | h | m | h | m | h | m |
| 1 | 22 | 52.1 | −8.2 | +7.8 | 2 | 20 | 50 | 2 | 12 | 7 | 29 |
| 11 | 22 | 51.2 | −8.2 | +7.8 | 2 | 20 | 10 | 1 | 31 | 6 | 48 |
| 21 | 22 | 50.2 | −8.3 | +7.8 | 2 | 19 | 31 | 0 | 51 | 6 | 08 |
| 31 | 22 | 49.2 | −8.5 | +7.8 | 2 | 18 | 51 | 0 | 11 | 5 | 27 |

# SEPTEMBER 2016

NINTH MONTH, 30 DAYS. *Septem* (seven), seventh month of Roman pre-Julian calendar

| | | | |
|---|---|---|---|
| 1 | *Thursday* | A bloodless military coup in Libya deposes King Idris 1969 | day 245 |
| 2 | *Friday* | The Treaty of Jaffa, between Saladin and Richard I, ends the hostilities of the 3rd Crusade 1192 | 246 |
| 3 | *Saturday* | Richard I (Coeur de Lion) is crowned at Westminster Abbey 1189 | 247 |
| 4 | *Sunday* | The French Third Republic is proclaimed following the overthrow of Napoleon III 1870 | 248 |

| | | | |
|---|---|---|---|
| 5 | *Monday* | Sam Houston is elected as the first president of the Republic of Texas 1836 | week 36 day 249 |
| 6 | *Tuesday* | Lithuania's independence is officially recognised by the Soviet Union 1991 | 250 |
| 7 | *Wednesday* | Henry Campbell-Bannerman, Liberal Prime Minister (1905–8) *b.* 1836 | 251 |
| 8 | *Thursday* | President of Chile Augusto Pinochet survives an assassination attempt 1986 | 252 |
| 9 | *Friday* | UK Ambassador Geoffrey Jackson is freed after being held for 8 months by rebels in Uruguay 1971 | 253 |
| 10 | *Saturday* | Mary Wollstonecraft, political theorist and advocate of women's rights *d.* 1797 | 254 |
| 11 | *Sunday* | Chilean president Salvador Allende commits suicide after his government is toppled in a military coup 1973 | 255 |

| | | | |
|---|---|---|---|
| 12 | *Monday* | Herbert Asquith, prime minister at the outbreak of the First World War *b.* 1852 | week 37 day 256 |
| 13 | *Tuesday* | Albania withdraws from the Warsaw Pact due to differences with the Soviet Union 1968 | 257 |
| 14 | *Wednesday* | Duke of Wellington (1st), leading military and political figure of the 19th century *d.* 1852 | 258 |
| 15 | *Thursday* | The Nuremberg Race Laws are unanimously passed by the Reichstag in Nazi Germany 1935 | 259 |
| 16 | *Friday* | Owain Glyndwr proclaims himself Prince of Wales and instigates a Welsh revolt against Henry IV 1400 | 260 |
| 17 | *Saturday* | The British National Party wins its first council seat in Millwall, London 1993 | 261 |
| 18 | *Sunday* | In a referendum the Welsh people vote in favour of a devolved National Assembly for Wales 1997 | 262 |

| | | | |
|---|---|---|---|
| 19 | *Monday* | New Zealand becomes the first country to grant all women aged 21 and over the right to vote 1893 | week 38 day 263 |
| 20 | *Tuesday* | The South Africa Act 1909 gains royal assent, creating the Union of South Africa | 264 |
| 21 | *Wednesday* | Britain formally annexes the islet of Rockall to prevent Soviet spying 1955 | 265 |
| 22 | *Thursday* | Sir Robert Walpole takes up residence at 10 Downing Street, the first prime minister to do so 1735 | 266 |
| 23 | *Friday* | Negotiations on the Karlstad Treaty end with an agreement to disunite Sweden and Norway 1905 | 267 |
| 24 | *Saturday* | The Rhodesian government agrees to introduce black majority rule 1974 | 268 |
| 25 | *Sunday* | Henry Pelham, Whig prime minister during the reign of George II *b.* 1694 | 269 |

| | | | |
|---|---|---|---|
| 26 | *Monday* | The first televised debate between US presidential candidates (Kennedy and Nixon) occurs 1960 | week 39 day 270 |
| 27 | *Tuesday* | For one day Lancaster, Pennsylvania becomes the capital of the American colonies 1777 | 271 |
| 28 | *Wednesday* | The Israeli-Palestinian Interim Agreement on the West Bank and the Gaza Strip is officially signed 1995 | 272 |
| 29 | *Thursday* | Lech Walesa, president of Poland and Nobel Peace Prize laureate *b.* 1943 | 273 |
| 30 | *Friday* | Neville Chamberlain makes his 'peace for our time' speech on the Munich Agreement 1938 | 274 |

## ASTRONOMICAL PHENOMENA

| d | h | |
|---|---|---|
| 1 | 09 | Annular eclipse of the Sun |
| 2 | 22 | Jupiter 0.4° South of the Moon |
| 2 | 17 | Neptune at opposition |
| 3 | 11 | Venus 1° South of the Moon |
| 8 | 21 | Saturn 4° South of the Moon |
| 16 | 19 | Penumbral eclipse of the Moon |
| 18 | 17 | Uranus 3° North of the Moon |
| 22 | 14 | Equinox |
| 28 | 19 | Mercury Greatest elongation West |
| 29 | 11 | Mercury 1° North of the Moon |
| 30 | 16 | Jupiter 1° South of the Moon |

## MINIMA OF ALGOL

| d | h | d | h | d | h |
|---|---|---|---|---|---|
| 1 | 05.4 | 12 | 16.6 | 24 | 03.9 |
| 4 | 02.2 | 15 | 13.5 | 27 | 00.7 |
| 6 | 23.0 | 18 | 10.3 | 29 | 21.5 |
| 9 | 19.8 | 21 | 07.1 | | |

## CONSTELLATIONS
The following constellations are near their meridian at

| | d | h | | d | h |
|---|---|---|---|---|---|
| August | 1 | 24 | September | 15 | 21 |
| August | 16 | 23 | October | 1 | 20 |
| September | 1 | 22 | October | 16 | 19 |

Draco, Cepheus, Lyra, Cygnus, Vulpecula, Sagitta, Delphinus, Equuleus, Aquila, Aquarius and Capricornus

## THE MOON

| Phases, Apsides and Node | d | h | m |
|---|---|---|---|
| ● New Moon | 1 | 09 | 03 |
| ◐ First Quarter | 9 | 11 | 49 |
| ○ Full Moon | 16 | 19 | 05 |
| ◑ Last Quarter | 23 | 09 | 56 |
| Apogee (405,055km) | 6 | 18 | 45 |
| Perigee (361,896km) | 18 | 17 | 00 |

Mean longitude of ascending node on 1st, 163°

# THE SUN

Diam. 31.8″

| Day | Right Ascension h | m | s | Dec. ° | Equation of time m | s | Rise 52° h | m | Rise 56° h | m | Transit h | m | Set 52° h | m | Set 56° h | m | Sidereal time h | m | s | Transit of first point of Aries h | m | s |
|---|---|---|---|---|---|---|---|---|---|---|---|---|---|---|---|---|---|---|---|---|---|---|
| 1 | 10 | 42 | 13 | +8.2 | −0 | 02 | 5 | 11 | 5 | 03 | 12 | 00 | 18 | 49 | 18 | 56 | 21 | 42 | 11 | 1 | 17 | 39 |
| 2 | 10 | 45 | 51 | +6.8 | +0 | 17 | 5 | 12 | 5 | 05 | 12 | 00 | 18 | 46 | 18 | 53 | 21 | 46 | 08 | 1 | 13 | 42 |
| 3 | 10 | 49 | 28 | +6.5 | +0 | 37 | 5 | 14 | 5 | 07 | 12 | 00 | 18 | 44 | 18 | 51 | 21 | 50 | 05 | 1 | 09 | 46 |
| 4 | 10 | 53 | 05 | +6.1 | +0 | 56 | 5 | 16 | 5 | 09 | 11 | 59 | 18 | 42 | 18 | 48 | 21 | 54 | 01 | 1 | 05 | 49 |
| 5 | 10 | 56 | 41 | +6.7 | +1 | 16 | 5 | 17 | 5 | 11 | 11 | 59 | 18 | 39 | 18 | 46 | 21 | 57 | 58 | 1 | 01 | 52 |
| 6 | 11 | 00 | 18 | +6.4 | +1 | 36 | 5 | 19 | 5 | 13 | 11 | 59 | 18 | 37 | 18 | 43 | 22 | 01 | 54 | 0 | 57 | 56 |
| 7 | 11 | 03 | 54 | +6.0 | +1 | 57 | 5 | 20 | 5 | 15 | 11 | 58 | 18 | 35 | 18 | 40 | 22 | 05 | 51 | 0 | 53 | 59 |
| 8 | 11 | 07 | 30 | +5.6 | +2 | 17 | 5 | 22 | 5 | 17 | 11 | 58 | 18 | 33 | 18 | 38 | 22 | 09 | 47 | 0 | 50 | 03 |
| 9 | 11 | 11 | 06 | +5.2 | +2 | 38 | 5 | 24 | 5 | 19 | 11 | 58 | 18 | 30 | 18 | 35 | 22 | 13 | 44 | 0 | 46 | 06 |
| 10 | 11 | 14 | 41 | +4.9 | +2 | 59 | 5 | 25 | 5 | 21 | 11 | 57 | 18 | 28 | 18 | 33 | 22 | 17 | 40 | 0 | 42 | 10 |
| 11 | 11 | 18 | 17 | +4.5 | +3 | 20 | 5 | 27 | 5 | 22 | 11 | 57 | 18 | 26 | 18 | 30 | 22 | 21 | 37 | 0 | 38 | 13 |
| 12 | 11 | 21 | 52 | +4.1 | +3 | 41 | 5 | 29 | 5 | 24 | 11 | 56 | 18 | 23 | 18 | 27 | 22 | 25 | 34 | 0 | 34 | 17 |
| 13 | 11 | 25 | 27 | +3.7 | +4 | 02 | 5 | 30 | 5 | 26 | 11 | 56 | 18 | 21 | 18 | 25 | 22 | 29 | 30 | 0 | 30 | 20 |
| 14 | 11 | 29 | 03 | +3.3 | +4 | 24 | 5 | 32 | 5 | 28 | 11 | 56 | 18 | 19 | 18 | 22 | 22 | 33 | 27 | 0 | 26 | 23 |
| 15 | 11 | 32 | 38 | +3.0 | +4 | 45 | 5 | 33 | 5 | 30 | 11 | 55 | 18 | 16 | 18 | 19 | 22 | 37 | 23 | 0 | 22 | 27 |
| 16 | 11 | 36 | 13 | +2.6 | +5 | 07 | 5 | 35 | 5 | 32 | 11 | 55 | 18 | 14 | 18 | 17 | 22 | 41 | 20 | 0 | 18 | 30 |
| 17 | 11 | 39 | 48 | +2.2 | +5 | 28 | 5 | 37 | 5 | 34 | 11 | 55 | 18 | 12 | 18 | 14 | 22 | 45 | 16 | 0 | 14 | 34 |
| 18 | 11 | 43 | 23 | +1.8 | +5 | 50 | 5 | 38 | 5 | 36 | 11 | 54 | 18 | 09 | 18 | 11 | 22 | 49 | 13 | 0 | 10 | 37 |
| 19 | 11 | 46 | 58 | +1.4 | +6 | 11 | 5 | 40 | 5 | 38 | 11 | 54 | 18 | 07 | 18 | 09 | 22 | 53 | 09 | 0 | 06 | 41 |
| 20 | 11 | 50 | 33 | +1.0 | +6 | 33 | 5 | 42 | 5 | 40 | 11 | 54 | 18 | 05 | 18 | 06 | 22 | 57 | 06 | 0 | 02 | 44 |
| 21 | 11 | 54 | 08 | +0.6 | +6 | 54 | 5 | 43 | 5 | 42 | 11 | 53 | 18 | 02 | 18 | 03 | 23 | 01 | 03 | 23 | 58 | 48 |
| 22 | 11 | 57 | 44 | +0.2 | +7 | 15 | 5 | 45 | 5 | 44 | 11 | 53 | 18 | 00 | 18 | 01 | 23 | 04 | 59 | 23 | 54 | 51 |
| 23 | 12 | 01 | 19 | −0.1 | +7 | 36 | 5 | 47 | 5 | 46 | 11 | 53 | 17 | 58 | 17 | 58 | 23 | 08 | 56 | 23 | 50 | 54 |
| 24 | 12 | 04 | 55 | −0.5 | +7 | 57 | 5 | 48 | 5 | 48 | 11 | 52 | 17 | 55 | 17 | 55 | 23 | 12 | 52 | 23 | 46 | 58 |
| 25 | 12 | 08 | 30 | −0.9 | +8 | 18 | 5 | 50 | 5 | 50 | 11 | 52 | 17 | 53 | 17 | 53 | 23 | 16 | 49 | 23 | 43 | 01 |
| 26 | 12 | 12 | 06 | −1.3 | +8 | 39 | 5 | 51 | 5 | 52 | 11 | 52 | 17 | 51 | 17 | 50 | 23 | 20 | 45 | 23 | 39 | 05 |
| 27 | 12 | 15 | 43 | −1.7 | +8 | 59 | 5 | 53 | 5 | 54 | 11 | 51 | 17 | 48 | 17 | 47 | 23 | 24 | 42 | 23 | 35 | 08 |
| 28 | 12 | 19 | 19 | −2.1 | +9 | 19 | 5 | 55 | 5 | 56 | 11 | 51 | 17 | 46 | 17 | 45 | 23 | 28 | 38 | 23 | 31 | 12 |
| 29 | 12 | 22 | 56 | −2.5 | +9 | 39 | 5 | 56 | 5 | 58 | 11 | 50 | 17 | 44 | 17 | 42 | 23 | 32 | 35 | 23 | 27 | 15 |
| 30 | 12 | 26 | 32 | −2.9 | +9 | 59 | 5 | 58 | 6 | 00 | 11 | 50 | 17 | 41 | 17 | 40 | 23 | 36 | 32 | 23 | 23 | 19 |

## DURATION OF TWILIGHT (in minutes)

| Latitude | 52° | 56° | 52° | 56° | 52° | 56° | 52° | 56° |
|---|---|---|---|---|---|---|---|---|
| | 1 September | | 11 September | | 21 September | | 31 September | |
| Civil | 35 | 39 | 34 | 38 | 34 | 37 | 34 | 37 |
| Nautical | 79 | 89 | 76 | 85 | 74 | 82 | 73 | 80 |
| Astronomical | 127 | 147 | 120 | 136 | 116 | 129 | 113 | 125 |

## THE NIGHT SKY

*Mercury* moves into the morning sky after inferior conjunction on the 13th. It is at greatest elongation west (18°) on the 28th and rises two hours before the Sun by the end of September. The Moon is nearby on the 29th.

Things improve a little for *Venus* but it will still be quite low all month. The Moon is nearby on the 3rd.

*Mars,* magnitude −0.3 to +0.1, now sets three hours after the Sun. It lies 7° below the Moon on the 9th. Mars crosses into Ophiuchus on the 3rd then Sagittarius on the 22nd.

*Jupiter* might be seen the first few days of September very low in the west after sunset but it is soon swamped by the twilight glow. The planet reaches conjunction on the 26th.

*Saturn,* magnitude +0.5, sets 3.25 hours after the Sun at the beginning of September but by an hour earlier on the 30th.

*Neptune* is at opposition on September 2nd when the magnitude 7.8 planet can be found in Aquarius.

*An annular solar eclipse* on September 1st sweeps across Central Africa and the northern part of Madagascar. Bordering countries will experience a partial solar eclipse.

*A penumbral lunar eclipse* on September 16th is visible from Eurasia, Africa, and Australia. The eclipse is in progress at moonrise from the UK. The Moon dips 90 per cent of the way into the southern part of the Earth's penumbral shadow so observers should notice a distinct dimming of the northern limb of the Moon.

# THE MOON

| Day | R.A. | | Dec. | Hor. Par. | Diam. | Sun's Co-Long. | PA of Br. Limb | Ph. | Age | Rise | | | | Transit | | Set | | | |
|---|---|---|---|---|---|---|---|---|---|---|---|---|---|---|---|---|---|---|---|
| | | | | | | | | | | 52° | | 56° | | | | 52° | | 56° | |
| | h | m | ° | ′ | ′ | ° | ° | % | d | h | m | h | m | h | m | h | m | h | m |
| 1 | 10 | 23 | +9.3 | 56.0 | 30.5 | 260 | 102 | 0 | 28.4 | 4 | 01 | 3 | 50 | 11 | 18 | 18 | 24 | 18 | 32 |
| 2 | 11 | 11 | +5.6 | 55.5 | 30.3 | 272 | 290 | 0 | 29.4 | 5 | 08 | 5 | 01 | 12 | 05 | 18 | 50 | 18 | 55 |
| 3 | 11 | 59 | +1.8 | 55.1 | 30.0 | 285 | 289 | 2 | 0.9 | 6 | 15 | 6 | 12 | 12 | 50 | 19 | 14 | 19 | 16 |
| 4 | 12 | 45 | −2.1 | 54.7 | 29.8 | 297 | 288 | 6 | 1.9 | 7 | 21 | 7 | 21 | 13 | 35 | 19 | 37 | 19 | 36 |
| 5 | 13 | 31 | −5.8 | 54.4 | 29.6 | 309 | 288 | 12 | 2.9 | 8 | 26 | 8 | 29 | 14 | 18 | 20 | 00 | 19 | 56 |
| 6 | 14 | 17 | −9.3 | 54.2 | 29.5 | 321 | 286 | 19 | 3.9 | 9 | 30 | 9 | 36 | 15 | 01 | 20 | 24 | 20 | 16 |
| 7 | 15 | 04 | −12.3 | 54.1 | 29.5 | 333 | 284 | 27 | 4.9 | 10 | 32 | 10 | 42 | 15 | 45 | 20 | 50 | 20 | 39 |
| 8 | 15 | 51 | −14.9 | 54.2 | 29.6 | 346 | 281 | 36 | 5.9 | 11 | 34 | 11 | 46 | 16 | 29 | 21 | 19 | 21 | 06 |
| 9 | 16 | 40 | −16.8 | 54.5 | 29.7 | 358 | 277 | 45 | 6.9 | 12 | 34 | 12 | 49 | 17 | 15 | 21 | 53 | 21 | 37 |
| 10 | 17 | 30 | −18.0 | 55.0 | 30.0 | 10 | 273 | 55 | 7.9 | 13 | 31 | 13 | 48 | 18 | 03 | 22 | 32 | 22 | 15 |
| 11 | 18 | 22 | −18.5 | 55.6 | 30.3 | 22 | 269 | 64 | 8.9 | 14 | 25 | 14 | 43 | 18 | 52 | 23 | 19 | 23 | 02 |
| 12 | 19 | 15 | −18.0 | 56.3 | 30.7 | 35 | 265 | 74 | 9.9 | 15 | 14 | 15 | 32 | 19 | 43 | — | | 23 | 56 |
| 13 | 20 | 09 | −16.5 | 57.2 | 31.1 | 47 | 261 | 82 | 10.9 | 15 | 57 | 16 | 14 | 20 | 34 | 0 | 14 | — | |
| 14 | 21 | 04 | −14.1 | 58.0 | 31.6 | 59 | 257 | 90 | 11.9 | 16 | 37 | 16 | 50 | 21 | 27 | 1 | 16 | 1 | 01 |
| 15 | 21 | 59 | −10.9 | 58.9 | 32.1 | 71 | 253 | 95 | 12.9 | 17 | 11 | 17 | 22 | 22 | 20 | 2 | 24 | 2 | 12 |
| 16 | 22 | 54 | −6.9 | 59.6 | 32.5 | 83 | 248 | 99 | 13.9 | 17 | 43 | 17 | 49 | 23 | 13 | 3 | 38 | 3 | 29 |
| 17 | 23 | 50 | −2.5 | 60.2 | 32.8 | 95 | 97 | 100 | 14.9 | 18 | 12 | 18 | 15 | — | | 4 | 55 | 4 | 50 |
| 18 | 0 | 46 | +2.2 | 60.5 | 33.0 | 108 | 76 | 98 | 15.9 | 18 | 40 | 18 | 39 | 0 | 07 | 6 | 15 | 6 | 14 |
| 19 | 1 | 43 | +6.8 | 60.6 | 33.0 | 120 | 75 | 93 | 16.9 | 19 | 10 | 19 | 05 | 1 | 01 | 7 | 36 | 7 | 39 |
| 20 | 2 | 40 | +10.9 | 60.4 | 32.9 | 132 | 77 | 86 | 17.9 | 19 | 41 | 19 | 32 | 1 | 56 | 8 | 56 | 9 | 04 |
| 21 | 3 | 39 | +14.3 | 60.0 | 32.7 | 144 | 80 | 77 | 18.9 | 20 | 17 | 20 | 05 | 2 | 52 | 10 | 16 | 10 | 28 |
| 22 | 4 | 38 | +16.8 | 59.5 | 32.4 | 156 | 84 | 67 | 19.9 | 20 | 58 | 20 | 42 | 3 | 49 | 11 | 32 | 11 | 47 |
| 23 | 5 | 37 | +18.2 | 58.8 | 32.1 | 168 | 88 | 55 | 20.9 | 21 | 45 | 21 | 27 | 4 | 46 | 12 | 41 | 12 | 58 |
| 24 | 6 | 35 | +18.4 | 58.2 | 31.7 | 181 | 93 | 44 | 21.9 | 22 | 39 | 22 | 21 | 5 | 43 | 13 | 43 | 14 | 01 |
| 25 | 7 | 32 | +17.6 | 57.5 | 31.4 | 193 | 97 | 33 | 22.9 | 23 | 40 | 23 | 22 | 6 | 39 | 14 | 36 | 14 | 53 |
| 26 | 8 | 26 | +15.9 | 56.9 | 31.0 | 205 | 102 | 24 | 23.9 | — | | — | | 7 | 33 | 15 | 20 | 15 | 35 |
| 27 | 9 | 19 | +13.3 | 56.4 | 30.7 | 217 | 106 | 16 | 24.9 | 0 | 44 | 0 | 29 | 8 | 25 | 15 | 56 | 16 | 09 |
| 28 | 10 | 09 | +10.2 | 55.8 | 30.4 | 229 | 109 | 9 | 25.9 | 1 | 51 | 1 | 38 | 9 | 14 | 16 | 27 | 16 | 37 |
| 29 | 10 | 58 | +6.7 | 55.4 | 30.2 | 242 | 113 | 4 | 26.9 | 2 | 58 | 2 | 49 | 10 | 01 | 16 | 54 | 17 | 00 |
| 30 | 11 | 45 | +2.9 | 55.0 | 30.0 | 254 | 119 | 1 | 27.9 | 4 | 04 | 3 | 59 | 10 | 47 | 17 | 18 | 17 | 21 |

# MERCURY

| Day | R.A. | | Dec | Mag. | Diam. | Phase | Rise | | Transit | | Set | |
|---|---|---|---|---|---|---|---|---|---|---|---|---|
| | h | m | ° | | ″ | % | h | m | h | m | h | m |
| 1 | 11 | 48.7 | −3.4 | +1.4 | 10 | 21 | 7 | 17 | 13 | 01 | 18 | 46 |
| 3 | 11 | 46.7 | −3.3 | +1.7 | 10 | 17 | 7 | 06 | 12 | 51 | 18 | 37 |
| 5 | 11 | 43.4 | −3.0 | +2.2 | 10 | 12 | 6 | 53 | 12 | 39 | 18 | 27 |
| 7 | 11 | 38.6 | −2.4 | +2.8 | 10 | 8 | 6 | 37 | 12 | 26 | 18 | 18 |
| 9 | 11 | 32.8 | −1.6 | +3.5 | 11 | 4 | 6 | 18 | 12 | 12 | 18 | 09 |
| 11 | 11 | 26.3 | −0.5 | +4.3 | 11 | 2 | 5 | 58 | 11 | 58 | 18 | 00 |
| 13 | 11 | 19.5 | +0.7 | +4.9 | 10 | 1 | 5 | 37 | 11 | 43 | 17 | 53 |
| 15 | 11 | 13.1 | +1.9 | +4.4 | 10 | 1 | 5 | 16 | 11 | 29 | 17 | 46 |
| 17 | 11 | 07.7 | +3.2 | +3.4 | 10 | 4 | 4 | 57 | 11 | 17 | 17 | 40 |
| 19 | 11 | 04.0 | +4.3 | +2.4 | 9 | 9 | 4 | 40 | 11 | 06 | 17 | 35 |
| 21 | 11 | 02.3 | +5.2 | +1.5 | 9 | 15 | 4 | 26 | 10 | 57 | 17 | 31 |
| 23 | 11 | 03.0 | +5.8 | +0.8 | 8 | 23 | 4 | 16 | 10 | 50 | 17 | 27 |
| 25 | 11 | 05.9 | +6.1 | +0.3 | 8 | 32 | 4 | 10 | 10 | 46 | 17 | 24 |
| 27 | 11 | 11.1 | +6.1 | −0.1 | 7 | 42 | 4 | 08 | 10 | 44 | 17 | 22 |
| 29 | 11 | 18.3 | +5.7 | −0.4 | 7 | 51 | 4 | 09 | 10 | 44 | 17 | 19 |

Rising and setting times are for latitude 54°

# VENUS

| Day | R.A. | | Dec | Mag. | Diam. | Phase | Rise | | Transit | | Set | |
|---|---|---|---|---|---|---|---|---|---|---|---|---|
| | h | m | ° | | ″ | % | h | m | h | m | h | m |
| 1 | 12 | 09.3 | +0.1 | −4.4 | 12 | 92 | 7 | 22 | 13 | 26 | 19 | 29 |
| 6 | 12 | 31.5 | −2.4 | −4.5 | 12 | 91 | 7 | 39 | 13 | 29 | 19 | 17 |
| 11 | 12 | 53.8 | −5.0 | −4.5 | 12 | 90 | 7 | 56 | 13 | 31 | 19 | 06 |
| 16 | 13 | 16.2 | −7.5 | −4.6 | 12 | 89 | 8 | 13 | 13 | 34 | 18 | 54 |
| 21 | 13 | 38.8 | −10.0 | −4.6 | 13 | 88 | 8 | 30 | 13 | 37 | 18 | 43 |
| 26 | 14 | 01.8 | −12.4 | −4.7 | 13 | 87 | 8 | 47 | 13 | 40 | 18 | 32 |

# MARS

| Day | R.A. | | Dec | Mag. | Diam. | Phase | Rise | | Transit | | Set | |
|---|---|---|---|---|---|---|---|---|---|---|---|---|
| | h | m | ° | | ″ | % | h | m | h | m | h | m |
| 1 | 16 | 47.8 | −25.2 | −0.3 | 10 | 85 | 14 | 40 | 18 | 05 | 21 | 30 |
| 6 | 17 | 00.3 | −25.4 | −0.2 | 10 | 85 | 14 | 35 | 17 | 57 | 21 | 20 |
| 11 | 17 | 13.3 | −25.7 | −0.2 | 10 | 85 | 14 | 30 | 17 | 51 | 21 | 12 |
| 16 | 17 | 26.8 | −25.8 | −0.1 | 10 | 85 | 14 | 25 | 17 | 44 | 21 | 04 |
| 21 | 17 | 40.7 | −25.9 | 0.0 | 9 | 85 | 14 | 19 | 17 | 39 | 20 | 58 |
| 26 | 17 | 55.0 | −25.9 | 0.0 | 9 | 85 | 14 | 14 | 17 | 33 | 20 | 52 |

# SUNRISE AND SUNSET

| | London 0° 05' 51° 30' | | Bristol 2° 35' 51° 28' | | Birmingham 1° 55' 52° 28' | | Manchester 2° 15' 53° 28' | | Newcastle 1° 37' 54° 59' | | Glasgow 4° 14' 55° 52' | | Belfast 5° 56' 54° 35' | |
|---|---|---|---|---|---|---|---|---|---|---|---|---|---|---|
| d | h m | h m | h m | h m | h m | h m | h m | h m | h m | h m | h m | h m | h m | h m |
| 1 | 5 13 | 18 46 | 5 24 | 18 56 | 5 19 | 18 55 | 5 19 | 18 58 | 5 13 | 18 58 | 5 22 | 19 10 | 5 31 | 19 14 |
| 2 | 5 15 | 18 44 | 5 25 | 18 54 | 5 21 | 18 52 | 5 21 | 18 55 | 5 15 | 18 55 | 5 24 | 19 07 | 5 33 | 19 12 |
| 3 | 5 17 | 18 41 | 5 27 | 18 51 | 5 23 | 18 50 | 5 22 | 18 53 | 5 17 | 18 53 | 5 26 | 19 05 | 5 35 | 19 09 |
| 4 | 5 18 | 18 39 | 5 28 | 18 49 | 5 24 | 18 48 | 5 24 | 18 51 | 5 19 | 18 50 | 5 28 | 19 02 | 5 37 | 19 07 |
| 5 | 5 20 | 18 37 | 5 30 | 18 47 | 5 26 | 18 45 | 5 26 | 18 48 | 5 21 | 18 48 | 5 30 | 19 00 | 5 39 | 19 04 |
| 6 | 5 21 | 18 35 | 5 31 | 18 45 | 5 28 | 18 43 | 5 27 | 18 46 | 5 23 | 18 45 | 5 32 | 18 57 | 5 41 | 19 02 |
| 7 | 5 23 | 18 32 | 5 33 | 18 42 | 5 29 | 18 41 | 5 29 | 18 43 | 5 25 | 18 43 | 5 34 | 18 55 | 5 42 | 19 00 |
| 8 | 5 25 | 18 30 | 5 35 | 18 40 | 5 31 | 18 38 | 5 31 | 18 41 | 5 26 | 18 40 | 5 36 | 18 52 | 5 44 | 18 57 |
| 9 | 5 26 | 18 28 | 5 36 | 18 38 | 5 32 | 18 36 | 5 33 | 18 39 | 5 28 | 18 38 | 5 38 | 18 49 | 5 46 | 18 55 |
| 10 | 5 28 | 18 25 | 5 38 | 18 35 | 5 34 | 18 34 | 5 34 | 18 36 | 5 30 | 18 35 | 5 40 | 18 47 | 5 48 | 18 52 |
| 11 | 5 29 | 18 23 | 5 39 | 18 33 | 5 36 | 18 31 | 5 36 | 18 34 | 5 32 | 18 33 | 5 42 | 18 44 | 5 50 | 18 49 |
| 12 | 5 31 | 18 21 | 5 41 | 18 31 | 5 37 | 18 29 | 5 38 | 18 31 | 5 34 | 18 30 | 5 43 | 18 41 | 5 52 | 18 47 |
| 13 | 5 33 | 18 19 | 5 43 | 18 29 | 5 39 | 18 27 | 5 40 | 18 29 | 5 36 | 18 27 | 5 45 | 18 39 | 5 53 | 18 44 |
| 14 | 5 34 | 18 16 | 5 44 | 18 26 | 5 41 | 18 24 | 5 41 | 18 26 | 5 38 | 18 25 | 5 47 | 18 36 | 5 55 | 18 42 |
| 15 | 5 36 | 18 14 | 5 46 | 18 24 | 5 42 | 18 22 | 5 43 | 18 24 | 5 39 | 18 22 | 5 49 | 18 33 | 5 57 | 18 39 |
| 16 | 5 37 | 18 12 | 5 47 | 18 22 | 5 44 | 18 19 | 5 45 | 18 21 | 5 41 | 18 20 | 5 51 | 18 31 | 5 59 | 18 37 |
| 17 | 5 39 | 18 09 | 5 49 | 18 19 | 5 46 | 18 17 | 5 47 | 18 19 | 5 43 | 18 17 | 5 53 | 18 28 | 6 01 | 18 34 |
| 18 | 5 41 | 18 07 | 5 51 | 18 17 | 5 47 | 18 15 | 5 48 | 18 16 | 5 45 | 18 15 | 5 55 | 18 26 | 6 03 | 18 32 |
| 19 | 5 42 | 18 05 | 5 52 | 18 15 | 5 49 | 18 12 | 5 50 | 18 14 | 5 47 | 18 12 | 5 57 | 18 23 | 6 04 | 18 29 |
| 20 | 5 44 | 18 02 | 5 54 | 18 12 | 5 51 | 18 10 | 5 52 | 18 12 | 5 49 | 18 09 | 5 59 | 18 20 | 6 06 | 18 27 |
| 21 | 5 45 | 18 00 | 5 55 | 18 10 | 5 52 | 18 08 | 5 54 | 18 09 | 5 51 | 18 07 | 6 01 | 18 18 | 6 08 | 18 24 |
| 22 | 5 47 | 17 58 | 5 57 | 18 08 | 5 54 | 18 05 | 5 55 | 18 07 | 5 53 | 18 04 | 6 03 | 18 15 | 6 10 | 18 22 |
| 23 | 5 49 | 17 56 | 5 59 | 18 05 | 5 56 | 18 03 | 5 57 | 18 04 | 5 54 | 18 02 | 6 05 | 18 12 | 6 12 | 18 19 |
| 24 | 5 50 | 17 53 | 6 00 | 18 03 | 5 57 | 18 01 | 5 59 | 18 02 | 5 56 | 17 59 | 6 07 | 18 10 | 6 14 | 18 16 |
| 25 | 5 52 | 17 51 | 6 02 | 18 01 | 5 59 | 17 58 | 6 01 | 17 59 | 5 58 | 17 57 | 6 09 | 18 07 | 6 15 | 18 14 |
| 26 | 5 53 | 17 49 | 6 03 | 17 59 | 6 01 | 17 56 | 6 02 | 17 57 | 6 00 | 17 54 | 6 11 | 18 04 | 6 17 | 18 11 |
| 27 | 5 55 | 17 46 | 6 05 | 17 56 | 6 03 | 17 53 | 6 04 | 17 55 | 6 02 | 17 52 | 6 13 | 18 02 | 6 19 | 18 09 |
| 28 | 5 57 | 17 44 | 6 07 | 17 54 | 6 04 | 17 51 | 6 06 | 17 52 | 6 04 | 17 49 | 6 15 | 17 59 | 6 21 | 18 06 |
| 29 | 5 58 | 17 42 | 6 08 | 17 52 | 6 06 | 17 49 | 6 08 | 17 50 | 6 06 | 17 46 | 6 17 | 17 57 | 6 23 | 18 04 |
| 30 | 6 00 | 17 40 | 6 10 | 17 50 | 6 08 | 17 46 | 6 09 | 17 47 | 6 08 | 17 44 | 6 19 | 17 54 | 6 25 | 18 01 |

## JUPITER

| Day | R.A. h m | Dec ° | Mag. | Diam. " | Rise h m | Transit h m | Set h m |
|---|---|---|---|---|---|---|---|
| 1 | 11 54.3 | +1.8 | −1.7 | 31 | 6 57 | 13 10 | 19 23 |
| 11 | 12 02.1 | +1.0 | −1.7 | 31 | 6 30 | 12 38 | 18 46 |
| 21 | 12 10.0 | +0.1 | −1.7 | 31 | 6 03 | 12 07 | 18 10 |

Equatorial Diam. 31", Polar Diam. 29"

## SATURN

| Day | R.A. h m | Dec ° | Mag. | Diam. " | Rise h m | Transit h m | Set h m |
|---|---|---|---|---|---|---|---|
| 1 | 16 33.7 | −20.4 | +0.5 | 17 | 13 47 | 17 48 | 21 50 |
| 11 | 16 35.2 | −20.5 | +0.5 | 16 | 13 10 | 17 11 | 21 11 |
| 21 | 16 37.4 | −20.6 | +0.6 | 16 | 12 34 | 16 34 | 20 33 |

Equatorial Diam. 16", Polar Diam. 15"
Rings – major axis 37" minor axis 16", Tilt 26°

## URANUS

| Day | R.A. h m | Dec ° | Mag. | Diam. " | Rise h m | Transit h m | Set h m |
|---|---|---|---|---|---|---|---|
| 1 | 1 29.2 | +8.7 | +6.0 | 4 | 19 55 | 2 46 | 9 38 |
| 11 | 1 28.2 | +8.6 | +6.0 | 4 | 19 15 | 2 06 | 8 57 |
| 21 | 1 26.9 | +8.4 | +6.0 | 4 | 18 32 | 1 25 | 8 15 |

## NEPTUNE

| Day | R.A. h m | Dec ° | Mag. | Diam. " | Rise h m | Transit h m | Set h m |
|---|---|---|---|---|---|---|---|
| 1 | 22 49.1 | −8.5 | +7.8 | 2 | 18 47 | 0 07 | 5 23 |
| 11 | 22 48.1 | −8.6 | +7.8 | 2 | 18 07 | 23 22 | 4 42 |
| 21 | 22 47.1 | −8.7 | +7.8 | 2 | 17 28 | 22 42 | 4 01 |

# OCTOBER 2016

TENTH MONTH, 31 DAYS. *Octo* (eighth), eighth month of Roman pre-Julian calendar

| 1 | *Saturday* | Oswald Mosley founds the British Union of Fascists 1932 | day 275 |
| 2 | *Sunday* | Mohandas Gandhi, leader of the Indian independence movement *b.* 1869 | 276 |

| 3 | *Monday* | The reunification of East and West Germany is formerly completed and celebrated 1990 | week 40 day 277 |
| 4 | *Tuesday* | Richard Cromwell, son of Oliver, and 2nd Lord Protector of the Commonwealth *b.* 1626 | 278 |
| 5 | *Wednesday* | 200 marchers set-out from Jarrow to walk to Westminster in protest at poverty and unemployment 1936 | 279 |
| 6 | *Thursday* | Anwar Sadat, president of Egypt, is assassinated during an annual victory parade in Cairo 1981 | 280 |
| 7 | *Friday* | Vladimir Putin, president of Russia who was formerly the country's prime minister *b.* 1952 | 281 |
| 8 | *Saturday* | Harold Macmillan leads the Conservatives to their third successive general election victory 1959 | 282 |
| 9 | *Sunday* | Marxist revolutionary Che Guevara is executed in Bolivia 1967 | 283 |

| 10 | *Monday* | Paul Kruger, 5th president of the South African Republic *b.* 1825 | week 41 day 284 |
| 11 | *Tuesday* | The Labour Party wins the second general election of the year with a three-seat majority 1974 | 285 |
| 12 | *Wednesday* | The USSR and USA fail to agree on disarmament at a summit in Reykjavik 1986 | 286 |
| 13 | *Thursday* | The British government loses its battle to prevent the publication of the book *Spycatcher* in the UK 1988 | 287 |
| 14 | *Friday* | George Grenville, Whig prime minister who was dismissed by King George III *b.* 1712 | 288 |
| 15 | *Saturday* | The Black Panther Party, a black nationalist organisation, is formed in California 1966 | 289 |
| 16 | *Sunday* | Much of the Palace of Westminster is destroyed by fire 1834 | 290 |

| 17 | *Monday* | Emperor Jacques I of Haiti is assassinated 1806 | week 42 day 291 |
| 18 | *Tuesday* | Henry John Temple, 3rd Viscount Palmerston, twice prime minister (1855–8 and 1859–65) *d.* 1865 | 292 |
| 19 | *Wednesday* | Conservative MPs vote at the Carlton Club to disband the coalition government 1922 | 293 |
| 20 | *Thursday* | The Dalai Lama arrives in the UK for the first time at the start of a 10-day tour 1973 | 294 |
| 21 | *Friday* | The Royal Navy defeats the combined fleets of the French and Spanish at the Battle of Trafalgar 1805 | 295 |
| 22 | *Saturday* | Hu Jintao is re-elected as General Secretary of the Communist Party of China 2007 | 296 |
| 23 | *Sunday* | Thousands attend a rally in Budapest, Hungary to demand an end to Soviet rule 1956 | 297 |

| 24 | *Monday* | The United Nations is officially established to promote international cooperation 1945 | week 43 day 298 |
| 25 | *Tuesday* | The general election is won by the Conservative Party led by Winston Churchill 1951 | 299 |
| 26 | *Wednesday* | The leaders of Israel and Jordon sign a peace treaty, ending 46 years of war 1994 | 300 |
| 27 | *Thursday* | Labour suffer its greatest defeat in the 1931 general election, losing 80 per cent of its seats | 301 |
| 28 | *Friday* | The USSR confirms the removal of missiles from Cuba, ending the Cuban Missile Crisis 1962 | 302 |
| 29 | *Saturday* | Sir Walter Raleigh was beheaded for conspiring against James I in 1618 | 303 |
| 30 | *Sunday* | In a referendum citizens in Quebec narrowly vote for the province to remain part of Canada 1995 | 304 |

| 31 | *Monday* | Indira Gandhi, prime minister of India, is assassinated by two of her bodyguards 1984 | week 44 day 305 |

## ASTRONOMICAL PHENOMENA

| d | h | |
|---|---|---|
| 6 | 08 | Saturn 4° South of the Moon |
| 11 | 04 | Jupiter 1° South of Mercury |
| 15 | 11 | Uranus at opposition |
| 16 | 02 | Uranus 3° North of the Moon |
| 21 | 05 | Ceres at opposition |
| 28 | 10 | Jupiter 1° South of the Moon |
| 30 | 08 | Saturn 3° North of Venus |
| 30 | 19 | Mercury 4° South of the Moon |

## MINIMA OF ALGOL

| d | h | d | h | d | h |
|---|---|---|---|---|---|
| 2 | 18.3 | 14 | 05.6 | 25 | 16.8 |
| 5 | 15.1 | 17 | 02.4 | 28 | 13.6 |
| 8 | 12.0 | 19 | 23.2 | 31 | 10.5 |
| 11 | 08.8 | 22 | 20.0 | | |

## CONSTELLATIONS

The following constellations are near their meridian at

| | d | h | | d | h |
|---|---|---|---|---|---|
| September | 1 | 24 | October | 16 | 21 |
| September | 15 | 23 | November | 1 | 20 |
| October | 1 | 22 | November | 15 | 19 |

Ursa Major (below the Pole), Cepheus, Cassiopeia, Cygnus, Lacerta, Andromeda, Pegasus, Capricornus, Aquarius and Piscis Austrinus

## THE MOON

| Phases, Apsides and Node | d | h | m |
|---|---|---|---|
| ● New Moon | 1 | 00 | 11 |
| ◐ First Quarter | 9 | 04 | 33 |
| ○ Full Moon | 16 | 04 | 23 |
| ◑ Last Quarter | 22 | 19 | 14 |
| ● New Moon | 30 | 17 | 38 |

| | d | h | m |
|---|---|---|---|
| Apogee (406,096km) | 4 | 11 | 03 |
| Perigee (357,861km) | 16 | 23 | 34 |
| Apogee (406,662km) | 31 | 19 | 29 |

Mean longitude of ascending node on 1st, 161°

# THE SUN

Diam. 32.1″

| Day | Right Ascension | | | Dec. − | Equation of time | | Rise 52° | | 56° | | Transit | | Set 52° | | 56° | | Sidereal time | | | Transit of first point of Aries | | |
|---|---|---|---|---|---|---|---|---|---|---|---|---|---|---|---|---|---|---|---|---|---|---|
| | h | m | s | ° | m | s | h | m | h | m | h | m | h | m | h | m | h | m | s | h | m | s |
| 1 | 12 | 30 | 10 | 3.3 | +10 | 18 | 6 | 00 | 6 | 02 | 11 | 50 | 17 | 39 | 17 | 37 | 23 | 40 | 28 | 23 | 19 | 22 |
| 2 | 12 | 33 | 47 | 3.6 | +10 | 37 | 6 | 01 | 6 | 04 | 11 | 50 | 17 | 37 | 17 | 34 | 23 | 44 | 25 | 23 | 15 | 25 |
| 3 | 12 | 37 | 25 | 4.0 | +10 | 56 | 6 | 03 | 6 | 06 | 11 | 49 | 17 | 34 | 17 | 32 | 23 | 48 | 21 | 23 | 11 | 29 |
| 4 | 12 | 41 | 03 | 4.4 | +11 | 15 | 6 | 05 | 6 | 08 | 11 | 49 | 17 | 32 | 17 | 29 | 23 | 52 | 18 | 23 | 07 | 32 |
| 5 | 12 | 44 | 41 | 4.8 | +11 | 33 | 6 | 06 | 6 | 10 | 11 | 49 | 17 | 30 | 17 | 26 | 23 | 56 | 14 | 23 | 03 | 36 |
| 6 | 12 | 48 | 20 | 5.2 | +11 | 51 | 6 | 08 | 6 | 12 | 11 | 48 | 17 | 27 | 17 | 24 | 0 | 00 | 11 | 22 | 59 | 39 |
| 7 | 12 | 51 | 59 | 5.6 | +12 | 08 | 6 | 10 | 6 | 14 | 11 | 48 | 17 | 25 | 17 | 21 | 0 | 04 | 07 | 22 | 55 | 43 |
| 8 | 12 | 55 | 39 | 5.9 | +12 | 25 | 6 | 12 | 6 | 16 | 11 | 48 | 17 | 23 | 17 | 19 | 0 | 08 | 04 | 22 | 51 | 46 |
| 9 | 12 | 59 | 19 | 6.3 | +12 | 42 | 6 | 13 | 6 | 18 | 11 | 47 | 17 | 21 | 17 | 16 | 0 | 12 | 01 | 22 | 47 | 50 |
| 10 | 13 | 02 | 59 | 6.7 | +12 | 58 | 6 | 15 | 6 | 20 | 11 | 47 | 17 | 18 | 17 | 14 | 0 | 15 | 57 | 22 | 43 | 53 |
| 11 | 13 | 06 | 40 | 7.1 | +13 | 13 | 6 | 17 | 6 | 22 | 11 | 47 | 17 | 16 | 17 | 11 | 0 | 19 | 54 | 22 | 39 | 56 |
| 12 | 13 | 10 | 21 | 7.5 | +13 | 29 | 6 | 18 | 6 | 24 | 11 | 47 | 17 | 14 | 17 | 08 | 0 | 23 | 50 | 22 | 36 | 00 |
| 13 | 13 | 14 | 03 | 7.8 | +13 | 43 | 6 | 20 | 6 | 26 | 11 | 46 | 17 | 12 | 17 | 06 | 0 | 27 | 47 | 22 | 32 | 03 |
| 14 | 13 | 17 | 45 | 8.2 | +13 | 58 | 6 | 22 | 6 | 28 | 11 | 46 | 17 | 10 | 17 | 03 | 0 | 31 | 43 | 22 | 28 | 07 |
| 15 | 13 | 21 | 28 | 8.6 | +14 | 11 | 6 | 24 | 6 | 30 | 11 | 46 | 17 | 07 | 17 | 01 | 0 | 35 | 40 | 22 | 24 | 10 |
| 16 | 13 | 25 | 12 | 8.9 | +14 | 24 | 6 | 25 | 6 | 32 | 11 | 46 | 17 | 05 | 16 | 58 | 0 | 39 | 36 | 22 | 20 | 14 |
| 17 | 13 | 28 | 56 | 9.3 | +14 | 37 | 6 | 27 | 6 | 34 | 11 | 45 | 17 | 03 | 16 | 56 | 0 | 43 | 33 | 22 | 16 | 17 |
| 18 | 13 | 32 | 40 | 9.7 | +14 | 49 | 6 | 29 | 6 | 36 | 11 | 45 | 17 | 01 | 16 | 53 | 0 | 47 | 30 | 22 | 12 | 21 |
| 19 | 13 | 36 | 26 | 10.0 | +15 | 00 | 6 | 31 | 6 | 38 | 11 | 45 | 16 | 59 | 16 | 51 | 0 | 51 | 26 | 22 | 08 | 24 |
| 20 | 13 | 40 | 11 | 10.4 | +15 | 11 | 6 | 32 | 6 | 40 | 11 | 45 | 16 | 57 | 16 | 49 | 0 | 55 | 23 | 22 | 04 | 27 |
| 21 | 13 | 43 | 58 | 10.8 | +15 | 21 | 6 | 34 | 6 | 42 | 11 | 45 | 16 | 55 | 16 | 46 | 0 | 59 | 19 | 22 | 00 | 31 |
| 22 | 13 | 47 | 45 | 11.1 | +15 | 30 | 6 | 36 | 6 | 44 | 11 | 45 | 16 | 52 | 16 | 44 | 1 | 03 | 16 | 21 | 56 | 34 |
| 23 | 13 | 51 | 33 | 11.5 | +15 | 39 | 6 | 38 | 6 | 47 | 11 | 44 | 16 | 50 | 16 | 41 | 1 | 07 | 12 | 21 | 52 | 38 |
| 24 | 13 | 55 | 22 | 11.8 | +15 | 47 | 6 | 39 | 6 | 49 | 11 | 44 | 16 | 48 | 16 | 39 | 1 | 11 | 09 | 21 | 48 | 41 |
| 25 | 13 | 59 | 11 | 12.2 | +15 | 54 | 6 | 41 | 6 | 51 | 11 | 44 | 16 | 46 | 16 | 37 | 1 | 15 | 05 | 21 | 44 | 45 |
| 26 | 14 | 03 | 01 | 12.5 | +16 | 01 | 6 | 43 | 6 | 53 | 11 | 44 | 16 | 44 | 16 | 34 | 1 | 19 | 02 | 21 | 40 | 48 |
| 27 | 14 | 06 | 52 | 12.8 | +16 | 06 | 6 | 45 | 6 | 55 | 11 | 44 | 16 | 42 | 16 | 32 | 1 | 22 | 59 | 21 | 36 | 52 |
| 28 | 14 | 10 | 43 | 13.2 | +16 | 11 | 6 | 47 | 6 | 57 | 11 | 44 | 16 | 40 | 16 | 30 | 1 | 26 | 55 | 21 | 32 | 55 |
| 29 | 14 | 14 | 36 | 13.5 | +16 | 16 | 6 | 48 | 6 | 59 | 11 | 44 | 16 | 38 | 16 | 27 | 1 | 30 | 52 | 21 | 28 | 58 |
| 30 | 14 | 18 | 29 | 13.8 | +16 | 19 | 6 | 50 | 7 | 01 | 11 | 44 | 16 | 37 | 16 | 25 | 1 | 34 | 48 | 21 | 25 | 02 |
| 31 | 14 | 22 | 23 | 14.2 | +16 | 22 | 6 | 52 | 7 | 03 | 11 | 44 | 16 | 35 | 16 | 23 | 1 | 38 | 45 | 21 | 21 | 05 |

## DURATION OF TWILIGHT (in minutes)

| Latitude | 52° | 56° | 52° | 56° | 52° | 56° | 52° | 56° |
|---|---|---|---|---|---|---|---|---|
| | 1 October | | 11 October | | 21 October | | 31 October | |
| Civil | 34 | 37 | 34 | 37 | 34 | 38 | 35 | 39 |
| Nautical | 73 | 80 | 73 | 80 | 74 | 81 | 75 | 83 |
| Astronomical | 113 | 125 | 112 | 124 | 113 | 124 | 114 | 126 |

## THE NIGHT SKY

*Mercury* rises 1.5 hours before the Sun and is favourably placed the first half of the month. It meets Jupiter on the 11th when both are less than 1° apart. Mercury passes through superior conjunction on the 27th.

*Venus,* magnitude −3.9, is still rather low in the west after sunset but should now be more easily seen given a clear horizon. The young Moon is 4° from Venus on the 3rd and the planet passes 3° from Saturn on the 30th.

*Mars,* magnitude +0.1 to +0.4, spends the month in the distinctive Teapot asterism of Sagittarius and on the 8th is close to the 2.8 magnitude star lambda Sagitarii marking the knob on the pot's lid. The Moon passes through the area on the nights of October 7th and 8th.

*Jupiter* should be picked up the second week of October after it muscles back into the morning sky. The magnitude −1.7 giant is rising a little more than 2.5 hours before the Sun by the 31st. Catch it close to Mercury on the 11th and 1.5° from the crescent Moon on the 28th.

*Saturn,* magnitude +0.5, is solely an evening sky object and sets about two hours after the Sun at the end of the month. The Moon is nearby on October 5th and 6th.

*Uranus* is at opposition in Pisces on the 15th when the magnitude 5.7 planet may be found in steadily held binoculars by referencing a good chart of its position.

# THE MOON

| Day | R.A. h | R.A. m | Dec. ° | Hor. Par. ' | Diam. ' | Sun's Co-Long. ° | PA of Br. Limb ° | Ph. % | Age d | Rise 52° h | Rise 52° m | Rise 56° h | Rise 56° m | Transit h | Transit m | Set 52° h | Set 52° m | Set 56° h | Set 56° m |
|---|---|---|---|---|---|---|---|---|---|---|---|---|---|---|---|---|---|---|---|
| 1 | 12 | 32 | −1.0 | 54.6 | 29.8 | 266 | 189 | 0 | 28.9 | 5 | 10 | 5 | 09 | 11 | 31 | 17 | 41 | 17 | 41 |
| 2 | 13 | 17 | −4.8 | 54.3 | 29.6 | 278 | 276 | 1 | 0.3 | 6 | 15 | 6 | 17 | 12 | 14 | 18 | 04 | 18 | 00 |
| 3 | 14 | 03 | −8.3 | 54.1 | 29.5 | 291 | 280 | 4 | 1.3 | 7 | 19 | 7 | 24 | 12 | 57 | 18 | 27 | 18 | 20 |
| 4 | 14 | 50 | −11.5 | 54.0 | 29.4 | 303 | 280 | 8 | 2.3 | 8 | 22 | 8 | 31 | 13 | 41 | 18 | 52 | 18 | 42 |
| 5 | 15 | 37 | −14.3 | 54.0 | 29.4 | 315 | 278 | 14 | 3.3 | 9 | 24 | 9 | 36 | 14 | 25 | 19 | 20 | 19 | 08 |
| 6 | 16 | 25 | −16.4 | 54.1 | 29.5 | 327 | 276 | 21 | 4.3 | 10 | 25 | 10 | 39 | 15 | 10 | 19 | 52 | 19 | 36 |
| 7 | 17 | 14 | −17.8 | 54.4 | 29.7 | 339 | 272 | 29 | 5.3 | 11 | 23 | 11 | 39 | 15 | 57 | 20 | 28 | 20 | 11 |
| 8 | 18 | 05 | −18.5 | 54.9 | 29.9 | 352 | 268 | 38 | 6.3 | 12 | 17 | 12 | 35 | 16 | 45 | 21 | 11 | 20 | 53 |
| 9 | 18 | 56 | −18.3 | 55.5 | 30.2 | 4 | 264 | 48 | 7.3 | 13 | 07 | 13 | 25 | 17 | 34 | 22 | 02 | 21 | 43 |
| 10 | 19 | 49 | −17.3 | 56.2 | 30.6 | 16 | 260 | 58 | 8.3 | 13 | 52 | 14 | 09 | 18 | 24 | 22 | 59 | 22 | 42 |
| 11 | 20 | 42 | −15.3 | 57.1 | 31.1 | 28 | 256 | 68 | 9.3 | 14 | 32 | 14 | 47 | 19 | 14 | — | | 23 | 48 |
| 12 | 21 | 36 | −12.4 | 58.0 | 31.6 | 40 | 252 | 77 | 10.3 | 15 | 07 | 15 | 20 | 20 | 06 | 0 | 03 | — | |
| 13 | 22 | 30 | −8.8 | 59.0 | 32.1 | 53 | 249 | 86 | 11.3 | 15 | 39 | 15 | 48 | 20 | 58 | 1 | 12 | 1 | 02 |
| 14 | 23 | 25 | −4.6 | 59.9 | 32.6 | 65 | 246 | 93 | 12.3 | 16 | 09 | 16 | 14 | 21 | 51 | 2 | 27 | 2 | 19 |
| 15 | 0 | 21 | +0.1 | 60.6 | 33.0 | 77 | 240 | 98 | 13.3 | 16 | 37 | 16 | 38 | 22 | 45 | 3 | 45 | 3 | 41 |
| 16 | 1 | 18 | +4.8 | 61.1 | 33.3 | 89 | 203 | 100 | 14.3 | 17 | 06 | 17 | 03 | 23 | 40 | 5 | 05 | 5 | 06 |
| 17 | 2 | 17 | +9.3 | 61.3 | 33.4 | 101 | 91 | 99 | 15.3 | 17 | 37 | 17 | 30 | — | | 6 | 28 | 6 | 33 |
| 18 | 3 | 16 | +13.2 | 61.1 | 33.3 | 113 | 85 | 95 | 16.3 | 18 | 12 | 18 | 01 | 0 | 37 | 7 | 50 | 8 | 00 |
| 19 | 4 | 17 | +16.2 | 60.7 | 33.1 | 125 | 86 | 89 | 17.3 | 18 | 51 | 18 | 36 | 1 | 35 | 9 | 11 | 9 | 25 |
| 20 | 5 | 18 | +18.0 | 60.0 | 32.7 | 138 | 90 | 80 | 18.3 | 19 | 37 | 19 | 20 | 2 | 34 | 10 | 27 | 10 | 44 |
| 21 | 6 | 19 | +18.6 | 59.2 | 32.3 | 150 | 94 | 70 | 19.3 | 20 | 31 | 20 | 13 | 3 | 34 | 11 | 35 | 11 | 53 |
| 22 | 7 | 17 | +18.1 | 58.3 | 31.8 | 162 | 98 | 59 | 20.3 | 21 | 31 | 21 | 13 | 4 | 32 | 12 | 33 | 12 | 50 |
| 23 | 8 | 14 | +16.5 | 57.5 | 31.3 | 174 | 103 | 49 | 21.3 | 22 | 35 | 22 | 19 | 5 | 28 | 13 | 20 | 13 | 37 |
| 24 | 9 | 07 | +14.1 | 56.7 | 30.9 | 186 | 106 | 38 | 22.3 | 23 | 42 | 23 | 29 | 6 | 22 | 13 | 59 | 14 | 13 |
| 25 | 9 | 58 | +11.1 | 56.0 | 30.5 | 198 | 109 | 28 | 23.3 | — | | — | | 7 | 12 | 14 | 31 | 14 | 42 |
| 26 | 10 | 47 | +7.6 | 55.4 | 30.2 | 211 | 112 | 20 | 24.3 | 0 | 49 | 0 | 39 | 8 | 00 | 14 | 59 | 15 | 06 |
| 27 | 11 | 34 | +3.9 | 54.9 | 29.9 | 223 | 114 | 13 | 25.3 | 1 | 56 | 1 | 50 | 8 | 45 | 15 | 24 | 15 | 28 |
| 28 | 12 | 20 | +0.0 | 54.6 | 29.7 | 235 | 117 | 7 | 26.3 | 3 | 02 | 2 | 59 | 9 | 30 | 15 | 47 | 15 | 47 |
| 29 | 13 | 06 | −3.8 | 54.3 | 29.6 | 247 | 121 | 3 | 27.3 | 4 | 06 | 4 | 07 | 10 | 13 | 16 | 09 | 16 | 07 |
| 30 | 13 | 51 | −7.5 | 54.1 | 29.5 | 259 | 134 | 1 | 28.3 | 5 | 10 | 5 | 14 | 10 | 55 | 16 | 31 | 16 | 26 |
| 31 | 14 | 37 | −10.8 | 53.9 | 29.4 | 272 | 227 | 0 | 29.3 | 6 | 13 | 6 | 21 | 11 | 39 | 16 | 56 | 16 | 47 |

# MERCURY

| Day | R.A. h m | Dec ° | Mag. | Diam. " | Phase % | Rise h m | Transit h m | Set h m |
|---|---|---|---|---|---|---|---|---|
| 1 | 11 27.1 | +5.1 | −0.7 | 7 | 60 | 4 14 | 10 45 | 17 17 |
| 3 | 11 37.2 | +4.3 | −0.8 | 6 | 68 | 4 21 | 10 48 | 17 15 |
| 5 | 11 48.3 | +3.3 | −0.9 | 6 | 75 | 4 30 | 10 51 | 17 12 |
| 7 | 12 00.0 | +2.1 | −1.0 | 6 | 81 | 4 41 | 10 55 | 17 09 |
| 9 | 12 12.2 | +0.8 | −1.0 | 6 | 86 | 4 52 | 11 00 | 17 06 |
| 11 | 12 24.6 | −0.6 | −1.1 | 5 | 90 | 5 05 | 11 04 | 17 03 |
| 13 | 12 37.2 | −2.0 | −1.1 | 5 | 93 | 5 17 | 11 09 | 17 00 |
| 15 | 12 49.8 | −3.5 | −1.2 | 5 | 95 | 5 30 | 11 14 | 16 57 |
| 17 | 13 02.4 | −5.0 | −1.2 | 5 | 97 | 5 43 | 11 19 | 16 53 |
| 19 | 13 15.0 | −6.4 | −1.2 | 5 | 98 | 5 56 | 11 23 | 16 50 |
| 21 | 13 27.6 | −7.9 | −1.3 | 5 | 99 | 6 09 | 11 28 | 16 46 |
| 23 | 13 40.1 | −9.3 | −1.3 | 5 | 100 | 6 22 | 11 33 | 16 43 |
| 25 | 13 52.5 | −10.7 | −1.4 | 5 | 100 | 6 34 | 11 37 | 16 39 |
| 27 | 14 05.0 | −12.0 | −1.4 | 5 | 100 | 6 47 | 11 42 | 16 36 |
| 29 | 14 17.4 | −13.4 | −1.3 | 5 | 100 | 6 59 | 11 46 | 16 32 |
| 31 | 14 29.8 | −14.6 | −1.2 | 5 | 100 | 7 12 | 11 51 | 16 29 |

Rising and setting times are for latitude 54°

# VENUS

| Day | R.A. h m | Dec ° | Mag. | Diam. " | Phase % | Rise h m | Transit h m | Set h m |
|---|---|---|---|---|---|---|---|---|
| 1 | 14 25.1 | −14.6 | −4.8 | 13 | 85 | 9 04 | 13 44 | 18 22 |
| 6 | 14 48.8 | −16.7 | −4.9 | 13 | 84 | 9 22 | 13 48 | 18 13 |
| 11 | 15 13.0 | −18.7 | −4.9 | 14 | 83 | 9 39 | 13 52 | 18 05 |
| 16 | 15 37.6 | −20.4 | −5.0 | 14 | 82 | 9 56 | 13 57 | 17 57 |
| 21 | 16 02.8 | −22.0 | −5.1 | 14 | 81 | 10 13 | 14 02 | 17 52 |
| 26 | 16 28.4 | −23.2 | −5.2 | 15 | 79 | 10 28 | 14 08 | 17 48 |
| 31 | 16 54.4 | −24.3 | −5.3 | 15 | 78 | 10 42 | 14 15 | 17 47 |

# MARS

| Day | R.A. h m | Dec ° | Mag. | Diam. " | Phase % | Rise h m | Transit h m | Set h m |
|---|---|---|---|---|---|---|---|---|
| 1 | 18 09.6 | −25.8 | +0.1 | 9 | 85 | 14 08 | 17 28 | 20 48 |
| 6 | 18 24.4 | −25.7 | +0.1 | 9 | 85 | 14 02 | 17 23 | 20 45 |
| 11 | 18 39.4 | −25.4 | +0.2 | 8 | 85 | 13 55 | 17 18 | 20 43 |
| 16 | 18 54.7 | −25.0 | +0.2 | 8 | 85 | 13 47 | 17 14 | 20 41 |
| 21 | 19 10.0 | −24.6 | +0.3 | 8 | 85 | 13 39 | 17 09 | 20 40 |
| 26 | 19 25.4 | −24.0 | +0.3 | 8 | 86 | 13 30 | 17 05 | 20 40 |
| 31 | 19 40.8 | −23.4 | +0.4 | 8 | 86 | 13 21 | 17 01 | 20 41 |

# SUNRISE AND SUNSET

| d | London 0° 05' / 51° 30' | | Bristol 2° 35' / 51° 28' | | Birmingham 1° 55' / 52° 28' | | Manchester 2° 15' / 53° 28' | | Newcastle 1° 37' / 54° 59' | | Glasgow 4° 14' / 55° 52' | | Belfast 5° 56' / 54° 35' | |
|---|---|---|---|---|---|---|---|---|---|---|---|---|---|---|
| | h m | h m | h m | h m | h m | h m | h m | h m | h m | h m | h m | h m | h m | h m |
| 1 | 6 02 | 17 37 | 6 11 | 17 47 | 6 09 | 17 44 | 6 11 | 17 45 | 6 09 | 17 41 | 6 20 | 17 51 | 6 27 | 17 59 |
| 2 | 6 03 | 17 35 | 6 13 | 17 45 | 6 11 | 17 42 | 6 13 | 17 42 | 6 11 | 17 39 | 6 22 | 17 49 | 6 28 | 17 56 |
| 3 | 6 05 | 17 33 | 6 15 | 17 43 | 6 13 | 17 39 | 6 15 | 17 40 | 6 13 | 17 36 | 6 24 | 17 46 | 6 30 | 17 54 |
| 4 | 6 06 | 17 30 | 6 16 | 17 40 | 6 14 | 17 37 | 6 17 | 17 38 | 6 15 | 17 34 | 6 26 | 17 43 | 6 32 | 17 51 |
| 5 | 6 08 | 17 28 | 6 18 | 17 38 | 6 16 | 17 35 | 6 18 | 17 35 | 6 17 | 17 31 | 6 28 | 17 41 | 6 34 | 17 49 |
| 6 | 6 10 | 17 26 | 6 20 | 17 36 | 6 18 | 17 32 | 6 20 | 17 33 | 6 19 | 17 29 | 6 30 | 17 38 | 6 36 | 17 46 |
| 7 | 6 11 | 17 24 | 6 21 | 17 34 | 6 20 | 17 30 | 6 22 | 17 30 | 6 21 | 17 26 | 6 32 | 17 36 | 6 38 | 17 44 |
| 8 | 6 13 | 17 22 | 6 23 | 17 32 | 6 21 | 17 28 | 6 24 | 17 28 | 6 23 | 17 24 | 6 34 | 17 33 | 6 40 | 17 42 |
| 9 | 6 15 | 17 19 | 6 25 | 17 29 | 6 23 | 17 26 | 6 26 | 17 26 | 6 25 | 17 21 | 6 36 | 17 31 | 6 42 | 17 39 |
| 10 | 6 16 | 17 17 | 6 26 | 17 27 | 6 25 | 17 23 | 6 27 | 17 23 | 6 27 | 17 19 | 6 39 | 17 28 | 6 44 | 17 37 |
| 11 | 6 18 | 17 15 | 6 28 | 17 25 | 6 27 | 17 21 | 6 29 | 17 21 | 6 29 | 17 16 | 6 41 | 17 26 | 6 46 | 17 34 |
| 12 | 6 20 | 17 13 | 6 30 | 17 23 | 6 28 | 17 19 | 6 31 | 17 19 | 6 31 | 17 14 | 6 43 | 17 23 | 6 47 | 17 32 |
| 13 | 6 21 | 17 11 | 6 31 | 17 21 | 6 30 | 17 17 | 6 33 | 17 16 | 6 33 | 17 12 | 6 45 | 17 21 | 6 49 | 17 29 |
| 14 | 6 23 | 17 08 | 6 33 | 17 18 | 6 32 | 17 14 | 6 35 | 17 14 | 6 35 | 17 09 | 6 47 | 17 18 | 6 51 | 17 27 |
| 15 | 6 25 | 17 06 | 6 35 | 17 16 | 6 34 | 17 12 | 6 37 | 17 12 | 6 37 | 17 07 | 6 49 | 17 16 | 6 53 | 17 25 |
| 16 | 6 27 | 17 04 | 6 37 | 17 14 | 6 35 | 17 10 | 6 38 | 17 10 | 6 39 | 17 04 | 6 51 | 17 13 | 6 55 | 17 22 |
| 17 | 6 28 | 17 02 | 6 38 | 17 12 | 6 37 | 17 08 | 6 40 | 17 07 | 6 41 | 17 02 | 6 53 | 17 11 | 6 57 | 17 20 |
| 18 | 6 30 | 17 00 | 6 40 | 17 10 | 6 39 | 17 06 | 6 42 | 17 05 | 6 43 | 17 00 | 6 55 | 17 08 | 6 59 | 17 18 |
| 19 | 6 32 | 16 58 | 6 42 | 17 08 | 6 41 | 17 03 | 6 44 | 17 03 | 6 45 | 16 57 | 6 57 | 17 06 | 7 01 | 17 15 |
| 20 | 6 33 | 16 56 | 6 43 | 17 06 | 6 43 | 17 01 | 6 46 | 17 01 | 6 47 | 16 55 | 6 59 | 17 03 | 7 03 | 17 13 |
| 21 | 6 35 | 16 54 | 6 45 | 17 04 | 6 44 | 16 59 | 6 48 | 16 58 | 6 49 | 16 53 | 7 01 | 17 01 | 7 05 | 17 11 |
| 22 | 6 37 | 16 52 | 6 47 | 17 02 | 6 46 | 16 57 | 6 50 | 16 56 | 6 51 | 16 50 | 7 03 | 16 59 | 7 07 | 17 08 |
| 23 | 6 39 | 16 50 | 6 49 | 17 00 | 6 48 | 16 55 | 6 52 | 16 54 | 6 53 | 16 48 | 7 05 | 16 56 | 7 09 | 17 06 |
| 24 | 6 40 | 16 48 | 6 50 | 16 58 | 6 50 | 16 53 | 6 53 | 16 52 | 6 55 | 16 46 | 7 07 | 16 54 | 7 11 | 17 04 |
| 25 | 6 42 | 16 46 | 6 52 | 16 56 | 6 52 | 16 51 | 6 55 | 16 50 | 6 57 | 16 44 | 7 09 | 16 52 | 7 13 | 17 02 |
| 26 | 6 44 | 16 44 | 6 54 | 16 54 | 6 53 | 16 49 | 6 57 | 16 48 | 6 59 | 16 41 | 7 12 | 16 49 | 7 15 | 17 00 |
| 27 | 6 46 | 16 42 | 6 56 | 16 52 | 6 55 | 16 47 | 6 59 | 16 46 | 7 01 | 16 39 | 7 14 | 16 47 | 7 17 | 16 57 |
| 28 | 6 47 | 16 40 | 6 57 | 16 50 | 6 57 | 16 45 | 7 01 | 16 44 | 7 03 | 16 37 | 7 16 | 16 45 | 7 19 | 16 55 |
| 29 | 6 49 | 16 38 | 6 59 | 16 48 | 6 59 | 16 43 | 7 03 | 16 42 | 7 05 | 16 35 | 7 18 | 16 43 | 7 21 | 16 53 |
| 30 | 6 51 | 16 36 | 7 01 | 16 46 | 7 01 | 16 41 | 7 05 | 16 40 | 7 07 | 16 33 | 7 20 | 16 40 | 7 23 | 16 51 |
| 31 | 6 53 | 16 34 | 7 03 | 16 45 | 7 03 | 16 39 | 7 07 | 16 38 | 7 09 | 16 31 | 7 22 | 16 38 | 7 25 | 16 49 |

## JUPITER

| Day | R.A. h m | Dec ° | Mag. | Diam. " | Rise h m | Transit h m | Set h m |
|---|---|---|---|---|---|---|---|
| 1 | 12 17.9 | -0.7 | -1.7 | 31 | 5 37 | 11 35 | 17 34 |
| 11 | 12 25.8 | -1.6 | -1.7 | 31 | 5 10 | 11 04 | 16 58 |
| 21 | 12 33.6 | -2.4 | -1.7 | 31 | 4 43 | 10 33 | 16 22 |
| 31 | 12 41.3 | -3.2 | -1.7 | 31 | 4 16 | 10 01 | 15 46 |

Equatorial Diam. 31", Polar Diam. 29"

## SATURN

| Day | R.A. h m | Dec ° | Mag. | Diam. " | Rise h m | Transit h m | Set h m |
|---|---|---|---|---|---|---|---|
| 1 | 16 40.2 | -20.7 | +0.6 | 16 | 11 58 | 15 57 | 19 56 |
| 11 | 16 43.5 | -20.9 | +0.6 | 16 | 11 23 | 15 21 | 19 19 |
| 21 | 16 47.3 | -21.0 | +0.6 | 16 | 10 49 | 14 45 | 18 43 |
| 31 | 16 51.5 | -21.1 | +0.6 | 15 | 10 14 | 14 10 | 18 06 |

Equatorial Diam. 16", Polar Diam. 14"
Rings – major axis 35" minor axis 16", Tilt 26°

## URANUS

| Day | R.A. h m | Dec ° | Mag. | Diam. " | Rise h m | Transit h m | Set h m |
|---|---|---|---|---|---|---|---|
| 1 | 1 25.5 | +8.3 | +6.0 | 4 | 17 52 | 0 45 | 7 34 |
| 11 | 1 24.0 | +8.1 | +6.0 | 4 | 17 12 | 0 04 | 6 52 |
| 21 | 1 22.5 | +8.0 | +6.0 | 4 | 16 32 | 23 19 | 6 11 |
| 31 | 1 21.0 | +7.8 | +6.0 | 4 | 15 52 | 22 38 | 5 29 |

## NEPTUNE

| Day | R.A. h m | Dec ° | Mag. | Diam. " | Rise h m | Transit h m | Set h m |
|---|---|---|---|---|---|---|---|
| 1 | 22 46.2 | -8.8 | +7.8 | 2 | 16 48 | 22 02 | 3 20 |
| 11 | 22 45.4 | -8.8 | +7.8 | 2 | 16 08 | 21 22 | 2 39 |
| 21 | 22 44.7 | -8.9 | +7.8 | 2 | 15 29 | 20 42 | 1 59 |
| 31 | 22 44.2 | -9.0 | +7.9 | 2 | 14 49 | 20 02 | 1 19 |

# NOVEMBER 2016

ELEVENTH MONTH, 30 DAYS. *Novem* (nine), ninth month of Roman pre-Julian calendar

| | | | |
|---|---|---|---|
| 1 | Tuesday | Geoffrey Howe resigns as deputy prime minister over the single currency 1990 | day 306 |
| 2 | Wednesday | The Balfour Declaration gives British support for a Jewish state in Palestine 1917 | 307 |
| 3 | Thursday | Lyndon B. Johnson defeats Barry Goldwater in the US presidential election 1964 | 308 |
| 4 | Friday | Former actor Ronald Reagan wins the US presidential election 1980 | 309 |
| 5 | Saturday | Woodrow Wilson wins the US presidential election in a rare four-way contest 1912 | 310 |
| 6 | Sunday | In a referendum Australia vote to retain the monarchy 1999 | 311 |
| 7 | Monday | Franklin D. Roosevelt is elected as the US president for a record fourth term 1944 | week 45 day 312 |
| 8 | Tuesday | Grover Cleveland wins his 2nd non-consecutive US presidential election 1892 | 313 |
| 9 | Wednesday | The dismantling of the Berlin Wall begins and border crossings are opened 1989 | 314 |
| 10 | Thursday | Mustafa Kemal Ataturk, founder and 1st president of the Republic of Turkey d. 1938 | 315 |
| 11 | Friday | Yasser Arafat, Palestinian leader and chair of the Palestine Liberation Organisation d. 2004 | 316 |
| 12 | Saturday | Akihito is enthroned as the 125th Emperor of Japan 1990 | 317 |
| 13 | Sunday | George Grenville, prime minister of Great Britain (1763–5) d. 1770 | 318 |
| 14 | Monday | The Scottish Nationalist Party contests its first general election 1935 | week 46 day 319 |
| 15 | Tuesday | William Pitt the Elder, prime minister during the Seven Years' War b. 1708 | 320 |
| 16 | Wednesday | Benazir Bhutto is elected prime minister of Pakistan, the first female head of an Islamic state 1988 | 321 |
| 17 | Thursday | 1st Duke of Newcastle, succeeded his younger brother Henry Pelham as prime minister d. 1768 | 322 |
| 18 | Friday | Chester A. Arthur, US president who succeeded the assassinated James Garfield d. 1886 | 323 |
| 19 | Saturday | Egyptian president Anwar Sadat becomes the first Arab leader to officially visit Israel 1977 | 324 |
| 20 | Sunday | Liberal MP Jeremy Thorpe is accused of conspiracy to kill his former lover Norman Scott 1978 | 325 |
| 21 | Monday | Voltaire, French Enlightenment writer, political philosopher and playwright b. 1694 | week 47 day 326 |
| 22 | Tuesday | US president John F. Kennedy is assassinated in Dallas, Texas by Lee Harvey Oswald 1963 | 327 |
| 23 | Wednesday | Eduard Shevardnadze, president of Georgia, retires from office following the Rose Revolution 2003 | 328 |
| 24 | Thursday | Zachary Taylor, US President who died sixteen months into his term b. 1784 | 329 |
| 25 | Friday | Augusto Pinochet, Chilean leader who came to power in 1973 in a violent coup b. 1915 | 330 |
| 26 | Saturday | Tony Blair becomes the first UK prime minister to address the Irish parliament 1998 | 331 |
| 27 | Sunday | Helen Clark is elected prime minister of New Zealand 1999 | 332 |
| 28 | Monday | In a referendum voters in Norway reject joining the European Union 1994 | week 48 day 333 |
| 29 | Tuesday | Jacques Chirac, former president and prime minister of France b. 1932 | 334 |
| 30 | Wednesday | Barbados becomes independent from the UK as granted under the Barbados Independence Act 1966 | 335 |

## ASTRONOMICAL PHENOMENA

d  h

2 19 Saturn 4° South of the Moon
12 11 Uranus 3° North of the Moon
24 01 Saturn 3° North of Mercury
25 02 Jupiter 2° South of the Moon
30 08 Saturn 4° South of the Moon

## MINIMA OF ALGOL

| d | h | d | h | d | h |
|---|---|---|---|---|---|
| 3 | 07.3 | 14 | 18.5 | 26 | 05.8 |
| 6 | 04.1 | 17 | 15.4 | 29 | 02.6 |
| 9 | 00.9 | 20 | 12.2 | | |
| 11 | 21.7 | 23 | 09.0 | | |

## CONSTELLATIONS

The following constellations are near their meridian at

| | d | h | | d | h |
|---|---|---|---|---|---|
| October | 1 | 24 | November | 15 | 21 |
| October | 16 | 23 | December | 1 | 20 |
| November | 1 | 22 | December | 16 | 19 |

Ursa Major (below the Pole), Cepheus, Cassiopeia, Andromeda, Pegasus, Pisces, Aquarius and Cetus

## THE MOON

| Phases, Apsides and Node | d | h | m |
|---|---|---|---|
| ◐ First Quarter | 7 | 19 | 51 |
| ○ Full Moon | 14 | 13 | 52 |
| ◑ Last Quarter | 21 | 08 | 33 |
| ● New Moon | 29 | 12 | 18 |
| Perigee (356,509km) | 14 | 11 | 21 |
| Apogee (406,554km) | 27 | 20 | 08 |

Mean longitude of ascending node on 1st, 159°

# THE SUN

Diam. 32.4″

| Day | Right Ascension | | | Dec. − | Equation of time | | Rise | | Transit | | Set | | | Sidereal time | | | Transit of first point of Aries | | |
|---|---|---|---|---|---|---|---|---|---|---|---|---|---|---|---|---|---|---|---|---|
| | | | | | | | 52° | 56° | | | 52° | | 56° | | | | | | |
| | h | m | s | ° | m | s | h | m | h | m | h | m | h | m | h | m | s | h | m | s |
| 1 | 14 | 26 | 27 | 14.5 | +16 | 24 | 6 55 | 7 08 | 11 | 44 | 16 | 31 | 16 | 19 | 2 | 42 | 51 | 21 | 17 | 09 |
| 2 | 14 | 30 | 23 | 14.8 | +16 | 25 | 6 57 | 7 10 | 11 | 44 | 16 | 29 | 16 | 16 | 2 | 46 | 48 | 21 | 13 | 12 |
| 3 | 14 | 34 | 19 | 15.1 | +16 | 25 | 6 59 | 7 12 | 11 | 44 | 16 | 27 | 16 | 14 | 2 | 50 | 44 | 21 | 09 | 16 |
| 4 | 14 | 38 | 16 | 15.4 | +16 | 24 | 7 01 | 7 14 | 11 | 44 | 16 | 26 | 16 | 12 | 2 | 54 | 41 | 21 | 05 | 19 |
| 5 | 14 | 42 | 14 | 15.7 | +16 | 23 | 7 03 | 7 16 | 11 | 44 | 16 | 24 | 16 | 10 | 2 | 58 | 37 | 21 | 01 | 23 |
| 6 | 14 | 46 | 13 | 16.0 | +16 | 21 | 7 04 | 7 18 | 11 | 44 | 16 | 22 | 16 | 08 | 3 | 02 | 34 | 20 | 57 | 26 |
| 7 | 14 | 50 | 12 | 16.3 | +16 | 18 | 7 06 | 7 20 | 11 | 44 | 16 | 20 | 16 | 06 | 3 | 06 | 31 | 20 | 53 | 29 |
| 8 | 14 | 54 | 13 | 16.6 | +16 | 14 | 7 08 | 7 23 | 11 | 44 | 16 | 19 | 16 | 04 | 3 | 10 | 27 | 20 | 49 | 33 |
| 9 | 14 | 58 | 14 | 16.9 | +16 | 09 | 7 10 | 7 25 | 11 | 44 | 16 | 17 | 16 | 02 | 3 | 14 | 24 | 20 | 45 | 36 |
| 10 | 15 | 02 | 16 | 17.2 | +16 | 04 | 7 12 | 7 27 | 11 | 44 | 16 | 16 | 16 | 00 | 3 | 18 | 20 | 20 | 41 | 40 |
| 11 | 15 | 06 | 19 | 17.5 | +15 | 57 | 7 13 | 7 29 | 11 | 44 | 16 | 14 | 15 | 59 | 3 | 22 | 17 | 20 | 37 | 43 |
| 12 | 15 | 10 | 23 | 17.7 | +15 | 50 | 7 15 | 7 31 | 11 | 44 | 16 | 13 | 15 | 57 | 3 | 26 | 13 | 20 | 33 | 47 |
| 13 | 15 | 14 | 27 | 18.0 | +15 | 42 | 7 17 | 7 33 | 11 | 44 | 16 | 11 | 15 | 55 | 3 | 30 | 10 | 20 | 29 | 50 |
| 14 | 15 | 18 | 33 | 18.3 | +15 | 33 | 7 19 | 7 35 | 11 | 45 | 16 | 10 | 15 | 53 | 3 | 34 | 06 | 20 | 25 | 54 |
| 15 | 15 | 22 | 39 | 18.5 | +15 | 24 | 7 20 | 7 37 | 11 | 45 | 16 | 08 | 15 | 52 | 3 | 38 | 03 | 20 | 21 | 57 |
| 16 | 15 | 26 | 46 | 18.8 | +15 | 13 | 7 22 | 7 39 | 11 | 45 | 16 | 07 | 15 | 50 | 3 | 42 | 00 | 20 | 18 | 00 |
| 17 | 15 | 30 | 54 | 19.0 | +15 | 02 | 7 24 | 7 41 | 11 | 45 | 16 | 06 | 15 | 48 | 3 | 45 | 56 | 20 | 14 | 04 |
| 18 | 15 | 35 | 03 | 19.3 | +14 | 50 | 7 26 | 7 43 | 11 | 45 | 16 | 04 | 15 | 47 | 3 | 49 | 53 | 20 | 10 | 07 |
| 19 | 15 | 39 | 12 | 19.5 | +14 | 37 | 7 27 | 7 45 | 11 | 45 | 16 | 03 | 15 | 45 | 3 | 53 | 49 | 20 | 06 | 11 |
| 20 | 15 | 43 | 23 | 19.7 | +14 | 23 | 7 29 | 7 47 | 11 | 46 | 16 | 02 | 15 | 44 | 3 | 57 | 46 | 20 | 02 | 14 |
| 21 | 15 | 47 | 34 | 20.0 | +14 | 08 | 7 31 | 7 49 | 11 | 46 | 16 | 01 | 15 | 42 | 4 | 01 | 42 | 19 | 58 | 18 |
| 22 | 15 | 51 | 46 | 20.2 | +13 | 52 | 7 32 | 7 51 | 11 | 46 | 16 | 00 | 15 | 41 | 4 | 05 | 39 | 19 | 54 | 21 |
| 23 | 15 | 55 | 59 | 20.4 | +13 | 36 | 7 34 | 7 53 | 11 | 47 | 15 | 59 | 15 | 40 | 4 | 09 | 35 | 19 | 50 | 25 |
| 24 | 16 | 00 | 13 | 20.6 | +13 | 19 | 7 35 | 7 55 | 11 | 47 | 15 | 58 | 15 | 38 | 4 | 13 | 32 | 19 | 46 | 28 |
| 25 | 16 | 04 | 27 | 20.8 | +13 | 01 | 7 37 | 7 57 | 11 | 47 | 15 | 57 | 15 | 37 | 4 | 17 | 29 | 19 | 42 | 31 |
| 26 | 16 | 08 | 42 | 21.0 | +12 | 42 | 7 38 | 7 58 | 11 | 47 | 15 | 56 | 15 | 36 | 4 | 21 | 25 | 19 | 38 | 35 |
| 27 | 16 | 12 | 58 | 21.2 | +12 | 23 | 7 40 | 8 00 | 11 | 48 | 15 | 55 | 15 | 35 | 4 | 25 | 22 | 19 | 34 | 38 |
| 28 | 16 | 17 | 15 | 21.3 | +12 | 03 | 7 41 | 8 02 | 11 | 48 | 15 | 54 | 15 | 34 | 4 | 29 | 18 | 19 | 30 | 42 |
| 29 | 16 | 21 | 33 | 21.5 | +11 | 42 | 7 43 | 8 04 | 11 | 48 | 15 | 54 | 15 | 33 | 4 | 33 | 15 | 19 | 26 | 45 |
| 30 | 16 | 25 | 51 | 21.7 | +11 | 20 | 7 44 | 8 05 | 11 | 49 | 15 | 53 | 15 | 32 | 4 | 37 | 11 | 19 | 22 | 49 |

## DURATION OF TWILIGHT (in minutes)

| Latitude | 52° | 56° | 52° | 56° | 52° | 56° | 52° | 56° |
|---|---|---|---|---|---|---|---|---|
| | 1 November | | 11 November | | 21 November | | 31 November | |
| Civil | 36 | 40 | 37 | 41 | 38 | 43 | 40 | 45 |
| Nautical | 75 | 84 | 78 | 87 | 80 | 90 | 82 | 93 |
| Astronomical | 115 | 127 | 117 | 130 | 120 | 134 | 123 | 138 |

## THE NIGHT SKY

*Mercury* sets before the end of civil twilight all month and so will not be seen.

*Venus,* magnitude −4.1, starts the month near Saturn in the evening sky but pulls away soon after and will slowly gain in altitude as the weeks pass. The slender crescent Moon nearby on the 2nd makes for an attractive sight when both Venus and Saturn ply the evening stage. Venus is setting nearly three hours after the Sun by the 30th.

*Mars* moves into Capricornus on the 8th where it spends the rest of the month crossing this bright-star poor group. The planet's magnitude declines a little more during November from magnitude +0.4 to +0.6 and it will set mid-evening. The Moon is nearby on the 6th.

*Jupiter,* magnitude −1.7, greets the early riser all month as it threads its way through Virgo. The Moon is quite close on the morning of the 25th when Jupiter is the sole planet on view during the small hours.

*Saturn* is now getting quite low in the southwest and will probably be lost to view during the last week of November by which time it is setting only about half an hour after the Sun.

# THE MOON

| Day | R.A. h | R.A. m | Dec. ° | Hor. Par. ′ | Diam. ′ | Sun's Co-Long. ° | PA of Br. Limb ° | Ph. % | Age d | Rise 52° h | Rise 52° m | Rise 56° h | Rise 56° m | Transit h | Transit m | Set 52° h | Set 52° m | Set 56° h | Set 56° m |
|---|---|---|---|---|---|---|---|---|---|---|---|---|---|---|---|---|---|---|---|
| 1 | 15 | 26 | −13.8 | 53.9 | 29.4 | 284 | 265 | 1 | 0.8 | 8 | 17 | 8 | 31 | 13 | 07 | 17 | 52 | 17 | 37 |
| 2 | 16 | 14 | −16.1 | 54.0 | 29.4 | 297 | 269 | 5 | 1.8 | 9 | 17 | 9 | 33 | 13 | 53 | 18 | 27 | 18 | 10 |
| 3 | 17 | 03 | −17.7 | 54.2 | 29.5 | 309 | 269 | 9 | 2.8 | 10 | 12 | 10 | 31 | 14 | 41 | 19 | 08 | 18 | 49 |
| 4 | 17 | 53 | −18.6 | 54.4 | 29.7 | 321 | 266 | 16 | 3.8 | 11 | 03 | 11 | 23 | 15 | 29 | 19 | 55 | 19 | 35 |
| 5 | 18 | 44 | −18.7 | 54.8 | 29.9 | 333 | 263 | 23 | 4.8 | 11 | 50 | 12 | 08 | 16 | 18 | 20 | 48 | 20 | 30 |
| 6 | 19 | 36 | −17.8 | 55.4 | 30.2 | 345 | 259 | 32 | 5.8 | 12 | 31 | 12 | 47 | 17 | 07 | 21 | 48 | 21 | 32 |
| 7 | 20 | 28 | −16.1 | 56.1 | 30.6 | 358 | 256 | 42 | 6.8 | 13 | 07 | 13 | 21 | 17 | 57 | 22 | 54 | 22 | 41 |
| 8 | 21 | 20 | −13.6 | 56.9 | 31.0 | 10 | 252 | 52 | 7.8 | 13 | 39 | 13 | 49 | 18 | 47 | — | | 23 | 55 |
| 9 | 22 | 12 | −10.3 | 57.8 | 31.5 | 22 | 249 | 62 | 8.8 | 14 | 08 | 14 | 15 | 19 | 37 | 0 | 04 | — | |
| 10 | 23 | 05 | −6.3 | 58.7 | 32.0 | 34 | 247 | 73 | 9.8 | 14 | 36 | 14 | 39 | 20 | 29 | 1 | 17 | 1 | 12 |
| 11 | 23 | 59 | −1.9 | 59.7 | 32.5 | 46 | 245 | 82 | 10.8 | 15 | 03 | 15 | 02 | 21 | 22 | 2 | 35 | 2 | 33 |
| 12 | 0 | 54 | +2.8 | 60.5 | 33.0 | 58 | 243 | 90 | 11.8 | 15 | 32 | 15 | 27 | 22 | 17 | 3 | 55 | 3 | 58 |
| 13 | 1 | 51 | +7.4 | 61.1 | 33.3 | 71 | 240 | 96 | 12.8 | 16 | 04 | 15 | 55 | 23 | 15 | 5 | 17 | 5 | 24 |
| 14 | 2 | 51 | +11.6 | 61.5 | 33.5 | 83 | 225 | 99 | 13.8 | 16 | 40 | 16 | 27 | — | | 6 | 40 | 6 | 51 |
| 15 | 3 | 52 | +15.1 | 61.5 | 33.5 | 95 | 117 | 100 | 14.8 | 17 | 24 | 17 | 08 | 0 | 15 | 8 | 00 | 8 | 16 |
| 16 | 4 | 55 | +17.6 | 61.1 | 33.3 | 107 | 97 | 97 | 15.8 | 18 | 15 | 17 | 57 | 1 | 16 | 9 | 15 | 9 | 34 |
| 17 | 5 | 57 | +18.7 | 60.5 | 33.0 | 119 | 97 | 91 | 16.8 | 19 | 15 | 18 | 56 | 2 | 17 | 10 | 21 | 10 | 40 |
| 18 | 6 | 59 | +18.6 | 59.6 | 32.5 | 131 | 100 | 84 | 17.8 | 20 | 20 | 20 | 03 | 3 | 17 | 11 | 15 | 11 | 33 |
| 19 | 7 | 58 | +17.3 | 58.7 | 32.0 | 143 | 103 | 74 | 18.8 | 21 | 28 | 21 | 14 | 4 | 14 | 11 | 58 | 12 | 14 |
| 20 | 8 | 54 | +15.0 | 57.7 | 31.4 | 155 | 107 | 64 | 19.8 | 22 | 37 | 22 | 26 | 5 | 07 | 12 | 35 | 12 | 47 |
| 21 | 9 | 47 | +12.1 | 56.8 | 30.9 | 168 | 110 | 54 | 20.8 | 23 | 46 | 23 | 38 | 5 | 57 | 13 | 04 | 13 | 13 |
| 22 | 10 | 37 | +8.6 | 56.0 | 30.5 | 180 | 112 | 44 | 21.8 | — | | — | | 6 | 44 | 13 | 30 | 13 | 36 |
| 23 | 11 | 25 | +4.8 | 55.3 | 30.1 | 192 | 113 | 34 | 22.8 | 0 | 52 | 0 | 48 | 7 | 29 | 13 | 53 | 13 | 55 |
| 24 | 12 | 11 | +1.0 | 54.8 | 29.8 | 204 | 115 | 25 | 23.8 | 1 | 58 | 1 | 57 | 8 | 12 | 14 | 15 | 14 | 14 |
| 25 | 12 | 57 | −2.9 | 54.4 | 29.6 | 216 | 115 | 17 | 24.8 | 3 | 02 | 3 | 05 | 8 | 54 | 14 | 37 | 14 | 33 |
| 26 | 13 | 42 | −6.6 | 54.1 | 29.5 | 229 | 116 | 11 | 25.8 | 4 | 05 | 4 | 11 | 9 | 37 | 15 | 01 | 14 | 53 |
| 27 | 14 | 28 | −10.1 | 54.0 | 29.4 | 241 | 117 | 6 | 26.8 | 5 | 08 | 5 | 18 | 10 | 21 | 15 | 26 | 15 | 15 |
| 28 | 15 | 14 | −13.1 | 53.9 | 29.4 | 253 | 121 | 2 | 27.8 | 6 | 10 | 6 | 23 | 11 | 05 | 15 | 54 | 15 | 40 |
| 29 | 16 | 02 | −15.6 | 54.0 | 29.4 | 265 | 143 | 0 | 28.8 | 7 | 10 | 7 | 26 | 11 | 51 | 16 | 27 | 16 | 11 |
| 30 | 16 | 51 | −17.5 | 54.1 | 29.5 | 277 | 234 | 0 | 0.3 | 8 | 08 | 8 | 26 | 12 | 38 | 17 | 06 | 16 | 47 |

## MERCURY

| Day | R.A. h | R.A. m | Dec ° | Mag. | Diam. ″ | Phase % | Rise h m | Transit h m | Set h m |
|---|---|---|---|---|---|---|---|---|---|
| 1 | 14 | 36.3 | −15.3 | −1.1 | 5 | 100 | 7 18 | 11 53 | 16 28 |
| 3 | 14 | 48.7 | −16.4 | −1.0 | 5 | 99 | 7 30 | 11 58 | 16 25 |
| 5 | 15 | 01.2 | −17.6 | −0.9 | 5 | 99 | 7 42 | 12 02 | 16 22 |
| 7 | 15 | 13.8 | −18.6 | −0.8 | 5 | 99 | 7 54 | 12 07 | 16 19 |
| 9 | 15 | 26.3 | −19.6 | −0.8 | 5 | 98 | 8 05 | 12 12 | 16 17 |
| 11 | 15 | 39.0 | −20.6 | −0.7 | 5 | 97 | 8 17 | 12 16 | 16 16 |
| 13 | 15 | 51.7 | −21.5 | −0.6 | 5 | 97 | 8 28 | 12 21 | 16 14 |
| 15 | 16 | 04.5 | −22.3 | −0.6 | 5 | 96 | 8 38 | 12 26 | 16 13 |
| 17 | 16 | 17.3 | −23.0 | −0.6 | 5 | 95 | 8 49 | 12 31 | 16 13 |
| 19 | 16 | 30.2 | −23.6 | −0.5 | 5 | 94 | 8 59 | 12 36 | 16 13 |
| 21 | 16 | 43.1 | −24.2 | −0.5 | 5 | 93 | 9 08 | 12 41 | 16 13 |
| 23 | 16 | 56.1 | −24.7 | −0.5 | 5 | 91 | 9 17 | 12 46 | 16 15 |
| 25 | 17 | 09.0 | −25.1 | −0.5 | 5 | 90 | 9 26 | 12 51 | 16 17 |
| 27 | 17 | 21.9 | −25.4 | −0.5 | 5 | 88 | 9 33 | 12 56 | 16 19 |
| 29 | 17 | 34.7 | −25.7 | −0.5 | 5 | 86 | 9 40 | 13 01 | 16 22 |

Rising and setting times are for latitude 54°

## VENUS

| Day | R.A. h | R.A. m | Dec ° | Mag. | Diam. ″ | Phase % | Rise h m | Transit h m | Set h m |
|---|---|---|---|---|---|---|---|---|---|
| 1 | 16 | 59.8 | −24.4 | −5.3 | 15 | 78 | 10 45 | 14 16 | 17 47 |
| 6 | 17 | 26.1 | −25.1 | −5.4 | 15 | 76 | 10 57 | 14 23 | 17 48 |
| 11 | 17 | 52.6 | −25.5 | −5.5 | 16 | 75 | 11 07 | 14 29 | 17 52 |
| 16 | 18 | 19.1 | −25.6 | −5.6 | 16 | 73 | 11 14 | 14 36 | 17 58 |
| 21 | 18 | 45.4 | −25.4 | −5.7 | 17 | 72 | 11 19 | 14 43 | 18 06 |
| 26 | 19 | 11.4 | −24.8 | −5.8 | 17 | 70 | 11 21 | 14 49 | 18 17 |

## MARS

| Day | R.A. h | R.A. m | Dec ° | Mag. | Diam. ″ | Phase % | Rise h m | Transit h m | Set h m |
|---|---|---|---|---|---|---|---|---|---|
| 1 | 19 | 44.0 | −23.3 | +0.4 | 7 | 86 | 13 19 | 17 00 | 20 41 |
| 6 | 19 | 59.4 | −22.5 | +0.4 | 7 | 86 | 13 09 | 16 56 | 20 43 |
| 11 | 20 | 14.8 | −21.6 | +0.5 | 7 | 87 | 12 58 | 16 51 | 20 44 |
| 16 | 20 | 30.1 | −20.7 | +0.5 | 7 | 87 | 12 47 | 16 47 | 20 47 |
| 21 | 20 | 45.3 | −19.7 | +0.5 | 7 | 87 | 12 35 | 16 42 | 20 49 |
| 26 | 21 | 00.3 | −18.6 | +0.6 | 7 | 88 | 12 23 | 16 38 | 20 52 |

# SUNRISE AND SUNSET

| | London 0° 05' | 51° 30' | Bristol 2° 35' | 51° 28' | Birmingham 1° 55' | 52° 28' | Manchester 2° 15' | 53° 28' | Newcastle 1° 37' | 54° 59' | Glasgow 4° 14' | 55° 52' | Belfast 5° 56' | 54° 35' |
|---|---|---|---|---|---|---|---|---|---|---|---|---|---|---|
| d | h m | h m | h m | h m | h m | h m | h m | h m | h m | h m | h m | h m | h m | h m |
| 1 | 6 54 | 16 33 | 7 04 | 16 43 | 7 04 | 16 37 | 7 09 | 16 36 | 7 11 | 16 28 | 7 24 | 16 36 | 7 27 | 16 47 |
| 2 | 6 56 | 16 31 | 7 06 | 16 41 | 7 06 | 16 35 | 7 11 | 16 34 | 7 13 | 16 26 | 7 26 | 16 34 | 7 29 | 16 45 |
| 3 | 6 58 | 16 29 | 7 08 | 16 39 | 7 08 | 16 34 | 7 13 | 16 32 | 7 15 | 16 24 | 7 28 | 16 32 | 7 31 | 16 43 |
| 4 | 7 00 | 16 27 | 7 10 | 16 37 | 7 10 | 16 32 | 7 14 | 16 30 | 7 17 | 16 22 | 7 31 | 16 30 | 7 33 | 16 41 |
| 5 | 7 02 | 16 26 | 7 11 | 16 36 | 7 12 | 16 30 | 7 16 | 16 28 | 7 19 | 16 20 | 7 33 | 16 28 | 7 35 | 16 39 |
| 6 | 7 03 | 16 24 | 7 13 | 16 34 | 7 14 | 16 28 | 7 18 | 16 26 | 7 21 | 16 18 | 7 35 | 16 26 | 7 37 | 16 37 |
| 7 | 7 05 | 16 22 | 7 15 | 16 32 | 7 15 | 16 27 | 7 20 | 16 25 | 7 23 | 16 17 | 7 37 | 16 24 | 7 39 | 16 35 |
| 8 | 7 07 | 16 21 | 7 17 | 16 31 | 7 17 | 16 25 | 7 22 | 16 23 | 7 25 | 16 15 | 7 39 | 16 22 | 7 41 | 16 33 |
| 9 | 7 09 | 16 19 | 7 18 | 16 29 | 7 19 | 16 23 | 7 24 | 16 21 | 7 27 | 16 13 | 7 41 | 16 20 | 7 43 | 16 32 |
| 10 | 7 10 | 16 18 | 7 20 | 16 28 | 7 21 | 16 22 | 7 26 | 16 19 | 7 29 | 16 11 | 7 43 | 16 18 | 7 45 | 16 30 |
| 11 | 7 12 | 16 16 | 7 22 | 16 26 | 7 23 | 16 20 | 7 28 | 16 18 | 7 31 | 16 09 | 7 45 | 16 16 | 7 47 | 16 28 |
| 12 | 7 14 | 16 15 | 7 24 | 16 25 | 7 25 | 16 19 | 7 30 | 16 16 | 7 33 | 16 08 | 7 47 | 16 14 | 7 49 | 16 26 |
| 13 | 7 15 | 16 13 | 7 25 | 16 23 | 7 26 | 16 17 | 7 31 | 16 15 | 7 35 | 16 06 | 7 50 | 16 12 | 7 51 | 16 25 |
| 14 | 7 17 | 16 12 | 7 27 | 16 22 | 7 28 | 16 16 | 7 33 | 16 13 | 7 37 | 16 04 | 7 52 | 16 11 | 7 53 | 16 23 |
| 15 | 7 19 | 16 10 | 7 29 | 16 21 | 7 30 | 16 14 | 7 35 | 16 12 | 7 39 | 16 03 | 7 54 | 16 09 | 7 55 | 16 22 |
| 16 | 7 21 | 16 09 | 7 31 | 16 19 | 7 32 | 16 13 | 7 37 | 16 10 | 7 41 | 16 01 | 7 56 | 16 07 | 7 57 | 16 20 |
| 17 | 7 22 | 16 08 | 7 32 | 16 18 | 7 33 | 16 11 | 7 39 | 16 09 | 7 43 | 15 59 | 7 58 | 16 06 | 7 58 | 16 19 |
| 18 | 7 24 | 16 07 | 7 34 | 16 17 | 7 35 | 16 10 | 7 41 | 16 07 | 7 45 | 15 58 | 8 00 | 16 04 | 8 00 | 16 17 |
| 19 | 7 26 | 16 05 | 7 36 | 16 16 | 7 37 | 16 09 | 7 42 | 16 06 | 7 47 | 15 57 | 8 02 | 16 03 | 8 02 | 16 16 |
| 20 | 7 27 | 16 04 | 7 37 | 16 14 | 7 39 | 16 08 | 7 44 | 16 05 | 7 49 | 15 55 | 8 04 | 16 01 | 8 04 | 16 14 |
| 21 | 7 29 | 16 03 | 7 39 | 16 13 | 7 40 | 16 06 | 7 46 | 16 03 | 7 51 | 15 54 | 8 06 | 16 00 | 8 06 | 16 13 |
| 22 | 7 31 | 16 02 | 7 40 | 16 12 | 7 42 | 16 05 | 7 48 | 16 02 | 7 52 | 15 52 | 8 07 | 15 58 | 8 08 | 16 12 |
| 23 | 7 32 | 16 01 | 7 42 | 16 11 | 7 44 | 16 04 | 7 49 | 16 01 | 7 54 | 15 51 | 8 09 | 15 57 | 8 10 | 16 10 |
| 24 | 7 34 | 16 00 | 7 44 | 16 10 | 7 45 | 16 03 | 7 51 | 16 00 | 7 56 | 15 50 | 8 11 | 15 56 | 8 11 | 16 09 |
| 25 | 7 35 | 15 59 | 7 45 | 16 09 | 7 47 | 16 02 | 7 53 | 15 59 | 7 58 | 15 49 | 8 13 | 15 55 | 8 13 | 16 08 |
| 26 | 7 37 | 15 58 | 7 47 | 16 08 | 7 48 | 16 01 | 7 55 | 15 58 | 8 00 | 15 48 | 8 15 | 15 53 | 8 15 | 16 07 |
| 27 | 7 38 | 15 57 | 7 48 | 16 08 | 7 50 | 16 00 | 7 56 | 15 57 | 8 01 | 15 47 | 8 17 | 15 52 | 8 16 | 16 06 |
| 28 | 7 40 | 15 57 | 7 50 | 16 07 | 7 52 | 16 00 | 7 58 | 15 56 | 8 03 | 15 46 | 8 18 | 15 51 | 8 18 | 16 05 |
| 29 | 7 41 | 15 56 | 7 51 | 16 06 | 7 53 | 15 59 | 7 59 | 15 55 | 8 05 | 15 45 | 8 20 | 15 50 | 8 20 | 16 04 |
| 30 | 7 43 | 15 55 | 7 53 | 16 05 | 7 55 | 15 58 | 8 01 | 15 54 | 8 06 | 15 44 | 8 22 | 15 49 | 8 21 | 16 03 |

## JUPITER

| Day | R.A. h m | Dec ° | Mag. | Diam. " | Rise h m | Transit h m | Set h m |
|---|---|---|---|---|---|---|---|
| 1 | 12 42.1 | −3.3 | −1.7 | 31 | 4 13 | 9 58 | 15 42 |
| 11 | 12 49.4 | −4.1 | −1.7 | 32 | 3 45 | 9 26 | 15 06 |
| 21 | 12 56.4 | −4.8 | −1.7 | 32 | 3 17 | 8 53 | 14 30 |

Equatorial Diam. 32", Polar Diam. 30"

## SATURN

| Day | R.A. h m | Dec ° | Mag. | Diam. " | Rise h m | Transit h m | Set h m |
|---|---|---|---|---|---|---|---|
| 1 | 16 51.9 | −21.1 | +0.6 | 15 | 10 11 | 14 07 | 18 03 |
| 11 | 16 56.5 | −21.3 | +0.5 | 15 | 9 37 | 13 32 | 17 27 |
| 21 | 17 01.3 | −21.4 | +0.5 | 15 | 9 04 | 12 57 | 16 51 |

Equatorial Diam. 15", Polar Diam. 14"
Rings – major axis 34" minor axis 15", Tilt 27°

## URANUS

| Day | R.A. h m | Dec ° | Mag. | Diam. " | Rise h m | Transit h m | Set h m |
|---|---|---|---|---|---|---|---|
| 1 | 1 20.8 | +7.8 | +6.0 | 4 | 15 48 | 22 34 | 5 25 |
| 11 | 1 19.5 | +7.7 | +6.0 | 4 | 15 08 | 21 54 | 4 43 |
| 21 | 1 18.3 | +7.6 | +6.0 | 4 | 14 28 | 21 13 | 4 02 |

## NEPTUNE

| Day | R.A. h m | Dec ° | Mag. | Diam. " | Rise h m | Transit h m | Set h m |
|---|---|---|---|---|---|---|---|
| 1 | 22 44.1 | −9.0 | +7.9 | 2 | 14 45 | 19 58 | 1 15 |
| 11 | 22 43.8 | −9.0 | +7.9 | 2 | 14 06 | 19 18 | 0 35 |
| 21 | 22 43.7 | −9.0 | +7.9 | 2 | 13 26 | 18 39 | 23 52 |

# DECEMBER 2016

TWELFTH MONTH, 31 DAYS. *Decem* (ten), tenth month of Roman pre-Julian calendar

| 1 | *Thursday* | Nancy Astor becomes the first woman to sit as an MP in the commons 1919 | day 336 |
| 2 | *Friday* | Fidel Castro takes office as president of Cuba 1976 | 337 |
| 3 | *Saturday* | The Eureka Rebellion between miners and UK colonial forces occurs in Australia 1854 | 338 |
| 4 | *Sunday* | Francisco Franco, autocratic head of Spain from 1939 until his death in 1975 *b.* 1892 | 339 |

| 5 | *Monday* | Herbert Asquith resigns as prime minister during the First World War 1916 | week 49 day 340 |
| 6 | *Tuesday* | David Lloyd George becomes the first Welsh prime minister of the UK 1916 | 341 |
| 7 | *Wednesday* | Noam Chomsky, American political commentator and linguist *b.* 1928 | 342 |
| 8 | *Thursday* | Russia, Belarus and Ukraine sign the Belavezha Accords dissolving the Soviet Union 1991 | 343 |
| 9 | *Friday* | Peter Kropotkin, Russian activist, anarchist and philosopher *b.* 1842 | 344 |
| 10 | *Saturday* | King Edward VIII signs his abdication notices in order to marry Wallace Simpson 1936 | 345 |
| 11 | *Sunday* | Mussolini declares Italy's withdrawal from the League of Nations 1937 | 346 |

| 12 | *Monday* | Delhi replaces Calcutta as the capital of the British Empire in India 1911 | week 50 day 347 |
| 13 | *Tuesday* | Saddam Hussein is captured by US soldiers near Tikrit, Iraq 2003 | 348 |
| 14 | *Wednesday* | The 1918 general election takes place with the lowest turnout since records began | 349 |
| 15 | *Thursday* | President Carter announces that the US will formally recognise communist China 1978 | 350 |
| 16 | *Friday* | MPs vote in favour for the permanent abolition of the death penalty for murder 1969 | 351 |
| 17 | *Saturday* | Simón Bolívar, Venezuelan military leader and politician *d.* 1830 | 352 |
| 18 | *Sunday* | Vaclav Havel, the first president of the Czech Republic *d.* 2011 | 353 |

| 19 | *Monday* | The 1910 general election sees the Liberal party win the highest number of seats | week 51 day 354 |
| 20 | *Tuesday* | Luis Carrero Blanco, the prime minister of Spain, is assassinated in Madrid 1973 | 355 |
| 21 | *Wednesday* | The 11-member Commonwealth of Independent States is formed 1991 | 356 |
| 22 | *Thursday* | The home of former prime minister, Edward Heath, is bombed by the IRA 1974 | 357 |
| 23 | *Friday* | Helmut Schmidt, Chancellor of West Germany (1974–82) *b.* 1918 | 358 |
| 24 | *Saturday* | MP John Stonehouse is found in Australia after disappearing in Miami, USA 1974 | 359 |
| 25 | *Sunday* | Nicolae Ceausescu, president and last Communist leader of Romania *d.* 1989 | 360 |

| 26 | *Monday* | Étienne Constantin de Gerlache, first prime minister of Belgium *b.* 1785 | week 52 day 361 |
| 27 | *Tuesday* | Benazir Bhutto, the former prime minister of Pakistan, is assassinated 2007 | 362 |
| 28 | *Wednesday* | Woodrow Wilson, 28th President of the USA (1913–21) *b.* 1856 | 363 |
| 29 | *Thursday* | William Gladstone, four-time prime minister of the UK *b.* 1809 | 364 |
| 30 | *Friday* | Grigori Rasputin, adviser to the Russian royal family, is murdered 1916 | 365 |
| 31 | *Saturday* | Queen Victoria names Ottawa as the capital of the Province of Canada 1857 | 366 |

## ASTRONOMICAL PHENOMENA

*d  h*
3  13  Venus 6° South of the Moon
5  11  Mars 3° South of the Moon
9  20  Uranus 3° North of the Moon
11  05  Mercury Greatest elongation East
13  –  Geminid meteor peak
21  11  Solstice
22  17  Jupiter 2° South of the Moon
27  21  Saturn 4° South of the Moon
29  05  Mercury 2° South of the Moon

## MINIMA OF ALGOL

| *d* | *h* | *d* | *h* | *d* | *h* |
|---|---|---|---|---|---|
| 1 | 23.4 | 13 | 10.7 | 24 | 22.0 |
| 4 | 20.3 | 16 | 07.5 | 27 | 18.8 |
| 7 | 17.1 | 19 | 04.4 | 30 | 15.6 |
| 10 | 13.9 | 22 | 01.2 | | |

## CONSTELLATIONS

The following constellations are near their meridian at

| | *d* | *h* | | *d* | *h* |
|---|---|---|---|---|---|
| November | 1 | 24 | December | 16 | 21 |
| November | 15 | 23 | January | 1 | 20 |
| December | 1 | 22 | January | 16 | 19 |

Ursa Major (below the Pole), Ursa Minor (below the Pole), Cassiopeia, Andromeda, Perseus, Triangulum, Aries, Taurus, Cetus and Eridanus

## THE MOON

| Phases, Apsides and Node | *d* | *h* | *m* |
|---|---|---|---|
| ◑ First Quarter | 7 | 09 | 03 |
| ○ Full Moon | 14 | 00 | 06 |
| ◐ Last Quarter | 21 | 01 | 56 |
| ● New Moon | 29 | 06 | 53 |
| Perigee (358,461km) | 12 | 23 | 29 |
| Apogee (405,870km) | 25 | 05 | 55 |

Mean longitude of ascending node on 1st, 158°

# THE SUN

Diam. 32.5″

| Day | Right Ascension | | | Dec. − ° | Equation of time m s | Rise 52° h m | 56° h m | Transit h m | Set 52° h m | 56° h m | Sidereal time h m s | Transit of first point of Aries h m s |
|---|---|---|---|---|---|---|---|---|---|---|---|---|
| | h | m | s | | | | | | | | | |
| 1 | 16 | 30 | 09 | 21.8 | +10 58 | 7 46 | 8 07 | 11 49 | 15 52 | 15 31 | 4 41 08 | 19 18 52 |
| 2 | 16 | 34 | 29 | 22.0 | +10 35 | 7 47 | 8 08 | 11 50 | 15 52 | 15 30 | 4 45 04 | 19 14 56 |
| 3 | 16 | 38 | 49 | 22.1 | +10 12 | 7 49 | 8 10 | 11 50 | 15 51 | 15 30 | 4 49 01 | 19 10 59 |
| 4 | 16 | 43 | 09 | 22.3 | +9 48 | 7 50 | 8 11 | 11 50 | 15 51 | 15 29 | 4 52 58 | 19 07 02 |
| 5 | 16 | 47 | 31 | 22.4 | +9 23 | 7 51 | 8 13 | 11 51 | 15 50 | 15 28 | 4 56 54 | 19 03 06 |
| 6 | 16 | 51 | 52 | 22.5 | +8 58 | 7 52 | 8 14 | 11 51 | 15 50 | 15 28 | 5 00 51 | 18 59 09 |
| 7 | 16 | 56 | 15 | 22.6 | +8 32 | 7 54 | 8 16 | 11 52 | 15 50 | 15 27 | 5 04 47 | 18 55 13 |
| 8 | 17 | 00 | 37 | 22.7 | +8 06 | 7 55 | 8 17 | 11 52 | 15 49 | 15 27 | 5 08 44 | 18 51 16 |
| 9 | 17 | 05 | 00 | 22.8 | +7 40 | 7 56 | 8 18 | 11 53 | 15 49 | 15 27 | 5 12 40 | 18 47 20 |
| 10 | 17 | 09 | 24 | 22.9 | +7 13 | 7 57 | 8 19 | 11 53 | 15 49 | 15 26 | 5 16 37 | 18 43 23 |
| 11 | 17 | 13 | 48 | 23.0 | +6 45 | 7 58 | 8 21 | 11 53 | 15 49 | 15 26 | 5 20 33 | 18 39 27 |
| 12 | 17 | 18 | 12 | 23.1 | +6 17 | 7 59 | 8 22 | 11 54 | 15 49 | 15 26 | 5 24 30 | 18 35 30 |
| 13 | 17 | 22 | 37 | 23.2 | +5 49 | 8 00 | 8 23 | 11 54 | 15 49 | 15 26 | 5 28 27 | 18 31 33 |
| 14 | 17 | 27 | 02 | 23.2 | +5 21 | 8 01 | 8 24 | 11 55 | 15 49 | 15 26 | 5 32 23 | 18 27 37 |
| 15 | 17 | 31 | 27 | 23.3 | +4 52 | 8 01 | 8 25 | 11 55 | 15 49 | 15 26 | 5 36 20 | 18 23 40 |
| 16 | 17 | 35 | 52 | 23.3 | +4 23 | 8 02 | 8 25 | 11 56 | 15 49 | 15 26 | 5 40 16 | 18 19 44 |
| 17 | 17 | 40 | 18 | 23.4 | +3 54 | 8 03 | 8 26 | 11 56 | 15 50 | 15 26 | 5 44 13 | 18 15 47 |
| 18 | 17 | 44 | 44 | 23.4 | +3 25 | 8 04 | 8 27 | 11 57 | 15 50 | 15 27 | 5 48 09 | 18 11 51 |
| 19 | 17 | 49 | 10 | 23.4 | +2 55 | 8 04 | 8 28 | 11 57 | 15 50 | 15 27 | 5 52 06 | 18 07 54 |
| 20 | 17 | 53 | 36 | 23.4 | +2 26 | 8 05 | 8 28 | 11 58 | 15 51 | 15 27 | 5 56 02 | 18 03 58 |
| 21 | 17 | 58 | 03 | 23.4 | +1 56 | 8 05 | 8 29 | 11 58 | 15 51 | 15 28 | 5 59 59 | 18 00 01 |
| 22 | 18 | 02 | 29 | 23.4 | +1 26 | 8 06 | 8 29 | 11 59 | 15 52 | 15 28 | 6 03 56 | 17 56 04 |
| 23 | 18 | 06 | 55 | 23.4 | +0 56 | 8 06 | 8 30 | 11 59 | 15 52 | 15 29 | 6 07 52 | 17 52 08 |
| 24 | 18 | 11 | 22 | 23.4 | +0 26 | 8 07 | 8 30 | 12 00 | 15 53 | 15 30 | 6 11 49 | 17 48 11 |
| 25 | 18 | 15 | 48 | 23.4 | −0 04 | 8 07 | 8 30 | 12 00 | 15 54 | 15 30 | 6 15 45 | 17 44 15 |
| 26 | 18 | 20 | 15 | 23.4 | −0 33 | 8 07 | 8 31 | 12 01 | 15 54 | 15 31 | 6 19 42 | 17 40 18 |
| 27 | 18 | 24 | 41 | 23.3 | −1 03 | 8 08 | 8 31 | 12 01 | 15 55 | 15 32 | 6 23 38 | 17 36 22 |
| 28 | 18 | 29 | 07 | 23.3 | −1 32 | 8 08 | 8 31 | 12 02 | 15 56 | 15 33 | 6 27 35 | 17 32 25 |
| 29 | 18 | 33 | 33 | 23.2 | −2 02 | 8 08 | 8 31 | 12 02 | 15 57 | 15 34 | 6 31 31 | 17 28 29 |
| 30 | 18 | 37 | 58 | 23.2 | −2 31 | 8 08 | 8 31 | 12 03 | 15 58 | 15 35 | 6 35 28 | 17 24 32 |
| 31 | 18 | 42 | 24 | 23.1 | −3 00 | 8 08 | 8 31 | 12 03 | 15 59 | 15 36 | 6 39 25 | 17 20 35 |

## DURATION OF TWILIGHT (in minutes)

| Latitude | 52° | 56° | 52° | 56° | 52° | 56° | 52° | 56° |
|---|---|---|---|---|---|---|---|---|
| | 1 December | | 11 December | | 21 December | | 31 December | |
| Civil | 40 | 45 | 41 | 47 | 41 | 47 | 41 | 47 |
| Nautical | 82 | 93 | 84 | 96 | 85 | 97 | 84 | 96 |
| Astronomical | 123 | 138 | 125 | 141 | 126 | 142 | 125 | 141 |

## THE NIGHT SKY

*Mercury* is at greatest elongation east (20°) on the 11th and low in the south-western evening sky until the third week of December. The Moon lies 8° above Mercury on the 1st. Mercury passes through inferior conjunction on December 28th and will be lost to view until the New Year.

*Venus*, magnitude −4.3, is a brilliant seasonal bauble hung above the south-western sky-line these evenings. The crescent Moon nearby on the 3rd makes for a lovely sight.

*Mars*, magnitude +0.9, is setting nearly 5.5 hours after the Sun by the end of December and moves into Aquarius on the 15th where it ends the year. Mars can be found 3.5° to the Moon's lower right on the 5th.

*Jupiter*, magnitude −1.8, rises during the early hours. The planet dominates the stars of Virgo where it currently lies, and the Moon in the area on the 22nd and 23rd will add to the scene.

*Saturn* passes through superior conjunction on the 10th and then surfaces in the morning sky, rising about 1.5 hours before the Sun by the end of 2016. The planet lies 6° to the right of the Moon on December 28th.

The *Geminids* are now considered the richest of the annual showers but have to contend with an almost Full Moon at their maximum on the night of December 13/14, meaning only the brighter members will be seen. Still, a watch of reasonable length should allow some Geminids to be logged.

## THE MOON

| Day | R.A. h | R.A. m | Dec. ° | Hor. Par. ′ | Diam. ′ | Sun's Co-Long. ° | PA of Br. Limb ° | Ph. % | Age d | Rise 52° h | Rise 52° m | Rise 56° h | Rise 56° m | Transit h | Transit m | Set 52° h | Set 52° m | Set 56° h | Set 56° m |
|---|---|---|---|---|---|---|---|---|---|---|---|---|---|---|---|---|---|---|---|
| 1 | 17 | 41 | −18.6 | 54.4 | 29.6 | 289 | 256 | 2 | 1.3 | 9 | 01 | 9 | 21 | 13 | 26 | 17 | 50 | 17 | 31 |
| 2 | 18 | 32 | −18.9 | 54.7 | 29.8 | 302 | 259 | 6 | 2.3 | 9 | 50 | 10 | 09 | 14 | 15 | 18 | 42 | 18 | 23 |
| 3 | 19 | 24 | −18.3 | 55.1 | 30.0 | 314 | 257 | 11 | 3.3 | 10 | 33 | 10 | 50 | 15 | 05 | 19 | 40 | 19 | 23 |
| 4 | 20 | 15 | −16.9 | 55.5 | 30.3 | 326 | 255 | 18 | 4.3 | 11 | 10 | 11 | 25 | 15 | 54 | 20 | 43 | 20 | 29 |
| 5 | 21 | 07 | −14.6 | 56.1 | 30.6 | 338 | 252 | 26 | 5.3 | 11 | 43 | 11 | 54 | 16 | 43 | 21 | 50 | 21 | 39 |
| 6 | 21 | 58 | −11.5 | 56.8 | 30.9 | 350 | 250 | 36 | 6.3 | 12 | 12 | 12 | 21 | 17 | 31 | 23 | 01 | 22 | 54 |
| 7 | 22 | 49 | −7.9 | 57.5 | 31.4 | 3 | 248 | 46 | 7.3 | 12 | 39 | 12 | 44 | 18 | 21 | — | | — | |
| 8 | 23 | 41 | −3.7 | 58.3 | 31.8 | 15 | 246 | 57 | 8.3 | 13 | 05 | 13 | 06 | 19 | 11 | 0 | 14 | 0 | 11 |
| 9 | 0 | 33 | +0.8 | 59.2 | 32.2 | 27 | 246 | 68 | 9.3 | 13 | 31 | 13 | 29 | 20 | 03 | 1 | 29 | 1 | 30 |
| 10 | 1 | 28 | +5.3 | 59.9 | 32.7 | 39 | 246 | 78 | 10.3 | 14 | 00 | 13 | 53 | 20 | 57 | 2 | 48 | 2 | 53 |
| 11 | 2 | 24 | +9.7 | 60.6 | 33.0 | 51 | 246 | 87 | 11.3 | 14 | 32 | 14 | 22 | 21 | 54 | 4 | 08 | 4 | 17 |
| 12 | 3 | 23 | +13.6 | 61.0 | 33.3 | 63 | 247 | 94 | 12.3 | 15 | 11 | 14 | 57 | 22 | 54 | 5 | 29 | 5 | 42 |
| 13 | 4 | 25 | +16.6 | 61.2 | 33.3 | 75 | 242 | 98 | 13.3 | 15 | 58 | 15 | 39 | 23 | 55 | 6 | 47 | 7 | 03 |
| 14 | 5 | 28 | +18.4 | 61.0 | 33.2 | 88 | 178 | 100 | 14.3 | 16 | 53 | 16 | 33 | — | | 7 | 58 | 8 | 18 |
| 15 | 6 | 31 | +18.9 | 60.5 | 33.0 | 100 | 110 | 99 | 15.3 | 17 | 57 | 17 | 38 | 0 | 57 | 9 | 00 | 9 | 20 |
| 16 | 7 | 33 | +18.2 | 59.8 | 32.6 | 112 | 106 | 94 | 16.3 | 19 | 06 | 18 | 50 | 1 | 57 | 9 | 51 | 10 | 08 |
| 17 | 8 | 32 | +16.3 | 58.9 | 32.1 | 124 | 107 | 88 | 17.3 | 20 | 18 | 20 | 05 | 2 | 54 | 10 | 33 | 10 | 47 |
| 18 | 9 | 28 | +13.5 | 58.0 | 31.6 | 136 | 109 | 80 | 18.3 | 21 | 29 | 21 | 19 | 3 | 48 | 11 | 06 | 11 | 17 |
| 19 | 10 | 21 | +10.1 | 57.0 | 31.1 | 148 | 111 | 71 | 19.3 | 22 | 38 | 22 | 32 | 4 | 38 | 11 | 34 | 11 | 41 |
| 20 | 11 | 10 | +6.3 | 56.1 | 30.6 | 160 | 113 | 61 | 20.3 | 23 | 45 | 23 | 43 | 5 | 25 | 11 | 59 | 12 | 02 |
| 21 | 11 | 58 | +2.3 | 55.4 | 30.2 | 172 | 113 | 51 | 21.3 | — | | — | | 6 | 09 | 12 | 22 | 12 | 22 |
| 22 | 12 | 44 | −1.6 | 54.8 | 29.9 | 185 | 114 | 41 | 22.3 | 0 | 51 | 0 | 52 | 6 | 52 | 12 | 44 | 12 | 41 |
| 23 | 13 | 30 | −5.4 | 54.4 | 29.6 | 197 | 113 | 32 | 23.3 | 1 | 55 | 2 | 00 | 7 | 35 | 13 | 06 | 13 | 00 |
| 24 | 14 | 15 | −9.0 | 54.1 | 29.5 | 209 | 112 | 23 | 24.3 | 2 | 58 | 3 | 06 | 8 | 18 | 13 | 30 | 13 | 21 |
| 25 | 15 | 02 | −12.2 | 54.0 | 29.4 | 221 | 111 | 16 | 25.3 | 4 | 00 | 4 | 12 | 9 | 02 | 13 | 57 | 13 | 45 |
| 26 | 15 | 49 | −14.9 | 54.1 | 29.5 | 233 | 109 | 10 | 26.3 | 5 | 01 | 5 | 16 | 9 | 47 | 14 | 28 | 14 | 13 |
| 27 | 16 | 38 | −17.0 | 54.2 | 29.5 | 246 | 109 | 5 | 27.3 | 6 | 00 | 6 | 18 | 10 | 34 | 15 | 05 | 14 | 47 |
| 28 | 17 | 28 | −18.4 | 54.5 | 29.7 | 258 | 111 | 2 | 28.3 | 6 | 56 | 7 | 15 | 11 | 22 | 15 | 47 | 15 | 28 |
| 29 | 18 | 19 | −19.0 | 54.8 | 29.9 | 270 | 142 | 0 | 29.3 | 7 | 48 | 8 | 06 | 12 | 12 | 16 | 36 | 16 | 17 |
| 30 | 19 | 11 | −18.6 | 55.1 | 30.1 | 282 | 238 | 0 | 0.8 | 8 | 34 | 8 | 51 | 13 | 01 | 17 | 32 | 17 | 15 |
| 31 | 20 | 03 | −17.4 | 55.6 | 30.3 | 294 | 250 | 3 | 1.8 | 9 | 13 | 9 | 29 | 13 | 51 | 18 | 35 | 18 | 20 |

## MERCURY

| Day | R.A. h | R.A. m | Dec ° | Mag. | Diam. ″ | Phase % | Rise h m | Transit h m | Set h m |
|---|---|---|---|---|---|---|---|---|---|
| 1 | 17 | 47.3 | −25.8 | −0.5 | 6 | 83 | 9 45 | 13 06 | 16 26 |
| 3 | 17 | 59.7 | −25.8 | −0.5 | 6 | 81 | 9 50 | 13 10 | 16 30 |
| 5 | 18 | 11.6 | −25.8 | −0.5 | 6 | 77 | 9 53 | 13 14 | 16 34 |
| 7 | 18 | 23.0 | −25.6 | −0.5 | 6 | 73 | 9 55 | 13 17 | 16 39 |
| 9 | 18 | 33.7 | −25.4 | −0.5 | 6 | 68 | 9 56 | 13 19 | 16 43 |
| 11 | 18 | 43.4 | −25.1 | −0.4 | 7 | 63 | 9 55 | 13 21 | 16 47 |
| 13 | 18 | 51.7 | −24.7 | −0.4 | 7 | 56 | 9 51 | 13 21 | 16 51 |
| 15 | 18 | 58.4 | −24.2 | −0.2 | 7 | 49 | 9 46 | 13 19 | 16 52 |
| 17 | 19 | 03.0 | −23.7 | 0.0 | 8 | 40 | 9 38 | 13 15 | 16 52 |
| 19 | 19 | 04.9 | −23.2 | +0.3 | 8 | 31 | 9 28 | 13 08 | 16 49 |
| 21 | 19 | 03.7 | −22.6 | +0.8 | 9 | 22 | 9 14 | 12 58 | 16 43 |
| 23 | 18 | 59.3 | −22.1 | +1.6 | 9 | 13 | 8 57 | 12 44 | 16 33 |
| 25 | 18 | 51.6 | −21.6 | +2.7 | 10 | 6 | 8 37 | 12 28 | 16 20 |
| 27 | 18 | 41.3 | −21.2 | +4.0 | 10 | 2 | 8 16 | 12 10 | 16 04 |
| 29 | 18 | 29.7 | −20.8 | +4.8 | 10 | 0 | 7 54 | 11 50 | 15 47 |
| 31 | 18 | 18.2 | −20.5 | +3.6 | 10 | 3 | 7 33 | 11 31 | 15 31 |

Rising and setting times are for latitude 54°

## VENUS

| Day | R.A. h | R.A. m | Dec ° | Mag. | Diam. ″ | Phase % | Rise h m | Transit h m | Set h m |
|---|---|---|---|---|---|---|---|---|---|
| 1 | 19 | 37.0 | −24.0 | −6.0 | 18 | 69 | 11 20 | 14 55 | 18 29 |
| 6 | 20 | 02.0 | −22.9 | −6.1 | 19 | 67 | 11 17 | 15 00 | 18 43 |
| 11 | 20 | 26.3 | −21.6 | −6.2 | 19 | 65 | 11 11 | 15 04 | 18 58 |
| 16 | 20 | 49.9 | −20.0 | −6.4 | 20 | 63 | 11 04 | 15 08 | 19 13 |
| 21 | 21 | 12.7 | −18.2 | −6.5 | 21 | 61 | 10 55 | 15 11 | 19 28 |
| 26 | 21 | 34.7 | −16.3 | −6.7 | 22 | 59 | 10 44 | 15 13 | 19 42 |
| 31 | 21 | 55.8 | −14.2 | −6.8 | 23 | 57 | 10 32 | 15 14 | 19 57 |

## MARS

| Day | R.A. h | R.A. m | Dec ° | Mag. | Diam. ″ | Phase % | Rise h m | Transit h m | Set h m |
|---|---|---|---|---|---|---|---|---|---|
| 1 | 21 | 15.3 | −17.4 | +0.6 | 7 | 88 | 12 10 | 16 33 | 20 55 |
| 6 | 21 | 30.1 | −16.2 | +0.7 | 6 | 88 | 11 57 | 16 28 | 20 59 |
| 11 | 21 | 44.8 | −14.9 | +0.7 | 6 | 89 | 11 44 | 16 23 | 21 02 |
| 16 | 21 | 59.3 | −13.5 | +0.8 | 6 | 89 | 11 31 | 16 18 | 21 05 |
| 21 | 22 | 13.7 | −12.1 | +0.8 | 6 | 89 | 11 17 | 16 12 | 21 08 |
| 26 | 22 | 27.9 | −10.7 | +0.8 | 6 | 90 | 11 03 | 16 07 | 21 11 |
| 31 | 22 | 42.0 | −9.2 | +0.9 | 6 | 90 | 10 49 | 16 01 | 21 14 |

# SUNRISE AND SUNSET

| d | London 0° 05′ / 51° 30′ h m | | Bristol 2° 35′ / 51° 28′ h m | | Birmingham 1° 55′ / 52° 28′ h m | | Manchester 2° 15′ / 53° 28′ h m | | Newcastle 1° 37′ / 54° 59′ h m | | Glasgow 4° 14′ / 55° 52′ h m | | Belfast 5° 56′ / 54° 35′ h m | |
|---|------|------|------|------|------|------|------|------|------|------|------|------|------|------|
| 1 | 7 44 | 15 55 | 7 54 | 16 05 | 7 56 | 15 57 | 8 02 | 15 54 | 8 08 | 15 43 | 8 24 | 15 48 | 8 23 | 16 03 |
| 2 | 7 45 | 15 54 | 7 55 | 16 04 | 7 57 | 15 57 | 8 04 | 15 53 | 8 09 | 15 42 | 8 25 | 15 48 | 8 25 | 16 02 |
| 3 | 7 47 | 15 54 | 7 57 | 16 04 | 7 59 | 15 56 | 8 05 | 15 52 | 8 11 | 15 42 | 8 27 | 15 47 | 8 26 | 16 01 |
| 4 | 7 48 | 15 53 | 7 58 | 16 03 | 8 00 | 15 56 | 8 07 | 15 52 | 8 12 | 15 41 | 8 28 | 15 46 | 8 27 | 16 00 |
| 5 | 7 49 | 15 53 | 7 59 | 16 03 | 8 01 | 15 55 | 8 08 | 15 51 | 8 14 | 15 40 | 8 30 | 15 45 | 8 29 | 16 00 |
| 6 | 7 51 | 15 52 | 8 00 | 16 02 | 8 03 | 15 55 | 8 09 | 15 51 | 8 15 | 15 40 | 8 31 | 15 45 | 8 30 | 15 59 |
| 7 | 7 52 | 15 52 | 8 02 | 16 02 | 8 04 | 15 54 | 8 10 | 15 51 | 8 17 | 15 39 | 8 33 | 15 44 | 8 32 | 15 59 |
| 8 | 7 53 | 15 52 | 8 03 | 16 02 | 8 05 | 15 54 | 8 12 | 15 50 | 8 18 | 15 39 | 8 34 | 15 44 | 8 33 | 15 59 |
| 9 | 7 54 | 15 52 | 8 04 | 16 02 | 8 06 | 15 54 | 8 13 | 15 50 | 8 19 | 15 39 | 8 35 | 15 44 | 8 34 | 15 58 |
| 10 | 7 55 | 15 51 | 8 05 | 16 02 | 8 07 | 15 54 | 8 14 | 15 50 | 8 20 | 15 38 | 8 36 | 15 43 | 8 35 | 15 58 |
| 11 | 7 56 | 15 51 | 8 06 | 16 01 | 8 08 | 15 54 | 8 15 | 15 50 | 8 21 | 15 38 | 8 38 | 15 43 | 8 36 | 15 58 |
| 12 | 7 57 | 15 51 | 8 07 | 16 01 | 8 09 | 15 54 | 8 16 | 15 50 | 8 23 | 15 38 | 8 39 | 15 43 | 8 37 | 15 58 |
| 13 | 7 58 | 15 51 | 8 08 | 16 01 | 8 10 | 15 54 | 8 17 | 15 50 | 8 24 | 15 38 | 8 40 | 15 43 | 8 38 | 15 58 |
| 14 | 7 59 | 15 51 | 8 09 | 16 02 | 8 11 | 15 54 | 8 18 | 15 50 | 8 25 | 15 38 | 8 41 | 15 43 | 8 39 | 15 58 |
| 15 | 8 00 | 15 52 | 8 10 | 16 02 | 8 12 | 15 54 | 8 19 | 15 50 | 8 25 | 15 38 | 8 42 | 15 43 | 8 40 | 15 58 |
| 16 | 8 01 | 15 52 | 8 10 | 16 02 | 8 13 | 15 54 | 8 20 | 15 50 | 8 26 | 15 38 | 8 43 | 15 43 | 8 41 | 15 58 |
| 17 | 8 01 | 15 52 | 8 11 | 16 02 | 8 14 | 15 54 | 8 20 | 15 50 | 8 27 | 15 38 | 8 43 | 15 43 | 8 42 | 15 58 |
| 18 | 8 02 | 15 52 | 8 12 | 16 02 | 8 14 | 15 55 | 8 21 | 15 50 | 8 28 | 15 39 | 8 44 | 15 43 | 8 43 | 15 58 |
| 19 | 8 03 | 15 53 | 8 12 | 16 03 | 8 15 | 15 55 | 8 22 | 15 51 | 8 28 | 15 39 | 8 45 | 15 44 | 8 43 | 15 59 |
| 20 | 8 03 | 15 53 | 8 13 | 16 03 | 8 16 | 15 55 | 8 22 | 15 51 | 8 29 | 15 39 | 8 45 | 15 44 | 8 44 | 15 59 |
| 21 | 8 04 | 15 54 | 8 14 | 16 04 | 8 16 | 15 56 | 8 23 | 15 52 | 8 30 | 15 40 | 8 46 | 15 45 | 8 44 | 16 00 |
| 22 | 8 04 | 15 54 | 8 14 | 16 04 | 8 17 | 15 56 | 8 23 | 15 52 | 8 30 | 15 41 | 8 46 | 15 45 | 8 45 | 16 00 |
| 23 | 8 05 | 15 55 | 8 14 | 16 05 | 8 17 | 15 57 | 8 24 | 15 53 | 8 30 | 15 41 | 8 47 | 15 46 | 8 45 | 16 01 |
| 24 | 8 05 | 15 55 | 8 15 | 16 05 | 8 17 | 15 58 | 8 24 | 15 53 | 8 31 | 15 42 | 8 47 | 15 47 | 8 46 | 16 02 |
| 25 | 8 05 | 15 56 | 8 15 | 16 06 | 8 18 | 15 58 | 8 25 | 15 54 | 8 31 | 15 43 | 8 47 | 15 47 | 8 46 | 16 02 |
| 26 | 8 06 | 15 57 | 8 15 | 16 07 | 8 18 | 15 59 | 8 25 | 15 55 | 8 31 | 15 43 | 8 48 | 15 48 | 8 46 | 16 03 |
| 27 | 8 06 | 15 58 | 8 16 | 16 08 | 8 18 | 16 00 | 8 25 | 15 56 | 8 31 | 15 44 | 8 48 | 15 49 | 8 46 | 16 04 |
| 28 | 8 06 | 15 58 | 8 16 | 16 09 | 8 18 | 16 01 | 8 25 | 15 57 | 8 32 | 15 45 | 8 48 | 15 50 | 8 46 | 16 05 |
| 29 | 8 06 | 15 59 | 8 16 | 16 09 | 8 18 | 16 02 | 8 25 | 15 58 | 8 32 | 15 46 | 8 48 | 15 51 | 8 46 | 16 06 |
| 30 | 8 06 | 16 00 | 8 16 | 16 10 | 8 18 | 16 03 | 8 25 | 15 59 | 8 31 | 15 47 | 8 48 | 15 52 | 8 46 | 16 07 |
| 31 | 8 06 | 16 01 | 8 16 | 16 11 | 8 18 | 16 04 | 8 25 | 16 00 | 8 31 | 15 48 | 8 47 | 15 53 | 8 46 | 16 08 |

## JUPITER

| Day | R.A. h m | Dec ° | Mag. | Diam. ″ | Rise h m | Transit h m | Set h m |
|-----|----------|-------|------|---------|----------|-------------|---------|
| 1 | 13 03.0 | −5.4 | −1.8 | 33 | 2 48 | 8 21 | 13 53 |
| 11 | 13 09.0 | −6.0 | −1.8 | 34 | 2 18 | 7 47 | 13 17 |
| 21 | 13 14.3 | −6.5 | −1.9 | 34 | 1 46 | 7 13 | 12 40 |
| 31 | 13 18.8 | −6.9 | −1.9 | 35 | 1 14 | 6 38 | 12 03 |

Equatorial Diam. 34″, Polar Diam. 32″

## SATURN

| Day | R.A. h m | Dec ° | Mag. | Diam. ″ | Rise h m | Transit h m | Set h m |
|-----|----------|-------|------|---------|----------|-------------|---------|
| 1 | 17 06.2 | −21.5 | +0.5 | 15 | 8 30 | 12 23 | 16 16 |
| 11 | 17 11.3 | −21.7 | +0.4 | 15 | 7 57 | 11 49 | 15 41 |
| 21 | 17 16.3 | −21.8 | +0.5 | 15 | 7 23 | 11 15 | 15 06 |
| 31 | 17 21.3 | −21.9 | +0.5 | 15 | 6 50 | 10 40 | 14 31 |

Equatorial Diam. 15″, Polar Diam. 14″
Rings – major axis 34″ minor axis 15″, Tilt 27°

## URANUS

| Day | R.A. h m | Dec ° | Mag. | Diam. ″ | Rise h m | Transit h m | Set h m |
|-----|----------|-------|------|---------|----------|-------------|---------|
| 1 | 1 17.3 | +7.5 | +6.1 | 4 | 13 48 | 20 33 | 3 21 |
| 11 | 1 16.5 | +7.4 | +6.1 | 4 | 13 09 | 19 53 | 2 41 |
| 21 | 1 16.1 | +7.4 | +6.1 | 4 | 12 29 | 19 13 | 2 01 |
| 31 | 1 16.0 | +7.4 | +6.1 | 4 | 11 50 | 18 34 | 1 21 |

## NEPTUNE

| Day | R.A. h m | Dec ° | Mag. | Diam. ″ | Rise h m | Transit h m | Set h m |
|-----|----------|-------|------|---------|----------|-------------|---------|
| 1 | 22 43.9 | −9.0 | +7.9 | 2 | 12 47 | 18 00 | 23 13 |
| 11 | 22 44.2 | −8.9 | +7.9 | 2 | 12 08 | 17 21 | 22 34 |
| 21 | 22 44.7 | −8.9 | +7.9 | 2 | 11 29 | 16 42 | 21 55 |
| 31 | 22 45.5 | −8.8 | +7.9 | 2 | 10 50 | 16 03 | 21 17 |

# TRANSIT OF MERCURY 9 MAY 2016

In the present epoch, transits of Mercury occur in May or November. May transits are roughly half as frequent as November transits and this is the last May transit until 2049. The dates of transits are gradually moving later in the year; in the early 1500s they were in April and October.

The interval between May transits is 13 or 33 years, and November transit intervals are 7, 13 or 33 years. For May transits, Mercury has a diameter of 12″ and occur at the descending node of Mercury's orbit. For November transits, Mercury has a diameter of 10″ and occur at the ascending node.

May transits are less frequent than November transits because during a May transit, Mercury is near aphelion whereas during a November transit, it is near perihelion.

Perihelion transits occur more frequently because Mercury moves faster in its orbit at perihelion and can reach the transit node more quickly, and at perihelion Mercury has less parallax as it is closer to the Sun.

Previous Mercury transits were in May 2003 and November 2006, the next are November 2019 and November 2032. For reference, the next Venus transit is not until 11 December 2117.

The transit is visible in its entirety from the UK, western Europe, eastern North America, most of South America and western Africa. No part is visible from Australasia, Japan, and Indonesia.

Times differ little throughout the world and even less from within the UK:

| Location | I | II | Greatest Transit (G) | III | IV | Duration |
|---|---|---|---|---|---|---|
| Geocentric | 11:12:18 | 11:15:30 | 14:57:25 | 18:39:12 | 18:42:24 | 7h 30m 06s |
| London | 11:12:23 | 11:15:35 | 14:56:17 | 18:37:21 | 18:40:33 | 7h 28m 10s |
| Glasgow | 11:12:26 | 11:15:37 | 14:56:22 | 18:37:23 | 18:40:35 | 7h 28m 09s |
| Belfast | 11:12:28 | 11:15:40 | 14:56:24 | 18:37:23 | 18:40:35 | 7h 28m 07s |
| Capetown | 11:12:16 | 11:15:26 | 14:56:43 | 15:58* | — | 4h 45m 30s |
| New York | 11:13:31 | 11:16:44 | 14:57:53 | 18:38:11 | 18:41:23 | 7h 27m 51s |
| Rio de Janeiro | 11:13:48 | 11:16:59 | 14:58:06 | 18:38:53 | 18:42:03 | 7h 28m 15s |
| Delhi | 11:10:42 | 11:13:53 | 13:28* | — | — | 2h 17m 17s |

* Transit ends at sunset

All times are given in Universal Time (GMT)
See diagram above and map below for positions of I, II, G, III and IV

Solar Semi-diameter: 15′ 50.4″
Mercury Semi-diameter: 0′ 06.0″

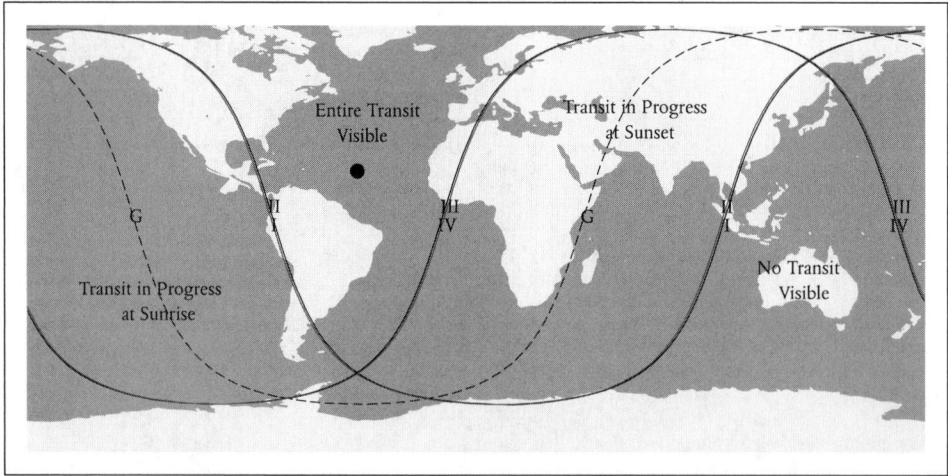

# ECLIPSES 2016

## ECLIPSES

During 2016 there will be four eclipses, two of the Sun and two of the Moon and a transit of Mercury.

1. A penumbral eclipse of the Moon on March 23 is visible from North and South America at moonset and eastern Asia at moonrise. Eastern Australia, New Zealand and the Pacific will see the whole eclipse. It should be noted that penumbral eclipses are not easy to observe.

2. A total eclipse of the Sun on March 9 is visible from Sumatra, Bangka Island, Palau Belitung, Central Kalimantan, Central Sulawesi, North Maluku and Woleai atoll, ending in the north Pacific Ocean. Partial phases are visable from northern Australia, Papua, Papua New Guinea, China and Alaska.

3. On 9 May a transit of Mercury will be visible in its entirety from the UK, western Europe, eastern North America and most of South America. No part of the transit is visible from Australasia and Japan (see page 1114).

4. An annular eclipse of the Sun on September 1 starts in the Gulf of Guinea and is visible from land on Annobon Island, central southern Africa (Gabon, Rep. of the Congo, Democratic Rep. of Congo, Tanzania and Mozambique) and into Madagascar, ending in the southern Indian Ocean.

5. A penumbral eclipse of the Moon on September 16 is visible from the UK and Europe at moonrise and visible in its entirety from eastern Africa and the whole of Asia. Australasia will see it at moonset.

## MEAN AND SIDEREAL TIME

The length of a sidereal day in mean time is 23h 56m 04s.09. Hence 1h MT = 1h+9$^s$.86 ST and 1h ST = 1h − 9$^s$.83 MT.

| Acceleration | | | | | | Retardation | | | | | |
|---|---|---|---|---|---|---|---|---|---|---|---|
| h | m | s | m | s | s | h | m | s | m | s | s |
| 1 | 0 | 10 | 0 | 00 | | 1 | 0 | 10 | 0 | 00 | |
| 2 | 0 | 20 | 3 | 02 | 0 | 2 | 0 | 20 | 3 | 03 | 0 |
| 3 | 0 | 30 | 9 | 07 | 1 | 3 | 0 | 29 | 9 | 09 | 1 |
| 4 | 0 | 39 | 15 | 13 | 2 | 4 | 0 | 39 | 15 | 15 | 2 |
| 5 | 0 | 49 | 21 | 18 | 3 | 5 | 0 | 49 | 21 | 21 | 3 |
| 6 | 0 | 59 | 27 | 23 | 4 | 6 | 0 | 59 | 27 | 28 | 4 |
| 7 | 1 | 09 | 33 | 28 | 5 | 7 | 1 | 09 | 33 | 34 | 5 |
| 8 | 1 | 19 | 39 | 34 | 6 | 8 | 1 | 19 | 39 | 40 | 6 |
| 9 | 1 | 29 | 45 | 39 | 7 | 9 | 1 | 28 | 45 | 46 | 7 |
| 10 | 1 | 39 | 51 | 44 | 8 | 10 | 1 | 38 | 51 | 53 | 8 |
| 11 | 1 | 48 | 57 | 49 | 9 | 11 | 1 | 48 | 57 | 59 | 9 |
| 12 | 1 | 58 | 60 | 00 | 10 | 12 | 1 | 58 | 60 | 00 | 10 |
| 13 | 2 | 08 | | | | 13 | 2 | 08 | | | |
| 14 | 2 | 18 | | | | 14 | 2 | 18 | | | |
| 15 | 2 | 28 | | | | 15 | 2 | 27 | | | |
| 16 | 2 | 38 | | | | 16 | 2 | 37 | | | |
| 17 | 2 | 48 | | | | 17 | 2 | 47 | | | |
| 18 | 2 | 57 | | | | 18 | 2 | 57 | | | |
| 19 | 3 | 07 | | | | 19 | 3 | 07 | | | |
| 20 | 3 | 17 | | | | 20 | 3 | 17 | | | |
| 21 | 3 | 27 | | | | 21 | 3 | 26 | | | |
| 22 | 3 | 37 | | | | 22 | 3 | 36 | | | |
| 23 | 3 | 47 | | | | 23 | 3 | 46 | | | |
| 24 | 3 | 57 | | | | 24 | 3 | 56 | | | |

To convert an interval of mean time to the corresponding interval of sidereal time, enter the acceleration table with the given mean time (taking the hours and the minutes and seconds separately) and add the acceleration obtained to the given mean time. To convert an interval of sidereal time to the corresponding interval of mean time, take out the retardation for the given sidereal time and subtract.

The columns for the minutes and seconds of the argument

are in the form known as critical tables. To use these tables, find in the appropriate left-hand column the two entries between which the given number of minutes and seconds lies; the quantity in the right-hand column between these two entries is the required acceleration or retardation. Thus the acceleration for 11m 26s (which lies between the entries 9m 07s and 15m 13s) is 2s. If the given number of minutes and seconds is a tabular entry, the required acceleration or retardation is the entry in the right-hand column above the given tabular entry, eg the retardation for 45m 46s is 7s.

*Example* – Convert 14h 27m 35s from ST to MT

| | h | m | s |
|---|---|---|---|
| Given ST | 14 | 27 | 35 |
| Retardation for 14h | | 2 | 18 |
| Retardation for 27m 35s | | | 5 |
| Corresponding MT | 14 | 25 | 12 |

For further explanation see pages 1118 and 1120

## EXPLANATION OF ASTRONOMICAL DATA

Positions of the heavenly bodies are given only to the degree of accuracy required by amateur astronomers for setting telescopes, or for plotting on celestial globes or star atlases. Where intermediate positions are required, linear interpolation may be employed.

Detailed definitions of the terms used cannot be given here. They must be sought in astronomical literature and textbooks.

A special feature has been made of the times when the Sun and Moon are visible in the British Isles. Since two columns, calculated for latitudes 52° and 56°, are devoted to risings and settings, the range 50° to 58° can be covered by interpolation and extrapolation. The times given in these columns are Greenwich Mean Times for the meridian of Greenwich. An observer west of this meridian must add his/her longitude (in time) and vice versa.

In accordance with the usual convention in astronomy, + and − indicate respectively north and south latitudes or declinations.

All data are, unless otherwise stated, for 0h Greenwich Mean Time (GMT), ie at the midnight at the beginning of the day named. Allowance must be made for British Summer Time during the period that this is in operation.

### PAGE ONE OF EACH MONTH

The calendar for each month is explained on page 1065.

Under the heading Astronomical Phenomena will be found particulars of the more important conjunctions of the Sun, Moon and planets with each other, and also the dates of other astronomical phenomena of special interest.

Times of Minima of Algol are approximate times of the middle of the period of diminished light.

The Constellations listed each month are those that are near the meridian at the beginning of the month at 22h local mean time. Allowance must be made for British Summer Time if necessary. The fact that any star crosses the meridian 4m earlier each night or 2h earlier each month may be used, in conjunction with the lists given each month, to find what constellations are favourably placed at any moment.

The principal phases of the Moon are the GMTs when the difference between the longitude of the Moon and that of the Sun is 0°, 90°, 180° or 270°. The times of perigee and apogee are those when the Moon is nearest to, and farthest from, the Earth, respectively. The nodes or points of intersection of the Moon's orbit and the ecliptic make a complete retrograde circuit of the ecliptic in about 19 years.

From a knowledge of the longitude of the ascending node and the inclination, whose value does not vary much from 5°, the path of the Moon among the stars may be plotted on a celestial globe or star atlas.

## PAGE TWO OF EACH MONTH

The Sun's diameter, in arc seconds, is given once a month.

The right ascension and declination (Dec.) is that of the true Sun. The right ascension of the mean Sun is obtained by applying the equation of time, with the sign given, to the right ascension of the true Sun, or, more easily, by applying 12h to the Sidereal Time. The direction in which the equation of time has to be applied in different problems is a frequent source of confusion and error. Apparent Solar Time is equal to the Mean Solar Time plus the Equation of Time. For example, at 12h GMT on August 8 the Equation of Time is −5m 44s and thus at 12h Mean Time on that day the Apparent Time is 12h − 5m 44s = 11h 54m 16s.

The Greenwich Sidereal Time at 0h and the Transit of the First Point of Aries (which is really the mean time when the sidereal time is 0h) are used for converting mean time to sidereal time and vice versa.

The GMT of transit of the Sun at Greenwich may also be taken as the local mean time (LMT) of transit in any longitude. It is independent of latitude. The GMT of transit in any longitude is obtained by adding the longitude to the time given if west, and vice versa.

## DECLINATION

The distance in degrees from the ecliptic (the Sun's apparent path through the sky and the path that the planets closely follow) is termed its *declination (Dec.)*. For northern latitudes, higher positive declination means the object is higher in the sky.

## LIGHTING-UP TIME

The legal importance of sunrise and sunset is that the Road Vehicles Lighting Regulations 1989 (SI 1989 No. 1796) as amended, make the use of front and rear position lamps on vehicles compulsory during the period between sunset and sunrise. Headlamps on vehicles are required to be used during the hours of darkness on unlit roads, on lit roads with a speed limit exceeding 30mph, or whenever visibility is seriously reduced. The hours of darkness are defined in these regulations as the period between half an hour after sunset and half an hour before sunrise.

In all laws and regulations 'sunset' refers to the local sunset, ie the time at which the Sun sets at the place in question. This common-sense interpretation has been upheld by legal tribunals.

## MAGNITUDE

Magnitudes of astronomical objects are measured in what may be considered the reverse to the obvious. Magnitude +3 is brighter than +4, magnitude −2 is brighter than magnitude −1. So from brighter to dimmer: −4, −3, −2, −1, 0, +1, +2, +3 etc, with +6 being the dimmest considered visible with the naked eye in very dark skies. Each magnitude is roughly 2.5 times brighter than the next, so a magnitude +1 object is 100 times brighter than a magnitude +6 object.

## SUNRISE AND SUNSET

The times of sunrise and sunset are those when the Sun's upper limb, as affected by refraction, is on the true horizon of an observer at sea-level. Assuming the mean refraction to be 34′, and the Sun's semi-diameter to be 16′, the time given is that when the true zenith distance of the Sun's centre is 90°+34′+16′ or 90° 50′, or, in other words, when the depression of the Sun's centre below the true horizon is 50′. The upper limb is then 34′ below the true horizon, but is

brought there by refraction. An observer on a ship might see the Sun for a minute or so longer, because of the dip of the horizon, while another viewing the sunset over hills or mountains would record an earlier time. Nevertheless, the moment when the true zenith distance of the Sun's centre is 90° 50′ is a precise time dependent only on the latitude and longitude of the place, and independent of its altitude above sea-level, the contour of its horizon, the vagaries of refraction or the small seasonal change in the Sun's diameter; this moment is suitable in every way as a definition of sunset (or sunrise) for all statutory purposes.

(For further information, *see* footnote on page 1117.)

## TWILIGHT

Light reaches us before sunrise and continues to reach us for some time after sunset. The interval between darkness and sunrise or sunset and darkness is called twilight. Astronomically speaking, twilight is considered to begin or end when the Sun's centre is 18° below the horizon, as no light from the Sun can then reach the observer. As thus defined twilight may last several hours; in high latitudes at the summer solstice the depression of 18° is not reached, and twilight lasts from sunset to sunrise.

The need for some sub-division of twilight is met by dividing the gathering darkness into four stages.

(1) *Sunrise or Sunset,* defined as above
(2) *Civil twilight,* which begins or ends when the Sun's centre is 6° below the horizon. This marks the time when operations requiring daylight may commence or must cease. In England it varies from about 30 to 60 minutes after sunset and the same interval before sunrise
(3) *Nautical twilight,* which begins or ends when the Sun's centre is 12° below the horizon. This marks the time when it is, to all intents and purposes, completely dark
(4) *Astronomical twilight,* which begins or ends when the Sun's centre is 18° below the horizon. This marks theoretical perfect darkness. It is of little practical importance, especially if nautical twilight is tabulated

To assist observers the durations of civil, nautical and astronomical twilights are given at intervals of ten days. The beginning of a particular twilight is found by subtracting the duration from the time of sunrise, while the end is found by adding the duration to the time of sunset. Thus the beginning of astronomical twilight in latitude 52°, on the Greenwich meridian, on March 11 is found as 06h 24m − 113m = 04h 31m and the end of civil twilight as 17h 57m +34m = 18h 31m. The letters TAN (twilight all night) are printed when twilight lasts all night.

Under the heading The Night Sky will be found notes describing the position and visibility of the planets and other phenomena.

## PAGE THREE OF EACH MONTH

The Moon moves so rapidly among the stars that its position is given only to the degree of accuracy that permits linear interpolation. The right ascension (RA) and declination (Dec.) are geocentric, ie for an imaginary observer at the centre of the Earth. To an observer on the surface of the Earth the position is always different, as the altitude is always less on account of parallax, which may reach 1°.

The lunar terminator is the line separating the bright from the dark part of the Moon's disk. Apart from irregularities of the lunar surface, the terminator is elliptical, because it is a circle seen in projection. It becomes the full circle forming the limb, or edge, of the Moon at New and Full Moon. The selenographic longitude of the terminator is measured from the mean centre of the visible disk, which may differ from the visible centre by as much as 8°, because of libration.

Instead of the longitude of the terminator the Sun's selenographic co-longitude (Sun's co-long.) is tabulated. It is numerically equal to the selenographic longitude of the morning terminator, measured eastwards from the mean centre of the disk. Thus its value is approximately 270° at New Moon, 360° at First Quarter, 90° at Full Moon and 180° at Last Quarter.

The Position Angle (PA) of the Bright Limb is the position angle of the midpoint of the illuminated limb, measured eastwards from the north point on the disk. The Phase column shows the percentage of the area of the Moon's disk illuminated; this is also the illuminated percentage of the diameter at right angles to the line of cusps. The terminator is a semi-ellipse whose major axis is the line of cusps, and whose semi-minor axis is determined by the tabulated percentage; from New Moon to Full Moon the east limb is dark, and vice versa.

The times given as moonrise and moonset are those when the upper limb of the Moon is on the horizon of an observer at sea-level. The Sun's horizontal parallax (Hor. par.) is about 9″, and is negligible when considering sunrise and sunset, but that of the Moon averages about 57′. Hence the computed time represents the moment when the true zenith distance of the Moon is 90° 50′ (as for the Sun) minus the horizontal parallax. The time required for the Sun or Moon to rise or set is about four minutes (except in high latitudes). *See also* the footnote below.

The GMT of transit of the Moon over the meridian of Greenwich is given; these times are independent of latitude but must be corrected for longitude. For places in the British Isles it suffices to add the longitude if west, and vice versa. For other places a further correction is necessary because of the rapid movement of the Moon relative to the stars. The entire correction is conveniently determined by first finding the west longitude $\lambda$ of the place. If the place is in west longitude, $\lambda$ is the ordinary west longitude; if the place is in east longitude $\lambda$ is the complement to 24h (or 360°) of the longitude and will be greater than 12h (or 180°). The correction then consists of two positive portions, namely $\lambda$ and the fraction $\lambda/24$ (or $\lambda°/360$) multiplied by the difference between consecutive transits. Thus for Christchurch, New Zealand, the longitude is 11h 31m east, so $\lambda$ = 12h 29m and the fraction $\lambda/24$ is 0.52. The transit on the local date 26 January 2016 is found as follows:

|  |  | d | h | m |
|---|---|---|---|---|
| GMT of transit at Greenwich | January | 25 | 0 | 54 |
| $\lambda$ |  |  | 12 | 29 |
| 0.52 × (01h 42m – 00h 54m) |  |  |  | 25 |
| GMT of transit at Christchurch |  | 25 | 13 | 48 |
| Corr. to NZ Standard Time |  |  | 12 | 00 |
| Local standard time of transit | January | 26 | 01 | 48 |

---

SUNRISE, SUNSET, MOONRISE AND MOONSET
The tables have been constructed for the meridian of Greenwich and for latitudes 52° and 56°. They give Greenwich Mean Time (GMT) throughout the year. To obtain the GMT of the phenomenon as seen from any other latitude and longitude in the British Isles, first interpolate or extrapolate for latitude by the usual rules of proportion. To the time thus found, the longitude (expressed in time) must be added if west (as it usually is in Great Britain) or subtracted if east. If the longitude is expressed in degrees and minutes of arc, it must be converted to time at the rate of 1° = 4m and 15′ = 1m.

The GMT at which the planet transits the Greenwich meridian is also given. The times of transit are to be corrected to local meridians in the usual way, as already described.

As is evident, for any given place the quantities $\lambda$ and the correction to local standard time may be combined permanently, being here 24h 29m.

Positions of Mercury are given for every second day, and those of Venus and Mars for every fifth day; they may be interpolated linearly. The diameter (Diam.) is given in seconds of arc. The phase is the illuminated percentage of the disk. In the case of the inner planets this approaches 100 at superior conjunction and 0 at inferior conjunction. When the phase is less than 50 the planet is crescent-shaped or horned; for greater phases it is gibbous. In the case of the exterior planet Mars, the phase approaches 100 at conjunction and opposition, and is a minimum at the quadratures.

To determine if a planet is visible or not, the transit time should be examined. If the transit time coincides with hours of darkness the planet should be easy to find, provided it is bright enough. If the time of transit is between 00h and 12h the planet should be visible above the eastern horizon; if between 12h and 24h, above the western horizon. The closer the transit time to midnight (0h) the longer it will be visible.

The inner planets – Mercury and Venus can never transit at midnight because they are too close to the Sun. If they transit close to noon (12h) then they will be too close to the Sun to be visible except during a large solar eclipse. The rise or set times should be examined to see if either is near sunrise or sunset. If this also coincides with a large positive declination (Dec.) then conditions are favourable for viewing.

Consulting The Night Sky paragraphs will also help determine observability.

## PAGE FOUR OF EACH MONTH

The GMTs of sunrise and sunset for seven cities, whose adopted positions in longitude (W.) and latitude (N.) are given immediately below the name, may be used not only for these phenomena, but also for lighting-up times (*see* page 1116 for a fuller explanation).

The particulars for the four outer planets resemble those for the planets on Page Three of each month, except that, because of the inferior brightness of Uranus and Neptune, these two planets require optical aids such as binoculars or a small telescope. The diameters given for the rings of Saturn are those of the major axis (in the plane of the planet's equator) and the minor axis respectively. The former has a small seasonal change due to the slightly varying distance of the Earth from Saturn, but the latter varies from zero when the Earth passes through the ring plane every 15 years to its maximum opening half-way between these periods. The rings were last open at their widest extent (and Saturn at its brightest) in 2002; this will occur again in 2017. The Earth passed through the ring plane in 2009.

## TIME

From the earliest ages, the natural division of time into recurring periods of day and night has provided the practical time-scale for the everyday activities of the human race. Indeed, if any alternative means of time measurement is adopted, it must be capable of adjustment so as to remain in general agreement with the natural time-scale defined by the diurnal rotation of the Earth on its axis. Ideally the rotation should be measured against a fixed frame of reference; in practice it must be measured against the background provided by the celestial bodies. If the Sun is chosen as the reference point, we obtain Apparent Solar Time, which is the time indicated by a sundial. It is not a uniform time but is subject to variations which amount to as much as a quarter of an hour in each direction. Such wide variations cannot be tolerated in a practical time-scale, and this has led to the concept of Mean Solar Time in which all the days are exactly the same length and equal to the average length of the Apparent Solar Day.

The positions of the stars in the sky are specified in relation to a fictitious reference point in the sky known as the First Point of Aries (or the Vernal Equinox). It is therefore convenient to adopt this same reference point when considering the rotation of the Earth against the background of the stars. The time-scale so obtained is known as Apparent Sidereal Time.

## GREENWICH MEAN TIME

The daily rotation of the Earth on its axis causes the Sun and the other heavenly bodies to appear to cross the sky from east to west. It is convenient to represent this relative motion as if the Sun really performed a daily circuit around a fixed Earth. Noon in Apparent Solar Time may then be defined as the time at which the Sun transits across the observer's meridian. In Mean Solar Time, noon is similarly defined by the meridian transit of a fictitious Mean Sun moving uniformly in the sky with the same average speed as the true Sun. Mean Solar Time observed on the meridian of the transit circle telescope of the Royal Observatory at Greenwich is called Greenwich Mean Time (GMT). The mean solar day is divided into 24 hours and, for astronomical and other scientific purposes, these are numbered 0 to 23, commencing at midnight. Civil time is usually reckoned in two periods of 12 hours, designated am (*ante meridiem,* ie before noon) and pm (*post meridiem,* ie after noon), although the 24 hour clock is increasingly being used.

## UNIVERSAL TIME

Before 1925 January 1, GMT was reckoned in 24 hours commencing at noon; since that date it has been reckoned from midnight. To avoid confusion in the use of the designation GMT before and after 1925, since 1928 astronomers have tended to use the term Universal Time (UT) or Weltzeit (WZ) to denote GMT measured from Greenwich Mean Midnight.

In precision work it is necessary to take account of small variations in Universal Time. These arise from small irregularities in the rotation of the Earth. Observed astronomical time is designated UT0. Observed time corrected for the effects of the motion of the poles (giving rise to a 'wandering' in longitude) is designated UT1. There is also a seasonal fluctuation in the rate of rotation of the Earth arising from meteorological causes, often called the annual fluctuation. UT1 corrected for this effect is designated UT2 and provides a time-scale free from short-period fluctuations. It is still subject to small secular and irregular changes.

## APPARENT SOLAR TIME

As mentioned above, the time shown by a sundial is called Apparent Solar Time. It differs from Mean Solar Time by an amount known as the Equation of Time, which is the total effect of two causes which make the length of the apparent solar day non-uniform. One cause of variation is that the orbit of the Earth is not a circle but an ellipse, having the Sun at one focus. As a consequence, the angular speed of the Earth in its orbit is not constant; it is greatest at the beginning of January when the Earth is nearest the Sun.

The other cause is due to the obliquity of the ecliptic; the plane of the equator (which is at right angles to the axis of rotation of the Earth) does not coincide with the ecliptic (the plane defined by the apparent annual motion of the Sun around the celestial sphere) but is inclined to it at an angle of 23° 26'. As a result, the apparent solar day is shorter than

average at the equinoxes and longer at the solstices. From the combined effects of the components due to obliquity and eccentricity, the equation of time reaches its maximum values in February (−14 minutes) and early November (+16 minutes). It has a zero value on four dates during the year, and it is only on these dates (approximately April 15, June 14, September 1 and December 25) that a sundial shows Mean Solar Time.

## SIDEREAL TIME

A sidereal day is the duration of a complete rotation of the Earth with reference to the First Point of Aries. The term sidereal (or 'star') time is a little misleading since the time-scale so defined is not exactly the same as that which would be defined by successive transits of a selected star, as there is a small progressive motion between the stars and the First Point of Aries due to the precession of the Earth's axis. This makes the length of the sidereal day shorter than the true period of rotation by 0.008 seconds. Superimposed on this steady precessional motion are small oscillations (nutation), giving rise to fluctuations in apparent sidereal time amounting to as much as 1.2 seconds. It is therefore customary to employ Mean Sidereal Time, from which these fluctuations have been removed. The conversion of GMT to Greenwich sidereal time (GST) may be performed by adding the value of the GST at 0h on the day in question (page two of each month) to the GMT converted to sidereal time using the table on page 1115.

*Example* – To find the GST at August 8d 02h 41m 11s GMT

|  | h | m | s |
|---|---|---|---|
| GST at 0h | 20 | 07 | 34 |
| GMT | 2 | 41 | 11 |
| Acceleration for 2h |  |  | 20 |
| Acceleration for 41m 11s |  |  | 7 |
| Sum = GST = | 22 | 49 | 12 |

If the observer is not on the Greenwich meridian then his/her longitude, measured positively westwards from Greenwich, must be subtracted from the GST to obtain Local Sidereal Time (LST). Thus, in the above example, an observer 5h east of Greenwich, or 19h west, would find the LST as 4h 49m 16s.

## EPHEMERIS TIME

An analysis of observations of the positions of the Sun, Moon and planets taken over an extended period is used in preparing ephemerides. (An ephemeris is a table giving the apparent position of a heavenly body at regular intervals of time, eg one day or ten days, and may be used to compare current observations with tabulated positions.) Discrepancies between the positions of heavenly bodies observed over a 300-year period and their predicted positions arose because the time-scale to which the observations were related was based on the assumption that the rate of rotation of the Earth is uniform. It is now known that this rate of rotation is variable. A revised time-scale, Ephemeris Time (ET), was devised to bring the ephemerides into agreement with the observations.

The second of ET is defined in terms of the annual motion of the Earth in its orbit around the Sun (1/31556925.9747 of the tropical year for 1900 January 0d 12h ET). The precise determination of ET from astronomical observations is a lengthy process as the requisite standard of accuracy can only be achieved by averaging over a number of years.

In 1976 the International Astronomical Union adopted Terrestrial Dynamical Time (TDT), a new dynamical time-scale for general use whose scale unit is the SI second (*see* Atomic Time, below). TDT was renamed Terrestrial Time (TT) in 1991. ET is now of little more than historical interest.

## TERRESTRIAL TIME
The uniform time system used in computing the ephemerides of the solar system is Terrestrial Time (TT), which has replaced ET for this purpose. Except for the most rigorous astronomical calculations, it may be assumed to be the same as ET. During 2016 the estimated difference TT − UT is about 68 seconds.

## ATOMIC TIME
The fundamental standards of time and frequency must be defined in terms of a periodic motion adequately uniform, enduring and measurable. Progress has made it possible to use natural standards, such as atomic or molecular oscillations. Continuous oscillations are generated in an electrical circuit, the frequency of which is then compared or brought into coincidence with the frequency characteristic of the absorption or emission by the atoms or molecules when they change between two selected energy levels. Since the 13th General Conference on Weights and Measures in October 1967, the unit of time, the second, has been defined in the International System of units (SI) as 'the duration of 9 192 631 770 periods of the radiation corresponding to the transition between the two hyperfine levels of the ground state of the caesium-133 atom'.

In the UK, the national time scale is maintained by the National Physical Laboratory (NPL), using an ensemble of atomic clocks based on either caesium or hydrogen atoms. In addition the NPL (along with several other national laboratories) has constructed and operates caesium fountain primary frequency standards, which utilise the cooling of caesium atoms by laser light to determine the duration of the SI second at the highest attainable level of accuracy. Caesium fountain primary standards typically achieve an accuracy of around 2 parts in 10 000 000 000 000 000, which is equivalent to one second in 158 million years.

Timekeeping worldwide is based on two closely related atomic time scales that are established through international collaboration. International Atomic Time (TAI) is formed by combining the readings of more than 400 atomic clocks located in more than 70 institutes and was set close to the astronomically based Universal Time (UT) near the beginning of 1958. It was formally recognised in 1971 and since 1988 January 1 has been maintained by the International Bureau of Weights and Measures (BIPM). Civil time in almost all countries is now based on Coordinated Universal Time (UTC), which differs from TAI by an integer number of seconds and was designed to make both atomic time and UT available with accuracy appropriate for most users. On 1 January 1972 UTC was set to be exactly 10 seconds behind TAI, and since then the UTC time-scale has been adjusted by the insertion (or, in principle, omission) of leap seconds in order to keep it within ±0.9 s of UT. These leap seconds are introduced, when necessary, at the same instant throughout the world, either at the end of December or at the end of June. The last leap second occurred immediately prior to 0h UTC on 2015 July 1, and was the 26th leap second. All leap seconds so far have been positive, with 61 seconds in the final minute of the UTC month. The time 23h 59m 60s UTC is followed one second later by 0h 0m 00s of the first day of the following month. Notices concerning the insertion of leap seconds are issued by the International Earth Rotation and Reference Systems Service (IERS).

The computation of UTC is carried out monthly by the BIPM and takes place in three stages. First, a weighted average known as Echelle Atomique Libre (EAL) is calculated from all of the contributing atomic clocks. In the second stage, TAI is generated by applying small corrections, derived from the results contributed by primary frequency standards, to the scale interval of EAL to maintain its value close to that of the SI second. Finally, UTC is formed from TAI by the addition of an integer number of seconds. The results are published monthly in the BIPM Circular T in the form of offsets at 5-day intervals between UTC and the time scales of contributing organisations.

## RADIO TIME-SIGNALS
UTC is made generally available through time-signals and standard frequency broadcasts such as MSF in the UK, CHU in Canada and WWV and WWVH in the USA. These are based on national time-scales that are maintained in close agreement with UTC and provide traceability to the national time-scale and to UTC. The markers of seconds in the UTC scale coincide with those of TAI.

To disseminate the national time-scale in the UK, special signals (call-sign MSF) are broadcast by the National Physical Laboratory. From April 1, 2007 the MSF service, previously broadcast from British Telecom's radio station at Rugby, has been transmitted from Anthorn radio station in Cumbria. The signals are controlled from a caesium beam atomic frequency standard and consist of a precise frequency carrier of 60 kHz which is switched off, after being on for at least half a second, to mark every second. The first second of the minute begins with a period of 500 ms with the carrier switched off, to serve as a minute marker. In the other seconds the carrier is always off for at least one tenth of a second at the start and then it carries an on-off code giving the British clock time and date, together with information identifying the start of the next minute. Changes to and from summer time are made following government announcements. Leap seconds are inserted as announced by the IERS and information provided by them on the difference between UTC and UT is also signalled. Other broadcast signals in the UK include the BBC six pips signal, the BT Timeline ('speaking clock'), the NPL telephone and internet time services for computers, and a coded time-signal on the BBC 198 kHz transmitters which is used for timing in the electricity supply industry. From 1972 January 1 the six pips on the BBC have consisted of five short pips from second 55 to second 59 (six pips in the case of a leap second) followed by one lengthened pip, the start of which indicates the exact minute. From 1990 February 5 these signals have been controlled by the BBC with seconds markers referenced to the satellite-based US navigation system GPS (Global Positioning System) and time and day referenced to the MSF transmitter. Formerly they were generated by the Royal Greenwich Observatory. The NPL telephone and internet time services are directly connected to the national time scale.

Accurate timing may also be obtained from the signals of international navigation systems such as the ground-based eLORAN, or the satellite-based American GPS or Russian GLONASS systems.

## STANDARD TIME
Since 1880 the standard time in Britain has been Greenwich Mean Time (GMT); a statute that year enacted that the word 'time' when used in any legal document relating to Britain meant, unless otherwise specifically stated, the mean time of the Greenwich meridian. Greenwich was adopted as the universal meridian on 13 October 1884. A system of standard time by zones is used worldwide, standard time in each zone differing from that of the Greenwich meridian by an integral number of hours or, exceptionally, half-hours or quarter-hours, either fast or slow. The large territories of

the USA and Canada are divided into zones approximately 7.5° on either side of central meridians.

Variations from the standard time of some countries occur during part of the year; they are decided annually and are usually referred to as Summer Time or Daylight Saving Time.

At the 180th meridian the time can be either 12 hours fast on Greenwich Mean Time or 12 hours slow, and a change of date occurs. The internationally recognised date or calendar line is a modification of the 180th meridian, drawn so as to include islands of any one group on the same side of the line, or for political reasons. The line is indicated by joining up the following coordinates:

| Lat. | Long. | Lat. | Long. |
|------|-------|------|-------|
| 90° S. | 180° | 48° N. | 180° |
| 51° S. | 180° | 53° N. | 170° E. |
| 45° S. | 172.5° W. | 65.5° N. | 169° W. |
| 15° S. | 172.5° W. | 68° N. | 169° W. |
| 5° S. | 180° | 90° N. | 180° |

Changes to the date line would require an international conference.

### BRITISH SUMMER TIME

In 1916 an Act ordained that during a defined period of that year the legal time for general purposes in Great Britain should be one hour in advance of Greenwich Mean Time. The Summer Time Acts 1922 and 1925 defined the period during which Summer Time was to be in force, stabilising practice until the Second World War.

During the Second World War (1941–5) and in 1947 Double Summer Time (two hours in advance of Greenwich Mean Time) was used for the period in which ordinary Summer Time would have been in force. During these years clocks were also kept one hour in advance of Greenwich Mean Time in the winter. After the war, ordinary Summer Time was invoked each year from 1948–68.

Between 1968 October 27 and 1971 October 31 clocks were kept one hour ahead of Greenwich Mean Time throughout the year. This was known as British Standard Time.

The most recent legislation is the Summer Time Act 1972, which enacted that 'the period of summer time for the purposes of this Act is the period beginning at two o'clock, Greenwich Mean Time, in the morning of the day after the third Saturday in March or, if that day is Easter Day, the day after the second Saturday in March, and ending at two o'clock, Greenwich Mean Time, in the morning of the day after the fourth Saturday in October.'

The duration of Summer Time can be varied by Order in Council and in recent years alterations have been made to synchronise the period of Summer Time in Britain with that used in Europe. The rule for 1981–94 defined the period of Summer Time in the UK as from the last Sunday in March to the day following the fourth Saturday in October and the hour of changeover was altered to 01h Greenwich Mean Time.

There was no rule for the dates of Summer Time between 1995–7. Since 1998 the 9th European Parliament and Council Directive on Summer Time has harmonised the dates on which Summer Time begins and ends across member states as the last Sundays in March and October respectively. Under the directive Summer Time begins and ends at 01hr Greenwich Mean Time in each member state. Amendments to the Summer Time Act to implement the directive came into force on 11 March 2002.

The duration of Summer Time in 2016 is:
March 27 01h GMT to October 30 01h GMT

## MEAN REFRACTION

| Alt. | Ref. | Alt. | Ref. | Alt. | Ref. |
|------|------|------|------|------|------|
| ° ′ | ′ | ° ′ | ′ | ° ′ | ′ |
| 1 20 | 21 | 3 12 | 13 | 7 54 | 6 |
| 1 30 | | 3 34 | | 9 27 | |
| 1 41 | 20 | 4 00 | 12 | 11 39 | 5 |
| 1 52 | 19 | 4 30 | 11 | 15 00 | 4 |
| 2 05 | 18 | 5 06 | 10 | 20 42 | 3 |
| 2 19 | 17 | 5 50 | 9 | 32 20 | 2 |
| 2 35 | 16 | 6 44 | 8 | 62 17 | 1 |
| 2 52 | 15 | 7 54 | 7 | 90 00 | 0 |
| 3 12 | 14 | | | | |

The refraction table is in the form of a critical table (see page 1115).

## ASTRONOMICAL CONSTANTS

| | |
|---|---|
| Solar parallax | 8″.794 |
| Astronomical unit | 149597870 km |
| Precession for the year 2016 | 50″.257 |
| Precession in right ascension | 3ˢ.075 |
| Precession in declination | 20″.043 |
| Constant of nutation | 9″.202 |
| Constant of aberration | 20″.496 |
| Mean obliquity of ecliptic (2009) | 23° 26′ 17″ |
| Moon's equatorial hor. parallax | 57′ 02″.70 |
| Velocity of light in vacuo per second | 299792.5 km |
| Solar motion per second | 20.0 km |
| Equatorial radius of the Earth | 6378.137 km |
| Polar radius of the Earth | 6356.752 km |

North galactic pole (IAU standard)
RA 12h 51m (2000.0). Dec. +27°.1 N.
Solar apex                        RA 18h 04m Dec. + 30°
Length of year (in mean solar days)

| | |
|---|---|
| Tropical | 365.24219 |
| Sidereal | 365.25636 |
| Anomalistic (perihelion to perihelion) | 365.25964 |
| Eclipse | 346.62003 |

| Length of month (mean values) | d | h | m | s |
|---|---|---|---|---|
| Synodic (new Moon to new Moon) | 29 | 12 | 44 | 02.0 |
| Sidereal | 27 | 07 | 43 | 43.2 |
| Anomalistic (perigee to perigee) | 27 | 13 | 18 | 51.8 |

## THE EARTH

The shape of the Earth is that of an oblate spheroid or solid of revolution whose meridian sections are ellipses not differing much from circles, while the sections at right angles are circles. The length of the equatorial axis is about 12,756 km, and that of the polar axis is 12,714 km. The mean density of the Earth is 5.5 times that of water, although that of the surface layer is less. The Earth and Moon revolve about their common centre of gravity in a lunar month; this centre in turn revolves round the Sun in a plane known as the ecliptic, that passes through the Sun's centre. The Earth's equator is inclined to this plane at an angle of 23.4°. This tilt is the cause of the seasons. In mid-latitudes, and when the Sun is high above the Equator, not only does the high noon altitude make the days longer, but the Sun's rays fall more directly on the Earth's surface; these effects combine to produce summer. In equatorial regions the noon altitude is large throughout the year, and there is little variation in the length of the day. In higher latitudes the noon altitude is lower, and the days in summer are appreciably longer than those in winter.

The average velocity of the Earth in its orbit is 30km a second. It makes a complete rotation on its axis in about 23h 56m of mean time, which is the sidereal day. Because of its annual revolution round the Sun, the rotation with respect to the Sun, or the solar day, is more than this by about four minutes. The extremity of the axis of rotation, or the North Pole of the Earth, is not rigidly fixed, but wanders over an area roughly 20 metres in diameter.

*Perihelion* is when the Earth is closest to the Sun, and *aphelion* when the Earth is furthest from the Sun:

| | | |
|---|---|---|
| Perihelion | January | 2d 22h 49m |
| | | (147,100,176km, 0.983303941au) |
| Aphelion | July | 4d 16h 24m |
| | | (152,103,776km, 1.016750939au) |

## TERRESTRIAL MAGNETISM

The Earth's main magnetic field corresponds approximately to that of a very strong small bar magnet near the centre of the Earth, but with appreciable smooth spatial departures. The origin of the main field is generally ascribed to electric currents associated with fluid motions in the Earth's core. As a result not only does the main field vary in strength and direction from place to place, but also with time. Superimposed on the main field are local and regional anomalies whose magnitudes may in places approach that of the main field; these are due to the influence of mineral deposits in the Earth's crust. A small proportion of the field is of external origin, mostly associated with electric currents in the ionosphere and magnetosphere. The configuration of the external field and the ionisation of the atmosphere depend on the incident particle and radiation flux from the Sun. There are, therefore, short-term and non-periodic as well as diurnal, 27-day, seasonal and approximate 11-year periodic changes in the magnetic field, dependent upon the position of the Sun, the degree of solar activity and the magnetic field embedded in the solar wind.

A magnetic compass points along the horizontal component of a magnetic line of force. These lines of force converge on the 'magnetic dip-poles', the places where the Earth's magnetic field is vertical. These poles move with time, and their present approximate adopted mean positions are 86.4° N., 166.4° W. and 64.2° S., 136.4° E. Compasses do not point directly, ie via great circle routes, to the dip-poles.

There is also a 'magnetic equator', at all points of which the vertical component of the Earth's magnetic field is zero and a magnetised needle remains horizontal. This line runs between 2° and 12° north of the geographical equator in Asia and Africa, turns sharply south in the Atlantic Ocean and crosses South America south of the geographical equator; it re-crosses the geographical equator in mid-Pacific.

Reference has already been made to secular changes in the Earth's field. The following table indicates the changes in magnetic declination (or variation of the compass relative to true north). Declination is the angle in the horizontal plane between the direction of true north and that in which a magnetic compass points. Similar, though much smaller, changes have occurred in 'dip' or magnetic inclination. Secular changes differ throughout the world.

*London (Greenwich)*

| | | | | | | |
|---|---|---|---|---|---|---|
| 1580 | 11° | 15′ | E. | 1900 | 16° | 29′ | W. |
| 1622 | 5° | 56′ | E. | 1925 | 13° | 10′ | W. |
| 1665 | 1° | 22′ | W. | 1950 | 9° | 07′ | W. |
| 1730 | 13° | 00′ | W. | 1975 | 6° | 39′ | W. |
| 1773 | 21° | 09′ | W. | 1998 | 3° | 32′ | W. |
| 1850 | 22° | 24′ | W. | | | |

In the British Isles, lines of equal declination (isogonics) now run approximately north–northeast to south–southwest. Though there are considerable local deviations due to geological causes, a rough value of magnetic declination may be obtained by assuming that at 50° N. on the meridian

of Greenwich, the value in 2016 is 0° 10′ west and allowing an increase of 11′ for each degree of latitude northwards and one of 26′ for each degree of longitude westwards. For example, at 53° N., 5° W., declination will be about 0° 10′ + 33′ + 130′, ie 2° 53′ west. The average annual change at the present time is about 11′ decrease. For navigation by compass using maps with the north lines from the British National Grid (as opposed to lines of equal longitude), account has to be taken of the difference between true north and grid north. This angle can be several degrees. In 2014 the variation of the compass relative to grid north become easterly for the first time in 350 years.

The number of magnetic observatories is about 180, irregularly distributed over the globe. There are three in the UK, run by the British Geological Survey: at Hartland, north Devon; at Eskdalemuir, Dumfries and Galloway; and at Lerwick, Shetland Islands. Some recent annual mean values of the magnetic elements for Hartland:

| Year | Declination West | | Dip or inclination | | Horizontal intensity nT | Vertical intensity nT |
|---|---|---|---|---|---|---|
| | ° | ′ | ° | ′ | | |
| 1960 | 9 | 58.8 | 66 | 43.9 | 18707 | 43504 |
| 1970 | 9 | 06.5 | 66 | 26.1 | 19033 | 43636 |
| 1980 | 7 | 43.8 | 66 | 10.3 | 19330 | 43768 |
| 1990 | 6 | 15.0 | 66 | 09.7 | 19539 | 43896 |
| 2000 | 4 | 43.6 | 66 | 06.9 | 19508 | 44051 |
| 2014 | 2 | 28.1 | 66 | 00.0 | 19728 | 44310 |

*nT = nanoTesla*

The magnetic field is also observed by a series of specialised satellites, the latest being a mission called Swarm. Three satellites were successfully launched by the European Space Agency in November 2013, each equipped with magnetometers and star cameras for accurate orientation. With the data from these satellites the Earth's magnetic field and its changes in time can be mapped to unprecedented accuracy.

Reliance on the Earth's magnetic field for navigation by compass is not restricted to land, maritime or aeronautical navigation (in the latter two usually as a fail-safe back-up system). It also extends underground with the oil industry using magnetic survey tools when drilling well-bores. Very accurate estimates of the local magnetic field are required for this, taking into account the crustal and external fields.

### MAGNETIC STORMS

Occasionally, sometimes with great suddenness, the Earth's magnetic field is subject for several hours to marked disturbance. During a severe storm in October 2003 the declination at Eskdalemuir changed by over 5° in six minutes. In many instances such disturbances are accompanied by widespread displays of auroras, marked changes in the incidence of cosmic rays, an increase in the reception of 'noise' from the Sun at radio frequencies, and rapid changes in the ionosphere and induced electric currents within the Earth. These can adversely affect satellite operations, telecommunications and electric power transmission systems. The disturbances are caused by changes in the stream of ionised particles which emanates from the Sun and through which the Earth is continuously passing. Some of these changes are associated with visible eruptions on the Sun, usually in the region of sun-spots. There is some tendency for disturbances to recur after intervals of about 27 days, the period of rotation of the Sun on its axis as seen from the Earth. But the sources of many disturbances are shorter lived than this. Predicting such disturbances with any useful accuracy remains challenging. The year 2016 is expected to be about two years after the most recent maximum of the approximate 11-year solar activity cycle. The peak in magnetic activity usually lags that in solar activity by at least two years.

## ELEMENTS OF THE SOLAR SYSTEM

| Orb | Mean distance from Sun (Earth = 1) | km 10⁶ | Sidereal period days | Synodic period days | Incl. of orbit to ecliptic ° ' | Diameter km | Mass (Earth = 1) | Period of rotation on axis days |
|---|---|---|---|---|---|---|---|---|
| Sun | — | — | — | — | — | 1,392,000 | 332,981 | 25–35* |
| Mercury | 0.39 | 58 | 88.0 | 116 | 7 00 | 4,879 | 0.0553 | 58.646 |
| Venus | 0.72 | 108 | 224.7 | 584 | 3 24 | 12,104 | 0.8150 | 243.019r |
| Earth | 1.00 | 150 | 365.3 | — | — | 12,756e | 1.0000 | 0.997 |
| Mars | 1.52 | 228 | 687.0 | 780 | 1 51 | 6,794e | 0.1074 | 1.026 |
| Jupiter | 5.20 | 778 | 4,334.4 | 399 | 1 18 | 142,984e 133,708p | 317.83 | 0.410e |
| Saturn | 9.55 | 1429 | 10,787.9 | 378 | 2 29 | 120,536e 108,728p | 95.16 | 0.426e |
| Uranus | 19.22 | 2875 | 30,773.3 | 370 | 0 46 | 51,118e | 14.54 | 0.718r |
| Neptune | 30.11 | 4504 | 60,349.2 | 367 | 1 46 | 49,528e | 17.15 | 0.671 |
| Pluto† | 39.80 | 5954 | 91,708.2 | 367 | 17 09 | 2,390 | 0.002 | 6.387 |

e equatorial, p polar, r retrograde, * depending on latitude, † reclassified as a dwarf planet since August 2006

## THE SATELLITES

| Name | Star mag. | Mean distance from primary km | Sidereal period of revolution d | Name | Star mag. | Mean distance from primary km | Sidereal period of revolution d |
|---|---|---|---|---|---|---|---|
| EARTH | | | | SATURN | | | |
| I Moon | — | 384,400 | 27.322 | VII Hyperion | 14 | 1,481,000 | 21.277 |
| | | | | VIII Iapetus | 11 | 3,561,300 | 79.330 |
| MARS | | | | IX Phoebe | 16 | 12,952,000 | 550.48r |
| I Phobos | 11 | 9,378 | 0.319 | | | | |
| II Deimos | 12 | 23,459 | 1.262 | URANUS | | | |
| | | | | VI Cordelia | 24 | 49,770 | 0.335 |
| JUPITER | | | | VII Ophelia | 24 | 53,790 | 0.376 |
| XVI Metis | 17 | 127,960 | 0.295 | VIII Bianca | 23 | 59,170 | 0.435 |
| XV Adrastea | 19 | 128,980 | 0.298 | IX Cressida | 22 | 61,780 | 0.464 |
| V Amalthea | 14 | 181,300 | 0.498 | X Desdemona | 22 | 62,680 | 0.474 |
| XIV Thebe | 16 | 221,900 | 0.675 | XI Juliet | 21 | 64,350 | 0.493 |
| I Io | 5 | 421,600 | 1.769 | XII Portia | 21 | 66,090 | 0.513 |
| II Europa | 5 | 670,900 | 3.551 | XIII Rosalind | 22 | 66,940 | 0.558 |
| III Ganymede | 5 | 1,070,000 | 7.155 | XIV Belinda | 22 | 75,260 | 0.624 |
| IV Callisto | 6 | 1,883,000 | 16.689 | XV Puck | 20 | 86,010 | 0.762 |
| XIII Leda | 20 | 11,165,000 | 240.92 | V Miranda | 16 | 129,390 | 1.413 |
| VI Himalia | 15 | 11,460,000 | 250.57 | I Ariel | 14 | 191,020 | 2.520 |
| X Lysithea | 18 | 11,717,000 | 259.22 | II Umbriel | 15 | 266,300 | 4.144 |
| VII Elara | 17 | 11,741,000 | 259.65 | III Titania | 14 | 435,910 | 8.706 |
| XII Ananke | 19 | 21,276,000 | 629.77r | IV Oberon | 14 | 583,520 | 13.463 |
| XI Carme | 18 | 23,404,000 | 734.17r | XVI Caliban | 22 | 7,230,000 | 579.5r |
| VIII Pasiphae | 17 | 23,624,000 | 743.68r | XX Stephano | 24 | 8,002,000 | 676.5r |
| IX Sinope | 18 | 23,939,000 | 758.90r | XVII Sycorax | 21 | 12,179,000 | 1,283.4r |
| | | | | XVIII Prospero | 23 | 16,418,000 | 1,992.8r |
| SATURN | | | | XIX Setebos | 23 | 17,459,000 | 2,202.2r |
| XVIII Pan | 20 | 133,583 | 0.575 | | | | |
| XV Atlas | 18 | 137,640 | 0.602 | NEPTUNE | | | |
| XVI Prometheus | 16 | 139,353 | 0.613 | III Naiad | 25 | 48,230 | 0.294 |
| XVII Pandora | 16 | 141,700 | 0.629 | IV Thalassa | 24 | 50,080 | 0.311 |
| XI Epimetheus | 15 | 151,422 | 0.694 | V Despina | 23 | 52,530 | 0.335 |
| X Janus | 14 | 151,472 | 0.695 | VI Galatea | 22 | 61,950 | 0.429 |
| I Mimas | 13 | 185,520 | 0.942 | VII Larissa | 22 | 73,550 | 0.555 |
| II Enceladus | 12 | 238,020 | 1.370 | VIII Proteus | 20 | 117,650 | 1.122 |
| III Tethys | 10 | 294,660 | 1.888 | I Triton | 13 | 354,760 | 5.877 |
| XIII Telesto | 19 | 294,660 | 1.888 | II Nereid | 19 | 5,513,400 | 360.136 |
| XIV Calypso | 19 | 294,660 | 1.888 | | | | |
| IV Dione | 10 | 377,400 | 2.737 | PLUTO | | | |
| XII Helene | 18 | 377,400 | 2.737 | I Charon | 17 | 19,600 | 6.387 |
| V Rhea | 10 | 527,040 | 4.518 | | | | |
| VI Titan | 8 | 1,221,850 | 15.945 | | | | |

The total number of satellites of the outer planets are: Jupiter 67, Saturn 62, Uranus 27, Neptune 14, Pluto 5.

# TIME MEASUREMENT AND CALENDARS

## MEASUREMENTS OF TIME

Measurements of time are based on the time taken by the Earth to rotate on its axis (day); by the Moon to revolve around the Earth (month); and by the Earth to revolve around the Sun (year). From these, which are not commensurable, certain average or mean intervals have been adopted for ordinary use.

### THE DAY
The day begins at midnight and is divided into 24 hours of 60 minutes, each of 60 seconds. The hours are counted from midnight up to 12 noon (when the Sun crosses the meridian), and these hours are designated am *(ante meridiem)*; and again from noon up to 12 midnight, which hours are designated pm *(post meridiem)*, except when the 24-hour reckoning is employed. The 24-hour reckoning ignores am and pm, numbering the hours 0 to 23 from midnight.

Colloquially the 24 hours are divided into day and night, day being the time while the Sun is above the horizon (including the four stages of twilight defined in the Astronomy section). Day is subdivided into morning, ending at noon; afternoon, from noon to about 6pm; and evening, which may be said to extend from 6pm until midnight. Night begins at the close of astronomical twilight (*see* the Astronomy section) and extends beyond midnight to sunrise the next day.

The names of the days are derived from Old English translations or adaptations of the Roman titles.

| | | |
|---|---|---|
| *Sunday* | Sol | Sun |
| *Monday* | Luna | Moon |
| *Tuesday* | Tiw/Tyr (god of war) | Mars |
| *Wednesday* | Woden/Odin | Mercury |
| *Thursday* | Thor | Jupiter |
| *Friday* | Frigga/Freyja (goddess of love) | Venus |
| *Saturday* | Saeterne | Saturn |

### THE MONTH
The month in the ordinary calendar is approximately the twelfth part of a year, but the lengths of the different months vary from 28 (or 29) days to 31.

### THE YEAR
The equinoctial or tropical year is the time that the Earth takes to revolve around the Sun from equinox to equinox, ie 365.24219 mean solar days, or 365 days 5 hours 48 minutes and 45 seconds.

The calendar year usually consists of 365 days but a year containing 366 days is called a bissextile (*see* Roman calendar) or leap year, one day being added to the month of February so that a date 'leaps over' a day of the week. In the Roman calendar the day that was repeated was the sixth day before the beginning of March, the equivalent of 24 February.

A year is a leap year if the date of the year is divisible by four without remainder, unless it is the last year of the century. The last year of a century is a leap year only if its number is divisible by 400 without remainder, eg the years 1800 and 1900 had only 365 days but the year 2000 had 366 days.

### THE SOLSTICE
A solstice is the point in the tropical year at which the Sun attains its greatest distance, north or south, from the Equator. In the northern hemisphere the furthest point north of the Equator marks the summer solstice and the furthest point south marks the winter solstice.

The date of the solstice varies according to locality. For example, if the summer solstice falls on 21 June late in the day by Greenwich time, that day will be the longest of the year at Greenwich, but it will fall on 22 June, local date, in Japan, and so 22 June will be the longest day there. The date of the solstice is also affected by the length of the tropical year, which is 365 days 6 hours less about 11 minutes 15 seconds. If a solstice happens late on 21 June in one year, it will be nearly 6 hours later in the next (unless the next year is a leap year), ie early on 22 June, and that will be the longest day.

This delay of the solstice does not continue because the extra day in a leap year brings it back a day in the calendar. However, because of the 11 minutes 15 seconds mentioned above, the additional day in a leap year brings the solstice back too far by 45 minutes, and the time of the solstice in the calendar is earlier, in a four-year pattern, as the century progresses. The last year of a century is in most cases not a leap year, and the omission of the extra day puts the date of the solstice later by about 6 hours. Compensation for this is made by the fourth centennial year being a leap year. The solstice became earlier in date throughout the last century and, because the year 2000 was a leap year, the solstice will get earlier still throughout the 21st century. The date of the winter solstice, the shortest day of the year, is affected by the same factors as the longest day.

At Greenwich the Sun sets at its earliest by the clock about ten days before the shortest day. The daily change in the time of sunset is due in the first place to the Sun's movement southwards at this time of the year, which diminishes the interval between the Sun's transit and its setting. However, the daily decrease of the Equation of Time causes the time of apparent noon to be continuously later day by day, which to some extent counteracts the first effect. The rates of the change of these two quantities are not equal or uniform; their combination causes the date of earliest sunset to be 12 or 13 December at Greenwich. In more southerly latitudes the effect of the movement of the Sun is less, and the change in the time of sunset depends on that of the Equation of Time to a greater degree, and the date of earliest sunset is earlier than it is at Greenwich, eg on the Equator it is about 1 November.

### THE EQUINOX
The equinox is the point at which the Sun crosses the Equator and day and night are of equal length all over the world. This occurs in March and September.

### DOG DAYS
The days about the heliacal rising of the Dog Star, noted from ancient times as the hottest period of the year in the northern hemisphere, are called the Dog Days. Their incidence has been variously calculated as depending on the Greater or Lesser Dog Star (Sirius or Procyon) and their duration has been reckoned as from 30 to 54 days. A generally accepted period is from 3 July to 15 August.

## CHRISTIAN CALENDAR

In the Christian chronological system the years are distinguished by cardinal numbers before or after the birth of Christ, the period being denoted by the letters BC (Before Christ) or, more rarely, AC *(Ante Christum)*, and AD *(Anno Domini* – In the Year of Our Lord); BCE (Before the Christian Era) and CE (Christian Era) are now sometimes used instead of BC and AD. The correlative dates of the epoch are the fourth year of the 194th Olympiad, the 753rd year from the foundation of Rome, AM 3761 in Jewish chronology, and the 4,714th year of the Julian period.

The system was introduced into Italy in the sixth century. Though first used in France in the seventh century, it was not universally established there until about the eighth century. It has been said that the system was introduced into England by St Augustine (AD 596), but it was probably not generally used until some centuries later. It was ordered to be used by the bishops at the Council of Chelsea (AD 816).

## THE JULIAN CALENDAR

In the Julian calendar (adopted by the Roman Empire in 45 BC) all the centennial years were leap years, and for this reason towards the close of the 16th century there was a difference of ten days between the tropical and calendar years; the equinox fell on 11 March of the calendar, whereas at the time of the Council of Nicaea (AD 325), it had fallen on 21 March. In 1582 Pope Gregory ordained that 5 October should be called 15 October and that of the end-century years only the fourth should be a leap year.

## THE GREGORIAN CALENDAR

The Gregorian calendar was adopted by Italy, France, Spain and Portugal in 1582, by Prussia, the Roman Catholic German states, Switzerland, Holland and Flanders on 1

January 1583, by Poland in 1586, Hungary in 1587, the Protestant German and Netherland states and Denmark in 1700, and by Great Britain and its Dominions (including the North American colonies) in 1752, by the omission of 11 days (3 September being reckoned as 14 September). Sweden omitted the leap day in 1700 but observed leap days in 1704 and 1708, and reverted to the Julian calendar by having two leap days in 1712; the Gregorian calendar was adopted in 1753 by the omission of 11 days (18 February being reckoned as 1 March). Japan adopted the calendar in 1872, China in 1912, Bulgaria in 1916, Turkey and Soviet Russia in 1918, Yugoslavia and Romania in 1919, and Greece in 1923.

In the same year that the change was made in England from the Julian to the Gregorian calendar, the start of the new year was also changed from 25 March to 1 January.

## THE ORTHODOX CHURCHES

Some Orthodox churches still use the Julian reckoning but the majority of Greek Orthodox churches and the Romanian Orthodox Church have adopted a modified 'New Calendar', observing the Gregorian calendar for fixed feasts and the Julian for movable feasts.

The Orthodox Church year begins on 1 September. There are four fast periods and, in addition to Pascha (Easter), twelve great feasts, as well as numerous commemorations of the saints of the Old and New Testaments throughout the year.

## EASTER DAYS AND DOMINICAL LETTERS 1500 TO 2040

Dates up to and including 1752 are according to the Julian calendar. For dominical letters in leap years, *see* note below

| | | 1500–1599 | 1600–1699 | 1700–1799 | 1800–1899 | 1900–1999 | 2000–2040 |
|---|---|---|---|---|---|---|---|
| *March* | | | | | | | |
| d | 22 | 1573 | 1668 | 1761 | 1818 | | |
| e | 23 | 1505/16 | 1600 | 1788 | 1845/56 | 1913 | 2008 |
| f | 24 | | 1611/95 | 1706/99 | | 1940 | |
| g | 25 | 1543/54 | 1627/38/49 | 1722/33/44 | 1883/94 | 1951 | 2035 |
| A | 26 | 1559/70/81/92 | 1654/65/76 | 1749/58/69/80 | 1815/26/37 | 1967/78/89 | |
| b | 27 | 1502/13/24/97 | 1608/87/92 | 1785/96 | 1842/53/64 | 1910/21/32 | 2005/16 |
| c | 28 | 1529/35/40 | 1619/24/30 | 1703/14/25 | 1869/75/80 | 1937/48 | 2027/32 |
| d | 29 | 1551/62 | 1635/46/57 | 1719/30/41/52 | 1807/12/91 | 1959/64/70 | |
| e | 30 | 1567/78/89 | 1651/62/73/84 | 1746/55/66/77 | 1823/34 | 1902/75/86/97 | |
| f | 31 | 1510/21/32/83/94 | 1605/16/78/89 | 1700/71/82/93 | 1839/50/61/72 | 1907/18/29/91 | 2002/13/24 |
| *April* | | | | | | | |
| g | 1 | 1526/37/48 | 1621/32 | 1711/16 | 1804/66/77/88 | 1923/34/45/56 | 2018/29/40 |
| A | 2 | 1553/64 | 1643/48 | 1727/38 | 1809/20/93/99 | 1961/72 | |
| b | 3 | 1575/80/86 | 1659/70/81 | 1743/63/68/74 | 1825/31/36 | 1904/83/88/94 | |
| c | 4 | 1507/18/91 | 1602/13/75/86/97 | 1708/79/90 | 1847/58 | 1915/20/26/99 | 2010/21 |
| d | 5 | 1523/34/45/56 | 1607/18/29/40 | 1702/13/24/95 | 1801/63/74/85/96 | 1931/42/53 | 2015/26/37 |
| e | 6 | 1539/50/61/72 | 1634/45/56 | 1729/35/40/60 | 1806/17/28/90 | 1947/58/69/80 | |
| f | 7 | 1504/77/88 | 1667/72 | 1751/65/76 | 1822/33/44 | 1901/12/85/96 | |
| g | 8 | 1509/15/20/99 | 1604/10/83/94 | 1705/87/92/98 | 1849/55/60 | 1917/28 | 2007/12 |
| A | 9 | 1531/42 | 1615/26/37/99 | 1710/21/32 | 1871/82 | 1939/44/50 | 2023/34 |
| b | 10 | 1547/58/69 | 1631/42/53/64 | 1726/37/48/57 | 1803/14/87/98 | 1955/66/77 | 2039 |
| c | 11 | 1501/12/63/74/85/96 | 1658/69/80 | 1762/73/84 | 1819/30/41/52 | 1909/71/82/93 | 2004 |
| d | 12 | 1506/17/28 | 1601/12/91/96 | 1789 | 1846/57/68 | 1903/14/25/36/98 | 2009/20 |
| e | 13 | 1533/44 | 1623/28 | 1707/18 | 1800/73/79/84 | 1941/52 | 2031/36 |
| f | 14 | 1555/60/66 | 1639/50/61 | 1723/34/45/54 | 1805/11/16/95 | 1963/68/74 | |
| g | 15 | 1571/82/93 | 1655/66/77/88 | 1750/59/70/81 | 1827/38 | 1900/06/79/90 | 2001 |
| A | 16 | 1503/14/25/36/87/98 | 1609/20/82/93 | 1704/75/86/97 | 1843/54/65/76 | 1911/22/33/95 | 2006/17/28 |
| b | 17 | 1530/41/52 | 1625/36 | 1715/20 | 1808/70/81/92 | 1927/38/49/60 | 2022/33 |
| c | 18 | 1557/68 | 1647/52 | 1731/42/56 | 1802/13/24/97 | 1954/65/76 | |
| d | 19 | 1500/79/84/90 | 1663/74/85 | 1747/67/72/78 | 1829/35/40 | 1908/81/87/92 | |
| e | 20 | 1511/22/95 | 1606/17/79/90 | 1701/12/83/94 | 1851/62 | 1919/24/30 | 2003/14/25 |
| f | 21 | 1527/38/49 | 1622/33/44 | 1717/28 | 1867/78/89 | 1935/46/57 | 2019/30 |
| g | 22 | 1565/76 | 1660 | 1739/53/64 | 1810/21/32 | 1962/73/84 | |
| A | 23 | 1508 | 1671 | | 1848 | 1905/16 | 2000 |
| b | 24 | 1519 | 1603/14/98 | 1709/91 | 1859 | | 2011 |
| c | 25 | 1546 | 1641 | 1736 | 1886 | 1943 | 2038 |

No dominical letter is placed against the intercalary day 29 February, but since it is still counted as a weekday and given a name, the series of letters moves back one day every leap year after intercalation. Thus, a leap year beginning with the dominical letter C will change to a year with the dominical letter B on 1 March

## MOVEABLE FEASTS TO THE YEAR 2040

| Year | Ash Wednesday | Easter | Ascension | Pentecost (Whit Sunday) | Advent Sunday |
|------|---------------|--------|-----------|-------------------------|---------------|
| 2016 | 10 February | 27 March | 5 May | 15 May | 27 November |
| 2017 | 1 March | 16 April | 25 May | 4 June | 3 December |
| 2018 | 14 February | 1 April | 10 May | 20 May | 2 December |
| 2019 | 6 March | 21 April | 30 May | 9 June | 1 December |
| 2020 | 26 February | 12 April | 21 May | 31 May | 29 November |
| 2021 | 17 February | 4 April | 13 May | 23 May | 28 November |
| 2022 | 2 March | 17 April | 26 May | 5 June | 27 November |
| 2023 | 22 February | 9 April | 18 May | 28 May | 3 December |
| 2024 | 14 February | 31 March | 9 May | 19 May | 1 December |
| 2025 | 5 March | 20 April | 29 May | 8 June | 30 November |
| 2026 | 18 February | 5 April | 14 May | 24 May | 29 November |
| 2027 | 10 February | 28 March | 6 May | 16 May | 28 November |
| 2028 | 1 March | 16 April | 25 May | 4 June | 3 December |
| 2029 | 14 February | 1 April | 10 May | 20 May | 2 December |
| 2030 | 6 March | 21 April | 30 May | 9 June | 1 December |
| 2031 | 26 February | 13 April | 22 May | 1 June | 30 November |
| 2032 | 11 February | 28 March | 6 May | 16 May | 28 November |
| 2033 | 2 March | 17 April | 26 May | 5 June | 27 November |
| 2034 | 22 February | 9 April | 18 May | 28 May | 3 December |
| 2035 | 7 February | 25 March | 3 May | 13 May | 2 December |
| 2036 | 27 February | 13 April | 22 May | 1 June | 30 November |
| 2037 | 18 February | 5 April | 14 May | 24 May | 29 November |
| 2038 | 10 March | 25 April | 3 June | 13 June | 28 November |
| 2039 | 23 February | 10 April | 19 May | 29 May | 27 November |
| 2040 | 15 February | 1 April | 10 May | 20 May | 2 December |

### NOTES

*Ash Wednesday* (first day in Lent) can fall at earliest on 4 February and at latest on 10 March

*Mothering Sunday* (fourth Sunday in Lent) can fall at earliest on 1 March and at latest on 4 April

*Easter Day* can fall at earliest on 22 March and at latest on 25 April

*Ascension Day* is forty days after Easter Day and can fall at earliest on 30 April and at latest on 3 June

*Pentecost (Whit Sunday)* is seven weeks after Easter and can fall at earliest on 10 May and at latest on 13 June

*Trinity Sunday* is the Sunday after Whit Sunday

*Corpus Christi* falls on the Thursday after Trinity Sunday

*Sundays after Pentecost* – there are not less than 18 and not more than 23

*Advent Sunday* is the Sunday nearest to 30 November

### THE DOMINICAL LETTER

The dominical letter is one of the letters A–G which are used to denote the Sundays in successive years. If the first day of the year is a Sunday the letter is A; if the second, B; the third, C; and so on. A leap year requires two letters, the first for 1 January to 29 February, the second for 1 March to 31 December. For the leap year 2016 the letter given in the table opposite is for the second part of the year (B) and the letter for the first part of the year will be the one given below (C); therefore the dominical letter for 2016 is CB (*see also* page 7).

### EPIPHANY

The feast of the Epiphany, commemorating the manifestation of Christ, later became associated with the offering of gifts by the Magi. The day was of great importance from the time of the Council of Nicaea (AD 325), as the primate of Alexandria was charged at every Epiphany feast with the announcement in a letter to the churches of the date of the forthcoming Easter. The day was also of importance in Britain as it influenced dates, ecclesiastical and lay, eg Plough Monday, when work was resumed in the fields, fell on the Monday in the first full week after Epiphany.

### LENT

The Teutonic word *Lent,* which denotes the fast preceding Easter, originally meant no more than the spring season; but from Anglo-Saxon times, at least, it has been used as the equivalent of the more significant Latin term *Quadragesima,* meaning the 'forty days' or, more literally, the fortieth day. Ash Wednesday is the first day of Lent, which ends at midnight before Easter Day.

### PALM SUNDAY

Palm Sunday, the Sunday before Easter and the beginning of Holy Week, commemorates the triumphal entry of Christ into Jerusalem.

### MAUNDY THURSDAY

Maundy Thursday is the day before Good Friday, the name itself being a corruption of *dies mandati* (day of the mandate) when Christ washed the feet of the disciples and gave them the mandate to love one another.

### EASTER DAY

Easter Day is the first Sunday after the full moon which happens on, or next after, the 21st day of March; if the full moon happens on a Sunday, Easter Day is the Sunday after.

This definition is contained in an Act of Parliament (24 Geo. II ch. 23) and explanation is given in the preamble to the Act that the day of full moon depends on certain tables that have been prepared. These tables are summarised in the early pages of the Book of Common Prayer. The moon referred to is not the real Moon of the heavens, but a hypothetical moon on whose 'full' the date of Easter depends, and the lunations of this 'calendar' moon consist of 29 and 30 days alternately, with certain necessary modifications to make the date of its full agree as nearly as possible with that of the real Moon, which is known as the Paschal Full Moon.

### A FIXED EASTER

In 1928 the House of Commons agreed to a motion for the third reading of a bill proposing that Easter Day shall, in the calendar year next but one after the commencement of the Act and in all subsequent years, be the first Sunday after the second Saturday in April. Easter would thus fall on the second or third Sunday in April, ie between 9 and 15 April (inclusive). A clause in the bill provided that before it shall come into operation, regard shall be had to any opinion expressed officially by the various Christian churches. Efforts by the World Council of Churches to secure a unanimous choice of date for Easter by its member churches have so far been unsuccessful.

## ROGATION DAYS
Rogation Days are the Monday, Tuesday and Wednesday preceding Ascension Day and from the fifth century were observed as public fasts with solemn processions and supplications. The processions were discontinued as religious observances at the Reformation, but survive in the ceremony known as 'beating the parish bounds'. Rogation Sunday is the Sunday before Ascension Day.

## EMBER DAYS
The Ember days occur on the Wednesday, Friday and Saturday of the same week, four times a year. Used for the ordination of clergy, these days are set aside for fasting and prayer. The weeks in which they fall are: (a) after the third Sunday in Advent, (b) before the second Sunday in Lent, (c) before Trinity Sunday and (d) after Holy Cross day.

## TRINITY SUNDAY
Trinity Sunday is eight weeks after Easter Day, on the Sunday following Pentecost (Whit Sunday). Subsequent Sundays are reckoned in the Book of Common Prayer calendar of the Church of England as 'after Trinity'.

Thomas Becket (1118–70) was consecrated Archbishop of Canterbury on the Sunday after Whit Sunday and his first act was to ordain that the day of his consecration should be held as a new festival in honour of the Holy Trinity.

## HINDU CALENDAR

The Hindu calendar is a luni-solar calendar of 12 months, each containing 29 days, 12 hours. Each month is divided into a light fortnight (Shukla or Shuddha) and a dark fortnight (Krishna or Vadya) based on the waxing and waning of the Moon. In most parts of India the month starts with the light fortnight, ie the day after the new moon, although in some regions it begins with the dark fortnight, ie the day after the full moon.

The new year according to the civil calendar begins on the first day of the month of Chaitra (March/April) and ends in the month of Phalgun (March). The financial new year begins on the first day of Kartik (Diwali day). For most Hindus, the first day of Chaitra and the first day of Kartik are equally important.

The 12 months – Chaitra, Vaishakh, Jyeshtha, Ashadh, Shravan, Bhadrapad, Ashvin, Kartik, Margashirsh, Paush, Magh and Phalgun – have Sanskrit names derived from 12 asterisms (constellations). There are regional variations to the names of the months but the Sanskrit names are understood throughout India.

Every lunar month that has a solar transit is termed pure (shuddha). The lunar month without a solar transit is impure (mala) and called an intercalary month. An intercalary month occurs approximately every 32 lunar months, whenever the difference between the Hindu year of 360 lunar days (354 days 8 hours solar time) and the 365 days 6 hours of the solar year reaches the length of one Hindu lunar month (29 days 12 hours).

The leap month, often referred to as Adhik Maas (extra month), may be added at any point in the Hindu year. The name given to the month varies according to when it occurs but is taken from the month immediately following it. There is no leap month in 2016; the next one will occur in 2018.

The days of the week are called Raviwar (Sunday), Somawar (Monday), Mangalwar (Tuesday), Budhawar (Wednesday), Guruwar (Thursday), Shukrawar (Friday) and Shaniwar (Saturday). The names are derived from the Sanskrit names of the Sun, the Moon and five planets, Mars, Mercury, Jupiter, Venus and Saturn.

Most fasts and festivals are based on the lunar calendar but a few are determined by the apparent movement of the Sun, eg Makar Sankranti and Pongal (in southern India), which are celebrated on 14/15 January to mark the start of the Sun's apparent journey northwards and a change of season.

Festivals celebrated throughout India are Chaitra (the New Year), Raksha-bandhan (the renewal of the kinship bond between brothers and sisters), Navaratri (a nine-night festival dedicated to the goddess Parvati), Dussehra (the victory of Rama over the demon army), Diwali (a festival of lights), Makar Sankranti, Shivaratri (dedicated to Shiva), and Holi (a spring festival). British Hindus commonly celebrate the festival of Diwali as the start of the financial new year.

Regional festivals are Durga-puja (dedicated to the goddess Durga (Parvati)), Sarasvati Puja (dedicated to the goddess Sarasvati), Ganesh Chaturthi (worship of Ganesh on the fourth day (Chaturthi) of the light half of Bhadrapad), Ram Navami (the birth festival of the god Rama) and Krishna Janmashtami (the birth festival of the god Krishna).

The main festivals celebrated in Britain are Navaratri, Dussehra, Durga-puja, Diwali, Holi, Sarasvati Puja, Ganesh Chaturthi, Raksha-bandhan, Ram Navami and Krishna Janmashtami. For dates of the main festivals in 2016, see page 7.

## JEWISH CALENDAR

The story of the Flood in the Book of Genesis indicates the use of a calendar of some kind and that the writers recognised 30 days as the length of a lunation. However, after the diaspora, Jewish communities were left in considerable doubt as to the times of fasts and festivals. This led to the formation of the Jewish calendar as used today. It is said that this was done in AD 358 by Rabbi Hillel II, though some assert that it did not happen until much later.

The calendar is luni-solar, and is based on the lengths of the lunation and of the tropical year as found by Hipparchus (c.120 BC), which differ little from those adopted at the present day. The year AM 5776 (2015–16) is the 19th year of the 304th Metonic (Minor or Lunar) cycle of 19 years and the 8th year of the 207th Solar (or Major) cycle of 28 years since the Era of the Creation. Jews hold that the Creation occurred at the time of the autumnal equinox in the year known in the Christian calendar as 3760 BC (954 of the Julian period). The epoch or starting point of Jewish chronology corresponds to 7 October 3761 BC. At the beginning of each solar cycle, the Tekufah of Nisan (the vernal equinox) returns to the same day and hour.

The hour is divided into 1,080 minims, and the month between one new moon and the next is reckoned as 29 days 12 hours 793 minims. The normal calendar year, called a regular common year, consists of 12 months of 30 days and 29 days alternately. Since 12 months such as these comprise only 354 days, in order that each of them shall not diverge greatly from an average place in the solar year, a 13th month is occasionally added after the fifth month of the civil year (which commences on the first day of the month Tishri), or as the penultimate month of the ecclesiastical year (which commences on the first day of the month Nisan). The years when this happens are called Embolismic or leap years.

Of the 19 years that form a Metonic cycle, seven are leap years; they occur at places in the cycle indicated by the numbers 3, 6, 8, 11, 14, 17 and 19, these places being chosen so that the accumulated excesses of the solar years should be as small as possible.

A Jewish year is of one of the following six types:

| | |
|---|---|
| minimal common | 353 days |
| regular common | 354 days |
| full common | 355 days |
| minimal leap | 383 days |
| regular leap | 384 days |
| full leap | 385 days |

The regular year has alternate months of 30 and 29 days. In a full year, Marcheshvan, the second month of the civil year, has 30 days instead of 29; in minimal years Kislev, the third month, has 29 instead of 30. The additional month in leap years is called Adar Sheni (Adar II) and follows the month called Adar Rishon; the usual Adar festivals are observed in Adar Sheni. In a leap year Adar I has 30 days, in all other years it has 29. None of the variations mentioned are allowed to change the number of days in the other months, which still follow the alternation of the normal 12.

These are the main features of the Jewish calendar, which must be considered permanent because as a Jewish law it cannot be altered except by a Great Sanhedrin.

The Jewish day begins between sunset and nightfall. The time used is that of the meridian of Jerusalem, which is 2h 21m in advance of Greenwich Mean Time. Rules for the beginning of sabbaths and festivals were laid down for the latitude of London in the 18th century and hours for nightfall are fixed annually by the Chief Rabbi.

## JEWISH CALENDAR 5776–77
AM 5776 is a full leap year of 13 months, 55 sabbaths and 385 days. AM 5777 is a minimal common year of 12 months, 50 sabbaths and 353 days.

| Month (length) | AM 5776 | AM 5777 |
|---|---|---|
| *Tishri* 1 (30) | 14 September 2015 | 3 October 2016 |
| *Marcheshvan* 1 | | |
| (30/29) | 14 October | 2 November |
| *Kislev* 1 (30/29) | 13 November | 1 December |
| *Tebet* 1 (29) | 13 December | 30 December |
| *Shebat* 1 (30) | 11 January 2016 | 28 January 2017 |
| *Adar Rishon* 1 (30) | 10 February | |
| *Adar Sheni* 1 | 11 March | |
| *Nisan* 1 (30) | 9 April | |
| *Iyar* 1 (29) | 9 May | |
| *Sivan* 1 (30) | 7 June | |
| *Tammuz* 1 (29) | 7 July | |
| *Ab* 1 (30) | 5 August | |
| *Elul* 1 (29) | 4 September | |

## JEWISH FASTS AND FESTIVALS
For dates of principal festivals in 2016, *see* page 7.

| | |
|---|---|
| *Tishri* 1–2 | Rosh Hashanah (New Year) |
| *Tishri* 3 | *Fast of Gedaliah |
| *Tishri* 10 | Yom Kippur (Day of Atonement) |
| *Tishri* 15–22 | Succot (Feast of Tabernacles) |
| *Tishri* 21 | Hoshana Rabba |
| *Tishri* 22 | Shemini Atseret (Solemn Assembly) |
| *Tishri* 23 | Simchat Torah (Rejoicing of the Law) |
| *Kislev* 25 | Hanukkah (Dedication of the Temple) begins |
| *Tebet* 10 | Fast of Tebet |
| †*Adar* 13 | §Fast of Esther |
| †*Adar* 14 | Purim |
| †*Adar* 15 | Shushan Purim |
| *Nisan* 15–22 | Pesach (Passover) |
| *Sivan* 6–7 | Shavuot (Feast of Weeks) |
| *Tammuz* 17 | *Fast of Tammuz |
| *Ab* 9 | *Fast of Ab |

\* If these dates fall on the sabbath the fast is kept on the following day
† Adar Sheni in leap years
§ This fast is observed on Adar 11 (or Adar Sheni 11 in leap years) if Adar 13 falls on a sabbath

## MUSLIM CALENDAR

The Muslim era is dated from the *Hijrah*, or flight of the Prophet Muhammad from Mecca to Medina, the corresponding date of which in the Julian calendar is 16 July AD 622. The lunar *hijri* calendar is used principally in Iran, Egypt, Malaysia, Pakistan, Mauritania, various Arab states and certain parts of India. Iran uses the solar hijri calendar as well as the lunar hijri calendar. The dating system was adopted about AD 639, commencing with the first day of the month Muharram.

The lunar calendar consists of 12 months of either 30 or 29 days, with the intercalation of one day at the end of the 12th month at stated intervals in each cycle of 30 years. The object of the intercalation is to reconcile the date of the first day of the month with the date of the actual new moon.

Some adherents still take the date of the evening of the first physical sighting of the crescent of the new moon as that of the first of the month. If cloud obscures the Moon the present month may be extended to 30 days, after which the new month will begin automatically regardless of whether the Moon has been seen. (Under religious law a month must have less than 31 days.) This means that the beginning of a new month and the date of religious festivals can vary from the published calendars.

In each cycle of 30 years, 19 years are common and contain 354 days, and 11 years are intercalary (leap years) of 355 days, the latter being called *kabisah*. The mean length of the Hijrah years is 354 days 8 hours 48 minutes and the period of mean lunation is 29 days 12 hours 44 minutes.

To ascertain if a year is common or kabisah, divide it by 30: the quotient gives the number of completed cycles and the remainder shows the place of the year in the current cycle. If the remainder is 2, 5, 7, 10, 13, 16, 18, 21, 24, 26 or 29, the year is kabisah and consists of 355 days.

## MUSLIM CALENDAR 1437–38
Hijrah 1437 (remainder 27) and Hijrah 1438 (remainder 28) are both common years. Calendar dates below are estimates based on calculations of moon phases.

| Month (length) | 1437 AH | 1438 AH |
|---|---|---|
| *Muharram* 1 | | |
| (30/30) | 14 October 2015 | 2 October 2016 |
| *Safar* 1 (29/29) | 13 November | 1 November |
| *Rabi' I* 1 (30/30) | 12 December | 30 November |
| *Rabi' II* 1 (30/30) | 11 January 2016 | 30 December |
| *Jumada I* 1 (29/30) | 10 February | 29 January 2017 |
| *Jumada II* 1 (29) | 10 March | |
| *Rajab* 1 (30) | 8 April | |
| *Sha'ban* 1 (29) | 8 May | |
| *Ramadan* 1 (30) | 6 June | |
| *Shawwal* 1 (29) | 6 July | |
| *Dhu'l Qa'da* 1 (29) | 4 August | |
| *Dhu'l Hijjah* 1 (30) | 2 September | |

## MUSLIM FESTIVALS

Ramadan is a month of fasting for all Muslims because it is the month in which the revelation of the *Qur'an* (Koran) began. During Ramadan, Muslims abstain from food, drink and sexual pleasure from dawn until after sunset.

The two major festivals are *Eid-ul-Fitr* and *Eid-ul-Adha*. Eid-ul-Fitr marks the end of the Ramadan fast and is celebrated on the day after the sighting of the new moon of the following month. Eid-ul-Adha, the festival of sacrifice (also known as the great festival), celebrates the submission of the Prophet Ibrahim (Abraham) to God. Eid-ul-Adha falls on the tenth day of Dhu'l-Hijjah, coinciding with the day when those on *hajj* (pilgrimage to Mecca) sacrifice animals.

Other days accorded special recognition are:

| | |
|---|---|
| *Muharram* 1 | New Year's Day |
| *Muharram* 10 | Ashura (the day Prophet Noah left the Ark and Prophet Moses was saved from Pharaoh (Sunni), the death of the Prophet's grandson Husain (Shi'ite)) |
| *Rabi'u-l-Awwal (Rabi' I)* 12 | Mawlid ul-Nabi (birthday of the Prophet Muhammad) |
| *Rajab* 27 | Laylat ul-Isra' wa'l-Mi'raj (The Night of Journey and Ascension) |
| *Ramadan*\* | Laylat ul-Qadr (Night of Power) |

\* Moveable feast

For dates of the major celebrations in 2015–16, *see* page 7.

## SIKH CALENDAR

The Sikh calendar is a lunar calendar of 365 days divided into 12 months. The length of the months varies between 29 and 32 days.

There are no prescribed feast days and no fasting periods. The main celebrations are Baisakhi (the new year and the anniversary of the founding of the Khalsa), Diwali Mela (festival of light), Hola Mohalla Mela (a spring festival held in the Punjab), and the Gurpurbs (anniversaries associated with the ten Gurus).

For dates of the major celebrations in 2016, *see* page 7.

## THAI CALENDAR

Thailand adopted the Suriyakati calendar, a modified version of the Gregorian calendar, during the reign of King Rama V in 1888, using 1 April as the first day of the year. In 1940 the date of the new year was changed to 1 January. The years are counted from the beginning of the Buddhist era (BE), which is calculated to have commenced upon the death of the Lord Buddha, taken to have occurred in 543 BC, so AD 2016 is BE 2559. The Chinese system of associating years with one of twelve animals is also in use in Thailand. The Chantarakati lunar calendar is used to determine religious holidays; the new year begins on the first day of the waxing moon in November or, if there is a leap month, in December.

## CIVIL AND LEGAL CALENDAR

### THE HISTORICAL YEAR

Before 1752, two calendar systems were used in England. The civil or legal year began on 25 March and the historical year on 1 January. Thus the civil or legal date 24 March 1658 was the same day as the historical date 24 March 1659; a date in that portion of the year is written as 24 March 1658/9, the earlier date showing the civil or legal year.

### THE NEW YEAR

In England in the seventh century, and as late as the 13th, the year was reckoned from Christmas Day, but in the 12th century the Church in England began the year with the feast of the Annunciation of the Blessed Virgin ('Lady Day') on 25 March, and this practice was adopted generally in the 14th century. The civil or legal year in the British dominions (exclusive of Scotland) began with Lady Day until 1751. But in and since 1752 the civil year has begun with 1 January. New Year's Day in Scotland was changed from 25 March to 1 January in 1600.

Elsewhere in Europe, 1 January was adopted as the first day of the year by Venice in 1522, German states in 1544, Spain, Portugal and the Roman Catholic Netherlands in 1556, Prussia, Denmark and Sweden in 1559, France in 1564, Lorraine in 1579, the Protestant Netherlands in 1583, Russia in 1725, and Tuscany in 1751.

### REGNAL YEARS

Regnal years are the years of a sovereign's reign and each begins on the anniversary of his or her accession, eg regnal year 65 of the present queen begins on 6 February 2016.

The system was used for dating Acts of Parliament until 1962. The Summer Time Act 1925, for example, is quoted as 15 and 16 Geo. V ch. 64, because it became law in the parliamentary session which extended over part of both of these regnal years. Acts of a parliamentary session during which a sovereign died were usually given two year numbers, the regnal year of the deceased sovereign and the regnal year of his or her successor, eg those passed in 1952 were dated 16 Geo. VI and 1 Elizabeth II. Since 1962 Acts of Parliament have been dated by the calendar year.

### QUARTER AND TERM DAYS

Holy days and saints days were the usual means in early times for setting the dates of future and recurrent appointments. The quarter days in England and Wales are the feast of the Nativity (25 December), the feast of the Annunciation (25 March), the feast of St John the Baptist (24 June) and the feast of St Michael and All Angels (29 September).

The term days in Scotland are Candlemas (the feast of the Purification), Whitsunday, Lammas (Loaf Mass) and Martinmas (St Martin's Day). These fell on 2 February, 15 May, 1 August and 11 November respectively. However, by the Term and Quarter Days (Scotland) Act 1990, the dates of the term days were changed to 28 February (Candlemas), 28 May (Whitsunday), 28 August (Lammas) and 28 November (Martinmas).

### RED-LETTER DAYS

Red-letter days were originally the holy days and saints days indicated in early ecclesiastical calendars by letters printed in red ink. The days to be distinguished in this way were approved at the Council of Nicaea in AD 325.

These days still have a legal significance, as judges of the Queen's Bench Division wear scarlet robes on red-letter days falling during the law sittings. The days designated as red-letter days for this purpose are:

*Holy and saints days*
The Conversion of St Paul, the Purification, Ash Wednesday, the Annunciation, the Ascension, the feasts of St Mark, SS Philip and James, St Matthias, St Barnabas, St John the Baptist, St Peter, St Thomas, St James, St Luke, SS Simon and Jude, All Saints, St Andrew.

*Civil calendar* (for dates, *see* page 7)
Includes the anniversaries of the Queen's accession, the Queen's birthday and the Queen's coronation, the Queen's official birthday, the birthday of the Duke of Edinburgh, the birthday of the Prince of Wales, St David's Day and Lord Mayor's Day.

## PUBLIC HOLIDAYS

Public holidays are divided into two categories, common law and statutory. Common law holidays are holidays 'by habit and custom'; in England, Wales and Northern Ireland these are Good Friday and Christmas Day.

Statutory public holidays, known as bank holidays, were first established by the Bank Holidays Act 1871. They were, literally, days on which the banks (and other public institutions) were closed and financial obligations due on that day were payable the following day. The legislation currently governing public holidays in the UK, which is the Banking and Financial Dealings Act 1971, stipulates the days that are to be public holidays in England, Wales, Scotland and Northern Ireland.

If a public holiday falls on a Saturday or a Sunday then another day will be given in lieu, usually the following Monday. For dates of public holidays in 2016 and 2017, *see* pages 8–9

# CHRONOLOGICAL CYCLES AND ERAS

### SOLAR (OR MAJOR) CYCLE
The solar cycle is a period of 28 years; in any corresponding year of each cycle the days of the week recur on the same day of the month.

### METONIC (LUNAR, OR MINOR) CYCLE
In 432 BC, Meton, an Athenian astronomer, found that 235 lunations are very nearly, though not exactly, equal in duration to 19 solar years and so after 19 years the phases of the Moon recur approximately on the same days of the month. The dates of full moon in a cycle of 19 years were inscribed in figures of gold on public monuments in Athens, and the number showing the position of a year in the cycle is called the golden number of that year.

### JULIAN PERIOD
The Julian period was proposed by Joseph Scaliger in 1582. The period is 7,980 Julian years, and its first year coincides with the year 4713 BC. The figure of 7,980 is the product of the number of years in the solar cycle, the Metonic cycle and the cycle of the Roman indiction ($28 \times 19 \times 15$).

### ROMAN INDICTION
The Roman indiction is a period of 15 years, instituted for fiscal purposes about AD 300.

### EPACT
The epact is the age of the calendar Moon, diminished by one day, on 1 January, in the ecclesiastical lunar calendar.

### CHINESE CALENDAR
A lunar calendar was the sole calendar in use in China until 1911, when the government adopted the new (Gregorian) calendar for official and most business activities. The Chinese tend to follow both calendars, the lunar calendar playing an important part in personal life, eg birth celebrations, festivals, marriages; and in rural villages the lunar calendar dictates the cycle of activities, denoting the change of weather and farming activities.

The lunar calendar is used in Hong Kong, Singapore, Malaysia, Tibet and elsewhere in south-east Asia. The calendar has a cycle of 60 years. The new year begins at the first new moon after the sun enters the sign of Aquarius, ie the new year falls between 21 January and 19 February in the Gregorian calendar.

Each year in the Chinese calendar is associated with one of 12 animals: the rat, the ox, the tiger, the rabbit, the dragon, the snake, the horse, the sheep, the monkey, the chicken or rooster, the dog, and the pig.

The date of the Chinese new year and the astrological sign for the years 2016–19 are:

| | | |
|---|---|---|
| 2016 | 8 February | Monkey |
| 2017 | 28 January | Rooster |
| 2018 | 16 February | Dog |
| 2019 | 5 February | Pig |

### COPTIC CALENDAR
In the Coptic calendar, which is used in parts of Egypt and Ethiopia, the year is made up of 12 months of 30 days each, followed, in general, by five complementary days. Every fourth year is an intercalary or leap year and in these years there are six complementary days. The intercalary year of the Coptic calendar immediately precedes the leap year of the Julian calendar. The era is that of Diocletian or the Martyrs, the origin of which is fixed at 29 August AD 284 (Julian date).

### INDIAN ERAS
In addition to the Muslim reckoning, other eras are used in India. The Saka era of southern India, dating from 3 March AD 78, was declared the national calendar of the Republic of India with effect from 22 March 1957, to be used concurrently with the Gregorian calendar. As revised, the year of the new Saka era begins at the spring equinox, with five successive months of 31 days and seven of 30 days in ordinary years, and six months of each length in leap years. The year AD 2016 is 1938 of the revised Saka era.

The year AD 2016 corresponds to the following years in other eras:

Year 2073 of the Vikram Samvat era
Year 1423 of the Bengali San era
Year 1192 of the Kollam era
Year 5117 of the Kaliyuga era
Year 2559 of the Buddha Nirvana era

### JAPANESE CALENDAR
The Japanese calendar is essentially the same as the Gregorian calendar, the years, months and weeks being of the same length and beginning on the same days as those of the Gregorian calendar. The numeration of the years is different, based on a system of epochs or periods, each of which begins at the accession of an emperor or other important occurrence. The method is not unlike the British system of regnal years, except that each year of a period closes on 31 December. The Japanese chronology begins about AD 650 and the three latest epochs are defined by the reigns of emperors, whose actual names are not necessarily used:

*Epoch*
Taisho – 1 August 1912 to 25 December 1926
Showa – 26 December 1926 to 7 January 1989
Heisei – 8 January 1989

The year Heisei 28 begins on 1 January 2016.

The months are known as First Month, Second Month, etc, First Month being equivalent to January. The days of the week are Nichiyobi (Sun-day), Getsuyobi (Moon-day), Kayobi (Fire-day), Suiyobi (Water-day), Mokuyobi (Wood-day), Kinyobi (Metal-day) and Doyobi (Earth-day).

### THE MASONIC YEAR
Two dates are quoted in warrants, dispensations, etc, issued by the United Grand Lodge of England, those for the current year being expressed as *Anno Domini* 2016 – *Anno Lucis* 6016. This *Anno Lucis* (year of light) is based on the Book of Genesis 1:3, the 4,000-year difference being derived, in modified form, from *Ussher's Notation*, published in 1654, which places the Creation of the World in 4004 BC.

## OLYMPIADS

Ancient Greek chronology was reckoned in Olympiads, cycles of four years corresponding with the Olympic Games held on the plain of Olympia, in Elis. The intervening years were the first, second, etc, of the Olympiad, which received the name of the victor at the Games. The first recorded Olympiad is that of Choroebus, 776 BC.

## ZOROASTRIAN CALENDAR

Zoroastrians, followers of the Iranian prophet Zarathushtra (known to the Greeks as Zoroaster) are mostly to be found in Iran and in India, where they are known as Parsees.

The Zoroastrian era dates from the coronation of the last Zoroastrian Sasanian king in AD 631. The Zoroastrian calendar is divided into 12 months, each comprising 30 days, followed by five holy days of the Gathas at the end of each year to make the year consist of 365 days.

In order to synchronise the calendar with the solar year of 365 days, an extra month was intercalated once every 120 years. However, this intercalation ceased in the 12th century and the new year, which had fallen in the spring, slipped back to August. Because intercalation ceased at different times in Iran and India, there was one month's difference between the calendar followed in Iran (Kadmi calendar) and that followed by the Parsees (Shenshai calendar). In 1906 a group of Zoroastrians decided to bring the calendar back in line with the seasons again and restore the new year to 21 March each year (Fasli calendar).

The Shenshai calendar (new year in August) is mainly used by Parsees. The Fasli calendar (new year, 21 March) is mainly used by Zoroastrians living in Iran, in the Indian subcontinent, or elsewhere.

# ROMAN CALENDAR

Roman historians adopted as an epoch the foundation of Rome, which is believed to have happened in the year 753 BC. The ordinal number of the years in Roman reckoning is followed by the letters AUC *(ab urbe condita)*, so that the year 2016 is 2769 AUC (MMDCCLXIX). The calendar that we know has developed from one said to have been established by Romulus using a year of 304 days divided into ten months, beginning with March. To this Numa added January and February, making the year consist of 12 months of 30 and 29 days alternately, with an additional day so that the total was 355. It is also said that Numa ordered an intercalary month of 22 or 23 days in alternate years, making 90 days in eight years, to be inserted after 23 February.

However, there is some doubt as to the origination and the details of the intercalation in the Roman calendar. In the year 46 BC Julius Caesar found that the calendar had been allowed to fall into some confusion. He sought the help of Egyptian astronomer Sosigenes, which led to the construction and adoption (45 BC) of the Julian calendar, and, by a slight alteration, to the Gregorian calendar now in use. The year 46 BC was made to consist of 445 days and is called the Year of Confusion.

In the Roman (Julian) calendar the days of the month were counted backwards from three fixed points, or days, and an intervening day was said to be so many days before the next coming point, the first and last being counted. These three points were the Kalends, the Nones and the Ides. Their positions in the months and the method of counting from them will be seen in the table below. The year containing 366 days was called *bissextilis annus*, as it had a doubled sixth day *(bissextus dies)* before the March Kalends on 24 February – *ante diem sextum Kalendas Martias*, or a.d. VI Kal. Mart.

| *Present days of the month* | *March, May, July, October have thirty-one days* | | *January, August, December have thirty-one days* | | *April, June, September, November have thirty days* | | *February has twenty-eight days, and in leap year twenty-nine* | |
|---|---|---|---|---|---|---|---|---|
| 1 | Kalendis | | Kalendis | | Kalendis | | Kalendis | |
| 2 | VI | ante | IV | ante | IV | ante | IV | ante |
| 3 | V | Nonas | III | Nonas | III | Nonas | III | Nonas |
| 4 | IV | | pridie Nonas | | pridie Nonas | | pridie Nonas | |
| 5 | III | | Nonis | | Nonis | | Nonis | |
| 6 | pridie Nonas | | VIII | | VIII | | VIII | |
| 7 | Nonis | | VII | | VII | | VII | |
| 8 | VIII | | VI | ante | VI | ante | VI | ante |
| 9 | VII | | V | Idus | V | Idus | V | Idus |
| 10 | VI | ante | IV | | IV | | IV | |
| 11 | V | Idus | III | | III | | III | |
| 12 | IV | | pridie Idus | | pridie Idus | | pridie Idus | |
| 13 | III | | Idibus | | Idibus | | Idibus | |
| 14 | pridie Idus | | XIX | | XVIII | | XVI | |
| 15 | Idibus | | XVIII | | XVII | | XV | |
| 16 | XVII | | XVII | | XVI | | XIV | |
| 17 | XVI | | XVI | | XV | | XIII | |
| 18 | XV | | XV | | XIV | | XII | |
| 19 | XIV | | XIV | | XIII | | XI | |
| 20 | XIII | | XIII | | XII | ante Kalendas | X | ante Kalendas |
| 21 | XII | | XII | ante Kalendas | XI | (of the month | IX | Martias |
| 22 | XI | ante Kalendas | XI | (of the month | X | following) | VIII | |
| 23 | X | (of the month | X | following) | IX | | VII | |
| 24 | IX | following) | IX | | VIII | | *VI | |
| 25 | VIII | | VIII | | VII | | V | |
| 26 | VII | | VII | | VI | | IV | |
| 27 | VI | | VI | | V | | III | |
| 28 | V | | V | | IV | | pridie Kalendas | |
| 29 | IV | | IV | | III | | Martias | |
| 30 | III | | III | | pridie Kalendas | | | |
| 31 | pridie Kalendas (Aprilis, Iunias, Sextilis, Novembris) | | pridie Kalendas (Februarias, Septembris, Ianuarias) | | (Maias, Quinctilis, Octobris, Decembris) | | | |

* Repeated in leap year

# CALENDAR FOR ANY YEAR 1780–2040

To select the correct calendar for any year between 1780 and 2040, consult the index below
* leap year

| | | | | | | | |
|---|---|---|---|---|---|---|---|
| 1780 N* | 1813 K | 1846 I | 1879 G | 1912 D* | 1945 C | 1978 A | 2011 M |
| 1781 C | 1814 M | 1847 K | 1880 J* | 1913 G | 1946 E | 1979 C | 2012 B* |
| 1782 E | 1815 A | 1848 N* | 1881 M | 1914 I | 1947 G | 1980 F* | 2013 E |
| 1783 G | 1816 D* | 1849 C | 1882 A | 1915 K | 1948 J* | 1981 I | 2014 G |
| 1784 J* | 1817 G | 1850 E | 1883 C | 1916 N* | 1949 M | 1982 K | 2015 I |
| 1785 M | 1818 I | 1851 G | 1884 F* | 1917 C | 1950 A | 1983 M | 2016 L* |
| 1786 A | 1819 K | 1852 J* | 1885 I | 1918 E | 1951 C | 1984 B* | 2017 A |
| 1787 C | 1820 N* | 1853 M | 1886 K | 1919 G | 1952 F* | 1985 E | 2018 C |
| 1788 F* | 1821 C | 1854 A | 1887 M | 1920 J* | 1953 I | 1986 G | 2019 E |
| 1789 I | 1822 E | 1855 C | 1888 B* | 1921 M | 1954 K | 1987 I | 2020 H* |
| 1790 K | 1823 G | 1856 F* | 1889 E | 1922 A | 1955 M | 1988 L* | 2021 K |
| 1791 M | 1824 J* | 1857 I | 1890 G | 1923 C | 1956 B* | 1989 A | 2022 M |
| 1792 B* | 1825 M | 1858 K | 1891 I | 1924 F* | 1957 E | 1990 C | 2023 A |
| 1793 E | 1826 A | 1859 M | 1892 L* | 1925 I | 1958 G | 1991 E | 2024 D* |
| 1794 G | 1827 C | 1860 B* | 1893 A | 1926 K | 1959 I | 1992 H* | 2025 G |
| 1795 I | 1828 F* | 1861 E | 1894 C | 1927 M | 1960 L* | 1993 K | 2026 I |
| 1796 L* | 1829 I | 1862 G | 1895 E | 1928 B* | 1961 A | 1994 M | 2027 K |
| 1797 A | 1830 K | 1863 I | 1896 H* | 1929 E | 1962 C | 1995 A | 2028 N* |
| 1798 C | 1831 M | 1864 L* | 1897 K | 1930 G | 1963 E | 1996 D* | 2029 C |
| 1799 E | 1832 B* | 1865 A | 1898 M | 1931 I | 1964 H* | 1997 G | 2030 E |
| 1800 G | 1833 E | 1866 C | 1899 A | 1932 L* | 1965 K | 1998 I | 2031 G |
| 1801 I | 1834 G | 1867 E | 1900 C | 1933 A | 1966 M | 1999 K | 2032 J* |
| 1802 K | 1835 I | 1868 H* | 1901 E | 1934 C | 1967 A | 2000 N* | 2033 M |
| 1803 M | 1836 L* | 1869 K | 1902 G | 1935 E | 1968 D* | 2001 C | 2034 A |
| 1804 B* | 1837 A | 1870 M | 1903 I | 1936 H* | 1969 G | 2002 E | 2035 C |
| 1805 E | 1838 C | 1871 A | 1904 L* | 1937 K | 1970 I | 2003 G | 2036 F* |
| 1806 G | 1839 E | 1872 D* | 1905 A | 1938 M | 1971 K | 2004 J* | 2037 I |
| 1807 I | 1840 H* | 1873 G | 1906 C | 1939 A | 1972 N* | 2005 M | 2038 K |
| 1808 L* | 1841 K | 1874 I | 1907 E | 1940 D* | 1973 C | 2006 A | 2039 M |
| 1809 A | 1842 M | 1875 K | 1908 H* | 1941 G | 1974 E | 2007 C | 2040 B* |
| 1810 C | 1843 A | 1876 N* | 1909 K | 1942 I | 1975 G | 2008 F* | |
| 1811 E | 1844 D* | 1877 C | 1910 M | 1943 K | 1976 J* | 2009 I | |
| 1812 H* | 1845 G | 1878 E | 1911 A | 1944 N* | 1977 M | 2010 K | |

## A

| | *January* | *February* | *March* |
|---|---|---|---|
| Sun. | 1  8 15 22 29 | 5 12 19 26 | 5 12 19 26 |
| Mon. | 2  9 16 23 30 | 6 13 20 27 | 6 13 20 27 |
| Tue. | 3 10 17 24 31 | 7 14 21 28 | 7 14 21 28 |
| Wed. | 4 11 18 25 | 1  8 15 22 | 1  8 15 22 29 |
| Thur. | 5 12 19 26 | 2  9 16 23 | 2  9 16 23 30 |
| Fri. | 6 13 20 27 | 3 10 17 24 | 3 10 17 24 31 |
| Sat. | 7 14 21 28 | 4 11 18 25 | 4 11 18 25 |

| | *April* | *May* | *June* |
|---|---|---|---|
| Sun. | 2  9 16 23 30 | 7 14 21 28 | 4 11 18 25 |
| Mon. | 3 10 17 24 | 1  8 15 22 29 | 5 12 19 26 |
| Tue. | 4 11 18 25 | 2  9 16 23 30 | 6 13 20 27 |
| Wed. | 5 12 19 26 | 3 10 17 24 31 | 7 14 21 28 |
| Thur. | 6 13 20 27 | 4 11 18 25 | 1  8 15 22 29 |
| Fri. | 7 14 21 28 | 5 12 19 26 | 2  9 16 23 30 |
| Sat. | 1  8 15 22 29 | 6 13 20 27 | 3 10 17 24 |

| | *July* | *August* | *September* |
|---|---|---|---|
| Sun. | 2  9 16 23 30 | 6 13 20 27 | 3 10 17 24 |
| Mon. | 3 10 17 24 31 | 7 14 21 28 | 4 11 18 25 |
| Tue. | 4 11 18 25 | 1  8 15 22 29 | 5 12 19 26 |
| Wed. | 5 12 19 26 | 2  9 16 23 30 | 6 13 20 27 |
| Thur. | 6 13 20 27 | 3 10 17 24 31 | 7 14 21 28 |
| Fri. | 7 14 21 28 | 4 11 18 25 | 1  8 15 22 29 |
| Sat. | 1  8 15 22 29 | 5 12 19 26 | 2  9 16 23 30 |

| | *October* | *November* | *December* |
|---|---|---|---|
| Sun. | 1  8 15 22 29 | 5 12 19 26 | 3 10 17 24 31 |
| Mon. | 2  9 16 23 30 | 6 13 20 27 | 4 11 18 25 |
| Tue. | 3 10 17 24 31 | 7 14 21 28 | 5 12 19 26 |
| Wed. | 4 11 18 25 | 1  8 15 22 29 | 6 13 20 27 |
| Thur. | 5 12 19 26 | 2  9 16 23 30 | 7 14 21 28 |
| Fri. | 6 13 20 27 | 3 10 17 24 | 1  8 15 22 29 |
| Sat. | 7 14 21 28 | 4 11 18 25 | 2  9 16 23 30 |

EASTER DAYS

| | |
|---|---|
| March 26 | 1815, 1826, 1837, 1967, 1978, 1989 |
| April 2 | 1809, 1893, 1899, 1961 |
| April 9 | 1871, 1882, 1939, 1950, 2023, 2034 |
| April 16 | 1786, 1797, 1843, 1854, 1865, 1911, 1922, 1933, 1995, 2006, 2017 |
| April 23 | 1905 |

## B (LEAP YEAR)

| | *January* | *February* | *March* |
|---|---|---|---|
| Sun. | 1  8 15 22 29 | 5 12 19 26 | 4 11 18 25 |
| Mon. | 2  9 16 23 30 | 6 13 20 27 | 5 12 19 26 |
| Tue. | 3 10 17 24 31 | 7 14 21 28 | 6 13 20 27 |
| Wed. | 4 11 18 25 | 1  8 15 22 29 | 7 14 21 28 |
| Thur. | 5 12 19 26 | 2  9 16 23 | 1  8 15 22 29 |
| Fri. | 6 13 20 27 | 3 10 17 24 | 2  9 16 23 30 |
| Sat. | 7 14 21 28 | 4 11 18 25 | 3 10 17 24 31 |

| | *April* | *May* | *June* |
|---|---|---|---|
| Sun. | 1  8 15 22 29 | 6 13 20 27 | 3 10 17 24 |
| Mon. | 2  9 16 23 30 | 7 14 21 28 | 4 11 18 25 |
| Tue. | 3 10 17 24 | 1  8 15 22 29 | 5 12 19 26 |
| Wed. | 4 11 18 25 | 2  9 16 23 30 | 6 13 20 27 |
| Thur. | 5 12 19 26 | 3 10 17 24 31 | 7 14 21 28 |
| Fri. | 6 13 20 27 | 4 11 18 25 | 1  8 15 22 29 |
| Sat. | 7 14 21 28 | 5 12 19 26 | 2  9 16 23 30 |

| | *July* | *August* | *September* |
|---|---|---|---|
| Sun. | 1  8 15 22 29 | 5 12 19 26 | 2  9 16 23 30 |
| Mon. | 2  9 16 23 30 | 6 13 20 27 | 3 10 17 24 |
| Tue. | 3 10 17 24 31 | 7 14 21 28 | 4 11 18 25 |
| Wed. | 4 11 18 25 | 1  8 15 22 29 | 5 12 19 26 |
| Thur. | 5 12 19 26 | 2  9 16 23 30 | 6 13 20 27 |
| Fri. | 6 13 20 27 | 3 10 17 24 31 | 7 14 21 28 |
| Sat. | 7 14 21 28 | 4 11 18 25 | 1  8 15 22 29 |

| | *October* | *November* | *December* |
|---|---|---|---|
| Sun. | 7 14 21 28 | 4 11 18 25 | 2  9 16 23 30 |
| Mon. | 1  8 15 22 29 | 5 12 19 26 | 3 10 17 24 31 |
| Tue. | 2  9 16 23 30 | 6 13 20 27 | 4 11 18 25 |
| Wed. | 3 10 17 24 31 | 7 14 21 28 | 5 12 19 26 |
| Thur. | 4 11 18 25 | 1  8 15 22 29 | 6 13 20 27 |
| Fri. | 5 12 19 26 | 2  9 16 23 30 | 7 14 21 28 |
| Sat. | 6 13 20 27 | 3 10 17 24 | 1  8 15 22 29 |

EASTER DAYS

| | |
|---|---|
| April 1 | 1804, 1888, 1956, 2040 |
| April 8 | 1792, 1860, 1928, 2012 |
| April 22 | 1832, 1984 |

## C

| | January | February | March |
|---|---|---|---|
| Sun. | 7 14 21 28 | 4 11 18 25 | 4 11 18 25 |
| Mon. | 1 8 15 22 29 | 5 12 19 26 | 5 12 19 26 |
| Tue. | 2 9 16 23 30 | 6 13 20 27 | 6 13 20 27 |
| Wed. | 3 10 17 24 31 | 7 14 21 28 | 7 14 21 28 |
| Thur. | 4 11 18 25 | 1 8 15 22 | 1 8 15 22 29 |
| Fri. | 5 12 19 26 | 2 9 16 23 | 2 9 16 23 30 |
| Sat. | 6 13 20 27 | 3 10 17 24 | 3 10 17 24 31 |

| | April | May | June |
|---|---|---|---|
| Sun. | 1 8 15 22 29 | 6 13 20 27 | 3 10 17 24 |
| Mon. | 2 9 16 23 30 | 7 14 21 28 | 4 11 18 25 |
| Tue. | 3 10 17 24 | 1 8 15 22 29 | 5 12 19 26 |
| Wed. | 4 11 18 25 | 2 9 16 23 30 | 6 13 20 27 |
| Thur. | 5 12 19 26 | 3 10 17 24 31 | 7 14 21 28 |
| Fri. | 6 13 20 27 | 4 11 18 25 | 1 8 15 22 29 |
| Sat. | 7 14 21 28 | 5 12 19 26 | 2 9 16 23 30 |

| | July | August | September |
|---|---|---|---|
| Sun. | 1 8 15 22 29 | 5 12 19 26 | 2 9 16 23 30 |
| Mon. | 2 9 16 23 30 | 6 13 20 27 | 3 10 17 24 |
| Tue. | 3 10 17 24 31 | 7 14 21 28 | 4 11 18 25 |
| Wed. | 4 11 18 25 | 1 8 15 22 29 | 5 12 19 26 |
| Thur. | 5 12 19 26 | 2 9 16 23 30 | 6 13 20 27 |
| Fri. | 6 13 20 27 | 3 10 17 24 31 | 7 14 21 28 |
| Sat. | 7 14 21 28 | 4 11 18 25 | 1 8 15 22 29 |

| | October | November | December |
|---|---|---|---|
| Sun. | 7 14 21 28 | 4 11 18 25 | 2 9 16 23 30 |
| Mon. | 1 8 15 22 29 | 5 12 19 26 | 3 10 17 24 31 |
| Tue. | 2 9 16 23 30 | 6 13 20 27 | 4 11 18 25 |
| Wed. | 3 10 17 24 31 | 7 14 21 28 | 5 12 19 26 |
| Thur. | 4 11 18 25 | 1 8 15 22 29 | 6 13 20 27 |
| Fri. | 5 12 19 26 | 2 9 16 23 30 | 7 14 21 28 |
| Sat. | 6 13 20 27 | 3 10 17 24 | 1 8 15 22 29 |

EASTER DAYS
| | |
|---|---|
| March 25 | 1883, 1894, 1951, 2035 |
| April 1 | 1866, 1877, 1923, 1934, 1945, 2018, 2029 |
| April 8 | 1787, 1798, 1849, 1855, 1917, 2007 |
| April 15 | 1781, 1827, 1838, 1900, 1906, 1979, 1990, 2001 |
| April 22 | 1810, 1821, 1962, 1973 |

## E

| | January | February | March |
|---|---|---|---|
| Sun. | 6 13 20 27 | 3 10 17 24 | 3 10 17 24 31 |
| Mon. | 7 14 21 28 | 4 11 18 25 | 4 11 18 25 |
| Tue. | 1 8 15 22 29 | 5 12 19 26 | 5 12 19 26 |
| Wed. | 2 9 16 23 30 | 6 13 20 27 | 6 13 20 27 |
| Thur. | 3 10 17 24 31 | 7 14 21 28 | 7 14 21 28 |
| Fri. | 4 11 18 25 | 1 8 15 22 | 1 8 15 22 29 |
| Sat. | 5 12 19 26 | 2 9 16 23 | 2 9 16 23 30 |

| | April | May | June |
|---|---|---|---|
| Sun. | 7 14 21 28 | 5 12 19 26 | 2 9 16 23 30 |
| Mon. | 1 8 15 22 29 | 6 13 20 27 | 3 10 17 24 |
| Tue. | 2 9 16 23 30 | 7 14 21 28 | 4 11 18 25 |
| Wed. | 3 10 17 24 | 1 8 15 22 29 | 5 12 19 26 |
| Thur. | 4 11 18 25 | 2 9 16 23 30 | 6 13 20 27 |
| Fri. | 5 12 19 26 | 3 10 17 24 31 | 7 14 21 28 |
| Sat. | 6 13 20 27 | 4 11 18 25 | 1 8 15 22 29 |

| | July | August | September |
|---|---|---|---|
| Sun. | 7 14 21 28 | 4 11 18 25 | 1 8 15 22 29 |
| Mon. | 1 8 15 22 29 | 5 12 19 26 | 2 9 16 23 30 |
| Tue. | 2 9 16 23 30 | 6 13 20 27 | 3 10 17 24 |
| Wed. | 3 10 17 24 31 | 7 14 21 28 | 4 11 18 25 |
| Thur. | 4 11 18 25 | 1 8 15 22 29 | 5 12 19 26 |
| Fri. | 5 12 19 26 | 2 9 16 23 30 | 6 13 20 27 |
| Sat. | 6 13 20 27 | 3 10 17 24 31 | 7 14 21 28 |

| | October | November | December |
|---|---|---|---|
| Sun. | 6 13 20 27 | 3 10 17 24 | 1 8 15 22 29 |
| Mon. | 7 14 21 28 | 4 11 18 25 | 2 9 16 23 30 |
| Tue. | 1 8 15 22 29 | 5 12 19 26 | 3 10 17 24 31 |
| Wed. | 2 9 16 23 30 | 6 13 20 27 | 4 11 18 25 |
| Thur. | 3 10 17 24 31 | 7 14 21 28 | 5 12 19 26 |
| Fri. | 4 11 18 25 | 1 8 15 22 29 | 6 13 20 27 |
| Sat. | 5 12 19 26 | 2 9 16 23 30 | 7 14 21 28 |

EASTER DAYS
| | |
|---|---|
| March 24 | 1799 |
| March 31 | 1782, 1793, 1839, 1850, 1861, 1907, 1918, 1929, 1991, 2002, 2013 |
| April 7 | 1822, 1833, 1901, 1985 |
| April 14 | 1805, 1811, 1895, 1963, 1974 |
| April 21 | 1867, 1878, 1889, 1935, 1946, 1957, 2019, 2030 |

## D (LEAP YEAR)

| | January | February | March |
|---|---|---|---|
| Sun. | 7 14 21 28 | 4 11 18 25 | 3 10 17 24 31 |
| Mon. | 1 8 15 22 29 | 5 12 19 26 | 4 11 18 25 |
| Tue. | 2 9 16 23 30 | 6 13 20 27 | 5 12 19 26 |
| Wed. | 3 10 17 24 31 | 7 14 21 28 | 6 13 20 27 |
| Thur. | 4 11 18 25 | 1 8 15 22 29 | 7 14 21 28 |
| Fri. | 5 12 19 26 | 2 9 16 23 | 1 8 15 22 29 |
| Sat. | 6 13 20 27 | 3 10 17 24 | 2 9 16 23 30 |

| | April | May | June |
|---|---|---|---|
| Sun. | 7 14 21 28 | 5 12 19 26 | 2 9 16 23 30 |
| Mon. | 1 8 15 22 29 | 6 13 20 27 | 3 10 17 24 |
| Tue. | 2 9 16 23 30 | 7 14 21 28 | 4 11 18 25 |
| Wed. | 3 10 17 24 | 1 8 15 22 29 | 5 12 19 26 |
| Thur. | 4 11 18 25 | 2 9 16 23 30 | 6 13 20 27 |
| Fri. | 5 12 19 26 | 3 10 17 24 31 | 7 14 21 28 |
| Sat. | 6 13 20 27 | 4 11 18 25 | 1 8 15 22 29 |

| | July | August | September |
|---|---|---|---|
| Sun. | 7 14 21 28 | 4 11 18 25 | 1 8 15 22 29 |
| Mon. | 1 8 15 22 29 | 5 12 19 26 | 2 9 16 23 30 |
| Tue. | 2 9 16 23 30 | 6 13 20 27 | 3 10 17 24 |
| Wed. | 3 10 17 24 31 | 7 14 21 28 | 4 11 18 25 |
| Thur. | 4 11 18 25 | 1 8 15 22 29 | 5 12 19 26 |
| Fri. | 5 12 19 26 | 2 9 16 23 30 | 6 13 20 27 |
| Sat. | 6 13 20 27 | 3 10 17 24 31 | 7 14 21 28 |

| | October | November | December |
|---|---|---|---|
| Sun. | 6 13 20 27 | 3 10 17 24 | 1 8 15 22 29 |
| Mon. | 7 14 21 28 | 4 11 18 25 | 2 9 16 23 30 |
| Tue. | 1 8 15 22 29 | 5 12 19 26 | 3 10 17 24 31 |
| Wed. | 2 9 16 23 30 | 6 13 20 27 | 4 11 18 25 |
| Thur. | 3 10 17 24 31 | 7 14 21 28 | 5 12 19 26 |
| Fri. | 4 11 18 25 | 1 8 15 22 29 | 6 13 20 27 |
| Sat. | 5 12 19 26 | 2 9 16 23 30 | 7 14 21 28 |

EASTER DAYS
| | |
|---|---|
| March 24 | 1940 |
| March 31 | 1872, 2024 |
| April 7 | 1844, 1912, 1996 |
| April 14 | 1816, 1968 |

## F (LEAP YEAR)

| | January | February | March |
|---|---|---|---|
| Sun. | 6 13 20 27 | 3 10 17 24 | 2 9 16 23 30 |
| Mon. | 7 14 21 28 | 4 11 18 25 | 3 10 17 24 31 |
| Tue. | 1 8 15 22 29 | 5 12 19 26 | 4 11 18 25 |
| Wed. | 2 9 16 23 30 | 6 13 20 27 | 5 12 19 26 |
| Thur. | 3 10 17 24 31 | 7 14 21 28 | 6 13 20 27 |
| Fri. | 4 11 18 25 | 1 8 15 22 29 | 7 14 21 28 |
| Sat. | 5 12 19 26 | 2 9 16 23 | 1 8 15 22 29 |

| | April | May | June |
|---|---|---|---|
| Sun. | 6 13 20 27 | 4 11 18 25 | 1 8 15 22 29 |
| Mon. | 7 14 21 28 | 5 12 19 26 | 2 9 16 23 30 |
| Tue. | 1 8 15 22 29 | 6 13 20 27 | 3 10 17 24 |
| Wed. | 2 9 16 23 30 | 7 14 21 28 | 4 11 18 25 |
| Thur. | 3 10 17 24 | 1 8 15 22 29 | 5 12 19 26 |
| Fri. | 4 11 18 25 | 2 9 16 23 30 | 6 13 20 27 |
| Sat. | 5 12 19 26 | 3 10 17 24 31 | 7 14 21 28 |

| | July | August | September |
|---|---|---|---|
| Sun. | 6 13 20 27 | 3 10 17 24 31 | 7 14 21 28 |
| Mon. | 7 14 21 28 | 4 11 18 25 | 1 8 15 22 29 |
| Tue. | 1 8 15 22 29 | 5 12 19 26 | 2 9 16 23 30 |
| Wed. | 2 9 16 23 30 | 6 13 20 27 | 3 10 17 24 |
| Thur. | 3 10 17 24 31 | 7 14 21 28 | 4 11 18 25 |
| Fri. | 4 11 18 25 | 1 8 15 22 29 | 5 12 19 26 |
| Sat. | 5 12 19 26 | 2 9 16 23 30 | 6 13 20 27 |

| | October | November | December |
|---|---|---|---|
| Sun. | 5 12 19 26 | 2 9 16 23 30 | 7 14 21 28 |
| Mon. | 6 13 20 27 | 3 10 17 24 | 1 8 15 22 29 |
| Tue. | 7 14 21 28 | 4 11 18 25 | 2 9 16 23 30 |
| Wed. | 1 8 15 22 29 | 5 12 19 26 | 3 10 17 24 31 |
| Thur. | 2 9 16 23 30 | 6 13 20 27 | 4 11 18 25 |
| Fri. | 3 10 17 24 31 | 7 14 21 28 | 5 12 19 26 |
| Sat. | 4 11 18 25 | 1 8 15 22 29 | 6 13 20 27 |

EASTER DAYS
| | |
|---|---|
| March 23 | 1788, 1856, 2008 |
| April 6 | 1828, 1980 |
| April 13 | 1884, 1952, 2036 |
| April 20 | 1924 |

## G

|  | January | February | March |
|---|---|---|---|
| Sun. | 5 12 19 26 | 2  9 16 23 | 2  9 16 23 30 |
| Mon. | 6 13 20 27 | 3 10 17 24 | 3 10 17 24 31 |
| Tue. | 7 14 21 28 | 4 11 18 25 | 4 11 18 25 |
| Wed. | 1  8 15 22 29 | 5 12 19 26 | 5 12 19 26 |
| Thur. | 2  9 16 23 30 | 6 13 20 27 | 6 13 20 27 |
| Fri. | 3 10 17 24 31 | 7 14 21 28 | 7 14 21 28 |
| Sat. | 4 11 18 25 | 1  8 15 22 | 1  8 15 22 29 |

|  | April | May | June |
|---|---|---|---|
| Sun. | 6 13 20 27 | 4 11 18 25 | 1  8 15 22 29 |
| Mon. | 7 14 21 28 | 5 12 19 26 | 2  9 16 23 30 |
| Tue. | 1  8 15 22 29 | 6 13 20 27 | 3 10 17 24 |
| Wed. | 2  9 16 23 30 | 7 14 21 28 | 4 11 18 25 |
| Thur. | 3 10 17 24 | 1  8 15 22 29 | 5 12 19 26 |
| Fri. | 4 11 18 25 | 2  9 16 23 30 | 6 13 20 27 |
| Sat. | 5 12 19 26 | 3 10 17 24 31 | 7 14 21 28 |

|  | July | August | September |
|---|---|---|---|
| Sun. | 6 13 20 27 | 3 10 17 24 31 | 7 14 21 28 |
| Mon. | 7 14 21 28 | 4 11 18 25 | 1  8 15 22 29 |
| Tue. | 1  8 15 22 29 | 5 12 19 26 | 2  9 16 23 30 |
| Wed. | 2  9 16 23 30 | 6 13 20 27 | 3 10 17 24 |
| Thur. | 3 10 17 24 31 | 7 14 21 28 | 4 11 18 25 |
| Fri. | 4 11 18 25 | 1  8 15 22 29 | 5 12 19 26 |
| Sat. | 5 12 19 26 | 2  9 16 23 30 | 6 13 20 27 |

|  | October | November | December |
|---|---|---|---|
| Sun. | 5 12 19 26 | 2  9 16 23 30 | 7 14 21 28 |
| Mon. | 6 13 20 27 | 3 10 17 24 | 1  8 15 22 29 |
| Tue. | 7 14 21 28 | 4 11 18 25 | 2  9 16 23 30 |
| Wed. | 1  8 15 22 29 | 5 12 19 26 | 3 10 17 24 31 |
| Thur. | 2  9 16 23 30 | 6 13 20 27 | 4 11 18 25 |
| Fri. | 3 10 17 24 31 | 7 14 21 28 | 5 12 19 26 |
| Sat. | 4 11 18 25 | 1  8 15 22 29 | 6 13 20 27 |

EASTER DAYS

| March 23 | 1845, 1913 |
|---|---|
| March 30 | 1823, 1834, 1902, 1975, 1986, 1997 |
| April 6 | 1806, 1817, 1890, 1947, 1958, 1969 |
| April 13 | 1800, 1873, 1879, 1941, 2031 |
| April 20 | 1783, 1794, 1851, 1862, 1919, 1930, 2003, 2014, 2025 |

## H (LEAP YEAR)

|  | January | February | March |
|---|---|---|---|
| Sun. | 5 12 19 26 | 2  9 16 23 | 1  8 15 22 29 |
| Mon. | 6 13 20 27 | 3 10 17 24 | 2  9 16 23 30 |
| Tue. | 7 14 21 28 | 4 11 18 25 | 3 10 17 24 31 |
| Wed. | 1  8 15 22 29 | 5 12 19 26 | 4 11 18 25 |
| Thur. | 2  9 16 23 30 | 6 13 20 27 | 5 12 19 26 |
| Fri. | 3 10 17 24 31 | 7 14 21 28 | 6 13 20 27 |
| Sat. | 4 11 18 25 | 1  8 15 22 29 | 7 14 21 28 |

|  | April | May | June |
|---|---|---|---|
| Sun. | 5 12 19 26 | 3 10 17 24 31 | 7 14 21 28 |
| Mon. | 6 13 20 27 | 4 11 18 25 | 1  8 15 22 29 |
| Tue. | 7 14 21 28 | 5 12 19 26 | 2  9 16 23 30 |
| Wed. | 1  8 15 22 29 | 6 13 20 27 | 3 10 17 24 |
| Thur. | 2  9 16 23 30 | 7 14 21 28 | 4 11 18 25 |
| Fri. | 3 10 17 24 | 1  8 15 22 29 | 5 12 19 26 |
| Sat. | 4 11 18 25 | 2  9 16 23 30 | 6 13 20 27 |

|  | July | August | September |
|---|---|---|---|
| Sun. | 5 12 19 26 | 2  9 16 23 30 | 6 13 20 27 |
| Mon. | 6 13 20 27 | 3 10 17 24 31 | 7 14 21 28 |
| Tue. | 7 14 21 28 | 4 11 18 25 | 1  8 15 22 29 |
| Wed. | 1  8 15 22 29 | 5 12 19 26 | 2  9 16 23 30 |
| Thur. | 2  9 16 23 30 | 6 13 20 27 | 3 10 17 24 |
| Fri. | 3 10 17 24 31 | 7 14 21 28 | 4 11 18 25 |
| Sat. | 4 11 18 25 | 1  8 15 22 29 | 5 12 19 26 |

|  | October | November | December |
|---|---|---|---|
| Sun. | 4 11 18 25 | 1  8 15 22 29 | 6 13 20 27 |
| Mon. | 5 12 19 26 | 2  9 16 23 30 | 7 14 21 28 |
| Tue. | 6 13 20 27 | 3 10 17 24 | 1  8 15 22 29 |
| Wed. | 7 14 21 28 | 4 11 18 25 | 2  9 16 23 30 |
| Thur. | 1  8 15 22 29 | 5 12 19 26 | 3 10 17 24 31 |
| Fri. | 2  9 16 23 30 | 6 13 20 27 | 4 11 18 25 |
| Sat. | 3 10 17 24 31 | 7 14 21 28 | 5 12 19 26 |

EASTER DAYS

| March 29 | 1812, 1964 |
|---|---|
| April 5 | 1896 |
| April 12 | 1868, 1936, 2020 |
| April 19 | 1840, 1908, 1992 |

## I

|  | January | February | March |
|---|---|---|---|
| Sun. | 4 11 18 25 | 1  8 15 22 | 1  8 15 22 29 |
| Mon. | 5 12 19 26 | 2  9 16 23 | 2  9 16 23 30 |
| Tue. | 6 13 20 27 | 3 10 17 24 | 3 10 17 24 31 |
| Wed. | 7 14 21 28 | 4 11 18 25 | 4 11 18 25 |
| Thur. | 1  8 15 22 29 | 5 12 19 26 | 5 12 19 26 |
| Fri. | 2  9 16 23 30 | 6 13 20 27 | 6 13 20 27 |
| Sat. | 3 10 17 24 31 | 7 14 21 28 | 7 14 21 28 |

|  | April | May | June |
|---|---|---|---|
| Sun. | 5 12 19 26 | 3 10 17 24 31 | 7 14 21 28 |
| Mon. | 6 13 20 27 | 4 11 18 25 | 1  8 15 22 29 |
| Tue. | 7 14 21 28 | 5 12 19 26 | 2  9 16 23 30 |
| Wed. | 1  8 15 22 29 | 6 13 20 27 | 3 10 17 24 |
| Thur. | 2  9 16 23 30 | 7 14 21 28 | 4 11 18 25 |
| Fri. | 3 10 17 24 | 1  8 15 22 29 | 5 12 19 26 |
| Sat. | 4 11 18 25 | 2  9 16 23 30 | 6 13 20 27 |

|  | July | August | September |
|---|---|---|---|
| Sun. | 5 12 19 26 | 2  9 16 23 30 | 6 13 20 27 |
| Mon. | 6 13 20 27 | 3 10 17 24 31 | 7 14 21 28 |
| Tue. | 7 14 21 28 | 4 11 18 25 | 1  8 15 22 29 |
| Wed. | 1  8 15 22 29 | 5 12 19 26 | 2  9 16 23 30 |
| Thur. | 2  9 16 23 30 | 6 13 20 27 | 3 10 17 24 |
| Fri. | 3 10 17 24 31 | 7 14 21 28 | 4 11 18 25 |
| Sat. | 4 11 18 25 | 1  8 15 22 29 | 5 12 19 26 |

|  | October | November | December |
|---|---|---|---|
| Sun. | 4 11 18 25 | 1  8 15 22 29 | 6 13 20 27 |
| Mon. | 5 12 19 26 | 2  9 16 23 30 | 7 14 21 28 |
| Tue. | 6 13 20 27 | 3 10 17 24 | 1  8 15 22 29 |
| Wed. | 7 14 21 28 | 4 11 18 25 | 2  9 16 23 30 |
| Thur. | 1  8 15 22 29 | 5 12 19 26 | 3 10 17 24 31 |
| Fri. | 2  9 16 23 30 | 6 13 20 27 | 4 11 18 25 |
| Sat. | 3 10 17 24 31 | 7 14 21 28 | 5 12 19 26 |

EASTER DAYS

| March 22 | 1818 |
|---|---|
| March 29 | 1807, 1891, 1959, 1970 |
| April 5 | 1795, 1801, 1863, 1874, 1885, 1931, 1942, 1953, 2015, 2026, 2037 |
| April 12 | 1789, 1846, 1857, 1903, 1914, 1925, 1998, 2009 |
| April 19 | 1829, 1835, 1981, 1987 |

## J (LEAP YEAR)

|  | January | February | March |
|---|---|---|---|
| Sun. | 4 11 18 25 | 1  8 15 22 29 | 7 14 21 28 |
| Mon. | 5 12 19 26 | 2  9 16 23 | 1  8 15 22 29 |
| Tue. | 6 13 20 27 | 3 10 17 24 | 2  9 16 23 30 |
| Wed. | 7 14 21 28 | 4 11 18 25 | 3 10 17 24 31 |
| Thur. | 1  8 15 22 29 | 5 12 19 26 | 4 11 18 25 |
| Fri. | 2  9 16 23 30 | 6 13 20 27 | 5 12 19 26 |
| Sat. | 3 10 17 24 31 | 7 14 21 28 | 6 13 20 27 |

|  | April | May | June |
|---|---|---|---|
| Sun. | 4 11 18 25 | 2  9 16 23 30 | 6 13 20 27 |
| Mon. | 5 12 19 26 | 3 10 17 24 31 | 7 14 21 28 |
| Tue. | 6 13 20 27 | 4 11 18 25 | 1  8 15 22 29 |
| Wed. | 7 14 21 28 | 5 12 19 26 | 2  9 16 23 30 |
| Thur. | 1  8 15 22 29 | 6 13 20 27 | 3 10 17 24 |
| Fri. | 2  9 16 23 30 | 7 14 21 28 | 4 11 18 25 |
| Sat. | 3 10 17 24 | 1  8 15 22 29 | 5 12 19 26 |

|  | July | August | September |
|---|---|---|---|
| Sun. | 4 11 18 25 | 1  8 15 22 29 | 5 12 19 26 |
| Mon. | 5 12 19 26 | 2  9 16 23 30 | 6 13 20 27 |
| Tue. | 6 13 20 27 | 3 10 17 24 31 | 7 14 21 28 |
| Wed. | 7 14 21 28 | 4 11 18 25 | 1  8 15 22 29 |
| Thur. | 1  8 15 22 29 | 5 12 19 26 | 2  9 16 23 30 |
| Fri. | 2  9 16 23 30 | 6 13 20 27 | 3 10 17 24 |
| Sat. | 3 10 17 24 31 | 7 14 21 28 | 4 11 18 25 |

|  | October | November | December |
|---|---|---|---|
| Sun. | 3 10 17 24 31 | 7 14 21 28 | 5 12 19 26 |
| Mon. | 4 11 18 25 | 1  8 15 22 29 | 6 13 20 27 |
| Tue. | 5 12 19 26 | 2  9 16 23 30 | 7 14 21 28 |
| Wed. | 6 13 20 27 | 3 10 17 24 | 1  8 15 22 29 |
| Thur. | 7 14 21 28 | 4 11 18 25 | 2  9 16 23 30 |
| Fri. | 1  8 15 22 29 | 5 12 19 26 | 3 10 17 24 31 |
| Sat. | 2  9 16 23 30 | 6 13 20 27 | 4 11 18 25 |

EASTER DAYS

| March 28 | 1880, 1948, 2032 |
|---|---|
| April 4 | 1920 |
| April 11 | 1784, 1852, 2004 |
| April 18 | 1824, 1976 |

## K

| | January | February | March |
|---|---|---|---|
| Sun. | 3 10 17 24 31 | 7 14 21 28 | 7 14 21 28 |
| Mon. | 4 11 18 25 | 1 8 15 22 | 1 8 15 22 29 |
| Tue. | 5 12 19 26 | 2 9 16 23 | 2 9 16 23 30 |
| Wed. | 6 13 20 27 | 3 10 17 24 | 3 10 17 24 31 |
| Thur. | 7 14 21 28 | 4 11 18 25 | 4 11 18 25 |
| Fri. | 1 8 15 22 29 | 5 12 19 26 | 5 12 19 26 |
| Sat. | 2 9 16 23 30 | 6 13 20 27 | 6 13 20 27 |

| | April | May | June |
|---|---|---|---|
| Sun. | 4 11 18 25 | 2 9 16 23 30 | 6 13 20 27 |
| Mon. | 5 12 19 26 | 3 10 17 24 31 | 7 14 21 28 |
| Tue. | 6 13 20 27 | 4 11 18 25 | 1 8 15 22 29 |
| Wed. | 7 14 21 28 | 5 12 19 26 | 2 9 16 23 30 |
| Thur. | 1 8 15 22 29 | 6 13 20 27 | 3 10 17 24 |
| Fri. | 2 9 16 23 30 | 7 14 21 28 | 4 11 18 25 |
| Sat. | 3 10 17 24 | 1 8 15 22 29 | 5 12 19 26 |

| | July | August | September |
|---|---|---|---|
| Sun. | 4 11 18 25 | 1 8 15 22 29 | 5 12 19 26 |
| Mon. | 5 12 19 26 | 2 9 16 23 30 | 6 13 20 27 |
| Tue. | 6 13 20 27 | 3 10 17 24 31 | 7 14 21 28 |
| Wed. | 7 14 21 28 | 4 11 18 25 | 1 8 15 22 29 |
| Thur. | 1 8 15 22 29 | 5 12 19 26 | 2 9 16 23 30 |
| Fri. | 2 9 16 23 30 | 6 13 20 27 | 3 10 17 24 |
| Sat. | 3 10 17 24 31 | 7 14 21 28 | 4 11 18 25 |

| | October | November | December |
|---|---|---|---|
| Sun. | 3 10 17 24 31 | 7 14 21 28 | 5 12 19 26 |
| Mon. | 4 11 18 25 | 1 8 15 22 29 | 6 13 20 27 |
| Tue. | 5 12 19 26 | 2 9 16 23 30 | 7 14 21 28 |
| Wed. | 6 13 20 27 | 3 10 17 24 | 1 8 15 22 29 |
| Thur. | 7 14 21 28 | 4 11 18 25 | 2 9 16 23 30 |
| Fri. | 1 8 15 22 29 | 5 12 19 26 | 3 10 17 24 31 |
| Sat. | 2 9 16 23 30 | 6 13 20 27 | 4 11 18 25 |

EASTER DAYS
| | |
|---|---|
| March 28 | 1869, 1875, 1937, 2027 |
| April 4 | 1790, 1847, 1858, 1915, 1926, 1999, 2010, 2021 |
| April 11 | 1819, 1830, 1841, 1909, 1971, 1982, 1993 |
| April 18 | 1802, 1813, 1897, 1954, 1965 |
| April 25 | 1886, 1943, 2038 |

## M

| | January | February | March |
|---|---|---|---|
| Sun. | 2 9 16 23 30 | 6 13 20 27 | 6 13 20 27 |
| Mon. | 3 10 17 24 31 | 7 14 21 28 | 7 14 21 28 |
| Tue. | 4 11 18 25 | 1 8 15 22 | 1 8 15 22 29 |
| Wed. | 5 12 19 26 | 2 9 16 23 | 2 9 16 23 30 |
| Thur. | 6 13 20 27 | 3 10 17 24 | 3 10 17 24 31 |
| Fri. | 7 14 21 28 | 4 11 18 25 | 4 11 18 25 |
| Sat. | 1 8 15 22 29 | 5 12 19 26 | 5 12 19 26 |

| | April | May | June |
|---|---|---|---|
| Sun. | 3 10 17 24 | 1 8 15 22 29 | 5 12 19 26 |
| Mon. | 4 11 18 25 | 2 9 16 23 30 | 6 13 20 27 |
| Tue. | 5 12 19 26 | 3 10 17 24 31 | 7 14 21 28 |
| Wed. | 6 13 20 27 | 4 11 18 25 | 1 8 15 22 29 |
| Thur. | 7 14 21 28 | 5 12 19 26 | 2 9 16 23 30 |
| Fri. | 1 8 15 22 29 | 6 13 20 27 | 3 10 17 24 |
| Sat. | 2 9 16 23 30 | 7 14 21 28 | 4 11 18 25 |

| | July | August | September |
|---|---|---|---|
| Sun. | 3 10 17 24 31 | 7 14 21 28 | 4 11 18 25 |
| Mon. | 4 11 18 25 | 1 8 15 22 29 | 5 12 19 26 |
| Tue. | 5 12 19 26 | 2 9 16 23 30 | 6 13 20 27 |
| Wed. | 6 13 20 27 | 3 10 17 24 31 | 7 14 21 28 |
| Thur. | 7 14 21 28 | 4 11 18 25 | 1 8 15 22 29 |
| Fri. | 1 8 15 22 29 | 5 12 19 26 | 2 9 16 23 30 |
| Sat. | 2 9 16 23 30 | 6 13 20 27 | 3 10 17 24 |

| | October | November | December |
|---|---|---|---|
| Sun. | 2 9 16 23 30 | 6 13 20 27 | 4 11 18 25 |
| Mon. | 3 10 17 24 31 | 7 14 21 28 | 5 12 19 26 |
| Tue. | 4 11 18 25 | 1 8 15 22 29 | 6 13 20 27 |
| Wed. | 5 12 19 26 | 2 9 16 23 30 | 7 14 21 28 |
| Thur. | 6 13 20 27 | 3 10 17 24 | 1 8 15 22 29 |
| Fri. | 7 14 21 28 | 4 11 18 25 | 2 9 16 23 30 |
| Sat. | 1 8 15 22 29 | 5 12 19 26 | 3 10 17 24 31 |

EASTER DAYS
| | |
|---|---|
| March 27 | 1785, 1842, 1853, 1910, 1921, 2005 |
| April 3 | 1825, 1831, 1983, 1994 |
| April 10 | 1803, 1814, 1887, 1898, 1955, 1966, 1977, 2039 |
| April 17 | 1870, 1881, 1927, 1938, 1949, 2022, 2033 |
| April 24 | 1791, 1859, 2011 |

## L (LEAP YEAR)

| | January | February | March |
|---|---|---|---|
| Sun. | 3 10 17 24 31 | 7 14 21 28 | 6 13 20 27 |
| Mon. | 4 11 18 25 | 1 8 15 22 | 7 14 21 28 |
| Tue. | 5 12 19 26 | 2 9 16 23 | 1 8 15 22 29 |
| Wed. | 6 13 20 27 | 3 10 17 24 | 2 9 16 23 30 |
| Thur. | 7 14 21 28 | 4 11 18 25 | 3 10 17 24 31 |
| Fri. | 1 8 15 22 29 | 5 12 19 26 | 4 11 18 25 |
| Sat. | 2 9 16 23 30 | 6 13 20 27 | 5 12 19 26 |

| | April | May | June |
|---|---|---|---|
| Sun. | 3 10 17 24 | 1 8 15 22 29 | 5 12 19 26 |
| Mon. | 4 11 18 25 | 2 9 16 23 30 | 6 13 20 27 |
| Tue. | 5 12 19 26 | 3 10 17 24 31 | 7 14 21 28 |
| Wed. | 6 13 20 27 | 4 11 18 25 | 1 8 15 22 29 |
| Thur. | 7 14 21 28 | 5 12 19 26 | 2 9 16 23 30 |
| Fri. | 1 8 15 22 29 | 6 13 20 27 | 3 10 17 24 |
| Sat. | 2 9 16 23 30 | 7 14 21 28 | 4 11 18 25 |

| | July | August | September |
|---|---|---|---|
| Sun. | 3 10 17 24 31 | 7 14 21 28 | 4 11 18 25 |
| Mon. | 4 11 18 25 | 1 8 15 22 29 | 5 12 19 26 |
| Tue. | 5 12 19 26 | 2 9 16 23 30 | 6 13 20 27 |
| Wed. | 6 13 20 27 | 3 10 17 24 31 | 7 14 21 28 |
| Thur. | 7 14 21 28 | 4 11 18 25 | 1 8 15 22 29 |
| Fri. | 1 8 15 22 29 | 5 12 19 26 | 2 9 16 23 30 |
| Sat. | 2 9 16 23 30 | 6 13 20 27 | 3 10 17 24 |

| | October | November | December |
|---|---|---|---|
| Sun. | 2 9 16 23 30 | 6 13 20 27 | 4 11 18 25 |
| Mon. | 3 10 17 24 31 | 7 14 21 28 | 5 12 19 26 |
| Tue. | 4 11 18 25 | 1 8 15 22 | 6 13 20 27 |
| Wed. | 5 12 19 26 | 2 9 16 23 30 | 7 14 21 28 |
| Thur. | 6 13 20 27 | 3 10 17 24 | 1 8 15 22 29 |
| Fri. | 7 14 21 28 | 4 11 18 25 | 2 9 16 23 30 |
| Sat. | 1 8 15 22 29 | 5 12 19 26 | 3 10 17 24 31 |

EASTER DAYS
| | |
|---|---|
| March 27 | 1796, 1864, 1932, 2016 |
| April 3 | 1836, 1904, 1988 |
| April 17 | 1808, 1892, 1960 |

## N (LEAP YEAR)

| | January | February | March |
|---|---|---|---|
| Sun. | 2 9 16 23 30 | 6 13 20 27 | 5 12 19 26 |
| Mon. | 3 10 17 24 31 | 7 14 21 28 | 6 13 20 27 |
| Tue. | 4 11 18 25 | 1 8 15 22 29 | 7 14 21 28 |
| Wed. | 5 12 19 26 | 2 9 16 23 | 1 8 15 22 29 |
| Thur. | 6 13 20 27 | 3 10 17 24 | 2 9 16 23 30 |
| Fri. | 7 14 21 28 | 4 11 18 25 | 3 10 17 24 31 |
| Sat. | 1 8 15 22 29 | 5 12 19 26 | 4 11 18 25 |

| | April | May | June |
|---|---|---|---|
| Sun. | 2 9 16 23 30 | 7 14 21 28 | 4 11 18 25 |
| Mon. | 3 10 17 24 | 1 8 15 22 29 | 5 12 19 26 |
| Tue. | 4 11 18 25 | 2 9 16 23 30 | 6 13 20 27 |
| Wed. | 5 12 19 26 | 3 10 17 24 31 | 7 14 21 28 |
| Thur. | 6 13 20 27 | 4 11 18 25 | 1 8 15 22 29 |
| Fri. | 7 14 21 28 | 5 12 19 26 | 2 9 16 23 30 |
| Sat. | 1 8 15 22 29 | 6 13 20 27 | 3 10 17 24 |

| | July | August | September |
|---|---|---|---|
| Sun. | 2 9 16 23 30 | 6 13 20 27 | 3 10 17 24 |
| Mon. | 3 10 17 24 31 | 7 14 21 28 | 4 11 18 25 |
| Tue. | 4 11 18 25 | 1 8 15 22 29 | 5 12 19 26 |
| Wed. | 5 12 19 26 | 2 9 16 23 30 | 6 13 20 27 |
| Thur. | 6 13 20 27 | 3 10 17 24 31 | 7 14 21 28 |
| Fri. | 7 14 21 28 | 4 11 18 25 | 1 8 15 22 29 |
| Sat. | 1 8 15 22 29 | 5 12 19 26 | 2 9 16 23 30 |

| | October | November | December |
|---|---|---|---|
| Sun. | 1 8 15 22 29 | 5 12 19 26 | 3 10 17 24 31 |
| Mon. | 2 9 16 23 30 | 6 13 20 27 | 4 11 18 25 |
| Tue. | 3 10 17 24 31 | 7 14 21 28 | 5 12 19 26 |
| Wed. | 4 11 18 25 | 1 8 15 22 29 | 6 13 20 27 |
| Thur. | 5 12 19 26 | 2 9 16 23 30 | 7 14 21 28 |
| Fri. | 6 13 20 27 | 3 10 17 24 | 1 8 15 22 29 |
| Sat. | 7 14 21 28 | 4 11 18 25 | 2 9 16 23 30 |

EASTER DAYS
| | |
|---|---|
| March 26 | 1780 |
| April 2 | 1820, 1972 |
| April 9 | 1944 |
| April 16 | 1876, 2028 |
| April 23 | 1848, 1916, 2000 |

# GEOLOGICAL TIME

| Era | Period | Epoch | Dates* | Evolutionary Stages |
|-----|--------|-------|--------|---------------------|
| Cenozoic | Quaternary | Holocene | 11,700 BP†–present | |
| | | Pleistocene | 2,588,000–11,700 BP | First humans |
| | Neogene | Pliocene | 5.332–2.588 Mya ‡ | } Majority of still existing species |
| | | Miocene | 23.03–5.332 Mya | |
| | Palaeogene | Oligocene | 33.9–23.03 Mya | |
| | | Eocene | 55.8–33.9 Mya | } First modern mammals |
| | | Palaeocene | 65.5–55.8 Mya | |
| Mesozoic | Cretaceous | | 145.5–65.5 Mya | |
| | Jurassic | | 199.6–145.5 Mya | First birds |
| | Triassic | | 251–199.6 Mya | First mammals |
| Palaeozoic | Permian | | 299–251 Mya | First reptiles |
| | Carboniferous | | 359.2–299 Mya | } First traces of land-living creatures |
| | Devonian | | 416–359.2 Mya | |
| | Silurian | | 443.7–416 Mya | |
| | Ordovician | | 488.3–443.7 Mya | First fish |
| | Cambrian | | 542–488.3 Mya | First invertebrates |
| Precambrian | Proterozoic | | 2,500–542 Mya | First primitive life forms, eg algae and bacteria |
| | Archaean | | 3,800–2,500 Mya | } Earth uninhabited |
| | Hadean | | 4,600–3,800 Mya | |

* approximate  † BP = Before Present  ‡ Mya = million years ago

## PALAEOZOIC ('ANCIENT LIFE')

*Cambrian* – Mainly sandstones, slate and shales; limestones in Scotland. Shelled fossils and invertebrates, eg trilobites and brachiopods, and the earliest known vertebrates (jawless fish) appear

*Ordovician* – Mainly shales and mudstones, eg in north Wales; limestones in Scotland. First fish

*Silurian* – Shales, mudstones and some limestones, found mostly in Wales and southern Scotland

*Devonian* – Old red sandstone, shale, limestone and slate, eg in south Wales and the West Country

*Carboniferous* – Coal-bearing rocks, millstone grit, limestone and shale. First traces of land-living creatures

*Permian* – Marls, sandstones and clays. First reptile fossils

There were two great phases of mountain building in the Palaeozoic era: the Caledonian, characterised in Britain by NE–SW lines of hills and valleys; and the later Hercynian, widespread in west Germany and adjacent areas, and in Britain exemplified in E–W lines of hills and valleys.

The end of the Palaeozoic era was marked by the extensive glaciations of the Permian period in the southern continents and the decline of amphibians. It was succeeded by an era of warm conditions.

## MESOZOIC ('MIDDLE FORMS OF LIFE')

*Triassic* – Mostly sandstone, eg in the W. Midlands; primitive mammals appear

*Jurassic* – Mainly limestones and clays, typically displayed in the Jura mountains, and in England in a NE–SW belt from Lincolnshire and the Wash to the Severn and the Dorset coast

*Cretaceous* – Mainly chalk, clay and sands, eg in Kent and Sussex

Giant reptiles were dominant during the Mesozoic era; marsupial mammals first appeared, as well as *Archaeopteryx lithographica,* the earliest known species of bird. Coniferous trees and flowering plants also developed during the era and, with the birds and the mammals, were the main species to survive into the Cenozoic era. The giant reptiles became extinct.

## CENOZOIC ('RECENT LIFE')

*Palaeocene* } The emergence of new forms of life, including
*Eocene* } existing species; primates appear

*Oligocene* – Fossils of a few still existing species

*Miocene* – Fossil remains show a balance of existing and extinct species

*Pliocene* } Fossil remains show a majority of still existing
*Pleistocene* } species

*Holocene* – The present, post-glacial period. Existing species only, except for a few exterminated by humans

In the last 25 million years, from the Miocene through the Pliocene periods, the Alpine-Himalayan and the circum-Pacific phases of mountain building reached their climax. During the Pleistocene period ice-sheets locked up masses of water as land ice, lowering the sea level by 100–200m. The glaciations and interglacials of the Ice Age are difficult to date and classify, but recent scientific opinion considers the Pleistocene period to have begun c.1.64 Mya. The last glacial retreat, merging into the Holocene period, was c.10,000 years ago.

# HUMAN DEVELOPMENT

All members of the human race belong to one species of animal, *Homo sapiens*, the definition of a species being in biological terms that all its members can interbreed. As a species of mammal it is possible to group humans with other similar types, known as the primates. Amongst these is found a sub-group, the apes, which includes, in addition to humans, the chimpanzees, gorillas, orangutans and gibbons. All lack a tail, have shoulder blades at the back, and a Y-shaped chewing pattern on the surface of their molars, as well as showing the more general primate characteristics of four incisors, a thumb which is able to touch the fingers of the same hand, and finger and toe nails instead of claws. However, there once lived creatures, now extinct, which were closer to modern man than the chimpanzees and gorillas, and which shared with modern man the characteristics of having flat faces (ie the absence of a pronounced muzzle), being bipedal, and possessing large brains.

The debate surrounding evidence for the oldest human ancestors is ongoing. The earliest putative hominin for which there is significant fossil evidence is *Ardipithecus ramidus*, for which an almost complete skeleton, dating to at least 4.4 million years ago (Mya), was discovered in the Afar Rift, Ethiopia in 1992. Analysis of the *Ardipithecus ramidus* skeleton suggests the creature had characteristics of both humans and apes; able to climb trees and walk on two feet.

The subsequent Australopithecines have left more numerous remains in south and east Africa, among which sub-groups may be detected. Living between 4.2 and 1.5 Mya, they were relatives of modern humans in the respect that they walked upright, did not have an extensive muzzle and had similar types of pre-molars. The first australopithecine remains were recognised at Taung in South Africa in 1924 and named *Australopithecus africanus*, dating between 3.3 and 2.3 Mya. The most impressive discovery was made at Hadar, Ethiopia, in 1974 when about half a skeleton of *Australopithecus afarensis*, known as 'Lucy', was found. Some 3.2 Mya, 'Lucy' (who is now considered to be male) certainly walked upright.

Also in east Africa, especially at Olduvai Gorge in Tanzania, between 2.5 and 1.8 Mya, lived a hominid group which not only walked upright, had a flat face, and a large brain case, but also made simple pebble and flake stone tools. Due to their distinctive characteristics, they have been grouped as a separate sub-species, now extinct, of the genus *Homo* and are known as *Homo habilis* or 'handy man'.

The use of fire, again a human characteristic, is associated with another group of extinct hominids whose remains, about a million years old, are found in south and east Africa, China, Indonesia, north Africa and Europe. The ability to make fire probably helped the colonisation of the colder northern areas and in this respect the site of Vertesszollos in Hungary is of particular importance. *Homo ergaster* in Africa and *Homo erectus* in Asia are the names given to this group of fossils and they relate to a number of famous individual discoveries, eg Solo Man, Heidelberg Man, and especially Peking Man who lived at the cave site at Choukoutien which has yielded evidence of fire and burnt bone.

The well-known group the Neanderthals, or *Homo neanderthalensis*, is an extinct form of human that lived between c.350,000 and c.24,000 years ago, spanning the last Ice Age and living alongside modern humans. The Neanderthals' ability to adapt to the cold climate on the edge of the ice-sheets is one of their characteristic features, with remains being found only in Europe, Asia and the Middle East. Complete Neanderthal skeletons were found during excavations at Tabun in Israel, together with evidence of tool-making and the use of fire. Distinguished by very large brains, it seems that Neanderthals were the first to develop recognisable social customs, especially deliberate burial rites. Why the Neanderthals became extinct is not clear but it may be connected with the climatic changes at the end of the Ice Ages, which would have seriously affected their food supplies; possibly they became too specialised for their own good.

The shin bone of Boxgrove Man found in 1993 – *Homo heidelbergensis* – and the Swanscombe skull are the best known early human fossil remains found in England. Some specialists prefer to group Swanscombe Man (or, more probably, woman) together with the Steinheim skull from Germany, seeing both as a separate sub-species. There is too little evidence as yet on which to form a final judgement.

Anatomically modern humans – *Homo sapiens sapiens* ('doubly wise man') – had evolved to our present physical condition and had colonised much of the world by about 40,000 years ago. There are many previously distinguished individual specimens, eg Cromagnon Man, the first early *Homo sapiens sapiens* of the European Upper Palaeolithic.

The discovery of the structure of DNA in 1953 has come to have a profound effect upon the study of human evolution. For example, it was claimed in 1987 that a common ancestor of all human beings was a person who lived in Africa some 200,000 years ago, thus encouraging the 'out of Africa' theory of hominid migration from east Africa to the Middle East and then throughout the world.

## CULTURAL DEVELOPMENT

The Three Age system, whereby prehistory was divided into a Stone Age, a Bronze Age and an Iron Age, was devised by Christian Thomsen, curator of the National Museum of Denmark in the early 19th century, to facilitate the classification of the museum's collections. The adjectives referred to the materials from which the implements and weapons were made and came to be regarded as the dominant features of the societies to which they related. The Three Age system remains a generally accepted concept in the popular mind. However, it is now seen by archaeologists as an inadequate model for human development. Common sense suggests that there were no complete breaks between one so-called Age and another. Nor can the Three Age system be applied universally. In some areas it is necessary to insert a Copper Age, while in South Africa there would seem to be no Bronze Age at all; in Australia, Old Stone Age societies survived, while in South America, New Stone Age communities exist into modern times.

The concept of the 'Neolithic revolution', associated with the domestication of plants and animals, was a development of particular importance in the human cultural pattern. It reflected a gradual change from the hunter-gatherer economies to a more settled agricultural way of life and therefore, so the argument goes, made possible the development of urban civilisation. Though it appears that the cultivation of wheat and barley was first undertaken, together with the domestication of cattle and goats/sheep, around 10,000 years ago in the Fertile Crescent (the area bounded by the rivers Tigris and Euphrates), there is evidence that sorghum was first domesticated in Africa, rice was first deliberately planted and pigs domesticated in South East Asia, maize first cultivated in Central America and llamas first domesticated in South America. Cultural change took place independently in different parts of the world at different rates and different times.

The Neolithic period of cultural development has been difficult to date reliably because it took place long before writing was invented. With the development and refinement of radio-carbon dating and other scientific methods of producing absolute chronologies, it may eventually be possible to obtain a reliable chronological framework, in terms of years, against which the cultural development of any particular area may be set.

# TIDES AND TIDAL PREDICTIONS

Tides are the periodic rise and fall of the sea-level caused mainly by the gravitational pull of the Moon and the Sun. This generates the tide raising force (TRF), of which the Moon accounts for approximately 70 per cent and the Sun 30 per cent. There is an 18-year interval between alignments generating the maximum TRF. Routinely when the Moon and the Sun are in line with the Earth they are said to be 'in conjunction' (or syzygy) and their TRFs combine. This produces the largest rise and fall of the tide, known as spring tides; they occur each month just after a full or new Moon. This is amplified when the Moon is at perigee, its closest point to the Earth. When coincident with spring tides (about once every 18 months) this gives rise to very high proxigean tides. The opposite effect, just after the Moon's first and last quarters, when the Sun and Moon are at an angle of 90°, produces neap tides, with a relatively small tidal range between high and low water.

A lunar day is about 24 hours and 50 minutes, giving two complete tidal cycles, with about 12 hours and 25 minutes between successive high waters. These are known as semi-diurnal tides and are applicable in the Atlantic Ocean and around the coasts of north-west Europe. Other parts of the world have diurnal tides, with only one high water and one low water each (lunar) day, or mixed tides which are partly diurnal and partly semi-diurnal.

Land and seabed conditions influence the tides locally. On the south coast of England, for example, double high waters occur between Swanage and Selsey Bill, and low water is much more sharply defined than high water. Tides can also be greatly affected by the Coriolis force, which is induced by the Earth's rotation and, in the northern hemisphere, tends to deflect any moving object to the right. Thus the easterly flood tidal stream in the English Channel is deflected towards the French coast causing higher high waters; on the ebb the opposite happens causing lower low waters. This, coupled with local geography, means that the mean spring range of the tide at St Malo is nearly 11m while the range on the English coast at Portland, 120 miles to the north, is a mere 2m.

Meteorological conditions also affect the tides. Prolonged strong winds and unusually high (or low) atmospheric pressure can significantly lower (or raise) the height of the tide; the drag of the wind alone (wind stress) can affect the predicted times of high and low water by as much as an hour. Variation of pressure by 34 millibars from the norm can cause a height difference of 0.3m.

## STORM SURGES AND SEICHES

On the east and west coasts of the UK there are about 20 events each year when surge levels exceed 0.6m. The semi-centennial surge is 1m in the Hebrides and at Land's End but up to 3m in the Thames estuary. Infrequently, surge peaks coincide with high water. The North Sea and the Thames estuary experience the most profound effects, often when a deep depression tracks south–easterly across the UK. Negative surges occur when strong southerly winds in the North Sea may lower tidal levels by 2m below prediction in these areas and the Dover Strait. Intense minor depressions, line squalls, or other abrupt changes in the weather can cause wave oscillations known as seiches. The wave period of a seiche can vary from a few hours to about 2 hours, with heights of up to a metre. Wick on the north-east coast of Scotland and Fishguard in south-west Wales are particularly prone to seiches.

## TIDAL STREAMS

Tidal streams are the horizontal movements of water caused by the rise and fall of the tide. They normally change direction about every 6 hours. Tidal streams should not be confused with ocean currents, such as the Gulf Stream, which run indefinitely in the same direction. The rate, or set, of the stream at any particular place is proportional to the range of the tide. Thus, the rate during spring tides is greater than that at neaps. In the central English Channel the maximum spring rate is nearly 5 knots while the neap rate at the same position is just 3 knots. As with tidal heights, local geography plays a significant role in the rate of the tidal stream. In the narrow waters of the Pentland Firth between mainland Scotland and the Orkney Islands, rates of 16 knots have been recorded.

The tidal stream does not necessarily turn at the same time as high or low water. In the English Channel the stream turns at approximately high and low water at Dover. However, high water at Dover is at about the same time as low water at Plymouth, and vice versa.

Around the UK, the main flood tidal stream sets eastward up the English Channel, north-east into the Bristol Channel, and north up the west coasts of Ireland and Scotland. However, the flood sets south-east through the North Channel and south into the Irish Sea, where it meets the northerly flood through St George's Channel at the Isle of Man. Off the east coasts of Scotland and England the stream sets south as far as the Thames estuary before meeting the north-going stream from the eastern part of the Dover Strait.

## DEFINITIONS

**Highest Astronomical Tide (HAT)** and **Lowest Astronomical Tide (LAT)** are the highest and lowest tide levels predicted to occur under average meteorological, and any combination of astronomical, conditions. For a given area, **Chart Datum (CD)** is the level, as close as possible to LAT, below which charted depths are given. It is also the reference for tidal predictions: the total depth at a given time being equal to the charted depth plus the height of the tide. **Ordnance Datum (OD)** at Newlyn is the datum level of land survey on mainland England, Scotland and Wales, from which heights on UK land maps are measured. CD depends on the tidal range and varies around the UK from about 5m above OD to about 6.5m below. The differences are noted in tide tables, allowing comparison of the tide levels along the coast and reference to Ordnance Survey data. **Duration** of the tide is the interval between low water and the next high water. It can be used to calculate the approximate time of low water when only the time of high water is known. **Mean Sea Level (MSL or ML)** is the average level of the sea's surface over a long period, normally observed over 18.6 years. The **Range** of the tide is the difference in height between successive high and low waters. It is greatest at spring tides, least at neaps. The range may be indicated by **Tidal Coefficients** which are proportional to, but not the same as, the range on a particular day. A coefficient of 95 indicates an average spring tide, while 45 is an average neap tide.

## PREDICTIONS

The data which follows gives the daily predictions of the time (Greenwich Mean Time) and height of high water at four ports. For the months when British Summer Time is in operation the hour's time difference should be added. The datum of predictions is the difference of height, in metres, of CD from Ordnance datum (Newlyn).

Tidal predictions for London Bridge, Liverpool, Greenock and Leith © Crown Copyright and/or database rights. Reproduced by permission of the Controller of Her Majesty's Stationery Office and the UK Hydrographic Office (W www.ukho.gov.uk). The section was compiled with the assistance of Chris Stevens and Perrin Towler.

## JANUARY 2016   *High Water*   GMT

| | | LONDON BRIDGE Datum of Predictions 3.20m below | | | | LIVERPOOL (Gladstone Dock) Datum of Predictions 4.93m below | | | | GREENOCK Datum of Predictions 1.62m below | | | | LEITH Datum of Predictions 2.90m below | | | |
|---|---|---|---|---|---|---|---|---|---|---|---|---|---|---|---|---|---|
| | | hr | ht m | hr | ht m | hr | ht m | hr | ht m | hr | ht m | hr | ht m | hr | ht m | hr | ht m |
| F | 1 | 05 47 | 6.3 | 18 16 | 6.2 | 03 14 | 8.0 | 15 34 | 8.1 | 04 51 | 3.1 | 16 45 | 3.4 | 07 08 | 4.7 | 19 30 | 4.8 |
| SA | 2 | 06 24 | 6.0 | 19 00 | 6.0 | 04 04 | 7.6 | 16 29 | 7.7 | 05 38 | 3.0 | 17 30 | 3.3 | 07 57 | 4.6 | 20 23 | 4.6 |
| SU | 3 | 07 12 | 5.8 | 19 58 | 5.8 | 05 04 | 7.3 | 17 34 | 7.4 | 06 30 | 2.9 | 18 22 | 3.1 | 08 50 | 4.4 | 21 21 | 4.5 |
| M | 4 | 08 29 | 5.6 | 21 08 | 5.8 | 06 12 | 7.3 | 18 43 | 7.4 | 07 32 | 2.9 | 19 22 | 3.0 | 09 48 | 4.4 | 22 22 | 4.4 |
| TU | 5 | 09 46 | 5.7 | 22 14 | 5.9 | 07 20 | 7.4 | 19 48 | 7.6 | 08 42 | 3.0 | 20 31 | 3.0 | 10 49 | 4.5 | 23 25 | 4.6 |
| W | 6 | 10 49 | 6.0 | 23 16 | 6.2 | 08 19 | 7.8 | 20 44 | 7.9 | 09 48 | 3.1 | 21 39 | 3.1 | 11 50 | 4.7 | — | — |
| TH | 7 | 11 46 | 6.3 | — | — | 09 08 | 8.2 | 21 31 | 8.3 | 10 41 | 3.3 | 22 36 | 3.2 | 00 24 | 4.7 | 12 45 | 4.9 |
| F | 8 | 00 11 | 6.5 | 12 36 | 6.6 | 09 51 | 8.6 | 22 12 | 8.6 | 11 25 | 3.4 | 23 24 | 3.3 | 01 15 | 5.0 | 13 31 | 5.2 |
| SA | 9 | 01 00 | 6.7 | 13 21 | 6.8 | 10 31 | 9.0 | 22 52 | 8.9 | 12 04 | 3.5 | — | — | 01 58 | 5.2 | 14 12 | 5.4 |
| SU | 10 | 01 45 | 6.8 | 14 04 | 7.0 | 11 10 | 9.3 | 23 32 | 9.1 | 00 08 | 3.4 | 12 40 | 3.6 | 02 38 | 5.4 | 14 50 | 5.5 |
| M | 11 | 02 27 | 6.9 | 14 46 | 7.2 | 11 49 | 9.5 | — | — | 00 52 | 3.4 | 13 16 | 3.7 | 03 17 | 5.5 | 15 28 | 5.6 |
| TU | 12 | 03 08 | 7.0 | 15 28 | 7.3 | 00 12 | 9.3 | 12 31 | 9.6 | 01 35 | 3.5 | 13 54 | 3.8 | 03 56 | 5.6 | 16 06 | 5.7 |
| W | 13 | 03 48 | 7.0 | 16 10 | 7.3 | 00 55 | 9.3 | 13 14 | 9.6 | 02 18 | 3.5 | 14 34 | 3.8 | 04 37 | 5.6 | 16 47 | 5.7 |
| TH | 14 | 04 27 | 7.0 | 16 52 | 7.1 | 01 38 | 9.2 | 13 58 | 9.5 | 03 01 | 3.5 | 15 17 | 3.8 | 05 20 | 5.6 | 17 31 | 5.6 |
| F | 15 | 05 08 | 6.9 | 17 37 | 6.9 | 02 24 | 9.0 | 14 46 | 9.2 | 03 44 | 3.5 | 16 01 | 3.7 | 06 07 | 5.4 | 18 18 | 5.5 |
| SA | 16 | 05 51 | 6.8 | 18 26 | 6.7 | 03 14 | 8.7 | 15 39 | 8.9 | 04 29 | 3.4 | 16 48 | 3.6 | 06 58 | 5.2 | 19 12 | 5.3 |
| SU | 17 | 06 41 | 6.6 | 19 24 | 6.5 | 04 11 | 8.3 | 16 40 | 8.5 | 05 16 | 3.3 | 17 42 | 3.4 | 07 58 | 5.0 | 20 17 | 5.0 |
| M | 18 | 07 43 | 6.4 | 20 32 | 6.3 | 05 18 | 8.0 | 17 51 | 8.3 | 06 11 | 3.2 | 18 50 | 3.2 | 09 07 | 4.8 | 21 33 | 4.9 |
| TU | 19 | 08 59 | 6.3 | 21 42 | 6.3 | 06 34 | 7.9 | 19 06 | 8.2 | 07 24 | 3.0 | 20 19 | 3.1 | 10 18 | 4.8 | 22 47 | 4.9 |
| W | 20 | 10 13 | 6.3 | 22 55 | 6.3 | 07 48 | 8.1 | 20 18 | 8.4 | 08 57 | 3.1 | 21 44 | 3.1 | 11 27 | 4.9 | 23 56 | 5.0 |
| TH | 21 | 11 25 | 6.5 | — | — | 08 53 | 8.5 | 21 20 | 8.6 | 10 09 | 3.2 | 22 49 | 3.3 | 12 29 | 5.1 | — | — |
| F | 22 | 00 05 | 6.5 | 12 29 | 6.7 | 09 48 | 8.8 | 22 13 | 8.9 | 11 05 | 3.4 | 23 43 | 3.4 | 00 57 | 5.2 | 13 24 | 5.3 |
| SA | 23 | 01 02 | 6.7 | 13 23 | 6.9 | 10 36 | 9.1 | 22 59 | 9.1 | 11 52 | 3.5 | — | — | 01 49 | 5.3 | 14 11 | 5.5 |
| SU | 24 | 01 50 | 6.8 | 14 09 | 7.0 | 11 18 | 9.3 | 23 40 | 9.2 | 00 32 | 3.4 | 12 35 | 3.6 | 02 35 | 5.4 | 14 54 | 5.6 |
| M | 25 | 02 33 | 6.9 | 14 51 | 7.1 | 11 56 | 9.4 | — | — | 01 16 | 3.4 | 13 14 | 3.7 | 03 16 | 5.5 | 15 35 | 5.6 |
| TU | 26 | 03 11 | 7.0 | 15 29 | 7.1 | 00 17 | 9.2 | 12 33 | 9.4 | 01 55 | 3.3 | 13 51 | 3.7 | 03 56 | 5.5 | 16 14 | 5.5 |
| W | 27 | 03 45 | 6.9 | 16 04 | 7.0 | 00 52 | 9.1 | 13 06 | 9.2 | 02 31 | 3.3 | 14 26 | 3.7 | 04 34 | 5.4 | 16 51 | 5.4 |
| TH | 28 | 04 17 | 6.9 | 16 36 | 6.8 | 01 25 | 8.9 | 13 39 | 9.0 | 03 04 | 3.3 | 15 01 | 3.7 | 05 10 | 5.2 | 17 27 | 5.3 |
| F | 29 | 04 47 | 6.7 | 17 07 | 6.6 | 01 59 | 8.6 | 14 13 | 8.7 | 03 40 | 3.3 | 15 37 | 3.6 | 05 47 | 5.0 | 18 04 | 5.1 |
| SA | 30 | 05 17 | 6.5 | 17 38 | 6.4 | 02 35 | 8.3 | 14 50 | 8.3 | 04 17 | 3.2 | 16 14 | 3.5 | 06 25 | 4.9 | 18 44 | 4.9 |
| SU | 31 | 05 49 | 6.3 | 18 13 | 6.2 | 03 14 | 7.9 | 15 32 | 7.9 | 04 57 | 3.1 | 16 54 | 3.3 | 07 08 | 4.7 | 19 29 | 4.6 |

## FEBRUARY 2016   *High Water*   GMT

| | | LONDON BRIDGE | | | | LIVERPOOL (Gladstone Dock) | | | | GREENOCK | | | | LEITH | | | |
|---|---|---|---|---|---|---|---|---|---|---|---|---|---|---|---|---|---|
| M | 1 | 06 26 | 6.1 | 18 54 | 6.0 | 04 02 | 7.5 | 16 24 | 7.5 | 05 40 | 3.0 | 17 39 | 3.1 | 07 56 | 4.5 | 20 24 | 4.4 |
| TU | 2 | 07 13 | 5.8 | 19 50 | 5.7 | 05 03 | 7.2 | 17 34 | 7.2 | 06 31 | 2.9 | 18 33 | 3.0 | 08 53 | 4.4 | 21 27 | 4.3 |
| W | 3 | 08 21 | 5.6 | 21 15 | 5.7 | 06 18 | 7.2 | 18 54 | 7.2 | 07 36 | 2.8 | 19 37 | 2.9 | 09 57 | 4.4 | 22 36 | 4.4 |
| TH | 4 | 09 57 | 5.7 | 22 31 | 5.9 | 07 32 | 7.4 | 20 06 | 7.5 | 08 58 | 2.9 | 20 53 | 2.9 | 11 04 | 4.5 | 23 45 | 4.5 |
| F | 5 | 11 07 | 6.1 | 23 38 | 6.3 | 08 34 | 7.9 | 21 03 | 8.0 | 10 08 | 3.0 | 22 07 | 3.0 | 12 10 | 4.7 | — | — |
| SA | 6 | 12 06 | 6.5 | — | — | 09 24 | 8.4 | 21 51 | 8.5 | 10 59 | 3.2 | 23 05 | 3.1 | 00 46 | 4.8 | 13 05 | 5.0 |
| SU | 7 | 00 35 | 6.6 | 12 58 | 6.8 | 10 09 | 8.9 | 22 34 | 8.9 | 11 41 | 3.4 | 23 53 | 3.3 | 01 35 | 5.1 | 13 50 | 5.3 |
| M | 8 | 01 25 | 6.9 | 13 46 | 7.1 | 10 51 | 9.4 | 23 15 | 9.3 | 12 20 | 3.5 | — | — | 02 18 | 5.4 | 14 30 | 5.6 |
| TU | 9 | 02 10 | 7.0 | 14 30 | 7.3 | 11 32 | 9.7 | 23 57 | 9.6 | 00 37 | 3.3 | 13 00 | 3.6 | 02 57 | 5.6 | 15 09 | 5.8 |
| W | 10 | 02 53 | 7.2 | 15 14 | 7.4 | 12 14 | 9.9 | — | — | 01 23 | 3.3 | 13 40 | 3.7 | 03 37 | 5.8 | 15 48 | 5.9 |
| TH | 11 | 03 34 | 7.3 | 15 56 | 7.4 | 00 39 | 9.7 | 12 58 | 10.0 | 02 04 | 3.5 | 14 22 | 3.8 | 04 18 | 5.8 | 16 29 | 5.9 |
| F | 12 | 04 14 | 7.3 | 16 38 | 7.3 | 01 22 | 9.6 | 13 41 | 9.9 | 02 45 | 3.5 | 15 04 | 3.8 | 05 01 | 5.7 | 17 13 | 5.9 |
| SA | 13 | 04 54 | 7.2 | 17 21 | 7.0 | 02 06 | 9.3 | 14 27 | 9.5 | 03 27 | 3.5 | 15 47 | 3.7 | 05 46 | 5.6 | 18 00 | 5.7 |
| SU | 14 | 05 35 | 7.0 | 18 06 | 6.7 | 02 52 | 8.9 | 15 16 | 9.1 | 04 08 | 3.5 | 16 32 | 3.6 | 06 35 | 5.3 | 18 52 | 5.4 |
| M | 15 | 06 22 | 6.8 | 18 58 | 6.4 | 03 45 | 8.5 | 16 14 | 8.5 | 04 51 | 3.3 | 17 21 | 3.4 | 07 32 | 5.0 | 19 56 | 5.0 |
| TU | 16 | 07 19 | 6.5 | 20 02 | 6.2 | 04 49 | 8.0 | 17 26 | 8.0 | 05 39 | 3.2 | 18 19 | 3.1 | 08 40 | 4.7 | 21 13 | 4.8 |
| W | 17 | 08 31 | 6.3 | 21 15 | 6.0 | 06 08 | 7.7 | 18 47 | 7.8 | 06 38 | 3.0 | 19 55 | 2.9 | 09 55 | 4.6 | 22 31 | 4.7 |
| TH | 18 | 09 50 | 6.2 | 22 35 | 6.1 | 07 30 | 7.8 | 20 07 | 7.9 | 08 25 | 2.9 | 21 40 | 2.9 | 11 10 | 4.7 | 23 48 | 4.8 |
| F | 19 | 11 10 | 6.3 | 23 51 | 6.3 | 08 41 | 8.2 | 21 12 | 8.3 | 09 54 | 3.0 | 22 44 | 3.1 | 12 20 | 4.9 | — | — |
| SA | 20 | 12 18 | 6.6 | — | — | 09 37 | 8.6 | 22 04 | 8.6 | 10 51 | 3.2 | 23 35 | 3.2 | 00 53 | 5.0 | 13 16 | 5.1 |
| SU | 21 | 00 49 | 6.6 | 13 12 | 6.8 | 10 23 | 8.9 | 22 46 | 8.9 | 11 38 | 3.4 | — | — | 01 43 | 5.2 | 14 01 | 5.3 |
| M | 22 | 01 36 | 6.8 | 13 56 | 7.0 | 11 02 | 9.2 | 23 23 | 9.1 | 00 20 | 3.3 | 12 21 | 3.5 | 02 24 | 5.3 | 14 41 | 5.5 |
| TU | 23 | 02 16 | 6.9 | 14 35 | 7.1 | 11 37 | 9.3 | 23 56 | 9.1 | 01 00 | 3.3 | 12 58 | 3.6 | 03 00 | 5.4 | 15 17 | 5.5 |
| W | 24 | 02 51 | 7.0 | 15 09 | 7.0 | 12 10 | 9.3 | — | — | 01 36 | 3.3 | 13 32 | 3.6 | 03 34 | 5.4 | 15 52 | 5.4 |
| TH | 25 | 03 23 | 7.0 | 15 39 | 7.0 | 00 27 | 9.1 | 12 41 | 9.2 | 02 07 | 3.3 | 14 04 | 3.6 | 04 07 | 5.3 | 16 25 | 5.4 |
| F | 26 | 03 52 | 7.0 | 16 07 | 6.9 | 00 58 | 9.0 | 13 12 | 9.1 | 02 37 | 3.3 | 14 36 | 3.6 | 04 40 | 5.2 | 16 58 | 5.3 |
| SA | 27 | 04 20 | 6.9 | 16 35 | 6.8 | 01 28 | 8.8 | 13 42 | 8.8 | 03 09 | 3.3 | 15 10 | 3.5 | 05 13 | 5.1 | 17 31 | 5.2 |
| SU | 28 | 04 50 | 6.8 | 17 05 | 6.6 | 02 00 | 8.6 | 14 13 | 8.5 | 03 43 | 3.3 | 15 45 | 3.5 | 05 49 | 5.0 | 18 07 | 5.0 |
| M | 29 | 05 20 | 6.6 | 17 38 | 6.4 | 02 34 | 8.2 | 14 48 | 8.1 | 04 18 | 3.2 | 16 23 | 3.3 | 06 27 | 4.8 | 18 48 | 4.7 |

## MARCH 2016   *High Water*   GMT

|  | | LONDON BRIDGE<br>Datum of Predictions<br>3.20m below | | | | | LIVERPOOL<br>(Gladstone Dock)<br>Datum of Predictions<br>4.93m below | | | | | GREENOCK<br>Datum of Predictions<br>1.62m below | | | | | LEITH<br>Datum of Predictions<br>2.90m below | | | | |
|---|---|---|---|---|---|---|---|---|---|---|---|---|---|---|---|---|---|---|---|---|---|
|  |  | hr | m | ht | hr | m | hr | m | ht | hr | m | hr | m | ht | hr | m | hr | m | ht | hr | m |
| TU | 1 | 05 | 55 | 6.3 | 18 | 15 | 6.1 | 03 | 13 | 7.8 | 15 | 30 | 7.6 | 04 | 56 | 3.1 | 17 | 05 | 3.1 | 07 | 10 | 4.6 | 19 | 36 | 4.5 |
| W | 2 | 06 | 37 | 6.1 | 19 | 02 | 5.9 | 04 | 04 | 7.4 | 16 | 30 | 7.2 | 05 | 39 | 2.9 | 17 | 55 | 2.9 | 08 | 03 | 4.4 | 20 | 37 | 4.3 |
| TH | 3 | 07 | 31 | 5.8 | 20 | 09 | 5.7 | 05 | 17 | 7.1 | 17 | 56 | 7.0 | 06 | 37 | 2.7 | 18 | 56 | 2.8 | 09 | 08 | 4.3 | 21 | 51 | 4.3 |
| F | 4 | 08 | 56 | 5.7 | 21 | 45 | 5.7 | 06 | 42 | 7.2 | 19 | 24 | 7.3 | 07 | 56 | 2.7 | 20 | 12 | 2.8 | 10 | 21 | 4.3 | 23 | 06 | 4.4 |
| SA | 5 | 10 | 26 | 6.0 | 23 | 03 | 6.1 | 07 | 56 | 7.7 | 20 | 32 | 7.8 | 09 | 27 | 2.8 | 21 | 40 | 2.9 | 11 | 34 | 4.6 | — | — | |
| SU | 6 | 11 | 35 | 6.5 | — | — | | 08 | 54 | 8.3 | 21 | 25 | 8.4 | 10 | 28 | 3.1 | 22 | 45 | 3.1 | 00 | 15 | 4.7 | 12 | 36 | 4.9 |
| M | 7 | 00 | 06 | 6.6 | 12 | 33 | 6.9 | 09 | 43 | 8.9 | 22 | 11 | 9.0 | 11 | 15 | 3.3 | 23 | 34 | 3.2 | 01 | 09 | 5.1 | 13 | 24 | 5.3 |
| TU | 8 | 01 | 00 | 6.9 | 13 | 23 | 7.2 | 10 | 28 | 9.5 | 22 | 54 | 9.5 | 11 | 57 | 3.5 | — | — | | 01 | 53 | 5.5 | 14 | 06 | 5.6 |
| W | 9 | 01 | 47 | 7.2 | 14 | 10 | 7.4 | 11 | 11 | 9.9 | 23 | 37 | 9.8 | 00 | 19 | 3.3 | 12 | 41 | 3.6 | 02 | 34 | 5.7 | 14 | 46 | 5.9 |
| TH | 10 | 02 | 31 | 7.4 | 14 | 54 | 7.5 | 11 | 54 | 10.1 | — | — | | 01 | 03 | 3.4 | 13 | 24 | 3.7 | 03 | 15 | 5.9 | 15 | 27 | 6.1 |
| F | 11 | 03 | 13 | 7.5 | 15 | 37 | 7.5 | 00 | 19 | 9.9 | 12 | 38 | 10.2 | 01 | 45 | 3.5 | 14 | 07 | 3.8 | 03 | 56 | 5.9 | 16 | 10 | 6.1 |
| SA | 12 | 03 | 55 | 7.5 | 16 | 19 | 7.4 | 01 | 02 | 9.8 | 13 | 22 | 10.0 | 02 | 26 | 3.5 | 14 | 50 | 3.8 | 04 | 40 | 5.8 | 16 | 55 | 6.0 |
| SU | 13 | 04 | 35 | 7.5 | 17 | 01 | 7.1 | 01 | 45 | 9.5 | 14 | 07 | 9.6 | 03 | 06 | 3.6 | 15 | 33 | 3.7 | 05 | 25 | 5.6 | 17 | 44 | 5.7 |
| M | 14 | 05 | 18 | 7.2 | 17 | 45 | 6.7 | 02 | 31 | 9.1 | 14 | 56 | 9.1 | 03 | 46 | 3.5 | 16 | 17 | 3.5 | 06 | 14 | 5.3 | 18 | 37 | 5.4 |
| TU | 15 | 06 | 04 | 6.9 | 18 | 34 | 6.4 | 03 | 21 | 8.5 | 15 | 53 | 8.4 | 04 | 27 | 3.4 | 17 | 04 | 3.3 | 07 | 09 | 5.0 | 19 | 41 | 5.0 |
| W | 16 | 06 | 58 | 6.6 | 19 | 33 | 6.1 | 04 | 24 | 8.0 | 17 | 05 | 7.8 | 05 | 13 | 3.2 | 18 | 00 | 2.9 | 08 | 17 | 4.7 | 20 | 56 | 4.7 |
| TH | 17 | 08 | 08 | 6.3 | 20 | 48 | 5.9 | 05 | 44 | 7.6 | 18 | 30 | 7.5 | 06 | 07 | 2.9 | 19 | 41 | 2.7 | 09 | 33 | 4.5 | 22 | 14 | 4.6 |
| F | 18 | 09 | 27 | 6.1 | 22 | 11 | 5.9 | 07 | 09 | 7.6 | 19 | 52 | 7.7 | 07 | 47 | 2.8 | 21 | 30 | 2.8 | 10 | 50 | 4.6 | 23 | 34 | 4.7 |
| SA | 19 | 10 | 50 | 6.3 | 23 | 29 | 6.2 | 08 | 22 | 8.0 | 20 | 57 | 8.1 | 09 | 32 | 2.9 | 22 | 29 | 3.0 | 12 | 02 | 4.8 | — | — | |
| SU | 20 | 11 | 59 | 6.6 | — | — | | 09 | 18 | 8.4 | 21 | 46 | 8.5 | 10 | 30 | 3.1 | 23 | 16 | 3.1 | 00 | 40 | 4.9 | 13 | 00 | 5.0 |
| M | 21 | 00 | 28 | 6.6 | 12 | 52 | 6.8 | 10 | 02 | 8.7 | 22 | 25 | 8.8 | 11 | 17 | 3.3 | 23 | 58 | 3.2 | 01 | 28 | 5.1 | 13 | 44 | 5.2 |
| TU | 22 | 01 | 14 | 6.8 | 13 | 35 | 6.9 | 10 | 40 | 9.0 | 22 | 59 | 9.0 | 11 | 58 | 3.4 | — | — | | 02 | 06 | 5.2 | 14 | 21 | 5.3 |
| W | 23 | 01 | 52 | 6.9 | 14 | 11 | 6.9 | 11 | 13 | 9.1 | 23 | 30 | 9.1 | 00 | 36 | 3.3 | 12 | 36 | 3.4 | 02 | 39 | 5.3 | 14 | 56 | 5.4 |
| TH | 24 | 02 | 26 | 7.0 | 14 | 43 | 7.0 | 11 | 44 | 9.2 | — | — | | 01 | 09 | 3.3 | 13 | 08 | 3.4 | 03 | 10 | 5.3 | 15 | 28 | 5.4 |
| F | 25 | 02 | 56 | 7.0 | 15 | 11 | 7.0 | 00 | 00 | 9.1 | 12 | 15 | 9.1 | 01 | 39 | 3.3 | 13 | 39 | 3.4 | 03 | 40 | 5.3 | 15 | 59 | 5.4 |
| SA | 26 | 03 | 24 | 7.1 | 15 | 37 | 7.0 | 00 | 30 | 9.1 | 12 | 45 | 9.0 | 02 | 08 | 3.4 | 14 | 10 | 3.4 | 04 | 11 | 5.3 | 16 | 31 | 5.3 |
| SU | 27 | 03 | 53 | 7.0 | 16 | 06 | 6.9 | 01 | 00 | 8.9 | 13 | 14 | 8.8 | 02 | 39 | 3.4 | 14 | 43 | 3.4 | 04 | 43 | 5.2 | 17 | 04 | 5.2 |
| M | 28 | 04 | 23 | 6.9 | 16 | 37 | 6.7 | 01 | 30 | 8.7 | 13 | 44 | 8.5 | 03 | 10 | 3.3 | 15 | 18 | 3.4 | 05 | 17 | 5.0 | 17 | 39 | 5.0 |
| TU | 29 | 04 | 55 | 6.7 | 17 | 10 | 6.5 | 02 | 02 | 8.4 | 14 | 17 | 8.2 | 03 | 42 | 3.3 | 15 | 55 | 3.3 | 05 | 54 | 4.9 | 18 | 18 | 4.8 |
| W | 30 | 05 | 30 | 6.5 | 17 | 46 | 6.2 | 02 | 39 | 8.1 | 14 | 58 | 7.8 | 04 | 17 | 3.1 | 16 | 37 | 3.1 | 06 | 35 | 4.7 | 19 | 03 | 4.6 |
| TH | 31 | 06 | 11 | 6.3 | 18 | 31 | 6.0 | 03 | 26 | 7.7 | 15 | 53 | 7.4 | 04 | 56 | 3.0 | 17 | 25 | 2.9 | 07 | 22 | 4.5 | 20 | 00 | 4.4 |

## APRIL 2016   *High Water*   GMT

|  | | LONDON BRIDGE | | | | | LIVERPOOL<br>(Gladstone Dock) | | | | | GREENOCK | | | | | LEITH | | | | |
|---|---|---|---|---|---|---|---|---|---|---|---|---|---|---|---|---|---|---|---|---|---|
| F | 1 | 07 | 03 | 6.0 | 19 | 31 | 5.8 | 04 | 33 | 7.4 | 17 | 12 | 7.1 | 05 | 47 | 2.8 | 18 | 24 | 2.8 | 08 | 24 | 4.4 | 21 | 11 | 4.3 |
| SA | 2 | 08 | 16 | 5.9 | 21 | 01 | 5.8 | 05 | 57 | 7.3 | 18 | 42 | 7.3 | 07 | 01 | 2.7 | 19 | 38 | 2.7 | 09 | 40 | 4.4 | 22 | 29 | 4.5 |
| SU | 3 | 09 | 49 | 6.1 | 22 | 26 | 6.1 | 07 | 16 | 7.7 | 19 | 57 | 7.8 | 08 | 38 | 2.8 | 21 | 08 | 2.8 | 10 | 56 | 4.5 | 23 | 40 | 4.8 |
| M | 4 | 11 | 02 | 6.5 | 23 | 34 | 6.6 | 08 | 21 | 8.3 | 20 | 56 | 8.5 | 09 | 52 | 3.0 | 22 | 18 | 3.0 | 12 | 01 | 4.9 | — | — | |
| TU | 5 | 12 | 03 | 6.9 | — | — | | 09 | 14 | 9.0 | 21 | 45 | 9.1 | 10 | 44 | 3.2 | 23 | 10 | 3.2 | 00 | 38 | 5.1 | 12 | 53 | 5.3 |
| W | 6 | 00 | 31 | 7.0 | 12 | 57 | 7.2 | 10 | 02 | 9.5 | 22 | 30 | 9.5 | 11 | 31 | 3.4 | 23 | 56 | 3.3 | 01 | 26 | 5.5 | 13 | 39 | 5.6 |
| TH | 7 | 01 | 21 | 7.2 | 13 | 46 | 7.4 | 10 | 47 | 9.9 | 23 | 14 | 9.9 | 12 | 17 | 3.6 | — | — | | 02 | 09 | 5.8 | 14 | 22 | 5.9 |
| F | 8 | 02 | 07 | 7.5 | 14 | 32 | 7.5 | 11 | 32 | 10.2 | 23 | 57 | 10.0 | 00 | 40 | 3.4 | 13 | 04 | 3.6 | 02 | 51 | 5.9 | 15 | 06 | 6.1 |
| SA | 9 | 02 | 50 | 7.6 | 15 | 16 | 7.5 | 12 | 17 | 10.2 | — | — | | 01 | 23 | 3.5 | 13 | 50 | 3.7 | 03 | 34 | 6.0 | 15 | 51 | 6.1 |
| SU | 10 | 03 | 34 | 7.7 | 15 | 59 | 7.3 | 00 | 41 | 9.9 | 13 | 03 | 9.9 | 02 | 05 | 3.6 | 14 | 35 | 3.7 | 04 | 18 | 5.9 | 16 | 39 | 6.0 |
| M | 11 | 04 | 17 | 7.6 | 16 | 42 | 7.1 | 01 | 25 | 9.6 | 13 | 50 | 9.5 | 02 | 45 | 3.6 | 15 | 20 | 3.6 | 05 | 05 | 5.6 | 17 | 29 | 5.7 |
| TU | 12 | 05 | 01 | 7.3 | 17 | 26 | 6.7 | 02 | 11 | 9.1 | 14 | 39 | 8.9 | 03 | 25 | 3.6 | 16 | 04 | 3.4 | 05 | 55 | 5.3 | 18 | 24 | 5.3 |
| W | 13 | 05 | 48 | 7.0 | 18 | 13 | 6.4 | 03 | 02 | 8.6 | 15 | 35 | 8.3 | 04 | 06 | 3.4 | 16 | 53 | 3.2 | 06 | 51 | 5.0 | 19 | 27 | 5.0 |
| TH | 14 | 06 | 41 | 6.6 | 19 | 08 | 6.1 | 04 | 03 | 8.0 | 16 | 44 | 7.7 | 04 | 51 | 3.2 | 17 | 50 | 2.9 | 07 | 57 | 4.7 | 20 | 37 | 4.7 |
| F | 15 | 07 | 46 | 6.3 | 20 | 19 | 5.9 | 05 | 18 | 7.7 | 18 | 03 | 7.5 | 05 | 45 | 3.0 | 19 | 22 | 2.7 | 09 | 09 | 4.6 | 21 | 49 | 4.5 |
| SA | 16 | 09 | 00 | 6.1 | 21 | 38 | 5.9 | 06 | 37 | 7.6 | 19 | 23 | 7.6 | 07 | 08 | 2.8 | 21 | 02 | 2.7 | 10 | 21 | 4.5 | 23 | 05 | 4.6 |
| SU | 17 | 10 | 18 | 6.2 | 22 | 55 | 6.1 | 07 | 50 | 7.8 | 20 | 29 | 7.9 | 08 | 56 | 2.9 | 22 | 01 | 2.9 | 11 | 32 | 4.7 | — | — | |
| M | 18 | 11 | 29 | 6.5 | 23 | 56 | 6.4 | 08 | 48 | 8.2 | 21 | 17 | 8.3 | 09 | 58 | 3.1 | 22 | 47 | 3.1 | 00 | 11 | 4.7 | 12 | 31 | 4.9 |
| TU | 19 | 12 | 23 | 6.7 | — | — | | 09 | 33 | 8.5 | 21 | 56 | 8.6 | 10 | 47 | 3.2 | 23 | 28 | 3.2 | 01 | 01 | 4.9 | 13 | 17 | 5.0 |
| W | 20 | 00 | 43 | 6.7 | 13 | 06 | 6.8 | 10 | 11 | 8.7 | 22 | 30 | 8.8 | 11 | 28 | 3.3 | — | — | | 01 | 39 | 5.1 | 13 | 55 | 5.2 |
| TH | 21 | 01 | 23 | 6.8 | 13 | 42 | 6.8 | 10 | 44 | 8.9 | 23 | 01 | 8.9 | 00 | 05 | 3.2 | 12 | 06 | 3.3 | 02 | 12 | 5.2 | 14 | 30 | 5.3 |
| F | 22 | 01 | 57 | 6.9 | 14 | 14 | 6.9 | 11 | 17 | 8.9 | 23 | 32 | 9.0 | 00 | 39 | 3.3 | 12 | 39 | 3.3 | 02 | 43 | 5.2 | 15 | 02 | 5.3 |
| SA | 23 | 02 | 28 | 7.0 | 14 | 42 | 6.9 | 11 | 49 | 9.0 | — | — | | 01 | 10 | 3.3 | 13 | 10 | 3.3 | 03 | 13 | 5.3 | 15 | 34 | 5.3 |
| SU | 24 | 02 | 58 | 7.1 | 15 | 10 | 6.9 | 00 | 03 | 9.0 | 12 | 19 | 8.9 | 01 | 40 | 3.4 | 13 | 42 | 3.3 | 03 | 44 | 5.3 | 16 | 06 | 5.2 |
| M | 25 | 03 | 28 | 7.1 | 15 | 41 | 6.9 | 00 | 34 | 8.9 | 12 | 50 | 8.7 | 02 | 09 | 3.4 | 14 | 16 | 3.4 | 04 | 17 | 5.2 | 16 | 40 | 5.2 |
| TU | 26 | 04 | 00 | 7.0 | 16 | 14 | 6.7 | 01 | 05 | 8.8 | 13 | 22 | 8.5 | 02 | 40 | 3.4 | 14 | 53 | 3.3 | 04 | 51 | 5.1 | 17 | 16 | 5.0 |
| W | 27 | 04 | 34 | 6.8 | 16 | 48 | 6.5 | 01 | 39 | 8.6 | 13 | 57 | 8.3 | 03 | 12 | 3.4 | 15 | 32 | 3.3 | 05 | 27 | 5.0 | 17 | 56 | 4.9 |
| TH | 28 | 05 | 11 | 6.6 | 17 | 26 | 6.3 | 02 | 17 | 8.3 | 14 | 39 | 8.0 | 03 | 46 | 3.3 | 16 | 14 | 3.2 | 06 | 07 | 4.8 | 18 | 41 | 4.7 |
| F | 29 | 05 | 54 | 6.4 | 18 | 11 | 6.1 | 03 | 04 | 8.0 | 15 | 33 | 7.6 | 04 | 25 | 3.1 | 17 | 02 | 3.0 | 06 | 54 | 4.7 | 19 | 35 | 4.6 |
| SA | 30 | 06 | 45 | 6.2 | 19 | 08 | 5.9 | 04 | 06 | 7.7 | 16 | 44 | 7.4 | 05 | 12 | 3.0 | 17 | 58 | 2.9 | 07 | 51 | 4.5 | 20 | 40 | 4.5 |

# MAY 2016    *High Water*    GMT

**LONDON BRIDGE** — Datum of Predictions 3.20m below
**LIVERPOOL (Gladstone Dock)** — Datum of Predictions 4.93m below
**GREENOCK** — Datum of Predictions 1.62m below
**LEITH** — Datum of Predictions 2.90m below

| Day | LB hr m | ht | LB hr m | ht | LIV hr m | ht | LIV hr m | ht | GRE hr m | ht | GRE hr m | ht | LEI hr m | ht | LEI hr m | ht |
|---|---|---|---|---|---|---|---|---|---|---|---|---|---|---|---|---|
| SU 1 | 07 53 | 6.1 | 20 27 | 5.9 | 05 23 | 7.7 | 18 06 | 7.5 | 06 20 | 2.8 | 19 08 | 2.8 | 09 02 | 4.5 | 21 55 | 4.6 |
| M 2 | 09 18 | 6.2 | 21 52 | 6.2 | 06 39 | 7.9 | 19 21 | 8.0 | 07 52 | 2.8 | 20 31 | 2.9 | 10 19 | 4.6 | 23 06 | 4.8 |
| TU 3 | 10 30 | 6.6 | 23 01 | 6.6 | 07 46 | 8.4 | 20 24 | 8.5 | 09 13 | 3.0 | 21 45 | 3.1 | 11 25 | 4.9 | — | — |
| W 4 | 11 34 | 6.9 | — | — | 08 43 | 9.0 | 21 17 | 9.0 | 10 13 | 3.2 | 22 41 | 3.2 | 00 06 | 5.2 | 12 22 | 5.3 |
| TH 5 | 00 01 | 6.9 | 12 31 | 7.2 | 09 35 | 9.4 | 22 05 | 9.5 | 11 05 | 3.4 | 23 30 | 3.4 | 00 57 | 5.5 | 13 12 | 5.6 |
| F 6 | 00 54 | 7.2 | 13 22 | 7.3 | 10 24 | 9.8 | 22 51 | 9.7 | 11 54 | 3.5 | — | — | 01 43 | 5.7 | 13 59 | 5.9 |
| SA 7 | 01 42 | 7.4 | 14 10 | 7.3 | 11 12 | 10.0 | 23 37 | 9.9 | 00 16 | 3.5 | 12 44 | 3.6 | 02 28 | 5.9 | 14 46 | 6.0 |
| SU 8 | 02 29 | 7.6 | 14 55 | 7.3 | 11 59 | 9.9 | — | — | 01 01 | 3.6 | 13 33 | 3.6 | 03 13 | 5.9 | 15 34 | 6.0 |
| M 9 | 03 14 | 7.6 | 15 40 | 7.2 | 00 22 | 9.8 | 12 47 | 9.7 | 01 44 | 3.6 | 14 20 | 3.6 | 03 59 | 5.8 | 16 24 | 5.9 |
| TU 10 | 03 59 | 7.5 | 16 24 | 7.0 | 01 08 | 9.5 | 13 34 | 9.3 | 02 25 | 3.6 | 15 07 | 3.5 | 04 48 | 5.6 | 17 16 | 5.6 |
| W 11 | 04 45 | 7.3 | 17 08 | 6.7 | 01 54 | 9.1 | 14 23 | 8.8 | 03 06 | 3.6 | 15 53 | 3.3 | 05 38 | 5.4 | 18 10 | 5.3 |
| TH 12 | 05 32 | 7.0 | 17 54 | 6.4 | 02 43 | 8.7 | 15 16 | 8.3 | 03 48 | 3.5 | 16 42 | 3.1 | 06 34 | 5.1 | 19 09 | 5.0 |
| F 13 | 06 23 | 6.6 | 18 44 | 6.1 | 03 40 | 8.2 | 16 17 | 7.8 | 04 33 | 3.3 | 17 38 | 2.9 | 07 35 | 4.8 | 20 10 | 4.7 |
| SA 14 | 07 21 | 6.3 | 19 46 | 5.9 | 04 45 | 7.8 | 17 26 | 7.5 | 05 24 | 3.1 | 18 47 | 2.7 | 08 39 | 4.7 | 21 14 | 4.5 |
| SU 15 | 08 27 | 6.1 | 20 57 | 5.9 | 05 55 | 7.6 | 18 38 | 7.5 | 06 30 | 2.9 | 20 09 | 2.7 | 09 44 | 4.6 | 22 21 | 4.5 |
| M 16 | 09 35 | 6.1 | 22 07 | 6.0 | 07 05 | 7.7 | 19 45 | 7.7 | 07 58 | 2.9 | 21 16 | 2.8 | 10 50 | 4.6 | 23 26 | 4.6 |
| TU 17 | 10 43 | 6.2 | 23 11 | 6.2 | 08 06 | 7.9 | 20 38 | 8.0 | 09 13 | 3.0 | 22 07 | 3.0 | 11 50 | 4.7 | — | — |
| W 18 | 11 42 | 6.4 | — | — | 08 55 | 8.1 | 21 21 | 8.3 | 10 07 | 3.1 | 22 51 | 3.1 | 00 21 | 4.7 | 12 42 | 4.8 |
| TH 19 | 00 04 | 6.5 | 12 30 | 6.6 | 09 37 | 8.4 | 21 58 | 8.6 | 10 52 | 3.2 | 23 30 | 3.2 | 01 04 | 4.9 | 13 24 | 5.0 |
| F 20 | 00 48 | 6.7 | 13 09 | 6.7 | 10 14 | 8.6 | 22 32 | 8.8 | 11 31 | 3.2 | — | — | 01 45 | 5.0 | 14 01 | 5.1 |
| SA 21 | 01 26 | 6.8 | 13 44 | 6.8 | 10 49 | 8.7 | 23 05 | 8.9 | 00 07 | 3.3 | 12 07 | 3.2 | 02 14 | 5.2 | 14 36 | 5.2 |
| SU 22 | 02 01 | 6.9 | 14 16 | 6.8 | 11 23 | 8.8 | 23 38 | 9.0 | 00 41 | 3.4 | 12 40 | 3.2 | 02 46 | 5.2 | 15 10 | 5.2 |
| M 23 | 02 34 | 7.0 | 14 48 | 6.9 | 11 56 | 8.8 | — | — | 01 13 | 3.4 | 13 14 | 3.3 | 03 20 | 5.3 | 15 45 | 5.2 |
| TU 24 | 03 06 | 7.0 | 15 22 | 6.8 | 00 11 | 9.0 | 12 30 | 8.7 | 01 43 | 3.5 | 13 51 | 3.3 | 03 54 | 5.3 | 16 20 | 5.2 |
| W 25 | 03 41 | 7.0 | 15 57 | 6.7 | 00 46 | 8.9 | 13 05 | 8.6 | 02 14 | 3.5 | 14 30 | 3.3 | 04 29 | 5.2 | 16 57 | 5.1 |
| TH 26 | 04 18 | 6.9 | 16 34 | 6.6 | 01 22 | 8.8 | 13 44 | 8.4 | 02 48 | 3.5 | 15 12 | 3.3 | 05 06 | 5.1 | 17 37 | 5.0 |
| F 27 | 04 58 | 6.7 | 17 13 | 6.4 | 02 03 | 8.6 | 14 27 | 8.2 | 03 25 | 3.4 | 15 55 | 3.2 | 05 47 | 5.0 | 18 23 | 4.9 |
| SA 28 | 05 42 | 6.6 | 17 58 | 6.3 | 02 50 | 8.3 | 15 19 | 8.0 | 04 04 | 3.3 | 16 43 | 3.1 | 06 33 | 4.9 | 19 14 | 4.8 |
| SU 29 | 06 32 | 6.4 | 18 52 | 6.2 | 03 48 | 8.1 | 16 23 | 7.8 | 04 51 | 3.2 | 17 36 | 3.0 | 07 26 | 4.8 | 20 15 | 4.7 |
| M 30 | 07 35 | 6.3 | 20 01 | 6.1 | 04 55 | 8.1 | 17 35 | 7.8 | 05 51 | 3.0 | 18 39 | 3.0 | 08 31 | 4.7 | 21 24 | 4.8 |
| TU 31 | 08 51 | 6.4 | 21 20 | 6.3 | 06 06 | 8.2 | 18 47 | 8.1 | 07 13 | 3.0 | 19 53 | 3.0 | 09 44 | 4.8 | 22 33 | 4.9 |

# JUNE 2016    *High Water*    GMT

**LONDON BRIDGE**    **LIVERPOOL (Gladstone Dock)**    **GREENOCK**    **LEITH**

| Day | LB hr m | ht | LB hr m | ht | LIV hr m | ht | LIV hr m | ht | GRE hr m | ht | GRE hr m | ht | LEI hr m | ht | LEI hr m | ht |
|---|---|---|---|---|---|---|---|---|---|---|---|---|---|---|---|---|
| W 1 | 10 01 | 6.6 | 22 30 | 6.6 | 07 14 | 8.5 | 19 53 | 8.5 | 08 36 | 3.1 | 21 09 | 3.1 | 10 53 | 5.0 | 23 35 | 5.1 |
| TH 2 | 11 06 | 6.8 | 23 33 | 6.9 | 08 15 | 8.9 | 20 51 | 8.9 | 09 44 | 3.2 | 22 12 | 3.2 | 11 54 | 5.3 | — | — |
| F 3 | 12 06 | 7.0 | — | — | 09 12 | 9.2 | 21 43 | 9.2 | 10 41 | 3.4 | 23 06 | 3.3 | 00 30 | 5.4 | 12 49 | 5.5 |
| SA 4 | 00 30 | 7.1 | 13 01 | 7.1 | 10 05 | 9.5 | 22 32 | 9.5 | 11 35 | 3.4 | 23 55 | 3.5 | 01 21 | 5.6 | 13 41 | 5.7 |
| SU 5 | 01 22 | 7.3 | 13 51 | 7.1 | 10 55 | 9.6 | 23 20 | 9.6 | 12 26 | 3.5 | — | — | 02 08 | 5.7 | 14 31 | 5.8 |
| M 6 | 02 11 | 7.4 | 14 39 | 7.2 | 11 44 | 9.6 | — | — | 00 41 | 3.5 | 13 18 | 3.5 | 02 56 | 5.8 | 15 21 | 5.8 |
| TU 7 | 02 59 | 7.5 | 15 25 | 7.1 | 00 06 | 9.6 | 12 32 | 9.5 | 01 25 | 3.6 | 14 07 | 3.4 | 03 43 | 5.7 | 16 11 | 5.7 |
| W 8 | 03 45 | 7.4 | 16 09 | 7.0 | 00 52 | 9.5 | 13 19 | 9.2 | 02 08 | 3.6 | 14 54 | 3.3 | 04 32 | 5.6 | 17 01 | 5.5 |
| TH 9 | 04 31 | 7.2 | 16 52 | 6.8 | 01 37 | 9.2 | 14 05 | 8.8 | 02 49 | 3.6 | 15 40 | 3.2 | 05 22 | 5.4 | 17 52 | 5.3 |
| F 10 | 05 16 | 6.9 | 17 34 | 6.5 | 02 23 | 8.8 | 14 52 | 8.4 | 03 30 | 3.5 | 16 27 | 3.1 | 06 13 | 5.2 | 18 44 | 5.0 |
| SA 11 | 06 02 | 6.6 | 18 18 | 6.3 | 03 11 | 8.4 | 15 42 | 8.0 | 04 13 | 3.4 | 17 15 | 3.0 | 07 06 | 5.0 | 19 36 | 4.8 |
| SU 12 | 06 51 | 6.3 | 19 09 | 6.0 | 04 05 | 8.0 | 16 39 | 7.6 | 04 59 | 3.2 | 18 06 | 2.9 | 08 03 | 4.8 | 20 31 | 4.6 |
| M 13 | 07 47 | 6.1 | 20 10 | 5.9 | 05 06 | 7.7 | 17 42 | 7.4 | 05 51 | 3.0 | 19 04 | 2.8 | 09 00 | 4.6 | 21 27 | 4.5 |
| TU 14 | 08 47 | 6.0 | 21 16 | 5.9 | 06 10 | 7.6 | 18 48 | 7.4 | 06 53 | 2.9 | 20 07 | 2.8 | 09 58 | 4.5 | 22 26 | 4.5 |
| W 15 | 09 48 | 6.0 | 22 19 | 6.0 | 07 14 | 7.6 | 19 49 | 7.7 | 08 04 | 2.9 | 21 11 | 2.9 | 10 58 | 4.5 | 23 25 | 4.6 |
| TH 16 | 10 49 | 6.1 | 23 18 | 6.3 | 08 12 | 7.8 | 20 41 | 8.0 | 09 12 | 2.9 | 22 06 | 3.0 | 11 56 | 4.6 | — | — |
| F 17 | 11 45 | 6.4 | — | — | 09 01 | 8.0 | 21 24 | 8.3 | 10 08 | 3.0 | 22 54 | 3.2 | 00 19 | 4.7 | 12 48 | 4.8 |
| SA 18 | 00 10 | 6.5 | 12 34 | 6.6 | 09 44 | 8.3 | 22 03 | 8.6 | 10 53 | 3.1 | 23 36 | 3.3 | 01 05 | 4.9 | 13 31 | 4.9 |
| SU 19 | 00 56 | 6.7 | 13 16 | 6.7 | 10 23 | 8.5 | 22 40 | 8.8 | 11 33 | 3.1 | — | — | 01 45 | 5.1 | 14 11 | 5.1 |
| M 20 | 01 36 | 6.8 | 13 55 | 6.8 | 11 00 | 8.6 | 23 15 | 8.9 | 00 14 | 3.4 | 12 11 | 3.2 | 02 22 | 5.2 | 14 48 | 5.2 |
| TU 21 | 02 13 | 6.9 | 14 32 | 6.8 | 11 36 | 8.7 | 23 52 | 9.1 | 00 48 | 3.4 | 12 49 | 3.2 | 02 58 | 5.3 | 15 24 | 5.3 |
| W 22 | 02 50 | 7.0 | 15 09 | 6.8 | 12 12 | 8.8 | — | — | 01 20 | 3.5 | 13 29 | 3.2 | 03 34 | 5.4 | 16 01 | 5.3 |
| TH 23 | 03 27 | 7.0 | 15 46 | 6.8 | 00 29 | 9.1 | 12 51 | 8.8 | 01 53 | 3.5 | 14 11 | 3.3 | 04 10 | 5.4 | 16 39 | 5.3 |
| F 24 | 04 06 | 7.0 | 16 24 | 6.7 | 01 09 | 9.0 | 13 32 | 8.7 | 02 29 | 3.5 | 14 54 | 3.3 | 04 48 | 5.3 | 17 20 | 5.3 |
| SA 25 | 04 47 | 6.9 | 17 03 | 6.6 | 01 51 | 8.9 | 14 16 | 8.6 | 03 08 | 3.5 | 15 38 | 3.3 | 05 29 | 5.3 | 18 05 | 5.2 |
| SU 26 | 05 30 | 6.8 | 17 46 | 6.5 | 02 37 | 8.8 | 15 05 | 8.4 | 03 49 | 3.5 | 16 24 | 3.2 | 06 14 | 5.2 | 18 54 | 5.1 |
| M 27 | 06 18 | 6.6 | 18 35 | 6.4 | 03 29 | 8.6 | 16 01 | 8.2 | 04 34 | 3.4 | 17 14 | 3.2 | 07 05 | 5.1 | 19 50 | 4.9 |
| TU 28 | 07 15 | 6.5 | 19 35 | 6.3 | 04 29 | 8.4 | 17 06 | 8.1 | 05 28 | 3.2 | 18 10 | 3.1 | 08 04 | 5.0 | 20 55 | 4.9 |
| W 29 | 08 24 | 6.4 | 20 50 | 6.3 | 05 36 | 8.3 | 18 17 | 8.1 | 06 37 | 3.1 | 19 15 | 3.0 | 09 15 | 4.9 | 22 04 | 4.9 |
| TH 30 | 09 33 | 6.4 | 22 02 | 6.5 | 06 46 | 8.4 | 19 26 | 8.3 | 08 01 | 3.1 | 20 33 | 3.0 | 10 26 | 5.0 | 23 09 | 5.0 |

## JULY 2016   *High Water*   GMT

| | | LONDON BRIDGE Datum of Predictions 3.20m below | | | | LIVERPOOL (Gladstone Dock) Datum of Predictions 4.93m below | | | | GREENOCK Datum of Predictions 1.62m below | | | | LEITH Datum of Predictions 2.90m below | | | |
|---|---|---|---|---|---|---|---|---|---|---|---|---|---|---|---|---|---|
| | | hr m | ht | hr m | ht | hr m | ht | hr m | ht | hr m | ht | hr m | ht | hr m | ht | hr m | ht |
| F | 1 | 10 40 | 6.5 | 23 08 | 6.7 | 07 53 | 8.6 | 20 30 | 8.6 | 09 19 | 3.1 | 21 46 | 3.1 | 11 33 | 5.1 | — | — |
| SA | 2 | 11 46 | 6.7 | — | — | 08 55 | 8.9 | 21 27 | 8.9 | 10 25 | 3.2 | 22 46 | 3.3 | 00 09 | 5.2 | 12 34 | 5.3 |
| SU | 3 | 00 11 | 6.9 | 12 46 | 6.8 | 09 52 | 9.1 | 22 19 | 9.2 | 11 22 | 3.3 | 23 39 | 3.4 | 01 04 | 5.4 | 13 29 | 5.5 |
| M | 4 | 01 08 | 7.1 | 13 39 | 6.9 | 10 44 | 9.3 | 23 07 | 9.4 | 12 16 | 3.4 | — | — | 01 55 | 5.6 | 14 20 | 5.6 |
| TU | 5 | 01 59 | 7.2 | 14 27 | 7.0 | 11 33 | 9.3 | 23 53 | 9.5 | 00 26 | 3.5 | 13 07 | 3.3 | 02 43 | 5.7 | 15 09 | 5.7 |
| W | 6 | 02 47 | 7.3 | 15 12 | 7.1 | 12 18 | 9.3 | — | — | 01 11 | 3.6 | 13 55 | 3.3 | 03 30 | 5.7 | 15 56 | 5.6 |
| TH | 7 | 03 32 | 7.3 | 15 54 | 7.0 | 00 36 | 9.4 | 13 01 | 9.1 | 01 52 | 3.6 | 14 40 | 3.2 | 04 16 | 5.6 | 16 42 | 5.5 |
| F | 8 | 04 15 | 7.2 | 16 33 | 6.9 | 01 18 | 9.2 | 13 42 | 8.8 | 02 31 | 3.6 | 15 22 | 3.2 | 05 01 | 5.5 | 17 27 | 5.3 |
| SA | 9 | 04 56 | 7.0 | 17 11 | 6.7 | 01 57 | 8.9 | 14 21 | 8.5 | 03 10 | 3.6 | 16 01 | 3.1 | 05 47 | 5.3 | 18 12 | 5.1 |
| SU | 10 | 05 35 | 6.7 | 17 48 | 6.4 | 02 38 | 8.6 | 15 03 | 8.2 | 03 49 | 3.5 | 16 42 | 3.0 | 06 32 | 5.1 | 18 57 | 4.9 |
| M | 11 | 06 14 | 6.4 | 18 26 | 6.2 | 03 22 | 8.2 | 15 49 | 7.8 | 04 29 | 3.3 | 17 25 | 3.0 | 07 19 | 4.9 | 19 43 | 4.7 |
| TU | 12 | 06 58 | 6.1 | 19 14 | 6.0 | 04 12 | 7.8 | 16 44 | 7.5 | 05 12 | 3.2 | 18 11 | 2.9 | 08 10 | 4.7 | 20 34 | 4.5 |
| W | 13 | 07 51 | 5.9 | 20 18 | 5.8 | 05 11 | 7.5 | 17 47 | 7.3 | 06 01 | 3.0 | 19 04 | 2.8 | 09 04 | 4.5 | 21 28 | 4.4 |
| TH | 14 | 08 52 | 5.8 | 21 27 | 5.8 | 06 18 | 7.3 | 18 55 | 7.4 | 06 57 | 2.9 | 20 06 | 2.8 | 10 02 | 4.4 | 22 26 | 4.5 |
| F | 15 | 09 56 | 5.9 | 22 31 | 6.0 | 07 26 | 7.4 | 19 58 | 7.6 | 08 04 | 2.8 | 21 15 | 2.9 | 11 04 | 4.5 | 23 27 | 4.6 |
| SA | 16 | 10 59 | 6.1 | 23 32 | 6.3 | 08 26 | 7.7 | 20 51 | 8.0 | 09 15 | 2.9 | 22 17 | 3.1 | 12 06 | 4.6 | — | — |
| SU | 17 | 11 58 | 6.4 | — | — | 09 16 | 8.0 | 21 36 | 8.4 | 10 16 | 3.0 | 23 07 | 3.2 | 00 26 | 4.8 | 13 01 | 4.8 |
| M | 18 | 00 25 | 6.6 | 12 49 | 6.6 | 09 59 | 8.3 | 22 16 | 8.7 | 11 05 | 3.1 | 23 48 | 3.3 | 01 16 | 5.0 | 13 46 | 5.0 |
| TU | 19 | 01 11 | 6.8 | 13 34 | 6.8 | 10 39 | 8.6 | 22 55 | 9.0 | 11 47 | 3.1 | — | — | 01 59 | 5.2 | 14 26 | 5.2 |
| W | 20 | 01 54 | 6.9 | 14 15 | 6.9 | 11 17 | 8.8 | 23 33 | 9.2 | 00 25 | 3.4 | 12 29 | 3.2 | 02 38 | 5.4 | 15 04 | 5.4 |
| TH | 21 | 02 34 | 7.1 | 14 55 | 7.0 | 11 56 | 9.0 | — | — | 00 59 | 3.5 | 13 10 | 3.2 | 03 15 | 5.5 | 15 42 | 5.5 |
| F | 22 | 03 14 | 7.2 | 15 34 | 7.0 | 00 12 | 9.4 | 12 36 | 9.1 | 01 35 | 3.6 | 13 53 | 3.3 | 03 52 | 5.6 | 16 20 | 5.5 |
| SA | 23 | 03 54 | 7.2 | 16 12 | 7.0 | 00 53 | 9.4 | 13 17 | 9.1 | 02 13 | 3.6 | 14 36 | 3.3 | 04 30 | 5.6 | 17 01 | 5.5 |
| SU | 24 | 04 34 | 7.1 | 16 50 | 6.9 | 01 35 | 9.4 | 14 00 | 9.0 | 02 53 | 3.6 | 15 20 | 3.3 | 05 11 | 5.6 | 17 45 | 5.4 |
| M | 25 | 05 16 | 7.0 | 17 31 | 6.8 | 02 20 | 9.2 | 14 46 | 8.7 | 03 34 | 3.6 | 16 04 | 3.3 | 05 55 | 5.5 | 18 33 | 5.3 |
| TU | 26 | 06 00 | 6.7 | 18 15 | 6.7 | 03 08 | 9.0 | 15 38 | 8.5 | 04 18 | 3.5 | 16 50 | 3.3 | 06 44 | 5.3 | 19 25 | 5.1 |
| W | 27 | 06 52 | 6.5 | 19 10 | 6.5 | 04 04 | 8.6 | 16 38 | 8.2 | 05 07 | 3.3 | 17 39 | 3.2 | 07 41 | 5.1 | 20 28 | 4.9 |
| TH | 28 | 07 56 | 6.3 | 20 20 | 6.4 | 05 10 | 8.3 | 17 51 | 8.0 | 06 06 | 3.1 | 18 38 | 3.1 | 08 51 | 5.0 | 21 39 | 4.8 |
| F | 29 | 09 07 | 6.2 | 21 36 | 6.4 | 06 24 | 8.1 | 19 06 | 8.0 | 07 28 | 3.0 | 19 57 | 3.0 | 10 07 | 4.9 | 22 49 | 4.9 |
| SA | 30 | 10 18 | 6.3 | 22 49 | 6.5 | 07 39 | 8.2 | 20 17 | 8.3 | 09 04 | 3.0 | 21 26 | 3.0 | 11 19 | 5.0 | 23 55 | 5.1 |
| SU | 31 | 11 31 | 6.4 | 23 59 | 6.7 | 08 47 | 8.5 | 21 18 | 8.7 | 10 19 | 3.1 | 22 34 | 3.2 | 12 26 | 5.1 | — | — |

## AUGUST 2016   *High Water*   GMT

| | | LONDON BRIDGE | | | | LIVERPOOL (Gladstone Dock) | | | | GREENOCK | | | | LEITH | | | |
|---|---|---|---|---|---|---|---|---|---|---|---|---|---|---|---|---|---|
| M | 1 | 12 36 | 6.7 | — | — | 09 46 | 8.8 | 22 10 | 9.1 | 11 17 | 3.2 | 23 27 | 3.4 | 00 54 | 5.3 | 13 23 | 5.3 |
| TU | 2 | 00 59 | 7.0 | 13 29 | 6.9 | 10 36 | 9.0 | 22 56 | 9.3 | 12 09 | 3.3 | — | — | 01 46 | 5.5 | 14 12 | 5.5 |
| W | 3 | 01 50 | 7.1 | 14 15 | 7.0 | 11 21 | 9.2 | 23 38 | 9.4 | 00 14 | 3.5 | 12 57 | 3.3 | 02 31 | 5.6 | 14 56 | 5.6 |
| TH | 4 | 02 35 | 7.2 | 14 57 | 7.1 | 12 01 | 9.2 | — | — | 00 57 | 3.6 | 13 41 | 3.2 | 03 15 | 5.7 | 15 39 | 5.5 |
| F | 5 | 03 17 | 7.2 | 15 35 | 7.1 | 00 17 | 9.4 | 12 39 | 9.1 | 01 35 | 3.6 | 14 20 | 3.2 | 03 56 | 5.6 | 16 20 | 5.5 |
| SA | 6 | 03 55 | 7.2 | 16 10 | 7.0 | 00 53 | 9.3 | 13 14 | 8.9 | 02 11 | 3.6 | 14 54 | 3.2 | 04 37 | 5.5 | 16 58 | 5.3 |
| SU | 7 | 04 30 | 7.0 | 16 43 | 6.9 | 01 28 | 9.1 | 13 48 | 8.7 | 02 46 | 3.6 | 15 28 | 3.1 | 05 16 | 5.4 | 17 36 | 5.1 |
| M | 8 | 05 03 | 6.8 | 17 14 | 6.7 | 02 02 | 8.8 | 14 23 | 8.4 | 03 21 | 3.5 | 16 04 | 3.1 | 05 55 | 5.2 | 18 15 | 5.0 |
| TU | 9 | 05 34 | 6.5 | 17 46 | 6.4 | 02 39 | 8.4 | 15 03 | 8.1 | 03 58 | 3.4 | 16 43 | 3.1 | 06 35 | 5.0 | 18 57 | 4.8 |
| W | 10 | 06 07 | 6.2 | 18 21 | 6.2 | 03 20 | 8.0 | 15 49 | 7.7 | 04 36 | 3.3 | 17 25 | 3.0 | 07 20 | 4.7 | 19 44 | 4.6 |
| TH | 11 | 06 46 | 6.0 | 19 06 | 5.9 | 04 11 | 7.5 | 16 46 | 7.3 | 05 19 | 3.1 | 18 13 | 2.9 | 08 12 | 4.5 | 20 37 | 4.4 |
| F | 12 | 07 40 | 5.7 | 20 15 | 5.7 | 05 17 | 7.2 | 17 58 | 7.2 | 06 11 | 2.9 | 19 10 | 2.8 | 09 12 | 4.4 | 21 37 | 4.4 |
| SA | 13 | 08 59 | 5.6 | 21 42 | 5.7 | 06 35 | 7.1 | 19 13 | 7.4 | 07 13 | 2.8 | 20 21 | 2.8 | 10 16 | 4.3 | 22 42 | 4.5 |
| SU | 14 | 10 14 | 5.8 | 22 52 | 6.0 | 07 49 | 7.3 | 20 17 | 7.8 | 08 26 | 2.8 | 21 38 | 3.0 | 11 24 | 4.5 | 23 48 | 4.7 |
| M | 15 | 11 23 | 6.2 | 23 53 | 6.4 | 08 48 | 7.8 | 21 08 | 8.3 | 09 44 | 2.9 | 22 37 | 3.1 | 12 28 | 4.7 | — | — |
| TU | 16 | 12 21 | 6.5 | — | — | 09 36 | 8.2 | 21 52 | 8.8 | 10 43 | 3.0 | 23 22 | 3.3 | 00 46 | 4.9 | 13 20 | 5.0 |
| W | 17 | 00 44 | 6.8 | 13 10 | 6.8 | 10 17 | 8.7 | 22 32 | 9.2 | 11 29 | 3.1 | — | — | 01 34 | 5.2 | 14 02 | 5.3 |
| TH | 18 | 01 31 | 7.0 | 13 54 | 7.0 | 10 57 | 9.1 | 23 12 | 9.5 | 00 01 | 3.4 | 12 11 | 3.2 | 02 14 | 5.5 | 14 41 | 5.5 |
| F | 19 | 02 14 | 7.2 | 14 35 | 7.1 | 11 36 | 9.3 | 23 52 | 9.7 | 00 38 | 3.5 | 12 53 | 3.3 | 02 52 | 5.7 | 15 20 | 5.7 |
| SA | 20 | 02 55 | 7.3 | 15 15 | 7.2 | 12 16 | 9.5 | — | — | 01 17 | 3.6 | 13 35 | 3.3 | 03 29 | 5.8 | 15 59 | 5.8 |
| SU | 21 | 03 36 | 7.4 | 15 54 | 7.3 | 00 33 | 9.8 | 12 58 | 9.5 | 01 57 | 3.7 | 14 17 | 3.4 | 04 09 | 5.9 | 16 40 | 5.8 |
| M | 22 | 04 16 | 7.3 | 16 32 | 7.2 | 01 16 | 9.8 | 13 40 | 9.3 | 02 38 | 3.7 | 14 59 | 3.4 | 04 51 | 5.9 | 17 23 | 5.6 |
| TU | 23 | 04 57 | 7.1 | 17 12 | 7.1 | 02 00 | 9.5 | 14 25 | 9.0 | 03 19 | 3.7 | 15 41 | 3.4 | 05 36 | 5.7 | 18 10 | 5.4 |
| W | 24 | 05 40 | 6.8 | 17 56 | 6.9 | 02 47 | 9.2 | 15 15 | 8.6 | 04 02 | 3.6 | 16 24 | 3.4 | 06 24 | 5.5 | 19 01 | 5.2 |
| TH | 25 | 06 27 | 6.5 | 18 47 | 6.6 | 03 42 | 8.7 | 16 14 | 8.2 | 04 48 | 3.4 | 17 11 | 3.3 | 07 22 | 5.2 | 20 04 | 4.9 |
| F | 26 | 07 27 | 6.2 | 19 54 | 6.4 | 04 49 | 8.2 | 17 30 | 7.8 | 05 42 | 3.1 | 18 06 | 3.1 | 08 34 | 4.9 | 21 18 | 4.8 |
| SA | 27 | 08 41 | 6.0 | 21 15 | 6.3 | 06 09 | 7.9 | 18 52 | 7.8 | 07 02 | 2.9 | 19 23 | 3.0 | 09 54 | 4.8 | 22 33 | 4.8 |
| SU | 28 | 09 59 | 6.1 | 22 34 | 6.4 | 07 31 | 7.9 | 20 08 | 8.2 | 09 04 | 2.9 | 21 13 | 3.0 | 11 12 | 4.8 | 23 45 | 5.0 |
| M | 29 | 11 18 | 6.3 | 23 48 | 6.7 | 08 42 | 8.3 | 21 09 | 8.6 | 10 17 | 3.0 | 22 22 | 3.2 | 12 22 | 5.0 | — | — |
| TU | 30 | 12 24 | 6.6 | — | — | 09 39 | 8.6 | 21 59 | 9.0 | 11 11 | 3.2 | 23 14 | 3.4 | 00 46 | 5.2 | 13 17 | 5.2 |
| W | 31 | 00 48 | 7.0 | 13 16 | 6.9 | 10 25 | 8.9 | 22 41 | 9.2 | 11 58 | 3.3 | 23 58 | 3.5 | 01 36 | 5.4 | 14 02 | 5.4 |

## SEPTEMBER 2016 — *High Water*    GMT

| | LONDON BRIDGE<br>Datum of Predictions<br>3.20m below | | | | | | LIVERPOOL<br>(Gladstone Dock)<br>Datum of Predictions<br>4.93m below | | | | | | GREENOCK<br>Datum of Predictions<br>1.62m below | | | | | | LEITH<br>Datum of Predictions<br>2.90m below | | | | | |
|---|---|---|---|---|---|---|---|---|---|---|---|---|---|---|---|---|---|---|---|---|---|---|---|---|
| | hr | m | ht | hr | m | ht | hr | m | ht | hr | m | ht | hr | m | ht | hr | m | ht | hr | m | ht | hr | m | ht |
| TH 1 | 01 | 37 | 7.1 | 13 | 59 | 7.0 | 11 | 04 | 9.1 | 23 | 19 | 9.4 | 12 | 40 | 3.3 | — | | — | 02 | 18 | 5.6 | 14 | 41 | 5.5 |
| F 2 | 02 | 18 | 7.2 | 14 | 37 | 7.1 | 11 | 40 | 9.2 | 23 | 53 | 9.4 | 00 | 38 | 3.6 | 13 | 19 | 3.3 | 02 | 57 | 5.6 | 15 | 17 | 5.5 |
| SA 3 | 02 | 56 | 7.2 | 15 | 11 | 7.1 | 12 | 12 | 9.2 | — | | — | 01 | 15 | 3.6 | 13 | 52 | 3.2 | 03 | 34 | 5.6 | 15 | 52 | 5.4 |
| SU 4 | 03 | 29 | 7.1 | 15 | 42 | 7.1 | 00 | 26 | 9.3 | 12 | 44 | 9.1 | 01 | 48 | 3.6 | 14 | 22 | 3.2 | 04 | 09 | 5.5 | 16 | 26 | 5.4 |
| M 5 | 03 | 59 | 7.0 | 16 | 12 | 7.0 | 00 | 57 | 9.1 | 13 | 15 | 8.9 | 02 | 20 | 3.6 | 14 | 53 | 3.3 | 04 | 44 | 5.4 | 17 | 01 | 5.2 |
| TU 6 | 04 | 27 | 6.8 | 16 | 41 | 6.8 | 01 | 28 | 8.9 | 13 | 47 | 8.6 | 02 | 53 | 3.6 | 15 | 27 | 3.3 | 05 | 19 | 5.2 | 17 | 37 | 5.1 |
| W 7 | 04 | 56 | 6.6 | 17 | 11 | 6.6 | 02 | 01 | 8.5 | 14 | 22 | 8.3 | 03 | 27 | 3.5 | 16 | 03 | 3.2 | 05 | 56 | 5.0 | 18 | 15 | 4.9 |
| TH 8 | 05 | 26 | 6.4 | 17 | 44 | 6.3 | 02 | 36 | 8.1 | 15 | 01 | 7.9 | 04 | 04 | 3.4 | 16 | 42 | 3.1 | 06 | 38 | 4.8 | 18 | 59 | 4.7 |
| F 9 | 06 | 01 | 6.1 | 18 | 23 | 6.1 | 03 | 18 | 7.6 | 15 | 50 | 7.5 | 04 | 45 | 3.2 | 17 | 27 | 3.0 | 07 | 26 | 4.6 | 19 | 50 | 4.5 |
| SA 10 | 06 | 44 | 5.8 | 19 | 13 | 5.8 | 04 | 16 | 7.2 | 17 | 01 | 7.2 | 05 | 35 | 3.0 | 18 | 21 | 2.9 | 08 | 25 | 4.4 | 20 | 52 | 4.4 |
| SU 11 | 07 | 45 | 5.6 | 20 | 32 | 5.6 | 05 | 40 | 6.9 | 18 | 25 | 7.2 | 06 | 35 | 2.8 | 19 | 29 | 2.8 | 09 | 33 | 4.3 | 22 | 00 | 4.4 |
| M 12 | 09 | 23 | 5.6 | 22 | 07 | 5.9 | 07 | 08 | 7.1 | 19 | 39 | 7.6 | 07 | 49 | 2.8 | 20 | 54 | 2.9 | 10 | 45 | 4.4 | 23 | 10 | 4.6 |
| TU 13 | 10 | 43 | 6.0 | 23 | 16 | 6.3 | 08 | 17 | 7.7 | 20 | 37 | 8.2 | 09 | 16 | 2.9 | 22 | 03 | 3.1 | 11 | 54 | 4.7 | — | | — |
| W 14 | 11 | 47 | 6.5 | — | | — | 09 | 09 | 8.3 | 21 | 24 | 8.8 | 10 | 22 | 3.1 | 22 | 51 | 3.3 | 00 | 13 | 4.9 | 12 | 50 | 5.1 |
| TH 15 | 00 | 13 | 6.8 | 12 | 40 | 6.8 | 09 | 52 | 8.8 | 22 | 07 | 9.4 | 11 | 10 | 3.2 | 23 | 33 | 3.5 | 01 | 04 | 5.3 | 13 | 35 | 5.4 |
| F 16 | 01 | 03 | 7.1 | 13 | 26 | 7.1 | 10 | 33 | 9.3 | 22 | 48 | 9.8 | 11 | 52 | 3.3 | — | | — | 01 | 47 | 5.6 | 14 | 15 | 5.7 |
| SA 17 | 01 | 48 | 7.3 | 14 | 10 | 7.3 | 11 | 13 | 9.6 | 23 | 29 | 10.0 | 00 | 14 | 3.6 | 12 | 33 | 3.4 | 02 | 26 | 5.8 | 14 | 54 | 5.9 |
| SU 18 | 02 | 32 | 7.5 | 14 | 51 | 7.4 | 11 | 54 | 9.8 | — | | — | 00 | 56 | 3.7 | 13 | 14 | 3.5 | 03 | 05 | 6.0 | 15 | 34 | 6.0 |
| M 19 | 03 | 14 | 7.5 | 15 | 31 | 7.5 | 00 | 11 | 10.1 | 12 | 36 | 9.8 | 01 | 39 | 3.8 | 13 | 56 | 3.5 | 03 | 46 | 6.1 | 16 | 16 | 5.9 |
| TU 20 | 03 | 55 | 7.4 | 16 | 11 | 7.5 | 00 | 55 | 10.0 | 13 | 19 | 9.6 | 02 | 22 | 3.8 | 14 | 37 | 3.6 | 04 | 30 | 6.0 | 17 | 00 | 5.8 |
| W 21 | 04 | 36 | 7.1 | 16 | 52 | 7.3 | 01 | 40 | 9.7 | 14 | 04 | 9.2 | 03 | 05 | 3.8 | 15 | 19 | 3.6 | 05 | 17 | 5.8 | 17 | 47 | 5.5 |
| TH 22 | 05 | 18 | 6.8 | 17 | 37 | 7.0 | 02 | 28 | 9.2 | 14 | 54 | 8.7 | 03 | 48 | 3.6 | 16 | 01 | 3.5 | 06 | 08 | 5.5 | 18 | 40 | 5.2 |
| F 23 | 06 | 05 | 6.4 | 18 | 28 | 6.7 | 03 | 23 | 8.6 | 15 | 54 | 8.2 | 04 | 34 | 3.4 | 16 | 47 | 3.4 | 07 | 08 | 5.2 | 19 | 44 | 4.9 |
| SA 24 | 07 | 02 | 6.1 | 19 | 35 | 6.4 | 04 | 33 | 8.0 | 17 | 12 | 7.8 | 05 | 27 | 3.1 | 17 | 41 | 3.2 | 08 | 22 | 4.9 | 21 | 01 | 4.7 |
| SU 25 | 08 | 16 | 5.9 | 20 | 55 | 6.2 | 05 | 56 | 7.7 | 18 | 36 | 7.8 | 06 | 53 | 2.8 | 18 | 57 | 3.0 | 09 | 42 | 4.7 | 22 | 17 | 4.7 |
| M 26 | 09 | 39 | 6.0 | 22 | 16 | 6.3 | 07 | 21 | 7.8 | 19 | 53 | 8.1 | 09 | 01 | 2.9 | 20 | 55 | 3.0 | 11 | 01 | 4.8 | 23 | 30 | 4.9 |
| TU 27 | 10 | 59 | 6.2 | 23 | 31 | 6.7 | 08 | 31 | 8.2 | 20 | 54 | 8.5 | 10 | 06 | 3.1 | 22 | 02 | 3.2 | 12 | 11 | 5.0 | — | | — |
| W 28 | 12 | 04 | 6.6 | — | | — | 09 | 24 | 8.6 | 21 | 41 | 8.9 | 10 | 55 | 3.3 | 22 | 53 | 3.4 | 00 | 31 | 5.2 | 13 | 04 | 5.2 |
| TH 29 | 00 | 30 | 7.0 | 12 | 54 | 6.9 | 10 | 06 | 8.9 | 22 | 21 | 9.1 | 11 | 38 | 3.4 | 23 | 36 | 3.5 | 01 | 19 | 5.4 | 13 | 45 | 5.3 |
| F 30 | 01 | 16 | 7.1 | 13 | 36 | 7.0 | 10 | 42 | 9.1 | 22 | 55 | 9.3 | 12 | 16 | 3.4 | — | | — | 01 | 59 | 5.5 | 14 | 20 | 5.4 |

## OCTOBER 2016 — *High Water*    GMT

| | LONDON BRIDGE | | | | | | LIVERPOOL<br>(Gladstone Dock) | | | | | | GREENOCK | | | | | | LEITH | | | | | |
|---|---|---|---|---|---|---|---|---|---|---|---|---|---|---|---|---|---|---|---|---|---|---|---|---|
| SA 1 | 01 | 55 | 7.1 | 14 | 11 | 7.0 | 11 | 14 | 9.2 | 23 | 27 | 9.3 | 00 | 15 | 3.6 | 12 | 51 | 3.4 | 02 | 35 | 5.5 | 14 | 53 | 5.5 |
| SU 2 | 02 | 29 | 7.1 | 14 | 43 | 7.1 | 11 | 45 | 9.2 | 23 | 58 | 9.2 | 00 | 50 | 3.6 | 13 | 21 | 3.4 | 03 | 09 | 5.5 | 15 | 24 | 5.4 |
| M 3 | 02 | 59 | 7.1 | 15 | 12 | 7.1 | 12 | 14 | 9.2 | — | | — | 01 | 21 | 3.6 | 13 | 49 | 3.4 | 03 | 42 | 5.5 | 15 | 56 | 5.4 |
| TU 4 | 03 | 26 | 7.0 | 15 | 41 | 7.1 | 00 | 28 | 9.1 | 12 | 45 | 9.0 | 01 | 53 | 3.6 | 14 | 20 | 3.4 | 04 | 15 | 5.4 | 16 | 28 | 5.3 |
| W 5 | 03 | 54 | 6.9 | 16 | 11 | 6.9 | 00 | 59 | 8.9 | 13 | 16 | 8.8 | 02 | 25 | 3.6 | 14 | 53 | 3.5 | 04 | 49 | 5.2 | 17 | 02 | 5.2 |
| TH 6 | 04 | 23 | 6.7 | 16 | 42 | 6.7 | 01 | 30 | 8.6 | 13 | 48 | 8.5 | 03 | 00 | 3.5 | 15 | 27 | 3.4 | 05 | 25 | 5.1 | 17 | 39 | 5.0 |
| F 7 | 04 | 54 | 6.5 | 17 | 15 | 6.5 | 02 | 03 | 8.2 | 14 | 24 | 8.1 | 03 | 37 | 3.4 | 16 | 04 | 3.3 | 06 | 05 | 4.9 | 18 | 20 | 4.8 |
| SA 8 | 05 | 27 | 6.2 | 17 | 53 | 6.2 | 02 | 42 | 7.8 | 15 | 09 | 7.7 | 04 | 18 | 3.3 | 16 | 45 | 3.2 | 06 | 50 | 4.6 | 19 | 08 | 4.6 |
| SU 9 | 06 | 08 | 6.0 | 18 | 40 | 6.0 | 03 | 34 | 7.4 | 16 | 12 | 7.4 | 05 | 05 | 3.1 | 17 | 36 | 3.0 | 07 | 45 | 4.5 | 20 | 07 | 4.5 |
| M 10 | 07 | 02 | 5.7 | 19 | 44 | 5.8 | 04 | 50 | 7.1 | 17 | 36 | 7.3 | 06 | 03 | 2.9 | 18 | 43 | 2.9 | 08 | 52 | 4.4 | 21 | 18 | 4.5 |
| TU 11 | 08 | 22 | 5.6 | 21 | 19 | 5.9 | 06 | 21 | 7.2 | 18 | 56 | 7.7 | 07 | 16 | 2.8 | 20 | 05 | 2.9 | 10 | 06 | 4.5 | 22 | 31 | 4.6 |
| W 12 | 09 | 58 | 5.9 | 22 | 36 | 6.3 | 07 | 38 | 7.7 | 20 | 00 | 8.2 | 08 | 44 | 2.9 | 21 | 22 | 3.1 | 11 | 17 | 4.8 | 23 | 37 | 4.9 |
| TH 13 | 11 | 08 | 6.4 | 23 | 38 | 6.8 | 08 | 36 | 8.3 | 20 | 52 | 8.9 | 09 | 55 | 3.1 | 22 | 17 | 3.4 | 12 | 16 | 5.1 | — | | — |
| F 14 | 12 | 05 | 6.8 | — | | — | 09 | 23 | 9.0 | 21 | 38 | 9.5 | 10 | 45 | 3.3 | 23 | 04 | 3.5 | 00 | 33 | 5.3 | 13 | 05 | 5.5 |
| SA 15 | 00 | 32 | 7.2 | 12 | 56 | 7.2 | 10 | 07 | 9.5 | 22 | 22 | 9.9 | 11 | 28 | 3.5 | 23 | 49 | 3.7 | 01 | 17 | 5.6 | 13 | 48 | 5.8 |
| SU 16 | 01 | 21 | 7.4 | 13 | 42 | 7.4 | 10 | 49 | 9.8 | 23 | 06 | 10.2 | 12 | 10 | 3.6 | — | | — | 01 | 59 | 5.9 | 14 | 28 | 6.0 |
| M 17 | 02 | 06 | 7.5 | 14 | 26 | 7.6 | 11 | 32 | 10.0 | 23 | 50 | 10.2 | 00 | 35 | 3.8 | 12 | 53 | 3.6 | 02 | 41 | 6.1 | 15 | 10 | 6.1 |
| TU 18 | 02 | 51 | 7.5 | 15 | 09 | 7.6 | 12 | 15 | 10.0 | — | | — | 01 | 21 | 3.8 | 13 | 35 | 3.7 | 03 | 25 | 6.2 | 15 | 53 | 6.0 |
| W 19 | 03 | 34 | 7.4 | 15 | 51 | 7.6 | 00 | 35 | 10.1 | 12 | 59 | 9.7 | 02 | 06 | 3.8 | 14 | 17 | 3.7 | 04 | 12 | 6.1 | 16 | 39 | 5.8 |
| TH 20 | 04 | 17 | 7.1 | 16 | 35 | 7.4 | 01 | 23 | 9.7 | 13 | 45 | 9.4 | 02 | 51 | 3.8 | 14 | 59 | 3.7 | 05 | 01 | 5.9 | 17 | 28 | 5.6 |
| F 21 | 05 | 00 | 6.8 | 17 | 22 | 7.1 | 02 | 12 | 9.2 | 14 | 36 | 8.8 | 03 | 36 | 3.6 | 15 | 42 | 3.6 | 05 | 55 | 5.5 | 18 | 22 | 5.3 |
| SA 22 | 05 | 46 | 6.4 | 18 | 14 | 6.7 | 03 | 08 | 8.5 | 15 | 37 | 8.3 | 04 | 24 | 3.4 | 16 | 28 | 3.5 | 06 | 56 | 5.2 | 19 | 27 | 5.0 |
| SU 23 | 06 | 41 | 6.1 | 19 | 18 | 6.4 | 04 | 16 | 8.0 | 16 | 51 | 7.9 | 05 | 21 | 3.1 | 17 | 21 | 3.3 | 08 | 08 | 4.9 | 20 | 41 | 4.8 |
| M 24 | 07 | 51 | 5.9 | 20 | 32 | 6.2 | 05 | 36 | 7.6 | 18 | 11 | 7.8 | 06 | 48 | 2.9 | 18 | 34 | 3.1 | 09 | 23 | 4.7 | 21 | 54 | 4.8 |
| TU 25 | 09 | 10 | 5.9 | 21 | 48 | 6.3 | 06 | 57 | 7.7 | 19 | 26 | 8.0 | 08 | 37 | 2.9 | 20 | 19 | 3.1 | 10 | 37 | 4.7 | 23 | 04 | 4.9 |
| W 26 | 10 | 27 | 6.1 | 23 | 02 | 6.5 | 08 | 07 | 8.0 | 20 | 27 | 8.4 | 09 | 40 | 3.1 | 21 | 31 | 3.2 | 11 | 46 | 4.9 | — | | — |
| TH 27 | 11 | 33 | 6.4 | — | | — | 08 | 59 | 8.4 | 21 | 15 | 8.7 | 10 | 28 | 3.3 | 22 | 23 | 3.4 | 00 | 05 | 5.1 | 12 | 40 | 5.1 |
| F 28 | 00 | 02 | 6.8 | 12 | 25 | 6.7 | 09 | 41 | 8.7 | 21 | 54 | 8.9 | 11 | 10 | 3.4 | 23 | 07 | 3.5 | 00 | 55 | 5.2 | 13 | 21 | 5.2 |
| SA 29 | 00 | 49 | 6.9 | 13 | 06 | 6.8 | 10 | 16 | 8.9 | 22 | 29 | 9.1 | 11 | 47 | 3.5 | 23 | 46 | 3.5 | 01 | 35 | 5.3 | 13 | 55 | 5.3 |
| SU 30 | 01 | 27 | 6.9 | 13 | 42 | 6.9 | 10 | 47 | 9.1 | 23 | 01 | 9.1 | 12 | 20 | 3.5 | — | | — | 02 | 11 | 5.4 | 14 | 27 | 5.4 |
| M 31 | 02 | 00 | 7.0 | 14 | 14 | 7.0 | 11 | 18 | 9.2 | 23 | 32 | 9.1 | 00 | 21 | 3.5 | 12 | 51 | 3.5 | 02 | 45 | 5.4 | 14 | 57 | 5.4 |

# NOVEMBER 2016   *High Water*   GMT

| | LONDON BRIDGE<br>Datum of Predictions<br>3.20m below | | | | | | LIVERPOOL<br>(Gladstone Dock)<br>Datum of Predictions<br>4.93m below | | | | | | GREENOCK<br>Datum of Predictions<br>1.62m below | | | | | | LEITH<br>Datum of Predictions<br>2.90m below | | | | | |
|---|---|---|---|---|---|---|---|---|---|---|---|---|---|---|---|---|---|---|---|---|---|---|---|---|---|
| | hr | m | hr | m | ht | | hr | m | hr | m | ht | | hr | m | hr | m | ht | | hr | m | hr | m | ht | |
| TU 1 | 02 | 29 | 7.0 | 14 44 | 7.1 | | 11 48 | 9.2 | — | — | | | 00 54 | 3.5 | 13 21 | 3.6 | | | 03 17 | 5.4 | 15 28 | 5.4 | | |
| W 2 | 02 | 57 | 7.0 | 15 14 | 7.1 | | 00 03 | 9.0 | 12 19 | 9.1 | | | 01 26 | 3.5 | 13 52 | 3.6 | | | 03 50 | 5.3 | 16 00 | 5.4 | | |
| TH 3 | 03 | 26 | 6.9 | 15 45 | 7.0 | | 00 35 | 8.9 | 12 50 | 8.9 | | | 02 00 | 3.5 | 14 24 | 3.6 | | | 04 24 | 5.2 | 16 34 | 5.3 | | |
| F 4 | 03 | 57 | 6.8 | 16 17 | 6.8 | | 01 07 | 8.6 | 13 23 | 8.7 | | | 02 36 | 3.5 | 14 58 | 3.6 | | | 05 00 | 5.1 | 17 10 | 5.1 | | |
| SA 5 | 04 | 29 | 6.6 | 16 53 | 6.6 | | 01 40 | 8.3 | 13 59 | 8.4 | | | 03 14 | 3.5 | 15 33 | 3.5 | | | 05 39 | 5.0 | 17 49 | 5.0 | | |
| SU 6 | 05 | 04 | 6.4 | 17 32 | 6.4 | | 02 20 | 8.0 | 14 43 | 8.1 | | | 03 55 | 3.3 | 16 12 | 3.3 | | | 06 23 | 4.8 | 18 35 | 4.8 | | |
| M 7 | 05 | 44 | 6.2 | 18 19 | 6.2 | | 03 09 | 7.7 | 15 40 | 7.8 | | | 04 41 | 3.2 | 16 59 | 3.2 | | | 07 15 | 4.6 | 19 29 | 4.6 | | |
| TU 8 | 06 | 34 | 5.9 | 19 17 | 6.1 | | 04 14 | 7.4 | 16 54 | 7.6 | | | 05 35 | 3.0 | 18 00 | 3.1 | | | 08 16 | 4.6 | 20 35 | 4.6 | | |
| W 9 | 07 | 41 | 5.8 | 20 37 | 6.1 | | 05 36 | 7.4 | 18 12 | 7.8 | | | 06 43 | 3.0 | 19 17 | 3.1 | | | 09 28 | 4.6 | 21 50 | 4.7 | | |
| TH 10 | 09 | 12 | 5.9 | 21 57 | 6.4 | | 06 54 | 7.8 | 19 20 | 8.3 | | | 08 04 | 3.0 | 20 37 | 3.2 | | | 10 39 | 4.8 | 22 58 | 4.9 | | |
| F 11 | 10 | 28 | 6.3 | 23 02 | 6.8 | | 07 59 | 8.3 | 20 18 | 8.9 | | | 09 19 | 3.2 | 21 42 | 3.4 | | | 11 41 | 5.1 | 23 56 | 5.3 | | |
| SA 12 | 11 | 30 | 6.8 | — | — | | 08 53 | 8.9 | 21 10 | 9.4 | | | 10 15 | 3.4 | 22 36 | 3.6 | | | 12 33 | 5.5 | — | — | | |
| SU 13 | 00 | 01 | 7.1 | 12 25 | 7.1 | | 09 41 | 9.4 | 21 58 | 9.8 | | | 11 03 | 3.5 | 23 26 | 3.7 | | | 00 47 | 5.6 | 13 20 | 5.8 | | |
| M 14 | 00 | 54 | 7.3 | 13 15 | 7.4 | | 10 26 | 9.8 | 22 45 | 10.1 | | | 11 48 | 3.7 | — | — | | | 01 34 | 5.9 | 14 04 | 6.0 | | |
| TU 15 | 01 | 43 | 7.4 | 14 02 | 7.6 | | 11 12 | 10.0 | 23 33 | 10.1 | | | 00 15 | 3.8 | 12 33 | 3.7 | | | 02 21 | 6.1 | 14 48 | 6.0 | | |
| W 16 | 02 | 30 | 7.4 | 14 49 | 7.6 | | 11 57 | 10.0 | — | — | | | 01 04 | 3.8 | 13 17 | 3.8 | | | 03 08 | 6.1 | 15 34 | 6.0 | | |
| TH 17 | 03 | 15 | 7.3 | 15 35 | 7.6 | | 00 20 | 10.0 | 12 43 | 9.8 | | | 01 53 | 3.8 | 14 00 | 3.9 | | | 03 57 | 6.0 | 16 21 | 5.9 | | |
| F 18 | 04 | 00 | 7.1 | 16 21 | 7.4 | | 01 09 | 9.6 | 13 30 | 9.5 | | | 02 40 | 3.7 | 14 43 | 3.8 | | | 04 48 | 5.8 | 17 11 | 5.6 | | |
| SA 19 | 04 | 45 | 6.8 | 17 09 | 7.1 | | 01 59 | 9.1 | 14 21 | 9.0 | | | 03 27 | 3.5 | 15 26 | 3.7 | | | 05 42 | 5.5 | 18 05 | 5.3 | | |
| SU 20 | 05 | 31 | 6.5 | 18 00 | 6.8 | | 02 53 | 8.6 | 15 17 | 8.5 | | | 04 17 | 3.4 | 16 12 | 3.6 | | | 06 41 | 5.2 | 19 07 | 5.1 | | |
| M 21 | 06 | 21 | 6.2 | 18 57 | 6.4 | | 03 53 | 8.1 | 16 21 | 8.1 | | | 05 12 | 3.1 | 17 04 | 3.4 | | | 07 45 | 4.9 | 20 15 | 4.9 | | |
| TU 22 | 07 | 22 | 6.0 | 20 02 | 6.2 | | 05 01 | 7.7 | 17 32 | 7.9 | | | 06 22 | 3.0 | 18 06 | 3.2 | | | 08 52 | 4.7 | 21 22 | 4.8 | | |
| W 23 | 08 | 32 | 5.9 | 21 10 | 6.2 | | 06 15 | 7.6 | 18 43 | 7.9 | | | 07 46 | 2.9 | 19 26 | 3.1 | | | 09 59 | 4.7 | 22 27 | 4.8 | | |
| TH 24 | 09 | 43 | 6.0 | 22 18 | 6.3 | | 07 26 | 7.8 | 19 48 | 8.0 | | | 08 57 | 3.0 | 20 44 | 3.2 | | | 11 05 | 4.7 | 23 29 | 4.9 | | |
| F 25 | 10 | 50 | 6.2 | 23 22 | 6.4 | | 08 23 | 8.1 | 20 40 | 8.3 | | | 09 51 | 3.2 | 21 45 | 3.3 | | | 12 03 | 4.9 | — | — | | |
| SA 26 | 11 | 46 | 6.4 | — | — | | 09 09 | 8.4 | 21 24 | 8.5 | | | 10 35 | 3.3 | 22 33 | 3.4 | | | 00 22 | 5.0 | 12 49 | 5.0 | | |
| SU 27 | 00 | 13 | 6.6 | 12 32 | 6.6 | | 09 46 | 8.7 | 22 02 | 8.7 | | | 11 15 | 3.5 | 23 15 | 3.4 | | | 01 08 | 5.1 | 13 27 | 5.2 | | |
| M 28 | 00 | 55 | 6.7 | 13 12 | 6.8 | | 10 21 | 8.9 | 22 37 | 8.9 | | | 11 51 | 3.5 | 23 53 | 3.4 | | | 01 47 | 5.2 | 14 01 | 5.3 | | |
| TU 29 | 01 | 31 | 6.8 | 13 47 | 6.9 | | 10 53 | 9.0 | 23 10 | 8.9 | | | 12 25 | 3.6 | — | — | | | 02 22 | 5.3 | 14 33 | 5.4 | | |
| W 30 | 02 | 03 | 6.9 | 14 20 | 7.0 | | 11 25 | 9.1 | 23 43 | 8.9 | | | 00 27 | 3.5 | 12 58 | 3.6 | | | 02 56 | 5.3 | 15 05 | 5.4 | | |

# DECEMBER 2016   *High Water*   GMT

| | LONDON BRIDGE | | | | | | LIVERPOOL<br>(Gladstone Dock) | | | | | | GREENOCK | | | | | | LEITH | | | | | |
|---|---|---|---|---|---|---|---|---|---|---|---|---|---|---|---|---|---|---|---|---|---|---|---|---|---|
| TH 1 | 02 | 33 | 6.9 | 14 51 | 7.0 | | 11 58 | 9.1 | — | — | | | 01 02 | 3.5 | 13 29 | 3.7 | | | 03 30 | 5.3 | 15 38 | 5.4 | | |
| F 2 | 03 | 05 | 6.9 | 15 24 | 7.0 | | 00 16 | 8.8 | 12 31 | 9.0 | | | 01 38 | 3.5 | 14 01 | 3.7 | | | 04 04 | 5.3 | 16 12 | 5.3 | | |
| SA 3 | 03 | 38 | 6.8 | 15 59 | 6.9 | | 00 50 | 8.7 | 13 06 | 8.9 | | | 02 15 | 3.5 | 14 35 | 3.7 | | | 04 40 | 5.2 | 16 48 | 5.2 | | |
| SU 4 | 04 | 13 | 6.7 | 16 36 | 6.8 | | 01 25 | 8.5 | 13 43 | 8.7 | | | 02 55 | 3.5 | 15 11 | 3.6 | | | 05 19 | 5.1 | 17 26 | 5.1 | | |
| M 5 | 04 | 49 | 6.5 | 17 17 | 6.6 | | 02 05 | 8.3 | 14 25 | 8.5 | | | 03 36 | 3.4 | 15 50 | 3.5 | | | 06 02 | 5.0 | 18 09 | 5.0 | | |
| TU 6 | 05 | 29 | 6.4 | 18 02 | 6.5 | | 02 51 | 8.0 | 15 16 | 8.2 | | | 04 21 | 3.3 | 16 34 | 3.4 | | | 06 50 | 4.9 | 18 58 | 4.9 | | |
| W 7 | 06 | 16 | 6.2 | 18 55 | 6.3 | | 03 48 | 7.8 | 16 19 | 8.1 | | | 05 10 | 3.2 | 17 26 | 3.3 | | | 07 45 | 4.8 | 19 57 | 4.8 | | |
| TH 8 | 07 | 13 | 6.1 | 20 03 | 6.2 | | 04 57 | 7.7 | 17 30 | 8.1 | | | 06 08 | 3.1 | 18 33 | 3.2 | | | 08 51 | 4.7 | 21 07 | 4.8 | | |
| F 9 | 08 | 29 | 6.1 | 21 21 | 6.4 | | 06 11 | 7.9 | 18 41 | 8.3 | | | 07 19 | 3.1 | 19 53 | 3.2 | | | 10 01 | 4.9 | 22 20 | 4.9 | | |
| SA 10 | 09 | 50 | 6.3 | 22 29 | 6.6 | | 07 22 | 8.3 | 19 46 | 8.7 | | | 08 37 | 3.2 | 21 08 | 3.3 | | | 11 06 | 5.1 | 23 25 | 5.2 | | |
| SU 11 | 10 | 57 | 6.6 | 23 32 | 6.8 | | 08 23 | 8.7 | 20 45 | 9.1 | | | 09 44 | 3.3 | 22 11 | 3.5 | | | 12 04 | 5.3 | — | — | | |
| M 12 | 11 | 58 | 7.0 | — | — | | 09 18 | 9.2 | 21 39 | 9.5 | | | 10 39 | 3.5 | 23 07 | 3.6 | | | 00 22 | 5.5 | 12 57 | 5.6 | | |
| TU 13 | 00 | 30 | 7.0 | 12 53 | 7.2 | | 10 08 | 9.5 | 22 30 | 9.7 | | | 11 29 | 3.6 | — | — | | | 01 15 | 5.7 | 13 45 | 5.8 | | |
| W 14 | 01 | 23 | 7.1 | 13 44 | 7.4 | | 10 56 | 9.8 | 23 20 | 9.8 | | | 00 00 | 3.7 | 12 17 | 3.7 | | | 02 05 | 5.9 | 14 31 | 5.9 | | |
| TH 15 | 02 | 13 | 7.2 | 14 33 | 7.5 | | 11 44 | 9.9 | — | — | | | 00 52 | 3.7 | 13 02 | 3.8 | | | 02 55 | 6.0 | 15 18 | 5.9 | | |
| F 16 | 03 | 01 | 7.2 | 15 22 | 7.5 | | 00 09 | 9.8 | 12 31 | 9.8 | | | 01 41 | 3.7 | 13 46 | 3.9 | | | 03 45 | 5.9 | 16 06 | 5.8 | | |
| SA 17 | 03 | 47 | 7.1 | 16 09 | 7.4 | | 00 57 | 9.5 | 13 17 | 9.5 | | | 02 30 | 3.6 | 14 29 | 3.9 | | | 04 35 | 5.8 | 16 56 | 5.7 | | |
| SU 18 | 04 | 32 | 6.9 | 16 55 | 7.1 | | 01 44 | 9.2 | 14 04 | 9.2 | | | 03 17 | 3.5 | 15 12 | 3.8 | | | 05 26 | 5.5 | 17 47 | 5.5 | | |
| M 19 | 05 | 15 | 6.7 | 17 42 | 6.8 | | 02 32 | 8.7 | 14 52 | 8.8 | | | 04 04 | 3.3 | 15 56 | 3.7 | | | 06 19 | 5.2 | 18 42 | 5.2 | | |
| TU 20 | 05 | 59 | 6.4 | 18 31 | 6.5 | | 03 21 | 8.3 | 15 44 | 8.4 | | | 04 52 | 3.2 | 16 43 | 3.5 | | | 07 14 | 5.0 | 19 40 | 5.0 | | |
| W 21 | 06 | 47 | 6.1 | 19 23 | 6.2 | | 04 16 | 7.8 | 16 43 | 8.0 | | | 05 43 | 3.1 | 17 33 | 3.3 | | | 08 11 | 4.7 | 20 40 | 4.8 | | |
| TH 22 | 07 | 45 | 5.9 | 20 22 | 6.0 | | 05 19 | 7.6 | 17 48 | 7.7 | | | 06 41 | 3.0 | 18 30 | 3.2 | | | 09 09 | 4.6 | 21 40 | 4.7 | | |
| F 23 | 08 | 50 | 5.8 | 21 23 | 6.0 | | 06 27 | 7.5 | 18 55 | 7.7 | | | 07 47 | 2.9 | 19 36 | 3.1 | | | 10 09 | 4.5 | 22 41 | 4.6 | | |
| SA 24 | 09 | 55 | 5.9 | 22 22 | 6.0 | | 07 34 | 7.6 | 19 58 | 7.8 | | | 08 55 | 3.0 | 20 48 | 3.1 | | | 11 10 | 4.6 | 23 41 | 4.7 | | |
| SU 25 | 10 | 58 | 6.1 | 23 27 | 6.2 | | 08 30 | 7.9 | 20 51 | 8.1 | | | 09 54 | 3.2 | 21 52 | 3.2 | | | 12 08 | 4.7 | — | — | | |
| M 26 | 11 | 54 | 6.3 | — | — | | 09 16 | 8.3 | 21 36 | 8.3 | | | 10 42 | 3.3 | 22 43 | 3.2 | | | 00 35 | 4.8 | 12 56 | 4.9 | | |
| TU 27 | 00 | 19 | 6.4 | 12 41 | 6.6 | | 09 55 | 8.6 | 22 15 | 8.5 | | | 11 24 | 3.5 | 23 26 | 3.3 | | | 01 21 | 5.0 | 13 36 | 5.1 | | |
| W 28 | 01 | 02 | 6.6 | 13 22 | 6.7 | | 10 32 | 8.8 | 22 51 | 8.7 | | | 12 03 | 3.6 | — | — | | | 02 01 | 5.1 | 14 12 | 5.3 | | |
| TH 29 | 01 | 41 | 6.7 | 13 59 | 6.8 | | 11 06 | 9.0 | 23 26 | 8.8 | | | 00 05 | 3.3 | 12 38 | 3.6 | | | 02 37 | 5.2 | 14 47 | 5.4 | | |
| F 30 | 02 | 17 | 6.8 | 14 34 | 6.9 | | 11 41 | 9.1 | — | — | | | 00 43 | 3.4 | 13 10 | 3.7 | | | 03 12 | 5.3 | 15 21 | 5.4 | | |
| SA 31 | 02 | 51 | 6.8 | 15 09 | 7.0 | | 00 00 | 8.9 | 12 16 | 9.2 | | | 01 20 | 3.4 | 13 42 | 3.7 | | | 03 46 | 5.3 | 15 55 | 5.4 | | |

# ABBREVIATIONS AND ACRONYMS

**A**
AAA    Amateur Athletic Association
ABA    Amateur Boxing Association
abr    abridged
ac    alternating current
AC    *ante Christum* before Christ
   Companion, Order of Australia
ADC    Aide-de-Camp
ADC (P)    Personal ADC to the Queen
Adj.    Adjutant
Adj. Gen.    Adjutant General
Adm.    Admiral
AE    Air Efficiency award
AEM    Air Efficiency Medal
aet    after extra time
AFC    Air Force Cross
AFM    Air Force Medal
AG    Attorney-General
AH    *anno Hegirae* in the year of the Hegira
AM    Assembly Member (Wales)
ANC    African National Congress
AO    Air Officer
   Officer, Order of Australia
AOC    Air Officer Commanding
apptd    appointed
APR    annual percentage rate
ASBO    antisocial behaviour order
AUC    *ab urbe condita* from the foundation of Rome
   *anno urbis conditae* from the founding of the city

**B**
b.    born
   bowled (cricket)
BAF    British Athletics Federation
BAFTA    British Academy of Film and Television Arts
BAS    Bachelor in Agricultural Science
   British Antarctic Survey
BBA    British Bankers' Association
BBFC    British Board of Film Classification
BCH (D)    Bachelor of (Dental) Surgery
BCL    Bachelor of Civil Law
BCOM    Bachelor of Commerce
BD    Bachelor of Divinity
BDA    British Dental Association
BDS    Bachelor of Dental Surgery
BED    Bachelor of Education
BEM    British Empire Medal
BENG    Bachelor of Engineering
BFPO    British Forces Post Office
BLIT    Bachelor of Literature
BLITT    Bachelor of Letters
BM    Bachelor of Medicine
BMA    British Medical Association
BMUS    Bachelor of Music
Bp    Bishop
BPHARM    Bachelor of Pharmacy
BPHIL    Bachelor of Philosophy
BPS    British Psychological Society

Brig.    Brigadier
BSI    British Standards Institution
BST    British Summer Time
Bt.    Baronet
BTEC    Business and Technology Education Council
BVMS    Bachelor of Veterinary Medicine and Surgery

**C**
c.    *circa* about
C.    Conservative
Cantuar:    of Canterbury (Archbishop)
Capt.    Captain
Carliol    of Carlisle (Bishop)
CB    Companion, Order of the Bath
CBE    Commander, Order of the British Empire
CC    Companion, Order of Canada
CCF    Combined Cadet Force
CCHEM    chartered chemist
CD    Civil Defence
   Corps Diplomatique
Cdr    Commander
Cdre    Commodore
CDS    Chief of the Defence Staff
CE    civil engineer
   Common (or Christian) Era
CENG    chartered engineer
Cestr:    of Chester (Bishop)
CET    Central European Time
cf    *confer* compare
CGC    Conspicuous Gallantry Cross
CGEOL    chartered geologist
CGM    Conspicuous Gallantry Medal
CGS    Chief of General Staff
CH    Companion of Honour
CHB/M    Bachelor/Master of Surgery
CI    Channel Islands
Cicestr:    of Chichester (Bishop)
CID    Criminal Investigation Department
CIE    Companion, Order of the Indian Empire
C-in-C    Commander-in-Chief
CILIP    Chartered Institute of Library and Information Professionals
CIPFA    Chartered Institute of Public Finance and Accountancy
CIS    Commonwealth of Independent States
CLJ    Commander, Order of St Lazarus of Jerusalem
CM    *Chirurgiae Magister* Master of Surgery
CMG    Companion, Order of St Michael and St George
CO    Commanding Officer
C of E    Church of England
Col.    Colonel
cons.    consecrated
Cpl.    Corporal
CPM    Colonial Police Medal

CPS    Crown Prosecution Service
CSI    Companion, Order of the Star of India
CVO    Commander, Royal Victorian Order

**D**
d    *denarius* penny
d.    died
DAB    Digital Audio Broadcasting
DBE    Dame Commander, Order of the British Empire
DCB    Dame Commander, Order of the Bath
D CH    *Doctor Chirurgiae* Doctor of Surgery
DCL    Doctor of Civil Law
DCM    Distinguished Conduct Medal
DCMG    Dame Commander, Order of St Michael and St George
DCVO    Dame Commander, Royal Victorian Order
DD    Doctor of Divinity
DDS    Doctor of Dental Surgery
DDT    dichlorodiphenyl trichloroethane
DFC    Distinguished Flying Cross
DFM    Distinguished Flying Medal
DIP ED    Diploma in Education
DIP HE    Diploma in Higher Education
DL    Deputy Lieutenant
DLIT    Doctor of Literature
DLITT    Doctor of Letters
DLR    Docklands Light Railway
DMUS    Doctor of Music
DNA    deoxyribonucleic acid
DPH *or*    Doctor of Philosophy
DPHIL
DPP    Director of Public Prosecutions
DSC    Distinguished Service Cross
DSc    Doctor of Science
DSM    Distinguished Service Medal
DSO    Companion, Distinguished Service Order
Dunelm:    of Durham (Bishop)
DUP    Democratic Unionist Party
**E**
Ebor:    of York (Archbishop)
EC    Elizabeth Cross
   European Community
ECG    electrocardiogram
ED    Efficiency Decoration
EEG    electroencephalogram
EEU    Eurasian Economic Union
EIB    European Investment Bank
ER    *Elizabetha Regina* Queen Elizabeth
ERM    exchange rate mechanism
ESA    European Space Agency
ETA    *Euzkadi ta Askatasuna* Basque separatist organisation

et seq    *et sequentia* and the following

Exon:    of Exeter (Bishop)

**F**

FANY    First Aid Nursing Yeomanry

FAQ    frequently asked questions

FARC    *Fuerzas Armadas Revolucionarias de Colombia* Revolutionary Armed Forces of Colombia

FBA    Fellow, British Academy

FBAA    Fellow, British Association of Accountants and Auditors

FBS    Fellow, Botanical Society

FBU    Fire Brigades Union

FCA    Fellow, Institute of Chartered Accountants in England and Wales

FCCA    Fellow, Chartered Association of Certified Accountants

FCGI    Fellow, City and Guilds of London Institute

FCIA    Fellow, Corporation of Insurance Agents

FCIARB    Fellow, Chartered Institute of Arbitrators

FCIB    Fellow, Chartered Institute of Bankers

   Fellow, Corporation of Insurance Brokers

FCIBSE    Fellow, Chartered Institution of Building Services Engineers

FCII    Fellow, Chartered Insurance Institute

FCIPS    Fellow, Chartered Institute of Purchasing and Supply

FCIS    Fellow, Institute of Chartered Secretaries and Administrators

FCIT    Fellow, Chartered Institute of Transport

FCMA    Fellow, Chartered Institute of Management Accountants

FCP    Fellow, College of Preceptors

FD    *Fidei Defensor* Defender of the Faith

FE    further education

FFA    Fellow, Faculty of Actuaries (Scotland)

   Fellow, Institute of Financial Accountants

FFAS    Fellow, Faculty of Architects and Surveyors

FFCM    Fellow, Faculty of Community Medicine

FFPHM    Fellow, Faculty of Public Health Medicine

FGS    Fellow, Geological Society

FHS    Fellow, Heraldry Society

FHSM    Fellow, Institute of Health Service Management

FIA    Fellow, Institute of Actuaries

FIBIOL    Fellow, Institute of Biology

FICE    Fellow, Institution of Civil Engineers

FICS    Fellow, Institution of Chartered Shipbrokers

FIEE    Fellow, Institution of Electrical Engineers

FIERE    Fellow, Institution of Electronic and Radio Engineers

FIM    Fellow, Institute of Metals

FIMGT    Fellow, Institute of Management

FIMM    Fellow, Institution of Mining and Metallurgy

FINSTF    Fellow, Institute of Fuel

FINSTP    Fellow, Institute of Physics

FIQS    Fellow, Institute of Quantity Surveyors

FIS    Fellow, Institute of Statisticians

FJI    Fellow, Institute of Journalists

FLS    Fellow, Linnean Society

FMEDSCI    Fellow, Academy of Medical Sciences

fo    folio

FPHS    Fellow, Philosophical Society

FRAD    Fellow, Royal Academy of Dancing

FRAES    Fellow, Royal Aeronautical Society

FRAGS    Fellow, Royal Agricultural Societies

FRAI    Fellow, Royal Anthropological Institute

FRAM    Fellow, Royal Academy of Music

FRAS    Fellow, Royal Asiatic Society

   Fellow, Royal Astronomical Society

FRBS    Fellow, Royal Botanic Society

   Fellow, Royal Society of British Sculptors

FRCA    Fellow, Royal College of Anaesthetists

FRCGP    Fellow, Royal College of General Practitioners

FRCM    Fellow, Royal College of Music

FRCO    Fellow, Royal College of Organists

FRCOG    Fellow, Royal College of Obstetricians and Gynaecologists

FRCP    Fellow, Royal College of Physicians, London

FRCPATH    Fellow, Royal College of Pathologists

FRCPE *or* FRCPED    Fellow, Royal College of Physicians, Edinburgh

FRCPI    Fellow, Royal College of Physicians, Ireland

FRCPSYCH    Fellow, Royal College of Psychiatrists

FRCR    Fellow, Royal College of Radiologists

FRCS    Fellow, Royal College of Surgeons of England

FRCSE *or* FRCSED    Fellow, Royal College of Surgeons of Edinburgh

FRCSGLAS    Fellow, Royal College of Physicians and Surgeons of Glasgow

FRCSI    Fellow, Royal College of Surgeons in Ireland

FRCVS    Fellow, Royal College of Veterinary Surgeons

FRECONS    Fellow, Royal Economic Society

FRENG    Fellow, Royal Academy of Engineering

FRGS    Fellow, Royal Geographical Society

FRHISTS    Fellow, Royal Historical Society

FRHS    Fellow, Royal Horticultural Society

FRIBA    Fellow, Royal Institute of British Architects

FRICS    Fellow, Royal Institution of Chartered Surveyors

FRMETS    Fellow, Royal Meteorological Society

FRMS    Fellow, Royal Microscopical Society

FRNS    Fellow, Royal Numismatic Society

FRPHARMS    Fellow, Royal Pharmaceutical Society

FRPS    Fellow, Royal Photographic Society

FRS    Fellow, Royal Society

FRSA    Fellow, Royal Society of Arts

FRSC    Fellow, Royal Society of Chemistry

FRSE    Fellow, Royal Society of Edinburgh

FRSH    Fellow, Royal Society of Health

FRSL    Fellow, Royal Society of Literature

FRTPI    Fellow, Royal Town Planning Institute

FSA    Fellow, Society of Antiquaries

FSS    Fellow, Royal Statistical Society

FSVA    Fellow, Incorporated Society of Valuers and Auctioneers

FTI    Fellow, Textile Institute

FTII    Fellow, Chartered Institute of Taxation

FZS    Fellow, Zoological Society

**G**

GBE    Dame/Knight Grand Cross, Order of the British Empire

GC    George Cross

GCB    Dame/Knight Grand Cross, Order of the Bath

GCLJ    Knight Grand Cross, Order of St Lazarus of Jerusalem

GCMG    Dame/Knight Grand Cross, Order of St Michael and St George

GCSI    Knight Grand Commander, Order of the Star of India

GCVO    Dame/Knight Grand Cross, Royal Victorian Order

Gen.    General

GHQ    general headquarters

GLA    Greater London Authority

GM    George Medal

| | | | | | | |
|---|---|---|---|---|---|---|
| GMB | Britain's General Union | **K** | | MCH(D) | Master of (Dental) Surgery |
| GOC | General Officer Commanding | KBE | Knight Commander, Order of the British Empire | MDS | Master of Dental Surgery |
| Gp Capt. | Group Captain | KCB | Knight Commander, Order of the Bath | ME | Middle English |
| GPS | Global Positioning System | | | | myalgic encephalomyelitis |
| **H** | | KCLJ | Knight Commander, Order of St Lazarus of Jerusalem | MED | Master of Education |
| HB | His Beatitude | | | Mgr | Monsignor |
| HBM | Her/His Britannic Majesty('s) | KCMG | Knight Commander, Order of St Michael and St George | MIT | Massachusetts Institute of Technology |
| HCF | Honorary Chaplain to the Forces | | | MLA | Member of Legislative Assembly (NI) |
| HE | Her/His Excellency | KCSI | Knight Commander, Order of the Star of India | | Museums, Libraries and Archives Council |
| | higher education | | | | |
| | His Eminence | KCVO | Knight Commander, Royal Victorian Order | MLITT | Master of Letters |
| HH | Her/His Highness | | | Mlle | Mademoiselle |
| | Her/His Honour | KG | Knight of the Garter | MM | Military Medal |
| | His Holiness | KGB | *Komitet Gosudarstvennoi Bezopasnosti* Committee of State Security (USSR) | Mme | Madame |
| HIM | Her/His Imperial Majesty | | | MMR | measles, mumps and rubella (vaccine) |
| HJS | *hic jacet sepultus* here lies buried | | | | |
| | | KLJ | Knight, Order of St Lazarus of Jerusalem | MN | Merchant Navy |
| HM | Her/His Majesty('s) | | | MPHIL | Master of Philosophy |
| HMAS | Her/His Majesty's Australian Ship | KP | Knight, Order of St Patrick | MR | Master of the Rolls |
| | | KStJ | Knight, Order of St John of Jerusalem | MRI | magnetic resonance imaging |
| HMC | Headmasters' and Headmistresses' Conference | | | MRSA | methicillin-resistant staphylococcus aureus |
| | | Kt. | Knight | | |
| HMI | Her/His Majesty's Inspector | KT | Knight of the Thistle | MS | manuscript (*pl* MSS) |
| | | **L** | | | Master of Surgery |
| HMS | Her/His Majesty's Ship | Lab. | Labour | | multiple sclerosis |
| Hon. | Honorary | Lat. | Latitude | MSP | Member of Scottish Parliament |
| | Honourable | lbw | leg before wicket (cricket) | | |
| HRH | Her/His Royal Highness | lc | lower case (printing) | MUSB/D | Bachelor/Doctor of Music |
| HRT | hormone replacement therapy | LCJ | Lord Chief Justice | | |
| | | LCM | least/lowest common multiple | MVO | Member, Royal Victorian Order |
| HSE | *hic sepultus est* here is buried | LD | Liberal Democrat | **N** | |
| | | LDS | Licentiate in Dental Surgery | NAAFI | Navy, Army and Air Force Institutes |
| HSH | Her/His Serene Highness | LHD | *Literarum Humaniorum Doctor* Doctor of Humane Letters/Literature | | |
| **I** | | | | NAFTA | North American Free Trade Agreement |
| IB | International Baccalaureate | | | | |
| IBF | International Boxing Federation | | | NAO | National Audit Office |
| | | Lib. | Liberal | NCO | non-commissioned officer |
| ICC | International Cricket Council | LITT D | Doctor of Letters | NDPB | non-departmental public body |
| | | LJ | Lord Justice | | |
| | International Criminal Court | LLB | Bachelor of Laws | NFU | National Farmers' Union |
| | | LLD | Doctor of Laws | non seq | *non sequitur* it does not follow |
| ICJ | International Court of Justice | LLM | Master of Laws | | |
| | | loc cit | *loco citato* in the place cited | Norvic: | of Norwich (Bishop) |
| id | *idem* the same | | | NP | Notary Public |
| IP | intellectual property | Londin: | of London (Bishop) | NSW | New South Wales (Australia) |
| | internet protocol | Long. | longitude | | |
| IPSA | Independent Parliamentary Standards Authority | lsd | *librae, solidi, denarii* pounds, shillings and pence | NUJ | National Union of Journalists |
| | | | | | |
| iPSC | induced pluripotent stem cell | Lt. | Lieutenant | NUS | National Union of Students |
| | | LTA | Lawn Tennis Association | NUT | National Union of Teachers |
| IRA | Irish Republican Army | LVO | Lieutenant, Royal Victorian Order | **O** | |
| IRB | International Rugby Board | | | Ob *or* obit | died |
| IRC | International Rescue Committee | **M** | | OBE | Officer, Order of the British Empire |
| | | m. | married | | |
| Is | Islands | M | Monsieur | OBR | Office for Budget Responsibility |
| IS | Islamic State | Maj. | Major | | |
| ISO | Imperial Service Order | MB | *Medicinae Baccalaureus* Bachelor of Medicine | OE | Old English |
| | International Organisation for Standardisation | | | OED | *Oxford English Dictionary* |
| | | MBA | Master of Business Administration | OHMS | On Her/His Majesty's Service |
| ISP | internet service provider | | | | |
| ISSN | International Standard Serial Number | MBC | Metropolitan Borough Council | OM | Order of Merit |
| | | | | ono | or near(est) offer |
| ITU | International Telecommunication Union | MBE | Member, Order of the British Empire | op | *opus* work |
| | | | | op cit | *opere citato* in the work cited |
| **J** | | MBO | management buy-out | | |
| J | Judge | MC | Master of Ceremonies | | |
| | Justice | | Military Cross | OS | Ordnance Survey |
| JP | Justice of the Peace | MCB | Muslim Council of Britain | OStJ | Officer, Order of St John of Jerusalem |
| | | MCC | Marylebone Cricket Club | | |

**P**

| | |
|---|---|
| PC | Plaid Cymru |
| | Police Constable |
| | Privy Counsellor |
| Petriburg: | of Peterborough (Bishop) |
| PG | parental guidance |
| | postgraduate |
| PHD | Doctor of Philosophy |
| pl | plural |
| PLO | Palestine Liberation Organisation |
| PM | post mortem |
| | Prime Minister |
| PO | Petty Officer |
| | Pilot Officer |
| | post office |
| | postal order |
| | *per procurationem* by proxy |
| PPS | Parliamentary Private Secretary |
| PR | proportional representation |
| PRA | President of the Royal Academy |
| pro tem | *pro tempore* for the time being |
| prox | *proximo* next month |
| PRS | President of the Royal Society |
| PRSE | President of the Royal Society of Edinburgh |
| Pte. | Private |

**Q**

| | |
|---|---|
| QBD | Queen's Bench Division |
| QC | Queen's Counsel |
| QE | quantitative easing |
| QED | *quod erat demonstrandum* which was to be proved |
| QGM | Queen's Gallantry Medal |
| QHC | Queen's Honorary Chaplain |
| QHDS | Queen's Honorary Dental Surgeon |
| QHNS | Queen's Honorary Nursing Sister |
| QHP | Queen's Honorary Physician |
| QHS | Queen's Honorary Surgeon |
| QMG | Quartermaster-General |
| QPM | Queen's Police Medal |
| QSO | quasi-stellar object *(quasar)* |
| | Queen's Service Order |
| quango | quasi-autonomous non-governmental organisation |
| qv | *quod vide* which see |

**R**

| | |
|---|---|
| r. | *recto* on the right-hand page |
| R | *Regina* Queen |
| | *Rex* King |
| RA | Royal Academy/Academician |
| | Royal Artillery |
| RAC | Royal Armoured Corps |
| | Royal Automobile Club |
| RADA | Royal Academy of Dramatic Art |
| RADC | Royal Army Dental Corps |
| RAEC | Royal Army Educational Corps |
| RAES | Royal Aeronautical Society |
| RAM | Royal Academy of Music |

| | |
|---|---|
| RAMC | Royal Army Medical Corps |
| RAN | Royal Australian Navy |
| RAOC | Royal Army Ordnance Corps |
| RAPC | Royal Army Pay Corps |
| RAVC | Royal Army Veterinary Corps |
| RBS | Royal Society of British Sculptors |
| RC | Red Cross |
| | Roman Catholic |
| RCN | Royal College of Nursing |
| RCT | Royal Corps of Transport |
| RD | Royal Naval and Royal Marine Forces Reserve Decoration |
| | Rural Dean |
| RE | Royal Engineers |
| REME | Royal Electrical and Mechanical Engineers |
| Rep | Republican |
| Rep. | Republic |
| Revd | Reverend |
| RGS | Royal Geographical Society |
| RHS | Royal Horticultural Society |
| RI | Royal Institute of Painters in Watercolours |
| | Royal Institution |
| RIR | Royal Irish Regiment |
| RM | Royal Marines |
| RMA | Royal Military Academy |
| RMT | National Union of Rail, Maritime and Transport Workers |
| RNIB | Royal National Institute of Blind People |
| RNID | Royal National Institute for Deaf People |
| RNR | Royal Naval Reserve |
| RNVR | Royal Naval Volunteer Reserve |
| RNXS | Royal Naval Auxiliary Service |
| Roffen: | of Rochester (Bishop) |
| RPA | Rural Payments Agency |
| RSA | Royal Scottish Academician |
| | Royal Society of Arts |
| RSC | Royal Shakespeare Company |
| RSE | Royal Society of Edinburgh |
| Rt. Hon. | Right Honourable |
| RUC | Royal Ulster Constabulary |

**S**

| | |
|---|---|
| s | section (Public Acts) |
| | *solidus* shilling |
| Salop | Shropshire |
| Sarum: | of Salisbury (Bishop) |
| SCD | Doctor of Science |
| SDLP | Social Democratic and Labour Party |
| SEAQ | Stock Exchange Automated Quotations system |
| SEN | special educational needs |
| | State Enrolled Nurse |
| SF | Sinn Fein |
| SFO | Serious Fraud Office |
| SI | statutory instrument |
| | *Système International d'Unités* International System of Units |

| | |
|---|---|
| sic | *sic* so written |
| sig | signature |
| | Signor |
| SLD | Social and Liberal Democrats |
| SOE | Special Operations Executive |
| sp | *sine prole* without issue |
| Sr | Senior |
| | Sister (title) |
| SS | steamship |
| SSN | standard serial number |
| stet | *stet* let it stand (printing) |
| Sub Lt. | sub-lieutenant |

**T**

| | |
|---|---|
| TD | Territorial Decoration |
| TEFL | teaching English as a foreign language |
| TNT | trinitrotoluene (explosive) |
| *trans.* | translated |
| TRH | Their Royal Highnesses |
| trs | transpose (printing) |

**U**

| | |
|---|---|
| U | Unionist |
| uc | upper case (printing) |
| UDA | Ulster Defence Association |
| UG | undergraduate |
| USB | universal serial bus |
| UTC | *Temps Universel Coordonné* coordinated universal time |
| UVF | Ulster Volunteer Force |

**V**

| | |
|---|---|
| v | *versus* against |
| v. | *verso* on the left-hand page |
| | Victoria and Albert Order |
| VAD | Voluntary Aid Detachment (nursing) |
| VC | Victoria Cross |
| VD | Volunteer Officers' Decoration |
| Ven. | Venerable |
| VRD | Royal Naval Volunteer Reserve Officers' Decoration |
| VSO | Voluntary Service Overseas |

**W**

| | |
|---|---|
| w. | widowed |
| WBC | World Boxing Council |
| WBO | World Boxing Organisation |
| WCC | World Council of Churches |
| WFTU | World Federation of Trade Unions |
| Winton: | of Winchester (Bishop) |
| WO | Warrant Officer |
| WRAC | Women's Royal Army Corps |
| WRAF | Women's Royal Air Force |
| WRNS | Women's Royal Naval Service |
| WRVS | Women's Royal Voluntary Service |
| WS | Writer to the Signet |

**Y**

| | |
|---|---|
| YMCA | Young Men's Christian Association |
| YWCA | Young Women's Christian Association |

**Z**

| | |
|---|---|
| ZANU-PF | Zimbabwean African National Union-Patriotic Front |

# INDEX